THE AMERICAN BENCH

JUDGES OF THE NATION

MARIE T. FINN
Executive Vice President —
Electronic Publishing Systems

DIANA R. IRVINE
Editor-in-Chief

MARY LEE BLISS
Editor

ROBERT KLUVER
Assistant Editor

ALESSANDRA RENTERIA
GINA L. PRATTON
CYNTHIA KNIERIM
JOANNA BAKER
Editorial Staff

FOURTEENTH EDITION

2003/2004

Published by
FORSTER-LONG, INC.
Sacramento, California

Other biographical reference books published
by Forster-Long, Inc. include

THE AMERICAN BAR including
The Canadian Bar, The Mexican Bar
and The International Bar

Listing only the best since 1918

and its companion

The American Bar Reference Handbook
including The Canadian Bar, The Mexican Bar and The International Bar

as well as the exciting series

WHO RUNS PROFESSIONAL SPORTS—THE NBA

WHO RUNS PROFESSIONAL SPORTS—Major League Baseball

WHO RUNS PROFESSIONAL SPORTS—THE NFL

ISBN 0-931398-48-7
ISSN 0160-2578
Library of Congress Catalog Card Number: 78-640695

FOREWORD

THE AMERICAN BENCH, published by Forster-Long, Inc., constitutes a comprehensive biographical reference guide to the American judiciary. For more than eighty-five years the annual editions of our book ***THE AMERICAN BAR including The Canadian Bar, The Mexican Bar and The International Bar*** have provided a selective directory of highly prestigious lawyers and law firms of the world.

THE AMERICAN BENCH, now in its fourteenth edition, is the only directory combining biographical information on over 19,000 judges from all levels of federal and state courts with jurisdictional, structural and geographical facts on the courts they serve, as provided by federal sources and by the individual states. All data received as of May 15, 2003 has been incorporated into this fourteenth edition. This volume, as well as future annual editions, should prove invaluable to lawyers and litigants, librarians, law students, businesses, universities and high schools, the general public and the judiciary itself.

The book is thumb-indexed and designed to facilitate access to information. It is divided into fifty-two sections: one section for the United States Courts and one for each of the fifty states and the District of Columbia. Each section is subdivided into three parts:

The first part contains descriptive information on each court in the state including method of selection of judges, jurisdiction and court location. Judges are listed with the courts they serve. A list of counties and county seats is provided where applicable.

The second part includes maps showing the judicial boundaries for the United States Courts of Appeals (in the United States section) and the United States District Courts (in each state's section). Additional maps show the judicial boundaries for many state courts. Maps are not included for those courts whose boundaries do not coincide with county lines or which are used solely for electoral purposes.

The third part provides biographies of the judges arranged alphabetically. Each biography includes title, court level served and office address. Full biographies, which are contributed by the judges, may contain information about the judges' educational background, legal background, current and previous judgeships, important decisions, authorships, posts of honor, awards, civic organizations, military service, personal interests and other pertinent facts. If available, information regarding retired judges who continue to serve is listed. Some judges serving minor courts in small communities or rural areas have been omitted, usually due to unavailability of information.

An alphabetical name index is located in the front of the book listing name, title, court and state of each judge. This index enables the user to locate quickly any judge with only the name as a reference point.

A glossary provides definitions of common legal and judicial terms found in ***THE AMERICAN BENCH***.

Annual revisions of ***THE AMERICAN BENCH*** ensure information is as up-to-date as possible. Court activities and statute revisions will be monitored so that jurisdictional and personnel changes can be incorporated into each subsequent edition. Past editions will assume historical significance as they become a comprehensive record of change within the judiciary and a permanent biographical record of former American judges.

We wish to acknowledge and thank the judges, court administrators and clerks across the country who readily cooperated with us in our efforts to produce this book.

We encourage suggestions and contributions that will expand our listings and enable us to provide a more complete record of the American judiciary. Every effort has been made to assure the information contained in ***THE AMERICAN BENCH*** has the highest possible degree of accuracy. We are confident that the users of this publication will find it a valuable reference work.

Information from previous editions of ***THE AMERICAN BENCH***, as well as from our legal directory, ***THE AMERICAN BAR including The Canadian Bar, The Mexican Bar and The International Bar*** is available through our research service. Please contact us directly for specific information, including research fees, at Forster-Long, Inc., 3280 Ramos Circle, Sacramento, California 95827. Telephone: (916) 362-3276. Toll-free: (800) 328-5091. Facsimile: (916) 362-5643. E-mail: editorial@forster-long.com. You can also submit requests and find additional information at www.americanbar.com.

Jay W. Long
Publisher

CONTENTS

USER'S GUIDE

THE AMERICAN BENCH has been organized into two main categories to enable our readers to locate information on the American judicial system quickly and efficiently: the Alphabetical Name Index and the Structure of Court Systems in the United States including Maps and Biographies.

The Alphabetical Name Index, located at the beginning of the book, provides instant access to any of the over 19,000 judges listed. It includes judges' names, their titles and the court and state they serve, allowing the reader to locate any judge included in the publication with only the name as a reference point.

The Structure of Court Systems in the United States including Maps and Biographies is divided into fifty state sections plus special sections for the United States Courts and the District of Columbia Courts. Each of these fifty-two sections includes Court Outlines, Judicial Boundary Maps and Biographical Data.

The United States Courts section consists of the U.S. Supreme Court, U.S. Courts of Appeals, U.S. District Courts, U.S. Court of International Trade, U.S. Court of Federal Claims, U.S. Court of Appeals for the Armed Forces, U.S. Court of Appeals for Veterans Claims, U.S. Tax Court and descriptive information on the Native American Indian Courts of Law.

Judges serving these courts are listed in the United States Courts section. Information regarding U.S. District Court judges serving Puerto Rico or the territorial district courts is also included here. All other U.S. District Court judges are listed under the individual states in which they serve.

Judges who serve the Bankruptcy Appellate Panels may also serve U.S. Bankruptcy Courts and thus have entries under both the United States Courts section and their individual states for easy reference.

Court Outlines depict the judicial structure of each state by providing descriptions of judge selection methods, jurisdiction, geographic boundaries and lists of judges serving the courts. We include contact information for all Federal court clerks as well as all state supreme court clerks. County and county seat information is provided where applicable.

Judicial Boundary Maps offer clear illustrations of U.S. Courts of Appeals Circuits (located in the United States Courts section) and U.S. District Courts of each state as well as selected state courts. Maps have not been included for state courts whose boundaries do not follow county lines or are used strictly for electoral purposes.

Biographical Data arranges judges alphabetically and includes judge title, court name and office address. Biographies, submitted by the judges themselves, may further contain other pertinent facts such as how and when a judge assumed office, educational background, court admissions, previous judgeships, legal and professional positions, authorships, important judicial decisions, teaching positions, awards and honors, military service and political and civic affiliations.

Common legal terms found in ***THE AMERICAN BENCH*** are defined in a *Glossary* at the end of the book.

ALPHABETICAL NAME INDEX

Aandal, Donald J.-Judge, Minnesota District Court Ninth Judicial District-Minn.

Aaron, Cynthia G.-Associate Justice, California Court of Appeal Fourth District Division One-Calif.

Aaron, Ezra J.-Chief Magistrate, Magistrate Court of Toombs County-Ga.

Abascal, Amado, III-Judge, Texas District Court 365th Judicial District-Tex.

Abbatangelo, Anthony L.-Justice of the Peace, Las Vegas Justices' Court-Nev.

Abbott, David W.-Judge, Superior Court of California County of Sacramento-Calif.

Abbott, H. T., III-Judge, South Carolina Family Court Fifteenth Judicial Circuit-S.C.

Abbott, Louisa-Judge, Superior Court of Georgia Eastern Judicial Circuit-Ga.

Abbott, Steven Luse-Judge, Wisconsin Circuit Court Monroe Circuit-Wis.

Abdallah, George J., Jr.-Judge, Superior Court of California County of San Joaquin-Calif.

Abdella, Charles A.-First Justice, Trial Court of Massachusetts District Court Department Worcester County East Brookfield Division and Justice, Worcester Division-Mass.

Abdella, James-Judge, Jamestown City Court-N.Y.

Abdus Salaam, Sheila-Justice, New York Supreme Court First Judicial District-N.Y.

Abel, Gordon C.-District Judge, Iowa District Court Fourth Judicial District-Ia.

Abel, Mark R.-Magistrate Judge, United States District Court Southern District of Ohio-Ohio

Abel, S. William-Judge, Superior Court of California County of Colusa-Calif.

Abele, Peter B.-Judge, Ohio Court of Appeals Fourth District-Ohio

Abernethy, Pamela L.-Judge, Oregon Circuit Court Third Judicial District-Ore.

Abery-Wetstone, Holly-Judge, Connecticut Superior Court-Conn.

Ableman, Peggy L.-Associate Judge, Delaware Superior Court New Castle County-Del.

Ables, Stephen B.-Judge, Texas District Court 216th Judicial District-Tex.

Abney, Robert-Judge, Des Arc District Court-Ark.

Abraham, Kenneth A.-Associate Judge, Illinois Circuit Court Eighteenth Judicial Circuit-Ill.

Abrahamson, Shirley Schlanger-Chief Justice, Wisconsin Supreme Court-Wis.

Abrams, Judith-Judge, Superior Court of California County of Los Angeles-Calif.

Abrams, Karen H.-Associate Judge, Circuit Court for St. Mary's County, Seventh Judicial Circuit-Md.

Abrams, Paul L.-Magistrate Judge, United States District Court Central District of California-Calif.

Abramson, Gilbert L.-Judge, Saratoga County Family Court-N.Y.

Abramson, Gillian L.-Associate Justice, New Hampshire Superior Court-N.H.

Abramson, Harold C.-Recalled Judge, United States Bankruptcy Court Northern District of Texas-Tex.

Abramson, Howland W.-Judge, Pennsylvania Court of Common Pleas First Judicial District-Pa.

Abramson, Lisabeth Hughes-Judge, Kentucky Circuit Court Thirtieth Judicial Circuit-Ky.

Abrashkin, William H.-First Justice, Trial Court of Massachusetts Housing Court Department Western Division-Mass.

Abrecht, Mary Ellen-Associate Judge, Superior Court of the District of Columbia-D.C.

Abruzzo, David N.-Judge, Ohio Court of Common Pleas Preble County-Ohio

Aceto, Mark F.-Judge, Superior Court of Arizona Maricopa County-Ariz.

Acey, William D.-Judge, Washington Superior Court Asotin-Columbia-Garfield Counties-Wash.

Acker, William M., Jr.-Senior Judge, United States District Court Northern District of Alabama-Ala.

Ackerman, Daniel J.-President Judge, Pennsylvania Court of Common Pleas Tenth Judicial District-Pa.

Ackerman, David B.-Judge, Escambia County Court-Fla.

Ackerman, Harold A.-Senior Judge, United States District Court District of New Jersey-N.J.

Ackerman, John D.-District Judge, Iowa District Court Third Judicial District-Ia.

Ackerman, Norman-Judge, Pennsylvania Court of Common Pleas First Judicial District-Pa.

Ackerson, David E.-Judge, Minnesota District Court Sixth Judicial District-Minn.

Acoba, Simeon R., Jr.-Associate Justice, Hawaii Supreme Court-Hi.

Acosta, Raymond L.-Senior Judge, United States District Court District of Puerto Rico

Acosta, Rolando T.-Justice, New York Supreme Court First Judicial District-N.Y.

Acree, William B., Jr.-Judge, Tennessee Circuit Court Twenty-seventh Judicial District-Tenn.

Acuña, Edgar B.-Judge, Superior Court of Arizona Pima County-Ariz.

Adair, James P.-Judge, Michigan Circuit Court Thirty-first Judicial Circuit-Mich.

Adair, Robin W.-Special Judge, Oklahoma District Court Fifteenth Judicial District-Okla.

Adair, Valerie-Judge, Nevada District Court Eighth Judicial District-Nev.

Adajian, Jacob-Judge, Superior Court of California County of Los Angeles-Calif.

Adams, Alfred Harris-Judge, Court of Appeals of Georgia-Ga.

Adams, Alton M.-Judge, State Court of Stephens County-Ga.

Adams, Brent T.-Judge, Nevada District Court Second Judicial District-Nev.

Adams, Chad-Judge, Ellis County Court-Tex.

Adams, Charles B.-Judge, Louisiana District Court Eleventh Judicial District-La.

Adams, Charles D.-Judge, Superior Court of Arizona Coconino County-Ariz.

Adams, Dale-Judge, Probate Court of Murray County-Ga.

Adams, David H.-Judge, United States Bankruptcy Court Eastern District of Virginia-Va.

Adams, Deborah Ross-Judge, Michigan District Court District Thirty-six-Mich.

Adams, Durand J.-Judge, Florida Circuit Court Twelfth Judicial Circuit-Fla.

Adams, Eric R.-Judge, Genesee County Family Court-N.Y.

Adams, Gail-Judge, Florida Circuit Court Ninth Judicial Circuit-Fla.

Adams, Glenn D.-Judge, Oklahoma Court of Civil Appeals-Okla.

Adams, Gordon G.-Judge, Texas District Court 169th Judicial District-Tex.

Adams, Gregory A.-Judge, Juvenile Court of Georgia Stone Mountain Judicial Circuit-Ga.

Adams, H. Greg-Judge, Probate Court of Walton County-Ga.

Adams, Henry Lee, Jr.-Judge, United States District Court Middle District of Florida-Fla.

Adams, Herbert E.-Judge, Sandusky County Court-Ohio

Adams, J. Scott-Judge, Morrilton District Court-Ark.

Adams, James G., Jr.-Judge, Kentucky District Court Third Judicial District-Ky.

Adams, James R.-Judge, Lee County Court-Fla.

Adams, Jody-Judge, New York City Family Court-N.Y.

Adams, John B.-Judge, Juvenile Court of Georgia Waycross Judicial Circuit-Ga.

Adams, John C.-Judge, Burlington Town Court-Ind.

Adams, John H., Sr.-Judge, Florida Circuit Court Ninth Judicial Circuit-Fla.

Adams, John R.-Judge, Kentucky Circuit Court Twenty-second Judicial Circuit-Ky.

Adams, John R.-Judge, United States District Court Northern District of Ohio-Ohio

Adams, John S.-Judge, Superior Court of California County of Orange-Calif.

Adams, Julia Hylton-Judge, Kentucky Circuit Court Twenty-fifth Judicial Circuit-Ky.

Adams, Rachel Amy-Judge, The Civil Court of the City of New York-N.Y.

Adams, Robert B.-Judge, Superior Court of Georgia Conasauga Judicial Circuit-Ga.

Adams, Samuel D.-Deputy Presiding Judge, Alaska District Court Third Judicial District-Alas.

Adams, Taggart D.-Judge, Connecticut Superior Court-Conn.

Adams, Thomas A.-Associate Justice, New York Supreme Court Appellate Division Second Judicial Department-N.Y.

Adams, Thomas R.-Judge, Superior Court of California County of Santa Barbara-Calif.

Adams, Verna A.-Judge, Superior Court of California County of Marin-Calif.

Adams, William-Judge, Aransas County Court at Law-Tex.

Adams, William P.-Judge, State Court of Bibb County-Ga.

Adams-Jarrell, Ann Frye-Judge, Probate Court of Habersham County-Ga.

Adamson, Robert W.-Chief Judge, Superior Court of Georgia Piedmont Judicial Circuit-Ga.

Adderly, A. Leo-Judge, Dade County Court-Fla.

Addy, Frank R., Jr.-Judge, Greenwood County Probate Court-S.C.

Adelman, Lynn-Judge, United States District Court Eastern District of Wisconsin-Wis.

Adelman, Terry I.-Magistrate Judge, United States District Court Eastern District of Missouri-Mo.

Aderholt, Bobby R.-Presiding Judge, Alabama Circuit Court Twenty-fifth Judicial Circuit-Ala.

Adkins, Daren L.-Associate Circuit Judge, Missouri Circuit Court Forty-third Judicial Circuit-Mo.

Adkins, John C.-Senior Judge, Brevard County Court-Fla.

Adkins, John R.-Judge, Circleville Municipal Court-Ohio

Adkins, Sally Denison-Associate Judge, Court of Special Appeals of Maryland-Md.

Adkins, William H., III-Associate Judge, Maryland District Court District Three-Md.

Adler, Harold A.-Judge, The Civil Court of the City of New York-N.Y.

Adler, Lester B.-Judge, Westchester County Court-N.Y.

Adler, Louise DeCarl-Judge, United States Bankruptcy Court Southern District of California-Calif.

Adler, Michael-Judge, Oregon Circuit Court Eleventh Judicial District-Ore.

Adler, Phillip I.-Judge, Vigo Superior Court-Ind.

Adler, Richard A.-Judge, Superior Court of California County of Los Angeles-Calif.

Admire, David S.-Judge, King District Court East Division King County-Wash.

Adrine, Ronald Bruce-Judge, Cleveland Municipal Court-Ohio

Affronti, Francis A.-Justice, New York Supreme Court Seventh Judicial District-N.Y.

Africk, Lance M.-Judge, United States District Court Eastern District of Louisiana-La.

Agan, Jerry-Judge, Presidio County Court-Tex.

Agate, Augustus C.-Judge, The Civil Court of the City of New York-N.Y.

Agati, Salvatore C.-Judge, Connecticut Superior Court-Conn.

Agee, G. Steven-Justice, Supreme Court of Virginia-Va.

Agerter, Lawrence E.-Judge, Minnesota District Court Third Judicial District-Minn.

Agid, Susan R.-Judge, Washington Court of Appeals Division I-Wash.

Agin, William-Judge, Madison County Court-Miss.

Agner, John R.-Senior Judge, Florida Circuit Court Third Judicial Circuit-Fla.

Agnes, Peter W., Jr.-Associate Justice, Trial Court of Massachusetts Superior Court Department-Mass.

Agosti, Deborah A.-Chief Justice, Nevada Supreme Court-Nev.

Agostini, John A.-Associate Justice, Trial Court of Massachusetts Superior Court Department-Mass.

Agran, Martin S.-Circuit Judge, Illinois Circuit Court of Cook County-Ill.

Aguilar, Luis-Judge, Texas District Court 120th Judicial District-Tex.

Aguirre, Frederick P.-Judge, Superior Court of California County of Orange-Calif.

Aguirre, Richard-Associate Judge, Illinois Circuit Court Twentieth Judicial Circuit-Ill.

Ahart, Alan M.-Judge, United States Bankruptcy Court Central District of California-Calif.

Ahern, Daniel J.-Judge, Oregon Circuit Court Twenty-second Judicial District-Ore.

ALPHABETICAL NAME INDEX

ALPHABETICAL NAME INDEX

Alley, Nancy F.-Judge, Florida Circuit Court Eighteenth Judicial Circuit-Fla.
Alley, Thomas R.-Associate Circuit Judge, Missouri Circuit Court Third Judicial Circuit-Mo.
Alley, Wayne E.-Senior Judge, United States District Court Western District of Oklahoma-Okla.
Allgood, Robert L.-Judge, Superior Court of Georgia Augusta Judicial Circuit-Ga.
Alling, Kathleen M.-Associate Judge, Illinois Circuit Court Second Judicial Circuit-Ill.
Allison, James S.-Judge, Powell Municipal Court-Wyo.
Allison, Kaye A.-Associate Judge, Circuit Court for Baltimore City, Eighth Judicial Circuit-Md.
Allison, Paul K.-Judge, Pennsylvania Court of Common Pleas Second Judicial District-Pa.
Allman, Richard N.-Judge, The Civil Court of the City of New York-N.Y.
Allphin, Michael G.-Judge, Utah District Court Second Judicial District-Utah
Allred, Clark B.-Magistrate Judge, United States District Court District of Utah-Utah
Allred, Don R.-Judge, Oldham County Court-Tex.
Alm, Steven S.-Family Court Judge, Hawaii Circuit Court First Judicial Circuit-Hi.
Almasy, John P.-Judge, Campbell Municipal Court-Ohio
Almeida, John A.-Judge, New Jersey Superior Court Vicinage Three-N.J.
Almeida, Lillian M.-Judge, Rhode Island Traffic Tribunal-R.I.
Almon, S. Brent-Judge, Posey Superior Court-Ind.
Aloi, Anthony F.-Judge, Onondaga County Court-N.Y.
Aloise, Michael B.-Judge, The Civil Court of the City of New York-N.Y.
Alonso, Alfonso E., Jr.-Judge, Bexar County Court at Law No. 1-Tex.
Alonzo, Gerard J., Jr.-Judge, Livingston County Court-N.Y.
Alper, Joanne F.-Judge, Virginia Circuit Court Seventeenth Judicial Circuit-Va.
Alpers, Bobbi M.-District Judge, Iowa District Court Seventh Judicial District-Ia.
Alpert, Allen G.-Judge, The Criminal Court of the City of New York-N.Y.
Alpert, Bruce D.-Justice, New York Supreme Court Tenth Judicial District-N.Y.
Alprin, Geoffrey M.-Associate Judge, Superior Court of the District of Columbia-D.C.
Alsbrooks, John H., Jr.-Judge, Jefferson County District Court Birmingham Division-Ala.
Alsdorf, Robert H.-Judge, Washington Superior Court King County-Wash.
Alsop, Donald D.-Senior Judge, United States District Court District of Minnesota-Minn.
Alsop, Jack-Judge, West Virginia Circuit Court Fourteenth Judicial Circuit-W.Va.
Alspach, Deborah A.-Judge, Ohio Court of Common Pleas Marion County-Ohio
Alston, Craig D.-Chief Judge, Michigan District Court District Seventy-four-Mich.
Alston, Rossie D., Jr.-Judge, Virginia Circuit Court Thirty-first Judicial Circuit-Va.
Alsup, William-Judge, United States District Court Northern District of California-Calif.
Altenberger, William V.-Recalled Judge, United States Bankruptcy Court Central District of Illinois-Ill.
Altenbernd, Chris W.-Chief Judge, Florida District Court of Appeal Second District-Fla.
Altice, Robert R., Jr.-Judge, Marion Superior Court-Ind.
Altman, Brian-Judge, East District Court Klickitat County-Wash.
Altman, Harry Jay, II-Judge, Superior Court of Georgia Southern Judicial Circuit-Ga.
Altman, Herbert I.-Judge, The Criminal Court of the City of New York-N.Y.
Altman, Myriam J.-Associate Justice, New York Supreme Court Appellate Division Second Judicial Department-N.Y.
Alton, Ann L.-Judge, Minnesota District Court Fourth Judicial District-Minn.
Altonaga, Cecilia Maria-Judge, Florida Circuit Court Eleventh Judicial Circuit-Fla.
Altoon, Alice E.-Judge, Superior Court of California County of Los Angeles-Calif.
Alvarado, Efrain L.-Judge, The Criminal Court of the City of New York-N.Y.
Alvarado, Paul H.-Judge, Superior Court of California City and County of San Francisco-Calif.
Alvarez, Carmen H.-Judge, New Jersey Superior Court Vicinage One-N.J.
Alvarez, Donald R.-Judge, Superior Court of California County of San Bernardino-Calif.
Alvarez, Javier-Judge, El Paso County Court at Law No. 3-Tex.
Alvarez, Jesus Maria-Judge, Starr County Court at Law-Tex.
Alvarez, Manny D.-Judge, Texas Criminal District Court No. 5 Dallas County-Tex.
Alvarez, Ronald V.-Judge, Florida Circuit Court Fifteenth Judicial Circuit-Fla.
Alvey, Joseph C.-Judge, Rockport City Court-Ind.
Alvord, Bethany J.-Judge, Connecticut Superior Court-Conn.
Alvord, Don L.-Magistrate Judge, Kansas District Court Twentieth Judicial District-Kan.
Amato, Dominic S.-Judge, Wisconsin Circuit Court Milwaukee Circuit-Wis.
Ambrecht, Michael R.-Judge, New York Court of Claims-N.Y.
Ambro, Thomas L.-Judge, United States Court of Appeals Third Circuit
Ambrose, Donetta W.-Chief Judge, United States District Court Western District of Pennsylvania-Pa.
Ambrose, Janice Rodnick-Associate Judge, Maryland District Court District Eleven-Md.
Ambrose, Robert Lawrence-Judge, Superior Court of California County of Santa Clara-Calif.
Ambrosio, Michael A.-Judge, New York City Family Court-N.Y.
Ames, Jack B.-Senior Judge, Nevada District Court-Nev.
Ames, William F.-Judge, Cortland County Court-N.Y.
Amestoy, Jeffrey L.-Chief Justice, Vermont Supreme Court-Vt.
Amirante, Sam L.-Associate Judge, Illinois Circuit Court of Cook County-Ill.
Amiton, Marshall L.-Judge, Oregon Circuit Court Fourth Judicial District-Ore.
Ammerman, Fredric J.-Judge, Pennsylvania Court of Common Pleas Forty-sixth Judicial District-Pa.
Ammerman, James Harry, II-Judge, Harrison County Court at Law-Tex.
Ammons, James Floyd, Jr.-Resident Judge, North Carolina Superior Court Fourth Judicial Division District 12-N.C.
Ammons, Thomas M., III-Judge, Virginia General District Court Second Judicial District-Va.
Amodeo, Damian J.-Judge, Dutchess County Family Court-N.Y.
Amodeo, Thomas P.-Chief Judge, Buffalo City Court-N.Y.
Amon, Carol Bagley-Judge, United States District Court Eastern District of New York-N.Y.
Amos, Edgar Allen-Judge, Concho County Court-Tex.
Amos, Eugene Mac, Jr.-Judge, Superior Court of California County of San Diego-Calif.
Amy, Marc T.-Judge, Louisiana Court of Appeal Third Circuit-La.
Anastor, Peter-Judge, Michigan District Court District Sixty-eight-Mich.
Anchondo, Robert-Judge, El Paso County Criminal Court at Law No. 2-Tex.
Anctil, Wallace J.-Justice, Berlin District Court and Special Justice, Gorham District Court-N.H.
Anderegg, Michael John-Chief Judge, Marquette County Probate Court-Mich.
Anderle, Thomas Pearce-Judge, Superior Court of California County of Santa Barbara-Calif.
Anders, Scott S.-Judge, Clark District Court Clark County and Judge, Camas-Washougal Municipal Court-Wash.
Andersen, Deborah-Judge, Probate Court of Paulding County-Ga.
Andersen, James W.-Justice of the Peace, Austin Justices' Court-Nev.
Andersen, Wayne R.-Judge, United States District Court Northern District of Illinois-Ill.
Anderson, A. E.-Judge, Fort Benton City Court-Mont.
Anderson, Adele K.-Judge, Pueblo County Court-Colo.
Anderson, Allen M.-Associate Judge, Illinois Circuit Court Sixteenth Judicial Circuit-Ill.
Anderson, Anthony A.-Judge, Superior Court of California County of Shasta-Calif.
Anderson, Arthur T.-Judge, Superior Court of Arizona Maricopa County-Ariz.
Anderson, Barry R.-Circuit Judge, Illinois Circuit Court Fifteenth Judicial Circuit-Ill.
Anderson, Betty J.-Judge, Probate Court of Wilcox County-Ga.
Anderson, Carl B., Jr.-Judge, Kansas District Court Ninth Judicial District-Kan.
Anderson, Carol S.-Judge, Bridger, Fromberg, Joliet and Red Lodge City Courts-Mont.
Anderson, Catherine L.-Judge, Minnesota District Court Fourth Judicial District-Minn.
Anderson, Charles T. L.-Judge, North Carolina District Court District 15B-N.C.
Anderson, Charlotte W.-Judge, Hillsborough County Court-Fla.
Anderson, Claudia J.-Circuit Judge, Illinois Circuit Court Fifth Judicial Circuit-Ill.
Anderson, Clifford R., III-Judge, Superior Court of California County of Santa Barbara-Calif.
Anderson, Daniel P.-Judge, Wisconsin Court of Appeals District Two-Wis.
Anderson, David L.-Judge, Panola County Court-Tex.
Anderson, Deb-Magistrate Judge, Kansas District Court Seventeenth Judicial District-Kan.
Anderson, Dudley N.-Judge, Pennsylvania Court of Common Pleas Twenty-ninth Judicial District-Pa.
Anderson, E. Riley-Associate Justice, Tennessee Supreme Court-Tenn.
Anderson, G. Barry-Judge, Minnesota Court of Appeals-Minn.
Anderson, G. Ross, Jr.-Judge, United States District Court District of South Carolina-S.C.
Anderson, Gary K.-District Associate Judge, Iowa District Court Fourth Judicial District-Ia.
Anderson, Georgia V.-Judge, South Carolina Family Court Seventh Judicial Circuit-S.C.
Anderson, Gregory S.-Judge, Idaho District Court Seventh Judicial District-Ida.
Anderson, Isaac, Jr.-Judge, Florida Circuit Court Twentieth Judicial Circuit-Fla.
Anderson, James E.-Judge, Harris County Criminal Court at Law No. 4-Tex.
Anderson, James W.-Judge, Randall County Court at Law-Tex.
Anderson, James Wallace-Judge, South Dakota Circuit Court Sixth Judicial Circuit-S.D.
Anderson, Jeanne W.-Judge, Limestone County District Court-Ala.
Anderson, John, III-Judge, Kansas District Court Tenth Judicial District-Kan.
Anderson, John P.-Judge, Wisconsin Circuit Court Adams Circuit-Wis.
Anderson, John R.-Judge, Utah District Court Eighth Judicial District-Utah
Anderson, John S.-Justice, Texas Court of Appeals Fourteenth District-Tex.
Anderson, Joseph F., Jr.-Chief Judge, United States District Court District of South Carolina-S.C.
Anderson, Joseph W.-Judge, Utah Juvenile Court Third Judicial District-Utah
Anderson, Keith Alexander-Judge, Dallas County Criminal Court at Law No. 9-Tex.
Anderson, Ken-Judge, Texas District Court 277th Judicial District-Tex.
Anderson, Larry K.-Presiding Judge, Alabama Circuit Court Twentieth Judicial Circuit-Ala.
Anderson, Lawrence O.-Magistrate Judge, United States District Court District of Arizona-Ariz.
Anderson, Lee-Judge, South Dakota Circuit Court First Judicial Circuit-S.D.
Anderson, Leland P.-Judge, Colorado District Court First Judicial District-Colo.
Anderson, Lyle R.-Judge, Utah District Court Seventh Judicial District-Utah
Anderson, Margaret R.-Judge, Superior Court of California County of Orange-Calif.
Anderson, Martha-Judge, Michigan Circuit Court Sixth Judicial Circuit-Mich.

ALPHABETICAL NAME INDEX

Anderson, Matthew S.-Judge, Superior Court of California County of Orange-Calif.

Anderson, Melinda-Chief Magistrate, Magistrate Court of Liberty County-Ga.

Anderson, Mike-Judge, Texas District Court 262nd Judicial District-Tex.

Anderson, P. Hunter-Judge, Minnesota District Court Tenth Judicial District-Minn.

Anderson, Paul H.-Associate Justice, Minnesota Supreme Court-Minn.

Anderson, Percy-Judge, United States District Court Central District of California-Calif.

Anderson, R. Lanier, III-Judge, United States Court of Appeals Eleventh Circuit

Anderson, R. Peter-First Justice, Trial Court of Massachusetts District Court Department Suffolk County Brighton Division-Mass.

Anderson, Ralph King, Jr.-Associate Judge, South Carolina Court of Appeals-S.C.

Anderson, Richard D.-Chief Judge, Kansas District Court Third Judicial District-Kan.

Anderson, Richard D.-Judge, Louisiana District Court Nineteenth Judicial District-La.

Anderson, Richard W.-Magistrate Judge, United States District Court District of Montana-Mont.

Anderson, Robert J.-Circuit Judge, Illinois Circuit Court Eighteenth Judicial Circuit-Ill.

Anderson, Ronald-Judge, West Virginia Family Court Circuit Six-W.Va.

Anderson, Russell A.-Associate Justice, Minnesota Supreme Court-Minn.

Anderson, Stephen H.-Senior Judge, United States Court of Appeals Tenth Circuit

Anderson, Susan H.-Judge, Clark County Municipal Court-Ohio

Anderson, Thor-Judge, Minnesota District Court Fourth Judicial District-Minn.

Anderson, W. Mark, III-Judge, Alabama Circuit Court Fifteenth Judicial Circuit-Ala.

Anderson, William E.-Judge, United States Bankruptcy Court Western District of Virginia-Va.

Anderson, William R.-Judge, Maine District Court-Me.

Anderson, William Roy, Jr.-Judge, Johnson County Court at Law No. 2-Tex.

Anderson, Zane C.-Judge, North Dakota District Court Southwest Judicial District-N.D.

Anderton, James P.-Associate Circuit Judge, Missouri Circuit Court Thirtieth Judicial Circuit-Mo.

Andler, Gail A.-Judge, Superior Court of California County of Orange-Calif.

Andre, John W., Jr.-Chief Magistrate, Magistrate Court of Chatham County-Ga.

Andrew, Stewart R.-Judge, San Juan District Court San Juan County-Wash.

Andrews, Bradford L.-Judge, Superior Court of California County of Los Angeles-Calif.

Andrews, Charles, Jr.-Judge, Kansas District Court Third Judicial District-Kan.

Andrews, Daniel True-Senior Judge, Florida Circuit Court Tenth Judicial Circuit-Fla.

Andrews, Deborah B.-Judge, Superior Court of California County of Los Angeles-Calif.

Andrews, Gary B.-Judge, Court of Appeals of Georgia-Ga.

Andrews, H. Dean-Circuit Judge, Illinois Circuit Court Fifth Judicial Circuit-Ill.

Andrews, Horace A.-Senior Judge, Florida Circuit Court Sixth Judicial Circuit-Fla.

Andrews, Michael F.-Judge, Pinellas County Court-Fla.

Andrews, Robert Lance-Judge, Florida Circuit Court Seventeenth Judicial Circuit-Fla.

Andrews, Stephen H.-Judge, Juvenile Court of Georgia Southern Judicial Circuit-Ga.

Andrews, Steven N.-Judge, Michigan Circuit Court Sixth Judicial Circuit-Mich.

Andrews, Virginia-Judge, Probate Court of Worth County-Ga.

Andrews, William Chapman, III-Judge, Virginia Circuit Court Eighth Judicial Circuit-Va.

Andrias, Richard T.-Associate Justice, New York Supreme Court Appellate Division First Judicial Department-N.Y.

Andringa, Henry J.-Judge, Pinellas County Court-Fla.

Andrus, J. Mark-Judge, Utah Juvenile Court Second Judicial District-Utah

Anello, Michael M.-Judge, Superior Court of California County of San Diego-Calif.

Angel, Carven D.-Judge, Florida Circuit Court Fifth Judicial Circuit-Fla.

Angelini, Karen-Justice, Texas Court of Appeals Fourth District-Tex.

Angelini, Raymond C.-Judge, Texas District Court 187th Judicial District-Tex.

Angell, M. Faith-Magistrate Judge, United States District Court Eastern District of Pennsylvania-Pa.

Angelle, Randy P.-Judge, Breaux Bridge City Court-La.

Angelos, Cynthia G.-Judge, Florida Circuit Court Nineteenth Judicial Circuit-Fla.

Angiolillo, Daniel D.-Justice, New York Supreme Court Ninth Judicial District-N.Y.

Angle, Loren E.-Associate District Judge, Oklahoma District Court Fourth Judicial District-Okla.

Angle, Stephen-Associate Circuit Judge, Missouri Circuit Court Seventeenth Judicial Circuit-Mo.

Anglin, David-Judge, Probate Court of Oconee County-Ga.

Annunziata, Rosemarie P.-Judge, Court of Appeals of Virginia-Va.

Anspach, Robert J.-Judge, Superior Court of California County of Kern-Calif.

Anstead, Harry Lee-Chief Justice, Florida Supreme Court-Fla.

Antell, Melvin P.-Retired Judge, New Jersey Superior Court Appellate Division-N.J.

Anthony, Carol Crafton-Judge, Arkansas Circuit Court Thirteenth Judicial Circuit-Ark.

Anthony, Fred J.-Judge, Shelton District Probate Court-Conn.

Anthony, Fred P.-Judge, Pennsylvania Court of Common Pleas Sixth Judicial District-Pa.

Antolini, Lawrence G.-Judge, Superior Court of California County of Sonoma-Calif.

Antonietti, Edward A.-Associate Judge, Illinois Circuit Court of Cook County-Ill.

Antonin, Frances Lawrence-Judge, New Jersey Superior Court Vicinage Six-N.J.

Antoon, John, II-Judge, United States District Court Middle District of Florida-Fla.

Antosz, John M.-Judge, Washington Superior Court Grant County-Wash.

Anzaldi, Ross R.-Judge, New Jersey Superior Court Vicinage Twelve-N.J.

Aparicio, Edward G.-Judge, Texas District Court 92nd Judicial District-Tex.

Apgar, Jonathan M.-Judge, Virginia Circuit Court Twenty-third Judicial Circuit-Va.

Appel, Claude W.-Chief Judge, Colorado District Court Third Judicial District-Colo.

Appel, Michelle Friedman-Judge, Michigan District Court District Forty-five B-Mich.

Appelwick, Marlin J.-Judge, Washington Court of Appeals Division I-Wash.

Appleton, Thomas R.-Circuit Judge, Illinois Circuit Court Seventh Judicial Circuit-Ill.

Apte, Alan S.-Judge, Florida Circuit Court Ninth Judicial Circuit-Fla.

Aquilino, Thomas J., Jr.-Judge, United States Court of International Trade

Aragon, Conrad Richard-Judge, Superior Court of California County of Los Angeles-Calif.

Aramony, Susan-Judge, Florida Circuit Court Seventeenth Judicial Circuit-Fla.

Aranda, Jose A., Jr.-Judge, Maverick County Court-Tex.

Araneta, Louis A.-Judge, Superior Court of Arizona Maricopa County-Ariz.

Arb, Susan C.-Judge, Moxee City Municipal Court-Wash.

Arcara, Richard J.-Chief Judge, United States District Court Western District of New York-N.Y.

Arce-Flores, Adriana-Magistrate Judge, United States District Court Southern District of Texas-Tex.

Arceneaux, David W.-Judge, Louisiana District Court Thirty-second Judicial District-La.

Archbold, Carolyn A.-Chief Judge, Michigan District Court District Twenty-nine-Mich.

Archer, Glenn L., Jr.-Senior Judge, United States Court of Appeals Federal Circuit

Archer, Theresa J.-Judge, Medicine Bow Municipal Court-Wyo.

Archer, Trudy DunCombe-Judge, Michigan District Court District Thirty-six-Mich.

Archibald, James P.-Active Retired Justice, Maine Supreme Judicial Court-Me.

Archibald, R. James-Judge, Idaho District Court Seventh Judicial District Magistrate Division-Ida.

Archuleta, David Anthony-Judge, Boulder County Court-Colo.

Archuleta, Judy L.-Judge, Jefferson County Court-Colo.

Ardaiz, James A.-Administrative Presiding Justice, California Court of Appeal Fifth District and Presiding Justice, California Court of Appeal Fifth District-Calif.

Arellano, Silvia R.-Judge, Superior Court of Arizona Maricopa County-Ariz.

Arena, Salvatore F.-Senior Judge, Connecticut Superior Court-Conn.

Arenas, Justo-Magistrate Judge, United States District Court District of Puerto Rico

Arend, Stephanie A.-Judge, Washington Superior Court Pierce County-Wash.

Argento, Phillip J.-Judge, Superior Court of California County of Los Angeles-Calif.

Argetsinger, J. C.-Judge, Schuyler County Court-N.Y.

Argo, Doyle W.-Magistrate Judge, United States District Court Western District of Oklahoma-Okla.

Arias, Roberto A.-Judge, Duval County Court-Fla.

Ark, John J.-Justice, New York Supreme Court Seventh Judicial District-N.Y.

Arkin, Angela-Judge, Colorado District Court Eighteenth Judicial District-Colo.

Arleo, Madeline Cox-Magistrate Judge, United States District Court District of New Jersey-N.J.

Armatas, Andrew S.-Judge, Denver County Court-Colo.

Armen, Robert N., Jr.-Special Trial Judge, United States Tax Court

Armijo, M. Christina-Judge, United States District Court District of New Mexico-N.Mex.

Armijo, Sergio-Judge, Washington Superior Court Pierce County-Wash.

Armstrong, Christopher J.-Chief Justice, Massachusetts Appeals Court-Mass.

Armstrong, David-Judge, Washington Court of Appeals Division II-Wash.

Armstrong, Donald E., Jr.-Judge, Kentucky District Court Thirtieth Judicial District-Ky.

Armstrong, Ernie B.-Judge, Texas District Court 132nd Judicial District-Tex.

Armstrong, Joan Bernard-Judge, Louisiana Court of Appeal Fourth Circuit-La.

Armstrong, Linda S.-Judge, Kentucky District Court Fifty-third Judicial District-Ky.

Armstrong, Mark W.-Judge, Superior Court of Arizona Maricopa County-Ariz.

Armstrong, Orville A.-Associate Justice, California Court of Appeal Second District Division Five-Calif.

Armstrong, Paul W.-Judge, New Jersey Superior Court Vicinage Thirteen-N.J.

Armstrong, Rex-Judge, Oregon Court of Appeals-Ore.

Armstrong, Robert Morgan-Chief Judge, Virginia General District Court Twenty-first Judicial District-Va.

Armstrong, Robert R., Jr.-Magistrate Judge, United States District Court Northern District of Alabama-Ala.

Armstrong, Robert S.-Judge, South Carolina Family Court Fourteenth Judicial Circuit-S.C.

Armstrong, Saundra Brown-Judge, United States District Court Northern District of California-Calif.

Armstrong, Sharon-Judge, Washington Superior Court King County-Wash.

Armstrong, Thomas George-Judge, Minnesota District Court Tenth Judicial District-Minn.

Armstrong, Valerie H.-Assignment Judge, New Jersey Superior Court Vicinage One-N.J.

Armstrong, Vernelis K.-Magistrate Judge, United States District Court Northern District of Ohio-Ohio

Arner, James G.-President Judge, Pennsylvania Court of Common Pleas Eighteenth Judicial District-Pa.

Arnold, C. Jeffery-Judge, Orange County Court-Fla.

ALPHABETICAL NAME INDEX

Arnold, Charles W., Jr.-Judge, Florida Circuit Court Fourth Judicial Circuit-Fla.

Arnold, Ellen L.-Special Justice, Henniker District Court-N.H.

Arnold, Gary M.-Judge, Arkansas Circuit Court Twenty-second Judicial Circuit-Ark.

Arnold, Harold C.-Judge, Duval County Court-Fla.

Arnold, J. Kelley-Magistrate Judge, United States District Court Western District of Washington-Wash.

Arnold, Jack T.-Chief Judge, Gratiot County Probate Court-Mich.

Arnold, James D.-Judge, Florida Circuit Court Thirteenth Judicial Circuit-Fla.

Arnold, John P.-Associate Justice, New Hampshire Superior Court-N.H.

Arnold, Mark S.-Judge, Superior Court of California County of Los Angeles-Calif.

Arnold, Morris Sheppard-Judge, United States Court of Appeals Eighth Circuit

Arnold, Nancy J.-Circuit Judge, Illinois Circuit Court of Cook County-Ill.

Arnold, Philip-Judge, Oregon Circuit Court First Judicial District-Ore.

Arnold, Richard E.-Judge, Connecticut Superior Court-Conn.

Arnold, Richard Sheppard-Senior Judge, United States Court of Appeals Eighth Circuit

Arnold, W. H. "Dub"-Chief Justice, Arkansas Supreme Court-Ark.

Arnold, Ward S.-Circuit Judge, Illinois Circuit Court Nineteenth Judicial Circuit-Ill.

Arnot, William G. "Bud", III-Chief Justice, Texas Court of Appeals Eleventh District-Tex.

Aronin, Gloria Cohen-Justice, New York Supreme Court Second Judicial District-N.Y.

Aronson, Arnold W.-Judge Referee, Connecticut Superior Court-Conn.

Aronson, Richard M.-Associate Justice, California Court of Appeal Fourth District Division Three-Calif.

Aronson, Stephen D.-Judge, Canandaigua City Court-N.Y.

Aronson, Terrence M.-Judge, Minnesota District Court Sixth Judicial District-Minn.

Arp, Randal R.-Judge, Wyoming Circuit Court Eighth Judicial District, Goshen, Niobrara and Platte Counties-Wyo.

Arredondo, Lorenzo-Judge, Lake Circuit Court-Ind.

Arreola, Rafael A.-Judge, Superior Court of California County of San Diego-Calif.

Arrigan, Robert F.-Chief Judge, Rhode Island Workers' Compensation Court-R.I.

Arrington, David-Judge, West Virginia Family Court Circuit Twenty-five-W.Va.

Arrington, Marvin S., Jr.-Judge, Superior Court of Georgia Atlanta Judicial Circuit-Ga.

Arterton, Janet Bond-Judge, United States District Court District of Connecticut-Conn.

Arthur, James R.-Judge, Comanche County Court-Tex.

Arthur, Robert L.-Judge, Daviess Circuit Court-Ind.

Artigliere, Ralph-Judge, Florida Circuit Court Tenth Judicial Circuit-Fla.

Asadoorian, Lisa L.-Judge, Michigan District Court District Fifty-two Division Three-Mich.

Asarch, Joel K.-Judge, Nassau County District Court-N.Y.

Asel, Jodie Capshaw-Associate Circuit Judge, Missouri Circuit Court Thirteenth Judicial Circuit-Mo.

Ash, David-Associate Circuit Judge, Missouri Circuit Court Forty-fifth Judicial Circuit-Mo.

Ash, Don R.-Judge, Tennessee Circuit Court Sixteenth Judicial District-Tenn.

Ash, Tommy Walton-Judge, Probate Court of Ben Hill County-Ga.

Ashby, Anne-Judge, Texas District Court 134th Judicial District-Tex.

Ashby, Karen-Presiding Judge, Denver Juvenile Court-Colo.

Asher, Martin J.-Judge, Kansas District Court First Judicial District-Kan.

Ashford, W. Mark-Judge, Nebraska District Court Fourth Judicial District-Neb.

Ashley, Carl-Judge, Wisconsin Circuit Court Milwaukee Circuit-Wis.

Ashley, Nancy-Judge, Superior Court of California County of Stanislaus-Calif.

Ashman, Martin C.-Magistrate Judge, United States District Court Northern District of Illinois-Ill.

Ashmann-Gerst, Judith-Associate Justice, California Court of Appeal Second District Division Two-Calif.

Ashmanskas, Donald C.-Magistrate Judge, United States District Court District of Oregon-Ore.

Ashrafi, Victor-Judge, New Jersey Superior Court Vicinage Thirteen-N.J.

Ashworth, David L.-Judge, Pennsylvania Court of Common Pleas Second Judicial District-Pa.

Ashworth, Stephen H.-Judge, Superior Court of California County of San Bernardino-Calif.

Askew, Stephen J.-Judge, Minnesota District Court Tenth Judicial District-Minn.

Askew, W. Ken-Chief Magistrate, Magistrate Court of Harris County-Ga.

Askey, William Hartman-Magistrate Judge, United States District Court Middle District of Pennsylvania-Pa.

Askren, Kenton G.-Associate Circuit Judge, Missouri Circuit Court Eighteenth Judicial Circuit-Mo.

Aspen, Marvin E.-Senior Judge, United States District Court Northern District of Illinois-Ill.

Asphaug, Karen-Judge, Minnesota District Court First Judicial District-Minn.

Aspinwall, Nancy K.-Judge, Probate Court of Liberty County-Ga.

Asquith, Patricia K.-Magistrate, Rhode Island Family Court-R.I.

Assad, George-Judge, Las Vegas Municipal Court-Nev.

Assini, Jo Anne-Judge, Schenectady County Family Court-N.Y.

Atack, Robert B.-Judge, Superior Court of California County of Santa Cruz-Calif.

Atack, Sharon-Judge, Flagler County Court-Fla.

Atchinson, William K., Jr.-Judge, Oneonta City Court-N.Y.

Atherton, Judith S. H.-Judge, Utah District Court Third Judicial District-Utah

Atkins, Edna-Judge, Nebraska County Court Fourth Judicial District-Neb.

Atkins, John L.-Judge, Kentucky Circuit Court Third Judicial Circuit-Ky.

Atkins, Marylin E.-Chief Judge, Michigan District Court District Thirty-six-Mich.

Atkinson, Christine J.-Judge, Zionsville Town Court-Ind.

Atkinson, Dale-Judge, Sumter County Probate Court-S.C.

Atkinson, Lynn C.-Judge, Superior Court of California County of Kings-Calif.

Atkinson, Mark-Judge, Harris County Criminal Court at Law No. 13-Tex.

Atkinson, T. Carroll-Judge, Marion County Probate Court-S.C.

Atkinson, William M.-Judge, Wisconsin Circuit Court Brown Circuit-Wis.

Atlas, Jeffrey M.-Judge, The Criminal Court of the City of New York-N.Y.

Atlas, Nancy F.-Judge, United States District Court Southern District of Texas-Tex.

Atlee, Isabel Hall-Chief Judge, Virginia Juvenile and Domestic Relations District Court Ninth Judicial District-Va.

Atwell, Charles E.-Circuit Judge, Missouri Circuit Court Sixteenth Judicial Circuit-Mo.

Atwood, John R.-Justice, Maine Superior Court-Me.

Aubry, Kathleen A.-Judge, Ohio Court of Common Pleas Wyandot County-Ohio

Aug, J. Vincent, Jr.-Judge, Bankruptcy Appellate Panel Sixth Circuit and Judge, United States Bankruptcy Court Southern District of Ohio-Ohio

Augello, Joseph M.-Judge, Pennsylvania Court of Common Pleas Eleventh Judicial District-Pa.

August, Joel E.-Judge, Hawaii Circuit Court Second Judicial Circuit-Hi.

Augustine, Cary-Associate Circuit Judge, Missouri Circuit Court Thirteenth Judicial Circuit-Mo.

Aukstik, William J.-Associate Judge, Illinois Circuit Court of Cook County-Ill.

Aulisi, Richard T.-Justice, New York Supreme Court Fourth Judicial District-N.Y.

Ault, David A.-Judge, Montgomery Superior Court-Ind.

Ault, J. Peter-Circuit Judge, Illinois Circuit Court Tenth Judicial Circuit-Ill.

Ault, Jerry E.-Judge, Mansfield Municipal Court-Ohio

Auna, Aley K., Jr.-Family Court Judge, Hawaii District Court Third Judicial Circuit-Hi.

Aurigemma, Julia L.-Judge, Connecticut Superior Court-Conn.

Austin, Andrew W.-Magistrate Judge, United States District Court Western District of Texas-Tex.

Austin, C. Stanley-Circuit Judge, Illinois Circuit Court Eighteenth Judicial Circuit-Ill.

Austin, Eugene H.-Judge, New Jersey Superior Court Vicinage Two-N.J.

Austin, Gary S.-Judge, Superior Court of California County of Fresno-Calif.

Austin, Hadley W.-Judge Referee, Connecticut Superior Court-Conn.

Austin, John-Judge, Warren County Court-N.Y.

Austin, Kyle David-Judge, North Carolina District Court District 24-N.C.

Austin, Leonard B.-Justice, New York Supreme Court Tenth Judicial District-N.Y.

Austin, Robert D.-Judge, Washington Superior Court Spokane County-Wash.

Austin, Robert E.-Presiding Judge, Alabama Circuit Court Forty-first Judicial Circuit-Ala.

Austin, Russell Parker-Judge, Harris County Probate Court No. 1-Tex.

Austin, Steven K.-Judge, Superior Court of California County of Contra Costa-Calif.

Austria, Anthony G., Jr.-Judge, Newburgh City Court-N.Y.

Autrey, Henry Edward-Judge, United States District Court Eastern District of Missouri-Mo.

Avadenka, Edward-Judge, Michigan District Court District Forty-eight-Mich.

Avera, Fred E.-Judge, Oregon Circuit Court Twelfth Judicial District-Ore.

Averitte, Clinton E.-Magistrate Judge, United States District Court Northern District of Texas-Tex.

Avery, David J.-Judge, Allen Superior Court-Ind.

Avery, Emerson R., Jr.-Judge, Cortland County Court-N.Y.

Avery, Richard Moore, Jr.-Judge, Perry County District Court-Ala.

Avritt, James L.-Judge, Kentucky District Court Eleventh Judicial District-Ky.

Axel, Neil E.-Associate Judge, Maryland District Court District Ten-Md.

Axelrad, Francine I.-Judge, New Jersey Tax Court-N.J.

Axelrod, Sidney-Judge Referee, Connecticut Superior Court-Conn.

Axley, W. Fred-Judge, Tennessee Criminal Court Thirtieth Judicial District-Tenn.

Ayabe, Bert I.-Judge, Hawaii District Court First Judicial Circuit-Hi.

Ayala, Juan C.-Associate Judge, Juvenile Court of Georgia Eastern Judicial Circuit-Ga.

Aycock, E. Burt, Jr.-Emergency Judge, North Carolina District Court-N.C.

Aycock, Keith Byron-District Judge, Oklahoma District Court Fifth Judicial District-Okla.

Aycock, Sharion-Judge, Mississippi Circuit Court First Judicial District-Miss.

Ayers, Cynthia J.-Judge, Marion Superior Court-Ind.

Ayers, Mike-Judge, Kahlotus Municipal Court-Wash.

Aylsworth, Robert R.-Judge, Warrick Superior Court-Ind.

Azrack, Joan Marie-Magistrate Judge, United States District Court Eastern District of New York-N.Y.

Babb, Linda H.-Judge, Florida Circuit Court Sixth Judicial Circuit-Fla.

Babb, Rhonda E.-Judge, Brevard County Court-Fla.

ALPHABETICAL NAME INDEX

Babcock, Lewis T.-Chief Judge, United States District Court District of Colorado-Colo.

Baber, Mark A.-Judge, New Jersey Superior Court Vicinage Six-N.J.

Babiarz, John E., Jr.-Associate Judge, Delaware Superior Court New Castle County-Del.

Babler, James C.-Judge, Wisconsin Circuit Court Barron Circuit-Wis.

Baca, Anna M.-Judge, Superior Court of Arizona Maricopa County-Ariz.

Baca, José J.-Judge, El Paso County Court at Law No. 7-Tex.

Baca, Marie A.-Judge, New Mexico District Court Second Judicial District-N.Mex.

Baca, Ted-Judge, New Mexico District Court Second Judicial District-N.Mex.

Baca, Theresa M.-Judge, New Mexico District Court Second Judicial District-N.Mex.

Bach, Mercedes A.-Judge, Dade County Court-Fla.

Bacharach, Robert-Magistrate Judge, United States District Court Western District of Oklahoma-Okla.

Bachman, L. Kent-Judge, Utah Juvenile Court Second Judicial District-Utah

Bachner, Monica-Judge, Superior Court of California County of Los Angeles-Calif.

Bacigalupo, Paul A.-Judge, Superior Court of California County of Los Angeles-Calif.

Back, Brian John-Judge, Superior Court of California County of Ventura-Calif.

Backes, Norman J.-Presiding Judge, North Dakota District Court East Central Judicial District-N.D.

Backlund, John C.-Judge, Utah District Court Fourth Judicial District-Utah

Backman, Paul L.-Judge, Florida Circuit Court Seventeenth Judicial Circuit-Fla.

Bacon, Max E.-Associate Circuit Judge, Missouri Circuit Court Thirty-first Judicial Circuit-Mo.

Bacus, Thomas Hays-Judge, Wichita County Court at Law No. 2-Tex.

Bade, Bruce C.-Judge, Blackford Circuit Court-Ind.

Badeaux, Reginald T., III-Judge, Louisiana District Court Twenty-second Judicial District-La.

Badger, Barbara Jean-Associate Judge, Illinois Circuit Court Twelfth Judicial Circuit-Ill.

Baer, Harold, Jr.-Judge, United States District Court Southern District of New York-N.Y.

Baer, Max-Judge, Pennsylvania Court of Common Pleas Fifth Judicial District-Pa.

Baety, Edward L.-Chief Judge, City Court of Atlanta-Ga.

Bagley, Jeffrey S.-Judge, Superior Court of Georgia Bell-Forsyth Judicial Circuit-Ga.

Bagley, Jerald-Judge, Florida Circuit Court Eleventh Judicial Circuit-Fla.

Bagneris, Dennis Raymond, Sr.-Judge, Louisiana Court of Appeal Fourth Circuit-La.

Bagneris, Michael G.-Judge, Louisiana District Court Orleans Parish Civil District-La.

Bahakel, Alfred-Judge, Alabama Circuit Court Tenth Judicial Circuit Birmingham Division-Ala.

Bahakel, Gloria T.-Judge, Alabama Circuit Court Tenth Judicial Circuit Birmingham Division-Ala.

Bahakel, S. Phillip-Judge, Jefferson County District Court Birmingham Division-Ala.

Bail, Deborah A.-Judge, Idaho District Court Fourth Judicial District-Ida.

Bailey, Amanda-Judge, Colorado District Court Twenty-first Judicial District-Colo.

Bailey, D'Army-Judge, Tennessee Circuit Court Thirtieth Judicial District-Tenn.

Bailey, Jennifer D.-Judge, Florida Circuit Court Eleventh Judicial Circuit-Fla.

Bailey, Jim-Justice, Ravalli County Justice of the Peace Court-Mont.

Bailey, John H., Jr.-Chief Judge, Superior Court of Georgia Northern Judicial Circuit-Ga.

Bailey, Kris D.-Judge, North Carolina District Court District 10-N.C.

Bailey, L. Mark-Judge, Indiana Court of Appeals First District-Ind.

Bailey, Nelson-Judge, Palm Beach County Court-Fla.

Bailey, Robert-Judge, Mississippi Circuit Court Tenth Judicial District-Miss.

Bailey, Sarah P.-Emergency Judge, North Carolina District Court-N.C.

Bailey, Terry Douglas-Judge, Panola County Court at Law-Tex.

Bailin, Roxanne-Chief Judge, Colorado District Court Twentieth Judicial District-Colo.

Baily-Schiffman, Loren-Judge, The Civil Court of the City of New York-N.Y.

Baime, David S.-Retired Judge, New Jersey Superior Court Appellate Division-N.J.

Bain, Dorothy L.-Judge, Wisconsin Circuit Court Marathon Circuit-Wis.

Baines, Robert A.-Judge, Superior Court of California County of Santa Clara-Calif.

Baird, Laura-Judge, Michigan Circuit Court Thirtieth Judicial Circuit-Mich.

Baird, Lourdes G.-Judge, United States District Court Central District of California-Calif.

Baird, Michael P.-Chief Magistrate, Magistrate Court of Clayton County-Ga.

Baird, William Douglas-Judge, Florida Circuit Court Sixth Judicial Circuit-Fla.

Baird, William R.-Judge, Ohio Court of Appeals Ninth District-Ohio

Baisinger, Glen D.-Judge, Oregon Circuit Court Twenty-third Judicial District-Ore.

Baisley, Paul J., Jr.-Justice, New York Supreme Court Tenth Judicial District-N.Y.

Bajorek, David A.-Chief Judge, Michigan District Court District Twenty-five-Mich.

Bakalis, George J.-Circuit Judge, Illinois Circuit Court Eighteenth Judicial Circuit-Ill.

Bakarich, Gerald S. "Jerry"-Judge, Superior Court of California County of Sacramento-Calif.

Baker, Andrew C.-Judge, Mississippi Circuit Court Seventeenth Judicial District-Miss.

Baker, Carl D.-District Judge, Iowa District Court Second Judicial District-Ia.

Baker, Caroline E.-Judge, Texas District Court 151st Judicial District-Tex.

Baker, David A.-Magistrate Judge, United States District Court Middle District of Florida-Fla.

Baker, David M.-Presiding Judge, West Virginia Court of Claims-W.Va.

Baker, Dorothy-Judge, Oregon Circuit Court Fourth Judicial District-Ore.

Baker, Evelyn M.-Circuit Judge, Missouri Circuit Court Twenty-second Judicial Circuit-Mo.

Baker, Franklin G.-Judge, Florida Circuit Court Twentieth Judicial Circuit-Fla.

Baker, Garrison-Judge, Probate Court of White County-Ga.

Baker, Harold Albert-Senior Judge, United States District Court Central District of Illinois-Ill.

Baker, Henry A.-Judge, Probate Court of Newton County and Chief Magistrate, Magistrate Court of Newton County-Ga.

Baker, James Edgar-Associate Judge, United States Court of Appeals for the Armed Forces

Baker, James L., Jr.-Resident Judge, North Carolina Superior Court Eighth Judicial Division District 24-N.C.

Baker, James T.-Judge, Probate Court of Douglas County-Ga.

Baker, John Gatch-Judge, Indiana Court of Appeals First District-Ind.

Baker, Karen-Judge, Arkansas Court of Appeals-Ark.

Baker, Larry O.-Circuit Judge, Illinois Circuit Court Second Judicial Circuit-Ill.

Baker, Lee F.-Judge, Pike Circuit Court-Ind.

Baker, Matthew J.-Judge, Kentucky Court of Appeals-Ky.

Baker, Max A.-Judge, New Jersey Superior Court Vicinage One-N.J.

Baker, Moses, Jr.-Judge, Florida Circuit Court Fifteenth Judicial Circuit-Fla.

Baker, Nannette A.-Circuit Judge, Missouri Circuit Court Twenty-second Judicial Circuit-Mo.

Baker, Rebecca M.-Judge, Washington Superior Court Ferry-Pend Oreille-Stevens Counties-Wash.

Baker, Reginald H.-Associate Judge, Illinois Circuit Court of Cook County-Ill.

Baker, Robert M.-Judge, Limestone County District Court-Ala.

Baker, Stephen J.-Associate Judge, Maryland District Court District Three-Md.

Baker, Thomas F.-Associate Judge, Illinois Circuit Court Nineteenth Judicial Circuit-Ill.

Baker, Tim A.-Magistrate Judge, United States District Court Southern District of Indiana-Ind.

Baker, Valerie L.-Judge, Superior Court of California County of Los Angeles-Calif.

Baker, William W.-Judge, Washington Court of Appeals Division I-Wash.

Baland, Timothy James-Judge, Minnesota District Court Seventh Judicial District-Minn.

Balbick, Robert J.-Judge, Batavia City Court-N.Y.

Baldock, Bobby R.-Senior Judge, United States Court of Appeals Tenth Circuit

Baldoni, Paul J.-Judge, La Porte Superior Court-Ind.

Baldwin, Cynthia A.-Judge, Pennsylvania Court of Common Pleas Fifth Judicial District-Pa.

Baldwin, Marc M.-Judge, New Jersey Superior Court Vicinage Three-N.J.

Baldwin, Maurice W., Jr.-Associate Judge, Circuit Court for Harford County, Third Judicial Circuit-Md.

Baldwin, Parley R.-Judge, Utah District Court Second Judicial District-Utah

Baldwin, Quillian, Jr.-Judge, Superior Court of Georgia Coweta Judicial Circuit-Ga.

Baldwin, Richard C.-Judge, Oregon Circuit Court Fourth Judicial District-Ore.

Baldwin, Thayer, Jr.-Judge, Connecticut Superior Court-Conn.

Baldwin, William E.-President Judge, Pennsylvania Court of Common Pleas Twenty-first Judicial District-Pa.

Baler, Gregory R.-Justice, Trial Court of Massachusetts District Court Department Norfolk County Quincy Division-Mass.

Balestri, William P.-Associate Judge, Illinois Circuit Court Thirteenth Judicial Circuit-Ill.

Balivet, Ernest T.-Judge, Caledonia District Probate Court-Vt.

Balkin, Ruth C.-Judge, Nassau County Family Court-N.Y.

Ball, Carol S.-Associate Justice, Trial Court of Massachusetts Superior Court Department-Mass.

Ball, Richard D.-Chief Judge, Michigan District Court District Fifty-four B-Mich.

Ball, Sanborn N.-Associate Circuit Judge, Missouri Circuit Court Forty-second Judicial Circuit-Mo.

Ball, Thomas H.-Magistrate Judge, Kansas District Court Eighth Judicial District-Kan.

Ballance, Garey M.-Judge, North Carolina District Court District 9-N.C.

Ballard, Mark J.-Associate Judge, Illinois Circuit Court of Cook County-Ill.

Ballati, David Louis-Judge, Superior Court of California City and County of San Francisco-Calif.

Ballen, Myron R.-Judge Referee, Connecticut Superior Court-Conn.

Ballinger, Eddward, Jr.-Judge, Superior Court of Arizona Maricopa County-Ariz.

Ballinger, Raima H.-Judge, Superior Court of California County of Sonoma-Calif.

Ballinger, Richard T.-Chief Judge, Kansas District Court Eighteenth Judicial District-Kan.

Ballou, Dan-Judge, Kentucky District Court Thirty-fourth Judicial District-Ky.

Ballou-Watts, Vicki-Associate Judge, Circuit Court for Baltimore County, Third Judicial Circuit-Md.

Balmer, Thomas A.-Justice, Oregon Supreme Court-Ore.

Balog, Steve A.-Special Judge, North Carolina Superior Court-N.C.

Balter, Bruce M.-Judge, The Civil Court of the City of New York-N.Y.

Baltimore, Joseph N.-Judge, Michigan District Court District Thirty-six-Mich.

Balzano, John S.-Judge, Utica City Court-N.Y.

Bamattre-Manoukian, Patricia-Associate Justice, California Court of Appeal Sixth District-Calif.

Bamberger, Joseph F.-Judge, Kentucky Circuit Court Fifty-fourth Judicial Circuit-Ky.

Bamberger, Phylis S.-Judge, New York Court of Claims-N.Y.

Bamberger, Thomas E.-Associate Justice, Nashua District Court-N.H.

ALPHABETICAL NAME INDEX

Banales, J. Manuel-Judge, Texas District Court 105th Judicial District-Tex.

Bandstra, Richard A.-Judge, Michigan Court of Appeals-Mich.

Bandstra, Ted E.-Magistrate Judge, United States District Court Southern District of Florida-Fla.

Banich, William R.-Associate Judge, Illinois Circuit Court Thirteenth Judicial Circuit-Ill.

Banina, Daniel C.-Judge, Miami Superior Court-Ind.

Banke, Karlton Van-Judge, Juvenile Court of Georgia Clayton Judicial Circuit-Ga.

Banks, Andrew P.-Judge, Superior Court of California County of Orange-Calif.

Banks, Henry D.-Chief Magistrate, Magistrate Court of Banks County-Ga.

Banks, J. Henry-Judge, North Carolina District Court District 9-N.C.

Banks, Julian D.-Judge, Alabama Circuit Court Thirteenth Judicial Circuit-Ala.

Banks, Patricia-Circuit Judge, Illinois Circuit Court of Cook County-Ill.

Banks, Rufus A., Jr.-Chief Judge, Virginia Juvenile and Domestic Relations District Court First Judicial District-Va.

Bankston, Michael-Judge, State Court of Mitchell County-Ga.

Bannister, Richard J.-Judge, Vandalia Municipal Court-Ohio

Bantz, Linda F.-Chief Magistrate, Magistrate Court of Randolph County-Ga.

Barajas, Johnny C.-Judge, Denver County Court-Colo.

Barajas, Richard-Chief Justice, Texas Court of Appeals Eighth District-Tex.

Barall, Herbert-Judge Referee, Connecticut Superior Court-Conn.

Baranco, Gordon S.-Judge, Superior Court of California County of Alameda-Calif.

Barasch, Melvin S.-Justice, New York Supreme Court Second Judicial District-N.Y.

Baratta, Stephen G.-Judge, Pennsylvania Court of Common Pleas Third Judicial District-Pa.

Barbadoro, Paul J.-Chief Judge, United States District Court District of New Hampshire-N.H.

Barbalunga, Alfred A.-First Justice, Trial Court of Massachusetts District Court Department Berkshire County Pittsfield Division-Mass.

Barbaro, Frank J.-Justice, New York Supreme Court Second Judicial District-N.Y.

Barbas, Rex-Judge, Florida Circuit Court Thirteenth Judicial Circuit-Fla.

Barbee, Mills-Judge, DeSoto County Court-Miss.

Barber, Alan M.-Judge, Winchester District Probate Court-Conn.

Barber, Catherine M.-Judge, Fairborn Municipal Court-Ohio

Barber, David-Judge, Kentucky Court of Appeals-Ky.

Barber, Herman L., Jr.-Judge, Crown Point City Court-Ind.

Barber, James E.-Judge, Ohio Court of Common Pleas Fulton County-Ohio

Barber, James R., III-Judge-at-Large, South Carolina Circuit Court-S.C.

Barber, Jesse C.-Senior Judge, Polk County Court-Fla.

Barber, Richard D.-Judge, Oregon Circuit Court Third Judicial District-Ore.

Barber, Wade, Jr.-Resident Judge, North Carolina Superior Court Third Judicial Division District 15B-N.C.

Barbera, Jerome J., III-Judge, Louisiana District Court Seventeenth Judicial District-La.

Barbera, Mary Ellen-Associate Judge, Court of Special Appeals of Maryland-Md.

Barbier, Carl J.-Judge, United States District Court Eastern District of Louisiana-La.

Barbosa, Manuel-Judge, United States Bankruptcy Court Northern District of Illinois-Ill.

Barbour, William H., Jr.-Judge, United States District Court Southern District of Mississippi-Miss.

Barclay, Elise D.-Judge, Jefferson County District Court Birmingham Division-Ala.

Barcus, Marc-Special Judge, Oklahoma District Court Fourteenth Judicial District-Okla.

Bardach, Gail Z.-Judge, Carmel City Court-Ind.

Barden, Jim-Judge, Medina County Court-Tex.

Barefoot, N. Vince-Associate District Judge, Oklahoma District Court Fourth Judicial District-Okla.

Barefoot, Napoleon B., Sr.-Emergency Judge, North Carolina Superior Court-N.C.

Barefoot, Napoleon Bonaparte, Jr.-Judge, North Carolina District Court District 13-N.C.

Barela, Henry T.-Judge, Superior Court of California County of Los Angeles-Calif.

Barfield, Edward T.-Judge, Florida District Court of Appeal First District-Fla.

Barfield, W. Leon-Magistrate Judge, United States District Court Southern District of Georgia-Ga.

Barger, Gary D.-Special Judge, Oklahoma District Court Twenty-first Judicial District-Okla.

Barglind, Mary Brouillette-Chief Judge, Michigan Circuit Court Forty-first Judicial Circuit-Mich.

Barina, Harry John, Jr.-Judge, Bell County Court at Law No. 2-Tex.

Barisonek, Walter R.-Judge, New Jersey Superior Court Vicinage Twelve-N.J.

Barkdull, Thomas H., III-Judge, Florida Circuit Court Fifteenth Judicial Circuit-Fla.

Barker, Daniel A.-Judge, Arizona Court of Appeals Division One-Ariz.

Barker, Jeffrey-Judge, East Wenatchee Municipal Court-Wash.

Barker, John E.-Magistrate Judge, Kansas District Court Eighth Judicial District-Kan.

Barker, Phil-Judge, Dallas County Criminal Court at Law No. 6-Tex.

Barker, S. H.-Chief Magistrate, Magistrate Court of Berrien County-Ga.

Barker, Sarah Evans-Judge, United States District Court Southern District of Indiana-Ind.

Barker, William M. "Mickey"-Associate Justice, Tennessee Supreme Court-Tenn.

Barkett, Rosemary-Judge, United States Court of Appeals Eleventh Circuit

Barkley, William G.-Judge, Virginia General District Court Sixteenth Judicial District-Va.

Barksdale, Rhesa H.-Judge, United States Court of Appeals Fifth Circuit

Barland, Thomas H.-Reserve Judge, Wisconsin Circuit Court-Wis.

Barlow, Glenn-Judge, Mississippi Chancery Court Sixteenth Judicial District-Miss.

Barlow, T. Mitchell-Judge, Florida Circuit Court Eighteenth Judicial Circuit-Fla.

Barnard, Geoffrey W.-Magistrate Judge, United States District Court District of the Virgin Islands

Barnard, J. Myron-Judge, Marion County Small Claims Court Perry Township Division-Ind.

Barnard, Laura Cheger-Judge, Michigan District Court District Seventy-one A-Mich.

Barnes, Anne Elizabeth-Judge, Court of Appeals of Georgia-Ga.

Barnes, Donald-Presiding Judge, Missouri Circuit Court Eighteenth Judicial Circuit-Mo.

Barnes, Edgar L.-Judge, North Carolina District Court District 1-N.C.

Barnes, Harry F.-Judge, United States District Court Western District of Arkansas-Ark.

Barnes, Margaret-Judge, Denton County Court at Law No. 2-Tex.

Barnes, Michael P.-Judge, Indiana Court of Appeals Third District-Ind.

Barnes, Rowland W.-Judge, Superior Court of Georgia Atlanta Judicial Circuit-Ga.

Barnes, Vicki-Judge, Mississippi Chancery Court Ninth Judicial District-Miss.

Barnet, Robert L., Jr.-Judge, Delaware Circuit Court-Ind.

Barnett, Bill-Judge, Hinds County Court-Miss.

Barnett, David A.-Associate District Judge, Oklahoma District Court Third Judicial District-Okla.

Barnett, Suzanne M.-Judge, Washington Superior Court King County-Wash.

Barnette, Henry V., Jr.-Emergency Judge, North Carolina Superior Court-N.C.

Barney, Robert S.-Judge, Missouri Court of Appeals Southern District-Mo.

Barnum, Kenneth Paul-Judge, Superior Court of California County of Santa Clara-Calif.

Barnwell, Jon M.-Judge, Mississippi Chancery Court Seventh Judicial District-Miss.

Baron, Jean Szekeres-Associate Judge, Maryland District Court District Five-Md.

Baron, Robert J.-Associate Judge, Illinois Circuit Court Twelfth Judicial Circuit-Ill.

Barone, John A.-Justice, New York Supreme Court Twelfth Judicial District-N.Y.

Barone, Louis A.-Justice, New York Supreme Court Ninth Judicial District-N.Y.

Baronzzi, Thomas M.-Judge, Ohio Court of Common Pleas Columbiana County-Ohio

Barr, James N.-Judge, United States Bankruptcy Court Central District of California-Calif.

Barr, Jeannine S.-Judge, Texas District Court 182nd Judicial District-Tex.

Barr, Jerry M.-Judge, Hamilton Superior Court-Ind.

Barr, Kenneth-Judge, Superior Court of California County of San Bernardino-Calif.

Barr, Robert W.-Judge, Alabama Circuit Court Twelfth Judicial Circuit-Ala.

Barra, John A.-Chief Judge, Illinois Circuit Court Tenth Judicial Circuit-Ill.

Barrasse, Michael J.-Judge, Pennsylvania Court of Common Pleas Forty-fifth Judicial District-Pa.

Barreto, Antonio, Jr.-Judge, Superior Court of California County of Los Angeles-Calif.

Barrett, David Eugene-Judge, Superior Court of Georgia Enotah Judicial Circuit-Ga.

Barrett, John W.-Senior Judge, Nevada District Court-Nev.

Barrett, Lawrence E.-Judge, Nebraska County Court Fourth Judicial District-Neb.

Barrett, R. Stephen-Judge, Pennsylvania Court of Common Pleas Thirty-eighth Judicial District-Pa.

Barrett, Steven L.-Judge, The Criminal Court of the City of New York-N.Y.

Barrett, Thang Nguyen-Judge, Superior Court of California County of Santa Clara-Calif.

Barrett, Thomas S.-Justice, Trial Court of Massachusetts District Court Department Bristol County Attleboro Division-Mass.

Barrett, William W.-Judge, Utah District Court Third Judicial District-Utah

Barron, G. Robert-Judge, Florida Circuit Court First Judicial Circuit-Fla.

Barron, Michael J.-Reserve Judge, Wisconsin Circuit Court-Wis.

Barron, Patricia D.-Chief Magistrate, Magistrate Court of Clarke County-Ga.

Barron, Richard L.-Presiding Judge, Oregon Circuit Court Fifteenth Judicial District-Ore.

Barros, Betsy-Justice, New York Supreme Court Second Judicial District-N.Y.

Barry, David M.-Judge Referee, Connecticut Superior Court-Conn.

Barry, David Michael-Justice, New York Supreme Court Seventh Judicial District-N.Y.

Barry, Dennis J.-Judge, Wisconsin Circuit Court Racine Circuit-Wis.

Barry, James J., Jr.-Associate Justice, New Hampshire Superior Court-N.H.

Barry, John O'Keefe-Judge, Collin County Court at Law No. 3-Tex.

Barry, Kathleen Sendley-Judge, Plainfield District Probate Court-Conn.

Barry, Maryanne Trump-Judge, United States Court of Appeals Third Circuit

Barry, Thomas T.-Special Justice, Hillsborough District Court-N.H.

Barry, Tobias "Toby"-Judge, Illinois Appellate Court Third Judicial District-Ill.

Barry, William P.-Judge, Superior Court of California County of Los Angeles-Calif.

Barstow, Jeffrey G.-Chief Judge, Michigan District Court District Ninety-five A-Mich.

Barta, James J.-Chief Judge, United States Bankruptcy Court Eastern District of Missouri-Mo.

Bartell, Angela Gina Baldi-Judge, Wisconsin Circuit Court Dane Circuit-Wis.

Bartheld, Thomas M.-Associate District Judge, Oklahoma District Court Eighteenth Judicial District-Okla.

Bartholomew, John G.-Reserve Judge, Wisconsin Circuit Court-Wis.

Bartholomew, Judith-Judge, Kentucky District Court Thirtieth Judicial District-Ky.

Bartkowicz, Ronald F.-Circuit Judge, Illinois Circuit Court of Cook County-Ill.

Bartle, Harvey, III-Judge, United States District Court Eastern District of Pennsylvania-Pa.

ALPHABETICAL NAME INDEX

Bartles, William P.-Judge, Juvenile Court of Georgia Flint Judicial Circuit-Ga.

Bartlett, Ann Reynolds-Judge, New Jersey Superior Court Vicinage Thirteen-N.J.

Bartlett, George R., III-Judge, Schoharie County Court-N.Y.

Bartlett, Gregory-Judge, Kentucky Circuit Court Sixteenth Judicial Circuit-Ky.

Bartlett, Randolph A.-Associate Presiding Judge, Superior Court of Arizona Mohave County-Ariz.

Bartlett, Stephen S.-Judge, South Carolina Family Court Thirteenth Judicial Circuit-S.C.

Bartley, A. Kirke, Jr.-Judge, The Criminal Court of the City of New York-N.Y.

Bartnoff, Judith-Associate Judge, Superior Court of the District of Columbia-D.C.

Barton, Charles M.-Judge, Colorado District Court Eleventh Judicial District-Colo.

Barton, James, III-Judge, Florida Circuit Court Thirteenth Judicial Circuit-Fla.

Barton, Janet-Judge, Superior Court of Arizona Maricopa County-Ariz.

Barton, Jeffrey-Judge, Superior Court of California County of San Diego-Calif.

Barton, Kevin-Judge, Johnson Superior Court-Ind.

Barton, M. L.-Judge, Hudson Municipal Court-Wyo.

Barton, Michael Einum-Judge, Superior Court of California County of Santa Cruz-Calif.

Barton, Patrick J.-Judge, Suffolk County District Court-N.Y.

Barton, Timothy L.-Chief Magistrate, Magistrate Court of Glynn County-Ga.

Barwick, Tripp-Judge, Probate Court of Decatur County-Ga.

Barz, Diane G.-Judge, Montana District Court Thirteenth Judicial District-Mont.

Barzee, Mary R.-Judge, Florida Circuit Court Eleventh Judicial Circuit-Fla.

Barzilay, Judith M.-Judge, United States Court of International Trade

Baschab, Pamela Willis-Judge, Alabama Court of Criminal Appeals-Ala.

Bascue, James Allen-Judge, Superior Court of California County of Los Angeles-Calif.

Bashant, Cynthia Ann-Judge, Superior Court of California County of San Diego-Calif.

Basinger, Randall L.-Judge, Ohio Court of Common Pleas Putnam County-Ohio

Basinski, David A.-Judge, Ohio Court of Common Pleas Lorain County-Ohio

Baskervill, Pamela S.-Judge, Virginia Circuit Court Eleventh Judicial Circuit-Va.

Baskfield, Allison Krehbiel-Judge, Minnesota District Court Fifth Judicial District-Minn.

Baskin, Barry-Judge, Superior Court of California County of Contra Costa-Calif.

Baskir, Lawrence M.-Judge, United States Court of Federal Claims

Bass, H. Gary-Associate Judge, Maryland District Court District One-Md.

Bass, J. Martin-Judge, Virginia Juvenile and Domestic Relations District Court Fifteenth Judicial District-Va.

Bass, James F., Jr.-Judge, Superior Court of Georgia Eastern Judicial Circuit-Ga.

Bass, Jerry D.-District Judge, Oklahoma District Court Seventh Judicial District-Okla.

Bass, John W., Sr.-Judge, State Court of Grady County-Ga.

Bass-Jones, Tammy-District Judge, Oklahoma District Court Seventh Judicial District-Okla.

Bassick, Edgar W., III-Judge Referee, Connecticut Superior Court-Conn.

Bassler, William G.-Judge, United States District Court District of New Jersey-N.J.

Bastian, Gary W.-Judge, Minnesota District Court Second Judicial District-Minn.

Bastian, John-Judge, South Dakota Circuit Court Fourth Judicial Circuit-S.D.

Bastianelli, David Mark-Judge, Wisconsin Circuit Court Kenosha Circuit-Wis.

Bastine, Paul A.-Judge, Washington Superior Court Spokane County-Wash.

Bastone, Robert P.-Associate Judge, Illinois Circuit Court of Cook County-Ill.

Bataillon, Joseph F.-Judge, United States District Court District of Nebraska-Neb.

Bataillon, Peter C.-Judge, Nebraska District Court Fourth Judicial District-Neb.

Batchelder, Alice M.-Judge, United States Court of Appeals Sixth Circuit

Batchelder, Joanne-Assistant Judge, Vermont Trial Court Lamoille County-Vt.

Batchelder, William G.-Judge, Ohio Court of Appeals Ninth District-Ohio

Batchik, Michael-Judge, Michigan District Court District Fifty-two Division One-Mich.

Bateman, Thomas H., III-Judge, Florida Circuit Court Second Judicial Circuit-Fla.

Bates, James D.-Judge, Ohio Court of Common Pleas Lucas County-Ohio

Bates, John D.-Judge, United States District Court District of Columbia-D.C.

Bates, Kay-Judge, Louisiana District Court Nineteenth Judicial District-La.

Bates, Stephen L.-Judge, Kentucky Circuit Court Fifteenth Judicial Circuit-Ky.

Bathum, Rick-Judge, King District Court South Division King County-Wash.

Batiste, Alvin, Jr.-Judge, Louisiana District Court Eighteenth Judicial District-La.

Batt, John F.-Judge, Niagara County Family Court-N.Y.

Battaglia, Anthony J.-Magistrate Judge, United States District Court Southern District of California-Calif.

Battaglia, Jack M.-Judge, The Civil Court of the City of New York-N.Y.

Battaglia, Lynne A.-Associate Judge, Court of Appeals of Maryland-Md.

Battani, Marianne O.-Judge, United States District Court Eastern District of Michigan-Mich.

Batten, Raymond A.-Judge, New Jersey Superior Court Vicinage One-N.J.

Battershell, John J.-Judge, Nebraska District Court Eleventh Judicial District-Neb.

Battey, David R.-Judge, Minnesota District Court Seventh Judicial District-Minn.

Battey, Richard H.-Senior Judge, United States District Court District of South Dakota-S.D.

Battle, Joseph L.-Judge, Alabama Circuit Court Twenty-third Judicial Circuit-Ala.

Battles, Emmett Lamar-Judge, Florida Circuit Court Thirteenth Judicial Circuit-Fla.

Batton, Robert-Judge, Jacksonville District Court-Ark.

Batts, Deborah A.-Judge, United States District Court Southern District of New York-N.Y.

Batzer, James M.-Chief Judge, Michigan Circuit Court Nineteenth Judicial Circuit-Mich.

Bauch, James C.-District Judge, Iowa District Court First Judicial District-Ia.

Bauer, Charles W.-Judge, Burlington District Probate Court-Conn.

Bauer, Daniel J.-Judge, Fernley Municipal Court-Nev.

Bauer, Henry R.-Judge, Troy City Court-N.Y.

Bauer, Ronald L.-Judge, Superior Court of California County of Orange-Calif.

Bauer, Thomas G.-Judge, Lawrenceburg City Court-Ind.

Bauer, William J.-Senior Judge, United States Court of Appeals Seventh Circuit

Bauercamper, John J.-District Judge, Iowa District Court First Judicial District-Ia.

Baugh, G. Todd-Judge, Montana District Court Thirteenth Judicial District-Mont.

Baughman, William H., Jr.-Magistrate Judge, United States District Court Northern District of Ohio-Ohio

Baum, Redfield T., Sr.-Judge, United States Bankruptcy Court District of Arizona-Ariz.

Baumann, Herbert, Jr.-Judge, Florida Circuit Court Thirteenth Judicial Circuit-Fla.

Baumgartner, Michael J.-Chief Judge, Michigan Circuit Court Thirty-fourth Judicial Circuit-Mich.

Baumgartner, Nancy A.-District Associate Judge, Iowa District Court Sixth Judicial District-Ia.

Baumgartner, Richard R.-Judge, Tennessee Criminal Court Sixth Judicial District-Tenn.

Bautista, Diana-Judge, Atascosa County Court-Tex.

Baverman, Alan J.-Magistrate Judge, United States District Court Northern District of Georgia-Ga.

Baxley, John Michael-Judge, South Carolina Circuit Court Fourth Judicial Circuit-S.C.

Baxley, Thomas H.-Judge, State Court of Early County-Ga.

Baxter, Floyd V.-Judge, Superior Court of California County of Los Angeles-Calif.

Baxter, Gregory L.-Presiding Judge, Oregon Circuit Court Eighth Judicial District-Ore.

Baxter, James Thomas-Judge, Alabama Circuit Court First Judicial Circuit-Ala.

Baxter, Jerry W.-Judge, Superior Court of Georgia Atlanta Judicial Circuit-Ga.

Baxter, Linda G.-Judge, New Jersey Superior Court Vicinage Four-N.J.

Baxter, Marvin R.-Associate Justice, California Supreme Court-Calif.

Baxter, Randolph-Judge, Bankruptcy Appellate Panel Sixth Circuit and Judge, United States Bankruptcy Court Northern District of Ohio-Ohio

Baxter, Susan Paradise-Magistrate Judge, United States District Court Western District of Pennsylvania-Pa.

Baxter, Wendy M.-Judge, Michigan Circuit Court Third Judicial Circuit-Mich.

Bayless, H. Jeffrey-Chief Judge, Colorado District Court Second Judicial District-Colo.

Bayley, Edgar B.-Judge, Pennsylvania Court of Common Pleas Ninth Judicial District-Pa.

Baylor, Robert E.-Justice, Trial Court of Massachusetts District Court Department Plymouth County Brockton Division-Mass.

Baylson, Michael M.-Judge, United States District Court Eastern District of Pennsylvania-Pa.

Bayly, John H., Jr.-Associate Judge, Superior Court of the District of Columbia-D.C.

Bayne, Bernadette-Judge, The Civil Court of the City of New York-N.Y.

Baynes, Thomas E.-Chief Judge, United States Bankruptcy Court Middle District of Florida-Fla.

Bayneum, Joann-Chief Magistrate, Magistrate Court of Fulton County-Ga.

Bayorgeon, James T.-Judge, Wisconsin Circuit Court Outagamie Circuit-Wis.

Baysinger, Robert F.-Judge, Superior Court of California County of San Joaquin-Calif.

Bea, Carlos-Judge, Superior Court of California City and County of San Francisco-Calif.

Beach, Harry A.-Judge, Michigan Circuit Court Forty-eighth Judicial Circuit-Mich.

Beach, Marcia-Judge, Florida Circuit Court Seventeenth Judicial Circuit-Fla.

Beach, Robert E.-Senior Judge, Florida Circuit Court Sixth Judicial Circuit-Fla.

Beach, Robert E., Jr.-Judge, Connecticut Superior Court-Conn.

Beacham, G. Rand-Judge, Utah District Court Fifth Judicial District-Utah

Beachley, Donald E.-Associate Judge, Circuit Court for Washington County, Fourth Judicial Circuit-Md.

Beacom, Richard-Judge, Texas District Court 354th Judicial District-Tex.

Beagle, Duncan M.-Judge, Michigan Circuit Court Seventh Judicial Circuit-Mich.

Beaird, Hugh-Presiding Judge, Alabama Circuit Court Fourteenth Judicial Circuit-Ala.

Beaird, Robert-Associate Circuit Judge, Missouri Circuit Court Sixteenth Judicial Circuit-Mo.

Beal, Beverly Tate-Resident Judge, North Carolina Superior Court Seventh Judicial Division District 25A-N.C.

Beale, Michael Earle-Resident Judge, North Carolina Superior Court Sixth Judicial Division District 20A-N.C.

Beam, Clarence Arlen-Senior Judge, United States Court of Appeals Eighth Circuit

Beam, John W., Jr.-Judge, Juvenile Court of Georgia Eastern Judicial Circuit-Ga.

Beaman, Grafton G.-Chief Judge, North Carolina District Court District 1-N.C.

Beaman, William C.-Magistrate Judge, United States District Court District of Wyoming-Wyo.

Bean, C. Christopher-Judge, North Carolina District Court District 1-N.C.

Bean, James Roy-Chief Judge, Florida Circuit Court Third Judicial Circuit-Fla.

Beard, David H.-Emergency Judge, North Carolina Superior Court-N.C.

ALPHABETICAL NAME INDEX

Beard, DeLawrence-Associate Judge, Circuit Court for Montgomery County, Sixth Judicial Circuit-Md.
Beard, Val Clark-Judge, Brewster County Court-Tex.
Bearden, D. Larry-Chief Magistrate, Magistrate Court of Grady County-Ga.
Bearden, Frank L.-Judge, Oregon Circuit Court Fourth Judicial District-Ore.
Bearden, J. Lane-Judge, Juvenile Court of Georgia Cherokee Judicial Circuit-Ga.
Bearden, Jerry M.-Judge, Mason County Court-Tex.
Bearden, Judith-Judge, Marion County District Court-Ark.
Bearden, Mary Ann-Presiding Judge, Oregon Circuit Court Second Judicial District-Ore.
Bearse, Edward W.-Judge, Minnesota District Court Tenth Judicial District-Minn.
Beasley, Charles Elliot-Judge, Probate Court of Candler County-Ga.
Beasley, Cheri L.-Judge, North Carolina District Court District 12-N.C.
Beasley, Dorothy Toth-Senior Judge, Court of Appeals of Georgia-Ga.
Beasley, James C., Jr.-Judge, Tennessee Criminal Court Thirtieth Judicial District-Tenn.
Beasley, Stephen B.-Judge, Louisiana District Court Eleventh Judicial District-La.
Beason, Candace J.-Judge, Superior Court of California County of Los Angeles-Calif.
Beaton, John M.-Associate Circuit Judge, Missouri Circuit Court Thirty-fifth Judicial Circuit-Mo.
Beattie, Philip A.-Circuit Justice, Trial Court of Massachusetts District Court Department-Mass.
Beatty, Donald W.-Associate Judge, South Carolina Court of Appeals-S.C.
Beatty, Joseph F.-Circuit Judge, Illinois Circuit Court Fourteenth Judicial Circuit-Ill.
Beatty, Prudence Carter-Judge, United States Bankruptcy Court Southern District of New York-N.Y.
Beaty, James Arthur, Jr.-Judge, United States District Court Middle District of North Carolina-N.C.
Beauchesne, Roger M.-Judge, Superior Court of California County of Stanislaus-Calif.
Beaudin, Bruce D.-Senior Judge, Superior Court of the District of Columbia-D.C.
Beaudoin, Roland-Judge, Maine District Court-Me.
Beauregard, Rosemary B.-Associate Judge, Delaware Court of Common Pleas Sussex County-Del.
Beavers, Graten D.-Judge, Nebraska County Court Ninth Judicial District-Neb.
Beavers, Tonny S.-Judge, Superior Court of Georgia Paulding Judicial Circuit-Ga.
Beavers, Wm. Rex-Associate Circuit Judge, Missouri Circuit Court Fourth Judicial Circuit-Mo.
Bebb, Robert Steven-Judge, Tennessee Criminal Court Tenth Judicial District-Tenn.
Bechtold, Paula-Judge, Oregon Circuit Court Fifteenth Judicial District-Ore.
Beck, Barbara J.-Judge, Superior Court of California County of Santa Barbara-Calif.
Beck, Dan R.-Judge, Texas District Court 155th Judicial District-Tex.
Beck, Dennis L.-Magistrate Judge, United States District Court Eastern District of California-Calif.
Beck, G. Richard-Chief Judge, Virginia General District Court Eleventh Judicial District-Va.
Beck, R. Jerry-Judge, Tennessee Circuit Court Second Judicial District-Tenn.
Beck, Raymond E., Sr.-Associate Judge, Circuit Court for Carroll County, Fifth Judicial Circuit-Md.
Beck, Ronna L.-Associate Judge, Superior Court of the District of Columbia-D.C.
Beck, Susan S.-Associate Justice, Massachusetts Appeals Court-Mass.
Becker, Carl F.-Judge, Delaware County Court-N.Y.
Becker, Cynthia C.-Judge, Avon District Probate Court-Conn.
Becker, Cynthia J.-Judge, Superior Court of Georgia Stone Mountain Judicial Circuit-Ga.
Becker, Edward R.-Chief Judge, United States Court of Appeals Third Circuit
Becker, Louis A., III-Associate Judge, Maryland District Court District Ten-Md.
Becker, Mary Kay-Chief Judge, Washington Court of Appeals Division I-Wash.
Becker, Nancy A.-Justice, Nevada Supreme Court-Nev.
Becker, Richard T.-Reserve Judge, Wisconsin Circuit Court-Wis.
Becker, Steven R.-Chief Judge, Kansas District Court Twenty-seventh Judicial District-Kan.
Becker, William A.-Judge, Virginia Juvenile and Domestic Relations District Court Thirty-first Judicial District-Va.
Becker, William J.-Associate Judge, Illinois Circuit Court Fourth Judicial Circuit-Ill.
Becker-Painter, Ruth-Judge, Monroe County Court-Fla.
Beckham, Gail D.-Justice, Rosebud County Justice of the Peace Court-Mont.
Beckman, Charles T.-Associate Judge, Illinois Circuit Court Fifteenth Judicial Circuit-Ill.
Beckman, Douglas-Judge, Oregon Circuit Court Fourth Judicial District-Ore.
Beckner, James E.-Judge, Tennessee Criminal Court Third Judicial District-Tenn.
Beckstead, Kathleen Leonard-Associate Judge, Circuit Court for Wicomico County, First Judicial Circuit-Md.
Beckum, Peggy J.-Judge, Green River Municipal Court-Wyo.
Beckwith, Daniel J.-Judge, Nebraska County Court Sixth Judicial District-Neb.
Beckwith, Sandra S.-Judge, United States District Court Southern District of Ohio-Ohio
Becnel, Mary Hotard-Judge, Louisiana District Court Fortieth Judicial District-La.
Bedell, Thomas A.-Judge, West Virginia Circuit Court Fifteenth Judicial Circuit-W.Va.
Bedford, T. Jackson, Jr.-Judge, Superior Court of Georgia Atlanta Judicial Circuit-Ga.
Bednar, Mary E.-Judge, New York City Family Court-N.Y.
Bednar, Michael C.-Judge, Jefferson County Court-Ohio
Bednar, Robert J.-Judge, Kansas District Court First Judicial District-Kan.
Bednar, Wilburn E.-Judge, Glasscock County Court-Tex.
Bedoya, Consuelo E.-Associate Judge, Illinois Circuit Court of Cook County-Ill.
Bedrosian, Haiganush R.-Associate Justice, Rhode Island Family Court-R.I.
Bedsworth, William W.-Associate Justice, California Court of Appeal Fourth District Division Three-Calif.
Beebe, Mark-Judge, Idaho District Court Sixth Judicial District Magistrate Division-Ida.
Beeghly, James L.-District Judge, Iowa District Court First Judicial District-Ia.
Beeler, Harold B.-Judge, The Civil Court of the City of New York-N.Y.
Beeman, Paul Lloyd-Judge, Superior Court of California County of Solano-Calif.
Beer, James R.-Judge, Wisconsin Circuit Court Green Circuit-Wis.
Beer, Peter H.-Senior Judge, United States District Court Eastern District of Louisiana-La.
Beezer, Robert R.-Senior Judge, United States Court of Appeals Ninth Circuit
Befort, Richard-Magistrate Judge, Kansas District Court Thirtieth Judicial District-Kan.
Begen, Loretta Murphy-Judge, Superior Court of California County of Stanislaus-Calif.
Beghe, Renato-Judge, United States Tax Court
Beglin, Edward W., Jr.-Assignment Judge, New Jersey Superior Court Vicinage Twelve-N.J.
Behar, Stephen M., Sr.-Judge, Suffolk County District Court-N.Y.
Behle, Donald A.-Associate Judge, Illinois Circuit Court Eleventh Judicial Circuit-Ill.
Behn, Richard E.-Judge, Superior Court of California County of Orange-Calif.
Behnke, Debra-Judge, Florida Circuit Court Thirteenth Judicial Circuit-Fla.
Behrens, Charles-Judge, Utah Juvenile Court Third Judicial District-Utah
Beier, Carol A.-Judge, Kansas Court of Appeals-Kan.
Beighle, Paul-Magistrate, Seattle Municipal Court-Wash.
Beistline, Ralph R.-Judge, United States District Court District of Alaska-Alas.
Beitz, Bob L.-Justice, Sanders County Justice of the Peace Court and Judge, Hot Springs, Plains and Thompson Falls City Courts-Mont.
Bekken, James M.-Judge, North Dakota District Court Southeast Judicial District-N.D.
Belcher, George K.-Judge, Washington District Probate Court-Vt.
Belden, Stephen F.-Judge, Canton Municipal Court-Ohio
Beldock, Ovid R.-Judge, Adams County Court-Colo.
Belen, Ariel E.-Justice, New York Supreme Court Second Judicial District-N.Y.
Belfi, Donald E.-Judge, Nassau County Court-N.Y.
Beliveau, John B.-Judge, Maine District Court-Me.
Bell, Alfred B.-Judge, Pennsylvania Court of Common Pleas Tenth Judicial District-Pa.
Bell, Bill-Judge, Rockwall County Court-Tex.
Bell, Charles Byron-Judge, Foard County Court-Tex.
Bell, Frank L.-Judge, Florida Circuit Court First Judicial Circuit-Fla.
Bell, James Gregory-Judge, North Carolina District Court District 16B-N.C.
Bell, John L.-Associate Judge, Illinois Circuit Court Fourteenth Judicial Circuit-Ill.
Bell, Kathleen-Judge, Arkansas Circuit Court First Judicial Circuit-Ark.
Bell, Kenneth B.-Justice, Florida Supreme Court-Fla.
Bell, Lisa C.-Judge, North Carolina District Court District 26-N.C.
Bell, Lois A.-Circuit Judge, Illinois Circuit Court Seventh Judicial Circuit-Ill.
Bell, Marie White-Judge, New Jersey Superior Court Vicinage Three-N.J.
Bell, Peter A.-Judge, Charlotte County Court-Fla.
Bell, Richard-Senior Judge, Supreme Court of Georgia-Ga.
Bell, Robert Holmes-Chief Judge, United States District Court Western District of Michigan-Mich.
Bell, Robert M.-Chief Judge, Court of Appeals of Maryland-Md.
Bell, Samuel H.-Senior Judge, United States District Court Northern District of Ohio-Ohio
Bell, Sharon J.-Chancellor, Tennessee Chancery Court Sixth Judicial District-Tenn.
Bell, Stewart L.-Judge, Nevada District Court Eighth Judicial District-Nev.
Bell, W. Robert-Resident Judge, North Carolina Superior Court Seventh Judicial Division District 26-N.C.
Bell, William K.-Judge, Alabama Circuit Court Twenty-third Judicial Circuit-Ala.
Bellamy, James T.-Associate Circuit Judge, Missouri Circuit Court Fifteenth Judicial Circuit-Mo.
Bellamy, Michael J.-Judge, Russell County District Court-Ala.
Bellantoni, Orazio R.-Justice, New York Supreme Court Ninth Judicial District-N.Y.
Bellini, Elma A.-Judge, Monroe County Court-N.Y.
Bellows, Carole K.-Circuit Judge, Illinois Circuit Court of Cook County-Ill.
Bellows, Randy I.-Judge, Virginia Circuit Court Nineteenth Judicial Circuit-Va.
Belois, Patricia L.-Judge, Minnesota District Court Fourth Judicial District-Minn.
Belot, Monti L.-Judge, United States District Court District of Kansas-Kan.
Belskis, Lawrence A.-Judge, Ohio Court of Common Pleas Franklin County-Ohio
Belsome, Roland L.-Judge, Louisiana District Court Orleans Parish Civil District-La.
Belson, James A.-Senior Judge, District of Columbia Court of Appeals-D.C.
Bembry, David Edgar-Judge, Hamilton County Court-Fla.
Benavides, Fortunato P.-Judge, United States Court of Appeals Fifth Circuit
Bench, Russell W.-Judge, Utah Court of Appeals-Utah

ALPHABETICAL NAME INDEX

Bencze, Alex R.-Judge, Arapahoe County Court-Colo.

Bender, Dennis F.-Judge, Seneca County Court-N.Y.

Bender, Gerald C.-Circuit Judge, Illinois Circuit Court of Cook County-Ill.

Bender, John T.-Judge, The Superior Court of Pennsylvania-Pa.

Bender, Michael L.-Justice, Colorado Supreme Court-Colo.

Bender, Thomas L.-Judge, Superior Court of California County of Madera-Calif.

Bendix, Helen I.-Judge, Superior Court of California County of Los Angeles-Calif.

Benefield, Deborah C.-Judge, Superior Court of Georgia Clayton Judicial Circuit-Ga.

Benefield, Harold G.-Judge, State Court of Clayton County-Ga.

Benge, Joan S.-Judge, Louisiana District Court Twenty-fourth Judicial District-La.

Bengtson, Larry E.-Judge, Kansas District Court Eighth Judicial District-Kan.

Benham, Robert-Justice, Supreme Court of Georgia-Ga.

Benitez, Peter J.-Judge, The Criminal Court of the City of New York-N.Y.

Benitez, Roger T.-Magistrate Judge, U.S. District Court Southern District of California-Calif.

Benke, Patricia D.-Associate Justice, California Court of Appeal Fourth District Division One-Calif.

Bennet, Helen B.-Judge, Saybrook District Probate Court-Conn.

Bennett, Arthur Thomas-Judge, Tennessee Criminal Court Thirtieth Judicial District-Tenn.

Bennett, Brenda P.-Judge, Allendale County Probate Court-S.C.

Bennett, Bruce Charles-Judge, Louisiana District Court Twenty-first Judicial District-La.

Bennett, Douglas J.-Judge, Athens County Municipal Court-Ohio

Bennett, Jack A.-Associate Circuit Judge, Missouri Circuit Court Twenty-sixth Judicial Circuit-Mo.

Bennett, John P.-Judge, Kansas District Court Tenth Judicial District-Kan.

Bennett, Mark W.-Chief Judge, United States District Court Northern District of Iowa-Ia.

Bennett, Marshal Jay-Judge, Fisher County Court-Tex.

Bennett, Richard A.-Judge, Superior Court of California County of Napa-Calif.

Bennett, Richard D.-Judge, United States District Court District of Maryland-Md.

Bennett, Robert B., Jr.-Chief Judge, Florida Circuit Court Twelfth Judicial Circuit-Fla.

Bennett, Robert J.-Justice of the Peace, Canal Justices' Court-Nev.

Bennett, Robert L.-Judge, Washington Circuit Court-Ind.

Bennett, Robert T.-Judge, Probate Court of Quitman County and Chief Magistrate, Magistrate Court of Quitman County-Ga.

Bennett, Roger A.-Judge, Washington Superior Court Clark County-Wash.

Bennett, Thomas B.-Judge, United States Bankruptcy Court Northern District of Alabama-Ala.

Bennett, William J.-Judge, Louisiana District Court Twelfth Judicial District-La.

Bennett-Haron, Karen-Justice of the Peace, Las Vegas Justices' Court-Nev.

Bennington, Barry A.-Chief Judge, Kansas District Court Twentieth Judicial District-Kan.

Benshoof, Paul T.-Judge, Minnesota District Court Ninth Judicial District-Minn.

Benson, Dee V.-Chief Judge, United States District Court District of Utah-Utah

Benson, Jerome T.-Judge, Superior Court of California City and County of San Francisco-Calif.

Benson, Quinn E.-Judge, Michigan District Court District Eight Division One-Mich.

Benson, Robert R.-Judge, Minnesota District Court Third Judicial District-Minn.

Benson, Stephen E.-Judge, Superior Court of California County of Butte-Calif.

Bensten, Ronald E.-Chief Judge, Virginia Juvenile and Domestic Relations District Court Seventh Judicial District-Va.

Bentivegna, James M.-Judge, Connecticut Superior Court-Conn.

Bentley, Bascom W., III-Judge, Texas District Court 369th Judicial District-Tex.

Bentley, Danny C.-Chief Magistrate, Magistrate Court of Upson County-Ga.

Bentley, Edward R.-Senior Judge, Florida Circuit Court Tenth Judicial Circuit-Fla.

Bentley, John H.-Judge, Alabama Circuit Court Twenty-fifth Judicial Circuit-Ala.

Benton, Duane-Judge, Supreme Court of Missouri-Mo.

Benton, James W., Jr.-Judge, Court of Appeals of Virginia-Va.

Benton, Levi James-Judge, Texas District Court 215th Judicial District-Tex.

Benton, Monica J.-Magistrate Judge, United States District Court Western District of Washington-Wash.

Benton, Robert T., II-Judge, Florida District Court of Appeal First District-Fla.

Benton, William-Judge, Arkansas Circuit Court Eleventh West Judicial Circuit-Ark.

Bentz, Warren W.-Recalled Judge, United States Bankruptcy Court Western District of Pennsylvania-Pa.

Benza, Louis C.-Justice, New York Supreme Court Twelfth Judicial District-N.Y.

Berch, Rebecca-Justice, Supreme Court of Arizona-Ariz.

Berchelmann, David A., Jr.-Judge, Texas District Court 37th Judicial District-Tex.

Berdon, Robert I.-Judge Referee, Connecticut Superior Court-Conn.

Bereola, Gail Brewster-Judge, Superior Court of California County of Alameda-Calif.

Berg, Jeffrey A.-Judge, Marion County Small Claims Court Decatur Township Division-Ind.

Berger, Carolyn-Justice, Delaware Supreme Court-Del.

Berger, Helaine L.-Associate Judge, Illinois Circuit Court of Cook County-Ill.

Berger, Irene C.-Judge, West Virginia Circuit Court Thirteenth Judicial Circuit-W.Va.

Berger, Marshall K., Jr.-Judge, Connecticut Superior Court-Conn.

Berger, Paul F.-Chief Judge, Michigan District Court District Fifty-six A-Mich.

Berger, Peter A.-Judge, Superior Court of California County of Contra Costa-Calif.

Berger, Stuart R.-Associate Judge, Circuit Court for Baltimore City, Eighth Judicial Circuit-Md.

Berger, William J.-Judge, Florida Circuit Court Fifteenth Judicial Circuit-Fla.

Bergerman, George M.-Justice, New York Supreme Court Ninth Judicial District-N.Y.

Bergeron, Joseph E.-Judge, Superior Court of California County of San Mateo-Calif.

Bergeron, Ronald M.-Chief Judge, Michigan Circuit Court Twenty-third Judicial Circuit-Mich.

Bergeson, George W.-District Judge, Iowa District Court Fifth Judicial District-Ia.

Bergin, Eugene W.-Justice, New York Supreme Court Seventh Judicial District-N.Y.

Berglund, Thomas C.-Associate Judge, Illinois Circuit Court Fourteenth Judicial Circuit-Ill.

Bergman, Linda L.-Judge, Oregon Circuit Court Fourth Judicial District-Ore.

Bergmann, Charles E.-Judge, Florida Circuit Court Thirteenth Judicial Circuit-Fla.

Bergson, Howard M.-Judge, Suffolk County District Court-N.Y.

Bergstedt, Scott J.-Judge, Albion and Colfax Municipal Courts-Wash.

Berke, Philip A.-Judge, Washington County Court-N.Y.

Berkemeyer, John B.-Associate Circuit Judge, Missouri Circuit Court Twentieth Judicial Circuit-Mo.

Berkman, Carol-Judge, The Criminal Court of the City of New York-N.Y.

Berkowitz, Meryl J.-Judge, Nassau County Court-N.Y.

Berland, Richard B.-Circuit Judge, Illinois Circuit Court of Cook County-Ill.

Berle, Elihu M.-Judge, Superior Court of California County of Los Angeles-Calif.

Berler, Howard-Justice, New York Supreme Court Tenth Judicial District-N.Y.

Berling, Amy-Judge, Toledo Municipal Court-Ohio

Berman, Andrew-Circuit Judge, Illinois Circuit Court of Cook County-Ill.

Berman, Fred-Judge, Broward County Court-Fla.

Berman, Glenn J.-Judge, New Jersey Superior Court Vicinage Eight-N.J.

Berman, Richard M.-Judge, United States District Court Southern District of New York-N.Y.

Bernabei, Marc-Circuit Judge, Illinois Circuit Court Thirteenth Judicial Circuit-Ill.

Bernal, Margaret Miller-Judge, Superior Court of California County of Los Angeles-Calif.

Bernal, Paul R.-Judge, Superior Court of California County of Santa Clara-Calif.

Bernard, Julie J.-Justice, Trial Court of Massachusetts District Court Department Bristol County New Bedford Division-Mass.

Bernard, Marielsa A.-Associate Judge, Circuit Court for Montgomery County, Sixth Judicial Circuit-Md.

Bernard, Michael A.-Judge, Girard Municipal Court-Ohio

Bernardi, Donald D.-Circuit Judge, Illinois Circuit Court Eleventh Judicial Circuit-Ill.

Bernardini, Susan-Judge, Superior Court of California County of Santa Clara-Calif.

Berner, David A.-Judge, Enumclaw Municipal Court-Wash.

Bernhard, Edmund R.-Judge, New Jersey Superior Court Vicinage Thirteen-N.J.

Bernini, Deborah-Judge, Superior Court of Arizona Pima County-Ariz.

Bernstein, Lauren Weiss-Judge, Superior Court of California County of Los Angeles-Calif.

Bernstein, Lawrence H.-Justice, New York Supreme Court Twelfth Judicial District-N.Y.

Bernstein, Mark Israel-Judge, Pennsylvania Court of Common Pleas First Judicial District-Pa.

Bernstein, Patricia E.-Associate Justice, Trial Court of Massachusetts Boston Municipal Court Department-Mass.

Bernstein, Scott-Judge, Florida Circuit Court Eleventh Judicial Circuit-Fla.

Bernstein, Stan-Judge, United States Bankruptcy Court Eastern District of New York-N.Y.

Bernstein, Stephen J.-Judge, New Jersey Superior Court Vicinage Five-N.J.

Bernstein, Stuart M.-Chief Judge, United States Bankruptcy Court Southern District of New York-N.Y.

Bernthal, David G.-Magistrate Judge, United States District Court Central District of Illinois-Ill.

Berrigan, Helen G.-Chief Judge, United States District Court Eastern District of Louisiana-La.

Berry, Annette J.-Judge, Michigan Circuit Court Third Judicial Circuit-Mich.

Berry, Edward DeJarnette-Chief Judge, Virginia Juvenile and Domestic Relations District Court Sixteenth Judicial District-Va.

Berry, Elizabeth-Judge, Texas Criminal District Court No. 3 Tarrant County-Tex.

Berry, J. Martin-Associate Judge, Illinois Circuit Court of Cook County-Ill.

Berry, Janet J.-Judge, Nevada District Court Second Judicial District-Nev.

Berry, Janis M.-Associate Justice, Massachusetts Appeals Court-Mass.

Berry, Jeffrey G.-Judge, Orange County Court-N.Y.

Berry, Joe R.-Judge, Angelina County Court-Tex.

Berry, Willis W., Jr.-Judge, Pennsylvania Court of Common Pleas First Judicial District-Pa.

Berryhill, Jack W.-Judge, Colorado District Court First Judicial District-Colo.

Berschauer, Daniel J.-Judge, Washington Superior Court Thurston County-Wash.

Bertani-Tomczak, Amy M.-Circuit Judge, Illinois Circuit Court Twelfth Judicial Circuit-Ill.

Bertelsman, William O.-Senior Judge, United States District Court Eastern District of Kentucky-Ky.

Bertin, Emanuel A.-Judge, Pennsylvania Court of Common Pleas Thirty-eighth Judicial District-Pa.

Bertness, Janette A.-Associate Judge, Rhode Island Workers' Compensation Court-R.I.

ALPHABETICAL NAME INDEX

Bertoli, James Gordon-Judge, Superior Court of California County of Sonoma-Calif.

Bertram, Allan Ray-Judge, Kentucky Circuit Court Eleventh Judicial Circuit-Ky.

Bertucci, Robert W.-Circuit Judge, Illinois Circuit Court of Cook County-Ill.

Berzon, Marsha L.-Judge, United States Court of Appeals Ninth Circuit

Bessen, Diane E.-Judge, State Court of Fulton County-Ga.

Bessey, John P.-Judge, Ohio Court of Common Pleas Franklin County-Ohio

Bessonette, George A.-Judge, Juvenile Court of Georgia Alapaha Judicial Circuit-Ga.

Best, Hollis G.-Magistrate Judge, United States District Court Eastern District of California-Calif.

Best, James J.-Judge, Louisiana District Court Eighteenth Judicial District-La.

Best, Robert P.-Justice, New York Supreme Court Fourth Judicial District-N.Y.

Betar, Samuel J., III-Associate Judge, Illinois Circuit Court of Cook County-Ill.

Bethancourt, Randy-Judge, Louisiana District Court Thirty-second Judicial District-La.

Bethel, Winston P.-Chief Magistrate, Magistrate Court of DeKalb County-Ga.

Betleski, Mark A.-Judge, Ohio Court of Common Pleas Lorain County-Ohio

Betts, Lowry M.-Retired-Recalled Judge, North Carolina District Court-N.C.

Betzner, David G.-Judge, Bunker Hill Town Court-Ind.

Bevens, William Wray-Judge, Ohio Court of Common Pleas Pike County-Ohio

Beverly, Virginia Q.-Senior Judge, Florida Circuit Court Fourth Judicial Circuit-Fla.

Beverly, William C., Jr.-Judge, Superior Court of California County of Los Angeles-Calif.

Bevil, Stephen M.-Judge, Tennessee Criminal Court Eleventh Judicial District-Tenn.

Bevis, Thomas E.-Judge, Volusia County Court-Fla.

Biafore, Joseph F., Jr.-Judge, Superior Court of California County of Santa Clara-Calif.

Bianchini, Victor E.-Recalled Magistrate Judge, United States District Court Western District of New York-N.Y.

Bianco, Vito L.-Judge, New Jersey Tax Court-N.J.

Bibb, David H.-Judge, Morgan County District Court-Ala.

Bibus, Thomas-Judge, Minnesota District Court First Judicial District-Minn.

Bickel, James R.-Presiding Judge, Missouri Circuit Court Twenty-eighth Judicial Circuit-Mo.

Biddlecome, George W.-Judge, Elkhart Superior Court-Ind.

Biebel, Paul P., Jr.-Circuit Judge, Illinois Circuit Court of Cook County-Ill.

Biehn, Kenneth G.-Judge, Pennsylvania Court of Common Pleas Seventh Judicial District-Pa.

Bielamowicz, Maryann K.-Judge, New Jersey Superior Court Vicinage Seven-N.J.

Bielawski, Lawrence M.-Chief Judge, Michigan Circuit Court Eighteenth Judicial Circuit-Mich.

Bielstein, R. H. "Sandy"-Judge, Fort Bend County Court at Law No. 4-Tex.

Bieluch, William C.-Judge Referee, Connecticut Superior Court-Conn.

Bierman, Janice L.-Circuit Judge, Illinois Circuit Court of Cook County-Ill.

Biernat, James M., Sr.-Judge, Michigan Circuit Court Sixteenth Judicial Circuit-Mich.

Biery, Fred-Judge, United States District Court Western District of Texas-Tex.

Bieter, Christopher M.-Judge, Idaho District Court Fourth Judicial District Magistrate Division-Ida.

Bigelow, Raymond C.-Judge, Louisiana District Court Orleans Parish Criminal District-La.

Bigelow, Tricia Ann-Judge, Superior Court of California County of Los Angeles-Calif.

Bigge, Douglas-Magistrate Judge, Kansas District Court Twenty-third Judicial District-Kan.

Biggers, Neal B., Jr.-Senior Judge, United States District Court Northern District of Mississippi-Miss.

Biggs, Carl-Judge, Superior Court of California County of Orange-Calif.

Bigham, Robert G.-Judge, Pennsylvania Court of Common Pleas Fifty-first Judicial District-Pa.

Bigley, Garland L.-Judge, Virginia General District Court Eleventh Judicial District-Va.

Bigley, Gerard M.-Judge, Pennsylvania Court of Common Pleas Fifth Judicial District-Pa.

Bihary, Joyce-Judge, United States Bankruptcy Court Northern District of Georgia-Ga.

Bilder, Lawrence-Retired Judge, New Jersey Superior Court Appellate Division-N.J.

Bill, Gregory D.-Judge, Michigan Circuit Court Third Judicial Circuit-Mich.

Billik, Richard J., Jr.-Circuit Judge, Illinois Circuit Court of Cook County-Ill.

Billings, Bruce-Judge, Las Animas County Court-Colo.

Billings, Jack A.-Judge, Oregon Circuit Court Second Judicial District-Ore.

Billings, Judith M.-Judge, Utah Court of Appeals-Utah

Billings, Lucy A.-Judge, The Civil Court of the City of New York-N.Y.

Billings, Thomas P.-Associate Justice, Trial Court of Massachusetts Superior Court Department-Mass.

Bilski, Carolyn Cerny-Judge, Austin County Court-Tex.

Bimson, J. Dale-Judge, Virginia General District Court Second Judicial District-Va.

Binder, Charles E.-Magistrate Judge, United States District Court Eastern District of Michigan-Mich.

Bingham, James F.-Judge Referee, Connecticut Superior Court-Conn.

Bingham, John L.-Magistrate Judge, Kansas District Court Twelfth Judicial District-Kan.

Birbrower, Barry-Judge, Peekskill City Court-N.Y.

Birch, Adolpho A., Jr.-Associate Justice, Tennessee Supreme Court-Tenn.

Birch, Stanley F., Jr.-Judge, United States Court of Appeals Eleventh Circuit

Bird, Daniel Woodrow, Jr.-Chief Judge, Virginia General District Court Twenty-seventh Judicial District-Va.

Bird, David-Judge, Gonzales County Court-Tex.

Bird, Sam N.-Judge, Arkansas Court of Appeals-Ark.

Bird, Steven R.-Judge, Ohio Court of Common Pleas Williams County-Ohio

Birdsall, William C.-Chief Judge, New Mexico District Court Eleventh Judicial District-N.Mex.

Birken, Arthur M.-Judge, Florida Circuit Court Seventeenth Judicial Circuit-Fla.

Birkenholz, James D.-District Associate Judge, Iowa District Court Fifth Judicial District-Ia.

Birnbaum, Arthur-Judge, The Civil Court of the City of New York-N.Y.

Birnbaum, Robert-Judge, Minnesota District Court Third Judicial District-Minn.

Birney, William J.-Judge, Superior Court of California County of Los Angeles-Calif.

Bischel, Sue E.-Judge, Wisconsin Circuit Court Brown Circuit-Wis.

Biscoe, Sam-Judge, Travis County Court-Tex.

Bise, Carter-Judge, Mississippi Chancery Court Eighth Judicial District-Miss.

Bishop, Fred A., Jr.-Judge, Superior Court of Georgia Gwinnett Judicial Circuit-Ga.

Bishop, Jody W.-Judge, Baldwin County District Court-Ala.

Bishop, Joe C.-Chief Judge, Superior Court of Georgia Pataula Judicial Circuit-Ga.

Bishop, Robert L.-Judge, Kansas District Court Nineteenth Judicial District-Kan.

Bishop, Stephen-Judge, Tekoa Municipal Court-Wash.

Bishop, Thomas A.-Judge, Connecticut Appellate Court-Conn.

Bishop, Wm. Thurmond-Chief Judge, United States Bankruptcy Court District of South Carolina-S.C.

Bisig, Angela McCormick-Judge, Kentucky District Court Thirtieth Judicial District-Ky.

Bispham, Carol R.-Judge, Oregon Circuit Court Twenty-third Judicial District-Ore.

Bissell, John W.-Chief Judge, United States District Court District of New Jersey-N.J.

Bissell, Ronald L.-Judge, Belt City Court-Mont.

Bissig, Louis F.-Judge, Superior Court of California County of Kings-Calif.

Bissonnette, Andrew P.-Judge, Wisconsin Circuit Court Dodge Circuit-Wis.

Bitting, Terry H.-Special Judge, Oklahoma District Court Fourteenth Judicial District-Okla.

Bivona, Andrew P.-Judge, Orange County Family Court-N.Y.

Bivona, John C.-Justice, New York Supreme Court Tenth Judicial District-N.Y.

Bixler, James M.-Justice of the Peace, Las Vegas Justices' Court-Nev.

Bjork, B. J.-Judge, Superior Court of California County of Riverside-Calif.

Bjorkman, Louise Dovre-Judge, Minnesota District Court Second Judicial District-Minn.

Black, Alan M.-Judge, Pennsylvania Court of Common Pleas Thirty-first Judicial District-Pa.

Black, Anthony K.-Judge, Florida Circuit Court Thirteenth Judicial Circuit-Fla.

Black, Bruce Douglas-Judge, United States District Court District of New Mexico-N.Mex.

Black, Bruce W.-Judge, United States Bankruptcy Court Northern District of Illinois-Ill.

Black, Donald S.-Judge, Superior Court of California County of Fresno-Calif.

Black, Harold A.-Judge, Virginia General District Court Twenty-fourth Judicial District-Va.

Black, Horace Dickson, Jr.-Judge, Texas District Court 77th Judicial District-Tex.

Black, John William-Magistrate Judge, United States District Court Southern District of Texas-Tex.

Black, K. Dean-Judge, North Carolina District Court District 27B-N.C.

Black, Kenneth A.-Judge, Superior Court of California County of Los Angeles-Calif.

Black, Mary A.-Special Judge, Oklahoma District Court Twenty-third Judicial District-Okla.

Black, Marylouise S.-Judge, Connecticut Superior Court-Conn.

Black, Phyllis-Justice of the Peace, Jackpot Justices' Court-Nev.

Black, Robert J.-Judge, Bogalusa City Court-La.

Black, Susan Harrell-Judge, United States Court of Appeals Eleventh Circuit

Black, Timothy S.-Judge, Hamilton County Municipal Court-Ohio

Black, Virgil C.-District Judge, Oklahoma District Court Seventh Judicial District-Okla.

Black, Walter E., Jr.-Senior Judge, United States District Court District of Maryland-Md.

Blackburn, Audrey Hope Peyton-Judge, New Jersey Superior Court Vicinage Seven-N.J.

Blackburn, Cheryl A.-Judge, Tennessee Criminal Court Twentieth Judicial District-Tenn.

Blackburn, G. Alan-Judge, Court of Appeals of Georgia-Ga.

Blackburn, Robert E.-Judge, United States District Court District of Colorado-Colo.

Blackburn, Sharon Lovelace-Judge, United States District Court Northern District of Alabama-Ala.

Blackburne, Laura D.-Justice, New York Supreme Court Eleventh Judicial District-N.Y.

Blackburne-Rigsby, Anna-Associate Judge, Superior Court of the District of Columbia-D.C.

Blackett, Carolyn Wade-Judge, Tennessee Criminal Court Thirtieth Judicial District-Tenn.

Blackmer, James F.-Judge, New Mexico District Court Second Judicial District-N.Mex.

Blackmon, Patricia Ann-Judge, Ohio Court of Appeals Eighth District-Ohio

Blackmore, Rebecca W.-Judge, North Carolina District Court District 5-N.C.

Blackshear, Cornelius-Judge, United States Bankruptcy Court Southern District of New York-N.Y.

Blackstock, James A.-Judge, Brazoria County Court at Law No. 3-Tex.

Blackwell, Carroll M.-Associate Circuit Judge, Missouri Circuit Court Tenth Judicial Circuit-Mo.

Blackwell, Penny L.-Judge, Pennsylvania Court of Common Pleas Nineteenth Judicial District-Pa.

Blackwell, Todd A.-Judge, Probate Court of Baldwin County-Ga.

Blackwell, Walter L., III-Judge, Superior Court of California County of San Bernardino-Calif.

ALPHABETICAL NAME INDEX

Blackwell, William-Chief Judge, Florida Circuit Court Twentieth Judicial Circuit-Fla.

Blackwell-Hatcher, June E.-Judge, Wayne County Probate Court-Mich.

Blackwood, Alan G.-Associate Judge, Illinois Circuit Court Fourteenth Judicial Circuit-Ill.

Blackwood, Jon Kerry-Judge, Tennessee Circuit Court Twenty-fifth Judicial District-Tenn.

Blackwood, William B., Jr.-Judge, Pinellas County Court-Fla.

Blaeser, Robert A.-Judge, Minnesota District Court Fourth Judicial District-Minn.

Blahovec, John E.-Judge, Pennsylvania Court of Common Pleas Tenth Judicial District-Pa.

Blair, H. Wetzel-Judge, Madison County Court-Fla.

Blair, Jolene C.-Judge, Colorado District Court Eighth Judicial District-Colo.

Blair, Roy-Judge, Coke County Court-Tex.

Blair, Steven E.-Judge, Alabama Circuit Court Twelfth Judicial Circuit-Ala.

Blake, Archie E.-Judge, Nevada District Court Third Judicial District-Nev.

Blake, Catherine C.-Judge, United States District Court District of Maryland-Md.

Blake, Donna L. J.-Magistrate Judge, Kansas District Court Twenty-fifth Judicial District-Kan.

Blake, Stanford-Judge, Florida Circuit Court Eleventh Judicial Circuit-Fla.

Blakely, Timothy L.-Judge, Minnesota District Court First Judicial District-Minn.

Blakey, Craig A., II-Judge, Superior Court of Arizona Maricopa County-Ariz.

Blalock, Candace Landers-District Judge, Oklahoma District Court Twenty-first Judicial District-Okla.

Blanc, Erik I.-Associate Judge, Illinois Circuit Court Tenth Judicial Circuit-Ill.

Blanc, Peter D.-Judge, Florida Circuit Court Fifteenth Judicial Circuit-Fla.

Blanchard, James G., Jr.-Judge, Superior Court of Georgia Augusta Judicial Circuit-Ga.

Blanchard, Richard L.-Presiding Judge, Oklahoma Workers' Compensation Court-Okla.

Blanchet, David-Judge, Louisiana District Court Fifteenth Judicial District-La.

Bland, Jane Nenninger-Judge, Texas District Court 281st Judicial District-Tex.

Bland, Jim D.-Special Judge, Oklahoma District Court Eighteenth Judicial District-Okla.

Bland, Thomas Steven-Judge, Kentucky Circuit Court Ninth Judicial Circuit-Ky.

Blane, Richard G., II-District Judge, Iowa District Court Fifth Judicial District-Ia.

Blankenship, Alan-Associate Circuit Judge, Missouri Circuit Court Thirty-ninth Judicial Circuit-Mo.

Blankenship, Patrick B.-Judge, Pulaski Superior Court-Ind.

Blanton, Larry R.-Judge, Orange Circuit Court-Ind.

Blanton, Lewis M.-Magistrate Judge, United States District Court Eastern District of Missouri-Mo.

Blanton, Richard S.-Judge, Virginia Circuit Court Tenth Judicial Circuit-Va.

Blass, Gregory J.-Judge, Suffolk County Family Court-N.Y.

Blatt, Sol, Jr.-Senior Judge, United States District Court District of South Carolina-S.C.

Blatz, Kathleen A.-Chief Justice, Minnesota Supreme Court-Minn.

Blau, Cecile A.-Judge, Clark Superior Court-Ind.

Blau, George G., III-Associate Judge, Juvenile Court of Georgia Atlanta Judicial Circuit-Ga.

Blauvelt, Arthur A., III-Judge, McCleary and Montesano Municipal Courts-Wash.

Blaylock, Connie Maples-Judge, Juvenile Court of Georgia Conasauga Judicial Circuit-Ga.

Blea, Jacob, III-Judge, Superior Court of California County of Alameda-Calif.

Blease, Coleman A.-Associate Justice, California Court of Appeal Third District-Calif.

Blechman, Deb S.-Judge, Orange County Court-Fla.

Bledsoe, Joseph-Judge, Probate Court of Heard County-Ga.

Bleil, Charles-Magistrate Judge, United States District Court Northern District of Texas-Tex.

Blewitt, Thomas M.-Magistrate Judge, United States District Court Middle District of Pennsylvania-Pa.

Blick, Joseph A., Jr.-Judge, North Carolina District Court District 3A-N.C.

Blink, Robert J.-District Judge, Iowa District Court Fifth Judicial District-Ia.

Blitch, Brooks E., III-Chief Judge, Superior Court of Georgia Alapaha Judicial Circuit-Ga.

Blitzman, Jay D.-Associate Justice, Trial Court of Massachusetts Juvenile Court Department Middlesex County Division-Mass.

Bloch, Alan N.-Senior Judge, United States District Court Western District of Pennsylvania-Pa.

Bloch, Eric J.-Judge, Oregon Circuit Court Fourth Judicial District-Ore.

Block, Cathy-Associate Judge, Illinois Circuit Court Twelfth Judicial Circuit-Ill.

Block, Daniel L.-Associate Juvenile Judge, Iowa District Court First Judicial District-Ia.

Block, Frederic-Judge, United States District Court Eastern District of New York-N.Y.

Block, Gary Michael-Judge, Harris County Civil Court at Law No. 2-Tex.

Block, Jack-Senior Judge, Dade County Court-Fla.

Block, Lawrence J.-Judge, United States Court of Federal Claims

Block, Robert N.-Magistrate Judge, United States District Court Central District of California-Calif.

Block, Susan-Circuit Judge, Missouri Circuit Court Twenty-first Judicial Circuit-Mo.

Blocker, Charles T. "Corky"-Judge, Martin County Court-Tex.

Blockman, Arnold F.-Circuit Judge, Illinois Circuit Court Sixth Judicial Circuit-Ill.

Blomgren, James Q.-Chief Judge, Iowa District Court Eighth Judicial District-Ia.

Blondin, Karen-Deputy Chief Judge, Hawaii Circuit Court First Judicial Circuit-Hi.

Bloodworth, John-Associate Circuit Judge, Missouri Circuit Court Thirty-sixth Judicial Circuit-Mo.

Bloom, Beth-Judge, Dade County Court-Fla.

Bloom, Jay M.-Judge, Superior Court of California County of San Diego-Calif.

Bloom, Karl Barney-Assistant Judge, Vermont Trial Court Washington County-Vt.

Bloom, Lois S.-Magistrate Judge, United States District Court Eastern District of New York-N.Y.

Bloom, Louis H.-Judge, West Virginia Circuit Court Thirteenth Judicial Circuit-W.Va.

Bloom, Stephen M.-Magistrate Judge, United States District Court District of Oregon-Ore.

Bloomquist, Timothy R.-Judge, Minnesota District Court Tenth Judicial District-Minn.

Blount, Clarence D.-Chief Judge, Superior Court of Georgia Waycross Judicial Circuit-Ga.

Blount, Nancy McCaughan-Judge, Michigan District Court District Thirty-six-Mich.

Blow, Randall M.-Judge, Virginia Juvenile and Domestic Relations District Court Second Judicial District-Va.

Blower, Earl-Judge, Idaho District Court Seventh Judicial District Magistrate Division-Ida.

Bloxom, Richard R.-Associate Judge, Maryland District Court District Two-Md.

Blue, Daryl-Judge, Monroe City Court-La.

Blue, Jon C.-Judge, Connecticut Superior Court-Conn.

Bluebond, Sheri-Judge, United States Bankruptcy Court Central District of California-Calif.

Blumenfeld, Joel L.-Judge, The Criminal Court of the City of New York-N.Y.

Blydenburgh, Donald R.-Justice, New York Supreme Court Tenth Judicial District-N.Y.

Boagni, Kenneth, Jr.-Judge, Opelousas City Court-La.

Boal, David W.-Judge, Kansas District Court Twenty-ninth Judicial District-Kan.

Board, John B.-Judge, Texas District Court 181st Judicial District-Tex.

Boardman, William M.-Assistant Judge, Vermont Trial Court Windsor County-Vt.

Boasberg, James E.-Associate Judge, Superior Court of the District of Columbia-D.C.

Boatright, Brian-Judge, Colorado District Court First Judicial District-Colo.

Boatright, Joe-Judge, Probate Court of Bacon County and Chief Magistrate, Magistrate Court of Bacon County-Ga.

Bobb, Aviva Koenigsberg-Judge, Superior Court of California County of Los Angeles-Calif.

Bobbink, Michael-Judge, Blaine, Everson-Nooksack and Sumas Municipal Courts-Wash.

Bobbitt, Joe A.-Judge, Hunt County Court-Tex.

Bobbitt, Thomas C., III-Chief Magistrate, Magistrate Court of Laurens County-Ga.

Bobo, J. A. "Jim"-Judge, Ector County Court at Law-Tex.

Bobrick, Edward A.-Magistrate Judge, United States District Court Northern District of Illinois-Ill.

Bocanegra, Arthur-Judge, Superior Court of California County of Santa Clara-Calif.

Bockman, Harlan R.-Chief Judge, Colorado District Court Seventeenth Judicial District-Colo.

Bodiford, James G.-Judge, Superior Court of Georgia Cobb Judicial Circuit-Ga.

Bodiford, Larry A.-Magistrate Judge, United States District Court Northern District of Florida-Fla.

Bodoh, William T.-Judge, Bankruptcy Appellate Panel Sixth Circuit and Chief Judge, United States Bankruptcy Court Northern District of Ohio-Ohio

Boeckman, Bradley L.-Judge, Superior Court of California County of Shasta-Calif.

Boedeker, Joseph F.-Chief Judge, Michigan District Court District Thirty-nine-Mich.

Boeding, Thomas L.-Judge, Kansas District Court Twenty-ninth Judicial District-Kan.

Boehm, Theodore R.-Associate Justice, Indiana Supreme Court-Ind.

Bogacz, Stephen J.-Judge, New York City Family Court-N.Y.

Bogen, Eugene M.-Magistrate Judge, United States District Court Northern District of Mississippi-Miss.

Bogen, Mark R.-Judge, Lebanon Municipal Court-Ohio

Boggia, Peter F.-Judge, New Jersey Superior Court Vicinage Two-N.J.

Boggins, John F.-Judge, Ohio Court of Appeals Fifth District-Ohio

Boggs, Danny J.-Judge, United States Court of Appeals Sixth Circuit

Boggs, John S.-Special Judge, Oklahoma District Court Tenth Judicial District-Okla.

Bogue, Andrew W.-Senior Judge, United States District Court District of South Dakota-S.D.

Bohanon, Richard L.-Judge, Bankruptcy Appellate Panel Tenth Circuit and Judge, United States Bankruptcy Court Western District of Oklahoma-Okla.

Bohling, William B.-Judge, Utah District Court Third Judicial District-Utah

Bohlman, Bruce E.-Judge, North Dakota District Court Northeast Central Judicial District-N.D.

Bohn, Robert H., Jr.-Associate Justice, Trial Court of Massachusetts Superior Court Department-Mass.

Bohning, Larry L.-Judge, Denver County Court-Colo.

Bohren, Michael O.-Judge, Wisconsin Circuit Court Waukesha Circuit-Wis.

Boice, William G.-Judge, Virginia Juvenile and Domestic Relations District Court Fourteenth Judicial District-Va.

Boie, Mark Monroe-Circuit Judge, Illinois Circuit Court First Judicial Circuit-Ill.

Boklund, William J.-Judge, La Porte Superior Court-Ind.

Bokos, C. Charles-Chief Judge, Michigan District Court District Eighteen-Mich.

Boland, Bernard E.-Judge, Minnesota District Court Seventh Judicial District-Minn.

Boland, Boyd N.-Magistrate Judge, United States District Court District of Colorado-Colo.

Boland, Paul-Associate Justice, California Court of Appeal Second District Division Eight-Calif.

Boles, Jeffrey V.-Judge, Hendricks Circuit Court-Ind.

Boles, Pamela-Judge, Juvenile Court of Georgia Bell-Forsyth Judicial Circuit-Ga.

ALPHABETICAL NAME INDEX

Bolger, Joel H.-Judge, Alaska District Court Third Judicial District-Alas.

Bolger, John D.-Associate Judge, Illinois Circuit Court Nineteenth Judicial Circuit-Ill.

Bolgert, James J.-Judge, Wisconsin Circuit Court Sheboygan Circuit-Wis.

Bolin, Bruce M.-Judge, Louisiana District Court Twenty-sixth Judicial District-La.

Boling, Larry-Judge, Arkansas Circuit Court Second Judicial Circuit-Ark.

Bolk, David R.-Judge, Vigo Circuit Court-Ind.

Bolle, William E.-Judge, Michigan District Court District Fifty-two Division Four-Mich.

Bollinger, Thomas J., Sr.-Associate Judge, Circuit Court for Baltimore County, Third Judicial Circuit-Md.

Bollinger, William A.-Judge, Palm Beach County Court-Fla.

Bollman, J. Michael-Judge, Superior Court of California County of San Diego-Calif.

Bolt-Meredith, Cassandra S.-Judge, Ohio Court of Common Pleas Pike County-Ohio

Bolton, Susan Ritchie-Judge, United States District Court District of Arizona-Ariz.

Bommer, Timothy J.-Magistrate Judge, United States District Court District of Wyoming-Wyo.

Bonapfel, Paul W.-Judge, United States Bankruptcy Court Northern District of Georgia-Ga.

Bonaventura, Mary Beth-Judge, Lake Superior Court-Ind.

Bonaventure, Joseph T.-Judge, Nevada District Court Eighth Judicial District-Nev.

Bond, James O.-Judge, Tennessee Criminal Court Fifteenth Judicial District-Tenn.

Bond, Jane-Judge, Ohio Court of Common Pleas Summit County-Ohio

Bondy, Robert-Judge, Michigan District Court District Fifty-two Division One-Mich.

Boner, Richard D.-Judge, North Carolina Superior Court Seventh Judicial Division District 26-N.C.

Bonfiglio, David-Judge, Elkhart Superior Court-Ind.

Bongiorno, Joseph S.-Associate Judge, Illinois Circuit Court Eighteenth Judicial Circuit-Ill.

Bongiovanni, Tonianne J.-Magistrate Judge, United States District Court District of New Jersey-N.J.

Boniello, Ralph A., III-Justice, New York Supreme Court Eighth Judicial District-N.Y.

Bonin, Paul A.-Judge, New Orleans Traffic Court-La.

Bonner, Alice D.-Judge, Superior Court of Georgia Atlanta Judicial Circuit-Ga.

Bonner, Fred-Judge, Seattle Municipal Court-Wash.

Bonner, Kimberly C.-Judge, Sarasota County Court-Fla.

Bonnoitt, H. E., Jr.-Judge, South Carolina Family Court Fifteenth Judicial Circuit-S.C.

Boochever, Robert-Senior Judge, United States Court of Appeals Ninth Circuit

Boohaker, Joseph L.-Judge, Alabama Circuit Court Tenth Judicial Circuit Birmingham Division-Ala.

Bookbinder, Ronald E.-Judge, New Jersey Superior Court Vicinage Three-N.J.

Boomer, Henry R.-Judge, Idaho District Court Fourth Judicial District Magistrate Division-Ida.

Boone, A. Gordon, Jr.-Associate Judge, Maryland District Court District Eight-Md.

Boone, Billy W.-Magistrate Judge, United States District Court Northern District of Texas-Tex.

Boone, Donald L.-Emergency Judge, North Carolina District Court-N.C.

Boone, Patrick J.-Judge, Texas District Court 57th Judicial District-Tex.

Boone, W. Kennedy, III-Associate Judge, Circuit Court for Washington County, Fourth Judicial Circuit-Md.

Booras, James K.-Circuit Judge, Illinois Circuit Court Nineteenth Judicial Circuit-Ill.

Boorstein, Beverly W.-Acting First Justice, Trial Court of Massachusetts Probate and Family Court Department Middlesex County Division-Mass.

Booth, Anne Cawthon-Judge, Florida District Court of Appeal First District-Fla.

Booth, Janet Carroll-Judge, Kentucky District Court Thirteenth Judicial District-Ky.

Booth, John W.-Senior Judge, Florida Circuit Court Fifth Judicial Circuit-Fla.

Booth, Joseph H.-Judge, Superior Court of Georgia Piedmont Judicial Circuit-Ga.

Booth, Kevin E.-Judge, Connecticut Superior Court-Conn.

Booth, Peter W.-Judge, Colorado District Court Fourth Judicial District-Colo.

Boothe, Leo-Judge, Louisiana District Court Seventh Judicial District-La.

Borack, Jerilyn L.-Judge, Superior Court of California County of Sacramento-Calif.

Borba, Joan Marie-Judge, Superior Court of California County of San Bernardino-Calif.

Borbely, James K.-Associate Judge, Illinois Circuit Court Fifth Judicial Circuit-Ill.

Borchard, Fred L.-Judge, Michigan Circuit Court Tenth Judicial Circuit-Mich.

Borde, Charles W., Jr.-Judge, Denham Springs City Court-La.

Borden, David M.-Associate Justice, Connecticut Supreme Court-Conn.

Borden, Stuart P.-Circuit Judge, Illinois Circuit Court Tenth Judicial Circuit-Ill.

Borders, Bettina-Associate Justice, Trial Court of Massachusetts Juvenile Court Department Bristol County Division-Mass.

Bordner, Steven R.-Associate Judge, Illinois Circuit Court Ninth Judicial Circuit-Ill.

Borek, Ted B.-Judge, Superior Court of Arizona Pima County-Ariz.

Boren, Roger W.-Presiding Justice, California Court of Appeal Second District Division Two-Calif.

Boren, Terrence R.-Judge, Superior Court of California County of Marin-Calif.

Borene, Bernard E.-Judge, Minnesota District Court Third Judicial District-Minn.

Borenstein, Isaac-Associate Justice, Trial Court of Massachusetts Superior Court Department-Mass.

Borman, Paul D.-Judge, United States District Court Eastern District of Michigan-Mich.

Borman, Susan D.-Judge, Michigan Circuit Court Third Judicial Circuit-Mich.

Bormann, Donald J.-District Associate Judge, Iowa District Court Third Judicial District-Ia.

Born, David P.-Judge, West Virginia Family Court Circuit Nineteen-W.Va.

Bornholdt, Thomas H.-Judge, Kansas District Court Tenth Judicial District-Kan.

Bornstein, Peter H.-Justice, Gorham and Lancaster District Courts and Special Justice, Berlin District Court-N.H.

Boroff, Henry Jack-Judge, Bankruptcy Appellate Panel First Circuit and Judge, United States Bankruptcy Court District of Massachusetts-Mass.

Boros, Debra L.-Judge, Ohio Court of Common Pleas Lorain County-Ohio

Borowski, David L.-Judge, Wisconsin Circuit Court Milwaukee Circuit-Wis.

Borrello, Leopold P.-Chief Judge, Michigan Circuit Court Tenth Judicial Circuit-Mich.

Borrello, Stephen L.-Judge, Michigan Court of Appeals-Mich.

Borresen, Thomas H.-Judge, Idaho District Court Fifth Judicial District Magistrate Division-Ida.

Borris, Thomas James-Judge, Superior Court of California County of Orange-Calif.

Borron, John A., Jr.-Circuit Judge, Missouri Circuit Court Sixteenth Judicial Circuit-Mo.

Borst, Philip W.-Judge, Washington Superior Court Lincoln County-Wash.

Bosa, Gordon J.-Judge, Conejos County Court-Colo.

Bosch, Carmen-Judge, Baldwin County District Court-Ala.

Bosman, Calvin L.-Judge, Michigan Circuit Court Twentieth Judicial Circuit-Mich.

Bosson, Richard C.-Justice, New Mexico Supreme Court-N.Mex.

Bostwick, Donald W.-Magistrate Judge, United States District Court District of Kansas-Kan.

Bostwick, Jeffrey-Judge, Superior Court of California County of San Diego-Calif.

Boswell, G. Harvey-Judge, United States Bankruptcy Court Western District of Tennessee-Tenn.

Boswell, George Timothy-Judge, Texas District Court 402nd Judicial District-Tex.

Boswell, Stephen Edwin-Senior Judge, Superior Court of Georgia-Ga.

Boteler, Charles W., Jr.-Judge, Kentucky Circuit Court Fourth Judicial Circuit-Ky.

Botley, Calvin-Magistrate Judge, United States District Court Southern District of Texas-Tex.

Botsford, Margot-Associate Justice, Trial Court of Massachusetts Superior Court Department-Mass.

Bottger, David A.-Judge, Colorado District Court Twenty-first Judicial District-Colo.

Boudin, Michael-Chief Judge, United States Court of Appeals First Circuit

Boudreau, Daniel J.-Justice, Supreme Court of Oklahoma-Okla.

Bouillion, Frances Moran-Judge, Lafayette City Court-La.

Bouker, Edward-Chief Judge, Kansas District Court Twenty-third Judicial District-Kan.

Boulden, Judith A.-Judge, Bankruptcy Appellate Panel Tenth Circuit and Judge, United States Bankruptcy Court District of Utah-Utah

Bouldin, Marygale-Judge, Canton District Probate Court-Conn.

Bouliane, Anne-Judge, Superior Court of California City and County of San Francisco-Calif.

Bounds, Joseph Phillips-Chief Judge, Virginia Juvenile and Domestic Relations District Court Twenty-third Judicial District-Va.

Bourgeois, Adam D., Jr.-Associate Judge, Illinois Circuit Court of Cook County-Ill.

Bourke, Terence-Judge, Wisconsin Circuit Court Sheboygan Circuit-Wis.

Bourne, Don-Judge, Russellville District Court-Ark.

Bousman, Monica M.-Judge, North Carolina District Court District 10-N.C.

Bouton, Daniel R.-Chief Judge, Virginia Circuit Court Sixteenth Judicial Circuit-Va.

Bovino, Salvatore-Judge, New Jersey Superior Court Vicinage Six-N.J.

Bowden, Aaron K.-Judge, Florida Circuit Court Fourth Judicial Circuit-Fla.

Bowden, George N.-Judge, Washington Superior Court Snohomish County-Wash.

Bowden, Robert L.-Judge, Barbour County District Court-Ala.

Bowdre, Karon O.-Judge, United States District Court Northern District of Alabama-Ala.

Bowen, Dudley H., Jr.-Chief Judge, United States District Court Southern District of Georgia-Ga.

Bowen, G. Thomas-Judge, New Jersey Superior Court Vicinage Fifteen-N.J.

Bowen, Robert O.-Judge, Marshall Superior Court-Ind.

Bowen, Wiley F.-Resident Judge, North Carolina Superior Court Fourth Judicial Division District 11A-N.C.

Bower, Frederick J.-Associate Judge, Maryland District Court District Eleven-Md.

Bower, N. Russell-Senior Judge, Florida Circuit Court Fourteenth Judicial Circuit-Fla.

Bower, Thomas N.-District Judge, Iowa District Court First Judicial District-Ia.

Bowers, Bob S., Jr.-Judge, Superior Court of California County of Los Angeles-Calif.

Bowers, Kathleen M.-Judge, Denver County Court-Colo.

Bowers, Scott R.-Judge, Vanderburgh Superior Court-Ind.

Bowers, Shellie F.-Associate Judge, Superior Court of the District of Columbia-D.C.

Bowes, Mary Jane-Judge, The Superior Court of Pennsylvania-Pa.

Bowie, Peter W.-Judge, United States Bankruptcy Court Southern District of California-Calif.

Bowie, Preston L., Jr.-Associate Judge, Illinois Circuit Court of Cook County-Ill.

Bowler, Marianne B.-Magistrate Judge, United States District Court District of Massachusetts-Mass.

Bowler, Patrick C.-Judge, Michigan District Court District Sixty-one-Mich.

Bowles, Jerry-Judge, Kentucky Circuit Court Thirtieth Judicial Circuit-Ky.

Bowling, James L.-Judge, Kentucky Circuit Court Forty-fourth Judicial Circuit-Ky.

Bowman, Donna-Judge, Ohio Court of Appeals Tenth District-Ohio

Bowman, J. Ronald-Judge, Ohio Court of Common Pleas Lucas County-Ohio

Bowman, Janice L.-Justice, New York Supreme Court Twelfth Judicial District-N.Y.

Bowman, John B.-Judge, Florida Circuit Court Seventeenth Judicial Circuit-Fla.

Bowman, John J.-Judge, Illinois Appellate Court Second Judicial District-Ill.

Bowman, Leo-Chief Judge, Michigan District Court District Fifty-Mich.

Bowman, Murry-Chief Magistrate, Magistrate Court of Jefferson County-Ga.

Bowman, Pasco M., II-Judge, United States Court of Appeals Eighth Circuit

Bownes, Hugh H.-Senior Judge, United States Court of Appeals First Circuit

Box, Gaylen L.-Judge, Idaho District Court Sixth Judicial District Magistrate Division-Ida.

Boyack, Douglas C.-Judge, Superior Court of California County of Tuolumne-Calif.

Boyd, Christopher S.-Judge, Michigan District Court District Seventy Division Two-Mich.

Boyd, D. W.-District Judge, Oklahoma District Court Eighth Judicial District-Okla.

Boyd, Delores R.-Magistrate Judge, United States District Court Middle District of Alabama-Ala.

Boyd, Donald W.-Judge, Probate Court of Troup County-Ga.

Boyd, James Berkley-Judge, Colorado District Court Ninth Judicial District-Colo.

Boyd, Jean Hudson-Judge, Texas Family District Court 323rd Judicial District-Tex.

Boyd, Jim-Judge, Prairie Grove District Court-Ark.

Boyd, Lauri McIntire-Judge, Selah Municipal Court-Wash.

Boyd, Robert S.-Judge, Superior Court of California County of Sonoma-Calif.

Boyd, William Stewart-Associate Judge, Illinois Circuit Court of Cook County-Ill.

Boyden, Ann-Judge, Utah District Court Third Judicial District-Utah

Boyer, Bruce-Judge, Florida Circuit Court Sixth Judicial Circuit-Fla.

Boyer, Danny D.-Judge, Kansas District Court Twenty-eighth Judicial District-Kan.

Boyer, Nancy Eshcoff-Judge, Allen Superior Court-Ind.

Boyer, Ryan W.-Judge, Idaho District Court Seventh Judicial District Magistrate Division-Ida.

Boyer, Susan E.-Judge, Ohio Court of Common Pleas Washington County-Ohio

Boyer, Tyrie W.-Judge, Duval County Court-Fla.

Boyett, William T.-Chief Judge, Superior Court of Georgia Conasauga Judicial Circuit-Ga.

Boykin, Ulysses W.-Judge, Michigan Circuit Court Third Judicial Circuit-Mich.

Boyko, Chris-Judge, Ohio Court of Common Pleas Cuyahoga County-Ohio

Boylan, Arthur J.-Magistrate Judge, United States District Court District of Minnesota-Minn.

Boyle, Denis John-Judge, The Criminal Court of the City of New York-N.Y.

Boyle, E. Thomas-Magistrate Judge, United States District Court Eastern District of New York-N.Y.

Boyle, Gary W.-Judge, Probate Court of New Hampshire Grafton County-N.H.

Boyle, John M.-Retired Judge, New Jersey Superior Court Appellate Division-N.J.

Boyle, Larry M.-Magistrate Judge, United States District Court District of Idaho-Ida.

Boyle, Mary J.-Judge, Ohio Court of Common Pleas Cuyahoga County-Ohio

Boyle, Terrence W.-Chief Judge, United States District Court Eastern District of North Carolina-N.C.

Boyle, William J.-Justice, Trial Court of Massachusetts District Court Department Hampden County Springfield Division-Mass.

Boyles, Stephen L.-Senior Judge, Florida Circuit Court Seventh Judicial Circuit-Fla.

Boylston, Richard-Judge, Lake County Court-Fla.

Boylston, Robert J.-Senior Judge, Florida Circuit Court Twelfth Judicial Circuit-Fla.

Boynton, Jay C.-Special Justice, Franklin District Court-N.H.

Bozeman, Terri L.-Judge, Lowndes County District Court-Ala.

Bozonelis, B. Theodore-Assignment Judge, New Jersey Superior Court Vicinage Ten-N.J.

Bozza, John A.-Judge, Pennsylvania Court of Common Pleas Sixth Judicial District-Pa.

Bozza, Mary Kaye-Judge, Lyndhurst Municipal Court-Ohio

Bozzuto, Elizabeth A.-Judge, Connecticut Superior Court-Conn.

Braaten, Karen Kosanda-Judge, North Dakota District Court Northeast Central Judicial District-N.D.

Brabham, David-Judge, Texas District Court 188th Judicial District-Tex.

Brace, A. Keith-Judge, Okaloosa County Court-Fla.

Bracewell, Michael Frederick-Judge, Probate Court of Morgan County-Ga.

Brack, Robert C.-Chief Judge, New Mexico District Court Ninth Judicial District-N.Mex.

Brackett, Charles Dwain-Judge, Probate Court of Union County-Ga.

Brackley, John C.-Judge, Wyoming District Court Fourth Judicial District-Wyo.

Bradberry, Guy E.-Judge, Louisiana District Court Fourteenth Judicial District-La.

Bradberry, James E.-Magistrate Judge, United States District Court Eastern District of Virginia-Va.

Bradbury, John-Judge, Idaho District Court Second Judicial District-Ida.

Bradbury, Stephen Douglas-Judge, Superior Court of California County of Lassen-Calif.

Braddy, Galen-Judge, North Carolina District Court District 3A-N.C.

Braden, Paul-Judge, Kentucky Circuit Court Thirty-fourth Judicial Circuit-Ky.

Bradfield, David Martin-Judge, Michigan District Court District Thirty-six-Mich.

Bradford, Cale J.-Judge, Marion Superior Court-Ind.

Bradford, Carl O.-Active Retired Justice, Maine Superior Court-Me.

Bradford, Harold-Judge, Superior Court of California County of Alpine-Calif.

Bradford, Roger V.-Judge, Porter Superior Court-Ind.

Bradley, Ann Walsh-Justice, Wisconsin Supreme Court-Wis.

Bradley, E. Scott-Associate Judge, Delaware Superior Court Sussex County-Del.

Bradley, Harry J.-Judge, Pennsylvania Court of Common Pleas Thirty-second Judicial District-Pa.

Bradley, Jane S.-Judge, Maine District Court-Me.

Bradley, Jaye-Judge, Mississippi Chancery Court Sixteenth Judicial District-Miss.

Bradley, John A. K.-Judge, The Civil Court of the City of New York-N.Y.

Bradley, Len W.-Judge, Clarksville District Court-Ark.

Bradley, Roger E.-Judge, Superior Court of Georgia Appalachian Judicial Circuit-Ga.

Bradley, Vikki-Judge, Upton County Court-Tex.

Bradley, Vincent G.-Justice, New York Supreme Court Third Judicial District-N.Y.

Bradley, William C., Jr.-Associate Judge, Delaware Court of Common Pleas New Castle County-Del.

Bradshaw-Hull, Lynn-Judge, Harris County Civil Court at Law No. 3-Tex.

Bradstreet, Peter C.-Judge, Steuben County Court-N.Y.

Brady, Alta J.-Judge, Oregon Circuit Court Eleventh Judicial District-Ore.

Brady, Edward T.-Associate Justice, Supreme Court of North Carolina-N.C.

Brady, James-Judge, Michigan District Court District Forty-seven-Mich.

Brady, James J.-Judge, United States District Court Middle District of Louisiana-La.

Brady, Laurel S.-Judge, Superior Court of California County of Contra Costa-Calif.

Brady, Michael L.-Judge, Ohio Court of Common Pleas Logan County-Ohio

Brady, Patrick F.-Associate Justice, Trial Court of Massachusetts Superior Court Department-Mass.

Brady, Patrick Michael-Judge, Wisconsin Circuit Court Marathon Circuit-Wis.

Brady, Robert Monroe-Chief Judge, North Carolina District Court District 25-N.C.

Brady, Terrence J.-Associate Judge, Illinois Circuit Court Nineteenth Judicial Circuit-Ill.

Bragg, Christopher W.-Judge, North Carolina District Court District 20-N.C.

Bragg, Susan W.-District Judge, Oklahoma District Court Seventh Judicial District-Okla.

Bragunier, Amy Janel-Associate Judge, Circuit Court for Charles County, Seventh Judicial Circuit-Md.

Brahney, Thomas M., III-Chief Judge, United States Bankruptcy Court Eastern District of Louisiana-La.

Brainard, Larrie R.-Judge, Superior Court of California County of San Diego-Calif.

Braithwaite, Dennis J.-Judge, New Jersey Superior Court Appellate Division-N.J.

Braman, Leonard-Senior Judge, Superior Court of the District of Columbia-D.C.

Bramblett, Mary Anne-Judge, Texas District Court 41st Judicial District-Tex.

Bramlage, Linda Rae-Judge, Kentucky Circuit Court Fifty-fourth Judicial Circuit-Ky.

Bramlette, David C.-Judge, United States District Court Southern District of Mississippi-Miss.

Brammer, J. William, Jr.-Judge, Arizona Court of Appeals Division Two-Ariz.

Branam, Richard E.-Associate District Judge, Oklahoma District Court Twenty-fifth Judicial District-Okla.

Branca, Thomas C.-Judge, Pennsylvania Court of Common Pleas Thirty-eighth Judicial District-Pa.

Brandenburg, Lynn-Judge, Probate Court of Pike County-Ga.

Brandlin, James R.-Judge, Superior Court of California County of Los Angeles-Calif.

Brandolino, Joseph A.-Judge, Superior Court of California County of Los Angeles-Calif.

Brandon, Merwin M., Jr.-Judge, Bastrop City Court-La.

Brandon, Walter C., Jr.-Associate Judge, Illinois Circuit Court Twentieth Judicial Circuit-Ill.

Brands, James V.-Justice, New York Supreme Court Ninth Judicial District-N.Y.

Brandt, Dorothy Chin-Judge, The Civil Court of the City of New York-N.Y.

Brandt, Gregory D.-District Associate Judge, Iowa District Court Fifth Judicial District-Ia.

Brandt, Michael E.-Circuit Judge, Illinois Circuit Court Tenth Judicial Circuit-Ill.

Brandt, Michael R.-Judge, North Haven District Probate Court-Conn.

Brandt, Michael T.-Judge, Franklin County Municipal Court-Ohio

Brandt, Philip H.-Judge, Bankruptcy Appellate Panel Ninth Circuit and Chief Judge, United States Bankruptcy Court Western District of Washington-Wash.

Brandveen, Antonio I.-Judge, New York Court of Claims-N.Y.

Branford, Thomas O.-Judge, Oregon Circuit Court Seventeenth Judicial District-Ore.

Brannen, Perry, Jr.-Chief Judge, Superior Court of Georgia Eastern Judicial Circuit-Ga.

Brannon, Anthony M.-Emergency Judge, North Carolina Superior Court-N.C.

Bransford, Tanya M.-Judge, Minnesota District Court Fourth Judicial District-Minn.

Branson, Albert H.-Magistrate Judge, United States District Court District of Alaska-Alas.

Bransten, Eileen C.-Justice, New York Supreme Court First Judicial District-N.Y.

Brant, Jonathan-Justice, Trial Court of Massachusetts District Court Department Middlesex County Cambridge Division-Mass.

Brantley, David B.-Judge, North Carolina District Court District 8-N.C.

Brantley, Ellen B.-Judge, Arkansas Circuit Court Sixth Judicial Circuit-Ark.

ALPHABETICAL NAME INDEX

Branton, Wiley-Judge, Arkansas Circuit Court Sixth Judicial Circuit-Ark.

Brasfield, Martha B.-Chancellor, Tennessee Chancery Court Twenty-fifth Judicial District-Tenn.

Brash, William W., III-Judge, Wisconsin Circuit Court Milwaukee Circuit-Wis.

Braslow, Stephen L.-Judge, Suffolk County Court-N.Y.

Brassard, Raymond J.-Associate Justice, Trial Court of Massachusetts Superior Court Department-Mass.

Braswell, Jerry-Resident Judge, North Carolina Superior Court Second Judicial Division District 8B-N.C.

Braswell, June B.-Chief Magistrate, Magistrate Court of Bulloch County-Ga.

Braswell, Morris E.-Judge, State Court of Clayton County-Ga.

Braswell, Roy O., Jr.-Judge, Probate Court of Wheeler County and Chief Magistrate, Magistrate Court of Wheeler County-Ga.

Bratton, Bruce F.-Judge, Pennsylvania Court of Common Pleas Twelfth Judicial District-Pa.

Braud, Walter D.-Circuit Judge, Illinois Circuit Court Fourteenth Judicial Circuit-Ill.

Brauer, Timothy A.-Special Judge, Oklahoma District Court Sixth Judicial District-Okla.

Braun, Evelyn L.-Justice, New York Supreme Court Eleventh Judicial District-N.Y.

Braun, Leon M., Jr.-Judge, State Court of Liberty County-Ga.

Braun, Richard Fredric-Judge, The Civil Court of the City of New York-N.Y.

Braunlich, Mark S.-Judge, Michigan District Court District One-Mich.

Braverman, Nathan-Associate Judge, Maryland District Court District One-Md.

Bravo, Carmine M.-Judge, Seminole County Court-Fla.

Brawka, Judith M.-Circuit Judge, Illinois Circuit Court Sixteenth Judicial Circuit-Ill.

Braxton, H. Harrison, Jr.-Judge, Virginia General District Court Fifteenth Judicial District-Va.

Braxton, Margie R.-Judge, Michigan Circuit Court Third Judicial Circuit-Mich.

Bray, Susan Elizabeth-Judge, North Carolina District Court District 18-N.C.

Bray, W. Lowell, Jr.-Judge, Florida Circuit Court Sixth Judicial Circuit-Fla.

Brazier, Jimmy B.-Judge, Probate Court of Stewart County-Ga.

Brazil, Timothy E.-Judge, Kansas District Court Thirty-first Judicial District-Kan.

Brazil, Wayne D.-Magistrate Judge, United States District Court Northern District of California-Calif.

Brazile, Kevin Clement-Judge, Superior Court of California County of Los Angeles-Calif.

Breall, Susan M.-Judge, Superior Court of California City and County of San Francisco-Calif.

Breaux, Terry G.-Judge, Franklin City Court-La.

Breckenridge, Patricia-Judge, Missouri Court of Appeals Western District-Mo.

Bredar, James K.-Magistrate Judge, United States District Court District of Maryland-Md.

Breeden, John L., Jr.-Judge, South Carolina Circuit Court Fifteenth Judicial Circuit-S.C.

Breen, Fredrick Edward-District Associate Judge, Iowa District Court Second Judicial District-Ia.

Breen, J. Daniel-Judge, United States District Court Western District of Tennessee-Tenn.

Breen, J. Timothy-Judge, Warren County Family Court-N.Y.

Breen, Peter I.-Judge, Nevada District Court Second Judicial District-Nev.

Breese, James B.-Judge, Denver County Court-Colo.

Breger, Eli-Senior Judge, Dade County Court-Fla.

Breithaupt, Henry C.-Judge, Oregon Tax Court-Ore.

Breland, David J.-Judge, Morgan County District Court-Ala.

Breland, Jan-Judge, Travis County Court at Law No. 6-Tex.

Bremer, Celeste F.-Magistrate Judge, United States District Court Southern District of Iowa-Ia.

Bremer, John E.-Magistrate Judge, Kansas District Court Seventeenth Judicial District-Kan.

Brennan, Arthur D.-Associate Justice, New Hampshire Superior Court-N.H.

Brennan, Daniel E., Jr.-Judge, Connecticut Superior Court-Conn.

Brennan, Dennis J.-Justice, Trial Court of Massachusetts District Court Department Worcester County Worcester Division-Mass.

Brennan, G. Arthur-Justice, Maine Superior Court-Me.

Brennan, James A.-Senior Judge, Nevada District Court-Nev.

Brennan, John D.-Judge Referee, Connecticut Superior Court-Conn.

Brennan, Kitty K.-Judge, Wisconsin Circuit Court Milwaukee Circuit-Wis.

Brennan, Lawrence J.-Judge, Nassau County Family Court-N.Y.

Brennan, Margaret Ann-Circuit Judge, Illinois Circuit Court of Cook County-Ill.

Brennan, Martha A.-First Justice, Trial Court of Massachusetts District Court Department Worcester County Clinton Division-Mass.

Brennan, Michael Brian-Judge, Wisconsin Circuit Court Milwaukee Circuit-Wis.

Brennan, Michael J.-Justice, New York Supreme Court Second Judicial District-N.Y.

Brennan, Michael W.-Reserve Judge, Wisconsin Circuit Court-Wis.

Brennan, Patrick J.-Judge, Michigan Circuit Court Sixth Judicial Circuit-Mich.

Brennan, Robert A.-Justice, Trial Court of Massachusetts District Court Department Essex County Gloucester Division-Mass.

Brennan, Shirley M.-Judge, Okeechobee County Court-Fla.

Brennan, Terrence H.-Judge, Michigan District Court District Forty-four-Mich.

Brennan, Thomas Emmett, Jr.-Chief Judge, Michigan District Court District Fifty-five-Mich.

Brennan, Thomas M.-Justice, Trial Court of Massachusetts District Court Department Middlesex County Newton Division-Mass.

Brennan, Timothy S.-Chief Judge, Baraga County Probate Court-Mich.

Brennan, W. John-Chief Judge, New Mexico District Court Second Judicial District-N.Mex.

Brenneman, Frederica S.-Judge Referee, Connecticut Superior Court-Conn.

Brenneman, Hugh W., Jr.-Magistrate Judge, United States District Court Western District of Michigan-Mich.

Brenner, Hugh Michael-Judge, Superior Court of California County of Orange-Calif.

Brenner, Lawrence J.-Judge, Pennsylvania Court of Common Pleas Thirty-first Judicial District-Pa.

Brescher, George Angen-Judge, Florida Circuit Court Seventeenth Judicial Circuit-Fla.

Breslin, Thomas A.-Judge, Albany County Court-N.Y.

Bressler, H. J.-Judge, Ohio Court of Common Pleas Butler County-Ohio

Brett, Charlie-Judge, Lee County Court-Miss.

Brewe, Franklin D.-Associate Judge, Illinois Circuit Court Sixteenth Judicial Circuit-Ill.

Brewer, Charles G.-Chief Magistrate, Magistrate Court of Emanuel County-Ga.

Brewer, Cynthia Lee-Judge, Madison County Court-Miss.

Brewer, Dallas-Judge, Yoakum County Court-Tex.

Brewer, David-Judge, Oregon Court of Appeals-Ore.

Brewer, Eileen M.-Circuit Judge, Illinois Circuit Court of Cook County-Ill.

Brewer, Jerry L.-Judge, Orange County Court-Fla.

Brewer, Scott T.-Judge, North Carolina District Court District 20-N.C.

Brewster, Daniel L.-Judge, Kansas District Court Eleventh Judicial District-Kan.

Brewster, David F.-Judge, Kansas District Court Eleventh Judicial District-Kan.

Brewster, Rudi M.-Senior Judge, United States District Court Southern District of California-Calif.

Breyer, Charles R.-Judge, United States District Court Northern District of California-Calif.

Breyer, Stephen-Associate Justice, The Supreme Court of the United States

Brian, Bard Kevin-Judge, Kentucky District Court Second Judicial District-Ky.

Brian, Pat B.-Judge, Utah District Court Third Judicial District-Utah

Bribiesca, Joseph-Judge, Kansas District Court Eighteenth Judicial District-Kan.

Brice, Janice Justina-Judge, Virginia Juvenile and Domestic Relations District Court Thirty-first Judicial District-Va.

Brice, Lynn S.-Judge, Virginia Juvenile and Domestic Relations District Court Twelfth Judicial District-Va.

Brick, Steven A.-Judge, Superior Court of California County of Alameda-Calif.

Bridenstine, Paul J.-Judge, Michigan District Court District Eight Division Three-Mich.

Bridewell, D. Wayne-Judge, Texas District Court 249th Judicial District-Tex.

Bridge, Bobbe J.-Justice, Washington Supreme Court-Wash.

Bridges, Billy G.-Judge, Court of Appeals of Mississippi-Miss.

Bridges, David L.-Justice, Texas Court of Appeals Fifth District-Tex.

Bridges, Douglas R.-Judge, Monroe Circuit Court-Ind.

Bridges, Forrest Donald-Resident Judge, North Carolina Superior Court Seventh Judicial Division District 27B-N.C.

Bridges, George-Associate Judge, Illinois Circuit Court Nineteenth Judicial Circuit-Ill.

Bridges, Joe D.-Judge, Denton County Criminal Court at Law No. 4-Tex.

Bridges, John E.-Judge, Washington Superior Court Chelan County-Wash.

Bridges, Judy C.-Judge, South Carolina Family Court Ninth Judicial Circuit-S.C.

Bridges, Kevin M.-Judge, North Carolina District Court District 20-N.C.

Bridges, Laura J.-Judge, North Carolina District Court District 29-N.C.

Bridgewater, C. C.-Judge, Washington Court of Appeals Division II-Wash.

Bridgforth, Stephen-Judge, New Mexico District Court Third Judicial District-N.Mex.

Brieant, Charles L.-Judge, United States District Court Southern District of New York-N.Y.

Briese, Shawn L.-Judge, Florida Circuit Court Seventh Judicial Circuit-Fla.

Brigantti-Hughes, Mary Ann-Judge, The Civil Court of the City of New York-N.Y.

Briggs, Barbara B.-Judge, Sarasota County Court-Fla.

Briggs, Bruce B.-Judge, North Carolina District Court District 24-N.C.

Briggs, Don F.-Judge, Florida Circuit Court Fifth Judicial Circuit-Fla.

Bright, Gwendolyn N.-Judge, Pennsylvania Court of Common Pleas First Judicial District-Pa.

Bright, Izetta F.-Judge, Michigan District Court District Thirty-six-Mich.

Bright, Lynn Clardy-Judge, Montgomery County District Court-Ala.

Bright, Myron H.-Senior Judge, United States Court of Appeals Eighth Circuit

Brill, Gerrilyn G.-Magistrate Judge, United States District Court Northern District of Georgia-Ga.

Brillhart, Michael J.-Judge, Pennsylvania Court of Common Pleas Nineteenth Judicial District-Pa.

Brim, Cynthia-Circuit Judge, Illinois Circuit Court of Cook County-Ill.

Brimmer, Clarence A.-Judge, United States District Court District of Wyoming-Wyo.

Briner, Karl D.-District Judge, Iowa District Court First Judicial District-Ia.

Brinkema, Leonie M.-Judge, United States District Court Eastern District of Virginia-Va.

Brinkley, Genece E.-Judge, Pennsylvania Court of Common Pleas First Judicial District-Pa.

Brinkley, Stanley A.-Chief Judge, Colorado District Court Fifteenth Judicial District-Colo.

Brinkman, Jack L.-Judge, Madison Superior Court-Ind.

Brinn, Michael P.-Associate Judge, Illinois Circuit Court Fourteenth Judicial Circuit-Ill.

Brinson, Benjamin P.-Judge, Juvenile Court of Georgia Atlantic Judicial Circuit-Ga.

Brintnall, George L. W.-Judge, Battle Ground Municipal Court-Wash.

ALPHABETICAL NAME INDEX

Briones, David-Judge, United States District Court Western District of Texas-Tex.

Briones, Dolores-Judge, El Paso County Court-Tex.

Brisco, Joseph R.-Judge, Superior Court of California County of San Bernardino-Calif.

Briscoe, Joseph R., Jr.-Circuit Judge, Missouri Circuit Court Eleventh Judicial Circuit-Mo.

Briscoe, Mary Beck-Judge, United States Court of Appeals Tenth Circuit

Brisebill, Tina-Justice of the Peace, Pahrump Justices' Court-Nev.

Briseño, Francisco Pedro-Judge, Superior Court of California County of Orange-Calif.

Briskman, Arthur B.-Judge, United States Bankruptcy Court Middle District of Florida-Fla.

Brister, Scott A.-Chief Justice, Texas Court of Appeals Fourteenth District-Tex.

Bristol, Alan M.-Judge, Navarro County Court-Tex.

Britt, John M.-Judge, North Carolina District Court District 7-N.C.

Britt, W. Earl-Senior Judge, United States District Court Eastern District of North Carolina-N.C.

Brizendine, Robert E.-Judge, United States Bankruptcy Court Northern District of Georgia-Ga.

Broadhurst, William D.-Judge, Virginia Circuit Court Twenty-third Judicial Circuit-Va.

Broadrick, Ray-Judge, Probate Court of Whitfield County-Ga.

Broadwater, W. Craig-Judge, United States District Court Northern District of West Virginia-W.Va.

Broberg, James E.-Judge, Minnesota District Court Third Judicial District-Minn.

Brock, David Allen-Chief Justice, New Hampshire Supreme Court-N.H.

Brock, Gary L.-Special Judge, Oklahoma District Court Seventeenth Judicial District-Okla.

Brock, Jeffrey T.-Judge, Conecuh County District Court-Ala.

Brock, Jerome E.-Judge, Superior Court of California County of Santa Clara-Calif.

Brock, Kathryn A.-Judge, New Jersey Superior Court Vicinage Twelve-N.J.

Brockway, David M.-Judge, Chemung County Family Court-N.Y.

Brodbeck, Alan L.-Judge, Nebraska County Court Eighth Judicial District-Neb.

Broderick, John T., Jr.-Associate Justice, New Hampshire Supreme Court-N.H.

Broderick, Michael F.-Family Court Judge, Hawaii District Court First Judicial Circuit-Hi.

Broderick, Patricia A.-Associate Judge, Superior Court of the District of Columbia-D.C.

Broderick, Peter L., Sr.-Judge, Niagara County Court-N.Y.

Brodhay, Stephen Y.-Associate Judge, Illinois Circuit Court of Cook County-Ill.

Brodie, Edward F.-Judge, Superior Court of California County of Ventura-Calif.

Brody, Anita B.-Judge, United States District Court Eastern District of Pennsylvania-Pa.

Brody, George-Recalled Judge, United States Bankruptcy Court Eastern District of Michigan-Mich.

Brogan, James A.-Judge, Ohio Court of Appeals Second District-Ohio

Brogan, Thomas F.-Judge, New Jersey Superior Court Vicinage Eleven-N.J.

Brogden, Joseph B.-Judge, Alabama Circuit Court Twenty-first Judicial Circuit-Ala.

Brogdon, James E., Jr.-Judge-at-Large, South Carolina Circuit Court-S.C.

Brogdon, M. Gino, Sr.-Judge, Superior Court of Georgia Atlanta Judicial Circuit-Ga.

Broker, Phyllis J.-Justice, Trial Court of Massachusetts District Court Department Middlesex County Woburn Division-Mass.

Bromiley, J. Kirk-Judge, Cashmere and Leavenworth Municipal Courts-Wash.

Bromley, Rebecca S.-Judge, Colorado District Court Fourth Judicial District-Colo.

Bronson, Neal B.-Judge, Ohio Court of Common Pleas Warren County-Ohio

Bronson, Terrence P.-Judge, Michigan District Court District One-Mich.

Bronson, Theotis-Judge, Florida Circuit Court Ninth Judicial Circuit-Fla.

Bronstein, Peter H.-Special Justice, Plaistow District Court-N.H.

Bronstein, Philip L.-Circuit Judge, Illinois Circuit Court of Cook County-Ill.

Brook, Sanford Michael-Chief Judge, Indiana Court of Appeals and Presiding Judge, Indiana Court of Appeals Third District-Ind.

Brooke, Alban E.-Senior Judge, Florida Circuit Court Fourth Judicial Circuit-Fla.

Brooker, Richard-Associate Judge, Juvenile Court of Georgia Dougherty Judicial Circuit-Ga.

Brooks, Charles C.-Judge, Recorder's Court of Chatham County-Ga.

Brooks, Daniel T.-Judge, Kansas District Court Eighteenth Judicial District-Kan.

Brooks, James M.-Judge, Superior Court of California County of Orange-Calif.

Brooks, John-Judge, Wyoming District Court Eighth Judicial District-Wyo.

Brooks, Larry R.-Associate District Judge, Oklahoma District Court Ninth Judicial District-Okla.

Brooks, Michael J.-Justice, Trial Court of Massachusetts District Court Department Middlesex County Natick Division-Mass.

Brooks, Rodney Hughes-Circuit Judge, Illinois Circuit Court of Cook County-Ill.

Brooks, Ruben-Magistrate Judge, United States District Court Southern District of California-Calif.

Brooks, Sidney B.-Chief Judge, United States Bankruptcy Court District of Colorado-Colo.

Brooks, Suzanne-Judge, Williamson County Court at Law No. 1-Tex.

Broome, Thomas H.-Judge, Rankin County Court-Miss.

Broomfield, Robert C.-Senior Judge, United States District Court District of Arizona-Ariz.

Brorby, Wade-Senior Judge, United States Court of Appeals Tenth Circuit

Brosey, Richard L.-Judge, Washington Superior Court Lewis County-Wash.

Brosnahan, Carol S.-Judge, Superior Court of California County of Alameda-Calif.

Brosnahan, Janet Adams-Circuit Judge, Illinois Circuit Court of Cook County-Ill.

Brosnahan, Mary M.-Circuit Judge, Illinois Circuit Court of Cook County-Ill.

Brothers, Thomas White-Judge, Tennessee Circuit Court Twentieth Judicial District-Tenn.

Brotherton, James C.-Judge, Alabama Circuit Court Fourteenth Judicial Circuit-Ala.

Brotherton, Robert P.-Judge, Texas District Court 30th Judicial District-Tex.

Brotman, Stanley S.-Senior Judge, United States District Court District of New Jersey-N.J.

Brotmann, Andrew K.-Judge, White Plains City Court-N.Y.

Broughton, Frank-Assistant Judge, Vermont Trial Court Addison County-Vt.

Broussard, Edward B.-Judge, Abbeville City Court-La.

Brousseau, Theodore H.-Judge, Florida Circuit Court Twentieth Judicial Circuit-Fla.

Brower, Orene Lynn-Judge, Idaho District Court Sixth Judicial District Magistrate Division-Ida.

Brown, Anna J.-Judge, United States District Court District of Oregon-Ore.

Brown, Archie Cameron-Chief Judge, Michigan Circuit Court Twenty-second Judicial Circuit-Mich.

Brown, Audrey-Justice, Pondera County Justice of the Peace Court-Mont.

Brown, Bert M.-Judge, Las Vegas Municipal Court-Nev.

Brown, Brandy Oliver-Judge, Kentucky District Court Twenty-fifth Judicial District-Ky.

Brown, Carl C., Jr.-Judge, Superior Court of Georgia Augusta Judicial Circuit-Ga.

Brown, Carolyn A.-Judge, Washington Superior Court Benton-Franklin Counties-Wash.

Brown, Cecil H.-Senior Judge, Florida Circuit Court Ninth Judicial Circuit-Fla.

Brown, Charles B.-Judge, Juvenile Court of Georgia Enotah Judicial Circuit-Ga.

Brown, Charles C., Jr.-President Judge, Pennsylvania Court of Common Pleas Forty-ninth Judicial District-Pa.

Brown, Charles E., Jr.-Judge, Ohio Court of Common Pleas Stark County-Ohio

Brown, Charles Lee-Judge, Florida Circuit Court Tenth Judicial Circuit-Fla.

Brown, Charlie-Chief Judge, North Carolina District Court District 19C-N.C.

Brown, Cheryl H.-Judge, Tolland District Probate Court-Conn.

Brown, Christopher C.-Judge, Michigan District Court District Fifty-Mich.

Brown, Colleen A.-Judge, United States Bankruptcy Court District of Vermont-Vt.

Brown, Craig B.-Judge, North Carolina District Court District 14-N.C.

Brown, Elizabeth E.-Judge, United States Bankruptcy Court District of Colorado-Colo.

Brown, Elwood L.-Judge, St. Clair County Probate Court-Mich.

Brown, Emanuel-Associate Judge, Maryland District Court District One-Md.

Brown, F. Keith-Circuit Judge, Illinois Circuit Court Sixteenth Judicial Circuit-Ill.

Brown, Frank A.-Judge, Superior Court of California County of San Diego-Calif.

Brown, Frank R.-Resident Judge, North Carolina Superior Court First Judicial Division District 7C-N.C.

Brown, Frederick L.-Associate Justice, Massachusetts Appeals Court-Mass.

Brown, Garrett E., Jr.-Judge, United States District Court District of New Jersey-N.J.

Brown, George A.-Judge, Mobile County District Court-Ala.

Brown, George E.-Judge, LaGrange Superior Court-Ind.

Brown, George H., Jr.-Judge, Tennessee Circuit Court Thirtieth Judicial District-Tenn.

Brown, George K., Jr.-Judge, Manatee County Court-Fla.

Brown, Gerald M.-Judge, Bell County Court at Law No. 3-Tex.

Brown, Geraldine Soat-Magistrate Judge, United States District Court Northern District of Illinois-Ill.

Brown, Gerard S.-Judge, Superior Court of California County of San Bernardino-Calif.

Brown, Gilbert T.-Judge, Superior Court of California County of Santa Clara-Calif.

Brown, Harold M.-Judge, Alaska Superior Court Third Judicial District-Alas.

Brown, Helen E.-Judge, Michigan Circuit Court Third Judicial Circuit-Mich.

Brown, Henry N., Jr.-Chief Judge, Louisiana Court of Appeal Second Circuit-La.

Brown, Houston L.-Judge, Alabama Circuit Court Tenth Judicial Circuit Birmingham Division-Ala.

Brown, Irma Jean-Judge, Superior Court of California County of Los Angeles-Calif.

Brown, J. Michael-Judge, Superior Court of California County of Humboldt-Calif.

Brown, James R.-Circuit Judge, Illinois Circuit Court of Cook County-Ill.

Brown, James W.-Judge, Superior Court of California County of Santa Barbara-Calif.

Brown, Janice R.-Associate Justice, California Supreme Court-Calif.

Brown, Jean Williams-Associate Justice, Alabama Supreme Court-Ala.

Brown, Jeffrey S.-Judge, Nassau County Court-N.Y.

Brown, Jeffrey V.-Judge, Texas District Court 55th Judicial District-Tex.

Brown, Jerry A.-Judge, United States Bankruptcy Court Eastern District of Louisiana-La.

Brown, Jim D.-Judge, Hansford County Court-Tex.

Brown, Jo Robin-Judge, Harris County Criminal Court at Law No. 12-Tex.

Brown, Joan A.-Judge, Pennsylvania Court of Common Pleas First Judicial District-Pa.

Brown, Joe B.-Magistrate Judge, United States District Court Middle District of Tennessee-Tenn.

Brown, Joel H.-Judge, Florida Circuit Court Eleventh Judicial Circuit-Fla.

Brown, Josef B.-Associate Judge, Maryland District Court District Five-Md.

Brown, Joyce Albright-Judge, North Carolina District Court District 27A-N.C.

ALPHABETICAL NAME INDEX

Brown, Karen Kennedy-Judge, United States Bankruptcy Court Southern District of Texas-Tex.
Brown, Kenneth D.-Judge, Pennsylvania Court of Common Pleas Twenty-ninth Judicial District-Pa.
Brown, Kenneth G.-Judge, New Mexico District Court Thirteenth Judicial District-N.Mex.
Brown, Kevin L.-Judge, Superior Court of California County of Los Angeles-Calif.
Brown, L. Elizabeth-Associate District Judge, Oklahoma District Court Fifteenth Judicial District-Okla.
Brown, Leslie D.-Judge, Utah Juvenile Court Fourth Judicial District-Utah
Brown, Leslie E.-Judge, Superior Court of California County of Los Angeles-Calif.
Brown, Lillis J.-Judge, Probate Court of Rockdale County-Ga.
Brown, Linda E.-Judge, Marion Superior Court-Ind.
Brown, Lisa-Judge, Nevada District Court Eighth Judicial District-Nev.
Brown, Lucy Chernow-Judge, Florida Circuit Court Fifteenth Judicial Circuit-Fla.
Brown, Lynn W.-Judge, Tennessee Criminal Court First Judicial District-Tenn.
Brown, Mary Ann-District Judge, Iowa District Court Eighth Judicial District-Ia.
Brown, Michael-Associate Judge, Illinois Circuit Court of Cook County-Ill.
Brown, Michael D.-Judge, Tom Green County Court-Tex.
Brown, Nancy-Judge, Superior Court of California County of Los Angeles-Calif.
Brown, Pamila J.-Associate Judge, Maryland District Court District Ten-Md.
Brown, Paul N.-Senior Judge, United States District Court Eastern District of Texas-Tex.
Brown, Richard S.-Judge, Wisconsin Court of Appeals District Two-Wis.
Brown, Richard T.-Judge, North Carolina District Court District 16A-N.C.
Brown, Rick S.-Judge, Superior Court of California County of Santa Barbara-Calif.
Brown, Robert E.-Judge, Holmes County Court-Fla.
Brown, Robert J.-Judge, Ohio Court of Common Pleas Wayne County-Ohio
Brown, Robert L.-Associate Justice, Arkansas Supreme Court-Ark.
Brown, Ronald-Judge, Superior Court of California County of Mendocino-Calif.
Brown, Ronald L.-Judge, Nebraska Workers' Compensation Court-Neb.
Brown, Ronda R.-Judge, Parke Circuit Court-Ind.
Brown, S. Phillip-Judge, Superior Court of Georgia Macon Judicial Circuit-Ga.
Brown, Samuel E.-Justice, Granite County Justice of the Peace Court and Judge, Philipsburg City Court-Mont.
Brown, Sherrie W.-Judge, Alabama Circuit Court Eighth Judicial Circuit-Ala.
Brown, Shirley Hastings-Judge, North Carolina District Court District 28-N.C.
Brown, Spencer Whitewood-Judge, Kerr County Court at Law-Tex.
Brown, Stephen E.-Judge, Grays Harbor District Court No. 1 Grays Harbor County-Wash.
Brown, Stephen M.-Chief Judge, Washington Court of Appeals Division III-Wash.
Brown, Stephen T.-Magistrate Judge, United States District Court Southern District of Florida-Fla.
Brown, Steven-Judge, Wyoming Circuit Court Seventh Judicial District, Natrona County-Wyo.
Brown, Susan-Judge, Ohio Court of Appeals Tenth District-Ohio
Brown, Susan-Judge, Texas District Court 185th Judicial District-Tex.
Brown, T. Lynn-Associate Circuit Judge, Missouri Circuit Court Thirty-third Judicial Circuit-Mo.
Brown, Tammy S.-Judge, Probate Court of Barrow County-Ga.
Brown, Thomas, III-Presiding Judge, Missouri Circuit Court Nineteenth Judicial Circuit-Mo.
Brown, Thomas A., Jr.-Judge, New Jersey Superior Court Vicinage Four-N.J.
Brown, Thomas C.-Judge, New Jersey Superior Court Vicinage Five-N.J.
Brown, Thomas E.-Judge, Arkansas Circuit Court Eleventh West Judicial Circuit-Ark.
Brown, Thomas Leo-Judge, Michigan Circuit Court Thirtieth Judicial Circuit-Mich.
Brown, Thomas Paul-Judge, Allegany County Court-N.Y.
Brown, Timothy L.-Judge, South Carolina Family Court Thirteenth Judicial Circuit-S.C.
Brown, Trish M.-Judge, United States Bankruptcy Court District of Oregon-Ore.
Brown, W. Frank, III-Chancellor, Tennessee Chancery Court Eleventh Judicial District-Tenn.
Brown, Walter B., Jr.-Judge, South Carolina Family Court Sixth Judicial Circuit-S.C.
Brown, Waymond-Judge, Pine Bluff District Court-Ark.
Brown, Wesley Ernest-Senior Judge, United States District Court District of Kansas-Kan.
Brown, Wesley L.-Judge, South Carolina Family Court Seventh Judicial Circuit-S.C.
Brown, William Houston-Judge, United States Bankruptcy Court Western District of Tennessee-Tenn.
Browne, Joe-Senior Judge, City Court of Atlanta-Ga.
Browne, Kim Alana-Judge, Ohio Court of Common Pleas Franklin County-Ohio
Browne, Robert L.-Judge, Sterling County Court-Tex.
Brownell, Scott MacKenzie-Judge, Florida Circuit Court Twelfth Judicial Circuit-Fla.
Brownell, Thomas F.-First Justice, Trial Court of Massachusetts District Court Department Plymouth County Plymouth Division-Mass.
Brownell, William S.-Magistrate Judge, United States District Court District of Maine-Me.
Brownfield, Gary L.-Associate Judge, Illinois Circuit Court of Cook County-Ill.
Brownfield, Thomas L.-Chief Judge, Illinois Circuit Court Eighth Judicial Circuit-Ill.
Brownhill, Paula J.-Presiding Judge, Oregon Circuit Court Eighteenth Judicial District-Ore.
Browning, Christopher C.-Judge, Superior Court of Arizona Pima County-Ariz.
Browning, Edwin B., Jr.-Judge, Florida District Court of Appeal First District-Fla.
Browning, James R.-Senior Judge, United States Court of Appeals Ninth Circuit
Browning, R. Mark-Family Court Judge, Hawaii District Court First Judicial Circuit-Hi.
Browning, Renona Carol-Judge, Kentucky District Court Thirty-eighth Judicial District-Ky.
Browning, Sue Carol-Judge, Kentucky District Court Seventh Judicial District-Ky.
Browning, William Docker-Senior Judge, United States District Court District of Arizona-Ariz.
Bruce, David S.-Associate Judge, Circuit Court for Anne Arundel County, Fifth Judicial Circuit-Md.
Bruce, Gary J.-Judge, Michigan District Court District Five-Mich.
Bruce, Raymond L.-Judge, The Civil Court of the City of New York-N.Y.
Bruce-Lyle, Desiree-Judge, Superior Court of California County of San Diego-Calif.
Brudie, Jeff M.-Judge, Idaho District Court Second Judicial District-Ida.
Brueher, Gary John-Judge, Othello District Court Adams County-Wash.
Bruggink, Eric G.-Senior Judge, United States Court of Federal Claims
Brugnaux, Barbara L.-Judge, Vigo Superior Court-Ind.
Bruguera, Soussan G.-Judge, Superior Court of California County of Los Angeles-Calif.
Bruhn, J. Michael-Judge, Ulster County Court-N.Y.
Bruiniers, Terence L.-Judge, Superior Court of California County of Contra Costa-Calif.
Brumbach, Charles P.-Judge, Idaho District Court Fifth Judicial District Magistrate Division-Ida.
Brun, Roy L.-Judge, Louisiana District Court First Judicial District-La.
Bruner, Cindy Hull-Judge, Adams County Court-Colo.
Brunetti, John J.-Judge, New York Court of Claims-N.Y.
Brunetti, Melvin T.-Senior Judge, United States Court of Appeals Ninth Circuit
Brunetti, Robert C.-Judge, Connecticut Superior Court-Conn.
Bruni, Louis H.-Judge, Webb County Court-Tex.
Brunner, Edward R.-Judge, Wisconsin Circuit Court Barron Circuit-Wis.
Brunner, H. Frank-Judge, Alabama Circuit Court Thirty-second Judicial Circuit-Ala.
Brunner, Jennifer L.-Judge, Ohio Court of Common Pleas Franklin County-Ohio
Brunnock, Thomas P.-Judge, Waterbury District Probate Court-Conn.
Bruno, Joseph F.-Justice, New York Supreme Court Second Judicial District-N.Y.
Bruns, David E.-Judge, Kansas District Court Third Judicial District-Kan.
Brunson, Catherine M.-Judge, Florida Circuit Court Fifteenth Judicial Circuit-Fla.
Brunton, Diane L.-Associate Judge, Illinois Circuit Court Seventh Judicial Circuit-Ill.
Brusatte, James L.-Associate Judge, Illinois Circuit Court Thirteenth Judicial Circuit-Ill.
Brutinel, Robert-Judge, Superior Court of Arizona Yavapai County-Ariz.
Bruzzese, Joseph J., Jr.-Judge, Ohio Court of Common Pleas Jefferson County-Ohio
Bryan, Albert V., Jr.-Senior Judge, United States District Court Eastern District of Virginia-Va.
Bryan, Andrea Y.-Judge, Superior Court of California County of Santa Clara-Calif.
Bryan, Ben L., Jr.-Judge, Florida Circuit Court Nineteenth Judicial Circuit-Fla.
Bryan, Berry-Judge, Angelina County Court at Law No. 2-Tex.
Bryan, Carl F., II-Judge, Superior Court of California County of Nevada-Calif.
Bryan, Daniel E., Jr.-Judge, Nebraska District Court First Judicial District-Neb.
Bryan, Howard F., IV-Presiding Judge, Alabama Circuit Court Fifth Judicial Circuit-Ala.
Bryan, Paul S.-Judge, Florida Circuit Court Third Judicial Circuit-Fla.
Bryan, Robert J.-Senior Judge, United States District Court Western District of Washington-Wash.
Bryant, George H.-Senior Judge, Superior Court of Georgia-Ga.
Bryant, Jerri S.-Chancellor, Tennessee Chancery Court Tenth Judicial District-Tenn.
Bryant, Lucy J.-Judge, Probate Court of Warren County-Ga.
Bryant, Malcolm F., Jr.-Judge, State Court of Toombs County-Ga.
Bryant, Paul M., Jr.-Judge, Superior Court of California County of San Bernardino-Calif.
Bryant, Peggy L.-Judge, Ohio Court of Appeals Tenth District-Ohio
Bryant, Quillian L., Jr.-Judge, Probate Court of Jefferson County-Ga.
Bryant, Robert A.-Associate Circuit Judge, Missouri Circuit Court Eighth Judicial Circuit-Mo.
Bryant, Steven J.-Judge, North Carolina District Court District 30-N.C.
Bryant, Thomas F.-Judge, Ohio Court of Appeals Third District-Ohio
Bryant, Vanessa L.-Judge, Connecticut Superior Court-Conn.
Bryant, Wanda G.-Associate Judge, North Carolina Court of Appeals-N.C.
Bryant, William Benson-Senior Judge, United States District Court District of Columbia-D.C.
Bryant-Deason, Susan-Judge, Superior Court of California County of Los Angeles-Calif.
Bryner, Alexander O.-Associate Justice, Alaska Supreme Court-Alas.
Bryner, Bryce K.-Presiding Judge, Utah District Court Seventh Judicial District-Utah
Bryson, Fred L.-Senior Judge, Florida Circuit Court Sixth Judicial Circuit-Fla.
Bryson, Larry A.-Associate Circuit Judge, Missouri Circuit Court Thirteenth Judicial Circuit-Mo.
Bryson, William C.-Judge, United States Court of Appeals Federal Circuit
Brzezinski, Robert B.-Chief Judge, Michigan District Court District Sixteen-Mich.
Bubenik, Sharron M.-District Judge, Oklahoma District Court Fourteenth Judicial District-Okla.
Bucaria, Stephen A.-Justice, New York Supreme Court Tenth Judicial District-N.Y.

Bucci, Elaine T.-Associate Judge, Rhode Island District Court-R.I.

Buchan, Mary E.-Judge, South Carolina Family Court Twelfth Judicial Circuit-S.C.

Buchanan, A. Deane-Judge, Cleveland Heights Municipal Court-Ohio

Buchanan, Barbara A.-Judge, Idaho District Court First Judicial District Magistrate Division-Ida.

Buchanan, Doris S.-Judge, Bennington District Probate Court-Vt.

Buchanan, Robert L., Jr.-Magistrate Judge, United States District Court District of South Carolina-S.C.

Buchanan, Theresa Carroll-Magistrate Judge, United States District Court Eastern District of Virginia-Va.

Buchmeyer, Jerry-Judge, United States District Court Northern District of Texas-Tex.

Buchter, Richard Lance-Justice, New York Supreme Court Eleventh Judicial District-N.Y.

Buchwald, Naomi Reice-Judge, United States District Court Southern District of New York-N.Y.

Buck, Michael L.-Chief Judge, Allegan County Probate Court-Mich.

Bucki, Carl L.-Judge, United States Bankruptcy Court Western District of New York-N.Y.

Buckingham, David C.-Judge, Kentucky Court of Appeals-Ky.

Buckles, Frederick R.-Magistrate Judge, United States District Court Eastern District of Missouri-Mo.

Bucklew, Susan C.-Judge, United States District Court Middle District of Florida-Fla.

Buckley, Daniel J.-Judge, Superior Court of California County of Los Angeles-Calif.

Buckley, Dennis J.-Judge, Superior Court of California County of Yuba-Calif.

Buckley, John P.-Reserve Judge, Wisconsin Circuit Court-Wis.

Buckley, John T.-Presiding Justice, New York Supreme Court Appellate Division First Judicial Department-N.Y.

Buckley, Paul V.-Justice, Trial Court of Massachusetts District Court Department Suffolk County Brighton Division-Mass.

Buckley, Peter C.-Judge, Chemung County Court-N.Y.

Buckley, Robert A.-Judge, Louisiana District Court Thirty-fourth Judicial District-La.

Buckley, Tim S.-Associate Justice, California Court of Appeal Fifth District-Calif.

Buckley, Timothy J.-Judge, Geneva City Court-N.Y.

Bucklo, Elaine E.-Judge, United States District Court Northern District of Illinois-Ill.

Buckner, Alan-Judge, Superior Court of California County of Los Angeles-Calif.

Buckner, Joseph Moody-Chief Judge, North Carolina District Court District 15B-N.C.

Buckner, Mary A.-Judge, Recorder's Court of Columbus-Muscogee County-Ga.

Buckner, Perry M.-Judge, South Carolina Circuit Court Fourteenth Judicial Circuit-S.C.

Buckner, Rosanne-Judge, Washington Superior Court Pierce County-Wash.

Buckwalter, Ronald L.-Judge, United States District Court Eastern District of Pennsylvania-Pa.

Buckworth, Mark D.-Associate Judge, Delaware Family Court New Castle County-Del.

Buczynski, Frank A., Jr.-Judge, New Jersey Superior Court Vicinage Fourteen-N.J.

Buday, Lynne Marie-Judge, Kalkaska County Probate Court-Mich.

Budney, Walter R.-Judge Referee, Connecticut Superior Court-Conn.

Budnick, Martin-Senior Judge, Florida Circuit Court Eighteenth Judicial Circuit-Fla.

Budoff, Robert-Judge, Superior Court of Arizona Maricopa County-Ariz.

Budzinski, Henry A.-Recalled Circuit Judge, Illinois Circuit Court of Cook County-Ill.

Bueltel, Joseph A.-Judge, Minnesota District Court Third Judicial District-Minn.

Buettner, Kenneth L.-Judge, Oklahoma Court of Civil Appeals-Okla.

Buffington, Larry-Judge, Mississippi Chancery Court Thirteenth Judicial District-Miss.

Buffington, William David-Chief Magistrate, Magistrate Court of Franklin County-Ga.

Bufford, Samuel L.-Judge, United States Bankruptcy Court Central District of California-Calif.

Buhl, Paul D.-Judge, East Haddam District Probate Court-Conn.

Buhl, William C.-Judge, Michigan Circuit Court Thirty-sixth Judicial Circuit-Mich.

Buis, J. Stephen-Judge, Virginia Juvenile and Domestic Relations District Court Thirteenth Judicial District-Va.

Bukaty, John J., Jr.-Judge, Kansas District Court Twenty-ninth Judicial District-Kan.

Bulkeley, Harry Clifford-Circuit Judge, Illinois Circuit Court Ninth Judicial Circuit-Ill.

Bull, Diane-Judge, Harris County Criminal Court at Law No. 11-Tex.

Bullard, James L.-Senior Judge, Superior Court of Georgia-Ga.

Bullard, Valerie-Judge, Nassau County District Court-N.Y.

Bullerdieck, Michael-Associate Circuit Judge, Missouri Circuit Court Thirty-second Judicial Circuit-Mo.

Bullock, Frank W., Jr.-Judge, United States District Court Middle District of North Carolina-N.C.

Bullock, Stafford G.-Resident Judge, North Carolina Superior Court Third Judicial Division District 10-N.C.

Bullock, Terry L.-Judge, Kansas District Court Third Judicial District-Kan.

Bumb, Michael J.-Judge, Ohio Court of Common Pleas Fulton County-Ohio

Bumgardner, Rudolph, III-Judge, Court of Appeals of Virginia-Va.

Bunch, Max W.-Justice of the Peace, Argenta Justices' Court-Nev.

Bunch, Thomas E.-Judge, Chillicothe Municipal Court-Ohio

Bunnell, Helen Ruwet-Judge, Litchfield District Probate Court-Conn.

Bunnell, Kimberly N.-Judge, Kentucky Circuit Court Twenty-second Judicial Circuit-Ky.

Bunning, David L.-Judge, United States District Court Eastern District of Kentucky-Ky.

Bunyan, Bert A.-Justice, New York Supreme Court Second Judicial District-N.Y.

Buras, Camille-Judge, Louisiana District Court Orleans Parish Criminal District-La.

Burbank, Jeffrey "R"-Presiding Judge, Utah Juvenile Court First Judicial District-Utah

Burch, Christine-Judge, Probate Court of Wayne County-Ga.

Burch, Joe-Associate District Judge, Oklahoma District Court Second Judicial District-Okla.

Burch, Paul M.-Judge, South Carolina Circuit Court Fourth Judicial Circuit-S.C.

Burch, Robert E.-Judge, Tennessee Circuit Court Twenty-third Judicial District-Tenn.

Burch, Susan R.-Judge, North Carolina District Court District 18-N.C.

Burchard, Jack-Judge, Washington Superior Court Okanogan County-Wash.

Burchett, Dewey E., Jr.-Judge, Louisiana District Court Twenty-sixth Judicial District-La.

Burd, Doris E.-Judge, Denver County Court-Colo.

Burdette, J. Dexter-Judge, Kansas District Court Twenty-ninth Judicial District-Kan.

Burdick, Roger S.-Justice, Idaho Supreme Court-Ida.

Burditt, Larry M.-Associate Circuit Judge, Missouri Circuit Court Thirtieth Judicial Circuit-Mo.

Burgasser, R. Thomas-Judge, North Tonawanda City Court-N.Y.

Burger, Joan M.-Circuit Judge, Missouri Circuit Court Twenty-second Judicial Circuit-Mo.

Burger-Plavan, Trena H.-Judge, Superior Court of California County of Sacramento-Calif.

Burgess, A. Franklin, Jr.-Associate Judge, Superior Court of the District of Columbia-D.C.

Burgess, Ben-Judge, Kansas District Court Eighteenth Judicial District-Kan.

Burgess, Brian L.-Judge, Vermont Trial Court-Vt.

Burgess, Don-Justice, Texas Court of Appeals Ninth District-Tex.

Burgess, Franklin D.-Judge, United States District Court Western District of Washington-Wash.

Burgess, Harold W., Jr.-Chief Judge, Virginia Juvenile and Domestic Relations District Court Twelfth Judicial District-Va.

Burgess, James L.-Judge, Kansas District Court Eighteenth Judicial District-Kan.

Burgess, Lowell, Jr.-Associate District Judge, Oklahoma District Court Seventeenth Judicial District-Okla.

Burgess, Ralph K.-Judge, Texas District Court 5th Judicial District-Tex.

Burgess, Robert E.-Judge, Louisiana District Court Eleventh Judicial District-La.

Burgett, Keith E.-District Judge, Iowa District Court Fourth Judicial District-Ia.

Burk, Richard B.-Senior Judge, Florida Circuit Court Fifteenth Judicial Circuit-Fla.

Burk, Warren-Judge, Florida Circuit Court Eighteenth Judicial Circuit-Fla.

Burke, Anne M.-Judge, Illinois Appellate Court First Judicial District Division Two-Ill.

Burke, Barbara Lee-Judge, Superior Court of California County of Los Angeles-Calif.

Burke, Dennis J.-Associate Judge, Illinois Circuit Court of Cook County-Ill.

Burke, Earle Jeffrey-Judge, Superior Court of California County of San Luis Obispo-Calif.

Burke, Edward D.-Judge, New York Court of Claims-N.Y.

Burke, Edward O.-Judge, Superior Court of Arizona Maricopa County-Ariz.

Burke, James-Judge, Wyoming District Court First Judicial District-Wyo.

Burke, James M.-Judge, The Criminal Court of the City of New York-N.Y.

Burke, John W.-Justice, New York Supreme Court Tenth Judicial District-N.Y.

Burke, Kevin S.-Judge, Minnesota District Court Fourth Judicial District-Minn.

Burke, Kim Wilson-Judge, Ohio Court of Common Pleas Hamilton County-Ohio

Burke, L. Todd-Resident Judge, North Carolina Superior Court Fifth Judicial Division District 21-N.C.

Burke, LeRoy, III-Judge, Recorder's Court of Chatham County-Ga.

Burke, Marlene R.-Assistant Judge, Vermont Trial Court Rutland County-Vt.

Burke, Michael J.-Presiding Judge, Superior Court of Arizona La Paz County-Ariz.

Burke, Michael J.-Circuit Judge, Illinois Circuit Court Eighteenth Judicial Circuit-Ill.

Burke, Richard E.-Judge, Connecticut Superior Court-Conn.

Burke, Rosemary Higgins-Judge, Miami Circuit Court-Ind.

Burke, Thomas F., Jr.-Judge, Pennsylvania Court of Common Pleas Eleventh Judicial District-Pa.

Burke, Wanda-Judge, Probate Court of Jenkins County-Ga.

Burke, William J., III-Judge, Suffolk County District Court-N.Y.

Burkemper, T. Bennett, Jr.-Associate Circuit Judge, Missouri Circuit Court Forty-fifth Judicial Circuit-Mo.

Burkett, Michael L.-Judge, Fremont Municipal Court-Ohio

Burkhalter, Lisa G.-Judge, Angelina County Court at Law No. 1-Tex.

Burkhalter, Steven-Judge, Probate Court of Floyd County-Ga.

Burkhalter, Terri-Associate Judge, Juvenile Court of Georgia Rome Judicial Circuit-Ga.

Burkhard, Robert V.-Judge, Nebraska District Court Fourth Judicial District-Neb.

Burkhart, Gordon R.-Judge, Superior Court of California County of Riverside-Calif.

Burlew, John H.-Judge, Hamilton County Municipal Court-Ohio

Burling, Jean K.-Associate Justice, New Hampshire Superior Court-N.H.

Burnes, Nonnie S.-Associate Justice, Trial Court of Massachusetts Superior Court Department-Mass.

Burnett, Arthur L., Sr.-Senior Judge, Superior Court of the District of Columbia-D.C.

Burnett, David-Judge, Arkansas Circuit Court Second Judicial Circuit-Ark.

ALPHABETICAL NAME INDEX

Burnett, E. C., III-Associate Justice, South Carolina Supreme Court-S.C.

Burnett, Ralph M.-Associate Judge, Maryland District Court District Twelve-Md.

Burnette, R. Edwin, Jr.-Judge, Virginia General District Court Twenty-fourth Judicial District-Va.

Burnette, Vickie-Judge, Probate Court of Thomas County-Ga.

Burney, Janet E.-Judge, Ohio Court of Common Pleas Cuyahoga County-Ohio

Burnham, Christopher L.-Judge, Morgan Superior Court-Ind.

Burnham, Donna Jean-Chief Magistrate, Magistrate Court of Heard County-Ga.

Burningham, Guy R.-Judge, Utah District Court Fourth Judicial District-Utah

Burns, Brian D.-Judge, Otsego County Court-N.Y.

Burns, Charles P.-Circuit Judge, Illinois Circuit Court of Cook County-Ill.

Burns, Christopher J.-Associate Justice, New York Supreme Court Appellate Division Fourth Judicial Department-N.Y.

Burns, Don C.-Judge, Louisiana District Court Thirty-seventh Judicial District-La.

Burns, Elizabeth-Judge, Cortland City Court-N.Y.

Burns, Ellen Bree-Senior Judge, United States District Court District of Connecticut-Conn.

Burns, Gloria M.-Judge, United States Bankruptcy Court District of New Jersey-N.J.

Burns, James S.-Chief Judge, Hawaii Intermediate Court of Appeals-Hi.

Burns, Kenneth M.-Judge, Mississippi Chancery Court Fourteenth Judicial District-Miss.

Burns, Larry A.-Magistrate Judge, United States District Court Southern District of California-Calif.

Burns, Leon C., Jr.-Judge, Tennessee Criminal Court Thirteenth Judicial District-Tenn.

Burns, Luke K., Jr.-Associate Judge, Circuit Court for Carroll County, Fifth Judicial Circuit-Md.

Burns, Patrick R.-Judge, Auburn Municipal Court-Wash.

Burns, Robert P.-Judge Referee, Connecticut Superior Court-Conn.

Burns, Steven D.-Judge, Nebraska District Court Third Judicial District-Neb.

Burnside, Janet R.-Judge, Ohio Court of Common Pleas Cuyahoga County-Ohio

Burnside, Robert A., Jr.-Judge, West Virginia Circuit Court Tenth Judicial Circuit-W.Va.

Burnstein, Miette K.-Judge, Florida Circuit Court Seventeenth Judicial Circuit-Fla.

Burr, Charles B., II-Judge, Pennsylvania Court of Common Pleas Thirty-second Judicial District-Pa.

Burr, Edward R.-Circuit Judge, Illinois Circuit Court of Cook County-Ill.

Burr, Jack L.-Chief Judge, Kansas District Court Fifteenth Judicial District-Kan.

Burr, Kenneth Mark-Judge, Superior Court of California County of Alameda-Calif.

Burr, Rodney T.-Justice of the Peace, Henderson Justices' Court-Nev.

Burr, Theodore J., Jr.-Judge, Virginia General District Court Sixth Judicial District-Va.

Burrell, Anthony L.-Circuit Judge, Illinois Circuit Court of Cook County-Ill.

Burrell, Don E., Jr.-Circuit Judge, Missouri Circuit Court Thirty-first Judicial Circuit-Mo.

Burrell, Garland E., Jr.-Judge, United States District Court Eastern District of California-Calif.

Burress, Daniel A.-Judge, Michigan Circuit Court Forty-fourth Judicial Circuit-Mich.

Burris, William J.-Judge, Louisiana District Court Twenty-second Judicial District-La.

Burroughs, Robert M., Sr.-Emergency Judge, North Carolina Superior Court-N.C.

Burrows, Jon-Judge, Bell County Court-Tex.

Burson, Lynn-Judge, Dallas County Criminal Court of Appeals No. 2-Tex.

Burt, Forrest W.-Judge, Ohio Court of Common Pleas Geauga County-Ohio

Burt, Jennifer Evans-Judge, Probate Court of Dawson County-Ga.

Burton, Charles-Judge, Palm Beach County Court-Fla.

Burton, David-Judge, Kentucky District Court Thirty-fourth Judicial District-Ky.

Burton, Freddie G., Jr.-Judge, Wayne County Probate Court-Mich.

Burton, Jim-Judge, Probate Court of Wilkes County-Ga.

Burton, Michael D.-Associate Circuit Judge, Missouri Circuit Court Twenty-first Judicial Circuit-Mo.

Burton, Michael K.-Judge, Utah District Court Third Judicial District-Utah

Burton, Robert B.-Judge, Idaho District Court First Judicial District Magistrate Division-Ida.

Burton, Susanne-Judge, Juvenile Court of Georgia Northern Judicial Circuit-Ga.

Burwell, Gladys B.-Judge, Galveston County Probate Court-Tex.

Bury, David C.-Judge, United States District Court District of Arizona-Ariz.

Buscaglia, Russell P.-Judge, New York Court of Claims-N.Y.

Busch, David L.-Associate Circuit Judge, Missouri Circuit Court Eighth Judicial Circuit-Mo.

Busch, Peter J.-Judge, Superior Court of California City and County of San Francisco-Calif.

Busch, Thomas H.-Judge, Tippecanoe Superior Court-Ind.

Bush, Bernetta D.-Circuit Judge, Illinois Circuit Court of Cook County-Ill.

Bush, David A.-Judge, Nebraska County Court Ninth Judicial District-Neb.

Bush, Jerri-Associate Circuit Judge, Missouri Circuit Court Third Judicial Circuit-Mo.

Bush, John B.-Presiding Judge, Alabama Circuit Court Nineteenth Judicial Circuit-Ala.

Bush, Julian L.-Circuit Judge, Missouri Circuit Court Twenty-second Judicial Circuit-Mo.

Bush, Leland O.-Judge, Minnesota District Court Fifth Judicial District-Minn.

Bush, Lynn Jeanne-Judge, United States Court of Federal Claims

Bush, Michael G.-Judge, Superior Court of California County of Kern-Calif.

Bush, Philip D.-Judge, Minnesota District Court Fourth Judicial District-Minn.

Bush, Russell Keith-Judge, Lee County District Court-Ala.

Bush, Zoe-Associate Judge, Superior Court of the District of Columbia-D.C.

Bushur, Jeffrey L.-Associate Circuit Judge, Missouri Circuit Court Sixteenth Judicial Circuit-Mo.

Buslee, Henry B.-Reserve Judge, Wisconsin Circuit Court-Wis.

Buss, Charles A.-Chief Judge, Colorado District Court Twenty-first Judicial District-Colo.

Busskohl, Patrick-Judge, Edgerton and Midwest Municipal Courts-Wyo.

Bustamante, Michael D.-Judge, New Mexico Court of Appeals-N.Mex.

Buster, David-Magistrate Judge, Kansas District Court Twenty-fourth Judicial District-Kan.

Butanis, Victor K.-Administrative Judge, Maryland District Court District Nine-Md.

Buter, David J.-Chief Judge, Michigan District Court District Sixty-one-Mich.

Buth, George S.-Chief Judge, Michigan Circuit Court Seventeenth Judicial Circuit-Mich.

Butler, Charles R., Jr.-Chief Judge, United States District Court Southern District of Alabama-Ala.

Butler, Denis J.-Judge, The Civil Court of the City of New York-N.Y.

Butler, Elizabeth-Associate Justice, Trial Court of Massachusetts Superior Court Department-Mass.

Butler, James F.-Chancellor, Tennessee Chancery Court Twenty-sixth Judicial District-Tenn.

Butler, John F.-Judge, Alabama Circuit Court Thirteenth Judicial Circuit-Ala.

Butler, Lewis Hayden-Judge, Knightstown Town Court-Ind.

Butler, Louis B., Jr.-Judge, Wisconsin Circuit Court Milwaukee Circuit-Wis.

Butler, Sophia C.-Associate Judge, Juvenile Court of Georgia Brunswick Judicial Circuit-Ga.

Butner, George W.-District Judge, Oklahoma District Court Twenty-second Judicial District-Okla.

Butterfield, G. K., Jr.-Special Judge, North Carolina Superior Court-N.C.

Butterworth, James N.-Chief Magistrate, Magistrate Court of Habersham County-Ga.

Butterworth, Robert A.-Senior Judge, Florida Circuit Court Seventeenth Judicial Circuit-Fla.

Buttner, Frederic A.-Judge, Florida Circuit Court Fourth Judicial Circuit-Fla.

Buttorff, Karla-Judge, Pierce District Court Pierce County-Wash.

Buttrick, John A.-Judge, Superior Court of Arizona Maricopa County-Ariz.

Buttrill, Del-Judge, Probate Court of Henry County-Ga.

Butts, Angela T.-Judge, Recorder's Court of DeKalb County-Ga.

Butts, John W.-Judge, Salem District Probate Court-Conn.

Butts, Nancy L.-Judge, Pennsylvania Court of Common Pleas Twenty-ninth Judicial District-Pa.

Butts, Robert John-Chief Judge, Cheboygan County Probate Court-Mich.

Butz, M. Kathleen-Judge, Superior Court of California County of Nevada-Calif.

Buxton, Mary Jo-Judge, Probate Court of Johnson County-Ga.

Buxton, William B.-Special Judge, Oklahoma District Court Fifth Judicial District-Okla.

Buyske, Marc G.-Judge, Montana District Court Ninth Judicial District-Mont.

Buzzard, Steven R.-Judge, Chehalis, Napavine, Vader and Winlock Municipal Courts-Wash.

Bybee, Jay S.-Judge, United States Court of Appeals Ninth Circuit

Bye, Kermit E.-Judge, United States Court of Appeals Eighth Circuit

Byer, Joan L.-Judge, Kentucky Circuit Court Thirtieth Judicial Circuit-Ky.

Byers, Gary L.-Judge, Maumee Municipal Court-Ohio

Byers, John K.-Senior Judge, Tennessee Appellate and Trial Courts-Tenn.

Byers-Emmerling, Melissa-Judge, East Liverpool Municipal Court-Ohio

Bynon, Robert P., Jr.-Judge, Jefferson County District Court Birmingham Division-Ala.

Byrd, Clara W.-Judge, Tennessee Circuit Court Fifteenth Judicial District-Tenn.

Byrd, David V.-Judge, North Carolina District Court District 23-N.C.

Byrd, Donald Cole-Judge, Superior Court of California County of Glenn-Calif.

Byrd, Duncan M., Jr.-Chief Judge, Virginia Circuit Court Twenty-fifth Judicial Circuit-Va.

Byrd, Sandy L. V.-Judge, Pennsylvania Court of Common Pleas First Judicial District-Pa.

Byrne, Bradley E.-Presiding Judge, Alabama Circuit Court Twenty-first Judicial Circuit-Ala.

Byrne, Darlene-Judge, Texas District Court 126th Judicial District-Tex.

Byrne, J. Michael-Judge, Superior Court of California County of Los Angeles-Calif.

Byrne, John M.-Judge Referee, Connecticut Superior Court-Conn.

Byrne, John N.-Judge, The Criminal Court of the City of New York-N.Y.

Byrne, Maureen A.-Acting Judge, Norwich City Court-N.Y.

Byrne, Robert E.-Circuit Judge, Illinois Circuit Court Eighteenth Judicial Circuit-Ill.

Byrne, Wm. Matthew, Jr.-Senior Judge, United States District Court Central District of California-Calif.

Byrnes, J. Norris-Associate Judge, Circuit Court for Baltimore County, Third Judicial Circuit-Md.

Byrnes, Marjorie L.-Judge, Rochester City Court-N.Y.

Byrnes, William H., III-Chief Judge, Louisiana Court of Appeal Fourth Circuit-La.

Byron, Michael J.-Judge, Wisconsin Circuit Court Rock Circuit-Wis.

Byron, Nicholas G.-Circuit Judge, Illinois Circuit Court Third Judicial Circuit-Ill.

Bysshe, Frederick H., Jr.-Judge, Superior Court of California County of Ventura-Calif.

Cable, Cindy L.-Justice of the Peace, Lane County Justice Court-Ore.

Cabranes, José A.-Judge, United States Court of Appeals Second Circuit

Cabrera, Carlos A.-Judge, Superior Court of California County of Fresno-Calif.

ALPHABETICAL NAME INDEX

Cabrinha, Neal Anthony-Judge, Superior Court of California County of Santa Clara-Calif.
Cacheris, James C.-Senior Judge, United States District Court Eastern District of Virginia-Va.
Cadagin, Donald M.-Circuit Judge, Illinois Circuit Court Seventh Judicial Circuit-Ill.
Caddel, Jerry D.-Judge, Ector County Court-Tex.
Caddell, Jack-Judge, United States Bankruptcy Court Northern District of Alabama-Ala.
Caddell, Patrick K.-Judge, Pinellas County Court-Fla.
Cade, Herbert A.-Judge, Louisiana District Court Orleans Parish Civil District-La.
Cadei, Raymond M.-Judge, Superior Court of California County of Sacramento-Calif.
Cadigan, Robert E.-Associate Judge, Circuit Court for Baltimore County, Third Judicial Circuit-Md.
Cadle, James E.-Judge, Superior Court of California County of San Joaquin-Calif.
Cady, Mark S.-Justice, Iowa Supreme Court-Ia.
Caeton, A. Dennis-Judge, Superior Court of California County of Fresno-Calif.
Cagle, Jack-Judge, Harris County Civil Court at Law No. 1-Tex.
Cahalan, William Leo-Judge, Michigan Circuit Court Third Judicial Circuit-Mich.
Cahill, Peter-Judge, Superior Court of Arizona Gila County-Ariz.
Cahill, Robert-Judge, Illinois Appellate Court First Judicial District Division Two-Ill.
Cahill, Robert Edward, Jr.-Associate Judge, Maryland District Court District Eight-Md.
Cahill, Robert G.-Judge, Jefferson County District Court Birmingham Division-Ala.
Cahn, Herman-Justice, New York Supreme Court First Judicial District-N.Y.
Cahoj, John-Magistrate Judge, Kansas District Court Fifteenth Judicial District-Kan.
Cahraman, Thomas H.-Judge, Superior Court of California County of Riverside-Calif.
Caiazza, Francis X.-Magistrate Judge, United States District Court Western District of Pennsylvania-Pa.
Cain, Chap, III-Judge, Texas District Court 253rd Judicial District-Tex.
Cain, David E.-Judge, Ohio Court of Common Pleas Franklin County-Ohio
Cain, Thomas W.-Judge, Superior Court of California County of Santa Clara-Calif.
Cain, Timothy M.-Judge, South Carolina Family Court Tenth Judicial Circuit-S.C.
Cain, William Bryan-Judge, Tennessee Court of Appeals Middle Division-Tenn.
Cain, William T.-Judge, Kentucky Circuit Court Twenty-eighth Judicial Circuit-Ky.
Calabrese, Alex M.-Judge, The Criminal Court of the City of New York-N.Y.
Calabrese, Anthony O., Jr.-Judge, Ohio Court of Appeals Eighth District-Ohio
Calabrese, Domenick-Judge, Woodbury District Probate Court-Conn.
Calabrese, Joseph C.-Judge, Nassau County Court-N.Y.
Calabresi, Guido-Judge, United States Court of Appeals Second Circuit
Calabria, Ann Marie-Associate Judge, North Carolina Court of Appeals-N.C.
Calagione, Robert B.-Justice, Trial Court of Massachusetts District Court Department Worcester County Westborough Division-Mass.
Caldwell, Charles M.-Judge, United States Bankruptcy Court Southern District of Ohio-Ohio
Caldwell, Donald Ray-Chief Magistrate, Magistrate Court of Catoosa County-Ga.
Caldwell, Gregory L.-Judge, Noblesville City Court-Ind.
Caldwell, Jesse B., III-Resident Judge, North Carolina Superior Court Seventh Judicial Division District 27A-N.C.
Caldwell, Johnnie L., Jr.-Judge, Superior Court of Georgia Griffin Judicial Circuit-Ga.
Caldwell, Karen K.-Judge, United States District Court Eastern District of Kentucky-Ky.
Caldwell, Kathleen-Judge, South Dakota Circuit Court Second Judicial Circuit-S.D.
Caldwell, Mary Ann-Judge, Jamestown Town Court-Ind.
Caldwell, Michael T.-Circuit Judge, Illinois Circuit Court Nineteenth Judicial Circuit-Ill.
Caldwell, R. Michael-Judge, Louisiana District Court Nineteenth Judicial District-La.
Caldwell, William W.-Senior Judge, United States District Court Middle District of Pennsylvania-Pa.
Caldwell, Wylie H., Jr.-Judge, South Carolina Family Court Twelfth Judicial Circuit-S.C.
Cales, James A., Jr.-Judge, Virginia Circuit Court Third Judicial Circuit-Va.
Calfee, Robert-Judge, West Virginia Family Court Circuit Eight-W.Va.
Calhoon, Jerry L.-Judge, Texas District Court 349th Judicial District-Tex.
Calhoun, Donald E., Jr.-Recalled Judge, United States Bankruptcy Court Southern District of Ohio-Ohio
Calhoun, John C.-Judge, Alabama Circuit Court Tenth Judicial Circuit Birmingham Division-Ala.
Calhoun, Stephen L.-Judge, Idaho District Court Second Judicial District Magistrate Division-Ida.
Calkins, Susan W.-Associate Justice, Maine Supreme Judicial Court-Me.
Callahan, Bill-Judge, Michigan Circuit Court Third Judicial Circuit-Mich.
Callahan, Connie M.-Associate Justice, California Court of Appeal Third District-Calif.
Callahan, John J.-Retired Judge, New Jersey Superior Court-N.J.
Callahan, Kenneth R.-Judge, Ohio Court of Common Pleas Cuyahoga County-Ohio
Callahan, Kevin G.-Judge, New Jersey Superior Court Vicinage Six-N.J.
Callahan, Lynne S.-Judge, Akron Municipal Court-Ohio
Callahan, Michael James-Judge, Michigan Circuit Court Third Judicial Circuit-Mich.
Callahan, Nathan A.-District Associate Judge, Iowa District Court First Judicial District-Ia.
Callahan, Richard-Circuit Judge, Missouri Circuit Court Nineteenth Judicial Circuit-Mo.
Callahan, Robert J.-Judge Referee, Connecticut Superior Court-Conn.
Callahan, Thomas J.-Judge, Yuma County Court-Colo.
Callahan, William E., Jr.-Magistrate Judge, United States District Court Eastern District of Wisconsin-Wis.
Callaway, Stephen V.-Judge, United States Bankruptcy Court Western District of Louisiana-La.
Callis, Ann-Circuit Judge, Illinois Circuit Court Third Judicial Circuit-Ill.
Calloway, Curtis A.-Judge, Louisiana District Court Nineteenth Judicial District-La.
Callum, Thomas E.-Judge, Illinois Appellate Court Second Judicial District-Ill.
Calogero, Pascal F., Jr.-Chief Justice, Supreme Court of Louisiana-La.
Calton, Patricia-Justice of the Peace, Wells Justices' Court and Judge, Wells Municipal Court-Nev.
Calvaruso, Edmund A.-Surrogate, Monroe County Surrogate's Court-N.Y.
Calvert, A. Gene, Jr.-Judge, Ellis County Court at Law No. 2-Tex.
Calvert, Logan-Judge, Kentucky District Court Fourth Judicial District-Ky.
Calvin, Michael B.-Circuit Judge, Missouri Circuit Court Twenty-second Judicial Circuit-Mo.
Camacho, Fernando M.-Judge, The Criminal Court of the City of New York-N.Y.
Camerer, G. Glenn-Judge, Nebraska County Court Twelfth Judicial District-Neb.
Cameron, Brenda-Judge, Kansas District Court Tenth Judicial District-Kan.
Cameron, Roderick A.-Judge, Wisconsin Circuit Court Chippewa Circuit-Wis.
Cameron, William M. "Mac", III-Judge, North Carolina District Court District 4-N.C.
Camp, Daniel P.-Judge, Juvenile Court of Georgia Coweta Judicial Circuit-Ga.
Camp, Jack T.-Judge, United States District Court Northern District of Georgia-Ga.
Camp, Laurie Smith-Judge, United States District Court District of Nebraska-Neb.
Camp, Richard C.-Judge, New Jersey Superior Court Vicinage Five-N.J.
Camp, Susan S.-Chief Magistrate, Magistrate Court of Douglas County-Ga.
Campanella, James W.-Circuit Judge, Illinois Circuit Court Twentieth Judicial Circuit-Ill.
Campbell, A. Bruce-Judge, United States Bankruptcy Court District of Colorado-Colo.
Campbell, Brian T.-Judge, Denver County Court-Colo.
Campbell, Bridgette-Judge, State Court of Cobb County-Ga.
Campbell, Calvin C.-Judge, Illinois Appellate Court First Judicial District Division Five-Ill.
Campbell, Cecil Paxton, II-Judge, Louisiana District Court Twenty-sixth Judicial District-La.
Campbell, Charles W., Jr.-Judge, Superior Court of California County of Ventura-Calif.
Campbell, Colin F.-Presiding Judge, Superior Court of Arizona Maricopa County-Ariz.
Campbell, Donald F.-Judge, New Jersey Superior Court Vicinage Fourteen-N.J.
Campbell, J. Colin, Sr.-Judge, Virginia Circuit Court Twenty-seventh Judicial Circuit-Va.
Campbell, J. Richard-Judge, Hamilton Superior Court-Ind.
Campbell, James T.-Justice, Texas Court of Appeals Seventh District-Tex.
Campbell, Joan-Judge, Texas District Court 248th Judicial District-Tex.
Campbell, John C.-Judge, Minden City Court-La.
Campbell, John MacLaughlin-Associate Judge, Superior Court of the District of Columbia-D.C.
Campbell, Joseph Timothy-Judge, Ohio Court of Common Pleas Greene County-Ohio
Campbell, Joyce A.-Judge, Fairfield Municipal Court-Ohio
Campbell, Kari-Judge, Moore County Court-Tex.
Campbell, Kevin G.-Magistrate Judge, Kansas District Court Twenty-fifth Judicial District-Kan.
Campbell, Levin Hicks-Senior Judge, United States Court of Appeals First Circuit
Campbell, Louis K.-Chief Judge, Virginia General District Court Twenty-fifth Judicial District-Va.
Campbell, Mary Ann-Judge, Pennsylvania Court of Common Pleas Twenty-third Judicial District-Pa.
Campbell, Nancy M.-Judge, State Court of Cobb County-Ga.
Campbell, Nancy W.-Judge, Oregon Circuit Court Twentieth Judicial District-Ore.
Campbell, Patricia B.-Judge, Wayne County Probate Court-Mich.
Campbell, Phil W.-Judge, Van Wert Municipal Court-Ohio
Campbell, Richard D.-Judge, State Court of Elbert County-Ga.
Campbell, Samuel E.-Judge, Virginia Juvenile and Domestic Relations District Court Sixth Judicial District-Va.
Campbell, Tena-Judge, United States District Court District of Utah-Utah
Campbell, Thomas-Associate Circuit Judge, Missouri Circuit Court Seventeenth Judicial Circuit-Mo.
Campbell, Thomas-Judge, Wyoming Circuit Court First Judicial District, Laramie County-Wyo.
Campbell, Thomas A.-Judge, Trumbull County Court-Ohio
Campbell, Todd J.-Judge, United States District Court Middle District of Tennessee-Tenn.
Campbell, Victoria Brace-Judge, Port Jervis City Court-N.Y.
Camplese, Albert S.-Judge, Ashtabula Municipal Court-Ohio
Camposeo, Elaine N.-Judge, Andover District Probate Court-Conn.
Campoy, Hector E.-Judge, Superior Court of Arizona Pima County-Ariz.
Canada, Andrew Joseph, Jr.-Judge, Virginia Circuit Court Second Judicial Circuit-Va.
Canaday, G. Michael-Judge, Louisiana District Court Fourteenth Judicial District-La.
Canaday, Russell D.-Judge, Kansas District Court Fourteenth Judicial District-Kan.
Canady, Charles T.-Judge, Florida District Court of Appeal Second District-Fla.
Canales, Adolph-Judge, Texas District Court 298th Judicial District-Tex.

ALPHABETICAL NAME INDEX

Canales, Paul-Judge, Bexar County Court at Law No. 2-Tex.

Canales, Terry A.-Judge, Texas District Court 79th Judicial District-Tex.

Canan, Russell F.-Associate Judge, Superior Court of the District of Columbia-D.C.

Canby, William C., Jr.-Senior Judge, United States Court of Appeals Ninth Circuit

Candee, Roland L.-Judge, Superior Court of California County of Sacramento-Calif.

Candelaria, Neil C.-Judge, New Mexico District Court Second Judicial District-N.Mex.

Candon, Kevin-Judge, Rutland District Probate Court-Vt.

Cane, Thomas-Chief Judge, Wisconsin Court of Appeals and Judge, Wisconsin Court of Appeals District Three-Wis.

Canepa, Theresa J.-Judge, Superior Court of California County of Contra Costa-Calif.

Canfield, James B.-Justice, New York Supreme Court Third Judicial District-N.Y.

Caniglia, Joseph P.-Judge, Nebraska County Court Fourth Judicial District-Neb.

Cannella, James L.-Judge, Louisiana Court of Appeal Fifth Circuit-La.

Cannizzaro, Joseph R.-Justice, New York Supreme Court Third Judicial District-N.Y.

Cannizzaro, Leon A., Jr.-Judge, Louisiana Court of Appeal Fourth Circuit-La.

Cannon, Diane Gordon-Circuit Judge, Illinois Circuit Court of Cook County-Ill.

Cannon, Evelyn Omega-Associate Judge, Circuit Court for Baltimore City, Eighth Judicial Circuit-Md.

Cannon, James F.-Judge, Dayton Municipal Court-Ohio

Cannon, Jonathan H.-Judge, Superior Court of California County of Orange-Calif.

Cannon, Julia Taylor-Judge, Virginia General District Court Twentieth Judicial District-Va.

Cannon, Larry E.-Judge, Probate Court of Rabun County-Ga.

Cannon, William H.-Judge, Michigan District Court District Forty-one B-Mich.

Cannon, William S.-Judge, Superior Court of California County of San Diego-Calif.

Cano-Garcia, Sylvia-Judge, New Mexico District Court Third Judicial District-N.Mex.

Canova, Greg-Judge, Washington Superior Court King County-Wash.

Canter, Zel-Judge, Superior Court of California County of Santa Barbara-Calif.

Cantero, Raoul G., III-Justice, Florida Supreme Court-Fla.

Cantil-Sakauye, Tani Gorre-Judge, Superior Court of California County of Sacramento-Calif.

Cantor, Jane B.-Judge, New Jersey Superior Court Vicinage Eight-N.J.

Cantrell, Ben H.-Judge, Tennessee Court of Appeals Middle Division-Tenn.

Cantrell, Damon H.-Special Judge, Oklahoma District Court Fourteenth Judicial District-Okla.

Cantrell, Daphene L.-Retired-Recalled Judge, North Carolina District Court-N.C.

Cantrell, Julie N.-Judge, Lake Superior Court-Ind.

Cantu, Arnoldo-Judge, Hidalgo County Court at Law No. 5-Tex.

Capeheart, Ted C.-Judge, Arkansas Circuit Court Ninth West Judicial Circuit-Ark.

Capel, Wallace, Jr.-Magistrate Judge, United States District Court Eastern District of Michigan-Mich.

Capell, John L., III-Judge, Alabama Circuit Court Fifteenth Judicial Circuit-Ala.

Capelle, Stephen H.-Magistrate Judge, United States District Court Western District of Texas-Tex.

Caperton, Michael-Judge, Kentucky District Court Twenty-seventh Judicial District-Ky.

Caperton, Tracy K.-Magistrate Judge, United States District Court Southern District of Texas-Tex.

Capineri, Stephen J.-Associate Justice, Rhode Island Family Court-R.I.

Caposela, Ernest M.-Judge, New Jersey Superior Court Vicinage Eleven-N.J.

Capper, Donald R.-Judge, Lawrence County Municipal Court-Ohio

Capper, Thomas J.-Judge, Ohio Court of Common Pleas Clark County-Ohio

Cappiello, Daniel M.-Special Justice, Rochester District Court-N.H.

Cappy, Ralph J.-Chief Justice, The Supreme Court of Pennsylvania-Pa.

Caprathe, William Joseph-Judge, Michigan Circuit Court Eighteenth Judicial Circuit-Mich.

Caputo, A. Richard-Judge, United States District Court Middle District of Pennsylvania-Pa.

Capuzzi, Conrad B.-President Judge, Pennsylvania Court of Common Pleas Fourteenth Judicial District-Pa.

Caracappa, Linda K.-Magistrate Judge, United States District Court Eastern District of Pennsylvania-Pa.

Carangelo, John J.-Judge, Orange District Probate Court-Conn.

Caraway, Billy B.-Judge, Hardin County Court-Tex.

Caraway, J. Jay-Judge, Louisiana Court of Appeal Second Circuit-La.

Carbo, John C., III-Judge, State Court of Clayton County-Ga.

Carbon, Susan B.-Special Justice, Concord District Court-N.H.

Carchman, Philip S.-Judge, New Jersey Superior Court Appellate Division-N.J.

Card, Larry D.-Judge, Alaska Superior Court Third Judicial District-Alas.

Card, Lee-Associate District Judge, Oklahoma District Court Twentieth Judicial District-Okla.

Cardamone, Richard J.-Senior Judge, United States Court of Appeals Second Circuit

Cardello, Bruce A.-Justice, Newport District Court-N.H.

Carden, Mary R.-Associate Judge, Juvenile Court of Georgia Northeastern Judicial Circuit-Ga.

Cardona, Anthony V.-Presiding Justice, New York Supreme Court Appellate Division Third Judicial Department-N.Y.

Cardonne Ely, Gisela-Judge, Florida Circuit Court Eleventh Judicial Circuit-Fla.

Cardoza, Jane-Judge, Superior Court of California County of Fresno-Calif.

Cardoza, Joseph E.-Judge, Hawaii Circuit Court Second Judicial Circuit-Hi.

Cardwell, Timothy Lee-Judge, Ohio Court of Common Pleas Huron County-Ohio

Cardwell, William W.-Presiding Judge, Alabama Circuit Court Sixteenth Judicial Circuit-Ala.

Caretti, Richard L.-Judge, Michigan Circuit Court Sixteenth Judicial Circuit-Mich.

Carey, Chad L.-Judge, Clinton County Municipal Court-Ohio

Carey, Cheryl-Judge, Washington Superior Court King County-Wash.

Carey, Joan B.-Judge, New York Court of Claims-N.Y.

Carey, John K.-Judge, Florida Circuit Court Thirteenth Judicial Circuit-Fla.

Carey, Joseph W.-Judge, Carroll Circuit Court-Ind.

Carey, Kevin J.-Judge, United States Bankruptcy Court Eastern District of Pennsylvania-Pa.

Carey, Paula M.-Associate Justice, Trial Court of Massachusetts Probate and Family Court Department Norfolk County Division-Mass.

Carey, Richard J.-First Justice, Trial Court of Massachusetts District Court Department Hampshire County Northampton Division-Mass.

Carey, Richard P.-Judge, Ohio Court of Common Pleas Clark County-Ohio

Carey McCray, Margaret-Judge, Mississippi Circuit Court Fourth Judicial District-Miss.

Carhart, Judd J.-Associate Justice, Trial Court of Massachusetts Superior Court Department-Mass.

Carithers, Hugh, Jr.-Judge, Florida Circuit Court Fourth Judicial Circuit-Fla.

Carley, George H.-Justice, Supreme Court of Georgia-Ga.

Carlin, John S.-Judge, Florida Circuit Court Twentieth Judicial Circuit-Fla.

Carlisle, Elaine L.-Judge, Municipal Court of Atlanta-Ga.

Carlisle, M. Russell, Jr.-Judge, State Court of Cobb County-Ga.

Carlisle, Sheila A.-Judge, Marion Superior Court-Ind.

Carlo-Altieri, Gerardo A.-Judge, Bankruptcy Appellate Panel First Circuit and Chief Judge, United States Bankruptcy Court District of Puerto Rico

Carlow, James Marion-Judge, Bowie County Court-Tex.

Carlson, Charles D.-Judge, Oregon Circuit Court Second Judicial District-Ore.

Carlson, Cynthia-Judge, Oregon Circuit Court Second Judicial District-Ore.

Carlson, Gary L.-Judge, Wisconsin Circuit Court Taylor Circuit-Wis.

Carlson, George C., Jr.-Justice, Mississippi Supreme Court-Miss.

Carlson, James L.-Judge, Wisconsin Circuit Court Walworth Circuit-Wis.

Carlson, M. Randolph, II-Chief Judge, Virginia Juvenile and Domestic Relations District Court Fourth Judicial District-Va.

Carlson, Mary E.-Judge, Minnesota District Court Tenth Judicial District-Minn.

Carlson, Max E.-Judge, Sedgwick County Court-Colo.

Carlson, Monte B.-Judge, Idaho District Court Fifth Judicial District-Ida.

Carlson, Patricia-Judge, Bozeman Municipal Court-Mont.

Carlson, Theodore L.-Judge, Nebraska Court of Appeals-Neb.

Carlson, Thomas A.-Magistrate Judge, United States District Court Eastern District of Michigan-Mich.

Carlson, Thomas E.-Judge, United States Bankruptcy Court Northern District of California-Calif.

Carlton, Charles T.-Senior Judge, Florida Circuit Court Twentieth Judicial Circuit-Fla.

Carlton, Stephen P.-Associate Circuit Judge, Missouri Circuit Court Twenty-ninth Judicial Circuit-Mo.

Carluzzo, Lewis R.-Special Trial Judge, United States Tax Court

Carman, Gregory W.-Chief Judge, United States Court of International Trade

Carmical, J. Stanley-Chief Judge, North Carolina District Court District 16B-N.C.

Carmichael, Vicki L.-Judge, Jeffersonville City Court-Ind.

Carmichael, William G.-Judge, Louisiana District Court Twentieth Judicial District-La.

Carmody, Ellen S.-Magistrate Judge, United States District Court Western District of Michigan-Mich.

Carmody, Thomas F., Jr.-Circuit Judge, Illinois Circuit Court of Cook County-Ill.

Carmody, Thomas P.-Chief Judge, Illinois Circuit Court Seventh Judicial Circuit-Ill.

Carmody, William W.-Chief Judge, Alger-Schoolcraft Counties Probate Court District-Mich.

Carnes, Burt-Judge, Texas District Court 368th Judicial District-Tex.

Carnes, Ed-Judge, United States Court of Appeals Eleventh Circuit

Carnes, Julie E.-Judge, United States District Court Northern District of Georgia-Ga.

Carnes, Thomas J.-Judge, Ohio Court of Common Pleas Portage County-Ohio

Carney, Christine A.-Judge, Larimer County Court-Colo.

Carney, Cormac J.-Judge, Superior Court of California County of Orange-Calif.

Carney, Gerald J.-Special Justice, New London District Court-N.H.

Carney, Jack E., Jr.-Judge, State Court of Bryan County-Ga.

Carney, Patrick M.-Judge, Buffalo City Court-N.Y.

Carney, Robert B.-Judge, Florida Circuit Court Seventeenth Judicial Circuit-Fla.

Carney, Thomas M.-Judge, Florida Circuit Court Eleventh Judicial Circuit-Fla.

Carni, Edward D.-Justice, New York Supreme Court Fifth Judicial District-N.Y.

Carniak, Nancy Tolwin-Judge, Michigan District Court District Fifty-two Division Three-Mich.

Carolan, Robert F.-Judge, Minnesota District Court First Judicial District-Minn.

ALPHABETICAL NAME INDEX

Caroom, Philip T.-Associate Judge, Circuit Court for Anne Arundel County, Fifth Judicial Circuit-Md.
Carp, Ted-Judge, Oregon Circuit Court Second Judicial District-Ore.
Carpanini, Mark F.-Judge, Polk County Court-Fla.
Carparelli, Russell-Judge, Colorado Court of Appeals-Colo.
Carpeneti, Walter L. "Bud"-Associate Justice, Alaska Supreme Court-Alas.
Carpenter, Christine-Associate Circuit Judge, Missouri Circuit Court Thirteenth Judicial Circuit-Mo.
Carpenter, Don L.-Justice, Trial Court of Massachusetts District Court Department Barnstable County Barnstable Division-Mass.
Carpenter, George E.-Judge, Colbert County District Court-Ala.
Carpenter, Hiram A., III-Judge, Pennsylvania Court of Common Pleas Twenty-fourth Judicial District-Pa.
Carpenter, Nanaruth H.-Judge, Kent County Probate Court-Mich.
Carpenter, William C., Jr.-Associate Judge, Delaware Superior Court New Castle County-Del.
Carpenter, William R.-Judge, Pennsylvania Court of Common Pleas Thirty-eighth Judicial District-Pa.
Carper, Brian Allan-Judge, Texas Family District Court 324th Judicial District-Tex.
Carpinello, Anthony J.-Associate Justice, New York Supreme Court Appellate Division Third Judicial Department-N.Y.
Carr, Brent A.-Judge, Tarrant County Criminal Court at Law No. 9-Tex.
Carr, Dolores A.-Judge, Superior Court of California County of Santa Clara-Calif.
Carr, Donna J.-Judge, Ohio Court of Appeals Ninth District-Ohio
Carr, Gayl Branum-Judge, Virginia Juvenile and Domestic Relations District Court Nineteenth Judicial District-Va.
Carr, James G.-Judge, United States District Court Northern District of Ohio-Ohio
Carr, Patrick M.-District Judge, Iowa District Court Third Judicial District-Ia.
Carr, Robert Stuart-Magistrate Judge, United States District Court District of South Carolina-S.C.
Carr, William O.-Associate Judge, Circuit Court for Harford County, Third Judicial Circuit-Md.
Carrafiello, Matthew D.-Judge, Pennsylvania Court of Common Pleas First Judicial District-Pa.
Carraway, Lonnie W.-Judge, North Carolina District Court District 8-N.C.
Carriere, Edward E., Jr.-Judge, State Court of DeKalb County-Ga.
Carrig, Bart M.-Acting Judge, Little Falls City Court-N.Y.
Carrillo, Victor G.-Judge, Taylor County Court-Tex.
Carrington, Trey-Judge, Throckmorton County Court-Tex.
Carrion, Audrey J. S.-Associate Judge, Circuit Court for Baltimore City, Eighth Judicial Circuit-Md.
Carro, Gregory-Judge, New York Court of Claims-N.Y.
Carroll, Bob-Judge, Ellis County Court at Law-Tex.
Carroll, Dennis D.-Judge, Madison Superior Court-Ind.
Carroll, Earl H.-Senior Judge, United States District Court District of Arizona-Ariz.
Carroll, Ellen-Judge, United States Bankruptcy Court Central District of California-Calif.
Carroll, Harry G.-Judge, New Jersey Superior Court Vicinage Two-N.J.
Carroll, Jeanné-Judge, Kentucky District Court Forty-second Judicial District-Ky.
Carroll, Joe-Judge, Texas District Court 27th Judicial District-Tex.
Carroll, John J., III-Chief Judge, North Carolina District Court District 5-N.C.
Carroll, Karen R.-Judge, Vermont Trial Court-Vt.
Carroll, Pat-Magistrate Judge, Kansas District Court Fifteenth Judicial District-Kan.
Carroll, Patrick-Judge, Lakewood Municipal Court-Ohio
Carroll, Patrick L., III-Judge, Connecticut Superior Court-Conn.
Carroll, Peter H.-Judge, United States Bankruptcy Court Central District of California-Calif.
Carroll, Stephen P.-District Judge, Iowa District Court Second Judicial District-Ia.
Carroll, Thomas J.-Judge, Marion Superior Court-Ind.
Carroll, Thomas J.-Judge, New York Court of Claims-N.Y.
Carruth, James C.-Magistrate Judge, United States District Court District of Arizona-Ariz.
Carruthers, Catharine R.-Judge, United States Bankruptcy Court Middle District of North Carolina-N.C.
Carruthers, Richard D.-Judge, The Criminal Court of the City of New York-N.Y.
Carson, Wallace P., Jr.-Chief Justice, Oregon Supreme Court-Ore.
Carter, Allan P.-Judge, Superior Court of California County of Solano-Calif.
Carter, Blaine A.-Magistrate Judge, Kansas District Court Second Judicial District-Kan.
Carter, Burrell J.-Chief Judge, Louisiana Court of Appeal First Circuit-La.
Carter, Clarence W.-Emergency Judge, North Carolina Superior Court-N.C.
Carter, David O.-Judge, United States District Court Central District of California-Calif.
Carter, Gene-Senior Judge, United States District Court District of Maine-Me.
Carter, Jack-Justice, Texas Court of Appeals Sixth District-Tex.
Carter, James H.-Justice, Iowa Supreme Court-Ia.
Carter, Jerald S.-Judge, Nassau County Court-N.Y.
Carter, John B., Jr.-Judge, North Carolina District Court District 16B-N.C.
Carter, John W.-Judge, The Criminal Court of the City of New York-N.Y.
Carter, Joseph T.-Judge, Minnesota District Court First Judicial District-Minn.
Carter, Kathryn-Magistrate Judge, Kansas District Court Twelfth Judicial District-Kan.
Carter, Kevin M.-Judge, Erie County Family Court-N.Y.
Carter, Marjorie Laird-Judge, Superior Court of California County of Orange-Calif.
Carter, Robert L.-Chief Judge, Illinois Circuit Court Thirteenth Judicial Circuit-Ill.
Carter, Robert L.-Senior Judge, United States District Court Southern District of New York-N.Y.
Carter, Robert R.-Judge, Virginia General District Court First Judicial District-Va.
Carter, Stephen L.-Judge, Garfield County Court-Colo.
Carter, Wilford Dan-Judge, Louisiana District Court Fourteenth Judicial District-La.
Carter, William A.-Judge, Albany City Court-N.Y.
Carter, William B. Mitchell-Magistrate Judge, United States District Court Eastern District of Tennessee-Tenn.
Cartwright, Joan S.-Judge, Superior Court of California County of Alameda-Calif.
Caruso, Daniel F.-Judge, Fairfield District Probate Court-Conn.
Caruso, Gary P.-Judge, Pennsylvania Court of Common Pleas Tenth Judicial District-Pa.
Caruso, John R.-Judge, Connecticut Superior Court-Conn.
Caruso, Vito C.-Justice, New York Supreme Court Fourth Judicial District-N.Y.
Carver, Charles Dana-Judge, Texas Criminal District Court Jefferson County-Tex.
Carver, Larry G.-Justice, Judith Basin County Justice of the Peace Court and Judge, Hobson and Stanford City Courts-Mont.
Carver, Sheri-Judge, Cherokee County District Court-Ala.
Carver, William H.-Judge, Wisconsin Circuit Court Winnebago Circuit-Wis.
Cary, G. Keith-Judge, Florida Circuit Court Twentieth Judicial Circuit-Fla.
Cary, Lauri-Judge, Cascade City Court-Mont.
Casale, Michael R.-Judge, New Jersey Superior Court Vicinage Five-N.J.
Casanueva, Darryl C.-Judge, Florida District Court of Appeal Second District-Fla.
Casciato, Joseph N.-Associate Judge, Illinois Circuit Court of Cook County-Ill.
Cascio, John M.-Judge, Pennsylvania Court of Common Pleas Sixteenth Judicial District-Pa.
Cascio, Roy M.-Judge, Second Parish Court Jefferson Parish-La.
Case, Charles G., II-Judge, United States Bankruptcy Court District of Arizona-Ariz.
Case, I. Vincent, Jr.-Judge, Wyoming Circuit Court Eighth Judicial District; Converse, Niobrara and Platte Counties-Wyo.
Case, James R.-Judge, Florida Circuit Court Sixth Judicial Circuit-Fla.
Case, Stuart-Judge, Hampton District Probate Court-Conn.
Casebolt, James S.-Judge, Colorado Court of Appeals-Colo.
Casellas, Salvador E.-Judge, United States District Court District of Puerto Rico
Casement, David A.-Magistrate Judge, Kansas District Court Fourteenth Judicial District-Kan.
Casey, Frederick J.-Judge, Minnesota District Court Ninth Judicial District-Minn.
Casey, Paula-Judge, Washington Superior Court Thurston County-Wash.
Casey, Richard C.-Judge, United States District Court Southern District of New York-N.Y.
Cash, Gary S.-Chief Judge, North Carolina District Court District 28-N.C.
Cashion, James C.-Judge, Marion County District Court-Ala.
Cashman, David R.-Judge, Pennsylvania Court of Common Pleas Fifth Judicial District-Pa.
Cashman, Dennis K.-Circuit Judge, Illinois Circuit Court Eighth Judicial Circuit-Ill.
Cashman, Edward J.-Judge, Vermont Trial Court-Vt.
Cashwell, Narley L.-Resident Judge, North Carolina Superior Court Third Judicial Division District 10-N.C.
Casias, Edward J.-Judge, Summit County Court-Colo.
Caskey, Gregory M.-Judge, Superior Court of California County of Shasta-Calif.
Cason, Betty B.-Judge, Probate Court of Carroll County-Ga.
Cason, Laninya-Associate Judge, Illinois Circuit Court Twentieth Judicial Circuit-Ill.
Cass, John E.-Judge, Minnesota District Court Tenth Judicial District-Minn.
Cass, Stephen W.-Surrogate, Chautauqua County Surrogate's Court-N.Y.
Cassady, William E.-Magistrate Judge, United States District Court Southern District of Alabama-Ala.
Cassata, Joseph J., Jr.-Judge, Tonawanda City Court-N.Y.
Cassavechia, Gary R.-Judge, Probate Court of New Hampshire Strafford County-N.H.
Cassel, William B.-Judge, Nebraska District Court Eighth Judicial District-Neb.
Cassell, Paul G.-Judge, United States District Court District of Utah-Utah
Casserly, Timothy-Judge, Superior Court of California County of San Diego-Calif.
Cassidy, Karen M.-Judge, New Jersey Superior Court Vicinage Twelve-N.J.
Cassidy, Kevin P.-Judge, Idaho District Court Fifth Judicial District Magistrate Division-Ida.
Cassidy, Michael Joseph-Judge, Virginia General District Court Nineteenth Judicial District-Va.
Cassidy, Paul A.-Chief Judge, Michigan District Court District Forty-two and Judge, Michigan District Court District Forty-two Division Two-Mich.
Cassini, Joseph C., III-Judge, New Jersey Superior Court Vicinage Five-N.J.
Castagna, William John-Senior Judge, United States District Court Middle District of Florida-Fla.
Castelda, Roger A.-Judge, Tonasket Municipal Court-Wash.
Castellani, Robert J.-Judge, Superior Court of Georgia Stone Mountain Judicial Circuit-Ga.
Castellanos, Cecilia P.-Judge, Superior Court of California County of Alameda-Calif.
Castellanos, Jesus A.-Magistrate Judge, United States District Court District of Puerto Rico

ALPHABETICAL NAME INDEX

Castellanos, Roland R.-Judge, State Court of Cobb County-Ga.

Castiglione, Frank B.-Associate Judge, Illinois Circuit Court of Cook County-Ill.

Castille, Ronald D.-Justice, The Supreme Court of Pennsylvania-Pa.

Castillo, Celia Foy-Judge, New Mexico Court of Appeals-N.Mex.

Castillo, Errlinda-Justice, Texas Court of Appeals Thirteenth District-Tex.

Castillo, Ruben-Judge, United States District Court Northern District of Illinois-Ill.

Castle, Marilyn C.-Judge, Louisiana District Court Fifteenth Judicial District-La.

Castleberry, Ronald L.-Judge, Washington Superior Court Snohomish County-Wash.

Castlen, Joseph-Judge, Kentucky District Court Sixth Judicial District-Ky.

Castlen, Thomas O.-Judge, Kentucky Circuit Court Sixth Judicial Circuit-Ky.

Castor, Robert-Judge, Wyoming Circuit Court Second Judicial District, Albany County-Wyo.

Castro, Melchor E.-Judge, Rochester City Court-N.Y.

Caswell, Susan P.-District Judge, Oklahoma District Court Seventh Judicial District-Okla.

Catalano, Carol-Chancellor, Tennessee Chancery Court Nineteenth Judicial District-Tenn.

Cataldo, John-Judge, The Criminal Court of the City of New York-N.Y.

Cate, Jocelyn B.-Judge, South Carolina Family Court Ninth Judicial Circuit-S.C.

Catena, Felix J.-Judge, Montgomery County Court-N.Y.

Cates, Jeffrey S.-Judge, Superior Court of Arizona Maricopa County-Ariz.

Cates, Robert P.-Judge, Florida Circuit Court Eighth Judicial Circuit-Fla.

Cathell, Dale R.-Associate Judge, Court of Appeals of Maryland-Md.

Cathey, Samuel-Chief Judge, North Carolina District Court District 22-N.C.

Cato, A. Wallace-Chief Judge, Superior Court of Georgia South Georgia Judicial Circuit-Ga.

Catoe, William M., Jr.-Magistrate Judge, United States District Court District of South Carolina-S.C.

Caton, Betty-Judge, Texas District Court 296th Judicial District-Tex.

Catterson, James M.-Justice, New York Supreme Court Tenth Judicial District-N.Y.

Catterton, Randy-Judge, Texas District Court 231st Judicial District-Tex.

Caudill, Danny P.-Judge, Kentucky Circuit Court Thirty-first Judicial Circuit-Ky.

Caudill, J. Gentry-Resident Judge, North Carolina Superior Court Seventh Judicial Division District 26-N.C.

Caudill, John David-Judge, Kentucky Circuit Court Thirty-first Judicial Circuit-Ky.

Causey, William J., Jr.-Judge, Monroe County District Court-Ala.

Cauthron, Robin J.-Chief Judge, United States District Court Western District of Oklahoma-Okla.

Cavanagh, Mark J.-Judge, Michigan Court of Appeals-Mich.

Cavanagh, Michael F.-Justice, Michigan Supreme Court-Mich.

Cavanagh, Thomas W., Jr.-Judge, New Jersey Superior Court Vicinage Nine-N.J.

Cavanaugh, Dennis M.-Judge, United States District Court District of New Jersey-N.J.

Cavanaugh, Patrick-Associate Judge, Circuit Court for Baltimore County, Third Judicial Circuit-Md.

Cavanaugh, Rita L.-Chief Magistrate, Magistrate Court of Spalding County-Ga.

Cavaneau, Jerry W.-Magistrate Judge, United States District Court Eastern District of Arkansas-Ark.

Cavedo, Bradley B.-Judge, Virginia Circuit Court Thirteenth Judicial Circuit-Va.

Cavel, Michael P.-Judge, Nebraska Workers' Compensation Court-Neb.

Cavender, David L.-Chief Judge, Superior Court of Georgia Atlantic Judicial Circuit-Ga.

Cayce, James-Judge, Washington Superior Court King County-Wash.

Cayce, John H., Jr.-Chief Justice, Texas Court of Appeals Second District-Tex.

Cayer, David S.-Resident Judge, North Carolina Superior Court Seventh Judicial Division District 26-N.C.

Cebull, Richard F.-Judge, United States District Court District of Montana-Mont.

Cecava, Kristine R.-Judge, Nebraska District Court Twelfth Judicial District-Neb.

Ceci, Louis J.-Reserve Judge, Wisconsin Circuit Court-Wis.

Cecil, Thomas M.-Judge, Superior Court of California County of Sacramento-Calif.

Cecile, James H.-Judge, Syracuse City Court-N.Y.

Ceckowski, Valerie Boettle-Associate Judge, Illinois Circuit Court Nineteenth Judicial Circuit-Ill.

Cedarbaum, Miriam Goldman-Senior Judge, United States District Court Southern District of New York-N.Y.

Celebrezze, Frank Daniel, Jr.-Judge, Ohio Court of Appeals Eighth District-Ohio

Celebrezze, James P.-Judge, Ohio Court of Common Pleas Cuyahoga County-Ohio

Celello, Richard J.-Judge, Michigan Circuit Court Forty-first Judicial Circuit-Mich.

Celeste, Mary-Judge, Denver County Court-Colo.

Celotto, Donald W.-Judge Referee, Connecticut Superior Court-Conn.

Cena, David A.-Judge, Superior Court of California County of Santa Clara-Calif.

Cenerini, Frank J.-Associate Judge, Rhode Island District Court-R.I.

Centra, John V.-Justice, New York Supreme Court Fifth Judicial District-N.Y.

Cercone, David S.-Judge, United States District Court Western District of Pennsylvania-Pa.

Ceresia, George B., Jr.-Justice, New York Supreme Court Third Judicial District-N.Y.

Cerezo, Carmen Consuelo-Judge, United States District Court District of Puerto Rico

Cerrato, Robert C.-Judge, Yonkers City Court-N.Y.

Cervini, Donna L.-Associate Judge, Illinois Circuit Court of Cook County-Ill.

Chabot, Elizabeth-Justice of the Peace, Paradise Valley Justices' Court-Nev.

Chabot, Herbert L.-Senior Judge, United States Tax Court

Chabot, Rae Lee-Judge, Michigan Circuit Court Sixth Judicial Circuit-Mich.

Chadwick, Daniel L.-Associate Circuit Judge, Missouri Circuit Court Forty-third Judicial Circuit-Mo.

Chaffee, David R.-Judge, Superior Court of California County of Orange-Calif.

Chafin, James T., III-Judge, State Court of Henry County-Ga.

Chafin, Teresa M.-Chief Judge, Virginia Juvenile and Domestic Relations District Court Twenty-ninth Judicial District-Va.

Chaiet, Paul F.-Judge, New Jersey Superior Court Vicinage Nine-N.J.

Chaisson, Robert A.-Judge, Louisiana District Court Twenty-ninth Judicial District-La.

Chaitin, Ellen-Judge, Superior Court of California City and County of San Francisco-Calif.

Chalfant, James C.-Judge, Superior Court of California County of Los Angeles-Calif.

Chalfant, Jan L.-Judge, Randolph Circuit Court-Ind.

Chamberlain, Hans Q.-Presiding Judge, Utah Juvenile Court Fifth Judicial District-Utah

Chamberlain, Paul H.-Chief Judge, Michigan Circuit Court Twenty-first Judicial Circuit-Mich.

Chambers, Amy Piro-Judge, New Jersey Superior Court Vicinage Eight-N.J.

Chambers, Cheryl E.-Justice, New York Supreme Court Second Judicial District-N.Y.

Chambers, Rob-Judge, State Court of Hall County-Ga.

Chambers, Robert C.-Judge, United States District Court Southern District of West Virginia-W.Va.

Chambers, Rodney-Judge, Magnolia District Court-Ark.

Chambers, Rosemary D.-Judge, Alabama Circuit Court Thirteenth Judicial Circuit-Ala.

Chambers, Timothy J.-Associate Judge, Illinois Circuit Court of Cook County-Ill.

Chambers, Timothy J.-Judge, Kansas District Court Twenty-seventh Judicial District-Kan.

Chambers, Tom-Justice, Washington Supreme Court-Wash.

Chamblee, Roland W., Jr.-Judge, St. Joseph Superior Court-Ind.

Chamblin, James H.-Judge, Virginia Circuit Court Twentieth Judicial Circuit-Va.

Champagne, Judith L.-Judge, Superior Court of California County of Los Angeles-Calif.

Champagne, Norman E.-Associate Justice, Manchester District Court-N.H.

Chan, Derrick H. M.-Judge, Hawaii Circuit Court First Judicial Circuit-Hi.

Chance, Chester B.-Judge, Florida Circuit Court Eighth Judicial Circuit-Fla.

Chandler, Billy-Chief Magistrate, Magistrate Court of Jackson County-Ga.

Chandler, Christopher R.-Judge, Superior Court of California County of Sutter-Calif.

Chandler, David A.-Judge, Court of Appeals of Mississippi-Miss.

Chandler, Joel R.-Judge, Tuscaloosa County District Court-Ala.

Chandler, Larry-Judge, Arkansas Circuit Court Thirteenth Judicial Circuit-Ark.

Chandler, Tommy W.-Judge, Kentucky Circuit Court Fifth Judicial Circuit-Ky.

Chandler, William B., III-Chancellor, Delaware Court of Chancery-Del.

Chaney, Kim J.-Judge, Cullman County District Court-Ala.

Chaney, Richard G.-Judge, North Carolina District Court District 14-N.C.

Chaney, Victoria Gerrard-Judge, Superior Court of California County of Los Angeles-Calif.

Chang, Gary W. B.-Judge, Hawaii Circuit Court First Judicial Circuit-Hi.

Chang, James H.-Judge, Superior Court of California County of Santa Clara-Calif.

Chang, Kevin S. C.-Magistrate Judge, United States District Court District of Hawaii-Hi.

Chang, Shelleyanne W. L.-Judge, Superior Court of California County of Sacramento-Calif.

Chapala, Walter P.-Judge, La Porte Superior Court-Ind.

Chapel, Charles S.-Judge, Oklahoma Court of Criminal Appeals-Okla.

Chapin, Sidney P.-Judge, Superior Court of California County of Kern-Calif.

Chaplin, Anne Kenney-Circuit Justice, Trial Court of Massachusetts Housing Court Department-Mass.

Chapman, Arthur-Judge, King District Court West Division King County-Wash.

Chapman, Brenda-Judge, Comal County Court at Law-Tex.

Chapman, Charles L.-Judge, Texas District Court 39th Judicial District-Tex.

Chapman, Melissa A.-Judge, Illinois Appellate Court Fifth Judicial District-Ill.

Chapman, Rosalyn M.-Magistrate Judge, United States District Court Central District of California-Calif.

Chapman, Thomas William-Associate Judge, Illinois Circuit Court Third Judicial Circuit-Ill.

Chapman, William E., III-Judge, Mississippi Circuit Court Twentieth Judicial District-Miss.

Chapman, William L., Jr.-Associate Judge, Delaware Family Court New Castle County-Del.

Chappell, Sheri Polster-Magistrate Judge, United States District Court Middle District of Florida-Fla.

Chappelle, Carlos J.-Special Judge, Oklahoma District Court Fourteenth Judicial District-Okla.

Chappelle, Steven G.-Associate Judge, Circuit Court for Charles County, Seventh Judicial Circuit-Md.

Charles, Alfonso-Judge, Gregg County Court at Law No. 2-Tex.

Charles, Bradford H.-Judge, Pennsylvania Court of Common Pleas Fifty-second Judicial District-Pa.

Charnock, Jane-Judge, West Virginia Family Court Circuit Eleven-W.Va.

Charron, Raymond A.-Chief Judge, Michigan District Court District Twenty-six and Judge, Michi-

ALPHABETICAL NAME INDEX

gan District Court District Twenty-six Division One-Mich.

Chasanow, Deborah K.-Judge, United States District Court District of Maryland-Md.

Chase, Dale H.-Judge, Medina Municipal Court-Ohio

Chase, Joseph F.-Judge, Minnesota District Court Third Judicial District-Minn.

Chase, L. Bryce-Judge, Superior Court of California County of Kern-Calif.

Chase, Richard R.-Judge, Wise County Court-Tex.

Chasez, Alma L.-Magistrate Judge, United States District Court Eastern District of Louisiana-La.

Chason, Willard H.-Senior Judge, Superior Court of Georgia-Ga.

Chastain, Michael-Judge, Probate Court of Lumpkin County-Ga.

Chatigny, Robert N.-Chief Judge, United States District Court District of Connecticut-Conn.

Chatman, Sharon A.-Judge, Superior Court of California County of Santa Clara-Calif.

Chavez, Alfredo-Judge, Texas District Court 65th Judicial District-Tex.

Chavez, Edward L.-Justice, New Mexico Supreme Court-N.Mex.

Chavez, James Edward-Judge, Superior Court of Arizona Mohave County-Ariz.

Chávez, Victor E.-Judge, Superior Court of California County of Los Angeles-Calif.

Chavez, Victoria-Judge, Superior Court of California County of Los Angeles-Calif.

Chavies, Michael B.-Judge, Florida Circuit Court Eleventh Judicial Circuit-Fla.

Chavis, Jeffrey C.-Judge, Probate Court of Jeff Davis County-Ga.

Cheatham, Frank Sellars, Jr.-Senior Judge, Superior Court of Georgia-Ga.

Cheek, David Eugene, Sr.-Judge, Virginia General District Court Thirteenth Judicial District-Va.

Cheek, Leon B., III-Judge, Orange County Court-Fla.

Cheely, Selma-Chief Magistrate, Magistrate Court of Hart County-Ga.

Chehardy, Susan M.-Judge, Louisiana Court of Appeal Fifth Circuit-La.

Chen, Edward M.-Magistrate Judge, United States District Court Northern District of California-Calif.

Chen, Ida K.-Judge, Pennsylvania Court of Common Pleas First Judicial District-Pa.

Cheney, Janice Wilson-Chief Magistrate, Magistrate Court of Jenkins County-Ga.

Chernenko, Joyce-Judge, West Virginia Family Court Circuit One-W.Va.

Cherniske, Victoria M.-Judge, Washington District Probate Court-Conn.

Chernoff, Paul A.-Associate Justice, Trial Court of Massachusetts Superior Court Department-Mass.

Cheroske, John Joseph-Judge, Superior Court of California County of Los Angeles-Calif.

Cherry, Burford A.-Judge, North Carolina District Court District 25-N.C.

Cherry, J. Blair, Jr.-Judge, Texas District Court 72nd Judicial District-Tex.

Cherry, John F.-Judge, Pennsylvania Court of Common Pleas Twelfth Judicial District-Pa.

Cherry, Michael A.-Judge, Nevada District Court Eighth Judicial District-Nev.

Cherry, Michael H.-Chief Judge, Michigan Circuit Court Fifteenth Judicial Circuit-Mich.

Cherry, Patrick F.-Chief Judge, Michigan District Court District Fifty-four A-Mich.

Cherry, Paul R.-Judge, DeKalb Circuit Court-Ind.

Cherry, Solomon G.-Emergency Judge, North Carolina District Court-N.C.

Cheshire, M. Louise-Chief Magistrate, Magistrate Court of Brantley County-Ga.

Cheshire, Robert C.-Judge, Texas District Court 377th Judicial District-Tex.

Chesler, Stanley R.-Judge, United States District Court District of New Jersey-N.J.

Cheslock, Jerome P.-Judge, Pennsylvania Court of Common Pleas Forty-third Judicial District-Pa.

Chesney, Maxine Mackler-Judge, United States District Court Northern District of California-Calif.

Chesterman, John A.-Judge, Minnesota District Court Third Judicial District-Minn.

Cheuvront, Jeffre-Judge, Nebraska District Court Third Judicial District-Neb.

Chew, David Wellington-Justice, Texas Court of Appeals Eighth District-Tex.

Chew, Linda-Judge, Texas Family District Court 327th Judicial District-Tex.

Chew, Randall E.-Judge, Juvenile Court of Georgia South Georgia Judicial Circuit and Chief Magistrate, Magistrate Court of Mitchell County-Ga.

Chewning, Richard W., III-Judge, South Carolina Family Court Eleventh Judicial Circuit-S.C.

Chiapparelli, Charles A.-Associate Judge, Maryland District Court District One-Md.

Chidester, David L.-Judge, Porter Superior Court-Ind.

Chidsey, William R., Jr.-Judge, Superior Court of California County of Los Angeles-Calif.

Chiechi, Carolyn P.-Judge, United States Tax Court

Childers, Kimberly-Judge, Kentucky District Court Thirty-sixth Judicial District-Ky.

Childers, Robert L.-Judge, Tennessee Circuit Court Thirtieth Judicial District-Tenn.

Childres, Juanita-Chief Magistrate, Magistrate Court of Crawford County-Ga.

Childress, Raymond S.-Judge, Louisiana District Court Twenty-second Judicial District-La.

Childs, Daniel Boone-Judge, Cherokee County Court at Law-Tex.

Chin, Denny-Judge, United States District Court Southern District of New York-N.Y.

Chin, Ming W.-Associate Justice, California Supreme Court-Calif.

Chin, Richard J.-Associate Justice, Trial Court of Massachusetts Superior Court Department-Mass.

Chiola, Thomas R.-Circuit Judge, Illinois Circuit Court of Cook County-Ill.

Chiota, John P.-Judge, Trumbull District Probate Court-Conn.

Chirlin, Judith C.-Judge, Superior Court of California County of Los Angeles-Calif.

Chittick, Hilary A.-Judge, Superior Court of California County of Fresno-Calif.

Chitwood, Howard Lee-Judge, Virginia Juvenile and Domestic Relations District Court Twenty-seventh Judicial District-Va.

Chiuminatto, Martin J., Jr.-Judge, Kleberg County Court at Law-Tex.

Chmelewski, Mark A.-Judge, Kittitas Municipal Court-Wash.

Chmura, John M.-Judge, Michigan District Court District Thirty-seven-Mich.

Choate, D. Jeffrey-Judge, Kentucky District Court Fortieth Judicial District-Ky.

Choate, Dennis S.-Judge, Superior Court of California County of Orange-Calif.

Choate, Stephen-Judge, Arkansas Circuit Court Sixteenth Judicial Circuit-Ark.

Cholakis, Catherine-Judge, Rensselaer County Family Court-N.Y.

Chouteau, Rene Auguste-Judge, Superior Court of California County of Sonoma-Calif.

Chow, Mark C.-Judge, King District Court West Division King County-Wash.

Choy, Darryl Y. C.-Family Court Judge, Hawaii District Court First Judicial Circuit-Hi.

Choy, Herbert Y. C.-Senior Judge, United States Court of Appeals Ninth Circuit

Chrein, Aaron Simon-Magistrate Judge, United States District Court Eastern District of New York-N.Y.

Chrestman, Don-Judge, Texas District Court 43rd Judicial District-Tex.

Christen, Morgan-Judge, Alaska Superior Court Third Judicial District-Alas.

Christensen, David E.-Judge, Minnesota District Court Fifth Judicial District-Minn.

Christensen, David L.-District Judge, Iowa District Court Fifth Judicial District-Ia.

Christensen, J. Michael-Judge, Michigan District Court District Sixty-one-Mich.

Christensen, Patti Ann-Judge, St. Johns County Court-Fla.

Christenson, Karen E.-Judge, Wisconsin Circuit Court Milwaukee Circuit-Wis.

Christian, Casey J.-Judge, Minnesota District Court Third Judicial District-Minn.

Christian, Deborah L.-Judge, Superior Court of California County of Los Angeles-Calif.

Christian, Erik-Associate Judge, Superior Court of the District of Columbia-D.C.

Christian, Kaye K.-Associate Judge, Superior Court of the District of Columbia-D.C.

Christian, Martha C.-Judge, Superior Court of Georgia Macon Judicial Circuit-Ga.

Christian, M'Liss-Judge, Bexar County Court at Law No. 6-Tex.

Christian, Wayne Anthony, II-Judge, Bexar County Court at Law No. 9-Tex.

Christian, William A.-Emergency Judge, North Carolina District Court-N.C.

Christiansen, Robert G.-Judge, Ohio Court of Common Pleas Lucas County-Ohio

Christiansen, Terry L.-Judge, Utah District Court Third Judicial District-Utah

Christianson, Ronald M.-Judge, Superior Court of California County of San Bernardino-Calif.

Christie, David-Judge, King District Court South Division King County-Wash.

Christle, Ruthanna-Judge, Wabash City Court-Ind.

Christley, Judith A.-Judge, Ohio Court of Appeals Eleventh District-Ohio

Christofferson, Lee A.-Judge, North Dakota District Court Northeast Judicial District-N.D.

Christopher, Deborah Kim-Judge, Montana District Court Twentieth Judicial District-Mont.

Christopher, Tracy-Judge, Texas District Court 295th Judicial District-Tex.

Christopherson, Bruce W.-Judge, Minnesota District Court Eighth Judicial District-Minn.

Chronister, John H.-President Judge, Pennsylvania Court of Common Pleas Nineteenth Judicial District-Pa.

Chrystal, Lisa F.-Judge, New Jersey Superior Court Vicinage Twelve-N.J.

Chrzanowski, Mary A.-Judge, Michigan Circuit Court Sixteenth Judicial Circuit-Mich.

Chu, Regina M.-Judge, Minnesota District Court Fourth Judicial District-Minn.

Chun, Danny K.-Judge, The Criminal Court of the City of New York-N.Y.

Churchill, Vickie I.-Judge, Washington Superior Court Island-San Juan Counties-Wash.

Chushcoff, Bryan E.-Judge, Washington Superior Court Pierce County-Wash.

Chutz, Wayne Ray-Judge, Louisiana District Court Twenty-first Judicial District-La.

Chylinski, James R.-Judge, Michigan Circuit Court Third Judicial Circuit-Mich.

Cianca, Marc A.-Chief Judge, Florida Circuit Court Nineteenth Judicial Circuit-Fla.

Ciancia, James J.-Judge, New Jersey Superior Court Appellate Division-N.J.

Ciavarella, Mark A., Jr.-Judge, Pennsylvania Court of Common Pleas Eleventh Judicial District-Pa.

Ciccone, Yolanda-Judge, New Jersey Superior Court Vicinage Eight-N.J.

Cicconetti, Michael A.-Judge, Painesville Municipal Court-Ohio

Cicoria, Ronald A.-Judge, Livingston County Court-N.Y.

Cielinski, Michael P.-Judge, Recorder's Court of Columbus-Muscogee County-Ga.

Ciesar, William W., Jr.-Judge, Whiting City Court-Ind.

Cifelli, Alfonse J.-Judge, New Jersey Superior Court Vicinage Five-N.J.

Ciklin, Cory J.-Judge, Palm Beach County Court-Fla.

Cilley, Robert S.-Chief Judge, North Carolina District Court District 29-N.C.

Cindrich, Robert J.-Judge, United States District Court Western District of Pennsylvania-Pa.

Cini, Dale A.-Circuit Judge, Illinois Circuit Court Fifth Judicial Circuit-Ill.

Cinniger, Ronald E.-Judge, Oregon Circuit Court Fourth Judicial District-Ore.

Ciparick, Carmen Beauchamp-Associate Judge, New York Court of Appeals-N.Y.

Cirigliano, Caesar D.-Judge, New York Court of Claims-N.Y.

ALPHABETICAL NAME INDEX

Cirone, Albert J., Jr.-Justice, Lebanon District Court-N.H.
Cisneros, Theresa M.-Judge, Colorado District Court Fourth Judicial District-Colo.
Cissell, James Charles-Judge, Ohio Court of Common Pleas Hamilton County-Ohio
Cissna, Timothy Paul-Judge, Superior Court of California County of Humboldt-Calif.
Citta, James N.-Judge, New Jersey Superior Court Vicinage Fourteen-N.J.
Ciullo, Albert R.-Judge, Rhode Island Traffic Tribunal-R.I.
Ciungan, Michael F.-Judge, Michigan District Court District Twenty-six Division Two-Mich.
Clabuesch, David L.-Chief Judge, Huron County Probate Court-Mich.
Clagett, Marjorie L.-Associate Judge, Circuit Court for Calvert County, Seventh Judicial Circuit-Md.
Clagett, Stephen L.-Administrative Judge, Maryland District Court District Four-Md.
Claire, Judith S.-Judge, Chautauqua County Family Court-N.Y.
Clancy, Daniel Patrick-Judge, Dallas County Criminal Court at Law No. 1-Tex.
Clancy, Margaret L.-Judge, New York Court of Claims-N.Y.
Clapp, Douglas A.-Judge, Maine District Court-Me.
Claps, Joseph M.-Associate Judge, Illinois Circuit Court of Cook County-Ill.
Clark, Alice P.-Associate Judge, Maryland District Court District Ten-Md.
Clark, Brian-Judge, Alaska District Court Third Judicial District-Alas.
Clark, Bruce A.-Judge, Superior Court of California County of Ventura-Calif.
Clark, Carlton E.-Judge, Nebraska County Court Eleventh Judicial District-Neb.
Clark, Carole W.-Judge, Texas Family District Court 321st Judicial District-Tex.
Clark, Cloyd-Judge, Nebraska County Court Eleventh Judicial District-Neb.
Clark, Darcel D.-Judge, The Criminal Court of the City of New York-N.Y.
Clark, David-Judge, Bairoil and Sinclair Municipal Courts-Wyo.
Clark, David C.-Senior Judge, Palm Beach County Court-Fla.
Clark, Dougald, Jr.-Judge, North Carolina District Court District 12-N.C.
Clark, Ellen K.-Judge, Washington Superior Court Spokane County-Wash.
Clark, Eugene-Judge, Kentucky Circuit Court Forty-first Judicial Circuit-Ky.
Clark, Giles R.-Retired-Recalled Judge, North Carolina Superior Court-N.C.
Clark, Glen E.-Judge, Bankruptcy Appellate Panel Tenth Circuit and Chief Judge, United States Bankruptcy Court District of Utah-Utah
Clark, H. David, II-Judge, Mississippi Chancery Court Second Judicial District-Miss.
Clark, James H., Jr.-Judge, Minnesota District Court Second Judicial District-Minn.
Clark, Janice G.-Judge, Louisiana District Court Nineteenth Judicial District-La.
Clark, Jeanette-Associate Judge, Superior Court of the District of Columbia-D.C.
Clark, Jill-Judge, Kentucky District Court Fifty-sixth Judicial District-Ky.
Clark, John T., III-Associate Judge, Maryland District Court District Three-Md.
Clark, Joseph T.-Judge, Ohio Court of Common Pleas Fairfield County-Ohio
Clark, Kenneth S., Jr.-Associate Judge, Delaware Court of Common Pleas Sussex County-Del.
Clark, Kim Berkeley-Judge, Pennsylvania Court of Common Pleas Fifth Judicial District-Pa.
Clark, Lawrence F., Jr.-Judge, Pennsylvania Court of Common Pleas Twelfth Judicial District-Pa.
Clark, Leif M.-Judge, United States Bankruptcy Court Western District of Texas-Tex.
Clark, Letitia Z.-Judge, United States Bankruptcy Court Southern District of Texas-Tex.
Clark, Marcus R.-Judge, Louisiana District Court Fourth Judicial District-La.
Clark, Margaret A.-Judge, Ohio Court of Common Pleas Brown County-Ohio
Clark, Margie I.-Justice of the Peace, Verdi Justices' Court-Nev.
Clark, Marilyn C.-Judge, New Jersey Superior Court Vicinage Eleven-N.J.
Clark, Martin F., Jr.-Judge, Virginia Circuit Court Twenty-first Judicial Circuit-Va.
Clark, Marty K.-Magistrate Judge, Kansas District Court Twentieth Judicial District-Kan.
Clark, Michael C.-Judge, Superior Court of Georgia Gwinnett Judicial Circuit-Ga.
Clark, Nancy Lynn-Judge, Orange County Court-Fla.
Clark, Nikki Ann-Judge, Florida Circuit Court Second Judicial Circuit-Fla.
Clark, Patricia-Judge, Washington Superior Court King County-Wash.
Clark, Patrick Allen-Judge, Texas District Court 128th Judicial District-Tex.
Clark, Paul W.-Judge, Kansas District Court Eighteenth Judicial District-Kan.
Clark, Robert F.-Judge, New York City Family Court-N.Y.
Clark, Ronald H.-Judge, United States District Court Eastern District of Texas-Tex.
Clark, Sarah Tunnell-Judge, Houston County Court at Law-Tex.
Clark, Tama Myers-Judge, Pennsylvania Court of Common Pleas First Judicial District-Pa.
Clark, Terry L.-Chief Judge, Michigan District Court District Seventy and Judge, Michigan District Court District Seventy Division One-Mich.
Clark, Thomas C.-Circuit Judge, Missouri Circuit Court Sixteenth Judicial Circuit-Mo.
Clark, Thomas L.-Judge, Kentucky Circuit Court Twenty-second Judicial Circuit-Ky.
Clark, Vernon B.-Judge, Louisiana District Court Thirtieth Judicial District-La.
Clark, William A.-Recalled Judge, United States Bankruptcy Court Southern District of Ohio-Ohio
Clarke, Arthur H., III-Judge, Michigan District Court District Seven-Mich.
Clarke, Cathleen B.-Judge, Brevard County Court-Fla.
Clarke, Dorothy H.-Judge, Virginia General District Court Seventeenth Judicial District-Va.
Clarke, Harold D., III-Judge, Spokane District Court Spokane County and Judge, Spokane Municipal Court-Wash.
Clarke, J. Calvitt, Jr.-Senior Judge, United States District Court Eastern District of Virginia-Va.
Clarke, Joseph M., II-Judge, Virginia Juvenile and Domestic Relations District Court Twenty-third Judicial District-Va.
Clarke, Mark H.-Circuit Judge, Illinois Circuit Court First Judicial Circuit-Ill.
Clarke, Stephen C.-District Judge, Iowa District Court First Judicial District-Ia.
Clarke, Toni E.-Associate Judge, Circuit Court for Prince George's County, Seventh Judicial Circuit-Md.
Clarke, Walter J., II-Judge, Probate Court of Gwinnett County-Ga.
Clarkson, Mary Ann-Assistant Judge, Vermont Trial Court Windham County-Vt.
Clarkson, Ward L.-Chief Judge, Michigan District Court District Sixty-six-Mich.
Clarkson, William J.-Associate Circuit Judge, Missouri Circuit Court Thirty-sixth Judicial Circuit-Mo.
Clary, Jerry L.-Judge, Fayette County District Court-Ala.
Clary, Michael D.-Circuit Judge, Illinois Circuit Court Fifth Judicial Circuit-Ill.
Clason, Jenifer Ward-Judge, Louisiana District Court Second Judicial District-La.
Clatterbaugh, James R.-Chief Judge, Shiawassee County Probate Court-Mich.
Clause, Herman C.-Judge, Louisiana District Court Fifteenth Judicial District-La.
Claver, H. Michael-Associate District Judge, Oklahoma District Court Twenty-fourth Judicial District-Okla.
Claville, Vernon-Judge, Caddo Parish Juvenile Court-La.
Clawges, Russell M., Jr.-Chief Judge, West Virginia Circuit Court Seventeenth Judicial Circuit-W.Va.
Clawson, Charles E., Jr.-Judge, Arkansas Circuit Court Twentieth Judicial Circuit-Ark.
Clay, Charles Q., III-Judge, Superior Court of California County of Los Angeles-Calif.
Clay, Eric L.-Judge, United States Court of Appeals Sixth Circuit
Clay, Evelyn B.-Circuit Judge, Illinois Circuit Court of Cook County-Ill.
Clayton, Bonnie Jean-Judge, Parmer County Court-Tex.
Clayton, Denise G.-Judge, Kentucky Circuit Court Thirtieth Judicial Circuit-Ky.
Clayton, James Keeble, Jr.-Judge, Tennessee Circuit Court Sixteenth Judicial District-Tenn.
Clayton, James R.-Judge, Florida Circuit Court Seventh Judicial Circuit-Fla.
Clayton, John-Associate Circuit Judge, Missouri Circuit Court Twenty-fifth Judicial Circuit-Mo.
Clayton, Melodie Howard-Judge, State Court of Cobb County-Ga.
Clayton, Robert M., II-Presiding Judge, Missouri Circuit Court Tenth Judicial Circuit-Mo.
Cleary, Edward J.-Judge, Minnesota District Court Second Judicial District-Minn.
Cleary, Patricia DelBueno-Judge, New Jersey Superior Court Vicinage Nine-N.J.
Cleary, Paul J.-Magistrate Judge, United States District Court Northern District of Oklahoma-Okla.
Clebowicz, Walter A.-Judge, Berlin District Probate Court-Conn.
Cleland, John M.-President Judge, Pennsylvania Court of Common Pleas Forty-eighth Judicial District-Pa.
Cleland, Robert H.-Judge, United States District Court Eastern District of Michigan-Mich.
Clem, Harry E.-Circuit Judge, Illinois Circuit Court Sixth Judicial Circuit-Ill.
Clem, Thomas L.-Judge, Madison County Court-Ind.
Clement, Edith Brown-Judge, United States Court of Appeals Fifth Circuit
Clement, Frank, Jr.-Judge, Tennessee Circuit Court Twentieth Judicial District-Tenn.
Clemente, Nicholas A.-Justice, New York Supreme Court Second Judicial District-N.Y.
Clements, Jean Harrison-Judge, Court of Appeals of Virginia-Va.
Clements, Marshall M.-Judge, Dixie County Court-Fla.
Clemon, U. W.-Chief Judge, United States District Court Northern District of Alabama-Ala.
Clemons, Holly F.-Associate Judge, Illinois Circuit Court Sixth Judicial Circuit-Ill.
Clerkin, John R.-Associate Judge, Illinois Circuit Court Ninth Judicial Circuit-Ill.
Cleve, Mark D.-District Judge, Iowa District Court Seventh Judicial District-Ia.
Clevenger, Raymond C., III-Judge, United States Court of Appeals Federal Circuit
Clevert, Charles N., Jr.-Judge, United States District Court Eastern District of Wisconsin-Wis.
Cliff, Carolyn-Judge, Langley Municipal Court-Wash.
Clifford, Patrick-Associate Circuit Judge, Missouri Circuit Court Twenty-first Judicial Circuit-Mo.
Clifford, Patrick J.-Judge, Connecticut Superior Court-Conn.
Clifford, Robert W.-Associate Justice, Maine Supreme Judicial Court-Me.
Clifton, Edward C.-Associate Justice, Rhode Island Superior Court-R.I.
Clifton, Richard R.-Judge, United States Court of Appeals Ninth Circuit
Cline, James Levi, Jr.-Judge, Superior Court of Georgia Ocmulgee Judicial Circuit-Ga.
Cline, Richard G.-Judge, Superior Court of California County of San Diego-Calif.
Clinger, David-Judge, Arkansas Circuit Court Nineteenth West Judicial Circuit-Ark.
Clingman, Gary L.-Judge, New Mexico District Court Fifth Judicial District-N.Mex.
Clogg, Richard B.-District Associate Judge, Iowa District Court Fifth Judicial District-Ia.

ALPHABETICAL NAME INDEX

ALPHABETICAL NAME INDEX

Cole, Ransey Guy, Jr.-Judge, United States Court of Appeals Sixth Circuit
Cole, Robert H., Sr.-Acting Judge, Corning City Court-N.Y.
Cole, Robert P.-Judge, Pasco County Court-Fla.
Cole, Roland A.-Justice, Maine Superior Court-Me.
Cole, Russell A., Jr.-Senior Judge, Florida Circuit Court Fourteenth Judicial Circuit-Fla.
Cole, Stephen E.-Magistrate Judge, United States District Court District of Wyoming-Wyo.
Cole, Susan S.-Magistrate Judge, United States District Court Northern District of Georgia-Ga.
Cole, Terry K.-Judge, Superior Court of California County of Stanislaus-Calif.
Cole, Tom C.-Presiding Judge, Superior Court of Arizona Yuma County-Ariz.
Coleman, Alonzo Brown, Jr.-Judge, North Carolina District Court District 15B-N.C.
Coleman, Cheryl F.-Judge, Albany City Court-N.Y.
Coleman, Claude M.-Judge, New Jersey Superior Court Vicinage Five-N.J.
Coleman, David H.-Judge, Hendricks Superior Court-Ind.
Coleman, Donald-Judge, Michigan District Court District Thirty-six-Mich.
Coleman, Donald D.-Judge, Superior Court of California County of Ventura-Calif.
Coleman, Eddy-Judge, Kentucky Circuit Court Thirty-fifth Judicial Circuit-Ky.
Coleman, Edward M.-Judge, New Jersey Superior Court Vicinage Thirteen-N.J.
Coleman, Frank M.-Judge, Lauderdale County Court-Miss.
Coleman, H. Joseph-Judge, Washington Court of Appeals Division I-Wash.
Coleman, Janet P.-Judge, Kentucky Circuit Court Ninth Judicial Circuit-Ky.
Coleman, JoAnn Spinks-Judge, Kentucky District Court Eighth Judicial District-Ky.
Coleman, Ralph E., Jr.-Judge, Jefferson County District Court Bessemer Division-Ala.
Coleman, Rudy B.-Judge, New Jersey Superior Court Vicinage Twelve-N.J.
Coleman, Sharon Johnson-Circuit Judge, Illinois Circuit Court of Cook County-Ill.
Coleman, Susan M.-Associate Judge, Illinois Circuit Court of Cook County-Ill.
Coleman, Ted P.-Senior Judge, Florida Circuit Court Ninth Judicial Circuit-Fla.
Coleman, Thomas B.-Judge, Columbia County Court-Fla.
Colins, James Gardner-President Judge, The Commonwealth Court of Pennsylvania-Pa.
Colins, Mary D.-Judge, Pennsylvania Court of Common Pleas First Judicial District-Pa.
Collester, Donald G., Jr.-Judge, New Jersey Superior Court Appellate Division-N.J.
Collette, William E.-Chief Judge, Michigan Circuit Court Thirtieth Judicial Circuit-Mich.
Collier, Albert-Judge, Superior Court of Georgia Clayton Judicial Circuit-Ga.
Collier, Christopher-Resident Judge, North Carolina Superior Court Sixth Judicial Division District 22-N.C.
Collier, Christopher-Judge, Ohio Court of Common Pleas Medina County-Ohio
Collier, Curtis L.-Judge, United States District Court Eastern District of Tennessee-Tenn.
Collier, Edward Ross-Judge, Juvenile Court of Georgia Pataula Judicial Circuit-Ga.
Collier, Glenn H.-Associate Judge, Illinois Circuit Court Tenth Judicial Circuit-Ill.
Collier, Jake-Judge, Texas District Court 158th Judicial District-Tex.
Collier, John S.-Judge, Napoleon Municipal Court-Ohio
Collier, Lacey A.-Judge, United States District Court Northern District of Florida-Fla.
Collier, Linda-Judge, Arkansas Circuit Court Twentieth Judicial Circuit-Ark.
Collier, Robert W.-Associate District Judge, Oklahoma District Court Fourth Judicial District-Okla.
Collings, Robert Biddlecombe-Magistrate Judge, United States District Court District of Massachusetts-Mass.
Collini, Robert J.-Judge, New York Court of Claims-N.Y.
Collins, Audrey Brodie-Judge, United States District Court Central District of California-Calif.
Collins, Barbara A.-Judge, Marion Superior Court-Ind.
Collins, Beverly M.-Judge, State Court of Cobb County-Ga.
Collins, Denise-Judge, Texas District Court 208th Judicial District-Tex.
Collins, Francis T.-Judge, New York Court of Claims-N.Y.
Collins, James G.-Circuit Justice, Trial Court of Massachusetts Juvenile Court Department-Mass.
Collins, Jim-Magistrate Judge, Kansas District Court Twenty-fifth Judicial District-Kan.
Collins, Jo Ann K.-Judge, Probate Court of Brooks County-Ga.
Collins, John B.-Chief Judge, Michigan District Court District Fourteen B-Mich.
Collins, John L.-Presiding Judge, Oregon Circuit Court Twenty-fifth Judicial District-Ore.
Collins, John P.-Judge, The Criminal Court of the City of New York-N.Y.
Collins, Julian E.-Judge, Florida Circuit Court Third Judicial Circuit-Fla.
Collins, Lawrence T.-Judge, Minnesota District Court Third Judicial District-Minn.
Collins, Michael-Judge, Kentucky District Court Fifty-fourth Judicial District-Ky.
Collins, Oakley C., Jr.-Judge, Ironton Municipal Court-Ohio
Collins, Patricia A.-Judge, Alaska Superior Court First Judicial District-Alas.
Collins, Patricia L.-Judge, Superior Court of California County of Los Angeles-Calif.
Collins, Randy E.-Judge, Shreveport City Court-La.
Collins, Raner C.-Judge, United States District Court District of Arizona-Ariz.
Collins, Richard L., Jr.-Judge, Ohio Court of Common Pleas Lake County-Ohio
Collins, Robert O.-Senior Judge, Florida Circuit Court Seventeenth Judicial Circuit-Fla.
Collins, Rosemary-Circuit Judge, Illinois Circuit Court Seventeenth Judicial Circuit-Ill.
Collins, Samuel W., Jr.-Active Retired Justice, Maine Supreme Judicial Court-Me.
Collins, Sheila Anne-Judge, Kentucky District Court Thirtieth Judicial District-Ky.
Collins, Thomas E.-Presiding Judge, Superior Court of Arizona Cochise County-Ariz.
Collins, William B.-Associate Circuit Judge, Missouri Circuit Court Seventeenth Judicial Circuit-Mo.
Collyer, Rosemary M.-Judge, United States District Court District of Columbia-D.C.
Colom, Dorothy W.-Judge, Mississippi Chancery Court Fourteenth Judicial District-Miss.
Colombo, Robert J., Jr.-Judge, Michigan Circuit Court Third Judicial Circuit-Mich.
Coloutti, Jean-Assistant Judge, Vermont Trial Court Rutland County-Vt.
Colston, Tami P.-Judge, Superior Court of Georgia Rome Judicial Circuit-Ga.
Colt, Edward S., II-Judge, Colorado District Court Fourth Judicial District-Colo.
Coltharp, James-Judge, Baylor County Court-Tex.
Colton, John P., Jr.-Judge, Tennessee Criminal Court Thirtieth Judicial District-Tenn.
Colton, Roger B.-Judge, Florida Circuit Court Fifteenth Judicial Circuit-Fla.
Colver, David O.-Judge, Phillips County Court-Colo.
Colville, Robert E.-Judge, Pennsylvania Court of Common Pleas Fifth Judicial District-Pa.
Colville, Robert J.-Judge, Pennsylvania Court of Common Pleas Fifth Judicial District-Pa.
Colvin, Dean A.-Judge, Marshall Superior Court-Ind.
Colvin, Gus W., Jr.-Judge, Calhoun County District Court-Ala.
Colvin, Ira B.-Judge, Pickens County District Court-Ala.
Colvin, James-Assistant Judge, Vermont Trial Court Bennington County-Vt.
Colvin, John O.-Judge, United States Tax Court
Colvin, Juanita M.-Justice of the Peace, Esmeralda Justices' Court-Nev.
Colwell, Michael J.-Circuit Judge, Illinois Circuit Court Sixteenth Judicial Circuit-Ill.
Combest, Preston-Judge, Camp County Court-Tex.
Combs, Douglas C.-Judge, Kentucky Circuit Court Thirty-third Judicial Circuit-Ky.
Combs, Douglas L.-District Judge, Oklahoma District Court Twenty-third Judicial District-Okla.
Combs, Frederick H.-Chief Judge, Virginia General District Court Twenty-ninth Judicial District-Va.
Combs, Roger E.-Associate Circuit Judge, Missouri Circuit Court Fourth Judicial Circuit-Mo.
Combs, Sara Walter-Judge, Kentucky Court of Appeals-Ky.
Combs Greene, Natalia-Associate Judge, Superior Court of the District of Columbia-D.C.
Comeaux, Keith R. J.-Judge, Louisiana District Court Sixteenth Judicial District-La.
Comerford, Richard F., Jr.-Judge, Connecticut Superior Court-Conn.
Comparet-Cassani, Joan-Judge, Superior Court of California County of Los Angeles-Calif.
Compton, Virginia-Judge, Dillon City Court-Mont.
Comstock, Mark A.-Judge, Berea Municipal Court-Ohio
Comstock, Russell A.-Judge, Idaho District Court Fourth Judicial District Magistrate Division-Ida.
Conaboy, Richard P.-Senior Judge, United States District Court Middle District of Pennsylvania-Pa.
Conahan, Michael T.-President Judge, Pennsylvania Court of Common Pleas Eleventh Judicial District-Pa.
Conboy, Carol Ann-Associate Justice, New Hampshire Superior Court-N.H.
Condon, Irvin G.-Judge, Charleston County Probate Court-S.C.
Condon, Joseph P.-Associate Judge, Illinois Circuit Court Nineteenth Judicial Circuit-Ill.
Condon, Thomas J.-Associate Judge, Illinois Circuit Court of Cook County-Ill.
Condren, Sheila A.-Special Judge, Oklahoma District Court Twelfth Judicial District-Okla.
Condron, Linda R.-Judge, Superior Court of California County of Santa Clara-Calif.
Conen, Jeffrey A.-Judge, Wisconsin Circuit Court Milwaukee Circuit-Wis.
Conery, John E.-Judge, Louisiana District Court Sixteenth Judicial District-La.
Conforti, N. Peter-Judge, New Jersey Superior Court Vicinage Ten-N.J.
Conger, Julie-Judge, Superior Court of California County of Alameda-Calif.
Conkel, Terrence E.-Judge, Minnesota District Court First Judicial District-Minn.
Conklin, J. Dan-Associate Circuit Judge, Missouri Circuit Court Thirty-first Judicial Circuit-Mo.
Conklin, John Riggs-Magistrate Judge, Kansas District Court Fifth Judicial District-Kan.
Conklin, Thomas R.-Judge, Kansas District Court Third Judicial District-Kan.
Conley, Erminie L.-Judge, New Jersey Superior Court Appellate Division-N.J.
Conley, Jane-Judge, Marion Superior Court-Ind.
Conley, John-Judge, Superior Court of California County of Orange-Calif.
Conley, Robert B.-Judge, Kentucky District Court Twentieth Judicial District-Ky.
Conliffe, Ken-Judge, Kentucky Circuit Court Thirtieth Judicial Circuit-Ky.
Conlin, Richard E.-Judge, Michigan District Court District Fourteen A-Mich.
Conlon, Albert S.-Circuit Justice, Trial Court of Massachusetts District Court Department-Mass.
Conlon, Claudia-Circuit Judge, Illinois Circuit Court of Cook County-Ill.
Conlon, Patricia Nedwicki-Judge, Kalamazoo County Probate Court-Mich.
Conlon, Suzanne B.-Judge, United States District Court Northern District of Illinois-Ill.
Conmey, Larry J.-District Judge, Iowa District Court Sixth Judicial District-Ia.
Conmy, Patrick A.-Senior Judge, United States District Court District of North Dakota-N.D.
Conn, Natalie R.-Judge, Grant Superior Court-Ind.
Conn, Steven F.-Judge, Superior Court of Arizona Mohave County-Ariz.
Connally, C. Ellen-Judge, Cleveland Municipal Court-Ohio

ALPHABETICAL NAME INDEX

ALPHABETICAL NAME INDEX

Cooper, Reinette W.-Judge, Hawaii District Court Second Judicial Circuit-Hi.
Cooper, Richard A.-Associate Judge, Maryland District Court District Four-Md.
Cooper, Richard I.-Chief Judge, Michigan Circuit Court Fifty-first Judicial Circuit-Mich.
Cooper, Rosalie B.-Retired Judge, New Jersey Superior Court-N.J.
Cooper, Samuel V.-Judge, Nebraska County Court Fourth Judicial District-Neb.
Cooper, Stephen C.-Chief Judge, Michigan District Court District Forty-six-Mich.
Cooper, Thomas R.-Judge, Wisconsin Circuit Court Milwaukee Circuit-Wis.
Cooper, Thomas W., Jr.-Judge, South Carolina Circuit Court Third Judicial Circuit-S.C.
Cooper, William-Justice, Kentucky Supreme Court-Ky.
Cooper-Hill, Jane-Magistrate Judge, United States District Court Southern District of Texas-Tex.
Cooperman, Amanda-Judge, Pennsylvania Court of Common Pleas First Judicial District-Pa.
Cooperman, Arthur J.-Justice, New York Supreme Court Eleventh Judicial District-N.Y.
Cooperrider, Luann-Judge, Ohio Court of Common Pleas Perry County-Ohio
Cope, Charles W.-Judge, Florida Circuit Court Sixth Judicial Circuit-Fla.
Cope, Gerald B., Jr.-Judge, Florida District Court of Appeal Third District-Fla.
Cope, Mark Ashton-Judge, Superior Court of California County of Riverside-Calif.
Copelan, Jesse, Jr.-Judge, State Court of Putnam County-Ga.
Copeland, Fred W.-Presiding Judge, Missouri Circuit Court Thirty-fourth Judicial Circuit-Mo.
Copeland, Richard Dennis-Associate Circuit Judge, Missouri Circuit Court Twenty-ninth Judicial Circuit-Mo.
Copeland, Weldon S., Jr.-Judge, Collin County Probate Court-Tex.
Copenhaver, John T., Jr.-Judge, United States District Court Southern District of West Virginia-W.Va.
Copenhaver, Ronald D.-Judge, Laramie Municipal Court-Wyo.
Copertino, John-Justice, New York Supreme Court Tenth Judicial District-N.Y.
Coplan, Robert G.-Associate Judge, Illinois Circuit Court Seventeenth Judicial Circuit-Ill.
Copland, Thomas A.-Judge, Grays Harbor District Court No. 2 Grays Harbor County-Wash.
Coppeto, Barbara A.-Senior Judge, Connecticut Superior Court-Conn.
Coppola, Carol L.-District Associate Judge, Iowa District Court Fifth Judicial District-Ia.
Copsey, Cheri C.-Judge, Idaho District Court Fourth Judicial District-Ida.
Corabi, Joseph M.-Judge, Jefferson County Court-Ohio
Corbett, Albert A., Jr.-Chief Judge, North Carolina District Court District 11-N.C.
Corbett, Donald J., Jr.-Judge, New York Court of Claims-N.Y.
Corbett, John P.-Associate Justice, Trial Court of Massachusetts Juvenile Court Department Plymouth County Division-Mass.
Corbett, Patricia-Judge, Pennsylvania Court of Common Pleas Forty-fifth Judicial District-Pa.
Corbin, Donald L.-Associate Justice, Arkansas Supreme Court-Ark.
Corbin, R. Thomas-Judge, Florida Circuit Court Twentieth Judicial Circuit-Fla.
Corbin, Robert Alan-Judge, Ohio Court of Common Pleas Brown County-Ohio
Corbo, Frank J., Jr.-Judge, Marlborough District Probate Court-Conn.
Corcoran, C. Timothy, III-Judge, United States Bankruptcy Court Middle District of Florida-Fla.
Cordes, Richard-Judge, Menard County Court-Tex.
Cordova, Alma-Judge, New York City Family Court-N.Y.
Cordy, Robert J.-Associate Justice, Massachusetts Supreme Judicial Court-Mass.
Corlew, Robert Ewing, III-Chancellor, Tennessee Chancery Court Sixteenth Judicial District-Tenn.
Corley, Phillip C.-Special Judge, Oklahoma District Court Ninth Judicial District-Okla.
Corn, Roger-Judge, Callahan County Court-Tex.
Cornejo-Lopez, Elia-Judge, Cameron County Court at Law No. 2-Tex.
Cornelio, Carmine-Judge, Superior Court of Arizona Pima County-Ariz.
Cornelius, Lon S., Jr.-Senior Judge, Florida Circuit Court Ninth Judicial Circuit-Fla.
Cornelius, Preston-Emergency Judge, North Carolina Superior Court-N.C.
Cornelius, Raymond E.-Justice, New York Supreme Court Seventh Judicial District-N.Y.
Cornell, Dennis A.-Associate Justice, California Court of Appeal Fifth District-Calif.
Cornett, Patti Palmour-Judge, Probate Court of Hall County-Ga.
Cornetta, Robert A.-Acting First Justice, Trial Court of Massachusetts District Court Department Essex County Salem Division and Justice, Ipswich Division-Mass.
Corning, Peter E.-Judge, Cayuga County Court-N.Y.
Cornish, Tom R.-Judge, Bankruptcy Appellate Panel Tenth Circuit and Judge, United States Bankruptcy Court Eastern District of Oklahoma-Okla.
Cornwell, James E., Jr.-Judge, Superior Court of Georgia Mountain Judicial Circuit-Ga.
Cornwell, Wayne-Judge, Whitestown Town Court-Ind.
Corodemus, Marina-Judge, New Jersey Superior Court Vicinage Eight-N.J.
Corpening, J. H., II-Judge, North Carolina District Court District 5-N.C.
Corradino, Thomas J.-Judge, Connecticut Superior Court-Conn.
Correll, David M.-Circuit Judge, Illinois Circuit Court Second Judicial Circuit-Ill.
Corriero, Michael A.-Judge, New York Court of Claims-N.Y.
Corrigan, Brian J.-Judge, Ohio Court of Common Pleas Cuyahoga County-Ohio
Corrigan, Carol A.-Associate Justice, California Court of Appeal First District Division Three-Calif.
Corrigan, John E.-Judge, Ohio Court of Common Pleas Cuyahoga County-Ohio
Corrigan, Maura D.-Chief Justice, Michigan Supreme Court-Mich.
Corrigan, Michael-Judge, Kansas District Court Eighteenth Judicial District-Kan.
Corrigan, Michael J.-Judge, Ohio Court of Appeals Eighth District-Ohio
Corrigan, Patrick F.-Judge, Ohio Court of Common Pleas Cuyahoga County-Ohio
Corrigan, Thomas H.-Judge Referee, Connecticut Superior Court-Conn.
Corrigan, Timothy J.-Judge, United States District Court Middle District of Florida-Fla.
Corsaro, Kimberly A.-Judge, Superior Court of Arizona Santa Cruz County-Ariz.
Corsiglia, George R.-Chief Judge, Michigan Circuit Court Forty-eighth Judicial Circuit-Mich.
Corso, S. Gerald-President Judge, Pennsylvania Court of Common Pleas Thirty-eighth Judicial District-Pa.
Corsones, Nancy-Judge, Vermont Trial Court-Vt.
Cortese, Philip V.-Judge, Montgomery County Family Court-N.Y.
Corwin, Charles D.-Chief Judge, Michigan Circuit Court Twenty-eighth Judicial Circuit-Mich.
Cory, Charles J.-Judge, Superior Court of California County of Santa Clara-Calif.
Coryell, James-Associate Judge, Illinois Circuit Court Sixth Judicial Circuit-Ill.
Corzine, William J.-Judge, Ohio Court of Common Pleas Ross County-Ohio
Cosbey, Roger B.-Magistrate Judge, United States District Court Northern District of Indiana-Ind.
Cosby, Donald J.-Judge, Texas District Court 67th Judicial District-Tex.
Coselli, John A.-Judge, Texas District Court 125th Judicial District-Tex.
Cosetti, Joseph L.-Recalled Judge, United States Bankruptcy Court Western District of Pennsylvania-Pa.
Cosgrove, Emmet L.-Judge, Connecticut Superior Court-Conn.
Cosgrove, John L.-Judge, Superior Court of California County of Placer-Calif.
Cosgrove, Nelson H.-Justice, New York Supreme Court Eighth Judicial District-N.Y.
Cosgrove, Patricia A.-Judge, Ohio Court of Common Pleas Summit County-Ohio
Cosper, Caprice-Judge, Texas District Court 339th Judicial District-Tex.
Costanzo, Robert Vincent-Judge, Kentucky District Court Forty-fourth Judicial District-Ky.
Costello, Dedee S.-Judge, Florida Circuit Court Fourteenth Judicial Circuit-Fla.
Costello, Dennis D.-Reserve Judge, Wisconsin Circuit Court-Wis.
Costello, Joseph Anthony, Jr.-Chief Judge, Michigan Circuit Court Thirty-eighth Judicial Circuit-Mich.
Costello, Leonard W.-Judge, Washington Superior Court Kitsap County-Wash.
Costello, Patricia K.-Judge, New Jersey Superior Court Vicinage Six-N.J.
Costello, Ralph F.-Justice, New York Supreme Court Tenth Judicial District-N.Y.
Costine, J. Mark-Judge, Ohio Court of Common Pleas Belmont County-Ohio
Cota, Raymond-Judge, Superior Court of California County of Imperial-Calif.
Cote, Denise-Judge, United States District Court Southern District of New York-N.Y.
Cote, Kenneth J., Jr.-Justice, Trial Court of Massachusetts District Court Department Hampden County Palmer Division-Mass.
Cote, Paul A., Jr.-Judge, Maine District Court-Me.
Cotnoir, Ernest J.-Judge, Putnam District Probate Court-Conn.
Cotten, Vernon-Judge, Mississippi Circuit Court Eighth Judicial District-Miss.
Cotter, Daniel J.-Judge, Nassau County Court-N.Y.
Cotter, Patricia-Justice, Montana Supreme Court-Mont.
Cotton, C. John-Judge, Wright Municipal Court-Wyo.
Cotton, Lyle J.-Judge, Bluffton City Court-Ind.
Cotton, Stacey W.-Chief Judge, United States Bankruptcy Court Northern District of Georgia-Ga.
Cottrell, Gary-Judge, Arkansas Circuit Court Twenty-first Judicial Circuit-Ark.
Cottrell, Patricia J.-Judge, Tennessee Court of Appeals Middle Division-Tenn.
Cottrill, Kelly J.-Judge, Muskingum County Court-Ohio
Couch, Valerie K.-Magistrate Judge, United States District Court Western District of Oklahoma-Okla.
Coughenour, John C.-Chief Judge, United States District Court Western District of Washington-Wash.
Coughlin, John W.-Judge, Colorado District Court Second Judicial District-Colo.
Couillard, Ronn M.-Judge, Superior Court of California County of Tulare-Calif.
Council, Gerald J.-Judge, New Jersey Superior Court Vicinage Seven-N.J.
Counsell, Jon M.-Judge, Wisconsin Circuit Court Clark Circuit-Wis.
Counts, James Waylon-Judge, New Mexico District Court Twelfth Judicial District-N.Mex.
Coursey, Daniel M., Jr.-Judge, Superior Court of Georgia Stone Mountain Judicial Circuit-Ga.
Courtney, Don E.-District Judge, Iowa District Court Third Judicial District-Ia.
Courtney, James P., Jr.-Judge, New Jersey Superior Court Vicinage Fourteen-N.J.
Courtright, John T.-Chief Judge, Michigan District Court District Twenty-four-Mich.
Couvillion, D. Irvin-Special Trial Judge, United States Tax Court
Couzens, J. Richard-Judge, Superior Court of California County of Placer-Calif.
Covarrubias, Manuel J.-Judge, Superior Court of California County of Ventura-Calif.
Covello, Alfred V.-Senior Judge, United States District Court District of Connecticut-Conn.

ALPHABETICAL NAME INDEX

Covello, Joseph-Justice, New York Supreme Court Tenth Judicial District-N.Y.
Coven, Mark S.-First Justice, Trial Court of Massachusetts District Court Department Norfolk County Quincy Division and Justice, Middlesex County Somerville Division-Mass.
Covie-Leese, Cynthia-Judge, New Jersey Superior Court Vicinage Three-N.J.
Covington, Mary F.-Judge, North Carolina District Court District 22-N.C.
Covington, Suzanne-Judge, Texas District Court 201st Judicial District-Tex.
Covington, Virginia M. Hernandez-Judge, Florida District Court of Appeal Second District-Fla.
Cowart, Gary R.-Judge, Broward County Court-Fla.
Cowart, Louise-Judge, Probate Court of Cook County-Ga.
Cowart, Richard M.-Judge, Superior Court of Georgia Southern Judicial Circuit-Ga.
Cowell, Michael A.-Judge, Superior Court of California County of Los Angeles-Calif.
Cowen, Linda S.-Judge, State Court of Clayton County-Ga.
Cowen, Robert E.-Senior Judge, United States Court of Appeals Third Circuit
Cowett, Patricia A. Y.-Judge, Superior Court of California County of San Diego-Calif.
Cowhey, James R.-Justice, New York Supreme Court Ninth Judicial District-N.Y.
Cowin, Judith Arnold-Associate Justice, Massachusetts Supreme Judicial Court-Mass.
Cowin, William I.-Associate Justice, Massachusetts Appeals Court-Mass.
Cowsert, Kenneth L.-Judge, Washington Superior Court Snohomish County-Wash.
Cox, Campbell, II-Judge, Texas District Court 145th Judicial District-Tex.
Cox, Cynthia L.-Judge, Florida Circuit Court Nineteenth Judicial Circuit-Fla.
Cox, Emmett Ripley-Senior Judge, United States Court of Appeals Eleventh Circuit
Cox, Frank R.-Chief Magistrate, Magistrate Court of Cobb County-Ga.
Cox, Fred-Judge, Hamilton County Court-Tex.
Cox, J. Craig-Judge, Pennsylvania Court of Common Pleas Fifty-third Judicial District-Pa.
Cox, J. Steven-Judge, Franklin Circuit Court-Ind.
Cox, Jacqueline P.-United States Bankruptcy Court Northern District of Illinois-Ill.
Cox, James A.-Judge, Superior Court of California County of Riverside-Calif.
Cox, James B. "J. B."-Chancellor, Tennessee Chancery Court Seventeenth Judicial District-Tenn.
Cox, John R.-Judge, Kentucky District Court Twenty-first Judicial District-Ky.
Cox, Joseph M.-Judge, Texas District Court 160th Judicial District-Tex.
Cox, Kathleen Gallogly-Associate Judge, Circuit Court for Baltimore County, Third Judicial Circuit-Md.
Cox, Marilyn Kay-Judge, Bailey County Court-Tex.
Cox, Michael A.-Judge, Adams County Court-Colo.
Cox, Ronald E.-Acting Chief Judge, Washington Court of Appeals Division I-Wash.
Cox, Sean F.-Judge, Michigan Circuit Court Third Judicial Circuit-Mich.
Cox, Walter Thompson, III-Senior Judge, United States Court of Appeals for the Armed Forces
Coxsey, Kent-Judge, Berryville District Court-Ark.
Coyle, David T.-Chief Judge, Michigan District Court District Three A-Mich.
Coyle, John J., Jr.-Judge, New Jersey Superior Court Vicinage Thirteen-N.J.
Coyle, Robert E.-Senior Judge, United States District Court Eastern District of California-Calif.
Coyler, Bruce-Associate Circuit Judge, Missouri Circuit Court Twenty-sixth Judicial Circuit-Mo.
Coyne, Michael J.-Associate Justice, Trial Court of Massachusetts Boston Municipal Court Department-Mass.
Coyne, William J.-Judge, Ohio Court of Common Pleas Cuyahoga County-Ohio
Cozier, Barry A.-Associate Justice, New York Supreme Court Appellate Division Second Judicial Department-N.Y.
Cozza, Salvatore "Sam" F.-Judge, Washington Superior Court Spokane County-Wash.
Cozzens, R. Bruce, Jr.-Justice, New York Supreme Court Tenth Judicial District-N.Y.
Crabb, Barbara B.-Chief Judge, United States District Court Western District of Wisconsin-Wis.
Crabtree, C. Scott-Judge, Colorado District Court Seventeenth Judicial District-Colo.
Crabtree, Michael R.-Judge, Idaho District Court Fifth Judicial District Magistrate Division-Ida.
Crabtree, Terry-Judge, Arkansas Court of Appeals-Ark.
Craddick, Judith S.-Judge, Superior Court of California County of Contra Costa-Calif.
Craft, Chris-Judge, Tennessee Criminal Court Thirtieth Judicial District-Tenn.
Craft, Ronald Richard-Judge, Ohio Court of Common Pleas Butler County-Ohio
Crahan, Lawrence G.-Judge, Missouri Court of Appeals Eastern District-Mo.
Craig, Carla E.-Judge, United States Bankruptcy Court Eastern District of New York-N.Y.
Craig, George T.-Presiding Judge, Alabama Circuit Court Thirty-ninth Judicial Circuit-Ala.
Craig, John O., III-Resident Judge, North Carolina Superior Court Fifth Judicial Division District 18-N.C.
Craig, William H.-Chief Judge, Superior Court of Georgia Flint Judicial Circuit-Ga.
Crain, David-Judge, Travis County Court at Law No. 3-Tex.
Crain, Patricia-Judge, Oregon Circuit Court First Judicial District-Ore.
Cram, Joyce M.-Judge, Superior Court of California County of Contra Costa-Calif.
Cramer, William D., Jr.-Presiding Judge, Oregon Circuit Court Twenty-fourth Judicial District-Ore.
Cramin, Corey Scott-Judge, Superior Court of California County of Orange-Calif.
Cramp, David S.-Judge, New Jersey Superior Court Vicinage Ten-N.J.
Crampton, Rebekah J.-Associate Justice, Trial Court of Massachusetts Juvenile Court Department Hampden County Division-Mass.
Crancer, Barbara A.-Associate Circuit Judge, Missouri Circuit Court Twenty-first Judicial Circuit-Mo.
Crandall, Donna L.-Judge, Superior Court of California County of Orange-Calif.
Crandall, Virginia Lea-Judge, Hawaii Circuit Court First Judicial Circuit-Hi.
Crandall, William H., Jr.-Judge, Missouri Court of Appeals Eastern District-Mo.
Crane, Clayton J.-Circuit Judge, Illinois Circuit Court of Cook County-Ill.
Crane, Kathianne Knaup-Judge, Missouri Court of Appeals Eastern District-Mo.
Crane, Randy-Judge, United States District Court Southern District of Texas-Tex.
Crane, Shawn-Judge, Pinellas County Court-Fla.
Crane, Stephen G.-Associate Justice, New York Supreme Court Appellate Division Second Judicial Department-N.Y.
Crane, William A.-Judge, Michigan Circuit Court Tenth Judicial Circuit-Mich.
Crane, William E.-Reserve Judge, Wisconsin Circuit Court-Wis.
Craney, Jane Spencer-Judge, Morgan Superior Court-Ind.
Cranford, Dwight L.-Resident Judge, North Carolina Superior Court First Judicial Division District 6A-N.C.
Cranford, John Herbert-Judge, State Court of Coweta County-Ga.
Cranford, Mary T.-Judge, Probate Court of Coweta County-Ga.
Cranna, William F.-Judge, Hudson City Court-N.Y.
Crapitto, Mary Nell-Judge, Galveston County Court at Law No. 1-Tex.
Cratsley, John C.-Associate Justice, Trial Court of Massachusetts Superior Court Department-Mass.
Craven, Caroline M.-Magistrate Judge, United States District Court Eastern District of Texas-Tex.
Craven, John J., Jr.-Associate Justice, Trial Court of Massachusetts Juvenile Court Department Suffolk County Division-Mass.
Craven, T. Peter-Judge, Colorado District Court Ninth Judicial District and Judge, Colorado Water Court Division Five-Colo.
Craven, Terry M.-Associate Justice, Trial Court of Massachusetts Juvenile Court Department Suffolk County Division-Mass.
Craven, Thomas L.-Associate Judge, Maryland District Court District Six-Md.
Cravens, David-Judge, Paris District Court-Ark.
Cravinho, Paul E.-Judge, Stonington District Probate Court-Conn.
Crawford, Dale A.-Judge, Ohio Court of Common Pleas Franklin County-Ohio
Crawford, Dan J.-Associate Circuit Judge, Missouri Circuit Court Thirty-fifth Judicial Circuit-Mo.
Crawford, Geoffrey W.-Judge, Vermont Trial Court-Vt.
Crawford, Juliett L.-Judge, Connecticut Superior Court-Conn.
Crawford, Linton Kim, Jr.-Judge, State Court of Habersham County-Ga.
Crawford, Rick-Chief Magistrate, Magistrate Court of Polk County-Ga.
Crawford, Stephen O'Neal-Judge, Texas District Court 90th Judicial District-Tex.
Crawford, Susan J.-Chief Judge, United States Court of Appeals for the Armed Forces
Crawford, W. Frank-Judge, Tennessee Court of Appeals Western Division-Tenn.
Crawford, William C.-Circuit Judge, Missouri Circuit Court Twenty-ninth Judicial Circuit-Mo.
Crawford, William H., II-Judge, Michigan District Court District Sixty-eight-Mich.
Crawley, John B.-Judge, Alabama Court of Civil Appeals-Ala.
Creager, Donald C.-Judge, Loving County Court-Tex.
Creany, Timothy P.-Judge, Pennsylvania Court of Common Pleas Forty-seventh Judicial District-Pa.
Creech, Wayne M.-Judge, South Carolina Family Court Ninth Judicial Circuit-S.C.
Creech, William A.-Retired-Recalled Judge, North Carolina District Court-N.C.
Creedon, Michael C.-Circuit Justice, Trial Court of Massachusetts District Court Department and First Justice, Barnstable County Falmouth Division-Mass.
Creekmore, Frederick Hillary, Sr.-Judge, Virginia Circuit Court First Judicial Circuit-Va.
Crehan, Matthew J.-Judge, Ohio Court of Common Pleas Butler County-Ohio
Creighton, Lee-Judge, Olympia Municipal Court-Wash.
Creitz, Daniel D.-Judge, Kansas District Court Thirty-first Judicial District-Kan.
Cremins, William T.-Judge, Connecticut Superior Court-Conn.
Crenshaw, Jeanne Dawes-Judge, Alachua County Court-Fla.
Crenshaw, Marva L.-Judge, Florida Circuit Court Thirteenth Judicial Circuit-Fla.
Crenshaw, McCarthy, Jr.-Judge, Florida Circuit Court Fourth Judicial Circuit-Fla.
Cresap, Wayne George-Judge, Louisiana District Court Thirty-fourth Judicial District-La.
Crespo, Manuel A.-Judge, Florida Circuit Court Eleventh Judicial Circuit-Fla.
Creswell, Kathryn E.-Circuit Judge, Illinois Circuit Court Eighteenth Judicial Circuit-Ill.
Cretella, Albert W., Jr.-Judge Referee, Connecticut Superior Court-Conn.
Creuzot, John Coleman-Judge, Texas Criminal District Court No. 4 Dallas County-Tex.
Crew, D. Bruce, III-Associate Justice, New York Supreme Court Appellate Division Third Judicial Department-N.Y.
Crew, Robert B., Jr.-Judge, Denver County Court-Colo.
Crews, Johnnie E.-Judge, Probate Court of Brantley County-Ga.
Cribbs, Graham Anderson-Judge, Superior Court of California County of Riverside-Calif.
Crichton, Scott J.-Judge, Louisiana District Court First Judicial District-La.
Crigler, B. Waugh-Magistrate Judge, United States District Court Western District of Virginia-Va.

ALPHABETICAL NAME INDEX

ALPHABETICAL NAME INDEX

Curless, Charles-Associate Circuit Judge, Missouri Circuit Court Twenty-eighth Judicial Circuit-Mo.

Curley, Patricia S.-Judge, Wisconsin Court of Appeals District One-Wis.

Curley, Sarah S.-Chief Judge, United States Bankruptcy Court District of Arizona-Ariz.

Curley, Thomas J., Jr.-Associate Justice, Trial Court of Massachusetts Superior Court Department-Mass.

Curnan, Robert J.-District Judge, Iowa District Court First Judicial District-Ia.

Curran, Barbara A.-Judge, New Jersey Superior Court Vicinage Six-N.J.

Curran, Dennis J.-Justice, Trial Court of Massachusetts District Court Department Norfolk County Stoughton Division-Mass.

Curran, Hugh C.-Judge Referee, Connecticut Superior Court-Conn.

Curran, John J., Jr.-First Justice, Trial Court of Massachusetts District Court Department Worcester County Leominster Division-Mass.

Curran, Thomas J.-Senior Judge, United States District Court Eastern District of Wisconsin-Wis.

Currence, Elizabeth M.-Judge, North Carolina District Court District 26-N.C.

Currie, Cameron McGowan-Judge, United States District Court District of South Carolina-S.C.

Currie, W. Keith-Associate Circuit Judge, Missouri Circuit Court Thirty-fourth Judicial Circuit-Mo.

Currier, Charles C.-Judge, New Mexico District Court Fifth Judicial District-N.Mex.

Curry, Charles B.-Chief Judge, Florida Circuit Court Tenth Judicial Circuit-Fla.

Curry, Daniel A.-Associate Justice, California Court of Appeal Second District Division Four-Calif.

Curry, George S.-Judge, Wisconsin Circuit Court Grant Circuit-Wis.

Curry, James L.-Judge, Superior Court of California County of Yuba-Calif.

Curry, Kenneth Charles-Judge, Texas District Court 153rd Judicial District-Tex.

Curry, Thomas J.-Judge, Colorado District Court Eighteenth Judicial District-Colo.

Curtin, Aymer L.-Judge, Alachua County Court-Fla.

Curtin, John T.-Senior Judge, United States District Court Western District of New York-N.Y.

Curtin, Patricia G.-Justice, Trial Court of Massachusetts District Court Department Middlesex County Concord Division-Mass.

Curtis, Daphne Means-Judge, Michigan Circuit Court Third Judicial Circuit-Mich.

Curtis, Herbert, III-Judge, Superior Court of California County of Ventura-Calif.

Curtis, Katherine R.-Judge, Montana District Court Eleventh Judicial District-Mont.

Curtis, Richard M.-Judge, Superior Court of California County of Monterey-Calif.

Cusack, Robert E.-Recalled Circuit Judge, Illinois Circuit Court of Cook County-Ill.

Cushenberry, Harold, Jr.-Associate Judge, Superior Court of the District of Columbia-D.C.

Cusimano, Charles V., II-Judge, Louisiana District Court Twenty-fourth Judicial District-La.

Cuthbertson, Frank-Judge, Washington Superior Court Pierce County-Wash.

Cutler, Beverly Winslow-Judge, Alaska Superior Court Third Judicial District-Alas.

Cutrer, Lilynn A.-Judge, Louisiana District Court Fourteenth Judicial District-La.

Cutrona, Anthony J.-Justice, New York Supreme Court Second Judicial District-N.Y.

Cutsumpas, Lloyd-Judge, Connecticut Superior Court-Conn.

Cybulski, David-Judge, Montana District Court Fifteenth Judicial District-Mont.

Cyganowski, Melanie L.-Judge, United States Bankruptcy Court Eastern District of New York-N.Y.

Cypher, Elspeth B.-Associate Justice, Massachusetts Appeals Court-Mass.

Cyr, Conrad K.-Senior Judge, United States Court of Appeals First Circuit.

Cyr, Cynthia-Assistant Judge, Vermont Trial Court Washington County-Vt.

Cyr, John P.-Justice, Littleton District Court-N.H.

Czajka, Paul-Judge, Columbia County Court-N.Y.

Czamanske, Daniel M.-Associate Circuit Judge, Missouri Circuit Court Sixth Judicial Circuit-Mo.

Czuleger, J. Stephen-Judge, Superior Court of California County of Los Angeles-Calif.

Czygier, John M., Jr.-Surrogate, Suffolk County Surrogate's Court-N.Y.

Dabiri, Gloria M.-Justice, New York Supreme Court Second Judicial District-N.Y.

Dabney, James R.-Judge, Superior Court of California County of Los Angeles-Calif.

Dabrowski, Albert S.-Judge, United States Bankruptcy Court District of Connecticut-Conn.

Dadd, Mark H.-Judge, Wyoming County Court-N.Y.

D'Addabbo, Frank M., Jr.-Judge, Connecticut Superior Court-Conn.

Daffron, Philip V.-Chief Judge, Virginia General District Court Twelfth Judicial District-Va.

D'Agostini, Diane-Judge, Michigan District Court District Forty-eight-Mich.

Dahl, Stephen J.-Justice of the Peace, North Las Vegas Justices' Court-Nev.

Dahlberg, Edwin C.-Reserve Judge, Wisconsin Circuit Court-Wis.

Dahlen, Kimberly L.-Associate Judge, Illinois Circuit Court First Judicial Circuit-Ill.

Daigh, Gary E.-Judge, Superior Court of California County of Los Angeles-Calif.

Daigle, Ronald A.-Judge, Maine District Court-Me.

Dailey, John Daniel-Judge, Colorado Court of Appeals-Colo.

Dailey, Joseph B.-Judge, Tennessee Criminal Court Thirtieth Judicial District-Tenn.

Dailey, Richard A.-Judge, Delaware Circuit Court-Ind.

Daily, Kirk A.-District Associate Judge, Iowa District Court Eighth Judicial District-Ia.

Dairman, Dennis W.-Judge, Superior Court of Arizona Maricopa County-Ariz.

Daisy, William L.-Chief Judge, North Carolina District Court District 18-N.C.

Dakan, Stephen L.-Senior Judge, Florida Circuit Court Twelfth Judicial Circuit-Fla.

Dakis, Linda N.-Judge, Dade County Court-Fla.

Dalby, Carol Cannedy-Judge, Miller County and Texarkana District Courts-Ark.

Dalby, Docia L.-Magistrate Judge, United States District Court Middle District of Louisiana-La.

Dalby, Giles W.-Judge, Garza County Court-Tex.

Dale, Robert P.-Judge, Superior Court of California County of Sonoma-Calif.

Dale, Sebe, Jr.-Judge, Mississippi Chancery Court Tenth Judicial District-Miss.

D'Alessandro, Nicholas M.-Judge, Pennsylvania Court of Common Pleas First Judicial District-Pa.

Daley, James P.-Judge, Wisconsin Circuit Court Rock Circuit-Wis.

Daley, Michael E.-Justice, New York Supreme Court Fifth Judicial District-N.Y.

Daley, Roger W.-Judge, New Jersey Superior Court Vicinage Eight-N.J.

Daley, Thomas F.-Judge, Louisiana Court of Appeal Fifth Circuit-La.

Dalianis, Linda Stewart-Associate Justice, New Hampshire Supreme Court-N.H.

Dalis, John S.-Chief Judge, United States Bankruptcy Court Southern District of Georgia-Ga.

Dallas, Denise-Judge, Probate Court of Glascock County-Ga.

Dally, David C.-Presiding Judge, Missouri Circuit Court Twenty-ninth Judicial Circuit-Mo.

D'Alton, James F., Jr.-Judge, Virginia Circuit Court Eleventh Judicial Circuit-Va.

Dalton, Robert E., Jr.-President Judge, Pennsylvania Court of Common Pleas Fourth Judicial District-Pa.

Dalton, Wesley C.-Associate Circuit Judge, Missouri Circuit Court Twelfth Judicial Circuit-Mo.

Daly, Margaret A.-Judge, Minnesota District Court Fourth Judicial District-Minn.

Daly, Noreen M.-Associate Judge, Illinois Circuit Court of Cook County-Ill.

Daly, Thomas R.-Judge, Yonkers City Court-N.Y.

Dalzell, Stewart-Judge, United States District Court Eastern District of Pennsylvania-Pa.

Dameron, E. Penn, Jr.-Resident Judge, North Carolina Superior Court Eighth Judicial Division District 29-N.C.

Damiani, Richard A.-Judge, Connecticut Superior Court-Conn.

Damich, Edward J.-Chief Judge, United States Court of Federal Claims

D'Amico, Michael L.-Judge, Erie County Court-N.Y.

Damico, Paul Anthony-Judge, Palm Beach County Court-Fla.

Damis, Spirro-Judge, Steilacoom Municipal Court-Wash.

Damon, John A.-Judge, Wisconsin Circuit Court Trempealeau Circuit-Wis.

Damon, Patricia L.-Judge, Deep River District Probate Court-Conn.

Damoorgian, Dorian-Judge, Florida Circuit Court Seventeenth Judicial Circuit-Fla.

Damrath, Joseph Edward-Judge, Hornell City Court-N.Y.

Damrell, Frank C., Jr.-Judge, United States District Court Eastern District of California-Calif.

Damron, Robert H.-Judge, Superior Court of California County of Sutter-Calif.

Dana, Howard H., Jr.-Associate Justice, Maine Supreme Judicial Court-Me.

Danahy, Paul W., Jr.-Senior Judge, Florida District Court of Appeal-Fla.

Dancy, Bonita J.-Associate Judge, Circuit Court for Baltimore City, Eighth Judicial Circuit-Md.

D'Andrea, Frank H., Jr.-Judge Referee, Connecticut Superior Court-Conn.

Dandurand, Joseph-Presiding Judge, Missouri Circuit Court Seventeenth Judicial Circuit-Mo.

Dangler, John B.-Judge, New Jersey Superior Court Vicinage Ten-N.J.

Daniel, Donald L.-Judge, Tippecanoe Circuit Court-Ind.

Daniel, Duane-Judge, King County Court-Tex.

Daniel, Jerry-Judge, State Court of Burke County-Ga.

Daniel, Joseph S. "Steve"-Judge, Tennessee Circuit Court Sixteenth Judicial District-Tenn.

Daniel, Kimberly J.-Judge, Virginia Juvenile and Domestic Relations District Court Nineteenth Judicial District-Va.

Daniel, Louis R.-Judge, Louisiana District Court Nineteenth Judicial District-La.

Daniel, Roxann Gray-Judge, Superior Court of Georgia Chattahoochee Judicial Circuit-Ga.

Daniel, Wiley Y.-Judge, United States District Court District of Colorado-Colo.

Daniele, Rhonda Lee-Judge, Pennsylvania Court of Common Pleas Thirty-eighth Judicial District-Pa.

Daniels, Annette-Justice of the Peace, Virginia City Justices' Court-Nev.

Daniels, George B.-Judge, United States District Court Southern District of New York-N.Y.

Daniels, Lawrence R.-Associate Judge, Circuit Court for Baltimore County, Third Judicial Circuit-Md.

Daniels, Paula-Chief Magistrate, Magistrate Court of Irwin County-Ga.

Daniels, Vernon-Judge, Douglas County Separate Juvenile Court-Neb.

Daniels, Wendel E.-Judge, New Jersey Superior Court Vicinage Fourteen-N.J.

Danielsen, David John-Judge, Superior Court of California County of San Diego-Calif.

Danielson, Brent V.-Chief Judge, Michigan District Court District Eighty-five-Mich.

Danielson, Cynthia Howard-District Judge, Iowa District Court Eighth Judicial District-Ia.

Danielson, Paul-Judge, Arkansas Circuit Court Fifteenth Judicial Circuit-Ark.

Danikolas, James-Judge, Lake Superior Court-Ind.

Danilson, David R.-District Judge, Iowa District Court Second Judicial District-Ia.

Dannan, Ed-Justice of the Peace, Reno Justices' Court-Nev.

Dannehy, Joseph F.-Judge Referee, Connecticut Superior Court-Conn.

Dannehy, Michael R.-Judge, Connecticut Superior Court-Conn.

ALPHABETICAL NAME INDEX

Dannel, Dennis Jude-Judge, New Orleans Traffic Court-La.
Danner, Alden E.-Judge, Superior Court of California County of Santa Clara-Calif.
Danner, Arthur-Judge, Superior Court of California County of Santa Cruz-Calif.
Danser, William R.-Judge, Superior Court of California County of Santa Clara-Calif.
D'Apolito, David-Judge, Mahoning County Court-Ohio
Darby, Richard B.-District Judge, Oklahoma District Court Third Judicial District-Okla.
Darbyshire, J. Hobart-District Judge, Iowa District Court Seventh Judicial District-Ia.
Darcy, Daniel P.-Circuit Judge, Illinois Circuit Court of Cook County-Ill.
Darden, Carr L.-Presiding Judge, Indiana Court of Appeals Fourth District-Ind.
Darden, David-Judge, State Court of Cobb County-Ga.
Darden, Linnie, III-Judge, Juvenile Court of Georgia Atlantic Judicial Circuit-Ga.
Darigan, Francis J., Jr.-Associate Justice, Rhode Island Superior Court-R.I.
Darling, Deanne L.-Judge, Oregon Circuit Court Fifth Judicial District-Ore.
Darlington, John H.-Judge, Superior Court of California County of Nevada-Calif.
Darnell, Jim Bob-Judge, Texas District Court 140th Judicial District-Tex.
Darrah, John W.-Judge, United States District Court Northern District of Illinois-Ill.
Dartt, Denise Ann-Judge, Toledo Municipal Court-Ohio
Dau, Ralph W.-Judge, Superior Court of California County of Los Angeles-Calif.
Dauber, Ellen A.-Associate Judge, Illinois Circuit Court Twentieth Judicial Circuit-Ill.
Daughaday, John T.-Judge, Kentucky Circuit Court Fifty-second Judicial Circuit-Ky.
Daugherity, Eugene P.-Circuit Judge, Illinois Circuit Court Thirteenth Judicial Circuit-Ill.
Daugherty, E. Duane-Judge, Jasper Circuit Court-Ind.
Daugherty, Hunter-Judge, Kentucky Circuit Court Thirteenth Judicial Circuit-Ky.
Daugherty, Jay A.-Presiding Judge, Missouri Circuit Court Sixteenth Judicial Circuit-Mo.
Daughtrey, Martha Craig-Judge, United States Court of Appeals Sixth Circuit
Dauksch, James C., Jr.-Senior Judge, Florida District Court of Appeal-Fla.
Daum, Elliot-Judge, Superior Court of California County of Sonoma-Calif.
Dauphiné, Susan M.-Judge, Superior Court of California County of Monterey-Calif.
Dauphinot, Lee Ann-Justice, Texas Court of Appeals Second District-Tex.
Davenport, Amy M.-Judge, Vermont Trial Court-Vt.
Davenport, Chris A.-Chief Magistrate, Magistrate Court of Jeff Davis County-Ga.
Davenport, Mitchell Grant-Judge, Jack County Court-Tex.
Davey, P. Kevin-Judge, Florida Circuit Court Second Judicial Circuit-Fla.
David, Michael P.-Presiding Judge, Missouri Circuit Court Twenty-second Judicial Circuit-Mo.
David, Steve-Judge, Boone Circuit Court-Ind.
Davidowitz, Edward M.-Justice, New York Supreme Court Twelfth Judicial District-N.Y.
Davidson, Glen H.-Chief Judge, United States District Court Northern District of Mississippi-Miss.
Davidson, Janice B.-Chief Judge, Colorado Court of Appeals-Colo.
Davidson, John L.-Judge, Superior Court of California County of San Diego-Calif.
Davidson, Lisa-Judge, Florida Circuit Court Eighteenth Judicial Circuit-Fla.
Davidson, Mark-Judge, Texas District Court 11th Judicial District-Tex.
Davidson, Rachel N.-Judge, New Jersey Superior Court Vicinage Five-N.J.
Davidson, Robert S.-Judge, Ohio Court of Common Pleas Marion County-Ohio
Davies, Carol G.-Judge, Texas District Court 177th Judicial District-Tex.
Davies, Doyle-Judge, Lusk Municipal Court-Wyo.
Davies, Jean A.-Judge, Minnesota District Court First Judicial District-Minn.
Davies, Robert E. Lee-Judge, Tennessee Circuit Court Twenty-first Judicial District-Tenn.
Davila, Edward J.-Judge, Superior Court of California County of Santa Clara-Calif.
Davilla, Raymond J., Jr.-Judge, Superior Court of California County of Santa Clara-Calif.
Davis, Allan H.-Judge, Ohio Court of Common Pleas Hancock County-Ohio
Davis, Alton T., Jr.-Chief Judge, Michigan Circuit Court Forty-sixth Judicial Circuit-Mich.
Davis, Andre Maurice-Judge, United States District Court District of Maryland-Md.
Davis, Arrie W.-Associate Judge, Court of Special Appeals of Maryland-Md.
Davis, Bonnie C.-Judge, Virginia Juvenile and Domestic Relations District Court Twelfth Judicial District-Va.
Davis, Brian Jordan-Judge, Florida Circuit Court Fourth Judicial Circuit-Fla.
Davis, Charles A., Jr.-Judge, Florida District Court of Appeal Second District-Fla.
Davis, Chester C.-Judge, North Carolina District Court District 21-N.C.
Davis, Chris-Judge, Cherokee County Court-Tex.
Davis, D. William, Jr.-Judge, Belmont County Court-Ohio
Davis, Danny E.-Judge, North Carolina District Court District 30-N.C.
Davis, David C.-Judge, Haskell County Court-Tex.
Davis, David P.-Judge, Ohio Court of Common Pleas Hamilton County-Ohio
Davis, Donald C.-Associate Judge, Circuit Court for Wicomico County, First Judicial Circuit-Md.
Davis, E. Purnell, II-Chief Judge, Superior Court of Georgia Toombs Judicial Circuit-Ga.
Davis, Edwin Malloy-Judge, Chesterfield County Probate Court-S.C.
Davis, Elaine L.-Judge, New Jersey Superior Court Vicinage Six-N.J.
Davis, Fred D.-Judge, Arkansas Circuit Court Eleventh West Judicial Circuit-Ark.
Davis, Fred W.-Judge, Texas District Court 17th Judicial District-Tex.
Davis, Gary W.-Judge, Kiowa County Court-Colo.
Davis, George W.-Judge, Kentucky District Court Thirty-second Judicial District-Ky.
Davis, Giles Jackson, Jr.-Judge, Ohio Court of Common Pleas Montgomery County-Ohio
Davis, Gordon Miles-Magistrate Judge, United States District Court Northern District of Florida-Fla.
Davis, Harwell G., III-Magistrate Judge, United States District Court Northern District of Alabama-Ala.
Davis, Henry E.-Judge, Florida Circuit Court Fourth Judicial Circuit-Fla.
Davis, J. Harvey-Judge, Superior Court of Georgia Tifton Judicial Circuit-Ga.
Davis, J. Maston-Chief Judge, Virginia Juvenile and Domestic Relations District Court Fifteenth Judicial District-Va.
Davis, James C.-Retired-Recalled Judge, North Carolina Superior Court-N.C.
Davis, James Franklin-Judge, Kansas District Court Tenth Judicial District-Kan.
Davis, James Z.-Judge, Utah Court of Appeals-Utah
Davis, Jeff W.-Judge, South Dakota Circuit Court Seventh Judicial Circuit-S.D.
Davis, Jerry A.-Magistrate Judge, United States District Court Northern District of Mississippi-Miss.
Davis, Joel G.-Judge, Louisiana District Court Thirty-third Judicial District-La.
Davis, John E.-Judge, Superior Court of Arizona Pima County-Ariz.
Davis, John P.-Judge, Nevada District Court Fifth Judicial District-Nev.
Davis, John Paul-Judge, Jefferson County Court at Law No. 3-Tex.
Davis, K. Elizabeth-Associate Circuit Judge, Missouri Circuit Court Seventh Judicial Circuit-Mo.
Davis, Keith D.-Judge, Superior Court of California County of San Bernardino-Calif.
Davis, Kenneth-Judge, Hill County Court-Tex.
Davis, Kenneth A.-Justice, New York Supreme Court Tenth Judicial District-N.Y.
Davis, Lamar W., Jr.-Judge, United States Bankruptcy Court Southern District of Georgia-Ga.
Davis, Laura Prosser-Judge, Baton Rouge City Court-La.
Davis, Legrome D.-Judge, United States District Court Eastern District of Pennsylvania-Pa.
Davis, Leonard E.-Judge, United States District Court Eastern District of Texas-Tex.
Davis, Linda-Chief Judge, Michigan District Court District Forty-one B-Mich.
Davis, Linda K.-Judge, Probate Court of Fannin County-Ga.
Davis, Linda Kay-Associate Judge, Superior Court of the District of Columbia-D.C.
Davis, Lindsay R., Jr.-Resident Judge, North Carolina Superior Court Fifth Judicial Division District 18-N.C.
Davis, Lynn W.-Judge, Utah District Court Fourth Judicial District-Utah
Davis, Mac-Judge, Wisconsin Circuit Court Waukesha Circuit-Wis.
Davis, Marguerite "Ditti"-Judge, Florida District Court of Appeal First District-Fla.
Davis, Mark S.-Judge, Virginia Circuit Court Third Judicial Circuit-Va.
Davis, Michael J.-Judge, United States District Court District of Minnesota-Minn.
Davis, Nancy-Judge, Superior Court of California City and County of San Francisco-Calif.
Davis, Norman J.-Judge, Superior Court of Arizona Maricopa County-Ariz.
Davis, Paul R., Jr.-Judge, Texas District Court 200th Judicial District-Tex.
Davis, R. Scott-Associate Judge, Maryland District Court District Two-Md.
Davis, Randall J.-Judge, Broomfield County Court-Colo.
Davis, Rex D.-Chief Justice, Texas Court of Appeals Tenth District-Tex.
Davis, Richard W. B.-Judge, Texas District Court 272nd Judicial District-Tex.
Davis, Robert E.-Justice, Kansas Supreme Court-Kan.
Davis, Robert E.-Special Judge, Oklahoma District Court Twenty-sixth Judicial District-Okla.
Davis, Robin Jean-Justice, West Virginia Supreme Court of Appeals-W.Va.
Davis, Rodney-Associate Justice, California Court of Appeal Third District-Calif.
Davis, Roger D.-Judge, Harrison Superior Court-Ind.
Davis, Ronald S.-Associate Judge, Illinois Circuit Court of Cook County-Ill.
Davis, S. Joseph, Jr.-Senior Judge, Florida Circuit Court Eighteenth Judicial Circuit-Fla.
Davis, Sam, Jr.-Judge, Probate Court of Bryan County-Ga.
Davis, Stephen T.-Chief Judge, Michigan Circuit Court Forty-seventh Judicial Circuit-Mich.
Davis, Stewart P.-Judge, Virginia General District Court Nineteenth Judicial District-Va.
Davis, Theodore Z.-Judge, New Jersey Superior Court Vicinage Four-N.J.
Davis, W. Eugene-Judge, United States Court of Appeals Fifth Circuit
Davis, Warren P.-Chief Magistrate, Magistrate Court of Gwinnett County-Ga.
Davis, William E.-Judge, Lake Superior Court-Ind.
Davis, William J.-Judge, Superior Court of California County of Siskiyou-Calif.
Davis, William J.-Justice, New York Supreme Court First Judicial District-N.Y.
Davis-Loomis, Nancy L.-Associate Judge, Circuit Court for Anne Arundel County, Fifth Judicial Circuit-Md.
Davy, Thomas M.-Circuit Judge, Illinois Circuit Court of Cook County-Ill.
Dawkins, Nolan Boyd-Judge, Virginia Juvenile and Domestic Relations District Court Eighteenth Judicial District-Va.
Dawley, Paul C.-Justice, Trial Court of Massachusetts District Court Department Plymouth County Brockton Division-Mass.
Dawson, Betty L.-Judge, Superior Court of California County of Merced-Calif.

ALPHABETICAL NAME INDEX

Dawson, Daniel P.-Judge, Florida Circuit Court Ninth Judicial Circuit-Fla.

Dawson, Georgia-Judge, North Dakota District Court East Central Judicial District-N.D.

Dawson, Glen R.-Judge, Utah District Court Second Judicial District-Utah

Dawson, Herman C.-Associate Judge, Circuit Court for Prince George's County, Seventh Judicial Circuit-Md.

Dawson, Howard A., Jr.-Senior Judge, United States Tax Court

Dawson, James P.-Justice, New York Supreme Court Fourth Judicial District-N.Y.

Dawson, Joseph J.-Judge, The Criminal Court of the City of New York-N.Y.

Dawson, Kent J.-Judge, United States District Court District of Nevada-Nev.

Dawson, Michael-Associate Circuit Judge, Missouri Circuit Court Twenty-seventh Judicial Circuit-Mo.

Dawson, Robert T.-Judge, United States District Court Western District of Arkansas-Ark.

Dawson, Tandra L.-Judge, New York City Family Court-N.Y.

Dawson, Thomas B.-Judge, Lancaster County Separate Juvenile Court-Neb.

Day, Charles B.-Magistrate Judge, United States District Court District of Maryland-Md.

Day, David E.-Judge, Idaho District Court Fourth Judicial District Magistrate Division-Ida.

Day, Gary L.-Judge, Montana District Court Sixteenth Judicial District-Mont.

Day, James W.-Circuit Judge, Illinois Circuit Court Seventh Judicial Circuit-Ill.

Day, Jeffrey K.-Judge, Orting Municipal Court-Wash.

Day, Jerry-Chief Magistrate, Magistrate Court of Walker County-Ga.

Day, Lance M.-Judge, Florida Circuit Court Fourth Judicial Circuit-Fla.

Day, Sam-Justice, Texas Court of Appeals Second District-Tex.

Day, Timothy Charles-Judge, Wyoming Circuit Court Ninth Judicial District, Teton County-Wyo.

Deadwyler, Margaret-Judge, Probate Court of Jackson County-Ga.

De Alba, David-Judge, Superior Court of California County of Sacramento-Calif.

Dean, Amy N.-Senior Judge, Florida Circuit Court Eleventh Judicial Circuit-Fla.

Dean, Gary J.-Special Judge, Oklahoma District Court Twelfth Judicial District-Okla.

Dean, John A., Jr.-Judge, New Mexico District Court Eleventh Judicial District-N.Mex.

Dean, John F.-Special Trial Judge, United States Tax Court

Dean, K. Preston-Circuit Judge, Missouri Circuit Court Sixteenth Judicial Circuit-Mo.

Dean, Keith-Judge, Texas District Court 265th Judicial District-Tex.

Dean-Walker, Becky-Judge, Hudspeth County Court-Tex.

De Angelis, Guido A.-Judge, Pennsylvania Court of Common Pleas Fifth Judicial District-Pa.

Dearie, Raymond J.-Judge, United States District Court Eastern District of New York-N.Y.

Dearing, Peter L.-Judge, Florida Circuit Court Fourth Judicial Circuit-Fla.

Dearman, John E.-Judge, Superior Court of California City and County of San Francisco-Calif.

DeArmond, Craig H.-Circuit Judge, Illinois Circuit Court Fifth Judicial Circuit-Ill.

Deason, Donald-Special Judge, Oklahoma District Court Seventh Judicial District-Okla.

Deasy, J. Michael-Judge, United States Bankruptcy Court District of New Hampshire-N.H.

Deatherage, Susan N.-Chief Judge, Virginia Juvenile and Domestic Relations District Court Twenty-first Judicial District-Va.

Deats, Paul E.-Chief Judge, Michigan District Court District Four-Mich.

Deaver, Danny R.-Associate District Judge, Oklahoma District Court Third Judicial District-Okla.

Debelius, John William, III-Associate Judge, Circuit Court for Montgomery County, Sixth Judicial Circuit-Md.

de Bellefeuille, Denise-Judge, Superior Court of California County of Santa Barbara-Calif.

De Bello, Lawrence P.-Judge, New Jersey Superior Court Vicinage Six-N.J.

DeBerry, Michael D.-Associate District Judge, Oklahoma District Court Seventeenth Judicial District-Okla.

Debevoise, Dickinson R.-Senior Judge, United States District Court District of New Jersey-N.J.

DeBoni, Frank-Associate Judge, Illinois Circuit Court of Cook County-Ill.

DeCardy, William D.-Associate Judge, Illinois Circuit Court Eleventh Judicial Circuit-Ill.

DeChambeau, Robert A.-Judge, Wisconsin Circuit Court Dane Circuit-Wis.

Decker, Tarrell-Judge, Port Orchard Municipal Court-Wash.

deCordova, Donald W.-Judge, New Jersey Superior Court Vicinage Two-N.J.

DeCourcy, Michael T.-Judge, Minnesota District Court Second Judicial District-Minn.

Decuir, Oswald A.-Judge, Louisiana Court of Appeal Third Circuit-La.

Deddeh, Peter C.-Judge, Superior Court of California County of San Diego-Calif.

Deddens, Robert L.-Judge, Oakwood Municipal Court-Ohio

Deegan, Joseph E.-Chief Judge, Leelanau County Probate Court-Mich.

Deegan, Peter E.-Chief Judge, Michigan Circuit Court Thirty-first Judicial Circuit-Mich.

Deehl, Robert M.-Senior Judge, Dade County Court-Fla.

Deen, Braswell D., Jr.-Senior Judge, Court of Appeals of Georgia-Ga.

Deering, Randy D.-Judge, Pike County Court-Ohio

Dees, Harry C., Jr.-Chief Judge, United States Bankruptcy Court Northern District of Indiana-Ind.

Deets, Darryl W.-Judge, Wisconsin Circuit Court Manitowoc Circuit-Wis.

DeFeo, William P.-Judge, New Fairfield District Probate Court-Conn.

DeFino-Nastasi, Rose Marie-Judge, Pennsylvania Court of Common Pleas First Judicial District-Pa.

DeFuria, Frederick A.-Judge, Florida Circuit Court Twelfth Judicial Circuit-Fla.

DeGenaro, Mary-Judge, Ohio Court of Appeals Seventh District-Ohio

DeGrasse, Leland G.-Justice, New York Supreme Court First Judicial District-N.Y.

DeGroot, John W.-Judge, Superior Court of California County of Madera-Calif.

DeHart, Kenneth Daly-Judge, Texas District Court 394th Judicial District-Tex.

Dehn, James E.-Judge, Minnesota District Court Tenth Judicial District-Minn.

De Hoyos, Jo-Ann Sylvia-Judge, Bexar County Court at Law No. 11-Tex.

Dein, Judith Gail-Magistrate Judge, United States District Court District of Massachusetts-Mass.

Deininger, David G.-Judge, Wisconsin Court of Appeals District Four-Wis.

Deister, Thomas M.-Judge, Mesa County Court-Colo.

Deiter, Charles J.-Judge, Marion Superior Court-Ind.

Deits, Mary J.-Chief Judge, Oregon Court of Appeals-Ore.

De Jesus, Sara E.-Judge, Bankruptcy Appellate Panel First Circuit and Judge, United States Bankruptcy Court District of Puerto Rico

DeJoseph, Brian F.-Justice, New York Supreme Court Fifth Judicial District-N.Y.

Dekker, Kathleen F.-Judge, Florida Circuit Court Second Judicial Circuit-Fla.

Dekreon, Gail-Judge, Superior Court of California City and County of San Francisco-Calif.

de la Carrera, Miguel-Judge, New Jersey Superior Court Vicinage Eleven-N.J.

De La Cruz, Estela M.-Judge, New Jersey Superior Court Vicinage Two-N.J.

De La Garza, Pete-Judge, Kleberg County Court-Tex.

Delahanty, Kevin-Judge, Kentucky District Court Thirtieth Judicial District-Ky.

Delahanty, Sean-Judge, Kentucky District Court Thirtieth Judicial District-Ky.

Delahanty, Thomas E., II-Justice, Maine Superior Court-Me.

DeLamatre, Robert C.-Judge, Ohio Court of Common Pleas Erie County-Ohio

Delaney, John J.-Judge, South Dakota Circuit Court Seventh Judicial Circuit-S.D.

DeLapp, Curtis L.-Associate District Judge, Oklahoma District Court Eleventh Judicial District-Okla.

deLaroche, Steven-Judge, Volusia County Court-Fla.

DeLaughter, Bobby B.-Judge, Mississippi Circuit Court Seventh Judicial District-Miss.

Delaurenti, Charles J., II-Judge, King District Court South Division King County-Wash.

DeLaurentiis, Joseph H.-Judge, Michigan District Court District Twenty-five-Mich.

Delbridge, Jane Pritchard-Judge, Virginia Juvenile and Domestic Relations District Court Nineteenth Judicial District-Va.

DelCampo, J. Antonio-Judge, State Court of DeKalb County-Ga.

Delehey, Charles A.-Judge, New Jersey Superior Court Vicinage Seven-N.J.

Delforge, Richard D.-Judge, Wisconsin Circuit Court Oconto Circuit-Wis.

Delgado, David-Circuit Judge, Illinois Circuit Court of Cook County-Ill.

Delgado, Katherine R.-Judge, Colorado District Court Seventeenth Judicial District-Colo.

Delgado, Rodolfo-Judge, Texas District Court 93rd Judicial District-Tex.

Delgado-Colon, Aida M.-Magistrate Judge, United States District Court District of Puerto Rico

Del Giudice, Vincent M.-Judge, New York Court of Claims-N.Y.

DeLissa, Janna K.-Magistrate Judge, Kansas District Court Twenty-fifth Judicial District-Kan.

Delk, Rodham T., Jr.-Judge, Virginia Circuit Court Fifth Judicial Circuit-Va.

Dell, John W.-Senior Judge, Florida District Court of Appeal-Fla.

Della Vecchia, Michael A.-Judge, Pennsylvania Court of Common Pleas Fifth Judicial District-Pa.

Dellick, F. Theresa-Judge, Ohio Court of Common Pleas Mahoning County-Ohio

Del Muro, Justine E.-Circuit Judge, Missouri Circuit Court Sixteenth Judicial Circuit-Mo.

DeLoach, Lee H.-Judge, Probate Court of Bulloch County-Ga.

Delorenzo, William R., Jr.-Judge, New Jersey Superior Court Vicinage Two-N.J.

Del Pesco, Susan C.-Associate Judge, Delaware Superior Court New Castle County-Del.

Del Pozzo, Ron M.-Judge, Superior Court of California County of Santa Clara-Calif.

DelRicci, Thomas M.-Judge, Pennsylvania Court of Common Pleas Thirty-eighth Judicial District-Pa.

Del Rosario, Dexter D.-Judge, Hawaii Circuit Court First Judicial Circuit-Hi.

Del Sole, Joseph A.-President Judge, The Superior Court of Pennsylvania-Pa.

DeLuca, Frank J.-Judge, Michigan District Court District Fifty-four A-Mich.

DeLuca, Steven P.-Judge, Broward County Court-Fla.

De Luccia, Ralph L., Jr.-Judge, New Jersey Superior Court Vicinage Eleven-N.J.

Del Vecchio, Nicholas Anthony-Judge, Nevada District Court Eighth Judicial District-Nev.

DelVecchio, Suzanne V.-Chief Justice, Trial Court of Massachusetts Superior Court Department-Mass.

Del Vero, Frank R.-Judge, Michigan District Court District Fifty-three-Mich.

deMahy, Paul J.-Judge, Louisiana District Court Sixteenth Judicial District-La.

DeMarce, Karl A. W.-Associate Circuit Judge, Missouri Circuit Court First Judicial Circuit-Mo.

Demarest, Carolyn E.-Justice, New York Supreme Court Second Judicial District-N.Y.

Demarest, David R.-Justice, New York Supreme Court Fourth Judicial District-N.Y.

DeMaro, Joseph A.-Justice, New York Supreme Court Tenth Judicial District-N.Y.

DeMayo, Anthony V.-Judge Referee, Connecticut Superior Court-Conn.

Dembe, Pamela Pryor-Judge, Pennsylvania Court of Common Pleas First Judicial District-Pa.

ALPHABETICAL NAME INDEX

DeMent, Ira-Senior Judge, United States District Court Middle District of Alabama-Ala.

Demers, David A.-Chief Judge, Florida Circuit Court Sixth Judicial Circuit-Fla.

Demetras, Stephen G.-Judge, Superior Court of California County of San Joaquin-Calif.

DeMeyer, Gary D.-Judge, Idaho District Court Third Judicial District Magistrate Division-Ida.

D'Emic, Matthew J.-Judge, New York Court of Claims-N.Y.

Demling, John W.-Associate Judge, Illinois Circuit Court Eighteenth Judicial Circuit-Ill.

Demlow, James C.-Judge, Jefferson County Court-Colo.

DeMoss, Harold R., Jr.-Judge, United States Court of Appeals Fifth Circuit

Dempsey, Alford J., Jr.-Judge, Superior Court of Georgia Atlanta Judicial Circuit-Ga.

Dempsey, Becky-Judge, Smith County Court-Tex.

Dempsey, Thomas E.-Judge, Pennsylvania Court of Common Pleas First Judicial District-Pa.

Dempster, Georgia-Judge, Texas Family District Court 308th Judicial District-Tex.

De Muniz, Paul J.-Justice, Oregon Supreme Court-Ore.

Denhardt, Robert Brim-Judge, Wyoming Circuit Court Ninth Judicial District, Fremont County and Judge, Dubois and Fremont Municipal Courts-Wyo.

Denkin, David L.-Judge, Sarasota County Court-Fla.

Denlow, Morton-Magistrate Judge, United States District Court Northern District of Illinois-Ill.

Dennard, R. Michael-Judge, Idaho District Court Fourth Judicial District Magistrate Division-Ida.

Denner, Richard E.-Judge, Superior Court of California County of Los Angeles-Calif.

Denney, Barry V.-Associate District Judge, Oklahoma District Court Thirteenth Judicial District-Okla.

Dennis, James Leon-Judge, United States Court of Appeals Fifth Circuit

Dennis, Maria E.-Judge, Florida Circuit Court Eleventh Judicial Circuit-Fla.

Dennis, Maureen D.-Judge, Connecticut Superior Court-Conn.

Dennis, R. Markley, Jr.-Judge-at-Large, South Carolina Circuit Court-S.C.

Dent, Judd-Chief Judge, Kansas District Court Fourteenth Judicial District-Kan.

Denton, Allen D.-Judge, Juvenile Court of Georgia Southern Judicial Circuit-Ga.

Denton, Mark R.-Judge, Nevada District Court Eighth Judicial District-Nev.

Denton, Mike-Judge, Travis County Court at Law No. 4-Tex.

Denton, Steven R.-Judge, Superior Court of California County of San Diego-Calif.

Denvir, James E.-Judge, Archuleta County Court-Colo.

DePanfilis, Anthony-Judge, Norwalk District Probate Court-Conn.

DePascale, Paul M.-Judge, New Jersey Superior Court Vicinage Six-N.J.

De Phillips, Guy P.-Judge, New York City Family Court-N.Y.

DePriest, Tommy W., Jr.-Circuit Judge, Missouri Circuit Court Twenty-first Judicial Circuit-Mo.

DeRamus, Judson Davie, Jr.-Resident Judge, North Carolina Superior Court Fifth Judicial Division District 21-N.C.

Derbigny, Darryl-Judge, Louisiana District Court Orleans Parish Criminal District-La.

Derby, E. Stephen-Judge, United States Bankruptcy Court District of Maryland-Md.

Derbyshire, Pam-Judge, Harris County Criminal Court at Law No. 7-Tex.

Deren, Joseph V.-Acting Judge, Lackawanna City Court-N.Y.

DeRiggi, Donald P.-Judge, Nassau County Court-N.Y.

Deriso, Susan-Justice of the Peace, Sparks Justices' Court-Nev.

Derke, Eleni Elia-Judge, Duval County Court-Fla.

Derman, Harriet E.-Judge, New Jersey Superior Court Vicinage Eight-N.J.

Dermott, Jon A.-Circuit Judge, Missouri Circuit Court Twenty-ninth Judicial Circuit-Mo.

Dernbach, Dennis A.-Associate Judge, Illinois Circuit Court of Cook County-Ill.

DeRobbio, Albert E.-Chief Judge, Rhode Island District Court-R.I.

DeRosa, Nicholas-Judge, Orange County Court-N.Y.

Derr, J. Russell-Judge, Nebraska District Court Fourth Judicial District-Neb.

Derr, Jacque D.-Judge, Winnfield City Court-La.

Derr, Sara-Judge, Spokane District Court Spokane County and Judge, Deer Park and Spokane Municipal Courts-Wash.

DeSantis, Vincent-Judge, Gloversville City Court-N.Y.

Desens, Stephen M.-Judge, Superior Court of Arizona Cochise County-Ariz.

Deshazer, Ellen Carol-Judge, Superior Court of California County of Los Angeles-Calif.

DeShazo, Nikki Towry-Judge, Dallas County Probate Court-Tex.

Deshler, Dana-Judge, Ohio Court of Appeals Tenth District-Ohio

Des Jardins, John A.-Judge, Wisconsin Circuit Court Outagamie Circuit-Wis.

Desjardins, Paul D.-Justice, Colebrook District Court-N.H.

Desmond, Leo T.-Associate Judge, Illinois Circuit Court Second Judicial Circuit-Ill.

DeSoto, Hector E.-Judge, New Jersey Superior Court Vicinage Five-N.J.

Despotopulos, David P.-Justice, Trial Court of Massachusetts District Court Department Worcester County Worcester Division-Mass.

Dest, Michael M.-Judge, Superior Court of California County of San Bernardino-Calif.

De Stefano, Francis P.-Judge, New Jersey Superior Court Vicinage Nine-N.J.

DeStefano, Peter L., Jr.-Judge, Jasper District Court-Ark.

Desvousges, Shelley H.-Judge, North Carolina District Court District 10-N.C.

Detamore, James R.-Judge, Boone Superior Court-Ind.

Detjen, Jennifer R. S.-Judge, Superior Court of California County of Madera-Calif.

Dettmering, W. O'Neal, Jr.-Judge, State Court of Douglas County-Ga.

Devaney, Leonard, III-Judge, Alaska Superior Court Fourth Judicial District-Alas.

De Vanon, Joseph F.-Judge, Superior Court of California County of Los Angeles-Calif.

DeVasto, Diane Vinson-Justice, Texas Court of Appeals Twelfth District-Tex.

Deveaux, Clinton E.-Judge, Municipal Court of Atlanta-Ga.

Dever, Joseph I.-First Justice, Trial Court of Massachusetts District Court Department Essex County Lynn Division-Mass.

Dever, L. A.-Judge, Utah District Court Third Judicial District-Utah

DeVesa, Frederick P.-Judge, New Jersey Superior Court Vicinage Eight-N.J.

deVilla, Francis-Magistrate, Seattle Municipal Court-Wash.

Devine, Bernard M.-Active Retired Judge, Maine District Court-Me.

Devine, James J.-Judge, Connecticut Superior Court-Conn.

DeVine, M. Patricia-Judge, North Carolina District Court District 15B-N.C.

Devine, Myles J.-Magistrate Judge, United States District Court District of South Dakota-S.D.

Devine, Thomas J.-Magistrate, Vermont Trial Court-Vt.

Devlin, Diane Y.-Judge, Buffalo City Court-N.Y.

Devlin, Donald M.-Circuit Judge, Illinois Circuit Court of Cook County-Ill.

Devlin, Robert J., Jr.-Judge, Connecticut Superior Court-Conn.

DeVore, David L.-Judge, Superior Court of California County of Alpine-Calif.

DeVries, John R.-Chief Judge, Manistee County Probate Court-Mich.

DeVries, Sharon N.-Special Justice, Portsmouth District Court-N.H.

Deweese, Deborah-Judge, Kentucky District Court Thirtieth Judicial District-Ky.

DeWeese, James-Judge, Ohio Court of Common Pleas Richland County-Ohio

Dewey, John P.-Judge, Sandusky County Court-Ohio

Dewey, Julia DiCocco-Judge, Connecticut Superior Court-Conn.

DeWitt, John W.-Special Judge, Oklahoma District Court Seventeenth Judicial District-Okla.

Dezern, Ray Wilbur, Jr.-Judge, Virginia General District Court Fourth Judicial District-Va.

Dezso, Carol J.-Judge, Ohio Court of Common Pleas Summit County-Ohio

Dial, Gary-Presiding Judge, Missouri Circuit Court First Judicial Circuit-Mo.

Diamond, Gustave-Senior Judge, United States District Court Western District of Pennsylvania-Pa.

Diamond, Kenneth S.-Judge, Nassau County Family Court-N.Y.

Diamond, Marylin G.-Judge, The Civil Court of the City of New York-N.Y.

Diamond, Michael K.-Judge, New Jersey Superior Court Vicinage Eleven-N.J.

Diamond, Scott B.-Associate Judge, Illinois Circuit Court Sixth Judicial Circuit-Ill.

Diaz, Albert-Special Judge, North Carolina Superior Court-N.C.

Diaz, Marta S.-Judge, Superior Court of California County of San Mateo-Calif.

Diaz, Oliver E., Jr.-Justice, Mississippi Supreme Court-Miss.

Diaz, Rafael-Associate Judge, Superior Court of the District of Columbia-D.C.

Diaz, Robert F.-Judge, Broward County Court-Fla.

Diaz, Rudolph A.-Judge, Superior Court of California County of Los Angeles-Calif.

DiBianco, Gustave J.-Magistrate Judge, United States District Court Northern District of New York-N.Y.

Dibiaso, Nickolas J.-Associate Justice, California Court of Appeal Fifth District-Calif.

DiBlasi, John P.-Justice, New York Supreme Court Ninth Judicial District-N.Y.

DiBona, Alfred J., Jr.-Judge, Pennsylvania Court of Common Pleas First Judicial District-Pa.

Dibrell, C. G. "Trey", III-Judge, Galveston County Court at Law No. 2-Tex.

Di Camillo, Angelo J.-Judge, New Jersey Tax Court-N.J.

Di Cesare, James J.-Judge, Superior Court of California County of Orange-Calif.

Dick, Patricia Macke-Judge, Kansas District Court Twenty-seventh Judicial District-Kan.

Dickerson, Henry R., Jr.-Judge, Oregon Circuit Court Twenty-first Judicial District-Ore.

Dickerson, Mary-Circuit Judge, Missouri Circuit Court Twenty-sixth Judicial Circuit-Mo.

Dickerson, Thomas A.-Justice, New York Supreme Court Ninth Judicial District-N.Y.

Dickert, Neal W.-Judge, Superior Court of Georgia Augusta Judicial Circuit-Ga.

Dickey, Alan A.-Judge, Florida Circuit Court Eighteenth Judicial Circuit-Fla.

Dickey, Don A.-Judge, Oregon Circuit Court Third Judicial District-Ore.

Dickinson, A. James-Judge, Minnesota District Court Second Judicial District-Minn.

Dickinson, David L.-Judge, Colorado District Court Sixth Judicial District and Judge, Colorado Water Court Division Seven-Colo.

Dickinson, David L.-Judge, State Court of Forsyth County-Ga.

Dickinson, Marty Joe-Judge, Kansas District Court Ninth Judicial District-Kan.

Dickler, Grace G.-Associate Judge, Illinois Circuit Court of Cook County-Ill.

Dickman, Toby L.-Judge, Pennsylvania Court of Common Pleas Thirty-eighth Judicial District-Pa.

Dickson, Brent E.-Associate Justice, Indiana Supreme Court-Ind.

Dickson, John W.-Judge, North Carolina District Court District 12-N.C.

Dickson, Vanessa-Judge, Kentucky District Court Fourteenth Judicial District-Ky.

Dickstein, Mel I.-Judge, Minnesota District Court Fourth Judicial District-Minn.

ALPHABETICAL NAME INDEX

DiClerico, Joseph Anthony, Jr.-Judge, United States District Court District of New Hampshire-N.H.
Didier, Daniel J.-Judge, Superior Court of California County of Orange-Calif.
Diem, Terri Sue-Judge, Eagle County Court-Colo.
Dier, Larry L.-Judge, Superior Court of California County of Modoc-Calif.
Dierker, Robert H., Jr.-Circuit Judge, Missouri Circuit Court Twenty-second Judicial Circuit-Mo.
Dieterich, Michael G.-District Associate Judge, Iowa District Court Eighth Judicial District-Ia.
Dietrich, Glen-Associate Circuit Judge, Missouri Circuit Court Fourth Judicial Circuit-Mo.
Dietz, John K.-Judge, Texas District Court 250th Judicial District-Tex.
Dietz, Richard J.-Judge, Wisconsin Circuit Court Brown Circuit-Wis.
Difanis, Thomas J.-Circuit Judge, Illinois Circuit Court Sixth Judicial Circuit-Ill.
DiFiglia, Vincent P.-Judge, Superior Court of California County of San Diego-Calif.
DiFiore, Janet-Justice, New York Supreme Court Ninth Judicial District-N.Y.
DiGangi, Peter C.-Circuit Justice, Trial Court of Massachusetts Probate and Family Court Department-Mass.
DiGirolamo, Thomas M.-Magistrate Judge, United States District Court District of Maryland-Md.
Diglio, Salvatore L.-Judge, Hamden District Probate Court-Conn.
Dignan, Terrance P.-Judge, Michigan District Court District Sixty-six-Mich.
Dilday, Judith Nelson-Associate Justice, Trial Court of Massachusetts Probate and Family Court Department Middlesex County Division-Mass.
Dildine, Dan-Presiding Judge, Missouri Circuit Court Forty-fifth Judicial Circuit-Mo.
DiLeo, Lucille A.-Circuit Justice, Trial Court of Massachusetts Probate and Family Court Department-Mass.
Dillard, Denver D.-District Judge, Iowa District Court Sixth Judicial District-Ia.
Dillin, S. Hugh-Senior Judge, United States District Court Southern District of Indiana-Ind.
Dillon, Daniel T.-Judge, Wisconsin Circuit Court Rock Circuit-Wis.
Dillon, James H.-Judge, Erie County Family Court-N.Y.
Dillon, Kevin M.-Justice, New York Supreme Court Eighth Judicial District-N.Y.
Dillon, Lawrence G.-Judge, Recorder's Court of Chatham County-Ga.
Dillon, Mark C.-Justice, New York Supreme Court Ninth Judicial District-N.Y.
Dillon, Richard-Assistant Judge, Vermont Trial Court Lamoille County-Vt.
Dillon, William B., III-Judge, Idaho District Court Third Judicial District Magistrate Division-Ida.
DiLoreto, Joseph E.-Judge, Superior Court of California County of Los Angeles-Calif.
Dilts, Thomas H.-Judge, New Jersey Superior Court Vicinage Thirteen-N.J.
Diltz, Peter C.-Judge, Wisconsin Circuit Court Door Circuit-Wis.
Dilworth, Jay D.-Judge, Reno Municipal Court-Nev.
DiMango, Patricia M.-Justice, New York Supreme Court Second Judicial District-N.Y.
DiMarzio, Philip L.-Chief Judge, Illinois Circuit Court Sixteenth Judicial Circuit-Ill.
DiMauro, Theresa S.-Judge, Vermont Trial Court-Vt.
Di Miceli, Elaine W.-Judge, Louisiana District Court Twenty-second Judicial District-La.
Dimitri, William A., Jr.-Associate Justice, Rhode Island Superior Court-R.I.
Dimitrouleas, William P.-Judge, United States District Court Southern District of Florida-Fla.
Dimkoff, Graydon W.-Chief Judge, Newaygo County Probate Court-Mich.
Dimmick, Carolyn R.-Senior Judge, United States District Court Western District of Washington-Wash.
Dimos, Jimmy N.-Judge, Louisiana District Court Fourth Judicial District-La.
Dimotsis, Jane G.-Judge, Vermont Trial Court-Vt.
DiMotto, Jean W.-Judge, Wisconsin Circuit Court Milwaukee Circuit-Wis.
DiMotto, John J.-Judge, Wisconsin Circuit Court Milwaukee Circuit-Wis.
DiMuro, George N.-Magistrate, Rhode Island Family Court-R.I.
Dinan, Daniel J.-Special Trial Judge, United States Tax Court
Dingell, Christopher D.-Judge, Michigan Circuit Court Third Judicial Circuit-Mich.
Dinkelacker, Patrick T.-Judge, Ohio Court of Common Pleas Hamilton County-Ohio
Dinneen, James F. X.-Circuit Justice, Trial Court of Massachusetts District Court Department-Mass.
DiNubile, Victor J., Jr.-Judge, Pennsylvania Court of Common Pleas First Judicial District-Pa.
DiPentima, Alexandra D.-Judge, Connecticut Appellate Court-Conn.
DiSandro, Domenic A., III-Magistrate, Rhode Island Traffic Tribunal-R.I.
DiSantis, Ernest J., Jr.-Judge, Pennsylvania Court of Common Pleas Sixth Judicial District-Pa.
DiSegna, Debra E.-Magistrate, Rhode Island Family Court-R.I.
Dishowitz, Martin R.-Judge, Broward County Court-Fla.
Diskey, Daniel D.-Judge, Florida Circuit Court Sixth Judicial Circuit-Fla.
Disko, Barbara J.-Circuit Judge, Illinois Circuit Court of Cook County-Ill.
DiStefano, Biagio J.-Judge, Madison County Court-N.Y.
D'Italia, Arthur N.-Assignment Judge, New Jersey Superior Court Vicinage Six-N.J.
Ditsworth, John-Judge, Superior Court of Arizona Maricopa County-Ariz.
Ditter, J. William, Jr.-Senior Judge, United States District Court Eastern District of Pennsylvania-Pa.
DiTullio, Sheila A.-Judge, Erie County Court-N.Y.
Di Vito, Gary F.-Judge, Pennsylvania Court of Common Pleas First Judicial District-Pa.
Dixon, Beth Spencer-Judge, North Carolina District Court District 19C-N.C.
Dixon, Bryan C.-District Judge, Oklahoma District Court Seventh Judicial District-Okla.
Dixon, Donna K.-Judge, Minnesota District Court Ninth Judicial District-Minn.
Dixon, Donna L.-Judge, Kentucky District Court Second Judicial District-Ky.
Dixon, Herbert B., Jr.-Associate Judge, Superior Court of the District of Columbia-D.C.
Dixon, James P.-Judge, Grimes County Court-Tex.
Dixon, Myra H.-Judge, State Court of Fulton County-Ga.
Dixon, Wallace W.-Recalled Magistrate Judge, United States District Court Middle District of North Carolina-N.C.
Dixson, Ann L.-Magistrate Judge, Kansas District Court Sixteenth Judicial District-Kan.
Dlott, Susan J.-Judge, United States District Court Southern District of Ohio-Ohio
Doak, D. Fred-Special Judge, Oklahoma District Court Seventh Judicial District-Okla.
Doan, Rupert A.-Judge, Ohio Court of Appeals First District-Ohio
Dobberpuhl, Eugene E.-Presiding Judge, South Dakota Circuit Court Fifth Judicial Circuit-S.D.
Dobbins, Mark L.-Associate District Judge, Oklahoma District Court Fifteenth Judicial District-Okla.
Dobrescu, Steve L.-Judge, Nevada District Court Seventh Judicial District-Nev.
Dobrich, Susan L.-Chief Judge, Cass County Probate Court-Mich.
Dobroth, John E.-Judge, Superior Court of California County of Ventura-Calif.
Dobson, John J.-Judge, Blount County District Court-Ala.
Dobson, T. Yates, Jr.-Retired-Recalled Judge, North Carolina District Court-N.C.
Dobson, Thomas R.-Judge, Pennsylvania Court of Common Pleas Thirty-fifth Judicial District-Pa.
Dobson, Tommy R.-Judge, Talladega County District Court-Ala.
Dockery, Peter J.-Associate Judge, Illinois Circuit Court Eighteenth Judicial Circuit-Ill.
Docter, James-Judge, Bremerton Municipal Court-Wash.
Dodd, David-Judge, Probate Court of Cobb County-Ga.
Dodd, Douglas D.-Judge, United States Bankruptcy Court Middle District of Louisiana-La.
Dodd, Ron L.-Justice of the Peace, Mesquite Justices' Court and Judge, Mesquite Municipal Court-Nev.
Dodge, Michael E.-Chief Judge, Michigan Circuit Court Forty-third Judicial Circuit-Mich.
Doerfer, Gordon L.-Associate Justice, Massachusetts Appeals Court-Mass.
Doerfler, John Christian-Judge, Williamson County Court-Tex.
Doern, James E. D.-Judge, Saratoga Springs City Court-N.Y.
Doerr, Thomas J.-President Judge, Pennsylvania Court of Common Pleas Fiftieth Judicial District-Pa.
Doerty, James A.-Judge, Washington Superior Court King County-Wash.
Doggett, Monty L.-Judge, Louisiana District Court Tenth Judicial District-La.
Doherty, Frances-Judge, Nevada District Court Second Judicial District-Nev.
Doherty, Joseph W.-Judge, Connecticut Superior Court-Conn.
Doherty, Mark-Judge, Orleans Parish Juvenile Court-La.
Doherty, Rebecca F.-Judge, United States District Court Western District of Louisiana-La.
Doherty, Robert P., Jr.-Chief Judge, Virginia Circuit Court Twenty-third Judicial Circuit-Va.
Dohnal, Dennis W.-Magistrate Judge, United States District Court Eastern District of Virginia-Va.
Doi, David Isumu-Judge, Superior Court of California County of Los Angeles-Calif.
Dolan, Colleen-Circuit Judge, Missouri Circuit Court Twenty-first Judicial Circuit-Mo.
Dolan, David A.-Presiding Judge, Missouri Circuit Court Thirty-third Judicial Circuit-Mo.
Dolan, Francis J.-Circuit Judge, Illinois Circuit Court of Cook County-Ill.
Dolan, Thomas J.-Judge, Dutchess County Court-N.Y.
Dolbin, Cyrus Palmer-Judge, Pennsylvania Court of Common Pleas Twenty-first Judicial District-Pa.
Dolehanty, Darrin M.-Judge, Wayne Superior Court-Ind.
Dolgener, Richard H.-Judge, Andrews County Court-Tex.
Dolinger, Michael H.-Magistrate Judge, United States District Court Southern District of New York-N.Y.
Dollard, James P.-Justice, New York Supreme Court Eleventh Judicial District-N.Y.
Dollison, Fred R.-Judge, Wyoming Circuit Court Sixth Judicial District, Crook and Weston Counties-Wyo.
Domalakes, John E.-Judge, Pennsylvania Court of Common Pleas Twenty-first Judicial District-Pa.
Dombrink, Stephen Allen-Judge, Superior Court of California County of Alameda-Calif.
Dominguez, Daniel R.-Judge, United States District Court District of Puerto Rico
Dominguez, James V.-Judge, Hillsborough County Court-Fla.
Domitrovich, Stephanie-Judge, Pennsylvania Court of Common Pleas Sixth Judicial District-Pa.
Dommerich, John W.-Judge, Lee County Court-Fla.
Domnarski, Edward S.-Judge, Connecticut Superior Court-Conn.
Domnitz, H. Ronald-Judge, Superior Court of California County of San Diego-Calif.
Donahoe, Gary E.-Judge, Superior Court of Arizona Maricopa County-Ariz.
Donahue, Daniel Francis-Judge, Clark Circuit Court-Ind.
Donahue, Kenneth Ray-Judge, Ochiltree County Court-Tex.

ALPHABETICAL NAME INDEX

ALPHABETICAL NAME INDEX

Doyle, Carol A.-Judge, United States Bankruptcy Court Northern District of Illinois-Ill.
Doyle, Cathryn M.-Surrogate, Albany County Surrogate's Court-N.Y.
Doyle, Dennis B.-Circuit Judge, Illinois Circuit Court Twentieth Judicial Circuit-Ill.
Doyle, James E., IV-Judge, Nebraska District Court Eleventh Judicial District-Neb.
Doyle, James F. X.-Judge, Suffolk County Court-N.Y.
Doyle, James T.-Circuit Judge, Illinois Circuit Court Sixteenth Judicial Circuit-Ill.
Doyle, John P.-Judge, Superior Court of California County of Los Angeles-Calif.
Doyle, John T.-Judge, Superior Court of California County of Los Angeles-Calif.
Doyle, John V.-Judge, Florida Circuit Court Seventh Judicial Circuit-Fla.
Doyle, Mary L.-Judge, Nebraska County Court Third Judicial District-Neb.
Doyle, Peter F.-First Justice, Trial Court of Massachusetts District Court Department Essex County Newburyport Division and Justice, Haverhill Division-Mass.
Doyle, Robert W.-Justice, New York Supreme Court Tenth Judicial District-N.Y.
Doyle, Theresa-Judge, Seattle Municipal Court-Wash.
Doyle, Vincent E., Jr.-Justice, New York Supreme Court Eighth Judicial District-N.Y.
Doyne, Peter E.-Judge, New Jersey Superior Court Vicinage Two-N.J.
Doyscher, David E.-Judge, Minnesota District Court Tenth Judicial District-Minn.
Dozier, Ronald C.-Circuit Judge, Illinois Circuit Court Eleventh Judicial Circuit-Ill.
Dozier, Steve R.-Judge, Tennessee Criminal Court Twentieth Judicial District-Tenn.
Dozor, Barry C.-Judge, Pennsylvania Court of Common Pleas Thirty-second Judicial District-Pa.
Drag, Walter F.-Judge, Dunkirk City Court-N.Y.
Drager, Laura E.-Judge, The Criminal Court of the City of New York-N.Y.
Drago, Karen A.-Judge, Schenectady City Court-N.Y.
Dragon, Gary J.-Judge, Slidell City Court-La.
Drain, Gershwin Allen-Judge, Michigan Circuit Court Third Judicial Circuit-Mich.
Drain, Robert D.-Judge, United States Bankruptcy Court Southern District of New York-N.Y.
Drake, Ernest G., Jr.-Judge, Louisiana District Court Twenty-first Judicial District-La.
Drake, H. Kevin-Chief Judge, Michigan District Court District Seventy-eight-Mich.
Drake, Judd-Chief Magistrate, Magistrate Court of Candler County-Ga.
Drake, Maggie-Judge, Michigan Circuit Court Third Judicial Circuit-Mich.
Drake, W. Homer, Jr.-Judge, United States Bankruptcy Court Northern District of Georgia-Ga.
Drange, Steven E.-Judge, Minnesota District Court Eighth Judicial District-Minn.
Dranginis, Anne C.-Judge, Connecticut Appellate Court-Conn.
Draper, Carol E.-Judge, Osceola County Court-Fla.
Draper, David R.-Judge, Washington Superior Court Lewis County-Wash.
Draper, George W., III-Judge, Missouri Court of Appeals Eastern District-Mo.
Drayer, Calvin S., Jr.-Judge, Pennsylvania Court of Common Pleas Thirty-eighth Judicial District-Pa.
Drayton-Harris, Pauline M.-Judge, Duval County Court-Fla.
Drazewski, Scott D.-Associate Judge, Illinois Circuit Court Eleventh Judicial Circuit-Ill.
Dreher, Nancy C.-Judge, Bankruptcy Appellate Panel Eighth Circuit and Judge, United States Bankruptcy Court District of Minnesota-Minn.
Dreiling, Janice P.-District Judge, Oklahoma District Court Eleventh Judicial District-Okla.
Drell, David-Judge, Bar Nunn Municipal Court-Wyo.
Drescher, Stephen W.-Judge, Idaho District Court Third Judicial District-Ida.
Dresnick, Ronald Charles-Judge, Florida Circuit Court Eleventh Judicial Circuit-Fla.
Drew, James M.-District Judge, Iowa District Court Second Judicial District-Ia.
Drew, R. Harmon, Jr.-Judge, Louisiana Court of Appeal Second Circuit-La.
Drew, Stephen-Judge, Superior Court of California County of Tulare-Calif.
Dreyer, David J.-Judge, Marion Superior Court-Ind.
Dreyfus, Lee S.-Judge, Wisconsin Circuit Court Waukesha Circuit-Wis.
Driesel, Willard-District Judge, Oklahoma District Court Seventeenth Judicial District-Okla.
Drinkard, Wesley Wade-Judge, Marengo County District Court-Ala.
Driscoll, Allan T.-Judge, East Hartford District Probate Court-Conn.
Driscoll, John C.-Judge, Connecticut Superior Court-Conn.
Driscoll, John J.-Judge, Pennsylvania Court of Common Pleas Tenth Judicial District-Pa.
Driscoll, Mary Ann-Justice, Trial Court of Massachusetts District Court Department Suffolk County South Boston Division-Mass.
Driskell, Jackie O.-Judge, Probate Court of Toombs County-Ga.
Droney, Christopher F.-Judge, United States District Court District of Connecticut-Conn.
Drowota, Frank F., III-Chief Justice, Tennessee Supreme Court-Tenn.
Drozd, Dale A.-Magistrate Judge, United States District Court Eastern District of California-Calif.
Druke, William E.-Judge, Arizona Court of Appeals Division Two-Ariz.
Drum, Teresa-Judge, Texas District Court 294th Judicial District-Tex.
Drumm, Bernhardt C., Jr.-Circuit Judge, Missouri Circuit Court Twenty-first Judicial Circuit-Mo.
Drummond, Mark A.-Associate Judge, Illinois Circuit Court Eighth Judicial Circuit-Ill.
Drury, Dennis C.-Judge, Michigan District Court District Fifty-two Division Four-Mich.
Drury, Timothy J.-Judge, Erie County Court-N.Y.
Druzinski, Diane M.-Judge, Michigan Circuit Court Sixteenth Judicial Circuit-Mich.
Dry, Robert T., Jr.-Judge, Texas District Court 199th Judicial District-Tex.
Dryden, James W.-Administrative Judge, Maryland District Court District Seven-Md.
Dubay, Kevin G.-Judge, Connecticut Superior Court-Conn.
Dubberly, B. Daniel, III-Judge, State Court of Tattnall County-Ga.
Dube, Robert L.-Magistrate Judge, United States District Court Southern District of Florida-Fla.
Dubensky, Peter A.-Judge, Florida Circuit Court Twelfth Judicial Circuit-Fla.
Duber, Robert, II-Presiding Judge, Superior Court of Arizona Gila County-Ariz.
Duberstein, Conrad B.-Chief Judge, United States Bankruptcy Court Eastern District of New York-N.Y.
Dubicki, David J.-Associate Judge, Illinois Circuit Court Tenth Judicial Circuit-Ill.
Dubina, Joel F.-Judge, United States Court of Appeals Eleventh Circuit
Dubofsky, Frank-Judge, Colorado District Court Twentieth Judicial District-Colo.
Dubois, Jan E.-Senior Judge, United States District Court Eastern District of Pennsylvania-Pa.
Dubose, Willie Bryan-Judge, Texas District Court 385th Judicial District-Tex.
Dubuisson, Susan A.-Judge, Thurston District Court Thurston County-Wash.
Dubuque, Joan-Judge, Washington Superior Court King County-Wash.
Dudgeon, Thomas C.-Associate Judge, Illinois Circuit Court Eighteenth Judicial Circuit-Ill.
Dudley, James B.-Associate Judge, Circuit Court for Howard County, Fifth Judicial Circuit-Md.
Duehr, John H.-Judge, Troy City Court-Mont.
Dues, Wilfrid Gavin-Judge, Ohio Court of Common Pleas Preble County-Ohio
Duff, Brian Barnett-Senior Judge, United States District Court Northern District of Illinois-Ill.
Duff, Ellar-Associate Judge, Illinois Circuit Court Third Judicial Circuit-Ill.
Duff, Larry R.-Judge, Idaho District Court Fifth Judicial District Magistrate Division-Ida.
Duffey, Aubrey-Judge, Superior Court of Georgia Coweta Judicial Circuit-Ga.
Duffey, Charles-Magistrate, Seattle Municipal Court-Wash.
Dufficy, Michael B.-Judge, Superior Court of California County of Marin-Calif.
Dufficy, Timothy J.-Judge, The Civil Court of the City of New York-N.Y.
Duffly, Fernande R. V.-Associate Justice, Massachusetts Appeals Court-Mass.
Duffy, Colleen-Judge, Mount Vernon City Court-N.Y.
Duffy, David M.-Judge, Minnesota District Court Fourth Judicial District-Minn.
Duffy, James E., Jr.-Associate Justice, Hawaii Supreme Court-Hi.
Duffy, John P.-District Judge, Iowa District Court Third Judicial District-Ia.
Duffy, Kevin Thomas-Senior Judge, United States District Court Southern District of New York-N.Y.
Duffy, Michael L.-Judge, Superior Court of California County of San Luis Obispo-Calif.
Duffy, Patrick Michael-Judge, United States District Court District of South Carolina-S.C.
Duffy, Wendy Clark-Judge, Superior Court of California County of Monterey-Calif.
Duffy, William J.-Reserve Judge, Wisconsin Circuit Court-Wis.
Duffy-Lewis, Maureen-Judge, Superior Court of California County of Los Angeles-Calif.
Dufresne, Edward A., Jr.-Chief Judge, Louisiana Court of Appeal Fifth Circuit-La.
Dufresne, Mary Steenson-Judge, Minnesota District Court Fourth Judicial District-Minn.
Dugan, Joseph Aloysius, Jr.-Associate Judge, Circuit Court for Montgomery County, Sixth Judicial Circuit-Md.
Dugan, L. Becky-Judge, Superior Court of California County of Riverside-Calif.
Dugan, Robert N.-Associate Judge, Circuit Court for Baltimore County, Third Judicial Circuit-Md.
Dugan, Timothy G.-Judge, Wisconsin Circuit Court Milwaukee Circuit-Wis.
Dugan, W. David-Judge, Florida Circuit Court Eighteenth Judicial Circuit-Fla.
Duggan, James E.-Associate Justice, New Hampshire Supreme Court-N.H.
Duggan, Michael M.-Judge, Superior Court of California County of Los Angeles-Calif.
Duggan, Patrick J.-Senior Judge, United States District Court Eastern District of Michigan-Mich.
Duggan, W. Dennis-Judge, Albany County Family Court-N.Y.
Dugger, Jay Edward-Judge, Virginia Juvenile and Domestic Relations District Court Eighth Judicial District-Va.
Duhe, John M., Jr.-Senior Judge, United States Court of Appeals Fifth Circuit
Duke, Patrick L.-Circuit Judge, Illinois Circuit Court Fourth Judicial Circuit-Ill.
Duke, Shirley S.-Chief Magistrate, Magistrate Court of Sumter County-Ga.
Duke, W. Russell, Jr.-Resident Judge, North Carolina Superior Court First Judicial Division District 3A-N.C.
Dukes, Robert A.-Judge, Superior Court of California County of Los Angeles-Calif.
Duket, Tim A.-Judge, Wisconsin Circuit Court Marinette Circuit-Wis.
Dull, Robert J.-District Associate Judge, Iowa District Court Third Judicial District-Ia.
Dumont, W. Hunt-Judge, New Jersey Superior Court Vicinage Ten-N.J.
Dunagan, Danny A.-Circuit Judge, Illinois Circuit Court Fourteenth Judicial Circuit-Ill.
Dunaway, Roger W., Jr.-Judge, Superior Court of Georgia Toombs Judicial Circuit-Ga.
Dunbar, Patricia A.-Circuit Justice, Trial Court of Massachusetts Juvenile Court Department-Mass.
Duncan, Daniel-Judge, Kansas District Court Twenty-ninth Judicial District-Kan.
Duncan, David K.-Magistrate Judge, United States District Court District of Arizona-Ariz.
Duncan, E. David-Judge, Albany City Court-N.Y.

ALPHABETICAL NAME INDEX

Duncan, Edward R., Jr.-Circuit Judge, Illinois Circuit Court Eighteenth Judicial Circuit-Ill.

Duncan, Jacqueline P.-Associate District Judge, Oklahoma District Court Second Judicial District-Okla.

Duncan, Joey E.-Magistrate Judge, Kansas District Court Sixteenth Judicial District-Kan.

Duncan, Sarah B.-Justice, Texas Court of Appeals Fourth District-Tex.

Duncan, Terrance R.-Judge, Superior Court of California County of Monterey-Calif.

Duncan, Xollie-Judge, Arkansas Circuit Court Nineteenth West Judicial Circuit-Ark.

Duncan-Brice, Jennifer-Circuit Judge, Illinois Circuit Court of Cook County-Ill.

Duncan-Peters, Stephanie-Associate Judge, Superior Court of the District of Columbia-D.C.

Dunevant, Thomas, III-Judge, Superior Court of Arizona Maricopa County-Ariz.

Dunlap, Jim-Judge, Lepanto, Marked Tree and Tyronza District Courts-Ark.

Dunlavey, Michael E.-Judge, Pennsylvania Court of Common Pleas Sixth Judicial District-Pa.

Dunlop, Roberta L.-Justice, New York Supreme Court Eleventh Judicial District-N.Y.

Dunn, Aileen H.-Judge, Probate Court of Colquitt County-Ga.

Dunn, Deborah A.-Justice, Trial Court of Massachusetts District Court Department Nantucket County Nantucket Division-Mass.

Dunn, James R.-Judge, Superior Court of California County of Los Angeles-Calif.

Dunn, John J.-Justice, New York Supreme Court Tenth Judicial District-N.Y.

Dunn, Larry D.-Circuit Judge, Illinois Circuit Court Second Judicial Circuit-Ill.

Dunn, Leslie A.-Judge, Superior Court of California County of Los Angeles-Calif.

Dunn, Michael A.-Judge, Gig Harbor Municipal Court-Wash.

Dunn, Philip R.-Judge Referee, Connecticut Superior Court-Conn.

Dunn, Randall Lawson-Judge, United States Bankruptcy Court District of Oregon-Ore.

Dunn, Thomas A.-Associate Judge, Illinois Circuit Court Twelfth Judicial Circuit-Ill.

Dunn, Thomas Arthur-Judge, Smith County Court at Law No. 1-Tex.

Dunn, Wallace B.-Associate Judge, Illinois Circuit Court Nineteenth Judicial Circuit-Ill.

Dunne, John P.-Justice, New York Supreme Court Tenth Judicial District-N.Y.

Dunnell, Christina G.-Judge, Connecticut Superior Court-Conn.

Dunnigan, Janette C.-Judge, Florida Circuit Court Twelfth Judicial Circuit-Fla.

Dunnigan, John L.-Associate Judge, Maryland District Court District Nine-Md.

Dunning, Kim Garlin-Judge, Superior Court of California County of Orange-Calif.

Dunning, Mary L.-Judge, Parma Municipal Court-Ohio

Dunphy, Sean M.-Chief Justice, Trial Court of Massachusetts Probate and Family Court Department-Mass.

Duplantier, Adrian G.-Senior Judge, United States District Court Eastern District of Louisiana-La.

Duplantier, Thomas R.-Judge, Louisiana District Court Fifteenth Judicial District-La.

Dupont, Antoinette L.-Judge Referee, Connecticut Superior Court-Conn.

Dupont, Thomas E., Sr.-Judge, Killingly District Probate Court-Conn.

Dupont, William C.-Judge, Plaquemine City Court-La.

Dupras, Fred-Judge, Superior Court of California County of Fresno-Calif.

Dupuis, Katherine R.-Judge, New Jersey Superior Court Vicinage Twelve-N.J.

Duran, Grace B.-Judge, New Mexico District Court Third Judicial District-N.Mex.

Durante, Joan Marie-Justice, New York Supreme Court Eleventh Judicial District-N.Y.

Durden, Nelson T.-Chief Judge, Virginia Juvenile and Domestic Relations District Court Eighth Judicial District-Va.

Durham, Christine Meaders-Chief Justice, Utah Supreme Court-Utah

Durham, Kathrynann W.-Judge, Pennsylvania Court of Common Pleas Thirty-second Judicial District-Pa.

Durham, Robert D.-Justice, Oregon Supreme Court-Ore.

Durham, Samuel I., Jr.-Judge, Michigan District Court District Ten-Mich.

Durkin, John M.-Judge, Ohio Court of Common Pleas Mahoning County-Ohio

Durkin, Kathleen A.-Judge, Pennsylvania Court of Common Pleas Fifth Judicial District-Pa.

Durocher, Daniel-Special Judge, Oklahoma District Court Seventh Judicial District-Okla.

Durrance, Julian Dale-Judge, Florida Circuit Court Tenth Judicial Circuit-Fla.

Durrant, Matthew B.-Associate Chief Justice, Utah Supreme Court-Utah

Duryee, Lynn-Judge, Superior Court of California County of Marin-Calif.

Dusek-Gomez, Nancy-First Justice, Trial Court of Massachusetts District Court Department Hampshire County Ware Division and Justice, Hampden County Springfield Division-Mass.

Dutcher, John F.-Judge, Idaho District Court Fourth Judicial District Magistrate Division-Ida.

Du Temple, Eric L.-Judge, Superior Court of California County of Tuolumne-Calif.

Dutson, Roger S.-Judge, Utah District Court Second Judicial District-Utah

Duval, Stanwood R., Jr.-Judge, United States District Court Eastern District of Louisiana-La.

Dwyer, G. Edward, Jr.-Associate Judge, Circuit Court for Frederick County, Sixth Judicial Circuit-Md.

Dwyer, Mark W.-Associate Judge, Illinois Circuit Court Eighteenth Judicial Circuit-Ill.

Dwyer, Michael J.-Judge, Wisconsin Circuit Court Milwaukee Circuit-Wis.

Dwyer, Michael L.-Judge, Oneida County Court-N.Y.

Dwyer, Stephen J.-Judge, Snohomish District Court South Division Snohomish County-Wash.

Dyal, Margaret N.-Judge, Juvenile Court of Georgia Northern Judicial Circuit-Ga.

Dych, Joseph A.-Judge, Pennsylvania Court of Common Pleas First Judicial District-Pa.

Dyche, R. W., III-Judge, Kentucky Court of Appeals-Ky.

Dye, Luther V.-Justice, New York Supreme Court Eleventh Judicial District-N.Y.

Dyer, Dee Rule-Judge, Wisconsin Circuit Court Outagamie Circuit-Wis.

Dyer, Richard W.-Judge, Connecticut Superior Court-Conn.

Dyk, Timothy B.-Judge, United States Court of Appeals Federal Circuit

Dyke, Ann-Judge, Ohio Court of Appeals Eighth District-Ohio

Dyke, William D.-Judge, Wisconsin Circuit Court Iowa Circuit-Wis.

Dykman, Charles P.-Judge, Wisconsin Court of Appeals District Four-Wis.

Dylina, Steven L.-Judge, Superior Court of California County of San Mateo-Calif.

Dymant, Anita H.-Judge, Superior Court of California County of Los Angeles-Calif.

Dywan, Jeffery J.-Judge, Lake Superior Court-Ind.

Eade, Richard D.-Judge, Florida Circuit Court Seventeenth Judicial Circuit-Fla.

Eadie, Richard D.-Judge, Washington Superior Court King County-Wash.

Eadie-Daniels, Loretta-Circuit Judge, Illinois Circuit Court of Cook County-Ill.

Eagan, Claire V.-Judge, United States District Court Northern District of Oklahoma-Okla.

Eagles, Catherine C.-Resident Judge, North Carolina Superior Court Fifth Judicial Division District 18-N.C.

Eagles, Sidney S., Jr.-Chief Judge, North Carolina Court of Appeals-N.C.

Eagloski, N. Edward, II-Chief Judge, West Virginia Circuit Court Twenty-ninth Judicial Circuit-W.Va.

Eagon, Diana-Judge, Minnesota District Court Fourth Judicial District-Minn.

Eakin, J. Michael-Justice, The Supreme Court of Pennsylvania-Pa.

Earl, Allan R.-Judge, Nevada District Court Eighth Judicial District-Nev.

Earle, Elisabeth A.-Judge, Travis County Court at Law No. 7-Tex.

Earles, Kristian-Judge, Louisiana District Court Fifteenth Judicial District-La.

Early, Sean P.-Judge, New Orleans Municipal Court-La.

Earnest, J. E.-Judge, Probate Court of Seminole County and Chief Magistrate, Magistrate Court of Seminole County-Ga.

Easley, Charles D., Jr.-Justice, Mississippi Supreme Court-Miss.

Eason, Carl E., Jr.-Judge, Virginia Circuit Court Fifth Judicial Circuit-Va.

Eastaugh, Robert L.-Associate Justice, Alaska Supreme Court-Alas.

Easter, Timothy L.-Judge, Tennessee Circuit Court Twenty-first Judicial District-Tenn.

Easterbrook, Frank H.-Judge, United States Court of Appeals Seventh Circuit

Eastmoore, E. L. "Gene"-Senior Judge, Florida Circuit Court Seventh Judicial Circuit-Fla.

Easton, Burton C.-Senior Judge, Pinellas County Court-Fla.

Easton, Kelly Mark-Judge, Kentucky Circuit Court Ninth Judicial Circuit-Ky.

Eaton, Douglas F.-Magistrate Judge, United States District Court Southern District of New York-N.Y.

Eaton, Kim D.-Judge, Pennsylvania Court of Common Pleas Fifth Judicial District-Pa.

Eaton, Lynda C.-Judge, Ferry District Court Ferry County-Wash.

Eaton, Merle R.-Judge, Superior Court of California County of Contra Costa-Calif.

Eaton, O. H. "Bill", Jr.-Judge, Florida Circuit Court Eighteenth Judicial Circuit-Fla.

Eaton, Richard K.-Judge, United States Court of International Trade

Eaton, Robert E.-Judge, Wisconsin Circuit Court Ashland Circuit-Wis.

Eaton, William Kenneth-Judge, Florence County Probate Court-S.C.

Eaves, Angela M.-Associate Judge, Maryland District Court District Nine-Md.

Ebel, David M.-Judge, United States Court of Appeals Tenth Circuit

Ebenger, David-Judge, Twisp and Winthrop Municipal Courts-Wash.

Ebert, Steven D.-Judge, Wisconsin Circuit Court Dane Circuit-Wis.

Eblen, E. Eugene-Judge, Tennessee Criminal Court Ninth Judicial District-Tenn.

Eby, Robert J.-President Judge, Pennsylvania Court of Common Pleas Fifty-second Judicial District-Pa.

Echarte, Pedro P., Jr.-Judge, Florida Circuit Court Eleventh Judicial Circuit-Fla.

Echols, Douglas A.-Judge, New Mexico District Court Eleventh Judicial District-N.Mex.

Echols, Robert L.-Chief Judge, United States District Court Middle District of Tennessee-Tenn.

Eckelkamp, Cindy-Associate Circuit Judge, Missouri Circuit Court Twentieth Judicial Circuit-Mo.

Eckels, Robert A.-Judge, Harris County Court-Tex.

Eckert, Annette A.-Circuit Judge, Illinois Circuit Court Twentieth Judicial Circuit-Ill.

Eckert, Jacquelyn Poole-Judge, Kentucky District Court Thirtieth Judicial District-Ky.

Eckert, Matthew K.-Judge, Kentucky District Court Thirtieth Judicial District-Ky.

Eckiss, Ronald R.-Circuit Judge, Illinois Circuit Court First Judicial Circuit-Ill.

Eckrich, Jerome-Judge, South Dakota Circuit Court Fourth Judicial Circuit-S.D.

Eckstein, Steven Douglas-Judge, Ohio Court of Common Pleas Crawford County-Ohio

Eckstrom, Daniel R.-Judge, Lexington County Probate Court-S.C.

Economou, Deno G.-Judge, Florida Circuit Court Twelfth Judicial Circuit-Fla.

Economus, Peter C.-Judge, United States District Court Northern District of Ohio-Ohio

Economy, R. George-Chief Judge, Ingham County Probate Court-Mich.

Eddinger, Kevin G.-Judge, North Carolina District Court District 19C-N.C.

ALPHABETICAL NAME INDEX

Eddy, David B.-Judge, Florida Circuit Court Fifth Judicial Circuit-Fla.
Edelman, Richard H.-Justice, Texas Court of Appeals Fourteenth District-Tex.
Edelstein, Charles D.-Senior Judge, Dade County Court-Fla.
Eden, Ben F.-Judge, Gunnison County Court-Colo.
Edenfield, Berry Avant-Judge, United States District Court Southern District of Georgia-Ga.
Eder, James J.-Associate Judge, Illinois Circuit Court Fourth Judicial Circuit-Ill.
Edgar, Alfred L.-Justice of the Peace, Klamath County Justice Court-Ore.
Edgar, R. Allan-Chief Judge, United States District Court Eastern District of Tennessee-Tenn.
Edgar, William J. "Sam"-Judge, State Court of Bacon County-Ga.
Edgerton, Michael F.-Associate Justice, Trial Court of Massachusetts Juvenile Court Department Essex County Division-Mass.
Edlitz, Sandra B.-Judge, Westchester County Family Court-N.Y.
Edmead, Carol Robinson-Justice, New York Supreme Court First Judicial District-N.Y.
Edmon, Lee Smalley-Judge, Superior Court of California County of Los Angeles-Calif.
Edmonds, Deirdre-Judge, Horry County Probate Court-S.C.
Edmonds, Glenda E.-Magistrate Judge, United States District Court District of Arizona-Ariz.
Edmonds, Walter I., Jr.-Judge, Oregon Court of Appeals-Ore.
Edmonds, William L.-Judge, United States Bankruptcy Court Northern District of Iowa-Ia.
Edmondson, J. L.-Chief Judge, United States Court of Appeals Eleventh Circuit
Edmondson, James E.-District Judge, Oklahoma District Court Fifteenth Judicial District-Okla.
Edmondson, Wiley W.-Associate Judge, Illinois Circuit Court Sixteenth Judicial Circuit-Ill.
Edmunds, Nancy G.-Judge, United States District Court Eastern District of Michigan-Mich.
Edmunds, Robert Holt, Jr.-Associate Justice, Supreme Court of North Carolina-N.C.
Edwards, Anthony C.-Judge, Superior Court of California County of Trinity-Calif.
Edwards, C. Thomas-Judge, North Carolina District Court District 25-N.C.
Edwards, Christopher C.-Judge, Superior Court of Georgia Griffin Judicial Circuit-Ga.
Edwards, David S.-Judge, Okanogan District Court Okanogan County-Wash.
Edwards, Deborah A.-Judge, Juvenile Court of Georgia Houston Judicial Circuit-Ga.
Edwards, Durwood-Magistrate Judge, United States District Court Western District of Texas-Tex.
Edwards, Ellen C.-Judge, Oklahoma Workers' Compensation Court-Okla.
Edwards, Ersel L.-Judge, Superior Court of California County of Nevada-Calif.
Edwards, Frederick E.-Judge, Texas District Court 9th Judicial District-Tex.
Edwards, Harry T.-Judge, United States Court of Appeals District of Columbia Circuit
Edwards, James-Judge, Gillette Municipal Court-Wyo.
Edwards, James A.-Judge, Superior Court of California County of San Bernardino-Calif.
Edwards, James R.-Associate Judge, Illinois Circuit Court Sixteenth Judicial Circuit-Ill.
Edwards, Jimmie M.-Circuit Judge, Missouri Circuit Court Twenty-second Judicial Circuit-Mo.
Edwards, Jules D., III-Judge, Louisiana District Court Fifteenth Judicial District-La.
Edwards, Julie A.-Judge, Ohio Court of Appeals Fifth District-Ohio
Edwards, Leonard P.-Judge, Superior Court of California County of Santa Clara-Calif.
Edwards, Marion F.-Judge, Louisiana Court of Appeal Fifth Circuit-La.
Edwards, Mildred M.-Associate Judge, Superior Court of the District of Columbia-D.C.
Edwards, Prentis-Judge, Michigan Circuit Court Third Judicial Circuit-Mich.
Edwards, Raymond, Jr.-Judge, Superior Court of California County of San Diego-Calif.
Edwards, Robert-Judge, Arkansas Circuit Court Seventeenth Judicial Circuit-Ark.
Edwards, Robert B.-Chief Judge, Virginia General District Court Fifth Judicial District-Va.
Edwards, Thomas C.-Judge, Superior Court of California County of Santa Clara-Calif.
Edwards, Tommy B.-Judge, South Carolina Family Court Tenth Judicial Circuit-S.C.
Edwards, Wilbur P., Jr.-Associate Justice, Trial Court of Massachusetts Housing Court Department Southeastern Division-Mass.
Edwards, William-Judge, Mount Vernon City Court-N.Y.
Edwards, William S.-Judge, Wyoming Circuit Court Sixth Judicial District, Campbell County-Wyo.
Edwards-Stephens, Sandra-Judge, Florida Circuit Court Fifth Judicial Circuit-Fla.
Effron, Andrew S.-Associate Judge, United States Court of Appeals for the Armed Forces
Egan, David Daniel-Justice, New York Supreme Court Seventh Judicial District-N.Y.
Egan, James D.-Circuit Judge, Illinois Circuit Court of Cook County-Ill.
Egan, John C., Jr.-Judge, Albany City Court-N.Y.
Egan, Joseph A., Jr.-Judge, Ridgefield District Probate Court-Conn.
Egan, Lynn M.-Circuit Judge, Illinois Circuit Court of Cook County-Ill.
Egan, Marilyn-Judge, Runnels County Court-Tex.
Egebakken, Richard-Justice, Wheatland County Justice of the Peace Court and Judge, Harlowton City Court-Mont.
Egeland, Deanna G.-Justice, Park County Justice of the Peace Court-Mont.
Egelhoff, Martin F.-Judge, Colorado District Court Second Judicial District-Colo.
Egerton, Anne Harwood-Judge, Superior Court of California County of Los Angeles-Calif.
Eggers, Robert J.-Circuit Judge, Illinois Circuit Court Seventh Judicial Circuit-Ill.
Eggert, E. Paul-Judge, Maine District Court-Me.
Eginton, Warren W.-Senior Judge, United States District Court District of Connecticut-Conn.
Egly, Carol S.-District Associate Judge, Iowa District Court Fifth Judicial District-Ia.
Ehlers, D. Todd-Judge, Wisconsin Circuit Court Door Circuit-Wis.
Ehlmann, Steve-Circuit Judge, Missouri Circuit Court Eleventh Judicial Circuit-Mo.
Ehrlich, Susan A.-Judge, Arizona Court of Appeals Division One-Ariz.
Eich, William F.-Reserve Judge, Wisconsin Circuit Court-Wis.
Eichen, Naomi G.-Judge, New Jersey Superior Court Appellate Division-N.J.
Eick, Charles F.-Magistrate Judge, United States District Court Central District of California-Calif.
Eide, D. Mark-Judge, King District Court South Division King County-Wash.
Eide, Kevin W.-Judge, Minnesota District Court First Judicial District-Minn.
Eidens, Michael C.-Judge, Schenectady County Court-N.Y.
Eiesland, Kenneth R.-Judge, Clark District Court Clark County and Judge, Camas-Washougal Municipal Court-Wash.
Eiffert, James-Presiding Judge, Missouri Circuit Court Thirty-eighth Judicial Circuit-Mo.
Eikleberry, Jane L.-Judge, Superior Court of Arizona Pima County-Ariz.
Eiler, Judith R.-Judge, King District Court South Division King County-Wash.
Eilperin, Stephen Francis-Senior Judge, Superior Court of the District of Columbia-D.C.
Einhorn, Ann A.-Associate Judge, Illinois Circuit Court Sixth Judicial Circuit-Ill.
Einhorn, John S.-Judge, Superior Court of California County of San Diego-Calif.
Eisele, Garnett Thomas-Senior Judge, United States District Court Eastern District of Arkansas-Ark.
Eisenberg, Dorothy-Judge, United States Bankruptcy Court Eastern District of New York-N.Y.
Eisenberg, Russell A.-Chief Judge, United States Bankruptcy Court Eastern District of Wisconsin-Wis.
Eisenhauer, Larry J.-Judge, Iowa Court of Appeals-Ia.
Eisman, Julianne S.-Judge, Nassau County Family Court-N.Y.
Eismann, Daniel T.-Justice, Idaho Supreme Court-Ida.
Eitzen, Tari S.-Judge, Washington Superior Court Spokane County-Wash.
El-Amin, Hassan Ali-Associate Judge, Maryland District Court District Five-Md.
Elder, Larry G.-Judge, Court of Appeals of Virginia-Va.
Eldred, Michael H.-Judge, Vigo Superior Court-Ind.
Eldridge, Frank M.-Judge, Court of Appeals of Georgia-Ga.
Eldridge, John C.-Associate Judge, Court of Appeals of Maryland-Md.
Eldridge, John D., III-Judge, Augusta District Court-Ark.
Elfvin, John T.-Senior Judge, United States District Court Western District of New York-N.Y.
Elfving, William J.-Judge, Superior Court of California County of Santa Clara-Calif.
Elgee, Robert J.-Judge, Idaho District Court Fifth Judicial District Magistrate Division-Ida.
Elia, Franklin D.-Associate Justice, California Court of Appeal Sixth District-Calif.
Elias, Emilie Harris-Judge, Superior Court of California County of Los Angeles-Calif.
Elias, Harry M.-Judge, Superior Court of California County of San Diego-Calif.
Eliason, Russell A.-Magistrate Judge, United States District Court Middle District of North Carolina-N.C.
Elkin, Sydney W.-Judge, West Hartford District Probate Court-Conn.
Elkins, Lee Hand-Judge, New York City Family Court-N.Y.
Elkins, Mike B.-Judge, Reagan County Court-Tex.
Elledge, Steve-Judge, Clarendon District Court-Ark.
Ellender, Timothy Claude-Judge, Louisiana District Court Thirty-second Judicial District-La.
Eller, Stan-Judge, Superior Court of California County of Mono-Calif.
Ellerbee, O. Wayne-Judge, Juvenile Court of Georgia Southern Judicial Circuit-Ga.
Ellerin, Betty Weinberg-Associate Justice, New York Supreme Court Appellate Division First Judicial Department-N.Y.
Ellinghaus-Jones, JoAnn M.-Administrative Judge, Maryland District Court District Ten-Md.
Ellington, Anne L.-Judge, Washington Court of Appeals Division I-Wash.
Ellington, B. Janice-Magistrate Judge, United States District Court Southern District of Texas-Tex.
Ellington, Edward-Chief Judge, United States Bankruptcy Court Southern District of Mississippi-Miss.
Ellington, John J.-Judge, Court of Appeals of Georgia-Ga.
Ellington, Thomas-Judge, Roy Municipal Court-Wash.
Ellinor, Thomas R.-Senior Judge, Bay County Court-Fla.
Elliot, David-Judge, The Civil Court of the City of New York-N.Y.
Elliot, Roger-Judge, Kentucky District Court Twenty-ninth Judicial District-Ky.
Elliott, Archie, Jr.-Judge, Virginia General District Court Third Judicial District-Va.
Elliott, Brady Gifford-Judge, Texas District Court 268th Judicial District-Tex.
Elliott, Fred-Judge, Robertson County Court-Tex.
Elliott, Gerald T.-Judge, Kansas District Court Tenth Judicial District-Kan.
Elliott, Jennifer-Judge, Nevada District Court Eighth Judicial District-Nev.
Elliott, Jerry G.-Judge, Kansas Court of Appeals-Kan.
Elliott, John J.-Surrogate, Oswego County Surrogate's Court-N.Y.
Elliott, Kate Ford-Judge, The Superior Court of Pennsylvania-Pa.
Elliott, Kathy Bradshaw-Circuit Judge, Illinois Circuit Court Twenty-first Judicial Circuit-Ill.

ALPHABETICAL NAME INDEX

ALPHABETICAL NAME INDEX

ALPHABETICAL NAME INDEX

Fallin, Glenn-Judge, Louisiana District Court Second Judicial District-La.
Fallon, Eldon E.-Judge, United States District Court Eastern District of Louisiana-La.
Falls, Thomas-Judge, Superior Court of California County of Los Angeles-Calif.
Falvey, Mary A.-Judge, Canton Municipal Court-Ohio
Falvey, W. Patrick-Judge, Yates County Court-N.Y.
Fambrough, Tim D.-Judge, Nolan County Court-Tex.
Famiglietti, Heidi-Judge, Plainville District Probate Court-Conn.
Fancher, Eric M.-Judge, Jefferson County District Court Bessemer Division-Ala.
Fandrich, Mark H.-Surrogate, Cayuga County Surrogate's Court-N.Y.
Fanguy, Jude Thaddeus-Judge, Houma City Court-La.
Fanning, Morris "Moe"-Justice of the Peace, Mina Justices' Court-Nev.
Fansler, Daryl R.-Chancellor, Tennessee Chancery Court Sixth Judicial District-Tenn.
Fantasia, Annette-Judge, West Virginia Family Court Circuit Three-W.Va.
Faragher, Patrick J.-Judge, Wisconsin Circuit Court Washington Circuit-Wis.
Farah, Joseph J.-Judge, Michigan Circuit Court Seventh Judicial Circuit-Mich.
Farber, James A.-Judge, New Jersey Superior Court Vicinage Ten-N.J.
Farber, Thomas A.-Judge, The Criminal Court of the City of New York-N.Y.
Farina, Joseph P.-Chief Judge, Florida Circuit Court Eleventh Judicial Circuit-Fla.
Farina, Louis J.-Judge, Pennsylvania Court of Common Pleas Second Judicial District-Pa.
Faris, Robert J.-Judge, United States Bankruptcy Court District of Hawaii-Hi.
Farley, John J., III-Judge, United States Court of Appeals for Veterans Claims
Farley, Michael H.-Magistrate Judge, Kansas District Court Tenth Judicial District-Kan.
Farmer, David R.-Judge, Tennessee Court of Appeals Western Division-Tenn.
Farmer, Drue-Judge, Lubbock County Court at Law No. 2-Tex.
Farmer, Gary M.-Judge, Florida District Court of Appeal Fourth District-Fla.
Farmer, John M.-Judge, Virginia Juvenile and Domestic Relations District Court Twenty-ninth Judicial District-Va.
Farmer, Nancy A.-Judge, Michigan District Court District Thirty-six-Mich.
Farmer, Robert L.-Emergency Judge, North Carolina Superior Court-N.C.
Farmer, Sheila G.-Judge, Ohio Court of Appeals Fifth District-Ohio
Farnan, Joseph J., Jr.-Judge, United States District Court District of Delaware-Del.
Farnell, Crockett-Judge, Florida Circuit Court Sixth Judicial Circuit-Fla.
Farnell, Dee Anna-Judge, Florida Circuit Court Sixth Judicial Circuit-Fla.
Farneti, Joseph-Judge, Suffolk County Court-N.Y.
Farnum, Mark J., Jr.-Reserve Judge, Wisconsin Circuit Court-Wis.
Farragut-Hemphill, Sandra-Associate Circuit Judge, Missouri Circuit Court Twenty-first Judicial Circuit-Mo.
Farrance, Robert A.-Judge, Manatee County Court-Fla.
Farrar, Cherri-Judge, Oklahoma Workers' Compensation Court-Okla.
Farrar, Dean E.-Judge, Superior Court of California County of Los Angeles-Calif.
Farrar, Kenneth W.-Chief Judge, Virginia Juvenile and Domestic Relations District Court Twenty-fourth Judicial District-Va.
Farrell, John P.-Judge, Superior Court of California County of Los Angeles-Calif.
Farrell, Michael J.-Judge, Superior Court of California County of Los Angeles-Calif.
Farrell, Michael W.-Associate Judge, District of Columbia Court of Appeals-D.C.
Farrell, Terry-Justice of the Peace, Grant County Justice Court-Ore.
Farrell, Timothy G.-Judge, New Jersey Superior Court Vicinage Fifteen-N.J.
Farren, Michael D.-Judge, New Jersey Superior Court Vicinage Nine-N.J.
Farris, Anita L.-Judge, Washington Superior Court Snohomish County-Wash.
Farris, Jerome-Senior Judge, United States Court of Appeals Ninth Circuit
Farris, Lon Edward-Judge, Virginia General District Court Thirty-first Judicial District-Va.
Farris, Sheila Nunley-Judge, Kentucky Circuit Court Fifty-first Judicial Circuit-Ky.
Farris, William C.-Judge, North Carolina District Court District 7-N.C.
Fasano, Roland D.-Judge, Connecticut Superior Court-Conn.
Fasel, Frank F.-Judge, Superior Court of California County of Orange-Calif.
Fasing, Timothy L.-Judge, Colorado District Court Eighteenth Judicial District-Colo.
Faske, Adele Segall-Senior Judge, Florida Circuit Court Eleventh Judicial Circuit-Fla.
Fast, Mahlon L.-Judge, New Jersey Superior Court Vicinage Five-N.J.
Faubion, William J.-Judge, Wahkiakum District Court Wahkiakum County-Wash.
Faucher, David E.-Magistrate Judge, United States District Court District of Hawaii-Hi.
Faulkner, David C.-Judge, Ohio Court of Common Pleas Hardin County-Ohio
Faulkner, Debora-Judge, Greenville County Probate Court-S.C.
Faunce, Jennifer-Judge, Michigan District Court District Thirty-seven-Mich.
Fautsch, Lawrence H.-District Judge, Iowa District Court First Judicial District-Ia.
Fauver, Peter Hofstra-Associate Justice, New Hampshire Superior Court-N.H.
Favreau, Dan W.-Judge, Ohio Court of Common Pleas Morgan County-Ohio
Fawell, Blanche Hill-Associate Judge, Illinois Circuit Court Eighteenth Judicial Circuit-Ill.
Fawke, W. Robert-Judge, Superior Court of California County of San Bernardino-Calif.
Fawsett, Patricia C.-Chief Judge, United States District Court Middle District of Florida-Fla.
Fay, Peter T.-Senior Judge, United States Court of Appeals Eleventh Circuit
Fearey, Margaret S.-Associate Justice, Trial Court of Massachusetts Juvenile Court Department Middlesex County Division-Mass.
Fecarotta, Thomas P., Jr.-Circuit Judge, Illinois Circuit Court of Cook County-Ill.
Fecteau, Francis R.-Associate Justice, Trial Court of Massachusetts Superior Court Department-Mass.
Feder, Richard Yale-Senior Judge, Florida Circuit Court Eleventh Judicial Circuit-Fla.
Federico, Philip J.-Judge, Florida Circuit Court Sixth Judicial Circuit-Fla.
Federman, Arthur B.-Judge, Bankruptcy Appellate Panel Eighth Circuit and Chief Judge, United States Bankruptcy Court Western District of Missouri-Mo.
Fee, William C.-Judge, Steuben Superior Court-Ind.
Feeney, Charles M., III-Associate Judge, Illinois Circuit Court Eleventh Judicial Circuit-Ill.
Feeney, Edward T.-Judge, Kingston City Court-N.Y.
Feeney, Joan N.-Judge, Bankruptcy Appellate Panel First Circuit and Chief Judge, United States Bankruptcy Court District of Massachusetts-Mass.
Feeney, John T.-Judge, Superior Court of California County of Humboldt-Calif.
Feeney, Kathleen A.-Judge, Michigan Circuit Court Seventeenth Judicial Circuit-Mich.
Feeney, Michael R.-Judge, Probate Court of New Hampshire Sullivan County-N.H.
Feess, Gary-Judge, United States District Court Central District of California-Calif.
Feffer, Irving S.-Judge, Superior Court of California County of Los Angeles-Calif.
Feick, John M.-Judge, Delaware Circuit Court-Ind.
Feikens, John-Senior Judge, United States District Court Eastern District of Michigan-Mich.
Feiler, Loree S.-Senior Judge, Dade County Court-Fla.
Fein, Dina-Associate Justice, Trial Court of Massachusetts Housing Court Department Western Division-Mass.
Fein, Roger G.-Circuit Judge, Illinois Circuit Court of Cook County-Ill.
Feinberg, Linda R.-Assignment Judge, New Jersey Superior Court Vicinage Seven-N.J.
Feinberg, Michael H.-Surrogate, Kings County Surrogate's Court-N.Y.
Feinberg, Wilfred-Senior Judge, United States Court of Appeals Second Circuit
Feiner, Leonard-Judge, Broward County Court-Fla.
Feinman, Paul G.-Judge, The Civil Court of the City of New York-N.Y.
Feinman, Thomas-Judge, Nassau County District Court-N.Y.
Feinstein, Katherine A.-Judge, Superior Court of California City and County of San Francisco-Calif.
Feldman, Anne G.-Justice, New York Supreme Court Second Judicial District-N.Y.
Feldman, Ethan D.-Judge, Arapahoe County Court-Colo.
Feldman, Joel M.-Magistrate Judge, United States District Court Northern District of Georgia-Ga.
Feldman, Jonathan W.-Magistrate Judge, United States District Court Western District of New York-N.Y.
Feldman, Martin L. C.-Judge, United States District Court Eastern District of Louisiana-La.
Feldstein, S. Peter-Judge, Hamilton County Court-N.Y.
Felice, Lee Phillip-Judge, Superior Court of California County of Kern-Calif.
Felice, Peter A.-Circuit Judge, Illinois Circuit Court of Cook County-Ill.
Fell, Sheila-Judge, Superior Court of California County of Orange-Calif.
Feller, Jerome-Judge, United States Bankruptcy Court Eastern District of New York-N.Y.
Felnagle, Thomas-Judge, Washington Superior Court Pierce County-Wash.
Felsenthal, Steven A.-Chief Judge, United States Bankruptcy Court Northern District of Texas-Tex.
Felton, Dan, III-Judge, Marianna District Court-Ark.
Felton, Walter S., Jr.-Judge, Court of Appeals of Virginia-Va.
Felts, Thomas J.-Judge, Allen Circuit Court-Ind.
Fender, Jane D.-Judge, South Carolina Family Court Fourteenth Judicial Circuit-S.C.
Fendlason, Donald M.-Judge, Louisiana District Court Twenty-second Judicial District-La.
Fennelly, John E.-Judge, Florida Circuit Court Nineteenth Judicial Circuit-Fla.
Fenner, Gary A.-Judge, United States District Court Western District of Missouri-Mo.
Fennessy, Michael A.-Judge, State Court of Sumter County-Ga.
Fenzel, Alfred M.-Judge, Superior Court of Arizona Maricopa County-Ariz.
Ferchill, Patrick W.-Judge, Tarrant County Probate Court No. 2-Tex.
Ferdinand, JoAnn-Judge, The Criminal Court of the City of New York-N.Y.
Ferencz, Bradley J.-Judge, New Jersey Superior Court Vicinage Eight-N.J.
Ferentz, Carol A.-Judge, New Jersey Superior Court Vicinage Five-N.J.
Fergus, Wiliam Lee-Judge, Arkansas Circuit Court Second Judicial Circuit-Ark.
Ferguson, Alfred E.-Judge, West Virginia Circuit Court Sixth Judicial Circuit-W.Va.
Ferguson, Darryl B.-Judge, Superior Court of California County of Tulare-Calif.
Ferguson, Edward C.-Chief Judge, Illinois Circuit Court Third Judicial Circuit-Ill.
Ferguson, Emmet F., III-Judge, Duval County Court-Fla.
Ferguson, George H.-Judge, Elyria Municipal Court-Ohio
Ferguson, Gibbs-Judge, McGehee District Court-Ark.

ALPHABETICAL NAME INDEX

Ferguson, Iris Golliday-Associate Circuit Judge, Missouri Circuit Court Twenty-second Judicial Circuit-Mo.

Ferguson, John B.-Judge, Virginia Juvenile and Domestic Relations District Court Twenty-third Judicial District-Va.

Ferguson, Kathryn C.-Judge, United States Bankruptcy Court District of New Jersey-N.J.

Ferguson, Ralph A., Jr.-Judge, Alabama Circuit Court Tenth Judicial Circuit Birmingham Division-Ala.

Ferguson, Warren J.-Senior Judge, United States Court of Appeals Ninth Circuit

Ferguson, William I.-Associate Judge, Illinois Circuit Court Eighteenth Judicial Circuit-Ill.

Fernandes, Armand, Jr.-Associate Justice, Trial Court of Massachusetts Probate and Family Court Department Bristol County Division-Mass.

Fernandez, Alfonso-Judge, Superior Court of California County of Santa Clara-Calif.

Fernandez, Ellis T., Jr.-Senior Judge, Florida Circuit Court Fourth Judicial Circuit-Fla.

Fernandez, Fé-Associate Judge, Illinois Circuit Court of Cook County-Ill.

Fernandez, Ferdinand F.-Senior Judge, United States Court of Appeals Ninth Circuit

Fernandez, Gaston J.-Judge, Hillsborough County Court-Fla.

Fernandez, Ivan F.-Judge, Florida Circuit Court Eleventh Judicial Circuit-Fla.

Fernandez, Manuel A.-Judge, Louisiana District Court Thirty-fourth Judicial District-La.

Fernandez, Mike L.-Judge, Val Verde County Court-Tex.

Fernandez-Ely, Erin-Judge, Pitkin County Court-Colo.

Ferns, Edward A.-Judge, Superior Court of California County of Los Angeles-Calif.

Ferradino, Stephen A.-Justice, New York Supreme Court Fourth Judicial District-N.Y.

Ferrari, Gary J.-Judge, Superior Court of California County of Los Angeles-Calif.

Ferrell, Eudon-Judge, Superior Court of California County of Los Angeles-Calif.

Ferren, John M.-Senior Judge, District of Columbia Court of Appeals-D.C.

Ferrer, Alex E.-Judge, Florida Circuit Court Eleventh Judicial Circuit-Fla.

Ferris, Janet E.-Judge, Florida Circuit Court Second Judicial Circuit-Fla.

Fertig, John W., Jr.-Judge, Oxford District Probate Court-Conn.

Fetsch, Michael F.-Judge, Minnesota District Court Second Judicial District-Minn.

Fettel, Douglas Alan-Judge, Superior Court of California County of San Bernardino-Calif.

Feucht, Lynette Young-Judge, Eunice City Court-La.

Feuerstein, Sandra J.-Associate Justice, New York Supreme Court Appellate Division Second Judicial Department-N.Y.

Few, John C.-Judge, South Carolina Circuit Court Thirteenth Judicial Circuit-S.C.

Feyen, Mark A.-Chief Judge, Ottawa County Probate Court-Mich.

Ficarrotta, Ronald N.-Judge, Florida Circuit Court Thirteenth Judicial Circuit-Fla.

Fidler, Larry Paul-Judge, Superior Court of California County of Los Angeles-Calif.

Fiechter, Michael A.-Judge, Nassau County District Court-N.Y.

Fiedler, Patrick J.-Judge, Wisconsin Circuit Court Dane Circuit-Wis.

Field, Charles D.-Judge, Superior Court of California County of Riverside-Calif.

Field, David D.-Judge, Dallam County Court-Tex.

Field, Joseph H.-Judge, Maine District Court-Me.

Field, Myrna P.-Judge, Pennsylvania Court of Common Pleas First Judicial District-Pa.

Fielder, John L.-Judge, Superior Court of California County of Kern-Calif.

Fielding, Jerry L.-Presiding Judge, Alabama Circuit Court Twenty-ninth Judicial Circuit-Ala.

Fields, John N.-Judge, Michigan Circuit Court Second Judicial Circuit-Mich.

Fields, Kenneth L.-Judge, Superior Court of Arizona Maricopa County-Ariz.

Fields, Michael R.-Judge, Harris County Criminal Court at Law No. 14-Tex.

Fields, Michael S.-Judge, Superior Court of California County of Monterey-Calif.

Fields, Richard S.-Judge, Superior Court of Arizona Pima County-Ariz.

Fields, Richard Todd-Judge, Superior Court of California County of Riverside-Calif.

Fields, Wilson-Judge, Louisiana District Court Nineteenth Judicial District-La.

Fierro, Eugene J.-Judge, Florida Circuit Court Eleventh Judicial Circuit-Fla.

Figarola, Rosa C.-Judge, Dade County Court-Fla.

Figler, Dayvid-Judge, Las Vegas Municipal Court-Nev.

Figueroa, Gilberto V.-Judge, Superior Court of Arizona Pinal County-Ariz.

Figueroa, Nicholas-Justice, New York Supreme Court First Judicial District-N.Y.

Figueroa, Raymond A.-Circuit Judge, Illinois Circuit Court of Cook County-Ill.

Fike, Eugene E., II-President Judge, Pennsylvania Court of Common Pleas Sixteenth Judicial District-Pa.

Filan, Denise K.-Circuit Judge, Illinois Circuit Court of Cook County-Ill.

Filer, Kelvin D.-Judge, Superior Court of California County of Los Angeles-Calif.

Filiberto, Patricia M.-Judge, Suffolk County District Court-N.Y.

Filice, Charles F.-Judge, Michigan District Court District Fifty-four A-Mich.

Filippine, Edward L.-Senior Judge, United States District Court Eastern District of Missouri-Mo.

Filmore, William H.-Judge, Dale County District Court-Ala.

Filosa, Jimmy D.-Judge, Oklahoma Workers' Compensation Court-Okla.

Filson, Anita D.-Judge, Virginia Juvenile and Domestic Relations District Court Twenty-fifth Judicial District-Va.

Finan, W. Timothy-Associate Judge, Circuit Court for Allegany County, Fourth Judicial Circuit-Md.

Finch, Daniel F.-Judge, North Carolina District Court District 9-N.C.

Finch, Gaylord L., Jr.-Judge, Virginia Circuit Court Nineteenth Judicial Circuit-Va.

Finch, Jay-Judge, Arkansas Circuit Court Nineteenth West Judicial Circuit-Ark.

Finch, Raymond L.-Chief Judge, United States District Court District of the Virgin Islands

Findley, J. Emory-Senior Judge, Superior Court of Georgia-Ga.

Fine, Edward H.-Chief Judge, Florida Circuit Court Fifteenth Judicial Circuit-Fla.

Fine, Lawrence J.-Judge, North Carolina District Court District 21-N.C.

Fine, Ralph Adam-Judge, Wisconsin Court of Appeals District One-Wis.

Fines, Gerald D.-Chief Judge, United States Bankruptcy Court Central District of Illinois-Ill.

Finifter, Michael J.-Associate Judge, Circuit Court for Baltimore County, Third Judicial Circuit-Md.

Fink, Howard Lewis-Associate Judge, Illinois Circuit Court of Cook County-Ill.

Finlay, Amber L.-Judge, Shelton Municipal Court-Wash.

Finley, Barbara K.-Justice of the Peace, Reno Justices' Court-Nev.

Finley, John C., III-Judge, Ashdown District Court-Ark.

Finley, John T.-Judge, Minnesota District Court Second Judicial District-Minn.

Finn, John V.-Judge, Wisconsin Circuit Court Portage Circuit-Wis.

Finn, Timothy J.-District Judge, Iowa District Court Second Judicial District-Ia.

Finnegan, William R.-Judge, Marion Municipal Court-Ohio

Fiora, Nancy-Magistrate Judge, United States District Court District of Arizona-Ariz.

Fiore, Thomas J.-Judge, Stafford District Probate Court-Conn.

Fiorella, Joseph A.-Judge, Buffalo City Court-N.Y.

Fiorenza, Clare L.-Judge, Wisconsin Circuit Court Milwaukee Circuit-Wis.

Fiorenza, John A.-Reserve Judge, Wisconsin Circuit Court-Wis.

Firestone, Nancy B.-Judge, United States Court of Federal Claims

Firetog, Neil Jon-Judge, The Criminal Court of the City of New York-N.Y.

Firmat, Francisco F.-Judge, Superior Court of California County of Orange-Calif.

Firtel, Leon M.-Judge, Florida Circuit Court Eleventh Judicial Circuit-Fla.

Fisch, Joseph-Judge, New York Court of Claims-N.Y.

Fischer, Brian T.-Judge, Connecticut Superior Court-Conn.

Fischer, Dale S.-Judge, Superior Court of California County Los Angeles-Calif.

Fischer, Jack W.-Judge, Connecticut Superior Court-Conn.

Fish, A. Joe-Chief Judge, United States District Court Northern District of Texas-Tex.

Fisher, Clarkson S., Jr.-Judge, New Jersey Superior Court Vicinage Nine-N.J.

Fisher, Fern A.-Justice, New York Supreme Court First Judicial District-N.Y.

Fisher, Gerald I.-Associate Judge, Superior Court of the District of Columbia-D.C.

Fisher, James H.-Chief Judge, Michigan Circuit Court Fifth Judicial Circuit-Mich.

Fisher, Jeff-Judge, Van Zandt County Court-Tex.

Fisher, John S.-Judge, Superior Court of California County of Los Angeles-Calif.

Fisher, Kenneth R.-Justice, New York Supreme Court Seventh Judicial District-N.Y.

Fisher, Marilyn Lassman-Judge, East Windsor District Probate Court-Conn.

Fisher, Michael Brooke-Judge, New Jersey Superior Court Vicinage Fifteen-N.J.

Fisher, Michael S.-Judge, Wisconsin Circuit Court Kenosha Circuit-Wis.

Fisher, Raymond C.-Judge, United States Court of Appeals Ninth Circuit

Fisher, Roger M.-Judge, Snohomish District Court Everett Division Snohomish County-Wash.

Fisher, Steven W.-Justice, New York Supreme Court Eleventh Judicial District-N.Y.

Fisher, Thomas G.-Judge, Indiana Tax Court-Ind.

Fisher, Timothy S.-Chief Judge, Virginia General District Court Seventh Judicial District-Va.

Fisher, Truston Lee-Judge, Lincoln County Court-Colo.

Fishman, Jane D.-Judge, Broward County Court-Fla.

Fishman, Kenneth J.-Associate Justice, Trial Court of Massachusetts Superior Court Department-Mass.

Fiss, Jan V.-Chief Judge, Illinois Circuit Court Twentieth Judicial Circuit-Ill.

Fister, Jon C.-District Judge, Iowa District Court First Judicial District-Ia.

Fitch, Milton F., Jr.-Resident Judge, North Carolina Superior Court First Judicial Division District 7B-N.C.

Fitch, Rod-Judge, Yakima District Court Yakima County-Wash.

Fitch, Thomas G.-Judge, New Mexico District Court Seventh Judicial District-N.Mex.

Fitterer, Richard C.-Judge, Grant District Court Grant County and Judge, Coulee City, Electric City, Grand Coulee, Mattawa, Moses Lake, Quincy, Royal City and Warden Municipal Courts-Wash.

FitzGerald, Daniel P.-Judge, The Criminal Court of the City of New York-N.Y.

Fitzgerald, E. Thomas-Judge, Michigan Court of Appeals-Mich.

Fitzgerald, Edmund G., Jr.-Judge, Yonkers City Court-N.Y.

Fitzgerald, Edward, III-Associate Justice, New Hampshire Superior Court-N.H.

Fitzgerald, J. Michael-Judge, Nebraska Workers' Compensation Court-Neb.

Fitzgerald, James J., III-Judge, Pennsylvania Court of Common Pleas First Judicial District-Pa.

Fitzgerald, James M.-Senior Judge, United States District Court District of Alaska-Alas.

Fitzgerald, Judith K.-Chief Judge, United States Bankruptcy Court Western District of Pennsylvania-Pa.

FitzGerald, Kerry-Justice, Texas Court of Appeals Fifth District-Tex.

ALPHABETICAL NAME INDEX

Fitzgerald, Kevin P.-Associate Judge, Illinois Circuit Court Eleventh Judicial Circuit-Ill.

Fitzgerald, Patty Walker-Judge, Kentucky Circuit Court Thirtieth Judicial Circuit-Ky.

Fitzgerald, Paula-Judge, Kentucky District Court Thirtieth Judicial District-Ky.

Fitzgerald, Richard T.-Judge, Salisbury District Probate Court-Conn.

Fitzgerald, Thomas R.-Justice, Supreme Court of Illinois-Ill.

Fitzgibbon, Madeleine A.-Judge, Suffolk County District Court-N.Y.

Fitzhugh, J. Michael-Judge, Arkansas Circuit Court Twelfth Judicial Circuit-Ark.

Fitzmaurice, Mary Ellen-Judge, New York City Family Court-N.Y.

Fitzpatrick, Diane L.-Judge, New York Court of Claims-N.Y.

Fitzpatrick, Duross-Senior Judge, United States District Court Middle District of Georgia-Ga.

Fitzpatrick, Johanna L.-Chief Judge, Court of Appeals of Virginia-Va.

Fitzpatrick, Maureen F.-Judge, Pennsylvania Court of Common Pleas Thirty-second Judicial District-Pa.

Fitzpatrick, Patrick F. X.-Judge, New Jersey Superior Court Vicinage Two-N.J.

Fitzpatrick, Philip J.-Judge, Lamoille District Probate Court-Vt.

Fitzsimmons, Brady M.-Judge, Louisiana Court of Appeal First Circuit-La.

Fitzsimmons, Donna Congeni-Judge, Rocky River Municipal Court-Ohio

Fitzsimmons, Holly B.-Magistrate Judge, United States District Court District of Connecticut-Conn.

Fitzsimmons, Mark E.-Associate Circuit Judge, Missouri Circuit Court Thirty-first Judicial Circuit-Mo.

Fitzwater, Sidney A.-Judge, United States District Court Northern District of Texas-Tex.

Flaherty, Francis X.-Associate Justice, Rhode Island Supreme Court-R.I.

Flaherty, Michael F.-Associate Justice, Trial Court of Massachusetts Boston Municipal Court Department-Mass.

Flaherty, Susan F.-Associate Juvenile Judge, Iowa District Court Sixth Judicial District-Ia.

Flaherty, Timothy J.-Justice, New York Supreme Court Eleventh Judicial District-N.Y.

Flaigle, Harold E.-Judge, Kansas District Court Eighteenth Judicial District-Kan.

Flake, Gail C.-Judge, Superior Court of Georgia Stone Mountain Judicial Circuit-Ga.

Flanagan, David T.-Judge, Wisconsin Circuit Court Dane Circuit-Wis.

Flanagan, Douglas J.-Judge, Juvenile Court of Georgia Augusta Judicial Circuit-Ga.

Flanagan, Hugh-Judge, Superior Court of California County of Merced-Calif.

Flanagan, John C.-Judge Referee, Connecticut Superior Court-Conn.

Flanagan, Kathy M.-Circuit Judge, Illinois Circuit Court of Cook County-Ill.

Flanagan, Louise W.-Magistrate Judge, United States District Court Eastern District of North Carolina-N.C.

Flanagan, Mel-Judge, Wisconsin Circuit Court Milwaukee Circuit-Wis.

Flanagan, Thomas E.-Circuit Judge, Illinois Circuit Court of Cook County-Ill.

Flanagan, Timothy M.-Judge, Ohio Court of Common Pleas Cuyahoga County-Ohio

Flancher, Faye M.-Judge, Wisconsin Circuit Court Racine Circuit-Wis.

Flanders, H. Gibbs, Jr.-Chief Judge, Superior Court of Georgia Dublin Judicial Circuit-Ga.

Flanders, Judith J.-Judge, Florida Circuit Court Tenth Judicial Circuit-Fla.

Flanders, Robert G., Jr.-Associate Justice, Rhode Island Supreme Court-R.I.

Flannagan, Charles B., II-Chief Judge, Virginia Circuit Court Twenty-eighth Judicial Circuit-Va.

Flannagan, John T.-Judge, United States Bankruptcy Court District of Kansas-Kan.

Flannell, Dan L.-Circuit Judge, Illinois Circuit Court Sixth Judicial Circuit-Ill.

Flannery, James Larry-Judge, Ohio Court of Common Pleas Warren County-Ohio

Flannery, James P., Jr.-Circuit Judge, Illinois Circuit Court of Cook County-Ill.

Flannery, Thomas A.-Senior Judge, United States District Court District of Columbia-D.C.

Flatley, Ellen-Justice, Trial Court of Massachusetts District Court Department Essex County Gloucester Division-Mass.

Flaum, Joel M.-Chief Judge, United States Court of Appeals Seventh Circuit

Flax, Richard-Magistrate Judge, Kansas District Court Twenty-third Judicial District-Kan.

Fleck, Deborah-Judge, Washington Superior Court King County-Wash.

Fleece, Steven Michael-Judge, Clark Superior Court-Ind.

Fleegle, Mark C.-Judge, Ohio Court of Common Pleas Muskingum County-Ohio

Fleet, Erwin-Senior Judge, Florida Circuit Court First Judicial Circuit-Fla.

Fleet, J. Leonard-Judge, Florida Circuit Court Seventeenth Judicial Circuit-Fla.

Fleetwood, James-Judge, Kansas District Court Eighteenth Judicial District-Kan.

Fleischer, Barbara-Judge, Florida Circuit Court Thirteenth Judicial Circuit-Fla.

Fleishauer, Frederic W.-Judge, Wisconsin Circuit Court Portage Circuit-Wis.

Fleisher, Leslie-Judge, Pennsylvania Court of Common Pleas First Judicial District-Pa.

Fleissig, Audrey G.-Magistrate Judge, United States District Court Eastern District of Missouri-Mo.

Fleming, Charles W., Jr.-Judge, Geneva County District Court-Ala.

Fleming, Frederick W.-Judge, Washington Superior Court Pierce County-Wash.

Fleming, Jeffrey M.-Judge, Orange County Court-Fla.

Fleming, John J.-Circuit Judge, Illinois Circuit Court of Cook County-Ill.

Fleming, Marion Lucas-Judge, Florida Circuit Court Sixth Judicial Circuit-Fla.

Fleming, Robert J.-Judge, Kansas District Court Eleventh Judicial District-Kan.

Fleming, Susan G.-Circuit Judge, Illinois Circuit Court of Cook County-Ill.

Fleming, Victor A. "Vic"-Judge, Little Rock District Court-Ark.

Fleming, William M., Jr.-Chief Judge, Superior Court of Georgia Augusta Judicial Circuit-Ga.

Flemmer, Jon-Judge, South Dakota Circuit Court Fifth Judicial Circuit-S.D.

Flenniken, Terry-Judge, Texas District Court 21st Judicial District-Tex.

Fletcher, Betty B.-Senior Judge, United States Court of Appeals Ninth Circuit

Fletcher, Darryl G.-Associate Judge, Maryland District Court District Eight-Md.

Fletcher, John-Judge, Florida District Court of Appeal Third District-Fla.

Fletcher, Norman S.-Chief Justice, Supreme Court of Georgia-Ga.

Fletcher, William A.-Judge, United States Court of Appeals Ninth Circuit

Fleuret, Jules E.-Judge, Superior Court of California County of San Bernardino-Calif.

Flickinger, Joseph F., III-Associate Judge, Delaware Court of Common Pleas New Castle County-Del.

Flier, Madeleine-Judge, Superior Court of California County of Los Angeles-Calif.

Flier, Richard S.-Judge, Superior Court of California County of Contra Costa-Calif.

Flinn, David B.-Judge, Superior Court of California County of Contra Costa-Calif.

Flood, Lawrence E.-Associate Judge, Illinois Circuit Court of Cook County-Ill.

Florendo, Joseph P., Jr.-Judge, Hawaii District Court Third Judicial Circuit-Hi.

Flores, Aida Salinas-Judge, Texas District Court 398th Judicial District-Tex.

Flores, G. R. "Lupe"-Judge, Jefferson County Court at Law No. 2-Tex.

Flores, Joseph A.-Judge, Ohio Court of Common Pleas Lucas County-Ohio

Flores, Manuel R.-Judge, Texas District Court 49th Judicial District-Tex.

Flores, Rogelio R.-Judge, Superior Court of California County of Santa Barbara-Calif.

Florey, James B.-Judge, Minnesota District Court Sixth Judicial District-Minn.

Flòrez, M. Jan-Judge, Arizona Court of Appeals Division Two-Ariz.

Floria, Sallyanne-Judge, New Jersey Superior Court Vicinage Five-N.J.

Florio, Anita R.-Associate Justice, New York Supreme Court Appellate Division Second Judicial Department-N.Y.

Florom, Kent E.-Judge, Nebraska County Court Eleventh Judicial District-Neb.

Flournoy, Robert, III-Judge, Superior Court of Georgia Cobb Judicial Circuit-Ga.

Flournoy, Robert E., Jr.-Senior Judge, Superior Court of Georgia-Ga.

Flower, Gary-Judge, Duval County Court-Fla.

Flowers, Karen B.-Judge, Nebraska District Court Third Judicial District-Neb.

Flowers, Wilford-Judge, Texas District Court 147th Judicial District-Tex.

Floyd, Alison L. "Nelson"-Judge, Ohio Court of Common Pleas Cuyahoga County-Ohio

Floyd, Charles-Chief Magistrate, Magistrate Court of Fayette County-Ga.

Floyd, Donald J.-Judge, Texas District Court 172nd Judicial District-Tex.

Floyd, George C.-Judge, State Court of Decatur County-Ga.

Floyd, Henry F.-Judge, South Carolina Circuit Court Thirteenth Judicial Circuit-S.C.

Floyd, Joseph L. "Lang"-Judge, Alabama Circuit Court Twenty-eighth Judicial Circuit-Ala.

Floyd, R. G.-Judge, Llano County Court-Tex.

Floyd, Robert F., Jr.-Resident Judge, North Carolina Superior Court Fourth Judicial Division District 16B-N.C.

Floyd, Terry K.-Judge, Juvenile Court of Georgia Brunswick Judicial Circuit-Ga.

Flug, Phyllis Orlikoff-Justice, New York Supreme Court Eleventh Judicial District-N.Y.

Flugaur, Thomas T.-Judge, Wisconsin Circuit Court Portage Circuit-Wis.

Flynn, Dennis J.-Reserve Judge, Wisconsin Circuit Court-Wis.

Flynn, Gregory C.-First Justice, Trial Court of Massachusetts District Court Department Middlesex County Waltham Division-Mass.

Flynn, Jeffrey L.-Judge, Minnesota District Court Fifth Judicial District-Minn.

Flynn, Jerry D.-Circuit Judge, Illinois Circuit Court Twentieth Judicial Circuit-Ill.

Flynn, John L., III-Judge, Superior Court of California County of Orange-Calif.

Flynn, Joseph P.-Judge, Connecticut Appellate Court-Conn.

Flynn, Margaret-Judge, Fairview City Court-Mont.

Flynn, Maurice R., III-Justice, Trial Court of Massachusetts District Court Department Middlesex County Malden Division-Mass.

Flynn, Patricia A.-Associate Justice, Trial Court of Massachusetts Juvenile Court Department Middlesex County Division-Mass.

Flynn, Paul G.-Judge, Superior Court of California County of Los Angeles-Calif.

Flynn, Paulette K.-Judge, Minnesota District Court Second Judicial District-Minn.

Flynn, Peter-Circuit Judge, Illinois Circuit Court of Cook County-Ill.

Flynn, Terence P.-Judge, New Jersey Superior Court Vicinage Five-N.J.

Foellger, Michael-Judge, Kentucky Circuit Court Seventeenth Judicial Circuit-Ky.

Fogan, Robert J.-Senior Judge, Florida Circuit Court Seventeenth Judicial Circuit-Fla.

Fogel, Jeremy D.-Judge, United States District Court Northern District of California-Calif.

Fogleman, John N.-Judge, Arkansas Circuit Court Second Judicial Circuit-Ark.

Foil, Frank-Judge, Louisiana Court of Appeal First Circuit-La.

Foiles, Robert D.-Judge, Superior Court of California County of San Mateo-Calif.

Foley, Charles B.-Chief Judge, Virginia General District Court Twentieth Judicial District-Va.

ALPHABETICAL NAME INDEX

Foley, Christopher R.-Judge, Wisconsin Circuit Court Milwaukee Circuit-Wis.
Foley, Daniel R.-Associate Judge, Hawaii Intermediate Court of Appeals-Hi.
Foley, Francis J., III-Judge, Connecticut Superior Court-Conn.
Foley, John F.-Reserve Judge, Wisconsin Circuit Court-Wis.
Foley, Maurice B.-Judge, United States Tax Court
Foley, Robert Michael-Judge, Superior Court of California County of Santa Clara-Calif.
Folino, Ronald W.-Judge, Pennsylvania Court of Common Pleas Fifth Judicial District-Pa.
Folk, Joe N.-Judge, Jasper County Court-Tex.
Follett, William H.-Judge, Superior Court of California County of Del Norte-Calif.
Follis, Frank-Judge, Guadalupe County Court at Law No. 2-Tex.
Followill, Kenneth B.-Chief Judge, Superior Court of Georgia Chattahoochee Judicial Circuit-Ga.
Folsom, David-Judge, United States District Court Eastern District of Texas-Tex.
Folsom, William R.-Judge, State Court of Brooks County-Ga.
Foltz, Harry Albers-Judge, Arkansas Circuit Court Twelfth Judicial Circuit-Ark.
Fontaine, Laurie A.-Judge, North Dakota District Court Northeast Judicial District-N.D.
Fontenot, Elvin C., Jr.-Judge, Leesville City Court-La.
Fontenot, H. Ward-Judge, Louisiana District Court Thirty-eighth Judicial District-La.
Fonvielle, J. Keaton-Emergency Judge, North Carolina District Court-N.C.
Foor, Peter B.-Judge, Superior Court of California County of Solano-Calif.
Foote, Gregory G.-Judge, Oregon Circuit Court Second Judicial District-Ore.
Foote, W. Ross-Judge, Louisiana District Court Ninth Judicial District-La.
Foradora, John H.-President Judge, Pennsylvania Court of Common Pleas Fifty-fourth Judicial District-Pa.
Foran, Leo K.-Chief Judge, Michigan District Court District Twenty-Mich.
Forbes, Jay W.-Chief Judge, New Mexico District Court Fifth Judicial District-N.Mex.
Forcum, John W.-Judge, Blackford Superior Court-Ind.
Forcum, Mark R.-Judge, Superior Court of California County of San Mateo-Calif.
Ford, Aubrey, Jr.-Judge, Macon County District Court-Ala.
Ford, Bradly S.-Judge, Idaho District Court Third Judicial District Magistrate Division-Ida.
Ford, Daniel A.-Associate Justice, Trial Court of Massachusetts Superior Court Department-Mass.
Ford, Donald R.-Judge, Ohio Court of Appeals Eleventh District-Ohio
Ford, G. Sarsfield-Judge, Connecticut Superior Court-Conn.
Ford, Jeffrey B.-Associate Judge, Illinois Circuit Court Sixth Judicial Circuit-Ill.
Ford, John C.-Judge, Louisiana District Court Thirtieth Judicial District-La.
Ford, Larry G.-Resident Judge, North Carolina Superior Court Sixth Judicial Division District 19C-N.C.
Ford, Marlene Lynch-Judge, New Jersey Superior Court Vicinage Fourteen-N.J.
Ford, Nicholas R.-Circuit Judge, Illinois Circuit Court of Cook County-Ill.
Ford, Richard T.-Recalled Judge, United States Bankruptcy Court Eastern District of California-Calif.
Ford, Steven E.-Chief Judge, Michigan District Court District Ninety-two-Mich.
Ford, William E.-Judge, Pennsylvania Court of Common Pleas Thirty-first Judicial District-Pa.
Forde, Annette-Associate Justice, Trial Court of Massachusetts Boston Municipal Court Department-Mass.
Forehand, Dwayne D.-Judge, Probate Court of Dooly County-Ga.
Forehand, V. Thomas, Jr.-Chief Judge, Virginia Circuit Court First Judicial Circuit-Va.
Foreman, James L.-Senior Judge, United States District Court Southern District of Illinois-Ill.
Foreman, John F.-Judge, Superior Court of Arizona Maricopa County-Ariz.
Foreman, Lester D.-Circuit Judge, Illinois Circuit Court of Cook County-Ill.
Forester, Karl S.-Chief Judge, United States District Court Eastern District of Kentucky-Ky.
Forester, William L.-Judge, New Jersey Superior Court Vicinage Fifteen-N.J.
Forgety, Telford E., Jr.-Chancellor, Tennessee Chancery Court Fourth and Fifth Judicial Districts-Tenn.
Forgione, Frank J.-Judge, North Branford District Probate Court-Conn.
Forma, Joseph S.-Justice, New York Supreme Court Eighth Judicial District-N.Y.
Forman, Peter M.-Judge, Dutchess County Family Court-N.Y.
Forman, Walter J.-Judge, Cohoes City Court-N.Y.
Fornelli, Francis J.-President Judge, Pennsylvania Court of Common Pleas Thirty-fifth Judicial District-Pa.
Forneret, Rodney G.-Judge, Superior Court of California County of Los Angeles-Calif.
Fornof-Lippencott, Susan J.-Judge, Champaign County Municipal Court-Ohio
Forrest, Steven W.-Judge, Elmira City Court-N.Y.
Forrester, F. Lee-Judge, New Jersey Superior Court Vicinage Seven-N.J.
Forrester, J. Owen-Judge, United States District Court Northern District of Georgia-Ga.
Forrester, Jim L.-Judge, Collingsworth County Court-Tex.
Forrester, Whitfield R.-Chief Judge, Superior Court of Georgia Cordele Judicial Circuit-Ga.
Forsling, Susan B.-Judge, State Court of Fulton County-Ga.
Forstenzer, Edward-Judge, Superior Court of California County of Mono-Calif.
Forster, John F., Jr.-Magistrate Judge, United States District Court Eastern District of Arkansas-Ark.
Forte, Michael B.-Associate Justice, Rhode Island Family Court-R.I.
Forte, Stephen P.-Justice of the Peace, Deschutes County Justice Court-Ore.
Fortinberry, Dana-Judge, Michigan District Court District Fifty-two Division Two-Mich.
Fortney, Rex D.-Judge, Ohio Court of Common Pleas Van Wert County-Ohio
Fortunato, Stephen J., Jr.-Associate Justice, Rhode Island Superior Court-R.I.
Foschio, Leslie G.-Magistrate Judge, United States District Court Western District of New York-N.Y.
Foscue, David E.-Judge, Washington Superior Court Grays Harbor County-Wash.
Foskey, Carnell T.-Judge, Nassau County Family Court-N.Y.
Foss, Janet A.-Special Judge, Oklahoma District Court Twenty-first Judicial District-Okla.
Fostel, John H.-Judge, Texas District Court 271st Judicial District-Tex.
Foster, Alan W.-Judge, Adams County Court-Ohio
Foster, Anna F.-Judge, North Carolina District Court District 27B-N.C.
Foster, Aundria Deloris-Judge, Virginia Juvenile and Domestic Relations District Court Seventh Judicial District-Va.
Foster, Christine-Judge, Maine District Court-Me.
Foster, Clinton E.-Senior Judge, Florida Circuit Court Fourteenth Judicial Circuit-Fla.
Foster, Don Al-Circuit Judge, Illinois Circuit Court Second Judicial Circuit-Ill.
Foster, James L.-Judge, Nebraska County Court Third Judicial District-Neb.
Foster, John C.-Judge, Michigan District Court District Forty-one B-Mich.
Foster, Joseph L.-Judge, New Jersey Tax Court-N.J.
Foster, Kathryn W.-Judge, Wisconsin Circuit Court Waukesha Circuit-Wis.
Foster, Kennard P.-Recalled Magistrate Judge, United States District Court Southern District of Indiana-Ind.
Foster, Lisa-Judge, Superior Court of California County of San Diego-Calif.
Foster, Phil-Judge, Camden District Court-Ark.
Foster, Robert A.-Judge, Florida Circuit Court Thirteenth Judicial Circuit-Fla.
Foster, Robert M.-Judge, Florida Circuit Court Fourth Judicial Circuit-Fla.
Foster, Terry J.-Circuit Judge, Illinois Circuit Court First Judicial Circuit-Ill.
Foster, Thomas E.-Judge, Kansas District Court Tenth Judicial District-Kan.
Foster, Thomas G., Jr.-Judge, North Carolina District Court District 18-N.C.
Foster, William A., III-Chief Judge, Superior Court of Georgia Paulding Judicial Circuit-Ga.
Foti, Paul M.-Judge, Connecticut Appellate Court-Conn.
Foughty, Donovan J.-Judge, North Dakota District Court Northeast Judicial District-N.D.
Foust, C. William-Judge, Wisconsin Circuit Court Dane Circuit-Wis.
Foust, Dennis R.-Judge, Kentucky Circuit Court Forty-second Judicial Circuit-Ky.
Foutz, Grant L.-Judge, New Mexico District Court Eleventh Judicial District-N.Mex.
Fowler, Craig-Judge, Texas District Court 255th Judicial District-Tex.
Fowler, Dean-Judge, Upshur County Court-Tex.
Fowler, Eddy-Judge, Probate Court of Franklin County-Ga.
Fowler, H. Gregory-Judge, State Court of Chatham County-Ga.
Fowler, Kenneth E.-Chief Magistrate, Magistrate Court of Twiggs County-Ga.
Fowler, Susan L.-Judge, Chittenden District Probate Court-Vt.
Fowler, W. Lee-Judge, Kansas District Court Fifth Judicial District-Kan.
Fowler, Wanda McKee-Justice, Texas Court of Appeals Fourteenth District-Tex.
Fox, Bruce I.-Chief Judge, United States Bankruptcy Court Eastern District of Pennsylvania-Pa.
Fox, David Kennedy-Judge, North Carolina District Court District 29-N.C.
Fox, Douglas T.-Judge, Wisconsin Circuit Court Price Circuit-Wis.
Fox, Elden S.-Judge, Superior Court of California County of Los Angeles-Calif.
Fox, Fred L., II-Chief Judge, West Virginia Circuit Court Sixteenth Judicial Circuit-W.Va.
Fox, Gerald M., Jr.-Judge, Stamford District Probate Court-Conn.
Fox, Idee C.-Judge, Pennsylvania Court of Common Pleas First Judicial District-Pa.
Fox, James C.-Senior Judge, United States District Court Eastern District of North Carolina-N.C.
Fox, Kenneth P.-Judge, Bellevue Municipal Court-Ohio
Fox, Kevin Nathaniel-Magistrate Judge, United States District Court Southern District of New York-N.Y.
Fox, Lawrence P.-Associate Judge, Illinois Circuit Court of Cook County-Ill.
Fox, Lisa-Judge, Dallas County Criminal Court at Law No. 10-Tex.
Fox, Mark D.-Magistrate Judge, United States District Court Southern District of New York-N.Y.
Fox, Michael J.-Judge, Washington Superior Court King County-Wash.
Fox, Patrick A.-First Justice, Trial Court of Massachusetts District Court Department Worcester County Gardner Division, First Justice, Winchendon Division and Justice, East Brookfield Division-Mass.
Fox, Tim-Judge, Arkansas Circuit Court Sixth Judicial Circuit-Ark.
Fox, William Gobin-Judge, Fremont County Court-Colo.
Foxman, S. James-Judge, Florida Circuit Court Seventh Judicial Circuit-Fla.
Foy, Louis F., Jr.-Judge, North Carolina District Court District 4-N.C.
Fracasse, Ronald J.-Judge Referee, Connecticut Superior Court-Conn.
Fraley, James F., Jr.-Judge, South Carolina Family Court Seventh Judicial Circuit-S.C.
Frame, Glenn-Judge, Ronan City Court-Mont.
France, Mary D.-Judge, United States Bankruptcy Court Middle District of Pennsylvania-Pa.

ALPHABETICAL NAME INDEX

France, Ralph H., II-Associate Judge, Maryland District Court District Eleven-Md.
Francis, Charles A.-Judge, Florida Circuit Court Second Judicial Circuit-Fla.
Francis, James C., IV-Magistrate Judge, United States District Court Southern District of New York-N.Y.
Francis, Mary Jo-Judge, Dade County Court-Fla.
Francis, Molly Meredith-Justice, Texas Court of Appeals Fifth District-Tex.
Francis, Nancy C.-Judge, Washtenaw County Probate Court-Mich.
Francis, Robert E.-Judge, New Jersey Superior Court Vicinage Fifteen-N.J.
Francis, Robert W.-Judge, Texas Criminal District Court No. 3 Dallas County-Tex.
Francis, Travis L.-Judge, New Jersey Superior Court Vicinage Eight-N.J.
Franco, Ralph P.-Justice, New York Supreme Court Tenth Judicial District-N.Y.
Franczyk, Thomas P.-Judge, Buffalo City Court-N.Y.
Frank, Charles H.-Associate Judge, Illinois Circuit Court Eleventh Judicial Circuit-Ill.
Frank, Donovan W.-Judge, United States District Court District of Minnesota-Minn.
Frank, Robert P.-Judge, Court of Appeals of Virginia-Va.
Frank, Steven H.-Judge, Marion Superior Court-Ind.
Frank Kelly, Kirsten-Judge, Michigan Court of Appeals-Mich.
Franke, John-Judge, Wisconsin Circuit Court Milwaukee Circuit-Wis.
Frankel, Deborah Kochiss-Judge, Connecticut Superior Court-Conn.
Frankel, Kimberly C.-Judge, Oregon Circuit Court Fourth Judicial District-Ore.
Frankland, David K.-Circuit Judge, Illinois Circuit Court Second Judicial Circuit-Ill.
Franklin, Beverly Mitchell-Judge, Lowndes County Court-Miss.
Franklin, H. G.-Judge, Lynn County Court-Tex.
Franklin, Humes J., Jr.-Judge, Virginia Circuit Court Twenty-fifth Judicial Circuit-Va.
Franklin, James A., Jr.-Presiding Judge, Missouri Circuit Court Twenty-sixth Judicial Circuit-Mo.
Franklin, Ronald G.-District Judge, Oklahoma District Court Fourth Judicial District-Okla.
Franklin, Sheldon R.-Judge, New Jersey Superior Court Vicinage Fourteen-N.J.
Franklin, Stephen J.-Judge, Eureka City Court-Mont.
Franks, Bill-Justice, Wibaux County Justice of the Peace Court and Judge, Wibaux City Court-Mont.
Franks, Helen R.-Associate Judge, Illinois Circuit Court Nineteenth Judicial Circuit-Ill.
Franks, Herschel P.-Judge, Tennessee Court of Appeals Eastern Division-Tenn.
Franks, Pamela J.-Judge, Superior Court of Arizona Maricopa County-Ariz.
Franks, Ruth Ann-Judge, Ohio Court of Common Pleas Lucas County-Ohio
Fransein, Doris L.-District Judge, Oklahoma District Court Fourteenth Judicial District-Okla.
Frantz, Julie-Judge, Oregon Circuit Court Fourth Judicial District-Ore.
Franzen, Stephen E.-Judge, Juvenile Court of Georgia Gwinnett Judicial Circuit-Ga.
Fraser, Jeffrey F.-Judge, Superior Court of California County of San Diego-Calif.
Frasher, James H., Jr.-Judge, Colorado District Court Tenth Judicial District-Colo.
Frasier, Francis J.-Justice, Hampton District Court-N.H.
Fratarcangeli, Mark A.-Judge, Michigan District Court District Forty-Mich.
Frates, Gregory F.-Judge, Idaho District Court Third Judicial District Magistrate Division-Ida.
Fratto, John A.-Judge, New Jersey Superior Court Vicinage Four-N.J.
Fratto, Joseph C., Jr.-Judge, Utah District Court Third Judicial District-Utah
Frawley, Thomas J.-Circuit Judge, Missouri Circuit Court Twenty-second Judicial Circuit-Mo.
Frawley, Timothy M.-Judge, Superior Court of California County of Sacramento-Calif.
Frazee, Evelyn-Justice, New York Supreme Court Seventh Judicial District-N.Y.
Frazee, Richard O., Sr.-Judge, Superior Court of California County of Orange-Calif.
Frazier, David J.-Judge, Washington Superior Court Whitman County-Wash.
Frazier, Douglas N.-Magistrate Judge, United States District Court Middle District of Florida-Fla.
Frazier, John A.-Senior Judge, Superior Court of Georgia-Ga.
Frazier, John R.-Judge, West Virginia Circuit Court Ninth Judicial Circuit-W.Va.
Frazier, Philip M.-Magistrate Judge, United States District Court Southern District of Illinois-Ill.
Frazier, Stephen N.-Judge, Kentucky Circuit Court Twenty-fourth Judicial Circuit-Ky.
Frazzini, Stephen F.-Judge, Connecticut Superior Court-Conn.
Frederick, J. Dennis-Judge, Utah District Court Third Judicial District-Utah
Frederick, Robert G.-Judge, Illinois Court of Claims-Ill.
Frederick, Robert J.-Judge, Kansas District Court Twenty-fifth Judicial District-Kan.
Fredericksen, Chris L.-Associate Judge, Illinois Circuit Court Tenth Judicial Circuit-Ill.
Fredricks, Josh M.-Judge, Superior Court of California County of Los Angeles-Calif.
Free, J. Robin-Judge, Louisiana District Court Eighteenth Judicial District-La.
Freed, Samuel-Judge Referee, Connecticut Superior Court-Conn.
Freedberg, Robert A.-President Judge, Pennsylvania Court of Common Pleas Third Judicial District-Pa.
Freedman, Frank H.-Senior Judge, United States District Court District of Massachusetts-Mass.
Freedman, Frederick A.-Judge Referee, Connecticut Superior Court-Conn.
Freedman, Helen E.-Justice, New York Supreme Court First Judicial District-N.Y.
Freedman, Philip M.-Retired Judge, New Jersey Superior Court-N.J.
Freedman, Robert Brandeis-Judge, Superior Court of California County of Alameda-Calif.
Freedman, Samuel S.-Judge Referee, Connecticut Superior Court-Conn.
Freeland, Janice-Justice, Toole County Justice of the Peace Court and Judge, Shelby City Court-Mont.
Freelove, Michael A.-Magistrate Judge, Kansas District Court Sixteenth Judicial District-Kan.
Freeman, Allen A.-Recalled Circuit Judge, Illinois Circuit Court of Cook County-Ill.
Freeman, Beth Labson-Judge, Superior Court of California County of San Mateo-Calif.
Freeman, Bill-Judge, Cooke County Court-Tex.
Freeman, Carolyn B.-Judge, Orange County Court-Fla.
Freeman, Charles E.-Justice, Supreme Court of Illinois-Ill.
Freeman, Clifford L.-Judge, Oregon Circuit Court Fourth Judicial District-Ore.
Freeman, Debra-Magistrate Judge, United States District Court Southern District of New York-N.Y.
Freeman, Gill S.-Judge, Florida Circuit Court Eleventh Judicial Circuit-Fla.
Freeman, Isaac St. C.-Judge, Virginia General District Court Twenty-eighth Judicial District-Va.
Freeman, Kenneth R.-Judge, Superior Court of California County of Los Angeles-Calif.
Freeman, Linda-Chief Magistrate, Magistrate Court of Terrell County-Ga.
Freeman, Nora L.-Judge, New York City Family Court-N.Y.
Freeman, Ronald J.-Judge, New Jersey Superior Court Vicinage Four-N.J.
Freeman, Thomas-Judge, Florida Circuit Court Eighteenth Judicial Circuit-Fla.
Freeman, Thomas B.-Judge, Pinellas County Court-Fla.
Freese, Chris E.-Associate Judge, Illinois Circuit Court Sixth Judicial Circuit-Ill.
Freese, John P.-Chief Judge, Illinois Circuit Court Eleventh Judicial Circuit-Ill.
Freese, Robert W.-Judge, Hendricks Superior Court-Ind.
Freesemann, Penny Haas-Judge, Superior Court of Georgia Eastern Judicial Circuit-Ga.
Fregiato, Frank A.-Judge, Belmont County Court-Ohio
Freitag, Paul W.-Justice of the Peace, Sparks Justices' Court-Nev.
Freitag, Robert L.-Associate Judge, Illinois Circuit Court Eleventh Judicial Circuit-Ill.
French, Charles S.-Judge, Washington Superior Court Snohomish County-Wash.
French, Dorothy F.-Associate Judge, Illinois Circuit Court Eighteenth Judicial Circuit-Ill.
French, Rae Ann-Judge, Maine District Court-Me.
Frerking, John-Associate Circuit Judge, Missouri Circuit Court Fifteenth Judicial Circuit-Mo.
Fresard, Patricia Susan-Judge, Michigan Circuit Court Third Judicial Circuit-Mich.
Frese, J. Jerome-Judge, St. Joseph Superior Court-Ind.
Freundlich, David-Judge, Suffolk County Family Court-N.Y.
Fricano, Amy J.-Justice, New York Supreme Court Eighth Judicial District-N.Y.
Fridline, Jacob M.-Judge, Ashland Municipal Court-Ohio
Fridy, Kaye W.-Judge, Laurens County Probate Court-S.C.
Fried, Bernard J.-Judge, The Criminal Court of the City of New York-N.Y.
Friedel, Karl W.-Judge, Kansas District Court Eighteenth Judicial District-Kan.
Friedland, Carolyn B.-Judge, Ohio Court of Common Pleas Cuyahoga County-Ohio
Friedland, Kenneth-Judge, Brevard County Court-Fla.
Friedlander, Ezra H.-Presiding Judge, Indiana Court of Appeals Second District-Ind.
Friedman, Bernard A.-Judge, United States District Court Eastern District of Michigan-Mich.
Friedman, Daniel M.-Senior Judge, United States Court of Appeals Federal Circuit
Friedman, David-Associate Justice, New York Supreme Court Appellate Division First Judicial Department-N.Y.
Friedman, Gary T.-Judge, Superior Court of California County of Kern-Calif.
Friedman, Jerome B.-Judge, United States District Court Eastern District of Virginia-Va.
Friedman, Judith L. A.-Judge, Pennsylvania Court of Common Pleas Fifth Judicial District-Pa.
Friedman, Marcy S.-Judge, The Civil Court of the City of New York-N.Y.
Friedman, Paul L.-Judge, United States District Court District of Columbia-D.C.
Friedman, Rhea G.-Judge, New York City Family Court-N.Y.
Friedman, Rochelle S.-Judge, The Commonwealth Court of Pennsylvania-Pa.
Friedman, Ronald M.-Judge, Florida Circuit Court Eleventh Judicial Circuit-Fla.
Friedman, Steven H.-Judge, United States Bankruptcy Court Southern District of Florida-Fla.
Friedman, Stuart A.-Judge, Ohio Court of Common Pleas Cuyahoga County-Ohio
Friedman, Terry-Judge, Superior Court of California County of Los Angeles-Calif.
Friedmann, William D.-Associate Justice, New York Supreme Court Appellate Division Second Judicial Department-N.Y.
Friedrich, Dennis P.-Judge, Colorado District Court Seventh Judicial District-Colo.
Friend, Kelsey Evans-Judge, Kentucky District Court Thirty-fifth Judicial District-Ky.
Friend, L. Edward, II-Judge, United States Bankruptcy Court Northern District of West Virginia-W.Va.
Frierson, Thomas R., II-Chancellor, Tennessee Chancery Court Third Judicial District-Tenn.
Friia, Jo Ann-Judge, White Plains City Court-N.Y.
Friot, Stephen P.-Judge, United States District Court Western District of Oklahoma-Okla.
Fritts, David T.-Circuit Judge, Illinois Circuit Court Fifteenth Judicial Circuit-Ill.
Fritz, Michael John-Associate Judge, Illinois Circuit Court Nineteenth Judicial Circuit-Ill.
Fritzler, Randal Brandt-Judge, Clark District Court Clark County and Judge, Camas-Washougal Municipal Court-Wash.

ALPHABETICAL NAME INDEX

Fritzsche, Paul A.-Justice, Maine Superior Court-Me.

Frizzell, Gregory Kent-District Judge, Oklahoma District Court Fourteenth Judicial District-Okla.

Frobish, Harold J.-Circuit Judge, Illinois Circuit Court Eleventh Judicial Circuit-Ill.

Froeberg, William R.-Judge, Superior Court of California County of Orange-Calif.

Froehlich, Harold V.-Judge, Wisconsin Circuit Court Outagamie Circuit-Wis.

Froehlich, Mark S.-Judge, Franklin County Municipal Court-Ohio

Froehlich, Peter-Judge, Alaska District Court First Judicial District-Alas.

Froelich, Jeffrey E.-Judge, Ohio Court of Common Pleas Montgomery County-Ohio

Froeschner, John Robert-Magistrate Judge, United States District Court Southern District of Texas-Tex.

Fromholz, Haley J.-Judge, Superior Court of California County of Los Angeles-Calif.

Fromme, Phillip M.-Judge, Kansas District Court Fourth Judicial District-Kan.

Frost, Gregory Lynn-Judge, United States District Court Southern District of Ohio-Ohio

Frost, Kem Thompson-Justice, Texas Court of Appeals Fourteenth District-Tex.

Frost, Mark A.-Judge, Columbiana County Municipal Court-Ohio

Fruin, Richard L., Jr.-Judge, Superior Court of California County of Los Angeles-Calif.

Frusciante, John A.-Judge, Florida Circuit Court Seventeenth Judicial Circuit-Fla.

Fry, Cynthia A.-Judge, New Mexico Court of Appeals-N.Mex.

Fry, Harvey L.-Chief Magistrate, Magistrate Court of Camden County-Ga.

Fry, James R.-Judge, Texas District Court 15th Judicial District-Tex.

Fry, Lawrence W.-Judge, Superior Court of California County of Riverside-Calif.

Frye, Andrew N., Jr.-Chief Judge, West Virginia Circuit Court Twenty-first Judicial Circuit-W.Va.

Frye, Helen J.-Senior Judge, United States District Court District of Oregon-Ore.

Frye, Henry E., Jr.-Resident Judge, North Carolina Superior Court Fifth Judicial Division District 18-N.C.

Fryefield, Peter-Judge, Florida Circuit Court Fourth Judicial Circuit-Fla.

Fryer, Joel James-Senior Judge, Superior Court of Georgia-Ga.

Fryer, Nancy-Judge, Probate Court of Terrell County-Ga.

Fuchs, Alicia A.-Judge, Oregon Circuit Court Fourth Judicial District-Ore.

Fuchs, Dennis M.-Judge, Utah District Court Third Judicial District-Utah

Fudenna, Keith H.-Judge, Superior Court of California County of Alameda-Calif.

Fudger, Arthur W.-Senior Judge, Superior Court of Georgia-Ga.

Fuente, William-Judge, Florida Circuit Court Thirteenth Judicial Circuit-Fla.

Fuentes, Jose L.-Judge, New Jersey Superior Court Appellate Division-N.J.

Fuentes, Julio M.-Judge, United States Court of Appeals Third Circuit

Fuerst, Nancy A.-Judge, Ohio Court of Common Pleas Cuyahoga County-Ohio

Fuger, Stanley T., Jr.-Judge, Connecticut Superior Court-Conn.

Fugit, Larry F.-Judge, Nebraska County Court Second Judicial District-Neb.

Fujioka, Fred J.-Judge, Superior Court of California County of Los Angeles-Calif.

Fullam, John P.-Senior Judge, United States District Court Eastern District of Pennsylvania-Pa.

Fuller, A. Peter-Judge, South Dakota Circuit Court Seventh Judicial Circuit-S.D.

Fuller, Ben A.-Judge, Alabama Circuit Court Nineteenth Judicial Circuit-Ala.

Fuller, C. Andrew-Chief Judge, Superior Court of Georgia Northeastern Judicial Circuit-Ga.

Fuller, David M.-Judge, State Court of Gwinnett County-Ga.

Fuller, David M.-Associate Justice, Trial Court of Massachusetts Probate and Family Court Department Hampden County Division-Mass.

Fuller, Gary L.-Judge, Stephens County Court-Tex.

Fuller, Hilton-Judge, Superior Court of Georgia Stone Mountain Judicial Circuit-Ga.

Fuller, Mark E.-Judge, United States District Court Middle District of Alabama-Ala.

Fuller, Mary E.-Judge, Superior Court of California County of San Bernardino-Calif.

Fuller, Max-Chief Magistrate, Magistrate Court of Gordon County-Ga.

Fuller, Tom-Judge, Dallas County Criminal Court at Law No. 5-Tex.

Fullerton, Judith A.-Judge, Michigan Circuit Court Seventh Judicial Circuit-Mich.

Fullerton, Walt-Judge, Pinellas County Court-Fla.

Fullilove, Harold W.-Judge, New Jersey Superior Court Vicinage Five-N.J.

Fullwood, Ernest Berlin-Resident Judge, North Carolina Superior Court Second Judicial Division District 5-N.C.

Fullwood, James R.-Judge, North Carolina District Court District 10-N.C.

Fulmer, Carolyn K.-Judge, Florida District Court of Appeal Second District-Fla.

Fulton, Junius P., III-Judge, Virginia Circuit Court Fourth Judicial Circuit-Va.

Fulton, Kenton W.-Judge, Oklahoma Workers' Compensation Court-Okla.

Fulton, Suzanne Kuczko-Chief Judge, Virginia General District Court Thirtieth Judicial District-Va.

Fulton, Thomas H.-Judge, United States Bankruptcy Court Western District of Kentucky-Ky.

Fultz, Karla J.-Associate Juvenile Judge, Iowa District Court Fifth Judicial District-Ia.

Funderburk, Eric B.-Judge, Russell County District Court-Ala.

Funderburk, Paul S.-Judge, Mississippi Circuit Court First Judicial District-Miss.

Funderburk, Raymond-Circuit Judge, Illinois Circuit Court of Cook County-Ill.

Funk, J. Brad-Associate Circuit Judge, Missouri Circuit Court Third Judicial Circuit-Mo.

Funk, Jerry A.-Judge, United States Bankruptcy Court Middle District of Florida-Fla.

Funk, Raymond-Judge, Alaska District Court Fourth Judicial District-Alas.

Funk, Thomas-Judge, Kentucky District Court Fifteenth Judicial District-Ky.

Funke, James, Jr.-Judge, Jennings Superior Court-Ind.

Furber, William J., Jr.-Judge, Pennsylvania Court of Common Pleas Thirty-eighth Judicial District-Pa.

Furfure, Marianne-Surrogate, Steuben County Surrogate's Court-N.Y.

Furgeson, Royal, Jr.-Judge, United States District Court Western District of Texas-Tex.

Fusco, John A.-Surrogate, Richmond County Surrogate's Court-N.Y.

Fuselier, Perrell-Judge, Oakdale City Court-La.

Fuselier, Thomas F.-Judge, Louisiana District Court Thirteenth Judicial District-La.

Fuste, Jose Antonio-Judge, United States District Court District of Puerto Rico

Futch, John E.-Judge, Marion County Court-Fla.

Futch, M. Daniel, Jr.-Senior Judge, Florida Circuit Court Seventeenth Judicial Circuit-Fla.

Futey, Bohdan A.-Senior Judge, United States Court of Federal Claims

Fybel, Richard David-Associate Justice, California Court of Appeal Fourth District Division Three-Calif.

Fye, Susan-Justice of the Peace, Beowawe Justices' Court-Nev.

Gabbard, Doug, II-District Judge, Oklahoma District Court Twenty-fifth Judicial District-Okla.

Gabbert, A. Rex-Associate Circuit Judge, Missouri Circuit Court Seventh Judicial Circuit-Mo.

Gabert, Alex W.-Judge, Texas District Court 229th Judicial District-Tex.

Gable, Dale Moore-Judge, South Carolina Family Court Second Judicial Circuit-S.C.

Gableman, Michael J.-Judge, Wisconsin Circuit Court Burnett Circuit-Wis.

Gabler, William J.-Acting Judge, Salamanca City Court-N.Y.

Gabler, William M.-Judge, Wisconsin Circuit Court Eau Claire Circuit-Wis.

Gabriel, E. Lee-Judge, Texas District Court 367th Judicial District-Tex.

Gabriel, John D.-Judge, Texas District Court 131st Judicial District-Tex.

Gaddis, Ben H.-Family Court Judge, Hawaii District Court Third Judicial Circuit-Hi.

Gaddis, Larry D.-Judge, Superior Court of California County of Placer-Calif.

Gaden, Barbara J.-Judge, Virginia General District Court Thirteenth Judicial District-Va.

Gadola, John A.-Judge, Michigan Circuit Court Seventh Judicial Circuit-Mich.

Gadola, Paul V.-Senior Judge, United States District Court Eastern District of Michigan-Mich.

Gadola, Thomas L.-Judge, Genesee County Probate Court-Mich.

Gaertner, Gary M., Jr.-Circuit Judge, Missouri Circuit Court Twenty-first Judicial Circuit-Mo.

Gaertner, Gary M., Sr.-Judge, Missouri Court of Appeals Eastern District-Mo.

Gaeta, Bruce A.-Judge, New Jersey Superior Court Vicinage Two-N.J.

Gaeta, Sebastian, Jr.-Judge, New Jersey Superior Court Vicinage Two-N.J.

Gaffney, Bernard D.-Judge Referee, Connecticut Superior Court-Conn.

Gaffney, Kevin J.-Justice, Trial Court of Massachusetts District Court Department Norfolk County Dedham Division-Mass.

Gage, Hilda R.-Judge, Michigan Court of Appeals-Mich.

Gage, Michael W.-Judge, Wisconsin Circuit Court Outagamie Circuit-Wis.

Gage, Walter C.-Judge, Geneva City Court-N.Y.

Gahagan, Fred S.-Judge, Natchitoches City Court-La.

Gaidry, Edward J. "Jimmy"-Judge, Louisiana Court of Appeal First Circuit-La.

Gailey, Timothy H.-Circuit Justice, Trial Court of Massachusetts District Court Department and First Justice, Suffolk County Chelsea Division-Mass.

Gain, Brian D.-Judge, Washington Superior Court King County-Wash.

Gainer, Thomas V., Jr.-Recalled Circuit Judge, Illinois Circuit Court of Cook County-Ill.

Gaines, Crystal-Judge, City Court of Atlanta-Ga.

Gaines, Edward R.-Judge, United States Bankruptcy Court Southern District of Mississippi-Miss.

Gaines, Joseph J.-Senior Judge, Superior Court of Georgia-Ga.

Gaines, Pendleton-Judge, Superior Court of Arizona Maricopa County-Ariz.

Gaitan, Fernando J., Jr.-Judge, United States District Court Western District of Missouri-Mo.

Gajarsa, Arthur J.-Judge, United States Court of Appeals Federal Circuit

Galasso, John Michael-Judge, Nassau County Court-N.Y.

Galasso, Nicholas J.-Associate Judge, Illinois Circuit Court Eighteenth Judicial Circuit-Ill.

Galati, Frank T.-Judge, Superior Court of Arizona Maricopa County-Ariz.

Galbraith, Robert H.-Special Judge, Oklahoma District Court Eighth Judicial District-Okla.

Galchinsky, Herbert H.-Judge, Denver County Court-Colo.

Gale, Edwin J.-Associate Justice, Rhode Island Superior Court-R.I.

Gale, Joseph H.-Judge, United States Tax Court

Gale, Nancy M.-Judge, Woodstock District Probate Court-Conn.

Galeotos, Paul-Judge, Cheyenne Municipal Court-Wyo.

Galewyrick, Molly E.-Judge, Wisconsin Circuit Court Polk Circuit-Wis.

Galik, Annette-Judge, Texas District Court 245th Judicial District-Tex.

Galindo, Jimmy B.-Judge, Reeves County Court-Tex.

Gallagher, Catherine A.-Judge, Superior Court of California County of Santa Clara-Calif.

ALPHABETICAL NAME INDEX

Gallagher, Daniel E.-Senior Judge, Florida Circuit Court Thirteenth Judicial Circuit-Fla.
Gallagher, Eileen-Judge, Ohio Court of Common Pleas Cuyahoga County-Ohio
Gallagher, Elizabeth A.-Judge, Connecticut Superior Court-Conn.
Gallagher, George W.-Judge, Texas District Court 396th Judicial District-Tex.
Gallagher, John W.-Judge, Ohio Court of Common Pleas Cuyahoga County-Ohio
Gallagher, Michael J.-Judge, Illinois Appellate Court First Judicial District Division Six-Ill.
Gallagher, Peter-Judge, Superior Court of California County of San Diego-Calif.
Gallagher, Sean C.-Judge, Ohio Court of Appeals Eighth District-Ohio
Gallagher, Thomas-Judge, Butte City Court-Mont.
Gallagher, Thomas J.-Reserve Judge, Wisconsin Circuit Court-Wis.
Gallagher, William D.-Judge, Superior Court of California County of Shasta-Calif.
Gallahue, Thomas E.-Judge, Virginia General District Court Nineteenth Judicial District-Va.
Gallas, James S.-Magistrate Judge, United States District Court Northern District of Ohio-Ohio
Gallegos, Nicholas-Judge, Edwards County Court-Tex.
Gallen, Thomas M.-Senior Judge, Florida Circuit Court Twelfth Judicial Circuit-Fla.
Galler, Gregory G.-Judge, Minnesota District Court Tenth Judicial District-Minn.
Galley, Kevin R.-Circuit Judge, Illinois Circuit Court Tenth Judicial Circuit-Ill.
Gallina, Scott-Judge, Colton and Uniontown Municipal Courts-Wash.
Gallinger, Art-Justice, Garfield County Justice of the Peace Court and Judge, Jordan City Court-Mont.
Gallipoli, Maurice J.-Judge, New Jersey Superior Court Vicinage Six-N.J.
Gallivan, Robert H.-Judge, Superior Court of California County of Orange-Calif.
Gallo, Robert C.-Judge, Pennsylvania Court of Common Pleas Fifth Judicial District-Pa.
Galloway, Harold L.-Justice, New York Supreme Court Seventh Judicial District-N.Y.
Galloway, Mark E.-Chief Judge, North Carolina District Court District 9A-N.C.
Galloway, Michael M.-Associate Judge, Circuit Court for Carroll County, Fifth Judicial Circuit-Md.
Galstad, Richard D.-Reserve Judge, Wisconsin Circuit Court-Wis.
Galton, Sid A.-Judge, Oregon Circuit Court Fourth Judicial District-Ore.
Galvan, Joe H.-Recalled Magistrate Judge, United States District Court District of New Mexico-N.Mex.
Galway, Richard E.-Associate Justice, New Hampshire Superior Court-N.H.
Gama, J. Richard-Judge, Superior Court of Arizona Maricopa County-Ariz.
Gambardella, Rosemary-Chief Judge, United States Bankruptcy Court District of New Jersey-N.J.
Gamber, Terry H.-Circuit Judge, Illinois Circuit Court Second Judicial Circuit-Ill.
Gambill, Bruce David-Associate District Judge, Oklahoma District Court Tenth Judicial District-Okla.
Gambill, C. Cleveland-Magistrate Judge, United States District Court Western District of Kentucky-Ky.
Gamble, Arthur E.-Chief Judge, Iowa District Court Fifth Judicial District-Ia.
Gamble, Brent-Judge, Texas District Court 270th Judicial District-Tex.
Gamble, David R.-Judge, Nevada District Court Ninth Judicial District-Nev.
Gamble, J. Michael-Judge, Virginia Circuit Court Twenty-fourth Judicial Circuit-Va.
Gamble, Rudell M.-Judge, Williamsburg County Probate Court-S.C.
Gambrell, Richard H.-Associate Judge, Illinois Circuit Court Ninth Judicial Circuit-Ill.
Gammerman, Ira-Justice, New York Supreme Court First Judicial District-N.Y.
Gamon, Lucy J.-District Associate Judge, Iowa District Court Eighth Judicial District-Ia.
Gams, Sylvia-Judge, Lovell Municipal Court-Wyo.
Gangel-Jacob, Phyllis B.-Justice, New York Supreme Court First Judicial District-N.Y.
Gangnes, Hilary Benson-Judge, Hawaii District Court First Judicial Circuit-Hi.
Ganim, Paul J.-Judge, Bridgeport District Probate Court-Conn.
Gannon, Edward V.-Judge, New Jersey Superior Court Vicinage Eleven-N.J.
Gannon, John C.-Judge, Rome City Court-N.Y.
Gano, G. Allen-Judge, Ohio Court of Common Pleas Clinton County-Ohio
Gàns, Louise Gruner-Judge, The Civil Court of the City of New York-N.Y.
Gant, Timothy-Judge, Yorktown Town Court-Ind.
Gants, Ralph D.-Associate Justice, Trial Court of Massachusetts Superior Court Department-Mass.
Ganucheau, Anita Hamann-Judge, Orleans Parish Juvenile Court-La.
Garaufis, Nicholas G.-Judge, United States District Court Eastern District of New York-N.Y.
Garaventa, John J.-Judge, Superior Court of California County of Tehama-Calif.
Garbarino, William F.-Judge, Arizona Court of Appeals Division One-Ariz.
Garber, Barry L.-Magistrate Judge, United States District Court Southern District of Florida-Fla.
Garber, Bernard J.-Judge, Superior Court of California County of San Joaquin-Calif.
Garber, Eleanore-Judge, Kentucky Circuit Court Thirtieth Judicial Circuit-Ky.
Garber, Sheldon C.-Associate Judge, Illinois Circuit Court of Cook County-Ill.
Garbis, Marvin J.-Senior Judge, United States District Court District of Maryland-Md.
Garbolino, James Daley-Judge, Superior Court of California County of Placer-Calif.
Garbrecht, Allen L.-Chief Judge, Michigan Circuit Court Thirty-seventh Judicial Circuit-Mich.
Garcia, Carlos A.-Judge, Frio County Court-Tex.
Garcia, David-Judge, Denton County Criminal Court at Law No. 3-Tex.
Garcia, David A.-Judge, Superior Court of California City and County of San Francisco-Calif.
Garcia, Edmundo B., Jr.-Judge, Duval County Court-Tex.
Garcia, Edward J.-Senior Judge, United States District Court Eastern District of California-Calif.
Garcia, Gonzalo-Judge, Texas District Court 210th Judicial District-Tex.
Garcia, Joe B.-Judge, Brooks County Court-Tex.
Garcia, Joseph Alexander, Jr.-Judge, Kenedy County Court-Tex.
Garcia, Lorenzo F.-Magistrate Judge, United States District Court District of New Mexico-N.Mex.
Garcia, Luis M.-Judge, Florida Circuit Court Sixteenth Judicial Circuit-Fla.
Garcia, Michael T.-Judge, Superior Court of California County of Sacramento-Calif.
Garcia, Orlando L.-Judge, United States District Court Western District of Texas-Tex.
Garcia, Patrick Michael-Judge, Texas District Court 384th Judicial District-Tex.
Garcia, Peter J.-Judge, Louisiana District Court Twenty-second Judicial District-La.
Garcia, Ramon-Judge, Hidalgo County Court-Tex.
Garcia, Richard Joseph-Judge, Ingham County Probate Court-Mich.
Garcia, Rodolfo-Circuit Judge, Illinois Circuit Court of Cook County-Ill.
Garcia, Tim-Judge, New Mexico District Court First Judicial District-N.Mex.
Garcia-Gregory, Jay A.-Judge, United States District Court District of Puerto Rico
Gardiner, Ana Isabel-Judge, Florida Circuit Court Seventeenth Judicial Circuit-Fla.
Gardner, Anne-Justice, Texas Court of Appeals Second District-Tex.
Gardner, Hugh C., III-Judge, Superior Court of California County of Los Angeles-Calif.
Gardner, James Knoll-Judge, United States District Court Eastern District of Pennsylvania-Pa.
Gardner, John D.-Associate District Judge, Oklahoma District Court Twenty-third Judicial District-Okla.
Gardner, Mark-Judge, Oregon Circuit Court Twentieth Judicial District-Ore.
Gardner, Patricia D.-Judge, Kent County Probate Court-Mich.
Gardner, Richard-Judge, Arkansas Circuit Court Fifth Judicial Circuit-Ark.
Gardner, Robert W., Jr.-Justice, Trial Court of Massachusetts District Court Department Worcester County Clinton Division-Mass.
Gardner, Sheldon-Circuit Judge, Illinois Circuit Court of Cook County-Ill.
Gardner, Thomas J., III-Judge, Mississippi Circuit Court First Judicial District-Miss.
Gardner, Wendell P., Jr.-Associate Judge, Superior Court of the District of Columbia-D.C.
Gardner, William D.-Reserve Judge, Wisconsin Circuit Court-Wis.
Garfield, Mary-Justice, McCone County Justice of the Peace Court and Judge, Circle City Court-Mont.
Garfinkel, Paul W.-Judge, South Carolina Family Court Ninth Judicial Circuit-S.C.
Garfinkel, William I.-Magistrate Judge, United States District Court District of Connecticut-Conn.
Garibaldi, Colette Y.-Deputy Chief Judge, Hawaii District Court First Judicial Circuit-Hi.
Garibaldi, John J.-Judge, Superior Court of California County of Santa Clara-Calif.
Gariglietti, John C.-Chief Judge, Kansas District Court Eleventh Judicial District-Kan.
Garinger, Gail-First Justice, Trial Court of Massachusetts Juvenile Court Department Middlesex County Division-Mass.
Garland, Grace D.-Chief Magistrate, Magistrate Court of Thomas County-Ga.
Garland, Merrick B.-Judge, United States Court of Appeals District of Columbia Circuit
Garman, Mary B.-Judge, Moorcroft, Sundance and Upton Municipal Courts-Wyo.
Garman, Rita B.-Justice, Supreme Court of Illinois-Ill.
Garmon, Johnnie M.-Chief Magistrate, Magistrate Court of Union County-Ga.
Garner, Carla W.-Judge, Sutton County Court-Tex.
Garner, David Edward-Judge, Texas District Court 10th Judicial District-Tex.
Garner, Robert "Bob"-Judge, Bradley County District Court-Ark.
Garnett, William E.-Judge, The Criminal Court of the City of New York-N.Y.
Garney, Norbert J.-Magistrate Judge, United States District Court Western District of Texas-Tex.
Garofolo, Albert J.-Judge, New Jersey Superior Court Vicinage One-N.J.
Garrahan, Sarah E.-Judge, Bexar County Court at Law No. 4-Tex.
Garrecht, James H.-Judge, Routt County Court-Colo.
Garrett, Jeanette G.-Judge, Louisiana District Court First Judicial District-La.
Garrett, John A.-Judge, Virginia General District Court Fourteenth Judicial District-Va.
Garrett, John C.-District Judge, Oklahoma District Court Fifteenth Judicial District-Okla.
Garrett, Michael-Associate Circuit Judge, Missouri Circuit Court Thirty-ninth Judicial Circuit-Mo.
Garrett, R. Jack-Presiding Judge, Missouri Circuit Court Thirty-seventh Judicial Circuit-Mo.
Garrett, Ramona Joyce-Judge, Superior Court of California County of Solano-Calif.
Garrett, Robert-Judge, Arkansas Circuit Court Twenty-second Judicial Circuit-Ark.
Garrett, Ruth Ann-Judge, Michigan District Court District Thirty-six-Mich.
Garrett, Wayne-Judge, Probate Court of Towns County and Chief Magistrate, Magistrate Court of Towns County-Ga.
Garrigan, Michael N.-Judge, Superior Court of California County of San Joaquin-Calif.
Garrison, Edward A.-Judge, Florida Circuit Court Fifteenth Judicial Circuit-Fla.
Garrison, James E.-Associate Judge, Illinois Circuit Court Twelfth Judicial Circuit-Ill.

ALPHABETICAL NAME INDEX

Garrison, Phillip R.-Judge, Missouri Court of Appeals Southern District-Mo.
Garrow, Janet E.-Judge, King District Court East Division King County-Wash.
Garruto, Bryan D.-Judge, New Jersey Superior Court Vicinage Eight-N.J.
Garry, William J.-Justice, New York Supreme Court Second Judicial District-N.Y.
Garsh, E. Susan-Associate Justice, Trial Court of Massachusetts Superior Court Department-Mass.
Garson, Gerald P.-Justice, New York Supreme Court Second Judicial District-N.Y.
Garson, Michael J.-Justice, New York Supreme Court Second Judicial District-N.Y.
Garson, Robin S.-Judge, The Civil Court of the City of New York-N.Y.
Garth, Lance J.-Justice, Trial Court of Massachusetts District Court Department Barnstable County Orleans Division-Mass.
Garth, Leonard I.-Senior Judge, United States Court of Appeals Third Circuit
Gartner, Kenneth L.-Judge, Nassau County District Court-N.Y.
Gartner, Shelley J.-Magistrate, Vermont Trial Court-Vt.
Garvey, John F.-Associate Circuit Judge, Missouri Circuit Court Twenty-second Judicial Circuit-Mo.
Garvey, Kevin L.-Judge, Kentucky Circuit Court Thirtieth Judicial Circuit-Ky.
Garvey, Margaret-Judge, Rockland County Family Court-N.Y.
Garwood, William L.-Senior Judge, United States Court of Appeals Fifth Circuit
Gary, Michael A.-Judge, The Criminal Court of the City of New York-N.Y.
Gary, William L.-Chief Judge, Florida Circuit Court Second Judicial Circuit-Fla.
Garza, Donna G.-Judge, Superior Court of California County of San Bernardino-Calif.
Garza, Dori Contreras-Justice, Texas Court of Appeals Thirteenth District-Tex.
Garza, Emilio M.-Judge, United States Court of Appeals Fifth Circuit
Garza, Federico "Fred"-Judge, Hidalgo County Court at Law No. 4-Tex.
Garza, G. Jaime-Judge, Hidalgo County Court at Law No. 2-Tex.
Garza, Homero-Judge, Hidalgo County Probate Court-Tex.
Garza, Jesus-Judge, Webb County Court at Law No. 2-Tex.
Garza, Reynaldo G.-Senior Judge, United States Court of Appeals Fifth Circuit
Garza, Robert-Judge, Texas District Court 138th Judicial District-Tex.
Gasaway, Grace Bennett-Judge, Hammond City Court-La.
Gasaway, John H., III-Judge, Tennessee Circuit Court Nineteenth Judicial District-Tenn.
Gasdia, Brian F.-Judge, Superior Court of California County of Los Angeles-Calif.
Gash, Robert T.-Retired-Recalled Judge, North Carolina District Court-N.C.
Gasiorowski, Francis W.-Judge, New Jersey Superior Court Vicinage Thirteen-N.J.
Gaskill, Jay P.-Judge, Idaho District Court Second Judicial District Magistrate Division-Ida.
Gaskins, Gay C.-Judge, Louisiana Court of Appeal Second Circuit-La.
Gasparovic, Gary S.-Associate Judge, Maryland District Court District Four-Md.
Gassaway, Michael Brandon-Judge, McLennan County Court at Law No. 2-Tex.
Gassett, J. Michael-District Judge, Oklahoma District Court Fourteenth Judicial District-Okla.
Gaston, Harley Black, Jr.-Retired-Recalled Judge, North Carolina District Court-N.C.
Gaston, Reginald D.-Special Judge, Oklahoma District Court Twenty-first Judicial District-Okla.
Gaston, Robert E.-Judge, Nevada District Court Eighth Judicial District-Nev.
Gately, Francis A., Jr.-Judge, Superior Court of California County of Los Angeles-Calif.
Gates, Lee A.-Judge, Nevada District Court Eighth Judicial District-Nev.
Gates, Michael L.-Judge, Florida Circuit Court Seventeenth Judicial Circuit-Fla.
Gatewood, Askew W., Jr.-Associate Judge, Maryland District Court District One-Md.
Gatterman, Bruce T.-Chief Judge, Kansas District Court Twenty-fourth Judicial District-Kan.
Gatzert, Norman Joseph-Judge, Superior Court of California County of San Mateo-Calif.
Gaughan, Martin J.-Judge, West Virginia Circuit Court First Judicial Circuit-W.Va.
Gaughan, Patricia Anne-Judge, United States District Court Northern District of Ohio-Ohio
Gaughan, Vincent M.-Circuit Judge, Illinois Circuit Court of Cook County-Ill.
Gaul, Daniel-Judge, Ohio Court of Common Pleas Cuyahoga County-Ohio
Gault, Richard S.-Chief Judge, Superior Court of Georgia Bell-Forsyth Judicial Circuit-Ga.
Gaultney, David B.-Justice, Texas Court of Appeals Ninth District-Tex.
Gausselin, Edwin A., Jr.-Associate Judge, Illinois Circuit Court of Cook County-Ill.
Gaut, Barton C.-Associate Justice, California Court of Appeal Fourth District Division Two-Calif.
Gauvey, Susan K.-Magistrate Judge, United States District Court District of Maryland-Md.
Gavin, F. James-Judge, Washington Superior Court Yakima County-Wash.
Gavin, James J.-Circuit Judge, Illinois Circuit Court of Cook County-Ill.
Gavin, Lee W.-Judge, North Carolina District Court District 19B-N.C.
Gavin, Thomas G.-Judge, Pennsylvania Court of Common Pleas Fifteenth Judicial District-Pa.
Gavrin, Darrell Lori-Judge, The Civil Court of the City of New York-N.Y.
Gayden, Hamilton, Jr.-Judge, Tennessee Circuit Court Twentieth Judicial District-Tenn.
Gaylord, John M.-Judge, Superior Court of Arizona Maricopa County-Ariz.
Gaylord, Shelley-Judge, Wisconsin Circuit Court Dane Circuit-Wis.
Gaynor, Robert E.-Retired Judge, New Jersey Superior Court Appellate Division-N.J.
Gazzara, Anthony V.-Judge, The Civil Court of the City of New York-N.Y.
Gazzillo, Ralph T.-Judge, Suffolk County Court-N.Y.
Gearhart, Van-Judge, Mountain Home District Court-Ark.
Gearin, Kathleen R.-Judge, Minnesota District Court Second Judicial District-Minn.
Geary, James M., Jr.-Justice, Trial Court of Massachusetts District Court Department Middlesex County Ayer Division-Mass.
Gebelein, Richard S.-Associate Judge, Delaware Superior Court New Castle County-Del.
Gebhardt, S. "Shay"-Judge, Bexar County Court at Law No. 3-Tex.
Gebo, A. Michael-Judge, Ogdensburg City Court-N.Y.
Gee, Delbert C.-Judge, Superior Court of California County of Alameda-Calif.
Geeker, Nickolas P.-Judge, Florida Circuit Court First Judicial Circuit-Fla.
Geenty, John Conrad-Justice, Trial Court of Massachusetts District Court Department Worcester County Dudley Division-Mass.
Geer, Martha A.-Associate Judge, North Carolina Court of Appeals-N.C.
Geer, Todd A.-District Judge, Iowa District Court First Judicial District-Ia.
Geeter, Shane-Chief Magistrate, Magistrate Court of Baldwin County-Ga.
Gehl, Peggy-Judge, Broward County Court-Fla.
Gehres, Daniel G.-Judge, Dayton Municipal Court-Ohio
Geiger, Donald H.-Associate Judge, Illinois Circuit Court Nineteenth Judicial Circuit-Ill.
Geiger, Dwight Luther-Judge, Florida Circuit Court Nineteenth Judicial Circuit-Fla.
Geiger, M. Richard-Presiding Judge, North Dakota District Court Northeast Judicial District-N.D.
Geiger, Richard J.-Judge, New Jersey Superior Court Vicinage Fifteen-N.J.
Geisler, Brett L.-Judge, Virginia Circuit Court Twenty-seventh Judicial Circuit-Va.
Gelade, Melvin L.-Judge, New Jersey Superior Court Vicinage Eight-N.J.
Gelber, Seymour-Senior Judge, Florida Circuit Court Eleventh Judicial Circuit-Fla.
Gelfman, Lenore R.-Associate Judge, Circuit Court for Howard County, Fifth Judicial Circuit-Md.
Gelinas, Andre A.-Associate Justice, Massachusetts Appeals Court-Mass.
Gelpi, Gustavo A., Jr.-Magistrate Judge, United States District Court District of Puerto Rico
Gemello, Linda Marino-Associate Justice, California Court of Appeal First District Division Five-Calif.
Gemmill, John C.-Vice Chief Judge, Arizona Court of Appeals Division One-Ariz.
Gempeler, Mark S.-Judge, Wisconsin Circuit Court Waukesha Circuit-Wis.
Genchi, Joan M.-Judge, Suffolk County Family Court-N.Y.
Genden, Michael A.-Judge, Florida Circuit Court Eleventh Judicial Circuit-Fla.
Gendler, Lawrence D.-Judge, Sarpy County Separate Juvenile Court-Neb.
Genesta, George-Judge, Superior Court of California County of Los Angeles-Calif.
Genovese, James T.-Judge, Louisiana District Court Twenty-seventh Judicial District-La.
Gensweider, Leo-Magistrate Judge, Kansas District Court Thirty-first Judicial District-Kan.
Gent, James Wayne-Judge, Kaufman County Court-Tex.
Gentry, L. Michael-Judge, North Carolina District Court District 9A-N.C.
Geoffrion, Anne M.-Circuit Justice, Trial Court of Massachusetts Probate and Family Court Department-Mass.
George, Daniel S.-Judge, Wisconsin Circuit Court Columbia Circuit-Wis.
George, Doughlas M.-Judge, Kentucky Circuit Court Eleventh Judicial Circuit-Ky.
George, Hulane Evans-Judge, Superior Court of Georgia Ocmulgee Judicial Circuit-Ga.
George, Kathryn A.-Judge, Macomb County Probate Court-Mich.
George, Lloyd D.-Senior Judge, United States District Court District of Nevada-Nev.
George, Michael A.-Judge, Pennsylvania Court of Common Pleas Fifty-first Judicial District-Pa.
George, Ronald M.-Chief Justice, California Supreme Court-Calif.
George, Stephanie-Judge, Superior Court of California County of Orange-Calif.
George, Stephen-Justice of the Peace, Henderson Justices' Court-Nev.
George, Stephen M.-Judge, Kentucky Circuit Court Thirtieth Judicial Circuit-Ky.
Georgelis, Michael A.-President Judge, Pennsylvania Court of Common Pleas Second Judicial District-Pa.
Gerace, Joseph-Justice, New York Supreme Court Eighth Judicial District-N.Y.
Geraci, Frank P., Jr.-Judge, Monroe County Court-N.Y.
Gerald, Lenora-Judge, The Civil Court of the City of New York-N.Y.
Gerald, Lynn F., Jr.-Judge, Florida Circuit Court Twentieth Judicial Circuit-Fla.
Gerard, Stephen C., II-District Associate Judge, Iowa District Court Sixth Judicial District-Ia.
Gerber, Joel-Judge, United States Tax Court
Gerber, Jonathan D.-Judge, Palm Beach County Court-Fla.
Gerber, Robert E.-Judge, United States Bankruptcy Court Southern District of New York-N.Y.
Gerges, Abraham G.-Justice, New York Supreme Court Second Judicial District-N.Y.
Gericke, Douglas N.-Judge, Superior Court of California County of San Bernardino-Calif.
Gerken, Thomas H.-Judge, Ohio Court of Common Pleas Hocking County-Ohio
Gerling, Stephen D.-Chief Judge, United States Bankruptcy Court Northern District of New York-N.Y.
German, Marjory A. C.-Associate Justice, Trial Court of Massachusetts Juvenile Court Department Suffolk County Division-Mass.
Germelman, Carle F., Jr.-Judge, Virginia Juvenile and Domestic Relations District Court Twenty-sixth Judicial District-Va.

ALPHABETICAL NAME INDEX

Gernant, David-Judge, Oregon Circuit Court Fourth Judicial District-Ore.
Gernon, Robert-Justice, Kansas Supreme Court-Kan.
Geroff, Steven R.-Judge, Pennsylvania Court of Common Pleas First Judicial District-Pa.
Gerou, Michael J.-Judge, Michigan District Court District Thirty-five-Mich.
Geroulo, Vito P.-Judge, Pennsylvania Court of Common Pleas Forty-fifth Judicial District-Pa.
Gerrard, John M.-Associate Justice, Nebraska Supreme Court-Neb.
Gerschutz, Daniel Richard-Judge, Ohio Court of Common Pleas Putnam County-Ohio
Gershengorn, Wendie I.-Associate Justice, Trial Court of Massachusetts Superior Court Department-Mass.
Gershon, Nina-Judge, United States District Court Eastern District of New York-N.Y.
Gerson, Alfred Sterling-Judge, Jefferson County Court at Law No. 1-Tex.
Gerst, Stephen A.-Judge, Superior Court of Arizona Maricopa County-Ariz.
Gerstein, Norman S.-Judge, Florida Circuit Court Eleventh Judicial Circuit-Fla.
Gersten, Carol R.-Senior Judge, Florida Circuit Court Eleventh Judicial Circuit-Fla.
Gersten, David M.-Judge, Florida District Court of Appeal Third District-Fla.
Gertner, Nancy-Judge, United States District Court District of Massachusetts-Mass.
Gesner, Beth P.-Magistrate Judge, United States District Court District of Maryland-Md.
Gessele, Melody-Justice, Granite County Justice of the Peace Court and Judge, Drummond City Court-Mont.
Gessner, Paul G.-Judge, North Carolina District Court District 10-N.C.
Getachew-Smith, David-Associate Judge, Juvenile Court of Georgia Atlanta Judicial Circuit-Ga.
Geter, Melanie M. Shaw-Associate Judge, Circuit Court for Prince George's County, Seventh Judicial Circuit-Md.
Getker, Sarah K. "Pete"-Justice of the Peace, Meadow Valley Justices' Court-Nev.
Gettleman, Robert W.-Judge, United States District Court Northern District of Illinois-Ill.
Gettys, John P.-Judge, York County Probate Court-S.C.
Getz, Floyd Thomas-Judge, Smith County Court at Law No. 3-Tex.
Gevedon, Kimberly I.-Judge, Kentucky District Court Thirty-seventh Judicial District-Ky.
Gex, Walter J., III-Judge, United States District Court Southern District of Mississippi-Miss.
Giacobbe, Anthony I.-Judge, New York Court of Claims-N.Y.
Giacobbe, George W.-Judge, First Parish Court Jefferson Parish-La.
Giammittorio, E. Robert-Chief Judge, Virginia General District Court Eighteenth Judicial District-Va.
Giardino, Richard C.-Judge, Fulton County Court-N.Y.
Giarrusso, Robin M.-Judge, Louisiana District Court Orleans Parish Civil District-La.
Gibb, Colin R.-Judge, Virginia Circuit Court Twenty-seventh Judicial Circuit-Va.
Gibbons, James D.-Judge, The Criminal Court of the City of New York-N.Y.
Gibbons, Julia Smith-Judge, United States Court of Appeals Sixth Circuit
Gibbons, Mark-Justice, Nevada Supreme Court-Nev.
Gibbons, Michael P.-Judge, Nevada District Court Ninth Judicial District-Nev.
Gibbs, Michael S.-Judge, Wisconsin Circuit Court Walworth Circuit-Wis.
Gibler, Fred M.-Judge, Idaho District Court First Judicial District-Ida.
Gibney, Alice Bridget-Associate Justice, Rhode Island Superior Court-R.I.
Gibson, Bynum-Judge, Arkansas Circuit Court Tenth Judicial Circuit-Ark.
Gibson, Carl G.-Associate District Judge, Oklahoma District Court Eleventh Judicial District-Okla.
Gibson, Carlette W.-Chief Magistrate, Magistrate Court of Pulaski County-Ga.
Gibson, Chuck-Judge, Dermott District Court-Ark.
Gibson, Denny Rodney-Judge, Probate Court of Pickens County-Ga.
Gibson, Dorothy M.-Associate Justice, Trial Court of Massachusetts Probate and Family Court Department Middlesex County Division-Mass.
Gibson, Douglas L.-Judge, State Court of Ware County-Ga.
Gibson, Jay-Judge, Texas District Court 70th Judicial District-Tex.
Gibson, John B.-Judge, Superior Court of California County of San Bernardino-Calif.
Gibson, John R.-Senior Judge, United States Court of Appeals Eighth Circuit
Gibson, Kim R.-Judge, Pennsylvania Court of Common Pleas Sixteenth Judicial District-Pa.
Gibson, Mike-Judge, Osceola District Court-Ark.
Gibson, Reginald W.-Senior Judge, United States Court of Federal Claims
Giddens, Marie M.-Judge, Probate Court of Schley County-Ga.
Giddings, James R.-Judge, Michigan Circuit Court Thirtieth Judicial Circuit-Mich.
Gideon, David S.-Acting Judge, Syracuse City Court-N.Y.
Gienapp, David-Judge, South Dakota Circuit Court Third Judicial Circuit-S.D.
Gierbolini-Ortiz, Gilberto-Senior Judge, United States District Court District of Puerto Rico
Gieringer, Raymond E.-Reserve Judge, Wisconsin Circuit Court-Wis.
Gierke, Herman Frederick "Sparky", III-Associate Judge, United States Court of Appeals for the Armed Forces
Giesler, Kathleen Luebke-Judge, Ohio Court of Common Pleas Ottawa County-Ohio
Gifford, Jack-Judge, Superior Court of California County of Alameda-Calif.
Gifford, Patricia J.-Judge, Marion Superior Court-Ind.
Gigante, Robert J.-Justice, New York Supreme Court Second Judicial District-N.Y.
Giglio, J. Michael-Judge, Juvenile Court of Georgia Lookout Mountain Judicial Circuit-Ga.
Gilardi, Richard P.-Judge, Connecticut Superior Court-Conn.
Gilbert, Arthur-Presiding Justice, California Court of Appeal Second District Division Six-Calif.
Gilbert, David A.-Judge, Colorado District Court Fourth Judicial District-Colo.
Gilbert, Hugh A.-Justice, New York Supreme Court Fifth Judicial District-N.Y.
Gilbert, J. Phil-Judge, United States District Court Southern District of Illinois-Ill.
Gilbert, James H.-Associate Justice, Minnesota Supreme Court-Minn.
Gilbert, John M.-Senior Judge, Florida Circuit Court Thirteenth Judicial Circuit-Fla.
Gilbert, Quintress J.-Judge, Juvenile Court of Georgia Macon Judicial Circuit-Ga.
Gilbert, Roger G.-Judge, Superior Court of California County of Butte-Calif.
Gilbert, Thomas S.-Judge, Michigan District Court District Eighty-six-Mich.
Gilbertson, David-Chief Justice, South Dakota Supreme Court-S.D.
Gilbride, Mary C.-Judge, Nebraska District Court Fifth Judicial District-Neb.
Gilding, William-Assistant Judge, Vermont Trial Court Orleans County-Vt.
Gildner, Stephen P.-Judge, Superior Court of California County of Kern-Calif.
Giles, F. Michael-Judge, New Jersey Superior Court Vicinage Five-N.J.
Giles, James T.-Chief Judge, United States District Court Eastern District of Pennsylvania-Pa.
Giles, Linda E.-Associate Justice, Trial Court of Massachusetts Superior Court Department-Mass.
Gill, Charles D.-Senior Judge, Connecticut Superior Court-Conn.
Gill, Charles Raymond-Judge, Superior Court of California County of San Diego-Calif.
Gill, David M.-Judge, Superior Court of California County of San Diego-Calif.
Gill, Herbert Cogbill, Jr.-Judge, Virginia Circuit Court Twelfth Judicial Circuit-Va.
Gill, Robert K.-Judge, Texas District Court 213th Judicial District-Tex.
Gill, Timothy R.-Circuit Judge, Illinois Circuit Court Seventeenth Judicial Circuit-Ill.
Gill, Tyler L.-Judge, Kentucky Circuit Court Seventh Judicial Circuit-Ky.
Gill-Jefferson, Carolyn W.-Judge, Louisiana District Court Orleans Parish Civil District-La.
Gilleran Johnson, Barbara-Judge, Illinois Appellate Court Second Judicial District-Ill.
Gillert, Tom C.-District Judge, Oklahoma District Court Fourteenth Judicial District-Okla.
Gilles, George D.-Judge, Texas District Court 142nd Judicial District-Tex.
Gillespie, Daniel T.-Associate Judge, Illinois Circuit Court of Cook County-Ill.
Gillespie, Michael J.-Judge, Oregon Circuit Court Fifteenth Judicial District-Ore.
Gillette, Martin-Judge, Probate Court of Camden County-Ga.
Gillette, W. Michael-Justice, Oregon Supreme Court-Ore.
Gilliard, Maryanne G.-Judge, Superior Court of California County of Sacramento-Calif.
Gilligan, Brian F.-Justice, Trial Court of Massachusetts District Court Department Worcester County Milford Division-Mass.
Gilligan, Timothy P.-Judge, Parma Municipal Court-Ohio
Gillis, Donald-Judge, State Court of Treutlen County-Ga.
Gillis, Dwayne Hamilton-Judge, Superior Court of Georgia Waycross Judicial Circuit-Ga.
Gillis, Gregory B.-Associate Circuit Judge, Missouri Circuit Court Sixteenth Judicial Circuit-Mo.
Gillis, John H., Jr.-Judge, Michigan Circuit Court Third Judicial Circuit-Mich.
Gillis, Susan Fox-Associate Judge, Illinois Circuit Court of Cook County-Ill.
Gillison, David F., Jr.-Judge, Lake Village District Court-Ark.
Gillman, Marvin H.-Senior Judge, Dade County Court-Fla.
Gillmor, Helen W.-Judge, United States District Court District of Hawaii-Hi.
Gillum, Forrest E. "Skip"-Judge, Evansville Municipal Court-Wyo.
Gilman, Larry E.-Judge, Virginia Juvenile and Domestic Relations District Court Fifteenth Judicial District-Va.
Gilman, Ronald Lee-Judge, United States Court of Appeals Sixth Circuit
Gilman, Shelley I.-Judge, Colorado District Court Second Judicial District-Colo.
Gilmore, David L.-President Judge, Pennsylvania Court of Common Pleas Twenty-seventh Judicial District-Pa.
Gilmore, Robert W., Jr.-Judge, La Porte Circuit Court-Ind.
Gilmore, Terence-Judge, Colorado District Court Eighth Judicial District-Colo.
Gilmore, Vanessa D.-Judge, United States District Court Southern District of Texas-Tex.
Gilmour, Richard H.-Judge, Superior Court of California County of Sacramento-Calif.
Gilner, Marc-Judge, Florida Circuit Court Twelfth Judicial Circuit-Fla.
Gilpatric, James P.-Judge, Kingston City Court-N.Y.
Gilroy, Patrick D.-Judge, Oregon Circuit Court Fifth Judicial District-Ore.
Gilroy, William P.-Judge, New Jersey Superior Court Vicinage Nine-N.J.
Gindin, William H.-Recalled Judge, United States Bankruptcy Court District of New Jersey-N.J.
Ginex, Gregory R.-Associate Judge, Illinois Circuit Court of Cook County-Ill.
Gingles, Ralph C., Jr.-Judge, North Carolina District Court District 27A-N.C.
Gini, Eugene S., Jr.-Judge, Superior Court of California County of Placer-Calif.
Ginn, Charles Philip-Resident Judge, North Carolina Superior Court Eighth Judicial Division District 24-N.C.
Ginocchio, James P.-Judge, Connecticut Superior Court-Conn.
Ginsberg, Harvey C.-Judge, Minnesota District Court Fourth Judicial District-Minn.

Ginsberg, Robert E.-Recalled Judge, United States Bankruptcy Court Northern District of Illinois-Ill.
Ginsberg, Ronald E.-Judge, State Court of Chatham County-Ga.
Ginsburg, Douglas H.-Chief Judge, United States Court of Appeals District of Columbia Circuit
Ginsburg, Ruth Bader-Associate Justice, The Supreme Court of the United States
Giordano, Raymond J.-Judge, Superior Court of California County of Sonoma-Calif.
Giovan, William J.-Judge, Michigan Circuit Court Third Judicial Circuit-Mich.
Giovine, Peter J.-Judge, New Jersey Superior Court Vicinage Fourteen-N.J.
Girard, Dennis H.-Chief Judge, Michigan District Court District Ninety-six-Mich.
Girardeau, John E.-Judge, Superior Court of Georgia Northeastern Judicial Circuit-Ga.
Girolami, Aldo-Judge, Superior Court of California County of Stanislaus-Calif.
Gische, Judith J.-Judge, The Civil Court of the City of New York-N.Y.
Giss, Harvey-Judge, Superior Court of California County of Los Angeles-Calif.
Gist, Richard D.-Magistrate Judge, United States District Court District of Wyoming-Wyo.
Giulio, Dennis H.-Justice, Jefferson County Justice of the Peace Court and Judge, Boulder and Whitehall City Courts-Mont.
Giunta, Maurice V.-Judge, Florida Circuit Court Eighth Judicial Circuit-Fla.
Givens, Debra L.-Judge, Buffalo City Court-N.Y.
Givhan, Margaret-Judge, Montgomery County District Court-Ala.
Gladstone, William E.-Senior Judge, Florida Circuit Court Eleventh Judicial Circuit-Fla.
Gladwin, Robert-Judge, Arkansas Court of Appeals-Ark.
Glant, David A.-Judge, Florida Circuit Court Eighth Judicial Circuit-Fla.
Glaspie, Kim David-Chief Judge, Michigan District Court District Seventy-one B-Mich.
Glass, Geoffrey T.-Judge, Superior Court of California County of Orange-Calif.
Glass, Jackie-Judge, Nevada District Court Eighth Judicial District-Nev.
Glasser, I. Leo-Senior Judge, United States District Court Eastern District of New York-N.Y.
Glasser, Thomas Daniel-Judge, Superior Court of California County of San Bernardino-Calif.
Glasson, Richard-Justice of the Peace, Tahoe Justices' Court-Nev.
Glatt, James, Jr.-Judge, Orange County Court-Fla.
Glavas, Kosma J.-Judge, Ohio Court of Common Pleas Lorain County-Ohio
Glaze, Tom-Associate Justice, Arkansas Supreme Court-Ark.
Glazebrook, James G.-Magistrate Judge, United States District Court Middle District of Florida-Fla.
Glazer, Gary S.-Judge, Pennsylvania Court of Common Pleas First Judicial District-Pa.
Glazer, Mindy S.-Judge, Florida Circuit Court Eleventh Judicial Circuit-Fla.
Gleason, James T.-Judge, Nebraska District Court Fourth Judicial District-Neb.
Gleason, Richard R.-District Associate Judge, Iowa District Court First Judicial District-Ia.
Gleason, Sharon-Judge, Alaska Superior Court Third Judicial District-Alas.
Gleeson, John-Judge, United States District Court Eastern District of New York-N.Y.
Gleinser, Harold F.-Judge, Goliad County Court-Tex.
Glenn, Alan E.-Judge, Tennessee Court of Criminal Appeals Western Division-Tenn.
Glenn, James R.-Chief Judge, Illinois Circuit Court Fifth Judicial Circuit-Ill.
Glenn, Paul M.-Judge, United States Bankruptcy Court Middle District of Florida-Fla.
Glennon, Bert, Jr.-Judge, Superior Court of California County of Los Angeles-Calif.
Glennon, Charles Edward-Recalled Circuit Judge, Illinois Circuit Court Twenty-first Judicial Circuit-Ill.
Gless, Alan G.-Judge, Nebraska District Court Fifth Judicial District-Neb.
Glick, Leonard E.-Judge, Florida Circuit Court Eleventh Judicial Circuit-Fla.
Glickman, Stephen-Associate Judge, District of Columbia Court of Appeals-D.C.
Globerman, Ira R.-Judge, The Civil Court of the City of New York-N.Y.
Glonek, George L.-Judge, Wisconsin Circuit Court Douglas Circuit-Wis.
Glover, David Mac-Judge, Malvern District Court-Ark.
Glover, Don E.-Judge, Arkansas Circuit Court Tenth Judicial Circuit-Ark.
Glover, Irma-Judge, State Court of Cobb County-Ga.
Glover, Thomas T.-Judge, United States Bankruptcy Court Western District of Washington-Wash.
Glover, William T.-Justice, New York Supreme Court Eleventh Judicial District-N.Y.
Glowacki, Francis W.-Circuit Judge, Illinois Circuit Court of Cook County-Ill.
Glowinsky, Carol-Judge, Colorado District Court Twentieth Judicial District-Colo.
Glownia, Joseph R.-Justice, New York Supreme Court Eighth Judicial District-N.Y.
Gluchowski, Paul F.-Judge, Virginia Juvenile and Domestic Relations District Court Thirty-first Judicial District-Va.
Glusman, Robert A.-Judge, Superior Court of California County of Butte-Calif.
Glynn, John M.-Associate Judge, Circuit Court for Baltimore City, Eighth Judicial Circuit-Md.
Go, Marilyn D.-Magistrate Judge, United States District Court Eastern District of New York-N.Y.
Gober, Bob Wayne-Judge, Hemphill County Court-Tex.
Gober, C. J., Jr.-Judge, State Court of Cherokee County-Ga.
Godbey, David C.-Judge, United States District Court Northern District of Texas-Tex.
Godbold, John C.-Senior Judge, United States Court of Appeals Eleventh Circuit
Goddard, Houston M.-Judge, Tennessee Court of Appeals Eastern Division-Tenn.
Goderich, Mario P.-Judge, Florida District Court of Appeal Third District-Fla.
Godfrey, Gordon L.-Judge, Washington Superior Court Grays Harbor County-Wash.
Godich, John Paul-Recalled Magistrate Judge, United States District Court Southern District of Indiana-Ind.
Godwin, George H.-Judge, Texas District Court 174th Judicial District-Tex.
Godzala, Thomas A.-Judge, Minnesota District Court Seventh Judicial District-Minn.
Goebel, E. Robert-Magistrate Judge, United States District Court Western District of Kentucky-Ky.
Goebel, Robert E., Jr.-Chief Judge, Delta County Probate Court-Mich.
Goeke, Joseph A., III-Associate Circuit Judge, Missouri Circuit Court Twenty-first Judicial Circuit-Mo.
Goelz, Douglas-Judge, South District Court Pacific County-Wash.
Goethals, Thomas M.-Judge, Superior Court of California County of Orange-Calif.
Goettel, Gerard L.-Senior Judge, United States District Court Southern District of New York-N.Y.
Goetz, C. Robert-Judge, Glendo Municipal Court-Wyo.
Goger, John J.-Judge, Superior Court of Georgia Atlanta Judicial Circuit-Ga.
Goggins, David J.-Judge, Michigan District Court District Sixty-seven Division One-Mich.
Goggins, W. Michael-Justice, Trial Court of Massachusetts District Court Department Hampshire County Northampton Division-Mass.
Gohman, Cheryl Anne-Judge, North Manchester Town Court-Ind.
Golar, Simeon-Justice, New York Supreme Court Eleventh Judicial District-N.Y.
Gold, Alan S.-Judge, United States District Court Southern District of Florida-Fla.
Gold, David P.-Judge, Connecticut Superior Court-Conn.
Gold, Lila P.-Judge, The Civil Court of the City of New York-N.Y.
Gold, Marc H.-Judge, Florida Circuit Court Seventeenth Judicial Circuit-Fla.
Gold, Steven M.-Magistrate Judge, United States District Court Eastern District of New York-N.Y.
Goldberg, Allen S.-Circuit Judge, Illinois Circuit Court of Cook County-Ill.
Goldberg, Arlene D.-Judge, The Criminal Court of the City of New York-N.Y.
Goldberg, Hank-Judge, Superior Court of California County of Los Angeles-Calif.
Goldberg, Joel M.-Judge, The Criminal Court of the City of New York-N.Y.
Goldberg, Joseph H.-Judge Referee, Connecticut Superior Court-Conn.
Goldberg, Martin R.-Magistrate Judge, United States District Court Southern District of New York-N.Y.
Goldberg, Maureen McKenna-Associate Justice, Rhode Island Supreme Court-R.I.
Goldberg, Mitchel Roy-Judge, United States Bankruptcy Court Central District of California-Calif.
Goldberg, Richard W.-Senior Judge, United States Court of International Trade
Goldberg, Stanley J.-Special Trial Judge, United States Tax Court
Goldberger, Kim H.-Judge, Jefferson County Court-Colo.
Golden, Joe Bob-Judge, Texas District Court 1st Judicial District-Tex.
Golden, Patricia P.-Associate Judge, Illinois Circuit Court Sixteenth Judicial Circuit-Ill.
Golden, Thomas Michael-Justice, Wyoming Supreme Court-Wyo.
Goldenberg, Renee-Judge, Florida Circuit Court Seventeenth Judicial Circuit-Fla.
Goldenhersh, Richard P.-Judge, Illinois Appellate Court Fifth Judicial District-Ill.
Goldgar, A. Benjamin-Judge, United States Bankruptcy Court Northern District of Illinois-Ill.
Goldie, Susan L.-Judge, Xenia Municipal Court-Ohio
Goldin, Arnold-Chancellor, Tennessee Chancery Court Thirtieth Judicial District-Tenn.
Goldman, Donald S.-Judge, New Jersey Superior Court Vicinage Five-N.J.
Goldman, Judith M.-Judge, Sarasota County Court-Fla.
Goldman, Marc L.-Magistrate Judge, United States District Court Central District of California-Calif.
Goldman, Murray-Senior Judge, Florida Circuit Court Eleventh Judicial Circuit-Fla.
Goldman, Steven H.-Circuit Judge, Missouri Circuit Court Twenty-first Judicial Circuit-Mo.
Goldsberry, L. Alan-Judge, Ohio Court of Common Pleas Athens County-Ohio
Goldsmith, Brooks P.-Judge, South Carolina Family Court Sixth Judicial Circuit-S.C.
Goldsmith, Christine K.-Judge, Superior Court of California County of San Diego-Calif.
Goldsmith, Ernest H.-Judge, Superior Court of California City and County of San Francisco-Calif.
Goldsmith, Jan-Judge, Superior Court of California County of San Diego-Calif.
Goldstein, Barry E.-Judge, Florida Circuit Court Seventeenth Judicial Circuit-Fla.
Goldstein, Carl-Associate Judge, Delaware Superior Court New Castle County-Del.
Goldstein, Daniel B.-Judge, Superior Court of California County of San Diego-Calif.
Goldstein, David-Justice, New York Supreme Court Eleventh Judicial District-N.Y.
Goldstein, Ferne J.-Judge, The Civil Court of the City of New York-N.Y.
Goldstein, Gloria-Associate Justice, New York Supreme Court Appellate Division Second Judicial Department-N.Y.
Goldstein, Samuel S.-Judge Referee, Connecticut Superior Court-Conn.
Goldwater, Bert M.-Recalled Judge, United States Bankruptcy Court District of Nevada-Nev.
Golia, James J.-Judge, The Civil Court of the City of New York-N.Y.

ALPHABETICAL NAME INDEX

ALPHABETICAL NAME INDEX

Graffeo, Victoria A.-Associate Judge, New York Court of Appeals-N.Y.

Graham, Dennis A.-Judge, Colorado Court of Appeals-Colo.

Graham, Donald L.-Judge, United States District Court Southern District of Florida-Fla.

Graham, Gordon E.-Associate Judge, Illinois Circuit Court Nineteenth Judicial Circuit-Ill.

Graham, James E.-Magistrate Judge, United States District Court Southern District of Georgia-Ga.

Graham, James L.-Judge, United States District Court Southern District of Ohio-Ohio

Graham, James T.-Judge, Connecticut Superior Court-Conn.

Graham, Jeanne J.-Judge, Minnesota District Court Fourth Judicial District-Minn.

Graham, John Stephen-Judge, Superior Court of California County of Marin-Calif.

Graham, L. Dale-Judge, North Carolina District Court District 22-N.C.

Graham, R. Malcolm-Associate Justice, Trial Court of Massachusetts Superior Court Department-Mass.

Graham, Richard S.-Judge, Florida Circuit Court Seventh Judicial Circuit-Fla.

Graham, Terry-Justice of the Peace, Wadsworth Justices' Court-Nev.

Graham, Thomas W. "Rusty"-Judge, Tennessee Circuit Court Twelfth Judicial District-Tenn.

Graham, Tracy-Judge, Juvenile Court of Georgia Clayton Judicial Circuit-Ga.

Graham, Wendell M.-Judge, Dade County Court-Fla.

Graham, William Louis-Judge, Kentucky Circuit Court Forty-eighth Judicial Circuit-Ky.

Graham, William T., Jr.-Judge, North Carolina District Court District 21-N.C.

Graham Harrell, Kimbara-Associate Judge, Illinois Circuit Court Second Judicial Circuit-Ill.

Grall, Jane-Judge, New Jersey Superior Court Vicinage Seven-N.J.

Gram, Laurence C.-Reserve Judge, Wisconsin Circuit Court-Wis.

Gramlich, Charles J.-Associate Judge, Illinois Circuit Court Seventh Judicial Circuit-Ill.

Granade, Callie V.-Judge, United States District Court Southern District of Alabama-Ala.

Granger, Russell H.-Judge, Clear Creek County Court-Colo.

Granier, Kirk R.-Judge, Louisiana District Court Twenty-ninth Judicial District-La.

Grant, Barry M.-Judge, Oakland County Probate Court-Mich.

Grant, Cheryl D.-Judge, Hamilton County Municipal Court-Ohio

Grant, Cy A.-Resident Judge, North Carolina Superior Court First Judicial Division District 6B-N.C.

Grant, Edward-Judge, Wyoming District Court First Judicial District-Wyo.

Grant, Edward J.-Judge, Michigan Circuit Court Fourth Judicial Circuit-Mich.

Grant, Garrett J.-Judge, Superior Court of California County of Contra Costa-Calif.

Grant, Glenn A.-Judge, New Jersey Superior Court Vicinage Five-N.J.

Grant, Jo Ellen-Judge, Louisiana District Court Twenty-fourth Judicial District-La.

Grant, John S., III-Judge, Mississippi Chancery Court Twentieth Judicial District-Miss.

Grant, Joshua F.-Judge, Lincoln District Court Lincoln County-Wash.

Grant, Laura-Justice of the Peace, East Line Justices' Court and Judge, West Wendover Municipal Court-Nev.

Grant, Linda K.-Judge, Freestone County Court-Tex.

Grant, Nanci J.-Judge, Michigan Circuit Court Sixth Judicial Circuit-Mich.

Grant, Robert E.-Judge, United States Bankruptcy Court Northern District of Indiana-Ind.

Grant, Susan H.-Chief Judge, Michigan District Court District Seventy-seven-Mich.

Granville, Warren J.-Judge, Superior Court of Arizona Maricopa County-Ariz.

Grasso, Joseph A., Jr.-Associate Justice, Massachusetts Appeals Court-Mass.

Grasso, Vincent J.-Judge, New Jersey Superior Court Vicinage Fourteen-N.J.

Grathwohl, Casper O.-Judge, Michigan Circuit Court Second Judicial Circuit-Mich.

Grau, Gregory E.-Judge, Wisconsin Circuit Court Marathon Circuit-Wis.

Graulty, Reynaldo D.-Judge, Hawaii Circuit Court First Judicial Circuit-Hi.

Gravens, Maureen A.-Judge, Rocky River Municipal Court-Ohio

Graves, Calvin S.-Judge, City Court of Atlanta-Ga.

Graves, Dennis-Judge, Oregon Circuit Court Third Judicial District-Ore.

Graves, James E., Jr.-Justice, Mississippi Supreme Court-Miss.

Graves, James M., Jr.-Judge, Michigan Circuit Court Fourteenth Judicial Circuit-Mich.

Graves, John William "Bill"-Justice, Kentucky Supreme Court-Ky.

Graves, Leslie J.-Circuit Judge, Illinois Circuit Court Seventh Judicial Circuit-Ill.

Graves, Ronald B.-Judge, New Jersey Superior Court Vicinage Ten-N.J.

Graves, T. Henley-Resident Judge, Delaware Superior Court Sussex County-Del.

Grawey, Richard E.-Circuit Judge, Illinois Circuit Court Tenth Judicial Circuit-Ill.

Gray, Alcide J.-Judge, Louisiana District Court Fourteenth Judicial District-La.

Gray, Alice Sprinkle-Judge, Arkansas Circuit Court Sixth Judicial Circuit-Ark.

Gray, Charlotte S.-Justice of the Peace, Morrow County Justice Court-Ore.

Gray, Dudley W., II-Judge, Superior Court of California County of Los Angeles-Calif.

Gray, Ernestine S.-Judge, Orleans Parish Juvenile Court-La.

Gray, G. Thomas-Judge, Morgan Superior Court-Ind.

Gray, James P.-Judge, Superior Court of California County of Orange-Calif.

Gray, Jane Powell-Judge, North Carolina District Court District 10-N.C.

Gray, Jerry C.-Judge, State Court of Jackson County-Ga.

Gray, Jimmylee-Judge, Michigan District Court District Thirty-six-Mich.

Gray, Joe S.-Judge, Superior Court of California County of Sacramento-Calif.

Gray, Jon R.-Circuit Judge, Missouri Circuit Court Sixteenth Judicial Circuit-Mo.

Gray, Karla M.-Chief Justice, Montana Supreme Court-Mont.

Gray, Lawrence C.-Associate Judge, Illinois Circuit Court Twelfth Judicial Circuit-Ill.

Gray, Loring Albert, Jr.-Chief Judge, Superior Court of Georgia Dougherty Judicial Circuit-Ga.

Gray, Marvin Kenneth-Retired-Recalled Judge, North Carolina Superior Court-N.C.

Gray, Mauri DeWaun-Associate Judge, Juvenile Court of Georgia Middle Judicial Circuit-Ga.

Gray, Thomas E.-Chancellor, Tennessee Chancery Court Eighteenth Judicial District-Tenn.

Gray, Thomas W.-Justice, Texas Court of Appeals Tenth District-Tex.

Gray, Twyla Mason-District Judge, Oklahoma District Court Seventh Judicial District-Okla.

Grays, Marguerite A.-Justice, New York Supreme Court Eleventh Judicial District-N.Y.

Grayson, Greg-Judge, Probate Court of Catoosa County-Ga.

Graziani, Edward C.-Judge, Connecticut Superior Court-Conn.

Graziano, Anthony J.-Judge, New Jersey Superior Court Vicinage Eleven-N.J.

Greaney, John M.-Associate Justice, Massachusetts Supreme Judicial Court-Mass.

Greanias, John K.-Circuit Judge, Illinois Circuit Court Sixth Judicial Circuit-Ill.

Greco, Robert V.-First Justice, Trial Court of Massachusetts District Court Department Middlesex County Framingham Division-Mass.

Greeley, Timothy P.-Magistrate Judge, United States District Court Western District of Michigan-Mich.

Green, Alan J.-Judge, Louisiana District Court Twenty-fourth Judicial District-La.

Green, Alvin E., Jr.-Judge, Superior Court of California County of San Diego-Calif.

Green, Brenda-Judge, Texas District Court 256th Judicial District-Tex.

Green, Clifford Scott-Senior Judge, United States District Court Eastern District of Pennsylvania-Pa.

Green, David Walker-Judge, Walton County Court-Fla.

Green, Dennis G.-Magistrate Judge, United States District Court Western District of Texas-Tex.

Green, Gordon Houston-Judge, Texas District Court 287th Judicial District-Tex.

Green, Henry W., Jr.-Judge, Kansas Court of Appeals-Kan.

Green, J. W., Jr.-Judge, Stuttgart District Court-Ark.

Green, James E.-Judge, Franklin County Municipal Court-Ohio

Green, Jennifer M.-Judge, North Carolina District Court District 10-N.C.

Green, Larry J.-Judge, Louisiana District Court Twenty-second Judicial District-La.

Green, Leo Edward, Jr.-Associate Judge, Maryland District Court District Five-Md.

Green, Mark V.-Associate Justice, Massachusetts Appeals Court-Mass.

Green, Mary Catherine-Judge, Polk County Court-Fla.

Green, Melvia B.-Judge, Florida District Court of Appeal Third District-Fla.

Green, Nancy Hand-Judge, Bamberg County Probate Court-S.C.

Green, Oliver L., Jr.-Senior Judge, Florida District Court of Appeal-Fla.

Green, Paul W.-Justice, Texas Court of Appeals Fourth District-Tex.

Green, R. A., Jr.-Senior Judge, Florida Circuit Court Eighth Judicial Circuit-Fla.

Green, Samuel L.-Associate Justice, New York Supreme Court Appellate Division Fourth Judicial Department-N.Y.

Green, Stanley B.-Judge, The Civil Court of the City of New York-N.Y.

Green, Terry A.-Judge, Superior Court of California County of Los Angeles-Calif.

Green, Tina Brooks-Chief Judge, Michigan District Court District Thirty-four-Mich.

Green, Tomie T.-Judge, Mississippi Circuit Court Seventh Judicial District-Miss.

Greenacre, Charles R.-Judge, Colorado District Court Seventh Judicial District and Judge, Colorado Water Court Division Four-Colo.

Greenaway, Joseph A., Jr.-Judge, United States District Court District of New Jersey-N.J.

Greenberg, Ethan-Judge, The Criminal Court of the City of New York-N.Y.

Greenberg, Mark-Judge, Dallas County Court at Law No. 5-Tex.

Greenberg, Martin L.-Retired Judge, New Jersey Superior Court-N.J.

Greenberg, Mel L.-Associate Justice, Massachusetts Appeals Court-Mass.

Greenberg, Morton I.-Senior Judge, United States Court of Appeals Third Circuit

Greenberg, Myron S.-Judge, Minnesota District Court Fourth Judicial District-Minn.

Greendyke, William R.-Chief Judge, United States Bankruptcy Court Southern District of Texas-Tex.

Greene, Charles M.-Judge, Florida Circuit Court Seventeenth Judicial Circuit-Fla.

Greene, Clayton, Jr.-Associate Judge, Court of Special Appeals of Maryland-Md.

Greene, Deborah S.-Judge, Municipal Court of Atlanta-Ga.

Greene, George R.-Judge, Alabama Circuit Court Twenty-sixth Judicial Circuit-Ala.

Greene, Henry F.-Senior Judge, Superior Court of the District of Columbia-D.C.

Greene, J. Mike-Judge, Probate Court of Jones County and Chief Magistrate, Magistrate Court of Jones County-Ga.

Greene, J. Thomas-Senior Judge, United States District Court District of Utah-Utah

Greene, Joseph F., Jr.-Retired Judge, New Jersey Superior Court-N.J.

Greene, Karen Jane-Judge, Texas District Court 282nd Judicial District-Tex.

ALPHABETICAL NAME INDEX

Greene, Lillian J.-Judge, Ohio Court of Common Pleas Cuyahoga County-Ohio
Greene, Mathew H.-Judge, New London District Probate Court-Conn.
Greene, Michael-Judge, Recorder's Court of Gwinnett County-Ga.
Greene, Paul W.-Magistrate Judge, United States District Court Northern District of Alabama-Ala.
Greene, Richard-Judge, Kansas Court of Appeals-Kan.
Greene, Warren G.-Judge, Superior Court of California County of Los Angeles-Calif.
Greene, William P., Jr.-Judge, United States Court of Appeals for Veterans Claims
Greene-Thapedi, Llwellyn-Circuit Judge, Illinois Circuit Court of Cook County-Ill.
Greenlee, John K.-Judge, North Carolina District Court District 27A-N.C.
Greenlief, Richard D.-Circuit Judge, Illinois Circuit Court Eighth Judicial Circuit-Ill.
Greenspan, Jane Cutler-Judge, Pennsylvania Court of Common Pleas First Judicial District-Pa.
Greenwald, Arthur M.-Judge, United States Bankruptcy Court Central District of California-Calif.
Greenwalt, J. Frank, Jr.-Judge, Virginia General District Court Twenty-first Judicial District-Va.
Greenwell, Tom-Judge, Texas Family District Court 319th Judicial District-Tex.
Greenwood, John E.-Judge, North Dakota District Court Southeast Judicial District-N.D.
Greenwood, Pamela T.-Judge, Utah Court of Appeals-Utah
Greenwood, Richard G.-Reserve Judge, Wisconsin Circuit Court-Wis.
Greenwood, Theodore-Judge, Newcastle Municipal Court-Wyo.
Greer, George W.-Judge, Florida Circuit Court Sixth Judicial Circuit-Fla.
Greer, Kevin L.-Judge, Ohio Court of Common Pleas Highland County-Ohio
Greeson, Howard R., Jr.-Emergency Judge, North Carolina Superior Court-N.C.
Grefer, Stephen-Judge, Second Parish Court Jefferson Parish-La.
Gregg, James D.-Chief Judge, United States Bankruptcy Court Western District of Michigan-Mich.
Gregg, John-Judge, Batesville District Court-Ark.
Gregg, Sherry L. Biddinger-Judge, Knox Circuit Court-Ind.
Gregory, Edgar B.-Chief Judge, North Carolina District Court District 23-N.C.
Gregory, Jackson V.-Judge, South Carolina Circuit Court Fourteenth Judicial Circuit-S.C.
Gregory, Lewis J.-Judge, Greenwood City Court-Ind.
Gregory, Roger L.-Judge, United States Court of Appeals Fourth Circuit
Gregory, Toy R.-Judge, Las Vegas Municipal Court-Nev.
Greiman, Alan J.-Circuit Judge, Illinois Circuit Court of Cook County-Ill.
Gremillion, Glenn B.-Judge, Louisiana Court of Appeal Third Circuit-La.
Grendell, Diane V.-Judge, Ohio Court of Appeals Eleventh District-Ohio
Gretick, Anthony L.-Judge, Ohio Court of Common Pleas Williams County-Ohio
Gretkowski, Elizabeth-Assistant Judge, Vermont Trial Court Chittenden County-Vt.
Gribetz, Sidney H.-Judge, New York City Family Court-N.Y.
Grider, Ralph H.-Judge, Jackson County District Court-Ala.
Gridley, William C.-Judge, Florida Circuit Court Ninth Judicial Circuit-Fla.
Griesa, Thomas P.-Senior Judge, United States District Court Southern District of New York-N.Y.
Griesbach, William C.-Judge, United States District Court Eastern District of Wisconsin-Wis.
Griesbaum, John M.-Judge, Florida Circuit Court Eighteenth Judicial Circuit-Fla.
Griffen, Wendell L.-Judge, Arkansas Court of Appeals-Ark.
Griffin, Belinda F.-Judge, Probate Court of Crisp County-Ga.
Griffin, Brian T.-Judge, Windsor District Probate Court-Conn.
Griffin, Burt W.-Judge, Ohio Court of Common Pleas Cuyahoga County-Ohio
Griffin, Frank-Judge, Brown County Court at Law No. 1-Tex.
Griffin, Guy William-Judge, Texas District Court 123rd Judicial District-Tex.
Griffin, Hendon H.-Chief Magistrate, Magistrate Court of Chattahoochee County-Ga.
Griffin, Henry McHenry, III-Judge, Kentucky Circuit Court Sixth Judicial Circuit-Ky.
Griffin, Jacqueline R.-Judge, Florida District Court of Appeal Fifth District-Fla.
Griffin, James P.-Judge, The Criminal Court of the City of New York-N.Y.
Griffin, Joe E.-Judge, Arkansas Circuit Court Eighth South Judicial Circuit-Ark.
Griffin, John E., Jr.-Judge, Superior Court of California County of Stanislaus-Calif.
Griffin, Johnny Frank-Judge, Schleicher County Court-Tex.
Griffin, Juliet-Magistrate Judge, United States District Court Middle District of Tennessee-Tenn.
Griffin, Linda C.-Judge, Rensselaer County Family Court-N.Y.
Griffin, Michael J.-Judge, Idaho District Court Second Judicial District Magistrate Division-Ida.
Griffin, Michael R.-Judge, Nevada District Court First Judicial District-Nev.
Griffin, Piper D.-Judge, Louisiana District Court Orleans Parish Civil District-La.
Griffin, Richard Allen-Judge, Michigan Court of Appeals-Mich.
Griffin, Stephen K.-Presiding Judge, Missouri Circuit Court Forty-third Judicial Circuit-Mo.
Griffin, William C., Jr.-Resident Judge, North Carolina Superior Court First Judicial Division District 2-N.C.
Griffis, T. Kenneth-Judge, Court of Appeals of Mississippi-Miss.
Griffith, Carl R., Jr.-Judge, Jefferson County Court-Tex.
Griffith, Charles D., Jr.-Judge, Virginia Circuit Court Fourth Judicial Circuit-Va.
Griffith, James R.-Judge, Oneida County Family Court-N.Y.
Griffith, Michael F.-Judge, Wyoming County Court-N.Y.
Griffith, Sam-Justice, Texas Court of Appeals Twelfth District-Tex.
Griffiths, David B.-Judge, Maine District Court-Me.
Grignon, Margaret M.-Associate Justice, California Court of Appeal Second District Division Five-Calif.
Grigsby, Michael-Judge, Marysville Municipal Court-Ohio
Grilli, Mary Ann-Judge, Superior Court of California County of Santa Clara-Calif.
Grillo, N. Robert-Judge, Ohio Court of Common Pleas Vinton County-Ohio
Grim, Arthur E.-Judge, Pennsylvania Court of Common Pleas Twenty-third Judicial District-Pa.
Grimes, Elizabeth A.-Judge, Superior Court of California County of Los Angeles-Calif.
Grimes, H. Terry-President Judge, Pennsylvania Court of Common Pleas Thirteenth Judicial District-Pa.
Grimes, Hubert L.-Judge, Florida Circuit Court Seventh Judicial Circuit-Fla.
Grimes, J. Kevin-Judge, Alabama Circuit Court Ninth Judicial Circuit-Ala.
Grimes, Samuel G.-Judge, North Carolina District Court District 2-N.C.
Grimm, Fredric A., Jr.-Judge, Michigan District Court District Sixty-Mich.
Grimm, Hadley E.-Presiding Judge, Missouri Circuit Court Forty-first Judicial Circuit-Mo.
Grimm, John W.-Circuit Judge, Missouri Circuit Court Thirty-second Judicial Circuit-Mo.
Grimm, Paul W.-Magistrate Judge, United States District Court District of Maryland-Md.
Grimm, Peter L.-Judge, Wisconsin Circuit Court Fond du Lac Circuit-Wis.
Grimmer, Dan-Judge, Superior Court of California County of Alameda-Calif.
Grincewicz, Donald E.-Judge, Florida Circuit Court Ninth Judicial Circuit-Fla.
Grine, David E.-Judge, Pennsylvania Court of Common Pleas Forty-ninth Judicial District-Pa.
Griner, Susan W.-Judge, Probate Court of Berrien County-Ga.
Grisham, Ray Felty-Judge, Texas District Court 336th Judicial District-Tex.
Gritt, Franklin L., Jr.-Judge, West Virginia Court of Claims-W.Va.
Gritton, Thomas J.-Judge, Wisconsin Circuit Court Winnebago Circuit-Wis.
Gritzner, James E.-Judge, United States District Court Southern District of Iowa-Ia.
Grodner, Teena D.-Judge, Virginia Juvenile and Domestic Relations District Court Nineteenth Judicial District-Va.
Grodnik, Charles H.-Judge, Elkhart City Court-Ind.
Groff, William J.-Associate Justice, New Hampshire Superior Court-N.H.
Grogan, J. B.-Associate Judge, Illinois Circuit Court of Cook County-Ill.
Grogins, Jack L.-Judge Referee, Connecticut Superior Court-Conn.
Grometer, R. Peter-Circuit Judge, Illinois Circuit Court Sixteenth Judicial Circuit-Ill.
Groneman, George A.-Judge, Kansas District Court Twenty-ninth Judicial District-Kan.
Groner, David Alan-Judge, Michigan Circuit Court Third Judicial Circuit-Mich.
Gropper, Allan L.-Judge, United States Bankruptcy Court Southern District of New York-N.Y.
Grosko, Michael-Judge, Kansas District Court Twenty-ninth Judicial District-Kan.
Gross, Bruce F.-Judge, Minnesota District Court Fifth Judicial District-Minn.
Gross, David A.-Judge, Nassau County District Court-N.Y.
Gross, Lisa M.-Judge, State Court of Screven County-Ga.
Gross, Maynard "Skip"-Judge, Florida Circuit Court Eleventh Judicial Circuit-Fla.
Gross, Michael A.-Judge, The Criminal Court of the City of New York-N.Y.
Gross, Raymond O.-Judge, Florida Circuit Court Sixth Judicial Circuit-Fla.
Gross, Robert M.-Judge, Florida District Court of Appeal Fourth District-Fla.
Grosse, C. Kenneth-Judge, Washington Court of Appeals Division I-Wash.
Grossi, Gilbert J.-Associate Judge, Illinois Circuit Court of Cook County-Ill.
Grossi, Patrick S.-Circuit Judge, Illinois Circuit Court of Cook County-Ill.
Grossman, Harlan G.-Judge, Superior Court of California County of Contra Costa-Calif.
Grossman, Mel-Judge, Florida Circuit Court Seventeenth Judicial Circuit-Fla.
Grosso, Joseph A.-Judge, The Criminal Court of the City of New York-N.Y.
Grosvenor, Paul H.-Judge, New York City Family Court-N.Y.
Grosz, Richard W.-Judge, North Dakota District Court Southeast Judicial District-N.D.
Grothaus, Douglas-Judge, Kentucky District Court Sixteenth Judicial District-Ky.
Groton, Thomas C., III-Associate Judge, Circuit Court for Worcester County, First Judicial Circuit-Md.
Grove, Ted E.-Judge, Oregon Circuit Court Nineteenth Judicial District-Ore.
Grover, Adrienne M.-Judge, Superior Court of California County of Monterey-Calif.
Grover, Kevin-Judge, Calhoun County Court-Fla.
Grover, Thomas G.-Judge, Wisconsin Circuit Court Shawano-Menominee Circuit-Wis.
Groves, Emanuella D.-Judge, Cleveland Municipal Court-Ohio
Grow, John W.-Justice, New York Supreme Court Fifth Judicial District-N.Y.
Grubb, George E.-Judge, Jeff Davis County Court-Tex.
Grubb, Gerald F.-Chief Judge, Illinois Circuit Court Seventeenth Judicial Circuit-Ill.
Grubb, Janet A.-Judge, Franklin County Municipal Court-Ohio
Grubbs, Adele-Judge, Superior Court of Georgia Cobb Judicial Circuit-Ga.
Grubbs, Ray Wilson-Judge, Virginia Circuit Court Twenty-seventh Judicial Circuit-Va.

ALPHABETICAL NAME INDEX

Grube, James R.-Judge, United States Bankruptcy Court Northern District of California-Calif.
Grube, Karl B.-Judge, Pinellas County Court-Fla.
Gruber, Rita-Judge, Arkansas Circuit Court Sixth Judicial Circuit-Ark.
Gruber, Wayne-Judge, Pulaski County District Court-Ark.
Gruenburg, Dawnn M.-Judge, Michigan District Court District Thirty-seven-Mich.
Gruendel, F. Herbert-Judge, Connecticut Superior Court-Conn.
Grupp, Carlynn D.-District Associate Judge, Iowa District Court Second Judicial District-Ia.
Grussel, Susan Ruscitti-Circuit Judge, Illinois Circuit Court of Cook County-Ill.
Guadagni, Raymond A.-Judge, Superior Court of California County of Napa-Calif.
Guaderrama, David C.-Judge, Texas District Court 243rd Judicial District-Tex.
Gubbay, Joseph E.-Judge, The Criminal Court of the City of New York-N.Y.
Gubow, David M.-Chief Judge, Michigan District Court District Forty-five B-Mich.
Guckenberger, Guy C.-Judge, Hamilton County Municipal Court-Ohio
Guenther, Mark-Judge, Montana District Court Eighteenth Judicial District-Mont.
Guertin, Richard J.-Judge, Middletown City Court-N.Y.
Guess, Robert E.-Judge, South Carolina Family Court Sixteenth Judicial Circuit-S.C.
Guess, William Marion, Jr.-Judge, Probate Court of DeKalb County-Ga.
Guice, Zoro J., Jr.-Resident Judge, North Carolina Superior Court Eighth Judicial Division District 29-N.C.
Guido, Edward E.-Judge, Pennsylvania Court of Common Pleas Ninth Judicial District-Pa.
Guidry, Greg Gerard-Judge, Louisiana District Court Twenty-fourth Judicial District-La.
Guidry, John Michael-Judge, Louisiana Court of Appeal First Circuit-La.
Guidry, Kevin J.-Judge, Juvenile Court of Georgia Piedmont Judicial Circuit-Ga.
Guidry-Whipple, Vanessa-Judge, Louisiana Court of Appeal First Circuit-La.
Guidugli, Daniel T.-Judge, Kentucky Court of Appeals-Ky.
Guiliani, Richard J.-Judge, Superior Court of California County of San Joaquin-Calif.
Guillory, Glenn D.-Judge, Aransas County Court-Tex.
Guimond, Joseph C.-Judge, Oregon Circuit Court Third Judicial District-Ore.
Guin, James C., III-Judge, Tuscaloosa County District Court-Ala.
Guin, Junius Foy, Jr.-Senior Judge, United States District Court Northern District of Alabama-Ala.
Guinn, Julian P.-Judge, Tennessee Circuit Court Twenty-fourth Judicial District-Tenn.
Guirola, Louis, Jr.-Magistrate Judge, United States District Court Southern District of Mississippi-Miss.
Guliani, Richard J.-Judge, Portland District Probate Court-Conn.
Gull, Frances C.-Judge, Allen Superior Court-Ind.
Gullett, Julia Shuping-Judge, North Carolina District Court District 22-N.C.
Gulotta, Frank A., Jr.-Judge, Nassau County Court-N.Y.
Gunn, J. Michael-Judge, Superior Court of California County of San Bernardino-Calif.
Gunn, Mary Ann-Judge, Arkansas Circuit Court Fourth Judicial Circuit-Ark.
Gunnarsson, Val-Circuit Judge, Illinois Circuit Court Fifteenth Judicial Circuit-Ill.
Gunnell, C. Steve-Judge, Jennings City Court-La.
Gunter, Alan B.-Judge, Connell Municipal Court-Wash.
Gunter, Jack N.-Senior Judge, Superior Court of Georgia-Ga.
Gunter, James H., Jr.-Judge, Arkansas Circuit Court Eighth North Judicial Circuit-Ark.
Gunther, Bobby W.-Judge, Florida District Court of Appeal Fourth District-Fla.
Gunther, Jeffrey L.-Judge, Superior Court of California County of Sacramento-Calif.
Gunther, Jessie B.-Judge, Maine District Court-Me.
Guolee, Michael D.-Judge, Wisconsin Circuit Court Milwaukee Circuit-Wis.
Guresz, Caroline-Judge, Cohoes City Court-N.Y.
Gurich, Noma Diane-District Judge, Oklahoma District Court Seventh Judicial District-Okla.
Gurrola, Barbara-Judge, Florida Circuit Court Fifth Judicial Circuit-Fla.
Guss, Mary E.-Magistrate Judge, United States District Court District of Alaska-Alas.
Guthrie, Bill-Judge, Blanco County Court-Tex.
Guthrie, David-Judge, Arkansas Circuit Court Thirteenth Judicial Circuit-Ark.
Guthrie, Frank W.-Judge, Jackson Superior Court-Ind.
Guthrie, Judith K.-Magistrate Judge, United States District Court Eastern District of Texas-Tex.
Guthrie, Nancy-Judge, Wyoming District Court Ninth Judicial District-Wyo.
Gutierrez, Annie M.-Judge, Superior Court of California County of Imperial-Calif.
Gutierrez, Arturo F.-Judge, Superior Court of California County of Ventura-Calif.
Gutierrez, Gilbert A.-Judge, Colorado District Court Nineteenth Judicial District-Colo.
Gutierrez, Philip S.-Judge, Superior Court of California County of Los Angeles-Calif.
Gutierrez, Sergio A.-Judge, Idaho Court of Appeals-Ida.
Gutman, Paul-Judge, Superior Court of California County of Los Angeles-Calif.
Gutmann, Elizabeth Simms-Judge, Miami County Municipal Court-Ohio
Guy, Ralph B., Jr.-Senior Judge, United States Court of Appeals Sixth Circuit
Guy-Schall, Lisa-Judge, Superior Court of California County of San Diego-Calif.
Guzman, Eva M.-Justice, Texas Court of Appeals Fourteenth District-Tex.
Guzman, Nestor F.-Judge, New Jersey Superior Court Vicinage Eleven-N.J.
Guzman, Raymond-Judge, The Civil Court of the City of New York-N.Y.
Guzman, Ronald A.-Judge, United State District Court Northern District of Illinois-Ill.
Guzman, Wilma-Judge, The Civil Court of the City of New York-N.Y.
Gwin, James S.-Judge, United States District Court Northern District of Ohio-Ohio
Gwin, W. Scott-Judge, Ohio Court of Appeals Fifth District-Ohio
Gwyn, Hunt-Judge, North Carolina District Court District 20-N.C.
Gysegem, Thomas P.-Judge, Warren Municipal Court-Ohio
Haas, John G.-Judge, Ohio Court of Common Pleas Stark County-Ohio
Haase, Herman S.-Circuit Judge, Illinois Circuit Court Twelfth Judicial Circuit-Ill.
Haase, Robert A.-Judge, Wisconsin Circuit Court Winnebago Circuit-Wis.
Habeck, James Roy-Judge, Wisconsin Circuit Court Shawano-Menominee Circuit-Wis.
Haber, Alan B.-Judge, Superior Court of California County of Los Angeles-Calif.
Haberkorn, Catherine M.-Circuit Judge, Illinois Circuit Court of Cook County-Ill.
Haberly, M. Karlynn-Judge, Washington Superior Court Kitsap County-Wash.
Hackeling, Steven-Judge, Suffolk County District Court-N.Y.
Hacker, Aleta-Judge, Texas Family District Court 326th Judicial District-Tex.
Hackett, James-Associate Judge, Illinois Circuit Court Third Judicial Circuit-Ill.
Hackett, Robert N., Jr.-Judge, Washington Superior Court Yakima County-Wash.
Hackner, Paul A.-Associate Judge, Circuit Court for Anne Arundel County, Fifth Judicial Circuit-Md.
Hadacek, John D.-Judge, Fostoria Municipal Court-Ohio
Haddad, Victor M.-Judge, Clermont County Municipal Court-Ohio
Haddad, William J.-Circuit Judge, Illinois Circuit Court of Cook County-Ill.
Hadden, Arthur-Judge, Connecticut Superior Court-Conn.
Hadden, William L., Jr.-Judge Referee, Connecticut Superior Court-Conn.
Haddock, Donald M.-Chief Judge, Virginia Circuit Court Eighteenth Judicial Circuit-Va.
Haddock, Lawrence Page-Judge, Florida Circuit Court Fourth Judicial Circuit-Fla.
Haddock, Steven E.-Presiding Judge, Alabama Circuit Court Eighth Judicial Circuit-Ala.
Haddon, Sam E.-Judge, United States District Court District of Montana-Mont.
Haden, Charles H., II-Judge, United States District Court Southern District of West Virginia-W.Va.
Haden, J. Richard-Judge, Superior Court of California County of San Diego-Calif.
Hadfield, Ben H.-Judge, Utah District Court First Judicial District-Utah
Hadley, Scott M.-Judge, Utah District Court Second Judicial District-Utah
Hadwiger, Mickey J.-Associate District Judge, Oklahoma District Court Fourth Judicial District-Okla.
Haeger, Robert E.-Judge, Huerfano County Court-Colo.
Haerle, Paul R.-Associate Justice, California Court of Appeal First District Division Two-Calif.
Haese, William J.-Reserve Judge, Wisconsin Circuit Court-Wis.
Hafele, Donald-Judge, Palm Beach County Court-Fla.
Hafner, Walter W., Jr.-Judge, Oswego County Court-N.Y.
Hagen, Dale B.-District Judge, Iowa District Court Fifth Judicial District-Ia.
Hagen, David W.-Judge, United States District Court District of Nevada-Nev.
Hagerman, C. David-Judge, Kentucky Circuit Court Thirty-second Judicial Circuit-Ky.
Hagerty, Gail-Judge, North Dakota District Court South Central Judicial District-N.D.
Haggerty, Ancer L.-Chief Judge, United States District Court District of Oregon-Ore.
Haggerty, S. Jane-Associate Justice, Trial Court of Massachusetts Superior Court Department-Mass.
Hagler, Brooks H.-Judge, Texas District Court 259th Judicial District-Tex.
Hagler, John Brown-Judge, Tennessee Circuit Court Tenth Judicial District-Tenn.
Hagler, Robert A.-Judge, Ohio Court of Common Pleas Greene County-Ohio
Hagopian, Jacob-Recalled Magistrate Judge, United States District Court District of Rhode Island-R.I.
Hague, Andrew S.-Judge, Dade County Court-Fla.
Hague, Charles G.-Judge, Ohio Court of Common Pleas Ashtabula County-Ohio
Hague, Douglas T.-Judge, New Jersey Superior Court Vicinage Eight-N.J.
Hagy, C. Christopher-Magistrate Judge, United States District Court Northern District of Georgia-Ga.
Hahn, Buddie J.-Judge, Texas District Court 260th Judicial District-Tex.
Hahn, Dale A.-Judge, Superior Court of California County of San Mateo-Calif.
Hahn, Gary R.-Judge, Superior Court of California County of Los Angeles-Calif.
Hahn, Susan L.-Judge, Washington Superior Court Yakima County-Wash.
Haight, Charles S., Jr.-Senior Judge, United States District Court Southern District of New York-N.Y.
Haight, Lois-Judge, Superior Court of California County of Contra Costa-Calif.
Haigwood, Thomas D.-Special Judge, North Carolina Superior Court-N.C.
Haik, Richard T.-Chief Judge, United States District Court Western District of Louisiana-La.
Hain, Trish-Assistant Judge, Vermont Trial Court Windham County-Vt.
Haines, Charles F.-Judge, Superior Court of California City and County of San Francisco-Calif.
Haines, James B., Jr.-Judge, Bankruptcy Appellate Panel First Circuit and Chief Judge, United States Bankruptcy Court District of Maine-Me.

ALPHABETICAL NAME INDEX

Haines, Randolph J.-Judge, United States Bankruptcy Court District of Arizona-Ariz.
Hair, John S., Jr.-Judge, North Carolina District Court District 12-N.C.
Hair, Mattox S.-Senior Judge, Florida Circuit Court Fourth Judicial Circuit-Fla.
Hairston, Andrew J.-Judge, City Court of Atlanta-Ga.
Hajek, David Wayne-Judge, Texas District Court 50th Judicial District-Tex.
Hake, Kenneth L.-Judge, Superior Court of California County of Sacramento-Calif.
Halbach, Joseph James, Jr.-Judge, Texas District Court 333rd Judicial District-Tex.
Halbrooks, Jill Flaskamp-Judge, Minnesota Court of Appeals-Minn.
Hale, Barbara Wade-Judge, Walker County Court at Law-Tex.
Hale, Daniel C.-Judge, Colorado District Court Twentieth Judicial District-Colo.
Hale, Eugene-Judge, Prescott District Court-Ark.
Hale, Harland Hanna-Judge, Franklin County Municipal Court-Ohio
Hale, Harlin DeWayne-Judge, United States Bankruptcy Court Northern District of Texas-Tex.
Hale, Milas Howard, II-Judge, Sherwood District Court-Ark.
Hale, Robert J.-Judge Referee, Connecticut Superior Court-Conn.
Haley, Donald D.-Judge, Washington Superior Court King County-Wash.
Haley, James W., Jr.-Judge, Virginia Circuit Court Fifteenth Judicial Circuit-Va.
Haley, Michael J.-Chief Judge, Michigan District Court District Eighty-six-Mich.
Halgren, Laura-Judge, Superior Court of California County of San Diego-Calif.
Halker, Janis-Judge, Orange County Court-Fla.
Hall, Brett-Judge, Texas District Court 382nd Judicial District-Tex.
Hall, Courtenay W.-Judge, Saratoga County Family Court-N.Y.
Hall, Cynthia Holcomb-Senior Judge, United States Court of Appeals Ninth Circuit
Hall, David M.-Circuit Judge, Illinois Circuit Court Nineteenth Judicial Circuit-Ill.
Hall, Derrell-Judge, Fannin County Court-Tex.
Hall, Diana R.-Judge, Superior Court of California County of Santa Barbara-Calif.
Hall, Don T.-Judge, DeSoto County Court-Fla.
Hall, Donald-Judge, Wyoming Circuit Court Ninth Judicial District, Fremont County-Wyo.
Hall, Eric D.-Judge, Kentucky District Court Thirty-first Judicial District-Ky.
Hall, Glenna-Judge, Washington Superior Court King County-Wash.
Hall, H. John-Judge, Washington Superior Court Lewis County-Wash.
Hall, Howard E.-Judge, Ohio Court of Common Pleas Morrow County-Ohio
Hall, J. Lewis, Jr.-Senior Judge, Florida Circuit Court Second Judicial Circuit-Fla.
Hall, Jack-Judge, Donley County Court-Tex.
Hall, James A.-Chief Judge, New Mexico District Court First Judicial District-N.Mex.
Hall, James R.-Associate Circuit Judge, Missouri Circuit Court Thirty-sixth Judicial Circuit-Mo.
Hall, Janet C.-Judge, United States District Court District of Connecticut-Conn.
Hall, Judy A.-Judge, Kentucky Circuit Court Third Judicial Circuit-Ky.
Hall, Karen Kimbrell-Judge, Madison County District Court-Ala.
Hall, L. Priscilla-Justice, New York Supreme Court Second Judicial District-N.Y.
Hall, Lysle G., Jr.-Judge, Michigan District Court District Twelve-Mich.
Hall, Margot S.-Judge, Newtown District Probate Court-Conn.
Hall, Michael T.-Judge, Ohio Court of Common Pleas Montgomery County-Ohio
Hall, Philip L.-Judge, Arizona Court of Appeals Division One-Ariz.
Hall, Richard V.-Judge, Colorado District Court Fourth Judicial District-Colo.
Hall, Robert M.-Judge, Warren Circuit Court-Ind.
Hall, Robert T.-Associate Judge, Illinois Circuit Court Seventh Judicial Circuit-Ill.
Hall, Russell D.-Special Judge, Oklahoma District Court Seventh Judicial District-Okla.
Hall, Sharon L.-Judge, Minnesota District Court Tenth Judicial District-Minn.
Hall, Shelvin Louise Marie-Judge, Illinois Appellate Court First Judicial District Division Three-Ill.
Hall, Sophia H.-Circuit Judge, Illinois Circuit Court of Cook County-Ill.
Hall, Stephen M.-Judge, Superior Court of California County of San Mateo-Calif.
Hall, Vincent T.-Senior Judge, Florida District Court of Appeal-Fla.
Hall, W. Q.-Judge, Huntsville District Court-Ark.
Hall, Wallace Haile-Senior Judge, Florida Circuit Court Eighteenth Judicial Circuit-Fla.
Hallanan, Elizabeth Virginia-Senior Judge, United States District Court Southern District of West Virginia-W.Va.
Hallenbeck, Terry C.-Judge, Minnesota District Court Sixth Judicial District-Minn.
Haller, Carol M.-Judge, Weld County Court-Colo.
Haller, Judith Lynnette-Associate Justice, California Court of Appeal Fourth District Division One-Calif.
Halliday, Bruce K.-Judge, Utah District Court Seventh Judicial District-Utah
Hallman, Diane-Judge, Probate Court of Appling County-Ga.
Hallman, Ron-Judge, State Court of Evans County-Ga.
Hallmark, Linda S.-Chief Judge, Oakland County Probate Court-Mich.
Hallock, James C.-Associate Judge, Illinois Circuit Court Sixteenth Judicial Circuit-Ill.
Halloran, Andrew-Judge, Essex County Court-N.Y.
Halloran, Richard B., Jr.-Judge, Michigan Circuit Court Third Judicial Circuit-Mich.
Halpern, James S.-Judge, United States Tax Court
Halpert, Helen L.-Judge, Washington Superior Court King County-Wash.
Halsey, Stephen M.-Judge, Minnesota District Court Tenth Judicial District-Minn.
Halstead, Donald R.-Chief Judge, Kalamazoo County Probate Court-Mich.
Hamblen, William D.-Chief Judge, Virginia Circuit Court Thirty-first Judicial Circuit-Va.
Hamby, Gary-Judge, Probate Court of Upson County-Ga.
Hamby, William G., Jr.-Chief Judge, North Carolina District Court District 19A-N.C.
Hamer, Donald L.-Judge, Glastonbury District Probate Court-Conn.
Hamer, Ted-Circuit Judge, Illinois Circuit Court Fourteenth Judicial Circuit-Ill.
Hamil, R. Timothy-Judge, Superior Court of Georgia Gwinnett Judicial Circuit-Ga.
Hamill, Bryanne A.-Judge, New York City Family Court-N.Y.
Hamilton, Barry A.-Associate Judge, Maryland District Court District Six-Md.
Hamilton, Clyde Henry-Senior Judge, United States Court of Appeals Fourth Circuit
Hamilton, David F.-Judge, United States District Court Southern District of Indiana-Ind.
Hamilton, Eugene N.-Senior Judge, Superior Court of the District of Columbia-D.C.
Hamilton, Gene-Presiding Judge, Missouri Circuit Court Thirteenth Judicial Circuit-Mo.
Hamilton, Glenn S.-Judge, Ohio Court of Common Pleas Madison County-Ohio
Hamilton, Jean C.-Judge, United States District Court Eastern District of Missouri-Mo.
Hamilton, Jim-Judge, North Little Rock District Court-Ark.
Hamilton, Jim T.-Judge, Tennessee Circuit Court Twenty-second Judicial District-Tenn.
Hamilton, John D.-Chief Judge, Iosco County Probate Court-Mich.
Hamilton, Joyce Amelia-Chief Judge, North Carolina District Court District 10-N.C.
Hamilton, Kathleen A.-Judge, Texas District Court 359th Judicial District-Tex.
Hamilton, Laura W.-Judge, Alabama Circuit Court Twenty-third Judicial Circuit-Ala.
Hamilton, Lee-Judge, Texas District Court 104th Judicial District-Tex.
Hamilton, Phyllis J.-Judge, United States District Court Northern District of California-Calif.
Hamilton, R. Morgan-Associate Judge, Illinois Circuit Court of Cook County-Ill.
Hamilton, Robert W.-Judge, South Prairie and Wilkeson Municipal Courts-Wash.
Hamlett, Linda R.-Associate Circuit Judge, Missouri Circuit Court Twelfth Judicial Circuit-Mo.
Hamlett, William C.-Judge, Idaho District Court Second Judicial District Magistrate Division-Ida.
Hamlin, Sandra L.-Associate Justice, Trial Court of Massachusetts Superior Court Department-Mass.
Hamlin, William Kent-Judge, Superior Court of California County of Fresno-Calif.
Hamm, Phillip-Judge, Kentucky District Court Twenty-sixth Judicial District-Ky.
Hammel, John W.-Judge, Marion Superior Court-Ind.
Hammer, Harry-Judge Referee, Connecticut Superior Court-Conn.
Hammer, Richard L., Jr.-Chief Judge, Michigan District Court District Twenty-one-Mich.
Hammerstone, James E., Jr.-Judge, Superior Court of California County of San Joaquin-Calif.
Hammes, Laura Palmer-Judge, Superior Court of California County of San Diego-Calif.
Hammond, Catherine Currin-Judge, Virginia Circuit Court Fourteenth Judicial Circuit-Va.
Hammond, John T.-Judge, Michigan Circuit Court Second Judicial Circuit-Mich.
Hammond, Kim C.-Judge, Florida Circuit Court Seventh Judicial Circuit-Fla.
Hammond, Lawrence T., Jr.-Emergency Judge, North Carolina District Court-N.C.
Hammond, Lisa K.-Special Judge, Oklahoma District Court Seventh Judicial District-Okla.
Hammond, Nancy D.-Judge, Ohio Court of Common Pleas Fayette County-Ohio
Hammontree, Jack-Associate District Judge, Oklahoma District Court Fourth Judicial District-Okla.
Hamner, Herschel T., Jr.-Judge, Alabama Circuit Court Sixth Judicial Circuit-Ala.
Hampe, Richard A.-Judge, Probate Court of New Hampshire Merrimack County-N.H.
Hampsey, Bernard J., Jr.-Associate Justice, New Hampshire Superior Court-N.H.
Hampton, Steve-Chief Magistrate, Magistrate Court of Murray County-Ga.
Hampton, Van Z.-Judge, Kansas District Court Sixteenth Judicial District-Kan.
Hamre, Paul E.-Chief Judge, Michigan Circuit Court Thirty-sixth Judicial Circuit-Mich.
Hamrick, Gayle B.-Judge, State Court of Richmond County-Ga.
Hamrick, H. Pope, Jr.-Judge, Volusia County Court-Fla.
Hancher, George H.-Judge, Pennsylvania Court of Common Pleas Fiftieth Judicial District-Pa.
Hancock, Alan R.-Judge, Washington Superior Court Island-San Juan Counties-Wash.
Hancock, George E.-Chief Magistrate, Magistrate Court of Stewart County-Ga.
Hancock, J. Phillip-Judge, Recorder's Court of DeKalb County-Ga.
Hancock, James H.-Senior Judge, United States District Court Northern District of Alabama-Ala.
Hancock, Karla-Judge, Minnesota District Court Tenth Judicial District-Minn.
Hancock, Mackey K.-Judge, Texas District Court 99th Judicial District-Tex.
Hancock, Michael E.-Chief Judge, Superior Court of Georgia Stone Mountain Judicial Circuit-Ga.
Hancock, Patricia-Judge, Texas District Court 113th Judicial District-Tex.
Hand, Kernan A.-Judge, Louisiana District Court Twenty-fourth Judicial District-La.
Hand, Robert J., Jr.-Judge, Casper Municipal Court-Wyo.
Hand, William Brevard-Senior Judge, United States District Court Southern District of Alabama-Ala.
Handwork, Peter M.-Judge, Ohio Court of Appeals Sixth District-Ohio
Handy, Althea M.-Associate Judge, Circuit Court for Baltimore City, Eighth Judicial Circuit-Md.

ALPHABETICAL NAME INDEX

ALPHABETICAL NAME INDEX

ALPHABETICAL NAME INDEX

ALPHABETICAL NAME INDEX

Hebert, Donald W.-Judge, Louisiana District Court Twenty-seventh Judicial District-La.
Hébert, J. Byron-Judge, Louisiana District Court Fifteenth Judicial District-La.
Hebert, Robert E.-Judge, Fort Bend County Court-Tex.
Hecht, Daryl L.-Judge, Iowa Court of Appeals-Ia.
Hecht, Nathan L.-Justice, Texas Supreme Court-Tex.
Heckerman, James S.-District Judge, Iowa District Court Fourth Judicial District-Ia.
Heckler, David W.-Judge, Pennsylvania Court of Common Pleas Seventh Judicial District-Pa.
Hedge, Brook-Associate Judge, Superior Court of the District of Columbia-D.C.
Hedger, Douglas-Judge, Henderson Municipal Court-Nev.
Hedges, Adele-Justice, Texas Court of Appeals First District-Tex.
Hedges, Bryan R.-Judge, Onondaga County Family Court-N.Y.
Hedges, Patricia T.-Judge, Louisiana District Court Twenty-second Judicial District-La.
Hedges, Ronald J.-Magistrate Judge, United States District Court District of New Jersey-N.J.
Hedlund, Deborah-Judge, Minnesota District Court Fourth Judicial District-Minn.
Hedspeth, David J.-Associate Circuit Judge, Missouri Circuit Court Thirty-seventh Judicial Circuit-Mo.
Hedstrom, Edward-Judge, Florida Circuit Court Seventh Judicial Circuit-Fla.
Hedstrom, Stephen Owen-Judge, Superior Court of California County of Lake-Calif.
Heebe, Frederick Jacob Reagan-Senior Judge, United States District Court Eastern District of Louisiana-La.
Heffelfinger, Jeffrey R.-Judge, Huntington Superior Court-Ind.
Heffernan, Charles J., Jr.-Judge, The Criminal Court of the City of New York-N.Y.
Heffernan, E. Michael-Judge, West Haven District Probate Court-Conn.
Heffernan, Pamela G.-Judge, Utah District Court Second Judicial District-Utah
Heffernan, Paul P.-First Justice, Trial Court of Massachusetts District Court Department Middlesex County Somerville Division-Mass.
Heffron, Robert Wilson-Associate Judge, Maryland District Court District Five-Md.
Hefley, Jerry Dan-Judge, Wheeler County Court-Tex.
Heflin, Jack R.-Judge, Florida Circuit Court First Judicial Circuit-Fla.
Heflin, Joe-Judge, Crosby County Court-Tex.
Hegarty, Michael K.-Judge, Michigan District Court District Fifty-three-Mich.
Hegarty, Patrick J.-Judge, Superior Court of California County of Los Angeles-Calif.
Hegel, Joe L.-Judge, Montana District Court Sixteenth Judicial District and Judge, Montana Water Court Lower Missouri River Basin Division-Mont.
Hegge, Robert, II-Judge, Pine Haven Municipal Court-Wyo.
Heilman, Joseph B.-Judge, Superior Court of Arizona Maricopa County-Ariz.
Heimann, James A.-Judge, Adams Superior Court-Ind.
Heimann, Stephen R.-Judge, Bartholomew Circuit Court-Ind.
Heimlich, James C.-Judge, New Jersey Superior Court Vicinage Twelve-N.J.
Hein, Jonathan P.-Judge, Ohio Court of Common Pleas Darke County-Ohio
Heinrich, Walter R.-Judge, Hillsborough County Court-Fla.
Heise, Debra A.-Judge, Idaho District Court First Judicial District Magistrate Division-Ida.
Heiser, Larry W.-Associate Judge, Illinois Circuit Court Ninth Judicial Circuit-Ill.
Heitler, Sherry Klein-Justice, New York Supreme Court First Judicial District-N.Y.
Helander, Joel E.-Judge, Guilford District Probate Court-Conn.
Helbling, James J.-Judge, Bonney Lake Municipal Court-Wash.
Held, Gerald S.-Justice, New York Supreme Court Second Judicial District-N.Y.
Heldman, Russ-Judge, Tennessee Circuit Court Twenty-first Judicial District-Tenn.
Heldt, Carl A.-Judge, Vanderburgh Circuit Court-Ind.
Helfrich, Robert-Judge, Mississippi Circuit Court Twelfth Judicial District-Miss.
Heller, Ellen M.-Circuit Administrative Judge, Circuit Court for Baltimore City, Eighth Judicial Circuit-Md.
Heller, Ernest A.-Judge, Lakewood Municipal Court-Wash.
Heller, James R.-Judge, Pierce District Court Pierce County-Wash.
Heller, Robert M.-Associate Circuit Judge, Missouri Circuit Court Thirty-seventh Judicial Circuit-Mo.
Hellerstein, Alvin K.-Judge, United States District Court Southern District of New York-N.Y.
Hellmann, Juda Maria-Judge, Kentucky Circuit Court Thirtieth Judicial Circuit-Ky.
Hellmer, Jerome P.-Judge, Kansas District Court Twenty-eighth Judicial District-Kan.
Hellums, Bonnie Crane-Judge, Texas District Court 247th Judicial District-Tex.
Helm, Reagan C.-Judge, Harris County Criminal Court at Law No. 1-Tex.
Helmick, Dennis S.-Judge, Ohio Court of Common Pleas Hamilton County-Ohio
Helms, Michael Etna-Resident Judge, North Carolina Superior Court Fifth Judicial Division District 23-N.C.
Hely, Charles J.-Associate Justice, Trial Court of Massachusetts Superior Court Department-Mass.
Hemann, Patricia A.-Magistrate Judge, United States District Court Northern District of Ohio-Ohio
Hemingsen, Donald R.-Chief Judge, Michigan District Court District Sixty-four B-Mich.
Hemm, Michael W.-Judge, Miami County Municipal Court-Ohio
Hemmett, Gordon M., Jr.-Judge, Washington County Court-N.Y.
Hendel, Seymour L.-Judge Referee, Connecticut Superior Court-Conn.
Henderson, Christopher C.-Associate Judge, Circuit Court for Charles County, Seventh Judicial Circuit-Md.
Henderson, Curt B.-Judge, Texas District Court 219th Judicial District-Tex.
Henderson, David Earl-Judge, Ohio Court of Common Pleas Jefferson County-Ohio
Henderson, Donnie-Judge, Crane County Court-Tex.
Henderson, Doug-Judge, Manatee County Court-Fla.
Henderson, Frederick A.-Judge, Wisconsin Circuit Court Rusk Circuit-Wis.
Henderson, James-Judge, Grayson County Court at Law No. 1-Tex.
Henderson, James C.-Senior Judge, Florida Circuit Court Eleventh Judicial Circuit-Fla.
Henderson, John N.-Associate District Judge, Oklahoma District Court Sixteenth Judicial District-Okla.
Henderson, Karen LeCraft-Judge, United States Court of Appeals District of Columbia Circuit
Henderson, Mary Jane Nettles-Judge, Volusia County Court-Fla.
Henderson, Nancy S.-Judge, Plymouth District Probate Court-Conn.
Henderson, Richard James-Judge, Superior Court of California County of Mendocino-Calif.
Henderson, Roger E.-Judge, South Carolina Family Court Fourth Judicial Circuit-S.C.
Henderson, Susan Orr-Judge, Fountain Circuit Court-Ind.
Henderson, Thelton E.-Senior Judge, United States District Court Northern District of California-Calif.
Henderson, Timothy H.-Judge, Kansas District Court Eighteenth Judicial District-Kan.
Henderson, Walter P.-Retired-Recalled Judge, North Carolina District Court-N.C.
Henderson, William D.-Chief Judge, Illinois Circuit Court Ninth Judicial Circuit-Ill.
Henderson, William W., Jr.-Senior Judge, Escambia County Court-Fla.
Hendon, Sylvia Sieve-Judge, Ohio Court of Common Pleas Hamilton County-Ohio
Hendren, Jimm Larry-Chief Judge, United States District Court Western District of Arkansas-Ark.
Hendrick, Jerry, Jr.-Judge, Virginia Juvenile and Domestic Relations District Court Twelfth Judicial District-Va.
Hendricks, Angela-Judge, Probate Court of Baker County and Chief Magistrate, Magistrate Court of Baker County-Ga.
Hendricks, Bruce H.-Magistrate Judge, United States District Court District of South Carolina-S.C.
Hendrickson, Robert A.-Judge, Butler County Court-Ohio
Hendrix, Danna-Judge, Superior Court of Arizona Coconino County-Ariz.
Hendrix, Marcena M.-Judge, Nebraska County Court Fourth Judicial District-Neb.
Hendrix, Thomas C.-Judge, Superior Court of California County of San Diego-Calif.
Hendry, John V.-Chief Justice, Nebraska Supreme Court-Neb.
Hendry, William L.-Senior Judge, Florida Circuit Court Nineteenth Judicial Circuit-Fla.
Henenberg, Karen Anne-Judge, Virginia General District Court Seventeenth Judicial District-Va.
Henke, James Paul-Judge, Superior Court of California County of Sacramento-Calif.
Hennegan, John O.-Associate Judge, Circuit Court for Baltimore County, Third Judicial Circuit-Md.
Hennessey, Mary R.-Judge Referee, Connecticut Superior Court-Conn.
Hennessey, Sheila M.-Judge, Newington District Probate Court-Conn.
Hennessy, Francis X.-Judge Referee, Connecticut Superior Court-Conn.
Henning, John L.-Judge, Superior Court of California County of Los Angeles-Calif.
Henning, John L., Jr.-Chief Judge, West Virginia Circuit Court Twentieth Judicial Circuit-W.Va.
Henning, Patti Englander-Judge, Florida Circuit Court Seventeenth Judicial Circuit-Fla.
Henriksen, John E.-Associate Judge, Delaware Family Court Sussex County-Del.
Henriod, Stephen L.-Judge, Utah District Court Third Judicial District-Utah
Henry, Charles E.-Judge, Ohio Court of Common Pleas Geauga County-Ohio
Henry, Charles H.-Resident Judge, North Carolina Superior Court Second Judicial Division District 4B-N.C.
Henry, David-Judge, Arkansas Circuit Court Eleventh East Judicial Circuit-Ark.
Henry, Donald M.-Associate Circuit Judge, Missouri Circuit Court Thirty-seventh Judicial Circuit-Mo.
Henry, Eveleen-Judge, Oregon Circuit Court Second Judicial District-Ore.
Henry, F. Bryant, Jr.-Judge, Juvenile Court of Georgia Lookout Mountain Judicial Circuit-Ga.
Henry, James F.-Circuit Judge, Illinois Circuit Court of Cook County-Ill.
Henry, Kathy-Justice, Prairie County Justice of the Peace Court and Judge, Terry City Court-Mont.
Henry, Linda Lee-Judge, McMullen County Court-Tex.
Henry, Margaret-Judge, Superior Court of California County of Los Angeles-Calif.
Henry, Matthew D.-Associate District Judge, Oklahoma District Court Fourteenth Judicial District-Okla.
Henry, Michael L.-Judge, Kentucky District Court Twenty-eighth Judicial District-Ky.
Henry, Patrick-Justice, New York Supreme Court Tenth Judicial District-N.Y.
Henry, Paul D.-Judge, Eaton Municipal Court-Ohio
Henry, Robert Harlan-Judge, United States Court of Appeals Tenth Circuit
Hensal, James E.-Judge, Fulton County Court-Ohio
Henshaw, A. J., Jr.-Associate District Judge, Oklahoma District Court Fifteenth Judicial District-Okla.

ALPHABETICAL NAME INDEX

Henshaw, Michael J.-Chief Judge, Illinois Circuit Court First Judicial Circuit-Ill.

Hensley, Dan A.-Presiding Judge, Alaska Superior Court Third Judicial District-Alas.

Hensley, James A., Jr.-Judge, Montgomery County Court-Ohio

Hensley, James A., Sr.-Judge, Montgomery County Court-Ohio

Hensley, Paul M.-Judge, Suffolk County District Court-N.Y.

Hensley, Robert E.-Senior Judge, Florida Circuit Court Twelfth Judicial Circuit-Fla.

Hensley, Todd A.-District Associate Judge, Iowa District Court Third Judicial District-Ia.

Henson, James D.-Judge, Ohio Court of Common Pleas Richland County-Ohio

Henson, James E.-Judge, Florida Circuit Court Ninth Judicial Circuit-Fla.

Henson, John S.-Judge, Montana District Court Fourth Judicial District-Mont.

Hentchel, Robert T.-Chief Judge, Michigan District Court District Seven-Mich.

Hepner, Paula J.-Judge, New York City Family Court-N.Y.

Hereford, William E.-Presiding Judge, Alabama Circuit Court Thirtieth Judicial Circuit-Ala.

Herlihy, Jerome O.-Associate Judge, Delaware Superior Court New Castle County-Del.

Herlihy, John F.-Judge, Superior Court of California County of Santa Clara-Calif.

Herlihy, Kevin M.-First Justice, Trial Court of Massachusetts District Court Department Essex County Haverhill Division and Justice, Lawrence Division-Mass.

Herlong, Henry M., Jr.-Judge, United States District Court District of South Carolina-S.C.

Herman, Douglas W.-Judge, Pennsylvania Court of Common Pleas Thirty-ninth Judicial District-Pa.

Herman, Gary W.-Judge, Auglaize County Municipal Court-Ohio

Herman, Guy-Judge, Travis County Probate Court No. 1-Tex.

Herman, Larry D.-Justice, Yellowstone County Justice of the Peace Court-Mont.

Herman, Martin A.-Judge, New Jersey Superior Court Vicinage Fifteen-N.J.

Herman, Thomas K.-Judge, Superior Court of California County of Los Angeles-Calif.

Herman, Thomas R.-Judge, Clermont County Municipal Court-Ohio

Hermansen, Gerald-Judge, Superior Court of California County of Butte-Calif.

Hernandez, Alex R.-Judge, Calhoun County Court at Law-Tex.

Hernandez, Esteban-Judge, Superior Court of California County of San Diego-Calif.

Hernandez, George C., Jr.-Judge, Superior Court of California County of Alameda-Calif.

Hernandez, Helios "Joe"-Judge, Superior Court of California County of Riverside-Calif.

Hernandez, Ivan-Judge, Dade County Court-Fla.

Hernandez, Marco-Presiding Judge, Oregon Circuit Court Twentieth Judicial District-Ore.

Hernandez, Pedro R.-Justice, Yellowstone County Justice of the Peace Court-Mont.

Hernandez, Todd-Judge, Louisiana District Court Nineteenth Judicial District-La.

Herndon, David R.-Judge, United States District Court Southern District of Illinois-Ill.

Herndon, James C.-Administrative Judge, Idaho District Court Seventh Judicial District-Ida.

Herndon, John E.-Special Judge, Oklahoma District Court Sixth Judicial District-Okla.

Herndon, Robert D.-Judge, Oregon Circuit Court Fifth Judicial District-Ore.

Herod, Steven R.-Judge, Texas District Court 91st Judicial District-Tex.

Herr, Maria Teresa "Tessa"-Judge, Texas District Court 186th Judicial District-Tex.

Herr, Marilyn Rhyne-Judge, New Jersey Superior Court Vicinage Thirteen-N.J.

Herr, Mark Edward-Judge, Seminole County Court-Fla.

Herrera, Mike-Judge, Texas District Court 383rd Judicial District-Tex.

Herrera, Ricardo-Judge, El Paso County Court at Law No. 1-Tex.

Herrick, David W.-Judge, Superior Court of California County of Lake-Calif.

Herrick, Stephen W.-Judge, Albany County Court-N.Y.

Herring, Janet-Judge, Encampment and Riverside Municipal Courts-Wyo.

Herring, Ronald A.-Judge, Florida Circuit Court Tenth Judicial Circuit-Fla.

Herring, William W.-Judge, Broward County Court-Fla.

Herron, John W.-Judge, Pennsylvania Court of Common Pleas First Judicial District-Pa.

Herscovitz, Martin Larry-Judge, Superior Court of California County of Los Angeles-Calif.

Hersher, Judy Holzer-Judge, Superior Court of California County of Sacramento-Calif.

Hershey, Stewart R.-Judge, Martin County Court-Fla.

Hershner, Robert F., Jr.-Chief Judge, United States Bankruptcy Court Middle District of Georgia-Ga.

Hervey, Barbara Parker-Judge, Texas Court of Criminal Appeals-Tex.

Hess, Frederick J.-Judge, Illinois Court of Claims-Ill.

Hess, Glenn L.-Judge, Florida Circuit Court Fourteenth Judicial Circuit-Fla.

Hess, John R.-Senior Judge, Superior Court of the District of Columbia-D.C.

Hess, Joseph E.-Judge, Virginia General District Court Twenty-fifth Judicial District-Va.

Hess, Kevin A.-Judge, Pennsylvania Court of Common Pleas Ninth Judicial District-Pa.

Hess, Robert L.-Judge, Superior Court of California County of Los Angeles-Calif.

Hester, Joseph P., Jr.-Justice, New York Supreme Court Sixth Judicial District-N.Y.

Hester, Samuel D.-Justice, New York Supreme Court Fifth Judicial District-N.Y.

Hester, Sharon H.-Presiding Judge, Alabama Circuit Court Thirty-fourth Judicial Circuit-Ala.

Hetherington, William, Jr.-District Judge, Oklahoma District Court Twenty-first Judicial District-Okla.

Heuer, James R.-Judge, Whitley Circuit Court-Ind.

Heumann, Ronald R.-Judge, Superior Court of California County of Riverside-Calif.

Hewes, Gaston Henderson-Judge, Harrison County Court-Miss.

Hewett, Mark-Judge, Arkansas Circuit Court Twelfth Judicial Circuit-Ark.

Hewitt, Emily Clark-Judge, United States Court of Federal Claims

Heyburn, John G., II-Chief Judge, United States District Court Western District of Kentucky-Ky.

Hiatt, James H.-Chief Judge, Colorado District Court Eighth Judicial District-Colo.

Hibbler, William J.-Judge, United States District Court Northern District of Illinois-Ill.

Hibbs, Kristin L.-District Judge, Iowa District Court Sixth Judicial District-Ia.

Hickey, William F., Jr.-Judge Referee, Connecticut Superior Court-Conn.

Hickman, Paul Stewart-Judge, Reno Municipal Court-Nev.

Hickman, S. Barrett-Justice, New York Supreme Court Ninth Judicial District-N.Y.

Hickok, Philip H.-Judge, Superior Court of California County of Los Angeles-Calif.

Hicks, Bethany G.-Judge, Superior Court of Arizona Maricopa County-Ariz.

Hicks, Claude W., Jr.-Magistrate Judge, United States District Court Middle District of Georgia-Ga.

Hicks, Edward J., III-Special Judge, Oklahoma District Court Fourteenth Judicial District-Okla.

Hicks, Gary A.-Judge, Virginia Circuit Court Fourteenth Judicial Circuit-Va.

Hicks, Gary D.-Justice, Lincoln County Justice of the Peace Court-Mont.

Hicks, Gary E.-Associate Justice, New Hampshire Superior Court-N.H.

Hicks, Larry R.-Judge, United States District Court District of Nevada-Nev.

Hicks, Ralph-Senior Judge, Superior Court of Georgia-Ga.

Hicks, Richard D.-Judge, Washington Superior Court Thurston County-Wash.

Hicks, Robert C.-Judge, West Virginia Family Court Circuit Two-W.Va.

Hicks, Ross H.-Judge, Tennessee Circuit Court Nineteenth Judicial District-Tenn.

Hicks, Timothy G.-Chief Judge, Michigan Circuit Court Fourteenth Judicial Circuit-Mich.

Hickson, Nina-Judge, Juvenile Court of Georgia Atlanta Judicial Circuit-Ga.

Hifo, Eden Elizabeth-Judge, Hawaii Circuit Court First Judicial Circuit-Hi.

Higa, Robert J.-Judge, Superior Court of California County of Los Angeles-Calif.

Higbee, Carol E.-Judge, New Jersey Superior Court Vicinage One-N.J.

Higbee, Ronald P.-Judge, Duval County Court-Fla.

Higbee, Thomas M.-Judge, Utah Juvenile Court Fifth Judicial District-Utah

Higer, Nathan W.-Judge, Idaho District Court Fifth Judicial District-Ida.

Higginbotham, Don-Judge, Williamson County Court at Law No. 3-Tex.

Higginbotham, Patrick E.-Judge, United States Court of Appeals Fifth Circuit

Higginbotham, Paul B.-Judge, Wisconsin Circuit Court Dane Circuit-Wis.

Higginbotham, Toni M.-Judge, East Baton Rouge Parish Family Court-La.

Higgins, Michael A.-Associate Judge, Rhode Island District Court-R.I.

Higgins, Michael F.-Judge, Licking County Municipal Court-Ohio

Higgins, Michael P.-Judge, Michigan Circuit Court Fortieth Judicial Circuit-Mich.

Higgins, Thomas A.-Senior Judge, United States District Court Middle District of Tennessee-Tenn.

Higgins, Thomas W., Jr.-Judge, Syracuse City Court-N.Y.

Higgs, David C.-Judge, Minnesota District Court Second Judicial District-Minn.

Higgs, Max D.-Judge, El Paso County Probate Court-Tex.

Higgs, W. Otis, Jr.-Judge, Tennessee Criminal Court Thirtieth Judicial District-Tenn.

High, Michael K.-Presiding Judge, Nebraska Workers' Compensation Court-Neb.

Highberger, William Foster-Judge, Superior Court of California County of Los Angeles-Calif.

Highers, Alan E.-Judge, Tennessee Court of Appeals Western Division-Tenn.

Highsmith, Robert M.-Associate District Judge, Oklahoma District Court Twentieth Judicial District-Okla.

Highsmith, Shelby-Senior Judge, United States District Court Southern District of Florida-Fla.

Hight, Bob T.-Judge, Superior Court of California County of Los Angeles-Calif.

Hight, C. T.-Judge, Texas District Court 75th Judicial District-Tex.

Hight, Henry W., Jr.-Resident Judge, North Carolina Superior Court Third Judicial Division District 9-N.C.

Hightower, Judith-Judge, Seattle Municipal Court-Wash.

Hightower, William G.-Judge, Pike County District Court-Ala.

Higley, Laura Carter-Justice, Texas Court of Appeals First District-Tex.

Hilberman, Joe W.-Judge, Superior Court of California County of Los Angeles-Calif.

Hilburn, Patricia Gwynett-Judge, North Carolina District Court District 3A-N.C.

Hildebrandt, Lee H., Jr.-Judge, Ohio Court of Appeals First District-Ohio

Hilden, Ronald L.-Judge, North Dakota District Court Southwest Judicial District-N.D.

Hilder, Robert K.-Judge, Utah District Court Third Judicial District-Utah

Hill, Alice C.-Judge, Superior Court of California County of Los Angeles-Calif.

Hill, Belinda-Judge, Texas District Court 230th Judicial District-Tex.

Hill, Brad R.-Judge, Superior Court of California County of Fresno-Calif.

Hill, Brian-Judge, Superior Court of California County of Santa Barbara-Calif.

Hill, Charles G.-Special Judge, Oklahoma District Court Seventh Judicial District-Okla.

ALPHABETICAL NAME INDEX

Hill, Deirdre H.-Judge, Superior Court of California County of Los Angeles-Calif.

Hill, Evelyn W.-Resident Judge, North Carolina Superior Court Third Judicial Division District 10-N.C.

Hill, George W.-Judge, West Virginia Circuit Court Fourth Judicial Circuit-W.Va.

Hill, Glynnis D.-Judge, Pennsylvania Court of Common Pleas First Judicial District-Pa.

Hill, James Clinkscales-Senior Judge, United States Court of Appeals Eleventh Circuit

Hill, James E., Jr.-Judge, St. Clair County District Court-Ala.

Hill, James T.-Judge, North Carolina District Court District 14-N.C.

Hill, James V.-Associate Judge, Illinois Circuit Court Second Judicial Circuit-Ill.

Hill, Mark J.-Judge, Florida Circuit Court Fifth Judicial Circuit-Fla.

Hill, Randy-Judge, Arkadelphia District Court-Ark.

Hill, Reuben B.-Judge, Marion Superior Court-Ind.

Hill, Russell J.-Recalled Judge, United States Bankruptcy Court Southern District of Iowa-Ia.

Hill, Sharon N.-Associate Judge, Juvenile Court of Georgia Atlanta Judicial Circuit-Ga.

Hill, Sherry L.-Judge, Tarrant County Criminal Court at Law No. 1-Tex.

Hill, Stephen D.-Chief Judge, Kansas District Court Sixth Judicial District-Kan.

Hill, Victor-Judge, Arkansas Circuit Court Second Judicial Circuit-Ark.

Hill, William Alexander-Judge, Bankruptcy Appellate Panel Eighth Circuit and Judge, United States Bankruptcy Court District of North Dakota-N.D.

Hill, Wm. Ralph, Jr.-Judge, Superior Court of Georgia Lookout Mountain Judicial Circuit-Ga.

Hill, William U.-Chief Justice, Wyoming Supreme Court-Wyo.

Hillary, G. Patrick-Judge, Kent County Probate Court-Mich.

Hille, Adalia-Judge, Ritzville District Court Adams County-Wash.

Hillebrand, Robert J.-Circuit Judge, Illinois Circuit Court Twentieth Judicial Circuit-Ill.

Hiller, Arthur A.-Judge, Connecticut Superior Court-Conn.

Hillery, Judith A.-Justice, New York Supreme Court Ninth Judicial District-N.Y.

Hilliard, Ruth H.-Judge, Superior Court of Arizona Maricopa County-Ariz.

Hillis, John T.-Judge, Binghamton City Court-N.Y.

Hillman, Stephen J.-Magistrate Judge, United States District Court Central District of California-Calif.

Hillman, Timothy S.-Associate Justice, Trial Court of Massachusetts Superior Court Department-Mass.

Hillman, William C.-Judge, Bankruptcy Appellate Panel First Circuit and Judge, United States Bankruptcy Court District of Massachusetts-Mass.

Hillsman, Marvin C., Jr.-Judge, Virginia Juvenile and Domestic Relations District Court Twenty-sixth Judicial District-Va.

Hillyer, Brad L.-Judge, Tuscarawas County Court-Ohio

Hilton, Claude M.-Chief Judge, United States District Court Eastern District of Virginia-Va.

Hilton, Douglas-Judge, Superior Court of California County of San Luis Obispo-Calif.

Hilyer, Bruce W.-Judge, Washington Superior Court King County-Wash.

Himelein, Larry M.-Judge, Cattaraugus County Court-N.Y.

Himmelberger, John G., Jr.-Judge, New Jersey Superior Court Vicinage One-N.J.

Hinckley, Harry G., Jr.-Senior Judge, Florida Circuit Court Seventeenth Judicial Circuit-Fla.

Hinds-Radix, Sylvia O.-Judge, The Civil Court of the City of New York-N.Y.

Hines, Earl S.-Magistrate Judge, United States District Court Eastern District of Texas-Tex.

Hines, Elizabeth Pollard-Judge, Michigan District Court District Fifteen-Mich.

Hines, Geraldine S.-Associate Justice, Trial Court of Massachusetts Superior Court Department-Mass.

Hines, Preston Harris-Justice, Supreme Court of Georgia-Ga.

Hines, Robert Jeffrey-Judge, Kentucky Circuit Court Second Judicial Circuit-Ky.

Hines, W. Ashley-Judge, Mississippi Circuit Court Fourth Judicial District-Miss.

Hinesley, Harold A.-Judge, Juvenile Court of Georgia Toombs Judicial Circuit-Ga.

Hinkle, Margaret R.-Associate Justice, Trial Court of Massachusetts Superior Court Department-Mass.

Hinkle, Robert L.-Judge, United States District Court Northern District of Florida-Fla.

Hinnant, Patrice A.-Judge, North Carolina District Court District 18-N.C.

Hinojosa, Federico G.-Justice, Texas Court of Appeals Thirteenth District-Tex.

Hinojosa, Gilberto-Judge, Cameron County Court-Tex.

Hinojosa, Leticia-Judge, Texas District Court 139th Judicial District-Tex.

Hinojosa, Ricardo H.-Judge, United States District Court Southern District of Texas-Tex.

Hinrichs, C. Randall-Judge, Suffolk County Court-N.Y.

Hinton, Alma L.-Judge, North Carolina District Court District 6A-N.C.

Hintz, Steven-Judge, Superior Court of California County of Ventura-Calif.

Hippe, Robert Owen-Judge, Nebraska District Court Twelfth Judicial District-Neb.

Hirai, Colleen K.-Chief Judge, Hawaii Circuit Court First Judicial Circuit-Hi.

Hiramoto, Joni T.-Judge, Superior Court of California County of Contra Costa-Calif.

Hiroshige, Ernest M.-Judge, Superior Court of California County of Los Angeles-Calif.

Hissong, Candace-Justice of the Peace, Douglas County Justice Court-Ore.

Hitchcock, John W.-Judge, Oregon Circuit Court Twenty-fifth Judicial District-Ore.

Hitchens, Donna J.-Judge, Superior Court of California City and County of San Francisco-Calif.

Hitpas, Patrick J.-Circuit Judge, Illinois Circuit Court Fourth Judicial Circuit-Ill.

Hitt, Fredric M.-Senior Judge, Seminole County Court-Fla.

Hittner, David-Judge, United States District Court Southern District of Texas-Tex.

Hjelm, Jeffrey L.-Justice, Maine Superior Court-Me.

Hoag, M. Jean-Judge, Superior Court of Arizona Maricopa County-Ariz.

Hoak, Mary C.-Judge, Grand County Court-Colo.

Hobbs, Gregory J., Jr.-Justice, Colorado Supreme Court-Colo.

Hobbs, Jimmie-Judge, Coleman County Court-Tex.

Hobbs, Johnny R.-Judge, Bradford County Court-Fla.

Hobbs, Truman M.-Senior Judge, United States District Court Middle District of Alabama-Ala.

Hobbs, Truman M., Jr.-Judge, Alabama Circuit Court Fifteenth Judicial Circuit-Ala.

Hoberg, Gordon O.-Surrogate Judge, North Dakota District Court-N.D.

Hoberg, Jay J.-Judge, Pennsylvania Court of Common Pleas Second Judicial District-Pa.

Hobgood, Robert H.-Resident Judge, North Carolina Superior Court Third Judicial Division District 9-N.C.

Hochberg, Faith S.-Judge, United States District Court District of New Jersey-N.J.

Hockenbury, Jay D.-Resident Judge, North Carolina Superior Court Second Judicial Division District 5-N.C.

Hockett, Marshall York-Judge, Superior Court of California County of San Diego-Calif.

Hodgdon, Allen D.-Assistant Judge, Vermont Trial Court Essex County-Vt.

Hodge, Richard L.-Magistrate Judge, United States District Court Middle District of Georgia-Ga.

Hodges, Bryan T.-Judge, Oregon Circuit Court Second Judicial District-Ore.

Hodges, Charles G.-Associate Judge, Juvenile Court of Georgia Atlanta Judicial Circuit-Ga.

Hodges, George R.-Chief Judge, United States Bankruptcy Court Western District of North Carolina-N.C.

Hodges, Ralph B.-Justice, Supreme Court of Oklahoma-Okla.

Hodges, Robert H., Jr.-Judge, United States Court of Federal Claims

Hodges, Sandra-Judge, Rusk County Court-Tex.

Hodges, Thomas L.-Judge, Superior Court of Georgia Northern Judicial Circuit-Ga.

Hodges, William Terrell-Senior Judge, United States District Court Middle District of Florida-Fla.

Hodgson, Beverly J.-Judge, Connecticut Superior Court-Conn.

Hodgson, Richard J.-Judge, Pennsylvania Court of Common Pleas Thirty-eighth Judicial District-Pa.

Hodny, William F.-Surrogate Judge, North Dakota District Court-N.D.

Hodos, Herbert H.-First Justice, Trial Court of Massachusetts District Court Department Franklin County Greenfield Division-Mass.

Hoekstra, Joel P.-Judge, Michigan Court of Appeals-Mich.

Hoellrich, Gene R.-Judge, Darke County Court-Ohio

Hoens, Helen E.-Judge, New Jersey Superior Court Appellate Division-N.J.

Hoerning, Candy-Justice, Beaverhead County Justice of the Peace Court-Mont.

Hoeveler, William M.-Senior Judge, United States District Court Southern District of Florida-Fla.

Hoff, E. Michael-Judge, Monroe Circuit Court-Ind.

Hoff, Gary D.-Judge, Superior Court of California County of Fresno-Calif.

Hoff, Mary K.-Judge, Missouri Court of Appeals Eastern District-Mo.

Hoff, Michael R.-Judge, Superior Court of California County of Los Angeles-Calif.

Hoff, Peter A.-Judge, Minnesota District Court Eighth Judicial District-Minn.

Hoff, Renae-Judge, Idaho District Court Third Judicial District-Ida.

Hoffenberg, Earl B.-Associate Judge, Illinois Circuit Court of Cook County-Ill.

Hoffer, George E.-President Judge, Pennsylvania Court of Common Pleas Ninth Judicial District-Pa.

Hoffert, John R.-Judge, Nebraska Workers' Compensation Court-Neb.

Hoffman, Harvey J.-Judge, Michigan District Court District Fifty-six A-Mich.

Hoffman, John C.-Judge, Minnesota District Court Tenth Judicial District-Minn.

Hoffman, John E., Jr.-Judge, United States Bankruptcy Court Southern District of Ohio-Ohio

Hoffman, John R.-Judge, Ohio Court of Common Pleas Stark County-Ohio

Hoffman, Marilyn Lois-Judge, Superior Court of California County of Los Angeles-Calif.

Hoffman, Mitchell L.-Associate Judge, Illinois Circuit Court Nineteenth Judicial Circuit-Ill.

Hoffman, Morris B.-Judge, Colorado District Court Second Judicial District-Colo.

Hoffman, Ronald E.-Judge, New Jersey Superior Court Vicinage Fourteen-N.J.

Hoffman, Thomas E.-Judge, Illinois Appellate Court First Judicial District Division Three-Ill.

Hoffman, William B.-Judge, Ohio Court of Appeals Fifth District-Ohio

Hoffmann, John P.-Judge, Wisconsin Circuit Court Waupaca Circuit-Wis.

Hoffmeyer, Duane E.-District Judge, Iowa District Court Third Judicial District-Ia.

Hofmann, Yuri-Judge, Superior Court of California County of San Diego-Calif.

Hogan, Daniel T.-Judge, Ohio Court of Common Pleas Franklin County-Ohio

Hogan, Jim-Judge, Wichita County Court at Law No. 1-Tex.

Hogan, Michael J.-Circuit Judge, Illinois Circuit Court of Cook County-Ill.

Hogan, Michael J.-Judge, New Jersey Superior Court Vicinage Three-N.J.

Hogan, Michael R.-Judge, United States District Court District of Oregon-Ore.

Hogan, Michele B.-Justice, Trial Court of Massachusetts District Court Department Middlesex County Cambridge Division-Mass.

Hogan, Thomas F.-Chief Judge, United States District Court District of Columbia-D.C.

Hogan, Thomas L.-Circuit Judge, Illinois Circuit Court of Cook County-Ill.

Hogan, Timothy S.-Magistrate Judge, United States District Court Southern District of Ohio-Ohio

Hogan, Vicki L.-Judge, Washington Superior Court Pierce County-Wash.

Hogg, David A.-Chief Judge, Michigan District Court District Eighty-four-Mich.

Hoggatt, Wallace R.-Judge, Superior Court of Arizona Cochise County-Ariz.

Hogshead, Charles R.-Special Judge, Oklahoma District Court Fourteenth Judicial District-Okla.

Hogshire, Edward L.-Judge, Virginia Circuit Court Sixteenth Judicial Circuit-Va.

Hogue, Amy D.-Judge, Superior Court of California County of Los Angeles-Calif.

Hohman, John A., Jr.-Judge, Monroe County Probate Court-Mich.

Hohnhorst, John C.-Judge, Idaho District Court Fifth Judicial District-Ida.

Hoke, Jay M.-Chief Judge, West Virginia Circuit Court Twenty-fifth Judicial Circuit-W.Va.

Holahan, John L., Jr.-Judge, Minnesota District Court Fourth Judicial District-Minn.

Holbrook, John Kevin-Judge, Kentucky District Court Twenty-fourth Judicial District-Ky.

Holcomb, Charles M.-Judge, Florida Circuit Court Eighteenth Judicial Circuit-Fla.

Holcomb, Charles R.-Judge, Texas Court of Criminal Appeals-Tex.

Holcomb, Janet S.-Presiding Judge, Oregon Circuit Court Twenty-first Judicial District-Ore.

Holcomb, John E.-Judge, Akron Municipal Court-Ohio

Holcombe, Walter M.-Judge, Reeves County Court at Law-Tex.

Holden, Calvin-Circuit Judge, Missouri Circuit Court Thirty-first Judicial Circuit-Mo.

Holden, William-Judge, Connecticut Superior Court-Conn.

Holder, Annie Doris-Judge, Probate Court of Calhoun County and Chief Magistrate, Magistrate Court of Calhoun County-Ga.

Holder, Gregory P.-Judge, Florida Circuit Court Thirteenth Judicial Circuit-Fla.

Holder, Janice M.-Associate Justice, Tennessee Supreme Court-Tenn.

Holder, Marc-Judge, Brazoria County Court at Law No. 2-Tex.

Holderman, James F., Jr.-Judge, United States District Court Northern District of Illinois-Ill.

Holdridge, Guy-Judge, Louisiana District Court Twenty-third Judicial District-La.

Holdridge, William E.-Judge, Illinois Appellate Court Third Judicial District-Ill.

Holifield, George W.-Judge, Seattle Municipal Court-Wash.

Holland, H. Russel-Senior Judge, United States District Court District of Alaska-Alas.

Holland, Jack Humphrey-Judge, Texas District Court 173rd Judicial District-Tex.

Holland, John-Judge, State Court of Turner County-Ga.

Holland, Lauren S.-Judge, Oregon Circuit Court Second Judicial District-Ore.

Holland, Lesley D.-Judge, Superior Court of California County of San Joaquin-Calif.

Holland, Marcella A.-Associate Judge, Circuit Court for Baltimore City, Eighth Judicial Circuit-Md.

Holland, Randy J.-Justice, Delaware Supreme Court-Del.

Holland, Robert L., Jr.-Chief Judge, West Virginia Circuit Court Third Judicial Circuit-W.Va.

Hollander, Ellen Lipton-Associate Judge, Court of Special Appeals of Maryland-Md.

Hollar-Gregory, Michelle-Judge, New Jersey Superior Court Vicinage Five-N.J.

Hollars, Bill-Judge, Hale County Court-Tex.

Hollenbeck, Harold C.-Judge, New Jersey Superior Court Vicinage Two-N.J.

Hollenbeck, Holly A.-Judge, Benton District Court Benton County-Wash.

Hollenhorst, Thomas E.-Associate Justice, California Court of Appeal Fourth District Division Two-Calif.

Hollerich, William-Judge, Idaho District Court Seventh Judicial District Magistrate Division-Ida.

Holley, Joel G.-Judge, Chambers County District Court-Ala.

Holley, Tonya-Judge, Probate Court of Early County and Chief Magistrate, Magistrate Court of Early County-Ga.

Hollie, Ronald D.-Justice, New York Supreme Court Eleventh Judicial District-N.Y.

Holliger, Ronald R.-Judge, Missouri Court of Appeals Western District-Mo.

Hollis, Pamela S.-Judge, United States Bankruptcy Court Northern District of Illinois-Ill.

Hollman, James W.-Judge, Superior Court of California County of Tulare-Calif.

Holloway, Denny L.-Judge, Alabama Circuit Court Twentieth Judicial Circuit-Ala.

Holloway, Jesse Aaron-Judge, Texas District Court 350th Judicial District-Tex.

Holloway, Robert L., Jr.-Judge, Tennessee Circuit Court Twenty-second Judicial District-Tenn.

Holloway, Roy C.-Judge, Idaho District Court Fifth Judicial District Magistrate Division-Ida.

Holloway, William J., Jr.-Senior Judge, United States Court of Appeals Tenth Circuit

Hollowell, Eileen W.-Judge, United States Bankruptcy Court District of Arizona-Ariz.

Hollows, Gregory G.-Magistrate Judge, United States District Court Eastern District of California-Calif.

Hollums, John R.-Judge, Texas District Court 110th Judicial District-Tex.

Holly, Carter P.-Judge, Superior Court of California County of San Joaquin-Calif.

Holm, Carl W.-Judge, Superior Court of California County of San Mateo-Calif.

Holman, Dixon W.-Justice, Texas Court of Appeals Second District-Tex.

Holman, Evelyn R.-Judge, Sharpsville Town Court-Ind.

Holman, Gary R.-Judge, Michigan District Court District Fifty-six B-Mich.

Holman, Stephen J.-Judge, Bainbridge Island Municipal Court-Wash.

Holman, Thomas C.-Judge, United States Bankruptcy Court Eastern District of California-Calif.

Holmer, C. Anders-Judge, Superior Court of California County of Nevada-Calif.

Holmes, Dallas Scott-Judge, Superior Court of California County of Riverside-Calif.

Holmes, Elenor F.-Judge, Limestone County Court-Tex.

Holmes, Ilona M.-Judge, Florida Circuit Court Seventeenth Judicial Circuit-Fla.

Holmes, John R.-Chief Judge, Michigan District Court District Ten-Mich.

Holmes, Nicholas H., Jr.-Judge, Ohio Court of Common Pleas Ross County-Ohio

Holmes, Patricia B.-Associate Judge, Illinois Circuit Court of Cook County-Ill.

Holmes, Roger W.-Associate Judge, Illinois Circuit Court Seventh Judicial Circuit-Ill.

Holmes, Sven Erik-Judge, United States District Court Northern District of Oklahoma-Okla.

Holmgren, Janet R.-Circuit Judge, Illinois Circuit Court Seventeenth Judicial Circuit-Ill.

Holowka, Nick O.-Chief Judge, Michigan Circuit Court Fortieth Judicial Circuit-Mich.

Holschuh, John D.-Senior Judge, United States District Court Southern District of Ohio-Ohio

Holston, John S., Jr.-Judge, New Jersey Superior Court Vicinage Fifteen-N.J.

Holt, Cathy M.-Judge, Superior Court of Arizona Maricopa County-Ariz.

Holt, Connie J.-Chief Magistrate, Magistrate Court of Morgan County-Ga.

Holt, Elmo-Senior Judge, Superior Court of Georgia-Ga.

Holt, J. David-Judge, Greene Superior Court-Ind.

Holt, Jenifer C.-Judge, Alabama Circuit Court Thirty-eighth Judicial Circuit-Ala.

Holt, Joe D.-Associate Circuit Judge, Missouri Circuit Court Thirteenth Judicial Circuit-Mo.

Holt, Leo E.-Circuit Judge, Illinois Circuit Court of Cook County-Ill.

Holt, R. Douglas-Presiding Judge, Superior Court of Arizona Graham County-Ariz.

Holt, Richlyn D.-Judge, North Carolina District Court District 30-N.C.

Holt, Shelly Sveda-Judge, North Carolina District Court District 5-N.C.

Holt, Wayne-Judge, San Augustine County Court-Tex.

Holt-Stone, C. Yvonne-Associate Judge, Maryland District Court District One-Md.

Holte, Robert W.-Presiding Judge, North Dakota District Court Northwest Judicial District-N.D.

Holter, Robert M.-Recalled Magistrate Judge, United States District Court District of Montana-Mont.

Holter, Terrance C.-Judge, Minnesota District Court Ninth Judicial District-Minn.

Holthoff, Howard "Corky"-Judge, Dumas District Court-Ark.

Holton, Anne B.-Chief Judge, Virginia Juvenile and Domestic Relations District Court Thirteenth Judicial District-Va.

Holton, Nola A.-Justice of the Peace, Pahranagat Valley Justices' Court and Judge, Caliente Municipal Court-Nev.

Holum, Gary A.-Judge, North Dakota District Court Northwest Judicial District-N.D.

Holzapfel, Leonard F.-Judge, Ohio Court of Common Pleas Jackson County-Ohio

Holzberg, Robert L.-Judge, Connecticut Superior Court-Conn.

Holzman, Lee L.-Surrogate, Bronx County Surrogate's Court-N.Y.

Hom, Kenneth W.-Judge, City Court of Miles City-Mont.

Hom, Rose-Judge, Superior Court of California County of Los Angeles-Calif.

Hom, Russell L.-Judge, Superior Court of California County of Sacramento-Calif.

Homer, David R.-Magistrate Judge, United States District Court Northern District of New York-N.Y.

Honeycutt, James M.-Judge, North Carolina District Court District 22-N.C.

Honeycutt, Pamela-Judge, Arkansas Circuit Court Second Judicial Circuit-Ark.

Honeywell, Charlene Edwards-Judge, Florida Circuit Court Thirteenth Judicial Circuit-Fla.

Hong, Jeannie Jinkyung-Associate Judge, Maryland District Court District One-Md.

Honigfeld, Jared D.-Judge, New Jersey Superior Court Vicinage Five-N.J.

Honorof, Alan L.-Judge, New York Court of Claims-N.Y.

Honts, George E., III-Judge, Virginia Circuit Court Twenty-fifth Judicial Circuit-Va.

Honzel, Thomas C.-Judge, Montana District Court First Judicial District-Mont.

Hood, Denise Page-Judge, United States District Court Eastern District of Michigan-Mich.

Hood, E. Leigh-Judge, Kansas District Court Sixteenth Judicial District-Kan.

Hood, Garfield W.-Chief Judge, Michigan Circuit Court Twelfth Judicial Circuit-Mich.

Hood, John S.-Judge, Lake Charles City Court-La.

Hood, Joseph Martin-Judge, United States District Court Eastern District of Kentucky-Ky.

Hood, Karen M. Fort-Judge, Michigan Court of Appeals-Mich.

Hood, Martha Walsh-Judge, Onondaga County Family Court-N.Y.

Hood, Richard L.-Senior Judge, Gadsden County Court-Fla.

Hooks, D. Jack, Jr.-Special Judge, North Carolina Superior Court-N.C.

Hoolihan, James W.-Judge, Minnesota District Court Seventh Judicial District-Minn.

Hooper, Ben W., II-Judge, Tennessee Circuit Court Fourth Judicial District-Tenn.

Hooper, Jeffrey A.-Judge, Ohio Court of Common Pleas Muskingum County-Ohio

Hooper, Keith-Magistrate Judge, Kansas District Court Seventeenth Judicial District-Kan.

Hoort, David A.-Judge, Michigan Circuit Court Eighth Judicial Circuit-Mich.

Hooten, Carol-Judge, Minnesota District Court First Judicial District-Minn.

ALPHABETICAL NAME INDEX

Hoover, Frank Allen-Judge, Superior Court of California County of Kern-Calif.
Hoover, James L.-Judge, Crawford County Municipal Court-Ohio
Hoover, Kim R.-Judge, Cuyahoga Falls Municipal Court-Ohio
Hoover, Michael W.-Presiding Judge, Wisconsin Court of Appeals District Three-Wis.
Hoover, Robert H.-Judge, Ohio Court of Common Pleas Licking County-Ohio
Hoover, Thomas B.-Chief Judge, Virginia Circuit Court Ninth Judicial Circuit-Va.
Hoover, Todd A.-Judge, Pennsylvania Court of Common Pleas Twelfth Judicial District-Pa.
Hopf, Nancy A.-Judge, Colorado District Court Eighteenth Judicial District-Colo.
Hopkins, Jeffery P.-Judge, United States Bankruptcy Court Southern District of Ohio-Ohio
Hopkins, Robert M.-Circuit Judge, Illinois Circuit Court Second Judicial Circuit-Ill.
Hopkins, Terrence J.-Judge, Illinois Appellate Court Fifth Judicial District-Ill.
Hopkins, Vanessa A.-Circuit Judge, Illinois Circuit Court of Cook County-Ill.
Hopkinson, Richard-Judge, Ten Sleep Municipal Court-Wyo.
Hoppe, Craig L.-Judge, St. Ignatius City Court-Mont.
Hopper, David W.-Judge, Greenwich District Probate Court-Conn.
Hopper, David W.-Judge, Madison County Court-Ind.
Hopper, Lewis B.-Judge, Kentucky Circuit Court Twenty-seventh Judicial Circuit-Ky.
Hoppin, Charles T.-Judge, Jefferson County Court-Colo.
Hopwood, Donald D.-Judge, Alaska Superior Court Third Judicial District-Alas.
Hora, Peggy Fulton-Judge, Superior Court of California County of Alameda-Calif.
Horan, Charles E.-Judge, Superior Court of California County of Los Angeles-Calif.
Horan, Diana-Associate Justice, Trial Court of Massachusetts Housing Court Department Worcester County Division-Mass.
Horan, Marilyn J.-Judge, Pennsylvania Court of Common Pleas Fiftieth Judicial District-Pa.
Horan, Richard T.-Chief Judge, Virginia General District Court Nineteenth Judicial District-Va.
Horan, Thomas M.-District Judge, Iowa District Court Sixth Judicial District-Ia.
Horgan, Thomas C.-Associate Justice, Trial Court of Massachusetts Boston Municipal Court Department-Mass.
Horgos, Robert P.-Judge, Pennsylvania Court of Common Pleas Fifth Judicial District-Pa.
Horkan, Frank D.-Judge, Superior Court of Georgia Southern Judicial Circuit-Ga.
Horkan, George Arthur, Jr.-Senior Judge, Superior Court of Georgia-Ga.
Horn, Allwin E., III-Judge, Alabama Circuit Court Tenth Judicial Circuit Birmingham Division-Ala.
Horn, Carl, III-Magistrate Judge, United States District Court Western District of North Carolina-N.C.
Horn, Charles A., Jr.-Judge, North Carolina District Court District 27B-N.C.
Horn, Frederick Paul-Judge, Superior Court of California County of Orange-Calif.
Horn, Gregory A.-Judge, Wayne Superior Court-Ind.
Horn, H. Chester, Jr.-Judge, Superior Court of California County of Los Angeles-Calif.
Horn, Marian Blank-Senior Judge, United States Court of Federal Claims
Horn, Mary-Judge, Denton County Court-Tex.
Hornak, Kimberly K.-Judge, Utah Juvenile Court Third Judicial District-Utah
Hornbaker, Steven L.-Judge, Kansas District Court Eighth Judicial District-Kan.
Hornby, D. Brock-Judge, United States District Court District of Maine-Me.
Horne, Clarence R., Jr.-Chief Magistrate, Magistrate Court of Rockdale County-Ga.
Horne, Kevin M.-Judge, Kentucky District Court Twenty-second Judicial District-Ky.
Horne, Thomas D.-Chief Judge, Virginia Circuit Court Twentieth Judicial Circuit-Va.
Horne, William S.-Circuit Administrative Judge, Circuit Court for Talbot County, Second Judicial Circuit-Md.
Horner, Jeffrey W.-Judge, Superior Court of California County of Alameda-Calif.
Horner, William M.-Judge, Oregon Circuit Court Twelfth Judicial District-Ore.
Hornstine, Louis F.-Judge, New Jersey Superior Court Vicinage Four-N.J.
Horowitz, Alfred-Judge, Florida Circuit Court Seventeenth Judicial Circuit-Fla.
Horowitz, Nilda Morales-Judge, Westchester County Family Court-N.Y.
Horowitz, Robert Davis-Judge, Ohio Court of Common Pleas Stark County-Ohio
Horowitz, Robert H.-Judge, Woodbridge District Probate Court-Conn.
Horton, Andrew M.-Judge, Maine District Court-Me.
Horton, Clarence E., Jr.-Special Judge, North Carolina Superior Court-N.C.
Horton, Joel D.-Judge, Idaho District Court Fourth Judicial District-Ida.
Horvath, Frank J.-Judge, Ohio Court of Common Pleas Lorain County-Ohio
Horwitz, David Maxwell-Judge, Superior Court of California County of Los Angeles-Calif.
Hosack, Charles W.-Administrative Judge, Idaho District Court First Judicial District-Ida.
Hosford, Kenneth-Judge, Liberty County Court-Fla.
Hoskins, Jeffrey J.-Judge, Ohio Court of Common Pleas Highland County-Ohio
Hostetler, David L.-Judge, Coshocton Municipal Court-Ohio
Hostetter, Charles E.-Judge, Brownsburg Town Court-Ind.
Hotchkiss, John-Judge, Washington Superior Court Douglas County-Wash.
Hotchkiss, Russell-Assistant Judge, Vermont Trial Court Orange County-Vt.
Hotham, Jeffrey A.-Judge, Superior Court of Arizona Maricopa County-Ariz.
Hotten, Michele D.-Associate Judge, Circuit Court for Prince George's County, Seventh Judicial Circuit-Md.
Houck, C. Weston-Judge, United States District Court District of South Carolina-S.C.
Houck, Kent C.-Reserve Judge, Wisconsin Circuit Court-Wis.
Houdashell, Ernie-Judge, Randall County Court-Tex.
Houff, W. Dale-Chief Judge, Virginia General District Court Twenty-sixth Judicial District-Va.
Houghton, Elaine-Judge, Washington Court of Appeals Division II-Wash.
Houran, Steven M.-Associate Justice, New Hampshire Superior Court-N.H.
Hourigan, Francis J., III-Judge, Superior Court of California County of Los Angeles-Calif.
House, Judy-Judge, Gaines County Court-Tex.
House, Mary Thornton-Judge, Superior Court of California County of Los Angeles-Calif.
House, Oscar G.-Judge, Kentucky District Court Forty-first Judicial District-Ky.
House, Ted-Associate Circuit Judge, Missouri Circuit Court Eleventh Judicial Circuit-Mo.
Householter, J. Gregory-Circuit Judge, Illinois Circuit Court Twenty-first Judicial Circuit-Ill.
Houser, Ann-Associate Judge, Illinois Circuit Court of Cook County-Ill.
Houser, Barbara J.-Judge, United States Bankruptcy Court Northern District of Texas-Tex.
Houser, Joseph M.-Judge, Mahoning County Court-Ohio
Houser, Robert-Judge, Superior Court of Arizona Maricopa County-Ariz.
Houston, David W., III-Judge, United States Bankruptcy Court Northern District of Mississippi-Miss.
Houston, J. Gorman, Jr.-Associate Justice, Alabama Supreme Court-Ala.
Houston, Jeanie Reavis-Judge, North Carolina District Court District 23-N.C.
Houston, John A.-Magistrate Judge, United States District Court Southern District of California-Calif.
Houston, Julian T.-Associate Justice, Trial Court of Massachusetts Superior Court Department-Mass.
Hovland, Daniel L.-Chief Judge, United States District Court District of North Dakota-N.D.
Howald, J. Kent-Associate Circuit Judge, Missouri Circuit Court Forty-second Judicial Circuit-Mo.
Howard, Brenda-Judge, Probate Court of Pierce County-Ga.
Howard, David A.-Judge, Vermont Trial Court-Vt.
Howard, Fred D.-Judge, Utah District Court Fourth Judicial District-Utah
Howard, Garritt E.-Circuit Judge, Illinois Circuit Court of Cook County-Ill.
Howard, George, Jr.-Judge, United States District Court Eastern District of Arkansas-Ark.
Howard, Jeffrey R.-Judge, United States Court of Appeals First Circuit
Howard, John L. "Pete"-Justice, Teton County Justice of the Peace Court and Judge, Choteau, Dutton and Fairfield City Courts-Mont.
Howard, Joseph W.-Judge, Arizona Court of Appeals Division Two-Ariz.
Howard, Kenneth R.-Judge, Reno Municipal Court-Nev.
Howard, Lee J.-Judge, Mississippi Circuit Court Sixteenth Judicial District-Miss.
Howard, Malcolm J.-Judge, United States District Court Eastern District of North Carolina-N.C.
Howard, Patrice-Judge, Probate Court of Putnam County-Ga.
Howard, Richard-Judge, Florida Circuit Court Fifth Judicial Circuit-Fla.
Howard, Victor C.-Judge, Missouri Court of Appeals Western District-Mo.
Howard, Vincent K.-Judge, Wisconsin Circuit Court Marathon Circuit-Wis.
Howard, William L., Sr.-Associate Judge, South Carolina Court of Appeals-S.C.
Howard, William R.-Judge, Minnesota District Court Fourth Judicial District-Minn.
Howard, William S.-Chief Judge, United States Bankruptcy Court Eastern District of Kentucky-Ky.
Howarth, Robert L.-Justice, Trial Court of Massachusetts District Court Department Hampden County Palmer Division-Mass.
Howatt, William J., Jr.-Judge, Superior Court of California County of San Diego-Calif.
Howe, Barbara-Justice, New York Supreme Court Eighth Judicial District-N.Y.
Howe, Christopher-Judge, Fair Haven District Probate Court-Vt.
Howe, Donald B.-Judge, Superior Court of Georgia Douglas Judicial Circuit-Ga.
Howe, Thomas R.-Judge, Minnesota District Court First Judicial District-Minn.
Howell, Baxter C.-Chief Magistrate, Magistrate Court of Dougherty County-Ga.
Howell, R. Joseph-Judge, Martin Circuit Court-Ind.
Howell, Shepherd Lee-Chief Judge, Superior Court of Georgia Cherokee Judicial Circuit-Ga.
Howell, Steven J.-Judge, Superior Court of California County of Butte-Calif.
Howerton, Philip F., Jr.-Judge, North Carolina District Court District 26-N.C.
Howes, Mary E.-District Associate Judge, Iowa District Court Seventh Judicial District-Ia.
Howland, Ronald L.-Recalled Magistrate Judge, United States District Court Western District of Oklahoma-Okla.
Howorth, Andrew K.-Judge, Mississippi Circuit Court Third Judicial District-Miss.
Howorth, H. Philip-Justice, Nashua District Court-N.H.
Howsare, Daniel Lee-President Judge, Pennsylvania Court of Common Pleas Fifty-seventh Judicial District-Pa.
Howse, Nathaniel R., Jr.-Circuit Judge, Illinois Circuit Court of Cook County-Ill.
Hoy, John J.-Judge, Florida Circuit Court Fifteenth Judicial Circuit-Fla.
Hoye, Polly A.-Judge, Fulton County Court-N.Y.
Hoyer, Kevin L.-Judge, Washington County Court-Colo.
Hoying, Fred H.-Judge, Jefferson Superior Court-Ind.

ALPHABETICAL NAME INDEX

Hoyle, Angela G.-Judge, North Carolina District Court District 27A-N.C.

Hoyle, Clifford D.-Judge, Derby District Probate Court-Conn.

Hoyt, Christine-Magistrate, Vermont Trial Court-Vt.

Hoyt, Irvin N.-Chief Judge, United States Bankruptcy Court District of South Dakota-S.D.

Hoyt, Kenneth M.-Judge, United States District Court Southern District of Texas-Tex.

Hrko, John S.-Chief Judge, West Virginia Circuit Court Twenty-seventh Judicial Circuit-W.Va.

Hronek, Thomas R.-District Associate Judge, Iowa District Court Second Judicial District-Ia.

Hubbard, Arnette R.-Circuit Judge, Illinois Circuit Court of Cook County-Ill.

Hubbard, Carol Ann-Special Judge, Oklahoma District Court Seventh Judicial District-Okla.

Hubbard, Edward Lewis-Judge, Virginia Circuit Court Seventh Judicial Circuit-Va.

Hubbard, Philip G., Jr.-Judge, Washington Superior Court King County-Wash.

Hubbart, Gerald D.-Judge, Florida Circuit Court Eleventh Judicial Circuit-Fla.

Hubbell, Billy-Judge, Crossett District Court-Ark.

Hubbell, Gerald-Judge, Franklin County Court-Tex.

Hubbell, Martina M.-Magistrate Judge, Kansas District Court Thirteenth Judicial District-Kan.

Hubbell, Richard C.-Judge, Superior Court of California County of Los Angeles-Calif.

Hubel, Dennis J.-Magistrate Judge, United States District Court District of Oregon-Ore.

Huber, John E.-Judge, Nebraska County Court Fourth Judicial District-Neb.

Huber, Joseph-Judge, Superior Court of California County of Santa Clara-Calif.

Huber, Michael-Judge, Wyoming Circuit Court Seventh Judicial District, Natrona County-Wyo.

Huber, Raymond S.-Judge, Wisconsin Circuit Court Waupaca Circuit-Wis.

Hublar, Robert T.-Judge, Floyd County Court-Ind.

Hubsher, Muriel Shaff-Justice, New York Supreme Court Second Judicial District-N.Y.

Huck, Paul C.-Judge, United States District Court Southern District of Florida-Fla.

Huckleberry, Robert James-Presiding Judge, Oregon Circuit Court Seventeenth Judicial District-Ore.

Huddleston, Joseph Russell-Judge, Kentucky Court of Appeals-Ky.

Huddleston, Margaret R.-Judge, Kentucky Circuit Court Eighth Judicial Circuit-Ky.

Hudgins, W. Edward, Jr.-Judge, Virginia General District Court Second Judicial District-Va.

Hudock, Bruce P.-Judge, Connecticut Superior Court-Conn.

Hudock, Joseph A.-Judge, The Superior Court of Pennsylvania-Pa.

Hudson, Donald C.-Circuit Judge, Illinois Circuit Court Sixteenth Judicial Circuit-Ill.

Hudson, Henry E.-Judge, United States District Court Eastern District of Virginia-Va.

Hudson, J. Harvey-Justice, Texas Court of Appeals Fourteenth District-Tex.

Hudson, James C.-Judge, Suffolk County Court-N.Y.

Hudson, Jim-Judge, Arkansas Circuit Court Eighth South Judicial Circuit-Ark.

Hudson, John N.-Judge, Adams County Court-Miss.

Hudson, Natalie-Judge, Minnesota Court of Appeals-Minn.

Hudson, Orlando F., Jr.-Resident Judge, North Carolina Superior Court Third Judicial Division District 14-N.C.

Hudson, Robin E.-Associate Judge, North Carolina Court of Appeals-N.C.

Hudson, Steven D.-Associate Circuit Judge, Missouri Circuit Court Third Judicial Circuit-Mo.

Hudspeth, Harry Lee-Senior Judge, United States District Court Western District of Texas-Tex.

Hue, William F.-Judge, Wisconsin Circuit Court Jefferson Circuit-Wis.

Huey, Clark E.-Associate District Judge, Oklahoma District Court Third Judicial District-Okla.

Huey, Paul L.-Judge, Hillsborough County Court-Fla.

Huff, Carol E.-Justice, New York Supreme Court First Judicial District-N.Y.

Huff, David A.-Judge, Nevada District Court Third Judicial District-Nev.

Huff, Jim-Judge, Live Oak County Court-Tex.

Huff, Margaret E.-Judge, Probate Court of Gilmer County-Ga.

Huff, Marilyn L.-Chief Judge, United States District Court Southern District of California-Calif.

Huff, Thomas E.-Associate Judge, South Carolina Court of Appeals-S.C.

Huffaker, Stephen L.-Senior Judge, Nevada District Court-Nev.

Huffer, Duane G.-Judge, Kosciusko Superior Court-Ind.

Huffman, Joan-Judge, Texas District Court 183rd Judicial District-Tex.

Huffman, Mary Katherine-Judge, Ohio Court of Common Pleas Montgomery County-Ohio

Huffman, Richard D.-Associate Justice, California Court of Appeal Fourth District Division One-Calif.

Hufstetler, K. Randall-Judge, Texas Family District Court 300th Judicial District-Tex.

Hug, Procter, Jr.-Senior Judge, United States Court of Appeals Ninth Circuit

Hughes, Brian P.-Associate Judge, Illinois Circuit Court Nineteenth Judicial Circuit-Ill.

Hughes, Jack W.-Judge, Alabama Circuit Court Seventh Judicial Circuit-Ala.

Hughes, James F.-Acting Judge, Mechanicville City Court-N.Y.

Hughes, Jean Spradling-Judge, Harris County Criminal Court at Law No. 15-Tex.

Hughes, Jefferson D., III-Judge, Louisiana District Court Twenty-first Judicial District-La.

Hughes, Jeffrey R.-Judge, United States Bankruptcy Court Western District of Michigan-Mich.

Hughes, John J.-Magistrate Judge, United States District Court District of New Jersey-N.J.

Hughes, Lynn Nettleton-Judge, United States District Court Southern District of Texas-Tex.

Hughes, M. Douglas-Judge, Louisiana District Court Twenty-first Judicial District-La.

Hughes, Melvin R., Jr.-Chief Judge, Virginia Circuit Court Thirteenth Judicial Circuit-Va.

Hughes, R. O.-Judge, Jefferson County District Court Birmingham Division-Ala.

Hughes, Renée Cardwell-Judge, Pennsylvania Court of Common Pleas First Judicial District-Pa.

Hughes, Richard L.-Judge, Michigan District Court District Sixty-seven Division Two-Mich.

Hughes, T. Christopher-Judge, Juvenile Court of Georgia Cordele Judicial Circuit-Ga.

Hughes, Thomas M., III-Judge, Beebe District Court-Ark.

Hughes, William J.-Judge, Hamilton Superior Court-Ind.

Hughes, Yvonne-Judge, Orleans Parish Juvenile Court-La.

Hughston, Harold V., Jr.-Presiding Judge, Alabama Circuit Court Thirty-first Judicial Circuit-Ala.

Huguenin, David L.-Chief Magistrate, Magistrate Court of Columbia County-Ga.

Huguenor, Susan D.-Judge, Superior Court of California County of San Diego-Calif.

Huitink, Terry Lee-Judge, Iowa Court of Appeals-Ia.

Huizenga, Roger L.-Judge, Walkerton Town Court-Ind.

Hulbert, David F.-Judge, Washington Superior Court Snohomish County-Wash.

Huling, Valerie Mackie-Judge, New Mexico District Court Second Judicial District-N.Mex.

Hull, Donald W.-Judge, Oregon Circuit Court Seventh Judicial District-Ore.

Hull, Frank M.-Judge, United States Court of Appeals Eleventh Circuit

Hull, Harry E., Jr.-Associate Justice, California Court of Appeal Third District-Calif.

Hull, John A.-Judge, Coryell County Court-Tex.

Hull, LaVail Earl-Chief Judge, Mecosta-Osceola Counties Probate Court District-Mich.

Hull, Owens Lee, Jr.-Presiding Judge, Missouri Circuit Court Sixth Judicial Circuit-Mo.

Hull, Thomas G.-Senior Judge, United States District Court Eastern District of Tennessee-Tenn.

Hulse, Gregory A.-District Judge, Iowa District Court Fifth Judicial District-Ia.

Hulsey, Eddie-Judge, Probate Court of Haralson County-Ga.

Hultgren, David R.-Circuit Judge, Illinois Circuit Court Ninth Judicial Circuit-Ill.

Hultgren, William C.-Judge, Michigan District Court District Nineteen-Mich.

Humble, Charles G.-Special Judge, Oklahoma District Court Seventh Judicial District-Okla.

Hume, James E.-Chief Judge, Virginia Juvenile and Domestic Relations District Court Eleventh Judicial District-Va.

Hummel, Christian F.-Surrogate, Rensselaer County Surrogate's Court-N.Y.

Hummer, Wayne G., Jr.-Judge, Pennsylvania Court of Common Pleas Second Judicial District-Pa.

Humphrey, Charles M., III-District Judge, Oklahoma District Court Twenty-fourth Judicial District-Okla.

Humphrey, Colette M.-Judge, Superior Court of California County of Kern-Calif.

Humphrey, James D.-Judge, Dearborn-Ohio Circuit Court-Ind.

Humphrey, Kathleen-Judge, Ennis City Court-Mont.

Humphrey, Marion-Judge, Arkansas Circuit Court Sixth Judicial Circuit-Ark.

Humphrey, Thomas E.-Justice, Maine Superior Court-Me.

Humphreys, Burrell Ives-Retired Judge, New Jersey Superior Court-N.J.

Humphreys, Elizabeth-Judge, Superior Court of California County of San Joaquin-Calif.

Humphreys, Karen M.-Magistrate Judge, United States District Court District of Kansas-Kan.

Humphreys, Robert J.-Judge, Court of Appeals of Virginia-Va.

Humphries, Paula G.-Judge, Michigan District Court District Thirty-six-Mich.

Hunn, Eric-Judge, Idaho District Court Sixth Judicial District Magistrate Division-Ida.

Hunnicutt, Deborah W.-Judge, Probate Court of Peach County-Ga.

Hunstein, Carol W.-Justice, Supreme Court of Georgia-Ga.

Hunt, Derek W.-Judge, Superior Court of California County of Orange-Calif.

Hunt, J. Robin-Chief Judge, Washington Court of Appeals Division II-Wash.

Hunt, Jack P.-Judge, Superior Court of California County of Los Angeles-Calif.

Hunt, John-Judge, New York City Family Court-N.Y.

Hunt, Keith P.-Chief Judge, Michigan District Court District Forty-three-Mich.

Hunt, Richard V.-Judge, Jefferson County Family Court-N.Y.

Hunt, Roger L.-Judge, United States District Court District of Nevada-Nev.

Hunt, Thomas R.-Judge, Grant Circuit Court-Ind.

Hunt, Willis B., Jr.-Judge, United States District Court Northern District of Georgia-Ga.

Hunter, Alexander Wayman, Jr.-Justice, New York Supreme Court Twelfth Judicial District-N.Y.

Hunter, Arthur L., Jr.-Judge, Louisiana District Court Orleans Parish Criminal District-La.

Hunter, David E.-Judge, Superior Court of California County of Alameda-Calif.

Hunter, E. Allen-Justice, Maine Superior Court-Me.

Hunter, Henley A.-Judge, United States Bankruptcy Court Western District of Louisiana-La.

Hunter, J. Michael-Judge, Florida Circuit Court Tenth Judicial Circuit-Fla.

Hunter, Jack E.-Judge, Texas District Court 94th Judicial District-Tex.

Hunter, John G.-Judge, Crawford County Probate Court-Mich.

Hunter, Linda Warren-Judge, Superior Court of Georgia Stone Mountain Judicial Circuit-Ga.

Hunter, Robert "Bob" C.-Associate Judge, North Carolina Court of Appeals-N.C.

Hunter, Scott D.-Judge, Mahoning County Court-Ohio

Hunter, William D.-Judge, Louisiana District Court Sixteenth Judicial District-La.

ALPHABETICAL NAME INDEX

Hunter, William K.-Judge, North Carolina District Court District 18-N.C.
Huntington, Edward B.-Judge, Superior Court of California County of San Diego-Calif.
Huntsman, Jean L.-Judge, Lima City Court-Mont.
Huot, David O.-Justice, Laconia District Court-N.H.
Hupp, Dennis Lee-Judge, Virginia Circuit Court Twenty-sixth Judicial Circuit-Va.
Hupp, Harry L.-Senior Judge, United States District Court Central District of California-Calif.
Huppert, Lynda F.-Judge, Marion County Small Claims Court Washington Township Division-Ind.
Huppert, Michael-District Judge, Iowa District Court Fifth Judicial District-Ia.
Hupy, William A.-Chief Judge, Menominee County Probate Court-Mich.
Hurd, David N.-Judge, United States District Court Northern District of New York-N.Y.
Hurd, Peter G.-Justice, Plaistow District Court-N.H.
Hurkin-Torres, Allen Z.-Justice, New York Supreme Court Second Judicial District-N.Y.
Hurlbutt, Robert G.-Associate Justice, New York Supreme Court Appellate Division Fourth Judicial Department-N.Y.
Hurley, D. Michael-Judge Referee, Connecticut Superior Court-Conn.
Hurley, Daniel T. K.-Judge, United States District Court Southern District of Florida-Fla.
Hurley, Denis R.-Judge, United States District Court Eastern District of New York-N.Y.
Hurley, James P.-Judge, New Jersey Superior Court Vicinage Eight-N.J.
Hurley, Joseph-Judge, Superior Court of California County of Alameda-Calif.
Hurley, Patrick J.-First Justice, Trial Court of Massachusetts District Court Department Plymouth County Hingham Division-Mass.
Hurley, Roger L.-Judge, Darke County Court-Ohio
Hurley, Steven Leroy-Judge, Ohio Court of Common Pleas Greene County-Ohio
Hurley-Marks, Mary E.-First Justice, Trial Court of Massachusetts District Court Department Hampden County Chicopee Division-Mass.
Hursh, Terry N.-Judge, Marion County Small Claims Court Lawrence Township Division-Ind.
Hurst, Patricia A.-Associate Justice, Rhode Island Superior Court-R.I.
Hurt, Steve D.-Judge, Kentucky District Court Sixtieth Judicial District-Ky.
Hurtado, Michael S.-Judge, Seattle Municipal Court-Wash.
Hurwitz, Andrew D.-Justice, Supreme Court of Arizona-Ariz.
Huschen, John B.-Circuit Judge, Illinois Circuit Court Eleventh Judicial Circuit-Ill.
Huscher, Paul R.-District Judge, Iowa District Court Fifth Judicial District-Ia.
Husing, Sylvia L.-Judge, Superior Court of California County of San Bernardino-Calif.
Hussmann, William G., Jr.-Magistrate Judge, United States District Court Southern District of Indiana-Ind.
Husum, Carol A.-Judge, Michigan District Court District Eight Division One-Mich.
Hutchens, Pamela E.-Judge, Virginia General District Court Second Judicial District-Va.
Hutcherson, James W.-Justice, New York Supreme Court Second Judicial District-N.Y.
Hutcheson, R. Michael-Judge, Florida Circuit Court Seventh Judicial Circuit-Fla.
Hutcheson, Robert W.-Judge, Ohio Court of Common Pleas Greene County-Ohio
Hutchins, Laurie L.-Judge, North Carolina District Court District 21-N.C.
Hutchins, Miriam Brown-Associate Judge, Maryland District Court District One-Md.
Hutchins, Thomas J.-Judge, Superior Court of California County of Ventura-Calif.
Hutchinson, A'Lan S.-Judge, Eatonville Municipal Court-Wash.
Hutchinson, Lew-Judge, Lewis District Court Lewis County-Wash.
Hutchinson, Susan Fayette-Judge, Illinois Appellate Court Second Judicial District-Ill.
Hutchison, Brian D.-Judge, Jay Circuit Court-Ind.
Hutchison, John A.-Chief Judge, West Virginia Circuit Court Tenth Judicial Circuit-W.Va.
Hutchison, Robert A.-District Judge, Iowa District Court Fifth Judicial District-Ia.
Huth, Mark-Judge, Jefferson District Court Jefferson County-Wash.
Hutson, Robert Byron-Judge, Superior Court of California County of Orange-Calif.
Huttman, Howard, Jr.-Justice of the Peace, McDermitt Justices' Court-Nev.
Huttner, Richard D.-Justice, New York Supreme Court Second Judicial District-N.Y.
Hutton, Christopher W.-Chief Judge, Virginia Circuit Court Eighth Judicial Circuit-Va.
Hutton, Herbert J.-Judge, United States District Court Eastern District of Pennsylvania-Pa.
Hutton, James P.-Judge, Washington Superior Court Yakima County-Wash.
Hutton, Todd J.-Judge, Nebraska County Court Second Judicial District-Neb.
Huvelle, Ellen Segal-Judge, United States District Court District of Columbia-D.C.
Hyatt, Carey S.-Judge, Superior Court of Arizona Maricopa County-Ariz.
Hyatt, Darrell-Judge, Rusk County Court at Law-Tex.
Hyatt, Janet Marlene-Resident Judge, North Carolina Superior Court Eighth Judicial Division District 30B-N.C.
Hyatt, Robert S.-Judge, Colorado District Court Second Judicial District-Colo.
Hyde, D. Ronald-Judge, Superior Court of California County of Alameda-Calif.
Hyde, John Gary-Judge, Texas District Court 238th Judicial District-Tex.
Hyde, Stephen J.-Judge, Westport Municipal Court-Wash.
Hyde, Troy K.-Associate Circuit Judge, Missouri Circuit Court Twenty-fourth Judicial Circuit-Mo.
Hyland, Colleen A.-Associate Judge, Illinois Circuit Court of Cook County-Ill.
Hyman, Eugene M.-Judge, Superior Court of California County of Santa Clara-Calif.
Hyman, Paul G., Jr.-Judge, United States Bankruptcy Court Southern District of Florida-Fla.
Hymer, Allan D.-Judge, Superior Court of California County of Alameda-Calif.
Hynes, John J.-Associate Judge, Illinois Circuit Court of Cook County-Ill.
Hynes, Thomas J.-Judge, New Mexico District Court Eleventh Judicial District-N.Mex.
Hyslop, Peyton B.-Judge, Hernando County Court-Fla.
Iacovetta, Nicholas J.-Judge, The Criminal Court of the City of New York-N.Y.
Iadanza, Eugene A.-Judge, New Jersey Superior Court Vicinage Nine-N.J.
Iannazzone, Joseph-Judge, State Court of Gwinnett County-Ga.
Iannotti, Frank A.-Judge, Connecticut Superior Court-Conn.
Ibarra, Ronald-Chief Judge, Hawaii Circuit Court Third Judicial Circuit-Hi.
Icenogle, John Philip-Judge, Nebraska District Court Ninth Judicial District-Neb.
Ichikawa, Garry T.-Judge, Superior Court of California County of Solano-Calif.
Ide, Robert A.-Judge, Nebraska County Court Tenth Judicial District-Neb.
Ige, Douglas H.-Deputy Chief Judge, Hawaii District Court Second Judicial Circuit-Hi.
Iglehart, Richard B.-Judge, Superior Court of California County of Alameda-Calif.
Ikeda, Dale-Judge, Superior Court of California County of Fresno-Calif.
Ikola, Raymond J.-Associate Justice, California Court of Appeal Fourth District Division Three-Calif.
Iles, Pamela Lee-Judge, Superior Court of California County of Orange-Calif.
Illingworth, Stephen R.-Judge, Nebraska District Court Tenth Judicial District-Neb.
Illston, Susan Yvonne-Judge, United States District Court Northern District of California-Calif.
Im, Seung Woo-Judge, Pinellas County Court-Fla.
Imber, Annabelle Clinton-Associate Justice, Arkansas Supreme Court-Ark.
Imbornone, Charles A.-Judge, New Orleans First City Court-La.
Imbrogno, Cynthia-Magistrate Judge, United States District Court Eastern District of Washington-Wash.
Imler, Kyle L.-Judge, Oakville Municipal Court-Wash.
Inboden, Steve-Judge, Harrisburg and Trumann District Courts-Ark.
Inbody, Everett O., II-Judge, Nebraska Court of Appeals-Neb.
Indeglia, Gilbert V.-Associate Justice, Rhode Island Superior Court-R.I.
Inderlied, H. F., Jr.-Judge, Ohio Court of Common Pleas Geauga County-Ohio
Infante, Edward A.-Recalled Magistrate Judge, United States District Court Northern District of California-Calif.
Infantino, Jerald A.-Judge, Superior Court of California County of Santa Clara-Calif.
Ingle, Gary A.-Judge, Superior Court of California County of Kern-Calif.
Ingraham, Jeffrey R.-Judge, Ohio Court of Common Pleas Mercer County-Ohio
Ingram, Cheryl D.-Circuit Judge, Illinois Circuit Court of Cook County-Ill.
Ingram, Edith J.-Judge, Probate Court of Hancock County-Ga.
Ingram, G. Conley-Senior Judge, Supreme Court of Georgia-Ga.
Ingram, Mark A.-Judge, Idaho District Court Fifth Judicial District Magistrate Division-Ida.
Ingram, S. Lark-Judge, Superior Court of Georgia Cobb Judicial Circuit-Ga.
Ingram, Shirley R.-Chief Magistrate, Magistrate Court of Hancock County-Ga.
Ingvalson, Robert J.-Judge, Benton District Court Prosser Branch Benton County-Wash.
Injejikian, Maral-Judge, Superior Court of California County of Los Angeles-Calif.
Inman, Dennis H.-Magistrate Judge, United States District Court Eastern District of Tennessee-Tenn.
Inman, William H.-Senior Judge, Tennessee Appellate and Trial Courts-Tenn.
Inman-Campbell, Gail-Judge, Harrison District Court-Ark.
Innes, Paul-Judge, New Jersey Superior Court Vicinage Seven-N.J.
Inveen, Laura-Judge, Washington Superior Court King County-Wash.
Ionta, Robert W.-Magistrate Judge, United States District Court District of New Mexico-N.Mex.
Iosco, Anthony A.-Circuit Judge, Illinois Circuit Court of Cook County-Ill.
Ippolito, Joseph P., Jr.-Magistrate, Rhode Island District Court-R.I.
Irby, John C.-Judge, North Dakota District Court East Central Judicial District-N.D.
Ireland, Faith-Justice, Washington Supreme Court-Wash.
Ireland, Kathleen D.-Judge, Broward County Court-Fla.
Ireland, Roderick L.-Associate Justice, Massachusetts Supreme Judicial Court-Mass.
Irenas, Joseph E.-Senior Judge, United States District Court District of New Jersey-N.J.
Irigoin, Katherine M.-Judge, Montana District Court Seventh Judicial District-Mont.
Irion, Joan K.-Judge, Superior Court of California County of San Diego-Calif.
Irons, Robert A.-Chief Judge, West Virginia Circuit Court Thirty-first Judicial Circuit-W.Va.
Iroz, John M.-Judge, Nevada District Court Sixth Judicial District-Nev.
Irvin, J. C.-District Judge, Iowa District Court Fourth Judicial District-Ia.
Irvin, R. Lee-Judge, Shreveport City Court-La.
Irvine, Patrick G.-Judge, Arizona Court of Appeals Division One-Ariz.
Irvine, Peter-Judge, Minnesota District Court Seventh Judicial District-Minn.
Irving, Jane Ellen-Judge, Holmes County Court-Ohio
Irving, Tyree-Judge, Court of Appeals of Mississippi-Miss.
Irwin, Charles A.-Judge, Superior Court of Arizona Cochise County-Ariz.
Irwin, David B.-Judge, Superior Court of Georgia Rockdale Judicial Circuit-Ga.

ALPHABETICAL NAME INDEX

Irwin, Jay R.-Magistrate Judge, United States District Court District of Arizona-Ariz.

Irwin, John F.-Judge, Nebraska Court of Appeals-Neb.

Irwin, Michael E.-Judge, Heber Springs District Court-Ark.

Isaac, Sheila R.-Judge, Kentucky Circuit Court Twenty-second Judicial Circuit-Ky.

Isaacks, Vicki B.-Judge, Texas District Court 393rd Judicial District-Tex.

Isaacs, Paul F.-Judge, Kentucky Circuit Court Fourteenth Judicial Circuit-Ky.

Isaacson, Rodger J.-Judge, Oregon Circuit Court Thirteenth Judicial District-Ore.

Isabella, Joseph V.-Judge, New Jersey Superior Court Vicinage Five-N.J.

Isackson, Carol-Judge, Superior Court of California County of San Diego-Calif.

Isacoff, Susan Elizabeth-Judge, Superior Court of California County of Los Angeles-Calif.

Isbell, Gary B.-Judge, Arkansas Circuit Court Fourteenth Judicial Circuit-Ark.

Isenhour, William O., Jr.-Judge, Kansas District Court Tenth Judicial District-Kan.

Ishii, Anthony W.-Judge, United States District Court Eastern District of California-Calif.

Ishikawa, Brian K.-Judge, Superior Court of Arizona Maricopa County-Ariz.

Isman, James E.-Judge, New Jersey Tax Court-N.J.

Isom, Claudia Rickert-Judge, Florida Circuit Court Thirteenth Judicial Circuit-Fla.

Ison, William H.-Senior Judge, Superior Court of Georgia-Ga.

Israel, R. Ted-Judge, Idaho District Court Sixth Judicial District Magistrate Division-Ida.

Issenman, David J.-Judge, New Jersey Superior Court Vicinage Twelve-N.J.

Ito, Lance Allan-Judge, Superior Court of California County of Los Angeles-Calif.

Iuliani, Anthony J.-Retired Judge, New Jersey Superior Court-N.J.

Iuppa, Barney-Judge, El Paso County Court-Colo.

Ivanchak, Terry-Judge, Warren Municipal Court-Ohio

Ivers, Donald L.-Judge, United States Court of Appeals for Veterans Claims

Ives, Dan-Judge, East Camden District Court-Ark.

Iwanicki, Don B.-Judge, Batavia City Court-N.Y.

Iwasaki, Glenn K.-Judge, Utah District Court Third Judicial District-Utah

Iwasko, James F.-Judge, Superior Court of California County of Santa Barbara-Calif.

Jaaskelainen, James George-Chief Judge, Keweenaw County Probate Court-Mich.

Jabar, Joseph M.-Justice, Maine Superior Court-Me.

Jabour, Christine S.-Magistrate, Rhode Island District Court-R.I.

Jack, Janis Graham-Judge, United States District Court Southern District of Texas-Tex.

Jacke, Linda-Judge, King District Court East Division King County-Wash.

Jackson, Bonnie F.-Judge, Louisiana District Court Nineteenth Judicial District-La.

Jackson, Carol E.-Chief Judge, United States District Court Eastern District of Missouri-Mo.

Jackson, Darnell-Judge, Michigan District Court District Seventy Division Two-Mich.

Jackson, Donald Wayne-Judge, Harris County Criminal Court at Law No. 3-Tex.

Jackson, Dwight David-Associate Judge, Circuit Court for Prince George's County, Seventh Judicial Circuit-Md.

Jackson, Elizabeth-Judge, Pennsylvania Court of Common Pleas First Judicial District-Pa.

Jackson, Frank Y.-Judge, Superior Court of California County of Los Angeles-Calif.

Jackson, Gary E.-Judge, City Court of Atlanta-Ga.

Jackson, Gwendolyn Jones-Chief Judge, Virginia General District Court Fourth Judicial District-Va.

Jackson, J. Russell-Judge, Juvenile Court of Georgia Bell-Forsyth Judicial Circuit-Ga.

Jackson, James A.-Judge, North Carolina District Court District 27A-N.C.

Jackson, James L.-Judge, New Jersey Superior Court Vicinage One-N.J.

Jackson, Joe L.-Associate District Judge, Oklahoma District Court Second Judicial District-Okla.

Jackson, John H.-Judge, Texas District Court 13th Judicial District-Tex.

Jackson, John J.-Associate Circuit Judge, Missouri Circuit Court Tenth Judicial Circuit-Mo.

Jackson, June-Judge, Waller County Court at Law-Tex.

Jackson, K. Dawson-Chief Judge, Superior Court of Georgia Gwinnett Judicial Circuit-Ga.

Jackson, Kathy King-Judge, Mississippi Circuit Court Nineteenth Judicial District-Miss.

Jackson, Kenneth G.-Chief Magistrate, Magistrate Court of Jasper County-Ga.

Jackson, Lenwood A.-Judge, City Court of Atlanta-Ga.

Jackson, Linda E.-Judge, Probate Court of Randolph County-Ga.

Jackson, M. Randolph-Justice, New York Supreme Court Second Judicial District-N.Y.

Jackson, Marianne-Associate Judge, Illinois Circuit Court of Cook County-Ill.

Jackson, Niles L.-Judge, United States Bankruptcy Court Western District of Oklahoma-Okla.

Jackson, Norman H.-Presiding Judge, Utah Court of Appeals-Utah

Jackson, R. Brooke-Judge, Colorado District Court First Judicial District-Colo.

Jackson, Randall R.-Circuit Judge, Missouri Circuit Court Fifth Judicial Circuit-Mo.

Jackson, Raymond Alvin-Judge, United States District Court Eastern District of Virginia-Va.

Jackson, Richard Eli-Associate Judge, Circuit Court for Cecil County, Second Judicial Circuit-Md.

Jackson, Ronald E.-Judge, Shelby County District Court-Ala.

Jackson, S. Edward-Judge, Alabama Circuit Court Twentieth Judicial Circuit-Ala.

Jackson, S. Farrell-Judge, Ohio Court of Common Pleas Fairfield County-Ohio

Jackson, Sally-Judge, West Virginia Family Court Circuit Twenty-four-W.Va.

Jackson, Stephen L.-Judge, Superior Court of Georgia Waycross Judicial Circuit-Ga.

Jackson, Teri L.-Judge, Superior Court of California City and County of San Francisco-Calif.

Jackson, Thomas Edward-Judge, Michigan Circuit Court Third Judicial Circuit-Mich.

Jackson, Thomas P.-Senior Judge, United States District Court District of Columbia-D.C.

Jackson, William M.-Associate Judge, Superior Court of the District of Columbia-D.C.

Jackson-Thompson, Marie O.-First Justice, Trial Court of Massachusetts District Court Department Middlesex County Woburn Division and Justice, Cambridge Division-Mass.

Jackwig, Lee M.-Judge, United States Bankruptcy Court Southern District of Iowa-Ia.

Jacob, Avelina S.-Judge, Virginia Juvenile and Domestic Relations District Court Twentieth Judicial District-Va.

Jacobi, Jerry F.-Judge, Clark Superior Court-Ind.

Jacobius, Moshe-Circuit Judge, Illinois Circuit Court of Cook County-Ill.

Jacobs, Dennis G.-Judge, United States Court of Appeals Second Circuit

Jacobs, Donald M.-Emergency Judge, North Carolina Superior Court-N.C.

Jacobs, Gary W.-Circuit Judge, Illinois Circuit Court Fifth Judicial Circuit-Ill.

Jacobs, George-Associate Justice, Massachusetts Appeals Court-Mass.

Jacobs, Jack B.-Vice Chancellor, Delaware Court of Chancery-Del.

Jacobs, John-Associate Circuit Judge, Missouri Circuit Court Forty-fourth Judicial Circuit-Mo.

Jacobs, Julian I.-Senior Judge, United States Tax Court

Jacobs, Louise M.-District Associate Judge, Iowa District Court Fifth Judicial District-Ia.

Jacobs, Rolly W.-Judge, South Carolina Family Court Fifth Judicial Circuit-S.C.

Jacobs-May, Jamie A.-Judge, Superior Court of California County of Santa Clara-Calif.

Jacobsen, Donald G.-Judge, Florida Circuit Court Tenth Judicial Circuit-Fla.

Jacobson, Debra A.-Judge, Minnesota District Court Third Judicial District-Minn.

Jacobson, Edward A.-District Judge, Iowa District Court Third Judicial District-Ia.

Jacobson, Laura Lee-Justice, New York Supreme Court Second Judicial District-N.Y.

Jacobson, Marc-Chief Judge, Virginia Circuit Court Fourth Judicial Circuit-Va.

Jacobson, Mary C.-Judge, New Jersey Superior Court Vicinage Five-N.J.

Jacobus, Bruce W.-Chief Judge, Florida Circuit Court Eighteenth Judicial Circuit-Fla.

Jaeger, Karl W.-Judge, Superior Court of California County of Los Angeles-Calif.

Jaeger, Steven M.-Judge, Nassau County District Court-N.Y.

Jaeger, Steven R.-Judge, Kentucky Circuit Court Sixteenth Judicial Circuit-Ky.

Jaffe, Aaron-Circuit Judge, Illinois Circuit Court of Cook County-Ill.

Jaffe, Barbara-Judge, The Civil Court of the City of New York-N.Y.

Jaffe, Bernard R.-Senior Judge, Dade County Court-Fla.

Jaffe, Dana Mitchell-Judge, Nassau County District Court-N.Y.

Jagielski, Raymond L.-Circuit Judge, Illinois Circuit Court of Cook County-Ill.

Jahnke, Lawrence E.-Judge, North Dakota District Court Northeast Central Judicial District-N.D.

Jahr, Steven E.-Judge, Superior Court of California County of Shasta-Calif.

Jaklitsch, Michele Dane-Associate Judge, Circuit Court for Anne Arundel County, Fifth Judicial Circuit-Md.

Jakubowski, Ruth A.-Associate Judge, Circuit Court for Baltimore County, Third Judicial Circuit-Md.

Jakubowski, Walter A., Jr.-Chief Judge, Michigan District Court District Thirty-seven-Mich.

James, Debra A.-Judge, The Civil Court of the City of New York-N.Y.

James, Dennis Lee-Judge, Wrightsville District Court-Ark.

James, George E.-Judge, Pennsylvania Court of Common Pleas Thirty-sixth Judicial District-Pa.

James, Hilda-Chief Magistrate, Magistrate Court of Atkinson County-Ga.

James, Jay Paul-Associate Judge, Delaware Court of Common Pleas New Castle County-Del.

James, Jerome-Judge, Virginia Circuit Court Fourth Judicial Circuit-Va.

James, Jim D.-Judge, Ohio Court of Common Pleas Stark County-Ohio

James, Joseph M.-Judge, Pennsylvania Court of Common Pleas Fifth Judicial District-Pa.

James, Maria-Elena-Magistrate Judge, United States District Court Northern District of California-Calif.

James, Mary Lynne-Judge, Moffat County Court-Colo.

James, Nena R.-Judge, Wyoming District Court Third Judicial District-Wyo.

James, Richard L.-Judge, Ohio Court of Common Pleas Trumbull County-Ohio

James, Robert G.-Judge, United States District Court Western District of Louisiana-La.

James, Robert J.-Chief Judge, Superior Court of Georgia Douglas Judicial Circuit-Ga.

James, Sylvia A.-Chief Judge, Michigan District Court District Twenty-two-Mich.

James, Thomas A., Jr.-Judge, Pennsylvania Court of Common Pleas Twenty-sixth Judicial District-Pa.

James, Tom-Justice, Texas Court of Appeals Fifth District-Tex.

James, Wanda Dinius-Justice, Mineral County Justice of the Peace Court and Judge, Alberton and Superior City Courts-Mont.

Jameson, C. Robert-Judge, Superior Court of California County of Orange-Calif.

Jameson, Charles W.-Chief Judge, Lenawee County Probate Court-Mich.

Jamieson, Linda S.-Justice, New York Supreme Court Ninth Judicial District-N.Y.

Jamin, Matthew D.-Magistrate Judge, United States District Court District of Alaska-Alas.

ALPHABETICAL NAME INDEX

Jamison, Alfred G.-Judge, Colorado County Court-Tex.
Jamison, Birdie Hairston-Judge, Virginia General District Court Thirteenth Judicial District-Va.
Jamison, Leon-Judge, Arkansas Circuit Court Eleventh West Judicial Circuit-Ark.
Jamison, Martha Hill-Judge, Texas District Court 164th Judicial District-Tex.
Jamison, Michael T.-Associate Circuit Judge, Missouri Circuit Court Twenty-first Judicial Circuit-Mo.
Janas, Thomas W.-Judge, Ohio Court of Common Pleas Lorain County-Ohio
Janavs, Dzintra I.-Judge, Superior Court of California County of Los Angeles-Calif.
Janecka, Edward F.-Judge, Fayette County Court-Tex.
Janelle, Andre G.-Judge, Maine District Court-Me.
Janes, David R.-Judge, West Virginia Circuit Court Sixteenth Judicial Circuit-W.Va.
Janes, Robert L.-Associate Judge, Illinois Circuit Court Sixteenth Judicial Circuit-Ill.
Jann, Norma-Judge, Illinois Court of Claims-Ill.
Janow, Lawrence-Judge, Virginia Juvenile and Domestic Relations District Court Twenty-fourth Judicial District-Va.
Janowitz, Norman-Judge, Nassau County District Court-N.Y.
Jansen, James P.-Judge, Wisconsin Circuit Court Langlade Circuit-Wis.
Jansen, Kathleen-Judge, Michigan Court of Appeals-Mich.
Jansen, William D.-Justice of the Peace, Las Vegas Justices' Court-Nev.
Janura, Arthur L., Jr.-Associate Judge, Illinois Circuit Court of Cook County-Ill.
Januzzi, Thomas A.-Judge, Oberlin Municipal Court-Ohio
Janzen, Andrea Price-Judge, Jefferson Parish Juvenile Court-La.
Jarasitis, Allen J.-Justice, Trial Court of Massachusetts District Court Department Suffolk County Charlestown Division-Mass.
Jarboe, Carl F.-Chief Judge, Grosse Pointe Park Municipal Court-Mich.
Jarman, Timothy T.-District Associate Judge, Iowa District Court Third Judicial District-Ia.
Jaroslovsky, Alan-Judge, United States Bankruptcy Court Northern District of California-Calif.
Jarrell, Cynthia J.-Judge, West Virginia Family Court Circuit Ten-W.Va.
Jarrell, H. Thomas, Jr.-Judge, North Carolina District Court District 18-N.C.
Jarrett, Barbara M.-Judge, Superior Court of Arizona Maricopa County-Ariz.
Jarrett, Edward L.-Judge, Caldwell County Court at Law No. 1-Tex.
Jarrette, James C.-Judge, Kosciusko Superior Court-Ind.
Jarvey, John A.-Magistrate Judge, United States District Court Northern District of Iowa-Ia.
Jarvis, James H., II-Senior Judge, United States District Court Eastern District of Tennessee-Tenn.
Jasmine, Madeline-Judge, Louisiana District Court Fortieth Judicial District-La.
Jasper, Jenny Walker-Judge, Minnesota District Court Tenth Judicial District-Minn.
Jasper, Mabel M.-Judge, Cleveland Municipal Court-Ohio
Jasprica, Judy Rae-Judge, Pierce District Court Pierce County-Wash.
Jauch, Richard Morgan-Judge, Arapahoe County Court-Colo.
Jaynes, Ralph H.-Presiding Judge, Missouri Circuit Court Fourteenth Judicial Circuit-Mo.
Jean, Arthur H., Jr.-Judge, Superior Court of California County of Los Angeles-Calif.
Jeansonne, Mark Anthony-Judge, Louisiana District Court Twelfth Judicial District-La.
Jefferson, Deadra L.-Judge, South Carolina Circuit Court Ninth Judicial Circuit-S.C.
Jefferson, Patricia L.-Judge, Michigan District Court District Thirty-six-Mich.
Jefferson, Wallace B.-Justice, Texas Supreme Court-Tex.
Jeffery, Michael I.-Presiding Judge, Alaska Superior Court Second Judicial District-Alas.
Jeffrey, David L.-Associate Judge, Illinois Circuit Court Fifteenth Judicial Circuit-Ill.
Jeffreys, Gary-Chief Judge, New Mexico District Court Sixth Judicial District-N.Mex.
Jelderks, John A.-Magistrate Judge, United States District Court District of Oregon-Ore.
Jellen, Edward D.-Chief Judge, United States Bankruptcy Court Northern District of California-Calif.
Jenkins, Bruce-Judge, Franklin County Municipal Court-Ohio
Jenkins, Bruce S.-Senior Judge, United States District Court District of Utah-Utah
Jenkins, Clarence N., Jr.-Judge, Virginia Juvenile and Domestic Relations District Court Thirteenth Judicial District-Va.
Jenkins, Claude-Judge, DeWitt District Court-Ark.
Jenkins, Dale-Judge, State Court of McIntosh County-Ga.
Jenkins, David A.-Judge, Vermont Trial Court-Vt.
Jenkins, Elizabeth A.-Magistrate Judge, United States District Court Middle District of Florida-Fla.
Jenkins, Jack W.-Special Judge, North Carolina Superior Court-N.C.
Jenkins, Knox V., Jr.-Resident Judge, North Carolina Superior Court Fourth Judicial Division District 11B-N.C.
Jenkins, Martin J.-Judge, United States District Court Northern District of California-Calif.
Jenkins, Michael Grady-Chief Magistrate, Magistrate Court of Screven County-Ga.
Jenkins, Patricia H.-Judge, Pennsylvania Court of Common Pleas Thirty-second Judicial District-Pa.
Jenkins, Ray L.-Judge, Tennessee Criminal Court Sixth Judicial District-Tenn.
Jenkins, Robert N., Sr.-Judge, South Carolina Family Court Thirteenth Judicial Circuit-S.C.
Jenkins, Scott H.-Judge, Texas District Court 53rd Judicial District-Tex.
Jenkins, Thomas K.-Judge, Ohio Court of Common Pleas Marion County-Ohio
Jennemann, Karen S.-Judge, United States Bankruptcy Court Middle District of Florida-Fla.
Jennings, J. C.-Judge, Morris County Court-Tex.
Jennings, James B.-Judge, Superior Court of California County of Santa Barbara-Calif.
Jennings, Joseph W., III-Circuit Justice, Trial Court of Massachusetts District Court Department-Mass.
Jennings, Terry-Justice, Texas Court of Appeals First District-Tex.
Jennings, William D., III-Judge, Civil Court of Richmond County and Chief Magistrate, Magistrate Court of Richmond County-Ga.
Jennings, William T.-Judge, Kentucky Circuit Court Twenty-fifth Judicial Circuit-Ky.
Jenrette, Isaac-Senior Judge, Superior Court of Georgia-Ga.
Jensen, D. Lowell-Senior Judge, United States District Court Northern District of California-Calif.
Jensen, James D.-Judge, Ohio Court of Common Pleas Lucas County-Ohio
Jensen, Karen A. Murphy-Associate Judge, Circuit Court for Caroline County, Second Judicial Circuit-Md.
Jensen, Kathleen-Justice, Cascade County Justice of the Peace Court-Mont.
Jensen, Lance-Judge, Superior Court of California County of Orange-Calif.
Jent, Julia M.-Judge, Porter Superior Court-Ind.
Jeremiah, Jeremiah S., Jr.-Chief Judge, Rhode Island Family Court-R.I.
Jergins, Michael P.-Judge, Texas District Court 395th Judicial District-Tex.
Jernigan, David H.-Judge, Kentucky Circuit Court Forty-fifth Judicial Circuit-Ky.
Jernigan, E. Wayne-Judge, Juvenile Court of Georgia Chattahoochee Judicial Circuit-Ga.
Jerz, James W.-Associate Judge, Illinois Circuit Court Eighteenth Judicial Circuit-Ill.
Jeske, Larry L.-Judge, Wisconsin Circuit Court Oconto Circuit-Wis.
Jesse, Michael S.-Judge, Minnesota District Court Seventh Judicial District-Minn.
Jessen, Richard T.-Judge, Minnesota District Court Seventh Judicial District-Minn.
Jessop, Gerald C.-Judge, Superior Court of California County of San Diego-Calif.
Jessop, Morris T.-Judge, Pinesdale City Court-Mont.
Jessup, Stephen M.-Judge, Howard Superior Court-Ind.
Jewell, Angela-Judge, New Mexico District Court Second Judicial District-N.Mex.
Jewell, Tommy E.-Judge, New Mexico District Court Second Judicial District-N.Mex.
Jewell, Wallace-Justice, Lewis and Clark County Justice of the Peace Court-Mont.
Joannides, Stephanie-Judge, Alaska Superior Court Third Judicial District-Alas.
Joel, David J.-Magistrate Judge, United States District Court Northern District of West Virginia-W.Va.
Johansen, Scott-Presiding Judge, Utah Juvenile Court Seventh Judicial District-Utah
Johanson, Jill-Judge, Washington Superior Court Cowlitz County-Wash.
John, Joseph R., Sr.-Retired Judge, North Carolina Court of Appeals-N.C.
John, Steven H.-Judge, South Carolina Circuit Court Fifteenth Judicial Circuit-S.C.
Johns, Timothy Robert-Judge, South Dakota Circuit Court Fourth Judicial Circuit-S.D.
Johnson, Alan Bond-Judge, United States District Court District of Wyoming-Wyo.
Johnson, Albert L.-Presiding Judge, Alabama Circuit Court Twenty-sixth Judicial Circuit-Ala.
Johnson, Alton P.-Chief Magistrate, Magistrate Court of Carroll County-Ga.
Johnson, Alvin D.-Judge, South Carolina Family Court Thirteenth Judicial Circuit-S.C.
Johnson, Anthony H.-Judge, Florida Circuit Court Ninth Judicial Circuit-Fla.
Johnson, Barbara D.-Judge, Washington Superior Court Clark County-Wash.
Johnson, Barbara R.-Judge, Superior Court of California County of Los Angeles-Calif.
Johnson, Bernette Joshua-Justice, Supreme Court of Louisiana-La.
Johnson, Boyd T.-Judge, Superior Court of Arizona Pinal County-Ariz.
Johnson, Bradley F.-Judge, Whitefish City Court-Mont.
Johnson, Calvin-Judge, Louisiana District Court Orleans Parish Criminal District-La.
Johnson, Charles A.-Presiding Judge, Oklahoma Court of Criminal Appeals-Okla.
Johnson, Charles R.-Judge, Superior Court of California County of Kings-Calif.
Johnson, Charles Ray-Chief Justice, Trial Court of Massachusetts Boston Municipal Court Department-Mass.
Johnson, Charles W.-Chief Judge, Michigan Circuit Court Fifty-seventh Judicial Circuit-Mich.
Johnson, Charles W.-Associate Chief Justice, Washington Supreme Court-Wash.
Johnson, Cheryl-Judge, Texas Court of Criminal Appeals-Tex.
Johnson, David K.-Judge, Greene Circuit Court-Ind.
Johnson, David L.-Judge, Ohio Court of Common Pleas Franklin County-Ohio
Johnson, Denise R.-Associate Justice, Vermont Supreme Court-Vt.
Johnson, Derek Guy-Judge, Superior Court of California County of Orange-Calif.
Johnson, Diana A.-Justice, New York Supreme Court Second Judicial District-N.Y.
Johnson, Donald C.-Judge, Tippecanoe Superior Court-Ind.
Johnson, Donald F.-Associate Judge, Circuit Court for Dorchester County, First Judicial Circuit-Md.
Johnson, Donald R.-Judge, Louisiana District Court Nineteenth Judicial District-La.
Johnson, Donald T.-Judge, Louisiana District Court Ninth Judicial District-La.
Johnson, Donna Hedgepeth-Judge, North Carolina District Court District 19A-N.C.
Johnson, Douglas F.-Judge, Douglas County Separate Juvenile Court-Neb.
Johnson, Dwight D.-Judge, Virginia Juvenile and Domestic Relations District Court Sixteenth Judicial District-Va.

ALPHABETICAL NAME INDEX

Johnson, E. Lynn-Resident Judge, North Carolina Superior Court Fourth Judicial Division District 12-N.C.
Johnson, Earl, Jr.-Associate Justice, California Court of Appeal Second District Division Seven-Calif.
Johnson, Edward Hodgson-Judge, Court of Appeals of Georgia-Ga.
Johnson, Edward S.-Judge, Bell County Court at Law No. 1-Tex.
Johnson, Emmett P., Jr.-Judge, State Court of Appling County-Ga.
Johnson, Eric M.-Associate Judge, Circuit Court for Montgomery County, Sixth Judicial Circuit-Md.
Johnson, Ernest-Judge, Kansas District Court Twenty-ninth Judicial District-Kan.
Johnson, Faith-Judge, Texas District Court 363rd Judicial District-Tex.
Johnson, Forrest Al-Judge, Mississippi Circuit Court Sixth Judicial District-Miss.
Johnson, Foye L.-Judge, Probate Court of Walker County-Ga.
Johnson, Frank J.-Judge, Superior Court of California County of Los Angeles-Calif.
Johnson, G. Richard-Chancellor, Tennessee Chancery Court First Judicial District-Tenn.
Johnson, Gary L.-Chief Judge, West Virginia Circuit Court Twenty-eighth Judicial Circuit-W.Va.
Johnson, Gregg E.-Judge, Minnesota District Court Second Judicial District-Minn.
Johnson, Harold A., Jr.-Chief Judge, Michigan District Court District Eighty-nine-Mich.
Johnson, Harold U., Jr.-Judge, New Jersey Superior Court Vicinage Fifteen-N.J.
Johnson, Horace J., Jr.-Judge, Superior Court of Georgia Alcovy Judicial Circuit-Ga.
Johnson, Howard R.-Judge, Municipal Court of Atlanta-Ga.
Johnson, Hurl William, III-Judge, Superior Court of California County of Stanislaus-Calif.
Johnson, Inge P.-Judge, United States District Court Northern District of Alabama-Ala.
Johnson, J. Alexander-Judge, Juvenile Court of Georgia Brunswick Judicial Circuit-Ga.
Johnson, J. B., Jr.-Magistrate Judge, United States District Court Eastern District of Kentucky-Ky.
Johnson, J. G.-District Associate Judge, Iowa District Court First Judicial District-Ia.
Johnson, J. Ramsey-Associate Judge, Superior Court of the District of Columbia-D.C.
Johnson, J. Richardson-Chief Judge, Michigan Circuit Court Ninth Judicial Circuit-Mich.
Johnson, James W., Jr.-Judge, South Carolina Circuit Court Eighth Judicial Circuit-S.C.
Johnson, Jane L.-Judge, Superior Court of California County of Los Angeles-Calif.
Johnson, Jean M.-Judge, Florida Circuit Court Fourth Judicial Circuit-Fla.
Johnson, Jeffrey W.-Magistrate Judge, United States District Court Central District of California-Calif.
Johnson, Jerry E.-Judge, Superior Court of California County of Los Angeles-Calif.
Johnson, Joe S., Jr.-Judge, Probate Court of Talbot County and Chief Magistrate, Magistrate Court of Talbot County-Ga.
Johnson, Joel B.-Judge, Texas District Court 156th Judicial District-Tex.
Johnson, Justin M.-Judge, The Superior Court of Pennsylvania-Pa.
Johnson, Karen-Judge, Texas District Court 95th Judicial District-Tex.
Johnson, Kathy J.-Judge, Louisiana District Court Seventh Judicial District-La.
Johnson, Kenneth H.-Judge, Marion Superior Court-Ind.
Johnson, Kim Robert-Judge, Minnesota District Court Tenth Judicial District-Minn.
Johnson, Kirk D.-Judge, Arkansas Circuit Court Eighth South Judicial Circuit-Ark.
Johnson, Kurt D.-Judge, Minnesota District Court Fifth Judicial District-Minn.
Johnson, L. Craig-Judge, Tennessee Circuit Court Fourteenth Judicial District-Tenn.
Johnson, Laura S.-Judge, Palm Beach County Court-Fla.
Johnson, Lawrence R.-Judge, Minnesota District Court Tenth Judicial District-Minn.
Johnson, Lee A.-Judge, Kansas Court of Appeals-Kan.
Johnson, Lee G.-Circuit Justice, Trial Court of Massachusetts District Court Department and First Justice, Middlesex County Malden Division-Mass.
Johnson, Linnea R.-Magistrate Judge, United States District Court Southern District of Florida-Fla.
Johnson, Marcus L.-Resident Judge, North Carolina Superior Court Seventh Judicial Division District 26-N.C.
Johnson, Margaret-Judge, Superior Court of California County of Santa Clara-Calif.
Johnson, Margaret Shaw-Judge, Minnesota District Court Third Judicial District-Minn.
Johnson, Marion J.-Judge, Superior Court of California County of Los Angeles-Calif.
Johnson, Megan B.-Associate Judge, Maryland District Court District Seven-Md.
Johnson, Michael-Judge, Superior Court of California County of Los Angeles-Calif.
Johnson, Nancy K.-Magistrate Judge, United States District Court Southern District of Texas-Tex.
Johnson, Nely L.-Judge, Oregon Circuit Court Fourth Judicial District-Ore.
Johnson, Norma Holloway-Senior Judge, United States District Court District of Columbia-D.C.
Johnson, Norman E., Jr.-Associate Judge, Maryland District Court District One-Md.
Johnson, Orson L.-Judge, Jefferson County District Court Birmingham Division-Ala.
Johnson, Pamela Taylor-Judge, East Baton Rouge Parish Juvenile Court-La.
Johnson, Patrick Reynolds-Judge, Virginia General District Court Twenty-ninth Judicial District-Va.
Johnson, Phil-Chief Justice, Texas Court of Appeals Seventh District-Tex.
Johnson, R. Kinard, Jr.-Judge, South Carolina Family Court Thirteenth Judicial Circuit-S.C.
Johnson, Randall G.-Judge, Virginia Circuit Court Thirteenth Judicial Circuit-Va.
Johnson, Randall Lee-Judge, Grant Superior Court-Ind.
Johnson, Richard-Judge, Texas Family District Court 303rd Judicial District-Tex.
Johnson, Rick A.-Judge, Kentucky Court of Appeals-Ky.
Johnson, Robert W.-Emergency Judge, North Carolina District Court-N.C.
Johnson, Ron-Judge, Kentucky Circuit Court Twenty-sixth Judicial Circuit-Ky.
Johnson, Shelia R.-Judge, Michigan District Court District Forty-six-Mich.
Johnson, Stephen P.-Associate Judge, Maryland District Court District Six-Md.
Johnson, Sterling, Jr.-Judge, United States District Court Eastern District of New York-N.Y.
Johnson, Susan-Judge, Kentucky District Court Twenty-fourth Judicial District-Ky.
Johnson, T. Michael-Judge, Florida Circuit Court Fifth Judicial Circuit-Fla.
Johnson, Teresa D.-Judge, Rochester City Court-N.Y.
Johnson, Theodore O.-Chief Judge, Michigan District Court District Eighty-eight-Mich.
Johnson, Thomas E.-Judge, Escambia County Court-Fla.
Johnson, Thomas E.-Judge, Sullivan Superior Court-Ind.
Johnson, Thomas L.-Chief Judge, Minnesota Workers' Compensation Court of Appeals-Minn.
Johnson, Timothy F.-Judge, Bexar County Court at Law No. 5-Tex.
Johnson, Vernita King-Judge, Washington County Court-Miss.
Johnson, W. Arvid-Judge, Superior Court of California County of Yolo-Calif.
Johnson, Walter E.-Magistrate Judge, United States District Court Northern District of Georgia-Ga.
Johnson, Warren G.-Presiding Judge, South Dakota Circuit Court Fourth Judicial Circuit-S.D.
Johnson, William-Judge, Florida Circuit Court Eleventh Judicial Circuit-Fla.
Johnson, William A.-Judge, Minnesota District Court Third Judicial District-Minn.
Johnson, William C., Jr.-Senior Judge, Florida Circuit Court Seventh Judicial Circuit-Fla.
Johnson, William Clayton-Senior Judge, Florida Circuit Court Seventeenth Judicial Circuit-Fla.
Johnson, William Paul-Judge, United States District Court District of New Mexico-N.Mex.
Johnson Smith, Emogene-Acting First Justice, Trial Court of Massachusetts District Court Department Norfolk County Wrentham Division and Justice, Suffolk County Dorchester Division-Mass.
Johnson-Speh, Sandi G.-Associate Judge, Illinois Circuit Court of Cook County-Ill.
Johnston, Charles A.-Judge, Carroll County Court-Ohio
Johnston, D. Craig-Judge, Oklahoma Workers' Compensation Court-Okla.
Johnston, Donald A., III-Judge, Michigan Circuit Court Seventeenth Judicial Circuit-Mich.
Johnston, Gerald G.-Judge, Superior Court of California County of Orange-Calif.
Johnston, J. Samuel, Jr.-Judge, Virginia Circuit Court Twenty-fourth Judicial Circuit-Va.
Johnston, Joseph F.-Circuit Justice, Trial Court of Massachusetts Juvenile Court Department-Mass.
Johnston, Joseph S.-Judge, Alabama Circuit Court Thirteenth Judicial Circuit-Ala.
Johnston, Lawrence V.-Senior Judge, Florida Circuit Court Eighteenth Judicial Circuit-Fla.
Johnston, Lorene G.-Judge, Jackson County Municipal Court-Ohio
Johnston, Robert Glenn, III-Judge, Superior Court of Georgia Chattahoochee Judicial Circuit-Ga.
Johnston, Robert J.-Magistrate Judge, United States District Court District of Nevada-Nev.
Johnston, Robert P.-Resident Judge, North Carolina Superior Court Seventh Judicial Division District 26-N.C.
Johnston, Vicki W.-Judge, Probate Court of Butts County-Ga.
Johnston, William D.-Judge, Wisconsin Circuit Court Lafayette Circuit-Wis.
Johnstone, Douglas I.-Associate Justice, Alabama Supreme Court-Ala.
Johnstone, Edward H.-Senior Judge, United States District Court Western District of Kentucky-Ky.
Johnstone, Martin E.-Justice, Kentucky Supreme Court-Ky.
Joiner, Charles W.-Senior Judge, United States District Court Eastern District of Michigan-Mich.
Joiner, J. Michael-Judge, Alabama Circuit Court Eighteenth Judicial Circuit-Ala.
Jolles, Isaac-Judge, Probate Court of Richmond County-Ga.
Jolley, Allen T.-Presiding Judge, Alabama Circuit Court Twenty-seventh Judicial Circuit-Ala.
Jolliff, Cliff L.-Judge, Juvenile Court of Georgia Northeastern Judicial Circuit-Ga.
Jolliffe, Frank E.-Chief Judge, West Virginia Circuit Court Eleventh Judicial Circuit-W.Va.
Jolly, E. Grady-Judge, United States Court of Appeals Fifth Circuit
Jolly, Jerry Arnold-Chief Judge, North Carolina District Court District 13-N.C.
Jolly, John R., Jr.-Special Judge, North Carolina Superior Court-N.C.
Jonas, Susan A.-Chief Judge, Michigan District Court District Fifty-eight-Mich.
Jonas, Zelda-Justice, New York Supreme Court Tenth Judicial District-N.Y.
Jones, Abraham Penn-Resident Judge, North Carolina Superior Court Third Judicial Division District 10-N.C.
Jones, Alvin F.-Judge, New Mexico District Court Fifth Judicial District-N.Mex.
Jones, Ann I.-Judge, Superior Court of California County of Los Angeles-Calif.
Jones, Anne Gue-Judge, South Carolina Family Court First Judicial Circuit-S.C.
Jones, Aubrey L., Jr.-Judge, Henderson County Court-Tex.

ALPHABETICAL NAME INDEX

Jones, Barbara J. R.-Presiding Justice, California Court of Appeal First District Division Five-Calif.

Jones, Barbara S.-Judge, United States District Court Southern District of New York-N.Y.

Jones, Benjamin-Judge, Louisiana District Court Fourth Judicial District-La.

Jones, Berlin-Judge, Arkansas Circuit Court Eleventh West Judicial Circuit-Ark.

Jones, Beverly Stites-Magistrate Judge, United States District Court Western District of Arkansas-Ark.

Jones, Bonnie L.-Judge, Virginia General District Court Eighth Judicial District-Va.

Jones, Brock-Judge, Texas District Court 112th Judicial District-Tex.

Jones, C. Darnell, II-Judge, Pennsylvania Court of Common Pleas First Judicial District-Pa.

Jones, Carl B.-Judge, Oklahoma Court of Civil Appeals-Okla.

Jones, Carol A.-Judge, North Carolina District Court District 4-N.C.

Jones, Casey-Judge, West Fork District Court-Ark.

Jones, Charles E.-Chief Justice, Supreme Court of Arizona-Ariz.

Jones, Charles Robert-Judge, Louisiana Court of Appeal Fourth Circuit-La.

Jones, Clarance J.-Judge, Connecticut Superior Court-Conn.

Jones, Clyde E.-Judge, Alabama Circuit Court Tenth Judicial Circuit Birmingham Division-Ala.

Jones, Dianne-Judge, Dallas County Court at Law No. 11-Tex.

Jones, Donald Richard-Judge, Texas District Court 266th Judicial District-Tex.

Jones, Dorothy F.-Circuit Judge, Illinois Circuit Court of Cook County-Ill.

Jones, Doug-Chief Magistrate, Magistrate Court of Tift County-Ga.

Jones, Edith Hollan-Judge, United States Court of Appeals Fifth Circuit

Jones, Edward-Judge, Arkansas Circuit Court Thirteenth Judicial Circuit-Ark.

Jones, Edward-Judge, Oregon Circuit Court Fourth Judicial District-Ore.

Jones, Ernest W.-Judge, Utah District Court Second Judicial District-Utah

Jones, Franklin C.-Justice, Rochester District Court-N.H.

Jones, Franklin P.-Judge, Superior Court of California County of Fresno-Calif.

Jones, Gary R.-Magistrate Judge, United States District Court Middle District of Florida-Fla.

Jones, George A., Jr.-Chief Judge, Virginia General District Court Twenty-second Judicial District-Va.

Jones, Glenn M.-Special Judge, Oklahoma District Court Seventh Judicial District-Okla.

Jones, Guilford L. "Gil", III-Judge, Texas District Court 33rd Judicial District-Tex.

Jones, Henry Louis, Jr.-Magistrate Judge, United States District Court Eastern District of Arkansas-Ark.

Jones, James Parker-Judge, United States District Court Western District of Virginia-Va.

Jones, Jeffrey Bruce-Judge, Superior Court of California County of Imperial-Calif.

Jones, Jeffrey W.-Judge, Probate Court of Pulaski County-Ga.

Jones, John Bailey-Senior Judge, United States District Court District of South Dakota-S.D.

Jones, John E., III-Judge, United States District Court Middle District of Pennsylvania-Pa.

Jones, John J. J., Jr.-Justice, New York Supreme Court Tenth Judicial District-N.Y.

Jones, John R.-Judge, Crockett County Court-Tex.

Jones, Jon Stephen-Magistrate Judge, Kansas District Court Fourth Judicial District-Kan.

Jones, Joyce B.-Judge, Probate Court of Polk County-Ga.

Jones, Larry-Judge, Utah Juvenile Court First Judicial District-Utah

Jones, Larry A.-Judge, Cleveland Municipal Court-Ohio

Jones, Larry A.-Special Judge, Oklahoma District Court Seventh Judicial District-Okla.

Jones, Lawrence-Judge, Superior Court of California County of Fresno-Calif.

Jones, Linda Z.-Judge, Guadalupe County Court at Law-Tex.

Jones, Lisa A.-Judge, Kentucky District Court Sixth Judicial District-Ky.

Jones, Lisa C.-Judge, Juvenile Courts of Georgia Southwestern Judicial Circuit-Ga.

Jones, Mark H.-Judge, Florida Circuit Court Sixteenth Judicial Circuit-Fla.

Jones, Michael D.-Judge, Superior Court of Arizona Maricopa County-Ariz.

Jones, Michael E.-Special Justice, Salem District Court-N.H.

Jones, Michael Q.-Circuit Judge, Illinois Circuit Court Sixth Judicial Circuit-Ill.

Jones, Michael R.-Judge, Tennessee Circuit Court Nineteenth Judicial District-Tenn.

Jones, Michael T.-Judge, Alabama Circuit Court Eleventh Judicial Circuit-Ala.

Jones, Molly S.-Judge, Tarrant County Criminal Court at Law No. 6-Tex.

Jones, Morris Bruce-Judge, Superior Court of California County of Los Angeles-Calif.

Jones, Napoleon A., Jr.-Judge, United States District Court Southern District of California-Calif.

Jones, Paul L.-Resident Judge, North Carolina Superior Court Second Judicial Division District 8A-N.C.

Jones, Peggy D.-Justice, Powder River County Justice of the Peace Court-Mont.

Jones, Peggy Foley-Judge, Ohio Court of Common Pleas Cuyahoga County-Ohio

Jones, Peter B.-Associate Judge, Delaware Family Court Sussex County-Del.

Jones, Richard A.-Judge, Washington Superior Court King County-Wash.

Jones, Rickey-Circuit Judge, Illinois Circuit Court of Cook County-Ill.

Jones, Robert Clive-Judge, United States Bankruptcy Court District of Nevada-Nev.

Jones, Robert E.-Judge, New Orleans Traffic Court-La.

Jones, Robert E.-Senior Judge, United States District Court District of Oregon-Ore.

Jones, Robert L.-Judge, Tennessee Circuit Court Twenty-second Judicial District-Tenn.

Jones, Robert L.-Judge, United States Bankruptcy Court Northern District of Texas-Tex.

Jones, Robert S.-Associate Judge, Juvenile Court of Georgia Gwinnett Judicial Circuit and Judge, Recorder's Court of Gwinnett County-Ga.

Jones, Rosemary Usher-Senior Judge, Florida Circuit Court Eleventh Judicial Circuit-Fla.

Jones, Sanford J.-Judge, Juvenile Court of Georgia Atlanta Judicial Circuit-Ga.

Jones, Steve C.-Judge, Superior Court of Georgia Western Judicial Circuit-Ga.

Jones, Steven E.-Judge, Nevada District Court Eighth Judicial District-Nev.

Jones, T. Michael-Judge, Florida Circuit Court First Judicial Circuit-Fla.

Jones, Talmadge R.-Judge, Superior Court of California County of Sacramento-Calif.

Jones, Theodore T., Jr.-Justice, New York Supreme Court Second Judicial District-N.Y.

Jones, Thomas H.-Associate Judge, Illinois Circuit Court First Judicial Circuit-Ill.

Jones, Thomas O.-Chief Judge, Virginia General District Court Thirteenth Judicial District-Va.

Jones, Thomas R.-Judge, Alabama Circuit Court Fourth Judicial Circuit-Ala.

Jones, Thomas Rawles, Jr.-Magistrate Judge, United States District Court Eastern District of Virginia-Va.

Jones, Vera Massey-Judge, Michigan Circuit Court Third Judicial Circuit-Mich.

Jones, W. Blair-Judge, Montana District Court Twenty-second Judicial District-Mont.

Jones, William G.-Emergency Judge, North Carolina District Court-N.C.

Jones-Bradley, Vanesa F.-Judge, Michigan District Court District Thirty-six-Mich.

Jones-Osborne, Lillie-Judge, Greene County District Court-Ala.

Jongbloed, Barbara Bailey-Judge, Connecticut Superior Court-Conn.

Joplin, Larry E.-Chief Judge, Oklahoma Court of Civil Appeals-Okla.

Jopling, Wallace M.-Senior Judge, Florida Circuit Court Third Judicial Circuit-Fla.

Jordan, Adalberto J.-Judge, United States District Court Southern District of Florida-Fla.

Jordan, Claudia J.-Judge, Denver County Court-Colo.

Jordan, Daniel E.-Circuit Judge, Illinois Circuit Court of Cook County-Ill.

Jordan, Edward R.-Circuit Judge, Illinois Circuit Court of Cook County-Ill.

Jordan, Frank J., Jr.-Judge, Superior Court of Georgia Chattahoochee Judicial Circuit-Ga.

Jordan, J. David-Judge, Escambia County District Court-Ala.

Jordan, Kent A.-Judge, United States District Court District of Delaware-Del.

Jordan, Leon-Senior Judge, United States District Court Eastern District of Tennessee-Tenn.

Jordan, Lillian B.-Emergency Judge, North Carolina District Court-N.C.

Jordan, Philip B., Jr.-Judge, West Virginia Circuit Court Twenty-first Judicial Circuit-W.Va.

Jordan, Scott-Judge, Nevada District Court Second Judicial District-Nev.

Jordan, Thomas H.-Judge, Jackson Municipal Court-Wyo.

Jordan, William Alan-Judge, State Court of Cherokee County-Ga.

Jordon, David L.-Judge, Michigan District Court District Fifty-four B-Mich.

Jorgensen, Ann B.-Circuit Judge, Illinois Circuit Court Eighteenth Judicial Circuit-Ill.

Jorgensen, Donald L.-Judge, North Dakota District Court South Central Judicial District-N.D.

Jorgensen, Gerald R., Jr.-Judge, Nebraska County Court Ninth Judicial District-Neb.

Jorgensen, Kenneth L.-Judge, Washington Superior Court Grant County-Wash.

Jorgenson, Cindy K.-Judge, United States District Court District of Arizona-Ariz.

Jorgenson, James R.-Judge, Florida District Court of Appeal Third District-Fla.

Jorzak, James J.-Circuit Judge, Illinois Circuit Court of Cook County-Ill.

Joseph, Barbara A.-Judge, Pennsylvania Court of Common Pleas First Judicial District-Pa.

Joseph, Ben W.-Judge, Vermont Trial Court-Vt.

Joseph, Burton S.-Justice, New York Supreme Court Tenth Judicial District-N.Y.

Joseph, William D.-Judge, Zanesville Municipal Court-Ohio

Josephson, Bertha D.-Associate Justice, Trial Court of Massachusetts Superior Court Department-Mass.

Josey-Herring, Anita-Associate Judge, Superior Court of the District of Columbia-D.C.

Joslyn, Patrick Reed-Judge, Michigan Circuit Court Fifty-fourth Judicial Circuit-Mich.

Joy, Mark M.-Associate Judge, Illinois Circuit Court Fourth Judicial Circuit-Ill.

Joy, William H.-District Judge, Iowa District Court Fifth Judicial District-Ia.

Joyce, John F.-Associate Judge, Illinois Circuit Court Fifteenth Judicial Circuit-Ill.

Joyce, Michael T.-Judge, The Superior Court of Pennsylvania-Pa.

Joyce, Patricia S.-Circuit Judge, Missouri Circuit Court Nineteenth Judicial Circuit-Mo.

Joyner, J. Curtis-Judge, United States District Court Eastern District of Pennsylvania-Pa.

Joyner, Michael E.-Judge, Recorder's Court of Columbus-Muscogee County-Ga.

Joyner, Sam A.-Magistrate Judge, United States District Court Northern District of Oklahoma-Okla.

Joyner, Todd-Judge, Idaho District Court Third Judicial District Magistrate Division-Ida.

Juba, George E.-Recalled Magistrate Judge, United States District Court District of Oregon-Ore.

Judah, Weldon C.-Circuit Judge, Missouri Circuit Court Fifth Judicial Circuit-Mo.

Judkins, Clint S.-Judge, Utah District Court First Judicial District-Utah

Judkins, Robert J.-Judge, Highland County Court-Ohio

Juhas, Mark A.-Judge, Superior Court of California County of Los Angeles-Calif.

ALPHABETICAL NAME INDEX

Julian, John M.-Justice, Trial Court of Massachusetts District Court Department Dukes County Edgartown Division-Mass.

Julian, Justin W.-Judge, Idaho District Court First Judicial District Magistrate Division-Ida.

Julian, Robert F.-Justice, New York Supreme Court Fifth Judicial District-N.Y.

Julien, Ethel Simms-Judge, Louisiana District Court Orleans Parish Civil District-La.

Jung, Barbara R.-Associate Judge, Maryland District Court District Eight-Md.

Jung, David F.-Judge, Fulton County Family Court-N.Y.

Junke, John P.-Judge, Prescott Municipal Court-Wash.

Junkin, Peter J.-Judge, Bedford Municipal Court-Ohio

Jurado, Terry L.-Judge, Renton Municipal Court-Wash.

Jurden, Jan R.-Associate Judge, Delaware Superior Court New Castle County-Del.

Jurow, George L.-Judge, New York City Family Court-N.Y.

Jurrens, M. Randall-Judge, Michigan District Court District Seventy Division One-Mich.

Jury, Meredith A.-Judge, United States Bankruptcy Court Central District of California-Calif.

Justice, Rebecca L.-Judge, Hagerstown Town Court-Ind.

Justice, William Wayne-Senior Judge, United States District Court Eastern District of Texas-Tex.

Justin, James M.-Judge, Michigan District Court District Twelve-Mich.

Justus, James-Associate Circuit Judge, Missouri Circuit Court Thirty-eighth Judicial Circuit-Mo.

Kaczmarek, Robert L.-Judge, Michigan Circuit Court Tenth Judicial Circuit-Mich.

Kaddo, James A.-Judge, Superior Court of California County of Los Angeles-Calif.

Kafker, Scott L.-Associate Justice, Massachusetts Appeals Court-Mass.

Kagan, Spencer M.-Circuit Justice, Trial Court of Massachusetts Probate and Family Court Department-Mass.

Kahl, Christian M.-Associate Judge, Circuit Court for Baltimore County, Third Judicial Circuit-Md.

Kahl, David B.-Judge, Corning City Court-N.Y.

Kahn, Barbara R.-Judge, Suffolk County District Court-N.Y.

Kahn, Charles F., Jr.-Judge, Wisconsin Circuit Court Milwaukee Circuit-Wis.

Kahn, Charles J., Jr.-Judge, Florida District Court of Appeal First District-Fla.

Kahn, Harold E.-Judge, Superior Court of California City and County of San Francisco-Calif.

Kahn, Lawrence E.-Judge, United States District Court Northern District of New York-N.Y.

Kahn, Marcy L.-Justice, New York Supreme Court First Judicial District-N.Y.

Kahn, Roger M.-Judge, New Jersey Tax Court-N.J.

Kainrad, Joseph R.-Judge, Ohio Court of Common Pleas Portage County-Ohio

Kaiser, Erik Michael-Judge, Superior Court of California County of Riverside-Calif.

Kalashian, Joseph A.-Judge, Superior Court of California County of Tulare-Calif.

Kalbfleisch, Gregory K.-Judge, Idaho District Court Second Judicial District Magistrate Division-Ida.

Kalitowski, Thomas J.-Judge, Minnesota Court of Appeals-Minn.

Kalkin, Alan S.-Judge, Superior Court of California County of Los Angeles-Calif.

Kallan, Kathleen G.-Associate Judge, Illinois Circuit Court Twelfth Judicial Circuit-Ill.

Kallas, Paris-Judge, Washington Superior Court King County-Wash.

Kalmbach, Randy L.-Chief Judge, Michigan District Court District Twenty-seven and Judge, Michigan District Court District Twenty-seven Division One-Mich.

Kalokathis, Nicholas-Judge, Wyoming District Court First Judicial District-Wyo.

Kaman, Marilyn J.-Judge, Minnesota District Court Fourth Judicial District-Minn.

Kamansky, Craig S.-Judge, Superior Court of California County of San Bernardino-Calif.

Kaminetz, Marvin S.-Associate Judge, Circuit Court for St. Mary's County, Seventh Judicial Circuit-Md.

Kamins, Bernard J.-Judge, Superior Court of California County of Los Angeles-Calif.

Kammeyer, Daniel M.-Judge, Minnesota District Court Tenth Judicial District-Minn.

Kamp, Gary A.-Associate Circuit Judge, Missouri Circuit Court Thirty-second Judicial Circuit-Mo.

Kamp, Joel J.-District Associate Judge, Iowa District Court Eighth Judicial District-Ia.

Kams, Timothy A.-Judge, Superior Court of California County of Fresno-Calif.

Kanarek, Paul B.-Judge, Florida Circuit Court Nineteenth Judicial Circuit-Fla.

Kandrevas, James A.-Chief Judge, Michigan District Court District Twenty-eight-Mich.

Kane, Anthony T.-Associate Justice, New York Supreme Court Appellate Division Third Judicial Department-N.Y.

Kane, Harold M.-Judge, Pennsylvania Court of Common Pleas First Judicial District-Pa.

Kane, John Lawrence, Jr.-Senior Judge, United States District Court District of Colorado-Colo.

Kane, Joseph E.-Judge, New Jersey Superior Court Vicinage One-N.J.

Kane, Michael J.-Judge, Pennsylvania Court of Common Pleas Seventh Judicial District-Pa.

Kane, Raymond J., Jr.-Associate Judge, Circuit Court for Howard County, Fifth Judicial Circuit-Md.

Kane, Robert J.-Associate Justice, Trial Court of Massachusetts Superior Court Department-Mass.

Kane, Stephen Joseph-Judge, Superior Court of California County of Fresno-Calif.

Kane, Thomas Kelly-Judge, Colorado District Court Fourth Judicial District-Colo.

Kane, Yvette-Judge, United States District Court Middle District of Pennsylvania-Pa.

Kaneshiro, Gale E.-Judge, Superior Court of California County of San Diego-Calif.

Kaney, Frank N.-Senior Judge, Florida Circuit Court Ninth Judicial Circuit-Fla.

Kangas, Roger W.-Judge, Michigan District Court District Ninety-six-Mich.

Kanne, Michael S.-Judge, United States Court of Appeals Seventh Circuit

Kannen, Bernard A.-Retired Judge, New Jersey Superior Court-N.J.

Kanning, Philip T.-Judge, Minnesota District Court First Judicial District-Minn.

Kantar, Kristina C.-Judge, Lake Station City Court-Ind.

Kantor, Henry-Judge, Oregon Circuit Court Fourth Judicial District-Ore.

Kantrowitz, R. Marc-Associate Justice, Massachusetts Appeals Court-Mass.

Kapala, Frederick J.-Circuit Judge, Illinois Circuit Court Seventeenth Judicial Circuit-Ill.

Kapalko, Paul A.-Judge, New Jersey Superior Court Vicinage Nine-N.J.

Kapelke, Robert J.-Judge, Colorado Court of Appeals-Colo.

Kapetan, Jon N.-Judge, Superior Court of California County of Fresno-Calif.

Kapitulik, Sharon G.-Judge, Haddam District Probate Court-Conn.

Kaplan, Burton A.-Judge, Connecticut Superior Court-Conn.

Kaplan, Deborah A.-Judge, The Civil Court of the City of New York-N.Y.

Kaplan, Jeff-Magistrate Judge, United States District Court Northern District of Texas-Tex.

Kaplan, Jonathan J.-Judge, Connecticut Superior Court-Conn.

Kaplan, Jordan-Associate Judge, Illinois Circuit Court of Cook County-Ill.

Kaplan, Joseph H. H.-Associate Judge, Circuit Court for Baltimore City, Eighth Judicial Circuit-Md.

Kaplan, Leon S.-Judge, Superior Court of California County of Los Angeles-Calif.

Kaplan, Lewis A.-Judge, United States District Court Southern District of New York-N.Y.

Kaplan, Michael G.-Judge, Florida Circuit Court Seventeenth Judicial Circuit-Fla.

Kaplan, Michael J.-Judge, United States Bankruptcy Court Western District of New York-N.Y.

Kaplan, Randy J.-Circuit Justice, Trial Court of Massachusetts Probate and Family Court Department-Mass.

Kaplan, Stanton S.-Judge, Florida Circuit Court Seventeenth Judicial Circuit-Fla.

Kapnick, Barbara R.-Justice, New York Supreme Court First Judicial District-N.Y.

Kapsner, Carol Ronning-Justice, North Dakota Supreme Court-N.D.

Karahalios, Pamela G.-Associate Judge, Illinois Circuit Court of Cook County-Ill.

Karahan, Jay-Judge, Harris County Criminal Court at Law No. 8-Tex.

Karalunas, Deborah H.-Justice, New York Supreme Court Fifth Judicial District-N.Y.

Karan, Amy B.-Judge, Dade County Court-Fla.

Karasic, Ronald Alan-Associate Judge, Maryland District Court District One-Md.

Karasov, Patricia Kerr-Judge, Minnesota District Court Fourth Judicial District-Minn.

Karazin, Edward R., Jr.-Judge, Connecticut Superior Court-Conn.

Kardis, Phillip J.-Circuit Judge, Illinois Circuit Court Third Judicial Circuit-Ill.

Karesh, Jonathan E.-Judge, Superior Court of California County of San Mateo-Calif.

Karkula, Paul A.-Circuit Judge, Illinois Circuit Court of Cook County-Ill.

Karl, Mark A.-Chief Judge, West Virginia Circuit Court Second Judicial Circuit-W.Va.

Karlan, Craig D.-Judge, Superior Court of California County of Los Angeles-Calif.

Karlan, Sandy-Judge, Florida Circuit Court Eleventh Judicial Circuit-Fla.

Karlin, Janice Miller-Judge, United States Bankruptcy Court District of Kansas-Kan.

Karlton, Lawrence K.-Senior Judge, United States District Court Eastern District of California-Calif.

Karmeier, Lloyd A.-Circuit Judge, Illinois Circuit Court Twentieth Judicial Circuit-Ill.

Karner, Cheryl S.-Judge, Ohio Court of Common Pleas Cuyahoga County-Ohio

Karnezis, Themis N.-Circuit Judge, Illinois Circuit Court of Cook County-Ill.

Karopkin, Martin G.-Judge, The Criminal Court of the City of New York-N.Y.

Karowsky, Lynn J.-Judge, Weld County Court-Colo.

Karpf, Michael L.-Judge, Superior Court of Georgia Eastern Judicial Circuit-Ga.

Karpinski, Diane J.-Judge, Ohio Court of Appeals Eighth District-Ohio

Kase, Edmund H., III-Chief Judge, New Mexico District Court Seventh Judicial District-N.Mex.

Kassel, Michael-Judge, New Jersey Superior Court Vicinage Four-N.J.

Kaster, Robert F.-Judge, Superior Court of California County of Siskiyou-Calif.

Kate, Linda A.-Judge, Ohio Court of Common Pleas Tuscarawas County-Ohio

Kato, Eileen A.-Judge, King District Court West Division King County-Wash.

Kato, Kenneth H.-Acting Chief Judge, Washington Court of Appeals Division III-Wash.

Katz, Bertram D.-Justice, New York Supreme Court Twelfth Judicial District-N.Y.

Katz, David A.-Judge, United States District Court Northern District of Ohio-Ohio

Katz, Joette-Associate Justice, Connecticut Supreme Court-Conn.

Katz, Marvin-Senior Judge, United States District Court Eastern District of Pennsylvania-Pa.

Katz, Matthew I.-Judge, Vermont Trial Court-Vt.

Katz, Nancy J.-Associate Judge, Illinois Circuit Court of Cook County-Ill.

Katz, Paul A.-Judge, Superior Court of Arizona Maricopa County-Ariz.

Katz, Stanley B.-Justice, New York Supreme Court Eleventh Judicial District-N.Y.

Katz, Theodore H.-Magistrate Judge, United States District Court Southern District of New York-N.Y.

Katzmann, Robert Allen-Judge, United States Court of Appeals Second Circuit

ALPHABETICAL NAME INDEX

Kauffman, Andrew C.-Judge, Superior Court of California County of Los Angeles-Calif.

Kauffman, Bruce W.-Judge, United States District Court Eastern District of Pennsylvania-Pa.

Kauffmann, Kathleen O.-Associate Judge, Illinois Circuit Court Fifteenth Judicial Circuit-Ill.

Kaufman, David-Judge, Kansas District Court Eighteenth Judicial District-Kan.

Kaufman, Ira R.-Judge, Superior Court of California County of Plumas-Calif.

Kaufman, Tod J.-Chief Judge, West Virginia Circuit Court Thirteenth Judicial Circuit-W.Va.

Kauger, Yvonne-Justice, Supreme Court of Oklahoma-Okla.

Kaul, Alvin "Bud"-Justice, Daniels County Justice of the Peace Court and Judge, Scobey City Court-Mont.

Kaull, John S.-Magistrate Judge, United States District Court Northern District of West Virginia-W.Va.

Kaup, Daniel J.-Judge, Colorado District Court Eighth Judicial District and Judge, Colorado Water Court Division Six-Colo.

Kautz, Keith G.-Judge, Wyoming District Court Eighth Judicial District-Wyo.

Kautzmann, Dwight C. H.-Magistrate Judge, United States District Court District of North Dakota-N.D.

Kauvar, Jane F.-Deputy Presiding Judge, Alaska District Court Fourth Judicial District-Alas.

Kavanagh, E. Michael-Justice, New York Supreme Court Third Judicial District-N.Y.

Kavanewsky, John F., Jr.-Judge, Connecticut Superior Court-Conn.

Kavitt, Richard A.-Associate Judge, Illinois Circuit Court of Cook County-Ill.

Kawaichi, Ken Martin-Judge, Superior Court of California County of Alameda-Calif.

Kawamoto, Lynne-Associate Judge, Illinois Circuit Court of Cook County-Ill.

Kay, Alan-Magistrate Judge, United States District Court District of Columbia-D.C.

Kay, Alan C.-Senior Judge, United States District Court District of Hawaii-Hi.

Kay, Laurence Donald-Presiding Justice, California Court of Appeal First District Division Four-Calif.

Kay, Stuart S., Jr.-Judge, Louisiana District Court Thirty-sixth Judicial District-La.

Kay, Thomas L.-Judge, Utah District Court Second Judicial District-Utah

Kaye, Judith S.-Chief Judge, New York Court of Appeals-N.Y.

Kaye, Robert Paul-Senior Judge, Florida Circuit Court Eleventh Judicial Circuit-Fla.

Kaylor, Anne-Judge, Polk County Court-Fla.

Kayne, Richard B.-Judge, Medical Lake Municipal Court-Wash.

Kays, Greg-Associate Circuit Judge, Missouri Circuit Court Twenty-sixth Judicial Circuit-Mo.

Kays, Scott L.-Judge, Superior Court of California County of Solano-Calif.

Kazanjian, Debra-Judge, Superior Court of California County of Fresno-Calif.

Kazen, George P.-Chief Judge, United States District Court Southern District of Texas-Tex.

Kazen, Philip A., Jr.-Judge, Texas District Court 227th Judicial District-Tex.

Kazmierski, Joseph G., Jr.-Circuit Judge, Illinois Circuit Court of Cook County-Ill.

Keadle, Thomas Howard-Chief Judge, West Virginia Circuit Court Twenty-sixth Judicial Circuit-W.Va.

Keamy, Leilah A.-Associate Justice, Trial Court of Massachusetts Probate and Family Court Department Middlesex County Division-Mass.

Kean, Gene Paul-Judge, South Dakota Circuit Court Second Judicial Circuit-S.D.

Kean, Joyce S.-Judge, Pennsylvania Court of Common Pleas First Judicial District-Pa.

Kearney, Frances A.-Judge, Superior Court of California County of Placer-Calif.

Kearney, Jan-Judge, Superior Court of Arizona Pima County-Ariz.

Kearns, R. Jerome-Judge, Vigo Superior Court-Ind.

Kearse, Amalya Lyle-Senior Judge, United States Court of Appeals Second Circuit

Keary, Ann O'Regan-Associate Judge, Superior Court of the District of Columbia-D.C.

Keasler, Michael E.-Judge, Texas Court of Criminal Appeals-Tex.

Keaton, Edwin A.-Judge, Arkansas Circuit Court Thirteenth Judicial Circuit-Ark.

Keaty, Phyllis Montgomery-Judge, Louisiana District Court Fifteenth Judicial District-La.

Keeble, Allen B.-Judge, Superior Court of Georgia Coweta Judicial Circuit-Ga.

Keefe, Thomas K.-Judge, Albany City Court-N.Y.

Keegan, Thomas W.-Justice, New York Supreme Court Third Judicial District-N.Y.

Keehan, Michael R.-Circuit Judge, Illinois Circuit Court of Cook County-Ill.

Keel, Mary Lou-Judge, Texas District Court 232nd Judicial District-Tex.

Keel, Patrick O.-Judge, Texas District Court 345th Judicial District-Tex.

Keele, Michael D.-Judge, Marion Superior Court-Ind.

Keeler, Charles C.-Judge, Pennsylvania Court of Common Pleas Thirty-second Judicial District-Pa.

Keeley, Irene M.-Chief Judge, United States District Court Northern District of West Virginia-W.Va.

Keeley, J. Michael-Judge, Kansas District Court Twentieth Judicial District-Kan.

Keeling, Kenneth H.-Judge, Texas District Court 278th Judicial District-Tex.

Keenan, Barbara Milano-Justice, Supreme Court of Virginia-Va.

Keenan, John F.-Senior Judge, United States District Court Southern District of New York-N.Y.

Keenan, Richard A.-Judge, Monroe County Court-N.Y.

Keenon, Una H. R.-Judge, East Cleveland Municipal Court-Ohio

Keep, Judith N.-Judge, United States District Court Southern District of California-Calif.

Kees, Lester P.-Judge, Louisiana District Court Thirtieth Judicial District-La.

Keesley, William P.-Judge, South Carolina Circuit Court Eleventh Judicial Circuit-S.C.

Keeter, Harold-Judge, Swisher County Court-Tex.

Keeton, Robert E.-Senior Judge, United States District Court District of Massachusetts-Mass.

Keever, Anna Elizabeth-Chief Judge, North Carolina District Court District 12-N.C.

Kegley, Russell Dee-Judge, Portsmouth Municipal Court-Ohio

Kehm, Dennis J.-Circuit Judge, Missouri Circuit Court Twenty-third Judicial Circuit-Mo.

Kehoe, Dennis M.-Judge, Wayne County Court-N.Y.

Kehoe, L. Paul-Associate Justice, New York Supreme Court Appellate Division Fourth Judicial Department-N.Y.

Keiger, R. Kason-Emergency Judge, North Carolina District Court-N.C.

Keir, Duncan W.-Judge, United States Bankruptcy Court District of Maryland-Md.

Keis, R. Brent-Judge, Tarrant County Court at Law No. 1-Tex.

Keith, Damon Jerome-Senior Judge, United States Court of Appeals Sixth Circuit

Keith, Martin Langhorne-Judge, Virginia Circuit Court Nineteenth Judicial Circuit-Va.

Keith, Tom J.-Judge, Arkansas Circuit Court Nineteenth West Judicial Circuit-Ark.

Kelbley, Michael Paul-Judge, Ohio Court of Common Pleas Seneca County-Ohio

Keliher, Margaret-Judge, Dallas County Court-Tex.

Kellams, Marc R.-Judge, Monroe Circuit Court-Ind.

Kellegrew, Kent M.-Judge, Superior Court of California County of Ventura-Calif.

Kelleher, Robert J.-Senior Judge, United States District Court Central District of California-Calif.

Keller, Ann Murry-Judge, Jefferson Parish Juvenile Court-La.

Keller, Christine E.-Judge, Connecticut Superior Court-Conn.

Keller, Eddie T.-Judge, Superior Court of California County of El Dorado-Calif.

Keller, James E.-Justice, Kentucky Supreme Court-Ky.

Keller, Mark J.-Judge, Vermont Trial Court-Vt.

Keller, Patricia-Judge, West Virginia Family Court Circuit Six-W.Va.

Keller, Peter A.-District Judge, Iowa District Court Fifth Judicial District-Ia.

Keller, Richard O.-Judge, Superior Court of California County of Alameda-Calif.

Keller, Scott D.-Judge, Pennsylvania Court of Common Pleas Twenty-third Judicial District-Pa.

Keller, Sharon-Presiding Judge, Texas Court of Criminal Appeals-Tex.

Keller, William D.-Senior Judge, United States District Court Central District of California-Calif.

Kelley, Daniel J.-Circuit Judge, Illinois Circuit Court of Cook County-Ill.

Kelley, David O.-Judge, Warrick Circuit Court-Ind.

Kelley, James E.-District Judge, Iowa District Court Seventh Judicial District-Ia.

Kelley, James K.-Judge, Brooklyn District Probate Court-Conn.

Kelley, John-Judge, Probate Court of Dodge County-Ga.

Kelley, Kendall M.-Judge, Wisconsin Circuit Court Brown Circuit-Wis.

Kelley, Patrick W.-Circuit Judge, Illinois Circuit Court Seventh Judicial Circuit-Ill.

Kelley, Ralph Houston-Recalled Judge, United States Bankruptcy Court Eastern District of Tennessee-Tenn.

Kelley, Thomas J., Jr.-Chief Judge, Virginia General District Court Seventeenth Judicial District-Va.

Kelley, Timothy E.-Judge, Louisiana District Court Nineteenth Judicial District-La.

Kellison, Craig M.-Magistrate Judge, United States District Court Eastern District of California-Calif.

Kellogg, Daniel F.-Circuit Judge, Missouri Circuit Court Fifth Judicial Circuit-Mo.

Kellogg, Michael K.-Judge, Superior Court of California County of Los Angeles-Calif.

Kelly, Carol A.-Circuit Judge, Illinois Circuit Court of Cook County-Ill.

Kelly, Carroll J.-Judge, Dade County Court-Fla.

Kelly, Charles W.-Judge, Shreveport City Court-La.

Kelly, Christopher-Judge, Douglas County Separate Juvenile Court-Neb.

Kelly, Christopher S.-Associate Circuit Judge, Missouri Circuit Court Thirteenth Judicial Circuit-Mo.

Kelly, Daniel J.-Judge, Michigan Circuit Court Thirty-first Judicial Circuit-Mich.

Kelly, Edwin W.-Administrative Justice, New Hampshire District Court and Resident Justice, Plymouth District Court-N.H.

Kelly, Elizabeth K.-Judge, Pennsylvania Court of Common Pleas Sixth Judicial District-Pa.

Kelly, James H.-Associate Circuit Judge, Missouri Circuit Court Twenty-fourth Judicial Circuit-Mo.

Kelly, James McGirr-Senior Judge, United States District Court Eastern District of Pennsylvania-Pa.

Kelly, James P.-Judge, Colorado District Court Fourth Judicial District-Colo.

Kelly, John-Judge, Suffolk County District Court-N.Y.

Kelly, John F.-Judge, Superior Court of Arizona Pima County-Ariz.

Kelly, John I.-Judge, Superior Court of California County of Kern-Calif.

Kelly, John V.-Judge, Oregon Circuit Court Seventh Judicial District-Ore.

Kelly, Joseph Patrick-Judge, Texas District Court 24th Judicial District-Tex.

Kelly, Kevin F.-Judge, Pennsylvania Court of Common Pleas Thirty-second Judicial District-Pa.

Kelly, Larry E.-Chief Judge, United States Bankruptcy Court Western District of Texas-Tex.

Kelly, M. Marc-Judge, Superior Court of California County of Orange-Calif.

Kelly, Marilyn-Justice, Michigan Supreme Court-Mich.

Kelly, Mary Beth-Co-Chief Judge, Michigan Circuit Court Third Judicial Circuit-Mich.

ALPHABETICAL NAME INDEX

Kelly, Mike-Judge, West Virginia Family Court Circuit Eleven-W.Va.

Kelly, Patricia-Judge, Florida District Court of Appeal Second District-Fla.

Kelly, Paul J., Jr.-Judge, United States Court of Appeals Tenth Circuit

Kelly, Peter Joseph-Justice, New York Supreme Court Eleventh Judicial District-N.Y.

Kelly, Robert A.-President Judge, Pennsylvania Court of Common Pleas Fifth Judicial District-Pa.

Kelly, Robert F.-Senior Judge, United States District Court Eastern District of Pennsylvania-Pa.

Kelly, Sally A.-Associate Justice, Trial Court of Massachusetts Boston Municipal Court Department-Mass.

Kelly, Thomas E.-Judge, Superior Court of California County of Santa Cruz-Calif.

Kelly, Thomas E.-Judge, Snohomish District Court Everett Division Snohomish County-Wash.

Kelly, Thomas P.-Judge, New Jersey Superior Court Vicinage Seven-N.J.

Kelly, Thomas W.-Judge, Superior Court of California County of Butte-Calif.

Kelly, Timothy J.-Judge, Michigan District Court District Seventy-four-Mich.

Kelly, Virginia-Judge, Superior Court of Arizona Pima County-Ariz.

Kelly, William A.-Circuit Judge, Illinois Circuit Court Fifteenth Judicial Circuit-Ill.

Kelly, William A.-Judge, Rockland County Court-N.Y.

Kelly, William G.-Chief Judge, Michigan District Court District Sixty-two B-Mich.

Kelsey, Bruce R.-Associate Judge, Illinois Circuit Court Eighteenth Judicial Circuit-Ill.

Kelsey, Carmen-Judge, Texas District Court 289th Judicial District-Tex.

Kelsey, D. Arthur-Judge, Court of Appeals of Virginia-Va.

Kelsey, Reeve-Judge, Ohio Court of Common Pleas Wood County-Ohio

Kelton, David D.-Judge, Texas District Court 44th Judicial District-Tex.

Kemp, John Dan, Jr.-Judge, Arkansas Circuit Court Sixteenth Judicial Circuit-Ark.

Kemp, Margaret J.-Judge, Superior Court of California County of San Mateo-Calif.

Kemp, Terence P.-Magistrate Judge, United States District Court Southern District of Ohio-Ohio

Kendall, Alger H., Jr.-Judge, Karnes County Court-Tex.

Kendall, Robert G.-Presiding Judge, Alabama Circuit Court Thirteenth Judicial Circuit-Ala.

Kenderdine, Henry S., Jr.-Judge, Pennsylvania Court of Common Pleas Second Judicial District-Pa.

Kendig, Russ-Judge, United States Bankruptcy Court Northern District of Ohio-Ohio

Kendrick, Benjamin N. A.-Judge, Virginia Circuit Court Seventeenth Judicial Circuit-Va.

Kendrick, Larry L.-Circuit Judge, Missouri Circuit Court Twenty-first Judicial Circuit-Mo.

Kenefick, James G., Jr.-Judge, Connecticut Superior Court-Conn.

Kennard, Joyce Luther-Associate Justice, California Supreme Court-Calif.

Kennedy, Anthony M.-Associate Justice, The Supreme Court of the United States

Kennedy, Brenda P.-Judge, Texas District Court 403rd Judicial District-Tex.

Kennedy, Cornelia G.-Senior Judge, United States Court of Appeals Sixth Circuit

Kennedy, David S.-Chief Judge, United States Bankruptcy Court Western District of Tennessee-Tenn.

Kennedy, David W.-Judge, Kansas District Court Eighteenth Judicial District-Kan.

Kennedy, Faye-Judge, Washington Court of Appeals Division I-Wash.

Kennedy, George L.-Judge, Griswold District Probate Court-Conn.

Kennedy, Henry H., Jr.-Judge, United States District Court District of Columbia-D.C.

Kennedy, James A.-Judge, New Jersey Superior Court Vicinage Nine-N.J.

Kennedy, James W.-Circuit Judge, Illinois Circuit Court of Cook County-Ill.

Kennedy, John David-Judge, Maine District Court-Me.

Kennedy, John R.-Associate Judge, Illinois Circuit Court Sixth Judicial Circuit-Ill.

Kennedy, John S.-Judge, Pennsylvania Court of Common Pleas Nineteenth Judicial District-Pa.

Kennedy, John Todd-Associate Judge, Illinois Circuit Court Seventeenth Judicial Circuit-Ill.

Kennedy, John William-Judge, Superior Court of California County of Contra Costa-Calif.

Kennedy, Kathleen G.-Circuit Judge, Illinois Circuit Court of Cook County-Ill.

Kennedy, Kerry M.-Circuit Judge, Illinois Circuit Court of Cook County-Ill.

Kennedy, Kevin-Judge, Colchester District Probate Court-Conn.

Kennedy, Michael B.-Judge, Idaho District Court Seventh Judicial District Magistrate Division-Ida.

Kennedy, Patrick Gene-Judge, Florida Circuit Court Seventh Judicial Circuit-Fla.

Kennedy, Robert A., Jr.-Judge, Wisconsin Circuit Court Forest-Florence Circuit-Wis.

Kennedy, Robert A. P.-Reserve Judge, Wisconsin Circuit Court-Wis.

Kennedy, Robert J.-Judge, Wisconsin Circuit Court Walworth Circuit-Wis.

Kennedy, Roderick T.-Judge, New Mexico Court of Appeals-N.Mex.

Kennedy, Sharon L.-Judge, Ohio Court of Common Pleas Butler County-Ohio

Kennedy, Sue K.-Judge, Nacogdoches County Court-Tex.

Kennedy, Thomas L.-Judge, Colorado District Court Fourth Judicial District-Colo.

Kennedy, William H.-Judge, Superior Court of California County of San Diego-Calif.

Kennedy, William P.-Assistant Judge, Vermont Trial Court Caledonia County-Vt.

Kennedy-Powell, Kathleen-Judge, Superior Court of California County of Los Angeles-Calif.

Kennelly, Matthew F.-Judge, United States District Court Northern District of Illinois-Ill.

Kenner, Carol J.-Judge, Bankruptcy Appellate Panel First Circuit and Judge, United States Bankruptcy Court District of Massachusetts-Mass.

Kenney, James A., III-Associate Judge, Court of Special Appeals of Maryland-Md.

Kenney, Joan M.-Judge, The Civil Court of the City of New York-N.Y.

Kenney, Scott M.-Judge, Florida Circuit Court Nineteenth Judicial Circuit-Fla.

Kennon, Thomas J., Jr.-Judge, Florida Circuit Court Third Judicial Circuit-Fla.

Kennon, Warner L.-Judge, Juvenile Court of Georgia Chattahoochee Judicial Circuit-Ga.

Kenny, Camille M.-Judge, New Jersey Superior Court Vicinage Six-N.J.

Kenny, Michael P.-Judge, Superior Court of California County of Sacramento-Calif.

Kenny, Timothy Michael-Co-Chief Judge, Michigan Circuit Court Third Judicial Circuit-Mich.

Kent, Cynthia Stevens-Judge, Texas District Court 114th Judicial District-Tex.

Kent, David L.-Special Justice, Plymouth District Court-N.H.

Kent, Richard T.-Judge, State Court of Colquitt County-Ga.

Kent, Samuel B.-Judge, United States District Court Southern District of Texas-Tex.

Kent, W. Wallace, Jr.-Chief Judge, Tuscola County Probate Court-Mich.

Kent, William J., III-Justice, New York Supreme Court Tenth Judicial District-N.Y.

Kenton, Victor B.-Magistrate Judge, United States District Court Central District of California-Calif.

Kenworthy, David M.-Judge, Pierce District Court Pierce County-Wash.

Kenyon, A. Richard-Senior Judge, Superior Court of Georgia-Ga.

Keogh, D. Webster-Judge, Pennsylvania Court of Common Pleas First Judicial District-Pa.

Keosian, Gregory-Judge, Superior Court of California County of Los Angeles-Calif.

Keough, Joseph A.-Special Magistrate, Rhode Island Superior Court-R.I.

Keough, Kathleen A.-Judge, Cleveland Municipal Court-Ohio

Kepner, Rex W.-Judge, Benton Circuit Court-Ind.

Keppel, James H.-Judge, Superior Court of Arizona Maricopa County-Ariz.

Kepple, James R.-Magistrate Judge, Kansas District Court Twenty-fourth Judicial District-Kan.

Kerian, Jon R.-Surrogate Judge, North Dakota District Court-N.D.

Kerins, Martin J.-Judge, Suffolk County Court-N.Y.

Kerman, David D.-First Justice, Trial Court of Massachusetts Housing Court Department Northeastern Division-Mass.

Kern, Cynthia S.-Judge, The Civil Court of the City of New York-N.Y.

Kern, Janine-Judge, South Dakota Circuit Court Seventh Judicial Circuit-S.D.

Kern, John W., III-Senior Judge, District of Columbia Court of Appeals-D.C.

Kern, Leila R.-Associate Justice, Trial Court of Massachusetts Superior Court Department-Mass.

Kern, Robert J.-Judge, Texas District Court 387th Judicial District-Tex.

Kern, Terry C.-Chief Judge, United States District Court Northern District of Oklahoma-Okla.

Kernaghan, Herbert E.-Judge, Juvenile Court of Georgia Augusta Judicial Circuit-Ga.

Kerns, Cedric A.-Judge, Las Vegas Municipal Court-Nev.

Kerr, Jean-Judge, Laurel City Court-Mont.

Kerr, Samuel W.-Judge, Ohio Court of Common Pleas Jefferson County-Ohio

Kerr, William S.-Judge, Virginia Juvenile and Domestic Relations District Court Tenth Judicial District-Va.

Kerrick, Carl B.-Judge, Idaho District Court Second Judicial District-Ida.

Kerrick, Juneal-Judge, Idaho District Court Third Judicial District-Ida.

Kerrigan, Kevin J.-Judge, The Civil Court of the City of New York-N.Y.

Kersten, James Kurt-Chief Judge, Michigan District Court District Thirty-three-Mich.

Kessler, Donn-Judge, Arizona Court of Appeals Division One-Ariz.

Kessler, Gladys-Judge, United States District Court District of Columbia-D.C.

Kessler, John W.-Judge, Ohio Court of Common Pleas Montgomery County-Ohio

Kessler, Ronald-Judge, Washington Superior Court King County-Wash.

Kest, John Marshall-Judge, Florida Circuit Court Ninth Judicial Circuit-Fla.

Kestin, Howard H.-Judge, New Jersey Superior Court Appellate Division-N.J.

Ketterling, Lester S.-Judge, North Dakota District Court Northeast Judicial District-N.D.

Kettler, Richard T.-Judge, Massillon Municipal Court-Ohio

Key, Barbara Hart-Judge, Wisconsin Circuit Court Winnebago Circuit-Wis.

Key, Craig-Associate District Judge, Oklahoma District Court Twenty-third Judicial District-Okla.

Key, Michael-Judge, Juvenile Court of Georgia Coweta Judicial Circuit-Ga.

Key, Spencer G., Jr.-Judge, North Carolina District Court District 17B-N.C.

Keyes, Evelyn-Justice, Texas Court of Appeals First District-Tex.

Keyes, John A.-Judge, New Haven District Probate Court-Conn.

Keys, Arlander-Magistrate Judge, United States District Court Northern District of Illinois-Ill.

Keys, Linda-Justice of the Peace, Wheeler County Justice Court-Ore.

Khalil, Karen-Judge, Michigan District Court District Seventeen-Mich.

Khan, Abraham-Judge, Superior Court of California County of Los Angeles-Calif.

Khoury, Alvin G.-Judge, Texas District Court 124th Judicial District-Tex.

Khouzam, Nelly N.-Judge, Florida Circuit Court Sixth Judicial Circuit-Fla.

Kibe, Gerald H.-Judge, Hawaii District Court First Judicial Circuit-Hi.

Kick, Michael J.-Circuit Judge, Illinois Circuit Court Twenty-first Judicial Circuit-Ill.

Kida, Nancy A.-Chief Judge, Benzie County Probate Court-Mich.

ALPHABETICAL NAME INDEX

Kidd, Mack-Justice, Texas Court of Appeals Third District-Tex.

Kidd, Ronnie D.-Judge, McCormick County Probate Court-S.C.

Kidd, Winston L.-Judge, Mississippi Circuit Court Seventh Judicial District-Miss.

Kidwell, Wayne L.-Justice, Idaho Supreme Court-Ida.

Kiedaisch, Debra J.-Judge, Orange County Family Court-N.Y.

Kieffer, James Robert-Judge, Wisconsin Circuit Court Waukesha Circuit-Wis.

Kiesel, Diane R.-Judge, The Criminal Court of the City of New York-N.Y.

Kieser, Fred, Jr.-Judge, New Jersey Superior Court Vicinage Eight-N.J.

Kieser, William S.-Judge, Pennsylvania Court of Common Pleas Twenty-ninth Judicial District-Pa.

Kiger, William T.-Associate Presiding Judge, Superior Court of Arizona Yavapai County-Ariz.

Kilander, Robert K.-Chief Judge, Illinois Circuit Court Eighteenth Judicial Circuit-Ill.

Kilbane, Anne L.-Judge, Ohio Court of Appeals Eighth District-Ohio

Kilbane, Mary Eileen-Judge, Cleveland Municipal Court-Ohio

Kilbride, Thomas L.-Justice, Supreme Court of Illinois-Ill.

Kilburg, Paul J.-Chief Judge, United States Bankruptcy Court Northern District of Iowa-Ia.

Kilcrease, Irvin H., Jr.-Chancellor, Tennessee Chancery Court Twentieth Judicial District-Tenn.

Kiley, Michael P.-Circuit Judge, Illinois Circuit Court Fourth Judicial Circuit-Ill.

Kilgore, Collins-Judge, Arkansas Circuit Court Sixth Judicial Circuit-Ark.

Kilgore, Martha K.-Associate District Judge, Oklahoma District Court Twenty-second Judicial District-Okla.

Killian, Lewis M., Jr.-Judge, United States Bankruptcy Court Northern District of Florida-Fla.

Killian, Robert K., Jr.-Judge, Hartford District Probate Court-Conn.

Killian, William R.-Senior Judge, Superior Court of Georgia-Ga.

Killingsworth, Priscilla-Chief Magistrate, Magistrate Court of Pike County-Ga.

Kilmartin, Peter J.-First Justice, Trial Court of Massachusetts District Court Department Middlesex County Ayer Division-Mass.

Kilnoski, Kathleen A.-District Associate Judge, Iowa District Court Fourth Judicial District-Ia.

Kilpatrick, Kenneth-Senior Judge, Superior Court of Georgia-Ga.

Kim, Brian G.-Associate Judge, Maryland District Court District Six-Md.

Kim, Mark C.-Judge, Superior Court of California County of Los Angeles-Calif.

Kim, Marliese G.-Judge, Superior Court of California County of Santa Clara-Calif.

Kimball, Catherine D. "Kitty"-Justice, Supreme Court of Louisiana-La.

Kimball, Dale A.-Judge, United States District Court District of Utah-Utah

Kimble, Wayne G., Jr.-Judge, North Carolina District Court District 4-N.C.

Kimbler, James L.-Judge, Ohio Court of Common Pleas Medina County-Ohio

Kimbrough, Rickey C.-Judge, Grandview Municipal Court-Wash.

Kimbrough, William E.-Judge, Clarke County District Court-Ala.

Kimes, Gary G.-District Judge, Iowa District Court Fifth Judicial District-Ia.

Kimes, Russell A., Jr.-Judge, New Canaan District Probate Court-Conn.

Kimmel, E. Dan-Associate Judge, Illinois Circuit Court First Judicial Circuit-Ill.

Kimmelman, Irwin I.-Retired Judge, New Jersey Superior Court-N.J.

Kinard, J. Ernest, Jr.-Judge, South Carolina Circuit Court Fifth Judicial Circuit-S.C.

Kincaid, Matthew C.-Judge, Boone Superior Court-Ind.

Kincaid, Roger-Chief Magistrate, Magistrate Court of Gilmer County-Ga.

Kincaid, Timothy S.-Resident Judge, North Carolina Superior Court Seventh Judicial Division District 25B-N.C.

Kincannon, Ronald L.-Associate District Judge, Oklahoma District Court First Judicial District-Okla.

Kindig, Gloria-Judge, Superior Court of Arizona Navajo County-Ariz.

King, C. Hunter-Judge, Louisiana District Court Orleans Parish Civil District-La.

King, Carolyn Dineen-Chief Judge, United States Court of Appeals Fifth Circuit

King, Charles E.-Judge, West Virginia Circuit Court Thirteenth Judicial Circuit-W.Va.

King, Dan C., III-Judge, Alabama Circuit Court Tenth Judicial Circuit Bessemer Division-Ala.

King, David D.-Judge, Probate Court of New Hampshire Coos County-N.H.

King, David J.-Chief Judge, Kansas District Court First Judicial District-Kan.

King, Edward J., III-Judge, Superior Court of California County of Tehama-Calif.

King, Frances S.-Judge, Marion County Court-Fla.

King, Garr M.-Judge, United States District Court District of Oregon-Ore.

King, George Herbert-Judge, United States District Court Central District of California-Calif.

King, Howard P.-Judge, South Carolina Circuit Court Third Judicial Circuit-S.C.

King, James L.-Judge, Alexandria City Court-Ind.

King, James Lawrence-Senior Judge, United States District Court Southern District of Florida-Fla.

King, Janet F.-Magistrate Judge, United States District Court Northern District of Georgia-Ga.

King, Jeffrey-Associate Justice, California Court of Appeal Fourth District Division Two-Calif.

King, Judy-Judge, Ohio Court of Common Pleas Montgomery County-Ohio

King, Julian M.-Judge, Alabama Circuit Court Twenty-ninth Judicial Circuit-Ala.

King, Kevin N.-Judge, Arkansas Circuit Court Third Judicial Circuit-Ark.

King, Lawrence D.-Judge, Dade County Court-Fla.

King, Leslie D.-Presiding Judge, Court of Appeals of Mississippi-Miss.

King, Lloyd-Recalled Judge, United States Bankruptcy Court District of Hawaii-Hi.

King, Michael Patrick-Judge, New Jersey Superior Court Appellate Division-N.J.

King, Norah McCann-Magistrate Judge, United States District Court Southern District of Ohio-Ohio

King, Paul A.-Judge, Colorado District Court Eighteenth Judicial District-Colo.

King, Richard M.-Judge, Superior Court of California County of Orange-Calif.

King, Robert Bruce-Judge, United States Court of Appeals Fourth Circuit

King, Robert Henry, Jr.-Justice of the Peace, Jackson County Justice Court-Ore.

King, Robert R., Jr.-Judge, Minnesota District Court First Judicial District-Minn.

King, Ronald B.-Judge, United States Bankruptcy Court Western District of Texas-Tex.

King, Ronald W.-Associate Justice, Trial Court of Massachusetts Probate and Family Court Department Worcester County Division-Mass.

King, Roy Wheatley-Judge, Rochester City Court-N.Y.

King, Rufus G., III-Chief Judge, Superior Court of the District of Columbia-D.C.

King, Samuel Pailthorpe-Senior Judge, United States District Court District of Hawaii-Hi.

King, Steve M.-Judge, Tarrant County Probate Court No. 1-Tex.

King, Steven E.-Judge, La Porte Superior Court-Ind.

King, Tom, Jr.-Judge, Alabama Circuit Court Tenth Judicial Circuit Birmingham Division-Ala.

King, W. David-Magistrate Judge, United States District Court Western District of Kentucky-Ky.

King, Warren M.-Senior Judge, District of Columbia Court of Appeals-D.C.

King, William R.-Judge, Crenshaw County District Court-Ala.

Kinghorn, Clifford R., Jr.-Justice, Merrimack District Court-N.H.

Kingsbury, Kenneth R.-Judge, Superior Court of California County of Alameda-Calif.

Kingsbury, Suzanne N.-Judge, Superior Court of California County of El Dorado-Calif.

Kingsley, James C.-Judge, Michigan Circuit Court Thirty-seventh Judicial Circuit-Mich.

Kingsley, Kay T.-Judge, Superior Court of California County of Monterey-Calif.

Kinkaid, Robert W., Jr.-Judge, Texas District Court 64th Judicial District-Tex.

Kinkeade, Ed-Judge, United States District Court Northern District of Texas-Tex.

Kinker, Amy-Associate Circuit Judge, Missouri Circuit Court Forty-fifth Judicial Circuit-Mo.

Kinnaird, Dorothy Kirie-Circuit Judge, Illinois Circuit Court of Cook County-Ill.

Kinney, Baird-Judge, Arkansas Circuit Court First Judicial Circuit-Ark.

Kinney, Gerald R.-Circuit Judge, Illinois Circuit Court Twelfth Judicial Circuit-Ill.

Kinney, Robert E.-Judge, Wisconsin Circuit Court Oneida Circuit-Wis.

Kinnicutt, Harry S.-Judge, Superior Court of California County of Solano-Calif.

Kinon, Lisa A.-Judge, South Carolina Family Court Fifteenth Judicial Circuit-S.C.

Kinser, Cynthia D.-Justice, Supreme Court of Virginia-Va.

Kinsey, Mose M.-Chief Magistrate, Magistrate Court of Colquitt County-Ga.

Kinsey, Patricia A.-Judge, Escambia County Court-Fla.

Kintner, Janet Ide-Judge, Superior Court of California County of San Diego-Calif.

Kintz, John F.-Circuit Judge, Missouri Circuit Court Twenty-first Judicial Circuit-Mo.

Kinworthy, David R.-Judge, Ohio Court of Common Pleas Allen County-Ohio

Kipperman, Carol A.-Associate Judge, Illinois Circuit Court of Cook County-Ill.

Kirby, John P.-Circuit Judge, Illinois Circuit Court of Cook County-Ill.

Kirby, Michael E.-Judge, Louisiana Court of Appeal Fourth Circuit-La.

Kirby, Robert W.-Retired-Recalled Judge, North Carolina Superior Court-N.C.

Kirchman, Michael-Judge, Wisconsin Circuit Court Crawford Circuit-Wis.

Kirihara, John D.-Judge, Superior Court of California County of Merced-Calif.

Kirk, James D.-Magistrate Judge, United States District Court Western District of Louisiana-La.

Kirk, Michael L.-Judge, Minnesota District Court Seventh Judicial District-Minn.

Kirk, Patrick L.-Judge, Herkimer County Court-N.Y.

Kirk, Philip M.-Judge, Wisconsin Circuit Court Waupaca Circuit-Wis.

Kirkendall, John N.-Chief Judge, Washtenaw County Probate Court-Mich.

Kirkham, I. Lloyd-Judge, Liberty County Court-Tex.

Kirkland, Thomas R.-Judge, Orange County Court-Fla.

Kirkman, K. Michael-Judge, Superior Court of California County of San Diego-Calif.

Kirkpatrick, Harry L., III-Judge, West Virginia Circuit Court Tenth Judicial Circuit-W.Va.

Kirkwood, Carolyn-Judge, Superior Court of California County of Orange-Calif.

Kirkwood, Lawrence R.-Judge, Florida Circuit Court Ninth Judicial Circuit-Fla.

Kirsch, James S.-Judge, Indiana Court of Appeals Second District-Ind.

Kirsch, James Wilson-Judge, Ohio Court of Common Pleas Scioto County-Ohio

Kirscher, Ralph B.-Judge, United States Bankruptcy Court District of Montana-Mont.

Kirschner, Richard H.-Judge, Superior Court of California County of Los Angeles-Calif.

Kiser, Jackson L.-Senior Judge, United States District Court Western District of Virginia-Va.

Kishel, Gregory F.-Chief Judge, United States Bankruptcy Court District of Minnesota-Minn.

Kistler, Rives-Judge, Oregon Court of Appeals-Ore.

ALPHABETICAL NAME INDEX

Kistler, Thomas King-Judge, Pennsylvania Court of Common Pleas Forty-ninth Judicial District-Pa.

Kitchens, James T., Jr.-Judge, Mississippi Circuit Court Sixteenth Judicial District-Miss.

Kitching, Patti S.-Associate Justice, California Court of Appeal Second District Division Three-Calif.

Kite, Marilyn S.-Justice, Wyoming Supreme Court-Wyo.

Kithil, David L.-Judge, Burnet County Court-Tex.

Kitley, John-Judge, Marion County Small Claims Court Franklin Township Division-Ind.

Kitson, Donald-Judge, Suffolk County Court-N.Y.

Kittredge, John W.-Associate Judge, South Carolina Court of Appeals-S.C.

Kittrell, James Orvil-Judge, Montague County Court-Tex.

Kitts, Hannelore-Judge, Kansas District Court Twentieth Judicial District-Kan.

Kitzes, Orin R.-Justice, New York Supreme Court Eleventh Judicial District-N.Y.

Klaczak, Lawrence C.-Judge Referee, Connecticut Superior Court-Conn.

Klager, James E.-Judge, Nueces County Court at Law No. 4-Tex.

Klammer, Theodore Rudolph-Judge, Ohio Court of Common Pleas Lake County-Ohio

Klaphake, Roger M.-Judge, Minnesota Court of Appeals-Minn.

Klass, Jack E.-Retired-Recalled Judge, North Carolina District Court-N.C.

Klass, Mark E.-Resident Judge, North Carolina Superior Court Sixth Judicial Division District 22-N.C.

Klatt, William A.-Judge, Ohio Court of Appeals Tenth District-Ohio

Klausner, Robert G.-Judge, United States District Court Central District of California-Calif.

Kleifield, Steven J.-Judge, Superior Court of California County of Los Angeles-Calif.

Klein, Allen-Special Judge, Oklahoma District Court Fourteenth Judicial District-Okla.

Klein, Andrew G.-Judge, Superior Court of Arizona Maricopa County-Ariz.

Klein, Brett Carroll-Judge, Superior Court of California County of Los Angeles-Calif.

Klein, Carol S.-Judge, Orange County Family Court-N.Y.

Klein, Christopher M.-Judge, Bankruptcy Appellate Panel Ninth Circuit and Judge, United States Bankruptcy Court Eastern District of California-Calif.

Klein, Clifford-Judge, Superior Court of California County of Los Angeles-Calif.

Klein, David-Judge, Westchester County Family Court-N.Y.

Klein, Dyanne J.-First Justice, Trial Court of Massachusetts District Court Department Middlesex County Newton Division-Mass.

Klein, Edward S.-Senior Judge, Florida Circuit Court Eleventh Judicial Circuit-Fla.

Klein, Felix-Judge, Texas District Court 154th Judicial District-Tex.

Klein, Gerald J.-Senior Judge, Dade County Court-Fla.

Klein, Harriet Farber-Judge, New Jersey Superior Court Vicinage Five-N.J.

Klein, Joan Dempsey-Presiding Justice, California Court of Appeal Second District Division Three-Calif.

Klein, Karen K.-Magistrate Judge, United States District Court District of North Dakota-N.D.

Klein, Kurt-Circuit Judge, Illinois Circuit Court Sixteenth Judicial Circuit-Ill.

Klein, Larry-Judge, Florida District Court of Appeal Fourth District-Fla.

Klein, Lee David-Judge, Poughkeepsie City Court-N.Y.

Klein, Mary Kay-Magistrate Judge, United States District Court District of Minnesota-Minn.

Klein, Murray Z.-Senior Judge, Dade County Court-Fla.

Klein, Richard B.-Judge, The Superior Court of Pennsylvania-Pa.

Klein, Richard M.-Judge, New York Court of Claims-N.Y.

Klein, Roger A.-Chief Judge, Colorado District Court Nineteenth Judicial District and Judge, Colorado Water Court Division One-Colo.

Klein, Stanley P.-Judge, Virginia Circuit Court Nineteenth Judicial Circuit-Va.

Kleinberg, James P.-Judge, Superior Court of California County of Santa Clara-Calif.

Kleinfeld, Andrew J.-Judge, United States Court of Appeals Ninth Circuit

Kleinfelter, Joseph H.-President Judge, Pennsylvania Court of Common Pleas Twelfth Judicial District-Pa.

Kleinpeter, William T.-Judge, Port Allen City Court-La.

Kleopfer, James D., Jr.-Judge, Scott Circuit Court-Ind.

Kleri, Patricia Ann-Judge, South Euclid Municipal Court-Ohio

Kleven, Debbie Gordon-Presiding Judge, North Dakota District Court Northeast Central Judicial District-N.D.

Kleweno, Gilbert H.-Magistrate Judge, United States District Court Western District of Washington-Wash.

Kliebert, Thomas, Jr.-Judge, Louisiana District Court Twenty-third Judicial District-La.

Klim, David G.-Judge, Onondaga County Family Court-N.Y.

Kline, John Anthony-Presiding Justice, California Court of Appeal First District Division Two-Calif.

Kline, Judith Anne-Judge, Virginia Juvenile and Domestic Relations District Court Seventh Judicial District-Va.

Kline, Roger L.-Judge, Ohio Court of Appeals Fourth District-Ohio

Kline, Samuel A.-Judge, Pennsylvania Court of Common Pleas Fifty-second Judicial District-Pa.

Klinginsmith, Tracy D.-Chief Judge, Kansas District Court Second Judicial District-Kan.

Klobucher, John M.-Recalled Judge, United States Bankruptcy Court Eastern District of Washington-Wash.

Kloch, John E.-Judge, Virginia Circuit Court Eighteenth Judicial Circuit-Va.

Kloch, Richard C., Sr.-Judge, New York Court of Claims-N.Y.

Kloote, Richard J.-Judge, Michigan District Court District Fifty-eight-Mich.

Klopfer, Barry B.-Judge, Superior Court of California County of Ventura-Calif.

Klossner, Daniel W.-Judge, Wisconsin Circuit Court Dodge Circuit-Wis.

Klotz, Ruth B.-Associate Probate Judge, Iowa District Court Fifth Judicial District-Ia.

Klubock, Daniel-Circuit Justice, Trial Court of Massachusetts District Court Department-Mass.

Kluewer, Susan T.-Judge, Nassau County District Court-N.Y.

Kluger, Judy Harris-Judge, The Criminal Court of the City of New York-N.Y.

Kluka, Barbara A.-Judge, Wisconsin Circuit Court Kenosha Circuit-Wis.

Kluttz, William C., Jr.-Judge, North Carolina District Court District 19C-N.C.

Knapp, Thomas-Judge, Minnesota District Court Seventh Judicial District-Minn.

Knapp, Whitman-Senior Judge, United States District Court Southern District of New York-N.Y.

Knece, P. Randall-Judge, Ohio Court of Common Pleas Pickaway County-Ohio

Knecht, James A.-Judge, Illinois Appellate Court Fourth Judicial District-Ill.

Knepper, Richard W.-Judge, Ohio Court of Appeals Sixth District-Ohio

Knieps, Karla J.-Judge, Oregon Circuit Court Thirteenth Judicial District-Ore.

Knierim, Paul J.-Judge, Simsbury District Probate Court-Conn.

Knight, C. Edward, III-Judge, Virginia General District Court Eighth Judicial District-Va.

Knight, Edward R.-Magistrate Judge, United States District Court District of New Jersey-N.J.

Knight, Gerald L.-Judge, Washington Superior Court Snohomish County-Wash.

Knight, H. Lamar-Senior Judge, Superior Court of Georgia-Ga.

Knight, J. Douglas-Judge, Vanderburgh Superior Court-Ind.

Knight, John-Circuit Judge, Illinois Circuit Court Third Judicial Circuit-Ill.

Knight, Louise O.-Judge, Pennsylvania Court of Common Pleas Seventeenth Judicial District-Pa.

Knight, Michael E.-Judge, Superior Court of California County of Los Angeles-Calif.

Knight, Rebecca B.-Judge, North Carolina District Court District 28-N.C.

Knight, Ted A.-Associate District Judge, Oklahoma District Court Sixteenth Judicial District-Okla.

Knight, W. D.-Senior Judge, Superior Court of Georgia-Ga.

Knight, William J. "Rusty"-Judge, Louisiana District Court Twenty-second Judicial District-La.

Knipel, Lawrence S.-Justice, New York Supreme Court Second Judicial District-N.Y.

Knipps, Susan K.-Judge, The Civil Court of the City of New York-N.Y.

Knisely, MaryJane McCalla-Judge, Billings Municipal Court-Mont.

Knize, Gene-Judge, Texas District Court 40th Judicial District-Tex.

Knobel, Barry W.-Judge, South Carolina Family Court Tenth Judicial Circuit-S.C.

Knoblock, M. Richard-Chief Judge, Michigan Circuit Court Fifty-second Judicial Circuit-Mich.

Knoll, Bradley S.-Judge, Michigan District Court District Fifty-eight-Mich.

Knoll, Jeannette Theriot-Justice, Supreme Court of Louisiana-La.

Knopf, Stephen A.-Judge, The Civil Court of the City of New York-N.Y.

Knopf, Thomas John-Judge, Kentucky Circuit Court Thirtieth Judicial Circuit-Ky.

Knopf, William L.-Judge, Kentucky Court of Appeals-Ky.

Knowles, Daniel E., III-Magistrate Judge, United States District Court Eastern District of Louisiana-La.

Knowles, E. Clifton-Magistrate Judge, United States District Court Middle District of Tennessee-Tenn.

Knowles, Richard J.-Judge, New Mexico District Court Second Judicial District-N.Mex.

Knowlton, John O.-Judge, Walla Walla District Court Walla Walla County-Wash.

Knox, Michael G.-Judge, North Carolina District Court District 19A-N.C.

Knox, William A.-Magistrate Judge, United States District Court Western District of Missouri-Mo.

Knuck, Francis X.-Senior Judge, Florida Circuit Court Eleventh Judicial Circuit-Fla.

Knudson, David S.-Judge, Kansas Court of Appeals-Kan.

Knupp, Larry S.-Judge, Superior Court of California County of Los Angeles-Calif.

Knust, Daniel Max-Associate Circuit Judge, Missouri Circuit Court Thirtieth Judicial Circuit-Mo.

Kobayashi, Charles C.-Judge, Superior Court of California County of Sacramento-Calif.

Kobayashi, Leslie E.-Magistrate Judge, United States District Court District of Hawaii-Hi.

Kober, Marilyn-Justice, Stillwater County Justice of the Peace Court and Judge, Columbus City Court-Mont.

Koblitz, Ellen L.-Judge, New Jersey Superior Court Vicinage Two-N.J.

Kobly, Elizabeth A.-Judge, Youngstown Municipal Court-Ohio

Kocay, Andre M.-Judge, Connecticut Superior Court-Conn.

Koch, Dale R.-Presiding Judge, Oregon Circuit Court Fourth Judicial District-Ore.

Koch, Judith Kilbane-Judge, Ohio Court of Common Pleas Cuyahoga County-Ohio

Koch, William Conway, Jr.-Judge, Tennessee Court of Appeals Middle Division-Tenn.

Kochenburger, John E.-Judge, Larimer County Court-Colo.

Kocher, James F.-Judge, Marion City Court-Ind.

Kochi, Dan T.-Deputy Chief Judge, Hawaii Circuit Court First Judicial Circuit-Hi.

Kocoras, Charles P.-Chief Judge, United States District Court Northern District of Illinois-Ill.

Kocurek, Julie Harris-Judge, Texas District Court 390th Judicial District-Tex.

Koehler, Thomas L.-District Judge, Iowa District Court Sixth Judicial District-Ia.

ALPHABETICAL NAME INDEX

Koehn, John D.-Reserve Judge, Wisconsin Circuit Court-Wis.

Koeltl, John G.-Judge, United States District Court Southern District of New York-N.Y.

Koenig, Julie-Judge, Florida Circuit Court Seventeenth Judicial Circuit-Fla.

Koenig, Nancy M.-Magistrate Judge, United States District Court Northern District of Texas-Tex.

Koenig, Paul T., Jr.-Judge, New Jersey Superior Court Vicinage Seven-N.J.

Koenigs, Rita-Justice, Trial Court of Massachusetts District Court Department Berkshire County Pittsfield Division-Mass.

Koetter, Juergen "Skipper"-Judge, Texas District Court 267th Judicial District-Tex.

Koffman, Robert L.-Associate Circuit Judge, Missouri Circuit Court Eighteenth Judicial Circuit-Mo.

Kogan, Randye A.-Associate Judge, Illinois Circuit Court of Cook County-Ill.

Kohl, Thomas W.-Judge, Oregon Circuit Court Twentieth Judicial District-Ore.

Kohm, Robert C.-Justice, New York Supreme Court Eleventh Judicial District-N.Y.

Kohn, Barbara "Skip"-Judge, Darby and Stevensville City Courts-Mont.

Kohout, Joan S.-Judge, Monroe County Family Court-N.Y.

Kolberg, Thomas W.-Judge, Oregon Circuit Court Sixteenth Judicial District-Ore.

Kolenda, Dennis C.-Judge, Michigan Circuit Court Seventeenth Judicial Circuit-Mich.

Koletsky, Joseph Q.-Judge, Connecticut Superior Court-Conn.

Kolhoss, Ruth-Justice of the Peace, Moapa Justices' Court-Nev.

Kolin, William M.-Judge, Superior Court of California County of Contra Costa-Calif.

Kolkey, Daniel M.-Associate Justice, California Court of Appeal Third District-Calif.

Kolkoski, Elizabeth-Judge, Las Vegas Municipal Court-Nev.

Kollar-Kotelly, Colleen C.-Judge, United States District Court District of Columbia-D.C.

Kolomitz, M. Jon-Chief Judge, Colorado District Court Sixteenth Judicial District-Colo.

Kolostian, Richard G.-Judge, Superior Court of California County of Los Angeles-Calif.

Komanski, Walter-Judge, Florida Circuit Court Ninth Judicial Circuit-Fla.

Komar, Jack-Judge, Superior Court of California County of Santa Clara-Calif.

Komives, Paul J.-Recalled Magistrate Judge, United States District Court Eastern District of Michigan-Mich.

Kondo, C. Kimi-Judge, Seattle Municipal Court-Wash.

Konduros, Aphrodite K.-Judge, South Carolina Family Court Thirteenth Judicial Circuit-S.C.

Konenkamp, John K.-Associate Justice, South Dakota Supreme Court-S.D.

Konetski, James J.-Associate Judge, Illinois Circuit Court Eighteenth Judicial Circuit-Ill.

Kongable, Kirby-Judge, Superior Court of Arizona Yuma County-Ariz.

Konkol, Daniel L.-Judge, Wisconsin Circuit Court Milwaukee Circuit-Wis.

Konrad, Nancy Amato-Judge, Jefferson Parish Juvenile Court-La.

Kontos, Peter J.-Judge, Ohio Court of Common Pleas Trumbull County-Ohio

Koontz, Lawrence L., Jr.-Justice, Supreme Court of Virginia-Va.

Kopelman, David H.-First Justice, Trial Court of Massachusetts Probate and Family Court Department Norfolk County Division-Mass.

Kopf, Richard G.-Chief Judge, United States District Court District of Nebraska-Neb.

Kopowski, Leonard L.-Judge, Kentucky Circuit Court Seventeenth Judicial Circuit-Ky.

Kopp, Quentin L.-Judge, Superior Court of California County of San Mateo-Calif.

Kopriva, Jolene Grubb-Judge, Pennsylvania Court of Common Pleas Twenty-fourth Judicial District-Pa.

Korbey, John A.-Justice, Salem District Court-N.H.

Korda, Lawrence L.-Judge, Florida Circuit Court Seventeenth Judicial Circuit-Fla.

Koretz, Eileen-Judge, The Criminal Court of the City of New York-N.Y.

Korman, Edward R.-Chief Judge, United States District Court Eastern District of New York-N.Y.

Kornahrens, Keith, Sr.-Judge, Berkeley County Probate Court-S.C.

Kornblum, Allen-Senior Judge, Florida Circuit Court Eleventh Judicial Circuit-Fla.

Kornmann, Charles B.-Judge, United States District Court District of South Dakota-S.D.

Kornreich, Louis H.-Judge, United States Bankruptcy Court District of Maine-Me.

Kornreich, Shirley Werner-Judge, The Civil Court of the City of New York-N.Y.

Kornstein, Harvey-Judge, Florida Circuit Court Tenth Judicial Circuit-Fla.

Korslund, Paul W.-Judge, Nebraska District Court First Judicial District-Neb.

Korvick, Maria Marinello-Judge, Florida Circuit Court Eleventh Judicial Circuit-Fla.

Kosach, Steven R.-Judge, Nevada District Court Second Judicial District-Nev.

Koschnick, Randy R.-Judge, Wisconsin Circuit Court Jefferson Circuit-Wis.

Kosel, Roger T.-Judge, Superior Court of California County of Siskiyou-Calif.

Koselka, Harvey A.-Chief Judge, Michigan Circuit Court Thirty-ninth Judicial Circuit-Mich.

Koselka, Natalia M.-Judge, Michigan District Court District Two A-Mich.

Kosik, Edwin M.-Senior Judge, United States District Court Middle District of Pennsylvania-Pa.

Kosko, George C.-Magistrate Judge, United States District Court District of South Carolina-S.C.

Koss, David R.-Judge, Cowlitz District Court Cowlitz County-Wash.

Kotey, Phyllis D.-Judge, Alachua County Court-Fla.

Kottmyer, Diane M.-Associate Justice, Trial Court of Massachusetts Superior Court Department-Mass.

Kotyk, Frank-Judge, Idaho District Court Third Judicial District Magistrate Division-Ida.

Koudelis, George-Judge, Pennsylvania Court of Common Pleas Thirty-second Judicial District-Pa.

Kouri, Stephen A.-Circuit Judge, Illinois Circuit Court Tenth Judicial Circuit-Ill.

Kourlis, Rebecca Love-Justice, Colorado Supreme Court-Colo.

Kouros, Joan-Judge, Lake Superior Court-Ind.

Kovachevich, Elizabeth Anne-Judge, United States District Court Middle District of Florida-Fla.

Kovack, Mary R.-Judge, Ohio Court of Common Pleas Medina County-Ohio

Koval, Joseph P.-Circuit Judge, Illinois Circuit Court Seventh Judicial Circuit-Ill.

Kowalski, John F.-Judge, Michigan Circuit Court Twenty-sixth Judicial Circuit-Mich.

Kowalski, Robert J.-Circuit Judge, Illinois Circuit Court of Cook County-Ill.

Koyanagi, Faye M.-Judge, Hawaii District Court First Judicial Circuit-Hi.

Kozinski, Alex-Judge, United States Court of Appeals Ninth Circuit

Kracov, Melvin S.-Judge, New Jersey Superior Court Vicinage Six-N.J.

Kraetzer, John Frederick-Judge, Superior Court of California County of Alameda-Calif.

Krake, Allen A.-Judge, Louisiana District Court Thirty-fifth Judicial District-La.

Kraker, Michael J.-Judge, Minnesota District Court Ninth Judicial District-Minn.

Kram, Shirley Wohl-Senior Judge, United States District Court Southern District of New York-N.Y.

Kramer, Barry D.-Surrogate, Schenectady County Surrogate's Court-N.Y.

Kramer, C. William-Circuit Judge, Missouri Circuit Court Sixteenth Judicial Circuit-Mo.

Kramer, Gary P.-Circuit Judge, Missouri Circuit Court Twenty-third Judicial Circuit-Mo.

Kramer, Herbert-Justice, New York Supreme Court Second Judicial District-N.Y.

Kramer, Kenneth B.-Chief Judge, United States Court of Appeals for Veterans Claims

Kramer, Michael D.-Associate Judge, Illinois Circuit Court Twenty-first Judicial Circuit-Ill.

Kramer, Michael J.-Judge, Noble Superior Court-Ind.

Kramer, Noel Anketell-Associate Judge, Superior Court of the District of Columbia-D.C.

Kramer, Richard A.-Judge, Superior Court of California City and County of San Francisco-Calif.

Krant, Elisabeth B.-Judge, Superior Court of California County of Tulare-Calif.

Krashna, David M.-Judge, Superior Court of California County of Alameda-Calif.

Krathen, David H.-Judge, Florida Circuit Court Seventeenth Judicial Circuit-Fla.

Krauel, Roger W.-Judge, Superior Court of California County of San Diego-Calif.

Kraus, Karl E.-Chief Judge, Michigan District Court District Seventy-three B-Mich.

Krause, Amy Ronayne-Judge, Michigan District Court District Fifty-four A-Mich.

Krause, Robert D.-Associate Justice, Rhode Island Superior Court-R.I.

Krauser, Peter Brunswick-Associate Judge, Court of Special Appeals of Maryland-Md.

Krauser, Sherrie L.-Associate Judge, Circuit Court for Prince George's County, Seventh Judicial Circuit-Md.

Krausman, Gabriel M.-Associate Justice, New York Supreme Court Appellate Division Second Judicial Department-N.Y.

Krauss, Sarah L.-Judge, The Civil Court of the City of New York-N.Y.

Kravchuk, Margaret J.-Magistrate Judge, United States District Court District of Maine-Me.

Kravitch, Phyllis A.-Senior Judge, United States Court of Appeals Eleventh Circuit

Kravitz, Neal E.-Associate Judge, Superior Court of the District of Columbia-D.C.

Kravitz, Shelley J.-Judge, Dade County Court-Fla.

Kreber, Ronald Patrick-Judge, Superior Court of California County of Orange-Calif.

Krebs, Robert P.-Judge, Mississippi Circuit Court Nineteenth Judicial District-Miss.

Krechevsky, Robert L.-Recalled Judge, United States Bankruptcy Court District of Connecticut-Conn.

Kreeger, George H.-Judge, Superior Court of Georgia Cobb Judicial Circuit-Ga.

Kreeger, Judith L.-Judge, Florida Circuit Court Eleventh Judicial Circuit-Fla.

Kreindler, Robert S.-Justice, New York Supreme Court Second Judicial District-N.Y.

Kreizman, Ira E.-Judge, New Jersey Superior Court Vicinage Nine-N.J.

Kremer, Daniel J.-Administrative Presiding Justice, California Court of Appeal Fourth District and Presiding Justice, California Court of Appeal Fourth District Division One-Calif.

Kremers, Jeffrey A.-Judge, Wisconsin Circuit Court Milwaukee Circuit-Wis.

Kremski, Julius J.-Judge Referee, Connecticut Superior Court-Conn.

Krepela, Richard W.-Judge, Nebraska County Court Seventh Judicial District-Neb.

Krese, Linda C.-Judge, Washington Superior Court Snohomish County-Wash.

Kressel, Robert J.-Chief Judge, Bankruptcy Appellate Panel Eighth Circuit and Judge, United States Bankruptcy Court District of Minnesota-Minn.

Kreul, Richard J.-Judge, Wisconsin Circuit Court Racine Circuit-Wis.

Krichbaum, R. Scott-Judge, Ohio Court of Common Pleas Mahoning County-Ohio

Krieger, Marcia S.-Judge, United States District Court District of Colorado-Colo.

Kriegler, Sandy R.-Judge, Superior Court of California County of Los Angeles-Calif.

Kristianson, Larry M.-Judge, Washington Superior Court Ferry-Pend Oreille-Stevens Counties-Wash.

Kristovich, Marlene-Judge, Superior Court of California County of Los Angeles-Calif.

Krocker, Jan-Judge, Texas District Court 184th Judicial District-Tex.

ALPHABETICAL NAME INDEX

ALPHABETICAL NAME INDEX

ALPHABETICAL NAME INDEX

Lau, Linda-Judge, Washington Superior Court King County-Wash.

Lauber, William G.-Judge, Lima Municipal Court-Ohio

Laughlin, Lauren-Judge, Florida Circuit Court Sixth Judicial Circuit-Fla.

Laughrey, Nanette K.-Judge, United States District Court Western District of Missouri-Mo.

Launey, Donald J.-Judge, Ville Platte City Court-La.

Laur, G. David-Judge, Noble Circuit Court-Ind.

Lauranzano, Michael C.-Justice, Trial Court of Massachusetts District Court Department Essex County Salem Division-Mass.

Laurence, Kenneth-Associate Justice, Massachusetts Appeals Court-Mass.

Laurent, John F.-Judge, Florida Circuit Court Tenth Judicial Circuit-Fla.

Lauria, Joseph M.-Judge, New York City Family Court-N.Y.

Lauriat, Peter M.-Associate Justice, Trial Court of Massachusetts Superior Court Department-Mass.

Laurie, Anna M.-Judge, Washington Superior Court Kitsap County-Wash.

Laurie, John G.-Associate Judge, Illinois Circuit Court of Cook County-Ill.

Lauten, Frederick, Jr.-Judge, Florida Circuit Court Ninth Judicial Circuit-Fla.

La Vecchia, Jaynee-Associate Justice, Supreme Court of New Jersey-N.J.

Lavender, Robert E.-Justice, Supreme Court of Oklahoma-Okla.

LaVergne, Luke A.-Judge, East Baton Rouge Parish Family Court-La.

Lavery, Richard-Judge, Evanston, Lyman and Mountain View Municipal Courts-Wyo.

Lavery, Robert G.-Judge, Alliance Municipal Court-Ohio

Lavery, William J.-Chief Judge, Connecticut Appellate Court-Conn.

LaVille, Jeanine Nemesi-Judge, Michigan District Court District Sixty-one-Mich.

Lavin, Luis A.-Judge, Superior Court of California County of Los Angeles-Calif.

Lavine, Douglas S.-Judge, Connecticut Superior Court-Conn.

LaViolette, Diana-Judge, Putnam Circuit Court-Ind.

Lavorato, Louis A.-Chief Justice, Iowa Supreme Court-Ia.

LaVoy, Thomas Oliver-Judge, Superior Court of California County of San Diego-Calif.

LaVoy, William F.-Judge, Michigan Circuit Court Thirty-eighth Judicial Circuit-Mich.

Law, W. Kenneth-Chief Justice, Texas Court of Appeals Third District-Tex.

Law, William G., Jr.-Judge, Florida Circuit Court Fifth Judicial Circuit-Fla.

Law, William H.-Judge, San Jacinto County Court-Tex.

Lawler, Daniel J.-Judge, Pennsylvania Court of Common Pleas Seventh Judicial District-Pa.

Lawler, Patrick N.-Associate Judge, Illinois Circuit Court Nineteenth Judicial Circuit-Ill.

Lawless, Janelle A.-Judge, Michigan Circuit Court Thirtieth Judicial Circuit-Mich.

Lawlis, Monte D.-Judge, Texas District Court 1st Judicial District A-Tex.

Lawliss, Timothy J.-Judge, Clinton County Family Court-N.Y.

Lawrence, Jeffrey-Circuit Judge, Illinois Circuit Court of Cook County-Ill.

Lawrence, L. Arthur, Jr.-Senior Judge, Florida District Court of Appeal-Fla.

Lawrence, N. Kent-Judge, State Court of Clarke County-Ga.

Lawrence, Paul G.-Associate Judge, Illinois Circuit Court Eleventh Judicial Circuit-Ill.

Lawrence, Paul H.-Justice, Goffstown District Court-N.H.

Lawrence, Richard S.-Judge, Nassau County Family Court-N.Y.

Lawrence, Rick E.-Judge, Maine District Court-Me.

Lawrence, William T.-Magistrate Judge, United States District Court Southern District of Indiana-Ind.

Laws, Marjorie C.-Circuit Judge, Illinois Circuit Court of Cook County-Ill.

Laws, Victor H., III-Magistrate Judge, United States District Court District of Maryland-Md.

Lawson, C. Alan-Judge, Florida Circuit Court Ninth Judicial Circuit-Fla.

Lawson, David M.-Judge, United States District Court Eastern District of Michigan-Mich.

Lawson, Eugene E.-Judge, Probate Court of Clayton County-Ga.

Lawson, Hugh-Judge, United States District Court Middle District of Georgia-Ga.

Lawson, James-Judge, Kentucky District Court Fortieth Judicial District-Ky.

Lawson, Kindall T.-Judge, Tennessee Circuit Court Third Judicial District-Tenn.

Lawson, Lawrence M.-Assignment Judge, New Jersey Superior Court Vicinage Nine-N.J.

Lawson, Marvin I.-Judge, Darlington County Probate Court-S.C.

Lawton, John F.-Associate Justice, New York Supreme Court Appellate Division Fourth Judicial Department-N.Y.

Lawton, Mark Edward-Associate Justice, Trial Court of Massachusetts Juvenile Court Department Suffolk County Division-Mass.

Lawton, William C.-Judge, North Carolina District Court District 10-N.C.

Lax, Kathleen T.-Judge, United States Bankruptcy Court Central District of California-Calif.

Lay, Donald P.-Senior Judge, United States Court of Appeals Eighth Circuit

Laycock, Claudia-Judge, Utah District Court Fourth Judicial District-Utah

Lazard, Ridgely L.-Judge, Superior Court of California County of Lassen-Calif.

Lazarus, Anne E.-Judge, Pennsylvania Court of Common Pleas First Judicial District-Pa.

Lazarus, Cynthia C.-Judge, Ohio Court of Appeals Tenth District-Ohio

Lazarus, Joel-Judge, Broward County Court-Fla.

Lazzara, Richard A.-Judge, United States District Court Middle District of Florida-Fla.

Leach, Jeryl F.-Judge, Newton Circuit Court-Ind.

Leach, Leslie G.-Judge, The Criminal Court of the City of New York-N.Y.

Leadbetter, Bonnie Brigance-Judge, The Commonwealth Court of Pennsylvania-Pa.

Leafe, Joseph A.-Judge, Virginia Circuit Court Fourth Judicial Circuit-Va.

Leahey, F. Joseph-Judge, Pennsylvania Court of Common Pleas Forty-seventh Judicial District-Pa.

Leak, Barbara A.-Judge, White Plains City Court-N.Y.

Leal, Janet L.-Judge, Cameron County Court at Law No. 1-Tex.

Leal, Manuel D.-Judge, United States Bankruptcy Court Southern District of Texas-Tex.

Leaphart, W. William-Justice, Montana Supreme Court-Mont.

Leary, George F.-Associate Justice, Trial Court of Massachusetts Juvenile Court Department Worcester Division-Mass.

Leary, James H.-Special Justice, Nashua District Court-N.H.

Leary, Paul K.-Justice, Trial Court of Massachusetts District Court Department Norfolk County Brookline Division-Mass.

Leary, William C.-Judge, Windsor Locks District Probate Court-Conn.

Leary, William H.-Judge, Minnesota District Court Second Judicial District-Minn.

Leasure, Diane O.-Circuit Administrative Judge, Circuit Court for Howard County, Fifth Judicial Circuit-Md.

Leasure, Gary George-Associate Judge, Circuit Court for Allegany County, Fourth Judicial Circuit-Md.

Leath, Jack-Judge, Sabine County Court-Tex.

Leavell, William A., III-Judge, North Carolina District Court District 24-N.C.

Leavitt, Cecil R.-Justice of the Peace, Bunkerville Justices' Court-Nev.

Leavitt, Edward J.-Judge, Connecticut Superior Court-Conn.

Leavitt, Lawrence R.-Magistrate Judge, United States District Court District of Nevada-Nev.

Leavitt, M. Hannah-Judge, The Commonwealth Court of Pennsylvania-Pa.

Leavitt, Michael W.-Judge, Washington Superior Court Yakima County-Wash.

Leavitt, Michelle-Judge, Nevada District Court Eighth Judicial District-Nev.

Leavitt, Myron E.-Justice, Nevada Supreme Court-Nev.

Leavy, Edward-Senior Judge, United States Court of Appeals Ninth Circuit

Leban, Mark King-Judge, Dade County Court-Fla.

LeBarron, Deborah A.-Judge, Euclid Municipal Court-Ohio

Lebedeff, Diane Alexis-Judge, The Civil Court of the City of New York-N.Y.

Lebedoff, Jonathan G.-Magistrate Judge, United States District Court District of Minnesota-Minn.

Leben, Steve-Judge, Kansas District Court Tenth Judicial District-Kan.

LeBlanc, John E.-Judge, Louisiana District Court Seventeenth Judicial District-La.

LeBlon, Vincent-Judge, New Jersey Superior Court Vicinage Eight-N.J.

Le Bon, Patricia Richmond-Judge, New Jersey Superior Court Vicinage Three-N.J.

Lebous, Ferris D.-Judge, New York Court of Claims-N.Y.

Lebov, William S.-Judge, Superior Court of California County of Yolo-Calif.

Lebow, Susan L.-Judge, Florida Circuit Court Seventeenth Judicial Circuit-Fla.

Lebowitz, Alan L.-Justice, New York Supreme Court Second Judicial District-N.Y.

Lebowitz, Jeffrey D.-Judge, The Civil Court of the City of New York-N.Y.

LeChien, Robert P.-Circuit Judge, Illinois Circuit Court Twentieth Judicial Circuit-Ill.

Lechwar, Rodney B.-Circuit Judge, Illinois Circuit Court Twelfth Judicial Circuit-Ill.

Leck, Bonnie Sue-Judge, Winkler County Court-Tex.

Leck, Ronald L.-Judge, Lavaca County Court-Tex.

LeClerc, Lawrence A.-Judge, North Dakota District Court East Central Judicial District-N.D.

Ledbetter, William H., Jr.-Judge, Virginia Circuit Court Fifteenth Judicial Circuit-Va.

Leddy, Mary E.-Justice of the Peace, Elko Justices' Court and Judge, Elko Municipal Court-Nev.

Lederman, Cindy S.-Judge, Florida Circuit Court Eleventh Judicial Circuit-Fla.

Ledet, Rosemary-Judge, Louisiana District Court Orleans Parish Civil District-La.

Ledina, Burton-Judge, Sullivan County Court-N.Y.

LeDuc, Charles H., II-Judge, Minnesota District Court Ninth Judicial District-Minn.

LeDuc, Denis R.-Judge, Michigan District Court District Forty-two Division One-Mich.

Lee, Alison Renee-Judge-at-Large, South Carolina Circuit Court-S.C.

Lee, Caryl A.-Judge, Superior Court of California County of Orange-Calif.

Lee, Charles Carter-Judge, Superior Court of California County of Los Angeles-Calif.

Lee, Cynthia Ming-Mei-Judge, Superior Court of California City and County of San Francisco-Calif.

Lee, Donald J.-Senior Judge, United States District Court Western District of Pennsylvania-Pa.

Lee, Edward F.-Judge, Superior Court of California County of Santa Clara-Calif.

Lee, Gerald Bruce-Judge, United States District Court Eastern District of Virginia-Va.

Lee, Gibson W.-Judge, Superior Court of California County of Los Angeles-Calif.

Lee, Helen Shores-Judge, Alabama Circuit Court Tenth Judicial Circuit Birmingham Division-Ala.

Lee, Jacquelyn L.-Judge, North Carolina District Court District 11-N.C.

Lee, Joe-Recalled Judge, United States Bankruptcy Court Eastern District of Kentucky-Ky.

Lee, Jo-Lynne Q.-Judge, Superior Court of California County of Alameda-Calif.

Lee, Katherine-Judge, Glendive City Court-Mont.

Lee, Kenneth-Judge, Superior Court of Arizona Pima County-Ariz.

Lee, Kristi D.-Magistrate Judge, United States District Court Southern District of Alabama-Ala.

ALPHABETICAL NAME INDEX

Lee, L. Joseph-Judge, Court of Appeals of Mississippi-Miss.
Lee, Laurens C.-Chief Magistrate, Magistrate Court of Peach County-Ga.
Lee, Lono J.-Judge, Hawaii District Court First Judicial Circuit-Hi.
Lee, Robert-Justice, Silver Bow County Justice of the Peace Court-Mont.
Lee, Robert E., Jr.-Senior Judge, Florida Circuit Court Seventh Judicial Circuit-Fla.
Lee, Robert W.-Judge, Broward County Court-Fla.
Lee, Roberta K.-Justice of the Peace, Hood River County Justice Court-Ore.
Lee, Tammy D.-Judge, Monroe City Court-La.
Lee, Thomas C.-Judge, Ohio Court of Common Pleas Holmes County-Ohio
Lee, Thomas F.-Judge, Texas District Court 63rd Judicial District-Tex.
Lee, Tom Stewart-Chief Judge, United States District Court Southern District of Mississippi-Miss.
Lee, W. David-Resident Judge, North Carolina Superior Court Sixth Judicial Division District 20B-N.C.
Lee, W. Richard-Judge, United States Bankruptcy Court Eastern District of California-Calif.
Lee, William C.-Senior Judge, United States District Court Northern District of Indiana-Ind.
Lee, William Charles-Judge, Tennessee Circuit Court Seventeenth Judicial District-Tenn.
Lee, William F., Jr.-Chief Judge, Superior Court of Georgia Coweta Judicial Circuit-Ga.
Leech, David A.-Chief Judge, North Carolina District Court District 3A-N.C.
Leehy, B. Scott-Judge, Monroe City Court-La.
Leen, Peggy A.-Magistrate Judge, United States District Court District of Nevada-Nev.
Leesfield, Ellen-Judge, Florida Circuit Court Eleventh Judicial Circuit-Fla.
Leete, John B.-President Judge, Pennsylvania Court of Common Pleas Fifty-fifth Judicial District-Pa.
Lefelt, Steven L.-Judge, New Jersey Superior Court Appellate Division-N.J.
Leffler, B. Bert-Judge, Nebraska County Court Eleventh Judicial District-Neb.
Lefkow, Joan Humphrey-Judge, United States District Court Northern District of Illinois-Ill.
Lefkowitz, Joan B.-Justice, New York Supreme Court Ninth Judicial District-N.Y.
Lefkowitz, Linda K.-Judge, Superior Court of California County of Los Angeles-Calif.
Lefler, Herbert P., III-Judge, Minnesota District Court Fourth Judicial District-Minn.
LeFrancois, David G.-Justice, Auburn District Court-N.H.
Lefstein, Lori R.-Circuit Judge, Illinois Circuit Court Fourteenth Judicial Circuit-Ill.
Legendre, Ronald A.-Judge, Osceola County Court-Fla.
Legg, Benson Everett-Chief Judge, United States District Court District of Maryland-Md.
Leggat, Bonnie-Judge, Texas District Court 71st Judicial District-Tex.
Leggert, Terry Ann-Judge, Oregon Circuit Court Third Judicial District-Ore.
Leh, James R.-Judge, Colorado District Court Thirteenth Judicial District-Colo.
Lehan, Jonathan M.-Judge, Superior Court of California County of Mendocino-Calif.
Leheny, Sandra Vilardi-Judge, Connecticut Superior Court-Conn.
Lehman, Dudley L.-Judge, Suffolk County Family Court-N.Y.
Lehman, Jack-Senior Judge, Nevada District Court-Nev.
Lehman, Larry L.-Justice, Wyoming Supreme Court-Wyo.
Lehmann, Mary Anne-Judge, Binghamton City Court-N.Y.
Lehner, Edward H.-Justice, New York Supreme Court First Judicial District-N.Y.
Lehr, Myriam-Judge, Dade County Court-Fla.
Lehrer, Alexander D.-Judge, New Jersey Superior Court Vicinage Nine-N.J.
Lehrmann, Debra H.-Judge, Texas Family District Court 360th Judicial District-Tex.
Leib, Susan J.-Judge, Mooresville Town Court-Ind.
Leiber, Dennis B.-Judge, Michigan Circuit Court Seventeenth Judicial Circuit-Mich.
Leibovitz, Lynn-Associate Judge, Superior Court of the District of Columbia-D.C.
Leibowitz, Mary Beth-Judge, Tennessee Criminal Court Sixth Judicial District-Tenn.
Leick, Robert K.-Judge, Stevenson Municipal Court-Wash.
Leidig, Bonnie M.-Magistrate Judge, Kansas District Court Seventeenth Judicial District-Kan.
Leifeste, Rae-Judge, Texas District Court 340th Judicial District-Tex.
Leifman, Steven-Judge, Dade County Court-Fla.
Leighton, Ronald B.-Judge, United States District Court Western District of Washington-Wash.
Leinenweber, Harry Daniel-Senior Judge, United States District Court Northern District of Illinois-Ill.
Leineweber, Edward E.-Judge, Wisconsin Circuit Court Richland Circuit-Wis.
Leis, H. Patrick, III-Justice, New York Supreme Court Tenth Judicial District-N.Y.
Leisure, Peter K.-Senior Judge, United States District Court Southern District of New York-N.Y.
Leisy, Raymond E.-Judge, Ohio Court of Common Pleas Wayne County-Ohio
Leitner, John R.-Judge, Minnesota District Court Ninth Judicial District-Minn.
Lemelle, Ivan L. R.-Judge, United States District Court Eastern District of Louisiana-La.
Lemery, Neal C.-Justice of the Peace, Tillamook County Justice Court-Ore.
Lemhouse, Jad-Justice of the Peace, Linn County Justice Court-Ore.
Lemmon, Mary Ann Vial-Judge, United States District Court Eastern District of Louisiana-La.
LeMoine, Frank-Judge, Kaplan City Court-La.
Lemons, Donald W.-Justice, Supreme Court of Virginia-Va.
Lenard, Joan A.-Judge, United States District Court Southern District of Florida-Fla.
Lench, Lisa B.-Judge, Superior Court of California County of Los Angeles-Calif.
Lenderman, John C.-Judge, Florida Circuit Court Sixth Judicial Circuit-Fla.
Lenk, Barbara A.-Associate Justice, Massachusetts Appeals Court-Mass.
Lennington, Wayne J.-Judge, Delaware Circuit Court-Ind.
Lenox, Samuel D., Jr.-Retired Judge, New Jersey Superior Court-N.J.
Lentz, Judith P.-Judge, Killingworth District Probate Court-Conn.
Lenz, Paul J.-Judge, Wisconsin Circuit Court Eau Claire Circuit-Wis.
Leomporra, Tullio Gene-Recalled Magistrate Judge, United States District Court Eastern District of Pennsylvania-Pa.
Leon, Richard J.-Judge, United States District Court District of Columbia-D.C.
Leonard, C. Jerome, Jr.-Emergency Judge, North Carolina District Court-N.C.
Leonard, Edward M., Jr.-Judge, Louisiana District Court Sixteenth Judicial District-La.
Leonard, J. Rich-Chief Judge, United States Bankruptcy Court Eastern District of North Carolina-N.C.
Leonard, Jean Pfeiffer-Judge, Superior Court of California County of Riverside-Calif.
Leonard, Joe M.-Judge, Texas District Court 196th Judicial District-Tex.
Leonard, Kip Wethered-Judge, Oregon Circuit Court Second Judicial District-Ore.
Leonard, Timothy Dwight-Judge, United States District Court Western District of Oklahoma-Okla.
Leonardo, John S.-Presiding Judge, Superior Court of Arizona Pima County-Ariz.
Leopold, John P.-Chief Judge, Colorado District Court Eighteenth Judicial District-Colo.
LePage, John-Associate Circuit Judge, Missouri Circuit Court Fortieth Judicial Circuit-Mo.
Lerner, Alfred D.-Associate Justice, New York Supreme Court Appellate Division First Judicial Department-N.Y.
Lerner, Benjamin-Judge, Pennsylvania Court of Common Pleas First Judicial District-Pa.
Lerner, Louis R.-Judge, Virginia Circuit Court Eighth Judicial Circuit-Va.
Lerner-Wren, Ginger-Judge, Broward County Court-Fla.
Leroy, Jacques C.-Justice, Trial Court of Massachusetts District Court Department Hampden County Springfield Division-Mass.
Leskinen, Steve P.-Judge, Pennsylvania Court of Common Pleas Fourteenth Judicial District-Pa.
Lessen, Larry Lee-Judge, United States Bankruptcy Court Central District of Illinois-Ill.
Lesser, Jack I.-Associate Judge, Maryland District Court District One-Md.
Lessman, Sarah P.-Associate Judge, Illinois Circuit Court Nineteenth Judicial Circuit-Ill.
Lester, Betty Joan-Judge, New Jersey Superior Court Vicinage Five-N.J.
Lester, David A.-District Judge, Iowa District Court Third Judicial District-Ia.
Lester, Kenneth-Judge, Florida Circuit Court Eighteenth Judicial Circuit-Fla.
Leston, Patrick J.-Associate Judge, Illinois Circuit Court Eighteenth Judicial Circuit-Ill.
Letourneau, Donald R.-Judge, Oregon Circuit Court Twentieth Judicial District-Ore.
Lett, Thomas R.-Judge, Tipton Circuit Court-Ind.
Letts, Bradley B.-Judge, North Carolina District Court District 30-N.C.
Letts, J. Spencer-Senior Judge, United States District Court Central District of California-Calif.
Leuba, Robert C.-Judge Referee, Connecticut Superior Court-Conn.
Leuenberger, Jan W.-Judge, Kansas District Court Third Judicial District-Kan.
Leung, Tony N.-Judge, Minnesota District Court Fourth Judicial District-Minn.
Lev, Debra-Judge, Bellingham Municipal Court-Wash.
Leval, Pierre N.-Senior Judge, United States Court of Appeals Second Circuit
Levens, William P.-Judge, Florida Circuit Court Thirteenth Judicial Circuit-Fla.
Levenson, Barbara S.-Judge, Florida Circuit Court Eleventh Judicial Circuit-Fla.
Leventhal, John Michael-Justice, New York Supreme Court Second Judicial District-N.Y.
Leveque, Jerome-Judge, Washington Superior Court Spokane County-Wash.
Levi, David F.-Judge, United States District Court Eastern District of California-Calif.
Levin, Bruce L.-Judge, Connecticut Superior Court-Conn.
Levin, Ian H.-Magistrate Judge, United States District Court Northern District of Illinois-Ill.
Levin, Leonard L.-Recalled Circuit Judge, Illinois Circuit Court of Cook County-Ill.
Levin, Steven-Judge, Florida Circuit Court Nineteenth Judicial Circuit-Fla.
Le Vine, Alan-Justice, New York Supreme Court Eleventh Judicial District-N.Y.
Levine, George-Judge, Connecticut Superior Court-Conn.
Levine, Joseph S.-Justice, New York Supreme Court Second Judicial District-N.Y.
Levine, Paul A.-Judge, Pinellas County Court-Fla.
Levine, Stanley A.-Judge, Allen Superior Court-Ind.
Levinger, Mary Jo-Judge, Superior Court of California County of Santa Clara-Calif.
Levinson, Eric L.-Associate Judge, North Carolina Court of Appeals-N.C.
Levinson, Steven H.-Associate Justice, Hawaii Supreme Court-Hi.
Levis, W. Kent-Judge, Superior Court of California County of Fresno-Calif.
Levitt, Judith Anne-Judge, The Criminal Court of the City of New York-N.Y.
Levitt, Linda-Judge, Vermont Trial Court-Vt.
Levitz, Dana Mark-Associate Judge, Circuit Court for Baltimore County, Third Judicial Circuit-Md.
Levy, D. Bruce-Judge, Florida Circuit Court Eleventh Judicial Circuit-Fla.
Levy, David L.-Judge, Florida District Court of Appeal Third District-Fla.
Levy, Herbert I.-Associate Justice, California Court of Appeal Fifth Appellate District-Calif.
Levy, Jon D.-Associate Justice, Maine Supreme Judicial Court-Me.
Levy, Kenneth S.-Judge, New Jersey Superior Court Vicinage Five-N.J.

ALPHABETICAL NAME INDEX

Levy, Paul Gans-Retired Judge, New Jersey Superior Court Appellate Division-N.J.

Levy, Robert M.-Magistrate Judge, United States District Court Eastern District of New York-N.Y.

Levy-Siwak, Ellen-Associate Circuit Judge, Missouri Circuit Court Twenty-first Judicial Circuit-Mo.

Lew, Arthur M.-Judge, Superior Court of California County of Los Angeles-Calif.

Lew, Ronald S. W.-Judge, United States District Court Central District of California-Calif.

Lewandowski, David-Judge, Ohio Court of Common Pleas Lucas County-Ohio

Lewinn, Laura-Judge, New Jersey Superior Court Vicinage Seven-N.J.

Lewis, Alvin N.-Chief Magistrate, Magistrate Court of Evans County-Ga.

Lewis, Bernard M.-Judge, Orange District Probate Court-Vt.

Lewis, Carl E.-Judge, Nueces County Court at Law No. 5-Tex.

Lewis, Casandra-Circuit Judge, Illinois Circuit Court of Cook County-Ill.

Lewis, Daniel-Justice, New York Supreme Court Eleventh Judicial District-N.Y.

Lewis, David B.-District Judge, Oklahoma District Court Fifth Judicial District-Okla.

Lewis, David W.-Associate Judge, Illinois Circuit Court Fifth Judicial Circuit-Ill.

Lewis, Diana-Judge, Florida Circuit Court Fifteenth Judicial Circuit-Fla.

Lewis, Garry D.-Associate Circuit Judge, Missouri Circuit Court Second Judicial Circuit-Mo.

Lewis, Gregory H.-Judge, Superior Court of California County of Orange-Calif.

Lewis, Harris-Judge, Probate Court of Chatham County-Ga.

Lewis, Hugh B.-Judge, North Carolina District Court District 26-N.C.

Lewis, J. Dean-Judge, Virginia Juvenile and Domestic Relations District Court Fifteenth Judicial District-Va.

Lewis, Jannie M.-Judge, Mississippi Circuit Court Twenty-first Judicial District-Miss.

Lewis, Jerry-Judge, Collin County Court at Law No. 2-Tex.

Lewis, Jim-Judge, McLennan County Court-Tex.

Lewis, Joan Marie-Judge, Superior Court of California County of San Diego-Calif.

Lewis, John B.-Judge, Oregon Circuit Court Twentieth Judicial District-Ore.

Lewis, John B., Jr.-Retired Judge, North Carolina Court of Appeals-N.C.

Lewis, John M.-Associate Justice, New Hampshire Superior Court-N.H.

Lewis, Jordan D.-Magistrate Judge, United States District Court Southern District of Indiana-Ind.

Lewis, Joseph, Jr.-Judge, Florida District Court of Appeal First District-Fla.

Lewis, Kathryn Streeter-Judge, Pennsylvania Court of Common Pleas First Judicial District-Pa.

Lewis, Lantz-Judge, Superior Court of California County of San Diego-Calif.

Lewis, Larry-Judge, Mississippi Circuit Court Eleventh Judicial District-Miss.

Lewis, Leslie A.-Judge, Utah District Court Third Judicial District-Utah

Lewis, Linton D., Jr.-Judge, Ohio Court of Common Pleas Perry County-Ohio

Lewis, Loren "Larry" P.-Circuit Judge, Illinois Circuit Court Second Judicial Circuit-Ill.

Lewis, Marilea Whatley-Judge, Texas Family District Court 330th Judicial District-Tex.

Lewis, Michael B.-Judge, Superior Court of California County of Kern-Calif.

Lewis, Michael J.-Judge, Terre Haute City Court-Ind.

Lewis, Ola M.-Resident Judge, North Carolina Superior Court Fourth Judicial Division District 13-N.C.

Lewis, Patrice E.-Associate Judge, Maryland District Court District Five-Md.

Lewis, Paul D.-First Justice, Trial Court of Massachusetts Juvenile Court Department Suffolk County Division-Mass.

Lewis, Preston B., Jr.-Judge, Juvenile Court of Georgia Augusta Judicial Circuit-Ga.

Lewis, Preston B., III-Judge, Probate Court of Burke County-Ga.

Lewis, R. Fred-Justice, Florida Supreme Court-Fla.

Lewis, R. Larry-Judge, Virginia General District Court Thirtieth Judicial District-Va.

Lewis, Richard A.-Judge, Pennsylvania Court of Common Pleas Twelfth Judicial District-Pa.

Lewis, Robert Dobbins-Retired-Recalled Judge, North Carolina Superior Court-N.C.

Lewis, Robert J., Jr.-Judge, Kansas Court of Appeals-Kan.

Lewis, Robert W.-Associate Judge, Illinois Circuit Court Second Judicial Circuit-Ill.

Lewis, Stephen-Judge, West Virginia Family Court Circuit Seven-W.Va.

Lewis, Sylvia A.-District Associate Judge, Iowa District Court Sixth Judicial District-Ia.

Lewis, Terrance G.-Judge, Ferndale and Lynden Municipal Courts-Wash.

Lewis, Terry P.-Judge, Florida Circuit Court Second Judicial Circuit-Fla.

Lewis, Theodis P.-Associate Judge, Illinois Circuit Court Seventh Judicial Circuit-Ill.

Lewis, Thomas Richards-Judge, Kentucky Circuit Court Eighth Judicial Circuit-Ky.

Lewis, Tryon D.-Judge, Texas District Court 161st Judicial District-Tex.

Lewis, W. Rob, II-Judge, North Carolina District Court District 6B-N.C.

Lewis, William B.-Judge Referee, Connecticut Superior Court-Conn.

Lewis, William R.-Judge, North Tonawanda City Court-N.Y.

Lewis, Woodrow, Jr.-Judge, Virginia Juvenile and Domestic Relations District Court Second Judicial District-Va.

Lewis, Yvonne-Justice, New York Supreme Court Second Judicial District-N.Y.

Ley, Nancy Moate-Judge, Florida Circuit Court Sixth Judicial Circuit-Fla.

Leyte-Vidal, Henry-Judge, Florida Circuit Court Eleventh Judicial Circuit-Fla.

Lian, Joseph, Jr.-First Justice, Trial Court of Massachusetts Probate and Family Court Department Worcester County Division-Mass.

Lias, Katherine S.-Judge, Ohio Court of Common Pleas Franklin County-Ohio

Libutti, Michael R.-Judge, Superior Court of California County of San Bernardino-Calif.

Licari, Joseph A., Jr.-Judge, Connecticut Superior Court-Conn.

Lichtenstein, David G.-Circuit Judge, Illinois Circuit Court of Cook County-Ill.

Lichtenstein, David N.-Judge, Jefferson County District Court Birmingham Division-Ala.

Lichtman, Peter D.-Judge, Superior Court of California County of Los Angeles-Calif.

Lidums, O. Robert-Associate Judge, Circuit Court for Cecil County, Second Judicial Circuit-Md.

Lieb, Judith S.-Judge, The Civil Court of the City of New York-N.Y.

Lieberman, Peter-Judge, South Dakota Circuit Court Second Judicial Circuit-S.D.

Lieberman, Stephen B.-Judge, Pennsylvania Court of Common Pleas Twenty-third Judicial District-Pa.

Liebowitz, Richard B.-Judge, Yonkers City Court-N.Y.

Lifland, Burton R.-Recalled Judge, United States Bankruptcy Court Southern District of New York-N.Y.

Lifland, John C.-Senior Judge, United States District Court District of New Jersey-N.J.

Lifson, Robert A.-Justice, New York Supreme Court Tenth Judicial District-N.Y.

Liggett, Kenneth E.-Judge, Clay County Court-Tex.

Light, William R.-Judge, Virginia Juvenile and Domestic Relations District Court Twenty-fourth Judicial District-Va.

Lightfoot, Richard-Judge, Lyme District Probate Court-Conn.

Lihotz, Marie E.-Judge, New Jersey Tax Court-N.J.

Lile, Stephen E.-Vice Presiding Judge, Oklahoma Court of Criminal Appeals-Okla.

Liljeberg, Hans J.-Judge, Louisiana District Court Twenty-fourth Judicial District-La.

Lillard, Holly Kirby-Judge, Tennessee Court of Appeals Western Division-Tenn.

Lilley, Vincent Austin-Judge, Virginia General District Court Twenty-third Judicial District-Va.

Lilley, Virgil Edgar-Judge, Lampasas County Court-Tex.

Lilly, Paulette J.-Judge, Ohio Court of Common Pleas Lorain County-Ohio

Lilly, Roy M.-Senior Judge, Superior Court of Georgia-Ga.

Lim, Arnold-Judge, New York City Family Court-N.Y.

Lim, John-Associate Judge, Hawaii Intermediate Court of Appeals-Hi.

Lim, Lillian Y.-Judge, Superior Court of California County of San Diego-Calif.

Limas, Abel C.-Judge, Texas District Court 404th Judicial District-Tex.

Limbaugh, Stephen N.-Senior Judge, United States District Court Eastern District of Missouri-Mo.

Limbaugh, Stephen N., Jr.-Chief Justice, Supreme Court of Missouri-Mo.

Limbert, George J.-Magistrate Judge, United States District Court Northern District of Ohio-Ohio

Limon, Stephen M.-Associate Justice, Trial Court of Massachusetts Juvenile Court Department Suffolk County Division-Mass.

Linares, Jose L.-Judge, United States District Court District of New Jersey-N.J.

Lincoln, Charles F.-Judge, Virginia Juvenile and Domestic Relations District Court Twenty-eighth Judicial District-Va.

Lincoln, Frank W.-Circuit Judge, Illinois Circuit Court Sixth Judicial Circuit-Ill.

Lindamood, Rebecca-Magistrate Judge, Kansas District Court Thirteenth Judicial District-Kan.

Lindberg, Denise Posse-Blanco-Judge, Utah District Court Third Judicial District-Utah

Lindberg, George W.-Senior Judge, United States District Court Northern District of Illinois-Ill.

Lindberg, Thomas-Judge, Superior Court of Arizona Yavapai County-Ariz.

Linde, Barbara-Judge, King District Court West Division King County-Wash.

Lindeman, Robert J.-Judge, Ohio Court of Common Pleas Miami County-Ohio

Linder, Ray Dean-District Judge, Oklahoma District Court Fourth Judicial District-Okla.

Linder, Virginia L.-Judge, Oregon Court of Appeals-Ore.

Lindley, George Womack-District Judge, Oklahoma District Court Fifth Judicial District-Okla.

Lindley, Stephen K.-Judge, Rochester City Court-N.Y.

Lindley, Wendy-Judge, Superior Court of California County of Orange-Calif.

Lindman, Dale B.-Judge, Minnesota District Court Second Judicial District-Minn.

Lindner, Jack Burton-Judge, Nebraska County Court Third Judicial District-Neb.

Lindquist, Kent-Recalled Judge, United States Bankruptcy Court Northern District of Indiana-Ind.

Lindsay, Arlene Rosario-Magistrate Judge, United States District Court Eastern District of New York-N.Y.

Lindsay, Kay A.-Presiding Judge, Utah Juvenile Court Fourth Judicial District-Utah

Lindsay, Mark-Judge, Arkansas Circuit Court Fourth Judicial Circuit-Ark.

Lindsay, Reginald C.-Judge, United States District Court District of Massachusetts-Mass.

Lindsay, Sam A.-Judge, United States District Court Northern District of Texas-Tex.

Lindsay, Tony-Judge, Texas District Court 280th Judicial District-Tex.

Lindsey, Hubert R.-Judge, Florida Circuit Court Fifteenth Judicial Circuit-Fla.

Lindsey, Lewis R. "Bob"-Judge, Florida Circuit Court First Judicial Circuit-Fla.

Lindsey, Robert E., III-Judge, Mills County Court-Tex.

Lindsley, Elizabeth-Judge, Utah Juvenile Court Third Judicial District-Utah

Lindstrom, John C.-Judge, Minnesota District Court Eighth Judicial District-Minn.

ALPHABETICAL NAME INDEX

Line, Franklin K., Jr.-Judge, Michigan District Court District Ten-Mich.

Linebaugh, Stephen P.-Judge, Pennsylvania Court of Common Pleas Nineteenth Judicial District-Pa.

Linehan, Neil J.-Associate Judge, Illinois Circuit Court of Cook County-Ill.

Ling, Thomas S.-Judge, Pennsylvania Court of Common Pleas Fifty-seventh Judicial District-Pa.

Ling-Cohan, Doris-Justice, New York Supreme Court First Judicial District-N.Y.

Lingreen, Margaret L.-District Judge, Iowa District Court First Judicial District-Ia.

Link, Frederic L.-Judge, Superior Court of California County of San Diego-Calif.

Link, Jonathan H.-Judge, Alaska Superior Court Third Judicial District-Alas.

Link, Scott-Judge, Texas District Court 80th Judicial District-Tex.

Linn, James B.-Associate Judge, Illinois Circuit Court of Cook County-Ill.

Linn, John G.-District Judge, Iowa District Court Eighth Judicial District-Ia.

Linn, Richard-Judge, United States Court of Appeals Federal Circuit

Lintner, Jack L.-Judge, New Jersey Superior Court Appellate Division-N.J.

Lioi, Sara E.-Judge, Ohio Court of Common Pleas Stark County-Ohio

Lipez, Kermit V.-Judge, United States Court of Appeals First Circuit

Lipinski, Marcella Carmen-Circuit Judge, Illinois Circuit Court of Cook County-Ill.

Lipman, George-Associate Judge, Maryland District Court District One-Md.

Lippis, Deborah J.-Justice of the Peace, Las Vegas Justices' Court-Nev.

Lippitt, Elizabeth A.-Judge, Superior Court of California County of Los Angeles-Calif.

Lippman, Jonathan-Judge, New York Court of Claims-N.Y.

Lippmann, Robert D.-Judge, The Civil Court of the City of New York-N.Y.

Lipps, Thomas R.-Judge, Ohio Court of Common Pleas Hamilton County-Ohio

Lippstreu, Randall L.-Judge, Nebraska District Court Twelfth Judicial District-Neb.

Lipscomb, Paul J.-Presiding Judge, Oregon Circuit Court Third Judicial District-Ore.

Lipscomb, Thomas J.-Circuit Judge, Illinois Circuit Court of Cook County-Ill.

Lipscomb, Willie G., Jr.-Judge, Michigan District Court District Thirty-six-Mich.

Lipsey, Howard I.-Associate Justice, Rhode Island Family Court-R.I.

Lipton, Lois-Judge, New Jersey Superior Court Vicinage Two-N.J.

Lisa, Joseph F.-Judge, New Jersey Superior Court Appellate Division-N.J.

Lisboa, Severiano, III-Judge, New Jersey Superior Court Vicinage Six-N.J.

Lisenby, Philip N.-Judge, Alabama Circuit Court Sixth Judicial Circuit-Ala.

Lisi, Mary M.-Judge, United Stated District Court District of Rhode Island-R.I.

Lisk, Ronald T.-Judge, Superior Court of California County of Santa Clara-Calif.

Lisotto, Robert G.-Judge, Ohio Court of Common Pleas Mahoning County-Ohio

Liston, Robert-Associate Circuit Judge, Missouri Circuit Court Eighteenth Judicial Circuit-Mo.

Liston, Teresa L.-Judge, Franklin County Municipal Court-Ohio

Little, C. Lawson-Judge, Alabama Circuit Court Twentieth Judicial Circuit-Ala.

Little, Charles A.-Judge, New Jersey Superior Court Vicinage Four-N.J.

Little, Donna Alyson-Judge, Superior Court of California City and County of San Francisco-Calif.

Little, F. A., Jr.-Senior Judge, United States District Court Western District of Louisiana-La.

Little, Jeannette L.-Judge, State Court of Troup County-Ga.

Little, Loyd H., Jr.-Presiding Judge, Alabama Circuit Court Twenty-third Judicial Circuit-Ala.

Little, Perry A.-Judge, Florida Circuit Court Thirteenth Judicial Circuit-Fla.

Little, Thomas E.-Associate Judge, Illinois Circuit Court Sixth Judicial Circuit-Ill.

Little, Walter R.-Judge, Pennsylvania Court of Common Pleas Fifth Judicial District-Pa.

Littlefield, Alicia-Special Judge, Oklahoma District Court Thirteenth Judicial District-Okla.

Littlefield, Robert E., Jr.-Judge, United States Bankruptcy Court Northern District of New York-N.Y.

Littlehales, Charles P.-Judge, Oregon Circuit Court Seventeenth Judicial District-Ore.

Littlejohn, Bill C.-Judge, Dayton Municipal Court-Ohio

Littlejohn, Janet P.-Judge, Texas District Court 150th Judicial District-Tex.

Littlejohn, Joe O.-Judge, Superior Court of California County of San Diego-Calif.

Littlejohn, Talmadge D., Jr.-Judge, Mississippi Chancery Court First Judicial District-Miss.

Litynski, Warren E.-Judge, Minnesota District Court Fifth Judicial District-Minn.

Litzenberger, Marilyn-Judge, Oregon Circuit Court Fourth Judicial District-Ore.

Livaudais, Marcel, Jr.-Senior Judge, United States District Court Eastern District of Louisiana-La.

Lively, Tom-Judge, Kentucky District Court Forty-sixth Judicial District-Ky.

Livermore, Richard Clifton-Judge, Superior Court of California County of San Mateo-Calif.

Livingston, D. Matt-Judge, Henderson County Court at Law-Tex.

Livingston, James D.-Judge, Nebraska District Court Ninth Judicial District-Neb.

Livingston, Lora J.-Judge, Texas District Court 261st Judicial District-Tex.

Livingston, Terrie-Justice, Texas Court of Appeals Second District-Tex.

Livingstone, Michael J.-Associate Justice, Trial Court of Massachusetts Probate and Family Court Department Plymouth County Division-Mass.

Lloyd, H. Weldon, Jr.-Judge, North Carolina District Court District 9-N.C.

Lloyd, Howard R.-Magistrate Judge, United States District Court Northern District of California-Calif.

Lloyd, John D.-District Judge, Iowa District Court Fifth Judicial District-Ia.

Lloyd, Leonia J.-Judge, Michigan District Court District Thirty-six-Mich.

Lloyd, Mary Margaret-Judge, Vanderburgh Superior Court-Ind.

Lloyd, Reginald I.-Judge-at-Large, South Carolina Circuit Court-S.C.

Lo, David-Judge, Hawaii District Court First Judicial Circuit-Hi.

Lobaugh, Oliver J.-Judge, Pennsylvania Court of Common Pleas Twenty-eighth Judicial District-Pa.

Lober, Jere E.-Senior Judge, Florida Circuit Court Eighteenth Judicial Circuit-Fla.

Loberg, Harry J.-Judge, Superior Court of California County of Santa Barbara-Calif.

Lobis, Joan B.-Justice, New York Supreme Court First Judicial District-N.Y.

Loble, C. Bruce-Chief Judge, Montana Water Court-Mont.

Locallo, Daniel M.-Circuit Judge, Illinois Circuit Court of Cook County-Ill.

Locascio, Louis F.-Judge, New Jersey Superior Court Vicinage Nine-N.J.

Locke, David B.-Justice, Trial Court of Massachusetts District Court Department Worcester County Gardner Division-Mass.

Locke, Jeffrey A.-Associate Justice, Trial Court of Massachusetts Superior Court Department-Mass.

Locke, Jim-Judge, Brazos County Court at Law No. 2-Tex.

Locke, Judith A.-Circuit Justice, Trial Court of Massachusetts Juvenile Court Department-Mass.

Lockemy, James E.-Judge-at-Large, South Carolina Circuit Court-S.C.

Lockett, John R.-Judge, Alabama Circuit Court Thirteenth Judicial Circuit-Ala.

Lockette, Willie E.-Judge, Superior Court of Georgia Dougherty Judicial Circuit-Ga.

Lockhart, Ben Allen-Judge, Howard County Court-Tex.

Locklear, Gary Lynn-Resident Judge, North Carolina Superior Court Fourth Judicial Division District 16B-N.C.

Lockwood, Brocton D.-Associate Judge, Illinois Circuit Court First Judicial Circuit-Ill.

LoConto, Paul F.-First Justice, Trial Court of Massachusetts District Court Department Worcester County Fitchburg Division and Justice, East Brookfield Division-Mass.

Lodge, Edward J.-Judge, United States District Court District of Idaho-Ida.

Lodge, Joseph-Judge, Superior Court of California County of Santa Barbara-Calif.

Loeb, Alan-Judge, Colorado Court of Appeals-Colo.

Loehrer, Sally L.-Judge, Nevada District Court Eighth Judicial District-Nev.

Loftin, Brenda Stith-Associate Circuit Judge, Missouri Circuit Court Twenty-first Judicial Circuit-Mo.

Loftus, Richard J., Jr.-Judge, Superior Court of California County of Santa Clara-Calif.

LoGalbo, Emanuel-Judge, Sarasota County Court-Fla.

Logan, Andrew D.-Judge, Ohio Court of Common Pleas Trumbull County-Ohio

Logan, Ben H., II-Judge, Michigan District Court District Sixty-one-Mich.

Logan, Paul E.-Judge, Florida Circuit Court Twelfth Judicial Circuit-Fla.

Logan, Roger V., Jr.-Judge, Arkansas Circuit Court Fourteenth Judicial Circuit-Ark.

Logan, Walter D.-Judge, Florida Circuit Court Sixth Judicial Circuit-Fla.

Logan, William H., Jr.-Judge, Virginia Juvenile and Domestic Relations District Court Twenty-sixth Judicial District-Va.

Logering, Nancy-Judge, Minnesota District Court Tenth Judicial District-Minn.

Loggins, Joseph E.-Senior Judge, Superior Court of Georgia-Ga.

Logue, Jean Chenault-Judge, Kentucky Circuit Court Twenty-fifth Judicial Circuit-Ky.

Lohff, John R.-Judge, Alaska District Court Third Judicial District-Alas.

Lohman, Eugene E.-Chief Judge, Virginia Juvenile and Domestic Relations District Court Twenty-eighth Judicial District-Va.

Lohn, John Joseph-Judge, Ohio Court of Common Pleas Medina County-Ohio

Lohorn, Peggy Quint-Judge, Montgomery County Court-Ind.

Loiselle, Alva P.-Judge Referee, Connecticut Superior Court-Conn.

Loken, James B.-Chief Judge, United States Court of Appeals Eighth Circuit

Lokuta, Ann H.-Judge, Pennsylvania Court of Common Pleas Eleventh Judicial District-Pa.

Lolley, John Larry-Judge, Louisiana District Court Fourth Judicial District-La.

Lombard, Arthur J.-Judge, Michigan Circuit Court Third Judicial Circuit-Mich.

Lombard, Edwin A.-Judge, Louisiana Court of Appeal Fourth Circuit-La.

Lombardi, James J.-Associate Judge, Circuit Court for Prince George's County, Seventh Judicial Circuit-Md.

Lombardi, Leon J.-Justice, Trial Court of Massachusetts Land Court Department-Mass.

Lombardi, Sebastian P.-Judge, New Jersey Superior Court Vicinage Five-N.J.

Lombardi, Suzanne-Judge, Alaska District Court Third Judicial District-Alas.

Lomeli, George R. G.-Judge, Superior Court of California County of Los Angeles-Calif.

London, Brett-Judge, Superior Court of California County of Orange-Calif.

Loney, Michael E.-Associate Judge, Circuit Court for Anne Arundel County, Fifth Judicial Circuit-Md.

Long, Cheryl M.-Associate Judge, Superior Court of the District of Columbia-D.C.

Long, Daniel M.-Circuit Administrative Judge, Circuit Court for Somerset County, First Judicial Circuit-Md.

ALPHABETICAL NAME INDEX

ALPHABETICAL NAME INDEX

Ludgate, Linda K. Mowson-Judge, Pennsylvania Court of Common Pleas Twenty-third Judicial District-Pa.

Ludington, Spencer J.-Judge, Fulton City Court-N.Y.

Ludington, Thomas L.-Chief Judge, Michigan Circuit Court Forty-second Judicial Circuit-Mich.

Ludlum, Alia Moses-Judge, United States District Court Western District of Texas-Tex.

Ludvigsen, Cynthia Ann-Judge, Superior Court of California County of San Bernardino-Calif.

Ludwig, Edmund V.-Senior Judge, United States District Court Eastern District of Pennsylvania-Pa.

Ludwig, Stanley W.-Judge, Springdale District Court-Ark.

Ludwig, Victor V.-Judge, Virginia Juvenile and Domestic Relations District Court Twenty-fifth Judicial District-Va.

Luebke, Dennis C.-Judge, Wisconsin Circuit Court Outagamie Circuit-Wis.

Luebs, Roger A.-Judge, Superior Court of California County of Riverside-Calif.

Lueck, Robert W.-Judge, Nevada District Court Eighth Judicial District-Nev.

Luitjen, Mark R.-Judge, Texas District Court 144th Judicial District-Tex.

Luke, Colin W.-Judge, Idaho District Court Seventh Judicial District Magistrate Division-Ida.

Luke, Linda K.C.-Family Court Judge, Hawaii District Court First Judicial Circuit-Hi.

Lukemire, Edward D.-Judge, Superior Court of Georgia Houston Judicial Circuit-Ga.

Lukens, Terence-Judge, Washington Superior Court King County-Wash.

Lum, Dean S.-Judge, Washington Superior Court King County-Wash.

Lum, Jennifer T.-Magistrate Judge, United States District Court Central District of California-Calif.

Lumpkin, Gary L.-Judge, Oklahoma Court of Criminal Appeals-Okla.

Lumpkin, Julia W.-Judge, Probate Court of Muscogee County-Ga.

Luna, Ana Maria-Judge, Superior Court of California County of Los Angeles-Calif.

Luna, Joe-Judge, Zavala County Court-Tex.

Lund, Donna M.-Justice, Petroleum County Justice of the Peace Court and Judge, Winnett City Court-Mont.

Lund, Kevin-Judge, Minnesota District Court Third Judicial District-Minn.

Lundell, Eric J.-Judge, Wisconsin Circuit Court St. Croix Circuit-Wis.

Lundin, Keith M.-Judge, Bankruptcy Appellate Panel Sixth Circuit and Judge, United States Bankruptcy Court Middle District of Tennessee-Tenn.

Lundsten, Paul G.-Judge, Wisconsin Court of Appeals District Four-Wis.

Lundy, Jack E.-Judge, Glades County Court-Fla.

Lundy, Mitchell M., Jr.-Judge, Mississippi Chancery Court Third Judicial District-Miss.

Lungstrum, John W.-Chief Judge, United States District Court District of Kansas-Kan.

Lunn, Robert J.-Justice, New York Supreme Court Seventh Judicial District-N.Y.

Luoma, Mark E.-Chief Judge, Michigan District Court District Ninety-three-Mich.

Lupo, Mary Elisabeth-Judge, Florida Circuit Court Fifteenth Judicial Circuit-Fla.

Luros, Michael S.-Judge, Superior Court of California County of Los Angeles-Calif.

Luse, Jennifer-Judge, East Baton Rouge Parish Family Court-La.

Lussow, John H.-Judge, Wisconsin Circuit Court Rock Circuit-Wis.

Lust, C. James-Judge, Washington Superior Court Yakima County-Wash.

Luster, John Patrick-Judge, Idaho District Court First Judicial District-Ida.

Lustfeldt, Gordon Lee-Circuit Judge, Illinois Circuit Court Twenty-first Judicial Circuit-Ill.

Lustig, Patrick F.-Associate Judge, Illinois Circuit Court of Cook County-Ill.

Lutes, Ray D.-Judge, Asotin District Court Asotin County-Wash.

Luth, Nancy-Judge, Great Falls Municipal Court-Mont.

Luther, Teresa K.-Judge, Nebraska District Court Ninth Judicial District-Neb.

Luttig, J. Michael-Judge, United States Court of Appeals Fourth Circuit

Lutty, Paul F., Jr.-Judge, Pennsylvania Court of Common Pleas Fifth Judicial District-Pa.

Lutz, Robert-Judge, Marion County Small Claims Court Wayne Township Division-Ind.

Lutz, William J.-Judge, Mississippi Chancery Court Eleventh Judicial District-Miss.

Luukinen, Charles-Presiding Judge, Oregon Circuit Court Twelfth Judicial District-Ore.

Lux, Paul G.-Judge, Erie County Court-Ohio

Luzzo, John T.-Judge, Florida Circuit Court Seventeenth Judicial Circuit-Fla.

Lydon, Thomas J.-Senior Judge, United States Court of Federal Claims

Lyerla, Bill W.-Magistrate Judge, Kansas District Court Eleventh Judicial District-Kan.

Lyerly, Alexander-Chief Judge, North Carolina District Court District 24-N.C.

Lyle, Ellen Hobbs-Chancellor, Tennessee Chancery Court Twentieth Judicial District-Tenn.

Lyman, Gregory G.-Chief Judge, Colorado District Court Sixth Judicial District and Judge, Colorado Water Court Division Seven-Colo.

Lyman, John V.-Judge, Tenino and Tumwater Municipal Courts-Wash.

Lyman, Paul D.-Presiding Judge, Utah Juvenile Court Sixth Judicial District-Utah

Lyman, Richard W., Jr.-Judge, Superior Court of California County of Los Angeles-Calif.

Lympus, Ted O.-Judge, Montana District Court Eleventh Judicial District-Mont.

Lynaugh, Barbara-Judge, Suffolk County Family Court-N.Y.

Lynch, Arnold-Judge, Kentucky District Court Third Judicial District-Ky.

Lynch, Daniel J.-Circuit Judge, Illinois Circuit Court of Cook County-Ill.

Lynch, Daniel Joseph-Circuit Judge, Illinois Circuit Court of Cook County-Ill.

Lynch, Edward I.-Judge, Minnesota District Court First Judicial District-Minn.

Lynch, Frank J., Jr.-Magistrate Judge, United States District Court Southern District of Florida-Fla.

Lynch, Gary-Associate Circuit Judge, Missouri Circuit Court Thirtieth Judicial Circuit-Mo.

Lynch, Gerard E.-Judge, United States District Court Southern District of New York-N.Y.

Lynch, Harold J.-Judge, New York City Family Court-N.Y.

Lynch, Joan E.-Justice, Trial Court of Massachusetts District Court Department Barnstable County Barnstable Division-Mass.

Lynch, Mike F.-Judge, Texas District Court 167th Judicial District-Tex.

Lynch, Sandra L.-Judge, United States Court of Appeals First Circuit

Lynch, Thomas M., IV-Judge, Florida Circuit Court Seventeenth Judicial Circuit-Fla.

Lynch, William P.-Judge, New Mexico District Court Fifth Judicial District-N.Mex.

Lynchard, Percy L.-Judge, Mississippi Chancery Court Third Judicial District-Miss.

Lynn, Barbara M. G.-Judge, United States District Court Northern District of Texas-Tex.

Lynn, Dennis Michael-Judge, United States Bankruptcy Court Northern District of Texas-Tex.

Lynn, James Murray-Judge, Pennsylvania Court of Common Pleas First Judicial District-Pa.

Lynn, Robert H.-Judge, Minnesota District Court Fourth Judicial District-Minn.

Lynn, Robert J.-Associate Justice, New Hampshire Superior Court-N.H.

Lyon, Michael D.-Judge, Utah District Court Second Judicial District-Utah

Lyon, Patricia-Judge, Snohomish District Court Evergreen Division Snohomish County-Wash.

Lyons, Champ, Jr.-Associate Justice, Alabama Supreme Court-Ala.

Lyons, Marie E.-Associate Justice, Trial Court of Massachusetts Probate and Family Court Department Hampden County Division-Mass.

Lyons, Raymond T.-Judge, United States Bankruptcy Court District of New Jersey-N.J.

Lyons, Robert Hagen-Judge, Butler County Court-Ohio

Lyons, Thomas N.-Judge, New Jersey Superior Court Vicinage Twelve-N.J.

Lyons, William H.-Justice, Manchester District Court-N.H.

Lytton, Howard B., Jr.-Judge, Dubois Superior Court-Ind.

Lytton, Tom M.-Judge, Illinois Appellate Court Third Judicial District-Ill.

Maag, Gordon E.-Judge, Illinois Appellate Court Fifth Judicial District-Ill.

Maas, Ellen L.-Judge, Minnesota District Court Tenth Judicial District-Minn.

Maas, Frank-Magistrate Judge, United States District Court Southern District of New York-N.Y.

Maass, Elizabeth T.-Judge, Florida Circuit Court Fifteenth Judicial Circuit-Fla.

Mabley, Daniel H.-Judge, Minnesota District Court Fourth Judicial District-Minn.

Mabrey, Paula Adele-Judge, Superior Court of California County of Los Angeles-Calif.

Macaron, Mark A.-Judge, New Mexico District Court Second Judicial District-N.Mex.

Macaulay, Alexander S.-Judge, South Carolina Circuit Court Tenth Judicial Circuit-S.C.

Macaulay, Robert E.-Judge, Minnesota District Court Sixth Judicial District-Minn.

MacDonald, Diane R.-Judge, Boulder County Court-Colo.

MacDonald, Donald, IV-Chief Judge, United States Bankruptcy Court District of Alaska-Alas.

MacDonald, John E.-Chief Judge, Michigan District Court District Thirty-five-Mich.

Macdonald, Kathleen I.-Judge, Michigan Circuit Court Third Judicial Circuit-Mich.

MacDonald, Michael W.-Chief Judge, Michigan District Court District Ninety-one-Mich.

MacDonnell, Mark A.-Judge, Bent County Court-Colo.

MacEachen, Kellie-Judge, Superior Court of California County of Orange-Calif.

Macek, Julie-Judge, Montana District Court Eighth Judicial District-Mont.

Macellaio, Joseph M.-Associate Judge, Illinois Circuit Court of Cook County-Ill.

MacElree, James Paul, II-Judge, Pennsylvania Court of Common Pleas Fifteenth Judicial District-Pa.

Maceroni, Michael S.-Judge, Michigan District Court District Forty-one A-Mich.

Maceroni, Peter J.-Chief Judge, Michigan Circuit Court Sixteenth Judicial Circuit-Mich.

Machen, Donald E.-Judge, Pennsylvania Court of Common Pleas Fifth Judicial District-Pa.

Machida, Kenji-Judge, Superior Court of California County of Los Angeles-Calif.

Machnik, Thaddeus S.-Associate Judge, Illinois Circuit Court of Cook County-Ill.

Macias, Patricia A.-Judge, Texas District Court 388th Judicial District-Tex.

Maciel, Ronald-Judge, Superior Court of California County of Kings-Calif.

MacInnes, Nicole-Judge, Washington Superior Court King County-Wash.

Mack, Michael A.-Judge, Connecticut Superior Court-Conn.

Mack, Milton L., Jr.-Chief Judge, Wayne County Probate Court-Mich.

Mack, Peter, Jr.-Judge, North Carolina District Court District 3B-N.C.

MacKay, Kathleen H.-Judge, Virginia Circuit Court Nineteenth Judicial Circuit-Va.

Mackay, William J.-Judge, Oregon Circuit Court Fourteenth Judicial District-Ore.

Macken, James L.-Judge, Nebraska County Court Twelfth Judicial District-Neb.

MacKenzie, Brian W.-Judge, Michigan District Court District Fifty-two Division One-Mich.

MacKenzie, Carol-Judge, Suffolk County District Court-N.Y.

MacKenzie, Kenneth C.-Judge, New Jersey Superior Court Vicinage Ten-N.J.

MacKenzie, Lyle Michael-Judge, Superior Court of California County of Los Angeles-Calif.

Mackey, Alfred W.-Judge, Ohio Court of Common Pleas Ashtabula County-Ohio

ALPHABETICAL NAME INDEX

Mackey, David-Judge, Superior Court of Arizona Yavapai County-Ariz.

Mackey, John S.-District Judge, Iowa District Court Second Judicial District-Ia.

Mackey, Malcolm H.-Judge, Superior Court of California County of Los Angeles-Calif.

Mackey, Robert D.-Judge, Superior Court of California County of Los Angeles-Calif.

Mackie, James B.-Chief Judge, Michigan District Court District Sixty-five B-Mich.

Mackin, John F.-Judge, Avon Lake Municipal Court-Ohio

MacKinnon, Cynthia Z.-Judge, Florida Circuit Court Ninth Judicial Circuit-Fla.

Macklin, William E.-Judge, Minnesota District Court First Judicial District-Minn.

Macktaz, Pamela M.-Associate Justice, Rhode Island Family Court-R.I.

MacLaren, Ronni B.-Judge, Superior Court of California County of Los Angeles-Calif.

MacLaughlin, Harry H.-Senior Judge, United States District Court District of Minnesota-Minn.

MacLaughlin, William A.-Judge, Superior Court of California County of Los Angeles-Calif.

MacLeod, Bonnie H.-Associate Justice, Trial Court of Massachusetts Superior Court Department-Mass.

MacLeod, Lawrence A., Jr.-Special Justice, Lebanon District Court-N.H.

MacMichael, James E.-Judge, Maine District Court-Me.

MacNabb, Joseph P.-Judge, Juvenile Court of Georgia Coweta Judicial Circuit-Ga.

Macnish, James Martin, Jr.-Judge, Kansas District Court Third Judicial District-Kan.

MacRae, Sharon-Judge, Texas District Court 290th Judicial District-Tex.

Macrum, James F., Jr.-Judge, Colorado District Court Eighteenth Judicial District-Colo.

Macy, Joseph I.-Justice, Trial Court of Massachusetts District Court Department Bristol County Taunton Division-Mass.

Madden, Joan A.-Justice, New York Supreme Court First Judicial District-N.Y.

Madden, John K.-Circuit Judge, Illinois Circuit Court of Cook County-Ill.

Madden, John T.-Judge, West Virginia Circuit Court Second Judicial Circuit-W.Va.

Madden, Patrick J.-District Judge, Iowa District Court Seventh Judicial District-Ia.

Madden, Patrick J.-Judge, Wisconsin Circuit Court Iron Circuit-Wis.

Madden, Patrick John-Reserve Judge, Wisconsin Circuit Court-Wis.

Madden, Patrick T.-Judge, Superior Court of California County of Los Angeles-Calif.

Maddock, Thomas M.-Judge, Superior Court of California County of Contra Costa-Calif.

Maddox, Don-Judge, New Mexico District Court Fifth Judicial District-N.Mex.

Maddox, Hugh-Active Retired Associate Justice, Alabama Supreme Court-Ala.

Maddox, J. Cordell, Jr.-Judge, South Carolina Circuit Court Tenth Judicial Circuit-S.C.

Maddox, Lola P.-Associate Judge, Illinois Circuit Court Third Judicial Circuit-Ill.

Maddox, William A.-Judge, Nevada District Court First Judicial District-Nev.

Maddux, John J., Jr.-Judge, Tennessee Circuit Court Thirteenth Judicial District-Tenn.

Maddux, Tracy L.-Chief Magistrate, Magistrate Court of Chattooga County-Ga.

Maddux, William D.-Circuit Judge, Illinois Circuit Court of Cook County-Ill.

Madenspacher, Joseph C.-Judge, Pennsylvania Court of Common Pleas Second Judicial District-Pa.

Mader, Katherine-Judge, Superior Court of California County of Los Angeles-Calif.

Madsen, Barbara A.-Justice, Washington Supreme Court-Wash.

Madson, A. Scott-Associate Judge, Illinois Circuit Court Thirteenth Judicial Circuit-Ill.

Maes, Dennis-Chief Judge, Colorado District Court Tenth Judicial District and Judge, Colorado Water Court Division Two-Colo.

Maes, Petra Jimenez-Chief Justice, New Mexico Supreme Court and Senior Justice, New Mexico Supreme Court-N.Mex.

Maetani, Howard H.-Judge, Utah District Court Fourth Judicial District-Utah

Magdich, Tomas M.-Circuit Judge, Illinois Circuit Court Fifteenth Judicial Circuit-Ill.

Magee, Gerald W.-Associate Juvenile Judge, Iowa District Court Second Judicial District-Ia.

Magee, Yada T.-Judge, Louisiana District Court Orleans Parish Civil District-La.

Mager, Gerald-Senior Judge, Florida District Court of Appeal-Fla.

Magers, Patrick F.-Judge, Superior Court of California County of Riverside-Calif.

Maggio, Mike-Judge, Arkansas Circuit Court Twentieth Judicial Circuit-Ark.

Magill, Frank J.-Senior Judge, United States Court of Appeals Eighth Circuit

Magistrali, Michael F.-Judge, Torrington District Probate Court-Conn.

Magnus-Stinson, Jane-Judge, Marion Superior Court-Ind.

Magnuson, Paul A.-Senior Judge, United States District Court District of Minnesota-Minn.

Magoon, Kenneth-Assistant Judge, Vermont Trial Court Orleans County-Vt.

Magre, Ed-Judge, Texas District Court 20th Judicial District-Tex.

Maguire, Frederick-Judge, Superior Court of California County of San Diego-Calif.

Maguire, Walter Flippin-Judge, Kentucky District Court Twenty-eighth Judicial District-Ky.

Mahan, James C.-Judge, United States District Court District of Nevada-Nev.

Mahan, Robert E.-Judge, Iowa Court of Appeals-Ia.

Mahan, Stephen C.-Judge, Virginia Circuit Court Second Judicial Circuit-Va.

Maher, Cathie B.-Judge, Wayne County Probate Court-Mich.

Maher, Dennis P.-Judge, Cathlamet Municipal Court-Wash.

Maher, Jerelyn D.-Associate Judge, Illinois Circuit Court Tenth Judicial Circuit-Ill.

Maher, John R.-Judge, Probate Court of New Hampshire Rockingham County-N.H.

Maher, Martin T.-Judge, Wayne County Probate Court-Mich.

Maher, William L.-Judge, Peekskill City Court-N.Y.

Mahler, Glenn A.-Judge, Superior Court of California County of Orange-Calif.

Mahon, Eldon B.-Senior Judge, United States District Court Northern District of Texas-Tex.

Mahon, Roger F.-Judge, New Jersey Superior Court Vicinage Thirteen-N.J.

Mahon, Roy S.-Justice, New York Supreme Court Tenth Judicial District-N.Y.

Mahon, William P.-Judge, Pennsylvania Court of Common Pleas Fifteenth Judicial District-Pa.

Mahoney, David J.-Justice, New York Supreme Court Eighth Judicial District-N.Y.

Mahoney, Margaret A.-Judge, United States Bankruptcy Court Southern District of Alabama-Ala.

Mahoney, Margaret R.-Judge, Superior Court of Arizona Maricopa County-Ariz.

Mahoney, P. Michael-Magistrate Judge, United States District Court Northern District of Illinois-Ill.

Mahoney, Patrick J.-Judge, Superior Court of California City and County of San Francisco-Calif.

Mahoney, Paul F.-First Justice, Trial Court of Massachusetts District Court Department Suffolk County East Boston Division and Justice, Middlesex County Malden Division-Mass.

Mahoney, Timothy J.-Chief Judge, United States Bankruptcy Court District of Nebraska-Neb.

Maier, Eugene Edward J.-Judge, Pennsylvania Court of Common Pleas First Judicial District-Pa.

Main, Philip D.-Judge, Granby District Probate Court-Conn.

Main, Robert G., Jr.-Judge, Franklin County Court-N.Y.

Maino, Runston G.-Judge, Superior Court of California County of San Diego-Calif.

Mains, William-Judge, Kentucky Circuit Court Twenty-first Judicial Circuit-Ky.

Maiocco, John P., Jr.-Judge Referee, Connecticut Superior Court-Conn.

Majeed, A. B.-Judge, Brevard County Court-Fla.

Majhan, Thomas J.-Judge, Washington Superior Court Jefferson County-Wash.

Major, Charles T.-Justice, New York Supreme Court Fifth Judicial District-N.Y.

Makemson, Robert R.-Judge, Florida Circuit Court Nineteenth Judicial Circuit-Fla.

Maki, William O.-Circuit Judge, Illinois Circuit Court of Cook County-Ill.

Makino, Kazuharu-Judge, Superior Court of California County of Orange-Calif.

Makowski, Joseph G.-Justice, New York Supreme Court Eighth Judicial District-N.Y.

Malak, Jeffrey A.-Associate Judge, Illinois Circuit Court of Cook County-Ill.

Malarney, Amber D.-Judge, North Carolina District Court District 1-N.C.

Maldonado, Albert H.-Judge, Superior Court of California County of Monterey-Calif.

Maldonado, Diana L.-Acting First Justice, Trial Court of Massachusetts District Court Department Norfolk County Dedham Division and Justice, Suffolk County Chelsea Division-Mass.

Maley, John David-District Judge, Oklahoma District Court Twenty-fourth Judicial District-Okla.

Malicki, Catherine E.-Judge, Municipal Court of Atlanta-Ga.

Mallach, Barbara J.-Judge, Superior Court of California County of San Mateo-Calif.

Mallano, Robert M.-Associate Justice, California Court of Appeal Second District Division One-Calif.

Mallett, Richard M.-Judge, Superior Court of California County of San Joaquin-Calif.

Mallia, Wayne J.-Judge, Texas District Court 405th Judicial District-Tex.

Mallis, Robert P.-Judge, Superior Court of Georgia Stone Mountain Judicial Circuit-Ga.

Mallon, Michael-Circuit Judge, Illinois Circuit Court Fifteenth Judicial Circuit-Ill.

Mallory, William L., Jr.-Judge, Hamilton County Municipal Court-Ohio

Mallott, Lewis E.-Associate Judge, Illinois Circuit Court Third Judicial Circuit-Ill.

Malloy, Edward A., Jr.-Associate Judge, Maryland District Court District Twelve-Md.

Malloy, Paul V.-Judge, Wisconsin Circuit Court Ozaukee Circuit-Wis.

Malmstadt, Michael G.-Judge, Wisconsin Circuit Court Milwaukee Circuit-Wis.

Maloan, W. Michael-Chancellor, Tennessee Chancery Court Twenty-seventh Judicial District-Tenn.

Malone, Bernard J., Jr.-Justice, New York Supreme Court Third Judicial District-N.Y.

Malone, Charles R.-Judge, Alabama Circuit Court Sixth Judicial Circuit-Ala.

Malone, John F.-Judge, New Jersey Superior Court Vicinage Twelve-N.J.

Malone, Michael J.-Judge, Kansas District Court Seventh Judicial District-Kan.

Malone, Tom-Judge, Kansas Court of Appeals-Kan.

Maloney, Dennis Paul-Judge, Florida Circuit Court Tenth Judicial Circuit-Fla.

Maloney, John P.-Judge Referee, Connecticut Superior Court-Conn.

Maloney, Michael J.-Circuit Judge, Missouri Circuit Court Seventh Judicial Circuit-Mo.

Maloney, Paul L.-Chief Judge, Michigan Circuit Court Second Judicial Circuit-Mich.

Maloney, Robert B.-Senior Judge, United States District Court Northern District of Texas-Tex.

Maloney, Timothy P.-Judge, Ohio Court of Common Pleas Mahoning County-Ohio

Malphrus, Joseph N., Jr.-Judge, Jasper County Probate Court-S.C.

Maltby, R. Terry-Chief Judge, Sanilac County Probate Court-Mich.

Maltese, Joseph J.-Judge, New York Court of Claims-N.Y.

Mamiya, Ron A.-Judge, Seattle Municipal Court-Wash.

Manahan, Teresa-Assistant Judge, Vermont Trial Court Franklin County-Vt.

ALPHABETICAL NAME INDEX

Manck, Joseph P.-Associate Judge, Circuit Court for Anne Arundel County, Fifth Judicial Circuit-Md.

Mancuso, James V.-Justice of the Peace, Incline Village/Crystal Bay Justices' Court-Nev.

Mandabach, Frederick A.-Judge, Superior Court of California County of San Bernardino-Calif.

Mandell, Andrew L.-Justice, Trial Court of Massachusetts District Court Department Worcester County Fitchburg Division-Mass.

Manderfield, Paula J.-Judge, Michigan Circuit Court Thirtieth Judicial Circuit-Mich.

Manella, Nora-Judge, United States District Court Central District of California-Calif.

Maness, Jayrene R.-Judge, North Carolina District Court District 19B-N.C.

Maney, Gerard E.-Judge, Albany County Family Court-N.Y.

Maney, T. Patterson-Judge, Okaloosa County Court-Fla.

Manfredi, William J.-Judge, Pennsylvania Court of Common Pleas First Judicial District-Pa.

Mangano, Guy J., Jr.-Judge, New York Court of Claims-N.Y.

Mangerson, Mark A.-Judge, Wisconsin Circuit Court Oneida Circuit-Wis.

Mangones, Philip P.-Associate Justice, New Hampshire Superior Court-N.H.

Mangum, J. Kenneth-Judge, Superior Court of Arizona Maricopa County-Ariz.

Manian, Victor-Judge, Wisconsin Circuit Court Milwaukee Circuit-Wis.

Manier, Jenny Pitts-Judge, St. Joseph Superior Court-Ind.

Manion, Daniel A.-Judge, United States Court of Appeals Seventh Circuit

Manis, Stephanie B.-Judge, Superior Court of Georgia Atlanta Judicial Circuit-Ga.

Manley, M. Kathleen-Judge, Vermont Trial Court-Vt.

Manley, Mary-Judge, Utah Juvenile Court Seventh Judicial District-Utah

Manley, Stephen V.-Judge, Superior Court of California County of Santa Clara-Calif.

Mann, Arthur H.-Judge, Superior Court of California County of Lake-Calif.

Mann, David C.-Associate Circuit Judge, Missouri Circuit Court Thirty-third Judicial Circuit-Mo.

Mann, Elizabeth N.-Judge, Monroe Circuit Court-Ind.

Mann, Roanne L.-Magistrate Judge, United States District Court Eastern District of New York-N.Y.

Mannen, Ann T.-Judge, Ohio Court of Common Pleas Cuyahoga County-Ohio

Manners, Michael W.-Circuit Judge, Missouri Circuit Court Sixteenth Judicial Circuit-Mo.

Mannes, Paul-Judge, United States Bankruptcy Court District of Maryland-Md.

Mannheimer, David-Judge, Alaska Court of Appeals-Alas.

Manning, Blanche M.-Judge, United States District Court Northern District of Illinois-Ill.

Manning, C. Wendell-Judge, Louisiana District Court Fourth Judicial District-La.

Manning, Donald E.-Judge, Juvenile Court of Georgia Brunswick Judicial Circuit-Ga.

Manning, Howard E., Jr.-Resident Judge, North Carolina Superior Court Third Judicial Division District 10-N.C.

Manning, James L.-Judge, Montgomery County Court-Ohio

Manning, Jeffrey A.-Judge, Pennsylvania Court of Common Pleas Fifth Judicial District-Pa.

Manning, L. Casey-Judge, South Carolina Circuit Court Fifth Judicial Circuit-S.C.

Manning, Sheila Gibson-Judge, Michigan Circuit Court Third Judicial Circuit-Mich.

Mannion, John J.-Associate Judge, Illinois Circuit Court of Cook County-Ill.

Mannion, Malachy E.-Magistrate Judge, United States District Court Middle District of Pennsylvania-Pa.

Mannion, Thomas B.-Retired Judge, New Jersey Superior Court-N.J.

Manos, John M.-Senior Judge, United States District Court Northern District of Ohio-Ohio

Manoukian, Socrates Peter-Judge, Superior Court of California County of Santa Clara-Calif.

Manrique, Tanja K.-Judge, Minnesota District Court Fourth Judicial District-Minn.

Mansfield, Scott-Associate Judge, Illinois Circuit Court Twentieth Judicial Circuit-Ill.

Manske, Jeffrey C.-Magistrate Judge, United States District Court Western District of Texas-Tex.

Mantineo, Maureen B.-Judge, New Jersey Superior Court Vicinage Six-N.J.

Mantooth-Stricklin, Debbie-Judge, Texas District Court 180th Judicial District-Tex.

Manz, David M.-Judge, Buffalo City Court-N.Y.

Manzanares, Lawrence A.-Judge, Colorado District Court Second Judicial District-Colo.

Manzanares, Sylvia A.-Judge, El Paso County Court-Colo.

Manzanet, Sallie-Justice, New York Supreme Court Twelfth Judicial District-N.Y.

Manzi, Mary McCauley-Associate Justice, Trial Court of Massachusetts Probate and Family Court Department Essex County Division-Mass.

Mapp, Calvin R.-Senior Judge, Dade County Court-Fla.

Marabella, Anthony J., Jr.-Judge, Louisiana District Court Nineteenth Judicial District-La.

Marable, Herman, Jr.-Judge, Michigan District Court District Sixty-eight-Mich.

Marak, Joseph P., Jr.-Associate District Judge, Oklahoma District Court Fourth Judicial District-Okla.

Marano, Anthony F.-Justice, New York Supreme Court Tenth Judicial District-N.Y.

Marano, Eugene A.-Judge, Idaho District Court First Judicial District Magistrate Division-Ida.

Maras, Marcia-Circuit Judge, Illinois Circuit Court of Cook County-Ill.

Marben, Kurt J.-Judge, Minnesota District Court Ninth Judicial District-Minn.

Marber, Randy Sue-Judge, Nassau County District Court-N.Y.

Marblestone, Donald-Judge, Seminole County Court-Fla.

Marbley, Algenon L.-Judge, United States District Court Southern District of Ohio-Ohio

Marcelain, Thomas M.-Judge, Licking County Municipal Court-Ohio

Marchant, Bristow-Magistrate Judge, United States District Court District of South Carolina-S.C.

Marchiano, James J.-Presiding Justice, California Court of Appeal First District Division One-Calif.

Marchman, Sharon Ingram-Judge, Louisiana District Court Fourth Judicial District-La.

Marcucci, John M.-Judge, Denver County Court-Colo.

Marcus, Gregg-Judge, Superior Court of California County of Los Angeles-Calif.

Marcus, James A.-Chief Judge, Michigan District Court District Seventy-three A-Mich.

Marcus, Martin-Judge, New York Court of Claims-N.Y.

Marcus, Michael H.-Judge, Oregon Circuit Court Fourth Judicial District-Ore.

Marcus, Stanley-Judge, United States Court of Appeals Eleventh Circuit

Marcus, Stephen A.-Judge, Superior Court of California County of Los Angeles-Calif.

Marcuzzo, Jeffrey-Judge, Nebraska County Court Fourth Judicial District-Neb.

Marden, Donald H.-Justice, Maine Superior Court-Me.

Margines, Charles-Judge, Superior Court of California County of Orange-Calif.

Margolis, Joan G.-Magistrate Judge, United States District Court District of Connecticut-Conn.

Margolis, Lawrence S.-Senior Judge, United States Court of Federal Claims

Margolius, Richard V.-Senior Judge, Florida Circuit Court Eleventh Judicial Circuit-Fla.

Margulies, Sandra Lynn-Associate Justice, California Court of Appeal First District Division One-Calif.

Margulies, Seymour-Retired Judge, New Jersey Superior Court-N.J.

Mariano, Peter E.-Judge, Naugatuck District Probate Court-Conn.

Maricle, R. Cletus-Judge, Kentucky Circuit Court Forty-first Judicial Circuit-Ky.

Marietti, William C.-Judge, Michigan Circuit Court Fourteenth Judicial Circuit-Mich.

Marik, Wayne J.-Judge, Wisconsin Circuit Court Racine Circuit-Wis.

Marin, Alan C.-Judge, New York Court of Claims-N.Y.

Marinello, Scott G.-Judge, Columbia District Court Columbia County and Judge, Dayton Municipal Court-Wash.

Maring, Mary Muehlen-Justice, North Dakota Supreme Court-N.D.

Maring, Waldo A.-Judge, Georgetown County Probate Court-S.C.

Marini, Francis L.-Justice, Trial Court of Massachusetts District Court Department Plymouth County Hingham Division-Mass.

Marino, Joseph D.-Judge, Middletown District Probate Court-Conn.

Marion, James Patrick-Judge, Superior Court of California County of Orange-Calif.

Marion, Sandee Bryan-Justice, Texas Court of Appeals Fourth District-Tex.

Marion, Tori J.-Judge, Townsend City Court-Mont.

Marionneaux, Jack T.-Judge, Louisiana District Court Eighteenth Judicial District-La.

Mark, Kevin F.-Judge, Minnesota District Court First Judicial District-Minn.

Mark, Robert A.-Chief Judge, United States Bankruptcy Court Southern District of Florida-Fla.

Markey, Charles J.-Judge, The Civil Court of the City of New York-N.Y.

Markey, Jane E.-Judge, Michigan Court of Appeals-Mich.

Markman, Joy W.-Judge, Superior Court of California County of Orange-Calif.

Markman, Stephen J.-Justice, Michigan Supreme Court-Mich.

Markovitz, Bernard-Judge, United States Bankruptcy Court Western District of Pennsylvania-Pa.

Markow, Theodore J.-Judge, Virginia Circuit Court Thirteenth Judicial Circuit-Va.

Marks, J. Lewis, Jr.-Chief Judge, West Virginia Circuit Court Fifteenth Judicial Circuit-W.Va.

Marks, John G.-Judge, Nassau County Family Court-N.Y.

Marks, Patricia D.-Judge, Monroe County Court-N.Y.

Marks, Ronald Harris-Judge, Virginia Juvenile and Domestic Relations District Court Second Judicial District-Va.

Marks, Victoria S.-Judge, Hawaii Circuit Court First Judicial Circuit-Hi.

Markson, Paul A., Jr.-Judge, Colorado District Court Second Judicial District-Colo.

Marlar, James M.-Judge, Bankruptcy Appellate Panel Ninth Circuit and Judge, United States Bankruptcy Court District of Arizona-Ariz.

Marlette, Patrick-Judge, Superior Court of California County of Sacramento-Calif.

Marlow, George D.-Associate Justice, New York Supreme Court Appellate Division First Judicial Department-N.Y.

Marlow, Monica-Judge, Superior Court of California County of Shasta-Calif.

Marmo, Ronald G.-Judge, New Jersey Superior Court Vicinage Eleven-N.J.

Marnocha, John M.-Judge, St. Joseph Superior Court-Ind.

Maroc, Richard W.-Judge, Lake Superior Court-Ind.

Maron, Edward A.-Judge, Nassau County District Court-N.Y.

Marovich, George M.-Senior Judge, United States District Court Northern District of Illinois-Ill.

Marquardt, Christel E.-Judge, Kansas Court of Appeals-Kan.

Marquart, Keith-Associate Circuit Judge, Missouri Circuit Court Fifth Judicial Circuit-Mo.

Marquez, Alfredo C.-Senior Judge, United States District Court District of Arizona-Ariz.

Marquez, Jose D. L.-Judge, Colorado Court of Appeals-Colo.

Marra, Kenneth A.-Judge, United States District Court Southern District of Florida-Fla.

ALPHABETICAL NAME INDEX

Marrano, Frederic J.-Judge, Lackawanna City Court-N.Y.

Marrero, Louis John-Justice, New York Supreme Court Second Judicial District-N.Y.

Marrero, Victor-Judge, United States District Court Southern District of New York-N.Y.

Marrinan, Margaret M.-Judge, Minnesota District Court Second Judicial District-Minn.

Marriott, Frank, Jr.-Judge, Volusia County Court-Fla.

Marrs, Bruce F.-Judge, Superior Court of California County of Los Angeles-Calif.

Marrus, Alan D.-Judge, The Criminal Court of the City of New York-N.Y.

Marsaglia, Robert C.-Circuit Judge, Illinois Circuit Court Thirteenth Judicial Circuit-Ill.

Marschewski, Jim-Judge, Arkansas Circuit Court Twelfth Judicial Circuit-Ark.

Marsh, Donna-Justice, Musselshell County Justice of the Peace Court and Judge, Roundup City Court-Mont.

Marsh, Malcolm F.-Senior Judge, United States District Court District of Oregon-Ore.

Marsh, Melba D.-Judge, Ohio Court of Common Pleas Hamilton County-Ohio

Marshall, Christopher J.-Judge, Oregon Circuit Court Fourth Judicial District-Ore.

Marshall, Consuelo Bland-Chief Judge, United States District Court Central District of California-Calif.

Marshall, Dan E.-Judge, Hancock Superior Court-Ind.

Marshall, Donald W., Jr.-Judge, Colorado District Court Seventeenth Judicial District-Colo.

Marshall, Frederick J.-Justice, New York Supreme Court Eighth Judicial District-N.Y.

Marshall, Jacqueline-Magistrate Judge, United States District Court District of Arizona-Ariz.

Marshall, Julie G.-Judge, Colorado District Court Eleventh Judicial District-Colo.

Marshall, Margaret H.-Chief Justice, Massachusetts Supreme Judicial Court-Mass.

Marshall, Peter-Judge, Volusia County Court-Fla.

Marshall, Thomas E.-Associate Judge, Circuit Court for Harford County, Third Judicial Circuit-Md.

Marshall, Walter L., Jr.-Judge, New Jersey Superior Court Vicinage Fifteen-N.J.

Marshall, William T.-Judge, Ohio Court of Common Pleas Scioto County-Ohio

Marsili, Anthony G.-Judge, Pennsylvania Court of Common Pleas Tenth Judicial District-Pa.

Martell, Donald H.-Judge, Portage County Municipal Court-Ohio

Marten, John Thomas-Judge, United States District Court District of Kansas-Kan.

Martens, Kevin E.-Judge, Wisconsin Circuit Court Milwaukee Circuit-Wis.

Martin, Beverly B.-Judge, United States District Court Northern District of Georgia-Ga.

Martin, Boyce Ficklen, Jr.-Chief Judge, United States Court of Appeals Sixth Circuit

Martin, Chris Allen-Judge, Ohio Court of Common Pleas Fairfield County-Ohio

Martin, Daniel-Judge, New York Court of Claims-N.Y.

Martin, David L.-Magistrate Judge, United States District Court District of Rhode Island-R.I.

Martin, David N.-Associate District Judge, Oklahoma District Court Twenty-fourth Judicial District-Okla.

Martin, E. Mason, II-Judge, Montgomery County Court at Law No. 3-Tex.

Martin, Elizabeth H.-Judge, Minnesota District Court Tenth Judicial District-Minn.

Martin, Everett A., Jr.-Judge, Virginia Circuit Court Fourth Judicial Circuit-Va.

Martin, Faye Sanders-Senior Judge, Superior Court of Georgia-Ga.

Martin, Gerald C.-Judge, Minnesota District Court Sixth Judicial District-Minn.

Martin, Gordon A., Jr.-Justice, Trial Court of Massachusetts District Court Department Suffolk County Roxbury Division-Mass.

Martin, Gregory H.-Judge, Superior Court of Arizona Maricopa County-Ariz.

Martin, Holli G.-Judge, Juvenile Court of Georgia Tifton Judicial Circuit-Ga.

Martin, Jack-Judge, Hall County Court-Tex.

Martin, Janice-Judge, Kentucky District Court Thirtieth Judicial District-Ky.

Martin, Jerry Cash-Emergency Judge, North Carolina Superior Court-N.C.

Martin, John C.-Associate Judge, North Carolina Court of Appeals-N.C.

Martin, John E.-Judge, Superior Court of California County of Calaveras-Calif.

Martin, John Nevin-Judge, Superior Court of California County of San Bernardino-Calif.

Martin, John S., Jr.-Judge, United States District Court Southern District of New York-N.Y.

Martin, John W.-Judge, Brinkley District Court-Ark.

Martin, Jonathan H.-Judge, Yakima Municipal Court-Wash.

Martin, Karen L.-Judge, Florida Circuit Court Fifteenth Judicial Circuit-Fla.

Martin, Kathryn B.-Judge, Probate Court of Lamar County-Ga.

Martin, Krista K.-Judge, Minnesota District Court Tenth Judicial District-Minn.

Martin, Larnzell, Jr.-Associate Judge, Circuit Court for Prince George's County, Seventh Judicial Circuit-Md.

Martin, Larry D.-Justice, New York Supreme Court Second Judicial District-N.Y.

Martin, LaTia W.-Justice, New York Supreme Court Twelfth Judicial District-N.Y.

Martin, Lawrence D.-Judge, El Paso County Court-Colo.

Martin, Lawrence D.-Judge, Collier County Court-Fla.

Martin, Leonard Watson-Judge, Tennessee Circuit Court Twenty-third Judicial District-Tenn.

Martin, LeRoy K., Jr.-Circuit Judge, Illinois Circuit Court of Cook County-Ill.

Martin, Luise Krieger-Judge, Dade County Court-Fla.

Martin, Mac-Judge, Nebraska County Court Ninth Judicial District-Neb.

Martin, Mark D.-Associate Justice, Supreme Court of North Carolina-N.C.

Martin, Paula B.-Judge, Kansas District Court Seventh Judicial District-Kan.

Martin, Ray D.-Judge, Alabama Circuit Court Fifth Judicial Circuit-Ala.

Martin, Robert A.-Judge, Connecticut Superior Court-Conn.

Martin, Robert D.-Chief Judge, United States Bankruptcy Court Western District of Wisconsin-Wis.

Martin, Rosa Lee-Chief Magistrate, Magistrate Court of Wilkes County-Ga.

Martin, Steven E.-Judge, Ohio Court of Common Pleas Hamilton County-Ohio

Martin, Victoria L.-Associate Judge, Illinois Circuit Court Nineteenth Judicial Circuit-Ill.

Martin, Willard G., Jr.-Special Justice, Laconia District Court-N.H.

Martin, William F.-Judge, Superior Court of California County of Santa Clara-Calif.

Martin, William J.-Judge, Ohio Court of Common Pleas Carroll County-Ohio

Martin, William J.-President Judge, Pennsylvania Court of Common Pleas Fortieth Judicial District-Pa.

Martin Bishop, Patricia-Circuit Judge, Illinois Circuit Court of Cook County-Ill.

Martin-Clark, Miriam B.-Judge, Michigan District Court District Thirty-six-Mich.

Martinelli, Michael A.-Judge, Yonkers City Court-N.Y.

Martinez, Alex Joseph-Justice, Colorado Supreme Court-Colo.

Martinez, Donna F.-Magistrate Judge, United States District Court District of Connecticut-Conn.

Martinez, Elvin L.-Judge, Hillsborough County Court-Fla.

Martinez, Frank-Judge, Colorado District Court Second Judicial District-Colo.

Martinez, Gilbert A.-Chief Judge, Colorado District Court Fourth Judicial District-Colo.

Martinez, Jimmy-Judge, Bee County Court-Tex.

Martinez, John L.-Judge, Superior Court of California County of Los Angeles-Calif.

Martinez, Jose E.-Judge, United States District Court Southern District of Florida-Fla.

Martinez, Lourdes A.-Magistrate Judge, United States District Court District of New Mexico-N.Mex.

Martinez, Michael A.-Judge, Colorado District Court Second Judicial District-Colo.

Martinez, Philip Ray-Judge, United States District Court Western District of Texas-Tex.

Martinez, Ricardo S.-Magistrate Judge, United States District Court Western District of Washington-Wash.

Martinez, Robert M.-Judge, Superior Court of California County of Los Angeles-Calif.

Martinez, Sandy-Circuit Judge, Missouri Circuit Court Twenty-fourth Judicial Circuit-Mo.

Martinez, Wilfredo-Judge, Orange County Court-Fla.

Martinez-Olguin, Camille-Judge, New Mexico District Court Thirteenth Judicial District-N.Mex.

Martini, William J.-Judge, United States District Court District of New Jersey-N.J.

Martinotti, Brian R.-Judge, New Jersey Superior Court Vicinage Two-N.J.

Martlew, Jeffrey L.-Chief Judge, Michigan Circuit Court Twenty-ninth Judicial Circuit-Mich.

Martoche, Salvatore R.-Justice, New York Supreme Court Eighth Judicial District-N.Y.

Martone, Frederick J.-Judge, United States District Court District of Arizona-Ariz.

Martone, Michael A.-Judge, Michigan District Court District Fifty-two Division Four-Mich.

Martusewicz, Kim H.-Judge, Jefferson County Court-N.Y.

Marty, Karen L.-Magistrate Judge, United States District Court District of Wyoming-Wyo.

Marullo, Frank A., Jr.-Judge, Louisiana District Court Orleans Parish Criminal District-La.

Marvel, L. Paige-Judge, United States Tax Court

Marvin, Seth L.-Judge, The Criminal Court of the City of New York-N.Y.

Marx, Krista-Judge, Palm Beach County Court-Fla.

Maschari, Ann B.-Judge, Ohio Court of Common Pleas Erie County-Ohio

Maschman, Curtis L.-Judge, Nebraska County Court First Judicial District-Neb.

Masdon, Samuel L.-Judge, Winston County District Court-Ala.

Mashburn, Mike-Judge, Arkansas Circuit Court Fourth Judicial Circuit-Ark.

Mask, Jacqueline Estes-Judge, Mississippi Chancery Court First Judicial District-Miss.

Maslach, Joe-Justice of the Peace, Tonopah Justices' Court-Nev.

Mason, Corinne-Judge, Collin County Court at Law No. 1-Tex.

Mason, David C.-Circuit Judge, Missouri Circuit Court Twenty-second Judicial Circuit-Mo.

Mason, George, III-Judge, Virginia General District Court Fifteenth Judicial District-Va.

Mason, James M.-Judge, Wisconsin Circuit Court Wood Circuit-Wis.

Mason, James W.-Judge, Ohio Court of Common Pleas Franklin County-Ohio

Mason, Jerry G.-Judge, Mississippi Chancery Court Twelfth Judicial District-Miss.

Mason, John H.-Associate Justice, Massachusetts Appeals Court-Mass.

Mason, Mark W.-Judge, Attica City Court-Ind.

Mason, Mary Anne-Circuit Judge, Illinois Circuit Court of Cook County-Ill.

Mason, Michael D.-Associate Judge, Circuit Court for Montgomery County, Sixth Judicial Circuit-Md.

Mason, Michael T.-Magistrate Judge, United States District Court Northern District of Illinois-Ill.

Mason, Reynold N.-Justice, New York Supreme Court Second Judicial District-N.Y.

Mason, Richard G.-Judge, Oklahoma Workers' Compensation Court-Okla.

Mason, Tomar-Judge, Superior Court of California City and County of San Francisco-Calif.

Mason, Wesley R., III-Judge, Superior Court of California County of San Diego-Calif.

ALPHABETICAL NAME INDEX

ALPHABETICAL NAME INDEX

McAtee, William J.-Magistrate, Rhode Island Superior Court-R.I.

McAuliffe, Steven J.-Judge, United States District Court District of New Hampshire-N.H.

McAvoy, Thomas J.-Judge, United States District Court Northern District of New York-N.Y.

McBain, John G., Jr.-Judge, Michigan Circuit Court Fourth Judicial Circuit-Mich.

McBee, William A.-Judge, New Mexico District Court Fifth Judicial District-N.Mex.

McBeth, Gerald D.-Associate Circuit Judge, Missouri Circuit Court Twenty-eighth Judicial Circuit-Mo.

McBeth, Robert E.-Judge, King District Court South Division King County-Wash.

McBeth, Veronica Simmons-Judge, Superior Court of California County of Los Angeles-Calif.

McBride, James J.-Judge, Superior Court of California City and County of San Francisco-Calif.

McBride, Jerry R.-Judge, Ohio Court of Common Pleas Clermont County-Ohio

McBride, John D.-Judge, Pennsylvania Court of Common Pleas Thirty-sixth Judicial District-Pa.

McBride, John R.-Judge, Minnesota District Court Tenth Judicial District-Minn.

McBride, Margaret Stanton-Judge, Illinois Appellate Court First Judicial District Division Two-Ill.

McBride, Terry H.-Associate District Judge, Oklahoma District Court Twelfth Judicial District-Okla.

McBrien, Peter J.-Judge, Superior Court of California County of Sacramento-Calif.

McBroom, Douglas-Judge, Washington Superior Court King County-Wash.

McBryde, John H.-Judge, United States District Court Northern District of Texas-Tex.

McCabe, Edward G.-Justice, New York Supreme Court Tenth Judicial District-N.Y.

McCabe, Mark C.-Judge, Michigan District Court District Sixty-seven Division Four-Mich.

McCabe, Pamela J.-Judge, Michigan District Court District Fifty-five-Mich.

McCabe, Patrick J.-Judge, Louisiana District Court Twenty-fourth Judicial District-La.

McCafferty, Bridget M.-Judge, Ohio Court of Common Pleas Cuyahoga County-Ohio

McCaffrey, Francis B.-Administrative Judge, Vermont Trial Court-Vt.

McCahill, Burke F.-Judge, Virginia Circuit Court Twentieth Judicial Circuit-Va.

McCall, Charles Allen-District Judge, Oklahoma District Court Fifth Judicial District-Okla.

McCall, James L., Jr.-Chief Magistrate, Magistrate Court of Montgomery County-Ga.

McCall, Sharon J.-Judge, Probate Court of Tattnall County-Ga.

McCall, Terry-Justice, Texas Court of Appeals Eleventh District-Tex.

McCalla, Jon Phipps-Judge, United States District Court Western District of Tennessee-Tenn.

McCallum, Jay B.-Judge, Louisiana District Court Third Judicial District-La.

McCallum, Linda F.-Judge, Florida Circuit Court Fourth Judicial Circuit-Fla.

McCallum, Mary M.-First Justice, Trial Court of Massachusetts Juvenile Court Department Norfolk County Division-Mass.

McCallum, Paul J.-Justice, Trial Court of Massachusetts District Court Department Bristol County Attleboro Division-Mass.

McCann, John S.-Associate Justice, Trial Court of Massachusetts Superior Court Department-Mass.

McCann, Kathleen J.-Judge, Michigan District Court District Sixteen-Mich.

McCarroll, John R., Jr.-Judge, Tennessee Circuit Court Thirtieth Judicial District-Tenn.

McCarter, Dorothy-Judge, Montana District Court First Judicial District-Mont.

McCarter, Mike-Judge, Montana Workers' Compensation Court-Mont.

McCarthy, Barbara S.-Judge, Sparks Municipal Court-Nev.

McCarthy, Carol Pearce-Circuit Judge, Illinois Circuit Court of Cook County-Ill.

McCarthy, Frank H.-Magistrate Judge, United States District Court Northern District of Oklahoma-Okla.

McCarthy, Harry-Judge, Washington Superior Court King County-Wash.

McCarthy, J. Michael-Judge, Florida Circuit Court Tenth Judicial Circuit-Fla.

McCarthy, James P.-Circuit Judge, Illinois Circuit Court of Cook County-Ill.

McCarthy, James W.-Judge, Oswego County Court-N.Y.

McCarthy, John A.-Judge, Washington Superior Court Pierce County-Wash.

McCarthy, Katherine M.-Circuit Judge, Illinois Circuit Court Sixth Judicial Circuit-Ill.

McCarthy, Kathleen M.-Judge, Michigan Circuit Court Third Judicial Circuit-Mich.

McCarthy, Kevin M.-Judge, Superior Court of California City and County of San Francisco-Calif.

McCarthy, Michael G.-Judge, Yakima District Court Yakima County-Wash.

McCarthy, Thomas G.-Judge, Minnesota District Court First Judicial District-Minn.

McCarthy, Timothy P.-Judge, Florida Circuit Court Fifteenth Judicial Circuit-Fla.

McCartin, Michael-Judge, Superior Court of California County of Orange-Calif.

McCarty, Alison-Judge, Akron Municipal Court-Ohio

McCarty, Edward W., III-Justice, New York Supreme Court Tenth Judicial District-N.Y.

McCarty, John M.-Judge, Kentucky District Court Thirty-eighth Judicial District-Ky.

McCarty, Mack S.-Judge, Probate Court of Macon County-Ga.

McCarty, Patrick L.-Judge, Marion Superior Court-Ind.

McCarville, Brian S.-Judge, Superior Court of California County of San Bernardino-Calif.

McCarville, Stephen F.-Judge, Superior Court of Arizona Pinal County-Ariz.

McCaslin, William-Judge, Kentucky District Court Fifty-sixth Judicial District-Ky.

McCauley, F. Mark-Judge, Washington Superior Court Grays Harbor County-Wash.

McCauley, James A.-Senior Judge, Florida Circuit Court Seventeenth Judicial Circuit-Fla.

McCauley, Judith L.-Judge, Douglas District Court Douglas County-Wash.

McCaulie, William Gregg-Judge, Florida Circuit Court Fourth Judicial Circuit-Fla.

McClain, Larry-Judge, Kansas District Court Tenth Judicial District-Kan.

McClain, Richard B.-Associate District Judge, Oklahoma District Court Twenty-first Judicial District-Okla.

McClanahan, Elizabeth A.-Judge, Court of Appeals of Virginia-Va.

McClanahan, Ralph E., II-Judge, Kentucky District Court Twenty-third Judicial District-Ky.

McClean, John R., Jr.-Associate Judge, Illinois Circuit Court Fourteenth Judicial Circuit-Ill.

McClellan, Harry H.-Judge, Florida Circuit Court Fourteenth Judicial Circuit-Fla.

McClelland, Lee W.-Judge, Morrow County Municipal Court-Ohio

McClendon, Page-Judge, Louisiana Court of Appeal First Circuit-La.

McClennen, Crane-Judge, Superior Court of Arizona Maricopa County-Ariz.

McCleve, Sheila K.-Judge, Utah District Court Third Judicial District-Utah

McClintock, Gregory K.-Associate Judge, Illinois Circuit Court Ninth Judicial Circuit-Ill.

McClintock, John C., Jr.-Judge, North Dakota District Court Northeast Judicial District-N.D.

McCluan, William T.-Judge, Brevard County Court-Fla.

McClure, Ann Crawford-Justice, Texas Court of Appeals Eighth District-Tex.

McClure, James F., Jr.-Senior Judge, United States District Court Middle District of Pennsylvania-Pa.

McClure, Melvin, Jr.-Judge, Mississippi Chancery Court Third Judicial District-Miss.

McClurg, Michael Douglas-Judge, Ohio Court of Common Pleas Darke County-Ohio

McCluskey, Terry K.-Judge, Washington Superior Court Kitsap County-Wash.

McCollum, Alice O.-Judge, Ohio Court of Common Pleas Montgomery County-Ohio

McCollum, Elliott P., Jr.-Judge, State Court of Thomas County-Ga.

McCombs, Rufe E.-Senior Judge, Superior Court of Georgia-Ga.

McConaghy, Dennis A.-Judge, Superior Court of California County of Riverside-Calif.

McConduit, Bruce J.-Judge, New Orleans Municipal Court-La.

McConnell, C. Allen-Judge, Toledo Municipal Court-Ohio

McConnell, Judith D.-Associate Justice, California Court of Appeal Fourth District Division One-Calif.

McConnell, L. A., Jr.-Senior Judge, Superior Court of Georgia-Ga.

McConnell, Michael W.-Judge, United States Court of Appeals Tenth Circuit

McCooe, William P.-Justice, New York Supreme Court First Judicial District-N.Y.

McCooey, Brendan J.-Associate Judge, Illinois Circuit Court of Cook County-Ill.

McCooey, Tracy S.-Judge, Alabama Circuit Court Fifteenth Judicial Circuit-Ala.

McCord, Richard J.-Judge, Glen Cove City Court-N.Y.

McCorkle, Lamar-Judge, Texas District Court 133rd Judicial District-Tex.

McCormack, Joseph D.-Judge, Wisconsin Circuit Court Ozaukee Circuit-Wis.

McCormack, Michael-Associate Justice, Nebraska Supreme Court-Neb.

McCormack, Thomas M.-Judge, New Jersey Superior Court Vicinage Five-N.J.

McCormick, Ann Graf-Judge, New Jersey Superior Court Vicinage Eight-N.J.

McCormick, David H.-Judge, Arkansas Circuit Court Fifteenth Judicial Circuit-Ark.

McCormick, Edward H.-Judge, North Carolina District Court District 11-N.C.

McCormick, John A.-Judge, Oregon Circuit Court Twenty-third Judicial District-Ore.

McCormick, John E.-Judge, Wisconsin Circuit Court Milwaukee Circuit-Wis.

McCormick, Mary E.-Associate Judge, Maryland District Court District Six-Md.

McCormick, Michael W.-Judge, Alabama Circuit Court Tenth Judicial Circuit Birmingham Division-Ala.

McCormick, Patrick C.-District Associate Judge, Iowa District Court Third Judicial District-Ia.

McCormick, Richard E., Jr.-Judge, Pennsylvania Court of Common Pleas Tenth Judicial District-Pa.

McCormick, Rick J.-Presiding Judge, Oregon Circuit Court Twenty-third Judicial District-Ore.

McCormick, Timothy P.-Judge, Ohio Court of Common Pleas Cuyahoga County-Ohio

McCorvey, Gary C.-Chief Judge, Superior Court of Georgia Tifton Judicial Circuit-Ga.

McCoun, Thomas B., III-Magistrate Judge, United States District Court Middle District of Florida-Fla.

McCown, Frank J.-Judge, Ohio Court of Common Pleas Lawrence County-Ohio

McCoy, Bill-Judge, Texas District Court 358th Judicial District-Tex.

McCoy, Bob-Judge, Texas District Court 48th Judicial District-Tex.

McCoy, Carol L.-Chancellor, Tennessee Chancery Court Twentieth Judicial District-Tenn.

McCoy, Charles W., Jr.-Judge, Superior Court of California County of Los Angeles-Calif.

McCoy, Darin-Judge, Probate Court of Evans County-Ga.

McCoy, David M.-Judge, Texas District Court 100th Judicial District-Tex.

McCoy, Harold Paul, Jr.-Chief Judge, North Carolina District Court District 6A-N.C.

McCoy, Richard D.-Associate Judge, Illinois Circuit Court Tenth Judicial Circuit-Ill.

McCoy, Royce-Judge, Wood County Court-Tex.

McCree, Wade H.-Judge, Michigan District Court District Thirty-six-Mich.

McCrorey, Joseph R.-Magistrate Judge, United States District Court District of South Carolina-S.C.

McCue, Richard J.-Judge, Virginia General District Court Seventeenth Judicial District-Va.

ALPHABETICAL NAME INDEX

McCullin, Donald L.-Circuit Judge, Missouri Circuit Court Twenty-second Judicial Circuit-Mo.

McCulloch, Amy W.-Judge, Richland County Probate Court-S.C.

McCulloch, William C.-Judge, Harris County Probate Court No. 4-Tex.

McCullough, J. Douglas-Associate Judge, North Carolina Court of Appeals-N.C.

McCullough, John T.-Judge, Illinois Appellate Court Fourth Judicial District-Ill.

McCullough, LeRoy-Judge, Washington Superior Court King County-Wash.

McCullough, M. Bruce-Judge, United States Bankruptcy Court Western District of Pennsylvania-Pa.

McCully, Sharon P.-Judge, Utah Juvenile Court Third Judicial District-Utah

McCune, Robert James-Judge, Marion County Court-Fla.

McCurdy, Gary D.-Special Judge, Oklahoma District Court Twenty-sixth Judicial District-Okla.

McCurdy, Joseph P., Jr.-Associate Judge, Circuit Court for Baltimore City, Eighth Judicial Circuit-Md.

McCurn, Neal P.-Senior Judge, United States District Court Northern District of New York-N.Y.

McCuskey, Michael P.-Judge, Unites States District Court Central District of Illinois-Ill.

McDade, Joe Billy-Chief Judge, United States District Court Central District of Illinois-Ill.

McDade, Mary W.-Judge, Illinois Appellate Court Third Judicial District-Ill.

McDaniel, Donna Jo-Judge, Pennsylvania Court of Common Pleas Fifth Judicial District-Pa.

McDaniel, Frederic R.-Judge, New Jersey Superior Court Vicinage Twelve-N.J.

McDaniel, Kent-Judge, Rankin County Court-Miss.

McDaniel, Lana-Judge, Texas District Court 203rd Judicial District-Tex.

McDaniel, Robert E.-Judge, Superior Court of California County of Kern-Calif.

McDaniel, Ronald K., Jr.-Judge, Montville District Probate Court-Conn.

McDaniel, Terry R.-Judge, Idaho District Court Fourth Judicial District Magistrate Division-Ida.

McDermid, Ronald-Justice of the Peace, Sherman County Justice Court-Ore.

McDermott, Dennis K.-Judge, Madison County Court-N.Y.

McDermott, Edward J.-Special Justice, Hampton District Court-N.H.

McDermott, Patrick R.-Judge, Nebraska County Court Fifth Judicial District-Neb.

McDermott, Peter D.-Judge, Idaho District Court Sixth Judicial District-Ida.

McDermott, Richard-Judge, Washington Superior Court King County-Wash.

McDermott, William H.-Judge, Alabama Circuit Court Thirteenth Judicial Circuit-Ala.

McDonald, Alan A.-Senior Judge, United States District Court Eastern District of Washington-Wash.

McDonald, Alex C.-Associate Justice, California Court of Appeal Fourth District Division One-Calif.

McDonald, Barbara A.-Circuit Judge, Illinois Circuit Court of Cook County-Ill.

McDonald, C. Brian-Associate Justice, Trial Court of Massachusetts Superior Court Department-Mass.

McDonald, David P.-Judge, United States Bankruptcy Court Eastern District of Missouri-Mo.

McDonald, Douglas C.-District Associate Judge, Iowa District Court Seventh Judicial District-Ia.

McDonald, Francis M., Jr.-Judge Referee, Connecticut Superior Court-Conn.

McDonald, Frederick H.-Judge, Ohio Court of Common Pleas Lucas County-Ohio

McDonald, J. Michael-Judge, Louisiana Court of Appeal First Circuit-La.

McDonald, James E., Jr.-Judge, Juvenile Court of Georgia Western Judicial Circuit-Ga.

McDonald, John J.-Judge, Michigan Circuit Court Sixth Judicial Circuit-Mich.

McDonald, Louis P.-Chief Judge, New Mexico District Court Thirteenth Judicial District-N.Mex.

McDonald, Martin-Judge, Kentucky District Court Thirtieth Judicial District-Ky.

McDonald, Michael S.-Magistrate Judge, United States District Court Western District of Texas-Tex.

McDonald, Randall G.-Judge, Florida Circuit Court Tenth Judicial Circuit-Fla.

McDonald, Robert J.-Justice, New York Supreme Court Eleventh Judicial District-N.Y.

McDonald, Robert W., Jr.-Judge, Florida Circuit Court Twelfth Judicial Circuit-Fla.

McDonald, Roger J.-Judge, Florida Circuit Court Ninth Judicial Circuit-Fla.

McDonald, Ronnie-Judge, Bastrop County Court-Tex.

McDonald, Tom-Judge, Kentucky Circuit Court Thirtieth Judicial Circuit-Ky.

McDonald, Ysleta-Judge, Alachua County Court-Fla.

McDonald-Burkman, Judith-Judge, Kentucky Circuit Court Thirtieth Judicial Circuit-Ky.

McDonnell, Anne-Judge, New Jersey Superior Court Vicinage Fifteen-N.J.

McDonnell, Nancy R.-Judge, Ohio Court of Common Pleas Cuyahoga County-Ohio

McDonough, Donald Patrick-Judge, Virginia General District Court Nineteenth Judicial District-Va.

McDonough, Martin E.-Associate Judge, Illinois Circuit Court of Cook County-Ill.

McDonough, William B.-First Justice, Trial Court of Massachusetts District Court Department Hampden County Holyoke Division-Mass.

McDougal, Bart-Judge, Erath County Court at Law-Tex.

McDougall, Dan C.-Judge, Idaho District Court Sixth Judicial District Magistrate Division-Ida.

McDowell, John H.-Associate Judge, Circuit Court for Washington County, Fourth Judicial Circuit-Md.

McDowell, Paula B.-Judge, Franklin County District Court-Ala.

McDowell, Robert Scott-Judge, Texas District Court 62nd Judicial District-Tex.

McDunn, Susan J.-Circuit Judge, Illinois Circuit Court of Cook County-Ill.

McEachen, David Thomas-Judge, Superior Court of California County of Orange-Calif.

McEachen, Richard A.-Judge, Superior Court of California County of Shasta-Calif.

McElligott, Michael J.-Judge, Oregon Circuit Court Twentieth Judicial District-Ore.

McElrath, Terrence J.-Judge, New York City Family Court-N.Y.

McElroy, James B.-First Justice, Trial Court of Massachusetts District Court Department Berkshire County Southern Berkshire Division-Mass.

McElwain, Warren L.-Circuit Judge, Missouri Circuit Court Forty-third Judicial Circuit-Mo.

McElwee, John D.-Judge, Maine District Court-Me.

McElwee, Roma M.-Special Judge, Oklahoma District Court Seventh Judicial District-Okla.

McElyea, Ellen-Judge, Juvenile Court of Georgia Blue Ridge Judicial Circuit-Ga.

McEntarfer, James A.-Judge, Perry Circuit Court-Ind.

McEssey, Eugene F.-Reserve Judge, Wisconsin Circuit Court-Wis.

McEuen, Rebecca L.-Judge, Broadus City Court-Mont.

McEvoy, Christine M.-Associate Justice, Trial Court of Massachusetts Superior Court Department-Mass.

McEwen, Willard W., Jr.-Magistrate Judge, United States District Court Central District of California-Calif.

McFadden, F. P. Kimberly-Judge, Pennsylvania Court of Common Pleas Third Judicial District-Pa.

McFadden, Linda A.-Judge, Superior Court of California County of Stanislaus-Calif.

McFadden, Patrick R.-Judge, Idaho District Court First Judicial District Magistrate Division-Ida.

McFaddin, George M., Jr.-Judge, South Carolina Family Court Third Judicial Circuit-S.C.

McFarland, Kay-Chief Justice, Kansas Supreme Court-Kan.

McFarling, Bruce-Judge, Texas District Court 362nd Judicial District-Tex.

McFeeley, Mark B.-Chief Judge, Bankruptcy Appellate Panel Tenth Circuit and Judge, United States Bankruptcy Court District of New Mexico-N.Mex.

McFerrin, H. Edward-Presiding Judge, Alabama Circuit Court Second Judicial Circuit-Ala.

McGahey, Robert L., Jr.-Judge, Colorado District Court Second Judicial District-Colo.

McGann, James-Judge, New Jersey Superior Court Vicinage Nine-N.J.

McGann, Patrick E.-Circuit Judge, Illinois Circuit Court of Cook County-Ill.

McGann, Patrick J., Jr.-Retired Judge, New Jersey Superior Court-N.J.

McGann, Robert C.-Judge, The Criminal Court of the City of New York-N.Y.

McGarity, Arch W.-Judge, Superior Court of Georgia Flint Judicial Circuit-Ga.

McGarity, Margaret Dee-Judge, United States Bankruptcy Court Eastern District of Wisconsin-Wis.

McGaw, Ronald J.-Judge, Poughkeepsie City Court-N.Y.

McGee, Aaron Frank, III-Judge, Louisiana District Court Twenty-seventh Judicial District-La.

McGee, Charles M.-Judge, Nevada District Court Second Judicial District-Nev.

McGee, Daniel J.-Judge, Idaho District Court First Judicial District Magistrate Division-Ida.

McGee, Delwin T.-Judge, Moore County Court at Law-Tex.

McGee, Kevin J.-Judge, Superior Court of California County of Ventura-Calif.

McGee, Linda M.-Associate Judge, North Carolina Court of Appeals-N.C.

McGee, Martin B.-Judge, North Carolina District Court District 19A-N.C.

McGehee, W. Hollis-Judge, Mississippi Chancery Court Fourth Judicial District-Miss.

McGhee, Odell G.-District Associate Judge, Iowa District Court Fifth Judicial District-Ia.

McGill, Patrick R.-Judge, Clinton County Court-N.Y.

McGill, Paul L.-Justice, Trial Court of Massachusetts District Court Department Suffolk County Roxbury Division-Mass.

McGillis, Terry J.-Justice, Powell County Justice of the Peace Court and Judge, Deer Lodge City Court-Mont.

McGillivray, Roderick D.-Judge, Bartholomew Superior Court-Ind.

McGimpsey, Earl R.-Judge, Ohio Court of Common Pleas Huron County-Ohio

McGinity, Leo F.-Associate Justice, New York Supreme Court Appellate Division Second Judicial Department-N.Y.

McGinley, Bernard L.-Judge, The Commonwealth Court of Pennsylvania-Pa.

McGinley, C. Creed-Judge, Tennessee Circuit Court Twenty-fourth Judicial District-Tenn.

McGinley, Carol K.-Judge, Pennsylvania Court of Common Pleas Thirty-first Judicial District-Pa.

McGinn, Bernard J.-Judge, Nebraska District Court Third Judicial District-Neb.

McGinnis, Robert W.-Judge, Kentucky Circuit Court Eighteenth Judicial Circuit-Ky.

McGinnis, Sheila-Circuit Judge, Illinois Circuit Court of Cook County-Ill.

McGinty, Timothy J.-Judge, Ohio Court of Common Pleas Cuyahoga County-Ohio

McGivern, William T., Jr.-Judge, Superior Court of California County of Marin-Calif.

McGlynn, James A.-Associate Juvenile Judge, Iowa District Court Second Judicial District-Ia.

McGlynn, William F.-Associate Judge, Illinois Circuit Court of Cook County-Ill.

McGookey, Beverly K.-Judge, Ohio Court of Common Pleas Erie County-Ohio

McGough, Bobby Frank-Judge, Stonewall County Court-Tex.

McGough, Lynett-Judge, Ohio Court of Common Pleas Lorain County-Ohio

McGovern, Walter T.-Senior Judge, United States District Court Western District of Washington-Wash.

McGowan, Jeffery Paulk-Judge, Probate Court of Atkinson County-Ga.

ALPHABETICAL NAME INDEX

McGowan, Joseph W., III-Judge, South Carolina Family Court Eighth Judicial Circuit-S.C.
McGowan, Mary-Judge, Arkansas Circuit Court Sixth Judicial Circuit-Ark.
McGrady, J. Thomas-Judge, Florida Circuit Court Sixth Judicial Circuit-Fla.
McGrath, Bob-Judge, Texas District Court 342nd Judicial District-Tex.
McGrath, Brigid Mary-Associate Judge, Illinois Circuit Court of Cook County-Ill.
McGrath, John J., Jr.-Judge, Virginia Circuit Court Twenty-sixth Judicial Circuit-Va.
McGrath, Patrick J.-Judge, Rensselaer County Court-N.Y.
McGrath, Patrick M.-Judge, Ohio Court of Common Pleas Franklin County-Ohio
McGrath, William J., Jr.-Judge, Superior Court of California County of San Diego-Calif.
McGratty, A. Lee-Judge, Virginia General District Court Twenty-fifth Judicial District-Va.
McGraw, H. Suzanne-Judge, West Virginia Family Court Circuit Thirteen-W.Va.
McGraw, J. Philip-Judge, Jasper Superior Court-Ind.
McGraw, Joseph G.-Circuit Judge, Illinois Circuit Court Seventeenth Judicial Circuit-Ill.
McGraw, Patrick J.-Judge, Saginaw County Probate Court-Mich.
McGraw, Peggy Stevens-Circuit Judge, Missouri Circuit Court Sixteenth Judicial Circuit-Mo.
McGraw, Robert-Reserve Judge, Wisconsin Circuit Court-Wis.
McGraw, Tim-Judge, Grayson County Court-Tex.
McGraw, Warren R.-Justice, West Virginia Supreme Court of Appeals-W.Va.
McGregor, Cecelia J.-Judge, Goshen City Court-Ind.
McGregor, F. B. "Bob", Jr.-Judge, Texas District Court 66th Judicial District-Tex.
McGregor, Prudence M.-Associate Justice, Trial Court of Massachusetts Probate and Family Court Department Bristol County Division-Mass.
McGregor, Robert B.-Senior Judge, Florida Circuit Court Eighteenth Judicial Circuit-Fla.
McGregor, Ruth V.-Vice Chief Justice, Supreme Court of Arizona-Ariz.
McGroarty, John S.-Judge, Nevada District Court Eighth Judicial District-Nev.
McGuckian, Paul A.-Associate Judge, Circuit Court for Montgomery County, Sixth Judicial Circuit-Md.
McGuiness, William R.-Administrative Presiding Justice, California Court of Appeal First District and Presiding Justice, California Court of Appeal First District Division Three-Calif.
McGuinness, James H., Jr.-Justice, Trial Court of Massachusetts District Court Department Middlesex County Natick Division-Mass.
McGuire, Dennis M.-Circuit Judge, Illinois Circuit Court of Cook County-Ill.
McGuire, Frank L. "Trippy", III-Judge, Covington County District Court-Ala.
McGuire, James C.-Judge, Superior Court of California County of San Bernardino-Calif.
McGuire, John W.-Associate Judge, Illinois Circuit Court Fourth Judicial Circuit-Ill.
McGuire, Joseph D.-Justice, New York Supreme Court Fifth Judicial District-N.Y.
McGuire, Kathleen A.-Associate Justice, New Hampshire Superior Court-N.H.
McGuire, Michael O.-Judge, North Dakota District Court East Central Judicial District-N.D.
McGuire, Scott L.-Magistrate Judge, Kansas District Court Thirtieth Judicial District-Kan.
McGuirk, John K.-Justice, New York Supreme Court Ninth Judicial District-N.Y.
McGuirl, Susan E.-Associate Justice, Rhode Island Superior Court-R.I.
McGunnigle, George F.-Judge, Minnesota District Court Fourth Judicial District-Minn.
McGury, Kathleen M.-Circuit Judge, Illinois Circuit Court of Cook County-Ill.
McHugh, Dennis M.-Associate Judge, Circuit Court for Montgomery County, Sixth Judicial Circuit-Md.
McHugh, James F.-Associate Justice, Massachusetts Appeals Court-Mass.
McHugh, Kenneth R.-Associate Justice, New Hampshire Superior Court-N.H.
McHugh, Peter M.-Emergency Judge, North Carolina Superior Court-N.C.
McIff, K. L.-Presiding Judge, Utah District Court Sixth Judicial District-Utah
McIlvaine, Stephen B.-Judge, Wadsworth Municipal Court-Ohio
McIlwain, William C.-Judge, North Carolina District Court District 16A-N.C.
McIlwrath, Rolleen Kent-Judge, Superior Court of California County of San Joaquin-Calif.
McInerney, Patricia A.-Judge, Pennsylvania Court of Common Pleas First Judicial District-Pa.
McIntosh, Donna L.-Judge, Florida Circuit Court Eighteenth Judicial Circuit-Fla.
McIntosh, Mark A.-Judge, Huntington Circuit Court-Ind.
McIntosh, William M.-Judge, Juvenile Court of Georgia Southern Judicial Circuit-Ga.
McIntyre, Ann-Judge, Winnsboro City Court-La.
McIntyre, Edwin Rudolph, Jr.-Judge, Louisiana District Court Fifth Judicial District-La.
McIntyre, James A.-Associate Justice, California Court of Appeal Fourth District Division One-Calif.
McIntyre, Janice M.-Judge, Superior Court of California County of Riverside-Calif.
McIntyre, Maureen P.-Circuit Judge, Illinois Circuit Court Nineteenth Judicial Circuit-Ill.
McIntyre, Richard D., Sr.-Judge, Lawrence Circuit Court-Ind.
McIntyre, Robert J.-Judge, Superior Court of California County of Riverside-Calif.
McIver, William C.-Judge, Florida Circuit Court Twentieth Judicial Circuit-Fla.
McIvor, Marci B.-Judge, United States Bankruptcy Court Eastern District of Michigan-Mich.
McKathan, M. Ashley-Presiding Judge, Alabama Circuit Court Twenty-second Judicial Circuit-Ala.
McKay, Chesley, Jr.-Judge, Superior Court of California County of Los Angeles-Calif.
McKay, J. D.-Judge, Wisconsin Circuit Court Brown Circuit-Wis.
McKay, James F., III-Judge, Louisiana Court of Appeal Fourth Circuit-La.
McKay, Joseph Kevin-Judge, The Criminal Court of the City of New York-N.Y.
McKay, Monroe G.-Senior Judge, United States Court of Appeals Tenth Circuit
McKay, Patti Jo-Judge, Superior Court of California County of Los Angeles-Calif.
McKay, Walter W.-Judge, Ohio Court of Common Pleas Trumbull County-Ohio
McKeag, Jane Dickson-Judge, United States Bankruptcy Court Eastern District of California-Calif.
McKeague, David W.-Judge, United States District Court Western District of Michigan-Mich.
McKee, Graydon S., III-Associate Judge, Circuit Court for Prince George's County, Seventh Judicial Circuit-Md.
McKee, Harry W. "Peter"-Magistrate Judge, United States District Court Eastern District of Texas-Tex.
McKee, Roger Curtis-Recalled Magistrate Judge, United States District Court Southern District of California-Calif.
McKee, Teresa-Judge, Lander Municipal Court-Wyo.
McKee, Theodore A.-Judge, United States Court of Appeals Third Circuit
McKeeman, Larry E.-Judge, Washington Superior Court Snohomish County-Wash.
McKeithen, Steve-Chief Justice, Texas Court of Appeals Ninth District-Tex.
McKenna, David H.-Judge, Hillsboro Municipal Court-Ohio
McKenna, John Peter-Associate Judge, Maryland District Court District Seven-Md.
McKenna, Lawrence M.-Senior Judge, United States District Court Southern District of New York-N.Y.
McKenna, Robert J., Jr.-First Justice, Trial Court of Massachusetts District Court Department Middlesex County Concord Division and Justice, Suffolk County South Boston Division-Mass.
McKenna, Sabrina-Judge, Hawaii Circuit Court First Judicial Circuit-Hi.
McKenna, Timothy J.-Justice, Haverhill District Court-N.H.
McKenney, Jessie-Justice, Sweet Grass County Justice of the Peace Court and Judge, Big Timber City Court-Mont.
McKenney, Kevin E.-Judge, Superior Court of California County of Santa Clara-Calif.
McKenrick, Gary D.-District Judge, Iowa District Court Seventh Judicial District-Ia.
McKenzie, A. Donald-Retired Judge, New Jersey Superior Court-N.J.
McKenzie, Christopher P.-Judge, Hawaii District Court First Judicial Circuit-Hi.
McKenzie, Franklin C., Jr.-Judge, Mississippi Chancery Court Nineteenth Judicial District-Miss.
McKeon, Douglas E.-Justice, New York Supreme Court Twelfth Judicial District-N.Y.
McKeon, John C.-Judge, Montana District Court Seventeenth Judicial District-Mont.
McKeon, Michael F.-Judge, Auburn City Court-N.Y.
McKeown, M. Margaret-Judge, United States Court of Appeals Ninth Circuit
McKeown, Margaret T. Murphy-Judge, Pennsylvania Court of Common Pleas First Judicial District-Pa.
McKibben, Howard D.-Judge, United States District Court District of Nevada-Nev.
McKillip, Brian R.-Associate Judge, Illinois Circuit Court Eighteenth Judicial Circuit-Ill.
McKimm, William-Judge, Mount Ida District Court-Ark.
McKinley, Bryan H.-District Judge, Iowa District Court Second Judicial District-Ia.
McKinley, Joseph H., Jr.-Judge, United States District Court Western District of Kentucky-Ky.
McKinney, Anne C.-Judge, East Hampton District Probate Court-Conn.
McKinney, Carey G.-Judge, Anderson County Court-Tex.
McKinney, James C.-Administrative Judge, Maryland District Court District Three-Md.
McKinney, Langston C.-Judge, Syracuse City Court-N.Y.
McKinney, Larry J.-Chief Judge, United States District Court Southern District of Indiana-Ind.
McKinnon, Jon-Judge, Bicknell City Court-Ind.
McKinsey, E. Anne-Judge, Minnesota District Court Fourth Judicial District-Minn.
McKinster, Art W.-Associate Justice, California Court of Appeal Fourth District Division Two-Calif.
McKinstry, William A.-Judge, Superior Court of California County of Alameda-Calif.
McKittrick, Thomas M.-Judge, Montana District Court Eighth Judicial District-Mont.
McKnew, Thomas I., Jr.-Judge, Superior Court of California County of Los Angeles-Calif.
McKnight, Charles N.-Judge, Mobile County District Court-Ala.
McKnight, Gail-Judge, Michigan District Court District Eighteen-Mich.
McKnight, H. Brent-Magistrate Judge, United States District Court Western District of North Carolina-N.C.
McKnight, Maureen H.-Judge, Oregon Circuit Court Fourth Judicial District-Ore.
McKoski, Raymond J.-Circuit Judge, Illinois Circuit Court Nineteenth Judicial Circuit-Ill.
McKown, Ann E.-Judge, North Carolina District Court District 14-N.C.
McKoy-Mitchell, Rickye-Judge, North Carolina District Court District 26-N.C.
McLachlan, C. Ian-Judge, Connecticut Appellate Court-Conn.
McLafferty, J. William-Judge, Superior Court of California County of Santa Barbara-Calif.
McLane, H. Arthur-Chief Judge, Superior Court of Georgia Southern Judicial Circuit-Ga.
McLaren, Robert D.-Judge, Illinois Appellate Court Second Judicial District-Ill.
McLauchlin, Philip Ben, Jr.-Presiding Judge, Alabama Circuit Court Thirty-third Judicial Circuit-Ala.

ALPHABETICAL NAME INDEX

McLaughlin, David A.-Associate Justice, Trial Court of Massachusetts Superior Court Department-Mass.

McLaughlin, Dennis J.-Judge, Superior Court of California County of Alameda-Calif.

McLaughlin, Edward Jude-Judge, The Criminal Court of the City of New York-N.Y.

McLaughlin, John A.-Judge, New Jersey Superior Court Vicinage Six-N.J.

McLaughlin, Joseph M.-Senior Judge, United States Court of Appeals Second Circuit

McLaughlin, Mary A.-Judge, United States District Court Eastern District of Pennsylvania-Pa.

McLaughlin, Michael Robert-Judge, Idaho District Court Fourth Judicial District-Ida.

McLaughlin, Sean J.-Judge, United States District Court Western District of Pennsylvania-Pa.

McLaughlin, Thomas P.-Chief Judge, Clare-Gladwin Counties Probate Court District-Mich.

McLean, Edward P.-Judge, Montana District Court Fourth Judicial District-Mont.

McLean, Mitchell L.-Judge, North Carolina District Court District 23-N.C.

McLean, Rod B.-Justice of the Peace, Columbia County Justice Court-Ore.

McLees, William W., Jr.-Judge, North Dakota District Court Northwest Judicial District-N.D.

McLellan, John S., III-Judge, Tennessee Circuit Court Second Judicial District-Tenn.

McLemore, Lucie U.-Judge, Montgomery County District Court-Ala.

McLeod, James A. W.-Judge, Buffalo City Court-N.Y.

McLeod, Maureen A.-Judge, New York City Family Court-N.Y.

McLimans, Paul R.-Judge, Colorado District Court Fourteenth Judicial District-Colo.

McLin, J. C.-Judge, Tennessee Criminal Court Thirtieth Judicial District-Tenn.

McLin, Nancy Chapman-Judge, South Carolina Family Court First Judicial Circuit-S.C.

McLoughlin, John Michael-Associate Judge, Rhode Island District Court-R.I.

McMahon, Colleen-Judge, United States District Court Southern District of New York-N.Y.

McMahon, James W.-Magistrate Judge, United States District Court Central District of California-Calif.

McMahon, Judith N.-Judge, The Civil Court of the City of New York-N.Y.

McMahon, Kevin P.-Judge, Connecticut Superior Court-Conn.

McMahon, Patricia D.-Judge, Wisconsin Circuit Court Milwaukee Circuit-Wis.

McMaken, Michael E.-Judge, Mobile County District Court-Ala.

McManimon, F. Patrick-Judge, New Jersey Superior Court Vicinage Seven-N.J.

McManus, Clarence E.-Judge, Louisiana Court of Appeal Fifth Circuit-La.

McManus, Edward J.-Senior Judge, United States District Court Northern District of Iowa-Ia.

McManus, Michael S.-Chief Judge, United States Bankruptcy Court Eastern District of California-Calif.

McManus, Timothy J.-Judge, Minnesota District Court First Judicial District-Minn.

McMaster, Jean B.-Judge, New Jersey Superior Court Vicinage Fifteen-N.J.

McMaster, Loren E.-Judge, Superior Court of California County of Sacramento-Calif.

McMaster, Russell J.-Judge, Ohio Court of Common Pleas Paulding County-Ohio

McMeans, Walter S.-Judge, Fort Bend County Court at Law No. 2-Tex.

McMenamin, William G.-Associate Judge, Illinois Circuit Court Twelfth Judicial Circuit-Ill.

McMichael, Charles L.-Judge, Cass County Court-Tex.

McMillan, H. W. "Bucky"-Presiding Judge, Alabama Court of Criminal Appeals-Ala.

McMillan, Walter C., Jr.-Chief Judge, Superior Court of Georgia Middle Judicial Circuit-Ga.

McMillen, Alesia A.-Circuit Judge, Illinois Circuit Court Eighth Judicial Circuit-Ill.

McMillen, Phyllis C.-Chief Judge, Michigan District Court District Fifty-one-Mich.

McMillian, Theodore-Judge, United States Court of Appeals Eighth Circuit

McMillin, Roger H., Jr.-Chief Judge, Court of Appeals of Mississippi-Miss.

McMinimee, Gary L.-District Judge, Iowa District Court Second Judicial District-Ia.

McMonagle, Christine T.-Judge, Ohio Court of Common Pleas Cuyahoga County-Ohio

McMonagle, Richard J.-Judge, Ohio Court of Common Pleas Cuyahoga County-Ohio

McMonagle, Timothy E.-Judge, Ohio Court of Appeals Eighth District-Ohio

McMonigal, William M.-Judge, Wisconsin Circuit Court Green Lake Circuit-Wis.

McMorrow, Mary Ann G.-Chief Justice, Supreme Court of Illinois-Ill.

McMullen, John N.-Judge, Colorado District Court Second Judicial District-Colo.

McMurchie, Boyd Leiper-Judge, South Dakota Circuit Court First Judicial Circuit-S.D.

McMurray, William L., Jr.-Senior Judge, Court of Appeals of Georgia-Ga.

McNabb, Kenneth D.-Judge, Hardeman County Court-Tex.

McNally, Colleen A.-Judge, Superior Court of Arizona Maricopa County-Ariz.

McNally, John-Judge, Kansas District Court Twenty-ninth Judicial District-Kan.

McNally, Michael K.-Judge, Michigan District Court District Thirty-three-Mich.

McNamara, A. J.-Senior Judge, United States District Court Eastern District of Louisiana-La.

McNamara, Jeffrey A.-Judge, East Lyme District Probate Court-Conn.

McNamara, Paddy H.-Circuit Judge, Illinois Circuit Court of Cook County-Ill.

McNamara, Thomas J.-Judge, New York Court of Claims-N.Y.

McNamee, Stephen M.-Chief Judge, United States District Court District of Arizona-Ariz.

McNary, Myra Scott-Judge, Pinellas County Court-Fla.

McNatt, Bobby W.-Judge, Superior Court of California County of San Joaquin-Calif.

McNeal, Raymond T.-Judge, Florida Circuit Court Fifth Judicial Circuit-Fla.

McNease, Brenda G.-Judge, Probate Court of Miller County and Chief Magistrate, Magistrate Court of Miller County-Ga.

McNeil, C. B.-Judge, Montana District Court Twentieth Judicial District-Mont.

McNeill, John T., III-Judge, New Jersey Superior Court Vicinage Four-N.J.

McNeill, John Worthy-Judge, Kentucky Circuit Court Nineteenth Judicial Circuit-Ky.

McNerney, Dan-Judge, Superior Court of California County of Orange-Calif.

McNiff, Peter J.-Judge, United States Bankruptcy Court District of Wyoming-Wyo.

McNulty, Jill Kathleen-Judge, Illinois Appellate Court First Judicial District Division One-Ill.

McNulty, Marion T.-Judge, Suffolk County Family Court-N.Y.

McNulty, Michael J.-Judge, Barberton Municipal Court-Ohio

McNutt, Charles P.-Judge, Superior Court of California County of Kern-Calif.

McPeters, Roberta-Judge, Superior Court of California County of San Bernardino-Calif.

McPhail, Michael W.-Judge, Forrest County Court-Miss.

McPhee, Wm. Thomas-Judge, Washington Superior Court Thurston County-Wash.

McPherson, Vanzetta Penn-Magistrate Judge, United States District Court Middle District of Alabama-Ala.

McQuade, Colin J.-Judge, Fulton County Court-Ohio

McQuade, Thomas G.-Judge, Nebraska County Court Fourth Judicial District-Neb.

McQuaid, Robert A., Jr.-Magistrate Judge, United States District Court District of Nevada-Nev.

McQueen, Verna Kay-Magistrate Judge, Kansas District Court Twenty-sixth Judicial District-Kan.

McQuin, R. Scott-Judge, Kansas District Court Thirtieth Judicial District-Kan.

McRae, Carol A.-Judge, Snohomish District Court South Division Snohomish County-Wash.

McRae, Chuck-Presiding Justice, Mississippi Supreme Court-Miss.

McRae, Earl M., Jr.-Judge, State Court of Coffee County-Ga.

McRae, Ferrill David-Judge, Alabama Circuit Court Thirteenth Judicial Circuit-Ala.

McReynolds, Dana R.-Associate Judge, Illinois Circuit Court Fourteenth Judicial Circuit-Ill.

McSeveney, Robert-Judge, Kent Municipal Court-Wash.

McShane, John Q.-Judge, Minnesota District Court Fourth Judicial District-Minn.

McShane, Maura-Circuit Judge, Missouri Circuit Court Twenty-first Judicial Circuit-Mo.

McShane, Michael-Judge, Oregon Circuit Court Fourth Judicial District-Ore.

McSorley, Sandra K.-Judge, Florida Circuit Court Fifteenth Judicial Circuit-Fla.

McSpadden, Michael Thomas-Judge, Texas District Court 209th Judicial District-Tex.

McSwain, Lawrence-Judge, North Carolina District Court District 18-N.C.

McSweeney-Moore, Colleen-Circuit Judge, Illinois Circuit Court of Cook County-Ill.

McSweeny, William F., III-Associate Justice, Trial Court of Massachusetts Probate and Family Court Department Middlesex County Division-Mass.

McSwiney, F. Graham-Justice, New London District Court-N.H.

McVay, Kipling Louise-Judge, Probate Court of Cherokee County-Ga.

McVeigh, Margaret Mary-Judge, New Jersey Superior Court Vicinage Eleven-N.J.

McVerry, Terrence F.-Judge, United States District Court Western District of Pennsylvania-Pa.

McVey, Michael R.-Judge, Superior Court of Arizona Maricopa County-Ariz.

McWaters, Vickie Sue-Chief Magistrate, Magistrate Court of Troup County-Ga.

McWeeny, Michael P.-Chief Judge, Virginia Circuit Court Nineteenth Judicial Circuit-Va.

McWeeny, Robert F.-Judge, Connecticut Superior Court-Conn.

McWhorter, T. Penn-Senior Judge, Superior Court of Georgia-Ga.

McWhorter, Wayne-Judge, Harrison County Court-Tex.

McWhorter, William H., Jr.-Judge, State Court of Emanuel County-Ga.

McWilliams, Robert H.-Senior Judge, United States Court of Appeals Tenth Circuit

Meacham, Clifford L.-Associate Judge, Illinois Circuit Court of Cook County-Ill.

Mead, Andrew-Justice, Maine Superior Court-Me.

Meade, Lesley A.-Judge, Tippecanoe Superior Court-Ind.

Meadow, Frank S.-Judge Referee, Connecticut Superior Court-Conn.

Meadows, E. Richard, Jr.-District Judge, Iowa District Court Eighth Judicial District-Ia.

Meadows, Victoria-Judge, Mason District Court Mason County-Wash.

Meagher, Dermot-Associate Justice, Trial Court of Massachusetts Boston Municipal Court Department-Mass.

Mealey, Thomas F., Jr.-Judge, Wyoming Circuit Court Third Judicial District, Uinta County-Wyo.

Means, Rayford A.-Judge, Pennsylvania Court of Common Pleas First Judicial District-Pa.

Means, Terry R.-Judge, United States District Court Northern District of Texas-Tex.

Means, William T.-Judge, St. Joseph Superior Court-Ind.

Mecca, Daniel P.-Judge, New Jersey Superior Court Vicinage Two-N.J.

Meccariello, Bryan F.-Judge, Southington District Probate Court-Conn.

Medd, Joel Douglas-Judge, North Dakota District Court Northeast Central Judicial District-N.D.

Meddaugh, Mark M.-Judge, Sullivan County Family Court-N.Y.

Medina, Sam-Judge, Texas District Court 237th Judicial District-Tex.

Medler, Mary Ann L.-Magistrate Judge, United States District Court Eastern District of Missouri-Mo.

ALPHABETICAL NAME INDEX

ALPHABETICAL NAME INDEX

Michael, Robert F., Jr.-Senior Judge, Florida Circuit Court Sixth Judicial Circuit-Fla.

Michael, Stephen D.-Judge, Ohio Court of Common Pleas Jackson County-Ohio

Michael, Terrence L.-Judge, Bankruptcy Appellate Panel Tenth Circuit and Judge, United States Bankruptcy Court Northern District of Oklahoma-Okla.

Michael, Wayne L.-Judge, North Carolina District Court District 22-N.C.

Michaelson, Brian L.-Associate Juvenile Judge, Iowa District Court Third Judicial District-Ia.

Michalek, John A.-Justice, New York Supreme Court Eighth Judicial District-N.Y.

Michalik, James E.-Special Justice, Colebrook District Court-N.H.

Michalski, Peter A.-Judge, Alaska Superior Court Third Judicial District-Alas.

Michel, John J.-Judge, Montrose County Court-Colo.

Michel, Paul R.-Judge, United States Court of Appeals Federal Circuit

Michel, Randy-Judge, Brazos County Court at Law No. 1-Tex.

Micheletti, E. Benn-Judge, New Jersey Superior Court Vicinage Nine-N.J.

Michels, Steven L.-Judge, Sunnyside Municipal Court-Wash.

Michot, Patrick L. "Rick"-Judge, Louisiana District Court Fifteenth Judicial District-La.

Mickelsen, Vicki-Judge, Chugwater and Wheatland Municipal Courts-Wyo.

Mickelson, Richard K.-Judge, Oregon Circuit Court Fifteenth Judicial District-Ore.

Mickiewicz, John W.-Reserve Judge, Wisconsin Circuit Court-Wis.

Mickle, Andrew A.-Judge, Municipal Court of Atlanta-Ga.

Mickle, Stephan P.-Judge, United States District Court Northern District of Florida-Fla.

Midcalf, Robin Alfred-Judge, Harrison County Court-Miss.

Middaugh, Laura Gene-Judge, Washington Superior Court King County-Wash.

Middendorff, Dennis-Associate Judge, Illinois Circuit Court Fourth Judicial Circuit-Ill.

Middlebrooks, Donald M.-Judge, United States District Court Southern District of Florida-Fla.

Middlesworth, Charles, Jr.-Judge, New Jersey Superior Court Vicinage One-N.J.

Middleton, Jeffrey C.-Judge, Michigan District Court District Three B-Mich.

Middleton, Kennie E.-Judge, Mississippi Chancery Court Seventeenth Judicial District-Miss.

Middleton, Marie H.-Judge, Probate Court of Long County and Chief Magistrate, Magistrate Court of Long County-Ga.

Midelis, James W.-Judge, St. Lucie County Court-Fla.

Midey, Nicholas V., Jr.-Judge, New York Court of Claims-N.Y.

Midkiff, Sandra C.-Circuit Judge, Missouri Circuit Court Sixteenth Judicial Circuit-Mo.

Midyett, Michael L.-Associate Circuit Judge, Missouri Circuit Court Ninth Judicial Circuit-Mo.

Miech, Robert J.-Reserve Judge, Wisconsin Circuit Court-Wis.

Miel, Charles H.-Chief Judge, Michigan Circuit Court Eighth Judicial Circuit-Mich.

Mignano, Stephen J.-Judge, New York Court of Claims-N.Y.

Mihalakos, Socrates H.-Judge Referee, Connecticut Superior Court-Conn.

Mihara, Nathan D.-Associate Justice, California Court of Appeal Sixth District-Calif.

Mihm, Michael M.-Judge, United States District Court Central District of Illinois-Ill.

Mihok, A. Thomas-Judge, Florida Circuit Court Ninth Judicial Circuit-Fla.

Mihok, Mark-Judge, Lorain Municipal Court-Ohio

Mikell, Charles B., Jr.-Judge, Court of Appeals of Georgia-Ga.

Mikell, Gary L.-Judge, State Court of Bulloch County-Ga.

Mikesic, David P.-Judge, Kansas District Court Twenty-ninth Judicial District-Kan.

Milam, Bobby C.-Senior Judge, Superior Court of Georgia-Ga.

Milam, Joseph Walton, Jr.-Judge, Virginia Circuit Court Twenty-second Judicial Circuit-Va.

Milbourne, B. Bryan-Chief Judge, Virginia Juvenile and Domestic Relations District Court Second Judicial District A-Va.

Miles, Linda-Judge, Superior Court of Arizona Maricopa County-Ariz.

Miles, Marilyn B.-Judge, Superior Court of California County of Humboldt-Calif.

Miles, Susan R.-Judge, Minnesota District Court Tenth Judicial District-Minn.

Miles, Wendell Alverson-Senior Judge, United States District Court Western District of Michigan-Mich.

Miles-LaGrange, Vicki-Judge, United States District Court Western District of Oklahoma-Okla.

Milhouse, Donna R.-Judge, Michigan District Court District Thirty-six-Mich.

Milich, Robert P.-Judge, Youngstown Municipal Court-Ohio

Milks, Marie N.-Judge, Hawaii Circuit Court First Judicial Circuit-Hi.

Millard, E. David-Judge, New Jersey Superior Court Vicinage Three-N.J.

Millard, Lisa-Judge, Texas Family District Court 310th Judicial District-Tex.

Millenky, Robert G.-Judge, New Jersey Superior Court Vicinage Four-N.J.

Miller, Alan R.-Judge, Edgewood Town Court-Ind.

Miller, Barbara J.-Judge, Superior Court of California County of Alameda-Calif.

Miller, Barbara L.-Judge, Kent District Probate Court-Conn.

Miller, Ben J.-Senior Judge, Superior Court of Georgia-Ga.

Miller, Burnett, III-Judge, Virginia General District Court Fourteenth Judicial District-Va.

Miller, Charles M.-Judge, Pennsylvania Court of Common Pleas Twenty-first Judicial District-Pa.

Miller, Christine Odell Cook-Judge, United States Court of Federal Claims

Miller, Clarence A.-Judge, State Court of Worth County-Ga.

Miller, David-Judge, Melbourne District Court-Ark.

Miller, David C.-Judge, Florida Circuit Court Eleventh Judicial Circuit-Fla.

Miller, Donald G.-Judge, Michigan Circuit Court Sixteenth Judicial Circuit-Mich.

Miller, Donna F.-Judge, Lake County Court-Fla.

Miller, Douglas P.-Judge, Superior Court of California County of Riverside-Calif.

Miller, Edward W.-Judge, South Carolina Circuit Court Thirteenth Judicial Circuit-S.C.

Miller, Elijah L., Jr.-Judge, New Jersey Superior Court Vicinage Two-N.J.

Miller, Elizabeth D.-Judge, North Carolina District Court District 26-N.C.

Miller, Eve L.-Judge, Oregon Circuit Court Fifth Judicial District-Ore.

Miller, Franz E.-Judge, Superior Court of California County of Orange-Calif.

Miller, G. David-Judge, Colorado District Court Fourth Judicial District-Colo.

Miller, G. Paul-Judge, Garfield District Court Garfield County-Wash.

Miller, Gary E.-Associate District Judge, Oklahoma District Court Twenty-sixth Judicial District-Okla.

Miller, Gary L.-Judge, Marion Superior Court-Ind.

Miller, Gordon R.-President Judge, Pennsylvania Court of Common Pleas Thirtieth Judicial District-Pa.

Miller, Howard-Associate Justice, New York Supreme Court Appellate Division Second Judicial Department-N.Y.

Miller, Howard S.-Judge, Nassau County District Court-N.Y.

Miller, James Otto-Judge, Wisconsin Circuit Court Columbia Circuit-Wis.

Miller, James S.-Judge, Douglas County Court-Colo.

Miller, Jeffords D.-Judge, Florida Circuit Court Ninth Judicial Circuit-Fla.

Miller, Jeffrey T.-Judge, United States District Court Southern District of California-Calif.

Miller, John A.-Judge, Fircrest Municipal Court-Wash.

Miller, John C.-Judge, Iowa Court of Appeals-Ia.

Miller, John David-Special Judge, Oklahoma District Court Twenty-second Judicial District-Okla.

Miller, John F., Jr.-Judge, Texas District Court 102nd Judicial District-Tex.

Miller, John G.-Associate Circuit Judge, Missouri Circuit Court Fifteenth Judicial Circuit-Mo.

Miller, John Philip-Associate Judge, Circuit Court for Baltimore City, Eighth Judicial Circuit-Md.

Miller, Joseph W.-Magistrate Judge, United States District Court District of Alaska-Alas.

Miller, Karen M.-Judge, Florida Circuit Court Fifteenth Judicial Circuit-Fla.

Miller, Kevin-Judge, Alaska District Court First Judicial District-Alas.

Miller, Lauren Levy-Judge, Florida Circuit Court Twentieth Judicial Circuit-Fla.

Miller, Lawrance S., Jr.-Chief Judge, West Virginia Circuit Court Eighteenth Judicial Circuit-W.Va.

Miller, Leslie Beth-Judge, Superior Court of Arizona Pima County-Ariz.

Miller, Linda Lancet-Judge, Superior Court of California County of Orange-Calif.

Miller, Linda Wallach-Judge, Pennsylvania Court of Common Pleas Forty-third Judicial District-Pa.

Miller, M. Yvette-Judge, Court of Appeals of Georgia-Ga.

Miller, Marvin V.-Judge, Nebraska County Court Fifth Judicial District-Neb.

Miller, Mary E.-Judge, Texas District Court 194th Judicial District-Tex.

Miller, Michael D.-Senior Judge, Florida Circuit Court Fifteenth Judicial Circuit-Fla.

Miller, Michael Owen-Judge, Superior Court of Arizona Pima County-Ariz.

Miller, Nodine-Judge, Ohio Court of Common Pleas Franklin County-Ohio

Miller, Paul E.-Chief Judge, Kansas District Court Twenty-first Judicial District-Kan.

Miller, Perry-Justice, Blaine County Justice of the Peace Court and Judge, Chinook City Court-Mont.

Miller, Peter T.-Judge, Putnam County Court-Fla.

Miller, Phyllis H.-Judge, Tennessee Criminal Court Second Judicial District-Tenn.

Miller, Regan A.-Judge, North Carolina District Court District 26-N.C.

Miller, Richard A.-Associate District Judge, Oklahoma District Court Twentieth Judicial District-Okla.

Miller, Richard W.-Judge, Washington Superior Court Adams County-Wash.

Miller, Rita J.-Judge, Superior Court of California County of Los Angeles-Calif.

Miller, Robert Allen-Judge, Kentucky Circuit Court Forty-sixth Judicial Circuit-Ky.

Miller, Robert E.-Judge, Putnam County Court-N.Y.

Miller, Robert L., Jr.-Chief Judge, United States District Court Northern District of Indiana-Ind.

Miller, Ron-Judge, South Dakota Circuit Court First Judicial Circuit-S.D.

Miller, Rosalind H.-Justice, Trial Court of Massachusetts District Court Department Suffolk County Dorchester Division-Mass.

Miller, Russell C.-Special Judge, Oklahoma District Court Twenty-fourth Judicial District-Okla.

Miller, Sandra-Judge, Juvenile Court of Georgia Paulding Judicial Circuit-Ga.

Miller, Sandra K.-Judge, Delta County Court-Colo.

Miller, Sondra-Associate Justice, New York Supreme Court Appellate Division Second Judicial Department-N.Y.

Miller, Stephen Barry-Judge, Michigan Circuit Court Thirty-seventh Judicial Circuit-Mich.

Miller, Stephen E.-Magistrate Judge, United States District Court Central District of California-Calif.

Miller, Stuart K.-Judge, Wayne County Municipal Court-Ohio

Miller, Tommy E.-Magistrate Judge, United States District Court Eastern District of Virginia-Va.

Miller, Victor L.-Justice of the Peace, Boulder Justices' Court and Judge, Boulder City Municipal Court-Nev.

Miller, W. Michael-Judge, Orange County Court-Fla.

Miller, Walker D.-Judge, United States District Court District of Colorado-Colo.

ALPHABETICAL NAME INDEX

ALPHABETICAL NAME INDEX

Moran, William F.-Judge, Pennsylvania Court of Common Pleas Third Judicial District-Pa.

Morden, Thomas R.-Judge, Idaho District Court Fourth Judicial District Magistrate Division-Ida.

Mordue, Norman A.-Judge, United States District Court Northern District of New York-N.Y.

More, Angus S., Jr.-Associate Judge, Illinois Circuit Court Seventeenth Judicial Circuit-Ill.

Moreau, Stacey W.-Judge, Virginia Juvenile and Domestic Relations District Court Twenty-second Judicial District-Va.

Morehead, A. E., III-Judge, South Carolina Family Court Twelfth Judicial Circuit-S.C.

Moreno, Carlos R.-Associate Justice, California Supreme Court-Calif.

Moreno, Federico A.-Judge, United States District Court Southern District of Florida-Fla.

Moreno, Mark A.-Magistrate Judge, United States District Court District of South Dakota-S.D.

Moreno, Maryann-Judge, Washington Superior Court Spokane County-Wash.

Moreno, Tracy T.-Judge, Superior Court of California County of Los Angeles-Calif.

Morey, Dane F.-Judge, Wisconsin Circuit Court Buffalo-Pepin Circuit-Wis.

Morey, Marcia H.-Judge, North Carolina District Court District 14-N.C.

Morfitt, James C.-Administrative Judge, Idaho District Court Third Judicial District-Ida.

Morgan, C. Cloud-Senior Judge, Superior Court of Georgia-Ga.

Morgan, Clarence E. "Cem", III-Judge, Mississippi Circuit Court Fifth Judicial District-Miss.

Morgan, David C.-Judge, Indian River County Court-Fla.

Morgan, David W.-Judge, New Jersey Superior Court Vicinage Fifteen-N.J.

Morgan, Dorothy-Judge, Washington County Court-Tex.

Morgan, Henry Coke, Jr.-Judge, United States District Court Eastern District of Virginia-Va.

Morgan, Hugh J.-Magistrate Judge, United States District Court Southern District of Florida-Fla.

Morgan, J. Dean-Judge, Washington Court of Appeals Division II-Wash.

Morgan, J. Robert-Judge, Kentucky Circuit Court Thirty-sixth Judicial Circuit-Ky.

Morgan, Jack W.-Judge, Superior Court of California County of Los Angeles-Calif.

Morgan, James E.-Judge, Texas District Court 220th Judicial District-Tex.

Morgan, James W.-Resident Judge, North Carolina Superior Court Seventh Judicial Division District 27B-N.C.

Morgan, Jon B.-Judge, Osceola County Court-Fla.

Morgan, Marilyn-Judge, United States Bankruptcy Court Northern District of California-Calif.

Morgan, Melzer A. "Pat", Jr.-Resident Judge, North Carolina Superior Court Fifth Judicial Division District 17A-N.C.

Morgan, Michael R.-Judge, North Carolina District Court District 10-N.C.

Morgan, Philip R.-Judge, Kentucky District Court Fortieth Judicial District-Ky.

Morgan, Roy B., Jr.-Judge, Tennessee Circuit Court Twenty-sixth Judicial District-Tenn.

Morgan, Virginia M.-Magistrate Judge, United States District Court Eastern District of Michigan-Mich.

Morgan, W. Charles-Judge, Superior Court of California County of Riverside-Calif.

Morgan, William F.-Judge, Pennsylvania Court of Common Pleas Thirty-seventh Judicial District-Pa.

Morgenstern, Esther M.-Judge, The Civil Court of the City of New York-N.Y.

Morgenstern-Clarren, Pat E.-Judge, United States Bankruptcy Court Northern District of Ohio-Ohio

Mori, Richard A.-First Justice, Trial Court of Massachusetts District Court Department Essex County Gloucester Division and Justice, Middlesex County Malden Division-Mass.

Moriarty, Diane E.-Justice, Trial Court of Massachusetts District Court Department Plymouth County Wareham Division-Mass.

Moriarty, Elaine M.-Associate Justice, Trial Court of Massachusetts Probate and Family Court Department Suffolk County Division-Mass.

Moriarty, Joan L.-Circuit Judge, Missouri Circuit Court Twenty-second Judicial Circuit-Mo.

Morin, Bruce Q.-Associate Judge, Rhode Island Workers' Compensation Court-R.I.

Morin, Robert E.-Associate Judge, Superior Court of the District of Columbia-D.C.

Morinello, Angelo J.-Judge, Niagara Falls City Court-N.Y.

Moroney, Dennis P.-Judge, Wisconsin Circuit Court Milwaukee Circuit-Wis.

Morrill, Robert E. K.-Associate Justice, New Hampshire Superior Court-N.H.

Morris, Barney L.-Judge, Clarendon County Probate Court-S.C.

Morris, Carl W.-Judge, Superior Court of California County of Alameda-Calif.

Morris, Cecelia G.-Judge, United States Bankruptcy Court Southern District of New York-N.Y.

Morris, Elizabeth A.-Judge, Putnam County Court-Fla.

Morris, Geoffrey P.-Judge, Kentucky Circuit Court Thirtieth Judicial Circuit-Ky.

Morris, James B.-Judge, Ripley Superior Court-Ind.

Morris, James I.-Judge, Superior Court of California County of Sacramento-Calif.

Morris, Joan T.-Judge, Virginia General District Court Seventh Judicial District-Va.

Morris, John-Judge, Cooke County Court at Law-Tex.

Morris, Joseph B.-Justice, Texas Court of Appeals Fifth District-Tex.

Morris, Judson W., Jr.-Judge, Superior Court of California County of Los Angeles-Calif.

Morris, M. Cindy-Judge, Superior Court of Georgia Conasauga Judicial Circuit-Ga.

Morris, Melinda-Judge, Michigan Circuit Court Twenty-second Judicial Circuit-Mich.

Morris, Patrick Joseph-Judge, Superior Court of California County of San Bernardino-Calif.

Morris, Phillip M.-Judge, Superior Court of California County of San Bernardino-Calif.

Morris, Rick-Judge, Texas District Court 146th Judicial District-Tex.

Morris, Robert J., Jr.-Judge, Florida Circuit Court Sixth Judicial Circuit-Fla.

Morris, S. Lee-Chief Judge, Virginia General District Court Third Judicial District-Va.

Morris, Stan R.-Chief Judge, Florida Circuit Court Eighth Judicial Circuit-Fla.

Morris, Thomas E.-Magistrate Judge, United States District Court Middle District of Florida-Fla.

Morris, Walter M., Jr.-Judge, Vermont Trial Court-Vt.

Morrison, Dan F.-District Judge, Iowa District Court Eighth Judicial District-Ia.

Morrison, Fred K.-Associate Justice, California Court of Appeal Third District-Calif.

Morrison, John C., Jr.-Judge, Virginia Circuit Court Fourth Judicial Circuit-Va.

Morrison, Johnny E.-Judge, Virginia Circuit Court Third Judicial Circuit-Va.

Morrison, Norman deVere-Judge, Virginia General District Court Twenty-sixth Judicial District-Va.

Morrison, Robert H., III-Judge, Louisiana District Court Twenty-first Judicial District-La.

Morrison, Stephen M.-Special Justice, Dover District Court-N.H.

Morrison, Truman A., III-Senior Judge, Superior Court of the District of Columbia-D.C.

Morriss, Josh R., III-Chief Justice, Texas Court of Appeals Sixth District-Tex.

Morrissey, Dennis J.-Circuit Judge, Illinois Circuit Court of Cook County-Ill.

Morrissey, George M.-Associate Judge, Illinois Circuit Court of Cook County-Ill.

Morrissey, J. David-Judge, Farmington District Probate Court-Conn.

Morrissey, John Emmett-Circuit Judge, Illinois Circuit Court of Cook County-Ill.

Morrissey, Linda G.-District Judge, Oklahoma District Court Fourteenth Judicial District-Okla.

Morrissey, Michael A.-Judge, Tippecanoe Superior Court-Ind.

Morrow, Bruce U.-Judge, Michigan Circuit Court Third Judicial Circuit-Mich.

Morrow, James A.-Judge, Minnesota District Court Tenth Judicial District-Minn.

Morrow, Margaret M.-Judge, United States District Court Central District of California-Calif.

Morrow, William C.-Judge, Midland County Court-Tex.

Morse, Heather D.-Judge, Superior Court of California County of Santa Cruz-Calif.

Morse, J. Patrick-Associate Judge, Illinois Circuit Court of Cook County-Ill.

Morse, John E., Jr.-Judge, Superior Court of Georgia Eastern Judicial Circuit-Ga.

Morse, Patricia A.-Judge, Michigan District Court District Eighty-seven-Mich.

Morse, Thomas Rainbow-Judge, Rochester City Court-N.Y.

Morse, William-Judge, Alaska Superior Court Third Judicial District-Alas.

Mortimer, Wendell, Jr.-Judge, Superior Court of California County of Los Angeles-Calif.

Morton, Douglas B.-Judge, Fulton Circuit Court-Ind.

Morton, J. Bruce-Retired-Recalled Judge, North Carolina District Court-N.C.

Morton, Natasha J.-Justice, Big Horn County Justice of the Peace Court-Mont.

Morton, Roger L.-Chief Judge, Virginia General District Court Sixteenth Judicial District-Va.

Moruza, Christine K.-Judge, Superior Court of California County of Alameda-Calif.

Morvant, William A.-Judge, Louisiana District Court Nineteenth Judicial District-La.

Mosby, J. Leyburn, Jr.-Chief Judge, Virginia Circuit Court Twenty-fourth Judicial Circuit-Va.

Moscone, Philip J.-Judge, Superior Court of California City and County of San Francisco-Calif.

Moseley, James A.-Justice, Texas Court of Appeals Fifth District-Tex.

Moseley, Thomas E.-Chief Magistrate, Magistrate Court of Bartow County-Ga.

Mosely, John D., Jr.-Judge, Louisiana District Court First Judicial District-La.

Moser, Adam H.-Judge, Nassau County District Court-N.Y.

Moses, Richard T.-Associate Justice, Trial Court of Massachusetts Superior Court Department-Mass.

Moses, Sybil R.-Assignment Judge, New Jersey Superior Court Vicinage Two-N.J.

Mosk, Richard M.-Associate Justice, California Court of Appeal Second District Division Five-Calif.

Moskowitz, Barry Ted-Judge, United States District Court Southern District of California-Calif.

Moskowitz, Karla-Justice, New York Supreme Court First Judicial District-N.Y.

Moskwa, Pamela A.-Chief Judge, Monroe County Probate Court-Mich.

Mosley, Donald M.-Judge, Nevada District Court Eighth Judicial District-Nev.

Moss, Brent J.-Judge, Idaho District Court Seventh Judicial District-Ida.

Moss, Cheryl B.-Judge, Nevada District Court Eighth Judicial District-Nev.

Moss, Lee D.-Judge, Probate Court of Lincoln County and Chief Magistrate, Magistrate Court of Lincoln County-Ga.

Moss, Robert James-Judge, Superior Court of California County of Orange-Calif.

Moss, Sandra Mazer-Judge, Pennsylvania Court of Common Pleas First Judicial District-Pa.

Moss, Sheila Marie-Judge, Lake Superior Court-Ind.

Mossey, Dale E.-Judge, Minnesota District Court Tenth Judicial District-Minn.

Motes, T. David-Judge, Superior Court of Georgia Piedmont Judicial Circuit-Ga.

Motheral, Linda-Judge, Texas District Court 257th Judicial District-Tex.

Motley, Constance Baker-Senior Judge, United States District Court Southern District of New York-N.Y.

Motley, Thomas J.-Associate Judge, Superior Court of the District of Columbia-D.C.

Mott, J. Thomas-Judge, Minnesota District Court Second Judicial District-Minn.

ALPHABETICAL NAME INDEX

ALPHABETICAL NAME INDEX

Murphy, Lisa Ruble-Circuit Judge, Illinois Circuit Court of Cook County-Ill.
Murphy, Margaret H.-Judge, United States Bankruptcy Court Northern District of Georgia-Ga.
Murphy, Mark H.-Judge, Juvenile Court of Georgia Tallapoosa Judicial Circuit-Ga.
Murphy, Martin P.-Judge, New York City Family Court-N.Y.
Murphy, Mary-Judge, Texas District Court 14th Judicial District-Tex.
Murphy, Mary Ann-Judge, Superior Court of California County of Los Angeles-Calif.
Murphy, Michael B.-Judge, Ohio Court of Common Pleas Montgomery County-Ohio
Murphy, Michael J.-Circuit Judge, Illinois Circuit Court of Cook County-Ill.
Murphy, Michael L.-Chief Judge, Superior Court of Georgia Tallapoosa Judicial Circuit-Ga.
Murphy, Michael R.-Judge, United States Court of Appeals Tenth Circuit
Murphy, Paul S.-Circuit Judge, Illinois Circuit Court First Judicial Circuit-Ill.
Murphy, Robert C.-Judge, Binghamton City Court-N.Y.
Murphy, Robert M.-Judge, Louisiana District Court Twenty-fourth Judicial District-La.
Murphy, Robert M., Jr.-Associate District Judge, Oklahoma District Court Ninth Judicial District-Okla.
Murphy, Roger P.-Reserve Judge, Wisconsin Circuit Court-Wis.
Murphy, Sigurd E.-Judge, Alaska District Court Third Judicial District-Alas.
Murphy, Stephen-Judge, Taylor County Court-Fla.
Murphy, Thomas J.-Justice, New York Supreme Court Fifth Judicial District-N.Y.
Murphy, Thomas M.-Judge, Minnesota District Court First Judicial District-Minn.
Murphy, Tim-Senior Judge, Superior Court of the District of Columbia-D.C.
Murphy, Timothy D.-Associate Judge, Maryland District Court District One-Md.
Murphy, Vincent-Judge, Collier County Court-Fla.
Murphy, Walter L.-Chief Justice, New Hampshire Superior Court-N.H.
Murphy, William B.-Judge, Michigan Court of Appeals-Mich.
Murphy, William C.-Judge, Granger and Union Gap Municipal Courts-Wash.
Murphy Gorman, Joyce Marie-Circuit Judge, Illinois Circuit Court of Cook County-Ill.
Murrah, Watt-Judge, Medina County Court at Law-Tex.
Murray, Ann M.-Judge, Maine District Court-Me.
Murray, Bryan K.-Judge, Idaho District Court Sixth Judicial District Magistrate Division-Ida.
Murray, Christopher M.-Judge, Michigan Court of Appeals-Mich.
Murray, Clarence D.-Judge, Lake Superior Court-Ind.
Murray, Dana Elizabeth-Judge, Arapahoe County Court-Colo.
Murray, Dennis E.-Judge, Superior Court of California County of Tehama-Calif.
Murray, Francis J., Jr.-Associate Justice, Rhode Island Family Court-R.I.
Murray, George C., Jr.-Judge, Vidalia City Court-La.
Murray, Lynn-Judge, Howard Circuit Court-Ind.
Murray, Marshall B.-Judge, Wisconsin Circuit Court Milwaukee Circuit-Wis.
Murray, Menton, Jr.-Judge, Texas District Court 103rd Judicial District-Tex.
Murray, Michael J.-Associate Judge, Illinois Circuit Court of Cook County-Ill.
Murray, Patricia Rivet-Judge, Louisiana Court of Appeal Fourth Circuit-La.
Murray, Robert F.-First Justice, Trial Court of Massachusetts Juvenile Court Department Plymouth County Division-Mass.
Murray, Walter A., Jr.-Associate Circuit Judge, Missouri Circuit Court Twentieth Judicial Circuit-Mo.
Murray, William J., Jr.-Judge, Superior Court of California County of San Joaquin-Calif.
Murray, William P.-Judge, Connecticut Superior Court-Conn.
Murtha, J. Garvan-Judge, United States District Court District of Vermont-Vt.
Muse, Christopher J.-Associate Justice, Trial Court of Massachusetts Superior Court Department-Mass.
Muse, Elliott, Jr.-Circuit Judge, Illinois Circuit Court of Cook County-Ill.
Musgrave, R. Kenton-Senior Judge, United States Court of International Trade
Musleh, Victor J.-Chief Judge, Florida Circuit Court Fifth Judicial Circuit-Fla.
Musmanno, John L.-Judge, The Superior Court of Pennsylvania-Pa.
Musson, John R.-Judge, Elyria Municipal Court-Ohio
Mutter, John A.-Associate Justice, Rhode Island Family Court-R.I.
Myers, Deanne Smith-Judge, Superior Court of California County of Los Angeles-Calif.
Myers, Eric Renard-Judge, Hillsborough County Court-Fla.
Myers, H. Dennis-Judge, Superior Court of California County of Riverside-Calif.
Myers, Jimmy Laird-Judge, North Carolina District Court District 22-N.C.
Myers, Louis Keith-Judge, Kentucky District Court Fifty-ninth Judicial District-Ky.
Myers, Marion D.-Judge, South Carolina Family Court Third Judicial Circuit-S.C.
Myers, Terry L.-Judge, United States Bankruptcy Court District of Idaho-Ida.
Myers, William H.-Judge, Court of Appeals of Mississippi-Miss.
Myerscough, Sue E.-Judge, Illinois Appellate Court Fourth Judicial District-Ill.
Myles, Lonny A.-Judge, Zachary City Court-La.
Myles, Raymond-Associate Judge, Illinois Circuit Court of Cook County-Ill.
Myles, William F.-Judge, Michigan Circuit Court Twenty-third Judicial Circuit-Mich.
Mylrea, Jane M.-Associate Juvenile Judge, Iowa District Court First Judicial District-Ia.
Myse, Gordon-Reserve Judge, Wisconsin Circuit Court-Wis.
Nachbar, Keith-Judge, Casper Municipal Court-Wyo.
Nachman, Bernard-Judge, Florida Circuit Court Fourth Judicial Circuit-Fla.
Nachtigal, Gayle-Judge, Oregon Circuit Court Twentieth Judicial District-Ore.
Nadeau, Gilbert J., Jr.-First Justice, Trial Court of Massachusetts District Court Department Bristol County Fall River Division-Mass.
Nadeau, Joseph P.-Associate Justice, New Hampshire Supreme Court-N.H.
Nadeau, Thomas L.-Judge, Connecticut Superior Court-Conn.
Nadeau, Tina L.-Associate Justice, New Hampshire Superior Court-N.H.
Nadel, Norbert A.-Judge, Ohio Court of Common Pleas Hamilton County-Ohio
Nadel, S. Michael-Judge, New York Court of Claims-N.Y.
Nadelson, Eileen N.-Judge, The Civil Court of the City of New York-N.Y.
Nadler, Gary-Judge, Superior Court of California County of Sonoma-Calif.
Nadler, Jerome S.-Judge, Superior Court of California County of Santa Clara-Calif.
Nafziger, Gary L.-Judge, Kansas District Court Second Judicial District-Kan.
Nagata, Russel S.-Judge, Hawaii District Court First Judicial Circuit-Hi.
Nagle, David G., Jr.-First Justice, Trial Court of Massachusetts District Court Department Plymouth County Brockton Division-Mass.
Nagle, Margaret A.-Magistrate Judge, United States District Court Central District of California-Calif.
Nahman, Robert L.-Surrogate, Queens County Surrogate's Court-N.Y.
Nahra, John A.-Chief Judge, Iowa District Court Seventh Judicial District-Ia.
Nail, Michael E.-Judge, Superior Court of California County of Solano-Calif.
Nail, Tommy-Judge, Alabama Circuit Court Tenth Judicial Circuit Birmingham Division-Ala.
Naiser, Lawrence E.-Judge, Wharton County Court-Tex.
Najam, Edward W., Jr.-Presiding Judge, Indiana Court of Appeals First District-Ind.
Najemy, Jan L.-First Justice, Trial Court of Massachusetts Juvenile Court Department Worcester Division-Mass.
Nakahara, Vernon K.-Judge, Superior Court of California County of Alameda-Calif.
Nakamura, Greg-Judge, Hawaii Circuit Court Third Judicial Circuit-Hi.
Nakamura, Kirk H.-Judge, Superior Court of California County of Orange-Calif.
Nakata, Alicia H.-Judge, Chelan District Court Chelan County-Wash.
Nakata, Eric M.-Judge, Superior Court of California County of San Bernardino-Calif.
Nakayama, Paula A.-Associate Justice, Hawaii Supreme Court-Hi.
Nakazato, Arthur-Magistrate Judge, United States District Court Central District of California-Calif.
Nakea, Clifford L.-Judge, Hawaii Circuit Court Fifth Judicial Circuit-Hi.
Nalitz, William R.-Judge, Pennsylvania Court of Common Pleas Thirteenth Judicial District-Pa.
Nall, Rayburn M. "Rim", Jr.-Judge, Texas District Court 59th Judicial District-Tex.
Nalley, Robert C.-Associate Judge, Circuit Court for Charles County, Seventh Judicial Circuit-Md.
Nancarrow, Mark-Judge, Texas District Court 204th Judicial District-Tex.
Nance, Alfred-Associate Judge, Circuit Court for Baltimore City, Eighth Judicial Circuit-Md.
Nance, Wayne-Judge, Briscoe County Court-Tex.
Nance, William Mitchell-Judge, Kentucky Circuit Court Forty-third Judicial Circuit-Ky.
Nance Adams, Lydia-Judge, Michigan District Court District Thirty-six-Mich.
Nanovic, Roger N.-Judge, Pennsylvania Court of Common Pleas Fifty-sixth Judicial District-Pa.
Napoli, H. Jequita-Special Judge, Oklahoma District Court Twenty-first Judicial District-Okla.
Naranjo, Orlinda L.-Judge, Travis County Court at Law No. 2-Tex.
Naranjo, Richard-Judge, Superior Court of California County of Los Angeles-Calif.
Nardelli, Eugene L.-Associate Justice, New York Supreme Court Appellate Division First Judicial Department-N.Y.
Nardi, Frank Mattioda-Judge, Owen Circuit Court-Ind.
Nardi, Joseph M., Jr.-Retired Judge, New Jersey Superior Court-N.J.
Nardulli, Steven H.-Associate Judge, Illinois Circuit Court Seventh Judicial Circuit-Ill.
Nares, Gilbert-Associate Justice, California Court of Appeal Fourth District Division One-Calif.
Narsutis, John Keith-Judge, Texas District Court 16th Judicial District-Tex.
Nash, Lloyd M.-Judge, Superior Court of California County of Los Angeles-Calif.
Nash, Michael-Judge, Superior Court of California County of Los Angeles-Calif.
Nash, Nan-Judge, New Mexico District Court Second Judicial District-N.Mex.
Nash, Robin S.-Judge, Juvenile Court of Georgia Stone Mountain Judicial Circuit-Ga.
Nash, Steven M.-Associate Judge, Illinois Circuit Court Seventeenth Judicial Circuit-Ill.
Nasif, Kenneth P.-Associate Justice, Trial Court of Massachusetts Juvenile Court Department Bristol County Division-Mass.
Nastasi, Aldo A.-Justice, New York Supreme Court Ninth Judicial District-N.Y.
Natal, Samuel D.-Judge, New Jersey Superior Court Vicinage Four-N.J.
Nathanson, Rosanne-Judge, Minnesota District Court Second Judicial District-Minn.
Nation, Beverly W.-Judge, Probate Court of Oglethorpe County-Ga.
Nation, Sidney L.-Chief Judge, Superior Court of Georgia Rockdale Judicial Circuit-Ga.
Nation, Steven R.-Judge, Hamilton Superior Court-Ind.
Nau, Denise-Judge, Wyoming Circuit Court First Judicial District, Laramie County-Wyo.
Nau, John W.-Judge, Ohio Court of Common Pleas Noble County-Ohio

ALPHABETICAL NAME INDEX

Naughton, Michael J.-Judge, Superior Court of California County of Orange-Calif.
Naugle, David N.-Judge, United States Bankruptcy Court Central District of California-Calif.
Nauhaus, Lester G.-Judge, Pennsylvania Court of Common Pleas Fifth Judicial District-Pa.
Nault, Peter-Judge, King District Court East Division King County-Wash.
Naus, Scott W.-President Judge, Pennsylvania Court of Common Pleas Twenty-sixth Judicial District-Pa.
Navarro, Rene-Judge, Superior Court of California County of Santa Clara-Calif.
Naves, Larry J.-Judge, Colorado District Court Second Judicial District-Colo.
Naville, Michael G.-Magistrate Judge, United States District Court Southern District of Indiana-Ind.
Nazaretian, Nick-Judge, Hillsborough County Court-Fla.
Naze, Peter Joseph-Judge, Wisconsin Circuit Court Brown Circuit-Wis.
Neal, Curtis J.-Judge, Florida Circuit Court Fifth Judicial Circuit-Fla.
Neal, Olly-Judge, Arkansas Court of Appeals-Ark.
Neal, Vernon-Chancellor, Tennessee Chancery Court Thirteenth Judicial District-Tenn.
Nealis, Paul J.-Associate Judge, Illinois Circuit Court of Cook County-Ill.
Nealon, Terrence R.-Judge, Pennsylvania Court of Common Pleas Forty-fifth Judicial District-Pa.
Nealon, William J., Jr.-Senior Judge, United States District Court Middle District of Pennsylvania-Pa.
Neary, Jeffrey A.-District Judge, Iowa District Court Third Judicial District-Ia.
Neaves, Charles M., Jr.-Judge, North Carolina District Court District 17B-N.C.
Nebeker, Frank Q.-Senior Judge, District of Columbia Court of Appeals-D.C.
Nechtem, Amy L.-Associate Justice, Trial Court of Massachusetts Juvenile Court Department Middlesex County Division-Mass.
Neddenriep, Gary-Associate Judge, Illinois Circuit Court Nineteenth Judicial Circuit-Ill.
Needham, Henry E., Jr.-Judge, Superior Court of California County of Alameda-Calif.
Needham, Scott R.-Judge, Wisconsin Circuit Court St. Croix Circuit-Wis.
Neel, Stephen E.-Associate Justice, Trial Court of Massachusetts Superior Court Department-Mass.
Neely, Cecil N.-Judge, Madison County Court-Tex.
Neely, Ruth-Judge, Pinedale Municipal Court-Wyo.
Neely, Tom A.-Judge, Texas District Court 46th Judicial District-Tex.
Neely, William M.-Chief Judge, North Carolina District Court District 19B-N.C.
Neese, Donald R.-Justice, Custer County Justice of the Peace Court-Mont.
Neff, Janet T.-Judge, Michigan Court of Appeals-Mich.
Nega, Marya-Circuit Judge, Illinois Circuit Court of Cook County-Ill.
Nehring, Ronald E.-Justice, Utah Supreme Court-Utah
Neidorf, Richard-Judge, Superior Court of California County of Los Angeles-Calif.
Neiles, Joseph-Judge, South Dakota Circuit Court Second Judicial Circuit-S.D.
Neill, John Edward-Judge, Texas District Court 18th Judicial District-Tex.
Neill, Kenneth R.-Judge, Montana District Court Eighth Judicial District-Mont.
Neill, Margaret M.-Circuit Judge, Missouri Circuit Court Twenty-second Judicial Circuit-Mo.
Neill, Mark H.-Circuit Judge, Missouri Circuit Court Twenty-second Judicial Circuit-Mo.
Neilson, George W.-Presiding Judge, Oregon Circuit Court Twenty-second Judicial District-Ore.
Neilson, Susan Bieke-Judge, Michigan Circuit Court Third Judicial Circuit-Mich.
Neiman, Kenneth P.-Magistrate Judge, United States District Court District of Massachusetts-Mass.
Neithercut, Geoffrey L.-Judge, Michigan Circuit Court Seventh Judicial Circuit-Mich.
Nellermoe, Barbara Hanson-Judge, Texas District Court 45th Judicial District-Tex.
Nelms, John-Judge, Texas District Court 195th Judicial District-Tex.
Nelsen, Carol-Justice of the Peace, Lake Justices' Court-Nev.
Nelson, Allen J.-Chief Judge, Genesee County Probate Court-Mich.
Nelson, Charles A.-Chief Judge, Michigan Circuit Court Fourth Judicial Circuit-Mich.
Nelson, Charles E.-Chief Magistrate, Magistrate Court of Dodge County-Ga.
Nelson, David Aldrich-Senior Judge, United States Court of Appeals Sixth Circuit
Nelson, David W.-Judge, North Dakota District Court Northwest Judicial District-N.D.
Nelson, Debra Steinberg-Judge, Florida Circuit Court Eighteenth Judicial Circuit-Fla.
Nelson, Dorothy Wright-Senior Judge, United States Court of Appeals Ninth Circuit
Nelson, Edwin L.-Judge, United States District Court Northern District of Alabama-Ala.
Nelson, Forrest D.-Special Judge, Oklahoma District Court Fifteenth Judicial District-Okla.
Nelson, Frank B.-District Judge, Iowa District Court Third Judicial District-Ia.
Nelson, Frederick Dickson-Judge, Ohio Court of Common Pleas Hamilton County-Ohio
Nelson, G. Carey-Judge, Superior Court of Georgia Cherokee Judicial Circuit-Ga.
Nelson, Henry Kent-Judge, Superior Court of California County of Mendocino-Calif.
Nelson, Hugh F.-Reserve Judge, Wisconsin Circuit Court-Wis.
Nelson, James C.-Justice, Montana Supreme Court-Mont.
Nelson, James T.-Senior Judge, Florida Circuit Court Seventh Judicial Circuit-Fla.
Nelson, John N.-Judge, Superior Court of Arizona Yuma County-Ariz.
Nelson, Kathleen-Judge, Utah Juvenile Court Second Judicial District-Utah
Nelson, Kathryn J.-Judge, Washington Superior Court Pierce County-Wash.
Nelson, Mark G., Sr.-Judge, Superior Court of California County of Los Angeles-Calif.
Nelson, Mark J.-Judge, New Jersey Superior Court Vicinage Six-N.J.
Nelson, Michael C.-Presiding Judge, Superior Court of Arizona Apache County-Ariz.
Nelson, Michael J.-Judge, New Jersey Superior Court Vicinage Five-N.J.
Nelson, Paul A.-Judge, Minnesota District Court Eighth Judicial District-Minn.
Nelson, Peggy J.-Chief Judge, New Mexico District Court Eighth Judicial District-N.Mex.
Nelson, Philip L.-Judge, Oregon Circuit Court Eighteenth Judicial District-Ore.
Nelson, Rodney E.-Judge, Superior Court of California County of Los Angeles-Calif.
Nelson, S. Anderson-Judge, Virginia Juvenile and Domestic Relations District Court Tenth Judicial District-Va.
Nelson, Sheila M.-Justice of the Peace, Lane County Justice Court-Ore.
Nelson, Susan Richard-Magistrate Judge, United States District Court District of Minnesota-Minn.
Nelson, Thomas E.-Judge, Berrien County Probate Court-Mich.
Nelson, Thomas G.-Judge, United States Court of Appeals Ninth Circuit
Nelson, Valerie Brathwaite-Judge, The Civil Court of the City of New York-N.Y.
Nelson, William J.-Judge, Marion Superior Court-Ind.
Nelson, William John-Judge, Florida Circuit Court Twentieth Judicial Circuit-Fla.
Nelson, William K.-Judge, Rockland County Court-N.Y.
Nemenoff, Brian Mark-Associate Judge, Illinois Circuit Court Tenth Judicial Circuit-Ill.
Nemeth, Peter J.-Judge, St. Joseph Probate Court-Ind.
Nemoyer, Edgar Carroll-Judge, New York Court of Claims-N.Y.
Nemoyer, Patrick H.-Justice, New York Supreme Court Eighth Judicial District-N.Y.
Nenno, Michael L.-Judge, Cattaraugus County Court-N.Y.
Nesbitt, B. Woodrow, Jr.-Judge, Louisiana District Court First Judicial District-La.
Nesbitt, John B.-Judge, Wayne County Court-N.Y.
Nesbitt, Joseph-Senior Judge, Florida District Court of Appeal-Fla.
Nesi, Anthony R.-Associate Justice, Trial Court of Massachusetts Probate and Family Court Department Bristol County Division-Mass.
Nethery, Barbara J.-Justice of the Peace, Carlin Justices' Court and Judge, Carlin Municipal Court-Nev.
Nettesheim, Neal P.-Presiding Judge, Wisconsin Court of Appeals District Two-Wis.
Nettles-Nickerson, Beverley-Judge, Michigan Circuit Court Thirtieth Judicial Circuit-Mich.
Neufeld, Gerald C.-Presiding Judge, Oregon Circuit Court Fourteenth Judicial District-Ore.
Neuman, Linda K.-Justice, Iowa Supreme Court-Ia.
Neumann, William A.-Justice, North Dakota Supreme Court-N.D.
Neustadter, Robert-Retired Judge, New Jersey Superior Court-N.J.
Nevas, Alan H.-Senior Judge, United States District Court District of Connecticut-Conn.
Neville, Cara Lee-Judge, Minnesota District Court Fourth Judicial District-Minn.
Neville, M. Francis-Judge, Alaska District Court Third Judicial District-Alas.
Neville, P. Scott, Jr.-Circuit Judge, Illinois Circuit Court of Cook County-Ill.
Neville, Thomas F.-Judge, Idaho District Court Fourth Judicial District-Ida.
Neville, William J.-Senior Judge, Superior Court of Georgia-Ga.
Nevin, Jack F.-Judge, Pierce District Court Pierce County-Wash.
Nevitt, William R., Jr.-Judge, Superior Court of California County of San Diego-Calif.
Nevius, Eugene S.-Judge, Clark County Municipal Court-Ohio
New, Arnold L.-Judge, Pennsylvania Court of Common Pleas First Judicial District-Pa.
Newbern, Thomas R. J.-Judge, North Carolina District Court District 6B-N.C.
Newbold, Edmund W.-Senior Judge, Florida Circuit Court Eleventh Judicial Circuit-Fla.
Newcombe, Scott J.-Judge, Michigan District Court District Seventy-four-Mich.
Newcomer, Clarence C.-Senior Judge, United States District Court Eastern District of Pennsylvania-Pa.
Newell, Peter B.-District Associate Judge, Iowa District Court Second Judicial District-Ia.
Newkirk, Frank, Jr.-Judge, Washington Superior Court-Ind.
Newkirk, Henry M.-Judge, State Court of Fulton County-Ga.
Newlin, John C.-Judge, Ohio Court of Common Pleas Champaign County-Ohio
Newman, Barbara F.-Judge, The Criminal Court of the City of New York-N.Y.
Newman, Clifton-Judge-at-Large, South Carolina Circuit Court-S.C.
Newman, Edward H.-Magistrate, Rhode Island Family Court-R.I.
Newman, Edward K.-Judge, Dade County Court-Fla.
Newman, Jon O.-Senior Judge, United States Court of Appeals Second Circuit
Newman, Mark-Associate Justice, Trial Court of Massachusetts Juvenile Court Department Essex County Division-Mass.
Newman, Pauline-Judge, United States Court of Appeals Federal Circuit
Newman, Richard-Judge, New Jersey Superior Court Appellate Division-N.J.
Newman, Robert H.-Senior Judge, Florida Circuit Court Eleventh Judicial Circuit-Fla.
Newman, Sandra Schultz-Justice, The Supreme Court of Pennsylvania-Pa.
Newman, Theodore R., Jr.-Senior Judge, District of Columbia Court of Appeals-D.C.
Newman, Thomas, Jr.-Judge, Madison Superior Court-Ind.

ALPHABETICAL NAME INDEX

Newman, Wanda-Judge, Diamondville Municipal Court-Wyo.
Newman, William T., Jr.-Judge, Virginia Circuit Court Seventeenth Judicial Circuit-Va.
Newmeister, Michael J.-District Associate Judge, Iowa District Court Sixth Judicial District-Ia.
Newnam, George A.-Judge, Colorado District Court Third Judicial District-Colo.
Newsom, Robert E.-Judge, Texas District Court 8th Judicial District-Tex.
Newsome, Randall J.-Judge, United States Bankruptcy Court Northern District of California-Calif.
Newton, Arnaud-Judge, Colorado District Court Eighth Judicial District-Colo.
Newton, Dewey A.-Justice of the Peace, Harney County Justice Court-Ore.
Newton, Fred-Presiding Judge, Superior Court of Arizona Coconino County-Ariz.
Newton, Martha D.-Judge, Anderson County Probate Court-S.C.
Newton, Ronald L.-Chief Magistrate, Magistrate Court of Fannin County-Ga.
Newton, Thomas H.-Judge, Missouri Court of Appeals Western District-Mo.
Ney, Peter H.-Judge, Colorado Court of Appeals-Colo.
Ney, R. Terrence-Judge, Virginia Circuit Court Nineteenth Judicial Circuit-Va.
Nguyen, Jacqueline H.-Judge, Superior Court of California County of Los Angeles-Calif.
Nguyen, Nho Trong-Judge, Superior Court of California County of Orange-Calif.
Nibert, David-Chief Judge, West Virginia Circuit Court Fifth Judicial Circuit-W.Va.
Nibert, Deloris J.-Judge, West Virginia Family Court Circuit Five-W.Va.
Nicandri, Eugene L.-Judge, St. Lawrence County Court-N.Y.
Nicastro, Deborah J.-Judge, Garfield Heights Municipal Court-Ohio
Nichol, Gerald C.-Judge, Wisconsin Circuit Court Dane Circuit-Wis.
Nicholas, Edward-Judge, Florida Circuit Court Twelfth Judicial Circuit-Fla.
Nicholas, Stephen W.-Judge, Recorder's Court of DeKalb County-Ga.
Nicholas, William N.-Associate Judge, Delaware Family Court Kent County-Del.
Nicholas, William T.-Judge, Pennsylvania Court of Common Pleas Thirty-eighth Judicial District-Pa.
Nicholls, Lewis Dunn-Judge, Kentucky Circuit Court Twentieth Judicial Circuit-Ky.
Nichols, A. W., III-Judge, Florida Circuit Court Seventh Judicial Circuit-Fla.
Nichols, C. Philip, Jr.-Associate Judge, Circuit Court for Prince George's County, Seventh Judicial Circuit-Md.
Nichols, Colie, Jr.-Judge, Santa Rosa County Court-Fla.
Nichols, David A.-Judge, Washington Superior Court Whatcom County-Wash.
Nichols, John F.-Judge, Washington Superior Court Clark County-Wash.
Nichols, Leslie C.-Judge, Superior Court of California County of Santa Clara-Calif.
Nichols, O. T. "Terry"-Judge, Juvenile Court of Georgia Brunswick Judicial Circuit and Chief Magistrate, Magistrate Court of Wayne County-Ga.
Nichols, Richard D.-Judge, Superior Court of Arizona Pima County-Ariz.
Nichols, Robert D.-Judge, Ohio Court of Common Pleas Madison County-Ohio
Nichols, Rudy J.-Judge, Michigan Circuit Court Sixth Judicial Circuit-Mich.
Nicholson, David C.-Chief Judge, Michigan District Court District Seventy-two-Mich.
Nicholson, George-Associate Justice, California Court of Appeal Third District-Calif.
Nicholson, J. C. "Buddy", Jr.-Judge, South Carolina Circuit Court Tenth Judicial Circuit-S.C.
Nicholson, John M.-Judge, Cambridge Municipal Court-Ohio
Nicholson, Julie A.-Chief Judge, Michigan District Court District Fifty-two and Judge, Michigan District Court District Fifty-two Division Three-Mich.
Nicholson, Robert J.-Justice, New York Supreme Court Fifth Judicial District-N.Y.
Nickell, Bette R.-Judge, Montrose County Court-Colo.
Nickerson, Gary A.-Associate Justice, Trial Court of Massachusetts Superior Court Department-Mass.
Nickerson, William M.-Senior Judge, United States District Court District of Maryland-Md.
Nickinson, Edward P., III-Judge, Florida Circuit Court First Judicial Circuit-Fla.
Nickleach, Joseph A.-President Judge, Pennsylvania Court of Common Pleas Thirty-third Judicial District-Pa.
Nicks, Diane M.-Judge, Wisconsin Circuit Court Dane Circuit-Wis.
Nicola, George J.-Retired Judge, New Jersey Superior Court-N.J.
Nicolai, Francis A.-Justice, New York Supreme Court Ninth Judicial District-N.Y.
Nicols, Alfred G., Jr.-Magistrate Judge, United States District Court Southern District of Mississippi-Miss.
Niedermeier, Jerome J.-Magistrate Judge, United States District Court District of Vermont-Vt.
Niehaus, David J.-Judge, Ohio Court of Common Pleas Butler County-Ohio
Niehaus, Richard A.-Judge, Ohio Court of Common Pleas Hamilton County-Ohio
Nielsen, George B., Jr.-Judge, United States Bankruptcy Court District of Arizona-Ariz.
Nielsen, Richard A.-Judge, Florida Circuit Court Thirteenth Judicial Circuit-Fla.
Nielsen, Wm. Fremming-Judge, United States District Court Eastern District of Washington-Wash.
Nielson, Dale-Presiding Judge, Superior Court of Arizona Navajo County-Ariz.
Niemeier, Brett J.-Judge, Vanderburgh Superior Court-Ind.
Niemeyer, Joseph H.-Judge, Ohio Court of Common Pleas Hancock County-Ohio
Niemeyer, Paul Victor-Judge, United States Court of Appeals Fourth Circuit
Niemira, Thad F.-Associate Circuit Judge, Missouri Circuit Court Twenty-second Judicial Circuit-Mo.
Nieto, Henry E.-Judge, Colorado Court of Appeals-Colo.
Nieves, Dennis V.-Judge, New Jersey Superior Court Vicinage Eight-N.J.
Nigg, Randal J.-District Associate Judge, Iowa District Court First Judicial District-Ia.
Nightingale, Rebecca-District Judge, Oklahoma District Court Fourteenth Judicial District-Okla.
Nigro, Martin L.-Judge Referee, Connecticut Superior Court-Conn.
Nigro, Russell M.-Justice, The Supreme Court of Pennsylvania-Pa.
Nilon, James P.-Judge, Alachua County Court-Fla.
Niman, Ronald J.-Justice of the Peace, Ely Justices' Court and Judge, Ely Municipal Court-Nev.
Nimmons, Ralph W., Jr.-Judge, United States District Court Middle District of Florida-Fla.
Nims, Arthur L., III-Senior Judge, United States Tax Court
Ninfo, John Charles, II-Chief Judge, United States Bankruptcy Court Western District of New York-N.Y.
Nishimoto, Cary H.-Judge, Superior Court of California County of Los Angeles-Calif.
Nishimura, Rhonda-Judge, Hawaii Circuit Court First Judicial Circuit-Hi.
Nivison, John C.-Judge, Maine District Court-Me.
Nix, Kenneth O.-Judge, Superior Court of Georgia Cobb Judicial Circuit-Ga.
Nix, Michael A.-Judge, Lee County District Court-Ala.
Nix, William A.-Judge, North Bonneville Municipal Court-Wash.
Nixon, John T.-Senior Judge, United States District Court Middle District of Tennessee-Tenn.
Nixon, Lewis-Circuit Judge, Illinois Circuit Court of Cook County-Ill.
Nixon, W. Stephen-Circuit Judge, Missouri Circuit Court Sixteenth Judicial Circuit-Mo.
Niznik, Gilbert L.-Associate Judge, Illinois Circuit Court Twelfth Judicial Circuit-Ill.
Noble, G. William-Judge, Alabama Circuit Court Tenth Judicial Circuit Birmingham Division-Ala.
Noble, John W.-Vice Chancellor, Delaware Court of Chancery-Del.
Noble, Laurie A.-Judge, Rio Blanco County Court-Colo.
Noble, Mary C.-Judge, Kentucky Circuit Court Twenty-second Judicial Circuit-Ky.
Noble, Richard E.-Chief Judge, Michigan District Court District Eighty-two-Mich.
Nobles, Kelly Baker-Judge, Newberry County Probate Court-S.C.
Nobles, Linda Lee-Judge, Florida Circuit Court First Judicial Circuit-Fla.
Noce, David D.-Magistrate Judge, United States District Court Eastern District of Missouri-Mo.
Noecker, James P.-Chief Judge, Michigan Circuit Court Forty-fifth Judicial Circuit-Mich.
Noel, Frank G.-Judge, Utah District Court Third Judicial District-Utah
Noel, Franklin L.-Magistrate Judge, United States District Court District of Minnesota-Minn.
Noel, Thomas E.-Associate Judge, Circuit Court for Baltimore City, Eighth Judicial Circuit-Md.
Nolan, J. Michael-Judge, Wisconsin Circuit Court Lincoln Circuit-Wis.
Nolan, Michael Jeffrey-Judge, Michigan District Court District Sixty-Mich.
Nolan, Nan R.-Magistrate Judge, United States District Court Northern District of Illinois-Ill.
Nolan, Nancy J.-Judge, Alaska District Court Third Judicial District-Alas.
Nolan, Thomas D., Jr.-Justice, New York Supreme Court Fourth Judicial District-N.Y.
Noland, Christine A.-Magistrate Judge, United States District Court Middle District of Louisiana-La.
Noland, Donald R.-Judge, Kansas District Court Eleventh Judicial District-Kan.
Noland, Paul-Recalled Associate Judge, Illinois Circuit Court Eighteenth Judicial Circuit-Ill.
Nolen, Ben-Judge, Tom Green County Court at Law-Tex.
Noneman, Gary R.-District Associate Judge, Iowa District Court Eighth Judicial District-Ia.
Noonan, Daniel A.-Judge, Wisconsin Circuit Court Milwaukee Circuit-Wis.
Noonan, John T., Jr.-Senior Judge, United States Court of Appeals Ninth Circuit
Noonan, Mary T.-Judge, Utah Juvenile Court Fourth Judicial District-Utah
Noonan, Robert C.-Judge, Genesee County Court-N.Y.
Noonan, William T.-Magistrate, Rhode Island Traffic Tribunal-R.I.
Norblad, Albin W.-Judge, Oregon Circuit Court Third Judicial District-Ore.
Norcott, Flemming L., Jr.-Associate Justice, Connecticut Supreme Court-Conn.
Nord, Beryl A.-Judge, Minnesota District Court Fourth Judicial District-Minn.
Nord, Larry B.-Magistrate Judge, United States District Court Northern District of California-Calif.
Nordberg, John A.-Senior Judge, United States District Court Northern District of Illinois-Ill.
Nordby, Jack S.-Judge, Minnesota District Court Fourth Judicial District-Minn.
Nordlund, Lorraine-Judge, Virginia General District Court Nineteenth Judicial District-Va.
Nordquist, Steven L.-Associate Judge, Illinois Circuit Court Seventeenth Judicial Circuit-Ill.
Nordstrom, Robert P. M.-Chief Judge, Montmorency County Probate Court-Mich.
Norell, Peter H.-Judge, Superior Court of California County of San Bernardino-Calif.
Norelli, Nancy Black-Judge, North Carolina District Court District 26-N.C.
Norgle, Charles Ronald, Sr.-Judge, United States District Court Northern District of Illinois-Ill.
Norko, Raymond R.-Judge, Connecticut Superior Court-Conn.
Norman, Mary K K-Judge, New Orleans Second City Court-La.
Norman, Mike-District Judge, Oklahoma District Court Fifteenth Judicial District-Okla.
Norman, Seth W.-Judge, Tennessee Criminal Court Twentieth Judicial District-Tenn.
Norris, Alan E.-Senior Judge, United States Court of Appeals Sixth Circuit
Norris, Jim-Judge, West Monroe City Court-La.

ALPHABETICAL NAME INDEX

Norris, William A., Jr.-Senior Judge, Florida Circuit Court Tenth Judicial Circuit-Fla.

North, Douglass-Judge, Washington Superior Court King County-Wash.

North, Kent L.-Judge, Bryan Municipal Court-Ohio

North, Pamela L.-Associate Judge, Circuit Court for Anne Arundel County, Fifth Judicial Circuit-Md.

North, Thomas B.-Chief Judge, Luce-Mackinac Counties Probate Court District-Mich.

Northam, David E.-Judge, Rush Superior Court-Ind.

Northcutt, Stevan T.-Judge, Florida District Court of Appeal Second District-Fla.

Northridge, Yolanda N.-Judge, Superior Court of California County of Alameda-Calif.

Northrop, Albert Willis-Associate Judge, Maryland District Court District Five-Md.

Northrop, Edward Skottowe-Senior Judge, United States District Court District of Maryland-Md.

Northway, Diane-Judge, Superior Court of California County of Santa Clara-Calif.

Norton, David C.-Judge, United States District Court District of South Carolina-S.C.

Norton, Glenn-Judge, Missouri Court of Appeals Eastern District-Mo.

Norton, John L., III-Administrative Judge, Maryland District Court District Two-Md.

Norton, Richard W.-Judge, Vermont Trial Court-Vt.

Notaro, Peter J.-Justice, New York Supreme Court Eighth Judicial District-N.Y.

Nott, Michael Gordon-Associate Justice, California Court of Appeal Second District Division Two-Calif.

Nottingham, Edward W.-Judge, United States District Court District of Colorado-Colo.

Nottolini, Gene Louis-Circuit Judge, Illinois Circuit Court Sixteenth Judicial Circuit-Ill.

Notzon, Marcel C.-Magistrate Judge, United States District Court Southern District of Texas-Tex.

Novack, Stanley-Judge Referee, Connecticut Superior Court-Conn.

Novak, Joel D.-District Judge, Iowa District Court Fifth Judicial District-Ia.

Novak, Rita M.-Associate Judge, Illinois Circuit Court of Cook County-Ill.

Novoselsky, Benjamin E.-Recalled Circuit Judge, Illinois Circuit Court of Cook County-Ill.

Nowak, Henry J., Jr.-Judge, Buffalo City Court-N.Y.

Nowak, Nancy Stein-Magistrate Judge, United States District Court Western District of Texas-Tex.

Nowakowski, Michael-Judge, Wisconsin Circuit Court Dane Circuit-Wis.

Nowicki, Julia M.-Circuit Judge, Illinois Circuit Court of Cook County-Ill.

Nowinski, Peter A.-Magistrate Judge, United States District Court Eastern District of California-Calif.

Nowinski, Thomas E.-Circuit Judge, Illinois Circuit Court of Cook County-Ill.

Nowlin, James R.-Chief Judge, United States District Court Western District of Texas-Tex.

Nuchia, Samuel M.-Justice, Texas Court of Appeals First District-Tex.

Nudell, Karen Joy-Judge, Superior Court of California County of Los Angeles-Calif.

Nudelman, Stuart A.-Circuit Judge, Illinois Circuit Court of Cook County-Ill.

Nuechterlein, Christopher A.-Magistrate Judge, United States District Court Northern District of Indiana-Ind.

Nuessle, Peter R.-Judge, South Carolina Family Court Second Judicial Circuit-S.C.

Nuffer, David-Magistrate Judge, United States District Court District of Utah-Utah

Nugent, Donald Clark-Judge, United States District Court Northern District of Ohio-Ohio

Nugent, Robert E.-Judge, Bankruptcy Appellate Panel Tenth Circuit and Chief Judge, United States Bankruptcy Court District of Kansas-Kan.

Nugent, Stephen P.-Associate Justice, Rhode Island Superior Court-R.I.

Nugent, Thomas P.-Judge, Superior Court of California County of San Diego-Calif.

Nugent, William E.-Judge, New Jersey Superior Court Vicinage One-N.J.

Nunez, Gus-Judge, Lorain Municipal Court-Ohio

Nunez, Patricia M.-Judge, The Criminal Court of the City of New York-N.Y.

Nunez, Ralph-Judge, Superior Court of California County of Fresno-Calif.

Nunley, Troy L.-Judge, Superior Court of California County of Sacramento-Calif.

Nunn, George F., Jr.-Chief Judge, Superior Court of Georgia Houston Judicial Circuit-Ga.

Nunner, Michael K.-Judge, Ohio Court of Common Pleas Harrison County-Ohio

Nuss, Lawton R.-Justice, Kansas Supreme Court-Kan.

Nuss, Richard James-Judge, Wisconsin Circuit Court Fond du Lac Circuit-Wis.

Nuzum, Milt-Judge, Marietta Municipal Court-Ohio

Nye, Kenneth Wilson-Judge, Virginia General District Court Sixth Judicial District-Va.

Nye, Michael E.-Chief Judge, Hillsdale County Probate Court-Mich.

Nygaard, Richard L.-Judge, United States Court of Appeals Third Circuit

Nykamp, Wesley J.-Judge, Michigan Circuit Court Twentieth Judicial Circuit-Mich.

Oakes, James L.-Senior Judge, United States Court of Appeals Second Circuit

Oakley, Brian A.-Judge, Michigan District Court District Thirty-four-Mich.

Oakley, Bruce-Judge, Texas District Court 234th Judicial District-Tex.

Oakley, Gladys M.-Judge, Austin County Court at Law-Tex.

Oakley, Thomas D.-Senior Judge, Florida Circuit Court Fourth Judicial Circuit-Fla.

O'Banner-Owens, Jeanette-Judge, Michigan District Court District Thirty-six-Mich.

O'Bannon, John M.-Associate Circuit Judge, Missouri Circuit Court Twenty-seventh Judicial Circuit-Mo.

Obbish, James M.-Associate Judge, Illinois Circuit Court of Cook County-Ill.

Obendorf, Richard L.-Judge, Butler City Court-Ind.

Ober, Joelle Ann-Judge, Hillsborough County Court-Fla.

Ober, William J.-Judge, Pennsylvania Court of Common Pleas Tenth Judicial District-Pa.

Oberbillig, Robert H.-Judge, Superior Court of Arizona Maricopa County-Ariz.

Oberdorfer, Louis F.-Senior Judge, United States District Court District of Columbia-D.C.

Oberholtzer, David-Judge, Superior Court of California County of San Diego-Calif.

Oberholzer, Richard J.-Judge, Superior Court of California County of Kern-Calif.

O'Berry, Karleen S.-Judge, Probate Court of Clinch County-Ga.

Obland, Joyce-Judge, Colstrip City Court-Mont.

O'Briant, Eric H.-Judge, West Virginia Circuit Court Seventh Judicial Circuit-W.Va.

O'Brien, Colleen A.-Judge, Michigan Circuit Court Sixth Judicial Circuit-Mich.

O'Brien, Daniel Patrick-Judge, Michigan Circuit Court Sixth Judicial Circuit-Mich.

O'Brien, Dennis-Judge, Windham District Probate Court-Conn.

O'Brien, Dennis D.-Judge, United States Bankruptcy Court District of Minnesota-Minn.

O'Brien, Donald E.-Senior Judge, United States District Court Northern District of Iowa-Ia.

O'Brien, Donald J., Jr.-Circuit Judge, Illinois Circuit Court of Cook County-Ill.

O'Brien, Edward P.-Circuit Judge, Illinois Circuit Court of Cook County-Ill.

O'Brien, Emmett M.-Circuit Judge, Missouri Circuit Court Twenty-first Judicial Circuit-Mo.

O'Brien, Erich J.-Judge, Sandusky Municipal Court-Ohio

O'Brien, Francis J.-Judge Referee, Connecticut Superior Court-Conn.

O'Brien, Gerard J., Jr.-Senior Judge, Florida Circuit Court Sixth Judicial Circuit-Fla.

O'Brien, Gregory C., Jr.-Judge, Superior Court of California County of Los Angeles-Calif.

O'Brien, Gregory M.-Associate Judge, Illinois Circuit Court of Cook County-Ill.

O'Brien, Joan M.-Circuit Judge, Illinois Circuit Court of Cook County-Ill.

O'Brien, John D.-Judge, Bay County Court-Fla.

O'Brien, John J., Jr.-General Magistrate, Rhode Island Family Court-R.I.

O'Brien, Mark Thomas-Associate Judge, Maryland District Court District Five-Md.

O'Brien, Mary Grace-Judge, Virginia Juvenile and Domestic Relations District Court Thirty-first Judicial District-Va.

O'Brien, Peter J.-Judge, Pennsylvania Court of Common Pleas Forty-third Judicial District-Pa.

O'Brien, Sarah B.-Judge, Wisconsin Circuit Court Dane Circuit-Wis.

O'Brien, Sheila M.-Judge, Illinois Appellate Court First Judicial District Division Six-Ill.

O'Brien, Terrence L.-Judge, United States Court of Appeals Tenth Circuit

O'Brien, Thomas E.-Judge, New Jersey Superior Court Vicinage Fourteen-N.J.

O'Brien, Thomas S.-Retired Judge, New Jersey Superior Court Appellate Division-N.J.

O'Brien, W. Terrence-Judge, Pennsylvania Court of Common Pleas Fifth Judicial District-Pa.

O'Brien, William F., III-Justice, New York Supreme Court Sixth Judicial District-N.Y.

O'Brien, William J.-Judge, Nassau County District Court-N.Y.

O'Brien, William T.-Circuit Judge, Illinois Circuit Court of Cook County-Ill.

O'Bryan, Joe-Judge, Cabot District Court-Ark.

Obus, Michael J.-Judge, The Criminal Court of the City of New York-N.Y.

Ochoa, Frank J.-Judge, Superior Court of California County of Santa Barbara-Calif.

Ochoa, Joseph V.-Judge, Oregon Circuit Court Third Judicial District-Ore.

O'Connell, Edward Y.-Judge Referee, Connecticut Superior Court-Conn.

O'Connell, Geoffrey J.-Justice, New York Supreme Court Tenth Judicial District-N.Y.

O'Connell, Peter D.-Judge, Michigan Court of Appeals-Mich.

O'Connor, Amy-Judge, New Jersey Superior Court Vicinage Thirteen-N.J.

O'Connor, Charles D., Jr.-Judge, Shelby Circuit Court-Ind.

O'Connor, Edward T., Jr.-Judge, New Jersey Superior Court Vicinage Six-N.J.

O'Connor, James B.-Senior Judge, Superior Court of Georgia-Ga.

O'Connor, James B.-Magistrate Judge, Kansas District Court Twenty-second Judicial District-Kan.

O'Connor, Jeffrey W.-Chief Judge, Illinois Circuit Court Fourteenth Judicial Circuit-Ill.

O'Connor, Karen L.-Judge, Superior Court of Arizona Maricopa County-Ariz.

O'Connor, Kathleen M.-Judge, Washington Superior Court Spokane County-Wash.

O'Connor, Kathleen R.-Judge, Superior Court of California County of Yuba-Calif.

O'Connor, Marilyn L.-Judge, Monroe County Family Court-N.Y.

O'Connor, Mark S.-Judge, Ohio Court of Common Pleas Logan County-Ohio

O'Connor, Maureen-Justice, Supreme Court of Ohio-Ohio

O'Connor, Sandra Day-Associate Justice, The Supreme Court of the United States

Oddone, Frederic M.-Presiding Judge, Utah Juvenile Court Third Judicial District-Utah

O'Dea, Kevin J.-Justice, Trial Court of Massachusetts District Court Department Norfolk County Brookline Division-Mass.

Odell, Timothy B.-Judge, Everett Municipal Court-Wash.

O'Dell-Seneca, Debbie-Judge, Pennsylvania Court of Common Pleas Twenty-seventh Judicial District-Pa.

Odette, Christopher-Chief Judge, Michigan District Court District Sixty-seven and Judge, Michigan District Court District Sixty-seven Division Four-Mich.

Odlin, John E.-Justice, Missoula County Justice of the Peace Court-Mont.

Odom, Sheila-Judge, Hampton County Probate Court-S.C.

ALPHABETICAL NAME INDEX

O'Donnell, Joanne B.-Judge, Superior Court of California County of Los Angeles-Calif.
O'Donnell, John F.-Justice, New York Supreme Court Eighth Judicial District-N.Y.
O'Donnell, John Peter-Judge, Ohio Court of Common Pleas Cuyahoga County-Ohio
O'Donnell, Kimberly B.-Judge, Virginia Juvenile and Domestic Relations District Court Thirteenth Judicial District-Va.
O'Donoghue, Peter J.-Justice, New York Supreme Court Eleventh Judicial District-N.Y.
Oesterle, Nancy C.-Justice of the Peace, Las Vegas Justices' Court-Nev.
Oeth, Steven J.-District Associate Judge, Iowa District Court Second Judicial District-Ia.
O'Farrell, Edward Emmett-Judge, Ohio Court of Common Pleas Tuscarawas County-Ohio
O'Farrell, Robert A.-Judge, Superior Court of California County of Monterey-Calif.
Offner, Michael-Judge, Nebraska County Court Tenth Judicial District-Neb.
O'Flaherty, Ian Michael-Judge, Virginia General District Court Nineteenth Judicial District-Va.
O'Flaherty, Joseph-Judge, Superior Court of California County of Placer-Calif.
Oftedal, Richard L.-Judge, Florida Circuit Court Fifteenth Judicial Circuit-Fla.
O'Gara, Lawrence-Circuit Judge, Illinois Circuit Court of Cook County-Ill.
Ogden, E. Jeanette-Judge, Buffalo City Court-N.Y.
Ogden, Steven D.-Judge, Superior Court of California County of Los Angeles-Calif.
Ogle, Norma M. McGee-Judge, Tennessee Court of Criminal Appeals Eastern Division-Tenn.
Ogle, Rex Henry-Judge, Tennessee Circuit Court Fourth Judicial District-Tenn.
Oglesby, John D.-Judge, Superior Court of California County of Kern-Calif.
Ogletree, Laverne C.-Judge, Probate Court of Greene County and Chief Magistrate, Magistrate Court of Greene County-Ga.
O'Grady, Daniel W.-Judge, Bethel District Probate Court-Conn.
O'Grady, John J., Jr.-Judge, Pennsylvania Court of Common Pleas First Judicial District-Pa.
O'Grady, Kevin M.-Judge, Westport District Probate Court-Conn.
O'Grady, Liam-Magistrate Judge, United States District Court Eastern District of Virginia-Va.
O'Grady, Timothy-District Judge, Iowa District Court Fourth Judicial District-Ia.
O'Hagan, Robert W.-Judge, New Jersey Superior Court Vicinage Nine-N.J.
O'Halloran, Kevin M.-Retired Judge, New Jersey Superior Court-N.J.
Ohanesian, Gail D.-Judge, Superior Court of California County of Sacramento-Calif.
O'Hanlon, Dan P.-Chief Judge, West Virginia Circuit Court Sixth Judicial Circuit-W.Va.
O'Hara, James P.-Magistrate Judge, United States District Court District of Kansas-Kan.
O'Hara, Michael A.-Chief Judge, Colorado District Court Fourteenth Judicial District and Judge, Colorado Water Court Division Six-Colo.
O'Hara, Patrick J.-Judge, Superior Court of California County of Tulare-Calif.
O'Hara, Robert G., Jr.-Chief Judge, Virginia Circuit Court Sixth Judicial Circuit-Va.
O'Hara, Thomas J.-Associate Judge, Illinois Circuit Court of Cook County-Ill.
Ohlig, Louis J.-Judge, Suffolk County Court-N.Y.
Ohm, Ralph L.-Judge, Hot Springs District Court-Ark.
Ohmer, Steven R.-Circuit Judge, Missouri Circuit Court Twenty-second Judicial Circuit-Mo.
Ohta, Sam-Judge, Superior Court of California County of Los Angeles-Calif.
Okamoto, Melvin-Judge, Denver County Court-Colo.
Okamoto, Vincent H.-Judge, Superior Court of California County of Los Angeles-Calif.
O'Keefe, Joseph D.-Judge, Pennsylvania Court of Common Pleas First Judicial District-Pa.
O'Keefe, Thomas V., Jr.-Judge, Connecticut Superior Court-Conn.
O'Kelley, William C.-Senior Judge, United States District Court Northern District of Georgia-Ga.
Oki, Dan Thomas-Judge, Superior Court of California County of Los Angeles-Calif.
Olberding, Ronald D.-Judge, Nebraska District Court Eighth Judicial District-Neb.
Old, Thomas L.-Judge, Newton Falls Municipal Court-Ohio
Oldner, Chris-Judge, Collin County Court at Law No. 5-Tex.
Olds, Eileen Anita-Judge, Virginia Juvenile and Domestic Relations District Court First Judicial District-Va.
Olds, Marjorie Z.-Judge, Ithaca City Court-N.Y.
O'Leary, James J.-Justice, Trial Court of Massachusetts District Court Department Essex County Newburyport Division-Mass.
O'Leary, Kathleen E.-Associate Justice, California Court of Appeal Fourth District Division Three-Calif.
O'Leary, Susan T.-Circuit Judge, Illinois Circuit Court Twelfth Judicial Circuit-Ill.
Oleisky, Allen-Judge, Minnesota District Court Fourth Judicial District-Minn.
Oler, J. Wesley, Jr.-Judge, Pennsylvania Court of Common Pleas Ninth Judicial District-Pa.
Oles, Edward M.-Judge, New Jersey Superior Court Vicinage Fourteen-N.J.
Olguin, Fernando M.-Magistrate Judge, United States District Court Central District of California-Calif.
Olivares, Kathleen H.-Judge, Texas District Court 205th Judicial District-Tex.
Oliver, Bonnie Chessher-Judge, Superior Court of Georgia Northeastern Judicial Circuit-Ga.
Oliver, Eugene, Jr.-Judge, The Criminal Court of the City of New York-N.Y.
Oliver, George E.-Senior Judge, Superior Court of Georgia-Ga.
Oliver, Otis M. "Bud"-Chief Judge, North Carolina District Court District 17B-N.C.
Oliver, Robert H.-Judge, Superior Court of California County of Fresno-Calif.
Oliver, Robert Webster-Justice, New York Supreme Court Tenth Judicial District-N.Y.
Oliver, Solomon, Jr.-Judge, United States District Court Northern District of Ohio-Ohio
Oliver, William-Judge, Kentucky District Court Thirteenth Judicial District-Ky.
Olivier, Rebecca M.-Judge, First Parish Court Jefferson Parish-La.
Olivieri, Thomas P.-Judge, New Jersey Superior Court Vicinage Six-N.J.
Olliff, R. Hudson-Senior Judge, Florida Circuit Court Fourth Judicial Circuit-Fla.
Olmedo, Charlaine F.-Judge, Superior Court of California County of Los Angeles-Calif.
Olmstead, Wayne-Associate District Judge, Oklahoma District Court First Judicial District-Okla.
Olney, Garrett-Judge, Superior Court of California County of Plumas-Calif.
Olsen, Gary A.-Justice, Broadwater County Justice of the Peace Court-Mont.
Olsen, Rory R.-Judge, Harris County Probate Court No. 3-Tex.
Olsen, Tina-Judge, Jefferson County Court-Colo.
Olson, Everett Nels-Surrogate Judge, North Dakota District Court-N.D.
Olson, Gregory A.-Judge, Pennsylvania Court of Common Pleas Fortieth Judicial District-Pa.
Olson, Lynn C.-Judge, Minnesota District Court Tenth Judicial District-Minn.
Olson, Roy G., Jr.-Judge, Jefferson County Court-Colo.
Olson, Tim P.-Associate Judge, Illinois Circuit Court Seventh Judicial Circuit-Ill.
Olsson, Debra L.-Associate Judge, Rhode Island Workers' Compensation Court-R.I.
Olszewski, Peter Paul, Jr.-Judge, Pennsylvania Court of Common Pleas Eleventh Judicial District-Pa.
O'Malley, Catherine J.-Associate Judge, Maryland District Court District One-Md.
O'Malley, Daniel W.-Justice, Trial Court of Massachusetts District Court Department Norfolk County Wrentham Division-Mass.
O'Malley, Denise Margaret-Judge, Illinois Appellate Court First Judicial District Division One-Ill.
O'Malley, Jack-Judge, Illinois Appellate Court Second Judicial District-Ill.
O'Malley, James P.-Circuit Judge, Illinois Circuit Court of Cook County-Ill.
O'Malley, John R.-Circuit Judge, Missouri Circuit Court Sixteenth Judicial Circuit-Mo.
O'Malley, Kathleen-Judge, Ohio Court of Common Pleas Cuyahoga County-Ohio
O'Malley, Kathleen McDonald-Judge, United States District Court Northern District of Ohio-Ohio
O'Malley, Mary Ann-Judge, Superior Court of California County of Contra Costa-Calif.
O'Malley, Mary Ann-Justice, Madison County Justice of the Peace Court-Mont.
O'Malley, Michael E.-Judge, Putnam County Court-Ohio
O'Malley, Michael J.-Circuit Judge, Illinois Circuit Court Twentieth Judicial Circuit-Ill.
O'Malley, Pat-Judge, Pierce District Court Pierce County-Wash.
O'Malley, William-Judge, Superior Court of California County of Contra Costa-Calif.
O'Malley, William P.-Circuit Judge, Illinois Circuit Court of Cook County-Ill.
Omansky, Paula J.-Judge, The Civil Court of the City of New York-N.Y.
O'Mara Frossard, Margaret-Circuit Judge, Illinois Circuit Court of Cook County-Ill.
O'Meara, John Corbett-Judge, United States District Court Eastern District of Michigan-Mich.
O'Melia, Michael J.-Judge, Superior Court of Arizona Maricopa County-Ariz.
O'Neal, Elaine M.-Chief Judge, North Carolina District Court District 14-N.C.
O'Neal, Loyd-Judge, Oregon Circuit Court Fourteenth Judicial District-Ore.
O'Neal, Robert B.-Judge, Sarpy County Separate Juvenile Court-Neb.
O'Neal, William D.-Circuit Judge, Illinois Circuit Court of Cook County-Ill.
O'Neil, William J.-Presiding Judge, Superior Court of Arizona Pinal County-Ariz.
O'Neill, Christina M.-Judge, Probate Court of New Hampshire Belknap County-N.H.
O'Neill, Deborah (Piperni)-Judge, Ohio Court of Common Pleas Franklin County-Ohio
O'Neill, Harriet-Justice, Texas Supreme Court-Tex.
O'Neill, James D., III-Associate Justice, New Hampshire Superior Court-N.H.
O'Neill, Lawrence J.-Magistrate Judge, United States District Court Eastern District of California-Calif.
O'Neill, Michael J.-Justice, Texas Court of Appeals Fifth District-Tex.
O'Neill, Norris L.-Judge Referee, Connecticut Superior Court-Conn.
O'Neill, Richard-Judge, Ohio Court of Common Pleas Clark County-Ohio
O'Neill, Robert F.-Judge, Superior Court of California County of San Diego-Calif.
O'Neill, Robert P.-Judge, Superior Court of California County of Los Angeles-Calif.
O'Neill, Steven T.-Judge, Pennsylvania Court of Common Pleas Thirty-eighth Judicial District-Pa.
O'Neill, Thomas N., Jr.-Senior Judge, United States District Court Eastern District of Pennsylvania-Pa.
O'Neill, Vincent J., Jr.-Judge, Superior Court of California County of Ventura-Calif.
O'Neill, W. James-First Justice, Trial Court of Massachusetts District Court Department Nantucket County Nantucket Division-Mass.
O'Neill, William M.-Judge, Ohio Court of Appeals Eleventh District-Ohio
Oney, Patricia Shanes-Judge, Ohio Court of Common Pleas Butler County-Ohio
Ong, Tomson T.-Judge, Superior Court of California County of Los Angeles-Calif.
Ongkeko, Rafael A.-Judge, Superior Court of California County of Los Angeles-Calif.
Onofry, Robert A.-Judge, Port Jervis City Court-N.Y.
Opala, Marian P.-Vice Chief Justice, Supreme Court of Oklahoma-Okla.
Oppliger, James R.-Judge, Superior Court of California County of Fresno-Calif.
Orbach, Jerome M.-Associate Judge, Illinois Circuit Court of Cook County-Ill.

ALPHABETICAL NAME INDEX

ALPHABETICAL NAME INDEX

Padova, John R.-Judge, United States District Court Eastern District of Pennsylvania-Pa.
Padovano, Philip J.-Judge, Florida District Court of Appeal First District-Fla.
Padrick, Henry Thomas, Jr.-Judge, Virginia Circuit Court Second Judicial Circuit-Va.
Padro, Eduardo-Justice, New York Supreme Court First Judicial District-N.Y.
Paer, Gary S.-Judge, Superior Court of California County of Orange-Calif.
Paez, Richard A.-Judge, United States Court of Appeals Ninth Circuit
Pagano, George A.-Judge, Pennsylvania Court of Common Pleas Thirty-second Judicial District-Pa.
Page, Alan C.-Associate Justice, Minnesota Supreme Court-Minn.
Page, Leslie D.-Associate District Judge, Oklahoma District Court Eighth Judicial District-Okla.
Page, Robert W.-Judge, New Jersey Superior Court Vicinage Four-N.J.
Page, Rodney S.-Judge, Utah District Court Second Judicial District-Utah
Page, Roger Amos-Judge, Tennessee Circuit Court Twenty-sixth Judicial District-Tenn.
Page, Tina S.-Associate Justice, Trial Court of Massachusetts Superior Court Department-Mass.
Pagliaccetti, Gary J.-Judge, Minnesota District Court Sixth Judicial District-Minn.
Pagones, James D.-Surrogate, Dutchess County Surrogate's Court-N.Y.
Pagones, Timothy G.-Judge, Beacon City Court-N.Y.
Pahl, Ronald J.-Judge, Oregon Circuit Court Sixth Judicial District-Ore.
Paine, George C., II-Chief Judge, United States Bankruptcy Court Middle District of Tennessee-Tenn.
Paine, James C.-Senior Judge, United States District Court Southern District of Florida-Fla.
Paine, Theodore E.-Circuit Judge, Illinois Circuit Court Sixth Judicial Circuit-Ill.
Painter, David-Judge, Louisiana District Court Fourteenth Judicial District-La.
Painter, Mark P.-Judge, Ohio Court of Appeals First District-Ohio
Paisley, Lewis G.-Judge, Kentucky Court of Appeals-Ky.
Paist, Sallie Walker-Judge, Juvenile Court of Georgia Cobb Judicial Circuit-Ga.
Paja, Marilyn-Judge, Kitsap District Court Kitsap County-Wash.
Pajak, John J.-Special Trial Judge, United States Tax Court
Pajtas, Richard M.-Chief Judge, Michigan Circuit Court Thirty-third Judicial Circuit-Mich.
Pake, David L.-Judge, Maumelle District Court-Ark.
Palazuelos, Yvette M.-Judge, Superior Court of California County of Los Angeles-Calif.
Palermo, Peter R.-Recalled Magistrate Judge, United States District Court Southern District of Florida-Fla.
Paley, Phillip Lewis-Judge, New Jersey Superior Court Vicinage Eight-N.J.
Pallenberg, Philip M.-Magistrate Judge, United States District Court District of Alaska-Alas.
Pallmeyer, Rebecca R.-Judge, United States District Court Northern District of Illinois-Ill.
Palm, Frederick W., Jr.-Judge, Groton District Probate Court-Conn.
Palmer, Bill R.-Judge, Kendall County Court at Law-Tex.
Palmer, Charles F.-Judge, Superior Court of California County of Los Angeles-Calif.
Palmer, J. Larry-Chief Judge, Virginia General District Court Sixth Judicial District-Va.
Palmer, Kathy-Judge, Superior Court of Georgia Middle Judicial Circuit-Ga.
Palmer, Phillip G., Sr.-Circuit Judge, Illinois Circuit Court First Judicial Circuit-Ill.
Palmer, Richard N.-Associate Justice, Connecticut Supreme Court-Conn.
Palmer, Stuart E.-Circuit Judge, Illinois Circuit Court of Cook County-Ill.
Palmer, Walter H.-Judge, Gibson Circuit Court-Ind.
Palmer, William D.-Judge, Florida District Court of Appeal Fifth District-Fla.
Palmieri, Daniel-Judge, Nassau County Court-N.Y.
Palomino, Raul C., Jr.-Judge, Hillsborough County Court-Fla.
Palughi, Delano J.-Judge, Mobile County District Court-Ala.
Palumbo, Daniel R.-Acting Judge, Olean City Court-N.Y.
Palumbo, Richard Angelo-Associate Judge, Maryland District Court District Five-Md.
Panarese, Donald D., Jr.-Associate Judge, Illinois Circuit Court of Cook County-Ill.
Pancake, David M.-Judge, West Virginia Circuit Court Sixth Judicial Circuit-W.Va.
Pando, Ana Maria-Judge, Dade County Court-Fla.
Panella, Jack Anthony-Judge, Pennsylvania Court of Common Pleas Third Judicial District-Pa.
Panepinto, Barbara I.-Judge, The Civil Court of the City of New York-N.Y.
Panepinto, Paul P.-Judge, Pennsylvania Court of Common Pleas First Judicial District-Pa.
Pangman, William W.-Judge, Superior Court of California County of Sierra-Calif.
Panichi, Thomas P.-Circuit Judge, Illinois Circuit Court of Cook County-Ill.
Panici, Luciano-Associate Judge, Illinois Circuit Court of Cook County-Ill.
Panioto, Ronald A.-Judge, Ohio Court of Common Pleas Hamilton County-Ohio
Pannell, Charles A., Jr.-Judge, United States District Court Northern District of Georgia-Ga.
Panner, Owen M.-Senior Judge, United States District Court District of Oregon-Ore.
Panos, John-Judge, State Court of DeKalb County-Ga.
Pantle, Kathleen M.-Circuit Judge, Illinois Circuit Court of Cook County-Ill.
Panuthos, Peter J.-Special Trial Judge, United States Tax Court
Papa, Mario J.-Judge, Gloversville City Court-N.Y.
Papadakis, Harry N.-Judge, Superior Court of California County of Fresno-Calif.
Papalini, Joseph I.-Judge, Pennsylvania Court of Common Pleas First Judicial District-Pa.
Papandrea, John F.-Judge, Meriden District Probate Court-Conn.
Papas, Leo S.-Magistrate Judge, United States District Court Southern District of California-Calif.
Pape, Timothy A.-Judge, Juvenile Court of Georgia Rome Judicial Circuit-Ga.
Papez, Dan L.-Chief Judge, Nevada District Court Seventh Judicial District-Nev.
Pappas, Jim D.-Chief Judge, United States Bankruptcy Court District of Idaho-Ida.
Pappas, Peter G.-Reserve Judge, Wisconsin Circuit Court-Wis.
Paras, George-Judge, Merrillville Town Court-Ind.
Paravis, Sara-Judge, Probate Court of Crawford County-Ga.
Pardes, Sondra K.-Judge, Nassau County District Court-N.Y.
Parga, Anthony L.-Justice, New York Supreme Court Tenth Judicial District-N.Y.
Pariente, Barbara J.-Justice, Florida Supreme Court-Fla.
Parins, Robert J.-Reserve Judge, Wisconsin Circuit Court-Wis.
Paris, Anthony J.-Justice, New York Supreme Court Fifth Judicial District-N.Y.
Parish, Lauren L.-Judge, Texas District Court 115th Judicial District-Tex.
Parisi, Thomas G.-Judge, Pennsylvania Court of Common Pleas Twenty-third Judicial District-Pa.
Park, David B.-Judge, Wyoming District Court Seventh Judicial District-Wyo.
Park, Richard Kent-Judge, Superior Court of California County of Sacramento-Calif.
Parker, Barrington D., Jr.-Judge, United States Court of Appeals Second Circuit
Parker, Bill G.-Judge, United States Bankruptcy Court Eastern District of Texas-Tex.
Parker, Edward C.-Judge, Rhode Island Traffic Tribunal-R.I.
Parker, Fred I.-Judge, United States Court of Appeals Second Circuit
Parker, George-Judge, Mason Municipal Court-Ohio
Parker, J. Richard-Resident Judge, North Carolina Superior Court First Judicial Division District 1-N.C.
Parker, James A.-Chief Judge, United States District Court District of New Mexico-N.Mex.
Parker, James S.-Judge, Florida Circuit Court Twelfth Judicial Circuit-Fla.
Parker, Jeffrey W.-Judge, Virginia Circuit Court Twentieth Judicial Circuit-Va.
Parker, John V.-Senior Judge, United States District Court Middle District of Louisiana-La.
Parker, John W.-Judge, Superior Court of California County of San Joaquin-Calif.
Parker, Johnny R.-Judge, Probate Court of Gordon County-Ga.
Parker, Julian A.-Judge, Louisiana District Court Orleans Parish Criminal District-La.
Parker, Kelly W.-Associate Circuit Judge, Missouri Circuit Court Forty-second Judicial Circuit-Mo.
Parker, Laura-Judge, Texas District Court 386th Judicial District-Tex.
Parker, Lorraine C.-Judge, New Jersey Superior Court Appellate Division-N.J.
Parker, Marla E.-Chief Judge, Michigan District Court District Forty-seven-Mich.
Parker, Mike T.-Judge, Hinds County Court-Miss.
Parker, Perry-Judge, Superior Court of California County of Sutter-Calif.
Parker, Regina Rogers-Judge, North Carolina District Court District 2-N.C.
Parker, Ronnie A.-Judge, Probate Court of Taylor County and Chief Magistrate, Magistrate Court of Taylor County-Ga.
Parker, S. Ben-Chief Magistrate, Magistrate Court of Oconee County-Ga.
Parker, Sarah E.-Associate Justice, Supreme Court of North Carolina-N.C.
Parker, Sheryl L.-Judge, The Criminal Court of the City of New York-N.Y.
Parker, Thomas F.-Judge, Connecticut Superior Court-Conn.
Parker, Tim S.-Judge, Eureka Springs District Court-Ark.
Parker, Wayland A., II-Judge, Greenwood District Court-Ark.
Parker, Westbrook J.-Chief Judge, Virginia Circuit Court Fifth Judicial Circuit-Va.
Parkinson, Paul K.-Associate Circuit Judge, Missouri Circuit Court Forty-first Judicial Circuit-Mo.
Parks, Bob-Judge, Texas District Court 143rd Judicial District-Tex.
Parks, Floyd L.-Associate Judge, Maryland District Court District Three-Md.
Parks, Joy-Chief Magistrate, Magistrate Court of White County-Ga.
Parks, Martin O.-Judge, Ohio Court of Common Pleas Lake County-Ohio
Parnell, Joe Michael-Judge, Kaufman County Court at Law-Tex.
Parnell, Lorna-Judge, Superior Court of California County of Los Angeles-Calif.
Parnham, John T.-Judge, Florida Circuit Court First Judicial Circuit-Fla.
Parraguirre, Ronald D.-Judge, Nevada District Court Eighth Judicial District-Nev.
Parrilli, Joanne C.-Associate Justice, California Court of Appeal First District Division Three-Calif.
Parrillo, Anthony J.-Judge, New Jersey Superior Court Appellate Division-N.J.
Parrish, Jill N.-Justice, Utah Supreme Court-Utah
Parrish, John Edward-Judge, Missouri Court of Appeals Southern District-Mo.
Parrish, Nancy E.-Judge, Kansas District Court Third Judicial District-Kan.
Parrish, Patricia G.-Special Judge, Oklahoma District Court Seventh Judicial District-Okla.
Parrish, Wayne R.-Judge, Superior Court of California County of Mariposa-Calif.
Parro, Randolph H.-Judge, Louisiana Court of Appeal First Circuit-La.
Parrott, David M.-Judge, Michigan District Court District Thirty-four-Mich.
Parrott, John Lee-Judge, Superior Court of Georgia Ocmulgee Judicial Circuit-Ga.
Parrott, Richard E.-Judge, Ohio Court of Common Pleas Union County-Ohio

ALPHABETICAL NAME INDEX

Parrott, Vann K.-Associate Judge, Juvenile Court of Georgia Southern Judicial Circuit-Ga.

Parry, Dennis H.-Judge, Howard Superior Court-Ind.

Parsons, Charles-Chief Judge, Missaukee County Probate Court-Mich.

Parsons, Charles-Judge, West Virginia Family Court Circuit Twenty-three-W.Va.

Parsons, Craig L.-Judge, Superior Court of California County of San Mateo-Calif.

Parsons, Douglas Mac-Judge, Alabama Circuit Court Tenth Judicial Circuit Bessemer Division-Ala.

Parsons, George W., Jr.-Judge, New Jersey Superior Court Vicinage Two-N.J.

Parsons, James N., III-Judge, Texas District Court 3rd Judicial District-Tex.

Parsons, Karen L.-Judge, New Mexico District Court Twelfth Judicial District-N.Mex.

Parsons, Marcia Phillips-Judge, United States Bankruptcy Court Eastern District of Tennessee-Tenn.

Parsons, Stewart E.-Judge, Gadsden County Court-Fla.

Parsons, William A.-Judge, Florida Circuit Court Seventh Judicial Circuit-Fla.

Partain, Jack-Judge, Superior Court of Georgia Conasauga Judicial Circuit-Ga.

Partida, Juan R.-Judge, Texas District Court 275th Judicial District-Tex.

Partin, Charles C.-Judge, Alabama Circuit Court Twenty-eighth Judicial Circuit-Ala.

Partnow, Mark I.-Justice, New York Supreme Court Second Judicial District-N.Y.

Paruk, Paul J.-Chief Judge, Michigan District Court District Thirty-one-Mich.

Pasell, Dale T.-Judge, Wisconsin Circuit Court La Crosse Circuit-Wis.

Paseur, Deborah B.-Judge, Lauderdale County District Court-Ala.

Pask, Neil Edward-Judge, Dallas County Criminal Court at Law No. 2-Tex.

Paskay, Alexander L.-Recalled Judge, United States Bankruptcy Court Middle District of Florida-Fla.

Passenger, Don-Judge, Michigan District Court District Sixty-one-Mich.

Passero, Robert J.-Assignment Judge, New Jersey Superior Court Vicinage Eleven-N.J.

Pastor, Michael E.-Judge, Superior Court of California County of Los Angeles-Calif.

Pasula, Angela-Judge, Michigan District Court District Five-Mich.

Patchen, Michael N.-Judge, Wyoming Circuit Court Seventh Judicial District, Natrona County-Wyo.

Patchett, Randy-Judge, Illinois Court of Claims-Ill.

Pate, Christine V.-Judge, Superior Court of California County of San Diego-Calif.

Pate, Dorothy Harris-Senior Judge, Florida Circuit Court Fourth Judicial Circuit-Fla.

Pate, J. Gary-Judge, Alabama Circuit Court Tenth Judicial Circuit Birmingham Division-Ala.

Pate, Warren L.-Chief Judge, North Carolina District Court District 16A-N.C.

Pate, William C.-Judge, Superior Court of California County of San Diego-Calif.

Patel, Marilyn Hall-Chief Judge, United States District Court Northern District of California-Calif.

Pater, Charles Lloyd-Judge, Ohio Court of Common Pleas Butler County-Ohio

Patnode, Cris-Justice of the Peace, Gilliam County Justice Court-Ore.

Patrick, Albert W., III-Chief Judge, Virginia General District Court Eighth Judicial District-Va.

Patrick, Hunter H.-Judge, Wyoming District Court Fifth Judicial District-Wyo.

Patrick, Isadore W.-Judge, Mississippi Circuit Court Ninth Judicial District-Miss.

Patrick, J. Steven-Chief Judge, Colorado District Court Seventh Judicial District and Judge, Colorado Water Court Division Four-Colo.

Patrick, William R.-Judge, Superior Court of California County of Butte-Calif.

Patsalos, Jeanne M.-Judge, Newburgh City Court-N.Y.

Patsalos, Peter C.-Justice, New York Supreme Court Ninth Judicial District-N.Y.

Patten, Edward E., Jr.-Judge, Mississippi Chancery Court Fifteenth Judicial District-Miss.

Patten, James R.-Judge, Probate Court of New Hampshire Carroll County and Special Justice, Northern Carroll County District Court and Southern Carroll County District Court-N.H.

Patterson, Cecil B., Jr.-Judge, Arizona Court of Appeals Division One-Ariz.

Patterson, James S.-Judge, El Paso County Court-Colo.

Patterson, Jan Powell-Justice, Texas Court of Appeals Third District-Tex.

Patterson, Jay-Judge, Texas District Court 101st Judicial District-Tex.

Patterson, Jerry D.-Judge, Marshall District Court-Ark.

Patterson, Jimmy P.-Judge, La Salle County Court-Tex.

Patterson, John Malcolm-Active Retired Judge, Alabama Court of Criminal Appeals-Ala.

Patterson, John S.-Judge, Arkansas Circuit Court Fifth Judicial Circuit-Ark.

Patterson, Larry R.-Judge, South Carolina Circuit Court Thirteenth Judicial Circuit-S.C.

Patterson, Michelle Weston-Justice, New York Supreme Court Second Judicial District-N.Y.

Patterson, Peggy E.-Magistrate Judge, United States District Court Eastern District of Kentucky-Ky.

Patterson, Robert L.-Judge, Denver County Court-Colo.

Patterson, Robert P., Jr.-Senior Judge, United States District Court Southern District of New York-N.Y.

Patterson, Timothy J.-Presiding Judge, Missouri Circuit Court Twenty-third Judicial Circuit-Mo.

Patti, Philip J.-Judge, New York Court of Claims-N.Y.

Patti, Sebastian Thomas-Circuit Judge, Illinois Circuit Court of Cook County-Ill.

Patti, Timothy L.-Resident Judge, North Carolina Superior Court Seventh Judicial Division District 27A-N.C.

Pattinson, William J.-District Judge, Iowa District Court Second Judicial District-Ia.

Patton, Houston J.-Judge, Hinds County Court-Miss.

Patton, James A.-Chief Judge, Kansas District Court Twenty-second Judicial District-Kan.

Patton, Nan J.-Associate District Judge, Oklahoma District Court Seventh Judicial District-Okla.

Patton, Phillip-Judge, Kentucky Circuit Court Forty-third Judicial Circuit-Ky.

Patton, Wayne-Judge, Lake County Court-Colo.

Paul, Alfred J.-Associate Judge, Illinois Circuit Court of Cook County-Ill.

Paul, John A.-Judge, Virginia General District Court Twenty-sixth Judicial District-Va.

Paul, Maurice M.-Senior Judge, United States District Court Northern District of Florida-Fla.

Paul, Michael A.-Judge, North Carolina District Court District 2-N.C.

Paul, Roy L.-Judge, Superior Court of California County of Los Angeles-Calif.

Paul, Troy C.-Judge, Probate Court of Coffee County-Ga.

Paules, Lois-Judge, Fort Laramie Municipal Court-Wyo.

Pauley, William H., III-Judge, United States District Court Southern District of New York-N.Y.

Paulhus, Angela M. Bucci-Magistrate, Rhode Island Family Court-R.I.

Paulsen, Donna L.-District Judge, Iowa District Court Fifth Judicial District-Ia.

Paulson, John T.-Presiding Judge, North Dakota District Court Southeast Judicial District-N.D.

Pavlich, Scott L.-Chief Judge, Michigan Circuit Court Fifty-third Judicial Circuit-Mich.

Pavlick, Juanita-Judge, Texas District Court 89th Judicial District-Tex.

Pavlikowski, Joseph S.-Senior Judge, Nevada District Court-Nev.

Pawlenty, Mary E.-Judge, Minnesota District Court First Judicial District-Minn.

Paxson, Deborah M.-Judge, Virginia Juvenile and Domestic Relations District Court Second Judicial District-Va.

Paxton, Julie-Judge, Kentucky Circuit Court Thirty-first Judicial Circuit-Ky.

Payne, A. Lynn, Jr.-Presiding Judge, Utah District Court Eighth Judicial District-Utah

Payne, C. David-Judge, Ohio Court of Common Pleas Lawrence County-Ohio

Payne, David C.-Judge, Kentucky District Court Sixth Judicial District-Ky.

Payne, Don Ed-Associate District Judge, Oklahoma District Court Seventeenth Judicial District-Okla.

Payne, Edith K.-Judge, New Jersey Superior Court Appellate Division-N.J.

Payne, Gary D.-Judge, Kentucky Circuit Court Twenty-second Judicial Circuit-Ky.

Payne, H. Dudley, Jr.-Chief Judge, Virginia Juvenile and Domestic Relations District Court Twentieth Judicial District-Va.

Payne, James Hardy-Chief Judge, United States District Court Eastern District of Oklahoma-Okla.

Payne, James W.-Judge, Marion Superior Court-Ind.

Payne, John E.-Associate Judge, Illinois Circuit Court Fifteenth Judicial Circuit-Ill.

Payne, John M., Jr.-Justice, Trial Court of Massachusetts District Court Department Hampden County Chicopee Division-Mass.

Payne, Jonathan Marlin-Judge, Probate Court of Chattooga County-Ga.

Payne, Kibbie F.-Judge, The Civil Court of the City of New York-N.Y.

Payne, Pamela F.-Judge, Stevens District Court Stevens County-Wash.

Payne, Paul-Chief Magistrate, Magistrate Court of Dawson County-Ga.

Payne, Richard Gale-Chief Judge, Florida Circuit Court Sixteenth Judicial Circuit-Fla.

Payne, Robert E.-Judge, United States District Court Eastern District of Virginia-Va.

Payne, Ronald K.-Resident Judge, North Carolina Superior Court Eighth Judicial Division District 28-N.C.

Payne, Roy S.-Magistrate Judge, United States District Court Western District of Louisiana-La.

Payne, Samuel H.-Judge, Tennessee Circuit Court Eleventh Judicial District-Tenn.

Paynter, Steven W.-Judge, The Civil Court of the City of New York-N.Y.

Payton, J. Jeffrey-Special Judge, Oklahoma District Court Fifteenth Judicial District-Okla.

Payton, Jeff-Judge, Mansfield Municipal Court-Ohio

Peach, John Weston-Judge, Florida Circuit Court Third Judicial Circuit-Fla.

Peacock, Russel W.-Justice of the Peace, Lund Justices' Court-Nev.

Peacock, Sarah M.-Associate Judge, Juvenile Court of Georgia Middle Judicial Circuit-Ga.

Peagler, Desiree Sutton-Associate Judge, Juvenile Court of Georgia Stone Mountain Judicial Circuit-Ga.

Peagler, George M., Jr.-Judge, Superior Court of Georgia Southwestern Judicial Circuit-Ga.

Pearl, Deborah M.-Judge, Essex District Probate Court-Conn.

Pearl, Jane-Judge, New York City Family Court-N.Y.

Pearman, James Richard-District Judge, Oklahoma District Court Tenth Judicial District-Okla.

Pearson, Alan L.-Chief Judge, Iowa District Court First Judicial District-Ia.

Pearson, Amanda K.-Judge, Saguache County Court-Colo.

Pearson, Barbara S.-Justice, Trial Court of Massachusetts District Court Department Middlesex County Lowell Division-Mass.

Pearson, Dennis R.-Judge, Vermont Trial Court-Vt.

Pearson, Glenn A.-Chief Judge, Michigan District Court District Ninety-four-Mich.

Pearson, John E.-Judge, Minnesota District Court Seventh Judicial District-Minn.

Pearson, Linley E.-Judge, Clinton Circuit Court-Ind.

Pearson, Ronald G.-Judge, United States Bankruptcy Court Southern District of West Virginia-W.Va.

ALPHABETICAL NAME INDEX

Pearson, S. D.-Chief Magistrate, Magistrate Court of Warren County-Ga.

Pearson, Skipper J.-Judge, Minnesota District Court Seventh Judicial District-Minn.

Peart, James C.-Judge, Idaho District Court Third Judicial District Magistrate Division-Ida.

Pease, Prudence-Assistant Judge, Vermont Trial Court Orange County-Vt.

Peasley, Frank-Judge, Douglas Municipal Court-Wyo.

Peatross, Charles B.-Judge, Louisiana Court of Appeal Second Circuit-La.

Peatross, Paul M., Jr.-Judge, Virginia Circuit Court Sixteenth Judicial Circuit-Va.

Peavy, Stanley H., III-Judge, Young County Court-Tex.

Pechman, Marsha J.-Judge, United States District Court Western District of Washington-Wash.

Peck, A. Susan-Judge, Connecticut Superior Court-Conn.

Peck, Andrew J.-Magistrate Judge, United States District Court Southern District of New York-N.Y.

Peck, George R.-Judge, Nassau County Court-N.Y.

Peckham, Eugene E.-Surrogate, Broome County Surrogate's Court-N.Y.

Peckler, Darren W.-Judge, Kentucky Circuit Court Fiftieth Judicial Circuit-Ky.

Peden, Mark-Judge, Martinsville City Court-Ind.

Peden, Michael Parker-Judge, Texas District Court 285th Judicial District-Tex.

Peden, Michelle-Judge, Hillsborough County Court-Fla.

Pederson, William R.-Judge, Minnesota Workers' Compensation Court of Appeals-Minn.

Peebles, Barbara T.-Associate Circuit Judge, Missouri Circuit Court Twenty-second Judicial Circuit-Mo.

Peebles, David E.-Magistrate Judge, United States District Court Northern District of New York-N.Y.

Peed, F. Gates-Judge, Superior Court of Georgia Ogeechee Judicial Circuit-Ga.

Peek, Bill-Judge, Texas District Court 202nd Judicial District-Tex.

Peek, Powell W.-Judge, Red River County Court-Tex.

Peek, Richard H.-Judge, Mills Municipal Court-Wyo.

Peel, Colby-Judge, Washington County Court-Fla.

Peele, Stanley-Emergency Judge, North Carolina District Court-N.C.

Peeler, Clarence Lee, Jr.-Senior Judge, Superior Court of Georgia-Ga.

Peeler, Robert E.-Judge, Edgefield County Probate Court-S.C.

Peeples, Clayburn-Judge, Tennessee Circuit Court Twenty-eighth Judicial District-Tenn.

Peeples, David-Judge, Texas District Court 224th Judicial District-Tex.

Peeples, Rodney A.-Judge, South Carolina Circuit Court Second Judicial Circuit-S.C.

Peer, Norman J.-Judge, New Jersey Superior Court Vicinage Nine-N.J.

Peer, Steven-Judge, Van Buren District Court-Ark.

Peet, Richard-Judge, Gray County Court-Tex.

Peim, Stuart L.-Judge, New Jersey Superior Court Vicinage Twelve-N.J.

Pekowsky, Robert R.-Reserve Judge, Wisconsin Circuit Court-Wis.

Pelander, John-Vice Chief Judge, Arizona Court of Appeals Division Two-Ariz.

Pelican, Steven T.-Judge, Colorado District Court Fourth Judicial District-Colo.

Pelikan, Daniel-Associate Circuit Judge, Missouri Circuit Court Eleventh Judicial Circuit-Mo.

Pellecchia, Donald E.-Judge, Florida Circuit Court Twentieth Judicial Circuit-Fla.

Pellegrini, Dante R.-Judge, The Commonwealth Court of Pennsylvania-Pa.

Pellegrino, Joseph A.-Associate Justice, Trial Court of Massachusetts Juvenile Court Department Hampden County Division-Mass.

Pellegrino, Joseph H.-Judge, Connecticut Appellate Court-Conn.

Pelton, Charles H.-District Judge, Iowa District Court Seventh Judicial District-Ia.

Pemberton, Stephen C.-Chief Judge, Illinois Circuit Court Fifteenth Judicial Circuit-Ill.

Pena, Rosendo, Jr.-Judge, Superior Court of California County of Fresno-Calif.

Pendergrass, Carl-Judge, Texas District Court 83rd Judicial District-Tex.

Pendino, Sam-Judge, Florida Circuit Court Thirteenth Judicial Circuit-Fla.

Pendleton, Alan Frank-Judge, Minnesota District Court Tenth Judicial District-Minn.

Pengilly, Charles-Judge, Alaska Superior Court Fourth Judicial District-Alas.

Penick, Thomas E., Jr.-Judge, Florida Circuit Court Sixth Judicial Circuit-Fla.

Penkower, Alan S.-Judge, Pennsylvania Court of Common Pleas Fifth Judicial District-Pa.

Penn, John Garrett-Senior Judge, United States District Court District of Columbia-D.C.

Pennington, Mickey Ray-Judge, Texas District Court 38th Judicial District-Tex.

Penny, J. Curt, Jr.-Judge, Kit Carson County Court-Colo.

Penoyar, Elizabeth-Judge, North District Court Pacific County and Judge, Ilwaco, Long Beach, Raymond and South Bend Municipal Courts-Wash.

Penoyar, Joel Morris-Judge, Washington Superior Court Pacific-Wahkiakum Counties-Wash.

Penrod, Earl G.-Judge, Gibson Superior Court-Ind.

Pensinger, Michele-Judge, Portland City Court-Ind.

Pensis, Teresa A.-Judge, North Stonington District Probate Court-Conn.

Pentuic, Carol M.-Associate Judge, Illinois Circuit Court Fourteenth Judicial Circuit-Ill.

Peoples, Howell N.-Chancellor, Tennessee Chancery Court Eleventh Judicial District-Tenn.

Peoples, Thomas G., Jr.-President Judge, Pennsylvania Court of Common Pleas Twenty-fourth Judicial District-Pa.

Pepe, Steven D.-Magistrate Judge, United States District Court Eastern District of Michigan-Mich.

Pepper, W. Allen, Jr.-Judge, United States District Court Northern District of Mississippi-Miss.

Peppers, Charles Donald, Sr.-Judge, State Court of Walker County-Ga.

Pepple, Frederick D.-Judge, Ohio Court of Common Pleas Auglaize County-Ohio

Pera, John R.-Judge, Lake Superior Court-Ind.

Perachi, Paul E.-First Justice, Trial Court of Massachusetts Juvenile Court Department Berkshire County Division-Mass.

Pereksta, Darlene J.-Judge, New Jersey Superior Court Vicinage Fourteen-N.J.

Perelman, David S.-Recalled Magistrate Judge, United States District Court Northern District of Ohio-Ohio

Pereyra-Shuminer, Cristina-Judge, Dade County Court-Fla.

Perez, George W.-Chief Judge, Minnesota Tax Court-Minn.

Perez, Luis G.-Associate Justice, Trial Court of Massachusetts Juvenile Court Department Worcester Division-Mass.

Perez, Myrna M. Martinez-Judge, New York City Family Court-N.Y.

Perez, Nancy-Judge, Palm Beach County Court-Fla.

Perez-Gimenez, Juan M.-Judge, United States District Court District of Puerto Rico

Perezous, Michael J.-Judge, Pennsylvania Court of Common Pleas Second Judicial District-Pa.

Perfilio, Joseph P.-Judge, New Jersey Superior Court Vicinage Twelve-N.J.

Perigo, Timothy W.-Presiding Judge, Missouri Circuit Court Fortieth Judicial Circuit-Mo.

Perivolidis, Arthur C.-Associate Judge, Illinois Circuit Court of Cook County-Ill.

Perk, Ralph J., Jr.-Judge, Cleveland Municipal Court-Ohio

Perk, Steven L.-Judge, Superior Court of California County of Orange-Calif.

Perkins, Carson Dane-Judge, Superior Court of Georgia Alapaha Judicial Circuit-Ga.

Perkins, David W.-Judge, Superior Court of California County of Los Angeles-Calif.

Perkins, Edward L.-Judge, Oregon Circuit Court Eleventh Judicial District-Ore.

Perkins, Harold W.-Associate Justice, New Hampshire Superior Court-N.H.

Perkins, Richard C.-Judge, Minnesota District Court First Judicial District-Minn.

Perkins, Richard K.-Judge, Hawaii Circuit Court First Judicial Circuit-Hi.

Perkins, Robert Anton-Judge, Texas District Court 331st Judicial District-Tex.

Perkins, Stephen L.-Active Retired Justice, Maine Superior Court-Me.

Perkins, Thomas L.-Judge, United States Bankruptcy Court Central District of Illinois-Ill.

Perkinson, Charles A., Jr.-Chief Judge, Virginia Juvenile and Domestic Relations District Court Sixth Judicial District-Va.

Perlich, John J.-Judge, Wisconsin Circuit Court La Crosse Circuit-Wis.

Perlman, Burton-Recalled Judge, United States Bankruptcy Court Southern District of Ohio-Ohio

Perlman, Gail L.-First Justice, Trial Court of Massachusetts Probate and Family Court Department Hampshire County Division-Mass.

Perluss, Dennis M.-Presiding Justice, California Court of Appeal Second District Division Seven-Calif.

Perren, Steven Zalkind-Associate Justice, California Court of Appeal Second District Division Six-Calif.

Perretta, Charlotte Anne-Associate Justice, Massachusetts Appeals Court-Mass.

Perretti, Serena-Retired Judge, New Jersey Superior Court-N.J.

Perri, Jamie S.-Judge, New Jersey Superior Court Vicinage Nine-N.J.

Perris, Elizabeth L.-Judge, Bankruptcy Appellate Panel Ninth Circuit and Judge, United States Bankruptcy Court District of Oregon-Ore.

Perrone, Thomas C.-Judge, Cass Superior Court-Ind.

Perrow, Mosby Garland, III-Judge, Virginia Circuit Court Twenty-fourth Judicial Circuit-Va.

Perry, Belvin-Chief Judge, Florida Circuit Court Ninth Judicial Circuit-Fla.

Perry, Buddy D.-Judge, Tennessee Circuit Court Twelfth Judicial District-Tenn.

Perry, Catherine D.-Judge, United States District Court Eastern District of Missouri-Mo.

Perry, Courtland D., II-Active Retired Judge, Maine District Court-Me.

Perry, Daniel L.-Judge, Florida Circuit Court Thirteenth Judicial Circuit-Fla.

Perry, Darrel R.-Judge, Idaho Court of Appeals-Ida.

Perry, Edwin J., III-Judge, Juvenile Court of Georgia South Georgia Judicial Circuit-Ga.

Perry, James E.C.-Judge, Florida Circuit Court Eighteenth Judicial Circuit-Fla.

Perry, John-Judge, Wyoming District Court Sixth Judicial District-Wyo.

Perry, John R.-Judge, Michigan District Court District Thirty-six-Mich.

Perry, Matthew J., Jr.-Senior Judge, United States District Court District of South Carolina-S.C.

Perry, Morton Lee-Senior Judge, Dade County Court-Fla.

Perry, Nathaniel C., III-Chief Judge, Michigan District Court District Sixty-eight-Mich.

Perry, Richard McBee-Associate District Judge, Oklahoma District Court Fourth Judicial District-Okla.

Perry, Robert J.-Judge, Superior Court of California County of Los Angeles-Calif.

Perry, Roger L.-Chief Judge, West Virginia Circuit Court Seventh Judicial Circuit-W.Va.

Perskie, Steven P.-Judge, New Jersey Superior Court Vicinage One-N.J.

Person, Carol M.-Judge, Minnesota District Court Sixth Judicial District-Minn.

Person, Suzanne E.-Judge, Superior Court of California County of Los Angeles-Calif.

Persón, Victor H.-Judge, Superior Court of California County of Los Angeles-Calif.

Persons, Jim-Judge, Mississippi Chancery Court Eighth Judicial District-Miss.

Perszyk, Joyce-Judge, Havre City Court-Mont.

ALPHABETICAL NAME INDEX

ALPHABETICAL NAME INDEX

Picquet, Roger-Judge, Superior Court of California County of San Luis Obispo-Calif.
Pieper, Daniel F.-Judge, South Carolina Circuit Court Ninth Judicial Circuit-S.C.
Pieras, Jaime, Jr.-Senior Judge, United States District Court District of Puerto Rico
Pierce, C. Fenning-Judge, Ohio Court of Common Pleas Coshocton County-Ohio
Pierce, Cary B.-Associate Judge, Illinois Circuit Court Eighteenth Judicial Circuit-Ill.
Pierce, Dan F.-Chief Magistrate, Magistrate Court of Walton County-Ga.
Pierce, David M.-Chief Magistrate, Magistrate Court of Houston County-Ga.
Pierce, Ellen I.-Chief Magistrate, Magistrate Court of Putnam County-Ga.
Pierce, George H.-Senior Judge, Bradford County Court-Fla.
Pierce, Harriett P.-Judge, Kershaw County Probate Court-S.C.
Pierce, James B.-Judge, Superior Court of California County of Los Angeles-Calif.
Pierce, Lynne A.-Chief Judge, Grosse Pointe Shores and Grosse Pointe Woods Municipal Courts-Mich.
Pierce, Mackie-Judge, Arkansas Circuit Court Sixth Judicial Circuit-Ark.
Pierce, Robert D. "Danny"-Judge, Walker County Court-Tex.
Pierce, Steven D.-Associate Justice, Trial Court of Massachusetts Housing Court Department Boston Division-Mass.
Piergies, James D.-Judge, Montgomery County Court-Ohio
Pierron, George Joseph, Jr.-Judge, Kansas Court of Appeals-Kan.
Piersol, Lawrence L.-Chief Judge, United States District Court District of South Dakota-S.D.
Pierson, Paul J.-Judge, Sullivan Circuit Court-Ind.
Pierson-Treacy, Rebekah-Judge, Marion Superior Court-Ind.
Piester, David L.-Magistrate Judge, United States District Court District of Nebraska-Neb.
Pietrucha, Edward N.-Circuit Judge, Illinois Circuit Court of Cook County-Ill.
Pietruszka, Michael F.-Judge, Erie County Court-N.Y.
Pietrykowski, Mark L.-Judge, Ohio Court of Appeals Sixth District-Ohio
Piggotte, Julianne-Judge, Florida Circuit Court Seventh Judicial Circuit-Fla.
Pigman, Robert J.-Judge, Vanderburgh Superior Court-Ind.
Pigott, Eugene F., Jr.-Presiding Justice, New York Supreme Court Appellate Division Fourth Judicial Department-N.Y.
Pihlaja, Steven A.-Judge, Minnesota District Court Fourth Judicial District-Minn.
Pike, C. Ashley-Judge, Ohio Court of Common Pleas Columbiana County-Ohio
Pikkarainen, A. John-Chief Judge, Michigan District Court District Fifty-three-Mich.
Pileggi, William G.-Associate Judge, Illinois Circuit Court of Cook County-Ill.
Pille, Glenn E.-District Judge, Iowa District Court Fifth Judicial District-Ia.
Pilshaw, Rebecca L.-Judge, Kansas District Court Eighteenth Judicial District-Kan.
Pincus, S. Michael-Associate Judge, Circuit Court for Montgomery County, Sixth Judicial Circuit-Md.
Pine, Elizabeth W.-Associate Justice, New York Supreme Court Appellate Division Fourth Judicial Department-N.Y.
Pineda-Kirwan, Diccia T.-Judge, The Civil Court of the City of New York-N.Y.
Pineiro, Robert M.-Judge, Florida Circuit Court Eleventh Judicial Circuit-Fla.
Pineles, Dean B.-Judge, Vermont Trial Court-Vt.
Pines, Emily-Justice, New York Supreme Court Tenth Judicial District-N.Y.
Pines, Spero-Judge, Broome County Family Court-N.Y.
Pineschi, Alan V.-Judge, Superior Court of California County of Placer-Calif.
Piper, Gordon H.-Justice, Trial Court of Massachusetts Land Court Department-Mass.
Piquette, William J.-Senior Judge, Dade County Court-Fla.
Pirraglia, Robert K.-Associate Judge, Rhode Island District Court-R.I.
Pirrello, R. L.-Circuit Judge, Illinois Circuit Court Seventeenth Judicial Circuit-Ill.
Pirtle, Patrick A.-Judge, Texas District Court 251st Judicial District-Tex.
Pisano, Joel A.-Judge, United States District Court District of New Jersey-N.J.
Pisano, Ralph C., Jr.-Judge, Huron Municipal Court-Ohio
Pisansky, John-Judge, New Jersey Superior Court Vicinage Twelve-N.J.
Piscal, Francis P.-Judge, New Jersey Superior Court Vicinage Fourteen-N.J.
Pitch, Myron E.-Judge, Helena City Court-Mont.
Pitman, Henry B.-Magistrate Judge, United States District Court Southern District of New York-N.Y.
Pitman, Karen-Judge, Probate Court of Monroe County-Ga.
Pitre, Robert A.-Judge, Louisiana District Court Twenty-fourth Judicial District-La.
Pittman, Craig S.-Judge, Alabama Court of Civil Appeals-Ala.
Pittman, Edwin Lloyd-Chief Justice, Mississippi Supreme Court-Miss.
Pittman, Gregory Christopher-Judge, Muskegon County Probate Court-Mich.
Pittman, John Mauzy-Judge, Arkansas Court of Appeals-Ark.
Pittman, Judy Markham-Chief Judge, Florida Circuit Court Fourteenth Judicial Circuit-Fla.
Pittman, Laurie J.-Judge, Portage County Municipal Court-Ohio
Pittman, Patty Jenkins-Judge, Connecticut Superior Court-Conn.
Pittman, Virgil-Senior Judge, United States District Court Southern District of Alabama-Ala.
Pitts, Arthur G.-Justice, New York Supreme Court Tenth Judicial District-N.Y.
Pitts, Bernard-Judge, Burns and Pine Bluffs Municipal Courts-Wyo.
Pitts, Frances-Judge, Wayne County Probate Court-Mich.
Pizzo, Mark A.-Magistrate Judge, United States District Court Middle District of Florida-Fla.
Pizzuto, Peter D.-Judge, New Jersey Tax Court-N.J.
Plager, S. Jay-Senior Judge, United States Court of Appeals Federal Circuit
Plaines, Robert-Judge, Jefferson County Court-Fla.
Plaisance, Mark D.-Judge, Baker City Court-La.
Plantz, Charles-Judge, Nebraska County Court Twelfth Judicial District-Neb.
Platt, David R.-Judge, Kansas District Court Eighth Judicial District-Kan.
Platt, Katherine B. L.-Judge, Pennsylvania Court of Common Pleas Fifteenth Judicial District-Pa.
Platt, L. Stuart-Magistrate Judge, United States District Court Western District of Texas-Tex.
Platt, Michael E.-Judge, Superior Court of California County of San Joaquin-Calif.
Platt, Stephen E.-Judge, Elkhart Superior Court-Ind.
Platt, Steven I.-Associate Judge, Circuit Court for Prince George's County, Seventh Judicial Circuit-Md.
Platt, Thomas Collier, Jr.-Senior Judge, United States District Court Eastern District of New York-N.Y.
Platt, William H.-President Judge, Pennsylvania Court of Common Pleas Thirty-first Judicial District-Pa.
Platzer, Cynthia Siemen-Judge, Michigan District Court District Seventy-two-Mich.
Platzer, Victoria-Judge, Florida Circuit Court Eleventh Judicial Circuit-Fla.
Plaut, Frank-Judge, Colorado District Court First Judicial District-Colo.
Plawecki, Mark J.-Judge, Michigan District Court District Twenty-Mich.
Pleicones, Costa M.-Associate Justice, South Carolina Supreme Court-S.C.
Plese, Annette S.-Judge, Spokane District Court Spokane County and Judge, Spokane Municipal Court-Wash.
Pleus, Robert J., Jr.-Judge, Florida District Court of Appeal Fifth District-Fla.
Plewe, Todd J.-Judge, Montezuma County Court-Colo.
Plitt, Emory A., Jr.-Associate Judge, Circuit Court for Harford County, Third Judicial Circuit-Md.
Plogstedt, Antoinette-Judge, Orange County Court-Fla.
Plotkin, Barry L.-Judge, Superior Court of California County of San Bernardino-Calif.
Plotz, Kenneth M.-Chief Judge, Colorado District Court Eleventh Judicial District-Colo.
Pluim, Jan A.-Judge, Superior Court of California County of Los Angeles-Calif.
Plumadore, Jan H.-Justice, New York Supreme Court Fourth Judicial District-N.Y.
Plummer, Mary P.-Magistrate Judge, Kansas District Court Twenty-sixth Judicial District-Kan.
Plunk, Britt-Judge, Texas District Court 356th Judicial District-Tex.
Plunkett, Paul E.-Senior Judge, United States District Court Northern District of Illinois-Ill.
Poch, Thomas B.-Judge, Minnesota District Court First Judicial District-Minn.
Poche, Marcel B.-Judge, Superior Court of California County of Santa Clara-Calif.
Podgorski, Richard-Judge, Denton County Criminal Court at Law No. 5-Tex.
Poe, Ted-Judge, Texas District Court 228th Judicial District-Tex.
Poehler, Patricia T.-First Justice, Trial Court of Massachusetts District Court Department Hampden County Palmer Division and Justice, Westfield Division-Mass.
Pogarsky, Alan J.-Judge, New Jersey Superior Court Vicinage Fourteen-N.J.
Pogue, Donald C.-Judge, United States Court of International Trade
Pohl, Dale L.-Judge, Kansas District Court Thirteenth Judicial District-Kan.
Pohorelsky, Viktor V.-Magistrate Judge, United States District Court Eastern District of New York-N.Y.
Poindexter, Gammiel Gray-Judge, Virginia General District Court Sixth Judicial District-Va.
Poitras, Dennis R.-Judge, Ashford District Probate Court-Conn.
Pokorny, Gale-Judge, Nebraska County Court Third Judicial District-Neb.
Pokorny, Thomas J.-Judge, Ohio Court of Common Pleas Cuyahoga County-Ohio
Polaha, Jerome M.-Judge, Nevada District Court Second Judicial District-Nev.
Polen, Mark E.-Chief Judge, Florida District Court of Appeal Fourth District-Fla.
Polidori, Ruthanne N.-Judge, Colorado District Court First Judicial District-Colo.
Polito, William P.-Justice, New York Supreme Court Seventh Judicial District-N.Y.
Polizzi, Thomas V.-Justice, New York Supreme Court Eleventh Judicial District-N.Y.
Pollack, Milton-Senior Judge, United States District Court Southern District of New York-N.Y.
Pollack, Richard-Judge, Hawaii Circuit Court First Judicial Circuit-Hi.
Pollak, Cheryl L.-Magistrate Judge, United States District Court Eastern District of New York-N.Y.
Pollak, Louis H.-Senior Judge, United States District Court Eastern District of Pennsylvania-Pa.
Pollak, Stuart R.-Associate Justice, California Court of Appeal First District Division Three-Calif.
Pollard, Nancy A.-Judge, Superior Court of California County of Orange-Calif.
Pollex, Charles A.-Judge, Wisconsin Circuit Court Adams Circuit-Wis.
Pollex, Robert C.-Judge, Ohio Court of Common Pleas Wood County-Ohio
Polley, William G.-Judge, Superior Court of California County of Tuolumne-Calif.
Pollitt, H. William, Jr.-Judge, Franklin County Municipal Court-Ohio
Pollock, Jerry-Judge, Broward County Court-Fla.
Polos, Peter J.-Judge, Superior Court of California County of Orange-Calif.
Polozola, Frank J.-Chief Judge, United States District Court Middle District of Louisiana-La.
Polster, Dan Aaron-Judge, United States District Court Northern District of Ohio-Ohio

Polston, Ricky-Judge, Florida District Court of Appeal First District-Fla.

Pomaro, Nicholas T.-Associate Judge, Illinois Circuit Court of Cook County-Ill.

Pomarole, Michael J.-Justice, Trial Court of Massachusetts District Court Department Middlesex County Cambridge Division-Mass.

Pomeroy, Christine A.-Judge, Washington Superior Court Thurston County-Wash.

Pomponio, Denise Almeida-Judge, Florida Circuit Court Thirteenth Judicial Circuit-Fla.

Pomponio, Joseph-Judge, West Virginia Family Court Circuit Fifteen-W.Va.

Ponce, Francisco G.-Judge, Dimmit County Court-Tex.

Ponce De Leon, Edmund-Circuit Judge, Illinois Circuit Court of Cook County-Ill.

Ponder, Suzan S.-Judge, Baton Rouge City Court-La.

Pone, Edward A.-Judge, North Carolina District Court District 12-N.C.

Ponsor, Michael A.-Judge, United States District Court District of Massachusetts-Mass.

Ponterio, Frank V.-Justice, New York Supreme Court Second Judicial District-N.Y.

Pontious, Victor D., Jr.-Judge, Ohio Court of Common Pleas Fayette County-Ohio

Ponton, George G.-Judge, Frankfort City Court-Ind.

Pool, C. Randy-Judge, North Carolina District Court District 29-N.C.

Poole, Craig E.-Chief Magistrate, Magistrate Court of Turner County-Ga.

Poole, James Howard-Judge, Superior Court of California County of Orange-Calif.

Poole, Ronald-Judge, Oregon Circuit Court Sixteenth Judicial District-Ore.

Pooler, Catherine M.-Judge, Dade County Court-Fla.

Pooler, Rosemary S.-Judge, United States Court of Appeals Second Circuit

Poovey, Nathaniel J.-Resident Judge, North Carolina Superior Court Seventh Judicial Division District 25B-N.C.

Pope, John A., III-Judge, Texas District Court 381st Judicial District-Tex.

Pope, John William-Judge, New Mexico District Court Thirteenth Judicial District-N.Mex.

Pope, M. Carol-Circuit Judge, Illinois Circuit Court Eighth Judicial Circuit-Ill.

Pope, Marvin P., Jr.-Judge, North Carolina District Court District 28-N.C.

Pope, Michael J.-Associate Judge, Illinois Circuit Court of Cook County-Ill.

Pope, Robert Thomas-Senior Judge, Superior Court of Georgia-Ga.

Pope, Ronald R.-Judge, Texas Family District Court 328th Judicial District-Tex.

Pope, Samuel B.-Judge, Arkansas Circuit Court Tenth Judicial Circuit-Ark.

Popejoy, Kenneth L.-Associate Judge, Illinois Circuit Court Eighteenth Judicial Circuit-Ill.

Popeo, Gerald J.-Judge, Utica City Court-N.Y.

Popke, Lita Masini-Judge, Michigan Circuit Court Third Judicial Circuit-Mich.

Popovich, Gregory-Judge, Kentucky District Court Seventeenth Judicial District-Ky.

Popovich, John E., Jr.-Judge, Colorado District Court Seventeenth Judicial District-Colo.

Poppell, Ralph E.-Chief Magistrate, Magistrate Court of McIntosh County-Ga.

Poppiti, Vincent James-Chief Judge, Delaware Family Court-Del.

Poppy, Donald A.-Judge, Wisconsin Circuit Court Calumet Circuit-Wis.

Porada, Elizabeth A.-Associate Justice, Massachusetts Appeals Court-Mass.

Porcellino, Charles E.-Associate Judge, Illinois Circuit Court of Cook County-Ill.

Poretz, Barry R.-Magistrate Judge, United States District Court Eastern District of Virginia-Va.

Porfilio, John C.-Senior Judge, United States Court of Appeals Tenth Circuit

Poritz, Deborah T.-Chief Justice, Supreme Court of New Jersey-N.J.

Porteous, G. Thomas, Jr.-Judge, United States District Court Eastern District of Louisiana-La.

Porter, Charles A., Jr.-Judge, Minnesota District Court Fourth Judicial District-Minn.

Porter, Charles L.-Judge, Louisiana District Court Sixteenth Judicial District-La.

Porter, Dennis J.-Associate Judge, Illinois Circuit Court of Cook County-Ill.

Porter, Gene T.-Chief Judge, Nevada District Court Eighth Judicial District-Nev.

Porter, J. Frank-Judge, Lee County Court-Fla.

Porter, J. Richard, III-Judge, Superior Court of Georgia South Georgia Judicial Circuit-Ga.

Porter, Jesse E. "Rusty", Jr.-Judge, West Helena District Court-Ark.

Porter, Linda S.-Judge, Lancaster County Separate Juvenile Court-Neb.

Porter, Louisa-Magistrate Judge, United States District Court Southern District of California-Calif.

Porter, Patsy Y.-Judge, State Court of Fulton County-Ga.

Porter, Rick-Judge, Clallam District Court No. 1 Clallam County-Wash.

Porter, W. Michael-Judge, Baca County Court-Colo.

Porter, William Reed-Judge, Texas District Court 276th Judicial District-Tex.

Portley, Maurice-Judge, Arizona Court of Appeals Division One-Ariz.

Portnoy, Linda S.-Judge, Lake Forest Park Municipal Court-Wash.

Porzio, Ralph J.-Judge, New York City Family Court-N.Y.

Posner, Charles A.-Judge, The Criminal Court of the City of New York-N.Y.

Posner, Richard A.-Judge, United States Court of Appeals Seventh Circuit

Post, Cheryl L.-Judge, Colorado District Court Eighteenth Judicial District-Colo.

Post, Dynda Rose Parks-District Judge, Oklahoma District Court Twelfth Judicial District-Okla.

Post, Edward R.-Chief Judge, Michigan Circuit Court Twentieth Judicial Circuit-Mich.

Post, Kenneth David-Judge, Michigan District Court District Fifty-eight-Mich.

Poston, Charles Evans-Judge, Virginia Circuit Court Fourth Judicial Circuit-Va.

Poston, Janet Nordell-Judge, Minnesota District Court Fourth Judicial District-Minn.

Poston, McCracken "Ken"-Judge, Juvenile Court of Georgia Lookout Mountain Judicial Circuit-Ga.

Potkonjak, Theodore S.-Associate Judge, Illinois Circuit Court Nineteenth Judicial Circuit-Ill.

Potter, Barbara R.-Judge, St. Lawrence County Family Court-N.Y.

Potter, Brent J.-Judge, Kentucky District Court Eighth Judicial District-Ky.

Potter, Gregory J.-Judge, Wisconsin Circuit Court Wood Circuit-Wis.

Potter, John W.-Senior Judge, United States District Court Northern District of Ohio-Ohio

Potter, Richard B.-Judge, Virginia Circuit Court Thirty-first Judicial Circuit-Va.

Potter, Russell F., Jr.-Senior Judge, Connecticut Superior Court-Conn.

Potter, Sam C., Jr.-Judge, Kentucky District Court Eighth Judicial District-Ky.

Potterfield, Amanda P.-District Judge, Iowa District Court Sixth Judicial District-Ia.

Potts, Wendy Lynn-Judge, Michigan Circuit Court Sixth Judicial Circuit-Mich.

Potvin, Sherri-Assistant Judge, Vermont Trial Court Grand Isle County-Vt.

Poulos, John A.-Judge, Canton Municipal Court-Ohio

Pounders, William R.-Judge, Superior Court of California County of Los Angeles-Calif.

Powell, Bob-Judge, Probate Court of Twiggs County-Ga.

Powell, Carleton D.-Special Trial Judge, United States Tax Court

Powell, Charles-Judge, Cokeville Municipal Court-Wyo.

Powell, Cleo Elaine-Judge, Virginia Circuit Court Twelfth Judicial Circuit-Va.

Powell, David E.-Associate District Judge, Oklahoma District Court Sixth Judicial District-Okla.

Powell, Dennis-Judge, Texas District Court 163rd Judicial District-Tex.

Powell, Kenneth-Judge, Probate Court of Bleckley County-Ga.

Powell, Larry Scott-Judge, Ohio Court of Common Pleas Meigs County-Ohio

Powell, Mark A.-Associate Circuit Judge, Missouri Circuit Court Thirty-first Judicial Circuit-Mo.

Powell, Mark E.-Judge, North Carolina District Court District 29-N.C.

Powell, Michael E.-Judge, Ohio Court of Common Pleas Warren County-Ohio

Powell, Rom W.-Senior Judge, Florida Circuit Court Ninth Judicial Circuit-Fla.

Powell, Samuel T., III-Judge, Virginia Circuit Court Ninth Judicial Circuit-Va.

Powell, Stephen W.-Judge, Ohio Court of Appeals Twelfth District-Ohio

Powell, Tony-Judge, Kansas District Court Eighteenth Judicial District-Kan.

Power, David Edwin-Judge, Superior Court of California County of Solano-Calif.

Power, Thomas G.-Judge, Michigan Circuit Court Thirteenth Judicial Circuit-Mich.

Powers, Dallas P.-Judge, Warren County Court-Ohio

Powers, Dennis N.-Judge, Michigan District Court District Fifty-two Division One-Mich.

Powers, Jean A.-Chief Magistrate, Magistrate Court of Worth County-Ga.

Powers, Jim-Judge, Hays County Court-Tex.

Powers, John Y.-Recalled Magistrate Judge, United States District Court Eastern District of Tennessee-Tenn.

Powers, Keith A.-Judge, Maine District Court-Me.

Powers, Lewis W.-Judge, Carson County Court-Tex.

Powers, Margaret A.-Judge, Superior Court of California County of San Bernardino-Calif.

Powers, Mark L.-Judge, Schenectady County Family Court-N.Y.

Powers, Michael F.-Chief Judge, Kansas District Court Eighth Judicial District-Kan.

Powers, Rocky L.-Associate District Judge, Oklahoma District Court Nineteenth Judicial District-Okla.

Powers, Warren A.-First Justice, Trial Court of Massachusetts District Court Department Worcester County Milford Division and Justice, Norfolk County Quincy Division-Mass.

Poyfair, Edwin L.-Judge, Washington Superior Court Clark County-Wash.

Pozonsky, Paul M.-Judge, Pennsylvania Court of Common Pleas Twenty-seventh Judicial District-Pa.

Pozza, Karen H.-Judge, Texas District Court 407th Judicial District-Tex.

Pozzi, Donald R.-Judge, Victoria County Court-Tex.

Prado, Edward C.-Judge, United States District Court Western District of Texas-Tex.

Prager, Erica L.-Judge, Nassau County District Court-N.Y.

Prager, Ronald S.-Judge, Superior Court of California County of San Diego-Calif.

Prall, G. Michael-Circuit Judge, Illinois Circuit Court Eleventh Judicial Circuit-Ill.

Prather, Andy-Judge, State Court of Muscogee County-Ga.

Prather, Charles N.-Senior Judge, Florida Circuit Court Ninth Judicial Circuit-Fla.

Prather, Claude R.-Judge, Kentucky District Court Thirtieth Judicial District-Ky.

Prather, Sharon-Circuit Judge, Illinois Circuit Court Nineteenth Judicial Circuit-Ill.

Prats, Sheila M.-Judge, Connecticut Superior Court-Conn.

Pratt, Charles F.-Judge, Allen Superior Court-Ind.

Pratt, Daniel S.-Judge, Superior Court of California County of Los Angeles-Calif.

Pratt, Darrell-Chief Judge, West Virginia Circuit Court Twenty-fourth Judicial Circuit-W.Va.

Pratt, Eugene Franklin, III-Judge, Benton District Court Benton County-Wash.

Pratt, J. Burdette-Presiding Judge, Oregon Circuit Court Ninth Judicial District-Ore.

Pratt, Linda Raspolich-Judge, Broward County Court-Fla.

ALPHABETICAL NAME INDEX

Pratt, Ralph D.-President Judge, Pennsylvania Court of Common Pleas Fifty-third Judicial District-Pa.
Pratt, Robert W.-Judge, United States District Court Southern District of Iowa-Ia.
Pratt, Tanya Walton-Judge, Marion Superior Court-Ind.
Pratte, Kenneth W.-Presiding Judge, Missouri Circuit Court Twenty-fourth Judicial Circuit-Mo.
Prause, Ben E.-Judge, De Witt County Court-Tex.
Preckel, Allan J.-Judge, Superior Court of California County of San Diego-Calif.
Pregerson, Dean D.-Judge, United States District Court Central District of California-Calif.
Pregerson, Harry-Judge, United States Court of Appeals Ninth Circuit
Preisse, Dana S.-Judge, Ohio Court of Common Pleas Franklin County-Ohio
Preminger, Eve M.-Surrogate, New York County Surrogate's Court-N.Y.
Premo, Eugene M.-Associate Justice, California Court of Appeal Sixth District-Calif.
Prescott, Orlando Alberto-Judge, Dade County Court-Fla.
Preska, Loretta A.-Judge, United States District Court Southern District of New York-N.Y.
Presnell, Gregory A.-Judge, United States District Court Middle District of Florida-Fla.
Pressler, Sylvia B.-Presiding Judge for Administration, New Jersey Superior Court Appellate Division-N.J.
Pressman, Joel M.-Judge, Superior Court of California County of San Diego-Calif.
Prestley, Linda Pearce-Judge, Connecticut Superior Court-Conn.
Preston, Lee-Circuit Judge, Illinois Circuit Court of Cook County-Ill.
Preston, Vernon L.-Judge, Findlay Municipal Court-Ohio
Prevas, John N.-Associate Judge, Circuit Court for Baltimore City, Eighth Judicial Circuit-Md.
Prewitt, James K.-Judge, Missouri Court of Appeals Southern District-Mo.
Prewitt, Jo Beth-Associate Circuit Judge, Missouri Circuit Court Thirty-seventh Judicial Circuit-Mo.
Prezeau, Michael-Judge, Montana District Court Nineteenth Judicial District-Mont.
Price, Arnold N.-Justice, New York Supreme Court Eleventh Judicial District-N.Y.
Price, Charles-Presiding Judge, Alabama Circuit Court Fifteenth Judicial Circuit-Ala.
Price, Dan R., II-Judge, Wyoming District Court Sixth Judicial District-Wyo.
Price, J. Frederick-Associate Judge, Circuit Court for Kent County, Second Judicial Circuit-Md.
Price, J. Max-Presiding Judge, Missouri Circuit Court Forty-second Judicial Circuit-Mo.
Price, Jeffry-Judge, Peru City Court-Ind.
Price, John-Judge, Pike County Court-Miss.
Price, John S., Jr.-Judge, Warren County Court-Miss.
Price, Jonathan R.-Judge, Superior Court of California County of Monterey-Calif.
Price, Richard Lee-Justice, New York Supreme Court First Judicial District-N.Y.
Price, Robert E.-Judge, Dallas County Probate Court No. 2-Tex.
Price, Steven L.-Judge, Oregon Circuit Court Twentieth Judicial District-Ore.
Price, Tom-Judge, Texas Court of Criminal Appeals-Tex.
Price, William A.-District Associate Judge, Iowa District Court Fifth Judicial District-Ia.
Price, William Ray, Jr.-Judge, Supreme Court of Missouri-Mo.
Price-Testerman, Connie S.-Judge, Montgomery County Court-Ohio
Prichard, R. I., III-Judge, Mississippi Circuit Court Fifteenth Judicial District-Miss.
Prickett, Gregg L.-Judge, Superior Court of California County of Orange-Calif.
Pridgen, Elton C.-Retired-Recalled Judge, North Carolina District Court-N.C.
Pridgen, John C.-Judge, Superior Court of Georgia Cordele Judicial Circuit-Ga.
Prigge, William N.-Special Justice, Jaffrey-Peterborough District Court-N.H.
Prigmore, Gene-Judge, Oklahoma Workers' Compensation Court-Okla.
Primomo, John W.-Magistrate Judge, United States District Court Western District of Texas-Tex.
Prince, Richard G.-Judge, Florida Circuit Court Tenth Judicial Circuit-Fla.
Prince, William T.-Recalled Magistrate Judge, United States District Court Eastern District of Virginia-Va.
Pringle, James T., Jr.-Judge, Kansas District Court Nineteenth Judicial District-Kan.
Prior, William A., Jr.-Chief Judge, Superior Court of Georgia Ocmulgee Judicial Circuit-Ga.
Prisock, Edward C.-Judge, Mississippi Chancery Court Sixth Judicial District-Miss.
Pritchard, Marion C.-Judge, Juvenile Court of Georgia Waycross Judicial Circuit-Ga.
Pritchett, Susie-Associate District Judge, Oklahoma District Court Fourth Judicial District-Okla.
Privett, Caryl P.-Judge, Alabama Circuit Court Tenth Judicial Circuit Birmingham Division-Ala.
Pro, Philip M.-Chief Judge, United States District Court District of Nevada-Nev.
Probus, William-Judge, Kentucky District Court Eighteenth Judicial District-Ky.
Procaccini, Daniel A.-Associate Justice, Rhode Island Superior Court-R.I.
Prochaska, J. Edward-Associate Judge, Illinois Circuit Court Seventeenth Judicial Circuit-Ill.
Prochaska, Jane H.-Judge, Nebraska County Court Fourth Judicial District-Neb.
Proctor, Benjamin D.-Judge, Wisconsin Circuit Court Eau Claire Circuit-Wis.
Proctor, George L.-Judge, United States Bankruptcy Court Middle District of Florida-Fla.
Proctor, Grace B.-Judge, Probate Court of Treutlen County and Chief Magistrate, Magistrate Court of Treutlen County-Ga.
Proctor, Ken-Judge, Henderson Municipal Court-Nev.
Proctor, Nathaniel P.-Judge, North Carolina District Court District 26-N.C.
Proctor, Richard L.-Judge, Cotton Plant, McCrory and Wynne District Courts-Ark.
Proctor, Williard-Judge, Arkansas Circuit Court Sixth Judicial Circuit-Ark.
Prodgers, Toby Batson-Judge, State Court of Cobb County-Ga.
Proffitt, Judith S.-Judge, Hamilton Circuit Court-Ind.
Profitt, Kenny-Judge, Kentucky District Court Thirty-ninth Judicial District-Ky.
Prohl, Emil Karl-Judge, Texas District Court 198th Judicial District-Tex.
Prokes, Roger M.-Presiding Judge, Missouri Circuit Court Fourth Judicial Circuit-Mo.
Propst, Robert B.-Senior Judge, United States District Court Northern District of Alabama-Ala.
Prosser, David T., Jr.-Justice, Wisconsin Supreme Court-Wis.
Prosser, John R.-Judge, Virginia Circuit Court Twenty-sixth Judicial Circuit-Va.
Prost, Sharon-Judge, United States Court of Appeals Federal Circuit
Proud, Clifford J.-Magistrate Judge, United States District Court Southern District of Illinois-Ill.
Proud, Douglas B.-Judge, Superior Court of California County of El Dorado-Calif.
Proud, James F.-Judge, Pennsylvania Court of Common Pleas Thirty-second Judicial District-Pa.
Provence, Tiffany-Judge, Dorchester County Probate Court-S.C.
Provost, Eleanor-Judge, Superior Court of California County of Tuolumne-Calif.
Prudenti, A. Gail-Presiding Justice, New York Supreme Court Appellate Division Second Judicial Department-N.Y.
Prus, Eric I.-Judge, The Civil Court of the City of New York-N.Y.
Pryor, William C.-Senior Judge, District of Columbia Court of Appeals-D.C.
Ptacek, Gerald Paul-Judge, Wisconsin Circuit Court Racine Circuit-Wis.
Ptomey, William R., Jr.-Judge, Monroe County Court-Fla.
Pu, Robert M.-Judge, Marlboro District Probate Court-Vt.
Puccinelli, Andrew J.-Judge, Nevada District Court Fourth Judicial District-Nev.
Pucillo, Deborah Dale-Senior Judge, Palm Beach County Court-Fla.
Puckett, Lawrence Howard-Judge, Tennessee Circuit Court Tenth Judicial District-Tenn.
Puffenberger, Jack R.-Judge, Ohio Court of Common Pleas Lucas County-Ohio
Pugh, David F.-Judge, Virginia Circuit Court Seventh Judicial Circuit-Va.
Pugh, Douglas A.-Chief Judge, Alpena County Probate Court-Mich.
Puglio, Jeannette M.-Judge, Roxbury District Probate Court-Conn.
Puglisi, Richard L.-Magistrate Judge, United States District Court District of New Mexico-N.Mex.
Puig-Lugo, Hiram E.-Associate Judge, Superior Court of the District of Columbia-D.C.
Pullen, Douglas-Judge, Superior Court of Georgia Chattahoochee Judicial Circuit-Ga.
Pullen, Lorraine-Judge, New Jersey Superior Court Vicinage Eight-N.J.
Pullman, Terry L.-Judge, Kansas District Court Eighteenth Judicial District-Kan.
Pulver, George J., Jr.-Judge, Greene County Court-N.Y.
Pumilia, Gary-Associate Judge, Illinois Circuit Court Seventeenth Judicial Circuit-Ill.
Punch, James P.-Judge, Orleans County Court-N.Y.
Purcell, Catherine D.-Judge, Superior Court of California County of Kern-Calif.
Purcell, Gary M.-Magistrate Judge, United States District Court Western District of Oklahoma-Okla.
Purcell, James-Judge, Kentucky District Court Fifteenth Judicial District-Ky.
Purcell, Ricky D.-Chief Judge, New Mexico District Court Tenth Judicial District-N.Mex.
Purdom, Wayne M.-Judge, State Court of DeKalb County-Ga.
Purdy, William G.-Judge, Oregon Circuit Court First Judicial District-Ore.
Purham, Albert L., Jr.-Associate Judge, Illinois Circuit Court Tenth Judicial Circuit-Ill.
Purnell, O. James, III-Judge, Ellington District Probate Court-Conn.
Purnell, Roland N.-Judge, Superior Court of California County of Ventura-Calif.
Pursel, John H.-Judge, New Jersey Superior Court Vicinage Thirteen-N.J.
Purtill, Joseph J.-Judge Referee, Connecticut Superior Court-Conn.
Puryear, Cecil G.-Judge, Texas District Court 137th Judicial District-Tex.
Puryear, David-Justice, Texas Court of Appeals Third District-Tex.
Pusateri, James A.-Judge, Bankruptcy Appellate Panel Tenth Circuit and Judge, United States Bankruptcy Court District of Kansas-Kan.
Puskarich, Matthew Paul-Judge, Ohio Court of Common Pleas Harrison County-Ohio
Pustilnik, Robert A.-Judge, Virginia General District Court Thirteenth Judicial District-Va.
Putka, Edward J.-Judge, Cowlitz District Court Cowlitz County and Judge, Woodland Municipal Court-Wash.
Putman, John-Judge, Arkansas Circuit Court Fourteenth Judicial Circuit-Ark.
Putnam, R. L. "Chip"-Judge, Superior Court of California County of Fresno-Calif.
Putnam, Terry Michael-Magistrate Judge, United States District Court Northern District of Alabama-Ala.
Pyle, Charles R.-Magistrate Judge, United States District Court District of Arizona-Ariz.
Pyott, Mardi F.-Associate Judge, Delaware Family Court Kent County-Del.
Pyun, Matthew S. K.-Judge, Hawaii District Court Third Judicial Circuit-Hi.
Quackenbush, Justin L.-Senior Judge, United States District Court Eastern District of Washington-Wash.
Quaintance, Kathryn-Judge, Minnesota District Court Fourth Judicial District-Minn.

ALPHABETICAL NAME INDEX

Quall, Robert D.-Judge, Superior Court of California County of Merced-Calif.

Quarles, William D.-Judge, United States District Court District of Maryland-Md.

Quattlebaum, Kenneth W.-Judge, Alabama Circuit Court Thirty-third Judicial Circuit-Ala.

Quesada, Frank-Judge, Florida Circuit Court Sixth Judicial Circuit-Fla.

Quidachay, Ronald Evans-Judge, Superior Court of California City and County of San Francisco-Calif.

Quigless, Angela Turner-Circuit Judge, Missouri Circuit Court Twenty-second Judicial Circuit-Mo.

Quigley, John C., Jr.-Judge, Virginia General District Court Twenty-seventh Judicial District-Va.

Quigley, Keith B.-President Judge, Pennsylvania Court of Common Pleas Forty-first Judicial District-Pa.

Quince, Peggy A.-Justice, Florida Supreme Court-Fla.

Quinlan, James S., Jr.-Recalled Circuit Judge, Illinois Circuit Court of Cook County-Ill.

Quinlan, Patrick G.-Judge, Louisiana District Court Orleans Parish Criminal District-La.

Quinlan, Regina L.-Associate Justice, Trial Court of Massachusetts Superior Court Department-Mass.

Quinlen, John I.-Judge, Superior Court of California County of Kern-Calif.

Quinn, Anthony-Judge, Utah District Court Third Judicial District-Utah

Quinn, Barbara M.-Judge, Connecticut Superior Court-Conn.

Quinn, Brian P.-Justice, Texas Court of Appeals Seventh District-Tex.

Quinn, Christopher G.-Judge, Nassau County District Court-N.Y.

Quinn, John Patrick, Jr.-Judge, Ohio Court of Common Pleas Summit County-Ohio

Quinn, Joseph P.-Judge, New Jersey Superior Court Vicinage Nine-N.J.

Quinn, Linda B.-Judge, Superior Court of California County of San Diego-Calif.

Quinn, Patrick J.-Judge, Illinois Appellate Court First Judicial District Division Five-Ill.

Quinn, Paul M.-Judge, North Carolina District Court District 3B-N.C.

Quinn, R. Joseph-Judge, Minnesota District Court Tenth Judicial District-Minn.

Quinn, Robert J.-Circuit Judge, Illinois Circuit Court of Cook County-Ill.

Quinn, Stephen K.-Judge, New Mexico District Court Ninth Judicial District-N.Mex.

Quinn, Thomas P.-Circuit Judge, Illinois Circuit Court of Cook County-Ill.

Quinn-Brintnall, Christine J.-Acting Chief Judge, Washington Court of Appeals Division II-Wash.

Quinney, Marvin C.-Judge, Wilson County Court-Tex.

Quiñones Alejandro, Nitza I.-Judge, Pennsylvania Court of Common Pleas First Judicial District-Pa.

Quint, Michael L.-Judge, Kansas District Court Twenty-fifth Judicial District-Kan.

Quintanilla, Roy-Judge, Galveston County Court at Law No. 3-Tex.

Quintero, Henry R., Sr.-Judge, New Mexico District Court Sixth Judicial District-N.Mex.

Quirk, Madeline-Associate Judge, Rhode Island District Court-R.I.

Quirk, Thomas P.-Judge, Lake Charles City Court-La.

Quisenberry, Graham-Judge, Parker County Court at Law-Tex.

Quist, Darvid D.-Judge, Nebraska District Court Sixth Judicial District-Neb.

Quist, Gordon Jay-Judge, United States District Court Western District of Michigan-Mich.

Raab, Ira J.-Justice, New York Supreme Court Tenth Judicial District-N.Y.

Raccuglia, Cynthia M.-Circuit Judge, Illinois Circuit Court Thirteenth Judicial Circuit-Ill.

Race, John R.-Judge, Wisconsin Circuit Court Walworth Circuit-Wis.

Racek, Frank L.-Judge, North Dakota District Court East Central Judicial District-N.D.

Raciti, Robert M.-Judge, The Criminal Court of the City of New York-N.Y.

Radack, Sherry-Chief Justice, Texas Court of Appeals First District-Tex.

Radakovich, Nina M.-Judge, City Court of Atlanta-Ga.

Radcliffe, Albert E.-Chief Judge, United States Bankruptcy Court District of Oregon-Ore.

Radcliffe, Dale W.-Judge, Connecticut Superior Court-Conn.

Radcliffe, James M., III-Associate Judge, Illinois Circuit Court Twentieth Judicial Circuit-Ill.

Radcliffe, Robert W.-Reserve Judge, Wisconsin Circuit Court-Wis.

Rader, Randall R.-Judge, United States Court of Appeals Federal Circuit

Rader, Robert Blackwell-Judge, North Carolina District Court District 10-N.C.

Radford, Lillian S.-Judge, Probate Court of Tift County-Ga.

Radford, Wendell C.-Magistrate Judge, United States District Court Eastern District of Texas-Tex.

Radius, Karen M.-Family Court Judge, Hawaii District Court First Judicial Circuit-Hi.

Radosevich, John G.-Associate Judge, Illinois Circuit Court Nineteenth Judicial Circuit-Ill.

Radvansky, Joseph P.-Judge, Batesville City Court-Ind.

Radzibon, Kenneth A.-Chief Judge, Presque Isle County Probate Court-Mich.

Rafeedie, Edward-Senior Judge, United States District Court Central District of California-Calif.

Rafferty, Gerald-Judge, Colorado District Court Eighteenth Judicial District-Colo.

Rafferty, James E.-Judge, New Jersey Superior Court Vicinage Fifteen-N.J.

Raffetto, Shackley F.-Chief Judge, Hawaii Circuit Court Second Judicial Circuit-Hi.

Ragan, James Edward, III-Emergency Judge, North Carolina Superior Court-N.C.

Rager, Kurt-Judge, Nebraska County Court Sixth Judicial District-Neb.

Raggi, Reena-Judge, United States Court of Appeals Second Circuit

Ragland, Tom-Judge, McLennan County Court at Law No. 1-Tex.

Ragosta, Vincent A.-Associate Justice, Rhode Island Superior Court-R.I.

Ragusa, Anthony D., Jr.-Judge, Louisiana District Court Twenty-fifth Judicial District-La.

Rahhal, Franklin D.-District Judge, Oklahoma District Court Twenty-fourth Judicial District-Okla.

Rahill, Robert J.-Associate Judge, Rhode Island District Court-R.I.

Rahmeyer, Nancy Steffen-Chief Judge, Missouri Court of Appeals Southern District-Mo.

Rahn, Albert, III-Judge, Superior Court of Georgia Atlantic Judicial Circuit-Ga.

Raiden, Michael E.-Judge, Polk County Court-Fla.

Raikes, Larry D.-Judge, Kentucky Circuit Court Tenth Judicial Circuit-Ky.

Rainaud, Stephen M.-Circuit Justice, Trial Court of Massachusetts Probate and Family Court Department-Mass.

Raines, Albert M.-Judge, Kirkland Municipal Court-Wash.

Raines, Keith R.-Judge, Oregon Circuit Court Twentieth Judicial District-Ore.

Rainey, John D.-Judge, United States District Court Southern District of Texas-Tex.

Rainey, William P.-Judge, West Memphis District Court-Ark.

Rains, Brian-Judge, Texas District Court 176th Judicial District-Tex.

Rains, David A.-Judge, Alabama Circuit Court Ninth Judicial Circuit-Ala.

Rainwater, Tonya Baccus-Judge, Florida Circuit Court Eighteenth Judicial Circuit-Fla.

Raker, Irma S.-Associate Judge, Court of Appeals of Maryland-Md.

Rakoff, Jed S.-Judge, United States District Court Southern District of New York-N.Y.

Rakower, Eileen A.-Judge, The Civil Court of the City of New York-N.Y.

Raley, C. Clarke-Associate Judge, Circuit Court for St. Mary's County, Seventh Judicial Circuit-Md.

Ralston, Owen-Judge, Waller County Court-Tex.

Rambo, Richard B.-Judge, Oregon Circuit Court Thirteenth Judicial District-Ore.

Rambo, Sylvia H.-Senior Judge, United States District Court Middle District of Pennsylvania-Pa.

Rambo, Wilson-Judge, Louisiana District Court Fourth Judicial District-La.

Ramerman, Dale B.-Judge, Washington Superior Court King County-Wash.

Ramey, Jerry Don-Judge, Yell County District Court-Ark.

Ramey, Scott-Judge, Sylvania Municipal Court-Ohio

Ramich, Thomas E.-Judge, Elmira City Court-N.Y.

Ramirez, Daniel P.-Judge, Superior Court of California County of Los Angeles-Calif.

Ramirez, Irma C.-Magistrate Judge, United States District Court Northern District of Texas-Tex.

Ramirez, Juan, Jr.-Judge, Florida District Court of Appeal Third District-Fla.

Ramirez, Larry-Judge, New Mexico District Court Third Judicial District-N.Mex.

Ramirez, Manuel Angelo-Presiding Justice, California Court of Appeal Fourth District Division Two-Calif.

Ramirez, Mario E., Jr.-Judge, Texas District Court 332nd Judicial District-Tex.

Ramirez, Mary Berndt-Judge, Pasco Municipal Court-Wash.

Ramirez, Peter J.-Magistrate Judge, Kansas District Court Twenty-fifth Judicial District-Kan.

Ramirez, Ralph M.-Judge, Wisconsin Circuit Court Waukesha Circuit-Wis.

Rammell, Mark S.-Judge, Idaho District Court Seventh Judicial District Magistrate Division-Ida.

Ramos, Charles E.-Justice, New York Supreme Court First Judicial District-N.Y.

Ramos, Dorina-Magistrate Judge, United States District Court Southern District of Texas-Tex.

Ramos, Joe-Judge, Charleston and Ozark District Courts-Ark.

Ramsay, Charles R.-Judge, Texas District Court 22nd Judicial District-Tex.

Ramsberger, Peter R.-Judge, Florida Circuit Court Sixth Judicial Circuit-Fla.

Ramsdell, Jeffrey M.-Judge, Washington Superior Court King County-Wash.

Ramsey, Edward L.-Judge, Alabama Circuit Court Tenth Judicial Circuit Birmingham Division-Ala.

Ramsey, Nadine M.-Judge, Louisiana District Court Orleans Parish Civil District-La.

Ramstad, Sheryl A.-Judge, Minnesota Tax Court-Minn.

Rancourt, Robert G.-Judge, Minnesota District Court Tenth Judicial District-Minn.

Rand, Charles M.-Judge, New Jersey Superior Court Vicinage Four-N.J.

Rand, David B.-Judge, New Jersey Superior Court Vicinage Ten-N.J.

Rand, Michael Miller-Chief Judge, Virginia Juvenile and Domestic Relations District Court Tenth Judicial District-Va.

Rand, Ripley E.-Special Judge, North Carolina Superior Court-N.C.

Rand, Sheldon M.-Judge, New York City Family Court-N.Y.

Randa, Rudolph T.-Chief Judge, United States District Court Eastern District of Wisconsin-Wis.

Randall, Gary B.-Judge, Nebraska District Court Fourth Judicial District-Neb.

Randall, R. A. "Jim"-Judge, Minnesota Court of Appeals-Minn.

Randall, Roger D.-Judge, Superior Court of California County of Kern-Calif.

Randall, William C.-Chief Magistrate, Magistrate Court of Bibb County and Judge, Civil Court of Bibb County-Ga.

Randolph, A. Raymond-Judge, United States Court of Appeals District of Columbia Circuit

Randon, Mark A.-Judge, Michigan District Court District Thirty-six-Mich.

Randow, Harry F.-Judge, Louisiana District Court Ninth Judicial District-La.

Raney, Julian H., Jr.-Chief Judge, Virginia General District Court Twenty-third Judicial District-Va.

Rangel, Bonnie-Judge, Texas District Court 171st Judicial District-Tex.

Rankin, Michael Lee-Associate Judge, Superior Court of the District of Columbia-D.C.

ALPHABETICAL NAME INDEX

Rankin, Susan Amanda-Judge, Texas Family District Court 301st Judicial District-Tex.

Ransdell, Maria-Judge, Kentucky District Court Twenty-second Judicial District-Ky.

Ransom, Lillian Harris-Judge, Pennsylvania Court of Common Pleas First Judicial District-Pa.

Ransom, Robert M.-Chief Judge, Michigan Circuit Court Seventh Judicial Circuit-Mich.

Rantala, Jeffry S.-Judge, Minnesota District Court Sixth Judicial District-Minn.

Rapkin, Harry M.-Judge, Florida Circuit Court Twelfth Judicial Circuit-Fla.

Rapoport, Arnold C.-Magistrate Judge, United States District Court Eastern District of Pennsylvania-Pa.

Rapoza, Phillip-Associate Justice, Massachusetts Appeals Court-Mass.

Rapp, James S.-Judge, Ohio Court of Common Pleas Hardin County-Ohio

Rapp, Keith-Judge, Oklahoma Court of Civil Appeals-Okla.

Rapp, Stephen A.-Judge, Florida Circuit Court Fifteenth Judicial Circuit-Fla.

Rappa, Thomas A., Jr.-Special Justice, Plymouth District Court-N.H.

Rappaport, Edward M.-Justice, New York Supreme Court Second Judicial District-N.Y.

Rappaport, Sheila A.-Judge, Colorado District Court Second Judicial District-Colo.

Rappe, Curtis B.-Judge, Superior Court of California County of Los Angeles-Calif.

Rarick, Philip J.-Justice, Supreme Court of Illinois-Ill.

Rash, Andy-Judge, Hood County Court-Tex.

Rashid, James J.-Judge, Michigan Circuit Court Third Judicial Circuit-Mich.

Rasin, Gale E.-Associate Judge, Maryland District Court District One-Md.

Rasin, Martha F.-Associate Judge, Maryland District Court District Seven-Md.

Rasinsky, Marc G.-Associate Judge, Maryland District Court District Ten-Md.

Raslavich, Stephen-Judge, United States Bankruptcy Court Eastern District of Pennsylvania-Pa.

Rasmussen, Karsten H.-Judge, Oregon Circuit Court Second Judicial District-Ore.

Rasmussen, Paul D.-Judge, Florida Circuit Court First Judicial Circuit-Fla.

Rasmussen, Paul E.-Judge, Minnesota District Court Ninth Judicial District-Minn.

Rasmussen, Robert H.-Judge, Wisconsin Circuit Court Polk Circuit-Wis.

Rasure, Dana L.-Chief Judge, United States Bankruptcy Court Northern District of Oklahoma-Okla.

Ratner, Marvin-Judge, Michigan District Court District Ten-Mich.

Rau, Lisa M.-Judge, Pennsylvania Court of Common Pleas First Judicial District-Pa.

Raucci, Andrew-Chief Justice, Illinois Court of Claims-Ill.

Rauch, Lucy D.-Presiding Judge, Missouri Circuit Court Eleventh Judicial Circuit-Mo.

Rauh, John R.-Judge, New Jersey Superior Court Vicinage One-N.J.

Raven, Mark D.-Chief Judge, Mason County Probate Court-Mich.

Ravens, Gary E.-Presiding Judge, Missouri Circuit Court Ninth Judicial Circuit-Mo.

Ravin, Michael L.-Judge, New Jersey Superior Court Vicinage Five-N.J.

Rawlings, Tom-Judge, Juvenile Court of Georgia Middle Judicial Circuit-Ga.

Rawlins, Robert W., Jr.-Senior Judge, Florida Circuit Court Thirteenth Judicial Circuit-Fla.

Rawlinson, Johnnie B.-Judge, United States Court of Appeals Ninth Circuit

Rawls, Addie M. Harris-Judge, North Carolina District Court District 11-N.C.

Rawls, Deborah Louise-Chief Judge, Virginia Juvenile and Domestic Relations District Court Second Judicial District-Va.

Rawson, Henry A.-Judge, Omak and Riverside Municipal Courts-Wash.

Ray, Elizabeth-Judge, Texas District Court 165th Judicial District-Tex.

Ray, George H.-Associate Judge, Illinois Circuit Court Seventh Judicial Circuit-Ill.

Ray, Herbert B.-Judge, Broome County Family Court-N.Y.

Ray, J. Thomas-Magistrate Judge, United States District Court Eastern District of Arkansas-Ark.

Ray, James-Judge, Ohio Court of Common Pleas Lucas County-Ohio

Ray, Jerry D.-Judge, Texas District Court 29th Judicial District-Tex.

Ray, Larry-Chief Magistrate, Magistrate Court of Pickens County-Ga.

Ray, Raymond B.-Judge, United States Bankruptcy Court Southern District of Florida-Fla.

Ray, Thomas L.-Associate Circuit Judge, Missouri Circuit Court Twenty-fourth Judicial Circuit-Mo.

Ray, William M., II-Judge, Superior Court of Georgia Gwinnett Judicial Circuit-Ga.

Raye, Vance W.-Associate Justice, California Court of Appeal Third District-Calif.

Rayes, Donna-Judge, Texas District Court 81st Judicial District-Tex.

Rayes, Douglas-Judge, Superior Court of Arizona Maricopa County-Ariz.

Rayvis, Cynthia-Judge, Superior Court of California County of Los Angeles-Calif.

Rea, William J.-Senior Judge, United States District Court Central District of California-Calif.

Read, J. Milton, Jr.-Emergency Judge, North Carolina Superior Court-N.C.

Read, Susan Phillips-Associate Judge, New York Court of Appeals-N.Y.

Reade, Linda R.-Judge, United States District Court Northern District of Iowa-Ia.

Ready, George B.-Judge, Mississippi Circuit Court Seventeenth Judicial District-Miss.

Reagan, Michael J.-Judge, United States District Court Southern District of Illinois-Ill.

Reagan, Ronald E.-Judge, Nebraska District Court Second Judicial District-Neb.

Real, Manuel L.-Judge, United States District Court Central District of California-Calif.

Reams, Gerald Brock-Judge, Kentucky District Court Thirty-second Judicial District-Ky.

Rearden, John B., Jr.-Judge, Darien District Probate Court-Conn.

Reardon, Joseph J.-First Justice, Trial Court of Massachusetts District Court Department Barnstable County Barnstable Division-Mass.

Reardon, Patricia DiMeo-Special Justice, Exeter District Court-N.H.

Reardon, Thomas Matthew-Judge, Superior Court of California County of Alameda-Calif.

Reardon, Timothy A.-Associate Justice, California Court of Appeal First District Division Four-Calif.

Reasbeck, James Milton-Senior Judge, Florida Circuit Court Seventeenth Judicial Circuit-Fla.

Reasoner, Stephen M.-Senior Judge, United States District Court Eastern District of Arkansas-Ark.

Reavis, Don H.-Justice, Texas Court of Appeals Seventh District-Tex.

Reavis, Robert E., II-Associate District Judge, Oklahoma District Court Thirteenth Judicial District-Okla.

Reavley, Thomas Morrow-Senior Judge, United States Court of Appeals Fifth Circuit

Rebolini, William B.-Judge, Suffolk County District Court-N.Y.

Rebstock, Robert J.-Judge, Pennsylvania Court of Common Pleas First Judicial District-Pa.

Recana, Mel Red-Judge, Superior Court of California County of Los Angeles-Calif.

Recant, Donna G.-Judge, The Criminal Court of the City of New York-N.Y.

Recanzone, Mario G.-Senior Judge, Nevada District Court-Nev.

Recht, Arthur M.-Judge, West Virginia Circuit Court First Judicial Circuit-W.Va.

Recio, Felix, Jr.-Magistrate Judge, United States District Court Southern District of Texas-Tex.

Reck, Susan L.-Chief Judge, Livingston County Probate Court-Mich.

Redd, Edward-Justice, Trial Court of Massachusetts District Court Department Suffolk County Roxbury Division-Mass.

Redd, F. Bennion-Magistrate Judge, United States District Court District of Utah-Utah

Redden, James A.-Senior Judge, United States District Court District of Oregon-Ore.

Reddick, Ryan D.-Associate District Judge, Oklahoma District Court First Judicial District-Okla.

Reddin, Mark B.-Judge, Bowling Green Municipal Court-Ohio

Redford, James Robert-Judge, Michigan Circuit Court Seventeenth Judicial Circuit-Mich.

Redmond, Maurice S.-Judge, Nebraska District Court Sixth Judicial District-Neb.

Redmond, Norene S.-Judge, Eastpointe Municipal Court-Mich.

Redwine, James M.-Judge, Posey Circuit Court-Ind.

Redwing, Dennis J.-Chief Judge, North Carolina District Court District 27A-N.C.

Reed, Angélique A.-Judge, New Orleans First City Court-La.

Reed, Clyde Derek-Judge, Kentucky District Court Tenth Judicial District-Ky.

Reed, Edward C., Jr.-Senior Judge, United States District Court District of Nevada-Nev.

Reed, Frederick G.-Surrogate, Ontario County Surrogate's Court-N.Y.

Reed, Gary K.-Chief Judge, Calhoun County Probate Court-Mich.

Reed, Hugh-Judge, Armstrong County Court-Tex.

Reed, Jeffrey B.-Judge, West Virginia Circuit Court Fourth Judicial Circuit-W.Va.

Reed, Jeffrey L.-Judge, Ohio Court of Common Pleas Allen County-Ohio

Reed, Lowell A., Jr.-Senior Judge, United States District Court Eastern District of Pennsylvania-Pa.

Reed, Melinda Myrle-Judge, Superior Court of California County of Tulare-Calif.

Reed, Rex L.-Judge, Kosciusko Circuit Court-Ind.

Reed, Sheridan E.-Judge, Superior Court of California County of San Diego-Calif.

Reed, Steven B.-Judge, Oregon Circuit Court Nineteenth Judicial District-Ore.

Reed, Thomas Jefferson Boyd-Judge, Boulder County Court-Colo.

Reed, Thomas Wayne-Chief Magistrate, Magistrate Court of Dade County-Ga.

Reese, Eugene W.-Judge, Alabama Circuit Court Fifteenth Judicial Circuit-Ala.

Reese, John-Judge, Alaska Superior Court Third Judicial District-Alas.

Reese, Kern-Judge, Louisiana District Court Orleans Parish Civil District-La.

Reese, Robin W.-Judge, Utah District Court Third Judicial District-Utah

Reese, Thomas-Judge, Rolling Hills Municipal Court-Wyo.

Reese, Thomas S.-Judge, Florida Circuit Court Twentieth Judicial Circuit-Fla.

Reeves, Danny C.-Judge, United States District Court Eastern District of Kentucky-Ky.

Reeves, G. Daniel-Judge, Alabama Circuit Court Eighteenth Judicial Circuit-Ala.

Reeves, Judy-Judge, Probate Court of Sumter County-Ga.

Reeves, R. H., III-Judge, State Court of Jenkins County-Ga.

Register, Allen L.-Judge, Florida Circuit Court Fourteenth Judicial Circuit-Fla.

Regnier, Jim-Justice, Montana Supreme Court-Mont.

Rego, Thomas M.-Associate Judge, Juvenile Court of Georgia Tallapoosa Judicial Circuit-Ga.

Rehkamp, C. Joseph-Judge, Pennsylvania Court of Common Pleas Forty-first Judicial District-Pa.

Rehm, Carol H., Jr.-Judge, Superior Court of California County of Los Angeles-Calif.

Rehm, Richard L.-Judge, Wisconsin Circuit Court Columbia Circuit-Wis.

Rehmeier, Randall L.-Judge, Nebraska District Court Second Judicial District-Neb.

Rehnquist, William Hubbs-Chief Justice, The Supreme Court of the United States

Reibman, Edward D.-Judge, Pennsylvania Court of Common Pleas Thirty-first Judicial District-Pa.

Reich, A. Philip, II-Presiding Judge, Alabama Circuit Court Thirty-sixth Judicial Circuit-Ala.

Reichbach, Gustin L.-Justice, New York Supreme Court Second Judicial District-N.Y.

Reicher, Max H.-Judge Referee, Connecticut Superior Court-Conn.

ALPHABETICAL NAME INDEX

ALPHABETICAL NAME INDEX

ALPHABETICAL NAME INDEX

Roberts, Bernard E., III-Chief Magistrate, Magistrate Court of Hall County-Ga.
Roberts, Carol-Justice of the Peace, Douglas County Justice Court-Ore.
Roberts, Charles E.-Judge, Florida Circuit Court Twelfth Judicial Circuit-Fla.
Roberts, Charles E.-Associate District Judge, Oklahoma District Court Twentieth Judicial District-Okla.
Roberts, Debra-Judge, Pasco County Court-Fla.
Roberts, Delbert Ray-Judge, Kimble County Court-Tex.
Roberts, Edwin H., Jr.-Judge, Mississippi Chancery Court Eighteenth Judicial District-Miss.
Roberts, Gayle P.-Judge, New York City Family Court-N.Y.
Roberts, Glynn D.-Judge, Louisiana District Court Fifth Judicial District-La.
Roberts, Joel D.-Judge, Jay Superior Court-Ind.
Roberts, John D.-Magistrate Judge, United States District Court District of Alaska-Alas.
Roberts, Larry E.-Judge, Mississippi Circuit Court Tenth Judicial District-Miss.
Roberts, Lisa A.-Circuit Justice, Trial Court of Massachusetts Probate and Family Court Department-Mass.
Roberts, Penny Ann-Judge, Tom Green County Court at Law No. 2-Tex.
Roberts, Ramona M.-Judge, Michigan District Court District Sixty-eight-Mich.
Roberts, Richard W.-Judge, United States District Court District of Columbia-D.C.
Roberts, Robert C.-Judge, Columbiana County Municipal Court-Ohio
Roberts, Russell "Jack"-Judge, Conway District Court-Ark.
Roberts, Stephen H.-Special Justice, Dover District Court-N.H.
Roberts, Susan Wadsworth-Judge, Florida Circuit Court Tenth Judicial Circuit-Fla.
Roberts, Victoria A.-Judge, United States District Court Eastern District of Michigan-Mich.
Roberts, W. F. "Corky"-Judge, Potter County Court at Law No. 1-Tex.
Roberts, W. Milnor-Administrative Judge, Maryland District Court District Eleven-Md.
Roberts, William J.-Presiding Judge, Missouri Circuit Court Twenty-seventh Judicial Circuit-Mo.
Robertson, A. James, II-Judge, Superior Court of California City and County of San Francisco-Calif.
Robertson, Beverly C.-Justice of the Peace, Baker County Justice Court-Ore.
Robertson, Charles T., II-Chief Magistrate, Magistrate Court of Cherokee County-Ga.
Robertson, George R.-Judge, Kansas District Court Twenty-eighth Judicial District-Kan.
Robertson, James-Judge, United States District Court District of Columbia-D.C.
Robertson, Kelly Marie-Judge, Superior Court of Arizona Pinal County-Ariz.
Robertson, Marvin E.-Chief Judge, Clinton County Probate Court-Mich.
Robertson, Ralph B.-Judge, Virginia General District Court Thirteenth Judicial District-Va.
Robertson, Sally Ireland-Judge, Minnesota District Court Seventh Judicial District-Minn.
Robertson, Thomas-Justice, Sheridan County Justice of the Peace Court and Judge, Plentywood City Court-Mont.
Robertson, Vicki-District Judge, Oklahoma District Court Seventh Judicial District-Okla.
Robeson, James Bailey-Chief Judge, Virginia Juvenile and Domestic Relations District Court Thirty-first Judicial District-Va.
Robichaud, Kathleen Leahey-Judge, Rensselaer City Court-N.Y.
Robie, Ronald B.-Associate Justice, California Court of Appeal Third District-Calif.
Robilio, Kay Spalding-Judge, Tennessee Circuit Court Thirtieth Judicial District-Tenn.
Robins, Mathew-Judge, State Court of DeKalb County-Ga.
Robins New, Shelley-Judge, Pennsylvania Court of Common Pleas First Judicial District-Pa.
Robinson, A. Carl-Special Judge, Oklahoma District Court Fifteenth Judicial District-Okla.
Robinson, Alvin-Judge, Afton Municipal Court-Wyo.
Robinson, Charles E.-Judge, Alabama Circuit Court Thirtieth Judicial Circuit-Ala.
Robinson, David S., Jr.-Judge, Michigan District Court District Thirty-six-Mich.
Robinson, Deborah A.-Magistrate Judge, United States District Court District of Columbia-D.C.
Robinson, Dorothy A.-Judge, Superior Court of Georgia Cobb Judicial Circuit-Ga.
Robinson, Douglas B.-Judge, Whitman District Court Whitman County-Wash.
Robinson, Frederick W.-Judge, Calhoun County Probate Court-S.C.
Robinson, Ira S.-Judge, New Mexico Court of Appeals-N.Mex.
Robinson, John M.-Judge, Louisiana District Court Twenty-sixth Judicial District-La.
Robinson, Julie A.-Judge, United States District Court District of Kansas-Kan.
Robinson, L. Vern-District Judge, Iowa District Court Sixth Judicial District-Ia.
Robinson, Mary Lou-Judge, United States District Court Northern District of Texas-Tex.
Robinson, Mary Rudd-Judge, Broward County Court-Fla.
Robinson, Mike-Judge, Benton District Court-Ark.
Robinson, Muriel-Judge, Tennessee Circuit Court Twentieth Judicial District-Tenn.
Robinson, Palmer-Judge, Washington Superior Court King County-Wash.
Robinson, Paul R., Sr.-Judge, Nebraska County Court Sixth Judicial District-Neb.
Robinson, Richard A.-Judge, Connecticut Superior Court-Conn.
Robinson, Rosalyn K.-Judge, Pennsylvania Court of Common Pleas First Judicial District-Pa.
Robinson, Steven D.-Senior Judge, Florida Circuit Court Eleventh Judicial Circuit-Fla.
Robinson, Stuart-Judge, Mississippi Chancery Court Fifth Judicial District-Miss.
Robinson, Sue L.-Chief Judge, United States District Court District of Delaware-Del.
Robinson, Wilkes Coleman-Senior Judge, United States Court of Federal Claims
Robinson-Thomas, Angela C.-Judge, Connecticut Superior Court-Conn.
Robison, Craig E.-Judge, Superior Court of California County of Orange-Calif.
Robison, Geoff-Judge, New Haven City Court-Ind.
Robison, Jack Hollis-Judge, Texas District Court 207th Judicial District-Tex.
Robison, Norman C.-Senior Judge, Nevada District Court-Nev.
Robles, Daniel T.-Judge, Cameron County Court at Law No. 3-Tex.
Robles, Ernest M.-Judge, United States Bankruptcy Court Central District of California-Calif.
Robles, Robert E.-Chief Judge, New Mexico District Court Third Judicial District-N.Mex.
Robreno, Eduardo C.-Judge, United States District Court Eastern District of Pennsylvania-Pa.
Roby, Karen Wells-Magistrate Judge, United States District Court Eastern District of Louisiana-La.
Roby, Veronica Mia-Judge, Elwood City Court-Ind.
Roby, William-Judge, Florida Circuit Court Nineteenth Judicial Circuit-Fla.
Rocco, Kenneth A.-Judge, Ohio Court of Appeals Eighth District-Ohio
Rocha, Gilbert T.-Associate Justice, Rhode Island Family Court-R.I.
Roche, Renee A.-Judge, Florida Circuit Court Ninth Judicial Circuit-Fla.
Rochester, John E.-Presiding Judge, Alabama Circuit Court Fortieth Judicial Circuit-Ala.
Rochford, Mary K.-Associate Judge, Illinois Circuit Court of Cook County-Ill.
Rochman, Morton-Judge, Superior Court of California County of Los Angeles-Calif.
Rochon, L. Stephen-Judge, Maple Valley and Pacific Municipal Courts-Wash.
Rockett, Edward J.-Associate Justice, Trial Court of Massachusetts Probate and Family Court Department Essex County Division-Mass.
Rockwell, Frederick Gore, III-Judge, Virginia Circuit Court Twelfth Judicial Circuit-Va.
Roda, Peter L.-Judge, North Carolina District Court District 28-N.C.
Rodatus, Robert V.-Judge, Juvenile Court of Georgia Gwinnett Judicial Circuit-Ga.
Rodda, Steven H.-Judge, Superior Court of California County of Sacramento-Calif.
Roddey, Lois-Judge, Chester County Probate Court-S.C.
Rodeghiero, Roy C.-Judge, Montana Water Court Yellowstone River Basin Division-Mont.
Roden, Jane-Judge, Dallas County Criminal Court at Law No. 8-Tex.
Roden, Russell-Judge, Dallas County Court at Law No. 1-Tex.
Rodenberg, John R.-Judge, Minnesota District Court Fifth Judicial District-Minn.
Rodery, Rick-Judge, Corning, Piggott and Rector District Courts-Ark.
Rodgers, Carl L.-Judge, Probate Court of Echols County and Chief Magistrate, Magistrate Court of Echols County-Ga.
Rodgers, Edward-Senior Judge, Florida Circuit Court Fifteenth Judicial Circuit-Fla.
Rodgers, Frederic B.-Judge, Gilpin County Court-Colo.
Rodgers, Joseph F., Jr.-Presiding Justice, Rhode Island Superior Court-R.I.
Rodgers, Linda S.-Chief Magistrate, Magistrate Court of Macon County-Ga.
Rodgers, Margaret C.-Magistrate Judge, United States District Court Northern District of Florida-Fla.
Rodgers, Philip E., Jr.-Chief Judge, Michigan Circuit Court Thirteenth Judicial Circuit-Mich.
Rodovich, Andrew P.-Magistrate Judge, United States District Court Northern District of Indiana-Ind.
Rodríguez, Ariel A.-Judge, New Jersey Superior Court Appellate Division-N.J.
Rodriguez, Eddie, Jr.-Judge, Connecticut Superior Court-Conn.
Rodriguez, Jesus I.-Judge, Superior Court of California County of Los Angeles-Calif.
Rodriguez, Jose Manuel-Judge, Florida Circuit Court Eleventh Judicial Circuit-Fla.
Rodriguez, Jose R.-Judge, Florida Circuit Court Ninth Judicial Circuit-Fla.
Rodriguez, Joseph H.-Senior Judge, United States District Court District of New Jersey-N.J.
Rodriguez, Lina S.-Judge, Superior Court of Arizona Pima County-Ariz.
Rodriguez, Linda A.-Judge, Hays County Court at Law No. 2-Tex.
Rodriguez, Luis A.-Judge, Superior Court of California Court of Orange-Calif.
Rodriguez, Mathias E.-Judge, New Jersey Superior Court Vicinage Eight-N.J.
Rodriguez, Nelda V.-Justice, Texas Court of Appeals Thirteenth District-Tex.
Rodriguez, Rosa-Judge, Florida Circuit Court Eleventh Judicial Circuit-Fla.
Roe, Katherian D.-Judge, Minnesota District Court Fourth Judicial District-Minn.
Roe, Sue H.-Judge, Aiken County Probate Court-S.C.
Roe, William A.-Judge, Louisiana District Court Twenty-fifth Judicial District-La.
Roeder, James L.-Judge, Superior Court of California County of Placer-Calif.
Roehr, Ronald-Judge, South Dakota Circuit Court Third Judicial Circuit-S.D.
Roell, Wayne A.-Judge, Spencer Circuit Court-Ind.
Roemer, Victoria L.-Judge, North Carolina District Court District 21-N.C.
Roesch, Frank-Judge, Superior Court of California County of Alameda-Calif.
Roethe, John W.-Judge, Wisconsin Circuit Court Rock Circuit-Wis.
Roettger, Norman Charles, Jr.-Senior Judge, United States District Court Southern District of Florida-Fla.
Roewe, Michael P.-Judge, Lewis District Court Lewis County-Wash.
Rogers, C. L. "Buck"-Judge, Tennessee Circuit Court Eighteenth Judicial District-Tenn.
Rogers, Charles G.-Judge, Superior Court of California County of San Diego-Calif.

ALPHABETICAL NAME INDEX

Rogers, Chase T.-Judge, Connecticut Superior Court-Conn.
Rogers, Clark-Judge, Marion Superior Court-Ind.
Rogers, Gary B.-Judge, Biscoe, De Valls Bluff and Hazen District Courts-Ark.
Rogers, Jasper G.-Judge, Dillon County Probate Court-S.C.
Rogers, John M.-Judge, United States Court of Appeals Sixth Circuit
Rogers, Judith W.-Judge, United States Court of Appeals District of Columbia Circuit
Rogers, Kathleen Martin-Surrogate, St. Lawrence County Surrogate's Court-N.Y.
Rogers, Mark J.-Acting Judge, Plattsburgh City Court-N.Y.
Rogers, Norman E., Jr.-Judge, New Hartford District Probate Court-Conn.
Rogers, Pamela R.-Judge, Superior Court of California County of Los Angeles-Calif.
Rogers, Patrick G.-Judge, Nebraska District Court Seventh Judicial District-Neb.
Rogers, Peter F.-Judge, Pennsylvania Court of Common Pleas First Judicial District-Pa.
Rogers, Randall Lee-Judge, Smith County Court at Law No. 2-Tex.
Rogers, Randolph-Judge, Superior Court of California County of Los Angeles-Calif.
Rogers, Randy T.-Judge, Ohio Court of Common Pleas Butler County-Ohio
Rogers, Richard Dean-Senior Judge, United States District Court District of Kansas-Kan.
Rogers, Richard M.-Judge, Ohio Court of Common Pleas Marion County-Ohio
Rogers, Thomas E., III-Magistrate Judge, United States District Court District of South Carolina-S.C.
Rogers, William G.-Justice of the Peace, Dayton Justices' Court-Nev.
Roggensack, Patience D.-Justice, Wisconsin Supreme Court-Wis.
Rohde, George F., Jr.-Judge, New Jersey Superior Court Vicinage Eleven-N.J.
Rohr, Charlie-Judge, Airway Heights Municipal Court-Wash.
Rohrer, Erik S.-Judge, Clallam District Court No. 2 Clallam County-Wash.
Rohrs, John T., III-Judge, Defiance Municipal Court-Ohio
Roith, Michael J.-Judge, Minnesota District Court Tenth Judicial District-Minn.
Roldan, Marco-Circuit Judge, Missouri Circuit Court Sixteenth Judicial Circuit-Mo.
Rolefson, Jon R.-Judge, Superior Court of California County of Alameda-Calif.
Rolf, Dennis A.-Presiding Judge, Missouri Circuit Court Fifteenth Judicial Circuit-Mo.
Roll, John M.-Judge, United States District Court District of Arizona-Ariz.
Roll, Richard-Judge, Oregon Circuit Court Twenty-seventh Judicial District-Ore.
Rollins, Barbara B.-Judge, Taylor County Court at Law No. 2-Tex.
Rollins, John Wiley-Judge, Tennessee Circuit Court Fourteenth Judicial District-Tenn.
Roma, Patrick J.-Judge, New Jersey Superior Court Vicinage Two-N.J.
Roman, David J.-Judge, Oswego County Family Court-N.Y.
Roman, Mary D.-Judge, Texas District Court 175th Judicial District-Tex.
Roman, Nelson S.-Justice, New York Supreme Court Twelfth Judicial District-N.Y.
Roman, Richard Abram-Judge, Texas District Court 346th Judicial District-Tex.
Roman, Sheri S.-Justice, New York Supreme Court Eleventh Judicial District-N.Y.
Romanchak, Eric G.-Family Court Judge, Hawaii District Court Second Judicial Circuit-Hi.
Romani, Charles, Jr.-Circuit Judge, Illinois Circuit Court Third Judicial Circuit-Ill.
Romanick, Bruce A.-Judge, North Dakota District Court South Central Judicial District-N.D.
Romano, Bernadette T.-Judge, Oneida County Family Court-N.Y.
Romano, Karen A.-District Judge, Iowa District Court Fifth Judicial District-Ia.
Romano, Sabino E.-Judge, Adams County Court-Colo.
Romanoff, Marvin S.-Judge, Franklin County Municipal Court-Ohio
Rome, Richard-Judge, Kansas District Court Twenty-seventh Judicial District-Kan.
Romei, John V.-Judge, Maine District Court-Me.
Romeo, Jeffrey L.-Judge, Adams County Court-Colo.
Romero, Ernesto-Judge, New Mexico District Court Second Judicial District-N.Mex.
Romero, Richard R.-Judge, Superior Court of California County of Los Angeles-Calif.
Romines, Kenneth M.-Circuit Judge, Missouri Circuit Court Twenty-first Judicial Circuit-Mo.
Ronan, Emmet J.-Judge, Superior Court of Arizona Maricopa County-Ariz.
Ronan, John J.-Judge Referee, Connecticut Superior Court-Conn.
Rondolino, Anthony-Judge, Florida Circuit Court Sixth Judicial Circuit-Fla.
Roney, Paul H.-Senior Judge, United States Court of Appeals Eleventh Circuit
Ronk, James M.-Judge, Ohio Court of Common Pleas Knox County-Ohio
Ronquillo, Roberto, Jr.-Justice, Trial Court of Massachusetts District Court Department Suffolk County Dorchester Division-Mass.
Roof, Jay B.-Judge, Washington Superior Court Kitsap County-Wash.
Rooney, James T.-Judge, Putnam County Court-N.Y.
Rooney, Stephen J.-Judge, New York Court of Claims-N.Y.
Roos, Charles L.-Judge, Idaho District Court Seventh Judicial District Magistrate Division-Ida.
Root, Kathryn Joan-Chief Judge, Oscoda County Probate Court-Mich.
Root, Lawrence C.-Chief Judge, Michigan Circuit Court Forty-ninth Judicial Circuit-Mich.
Roper, Ellen S.-Circuit Judge, Missouri Circuit Court Thirteenth Judicial Circuit-Mo.
Roper, Glade F.-Judge, Superior Court of California County of Tulare-Calif.
Roper, John M., Sr.-Magistrate Judge, United States District Court Southern District of Mississippi-Miss.
Roper, Roy M.-Magistrate Judge, Kansas District Court Twenty-second Judicial District-Kan.
Ropp, Barlow-Judge, Kentucky District Court Forty-third Judicial District-Ky.
Rosa, Janice M.-Justice, New York Supreme Court Eighth Judicial District-N.Y.
Rosa, Joseph, Jr.-Judge, New Jersey Superior Court Vicinage Two-N.J.
Rosas, Salvador M.-Judge, Minnesota District Court Second Judicial District-Minn.
Rosato, Peter P.-Justice, New York Supreme Court Ninth Judicial District-N.Y.
Rosborough, Michael J.-Judge, Wisconsin Circuit Court Vernon Circuit-Wis.
Rose, Charles Paul, Jr.-Judge, Superior Court of Georgia Atlantic Judicial Circuit-Ga.
Rose, Edward J.-Judge, Little Falls City Court-N.Y.
Rose, Neal P.-Judge, Sherrill City Court-N.Y.
Rose, Robert E.-Justice, Nevada Supreme Court-Nev.
Rose, Robert S.-Associate Justice, New York Supreme Court Appellate Division Third Judicial Department-N.Y.
Rose, Thomas M.-Judge, United States District Court Southern District of Ohio-Ohio
Roseberry, Michael R.-Circuit Judge, Illinois Circuit Court Eighth Judicial Circuit-Ill.
Rosen, Eric S.-Judge, Kansas District Court Third Judicial District-Kan.
Rosen, Gerald E.-Judge, United States District Court Eastern District of Michigan-Mich.
Rosen, Irving-Judge, The Civil Court of the City of New York-N.Y.
Rosen, Joel B.-Magistrate Judge, United States District Court District of New Jersey-N.J.
Rosen, Marc I.-Judge, Kentucky Circuit Court Thirty-second Judicial Circuit-Ky.
Rosenbalm, Wheeler Armston-Judge, Tennessee Circuit Court Sixth Judicial District-Tenn.
Rosenbaum, James M.-Chief Judge, United States District Court District of Minnesota-Minn.
Rosenbaum, Marilyn Brown-Judge, Minnesota District Court Fourth Judicial District-Minn.
Rosenberg, David A.-Judge, New Jersey Superior Court Vicinage Eight-N.J.
Rosenberg, Gerald-Judge, Superior Court of California County of Los Angeles-Calif.
Rosenberg, Gerard H.-Justice, New York Supreme Court Second Judicial District-N.Y.
Rosenberg, Robert A.-Judge, Florida Circuit Court Seventeenth Judicial Circuit-Fla.
Rosenberg, Scott D.-District Judge, Iowa District Court Fifth Judicial District-Ia.
Rosenberger, Ernst H.-Associate Justice, New York Supreme Court Appellate Division First Judicial Department-N.Y.
Rosenblatt, Alan E.-Judge, Virginia Circuit Court Second Judicial Circuit-Va.
Rosenblatt, Albert M.-Associate Judge, New York Court of Appeals-N.Y.
Rosenblatt, Michelle R.-Judge, Superior Court of California County of Los Angeles-Calif.
Rosenblatt, Paul G.-Judge, United States District Court District of Arizona-Ariz.
Rosenblum, Ellen F.-Judge, Oregon Circuit Court Fourth Judicial District-Ore.
Rosenblum, Paul Weil-Judge, Kentucky Circuit Court Twelfth Judicial Circuit-Ky.
Rosenbohm, Kay F. Graves-Associate Circuit Judge, Missouri Circuit Court Fourth Judicial Circuit-Mo.
Rosenfield, Alan S.-Judge, Superior Court of California County of Los Angeles-Calif.
Rosenfield, Arnold D.-Judge, Superior Court of California County of Sonoma-Calif.
Rosengarten, Roger N.-Justice, New York Supreme Court Eleventh Judicial District-N.Y.
Rosenn, Max-Senior Judge, United States Court of Appeals Third Circuit
Rosenthal, Joel B.-Judge, United States Bankruptcy Court District of Massachusetts-Mass.
Rosenthal, Kate-Judge, Syracuse City Court-N.Y.
Rosenthal, Lee H.-Judge, United States District Court Southern District of Texas-Tex.
Rosenwasser, Stewart A.-Judge, Orange County Court-N.Y.
Rosenzweig, Joseph-Justice, New York Supreme Court Eleventh Judicial District-N.Y.
Rosinek, Jeffrey-Judge, Florida Circuit Court Eleventh Judicial Circuit-Fla.
Rosman, Jay B.-Judge, Florida Circuit Court Twentieth Judicial Circuit-Fla.
Rosmarin, John G.-Judge, Hamilton Municipal Court-Ohio
Ross, Allyne-Judge, United States District Court Eastern District of New York-N.Y.
Ross, Carl W.-Judge, Crowley County Court-Colo.
Ross, Carroll Lee-Judge, Tennessee Circuit Court Tenth Judicial District-Tenn.
Ross, Dale-Chief Judge, Florida Circuit Court Seventeenth Judicial Circuit-Fla.
Ross, David S.-First Justice, Trial Court of Massachusetts District Court Department Franklin County Orange Division and Justice, Hampden County Chicopee Division-Mass.
Ross, Donald R.-Senior Judge, United States Court of Appeals Eighth Circuit
Ross, Donald Rae-Justice, Texas Court of Appeals Sixth District-Tex.
Ross, Edward B.-Judge, Whatcom District Court Whatcom County-Wash.
Ross, Graham T.-Assignment Judge, New Jersey Superior Court Vicinage Thirteen-N.J.
Ross, Herbert A.-Recalled Judge, United States Bankruptcy Court District of Alaska-Alas.
Ross, John A.-Circuit Judge, Missouri Circuit Court Twenty-first Judicial Circuit-Mo.
Ross, John L.-Judge, Bellefontaine Municipal Court-Ohio
Ross, Kevin A.-Judge, Superior Court of California County of Los Angeles-Calif.
Ross, Margaret V.-Judge, Pierce District Court Pierce County-Wash.
Ross, Maurice-Associate Judge, Superior Court of the District of Columbia-D.C.
Ross, Neil E.-Judge, The Criminal Court of the City of New York-N.Y.
Ross, Robert A.-Justice, New York Supreme Court Tenth Judicial District-N.Y.
Ross, Sherman A.-Judge, Harris County Criminal Court at Law No. 10-Tex.

ALPHABETICAL NAME INDEX

Russell, Douglas S.-District Judge, Iowa District Court Sixth Judicial District-Ia.
Russell, Franklin Lee-Judge, Tennessee Circuit Court Seventeenth Judicial District-Tenn.
Russell, G. Darrell, Jr.-Associate Judge, Maryland District Court District Eight-Md.
Russell, Heather S.-Judge, Hamilton County Municipal Court-Ohio
Russell, Jacqueline L.-Judge, Pennsylvania Court of Common Pleas Twenty-first Judicial District-Pa.
Russell, James Franklin-Judge, Tennessee Circuit Court Thirtieth Judicial District-Tenn.
Russell, James MacDonald, Jr.-Judge, Butler County District Court-Ala.
Russell, Janice D.-Judge, Kansas District Court Tenth Judicial District-Kan.
Russell, Karen D.-Judge, New Jersey Superior Court Vicinage Ten-N.J.
Russell, Kerry L.-Judge, Texas District Court 7th Judicial District-Tex.
Russell, Mary Rhodes-Judge, Missouri Court of Appeals Eastern District-Mo.
Russell, Norman L.-Associate District Judge, Oklahoma District Court Third Judicial District-Okla.
Russell, Robert H., II-Judge, Colorado District Court Eighteenth Judicial District-Colo.
Russell, Robert L., III-Judge, Superior Court of Georgia Atlantic Judicial Circuit-Ga.
Russell, Robert T., Jr.-Judge, Buffalo City Court-N.Y.
Russell, Ronald D.-Judge, Maine District Court-Me.
Russell, Thomas B.-Judge, United States District Court Western District of Kentucky-Ky.
Russell, Thomas G.-Circuit Judge, Illinois Circuit Court Seventh Judicial Circuit-Ill.
Russell, Van P.-Judge, Franklin County Court-Fla.
Russell, William D., Jr.-Judge, Etowah County District Court-Ala.
Russello, Mark M.-Judge, New Jersey Superior Court Vicinage Two-N.J.
Russo, Anthony J.-Judge, Ohio Court of Common Pleas Cuyahoga County-Ohio
Russo, Joseph D.-Judge, Ohio Court of Common Pleas Cuyahoga County-Ohio
Russo, Joseph F.-Judge, Ohio Court of Common Pleas Cuyahoga County-Ohio
Russo, Michael Joseph-Judge, Ohio Court of Common Pleas Cuyahoga County-Ohio
Russo, Nancy Margaret-Judge, Ohio Court of Common Pleas Cuyahoga County-Ohio
Rustad, Gerald H.-Judge, North Dakota District Court Northwest Judicial District-N.D.
Rutberg, Fredric D.-Justice, Trial Court of Massachusetts District Court Department Berkshire County Southern Berkshire Division-Mass.
Ruth, James A.-Judge, Duval County Court-Fla.
Ruth, Kristin Holmquist-Judge, North Carolina District Court District 10-N.C.
Rutrough, Elizabeth-Associate Judge, Juvenile Court of Georgia Dublin Judicial Circuit-Ga.
Rutter, Edith R.-Associate Circuit Judge, Missouri Circuit Court Forty-second Judicial Circuit-Mo.
Ruttle, Ann-Judge, Kentucky District Court Sixteenth Judicial District-Ky.
Ruvolo, Ignazio "Nace" John-Associate Justice, California Court of Appeal First District Division Two-Calif.
Ruwe, Robert P.-Judge, United States Tax Court
Ruybalid, Ernest J.-Judge, Pueblo County Court-Colo.
Ruyle, Stephen W.-Judge, Ohio Court of Common Pleas Defiance County-Ohio
Ryan, Daniel P.-Judge, Michigan Circuit Court Third Judicial Circuit-Mich.
Ryan, David W.-Judge, Superior Court of California County of San Diego-Calif.
Ryan, Edward J.-Judge, New Jersey Superior Court Vicinage Eight-N.J.
Ryan, Gregory J.-Special Judge, Oklahoma District Court Seventh Judicial District-Okla.
Ryan, H. Chris, Jr.-Circuit Judge, Illinois Circuit Court Thirteenth Judicial Circuit-Ill.
Ryan, James J.-Associate Judge, Illinois Circuit Court of Cook County-Ill.
Ryan, James L.-Senior Judge, United States Court of Appeals Sixth Circuit
Ryan, James L.-Associate Judge, Circuit Court for Montgomery County, Sixth Judicial Circuit-Md.
Ryan, James T.-Circuit Judge, Illinois Circuit Court of Cook County-Ill.
Ryan, Jerry-Judge, Mena District Court-Ark.
Ryan, John E.-Chief Judge, Bankruptcy Appellate Panel Ninth Circuit and Judge, United States Bankruptcy Court Central District of California-Calif.
Ryan, John J. P.-Judge Referee, Connecticut Superior Court-Conn.
Ryan, Kevin K.-Judge, Clinton County Court-N.Y.
Ryan, Michael D.-Justice, Supreme Court of Arizona-Ariz.
Ryan, Michael J.-Special Justice, Goffstown District Court-N.H.
Ryan, Peter V.-Judge, New Jersey Superior Court Vicinage Five-N.J.
Ryan, Stephen P.-Judge, Kentucky Circuit Court Thirtieth Judicial Circuit-Ky.
Ryan, Thomas J.-Judge, Idaho District Court Third Judicial District Magistrate Division-Ida.
Ryan, Timothy P.-Judge, Snohomish District Court South Division Snohomish County-Wash.
Ryan, W. Michael-Justice, Trial Court of Massachusetts District Court Department Hampshire County Northampton Division-Mass.
Ryan, William A.-Judge, Hale County District Court-Ala.
Ryan, William C.-Judge, Superior Court of California County of Los Angeles-Calif.
Ryan, William P., Jr.-Judge, Kentucky District Court Thirtieth Judicial District-Ky.
Ryburn, Douglas Lee-Judge, Terry County Court-Tex.
Ryckman, Jere-Judge, Wyoming District Court Third Judicial District-Wyo.
Ryder, Byron-Judge, Leon County Court-Tex.
Ryder, Herboth S.-Senior Judge, Florida District Court of Appeal-Fla.
Rykken, Miriam P.-Judge, Minnesota Workers' Compensation Court of Appeals-Minn.
Rylaarsdam, William F.-Associate Justice, California Court of Appeal Fourth District Division Three-Calif.
Ryland, B. Dexter-Judge, Louisiana District Court Ninth Judicial District-La.
Rymell, Jennifer-Judge, Tarrant County Court at Law No. 2-Tex.
Rymer, Pamela Ann-Judge, United States Court of Appeals Ninth Circuit
Rynd, Frank-Judge, Texas Family District Court 309th Judicial District-Tex.
Rysavy, Donald E.-Judge, Minnesota District Court Third Judicial District-Minn.
Ryskamp, Kenneth L.-Senior Judge, United States District Court Southern District of Florida-Fla.
Ryu, Tammy Chung-Judge, Superior Court of California County of Los Angeles-Calif.
Saad, Henry William-Judge, Michigan Court of Appeals-Mich.
Sabaitis, Catherine P.-First Justice, Trial Court of Massachusetts Probate and Family Court Department Plymouth County Division-Mass.
Sabalos, Charles S.-Judge, Superior Court of Arizona Pima County-Ariz.
Sabatino, Jack M.-Judge, New Jersey Superior Court Vicinage Seven-N.J.
Sabbath, George E.-Judge, New Jersey Superior Court Vicinage Eleven-N.J.
Sabers, Richard W.-Associate Justice, South Dakota Supreme Court-S.D.
Sabet, Shahla S.-Judge, Superior Court of California County of San Bernardino-Calif.
Sabiston, Michael A.-Judge, North Carolina District Court District 19B-N.C.
Sabol, Lori Stein-Judge, West Lafayette City Court-Ind.
Sabra, Bernadette L.-First Justice, Trial Court of Massachusetts District Court Department Bristol County New Bedford Division and Justice, Fall River Division-Mass.
Sabraw, Bonnie Lewman-Judge, Superior Court of California County of Alameda-Calif.
Sabraw, Dana Makoto-Judge, Superior Court of California County of San Diego-Calif.
Sabraw, Ronald M.-Judge, Superior Court of California County of Alameda-Calif.
Sacavage, Robert B.-President Judge, Pennsylvania Court of Common Pleas Eighth Judicial District-Pa.
Sachs, Howard F.-Senior Judge, United States District Court Western District of Missouri-Mo.
Sachse, Thomas H.-Judge, Kansas District Court Fourth Judicial District-Kan.
Sack, Barry D.-Judge, Hudson City Court-N.Y.
Sack, Robert D.-Judge, United States Court of Appeals Second Circuit
Sackett, Robert A.-Judge, The Civil Court of the City of New York-N.Y.
Sackett, Rosemary Shaw-Chief Judge, Iowa Court of Appeals-Ia.
Sacks, David G.-First Justice, Trial Court of Massachusetts Probate and Family Court Department Hampden County Division-Mass.
Sacks, Stanley J.-Associate Judge, Illinois Circuit Court of Cook County-Ill.
Sadler, Alan B.-Judge, Montgomery County Court-Tex.
Sadler, Lisa L.-Judge, Ohio Court of Appeals Tenth District-Ohio
Sadler, Lucinda V.-Special Justice, Hooksett District Court-N.H.
Saenz, L. Arnoldo-Judge, Jim Wells County Court-Tex.
Saffold, Shirley Strickland-Judge, Ohio Court of Common Pleas Cuyahoga County-Ohio
Sage, Larry-Judge, Sparks Municipal Court-Nev.
Sage, Michael J.-Judge, Ohio Court of Common Pleas Butler County-Ohio
Sage, Robin D.-Judge, Texas Family District Court 307th Judicial District-Tex.
Sagstuen, Warren R.-Judge, Minnesota District Court Fourth Judicial District-Minn.
Sahagian, Maryanne-Circuit Justice, Trial Court of Massachusetts Probate and Family Court Department-Mass.
Sahagun, Raul Anthony-Judge, Superior Court of California County of Los Angeles-Calif.
Sahlstrom, R. Craig-Associate Judge, Illinois Circuit Court Seventeenth Judicial Circuit-Ill.
Saiers, K. Peter-Judge, Superior Court of California County of San Joaquin-Calif.
Sainsbury, Sterling B.-Judge, Utah Juvenile Court Fourth Judicial District-Utah
St. Arnold, Jack A.-Judge, Florida Circuit Court Sixth Judicial Circuit-Fla.
Saint Clair, J. Wesley-Judge, King District Court East Division King County-Wash.
St. Clair, James-Judge, Cochran County Court-Tex.
St. Clair, Richard T.-Judge, Idaho District Court Seventh Judicial District-Ida.
St. Eve, Amy J.-Judge, United States District Court Northern District of Illinois-Ill.
Saint-Evens, Angus-Judge, Superior Court of California County of Glenn-Calif.
St. Germaine, Curtis-Chief Magistrate, Magistrate Court of Burke County-Ga.
St. John, Stephen C.-Judge, United States Bankruptcy Court Eastern District of Virginia-Va.
St. Pierre, Emile R.-Judge, Louisiana District Court Twenty-ninth Judicial District-La.
Saitta, Nancy M.-Judge, Nevada District Court Eighth Judicial District-Nev.
Saitta, Wayne P.-Judge, The Civil Court of the City of New York-N.Y.
Sakamoto, Karl K.-Judge, Hawaii Circuit Court First Judicial Circuit-Hi.
Saks, Alan J.-Justice, New York Supreme Court Twelfth Judicial District-N.Y.
Salafia, Linda M.-Judge, Norwich District Probate Court-Conn.
Salazar, John Steven-Judge, Superior Court of California County of Santa Cruz-Calif.
Salcedo, Fidel-Justice of the Peace, Reno Justices' Court-Nev.
Salcido, DeAnn M.-Judge, Superior Court of California County of San Diego-Calif.
Salcines, E. J.-Judge, Florida District Court of Appeal Second District-Fla.

ALPHABETICAL NAME INDEX

ALPHABETICAL NAME INDEX

Savage, Drella-Circuit Judge, Illinois Circuit Court of Cook County-Ill.

Savage, Judith Colenback-Associate Justice, Rhode Island Superior Court-R.I.

Savage, Katherine D.-Associate Judge, Circuit Court for Montgomery County, Sixth Judicial Circuit-Md.

Savage, Ralph-Judge, Idaho District Court Seventh Judicial District Magistrate Division-Ida.

Savage, Randy-Judge, Burnet County Court at Law No. 1-Tex.

Savage, Timothy J.-Judge, United States District Court Eastern District of Pennsylvania-Pa.

Savell, Richard D.-Judge, Alaska Superior Court Fourth Judicial District-Alas.

Savignano, Richard D.-Justice, Trial Court of Massachusetts District Court Department Plymouth County Brockton Division-Mass.

Savoie, D. Kent-Judge, Louisiana District Court Fourteenth Judicial District-La.

Sawaya, Thomas D.-Judge, Florida District Court of Appeal Fifth District-Fla.

Sawicki, Daniel-Chief Judge, Michigan District Court District Forty-four-Mich.

Sawyer, C. David, Jr.-Judge, South Carolina Family Court Eleventh Judicial Circuit-S.C.

Sawyer, David H.-Judge, Michigan Court of Appeals-Mich.

Sawyer, James B., II-Judge, Washington Superior Court Mason County-Wash.

Sawyer, Laurence K.-Judge, Superior Court of California County of Sonoma-Calif.

Sawyer, Stephen G.-Circuit Judge, Illinois Circuit Court Second Judicial Circuit-Ill.

Sawyer, William R.-Chief Judge, United States Bankruptcy Court Middle District of Alabama-Ala.

Saxe, David B.-Associate Justice, New York Supreme Court Appellate Division First Judicial Department-N.Y.

Saxon, David P.-Judge, Fort Smith District Court-Ark.

Saxon, Stella H.-Judge, Texas District Court 218th Judicial District-Tex.

Saxton, Richard N., Jr.-President Judge, Pennsylvania Court of Common Pleas Twenty-fifth Judicial District-Pa.

Saxton, Thomas M., Jr.-Magistrate Judge, Kansas District Court Thirty-first Judicial District-Kan.

Saylor, Charles Horace-Judge, Pennsylvania Court of Common Pleas Eighth Judicial District-Pa.

Saylor, Thomas G.-Justice, The Supreme Court of Pennsylvania-Pa.

Sayre, Jeffrey D.-Associate Circuit Judge, Missouri Circuit Court Ninth Judicial Circuit-Mo.

Sazama, Thomas J.-Judge, Wisconsin Circuit Court Chippewa Circuit-Wis.

Scaggs, John H.-District Judge, Oklahoma District Court Twentieth Judicial District-Okla.

Scales, Juliette Wiltshire-Associate Judge, Juvenile Court of Georgia Atlanta Judicial Circuit-Ga.

Scalia, Antonin-Associate Justice, The Supreme Court of the United States

Scancarella, Joseph F.-Judge, New Jersey Superior Court Vicinage Eleven-N.J.

Scandurra, Robert A.-Associate Justice, Trial Court of Massachusetts Probate and Family Court Department Barnstable County Division-Mass.

Scanlon, Eugene F., Jr.-Judge, Pennsylvania Court of Common Pleas Fifth Judicial District-Pa.

Scarano, Jerry J.-Judge, Saratoga County Court-N.Y.

Scarborough, Vickie B.-Chief Magistrate, Magistrate Court of Telfair County-Ga.

Scarlett, Stephen G.-Judge, Superior Court of Georgia Brunswick Judicial Circuit-Ga.

Scarpellino, Philip A.-Judge, Connecticut Superior Court-Conn.

Scarpino, Anthony A., Jr.-Surrogate, Westchester County Surrogate's Court-N.Y.

Scarpone, David J.-Judge, Jefferson County Court-Ohio

Scarpulla, Saliann-Judge, The Civil Court of the City of New York-N.Y.

Schacht, Donald W.-Judge, Washington Superior Court Walla Walla County-Wash.

Schack, Arthur M.-Judge, The Civil Court of the City of New York-N.Y.

Schack, Larry-Judge, Florida Circuit Court Nineteenth Judicial Circuit-Fla.

Schacter, David Martin-Judge, Superior Court of California County of Los Angeles-Calif.

Schaefer, Donavon D.-District Associate Judge, Iowa District Court Third Judicial District-Ia.

Schaefer, John A.-Judge, Florida Circuit Court Sixth Judicial Circuit-Fla.

Schaefer, Jon Patrick-Judge, Shelby Municipal Court-Ohio

Schaefer, Philip D.-Judge, Michigan Circuit Court Ninth Judicial Circuit-Mich.

Schaeffer, Susan F.-Judge, Florida Circuit Court Sixth Judicial Circuit-Fla.

Schaeperkoetter, Jeff W.-Circuit Judge, Missouri Circuit Court Twentieth Judicial Circuit-Mo.

Schaff, Gail-Justice, Golden Valley County Justice of the Peace Court and Judge, Ryegate City Court-Mont.

Schafstall, Robert D.-Judge, Franklin City Court-Ind.

Schall, Alvin A.-Judge, United States Court of Appeals Federal Circuit

Schaller, Barry R.-Judge, Connecticut Appellate Court-Conn.

Schapira, Carol-Judge, Washington Superior Court King County-Wash.

Schapiro, Sheldon M.-Judge, Florida Circuit Court Seventeenth Judicial Circuit-Fla.

Schatz, Gregory M.-Judge, Nebraska District Court Fourth Judicial District-Neb.

Schaumann, Dennis M.-Circuit Judge, Missouri Circuit Court Twenty-second Judicial Circuit-Mo.

Scheb, John M.-Senior Judge, Florida District Court of Appeal-Fla.

Schechter, Sara P.-Judge, New York City Family Court-N.Y.

Schechtman, Ronald H.-Chief Judge, Iowa District Court Second Judicial District-Ia.

Scheel, Danny-Judge, Comal County Court-Tex.

Scheer, Donald A.-Magistrate Judge, United States District Court Eastern District of Michigan-Mich.

Scheer, James J.-Judge, Celina Municipal Court-Ohio

Scheffy, Brackett Leighton-Justice, Henniker District Court-N.H.

Schehr, Kevin-Associate Circuit Judge, Missouri Circuit Court Twenty-sixth Judicial Circuit-Mo.

Scheibenberger, Kenneth R.-Judge, Allen Superior Court-Ind.

Scheier, Karyn Faith-Chief Justice, Trial Court of Massachusetts Land Court Department-Mass.

Scheinblum, Howard-Judge, Connecticut Superior Court-Conn.

Scheindlin, Shira A.-Judge, United States District Court Southern District of New York-N.Y.

Schell, David Stanford-Judge, Virginia Juvenile and Domestic Relations District Court Nineteenth Judicial District-Va.

Schell, Richard A.-Judge, United States District Court Eastern District of Texas-Tex.

Schell, Tarey-Associate Judge, Juvenile Court of Georgia Griffin Judicial Circuit-Ga.

Schellhas, Heidi S.-Judge, Minnesota District Court Fourth Judicial District-Minn.

Schellinger, Jacqueline-Judge, Wisconsin Circuit Court Milwaukee Circuit-Wis.

Schemer, Jack M.-Judge, Florida Circuit Court Fourth Judicial Circuit-Fla.

Schempp, Darlene E.-Judge, Superior Court of California County of Los Angeles-Calif.

Schenkier, Sidney I.-Magistrate Judge, United States District Court Northern District of Illinois-Ill.

Scheper, Barbara Marie-Judge, Superior Court of California County of Los Angeles-Calif.

Scher, Preston S.-Judge, New Rochelle City Court-N.Y.

Scherer, John H.-Judge, Minnesota District Court Seventh Judicial District-Minn.

Scherer, Micki A.-Judge, The Criminal Court of the City of New York-N.Y.

Scherer, Richard S.-Judge, Minnesota District Court Fourth Judicial District-Minn.

Schermer, Barry S.-Judge, Bankruptcy Appellate Panel Eighth Circuit and Judge, United States Bankruptcy Court Eastern District of Missouri-Mo.

Scheuler, Richard-Judge, Superior Court of California County of Tehama-Calif.

Schiferl, Michael A.-Judge, Colorado District Court Sixteenth Judicial District-Colo.

Schiff, Gerald H.-Chief Judge, United States Bankruptcy Court Western District of Louisiana-La.

Schiff, Louis H.-Judge, Broward County Court-Fla.

Schiff, Ronald D.-Associate Judge, Circuit Court for Prince George's County, Seventh Judicial Circuit-Md.

Schiffner, Glenn D.-Judge, Kansas District Court Fifteenth Judicial District-Kan.

Schildknecht, Carter Tinsley-Judge, Texas District Court 106th Judicial District-Tex.

Schilleci, Vincent J., Jr.-Judge, Jefferson County District Court Bessemer Division-Ala.

Schiller, Berle M.-Judge, United States District Court Eastern District of Pennsylvania-Pa.

Schiller, James A. "J.R."-Judge, Idaho District Court Third Judicial District Magistrate Division-Ida.

Schiller, Stephen A.-Circuit Judge, Illinois Circuit Court of Cook County-Ill.

Schimelman, Stuart M.-Judge, Connecticut Superior Court-Conn.

Schindler, Ann-Judge, Washington Court of Appeals Division I-Wash.

Schingle, Michael J.-Judge, Morgan County Court-Colo.

Schiralli, Nicholas J.-Judge, Lake Superior Court-Ind.

Schisler, Richard T.-Judge, Portsmouth Municipal Court-Ohio

Schiveley, Mark-Presiding Judge, Oregon Circuit Court First Judicial District-Ore.

Schlaefer, Leo F.-Reserve Judge, Wisconsin Circuit Court-Wis.

Schlaegel, E. Lee-Judge, West Virginia Circuit Court Twenty-fifth Judicial Circuit-W.Va.

Schlatter, O. Edward-Magistrate Judge, United States District Court District of Colorado-Colo.

Schlesinger, Alice-Justice, New York Supreme Court First Judicial District-N.Y.

Schlesinger, Harvey Erwin-Judge, United States District Court Middle District of Florida-Fla.

Schlosser, Marvin E.-Judge, New Jersey Superior Court Vicinage Three-N.J.

Schlosstein, Gary B.-Reserve Judge, Wisconsin Circuit Court-Wis.

Schma, William G.-Judge, Michigan Circuit Court Ninth Judicial Circuit-Mich.

Schmalenberger, Allan L.-Presiding Judge, North Dakota District Court Southwest Judicial District-N.D.

Schmehl, Jeffrey L.-Judge, Pennsylvania Court of Common Pleas Twenty-third Judicial District-Pa.

Schmehl, Peter W.-Judge, Pennsylvania Court of Common Pleas Twenty-third Judicial District-Pa.

Schmenk, Joseph N.-Judge, Ohio Court of Common Pleas Defiance County-Ohio

Schmetterer, Jack B.-Judge, United States Bankruptcy Court Northern District of Illinois-Ill.

Schmidt, Bruce K.-Judge, Wisconsin Circuit Court Winnebago Circuit-Wis.

Schmidt, Daniel L.-Judge, Illinois Appellate Court Third Judicial District-Ill.

Schmidt, David I.-Judge, The Civil Court of the City of New York-N.Y.

Schmidt, Earl William-Reserve Judge, Wisconsin Circuit Court-Wis.

Schmidt, Frederick D.-Justice, New York Supreme Court Eleventh Judicial District-N.Y.

Schmidt, Jean M.-Judge, Kansas District Court Third Judicial District-Kan.

Schmidt, Kenneth W.-Judge, Michigan Circuit Court Eighteenth Judicial Circuit-Mich.

Schmidt, Richard Allan-Judge, Idaho District Court Fourth Judicial District Magistrate Division-Ida.

Schmidt, Richard S.-Judge, United States Bankruptcy Court Southern District of Texas-Tex.

ALPHABETICAL NAME INDEX

ALPHABETICAL NAME INDEX

Presiding Justice, California Court of Appeal Third District-Calif.

Scott, Charles R.-Judge, Louisiana District Court First Judicial District-La.

Scott, G. Lewis-Judge, West Yellowstone City Court-Mont.

Scott, Hugh B.-Magistrate Judge, United States District Court Western District of New York-N.Y.

Scott, James B., Jr.-Judge, Tennessee Circuit Court Seventh Judicial District-Tenn.

Scott, James D.-District Judge, Iowa District Court Third Judicial District-Ia.

Scott, Jeanne E.-Judge, United States District Court Central District of Illinois-Ill.

Scott, John R.-Judge, Arkansas Circuit Court Nineteenth West Judicial Circuit-Ark.

Scott, John Whittier, Jr.-Judge, Virginia Circuit Court Fifteenth Judicial Circuit-Va.

Scott, Joseph M., Jr.-Judge, United States Bankruptcy Court Eastern District of Kentucky-Ky.

Scott, Justus C.-Chief Judge, Lapeer County Probate Court-Mich.

Scott, Linda K.-Judge, Superior Court of Arizona Maricopa County-Ariz.

Scott, Robert C.-Senior Judge, Florida Circuit Court Seventeenth Judicial Circuit-Fla.

Scott, Robert H.-Magistrate Judge, United States District Court District of New Mexico-N.Mex.

Scott, Russell D.-Judge, Superior Court of California County of Monterey-Calif.

Scott, Steven-Judge, Washington Superior Court King County-Wash.

Scott, Susan Devlin-Judge, Pennsylvania Court of Common Pleas Seventh Judicial District-Pa.

Scott, Terry J.-Judge, Superior Court of California County of San Diego-Calif.

Scoville, Joseph G.-Magistrate Judge, United States District Court Western District of Michigan-Mich.

Scoville, Vernon E., III-Associate Circuit Judge, Missouri Circuit Court Sixteenth Judicial Circuit-Mo.

Scriven, Mary S.-Magistrate Judge, United States District Court Middle District of Florida-Fla.

Scrivener, Louise G.-Associate Judge, Circuit Court for Montgomery County, Sixth Judicial Circuit-Md.

Scroggins, Danny L.-Associate District Judge, Oklahoma District Court Twenty-fifth Judicial District-Okla.

Scuccimarra, Thomas H.-Judge, New York Court of Claims-N.Y.

Scudder, Henry J.-Associate Justice, New York Supreme Court Appellate Division Fourth Judicial Department-N.Y.

Scuderi, Peter B.-Recalled Magistrate Judge, United States District Court Eastern District of Pennsylvania-Pa.

Scullin, Frederick J., Jr.-Chief Judge, United States District Court Northern District of New York-N.Y.

Scully, Jack William-Chief Judge, Arenac County Probate Court-Mich.

Scully, Thomas F.-Judge, New Jersey Superior Court Vicinage Nine-N.J.

Scurlock, Don P., III-Judge, Choctaw County District Court-Ala.

Seals, James H.-Judge, Florida Circuit Court Twentieth Judicial Circuit-Fla.

Seaman, David E.-Judge, Niagara County Family Court-N.Y.

Seamans, Barbara G.-Judge, Canaan District Probate Court-Conn.

Seamans, Kenneth W.-President Judge, Pennsylvania Court of Common Pleas Thirty-fourth Judicial District-Pa.

Sear, Morey L.-Senior Judge, United States District Court Eastern District of Louisiana-La.

Searer, Timothy S.-President Judge, Pennsylvania Court of Common Pleas Fifty-eighth Judicial District-Pa.

Sears, Donald W.-Chief Magistrate, Magistrate Court of Appling County-Ga.

Sears, Leah-Presiding Justice, Supreme Court of Georgia-Ga.

Seaton, Sarah Cowen-Judge, North Carolina District Court District 4-N.C.

Seaver, William H.-Senior Judge, Pasco County Court-Fla.

Seay, Frank Howell-Judge, United States District Court Eastern District of Oklahoma-Okla.

Seay, Thomas W., Jr.-Retired-Recalled Judge, North Carolina Superior Court-N.C.

Seay, William C.-Circuit Judge, Missouri Circuit Court Forty-second Judicial Circuit-Mo.

Sebelius, K. Gary-Magistrate Judge, United States District Court District of Kansas-Kan.

Sebesta, Patrick E.-Judge, Texas District Court 239th Judicial District-Tex.

Seckinger, Frances Y.-Judge, Probate Court of Effingham County-Ga.

Secola, Joseph P.-Judge, Brookfield District Probate Court-Conn.

Sedita, Frank A., Jr.-Justice, New York Supreme Court Eighth Judicial District-N.Y.

Sedwick, John W.-Chief Judge, United States District Court District of Alaska-Alas.

See, Harold F.-Associate Justice, Alabama Supreme Court-Ala.

See, Ramona G.-Judge, Superior Court of California County of Los Angeles-Calif.

Seeborg, Richard-Magistrate Judge, United States District Court Northern District of California-Calif.

Seeley, Thomas J., Jr.-Judge, Tennessee Circuit Court First Judicial District-Tenn.

Seeliger, Clarence F.-Judge, Superior Court of Georgia Stone Mountain Judicial Circuit-Ga.

Seewald, Robert G.-Judge, The Criminal Court of the City of New York-N.Y.

Segal, John-Judge, Superior Court of California County of Los Angeles-Calif.

Segal, Marvin E.-Justice, New York Supreme Court Tenth Judicial District-N.Y.

Segal, Suzanne H.-Magistrate Judge, United States District Court Central District of California-Calif.

Segal, Vincent D.-Judge, New Jersey Superior Court Vicinage One-N.J.

Segars-Andrews, Frances P.-Judge, South Carolina Family Court Ninth Judicial Circuit-S.C.

Segura, Robert L.-Judge, New Iberia City Court-La.

Sehon, Thomas-Judge, Falls County Court-Tex.

Seibel, Gerald J.-Judge, Minnesota District Court Eighth Judicial District-Minn.

Seibert, Harry W., Jr.-Surrogate, Saratoga County Surrogate's Court-N.Y.

Seibert, James E.-Magistrate Judge, United States District Court Northern District of West Virginia-W.Va.

Seiden, Adam-Judge, Mount Vernon City Court-N.Y.

Seidler, I. Marshall-Associate Judge, Maryland District Court District Eight-Md.

Seidlin, Larry S.-Judge, Florida Circuit Court Seventeenth Judicial Circuit-Fla.

Seidman, Lee Jay-Judge, Broward County Court-Fla.

Seiffert, Johnny D.-Justice, Carbon County Justice of the Peace Court-Mont.

Seigel, Mark D.-Circuit Judge, Missouri Circuit Court Twenty-first Judicial Circuit-Mo.

Seinfeld, Karen Goodman-Judge, Washington Court of Appeals Division II-Wash.

Seitz, Joan G.-Presiding Judge, Oregon Circuit Court Sixteenth Judicial District-Ore.

Seitz, Patricia A.-Judge, United States District Court Southern District of Florida-Fla.

Seitz, Victoria-Judge, King District Court South Division King County-Wash.

Selander, Robert R.-Presiding Judge, Oregon Circuit Court Fifth Judicial District-Ore.

Selby, Kevin-Associate Circuit Judge, Missouri Circuit Court Fortieth Judicial Circuit-Mo.

Self, Ed-Judge, Texas District Court 242nd Judicial District-Tex.

Self, William J., II-Judge, Probate Court of Bibb County-Ga.

Selfridge, Shelley-Magistrate Judge, Kansas District Court Twenty-fourth Judicial District-Kan.

Sellers, Barbara Jackson-Judge, United States Bankruptcy Court Southern District of Ohio-Ohio

Sellers, Jefferson D.-District Judge, Oklahoma District Court Fourteenth Judicial District-Okla.

Sellman, John R.-Judge, Idaho District Court Fourth Judicial District Magistrate Division-Ida.

Sells, Lillie Ann-Judge, Tennessee Criminal Court Thirteenth Judicial District-Tenn.

Selman, Jerry K.-Judge, Alabama Circuit Court Fourteenth Judicial Circuit-Ala.

Selna, James V.-Judge, Superior Court of California County of Orange-Calif.

Selph, Steven-Judge, Polk County Court-Fla.

Selser, John E.-Judge, New Jersey Superior Court Vicinage Eleven-N.J.

Seltzer, Barry S.-Magistrate Judge, United States District Court Southern District of Florida-Fla.

Seltzer, George L.-Judge, New Jersey Superior Court Vicinage One-N.J.

Selya, Bruce M.-Judge, United States Court of Appeals First Circuit

Semento, Lawrence J.-Judge, Florida Circuit Court Fifth Judicial Circuit-Fla.

Senda, Trudy K.-Judge, Hawaii District Court Fifth Judicial Circuit-Hi.

Senechal, Alice R.-Magistrate Judge, United States District Court District of North Dakota-N.D.

Senne, Herbert H., Jr.-Judge, Kinney County Court-Tex.

Sens, Paul N.-Judge, New Orleans Municipal Court-La.

Sensenich, Ila Jeanne-Magistrate Judge, United States District Court Western District of Pennsylvania-Pa.

Sentelle, David B.-Judge, United States Court of Appeals District of Columbia Circuit

Senter, J. Larry-Judge, North Carolina District Court District 9-N.C.

Senter, L. T., Jr.-Senior Judge, United States District Court Northern District of Mississippi-Miss.

Senyk, Waldemar B.-Judge, Minnesota District Court Seventh Judicial District-Minn.

Sepulveda, Patricia K.-Associate Justice, California Court of Appeal First District Division Four-Calif.

Sequino, Karen Skromme Nash-Judge, Connecticut Superior Court-Conn.

Seraphin, Fred-Judge, Dade County Court-Fla.

Sergent, Birg E.-Judge, Virginia Circuit Court Thirtieth Judicial Circuit-Va.

Serkes, Joseph Michael-Chief Judge, Virginia General District Court Twenty-fourth Judicial District-Va.

Serna, Patricio M.-Justice, New Mexico Supreme Court-N.Mex.

Serpentelli, Eugene D.-Assignment Judge, New Jersey Superior Court Vicinage Fourteen-N.J.

Serra, Robert L.-Judge, Kansas District Court Twenty-ninth Judicial District-Kan.

Servaas, Steven Richard-Judge, Michigan District Court District Sixty-three Division One-Mich.

Servitto, Deborah A.-Judge, Michigan Circuit Court Sixteenth Judicial Circuit-Mich.

Servitto, Edward A., Jr.-Judge, Michigan Circuit Court Sixteenth Judicial Circuit-Mich.

Sessions, William K., III-Chief Judge, United States District Court District of Vermont-Vt.

Sestak, William G.-Judge, Pasco County Court-Fla.

Setzer, Joseph E.-Chief Judge, North Carolina District Court District 8-N.C.

Severson, Glen A.-Presiding Judge, South Dakota Circuit Court Second Judicial Circuit-S.D.

Sevier, Gerald F.-Judge, Superior Court of California County of Tulare-Calif.

Sewell, G. Bruce-District Judge, Oklahoma District Court Fifteenth Judicial District-Okla.

Sexton, Benjamin J.-Judge, Kansas District Court Eighth Judicial District-Kan.

Sexton, E. Shayne-Judge, Tennessee Criminal Court Eighth Judicial District-Tenn.

Sexton, Elizabeth Walter-Associate Judge, Illinois Circuit Court Eighteenth Judicial Circuit-Ill.

Sexton, George C.-Judge, Tennessee Circuit Court Twenty-third Judicial District-Tenn.

Sexton, Susan-Judge, Florida Circuit Court Thirteenth Judicial Circuit-Fla.

Sexton, Susan-Judge, Probate Court of Elbert County-Ga.

Seybert, Joanna-Judge, United States District Court Eastern District of New York-N.Y.

ALPHABETICAL NAME INDEX

Seybolt, Harry K.-Judge, New Jersey Superior Court Vicinage Thirteen-N.J.

Seymore, Charles W.-Justice, Texas Court of Appeals Fourteenth District-Tex.

Seymour, Margaret B.-Judge, United States District Court District of South Carolina-S.C.

Seymour, Stephanie Kulp-Judge, United States Court of Appeals Tenth Circuit

Seymour, Steven P.-Circuit Judge, Illinois Circuit Court Fourth Judicial Circuit-Ill.

Sferrazza, Samuel J.-Judge, Connecticut Superior Court-Conn.

Sgroi, Sandra L.-Justice, New York Supreme Court Tenth Judicial District-N.Y.

Sgueglia, Vincent A.-Judge, Tioga County Court-N.Y.

Shabaz, John C.-Judge, United States District Court Western District of Wisconsin-Wis.

Shackelford, Jan-Judge, Florida Circuit Court First Judicial Circuit-Fla.

Shadid, James E.-Circuit Judge, Illinois Circuit Court Tenth Judicial Circuit-Ill.

Shadoan, William L.-Judge, Kentucky Circuit Court First Judicial Circuit-Ky.

Shadrick, Thomas S.-Chief Judge, Virginia Circuit Court Second Judicial Circuit-Va.

Shadur, Milton I.-Senior Judge, United States District Court Northern District of Illinois-Ill.

Shafer, Abe-Circuit Judge, Missouri Circuit Court Sixth Judicial Circuit-Mo.

Shafer, Carson B.-Senior Judge, City Court of Atlanta-Ga.

Shafer, Marilyn-Judge, The Civil Court of the City of New York-N.Y.

Shafer, Robert T., Jr.-Senior Judge, Florida Circuit Court Twentieth Judicial Circuit-Fla.

Shaffer, Catherine-Judge, Washington Superior Court King County-Wash.

Shaffer, Craig B.-Magistrate Judge, United States District Court District of Colorado-Colo.

Shaffer, Ronald L.-District Judge, Oklahoma District Court Fourteenth Judicial District-Okla.

Shaffer, William R.-Judge, Pennsylvania Court of Common Pleas Fiftieth Judicial District-Pa.

Shaheed, David A.-Judge, Marion Superior Court-Ind.

Shaheen, Anthony F.-Justice, New York Supreme Court Fifth Judicial District-N.Y.

Shahood, George A.-Judge, Florida District Court of Appeal Fourth District-Fla.

Shake, Ann O'Malley-Judge, Kentucky Circuit Court Thirtieth Judicial Circuit-Ky.

Shake, James M.-Judge, Kentucky Circuit Court Thirtieth Judicial Circuit-Ky.

Shallcross, Deborah C.-District Judge, Oklahoma District Court Fourteenth Judicial District-Okla.

Shames, Mark I.-Judge, Florida Circuit Court Sixth Judicial Circuit-Fla.

Shamon, Thomas J.-Judge, Auburn City Court-N.Y.

Shamsie, Terry-Judge, Nueces County Court-Tex.

Shanahan, Thomas M.-Judge, United States District Court District of Nebraska-Neb.

Shands, Rodney E.-Judge, Mississippi Chancery Court First Judicial District-Miss.

Shannon, Cheryl Lee-Judge, Texas Family District Court 305th Judicial District-Tex.

Shanstrom, Jack D.-Senior Judge, United States District Court District of Montana-Mont.

Shapero, Kenneth L.-Judge, Superior Court of California County of Santa Clara-Calif.

Shapero, Walter-Recalled Judge, United States Bankruptcy Court Eastern District of Michigan-Mich.

Shapiro, Bernard S.-Judge, Florida Circuit Court Eleventh Judicial Circuit-Fla.

Shapiro, Fred L.-Judge, Westchester County Court-N.Y.

Shapiro, James Edward-Judge, United States Bankruptcy Court Eastern District of Wisconsin-Wis.

Shapiro, Martin-Judge, Dade County Court-Fla.

Shapiro, Marvin A.-Judge, Ohio Court of Common Pleas Summit County-Ohio

Shapiro, Norma L.-Senior Judge, United States District Court Eastern District of Pennsylvania-Pa.

Shapiro, Norman J.-Judge, Superior Court of California County of Los Angeles-Calif.

Shapiro, Robert B.-Judge, Connecticut Superior Court-Conn.

Shapiro, Sidney B.-Judge, Florida Circuit Court Eleventh Judicial Circuit-Fla.

Sharer, J. Frederick-Associate Judge, Court of Special Appeals of Maryland-Md.

Sharkey, Terrence V.-Associate Judge, Illinois Circuit Court of Cook County-Ill.

Sharp, Allen-Judge, United States District Court Northern District of Indiana-Ind.

Sharp, Alvin R.-Judge, Louisiana District Court Fourth Judicial District-La.

Sharp, Donald R.-Chief Judge, United States Bankruptcy Court Eastern District of Texas-Tex.

Sharp, George Kendall-Senior Judge, United States District Court Middle District of Florida-Fla.

Sharp, P. Trevor-Magistrate Judge, United States District Court Middle District of North Carolina-N.C.

Sharp, Philip D.-Judge, Superior Court of California County of San Diego-Calif.

Sharp, Stephen R.-Presiding Judge, Missouri Circuit Court Thirty-fifth Judicial Circuit-Mo.

Sharp, William W.-Chief Judge, Virginia Juvenile and Domestic Relations District Court Twenty-sixth Judicial District-Va.

Sharp, Winifred J.-Judge, Florida District Court of Appeal Fifth District-Fla.

Sharpe, Gary L.-Magistrate Judge, United States District Court Northern District of New York-N.Y.

Sharpe, Margaret L.-Emergency Judge, North Carolina District Court-N.C.

Sharpnack, John T.-Judge, Indiana Court of Appeals Fifth District-Ind.

Shartel, James R.-Justice of the Peace, Washington County Justice Court-Ore.

Shashy, William A.-Judge, Alabama Circuit Court Fifteenth Judicial Circuit-Ala.

Shattuck, Carolyn M.-Magistrate Judge, United States District Court District of Hawaii-Hi.

Shaughnessy, William-Judge Referee, Connecticut Superior Court-Conn.

Shaver, Donald E.-Judge, Superior Court of California County of Stanislaus-Calif.

Shavor, John D.-Judge, Cottle County Court-Tex.

Shaw, Booker T.-Judge, Missouri Court of Appeals Eastern District-Mo.

Shaw, Charles A.-Judge, United States District Court Eastern District of Missouri-Mo.

Shaw, Charles R.-Chief Magistrate, Magistrate Court of Lanier County-Ga.

Shaw, Greg-Judge, Alabama Court of Criminal Appeals-Ala.

Shaw, Leander J., Jr.-Senior Justice, Florida Supreme Court-Fla.

Shaw, Rex A.-Judge, Jackson County Court-Colo.

Shaw, Richard H.-Judge, Barry County Probate Court-Mich.

Shaw, Stephen R.-Judge, Ohio Court of Appeals Third District-Ohio

Shaw, Susanne S.-Judge, Superior Court of California County of Orange-Calif.

Shaw, William H., III-Judge, Virginia Circuit Court Ninth Judicial Circuit-Va.

Shawcross, Raymond E.-Associate Justice, Rhode Island Family Court-R.I.

Shay, Michael E.-Judge, Connecticut Superior Court-Conn.

Shea, David M.-Judge Referee, Connecticut Superior Court-Conn.

Shea, Edward F.-Judge, United States District Court Eastern District of Washington-Wash.

Shea, John A.-Judge, New Orleans Municipal Court-La.

Shea-Stonum, Marilyn-Judge, United States Bankruptcy Court Northern District of Ohio-Ohio

Shearer, Robin W.-Associate Judge, Juvenile Court of Georgia Western Judicial Circuit-Ga.

Shearing, Miriam-Justice, Nevada Supreme Court-Nev.

Shedd, Dennis W.-Judge, United States Court of Appeals Fourth Circuit

Sheedy, Barbara J.-Judge, Connecticut Superior Court-Conn.

Sheedy, Patrick T.-Reserve Judge, Wisconsin Circuit Court-Wis.

Sheehan, Colleen F.-Circuit Judge, Illinois Circuit Court of Cook County-Ill.

Sheehan, Joseph W.-Judge, Mechanicville City Court-N.Y.

Sheehan, Kevin M.-Circuit Judge, Illinois Circuit Court of Cook County-Ill.

Sheehan, Martin J.-Judge, Kentucky District Court Sixteenth Judicial District-Ky.

Sheehan, Nancy Drew-Circuit Judge, Illinois Circuit Court of Cook County-Ill.

Sheen, Terence M.-Associate Judge, Illinois Circuit Court Eighteenth Judicial Circuit-Ill.

Shefferly, Phillip J.-Judge, United States Bankruptcy Court Eastern District of Michigan-Mich.

Sheffield, Mary W.-Associate Circuit Judge, Missouri Circuit Court Twenty-fifth Judicial Circuit-Mo.

Sheldon, Charles D.-Judge, Superior Court of California County of Los Angeles-Calif.

Sheldon, Christopher J.-Judge, Superior Court of California County of Riverside-Calif.

Sheldon, Michael R.-Judge, Connecticut Superior Court-Conn.

Sheldon, Steven D.-Judge, Superior Court of Arizona Maricopa County-Ariz.

Sheldon, Timothy Q.-Circuit Judge, Illinois Circuit Court Sixteenth Judicial Circuit-Ill.

Sheldon, Toni A.-Judge, Washington Superior Court Mason County-Wash.

Shelfer, James O.-Judge, Leon County Court-Fla.

Shelton, Donald E.-Judge, Michigan Circuit Court Twenty-second Judicial Circuit-Mich.

Shelton, Marian R.-Judge, New York City Family Court-N.Y.

Shelton, Pat-Judge, Texas Family District Court 313th Judicial District-Tex.

Shelton, Phrasel L.-Judge, Superior Court of California County of San Mateo-Calif.

Shelton, Stephen R.-Judge, Puyallup and Sumner Municipal Courts-Wash.

Shemwell, Robert H.-Magistrate Judge, United States District Court Western District of Louisiana-La.

Shenkin, Robert J.-Judge, Pennsylvania Court of Common Pleas Fifteenth Judicial District-Pa.

Shepard, Clifford B., Jr.-Senior Judge, Florida Circuit Court Fourth Judicial Circuit-Fla.

Shepard, Jeanne L.-Magistrate, Rhode Island Family Court-R.I.

Shepard, Randall T.-Chief Justice, Indiana Supreme Court-Ind.

Shepard, Renard F.-Judge, Superior Court of California County of Sacramento-Calif.

Shepherd, Bobby E.-Magistrate Judge, United States District Court Western District of Arkansas-Ark.

Shepherd, Darrell G.-Associate District Judge, Oklahoma District Court Fifteenth Judicial District-Okla.

Shepherd, Douglas P.-Judge, Michigan District Court District Forty-one A-Mich.

Shepherd, E. Allen-Associate Judge, Circuit Court for Prince George's County, Seventh Judicial Circuit-Md.

Shepherd, Jean F.-Judge, Kansas District Court Seventh Judicial District-Kan.

Sheppard, Albert W., Jr.-Judge, Pennsylvania Court of Common Pleas First Judicial District-Pa.

Sheppard, Clayton C.-Chief Magistrate, Magistrate Court of Washington County-Ga.

Sheppard, Harry R.-Judge, Superior Court of California County of Alameda-Calif.

Sheppard, Lawrence E.-Judge, Kansas District Court Tenth Judicial District-Kan.

Sherbin, James L.-Associate Judge, Circuit Court for Garrett County, Fourth Judicial Circuit-Md.

Sherck, James Robert-Judge, Ohio Court of Common Pleas Sandusky County-Ohio

Sheridan, Edward A.-Judge, New York Court of Claims-N.Y.

Sheridan, James E.-Chief Judge, Michigan District Court District Two A-Mich.

Sheridan, Paul F.-Chief Judge, Virginia Circuit Court Seventeenth Judicial Circuit-Va.

Sheridan, Stephen E.-Chief Judge, Michigan District Court District Fifty-seven-Mich.

ALPHABETICAL NAME INDEX

Sherlock, Jeffrey M.-Judge, Montana District Court First Judicial District and Judge, Montana Water Court Upper Missouri River Basin Division-Mont.

Sherman, Howard E.-Judge, The Civil Court of the City of New York-N.Y.

Sherman, Louis A.-Judge, Virginia General District Court Fourth Judicial District-Va.

Sherman, M. John-Judge, Tompkins County Court-N.Y.

Sherman, Vilia-Judge, Superior Court of California County of Riverside-Calif.

Sherrill, Russell Graham, III-Emergency Judge, North Carolina District Court-N.C.

Sherrill, Trace C.-Special Judge, Oklahoma District Court Nineteenth Judicial District-Okla.

Sherrill, William C., Jr.-Magistrate Judge, United States District Court Northern District of Florida-Fla.

Sherrod, Martha L.-Judge, Madison County District Court-Ala.

Sherry, Thea A.-Associate Circuit Judge, Missouri Circuit Court Twenty-first Judicial Circuit-Mo.

Sherwood, William E.-Justice, New York Supreme Court Ninth Judicial District-N.Y.

Shevin, Robert L.-Judge, Florida District Court of Appeal Third District-Fla.

Sheward, Richard S.-Judge, Ohio Court of Common Pleas Franklin County-Ohio

Shewmaker, Terry C.-Judge, Elkhart Circuit Court-Ind.

Shick, Mitchell K.-Circuit Judge, Illinois Circuit Court Fifth Judicial Circuit-Ill.

Shields, Jack-Justice, Fergus County Justice of the Peace Court and Judge, Lewistown City Court-Mont.

Shields, Karen G.-Associate Judge, Illinois Circuit Court of Cook County-Ill.

Shields, Thomas J.-Magistrate Judge, United States District Court Southern District of Iowa-Ia.

Shields, V. Sue-Magistrate Judge, United States District Court Southern District of Indiana-Ind.

Shiff, Alan H. W.-Chief Judge, United States Bankruptcy Court District of Connecticut-Conn.

Shiffman, Stuart H.-Associate Judge, Illinois Circuit Court Seventh Judicial Circuit-Ill.

Shilts, Kim VanValer-Judge, Johnson Superior Court-Ind.

Shinabarger, Ronda-Justice, Meagher County Justice of the Peace Court and Judge, White Sulphur Springs City Court-Mont.

Shindurling, Jon J.-Judge, Idaho District Court Seventh Judicial District-Ida.

Shinholser, Olin W.-Judge, Florida Circuit Court Tenth Judicial Circuit-Fla.

Shinn, Steven E.-Chief Judge, Colorado District Court Thirteenth Judicial District-Colo.

Shipley, Marietta M.-Judge, Tennessee Circuit Court Twentieth Judicial District-Tenn.

Shipman, L. Dee-Judge, Texas District Court 211th Judicial District-Tex.

Shipp, Steve Henry-Judge, Hunt County Court at Law-Tex.

Shirley, C. Clifford-Magistrate Judge, United States District Court Eastern District of Tennessee-Tenn.

Shirron, Phillip H.-Judge, Arkansas Circuit Court Seventh Judicial Circuit-Ark.

Shivers, Melessa-Judge, Probate Court of Clay County-Ga.

Shockley, A. Bonwill-Judge, Virginia Circuit Court Second Judicial Circuit-Va.

Shockley, Doris L.-Judge, Superior Court of California County of Yolo-Calif.

Shoemaker, Wayne-Judge, Orange County Court-Fla.

Shoffner, Clarence P. "Phil"-Judge, Searcy District Court-Ark.

Sholden, John-Judge, Texas Family District Court 304th Judicial District-Tex.

Sholes, Ronald J.-Judge, New Orleans Traffic Court-La.

Shonkwiler, John P.-Chief Judge, Illinois Circuit Court Sixth Judicial Circuit-Ill.

Shoob, Marvin H.-Senior Judge, United States District Court Northern District of Georgia-Ga.

Shoob, Wendy L.-Judge, Superior Court of Georgia Atlanta Judicial Circuit-Ga.

Shook, John P.-Judge, Superior Court of California County of Los Angeles-Calif.

Shore, Brent D.-Judge, Duval County Court-Fla.

Shore, Brian Dean-Associate Judge, Illinois Circuit Court Seventeenth Judicial Circuit-Ill.

Shore, Howard H.-Judge, Superior Court of California County of San Diego-Calif.

Shore, Scott A.-Circuit Judge, Illinois Circuit Court Tenth Judicial Circuit-Ill.

Short, Charles A.-Judge, Alabama Circuit Court Twenty-second Judicial Circuit-Ala.

Short, Jim-Judge, Salem District Court-Ark.

Short, Paul E., Jr.-Judge, South Carolina Circuit Court Sixth Judicial Circuit-S.C.

Shortall, Joseph M.-Judge, Connecticut Superior Court-Conn.

Shreder, Steven P.-Magistrate Judge, United States District Court Eastern District of Oklahoma-Okla.

Shreeves-Johns, Karen-Judge, Pennsylvania Court of Common Pleas First Judicial District-Pa.

Shriver, James A.-Judge, Clermont County Municipal Court-Ohio

Shrum, Kenneth W.-Judge, Missouri Court of Appeals Southern District-Mo.

Shubb, William B.-Chief Judge, United States District Court Eastern District of California-Calif.

Shubin, Dorothy L.-Judge, Superior Court of California County of Los Angeles-Calif.

Shuff, Michael W.-Judge, Orange County Court at Law-Tex.

Shuff, Steve C.-Judge, Ohio Court of Common Pleas Seneca County-Ohio

Shuffield, Milton Gunn-Judge, Texas District Court 136th Judicial District-Tex.

Shuger, Nancy B.-Associate Judge, Maryland District Court District One-Md.

Shuker, Nan R.-Associate Judge, Superior Court of the District of Columbia-D.C.

Shuler, James L.-Judge, New Mexico District Court Fifth Judicial District-N.Mex.

Shull, James Michael-Judge, Virginia Juvenile and Domestic Relations District Court Thirtieth Judicial District-Va.

Shulman, Arnold-Senior Judge, Court of Appeals of Georgia-Ga.

Shulman, Martin-Judge, The Civil Court of the City of New York-N.Y.

Shulman, William S.-Chief Judge, United States Bankruptcy Court Southern District of Alabama-Ala.

Shults, David A.-Judge, Hornell City Court-N.Y.

Shultz, Lon W.-Circuit Judge, Illinois Circuit Court of Cook County-Ill.

Shumaker, Gordon W.-Judge, Minnesota Court of Appeals-Minn.

Shumaker, Thomas E.-Chief Judge, St. Joseph County Probate Court-Mich.

Shuman, D. Robert-Judge, Superior Court of California County of Sacramento-Calif.

Shuman, Gordon S.-Judge, Probate Court of McIntosh County-Ga.

Shumate, James L.-Judge, Utah District Court Fifth Judicial District-Utah

Shumate, Kimberly W.-Judge, Kentucky District Court Ninth Judicial District-Ky.

Shumsky, Rosemary-Judge, Superior Court of California County of Los Angeles-Calif.

Shurling, William M., III-Judge, Civil Court of Bibb County-Ga.

Shurn, Michael A.-Judge, Pulaski Circuit Court-Ind.

Shushan, Sally A.-Magistrate Judge, United States District Court Eastern District of Louisiana-La.

Shuster, Joe-Judge, Pecos County Court-Tex.

Shuster, Neil H.-Judge, New Jersey Superior Court Vicinage Seven-N.J.

Shuteran, Sharon Elaine-Judge, San Miguel County Court-Colo.

Shutter, Steven G.-Judge, Broward County Court-Fla.

Shwartz, Patty-Magistrate Judge, United States District Court District of New Jersey-N.J.

Sichel, Elisabeth-Judge, Superior Court of California County of Riverside-Calif.

Sickel, James R.-Magistrate Judge, United States District Court Eastern District of Wisconsin-Wis.

Sidel, Kevin-Judge, Elbert County Court-Colo.

Siebel, Richard A.-Circuit Judge, Illinois Circuit Court of Cook County-Ill.

Siebman, Carol M.-Judge, Grayson County Court at Law No. 2-Tex.

Siefert, John-Judge, Wisconsin Circuit Court Milwaukee Circuit-Wis.

Siefkin, Susan D.-Judge, Superior Court of California County of Stanislaus-Calif.

Sieg, Peter K.-Judge, Florida Circuit Court Eighth Judicial Circuit-Fla.

Siegal, Bernice Daun-Judge, The Civil Court of the City of New York-N.Y.

Siegel, Andrew L.-Judge, Florida Circuit Court Seventeenth Judicial Circuit-Fla.

Siegel, H. Warren-Judge, Superior Court of California County of Orange-Calif.

Siegel, Norman I.-Judge, New York Court of Claims-N.Y.

Siegel, Paul-Judge, Florida Circuit Court Eleventh Judicial Circuit-Fla.

Siegel, Richard J.-Circuit Judge, Illinois Circuit Court Twelfth Judicial Circuit-Ill.

Sierawski, Stephen S.-Chief Judge, Michigan District Court District Forty-one A-Mich.

Sierra, Monica L.-Judge, Florida Circuit Court Thirteenth Judicial Circuit-Fla.

Sieve, Philip L.-Chief Judge, Kansas District Court Twenty-ninth Judicial District-Kan.

Sievers, Charles F.-Judge, Virginia General District Court Thirty-first Judicial District-Va.

Sievers, Richard D.-Judge, Nebraska Court of Appeals-Neb.

Sifferman, Scott S.-Associate Circuit Judge, Missouri Circuit Court Thirty-ninth Judicial Circuit-Mo.

Sifton, Charles P.-Senior Judge, United States District Court Eastern District of New York-N.Y.

Sigalas, Sharon W.-Judge, Jackson County Court-Miss.

Sigler, Victoria S.-Judge, Florida Circuit Court Eleventh Judicial Circuit-Fla.

Sigmon, Amy R.-Judge, North Carolina District Court District 25-N.C.

Sigmund, Diane W.-Judge, United States Bankruptcy Court Eastern District of Pennsylvania-Pa.

Sikora, Mitchell J., Jr.-Associate Justice, Trial Court of Massachusetts Superior Court Department-Mass.

Sikora, Peter M.-Judge, Ohio Court of Common Pleas Cuyahoga County-Ohio

Silbar, Claudia-Judge, Superior Court of California County of Orange-Calif.

Silber, Debra-Judge, The Civil Court of the City of New York-N.Y.

Silberman, Laurence H.-Senior Judge, United States Court of Appeals District of Columbia Circuit

Silberman, Morris-Judge, Florida District Court of Appeal Second District-Fla.

Silbermann, Jacqueline W.-Justice, New York Supreme Court First Judicial District-N.Y.

Silbert, Jonathan E.-Judge, Connecticut Superior Court-Conn.

Siler, Eugene E., Jr.-Senior Judge, United States Court of Appeals Sixth Circuit

Silkworth, Ronald A.-Associate Judge, Circuit Court for Anne Arundel County, Fifth Judicial Circuit-Md.

Sill-Rogers, Christine T.-Associate Circuit Judge, Missouri Circuit Court Sixteenth Judicial Circuit-Mo.

Sillman, Stephen A.-Judge, Superior Court of California County of Monterey-Calif.

Sills, David George-Presiding Justice, California Court of Appeal Fourth District Division Three-Calif.

Silveira, Marie Sovey-Judge, Superior Court of California County of Stanislaus-Calif.

Silveira, William, Jr.-Judge, Superior Court of California County of Tulare-Calif.

Silver, George E.-Judge, Ogdensburg City Court-N.Y.

Silver, Gray, III-Judge, West Virginia Circuit Court Twenty-third Judicial Circuit-W.Va.

Silver, Howard R.-Justice, New York Supreme Court Twelfth Judicial District-N.Y.

Silver, Roger A.-Judge, Dade County Court-Fla.

ALPHABETICAL NAME INDEX

ALPHABETICAL NAME INDEX

Sklar, Daniel Richard-Judge, Texas Family District Court 329th Judicial District-Tex.
Sklar, Stanley L.-Justice, New York Supreme Court First Judicial District-N.Y.
Skoglund, Marilyn S.-Associate Justice, Vermont Supreme Court-Vt.
Skolnick, David W.-Judge, Connecticut Superior Court-Conn.
Skolnik, Peter-Judge, Broward County Court-Fla.
Skopil, Otto R., Jr.-Senior Judge, United States Court of Appeals Ninth Circuit
Skorupa, Frank J.-Judge, Nebraska County Court Fifth Judicial District-Neb.
Skow, William J.-Judge, Ohio Court of Common Pleas Lucas County-Ohio
Skowronski, Joseph P., Jr.-Associate Judge, Illinois Circuit Court Fifth Judicial Circuit-Ill.
Skretny, William M.-Judge, United States District Court Western District of New York-N.Y.
Skropos, Gus James-Judge, Superior Court of California County of San Bernardino-Calif.
Skupniewitz, Joseph W.-Magistrate Judge, United States District Court Western District of Wisconsin-Wis.
Skyers, Ronald V.-Judge, Superior Court of California County of Los Angeles-Calif.
Slaby, Lynn C.-Judge, Ohio Court of Appeals Ninth District-Ohio
Slaby, Richard A.-Judge, State Court of Richmond County-Ga.
Slade, John F., III-Associate Judge, Maryland District Court District Four-Md.
Slater, Allen R.-Judge, Kansas District Court Tenth Judicial District-Kan.
Slater, David W.-Associate Judge, Illinois Circuit Court Fourth Judicial Circuit-Ill.
Slater, Kent F.-Judge, Illinois Appellate Court Third Judicial District-Ill.
Slattery, John B.-Judge, Springhill City Court-La.
Slattery Boyle, Maura-Circuit Judge, Illinois Circuit Court of Cook County-Ill.
Slaughter, William R., II-Judge, Suwannee County Court-Fla.
Slavin, Timothy J.-Circuit Judge, Illinois Circuit Court Fourteenth Judicial Circuit-Ill.
Sledge, James S.-Judge, United States Bankruptcy Court Northern District of Alabama-Ala.
Sleet, Gregory M.-Judge, United States District Court District of Delaware-Del.
Sletta, Stephen J.-Judge, El Paso County Court-Colo.
Sleva, William G.-Judge, Lawrence Superior Court-Ind.
Slieter, Randall J.-Judge, Minnesota District Court Eighth Judicial District-Minn.
Slights, Joseph R., III-Associate Judge, Delaware Superior Court New Castle County-Del.
Sloan, James D.-Judge, Hendry County Court-Fla.
Slobod, Elaine-Surrogate, Orange County Surrogate's Court-N.Y.
Slocum, David K.-Circuit Judge, Illinois Circuit Court Eighth Judicial Circuit-Ill.
Slom, Samuel J.-Judge, Dade County Court-Fla.
Slone, O. Duane-Judge, Tennessee Circuit Court Fourth Judicial District-Tenn.
Sloop, John R.-Judge, Seminole County Court-Fla.
Sloviter, Dolores Korman-Judge, United States Court of Appeals Third Circuit
Smalkin, Frederic N.-Senior Judge, United States District Court District of Maryland-Md.
Small, A. Thomas-Judge, United States Bankruptcy Court Eastern District of North Carolina-N.C.
Small, Joseph C.-Presiding Judge, New Jersey Tax Court-N.J.
Small, Kimberly-Chief Judge, Michigan District Court District Forty-eight-Mich.
Small, T. W. "Chip"-Judge, Washington Superior Court Chelan County-Wash.
Smalls, Alex Jerome-Chief Judge, Delaware Court of Common Pleas-Del.
Smallwood, Tennant M., Jr.-Judge, Alabama Circuit Court Tenth Judicial Circuit Birmingham Division-Ala.
Smaltz, Lois Anderson-Judge, Superior Court of California County of Los Angeles-Calif.
Smart, James M., Jr.-Judge, Missouri Court of Appeals Western District-Mo.
Smeltzer, Rod W.-Judge, Wisconsin Circuit Court Dunn Circuit-Wis.
Smerling, Terry Lee-Judge, Superior Court of California County of Los Angeles-Calif.
Smierciak, Robert M.-Associate Judge, Illinois Circuit Court of Cook County-Ill.
Smiley, Elijah-Judge, Bay County Court-Fla.
Smiley, John R.-Judge, Superior Court of California County of Ventura-Calif.
Smiley, Prentis, Jr.-Judge, Virginia Circuit Court Ninth Judicial Circuit-Va.
Smith, Al-Judge, Mississippi Circuit Court Eleventh Judicial District-Miss.
Smith, Allen W.-Judge Referee, Connecticut Superior Court-Conn.
Smith, Amy McCorkle-Judge, Hopkins County Court at Law-Tex.
Smith, Arthur R.-Judge, Mesa County Court-Colo.
Smith, Bea Ann-Justice, Texas Court of Appeals Third District-Tex.
Smith, Berkeley A.-Presiding Judge, Oregon Circuit Court Nineteenth Judicial District-Ore.
Smith, Bernard-Judge, Oregon Circuit Court Seventh Judicial District-Ore.
Smith, Beth A.-Judge, Ohio Court of Common Pleas Mahoning County-Ohio
Smith, Bob-Judge, Probate Court of Hart County-Ga.
Smith, Bradley-Judge, Texas District Court 400th Judicial District-Tex.
Smith, C. McFerrin, III-Judge, Florida Circuit Court Seventh Judicial Circuit-Fla.
Smith, Carol E.-Associate Judge, Circuit Court for Baltimore City, Eighth Judicial Circuit-Md.
Smith, Carol Gibson-First Justice, Trial Court of Massachusetts Juvenile Court Department Barnstable/Town of Plymouth Division-Mass.
Smith, Charles B.-Magistrate Judge, United States District Court Eastern District of Pennsylvania-Pa.
Smith, Charles E.-Senior Judge, Florida Circuit Court Nineteenth Judicial Circuit-Fla.
Smith, Charles K. "C.K."-Chancellor, Tennessee Chancery Court Fifteenth Judicial District-Tenn.
Smith, Charles L., III-Chief Judge, Iowa District Court Fourth Judicial District-Ia.
Smith, Charles Lynwood, Jr.-Judge, United States District Court Northern District of Alabama-Ala.
Smith, Clancy C.-Special Judge, Oklahoma District Court Fourteenth Judicial District-Okla.
Smith, Clay M.-Judge, Superior Court of California County of Orange-Calif.
Smith, Clifford J.-Special Judge, Oklahoma District Court Fourteenth Judicial District-Okla.
Smith, Clinton W.-President Judge, Pennsylvania Court of Common Pleas Twenty-ninth Judicial District-Pa.
Smith, D. Brooks-Judge, United States Court of Appeals Third Circuit
Smith, Dale P.-Chief Magistrate, Magistrate Court of Stephens County-Ga.
Smith, Danny-Magistrate Judge, Kansas District Court Twenty-fourth Judicial District-Kan.
Smith, David K.-Judge, Superior Court of Georgia Cherokee Judicial Circuit-Ga.
Smith, Dennis-Associate Circuit Judge, Missouri Circuit Court Twenty-first Judicial Circuit-Mo.
Smith, Dennis J.-Judge, Virginia Circuit Court Nineteenth Judicial Circuit-Va.
Smith, Diana Becton-Judge, Superior Court of California County of Contra Costa-Calif.
Smith, Donald A., Jr.-Judge, New Jersey Superior Court Vicinage Fifteen-N.J.
Smith, Donald L.-Retired Judge, North Carolina Court of Appeals-N.C.
Smith, Douglas E.-Justice of the Peace, Las Vegas Justices' Court-Nev.
Smith, Douglas Joseph-Judge, King District Court East Division King County-Wash.
Smith, E. Byron-Chief Judge, Superior Court of Georgia Towaliga Judicial Circuit-Ga.
Smith, Ed D.-Judge, Motley County Court-Tex.
Smith, Edward G.-Judge, Pennsylvania Court of Common Pleas Third Judicial District-Pa.
Smith, Edwin H.-Judge, Missouri Court of Appeals Western District-Mo.
Smith, Edwin R.-Magistrate Judge, Kansas District Court Fourth Judicial District-Kan.
Smith, Eric-Judge, Alaska Superior Court Third Judicial District-Alas.
Smith, Erithe A.-Judge, United States Bankruptcy Court Central District of California-Calif.
Smith, Frederick D.-Judge, Florida Circuit Court Eighth Judicial Circuit-Fla.
Smith, Fredricka G.-Judge, Florida Circuit Court Eleventh Judicial Circuit-Fla.
Smith, G. R.-Magistrate Judge, United States District Court Southern District of Georgia-Ga.
Smith, Gail-Chief Magistrate, Magistrate Court of Oglethorpe County-Ga.
Smith, Gale-Associate District Judge, Oklahoma District Court Second Judicial District-Okla.
Smith, George Bundy-Associate Judge, New York Court of Appeals-N.Y.
Smith, George C.-Senior Judge, United States District Court Southern District of Ohio-Ohio
Smith, Gilbert A.-Senior Judge, Florida Circuit Court Twelfth Judicial Circuit-Fla.
Smith, Gordon L.-Justice, Gallatin County Justice of the Peace Court and Judge, Bozeman and Manhattan City Courts-Mont.
Smith, Greggory M.-Associate District Judge, Oklahoma District Court Twenty-second Judicial District-Okla.
Smith, Gregory E.-Judge, Pennsylvania Court of Common Pleas First Judicial District-Pa.
Smith, Herman J., Jr.-Associate Justice, Trial Court of Massachusetts Superior Court Department-Mass.
Smith, J. Curtis-Judge, Tennessee Circuit Court Twelfth Judicial District-Tenn.
Smith, J. D.-Chief Judge, Court of Appeals of Georgia-Ga.
Smith, J. Michael-Chief Judge, Kansas District Court Nineteenth Judicial District-Kan.
Smith, Jack-Judge, Alaska District Court Third Judicial District-Alas.
Smith, James G. Fitzgerald-Judge, Illinois Appellate Court First Judicial District Division One-Ill.
Smith, James H.-Judge, Virginia Juvenile and Domestic Relations District Court Ninth Judicial District-Va.
Smith, James J.-Chief Judge, Kansas District Court Fourth Judicial District-Kan.
Smith, James P.-Judge, Alabama Circuit Court Twenty-third Judicial Circuit-Ala.
Smith, James W., Jr.-Presiding Justice, Mississippi Supreme Court-Miss.
Smith, Jeffrey A.-President Judge, Pennsylvania Court of Common Pleas Forty-second Judicial District-Pa.
Smith, Jeffrey R.-Judge, Carroll Superior Court-Ind.
Smith, Jerry-Judge, Tennessee Court of Criminal Appeals Middle Division-Tenn.
Smith, Jerry E.-Judge, United States Court of Appeals Fifth Circuit
Smith, Joanne M.-Judge, Minnesota District Court Second Judicial District-Minn.
Smith, Joe E.-District Associate Judge, Iowa District Court Fifth Judicial District-Ia.
Smith, John P.-Judge, Minnesota District Court Ninth Judicial District-Minn.
Smith, John Roger-Judge, Volusia County Court-Fla.
Smith, John W.-Judge, North Carolina District Court District 5-N.C.
Smith, Joseph E.-Judge, Levy County Court-Fla.
Smith, Karen S.-Judge, The Civil Court of the City of New York-N.Y.
Smith, Kathryn M.-Judge, The Civil Court of the City of New York-N.Y.
Smith, Kathryn N.-Judge, Minnesota District Court Eighth Judicial District-Minn.
Smith, Kathy R.-Judge, Clinton Superior Court-Ind.
Smith, Ken W.-Judge, State Court of Jeff Davis County and Judge, Juvenile Court of Georgia Brunswick Judicial Circuit-Ga.
Smith, Kevin C.-Judge, Findlay Municipal Court-Ohio
Smith, Kim M.-Judge, Arkansas Circuit Court Fourth Judicial Circuit-Ark.

ALPHABETICAL NAME INDEX

Smith, Kirk-Surrogate Judge, North Dakota District Court-N.D.
Smith, L. Joe-Special Judge, Oklahoma District Court Twelfth Judicial District-Okla.
Smith, L. Ralph, Jr.-Judge, Florida Circuit Court Second Judicial Circuit-Fla.
Smith, Larry G.-Senior Judge, Florida District Court of Appeal-Fla.
Smith, Larry Mack-Judge, Alabama Circuit Court Eleventh Judicial Circuit-Ala.
Smith, Lavenski R.-Judge, United States Court of Appeals Eighth Circuit
Smith, Lawrence D.-Judge, New Jersey Superior Court Vicinage Two-N.J.
Smith, Leo-Judge, Terrell County Court-Tex.
Smith, Leslie C.-Magistrate Judge, United States District Court District of New Mexico-N.Mex.
Smith, Leslie Kim-Judge, Michigan Circuit Court Third Judicial Circuit-Mich.
Smith, Lisa Margaret-Magistrate Judge, United States District Court Southern District of New York-N.Y.
Smith, Lisa Young-Judge, City Court of Atlanta-Ga.
Smith, Loren A.-Senior Judge, United States Court of Federal Claims
Smith, M. Bruce-Judge, Superior Court of California County of Fresno-Calif.
Smith, Mark J.-District Judge, Iowa District Court Seventh Judicial District-Ia.
Smith, Mark R.-District Judge, Oklahoma District Court Fifth Judicial District-Okla.
Smith, Martin E.-Judge, Broome County Court-N.Y.
Smith, Martin J.-Chief Judge, Eastpointe Municipal Court-Mich.
Smith, Mary H.-Justice, New York Supreme Court Ninth Judicial District-N.Y.
Smith, Maura T.-Judge, Florida Circuit Court Ninth Judicial Circuit-Fla.
Smith, Michael A.-Judge, Superior Court of California County of San Bernardino-Calif.
Smith, Michael R.-Chief Judge, Michigan Circuit Court First Judicial Circuit-Mich.
Smith, Mike-Judge, Mississippi Circuit Court Fourteenth Judicial District-Miss.
Smith, N. Randy-Judge, Idaho District Court Sixth Judicial District-Ida.
Smith, Nancy E.-Associate Justice, New York Supreme Court Appellate Division Second Judicial Department-N.Y.
Smith, Norbert P.-Judge, Minnesota District Court Fifth Judicial District-Minn.
Smith, Norman P.-Judge, Ohio Court of Common Pleas Shelby County-Ohio
Smith, Ortrie D.-Judge, United States District Court Western District of Missouri-Mo.
Smith, Oscar D., Jr.-Senior Judge, Superior Court of Georgia-Ga.
Smith, Patricia M.-Judge, Shelby County District Court-Ala.
Smith, Paul A.-Associate Judge, Circuit Court for Baltimore City, Eighth Judicial Circuit-Md.
Smith, Peter W.-Associate Justice, New Hampshire Superior Court-N.H.
Smith, Philip C.-Judge, State Court of Forsyth County-Ga.
Smith, Phillip-Judge, Arkansas Circuit Court Third Judicial Circuit-Ark.
Smith, R. Michael-Judge, Superior Court of California County of Solano-Calif.
Smith, R. Rucker-Chief Judge, Superior Court of Georgia Southwestern Judicial Circuit-Ga.
Smith, R. Wayne-Judge, Louisiana District Court Third Judicial District-La.
Smith, Radford W.-Senior Judge, Pinellas County Court-Fla.
Smith, Ralph C., Jr.-Chief Magistrate, Magistrate Court of Decatur County-Ga.
Smith, Rebecca Beach-Judge, United States District Court Eastern District of Virginia-Va.
Smith, Richard-Judge, Mississippi Circuit Court Fourth Judicial District-Miss.
Smith, Richard M.-Judge, Kansas District Court Sixth Judicial District-Kan.
Smith, Robert B.-Judge, Logan County Court-Colo.
Smith, Robert J.-Judge, Virginia General District Court Nineteenth Judicial District-Va.
Smith, Rupert Jasen-Senior Judge, Florida Circuit Court Nineteenth Judicial Circuit-Fla.
Smith, Sarah D.-Special Judge, Oklahoma District Court Fourteenth Judicial District-Okla.
Smith, Spurgeon E.-Judge, Superior Court of California County of Los Angeles-Calif.
Smith, Stan-Judge, Superior Court of Georgia Dublin Judicial Circuit-Ga.
Smith, Stephen F., Jr.-Judge, New Jersey Superior Court Vicinage Ten-N.J.
Smith, Steve-Judge, Texas District Court 361st Judicial District-Tex.
Smith, Steven Wayne-Justice, Texas Supreme Court-Tex.
Smith, Terence B.-Associate Judge, Illinois Circuit Court of Cook County-Ill.
Smith, Thomas B.-Judge, Florida Circuit Court Ninth Judicial Circuit-Fla.
Smith, Thomas P.-Magistrate Judge, United States District Court District of Connecticut-Conn.
Smith, Thomas P.-Associate Judge, Circuit Court for Prince George's County, Seventh Judicial Circuit-Md.
Smith, Thomas S., Jr.-Judge, New Jersey Superior Court Vicinage Three-N.J.
Smith, Tom R.-Judge, Kansas District Court Twenty-sixth Judicial District-Kan.
Smith, Vann-Judge, Arkansas Circuit Court Sixth Judicial Circuit-Ark.
Smith, Vernon F.-Judge, Superior Court of California County of Marin-Calif.
Smith, W. Bruce-Judge, Florida Circuit Court Tenth Judicial Circuit-Fla.
Smith, W. Osmond, III-Resident Judge, North Carolina Superior Court Third Judicial Division District 9A-N.C.
Smith, Walter S., Jr.-Judge, United States District Court Western District of Texas-Tex.
Smith, William D.-Judge, Texas District Court 84th Judicial District-Tex.
Smith, William E.-Judge, United Stated District Court District of Rhode Island-R.I.
Smith, William J.-Senior Judge, Superior Court of Georgia-Ga.
Smith, Willis V.-Judge, Lipscomb County Court-Tex.
Smith, Winifred Younge-Judge, Superior Court of California County of Alameda-Calif.
Smith-Ribner, Doris A.-Judge, The Commonwealth Court of Pennsylvania-Pa.
Smith-Steward, Pamela-Judge, Superior Court of California County of Sacramento-Calif.
Smithart, Burt-Presiding Judge, Alabama Circuit Court Third Judicial Circuit-Ala.
Smitherman, Tom-Judge, Arkansas Circuit Court Eighteenth East Judicial Circuit-Ark.
Smithson, Andrew J.-Judge, New Jersey Superior Court Vicinage Seven-N.J.
Smoak, Gerald C., Jr.-Judge, South Carolina Family Court Fourteenth Judicial Circuit-S.C.
Smoak, I. A., III-Judge, Colleton County Probate Court-S.C.
Smoker, Thomas R.-Associate Judge, Illinois Circuit Court Nineteenth Judicial Circuit-Ill.
Smolenski, Michael R.-Chief Judge pro tem, Michigan Court of Appeals-Mich.
Smolenski, Sara J.-Chief Judge, Michigan District Court District Sixty-three and Judge, Michigan District Court District Sixty-three Division Two-Mich.
Smolkin, Stanley A.-Judge, Long Beach City Court-N.Y.
Smoot, John M.-First Justice, Trial Court of Massachusetts Probate and Family Court Department Suffolk County Division-Mass.
Smukler, Larry M.-Associate Justice, New Hampshire Superior Court-N.H.
Smyser, Howard D.-Judge, Idaho District Court Fifth Judicial District Magistrate Division-Ida.
Smyser, J. Andrew-Magistrate Judge, United States District Court Middle District of Pennsylvania-Pa.
Smyth, Joseph A., Jr.-Judge, Pennsylvania Court of Common Pleas Thirty-eighth Judicial District-Pa.
Smyth, Michael-Judge, Superior Court of California County of San Diego-Calif.
Snauffer, Mark Wood-Judge, Superior Court of California County of Fresno-Calif.
Sneed, Joseph Tyree-Senior Judge, United States Court of Appeals Ninth Circuit
Snider, Neil G.-First Justice, Trial Court of Massachusetts District Court Department Worcester County Dudley Division and Justice, Worcester Division-Mass.
Snite, Albert John, Jr.-Judge, Pennsylvania Court of Common Pleas First Judicial District-Pa.
Snow, Gary P.-District Judge, Oklahoma District Court Twenty-second Judicial District-Okla.
Snow, John J., Jr.-Chief Judge, North Carolina District Court District 30-N.C.
Snow, Lurana S.-Magistrate Judge, United States District Court Southern District of Florida-Fla.
Snow, Murray G.-Judge, Arizona Court of Appeals Division One-Ariz.
Snow, P. Thomas-Judge, Wayne Superior Court-Ind.
Snow, Terry K.-Judge, Hancock Superior Court-Ind.
Snowberger, Michelle-Judge, Belgrade City Court-Mont.
Snowden, W. Scott-Judge, Superior Court of California County of Napa-Calif.
Snowdy, J. Sterling-Judge, Louisiana District Court Fortieth Judicial District-La.
Snukals, Beverly W.-Judge, Virginia Circuit Court Thirteenth Judicial Circuit-Va.
Snyder, Arthur I.-Senior Judge, Florida Circuit Court Eleventh Judicial Circuit-Fla.
Snyder, Christina A.-Judge, United States District Court Central District of California-Calif.
Snyder, D. Mark-Judge, West Virginia Family Court Circuit Eleven-W.Va.
Snyder, Gregory M.-Judge, Pennsylvania Court of Common Pleas Nineteenth Judicial District-Pa.
Snyder, Harry G.-Judge, Wisconsin Court of Appeals District Two-Wis.
Snyder, Howard T.-Magistrate Judge, United States District Court Middle District of Florida-Fla.
Snyder, Irvin J.-Judge, New Jersey Superior Court Vicinage Four-N.J.
Snyder, Leslie Crocker-Judge, New York Court of Claims-N.Y.
Snyder, Paul B.-Judge, United States Bankruptcy Court Western District of Washington-Wash.
Snyder, Sandra-Magistrate Judge, United States District Court Eastern District of California-Calif.
So, Kenneth Kai-Young-Judge, Superior Court of California County of San Diego-Calif.
Sobecki, Dean A.-Judge, Daviess Superior Court-Ind.
Sobel, Jennifer B.-Special Justice, Haverhill, Lancaster and Littleton District Courts-N.H.
Sobotka, Virginia A.-Chief Judge, Michigan District Court District Nineteen-Mich.
Soden, Denis F.-Chief Judge, Virginia Juvenile and Domestic Relations District Court Fourteenth Judicial District-Va.
Soder, Robert F.-Judge, Kentucky District Court Fourth Judicial District-Ky.
Sodergren, Thomas-Associate Circuit Judge, Missouri Circuit Court Nineteenth Judicial Circuit-Mo.
Sogluizzo, Maureen P.-Judge, New Jersey Superior Court Vicinage Six-N.J.
Sognier, John W.-Senior Judge, Court of Appeals of Georgia-Ga.
Sohigian, Ronald M.-Judge, Superior Court of California County of Los Angeles-Calif.
Sokalski, Ronald B.-Judge, New Jersey Superior Court Vicinage Eleven-N.J.
Sokolov, Thomas R.-Judge, Superior Court of California County of Los Angeles-Calif.
Sokolovske, Mary Jane-District Judge, Iowa District Court Third Judicial District-Ia.
Solganick, Irwin J.-Circuit Judge, Illinois Circuit Court of Cook County-Ill.
Solien, John R.-Judge, Minnesota District Court Ninth Judicial District-Minn.
Solis, Jorge A.-Judge, United States District Court Northern District of Texas-Tex.

ALPHABETICAL NAME INDEX

ALPHABETICAL NAME INDEX

Spivey, Ronald E.-Resident Judge, North Carolina Superior Court Fifth Judicial Division District 21-N.C.

Spodek, Ellen M.-Judge, The Civil Court of the City of New York-N.Y.

Spodek, Jules L.-Justice, New York Supreme Court Second Judicial District-N.Y.

Spolzino, Robert A.-Justice, New York Supreme Court Ninth Judicial District-N.Y.

Spomer, Stephen L.-Circuit Judge, Illinois Circuit Court First Judicial Circuit-Ill.

Spon, Ronald-Judge, Ohio Court of Common Pleas Richland County-Ohio

Sposeep, Michael L.-Judge, Wabash Superior Court-Ind.

Spoto, Keith P.-Judge, Polk County Court-Fla.

Sprague, George R.-Justice, Trial Court of Massachusetts District Court Department Middlesex County Cambridge Division-Mass.

Sprecher, Jeffrey K.-Judge, Pennsylvania Court of Common Pleas Twenty-third Judicial District-Pa.

Sprengelmeyer, Victor V.-Associate Judge, Illinois Circuit Court Fifteenth Judicial Circuit-Ill.

Sprick, Gary G.-Associate Circuit Judge, Missouri Circuit Court Fourteenth Judicial Circuit-Mo.

Springer, Sarah P.-Judge, Mississippi Chancery Court Twelfth Judicial District-Miss.

Springmann, Theresa L.-Magistrate Judge, United States District Court Northern District of Indiana-Ind.

Springstead, Jack-Judge, Florida Circuit Court Fifth Judicial Circuit-Fla.

Sprinkel, George A., IV-Judge, Florida Circuit Court Ninth Judicial Circuit-Fla.

Sprinkle, Vincent G.-Judge, Tarrant County Court at Law No. 3-Tex.

Sprizzo, John E.-Senior Judge, United States District Court Southern District of New York-N.Y.

Sprouse, Dennis M.-Special Judge, Oklahoma District Court Fifteenth Judicial District-Okla.

Sprowls, Larry D.-Judge, Hockley County Court-Tex.

Spruell, Ray-Judge, Jonesboro and Lake City District Courts-Ark.

Spruill, James H., III-Judge, South Carolina Family Court Fourth Judicial Circuit-S.C.

Spurgeon, Paul E.-Judge, Mount Vernon Municipal Court-Ohio

Spurgin, Dale-Judge, Jones County Court-Tex.

Spurlock, Charles T.-Associate Justice, Trial Court of Massachusetts Superior Court Department-Mass.

Squatrito, Dominic J.-Judge, United States District Court District of Connecticut-Conn.

Squier, James-Judge, Texas Family District Court 312th Judicial District-Tex.

Squire, Carole R.-Judge, Ohio Court of Common Pleas Franklin County-Ohio

Squire, Orin Lee-Judge, Idaho District Court Second Judicial District Magistrate Division-Ida.

Squires, Donald B.-Judge, Superior Court of California County of Alameda-Calif.

Squires, John H.-Judge, United States Bankruptcy Court Northern District of Illinois-Ill.

Sragow, Roanne-Circuit Justice, Trial Court of Massachusetts District Court Department and First Justice, Middlesex County Cambridge Division-Mass.

Srstka, William-Judge, South Dakota Circuit Court Second Judicial Circuit-S.D.

Stacey, Rex D.-Judge, Minnesota District Court First Judicial District-Minn.

Stack, Daniel J.-Circuit Judge, Illinois Circuit Court Third Judicial Circuit-Ill.

Stack, Elaine Jackson-Justice, New York Supreme Court Tenth Judicial District-N.Y.

Stack, James F.-Associate Judge, Illinois Circuit Court of Cook County-Ill.

Stackhouse, John E. H.-Judge, The Civil Court of the City of New York-N.Y.

Stacy, Frances H.-Magistrate Judge, United States District Court Southern District of Texas-Tex.

Stadler, Stewart E.-Judge, Montana District Court Eleventh Judicial District-Mont.

Stadtmauer, David-Justice, New York Supreme Court Twelfth Judicial District-N.Y.

Stadtmueller, J. P.-Judge, United States District Court Eastern District of Wisconsin-Wis.

Staffel, Timothy J.-Judge, Superior Court of California County of Santa Barbara-Calif.

Staffier, Nancy-Associate Justice, Trial Court of Massachusetts Superior Court Department-Mass.

Stafford, Charles E., Jr.-Judge, Superior Court of California County of Riverside-Calif.

Stafford, Harrison, II-Judge, Jackson County Court-Tex.

Stafford, J. Steven-Chancellor, Tennessee Chancery Court Twenty-ninth Judicial District-Tenn.

Stafford, Leonard L.-Senior Judge, Florida Circuit Court Seventeenth Judicial Circuit-Fla.

Stafford, Richard H.-Reserve Judge, Wisconsin Circuit Court-Wis.

Stafford, Rodney J.-Judge, Superior Court of California County of Santa Clara-Calif.

Stafford, William Henry, Jr.-Senior Judge, United States District Court Northern District of Florida-Fla.

Stafsholt, Jon E.-Judge, Minnesota District Court Eighth Judicial District-Minn.

Stagg, Tom-Senior Judge, United States District Court Western District of Louisiana-La.

Stahl, Gayle-Justice, Phillips County Justice of the Peace Court and Judge, Malta City Court-Mont.

Stahl, Norman H.-Senior Judge, United States Court of Appeals First Circuit

Stahlin, Jeremy A.-Associate Justice, Trial Court of Massachusetts Probate and Family Court Department Suffolk County Division-Mass.

Stair, Richard S., Jr.-Judge, United States Bankruptcy Court Eastern District of Tennessee-Tenn.

Stakem, Paul J.-Administrative Judge, Maryland District Court District Twelve-Md.

Staker, Robert J.-Senior Judge, United States District Court Southern District of West Virginia-W.Va.

Staley, Harry Anthony-Judge, Superior Court of California County of Kern-Calif.

Staley, Mary Ellen-Judge, Superior Court of Georgia Cobb Judicial Circuit-Ga.

Staley, Matt C.-Judge, Ohio Court of Common Pleas Allen County-Ohio

Stallman, Michael D.-Judge, The Civil Court of the City of New York-N.Y.

Stallone, Albert A.-President Judge, Pennsylvania Court of Common Pleas Twenty-third Judicial District-Pa.

Stamp, Frederick P., Jr.-Judge, United States District Court Northern District of West Virginia-W.Va.

Stamp, Zack-Judge, Illinois Court of Claims-Ill.

Stamper, Russell Wright-Reserve Judge, Wisconsin Circuit Court-Wis.

Stanback, A. Leon, Jr.-Resident Judge, North Carolina Superior Court Third Judicial Division District 14-N.C.

Stanceu, Timothy C.-Judge, United States Court of International Trade

Stancil, Hale R.-Judge, Florida Circuit Court Fifth Judicial Circuit-Fla.

Standard, Leon-Judge, Irion County Court-Tex.

Stander, Thomas A.-Justice, New York Supreme Court Seventh Judicial District-N.Y.

Standish, William L.-Senior Judge, United States District Court Western District of Pennsylvania-Pa.

Standley, Larry-Judge, Harris County Criminal Court at Law No. 6-Tex.

Standridge, Brent-Judge, North Little Rock District Court-Ark.

Standridge, Richard E.-Associate Circuit Judge, Missouri Circuit Court Sixteenth Judicial Circuit-Mo.

Stanford, Richard W., Jr.-Judge, Superior Court of California County of Orange-Calif.

Stanger, George H., Jr.-Assignment Judge, New Jersey Superior Court Vicinage Fifteen-N.J.

Stanley, Jean A.-Judge, Tennessee Circuit Court First Judicial District-Tenn.

Stanley, Larry Barton, Jr.-Judge, Tennessee Circuit Court Thirty-first Judicial District and Chancellor, Tennessee Chancery Court Thirty-first Judicial District-Tenn.

Stanley, Mary E.-Magistrate Judge, United States District Court Southern District of West Virginia-W.Va.

Stanley, Trina Thompson-Judge, Superior Court of California County of Alameda-Calif.

Stansbury, Kim P.-Judge, City Court of Morgan City-La.

Stanton, Louis L.-Senior Judge, United States District Court Southern District of New York-N.Y.

Stapler, Evan Lee-Chief Magistrate, Magistrate Court of Haralson County-Ga.

Staples, Bernard C.-Judge, Maine District Court-Me.

Stapleton, Walter K.-Senior Judge, United States Court of Appeals Third Circuit

Starcher, Larry Victor-Chief Justice, West Virginia Supreme Court of Appeals-W.Va.

Starck, Christopher C.-Circuit Judge, Illinois Circuit Court Nineteenth Judicial Circuit-Ill.

Stark, Charles H.-Chief Judge, Michigan Circuit Court Eleventh Judicial Circuit-Mich.

Stark, Homer W.-Senior Judge, Superior Court of Georgia-Ga.

Stark, Isabel B.-Judge, New Jersey Superior Court Vicinage Two-N.J.

Stark, Lisa Kay-Judge, Wisconsin Circuit Court Eau Claire Circuit-Wis.

Starken, Raymond T.-Judge, Ash Flat and Cherokee Village District Courts-Ark.

Starkey, James G.-Justice, New York Supreme Court Second Judicial District-N.Y.

Starks, Cheryl A.-Circuit Judge, Illinois Circuit Court of Cook County-Ill.

Starling, Richard E., Jr.-Judge, Alexandria City Court-La.

Starnes, Hugh E.-Judge, Florida Circuit Court Twentieth Judicial Circuit-Fla.

Starr, Walter R.-Judge, Ohio Court of Common Pleas Monroe County-Ohio

Starrett, Keith-Judge, Mississippi Circuit Court Fourteenth Judicial District-Miss.

Starzynski, James S.-Chief Judge, United States Bankruptcy Court District of New Mexico-N.Mex.

Staskal, Douglas F.-District Judge, Iowa District Court Fifth Judicial District-Ia.

Statler, Peter-Associate Circuit Judge, Missouri Circuit Court Thirty-second Judicial Circuit-Mo.

Staton, Betty E.-Judge, New York City Family Court-N.Y.

Staton, Jon Tom-Associate District Judge, Oklahoma District Court Fifth Judicial District-Okla.

Staton, Louise-Judge, West Virginia Family Court Circuit Thirteen-W.Va.

Stauffer, Monica-Presiding Judge, Superior Court of Arizona Greenlee County-Ariz.

Staveley, John F.-Judge, Boulder County Court-Colo.

Staven, Martin W.-Judge, Superior Court of California County of Tulare-Calif.

Steadman, John M.-Associate Judge, District of Columbia Court of Appeals-D.C.

Steadman, Timothy J.-Associate Judge, Illinois Circuit Court Sixth Judicial Circuit-Ill.

Steady, B. Kevin-Assistant Judge, Vermont Trial Court Grand Isle County-Vt.

Steagall, Fred R.-Judge, Dale County District Court-Ala.

Stearns, Richard G.-Judge, United States District Court District of Massachusetts-Mass.

Stebner, Kenneth-Judge, Wyoming District Court Second Judicial District-Wyo.

Stecco, Larry-Judge, Michigan District Court District Sixty-seven Division Three-Mich.

Steckler, Sanford R.-Judge, Mississippi Chancery Court Eighth Judicial District-Miss.

Steckroth, Donald H.-Judge, United States Bankruptcy Court District of New Jersey-N.J.

Stedman, Juanita-Judge, Juvenile Court of Georgia Cobb Judicial Circuit-Ga.

Steedley, Annie Ruth-Chief Magistrate, Magistrate Court of Clinch County-Ga.

Steege, Peter O.-Judge, Pennsylvania Court of Common Pleas Thirty-sixth Judicial District-Pa.

Steeh, George C., III-Judge, United States District Court Eastern District of Michigan-Mich.

Steel, Cynthia Dianne-Judge, Nevada District Court Eighth Judicial District-Nev.

Steel, Gary L.-Judge, Texas District Court 274th Judicial District-Tex.

Steel, Jim Bob-Judge, Murfreesboro District Court-Ark.

Steele, Charles D.-Judge, Ohio Court of Common Pleas Van Wert County-Ohio

Steele, Janet F.-Judge, West Virginia Family Court Circuit Fourteen-W.Va.

Steele, John E.-Judge, United States District Court Middle District of Florida-Fla.

Steele, John O.-Circuit Judge, Illinois Circuit Court of Cook County-Ill.

Steele, Larry A.-Presiding Judge, Utah Juvenile Court Eighth Judicial District-Utah

Steele, Myron T.-Justice, Delaware Supreme Court-Del.

Steele, Rodney-Presiding Judge, South Dakota Circuit Court Third Judicial Circuit-S.D.

Steele, Russell E.-Presiding Judge, Missouri Circuit Court Second Judicial Circuit-Mo.

Steele, Wayne E.-Judge, Fulton Superior Court-Ind.

Steele, William H.-Magistrate Judge, United States District Court Southern District of Alabama-Ala.

Steelman, Sanford L., Jr.-Associate Judge, North Carolina Court of Appeals-N.C.

Steen, Wesley W.-Judge, United States Bankruptcy Court Southern District of Texas-Tex.

Steenland, Catherine B.-Judge, Michigan District Court District Thirty-nine-Mich.

Steenrod, Rebecca R.-Associate Judge, Illinois Circuit Court Tenth Judicial Circuit-Ill.

Steensland, M. John-Judge, Houston County District Court-Ala.

Stefaniak, Thomas P., Jr.-Judge, Lake Superior Court-Ind.

Steger, William M.-Senior Judge, United States District Court Eastern District of Texas-Tex.

Stegner, John R.-Administrative Judge, Idaho District Court Second Judicial District-Ida.

Steidley, J. Dwayne-Associate District Judge, Oklahoma District Court Twelfth Judicial District-Okla.

Steigmann, Robert James-Judge, Illinois Appellate Court Fourth Judicial District-Ill.

Stein, Harry-Senior Judge, Florida Circuit Court Eighteenth Judicial Circuit-Fla.

Stein, Kenneth R.-Retired Judge, New Jersey Superior Court-N.J.

Stein, Leslie E.-Justice, New York Supreme Court Third Judicial District-N.Y.

Stein, Linda S.-Judge, Dade County Court-Fla.

Stein, Sidney H.-Judge, United States District Court Southern District of New York-N.Y.

Stein, Taylor C.-Special Judge, Oklahoma District Court Fifth Judicial District-Okla.

Stein, William Douglas-Associate Justice, California Court of Appeal First District Division One-Calif.

Steinbeck, Margaret Ogilvie-Judge, Florida Circuit Court Twentieth Judicial Circuit-Fla.

Steinberg, Jonathan Robert-Judge, United States Court of Appeals for Veterans Claims

Steinberg, Joseph L.-Judge Referee, Connecticut Superior Court-Conn.

Steinberg, Marjorie S.-Judge, Superior Court of California County of Los Angeles-Calif.

Steinberg, Ralph-Senior Judge, Florida Circuit Court Thirteenth Judicial Circuit-Fla.

Steinberg, Robert J.-Associate Judge, Maryland District Court District Eight-Md.

Steinberg, Robert L.-Judge, Pennsylvania Court of Common Pleas Thirty-first Judicial District-Pa.

Steinberg, Stephen C.-First Justice, Trial Court of Massachusetts Probate and Family Court Department Dukes County Division and Associate Justice, Plymouth County Division-Mass.

Steiner, D. Gary-Judge, Washington Superior Court Pierce County-Wash.

Steiner, David A.-Judge, King District Court East Division King County-Wash.

Steiner, Russell A.-Judge, Ohio Court of Common Pleas Licking County-Ohio

Steiner, Samuel J.-Judge, United States Bankruptcy Court Western District of Washington-Wash.

Steinhardt, Marsha L.-Justice, New York Supreme Court Second Judicial District-N.Y.

Steinhardt, Raphael-Judge, Dade County Court-Fla.

Steinheider, John F.-Judge, Nebraska County Court Second Judicial District-Neb.

Steinheimer, Connie J.-Judge, Nevada District Court Second Judicial District-Nev.

Steinke, Robert R.-Judge, Nebraska District Court Fifth Judicial District-Neb.

Steinkruger, Niesje J.-Presiding Judge, Alaska Superior Court Fourth Judicial District-Alas.

Steinle, Roland J., III-Judge, Superior Court of Arizona Maricopa County-Ariz.

Steinmetz, Donald W.-Reserve Judge, Wisconsin Circuit Court-Wis.

Steinmeyer, F. E., III-Senior Judge, Florida Circuit Court Second Judicial Circuit-Fla.

Steketee, Peter W.-Chief Judge, Virginia General District Court Thirty-first Judicial District-Va.

Stella, Michael T., Jr.-First Justice, Trial Court of Massachusetts District Court Department Essex County Lawrence Division-Mass.

Stem, Robert Miller-Judge, Texas District Court 82nd Judicial District-Tex.

Stempien, Jeanne-Judge, Michigan Circuit Court Third Judicial Circuit-Mich.

Stengel, Bruce V.-Judge, Vermillion Circuit Court-Ind.

Stengel, Charles H.-Circuit Judge, Illinois Circuit Court Fourteenth Judicial Circuit-Ill.

Stengel, L. Edward-Judge, Wisconsin Circuit Court Sheboygan Circuit-Wis.

Stengel, Lawrence F.-Judge, Pennsylvania Court of Common Pleas Second Judicial District-Pa.

Stengel, Michele-Judge, Kentucky District Court Thirtieth Judicial District-Ky.

Stengel, Robert F.-Judge, Connecticut Superior Court-Conn.

Stephan, Kenneth C.-Associate Justice, Nebraska Supreme Court-Neb.

Stephan, Rebecca-Magistrate Judge, Kansas District Court Sixth Judicial District-Kan.

Stephen, Larry R. C.-Judge, The Criminal Court of the City of New York-N.Y.

Stephens, A. Douglas-Judge, Marion County Small Claims Court Pike Township Division-Ind.

Stephens, Booker T.-Judge, West Virginia Circuit Court Eighth Judicial Circuit-W.Va.

Stephens, Cynthia D.-Judge, Michigan Circuit Court Third Judicial Circuit-Mich.

Stephens, Debra Moses-Judge, Palm Beach County Court-Fla.

Stephens, Donald W.-Resident Judge, North Carolina Superior Court Third Judicial Division District 10-N.C.

Stephens, Douglas M.-Judge, Kentucky Circuit Court Sixteenth Judicial Circuit-Ky.

Stephens, Eddie A.-Associate Judge, Illinois Circuit Court of Cook County-Ill.

Stephens, Lawton E.-Chief Judge, Superior Court of Georgia Western Judicial Circuit-Ga.

Stephens, Leigh Anne-Judge, Kentucky District Court Thirty-third Judicial District-Ky.

Stephens, Ronald L.-Resident Judge, North Carolina Superior Court Third Judicial Division District 14-N.C.

Stephens, Sherry K.-Judge, Superior Court of Arizona Maricopa County-Ariz.

Stephens, Susan R.-Judge, Coryell County Court at Law-Tex.

Stephens, Trevor N.-Judge, Alaska Superior Court First Judicial District-Alas.

Stephenson, Brad-Judge, Eastland County Court-Tex.

Stephenson, Elizabeth D.-Judge, King District Court South Division King County-Wash.

Stephenson, Franklin M.-Judge, Superior Court of California County of San Joaquin-Calif.

Stephenson, Gene R.-Judge, Florida Circuit Court Eighteenth Judicial Circuit-Fla.

Stephenson, George T.-Judge, Minnesota District Court Second Judicial District-Minn.

Stephenson, Martha King-Judge, Probate Court of Fayette County-Ga.

Stephenson, Nancy Smith-Judge, Probate Court of Dougherty County-Ga.

Stepler, Mary Ann-Associate Judge, Circuit Court for Frederick County, Sixth Judicial Circuit-Md.

Steptoe, Thomas W., Jr.-Judge, West Virginia Circuit Court Twenty-third Judicial Circuit-W.Va.

Sterba, David P.-Circuit Judge, Illinois Circuit Court of Cook County-Ill.

Sterling, Janis Ann-Judge, Superior Court of Arizona Yavapai County-Ariz.

Sterling, William N.-Judge, Superior Court of California County of Los Angeles-Calif.

Stern, Edwin H.-Judge, New Jersey Superior Court Appellate Division-N.J.

Stern, Herbert L., III-Judge, Colorado District Court Second Judicial District-Colo.

Stern, Jacqueline Marion-Judge, Superior Court of California County of San Diego-Calif.

Stern, Kenneth D.-Judge, Florida Circuit Court Fifteenth Judicial Circuit-Fla.

Stern, Michael L.-Judge, Superior Court of California County of Los Angeles-Calif.

Stern, Morris-Judge, United States Bankruptcy Court District of New Jersey-N.J.

Stern, Rebecca J.-Judge, Tennessee Criminal Court Eleventh Judicial District-Tenn.

Stetson, Brad-Judge, Florida Circuit Court Fourth Judicial Circuit-Fla.

Stettin, Herbert-Senior Judge, Florida Circuit Court Eleventh Judicial Circuit-Fla.

Stevens, Barry Keith-Judge, Connecticut Superior Court-Conn.

Stevens, Catherine C.-Emergency Judge, North Carolina District Court-N.C.

Stevens, Correale F.-Judge, The Superior Court of Pennsylvania-Pa.

Stevens, Darrell W.-Judge, Superior Court of California County of Butte-Calif.

Stevens, Emily A.-Judge, Superior Court of California County of Los Angeles-Calif.

Stevens, Henry L., IV-Judge, North Carolina District Court District 4-N.C.

Stevens, John C., III-First Justice, Trial Court of Massachusetts Probate and Family Court Department Essex County Division-Mass.

Stevens, John Paul-Associate Justice, The Supreme Court of the United States

Stevens, John R.-Chief Judge, Virginia General District Court Fifteenth Judicial District-Va.

Stevens, Lawrence T.-Associate Justice, California Court of Appeal First District Division Five-Calif.

Stevens, Richard A.-Associate Judge, Illinois Circuit Court of Cook County-Ill.

Stevens, Richard L.-Judge, Ashtabula County Court-Ohio

Stevens, Samuel S.-Judge, Superior Court of California County of Santa Cruz-Calif.

Stevenson, Jo Ann C.-Judge, United States Bankruptcy Court Western District of Michigan-Mich.

Stevenson, Julie R.-Associate Judge, Circuit Court for Frederick County, Sixth Judicial Circuit-Md.

Stevenson, W. Matthew-Judge, Florida District Court of Appeal Fourth District-Fla.

Steverson, L. Neil-Chief Judge, Virginia General District Court Fourteenth Judicial District-Va.

Stewart, Brian T.-Judge, United States District Court District of Utah-Utah

Stewart, Bruce D.-Circuit Judge, Illinois Circuit Court First Judicial Circuit-Ill.

Stewart, C. Jean-Presiding Judge, Denver Probate Court-Colo.

Stewart, Carl E.-Judge, United States Court of Appeals Fifth Circuit

Stewart, Daniel-Judge, Fort Smith District Court-Ark.

Stewart, David A.-Judge, Little Rock District Court-Ark.

Stewart, David C.-Judge, Alaska Court of Appeals-Alas.

Stewart, Donald W.-Judge, Alabama Circuit Court Sixteenth Judicial Circuit-Ala.

Stewart, Frederick N.-Judge, Kansas District Court First Judicial District-Kan.

Stewart, Gary A.-Judge, Michigan District Court District Fifty-seven-Mich.

Stewart, Herman I.-Judge, Louisiana District Court Thirty-sixth Judicial District-La.

ALPHABETICAL NAME INDEX

Stewart, Howard-Judge, Elmer City Municipal Court-Wash.
Stewart, James B.-Circuit Judge, Illinois Circuit Court Ninth Judicial Circuit-Ill.
Stewart, James E., Sr.-Judge, Louisiana Court of Appeal Second Circuit-La.
Stewart, Janice M.-Magistrate Judge, United States District Court District of Oregon-Ore.
Stewart, Jeffrey F.-Chancellor, Tennessee Chancery Court Twelfth Judicial District-Tenn.
Stewart, John Kennedy-Judge, Superior Court of California City and County of San Francisco-Calif.
Stewart, Judith A.-Judge, Brown Circuit Court-Ind.
Stewart, Lynn Kellene-Associate Judge, Circuit Court for Baltimore City, Eighth Judicial Circuit-Md.
Stewart, Marcia-Judge, North Carolina District Court District 11-N.C.
Stewart, Michael R.-District Associate Judge, Iowa District Court Eighth Judicial District-Ia.
Stewart, Robert William-Judge, Ohio Court of Common Pleas Athens County-Ohio
Stewart, Victoria A.-Circuit Judge, Illinois Circuit Court of Cook County-Ill.
Stewart, William-Judge, Hoquiam Municipal Court-Wash.
Stewart, William C., Jr.-Judge, Wisconsin Circuit Court Dunn Circuit-Wis.
Stewart, William D.-Judge, Superior Court of California County of Los Angeles-Calif.
Stewart, William F.-Judge, Kentucky Circuit Court Fifty-third Judicial Circuit-Ky.
Stewart, William G.-Judge, North Carolina District Court District 7-N.C.
Stickel, Olga H.-Judge, Elkhart Superior Court-Ind.
Sticklen, Kathryn A.-Judge, Idaho District Court Fourth Judicial District-Ida.
Stickney, Paul D.-Magistrate Judge, United States District Court Northern District of Texas-Tex.
Stidham, Dan-Judge, Paragould District Court-Ark.
Stiehl, Robert J., III-Judge, North Carolina District Court District 12-N.C.
Stiehl, William D.-Senior Judge, United States District Court Southern District of Illinois-Ill.
Stigler, George L.-District Judge, Iowa District Court First Judicial District-Ia.
Stiles, Brian L.-Judge, Sedro-Woolley Municipal Court-Wash.
Stillman, F. Bradford-Magistrate Judge, United States District Court Eastern District of Virginia-Va.
Stillwell, Robert C.-Associate Circuit Judge, Missouri Circuit Court Twenty-fourth Judicial Circuit-Mo.
Stilson, C. Michael-Judge, United States Bankruptcy Court Northern District of Alabama-Ala.
Stilwell, H. Samuel-Associate Judge, South Carolina Court of Appeals-S.C.
Stilwell, Lee G.-Associate District Judge, Oklahoma District Court Twenty-second Judicial District-Okla.
Stilwell, M. Lee, Jr.-Judge, Virginia General District Court Twenty-second Judicial District-Va.
Stilz, Clifford L., Jr.-Judge, Thurston District Court Thurston County-Wash.
Stine, D. Michael-Judge, Pennsylvania Court of Common Pleas Twenty-first Judicial District-Pa.
Stinnett, R. Thomas-Judge, United States Bankruptcy Court Eastern District of Tennessee-Tenn.
Stinson, Betty Owen-Justice, New York Supreme Court Twelfth Judicial District-N.Y.
Stinson, Ford E., Jr.-Judge, Louisiana District Court Twenty-sixth Judicial District-La.
Stipp, Gordon R.-Associate Judge, Illinois Circuit Court Fifth Judicial Circuit-Ill.
Stirling, Lawrence W.-Judge, Superior Court of California County of San Diego-Calif.
Stirman, C. Edward-Judge, Larimer County Court-Colo.
Stites, Barbara-Magistrate Judge, Kansas District Court Seventeenth Judicial District-Kan.
Stith, Laura Denvir-Judge, Supreme Court of Missouri-Mo.
Stitham, Kevin L.-Judge, Maine District Court-Me.
Stitt, David T.-Judge, Virginia Circuit Court Nineteenth Judicial Circuit-Va.
Stiven, James F.-Magistrate Judge, United States District Court Southern District of California-Calif.
Stock, Nancy Wieben-Judge, Superior Court of California County of Orange-Calif.
Stockdale, David C.-Judge, Hamilton County Municipal Court-Ohio
Stocks, Agnes-Judge, Baggs and Dixon Municipal Courts-Wyo.
Stocks, William L.-Chief Judge, United States Bankruptcy Court Middle District of North Carolina-N.C.
Stoddard, Cecile D.-Judge, Pomfret District Probate Court-Conn.
Stoddard, Michael-Chief Judge, Superior Court of Georgia Cobb Judicial Circuit-Ga.
Stoddard, Ralph C.-Judge, Florida Circuit Court Thirteenth Judicial Circuit-Fla.
Stoddart, Douglas W.-Justice, Trial Court of Massachusetts District Court Department Middlesex County Framingham Division-Mass.
Stodolink, Edward F.-Judge Referee, Connecticut Superior Court-Conn.
Stoever, Thomas William-Judge, Superior Court of California County of Los Angeles-Calif.
Stofferahn, David A.-Judge, Minnesota Workers' Compensation Court of Appeals-Minn.
Stohr, Donald J.-Judge, United States District Court Eastern District of Missouri-Mo.
Stoker, Randy J.-Judge, Idaho District Court Fifth Judicial District Magistrate Division-Ida.
Stokes, Angela R.-Judge, Cleveland Municipal Court-Ohio
Stokes, Charles-Judge, Texas District Court 68th Judicial District-Tex.
Stokes, Richard F.-Associate Judge, Delaware Superior Court Sussex County-Del.
Stokinger, Carol A.-Judge, New York City Family Court-N.Y.
Stoll, Charles W.-Judge, Superior Court of California County of Los Angeles-Calif.
Stoll, Mark T.-Associate Circuit Judge, Missouri Circuit Court Twenty-third Judicial Circuit-Mo.
Stolte, Barbara Clarke-Judge, New Jersey Superior Court Vicinage Eight-N.J.
Stoltz, Kathryne A.-Judge, Superior Court of California County of Los Angeles-Calif.
Stolz, Katherine M.-Judge, Washington Superior Court Pierce County-Wash.
Stolz, Robert M.-Judge, The Civil Court of the City of New York-N.Y.
Stone, Barry J.-Judge, Florida District Court of Appeal Fourth District-Fla.
Stone, Catherine-Justice, Texas Court of Appeals Fourth District-Tex.
Stone, Charles M.-Judge, Virginia Circuit Court Twenty-first Judicial Circuit-Va.
Stone, Hugh W.-Chief Judge, Superior Court of Georgia Enotah Judicial Circuit-Ga.
Stone, Lewis Bart-Judge, New York Court of Claims-N.Y.
Stone, Martin E.-Judge, Oregon Circuit Court Fifteenth Judicial District-Ore.
Stone, Norman R., III-Associate Judge, Maryland District Court District Eight-Md.
Stone, Richard A.-Judge, Superior Court of California County of Los Angeles-Calif.
Stone, Richard W.-Chief Judge, North Carolina District Court District 17A-N.C.
Stone, Robert B.-Judge, West Virginia Circuit Court Seventeenth Judicial Circuit-W.Va.
Stone, Ronald W.-Judge, Oregon Circuit Court Twenty-fifth Judicial District-Ore.
Stone, William F.-Judge, Florida Circuit Court First Judicial Circuit-Fla.
Stone, William F., Jr.-Judge, United States Bankruptcy Court Western District of Virginia-Va.
Stoneburner, Terri-Judge, Minnesota Court of Appeals-Minn.
Stoner, Mark D.-Judge, Marion Superior Court-Ind.
Stonier, James J.-Judge, Washington Superior Court Cowlitz County-Wash.
Stoppa, Terry L.-Justice, Hill County Justice of the Peace Court-Mont.
Storck, John R.-Judge, Wisconsin Circuit Court Dodge Circuit-Wis.
Storey, William-Judge, Arkansas Circuit Court Fourth Judicial Circuit-Ark.
Storie, Tracy Lee-Associate Circuit Judge, Missouri Circuit Court Twenty-fifth Judicial Circuit-Mo.
Storm, Sandra H.-Judge, Alabama Circuit Court Tenth Judicial Circuit Birmingham Division-Ala.
Stormer, Elinore Marsh-Judge, Akron Municipal Court-Ohio
Stormes, Nita L.-Magistrate Judge, United States District Court Southern District of California-Calif.
Stortecky, Frederick R.-Judge, Johnstown City Court-N.Y.
Story, Bentley E.-Judge, Arkansas Circuit Court First Judicial Circuit-Ark.
Story, Richard W.-Judge, United States District Court Northern District of Georgia-Ga.
Story, Steven L.-Judge, Meigs County Court-Ohio
Stosberg, David T.-Judge, Bankruptcy Appellate Panel Sixth Circuit and Chief Judge, United States Bankruptcy Court Western District of Kentucky-Ky.
Stotler, Alicemarie H.-Judge, United States District Court Central District of California-Calif.
Stotler, James Allen-Judge, Superior Court of California County of Orange-Calif.
Stott, Gary D.-Presiding Judge, Utah District Court Fourth Judicial District-Utah
Stotts, Rita Laverne-Judge, Tennessee Circuit Court Thirtieth Judicial District-Tenn.
Stoudt, Bill-Judge, Gregg County Court-Tex.
Stoughton, George D.-Judge Referee, Connecticut Superior Court-Conn.
Stout, Dean-Judge, Superior Court of California County of Inyo-Calif.
Stout, Gary Creamer-Judge, Washington Court House Municipal Court-Ohio
Stout, Roderick P.-Judge, Alabama Circuit Court Thirteenth Judicial Circuit-Ala.
Stout, Walter W., III-Judge, Virginia Circuit Court Thirteenth Judicial Circuit-Va.
Stovall, Dennis J.-District Judge, Iowa District Court Fifth Judicial District-Ia.
Stovall, Suzanne-Judge, Texas District Court 221st Judicial District-Tex.
Stover, Earl, III-Judge, Texas District Court 88th Judicial District-Tex.
Stoverink, David F.-Circuit Judge, Illinois Circuit Court Ninth Judicial Circuit-Ill.
Stowe, David L.-Chief Judge, Grand Traverse County Probate Court-Mich.
Stralka, Paul-Circuit Judge, Illinois Circuit Court of Cook County-Ill.
Strand, Roger Gordon-Senior Judge, United States District Court District of Arizona-Ariz.
Straniere, Philip S.-Judge, The Civil Court of the City of New York-N.Y.
Strassburger, Eugene B., III-Judge, Pennsylvania Court of Common Pleas Fifth Judicial District-Pa.
Stratton, C. William-Associate District Judge, Oklahoma District Court Fifth Judicial District-Okla.
Stratton, Evelyn Lundberg-Justice, Supreme Court of Ohio-Ohio
Straub, Anna K.-Justice, Fallon County Justice of the Peace Court and Judge, Baker City Court-Mont.
Straub, Chester J.-Judge, United States Court of Appeals Second Circuit
Straus, Robert H.-Judge, The Criminal Court of the City of New York-N.Y.
Strauss, Charles J.-Judge, Virginia Circuit Court Twenty-second Judicial Circuit-Va.
Strauss, Gus J.-Judge, Texas District Court 2nd 25th Judicial District-Tex.
Strauss, Richard-Judge, Superior Court of California County of San Diego-Calif.
Strauss, Sidney F.-Justice, New York Supreme Court Eleventh Judicial District-N.Y.
Streepy, Jack B.-Magistrate Judge, United States District Court Northern District of Ohio-Ohio
Street, John B.-Judge, Chillicothe Municipal Court-Ohio
Street, Malcolm B., Jr.-Judge, Alabama Circuit Court Seventh Judicial Circuit-Ala.
Streger, Elaine-Judge, Superior Court of California County of Orange-Calif.

ALPHABETICAL NAME INDEX

ALPHABETICAL NAME INDEX

Sundt, Ann Newman-Associate Judge, Circuit Court for Montgomery County, Sixth Judicial Circuit-Md.

Sundvold, Stephen J.-Judge, Superior Court of California County of Orange-Calif.

Sunshine, Jeffrey S.-Judge, New York City Family Court-N.Y.

Suntag, David T.-Judge, Vermont Trial Court-Vt.

Superville, Maurice Charles, Jr.-Judge, Lamar County Court-Tex.

Supina, Gerald Joseph-Chief Judge, Ionia County Probate Court-Mich.

Supnick, Samuel L.-Retired Judge, New Jersey Superior Court-N.J.

Surbeck, John F., Jr.-Judge, Allen Superior Court-Ind.

Suria, Fred G., Jr.-Circuit Judge, Illinois Circuit Court of Cook County-Ill.

Suriano, Donald J.-Circuit Judge, Illinois Circuit Court of Cook County-Ill.

Surrick, R. Barclay-Judge, United States District Court Eastern District of Pennsylvania-Pa.

Susano, Charles D., Jr.-Judge, Tennessee Court of Appeals Eastern Division-Tenn.

Susco, Wendy W.-Judge, Connecticut Superior Court-Conn.

Sussman, Ruth Levine-Judge, The Criminal Court of the City of New York-N.Y.

Suster, Ronald-Judge, Ohio Court of Common Pleas Cuyahoga County-Ohio

Suter, Karen L.-Judge, New Jersey Superior Court Vicinage Three-N.J.

Sutherland, Keith M.-Presiding Judge, Missouri Circuit Court Twelfth Judicial Circuit-Mo.

Sutherland, Mike-Judge, Burleson County Court-Tex.

Sutherland, Patrice K.-Judge, Minnesota District Court First Judicial District-Minn.

Sutherland, Thomas M.-Judge, Kansas District Court Tenth Judicial District-Kan.

Sutherland, William J.-Chief Judge, Michigan District Court District Twenty-three-Mich.

Sutin, Jonathan B.-Judge, New Mexico Court of Appeals-N.Mex.

Sutker-Dermer, Shelley-Circuit Judge, Illinois Circuit Court of Cook County-Ill.

Sutnik, Thomas Michael-Judge, Southbury District Probate Court-Conn.

Sutro, John A., Jr.-Judge, Superior Court of California County of Marin-Calif.

Suttell, Paul A.-Associate Justice, Rhode Island Supreme Court-R.I.

Sutterfield, Dennis-Judge, Arkansas Circuit Court Fifth Judicial Circuit-Ark.

Suttle, Ned Michael-Presiding Judge, Alabama Circuit Court Eleventh Judicial Circuit-Ala.

Sutton, Berrien L.-Judge, State Court of Clinch County and Judge, Juvenile Court of Georgia Alapaha Judicial Circuit-Ga.

Sutton, Daniel L.-Chief Judge, Michigan District Court District Eighty-three-Mich.

Sutton, Frank-Chief Magistrate, Magistrate Court of Rabun County-Ga.

Sutton, James M., Jr.-Judge, Superior Court of California County of Los Angeles-Calif.

Sutton, Janet-Associate Circuit Judge, Missouri Circuit Court Seventh Judicial Circuit-Mo.

Sutton, Joe V.-Judge, Kosciusko Superior Court-Ind.

Sutton, Richard C.-Judge, Superior Court of Georgia Tallapoosa Judicial Circuit-Ga.

Sutton, Thomas H.-Circuit Judge, Illinois Circuit Court Second Judicial Circuit-Ill.

Sutula, John D.-Judge, Ohio Court of Common Pleas Cuyahoga County-Ohio

Sutula, Kathleen Ann-Judge, Ohio Court of Common Pleas Cuyahoga County-Ohio

Suzukawa, Steven C.-Judge, Superior Court of California County of Los Angeles-Calif.

Svaren, David A.-Judge, Skagit District Court Skagit County and Judge, Anacortes, Burlington and Mount Vernon Municipal Courts-Wash.

Svet, Don J.-Recalled Magistrate Judge, United States District Court District of New Mexico-N.Mex.

Svetanoff, Gerald N.-Judge, Lake Superior Court-Ind.

Svetkey, Susan M.-Judge, Oregon Circuit Court Fourth Judicial District-Ore.

Svoboda, Joseph V.-Judge, Carlisle, England and Ward District Courts-Ark.

Swager, Douglas E.-Associate Justice, California Court of Appeal First District Division One-Calif.

Swaim, Kristie-Associate Circuit Judge, Missouri Circuit Court Second Judicial Circuit-Mo.

Swain, L. Kevin-Judge, Idaho District Court Fourth Judicial District Magistrate Division-Ida.

Swain, Laura Taylor-Judge, United States District Court Southern District of New York-N.Y.

Swain, Leslie A.-Judge, Superior Court of California County of Los Angeles-Calif.

Swallow, Joseph P.-Chief Judge, Michigan Circuit Court Twenty-sixth Judicial Circuit-Mich.

Swan, Allen G.-First Justice, Trial Court of Massachusetts District Court Department Essex County Ipswich Division and Justice, Haverhill Division-Mass.

Swandal, William Nels-Judge, Montana District Court Sixth Judicial District-Mont.

Swank, Donald L.-Judge, Michigan District Court District Thirty-three-Mich.

Swann, William K., III-Judge, Tennessee Circuit Court Sixth Judicial District-Tenn.

Swanson, James R.-Judge, Virginia Circuit Court Twenty-third Judicial Circuit-Va.

Swanson, Joel E.-District Judge, Iowa District Court Second Judicial District-Ia.

Swanson, Ronald-Judge, Santa Rosa County Court-Fla.

Swanson, Stephen D.-Judge, Minnesota District Court Fourth Judicial District-Minn.

Swanstrom, Don L.-Judge, Idaho District Court First Judicial District Magistrate Division-Ida.

Swart, Coleman A.-Judge, Superior Court of California County of Los Angeles-Calif.

Swartwood, Charles B., III-Magistrate Judge, United States District Court District of Massachusetts-Mass.

Swartz, David Scott-Judge, Michigan Circuit Court Twenty-second Judicial Circuit-Mich.

Swartz, Jeffrey D.-Judge, Dade County Court-Fla.

Swartz, Stephen M.-Judge, Nebraska County Court Fourth Judicial District-Neb.

Sweat, David R.-Judge, Superior Court of Georgia Western Judicial Circuit-Ga.

Sweat, Marcus Lee, Jr.-Judge, Probate Court of Ware County-Ga.

Sweazea, Kevin-Judge, New Mexico District Court Seventh Judicial District-N.Mex.

Sween, Birger M.-Retired Judge, New Jersey Superior Court-N.J.

Sweeney, Constance M.-Associate Justice, Trial Court of Massachusetts Superior Court Department-Mass.

Sweeney, Dennis J.-Judge, Washington Court of Appeals Division III-Wash.

Sweeney, Dennis M.-Associate Judge, Circuit Court for Howard County, Fifth Judicial Circuit-Md.

Sweeney, Edward-Associate Circuit Judge, Missouri Circuit Court Twenty-second Judicial Circuit-Mo.

Sweeney, Francis E.-Justice, Supreme Court of Ohio-Ohio

Sweeney, J. Edward-Presiding Judge, Missouri Circuit Court Thirty-ninth Judicial Circuit-Mo.

Sweeney, J. Miles-Presiding Judge, Missouri Circuit Court Thirty-first Judicial Circuit-Mo.

Sweeney, James J.-Judge, Ohio Court of Appeals Eighth District-Ohio

Sweeney, John A.-Assignment Judge, New Jersey Superior Court Vicinage Three-N.J.

Sweeney, Kathleen M.-Associate Judge, Maryland District Court District One-Md.

Sweeney, Patrick A.-Judge, Suffolk County Family Court-N.Y.

Sweeney, Peter Paul-Judge, The Civil Court of the City of New York-N.Y.

Sweeney, Philip J.-Circuit Judge, Missouri Circuit Court Twenty-first Judicial Circuit-Mo.

Sweeny, John W., Jr.-Justice, New York Supreme Court Ninth Judicial District-N.Y.

Sweet, Michael W.-Judge, Superior Court of California County of Yolo-Calif.

Sweet, Robert Workman-Senior Judge, United States District Court Southern District of New York-N.Y.

Sweetland, Heather L.-Judge, Minnesota District Court Sixth Judicial District-Minn.

Sweigert, Philip Kerner-Recalled Magistrate Judge, United States District Court Western District of Washington-Wash.

Swenson, Douglas G.-Judge, Minnesota District Court Tenth Judicial District-Minn.

Swenson, James T.-Judge, Minnesota District Court Fourth Judicial District-Minn.

Swent, F. Rae-Judge, Louisiana District Court Ninth Judicial District-La.

Swersky, Alfred D.-Judge, Virginia Circuit Court Eighteenth Judicial Circuit-Va.

Swienton, Cynthia K.-Judge, Connecticut Superior Court-Conn.

Swietlik, Walter J.-Reserve Judge, Wisconsin Circuit Court-Wis.

Swift, Bert L.-Judge, Superior Court of California County of San Bernardino-Calif.

Swift, Pattie P.-Judge, Colorado District Court Twelfth Judicial District-Colo.

Swift, Stephen J.-Judge, United States Tax Court

Swift, Thomas A.-Judge, Ohio Court of Common Pleas Trumbull County-Ohio

Swigert, William Theron, Sr.-Judge, Florida Circuit Court Fifth Judicial Circuit-Fla.

Swiney, D. Michael-Judge, Tennessee Court of Appeals Eastern Division-Tenn.

Swinton, Barbara G.-District Judge, Oklahoma District Court Seventh Judicial District-Okla.

Swisher, Robert G.-Judge, Washington Superior Court Benton-Franklin Counties-Wash.

Switalski, Mark S.-Judge, Michigan Circuit Court Sixteenth Judicial Circuit-Mich.

Switalski, Matthew S.-Judge, Michigan Circuit Court Sixteenth Judicial Circuit-Mich.

Switzer, David-Judge, Arkansas Circuit Court Eighteenth East Judicial Circuit-Ark.

Swope, Derek C.-Chief Judge, West Virginia Circuit Court Ninth Judicial Circuit-W.Va.

Swope, Thomas A., Jr.-Judge, Pennsylvania Court of Common Pleas Forty-seventh Judicial District-Pa.

Sword, Dean W., Jr.-Chief Judge, Virginia Circuit Court Third Judicial Circuit-Va.

Swords, Daniel J.-First Justice, Trial Court of Massachusetts Juvenile Court Department Hampden County Division-Mass.

Swords, Patricia A.-Judge, Connecticut Superior Court-Conn.

Sykes, Diane S.-Justice, Wisconsin Supreme Court-Wis.

Syler, William L.-Presiding Judge, Missouri Circuit Court Thirty-second Judicial Circuit-Mo.

Sylvester, Esther R.-Judge, Pennsylvania Court of Common Pleas First Judicial District-Pa.

Sylvester, Joseph H.-Judge Referee, Connecticut Superior Court-Conn.

Sylvester, William B.-Judge, Colorado District Court Eighteenth Judicial District-Colo.

Sylvia, Jimmy-Judge, Chambers County Court-Tex.

Sypek, Maria Marinari-Judge, New Jersey Superior Court Vicinage Seven-N.J.

Sypolt, Diane Gilbert-Judge, United States Court of Federal Claims

Sypolt, Greg D.-Judge, Washington Superior Court Spokane County-Wash.

Szczur, Margaret O.-Judge, Erie County Family Court-N.Y.

Szumowski, David M.-Judge, Superior Court of California County of San Diego-Calif.

Szymanski, David J.-Judge, Wayne County Probate Court-Mich.

Tabbey, Kirk W.-Judge, Michigan District Court District Fourteen A-Mich.

Tabor, Gary-Judge, Washington Superior Court Thurston County-Wash.

Tabor, Nancy S.-District Judge, Iowa District Court Seventh Judicial District-Ia.

Tacha, Deanell Reece-Chief Judge, United States Court of Appeals Tenth Circuit

Tackett, Julia K.-Judge, Kentucky Court of Appeals-Ky.

ALPHABETICAL NAME INDEX

Tacoma, Kenneth L.-Chief Judge, Wexford County Probate Court-Mich.
Taddeo, Ann Marie-Judge, Monroe County Family Court-N.Y.
Tafoya, Robert S.-Judge, Superior Court of California County of Kern-Calif.
Taft, Franklin R.-Judge, Superior Court of California County of Solano-Calif.
Taft, Tim-Justice, Texas Court of Appeals First District-Tex.
Tafuri, Anthony A.-Judge, Suffolk County District Court-N.Y.
Taggart, Patrick J.-Judge, Wisconsin Circuit Court Sauk Circuit-Wis.
Tagle, Hilda Gloria-Judge, United States District Court Southern District of Texas-Tex.
Tahvonen, Randy L.-Judge, Michigan Circuit Court Twenty-ninth Judicial Circuit-Mich.
Taisey, Robert M., Jr.-Judge, Idaho District Court Third Judicial District Magistrate Division-Ida.
Taite, Ralph-Judge, Dallas County Criminal Court at Law No. 4-Tex.
Takasugi, Robert M.-Senior Judge, United States District Court Central District of California-Calif.
Talamante, David M.-Judge, Superior Court of Arizona Maricopa County-Ariz.
Talbert, Patricia Medina-Judge, New Jersey Superior Court Vicinage Five-N.J.
Talbot, Michael J.-Judge, Michigan Court of Appeals-Mich.
Talbot, Richard J.-Justice, Keene District Court-N.H.
Talevi, Jacqueline F. Ward-Judge, Virginia General District Court Twenty-third Judicial District-Va.
Taliaferro, Harry T., III-Judge, Virginia Circuit Court Fifteenth Judicial Circuit-Va.
Taliaferro, Viola J.-Judge, Monroe Circuit Court-Ind.
Talley, William A., Jr.-Judge, Virginia General District Court Sixteenth Judicial District-Va.
Tallman, C. Darren-Judge, West Virginia Family Court Circuit Three-W.Va.
Tallman, Howard R.-Judge, United States Bankruptcy Court District of Colorado-Colo.
Tallman, Paul D.-Judge, Colorado District Court Fifteenth Judicial District-Colo.
Tallman, Richard C.-Judge, United States Court of Appeals Ninth Circuit
Tallmer, Megan-Judge, The Criminal Court of the City of New York-N.Y.
Talton-Harris, Alfreda-Judge, Virginia Juvenile and Domestic Relations District Court Fifth Judicial District-Va.
Tan, Sen K.-Judge, Alaska Superior Court Third Judicial District-Alas.
Tandy, Jack A.-Judge, Shelby Superior Court-Ind.
Tanenbaum, Melvyn-Justice, New York Supreme Court Tenth Judicial District-N.Y.
Tang, Julie M.-Judge, Superior Court of California City and County of San Francisco-Calif.
Tang, Paul E.-Judge, Superior Court of Arizona Pima County-Ariz.
Tangeman, Martin J.-Judge, Superior Court of California County of San Luis Obispo-Calif.
Tanksley, Kathryn Johnson-Judge, State Court of Cobb County-Ga.
Tanner, Jack E.-Senior Judge, United States District Court Western District of Washington-Wash.
Tanner, Martha-Judge, Texas District Court 166th Judicial District-Tex.
Tanner, Sharon Howard-Judge, Duval County Court-Fla.
Tansil, Mark-Judge, Superior Court of California County of Sonoma-Calif.
Tanzer, Lois-Judge, Connecticut Superior Court-Conn.
Tapia, Fernando-Judge, The Civil Court of the City of New York-N.Y.
Tarantino, Richard P.-Judge, Glens Falls City Court-N.Y.
Tarbuck, Joseph Q.-Senior Judge, Florida Circuit Court First Judicial Circuit-Fla.
Targum, Anne E.-Justice, New York Supreme Court Twelfth Judicial District-N.Y.
Tarle, Norman Perry-Judge, Superior Court of California County of Los Angeles-Calif.
Tarnow, Arthur J.-Judge, United States District Court Eastern District of Michigan-Mich.
Tarrance, Carter William-Judge, Texas District Court 392nd Judicial District-Tex.
Tarrant, Kyle Higgs-Judge, Michigan District Court District Seventy Division Two-Mich.
Tashima, A. Wallace-Judge, United States Court of Appeals Ninth Circuit
Tate, Charles G.-Special Judge, Oklahoma District Court Twentieth Judicial District-Okla.
Tate, Douglas A.-Judge, Howard Superior Court-Ind.
Tate, Joseph Scott-Chief Judge, Virginia General District Court Twenty-eighth Judicial District-Va.
Tate, Samuel McDowell-Retired-Recalled Judge, North Carolina District Court-N.C.
Tate, Susan P.-Judge, Probate Court of Clarke County-Ga.
Tatel, David S.-Judge, United States Court of Appeals District of Columbia Circuit
Tatro, John-Justice of the Peace, Carson City Justices' Court and Judge, Carson City Municipal Court-Nev.
Tatum, Danny-Judge, Ruston City Court-La.
Tatum, Stephen R.-Judge, Kansas District Court Tenth Judicial District-Kan.
Taube, Gerald-Justice, Durham District Court-N.H.
Taubman, Daniel Marc-Judge, Colorado Court of Appeals-Colo.
Taul, Carl H.-Judge, Ripley Circuit Court-Ind.
Tauro, Joseph L.-Judge, United States District Court District of Massachusetts-Mass.
Taylor, A. Bailey-Judge, Kentucky District Court Fifty-fifth Judicial District-Ky.
Taylor, A. Blenn, Jr.-Senior Judge, Superior Court of Georgia-Ga.
Taylor, Alvin E.-Justice, Portsmouth District Court-N.H.
Taylor, Anna Diggs-Senior Judge, United States District Court Eastern District of Michigan-Mich.
Taylor, Anne-Judge, Franklin County Municipal Court-Ohio
Taylor, Arthur Howard-Senior Judge, Florida Circuit Court Eleventh Judicial Circuit-Fla.
Taylor, Barry A.-Judge, Superior Court of California County of Los Angeles-Calif.
Taylor, Bill-Circuit Judge, Illinois Circuit Court of Cook County-Ill.
Taylor, C. Hearn-Judge, Orleans Parish Juvenile Court-La.
Taylor, Carl E.-Judge, Connecticut Superior Court-Conn.
Taylor, Carole Y.-Judge, Florida District Court of Appeal Fourth District-Fla.
Taylor, Clayton K.-Judge, Tallapoosa County District Court-Ala.
Taylor, Clifford W.-Justice, Michigan Supreme Court-Mich.
Taylor, Don-Judge, Liberty County Court at Law-Tex.
Taylor, Donna F.-Judge, Nebraska County Court Seventh Judicial District-Neb.
Taylor, Eric C.-Judge, Superior Court of California County of Los Angeles-Calif.
Taylor, Eugene-Circuit Judge, Illinois Circuit Court Ninth Judicial Circuit-Ill.
Taylor, Gary L.-Judge, United States District Court Central District of California-Calif.
Taylor, Harold D.-Judge, Custer County Court-Colo.
Taylor, Hendrix Arthur, Jr.-Judge, Arkansas Circuit Court Eleventh West Judicial Circuit-Ark.
Taylor, James H.-Reserve Judge, Wisconsin Circuit Court-Wis.
Taylor, James R.-Judge, Utah District Court Fourth Judicial District-Utah
Taylor, Janice A.-Justice, New York Supreme Court Eleventh Judicial District-N.Y.
Taylor, Joe C.-Judge, Oklahoma Court of Civil Appeals-Okla.
Taylor, Joi Jeter-Judge, Virginia General District Court Thirteenth Judicial District-Va.
Taylor, Kimberly Susan-Resident Judge, North Carolina Superior Court Sixth Judicial Division District 22-N.C.
Taylor, L. Haldane-Judge, Florida Circuit Court Fourth Judicial Circuit-Fla.
Taylor, Lawton G., Sr.-Chief Magistrate, Magistrate Court of Ware County-Ga.
Taylor, Lydia Calvert-Judge, Virginia Circuit Court Fourth Judicial Circuit-Va.
Taylor, Lynn O'Malley-Judge, Superior Court of California County of Marin-Calif.
Taylor, Maurice G., Jr.-Magistrate Judge, United States District Court Southern District of West Virginia-W.Va.
Taylor, Meredith C.-Judge, Superior Court of California County of Los Angeles-Calif.
Taylor, Ramona D.-Judge, Virginia Juvenile and Domestic Relations District Court Second Judicial District-Va.
Taylor, Richard C.-Judge, Minnesota District Court Ninth Judicial District-Minn.
Taylor, Richard D.-Judge, United States Bankruptcy Courts Eastern and Western Districts of Arkansas-Ark.
Taylor, Richard D., Jr.-Judge, Virginia Circuit Court Thirteenth Judicial Circuit-Va.
Taylor, Robert Edward-Judge, Ohio Court of Common Pleas Hamilton County-Ohio
Taylor, Robert Gregory-Judge, Superior Court of California County of Riverside-Calif.
Taylor, Ronald E.-Associate Circuit Judge, Missouri Circuit Court Fifth Judicial Circuit-Mo.
Taylor, Ronald L.-Judge, Superior Court of California County of Riverside-Calif.
Taylor, Royce-Judge, Tennessee Circuit Court Sixteenth Judicial District-Tenn.
Taylor, Sandra F.-Judge, Florida Circuit Court Sixteenth Judicial Circuit-Fla.
Taylor, Steven W.-District Judge, Oklahoma District Court Eighteenth Judicial District-Okla.
Taylor, Susan-Judge, Probate Court of Mitchell County-Ga.
Taylor, Susan Chandler-Resident Judge, North Carolina Superior Court Sixth Judicial Division District 20B-N.C.
Taylor, Terry N.-Magistrate Judge, Kansas District Court Twelfth Judicial District-Kan.
Taylor, Valeria M.-Justice of the Peace, Baker Justices' Court-Nev.
Taylor, Wilford, Jr.-Judge, Virginia Circuit Court Eighth Judicial Circuit-Va.
Tchaikovsky, Leslie J.-Judge, United States Bankruptcy Court Northern District of California-Calif.
Teachout, Mary Miles-Judge, Vermont Trial Court-Vt.
Teahan, William W., Jr.-Justice, Trial Court of Massachusetts District Court Department Hampden County Springfield Division-Mass.
Teat, Jimmy C.-Judge, Louisiana District Court Second Judicial District-La.
Tedrick, Marjorie-Judge, Buckley Municipal Court-Wash.
Teel, Robert J., Jr.-Judge, Coosa County District Court-Ala.
Teel, S. Martin, Jr.-Judge, United States Bankruptcy Court District of Columbia-D.C.
Teeple, Donald A.-Chief Judge, Michigan Circuit Court Twenty-fourth Judicial Circuit-Mich.
Teilborg, James A.-Judge, United States District Court District of Arizona-Ariz.
Teitelman, Richard B.-Judge, Supreme Court of Missouri-Mo.
Tejada, Charles J.-Judge, New York Court of Claims-N.Y.
Telesca, Michael A.-Senior Judge, United States District Court Western District of New York-N.Y.
Telle, Jack-Judge, Kentucky District Court Fifty-eighth Judicial District-Ky.
Teller, Samuel H.-Senior Judge, Connecticut Superior Court-Conn.
Telsey, Norman-Retired Judge, New Jersey Superior Court-N.J.
Temin, Carolyn Engel-Judge, Pennsylvania Court of Common Pleas First Judicial District-Pa.
Temples, Coy H.-Senior Judge, Superior Court of Georgia-Ga.
Tench, Benjamin M.-Senior Judge, Florida Circuit Court Eighth Judicial Circuit-Fla.
Tench, Charles P.-Judge, Virginia Circuit Court Seventh Judicial Circuit-Va.
Teneyck, David-Judge, Minnesota District Court Ninth Judicial District-Minn.

ALPHABETICAL NAME INDEX

ALPHABETICAL NAME INDEX

Thompson, Stephen W.-Judge, New Jersey Superior Court Vicinage Four-N.J.

Thompson, Terry-Justice of the Peace, Malheur County Justice Court-Ore.

Thompson, William A., Jr.-Judge, Lamb County Court-Tex.

Thompson, William C.-Judge, Alabama Court of Civil Appeals-Ala.

Thomsen, Scott-Associate Circuit Judge, Missouri Circuit Court Thirty-second Judicial Circuit-Mo.

Thornbrugh, P. Thomas-District Judge, Oklahoma District Court Fourteenth Judicial District-Okla.

Thornburg, Lacy H.-Judge, United States District Court Western District of North Carolina-N.C.

Thorne, Larry-Judge, Texas Family District Court 317th Judicial District-Tex.

Thorne, William A., Jr.-Judge, Utah Court of Appeals-Utah

Thornsbury, Michael-Chief Judge, West Virginia Circuit Court Thirtieth Judicial Circuit-W.Va.

Thornton, Edward R., Jr.-Special Justice, Derry District Court-N.H.

Thornton, Jacqueline Ehret-Magistrate Judge, Kansas District Court Seventeenth Judicial District-Kan.

Thornton, Megan-Judge, Kentucky District Court Twenty-second Judicial District-Ky.

Thornton, Michael B.-Judge, United States Tax Court

Thornton, Ray-Associate Justice, Arkansas Supreme Court-Ark.

Thorpe, Janet C.-Judge, Florida Circuit Court Ninth Judicial Circuit-Fla.

Thorpe, Richard J.-Judge, Washington Superior Court Snohomish County-Wash.

Thorson, Toni G.-Judge, Lancaster County Separate Juvenile Court-Neb.

Thrash, Thomas W., Jr.-Judge, United States District Court Northern District of Georgia-Ga.

Thrasher, Thomas N.-Judge, Superior Court of California County of Orange-Calif.

Threadgill, Edward F.-Senior Judge, Florida District Court of Appeal-Fla.

Throesch, John-Judge, Pocahontas District Court-Ark.

Thrower, Alan W.-Judge, State Court of Baldwin County-Ga.

Thuet, William F.-Judge, Minnesota District Court First Judicial District-Minn.

Thums, Raymond F.-Judge, Wisconsin Circuit Court Marathon Circuit-Wis.

Thunberg, Melanie Wilk-Associate Justice, Rhode Island Superior Court-R.I.

Thurman, James R.-Chief Magistrate, Magistrate Court of Lee County-Ga.

Thurman, William T.-Judge, United States Bankruptcy Court District of Utah-Utah

Thurston, William J.-Circuit Judge, Illinois Circuit Court First Judicial Circuit-Ill.

Thynge, Mary Pat-Magistrate Judge, United States District Court District of Delaware-Del.

Tice, Douglas O., Jr.-Chief Judge, United States Bankruptcy Court Eastern District of Virginia-Va.

Tice, Merton B., Jr.-Judge, South Dakota Circuit Court Seventh Judicial Circuit-S.D.

Tichenor, Carroll J.-Judge, Oregon Circuit Court Twenty-fifth Judicial District-Ore.

Tidball, Jane A.-Judge, Colorado District Court First Judicial District-Colo.

Tidey, George F.-Judge, Virginia Circuit Court Fourteenth Judicial Circuit-Va.

Tidwell, G. Ernest-Senior Judge, United States District Court Northern District of Georgia-Ga.

Tidwell, Moody R.-Senior Judge, United States Court of Federal Claims

Tiede, Stuart L.-Judge, South Dakota Circuit Court Second Judicial Circuit-S.D.

Tiernan, John H.-Judge, Superior Court of California County of Colusa-Calif.

Tierney, Kevin-Judge, Connecticut Superior Court-Conn.

Tigar, Jon S.-Judge, Superior Court of California County of Alameda-Calif.

Tighe, Karen A.-Chief Judge, Bay County Probate Court-Mich.

Tignor, Robert S.-Senior Judge, Superior Court of the District of Columbia-D.C.

Tiktin, Stephen-Presiding Judge, Oregon Circuit Court Eleventh Judicial District-Ore.

Tillerson Adams, Sheila R.-Associate Judge, Circuit Court for Prince George's County, Seventh Judicial Circuit-Md.

Tillett, Jerry R.-Resident Judge, North Carolina Superior Court First Judicial Division District 1-N.C.

Tilley, N. Carlton, Jr.-Chief Judge, United States District Court Middle District of North Carolina-N.C.

Tilley, Velma-Judge, Juvenile Court of Georgia Cherokee Judicial Circuit-Ga.

Tills, Ronald H.-Judge, New York Court of Claims-N.Y.

Tilsen, Judith M.-Judge, Minnesota District Court Second Judicial District-Minn.

Tilson, Arthur R.-Judge, Pennsylvania Court of Common Pleas Thirty-eighth Judicial District-Pa.

Timberlake, George W.-Circuit Judge, Illinois Circuit Court Second Judicial Circuit-Ill.

Timko, Mary L.-Associate Juvenile Judge, Iowa District Court Third Judicial District-Ia.

Timlin, Robert James-Judge, United States District Court Central District of California-Calif.

Timm, Robert-Judge, South Dakota Circuit Court Third Judicial Circuit-S.D.

Timm, Steven B.-Judge, Nebraska County Court First Judicial District-Neb.

Timmer, Ann A. Scott-Judge, Arizona Court of Appeals Division One-Ariz.

Timmerman, Wayne S.-Judge, Florida Circuit Court Thirteenth Judicial Circuit-Fla.

Timmers, Steven M.-Chief Judge, Michigan District Court District Sixty-two A-Mich.

Timmons-Goodson, Patricia Ann-Associate Judge, North Carolina Court of Appeals-N.C.

Tin, Becky Thorne-Judge, North Carolina District Court District 26-N.C.

Tinder, John D.-Judge, United States District Court Southern District of Indiana-Ind.

Tindol, Lorene-Judge, Probate Court of Webster County and Chief Magistrate, Magistrate Court of Webster County-Ga.

Tingling, Milton A., Jr.-Justice, New York Supreme Court First Judicial District-N.Y.

Tingstad, Anders B., Jr.-Chief Judge, Michigan District Court District Ninety-eight-Mich.

Tinley, Pat-Judge, Kerr County Court-Tex.

Tinlin, Charles J.-Judge, St. Johns County Court-Fla.

Tipton, Joseph M.-Judge, Tennessee Court of Criminal Appeals Eastern Division-Tenn.

Tipton, Leland H.-Judge, Superior Court of California County of Los Angeles-Calif.

Tipton, Virgil R.-Special Judge, Oklahoma District Court Twenty-first Judicial District-Okla.

Tisdale, John H.-Associate Judge, Circuit Court for Frederick County, Sixth Judicial Circuit-Md.

Tisdale, Stephen-Judge, Eudora District Court-Ark.

Tise, Lindsay A., Jr.-Judge, Superior Court of Georgia Northern Judicial Circuit-Ga.

Tisher, Francisca P.-Judge, Superior Court of California County of Napa-Calif.

Titus, Becky A.-Judge, Florida Circuit Court Twelfth Judicial Circuit-Fla.

Titus, Kenneth C.-Resident Judge, North Carolina Superior Court Third Judicial Division District 14-N.C.

Titus, Linda S.-Judge, Minnesota District Court Fifth Judicial District-Minn.

Titus, Patricia J.-Judge, Superior Court of California County of Los Angeles-Calif.

Tjoflat, Gerald Bard-Judge, United States Court of Appeals Eleventh Circuit

Toal, Jean Hoefer-Chief Justice, South Carolina Supreme Court-S.C.

Tobias, Harry J.-Judge, Superior Court of California County of San Benito-Calif.

Tobias, Max N., Jr.-Judge, Louisiana Court of Appeal Fourth Circuit-La.

Tobias, Robert C.-Judge, Arapahoe County Court-Colo.

Tobin, Beverly Cipollo-Judge, Albany County Family Court-N.Y.

Tobin, David-Judge, Ohio Court of Common Pleas Columbiana County-Ohio

Tobin, David L.-Senior Judge, Florida Circuit Court Eleventh Judicial Circuit-Fla.

Tobin, David R.-Judge, Connecticut Superior Court-Conn.

Tobin, Karen T.-Circuit Judge, Illinois Circuit Court of Cook County-Ill.

Tobin, Richard J.-Judge, Connecticut Superior Court-Conn.

Tobin, Victor-Judge, Florida Circuit Court Seventeenth Judicial Circuit-Fla.

Tochka, Robert N.-Justice, Trial Court of Massachusetts District Court Department Essex County Lynn Division-Mass.

Todd, Alan C.-Judge, Orange County Court-Fla.

Todd, Daryl F., Sr.-Judge, New Jersey Superior Court Vicinage One-N.J.

Todd, Debra McCloskey-Judge, The Superior Court of Pennsylvania-Pa.

Todd, Gregory R.-Judge, Montana District Court Thirteenth Judicial District-Mont.

Todd, Jack A.-Chief Magistrate, Magistrate Court of Meriwether County-Ga.

Todd, James B.-Magistrate Judge, United States District Court Eastern District of Kentucky-Ky.

Todd, James D.-Chief Judge, United States District Court Western District of Tennessee-Tenn.

Todd, Jeffrey D.-Judge, Grant Superior Court-Ind.

Todd, Kathryn Doi-Associate Justice, California Court of Appeal Second District Division Two-Calif.

Todd, Kenneth G.-Judge, Monroe Circuit Court-Ind.

Todd, Randal B.-Judge, Pennsylvania Court of Common Pleas Fifth Judicial District-Pa.

Todd, Reginald F.-Chief Magistrate, Magistrate Court of Charlton County-Ga.

Todd, Ted R.-Judge, Jefferson-Switzerland Circuit Court-Ind.

Todd, William C., III-Judge, New Jersey Superior Court Vicinage One-N.J.

Todd, William F., Jr.-Judge, State Court of Rockdale County-Ga.

Todryk, Phillip P.-Reserve Judge, Wisconsin Circuit Court-Wis.

Toepfer, Thomas L.-Judge, Kansas District Court Twenty-third Judicial District-Kan.

Togliatti, Jennifer P.-Judge, Nevada District Court Eighth Judicial District-Nev.

Tognarelli, Richard L.-Associate Judge, Illinois Circuit Court Third Judicial Circuit-Ill.

Tolbert, Bruce E.-Judge, Westchester County Family Court-N.Y.

Tolbert, Susan Laker-Judge, Ohio Court of Common Pleas Hamilton County-Ohio

Tolen, Lynda A.-Judge, Michigan District Court District Five-Mich.

Tolentino, Shirley A.-Judge, New Jersey Superior Court Vicinage Six-N.J.

Toliver, Charles H., IV-Associate Judge, Delaware Superior Court New Castle County-Del.

Tollefson, Brian-Judge, Washington Superior Court Pierce County-Wash.

Tolman, Jeff-Judge, Poulsbo Municipal Court-Wash.

Tolson, Robert, Jr.-Judge, Pine Bluff District Court-Ark.

Tolton, William Jeremiah, Jr.-Judge, Florida Circuit Court First Judicial Circuit-Fla.

Tolub, Walter B.-Judge, The Civil Court of the City of New York-N.Y.

Tom, Peter-Associate Justice, New York Supreme Court Appellate Division First Judicial Department-N.Y.

Tomasello, John-Judge, New Jersey Superior Court Vicinage Fifteen-N.J.

Tomberlin, John M.-Judge, Superior Court of California County of San Bernardino-Calif.

Tombrink, Richard, Jr.-Judge, Florida Circuit Court Fifth Judicial Circuit-Fla.

Tomei, Albert-Justice, New York Supreme Court Second Judicial District-N.Y.

Tomlinson, Guy P.-Surrogate, Montgomery County Surrogate's Court-N.Y.

Tompkins, Harold-Justice, New York Supreme Court First Judicial District-N.Y.

Tompkins, James L., III-Judge, Virginia Juvenile and Domestic Relations District Court Twenty-seventh Judicial District-Va.

ALPHABETICAL NAME INDEX

Tompkins, Linda G.-Judge, Washington Superior Court Spokane County-Wash.
Tondreau, Patrick E.-Judge, Superior Court of California County of Santa Clara-Calif.
Toney, Amanda S.-Circuit Judge, Illinois Circuit Court of Cook County-Ill.
Tonigan, Henry C., III-Circuit Judge, Illinois Circuit Court Nineteenth Judicial Circuit-Ill.
Toohey, Richard-Judge, Superior Court of California County of Orange-Calif.
Toole, Elisabeth A.-Judge, Geneva City Court-N.Y.
Toole, Patrick J., Jr.-Judge, Pennsylvania Court of Common Pleas Eleventh Judicial District-Pa.
Toomer, Pinkie T.-Judge, Probate Court of Fulton County-Ga.
Toomey, John J., Jr.-Judge, Suffolk County District Court-N.Y.
Toomin, Michael P.-Circuit Judge, Illinois Circuit Court of Cook County-Ill.
Toor, Helen M.-Judge, Vermont Trial Court-Vt.
To'Oto'O, Fa'auuga-Judge, Hawaii District Court First Judicial Circuit-Hi.
Topf, William L., III-Judge, Superior Court of Arizona Maricopa County-Ariz.
Torack, Edward V.-Judge, New Jersey Superior Court Vicinage Two-N.J.
Torhorst, Allan "Pat"-Judge, Wisconsin Circuit Court Racine Circuit-Wis.
Torluemke, Kenneth W.-Associate Judge, Illinois Circuit Court Eighteenth Judicial Circuit-Ill.
Tormey, James C., III-Justice, New York Supreme Court Fifth Judicial District-N.Y.
Tornatta, Robert J.-Judge, Vanderburgh Superior Court-Ind.
Torpy, Vincent G., Jr.-Judge, Florida District Court of Appeal Fifth District-Fla.
Torreano, John A.-Chief Judge, Dickinson County Probate Court-Mich.
Torrence, John M.-Circuit Judge, Missouri Circuit Court Sixteenth Judicial Circuit-Mo.
Torres, Analisa-Judge, The Civil Court of the City of New York-N.Y.
Torres, Edwin-Justice, New York Supreme Court Twelfth Judicial District-N.Y.
Torres, Ernest C.-Chief Judge, United States District Court District of Rhode Island-R.I.
Torres, Isidore B.-Judge, Michigan Circuit Court Third Judicial Circuit-Mich.
Torres, Robert E.-Judge, The Civil Court of the City of New York-N.Y.
Torribio, John A.-Judge, Superior Court of California County of Los Angeles-Calif.
Torrisi, Fred-Judge, Alaska Superior Court Third Judicial District-Alas.
Torruella, Juan R.-Judge, United States Court of Appeals First Circuit
Toth, D. Richard-Judge, Colorado District Court Fourth Judicial District-Colo.
Tourtelot, John D.-Associate Judge, Illinois Circuit Court of Cook County-Ill.
Toussaint, Edward J., Jr.-Chief Judge, Minnesota Court of Appeals-Minn.
Toussaint, Wavny-Judge, The Civil Court of the City of New York-N.Y.
Tower, Timothy W.-Judge, Superior Court of California County of San Diego-Calif.
Tower, Winship C.-Judge, Virginia Juvenile and Domestic Relations District Court Second Judicial District-Va.
Towery, Roger E.-Judge, Texas District Court 97th Judicial District-Tex.
Town, Michael Anthony-Judge, Hawaii Circuit Court First Judicial Circuit-Hi.
Townes, Sandra L.-Associate Justice, New York Supreme Court Appellate Division Second Judicial Department-N.Y.
Townley, Thomas W.-Judge, Niles Municipal Court-Ohio
Townley-Tilson, W. H. Dale-Justice, Franklin District Court-N.H.
Townsend, J. G.-Circuit Judge, Illinois Circuit Court Sixth Judicial Circuit-Ill.
Townsend, Leonard-Judge, Michigan Circuit Court Third Judicial Circuit-Mich.
Townsend, Richard R.-Judge, Clay County Court-Fla.
Townsend, Sharon S.-Judge, Erie County Family Court-N.Y.
Townsend, Thomas N.-Judge, Superior Court of California County of Los Angeles-Calif.
Towslee, Harold Robert-Judge, Texas District Court 335th Judicial District-Tex.
Towson, William Malcolm, Sr.-Senior Judge, Superior Court of Georgia-Ga.
Tracey, Ann Marie-Judge, Ohio Court of Common Pleas Hamilton County-Ohio
Trachman, Lisa G.-Judge, Broward County Court-Fla.
Tracy, David-Judge, Federal Way Municipal Court-Wash.
Trader, Merrill C.-Associate Judge, Delaware Court of Common Pleas Kent County-Del.
Traficanti, Joseph J., Jr.-Surrogate, Ulster County Surrogate's Court-N.Y.
Trager, David G.-Judge, United States District Court Eastern District of New York-N.Y.
Trahan, John D.-Judge, Louisiana District Court Fifteenth Judicial District-La.
Trainor, Joseph A.-Associate Justice, Massachusetts Appeals Court-Mass.
Trainor, Kerry R.-Judge, Suffolk County Family Court-N.Y.
Trammell, T. A.-Judge, Basin Municipal Court-Wyo.
Tranbarger, Gary B.-Judge, Superior Court of California County of Riverside-Calif.
Trandahl, Kathleen F.-Judge, South Dakota Circuit Court Sixth Judicial Circuit-S.D.
Trapp, Robert Hill-Judge, Texas District Court 411th Judicial District-Tex.
Trask, Gloria Connor-Judge, Superior Court of California County of Riverside-Calif.
Trauger, Aleta A.-Judge, United States District Court Middle District of Tennessee-Tenn.
Travers, Wenda Kavanagh-Judge, Virginia General District Court Thirty-first Judicial District-Va.
Travis, Alan C.-Judge, Ohio Court of Common Pleas Franklin County-Ohio
Travis, Charles M.-Circuit Judge, Illinois Circuit Court of Cook County-Ill.
Travis, Neil Maurice-Judge, Livingston City Court-Mont.
Trawick, Daryl E.-Judge, Florida Circuit Court Eleventh Judicial Circuit-Fla.
Trawick, Gary E.-Special Judge, North Carolina Superior Court-N.C.
Traxler, William B., Jr.-Judge, United States Court of Appeals Fourth Circuit
Traylor, Chet D.-Justice, Supreme Court of Louisiana-La.
Traynor, J. Michael-Judge, Florida Circuit Court Seventh Judicial Circuit-Fla.
Trebesch, Dean-Judge, Superior Court of Arizona Maricopa County-Ariz.
Trebets, John Frank-Judge, Mentor Municipal Court-Ohio
Treece, Randolph F.-Magistrate Judge, United States District Court Northern District of New York-N.Y.
Trejo, Alma-Judge, El Paso County Criminal Court at Law No. 1-Tex.
Trembath, James R.-Judge, Superior Court of California County of Contra Costa-Calif.
Trent, Earl W., Jr.-Judge, Pennsylvania Court of Common Pleas First Judicial District-Pa.
Trentacosta, Robert J.-Judge, Superior Court of California County of San Diego-Calif.
Tressler, Paul W.-Judge, Pennsylvania Court of Common Pleas Thirty-eighth Judicial District-Pa.
Treu, Rolf Michael-Judge, Superior Court of California County of Los Angeles-Calif.
Triana, Gisela D.-Judge, Travis County Court at Law No. 5-Tex.
Triarsi, John S.-Judge, New Jersey Superior Court Vicinage Twelve-N.J.
Tribble, William L., Sr.-Judge, Juvenile Court of Georgia Dublin Judicial Circuit-Ga.
Trible, Peter L.-Judge, Virginia General District Court Fifteenth Judicial District-Va.
Trice, John A.-Judge, Superior Court of California County of San Luis Obispo-Calif.
Trickey, Michael-Judge, Washington Superior Court King County-Wash.
Trigg, Linda S.-Magistrate Judge, Kansas District Court Tenth Judicial District-Kan.
Trimble, James F.-Chief Magistrate, Magistrate Court of Butts County-Ga.
Trimble, James T., Jr.-Senior Judge, United States District Court Western District of Louisiana-La.
Trimble, Thomas-Presiding Judge, South Dakota Circuit Court Seventh Judicial Circuit-S.D.
Trimboli, Mary Grace-Judge, Toledo Municipal Court-Ohio
Triozzi, Robert J.-Judge, Cleveland Municipal Court-Ohio
Tripp, Alfred M.-Judge, Virginia General District Court Fourth Judicial District-Va.
Tripp, Gregory J.-Judge, Spokane District Court Spokane County and Judge, Cheney and Spokane Municipal Courts-Wash.
Tripp, Susan M.-Judge, Oregon Circuit Court Third Judicial District-Ore.
Triska, Richard E.-Justice of the Peace, Linn County Justice Court-Ore.
Tristano, Sandra-Circuit Judge, Illinois Circuit Court of Cook County-Ill.
Trivett, Larry M.-Judge, Marysville Municipal Court-Wash.
Trockman, Wayne S.-Judge, Vanderburgh Superior Court-Ind.
Troia, Joseph S.-Judge, Nebraska District Court Fourth Judicial District-Neb.
Troiano, James G.-Judge, New Jersey Superior Court Vicinage Five-N.J.
Trombley, Wilson J.-Judge, Connecticut Superior Court-Conn.
Trombly, Charles W.-Justice, Trial Court of Massachusetts Land Court Department-Mass.
Trompeter, Philip-Judge, Virginia Juvenile and Domestic Relations District Court Twenty-third Judicial District-Va.
Trosch, Louis A., Jr.-Judge, North Carolina District Court District 26-N.C.
Trott, Stephen S.-Judge, United States Court of Appeals Ninth Circuit
Trotto, Hertha C.-Judge, Suffolk County District Court-N.Y.
Trout, Linda Copple-Chief Justice, Idaho Supreme Court-Ida.
Trout, Robert L.-Associate Circuit Judge, Missouri Circuit Court Sixteenth Judicial Circuit-Mo.
Troutman, Conrad, Jr.-Judge, Tennessee Circuit Court Eighth Judicial District-Tenn.
Troutman, Shirley-Judge, Erie County Court-N.Y.
Trowbridge, C. Pfeiffer-Senior Judge, Florida Circuit Court Nineteenth Judicial Circuit-Fla.
Troy, Joseph M.-Judge, Wisconsin Circuit Court Outagamie Circuit-Wis.
Troy, Paul E.-Associate Justice, Trial Court of Massachusetts Superior Court Department-Mass.
Trucilla, John J.-Judge, Pennsylvania Court of Common Pleas Sixth Judicial District-Pa.
Trude, William W., Jr.-Judge, Kentucky Circuit Court Twenty-third Judicial Circuit-Ky.
Trudo, Martha Jane-Judge, Texas District Court 264th Judicial District-Tex.
Truitt, John R.-Associate Judge, Illinois Circuit Court Seventeenth Judicial Circuit-Ill.
Trujillo, Michael H.-Judge, Rio Grande County Court-Colo.
Trujillo, Richard J.-Judge, Superior Court of Arizona Maricopa County-Ariz.
Trujillo, Victor P.-Justice of the Peace, Hawthorne Justices' Court-Nev.
Trumbull, Patricia V.-Magistrate Judge, United States District Court Northern District of California-Calif.
Trump, Russell G.-Justice of the Peace, Douglas County Justice Court-Ore.
Trusty, Frank-Judge, Kentucky District Court Sixteenth Judicial District-Ky.
Tschiember, Georgia A.-Judge, Suffolk County District Court-N.Y.
Tsenin, Kay-Judge, Superior Court of California City and County of San Francisco-Calif.
Tsoucalas, Nicholas-Senior Judge, United States Court of International Trade
Tucker, Elton G.-Judge, North Carolina District Court District 5-N.C.

Tucker, Joseph B.-Senior Judge, Superior Court of Georgia-Ga.
Tucker, Josephine Staton-Judge, Superior Court of California County of Orange-Calif.
Tucker, Kimbrell Kelly-Judge, North Carolina District Court District 12-N.C.
Tucker, Loren-Judge, Montana District Court Fifth Judicial District-Mont.
Tucker, Marcus O., Jr.-Judge, Superior Court of California County of Los Angeles-Calif.
Tucker, Michael-Judge, Ohio Court of Common Pleas Montgomery County-Ohio
Tucker, Paul A.-Judge, Virginia Juvenile and Domestic Relations District Court Twenty-fifth Judicial District-Va.
Tucker, Petrese Brown-Judge, United States District Court Eastern District of Pennsylvania-Pa.
Tucker, Thomas J.-Judge, United States Bankruptcy Court Eastern District of Michigan-Mich.
Tucker, Thomas M.-Associate Judge, Illinois Circuit Court of Cook County-Ill.
Tucker, Tim-Judge, South Dakota Circuit Court Third Judicial Circuit-S.D.
Tuggle, Thomas M.-Chief Judge, Kansas District Court Twelfth Judicial District-Kan.
Tuitt, Alison Y.-Judge, The Civil Court of the City of New York-N.Y.
Tully, John Patrick-Judge, Illinois Appellate Court First Judicial District Division Six-Ill.
Tumas, Alison Whitmer-Associate Judge, Delaware Family Court New Castle County-Del.
Tungate, Sherri L. E.-Circuit Judge, Illinois Circuit Court Fourth Judicial Circuit-Ill.
Tungate, Susan Sumner-Circuit Judge, Illinois Circuit Court Twenty-first Judicial Circuit-Ill.
Tunheim, John R.-Judge, United States District Court District of Minnesota-Minn.
Tunis, Dava J.-Judge, Dade County Court-Fla.
Tunstall, Billy A., Jr.-Judge, South Carolina Family Court Eighth Judicial Circuit-S.C.
Turbeville, R. Wright-Judge, South Carolina Family Court Third Judicial Circuit-S.C.
Turbow, Daniel-Judge, New York City Family Court-N.Y.
Turchin, Carolyn-Magistrate Judge, United States District Court Central District of California-Calif.
Turcotte, David T.-Justice, Trial Court of Massachusetts District Court Department Bristol County Fall River Division-Mass.
Tureau, Ralph-Judge, Louisiana District Court Twenty-third Judicial District-La.
Turgeon, Jeannine-Judge, Pennsylvania Court of Common Pleas Twelfth Judicial District-Pa.
Turk, James Clinton-Senior Judge, United States District Court Western District of Virginia-Va.
Turk, Robert M. D.-Chief Judge, Virginia Circuit Court Twenty-seventh Judicial Circuit-Va.
Turkelson, Eugene I.-Chief Judge, Ogemaw County Probate Court-Mich.
Turkington, Edna M.-Circuit Judge, Illinois Circuit Court of Cook County-Ill.
Turnbach, Edward J.-Judge, New Jersey Superior Court Vicinage Fourteen-N.J.
Turnbull, John A.-Judge, Tennessee Circuit Court Thirteenth Judicial District-Tenn.
Turnbull, John Grason, II-Circuit Administrative Judge, Circuit Court for Baltimore County, Third Judicial Circuit-Md.
Turnbull, Kent D.-Judge, Nebraska County Court Eleventh Judicial District-Neb.
Turner, Alvin, Jr.-Judge, Louisiana District Court Twenty-third Judicial District-La.
Turner, David Jasper, Jr.-Judge, Juvenile Court of Georgia Coweta Judicial Circuit-Ga.
Turner, Debra Kaplan-Judge, Superior Court of Georgia Gwinnett Judicial Circuit-Ga.
Turner, Edward M., III-Judge, Virginia General District Court Twenty-seventh Judicial District-Va.
Turner, Eugene C.-Judge, Collier County Court-Fla.
Turner, George B.-Judge, Brevard County Court-Fla.
Turner, H. Haywood, III-Chief Magistrate, Magistrate Court of Muscogee County and Judge, Municipal Court of Columbus-Ga.
Turner, James T.-Judge, United States Court of Federal Claims
Turner, Jerold L.-Judge, Superior Court of California County of Kern-Calif.
Turner, Jerry L.-Judge, Washington County District Court-Ala.
Turner, John-Judge, Connecticut Superior Court-Conn.
Turner, John D., Jr.-Circuit Judge, Illinois Circuit Court of Cook County-Ill.
Turner, John R.-Judge, Superior Court of Georgia Ogeechee Judicial Circuit-Ga.
Turner, John W.-Judge, Illinois Appellate Court Fourth Judicial District-Ill.
Turner, Joseph E.-Judge, North Carolina District Court District 18-N.C.
Turner, Kelly D.-Judge, State Court of Lowndes County-Ga.
Turner, Larry Gibbs-Judge, Florida Circuit Court Eighth Judicial Circuit-Fla.
Turner, Linda D.-Associate Judge, Superior Court of the District of Columbia-D.C.
Turner, Louie H., Jr.-Judge, Alabama Circuit Court Seventh Judicial Circuit-Ala.
Turner, Matthew J.-Judge, Troy City Court-N.Y.
Turner, Paul A.-Presiding Justice, California Court of Appeal Second District Division Five-Calif.
Turner, R. Leslie-Judge, North Carolina District Court District 8-N.C.
Turner, Robert J.-Judge, Michigan District Court District Forty-three-Mich.
Turner, Thomas W.-Judge, Florida Circuit Court Ninth Judicial Circuit-Fla.
Turner, Valarie E.-Circuit Judge, Illinois Circuit Court of Cook County-Ill.
Turner, Virginia S.-Judge, Probate Court of Irwin County-Ga.
Turner, Wendell Ellis-Justice of the Peace, Searchlight Justices' Court-Nev.
Turnoff, William C.-Magistrate Judge, United States District Court Southern District of Florida-Fla.
Turpin, Bobby G.-Judge, Roanoke Town Court-Ind.
Turrentine, Howard B.-Senior Judge, United States District Court Southern District of California-Calif.
Turrone, Richard Charles-Judge, Superior Court of California County of Santa Clara-Calif.
Tusan, Gail S.-Judge, Superior Court of Georgia Atlanta Judicial Circuit-Ga.
Tuten, James R., Jr.-Chief Judge, Superior Court of Georgia Brunswick Judicial Circuit-Ga.
Twardowski, Thomas M.-Judge, United States Bankruptcy Court Eastern District of Pennsylvania-Pa.
Twerdy, Claire C.-Judge, Mansfield District Probate Court-Conn.
Twisselman, Kenneth C., II-Judge, Superior Court of California County of Kern-Calif.
Tygart, Frederick B.-Judge, Florida Circuit Court Fourth Judicial Circuit-Fla.
Tygrett, Howard-Judge, Texas District Court 86th Judicial District-Tex.
Tyler, Glen Allen-Judge, Virginia Circuit Court Second Judicial Circuit-Va.
Tyler, Kathy-Judge, Probate Court of Jasper County-Ga.
Tylwalk, John C.-Judge, Pennsylvania Court of Common Pleas Fifty-second Judicial District-Pa.
Tynan, Michael Anthony-Judge, Superior Court of California County of Los Angeles-Calif.
Tyner, Deborah G.-Judge, Michigan Circuit Court Sixth Judicial Circuit-Mich.
Tyre, Gwendolyn R.-Associate Justice, Trial Court of Massachusetts Juvenile Court Department Middlesex County Division-Mass.
Tyrrell, Natalie-Justice of the Peace, North Las Vegas Justices' Court-Nev.
Tyson, John Marsh-Associate Judge, North Carolina Court of Appeals-N.C.
Tyson, Ralph E.-Judge, United States District Court Middle District of Louisiana-La.
Uale, Bode Amilale-Family Court Judge, Hawaii District Court First Judicial Circuit-Hi.
Udall, David K.-Judge, Superior Court of Arizona Maricopa County-Ariz.
Ugast, Fred B.-Senior Judge, Superior Court of the District of Columbia-D.C.
Uhler, Ingrid Adamson-Judge, Superior Court of California County of San Bernardino-Calif.
Uhler, John C.-Judge, Pennsylvania Court of Common Pleas Nineteenth Judicial District-Pa.
Uhrig, Ira J.-Magistrate Judge, United States District Court Western District of Washington and Judge, Whatcom District Court Whatcom County-Wash.
Uhrmacher, Bette E.-Judge, New Jersey Superior Court Vicinage Nine-N.J.
Ulbricht, Heidi J.-Judge, Kalispell Municipal Court-Mont.
Ulfig, Cynthia L.-Judge, Superior Court of California County of Los Angeles-Calif.
Ullman, Michael S.-Judge, Superior Court of California County of Sacramento-Calif.
Ulloa, Juan-Judge, Superior Court of California County of Imperial-Calif.
Ullsvik, John M.-Judge, Wisconsin Circuit Court Jefferson Circuit-Wis.
Ulmer, Ray E., Jr.-Judge, Florida Circuit Court Sixth Judicial Circuit-Fla.
Ulrich, Lowell R.-Chief Judge, Chippewa County Probate Court-Mich.
Ulrich, Robert G.-Judge, Missouri Court of Appeals Western District-Mo.
Umhofer, Donald George-Judge, Superior Court of California County of San Luis Obispo-Calif.
Underhill, Stefan R.-Judge, United States District Court District of Connecticut-Conn.
Underwood, Bradley S.-Judge, Texas District Court 364th Judicial District-Tex.
Underwood, Olen-Judge, Texas District Court 284th Judicial District-Tex.
Underwood, William L., Jr.-Justice, New York Supreme Court Tenth Judicial District-N.Y.
Unfug, Charles-Judge, Weld County Court-Colo.
Ungaro-Benages, Ursula M.-Judge, United States District Court Southern District of Florida-Fla.
Unger, Cynda Riggins-Judge, Superior Court of California County of Solano-Calif.
Unpingco, John S.-Chief Judge, United States District Court District of Guam
Unruh, Brenda Burnham-Judge, Ohio Court of Common Pleas Summit County-Ohio
Unruh, Steve-Magistrate Judge, Kansas District Court Fifteenth Judicial District-Kan.
Unthank, G. Wix-Senior Judge, United States District Court Eastern District of Kentucky-Ky.
Upchurch, Margaret N.-Judge, Saluda County Probate Court-S.C.
Updike, James W., Jr.-Judge, Virginia Circuit Court Twenty-fourth Judicial Circuit-Va.
Uplinger, Karen M.-Judge, Syracuse City Court-N.Y.
Upp, Brian H.-Special Judge, Oklahoma District Court Seventh Judicial District-Okla.
Upson, Thomas F.-Judge, Connecticut Superior Court-Conn.
Upton, Suzanne M.-Judge, Oregon Circuit Court Twentieth Judicial District-Ore.
Uranga, Carlos A.-Judge, Superior Court of California County of Los Angeles-Calif.
Urbanek, Dale L.-Magistrate Judge, Kansas District Court Twentieth Judicial District-Kan.
Urbina, Ricardo Manuel-Judge, United States District Court District of Columbia-D.C.
Urbom, Warren K.-Senior Judge, United States District Court District of Nebraska-Neb.
Urdal, Ronald T.-Judge, Fayette Superior Court-Ind.
Ure, Jane-Judge, Superior Court of California County of Sacramento-Calif.
Urick, Walter Aleksy-Chief Judge, Oceana County Probate Court-Mich.
Ursin, Theresa L.-Associate Judge, Illinois Circuit Court Fifteenth Judicial Circuit-Ill.
Urso, Joseph J.-Circuit Judge, Illinois Circuit Court of Cook County-Ill.
Utschig, Thomas S.-Judge, United States Bankruptcy Court Western District of Wisconsin-Wis.
Utter, Terry-Justice, Lincoln County Justice of the Peace Court-Mont.
Uviller, Rena K.-Judge, New York Court of Claims-N.Y.
Vaa, Galen J.-Judge, Minnesota District Court Seventh Judicial District-Minn.

ALPHABETICAL NAME INDEX

Vaccaro, Dorothy L.-Judge, Pinellas County Court-Fla.
Vafiades, Vendean V.-Chief Judge, Maine District Court-Me.
Vahle, Chet W.-Associate Judge, Illinois Circuit Court Eighth Judicial Circuit-Ill.
Vahlenkamp, Virgil L., Jr.-Judge, Denton County Criminal Court at Law No. 2-Tex.
Vaidik, Nancy Harris-Judge, Indiana Court of Appeals Fifth District-Ind.
Vail, Sarah E.-Judge, Windsor District Probate Court-Vt.
Vaitheswaran, Anuradha-Judge, Iowa Court of Appeals-Ia.
Valasek, Kenneth G.-Judge, Pennsylvania Court of Common Pleas Thirty-third Judicial District-Pa.
Valbuena, Martin E.-Chief Magistrate, Magistrate Court of Paulding County-Ga.
Valdez, Andrew A.-Judge, Utah Juvenile Court Third Judicial District-Utah
Valdez, Rogelio-Chief Justice, Texas Court of Appeals Thirteenth District-Tex.
Valdriz, Geronimo, Jr.-Family Court Judge, Hawaii District Court Second Judicial Circuit-Hi.
Valen, Anthony-Judge, Ohio Court of Appeals Twelfth District-Ohio
Valentine, Jerald A.-Judge, New Mexico District Court Third Judicial District-N.Mex.
Valentine, Leo, Jr.-Judge, Superior Court of California County of San Diego-Calif.
Valentine, Michael J.-Judge, Virginia Juvenile and Domestic Relations District Court Nineteenth Judicial District-Va.
Valentino, Joseph D.-Justice, New York Supreme Court Seventh Judicial District-N.Y.
Van Akkeren, Timothy M.-Judge, Wisconsin Circuit Court Sheboygan Circuit-Wis.
Van Amburg, James W.-Associate Circuit Judge, Missouri Circuit Court Sixth Judicial Circuit-Mo.
Van Antwerpen, Franklin S.-Judge, United States District Court Eastern District of Pennsylvania-Pa.
Van Artsdalen, Donald W.-Senior Judge, United States District Court Eastern District of Pennsylvania-Pa.
Vanaskie, Thomas I.-Chief Judge, United States District Court Middle District of Pennsylvania-Pa.
Van Ausdall, Rice-Judge, Arkansas Circuit Court Second Judicial Circuit-Ark.
Van Bebber, G. Thomas-Senior Judge, United States District Court District of Kansas-Kan.
VanBenthuysen, Howard-Judge, Vermont Trial Court-Vt.
Van Camp, Brian R.-Judge, Superior Court of California County of Sacramento-Calif.
Vance, Richard Robert-Judge, Tennessee Circuit Court Fourth Judicial District-Tenn.
Vance, Robert S., Jr.-Judge, Alabama Circuit Court Tenth Judicial Circuit Birmingham Division-Ala.
Vance, Roy Carroll-Assistant Judge, Vermont Trial Court Caledonia County-Vt.
Vance, Sarah S.-Judge, United States District Court Eastern District of Louisiana-La.
Vance, William E.-Judge, Jackson Circuit Court-Ind.
Vance, William R.-Justice, Texas Court of Appeals Tenth District-Tex.
Vancil, David L., Jr.-Circuit Judge, Illinois Circuit Court Ninth Judicial Circuit-Ill.
Van Dam, Philip M.-Chief Judge, Michigan District Court District Seventy-five-Mich.
Van De Hey, Robert P.-Judge, Wisconsin Circuit Court Grant Circuit-Wis.
Van de North, John B. "Jack", Jr.-Judge, Minnesota District Court Second Judicial District-Minn.
Vanderbeck, James "Scott"-Judge, LaGrange Circuit Court-Ind.
Vandercook, Susan E.-Chief Judge, Jackson County Probate Court-Mich.
Van Deren, Marywave-Judge, Washington Superior Court Pierce County-Wash.
Vander Feer, John Peter-Judge, Superior Court of California County of San Bernardino-Calif.
Vandergriff, Tom J.-Judge, Tarrant County Court-Tex.
VanDerKarr, Scott D.-Judge, Franklin County Municipal Court-Ohio
Vander Lans, Judith A.-Judge, Superior Court of California County of Los Angeles-Calif.
Vanderpool, Daniel J.-Judge, Wabash Circuit Court-Ind.
Vanderpool, Janna L.-Judge, Superior Court of Arizona Pinal County-Ariz.
VanderSchoor, Vic L.-Judge, Washington Superior Court Benton-Franklin Counties-Wash.
Vandersnick, Larry S.-Circuit Judge, Illinois Circuit Court Fourteenth Judicial Circuit-Ill.
Vandervort, R. Clarke-Magistrate Judge, United States District Court Southern District of West Virginia-W.Va.
Vander Wall, David G.-Judge, Superior Court of California County of Stanislaus-Calif.
Van de Veer, Philip J.-Judge, Pend Oreille District Court Pend Oreille County-Wash.
VandeWalle, Gerald W.-Chief Justice, North Dakota Supreme Court-N.D.
Van De Water, Linda-Judge, Wisconsin Circuit Court Waukesha Circuit-Wis.
VandeWiele, Mark A.-Circuit Judge, Illinois Circuit Court Fourteenth Judicial Circuit-Ill.
van Doorninck, Kitty-Ann-Judge, Washington Superior Court Pierce County-Wash.
Van Dusen, Richard William-Judge, Superior Court of California County of Los Angeles-Calif.
Van Dyck, Richard G.-District Judge, Oklahoma District Court Sixth Judicial District-Okla.
Van Dyk, Douglas-Judge, Oregon Circuit Court Fifth Judicial District-Ore.
Van Dyke, Stephen A.-Judge, Utah Juvenile Court Second Judicial District-Utah
Vanerhoef, Tyler-Judge, Dayton Municipal Court-Wyo.
Vanes, Thomas W.-Judge, Lowell Town Court-Ind.
van Gestel, Allan-Associate Justice, Trial Court of Massachusetts Superior Court Department-Mass.
Van Graafeiland, Ellsworth A.-Senior Judge, United States Court of Appeals Second Circuit
Van Hook, George Ellis, Jr.-Judge, Union County District Court-Ark.
Van Horn, Carol L.-Judge, Pennsylvania Court of Common Pleas Thirty-ninth Judicial District-Pa.
Van Horn, Kenneth-Judge, Probate Court of Chattahoochee County-Ga.
Van Landschoot, Warren R.-Judge, North Las Vegas Municipal Court-Nev.
Vanmarel, Steven P.-District Associate Judge, Iowa District Court Second Judicial District-Ia.
VanMeter, Laurance-Judge, Kentucky Circuit Court Twenty-second Judicial Circuit-Ky.
VanMiddlesworth, Douglas H.-Judge, Wayne Circuit Court-Ind.
Van Norman, Laureen K.-Judge, Nebraska Workers' Compensation Court-Neb.
Van Nortwick, William A., Jr.-Judge, Florida District Court of Appeal First District-Fla.
Vannoy, Douglas R.-Judge, Colorado District Court Thirteenth Judicial District-Colo.
Van Nuys, Heather K.-Judge, Washington Superior Court Yakima County-Wash.
Vano, James F.-Judge, Kansas District Court Tenth Judicial District-Kan.
Van Oss, Terrence R.-Judge, Superior Court of California County of San Joaquin-Calif.
Vanover, Henry A.-Judge, Virginia Circuit Court Twenty-ninth Judicial Circuit-Va.
Van Pelt, Ralph, Jr.-Judge, Superior Court of Georgia Lookout Mountain Judicial Circuit-Ga.
Van Sharp, Carl-Judge, Louisiana District Court Fourth Judicial District-La.
Van Sickle, Fred-Chief Judge, United States District Court Eastern District of Washington-Wash.
Van Sicklen, Steven-Judge, Superior Court of California County of Los Angeles-Calif.
Van Stockum, Raymond P.-Judge, Superior Court of California County of San Bernardino-Calif.
Vanston, Brendan J.-President Judge, Pennsylvania Court of Common Pleas Forty-fourth Judicial District-Pa.
Van Strydonck, Thomas M.-Justice, New York Supreme Court Seventh Judicial District-N.Y.
Van Tine, Rena M.-Associate Judge, Illinois Circuit Court of Cook County-Ill.
Vantrease, E. Kyle-Circuit Judge, Illinois Circuit Court Second Judicial Circuit-Ill.
Van Ullen, Stephen J.-Judge, Cohoes City Court-N.Y.
Van Voorhis, Bruce-Judge, Superior Court of California County of Contra Costa-Calif.
Van Winkle, James-Judge, Reno Municipal Court-Nev.
Van Zee, Arlen J.-District Associate Judge, Iowa District Court Seventh Judicial District-Ia.
Varco, Robert B.-Judge, Minnesota District Court Tenth Judicial District-Minn.
Vardaro, Anthony J.-Judge, Pennsylvania Court of Common Pleas Thirtieth Judicial District-Pa.
Varga, James Michael-Circuit Judge, Illinois Circuit Court of Cook County-Ill.
Vargas, Luis Rafael-Judge, Superior Court of California County of San Diego-Calif.
Vargas, Robert J.-Judge, Nueces County Court at Law No. 1-Tex.
Varin, John F.-Judge, Idaho District Court Fifth Judicial District Magistrate Division-Ida.
Varlan, Thomas A.-Judge, United States District Court Eastern District of Tennessee-Tenn.
Varney, Robert Charles-Justice, Southern Carroll County District Court-N.H.
Varoutsos, George D.-Chief Judge, Virginia Juvenile and Domestic Relations District Court Seventeenth Judicial District-Va.
Vartabedian, Steven M.-Associate Justice, California Court of Appeal Fifth District-Calif.
Vasington, Paul M.-Judge Referee, Connecticut Superior Court-Conn.
Vasquez, Emily Elizabeth-Judge, Superior Court of California County of Sacramento-Calif.
Vasquez, Juan Flores-Judge, United States Tax Court
Vasquez, Raul-Judge, Texas District Court 111th Judicial District-Tex.
Vasquez-Gardner, Juanita A.-Judge, Texas District Court 399th Judicial District-Tex.
Vassar, Joe Sam-District Judge, Oklahoma District Court Twenty-fourth Judicial District-Okla.
Vassar, Paul-District Judge, Oklahoma District Court Twenty-third Judicial District-Okla.
Vaughan, Barry Leon-Circuit Judge, Illinois Circuit Court Second Judicial Circuit-Ill.
Vaughan, David B.-Justice, New York Supreme Court Second Judicial District-N.Y.
Vaughan, James N.-Chief Judge, Maryland District Court-Md.
Vaughan, Michelle-Judge, Juvenile Court of Georgia Enotah Judicial Circuit-Ga.
Vaughey, Cornelius J.-Administrative Judge, Maryland District Court District Six-Md.
Vaughn, Clarence R., Jr.-Senior Judge, Superior Court of Georgia-Ga.
Vaughn, Dan L.-Judge, Florida Circuit Court Nineteenth Judicial Circuit-Fla.
Vaughn, Donald G.-Judge, Thorntown Town Court-Ind.
Vaughn, James T., Jr.-Resident Judge, Delaware Superior Court Kent County-Del.
Vaughn, Kirk A.-Judge, Louisiana District Court Thirty-fourth Judicial District-La.
Vaughn, Mark W.-Judge, Bankruptcy Appellate Panel First Circuit and Chief Judge, United States Bankruptcy Court District of New Hampshire-N.H.
Vaughn, Thomas L.-Judge, Virginia General District Court Twelfth Judicial District-Va.
Vaughn, Timothy J.-Associate Justice, New Hampshire Superior Court-N.H.
Vaught, Larry D.-Judge, Arkansas Court of Appeals-Ark.
Vazquez, Martha-Judge, United States District Court District of New Mexico-N.Mex.
Vazquez, Peter J.-Judge, New Jersey Superior Court Vicinage Five-N.J.
Veals, Craig Elliott-Judge, Superior Court of California County of Los Angeles-Calif.
Veasey, E. Norman-Chief Justice, Delaware Supreme Court-Del.
Vecchiarelli, Nancy A.-Magistrate Judge, United States District Court Northern District of Ohio-Ohio
Vecchio, Steven G.-Associate Judge, Illinois Circuit Court Seventeenth Judicial Circuit-Ill.

Veenstra, Lynette B.-Associate Circuit Judge, Missouri Circuit Court Forty-fourth Judicial Circuit-Mo.
Vega, Raul-Circuit Judge, Illinois Circuit Court of Cook County-Ill.
Vega, Valorie-Judge, Nevada District Court Eighth Judicial District-Nev.
Vehlow, John C.-Judge, Idaho District Court Fourth Judicial District Magistrate Division-Ida.
Veiga, Aurendina G.-Magistrate, Rhode Island Traffic Tribunal-R.I.
Vela, Filemon B.-Senior Judge, United States District Court Southern District of Texas-Tex.
Vela, Rose-Judge, Texas District Court 148th Judicial District-Tex.
Velasco, Bernardo P.-Magistrate Judge, United States District Court District of Arizona-Ariz.
Velasquez, David Charles-Judge, Superior Court of California County of Orange-Calif.
Velasquez, Jose A.-Judge, Superior Court of California County of Monterey-Calif.
Velasquez, Juan, II-Judge, Victoria County Court at Law No. 2-Tex.
Velazquez, Hector R.-Judge, New Jersey Superior Court Vicinage Six-N.J.
Velis, Peter A.-Associate Justice, Trial Court of Massachusetts Superior Court Department-Mass.
Velure, Lyle C.-Judge, Oregon Circuit Court Second Judicial District-Ore.
Vena, Thomas R.-Judge, New Jersey Superior Court Vicinage Five-N.J.
Venezia, Deborah J.-Judge, New Jersey Superior Court Vicinage Eight-N.J.
Venezia, Donald R.-Judge, New Jersey Superior Court Vicinage Two-N.J.
Venne, Donald J.-Judge, Minnesota District Court Tenth Judicial District-Minn.
Venso, Norma-Judge, Texas District Court 56th Judicial District-Tex.
Venters, Daniel J.-Judge, Kentucky Circuit Court Twenty-eighth Judicial Circuit-Ky.
Venters, Jerry W.-Judge, United States Bankruptcy Court Western District of Missouri-Mo.
Venzer, Ellen Sue-Judge, Dade County Court-Fla.
Vera, Eloy-Judge, Starr County Court-Tex.
Veras, Sonia M.-Judge, Suffolk County District Court-N.Y.
Verby, Steven-Judge, Idaho District Court First Judicial District-Ida.
Vercillo, Damian J.-Judge, Ohio Court of Common Pleas Ashland County-Ohio
Verdin, Maria del Mar-Judge, Superior Court of Arizona Maricopa County-Ariz.
Vergeront, Margaret J.-Presiding Judge, Wisconsin Court of Appeals District Four-Wis.
Verhey, Elizabeth-Judge, Tacoma Municipal Court-Wash.
Verin, Eugene R.-Judge, Alabama Circuit Court Tenth Judicial Circuit Bessemer Division-Ala.
Verkamp, Stephen L.-Magistrate Judge, United States District Court District of Arizona-Ariz.
Verniero, Peter G.-Associate Justice, Supreme Court of New Jersey-N.J.
Vernon, Susan-Judge, Monroe County Court-Fla.
Versaci, Vincent W.-Judge, Schenectady City Court-N.Y.
Versluis, Peter P.-Chief Judge, Michigan District Court District Fifty-nine-Mich.
Vertefeuille, Christine S.-Associate Justice, Connecticut Supreme Court-Conn.
Vescovo, Diane K.-Magistrate Judge, United States District Court Western District of Tennessee-Tenn.
Vespa, Joe R.-Circuit Judge, Illinois Circuit Court Tenth Judicial Circuit-Ill.
Vettel, Ronald W.-Judge, Ohio Court of Common Pleas Ashtabula County-Ohio
Vettori, Diane S.-Judge, Mahoning County Court-Ohio
Viar, Robert C., Jr.-Chief Judge, Virginia Juvenile and Domestic Relations District Court Twenty-seventh Judicial District-Va.
Vican, Ronald E.-President Judge, Pennsylvania Court of Common Pleas Forty-third Judicial District-Pa.
Vicencia, Michael P.-Judge, Superior Court of California County of Los Angeles-Calif.
Vichness, Paul J.-Judge, New Jersey Superior Court Vicinage Five-N.J.
Vickers, Charles M.-Chief Judge, West Virginia Circuit Court Twelfth Judicial Circuit-W.Va.
Vickers, Larry Everett-Judge, Hinsdale County Court-Colo.
Victor, A. Rex-Judge, Superior Court of California County of San Bernardino-Calif.
Victor, Paul A.-Justice, New York Supreme Court Twelfth Judicial District-N.Y.
Victory, Jeffrey P.-Justice, Supreme Court of Louisiana-La.
Vidal, Frances R.-Justice of the Peace, Smith Valley Justices' Court and Judge, Yerington Municipal Court-Nev.
Vidal, Richard W.-Circuit Judge, Illinois Circuit Court Seventeenth Judicial Circuit-Ill.
Vidrine, J. Larry-Judge, Louisiana District Court Thirteenth Judicial District-La.
Vieregg, Arthur B., Jr.-Judge, Virginia Circuit Court Nineteenth Judicial Circuit-Va.
Vietor, Harold D.-Senior Judge, United States District Court Southern District of Iowa-Ia.
Vieux, Philip C.-Chief Judge, Kansas District Court Twenty-fifth Judicial District-Kan.
Vigil, Michael E.-Judge, New Mexico District Court First Judicial District-N.Mex.
Vigil, Barbara J.-Judge, New Mexico District Court First Judicial District-N.Mex.
Vigil, Carol J.-Judge, New Mexico District Court First Judicial District-N.Mex.
Vigil, John J.-Judge, Colorado District Court Seventeenth Judicial District-Colo.
Vigil, Michael E.-Judge, New Mexico Court of Appeals-N.Mex.
Vigna, Rosalie-Judge, Colorado District Court Tenth Judicial District-Colo.
Vilardi, Alice-Judge, Superior Court of California County of Alameda-Calif.
Villa, Carlos-Judge, El Paso County Court at Law No. 5-Tex.
Villalpando, Jesse M.-Judge, Lake Superior Court-Ind.
Villano, Barbara Ann-Judge, New Jersey Superior Court Vicinage Fourteen-N.J.
Villanti, Craig C.-Judge, Florida Circuit Court Sixth Judicial Circuit-Fla.
Villanueva, Charles E.-Retired Judge, New Jersey Superior Court-N.J.
Villanueva, Jose A.-Judge, Ohio Court of Common Pleas Cuyahoga County-Ohio
Villarreal, Luis Mario-Judge, Superior Court of California County of Solano-Calif.
Villarreal, Lydia-Judge, Superior Court of California County of Monterey-Calif.
Villarreal, Stephen C.-Judge, Superior Court of Arizona Pima County-Ariz.
Villegas, George R.-Judge, The Civil Court of the City of New York-N.Y.
Vincent, Charles M.-Judge, North Carolina District Court District 3A-N.C.
Vincent, David Lee, III-Circuit Judge, Missouri Circuit Court Twenty-first Judicial Circuit-Mo.
Vincent, Odessa F.-Associate Judge, Superior Court of the District of Columbia-D.C.
Vincent, Teresa H.-Judge, North Carolina District Court District 18-N.C.
Vines, Carlton H.-Judge, State Court of Chattooga County-Ga.
Vining, Mark-Judge, Kansas District Court Eighteenth Judicial District-Kan.
Vining, Robert L., Jr.-Senior Judge, United States District Court Northern District of Georgia-Ga.
Vinson, Roger-Chief Judge, United States District Court Northern District of Florida-Fla.
Vinson, Virginia A.-Judge, Alabama Circuit Court Tenth Judicial Circuit Birmingham Division-Ala.
Violante, Mark Anthony-Chief Judge, Niagara Falls City Court-N.Y.
Virga, Michael G.-Judge, Superior Court of California County of Sacramento-Calif.
Virzi, Vito A.-Justice, Trial Court of Massachusetts District Court Department Worcester County Winchendon Division-Mass.
Visalli, Joseph C.-Judge, New Jersey Superior Court Vicinage One-N.J.
Viscardi, Gerard C.-Judge, Rio Blanco County Court-Colo.
Visitacion-Lewis, Laura-Justice, New York Supreme Court First Judicial District-N.Y.
Vitale, Jack-Chief Judge, Michigan District Court District One-Mich.
Vitale, Linda-Judge, Florida Circuit Court Seventeenth Judicial Circuit-Fla.
Vitaliano, Eric N.-Judge, The Civil Court of the City of New York-N.Y.
Vittitow, Robert C.-Judge, Arkansas Circuit Court Tenth Judicial Circuit-Ark.
Vitunac, Ann E.-Magistrate Judge, United States District Court Southern District of Florida-Fla.
Viviano, Antonio P.-Judge, Michigan Circuit Court Sixteenth Judicial Circuit-Mich.
Vlack, Edward F., III-Judge, Wisconsin Circuit Court St. Croix Circuit-Wis.
Vlahos, Kosta N.-Judge, Mississippi Circuit Court Second Judicial District-Miss.
Vlavianos, Richard-Judge, Superior Court of California County of San Joaquin-Calif.
Voccola, Kathleen A.-Associate Justice, Rhode Island Family Court-R.I.
Vocke, Timothy Louis-Reserve Judge, Wisconsin Circuit Court-Wis.
Voelker, Raymond F.-Judge, Cheshire District Probate Court-Conn.
Voet, Raymond P.-Chief Judge, Michigan District Court District Sixty-four A-Mich.
Vogel, Charles S.-Administrative Presiding Justice, California Court of Appeal Second District and Presiding Justice, California Court of Appeal Second District Division Four-Calif.
Vogel, Christine K.-Judge, Hillsborough County Court-Fla.
Vogel, Gayle Nelson-Judge, Iowa Court of Appeals-Ia.
Vogel, Miriam A.-Associate Justice, California Court of Appeal Second District Division One-Calif.
Vogel, Netti C.-Associate Justice, Rhode Island Superior Court-R.I.
Vogel, Richard J.-District Judge, Iowa District Court Eighth Judicial District-Ia.
Vogell, Constance J.-Judge, Westbrook District Probate Court-Conn.
Vogelson, M. Allan-Judge, New Jersey Superior Court Vicinage Four-N.J.
Vogt, Eddie J.-Judge, Kendall County Court-Tex.
Vogt, JoAnn L.-Judge, Colorado Court of Appeals-Colo.
Vogt, John F.-Judge, Superior Court of California County of Fresno-Calif.
Voigt, Barton R.-Justice, Wyoming Supreme Court-Wyo.
Volden, Roseanna K.-Magistrate Judge, Kansas District Court Twenty-sixth Judicial District-Kan.
Volkert, Donald J., Jr.-Judge, New Jersey Superior Court Vicinage Five-N.J.
Volland, Phillip-Judge, Alaska Superior Court Third Judicial District-Alas.
Vollmer, Richard W., Jr.-Senior Judge, United States District Court Southern District of Alabama-Ala.
Vollor, Frank-Judge, Mississippi Circuit Court Ninth Judicial District-Miss.
Volz, Edward J., Jr.-Judge, Lee County Court-Fla.
von der Heydt, James A.-Senior Judge, United States District Court District of Alaska-Alas.
Von Doenhoff, Robert Christopher-Judge, Houston County Court-Tex.
Vonhof, Gary L.-Judge, Florida Circuit Court Fifteenth Judicial Circuit-Fla.
Von Wald, Jack R.-Judge, South Dakota Circuit Court Fifth Judicial Circuit-S.D.
Voorhees, Richard L.-Judge, United States District Court Western District of North Carolina-N.C.
Vorhees, Marianne L.-Judge, Delaware Circuit Court-Ind.
Voris, Michael J.-Judge, Ohio Court of Common Pleas Clermont County-Ohio
Vortmann, Paul Anthony-Judge, Superior Court of California County of Tulare-Calif.
Votendahl, Jerry A.-Judge, Walla Walla District Court Walla Walla County-Wash.
Votolato, Arthur N.-Chief Judge, Bankruptcy Appellate Panel First Circuit and Judge, United States Bankruptcy Court District of Rhode Island-R.I.

ALPHABETICAL NAME INDEX

Vowell, J. Scott-Presiding Judge, Alabama Circuit Court Tenth Judicial Circuit Birmingham Division-Ala.

Voy, William O.-Judge, Nevada District Court Eighth Judicial District-Nev.

Voyles, Sadie W.-Judge, Probate Court of Grady County-Ga.

Vrabel, Paul M.-Justice, Trial Court of Massachusetts District Court Department Berkshire County Northern Berkshire Division-Mass.

Vratil, Kathryn H.-Judge, United States District Court District of Kansas-Kan.

Vukovich, Joseph J.-Judge, Ohio Court of Appeals Seventh District-Ohio

Vuvunas, Emmanuel J.-Judge, Wisconsin Circuit Court Racine Circuit-Wis.

Wachs, Jeffrey Michael-Associate Judge, Maryland District Court District Seven-Md.

Wachter, A. J.-Judge, Kansas District Court Eleventh Judicial District-Kan.

Wacker, Robert A.-Judge, King District Court East Division King County-Wash.

Wadas, Kenneth J.-Circuit Judge, Illinois Circuit Court of Cook County-Ill.

Waddell, Jerry F.-Chief Judge, North Carolina District Court District 3B-N.C.

Waddell, Robert P. "Bobby"-Judge, Louisiana District Court First Judicial District-La.

Wade, Gary R.-Judge, Tennessee Court of Criminal Appeals Eastern Division-Tenn.

Wade, Henry, Jr.-Judge, Texas District Court 292nd Judicial District-Tex.

Wade, John P.-Judge, Superior Court of California County of San Bernardino-Calif.

Wade, Kristin-Judge, Dallas County Criminal Court of Appeals No. 1-Tex.

Wade, Len A.-Judge, Texas District Court 141st Judicial District-Tex.

Wadel, Peter J.-Chief Judge, Michigan District Court District Seventy-nine-Mich.

Wadleigh, Ralph N.-Judge, Otero County Court-Colo.

Wagenbach, Larry D.-Judge, Fort Bend County Court at Law No. 1-Tex.

Wages, Christopher-Judge, Buffalo Municipal Court-Wyo.

Wagner, A. J.-Judge, Ohio Court of Common Pleas Montgomery County-Ohio

Wagner, Annice M.-Chief Judge, District of Columbia Court of Appeals-D.C.

Wagner, Jeffrey A.-Judge, Wisconsin Circuit Court Milwaukee Circuit-Wis.

Wagner, Jerry-Judge Referee, Connecticut Superior Court-Conn.

Wagner, John F., Jr.-Judge, Pennsylvania Court of Common Pleas Fourteenth Judicial District-Pa.

Wagner, Lynnita K. C.-Judge, Ohio Court of Common Pleas Miami County-Ohio

Wagner, Marguerite L.-Judge, Superior Court of California County of San Diego-Calif.

Wagner, Mary K.-Judge, Wisconsin Circuit Court Kenosha Circuit-Wis.

Wagner, Richard-Judge, Nevada District Court Sixth Judicial District-Nev.

Wagoner, James R.-Judge, Superior Court of California County of El Dorado-Calif.

Waguespack, Zorraine M.-Judge, Louisiana District Court Twenty-first Judicial District-La.

Wahl, Eric J.-Judge, Wisconsin Circuit Court Eau Claire Circuit-Wis.

Waickowski, Paul S.-First Justice, Trial Court of Massachusetts District Court Department Worcester County Westborough Division-Mass.

Wainwright, Dale-Justice, Texas Supreme Court-Tex.

Wainwright, George L., Jr.-Associate Justice, Supreme Court of North Carolina-N.C.

Waite, Cheryl L.-Judge, Ohio Court of Appeals Seventh District-Ohio

Waite, D. Lanny-Justice of the Peace, Moapa Valley Justices' Court-Nev.

Waites, John E.-Judge, United States Bankruptcy Court District of South Carolina-S.C.

Wakefield, Dana U.-Judge, Denver Juvenile Court-Colo.

Wakefield, Elizabeth-Judge, Vermilion Municipal Court-Ohio

Wakefield, Frank-Judge, Kentucky District Court Forty-ninth Judicial District-Ky.

Waks, David-Judge, New Jersey Superior Court Vicinage Eleven-N.J.

Waldeck, Joseph R.-Associate Judge, Illinois Circuit Court Nineteenth Judicial Circuit-Ill.

Walden, Scott-Circuit Judge, Illinois Circuit Court Eighth Judicial Circuit-Ill.

Waldhausen, Bruce-Justice, Roosevelt County Justice of the Peace Court and Judge, Culbertson and Poplar City Courts-Mont.

Waldman, Daniel M.-Judge, New Jersey Superior Court Vicinage Nine-N.J.

Waldman, Jay C.-Judge, United States District Court Eastern District of Pennsylvania-Pa.

Waldon, Alton R., Jr.-Judge, New York Court of Claims-N.Y.

Waldorf, Marcia J.-Family Court Judge, Hawaii Circuit Court First Judicial Circuit-Hi.

Waldrip, Wade-Judge, Wyoming Circuit Court Second Judicial District, Carbon County and Judge, Dixon Municipal Court-Wyo.

Waldron, Dennis J.-Judge, Louisiana District Court Orleans Parish Criminal District-La.

Waldron, Stephen M.-Associate Judge, Circuit Court for Harford County, Third Judicial Circuit-Md.

Waldron, Thomas F.-Judge, Bankruptcy Appellate Panel Sixth Circuit and Chief Judge, United States Bankruptcy Court Southern District of Ohio-Ohio

Walke, Geary L.-Special Judge, Oklahoma District Court Seventh Judicial District-Okla.

Walker, Bradley C.-Judge, Minnesota District Court Fifth Judicial District-Minn.

Walker, David Seth-Senior Judge, Florida Circuit Court Sixth Judicial Circuit-Fla.

Walker, Deborah D.-Judge, New Mexico District Court Second Judicial District-N.Mex.

Walker, Dianne M.-Judge, Probate Court of Telfair County-Ga.

Walker, Edgar G.-Judge, The Civil Court of the City of New York-N.Y.

Walker, Hugh A.-Judge, Superior Court of California County of Alameda-Calif.

Walker, Jacob A., III-Judge, Alabama Circuit Court Thirty-seventh Judicial Circuit-Ala.

Walker, James D., Jr.-Judge, United States Bankruptcy Court Middle District of Georgia-Ga.

Walker, Jeff-Judge, Texas District Court 96th Judicial District-Tex.

Walker, Jennifer Bailey-Judge, West Virginia Circuit Court Thirteenth Judicial Circuit-W.Va.

Walker, Jill C.-Judge, Wakulla County Court-Fla.

Walker, John M., Jr.-Chief Judge, United States Court of Appeals Second Circuit

Walker, John R.-Judge, Louisiana District Court Thirty-second Judicial District-La.

Walker, John R.-President Judge, Pennsylvania Court of Common Pleas Thirty-ninth Judicial District-Pa.

Walker, Joseph H.-Judge, Tennessee Circuit Court Twenty-fifth Judicial District-Tenn.

Walker, Joseph M., III-Associate Justice, Trial Court of Massachusetts Superior Court Department-Mass.

Walker, Julie M. T.-Judge, City Court of Atlanta-Ga.

Walker, Karla K.-Judge, Three Forks City Court-Mont.

Walker, Keith M.-Judge, Idaho District Court Seventh Judicial District Magistrate Division-Ida.

Walker, Layne-Judge, Texas District Court 252nd Judicial District-Tex.

Walker, Linda T.-Magistrate Judge, United States District Court Northern District of Georgia-Ga.

Walker, Michael R.-Judge, Louisiana District Court First Judicial District-La.

Walker, Nathaniel-Judge, Dallas County District Court-Ala.

Walker, Neil J.-First Justice, Trial Court of Massachusetts District Court Department Middlesex County Lowell Division-Mass.

Walker, Peggy H.-Judge, Juvenile Court of Georgia Douglas Judicial Circuit-Ga.

Walker, R. Joy-Judge, Recorder's Court of DeKalb County-Ga.

Walker, Ralph A.-Retired Judge, North Carolina Court of Appeals-N.C.

Walker, Richard B.-Chief Judge, Kansas District Court Ninth Judicial District-Kan.

Walker, Robert D.-Judge, Minnesota District Court Fifth Judicial District-Minn.

Walker, Robert H.-Judge, Mississippi Circuit Court Second Judicial District-Miss.

Walker, Rodney L.-Judge, Superior Court of California County of Riverside-Calif.

Walker, Russell G., Jr.-Resident Judge, North Carolina Superior Court Fifth Judicial Division District 19B-N.C.

Walker, Sam D.-Judge, Westchester County Court-N.Y.

Walker, Sue-Justice, Texas Court of Appeals Second District-Tex.

Walker, Susan Russ-Magistrate Judge, United States District Court Middle District of Alabama-Ala.

Walker, Thomas S.-District Judge, Oklahoma District Court Twentieth Judicial District-Okla.

Walker, Tracey D.-Justice, Carter County Justice of the Peace Court and Judge, Alzada and Ekalaka City Courts-Mont.

Walker, Vaughn R.-Judge, United States District Court Northern District of California-Calif.

Walker, William-Judge, Ohio Court of Common Pleas Clermont County-Ohio

Walker, William E.-Judge, Minnesota District Court Seventh Judicial District-Minn.

Wall, Alex W.-Judge, Baton Rouge City Court-La.

Wall, Caroline E.-Associate District Judge, Oklahoma District Court Fourteenth Judicial District-Okla.

Wall, Chuck-Justice, Lake County Justice of the Peace Court-Mont.

Wall, David-Judge, Nevada District Court Eighth Judicial District-Nev.

Wall, Joseph R.-Judge, Wisconsin Circuit Court Milwaukee Circuit-Wis.

Wall, Mark W.-Judge, Middletown Municipal Court-Ohio

Wall, Patrick J.-Judge, Harwinton District Probate Court-Conn.

Wall, Robert Larry-Chief Magistrate, Magistrate Court of Schley County-Ga.

Wall, Roger-Associate Circuit Judge, Missouri Circuit Court Forty-fourth Judicial Circuit-Mo.

Wall, Sarah-Judge, Juvenile Court of Georgia Oconee Judicial Circuit-Ga.

Wall, William D.-Magistrate Judge, United States District Court Eastern District of New York-N.Y.

Wallace, Allen Wilson-Senior Judge, Tennessee Trial and Appellate Courts-Tenn.

Wallace, Arthur E.-Judge, Superior Court of California County of Kern-Calif.

Wallace, Barbara W.-Presiding Judge, Missouri Circuit Court Twenty-first Judicial Circuit-Mo.

Wallace, C. G.-Judge, Nebraska County Court Twelfth Judicial District-Neb.

Wallace, Gary G.-Associate Circuit Judge, Missouri Circuit Court Forty-first Judicial Circuit-Mo.

Wallace, J. Clifford-Senior Judge, United States Court of Appeals Ninth Circuit

Wallace, Jeff M.-Presiding Judge, Oregon Circuit Court Sixth Judicial District-Ore.

Wallace, Jim-Judge, Texas District Court 263rd Judicial District-Tex.

Wallace, John E., Jr.-Associate Justice, Supreme Court of New Jersey-N.J.

Wallace, Kevin P.-Judge, DeKalb Superior Court-Ind.

Wallace, Philip Arthur-Judge, Virginia Juvenile and Domestic Relations District Court Twenty-fourth Judicial District-Va.

Wallace, Sean D.-Associate Judge, Circuit Court for Prince George's County, Seventh Judicial Circuit-Md.

Wallace, Tanya T.-Chief Judge, North Carolina District Court District 20-N.C.

Wallace, Ted-Judge, Michigan District Court District Thirty-six-Mich.

Wallace, Waddell A., III-Judge, Florida Circuit Court Fourth Judicial Circuit-Fla.

Wallach, Evan J.-Judge, United States Court of International Trade

ALPHABETICAL NAME INDEX

ALPHABETICAL NAME INDEX

Watanabe, Corinne K. A.-Associate Judge, Hawaii Intermediate Court of Appeals-Hi.
Watanabe, Michael Jiro-Magistrate Judge, United States District Court District of Colorado-Colo.
Watanabe, Wilfred K.-Judge, Hawaii Circuit Court First Judicial Circuit-Hi.
Waters, Billy J.-Judge, Juvenile Court of Georgia Alcovy Judicial Circuit-Ga.
Waters, Bruce-Judge, Wyoming Circuit Court Fifth Judicial District, Park County-Wyo.
Waters, George-Judge, Charlestown City Court-Ind.
Waters, John M., Jr.-Judge, New Jersey Superior Court Vicinage Fifteen-N.J.
Waters, John S.-Associate Circuit Judge, Missouri Circuit Court Thirty-eighth Judicial Circuit-Mo.
Waters, Lee-Judge, Texas District Court 223rd Judicial District-Tex.
Waters, Robert A.-Chief Judge, West Virginia Circuit Court Fourth Judicial Circuit-W.Va.
Waters, Sharon J.-Judge, Superior Court of California County of Riverside-Calif.
Waterstone, Mary M.-Judge, Michigan Circuit Court Third Judicial Circuit-Mich.
Watkins, David D.-Judge, State Court of Richmond County-Ga.
Watkins, Gary L.-Judge, Texas District Court 244th Judicial District-Tex.
Watkins, Thomas D.-Judge, Pennsylvania Court of Common Pleas First Judicial District-Pa.
Watkins, Thomas P.-Judge, Idaho District Court Fourth Judicial District Magistrate Division-Ida.
Watkins, William M. "Chip"-Judge, West Virginia Family Court Circuit Twenty-six-W.Va.
Watson, Barbara Roush-Judge, Portage County Municipal Court-Ohio
Watson, Barry E.-Judge, Idaho District Court First Judicial District Magistrate Division-Ida.
Watson, Cyril J.-Circuit Judge, Illinois Circuit Court of Cook County-Ill.
Watson, Dennis D.-Judge, Montgomery County Court at Law No. 1-Tex.
Watson, Floyd A.-Judge, Shelby County Court-Tex.
Watson, John M.-Judge, Superior Court of California County of Orange-Calif.
Watson, John W., III-Judge, Florida Circuit Court Seventh Judicial Circuit-Fla.
Watson, Kenton J.-Judge, Kentucky District Court Fifty-first Judicial District-Ky.
Watson, Leo A., Jr.-Associate District Judge, Oklahoma District Court Fifth Judicial District-Okla.
Watson, Michael H.-Judge, Ohio Court of Common Pleas Franklin County-Ohio
Watson, Richard O.-Senior Judge, Florida Circuit Court Seventh Judicial Circuit-Fla.
Watson, W. Bruce, Jr.-Judge, Superior Court of California County of Humboldt-Calif.
Watson, William J.-Judge, Lockport City Court-N.Y.
Watt, David W., Jr.-Circuit Judge, Illinois Circuit Court First Judicial Circuit-Ill.
Watt, Joseph M.-Chief Justice, Supreme Court of Oklahoma-Okla.
Watters, Elaine-Judge, Superior Court of California County of Sonoma-Calif.
Watters, Susan P.-Judge, Montana District Court Thirteenth Judicial District-Mont.
Wattigny, Gerard B.-Judge, Louisiana District Court Sixteenth Judicial District-La.
Wattles, Bob-Judge, Florida Circuit Court Ninth Judicial Circuit-Fla.
Watts, Pat H., Jr.-Judge, Mississippi Chancery Court Sixteenth Judicial District-Miss.
Watts, Sandra-Judge, Texas District Court 117th Judicial District-Tex.
Watts, Shirley Marie-Associate Judge, Circuit Court for Baltimore City, Eighth Judicial Circuit-Md.
Waugh, Alexander P., Jr.-Judge, New Jersey Superior Court Vicinage Eight-N.J.
Waxman, Barbara Baer-Associate Judge, Maryland District Court District One-Md.
Waxse, David J.-Magistrate Judge, United States District Court District of Kansas-Kan.
Waxter, Thomas, Jr.-Associate Judge, Circuit Court for Baltimore City, Eighth Judicial Circuit-Md.
Way, Jan A.-Judge, Kansas District Court Twenty-ninth Judicial District-Kan.
Wayman, Scott L.-Judge, Idaho District Court First Judicial District Magistrate Division-Ida.
Wayne, Roger L.-Judge, Superior Court of California County of Madera-Calif.
Weatherby, Joseph J.-Judge, Colorado District Court Thirteenth Judicial District-Colo.
Weatherby, Michael-Judge, Florida Circuit Court Fourth Judicial Circuit-Fla.
Weatherford, James L.-Senior Judge, Tennessee Appellate and Trial Courts-Tenn.
Weatherly, Julia Beth-Associate Judge, Circuit Court for Prince George's County, Seventh Judicial Circuit-Md.
Weathersby, Jane R.-Judge, Mississippi Chancery Court Ninth Judicial District-Miss.
Weaver, Brenda S.-Chief Judge, Superior Court of Georgia Appalachian Judicial Circuit-Ga.
Weaver, Elizabeth A.-Justice, Michigan Supreme Court-Mich.
Weaver, James A.-District Associate Judge, Iowa District Court Seventh Judicial District-Ia.
Weaver, John F.-Chancellor, Tennessee Chancery Court Sixth Judicial District-Tenn.
Weaver, Raymond W., Jr.-Presiding Judge, Superior Court of Arizona Yavapai County-Ariz.
Weaver, T. M. "Mike"-Chief Judge, United States Bankruptcy Court Western District of Oklahoma-Okla.
Weaver, Tim-Judge, Arkansas Circuit Court Sixteenth Judicial Circuit-Ark.
Weaver, William W.-Judge, Ohio Court of Common Pleas Lake County-Ohio
Webb, Benjamin Hays, II-Judge, West Virginia Court of Claims-W.Va.
Webb, Gordon-Judge, Arkansas Circuit Court Fourteenth Judicial Circuit-Ark.
Webb, J. David-Judge, Ohio Court of Common Pleas Paulding County-Ohio
Webb, James M.-Resident Judge, North Carolina Superior Court Fifth Judicial Division District 19B-N.C.
Webb, John R.-Judge, Colorado Court of Appeals-Colo.
Webb, Richard W.-President Judge, Pennsylvania Court of Common Pleas Fifty-sixth Judicial District-Pa.
Webb, Rodney S.-Senior Judge, United States District Court District of North Dakota-N.D.
Webb, Tom B.-Magistrate Judge, Kansas District Court Twenty-sixth Judicial District-Kan.
Webb, William A.-Magistrate Judge, United States District Court Eastern District of North Carolina-N.C.
Webb, William R.-Judge, Florida Circuit Court Sixth Judicial Circuit-Fla.
Webber, Albert G.-Circuit Judge, Illinois Circuit Court Sixth Judicial Circuit-Ill.
Webber, E. Richard-Judge, United States District Court Eastern District of Missouri-Mo.
Webber, Paul R., III-Senior Judge, Superior Court of the District of Columbia-D.C.
Webber, Troy K.-Justice, New York Supreme Court First Judicial District-N.Y.
Weber, Daniel S.-Circuit Judge, Illinois Circuit Court of Cook County-Ill.
Weber, Frederic G.-Retired Judge, New Jersey Superior Court-N.J.
Weber, Gary J.-Judge, Suffolk County Court-N.Y.
Weber, Herman Jacob, Jr.-Senior Judge, United States District Court Southern District of Ohio-Ohio
Weber, Joan P.-Judge, Superior Court of California County of San Diego-Calif.
Weber, John R.-Judge, Michigan Circuit Court Twenty-fifth Judicial Circuit-Mich.
Weber, Joseph P.-Judge, Clarksville Town Court-Ind.
Weber, Michael R.-Circuit Judge, Illinois Circuit Court Fourth Judicial Circuit-Ill.
Weber, Raymond M.-Associate Circuit Judge, Missouri Circuit Court Twenty-fourth Judicial Circuit-Mo.
Webster, Allen Joseph, Jr.-Judge, Superior Court of California County of Los Angeles-Calif.
Webster, C. Edward, II-Judge, Cody Municipal Court-Wyo.
Webster, Edward D.-Judge, Superior Court of California County of Riverside-Calif.
Webster, Hollis L.-Circuit Judge, Illinois Circuit Court Eighteenth Judicial Circuit-Ill.
Webster, Jonathan W.-Judge, Jennings Circuit Court-Ind.
Webster, Peter-Judge, Florida District Court of Appeal First District-Fla.
Wechsler, James J.-Chief Judge, New Mexico Court of Appeals-N.Mex.
Wecker, Barbara Byrd-Judge, New Jersey Superior Court Appellate Division-N.J.
Weckstein, Clifford R.-Judge, Virginia Circuit Court Twenty-third Judicial Circuit-Va.
Weddle, James G.-Judge, Kentucky Circuit Court Twenty-ninth Judicial Circuit-Ky.
Wedemeyer, Robert W.-Judge, Tennessee Court of Criminal Appeals Middle Division-Tenn.
Wedemeyer, Ted E., Jr.-Presiding Judge, Wisconsin Court of Appeals District One-Wis.
Wedoff, Eugene R.-Chief Judge, United States Bankruptcy Court Northern District of Illinois-Ill.
Weech, Charles P.-Associate Judge, Illinois Circuit Court Nineteenth Judicial Circuit-Ill.
Weedon, Jill Carpenter-Special Judge, Oklahoma District Court Second Judicial District-Okla.
Weeks, Albert H.-Judge, Probate Court of New Hampshire Cheshire County-N.H.
Weeks, Gregory A.-Resident Judge, North Carolina Superior Court Fourth Judicial Division District 12-N.C.
Weeks, James H.-Senior Judge, Superior Court of Georgia-Ga.
Weeks, John Wilson-Judge, Texas District Court 42nd Judicial District-Tex.
Weeks, Larry-Presiding Judge, Alaska Superior Court First Judicial District-Alas.
Weeks, Orrelle R.-Judge, Denver Juvenile Court-Colo.
Weeks, Renee Jones-Judge, New Jersey Superior Court Vicinage Five-N.J.
Wefald, Robert O.-Judge, North Dakota District Court South Central Judicial District-N.D.
Wefing, Dorothea O'C.-Judge, New Jersey Superior Court Appellate Division-N.J.
Wegge, William J., Jr.-Associate Circuit Judge, Missouri Circuit Court Twenty-third Judicial Circuit-Mo.
Wegner, Grant Steven-Circuit Judge, Illinois Circuit Court Sixteenth Judicial Circuit-Ill.
Wehr, William J.-Judge, Kentucky Circuit Court Seventeenth Judicial Circuit-Ky.
Wehrman, J. Gregory-Magistrate Judge, United States District Court Eastern District of Kentucky-Ky.
Weigand, Michael L.-Judge, Barberton Municipal Court-Ohio
Weighall, Roberta "Bobbie"-Justice of the Peace, Tecoma Justices' Court-Nev.
Weikert, William E.-Judge, Dubois Circuit Court-Ind.
Weil, Lorraine Murphy-Judge, United States Bankruptcy Court District of Connecticut-Conn.
Weiler, Jennifer P.-Judge, Garfield Heights Municipal Court-Ohio
Weimer, John L.-Justice, Supreme Court of Louisiana-La.
Weinberg, Claire I.-Judge, Nassau County Court-N.Y.
Weinberg, John L.-Magistrate Judge, United States District Court Western District of Washington-Wash.
Weinberg, Richard G.-Senior Judge, Florida Circuit Court Seventh Judicial Circuit-Fla.
Weinberg, Richard M.-Judge, The Criminal Court of the City of New York-N.Y.
Weiner, Alfred J.-Surrogate, Rockland County Surrogate's Court-N.Y.
Weiner, Charles R.-Senior Judge, United States District Court Eastern District of Pennsylvania-Pa.
Weiner, Marie S.-Judge, Superior Court of California County of San Mateo-Calif.

Weingart, John L.-Judge, Kansas District Court Twenty-second Judicial District-Kan.
Weinke, Steven W.-Judge, Wisconsin Circuit Court Fond du Lac Circuit-Wis.
Weinman, Bernie-Judge, Tennessee Criminal Court Thirtieth Judicial District-Tenn.
Weinshienk, Zita Leeson-Senior Judge, United States District Court District of Colorado-Colo.
Weinstein, Halee F.-Associate Judge, Maryland District Court District One-Md.
Weinstein, Jack B.-Senior Judge, United States District Court Eastern District of New York-N.Y.
Weinstein, Jeremy S.-Justice, New York Supreme Court Eleventh Judicial District-N.Y.
Weinstein, Paul H.-Circuit Administrative Judge, Circuit Court for Montgomery County, Sixth Judicial Circuit-Md.
Weinstein, Peter M.-Judge, Florida Circuit Court Seventeenth Judicial Circuit-Fla.
Weinstein, Stewart H.-Judge, New York City Family Court-N.Y.
Weintraub, Debre Katz-Judge, Superior Court of California County of Los Angeles-Calif.
Weir, Kathleen A.-Judge, Minnesota District Court Seventh Judicial District-Minn.
Weir, Robert W.-Judge, Superior Court of California County of Del Norte-Calif.
Weir, William H.-Associate Judge, Illinois Circuit Court Sixteenth Judicial Circuit-Ill.
Weis, Joseph F., Jr.-Senior Judge, United States Court of Appeals Third Circuit
Weisberg, Frederick H.-Associate Judge, Superior Court of the District of Columbia-D.C.
Weisberg, Sheldon H.-Chief Judge, Arizona Court of Appeals Division One-Ariz.
Weisberg, Stanley Martin-Judge, Superior Court of California County of Los Angeles-Calif.
Weiser, Laura Ann-Judge, Victoria County Court at Law No. 1-Tex.
Weisfield, Robert Douglas-Judge, West District Court Klickitat County-Wash.
Weisman, William R.-Judge, Superior Court of California County of Los Angeles-Calif.
Weiss, Allan B.-Justice, New York Supreme Court Eleventh Judicial District-N.Y.
Weiss, Richard-Judge, Superior Court of Arizona Mohave County-Ariz.
Weiss, Robert E.-Judge, Genesee County Probate Court-Mich.
Weissbard, Harvey-Judge, New Jersey Superior Court Appellate Division-N.J.
Weissbrodt, Arthur S.-Judge, United States Bankruptcy Court Northern District of California-Calif.
Weitzman, Jamey H.-Associate Judge, Maryland District Court District One-Md.
Welbaum, Jeffrey M.-Judge, Ohio Court of Common Pleas Miami County-Ohio
Welborn, Michael E.-Judge, Texas District Court 36th Judicial District-Tex.
Welch, A. J., Jr.-Judge, Juvenile Court of Georgia Flint Judicial Circuit-Ga.
Welch, Bill D.-Associate District Judge, Oklahoma District Court Sixteenth Judicial District-Okla.
Welch, Charles W., III-Associate Judge, Delaware Court of Common Pleas Kent County-Del.
Welch, David L.-Judge, Monroe Circuit Court-Ind.
Welch, Elizabeth-Judge, Oregon Circuit Court Fourth Judicial District-Ore.
Welch, James Michael-Judge, Superior Court of California County of San Bernardino-Calif.
Welch, James R. "Bump"-Judge, Probate Court of Marion County and Chief Magistrate, Magistrate Court of Marion County-Ga.
Welch, Jewel E., Jr.-Judge, Louisiana District Court Nineteenth Judicial District-La.
Welch, JoAnne M.-Justice, Deer Lodge County Justice of the Peace Court and Judge, Anaconda City Court-Mont.
Welch, John K.-Associate Judge, Delaware Court of Common Pleas New Castle County-Del.
Welch, Joseph R.-Circuit Justice, Trial Court of Massachusetts District Court Department-Mass.
Welch, Martin P.-Associate Judge, Circuit Court for Baltimore City, Eighth Judicial Circuit-Md.
Welch, Richard E., III-Associate Justice, Trial Court of Massachusetts Superior Court Department-Mass.
Welch, Robert L.-Circuit Judge, Illinois Circuit Court Eighth Judicial Circuit-Ill.
Welch, Samuel H., Jr.-Presiding Judge, Alabama Circuit Court Thirty-fifth Judicial Circuit-Ala.
Welch, Thomas F.-Judge, Bay County Court-Fla.
Welch, Thomas M.-Judge, Illinois Appellate Court Fifth Judicial District-Ill.
Welker, James E.-Judge, Wisconsin Circuit Court Rock Circuit-Wis.
Wellerson, Craig L.-Judge, New Jersey Superior Court Vicinage Three-N.J.
Welles, David H.-Judge, Tennessee Court of Criminal Appeals Middle Division-Tenn.
Wellington, Michael D.-Judge, Superior Court of California County of San Diego-Calif.
Wellmann, Fred W.-Judge, Minnesota District Court Third Judicial District-Minn.
Wellons, William Lindley-Chief Judge, Virginia Circuit Court Tenth Judicial Circuit-Va.
Wells, Albert E. "Gene"-Judge, Probate Court of McDuffie County-Ga.
Wells, Carol Sandra-Magistrate Judge, United States District Court Eastern District of Pennsylvania-Pa.
Wells, Charles Talley-Justice, Florida Supreme Court-Fla.
Wells, Charlotte-Judge, Superior Court of Arizona Mohave County-Ariz.
Wells, Debbie-Judge, Probate Court of Screven County-Ga.
Wells, Harold B., III-Judge, New Jersey Superior Court Appellate Division-N.J.
Wells, Jimmy D.-Judge, Walker County District Court-Ala.
Wells, Judith G.-Judge, Texas Family District Court 325th Judicial District-Tex.
Wells, Judson W., Sr.-Judge, Mobile County District Court-Ala.
Wells, Kelvin C.-Judge, Okaloosa County Court-Fla.
Wells, Kerry-Judge, Superior Court of California County of San Diego-Calif.
Wells, Lee Edward-Judge, Wisconsin Circuit Court Milwaukee Circuit-Wis.
Wells, Lesley-Judge, United States District Court Northern District of Ohio-Ohio
Wells, Linda Ann-Judge, Florida District Court of Appeal Third District-Fla.
Wells, Peter N.-Surrogate, Onondaga County Surrogate's Court-N.Y.
Wells, Richard D.-Chief Judge, Michigan District Court District Sixty-five A-Mich.
Wells, Thomas B.-Chief Judge, United States Tax Court
Welsh, Diane M.-Magistrate Judge, United States District Court Eastern District of Pennsylvania-Pa.
Welsh, James E.-Presiding Judge, Missouri Circuit Court Seventh Judicial Circuit-Mo.
Welsh, Robert A., Jr.-First Justice, Trial Court of Massachusetts District Court Department Barnstable County Orleans Division-Mass.
Welter, Daniel G.-Associate Judge, Illinois Circuit Court of Cook County-Ill.
Welty, William D.-Chief Judge, Michigan District Court District Three B-Mich.
Wendt, David R.-Judge, Lockport City Court-N.Y.
Wenell, Gary E.-District Judge, Iowa District Court Third Judicial District-Ia.
Wennet, Richard I.-Judge, Florida Circuit Court Fifteenth Judicial Circuit-Fla.
Wenzel, Glenn R.-Judge, New Jersey Superior Court Vicinage Eleven-N.J.
Wenzelman, Kendall O.-Chief Judge, Illinois Circuit Court Twenty-first Judicial Circuit-Ill.
Werdegar, Kathryn Mickle-Associate Justice, California Supreme Court-Calif.
Werlein, Ewing, Jr.-Judge, United States District Court Southern District of Texas-Tex.
Werner, Lois-Magistrate Judge, Kansas District Court Twenty-third Judicial District-Kan.
Werner, Mary M.-Justice, New York Supreme Court Tenth Judicial District-N.Y.
Werner, Richard T.-Judge, Wisconsin Circuit Court Rock Circuit-Wis.
Wernette, Richard G.-Judge, College Place Municipal Court-Wash.
Wernick, Lawrence B.-Associate Justice, Trial Court of Massachusetts Superior Court Department-Mass.
Wernick, Mark S.-Judge, Minnesota District Court Fourth Judicial District-Minn.
Wertheim, Ronald P.-Senior Judge, Superior Court of the District of Columbia-D.C.
Wertheimer, William L'E.-Judge, New Jersey Superior Court Vicinage Twelve-N.J.
Wertman, William-Judge, West Virginia Family Court Circuit Twenty-four-W.Va.
Wesley, David S.-Judge, Superior Court of California County of Los Angeles-Calif.
Wesley, John P.-Judge, Vermont Trial Court-Vt.
Wesley, Richard C.-Associate Judge, New York Court of Appeals-N.Y.
Wessel, John D.-Judge, Florida Circuit Court Fifteenth Judicial Circuit-Fla.
West, C. Gregory-Judge, Oregon Circuit Court Third Judicial District-Ore.
West, Carl J.-Judge, Superior Court of California County of Los Angeles-Calif.
West, Ernest Ray, III-Judge, Brown County Court-Tex.
West, John Andrew-Judge, Ohio Court of Common Pleas Hamilton County-Ohio
West, Joseph K.-Justice, New York Supreme Court Ninth Judicial District-N.Y.
West, Katrina-Judge, Superior Court of California County of San Bernardino-Calif.
West, Kimberly E.-Magistrate Judge, United States District Court Eastern District of Oklahoma-Okla.
West, Lee R.-Senior Judge, United States District Court Western District of Oklahoma-Okla.
West, Mickey D.-Judge, Palo Pinto County Court-Tex.
West, Patricia L.-Judge, Virginia Circuit Court Second Judicial Circuit-Va.
West, Phillip R.-Chief Judge, Superior Court of Georgia Oconee Judicial Circuit-Ga.
West, Randolph T.-Judge, Virginia Circuit Court Seventh Judicial Circuit-Va.
West, Robert E., Jr.-Judge, Black Diamond Municipal Court-Wash.
West, Russell B.-Judge, Oregon Circuit Court Tenth Judicial District-Ore.
West, Thomas G.-Judge, Connecticut Appellate Court-Conn.
West, W. Brent-Presiding Judge, Utah District Court Second Judicial District-Utah
Westbrook, Marc H.-Judge, South Carolina Circuit Court Eleventh Judicial Circuit-S.C.
Westbrook, William Jerry-Judge, Juvenile Court of Georgia Lookout Mountain Judicial Circuit-Ga.
Westbrooke, Henry W., Jr.-Circuit Judge, Missouri Circuit Court Thirty-first Judicial Circuit-Mo.
Westcott, Michael N.-Judge, Maine District Court-Me.
Wester, Robert C.-Judge, Nebraska County Court Second Judicial District-Neb.
Westfall, David S.-Judge, Ouray County Court-Colo.
Westhafer, John A.-Judge, Decatur Circuit Court-Ind.
Westhoff, Fred-Associate Circuit Judge, Missouri Circuit Court Second Judicial Circuit-Mo.
Westmoreland, Greg Baer-Judge, Matagorda County Court-Tex.
Westmoreland, Melvin K.-Judge, Superior Court of Georgia Atlanta Judicial Circuit-Ga.
Westra, Clarence, Jr.-Judge, Superior Court of California County of Kern-Calif.
Westra, Vincent Castelli-Chief Judge, Michigan District Court District Eight and Judge, Michigan District Court District Eight Division Three-Mich.
Wetenkamp, Jean High-Judge, Superior Court of California County of Santa Clara-Calif.
Wetherell, Michael-Judge, Idaho District Court Fourth Judicial District-Ida.
Wetsel, John E., Jr.-Chief Judge, Virginia Circuit Court Twenty-sixth Judicial Circuit-Va.
Wettick, R. Stanton, Jr.-Judge, Pennsylvania Court of Common Pleas Fifth Judicial District-Pa.
Wetzel, William A.-Judge, New York Court of Claims-N.Y.
Wexler, Ben K.-Judge, Tennessee Circuit Court Third Judicial District-Tenn.

ALPHABETICAL NAME INDEX

Wickersham, S. Charles-Judge, Superior Court of California County of San Diego-Calif.

Widener, H. Emory, Jr.-Judge, United States Court of Appeals Fourth Circuit

Widick, Paul E.-Judge, Minnesota District Court Seventh Judicial District-Minn.

Widmoyer, David W.-Judge, Nappanee City Court-Ind.

Wiederstein, Robert-Judge, Kentucky District Court Fifty-first Judicial District-Ky.

Wieland, Charles A.-Judge, Superior Court of California County of Madera-Calif.

Wieland, Lucy Ann-Judge, Minnesota District Court Fourth Judicial District-Minn.

Wiener, Jacques L., Jr.-Judge, United States Court of Appeals Fifth Circuit

Wieners, Joseph F.-Judge, Minnesota District Court Third Judicial District-Minn.

Wierengo, Andrew-Chief Judge, Michigan District Court District Sixty-Mich.

Wiese, John P.-Senior Judge, United States Court of Federal Claims

Wiese, Peter E.-Judge, Connecticut Superior Court-Conn.

Wiesman, Melvyn Wade-Circuit Judge, Missouri Circuit Court Twenty-first Judicial Circuit-Mo.

Wiest, Mark K.-Judge, Ohio Court of Common Pleas Wayne County-Ohio

Wiest, Wm. Harvey-Judge, Pennsylvania Court of Common Pleas Eighth Judicial District-Pa.

Wigenton, Susan D.-Magistrate Judge, United States District Court District of New Jersey-N.J.

Wiggins, Brian-Judge, Kentucky District Court Forty-fifth Judicial District-Ky.

Wiggins, David C.-Judge, Florida Circuit Court Fourth Judicial Circuit-Fla.

Wiggins, Esther L.-Judge, Virginia Juvenile and Domestic Relations District Court Seventeenth Judicial District-Va.

Wiggins, John D.-Circuit Judge, Missouri Circuit Court Twenty-fifth Judicial Circuit-Mo.

Wiggins, Marvin Wayne-Presiding Judge, Alabama Circuit Court Fourth Judicial Circuit-Ala.

Wilbert, Warren-Judge, Kansas District Court Eighteenth Judicial District-Kan.

Wilborn, Carroll E., Jr.-Judge, Texas District Court 344th Judicial District-Tex.

Wilbur, Lori-Judge, South Dakota Circuit Court Sixth Judicial Circuit-S.D.

Wilcox, Bruce A.-Judge, Virginia General District Court Fourth Judicial District-Va.

Wilcox, Jon P.-Justice, Wisconsin Supreme Court-Wis.

Wilcox, Robert C.-Associate Judge, Maryland District Court District Seven-Md.

Wilcox, Tommy Day-Chief Judge, Superior Court of Georgia Macon Judicial Circuit-Ga.

Wild, Joe A.-Judge, Indian River County Court-Fla.

Wilde, Linda M.-Judge, Superior Court of California County of San Bernardino-Calif.

Wilder, Frank N., IV-Chief Magistrate, Magistrate Court of Monroe County-Ga.

Wilder, Kurtis T.-Judge, Michigan Court of Appeals-Mich.

Wiley, Dale M.-Judge, Virginia Juvenile and Domestic Relations District Court Twenty-second Judicial District-Va.

Wiley, Dennis M.-Judge, Michigan District Court District Five-Mich.

Wiley, Edwin B.-Judge, West Virginia Family Court Circuit Twelve-W.Va.

Wiley, Jim W.-Judge, Louisiana District Court Eighth Judicial District-La.

Wiley, John Shepard, Jr.-Judge, Superior Court of California County of Los Angeles-Calif.

Wilfong, Jaymie Godwin-Judge, West Virginia Family Court Circuit Twenty-two-W.Va.

Wilhoit, Henry Rupert, Jr.-Senior Judge, United States District Court Eastern District of Kentucky-Ky.

Wilk, S. Michael-Judge, Wisconsin Circuit Court Kenosha Circuit-Wis.

Wilke, Kurt L.-District Judge, Iowa District Court Second Judicial District-Ia.

Wilke, W. Michael-Judge, Decatur Superior Court-Ind.

Wilken, Claudia-Judge, United States District Court Northern District of California-Calif.

Wilkerson, Analia H.-Judge, Harris County Criminal Court at Law No. 9-Tex.

Wilkes, Christopher C.-Judge, West Virginia Circuit Court Twenty-third Judicial Circuit-W.Va.

Wilkes, Don E.-Judge, Probate Court of Emanuel County-Ga.

Wilkes, E. M., III-Judge, Superior Court of Georgia Brunswick Judicial Circuit-Ga.

Wilkes, William A.-Judge, Florida Circuit Court Fourth Judicial Circuit-Fla.

Wilking, Richard-Judge, Casper Municipal Court-Wyo.

Wilkins, Diane W.-Presiding Judge, Utah Juvenile Court Second Judicial District-Utah

Wilkins, Frederick B., Jr.-Judge, North Carolina District Court District 17A-N.C.

Wilkins, Lottie E.-Justice, New York Supreme Court First Judicial District-N.Y.

Wilkins, Michael J.-Justice, Utah Supreme Court-Utah

Wilkins, William W., Jr.-Chief Judge, United States Court of Appeals Fourth Circuit

Wilkinson, Charles W., Jr.-Chief Judge, North Carolina District Court District 9-N.C.

Wilkinson, J. Michael-Judge, Texas District Court 179th Judicial District-Tex.

Wilkinson, James Harvie, III-Judge, United States Court of Appeals Fourth Circuit

Wilkinson, Joseph C., Jr.-Magistrate Judge, United States District Court Eastern District of Louisiana-La.

Wilkinson, Michael O.-Judge, Superior Court of Arizona Maricopa County-Ariz.

Wilkinson, Norman-Judge, Arkansas Circuit Court Twelfth Judicial Circuit-Ark.

Wilkinson, Randell L.-Judge, Superior Court of California County of Orange-Calif.

Will, Joseph G.-Judge, Florida Circuit Court Seventh Judicial Circuit-Fla.

Will, Sharon B.-Judge, Virginia Juvenile and Domestic Relations District Court Fourteenth Judicial District-Va.

Willard, Benedict J.-Judge, Louisiana District Court Orleans Parish Criminal District-La.

Willard, William-Judge, Mississippi Chancery Court Seventh Judicial District-Miss.

Willcox, Stephen K.-Associate Circuit Judge, Missouri Circuit Court First Judicial Circuit-Mo.

Willett, Barry-Judge, Kentucky Circuit Court Thirtieth Judicial Circuit-Ky.

Willett, Eileen-Judge, Superior Court of Arizona Maricopa County-Ariz.

Willett, William G.-Judge, Superior Court of California County of Los Angeles-Calif.

Willhite, Thomas Lyle, Jr.-Judge, Superior Court of California County of Los Angeles-Calif.

Williams, Alexander, Jr.-Judge, United States District Court District of Maryland-Md.

Williams, Alexander H., III-Judge, Superior Court of California County of Los Angeles-Calif.

Williams, Alexandra N.-Administrative Judge, Maryland District Court District Eight-Md.

Williams, Amanda F.-Judge, Superior Court of Georgia Brunswick Judicial Circuit-Ga.

Williams, Amy M.-Judge, Pinellas County Court-Fla.

Williams, Ann Claire-Judge, United States Court of Appeals Seventh Circuit

Williams, Betty J.-Judge, The Civil Court of the City of New York-N.Y.

Williams, Branna Woodward-Judge, Barnwell County Probate Court-S.C.

Williams, Bruce E.-Judge, Alabama Circuit Court Twenty-third Judicial Circuit-Ala.

Williams, C. René-Judge, Kentucky District Court Fifth Judicial District-Ky.

Williams, Carolyn H.-Judge, Kalamazoo County Probate Court-Mich.

Williams, Charles E.-Judge, Florida Circuit Court Twelfth Judicial Circuit-Fla.

Williams, Chris E.-Judge, Arkansas Circuit Court Seventh Judicial Circuit-Ark.

Williams, Danita E.-District Judge, Oklahoma District Court Sixteenth Judicial District-Okla.

Williams, David L.-Judge, Virginia General District Court First Judicial District-Va.

Williams, David Victor-Chief Judge, Virginia Circuit Court Twenty-first Judicial Circuit-Va.

Williams, Debra-Justice, Silver Bow County Justice of the Peace Court-Mont.

Williams, Dwight H., Jr.-Judge, United States Bankruptcy Court Middle District of Alabama-Ala.

Williams, Elijah H.-Judge, Florida Circuit Court Seventeenth Judicial Circuit-Fla.

Williams, Felicia Toney-Judge, Louisiana Court of Appeal Second Circuit-La.

Williams, Frank B.-Justice, New York Supreme Court Fourth Judicial District-N.Y.

Williams, Frank J.-Chief Justice, Rhode Island Supreme Court-R.I.

Williams, Frank Vernon, III-Chancellor, Tennessee Chancery Court Ninth Judicial District-Tenn.

Williams, G. Randall-Associate Judge, Juvenile Court of Georgia Tallapoosa Judicial Circuit-Ga.

Williams, Gino W.-Judge, Virginia General District Court Twenty-seventh Judicial District-Va.

Williams, Glen Morgan-Senior Judge, United States District Court Western District of Virginia-Va.

Williams, H. Bruce-Judge, South Carolina Family Court Fifth Judicial Circuit-S.C.

Williams, H. Gregory-Justice, Trial Court of Massachusetts District Court Department Hampden County Springfield Division-Mass.

Williams, James C., Jr.-Judge, South Carolina Circuit Court First Judicial Circuit-S.C.

Williams, James P.-Associate Circuit Judge, Missouri Circuit Court Ninth Judicial Circuit-Mo.

Williams, James R.-Judge, Union Circuit Court-Ind.

Williams, James R.-Judge, Ohio Court of Common Pleas Summit County-Ohio

Williams, Jerry-Judge, Thermopolis Municipal Court-Wyo.

Williams, John Everett-Judge, Tennessee Court of Criminal Appeals Western Division-Tenn.

Williams, Johnny Lee-Judge, Mississippi Chancery Court Tenth Judicial District-Miss.

Williams, Joseph J.-Judge, North Carolina District Court District 20-N.C.

Williams, Joseph M.-Judge, Baker County Court-Fla.

Williams, Karen J.-Judge, United States Court of Appeals Fourth Circuit

Williams, Karen R.-Judge, Tennessee Circuit Court Thirtieth Judicial District-Tenn.

Williams, Keary R.-Chief Judge, Virginia Circuit Court Twenty-ninth Judicial Circuit-Va.

Williams, Kemper Stephen-Judge, Texas District Court 135th Judicial District-Tex.

Williams, Kenneth-Judge, Lonoke District Court-Ark.

Williams, Kenneth Day-Judge, Washington Superior Court Clallam County-Wash.

Williams, Kenneth L.-Judge, Florida Circuit Court First Judicial Circuit-Fla.

Williams, L. Marie-Judge, Tennessee Circuit Court Eleventh Judicial Circuit-Tenn.

Williams, Locke A.-Judge, Oregon Circuit Court Twenty-first Judicial District-Ore.

Williams, M. Edward-Circuit Judge, Missouri Circuit Court Twenty-third Judicial Circuit-Mo.

Williams, Marcus D.-Judge, Virginia Circuit Court Nineteenth Judicial Circuit-Va.

Williams, Mikel H.-Magistrate Judge, United States District Court District of Idaho-Ida.

Williams, Milton L.-Associate Justice, New York Supreme Court Appellate Division First Judicial Department-N.Y.

Williams, O. Edgar, Jr.-Senior Judge, Florida Circuit Court Seventeenth Judicial Circuit-Fla.

Williams, Patricia Anne-Judge, The Criminal Court of the City of New York-N.Y.

Williams, Patricia C.-Chief Judge, United States Bankruptcy Court Eastern District of Washington-Wash.

Williams, Paul X.-Judge, Booneville District Court-Ark.

Williams, Richard L.-Senior Judge, United States District Court Eastern District of Virginia-Va.

Williams, Robert E.-Judge, Nassau County Court-Fla.

Williams, Rose Vaughn-Judge, North Carolina District Court District 8-N.C.

ALPHABETICAL NAME INDEX

ALPHABETICAL NAME INDEX

Wintersheimer, Donald C.-Justice, Kentucky Supreme Court-Ky.
Winthrop, Lawrence-Judge, Arizona Court of Appeals Division One-Ariz.
Wirth, Charlotte L.-Chief Judge, Michigan District Court District Seventeen-Mich.
Wirtz, Robert J.-Judge, Wisconsin Circuit Court Fond du Lac Circuit-Wis.
Wisch, Scott-Judge, Texas District Court 372nd Judicial District-Tex.
Wise, Alisa K.-Judge, Alabama Court of Criminal Appeals-Ala.
Wise, Elizabeth-Judge, Perry County District Court-Ark.
Wise, Jill R.-Judge, Chelan Municipal Court-Wash.
Wise, Jo Ann-Judge, Kentucky Circuit Court Twenty-second Judicial Circuit-Ky.
Wise, John W.-Judge, Ohio Court of Appeals Fifth District-Ohio
Wise, Kenneth Price-Judge, Texas District Court 152nd Judicial District-Tex.
Wise, Patricia D.-Judge, Mississippi Chancery Court Fifth Judicial District-Miss.
Wiseman, Jane P.-District Judge, Oklahoma District Court Fourteenth Judicial District-Okla.
Wiseman, Rebecca A.-Associate Justice, California Court of Appeal Fifth District-Calif.
Wiseman, Russell Benson-Judge, Ohio Court of Common Pleas Crawford County-Ohio
Wiseman, Thomas A., Jr.-Senior Judge, United States District Court Middle District of Tennessee-Tenn.
Wisman, Jay F.-Judge, Snohomish District Court Cascade Division Snohomish County-Wash.
Wisner, Donald J.-Associate Justice, New York Supreme Court Appellate Division Fourth Judicial Department-N.Y.
Wiss, Mary E.-Judge, Superior Court of California City and County of San Francisco-Calif.
Wisser, Jon Neil-Judge, Texas District Court 299th Judicial District-Tex.
Wistrich, Andrew J.-Magistrate Judge, United States District Court Central District of California-Calif.
Witham, Robert-Judge, Henry Superior Court-Ind.
Witham, William L., Jr.-Associate Judge, Delaware Superior Court Kent County-Del.
Withers, Nelly F.-Judge, Recorder's Court of DeKalb County-Ga.
Witkowiak, Timothy M.-Judge, Wisconsin Circuit Court Milwaukee Circuit-Wis.
Witkowski, Aileen A.-Judge, Thompson District Probate Court-Conn.
Witt, Curwood-Judge, Tennessee Court of Criminal Appeals Eastern Division-Tenn.
Witt, Gary D.-Associate Circuit Judge, Missouri Circuit Court Sixth Judicial Circuit-Mo.
Witt, Gary R.-Judge, Superior Court of California County of Kern-Calif.
Witte, G. Michael-Judge, Dearborn Superior Court-Ind.
Witten, Fred N.-Judge, Gulf County Court-Fla.
Wittenberg, Charles S.-Judge, Ohio Court of Common Pleas Lucas County-Ohio
Witthoff, Earl J.-Judge, Nebraska District Court Third Judicial District-Neb.
Wittmayer, John-Judge, Oregon Circuit Court Fourth Judicial District-Ore.
Wittner, Bonnie G.-Judge, The Criminal Court of the City of New York-N.Y.
Wizmur, Judith H.-Judge, United States Bankruptcy Court District of New Jersey-N.J.
Woehrle, Carla M.-Magistrate Judge, United States District Court Central District of California-Calif.
Woelfel, Harold F., Jr.-President Judge, Pennsylvania Court of Common Pleas Seventeenth Judicial District-Pa.
Woessner, David E.-Judge, Ohio Court of Common Pleas Wood County-Ohio
Wofford, Charles A.-Senior Judge, Superior Court of Georgia-Ga.
Wogan, Cameron F.-Presiding Judge, Oregon Circuit Court Thirteenth Judicial District-Ore.
Wogan, Chris R.-Judge, Pennsylvania Court of Common Pleas First Judicial District-Pa.
Wojcik, Albert J.-Judge, Superior Court of California County of Riverside-Calif.
Wojcik, Eugene A.-Associate Judge, Illinois Circuit Court Eighteenth Judicial Circuit-Ill.
Wojkowski, Gregory J.-Circuit Judge, Illinois Circuit Court of Cook County-Ill.
Wojtecki, Leonard J.-Associate Judge, Illinois Circuit Court Sixteenth Judicial Circuit-Ill.
Wolaver, Stephen Arthur-Judge, Ohio Court of Common Pleas Greene County-Ohio
Wolf, Dale A.-Judge, Minnesota District Court Sixth Judicial District-Minn.
Wolf, Flora Barth-Judge, Pennsylvania Court of Common Pleas First Judicial District-Pa.
Wolf, Gerald J.-Judge, Minnesota District Court Third Judicial District-Minn.
Wolf, James R.-Judge, Florida District Court of Appeal First District-Fla.
Wolf, Linda Ralu Smith-Judge, Muncie City Court-Ind.
Wolf, Mark L.-Judge, United States District Court District of Massachusetts-Mass.
Wolf, Peter H.-Senior Judge, Superior Court of the District of Columbia-D.C.
Wolfe, Eugene-Associate Judge, Maryland District Court District Six-Md.
Wolfe, J. Stan-Judge, Gillette Municipal Court-Wyo.
Wolfe, James Boyd, Jr.-Recalled Judge, United States Bankruptcy Court Middle District of North Carolina-N.C.
Wolfe, Mark-Judge, Hillsborough County Court-Fla.
Wolfe, Norman H.-Special Trial Judge, United States Tax Court
Wolfe, Richard B.-Judge, Superior Court of California County of Los Angeles-Calif.
Wolfe, Virginia A.-Reserve Judge, Wisconsin Circuit Court-Wis.
Wolff, Michael A.-Judge, Supreme Court of Missouri-Mo.
Wolff, Nelson W.-Judge, Bexar County Court-Tex.
Wolff, William H., Jr.-Judge, Ohio Court of Appeals Second District-Ohio
Wolfgang, Penny M.-Justice, New York Supreme Court Eighth Judicial District-N.Y.
Wolfgram, Thomas R.-Judge, Wisconsin Circuit Court Ozaukee Circuit-Wis.
Wolfskill, Dave-Judge, Hulett Municipal Court-Wyo.
Wolfson, Freda L.-Judge, United States District Court District of New Jersey-N.J.
Wolfson, Lori M.-Recalled Circuit Judge, Illinois Circuit Court of Cook County-Ill.
Wolfson, Warren D.-Circuit Judge, Illinois Circuit Court of Cook County-Ill.
Wolin, Alfred M.-Senior Judge, United States District Court District of New Jersey-N.J.
Wolking, John L.-Special Judge, Oklahoma District Court Twenty-sixth Judicial District-Okla.
Wolle, Charles R.-Senior Judge, United States District Court Southern District of Iowa-Ia.
Wollenberg, William L.-Judge Referee, Connecticut Superior Court-Conn.
Wollheim, Robert-Judge, Oregon Court of Appeals-Ore.
Wollman, Paul L.-Judge, Amsterdam City Court-N.Y.
Wollman, Roger L.-Judge, United States Court of Appeals Eighth Circuit
Wolven, Carol A.-Judge, Connecticut Superior Court-Conn.
Wolverton, Michael-Judge, Alaska Superior Court Third Judicial District-Alas.
Womack, Dana M.-Judge, Texas District Court 348th Judicial District-Tex.
Womack, Paul-Judge, Texas Court of Criminal Appeals-Tex.
Womack, Stephen H.-Judge, New Jersey Superior Court Vicinage Eleven-N.J.
Wommack, Robert W., Jr.-Judge, State Court of Washington County-Ga.
Wong, Alvin T.-Judge, State Court of DeKalb County-Ga.
Wong, Cerena-Judge, Superior Court of California County of Sonoma-Calif.
Wong, Douglas S.-Judge, The Criminal Court of the City of New York-N.Y.
Wong, Frances Q. F.-Senior Family Court Judge, Hawaii Circuit Court First Judicial Circuit-Hi.
Wood, April C.-Judge, North Carolina District Court District 22-N.C.
Wood, Diane P.-Judge, United States Court of Appeals Seventh Circuit
Wood, Ellen-Chief Magistrate, Magistrate Court of Cook County-Ga.
Wood, Frederick L.-Chief Judge, Branch County Probate Court-Mich.
Wood, Gael D.-Presiding Judge, Missouri Circuit Court Twentieth Judicial Circuit-Mo.
Wood, George L.-Judge, Washington Superior Court Clallam County-Wash.
Wood, Harlington, Jr.-Senior Judge, United States Court of Appeals Seventh Circuit
Wood, James C.-Judge, Alabama Circuit Court Thirteenth Judicial Circuit-Ala.
Wood, James T.-Judge, Kentucky District Court Forty-seventh Judicial District-Ky.
Wood, Jerry-Chief Magistrate, Magistrate Court of Floyd County-Ga.
Wood, Jon B.-Chief Judge, Superior Court of Georgia Lookout Mountain Judicial Circuit-Ga.
Wood, Judith E.-Judge, Monon Town Court-Ind.
Wood, Kimba M.-Judge, United States District Court Southern District of New York-N.Y.
Wood, Kimberly L.-Judge, Costilla County Court-Colo.
Wood, Mark I.-Judge, Alaska Superior Court Fourth Judicial District-Alas.
Wood, Mike-Judge, Harris County Probate Court No. 2-Tex.
Wood, Phillip W.-Judge, Autauga County District Court-Ala.
Wood, R. Barry-Judge, Idaho District Court Fifth Judicial District-Ida.
Wood, Sharolyn P.-Judge, Texas District Court 127th Judicial District-Tex.
Wood, Thomas H.-Judge, Virginia Circuit Court Twenty-fifth Judicial Circuit-Va.
Wood, William-Judge, Milton Municipal Court-Wash.
Wood, William S.-Associate Judge, Illinois Circuit Court of Cook County-Ill.
Wood, William Z., Jr.-Resident Judge, North Carolina Superior Court Fifth Judicial Division District 21-N.C.
Woodall, Thomas A.-Associate Justice, Alabama Supreme Court-Ala.
Woodall, Thomas T.-Judge, Tennessee Court of Criminal Appeals Middle Division-Tenn.
Woodard, Beverly J.-Associate Judge, Maryland District Court District Five-Md.
Woodard, Billie Colombaro-Judge, Louisiana Court of Appeal Third Circuit-La.
Woodard, Cynthia T.-Judge, Louisiana District Court Third Judicial District-La.
Woodard, Michele M.-Justice, New York Supreme Court Tenth Judicial District-N.Y.
Woodard, Susan J.-Judge, Yakima Municipal Court-Wash.
Woodard, W. Wayne-Judge, Charlotte County Court-Fla.
Woodford, L. Thomas-Chief Judge, Colorado District Court First Judicial District-Colo.
Woodham, Charles W.-Judge, Henry County District Court-Ala.
Woodland, William H.-Judge, Idaho District Court Sixth Judicial District-Ida.
Woodliff, Duane A.-Special Judge, Oklahoma District Court Twenty-fourth Judicial District-Okla.
Woodlock, Douglas P.-Judge, United States District Court District of Massachusetts-Mass.
Woodlock, Jerry W.-Judge, Texas District Court 235th Judicial District-Tex.
Woodroof, James W., Jr.-Judge, Alabama Circuit Court Thirty-ninth Judicial Circuit-Ala.
Woodrum, William E., Jr.-Chief Judge, Superior Court of Georgia Ogeechee Judicial Circuit-Ga.
Woods, Carr-Associate Circuit Judge, Missouri Circuit Court Thirty-ninth Judicial Circuit-Mo.
Woods, E. H. "Bucky", III-Chief Judge, Superior Court of Georgia Mountain Judicial Circuit-Ga.
Woods, George E.-Senior Judge, United States District Court Eastern District of Michigan-Mich.
Woods, Henry T.-Judge, South Carolina Family Court Sixteenth Judicial Circuit-S.C.
Woods, Margie G.-Judge, Superior Court of California County of San Diego-Calif.

ALPHABETICAL NAME INDEX

Woods, Norvell "Fred", Jr.-Associate Justice, California Court of Appeal Second District Division Seven-Calif.

Woods, Robert J.-Associate Judge, Circuit Court for Prince George's County, Seventh Judicial Circuit-Md.

Woods-Skipper, Sheila A.-Judge, Pennsylvania Court of Common Pleas First Judicial District-Pa.

Woodson, J. William-Senior Judge, Florida Circuit Court Eighteenth Judicial Circuit-Fla.

Woodson, Robert G., Jr.-Chief Judge, Virginia General District Court Tenth Judicial District-Va.

Woodward, Ben-Judge, Texas District Court 119th Judicial District-Tex.

Woodward, James-Judge, Superior Court of California County of Trinity-Calif.

Woodward, Patrick L.-Associate Judge, Circuit Court for Montgomery County, Sixth Judicial Circuit-Md.

Woody, W. Bruce-Judge, Dallas County Court at Law No. 4-Tex.

Wool, Leon-Associate Judge, Illinois Circuit Court of Cook County-Ill.

Woolard, Charlotte Walter-Judge, Superior Court of California City and County of San Francisco-Calif.

Woolard, Diane M.-Judge, Washington Superior Court Clark County-Wash.

Wooldridge, John T.-Judge, Texas District Court 269th Judicial District-Tex.

Wooldridge, Robert W., Jr.-Judge, Virginia Circuit Court Nineteenth Judicial Circuit-Va.

Woolery, Richard A.-Special Judge, Oklahoma District Court Twenty-fourth Judicial District-Okla.

Wooleyhan, John C.-Associate Judge, Illinois Circuit Court Eighth Judicial Circuit-Ill.

Woolley, John C.-Judge, Superior Court of California County of Orange-Calif.

Woolley, William Sioux-Judge, Kansas District Court Eighteenth Judicial District-Kan.

Wooster, Evelyn-Judge, Castle Rock Municipal Court-Wash.

Wooten, Marvin R.-Recalled Judge, United States Bankruptcy Court Western District of North Carolina-N.C.

Wooten, Terry L.-Judge, United States District Court District of South Carolina-S.C.

Wootten, John D., Jr.-Judge, Tennessee Circuit Court Fifteenth Judicial District-Tenn.

Worcester, Dean S.-Judge, Virginia General District Court Twentieth Judicial District-Va.

Word, Cole-Judge, Bosque County Court-Tex.

Work, Jeff-Judge, Texas District Court 189th Judicial District-Tex.

Work, Mary MacMaster-Judge, Ulster County Family Court-N.Y.

Worke, Renee L.-Judge, Minnesota District Court Third Judicial District-Minn.

Workman, Anne-Judge, Superior Court of Georgia Stone Mountain Judicial Circuit-Ga.

Workman, Dale C.-Judge, Tennessee Circuit Court Sixth Judicial District-Tenn.

Workman, David A.-Judge, Superior Court of California County of Los Angeles-Calif.

Workman, RicKard A.-Judge, Lima Municipal Court-Ohio

Worsham, Jack Logan-Judge, Hutchinson County Court-Tex.

Worshtil, Joel D.-Associate Judge, Maryland District Court District Five-Md.

Worswick, Lisa R.-Judge, Washington Superior Court Pierce County-Wash.

Worth, Patricia G.-Judge, Maine District Court-Me.

Worthen, Freddie J.-Judge, Volusia County Court-Fla.

Worthen, James T.-Chief Justice, Texas Court of Appeals Twelfth District-Tex.

Worthington, Donald L.-District Judge, Oklahoma District Court Ninth Judicial District-Okla.

Worthington, Margherita Patti-Judge, Pennsylvania Court of Common Pleas Forty-third Judicial District-Pa.

Worthy, Kym L.-Judge, Michigan Circuit Court Third Judicial Circuit-Mich.

Wright, Carolyn I.-Justice, Texas Court of Appeals Fifth District-Tex.

Wright, Cynthia D.-Judge, Superior Court of Georgia Atlanta Judicial Circuit-Ga.

Wright, E. Kenneth, Jr.-Circuit Judge, Illinois Circuit Court of Cook County-Ill.

Wright, Frederick C., III-Circuit Administrative Judge, Circuit Court for Washington County, Fourth Judicial Circuit-Md.

Wright, Geoffrey D.-Judge, The Civil Court of the City of New York-N.Y.

Wright, H. T.-Judge, Caldwell County Court-Tex.

Wright, James L.-Judge, Superior Court of California County of Los Angeles-Calif.

Wright, Jim R.-Justice, Texas Court of Appeals Eleventh District-Tex.

Wright, John F.-Associate Justice, Nebraska Supreme Court-Neb.

Wright, John Homer-Judge, Arkansas Circuit Court Eighteenth East Judicial Circuit-Ark.

Wright, Karla Foreman-Judge, Polk County Court-Fla.

Wright, Melvin R.-Associate Judge, Superior Court of the District of Columbia-D.C.

Wright, Merideth-Judge, Vermont Environmental Court-Vt.

Wright, Milton L., Jr.-First Justice, Trial Court of Massachusetts District Court Department Suffolk County Roxbury Division-Mass.

Wright, Paul-Magistrate Judge, Kansas District Court Twenty-first Judicial District-Kan.

Wright, Philip A., Jr.-Judge, Wallingford District Probate Court-Conn.

Wright, Richard O.-Judge, Wisconsin Circuit Court Marquette Circuit-Wis.

Wright, Robert C.-Judge, Pennsylvania Court of Common Pleas Thirty-second Judicial District-Pa.

Wright, Samuel T.-Judge, Kentucky Circuit Court Forty-seventh Judicial Circuit-Ky.

Wright, Scott O.-Senior Judge, United States District Court Western District of Missouri-Mo.

Wright, Susan Webber-Chief Judge, United States District Court Eastern District of Arkansas-Ark.

Wright, Tim-Judge, Williamson County Court at Law No. 2-Tex.

Wright, Timothy S.-Judge, Virginia General District Court First Judicial District-Va.

Wright, Vicki-Associate Judge, Illinois Circuit Court Fourteenth Judicial Circuit-Ill.

Wright, Wilhelmina M.-Judge, Minnesota Court of Appeals-Minn.

Wright, William Leon-Judge, Florida Circuit Court Fourteenth Judicial Circuit-Fla.

Wright, Willie B.-Associate Judge, Illinois Circuit Court of Cook County-Ill.

Wright, Zebedee W.-Judge, Broward County Court-Fla.

Wrigley, Joseph-Special Judge, Oklahoma District Court Twenty-second Judicial District-Okla.

Wroble, Arthur G.-Judge, Florida Circuit Court Fifteenth Judicial Circuit-Fla.

Wu, George H.-Judge, Superior Court of California County of Los Angeles-Calif.

Wulle, John P.-Judge, Washington Superior Court Clark County-Wash.

Wunderlich, William M.-Associate Justice, California Court of Appeal Sixth District-Calif.

Wyatt, Harry M., III-Associate District Judge, Oklahoma District Court Twelfth Judicial District-Okla.

Wyatt, James Randall, Jr.-Judge, Tennessee Criminal Court Twentieth Judicial District-Tenn.

Wyatt, Merri S.-Judge, Oregon Circuit Court Fourth Judicial District-Ore.

Wyatt, Robert L.-Judge, Louisiana District Court Fourteenth Judicial District-La.

Wybo-Vopata, Gerri-Magistrate Judge, Kansas District Court Twenty-second Judicial District-Kan.

Wyckman, Scott-Justice, Gallatin County Justice of the Peace Court-Mont.

Wyde, Dan L.-Judge, Dallas County Criminal Court at Law No. 3-Tex.

Wyers, Jan G.-Judge, Oregon Circuit Court Fourth Judicial District-Ore.

Wyler, Stephanie-Judge, Ohio Court of Common Pleas Clermont County-Ohio

Wylie, Paul O.-Judge, Archer County Court-Tex.

Wylie, William J., Jr.-Judge, South Carolina Family Court First Judicial Circuit-S.C.

Wynn, James A., Jr.-Associate Judge, North Carolina Court of Appeals-N.C.

Wynn, Patricia A.-Senior Judge, Superior Court of the District of Columbia-D.C.

Wynn, Robert S.-Judge, Ashtabula County Court-Ohio

Wynne, Charles S.-Judge, State Court of Hall County-Ga.

Wynne, Thomas J.-Judge, Washington Superior Court Snohomish County-Wash.

Xanthos, Suzanne J.-Judge, Sharon District Probate Court-Conn.

Yackel, Norman L.-Judge, Wisconsin Circuit Court Sawyer Circuit-Wis.

Yacknin, Ellen-Judge, Rochester City Court-N.Y.

Yacucci, Philip J.-Judge, St. Lucie County Court-Fla.

Yaffe, David P.-Judge, Superior Court of California County of Los Angeles-Calif.

Yaggy, Carol-Judge, Superior Court of California City and County of San Francisco-Calif.

Yale, Guy D.-Judge, Bethany District Probate Court-Conn.

Yamin, Dianne E.-Judge, Danbury District Probate Court-Conn.

Yancey, James Alan-Judge, Polk County Court-Fla.

Yancey, Virginia E.-Justice, New York Supreme Court Second Judicial District-N.Y.

Yañez, Linda Reyna-Justice, Texas Court of Appeals Thirteenth District-Tex.

Yannotti, Joseph L.-Judge, New Jersey Superior Court Vicinage Two-N.J.

Yanthis, George A.-Magistrate Judge, United States District Court Southern District of New York-N.Y.

Yarbrough, James D.-Judge, Galveston County Court-Tex.

Yarbrough, Jan-Judge, Texas Family District Court 306th Judicial District-Tex.

Yardley, Laurie-Judge, Nebraska County Court Third Judicial District-Neb.

Yarnell, Michael A.-Judge, Superior Court of Arizona Maricopa County-Ariz.

Yashar, Marjorie R.-Judge, Rhode Island Traffic Tribunal-R.I.

Yates, Harvey-Judge, Arkansas Circuit Court First Judicial Circuit-Ark.

Yates, James A.-Justice, New York Supreme Court First Judicial District-N.Y.

Yates, Leslie Brock-Justice, Texas Court of Appeals Fourteenth District-Tex.

Yates, Reginald-Judge, Superior Court of California County of Los Angeles-Calif.

Yates, Sharon G.-Presiding Judge, Alabama Court of Civil Appeals-Ala.

Yawn, Theron A., Jr.-Senior Judge, Florida Circuit Court Eighth Judicial Circuit-Fla.

Yazinski, John J.-Justice, Claremont District Court-N.H.

Yeager, Christopher W.-Judge, Superior Court of California County of Imperial-Calif.

Yeager, S. Michael-Judge, Pennsylvania Court of Common Pleas Fiftieth Judicial District-Pa.

Yeager, Thomas M.-Judge, Louisiana District Court Ninth Judicial District-La.

Yeakel, Lee-Justice, Texas Court of Appeals Third District-Tex.

Yeargan, Charles A.-Judge, Arkansas Circuit Court Ninth West Judicial Circuit-Ark.

Yeates, Robert S.-Judge, Utah Juvenile Court Third Judicial District-Utah

Yeatts, Archer L., III-Judge, Virginia General District Court Fourteenth Judicial District-Va.

Yeatts, Fred L.-Judge, King District Court East Division King County-Wash.

Yegan, Kenneth R.-Associate Justice, California Court of Appeal Second District Division Six-Calif.

Yelton, Ernest E.-Judge, Clay Circuit Court-Ind.

Yenior, Allen C.-Chief Judge, Michigan District Court District Eighty-one-Mich.

Yent, Rufus L.-Judge, Superior Court of California County of San Bernardino-Calif.

Yeoman, Frank, Jr.-Judge, Kansas District Court Third Judicial District-Kan.

Yerger, W. Swan-Judge, Mississippi Circuit Court Seventh Judicial District-Miss.
Yerman, Mark J.-Judge, Citrus County Court-Fla.
Yetter, J. W.-Judge, Meeteetse Municipal Court-Wyo.
Yew, Erica R.-Judge, Superior Court of California County of Santa Clara-Calif.
Ynostroza, Carlos G.-Judge, Superior Court of California County of Alameda-Calif.
Yock, Robert J.-Senior Judge, United States Court of Federal Claims
Yocum, Tony-Judge, Hope District Court-Ark.
Yohn, William H., Jr.-Judge, United States District Court Eastern District of Pennsylvania-Pa.
Yonts, Robert B., Jr.-Judge, Superior Court of California County of Santa Cruz-Calif.
York, Jane A.-Judge, Superior Court of California County of Fresno-Calif.
York, Jim-Judge, Texas District Court 246th Judicial District-Tex.
York, Louis B.-Judge, The Civil Court of the City of New York-N.Y.
York, Van Lee-Judge, Borden County Court-Tex.
York, Wendy-Judge, New Mexico District Court Second Judicial District-N.Mex.
Yoshioka, Terence T.-Family Court Judge, Hawaii District Court Third Judicial Circuit-Hi.
Yost, Eric-Judge, Kansas District Court Eighteenth Judicial District-Kan.
Yost, Gary L.-Judge, Ohio Court of Common Pleas Ashtabula County-Ohio
Yost, LeRoy W.-Judge, Minnesota District Court First Judicial District-Minn.
Youck, David A.-Associate Judge, Illinois Circuit Court Twenty-first Judicial Circuit-Ill.
Young, Anthony L.-Circuit Judge, Illinois Circuit Court of Cook County-Ill.
Young, Cliff-Senior Justice, Nevada Supreme Court-Nev.
Young, David H.-Judge, Florida Circuit Court Eleventh Judicial Circuit-Fla.
Young, David W.-Associate Judge, Circuit Court for Baltimore City, Eighth Judicial Circuit-Md.
Young, Everett-Judge, Texas District Court 297th Judicial District-Tex.
Young, Frederick N.-Judge, Ohio Court of Appeals Second District-Ohio
Young, George C.-Senior Judge, United States District Court Middle District of Florida-Fla.
Young, H. David-Magistrate Judge, United States District Court Eastern District of Arkansas-Ark.
Young, Joan E.-Chief Judge, Michigan Circuit Court Sixth Judicial Circuit-Mich.
Young, Kevin G.-Judge, Syracuse City Court-N.Y.
Young, Lucien, III-Judge, Noble County Court-Ohio
Young, Marshall P.-Magistrate Judge, United States District Court District of South Dakota-S.D.
Young, Michael A.-Judge, Minnesota District Court First Judicial District-Minn.
Young, Norman E.-Judge, Wyoming District Court Ninth Judicial District-Wyo.
Young, Patricia G.-Judge, Idaho District Court Fourth Judicial District Magistrate Division-Ida.
Young, Patricia K.-Judge, North Carolina District Court District 28-N.C.
Young, Patrick H.-Judge, Paulding County Court-Ohio
Young, Patrick M.-Associate Judge, Illinois Circuit Court Twentieth Judicial Circuit-Ill.
Young, Paul-Judge, Caddo Parish Juvenile Court-La.
Young, Randy-Judge, McCulloch County Court-Tex.
Young, Richard L.-Judge, United States District Court Southern District of Indiana-Ind.
Young, Robert P., Jr.-Justice, Michigan Supreme Court-Mich.
Young, Roger M.-Judge, South Carolina Circuit Court Ninth Judicial Circuit-S.C.
Young, Ronald T. L.-Judge, Superior Court of California County of Napa-Calif.
Young, Tom F., Jr.-Judge, Alabama Circuit Court Fifth Judicial Circuit-Ala.
Young, W. Dale-Judge, Tennessee Circuit Court Fifth Judicial District-Tenn.
Young, William E.-Judge, Marion Superior Court-Ind.
Young, William G.-Chief Judge, United States District Court District of Massachusetts-Mass.
Young, William W.-Judge, Ohio Court of Appeals Twelfth District-Ohio
Youngblood, Carole F.-Judge, Michigan Circuit Court Third Judicial Circuit-Mich.
Younge, John Milton-Judge, Pennsylvania Court of Common Pleas First Judicial District-Pa.
Youngquist, Raymond C.-Judge, Superior Court of California County of San Bernardino-Calif.
Yu, Mary-Judge, Washington Superior Court King County-Wash.
Yuille, Richard B.-Judge, Michigan Circuit Court Seventh Judicial Circuit-Mich.
Yule, Dennis D.-Judge, Washington Superior Court Benton-Franklin Counties-Wash.
Yunck, Robert J.-Justice, Glacier County Justice of the Peace Court and Judge, Cut Bank City Court-Mont.
Zabel, Sarah-Judge, Florida Circuit Court Eleventh Judicial Circuit-Fla.
Zacharias, C. Michael-Special Judge, Oklahoma District Court Fourteenth Judicial District-Okla.
Zachman, Thomas F.-Judge, Brown County Municipal Court-Ohio
Zack, Robert S.-Judge, Broward County Court-Fla.
Zagel, James B.-Judge, United States District Court Northern District of Illinois-Ill.
Zagelow, Robert L.-Judge, Washington Superior Court Walla Walla County-Wash.
Zager, Bruce B.-District Judge, Iowa District Court First Judicial District-Ia.
Zahra, Brian K.-Judge, Michigan Court of Appeals-Mich.
Zainey, Jay C.-Judge, United States District Court Eastern District of Louisiana-La.
Zakaib, Paul, Jr.-Judge, West Virginia Circuit Court Thirteenth Judicial Circuit-W.Va.
Zaleski, Edward M.-Judge, Ohio Court of Common Pleas Lorain County-Ohio
Zaleski, Jerome A.-Judge, Pennsylvania Court of Common Pleas First Judicial District-Pa.
Zaleski, Margaret A.-Circuit Justice, Trial Court of Massachusetts District Court Department-Mass.
Zambelli, Barbara Gunther-Judge, Westchester County Court-N.Y.
Zampino, Thomas P.-Judge, New Jersey Superior Court Vicinage Five-N.J.
Zander, Barb-Magistrate, Vermont Trial Court-Vt.
Zapata, Frank R.-Judge, United States District Court District of Arizona-Ariz.
Zappa, Leo J., Jr.-Circuit Judge, Illinois Circuit Court Seventh Judicial Circuit-Ill.
Zappen, Edward F., Jr.-Judge, Wisconsin Circuit Court Wood Circuit-Wis.
Zarefsky, Ralph-Magistrate Judge, United States District Court Central District of California-Calif.
Zarella, Peter T.-Associate Justice, Connecticut Supreme Court-Conn.
Zastera, William B.-Judge, Nebraska District Court Second Judicial District-Neb.
Zatkoff, Lawrence P.-Chief Judge, United States District Court Eastern District of Michigan-Mich.
Zazzali, James-Associate Justice, Supreme Court of New Jersey-N.J.
Zebert, Thomas L.-Judge, Mississippi Chancery Court Twentieth Judicial District-Miss.
Zebre, Frank J.-Judge, Wyoming Circuit Court Third Judicial District, Lincoln County-Wyo.
Zeidwig, Howard M.-Judge, Florida Circuit Court Seventeenth Judicial Circuit-Fla.
Zeigler, Phillip-Judge, Texas District Court 52nd Judicial District-Tex.
Zeldon, Joan-Associate Judge, Superior Court of the District of Columbia-D.C.
Zelezinski, Frank G.-Circuit Judge, Illinois Circuit Court of Cook County-Ill.
Zeleznik, Joseph D.-Chief Judge, Ontonagon County Probate Court-Mich.
Zeller, Sharon L.-Judge, Broward County Court-Fla.
Zellerbach, Paul E.-Judge, Superior Court of California County of Riverside-Calif.
Zelman, Steven M.-Judge, Bloomfield District Probate Court-Conn.
Zelon, Laurie D.-Judge, Superior Court of California County of Los Angeles-Calif.
Zemaitis, Daniel V.-Judge, Michigan Circuit Court Seventeenth Judicial Circuit-Mich.
Zemmelman, Norman G.-Judge, Ohio Court of Common Pleas Lucas County-Ohio
Zeno, Melvin C.-Judge, Louisiana District Court Twenty-fourth Judicial District-La.
Zenoff, David-Senior Justice, Nevada Supreme Court-Nev.
Zenoff, Kathryn E.-Circuit Judge, Illinois Circuit Court Seventeenth Judicial Circuit-Ill.
Zent, Becky-Judge, Shoshoni Municipal Court-Wyo.
Zepkin, J. R.-Judge, Virginia General District Court Ninth Judicial District-Va.
Zerbi, Victor M., Jr.-Judge, Garfield County Court-Colo.
Zervos, Larry C.-Judge, Alaska Superior Court First Judicial District-Alas.
Zetusky, Edward J., Jr.-Judge, Pennsylvania Court of Common Pleas Thirty-second Judicial District-Pa.
Zide, Elliott L.-First Justice, Trial Court of Massachusetts District Court Department Worcester County Worcester Division and Justice, Fitchburg Division-Mass.
Ziegler, Annette K.-Judge, Wisconsin Circuit Court Washington Circuit-Wis.
Ziegler, Donald E.-Senior Judge, United States District Court Western District of Pennsylvania-Pa.
Ziemian, Robert P.-First Justice, Trial Court of Massachusetts District Court Department Suffolk County South Boston Division and Justice, West Roxbury Division-Mass.
Zigler, Greg A.-District Judge, Oklahoma District Court First Judicial District-Okla.
Zika, Patrick J.-Judge, Superior Court of California County of Alameda-Calif.
Zilly, Thomas S.-Judge, United States District Court Western District of Washington-Wash.
Zimbelman, Tamara L.-Magistrate Judge, Kansas District Court Fifteenth Judicial District-Kan.
Zimmer, Van D.-Judge, Iowa Court of Appeals-Ia.
Zimmerman, Ann E.-Justice of the Peace, Las Vegas Justices' Court-Nev.
Zimmerman, Bernard-Magistrate Judge, United States District Court Northern District of California-Calif.
Zimmerman, Darvin J.-Judge, Clark District Court Clark County and Judge, Camas-Washougal Municipal Court-Wash.
Zimmerman, James D.-Judge, Colorado District Court First Judicial District-Colo.
Zimmerman, Joseph-Judge, Superior Court of California County of Imperial-Calif.
Zimmerman, Lloyd B.-Judge, Minnesota District Court Fourth Judicial District-Minn.
Zimmerman, M. Patricia-Judge, Vermont Trial Court-Vt.
Zimmerman, Richard A.-Judge, Minnesota District Court Ninth Judicial District-Minn.
Zimmerman, Stacey-Judge, Arkansas Circuit Court Fourth Judicial Circuit-Ark.
Zinter, Steven-Associate Justice, South Dakota Supreme Court-S.D.
Ziolkowski, Robert L.-Judge, Michigan Circuit Court Third Judicial Circuit-Mich.
Zissman, Michael C.-Associate Judge, Illinois Circuit Court of Cook County-Ill.
Zitter, Mary Patricia-Judge, Ohio Court of Common Pleas Mercer County-Ohio
Zive, Gregg W.-Chief Judge, United States Bankruptcy Court District of Nevada-Nev.
Zloch, William J.-Chief Judge, United States District Court Southern District of Florida-Fla.
Zoarski, Howard F.-Judge Referee, Connecticut Superior Court-Conn.
Zobel, Rya W.-Judge, United States District Court District of Massachusetts-Mass.
Zoll, Samuel E.-Chief Justice, Trial Court of Massachusetts District Court Department and Justice, Essex County Salem Division-Mass.
Zone, Joseph-Judge, Cleveland Municipal Court-Ohio
Zopp, Gerald M., Jr.-Associate Judge, Illinois Circuit Court Nineteenth Judicial Circuit-Ill.
Zore, Gerald S.-Judge, Marion Superior Court-Ind.

UNITED STATES COURTS

THE SUPREME COURT OF THE UNITED STATES

The Supreme Court of the United States is the highest court in the land and the only court mandated by the Constitution of the United States. The court consists of a chief justice and eight associate justices nominated and appointed by the President with the advice and consent of the Senate to serve during good behavior. The justices also serve as circuit justices in the U.S. Courts of Appeals.

The Supreme Court has original and exclusive jurisdiction of all controversies between the states. The court has original jurisdiction over actions to which foreign ministers are party, all controversies between the United States and a state and actions or proceedings by a state against the citizens of another state or against aliens. Although the Supreme Court has original jurisdiction of the areas mentioned, litigants rarely attempt to have a case heard there in the first instance.

The Supreme Court has appellate jurisdiction as to law and fact over cases arising out of any court in the land, provided the case involves constitutional issues, federal laws, treaties or laws relating to navigable waters. The court may reverse, modify or affirm any lower court decision, or it may remand a case to a lower court. The court exercises its own discretion in accepting or rejecting cases by petition for certiorari. The court may issue other writs as necessary to exercise its jurisdiction. In their capacity as circuit justices, the justices may stay the execution of decisions reached in the U.S. Courts of Appeals. The United States is represented before the Supreme Court by the Solicitor General of the United States.

The court sits at Washington, D.C.

Chief Justice

William Hubbs Rehnquist
(District of Columbia, Fourth
And Federal Circuits)

Associate Justices

John Paul Stevens (Sixth and Seventh Circuits)
Sandra Day O'Connor (Ninth Circuit)
Antonin Scalia (Fifth Circuit)
Anthony M. Kennedy (Eleventh Circuit)
David Hackett Souter (First and Third Circuits)
Clarence Thomas (Eighth Circuit)
Ruth Bader Ginsburg (Second Circuit)
Stephen Breyer (Tenth Circuit)

Clerk

William K. Suter
U.S. Supreme Court Building
One First Street N.E.
Washington, D.C. 20543-0001
(202) 479-3011

Administrative Office of the U.S. Courts

Leonidas Ralph Mecham
Director
Washington, D.C. 20544
(202) 273-3000

UNITED STATES COURTS OF APPEALS

The United States Courts of Appeals are intermediate appellate courts originally created by an act of Congress in 1891 to relieve the U.S. Supreme Court of considering all appeals from the federal trial courts. The United States and its territories are now divided into twelve regional circuits and one national circuit with six to twenty-eight judges per circuit. Each circuit includes three or more states except the District of Columbia Circuit. One of the justices of the Supreme Court is assigned as circuit justice for each circuit; the circuit justice shall have precedence over circuit judges and shall preside at any session which he attends. Judges are nominated and appointed by the President with the advice and consent of the Senate to serve during good behavior. Except in the District of Columbia, each circuit judge must be a resident of the circuit at the time of appointment and thereafter while in active service. Each circuit judge of the Federal Circuit must reside within fifty miles of the District of Columbia. The chief judge of each circuit is the judge who has the longest service of those under sixty-five years of age and who has not previously served as chief judge. The chief judge serves for a term of seven years or until age seventy (whichever occurs first) and continues to serve after expiration of such term until another judge is qualified. Retired judges may serve by assignment as senior judges.

The twelve circuits with regional jurisdiction include the District of Columbia and First through Eleventh Circuits. These courts have original jurisdiction to review and enforce orders of many federal administrative agencies, such as the Securities and Exchange Commission and the National Labor Relations Board. These decisions are final except as they are subject to discretionary review by the Supreme Court. The courts also have original habeas corpus jurisdiction, although it is seldom used. The courts have appellate jurisdiction over the review of all final decisions and certain interlocutory decisions of the U.S. District Courts.

The Federal Circuit has national jurisdiction. It began operation on October 1, 1982, as a result of a merger between the appellate division of the former U.S. Court of Claims and the U.S. Court of Customs and Patent Appeals. The court hears appeals in patent, copyright and trademark cases from any U.S. District Court, all appeals from the U.S. Court of Federal Claims and U.S. Court of International Trade and certain other appeals including those from final decisions of the Merit Systems Protection Board. With the abolishment of the Temporary Emergency Court of Appeals of the United States on April 29, 1993, the Federal Circuit assumed

UNITED STATES COURTS OF APPEALS—*Continued*

that court's exclusive jurisdiction of all appeals from the U.S. District Courts in cases and controversies concerning the economic stabilization laws and the regulation of energy. This court differs from the other U.S. Courts of Appeals in that it takes cases by subject matter from any region of the country rather than hearing cases by region.

The courts usually convene in panels of three judges each but may also sit en banc. The courts hold regular sessions in each respective circuit at the locations indicated below and at other locations as each court may designate by rule.

The judicial council of a circuit may establish a Bankruptcy Appellate Panel, consisting of bankruptcy judges from districts within the circuit, to hear and determine appeals of bankruptcy cases upon consent of all parties. If authorized by the Judicial Conference of the United States, the judicial councils of two or more circuits may establish a Joint Bankruptcy Appellate Panel for the same purpose. Bankruptcy Appellate Panels have been established in the First, Sixth, Eighth, Ninth and Tenth Circuits. Appeals are to the Court of Appeals for that Circuit.

DISTRICT OF COLUMBIA CIRCUIT includes the District of Columbia. The court sits at Washington, D.C.

Chief Judge

Douglas H. Ginsburg

Judges

Harry T. Edwards
Karen LeCraft Henderson
David S. Tatel
David B. Sentelle
A. Raymond Randolph
Judith W. Rogers
Merrick B. Garland

Senior Judges

Laurence H. Silberman
Stephen F. Williams

Clerk

Mark J. Langer
5409 U.S. Courthouse
333 Constitution Avenue N.W.
Washington, D.C. 20001-2866
(202) 216-7300

FIRST CIRCUIT includes Maine, Massachusetts, New Hampshire, Rhode Island and Puerto Rico. The court sits at Boston, Massachusetts, and at other locations as ordered by the court.

Chief Judge

Michael Boudin

Judges

Juan R. Torruella
Bruce M. Selya
Sandra L. Lynch
Kermit V. Lipez
Jeffrey R. Howard

Senior Judges

Frank M. Coffin
Levin Hicks Campbell
Hugh H. Bownes
Conrad K. Cyr
Norman H. Stahl

Clerk

Richard C. Donovan
2500 U.S. Courthouse
One Courthouse Way
Boston, Massachusetts 02210-3002
(617) 748-9057

Bankruptcy Appellate Panel First Circuit

Chief Judge

Arthur N. Votolato

Judges

Carol J. Kenner
Sara E. De Jesus
William C. Hillman
Mark W. Vaughn
Gerardo A. Carlo-Altieri
Enrique S. Lamoutte
James B. Haines, Jr.
Joan N. Feeney
Henry Jack Boroff

Bankruptcy Appellate Panel Clerk

Phoebe D. Morse
1010 Federal Building
10 Causeway Street
Boston, Massachusetts 02222-1074
(617) 565-8942

SECOND CIRCUIT includes Connecticut, New York and Vermont. The court sits at New York, New York, and at other locations as ordered by the court.

Chief Judge

John M. Walker, Jr.

Judges

Dennis G. Jacobs
José A. Cabranes
Rosemary S. Pooler
Robert D. Sack
Robert Allen Katzmann
Reena Raggi
Guido Calabresi
Fred I. Parker
Chester J. Straub
Sonia Sotomayor
Barrington D. Parker, Jr.

Senior Judges

Wilfred Feinberg
Ellsworth A. Van Graafeiland
Jon O. Newman
Ralph K. Winter, Jr.
Joseph M. McLaughlin
James L. Oakes
Thomas Joseph Meskill
Amalya Lyle Kearse
Richard J. Cardamone
Roger J. Miner
Pierre N. Leval

Clerk

Roseann MacKechnie
1702 U.S. Courthouse
40 Centre Street
New York, New York 10007-1561
(212) 857-8585

THIRD CIRCUIT includes Delaware, New Jersey, Pennsylvania and the Virgin Islands. The court sits at Philadelphia, Pennsylvania, and at other locations as ordered by the court.

Chief Judge

Edward R. Becker

Judges

Dolores Korman Sloviter
Samuel A. Alito, Jr.
Theodore A. McKee
Maryanne Trump Barry
Julio M. Fuentes
Anthony J. Scirica
Richard L. Nygaard
Jane R. Roth
Marjorie O. Rendell
Thomas L. Ambro
D. Brooks Smith

UNITED STATES COURTS OF APPEALS—*Continued*

Senior Judges

Ruggero J. Aldisert
Joseph F. Weis, Jr.
Walter K. Stapleton
Robert E. Cowen
Max Rosenn
Leonard I. Garth
Morton I. Greenberg

Clerk

Marcia M. Waldron
21400 U.S. Courthouse
601 Market Street
Philadelphia, Pennsylvania 19106-1790
(267) 299-4901

FOURTH CIRCUIT includes Maryland, North Carolina, South Carolina, Virginia and West Virginia. The court sits at Asheville, North Carolina and Richmond, Virginia, and at other locations as ordered by the court.

Chief Judge

William W. Wilkins, Jr.

Judges

H. Emory Widener, Jr.
Paul Victor Niemeyer
J. Michael Luttig
M. Blane Michael
William B. Traxler, Jr.
Roger L. Gregory
James Harvie Wilkinson III
Karen J. Williams
Diana Gribbon Motz
Robert Bruce King
Dennis W. Shedd

Senior Judge

Clyde Henry Hamilton

Clerk

Patricia S. Connor
501 U.S. Courthouse Annex
1100 East Main Street
Richmond, Virginia 23219-3517
(804) 916-2700

FIFTH CIRCUIT includes Louisiana, Mississippi and Texas. The court sits at New Orleans, Louisiana; Jackson, Mississippi; and Fort Worth, Texas, and at other locations as ordered by the court.

Chief Judge

Carolyn Dineen King

Judges

E. Grady Jolly
W. Eugene Davis
Jerry E. Smith
Jacques L. Wiener, Jr.
Harold R. DeMoss, Jr.
Fortunato P. Benavides
Edith Brown Clement
Patrick E. Higginbotham
Edith Hollan Jones
Rhesa H. Barksdale
Emilio M. Garza
Carl E. Stewart
James Leon Dennis

Senior Judges

Reynaldo G. Garza
Thomas Morrow Reavley
William L. Garwood
John M. Duhe, Jr.

Clerk

Charles R. Fulbruge III
100 U.S. Court of Appeals Building
600 Camp Street
New Orleans, Louisiana 70130
(504) 310-7700

SIXTH CIRCUIT includes Kentucky, Michigan, Ohio and Tennessee. The court sits at Cincinnati, Ohio, and at other locations as ordered by the court.

Chief Judge

Boyce Ficklen Martin, Jr.

Judges

Danny J. Boggs
Martha Craig Daughtrey
Ransey Guy Cole, Jr.
Ronald Lee Gilman
John M. Rogers
Alice M. Batchelder
Karen Nelson Moore
Eric L. Clay
Julia Smith Gibbons

Senior Judges

Damon Jerome Keith
Cornelia G. Kennedy
David Aldrich Nelson
Ralph B. Guy, Jr.
Richard Suhrheinrich
Gilbert S. Merritt
Robert B. Krupansky
James L. Ryan
Alan E. Norris
Eugene E. Siler, Jr.

Clerk

Leonard Green
532 U.S. Courthouse
100 East Fifth Street
Cincinnati, Ohio 45202-3988
(513) 564-7000

Bankruptcy Appellate Panel Sixth Circuit

Chief Judge

Steven W. Rhodes

Judges

Keith M. Lundin
J. Vincent Aug, Jr.
Randolph Baxter
David T. Stosberg
Thomas F. Waldron
William T. Bodoh

Bankruptcy Appellate Panel Clerk

Leonard Green
532 U.S. Courthouse
100 East Fifth Street
Cincinnati, Ohio 45202-3988
(513) 564-7000

SEVENTH CIRCUIT includes Illinois, Indiana and Wisconsin. The court sits at Chicago, Illinois, and at other locations as ordered by the court.

Chief Judge

Joel M. Flaum

Judges

Richard A. Posner
Frank H. Easterbrook
Daniel A. Manion
Ilana Diamond Rovner
Terence T. Evans
John L. Coffey
Kenneth F. Ripple
Michael S. Kanne
Diane P. Wood
Ann Claire Williams

Senior Judges

Thomas E. Fairchild
William J. Bauer
Harlington Wood, Jr.
Richard D. Cudahy

Clerk

Gino J. Agnello
U.S. Courthouse
219 South Dearborn Street
Chicago, Illinois 60604
(312) 435-5850

UNITED STATES COURTS OF APPEALS—*Continued*

EIGHTH CIRCUIT includes Arkansas, Iowa, Minnesota, Missouri, Nebraska, North Dakota and South Dakota. The court sits at St. Paul, Minnesota; Kansas City and St. Louis, Missouri; and Omaha, Nebraska, and at other locations as ordered by the court.

Chief Judge
James B. Loken

Judges
Theodore McMillian
Roger L. Wollman
Diana E. Murphy
William Jay Riley
Lavenski R. Smith
Pasco M. Bowman II
Morris Sheppard Arnold
Kermit E. Bye
Michael J. Melloy

Senior Judges
Donald P. Lay
Myron H. Bright
Richard S. Arnold
George G. Fagg
Clarence Arlen Beam
Gerald W. Heaney
Donald R. Ross
John R. Gibson
Frank J. Magill
David R. Hansen

Clerk
Michael E. Gans
24.329 U.S. Courthouse
111 South Tenth Street
St. Louis, Missouri 63102
(314) 244-2400

Bankruptcy Appellate Panel Eighth Circuit

Chief Judge
Robert J. Kressel

Judges
William Alexander Hill
Barry S. Schermer
Nancy C. Dreher
Arthur B. Federman

Bankruptcy Appellate Panel Clerk
Michael E. Gans
24.329 U.S. Courthouse
111 South Tenth Street
St. Louis, Missouri 63102
(314) 244-2400

NINTH CIRCUIT includes Alaska, Arizona, California, Hawaii, Idaho, Montana, Nevada, Oregon, Washington, Guam and the Northern Mariana Islands. The court sits at Los Angeles and San Francisco, California; Honolulu, Hawaii; Portland, Oregon; and Seattle, Washington, and at other locations as ordered by the court.

Chief Judge
Mary M. Schroeder

Judges
Harry Pregerson
Alex Kozinski
Stephen S. Trott
Pamela Ann Rymer
Andrew J. Kleinfeld
A. Wallace Tashima
Barry G. Silverman
M. Margaret McKeown
William A. Fletcher
Ronald M. Gould
Marsha L. Berzon
Stephen Reinhardt
Diarmuid F. O'Scannlain
Thomas G. Nelson
Michael Daly Hawkins
Sidney R. Thomas
Susan P. Graber
Kim M. Wardlaw
Raymond C. Fisher
Richard A. Paez
Richard C. Tallman
Johnnie B. Rawlinson
Richard R. Clifton
Jay S. Bybee

Senior Judges
James R. Browning
Alfred T. Goodwin
Joseph Tyree Sneed
Otto R. Skopil, Jr.
Betty B. Fletcher
Warren J. Ferguson
William C. Canby, Jr.
Robert R. Beezer
Melvin T. Brunetti
John T. Noonan, Jr.
Ferdinand F. Fernandez
Herbert Y. C. Choy
J. Clifford Wallace
Procter Hug, Jr.
Jerome Farris
Arthur L. Alarcon
Dorothy Wright Nelson
Robert Boochever
Cynthia Holcomb Hall
David R. Thompson
Edward Leavy

Clerk
Cathy A. Catterson
P.O. Box 193939
San Francisco, California 94119-3939
(415) 556-9800

Bankruptcy Appellate Panel Ninth Circuit

Chief Judge
John E. Ryan

Judges
James M. Marlar
Dennis Montali
Elizabeth L. Perris
Christopher M. Klein
Philip H. Brandt

Bankruptcy Appellate Panel Clerk
Nancy B. Dickerson
Court of Appeals Building
125 South Grand Avenue
Pasadena, California 91105-1652
(626) 229-7224

TENTH CIRCUIT includes Colorado, Kansas, New Mexico, Oklahoma, Utah and Wyoming. The court sits at Denver, Colorado; Wichita, Kansas; and Oklahoma City, Oklahoma, and at other locations as ordered by the court.

Chief Judge
Deanell Reece Tacha

Judges
Stephanie Kulp Seymour
Paul J. Kelly, Jr.
Mary Beck Briscoe
Michael R. Murphy
Terrence L. O'Brien
David M. Ebel
Robert Harlan Henry
Carlos F. Lucero
Harris L. Hartz
Michael W. McConnell

Senior Judges
William Holloway, Jr.
Monroe G. McKay
Stephen H. Anderson
Wade Brorby
Robert H. McWilliams
John C. Porfilio
Bobby R. Baldock

Clerk
Patrick J. Fisher
U.S. Courthouse
1823 Stout Street
Denver, Colorado 80257
(303) 844-3157

UNITED STATES COURTS OF APPEALS—*Continued*

Bankruptcy Appellate Panel Tenth Circuit

Chief Judge
Mark B. McFeeley

Judges

Tom R. Cornish
Glen E. Clark
Judith A. Boulden
Robert E. Nugent
James A. Pusateri
Richard L. Bohanon
Terrence L. Michael

Bankruptcy Appellate Panel Clerk
Barbara A. Schermerhorn
U.S. Courthouse
1823 Stout Street
Denver, Colorado 80257
(303) 335-2900

ELEVENTH CIRCUIT includes Alabama, Florida and Georgia. The court sits at Montgomery, Alabama; Jacksonville, Florida; and Atlanta, Georgia, and at other locations as ordered by the court.

Chief Judge
J. L. Edmondson

Judges

Gerald Bard Tjoflat
Stanley F. Birch, Jr.
Susan Harrell Black
Rosemary Barkett
Stanley Marcus
R. Lanier Anderson, III
Joel F. Dubina
Ed Carnes
Frank M. Hull
Charles R. Wilson

Senior Judges

John C. Godbold
James Clinkscales Hill
Phyllis A. Kravitch
Paul H. Roney
Peter T. Fay
Emmett Ripley Cox

Clerk
Thomas K. Kahn
Court of Appeals Building
56 Forsyth Street N.W.
Atlanta, Georgia 30303
(404) 335-6100

FEDERAL CIRCUIT includes all federal judicial districts. The court sits at Washington, D.C., and at other locations as ordered by the court.

Chief Judge
H. Robert Mayer

Judges

Pauline Newman
Alan D. Lourie
Randall R. Rader
William C. Bryson
Richard Linn
Sharon Prost
Paul R. Michel
Raymond Clevenger III
Alvin A. Schall
Arthur J. Gajarsa
Timothy B. Dyk

Senior Judges
Byron G. Skelton
Daniel M. Friedman
Glenn L. Archer, Jr.
S. Jay Plager

Clerk
Jan Horbaly
National Courts Building
717 Madison Place N.W.
Washington, D.C. 20439-0002
(202) 312-5520

UNITED STATES DISTRICT COURTS

The United States District Courts are the trial courts of general federal jurisdiction. The fifty states are divided into eighty-nine district courts with each state having at least one district and as many as four districts. A district may be further divided into divisions. There is also a District Court in the District of Columbia and the Commonwealth of Puerto Rico. In addition, there are territorial District Courts in Guam, the Northern Mariana Islands and the Virgin Islands, which have local as well as federal jurisdiction. Except for the judges in Guam, the Northern Mariana Islands and the Virgin Islands, who serve ten-year terms, all District Court judges are appointed by the President with the approval of the Senate to serve during good behavior. The judge in each district who is senior in commission of those under sixty-five years of age and who has not previously served in that capacity is the chief judge. The chief judge serves for a nonrenewable term of seven years or until age seventy (whichever occurs first). Retired district judges may serve by assignment as senior judges. The term "magistrate" was changed to "magistrate judge" effective December 1, 1990. U.S. magistrate judges are appointed by majority vote of the district judges in each district to assist the judges with their judicial work. Full-time magistrate judges are appointed for a term of eight years, and part-time magistrate judges are appointed for a term of four years. In 1984, under the Bankruptcy Code, Congress created as a unit of the District Court a Bankruptcy Court for each district. Since passage of the 1984 Bankruptcy Act, Bankruptcy Court judges are appointed by the U.S. Court of Appeals judges of each circuit to serve fourteen-year terms. Retired magistrate judges and retired Bankruptcy Court judges may be recalled by the judicial council of a circuit to serve any judicial district within that circuit.

The District Courts have original jurisdiction of all civil actions arising under the Constitution, laws and treaties of the United States, cases of admiralty or maritime jurisdiction, civil cases against a foreign state and civil cases between citizens of different states or between the citizens of a state and subjects of a foreign state when the amount in controversy exceeds $50,000. The jurisdiction of magistrate judges is limited primarily to pretrial hearings and motions; they may also hear any civil case with or without a jury upon the consent of the parties, as well as criminal misdemeanor cases. Bankruptcy Court judges have jurisdiction as referred by the District Court in such matters as adjudging persons or firms bankrupt, causing the estates of debtors to be collected and appointing receivers or marshals to take charge of the property of debtors.

Usually only one judge hears a case in a District Court, but in rare cases it is required that three judges comprise the court. The courts sit in prescribed cities within districts.

Biographical information for District Court judges of the Commonwealth of Puerto Rico and the territorial District Courts of Guam, the Northern Mariana Islands

UNITED STATES DISTRICT COURTS—*Continued*

and the Virgin Islands is listed in the United States Courts section. Information regarding all other District Court judges is listed under the individual states.

DISTRICT OF GUAM sits at Hagåtña.

Chief Judge
John S. Unpingco

Clerk
Mary Lou Michels Moran
U.S. Courthouse, Fourth Floor
520 West Soledad Avenue
Hagåtña, Guam 96910
(671) 473-9100

DISTRICT OF THE NORTHERN MARIANA ISLANDS sits at Saipan.

Chief Judge
Alex R. Munson

Clerk
Galo Perez
P.O. Box 500687
Saipan, MP 96950-0687
(670) 236-2902

DISTRICT OF PUERTO RICO sits at San Juan.

Chief Judge
Hector M. Laffitte

Judges

Juan M. Perez-Gimenez	Carmen Consuelo Cerezo
Jose Antonio Fuste	Salvador E. Casellas
Daniel R. Dominguez	Jay A. Garcia-Gregory

Senior Judges
Gilberto Gierbolini-Ortiz
Jaime Pieras, Jr.
Raymond L. Acosta

Magistrate Judges
Jesus A. Castellanos
Justo Arenas
Aida M. Delgado-Colon
Gustavo A. Gelpi, Jr.

Clerk
Frances Rios de Moran
150 Federal Building
150 Carlos Chardon Avenue
San Juan, Puerto Rico 00918-1767
(787) 772-3000

Bankruptcy Court Chief Judge
Gerardo A. Carlo-Altieri

Bankruptcy Court Judges
Enrique S. Lamoutte
Sara E. De Jesus

Bankruptcy Clerk
Celestino Matta-Mendez
109 U.S. Courthouse
300 Recinto Sur Street
San Juan, Puerto Rico 00901
(787) 977-6000

DISTRICT OF THE VIRGIN ISLANDS sits at Charlotte Amalie, St. Thomas and Christiansted, St. Croix, and at other locations as ordered by the court.

Chief Judge
Raymond L. Finch

Judge
Thomas K. Moore

Magistrate Judges
Geoffrey W. Barnard
Jeffrey L. Resnick

Clerk
Wilfredo F. Morales
136 Federal Building Lot 13
3013 Estate Golden Rock
Christiansted
St. Croix, Virgin Islands 00820
(340) 773-1130

UNITED STATES COURT OF INTERNATIONAL TRADE

The United States Court of International Trade is a special court of nationwide jurisdiction dealing primarily with cases involving international trade and custom duties. Originally established as the Board of U.S. General Appraisers in 1890 and named the U.S. Customs Court in 1926, it was integrated into the federal court structure under Article III of the Constitution in 1956. On November 1, 1980, the U.S. Court of International Trade was created as the successor to the U.S. Customs Court. Judges are appointed by the President with the advice and consent of the Senate to serve during good behavior. Not more than five of the judges may belong to any one political party. The designation of the chief judge is governed by 28 U.S.C. § 258 and conforms to the seniority system applicable to the other Article III courts.

The court has exclusive jurisdiction of civil actions against the United States, its agencies and officers arising under the tariff laws. This includes controversies challenging duties the federal government has placed on imports as well as suits against federal "anti-dumping" duties. The court also has original jurisdiction over suits initiated by the United States concerning import transactions and federal statutes governing international trade and may review decisions by the secretaries of commerce and labor certifying which workers, businesses and communities are eligible for assistance because of economic injury caused by import competition. The court possesses all the powers in law and equity of, or as conferred by statute upon, a U.S. District Court and is authorized to conduct jury trials. Appeals are to the U.S. Court of Appeals for the Federal Circuit.

All cases are decided by a single judge except cases involving a constitutional issue or otherwise having broad and significant implications, which may be assigned by the chief judge to a three-judge panel. The court is located in New York City, but sessions may be held at any place within the jurisdiction of the United States. The court is also authorized to hold hearings in foreign countries.

Chief Judge
Gregory W. Carman

UNITED STATES COURT OF INTERNATIONAL TRADE—*Continued*

Judges

Jane A. Restani
Donald C. Pogue
Delissa A. Ridgway
Richard K. Eaton
Thomas J. Aquilino, Jr.
Evan J. Wallach
Judith M. Barzilay
Timothy C. Stanceu

Senior Judges

Nicholas Tsoucalas
R. Kenton Musgrave
Richard W. Goldberg

Clerk

Leo M. Gordon
One Federal Plaza
New York, New York 10278-0001
(212) 264-2814

UNITED STATES COURT OF FEDERAL CLAIMS

The United States Court of Federal Claims was originally established by Congress as the United States Court of Claims in 1855. The court has nationwide jurisdiction in suits against the federal government for money judgments and not sounding in tort, wherein Congress has waived the sovereign immunity of the United States. Aliens and foreign governments may bring suits in the court provided their courts give our citizens the same privilege. Judges are appointed by the President with the advice and consent of the Senate to fifteen-year terms. A chief judge is selected by the President to serve until age seventy or until another chief judge is designated. Retired judges may serve by assignment as senior judges.

The court has exclusive jurisdiction of cases involving patent and copyright infringements by the federal government. The court has original jurisdiction of all claims against the United States which are founded upon the Constitution, an act of Congress, any regulation of an executive department and any express or implied contract with the United States as well as claims for liquidated or unliquidated damages not sounding in tort. The court's jurisdiction extends to claims by or against contractors subject to the Contract Disputes Act of 1978. The court has jurisdiction concurrent with the U.S. District Courts of tax refund claims and any other civil action or claim against the United States not exceeding $10,000. The court has appellate jurisdiction of decisions rendered by the Indian Claims Commission. The court exercises its power by appropriate process, including the power of subpoena served anywhere the federal government exercises its domain. The judgments of the court are subject to review by the U.S. Court of Appeals for the Federal Circuit.

The court is headquartered in Washington, D.C., but the court sits throughout the U.S. for the convenience of the parties. Judicial power is exercised by a single judge.

Chief Judge

Edward J. Damich

Judges

Christine Odell Cook Miller
Diane Gilbert Sypolt
James T. Turner
Robert H. Hodges, Jr.
Lawrence M. Baskir
Lynn Jeanne Bush
Francis M. Allegra
Lawrence J. Block
Emily Clark Hewitt
Nancy B. Firestone

Senior Judges

Thomas J. Lydon
Reginald W. Gibson
Moody R. Tidwell
James F. Merow
Marian Blank Horn
Wilkes C. Robinson
Bohdan A. Futey
Kenneth R. Harkins
Lawrence S. Margolis
Robert J. Yock
Loren A. Smith
Eric G. Bruggink
John P. Wiese

Clerk

Margaret Mary Earnest
National Courts Building
717 Madison Place N.W.
Washington, D.C. 20005-1086
(202) 208-4968

UNITED STATES COURT OF APPEALS FOR THE ARMED FORCES

The United States Court of Appeals for the Armed Forces is a special United States court originally established in 1950 as the United States Court of Military Appeals. As of October 5, 1994 the court became known by its current name. The court consists of civilian judges who are appointed by the President with the advice and consent of the Senate for fifteen-year terms. The court is judicially independent and does not come under the purview of the Judicial Conference of the U.S. or the Administrative Office of the U.S. Courts.

The court has appellate jurisdiction of all criminal cases involving a court-martial in any of the armed services or the Coast Guard. The court hears appeals in matters of law under the Uniform Code of Military Justice which involve a general or a flag officer, the death penalty, a sentence of one year or more imprisonment and/or dismissal, a dishonorable or bad conduct discharge and cases certified by the Judge Advocates General of the armed services or the General Counsel of the Department of Transportation acting for the Coast Guard. The court also entertains petitions for extraordinary relief in aid of its jurisdiction. Although the court was previously the final appellate tribunal in the military justice system, as of August 1, 1984, decisions may be reviewed by the U.S. Supreme Court by writ of certiorari.

The court sits at Washington, D.C.

Chief Judge

Susan J. Crawford

Associate Judges

Herman Frederick "Sparky" Gierke, III
Andrew S. Effron
James Edgar Baker

Senior Judges

Walter Thompson Cox, III
Eugene R. Sullivan
Robinson O. Everett

Clerk

William A. DeCicco
450 E Street N.W.
Washington, D.C. 20442-0001
(202) 761-1448

UNITED STATES COURT OF APPEALS FOR VETERANS CLAIMS

The United States Court of Appeals for Veterans Claims was orginally established as the United States Court of Veterans Appeals on November 18, 1988 by the enactment of the Veteran's Judicial Review Act. It commenced operation in October 1989. The court became known by its current name on March 1, 1999, as a result of the Veterans Programs Enhancement Act of 1998. The court consists of a chief judge and at least three but not more than seven judges appointed by the President with the advice and consent of the Senate for fifteen-year terms. During the period from January 1, 2002 through August 15, 2005, the authorized number of judges of the court is increased by two. These two judges will serve for thirteen-year terms. The court is judicially independent and does not come under the purview of the Judicial Conference of the U.S. or the Administrative Office of the U.S. Courts.

The court has exclusive jurisdiction to review final decisions of the Board of Veterans Appeals, which is an administrative body within the Department of Veterans Affairs. Most appeals involve the entitlement to or amount of disability or survivor benefits, although a few may involve education benefits, life insurance, home loan foreclosure, or waiver of indebtedness. The court reviews the record which was made available to the Board. It does not hold new trials or receive new evidence. Decisions of the U.S. Court of Appeals for Veterans Claims may be appealed to the U.S. Court of Appeals for the Federal Circuit and subsequently reviewed by the U.S. Supreme Court.

The court sits at Washington, D.C., but may sit anywhere in the United States.

Chief Judge
Kenneth B. Kramer

Judges
John J. Farley, III
Donald L. Ivers
Jonathan Robert Steinberg
William P. Greene, Jr.

Executive Officer and Clerk
Norman Y. Herring
625 Indiana Avenue N.W., Suite 900
Washington, D.C. 20004-2950
(202) 501-5980

UNITED STATES TAX COURT

The United States Tax Court is a special court of record created under Article I of the Constitution. Originally called the U.S. Board of Tax Appeals and established as an independent agency in the executive branch in 1924, it became the Tax Court of the U.S. in 1942 and assumed its current name in 1969. Judges are appointed by the President with the advice and consent of the Senate for fifteen-year terms. A chief judge is elected by peer vote for a two-year term. The chief judge appoints special trial judges who hear cases in the Small Tax Division or serve as the court directs. The chief judge may also recall retired judges to perform judicial duties as senior judges. The court is judicially independent and does not come under the purview of the Judicial Conference of the U.S. or the Administrative Office of the U.S. Courts.

The court has jurisdiction over controversies between taxpayers and the Internal Revenue Service which involve deficiencies or overpayments in income, estate, gift and personal holding company surtaxes. Decisions of this court may be appealed to the appropriate U.S. Court of Appeals and subsequently reviewed by the U.S. Supreme Court on writ of certiorari. At the option of individual taxpayers, cases involving $50,000 or less may be tried under the simplified rules of the Small Tax Division, the decisions of which are final and cannot be appealed.

The court sits at Washington, D.C. and other cities as required for the convenience of the parties. Sessions are conducted by a single judge or special trial judge.

Chief Judge
Thomas B. Wells

Judges
Renato Beghe
Carolyn P. Chiechi
Mary Ann Cohen
John O. Colvin
Maurice B. Foley
Joseph H. Gale
Joel Gerber
James S. Halpern
David Laro
L. Paige Marvel
Robert P. Ruwe
Stephen J. Swift
Michael B. Thornton
Juan Flores Vasquez
Laurence J. Whalen

Senior Judges
Herbert L. Chabot
Howard A. Dawson, Jr.
Julian I. Jacobs
Arthur L. Nims III

Special Trial Judges
Robert N. Armen, Jr.
Lewis R. Carluzzo
D. Irvin Couvillion
John F. Dean
Daniel J. Dinan
Stanley J. Goldberg
John J. Pajak
Peter J. Panuthos
Carleton D. Powell
Norman H. Wolfe

Clerk
Charles S. Casazza
400 Second Street N.W.
Washington, D.C. 20217-0002
(202) 606-8754

NATIVE AMERICAN INDIAN COURTS OF LAW

Native American Indian Tribes have traditionally been dealt with as sovereign nations in this country. Hence, Indian law enforcement was a concern only when a non-Indian was involved. As Indians and non-Indians began living in closer proximity, the need arose to deal with Indians on an individual rather than a tribal basis. The post Civil War period marks the beginning of non-Indians' involvement in law enforcement in Indian country. In 1924 the legal status of Indians was changed when all Indians were granted United States citizenship. These factors and more, plus the many treaties and agreements between the United States and Indians, have all contributed to the evolution of the courts of Indian law.

Courts of Indian law are established as courts of limited jurisdiction on many Indian reservations in the United States. The courts may be established under tribal au-

NATIVE AMERICAN INDIAN COURTS OF LAW—*Continued*

thority or under the authority of Title 25 of the Code of Federal Regulations as courts of Indian offenses. The largest number of tribal justice systems are those known as tribal courts. In some states Indian matters and offenses are under the jurisdiction of state courts.

Courts may be established by a tribe on reservations which are under the jurisdiction of the United States government. If the tribe has a constitution and legal code, a tribal court may be established and may operate under tribal authority. In tribes without a constitution and legal code, courts are established and operate under the authority of Title 25 of the Code of Federal Regulations (CFR courts). These courts exist only when tribal law and custom have broken down and there is no adequate substitute under state or federal law. Among the courts under tribal authority, Pueblo Custom Courts are governed by customs that are centuries old.

Judges of tribal courts are either elected or chosen by the tribal council. Judges of CFR courts are appointed for four-year terms by the Bureau of Indian Affairs with tribal approval. A judge of an Indian court must be a member of that tribe and must not have a felony record or, within a year prior to appointment, have been convicted of a misdemeanor.

CFR courts have criminal jurisdiction over the offenses described in 25 CFR Part 11. Tribal courts have jurisdiction over crimes described in the tribal legal code or constitution. In both types of courts the criminal jurisdiction is over lesser offenses. Civil jurisdiction in both courts is generally limited to suits between tribal members. The courts may have jurisdiction over suits in which some, but not all, the parties are tribal members, provided the nonmembers agree to the courts' jurisdiction. In 1974 the U.S. District Court Western District of Washington upheld, in *Oliphant v. Schlie,* a tribal ordinance giving the tribe jurisdiction over non-Indians on the reservation. In 1976 this decision was upheld in the U.S. Court of Appeals for the Ninth Circuit. Some Indian courts maintain jurisdiction over all enlisted Indians as well as those living on the reservation. Indian court jurisdiction is concurrent, not exclusive, in any case where the offense is also under the jurisdiction of state or federal courts. Some Indian courts exercise jurisdiction over juvenile cases and appellate jurisdiction over other tribal courts.

Intertribal court systems have also been established in several locations. These court systems usually serve several different tribes within a specific geographical area. For example, The Intertribal Court of Appeals of South Dakota serves as an appellate court for three Sioux tribes: Crow Creek, Rosebud and Sisseton-Wahpeton. The CFR court system in Western Oklahoma serves several different tribes at four locations. The Northwest Intertribal Court System, a nonprofit private agency, serves fifteen tribes in the Northwest and acts primarily as a personnel services bank for member tribes which cannot afford a fully functioning court system of their own.

Indians on reservations are subject to the general federal laws, as are all Americans, and are also subject to federal laws which are applicable to federal enclaves other than the District of Columbia. The U.S. Supreme Court, in *William v. United States,* held that the Assimilative Crimes Act, 18 U.S.C. 13, gives the federal courts jurisdiction to try any person accused of violating a state law on an Indian reservation. Additionally, the Major Crimes Act, 18 U.S.C. 1153, gives the federal courts jurisdiction over thirteen specific crimes when committed by an Indian in Indian country. Other federal criminal statutes deal with specific subject matter offenses on Indian reservations.

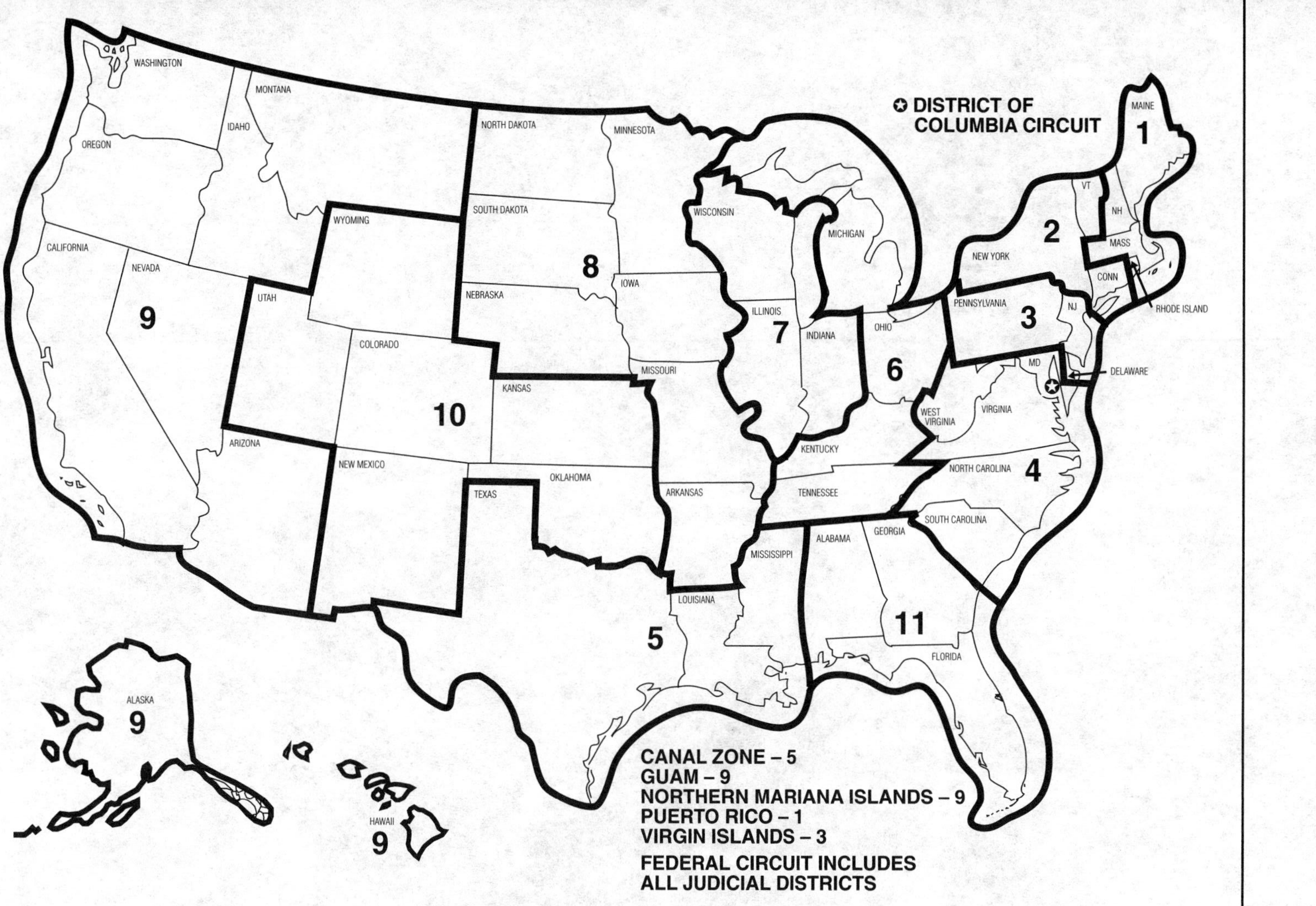
DISTRICT OF COLUMBIA CIRCUIT
WASHINGTON
MONTANA
OREGON
IDAHO
NORTH DAKOTA
MINNESOTA
MAINE
1
VT
NH
MASS
CONN
RHODE ISLAND
2
NEW YORK
WISCONSIN
MICHIGAN
WYOMING
SOUTH DAKOTA
CALIFORNIA
NEVADA
9
8
IOWA
UTAH
NEBRASKA
ILLINOIS
7
INDIANA
OHIO
PENNSYLVANIA
3
NJ
COLORADO
MISSOURI
MD
DELAWARE
6
KANSAS
10
WEST VIRGINIA
VIRGINIA
ARIZONA
NEW MEXICO
KENTUCKY
NORTH CAROLINA
4
OKLAHOMA
TEXAS
ARKANSAS
TENNESSEE
SOUTH CAROLINA
ALABAMA
GEORGIA
MISSISSIPPI
LOUISIANA
11
5
FLORIDA
ALASKA
9
HAWAII
9
CANAL ZONE – 5
GUAM – 9
NORTHERN MARIANA ISLANDS – 9
PUERTO RICO – 1
VIRGIN ISLANDS – 3
FEDERAL CIRCUIT INCLUDES
ALL JUDICIAL DISTRICTS

CIRCUITS OF UNITED STATES COURTS OF APPEALS

UNITED STATES COURTS

ACOSTA, Raymond L. *(Senior Judge, United States District Court District of Puerto Rico)* Appointed for life by President Ronald Reagan to term beginning Oct 14, 1982. Assumed Senior status June 1, 1994, serves by assignment. Born New York New York May 31, 1925. Educated at Princeton University 1948 and Rutgers University J.D. 1952. Member Delta Theta Phi. Admitted to practice New Jersey 1953, U.S. Supreme Court 1956 and Puerto Rico 1959. In legal practice Hackensack New Jersey 1953-54 and San Juan Puerto Rico 1961-66.

Assistant U.S. Attorney 1958-61. U.S. Attorney 1980-82. Author "The Application of the Employee Retirement Security Act of 1974 to Puerto Rico" Puerto Rico Bar Association L. Rev. May 1978. Member Federal Bar Association (Past President Puerto Rico Chapter). USN March 1943 to March 1946. Participant D-Day invasion of Normandy (Utah Beach) on June 6, 1944. Special Agent Federal Bureau of Investigation 1954-58. Alternate Delegate U.S.-Puerto Rico Commission on the Status of Puerto Rico (STACOM) 1962-63. Member Governor's Special Committee to Study the Structure and Organization of the Police Department of Puerto Rico 1969. President United Fund of Puerto Rico 1979.

Office: 348 Courthouse & Post Office Bldg., Third Floor, 300 Recinto Sur Street, San Juan, Puerto Rico 00901.

Telephone: (787) 977-6070.

ALARCON, Arthur L. *(Senior Judge, United States Court of Appeals Ninth Circuit)* Appointed for life by President Jimmy Carter to term beginning Nov 20, 1979. Assumed Senior status Nov 21, 1992, serves by assignment. Born Los Angeles California Aug 14, 1925. Catholic. Educated at University of California at Los Angeles 1946-48 and University of Southern California B.A. in Political Science 1949 LL.B. 1951. Editorial Board University of Southern California Law Review 1950-51. Law Clerk to Superior Court of California Los Angeles County. Admitted to practice California 1952. Began legal practice Los Angeles 1952. Judge, Superior Court of California Los Angeles County July 1, 1964 to June 8, 1978, appointed by Governor Edmund G. Brown, Sr. Associate Justice, California Court of Appeal Second District June 8, 1978 to Nov 20, 1979, appointed by Governor Edmund G. Brown, Jr.

Deputy District Attorney Los Angeles County June 23, 1952 to July 31, 1961. Legal Advisor and Clemency and Extradition Secretary Aug 1, 1961 to July 7, 1962 and Executive Assistant July 9, 1962 to March 14, 1964 to Governor Edmund G. Brown, Sr. Executive Secretary 1962 and temporary Chairman 1964 California Adult Authority. Author chapter on search and seizure problems *California Criminal Law Practice Handbook* California CEB 1964. Co-author with Anthony Murray and Gordon Ringer "Prison Reform: Backward or Forward?" 50 California State B. Jour. 356. Co-editor with Fricke *California Criminal Law* 10th ed., *California Criminal Evidence* 7th ed. and *California Criminal Proceedings* 7th ed. Former Adjunct Professor of Criminal Law Loyola University Law School. Former Lecturer University of Southern California Law Center. Director Special Study Commission on Narcotics 1960-61. Member State Bar of California (Past Chairman Select Committee on Criminal Justice) and Los Angeles County Bar Association (Past Chairman Committee on Criminal Justice). Faculty member California College of Trial Judges 1967-72 and California Judicial College 1973-81. Staff Sergeant U.S. Army Infantry 1943-46. Recipient Combat Infantry Badge, Purple Heart and four Battle Stars. Republican. Founding member and former Chairman Mexican-American Scholarship Foundation Assisting Careers in Law (MAS FACIL). Founder and former Board member Council on Mexican-American Affairs. Former member Board of Directors Coro Foundation Los Angeles Chapter, Los Angeles Boys and Girls Club and Performing Arts Council Los Angeles Music Center.

Office: 1607 U.S. Courthouse, 312 North Spring Street, Los Angeles, California 90012.

Telephone: (213) 894-2693.

ALDISERT, Ruggero J. *(Senior Judge, United States Court of Appeals Third Circuit)* Appointed for life by President Lyndon B. Johnson to term beginning Aug 8, 1968. Former Chief Judge. Assumed Senior status Dec 31, 1986, serves by assignment. Born Carnegie Pennsylvania Nov 10, 1919. Roman Catholic. Educated at University of Pittsburgh B.A. 1941 J.D. 1947. Admitted to practice Pennsylvania 1947. Began legal practice Pittsburgh 1947. Judge, Pennsylvania Court of Common Pleas Fifth Judicial District 1961-68.

Author *The Judicial Process, Text, Materials and Cases* West Publishing Co. 1996. Adjunct Professor of Law University of Pittsburgh 1964-86. Visiting Professor of Law University of Texas July 1972 to Aug 1972. Member Allegheny County, Pennsylvania, Federal and American Bar Associations. Board of Directors and Chairman Federal Appellate Judges Seminars Federal Judicial Center Washington D.C. 1974-80. Faculty member Senior Appellate Judges Conference New York University 1971-85. Major USMC 1942-46.

Office: 120 Cremona Drive, Suite D, Santa Barbara, California 93117-5511.

Telephone: (805) 685-7466.

ALITO, Samuel A., Jr. *(Judge, United States Court of Appeals Third Circuit)* Appointed for life by President George Bush to term beginning June 15, 1990. Born Trenton New Jersey April 1, 1950. Educated at Princeton University A.B. 1972 and Yale Law School J.D. 1975. Editor Yale Law Journal 1974-75. Law Clerk to Hon. Leonard I. Garth, U.S. Court of Appeals Third Circuit 1976-77. Admitted to practice New Jersey 1975.

Mailing address: P.O. Box 999, Newark, New Jersey 07101-0999.

Office: 357 U.S. Post Office & Courthouse, Newark, New Jersey 07102.

Telephone: (973) 645-2424.

ALLEGRA, Francis M. *(Judge, United States Court of Federal Claims)* Appointed by President Bill Clinton to term beginning Oct 16, 1998. Term expires Oct 2013. Educated at Borromeo College of Ohio 1978 and Cleve-

ALLEGRA, FRANCIS M.—*Continued*

land State University J.D. 1981. Law Clerk to Hon. Philip R. Miller, U.S. Court of Claims 1981-82. In legal practice Cleveland 1982-84.

Trial Attorney, Special Assistant to Assistant Attorney General and Counselor to Assistant Attorney General Tax Division U.S. Department of Justice 1984-94. Counselor to Associate Attorney General and Deputy Associate Attorney General U.S. Department of Justice 1994-98.

Office: National Courts Building, 717 Madison Place N.W., Washington, D.C. 20005-1086.

Telephone: (202) 219-1317.

AMBRO, Thomas L. *(Judge, United States Court of Appeals Third Circuit)* Appointed for life by President Bill Clinton to term beginning June 19, 2000. Born Cambridge Ohio Dec 27, 1949. Educated at Georgetown University B.A. 1971 J.D. 1975. Law Clerk to Chief Justice Daniel L. Herrmann, Delaware Supreme Court 1975-76. In legal practice 1976-2000.

Office: 5122 Federal Building, Lockbox 32, 844 North King Street, Wilmington, Delaware 19801.

Telephone: (302) 573-6500.

ANDERSON, R. Lanier, III *(Judge, United States Court of Appeals Eleventh Circuit)* Appointed to Fifth Circuit for life by President Jimmy Carter to term beginning Aug 6, 1979. Assigned to Eleventh Circuit Oct 1, 1981. Former Chief Judge. Born Macon Georgia Nov 12, 1936. Episcopalian. Educated at Yale University A.B. magna cum laude 1958 and Harvard University LL.B. 1961. Admitted to practice Georgia. Began legal practice Macon 1963.

Member American Judicature Society, State Bar of Georgia, Macon and American Bar Associations. Captain U.S. Army 1961-63.

Mailing address: P.O. Box 977, Macon, Georgia 31202-0977.

Telephone: (478) 752-8101.

ANDERSON, Stephen H. *(Senior Judge, United States Court of Appeals Tenth Circuit)* Appointed for life by President Ronald Reagan to term beginning 1985. Assumed Senior status Jan 1, 2000, serves by assignment. Born Salt Lake City Utah Jan 12, 1932. Educated at University of Utah College of Law LL.B. 1960. In legal practice Salt Lake City 1964-85.

Trial Attorney Tax Division U.S. Department of Justice 1960-64. U.S. Army 1953-55.

Office: 4201 Federal Building, 125 South State Street, Salt Lake City, Utah 84138-1102.

Telephone: (801) 524-6950.

AQUILINO, Thomas J., Jr. *(Judge, United States Court of International Trade)* Appointed for life by President Ronald Reagan.

Office: One Federal Plaza, New York, New York 10278-0001.

Telephone: (212) 264-2854.

ARCHER, Glenn L., Jr. *(Senior Judge, United States Court of Appeals Federal Circuit)* Appointed for life by President Ronald Reagan Oct 1985 to term beginning Dec 23, 1985. Chief Judge March 19, 1994 to Dec 24, 1997. Assumed Senior status Dec 24, 1997, serves by assignment. Born Densmore Kansas March 21, 1929. Educated at Yale University B.A. 1951 and George Washington University Law School J.D. with honors 1954. In legal practice Washington D.C. 1956-81.

Assistant Attorney General Tax Division U.S. Department of Justice Dec 1981 to Dec 1985.

Office: National Courts Building, 717 Madison Place N.W., Washington, D.C. 20439-0002.

Telephone: (202) 633-5846.

ARENAS, Justo *(Magistrate Judge, United States District Court District of Puerto Rico)* Appointed by U.S. District Court judges.

Office: 198 Federal Building, 150 Carlos Chardon Avenue, San Juan, Puerto Rico 00918-1760.

Telephone: (787) 772-3190.

ARMEN, Robert N., Jr. *(Special Trial Judge, United States Tax Court)* Appointed by U.S. Tax Court Chief Judge.

Office: 400 Second Street N.W., Washington, D.C. 20217-0002.

Telephone: (202) 874-6101.

ARNOLD, Morris Sheppard *(Judge, United States Court of Appeals Eighth Circuit)* Appointed for life by President George Bush to term beginning June 2, 1992. Born Texarkana Texas Oct 8, 1941. Episcopalian. Educated at Yale University 1959-61, University of Arkansas B.S.E.E. 1965 LL.B. 1968 and Harvard University LL.M. 1969 S.J.D. 1971. Honorary LL.D. University of Arkansas at Little Rock 1999. Knox Fellow University of London 1970-71. Editor-in-Chief Arkansas Law Review 1967. Member Sigma Pi, Theta Tau and Tau Beta Pi. Admitted to practice Arkansas 1968 and Pennsylvania 1984. In legal practice Texarkana Arkansas 1968. Judge, U.S. District Court Western District of Arkansas Dec 30, 1985 to June 1, 1992.

Author "Select Cases of Trespass from the King's Courts 1309-1399" Selden Society 1985 and 1988 and *Unequal Laws Unto a Savage Rule: European Legal Traditions in Arkansas 1686-1836* 1985, *Colonial Arkansas, 1686-1804: A Social and Cultural History* 1991 and *Rumble of a Distant Drum: The Quapaw and Old World Newcomers, 1673-1804* 2000 University of Arkansas Press. Professor of Law Indiana University 1971-77 and University of Pennsylvania 1977-81. Altheimer Distinguished Professor of Law University of Arkansas at Little Rock 1981-84. Visiting Professor Stanford Law School 1985. Dean Indiana University School of Law 1985. Member The American Law Institute. Recipient Chevalier dans l'Ordre des Palmes Academiques. General Counsel 1982 and State Chairman 1983 Republican Party of Arkansas. Chairman Scholars for Reagan Committee Pennsylvania 1984.

Mailing address: P.O. Box 2060, Little Rock, Arkansas 72203-2060.

Telephone: (501) 324-6880.

ARNOLD, Richard Sheppard *(Senior Judge, United States Court of Appeals Eighth Circuit)* Appointed to serve during good behavior by President Jimmy Carter to term beginning March 7, 1980. Former Chief Judge to April 18, 1998. Assumed Senior status April 1, 2001, serves by assignment. Born Texarkana Texas March 26, 1936. Episcopalian. Educated at Yale University B.A. summa cum laude 1957 and Harvard University LL.B. magna cum laude 1960. Case Editor Harvard Law Review 1959-60. Law Clerk to Hon. William J. Brennan, Jr., U.S. Supreme Court 1960-61. Member Phi Beta Kappa. Admitted to practice Arkansas 1960 and District

ARNOLD, RICHARD SHEPPARD—*Continued*

of Columbia 1961. In legal practice Washington D.C. 1961-64 and Texarkana Arkansas 1964-74. Judge, U.S. District Courts Eastern and Western Districts of Arkansas 1978-80.

Author "Consequences of Abstention by a Federal Court" 73 Harvard L. Rev. 1358, 1960; "The Power of State Courts to Enjoin Federal Officers" 73 Yale L. Jour. 1385, 1964; "State Power to Enjoin Federal Court Proceedings" 51 Virginia L. Rev. 59, 1965; "The Supreme Court and the Antitrust Laws" 34 ABA Antitrust L. Jour. 2, 1967; "An Ombudsman for Arkansas" 21 Arkansas L. Rev. 327, 1967; "The Substantive Right to Environmental Quality Under the National Environmental Policy Act" 3 Environmental Law Reporter 50028, 1973; "Judges and the Public" 9 No. 4 Litigation 5 Summer 1983; "Address of Circuit Judge Richard S. Arnold to the 1983 Judicial Conference" 5 Third Circuit Jour. 5-8 Spring 1984; "Mr. Justice Blackmun: An Appreciation" Hamline University L. Rev. Jan 1985; book review *The Role of Courts in American Society* 64 Washington University Law Quarterly 279, 1986; "Address of Judge Richard Arnold, United States Court of Appeals, Eighth Circuit" *Symposium on the Judiciary* Arkansas Bar Foundation 1989; "Mr. Justice Brennan—An Appreciation" 26 Harvard Civil Rights-Civil Liberties L. Rev. 7, 1991; "Justice Brennan and the State Courts" 26 Valparaiso University L. Rev. V 1991; "A Remembrance: Mr. Justice Brennan October Term 1960" J. Sup. Ct. Hist. 5, 1991; "A Tribute to Judge Donald P. Lay" 18 William Mitchell L. Rev. 561, 1992; "Trial by Jury: The Constitutional Right to a Jury of Twelve in Civil Trials" 22 Hofstra L. Rev. 1, 1993; "A Tribute to Justice Harry Blackmun" 108 Harvard L. Rev. 6, 1994; "Justice Harry A. Blackmun: Some Personal Notes" 43 American University L. Rev. 699, 1994; "L. Ralph Mecham: A Tribute" 44 American University L. Rev. 1479, 1995; "Mr. Justice Blackmun: A Reminiscence" 71 North Dakota L. Rev. 3, 1995; "Mr. Justice Blackmun—A Tribute" 28 Creighton L. Rev. 589, 1995; "The Future of the Federal Courts" 60 Missouri L. Rev. 533, 1995; chapter "William J. Brennan, Jr." *The Warren Court: A Retrospective* Bernard Schwartz ed. 1996; "Money, or the Relations of the Judicial Branch with the Other Two Branches, Legislative and Executive" 40 St. Louis University L. Jour. 19, 1996; "Judicial Politics Under President Washington" 38 Arizona L. Rev. 473, 1996; and "How James Madison Interpreted the Constitution" 72 New York University L. Rev. May 1997. Coauthor with Hon. Myron H. Bright "Oral Argument? It May Be Crucial!" 70 ABA Jour. 68 Sept 1984.

Part-time Instructor in Antitrust Practice University of Virginia 1962-64. Fellow American Bar Foundation. Member The American Law Institute (Council member), Pulaski County, Arkansas and American Bar Associations. Instructor Appellate Judges Seminar New York University since 1984. Named Texarkana's Outstanding Young Man 1971, one of Arkansas's Ten Outstanding Young Men by Jaycees 1971 and Conservationist of the Year by the Arkansas Wildlife Foundation 1973. Former Democrat. Legislative Secretary for Governor Dale Bumpers of Arkansas 1973-74. Staff Coordinator 1974 and Legislative Assistant to Senator Dale Bumpers 1975-78. Delegate Democratic National Convention 1968 and Arkansas Constitutional Convention 1969-70. Executive Committee Arkansas Democratic State Committee 1972-74. Board of Trustees University of Arkansas 1973-74. Visiting Committee Harvard University Law School 1973-74 and University of Chicago Law School 1983-86. Enjoys study of Hebrew and playing golf.

Office: 208 U.S. Courthouse, 600 West Capitol Avenue, Little Rock, Arkansas 72201-3336.

Telephone: (501) 604-5210.

AUG, J. Vincent, Jr. *(Judge, Bankruptcy Appellate Panel Sixth Circuit)* Selected by the Judicial Council of the Sixth Circuit. Term expires 2004. Also Judge, U.S. Bankruptcy Court Southern District of Ohio. Former Magistrate, U.S. District Court Southern District of Ohio.

Office: 800 Atrium II, 221 East Fourth Street, Cincinnati, Ohio 45202.

Telephone: (513) 684-2572.

BAKER, James Edgar *(Associate Judge, United States Court of Appeals for the Armed Forces)* Appointed by the President.

Office: 450 E Street N.W., Washington, D.C. 20442-0001.

Telephone: (202) 761-1459.

BALDOCK, Bobby R. *(Senior Judge, United States Court of Appeals Tenth Circuit)* Appointed for life by President Ronald Reagan to term beginning Jan 24, 1986. Assumed Senior status Jan 26, 2001, serves by assignment. Born Rocky Oklahoma Jan 24, 1936. Educated at New Mexico Military Institute 1956 and University of Arizona College of Law J.D. 1960. In legal practice Roswell 1960-83. Judge, U.S. District Court District of New Mexico 1983 to Jan 23, 1986, appointed by President Ronald Reagan.

Adjunct Professor Eastern New Mexico University 1962-81. Captain Adjutant General Staff New Mexico National Guard 1960-70.

Mailing address: P.O. Box 2388, Roswell, New Mexico 88202-2388.

Telephone: (505) 625-2388.

BARKETT, Rosemary *(Judge, United States Court of Appeals Eleventh Circuit)* Appointed for life by President Bill Clinton. Educated at Spring Hill College B.S. summa cum laude 1967 and University of Florida Law School J.D. 1970. Awarded honorary LL.D. Stetson University College of Law 1987, John Marshall Law School 1990, Nova University 1992 and Rollins College 1992, honorary Doctorate of Humane Letters Florida International University 1987 and University of South Florida 1990 and honorary Doctorate of Civil Laws Spring Hill College 1990. Recipient J. Hills Miller Memorial Award University of Florida Law School 1970. In legal practice West Palm Beach 1971-79. Judge 1979-84 and Chief Judge 1983-84, Florida Circuit Court Fifteenth Judicial Circuit. Judge, Florida District Court of Appeal Fourth District 1984-85, appointed by Governor Robert Graham. Former Justice and Chief Justice, Florida Supreme Court, appointed by Governor Robert Graham to term beginning 1985.

Editorial Board *The Florida Judges' Manual.* Board of Directors American Judicature Society. Member Florida Association of Women Lawyers, National Association of Women Judges, The Florida Bar and American Bar Association (Task Force on Death Penalty Habeas Corpus, Standing Committee on Lawyer Public Service Responsibility). Faculty Member Florida Judicial College and The National Judicial College. Recipient American

BARKETT, ROSEMARY—*Continued*

Academy of Matrimonial Lawyers Award 1984, Woman of Achievement Award from Palm Beach County Commission on the Status of Women 1985, Judicial Achievement Award for the State of Florida from The Association of Trial Lawyers of America 1986, Achievement Award from Academy of Florida Trial Lawyers 1988, Hannah G. Solomon Award from National Council of Jewish Women 1991 and Judge Mattie Belle Davis Award from Dade County Association of Women Lawyers 1991-92. Inducted into Florida Women's Hall of Fame 1986. Chair Child Care Welfare Study Commission, Child Support Study Commission and Study Commission on Guardianship Law. Member and former Chair Board of Trustees Palm Beach Marine Institute, Inc. Board of Governors Shepard Broad Law Center Nova University. Board of Advisors University of Florida Center for Governmental Responsibility. Board of Visitors St. Thomas University School of Law. Member Visiting Committee University of Miami School of Law. Member Florida Kids County Advisory Council, Gender Bias Study Implementation Commission and Commission on the Status of Women.

Office: 1223 Federal Justice Building, 99 N.E. Fourth Street, Miami, Florida 33132.

Telephone: (305) 536-7335.

BARKSDALE, Rhesa H. *(Judge, United States Court of Appeals Fifth Circuit)* Appointed for life by President George Bush to term beginning April 1, 1990. Born Jackson Mississippi Aug 8, 1944. Educated at U.S. Military Academy B.S. 1966 and University of Mississippi J.D. 1972. Law Clerk to Associate Justice Byron R. White, U.S. Supreme Court 1972-73. Admitted to practice Mississippi 1972. U.S. Army.

Office: 200 U.S. Courthouse, 245 East Capitol Street, Jackson, Mississippi 39201.

Telephone: (601) 965-5840.

BARNARD, Geoffrey W. *(Magistrate Judge, United States District Court District of the Virgin Islands)* Appointed by U.S. District Court judges.

Office: 345 Federal Building, 5500 Veterans Drive, Charlotte Amalie, St. Thomas, Virgin Islands 00802-6424.

Telephone: (340) 774-5480.

BARRY, Maryanne Trump *(Judge, United States Court of Appeals Third Circuit)* Appointed for life by President Bill Clinton to term beginning Oct 1999. Born New York New York April 5, 1937. Educated at Mount Holyoke College B.A. 1958, Columbia University M.A. 1962 and Hofstra University School of Law J.D. 1974. Judge, U.S. District Court District of New Jersey 1983 to Oct 1999, appointed by President Ronald Reagan.

Assistant U.S. Attorney Civil Division 1974-75, Deputy Chief 1976-77 and Chief 1977-82 Appeals Division, Executive Assistant U.S. Attorney 1981-82 and First Assistant U.S. Attorney 1981-83 U.S. Attorney's Office. Chair Criminal Law Committee Judicial Conference.

Mailing address: P.O. Box 999, Newark, New Jersey 07101-0999.

Office: 333 U.S. Post Office and Courthouse, Newark, New Jersey 07102.

Telephone: (973) 645-2133.

BARZILAY, Judith M. *(Judge, United States Court of International Trade)* Appointed for life by President Bill Clinton Jan 27, 1998 to term beginning June 3, 1998. Born Russell Kansas Jan 3, 1944. Jewish. Educated at Wichita State University B.S. 1965 and Rutgers University M.L.S. 1971 J.D. 1981. Law Clerk to Hon. Robert E. Tarleton, New Jersey Superior Court Law Division Vicinage Six 1981-82. Moot Court Board 1981. Admitted to practice New Jersey 1981, U.S. District Court District of New Jersey 1981, U.S. Court of International Trade 1983 and U.S. Court of Appeals Federal Circuit 1984. In legal practice Wayne New Jersey 1982-83 and New York New York 1986-88.

Senior Attorney 1988-90 and Vice President 1990-98 Sony Corporation.

Office: One Federal Plaza, New York, New York 10278-0001.

Telephone: (212) 264-5420.

E-mail address: judith_barzilay@cit.uscourts.gov

BASKIR, Lawrence M. *(Judge, United States Court of Federal Claims)* Appointed by President Bill Clinton to term beginning Oct 23, 1998. Term expires Oct 2013. Chief Judge July 11, 2000 to May 13, 2002. Educated at Princeton University B.A. and Harvard Law School LL.B.

Principal Deputy General Counsel U.S. Department of the Army 1994-98. Former Legislative Director Senator Bill Bradley. Former Deputy Assistant Secretary for Legislation U.S. Department of the Treasury. Chief Executive Officer and General Counsel Presidential Clemency Board for Draft Evaders and Deserters. Former Chief Counsel and Staff Director Constitutional Rights Subcommittee U.S. Senate Judiciary Committee.

Office: National Courts Building, 717 Madison Place N.W., Washington, D.C. 20005-1086.

Telephone: (202) 219-9565.

BATCHELDER, Alice M. *(Judge, United States Court of Appeals Sixth Circuit)* Appointed for life by President George Bush to term beginning Jan 1992. Born Wilmington Delaware Aug 15, 1944. Religious affiliation: Anglican. Educated at Ohio Wesleyan University B.A. 1964, University of Akron School of Law J.D. 1971 and University of Virginia LL.M. 1988. Admitted to practice Ohio 1971 and U.S. District Court Northern District of Ohio 1973. In legal practice Medina Ohio 1971-83. Bankruptcy Judge 1983-85 and Judge 1985-92, U.S. District Court Northern District of Ohio.

Member Ohio Board of Bar Examiners 1975-80 and Constitutional Law Drafting Committee Multi-State Bar Exam since 1980.

Office: 143 West Liberty Street, Medina, Ohio 44256.

Telephone: (330) 764-6026.

BAUER, William J. *(Senior Judge, United States Court of Appeals Seventh Circuit)* Appointed for life by President Gerald R. Ford to term beginning 1975. Chief Judge Sept 29, 1986 to Sept 28, 1993. Assumed Senior status Oct 31, 1994, serves by assignment. Born Chicago Illinois Sept 15, 1926. Educated at Elmhurst College A.B. with honors 1949 and DePaul University J.D. 1952. Awarded honorary LL.D. Elmhurst College 1969, Roosevelt University 1994 and DePaul University College of Law and LL.D. honoris causa John Marshall Law School 1987. Admitted to practice Illinois 1951. In legal practice 1953-64. Judge, Illinois Circuit Court Eighteenth Judicial Circuit 1964-70. Judge, U.S. District Court Northern District of Illinois 1971-75.

Assistant State's Attorney 1952-56, First Assistant State's Attorney 1956-58 and State's Attorney 1959-64

BAUER, WILLIAM J.—*Continued*

DuPage County. U.S. Attorney Northern District of Illinois 1970-71. Instructor in Business Law Elmhurst College 1952-59. Adjunct Professor of Law DePaul University 1978-91. Former member Illinois Supreme Court Committee on Pattern Criminal Jury Instructions, Governor's Council on the Diagnosis and Evaluation of Criminal Defendants, National District Attorneys Association, Illinois Association of Circuit and Appellate Court Judges and Illinois State's Attorneys Association (Past Director). Chairman Federal Criminal Jury Instruction Committee of the Seventh Circuit. Member Law Club of Chicago, Legal Club of Chicago, American Judicature Society, Chicago, DuPage County (Past President), Illinois State (Former Chairman Criminal Law Section), Federal (Former Director) and American Bar Associations. U.S. Army 1945-47. Law Advisory Board Loyola University. Board of Trustees Elmhurst College, DePaul University and Elmhurst Memorial Hospital. Board of Advisors Mercy Hospital. Member Union League Club of Chicago.

Office: U.S. Courthouse, 219 South Dearborn Street, Chicago, Illinois 60604.

Telephone: (312) 435-5810.

BAXTER, Randolph *(Judge, Bankruptcy Appellate Panel Sixth Circuit)* Selected by the Judicial Council of the Sixth Circuit. Also Judge, U.S. Bankruptcy Court Northern District of Ohio.

Office: 3205 Key Tower, 127 Public Square, Cleveland, Ohio 44114-1309.

Telephone: (216) 522-4373.

BEAM, Clarence Arlen *(Senior Judge, United States Court of Appeals Eighth Circuit)* Appointed for life by President Ronald Reagan to term beginning 1987. Assumed Senior status Feb 1, 2001. Born Stapleton Nebraska Jan 14, 1930. Presbyterian. Educated at University of Nebraska B.S. J.D. Member Delta Theta Phi and Alpha Gamma Rho. Admitted to practice Nebraska 1965, U.S. District Court District of Nebraska 1965, U.S. Supreme Court 1975, U.S. Court of Appeals Eighth Circuit 1976 and U.S. Tax Court 1979. Began legal practice Lincoln 1965. Former Judge and Chief Judge, U.S. District Court District of Nebraska, appointed by Ronald Reagan to term beginning Jan 8, 1982.

Commissioner Conference of Commissioners on Uniform State Laws since 1979. Member Lincoln, Omaha and Nebraska State Bar Association. Captain U.S. Army 1951-53. Republican.

Office: 435 U.S. Courthouse, 100 Centennial Mall North, Lincoln, Nebraska 68508.

Telephone: (402) 437-5420.

BECKER, Edward R. *(Chief Judge, United States Court of Appeals Third Circuit)* Appointed for life by President Ronald Reagan to term beginning Jan 22, 1982. Chief Judge since Jan 31, 1998. Born Philadelphia Pennsylvania May 4, 1933. Jewish. Educated at University of Pennsylvania B.A. 1954 and Yale Law School LL.B. 1957. Member Phi Beta Kappa. Admitted to practice Pennsylvania 1957. In legal practice Philadelphia Oct 1957 to Dec 1970. Judge, U.S. District Court Eastern District of Pennsylvania Dec 1970 to Jan 1982.

Author "Need for the Revitalization of the Private Practitioner in Law" 3 Loyola University L. Jour. 271, 1972; "The Judge's Perspective" 51 Antitrust L. Jour. 437-445, 1982; "Organization for Trial in Antitrust Cases" 51 Antitrust L. Jour. 239, 1982; "The Use of 'Law and Economics' by Judges" 33 Journal of Legal Education 306, 1983; "Form for Statement of Reason for Imposing Sentence and Accompanying Models" Committee on Criminal Law and Probation Administration Judicial Conference of the U.S. 1988; "Flexibility and Discretion Available to the Sentencing Judge Under the Guidelines Regime" *The Sentencing Reform Act of 1984 and Sentencing Guidelines* 55 No. 4 Federal Probation 10-15 Dec 1991; "Conference on the Federal Sentencing Guidelines: Summary of Proceedings" 101 Yale L. Rev. 2053 June 1992; "Is the Evidence All In?" 78 American Bar Association Journal Oct 1992; Sullivan Lecture "Insuring Reliable Fact Finding in Guidelines Sentencing: Must the Guarantees of the Confrontation and Due Process Clauses Be Applied?" Capital Law School Nov 11, 1992; and "In Praise of Footnotes" Washington University Law Quarterly Spring 1996. Coauthor with Calabresi, Coleman, Jr., Freedman, Greenburg, Higginbotham, et al. Dedication "In Honor of Louis H. Pollak" 127 University of Pennsylvania L. Rev. 283-315, 1978; with Wilson W. Herndon, Edward C. Schmidt, John B. Pegram, Ernest R. Higginbotham, A. Stephans Clay, Thomas B. Leary and William A. Sankbeil 51 "Panel Discussion on Antitrust Law" Antitrust L. Jour 451-458, 1982; with Patrick E. Higginbotham and William K. Slate, II "Why the Numbers Don't Add Up" 73 American Bar Association Journal 83 Oct 1987; and with Professor Aviva Orenstein "The Federal Rules of Evidence After Sixteen Years—The Effect of 'Plain Meaning' Jurisprudence, The Need for an Advisory Committee on the Rules of Evidence, and Suggestions for Selective Revision of the Rules" 60 George Washington L. Rev. 857 April 1992 reprinted in *Federal Rules Digest.* Board of Editors *Manual for Complex Litigation* 1981-90. Co-editor "Sample Jury Instructions in Civil Antitrust Cases" Task Force Section of Antitrust Law American Bar Association.

Lecturer on Law University of Pennsylvania Law School 1979-83. Jurist-in-Residence Villanova University School of Law March 21-24, 1988. Member The American Law Institute (Representative to ALI-ABA Committee, Member Advisory Committee for Restatement Conflict of Laws 2d), American Judicature Society, Philadelphia and American (Judicial Representative and Council Member Section of Antitrust Law 1983-86) Bar Associations. Member District Court Studies Project 1975-76, Faculty Member Seminar for Newly Appointed Judges since 1978, Member Committee on Sentencing, Probation and Pretrial Services 1985-90 and Board Member since March 28, 1991 Federal Judicial Center. Lecturer Federal Trial Evidence and Civil Practice since 1978, Conferee Arden House III Conference on Continuing Legal Education Nov 1978, Member Advisory Group for Trial Practice Committee on Continuing Legal Education, Advisory Group to Program Subcommittee and Committee on Continuing Professional Education ALI-ABA. Member Committee on Administration of the Probation System 1979-87, Chairman Committee on Criminal Law and Probation Administration Oct 1, 1987 to Oct 1, 1990, Member Committee on Long-Range Planning since Oct 1990 and Executive Committee since 1999 Judicial Conference of the U.S. Participant Conference on the Place of Economics in Legal Education Association of American Law Schools and Emory University Law and Economics Center, Denver Colorado Oct 28, 1982 and Federal Civil Appellate Jurisdiction Editor-

BECKER, EDWARD R.—*Continued*

ial Conference Duke University School of Law, Durham North Carolina March 11, 1983. Keynote Speaker "The Case for the Creation of a Judicial Conference Advisory Committee on the Rules of Evidence" Conference on Evidence Association of American Law Schools, Iowa City Iowa June 8-10, 1991. Faculty Member Appellate Judges Seminar Institute of Judicial Administration New York University School of Law July 6-10, 1992. Founder and Chair Professional Education Committee U.S. District Court Eastern District of Pennsylvania. Recipient Devitt Award from American Judicature Society 2002. Republican. Co-trustee Magna Carta Foundation of Philadelphia 1986-87. Member Visiting Committee University of Chicago Law School 1988-91.

Office: 19613 U.S. Courthouse, 601 Market Street, Philadelphia, Pennsylvania 19106-1782.

Telephone: (215) 597-9642.

BEEZER, Robert R. *(Senior Judge, United States Court of Appeals Ninth Circuit)* Appointed for life by President Ronald Reagan to term beginning 1984. Assumed Senior status July 31, 1996, serves by assignment. Born Seattle Washington July 21, 1928. Educated at University of Virginia B.A. 1951 LL.B. 1956. In legal practice Seattle 1956-84. Judge pro tem, Seattle Municipal Court 1962-76. Lieutenant USMCR 1951-53.

Office: 802 U.S. Courthouse, 1010 Fifth Avenue, Seattle, Washington 98104-1115.

Telephone: (206) 553-0384.

BEGHE, Renato *(Judge, United States Tax Court)* Appointed by President George Bush to term beginning March 26, 1991. Term expires March 26, 2006. Born Chicago Illinois March 12, 1933. Educated at University of Chicago A.B. 1951 J.D. 1954. Co-managing Editor University of Chicago Law Review 1953-54. Member Phi Beta Kappa and Order of the Coif. Admitted to practice New York 1955. In legal practice New York City 1954-89.

Important Decisions: Harper v. Commissioner (lawyer sanctions) T.C. 100 T.C. 533, 1992 and Estate of Mueller v. Commissioner (equitable recoupment) 101 T.C. 551 (maj. op.) 1993, 107 T.C. 189, 203 (dissent) 1996. Instructor "Tax Free Reorganizations" Graduate Estate Planning Program University of Miami School of Law Winter 1986. Member International Fiscal Association, The Association of the Bar of the City of New York (Chairman Art Law Committee 1980-83), New York State (Chairman Tax Section 1977-78, Co-chairman Joint Practice Committee of Lawyers and Accountants 1989-90), American (Section of Taxation) and International Bar Associations. Lecturer at tax conferences including New York University Federal Tax Institutes 1967 and 1978 and University of Chicago Federal Tax Institute 1974, 1980 and 1986. Republican. Member America-Italy Society, Inc. (Board of Directors 1980-92) and Honorable Order of Kentucky Colonels.

Office: 400 Second Street N.W., Washington, D.C. 20217-0002.

Telephone: (202) 606-8808.

BENAVIDES, Fortunato P. *(Judge, United States Court of Appeals Fifth Circuit)* Appointed for life by President Bill Clinton. Born Mission Texas Feb 3, 1947. Episcopalian. Educated at University of Houston B.B.A. 1968 J.D. 1972. Member Phi Delta Phi. Admitted to practice Texas 1972, U.S. District Court Southern District of Texas and U.S. Court of Appeals Fifth Circuit. In legal practice McAllen 1971-77. Judge, Hidalgo County Court at Law No. 2 1977-79. Judge, Texas District Court 92nd Judicial District 1981-84. Justice, Texas Court of Appeals Thirteenth District 1984-91, appointed by Governor Mark White. Former Judge, Texas Court of Criminal Appeals, appointed by Governor Ann W. Richards to term beginning 1991.

Former Member Texas State Juvenile Probation Commission. Member State Bar of Texas (Judicial and Family Law Sections). Former Director Hidalgo County Easter Seal Center. Board of Directors Texas Center for the Judiciary, Inc. Enjoys fishing and wildlife.

Office: 450 Thornberry Judicial Building, 903 San Jacinto Boulevard, Austin, Texas 78701.

Telephone: (512) 916-5796.

BERZON, Marsha L. *(Judge, United States Court of Appeals Ninth Circuit)* Appointed for life by President Bill Clinton to term beginning March 21, 2000. Born Cincinnati Ohio April 17, 1945. Educated at Radcliffe College B.A. 1966 and University of California Boalt Hall School of Law J.D. 1973. Law Clerk to Hon. James R. Browning, U.S. Court of Appeals Ninth Circuit 1973-74 and Hon. William J. Brennan, Jr., U.S. Supreme Court 1974-75. In legal practice Washington D.C. 1975-77 and San Francisco California 1978-2000.

Lecturer University of California at Berkeley 1992. Practitioner-in-Residence Cornell Law School 1994.

Mailing address: P.O. Box 193939, San Francisco, California 94119-3939.

Office: 243 U.S. Court of Appeals Building, 95 Seventh Street, San Francisco, California 94103-1526.

Telephone: (415) 556-7800.

BIRCH, Stanley F., Jr. *(Judge, United States Court of Appeals Eleventh Circuit)* Appointed for life by President George Bush. Born Langley Field Virginia Aug 29, 1945. Episcopalian. Educated at University of Virginia B.A. 1967 and Emory University J.D. 1970 LL.M. in Taxation 1976. Law Clerk to Chief Judge Sidney O. Smith, Jr., U.S. District Court Northern District of Georgia 1972-74. Admitted to practice Georgia 1970. In legal practice Gainesville 1974-85 and Atlanta 1985-90.

Member Old War Horse Lawyers Club, Lawyers Club of Atlanta and State Bar of Georgia. First Lieutenant U.S. Army Special Forces Vietnam 1970-72.

Office: Court of Appeals Building, 56 Forsyth Street N.W., Atlanta, Georgia 30303.

Telephone: (404) 335-6333.

BLACK, Susan Harrell *(Judge, United States Court of Appeals Eleventh Circuit)* Appointed for life by the President. Born Valdosta Georgia Oct 20, 1943. Episcopalian. Educated at Ohio Wesleyan University, Spring Hill College, Florida State University B.A. with honors 1964, University of Florida J.D. 1967 and University of Virginia LL.M. 1984. Recipient American Jurisprudence Award in Constitutional Law 1965. Member Phi Delta Phi, Delta Sigma Rho, Tau Kappa Alpha, Pi Sigma Alpha and Kappa Kappa Gamma. Admitted to practice Florida 1967. Began legal practice Jacksonville 1968. Judge, Duval County Court 1973-75. Judge, Florida Circuit Court Fourth Judicial Circuit 1975-79. Former Judge and Chief Judge, U.S. District Court Middle District of Florida, appointed by President Jimmy Carter to term beginning Aug 17, 1979.

Attorney U.S. Army Corps of Engineers 1968-69. Assistant State Attorney Fourth Judicial Circuit 1969-72.

BLACK, SUSAN HARRELL—*Continued*

Assistant General Counsel Jacksonville 1972-73. Author "Judicial Notice; Presumptions; Burden of Proof" *Evidence in Florida* 2nd ed. The Florida Bar CLE 1978, "Extradition" *Florida Criminal Rules and Practice* 2nd ed. The Florida Bar CLE 1978 and "A New Look at Preliminary Injunctions: Can Principles from the Past Offer Any Guidelines to Decision Makers in the Future?" Alabama L. Rev. Fall 1984. Important Decisions: National Life Insurance Company v. Southeast First National Bank of Miami 361 So. 2d 432 (Fla. 4th DCA 1978); Browne v. Monumental Properties of Florida, Inc. 361 So. 2d 433 (Fla. 4th DCA 1978); Port of Jacksonville Maritime, etc. v. Hayes (issuance of bridge permit) 485 F. Supp. 741 (M.D. Fla. 1980) aff'd 620 F.2d (5th Cir. 1980) reh'g denied 625 F.2d 1016 (5th Cir. 1980); Financial Dynamics, Ltd. v. United States (limited partnership) 531 F. Supp. 187 (M.D. Fla. 1980); Florida Health Care Assn. v. Pingree (Medicare and Medicaid services) 497 F. Supp. 107 (M.D. Fla. 1980); United States v. Spearin, Preston & Burrows, Inc. (Miller Act) 496 F. Supp. 816 (M.D. Fla. 1980); United States v. Cargo Service Stations, Inc. (antitrust case) 657 F.2d 676 (5th Cir. 1981) reh'g denied 664 F.2d 291 cert. denied 455 U.S. 1017 (1982); ITT Rayonier Inc. v. United States (EPA case) 651 F.2d 343 (5th Cir. 1981); Walter E. Heller & Co. S.E. Ga. v. Riviana Foods, Inc. (creditors' security interest) 648 F.2d 1059 (5th Cir. 1981); In re Grand Jury Subpoena 646 F.2d 963 (5th Cir. 1981); Seaboard Coast Line Railroad Company v. National Railroad Passenger Corporation (common carrier freight tariff rates) 645 F.2d 513 (5th Cir. 1981); Chaffin v. Taylor, etc. (aid to families with dependent children) 521 F. Supp. 1344 (M.D. Fla. 1981); United States v. Butts (jury selection process) 514 F. Supp. 1225 (M.D. Fla. 1981); Guardian Mortgage Investors v. Sunset Villas Phase III Condominium Assn., Inc. (In re Guardian Mortgage Investors) 15 Bankr. 284 (M.D. Fla. 1981); Grizzell v. Wainwright (evidence re jury's decision) 692 F.2d 722 (11th Cir. 1982) cert. denied 103 S. Ct. 2129 (1983); Dobbert v. Strickland (death sentence) 532 F. Supp. 545 (M.D. Fla. 1982) aff'd 718 F.2d 1518 (11th Cir. 1983) reh'g denied 720 F.2d 1294 (11th Cir. 1983) cert. denied 104 S. Ct. 3591 (1984); Silverberg v. Paine, Webber, Jackson & Curtis, Incorporated (common law fraud and negligence) 710 F.2d 678 (11th Cir. 1983); United States v. Helmich (espionage case) 704 F.2d 547 (11th Cir. 1983) cert. denied 104 S. Ct. 353 (1983); Ahern v. Boeing Company (tortious interference) 701 F.2d 142 (11th Cir. 1983); Lonray, Inc. v. Azucar, Inc. (contractual agreement) 568 F. Supp. 189 (M.D. Fla. 1983); Harris v. Great Southern Life Insurance Company (interpleader relief) 558 F. Supp. 689 (M.D. Fla. 1983); and Brown v. American Petrofina Marketing, Inc. (nonrenewal of lease agreements) 555 F. Supp. 1327 (M.D. Fla. 1983) aff'd 733 F.2d 906.

Assistant Project Director for Court Management Systems 1969-72. Chairman State Parole and Probation Qualifications Committee 1977-79. Member Criminal Justice Information System Steering Committee 1970-79, Governor's Metropolitan Criminal Justice Advisory Council 1973-79 (Chairman Courts Subcommittee 1973-79), Governor's Task Force on Florida's Correction System 1975-76, Judiciary Education Advisory Committee Florida Supreme Court 1976, Advisory Council Department of Offender Rehabilitation 1976-79, Florida Court Education Council 1978-79 and Supreme Court Committee on Standard Civil Jury Instructions 1978-79. Former Member Council of State Governments, Florida Prosecuting Attorneys Association, Florida Conference of County Court Judges (Criminal Law Committee 1973-74), Florida Conference of Circuit Court Judges (Chairman Education Committee 1976-79), National District Attorneys Association and National Institute of Municipal Law Officers. Associate Member The Maritime Law Institute of the U.S. Member Committee on Uniform Standards for Handling Removal Cases, Judicial Conference of the U.S. (Committee on Inns of Court since 1984), The U.S. District Judges Association Eleventh Circuit (Secretary-Treasurer since 1984), The Florida Bar (Member 1972-76 and Chairman Legislation Subcommittee 1975 Criminal Law Committee, Chairman CLE Steering Committee for Criminal Law Course 1976, CLE Steering Committee Manual on Florida Criminal Rules and Practice 1976-78 and Criminal Jury Instructions Committee 1978-79 and Member CLE Manual on Evidence 1976-78, Criminal Procedure Rules Committee 1976-79, Criminal Law Section 1976-79, Special Committee on Liaison with Judiciary and Trial Lawyers 1977-78 and Civil Procedure Rules Committee since 1979), Jacksonville (Co-editor Bar Bulletin 1972) and American (Member 1973-75 and Florida Membership Chairman 1974 National Conference of Special Court Judges, Member National Conference of State Trial Judges 1975-79, Convention Delegate 1977 and 1978, Member Judicial Administration Division) Bar Associations.

Vice Chairman Education Committee 1975-76 and Dean Jan 1978 and March 1979 College for New Judges and Instructor in Trial Advocacy Feb 9, 1979, Feb 22, 1980, Jan 30, 1981 and Nov 2, 1982 University of Florida. Faculty Member The National Judicial College 1977-79. Instructor Young Lawyers Orientation Seminar Jacksonville Bar Association Jan 7, 1981, Jan 7, 1982 and Jan 6, 1984; National Institute for Trial Advocacy University of North Carolina May 14-19, 1981; Criminal Trial Advocacy Course U.S. Attorney General's Advocacy Institute Feb 16-17, 1984; and Clinical Course in Commercial Practice Duke University School of Law April 14, 1984. Chairman Program Committee Workshop for Judges of the U.S. Eleventh Circuit 1982. Member Program Committee Workshop for Judges of the U.S. Fifth and Eleventh Circuits 1983. Lecturer "Court Management Using Information System" The Institute for Court Management June 9, 1975; Educational Seminars March 9-12, 1976 and March 19-22, 1978 and Evidence Seminar March 20-23, 1977 Florida Conference of Circuit Court Judges; "Role of the Bar and Judiciary in Corrections" National Conference on Community Corrections and Positive Education Programming April 13-15, 1976; "Commitment and Confidence in Corrections" Jan 30, 1977 and "From the Judge's Perspective" Sept 22, 1983 The Florida Bar CLE; "Technology and Court Management Systems Development," "Organizing and Conducting a Court Improvement Plan for Your Jurisdiction" and "Your Role in Initiating and Preparing Your Court for Change" National College for the State Judiciary April 20-22, 1977; "Sentencing" College for New Judges University of Florida Jan 22-25, 1978 and March 18-23, 1979; "Redesign of an Existing Information System" "Installing a Better System" and "Critique of Workshop Problem" The National Judicial College March 15-17, 1978 and Nov 12-17, 1978; and

BLACK, SUSAN HARRELL—*Continued*

"Judicial Techniques to Expedite Trials (Bankruptcy Judges)" Nov 17-19, 1982 and March 16-18, 1983 and "Judicial Techniques to Expedite Trials (Full-Time Magistrates)" Feb 23-25, 1983 Federal Judicial Center.

Recipient Florida Blue Key from University of Florida 1976, Outstanding Alumna Award from University of Florida Alumni Club of Jacksonville 1978, Kappa Gamma National Alumni Achievement Award 1980 and University of Florida Distinguished Alumnus Award 1982. Commencement Speaker University of Florida College of Law Spring 1977 and Florida State University College of Law Dec 1979. Former Member Northeast Florida District Mental Health Board. Member Medical Examiners Commission 1971-72, League of Women Voters 1972-76, Law Center Council University of Florida Law Center Association, Inc. 1972-78, Governor's Conference on Energy Supply and Use 1973, Governor's Commission on the Status of Women 1973-79 and Visiting Alumni Committee University of Florida College of Law 1981-82. Executive Board of Directors Probationers Residence Program, Inc. 1973-75. Board of Directors Jacksonville Adult Development Center Project 1975-77, Offender Assistance Through Community Colleges Project Advisory Committee 1975-78 and Leadership Jacksonville. Board of Trustees Jacksonville Hospital Educational Program 1977-79 and Jacksonville Council on Citizen Involvement, Inc. Advisory Board 1977-84, Member Public Relations Committee since 1977, Task Force on Nursing 1981-82 and Nominating Committee for Officers of Advisory Board 1983 Jacksonville Health Educations Programs, Inc. Member 1980 and Chairman 1981 Nominating Committee, Member Executive Committee 1981-82 and Award Committee since 1981 and Vice Chairman since 1981 Board of Trustees University of Florida Law Center Association, Inc. Enjoys travel and tennis.

Mailing address: P.O. Box 53135, Jacksonville, Florida 32201-3135.

Telephone: (904) 232-2496.

BLOCK, Lawrence J. *(Judge, United States Court of Federal Claims)* Appointed by President George W. Bush to term beginning Oct 11, 2002. Term expires Oct 2017.

Office: National Courts Building, 717 Madison Place N.W., Washington, D.C. 20005-1086.

Telephone: (202) 219-9660.

BODOH, William T. *(Judge, Bankruptcy Appellate Panel Sixth Circuit)* Selected by the Judicial Council of the Sixth Circuit to term beginning 2003. Also Chief Judge, United States Bankruptcy Court Northern District of Ohio. Appointed by U.S. Court of Appeals Sixth Circuit judges Feb 12, 1985 to term beginning June 10, 1985. Reappointed June 9, 1999, current term expires June 2013. Chief Judge since July 1, 2001. Born Newark Ohio Sept 5, 1938. Episcopalian. Educated at Ohio University B.S.C. 1961 and The Ohio State University College of Law J.D. 1964. Member Pi Kappa Alpha and Phi Delta Phi. Admitted to practice Ohio 1964, U.S. Supreme Court 1970, U.S. District Court Northern District of Ohio 1972 and U.S. Court of Appeals Sixth Circuit 1980. Began legal practice Columbus 1964. In legal practice Cleveland 1967-72 and Youngstown 1972-85.

Author *A Local Rules Guide for Ohio Northern District Bankruptcy Court* Professional Education Systems, Inc. 1988; "A Few Useful Provisions—The Adoption of the Bill of Rights" Ohio State Alumni Magazine Jan 1991; "The Parameters of the Non-Plan Liquidating Chapter 11: Refining the *Lionel* Standard" 9 Bankruptcy Development Journal 1, 1992; "On Judging Judges" 55 No. 4 Ohio State L. Jour. 889, 1994; "Protective Orders in the Bankruptcy Court: The Congressional Mandate of Bankruptcy Code Section 107 and Its Constitutional Implications" 24 Hastings Constitutional Law Quarterly 67 Fall 1996; "Inequality Among Creditors: The Unconstitutional Use of Successor Liability to Create a New Class of Priority Creditors" 4 American Bankruptcy Institute L. Rev. 325 Winter 1996; and "Bankruptcy Reform: An Orderly Development of Public Policy?"49 Cleveland State L. Rev. 191, 2001. Member ex officio Judicial Council of the Sixth Circuit 1990-93. Fellow American College of Bankruptcy. Member National Conference of Bankruptcy Judges (Board of Governors 1988-93) and American Bankruptcy Institute (Board of Directors since 1994). Former Member Advisory Board Salvation Army. Former Member Board of Trustees Easter Seal Society of Eastern Ohio. President Youngstown Symphony Society 1973-75. Member National Council College of Law since 1972, Former Member and Chair 1990-92 Alumni Advisory Council and President Law Alumni Association 1994-95 The Ohio State University. Interests include sailing, fly fishing, Civil War history and antique automobile restoration.

Mailing address: P.O. Box 147, Youngstown 44501-0147.

Office: 301 U.S. Courthouse, 10 East Commerce Street, Youngstown 44503.

Telephone: (330) 746-6829.

Fax: (330) 746-0480

E-mail address: william_bodoh@ohnb.uscourts.gov

BOGGS, Danny J. *(Judge, United States Court of Appeals Sixth Circuit)* Appointed for life by President Ronald Reagan to term beginning 1986. Born Havana Cuba Oct 23, 1944. Educated at Harvard University A.B. cum laude 1965 and University of Chicago J.D. 1968. Staff member University of Chicago Law Review 1966-67. Bigelow Fellow. Member Phi Delta Phi and Order of the Coif. Admitted to practice Illinois 1969, Kentucky 1969, U.S. District Court Western District of Kentucky 1972, U.S. Supreme Court 1973 and U.S. Court of Appeals District of Columbia Circuit 1974. Began legal practice Bowling Green Kentucky 1975. In legal practice Washington D.C. 1979-81.

Legal Counsel to Governor of Kentucky 1970-71. Assistant to Solicitor General of the U.S. 1973-75. Special Assistant to President of the U.S. 1981-83. Deputy Secretary U.S. Department of Energy 1983-86. Instructor University of Chicago 1968-69. Member Brandeis American Inns of Court, Kentucky and American Bar Associations.

Office: 220 U.S. Courthouse, 601 West Broadway, Louisville, Kentucky 40202.

Telephone: (502) 625-3900.

BOHANON, Richard L. *(Judge, Bankruptcy Appellate Panel Tenth Circuit)* Selected by the Judicial Council of the Tenth Circuit. Also Judge, U.S. Bankruptcy Court Western District of Oklahoma. Appointed by U.S. District Court judges to term beginning Dec 6, 1982. Reappointed by U.S. Court of Appeals Tenth Circuit judges May 12, 1986 and May 2000. Current term expires May 2014. Former Chief Judge Bankruptcy Court.

BOHANON, RICHARD L.—*Continued*

Born Oklahoma City Oklahoma Feb 9, 1935. Educated at Dartmouth College A.B. 1957, University of Oklahoma LL.B. 1960 and New York University LL.M. 1963. Law Clerk to Chief Judge A. P. Murrah, U.S. Court of Appeals Tenth Circuit 1960-61. Admitted to practice Oklahoma 1960. In legal practice Oklahoma City 1963-82.

Board of Governors National Conference of Bankruptcy Judges since 1982. President American Inn of Court XXIII.

Office: Old Post Office Building, 215 Dean A. McGee Avenue, Oklahoma City, Oklahoma 73102.

Telephone: (405) 609-5660, 231-5140.

BOOCHEVER, Robert *(Senior Judge, United States Court of Appeals Ninth Circuit)* Appointed for life by President Jimmy Carter to term beginning 1980. Assumed Senior status June 10, 1986, serves by assignment. Born New York New York Oct 2, 1917. Educated at Cornell University B.A. 1939 J.D. 1941. Recipient New York State Regents Scholarship and President's Scholarship. Awarded honorary Doctor of Humanities University of Alaska 1980. Admitted to practice New York 1944 and Alaska 1947. In legal practice 1947-72. Justice 1972-80 and Chief Justice 1975-78, Alaska Supreme Court.

Assistant U.S. Attorney Juneau 1946-47. Chairman Ninth Circuit Library Committee 1995-2001. Fellow American College of Trial Lawyers. Member Awards Jury Freedom Foundation at Valley Forge 1973, American Judicature Society (Director 1970-74), Alaska Judicial Qualifications Commission 1972-75, The American Law Institute, Alaska Judicial Council (Chairman 1975-78), Juneau (President 1972), Alaska (President 1962, Board of Governors 1958-62) and American Bar Associations. Attended New York University School of Law Appellate Judges Seminar 1975. Named Juneau Man of the Year 1974. Honored by University of California at Davis School of Law with creation of Boochever and Bird Chair for the Study and Teaching of Freedom and Equality 2001. Captain U.S. Army Infantry 1941-45. Vice President Alaska Chamber of Commerce 1952-53. Chairman American Red Cross Juneau Chapter 1953-56, Alaskans United 1963-66, Juneau Planning Commission 1964-69 and Explorers Club Juneau Chapter 1971-78. Board of Directors First National Bank of Juneau 1957-62 and Salvation Army 1965-69. Member Territory of Alaska Development Board 1948-53, Boy Scouts of America Council 1950-60, Juneau Chamber of Commerce (Board of Directors 1952-58, President 1952 and 1954), St. Ann's Hospital Board 1963-66 and Advisory Board National Bank of Alaska Juneau Branch 1963-71.

Office: Court of Appeals Building, 125 South Grand Avenue, Pasadena, California 91105-1652.

Telephone: (626) 229-7200.

BOROFF, Henry Jack *(Judge, Bankruptcy Appellate Panel First Circuit)* Selected by the Judicial Council of the First Circuit. Also Judge, U.S. Bankruptcy Court District of Massachusetts. Appointed by U.S. Court of Appeals First Circuit judges to term beginning Dec 10, 1993. Term expires Dec 10, 2007. Born Boston Massachusetts 1951. Educated at Boston University A.B. magna cum laude 1972 J.D. 1975. Admitted to practice Massachusetts 1975, U.S. District Court District of Massachusetts 1976, U.S. Court of Appeals First Circuit 1979 and U.S. Supreme Court 1987. In legal practice Boston 1976-93.

Author "Insurance Proceeds under § 9-306: Before and After" 1974 and "The Precedential Effect of Bankruptcy Appellate Decision" 1998 Commercial L. Jour. Adjunct Professor of Bankruptcy Law and Secured Transactions Western New England College School of Law since 1996 and Northeastern University 1998-2000. Former Member Commercial Law League of America (Chair New England District 1983-84). Member Boston (Member since 1976 and Chair 1987-90 Bankruptcy Committee) and Massachusetts Bar Associations. Lecturer on bankruptcy and related topics American Bankruptcy Institute, Boston Bar Association, Hampden County Bar Association and Massachusetts Bar Association. Listed in Massachusetts Bankruptcy Listings *Best Lawyers in America* Woodward and White 1987, 1989-90, 1991-92 and 1993-94.

Office: 595 Main Street, Worcester, Massachusetts 01608.

Telephone: (508) 770-8940.

Fax: (508) 793-0183

BOUDIN, Michael *(Chief Judge, United States Court of Appeals First Circuit)* Appointed for life by President George Bush to term beginning May 29, 1992. Chief Judge since June 16, 2001. Born New York New York Nov 29, 1939. Educated at Harvard College B.A. magna cum laude 1961 LL.B. magna cum laude 1964. Editor-in-Chief Harvard Law Review 1963-64. Law Clerk to Hon. Henry J. Friendly, U.S. Court of Appeals Second Circuit 1964-65 and Hon. John M. Harlan, U.S. Supreme Court 1965-66. Admitted to practice New York 1964 and District of Columbia 1967. In legal practice Washington D.C. 1966-87. Judge, U.S. District Court District of Columbia 1990-92.

Deputy Assistant Attorney General Antitrust Division U.S. Department of Justice 1987-90. Author "Common Sense in Law Practice" 34 Harvard Law School Bulletin 22 Spring 1983 and "Antitrust Doctrine and the Sway of Metaphor" 75 Georgetown L. Jour. 395, 1987. Visiting Professor from Law Practice Harvard Law School 1982-83. Lecturer Harvard Law School 1983-98 and University of Pennsylvania Law School 1984-85. Member The American Law Institute, The District of Columbia Bar, New York State and American Bar Associations.

Office: U.S. Courthouse, One Courthouse Way, Boston, Massachusetts 02210.

Telephone: (617) 748-4431.

Fax: (617) 748-4466

BOULDEN, Judith A. *(Judge, Bankruptcy Appellate Panel Tenth Circuit)* Selected by the Judicial Council of the Tenth Circuit. Also Judge, U.S. Bankruptcy Court District of Utah. Appointed by U.S. District Court judges. Reappointed by U.S. Court of Appeals Tenth Circuit judges.

Office: 330 U.S. Courthouse, 350 South Main Street, Salt Lake City, Utah 84101.

Telephone: (801) 524-5749.

BOWMAN, Pasco M., II *(Judge, United States Court of Appeals Eighth Circuit)* Appointed for life by President Ronald Reagan to term beginning Aug 1, 1983. Chief Judge April 18, 1998 to April 24, 1999. Born Harrisonburg Virginia Dec 20, 1933. Educated at Bridgewater College B.A. summa cum laude 1955, New York University School of Law J.D. 1958 and University of Virginia LL.M. 1986. Awarded honorary LL.D.

BOWMAN, PASCO M., II—*Continued*

Bridgewater College 1988. Fulbright Scholar London School of Economics and Political Science 1961-62. Managing Editor New York University Law Review 1957-58. Member Phi Delta Phi. Admitted to practice New York 1958, Georgia 1965, Missouri 1980 and U.S. Supreme Court. Began legal practice New York City 1958.

Author Comment "Interpretation and Enforcement of Trust Provisions Allocating Stock Dividends Elsewhere than to Principal of Trust" 32 New York University L. Rev. 878-885, 1957; "An Introduction to the New Georgia Corporation Law" 4 Georgia State B. Jour. 419-456, 1968; "Georgia's New Corporation Law" 10 The Georgia CPA 3, 1968-69; "Corporate Finance Under the Georgia Business Corporation Code of 1968" 3 Georgia L. Rev. 11-53, 1969; "The New Georgia Corporation Law: 1969 Amendments" 5 Georgia State B. Jour. 433-444, 1969; book review of Brown *Franchising: Trap for the Trusting* 4 Georgia L. Rev. 428-432, 1970; book review of Dam *The Gatt—Law and International Economic Organization* 1 Georgia Jour. of International and Comparative Law 190-195, 1970; "Agency and Business Associations" Annual Survey of Georgia Law 22 Mercer L. Rev. 51-77, 1971; "Liabilities of Corporate Officers and Directors: Indemnification" North Carolina Bar Association Institute on Business Organizations Jan 1972; book review of O'Neal *Close Corporations* Vol. 1, 2d ed. Duke L. Jour. 1278-1282, 1972; "Indemnifying Corporate Directors and Officers" Spring 1973 and "D & O Insurance—*Caveat Emptor*" Summer 1973 in "Developments in Corporate, Banking and Securities Law" State Bar of Georgia Section of Corporate and Banking Law; book review of Moore *Law and the Indo-China War* 3 Denver Jour. of International Law and Policy 147-151, 1973; and "Proof of Antitrust Causation—The Emerging Emphasis on Fact of Damage?" Antitrust in the 80's University of Missouri-Kansas City CLE, 1981. Reporter and Principal Draftsman "Proposed Georgia Business Corporation Act of 1968" 1965-67. Co-author with McQueen "Corporations—Formation: The Law in Georgia" 1980, with McQueen and Kelley "Corporations—Formation: The Law in Tennessee" 1981 and with McQueen and Downs "Corporations—Formation: The Law in Missouri" 1983.

Assistant Professor, Associate Professor and Professor of Law University of Georgia School of Law 1964-70. Dean and Professor of Law Wake Forest University School of Law 1970-78 and University of Missouri-Kansas City 1979-83. Visiting Professor of Law University of Virginia School of Law 1978-79. Member The Missouri Bar, State Bar of Georgia and New York State Bar Association. Listed in *Who's Who in America* since 1981 and *Who's Who in American Law* since 1981. Recipient The Macon Award from North Carolina Conservative Society 1979, Excellence in Teaching Award from Wake Forest University School of Law 1980, Chancellor's Citation from University of Missouri-Kansas City 1983 and Distinguished Alumnus Award from Bridgewater College 1984. Colonel USAR JAGC since 1959. Republican.

Office: 10-50 U.S. Courthouse, 400 East Ninth Street, Kansas City, Missouri 64106.

Telephone: (816) 512-5800.

BOWNES, Hugh H. *(Senior Judge, United States Court of Appeals First Circuit)* Appointed for life by President Jimmy Carter Nov 1977. Assumed Senior status Jan 1, 1990, serves by assignment. Born New York New York March 10, 1920. Educated at Columbia University B.A. 1941 LL.B. 1948. Admitted to practice New Hampshire 1948. Began legal practice Laconia 1948. Associate Justice, New Hampshire Superior Court 1966-68. Judge, U.S. District Court District of New Hampshire 1968-77.

Member Belknap County (President 1965), New Hampshire and American Bar Associations. Served from Private to Major USMCR 1941-46. Recipient Silver Star and Purple Heart. Member City Council 1953-57 and Mayor 1963-65 Laconia. Chairman Laconia Democratic Committee 1954-57. Member Democratic National Committee from New Hampshire 1963-66. Chairman Laconia Chapter American Red Cross 1951-52. President of Board Laconia Hospital Association 1963-64. Member Laconia Chamber of Commerce (Past President) and Lions Club (Past President Laconia).

Office: 6730 U.S. Courthouse, One Courthouse Way, Boston, Massachusetts 02210-3002.

Telephone: (617) 748-9007.

BRANDT, Philip H. *(Judge, Bankruptcy Appellate Panel Ninth Circuit)* Selected by the Judicial Council of the Ninth Circuit January 1998. Also Chief Judge, U.S. Bankruptcy Court Western District of Washington. Appointed by U.S. Court of Appeals Ninth Circuit judges to term beginning 1991. Term expires 2005. Chief Judge Bankruptcy Court since Oct 1, 2001. Educated at Harvard University B.A. in Economics 1966 and University of Washington J.D. 1972. In legal practice Tacoma 1976-91.

Attorney Department of Justice 1973 and Federal Maritime Commission 1973. Deputy Prosecutor Pierce County 1974. Important Decisions: In re Wallaert 149 B.R. 665, Bankr. W.D. Wash. Nov 30, 1992 (No. 92-32032, 92-33117); In re Ford 159 B.R. 930, 29 Bankr. Cas.2d (Collier) 1580, Bankr. W.D. Wash. 1983 (No. 93-32649); In re Orris 166 B.R. 935 Bankr. W.D. Wash. May 3, 1994 (No. 92-35604, 93-31676, 92-34171); In re Steffen 181 B.R. 981, Bankr. W.D. Wash. 1995 (No. 94-33752); In re Ehrle 189 B.R. 771, 28 U.C.C. Rep. Serv. 2d 691, 95 Daily Journal D.A.R 16,837, Bankr. 9th Cir. Cal. Nov 21, 1995 (No. CC-94-2546-BHO, SA93-14904-JB, SA93-1621-JB); In re Sheldon 196 B.R. 551 Bankr. W.D. Wash. April 4, 1996 (No. 95-34508); In re Penberthy 211 B.R. 391, 31 Bankr. Ct. Dec. (LRP) 503, Bankr. W.D. Wash. July 24, 1997 (No. 94-08427); In re Fernandez 227 B.R. 174, 98 Cal. Daily Op. Serv. 8485, 98 Daily Journal D.A.R. 11,825, 2 Cal. Bankr. Ct. Rep. 31, Bankr. 9th Cir. Cal.Nov 5, 1998 (No. CC-97-1628-BKME, LA97-02372-TD, CC-97-1863-BKME, LA97-25043-TD); In re Hough 239 B.R. 412 Bankr. L. Rep. (CCH) P78,012, 99 Cal. Daily Op. Serv. 8158, 1999 Daily Journal D.A.R. 10,453, 3 Cal. Bankr. Ct. Rep. 69 Bankr. 9th Cir. Idaho Sept 10, 1999 (No. ID-99-1092-BRP, 98-01101, 98-6172); In re Reinertson 241 B.R. 451, 1999 Daily Journal D.A.R. 11,953 Bankr. 9th Cir. Mont. Nov 2, 1999 (No. MT-98-1674-BHAP); and In re Foross 1999 WL 1270364, Bankr. 9th Cir. Cal. Nov. 30, 1999 (No. EC-98-1832-BMAR, 97-25921-A-13, 98-2325-A). Director Standards Project Governor's Committee on Law and Justice 1975-76. Member National Conference on Bankruptcy Judges, Tacoma-Pierce County, Washington State and American (Member Joint ad hoc Committee on Bankruptcy Court Structure and Insolvency Processes, National Conference of Federal Trial

BRANDT, PHILIP H.—*Continued*

Judges Judicial Division) Bar Associations. USN 1966-69. Captain USNR 1989 (retired). Former Board Member Whatcom Chamber of Commerce and Industry (Former Chairman Industrial/Port Committee). Member Economic Development Task Force Whatcom County Council 1982 and Bellingham School Board 1985. Former Board Member Martin Luther King Center. Former Member City Club of Tacoma and Tacoma-Pierce County Chamber of Commerce.

Office: 2100 U.S. Courthouse, 1717 Pacific Avenue, Tacoma, Washington 98402-3233.

Telephone: (253) 593-6310.

BREYER, Stephen *(Associate Justice, The Supreme Court of the United States)* Appointed for life by President Bill Clinton. Also Circuit Justice, U.S. Court of Appeals Tenth Circuit. Born San Francisco California Aug 15, 1938. Educated at Stanford University A.M. with highest honors 1959, Magdalen College Oxford University Marshall Scholar B.A. 1961 and Harvard Law School LL.B. magna cum laude 1964. Articles Editor Harvard Law Review. Law Clerk to Hon. Arthur J. Goldberg, U.S. Supreme Court 1964-65. Former Chief Judge, U.S. Court of Appeals First Circuit, appointed by President Jimmy Carter to term beginning 1981.

Special Assistant to Assistant Attorney General Antitrust Division U.S. Department of Justice 1965-67. Assistant Special Prosecutor Watergate Special Prosecution Force 1973. Special Counsel (Staff Director for Investigation of Civil Aeronautics Board) Administrative Practices Subcommittee U.S. Senate Judiciary Committee 1974-75. Chief Counsel U.S. Senate Judiciary Committee 1979-80. Author "The Uneasy Case for Copyright: A Study of Copyright in Books, Photocopies and Computer Programs" 84 Harvard L. Rev. 281, 1970 reprinted in *Technology and Copyright* Bush 1972, "The Ash Council's Report on the Independent Regulatory Agencies" 2 Bell Jour. of Economics and Management Science 628, 1971 reprinted in *Reforming Regulation* Noll 1971, "The Problem of the Honest Monopolist" 41 ABA Antitrust L. Jour. 194, 1975, "Five Questions about Australian Antitrust Law" 51 Australian L. Jour. 28, 1977, "Vermont Yankee and the Courts: Role in the Nuclear Energy Controversy" 91 Harvard L. Rev. 1833, 1978, "Taxes as a Substitute for Regulation" 10 Growth and Change 39, 1979, "Analyzing Regulatory Failure: Mismatches, Less Restrictive Alternatives and Reform" 92 Harvard L. Rev. 549, 1979, *Regulation and Its Reform* Harvard University Press 1982, "Economics for Lawyers and Judges" 33 Jour. of Legal Education 294, 1983 and "Two Models for Regulatory Reform" 34 South Carolina L. Rev. 629, 1983. Co-author with Paul MacAvoy "The Federal Power Commission and the Coordination Problem in the Electrical Power Industry" 46 Southern California L. Rev. 661, 1973, "The Natural Gas Shortage and the Regulation of Natural Gas Producers" 86 Harvard L. Rev. 941, 1973 reprinted in *Energy Supply and Government Policy* Kalter & Vogely 1976 and *The Federal Power Commission and the Regulation of Energy* Brookings 1974, with Richard Zeckhauser "The Regulation of Genetic Engineering" 1 Man and Medicine 1, 1975 reprinted in *Genetic Responsibility* Lipkin & Rowley 1975 and with Richard Stewart *Administrative Law and Regulatory Policy* Little, Brown and Co. 1979.

Assistant Professor of Law 1967-70, Professor of Law 1970-80 and Lecturer on Administrative Law and Economic Regulation since 1981 Harvard University Law School. Visiting Lecturer on Antitrust Law University of Sydney College of Law, Australia 1975. Professor Kennedy School of Government Harvard University 1977-80. Fellow American Bar Foundation. Member Council on Foreign Relations, The American Law Institute and American Bar Association. Member U.S. Sentencing Commission since 1986. Judicial Conference Representative to Administrative Conference of the U.S. Member Board of Trustees University of Massachusetts 1974-81. Trustee Dana Farber Cancer Institute (Jimmy Fund) since 1977. Fellow American Academy of Arts and Sciences.

Office: One First Street N.E., Washington, D.C. 20543-0001.

Telephone: (202) 479-3000.

BRIGHT, Myron H. *(Senior Judge, United States Court of Appeals Eighth Circuit)* Appointed for life by President Lyndon B. Johnson to term beginning 1968. Assumed Senior status June 1, 1985, serves by assignment. Born Eveleth Minnesota March 5, 1919. Educated at University of Minnesota B.S.L. 1941 J.D. 1947. Admitted to practice Minnesota and North Dakota. In legal practice Fargo North Dakota 1947-68.

Distinguished Professor of Law, Trial Advocacy and Appellate Practice St. Louis University School of Law 1985-95. Member American Judicature Society, Federal Judges Association, The Bar Association of Metropolitan St. Louis, State Bar Association of North Dakota, Cass County and American Bar Associations. Captain U.S. Army 1942-46.

Office: 340 U.S. Courthouse, 655 First Avenue North, Fargo, North Dakota 58102-4952.

Telephone: (701) 297-7260.

BRISCOE, Mary Beck *(Judge, United States Court of Appeals Tenth Circuit)* Appointed for life by President Bill Clinton to term beginning 1995. Born Council Grove Kansas 1947. Educated at University of Kansas B.A. 1969 J.D. 1973 and University of Virginia LL.M. 1990. Admitted to practice Kansas 1973, U.S. District Court District of Kansas 1973, U.S. Court of Appeals Tenth Circuit 1974 and U.S. Supreme Court 1980. Judge 1984-95 and Chief Judge 1990-95, Kansas Court of Appeals.

Attorney-Examiner Financial Division Interstate Commerce Commission 1973-74. Assistant U.S. Attorney U.S. Department of Justice, Wichita and Topeka Kansas 1974-84. Member and Fellow Kansas Bar Association and American Bar Association. Member Topeka Women Attorneys Association, American Judicature Society and Topeka Bar Association. Recipient Outstanding Service Award from Kansas Bar Association 1992.

Office: 645 Massachusetts Street, Suite 400, Lawrence, Kansas 66044-2235.

Telephone: (785) 843-4067.

BRORBY, Wade *(Senior Judge, United States Court of Appeals Tenth Circuit)* Appointed for life by President Ronald Reagan to term beginning 1988. Assumed Senior status May 25, 2001, serves by assignment. Born Omaha Nebraska May 23, 1934. Educated at University of Wyoming B.S. 1956 J.D. 1958. In legal practice Gillette 1961-88.

BRORBY, WADE—*Continued*

County and Prosecuting Attorney Campbell County 1963-70. USAF 1958-61.

Mailing address: P.O. Box 1028, Cheyenne, Wyoming 82003-1028.

Telephone: (307) 772-2885.

BROWNING, James R. *(Senior Judge, United States Court of Appeals Ninth Circuit)* Appointed for life by President John F. Kennedy to term beginning Oct 23, 1961. Chief Judge 1976-88. Assumed Senior status Sept 1, 2000, serves by assignment. Born Great Falls Montana Oct 1, 1918. Educated at Montana State University (now University of Montana) LL.B. with honors 1941. Awarded honorary LL.D. University of Montana 1978. Admitted to practice Montana 1941, District of Columbia 1950 and U.S. Supreme Court 1952. In legal practice Washington D.C. 1953-58. Clerk, U.S. Supreme Court 1958-61.

Special Attorney Antitrust Division 1941-43, Special Attorney 1946-48 and Assistant Chief 1949-51 General Litigation Section Antitrust Division, Chief Northwest Regional Office 1948-49 and First Assistant Civil Division 1951-52 U.S. Department of Justice. Executive Assistant to U.S. Attorney General 1952-53. Chief Executive Office for U.S. Attorneys 1953. Lecturer New York University School of Law 1953 and Georgetown University Law Center 1957-58. Member The American Law Institute, American Judicature Society (Director 1972), American Society for Legal History (Advisory Board Journal), State Bar of Montana, Federal and American Bar Associations. Recipient Devitt Distinguished Service to Justice Award 1990. U.S. Army 1943-46.

Mailing address: P.O. Box 193939, San Francisco, California 94119-3939.

Office: 316 U.S. Court of Appeals Building, 95 Seventh Street, San Francisco, California 94103.

Telephone: (415) 556-9600.

BRUGGINK, Eric G. *(Senior Judge, United States Court of Federal Claims)* Appointed by President Ronald Reagan to term beginning April 16, 1986. Assumed Senior status April 16, 2001, serves by assignment. Born Kalidjati Indonesia Sept 11, 1949. Christian. Educated at Auburn University B.A. cum laude 1971 M.A. 1972 and University of Alabama J.D. 1975. Note and Comment Editor University of Alabama Law Review 1973-75. Law Clerk to Hon. Frank McFadden, U.S. District Court Northern District of Alabama 1975-76. Admitted to practice Alabama 1975, District of Columbia 1986 and U.S. Court of Appeals Eleventh and Federal Circuits. In legal practice Dothan 1976-77 and Montgomery 1979-82.

Assistant Director Alabama Law Institute 1977-79. Director Office of Appeals U.S. Merit Systems Protection Board 1982-86. Author "Statutory Negligence in Alabama" Alabama L. Rev. 1975. Member Alabama State Bar, The District of Columbia Bar, Claims Court, Federal Circuit and Federal Bar Associations. President American Inn of Court 69, 1988-89.

Office: National Courts Building, 717 Madison Place N.W., Washington, D.C. 20005-1086.

Telephone: (202) 219-9612.

BRUNETTI, Melvin T. *(Senior Judge, United States Court of Appeals Ninth Circuit)* Appointed for life by President Ronald Reagan to term beginning April 5, 1985. Assumed Senior status Nov 11, 1999, serves by assignment. Born Reno Nevada Nov 10, 1933. Educated at University of Nevada, Reno 1960 and University of California Hastings College of the Law J.D. 1964. Admitted to practice Nevada 1964 and U.S. District Court District of Nevada 1964. In legal practice 1964-85.

Important Decisions: United States v. Hall 778 F.2d 1427, 1985; United States v. Martin 781 F.2d 671, 1986; Quantum Exploration, Inc. v. Clark 780 F.2d 1457, 1986; Adamson v. Ricketts 789 F.2d 722, 1986 (dissenting); Platero-Cortez v. INS 804 F.2d 1127, 1986; Duro v. Reina 821 F.2d 1358, 1987; United States v. General Dynamics 813 F.2d 1441, 1987 (dissenting); Turcios v. INS 821 F.2d 1396, 1987; Sierra Club v. NRC 825 F.2d 1356, 1987; Gaudiya Vaishnava Society v. San Francisco 900 F.2d 1369, 9th Cir. 1990; and Harris v. Vasquez 913 F.2d 606, 9th Cir. 1990. Member State Bar of Nevada (Board of Governors 1975-84, President 1984-85), Carson City, Washoe County and American Bar Associations. Member Nevada Army National Guard 1954-56. Member Council of Legal Advisors to Republican National Committee 1982-84.

Office: 506 U.S. Courthouse & Federal Bldg., 400 South Virginia Street, Reno, Nevada 89501-2193.

Telephone: (775) 686-5931.

BRYSON, William C. *(Judge, United States Court of Appeals Federal Circuit)* Appointed for life by President Bill Clinton June 1994 to term beginning Oct 7, 1994. Born Houston Texas Aug 19, 1945. Educated at Harvard University A.B. 1969 and University of Texas School of Law J.D. 1973. Law Clerk to Hon. Henry J. Friendly, U.S. Court of Appeals Second Circuit 1973-74 and Associate Justice Thurgood Marshall, U.S. Supreme Court 1974-75. In legal practice Washington D.C. 1975-78.

Attorney Office of the Solicitor General 1978-79 and 1986-94, Criminal Division U.S. Department of Justice 1979-86 and Office of the Associate Attorney General 1994.

Office: National Courts Building, 717 Madison Place N.W., Washington, D.C. 20439-0002.

Telephone: (202) 633-5808.

BUSH, Lynn Jeanne *(Judge, United States Court of Federal Claims)* Appointed by President Bill Clinton to term beginning Oct 26, 1998. Term expires Oct 2013. Educated at Antioch College 1970 and Georgetown University Law Center J.D. 1976. Administrative Judge, Board of Contract Appeals U.S. Department of Housing and Urban Development 1996-98.

Trial Attorney Commercial Litigation Branch Civil Division U.S. Department of Justice 1976-87. Senior Trial Attorney Naval Facilities Engineering Command 1987-89 and Counsel Engineering Field Activity Chesapeake Naval Facilities Engineering Command 1989-96 U.S. Department of the Navy.

Office: National Courts Building, 717 Madison Place N.W., Washington, D.C. 20005-1086.

Telephone: (202) 219-1269.

BYBEE, Jay S. *(Judge, United States Court of Appeals Ninth Circuit)* Appointed for life by President George W. Bush to term beginning March 28, 2003.

Mailing address: P.O. Box 193939, San Francisco, California 94119-3939.

Telephone: (415) 556-9800.

BYE, Kermit E. *(Judge, United States Court of Appeals Eighth Circuit)* Appointed for life by President Bill Clinton to term beginning 2000. Born Hatton North

BYE, KERMIT E.—*Continued*

Dakota Jan 13, 1937. Educated at University of North Dakota B.S. 1959 J.D. 1962. In legal practice Fargo 1968-2000.

Deputy Securities Commissioner 1962-64 and Special Assistant Attorney General 1964-66 North Dakota. Assistant U.S. Attorney District of North Dakota 1966-68.

Office: 330 U.S. Courthouse, 655 First Avenue North, Fargo, North Dakota 58102.

Telephone: (701) 297-7270.

CABRANES, José A. *(Judge, United States Court of Appeals Second Circuit)* Appointed for life by President Bill Clinton to term beginning Aug 12, 1994. Born Mayaguez Puerto Rico Dec 22, 1940. Roman Catholic. Educated at Columbia University A.B. 1961, Yale Law School J.D. 1965 and Cambridge University M.Litt. 1967. Admitted to practice New York 1968, District of Columbia 1975 and U.S. District Court District of Connecticut 1976. In legal practice New York City 1967-71. Judge and Chief Judge, U.S. District Court District of Connecticut Dec 21, 1979 to Aug 11, 1994, appointed by President Jimmy Carter.

Special Counsel to Governor of Puerto Rico and Head of Office of the Commonwealth of Puerto Rico Washington D.C. 1973-75. General Counsel Yale University 1975-79. Author *Citizenship and the American Empire* Yale University Press 1979. Co-author with Kate Stith *Fear of Judging: Sentencing Guidelines in the Federal Courts* University of Chicago Press 1998. Associate Professor of Law Rutgers University Law School 1971-73. President's Commission on Mental Health 1977-78. Public Member U.S. Delegation to Conference on Security and Cooperation in Europe Belgrade 1977-78. Member The American Law Institute and Connecticut Bar Association. Political affiliation: Independent. Trustee Colgate University 1981-90, Yale University 1987-97 and Columbia University since 2000.

Office: U.S. Courthouse, 141 Church Street, New Haven, Connecticut 06510.

Telephone: (203) 867-8782.

CALABRESI, Guido *(Judge, United States Court of Appeals Second Circuit)* Appointed for life by President Bill Clinton to term beginning 1994. Born Milan Italy Oct 18, 1932. Educated at Yale University B.S. 1953 LL.B. 1958 and Oxford University B.A. 1955 M.A. 1959. Honorary LL.D. University of Notre Dame 1979, Villanova University 1984, University of Toronto 1985, Boston College 1986, Catholic University of America 1986, University of Chicago 1988, Connecticut College 1988, Illinois Institute of Technology, Chicago-Kent College of Law 1989, William Mitchell College 1992, Princeton University 1992, University of Detroit Mercy School of Law 1994, Seton Hall University 1995, Albertus Magnus College 1995, Lewis & Clark College Northwestern School of Law 1996, St. John's University 1997, Pace University School of Law 1998, Iona College 1998, Roger Williams University School of Law 1999, Hofstra University School of Law 1999, New York Law School 1999, Skidmore College 2000, Colby College 2001 and University of San Diego School of Law 2001. Honorary Dott. Jur. Università di Pavia 1987, University of Bologna 1990, Stockholm University 1993 and University of Milan 1998. Rhodes Scholar 1953. Staff member 1955-57 and Note Editor 1957-58 Yale Law Journal. Law Clerk to Hon. Hugo Black, U.S. Supreme Court 1958-59. Member Phi Beta Kappa and Order of the Coif. Admitted to practice Connecticut 1958.

Author "Robinson-Patman Act and Functional Discounts" 66, 243, 1956, "Some Thoughts on Risk Distributions and the Law of Torts" 70, 499, 1961, "Retroactivity: Paramount Powers and Contractual Changes" 71, 1191, 1962 and "You Can Call It Thucydides or You Can Call It Mustard Plaster, but It's All Proximate Cause Just the Same—In Memory of Fleming James" 91, 1, 1981 Yale L. Jour.; "The Decision for Accidents: An Approach to Non-Fault Allocation of Costs" 78 Harvard L. Rev. 713, 1965; "Changes for Automobile Claims, Views, and Overviews, Rules" 1967 *Illinois Law Forum* 600-611, 1967; "Transaction Costs, Resource Allocation and Liability Rules" 11 Journal of Law & Economics 67, 1968; "Reflections on Medical Experimentation in Humans" 98 No. 2 *Daedalus: Proceedings of the American Academy of Arts and Sciences* 387 Spring 1969; *The Costs of Accidents: A Legal and Economic Analysis* Yale University Press Feb 1970; "The New York Plan: A Free Choice Modification" 71 Columbia L. Rev. 267, 1971; Comments "Preclinical Problems of New Drug Development" *Regulating New Drugs* edited by R. L. Landeau University of Chicago Press 1973; "Birth, Death, and the Law" 37 *Pharos* 39, 1974; "Concerning Cause and the Law of Torts: An Essay for Harry Kalven, Jr." 43 University of Chicago L. Rev. 69, 1975; "The Problem of Malpractice: Trying to Round Out the Circle" 27 University of Toronto L. Jour. 131, 1977 and *The Economics of Medical Malpractice* edited by S. Rottenberg American Enterprise Institute 1978; "Product Liability: Curse or Bulwark of Free Enterprise?" 27 Cleveland State L. Rev. 314, 1979; "About Law and Economics: A Letter to Ronald Dworkin" 8 Hofstra L. Rev. 553, 1980; *A Common Law for the Age of Statutes* Harvard University Press Jan 1982; "The New Economic Analysis of Law: Scholarship, Sophistry, or Self-Indulgence?" 68 *Proceedings of the British Academy* 85, 1982; Commentary "The Passage of Time: The Implications for Product Liability" 58 New York University L. Rev. 939, 1983; *Ideals, Beliefs, Attitudes and the Law: Private Law Perspectives on a Public Law Problem* Syracuse University Press May 1985; "In Memoriam, The Honorable Potter Stewart" *Proceedings Before the Supreme Court of the United States* 14 Washington D.C. 1986; "Jay Katz's Contributions to Law and Medicine at Yale" 16 Law, Medicine & Health Care 3-4, 1988; "What Clarence Thomas Knows" Op-ed *The New York Times* July 28, 1991; "Whatever the Next Step Is, the Scoundrels Win" *Los Angeles Times* Oct 8, 1991; "Do We Own Our Own Bodies?" 1 Health Matrix Journal of Law-Medicine 501, 1991; "Coals to Newcastle or Doggerel for a Poet: A Tribute to John Simon" 27 San Francisco L. Rev. 5, 1992; "What Makes a Judge Great: To A. Leon Higginbotham, Jr." 142 University of Pennsylvania L. Rev. 513, 1993; Comments "Is There a Threat to Judicial Independence in the United States Today?" XXVI Fordham Urban L. Jour. 1, 1998; and "Two Functions of Formalism" 67 University of Chicago L. Rev. 479, 2000.

Co-author with Kenneth C. Bass, III "Right Approach, Wrong Implications: A Critique of McKean on Products Liability" 38 University of Chicago L. Rev. 74 Fall 1970; with A. Douglas Melamed "Property Rules, Liability Rules and Inalienability: One View of the Cathedral" 85 Harvard L. Rev. 1089, 1972; with P. Bobbitt *Tragic Choices* W. W. Norton & Co. Jan 1978; with

CALABRESI, GUIDO—*Continued*

Alvin K. Klevorick "Four Tests for Liability in Torts" 14 Journal of Legal Studies 3, 1985; with Edward R. Becker and Stephen G. Breyer "The Federal Judicial Law Clerk Hiring Problem and the Modest March 1 Solution" 104 Yale L. Jour. 207, 1994; and with Jeffrey O. Cooper "New Directions in Tort Law" 859 Valparaiso University L. Rev. 30, 1996. Associate Professor of Law 1961-62, Professor of Law 1962-95 and Sterling Professor of Law Emeritus and Professorial Lecturer since 1995 Yale University. Dean Yale University Law School 1985-94. Visiting Professor Harvard University Law School 1969-70 and University of Padua May 1993.

Member Committee on Legal Issues in Medical Care 1970-76. Member Society of American Law Teachers, Association of American Law Schools (Executive Committee 1987-89, Committee on the Challenges of Diversity since 1991, Program Committee 1993-94), Canadian Institute for Advanced Legal Studies, National Association of Women Lawyers, The Association of Trial Lawyers of America, The American Law Institute, American Bar Foundation, Connecticut, National and American Bar Associations. Recipient Laetare Medal from University of Notre Dame 1985, Award for Outstanding Research in Law and Government from Fellows of the American Bar Foundation 1998, Thomas Jefferson Medal in Law from The Jefferson Foundation and University of Virginia School of Law 2000 and Morton A. Brody Distinguished Judicial Service Award 2001. Named Commendatore (Honorary Knight Commander) by Republic of Italy 1994.

Trustee Dixwell Community House 1962-70, Connecticut College 1972-81, Russell Sage Foundation 1975-81 and American International School of Florence 1992-94. Board of Education Town of Woodbridge 1967-69. Trustee 1970-80, President of Board 1976-80 and Honorary Trustee since 1980 Hopkins School. Member National Commission on Critical Choices for Americans 1973-76 and Academic Committee Haifa University Law School 1989-94. Council Member 1983-86 and Fellow American Academy of Arts and Sciences. Director Friends of Legal Services for South Central Connecticut 1987-94. Board of Advisors Georgetown University Law School 1991-99. Council Member National Italian American Foundation since 1993. Advisory Board Meiklejohn Institute for Legal Studies since 1994. Foreign Member Royal Swedish Academy of Sciences. Member Yale Club of New York City, Century Association, The Benchers, The Dissenters, Italian American Historical Society of New Haven, Catholic Commission on Intellectual and Cultural Affairs, American Philosophical Society and Connecticut Academy of Arts and Sciences.

Office: Connecticut Financial Center, 157 Church Street, New Haven, Connecticut 06510.

Telephone: (203) 773-2291.

Fax: (203) 773-2401

CAMPBELL, Levin Hicks *(Senior Judge, United States Court of Appeals First Circuit)* Appointed for life by President Richard M. Nixon to term beginning Aug 31, 1972. Chief Judge March 31, 1983 to March 31, 1990. Assumed Senior status Jan 3, 1992, serves by assignment. Born Summit New Jersey Jan 2, 1927. Protestant. Educated at Harvard University A.B. cum laude 1948 LL.B. 1951. Awarded honorary LL.D. Suffolk University 1975. Admitted to practice District of Columbia 1951 and Massachusetts 1954. In legal practice Boston 1954-64. Associate Justice, Superior Court of Massachusetts 1969-72. Judge, U.S. District Court District of Massachusetts Jan 1972 to Aug 1972.

Assistant Attorney General 1964, Special Assistant Attorney General 1966-67 and First Assistant Attorney General 1967-68 Massachusetts. Member Massachusetts Bar Foundation, American Bar Foundation, The American Law Institute, Boston, Massachusetts, Federal and American Bar Associations. Attended National College of the State Judiciary July 1970. Chairman Subcommittee on Supporting Personnel 1975-83; Member Committee on Court Administration 1980-83, Executive Committee 1984-90, ad hoc Committee to Study the Judicial Conference 1987; Member 1988-90 and Chairman Subcommittee on Administration and Structure 1988-90 Federal Courts Study Committee; and Chairman Committee to Review Circuit Council Conduct and Disability Orders 1989-94 Judicial Conference of the U.S. Member National Commission on Judicial Discipline and Removal 1991-93. Fellow 1968-69 and Study Group Leader "Imperial Judiciary" Fall 1980 Institute of Politics J. F. Kennedy School Harvard University. Faculty Chairman Law Session Salzburg Seminar in American Studies July 1981. Served to First Lieutenant U.S. Army JAGC 1951-54. Recipient Commendation Medal for Services in Korea 1953. Member House of Representatives Massachusetts 1963-64. Visiting Committee Harvard University Press 1958-65 and Harvard Extension 1968-76. President Cambridge Neighborhood 9 Association 1960-62 and Board of Overseers Shady Hill School 1969-70. Treasurer Cambridge Center for Adult Education 1961-64. Campaign Chairman Cambridge United Fund 1965. Vice President Cambridge Community Services. Board of Overseers Boston Symphony Orchestra 1969-75 and 1977-80. Corporation Member SEA Education Association since 1982. Trustee Colby College, Waterville Maine 1982-90 and 1991-99 and Asheville School, Asheville North Carolina 1987-95. Overseer USS Constitution Museum since 1992. President 2000-02 and Council Member since 2003 Massachusetts Historical Society. Board of Directors Salzburg Seminar Alumni Association. Enjoys sailing and the symphony.

Office: 6720 U.S. Courthouse, One Courthouse Way, Boston, Massachusetts 02210-3002.

Telephone: (617) 748-9002.

CANBY, William C., Jr. *(Senior Judge, United States Court of Appeals Ninth Circuit)* Appointed for life by President Jimmy Carter to term beginning 1980. Assumed Senior status May 23, 1996, serves by assignment. Born St. Paul Minnesota May 22, 1931. Educated at Yale University A.B. 1953 and University of Minnesota LL.B. 1956. Note Editor Minnesota Law Review 1955-56. Law Clerk to Justice Charles E. Whittaker, U.S. Supreme Court 1958-59. Member Phi Beta Kappa and Order of the Coif. Admitted to practice Minnesota 1956 and Arizona 1972. In legal practice St. Paul Minnesota 1959-62. Chief Justice, High Court of the Trust Territory of the Pacific Islands 1993-94.

Associate and Deputy Director Ethiopia 1962-64 and Director Uganda 1964-66 Peace Corps. Assistant to Senator Walter Mondale 1966 and to State University of New York President 1967. Author *American Indian Law* 1981. Professor of Law Arizona State University 1967-80. Fulbright Professor of Law Makerere University, Kampala Uganda 1970-71. Board of Directors Maricopa County Legal Aid Society 1972-78 and Arizona Center for Law in the Public Interest 1974-80. Member State

CANBY, WILLIAM C., JR.—*Continued*

Bar of Arizona and Minnesota State Bar Association. USAF 1956-58. Precinct and State Committeeman Democratic Party Arizona 1972-80. Board of Directors Central Arizona Coalition for Right to Choose 1976-80.

Office: 612 U.S. Courthouse, 401 West Washington Street SPC 55, Phoenix, Arizona 85003-2156.

Telephone: (602) 514-7300.

CARDAMONE, Richard J. *(Senior Judge, United States Court of Appeals Second Circuit)* Appointed for life by President Ronald Reagan to term beginning Nov 13, 1981. Assumed Senior status Nov 13, 1993, serves by assignment. Born Utica New York Oct 10, 1925. Roman Catholic. Educated at Harvard University B.A. 1948 and Syracuse University LL.B. 1952. Admitted to practice New York 1952. In legal practice Utica 1952-62. Justice, New York Supreme Court 1963-71. Associate Justice 1971-81 and Senior Associate Justice Jan 1, 1979 to 1981, New York Supreme Court Appellate Division Fourth Judicial Department.

President New York State Association of Supreme Court Justices 1977-78. Member New York State Commission on Judicial Conduct 1978-81, The American Law Institute, Oneida County and New York State Bar Associations. Lieutenant j.g. USNR PTO 1943-46. Trustee Syracuse University College of Law, Slocum Dickinson Foundation and St. Luke Hospital Center.

Office: 330 Federal Building, 10 Broad Street, Utica, New York 13501.

Telephone: (315) 793-8198.

CARLO-ALTIERI, Gerardo A. *(Judge, Bankruptcy Appellate Panel First Circuit and Chief Judge, United States Bankruptcy Court District of Puerto Rico)* Selected for Appellate Panel by Judicial Council of the First Circuit. Appointed to Bankruptcy Court by U.S. Court of Appeals First Circuit judges. Chief Judge Bankruptcy Court since March 1, 1999.

Office: 245 Federal Bldg. & U.S. Courthouse, 300 Recinto Sur Street, San Juan, Puerto Rico 00901.

Telephone: (787) 977-6040.

CARLUZZO, Lewis R. *(Special Trial Judge, United States Tax Court)* Appointed by U.S. Tax Court Chief Judge Lapsley W. Hamblen, Jr.

Office: 400 Second Street N.W., Washington, D.C. 20217-0002.

Telephone: (202) 874-6043.

CARMAN, Gregory W. *(Chief Judge, United States Court of International Trade)* Appointed for life by President Ronald Reagan to term beginning March 3, 1984. Born Farmingdale New York Jan 31, 1937. Episcopalian. Educated at University of Paris 1956-57, St. Lawrence University B.A. 1958, St. John's University School of Law J.D. with honors 1961, University of Virginia School of Law J.A.G. with honors 1962 and New York University School of Law LL.M. in Taxation. Staff member St. John's University Law Review 1961. Member Phi Delta Phi and Sigma Chi. Admitted to practice New York 1961, U.S. Court of Military Appeals 1962, U.S. District Courts Eastern 1966 and Southern 1966 Districts of New York, U.S. Courts of Appeals Second 1966 and District of Columbia 1982 Circuits and U.S. Supreme Court 1967. Began legal practice New York City 1961. In legal practice Farmingdale 1961.

Fellow American College of Mortgage Attorneys. President Protestant Lawyers Association of Long Island. Member Nassau Lawyers Association, New York State Defenders Association, Nassau County, New York State, Federal and American (Past President Savings & Loan League Committee New York Chapter) Bar Associations. Captain U.S. Army JAG 1958-64. Recipient Commendation Medal for Meritorious Service Jan 14, 1964. Member Nassau County Republican Committee. Councilman Town of Oyster Bay New York 1972-80. Member U.S. House of Representatives 97th Congress 1981-82. Former member of Vestry St. Thomas Episcopal Church. Charter Trustee and former President Farmingdale-Bethpage Historical Society. District Chairman United Cerebral Palsy. Member Rotary International since 1964, United Way (Chairman Town of Oyster Bay 1973-76), Elks, Boy Scouts of America (Past Vice Chairman Paumanok District, member District Committee Nassau County Council since 1964), Holland Society and Bicentennial Commission of Nassau County. Enjoys skiing, golf, tennis and gardening.

Office: One Federal Plaza, New York, New York 10278-0001.

Telephone: (212) 264-2842.

CARNES, Ed *(Judge, United States Court of Appeals Eleventh Circuit)* Appointed for life by President George Bush to term beginning Oct 2, 1992. Born Albertville Alabama June 3, 1950. Methodist. Educated at University of Alabama B.S. with honors 1972 and Harvard Law School J.D. with honors 1975. Admitted to practice Alabama 1975.

Assistant Attorney General Alabama 1975-92.

Office: 500-D Federal Courthouse Annex, One Church Street, Montgomery, Alabama 36104.

Telephone: (334) 954-3580.

CASELLAS, Salvador E. *(Judge, United States District Court District of Puerto Rico)* Appointed for life by President Bill Clinton Sept 29, 1994. Born San Juan Puerto Rico June 10, 1935. Educated at Georgetown University B.S.F.S. cum laude 1957, University of Puerto Rico LL.B. magna cum laude 1960 and Harvard Law School LL.M. 1961. Associate Editor University of Puerto Rico Law Review 1959-60. Admitted to practice Puerto Rico 1962, U.S. District Court District of Puerto Rico 1963, U.S. Court of Appeals First Circuit 1963, U.S. Customs Court 1964, U.S. Court of Customs and Patent Appeals 1968, U.S. Supreme Court 1977, District of Columbia 1979 and U.S. Tax Court 1981. In legal practice San Juan 1962-72 and 1977 to Oct 1994.

Commissioner Puerto Rico National Conference of Commissioners on Uniform State Laws 1967-72. Author Note "Mandatory Legal Easements" 93, 1959 and "Comments on New Horizontal Property Law" 301, 1959 XXVIII University of Puerto Rico L. Rev.; "Legal Effects of Wills Executed Outside of Puerto Rico" XX 307, 1960, "The Admiralty Jurisdiction in the Commonwealth of Puerto Rico" XXII No. 2, 165, 1962, "Recent Court Decisions on Tax Matters" XXVI 298, 1966 and "Federal and Commonwealth Jurisdiction in the Field of Maritime Law" XXVI No. 4, 259, 1966 Puerto Rico Bar Association L. Rev.; "Diplomatic Antecedents and Causes of the Spanish-American War: 1895-98" IX No. 1 Social Sciences Review 55 University of Puerto Rico 1965; and "Freedom of the Press and the Protection of Reputation" 1 No. 1 Review of the Puerto Rico Academy of Jurisprudence 27, 1989.

CASELLAS, SALVADOR E.—*Continued*

Director Puerto Rico Bar Association Foundation 1985-88. Fellow American Bar Foundation. Second Lieutenant U.S. Army 1961-62. First Lieutenant USAR JAGC 1963-67. Civilian Aide 1985-89 and Civilian Aide Emeritus since 1990 Secretary of the Army. Recipient Puerto Rico National Guard Medal 1992. Secretary of the Treasury Puerto Rico 1973-76. Vice Chairman Governor's Finance Council 1973-76. Member Governor's Economic Advisory Council 1986-89. Director Ana G. Méndez Educational Foundation 1980-83, Committee on Economic Development 1983-94, Puerto Rico Community Foundation 1984-87, Centros Sor Isolina Ferré 1989-94, Puerto Rico Legal Aid Society 1992-93, Alliance for a Drug Free Puerto Rico 1993-94 and Angel Ramos Foundation since 1993. President 1984-87 and Director 1984-94 Luis Muñoz Marín Foundation. Trustee Puerto Rico National Guard Trust 1991-92. Former Director First Federal Bank. Former Member Law School Evaluating Commission, Puerto Rico Crime Commission, Puerto Rico Commission on the Bicentennial of the U.S. Constitution, Puerto Rico Police Advisory Council and Municipal Reform Commission.

Office: CH-111 U.S. Courthouse, 150 Carlos Chardon Avenue, San Juan, Puerto Rico 00918-1761.

Telephone: (787) 772-3150.

CASTELLANOS, Jesus A. *(Magistrate Judge, United States District Court District of Puerto Rico)* Appointed by U.S. District Court judges March 21, 1980. Reappointed March 21, 1989 and March 21, 1996. Current term expires March 21, 2004. Born Puerto Rico Aug 19, 1942. Christian. Educated at Inter-American University of Puerto Rico B.A. 1963 LL.B. 1968. Member Phi Eta Mu. Admitted to practice Puerto Rico 1970. In legal practice San Juan 1974-76.

Attorney Water Resources Authority Puerto Rico 1970. Member Puerto Rico and Federal Bar Associations. Legislative Assistant U.S. House of Representatives 1971-72 and 1977-80. Enjoys arts and literature.

Office: 182 Federal Building, 150 Carlos Chardon Avenue, San Juan, Puerto Rico 00918-1759.

Telephone: (787) 772-3185.

CEREZO, Carmen Consuelo *(Judge, United States District Court District of Puerto Rico)* Appointed for life by President Jimmy Carter to term beginning 1980. Chief Judge 1993-99. Born San Juan Puerto Rico Aug 22, 1940. Educated at University of Puerto Rico B.A. 1963 J.D. 1966 and University of Virginia School of Law LL.M. 1988. Law Clerk to U.S. District Court District of Puerto Rico 1967-72. In legal practice Puerto Rico 1966-67. Judge, Puerto Rico Superior Court 1972-76. Judge, Puerto Rico Court of Intermediate Appeals 1976-80.

Office: CH-131 U.S. Courthouse, 150 Carlos Chardon Avenue, San Juan, Puerto Rico 00918-1764.

Telephone: (787) 772-3110.

CHABOT, Herbert L. *(Senior Judge, United States Tax Court)* Appointed by President Jimmy Carter to term beginning April 3, 1978. Reappointed by President Bill Clinton Oct 20, 1993. Assumed Senior status, serves by assignment. Born Bronx County New York July 17, 1931. Educated at City College of the City University of New York B.A. in Government cum laude 1952, Columbia University LL.B. 1957 and Georgetown University LL.M. in Taxation 1964. Law Clerk to Hon. Russell E. Train, U.S. Tax Court 1961-65. Admitted to practice New York 1958.

Legal staff American Jewish Congress 1957-61. Joint Committee on Internal Revenue Taxation U.S. Congress 1965-78. Adjunct Professor George Washington University National Law Center 1974-83. Member Federal and American (Section of Taxation) Bar Associations. Delegate Maryland Constitutional Convention 1967-68. Corporal U.S. Army 1953-55 and Sergeant First Class USAR 1955-63.

Office: 400 Second Street N.W., Washington, D.C. 20217-0002.

Telephone: (202) 606-8930.

CHIECHI, Carolyn P. *(Judge, United States Tax Court)* Appointed by President George Bush July 27, 1992 to term beginning Oct 1, 1992. Term expires Oct 1, 2007. Born Newark New Jersey Dec 6, 1943. Catholic. Educated at Georgetown University B.S. magna cum laude 1965 J.D. 1969 LL.M. in Taxation 1971. Law Clerk to Hon. Leo H. Irwin, U.S. Tax Court 1969-71. Admitted to practice District of Columbia 1969, U.S. District Court District of Columbia 1969, U.S. Courts of Appeals District of Columbia 1969, Federal 1982, Sixth 1985, Fifth 1987 and Ninth 1991 Circuits, U.S. Tax Court 1971, U.S. Supreme Court 1974 and U.S. Court of Federal Claims 1978. In legal practice Washington D.C. 1971-92.

Co-author *Private Foundations Before and After the Tax Reform Act of 1969* American Enterprise Institute for Public Policy Research Washington D.C. May 1974; and *T.M. Portfolio 338* 1976 revised *T.M. Portfolio 338-2nd* 1983 and *T.M. Portfolio 338-3rd* 1991 Tax Management, Inc. Authored over twenty articles in various publications including *The Journal of Taxation, The Tax Advisor, Trusts & Estates* and *Private Foundations—Section 4940 and Section 4944.* Department Editor *The Journal of Taxation* 1986-92. Fellow American College of Tax Counsel and American Bar Foundation. Former Member Federal Circuit Bar Association (Tax Appeals Committee 1988-92) and U.S. Court of Federal Claims Bar Association (Member 1987-92 and Vice Chairperson 1988-92 Committee on Practice and Procedure). Member American Judicature Society, Women's Bar Association of the District of Columbia, The District of Columbia Bar (Member 1980-82 and Chairman 1981-82 Steering Committee and Member since 1986 and Chairperson 1987-88 Tax Audits and Litigation Committee Tax Section), Federal (Section of Taxation, Judiciary Division) and American (Committee on Administrative Practice 1975-82, Committee on Regulated Investment Companies 1982-91, Committee on Court Procedure since 1991, Sections: Taxation, Litigation) Bar Associations. Board of Directors Stuart Stiller Memorial Foundation since 1986. National Law Alumni Board 1986-93 and Board of Regents since 1988 Georgetown University. Board of Governors Georgetown University Alumni Association since 1994.

Office: 400 Second Street N.W., Washington, D.C. 20217-0002.

Telephone: (202) 606-8855.

CHOY, Herbert Y. C. *(Senior Judge, United States Court of Appeals Ninth Circuit)* Appointed for life by President Richard M. Nixon to term beginning 1971. Assumed Senior status Oct 3, 1984, serves by assignment. Born Makaweli Kauai Hawaii Jan 6, 1916. Educated at University of Hawaii B.A. 1938 and Harvard

CHOY, HERBERT Y. C.—*Continued*
University J.D. 1941. Admitted to practice Hawaii 1941. In legal practice Honolulu 1946-71.
Territorial Guard Hawaii 1941-42. Attorney General Territory of Hawaii 1957-58. U.S. Army 1942-46. Recipient Order of Civil Merit (Korea). Trustee Hawaii Loa College 1963-79.
Mailing address: P.O. Box 50127, Honolulu, Hawaii 96850.
Office: C-305 Federal Building, 300 Ala Moana Boulevard, Honolulu, Hawaii 96850-0305.
Telephone: (808) 541-1801.

CLARK, Glen E. *(Judge, Bankruptcy Appellate Panel Tenth Circuit)* Selected by the Judicial Council of the Tenth Circuit. Also Chief Judge, U.S. Bankruptcy Court District of Utah. Appointed by U.S. District Court judges to term beginning July 1, 1982. Reappointed by U.S. Court of Appeals Tenth Circuit judges. Born Cedar Rapids Iowa Nov 23, 1943. Educated at University of Iowa B.A. 1966 and University of Utah College of Law J.D. 1971. Articles Editor Utah Law Review 1970-71. Member Order of the Coif. Admitted to practice Utah 1971, U.S. District Court District of Utah 1971 and U.S. Court of Appeals Tenth Circuit 1972. Began legal practice Salt Lake City 1971.
Office: 365 U.S. Courthouse, 350 South Main Street, Salt Lake City, Utah 84101.
Telephone: (801) 524-6549.

CLAY, Eric L. *(Judge, United States Court of Appeals Sixth Circuit)* Appointed for life by President Bill Clinton to term beginning 1997. Born Durham North Carolina Jan 18, 1948. Educated at University of North Carolina B.A. 1969 and Yale Law School J.D. 1972. Law Clerk to Hon. Damon J. Keith, U.S. District Court Eastern District of Michigan 1972-73. In legal practice Detroit 1973-97.
Office: 619 U.S. Courthouse, 231 West Lafayette Boulevard, Detroit, Michigan 48226.
Telephone: (313) 234-5260.

CLEMENT, Edith Brown *(Judge, United States Court of Appeals Fifth Circuit)* Appointed for life by President George W. Bush to term beginning Nov 27, 2001. Born Birmingham Alabama April 29, 1948. Catholic. Educated at University of Alabama B.A. 1969 and Tulane University School of Law J.D. 1972. Law Clerk to Hon. Herbert W. Christenberry, U.S. District Court Eastern District of Louisiana 1973-75. Admitted to practice Louisiana 1973, U.S. Courts of Appeals Fifth 1975 and Eleventh 1981 Circuits and U.S. Supreme Court 1978. In legal practice New Orleans 1975-91. Judge, U.S. District Court Eastern District of Louisiana 1991 to Nov 26, 2001, appointed by President George Bush.
Member The Maritime Law Association of the U.S., Louisiana State, Fifth Circuit, Eleventh Circuit, U.S. Supreme Court and Federal Bar Associations.
Office: 200 U.S. Court of Appeals Building, 600 Camp Street, New Orleans, Louisiana 70130.
Telephone: (504) 589-7530.

CLEVENGER, Raymond C., III *(Judge, United States Court of Appeals Federal Circuit)* Appointed for life by President George Bush Jan 24, 1990 to term beginning May 3, 1990. Born Topeka Kansas Aug 27, 1937. Educated at Yale University B.A. 1959 LL.B. 1966. Law Clerk to Associate Justice Byron Raymond White, U.S. Supreme Court Oct 1966 term. In legal practice Washington D.C. 1967-90.
Office: National Courts Building, 717 Madison Place N.W., Washington, D.C. 20439-0002.
Telephone: (202) 633-5909.

CLIFTON, Richard R. *(Judge, United States Court of Appeals Ninth Circuit)* Appointed for life by President George W. Bush to term beginning Aug 5, 2002. Born Framingham Massachusetts 1950. Educated at Princeton University A.B. 1972 and Yale Law School J.D. 1975. Law Clerk to Hon. Herbert Y. C. Choy, U.S. Court of Appeals Ninth Circuit 1975-76. In legal practice Honolulu 1977-2002.
Mailing address: 1132 Bishop Street, Suite 601, Honolulu, Hawaii 96813.
Telephone: (808) 522-7474.

COFFEY, John L. *(Judge, United States Court of Appeals Seventh Circuit)* Appointed for life by President Ronald Reagan to term beginning March 27, 1982. Born Milwaukee Wisconsin April 15, 1922. Educated at Marquette University B.A. 1943 J.D. 1948. Awarded honorary M.B.A. Spencerian Business College 1964. Member Alpha Sigma Nu, Phi Alpha Delta and Woolsack Society. Admitted to practice Wisconsin 1948, U.S. District Court 1948 and U.S. Supreme Court 1980. Judge, Milwaukee County Civil Court 1954-60. Judge, Milwaukee County Municipal Court 1960-62. Judge 1962-72, Senior Judge 1972-75 and Chief Presiding Judge Jan 1976 to Nov 1976 Criminal Division and Judge Civil Division Nov 1976 to Aug 2, 1978, Wisconsin Circuit Court Milwaukee County. Justice, Wisconsin Supreme Court Aug 1978 to March 1982.
Assistant City Attorney Milwaukee Aug 1949 to June 1954. Important Decisions 1983-89: United States v. Madison (sentencing) 689 F.2d 1300, 7th Cir. 1982, cert. denied 459 U.S. 1117, 103 S. Ct. 754, 74 L.Ed. 971, 1983; Quilici v. Village of Morton Grove (handgun control) 695 F.2d 261, 7th Cir. 1982, cert. denied 464 U.S. 863, 104 S. Ct. 194, 78 L.Ed.2d 170, 1983; Martin v. Helstad (due process) 699 F.2d 387, 7th Cir. 1983; Analytica, Inc. v. N.P.D. Research, Inc. (attorney disqualification) 708 F.2d 1263, 7th Cir. 1983; East Chicago Rehabilitation Center, Inc. v. N.L.R.B. (wildcat strikes) 710 F.2d 397, 7th Cir. 1983, cert. denied 465 U.S. 1065, 104 S. Ct. 1414, 79 L.Ed.2d 740, 1984; E.E.O.C. v. University of Notre Dame Du Lac 715 F.2d 331, 7th Cir. 1983; Hope, Inc. v. County of DuPage (housing discrimination) 738 F.2d 797, 7th Cir. 1984; Zbaraz v. Hartigan (abortion) 763 F.2d 1532, 7th Cir. 1985 (dissenting), aff'd 484 U.S. 171, 108 S. Ct. 479, 98 L.Ed.2d 478, 1987; Donovan v. Estate of Fitzsimmons (mismanagement of pension fund) 778 F.2d 298, 7th Cir. 1985 (dissenting), rev'd 805 F.2d 682, 1986; Larimore v. Comptroller of Currency (bank director liability) 789 F.2d 1244, 7th Cir. 1986; Schultz v. Frisby (first amendment, residential picketing) 807 F.2d 1339, 7th Cir. 1986 (dissenting), vacated 818 F.2d 1284, 7th Cir. 1987, aff'd 822 F.2d 642, 7th Cir. 1987, rev'd 108 S. Ct. 2495, 101 L.Ed.2d 420, 1988; State of Wisconsin v. Bowen (disallowance of Medicaid reimbursement) 797 F.2d 391, 55 U.S.L.W. 2086, 7th Cir. 1986 (dissenting), cert. granted 107 S. Ct. 926, 93 L.Ed.2d 978, 1987, cert. dismissed 108 S. Ct. 1495, 99 L.Ed.2d 879, 1988; Heller v. Equitable Life Association Society 833 F.2d 1253, 7th Cir. 1987; Greenberg v. Kmetko (civil rights) 811 F.2d 1057, 7th Cir. 1987 (dissenting), vacated 820 F.2d

COFFEY, JOHN L.—*Continued*

897, 7th Cir. 1987, rehearing 840 F.2d 467, 1988; Rakovich v. Wade 819 F.2d 1393, 7th Cir. 1987 (dissenting in part), vacated 850 F.2d 1179, 7th Cir. 1987, cert. denied 109 S. Ct. 497, 102 L.Ed.2d 534, 1988; Sherrod v. Berry 827 F.2d 195, 7th Cir. 1987 (dissenting), vacated 835 F.2d 1222, 7th Cir. 1988, rev'd 856 F.2d 802, 7th Cir. 1988; Teague v. Lane (habeas corpus, sixth amendment, jury selection) 820 F.2d 832, 7th Cir. 1987, aff'd 109 S. Ct. 1060, 103 L.Ed.2d 334, 1989; Eagan v. Duckworth (Miranda warnings, confessions) 843 F.2d 1554, 7th Cir. (dissenting) cert. granted 1988, rev'd 109 S. Ct. 2875, 1989; Ford v. Childers 855 F.2d 1271, 7th Cir. 1988; Ragsdale v. Turnock, 841 F.2d 1358, 7th Cir. 1988 (dissenting), appeal dismissed 112 S. Ct. 1309, 117 L.Ed.2d 510, 1992; G. Heileman Brewing Co., Inc. v. Joseph Oat Corp. 871 F.2d 648, 7th Cir. 1989 (dissenting); International Union v. Johnson Controls, Inc. 886 F.2d 871, 7th Cir. 1989, rev'd 499 U.S. 187, 111 S. Ct. 1522, 108 L.Ed.2d 762, 1991; and Mather v. Village of Mundelein 869 F.2d 356, 7th Cir. 1989.

Important Decisions 1990-94: Miller v. Civil City of South Bend 904 F.2d 1081, 7th Cir. 1990, rev'd sub nom Barnes v. Glen Theater, Inc. 501 U.S. 560, 111 S. Ct. 2456, 115 L.Ed.2d 504, 1991; K.H. through Murphy v. Morgan 914 F.2d 846, 7th Cir. 1990 (dissenting); Doe v. Village of Crestwood 917 F.2d 1476, 7th Cir. 1991 (dissenting), cert. denied 112 S. Ct. 3025, 120 L.Ed.2d 986, 1992; Shelton v. Old Ben Coal Co. 933 F.2d 504, 7th Cir. 1991 (dissenting); Collins v. Director, Office of Workers' Compensation Programs, United States Department of Labor 932 F.2d 1191, 7th Cir. 1991 (concurring); Compton v. Inland Steel Coal Co. 933 F.2d 477, 7th Cir. 1991 (concurring); Hunter v. Clark (no adverse inference instruction) 906 F.2d 302, 7th Cir. 1990, vacated and rehearing granted en banc 934 F.2d 856, 7th Cir. 1991; United States v. Leichtnam 948 F.2d 370, 7th Cir. 1991 (concurring in part, dissenting in part); South Suburban Housing Center v. Board of Realtors 935 F.2d 868, 7th Cir. 1991, cert. denied sub nom Greater South Suburban Board of Realtors v. City of Blue Island 502 U.S. 1074, 112 S. Ct. 971, 117 L.Ed.2d 136, 1992, vacated and rehearing granted 964 F.2d 611, 7th Cir. 1991; Doe v. Small (establishment clause) 934 F.2d 743, 7th Cir. 1991 (dissenting), vacated and rehearing granted 947 F.2d 256, rev'd 964 F.2d 611, 7th Cir. 1992; Senn v. United Dominion Ind. Inc. 951 F.2d 806, 7th Cir. 1992, rehearing denied 962 F.2d 655, 7th Cir. 1992, cert. denied 113 S. Ct. 2992, 115 L.Ed.2d 687, 1993; Banks v. NCAA 977 F.2d 1081, 7th Cir. 1992, cert. denied 113 S. Ct. 2336, 124 L.Ed.2d 247, 1993; Churchill v. Waters 977 F.2d 1114, 7th Cir. 1992, vacated 114 S. Ct. 1878, 128 L.Ed.2d 686, 1994; Phillips v. Lincoln Nat. Life Ins. Co. 978 F.2d 302, 7th Cir. 1992; Matter of Scarlata 979 F.2d 521, 7th Cir. 1992 (dissenting); Bebout v. Norfolk & W. Ry. 982 F.2d 1178, 7th Cir. 1993 (concurring in part, dissenting in part); American Dental Association v. Martin 984 F.2d 823, 7th Cir. 1993 (concurring), cert. denied sub nom 114 S. Ct. 172, 126 L.Ed.2d 132, 1993; United States v. Lechuga 994 F.2d 346, 7th Cir. 1993, cert. denied 114 S. Ct. 482, 126 L.Ed.2d 433, 1993; Welsh v. Boy Scouts 993 F.2d 1267, 7th Cir. 1993, cert. denied 114 S. Ct. 602, 126 L.Ed.2d 567, 1993; Reich v. Great Lakes Indian Fish and Wildlife Commission 4 F.3d 490, 7th Cir. 1993 (dissenting); Cuppett v. Duckworth 8 F.3d 1132, 7th Cir. 1993, cert. denied 114 S. Ct. 1226, 127 L.Ed.2d 571, 1994; and United States v. Hudspeth 42 F.3d 1015, 7th Cir. 1994.

Important Decisions since 1995: Carrie Jaffee, as Special Administrator for Ricky Allen, Sr. and Lechia Allen, Next Friend of Rickey Allen, Jr., and Brandon Allen v. Mary Lu Redmond and Village of Hoffman Estates 51 F.3d 1346, 7th Cir. 1995, aff'd S. Ct. June 13, 1996, 64 USLW 4490; United States v. Shannon 110 F.3d 382, 7th Cir. 1997; United States v. Jerez and Solis 108 F.3d 684, 7th Cir. 1997; Jansen v. Packaging and Ellerth v. Burlington 123 F.3d 490, 7th Cir. 1997; Gracia v. Volvo 112 F.3d 291, 7th Cir. 1997, rehearing denied June 10, 1997; Robb v. Norfolk 122 F.3d 354, 7th Cir. 1997 rehearing denied Sept 12, 1997; Smith v. Metropolitan School District 128 F.3d 1014, 7th Cir. 1997; United States v. Fawley 137 F.3d 458, 7th Cir. 1998; Doe v. Univ. of Ill. 138 F.3d 653, 7th Cir. 1997, concurring in part, dissenting in part, cert. granted, vacated by Board of Trustees of University of Illinois v. Doe 119 S. Ct. 2016, 143 L.Ed.2d 1028, 1999; Patterson v. Chicago Ass'n for Retarded Citizens 150 F.3d 719, 7th Cir. 1998; Herdrich v. Pegram 154 F.3d 362, 7th Cir. 1998, rehearing denied 170 F.3d 683, 7th Cir. 1999; United States v. Hall 142 F.3d 988, 7th Cir. 1998; Paters v. United States 159 F.3d 1043, 7th Cir. 1998, concurring in part, dissenting in part; Filipovic v. K & R Express Sys., Inc. 176 F.3d 390, 7th Cir. 1999; Wilson v. Williams 161 F.3d 1078, 7th Cir. 1998, aff'd 1999 WL 432591, 7th Cir. June 29, 1999; United States v. George Wilson, et al.; Indiana Civil Liberties Union v. O'Bannon 259 F.3d 766, 7th Cir. 2001; Linnemeir v. Board of Trustees of Purdue Univ. 260 F.3d 757, 7th Cir. 2001; McNair v. Coffey 279 F.3d 463, 7th Cir. 2002; Anheuser-Busch, Inc. v. Beer, Soft Drink, Water, Fruit Juice, et al. 280 F.3d 1133, 7th Cir. 2002; Driebel v. City of Milwaukee 298 F.3d 622, 7th Cir. 2002; Brown v. Sternes 304 F.3d 677, 7th Cir. 2002; and A Woman's Choice—East Side Women's Clinic v. Newman 305 F.3d 684, 7th Cir. 2002.

Fellow American Bar Foundation. Former member Wisconsin Board of Criminal Court Judges and Wisconsin Board of Circuit Court Judges. Member Wisconsin Lawyers Pro Bono Publico, American Judicature Society, National Lawyers Club, State Bar of Wisconsin, Illinois State, Seventh Circuit and American Bar Associations. Listed in *Who's Who in the Midwest, Who's Who in American Politics, Who's Who in America* and *Who's Who International.* Named Outstanding Young Man of the Year by Milwaukee Junior Chamber of Commerce 1951, one of Five Outstanding Young Men in the State by Wisconsin Junior Chamber of Commerce 1957 and Marquette University Outstanding Law Alumnus of the Year 1980. Recipient Distinguished Service Award from American Legion Cudworth Post 1973 and Distinguished Professional Achievement Merit Award from Marquette University 1985. USN 1943-46. Chairman St. Joseph's Home for Children Advisory Board 1958-65 and St. Eugene's School Board 1967-70. Member St. Mary's Hospital Advisory Board 1964-70. President St. Eugene's Church Council 1974. Former member Milwaukee County Department of Public Welfare Volunteer Services Advisory Committee, Board of Directors Marquette University "M" Club and Board of Directors and Executive Board Milwaukee-Waukesha Chapter American Red Cross. Member St. Monica's Congregation, American

COFFEY, JOHN L.—*Continued*

Legion Cudworth Post 23, Milwaukee County Council Boy Scouts of America and Marquette University Law Alumni.

Office: 619 U.S. Courthouse & Federal Bldg., 517 East Wisconsin Avenue, Milwaukee, Wisconsin 53202.

Telephone: (414) 297-4180.

COFFIN, Frank M. *(Senior Judge, United States Court of Appeals First Circuit)* Appointed for life by President Lyndon B. Johnson to term beginning Nov 22, 1965. Chief Judge 1972-83. Assumed Senior status Feb 1, 1989, serves by assignment. Born Lewiston Maine July 11, 1919. Educated at Bates College A.B. 1940 and Harvard University I.A. 1943 LL.B. 1947. Awarded honorary LL.D. Bates College 1959, University of Maine 1967, Bowdoin College 1969 and Colby College 1975. Law Clerk to U.S. District Court District of Maine 1947-49. In legal practice Lewiston 1947-52 and Portland 1952-56.

Corporation Counsel Lewiston 1949-52. Managing Director Department of State Development Loan Fund 1961. Deputy Administrator Agency for International Development 1961-64. U.S. Permanent Representative to Development Assistance Committee OECD 1964-65. Author *Witness for Aid* Houghton Mifflin Co. 1964, *The Ways of a Judge* Houghton Mifflin Co. 1980, *A Lexicon of Oral Advocacy* National Institute for Trial Advocacy 1984 and *On Appeal: Courts, Lawyering and Judging* W. W. Norton & Company 1994. Adjunct Professor of Appellate Advocacy University of Maine School of Law 1986-89. Member The American Law Institute, The Examiner Club, Institute of Judicial Administration, American Judicature Society and American Bar Association. Chairman Committee on the Judicial Branch Judicial Conference of the U.S. 1983-90. Director Governance Institute since 1987. Recipient Edwin T. Dahlberg Peace Award from American Baptist Convention May 16, 1970, Distinguished Service Award from Maine State Bar Association 1986, Benjamin E. Mays Award from Bates College June 1990 and Howard H. Dana, Jr. Award from Maine Bar Foundation 1997. Lieutenant s.g. USNR PTO 1943-46. Member U.S. House of Representatives 1957-60 (House Foreign Affairs Committee, Joint Economic Committee and Canada-U.S. Interparliamentary Group). Chairman Maine Democratic State Committee 1954-56. Member American Academy of Arts and Sciences and Lewiston School Board 1947-49. Enjoys sculpture, painting and boating.

Office: Federal Courthouse, 156 Federal Street, Portland, Maine 04101.

Telephone: (207) 780-3291.

COHEN, Mary Ann *(Judge, United States Tax Court)* Appointed by President Ronald Reagan July 1982 to term beginning Sept 24, 1982. Reappointed by President Bill Clinton Nov 7, 1997, current term expires Nov 6, 2012. Chief Judge June 1, 1996 to May 31, 2000. Born Albuquerque New Mexico July 16, 1943. Educated at University of California at Los Angeles B.S. 1964 and University of Southern California J.D. 1967. Admitted to practice California 1967. In legal practice Los Angeles 1967-82.

Member U.S. Attorney General's Advisory Committee on Tax Litigation U.S. Department of Justice 1979-80. Member American Bar Association (Section of Taxation, Judicial Administration Division).

Office: 400 Second Street N.W., Washington, D.C. 20217-0002.

Telephone: (202) 606-8821.

COLE, Ransey Guy, Jr. *(Judge, United States Court of Appeals Sixth Circuit)* Appointed for life by President Bill Clinton to term beginning Jan 1996. Born Birmingham Alabama May 23, 1951. Educated at Tufts University B.A. 1972 and Yale University Law School J.D. 1975. Admitted to practice Ohio 1975, U.S. District Court Southern District of Ohio 1977, U.S. Claims Court 1978 and District of Columbia 1982. In legal practice Columbus Ohio 1975-78, 1980-86 and 1993-95. Judge, U.S. Bankruptcy Court Southern District of Ohio 1987-93, appointed by President Ronald Reagan.

Trial Attorney Civil Division U.S. Department of Justice 1978-80. Board of Trustees Robert B. Elliott Law Club 1984-86. Board of Directors American Bankruptcy Board of Certification 1993-95 and Bankruptcy Arbitration and Mediation Services 1993-95. Member National Conference of Bankruptcy Judges 1983-95, Columbus (Board of Governors 1990-94), Ohio State (Council of Delegates 1989-91), American (Vice Chair Subcommittee on Membership—Women, Minorities and Young Lawyers Committee on Business Bankruptcy 1993-95) and National Bar Associations. Board of Directors Affiliated Mutual Funds of Nationwide Mutual Insurance Company 1984-86 and Community Health and Wellness Board U.S. Health Corporation 1994-95. Board of Trustees Buckeye Boys Ranch 1976-78, YMCA 1984-86, Central Ohio March of Dimes 1985-88, Neighborhood House 1985-88, The University Club 1989-92, Children's Hospital, Worthington Schools Education Foundation and "I Know I Can" (a college-bound program) Columbus City Schools. Member Urban Emphasis Program Boy Scouts of America 1982-83, Columbus Civil Service Commission 1986 and Mayor's Professional Sports Committee City of Columbus.

Office: 127 U.S. Courthouse, 85 Marconi Boulevard, Columbus, Ohio 43215.

Telephone: (614) 719-3350.

COLVIN, John O. *(Judge, United States Tax Court)* Appointed by President George Bush.

Office: 400 Second Street N.W., Washington, D.C. 20217-0002.

Telephone: (202) 606-8834.

CORNISH, Tom R. *(Judge, Bankruptcy Appellate Panel Tenth Circuit)* Selected by the Judicial Council of the Tenth Circuit to term beginning Feb 7, 1996. Also Judge, U.S. Bankruptcy Court Eastern District of Oklahoma.

Mailing address: P.O. Box 1347, Okmulgee, Oklahoma 74447-1347.

Telephone: (918) 758-0366.

COUVILLION, D. Irvin *(Special Trial Judge, United States Tax Court)* Appointed by U.S. Tax Court Chief Judge to term beginning July 1, 1985. Born Simmesport Louisiana Oct 27, 1934. Catholic. Educated at Louisiana State University B.S. 1956 J.D. 1959 and Georgetown University Law Center LL.M. in Taxation 1973. Admitted to practice Louisiana 1959. In legal practice Marksville 1959-66 and Baton Rouge 1974-85.

Member Louisiana State Bar Association. Administra-

COUVILLION, D. IRVIN—*Continued*

tive Assistant to U.S. Representative Speedy O. Long (D-La.) 1966-73.

Office: 400 Second Street N.W., Washington, D.C. 20217-0002.

Telephone: (202) 874-6097.

COWEN, Robert E. *(Senior Judge, United States Court of Appeals Third Circuit)* Appointed for life by President Ronald Reagan to term beginning Nov 9, 1987. Assumed Senior status Sept 4, 1998, serves by assignment. Born Newark New Jersey Sept 4, 1930. Educated at Drake University B.S. 1952 and Rutgers University LL.B. 1958. Law Clerk to Hon. Walter Conklin, Superior Court of New Jersey 1958-59. Admitted to practice New Jersey 1958, U.S. District Court District of New Jersey 1958 and U.S. Court of Appeals Third Circuit 1978. In legal practice Newark 1959-69. Director Ethics and Professional Services Administrative Office of the U.S. Courts, State of New Jersey 1973-78. Magistrate, U.S. District Court District of New Jersey Dec 1, 1978 to Nov 1985. Judge, U.S. District Court District of New Jersey Nov 1985 to Nov 1987.

Assistant County Prosecutor Essex County 1969-70. Deputy Attorney General New Jersey 1970-73. Ex officio Member Security and Facility Committee Judicial Council of the Third Circuit and Security and Facility Committee U.S. Court of Appeals Third Circuit. Advisory Board The Association of the Federal Bar of the State of New Jersey. Member New Jersey Supreme Court Commission on Ethics. Member Federal Judges Association, National Association of Bar Counsel, New Jersey State (Committee on Ethics and Federal Practice Committee) and American Bar Associations. Lecturer New Jersey ICLE since 1965. Chair Visiting Committee Rutgers Law School. Enjoys sailing, skiing, hiking, mountaineering and theater.

Office: 207 Federal Bldg. & U.S. Courthouse, 402 East State Street, Trenton, New Jersey 08608.

Telephone: (609) 989-2188.

COX, Emmett Ripley *(Senior Judge, United States Court of Appeals Eleventh Circuit)* Appointed for life by President Ronald Reagan to term beginning 1988. Assumed Senior status Dec 18, 2000, serves by assignment. Born Cottonwood Alabama Feb 13, 1935. Educated at University of Alabama B.A. 1957 LL.B. 1959. Member Omicron Delta Kappa, Phi Delta Phi, Alpha Tau Omega (President), Bench and Bar and Farrah Order of Jurisprudence. Admitted to practice Alabama U.S. Courts of Appeals Fifth, Eighth and Eleventh Circuits and U.S. Supreme Court. In legal practice Birmingham 1959-64 and Mobile 1964-81. Former Judge, U.S. District Court Southern District of Alabama, appointed by Ronald Reagan to term beginning Dec 2, 1981.

Member The Maritime Law Association of the U.S., Judicial Conference of the U.S. (Defender Services Committee, Committee on the Judicial Branch), Alabama State Bar, Mobile and Federal Bar Associations.

Office: 56 Forsyth Street N.W., Atlanta, Georgia 30303.

Telephone: (251) 690-2055.

COX, Walter Thompson, III *(Senior Judge, United States Court of Appeals for the Armed Forces)* Appointed by President Ronald Reagan July 26, 1984 to term beginning Sept 6, 1984. Chief Judge Oct 1, 1995 to Sept 30, 1999. Assumed Senior status Oct 1, 1999, serves by assignment. Born Anderson South Carolina Aug 13, 1942. Episcopalian. Educated at Clemson University B.S. 1964 and University of South Carolina J.D. cum laude 1967. Member Phi Alpha Delta. Admitted to practice South Carolina 1967, U.S. District Court District of South Carolina 1967, U.S. Court of Appeals Fourth Circuit 1973, U.S. Court of Military Appeals 1984 and U.S. Supreme Court 1987. In legal practice Anderson 1973-78. Judge, South Carolina Circuit Court Tenth Judicial Circuit 1978-84.

Author *The Constitution and the Army: The Courts—The Evolution of Military Justice Under the Constitution* U.S. Army War College Military History Institute 1988. Member South Carolina Trial Lawyers Association, Bar Association of the District of Columbia, South Carolina Bar (House of Delegates, Board of Grievances, Hearing Office Judicial Standards Commission), Anderson County, Federal (Judicial Administration Section) and American (Judicial Administration Division, Committee on Military Law) Bar Associations. Captain U.S. Army JAGC 1967-73.

Office: 450 E Street N.W., Washington, D.C. 20442-0001.

Telephone: (202) 761-1459.

CRAWFORD, Susan J. *(Chief Judge, United States Court of Appeals for the Armed Forces)* Appointed by President George Bush Feb 19, 1991 to term beginning Nov 18, 1991. Term expires Sept 30, 2006. Chief Judge since Oct 1, 1999. Born Pittsburgh Pennsylvania April 22, 1947. Presbyterian. Educated at Bucknell University B.A. 1969 and New England School of Law J.D. cum laude 1977. Admitted to practice Maryland 1977, District of Columbia 1980, U.S. Court of Appeals for the Armed Forces 1985 and U.S. Supreme Court 1993. In legal practice Oakland Maryland 1977-81.

Deputy General Counsel 1981-83 and General Counsel 1983-89 U.S. Department of the Army. Inspector General U.S. Department of Defense 1989-91. Important Decisions: United States v. Lopez 35 MJ 35, 1992; United States v. Houser 36 MJ 392, 1993 and United States v. MacCulloch 40 MJ 236, 1994. Instructor in Basic Law and American National Government Garrett County Community College 1979-81. Member Edward Bennett Williams American Inn of Court, The District of Columbia Bar, Maryland State Bar Association, Inc. and Federal Bar Association. Seminar Leader Judicial Conference U.S. Court of Appeals for the Armed Forces May 1993. Panel Moderator Standing Committee on Law and National Security American Bar Association Conference Oct 1994. Recipient Outstanding Alumni of the Year Award from New England School of Law 1987, Distinguished Service Medal from U.S. Department of the Army 1989, Award for Achievement in Chosen Profession 1989 and Alumni Athlete Achievement Award 1993 from Bucknell University and Meritorious Service Medal from U.S. Department of Defense 1991. Chair Garrett County Republican State Central Committee 1978-81. Member Maryland Forestry Advisory Commission 1978-81 and Maryland Commission for Women Garrett County 1980-83. Trustee Bucknell University since 1988 and New England School of Law since 1989. Enjoys recreational activities, reading and traveling.

Office: 450 E Street N.W., Washington, D.C. 20442-0001.

Telephone: (202) 761-1458.

CUDAHY, Richard D. *(Senior Judge, United States Court of Appeals Seventh Circuit)* Appointed for life by President Jimmy Carter. Assumed Senior status Aug 15, 1994, serves by assignment. Born Milwaukee Wisconsin Feb 2, 1926. Educated at U.S. Military Academy B.S. 1948 and Yale University LL.B. 1955. Honorary LL.D. Ripon College LL.D. 1981, DePaul University 1995, Wabash College 1996 and Stetson University 1998. Law Clerk to Chief Judge Charles E. Clark, U.S. Court of Appeals Second Circuit 1955-56. Member Order of the Coif. In legal practice Chicago Illinois 1956-61, Milwaukee Wisconsin 1972 and Washington D.C. 1976-79.

Assistant to Legal Advisor U.S. Department of State 1956-57. President and CEO Patrick Cudahy, Inc. Wisconsin 1960-71. Commissioner 1972-75 and Chairman 1975 Wisconsin Public Service Commission. Author "The Folklore of Deregulation" Yale Journal on Regulation 1998. Lecturer on Law Marquette University Law School 1962-66 and 1972-73. Visiting Professor of Law University of Wisconsin 1966-67. Professorial Lecturer George Washington University 1977-78. Adjunct Professor of Law DePaul University since 1995. President Law Club of Chicago 1992-93. Member Judicial Panel to Appoint Independent Counsels 1998-2002. Member The American Law Institute and American Bar Association (Council Section of Public Utility, Communications and Transportation Law). Faculty Member ALI/ABA Course on Energy and the Law. First Lieutenant U.S. Army 1948-51. Chairman Wisconsin Democratic Party 1967-68. Democratic Candidate for Wisconsin Attorney General 1968. Board Member National Institute on Political Communication 1969. Chairman Wisconsin Regional Export Expansion Council 1962-64. Commissioner Milwaukee Harbor 1964-66. President Milwaukee Urban League 1965-66. Board of Directors United Community Services Milwaukee 1965-66. Board Member and Chair Patrick & Anna M. Cudahy Fund since 1970. Board Member American Institute for Public Service 1972-98 and Environmental Defense Fund 1976-79. Chairman International Human Rights Law Institute DePaul University 1990-98. Member Advisory Committee Center for International Human Rights Northwestern University School of Law and Visiting Committee Divinity School Board University of Chicago.

Office: U.S. Courthouse, 219 South Dearborn Street, Chicago, Illinois 60604.

Telephone: (312) 435-5825.

CYR, Conrad K. *(Senior Judge, United States Court of Appeals First Circuit)* Appointed for life by President George Bush to term beginning Nov 20, 1989. Assumed Senior status Jan 31, 1997, serves by assignment. Born Limestone Maine Dec 9, 1931. Roman Catholic. Educated at College of the Holy Cross B.S. cum laude 1953 and Yale University J.D. 1956. Admitted to practice Maine 1956, U.S. District Court District of Maine 1959 and U.S. Court of Appeals First Circuit 1960. In legal practice Limestone 1956-59 and Bangor 1959-62. Bankruptcy Judge 1961-81, Chief Judge Bankruptcy Appellate Panel 1961-81, Judge 1981-83 and Chief Judge 1983-89, U.S. District Court District of Maine.

Assistant U.S. Attorney District of Maine 1959-61. Standing Special Master U.S. District Court District of Maine 1974-76. Editor-in-Chief American Bankruptcy L. Jour. 1970-81. Important Decisions: In re Herbert P. Vaillancourt March 26, 1970; In re Trans East Air, Inc. 1974 and 1975; Samoset Associates v. Trustees of Builders Investment Group 1976; Chemical Bank and First Pennsylvania Bank, N.A. v. American Kitchen Foods 1976; Trustees of Builders Investment Group v. Samoset Associates 1978; Sheck et al. v. Baileyville School Comm. (free speech, book banning) 1982; and Bangor Baptist Church et al. v. State of Maine et al. (freedom of religion, regulation of private church schools, justiciability, statutory construction) 1983. President National Conference of Bankruptcy Judges 1976-77. Member Judicial Conference Committee on the Administration of the Bankruptcy System since 1987, Judicial Council of the First Circuit, American Judicature Society, Aroostook County, Penobscot County and Maine State Bar Associations. Named Outstanding Young Man of Maine 1963. Recipient National Judge's Recognition Award 1979, Certificate of Appreciation from Kansas Bar Association 1979, Key to Town of Limestone Maine 1983 and Certificate of Appreciation from University of Maine at Presque Isle 1983.

Mailing address: P.O. Box 635, Bangor, Maine 04402-0635.

Telephone: (207) 941-8150.

DAMICH, Edward J. *(Chief Judge, United States Court of Federal Claims)* Appointed by President Bill Clinton to term beginning Dec 1, 1998. Term expires Dec 2013. Chief Judge since May 13, 2002. Educated at St. Stephen's College 1970, Catholic University of America School of Law J.D. 1976 and Columbia University School of Law LL.M. 1983 J.S.D. 1991.

Commissioner U.S. Copyright Royalty Tribunal 1992-93. Chief Intellectual Property Counsel U.S. Senate Judiciary Committee 1995.

Office: National Courts Building, 717 Madison Place N.W., Washington, D.C. 20005-1086.

Telephone: (202) 219-1433.

DAUGHTREY, Martha Craig *(Judge, United States Court of Appeals Sixth Circuit)* Appointed for life by President Bill Clinton to term beginning Nov 22, 1993. Born Covington Kentucky July 21, 1942. Educated at Vanderbilt University B.A. cum laude 1964 J.D. 1968. Member Phi Beta Kappa and Order of the Coif. Admitted to practice Tennessee 1968. Began legal practice Nashville 1968. Judge, Tennessee Court of Criminal Appeals 1975-90. Associate Justice, Tennessee Supreme Court April 23, 1990 to 1993, appointed by Governor Ned Ray McWherter.

Assistant U.S. Attorney Nashville 1968-69. Assistant District Attorney Nashville 1969-72. Author "Cross-Sectionalism in Jury Selection Procedures After *Taylor vs. Louisiana*" University of Tennessee L. Rev. 1975 and "State Court Activism and Other Symptoms of the New Federalism" University of Tennessee L. Rev. 1978. Board of Editors *ABA Journal* since 1996. Assistant Professor of Law 1972-75, Lecturer on Law 1976-82 and Adjunct Professor of Law 1988-91 Vanderbilt University. President Women Judges Fund for Justice 1983-84 and 1985-86, National Association of Women Judges 1984-85 and Lawyers Association for Women of Middle Tennessee 1986-87. Member Institute of Judicial Administration, American Judicature Society (Board of Directors 1988-92), Nashville (Board of Directors 1988-90), Tennessee, Federal and American (House of Delegates 1988-91, Chairman Appellate Judges' Conference 1984-85 and Chairman Judicial Administration Division 1989-90, Member Standing Committee on Continuing Education of the Bar 1991-94 and Commission on Women in the Profession 1994-97) Bar Associations. Executive

DAUGHTREY, MARTHA CRAIG—*Continued*

Committee Tennessee Judicial Conference 1977-80. Faculty Member New York University Appellate Judges Seminar 1977-90 and since 1994. Faculty Member The National Judicial College 1981 and 1989. Listed in *Who's Who in America.* Named one of Ten Outstanding Young Women of America 1976 and one of Thirty Women to Watch by Ladies Home Journal 1984. Nominee Ladies Home Journal Woman of the Year 1977. Recipient Cable Support Women Award 1983 and Athena Award 1991. Former Chairperson Nashville Women's Political Caucus. Member and former Vice President Council on Alcohol and Drug Abuse. Former Chairperson Board of Visitors University of Memphis School of Law.

Office: 300 U.S. Customs House, 701 Broadway, Nashville, Tennessee 37203.

Telephone: (615) 736-7678.

DAVIS, W. Eugene *(Judge, United States Court of Appeals Fifth Circuit)* Appointed for life by President Ronald Reagan Nov 16, 1983. Born Winfield Alabama Aug 18, 1936. Educated at Tulane University Law School LL.B. 1960 Judge, U.S. District Court Western District of Louisiana 1976-83, appointed by President Gerald R. Ford.

Office: 5100 U.S. Courthouse, 800 Lafayette Street, Lafayette, Louisiana 70501.

Telephone: (337) 593-5280.

DAWSON, Howard A., Jr. *(Senior Judge, United States Tax Court)* Appointed by President John F. Kennedy to term beginning Aug 21, 1962. Reappointed by President Richard M. Nixon May 21, 1970. Chief Judge 1973-77 and 1983-85. Assumed Senior status, serves by assignment. Born Okolona Arkansas Oct 23, 1922. Educated at University of North Carolina B.S.B.A. 1946 and George Washington University J.D. with honors 1949. Member Delta Theta Phi. President Case Club. Secretary-Treasurer Student Bar Association. In legal practice Washington D.C. 1949-50.

Attorney Office of Chief Counsel Civil Division 1950-53, Civil Advisory Counsel Atlanta District 1953-57, Regional Counsel Atlanta Region 1958, Personal Assistant to Chief Counsel Dec 1, 1958 to June 1, 1959 and Assistant Chief Counsel Administration June 1, 1959 to Aug 19, 1962 Internal Revenue Service. David Brennan Distinguished Visiting Professor of Law University of Akron Law Center Spring 1986. Professor of Law and Director Graduate Tax Program University of Baltimore School of Law 1986-89. Distinguished Visiting Professor of Law University of San Diego Spring 1991. Member The District of Columbia Bar, State Bar of Georgia, Federal and American (Section of Taxation) Bar Associations. U.S. Army Finance Corps ETO 1942-45. Captain USAR Finance Corps (retired). Member George Washington University Law Alumni Association.

Office: 400 Second Street N.W., Washington, D.C. 20217-0002.

Telephone: (202) 606-8791.

DEAN, John F. *(Special Trial Judge, United States Tax Court)* Appointed by U.S. Tax Court Chief Judge Lapsley W. Hamblen, Jr. to term beginning Aug 8, 1994. Born Washington D.C. Episcopalian. Educated at Michigan State University B.S. 1970, Catholic University of America J.D. 1975 and Georgetown University Law Center M.L.T. 1985. Admitted to practice District of Columbia 1975, U.S. Tax Court 1975 and U.S. District Courts Northern District of Texas 1976 and District of Maryland 1980.

With Office of Chief Counsel 1975-94 and Special Counsel International 1988-94 Internal Revenue Service. Adjunct Professor of Law Howard University School of Law since 1998. Member The District of Columbia Bar, Washington, National and American Bar Associations.

Office: 400 Second Street N.W., Washington, D.C. 20217-0002.

Telephone: (202) 874-6083.

De JESUS, Sara E. *(Judge, Bankruptcy Appellate Panel First Circuit and Judge, United States Bankruptcy Court District of Puerto Rico)* Selected for Appellate Panel by the Judicial Council of the First Circuit. Appointed to Bankruptcy Court by U.S. Court of Appeals First Circuit judges. Chief Judge Bankruptcy Court Jan 1, 1988 to March 16, 1999.

Office: 238 Federal Bldg. & U.S. Courthouse, 300 Recinto Sur Street, San Juan, Puerto Rico 00901.

Telephone: (787) 977-6020.

DELGADO-COLON, Aida M. *(Magistrate Judge, United States District Court District of Puerto Rico)* Appointed by U.S. District Court judges to term beginning Dec 23, 1993. Reappointed Dec 23, 2001, current term expires Dec 22, 2009. Educated at University of Puerto Rico B.B.A. cum laude 1977 and Catholic University of Puerto Rico Law School J.D. cum laude 1980. Editor of Jurisprudence and Member Board of Directors Catholic University of Puerto Rico Law Review. Admitted to practice Puerto Rico 1980, U.S. District Court District of Puerto Rico 1982, U.S. Court of Appeals First Circuit 1982, U.S. Court of International Trade 1983, U.S. Supreme Court 1984 and U.S. Court of Federal Claims 1993.

Assistant Federal Public Defender 1982-88, First Assistant Federal Public Defender 1988-93 and Acting Federal Public Defender March 1991 to Aug 1991 Office of Federal Public Defender. Member Criminal Justice Act Panel Selection Committee 1986-91. Member Federal Bar Examination Committee since 1986 and Local Rules Committee since 1991, Chairperson Interpreters and Court Reporters Committee since 1994, EEOC Coordinator 1995-99 and Alternate EDR Coordinator since 1999 U.S. District Court District of Puerto Rico. Former Member National Association of Criminal Defense Lawyers, Federal (Board of Directors 1994) and American Bar Associations. Founding Member and Secretary Puerto Rico Association of Criminal Defense Lawyers 1991-93. Member Women Judges Association, Federal Magistrates Judges Association and Puerto Rico Bar Association. Attended DNA Evidence and Death Penalty Trials Seminar March 1986 and Current Problems in Criminal Law Feb 1994 and Feb 1995 Federal Public Defenders Office; U.S. District Court Differentiated Case Management System Workshop Court Management Associates Feb 29, 1996 to March 1, 1996; Justice and Mental Health Symposium Fundación Puertorriqueña Pro Salud Mental Nov 1, 1996; Financial Statements in the Courtroom Workshop Federal Judicial Center May 2001 to June 2001; and Sentencing Guidelines Seminar U.S. Sentencing Commission San Juan Puerto Rico May 22, 2002. Speaker 'Women's Participation in the Justice System" Feb 1994 to March 1994 and "Courtroom as a Classroom" U.S. Court of Appeals for the First Circuit Nov 17, 2000 Interamerican University School of Law;

DELGADO-COLON, AIDA M.—*Continued*

"The Bail Reform Act: Practical Considerations" 1994 and "Do's and Don't's of Federal Practice Before a Federal Magistrate Judge" March 1999 Puerto Rico Chapter Federal Bar Association; "Practical Considerations and Legal Standards for the Application of Search and Arrest Warrants" Federal Law Enforcement Officers Association Aug 27, 1996; Criminal Justice Act Seminar June 27, 1997, "Effective Assistance of Counsel During the Initial Stages of a Case" Criminal Justice Act Seminar June 25, 1998 and Panel on "Preparation of CJA Vouchers" Oct 26, 2001 Federal Public Defender's Office; "Special Considerations in Representing Non-Citizen Defendants" June 17, 1999, "Role of the U.S. Magistrate Judges in the Federal Court" Feb 27. 2002 and "Courtroom as a Classroom" U.S. Court of Appeals First Circuit Feb 23, 2000 University of Puerto Rico Law School; "Bail Seminar" Sept 12, 2000 and "Role of the U.S. Magistrate Judges in the Federal Court" April 4, 2001 Catholic University School of Law; and "Money Laundering Statute Seminar" Panama City Panama July 2001. Coordinator "Identification Issues in the Courtroom" Federal Bar Association Annual Convention Sept 1997. Speaker and Coordinator "Getting to Know the Federal Court and Agencies" Catholic University School of Law April 24, 2002 and "Getting to Know the Federal Court and Related Agencies" Interamerican University Law School Oct 16, 2002. Investigator Sept 1980 to June 1981 and Director of Research July 1981 to Aug 1982 Governor's Advisory Council on Labor Law. Former Member National History Society of Puerto Rico, Sociedad de Espeleología de Puerto Rico and Cuerpo de Voluntarios Defensa Civil. Member Alumni Association Catholic University of Puerto Rico Law School.

Office: 495 Federal Building, 150 Carlos Chardon Avenue, San Juan, Puerto Rico 00918-1756.

Telephone: (787) 772-3195.

E-mail address: aida_delgado-colon@prd.uscourts.gov

DeMOSS, Harold R., Jr. *(Judge, United States Court of Appeals Fifth Circuit)* Appointed for life by President George Bush Dec 2, 1991. Born Houston Texas Dec 30, 1930. Educated at Rice University B.A. 1952 and University of Texas School of Law LL.B. 1955.

Office: 12015 U.S. Courthouse, 515 Rusk Avenue, Houston, Texas 77002.

Telephone: (713) 250-5462.

DENNIS, James Leon *(Judge, United States Court of Appeals Fifth Circuit)* Appointed for life by President Bill Clinton to term beginning Oct 2, 1995. Born Monroe Louisiana Jan 9, 1936. Methodist. Educated at Louisiana Tech University B.S. 1959, Louisiana State University J.D. with honors 1962 and University of Virginia LL.M. in Judicial Process 1984. Managing Editor Louisiana Law Review. Member Phi Delta Phi and Order of the Coif. Admitted to practice Louisiana 1962. In legal practice Monroe 1962-72. Judge, Louisiana District Court Fourth Judicial District 1972-74. Judge, Louisiana Court of Appeal Second Circuit 1974-75. Associate Justice, Supreme Court of Louisiana Dec 1975 to Oct 1995.

Author Note "Torts—Firearms—Liability for Sale to Minor in Violation of Criminal Statute" 20 Louisiana L. Rev. 796, 1960; Comment "State Involvement in Private Discrimination Under the Fourteenth Amendment" 21 Louisiana L. Rev. 433, 1961; Note "Automobiles—Community Mission—Burden of Proof" 21 Louisiana L. Rev. 647, 1961; Comment "Misstatements in Applications for Life and Health and Accident Insurance Under the Louisiana Insurance Code" 22 Louisiana L. Rev. 190, 1961; Note "Evidence—Unreasonable Search and Seizure—Pretrial Motion to Suppress" 22 Louisiana L. Rev. 842, 1962; "Use of Our Courts for Speedier Criminal Justice" 28 No. 1 Louisiana B. Jour. 39 June 1980; "A Practical Approach to the Use of Precedent Under the Louisiana Civil Code" May 1984; Chapter "Basic Principles of Manufacturers Liability Under the Civil Code of Québec" Conférences Sur Le Nouveau Code Civil Québec 1992; "Interpretation and Application of the Civil Code and the Evaluation of Judicial Precedent" 54 Louisiana L. Rev. 1, 1993; and "Judicial Power and the Administrative State" 62 Louisiana L. Rev. 59, 2001. Instructor Louisiana State University Law Center summer school 1980, 1981 and 1989 and Tulane University School of Law Greece Program 1986, 1999 and 2003. Adjunct Professor Tulane University School of Law 2003. Member Louisiana State and American (Committee on Appellate Practice) Bar Associations. Coordinator Louisiana Constitutional Revision Commission 1970-72. Chairman Judiciary Committee Louisiana Constitutional Convention 1973-74. Chairman Board of Governors Louisiana Judicial College 1976-80. Recipient Monroe Jaycee Distinguished Service Award 1970. Private First Class U.S. Army 1955-57. Democrat. Louisiana State Representative 1968-72. Chairman Louisiana Commission on the Bicentennial of the U.S. Constitution since 1986. Enjoys hunting and fishing.

Office: 219 U.S. Court of Appeals Building, 600 Camp Street, New Orleans, Louisiana 70130.

Telephone: (504) 310-8000.

DINAN, Daniel J. *(Special Trial Judge, United States Tax Court)* Appointed by U.S. Tax Court Chief Judge C. Moxley Featherston Feb 6, 1979. Born New Haven Connecticut March 21, 1929. Educated at Fairfield University B.S.S. in History 1952 and Georgetown University Law Center LL.B. 1960. Admitted to practice Virginia 1961.

Trial Attorney Tax Division 1961-70 and Assistant Chief Civil Trial Section Tax Division 1970 U.S. Department of Justice. Instructor in Trial Practice and Technique, Evidence and Civil Procedure Attorney General's Advocacy Institute 1977-79. USMC.

Office: 400 Second Street N.W., Washington, D.C. 20217-0002.

Telephone: (202) 874-6094.

DOMINGUEZ, Daniel R. *(Judge, United States District Court District of Puerto Rico)* Appointed for life by President Bill Clinton to term beginning 1994. Born San Juan Puerto Rico July 2, 1945. Educated at Boston University B.A. 1967 and University of Puerto Rico LL.B. 1970. In legal practice Hato Rey 1970-94. USAR 1967.

Office: CH-129 U.S. Courthouse, 150 Carlos Chardon Avenue, San Juan, Puerto Rico 00918-1766.

Telephone: (787) 772-3160.

DREHER, Nancy C. *(Judge, Bankruptcy Appellate Panel Eighth Circuit)* Selected by the Judicial Council of the Eighth Circuit to term beginning 1996. Also Judge, U.S. Bankruptcy Court District of Minnesota. Appointed by U.S. Court of Appeals Eighth Circuit judges to term beginning 1988. Reappointed Jan 2002, current term expires Jan 2016. Educated at University of Wis-

DREHER, NANCY C.—*Continued*
consin B.A. 1964 J.D. 1967. Articles Editor Wisconsin Law Review. In legal practice 1968-88.

Adjunct Professor of Advanced Civil Trial Practice William Mitchell College of Law 1981-82. Adjunct Professor University of Minnesota 1992-94.

Office: 7W U.S. Courthouse, 300 South Fourth Street, Minneapolis, Minnesota 55415.

Telephone: (612) 664-5260.

DUBINA, Joel F. *(Judge, United States Court of Appeals Eleventh Circuit)* Appointed for life by President George Bush to term beginning Oct 1990. Born Elkhart Indiana Oct 26, 1947. Educated at University of Alabama B.S. 1970 and Cumberland School of Law of Samford University J.D. 1973. Law Clerk to Hon. Robert Edward Varner, U.S. District Court Middle District of Alabama 1973-74. In legal practice Montgomery 1974-83. Magistrate Judge 1983-86 and Judge 1986 to Oct 1990, U.S. District Court Middle District of Alabama, appointed by President Ronald Reagan.

Mailing address: P.O. Box 867, Montgomery, Alabama 36101-0867.

Telephone: (334) 223-7126.

DUHE, John M., Jr. *(Senior Judge, United States Court of Appeals Fifth Circuit)* Appointed for life by President Ronald Reagan to term beginning Nov 9, 1988. Assumed Senior status April 7, 1999, serves by assignment. Born Iberia Parish Louisiana April 7, 1933. Catholic. Educated at University of Southwestern Louisiana 1951, Washington and Lee University 1951-53 and Tulane University B.S. 1955 LL.B. 1957. Associate Editor and Editor-in-Chief 1957 Tulane University Law Review. Member Kappa Sigma, Kappa Delta Phi, Omicron Delta Kappa and Order of the Coif. Admitted to practice Louisiana 1957, U.S. District Court 1957 and U.S. Supreme Court 1962. Began legal practice New Iberia 1957. Judge, Louisiana District Court Sixteenth Judicial District 1979-84. Judge, U.S. District Court Western District of Louisiana June 1984 to Nov 1988.

Former member Louisiana District Judges Association, Louisiana Association of Defense Counsel and Iberia Parish Bar Association (Secretary-Treasurer, President 1973-74). Member Louisiana State Bar Association. Listed in *Who's Who in America.* Inducted into Tulane University Hall of Fame. Republican. Former member Iberia Parish Republican Executive Committee. Enjoys sailing.

Office: 5200 U.S. Courthouse, 800 Lafayette Street, Lafayette, Louisiana 70501.

Telephone: (337) 593-5250.

DYK, Timothy B. *(Judge, United States Court of Appeals Federal Circuit)* Appointed for life by President Bill Clinton to term beginning June 9, 2000. Educated at Harvard University A.B. cum laude 1958 LL.B. magna cum laude 1961. Law Clerk to Hon. Harold H. Burton and Hon. Stanley F. Reed, U.S. Supreme Court 1961-62 and Chief Justice Earl Warren, U.S. Supreme Court 1962-63. In legal practice 1964-2000.

Special Assistant to Assistant Attorney General 1963-64. Adjunct Professor Yale Law School, University of Virginia School of Law and Georgetown University Law Center.

Office: National Courts Building, 717 Madison Place N.W., Washington, D.C. 20439-0002.

Telephone: (202) 633-8200.

EASTERBROOK, Frank H. *(Judge, United States Court of Appeals Seventh Circuit)* Appointed for life by President Ronald Reagan to term beginning April 10, 1985. Born Buffalo New York Sept 3, 1948. Educated at Swarthmore College B.A. with high honors 1970 and University of Chicago J.D. cum laude 1973. Topics and Comment Editor University of Chicago Law Review 1971-73. Law Clerk to Hon. Levin H. Campbell, U.S. Court of Appeals First Circuit 1973-74. Member Phi Beta Kappa and Order of the Coif. Admitted to practice District of Columbia 1975.

Assistant to the Solicitor General 1974-77. Deputy Solicitor General of the U.S. 1978-79. Co-author with Richard A. Posner *Antitrust* West Publishing Co. 1981 and with Daniel R. Fischel *The Economic Structure of Corporate Law* Harvard 1991. Editor Journal of Law and Economics 1982-91. Assistant Professor of Law 1979-81, Professor of Law 1981-84, Lee and Brena Freeman Professor of Law 1984-85 and Senior Lecturer since 1985 University of Chicago. Member The American Law Institute. Member American Academy of Arts and Sciences.

Office: U.S. Courthouse, 219 South Dearborn Street, Chicago, Illinois 60604.

Telephone: (312) 435-5808.

EATON, Richard K. *(Judge, United States Court of International Trade)* Appointed for life by President Bill Clinton to term beginning Jan 3, 2000. Born Walton New York. Educated at Ithaca College B.A. 1970 and Albany Law School of Union University J.D. 1974.

Chief of Staff U.S. Senator Daniel Patrick Moynihan 1983 and 1991-93.

Office: One Federal Plaza, New York, New York 10278-0001.

Telephone: (212) 264-2900.

EBEL, David M. *(Judge, United States Court of Appeals Tenth Circuit)* Appointed for life by President Ronald Reagan to term beginning April 1988. Born Wichita Kansas June 3, 1940. Educated at Northwestern University B.A. 1962 and University of Michigan Law School J.D. 1965. Law Clerk to Hon. Byron Raymond White, U.S. Supreme Court 1965-66. In legal practice Denver 1966-88.

Office: 109L U.S. Courthouse, 1823 Stout Street, Denver, Colorado 80257.

Telephone: (303) 844-3800.

E-mail address: David_M._Ebel@ca10.uscourts.gov

EDMONDSON, J. L. *(Chief Judge, United States Court of Appeals Eleventh Circuit)* Appointed for life by President Ronald Reagan to term beginning 1986. Chief Judge since June 1, 2002. Born Jasper Georgia July 14, 1947. Educated at Emory University B.A. 1968, University of Georgia School of Law J.D. 1971 and University of Virginia M.L. in Judicial Process 1990. Law Clerk to Hon. Sidney O. Smith, U.S. District Court Northern District of Georgia 1971-73. In legal practice Jasper 1973 and Lawrenceville 1973-86.

Instructor University of Georgia School of Law 1975-84.

Office: Court of Appeals Building, 56 Forsyth Street N.W., Atlanta, Georgia 30303.

Telephone: (404) 335-6230.

EDWARDS, Harry T. *(Judge, United States Court of Appeals District of Columbia Circuit)* Appointed for life by President Jimmy Carter to term beginning Feb 20,

EDWARDS, HARRY T.—*Continued*

1980. Former Chief Judge. Educated at Cornell University B.S. 1962 and University of Michigan J.D. with high distinction 1965. Staff member Michigan Law Review. Executive Committee Order of the Coif. In legal practice Chicago 1965-70.

Co-author *The Lawyer as a Negotiator* West Publishing Co. 1977, *Labor Relations Law in the Public Sector* 2nd ed. Michie/Bobbs-Merrill 1979, *Collective Bargaining and Labor Arbitration* 2nd ed. Michie/Bobbs-Merrill 1979, *Higher Education and the Law* Harvard University 1979, *Higher Education and the Unholy Crusade Against Governmental Regulation* Harvard University 1980 and *An Introduction to the American Legal System* Harvard University 1980. Professor of Law University of Michigan 1970-75 and 1977-80 and Harvard University 1975-77. Visiting Professor of Law Program for International Legal Cooperation University of Brussels Winter 1974. Faculty member Institute for Educational Management Harvard University 1976-82. Part-time Lecturer on Law Harvard University since 1984. Distinguished Lecturer on Law Duke University School of Law since 1984. Instructor in Federal Courts New York University School of Law. Board of Directors National Institute of Dispute Resolution. Member The American Law Institute, American Judicature Society and American Bar Association. Recipient Groat Alumni Award from Cornell University, Award for distinguished contributions to teaching and public service from Society of American Law Teachers and Whitney North Seymour Medal from American Arbitration Association. Former Chairman Board of Directors AMTRAK. Member Association of American Law Schools (Executive Committee), National Academy of Arbitrators (Vice President), President's National Commission on International Women's Year and American Academy of Arts and Sciences.

Office: 5400 U.S. Courthouse, 333 Constitution Avenue N.W., Washington, D.C. 20001-2866.

Telephone: (202) 216-7380.

EFFRON, Andrew S. *(Associate Judge, United States Court of Appeals for the Armed Forces)* Appointed by President Bill Clinton to term beginning 1996. Term expires 2011. Born Stamford Connecticut. Educated at Harvard College and Harvard Law School.

Former Attorney-Adviser Office of General Counsel Department of Defense. Former Staff Member Senate Armed Services Committee. U.S. Army JAGC. Former legislative aide to Representative William A. Steiger.

Office: 405 E Street N.W., Washington, D.C. 20442-0001.

Telephone (202) 761-5210.

EVANS, Terence T. *(Judge, United States Court of Appeals Seventh Circuit)* Appointed for life by President Bill Clinton. Born 1940. Educated at Marquette University B.A. 1962 J.D. 1967. Law Clerk to Wisconsin Supreme Court 1967-68. In legal practice Milwaukee 1970-74. Judge, Wisconsin County Court Milwaukee County 1974-78. Judge, Wisconsin Circuit Court Milwaukee Circuit 1978-79. Former Judge, U.S. District Court Eastern District of Wisconsin, appointed by President Jimmy Carter to term beginning 1979.

Assistant District Attorney Milwaukee County 1968-70. Member Milwaukee Young Lawyers Association, State Bar of Wisconsin and Milwaukee Bar Association.

Office: 721 U.S. Courthouse & Federal Bldg., 517 East Wisconsin Avenue, Milwaukee, Wisconsin 53202-4595.

Telephone: (414) 297-3222.

EVERETT, Robinson O. *(Senior Judge, United States Court of Appeals for the Armed Forces)* Appointed by President Jimmy Carter Feb 15, 1980 to term beginning April 15, 1980. Chief Judge April 16, 1980 to Oct 1, 1990. Assumed Senior status Oct 1, 1990, serves by assignment. Born Durham North Carolina 1928. Presbyterian. Educated at Harvard University A.B. magna cum laude 1947 J.D. magna cum laude 1950 and Duke University LL.M. 1959. Board of Editors Harvard Law Review 1957-59. Honorary member Delta Theta Phi. Admitted to practice North Carolina 1950, U.S. Court of Military Appeals 1953 and District of Columbia 1954. Began legal practice Durham 1955. In legal practice Raleigh and Washington D.C.

Counsel 1961-64 and Consultant 1964-66 U.S. Senate Subcommittee on Constitutional Rights Committee on the Judiciary. Author *Military Justice in the Armed Forces of the United States* Stackpole 1956. Important Decisions: U.S. v. Trottier (military jurisdiction) 9 M.J. 337 C.M.A. 1980. Law Faculty Duke Law School 1950-51 and since 1956. Member The American Law Institute, The North Carolina State Bar (Bar Council 1978-83) and Durham County Bar Association (President 1977). Chairman Durham Redevelopment Commission 1958-75. Commissioner on Uniform Laws 1961-73 and 1977-85. Colonel USAFR 1950-78. Democrat. Delegate to Kansas City Mini Convention 1974. Elder, First Presbyterian Church Durham North Carolina. Enjoys travel and sports.

Office: 450 E Street N.W., Washington, D.C. 20442-0001.

Telephone: (202) 761-5207.

FAGG, George G. *(Senior Judge, United States Court of Appeals Eighth Circuit)* Appointed for life by President Ronald Reagan to term beginning Nov 1, 1982. Assumed Senior status May 1, 1999, serves by assignment. Born Eldora Iowa April 30, 1934. Educated at Drake University B.S.B.A. with honors 1956 J.D. with honors 1958. Editor Drake Law Review 1957-58. Member Order of the Coif. Admitted to practice Iowa 1958. In legal practice Marshalltown 1958-72. Judge, Iowa District Court 1972-82, appointed by Governor Robert D. Ray.

Member American Judicature Society, Iowa State (Former member Committees on Iowa Uniform Court Instructions and Iowa Rules of Civil Procedure) and American Bar Associations. Attended The National Judicial College (Participant 1973 and 1977, Faculty Advisor 1978, Instructor 1979).

Office: 455 U.S. Courthouse Annex, 110 East Court Avenue, Des Moines, Iowa 50309-2051.

Telephone: (515) 284-6219.

FAIRCHILD, Thomas E. *(Senior Judge, United States Court of Appeals Seventh Circuit)* Appointed for life by President Lyndon B. Johnson to term beginning Aug 11, 1966. Chief Judge Feb 7, 1975 to July 1, 1981. Assumed Senior status Sept 1, 1981, serves by assignment. Born Milwaukee Wisconsin Dec 25, 1912. Educated at Deep Springs College 1929-31, Princeton University 1931-33, Cornell University B.A. 1934 and Uni-

FAIRCHILD, THOMAS E.—*Continued*
versity of Wisconsin Law School Class of 1937 LL.B. conferred 1938. Awarded honorary LL.D. St. Norbert College 1966, Carthage College 1972, University of Wisconsin 1975 and John Marshall Law School 1978. In legal practice Portage 1938-41 and Milwaukee 1945-48 and 1953-57. Justice, Wisconsin Supreme Court Jan 1957 to Aug 1966.

With Office of Price Administration Milwaukee and Chicago 1941-45. Attorney General of Wisconsin 1948-51. U.S. Attorney Western District of Wisconsin 1951-52. Chairman Governor's Commission on Constitutional Revision under Governors Nelson, Reynolds and Knowles. Member American Judicature Society, The American Law Institute (Council member), State Bar of Wisconsin, Milwaukee, Dane County, Seventh Circuit and American Bar Associations. Board of Directors and Treasurer Wisconsin Welfare Council 1955-61. Wisconsin State Chairman American Brotherhood Month 1959. Former Director United Nations Association of Dane County Wisconsin. Former member Committee on Administration of Probation System of the U.S. Board of Trustees Deep Springs College. Advisory Council Cornell Law School.

Office: U.S. Courthouse, 219 South Dearborn Street, Chicago, Illinois 60604.

Telephone: (312) 435-5800.

FARLEY, John J., III *(Judge, United States Court of Appeals for Veterans Claims)* Appointed by President George Bush to term beginning Sept 14, 1989. Term expires 2004. Educated at College of the Holy Cross A.B. 1964, Columbia University M.B.A. 1966 and Hofstra University School of Law J.D. cum laude 1973. Founding Editor-in-Chief Hofstra Law Review. Admitted to practice New York, District of Columbia, U.S. Court of Appeals District of Columbia Circuit and U.S. Supreme Court.

Trial Attorney Torts Section 1973-78 and Assistant Director—Official Immunity 1978-80 and Director 1980-89 Torts Branch Civil Division U.S. Department of Justice. Author "Personal Liability of Federal Investigators and Law Enforcement Officers" 2 *Investigators Journal* Fall 1986, "Senior Executives' Personal Liability" 7 No. 4 *Action* May 1987, "The Fallout from Westfall" 8 No. 3 *Action* May 1988, "From Liability to Immunity: The Roller Coaster Ride of 1988" 1 No. 1 *The Institute* Feb 1989, "The New Kid on the Block of Veteran's Law: The United States Court of Veterans Appeals" 38 No. 9 *Federal Bar News & Journal* Nov/Dec 1991 and "Robin Hood Jurisprudence: The Triumph of Equity in American Tort Law" 65 St. John's L. Rev. 997, 1991. Lecturer and Faculty Member Catholic University of America School of Law. Member Federal Bar Association (First Chairman Veterans Law Section 1990). Lecturer and Faculty Member Attorney General's Advocacy Institute, FBI Academy, Legal Education Institute, OPM Executive Seminar Centers, Federal Executive Institute, Government Affairs Institute and Federal Judicial Center. Recipient Department of Justice Special Achievement Award 1979, First Civil Division Special Award for Superior Performance 1980, Senior Executive Service Special Achievement Awards 1984 and 1988 and Distinguished Alumni Medal 1986 and Dean's Award for Distinguished Law School Alumni 1995 Hofstra University. Inducted into Massapequa High School Hall of Fame 1999. Captain U.S. Army 1966-70 (retired). Recipient Bronze Star with "V" device, 3 oak leaf clusters; Purple Heart Medal with oak leaf cluster; and Army Commendation Medal. Board of Directors Senior Executives Association 1986-90 and Amputee Coalition of America. Member John Carroll Society.

Office: 625 Indiana Avenue N.W., Suite 900, Washington, D.C. 20004-2950.

Telephone: (202) 501-5882.

FARRIS, Jerome *(Senior Judge, United States Court of Appeals Ninth Circuit)* Appointed for life by President Jimmy Carter Oct 16, 1979. Assumed Senior status March 4, 1995, serves by assignment. Born Birmingham Alabama March 4, 1930. Protestant. Educated at Morehouse College B.S. 1951, Atlanta University M.S.W. 1955 and University of Washington J.D. 1958. Awarded honorary LL.D. Morehouse College 1978. Staff member Law Review. Recipient William Wilshire Memorial Scholarship Award, Hearst Oratorical Scholarship, Pepsi-Cola Scholarship, National Mental Health Grant and Entering Freshman Scholarship Morehouse College. Member Oval Club and Order of the Coif. Admitted to practice Washington 1958. In legal practice Seattle 1958-69. Judge 1969-79, Chief Judge 1977-78 and First Presiding Chief Judge Jan 1977 to Jan 1978, Washington Court of Appeals Division One.

Former Lecturer University of Washington Law School and School of Social Work. Chairman State-Federal Judicial Council 1983-87. Fellow American Bar Foundation (Board of Directors since 1987, Executive Committee since 1989). Member Executive Committee and Chairman 1982-83 Appellate Judges Conference American Bar Association. Former Trustee Seattle-King County Bar Association. Former Chairman Washington Council on Crime and Delinquency. Member Judicial Conference Committee on International Judicial Relations 1997-2000 and U.S. Supreme Court Judicial Fellows Commission since 1997. Listed in *Outstanding Young Men of America* 1965-66. Recipient Distinguished Service Award from Seattle Jaycees 1965 and Clayton Frost Award 1966. U.S. Army Signal Corps 1952-53. Founder and Director First Union National Bank 1965-69. Founder Liberty Bank of Seattle. Democrat. Delegate to White House Conference on Children and Youth 1970. Member Visiting Committee University of Washington School of Social Work 1977-90 and Harvard Law School since 1996. Board of Regents University of Washington 1985-97. Board of Trustees Morehouse College since 1999. Member King County Youth Commission 1969-70 and State Child Welfare Advisory Committee. Past President Washington State Junior Chamber of Commerce. Former Board member United Way.

Office: 1030 U.S. Courthouse, 1010 Fifth Avenue, Seattle, Washington 98104-1181.

Telephone: (206) 553-2672.

FAY, Peter T. *(Senior Judge, United States Court of Appeals Eleventh Circuit)* Appointed to Fifth Circuit for life by President Gerald R. Ford to term beginning 1976. Assigned to Eleventh Circuit Oct 1, 1981. Assumed Senior status Jan 19, 1994, serves by assignment. Born Rochester New York Jan 18, 1929. Roman Catholic. Educated at Rollins College B.A. 1951 and University of Florida J.D. 1956. Member Order of the Coif, Phi Delta Phi (Past President), Omicron Delta Kappa (Past President), Pi Gamma Mu (Past President) and Phi Kappa Phi. Admitted to practice Florida 1956 and U.S. Supreme Court 1961. In legal practice Miami 1961-70.

FAY, PETER T.—*Continued*

Judge, U.S. District Court Southern District of Florida 1970-76.

Member Law Science Academy, Florida Academy of Trial Attorneys, The Florida Bar, Dade County, John Marshall (Past President) and American Bar Associations. Member Judicial Conference Committee for Implementation of Criminal Justice Act since 1974. Professor Florida Junior Bar Practical Legal Institute 1959-65. Lecturer Florida Bar Legal Institute since 1959. Faculty member Federal Judicial Center since 1974. USAF 1951-53. Republican. Member Orange Bowl Commission since 1974, Administrative Board Biscayne College since 1970, Miami Chamber of Commerce and Medico Legal Institute. District collector United Fund 1957-70. Director University of Florida Alumni Association.

Office: Federal Justice Building, 12th Floor, 99 N.E. Fourth Street, Miami, Florida 33132.

Telephone: (305) 536-5974.

FEDERMAN, Arthur B. *(Judge, Bankruptcy Appellate Panel Eighth Circuit)* Selected by the Judicial Council of the Eighth Circuit. Also Chief Judge, U.S. Bankruptcy Court Western District of Missouri. Appointed by U.S. Court of Appeals Eighth Circuit judges. Chief Judge Bankruptcy Court since Jan 1, 2000.

Office: 6552 U.S. Courthouse, 400 East Ninth Street, Kansas City, Missouri 64106.

Telephone: (816) 512-1910.

FEENEY, Joan N. *(Judge, Bankruptcy Appellate Panel First Circuit)* Selected by the Judicial Council of the First Circuit. Also Chief Judge, U.S. Bankruptcy Court District of Massachusetts. Appointed by U.S. Court of Appeals First Circuit judges. Chief Judge Bankruptcy Court since Dec 10, 2002.

Office: 1101 Federal Building, 10 Causeway Street, Boston, Massachusetts 02222-1074.

Telephone: (617) 565-6049.

FEINBERG, Wilfred *(Senior Judge, United States Court of Appeals Second Circuit)* Appointed for life by President Lyndon B. Johnson to term beginning March 18, 1966. Chief Judge 1980-88. Assumed Senior status Jan 31, 1991, serves by assignment. Educated at Columbia University A.B. 1940 LL.B. 1946. Awarded honorary LL.D. Columbia University 1985 and Syracuse University 1985. Editor-in-Chief Columbia Law Review. Member Phi Beta Kappa. Judge, U.S. District Court Southern District of New York Oct 16, 1961 to March 17, 1966.

Deputy Superintendent New York State Banking Department 1958. Author "Recent Developments in the Law of Privacy" 48 Columbia L. Rev. 713, 1948; "Arbitration and Antitrust—An Introduction" 44 New York University L. Rev. 1069, 1969; "Expediting Review of Felony Convictions" 59 American Bar Association Journal 1025, 1973; "Foreword: A National Court of Appeals?" 42 Brooklyn L. Rev. 611, 1976; "The National Court of Appeals: Is It Necessary?" 32 The Record 106, 1977; "Foreword: Judicial Administration: Stepchild of the Law" 52 St. John's L. Rev. 187, 1978; "Maritime Arbitration and the Federal Courts" 5 Fordham International L. Jour. 245, 1982; Introduction to *The Law and The Public* by A. Bartlett Giamatti 38 No. 1 The Record Jan-Feb 1983; "Address Before the New York Patent Law Association" 65 Journal of the Patent Office Society 221 April 1983; "The State of the Second Circuit" 38 The Record 363 May-June 1983; "Tribute: Hon. James D. Hopkins" 3 Pace L. Rev. 451, 1983; "Introduction: 'The Remarkable Hands—An Affectionate Portrait'" Federal Bar Association 1983; "The State of the Second Circuit" 39 The Record 178 April 1984; "Constraining 'The Least Dangerous Branch'; The Tradition of Attacks on Judicial Power" (Madison Lecture) 50 New York University L. Rev. 252 May 1984; "The Office of Chief Judge of a Federal Court of Appeals" (Sonnett Lecture) 53 Fordham L. Rev. 369, 1985; "Judicial Independence" 36 Syracuse L. Rev. 885, 1985; "Unique Customs and Practices of the Second Circuit" 14 Hofstra L. Rev. 297, 1986; "In Memoriam: Henry J. Friendly" 99 No. 8 Harvard L. Rev. June 1986; "The Coming Deterioration of the Federal Judiciary" 42 The Record 179 March 1987; Foreword "Senior Judges: A National Resource" 56 No. 2 Brooklyn L. Rev. 1990 "The Role of Judges" *The Grand Design of America's Justice System* 30 Series of Institute of Comparative Law Chuo University, Japan 81, 1995; and "A View from the Bench" 7 No. 1 *Experience* 22 Senior Lawyers Division American Bar Association Fall 1996. Board of Editors Judicial Writing Project Federal Judicial Center.

Madison Lecturer New York University Law School 1983. Sonnett Lecturer Fordham University Law School 1984. Former member Advisory Council for Appellate Justice. Member American Judicature Society, The American Law Institute, New York County Lawyers' Association, The Association of the Bar of the City of New York and American Bar Association (Task Force Updating ABA Standards for Administration of Criminal Justice). Member Judicial Conference of the U.S. (Advisory Committee on Civil Rules 1965-70, Subcommittee on Supporting Personnel 1969-71, Subcommittee on Judicial Statistics 1971-76, Chairman Executive Committee 1987-88, Committee on Long Range Planning) and Federal Judicial Center Advisory Committee on Experimentation in the Law. Recipient Learned Hand Medal for Excellence in Federal Jurisprudence 1982, Gold Medal Award for Distinguished Service in the Law from New York State Bar Association 1990 and Medal for Excellence from Columbia Law Alumni Association 1990. U.S. Army 1942-45. Member Devitt Award Committee 1989 and 1990.

Office: U.S. Courthouse, 40 Centre Street, New York, New York 10007.

Telephone: (212) 857-2100.

FERGUSON, Warren J. *(Senior Judge, United States Court of Appeals Ninth Circuit)* Appointed for life by President Jimmy Carter to term beginning Dec 20, 1979. Assumed Senior status July 31, 1986, serves by assignment. Born Eureka Nevada Oct 31, 1920. Roman Catholic. Educated at University of Nevada B.A. 1942 and University of Southern California LL.B. 1949. Member Theta Chi, Phi Beta Kappa and Phi Kappa Phi. Admitted to practice California 1950. Began legal practice Fullerton 1950. Judge, Anaheim-Fullerton Municipal Court 1959-61. Judge, Superior Court of California Orange County 1961-66. Judge, U.S. District Court Central District of California 1966-79.

City Attorney for Buena Park, Placentia, La Puente, Baldwin Park, Walnut, Rosemead and Santa Fe Springs 1953-59. Associate Professor of Psychiatry University of Southern California since 1971. Associate Professor of Law Loyola University 1976-77. Former member State Bar of California, Orange County and American Bar Associations. Member Federal Bar Association. Faculty

FERGUSON, WARREN J.—*Continued*
member Federal Judicial Center 1971-74 and Practising Law Institute 1973-77. Instructor Evidence Seminar at University of Iowa 1974, New York Law Journal Evidence Seminar 1975 and Law & Business Seminar 1983. Master Sergeant U.S. Army 1942-45. Democrat.

Office: 10080 Federal Building, 411 West Fourth Street, Santa Ana, California 92701-4500.

Telephone: (714) 338-4680.

FERNANDEZ, Ferdinand F. *(Senior Judge, United States Court of Appeals Ninth Circuit)* Appointed for life by President George Bush to term beginning 1989. Assumed Senior status June 1, 2002, serves by assignment. Born Pasadena California May 29, 1937. Educated at University of Southern California B.S. 1958 J.D. 1962 and Harvard Law School LL.M. 1963. Law Clerk to Hon. William Matthew Byrne, Jr., U.S. District Court Central District of California 1963-64. In legal practice Pomona 1964-80. Judge, Superior Court of California San Bernardino County 1980-85. Judge, U.S. District Court Central District of California 1985 to 1989, appointed by President Ronald Reagan.

Office: 602 Court of Appeals Building, 125 South Grand Avenue, Pasadena, California 91105-1644.

Telephone: (626) 229-7121.

FINCH, Raymond L. *(Chief Judge, United States District Court District of the Virgin Islands)* Appointed by President Bill Clinton to term beginning 1994. Term expires 2004. Chief Judge since 2000. Born Christiansted St. Croix Virgin Islands Oct 4, 1940. Educated at Howard University B.A. 1962 J.D. 1965. Law Clerk to Municipal Court of the Virgin Islands 1965-66. Moot Court Team 1964-65. In legal practice Virgin Islands 1971-75. Former Judge, Municipal Court of the Virgin Islands. Acting Presiding Judge July 28, 1978 to Aug 17, 1978 and Former Judge, Territorial Court of the Virgin Islands.

Instructor University of the Virgin Islands. Honorary Member Federal Bar Association. Member The American Law Institute, American Judges Association, Virgin Islands, National and American Bar Associations. Instructor American Banking Association 1965-78 and 45-hour course "Banking and the Law." Attended "Trial Judges Academy" Seminar 1976 and "The Practicalities of Judging: Jurisprudence and the Humanities" Seminar June 1978 American Academy of Judicial Education and "Criminal-Evidence" Oct 1976, Oct 1977, Oct 1978 and Oct 1979 and Federal Court Seminars since Sept 1994 The National Judicial College. Listed in *Personalities of the South* 1978-79 and Marquis *Who's Who in America* since 1978. Served to Captain U.S. Army 1966-69. Recipient Army Commendation Medal and Bronze Star Medal. Previously worked as Temporary Deputy Marshal U.S. Department of Justice and stock clerk Virgin Islands Corporation. Democrat. Board of Directors St. Croix Division Boys' Club since 1975. Supervisory Board Member Juvenile Justice and Prevention of Delinquency Committee. Member Law Enforcement Planning Commission and Donald Walker Scholarship Foundation. Interests include boating, flying, motorcycling, running, shortwave dxing, Ham Radio and travel.

Office: 3013 Estate Golden Rock, Christiansted, St. Croix, Virgin Islands 00820.

Telephone: (340) 773-5021.

FIRESTONE, Nancy B. *(Judge, United States Court of Federal Claims)* Appointed by President Bill Clinton to term beginning Dec 4, 1998. Term expires Dec 2013. Educated at Washington University at St. Louis 1973 and University of Missouri School of Law J.D. 1977. Judge, Environmental Appeals Board U.S. Environmental Protection Agency 1992-95.

Attorney 1977-84, Assistant Chief Policy Section 1984-85, Deputy Chief Enforcement Section 1985-89 and Deputy Assistant Attorney General 1995-98 Environmental and Natural Resources Division U.S. Department of Justice. Associate Deputy Administrator U.S. Environmental Protection Agency 1989-92.

Office: National Courts Building, 717 Madison Place N.W., Washington, D.C. 20005-1086.

Telephone: (202) 219-9616.

FISHER, Raymond C. *(Judge, United States Court of Appeals Ninth Circuit)* Appointed for life by President Bill Clinton to term beginning 1999. Born Oakland California July 12, 1939. Educated at University of California at Santa Barbara B.A. 1961 and Stanford Law School LL.B. 1966. President Stanford Law Review 1965-66. Law Clerk to Hon. J. Skelly Wright, U.S. Court of Appeals District of Columbia Circuit 1966-67 and Hon. William J. Brennan, Jr., U.S. Supreme Court 1967-68. Member Order of the Coif. In legal practice Los Angeles 1968-97.

Deputy General Counsel Independent Commission on the Los Angeles Police Department Christopher Commission 1990. Associate Attorney General U.S. Department of Justice 1997-99. Member Los Angeles City Civil Service Commission 1984-89. President Los Angeles Police Commission 1995-97.

Office: Court of Appeals Building, 125 South Grand Avenue, Pasadena, California 91105-1652.

Telephone: (626) 229-7110.

FLAUM, Joel M. *(Chief Judge, United States Court of Appeals Seventh Circuit)* Appointed for life by President Ronald Reagan May 5, 1983. Chief Judge since Aug 1, 2000. Born Hudson New York Nov 26, 1936. Jewish. Educated at Union College B.A. 1958 and Northwestern University School of Law J.D. 1963 LL.M. 1964. Honorary LL.D. John Marshall Law School 2002. Board of Editors Northwestern University Law Review. Judge, U.S. District Court Northern District of Illinois Jan 21, 1975 to May 31, 1983, appointed by President Gerald R. Ford.

Assistant State's Attorney Cook County Illinois 1965-69. Assistant Attorney General 1969-70 and First Assistant Attorney General 1970-72 Illinois. First Assistant U.S. Attorney Northern District of Illinois 1972-75. Adjunct Professor of Law Northwestern University School of Law 1967-69. Instructor DePaul University College of Law. Fellow Ford Foundation 1963-64. Life Fellow Chicago Bar Foundation and American Bar Foundation. Member Chicago Inn of Court (Counselor), Lawyers Club of Chicago, The American Law Institute (ex officio), The Maritime Law Association of the U.S., Navy-Marine Corps Retired Judge Advocates Association, Judicial Conference of the U.S. (Executive Committee), American Judicature Society, Chicago, Illinois State, Seventh Circuit, Federal and American Bar Associations. Lecturer on Federal Courts, Appellate Practice, Criminal Procedure and Military Justice USNR. Lieutenant Commander USNR JAGC 1981-92. Chairman Advisory Committee U.S. Coast Guard Academy and Visiting

FLAUM, JOEL M.—*Continued*
Committee Northwestern University School of Law. Member Naval Justice School Foundation and The Naval Reserve Association.
Office: U.S. Courthouse, 219 South Dearborn Street, Chicago, Illinois 60604.
Telephone: (312) 435-5626.

FLETCHER, Betty B. *(Senior Judge, United States Court of Appeals Ninth Circuit)* Appointed for life by President Jimmy Carter to term beginning Oct 15, 1979. Assumed Senior status Nov 1, 1998, serves by assignment. Born Tacoma Washington March 29, 1923. Educated at Stanford University B.A. with distinction 1943 and University of Washington LL.B. 1956. Staff member University of Washington Law Review. Member Phi Beta Kappa and Order of the Coif. Admitted to practice Washington 1956 and District of Columbia 1971. Began legal practice Seattle 1956.
President Federal Judges Association. Member American Judicature Society (Director 1978-80), Seattle-King County (President 1972-73) and Washington State (Governor 1975-78) Bar Associations. Member Children's Home Society of Washington (Past President) and Seattle Symphony (Former Trustee). Trustee Saul & Dayee G. Haas Foundation.
Office: 1000 U.S. Courthouse, 1010 Fifth Avenue, Seattle, Washington 98104-1180.
Telephone: (206) 553-2670.

FLETCHER, William A. *(Judge, United States Court of Appeals Ninth Circuit)* Appointed for life by President Bill Clinton to term beginning Feb 1, 1999. Born Philadelphia Pennsylvania June 6, 1945. Educated at Harvard College B.A. 1968, Oxford University B.A. 1970 and Yale Law School J.D. 1975. Law Clerk to Hon. Stanley A. Weigel, U.S. District Court Northern District of California 1975-76 and Hon. William J. Brennan, Jr., U.S. Supreme Court 1976-77.
Professor of Law University of California Boalt Hall School of Law 1977-98. Lieutenant USN 1970-72.
Mailing address: P.O. Box 193939, San Francisco, California 94119-3939.
Office: 95 Seventh Street, Suite 216, San Francisco, California 94103.
Telephone: (415) 556-9941.

FOLEY, Maurice B. *(Judge, United States Tax Court)* Appointed by President Bill Clinton March 17, 1995. Term expires April 10, 2010. Born Belleville Illinois March 28, 1960. Baptist. Educated at Swarthmore College B.A. 1982, University of California Boalt Hall School of Law J.D. 1985 and Georgetown University Law Center M.L.T. 1988. Admitted to practice California 1986.
Member State Bar of California.
Office: 400 Second Street N.W., Washington, D.C. 20217-0002.
Telephone: (202) 606-8800.

FRIEDMAN, Daniel M. *(Senior Judge, United States Court of Appeals Federal Circuit)* Assumed office Oct 1, 1982. Assumed Senior status Nov 1, 1989, serves by assignment. Born New York New York Feb 8, 1916. Educated at Columbia University A.B. in Government and History 1937 LL.B. 1940. Staff member Columbia Law Review. Kent Scholar. Admitted to practice New York 1941, U.S. Supreme Court 1948 and U.S. Courts of Appeals District of Columbia 1955, Ninth 1957 and Fourth 1959 Circuits. Began legal practice New York City 1940. Chief Judge, U.S. Court of Claims May 24, 1978 to Sept 30, 1982.
Author articles in Columbia and Harvard Law Reviews. Member Judicial Conference of the U.S. 1978-82, The American Law Institute, Federal and American Bar Associations. Recipient Attorney General's Exceptional Service Award 1969, Justice Tom C. Clark Award from Federal Bar Association District of Columbia Chapter 1976 and National Civil Service Career Service Award 1976. Master Sergeant Quartermaster Corps USAS 1942-46. Enjoys stamp collecting and photography.
Office: National Courts Building, 717 Madison Place N.W., Washington, D.C. 20439-0002.
Telephone: (202) 633-5836.

FUENTES, Julio M. *(Judge, United States Court of Appeals Third Circuit)* Appointed for life by President Bill Clinton to term beginning May 15, 2000. Born Humacao Puerto Rico Feb 16, 1946. Educated at Southern Illinois University B.A. 1971, New York University M.A. 1972, State University of New York at Buffalo J.D. 1975 and Rutgers University M.A. 1993. In legal practice Newark 1975-81. Judge, Newark Municipal Court 1979-87. Judge, New Jersey Superior Court Vicinage Five 1987-2000.
Office: 5032 Federal Bldg. & U.S. Courthouse, 50 Walnut Street, Newark, New Jersey 07102.
Telephone: (973) 645-3831.

FUSTE, Jose Antonio *(Judge, United States District Court District of Puerto Rico)* Appointed for life by President Ronald Reagan to term beginning Nov 8, 1985. Born San Juan Puerto Rico Nov 3, 1943. Educated at University of Puerto Rico B.B.A. 1965 LL.B. cum laude 1968. Associate Director Puerto Rico Law Review 1967-68. Admitted to practice Puerto Rico 1969, U.S. District Court District of Puerto Rico 1969 and U.S. Courts of Appeals First, Second, Third and Fifth Circuits 1969-78. In legal practice San Juan 1968-85.
Author "*People v. Hernández:* Mistake of Fact as a Defense in Statutory Rape Proceedings in Puerto Rico" 36 Puerto Rico L. Rev. 177, 1967 and "The Doctrine of Tacit Confirmation and Sections 91 and 1313 of the Civil Code" 37 Puerto Rico L. Rev. 87, 1968. Professor of Admiralty Law University of Puerto Rico 1972-85 and 1996-2002. Fellow The American Law Institute. Member Southeastern Admiralty Law Institute, The Maritime Law Association of the U.S., The Association of Trial Lawyers of America, American Judicature Society, Bar Association of the District of Columbia, Puerto Rico, Federal and American Bar Associations.
Office: CH-133 U.S. Courthouse, 150 Carlos Chardon Avenue, San Juan, Puerto Rico 00918-1758.
Telephone: (787) 772-3120.

FUTEY, Bohdan A. *(Senior Judge, United States Court of Federal Claims)* Appointed by President Ronald Reagan to term beginning May 28, 1987. Assumed Senior status May 6, 2002, serves by assignment. Born Ukraine June 28, 1939. Catholic. Educated at Case Western Reserve University B.A. 1962 M.A. 1964 and Cleveland Marshall Law School J.D. 1968. Admitted to practice Ohio, U.S. District Courts Northern District of Ohio and District of Columbia. In legal practice 1968-72 and 1975-84.
Chief Assistant Police Prosecutor Cleveland 1972-74. Executive Assistant to Mayor Cleveland 1974-75. Chair-

FUTEY, BOHDAN A.—*Continued*

man Foreign Claims Settlement Commission of the U.S. 1984-87. Member The District of Columbia Bar, Parma, Cleveland, Ukrainian-American and American Bar Associations. Attended U.S. Court of Appeals for the Federal Circuit Judicial Conference 1987 and U.S. Claims Court Judicial Conference 1987 and 1988. Republican. Enjoys reading, camping, swimming, traveling, soccer and football.

Office: National Courts Building, 717 Madison Place N.W., Washington, D.C. 20005-1086.

Telephone: (202) 219-9670.

GAJARSA, Arthur J. *(Judge, United States Court of Appeals Federal Circuit)* Appointed for life by President Bill Clinton April 18, 1996 to term beginning Sept 12, 1997. Born Norcia Italy March 1, 1941. Educated at Rensselaer Polytechnic Institute B.S.E.E. 1962, Catholic University of America M.A. in Economics 1968 and Georgetown University Law Center J.D. 1967. Law Clerk to Hon. Joseph McGarraghy, U.S. District Court District of Columbia 1967-68. Admitted to practice District of Columbia 1968, U.S. District Courts District of Columbia 1968 and Northern District of New York 1980, Connecticut 1969, U.S. Supreme Court 1971, U.S. Courts of Appeals Ninth 1974, Federal 1974 and Second 1984 Circuits and U.S. Patent and Trademark Office 1963. In legal practice 1971-97.

Patent Examiner U.S. Patent and Trademark Office 1962-63. Attorney Office of General Counsel Aetna Life and Casualty Co. 1968-69. Special Counsel and Assistant to the Commissioner of Indian Affairs Bureau of Indian Affairs U.S. Department of the Interior 1969-71. Member American Judicature Society, The District of Columbia Bar, Federal Circuit, Federal and American Bar Associations. Trustee Rensselaer Neuman Foundation since 1973, Foundation for Improving Understanding of the Arts 1982-96 and Outward Bound U.S.A. 1987-2001. Board of Directors 1976-99, General Counsel 1976-89, President 1989-92 and Vice Chair 1993-96 National Italian American Foundation. Trustee since 1994 and Vice Chairman of the Board since 1998 Rensselaer Polytechnic Institute. Board of Regents 1994-99, Board of Directors since 2000 and Chairman Law Committee Georgetown University.

Office: National Courts Building, 717 Madison Place N.W., Washington, D.C. 20439-0002.

Telephone: (202) 633-6570.

GALE, Joseph H. *(Judge, United States Tax Court)* Appointed by President Bill Clinton.

Office: 400 Second Street N.W., Washington, D.C. 20217-0002.

Telephone: (202) 606-8807.

GARCIA-GREGORY, Jay A. *(Judge, United States District Court District of Puerto Rico)* Appointed for life by President Bill Clinton to term beginning Aug 1, 2000. Born San Juan Puerto Rico Sept 19, 1944. Educated at Assumption College A.B. 1966, University of Madrid M.A. 1969 and University of Puerto Rico School of Law LL.B. 1972. Law Clerk to Hon. Hiram Cancio and Hon. Jose Toledo, U.S. District Court District of Puerto Rico 1973-74. In legal practice Puerto Rico 1974-2000.

Office: CH-151 U.S. Courthouse, 150 Carlos Chardon Avenue, San Juan, Puerto Rico 00918.

Telephone: (787) 772-3171.

GARLAND, Merrick B. *(Judge, United States Court of Appeals District of Columbia Circuit)* Appointed for life by President Bill Clinton to term beginning 1997. Educated at Harvard University A.B. summa cum laude 1974 J.D. magna cum laude 1977. Articles Editor Harvard Law Review. Law Clerk to Senior Judge Henry J. Friendly, U.S. Court of Appeals Second Circuit 1977-78 and Hon. William J. Brennan, Jr., U.S. Supreme Court 1978-79. Member Phi Beta Kappa. In legal practice Washington D.C. 1981-89 and 1992-93.

Special Assistant to Attorney General 1979-81. Assistant U.S. Attorney District of Columbia 1989-92. Deputy Assistant Attorney General Criminal Division 1993-94. Principal Associate Deputy Attorney General U.S. Department of Justice 1994-97. Author "Antitrust and State Action" 96 Yale L. Jour. 486, 1987, "Antitrust and Federalism" 96 Yale L. Jour. 1291, 1987 and "Deregulation and Judicial Review" 98 Harvard L. Rev. 505, 1985. Lecturer on Law Harvard Law School 1985-86. Co-chair Administrative Law Section The District of Columbia Bar 1991-94.

Office: 3836 U.S. Courthouse, 333 Constitution Avenue N.W., Washington, D.C. 20001-2866.

Telephone: (202) 216-7460.

GARTH, Leonard I. *(Senior Judge, United States Court of Appeals Third Circuit)* Appointed for life by President Richard M. Nixon to term beginning Aug 29, 1973. Assumed Senior status June 30, 1986, serves by assignment. Born Brooklyn New York April 7, 1921. Jewish. Educated at Columbia University B.A. 1942, National Institute of Public Affairs 1942-43 and Harvard University LL.B. 1952. Admitted to practice New Jersey 1952. In legal practice Paterson 1952-70. Judge, U.S. District Court District of New Jersey Jan 29, 1970 to Aug 28, 1973.

Former Lecturer and former Co-adjutant Faculty Member Rutgers University Law School and Seton Hall University School of Law. Former Member Committee on Revision of General and Admiralty Rules U.S. District Court District of New Jersey, Supreme Court Financial Disclosure Committee Judicial Conference of the U.S., New Jersey Board of Bar Examiners 1964-68, Passaic County (President 1967-68), Federal and American (Co-chair Committee on Appellate Practice Appellate Judges Conference) Bar Associations. Member The American Law Institute. Lecturer ICLE and Practising Law Institute. Advisory Board Federal Courts Study Committee. First Lieutenant U.S. Army 1943-46. Member Harvard Law School Association (National Vice President 1963-64) and Advisory Committee on Law and Society Ramapo College Mahwah New Jersey since 1986.

Newark office: 5040 Federal Courthouse, 50 Walnut Street, Newark, New Jersey 07102-3506.

Telephone: (973) 645-6521.

Fax: (973) 645-6119

Philadelphia office: 20613 U.S. Courthouse, Philadelphia, Pennsylvania 19106.

Telephone: (215) 597-3925.

GARWOOD, William L. *(Senior Judge, United States Court of Appeals Fifth Circuit)* Appointed for life by President Ronald Reagan to term beginning Nov 9, 1981. Assumed Senior status Jan 23, 1997, serves by assignment. Born Houston Texas Oct 29, 1931. Episcopalian. Educated at Princeton University A.B. 1952 and University of Texas LL.B. with honors 1955. Editorial

GARWOOD, WILLIAM L.—*Continued*

Board and Associate Note Editor Texas Law Review 1954-55. Law Clerk to Hon. John R. Brown, U.S. Court of Appeals Fifth Circuit 1955-56. Member Order of the Coif and Chancellors (Grand Chancellor). Admitted to practice Texas 1955, U.S. Court of Appeals Fifth Circuit 1956, U.S. District Courts Southern 1956 and Western 1960 Districts of Texas, U.S. Court of Military Appeals 1957 and U.S. Supreme Court 1959. Began legal practice Austin 1959. Justice, Texas Supreme Court 1979-80.

Director 1986-96 and President 1990-91 Texas Law Review Association. Life Fellow Texas Bar Foundation and American Bar Foundation. Member American Bar Association 1955-92. Life Member The American Law Institute. Member State Bar of Texas. Recipient Leon Green Award 1984 and Distinguished Lawyer Award from Travis County Bar Association 1997. First Lieutenant U.S. Army JAGC 1956-59. Recipient Army Commendation Ribbon 1959. Director and Trustee Child & Family Service of Austin 1965-73 (President 1970-71), Mental Health and Mental Retardation Center of Austin and Travis County 1966-69, Human Opportunities Corporation of Austin and Travis County 1966-70, Medical Dental Referral Service of Austin 1966-73, St. Andrew's Episcopal School (President 1972), Community Council of Austin and Travis County 1968-72 and United Fund of Austin and Travis County 1971-73. Advisory Board Salvation Army Austin Texas since 1972. Enjoys hunting and reading.

Office: 300 Thornberry Judicial Building, 903 San Jacinto Boulevard, Austin, Texas 78701.

Telephone: (512) 916-5113.

GARZA, Emilio M. *(Judge, United States Court of Appeals Fifth Circuit)* Appointed for life by President George Bush to term beginning June 7, 1991. Born San Antonio Texas Aug 1, 1947. Roman Catholic. Educated at University of Notre Dame B.A. 1969 M.A. 1970 and University of Texas J.D. 1976. Admitted to practice Texas 1976, U.S. District Court Western District of Texas 1977, U.S. Tax Court 1977 and U.S. Court of Appeals Fifth Circuit 1978. In legal practice San Antonio 1976-87. Judge, Texas District Court 225th Judicial District 1987-88. Judge, U.S. District Court Western District of Texas 1988-91.

Member State Bar of Texas and San Antonio Bar Association. Captain USMCR 1970-79 (active duty 1970-73). Member Century Club 1987-88. Board of Directors Symphony Society 1987-89. Member Fine Arts and Humanities Advisory Council University of Texas at San Antonio since 1992. Member Advisory Board Phoenix Institute since 1992.

Office: 501 Fountainhead One Building, 8200 Interstate 10 West, San Antonio, Texas 78230.

Telephone: (210) 525-2950.

GARZA, Reynaldo G. *(Senior Judge, United States Court of Appeals Fifth Circuit)* Appointed for life by President Jimmy Carter Aug 1, 1979. Assumed Senior status Aug 1, 1982, serves by assignment. Born Brownsville Texas July 7, 1915. Roman Catholic. Educated at Brownsville Junior College A.A. 1935 and University of Texas B.A. 1939 LL.B. 1939. Admitted to practice Texas 1939. Began legal practice Brownsville 1939. Judge April 1961 to Aug 1979 and Chief Judge Dec 1974 to Aug 1979, U.S. District Court Southern District of Texas. Chief Judge, Temporary Emergency Court of the United States Nov 8, 1982 to April 1993.

Member State Bar of Texas and Cameron County Bar Association. Recipient Medal Pro Ecclesia Et Pontifice from Pope Pius XII 1954. Knighted in the Order of St. Gregory the Great by Pope Pius XII 1955. USAS 1942-45. Democrat. Member City Commission Brownsville 1947. Member School Board Brownsville Independent District 1941, Boy Scouts of America and Knights of Columbus.

Office: 3086 Federal Bldg. & U.S. Courthouse, 600 East Harrison Street, Brownsville, Texas 78520-7114.

Telephone: (956) 548-2592.

GELPI, Gustavo A., Jr. *(Magistrate Judge, United States District Court District of Puerto Rico)* Appointed by U.S. District Court judges to term beginning June 29, 2001.

Office: 182 Federal Building, 150 Carlos Chardon Avenue, San Juan, Puerto Rico 00918.

Telephone: (787) 772-3103.

GERBER, Joel *(Judge, United States Tax Court)* Appointed by President Ronald Reagan to term beginning June 18, 1984. Reappointed by President Bill Clinton. Born Chicago Illinois July 16, 1940. Educated at Roosevelt University B.S.B.A. 1962, DePaul University J.D. 1965 and Boston University LL.M. in Taxation 1968. Admitted to practice Illinois 1965, Georgia 1974 and Tennessee 1978.

Trial Attorney Boston Massachusetts 1965-72, Staff Assistant to Regional Counsel and Senior Trial Attorney Atlanta Georgia 1972-76, District Counsel Nashville Tennessee 1976-80, Deputy Chief Counsel Washington D.C. 1980-84 and Acting Chief Counsel May 1983 to March 1984 Internal Revenue Service. Lecturer on Law Vanderbilt University 1976-80 and University of Miami 1986-87. Member American Bar Association (Section of Taxation, Chairman Special Committee on Lawyers in Government 1988-89). Recipient Presidential Meritorious Rank Award 1983 and Secretary of the Treasury's Exceptional Service Award 1984.

Office: 400 Second Street N.W., Washington, D.C. 20217-0002.

Telephone: (202) 606-8841.

GIBBONS, Julia Smith *(Judge, United States Court of Appeals Sixth Circuit)* Appointed for life by President George W. Bush to term beginning Aug 2, 2002. Born Pulaski Tennessee Dec 23, 1950. Educated at Vanderbilt University B.A. magna cum laude 1972 and University of Virginia School of Law J.D. 1975. Editorial Board Virginia Law Review. Law Clerk to Hon. William E. Miller, U.S. Court of Appeals Sixth Circuit 1975-76. Member Order of the Coif. Admitted to practice Tennessee 1975. In legal practice Memphis 1976-79. Judge, Tennessee Circuit Court 1981-83. First female trial judge of a court of record in Tennessee. Judge, U.S. District Court Western District of Tennessee June 1983 to Aug 1, 2002, appointed by President Ronald Reagan.

Legal Advisor to Governor Lamar Alexander 1979-81.

Office: 1157 Federal Building, 167 North Main Street, Memphis, Tennessee 38103.

Telephone: (901) 495-1265.

GIBSON, John R. *(Senior Judge, United States Court of Appeals Eighth Circuit)* Appointed for life by President Ronald Reagan to term beginning March 30, 1982. Assumed Senior status Jan 1, 1994, serves by as-

GIBSON, JOHN R.—*Continued*

signment. Born Springfield Missouri Dec 20, 1925. Educated at University of Missouri-Columbia A.B. 1949 J.D. 1952. In legal practice Kansas City 1952-81. Judge, U.S. District Court Western District of Missouri 1981 to March 29, 1982, appointed by President Ronald Reagan. Sergeant U.S. Army 1944-46.

Office: 10-40 U.S. Courthouse, 400 East Ninth Street, Kansas City, Missouri 64106.

Telephone: (816) 512-5830.

GIBSON, Reginald W. *(Senior Judge, United States Court of Federal Claims)* Appointed by President Ronald Reagan to term beginning Dec 15, 1982. Assumed Senior status, serves by assignment. Born Lynchburg Virginia July 31, 1927. Baptist. Educated at Virginia Union University B.S. 1952, University of Pennsylvania 1952-53 and Howard University School of Law LL.B. 1956. Member Kappa Alpha Psi. Admitted to practice District of Columbia 1957 and Illinois 1972. Began legal practice Washington D.C. 1961. In legal practice Chicago 1971.

Agent Internal Revenue Service 1957-61. Trial Attorney Tax Division Criminal Section U.S. Department of Justice 1961-71. Senior Tax Attorney and General Tax Attorney International Harvester Co. 1971-82. Member The District of Columbia Bar, Chicago, National, Federal and American Bar Associations. Recipient U.S. Attorney General's Certificate of Award 1969 and Special Commendation for Outstanding Service in the Tax Division U.S. Department of Justice 1970. Listed in *Who's Who in Black America* 1980 and *Who's Who in America* since 1983. Named Distinguished Alumni of the Year by Howard University School of Law 1984. Corporal U.S. Army 1946-47. Enjoys golfing and swimming.

Office: National Courts Building, 717 Madison Place N.W., Washington, D.C. 20005-1086.

Telephone: (202) 219-9578.

GIERBOLINI-ORTIZ, Gilberto *(Senior Judge, United States District Court District of Puerto Rico)* Appointed for life by President Jimmy Carter to term beginning 1980. Chief Judge 1991-93. Assumed Senior status Dec 27, 1993, serves by assignment. Born Coamo Puerto Rico Dec 22, 1926. Educated at University of Puerto Rico B.A. 1957 LL.B. 1961. In legal practice Puerto Rico 1973-80. Judge, Puerto Rico Superior Court 1966-69.

Assistant U.S. Attorney Commonwealth of Puerto Rico 1961-66. Assistant Commonwealth Attorney General for Antitrust Puerto Rico 1970-72. Sergeant 1943-46 and Captain 1951-57 U.S. Army. Assistant Secretary of Justice and Commonwealth Solicitor General Puerto Rico 1969-72. Chairman State Elections Board Commonwealth of Puerto Rico 1972.

Office: 342 U.S. Courthouse Third Floor, 300 Recinto Sur Street, San Juan, Puerto Rico 00901.

Telephone: (787) 977-6060.

GIERKE, Herman Frederick "Sparky", III *(Associate Judge, United States Court of Appeals for the Armed Forces)* Appointed by President George Bush to term beginning Nov 1991. Term expires 2006. Born Williston North Dakota March 13, 1943. Lutheran. Educated at University of North Dakota B.A. 1964 J.D. 1966. Member Blue Key and Phi Delta Phi. Admitted to practice North Dakota 1966, U.S. District Court District of North Dakota, U.S. Supreme Court and U.S. Court of Appeals for the Armed Forces. In legal practice Watford City April 1971 to Oct 1983. Justice, North Dakota Supreme Court Oct 1, 1983 to Nov 20, 1991. One of the youngest justices ever appointed to North Dakota Supreme Court.

State's Attorney McKenzie County 1974-82. City Attorney Watford City 1974-83. Former Attorney McKenzie Electric Cooperative, McKenzie County Grazing Association and McKenzie County Public School District. Adjunct Professor of Law George Washington University National Law Center, Catholic University of America School of Law and Barry University at Orlando. Fellow American College of Trust and Estate Counsel and American Bar Foundation. Charter Member North Dakota Council of School Attorneys and North Dakota Trial Lawyers Association (Board of Governors 1977-83). Board of Governors 1977-79 and 1981-84 and President 1982-83 State Bar Association of North Dakota. President Northwest Judicial District Bar Association 1977-79, Upper Missouri Bar Association 1978-79 and North Dakota State's Attorneys Association 1979-80. Board of Governors North Dakota Trial Lawyers Association 1979-80. Vice Chairman June 1989 to June 1991 and Chairman June 1991 to Nov 1991 North Dakota Judicial Conference. Member The Association of Trial Lawyers of America, American Judicature Society and American Bar Association. Recipient Governor's Award for outstanding service to the State of North Dakota 1984, North Dakota National Leadership Award of Excellence 1988 and 1991 and Sioux Award from University of North Dakota 1989. Named Man of the Year by Delta Mu Chapter Kappa Sigma 1989 and Outstanding Greek Alumnus by University of North Dakota 1989. Captain 1967-71 and Military Judge Dec 1969 to April 1971 U.S. Army JAGC. Recipient Bronze Star and Air Medal for Meritorious Service. Life Member Veterans of Foreign Wars, 40 et 8 and American Legion (Vietnam Era State Commander North Dakota American Legion 1983-84, National Vice Commander 1985-86, Vietnam Era National Commander 1988-89). Licensed private pilot. Interests include racquetball, golf, tennis, ranching and raising horses.

Office: 450 E Street N.W., Washington, D.C. 20442-0001.

Telephone: (202) 761-1458.

GILMAN, Ronald Lee *(Judge, United States Court of Appeals Sixth Circuit)* Appointed for life by President Bill Clinton to term beginning Nov 21, 1997. Born Memphis Tennessee Oct 16, 1942. Jewish. Educated at Massachusetts Institute of Technology B.S. and Harvard Law School J.D. cum laude. Admitted to practice Tennessee 1967. In legal practice Memphis 1967-97.

Author *Tennessee Corporations* Lawyers Cooperative Publishing Co. 1980 annual supplements through 1994; "The Holographic Codicil" Tennessee B. Jour. Aug 1982; "Dishonesty Alone Does Not Deck a Fidelity Insurer" *Insurance Counsel Journal* Oct 1984; "Planning for Disability" *The Practical Lawyer* March 1989; "Mediation: Prime ADR Tool of the '90s" Tennessee B. Jour. March 1994; "Resolving Commercial Cases through Alternative Dispute Resolution" 26 University of Memphis L. Rev. 1121 Spring 1996; and "Rookie Year on the Federal Bench" 60 Ohio State L. Jour. 1085, 1999. Adjunct Professor of Trial Advocacy University of Memphis School of Law 1980-97. Commercial Arbitrator and Mediator American Arbitration Association 1988-97. Securities Arbitrator National Association of

GILMAN, RONALD LEE—*Continued*

Securities Dealers 1993-97. Dalkon Shield Referee 1994-97. Life Member Judicial Conference of the Sixth Circuit. Fellow The American College of Trust and Estate Counsel. Member Tennessee Bar Foundation, American Bar Foundation, American Judicature Society, The American Law Institute, Memphis (President Young Lawyers Division 1974, President 1987), Tennessee (President Young Lawyers Conference 1978-79, Speaker House of Delegates 1985-87, President 1990-91) and American (House of Delegates 1990-97, Judicial Division since 1997) Bar Associations. Eagle Scout 1958. Recipient Sam A. Myar, Jr. Memorial Award for outstanding service to the legal profession and the community 1981. Listed in *Best Lawyers in America* 1983-97, *Who's Who in American Law* and *Who's Who in America.* Director and Treasurer Senior Citizens Services 1968-73. Regional Chair MIT Educational Council 1968-88. Director Memphis Jewish Home 1984-87. Graduate Leadership Memphis 1985. President Society of Memphis Magicians 1986. Board of Directors Capital Case Resource Center of Tennessee 1988-95. Board of Directors and Advisory Board Chickasaw Council Boy Scouts of America 1993-2000. Interests include magic.

Office: 1176 Federal Building, 167 North Main Street, Memphis, Tennessee 38103.

Telephone: (901) 495-1575.

Fax: (901) 495-1580

GINSBURG, Douglas H. *(Chief Judge, United States Court of Appeals District of Columbia Circuit)* Appointed for life by President Ronald Reagan to term beginning Nov 10, 1986. Chief Judge since July 16, 2001. Born Chicago Illinois May 25, 1946. Educated at Cornell University B.S. 1970 and University of Chicago Law School J.D. 1973. Law Clerk to Hon. Carl McGowan, U.S. Court of Appeals District of Columbia Circuit 1973-74 and Hon. Thurgood Marshall, U.S. Supreme Court 1974-75. Member Phi Kappa Phi. Admitted to practice Illinois 1973, Massachusetts 1982, U.S. Supreme Court 1984 and U.S. Court of Appeals Ninth Circuit 1986.

Deputy Assistant Attorney General Regulatory Affairs 1983-84 and Assistant Attorney General 1985-86 Antitrust Division U.S. Department of Justice. Administrator Information and Regulatory Affairs Office of Management and Budget Executive Office of the President 1984-85. Assistant Professor of Law 1975-81, Professor of Law 1975-81 and Lecturer on Law since 1987 Harvard Law School. Visiting Professor of Law Columbia University 1987-88. Foundation Professor of Law George Mason University since 1988. Charles J. Merriam Visiting Scholar and Senior Lecturer University of Chicago 1990. Member American Economic Association, Massachusetts and Illinois State Bar Associations.

Office: 5128 U.S. Courthouse, 333 Constitution Avenue N.W., Washington, D.C. 20001-2866.

Telephone: (202) 216-7190.

GINSBURG, Ruth Bader *(Associate Justice, The Supreme Court of the United States)* Appointed for life by President Bill Clinton. Also Circuit Justice, U.S. Court of Appeals Second Circuit. Born Brooklyn New York March 15, 1933. Educated at Cornell University B.A. with distinction 1954, Harvard Law School 1956-58 and Columbia University School of Law LL.B. 1959 replaced by J.D. Awarded honorary LL.D. Lund University, Sweden 1969, American University 1981, Vermont Law School 1984, Georgetown University 1985, DePaul University 1985, Brooklyn Law School 1987, Hebrew Union College 1988, Rutgers University 1991, Amherst College 1991 and Lewis & Clark College 1992. Kent Scholar. Staff member Harvard Law Review and Columbia Law Review. Law Secretary to Hon. Edmund L. Palmieri, U.S. District Court Southern District of New York 1959-61. Member Phi Beta Kappa (PBK Visiting Scholar 1973-74) and Phi Kappa Phi. Admitted to practice New York 1959, District of Columbia 1975, U.S. Supreme Court, U.S. Courts of Appeals Second, Fifth and District of Columbia Circuits and U.S. District Courts District of Columbia and Eastern and Southern Districts of New York. Former Judge, U.S. Court of Appeals District of Columbia Circuit, appointed by President Jimmy Carter to term beginning June 30, 1980.

Author "Special Findings and Jury Unanimity in the Federal Courts" 65 Columbia L. Rev. 256, 1965; "The Competent Court in Private International Law" 20 Rutgers L. Rev. 89, 1965; "Civil Procedure, Basic Features of the Swedish System" 14 American Journal of Comparative Law 336, 1965; "Proof of Foreign Law in Sweden" 14 International & Comparative Law Quarterly 277, 1965; "Recognition and Execution of Foreign Civil Judgments and Arbitration Awards" *Legal Thought in the United States Under Contemporary Pressures* 237-259, 1970; "Sex and Unequal Protection: Men and Women as Victims" 11 Journal of Family Law 347, 1971; "Men, Women, and the Constitution" 10 Columbia Journal of Law and Social Problems 91, 1973; "The Need for the Equal Rights Amendment" 59 American Bar Association Journal 1013, 1973; "Women as Full Members of the Club: An Evolving American Ideal" 6 Human Rights 1 Fall 1977; "From No Rights, to Half Rights, to Confusing Rights" 7 No. 1 Human Rights 12 May 1978; "The Equal Rights Amendment Is the Way" 1 Harvard Women's L. Jour. 19 Spring 1978; "A Feminist Lawyer Visits China" 4 Women's Agenda 5 Jan 1979; "Inviting Judicial Activism: A 'Liberal' or 'Conservative' Technique?" 15 Georgia L. Rev. 539, 1981; "Reflections on the Independence, Good Behavior, and Workload of Federal Judges" 55 University of Colorado L. Rev. 1, 1983; "Some Thoughts on Autonomy and Equality in Relation to *Roe v. Wade*" 63 North Carolina L. Rev. 375, 1985; "On Amending the Constitution: A Plea for Patience" 12 University of Arkansas at Little Rock L. Jour. 677, 1990; and "Styles of Collegial Judging" 39 Federal Bar News and Journal 199, 1992. Co-author with Anders Bruzelius *Civil Procedure in Sweden* 1965 and *Swedish Code of Judicial Procedure* 1968 and with Herma Hill Kay and Kenneth M. Davidson *Text, Cases, and Materials on Sex-Based Discrimination* 1974 and Supplement with Herma Hill Kay 1978. Volume Editor Volume 1 *Business Regulation in the Common Market Nations* 1969. Symposium Editor "The Status of Women" 20 American Journal of Comparative Law 585, 1972. Editorial Board American Journal of Comparative Law 1966-72 and *Encyclopedia of the American Constitution* National Endowment for the Humanities. Board of Editors American Bar Association Journal 1972-78. Editorial Board *Guide to American Law* 1978-80 and Advisory Board 1978-80 Law School Department West Publishing Company. Advisory Board "Constitution" Journal of the Foundation for the U.S. Constitution.

GINSBURG, RUTH BADER—*Continued*

Research Associate 1961-62 and Associate Director 1962-63 Project of International Procedure, Professor 1972-80 and Advisory Board Samuel Rubin Program for the Advancement of Liberty and Equality through Law Columbia University School of Law. Assistant Professor 1963-66, Associate Professor 1966-69 and Professor 1969-72 Rutgers University School of Law. Visiting Faculty New York University School of Law Spring 1968, Harvard Law School Fall 1971, University of Amsterdam, The Netherlands Summer 1975, University of Strasbourg, France Summer 1975, Salzburg Seminar in American Studies Summer 1984 and Aspen Institute Summer 1990. Academic Advisory Board Center for the Study of Human Rights 1977-80 and Advisory Board Program in Sex Roles and Social Change Center for the Study of Social Sciences 1977-80 Columbia University. Fellow Center for Advanced Study in the Behavioral Sciences Stanford University 1977-78. Fellow American Bar Foundation (Executive Committee 1989 and Secretary Board of Directors 1989). Honorary Member Board of Governors International Association of Jewish Lawyers and Jurists. Member Council on Foreign Relations, Federal Bar Council (Vice President 1978-80), The American Law Institute (Advisor Second Restatement of Judgments 1972-82 and Project on Complex Litigation, Council Member), American Foreign Law Association (Board of Directors 1970-77, Vice President 1973-76), The Association of the Bar of the City of New York (Foreign Law Committee 1966-69, Post Admission Legal Education Committee 1970-74, Executive Committee 1974-78, Sex and Law Committee 1978-79, Civil Rights Committee 1979-80) and American Bar Association (Member Committee on European Law 1967-72 and Chairman Committee on Comparative Procedure and Practice 1970-73 Section of International Law and Practice, Council Member Section of Individual Rights and Responsibilities 1975-81, Member Amicus Curiae Committee 1979-80 and Standing Committee on Federal Judicial Improvements). Member Committee on the Fifth International Appellate Judges Conference Judicial Conference of the U.S. 1988-90. Member Conference Planning and Program Committee 1976-80 and Council Advisory Committee on Planning for the District Courts 1979-80 Judicial Conference of the Second Circuit. Recipient Outstanding Teacher of Law Award from Society of American Law Teachers 1979 and Woman of Achievement Award from Barnard College 1980. Board of Directors Citizens Union 1972-74, Women's Law Fund 1972-80, Women's Action Alliance 1975-80 and National Woman's Party 1977-80. Director Women's Rights Project 1972-73, General Counsel 1973-80 and National Board of Directors 1974-80 American Civil Liberties Union. International Board Children's International Summer Villages 1963-67. Executive Committee 1972 and Nominating Committee 1979 Association of American Law Schools. Executive Committee 1975-77, Board of Governors 1975-77 and Vice President 1978-80 Society of American Law Teachers. Advisory Council Federation of Organizations for Professional Women 1977-80. National Advisory Board 1977-80 and Advisory Board to Legal Defense and Educational Fund 1977-80 Women's Equity Action League. Advisory Board Urban Institute Center for Policy Research on Women 1977-80. Member National Commission on Law and Social Action American Jewish Congress 1978-80. Fellow American Academy of Arts and Sciences. Presiding Member Historical Society of the District of Columbia Circuit.

Office: One First Street N.E., Washington, D.C. 20543-0001.

Telephone: (202) 479-3000.

GODBOLD, John C. *(Senior Judge, United States Court of Appeals Eleventh Circuit)* Appointed to Fifth Circuit for life by President Lyndon B. Johnson to term beginning 1966. Chief Judge Fifth Circuit Feb 2, 1981 to Sept 30, 1981. Assigned to Eleventh Circuit Oct 1, 1981. Chief Judge Eleventh Circuit 1981-86. Assumed Senior status Oct 23, 1987, serves by assignment. Born Coy Alabama March 24, 1920. Episcopalian. Educated at Auburn University B.S. 1940 and Harvard University J.D. 1948. Awarded honorary LL.D. Auburn University, Samford University and Stetson University. Member Omicron Delta Kappa and Phi Kappa Phi. Admitted to practice Alabama 1948 and U.S. District Court Middle District of Alabama 1948. In legal practice Montgomery 1948-66.

Author "Twenty Pages and Twenty Minutes—Effective Advocacy on Appeal" 30 Southwestern L. Jour. 801, 1976; "How to Communicate with the Bench" *Barrister* 1981; "Factfinding by Appellate Courts—An Available and Appropriate Power" 12, 365, 1982, "Scottsboro Comments" 28, 599, 1998 and "'Lawyer'—A Title of Honor" 29, 301, 1999 Cumberland L. Rev.; "Pro Bono Representation of Death Sentenced Inmates" 42 Record of The Association of the Bar of the City of New York 859, 871-876, 1987; and "Effective Legal Writing in Federal Court" Georgia State B. Jour. 1990. Instructor Auburn University 1945-46. Leslie Wright Professor of Law Cumberland School of Law of Samford University since 1990. Member Alabama State Bar, Montgomery County, Federal and American Bar Associations. Board of Directors 1976-81 and Director 1987-89 Federal Judicial Center. Recipient Edward J. Devitt Distinguished Service to Justice Award 1996 and Award for Significant Achievement in the Humanities from Auburn University. U.S. Army Field Artillery 1941-46.

Mailing address: P.O. Box 1589, Montgomery, Alabama 36102-1589.

Telephone: (334) 223-7210.

Fax: (334) 223-7544

GOLDBERG, Richard W. *(Senior Judge, United States Court of International Trade)* Appointed for life by President George Bush April 2, 1991. Assumed Senior status April 2, 2001, serves by assignment. Born Fargo North Dakota. Educated at University of Miami B.B.A. 1950 J.D. 1952. Admitted to practice Florida 1952, North Dakota 1952, U.S. Court of Appeals for the Armed Forces 1955, U.S. District Court District of Columbia 1958 and U.S. Supreme Court 1958. In legal practice Washington D.C. 1989-90.

State Senator North Dakota 1966-75. Acting Undersecretary and Deputy Undersecretary International and Commodity Programs U.S. Department of Agriculture 1983-89. Member State Bar Association of North Dakota, The District of Columbia Bar, The Florida Bar and American Bar Association. USAF JAGC 1953-56.

Office: One Federal Plaza, New York, New York 10278-0001.

Telephone: (212) 264-9741.

GOLDBERG, Stanley J. *(Special Trial Judge, United States Tax Court)* Appointed by U.S. Tax Court Chief Judge Samuel B. Sterrett Aug 4, 1985. Born Baltimore Maryland Feb 16, 1939. Educated at University of Maryland B.S. 1960 LL.B. 1964 and New York University. Admitted to practice Maryland 1964, New Jersey 1967 and U.S. District Courts District of Maryland 1964 and District of New Jersey 1967.

Tax Attorney General Litigation 1965-67 and Tax Litigation 1967-76, Special Trial Attorney 1976-84 and Assistant District Counsel Manhattan District 1984-85 Office of Chief Counsel Internal Revenue Service Department of the Treasury New York City.

Office: 400 Second Street N.W., Washington, D.C. 20217-0002.

Telephone: (202) 874-6059.

GOODWIN, Alfred T. *(Senior Judge, United States Court of Appeals Ninth Circuit)* Appointed for life by President Richard M. Nixon to term beginning Dec 17, 1971. Chief Judge June 15, 1988 to Jan 31, 1991. Assumed Senior status Feb 1, 1991, serves by assignment. Born Bellingham Washington June 29, 1923. Presbyterian. Educated at University of Oregon B.A. in Journalism 1947 J.D. 1951. Editor and contributor Oregon Law Review. Member Order of the Coif, Phi Delta Phi, Friars and Sigma Delta Chi. Awarded honorary LL.D. Lewis & Clark College 1976. Admitted to practice Oregon 1951. In legal practice Eugene 1951-55. Judge, Oregon Circuit Court (Lane County) July 1, 1955 to March 18, 1960, appointed by Governor Paul Patterson. Associate Justice, Oregon Supreme Court March 18, 1960 to Dec 22, 1969, appointed by Governor Mark O. Hatfield. Judge, U.S. District Court District of Oregon Dec 22, 1969 to Dec 17, 1971, appointed by President Richard M. Nixon.

Member Oregon Constitutional Revision Commission 1961-63. Member Committee on Court Administration Judicial Conference of the U.S., Oregon Bar-Press-Broadcasters Joint Committee (Chairman 1962-66), American Judicature Society, The American Law Institute, Oregon State Bar, Federal and American (Section of Legal Education and Chairman Legal Advisory Committee on Fair Trial-Free Press) Bar Associations. Served to Captain U.S. Army Infantry 1942-46 and Lieutenant Colonel USAR JAGC 1946-69 (retired). Editorial staff member and reporter Register Guard Eugene 1947-48 and part time 1949-50. President University of Oregon Alumni Association 1962-63. Board member University of Oregon Development Fund. Member Awards Jury Freedoms Foundation at Valley Forge 1964, Community Action Council, Salem Art Association, Central Lane YMCA, Salvation Army at Eugene and Human Relations Commission at Salem.

Office: Court of Appeals Building, 125 South Grand Avenue, Pasadena, California 91105-1652.

Telephone: (626) 229-7100.

GOULD, Ronald M. *(Judge, United States Court of Appeals Ninth Circuit)* Appointed for life by President Bill Clinton to term beginning Jan 3, 2000. Born St. Louis Missouri Oct 17, 1946. Educated at University of Pennsylvania B.S. 1968 and University of Michigan J.D. 1973. Law Clerk to Hon. Wade H. McCree, Jr., U.S. Court of Appeals Sixth Circuit 1973-74 and Hon. Potter Stewart, U.S. Supreme Court 1974-75. In legal practice Seattle 1975-99.

Adjunct Professor University of Washington School of Law 1986-89.

Office: Park Place Building 21st Floor, 1200 Sixth Avenue, Seattle, Washington 98101-3123.

Telephone: (206) 553-7344.

GRABER, Susan P. *(Judge, United States Court of Appeals Ninth Circuit)* Appointed for life by President Bill Clinton to term beginning April 1, 1998. Born Oklahoma City Oklahoma July 5, 1949. Jewish. Educated at Wellesley College B.A. with honors 1969 and Yale Law School J.D. 1972. Member Phi Beta Kappa. Admitted to practice New Mexico 1972, Ohio 1977 and Oregon 1978. In legal practice Santa Fe New Mexico 1974-75, Cincinnati Ohio 1975-78 and Portland Oregon 1978-88. Judge pro tem, Multnomah County District Court 1983-88. Judge, Oregon Court of Appeals 1988-90. Justice, Oregon Supreme Court May 2, 1990 to March 31, 1998, appointed by Governor Neil Goldschmidt.

Assistant Attorney General Bureau of Revenue New Mexico 1972-74. Arbitrator Oregon Circuit Court Fourth Judicial District 1985-88. Mediator U.S. District Court District of Oregon 1986-88. Chair Judicial Benefits Committee 1988-89. Governor's Advisory Council on Legal Services 1979-88. Co-chair Planning Committee Western Regional Conference on State-Federal Judicial Relationships. Author "Attorney Fees" *Civil Litigation* 1982, "Class Actions" *Civil Pleading and Practice* 1985, "Looking at Feminist Legal Theory from the Bench" 35 *The Advocate* Lewis & Clark College Northwestern School of Law Summer 1992, "Strategies for an Effective Brief" *Appeal and Review* 1993 and "Obiter Dictum: Substantive Legal Issues Create Tensions Between State and Federal Courts" 2 No. 7 *State-Federal Judicial Observer* joint publication of Federal Judicial Center and National Center for State Courts Oct 1994. Editorial Advisory Board *State-Federal Observer* 1994. Master American Inns of Court 1988-90. Board Member Oregon Law Foundation 1990-91. Member Magistrate Selection Committee U.S. District Court District of Oregon 1992. Member Oregon Women Lawyers, Oregon Judicial Conference (Chair Benefits Committee 1988-91, Member 1988-91 and Program Chair 1990 Education Committee, Member Retirement and Salary Committee since 1992), Oregon Appellate Judges Association (President 1992-93, Chair Education Committee 1993-94), State-Federal Judicial Council (Chair Subcommittee on Certification of State Law Questions 1994, Member Habeas Corpus Rules Committee since 1994), National Association of Women Judges, Judicial Conference of the Ninth Circuit (Lawyer Delegate 1982-84, Delegation Chair 1984-85, Chair Lawyer Representatives Coordinating Committee 1985-86, Program Subcommittee 1986-87 and Executive Committee 1987-88), Council on Court Procedures since 1989, The American Law Institute, Oregon State Bar (Member 1981-85 and Chair 1983-84 Legal Aid Committee, Chair Subcommittee on Trial Court Consolidation Judicial Administration Committee 1985-87, Member Committee on Pro Bono Service 1988-90) and American Bar Association.

Invitee to Symposia on State-Federal Judicial Relations American Judicature Society and State Justice Institute 1994. Recipient Founder's Award for Pro Bono Service Northwest Women's Law Center Seattle 1986. Listed in *Who's Who in the West, Who's Who of American Women, Who's Who in American Law* and *Who's Who in America.* Board of Governors 1981-83 and First/

GRABER, SUSAN P.—*Continued*

Second Vice President 1985-87 City Club of Portland. Member Jewish Community Relations Committee 1983-86. Director U.S. District Court District of Oregon Historical Society since 1985. Board of Visitors University of Oregon School of Law 1986-93 and Lewis & Clark College Northwestern University School of Law since 1994. Chair Rhodes Scholar Selection Committee Oregon since 1993. Member Temple Beth Israel.

Office: Pioneer Courthouse, 555 S.W. Yamhill Street, Portland, Oregon 97204-1396.

Telephone: (503) 326-7608.

GREENBERG, Morton I. *(Senior Judge, United States Court of Appeals Third Circuit)* Appointed for life by President Ronald Reagan to term beginning 1987. Assumed Senior status June 30, 2000, serves by assignment. Born Philadelphia Pennsylvania March 20, 1933. Jewish. Educated at University of Pennsylvania A.B. 1954 and Yale University LL.B. 1957. Board of Editors Yale Law Journal. Admitted to practice New Jersey 1958. In legal practice Cape May 1960-71. Judge, New Jersey Superior Court Appellate Division 1973-87, appointed by Governor William T. Cahill.

Deputy Attorney General Trenton 1958. County Attorney 1970-71 and First Assistant County Prosecutor 1971 Cape May County. Assistant Attorney General New Jersey 1971-73. Member Mercer County Bar Association.

Office: 219 Federal Bldg. & U.S. Courthouse, 402 East State Street, Trenton, New Jersey 08608.

Telephone: (609) 989-0436.

GREENE, William P., Jr. *(Judge, United States Court of Appeals for Veterans Claims)* Appointed by President Bill Clinton.

Office: 625 Indiana Avenue N.W., Suite 900, Washington, D.C. 20004-2950.

Telephone: (202) 501-5890.

GREGORY, Roger L. *(Judge, United States Court of Appeals Fourth Circuit)* Appointed for life by President Bill Clinton to term beginning Jan 18, 2001. Born Philadelphia Pennsylvania July 17, 1953. Educated at Virginia State University B.A. summa cum laude 1975 and University of Michigan J.D. 1978. Member Alpha Kappa Mu and Alpha Mu Gamma. Admitted to practice Michigan 1978 and Virginia 1980. In legal practice Detroit Michigan 1978-80 and Richmond Virginia 1980-2000.

Fellow Virginia Law Foundation. Member Virginia Association of Defense Attorneys (Board of Directors 1996-99), Fourth Circuit Judicial Conference, Old Dominion Bar Association (President 1990-92), Richmond (Board of Directors 1990-93), National and American Bar Associations. Recipient Alumnus of the Year Award from Leadership Metro Richmond Alumni Association 1991, Humanitarian Award from National Conference on Christians and Jews 1997 and President's Proclamation of Honor from Virginia State University. Former Chairman Industrial Development Authority of Richmond and Executive Committee Richmond Renaissance. Former Rector Virginia Commonwealth University. Former Member Board of Visitors Virginia State University and Board of Trustees Virginia State University Foundation. Board of Directors Christian Children's Fund.

Office: 212 U.S. Courthouse, 1000 East Main Street, Richmond, Virginia 23219.

Telephone: (804) 916-2607.

GUY, Ralph B., Jr. *(Senior Judge, United States Court of Appeals Sixth Circuit)* Appointed for life by President Ronald Reagan. Assumed Senior status Sept 1, 1994, serves by assignment. Born Aug 30, 1929. Educated at University of Michigan A.B. 1951 J.D. 1953. Member Phi Alpha Delta. In legal practice 1954-55. Former Judge, U.S. District Court Eastern District of Michigan, appointed by President Gerald R. Ford to term beginning June 7, 1976.

Assistant Corporation Counsel 1955-58 and Corporation Counsel 1958-69 City of Dearborn. Chief Assistant U.S. Attorney 1969-70 and U.S. Attorney 1970-76 Eastern District of Michigan. Member Federal Executive Board 1970-76 (Director 1971-73) and U.S. Attorney General's Advisory Committee (Chairman 1974-75). Member American Judicature Society, Sixth Circuit District Judges Association (President 1984-85), Federal Judges Association (Director since 1982), Michigan Association of Municipal Attorneys (President 1962-64), National Institute of Municipal Law Officers (Michigan State Chairman 1964-69), State Bar of Michigan (Chairman Public Corporation Law Section 1961-62, Representative Assembly 1972-75, Board of Commissioners 1975-87), Dearborn (President 1959-69), Federal (President 1974-75), and American (State Chairman Section of State, Urban and Local Government Law 1965-70) Bar Associations. Recipient Outstanding Young Man of 1961 Award from Dearborn Chamber of Commerce, Civic Achievement Award from Dearborn Rotary Club 1971 and Distinguished Alumni Award from University of Michigan Alumni Club of Dearborn 1972. Wayne County Board of Supervisors 1958-69. Election Commissioner 1958-69 and Public Health Commissioner 1958-69 City of Dearborn. Detroit Metropolitan Regional Planning Commission 1960-68 (Executive Council 1965-68). President Dearborn Housing Commission 1961-69. Detroit-Wayne County Building Authority Treasurer 1966-73. Member Dearborn Board of Education (Chairman, member College Study Committee 1970 and School Study Committee 1973-74), Michigan Municipal League (Board of Directors 1966-69), Out-County Supervisors Association (President 1965), Neighborhood Legal Services (Board of Directors 1965-71), YMCA (Board of Management 1965-73), Dearborn Rotary Club (President 1973-74) and University of Michigan Alumni Club of Dearborn (President 1961-62).

Mailing address: P.O. Box 7910, Ann Arbor, Michigan 48107-7910.

Telephone: (734) 741-2300.

HAINES, James B., Jr. *(Judge, Bankruptcy Appellate Panel First Circuit)* Selected by the Judicial Council of the First Circuit. Also Chief Judge, U.S. Bankruptcy Court District of Maine. Appointed by U.S. Court of Appeals First Circuit judges.

Office: 537 Congress Street, Portland, Maine 04101.

Telephone: (207) 780-3653.

HALL, Cynthia Holcomb *(Senior Judge, United States Court of Appeals Ninth Circuit)* Appointed for life by President Ronald Reagan to term beginning 1984. Assumed Senior status Aug 31, 1997, serves by assignment. Born Los Angeles California Feb 19, 1929. Episcopalian. Educated at Stanford University A.B. 1951 J.D. 1954 and New York University LL.M. in Taxation 1960. Law Clerk to Hon. Richard H. Chambers, U.S. Court of Appeals Ninth Circuit 1954-55. Research Assistant to Editor Tax Law Review 1959-60. Admitted to

HALL, CYNTHIA HOLCOMB—*Continued*

practice Arizona 1954 and California 1956. In legal practice Beverly Hills California 1966-72. Judge, U.S. Tax Court 1972-81. Judge, U.S. District Court Central District of California 1981-84.

Trial Attorney Trial Section of Tax Division Department of Justice 1960-64. Attorney-Adviser Office of Tax Legislative Counsel Treasury Department 1964-66. Member State Bar of Arizona, State Bar of California and American Bar Association. Lieutenant j.g. USNR Bureau of Naval Personnel and Office of Navy Judge Advocate General 1951-53. Republican.

Office: Court of Appeals Building, 125 South Grand Avenue, Pasadena, California 91105-1652.

Telephone: (626) 229-7300.

HALPERN, James S. *(Judge, United States Tax Court)* Appointed by the President.

Office: 400 Second Street N.W., Washington, D.C. 20217-0002.

Telephone: (202) 606-8881.

HAMILTON, Clyde Henry *(Senior Judge, United States Court of Appeals Fourth Circuit)* Appointed for life by the President. Assumed Senior status Nov 30, 1999, serves by assignment. Born Edgefield South Carolina Feb 8, 1934. Educated at Wofford College B.S. 1956 and George Washington University J.D. with honors 1961. Board of Editors George Washington Law Review 1959-60. Admitted to practice South Carolina 1961 and U.S. District Court District of South Carolina 1961. In legal practice Edgefield 1961-63 and Spartanburg 1963-81. Former Judge, U.S. District Court District of South Carolina, appointed by President Ronald Reagan to term beginning Jan 8, 1982.

Editorial Staff Cumulative Index of Congressional Committee Hearings 1955-58. Reference Assistant U.S. Senate Library 1958-61. Board of Directors 1969-76 and General Counsel 1969-80 Synalloy Corporation. Member South Carolina Bar. Board of Commissioners on Grievances and Discipline South Carolina Supreme Court 1980-81. Listed in *Who's Who in American Law*. First Lieutenant U.S. Army 1956-58. Captain USAR 1962. Delegate Spartanburg County Republican Convention 1976 and 1980, Fourth Congressional District Republican Convention 1976 and 1980 and South Carolina Republican Convention 1976 and 1980. Trustee Administrative Board 1980-83 and Former Chairman Finance Committee Trinity United Methodist Church. President Spartanburg County Arts Council 1971-73. President 1972-74 and Sustaining Trustee 1975-81 The Spartanburg Day School. Member Steering Committee, Undergraduate Merit Fellowship Program and Estate Planning Council Converse College. Trustee Spartanburg Methodist College 1979-84. Enjoys tennis, fishing and watching sports.

Office: 1250 Bank of America Plaza, 1901 Main Street Compartment 704, Columbia, South Carolina 29201-2435.

Telephone: (803) 765-5461.

HANSEN, David R. *(Senior Judge, United States Court of Appeals Eighth Circuit)* Appointed for life by President George Bush to term beginning Nov 18, 1991. Chief Judge Feb 1, 2002 to March 31, 2003. Assumed Senior status April 1, 2003, serves by assignment. Born Exira Iowa March 16, 1938. Episcopalian. Educated at Northwest Missouri State University B.A. with highest honors 1960 and George Washington University J.D. with honors 1963. Recipient Edward P. Morgan Citizenship Award as Outstanding Senior 1960. Member Tau Kappa Epsilon (President) and Phi Delta Phi (Vice President). Admitted to practice Iowa 1963, U.S. Court of Military Appeals 1964 and U.S. Supreme Court 1967. In legal practice Iowa Falls 1968-76. Judge, Iowa Falls Police Court 1969-73. District Judge, Iowa District Court Second Judicial District Sept 9, 1976 to March 11, 1986. Judge, U.S. District Court Northern District of Iowa March 11, 1986 to Nov 18, 1991.

Member Iowa State Bar Association. Captain U.S. Army JAGC 1964-68. Former speaker at training conferences for judges and magistrates. Republican. Assistant Clerk to Minority Appropriations Committee U.S. House of Representatives 1960-62. Administrative Aide to Congressman Ben F. Jensen 1962-63. Chairman Hardin County Republican Party 1975-76. Member Rotary Club 1968-76 and U.S. Capitol Historical Society. Enjoys woodworking and gardening.

Office: 304 Federal Bldg. & U.S. Courthouse, 101 First Street S.E., Cedar Rapids, Iowa 52401.

Telephone: (319) 364-5815.

HARKINS, Kenneth R. *(Senior Judge, United States Court of Federal Claims)* Appointed by President Ronald Reagan to term beginning Oct 1, 1982. Assumed Senior status Dec 1, 1986, serves by assignment. Born Cadiz Ohio Sept 1, 1921. Educated at The Ohio State University B.A. 1943 LL.B. 1948 J.D. 1967. Member Phi Eta Sigma, Phi Beta Kappa and Order of the Coif. Commissioner, U.S. Court of Claims 1971 to Sept 30, 1982.

Attorney-Advisor Housing and Home Finance Agency 1949-51. Trial Attorney U.S. Department of Justice 1951-55. U.S. Army 1943-46. Member Committee on the Judiciary House of Representatives 1955-60 and 1964-71.

Office: National Courts Building, 717 Madison Place N.W., Washington, D.C. 20005-1086.

Telephone: (202) 219-9548.

HARTZ, Harris L. *(Judge, United States Court of Appeals Tenth Circuit)* Appointed for life by President George W. Bush to term beginning Dec 11, 2001. Born Baltimore Maryland Jan 20, 1947. Jewish. Educated at Harvard University A.B. summa cum laude 1967 J.D. magna cum laude 1972. Developments Editor Harvard Law Review 1971-72. Admitted to practice New Mexico 1972. In legal practice Albuquerque 1972-88. Former Judge and Chief Judge, New Mexico Court of Appeals, appointed by Governor Garrey Carruthers to term beginning Oct 1988.

Assistant U.S. Attorney District of New Mexico 1972-75. Visiting Assistant Professor of Law University of Illinois College of Law 1976. Executive Director New Mexico Organized Crime Prevention Commission 1977-79. Advisor The American Law Institute Restatement of the Law (Third) Agency since 1977. Member American Judicature Society, The American Law Institute and American Bar Association (Advisory Committee, Standing Committee on Law and National Security 1995-97). Chairman New Mexico Racing Commission 1987-88. Republican Party Nominee New Mexico Supreme Court 1986, 1992 and 1996.

Office: 710 U.S. Courthouse, 333 Lomas Boulevard N.W., Albuquerque, New Mexico 87102.

Telephone: (505) 348-2350.

HAWKINS, Michael Daly *(Judge, United States Court of Appeals Ninth Circuit)* Appointed for life by President Bill Clinton to term beginning Sept 16, 1994. Born Winslow Arizona Feb 12, 1945. Lutheran. Educated at Arizona State University B.A. 1967 J.D. cum laude 1970 and University of Virginia LL.M. 1998. Comment Editor Arizona State Law Journal 1968-70. Admitted to practice Arizona 1970, U.S. Court of Military Appeals 1971, U.S. District Court District of Arizona 1973, U.S. Court of Appeals Ninth Circuit 1974 and U.S. Supreme Court 1974. In legal practice Phoenix 1973-77 and 1980-94. Judge pro tem, Arizona Court of Appeals Division One 1985-89 and 1993-94.

U.S. Attorney District of Arizona 1977-80. Special Prosecutor The Navajo Nation 1981-82 and 1987-89. Author Note "Resisting The Unlawful Taking of Blood" 288, 1969 and Book Review "Perjury: The Hiss-Chambers Case" by A. Weinstein 883, 1977 Arizona State L. Jour.; "Law Offices Searches: A Lawyer's Nightmare" May 1985 and "The Supreme Court & The Modern Prosecutor: Less Talk, Less Cop" Sept 1993 *The Maricopa Lawyer;* "The Grand Jury 200 Years Later" *Arizona Attorney* Aug-Sept 1991; "From the Bench—Your Worst Nightmare: Things That Can Go Bump on Appeal" 23 No. 3 *Litigation* American Bar Association Spring 1996; and "Dining with the Dogs: Reflections on the History of the Criticism of Judges" 57 Ohio State L. Jour. 1353-1364 Fall-Winter 1996. Co-author Comment "Voter Restrictions for Special Purpose Districts: A Case Study of the Salt River Project" Arizona State L. Jour. 636, 1969 and Paper "RCRA Enforcement: Avoiding Civil and Criminal Liability" *Environmental Management Review* Feb 1992. Important Decisions: United States v. Estrada-Plata 57 F.3d 757, 9th Cir. 1995; Erickson v. United States ex rel Dept. Health & Human Services 67 F.3d 858, 9th Cir. 1995; International Ambassador Programs v. Archexpo 68 F.3d 337, 9th Cir. 1995; United States v. Rubin 79 F.3d 109, 9th Cir. 1996; Northwest Forest Resources v. Glickman 82 F.3d 825, 9th Cir. 1996; Springfield v. United States 88 F.3d 750, 9th Cir. 1996; Smith v. Jackson 84 F.3d 1213, 9th Cir. 1996; Canseco v. Construction Laborers Pension Trust 93 F.3d 600, 9th Cir. 1996; United States v. Annigoni 96 F.3d 1132, 9th Cir. 1996; Federation of African American Contractors v. City of Oakland 96 F.3d 1204, 9th Cir. 1996; Amarel v. Connell 102 F.3d 1494, 9th Cir. 1997; Gabbert v. Conn 131 F.3d 793, 9th Cir. 1997; and AT&SF Ry. Co. v. Brown & Bryant 132 F.3d 1295, 9th Cir. 1997. Chairman U.S. Magistrates and Bankruptcy Judges Merit Selection Committee 1983-84 and Governor's Task Force on Juvenile Corrections 1990-91. Lawyer Representative and Chairman Arizona Delegation 1982-83 and Member Executive Committee 1983-86 Judicial Conference of the Ninth Circuit. Member Appellate Courts Merit Selection Commission 1985-89 and National Conference of Uniform State Law Commissioners 1989-92. Member Arizona Trial Lawyers Association (Secretary 1976-77, Board of Directors 1976-78), National Association of Former U.S. Attorneys (President 1989-90), State Bar of Arizona (Local Administrative Disciplinary Committee 1976-85, Continuing Legal Education Committee 1977-80, Federal Courts Committee 1980-86), Maricopa County (Board of Directors 1975-77 and 1981-89, President 1987-88) and Federal (President Arizona Chapter 1981-82) Bar Associations.

Lecturer and panelist at various Continuing Legal Education programs on Civil Trial Practice, Evidence and Criminal Procedure. Attended Appellate Judges Seminar for New Judges New York University School of Law July 8-14, 1995 and "The Community of Courts: The Compleat Appellate Judge" co-sponsored by State Justice Institute, Federal Judicial Center and Appellate Judges Conference Judicial Division American Bar Association, Washington D.C. March 28-31, 1996. Panelist "Ninth Circuit Civil, Criminal and Bankruptcy Practice: Everything You Always Wanted to Know About Circuit Appeals But Were Afraid to Ask" Appellate Practice Section State Bar of Arizona March 1, 1996. Listed in *Outstanding Young Men in America* 1978, *Who's Who in America* since 1978 and *Who's Who in American Law* since 1979. Recipient Distinguished Achievement Award from Arizona State University College of Law 1979 and Alumni Achievement Award from Arizona State University 1995. Served to Captain USMC 1970-73. Special Court Martial Military Judge 1973. Democrat. Public Member Administrative Conference of United States since 1989. Member Arizona Lottery Commission 1980-83, Centennial Commission Arizona State University 1981-85, Dean Search Committee Arizona State University College of Law 1988-89 and Oversight Committee on Community Behavioral Health and Substance Abuse Treatment 1992-93.

Office: 510 U.S. Courthouse, 401 West Washington Street, Phoenix, Arizona 85003-2151.

Telephone: (602) 322-7310.

HEANEY, Gerald W. *(Senior Judge, United States Court of Appeals Eighth Circuit)* Appointed for life by President Lyndon B. Johnson to term beginning Dec 1, 1966. Assumed Senior status Dec 31, 1988, serves by assignment. Born Goodhue Minnesota Jan 29, 1918. Catholic. Educated at St. Thomas College 1935-37 and University of Minnesota B.S.L. 1939 LL.B. 1941. Admitted to practice Minnesota. Began legal practice Duluth.

Author "Labor Relations—A National or a State Problem" 26 Minnesota L. Rev. 359, 1942 and "The Minnesota and National Labor Relations Acts—A Substantive and Procedural Comparison" 38 Minnesota L. Rev. 1954. Member Eleventh Judicial District, Minnesota State (Labor Law Section Chairman 1959) and American (Labor Law Section) Bar Associations. Captain USAS 1942-46. Democrat. Democratic National Committeeman from Minnesota 1955-60.

Office: 315 Federal Bldg. & U.S. Courthouse, 515 West First Street, Duluth, Minnesota 55802.

Telephone: (218) 529-3530.

HENDERSON, Karen LeCraft *(Judge, United States Court of Appeals District of Columbia Circuit)* Appointed for life by President George Bush to term beginning July 1990. Born Oberlin Ohio July 11, 1944. Educated at Duke University B.A. 1966 and University of North Carolina School of Law J.D. 1969. In legal practice Chapel Hill North Carolina 1969-70 and Charleston and Columbia South Carolina 1983-86. Judge, U.S. District Court District of South Carolina 1986-90, appointed by President Ronald Reagan.

Assistant Attorney General 1973-78, Senior Assistant Attorney General and Director Special Litigation Section

HENDERSON, KAREN LECRAFT—*Continued*

1978-82 and Deputy Attorney General and Director Criminal Division 1982-83 South Carolina.

Office: 3118 U.S. Courthouse, 333 Constitution Avenue N.W., Washington, D.C. 20001-2866.

Telephone: (202) 216-7370.

HENRY, Robert Harlan *(Judge, United States Court of Appeals Tenth Circuit)* Appointed for life by President Bill Clinton to term beginning May 16, 1994. Born Shawnee Oklahoma April 3, 1953. Educated at University of Oklahoma B.A. with high honors 1974 J.D. 1976. Honorary LL.D. Oklahoma City University 2000. Member Phi Beta Kappa and Phi Delta Phi. In legal practice Shawnee Oklahoma 1977-87.

Attorney General Oklahoma 1987-91. Co-author with J. Rarick "The Oklahoma Powers of Appointment Act of 1977" 32 Oklahoma L. Rev. 787, 1979. Author "A Black Hat for the Lone Ranger? The Attorney General as Defender of Tort Claims" *The Journal of State Government* 112 May-June 1988; Preface *Oklahoma Business Organizations* by Irving L. Faught Aspen Publishers 1990; "The Oklahoma Constitutional Revision Commission: A Call to Arms or the Sounding of Retreat?" 17 No. 1 Spring 1992 and "Forward into the Past: Observations Regarding George Anastaplo's 'Lectures for Students of Law'" 20 No. 1, 1995 Oklahoma City University L. Rev.; "An Independent Judiciary" 28 No. 1-2 Southwestern Association of Law Libraries 1996; "Catching the Jurisprudential Wave: Bernard Schwartz's *Main Currents in American Legal Thought*" 33 Tulsa L. Jour. 385, 1997; "The Lawyer Who Killed Jim Crow" *The American Lawyer* 128 Nov 1988; Chapter 2 "The Play and the Players" *The Burger Court: Counter-Revolution or Confirmation?* Oxford Press 1998; "Deliberations About Democracy: Revolutions, Republicanism, and Reform" 34 Willamette L. Rev. 533, 1998; Book Review "The Value(s) of Oliver Wendell Holmes, Jr.: Through a Magic Mirror Darkly" 5 Green Bag 2d 105, 2001; and Foreword *He Made it Safe to Murder, The Life of Moman Pruiett* by Howard K. Berry Oklahoma Heritage Association 2001. Important Decisions: Miller v. Gentry (In re Miller) No. 94-3225, 63 U.S.L.W. 2723 May 19, 1995; Gail v. United States No. 94-4243, 64 U.S.L.W. 2029 June 27, 1995; Shillinger v. Haworth No. 94-8062, 64 U.S.L.W. 2339 Nov 17, 1995; and Villanueva v. Carere No. 94-1454, 64 U.S.L.W. 2792 June 4, 1996.

Lecturer on Business Law Oklahoma Baptist University 1978-80 and Political Science Oklahoma City University 1993. Professor of Law 1991-94 and Dean 1993-94 Oklahoma City University School of Law. Commissioner National Conference of Commissioners on Uniform State Laws since 1982. Chair Oklahoma Constitutional Revision Committee 1991-92 and Lawyer's Advisory Committee since 1997 and History Committee since 1998 U.S. Court of Appeals Tenth Circuit. Member Civil Justice Reform Act Advisory Group Western District of Oklahoma 1993-94 and Judicial Outreach Program Institute on International Law in Public Affairs since 2000. Master William J. Holloway, Jr. Inn American Inns of Court. Former Member Oklahoma Trial Lawyers Association and National Association of Attorneys General (Supreme Court Advocacy Committee). Member The American Law Institute, American Society of International Law (Advisory Board Committee), Oklahoma County, Oklahoma and American (Committees on State Justice Initiatives since 2000 and Africa Law Initiative Council since 2000) Bar Associations. Named Humanitarian of the Year by Oklahoma City Region National Conference of Christians and Jews 1996. Recipient E. T. Dunlap Award for Public Service from Southeastern Oklahoma University 1998 and Federal Judge of the Year Award from Oklahoma Trial Lawyers Association 1999. State Representative Oklahoma House of Representatives 1976-86. Advisory Board Jasmine Moran Foundation Children's Museum since 1990. Board of Directors VERA Institute of Justice since 1999 and Oklahoma Medical Research Foundation since 2000.

Office: 2421 U.S. Courthouse, 200 N.W. Fourth Street, Oklahoma City, Oklahoma 73102.

Telephone: (405) 609-5440.

Fax: (405) 609-5449

HEWITT, Emily Clark *(Judge, United States Court of Federal Claims)* Appointed by President Bill Clinton to term beginning Oct 22, 1998. Term expires Oct 2013. Educated at Cornell University A.B. 1966, Union Theological Seminary M.Phil. 1975 and Harvard Law School J.D. 1978. In legal practice Boston 1978-93.

General Counsel U.S. General Services Administration 1993-98. Ordained Deacon 1972 and Ordained Priest 1974 Episcopal Church.

Office: National Courts Building, 717 Madison Place N.W., Washington, D.C. 20005.

Telephone: (202) 219-9992.

HIGGINBOTHAM, Patrick E. *(Judge, United States Court of Appeals Fifth Circuit)* Appointed for life by President Ronald Reagan to term beginning 1982. Born McCalla Alabama Dec 16, 1938. Educated at University of Texas and University of Alabama B.A., LL.B. Awarded honorary LL.D. Southern Methodist University 1989. Note Editor Alabama Law Review. Member Omicron Delta Kappa, Bench and Bar Honor Society and Order of the Coif. Began legal practice Dallas. Judge, U.S. District Court Northern District of Texas 1975-82, appointed by President Gerald R. Ford, becoming the youngest sitting federal judge in the U.S. at time of appointment.

Former Member Board of Editors *American Bar Journal.* Adjunct Professor of Law Southern Methodist University Law School. Instructor in Constitutional Law Louisiana State University program, Aix-en-Province France and University of Texas School of Law 1998. John Sparkman jurist in residence University of Alabama School of Law Fall 1995, 1997 and 1999. Member American Delegation assisting Albanian government to draft a constitution 1992. President American Inns of Court 1996-2000. Board of Overseers Institute for Civil Justice, RAND. Research Fellow, Trustee and Chair Board of Trustees The Center for American and International Law. Past President Dallas Inn of Court. Former Director Dallas Bar Association, Dallas Bar Foundation and American Judicature Society. Former Judicial Member Section Council Section of Antitrust Law and Former Chairman Appellate Judges Conference Judicial Administration Division American Bar Association. Former Member and Chairman Advisory Committee on Civil Rules Council of the Federal and State Judiciary. Former Advisor Study of Habeas Corpus National Center for State Courts. Fellow American Bar Foundation. Member The American Law Institute (Advisory Committee Complex Litigation Program) and The Maritime Law Association of the U.S. Faculty Member Federal

HIGGINBOTHAM, PATRICK E.—*Continued*

Judicial Center. Instructor National Institute for Trial Advocacy. Conferee "American Assembly on Law and the American Future" Stanford University 1975 and "Pound Conference" St. Paul Minnesota 1976. American Judiciary Representative lecturing on judicial interpretations of constitutional text Supreme Court of Brazil and Brazil's Constituent Assembly May 1988. Named Outstanding Alumnus by University of Texas at Arlington 1978 and One of the Nation's 100 Most Powerful Persons for the 80's by *Next* Magazine April 1981. Recipient Dan Meador Award for service to University of Alabama School of Law 1986, Samuel E. Gates Litigation Award for significant contributions to improvement of litigation process from American College of Trial Lawyers 1997 and The A. Sherman Christensen Award for leadership from American Inns of Court 2002. USAF JAGC 1961-64. Former Member Search Committee for Endowed Chairs and Board of Visitors Southern Methodist University. Former Member Board of Visitors University of Chicago. Member Philosophical Society of Texas. Lay Member and Former Member Administrative Board Highland Park United Methodist Church.

Office: 1302 Federal Bldg. & U.S. Courthouse, 1100 Commerce Street, Dallas, Texas 75242-1003.

Telephone: (214) 767-0793.

HILL, James Clinkscales *(Senior Judge, United States Court of Appeals Eleventh Circuit)* Appointed to Fifth Circuit for life by President Gerald R. Ford to term beginning May 26, 1976. Assigned to Eleventh Circuit Oct 1, 1981. Assumed Senior status Oct 15, 1989, serves by assignment. Born Darlington South Carolina Jan 8, 1924. Southern Baptist. Educated at University of South Carolina B.S.C. 1948 (class of 1944 interrupted by military service) and Emory University J.D. 1948. Admitted to practice Georgia 1948. In legal practice Atlanta 1948-74. Judge, U.S. District Court Northern District of Georgia 1974-76.

Life Fellow American Bar Foundation. Fellow American College of Trial Lawyers. Member American Judicature Society, The American Law Institute, World Association of Judges, Lawyers Club of Atlanta, Old War Horse Lawyers Club (Past President), State Bar of Georgia, Atlanta, Federal and American Bar Associations. Staff Sergeant USAAC 1943-45. Republican. Enjoys travel, golf, photography, flying, scuba diving and mountain climbing.

Mailing address: P.O. Box 52598, Jacksonville, Florida 32201-2598.

Telephone: (904) 232-2284.

HILL, William Alexander *(Judge, Bankruptcy Appellate Panel Eighth Circuit)* Selected by the Judicial Council of the Eighth Circuit to term beginning Sept 1996. Also Judge, U.S. Bankruptcy Court District of North Dakota. Appointed by U.S. District Court judges to term beginning March 21, 1984. Reappointed by U.S. Court of Appeals Eighth Circuit judges May 24, 1988. Born Carmel California Aug 21, 1946. Episcopalian. Educated at University of North Dakota B.S.B.A. 1968 J.D. 1971. Editorial staff member North Dakota Law Review 1969-71. Law Clerk to Chief Judge Paul Benson, U.S. District Court District of North Dakota 1972-74. Member Sigma Nu and Phi Alpha Delta. Admitted to practice North Dakota 1971, Minnesota 1974, U.S. District Court 1974, U.S. Court of Appeals Eighth Circuit 1974 and U.S. Tax Court 1978. In legal practice Fargo North Dakota 1974-83. Part-time Magistrate, U.S. District Court District of North Dakota 1975-83.

Deputy Secretary of State 1971-72. Member National Conference of Bankruptcy Judges, State Bar Association of North Dakota, Cass County and Minnesota State Bar Associations. Republican. Member Fargo Chamber of Commerce, Historical Society, Masons and Boy Scouts.

Office: 350 U.S. Courthouse, 655 First Avenue North, Fargo, North Dakota 58102-4952.

Telephone: (701) 297-7140.

HILLMAN, William C. *(Judge, Bankruptcy Appellate Panel First Circuit)* Selected by the Judicial Council of the First Circuit to term beginning 1996. Also Judge, U.S. Bankruptcy Court District of Massachusetts. Appointed by U.S. Court of Appeals First Circuit judges to term beginning 1991. Chief Judge Bankruptcy Court 1998-2002. Educated at University of Chicago and Boston University School of Law J.D. cum laude LL.M. Secretary and Note Editor Boston University Law Review. Admitted to practice Massachusetts, Rhode Island, U.S. District Courts District of Connecticut, District of Massachusetts and District of Rhode Island, U.S. Courts of Appeals First, Fifth and Eleventh Circuits and U.S Supreme Court. In legal practice Providence Rhode Island 1957-91. Judge of Probate Barrington Rhode Island 1974-84. Deputy Judge of Probate West Greenwich Rhode Island 1984-91 and Hopkinton Rhode Island 1990.

Author "What's in a Name: The UCC Filing System in Court" 44 Oklahoma L. Rev. 151, 1991; "Introductory Note: Symposium on Revised Article 9 of the Uniform Commercial Code" 73 Bankruptcy L. Jour. xi Winter 1999; and "Preview of Coming Attractions: Revised Article 9 of the UCC" Norton Bankruptcy Law Advisor 7 Sept 1999. Editorial Advisory Board American Bankruptcy L. Jour. 1993-98. Co-author with Hon. Joan N. Feeney "Property of the Estate" *Chapter 11 Theory & Practice: A Guide to Reorganization* LRP Publications 1994 and with Margaret M. Crouch *Bankruptcy Deskbook* and annual supplements PLI Press 2000. Adjunct Faculty of Bankruptcy Suffolk University Law School 1996-98 and Northeastern University School of Law since 1998 and Advanced Commercial Law Seminars Boston College Law School 1996 and 2001. Secretary 1969-95 and Commissioner since 1969 Rhode Island Commission on Uniform State Laws. Member 1975-80 and Secretary 1977-80 Disciplinary Board Rhode Island Supreme Court. Chairman 1982-84 and Director 1982-88 Rhode Island Law Institute. Honorary Consultant The Law Reform Commission Australia 1984-87. Member Article 9 Review Committee Uniform Commercial Code Permanent Editorial Board 1989-92. Life Member National Conference of Commissioners on Uniform State Laws (Chairman Uniform Marital Property Act Drafting Committee 1979-83 and Uniform Franchise and Business Opportunities Act Review Committee 1983-87, Member UCC Article 6 Revision Drafting Committee 1987-88, UCC Article 5 Revision Drafting Committee 1990-95, UCC Article 2 Revision Review Committee 1991-94, UCC Article 9 Revision Drafting Committee since 1993). Fellow American College of Bankruptcy. Presenter "Remedies for Breach of Contract," "The Law of Contracts" and "Secured Transactions" U.S. Agency for International Development 1996; "Revised Article 9 of the Uniform Commercial Code" ALI-ABA 1997; "Chapter 11 Case Administration" 1997, "Leases and Li-

HILLMAN, WILLIAM C.—*Continued*

censes" 1998 and "Bankruptcy Litigation Forum" 2000 American Bankruptcy Institute; "Bankruptcy Court Jurisdiction and Venue" 1999, "The Debtor's Duties" 2000 and "Workouts and Bankruptcies in the eCommerce Economy" 2001 Practising Law Institute; "Getting Ready for an Internet Company Bankruptcy" Business Law Section American Bar Association 2000; "First Day Orders" Federal Judicial Center 2000; "Revised Article 9: Transition Rules" State Bar of Idaho 2001; and "Revised Article 9: Scope and Terminology Changes" Glasser Legal Works 2001.

Office: 1101 Federal Building, 10 Causeway Street, Boston, Massachusetts 02222-1074.

Telephone: (617) 565-6097.

HODGES, Robert H., Jr. *(Judge, United States Court of Federal Claims)* Appointed by President George Bush to term beginning 1990. Term expires 2005. Born Columbia South Carolina Sept 11, 1944. Educated at University of South Carolina B.S. 1966 J.D. 1969.

Former Vice President and General Counsel First National Bank of South Carolina. Former Executive Vice President and General Counsel South Carolina Bankers Association. Former Legislative Aide to Senator Strom Thurmond. Former Legislative Assistant to Congressman Floyd Spence.

Office: National Courts Building, 717 Madison Place N.W., Washington, D.C. 20005-1086.

Telephone: (202) 219-9573.

HOLLOWAY, William J., Jr. *(Senior Judge, United States Court of Appeals Tenth Circuit)* Appointed for life by President Lyndon B. Johnson to term beginning Sept 26, 1968. Chief Judge 1984-91. Assumed Senior status May 31, 1992, serves by assignment. Born Hugo Oklahoma June 23, 1923. United Methodist. Educated at University of Oklahoma A.B. 1947 and Harvard Law School LL.B. 1950. Awarded honorary Doctor of Laws from Oklahoma City University Aug 1991. Admitted to practice Oklahoma 1950, U.S. Court of Appeals Tenth Circuit 1952 and U.S. Supreme Court 1958. In legal practice Oklahoma City 1952-68.

Important Decisions: Aspen Highlands Skiing Corp. v. Aspen Skiing Co. 738 F.2d 1509, 10th Cir. 1984 aff'd 472 U.S. 585, 1985; and Grant v. Meyer 828 F.2d 1446, 10th Cir. 1987 aff'd 486 U.S. 414, 1988. Member Oklahoma County, Oklahoma, Federal and American Bar Associations. Recipient President's Award from Oklahoma Bar Association 1988 and Award from Oklahoma City Chapter Phi Beta Kappa 1989. U.S. Army May 1943 to Aug 1946.

Mailing address: P.O. Box 1767, Oklahoma City, Oklahoma 73101-1767.

Telephone: (405) 609-5420.

HORN, Marian Blank *(Senior Judge, United States Court of Federal Claims)* Appointed by President Ronald Reagan to term beginning April 15, 1986. Assumed Senior status, serves by assignment. Educated at Columbia University and Fordham University School of Law J.D. Admitted to practice District of Columbia, New York and U.S. Supreme Court.

Former Deputy Chief Appeals Bureau District Attorney's Office Bronx County New York. Former Deputy Associate Solicitor for Surface Mining, Associate Solicitor for General Law, Acting Solicitor and Principal Deputy Solicitor U.S. Department of the Interior. Former Adjunct Professor of Law Washington College of Law of American University. Adjunct Professor of Trial Advocacy George Washington University National Law Center. Former Deputy Assistant General Counsel for Procurement and Financial Incentives, Senior Attorney Strategic Petroleum Reserve and Litigation Attorney U.S. Department of Energy.

Office: National Courts Building, 717 Madison Place N.W., Washington, D.C. 20005-1086.

Telephone: (202) 219-9576.

HOWARD, Jeffrey R. *(Judge, United States Court of Appeals First Circuit)* Appointed for life by President George W. Bush.

Office: 2500 U.S. Courthouse, One Courthouse Way, Boston, Massachusetts 02210.

Telephone: (603) 225-1525.

HUG, Procter, Jr. *(Senior Judge, United States Court of Appeals Ninth Circuit)* Appointed for life by President Jimmy Carter to term beginning Sept 16, 1977. Chief Judge March 1, 1996 to Dec 1, 2000. Assumed Senior status Jan 1, 2002, serves by assignment. Born Reno Nevada March 11, 1931. Catholic. Educated at University of Nevada B.S. with honors 1953 and Stanford University J.D. 1958. Staff member Stanford University Law Review. Admitted to practice Nevada 1958. Began legal practice Reno 1958.

Deputy Attorney General 1972-76. Author "Nevada Pattern Civil Jury Instructions" State Bar of Nevada. Member The American Law Institute, American Judicature Society, State Bar of Nevada and American Bar Association (State Delegate to House of Delegates 1972-78 and Board of Governors 1976-78). Board of Directors The National Judicial College 1977-78. Recipient Outstanding Alumnus Award from University of Nevada 1967, Distinguished Nevadan Award from University of Nevada 1982 and Alumnus of the Year Award from University of Nevada 1988. Lieutenant USN 1953-55. Democrat. Former member Nevada Democratic Central Committee. Director Reno Chamber of Commerce 1976-77. President University of Nevada Alumni Association. Regent University of Nevada 1962 (Chairman 1971-72). Enjoys skiing, tennis and sailing.

Office: 708 U.S. Courthouse & Federal Bldg., 400 South Virginia Street, Reno, Nevada 89501.

Telephone: (775) 686-5949.

HULL, Frank M. *(Judge, United States Court of Appeals Eleventh Circuit)* Appointed for life by President Bill Clinton to term beginning Sept 4, 1997. Born Augusta Georgia Dec 9, 1948. Episcopalian. Educated at Randolph-Macon Woman's College A.B. 1970, University of Reading, England 1968-69 and Emory University School of Law J.D. cum laude 1973. Notes and Comments Editor Emory Law Journal 1973. Law Clerk to Hon. Elbert P. Tuttle, U.S. Court of Appeals Fifth Circuit 1973-74. Member Order of the Coif and Pi Society. Admitted to practice Georgia 1973, U.S. District Court Northern District of Georgia 1974, U.S. Supreme Court 1977 and U.S. Court of Appeals Eleventh Circuit 1981. In legal practice Atlanta 1974-84. Judge, State Court of Fulton County 1984-90, appointed by Governor Joe Frank Harris. Former Judge, Superior Court of Georgia Atlanta Judicial Circuit, appointed by Governor Joe Frank Harris to term beginning Aug 22, 1990. Former

HULL, FRANK M.—*Continued*

Judge, U.S. District Court Northern District of Georgia, appointed for life by President Bill Clinton.

Author "Pyramid Marketing Plans and Consumer Protection: State and Federal Regulations" 21 Emory L. Jour. 445, 1972; "Civil Procedures—Application of Long-Arm Statute to Foreign Corporation" 8 Georgia State B. Jour. 414, 1972; "Bankruptcy of Principal: Reclamation and Other Common Problems Facing the Principal and Its Surety" 12 Forum 200, 1976 (presented at Annual Meeting Section of Tort and Insurance Practice American Bar Association, Atlanta 1976); "Surety's Liability for Attorneys' Fees and Court Costs Under Fidelity Bonds" 14 Forum 634, 1979 (presented at Annual Meeting Section of Tort and Insurance Practice American Bar Association, New York 1978); "The ABC's of Unidentifiable Employee Coverage" 15 Forum 948, 1980 (presented at Mid-Winter Meeting Section of Tort and Insurance Practice American Bar Association, New York 1980); "Who Is an Employee Covered by Fidelity Bonds" (presented at National Institute of Employee Dishonesty American Bar Association, New Orleans 1983); "An Overview of the Liability of the Contractor's Accountant to Third Parties in the Construction Industry" 4 No. 2 *The Construction Lawyer* 1983; and "Attorney's Fees and Court Costs Under Bankers' Blanket Bonds" (presented at Banking Law Institute Seminar, Chicago May 1984). Editorial staff *The Construction Lawyer* Forum Committee on the Construction Industry American Bar Association 1981-85.

Board of Directors 1977-79 and Chairman Northern District Casenotes Committee 1977-79 Atlanta Council of Younger Lawyers. Board of Directors Atlanta Volunteer Lawyers Foundation. Member Lawyers Club of Atlanta, Georgia Association of Women Lawyers, National Association of Women Judges, National Center for State Courts, American Judicature Society (Board of Directors since 1990), State Bar of Georgia (Committee on Women and Minorities in the Profession since 1988), North Fulton, South Fulton, Atlanta, Gate City and American (Vice Chairman Fidelity and Surety Law Committee 1978-85, Financial Secretary Section of Tort and Insurance Practice 1979-82 and Chairman Contract Documents Division Forum Committee on the Construction Industry 1983-84) Bar Associations. Board of Directors Metro Atlanta Mediation Center, Inc. (operates family counseling center The Bridge) 1976-79. Member Uniform Rules Committee 1987-90 and Program Committee 1987-90 Council of State Court Judges of Georgia and Georgia Commission on Gender Bias in the Judicial System since 1988. Participant Leadership Atlanta since 1986. Member Atlanta Speech School Guild, Atlanta Center for Puppetry Arts, The Atlanta Botanical Garden, American Association of University Women and Cathedral of St. Philip, Atlanta.

Office: 300 Court of Appeals Building, 56 Forsyth Street N.W., Atlanta, Georgia 30303.

Telephone: (404) 335-6550.

IVERS, Donald L. *(Judge, United States Court of Appeals for Veterans Claims)* Appointed by President George Bush to term beginning Aug 6, 1990. Term expires Aug 6, 2005. Born San Diego California May 6, 1941. Educated at New Mexico Military Institute, University of New Mexico, American University J.D. and Georgetown University. In legal practice Washington D.C. 1972-78.

Chief Counsel Republican National Committee 1978-81. Chief Counsel Federal Highway Administration 1981-85. Counselor to Secretary of Transportation 1984-85. General Counsel Veterans Administration 1985-90. Acting General Counsel Department of Veterans Affairs March 1990. Served to Lieutenant Colonel U.S. Army (active duty 1963-68, retired).

Office: 625 Indiana Avenue N.W., Suite 900, Washington, D.C. 20004-2950.

Telephone: (202) 501-5878.

JACOBS, Dennis G. *(Judge, United States Court of Appeals Second Circuit)* Appointed for life by President George Bush Dec 8, 1992. Born New York New York Feb 28, 1944. Educated at Queens College of the City University of New York B.A. 1964 and New York University M.A. 1965 J.D. 1973.

Member The Association of the Bar of the City of New York and The Federalist Society.

Office: 1702 U.S. Courthouse, 40 Centre Street, New York, New York 10007.

Telephone: (212) 857-2150.

JACOBS, Julian I. *(Senior Judge, United States Tax Court)* Appointed by President Ronald Reagan to term beginning March 30, 1984. Assumed Senior status, serves by assignment. Born Baltimore Maryland Aug 13, 1937. Educated at University of Maryland B.A. 1958 LL.B. 1960 and Georgetown University Law Center LL.M. in Taxation 1965. In legal practice Baltimore Maryland 1967-84.

With Internal Revenue Service Washington D.C. 1965-67. Trial Attorney Office of Regional Counsel Internal Revenue Service Buffalo New York 1965-67. Chairman Study Commission to Improve Quality of Maryland Tax Law, appointed by Governor Blair Lee III 1978. Member several study groups to consider changes in Maryland tax laws and Commissioner of Commission to Reorganize and Recodify Maryland Tax Laws, appointed by Governor Harry Roe Hughes 1978. Adjunct Professor Graduate Tax Program University of Baltimore since 1991. Former Chairman Tax Section Maryland State Bar Association, Inc.

Office: 400 Second Street N.W., Washington, D.C. 20217-0002.

Telephone: (202) 606-8811.

JOLLY, E. Grady *(Judge, United States Court of Appeals Fifth Circuit)* Appointed for life by President Ronald Reagan July 30, 1982. Born Louisville Mississippi Oct 3, 1937. Educated at University of Mississippi B.A. 1959 LL.B. 1962.

Office: 202 U.S. Courthouse, 245 East Capitol Street, Jackson, Mississippi 39201.

Telephone: (601) 965-4165.

JONES, Edith Hollan *(Judge, United States Court of Appeals Fifth Circuit)* Appointed for life by President Ronald Reagan April 4, 1985. Born Philadelphia Pennsylvania April 7, 1949. Educated at Cornell University B.A. 1971 and University of Texas School of Law J.D. 1974.

Office: 12505 U.S. Courthouse, 515 Rusk Avenue, Houston, Texas 77002-2655.

Telephone: (713) 250-5484.

KANNE, Michael S. *(Judge, United States Court of Appeals Seventh Circuit)* Appointed for life by President Ronald Reagan to term beginning May 21, 1987. Born

KANNE, MICHAEL S.—*Continued*
Rensselaer Indiana Dec 21, 1938. Roman Catholic. Educated at St. Joseph's College 1957-58, Indiana University B.S. 1962, Boston University 1962-63 and Indiana University at Bloomington J.D. 1968. Member Lambda Chi Alpha and Phi Delta Phi. Admitted to practice Indiana 1968 and U.S. District Court Northern District of Indiana 1968. In legal practice Rensselaer 1968-72. Judge, Indiana Circuit Court Jasper County 1972-82. Judge, U.S. District Court Northern District of Indiana 1982-87.

Co-author *United States Courts Design Guide* 1991. Important Decisions: G. Heileman Brewing Co. v. Joseph Oat Corp. 871 F.2d 648, 7th Cir. 1989; Freedom from Religion Foundation Inc. v. City of Marshfield, Wis. 203 F.3d 487, 7th Cir. 2000; and United States v. Andreas 216 F.3d 645, 7th Cir. 2000. Lecturer on Constitutional Law St. Joseph's College 1976-86 and St. Francis College 1989-90. Member Committee on Space and Facilities 1987-94 and Committee on Federal Defenders since 1997 Judicial Conference of the U.S. Member Indiana Bar Foundation (Elected 1985), Jasper County (President 1972-80) and Indiana State (Board of Managers 1977-79) Bar Associations. Instructor and lecturer for numerous conferences on topics from courtroom design to media relations. Recipient Distinguished Graduate Award from National Catholic Educational Association 1991, Distinguished Achievement Award from General Services Administration 1995 and Order of Achievement from Lambda Chi Alpha National Fraternity 1999. Named Outstanding Alumnus by *Today's Catholic Teacher* 1991 and Law Alumni Fellow by Indiana University 1999. First Lieutenant USAF 1962-65. Trustee St. Joseph's College since 1984. Board of Visitors School of Law since 1987 and School of Public and Environmental Affairs since 1991 Indiana University. Member Union Club of Chicago. Enjoys horseback riding and weight lifting.

Mailing address: P.O. Box 1340, Lafayette, Indiana 47902-1340.

Telephone: (765) 420-6200.

KATZMANN, Robert Allen *(Judge, United States Court of Appeals Second Circuit)* Appointed for life by President Bill Clinton July 16, 1999 to term beginning Sept 22, 1999. Born New York New York 1953. Educated at Columbia University A.B. summa cum laude 1973, Harvard University M.A. 1975 Ph.D. 1978 and Yale University J.D. 1980. Article and Book Editor Yale University Law Journal 1979-80. Law Clerk to Hon. Hugh H. Bownes, U.S. Court of Appeals First Circuit 1980-81. Member Phi Beta Kappa. Admitted to practice Massachusetts 1982, U.S. Court of Appeals First Circuit 1983, District of Columbia 1984 and U.S. District Court District of Massachusetts 1984.

Author *Regulatory Bureaucracy: The Federal Trade Commission and Antitrust Policy* 1980, *Institutional Disability* 1986 and *Courts and Congress* 1997. Co-editor *Managing Appeals in Federal Courts* 1988. Editor *Judges and Legislators* 1988 and *The Law Firm and the Public Good* 1995. Adjunct Professor of Law Public Policy 1984-92 and Professor of Law William J. Walsh Professional Government 1992-99 Georgetown University. Visiting Professor of Political Science Washington Program University of California at Los Angeles 1990-92. Visiting Chair Wayne Morse Center for Law and Politics University of Oregon 1992. Adjunct Professor of Law New York University since 2001. Member American Judicature Society (Board of Directors 1992-98) and American Bar Association (Vice Chair Committees on Government Operations and Separation of Powers Section of Administrative Law and Regulatory Practice 1991-94, Public Member Administration Conference 1992-95). Recipient Charles E. Merriam Award from American Political Science Association 2001. Research Associate 1981-85, Fellow 1985-99 and Acting Director of Government Studies 1998 Brookings Institution. President Governance Institute 1986-99. Member American Political Science Association and Association for Public Policy Analysis and Management.

Office: 40 Foley Square, New York, New York 10007-1502.

Telephone: (212) 857-2180.

KEARSE, Amalya Lyle *(Senior Judge, United States Court of Appeals Second Circuit)* Appointed for life by President Jimmy Carter to term beginning 1979. Assumed Senior status June 11, 2002, serves by assignment. Born Vauxhall New Jersey June 11, 1937. Educated at Wellesley College B.A. 1959 and University of Michigan J.D. cum laude 1962. Admitted to practice New York 1963 and U.S. Supreme Court 1967. In legal practice New York City 1962-79.

Lecturer on Evidence New York University Law School 1968-69. President's Commission on Selection of Federal Judicial Officers 1977-78. Member Lawyers Committee for Civil Rights Under Law, The American Law Institute, The Association of the Bar of the City of New York and American Bar Association. National Women's Pairs Bridge Champion 1971 and 1972. Trustee American Contract Bridge League National Laws Commission since 1975 and New York City YWCA 1976-79. Board of Directors Legal Defense and Educational Fund NAACP 1977-79 and National Urban League 1978-79. Author *Bridge Convention Complete* 1975 2nd ed. 1984 and *Bridge at Your Fingertips* 1980. Member Charles Goren Editorial Board since 1974. Editor *Official Encyclopedia of Bridge* 3rd ed. 1976. Translator and Editor *Bridge Analysis* 1979.

Office: U.S. Courthouse, 40 Centre Street, New York, New York 10007.

Telephone: (212) 857-2250.

KEITH, Damon Jerome *(Senior Judge, United States Court of Appeals Sixth Circuit)* Appointed for life by President Jimmy Carter. Assumed Senior status May 1, 1995, serves by assignment. Born Detroit Michigan July 4, 1922. Educated at West Virginia State College B.A. 1943, Howard University LL.B. 1949 and Wayne State University LL.M. in Labor Law 1956. Awarded honorary LL.D. West Virginia State College 1965, Wayne State University 1973, Howard University 1974, University of Michigan 1974, Lincoln University 1975, University of Detroit 1975, Atlanta University 1975, New York Law School 1978, Michigan State University 1978, Detroit College of Law 1978, Marygrove College, Detroit Institute of Technology, Shaw College, Central State University, Yale University, Loyola Law School, Eastern Michigan University, Virginia Union University and Central Michigan University. Admitted to practice Michigan 1950. In legal practice Detroit 1950-67. Judge 1967-77 and Chief Judge 1975-77, U.S. District Court Eastern District of Michigan.

Contributor on Family Law, Survey of Michigan Law Wayne L. Rev. 6 p. 152, 1959; 7 p. 209, 1960; 8 p.

KEITH, DAMON JEROME—*Continued*

243, 1961; 9 p. 227, 1962; 10 p. 249, 1963 and 11 p. 293, 1964. Author "Paladin of the People" in *From the Black Bar: Voices for Equal Justice* 313, G. P. Putnam and Sons 1976, "Civil Liberties and Criminal Law" in *Who Are the Guilty?: Crime, Justice and Punishment in America* Courses by Newspaper University of California Extension Program 1977 and "Equal Protection, the Standard of Review: The Path Taken and the Road Beyond" 57 No. 4 University of Detroit Journal of Urban Law 701. Important Decisions: The Pontiac School Decision 1970, The White Panther Wiretap Decision 1971, Morris v. Michigan State Board of Education 1972, The Hamtramck Case 1973, The Detroit Edison Case 1973, Zuch v. Hussey 1975 and The Detroit Police Layoff Case 1975. Important Opinions: United States v. Haulman 288 F. Supp. 775 E.D. Mich. 1968; Davis v. School District of Pontiac, Inc. 309 F. Supp. 734 E.D. Mich. 1970, aff'd 443 F.2d 573 6th Cir. 1970, cert. denied 404 U.S. 913, 1971; Madison Realty Co. v. Detroit 315 F. Supp. 367 E.D. Mich. 1970; Garrett v. City of Hamtramck 335 F. Supp. 16 E.D. Mich. 1971, 357 F. Supp. 925 E.D. Mich. 1973; Stamps v. Detroit Edison Co. 365 F. Supp. 87 E.D. Mich. 1973 aff'd in part and rev'd in part and remanded sub. nom., E.E.O.C. v. Detroit Edison Co. 515 F.2d 301, 6th Cir. 1975, vacated and remanded 431 U.S. 951, 1977; and Ghandi v. Police Department of Detroit 74 F.R.D. 115 E.D. Mich. 1977. Presiding Judge, John Fletcher Caskey Prize Trial, Yale Law School 1972. Lecturer in the Distinguished Visiting Lecturer Series 1972 and Guest Lecturer in the William H. Hastie Lecture Series 1981 Howard University. Former member National Panel of Arbitrators American Arbitration Association. Elected Sixth Circuit Delegate to Judicial Conference of the U.S. 1975-78. Member Committee on Codes of Conduct 1979 and Subcommittee on Supporting Personnel Committee on Court Administration 1983 Judicial Conference of the U.S. Member State Bar of Michigan (Commissioner 1960-67, Chairman Commission on Bail and Criminal Justice 1965), Wolverine, Detroit, National and American Bar Associations.

Recipient Michigan Chronicle Outstanding Citizen Award 1960, 1964 and 1974, Emancipation Freedom Award from Windsor Ontario, Layman of the Year Award from Detroit Council of Churches 1963, Citizen of the Year Award from Detroit Medical Society 1966, Annual Judicial Award from National Bar Association 1971, Judicial Independence Award from American Civil Liberties Union of Michigan 1973, Spingarn Medal from NAACP 1974, Judge of the Year Award from National Conference of Black Lawyers 1974, Distinguished Service Award from National Urban Coalition 1974, Federal Judge of the Year Award from Black American Law Students Association 1974, Award for Outstanding Contributions to the Black Community from National Association of Black Social Workers 1974, Distinguished Service Award from National Newspaper Publishers Association 1974, Outstanding Trial Judges Award from Michigan Trial Lawyers Association 1974, Distinguished Citizen Award from Michigan State University 1974, Equal Opportunity Award from Detroit Urban League 1975, Special Award for Judicial Excellence from Georgia Conference of Black Lawyers 1977, Scholarship and Dedication Award from National Association of Black Accountants 1977, The A. Philip Randolph Award from Detroit Coalition of Black Trade Unionists 1981, Human Rights Day Award from B'nai B'rith Women's Council of Metropolitan Detroit 1981, Robert L. Millender Award from Michigan Chapter of the Southern Christian Leadership Conference 1982, Award from Detroit Chapter of the National Association of Black Journalists 1982, Special Certificate of Appreciation from Black Law Students Association of Harvard University Law School 1982, Award from Minority Advisory Panel of the Michigan Bell Company 1982, Outstanding Service Award from West Virginia State College Detroit Alumni Chapter 1983 and Award for Distinguished Service to the Cause of Justice from the Optimist Club of Central Detroit 1983. Named One of the 100 Most Influential Black Americans by Ebony Magazine 1971-78 and Judge of the Year 1973 by National Conference of Black Lawyers. Damon J. Keith Elementary School 1974 and Damon J. Keith Middle School 1977 dedicated by Detroit Board of Education. Reception honoring Damon J. Keith sponsored by Women's Committee of the United Negro College Fund 1981.

Staff Sergeant USAS WWII. President Detroit Housing Commission 1958-67. Chairman Michigan Civil Rights Commission 1964-67. Past President Detroit Cotillion Club. Former Trustee Medical Corporation. General Co-chairman United Negro College Fund. Vice Chairman Detroit Symphony Orchestra. Deacon Tabernacle Baptist Church. Board of Trustees Cranbrook School, Interlochen Arts Academy and Detroit Arts Commission. Member Wayne County Board of Supervisors 1958-63, Michigan Committee on Manpower Development and Vocational Training and Coordinating 1964, Citizens Advisory Commission on Equal Opportunity Detroit Board of Education 1966, Mayor's Health Advisory Committee 1969, Visiting Committee Wayne State University Law School, Committee of Management Detroit YMCA, Detroit Area Council Boy Scouts of America and Detroit Arts Commission.

Office: 240 U.S. Courthouse, 231 West Lafayette Boulevard, Detroit, Michigan 48226.

Telephone: (313) 234-5245.

KELLY, Paul J., Jr. *(Judge, United States Court of Appeals Tenth Circuit)* Appointed for life by President George Bush to term beginning April 14, 1992. Born New York Dec 6, 1940. Educated at University of Notre Dame B.B.A. 1963 and Fordham University School of Law J.D. 1967. Admitted to practice New Mexico 1968. In legal practice Roswell 1967-82 and Santa Fe 1982-92.

Mailing address: P.O. Box 10113, Santa Fe, New Mexico 87504-6113.

Telephone: (505) 988-6541.

KENNEDY, Anthony M. *(Associate Justice, The Supreme Court of the United States)* Appointed for life by President Ronald Reagan to term beginning 1988. Also Circuit Justice, U.S. Court of Appeals Eleventh Circuit. Born Sacramento California July 23, 1936. Catholic. Educated at Stanford University B.A. 1958 and Harvard University LL.B. 1961. Admitted to practice California 1962. Began legal practice San Francisco 1962. In legal practice Sacramento 1963-75. Judge, U.S. Court of Appeals Ninth Circuit May 1975 to Jan 1988, appointed by President Gerald R. Ford.

Professor McGeorge School of Law 1964-88. Member Advisory Committee on Codes of Conduct 1979-87 and Chairman Pacific Territories Committee 1982-90 Judicial Conference of the U.S. Board member Federal Judicial

KENNEDY, ANTHONY M.—*Continued*

Center 1987-88. Member American Bar Association. Republican. Enjoys teaching, golf and tennis.
Office: One First Street N.E., Washington, D.C. 20543-0001.
Telephone: (202) 479-3000.

KENNEDY, Cornelia G. *(Senior Judge, United States Court of Appeals Sixth Circuit)* Appointed for life by President Jimmy Carter to term beginning 1979. Assumed Senior status March 1, 1999, serves by assignment. First woman from Michigan to serve as Federal Judge. Born Detroit Michigan Aug 4, 1923. Educated at University of Michigan B.A. with honors 1945 J.D. with distinction 1947. Board of Editors Michigan Law Review. Law Clerk to Hon. Harold M. Stephens, U.S. Court of Appeals 1947-48. Member Phi Beta Kappa and Phi Kappa Phi. Awarded honorary Doctor of Law from Northern Michigan University, Eastern Michigan University, Western Michigan University, Detroit College of Law 1980 and University of Detroit 1987. In legal practice Detroit 1948-66. Judge, Michigan Circuit Court Third Judicial Circuit Nov 8, 1966 to Oct 1970. Judge 1970-79 and Chief Judge 1977-79, U.S. District Court Eastern District of Michigan.
Member Federal Judicial Center (Board of Directors), Federal Judicial Fellows (Board of Directors), American Judicature Society, National Association of Women Lawyers, The Association of Trial Lawyers of America, State Bar of Michigan (Former Chairman Negligence Law Section), Detroit (Former Director), Federal and American (Former member Judicial Administration Division Council) Bar Associations. Member Advisory Committee on Judicial Activities and Joint Committee on Code of Judicial Conduct Judicial Conference of the U.S. Former Chairman National Conference of Federal Trial Judges (first woman elected to position). Appointed by the President to Commission of the Bicentennial for the U.S. Constitution.
Office: 744 U.S. Courthouse, 231 West Lafayette Boulevard, Detroit, Michigan 48226-2787.
Telephone: (313) 234-5240.

KENNER, Carol J. *(Judge, Bankruptcy Appellate Panel First Circuit)* Selected by the Judicial Council of the First Circuit. Also Judge, U.S. Bankruptcy Court District of Massachusetts. Former Chief Judge Bankruptcy Court.
Office: 1101 Federal Building, 10 Causeway Street, Boston, Massachusetts 02222-1074.
Telephone: (617) 565-6066.

KING, Carolyn Dineen *(Chief Judge, United States Court of Appeals Fifth Circuit)* Appointed for life by President Jimmy Carter to term beginning 1979. Born Syracuse New York Jan 30, 1938. Roman Catholic. Educated at Smith College A.B. summa cum laude 1959 and Yale University LL.B. 1962. Member Phi Beta Kappa. Admitted to practice District of Columbia 1962 and Texas 1963. In legal practice Houston 1962-79.
Member Dallas Regional Panel 1972-76 and Commission 1977 President's Commission on White House Fellowships. Member The American Law Institute (Council since 1991, Executive Committee 1997-99, Chair Membership Committee 1997-99, Adviser to Restatement of the Law Third—Torts: Products Liability, Adviser to Transnational Insolvency Project), Judicial Conference of the U.S. (Chairman Executive Committee), State Bar of Texas, Houston, Federal and American Bar Associations. Research Fellow The Center for American and International Law (formerly Southwestern Legal Foundation) since 1989. Recipient Smith College Medal 1997 and Outstanding Alumnus Award from Phi Beta Kappa Alumni of Greater Houston 1998. Trustee, member Executive Committee and Treasurer Houston Ballet Foundation 1967-70. Member Houston District Advisory Council Small Business Administration 1972-76. Board of Directors Houston Chapter American Heart Association 1978-79. National Trustee Palmer Drug Abuse Program 1978-79. Trustee, Secretary, Treasurer, Chairman Audit Committee and Finance Committee and member Management Committee United Way Texas Gulf Coast 1979-85. Trustee and Member Executive Committee 1988-98 and Chairman Board of Trustees 1994-98 University of St. Thomas. Member The Philosophical Society of Texas since 1995. Advisory Board Center for Thomistic Studies since Feb 1999.
Office: 11020 U.S. Courthouse, 515 Rusk Avenue, Houston, Texas 77002.
Telephone: (713) 250-5750.

KING, Robert Bruce *(Judge, United States Court of Appeals Fourth Circuit)* Appointed for life by President Bill Clinton June 24, 1998 to term beginning Oct 23, 1998. Born White Sulphur Springs West Virginia Jan 29, 1940. Presbyterian. Educated at West Virginia University B.A. 1961 J.D. 1968. Staff member West Virginia Law Review. Law Clerk to Chief Judge John A. Field, Jr., U.S. District Court Southern District of West Virginia 1969-70. Member Pi Sigma Alpha, Phi Alpha Delta and Order of the Coif. Admitted to practice West Virginia 1968, U.S. District Courts Southern 1968 and Northern 1972 Districts of West Virginia and Eastern District of Kentucky 1975, U.S. Court of Appeals Fourth Circuit 1970, U.S. Supreme Court 1974, U.S. Claims Court 1985 and U.S. Tax Court 1991. In legal practice Lewisburg 1969-70 and Charleston 1975-77 and 1981-98.
Assistant U.S. Attorney 1970-74 and U.S. Attorney 1977-81 Southern District of West Virginia. Member Judicial Investigation Commission of West Virginia 1990-94. Fellow American Bar Foundation and American College of Trial Lawyers. Member American Board of Trial Advocates (President West Virginia Chapter 1986-90), Judicial Conference of the Fourth Circuit, Federal Judges Association, Greenbrier County, Kanawha County, West Virginia (Board of Governors 1981-84, Committee on Legal Ethics 1984-87) and American Bar Associations. West Virginia National Guard 1957-59. Special Agent Office of Special Investigations USAF 1961-64. Teacher Greenbrier County West Virginia 1964-65. Assistant Manager Sam Snead All-American Golf Course Summer 1965. Research Assistant State and Community Planning Unit Office of Research and Development West Virginia University 1966-68. Member Visiting Committee West Virginia University College of Law since 1997. Member U.S. and West Virginia Golf Associations, West Virginia University Alumni Association, West Virginia Law School Association.
Office: 7602 U.S. Courthouse, 300 Virginia Street East, Charleston, West Virginia 25301-2523.
Telephone: (304) 347-3533.

KLEIN, Christopher M. *(Judge, Bankruptcy Appellate Panel Ninth Circuit)* Selected by the Judicial Coun-

KLEIN, CHRISTOPHER M.—*Continued*

cil of the Ninth Circuit. Also Judge, U.S. Bankruptcy Court Eastern District of California.

Office: 3-200 U.S. Courthouse, 501 I Street, Sacramento, California 95814-2322.

Telephone: (916) 930-4510.

KLEINFELD, Andrew J. *(Judge, United States Court of Appeals Ninth Circuit)* Appointed for life by President George Bush Sept 16, 1991. Born Bronx New York June 12, 1945. Jewish. Educated at Wesleyan University B.A. with honors 1966 and Harvard Law School J.D. with honors 1969. Law Clerk to Hon. Jay A. Rabinowitz, Alaska Supreme Court 1969-71. Admitted to practice Alaska 1970 and Massachusetts 1973. In legal practice Fairbanks 1971-86. Magistrate, U.S. District Court District of Alaska 1971-86. Judge, U.S. District Court District of Alaska July 14, 1986 to 1991, appointed by President Ronald Reagan.

Important Decisions: United States v. Castillo-Villagra (immigration) 972 F.2d 1017, 9th Cir. 1992; United States v. Fine (sentencing guidelines) 975 F.2d 596, 9th Cir. 1992; Longview Fibre Co. v. Rasmussen (environmental law) 980 F.2d 1307, 9th Cir. 1992; United States v. Unimex, Inc. (forfeitures) 991 F.2d 546, 9th Cir. 1993; Madera Irrigation District v. Hancock (reclamation, water rights) 985 F.2d 1397, 9th Cir. 1993; Sayles Hydro Associates v. Maughan (federal preemption, waters) 985 F.2d 451, 9th Cir. 1993; Freestone v. Cowen (dissent concluded "deadbeat dads" statute did not create a private cause of action to improve state compliance) 68 F.3d 1141, 9th Cir. 1995, rev'd Blessing v. Firestone 117 S. Ct. 1353, 1997; Finley v. National Endowment for the Arts (standards of decency; permissible majoritarian constraint upon government) 100 F.3d 671, 683, 9th Cir. 1996, cert. granted No. 97-371 Nov 26, 1997; Rennick v. O.P.T.I.O.N. Care, Inc. (contractual significance of shaking hands on a deal and letters of intent) 77 F.3d 309, 9th Cir. 1996; Compassion in Dying v. State of Washington (constitutional right to physician's assisted suicide; en banc, Kleinfeld dissenting) 79 F.3d 790, 857, 9th Cir. 1996, rev'd Washington v. Glucksberg 117 S. Ct. 2258, 1997; and Chandler v. U.S. Army (decision decodes an especially complex and impenetrable federal wire tapping statute) 125 F.3d 1296, 9th Cir. 1997. President Tanana Valley Bar Association 1976-77. Member Board of Governors 1980-83 and President 1981-82 Alaska Bar Association. Republican.

Office: 3-A Courthouse Square, 250 Cushman Street, Fairbanks, Alaska 99701.

Telephone: (907) 456-0564.

KOZINSKI, Alex *(Judge, United States Court of Appeals Ninth Circuit)* Appointed for life by President Ronald Reagan. Born Bucharest Romania July 23, 1950. Educated at University of California at Los Angeles A.B. cum laude 1972 J.D. with honors 1975. Managing Editor UCLA Law Review 1974-75. Law Clerk to Hon. Anthony M. Kennedy, U.S. Court of Appeals Ninth Circuit 1975-76 and Chief Justice Warren Earl Burger, U.S. Supreme Court 1976-77. Admitted to practice California 1975 and District of Columbia 1978. In legal practice Los Angeles 1977-79 and Washington D.C. 1979-81. Former Chief Judge, U.S. Claims Court, appointed by President Ronald Reagan to term beginning Oct 1, 1982.

Deputy Legal Counsel Office of President Elect Ronald Reagan Nov 1980 to Jan 1981. Assistant Counsel Office of Counsel to the President Jan to June 1981. Special Counsel Merit Systems Protection Board June 1981 to Aug 1982. Author "So You Want to Become a Federal Judge by 35?" *The National Law Journal* C6 Aug 19, 1996; "In Praise of Moot Court—Not!" 97 Columbia L. Rev. 178, 1997; "Tinkering with Death" *The New Yorker* Feb 10, 1997; "Brave New World" 30 University of California at Davis L. Rev. 997, 1997; "The Many Faces of Judicial Independence" 14 Georgia State University L. Rev. 861, 1998; "Constitutional Federalism Reborn" 22 Harvard Journal of Law and Public Policy 93, 1998; "Should Reading Legislative History Be an Impeachable Offense?" 31 Suffolk University L. Rev. 807, 1998; "Conduct Unbecoming" Book Review on *Closed Chambers* by Edward Lazarus 108 Yale L. Jour. 835, 1999; "The Case of the Speluncean Explorers: A Fiftieth Anniversary Symposium" 112 Harvard L. Rev. 1834, 1876, 1999; "Carthage Must Be Destroyed" 12 Federal Sentencing Reporter 67, 1999; "When the Written Word and Reality Diverge" Forward 17, Feb 4, 2000; "The Toyota Principle" 56 Washington and Lee L. Rev. 923, 1999; "Pull Down the Blinds" Book Review on *The Unwanted Gaze* by Jeffrey Rosen *The New York Times* Book Review Section 10 July 2, 2000; "How I Narrowly Escaped Insanity" 48 UCLA L. Rev. 1293, 2001; and "Privacy on Trial" *The Wall Street Journal* A22 Sept 4, 2001.

Important Decisions: Sussman v. American Broad. Cos., Inc. 186 F.3d 1200, 9th Cir. 1999 cert. denied 528 U.S. 1131, 2000; Wendt v. Host International 197 F.3d 1284, 9th Cir. 1999 (dissent from denial of reh'g en banc); Humanitarian Law Project v. Reno 205 F.3d 1130, 9th Cir. 2000 cert. denied 121 S. Ct. 1226, 2001; Brooks v. City of San Mateo 214 F.3d 1082, 9th Cir. 2000 amended and reh'g denied 229 F.3d 917, 9th Cir. 2000; United States v. Poehlman 217 F.3d 692, 9th Cir. 2000; United States v. Corey 232 F.3d 1166, 9th Cir. 2000 cert. denied 121 S. Ct. 198 Oct 1, 2001; Mozes v. Mozes 239 F.3d 1067 9th Cir. 2001; Odle v. Woodford 238 F.3d 1084, 9th Cir. cert. denied 122 S. Ct. 201, 2001; United States v. Johnson 256 F.3d 895, 9th Cir. 2001 (en banc); Abovian v. INS 257 F.3d 971, 9th Cir. 2001 (dissent from denial of reh'g en banc); United States v. Kaczynski 262 F.3d 1034, 9th Cir. 2001 (dissent from denial of reh'g en banc); Hart v. Massanari 266 F.3d 1155, 9th Cir. 2001; Summerlin v. Stewart 267 F.3d 926, 9th Cir. 2001 (dissent); and Swenson v. Potter 271 F.3d 1184, 9th Cir. 2001. Republican.

Mailing address: P.O. Box 91510, Pasadena, California 91105-1510.

Office: 200 Court of Appeals Building, 125 South Grand Avenue, Pasadena, California 91105-1652.

Telephone: (626) 229-7140.

KRAMER, Kenneth B. *(Chief Judge, United States Court of Appeals for Veterans Claims)* Appointed by President George Bush to term beginning 1989. Term expires 2004. Educated at University of Illinois B.A. 1963 and Harvard Law School J.D. 1966. Admitted to practice Colorado. In legal practice El Paso County Colorado 1970.

Former Deputy District Attorney El Paso County Colorado. Former Commissioner National Commission on Uniform States Laws. U.S. Army JAGC 1967-70. Former Assistant Secretary for Financial Management U.S. Army. Former Vice President Aries Properties, Inc. State Representative Colorado 1973-78. U.S. Representative (Colorado) 1978-86. Founder and Director U.S. Space

KRAMER, KENNETH B.—*Continued*

Foundation. Former Member Board of Visitors U.S. Air Force Academy. Former Director American Security Council Foundation, Mountain Valley Chapter March of Dimes and Pikes Peak Mental Health Center.

Office: 625 Indiana Avenue N.W., Suite 900, Washington, D.C. 20004-2950.

Telephone: (202) 501-5970.

KRAVITCH, Phyllis A. *(Senior Judge, United States Court of Appeals Eleventh Circuit)* Appointed to Fifth Circuit for life by President Jimmy Carter to term beginning March 1979. Assigned to Eleventh Circuit Oct 1, 1981. Assumed Senior status Dec 31, 1996, serves by assignment. Born Savannah Georgia Aug 23, 1920. Jewish. Educated at Goucher College A.B. 1941 and University of Pennsylvania LL.B. with honors 1943. Awarded honorary LL.D. Goucher College 1981 and Emory University 1998. Board of Editors Law Review. Admitted to practice Georgia 1943, U.S. District Court 1944, U.S. Supreme Court 1948 and U.S. Court of Appeals 1962. In legal practice Savannah 1944-76. Judge, Superior Court of Georgia Eastern Judicial Circuit 1977-79 (first woman judge Superior Court of Georgia).

Fellow American Bar Foundation. Member Rules Committee Judicial Conference 1994-2000. Member The American Law Institute, American Judicature Society, State Bar of Georgia, Savannah (President 1976) and American Bar Associations. Trustee Institute of Continuing Legal Education in Georgia 1979-82. Named Savannah's Most Influential Woman 1978. Recipient Hannah G. Solomon Award from National Council of Jewish Women 1978, Margaret Brent Award from American Bar Association 1991, James Wilson Award from University of Pennsylvania 1992, Arabella Babb Mansfield Award from National Association of Women Lawyers 1999, Trailblazer Award from Greater Atlanta Hadassah Attorneys' Council 2000, Kathleen Kessler Award from Georgia Association of Women Lawyers 2001 and Shining Star Award from Atlanta Women's Foundation 2002. Listed in *Jewish Women in America: An Historical Encyclopedia* 1999. Member Chatham County Board of Education 1949-55 and Law School Council Emory University School of Law since 1986. Visiting Committee University of Chicago Law School 1990-93 and Goucher College since 2000. Selection Panel Truman Scholars 1993-2000. Visitors Board Georgia State University School of Law since 1994.

Office: Court of Appeals Building, 56 Forsyth Street N.W., Atlanta, Georgia 30303.

Telephone: (404) 335-6300.

KRESSEL, Robert J. *(Chief Judge, Bankruptcy Appellate Panel Eighth Circuit)* Selected by the Judicial Council of the Eighth Circuit to term beginning Sept 10, 1996. Also Judge, U.S. Bankruptcy Court District of Minnesota. Appointed by U.S. District Court judges Dec 6, 1982. Reappointed by U.S. Court of Appeals Eighth Circuit judges Dec 5, 1986 and Dec 5, 2000. Current term expires Dec 4, 2014. Former Chief Judge Bankruptcy Court. Educated at University of Notre Dame A.B. in Mathematics cum laude 1969 and Harvard Law School J.D. 1972. In legal practice Minneapolis 1972-79. Referee, Hennepin County Conciliation Court 1979.

Bankruptcy Analyst U.S. Trustee's Office Minneapolis 1979-81. Assistant U.S. Trustee Districts of Minnesota, North Dakota and South Dakota July 26, 1981 to Dec 4, 1982. Author "Ethical Considerations in Representing Creditors and Debtors" *Hennepin Lawyer* March-April 1982, "Tardy Claims: The Congressional Solution to the Hausladen Problem" *Norton Bankruptcy Law Advisor* Jan 1995 and "Calculating the Present Value of Deferred Payment Under a Chapter 12 Plan: A New Twist to an Old Problem" 62 American Bankruptcy L. Jour. 313. Adjunct Professor of Law Hamline University School of Law 1983-84 and William Mitchell College of Law 1986-95. Member National Conference of Bankruptcy Judges (Board of Governors 1987-90), Hennepin County (Secretary 1979-80 and Chairman 1980-82 Debtor-Creditor Remedies Committee, Member Governing Council 1980-82 and Ethics Committee 1982-83), Minnesota State (Bankruptcy Section), Federal (President Minnesota Chapter 1989-90) and American Bar Associations.

Lecturer "Ten Most Common Mistakes Made in Bankruptcy Court" March 10, 1981 and "Effect of Bankruptcy on Real Estate Mortgage Foreclosures" Dec 1, 1992 Debtor-Creditor Remedies Committee Hennepin County Bar Association; "Selected Problems and Practical Considerations in Bankruptcy Practice" Dec 2-3, 1982 and "Bankruptcy Practice 1985" March 22, 1985 Advanced Legal Education Hamline University School of Law; "Divorce" Minnesota Trial Lawyers Association and American Academy of Matrimonial Lawyers Oct 11-13, 1984; "Continuing Education for Revenue Officers" March 28, 1985 and "Treatment of Creditors Who Tardily File Claims" April 19, 1994 Internal Revenue Service; "Debtors' and Creditors' Practice and Procedure" March 29, 1985, "Successfully Representing Financial Institutions" Nov 4, 1988, "Practicing Under the New Local and National Bankruptcy Rules" June 13, 1991 and "Family Law Institute" 1993, 1995 and 1996 Minnesota CLE; "What You Should Know About the United States Bankruptcy Court" Minnesota Association for Court Administration June 12, 1985; "Bankruptcy's Impact on Consumer Lending" Minneapolis Consumer Credit Association Oct 16, 1985; "Bankruptcy Institute" 1985-89 and 1991-96 and "Bankruptcy Practice and Appeals Under the New Local Rules" Feb 7, 1986 Minnesota CLE and Bankruptcy Section Minnesota State Bar Association; "Foreclosure and Repossession" May 9, 1986 and "Farm and Small Business Reorganization" July 21, 1986 National Business Institute; "Environmental Issues in Bankruptcy" June 16, 1987 and "Trustee's Liability for Environmental Cleanup and Abandonment of Property" Jan 17, 1989 Environmental Law Committee Hennepin County Bar Association; "Chapter 12 Review and Assessment Workshop for Bankruptcy Judges" Sept 20-22, 1987, "Bankruptcy Case Management Workshop" March 13-15, 1988, "Seminar for Bankruptcy Judges" Feb 22-24, 1989, "Workshop for Chief Bankruptcy Judges" Sept 18-20, 1989 and "Workshop for Bankruptcy Judges of the Eighth, Ninth and Tenth Circuits" Dec 4-6, 1989 Federal Judicial Center; "Federal Court Practice Seminar" Minnesota Chapter Federal Bar Association April 8, 1988; "The Bankruptcy Rules" Commercial Law League of America July 10, 1988; "Drafting and Confirming Reorganization Plans" Aug 12, 1988 and "Bankruptcy Litigation and Practice in Minnesota" Feb 17, 1989 Professional Education Systems, Inc.; "Strategic Uses of Chapter 11" Advanced Legal Education Sept 9, 1988; "Environmental Liability in Bankruptcy Cases" Hennepin County Bar Association March 8, 1990; "New Value on Cramdown" National Conference of Bankrupt-

KRESSEL, ROBERT J.—*Continued*
cy Judges Nov 10, 1990; "Cramdown After *Ahlers*" National Real Estate Development Center March 7, 1991; "Welcome to the Nineties: Bankruptcy Law and Practice for Everyone" University of Minnesota Law School March 22, 1992; "Bankruptcy Reform Act of 1994" Minnesota Institute for Legal Education Nov 30, 1994; "Child Support Seminar" Office of Administrative Hearings Oct 27, 1995; and "A Bankruptcy Primer for State Court Judges" Annual Conference of Judges Minnesota Supreme Court Dec 6, 1995.

Director 1975-81, Secretary 1977-79, Vice Chairman 1979-80 and Chairman Nominating Committee and Bylaws Committee Kidney Foundation of the Upper Midwest. Trustee National Kidney Foundation 1976-81. Member 1980-86 and Chairman 1982-83 Board of Trustees and Member Management Committee, Children's Center Advisory Committee and Program Council YWCA of Minneapolis.

Office: 8W U.S. Courthouse, 300 South Fourth Street, Minneapolis, Minnesota 55415.

Telephone: (612) 664-5250.

KRUPANSKY, Robert B. *(Senior Judge, United States Court of Appeals Sixth Circuit)* Appointed for life by President Ronald Reagan March 10, 1982 to term beginning April 19, 1982. Assumed Senior status July 1, 1991, serves by assignment. Born Cleveland Ohio Aug 15, 1921. Catholic. Educated at Western Reserve University (now Case Western Reserve University) B.A. 1942 LL.B. 1948 replaced by J.D. 1968. Admitted to practice Ohio 1948, U.S. District Court Northern District of Ohio 1950, U.S. Supreme Court 1956, U.S. Court of Customs and Patent Appeals 1956 and U.S. Court of Appeals Sixth Circuit 1969. In legal practice Cleveland 1948-52 and 1960-69. Judge, Ohio Court of Common Pleas Cuyahoga County 1958-59. Judge, U.S. District Court Northern District of Ohio 1970-82.

Assistant Attorney General State of Ohio 1951-57. Chief Counsel Department of Liquor Control 1951-57. Member Governor's Cabinet as Director Department of Liquor Control 1958 and Independence Charter Review Commission 1962. Director of Law Mayfield Heights Ohio 1960-64. U.S. Attorney Northern District of Ohio July 1969 to Oct 1970. Author "Patents—Damages for Infringement—Accident Law" chapter 97 sections 97.1-97.34 in *Federal Jury Practice and Instructions* Devitt & Blackmar and "The Federal Rules Are Alive and Well" Litigation Magazine Fall 1977 American Bar Association Section of Litigation.

Important Decisions: Lamb Enterprises, Inc. v. Toledo Blade Company (antitrust action) 461 F.2d 506, 6th Cir. 1972, cert. denied, 409 U.S. 1001, 93 S. Ct. 325, 1972; Ongoing Reorganization Proceedings of the Erie Lackawanna Railway Company since 1972; Sims v. Sheet Metal Workers International Association Local Union 65, 353 F. Supp. 22 N.D. Ohio 1972, 489 F.2d 1023, 6th Cir. 1973; Sykes et al. v. Kreiger et al. (rights of detainees in criminal detention facilities) Civil No. C71-1181; Cantrell v. Forest City Publishing Co. (invasion of privacy case) 484 F.2d 150, 6th Cir. 1973, 419 U.S. 245, 95 S. Ct. 465, 1974; Sperberg v. Goodyear Tire and Rubber Co. (patent case) 519 F.2d 708, 6th Cir. 1975; Ball v. E. I. du Pont de Nemours & Co. Inc. (product liability case) 512 F.2d 715, 6th Cir. 1975; U.S. v. Spaganlo (criminal conspiracy action with multiple defendants) Criminal No. CR73-600 aff'd 519 F.2d 1403, 6th Cir. 1975, cert. denied 44 U.S.L.W. 3263, 1975; White & White, Inc. v. American Hospital Supply Corp. 723 F.2d 495, 6th Cir. 1983; Bowen v. Tennessee 698 F.2d 241, 6th Cir. 1983 en banc; City of Cleveland v. The Cleveland Electric Illuminating Company (antitrust) 538 F. Supp. 1257, 1980, 734 F.2d 1157, 1984; Kelly v. Metropolitan County Board of Education 733 F.2d 677, 6th Cir. 1985 en banc; In re Erie Lackawanna Railway Co. No. B72-2838 N.D. Ohio June 18, 1985 aff'd 803 F.2d 881, 6th Cir. 1986; In re Art Materials Antitrust Litigation MDL No. 436; Rabidue v. Osceola Refining Co. 805 F.2d 611, 6th Cir. 1986; Murphy v. Sowders 801 F.2d 205, 6th Cir. 1986; United States v. Reeves 794 F.2d 1101, 6th Cir. 1986; United States v. One (1) Beechcraft Baron No. N242B5 788 F.2d 384, 6th Cir. 1986; United States v. Day 789 F.2d 1217, 6th Cir. 1986; United States v. Padin 787 F.2d 1071, 6th Cir. 1986; Beach v. Viking Sewing Machine Co. 784 F.2d 746, 6th Cir. 1986; Stone v. Beaumont Hospital 782 F.2d 609, 6th Cir. 1986; and Connaughton v. Harte Hanks Communications, Inc. 842 F.2d 825, 6th Cir. 1988, aff'd 109 S. Ct. 2678, 1989. Former Adjunct Professor of Law Case Western Reserve University. Member American Judicature Society, Bar Association of Greater Cleveland (Grievance Committee, Executive Committee, Committee on Civil Disorders, Special Committee on Law and Urban Affairs, Nominating Committee and former Chairman Municipal Courts Committee), Cuyahoga County, Ohio State and American Bar Associations. Pilot USAAC 1942-46. Colonel USAF 1946-72 (retired). Republican.

Office: U.S. Courthouse, 801 West Superior Avenue, Cleveland, Ohio 44113-1832.

Telephone: (216) 357-7180.

Fax: (216) 357-7184

LAFFITTE, Hector M. *(Chief Judge, United States District Court District of Puerto Rico)* Appointed for life by President Ronald Reagan to term beginning July 1983. Chief Judge since March 16, 1999. Born Ponce Puerto Rico April 13, 1934. Catholic. Educated at Polytechnic Institute of Puerto Rico B.A. 1955, University of Puerto Rico LL.B. 1959 and Georgetown University LL.M. 1960. Admitted to practice Puerto Rico 1959, U.S. District Court District of Puerto Rico 1959, U.S. Court of Appeals First Circuit 1959, U.S. Court of Military Appeals 1960 and U.S. Supreme Court 1976. In legal practice Puerto Rico 1970-83.

Member Governor's Advisory Committee on Judicial Appointments 1977-83 and Magistrate Judges Committee Judicial Conference 1992. Former Member Puerto Rico Bar Association. Member American Arbitration Association, Association of Labor Relations Practitioners, Institute of Judicial Administration, Federal and American Bar Associations. Member Governor's Advisory Committee on Labor Policy 1977-83. Advisor on Labor Practice and Procedures Government of U.S. Virgin Islands 1970. Member Civil Rights Commission of Puerto Rico 1969-72. Enjoys reading.

Office: CH-142 U.S. Courthouse, 150 Carlos Chardón Avenue, San Juan, Puerto Rico 00918-1757.

Telephone: (787) 772-3130.

LAMOUTTE, Enrique S. *(Judge, Bankruptcy Appellate Panel First Circuit and Judge, United States Bankruptcy Court District of Puerto Rico)* Selected for Ap-

LAMOUTTE, ENRIQUE S.—*Continued*

pellate Panel by U.S. Court of Appeals First Circuit judges. Former Chief Judge Bankruptcy Court.

Office: 251 Federal Bldg. & U.S. Courthouse, 300 Recinto Sur Street, San Juan, Puerto Rico 00901.

Telephone: (787) 977-6030.

LARO, David *(Judge, United States Tax Court)* Appointed by President George Bush Aug 17, 1992 to term beginning Nov 2, 1992. Term expires Nov 1, 2007. Born Flint Michigan March 3, 1942. Educated at University of Michigan B.A. 1964, University of Illinois College of Law J.D. 1967 and New York University School of Law LL.M. in Taxation 1970. First Place Moot Court Competition University of Illinois College of Law. Member Phi Delta Phi. Admitted to practice Michigan 1968. In legal practice Flint 1968-92 and Ann Arbor 1988-92.

Contributing Author American Bar Association Journal, University of Illinois L. Rev. and other publications. Important Decisions: Richard L. Simon and Fiona Simon (depreciation on two 19th century violin bows) 103 T.C. 15, 1994; Brian P. Liddle and Brenda H. Liddle (depreciation of a 17th century Ruggeri bass viol) 103 T.C. 16, 1994; Mandelbaum (lack of marketability discount); Wal-Mart (inventory shrinkage); ACM Partnership (corporate tax shelter); and Norwest (capitalization of salaries). Instructor Georgetown University Law Center 1993-94. Visiting Professor University of San Diego Law School. Fellow American College of Tax Counsel. Member State Bar of Michigan. Former Instructor Trial Advocacy Institute University of Virginia School of Law and National Institute for Trial Advocacy. Guest Speaker American Bar Association and American Institute of Certified Public Accountants. Lecturer to Russian judges on Tax Reform and Litigation Procedures Harvard Institute for International Development and Georgia State University, Moscow Russia May 1997 and Dec 1998. Commentator on draft laws of Uzbekistan, Kazakhstan, Slovakia, Ukraine, and Republic of Macedonia American Bar Association Central and East European Law Initiative. Board of Regents University of Michigan 1975-81. Chairman State Tenure Commission State Board of Education Michigan 1982-84. Former Director Ann Arbor Art Association. Former Member Holocaust Foundation and National Advisory Committee New York University School of Law.

Office: 400 Second Street N.W., Washington, D.C. 20217-0002.

Telephone: (202) 606-8893.

LAY, Donald P. *(Senior Judge, United States Court of Appeals Eighth Circuit)* Appointed for life by President Lyndon B. Johnson to term beginning Aug 26, 1966. Chief Judge Jan 1, 1980 to Jan 7, 1992. Assumed Senior status Jan 7, 1992, serves by assignment. Second youngest judge to be appointed to the U.S. Court of Appeals at time of appointment. Born Princeton Illinois Aug 24, 1926. Protestant. Educated at U.S. Naval Academy 1945-46 and University of Iowa B.A. 1949 J.D. 1951. Awarded honorary LL.D. William Mitchell College 1985. Member Order of the Coif. Admitted to practice Iowa 1951, Nebraska 1951 and Wisconsin 1953. In legal practice Milwaukee Wisconsin 1953-54 and Omaha Nebraska 1954-66.

Author "Mapping the Trial—Order of Proof" Am. Jur. Trials Vol. 5 1966, "Law and Order: Due Process of Law 1968" Trial Lawyers Forum Jan-Feb 1969, "Problems in Federal Habeas Corpus Involving State Prisoners" 45 Federal Rules Decisions 1968, "Post Conviction Remedies and the Overburdened Judiciary: Solutions Ahead" Creighton L. Rev. Vol. 3 1970, "The Law of Evidence: The Basic Discipline for the Legal Mind" Iowa Advocate Vol. X No. 3 Spring 1972, "Appellate Advocacy: Its Significance for Both Judge and Lawyer" The Arkansas Lawyer March 1973, "Corrections and the Courts: A Plea for Understanding and Implementation" Resolution Vol. 1 No. 1 Fall 1974, "Why Rush to Judgment? Some Second Thoughts on the Proposed National Court of Appeals" Judicature Vol. 59 No. 4 Nov 1975, "Reconciling Tradition with Reality: The Expedited Appeal" UCLA Review Vol. 23 No. 3 Feb 1976, "Exhaustion of Grievance Procedures for State Prisoners Under Section 1977e of the Civil Rights Act" 71 Iowa L. Rev. 1986, "The Writ of Habeas Corpus: A Complex Procedure for a Simple Process" 77 No. 5 Minnesota L. Rev. May 1993, *Law: A Human Process* West Publishing Co. 1996, "A Tribute to Dean James F. Hogg" 21 William Mitchell L. Rev. 639, 1996, "Tribute to Justice Warren Burger" 22 William Mitchell L. Rev. 25, 1996, "Tribute to Judge Gerald Heaney" 81 No. 5 Minnesota L. Rev. 1095 May 1997 and "Forward: The Importance of Law Reviews" 32 Creighton L. Rev. 779, 1999.

Instructor seminars on Supreme Court decisions Creighton University 1976 and 1977. Instructor William Mitchell College of Law 1982-2001. James A. Levee Professor of Criminal Procedure Law University of Minnesota since 1992. Consultant to Advisory Committee on State-Federal Relations Federal Judicial Center 1968-70. Member Judicial Conference Committee on Trial Practice and Technique 1969-70 and Advisory Committee on Appellate Rules 1973-78. Fellow International Academy of Trial Lawyers. Executive Board American Judicature Society 1979-82. Board of Directors National Board of Trial Advocacy. Board member Pretrial Resource Center. Honorary member Iowa Academy of Trial Lawyers and The Association of Trial Lawyers of America (Board of Governors 1963-65). Member Judicial Conference of the U.S. 1980-92. Member Law Science Academy (Vice President 1960), Iowa State, Nebraska State and American Bar Associations. Faculty member on Evidence National College of Trial Judges 1964-65. Recipient Hancher-Finkbine Award from University of Iowa, Judicial Achievement Award as Outstanding Federal Appellate Judge of the Year from The Association of Trial Lawyers of America 1982 and Herbert Harley Award from American Judicature Society Oct 18, 1988. USN 1944-45. Democrat. Enjoys golfing, skiing, fishing and hunting.

Office: 560 Federal Building, 316 North Robert Street, St. Paul, Minnesota 55101.

Telephone: (651) 848-1310.

LEAVY, Edward *(Senior Judge, United States Court of Appeals Ninth Circuit)* Appointed for life by President Ronald Reagan to term beginning 1987. Assumed Senior status May 19, 1997, serves by assignment. Born Oregon Aug 14, 1929. Catholic. Educated at University of Portland A.B. cum laude 1950 and University of Notre Dame LL.B. cum laude 1953. Judge, U.S. District Court District of Oregon 1984-87.

Office: 232 Pioneer Courthouse, 555 S.W. Yamhill Street, Portland, Oregon 97204-1396.

Telephone: (503) 326-5665.

LEVAL, Pierre N. *(Senior Judge, United States Court of Appeals Second Circuit)* Appointed for life by President Bill Clinton. Assumed Senior status Aug 16, 2002, serves by assignment. Born New York New York Sept 4, 1936. Educated at Harvard University B.A. cum laude 1959 J.D. magna cum laude 1963. Law Clerk to Hon. Henry J. Friendly, U.S. Court of Appeals Second Circuit 1963-64. Admitted to practice New York 1964, U.S. Court of Appeals Second Circuit 1964 and U.S. District Court Southern District of New York 1966. In legal practice New York City 1969-75. Former Judge, U.S. District Court Southern District of New York, appointed by President Jimmy Carter to term beginning 1977.

Assistant U.S. Attorney 1964-68 and Chief Appellate Attorney 1967-68 Southern District of New York. First Assistant District Attorney 1975-76 and Chief Assistant District Attorney 1976-77 New York County. Member The American Law Institute (Council), New York County Lawyers' Association and The Association of the Bar of the City of New York. U.S. Army 1959.

Office: 1901 U.S. Courthouse, 40 Centre Street, New York, New York 10007.

Telephone: (212) 857-2310.

LINN, Richard *(Judge, United States Court of Appeals Federal Circuit)* Appointed for life by President Bill Clinton to term beginning Jan 1, 2000. Born Brooklyn New York April 13, 1944. Educated at Rensselaer Polytechnic Institute B.E.E. 1965 and Georgetown University Law Center J.D. 1969. Admitted to practice Virginia 1969, District of Columbia 1970, New York 1994, U.S. District Courts District of Columbia and Eastern District of Virginia, U.S. Courts of Appeals Fourth, Sixth, District of Columbia and Federal Circuits and U.S. Supreme Court.

Patent Examiner U.S. Patent and Trademark Office 1965-68. Adjunct Professor of Law George Washington University National Law Center since 2001. Master Giles S. Rich American Inn of Court since 2000. Member American Intellectual Property Law Association, The District of Columbia Bar (Intellectual Property Section), Virginia State Bar (Chairman 1975 and Founding Member Board of Governors Section on Patent, Trademark and Copyright Law), Virginia (Intellectual Property Law Section) and Federal Circuit Bar Associations. Advisory Board George Washington University National Law Center since 2001.

Office: National Courts Building, 717 Madison Place N.W., Washington, D.C. 20439-0002.

Telephone: (202) 633-6575.

LIPEZ, Kermit V. *(Judge, United States Court of Appeals First Circuit)* Appointed for life by President Bill Clinton to term beginning July 1, 1998. Born Philadelphia Pennsylvania Aug 18, 1941. Educated at Haverford College B.A. 1963, Yale Law School LL.B. 1967 and University of Virginia School of Law LL.M. 1990. In legal practice Portland 1973-85. Justice, Maine Superior Court 1985-94. Associate Justice, Supreme Judicial Court of Maine 1994-98.

Staff Attorney Civil Rights Division Honor Program U.S. Department of Justice 1967-68. Special Assistant and Legal Counsel to Governor Kenneth Merwin Curtis 1968-71. Legislative Aide to U.S. Senator Edmund S. Muskie 1971-72.

Office: Federal Courthouse, 156 Federal Street, Portland, Maine 04101.

Telephone: (207) 822-0455.

LOKEN, James B. *(Chief Judge, United States Court of Appeals Eighth Circuit)* Appointed for life by President George Bush to term beginning Jan 1991. Chief Judge since April 1, 2003. Born Madison Wisconsin 1940. Educated at University of Wisconsin B.S. 1962 and Harvard University J.D. 1965. Admitted to practice New York 1966 and Minnesota 1968.

Office: 11W U.S. Courthouse, 300 South Fourth Street, Minneapolis, Minnesota 55415.

Telephone: (612) 664-5810.

LOURIE, Alan D. *(Judge, United States Court of Appeals Federal Circuit)* Appointed for life by President George Bush to term beginning April 11, 1990. Born Boston Massachusetts Jan 13, 1935. Educated at Harvard University B.A. 1956, University of Wisconsin M.S. 1958, University of Pennsylvania Ph.D. 1965 and Temple University J.D. 1970.

Former Vice President Corporate Patents and Trademarks and Associate General Counsel SmithKline Beecham Corporation. Member Committee on Financial Disclosure Judicial Conference 1990-98. Member American Intellectual Property Law Association and American Bar Association. Recipient Jefferson Medal for significant contributions to intellectual property law from New Jersey Intellectual Property Law Association 1998. Member Harvard Club of Washington.

Office: National Courts Building, 717 Madison Place N.W., Washington, D.C. 20439-0002.

Telephone: (202) 633-5851.

LUCERO, Carlos F. *(Judge, United States Court of Appeals Tenth Circuit)* Appointed for life by President Bill Clinton to term beginning 1995. Born Antonito Colorado Nov 23, 1940. Educated at Adams State College B.A. 1961 and George Washington University National Law Center 1964. Law Clerk to Hon. William E. Doyle, U.S. District Court District of Colorado 1964-65. In legal practice Alamosa 1966-95.

Adjunct Professor Adams State College 1968-95.

Office: 420 U.S. Courthouse, 1823 Stout Street, Denver, Colorado 80257.

Telephone: (303) 844-2200.

LUNDIN, Keith M. *(Judge, Bankruptcy Appellate Panel Sixth Circuit)* Selected by the Judicial Council of the Sixth Circuit. Also Judge, U.S. Bankruptcy Court Middle District of Tennessee.

Office: 260 Customs House, 701 Broadway, Nashville, Tennessee 37203.

Telephone: (615) 736-5586.

LUTTIG, J. Michael *(Judge, United States Court of Appeals Fourth Circuit)* Appointed for life by President George Bush Aug 2, 1991 to term beginning Oct 17, 1991. Born Tyler Texas June 13, 1954. Educated at Washington and Lee University B.A. 1976 and University of Virginia J.D. 1981. Aide U.S. Supreme Court 1976-78. Law Clerk to Hon. Antonin Scalia, U.S. Court of Appeals District of Columbia Circuit 1982-83. Law Clerk 1983-84 and Special Assistant 1984-85 to Chief Justice Warren Earl Burger, U.S. Supreme Court. In legal practice Washington D.C. 1985-89.

LUTTIG, J. MICHAEL—*Continued*

Assistant Counsel Office of the Counsel to the President 1981-82. Principal Deputy Assistant Attorney General March 1989 to 1990 and Assistant Attorney General 1990-91 Office of Legal Counsel U.S. Department of Justice. Counselor to Attorney General of the U.S. 1990-91. Member The District of Columbia Bar, Virginia and American Bar Associations.

Office: U.S. Courthouse, 401 Courthouse Square, Alexandria, Virginia 22314-5799.

Telephone: (703) 299-3380.

LYDON, Thomas J. *(Senior Judge, United States Court of Federal Claims)* Appointed by President Ronald Reagan to term beginning Oct 1, 1982. Assumed Senior status Aug 1, 1987, serves by assignment. Born Portland Maine June 3, 1927. Educated at University of Maine B.A. 1952 and Georgetown University Law Center LL.B. 1955 LL.M. 1957. Commissioner, U.S. Court of Claims 1972-82.

Supervisory Trial Attorney U.S. Department of Justice 1955-72. USN 1945-46.

Office: National Courts Building, 717 Madison Place N.W., Washington, D.C. 20005-1086.

Telephone: (202) 219-0061.

LYNCH, Sandra L. *(Judge, United States Court of Appeals First Circuit)* Appointed for life by President Bill Clinton to term beginning March 1995. Born Oak Park Illinois July 31, 1946. Educated at Wellesley College A.B. 1968 and Boston University School of Law J.D. cum laude 1971. Law Clerk to Hon. Raymond J. Pettine, U.S. District Court District of Rhode Island 1971-73. In legal practice Boston 1978-95.

Assistant Attorney General Massachusetts 1973-74. General Counsel Massachusetts Department of Education 1974-78. Special Counsel Judicial Conduct Commission of Massachusetts 1990-92. Instructor Boston University School of Law 1973-74.

Office: 8710 U.S. Courthouse, One Courthouse Way, Boston, Massachusetts 02210-3002.

Telephone: (617) 748-9014.

MAGILL, Frank J. *(Senior Judge, United States Court of Appeals Eighth Circuit)* Appointed for life by President Ronald Reagan to term beginning April 1, 1986. Assumed Senior status April 1, 1997, serves by assignment. Born Verona North Dakota June 3, 1927. Catholic. Educated at Georgetown University School of Foreign Service B.S. 1951, Columbia University M.A. 1953 and Georgetown University LL.B. 1955. Board of Editors North Dakota Law Review 1951-52. Member Delta Sigma Psi. Admitted to practice District of Columbia 1955 and North Dakota 1955. In legal practice Fargo 1955-86.

Author "Legal Aspects of Severance Taxes on Petroleum Resources" 29 North Dakota L. Rev. 279, 1953. Important Decision: Perpich v. U.S. Department of Defense, et al. 880 F.2d 11, 1989. Former Member Association of Transportation Practitioners, National Association of Railroad Trial Counsel, Trial Attorneys of America, American Counsel Association and Federal Bar Association. Member Ethics Committee 1965-70 and Chairman Legislative Committee 1975 State Bar Association of North Dakota. Chairman North Dakota Defense Research Institute 1965-78. President Cass County Bar Association 1970. Chairman Labor Law Committee 1981 and Member Governing Council 1982-85 Section of Public Utility Law American Bar Association. Honorary Fellow American College of Trial Lawyers. Member 1988-98 and Chairman 1993-98 Committee on Financial Disclosure Judicial Conference of the United States. U.S. Navy 1945-47. Republican. Former Parliamentarian Republican State Convention. Past President Fargo Public Library. Former Board Member North Dakota State Chamber of Commerce, Village Family Service, North Dakota Cancer Society and Montessori Preschool. Former Director Law Affairs Committee Georgetown University Law Center. Enjoys skiing, tennis and sailing.

Office: 320 U.S. Courthouse, 655 First Avenue North, Fargo, North Dakota 58102-4932.

Telephone: (701) 297-7250.

MANION, Daniel A. *(Judge, United States Court of Appeals Seventh Circuit)* Appointed for life by President Ronald Reagan to term beginning 1987. Educated at University of Notre Dame B.A. in Political Science 1964 and Indiana University at Indianapolis J.D. 1973. In legal practice 1974-86.

Deputy Attorney General Indiana 1973-74. State Senator Indiana 1978-82. Lieutenant U.S. Army 1965-66 Vietnam 1966. Director of Industrial Development Indiana Department of Commerce 1969-73. Board of Directors St. Joseph Bank & Trust Company 1979-86.

Office: 301 Federal Bldg. & U.S. Courthouse, 204 South Main Street, South Bend, Indiana 46601.

Telephone: (574) 246-8060.

MARCUS, Stanley *(Judge, United States Court of Appeals Eleventh Circuit)* Appointed for life by President Bill Clinton to term beginning 1997. Born New York New York March 27, 1946. Educated at Queens College of the City University of New York B.A. 1967 and Harvard Law School J.D. 1971. Law Clerk to Hon. John Ries Bartels, U.S. District Court Eastern District of New York 1971-73. In legal practice New York City 1974-75. Judge, U.S. District Court Southern District of Florida 1985-97, appointed by President Ronald Reagan.

Assistant U.S. Attorney Eastern District of New York 1975-78. Deputy Chief 1978-79 and Chief 1980-82 Organized Crime Strike Force U.S. Department of Justice. U.S. Attorney Southern District of Florida 1982-85.

Office: 1262 Federal Justice Building, 99 N.E. Fourth Street, Miami, Florida 33132.

Telephone: (305) 536-4841.

MARGOLIS, Lawrence S. *(Senior Judge, United States Court of Federal Claims)* Appointed by President Ronald Reagan Sept 27, 1982 to term beginning Dec 15, 1982. Assumed Senior status Dec 1997, serves by assignment. Born Philadelphia Pennsylvania March 13, 1935. Educated at Drexel Institute of Technology (now Drexel University) B.S. in Aeronautical and Mechanical Engineering 1957 and George Washington University National Law Center J.D. 1961. Member Phi Alpha Delta (Officer 1960). Admitted to practice District of Columbia 1963. Magistrate Judge, U.S. District Court District of Columbia 1971-82.

Patent Examiner U.S. Patent Office 1957-62. Patent Counsel Naval Ordnance Laboratory White Oak Maryland 1962-63. Assistant Corporation Counsel District of Columbia 1963-66. Consultant to President's National Crime Commission 1966-67. Attorney Criminal Division U.S. Department of Justice and Special Assistant U.S. Attorney District of Columbia 1966-68. Assistant U.S. Attorney 1968-71. Author "Some Answers to Your Criminal Law Problems—The American Bar Association

MARGOLIS, LAWRENCE S.—*Continued*

Criminal Justice Standards" District of Columbia B. Jour. Feb 1973 and "Federal Magistrates—Relief for the Federal Courts" *The Judges Journal* Oct 1973. Editor *Young Lawyers Newspaper* 1965-66 and District of Columbia B. Jour. 1966-73. Board of Editors *The District Lawyer* 1977-79 and *The Judges Journal*. Former Technical Editor Federal B. Jour. President Federal Bar Toastmasters 1960. President District of Columbia Chapter 1975-76 and National President 1983-84 George Washington Law Association. Fellow American Bar Foundation. Member Board of Directors National Council of U.S. Magistrates 1972-75 and 1977-79. Chair Alternative Dispute Resolution Committee 2000 and Space and Building Committee 2000 U.S. Court of Federal Claims. Member District of Columbia Judicial Conference since 1968 and National Conference of Special Court Judges (Executive Committee since 1973, President 1977-78). Member Bar Association of the District of Columbia (Executive Council Young Lawyers Section 1965-68, Board of Directors Research Foundation 1968-69, Board of Directors 1970-72, Co-founder and Chairman Big Brothers Program for Federal Juvenile Offenders, Program Chairman and Moderator for radio and television programs) and American Bar Association (Criminal Justice Standards Committee 1973-76, Chairman Judicial Administration Division 1980-81). Lecturer Seminars for Prosecutors, U.S. Marshals and Narcotics Agents 1967-72, The District of Columbia Bar Criminal Practice Institute for defense attorneys and prosecutors 1972-73, Federal Judicial Center since 1972, American Bar Association Section of Criminal Law National Institute 1974 and U.S. Attorney General's Trial Advocacy Institute. Moot Court Judge Georgetown University, George Washington University and National Institute of Trial Advocacy.

Recipient Letters of Commendation from President's National Crime Commission 1966, U.S. Attorney General and Assistant Attorney General Criminal Division 1966-68, District of Columbia Bureau of Prisoner Rehabilitation and American Bar Association for Outstanding Publication. Recipient Boy Scouts Service Award, District of Columbia Jaycees Award, Legal Aid Award from George Washington University National Law Center, Award from Phi Alpha Delta, Alumni Service Award 1976 and Distinguished Alumni Achievement Award 1985 from George Washington University, Award from The District of Columbia Bar Young Lawyers Section 1983, Award from Alternative Dispute Resolution Center for Public Resources 1987, Distinguished Alumni Achievement Award from Drexel University 1988, Outstanding District President Award from Washington D.C. Rotary Club 1989 and Award for Outstanding Work Chairing Alternative Dispute Resolution Task Force U.S. Court of Federal Claims 1997. Named Outstanding Committee Chairman for Service as Editor District of Columbia Bar Journal 1972-73, Rotarian of the Year 1984 and one of "Drexel 100" (top 100 graduates in 100 year history) Drexel University 1992. Board of Governors George Washington University General Alumni Association 1978-86. Trustee Drexel University since 1983. Board of Directors since 1984, President 1988-89 and District Governor 1991-92 Washington D.C. Rotary Club.

Office: National Courts Building, 717 Madison Place N.W., Washington, D.C. 20005-1086.
Telephone: (202) 219-9581.

MARLAR, James M. *(Judge, Bankruptcy Appellate Panel Ninth Circuit)* Selected by the Judicial Council of the Ninth Circuit. Also Judge, U.S. Bankruptcy Court District of Arizona. Appointed by U.S. Court of Appeals Ninth Circuit judges.

Office: 110 South Church Avenue, Suite 8112, Tucson, Arizona 85701-1608.
Telephone: (520) 620-7500.

MARTIN, Boyce Ficklen, Jr. *(Chief Judge, United States Court of Appeals Sixth Circuit)* Appointed for life by President Jimmy Carter to term beginning 1979. Born Boston Massachusetts Oct 23, 1935. Episcopalian. Educated at Davidson College A.B. 1957 and University of Virginia J.D. 1963. Law Clerk to Chief Judge Shackelford Miller Jr., U.S. Court of Appeals Sixth Circuit 1963-64. Admitted to practice Kentucky 1963. In legal practice Louisville 1965-74. Magistrate, U.S. District Court Western District of Kentucky 1965-67. Judge, Kentucky Circuit Court Thirtieth Judicial Circuit Aug 1974 to Aug 1976. Chief Judge, Kentucky Court of Appeals Aug 1976 to Sept 1979.

Assistant U.S. District Attorney 1964-65. U.S. Attorney Western District of Kentucky 1965. Principal Assistant Jefferson County Attorney 1970-74. Member Louisville, Kentucky, Federal and American Bar Associations. Captain USAR 1957-65. Democrat. Former Chairman Louisville Zoological Commission. Former Secretary and Board member Metropolitan YMCA of Jefferson County and YMCA Blue Ridge Assembly, Black Mountain North Carolina. Former Trustee Blackacre Foundation, Louisville Kentucky and Davidson College, Davidson North Carolina. Chairman Board of Trustees Hanover College, Hanover Indiana.

Office: 209 U.S. Courthouse, 601 West Broadway, Louisville, Kentucky 40202.
Telephone: (502) 625-3800.

MARVEL, L. Paige *(Judge, United States Tax Court)* Appointed by President Bill Clinton Feb 24, 1998 to term beginning April 6, 1998. Term expires April 5, 2013. Born Easton Maryland Dec 6, 1949. Catholic. Educated at College of Notre Dame B.A. magna cum laude 1971 and University of Maryland School of Law J.D. with honors 1974. Staff member Maryland Law Review 1972-74. Member Order of the Coif. Admitted to practice Maryland 1974, U.S. District Court District of Maryland, U.S. Courts of Appeals District of Columbia and Fourth Circuits, U.S. Court of Federal Claims, U.S. Tax Court and U.S. Supreme Court. In legal practice 1974-88.

Author "Tax Aspects of Divorce and Separation" *Maryland Divorce and Separation Law* 1979, 1982, 1985, 1987, 1992 and 1996 and "Admissions and Amusement Tax" *Maryland Taxes* 1982 MICPEL; "A Checklist for Litigating the Civil Fraud Penalty Case" 4 The Practical Litigator 71 July 1993; and "Refund Claims and Forum Selection After *Lundy*" 84 Journal of Taxation 303 May 1996. Co-editor Procedure Department The Journal of Taxation since 1990. Contributor "What Every Lawyer Needs to Know (An Internal Revenue Audit)" American Bar Association Journal 64, 66 Aug 1996. Member Executive Council Baltimore City Bar Association 1977-78 and 1992-93. Council Member Tax Section Federal Bar Association 1984-90. Barrister

MARVEL, L. PAIGE—*Continued*

J. Edgar Murdock Inn of Court American Inns of Court 1988-93. Former Member National Association of Criminal Defense Lawyers, Inc. and Maryland Association of Criminal Defense Lawyers. Fellow American College of Tax Counsel (Regent 1996-98), American Bar Foundation and Maryland Bar Foundation. Member The American Law Institute (Adviser Restatement of the Law Third—The Law Governing Lawyers 1988-99), Maryland State Bar Association, Inc. (Council Member 1978-80 and Chair 1982-83 Taxation Section, Board of Governors 1988-90 and 1996-98) and American Bar Association (Council Director 1989-92 and Vice Chair Committee Operations 1993-95 Section of Taxation). Lecturer Domestic Relations Tax Workshop 1983, 1986, 1990 and 1992; United States Tax Court Judicial Conference 1986, 1988, 1990, 1992, 1994 and 1996; Virginia Conference on Federal Taxation 1989, 1994, 1995 and 1997; Tax Practitioners Technical Roundtable ABA/AICPA/IRS National Office 1990 and 1992; Invitational Conference on Professionalism in Tax Practice 1993; NYU Institute on Closely Held Businesses 1995; Annual Symposium on Accounting and Taxation North Carolina Association of Certified Public Accountants 1995 and 1997; Notre Dame Tax and Estate Planning Institute 1997; and "How to Handle a Tax Controversy" annual program ALI-ABA. Instructor and Supervising Attorney Federal District Court Practice Course 1984-85. Named one of Baltimore Magazine's "81 People to Watch in 81" Jan 1981 and one of "Maryland's Top 100 Women" 1998. Recipient Distinguished Service Award from Maryland State Bar Association, Inc. 1982-83 and Certificate of Recognition May 1987 and Distinguished Service Award May 1995 from Section of Taxation American Bar Association. Listed in *Best Lawyers in America* 1991-92, 1993-94, 1995-96 and 1997-98; *Who's Who in American Law* 1994-95, 1996-97, 1998-99 and 2000-01; *Who's Who in America* 1997-2000; and *Who's Who in the East* 2000-01. Member Keswick Improvement Association 1977-82, Advisory Commission to the Maryland State Department of Economic and Community Development 1978-81, Women's Banking Advisory Commission to Suburban Trust Bank 1980-81 and Advisory Committee University of Baltimore Graduate Tax Program 1986-98. Board of Visitors University of Maryland Law School since 1995. Board of Trustees Loyola-Notre Dame Library, Inc. since Feb 1996. Member The Women's Law Center and Stoneleigh Improvement Association.

Office: 400 Second Street N.W., Washington, D.C. 20217-0002.

Telephone: (202) 606-8871.

MAYER, H. Robert *(Chief Judge, United States Court of Appeals Federal Circuit)* Appointed for life by President Ronald Reagan to term beginning June 19, 1987. Chief Judge since Dec 25, 1997. Born Buffalo New York Feb 21, 1941. Catholic. Educated at U.S. Military Academy B.S. 1963 and College of William & Mary Marshall-Wythe School of Law J.D. 1971. Recipient William A. R. Goodwin Scholarships 1969-71, West Publishing Company Scholarship Award 1969-70, American Jurisprudence Awards for Corporation Law, Torts and Creditors' Rights and Debtors' Remedies and Outstanding Law Review Candidate Award 1969. Editor-in-Chief William & Mary Law Review 1970-71. Law Clerk to Hon. John D. Butzner, Jr., U.S. Court of Appeals Fourth Circuit 1971-72. Member Omicron Delta Kappa. Admitted to practice Virginia 1971, U.S. Court of Appeals Fourth Circuit 1972, U.S. District Court Eastern District of Virginia 1972, U.S. Court of Military Appeals 1973, U.S. Court of Military Review 1973, U.S. Supreme Court 1977 and District of Columbia 1980. In legal practice Charlottesville 1975-77 and Washington D.C. 1980-81. Judge, U.S. Claims Court 1982-87, appointed by President Ronald Reagan.

Special Assistant to U.S. Supreme Court Chief Justice Warren Earl Burger 1977-80. Deputy Special Counsel and Acting Special Counsel U.S. Merit Systems Protection Board 1981-82. Author Comment 10 William & Mary L. Rev. 767 and 997, 1969, Comment 11 William & Mary L. Rev. 261 and Note "Preventive Detention and the Proposed Amendment to the Bail Reform Act of 1966" 11 William & Mary L. Rev. 525. Lecturer University of Virginia School of Law 1975-77. Member Judicial Conference of the U.S. (Committee on International Appellate Judges Conference). Major U.S. Army 1963-75. Lieutenant Colonel USAR (retired). Recipient Bronze Star, Meritorious Service Medal, two Commendation Medals, Combat Infantryman Badge, Campaign and Service Ribbons, Ranger Tab, Parachutist Badge and Ranger Combat Badge. Republican. Board of Directors William & Mary Law School Association 1979-85, West Point Association of Graduates, Army Athletic Association and West Point Society of D.C.

Office: National Courts Building, 717 Madison Place N.W., Washington, D.C. 20439-0002.

Telephone: (202) 312-5581.

McCONNELL, Michael W. *(Judge, United States Court of Appeals Tenth Circuit)* Appointed for life by President George W. Bush to term beginning Dec 5, 2002. Born Louisville Kentucky 1955. Educated at Michigan State University B.A. 1976 and University of Chicago Law School J.D. 1979. Law Clerk to Hon. J. Skelly Wright, U.S. Court of Appeals District of Columbia Circuit 1979-80 and Hon. William J. Brennan, Jr., U.S. Supreme Court 1980-81.

Office: 6404 Federal Building, 125 South State Street, Salt Lake City, Utah 84138.

Telephone: (801) 524-5145.

McFEELEY, Mark B. *(Chief Judge, Bankruptcy Appellate Panel Tenth Circuit)* Selected by the Judicial Council of the Tenth Circuit. Chief Judge Appellate Panel since June 3, 1999. Also Judge, U.S. Bankruptcy Court District of New Mexico. Appointed by U.S. District Court judges Sept 28, 1981. Reappointed by U.S. Court of Appeals Tenth Circuit judges. Former Chief Judge Bankruptcy Court. Born Orlando Florida May 5, 1944. Presbyterian. Educated at U.S. Merchant Marine Academy B.S. 1966 and University of New Mexico J.D. cum laude 1972. Editor New Mexico Law Review 1971-72. Law Clerk to Hon. Oliver Seth, U.S. Court of Appeals Tenth Circuit 1972-73. Member Phi Kappa Phi. Admitted to practice New Mexico 1972, U.S. District Court District of New Mexico 1972 and U.S. Court of Appeals Tenth Circuit 1972. Began legal practice Santa Fe 1974.

Member American Bankruptcy Institute, National Conference of Bankruptcy Judges and State Bar of New Mexico. Democrat.

Mailing address: P.O. Box 546, Albuquerque, New Mexico 87103-0546.

Telephone: (505) 348-2525.

McKAY, Monroe G. *(Senior Judge, United States Court of Appeals Tenth Circuit)* Appointed for life by President Jimmy Carter to term beginning Dec 1977. Former Chief Judge. Assumed Senior status Dec 31, 1993, serves by assignment. Born Huntsville Utah May 30, 1928. Church of Jesus Christ of Latter-Day Saints. Educated at Brigham Young University B.S. 1957 and University of Chicago J.D. 1960. Member Order of the Coif, Blue Key and Phi Kappa Phi. Law Clerk to Arizona Supreme Court 1960-61. Admitted to practice Arizona 1961. In legal practice Phoenix 1961-66 and 1968-74.

Associate Professor 1974-76 and Professor of Law 1976-77 Brigham Young University. Member The American Law Institute, State Bar of Arizona and Maricopa County Bar Association. Member Board of Directors and President Maricopa County Legal Aid Society 1972-74. Director Peace Corps Malawi Africa 1966-68. USMC 1946-48. President Arizona Association for Health and Welfare 1970-72.

Office: 6012 Federal Building, 125 South State Street, Salt Lake City, Utah 84138-1181.

Telephone: (801) 524-5252.

McKEE, Theodore A. *(Judge, United States Court of Appeals Third Circuit)* Appointed for life by President Bill Clinton to term beginning June 1994. Born Rochester New York June 5, 1947. Educated at State University of New York at Cortland B.A. 1969 and Syracuse University College of Law J.D. 1975. In legal practice Philadelphia 1975-77. Judge, Pennsylvania Court of Common Pleas First Judicial District 1984-94.

Assistant U.S. Attorney Eastern District of Pennsylvania 1977-80. Deputy City Solicitor Philadelphia 1980-83. General Counsel Philadelphia Parking Authority 1983. Lecturer Rutgers University School of Law 1980-91.

Office: 20614 U.S. Courthouse, 601 Market Street, Philadelphia, Pennsylvania 19106-1715.

Telephone: (215) 597-9601.

McKEOWN, M. Margaret *(Judge, United States Court of Appeals Ninth Circuit)* Appointed for life by President Bill Clinton to term beginning May 28, 1998. Born Casper Wyoming May 11, 1951. Protestant. Educated at University of Wyoming B.A. 1971, University of Madrid, Spain Certificate in Hispanic Studies 1971 and Georgetown University Law Center J.D. 1975. Editor Journal of Law and Policy in International Business. Member Phi Beta Kappa. Admitted to practice Washington 1975 and District of Columbia 1980. In legal practice Seattle Washington 1975-79 and 1981-98 and Washington D.C. 1979-80 and 1995-96.

Project Director *Women and the Law in Washington State* Seattle Madrona Press 1977. Consulting Editor *Family Law Desk Book* Washington State Bar Association 1992. Author "Trial Techniques in Trade Secret Litigation" *Intellectual Counseling and Litigation* Matthew Bender 1992; "Rule 65 Injunctions" *Washington Civil Procedure Deskbook* Washington State Bar Association 1992; "Alternate Dispute Resolution—Hybrid Solutions—How to get your case out of litigation and into mediation, arbitration or other ADR forum" 1992; "Trade Secret Protection in Japan: A New Era" 2 *International Computer Lawyer* 19 Jan 1994; and "Trade Secret Litigation in the United States" New York Bar Association 1995. Co-author with Peter Cowhey "The Promise of a New World Information Order" *The Knowledge Economy* Aspen Institute 1993, reprinted U.S. Information Agency; and with Ping Kiang "China Begins Revolution in Intellectual Property" *The National Law Journal* Oct 31, 1994 and "The Road to China—Navigating the Intellectual Property Maze in China" *Road to Asia—New Dimensions in Entertainment* 1994. Contributing Author *Covenants Not to Compete* TechLaw Group 1994 and *Business and Commercial Litigation in Federal Courts* West 1998.

Important Decisions: County of Lewis v. Allen (tribal jurisdiction; en banc), 163 F.3d 509, 9th Cir. 1998; Carson Harbor Village, Ltd. v. Unocal Corp. 270 F.3d 863, 9th Cir. 2001 (en banc; held that the passive migration of contaminants does not fall within Comprehensive Environmental Response, Compensation and Liability Act's definition of "disposal" and thus affirmed the district court's award of summary judgment for certain defendants); Swinton v. Potomac Corp. 270 F.3d 794, 9th Cir. 2001 (upheld jury verdict in race discrimination case and upheld significant punitive damages award); and United States v. Idaho 210 F.3d 1067, 9th Cir. 2000 aff'd 121 S. Ct. 2135, 2001 (extensive historical and legal analysis in upholding Indians' claim to certain lands underlying Lake Coeur d'Alene).

Adjunct Professor University of Washington School of Law 2000-01. Member Code of Conduct Committee Judicial Conference of the U.S. since 2001, Ninth Circuit Executive Committee since 2000, Board of Directors American Judicature Society since 2000, The American Law Institute since 1996 and National Association of Women Judges since 1998. Board of Directors The Public Defender 1982-83. Board of Directors and President Legal Foundation of Washington 1986-91. Board of Trustees and President Western Washington Chapter Federal Bar Association 1986-89. Special Counsel Washington Commission on Judicial Conduct. Lawyer Representative to Judicial Conference of the Ninth Circuit. Member Ninth Circuit Gender Bias Task Force. Member Pro Bono Panel and Federal Judicial Nomination Commission Western District of Washington. Fellow American Bar Foundation. Member Washington Women Lawyers (Co-President 1979), American Intellectual Property Law Association, King County (Board of Trustees Young Lawyers 1979-80, Member and Secretary Board of Trustees 1984-87, Member Judicial Evaluation Committee, Judicial Conferencing Committee), Washington State (Chair Judicial Recommendation Committee 1990) and American (House of Delegates 1990-96) Bar Associations. Former Faculty Member National Institute for Trial Advocacy.

Named Outstanding Lawyer of the Year by King County Bar Association 1992 and One of 50 Most Influential Women Lawyers in America by *The National Law Journal* 1998. Recipient Big Sisters Mentor Award 1998, Distinguished Alumni Award from University of Wyoming College of Arts and Sciences 1999 and Alumnae Achievement Award from Georgetown University Law Center 2000. Listed in *Who's Who of American Women, Who's Who in American Law* and *Who's Who in America.* White House Fellow (Special Assistant to Secretary of the Interior and to Counselor to the President) 1980-81. Board of Directors White House Fellows Foundation (Former Chair).

Former Member Board of Trustees and Executive Committee Corporate Council for the Arts. Former Member and Secretary National Board of Directors Girl Scouts. Former General Counsel and Board of Directors Downtown Seattle Association. Former Member Board of Directors Family Services of King County and

MCKEOWN, M. MARGARET—*Continued*

YMCA of Greater Seattle. Former Member Advisory Committee Children's Museum Campaign. Former Member Executive Committee Washington Council on International Trade. Former Member Seattle Center Advisory Commission, Leadership Tomorrow United Way Leadership Program and Washington State Women's Council.

Office: 401 West A Street, Suite 2000, San Diego, California 92101.

Telephone: (619) 557-5300.

E-mail address: judge_McKeown@ca9.uscourts.gov

McLAUGHLIN, Joseph M. *(Senior Judge, United States Court of Appeals Second Circuit)* Appointed for life by President George Bush to term beginning Oct 18, 1990. Assumed Senior status March 20, 1998, serves by assignment. Born Brooklyn New York March 20, 1933. Educated at Fordham University A.B. 1954 LL.B. 1959 and New York University School of Law LL.M. 1964. Honorary LL.D. Mercy College 1981 and Fordham University 1997. Editor-in-Chief Fordham Law Review 1958-59. National Moot Court Team. In legal practice New York City 1959-61. Judge, U.S. District Court Eastern District of New York Oct 13, 1981 to Oct 17, 1990, appointed by President Ronald Reagan.

Author *McKinney's Practice Commentaries to Civil Practice Law and Rules* Edward Thompson & Co. 1963, "New York Trial Practice: Trends, Development" monthly article New York L. Jour. 1971-81 and *New York and Federal Law of Evidence* Practising Law Institute. Coauthor with H. Peterfreund *Cases on New York Practice* 1978. Editor-in-Chief *Practical Trial Evidence* Matthew Bender and Co. 1989. Lecturer New York Practice Practising Law Institute Harvard Law School and Columbia University School of Law 1963-71. Professor of Law 1961-81 and Dean 1971-81 Fordham Law School. Executive Secretary 1962-66 and member 1973-77 Mayor's Committee on the Judiciary. Counsel Suffolk District Court Investigation 1967. Special Mediator Medical Malpractice Panel 1975-81. Chairman New York State Law Revision Commission 1975-82. Member Committee on Modern Courts 1971-81, New York City Police Department Academic Advisory Committee 1972-75, Committee on Qualifications to Practice in Federal Courts (Clare Committee) 1973-75, Judicial Conference Committee on Standards for Admission to Practice in the Federal Courts (Devitt Committee) 1976-79 and Advisory Committee on Civil Practice New York Judicial Conference 1978-81. Fellow American Bar Foundation and New York Bar Foundation. Member The Association of the Bar of the City of New York (Committee on Law Reform 1965-66, Committee on Law and Medicine 1969-70), New York State (Executive Committee Section of Insurance Negligence and Compensation 1964-68, Committee on Continuing Legal Education since 1966, Chairman Committee on Courts and the Community 1974-82, House of Delegates 1978-80) and American Bar Associations. Captain U.S. Army Corps of Engineers Korea 1955-57. Assistant Counsel New York City Charter Revision Commission 1961. Advisory Board New York Local Coalition for Soviet Jewry 1975-81.

Office: 2402 U.S. Courthouse, 40 Centre Street, New York, New York 10007.

Telephone: (212) 857-2200.

McMILLIAN, Theodore *(Judge, United States Court of Appeals Eighth Circuit)* Appointed for life by President Jimmy Carter to term beginning Oct 2, 1978. Born St. Louis Missouri Jan 28, 1919. Educated at Lincoln University B.S. 1941 and St. Louis University J.D. 1949. Awarded honorary D.H. University of Missouri-St. Louis and honorary LL.D. St. Louis University. Member Alpha Sigma Nu. Admitted to practice Missouri 1949. Began legal practice St. Louis 1949. Judge, Missouri Circuit Court Twenty-second Judicial Circuit 1956-72. Judge, Missouri Court of Appeals St. Louis District 1972-78.

Assistant Circuit Attorney 1953-56. Author "Recommendations for Combating Juvenile Delinquency" 16 St. Louis B. Jour. 2, 1969 and "Violence and Security" 16 St. Louis B. Jour. 3, 1970. Lecturer on Law St. Louis University 1957-72. Associate Professor University of Missouri-St. Louis since 1970 and Webster College since 1977. Member American Judicature Society, Lawyers Association of Kansas City, National Council of Juvenile and Family Court Judges (Past President), John Jay Steering Committee Academy of Criminal Justice Sciences, Missouri Council of Law Enforcement Assistance 1968-70, National Advisory Board of Law Enforcement Administration 1968-70, National Legal Aid Advisory Board 1968-70, The Missouri Bar and Mound City Bar Association. Faculty member National College of the State Judiciary 1964-77 and National College of Juvenile Justice since 1972. Recipient Alumni Merit Award from St. Louis University 1965, Award of Honor (Jurist) from St. Louis Lawyers Association 1970 and Foundation Award from The Bar Association of Metropolitan St. Louis 1992. Phi Delta Phi honor initiate 1968. Named Man of the Year by Frontier International 1970. Appointed to Phi Beta Kappa by Dean of St. Louis University 1972. First Lieutenant Signal Corps USAS ETO 1942-46. Member National Council on Crime and Delinquency, Missouri Social Welfare Association, Urban League of St. Louis (Executive Committee, Past President), Herbert Hoover Boys Club of St. Louis (Chairman Advisory Board), St. Louis Minority Economic Development Agency (Board Chairman), President's Council St. Louis University, Board of Trustees Blue Cross, Advisory Council Danforth Foundation and Board of Directors Tower Village. Board Chairman Human Development Corporation 1965-77. Member Catholic Charities of St. Louis 1965-69 and Executive Committee St. Louis Crime Commission 1968-70. Subdivision Chairman "Challenge of the Seventies" Social Division 1968-70. Board of Directors St. Louis Spirit of '76, Inc. 1976-77. Enjoys reading periodicals and books relevant to the judiciary. Interested in Egyptology, Civil War, art, sports cars, music, concerts, travel and historical sites.

Office: 25.162 U.S. Courthouse, 111 South Tenth Street, St. Louis, Missouri 63102.

Telephone: (314) 244-2500.

McWILLIAMS, Robert H. *(Senior Judge, United States Court of Appeals Tenth Circuit)* Appointed for life by President Richard M. Nixon to term beginning Nov 5, 1970. Assumed Senior status Aug 1, 1984, serves by assignment. Born Salina Kansas April 27, 1916. Episcopalian. Educated at University of Denver A.B. 1938 LL.B. 1941. Admitted to practice Colorado 1941. Began legal practice Denver 1941. Judge, Denver Municipal Court 1949-52. Judge, Colorado District Court 1952-61. Justice, Colorado Supreme Court 1961-70.

Instructor University of Denver 1954-60. Member

MCWILLIAMS, ROBERT H.—*Continued*

Colorado and American Bar Associations. Sergeant OSS U.S. Army 1945-46. Republican.

Office: 216 U.S. Courthouse, 1823 Stout Street, Denver, Colorado 80257.

Telephone: (303) 844-3430.

MELLOY, Michael J. *(Judge, United States Court of Appeals Eighth Circuit)* Appointed for life by President George W. Bush to term beginning Feb 26, 2002. Born Dubuque Iowa Jan 15, 1948. Educated at Loras College B.A. 1970 and University of Iowa College of Law J.D. 1974. In legal practice Dubuque 1974-86. Judge, U.S. Bankruptcy Court Northern District of Iowa 1986-92. Judge 1992-2002 and Chief Judge 1992-99, U.S. District Court Northern District of Iowa, appointed by President George Bush. U.S. Army 1970-72. USAR 1972-76.

Office: 625 First Street S.E., Suite 200, Cedar Rapids, Iowa 52401.

Telephone: (319) 363-7580.

MEROW, James F. *(Senior Judge, United States Court of Federal Claims)* Assumed office Oct 1, 1982. Assumed Senior status Aug 5, 1998, serves by assignment. Born Salamanca New York March 16, 1932. Educated at George Washington University A.B. with distinction 1953 J.D. with distinction 1956. Board of Editors George Washington Law Review. Member Phi Beta Kappa, Omicron Delta Kappa and Order of the Coif. Trial Judge, U.S. Court of Claims 1978 to Sept 30, 1982.

Trial Attorney and Branch Director Civil Division Department of Justice 1956 and 1959-78. Member The District of Columbia Bar, Virginia State Bar, Federal and American Bar Associations. Recipient John Marshall Award from Department of Justice 1976. U.S. Army JAGC 1956-59.

Office: National Courts Building, 717 Madison Place N.W., Washington, D.C. 20005-1086.

Telephone: (202) 219-9787.

MERRITT, Gilbert S. *(Senior Judge, United States Court of Appeals Sixth Circuit)* Appointed for life by President Jimmy Carter to term beginning Nov 18, 1977. Chief Judge 1989-96. Assumed Senior status Jan 17, 2001, serves by assignment. Born Nashville Tennessee Jan 17, 1936. Episcopalian. Educated at Yale University B.A. 1957, Vanderbilt University LL.B. 1960 and Harvard University LL.M. 1962. Managing Editor Vanderbilt Law Review 1959-60. Member Order of the Coif. Admitted to practice Tennessee 1960. In legal practice Nashville 1962-63 and 1970-77.

Associate Director of Law Nashville Metropolitan Government 1963-65. City Attorney Nashville 1963-66. U.S. District Attorney Middle District of Tennessee 1966-69. Executive Secretary Tennessee Code Commission 1977. Assistant Dean and Instructor 1960-61, Lecturer 1962-76 and Associate Professor of Law 1969-70 Vanderbilt University Law School. Member The American Law Institute, Nashville, Tennessee, Federal and American Bar Associations. Democrat. Delegate Tennessee Constitutional Convention 1965. Treasurer Tennessee Democratic Executive Committee 1973-75. Chairman Board of Trustees Vanderbilt Institute of Public Policy Studies. Trustee Fisk University. Member Vanderbilt Law Alumni Association (President 1979-80).

Office: 303 U.S. Customs House, 701 Broadway, Nashville, Tennessee 37203.

Telephone: (615) 736-5957.

MESKILL, Thomas Joseph *(Senior Judge, United States Court of Appeals Second Circuit)* Appointed for life by President Gerald R. Ford to term beginning April 24, 1975. Former Chief Judge. Assumed Senior status June 30, 1993, serves by assignment. Born New Britain Connecticut Jan 30, 1928. Roman Catholic. Educated at Trinity College B.S. 1950, New York University School of Law and University of Connecticut J.D. 1956. Editor Law Review. Awarded honorary LL.D. University of Bridgeport 1971, Trinity College 1972 and University of New Haven 1974. Admitted to practice Connecticut 1956, Florida 1957, U.S. Court of Appeals Second Circuit and U.S. Supreme Court 1967. Began legal practice New Britain Connecticut 1956.

Assistant Corporation Counsel 1960-62 and Corporation Counsel 1965-66 New Britain. Member The Florida Bar, New Britain, Hartford County, Connecticut and American Bar Associations. Member Constitutional Convention Hartford 1965. Recipient Distinguished Service Award of the Junior Chamber of Commerce 1964. Officer USAF Korea. Mayor New Britain 1962-64. Elected to Congress 1966 and 1968. Served on Judiciary Committee, Subcommittee on Claims and Subcommittee on Immigration (Ranking Minority member). Governor of Connecticut 1971-75. Vice Chairman Republican Governor's Association 1973. Corporator New Britain General Hospital. Past President Junior Chamber of Commerce and New Britain Council of Social Agencies. Member Executive Committee National Governor's Conference 1971-72, President's Committee on Mental Retardation 1973-75, Daly Council Knights of Columbus and New Britain Lodge of Elks. Enjoys skiing, flying (commercial pilot license), golfing and fishing.

Office: 204 Old Post Office Plaza, 114 West Main Street, New Britain, Connecticut 06051.

Telephone: (860) 224-2617.

MICHAEL, M. Blane *(Judge, United States Court of Appeals Fourth Circuit)* Appointed for life by President Bill Clinton Aug 6, 1993. Born Charleston South Carolina Feb 17, 1943. Educated at West Virginia University A.B. 1965 and New York University School of Law J.D. 1968. In legal practice New York City 1968-71, Petersburg West Virginia 1973-75 and Charleston West Virginia 1981-93.

Assistant U.S. Attorney Southern District of New York 1971-72. Special Assistant U.S. Attorney Northern District of West Virginia 1972. Law Clerk to Hon. Robert Earl Maxwell, U.S. District Court Northern District of West Virginia 1975-76. Counsel to Governor John D. Rockefeller IV West Virginia 1977-80.

Office: 7404 U.S. Courthouse, 300 Virginia Street East, Charleston, West Virginia 25301-2523.

Telephone: (304) 347-3516.

MICHAEL, Terrence L. *(Judge, Bankruptcy Appellate Panel Tenth Circuit)* Selected by the Judicial Council of the Tenth Circuit to term beginning June 7, 2000. Also Judge, U.S. Bankruptcy Court Northern District of Oklahoma. Appointed by U.S. Court of Appeals Tenth Circuit judges to term beginning June 9, 1997. Term expires June 8, 2011. Chief Judge Bankruptcy Court June 2, 1999 to June 1, 2001. Educated at Doane College

MICHAEL, TERRENCE L.—*Continued*
B.A. magna cum laude 1980 and University of Southern California J.D. 1983. Admitted to practice Nebraska 1983. In legal practice Omaha Nebraska 1983-97.

Member American Inns of Court (President Johnson/Sontag Chapter), National Conference of Bankruptcy Judges and Nebraska State Bar Association.

Office: 123 Federal Building, 224 South Boulder Avenue, Tulsa 74103-3015.

Telephone: (918) 699-4065.

Fax: (918) 699-4061

MICHEL, Paul R. *(Judge, United States Court of Appeals Federal Circuit)* Appointed for life by President Ronald Reagan to term beginning March 8, 1988. Born Philadelphia Pennsylvania Feb 3, 1941. Educated at Williams College B.A. 1963 and University of Virginia School of Law J.D. 1966. Admitted to practice Pennsylvania 1967 and U.S. Supreme Court 1970.

Assistant District Attorney Philadelphia 1967-71. Deputy District Attorney for Investigations 1972-74. Assistant Watergate Special Prosecutor 1974-75. Assistant Counsel Senate Intelligence Committee 1975-76. Deputy Chief Public Integrity Section Criminal Division U.S. Department of Justice 1976-78. "Koreagate" Prosecutor 1976-78. Associate Deputy Attorney General 1978-81 and Acting Deputy Attorney General Dec 1979 to Feb 1980. Counsel and Administrative Assistant to Senator Arlen Specter 1981-88.

Office: National Courts Building, 717 Madison Place N.W., Washington, D.C. 20439-0002.

Telephone: (202) 633-6297.

MILLER, Christine Odell Cook *(Judge, United States Court of Federal Claims)* Appointed by President Ronald Reagan Dec 10, 1982 to term beginning Jan 24, 1983. Reappointed by President Bill Clinton Feb 4, 1998, current term expires Dec 2013. Born Oakland California Aug 26, 1944. Presbyterian. Educated at Stanford University B.A. 1966 and University of Utah College of Law J.D. 1969. Reginald Heber Smith Scholar. Comment Editor Utah Law Review 1968-69. Law Clerk to Chief Judge David T. Lewis, U.S. Court of Appeals Tenth Circuit 1969-70. Former Stanford-in-Washington Intern with Hon. Don H. Clausen, Stanford-in-Italy VIII and People-to-People Student Ambassador to England. Member Order of the Coif. Admitted to practice Utah 1969, District of Columbia 1972, California 1982, U.S. Claims Court and U.S. Supreme Court. In legal practice Washington D.C. March 1980 to Jan 1983.

Special Counsel Pension Benefit Guaranty Corporation 1976-78. Trial Attorney Foreign Litigation Unit Court of Claims Section Civil Division U.S. Department of Justice. Team Leader Attorney Bureau of Consumer Protection Division Federal Trade Commission. Assistant General Counsel U.S. Railway Association. Member The District of Columbia Bar, State Bar of California and American Bar Association. Republican. Certified gemologist. Member Cosmos Club and University Club (Board of Governors).

Office: National Courts Building, 717 Madison Place N.W., Washington, D.C. 20005-1086.

Telephone: (202) 219-9546.

MINER, Roger J. *(Senior Judge, United States Court of Appeals Second Circuit)* Appointed for life by President Ronald Reagan to term beginning Aug 2, 1985. Assumed Senior status Jan 1, 1997, serves by assignment. Born Hudson New York April 14, 1934. Jewish. Educated at Columbia College, State University of New York B.S. and New York Law School LL.B. cum laude 1956. Honorary LL.D. New York Law School, Syracuse University and Albany Law School. Managing Editor New York Law School Law Review. Admitted to practice New York 1956, U.S. Court of Military Appeals 1956, Republic of Korea 1958 and U.S. District Courts Eastern 1959 and Southern 1959 Districts of New York. In legal practice Hudson 1959-75. Justice, New York Supreme Court Third Judicial District 1976-81. Judge, U.S. District Court Northern District of New York 1981-85.

Corporation Counsel City of Hudson 1961-64. Assistant District Attorney 1964 and District Attorney 1968-75 Columbia County. Author "Research in Judicial Administration: A Judge's Perspective" 12 *Justice System Journal* 8, 1987; "Federal Courts at the Crossroads" 4 *Constitutional Commentary* 251, 1987; "Preemptive Strikes on State Autonomy: The Role of Congress" 99 *The Heritage Lectures* 1987; "Federal Courts, Federal Crimes, and Federalism" 10 Harvard Journal of Law and Public Policy 117, 1987; "Should Lawyers Be More Critical of Courts?" 71 *Judicature* 134, 1987, reprinted in *Trial* 82 May 1988 and *Case & Comment* 40 May-June 1988; "The Tensions of a Dual Court System and Some Prescriptions for Relief" 51 Albany L. Rev. 151, 1987 (11th Annual Lewis H. Case Memorial Lecture); "The Don'ts of Oral Argument" 14 *Litigation* 3 Summer 1988, reprinted in *Appellate Practice Manual* 263 American Bar Association 1992; "Appellate Practice in the United States Court of Appeals for the Second Circuit" *Appellate Practice Coursebook* New York State Bar Association Committee on Continuing Legal Education Fall 1988; "Lawyers Owe One Another" *The National Law Journal* 13 col. 1 Dec 19, 1988; "Exploiting Stolen Text: Fair Use or Foul Play" 37 *Journal of Copyright Society* 1, 1989; "Confronting the Communication Crisis in the Legal Profession" 34 New York Law School L. Rev. 1989; "One Hundred Years of Influence on National Jurisprudence: Second Circuit Court of Appeals Decisions Reviewed by the United States Supreme Court" reprinted in *United States Courts in the Second Circuit* 138 Federal Bar Council 1992; "Crime and Punishment in the Federal Courts" 43 Syracuse L. Rev. 681, 1992; book review "Rewriting the History of the Judiciary Act of 1789: Exposing Myths, Challenging Premises, and Using New Evidence" 36 New York Law School L. Rev. 525, 1992; "Advice and Consent in Theory and Practice" 41 American University L. Rev. 1075, 1992, reprinted in *Judges on Judging: Views from the Bench* 53 David M. O'Brien, ed. 1997; "Eye on Justice" 67 New York State B. Jour. Feb 1995; "The Reception of Foreign Law in the U.S. Federal Courts" 43 *American Journal of Comparative Law* 581, Fall 1995; Book Review "The Federal Courts: Challenge and Reform by Richard A. Posner" 46 Catholic University L. Rev. 1189, Summer 1997; "Professional Responsibility in Appellate Practice: A View from the Bench" 19 Pace L. Rev. 323, Spring 1999; "Frank X. Altimari—Humanist Judge" 15 Touro L. Rev. 4 Summer 1999; "Common Disorders of the Appendix and Their Treatment" 3 Journal of Appellate Practice & Process 39, 2001; and "What Terrorists Have Cause to Fear" New York L. Jour. 2 Oct 11, 2001. Co-author with Jacqueline Miner "Travels in Baja California" 9 *Experience* 30 Fall 1998.

Important Decisions: The Beer Institute v. Healy 849

MINER, ROGER J.—*Continued*

F.2d 753, 2d Cir. 1988, aff'd 491 U.S. 324, 1989; United States v. Starrett City Associates 840 F.2d 1096, 2d Cir. cert. denied 488 U.S. 946, 1988; New Era Publications International, ApS v. Henry Holt & Co. 873 F.2d 576, 2d Cir. 1989, cert. denied 493 U.S. 1094, 1990; EEOC v. State of New York 907 F.2d 316, 2d Cir. 1990; Planned Parenthood Federation of America, Inc. v. Agency for International Development 915 F.2d 59, 2d Cir. 1990, cert. denied 500 U.S. 952, 1991; Morgan Guarantee Trust Co. of New York v. Republic of Palau 924 F.2d 1237, 2d Cir. 1991; Dial Information Services Corp. of New York v. Thornburgh 938 F.2d 1535, 2d Cir. 1991, cert. denied 502 U.S. 1072, 1992; Lamb's Chapel v. Center Moriches Union Free School District 959 F.2d 381, 2d Cir. 1992 rev'd 508 U.S. 384, 1993; Quill v. Vacco 80 F.3d 716, 2d Cir. 1996, rev'd 521 U.S. 793, 1997; Kaplan v. Rand 192 F.3d 60, 2d Cir. 1999; and Commack Self-Serv. Kosher Meats v. Weiss 294 F.3d 415, 2d Cir. 2002.

Adjunct Associate Professor Columbia Greene Community College 1974-79. Lecturer State University of New York at Albany 1985. Adjunct Professor New York Law School 1986-96 and Albany Law School since 1997. Former member National District Attorneys Association. Member New York District Attorneys Association 1968-75, New York Supreme Court Justices Association 1976-81 and Association of Trial Judges Third Judicial District 1979-81. President Albany Law School American Inn of Court 1987-88. Member State/Federal Judicial Council of New York 1986-91 and Committee on Federal-State Jurisdiction Judicial Conference of the U.S. 1988-92. Member American Society of Writers on Legal Subjects (Scribes), The American Law Institute, American Judicature Society, Federal Judges Association, The Association of the Bar of the City of New York, Columbia County, New York State and American Bar Associations. Lecturer on Federal Trial and Appellate Practice in various programs of New York State Bar Association and American Bar Association. Listed in *Who's Who in American Law* and *Who's Who in America.* Recipient Distinguished Alumnus Award from New York Law School Alumni Association, Dean's Medal for Distinguished Professional Service from New York Law School, Albany Jewish Federation Award, Abraham Lincoln Award, Outstanding Elk Award, Award for Community Service from Kiwanis, Man of the Year Award from Columbia County Rotary Club 1984 and Dedication of 30th Volume New York Law School Law Review 30 New York Law School L. Rev. 693, 1985. First Lieutenant U.S. Army 1956-59. Captain USAR JAGC 1960-64. Republican. Board of Trustees New York Law School. Member Supreme Court Historical Society, Second Circuit Historical Committee (Chairman 1989-94), Northern District Historical Committee, Columbia County Historical Society, New York Law School Alumni Association, Isaiah Lodge B'nai B'rith, Congregation Anshe Emeth and Hudson Lodge of Elks (Past Exalted Ruler).

Office: 414 U.S. Courthouse, 445 Broadway, Albany, New York 12207.

Telephone: (518) 431-0401.

MONTALI, Dennis *(Judge, Bankruptcy Appellate Panel Ninth Circuit)* Selected by the Judicial Council of the Ninth Circuit. Also Judge, U.S. Bankruptcy Court Northern District of California. Appointed by U.S. Court of Appeals Ninth Circuit judges to term beginning April 23, 1993. Educated at University of Notre Dame B.A. 1961 and University of California at Berkeley J.D. 1968.

Mailing address: P.O. Box 7341, San Francisco, California 94120-7341.

Telephone: (415) 268-2320.

MOORE, Karen Nelson *(Judge, United States Court of Appeals Sixth Circuit)* Appointed for life by President Bill Clinton to term beginning 1995. Educated at Radcliffe College A.B. magna cum laude 1970 and Harvard Law School J.D. magna cum laude 1973. Staff member Harvard Law Review 1971-73. Member Phi Beta Kappa. Law Clerk to Hon. Malcolm Richard Wilkey, U.S. Court of Appeals District of Columbia Circuit 1973-74 and Associate Justice Harry A. Blackmun, U.S. Supreme Court 1974-75. Admitted to practice District of Columbia 1973, Ohio 1976, U.S. District Courts District of Columbia and Northern District of Ohio, U.S. Courts of Appeals Sixth and District of Columbia Circuits and U.S. Supreme Court 1980. In legal practice Cleveland 1975-77.

Author "Procedural Due Process in Quasi In Rem Actions After Shaffer v. Heitner" 20 William & Mary L. Rev. 157, 1978; "Collateral Attack on Subject Matter Jurisdiction: A Critique of the Restatement (Second) of Judgments" 66 Cornell L. Rev. 534, 1981; "Appellate Review of Judicial Disqualification Decisions in the Federal Courts" 35 Hastings L. Jour. 829, 1984; "Justice Blackmun's Contributions on the Court: The Commercial Speech and State Tax Examples" 8 Hamline L. Rev. 29, 1985; "The Foreign Tax Credit for Foreign Taxes Paid in Lieu of Income Taxes: An Evaluation of the Rationale and a Reform Proposal" 7 American Journal of Tax Policy 207, 1988; "The Sham Transaction Doctrine: An Outmoded and Unnecessary Approach to Combating Tax Avoidance" 41 Florida L. Rev. 659, 1989; "The Supplemental Jurisdiction Statute: An Important But Controversial Supplement to Federal Jurisdiction" 41 Emory L. Jour. 31, 1992; "The Supreme Court's Role in Interpreting the Federal Rules of Civil Procedure" 44 Hastings L. Jour. 1039, 1993; and "Justice Blackmun and Preclusion in the State-Federal Context" 97 Dickinson L. Rev. 465, 1993. Assistant Professor of Law 1977-80, Associate Professor of Law 1980-82, Professor of Law 1982-95 and Arthur E. Petersilge Professor of Law (endowed chair) 1994-95 Case Western Reserve University School of Law. Visiting Professor of Law Harvard Law School 1990-91. Member Standing Committee on Judicial Selection, Tenure and Compensation American Bar Association 1978-82. Trustee Cleveland Bar Association 1979-82. Master Bencher Judge Anthony J. Celebrezze Inn of Court since 1989. Fellow American Bar Foundation. Member Association of American Law Schools (Chair Civil Procedure Section 1985-86 and Member 1985-89 and Chair 1987-89 Committee on Academic Freedom and Tenure, Member Special Committee on Tenure and the Tenuring Process 1988-91) and The American Law Institute (Members Consultative Group Complex Litigation Project 1989-93). Chair Workshop for New Law Teachers 1986 and Workshop on Civil Procedure 1994-95 Association of American Law Schools. Recipient Teacher of the Year Award from Student Bar Association 1988 and Distinguished Teacher Award from Law Alumni Association 1990 Case Western Reserve University. Director Radcliffe College Alumnae Association 1977-80. Trustee Lakewood Hospital 1978-85 and Radcliffe College 1980-84.

MOORE, KAREN NELSON—*Continued*

Director 1984-87 and Vice President 1994-96 Harvard Alumni Association. Chair University Committee on the Status of Women Faculty Case Western Reserve University 1991-93.

Office: U.S. Courthouse, 100 East Fifth Street, Cincinnati, Ohio 45202-3988.

Telephone: (513) 564-7000.

MOORE, Thomas K. *(Judge, United States District Court District of the Virgin Islands)* Appointed by President George Bush June 30, 1992 to term beginning Aug 14, 1992. Reappointed by President George W. Bush 2002, current term expires June 2012. Former Chief Judge. Born Idaho Falls Idaho Jan 15, 1938. Protestant. Educated at Harvard University B.A. 1961 and Georgetown University Law Center J.D. 1967. Editor-in-Chief Georgetown Law Journal 1966-67. Law Clerk to Hon. John A. Danaher, U.S. Court of Appeals District of Columbia Circuit 1967-68. Admitted to practice Virginia 1967, U.S. District Courts Eastern District of Virginia 1967 and District of the Virgin Islands 1977, District of Columbia 1969, U.S. Courts of Appeals District of Columbia 1969, Fourth 1971 and Third 1977 Circuits and Virgin Islands 1977. In legal practice Washington D.C. 1969-70 and St. Thomas Virgin Islands 1978-92.

Staff Attorney U.S. Department of Transportation 1968-69. Assistant U.S. Attorney District of Columbia 1970-71, Eastern District of Virginia 1971-76 and District of the Virgin Islands 1976-78. Member American Bar Association. Attended Sentencing Institute Seminar Tallahassee Florida Oct 27-30, 1992, Seminar on Juror Utilization and Management Rancho Mirage California April 4-7, 1993, National Workshop for District Judges San Francisco California Sept 2-4, 1993, National Alternative Dispute Resolution Institute for Federal Judges Cambridge Massachusetts Nov 12-13, 1993, Workshop for Judges Third and Fourth Circuits Charlottesville Virginia March 21-23, 1994, National Court Management Conference Fort Lauderdale Florida April 24-28, 1994 and Scientific Evidence Program San Francisco California Jan 23-24, 1995 Federal Judicial Center; Budget Decentralization Workshop Administrative Office Atlanta Georgia March 21-22, 1993; Judicial Conference of the Third Circuit Baltimore Maryland April 18-19, 1993; First Judicial Conference for the Virgin Islands, Virgin Islands Judicial Council March 11, 1994; and Financial Statements in the Courtroom Workshop Federal Judicial Center and American Institute of Certified Public Accountants Orlando Florida Jan 4-6, 1995. Lieutenant USAF 1961-64. Republican. Member St. Thomas Yacht Club, St. Thomas Council of the Arts, St. Thomas Humane Society and American Association of Retired Persons. Enjoys tennis, swimming and sailing.

Office: 310 Federal Building, 5500 Veterans Drive, Charlotte Amalie, St. Thomas, Virgin Islands 00802-6424.

Telephone: (340) 774-1800.

MOTZ, Diana Gribbon *(Judge, United States Court of Appeals Fourth Circuit)* Appointed for life by President Bill Clinton to term beginning June 1994. Born Washington D.C. July 15. Roman Catholic. Educated at Vassar College B.A. with honors 1965 and University of Virginia LL.B. with honors 1968. Editorial Board Virginia Law Review 1967-68. Member Lychnos Society. Admitted to practice Maryland 1969, U.S. District Court District of Maryland 1969, U.S. Court of Appeals Fourth Circuit 1973 and U.S. Supreme Court 1980. In legal practice Baltimore 1969-71 and 1986-91. Associate Judge, Court of Special Appeals of Maryland May 22, 1991 to June 1994, appointed by Governor William D. Schaefer.

Assistant Attorney General 1972-82 and Chief of Litigation 1982-86 Attorney General's Office Maryland. Member Federal Courts Study Committee 1989-90. Member The American Law Institute, Maryland Bar Foundation, American Bar Foundation, Maryland State Bar Association, Inc. and American Bar Association. Democrat.

Office: 920 Federal Bldg. & U.S. Courthouse, 101 West Lombard Street, Baltimore, Maryland 21201-2690.

Telephone: (410) 962-3606.

MUNSON, Alex R. *(Chief Judge, United States District Court District of the Northern Mariana Islands)* Appointed by President Ronald Reagan to term beginning Nov 17, 1988. Reappointed by President Bill Clinton 1998, current term expires Nov 2008. Also Associate Justice, Supreme Court of the Republic of Palau since 1990. Born Los Angeles California Sept 25, 1941. Educated at Long Beach State College B.A. 1964 M.A. 1965, University of Southern California Ed.D. 1970 and Loyola Law School J.D. 1975. Admitted to practice California 1975, U.S. District Courts Central District of California 1977 and District of the Northern Mariana Islands 1983 and U.S. Supreme Court 1982. In legal practice Los Angeles 1977-82. Chief Justice, High Court of the Trust Territory of the Pacific Islands 1982-93.

Member State Bar of California and American Bar Association. Republican.

Mailing address: P.O. Box 500687, Saipan, MP 96950-0687.

Telephone: (670) 236-2900.

MURPHY, Diana E. *(Judge, United States Court of Appeals Eighth Circuit)* Appointed for life by President Bill Clinton. Educated at University of Minnesota B.A. magna cum laude 1954 J.D. magna cum laude 1974. Fulbright Scholar Johannes Gutenberg University, Mainz Germany 1954-55. Staff member 1972-73 and Editor 1973-74 Minnesota Law Review. Member Phi Beta Kappa and Order of the Coif. In legal practice Minneapolis 1974-76. Judge, Hennepin County Municipal Court 1976-78. Judge, Minnesota District Court Fourth Judicial District May 1978 to Feb 1980. Former Judge and Chief Judge, U.S. District Court District of Minnesota, appointed by President Jimmy Carter to term beginning Feb 1980.

Author "Minneapolis Works for Equal Opportunity" Minneapolis League of Women Voters 1965; Comment 57 Minnesota L. Rev. 603, 1973; Note "An Effort to Revise the Minnesota Bill of Rights" 58 Minnesota L. Rev. 157, 1973; Bill of Rights Committee Report Minnesota Constitutional Study Commission Feb 1973; Introductory Remarks "Women and the Constitution" VI *Law and Inequality* May 1988; "Report, U.S. District Court for Minnesota" 45 *Bench & Bar of Minnesota* 6, Aug 1988; "The Judicial Improvements Act of 1990: The Concerns of Federal Judges" 74 *Judicature* 112, Aug-Sept 1990; "Leading the Federal Judges Association into the 1990s" 22 No. 10 *The Third Branch* Oct 1990; "Unified and Consolidated Complaints in Multidistrict Litigation" 132 F.R.D. 597, 1990; and "A Tribute to U.S. Magistrate Bernard P. Becker" 17 William Mitchell

MURPHY, DIANA E.—*Continued*

L. Rev. 395, 1991. Co-author "The Minnesota Federal Court Embarks on Bicentennial Projects" 56 *The Hennepin Lawyer* 5 May-June 1987 and "Impeaching Federal Judges: Where Are We and Where Are We Going?" 72 *Judicature* 359, April-May 1989. Instructor in Trial Practice and Moot Court University of Minnesota School of Law. Fellow American Bar Foundation. Board of Directors since 1982 and former Vice President and President Federal Judges Association. Board of Directors since 1982, Vice President 1985-88 and Treasurer since 1988 American Judicature Society. Director Federal Judicial Center. Member Hennepin County Bar Foundation (Board of Directors since 1981, President 1983-84), Minnesota Women Lawyers, Eighth Judicial Circuit Judges Association (Program Committee 1981-82), National Association of Women Judges, The American Law Institute, Hennepin County (Governing Council 1976-81 and 1983-84, Chair Election Committee 1978, Co-chair Program Committee 1978-79, Member Bylaws and Long Range Planning Committee 1979-80, Executive Committee 1979-80), Minnesota State (Board of Governors 1976-81, Long Range Planning Committee 1978-81, Nominating Committee 1980, Litigation Section) and American (Judges Advisory Committee Ethics and Responsibility Standing Committee 1981-88, Standing Committee on Judicial Selection, Tenure and Compensation Section of Litigation, Judicial Administration Division) Bar Associations.

Lecturer Federal Practice Seminars Federal Bar Association and U.S. Attorney General's Advocacy Institute. Recipient Amicus Founder's Award 1980, Outstanding Achievement Award from YWCA 1981 and University of Minnesota 1983 and Distinguished Citizen Award from Alpha Gamma Delta 1985. Bench Representative on Urban Coalition Task Force on Sentencing. Charter Member Minnesota Women's Caucus and Minnesota DFL Feminist Caucus. Executive Advisory Board Victim Crisis Center. Board of Regents, Executive Committee, Chair Academic and Student Affairs Committee St. John's University. Board of Directors Operation DeNovo 1971-76 (Chairman 1974-75), Minnesota Civil Liberties Union 1973-75, Amicus 1976-80, Minneapolis United Way since 1985, Twin Cities Public Television since 1986 (Executive Committee), Minnesota Science Museum since 1988, University of Minnesota Alumni Association (President 1981-82, former Secretary and Member Executive Committee), Spring Hill Conference Center, St. Paul Chamber Orchestra, Harriet Tubman Shelter, Center for New Democratic Processes, The Arthritis Foundation and Bush Foundation (Chair). Trustee University of St. Thomas. Member Minnesota Women's Economic Roundtable and NTL Council on Foundations.

Office: 11E U.S. Courthouse, 300 South Fourth Street, Minneapolis, Minnesota 55415.

Telephone: (612) 664-5820.

MURPHY, Michael R. *(Judge, United States Court of Appeals Tenth Circuit)* Appointed for life by President Bill Clinton. Born Denver Colorado Aug 6, 1947. Catholic. Educated at Creighton University B.A. 1969 and University of Wyoming J.D. with honors 1972. Editor-in-Chief Land and Water Law Review 1971-72. Law Clerk to Chief Judge David T. Lewis, U.S. Court of Appeals Tenth Circuit 1972-73. Admitted to practice Wyoming 1972, Utah 1973, U.S. Courts of Appeals Fifth, Ninth, Tenth and Federal Circuits and U.S. Tax Court. In legal practice Salt Lake City Utah 1973-86. Former Judge and Presiding Judge, Utah District Court Third Judicial District, appointed by Governor Norman H. Bangerter to term beginning Oct 3, 1986.

Editorial Board *The Judges' Journal* American Bar Association 1997-99. Member Committee on Federal-State Jurisdiction Judicial Conference of the U.S. since 2001. Fellow American Bar Foundation since 1996. Member Utah State Bar, Wyoming State Bar and American Bar Association. Recipient Freedom of Information Award from Society of Professional Journalists 1989, Judge of the Year Award from Utah State Bar 1992, Utah Minority Bar Association Award 1995 and Alumni Achievement Citation from Creighton University 1997.

Office: 5438 Federal Building, 125 South State Street, Salt Lake City, Utah 84138-1181.

Telephone: (801) 524-5955.

MUSGRAVE, R. Kenton *(Senior Judge, United States Court of International Trade)* Appointed for life by President Ronald Reagan July 1, 1987 to term beginning Nov 13, 1987. Assumed Senior status Nov 14, 1997, serves by assignment. Born Clearwater Florida Sept 7, 1927. Educated at University of Washington B.A. 1948 and Emory University J.D. with distinction 1953. Staff member Journal of International Law 1953. Admitted to practice Georgia 1953, California 1962, U.S. Supreme Court 1962, U.S. Customs Court 1967 and U.S. Court of International Trade 1980. In legal practice 1972-75.

Assistant General Counsel Lockheed Aircraft and Lockheed International 1953-62. Vice President and General Counsel Mattel, Inc. 1963-71. Counsel League of Women Voters 1964-66. Assistant General Counsel Pacific Enterprises 1975-81. Vice President, General Counsel and Secretary Vivitar Corporation 1981-85. Member State Bar of California, State Bar of Georgia and Los Angeles County Bar Association (Chairman Corporate Law Departments Section 1965-66). Vice President and Director South Bay Social Services Group 1963-1970 and Santa Barbara Applied Research Corporation 1982-87. Director Ringling Bros. and Barnum & Bailey Combined Shows, Inc. 1968-72, Orlando Bank and Trust 1970-73, Palos Verdes Community Arts Association 1973-79, Morris Animal Foundation since 1981, Dolphins of Shark Bay Foundation, Australia since 1985 and The Dian Fossey Gorilla Fund since 1987. Member Florida Council of 100, 1970-73, appointed by governor. Director Emeritus Pet Protection Society since 1981.

Office: One Federal Plaza, New York, New York 10278-0001.

Telephone: (212) 264-2819.

NELSON, David Aldrich *(Senior Judge, United States Court of Appeals Sixth Circuit)* Appointed for life by President Ronald Reagan Oct 17, 1985. Assumed Senior status Oct 1, 1999. Born Watertown New York 1932. Educated at Hamilton College A.B. 1954, Cambridge University, England First Class Honours 1954-55 and Harvard University Law School LL.B. cum laude 1958. Valedictorian Hamilton College 1954. Fulbright Scholar. Member Phi Beta Kappa and Emerson Literary Society. Admitted to practice Ohio 1958, U.S. Supreme Court 1962, U.S. Court of Appeals Sixth Circuit 1963 and New York 1982. In legal practice Cleveland Ohio 1958-59, 1962-69 and 1972-85.

Attorney-Advisor Office of Secretary of the Air Force 1959-62. General Counsel U.S. Post Office Department

NELSON, DAVID ALDRICH—*Continued*

1969-71. Senior Assistant Postmaster General and General Counsel U.S. Postal Service 1971. Fellow American College of Trial Lawyers and Ohio State Bar Foundation. Member Cincinnati, Ohio State and Federal Bar Associations. Recipient Benjamin Franklin Award 1969. First Lieutenant USAFR 1959-62. Trustee Hamilton College 1984-88. Member National Council Ohio State University College of Law 1988-98.

Office: Potter Stewart U.S. Courthouse, 100 East Fifth Street, Cincinnati, Ohio 45202.

Telephone: (513) 564-7414.

NELSON, Dorothy Wright *(Senior Judge, United States Court of Appeals Ninth Circuit)* Appointed for life by President Jimmy Carter to term beginning 1980. Assumed Senior status Jan 1, 1995, serves by assignment. Born San Pedro California Sept 30, 1928. Educated at University of California at Los Angeles B.A. 1950 J.D. 1953 and University of Southern California LL.M. 1956. Member Phi Beta Kappa and Order of the Coif (National Vice President 1974-76). Admitted to practice California 1954.

Consultant STAR, Law Enforcement Assistant Administration. Author "Judicial Administration and the Administration of Justice" 1973. Contributor of articles to professional journals. Research Associate Fellow 1953-56, Instructor 1957, Assistant Professor 1958-61, Associate Professor 1961-67, Associate Dean 1965-67, Professor 1967 and Dean 1967-80 University of Southern California. Fellow American Bar Foundation. Advisory Board for State Courts 1971-73. Board of Directors Council on Legal Education for Professional Responsibility 1971-80, Constitutional Rights Foundation and American National Institute for Social Advancement. Co-chairman "Confronting Myths in Education" President Richard M. Nixon's White House Conference on Children and President Jimmy Carter's Commission on Pension Policy 1974-80. Member American Judicature Society (Director), State Bar of California (Board of Directors CLE Committee 1967-74) and American Bar Association (Chairman Committee on Education in Judicial Administration Judicial Administration Division since 1973). Chairman Committee on Education in Judicial Administration Association of American Law Schools. Committee to Consider Standards for Admission to Practice in Federal Courts Judicial Conference of U.S. 1976-79. Named Law Alumnus of the Year by University of California at Los Angeles 1967, Times Woman of the Year 1968, and Distinguished Jurist by Indiana University School of Law-Indianapolis 1994. Recipient Professional Achievement Award 1969, AWARE International Award 1970, Ernestine Stalhut Outstanding Woman Lawyer Award 1972, University of Judaism Humanitarian Award 1973, Coro Award for Education 1978, Medal of Honor from University of California at Los Angeles May 1993, Emil Gumpert Judicial ADR Recognition Award from Los Angeles County Bar Association 1996, Julia Morgan "Trail Blazing Architect for Racial Justice" Award from YWCA Pasadena 1997, Samuel E. Gates Litigation Award from American College of Trial Lawyers 1999, D'Alemberte/Raven Award from Section of Dispute Resolution American Bar Association April 2000, Bernard E. Witkin Award from State Bar of California Sept 2000 and Judge of the Year Award from Pasadena Bar Association Oct 2002. Board of Visitors U.S. Air Force Academy 1978. Fellow Davenport College and Yale University.

Office: Court of Appeals Building, 125 South Grand Avenue, Pasadena, California 91105-1652.

Telephone: (626) 229-7400.

NELSON, Thomas G. *(Judge, United States Court of Appeals Ninth Circuit)* Appointed for life by President George Bush to term beginning Oct 17, 1990. Born Idaho Falls Idaho Nov 14, 1936. Educated at University of Idaho College of Law LL.B. 1962. In legal practice Twin Falls 1965-90.

Assistant Attorney General and Chief Deputy Attorney General Idaho 1963-65. USAR 1965-68.

Mailing address: P.O. Box 1339, Boise, Idaho 83701-1339.

Telephone: (208) 334-9744.

NEWMAN, Jon O. *(Senior Judge, United States Court of Appeals Second Circuit)* Appointed for life by President Jimmy Carter to term beginning June 25, 1979. Former Chief Judge. Assumed Senior status July 1, 1997, serves by assignment. Born New York New York May 2, 1932. Jewish. Educated at Princeton University A.B. magna cum laude 1953 and Yale University LL.B. 1956. Law Clerk to Judge Washington 1956-57. Senior Law Clerk to Chief Justice Earl Warren, U.S. Supreme Court 1957-58. Admitted to practice Connecticut 1956. Former Judge, U.S. District Court District of Connecticut, appointed by President Richard M. Nixon to term beginning Jan 17, 1972.

U.S. Attorney District of Connecticut 1964-69. Instructor University of Connecticut Law School since 1971. Member Connecticut Bar Association. Democrat.

Office: Federal Bldg. & U.S. Courthouse, 450 Main Street, Hartford, Connecticut 06103.

Telephone: (860) 240-3260.

NEWMAN, Pauline *(Judge, United States Court of Appeals Federal Circuit)* Appointed for life by President Ronald Reagan to term beginning May 7, 1984. Born New York New York June 20, 1927. Educated at Vassar College B.A. 1947, Columbia University M.A. 1948, Yale University Ph.D. in Chemistry 1952 and New York University School of Law LL.B. 1958. Admitted to practice New York 1958 and Pennsylvania 1979.

Patent Attorney and House Counsel 1954-84 and Director Patent, Trademark and Licensing Department 1969-84 FMC Corp. Board of Directors American Institute of Chemists 1960-66 and 1970-76; American Chemical Society 1973-75, 1976-78 and 1979-81; and Philadelphia College of Pharmacy and Science 1983-84. National Board Medical College of Pennsylvania 1975-84. Member U.S. Delegation to Diplomatic Conference on the Revision of Paris Convention for the Protection of Industrial Property 1982-84. Patent Policy Board State University of New York 1983-84. Board of Governors New York Patent Law Association 1970-74. Board of Directors 1975-76 and 1977-79 and Vice President 1978-79 U.S. Trademark Association. Board of Directors American Patent Law Association 1981-84. Section Council Section of Patent, Trademark and Copyright Law American Bar Association 1982-84.

Office: National Courts Building, 717 Madison Place N.W., Washington, D.C. 20439-0002.

Telephone: (202) 633-5841.

NIEMEYER, Paul Victor *(Judge, United States Court of Appeals Fourth Circuit)* Appointed for life by

NIEMEYER, PAUL VICTOR—*Continued*

President George Bush to term beginning 1990. Born Princeton New Jersey April 5, 1941. Episcopalian. Educated at Kenyon College A.B. 1962, University of Munich, Germany 1962-63 and University of Notre Dame J.D. 1966. Admitted to practice Maryland 1966, U.S. District Courts District of Maryland 1967 and Southern District of Texas 1977, U.S. Courts of Appeals Fourth 1968, Fifth 1978 and Third 1980 Circuits and U.S. Supreme Court 1970. In legal practice Baltimore 1966-88. Judge, U.S. District Court District of Maryland 1988-90, appointed by President Ronald Reagan.

Co-author *Maryland Rules Commentary* 1984 supplement 1988 and 2nd ed. 1992. Contributor of articles to professional journals. Lecturer on Advanced Business Law Johns Hopkins University 1971-75. Senior Lecturing Fellow Duke University School of Law since 1994. Fellow American College of Trial Lawyers, American Bar Foundation and Maryland Bar Foundation. Member Standing Committee on Rules of Practice and Procedure for Courts of Appeals 1973-88, Hearing Panel Attorney Grievance Committee 1978-81 and Select Committee on Professional Conduct 1983-85. Member since 1993 and Chairman since 1996 Civil Rules Advisory Committee. Member Wednesday Law Club, Lawyers Round Table, The American Law Institute and Maryland State Bar Association, Inc. Lecturer Maryland Judicial Conference. Recipient Distinguished Service Award from Litigation Section Maryland State Bar Association, Inc. 1981 and Special Merit Citation from American Judicature Society 1987. Republican.

Office: 910 Federal Bldg. & U.S. Courthouse, 101 West Lombard Street, Baltimore, Maryland 21201-2611.

Telephone: (410) 962-4210.

NIMS, Arthur L., III *(Senior Judge, United States Tax Court)* Appointed by President Jimmy Carter to term beginning June 29, 1979. Chief Judge June 1, 1988 to May 31, 1992. Assumed Senior status June 1, 1992, serves under recall. Born Oklahoma City Oklahoma Jan 3, 1923. Educated at Williams College B.A., University of Georgia School of Law LL.B. and New York University School of Law LL.M. in Taxation. Admitted to practice Georgia 1949 and New Jersey 1955. In legal practice Macon Georgia 1949-51 and Newark New Jersey 1955-79.

Special Attorney Office of the District Counsel New York City 1951-54 and Attorney Legislation and Regulations Division Chief Counsel's Office Washington D.C. 1954-55 Internal Revenue Service. Member The American Law Institute, New Jersey State (Chairman Section of Taxation 1969-71) and American (Secretary Section of Taxation 1977-79) Bar Associations. Lieutenant j.g. active duty USNR PTO WWII.

Office: 400 Second Street N.W., Washington, D.C. 20217-0002.

Telephone: (202) 606-8761.

NOONAN, John T., Jr. *(Senior Judge, United States Court of Appeals Ninth Circuit)* Appointed for life by President Ronald Reagan Oct 16, 1985. Assumed Senior status Dec 27, 1996, serves by assignment. Born Boston Massachusetts Oct 24, 1926. Educated at Harvard University B.A. 1946 LL.B. 1954 and Catholic University of America M.A. 1949 Ph.D. 1951. In legal practice Boston 1955-60.

Special Staff/Assistant to Robert Cutler National Security Council 1954-55. Associate Professor of Law 1961-63 and Professor of Law 1963-66 Notre Dame Law School. Professor of Law University of California Boalt Hall School of Law 1966-86.

Mailing address: P.O. Box 193939, San Francisco, California 94119-3939.

Office: 331 U.S. Court of Appeals Building, 95 Seventh Street, San Francisco, California 94103.

Telephone: (415) 556-9636.

NORRIS, Alan E. *(Senior Judge, United States Court of Appeals Sixth Circuit)* Appointed for life by President Ronald Reagan to term beginning July 1, 1986. Assumed Senior status July 1, 2001, serves by assignment. Born Columbus Ohio Aug 15, 1935. Educated at La Sorbonne University of Paris Certificate 1956, Otterbein College B.A. with honors 1957, New York University School of Law LL.B. 1960 and University of Virginia School of Law LL.M. 1986. Honorary L.H.D. Otterbein College 1991. Honorary LL.D. Capital University Law School 2001. Root-Tilden Scholar New York University 1960. Law Clerk to Chief Justice Kingsley A. Taft, Ohio Supreme Court 1960-61. Admitted to practice Ohio 1960. In legal practice Columbus 1961-62 and Westerville 1962-80. Judge, Ohio Court of Appeals Tenth District 1981-86.

City Prosecutor City of Westerville 1962-66. Author book review "Delay in Court" Ohio Bar April 25, 1960, "The Law's Delay in Ohio: Remedy Without New Legislation" Ohio Bar July 18, 1960, Statehouse Report weekly column published in legislative district weekly newspapers 1967-80, "Ohio's New Criminal Code" Ohio Bar Feb 5, 1973, "Legislative History of Ohio's New Criminal Code" Cleveland State L. Rev. Winter 1974, "Divorce Reform, Ohio Style" Ohio Bar Sept 16, 1974, "Divorce Reform: Ohio's Alternative to No-Fault" State Government Winter 1975, "Cons of the Lottery Game" Sunday Plain Dealer Magazine Aug 22, 1976, "And Still Counting" The Columbus Dispatch Magazine Sept 19, 1976 reprinted Ohio Township News Dec 1976, "Modern Courts: The Next Step" Ohio Bar Nov 15, 1976, "Financing Alcohol Abuse Programs—Where Do We Go From Here?" *Ohio's Health* March-April 1977, "Shock Treatment for Felons in Ohio" State Government Winter 1977, "How Do You Feel About Shock Parole?" The Columbus Dispatch April 5, 1977, "Public Financing of Campaigns is a Hoax" The Columbus Citizen-Journal May 9, 1977, "Divorce Reform Revisited" Ohio Bar June 27, 1977, "Should Ohio Repeal Its 'Little Hatch Act'?" The Columbus Dispatch Dec 26, 1977, "Bringing Federal Judges to Account" *Ohio Pharmacist* Nov 1978, "Ohio Has Its Own Unknown Soldier" The Columbus Dispatch Magazine Dec 10, 1978, "How to Check the Power of Our Federal Judiciary" State Legislatures Jan 1979, "Dog Racing—Who Needs It?" The Columbus Dispatch May 14, 1979, "A New Bill for Public-Sector Collective Bargaining in Ohio" Agenda For Management Spring 1979, "Ohioans Better Served by Citizen Legislators" The Public Employee News July 1979, "Issue Two Ignores Spending Hikes by Government" The Columbus Dispatch May 12, 1980, "The Battle of Piqua" The Columbus Dispatch Magazine Aug 3, 1980, "Ohio Domestic Relations Law, Chapter 69, Appeals: Review Basis" Banks-Baldwin Law Publishing Company 1984, "Equal Justice: Where Promise is Eroded by Practice" *Ohio Bar* July 28, 1986, "Ohio's Divorce Reform Act—Expectation and Realization" 13 Ohio Northern University L. Rev. 173, 1986 and "The Bicentennial of Judicial

NORRIS, ALAN E.—*Continued*

Federalism" 53 Ohio Official Reports LVII 1990. Editor "Title 31, Domestic Relations—Children" *Ohio's Revised Code Annotated* Banks-Baldwin Law Publishing Company Sept 10, 1976.

Instructor in Business Law Otterbein College 1976-80. Member Council of State Governments (Committee on Suggested State Legislation 1967-76, Executive Subcommittee 1969-76), Ohio Constitutional Revision Commission 1971-77 (Chairman Grand and Petit Jury Committee 1975-76), Ohio Comprehensive Health Planning Council 1971-72, Federal Elections Commission Advisory Panel 1976-77, National Legislative Conference (Member 1973-76 and Chairman 1974-76 Reapportionment Committee), Dangerous Offender Project Academy for Contemporary Problems (Advisory Committee 1975-78), National Conference of State Legislatures (Committee on Ethics, Elections and Reapportionment 1976-80, Chairman Subcommittee on Voters, Candidates and Equipment 1979-80), Ohio Judicial Conference (Chairman Subcommittee on Plain Language Jury Instructions since 1983), American Judicature Society, Institute of Judicial Administration, Court of Appeals Association (Co-chairman Legislative Committee since 1983), Columbus (Professional Ethics Committee 1961-64, Real Property Committee 1964-67, member 1967-72 and Chairman 1969-70 Committee on the Judiciary, member Legislative Committee 1972-74 and ad hoc Committee 1976-78), Ohio State (Modern Courts Committee 1961-64, Electronics Reporting Committee 1970) and American (Sections: General Practice and Family Law 1976-80) Bar Associations. Attended Seminar for Outstanding State Legislators Eagleton Institute Rutgers University 1969 and Intermediate Appellate Judges' Seminar Institute of Judicial Administration New York University School of Law 1981. Lecturer at CLE Seminars Ohio State Bar Association and Ohio Academy of Trial Lawyers. Lecturer at CLE Seminars and Noon Luncheon Series Columbus Bar Association. Lecturer Ohio Judicial Conference and Buckeye Girls' State.

Named Outstanding Young Man by Jaycees 1967, Honorary Kentucky Colonel 1971 and Legislator of the Year Award by Ohio Academy of Trial Lawyers 1972. Recipient Public Resolution of Honor from Ohio Prosecuting Attorneys Association 1971 and Special Achievement Award from Otterbein College 1973. Listed in *Who's Who in America, Who's Who in Ohio, Who's Who in Government, Who's Who in American Politics, Who's Who in the Midwest, Who's Who Among Authors and Journalists, Who's Who in American Law, Who's Who of American Lawyers, Outstanding Americans, Community Leaders and Noteworthy Americans, Notable Americans, Dictionary of International Biography, Personalities of the West and Midwest, International Who's Who in Community Service, The Best Lawyers in America, Men of Achievement, Two Thousand Notable Americans, Blue Book of Franklin County, Directory of Distinguished Americans* and *5,000 Personalities of the World.* Member Ohio House of Representatives Jan 1, 1967 to Dec 31, 1980. House Minority Whip Jan 1, 1973 to Dec 31, 1980. Member Franklin County Republican Central Committee 1962-80 (Chairman Rules Committee 1976-78). Member Special Finance Committee 1976-78 and Federal Judiciary Task Force 1979-80 Ohio Republican Party. Member 1962-66 and Chairman 1966 Westerville Zoning Board of Appeals. Member 1970-80, Vice Chairman 1971-75 and Chairman 1975-80 Ohio American Revolution Bicentennial Commission. Member Central Ohio American Revolution Bicentennial Commission 1974-80 and Blendon Township American Revolution Bicentennial Commission 1974-80. Member Pi Kappa Phi Alumni Association (President 1962-64, Trustee 1963-80), Alumni Council 1963-67, Development Board since 1965 and Administrative Council 1971 Otterbein College. President Otterbein College Alumni Association 1971-72. Trustee United Methodist Children's Home Worthington 1970-82. Board of Directors Maryhaven, Inc. 1975-78. Board of Governors The Westerville Fund (administered by Columbus Foundation) since 1981. Scoutmaster Post 39, 1961-63, Merit Badge Counselor since 1965, member Arrowhead District Central Ohio Council since 1981 and Chairman Nominating Committee 1982-83 Boy Scouts of America. President Emerson School PTA 1972-73. Member Westerville Historical Society since 1961 (President 1967-69), Advisory Board of Management North Branch YMCA, Westerville Area Council of Churches 1968-71, Church of the Master United Methodist Church (Board of Trustees 1971-76 and 1978-80, Finance Committee 1973-75 and since 1984, Pastor-Parish Relations Committee 1981-83, Sunday School teacher and usher), Ohio Historical Society, Sons of the American Revolution, Kiwanis (Member 1962-79 and Chairman Division 10E Support of Churches Program 1965-66, Charter member and President 1964 Westerville Club) and Masons (Master Blendon Lodge 339 R. & A.M. 1966, Worthy Patron Mizpah Chapter 38 Order Eastern Star 1967, Commissioner of Trials Grand Lodge of Ohio 1972-78, member Horeb Chapter 3 R.A.M., Zabud Council 99 R. & S.M. and Mount Vernon Commandry 1 K.T.).

Office: 328 U.S. Courthouse, 85 Marconi Boulevard, Columbus, Ohio 43215.

Telephone: (614) 719-3330.

NUGENT, Robert E. *(Judge, Bankruptcy Appellate Panel Tenth Circuit)* Selected by the Judicial Council of the Tenth Circuit to term beginning March 5, 2002. Also Chief Judge, U.S. Bankruptcy Court District of Kansas. Appointed by U.S. Court of Appeals Tenth Circuit judges to term beginning June 14, 2000. Term expires June 14, 2014. Chief Judge Bankruptcy Court since Oct 28, 2002. Born May 2, 1955. Educated at University of Kansas B.A. 1977 J.D. 1980.

Office: 104 U.S. Courthouse, 401 North Market Street, Wichita, Kansas 67202.

Telephone: (316) 269-6404.

NYGAARD, Richard L. *(Judge, United States Court of Appeals Third Circuit)* Appointed for life by President Ronald Reagan to term beginning Nov 7, 1988. Born Thief River Falls Minnesota July 9, 1940. Educated at University of Southern California B.S. cum laude 1969 and University of Michigan J.D. 1971. Honorary LL.D. Edinboro University 1993. Judge, Pennsylvania Court of Common Pleas Sixth Judicial District 1981 to Nov 7, 1988.

Faculty Member, Director Institute for Behavioral Research and Lecturer on Genetics and the Law Pennsylvania State University. Lecturer on Genetics and the Law University of Chicago Law School. Constitutional Consultant Albania, Lithuania, Ukraine, Russia, Kazakhstan, Azerbaijan and Croatia. Member Committee on Automation Technology for the U.S. Courts (Chairman Long Range Planning Subcommittee), Erie County, Pennsylva-

NYGAARD, RICHARD L.—*Continued*
nia and Federal Bar Associations. Lecturer on Genetics and the Law Mid-Georgia Educational Foundation and American Society of Criminologists. County Councilman 1977-81. Board of Visitors Regent University School of Law. Life Member NAACP.
Office: 717 State Street, Suite 500, Erie, Pennsylvania 16501.
Telephone: (814) 454-2304.

OAKES, James L. *(Senior Judge, United States Court of Appeals Second Circuit)* Appointed for life by President Richard M. Nixon to term beginning May 27, 1971. Chief Judge Jan 1, 1989 to July 1, 1992. Assumed Senior status July 1, 1992, serves by assignment. Born Springfield Illinois Feb 21, 1924. Educated at Harvard University A.B. cum laude 1945 LL.B. cum laude 1947. Awarded honorary LL.D. New England College 1976, Suffolk University 1980 and Vermont Law School 1995. Law Clerk to Hon. Harrie B. Chase, U.S. Court of Appeals 1947-48 and 1949-50. Admitted to practice California 1949 and Vermont 1950. Began legal practice San Francisco California 1949. In legal practice Brattleboro Vermont 1950-66 and 1969-70. Judge, U.S. District Court District of Vermont 1970-71.
Attorney General Vermont 1967-69. Counsel Vermont Statutory Revision Commission 1957-60. Special Counsel Public Service Commission 1959-60. Adjunct Professor of First Year Ethics Duke University School of Law 1985-90 and 1992-96. Adjunct Professor of Professional Responsibility Iowa University College of Law 1993-97. Life Member The American Law Institute. Member Vermont Trial Lawyers Association (President 1965-66), American Bar Foundation, American Judicature Society, Institute of Judicial Administration and Vermont Bar Association (President 1971-72). Recipient Learned Hand Award for Excellence in Jurisprudence from Federal Bar Council 1983; Environmental Law Institute Award 1989; Louis Dembitz Brandeis Medal for Distinguished Legal Service from Brandeis University 1991; William J. Brennan, Jr. Award for Commitment to Individual Rights and Civil Liberties from New York State Association of Criminal Defense Lawyers 1992; Gold Medal Award for Distinguished Service in the Law from New York State Bar Association 1992; and Edward Weinfeld Award for Distinguished Contribution to the Administration of Justice 1992 and Distinguished Public Service Award 1994 from New York County Lawyers' Association. Member State Senate Vermont 1961-65.
Mailing address: P.O. Box 696, Brattleboro, Vermont 05302-0696.
Telephone: (802) 254-5000.

O'BRIEN, Terrence L. *(Judge, United States Court of Appeals Tenth Circuit)* Appointed for life by President George W. Bush to term beginning April 23, 2002. Born Lincoln Nebraska Aug 8, 1943. Catholic. Educated at University of Wyoming B.S. 1965 J.D. with honors 1972. Staff member 1970 and Wyoming Division Editor 1971-72 Land & Water Law Review. Member Phi Kappa Phi. Admitted to practice Wyoming 1972, U.S. District Court District of Wyoming 1972, U.S. Courts of Appeals Second, Fourth, Fifth, Seventh, Eighth, Ninth, Tenth and District of Columbia Circuits 1972-74 and U.S. Supreme Court 1975. In legal practice Buffalo 1974-80. Justice of the Peace, Johnson County Justice Court Nov 1975 to Aug 1980. Former Judge, Wyoming District Court Sixth Judicial District, appointed by Governor Ed Herschler to term beginning Aug 15, 1980.
With Land and Natural Resources Division U.S. Department of Justice Washington D.C. 1972-74. Instructor in Business Law University of Wyoming 1971-72 and Sheridan College 1976. Member Wyoming State Bar. Attended The National Judicial College. Captain USAR 1966-69. Republican.
Office: 2120 Capitol Avenue, Room 20212, Cheyenne, Wyoming 82001.
Telephone: (307) 772-2660.

O'CONNOR, Sandra Day *(Associate Justice, The Supreme Court of the United States)* Appointed for life by President Ronald Reagan to term beginning Sept 21, 1981. Also Circuit Justice, U.S. Court of Appeals Ninth Circuit. Born El Paso Texas March 26, 1930. Protestant. Educated at Stanford University A.B. magna cum laude 1950 LL.B. 1952. Board of Editors Stanford Law Review. Member Order of the Coif and Cap and Gown. Admitted to practice California 1952 and Arizona 1957. Judge, Superior Court of Arizona 1974-79. Judge, Arizona Court of Appeals 1979-81.
Former member State Bar of California. Member State Bar of Arizona and American Bar Association. Recipient Phoenix Ad Club Woman of the Year Award 1972 and National Conference of Christians and Jews Humanitarian Award 1974. Republican. Member State Senate Arizona 1969-75. Board of Trustees Stanford University, Heard Museum and Phoenix Historical Society. Member Salvation Army Advisory Board, Taft Institute, Junior Achievement and National Defense Advisory Committee on Women in the Service 1973-76. Enjoys tennis, skiing and golf.
Office: One First Street N.E., Washington, D.C. 20543-0001.
Telephone: (202) 479-3000.

O'SCANNLAIN, Diarmuid F. *(Judge, United States Court of Appeals Ninth Circuit)* Appointed for life by President Ronald Reagan Sept 26, 1986 to term beginning Nov 25, 1986. Born New York New York March 28, 1937. Catholic. Educated at St. John's University B.A. 1957, Harvard University J.D. 1960 and University of Virginia School of Law LL.M. in Judicial Process 1992. Honorary LL.D. University of Notre Dame 2002. Admitted to practice New York 1964 and Oregon 1965. Began legal practice New York 1963. In legal practice Portland Oregon 1965-86.
Deputy Attorney General Oregon 1969-71. Public Utility Commissioner Oregon 1971-73. Director Department of Environmental Quality Oregon 1973-74. Adjunct Professor Lewis & Clark College Northwestern School of Law. Member Federal Judges Association, Oregon State Bar, New York State, Federal and American (Committee on Appellate Practice and Ninth Appellate Practice Institute, Past Chair Appellate Judges Conference, Immediate Past Chair Judicial Division) Bar Associations. Faculty Member Institute for Judicial Administration New York University School of Law. Major U.S. Army JAGC 1955-78. Republican. Member Republican National Committee 1983-86. Moot Court Judge Harvard Law School, Stanford Law School, University of California Boalt Hall School of Law, University of Virginia, Cornell University, University of Notre Dame, Fordham University, University of Alabama, University of Southern California, University of California at Davis and

O'SCANNLAIN, DIARMUID F.—*Continued*

Loyola Marymount University. Member Harvard Law School Association.

Office: 313 Pioneer Courthouse, 555 S.W. Yamhill Street, Portland, Oregon 97204-1396.

Telephone: (503) 326-2187.

PAEZ, Richard A. *(Judge, United States Court of Appeals Ninth Circuit)* Appointed for life by President Bill Clinton to term beginning March 17, 2000. Born Salt Lake City Utah May 5, 1947. Church of Jesus Christ of Latter-Day Saints. Educated at University of California at Irvine 1966-67, Brigham Young University B.A. 1969 and University of California Boalt Hall School of Law J.D. 1972. Admitted to practice California 1972, U.S. District Courts Eastern 1972, Central 1973, Northern and Southern Districts of California, U.S. Court of Appeals Ninth Circuit 1975 and U.S. Supreme Court 1977. Judge April 6, 1981 to 1994, Assistant Presiding Judge 1987 and Presiding Judge 1988, Los Angeles Municipal Court Los Angeles County. Temporary Judge, California Court of Appeal Second District Division Seven June 1983 to July 1983. Judge, U.S. District Court Central District of California June 16, 1994 to 2000, appointed by President Bill Clinton.

Staff Attorney Western Center on Law and Poverty, Inc. 1974-76. Director of Litigation/Senior Counsel Oct 1976 to Dec 1980 and Acting Executive Director Jan 1981 to May 1981 Legal Aid Foundation of Los Angeles. Member California Judges' Association 1981-94, Los Angeles County Criminal Justice Coordinating Committee 1988 and 1990-91, Los Angeles County Judicial Procedures Commission 1988 and 1990-91, California Judicial Council Feb 1991 to July 1994 (Court Management and Municipal and Justice Courts Committee 1991-93, Executive Committee 1993), Ad Hoc Superior and Municipal Courts Administrative Consolidation Committee 1993 and Ad Hoc Los Angeles Superior Court Civil Rules Committee 1993. Board of Directors Public Counsel 1984-87. Chair Los Angeles County Municipal Courts Marshal's Committee 1986-88 and Los Angeles County Municipal Court Judges' Association 1990-91. Member Los Angeles County/City Criminal Justice Group, Mexican-American Bar Association of Los Angeles (Board of Trustees 1981) and Los Angeles County Bar Association (Special Committee on California Rape Laws 1978, Economical Litigation Committee 1983-84, State Courts Committee 1988-94). Lecturer Landlord-Tenant Litigation Rutter Group 1984 and 1990. Instructor Civil Institute 1985 and 1986 and California Continuing Judicial Studies Program 1985-87 and 1990 and Member New Judge Education Planning Committee 1988-91 and Civil Procedures Bench Book Planning Committee California Center for Judicial Education and Research. Instructor Civil Law and Motion 1985-87 and 1990-91 California Judicial College. Recipient Benito Juarez Award for Outstanding Legal Accomplishments from Mexican-American Bar Association of Los Angeles 1980.

Mailing address: P.O. Box 91510, Pasadena, California 91109-1510.

Office: 204 U.S. Courthouse, 125 South Grand Avenue, Pasadena, California 91105-1652.

Telephone: (626) 229-7180.

PAJAK, John J. *(Special Trial Judge, United States Tax Court)* Appointed by U.S. Tax Court Chief Judge C. Moxley Featherston May 31, 1979. Liaison Special Trial Judge 1984-85. Chief Special Trial Judge 1985-87. Born Buffalo New York Aug 24, 1932. Educated at Syracuse University B.A. in American Studies magna cum laude 1954 LL.B. 1956 replaced by J.D. Notes Editor Syracuse Law Review. Member Phi Beta Kappa, Orange Key (Former Vice President) and Order of the Coif. Admitted to practice New York 1956, District of Columbia 1961, U.S. Supreme Court, U.S. Courts of Appeals First, Fourth and Ninth Circuits, U.S. Claims Court and U.S. Tax Court. In legal practice Washington D.C. 1961-79.

With Attorney General's Recruitment Program for Honor Law Graduates Office of Alien Property Litigation Section 1956-58 and Tax Division Appellate Section 1958-61 U.S. Department of Justice. Member The District of Columbia Bar, Federal and American (Section of Taxation) Bar Associations.

Office: 400 Second Street N.W., Washington, D.C. 20217-0002.

Telephone: (202) 874-6079.

PANUTHOS, Peter J. *(Special Trial Judge, United States Tax Court)* Appointed by U.S. Tax Court Chief Judge Theodore Tannenwald, Jr. to term beginning June 13, 1983. Currently serves as Chief Special Trial Judge. Educated at Bernard Baruch School of Business City College of the City University of New York, Bryant College B.S. 1966, Suffolk University Law School J.D. 1969 and Boston University School of Law LL.M. in Taxation 1972. Staff member Suffolk University Law Review. Admitted to practice Massachusetts 1969, District of Columbia 1999 and U.S. Supreme Court.

Trial Lawyer and Assistant District Counsel Boston Office of Chief Counsel Internal Revenue Service 1970-83. Adjunct Professor Bentley College, Catholic University of America School of Law and University of the District of Columbia School of Law. Member American Inns of Court, Federal (Former Officer Boston Chapter) and American Bar Associations. Faculty Member Trial Training Program National Institute for Trial Advocacy for six years.

Office: 400 Second Street N.W., Washington, D.C. 20217-0002.

Telephone: (202) 874-6075.

PARKER, Barrington D., Jr. *(Judge, United States Court of Appeals Second Circuit)* Appointed for life by President George W. Bush to term beginning Oct 18, 2001. Born Washington D.C. Aug 21, 1944. Educated at Yale University B.A. 1965 LL.B. 1969. Law Clerk to Hon. Aubrey E. Robinson, Jr., U.S. District Court District of Columbia 1969-70. In legal practice New York City 1970-94. Judge, U.S. District Court Southern District of New York 1994 to Oct 17, 2001, appointed by President Bill Clinton.

Office: Two Stamford Plaza, 281 Tresser Boulevard, Stamford, Connecticut 06901.

Telephone: (203) 328-8080.

PARKER, Fred I. *(Judge, United States Court of Appeals Second Circuit)* Appointed for life by President Bill Clinton Oct 11, 1994. Born Boston Massachusetts Feb 2, 1938. Educated at University of Massachusetts B.A. cum laude 1962 and Georgetown University Law Center LL.B. 1965. Managing Editor Georgetown Law Journal. In legal practice Middlebury 1972-90. Judge 1990-94 and Chief Judge 1991-94, U.S. District Court District of Vermont.

Deputy Attorney General Vermont 1969-72. Chair

PARKER, FRED I.—*Continued*

Vermont Criminal Justice Training Counsel 1973-79. Member Professional Conduct Board Vermont Supreme Court 1975-79. Member Judicial Conduct Board of Vermont 1982-89. Member American Board of Trial Advocates, Chittenden County and Vermont (Chair Special Committee on the Reform of the Judiciary 1988-89) Bar Associations. USMCR 1956-62.

Mailing address: P.O. Box 392, Burlington, Vermont 05402.

Telephone: (802) 951-6401.

PEREZ-GIMENEZ, Juan M. *(Judge, United States District Court District of Puerto Rico)* Magistrate 1975-79. Appointed Judge for life by President Jimmy Carter Oct 23, 1979. Chief Judge 1984-91. Born San Juan Puerto Rico March 28, 1941. Educated at University of Puerto Rico B.A. 1963 LL.B. 1968 and George Washington University M.B.A. 1965. In legal practice San Juan 1968-71.

Assistant U.S. Attorney District of Puerto Rico 1971-75.

Office: CH-125 U.S. Courthouse, 150 Carlos Chardon Avenue, San Juan, Puerto Rico 00918-1765.

Telephone: (787) 772-3140.

PERRIS, Elizabeth L. *(Judge, Bankruptcy Appellate Panel Ninth Circuit)* Selected by the Judicial Council of the Ninth Circuit. Also Judge, U.S. Bankruptcy Court District of Oregon.

Office: 1001 S.W. Fifth Avenue, Room 700, Portland, Oregon 97204.

Telephone: (503) 326-4173.

PIERAS, Jaime, Jr. *(Senior Judge, United States District Court District of Puerto Rico)* Appointed for life by President Ronald Reagan to term beginning July 23, 1982. Assumed Senior status, serves by assignment. Born San Juan Puerto Rico May 19, 1924. Catholic. Educated at Catholic University of America B.A. 1945 and Georgetown University J.D. 1948. Member Phi Delta Phi. Admitted to practice Puerto Rico 1949, U.S. Court of Appeals First Circuit 1950, District of Columbia 1983 and U.S. Supreme Court 1984. In legal practice San Juan 1949-82.

Author "Judicial Economy and Efficiency Through the Initial Scheduling Conference: The Method" 35 Catholic University L. Rev. 943, 1986. Member Committee on the Bicentennial of the Constitution Judicial Conference of U.S., The District of Columbia Bar, Puerto Rico and American (Executive Committee Judicial Administration Division 1987) Bar Associations. Lieutenant U.S. Army 1950-55. Member Republican National Committee Puerto Rico 1966-80. Member Rotary Club. Enjoys reading.

Office: 353 U.S. Courthouse Third Floor, 300 Recinto Sur Street, San Juan, Puerto Rico 00901.

Telephone: (787) 977-6050.

PLAGER, S. Jay *(Senior Judge, United States Court of Appeals Federal Circuit)* Appointed for life by President George Bush to term beginning Nov 11, 1989. Assumed Senior status Nov 30, 2000, serves by assignment. Born Long Branch New Jersey May 16, 1931. Educated at University of North Carolina A.B. 1952, University of Florida J.D. with high honors 1958 and Columbia University LL.M. 1961. Editor-in-Chief University of Florida Law Review. Member Phi Beta Kappa, Phi Kappa Phi and Order of the Coif. Admitted to practice Florida 1958 and Illinois 1964.

Co-author with A. V. Kendall "Severance Damage in Eminent Domain Proceedings" 10 University of Florida L. Rev. 1, 1957; with F. E. Maloney "Florida's Ground Water: Legal Problems in Managing a Precious Resource" 21 University of Miami L. Rev. 751, 1967 and "Multiple Interests in Riparian Land, Subdivision Platting, and the Allocation of Riparian Rights" 46 Journal of Urban Law 41, 1968; with F. E. Maloney and F. N. Baldwin "Water Pollution—Attempts to Decontaminate Florida Law" 20 University of Florida L. Rev. 131, 1967 and *Water Law and Administration* University of Florida Press 1968; with F. E. Maloney, R. C. Ausness and B. D. E. Canter *Florida Water Law* revised ed. 1980; with I. Nagel "RICO, Past and Future: Some Observations and Conclusions" 52 Cincinnati L. Rev. 456, 1983; with B. Garth and I. Nagel "The Institution of the Private Attorney General: Perspectives from an Empirical Study of Class Action Litigation" 61 Southern California L. Rev. 353, 1988; and with Stephen B. Burbank "Foreword: The Law of Federal Judicial Discipline and the Lessons of Social Science" No. 1 University of Pennsylvania L. Rev. 142, 1993. Author "The Spouse's Nonbarrable Share: A Solution in Search of a Problem" 33 University of Chicago L. Rev. 681, 1966; "The Planning/Land Use Control Relationship: A Look at Some Alternatives" 3 Land-Use Controls Quarterly 26, 1969; *Social Justice Through Law—New Approaches in the Law of Property* Foundation Press 1970; "Policy, Planning and the Courts" 37 Journal of the American Institute of Planners 174, 1971; "Agency Diplomacy: Relations with Congress and the White House, and Ethics in the Administrative Process" 4 Administrative L. Jour. 1, 1990; "The United States Courts of Appeals, the Federal Circuit, and the Non-Regional Subject Matter Concept: Reflections on the Search for a Model" 39 American University L. Rev. 4, 1990; "Takings Law and Appellate Decision Making" 25 Environmental Law 161 Winter 1995; and "Challenges for Intellectual Property Law in the Twenty-first Century: Indeterminacy and Other Problems" University of Illinois L. Rev. 69, 2001. Assistant Professor of Law 1958-62 and Associate Professor of Law 1962-64 University of Florida College of Law. Visiting Associate Professor of Law 1963-64, Associate Professor of Law 1964-65 and Professor of Law 1965-77 University of Illinois College of Law. Visiting Research Professor of Law University of Wisconsin 1967-68. Dean 1977-84 and Professor of Law 1977-90 Indiana University School of Law. Visiting Professor of Law and Visiting Fellow Cambridge University, England Fall 1980, Trinity College, England Fall 1980 and Rockefeller Foundation Research Center, Bellagio Italy Fall 1980. Vice Chairman National Commission on Judicial Discipline and Removal 1991-93. Member Judicial Conference Budget Committee. Served to Commander USN 1948-71 (active duty 1952-55). Counselor to Under Secretary U.S. Department of Health and Human Services 1986-87. Associate Director 1987-88 and Administrator 1988-89 Office of Information and Regulatory Affairs Office of Management and Budget.

Office: National Courts Building, 717 Madison Place N.W., Washington, D.C. 20439-0002.

Telephone: (202) 633-5866.

POGUE, Donald C. *(Judge, United States Court of International Trade)* Appointed for life by President Bill Clinton 1995. Educated at Dartmouth College magna

POGUE, DONALD C.—*Continued*

cum laude, Yale University Masters of Philosophy J.D. and University of Essex, England. Member Phi Beta Kappa. In legal practice Hartford 15 years. Judge, Connecticut Superior Court 1994-95.

Commissioner and Chairman Connecticut Commission on Hospitals and Health Care 1989-94. Chair Long Range Planning Committee and Member Education and Technology Committee U.S. Court of International Trade.

Office: One Federal Plaza, New York, New York 10278-0001.

Telephone: (212) 264-2126.

POOLER, Rosemary S. *(Judge, United States Court of Appeals Second Circuit)* Appointed for life by President Bill Clinton June 19, 1998. Born New York New York June 21, 1938. Educated at Brooklyn College B.A. 1959, University of Connecticut M.A. 1961, University of Michigan Law School J.D. 1965, Harvard University Program for Senior Managers in Government 1978 and State University of New York at Albany Certificate in Regulatory Economics 1986. In legal practice Syracuse 1966-72. Justice, New York Supreme Court Fifth Judicial District 1991-94. Judge, U.S. District Court Northern District of New York 1994-98, appointed by President Bill Clinton.

Commissioner New York State Public Service Commission 1981-86. Visiting Professor of Law Syracuse University College of Law 1987-88. Secretary and Member Executive Committee Association of Supreme Court Justices of the State of New York, Women's Bar Association of the State of New York, Onondaga County and New York State (Council of Judicial Associations) Bar Associations. Staff Director Subcommittee on Utility, Structure and Management Committee on Corporations, Authorities and Commissions New York State Assembly 1987. Member New York Public Interest Research Group 1974-76. Chair and Executive Director New York State Consumer Protection Board 1976-81. Board of Directors Loretto Geriatric Center. Member YWCA.

Mailing address: P.O. Box 7395, Syracuse, New York 13261-7395.

Telephone: (315) 448-0420.

PORFILIO, John C. *(Senior Judge, United States Court of Appeals Tenth Circuit)* Appointed for life by President Ronald Reagan. Assumed Senior status Oct 15, 1999, serves by assignment. Born Denver Colorado Oct 14, 1934. Roman Catholic. Educated at Stanford University 1952-54 and University of Denver B.A. 1956 LL.B. 1959. Admitted to practice Colorado 1959 and U.S. Supreme Court 1968. Began legal practice Denver 1959. Judge, U.S. Bankruptcy Court District of Colorado Jan 1975 to July 1982. Former Judge, U.S. District Court District of Colorado, appointed by President Ronald Reagan to term beginning July 2, 1982.

Assistant Attorney General 1962-68, Deputy Attorney General 1968-72 and Attorney General 1972-74 Colorado. Instructor Colorado Law Enforcement Training Academy 1966-70. Member American Bar Association. Enjoys music and cooking.

Office: 102G U.S. Courthouse, 1823 Stout Street, Denver, Colorado 80257.

Telephone: (303) 844-6346.

POSNER, Richard A. *(Judge, United States Court of Appeals Seventh Circuit)* Appointed for life by President Ronald Reagan Dec 4, 1981. Former Chief Judge. Born New York New York Jan 11, 1939. Educated at Yale College summa cum laude 1959 and Harvard University Law School 1962. President Harvard Law Review. Law Clerk to Hon. William J. Brennan, Jr., U.S. Supreme Court. Member Phi Beta Kappa.

Former Assistant to Commissioner Philip Elman Federal Trade Commission and U.S. Solicitor General Thurgood Marshall. Former General Counsel President Lyndon B. Johnson's Task Force on Communications Policy. President Lexecon Inc. 1977-81. Author of 30 books and more than 300 articles mainly exploring the application of economic analysis to law in a variety of fields. Former Editor Journal of Legal Studies. Associate Professor of Law Stanford University 1968. Professor of Law 1969, Lee and Brena Freeman Professor of Law 1970-81 and part-time Senior Lecturer since 1981 University of Chicago. Member American Economic Association, American Academy of Arts and Sciences and The American Law Institute.

Office: U.S. Courthouse, 219 South Dearborn Street, Chicago, Illinois 60604.

Telephone: (312) 435-5806.

POWELL, Carleton D. *(Special Trial Judge, United States Tax Court)* Appointed by U.S. Tax Court Chief Judge Samuel Black Sterrett to term beginning Aug 25, 1985.

Office: 400 Second Street N.W., Washington, D.C. 20217-0002.

Telephone: (202) 874-6063.

PREGERSON, Harry *(Judge, United States Court of Appeals Ninth Circuit)* Appointed for life by President Jimmy Carter to term beginning Nov 6, 1979. Born Los Angeles California Oct 13, 1923. Educated at University of California at Los Angeles B.A. 1947 and Boalt Hall School of Law LL.B. 1950. Admitted to practice California 1951. In legal practice Van Nuys 1953-65. Judge, Los Angeles Municipal Court Los Angeles County 1965-66. Judge, Superior Court of California Los Angeles County 1966-67. Judge, U.S. District Court Central District of California 1967-79.

Important Decisions: Soria v. Oxnard School District Board of Trustees (school desegregation) 328 F. Supp. 155 C.D. Cal. 1971, vacated and remanded 488 F.2d 579, 9th Cir. 1973, on remand 386 F. Supp. 539 C.D. Cal. 1974; In re Equity Funding Corp. of America (bankruptcy reorganization) 391 F. Supp. 768, C.D. Cal., further proceedings 396 F. Supp. 1266 C.D. Cal., further proceedings 416 F. Supp. 132 C.D. Cal. 1975; Manhart v. Los Angeles Department of Water & Power (sex discrimination) 387 F. Supp. 980 C.D. Cal. 1975, aff'd 553 F.2d 981, 9th Cir. 1976, vacated and remanded 435 U.S. 702, 1978; Keith v. Volpe (environmental law) 352 F. Supp. 1324 C.D. Cal. 1972, aff'd en banc 506 F.2d 696, 9th Cir. 1974, cert. denied 420 U.S. 908, 1975; and Chevron USA, Inc. v. Hammond (does federal regulation preempt state law?) No. 81-3700, 9th Cir. Feb 3, 1984. Member State Bar of California, San Fernando Valley, Los Angeles County and American (Vice Chairman Committee on Federal Rules of Criminal Procedure and Evidence Section of Criminal Law since 1972) Bar Associations. Lecturer Seminars for Newly Appointed Federal Judges Federal Judicial Center Oct 1970 to March 1971 and Institute for Court Management since 1973. Speaker Fourth Annual Continuing Education of the Bar Federal Practice Institute June 1981, "Bridging the Gap

PREGERSON, HARRY—*Continued*

in Federal Court" Federal Bar Association Los Angeles Chapter Feb 1982 and Ninth Annual Continuing Education of the Bar Federal Practice Institute June 1986. Panelist "Will the Judiciary Be Ready for the 1990's or Even the Year 2000?" International Academy of Trial Lawyers Oct 1983. Recipient Promotion of Justice Civic Award from City of San Fernando 1965, Award from San Fernando Valley Jewish Federation Council 1966, Service Award from Greater Los Angeles Council Marine Corps Reserve Officers Association 1969, Alumnus of the Year Award from Jewish Big Brothers Association 1970, Champion of Justice "Por la Raza" Award from Latin American Civic Association of San Fernando 1973, Bicentennial Distinguished Alumnus Award from Roosevelt High School Los Angeles Unified School District 1976, Professional Achievement Award from Los Angeles Athletic Club 1980, Winston Crouch Award from American Society of Public Administrators 1983 and Appreciation Awards from International Academy of Trial Lawyers 1982 and 1983. Naval ROTC V-12 Program Sept 1941 to Feb 1944. First Lieutenant USMCR Feb 1944 to Dec 1946. Recipient Purple Heart May 1945. President Marine Corps Reserve Officers Association since 1966. Advisory Board International Orphans, Inc. since 1966 and Jewish Big Brothers Association since 1970.

Office: 21800 Oxnard Street, Suite 1140, Woodland Hills, California 91367-3633.

Telephone: (818) 710-7791.

PROST, Sharon *(Judge, United States Court of Appeals Federal Circuit)* Appointed for life by President George W. Bush to term beginning Oct 3, 2001. Born Newburyport Massachusetts. Educated at Cornell University B.S. 1973, George Washington University M.B.A. 1975 LL.M. 1984 and Washington College of Law of American University J.D. 1975.

Office: National Courts Building, 717 Madison Place N.W., Washington, D.C. 20439-0002.

Telephone: (202) 312-5520.

PUSATERI, James A. *(Judge, Bankruptcy Appellate Panel Tenth Circuit)* Selected by the Judicial Council of the Tenth Circuit. Also Judge, U.S. Bankruptcy Court District of Kansas. Appointed by U.S. District Court judges Dec 27, 1976. Reappointed Dec 15, 1986. Former Chief Judge Bankruptcy Court. Born Kansas City Missouri May 20, 1938. Roman Catholic. Educated at University of Kansas B.A. 1960 J.D. 1963. Member Sigma Alpha Epsilon. Admitted to practice Kansas 1963, U.S. District Court District of Kansas 1963 and U.S. Court of Appeals Tenth Circuit 1965. In legal practice Olathe 1963-65, Prairie Village 1965-69 and Kansas City 1969-76.

City Councilman Prairie Village 1967-69. Assistant U.S. Attorney Kansas City Kansas 1969-76. Author "Section 1111(b) of the Bankruptcy Code: How Much Does the Debtor Have to Pay and When Should the Creditor Elect" American Bankruptcy L. Jour. Spring 1984. Member National Conference of Bankruptcy Judges, American Bankruptcy Institute, Topeka and Kansas Bar Associations.

Office: 215 U.S. Courthouse, 444 S.E. Quincy Street, Topeka, Kansas 66683-3502.

Telephone: (785) 295-2786.

RADER, Randall R. *(Judge, United States Court of Appeals Federal Circuit)* Appointed for life by President George Bush to term beginning Aug 14, 1990. Born Hastings Nebraska April 21, 1949. Mormon. Educated at Brigham Young University B.A. with honors 1974 and George Washington Law School J.D. with honors 1978. Admitted to practice District of Columbia 1978, U.S. Supreme Court 1984 and U.S. Court of Federal Claims 1988. Judge, U.S. Claims Court (now U.S. Court of Federal Claims) Oct 1988 to Aug 1990, appointed by President Ronald Reagan.

Co-author *Patent Law* West Publishing 1998. Instructor in Patent Law I and II University of Virginia School of Law 1993-99, in Comparative Intellectual Property Law Georgetown University Law Center 1998-99, and in Patent Law George Washington University since 1999. Member U.S. Judicial Conference Committee on the Judicial Branch. Enjoys basketball and tennis.

Office: National Courts Building, 717 Madison Place N.W., Washington, D.C. 20439-0002.

Telephone: (202) 633-5861.

RAGGI, Reena *(Judge, United States Court of Appeals Second Circuit)* Appointed for life by President George W. Bush to term beginning Oct 7, 2002. Born Jersey City New Jersey May 11, 1951. Educated at Wellesley College B.A. 1973 and Harvard Law School J.D. 1976. Law Clerk to Hon. Thomas E. Fairchild, U.S. Court of Appeals Seventh Circuit 1976-77. In legal practice New York City 1977-79 and 1986-87. Judge, U.S. District Court Eastern District of New York 1987 to Oct 6, 2002, appointed by President Ronald Reagan.

Assistant U.S. Attorney 1979-86 (Chief Narcotics Division 1982-84 and Special Prosecutions Division 1984-86) and U.S. Attorney 1986 Eastern District of New York.

Office: U.S. Courthouse, 40 Centre Street, New York, New York 10007.

Telephone: (212) 857-2292.

RANDOLPH, A. Raymond *(Judge, United States Court of Appeals District of Columbia Circuit)* Appointed for life by President George Bush to term beginning July 20, 1990. Born Riverside New Jersey Nov 1, 1943. Educated at Drexel University B.S. 1966 and University of Pennsylvania Law School J.D. summa cum laude 1969. Managing Editor University of Pennsylvania Law Review. Law Clerk to Hon. Henry J. Friendly, U.S. Court of Appeals Second Circuit 1969-70. Admitted to practice California 1970, District of Columbia 1973, U.S. Courts of Appeals Sixth 1971, District of Columbia 1973, Fourth 1979, Fifth 1980, Seventh 1981, Eleventh 1981, Ninth 1983, First 1984, Second 1987 and Eighth 1989 Circuits, U.S. Supreme Court 1973, U.S. District Courts District of Columbia 1973, Southern District of Illinois 1974, Central District of California 1984 and District of Maryland 1986 and U.S. Tax Court 1974. In legal practice Los Angeles California 1969 and Washington D.C. 1973-75 and 1977-90.

Adjunct Professor of Civil Procedure and Injunctions Georgetown University 1974-78. Adjunct Professor of Constitutional Law 1992 and Distinguished Adjunct Professor of Law since 1998 George Mason University School of Law. Chairman Codes of Conduct Committee Judicial Conference 1995-98. Member The American

RANDOLPH, A. RAYMOND—*Continued*

Law Institute, The Association of Trial Lawyers of America and American Bar Association.

Office: 3108 U.S. Courthouse, 333 Constitution Avenue N.W., Washington, D.C. 20001-2866.

Telephone: (202) 216-7425.

RAWLINSON, Johnnie B. *(Judge, United States Court of Appeals Ninth Circuit)* Appointed for life by President Bill Clinton to term beginning July 2000. Born Concord North Carolina Dec 16, 1952. Educated at North Carolina Agricultural & Technical State University B.S. 1974 and McGeorge School of Law University of the Pacific J.D. 1979. In legal practice Las Vegas 1979-80. Judge, U.S. District Court District of Nevada 1998 to July 2000, appointed by President Bill Clinton.

Staff Attorney Nevada Legal Services 1980. Deputy District Attorney 1980-89, Chief Deputy District Attorney 1989-95 and Assistant District Attorney 1995-98 Las Vegas.

Office: 7072 U.S. Courthouse, 333 Las Vegas Boulevard South, Las Vegas, Nevada 89101-7074.

Telephone: (702) 464-5670.

REAVLEY, Thomas Morrow *(Senior Judge, United States Court of Appeals Fifth Circuit)* Appointed for life by President Jimmy Carter to term beginning 1979. Assumed Senior status Aug 1, 1990, serves by assignment. Born Quitman Texas June 21, 1921. Educated at University of Texas B.A. 1942, Harvard University J.D. 1948 and University of Virginia LL.M. 1983. Awarded honorary LL.D. Austin College 1974, Southwestern University 1977, Texas Wesleyan College 1982 and Pepperdine University 1993. Admitted to practice Texas 1948. In legal practice Nacogdoches 1949-51, Jasper 1952-55 and Austin Texas 1957-64. Judge, Texas District Court Austin District 1964-68. Justice, Texas Supreme Court 1968-77.

Assistant District Attorney Dallas 1948-49. County Attorney Nacogdoches County 1951. Adjunct Professor University of Texas School of Law 1958-59 and since 1978. Lecturer Baylor University School of Law since 1976. Visiting Professor of Law Pepperdine University School of Law 1990. M. D. Anderson Distinguished Visiting Professor Texas Tech University School of Law 1998. President Texas Judicial Council 1971-76. Recipient Rosewood Gavel Award from St. Mary's University of San Antonio School of Law 1985, Outstanding Texas Jurist Award from Texas Bar Foundation 1991 and Leon Green Award from Texas Law Review 1996. Lieutenant USNR 1943-45. Secretary of State Texas 1955-57. 33° Mason.

Office: 434 Thornberry Judicial Building, 903 San Jacinto Boulevard, Austin, Texas 78701.

Telephone: (512) 916-5871.

REHNQUIST, William Hubbs *(Chief Justice, The Supreme Court of the United States)* Appointed for life by President Richard M. Nixon Oct 21, 1971 to term beginning Jan 7, 1972. Chief Justice since 1986. Also Circuit Justice, U.S. Courts of Appeals District of Columbia, Fourth and Federal Circuits. Born Milwaukee Wisconsin Oct 1, 1924. Educated at Stanford University B.A. M.A. 1948 LL.B. 1952 and Harvard University M.A. 1950. Law Clerk to Hon. Robert H. Jackson, U.S. Supreme Court Feb 1952 to June 1953. Board of Editors Stanford Law Review. Member Phi Beta Kappa and Order of the Coif. In legal practice Phoenix Arizona 1953-69.

Assistant Attorney General Office of Legal Counsel, appointed by President Richard M. Nixon 1969. Contributor of articles on legal subjects to various periodicals. Sergeant USAAC 1943-46. Member Emmanuel Lutheran Church. Active in professional, civic and church affairs.

Office: One First Street N.E., Washington, D.C. 20543-0001.

Telephone: (202) 479-3000.

REINHARDT, Stephen *(Judge, United States Court of Appeals Ninth Circuit)* Appointed for life by President Jimmy Carter to term beginning Sept 17, 1980. Born New York New York March 27, 1931. Educated at Pomona College B.A. cum laude 1951 and Yale Law School LL.B. 1954. Law Clerk to Hon. Luther W. Youghdahl, U.S. District Court District of Columbia 1955-57. Member Order of the Coif. Admitted to practice District of Columbia 1954, California 1958 and U.S. Supreme Court 1960. Began legal practice Los Angeles 1957.

Member 1962-69 and Vice Chairman 1969-74 California Advisory Committee to U.S. Commission on Civil Rights. Member State Bar of California (Committee on Legislation 1973-77), Los Angeles County 1974-80 and American Bar Associations. First Lieutenant USAF 1954-56. President Los Angeles City Recreation and Parks Commission 1974-75. Board of Directors Amateur Athletic Foundation of Los Angeles 1984-92. Member Los Angeles Coliseum Commission 1974-75, Los Angeles Police Commission 1975-80 (President 1978-80) and Executive Committee 1984 Olympic Organizing Committee 1979-84.

Office: 1747 U.S. Courthouse, 312 North Spring Street, Los Angeles, California 90012-4701.

Telephone: (213) 894-3639.

RENDELL, Marjorie O. *(Judge, United States Court of Appeals Third Circuit)* Appointed for life by President Bill Clinton to term beginning Nov 1997. Born Wilmington Delaware Dec 20, 1947. Educated at University of Pennsylvania B.A. 1969 and Villanova University School of Law J.D. 1973. In legal practice Philadelphia 1973-93. Judge, U.S. District Court Eastern District of Pennsylvania 1994 to Nov 1997, appointed by President Bill Clinton.

Office: 21613 U.S. Courthouse, 601 Market Street, Philadelphia, Pennsylvania 19106-1598.

Telephone: (215) 597-3015.

RESNICK, Jeffrey L. *(Magistrate Judge, United States District Court District of the Virgin Islands)* Appointed Part-time Magistrate by U.S. District Court judges to term beginning May 23, 1989. Appointed Magistrate Judge by U.S. District Court judges to term beginning Feb 1991. Reappointed 1999, current term expires 2007. Born Brooklyn New York. Jewish. Educated at University of Connecticut B.A. 1964 LL.B. 1967. Admitted to practice Connecticut 1967, Virgin Islands 1968, New York 1968, U.S. Court of Appeals Third Circuit 1969 and District of Columbia 1979. In legal practice Christiansted, St. Croix 1968-69 and 1973-89.

Assistant Attorney General Virgin Islands 1969-73.

RESNICK, JEFFREY L.—*Continued*

Member American Bar Association. Member Virgin Islands Bridge Team.

Office: 295 Federal Building, 3013 Estate Golden Rock, Christiansted, St. Croix, Virgin Islands 00820-4355.

Telephone: (340) 773-1601.

RESTANI, Jane A. *(Judge, United States Court of International Trade)* Appointed for life by President Ronald Reagan to term beginning Nov 16, 1983. Born San Francisco California Feb 27, 1948. Educated at University of California at Berkeley B.A. with distinction 1969 and University of California at Davis J.D. 1973. Articles Editor University of California at Davis Law Review. Member Phi Kappa Phi and Order of the Coif. Admitted to practice California 1973.

Trial Attorney Attorney General's Honor Program 1973-76, Assistant Chief Commercial Litigation Section 1976-80 and Director Commercial Litigation Branch 1980-83 Civil Division Department of Justice.

Office: One Federal Plaza, New York, New York 10278-0001.

Telephone: (212) 264-3668.

RHODES, Steven W. *(Chief Judge, Bankruptcy Appellate Panel Sixth Circuit)* Selected by the Judicial Council of the Sixth Circuit. Also Chief Judge, U.S. Bankruptcy Court Eastern District of Michigan. Born New York New York Dec 27, 1948. Jewish. Educated at Purdue University B.S.M.E. 1970 and University of Michigan J.D. 1972. Law Clerk to Hon. John Feikens, U.S. District Court Eastern District of Michigan 1973. Admitted to practice Michigan 1973. Began legal practice Detroit 1974. In legal practice Ann Arbor 1977-81. Former Magistrate Judge, U.S. District Court Eastern District of Michigan.

Member State Bar of Michigan and Federal Bar Association.

Office: 211 West Fort Street, Suite 1800, Detroit, Michigan 48226-3211.

Telephone: (313) 234-0020.

RIDGWAY, Delissa A. *(Judge, United States Court of International Trade)* Appointed for life by President Bill Clinton March 17, 1998 to term beginning May 29, 1998. Born Kirksville Missouri June 28, 1955. Roman Catholic. Educated at University of Missouri-Columbia B.A. with honors 1976 and Northeastern University School of Law J.D. 1979. Law Clerk to Hon. June L. Green, U.S. District Court District of Columbia 1979. Admitted to practice District of Columbia 1979, U.S. District Court District of Columbia 1980, U.S. Courts of Appeals District of Columbia 1980 and First 1988 Circuits and U.S. Supreme Court 1983. In legal practice Washington D.C. 1979-94.

Chair Foreign Claims Settlement Commission of the U.S. 1994-98. Author "Dispute Resolution in World Financial Institutions" 10 *Journal of International Arbitration* 73, 1993; "The Legal Legacy of the Gulf War—Claims Against Iraq" 13 *Journal of International Arbitration* 5, 1996; "The Genocide Convention After Fifty Years: Contemporary Strategies for Combating a Crime Against Humanity" Proceedings of 92nd Annual Meeting American Society of International Law 1998; "International Arbitration: The Next Growth Industry" *Dispute Resolution Journal* American Arbitration Association Feb 1999; and "Justice for the 'Forgotten Victims': U.S. Survivors of the Holocaust" IX Brooklyn Law School Journal of Law and Policy 767, 2001. Adjunct Professor of International Arbitration and International Business Transactions Washington College of Law of American University 1992-94 and Cornell Law School 1999-2001. President Charlotte E. Ray American Inn of Court 1997-98. Charter Fellow Federal Bar Foundation. Fellow American Bar Foundation. Member The American Law Institute, Women's Bar Association of the District of Columbia (President 1992-93), The District of Columbia Bar (Secretary 1991-92, Board of Governors 1991-98), Federal (National Council since 1993) and American (Commission on Women in the Profession since 2002) Bar Associations. Frequent speaker on topics ranging from customs and international trade law, international arbitration, international commercial law and international claims, to cross-cultural communication, law practice management, career planning/development and women and minorities in the profession. Recipient Frederick B. Abramson Award from The District of Columbia Bar 1996, Best Bar Project from National Council of Bar Presidents 1996 and Earl W. Kintner Award from Federal Bar Association 2000. Named Distinguished Woman in International Law by Federal Bar Association 1997 and Woman Lawyer of the Year for Washington D.C. 2001. Enjoys films, skiing and cooking.

Office: One Federal Plaza, New York, New York 10278-0001.

Telephone: (212) 264-5480.

RILEY, William Jay *(Judge, United States Court of Appeals Eighth Circuit)* Appointed for life by President George W. Bush to term beginning Aug 16, 2001. Born Lincoln Nebraska 1947. Educated at University of Nebraska B.A. 1969 J.D. 1972. Law Clerk to Hon. Donald P. Lay, U.S. Court of Appeals Eighth Circuit 1972-73. In legal practice Nebraska 1973-2001.

Adjunct Professor Creighton University College of Law since 1991.

Office: 4179 U.S. Courthouse, 111 South Eighteenth Plaza, Omaha, Nebraska 68102-1322.

Telephone: (402) 661-7593.

RIPPLE, Kenneth F. *(Judge, United States Court of Appeals Seventh Circuit)* Appointed for life by President Ronald Reagan May 10, 1985 to term beginning June 10, 1985. Born Pittsburgh Pennsylvania May 19, 1943. Educated at Fordham University A.B. summa cum laude 1965, University of Virginia School of Law J.D. 1968, George Washington University National Law Center LL.M. summa cum laude 1972 and University of Paris, France. Honorary LL.D. George Washington University 1992. Member Phi Beta Kappa. Admitted to practice District of Columbia, Indiana, New York, Virginia, U.S. District Court Northern District of Indiana, U.S. Courts of Appeals Seventh and District of Columbia Circuits, U.S. Court of Appeals for the Armed Forces and U.S. Supreme Court.

Attorney Office of the General Counsel IBM Aug 1968 to Oct 1968. Legal Officer Sept 1972 to July 1973 and Special Assistant to Chief Justice July 1973 to Sept 1977 U.S. Supreme Court. Consultant California Board of Bar Examiners 1981 and Alabama Supreme Court 1983. Special Assistant Attorney General Michigan 1984. Professor of Law University of Notre Dame since 1977. Reporter 1978-85, Member 1985-90 and Chair 1990-93 Advisory Committee on the Federal Appellate Rules. Member The American Law Institute, New York

RIPPLE, KENNETH F.—*Continued*

State, Federal and American Bar Associations. Chair Committee on Appellate Judge Education Federal Judicial Center since 1996. Recipient Professor of the Year Award 1978-80 and 1984-85 and Special Presidential Award 1985. Commander USNR JAGC (active duty 1968-72; retired). Recipient Navy Commendation Medal. Member Military Justice Act of 1983 Advisory Commission 1984. Board of Visitors Brigham Young University School of Law 1990-92. Consultant Sept 1977 and Member American Team 1980 Anglo-American Judicial Exchange. Member Advisory Committee on the Bill of Rights Commission on the Bicentennial of the Constitution.

Office: 208 Federal Bldg. & U.S. Courthouse, 204 South Main Street, South Bend, Indiana 46601.

Telephone: (574) 246-8150.

ROBINSON, Wilkes Coleman *(Senior Judge, United States Court of Federal Claims)* Appointed by President Ronald Reagan May 7, 1987 to term beginning July 10, 1987. Assumed Senior status 1997, serves by assignment. Born Anniston Alabama Sept 30, 1925. Episcopalian. Educated at University of Alabama B.A. with honors 1948 and University of Virginia J.D. 1951. Member Phi Beta Kappa, Phi Eta Sigma and Phi Alpha Theta. Admitted to practice Alabama 1951, Virginia 1961, Missouri 1966, Kansas 1983, U.S. District Courts, U.S. Courts of Appeals and U.S. Supreme Court. In legal practice Anniston Alabama 1951-54, Mobile Alabama 1956-58, Richmond Virginia 1958-66, St. Louis Missouri 1966-70 and Kansas City Missouri 1970-87. Judge, Recorder's Court Anniston Alabama 1953-55. Judge, Juvenile and Domestic Relations Court Calhoun County Alabama 1954-56.

Government Appeal Agent Draft Board 1951-54. Important Decision: Shimota v. United States 21 Cl. Ct. 510, 1990. Former Member Kansas Bar Association. Member The Missouri Bar, Alabama State Bar, Virginia State Bar, Virginia and U.S. Claims Court Bar Associations. Seaman First Class USNR 1943-44. Vice President SR Financial Corporation 1986-87. Listed in *Who's Who in America.* Republican. Former Member Board of Directors Kansas City Philharmonic Orchestra. Former Member Rotary Club. Member Masons, Scottish Rite, Indian Bayou Golf and Country Club and Destin Racquet and Fitness Club. Enjoys travel, golf and tennis.

Office: National Courts Building, 717 Madison Place N.W., Washington, D.C. 20005-1086.

Telephone: (202) 219-9992.

ROGERS, John M. *(Judge, United States Court of Appeals Sixth Circuit)* Appointed for life by President George W. Bush to term beginning Nov 27, 2002.

Office: 100 East Vine Street, Suite 400, Lexington, Kentucky 40507.

Telephone: (859) 233-2680.

ROGERS, Judith W. *(Judge, United States Court of Appeals District of Columbia Circuit)* Appointed for life by President Bill Clinton. Educated at Radcliffe College B.A. with honors 1961, Harvard Law School LL.B. 1964 and University of Virginia LL.M. 1988. Member Phi Beta Kappa. Admitted to practice District of Columbia 1965. Former Judge and Former Chief Judge, District of Columbia Court of Appeals, appointed by President Ronald Reagan to term beginning Sept 15, 1983.

Assistant U.S. Attorney District of Columbia 1965-68. Office of Deputy Attorney General U.S. Department of Justice 1968-69. General Counsel to Congressional Commission on Organization of District of Columbia 1971-72. Corporation Counsel District of Columbia 1979-83. Instructor Poverty Law Clinic University of California Boalt Hall 1968-69. Fellow American Bar Association. Member National Association of Women Judges, Bar Association of the District of Columbia and The District of Columbia Bar. Recipient Outstanding Service Award from Mayor Walter E. Washington 1973, Distinguished Public Service Award 1983, Charlotte Ray Award from Greater Washington Women's Division National Bar Association 1989 and Woman Lawyer of the Year Award from Women's Bar Association 1990. Legislative Assistant to Mayor Walter E. Washington 1972-79.

Office: 5800 U.S. Courthouse, 333 Constitution Avenue N.W., Washington, D.C. 20001-2866.

Telephone: (202) 216-7260.

RONEY, Paul H. *(Senior Judge, United States Court of Appeals Eleventh Circuit)* Appointed for life to Fifth Circuit by President Richard M. Nixon to term beginning Nov 23, 1970. Assigned to Eleventh Circuit Oct 1, 1981. Chief Judge Sept 3, 1986 to Sept 30, 1989. Assumed Senior status Oct 1, 1989, serves by assignment. Born Olney Illinois Sept 5, 1921. Educated at St. Petersburg Junior College 1938-40, University of Pennsylvania B.S. in Economics 1942, Harvard University LL.B. 1948 and University of Virginia LL.M. 1984. Awarded honorary LL.D. Stetson University 1977. Admitted to practice New York 1949 and Florida 1950. In legal practice New York City 1948-50 and St. Petersburg Florida 1950-70.

Lecturer on Law Stetson University 1957, 1965 and 1966. Fellow American Bar Foundation 1975. Member Judicial Conference of the U.S. (Executive Committee 1986-89), American Judicature Society (Director 1972-76), The American Law Institute, The Florida Bar (Chairman Continuing Legal Education Committee 1969-71, Budget Committee 1969-70 and Group Legal Services 1969-70; member Board of Governors 1967-70 and Executive Committee 1969-71), St. Petersburg (President 1964-65) and American (Chairman Legal Advisory Committee on Fair Trial-Free Press 1973-76, member Task Force on Courts & the Public 1973-76 and Chairman Appellate Judges Conference 1978-79 Judicial Administration Division; Vice Chairman Action Committee on Vital Issues in Criminal Justice Criminal Justice Section 1977-78) Bar Associations. Former member Pinellas County Trial Lawyers Association. Faculty member National College of the State Judiciary 1974-75. U.S. Army 1943-46. Member St. Petersburg Council of Human Relations (President 1951-53), St. Petersburg Junior Chamber of Commerce (President 1954-55), Family and Children's Service Bureau (President 1961) and Community Welfare Council (President 1962-64). Former member American Red Cross Chapter of South Pinellas (Former Director and Vice President), Suncoasters (Festival of States), American Cancer Society, St. Petersburg Chamber of Commerce, Child Guidance Clinic, Science Center of St. Petersburg, Museum of Fine Arts, All Children's Hospital (Co-chairman Fund Drive 1966-67) and United Fund (Chairman Professional Division 1965). Co-chairman Fund Drive Florida Presbyterian College (now Eckerd College) 1963-64.

Office: 1220 Bank of America Building, One Progress Plaza, 200 Central Avenue, St. Petersburg, Florida 33701-3326.

Telephone: (727) 893-3296.

ROSENN, Max *(Senior Judge, United States Court of Appeals Third Circuit)* Appointed for life by President Richard M. Nixon to term beginning 1970. Assumed Senior status Jan 21, 1981, serves by assignment. Born Plains Pennsylvania Feb 4, 1910. Jewish. Educated at Cornell University B.A. 1929 and University of Pennsylvania LL.B. 1932. Awarded honorary degrees Dickinson School of Law, King's College and College Misericordia. Admitted to practice Pennsylvania 1932, U.S. Supreme Court and Philippines. In legal practice Wilkes-Barre Pennsylvania 1932-70.

Special Counsel Pennsylvania Department of Justice 1939. Assistant District Attorney Luzerne County 1942-44. Secretary Pennsylvania Department of Public Welfare 1966-67. Fellow American College of Trial Lawyers and International Academy of Trial Lawyers. Member Criminal Procedure Rules Committee Pennsylvania Supreme Court 1958-85 and Pennsylvania Commission to Revise Public Employee Laws 1968-69. Member Luzerne County, Pennsylvania (Chairman Industrial Relations Section) and American Bar Associations. Recipient Distinguished Award from Wyoming Seminary. First Lieutenant U.S. Army WWII. Alternate Delegate Republican National Convention 1964. Former Director Wyoming National Bank of Wilkes-Barre. Director and Solicitor Franklin Federal Savings & Loan Association 1937-70. Chairman Governor's Hospital Study Commission, Governor's Council for Human Services 1966-67, Commission on Metropolitan Government 1957-58, Pennsylvania Human Relations Commission 1969-70, Pennsylvania Committee on Children and Youth 1968-70 and Legislative Task Force Structure Pennsylvania Department of Human Services 1970. Member Pennsylvania Board of Public Welfare 1963-66 and Executive Board Commonwealth of Pennsylvania 1966-67. President Wyoming Valley Jewish Committee 1941-42 and Property Owners Association Luzerne County 1955-57. Trustee Wilkes-Barre Jewish Community Center. Member Anti-Defamation League (President Pennsylvania-West Virginia-Delaware Board 1955-58, National Commissioner 1964-66), Shriners, 33° Masons and B'nai B'rith (President District Grand Lodge 1947-48, Life Governor).

Office: 235 Max Rosenn U.S. Courthouse, 197 South Main Street, Wilkes-Barre, Pennsylvania 18701.

Telephone: (570) 826-6424.

ROSS, Donald R. *(Senior Judge, United States Court of Appeals Eighth Circuit)* Appointed for life by President Richard M. Nixon to term beginning Jan 25, 1971. Assumed Senior status June 13, 1987, serves by assignment. Born Orleans Nebraska June 8, 1922. Protestant. Educated at University of Nebraska J.D. 1948. Awarded honorary LL.D. University of Nebraska 1990. Admitted to practice Nebraska 1948. Began legal practice Lexington 1948. In legal practice Omaha 1956-71.

Mayor of Lexington 1953. U.S. Attorney District of Nebraska 1953-56. Member Omaha and Nebraska State Bar Associations. Recipient Herbert Harley Award from American Judicature Society Oct 30, 1987. Major USAF 1942-46. Republican.

Office: 4226 U.S. Courthouse, 111 South 18th Plaza, Omaha, Nebraska 68102-1322.

Telephone: (402) 661-7580.

ROTH, Jane R. *(Judge, United States Court of Appeals Third Circuit)* Appointed for life by President George Bush to term beginning 1991. Born Philadelphia Pennsylvania June 16, 1935. Episcopalian. Educated at Smith College B.A. 1956 and Harvard Law School LL.B. cum laude 1965. Admitted to practice Delaware 1965, U.S. District Court District of Delaware 1966 and U.S. Court of Appeals Third Circuit 1974. In legal practice Wilmington 1965-85. Judge, U.S. District Court District of Delaware 1985-91, appointed by President Ronald Reagan.

Former Member Committee on the Judicial Branch and Chairman Committee on Security and Facilities Judicial Conference of the U.S. Fellow The American Bar Foundation. Member Federal Judges Association, The Delaware State and American Bar Associations.

Office: 5100 Federal Building, Lockbox 12, 844 North King Street, Wilmington, Delaware 19801-3595.

Telephone: (302) 573-6104.

ROVNER, Ilana Diamond *(Judge, United States Court of Appeals Seventh Circuit)* Appointed for life by President George H. W. Bush to term beginning Aug 17, 1992. Born Riga Latvia 1938. Jewish. Educated at Villanova University 1958, Bryn Mawr College A.B. 1960, Exeter College Oxford University, England 1960, King's College University of London, England 1960-61, Georgetown University Law Center 1961-64, New York University Law School 1962 and Illinois Institute of Technology, Chicago-Kent College of Law J.D. 1966. Awarded honorary Litt.D. Mundelein College 1989 and Rosary College 1989 and honorary D.H.L. from Spertus College of Judaica 1992. Member Kappa Beta Pi. Admitted to practice Illinois 1972, U.S. District Court Northern District of Illinois 1972, U.S. Court of Appeals Seventh Circuit 1977, U.S. Supreme Court 1981 and Trial Bar of U.S. District Court Northern District of Illinois 1982. Began legal practice Chicago. Judge, U.S. District Court Northern District of Illinois Nov 1, 1984 to Aug 17, 1992.

Law Clerk to Hon. James B. Parsons, U.S. District Court Northern District of Illinois May 1972 to Aug 1973. Assistant U.S. Attorney Aug 1973 to Aug 1977 and Deputy Chief Jan 1975 to March 1976 and Chief April 1976 to Aug 1977 Public Protection Unit U.S. Attorney's Office Northern District of Illinois. Deputy Governor and Legal Counsel to Governor James R. Thompson Aug 1977 to Oct 1984. Important Decisions: Suburban O'Hare Commission, et al. v. Elizabeth Hanford Dole 603 F. Supp. 1013 N.D. Ill. 1985; Beck v. Cantor, Fitzgerald & Co. 621 F. Supp. 1547 N.D. Ill. 1985; Thomas J. Marzen v. U.S. Department of Health and Human Services 632 F. Supp. 785 N.D. Ill 1986, aff'd 825 F.2d 1148, 7th Cir. 1987; Koefoot v. American College of Surgeons 692 F. Supp. 843 N.D. Ill. 1988; United States v. Finley 705 F. Supp. 1272 N.D. Ill. 1988; Scadron v. City of Des Plaines 734 F. Supp. 1437 N.D. Ill. 1990, aff'd 989 F.2d 502, 7th Cir. 1993; Welsh v. Boy Scouts of America 787 F. Supp. 1511 N.D. Ill. 1992, aff'd 993 F.2d 1267, 7th Cir. 1993, cert. denied 114 S. Ct. 602, 1993; Henry v. I.N.S. 8 F.3d 426, 7th Cir. 1993; Lisek v. Norfolk and Western Ry. Co. 30 F.3d 823, 7th Cir. 1994, cert. denied 115 S. Ct. 904, 1995; LaSalle Bank Lake View v. Seguban 54 F.3d 387, 7th Cir. 1995; Youakim v. McDonald 71 F.3d 1274, 7th Cir. 1995, cert. denied 116 S. Ct. 2571, 1996; United States v. Hernandez 79 F.3d 584, 7th Cir. 1996, cert. denied 117 S. Ct. 2407; Veprinsky v. Fluor Daniel, Inc. 87 F.3d 881, 7th Cir. 1996; Bracy v. Gramley 81 F.3d 684, 7th Cir. 1996, (dissent), rev'd 520 U.S. 899, 117 S. Ct. 726, 1997; Schleibaum v. Kmart Corp. 153

ROVNER, ILANA DIAMOND—*Continued*
F.3d 496, 7th Cir. 1998, cert. denied 119 S. Ct. 872; Gillespie v. City of Indianapolis 185 F.3d 693, 7th Cir. 1999, cert. denied WL29384; and Shepherd v. Slater Steels 168 F.3d 998, 7th Cir. 1999.

Member District Performance Committee 1982-84, Executive Committee Sept 1989 to Aug 1992 and Civil Justice Reform Act Advisory Committee March 1991 to Aug 1992 U.S. District Court Northern District of Illinois. Member Race and Gender Fairness Committee Seventh Circuit since 1993, Gender Study Task Force 1995-96 and Fairness Committee since 1996 U.S. Court of Appeals. Member Decalogue Society, Chicago Council of Lawyers, National Association of Women Judges, Federal Judges Association, International Association of Jewish Lawyers and Jurists, Judicial Conference of the Seventh Circuit, Judicial Conference of the U.S. (Committee on Court Administration and Case Management since 2000), Women's Bar Association of Illinois, Chicago, Seventh Circuit, Federal (Judicial Selection Committee 1977-80, Treasurer 1978-79 and Secretary 1979-80; Second Vice President 1980-81, Vice President 1981-82 and President 1982-83 Chicago Chapter; Second Vice President 1983-84 and Vice President 1984-85 Seventh Circuit) and American Bar Associations. Named Today's Chicago Woman of the Year 1985, Woman of the Year by The Chicago Woman's Club 1986, one of Chicago's 100 Most Influential Women by Crain's Chicago Business 1996 and one of 15 Women of the Century by Chicago Sun-Times 1999. Honored by Midwest Women's Center 1986, Chicago Foundation for Women 1990, Hebrew Immigrant Aid Society of Chicago 1996 and Chicago Attorney's Council of Hadassah 1999. Recipient Special Commendation Award from U.S. Department of Justice 1975, Annual National Law and Social Justice Leadership Award from The League to Improve Community 1975, Special Achievement Award from U.S. Department of Justice 1976, Annual Guardian Police Award 1977, Professional Achievement Award from Illinois Institute of Technology, Chicago-Kent College of Law 1986, Defense of Prisoners Committee Commendation from Chicago Bar Association 1987, Service Award from Spertus College of Judaica 1987, ORT Women's American Community Service Award 1987-88, Annual Award from Women's Bar Association of Illinois 1989, Citation of Honor from Decalogue Society 1991, Full Circle Award from Sculpture Chicago 1993, Louis Dembitz Brandeis Medal for Distinguished Legal Service from Brandeis University 1993, First Women Award from Valparaiso University 1993, Myra Bradwell Woman of Achievement Award from Women's Bar Association of Illinois 1994, Outstanding New Citizen Award from Citizenship Council of Metropolitan Chicago 1995, Merit Award from Decalogue Society of Lawyers 1997, Arabella Babb Mansfield Award from National Association of Women Lawyers 1998 and First Woman Award from Women's Bar Association of Illinois, Chicago Bar Association Alliance for Women 2000 and Georgetown University Law Center 2001. Listed in *Who's Who of American Women* since 1981, *Who's Who in American Law* since 1985, *Who's Who in America* since 1988 and *Who's Who in the Midwest* since 1988. Ilana Diamond Rovner Appellate Advocacy Program and Moot Court Competition inaugurated by Chicago-Kent College of Law 1992. Ilana Diamond Rovner Scholarship established by Illinois Institute of Technology, Chicago-Kent College of Law and Decalogue Foundation 1998. Republican. Board of Trustees Anshe Emet Synagogue 1980-88, Bryn Mawr College 1983-89 and Illinois Institute of Technology since 1989. Board of Overseers Illinois Institute of Technology, Chicago-Kent College of Law since 1983. Advisory Council Rush Center for Sports Medicine 1991-93. Board of Visitors Northern Illinois University College of Law 1992-94, University of Chicago Law School 1993-96 and since 2000 and Northwestern University School of Law 1993-98. Chair Illinois State Selection Committee The Rhodes Scholarship Trust 1998-2000. Board of Directors Rehabilitation Institute of Chicago since 1998.

Office: U.S. Courthouse, 219 South Dearborn Street, Chicago, Illinois 60604.

Telephone: (312) 435-5608.

RUWE, Robert P. *(Judge, United States Tax Court)* Appointed by President George Bush.

Office: 400 Second Street N.W., Washington, D.C. 20217-0002.

Telephone: (202) 606-8831.

RYAN, James L. *(Senior Judge, United States Court of Appeals Sixth Circuit)* Appointed for life by President Ronald Reagan. Assumed Senior status Jan 1, 2000, serves by assignment. Born Detroit Michigan Nov 19, 1932. Roman Catholic. Educated at University of Detroit LL.B. 1956 B.A. 1992. Redford Township Justice of the Peace 1963-66. Judge, Michigan Circuit Court Third Judicial Circuit 1966-75. Former Justice, Michigan Supreme Court, assumed office 1975.

Member Naval Reserve Lawyers Association, American Judicature Society, National Conference of Appellate Court Judges, State Bar of Michigan and Federal Bar Association. Supervising Justice Michigan Judicial Institute 1976-86. Captain USNR (retired). Board of Governors Ave Maria School of Law. Member Knights of Columbus and Knights of Malta.

Office: 611 U.S. Courthouse, 231 West Lafayette Boulevard, Detroit, Michigan 48226.

Telephone: (313) 234-5250.

RYAN, John E. *(Chief Judge, Bankruptcy Appellate Panel Ninth Circuit)* Selected by the Judicial Council of the Ninth Circuit. Also Judge, U.S. Bankruptcy Court Central District of California. Appointed by U.S. Court of Appeals Ninth Circuit judges to term beginning 1986. Reappointed 2000, current term expires 2014. Born Boston Massachusetts Jan 22, 1941. Catholic. Educated at U.S. Naval Academy B.S. 1963 and Georgetown University LL.B. 1972. Articles Editor Georgetown Law Journal 1971-72. Admitted to practice Massachusetts 1972 and California 1976. In legal practice Boston Massachusetts 1972-75 and San Diego California 1984-86.

Attorney CF Braun 1976-78. Senior Attorney Oak Industries 1979-83. Fellow American College of Bankruptcy. Member National Conference of Bankruptcy Judges, State Bar of California and Massachusetts Bar Association. USN 1963-72. Enjoys camping and kayaking. Personal Statement or Quote: "When you come to court, be prepared, be cordial, and be honest."

Office: 411 West Fourth Street, Santa Ana, California 92701.

Telephone: (714) 338-5450.

Fax: (714) 338-5459

E-mail address: john_ryan@cacb.uscourts.gov

RYMER, Pamela Ann *(Judge, United States Court of Appeals Ninth Circuit)* Appointed for life by President George Bush to term beginning May 24, 1989. Born Knoxville Tennessee Jan 6, 1941. Presbyterian. Educated at Vassar College A.B. 1961 and Stanford University LL.B. 1964. Awarded honorary LL.D. Pepperdine University 1988. Admitted to practice California 1966, U.S. Courts of Appeals Ninth 1966 and Tenth 1966 Circuits and U.S. Supreme Court. In legal practice Los Angeles 1966-83. Judge, U.S. District Court Central District of California Feb 28, 1983 to May 23, 1989, appointed by President Ronald Reagan.

Author "A Trial Lawyer's Problem in Antitrust" Association of Business Trial Lawyers Feb 18, 1976; "The Economist as an Expert Witness in Antitrust Litigation" 52 Los Angeles B. Jour. 114, 1976; "Forward to the Past—Or, When Do Predicate Acts a Pattern Make" 4 Trial Lawyers Section Newsletter 1986; "Integrity First" 11 No. 10 Los Angeles Lawyer 1989; "High Road, Low Road—Legal Profession at the Crossroads" Trial Oct 1989; "How Big Is Too Big?" 15 Journal of Law & Politics 383, 1999; "The Trials of Judging" 4 Green Bag 2d 57, 2000; and "Implications of the White Commission" 34 University of California at Davis L. Rev. 351, 2000. Member Committee on Summer Educational Programs 1987-88 and Committee on Appellate Judge Education 1996-99 Federal Judicial Center; and Commission of Structural Alternatives for the Federal Courts of Appeals 1997-98. Chair Judicial Conference of the Ninth Circuit 1990. Board of Governors Association of Business Trial Lawyers 1990-92. Member ad hoc Committee on Gender-Based Violence 1991-94 and Committee on Federal-State Jurisdiction 1993-96 Judicial Conference of the U.S. Member State Bar of California (Los Angeles Delegate Conference of Delegates 1982, Member Executive Committee Antitrust and Trade Regulation Section 1990-92), Los Angeles County (Member Judicial Appointments Committee 1979-82 and Committee on Professionalism since 1988, Chair Antitrust Section 1981-82, Chairman Subcommittee on Peer Review and Counseling Committee on Federal Courts Practice Standards 1981-83) and American (Editorial Board *Judges Journal* Appellate Judges Conference 1989-91, Member Coordinating Committee on the Agenda for Civil Justice Reform in America 1991 and Task Force on Civil Justice Reform 1991-93 Judicial Administration Division) Bar Associations. Faculty Member Managing Complex Litigation The National Judicial College 1986-88 and New Judges Orientation Federal Judicial Center. Recipient Outstanding Trial Jurist Award from Los Angeles County Bar Association 1988. Named David T. Lewis Distinguished Jurist-in-Residence University of Utah College of Law 1992. Member 1976-84 and Chair 1980-84 California Postsecondary Education Commission. Board of Directors Constitutional Rights Foundation since 1985, California Higher Education Policy Center 1992-97 and Pacific Council on International Policy since 1995. Member since 1986 and Chair 1993-96 Board of Visitors Stanford Law School. Member Education Commission of the States Task Force on State Policy and Independent Higher Education 1987-89 and Carnegie Commission Task Force on Science and Technology in Judicial and Regulatory Decisionmaking 1990-93. Board of Visitors Pepperdine Law School since 1987. Member Board of Trustees since 1991 and Chair Committee on Academic Policy, Planning and Management and ad hoc Committee on Athletics Stanford University. Member Commission on Substance Abuse on College and University Campuses 1992-94 and Commission on Substance Abuse at High Schools 1995-97 Center on Addiction and Substance Abuse Columbia University. Chair Court Appointed Scientific Experts Advisory Committee American Association for the Advancement of Science since 1999.

Mailing address: P.O. Box 91510, Pasadena, California 91109-1510.

Office: 600 Court of Appeals Building, 125 South Grand Avenue, Pasadena, California 91105-1652.

Telephone: (626) 229-7210.

SACK, Robert D. *(Judge, United States Court of Appeals Second Circuit)* Appointed for life by President Bill Clinton June 16, 1998 to term beginning Aug 6, 1998. Educated at University of Rochester 1960 and Columbia University School of Law 1963. Law Clerk to Hon. Arthur S. Lane, U.S. District Court District of New Jersey. In legal practice New York City 1964-98.

Advisory Board *Media Law Reporter* Bureau of National Affairs and *Communications Lawyer* Forum on Communications Law American Bar Association 1980-88. Author *Sack on Defamation: Libel, Slander, and Related Problems* 3rd ed. 1999 and "Protection of Opinion Under the First Amendment: Reflections on Alfred Hill, 'Defamation and Privacy Under the First Amendment'" 100th Anniversary issue Columbia L. Rev. Co-author *Advertising and Commercial Speech: A First Amendment Guide* 1999. Lecturer on Law Columbia University School of Law. Chairman National Council on Crime and Delinquency 1982-83. Fellow American Bar Foundation. Member The Association of the Bar of the City of New York and American Bar Association. Senior Associate Special Counsel to Impeachment Inquiry Staff U.S. House of Representatives 1974. Board of Trustees Columbia University Seminars on Media and Society 1985-92. Director William F. Kerby and Robert S. Potter Fund. Board of Visitors Columbia University School of Law.

Office: U.S. Courthouse, 40 Centre Street, New York, New York 10007.

Telephone: (212) 857-2140.

SCALIA, Antonin *(Associate Justice, The Supreme Court of the United States)* Appointed for life by President Ronald Reagan to term beginning 1986. Also Circuit Justice, U.S. Court of Appeals Fifth Circuit. Born Trenton New Jersey March 11, 1936. Roman Catholic. Educated at University of Fribourg, Switzerland, Georgetown University A.B. summa cum laude 1957 and Harvard University Law School LL.B. magna cum laude 1960. Note Editor Harvard Law Review 1959-60. Sheldon Fellow Harvard University 1960-61. Admitted to practice Ohio 1962 and Virginia 1970. In legal practice Cleveland Ohio 1962-67. Judge, U.S. Court of Appeals District of Columbia Circuit 1982-86.

General Counsel Office of Telecommunications Policy Executive Office of the President March 1971 to Sept 1972. Chairman Administrative Conference of the U.S. Sept 1972 to Aug 1974. Assistant Attorney General Office of Legal Counsel U.S. Department of Justice Aug 1974 to Jan 1977. Editor Regulation Magazine 1979-82. Professor of Law University of Virginia 1967-74 (on leave 1971-74) and University of Chicago 1977-82. Visiting Professor of Law Georgetown University 1977 and Stanford University 1980-81. Member American Bar Association (Chairman Section of Administrative Law

SCALIA, ANTONIN—*Continued*

1981-82 and Conference of Section Chairmen 1982-83). Scholar in Residence American Enterprise Institute 1977. Board of Visitors Brigham Young University J. Reuben Clark Law School 1978-81.

Office: One First Street N.E., Washington, D.C. 20543-0001.

Telephone: (202) 479-3000.

SCHALL, Alvin A. *(Judge, United States Court of Appeals Federal Circuit)* Appointed for life by President George Bush to term beginning Aug 19, 1992. Born New York New York April 4, 1944. Educated at Princeton University B.A. 1966 and Tulane University School of Law J.D. 1969. Admitted to practice New York 1970 and District of Columbia 1980. In legal practice New York New York 1970-73 and Washington D.C. 1987-88.

Author Chapter 9 "Federal Contract Disputes and Forums" *Construction Litigation: Strategies and Techniques* ed. by Barry A. Bramble and Albert E. Phillips Wiley Law Publications John Wiley & Sons 1989.

Office: National Courts Building, 717 Madison Place N.W., Washington, D.C. 20439-0002.

Telephone: (202) 633-6562.

SCHERMER, Barry S. *(Judge, Bankruptcy Appellate Panel Eighth Circuit)* Selected by the Judicial Council of the Eighth Circuit to term beginning 1996. Also Judge, U.S. Bankruptcy Court Eastern District of Missouri. Appointed by U.S. Court of Appeals Eighth Circuit judges to term beginning 1986. Reappointed 2000, current term expires 2014. Former Chief Judge Bankruptcy Court. Educated at Washington University J.D. 1973.

Adjunct Professor Washington University School of Law.

Office: U.S. Courthouse, 111 South Tenth Street, St. Louis, Missouri 63102.

Telephone: (314) 244-4531.

SCHROEDER, Mary M. *(Chief Judge, United States Court of Appeals Ninth Circuit)* Appointed for life by President Jimmy Carter to term beginning Oct 12, 1979. Chief Judge since Dec 1, 2000. Born Boulder Colorado Dec 4, 1940. Educated at Swarthmore College B.A. 1962 and University of Chicago J.D. 1965. Law Clerk to Justice Jesse A. Udall, Supreme Court of Arizona 1970. Admitted to practice District of Columbia 1966, Illinois 1966 and Arizona 1970. In legal practice Phoenix Arizona 1971-75. Judge, Arizona Court of Appeals Division One 1975-79, appointed by Governor Raul Castro.

With Civil Division U.S. Department of Justice 1965-69. Co-author book reviews of Wright & Miller *Federal Practice & Procedure* 87 Harvard L. Rev. 315, 1973 and *Encyclopaedia Britannica III* ABA Jour. 1974. Visiting Instructor Arizona State University 1974, 1976 and 1978. Member Arizona Association of Women Lawyers, National Association of Women Lawyers, National Association of Women Judges (President 1998-99), The American Law Institute, The District Columbia Bar, State Bar of Arizona, Illinois State, Federal and American Bar Associations. Recipient Distinguished Achievement Award from Arizona State University 1977. Democrat. Former Democratic Precinct Committeeman. Former member Democratic State Committee, Arizona Women's Political Caucus and Women Lawyers for the ERA. Member Soroptimists International.

Office: 610 U.S. Courthouse, 401 West Washington Street, Phoenix, Arizona 85003-2156.

Telephone: (602) 322-7320.

SCIRICA, Anthony J. *(Judge, United States Court of Appeals Third Circuit)* Appointed for life by President Ronald Reagan Aug 6, 1987. Born Norristown Pennsylvania Dec 16, 1940. Educated at Wesleyan University B.A. 1962 and University of Michigan J.D. 1965. Former Judge, Pennsylvania Court of Common Pleas. Judge, U.S. District Court Eastern District of Pennsylvania 1984-87.

Chair Committee on Rules of Practice and Procedure Judicial Conference of the U.S.

Office: 22614 U.S. Courthouse, 601 Market Street, Philadelphia, Pennsylvania 19106-1746.

Telephone: (215) 597-2399.

SELYA, Bruce M. *(Judge, United States Court of Appeals First Circuit)* Appointed for life by President Ronald Reagan to term beginning Nov 23, 1986. Born Providence Rhode Island May 27, 1934. Jewish. Member Temple Beth El. Educated at Harvard University A.B. magna cum laude 1955 LL.B. magna cum laude 1958. Recipient Smith Foundation Scholarship. Named John Harvard Scholar. Law Clerk to Chief Judge Edward W. Day, U.S. District Court District of Rhode Island 1958-60. Admitted to practice District of Columbia 1959 and Rhode Island 1960. In legal practice Providence 1960-82. Judge, Lincoln Probate Court 1965-72. Judge, U.S. District Court District of Rhode Island 1982-86.

Important Decisions: Scuncio Motors v. Subaru (first impression dealer's law) 1982; Seveney v. U.S. (rights of former military personnel) 1982; Milene Music v. Gatauco (copyright) 1982; Brown v. Dean (minority voting rights) 1982; United Nuclear Corporation v. Cannon (nuclear power industry regulation) 1982; Plummer v. Abbott Laboratories (DES litigation) 1983; Muniz Ramirez v. Puerto Rico Fire Service (constitutional amendment conflict) 1983; Gonsalves v. Alpine Country Club (first impression) 1983; Fifth Senatorial District Committee v. Quattrocchi (political committees) 1983; Belcher v. Mansi (novel impression) 1983; Calenda v. Board of Medical Review (medical professionals) 1983; Smith v. Harris (public school teachers) 1983; Burney v. Pawtucket (sex discrimination) 1983; Breest v. Moran (interstate prisoner transfers) 1983; Linder v. Berge (fair representation) 1983; Woo v. Glantz (self-incrimination) 1983; Fuentes v. Moran (waiver of counsel) 1983; United States v. Puerto Rico (novel impression) 1983; Marcello v. Regan (federal tax intercept program) 1984; Fischer v. McGowan (initial judicial interpretation of press shield law) 1984; Chang v. U.R.I. (sex discrimination) 1985; and U.S. v. Meyer (Export-Import Act) 1987.

Member Rhode Island Judicial Council 1964-72 (Secretary 1965-70, Chairman 1971-72), Governor's Commission on Crime and Administration of Justice 1967-69, Federal Judges Association, American Arbitration Association, Rhode Island Bar Foundation, Rhode Island (Chairman Committee on Continuing Legal Education 1971-74, Vice Chairman Committee on Banks and Trusts 1977-80, member Committee on Professional Ethics and Responsibility 1979-82, Federal Bench/Bar Committee since 1982 and Joint Liaison Committee), Federal

SELYA, BRUCE M.—*Continued*

and American Bar Associations. Delegate National Conference on Revisions to Federal Appellate Practice 1968-82. Member Republican State Executive Committee 1965-82 (General Counsel 1965-69, Vice Chairman 1969-74). Trustee since 1982 and Chairman of the Board since 1986 Bryant College. Board of Directors Jewish Federation of Rhode Island and Jewish Home for the Aged. Co-founder and first Chairman Jewish Community Relations of Rhode Island. Corporator Rhode Island Hospital, Butler Hospital, Roger Williams General Hospital and Narragansett Foundation. Member Anti-Defamation League (Rhode Island Area Chairman 1974-78, Regional Vice President New England 1978-82), Rhode Island Historical Society, Harvard Club of Rhode Island, Harvard Law School Association of Rhode Island and University Club. Enjoys reading, poetry and tennis. Interested in the human condition.

Office: 316 Federal Bldg. & U.S. Courthouse, One Exchange Terrace, Providence, Rhode Island 02903-1755.

Telephone: (401) 752-7140.

SENTELLE, David B. *(Judge, United States Court of Appeals District of Columbia Circuit)* Appointed for life by President Ronald Reagan to term beginning 1988. Former Judge, U.S. District Court Western District of North Carolina.

Office: 5818 U.S. Courthouse, 333 Constitution Avenue N.W., Washington, D.C. 20001-2866.

Telephone: (202) 216-7330.

SEYMOUR, Stephanie Kulp *(Judge, United States Court of Appeals Tenth Circuit)* Appointed for life by President Jimmy Carter to term beginning 1979. Chief Judge Jan 1, 1994 to Dec 31, 2000. Born Battle Creek Michigan Oct 16, 1940. Educated at Smith College B.A. magna cum laude 1962 and Harvard University J.D. 1965. Member Phi Beta Kappa. Admitted to practice Oklahoma 1965. In legal practice Boston Massachusetts 1965-66, Tulsa Oklahoma 1966-67 and 1971-79 and Houston Texas 1968-69.

Legal Advisory Panel Tulsa Task Force on Battered Women 1971-77. Member various task forces Tulsa Human Rights Commission 1972-76. Associate Bar Examiner Oklahoma Bar Association 1973-79. Trustee Tulsa County Law Library 1977-78. Member 1985-90 and Chair 1987-90 Committee on Defender Services and Member Committee to Review Circuit Council and Disability Orders since 1996 Judicial Conference of the U.S. Member Oklahoma State-Federal-Tribal Council since 1993 and Joint Federal-Tribal Relations Committee Ninth and Tenth Circuits 1993-94. Member Oak Chapter Council American Inns of Court. Member National Association of Women Judges, Tulsa County, Oklahoma and American Bar Associations.

Office: 4-562 Federal Bldg. & U.S. Courthouse, 333 West Fourth Street, Tulsa, Oklahoma 74103-3877.

Telephone: (918) 699-4745.

SHEDD, Dennis W. *(Judge, United States Court of Appeals Fourth Circuit)* Appointed for life by President George W. Bush to term beginning Dec 10, 2002. Born Cordova South Carolina Jan 28, 1953. Educated at Wofford College B.A. 1975, University of South Carolina School of Law J.D. 1978 and Georgetown University Law Center LL.M. 1980. In legal practice Columbia 1988-90. Former Judge, U.S. District Court District of South Carolina, appointed by President George Bush to term beginning 1990.

Staff Member 1978-88 and Administrative Assistant 1982-84 to U.S. Senator Strom Thurmond. Chief Counsel and Staff Director Committee on the Judiciary U.S. Senate 1985-86.

Office: Federal Courthouse, 1845 Assembly Street, Columbia, South Carolina 29201-2431.

Telephone: (803) 253-3688.

SILBERMAN, Laurence H. *(Senior Judge, United States Court of Appeals District of Columbia Circuit)* Appointed for life by President Ronald Reagan Sept 11, 1985. Assumed Senior status Nov 1, 2000, serves by assignment. Born York Pennsylvania Oct 12, 1935. Educated at Dartmouth College A.B. 1957 and Harvard Law School LL.B. 1961. In legal practice Honolulu Hawaii 1961-67 and Washington D.C. 1973-74, 1978-79 and 1983-85.

Attorney Appellate Division National Labor Relations Board 1967-69. Solicitor of Labor U.S. Department of Labor 1969-70. Deputy Attorney General of the U.S. 1974-75. Lecturer University of Hawaii School of Law 1962-63. Adjunct Professor of Law Georgetown University Law Center since 1987. Private U.S. Army 1957-58. Executive Vice President of Strategic Planning Legal and Government Affairs Crocker National Bank 1979-83. Ambassador to Yugoslavia 1975-77. President's Special Envoy on ILO Affairs 1976. Senior Fellow 1977-78 and Visiting Fellow 1978-85 American Enterprise Institute.

Office: 3400 U.S. Courthouse, 333 Constitution Avenue N.W., Washington, D.C. 20001-2866.

Telephone: (202) 216-7353.

SILER, Eugene E., Jr. *(Senior Judge, United States Court of Appeals Sixth Circuit)* Appointed for life by President George Bush to term beginning Sept 16, 1991. Assumed Senior status Dec 31, 2001, serves by assignment. Born Williamsburg Kentucky Oct 19, 1936. Baptist. Educated at Vanderbilt University B.A. cum laude 1958, University of Virginia LL.B. 1963 LL.M. 1995 and Georgetown University LL.M. 1964. Staff member University of Virginia Law Review. Admitted to practice Kentucky 1963, District of Columbia 1963 and Virginia 1963. Began legal practice Washington D.C. 1963. In legal practice Williamsburg Kentucky 1964-70. Judge, U.S. District Courts Eastern and Western Districts of Kentucky Dec 8, 1975 to Sept 15, 1991. Chief Judge, U.S. District Court Eastern District of Kentucky 1984-91.

Whitley County Attorney at Williamsburg 1965-70. U.S. Attorney Eastern District of Kentucky at Lexington 1970-75. Member The District of Columbia Bar, Virginia State Bar and Kentucky Bar Association. Recipient Outstanding Judge Award from Kentucky Bar Association 1992. Lieutenant j.g. USN 1958-60 and USNR 1960-83. Republican. Alternate Delegate to Republican National Convention 1968. Co-chairman Fifth Congressional District Campaign 1966 for Senator John Sherman Cooper and Congressman Tim Lee Carter. Member Regional Mental Health Board at London Kentucky 1966-70. Trustee Cumberland College 1966-74 and 1980-88. First Vice President Kentucky Baptist Convention 1986-

SILER, EUGENE E., JR.—*Continued*

87 and 2002-03. Director Baptist Healthcare System 1990-99 and since 2001.

Office: 310 South Main Street, Suite 333, London, Kentucky 40741.

Telephone: (606) 877-7930.

SILVERMAN, Barry G. *(Judge, United States Court of Appeals Ninth Circuit)* Appointed for life by President Bill Clinton to term beginning Feb 6, 1998. Born New York New York Oct 11, 1951. Educated at Arizona State University B.A. summa cum laude 1973 J.D. 1976. Staff member Arizona State University Law Journal 1974-75. Admitted to practice Arizona 1976, U.S. District Court District of Arizona 1976, U.S. Court of Appeals Ninth Circuit 1976 and U.S. Supreme Court 1980. Court Commissioner 1979-84 and Judge Sept 4, 1984 to Jan 20, 1995, Superior Court of Arizona Maricopa County. Magistrate Judge, U.S. District Court District of Arizona Jan 21, 1995 to Feb 5, 1998.

Assistant City Prosecutor Phoenix 1976-77. Deputy Attorney Maricopa County 1977-79. Author "A Judge's Mailbox" 18 *Litigation* 43 Fall 1991 and "Out of Order" *Arizona Attorney* 1991. Instructor in Constitutional Law Spring 1983 and Adjunct Professor of Advanced Criminal Procedure Spring 1989 Arizona State University College of Law. Lecturer on Community Property BAR/BRI Arizona, Idaho and Nevada Bar Review Course since 1989. Member State Bar of Arizona, Maricopa County and American Bar Associations. Recipient Henry Stevens Award from Maricopa County Bar Association 1991 and Exel Award from Society of National Association Publications 1992.

Office: 401 West Washington Street, SPC 78, Phoenix, Arizona 85003.

Telephone: (602) 322-7330.

SKELTON, Byron G. *(Senior Judge, United States Court of Appeals Federal Circuit)* Appointed to U.S. Court of Claims for life by President Lyndon B. Johnson to term beginning Nov 9, 1966. Assumed Senior status June 1, 1977, serves by assignment. U.S. Court of Claims appellate division merged with U.S. Court of Customs and Patent Appeals to become U.S. Court of Appeals Federal Circuit Oct 1, 1982. Born Florence Texas Sept 1, 1905. Educated at University of Texas B.A. 1927 M.A. 1928 LL.B. 1931. Member Phi Beta Kappa, Pi Sigma Alpha and Sigma Delta Pi. Honorary member Delta Theta Phi. Admitted to practice Texas 1931, U.S. Court of Appeals Fifth Circuit 1937, U.S. Supreme Court 1946, Federal Communications Commission 1950, U.S. Tax Court 1952, U.S. Treasury Department 1952 and Interstate Commerce Commission 1953. In legal practice Temple 1931-34, 1938-42 and 1945-66.

County Attorney Bell County 1934-38. Special Assistant to U.S. Ambassador to Argentina in Buenos Aires 1942-45. City Attorney Temple 1945-60. Member The American Law Institute, American Judicature Society, State Bar of Texas (Grievance Committee, Committee on Administration of Justice and Legislative Committee) and American Bar Association. Past President Bell-Lampasas-Mills Counties Bar Association. Listed in *Who's Who in the Southwest* 1956-64 and *Who's Who in America* 1958 and since 1960. Recipient DeMolay Legion of Honor Award 1978. Named Outstanding Citizen of Temple Texas by Junior Chamber of Commerce 1984. Democrat. Delegate to Democratic National Conventions 1948, 1956, 1960 and 1964 and to State Democratic Conventions 1946-60. Chairman Democratic Advisory Council 1955-56 and Executive Committee of Texas Democratic Advisory Council 1954-55. Democratic National Committeeman for Texas 1956-64. Member Credentials Committee of Democratic National Committee 1956-64. Chairman Texas Inaugural Committee 1961. Director First National Bank of Temple. Director and Past President Temple Chamber of Commerce. Past President Temple Kiwanis Club, YMCA, USO Council and Ex-Students Association of University of Texas. President University of Texas Ex-Students of Washington D.C. 1970-71. Past Worshipful Master and D.D.G.M. of Masonic Lodge. Shriner. Former Trustee and member Board of Stewards First Methodist Church of Temple. Speaks, reads and writes Spanish.

Office: 305 Federal Building, 101 South Main Street, Temple, Texas 76501.

Telephone: (254) 298-1276.

SKOPIL, Otto R., Jr. *(Senior Judge, United States Court of Appeals Ninth Circuit)* Appointed for life by President Jimmy Carter to term beginning Oct 20, 1979. Assumed Senior status June 30, 1986, serves by assignment. Born Portland Oregon June 3, 1919. Baptist. Educated at Willamette University B.A. 1941 LL.B. 1946 replaced by J.D. and Harvard University Graduate School of Business (Navy Supply Corps). Awarded honorary LL.D. Willamette University 1983. Admitted to practice Oregon 1946, U.S. District Court District of Oregon 1946, U.S. Court of Appeals Ninth Circuit 1966 and U.S. Supreme Court 1967. Began legal practice Salem 1946. Judge 1972-79 and Chief Judge 1976-79, U.S. District Court District of Oregon.

Important Decisions: SEC v. Glenn W. Turner Enterprises 1972; Browder v. USA 1975; Port of Astoria v. Hodel 1975; U.S. v. Truckee-Carson Irrigation District, State of Nevada 649 F.2d 1286, 1981; U.S. v. Powers 629 F.2d 619, 1980; U.S. v. Underwood 717 F.2d 482, 1983 (dissent); and Ashelman v. Pope 793 F.2d 1072, 1986. Member The Maritime Law Association of the U.S., International Society of Barristers, Oregon State Bar (Board of Governors 1960-63), Marion County and American (Committee to Achieve Justice Through the Adversary System) Bar Associations. Board of Directors Federal Judicial Center 1979. Chairman Committee on Administration of Magistrate System 1980-86 and Committee on Long Range Planning since 1991 Judicial Conference of the U.S. Named Oregon Legal Citizen of the Year 1986 and Distinguished Alumni by Willamette University College of Law 1988. Lieutenant USNR Supply Corps 1942-46. Republican. Founder Oregon Chapter American Leadership Forum. Board of Elders Mount Park Church Lake Oswego 1979-81. Fellowship Council of the Prayer Breakfast Movement. Member Willamette University Board of Trustees, Salem Citizens Advisory Committee and State of Oregon Governor's Committee on Staffing of Mental Institutions (Chairman).

Office: 827 U.S. Courthouse, 1000 Southwest Third Avenue, Portland, Oregon 97204-2902.

Telephone: (503) 326-8390.

SLOVITER, Dolores Korman *(Judge, United States Court of Appeals Third Circuit)* Appointed for life by President Jimmy Carter to term beginning 1979. Chief Judge 1991 to Jan 30, 1998. Born Philadelphia Pennsylvania Sept 5, 1932. Educated at Temple University A.B. in Economics with distinction 1953 and University of

SLOVITER, DOLORES KORMAN—*Continued*
Pennsylvania LL.B. magna cum laude 1956. Awarded honorary LL.D. Dickinson School of Law 1984, University of Richmond May 1992 and Widener University 1994 and honorary L.H.D. Temple University 1986. Member Phi Beta Kappa and Order of the Coif (President University of Pennsylvania Chapter 1975-77). Admitted to practice Pennsylvania 1957. In legal practice Philadelphia 1957-72.

Associate Professor and Professor of Law Temple University School of Law 1972-79. Disciplinary Board Pennsylvania Supreme Court 1978-79. Member The American Law Institute, National Association of Women Judges, Federal Judges Association, American Judicature Society (Board of Directors), Philadelphia (Board of Governors 1976-78), Federal and American Bar Associations. Pennsylvania Governor's Council on Aging Southeastern Region 1976-79. Member "Committee of 70" 1976-79. Board of Overseers University of Pennsylvania.

Office: 18614 U.S. Courthouse, 601 Market Street, Philadelphia, Pennsylvania 19106-1786.

Telephone: (215) 597-1588.

SMITH, D. Brooks *(Judge, United States Court of Appeals Third Circuit)* Appointed for life by President George W. Bush to term beginning Sept 23, 2002. Born Altoona Pennsylvania Dec 4, 1951. Roman Catholic. Educated at Franklin & Marshall College B.A. 1973 and Dickinson School of Law J.D. 1976. Member Phi Gamma Mu. Admitted to practice Pennsylvania 1976 and U.S. District Courts Western 1978 and Middle 1983 Districts of Pennsylvania. In legal practice Altoona 1976-84. Judge, Pennsylvania Court of Common Pleas Twenty-fourth Judicial District 1984-88. Judge Nov 1, 1988 to Jan 30, 2001 and Chief Judge Jan 31, 2001 to Sept 22, 2002, U.S. District Court Western District of Pennsylvania, appointed by President Ronald Reagan.

Assistant District Attorney 1977-79 and District Attorney 1983-84 Blair County. Special Assistant District Attorney 1981-83. Instructor Pennsylvania State University 1977-88 and St. Francis College 1986-88. Member The American Law Institute, Federal Judges Association (Board of Directors), American Judicature Society, Allegheny County (Federal Section) and Pennsylvania Bar Associations. Recipient Law Enforcement Commendation Medal from Sons of the American Revolution. Republican. Former Board Member Blair County Legal Services Corporation, Family and Children's Services of Blair County, Domestic Abuse Project, Altoona Symphony Society and Blair County Society for Crippled Children and Adults. Vice Chair Board of Trustees St. Francis University. Enjoys flyfishing, sailing and walking.

Office: 104 Penn Traffic Building, 319 Washington Street, Johnstown, Pennsylvania 15901.

Telephone: (814) 533-4514.

SMITH, Jerry E. *(Judge, United States Court of Appeals Fifth Circuit)* Appointed for life by President Ronald Reagan to term beginning Jan 7, 1988. Born Del Rio Texas Nov 7, 1946. Methodist. Educated at Yale University B.A. 1969 J.D. 1972. Law Clerk to Hon. Halbert O. Woodward, U.S. District Court Northern District of Texas 1972-73. In legal practice Houston 1973-84.

City Attorney Houston 1984-88. Chair Advisory Committee on Federal Rules of Evidence since 2002. Member State Bar of Texas. Member Texas State Republican Executive Committee 1976-87. Chairman Harris County Republican Party 1977-78. Board of Directors Harris County Housing Authority 1978-80. Chairman Houston Civil Service Commission 1982-84.

Office: 12621 U.S. Courthouse, 515 Rusk Avenue, Houston, Texas 77002-2698.

Telephone: (713) 250-5101.

SMITH, Lavenski R. *(Judge, United States Court of Appeals Eighth Circuit)* Appointed for life by President George W. Bush to term beginning July 19, 2002.

Office: 600 West Capitol Avenue, Suite 302, Little Rock, Arkansas 72201.

Telephone: (501) 604-5130.

SMITH, Loren A. *(Senior Judge, United States Court of Federal Claims)* Appointed by President Ronald Reagan July 11, 1985 to term beginning Sept 12, 1985. Chief Judge Jan 14, 1986 to July 11, 2000. Assumed Senior status July 11, 2000, serves by assignment. Born Chicago Illinois Dec 22, 1944. Jewish. Educated at Northwestern University B.A. 1966 J.D. 1969. Awarded honorary LL.D. John Marshall Law School 1995, Capital University Law School 1996 and Campbell University 1997. Admitted to practice Illinois, U.S. Court of Military Appeals, U.S. Courts of Appeals District of Columbia and Federal Circuits, U.S. Supreme Court and U.S. Court of Federal Claims. In legal practice Chicago 1972-73.

General Attorney Federal Communications Commission 1973. Assistant to the Special Counsel to President Richard M. Nixon 1973-74. Special Assistant U.S. Attorney District of Columbia 1974-75. Chairman Administrative Conference of the U.S. 1981-85 (Member President's Cabinet Councils on Legal Policy and on Management and Administration; Chairman Council of Independent Regulatory Agencies). Author "Business, Buck$ & Bull: The Corporation, the First Amendment & the Corrupt Practices Law" 4 Delaware Journal of Corporate Law 1, 1978; "Judicialization: The Twilight of Administrative Law" 85 Duke L. Jour. 2, 1985; "Vision of the Exchange" William & Mary L. Rev. 1986; "Judicialization of the Administrative Process: The Fine Print" National Legal Center for the Public Interest 1986; "The End of the Constitution" 4 Detroit College of Law Rev. 1147, 1986; "Administration: An Idea Whose Time May Have Passed" *The Fettered Presidency* edited by L. Gordon Crovitz and Jeremy A. Rabkin 1989; "A Spring Thaw in Estonia" *The Washington Times* April 11, 1992; "Renovation of an Old Court" Federal Bar News and Journal Sept 1993; "The Morality of Regulation" William & Mary Environmental Law and Policy Review 1998; and "The Aging of Administrative Law: The Administrative Conference Reaches Early Retirement" Arizona State L. Jour. 1998. Co-author "Black America and Organized Labor: A Fair Deal?" Lincoln Institute for Research and Education 1979. Adjunct Professor The International School of Law (now George Mason University School of Law) 1973-74, Washington College of Law of American University, Georgetown University Law Center and Catholic University of America School of Law. Professor of Constitutional Law, Federal Election Law and Equity and Administrative Law Delaware Law School of Widener University 1976-84. First Distinguished Jurist-in-Residence University of Denver College of Law 1993. Presented with Allen Chair University of Richmond School of Law 1995. Honorary Member Bar Association of the District of Columbia. Spoken and ap-

SMITH, LOREN A.—*Continued*

peared on TV and radio in Estonia, Republic of South Africa, Zambia, Kenya, Czech Republic, Hungary, Turkey, Egypt, Pakistan, Philippines, Singapore, Italy, Germany, England, Canada, Spain, Switzerland and Ukraine on behalf of U.S. Information Agency and other groups. Named Member of the Year by The University Club of Washington D.C. 1991. Recipient Presidential Medal from Catholic University of America School of Law May 29, 1993, Romanian Medal of Justice from Romanian Minister of Justice 1995 and Ronald Reagan Public Service Award from National Property Rights Conference 1997. Host "What's Best for America?" radio talk show 1972. Previously worked as campaign consultant, corporate officer and lecturer. Candidate Illinois General Assembly 1970. Chief Counsel Reagan for President campaigns 1976 and 1980. Deputy Director Executive Branch Management Office of the Presidential Transition Nov 1980 to Jan 1981. Honorary Member The University Club of Washington D.C. (Chairman Centennial Committee). Member Community Advisory Board WETA Public Television and Radio.

Office: National Courts Building, 717 Madison Place N.W., Washington, D.C. 20005-1086.

Telephone: (202) 219-9567.

SNEED, Joseph Tyree *(Senior Judge, United States Court of Appeals Ninth Circuit)* Appointed for life by President Richard M. Nixon to term beginning Aug 24, 1973. Assumed Senior status July 21, 1987, serves by assignment. Born Calvert Texas July 21, 1920. Episcopalian. Educated at Southwestern University B.B.A. 1941, University of Texas LL.B. 1947 and Harvard University S.J.D. 1958. Awarded honorary LL.D. Southwestern University 1968. Member Order of the Coif.

Deputy Attorney General U.S. Department of Justice 1973. Author *Configuration of Gross Income* Ohio State University Press 1967. Assistant Professor 1947-51, Associate Professor 1951-54 and Professor of Law 1954-57 University of Texas School of Law. Professor of Law Cornell University 1957-62, Stanford University 1962-71 and Duke University (also Dean) 1971-73. Member Executive Committee Association of American Law Schools 1965-66 (President 1968), California Law Revision Commission 1970, Advisory Committee National Institute of Law Enforcement and Criminal Justice 1974-75, The American Law Institute, American Judicature Society (Board of Directors 1976-77), State Bar of Texas, New York State, Federal and American (Judges Advisory Committee, Standing Committee on Ethics and Professional Responsibility 1976-77) Bar Associations. Republican. Trustee College Retirement Equities Fund and Teachers Insurance and Annuity Association of America 1967-71. Board of Visitors Hastings College of the Law 1974-75 and Duke University 1973-76. Member Harvard Club of San Francisco.

Mailing address: P.O. Box 193939, San Francisco, California 94119-3939.

Office: 326 U.S. Court of Appeals Building, 95 Seventh Street, San Francisco, California 94103.

Telephone: (415) 556-9666.

SOTOMAYOR, Sonia *(Judge, United States Court of Appeals Second Circuit)* Appointed for life by President Bill Clinton Nov 6, 1998. Born Bronx New York June 25, 1954. Educated at Princeton University A.B. summa cum laude 1976 and Yale Law School J.D. 1979. Editor Yale L. Jour. Judge, U.S. District Court Southern District of New York 1992-98.

Assistant District Attorney New York County 1979-84. Member Association of Judges of Hispanic Heritage, Hispanic National Bar Association, Puerto Rican and American Bar Associations. Member New York City Campaign Finance Board. Former Member Board of Directors State of New York Mortgage Agency. Board of Directors Puerto Rican Legal Defense and Education Fund and Maternity Center Association.

Office: 410 U.S. Courthouse, 40 Centre Street, New York, New York 10007.

Telephone: (212) 857-2420.

SOUTER, David Hackett *(Associate Justice, The Supreme Court of the United States)* Appointed for life by President George Bush to term beginning Oct 8, 1990. Also Circuit Justice, U.S. Courts of Appeals First and Third Circuits. Born Melrose Massachusetts Sept 17, 1939. Episcopalian. Educated at Harvard University B.A. 1961 LL.B. 1966 and Oxford University, England 1961-63. Rhodes Scholar. Member Phi Beta Kappa. Admitted to practice New Hampshire. In legal practice Concord 1966-68. Associate Justice, New Hampshire Superior Court 1978-83. Associate Justice, New Hampshire Supreme Court 1983-90.

Assistant Attorney General 1968-71, Deputy Attorney General 1971-76 and Attorney General 1976-78 New Hampshire. Member New Hampshire and American Bar Associations. Republican. Trustee Concord Hospital 1973-85 (President Board of Trustees 1978-84). Board of Overseers Dartmouth Medical School since 1981. Member New Hampshire Historical Society (Trustee 1976-85, Vice President 1980-85).

Office: One First Street N.E., Washington, D.C. 20543-0001.

Telephone: (202) 479-3000.

STAHL, Norman H. *(Senior Judge, United States Court of Appeals First Circuit)* Appointed for life by President George Bush to term beginning Aug 3, 1992. Assumed Senior status April 16, 2001, serves by assignment. Born Manchester New Hampshire Jan 30, 1931. Educated at Tufts University B.A. magna cum laude 1952 and Harvard Law School LL.B. 1955. Law Clerk to Hon. John V. Spalding, Massachusetts Supreme Court 1955-56. Admitted to practice Massachusetts 1955, New Hampshire 1956 and U.S. District Court District of New Hampshire 1956. In legal practice Manchester New Hampshire 1956-90. Judge, U.S. District Court District of New Hampshire 1990-92, appointed by President George Bush.

Office: 8730 U.S. Courthouse, One Courthouse Way, Boston, Massachusetts 02210.

Telephone: (617) 748-4596.

STANCEU, Timothy C. *(Judge, United States Court of International Trade)* Appointed for life by President George W. Bush to term beginning April 15, 2003.

Office: One Federal Plaza, New York, New York 10278-0001.

Telephone: (212) 264-2877.

STAPLETON, Walter K. *(Senior Judge, United States Court of Appeals Third Circuit)* Appointed for life by President Ronald Reagan. Assumed Senior status June 2, 1999, serves by assignment. Born Cuthbert Georgia June 2, 1934. Baptist. Educated at Princeton University B.A. cum laude 1956, Harvard University

STAPLETON, WALTER K.—*Continued*

LL.B. cum laude 1959 and University of Virginia Law School M.J.P. 1984. Admitted to practice Delaware. In legal practice Wilmington 1959-70. Former Judge and Chief Judge, U.S. District Court District of Delaware, appointed by President Richard M. Nixon to term beginning 1970.

Deputy Attorney General Delaware 1964. Member The Delaware State and American Bar Associations.

Office: 5323 Federal Building, Lockbox 33, 844 North King Street, Wilmington, Delaware 19801-3587.

Telephone: (302) 573-6165.

STEINBERG, Jonathan Robert *(Judge, United States Court of Appeals for Veterans Claims)* Appointed by President George Bush to term beginning Aug 1990. Term expires 2005. Educated at Cornell University B.A. 1960 and University of Pennsylvania Law School J.D. cum laude 1963. Law Clerk to Hon. Warren E. Burger, U.S. Court of Appeals District of Columbia Circuit 1963-64. Member Order of the Coif.

Former Research Assistant The American Law Institute. Attorney-Advisor 1964-68 and Deputy General Counsel 1968-69 Peace Corps. Counsel Subcommittee on Veterans' Affairs, Subcommittee on Railroad Retirement and Special Subcommittee on Human Resources Committee on Labor and Public Welfare 1969-77; and Chief Counsel and Staff Director 1977-81 and 1987-90 and Minority Chief Counsel and Staff Director 1981-87 Committee on Veterans' Affairs U.S. Senate.

Office: 625 Indiana Avenue N.W., Suite 900, Washington, D.C. 20004-2950.

Telephone: (202) 501-5874.

STEVENS, John Paul *(Associate Justice, The Supreme Court of the United States)* Appointed for life by President Gerald R. Ford to term beginning Dec 19, 1975. Also Circuit Justice, U.S. Courts of Appeals Sixth and Seventh Circuits. Born Chicago Illinois April 20, 1920. Educated at University of Chicago A.B. 1941 and Northwestern University J.D. 1947. Law Clerk to Justice Wiley Rutledge 1947-48. Admitted to practice Illinois 1949. Began legal practice Chicago 1949. Judge, U.S. Court of Appeals Seventh Circuit 1970-75.

Member Attorney General's National Committee to Study Antitrust Laws 1953-55. Member The American Law Institute, Chicago, Illinois State and Federal Bar Associations. USN 1942-45. Recipient Bronze Star. U.S. House of Representatives 1951-52 (Associate Counsel Subcommittee on the Study of Monopoly Power Judiciary Committee).

Office: One First Street N.E., Washington, D.C. 20543-0001.

Telephone: (202) 479-3000.

STEWART, Carl E. *(Judge, United States Court of Appeals Fifth Circuit)* Appointed for life by President Bill Clinton to term beginning May 12, 1994. Born Shreveport Louisiana Jan 2, 1950. United Methodist. Educated at Dillard University B.A. magna cum laude 1971, Loyola University School of Law J.D. 1974 and Harvard University. Member Omega Psi Phi. Admitted to practice Louisiana 1974. In legal practice Shreveport 1977-78 and 1983-85. Judge, Louisiana District Court First Judicial District 1985-91. Judge, Louisiana Court of Appeal Second Circuit 1991-94.

Staff Attorney Louisiana Attorney General's Office Jan 1978 to April 1979. Assistant U.S. Attorney Western District of Louisiana April 1979 to Nov 1983. Member Black Lawyers Association of Shreveport-Bossier, Louisiana District Judges Association, American Inns of Court (Harry V. Booth Chapter), Shreveport, Louisiana State, National (Judicial Council) and American (Judicial Division) Bar Associations. Named Black Leader of the Year by Southern University Afro-American Society, Outstanding Young Man by Shreveport Jaycees 1983, Outstanding Young Man by Louisiana Jaycees 1984 and Distinguished Alumnus by Dillard University 1986. Captain U.S. Army JAGC 1975-77. Enjoys reading novels and traveling.

Office: 2299 U.S. Courthouse, 300 Fannin Street, Shreveport, Louisiana 71101-3074.

Telephone: (318) 676-3765.

STOSBERG, David T. *(Judge, Bankruptcy Appellate Panel Sixth Circuit)* Selected by the Judicial Council of the Sixth Circuit. Also Chief Judge, U.S. Bankruptcy Court Western District of Kentucky. Appointed by U.S. Court of Appeals Sixth Circuit judges.

Office: 533 U.S. Courthouse, 601 West Broadway, Louisville, Kentucky 40202-2264.

Telephone: (502) 627-5575.

STRAUB, Chester J. *(Judge, United States Court of Appeals Second Circuit)* Appointed for life by President Bill Clinton to term beginning July 15, 1998. Born Brooklyn New York May 12, 1937. Educated at St. Peter's College B.A. 1958 and University of Virginia School of Law LL.B. 1961. Editor Virginia Law Review. In legal practice New York City 1963-98. Mediator, U.S. District Court Southern District of New York 1993-98. Neutral Evaluator, U.S. District Court Eastern District of New York 1994-98.

Member The Association of the Bar of the City of New York, New York State and American (Section of Litigation) Bar Associations. Recipient Certificate of Appreciation for Exemplary Public Service from State of New York. First Lieutenant U.S. Army 1961-63. Member State Assembly 1967-72 and State Senate 1973-75 New York. Member Senator Daniel Patrick Moynihan's Judicial Selection Committee 1996-98. Trustee Lenox Hill Hospital since 1983 and Joseph Collins Foundation 1986-98. Member Cardinal's Committee for the Laity Catholic Charities of the Archdiocese of New York.

Office: 2530 U.S. Courthouse, 500 Pearl Street, New York, New York 10007-1312.

Telephone: (212) 857-2130.

SUHRHEINRICH, Richard F. *(Senior Judge, United States Court of Appeals Sixth Circuit)* Appointed for life by President George Bush to term beginning June 28, 1990. Assumed Senior status Aug 15, 2001, serves by assignment. Born Lincoln City Indiana Aug 15, 1936. Educated at Wayne State University B.S. 1960 and Detroit College of Law J.D. cum laude 1963. Member Delta Theta Phi and Delta Chi. Admitted to practice Michigan 1963 and U.S. Court of Appeals Sixth Circuit 1978. In legal practice Detroit 1963-84. Judge, U.S. District Court Eastern District of Michigan Oct 23, 1984 to June 27, 1990, appointed by President Ronald Reagan.

Assistant Prosecuting Attorney Macomb County 1967. Important Decisions: J. Edinger and Son, Inc. v. City of Louisville (civil rights) 802 F.2d 213, 6th Cir. 1986; Taylor v. Watters (civil rights) 636 F. Supp. 181 E.D. Mich. 1986; and Oakland County by Kuhn v. City of Detroit (monopolies) 620 F. Supp. 1399, 628 F. Supp. 610 E.D. Mich. 1986. Associate Professor of Law De-

SUHRHEINRICH, RICHARD F.—*Continued*

troit College of Law 1975-85. Executive Board Federal Bar Association. Member State Bar of Michigan, Macomb County and American Bar Associations. Board of Trustees Detroit College of Law, Hutzel Hospital and Southwest Detroit Hospital Corp. Board of Directors Family Service of Detroit and Wayne County and Sparrow, Inc.

Office: 241 Federal Building, 315 West Allegan Street, Lansing, Michigan 48933.

Telephone: (517) 377-1513.

SULLIVAN, Eugene R. *(Senior Judge, United States Court of Appeals for the Armed Forces)* Appointed by President Ronald Reagan to term beginning May 27, 1986. Chief Judge Oct 1, 1990 to Oct 1, 1995. Assumed Senior status, serves by assignment. Born St. Louis Missouri Aug 2, 1941. Roman Catholic. Educated at U.S. Military Academy B.S. 1964 and Georgetown University Law Center J.D. 1971. Editor Georgetown Law Journal 1971. Law Clerk to U.S. Court of Appeals Eighth Circuit 1971-72. Admitted to practice District of Columbia 1972 and Missouri 1972. In legal practice Washington D.C. 1972-74.

Assistant Special Counsel to White House 1974. Trial Attorney U.S. Department of Justice 1974-82. Deputy General Counsel 1982-84 and General Counsel 1984-86 Department of U.S. Air Force. Author "Practice Before U.S. Court of Appeals" *Missouri Bar Handbook* The Missouri Bar 1974-78 and "Procurement Fraud" 95 Military L. Rev. 117 Winter 1982. Member The District of Columbia Bar and The Missouri Bar. Recipient Professional Writing Award 1982 and Exceptional Civilian Service Medal USAF. Captain U.S. Army 1964-69. Recipient Bronze Star, Air Medal, Army Commendation Medal, Ranger Badge and Parachutist Badge. Enjoys lacrosse, squash and legal debates.

Office: 450 E Street N.W., Washington, D.C. 20442-0001.

Telephone: (202) 761-1458.

SWIFT, Stephen J. *(Judge, United States Tax Court)* Appointed by President Ronald Reagan to term beginning Aug 16, 1983. Reappointed by President Bill Clinton Sept 12, 2000. Born Salt Lake City Utah Sept 7, 1943. Mormon. Educated at Brigham Young University B.S. in Political Science 1967 and George Washington University J.D. with honors 1970. Admitted to practice District of Columbia 1970 and California 1975.

Honors Program Trial Attorney Tax Division U.S. Department of Justice 1970-74. Assistant U.S. Attorney Tax Division U.S. Attorney's Office 1974-77. Vice President and Senior Tax Counsel Bank of America N.T. & S.A. 1977-83. Adjunct Professor Golden Gate University Graduate Tax Program 1977-83 and University of Baltimore Graduate Tax Program since 1987. Member The District of Columbia Bar, State Bar of California and American Bar Association (Section of Taxation, Judicial Administration Division). Republican.

Office: 400 Second Street N.W., Washington, D.C. 20217-0002.

Telephone: (202) 606-8731.

SYPOLT, Diane Gilbert *(Judge, United States Court of Federal Claims)* Appointed by President George Bush to term beginning Oct 22, 1990. Term expires 2005. Born Rochester New York June 14, 1947. Educated at Smith College B.A. 1969 and Boston University J.D. 1979. Law Clerk to Hon. Catherine B. Kelly, District of Columbia Court of Appeals 1979-80. Admitted to practice District of Columbia 1979, Massachusetts 1979 and U.S. Courts of Appeals District of Columbia 1980 and Third 1983 Circuits. In legal practice Washington D.C. 1979-83.

Assistant General Counsel Office of Management and Budget 1983-86. Deputy General Counsel and Acting General Counsel U.S. Department of Education 1986-89. Counselor to Vice President Dan Quayle and Counsel President's Council on Competitiveness 1989-90. Master Federal American Inn of Court (President 1997-98). Recipient Young Lawyers Award from Boston University School of Law 1989. Republican. Director Democracy Development Institute. Member Federalist Society and University Club. Volunteer Hospice of Washington.

Office: National Courts Building, 717 Madison Place N.W., Washington, D.C. 20005-1086.

Telephone: (202) 219-9655.

TACHA, Deanell Reece *(Chief Judge, United States Court of Appeals Tenth Circuit)* Appointed for life by President Ronald Reagan to term beginning Dec 16, 1985. Chief Judge since Jan 1, 2001. Born Goodland Kansas Jan 26, 1946. Methodist. Educated at University of Kansas B.A. in American Studies 1968 and University of Michigan Law School J.D. 1971. Member Gamma Phi Beta. Admitted to practice Missouri 1971, Kansas 1973 and District of Columbia 1973. In legal practice Washington D.C. 1972-73 and Concordia Kansas 1973-74.

U.S. Sentencing Commissioner 1994-98. Author "Title IX: An Expanded Concept of Affirmative Action Against Sex Discrimination in Education" *New Directions in Legal Education* NOLPE 1975; "The Kansas Open Meetings Law: Sunshine on the Sunflower State" 27 No. 2 Kansas L. Rev. Winter 1977; "Judges and Legislators: Renewing the Relationship" 52 No. 1 Ohio State L. Jour. 1991; "Renewing Our Civic Commitment: Lawyers and Judges as Painters of the 'Big Picture'" 41 Kansas L. Rev. 481, 1993; "Tenth Circuit Procedure and Expectations" 33 Washburn L. Jour. 43, 1993; "'W' Stories: Women in Leadership Positions in the Judiciary" 97 West Virginia L. Rev. 683, 1995; "James K. Logan: Colleague, Mentor, Friend, Jurist, Scholar, Teacher, Small-Town Kansas Kid" 43 Kansas L. Rev. 493, 1995; "The 'C' Word: On Collegiality" 56 Ohio State L. Jour. 585, 1995; "Independence of the Judiciary for the Third Century" 46 Mercer L. Rev. 645, 1995; and "Judges and Legislators: Enhancing the Relationship" 44 American University L. Rev. 1537, 1995. Director Legal Aid Clinic Sept 1974 to July 1977, Professor of Law 1974-86, Associate Dean School of Law July 1977 to July 1979, Associate Vice Chancellor for Academic Affairs 1979-81, Vice Chancellor for Academic Affairs May 1981 to Dec 1985 and President Alumni Association 1988-89 University of Kansas. Chair Committee on the Judicial Branch Judicial Conference of the U.S. 1990-94 and since 2001. Member Kansas and American Bar Associations. Board of Trustees St. Paul School of Theology and Kansas Health Foundation. Board of Visitors Brigham Young University J. Reuben Clark Law School. Member Committee of Visitors University of Michigan Law School.

Office: 643 Massachusetts Street, Suite 301, Lawrence, Kansas 66044-2292.

Telephone: (785) 842-8556.

TALLMAN, Richard C. *(Judge, United States Court of Appeals Ninth Circuit)* Appointed for life by President Bill Clinton to term beginning June 30, 2000. Born Oakland California March 3, 1953. Educated at University of Santa Clara B.S.C. 1975 and Northwestern University School of Law J.D. 1978. Law Clerk to Hon. Morell E. Sharp, U.S. District Court Western District of Washington 1978-79. In legal practice Seattle 1983-2000.

Trial Attorney Criminal Division U.S. Department of Justice 1979-80. Assistant U.S. Attorney Western District of Washington 1980-83.

Office: Park Place Building 21st Floor, 1200 Sixth Avenue, Seattle, Washington 98101.

Telephone: (206) 553-6300.

TASHIMA, A. Wallace *(Judge, United States Court of Appeals Ninth Circuit)* Appointed for life by President Bill Clinton to term beginning Jan 1996. Born Santa Maria California June 24, 1934. Educated at University of California at Los Angeles B.A. 1958 and Harvard Law School LL.B. 1961. In legal practice Los Angeles 1977-80. Judge, U.S. District Court Central District of California 1980 to Jan 1996, appointed by President Jimmy Carter.

Deputy Attorney General California 1961-67. Attorney Spreckels Sugar Division 1968-72 and General Attorney and Vice President 1972-77 Amstar Corporation. Sergeant USMC 1953-56.

Mailing address: P.O. Box 91510, Pasadena, California 91109-1510.

Office: 406 Court of Appeals Building, 125 South Grand Avenue, Pasadena, California 91105.

Telephone: (626) 229-7373.

TATEL, David S. *(Judge, United States Court of Appeals District of Columbia Circuit)* Appointed for life by President Bill Clinton to term beginning Oct 11, 1994. Educated at University of Michigan B.A. in Political Science 1963 and University of Chicago Law School J.D. 1966. Editorial Board University of Chicago Law Review. Admitted to practice Illinois 1966 and District of Columbia 1970. In legal practice Chicago 1967-69 and District of Columbia 1970-72, 1974-77 and 1979-94.

Director Chicago Lawyers' Committee for Civil Rights Under Law 1969-70 and Office for Civil Rights U.S. Department of Health, Education and Welfare 1977-79. Director 1972-74 and Co-Chair 1989-91 National Lawyers' Committee for Civil Rights Under Law. Lecturer Stanford University Law School 1991-92. Chair Board of Directors Spencer Foundation 1987-97. Board Member Carnegie Foundation for the Advancement of Teaching since 1998. Director National Board of Professional Teaching Standards 1995-98.

Office: 3818 U.S. Courthouse, 333 Constitution Avenue N.W., Washington, D.C. 20001-2866.

Telephone: (202) 216-7160.

THOMAS, Clarence *(Associate Justice, The Supreme Court of the United States)* Appointed for life by President George Bush to term beginning 1991. Also Circuit Justice, U.S. Court of Appeals Eighth Circuit. Born Savannah Georgia 1948. Educated at College of the Holy Cross B.A. with honors and Yale Law School J.D. 1974. Admitted to practice Missouri 1974. Judge, U.S. Court of Appeals District of Columbia Circuit 1990-91.

With Office of Attorney General Missouri 1974-77. Attorney Law Department Monsanto Company 1977-79. Legislative Assistant to U.S. Senator John C. Danforth (Missouri) 1979-81. Assistant Secretary for Civil Rights U.S. Department of Education 1981-82. Chairman U.S. Equal Employment Opportunity Commission May 1982 to March 1990.

Office: One First Street N.E., Washington, D.C. 20543-0001.

Telephone: (202) 479-3000.

THOMAS, Sidney R. *(Judge, United States Court of Appeals Ninth Circuit)* Appointed for life by President Bill Clinton to term beginning 1996. Born Bozeman Montana Aug 14, 1953. Educated at Montana State University B.A. 1975 and University of Montana School of Law J.D. 1978. Legal Intern to Hon. William Wallace Lessley, Montana District Court Eighteenth Judicial District. In legal practice Billings 1978-95.

Adjunct Instructor in Law Rocky Mountain College 1982-95.

Mailing address: P.O. Box 31478, Billings, Montana 59107-1478.

Office: 301 North 27th Street, Suite 200, Billings, Montana 59101.

Telephone: (406) 657-5950.

THOMPSON, David R. *(Senior Judge, United States Court of Appeals Ninth Circuit)* Appointed for life by President Ronald Reagan Oct 7, 1985. Assumed Senior status Dec 31, 1998, serves by assignment. Born San Diego California Dec 26, 1930. Educated at University of Southern California B.S. 1952 LL.B. 1955. In legal practice San Diego 1957-85. USN 1955-57.

Office: 2193 U.S. Courthouse, 940 Front Street, San Diego, California 92101-8919.

Telephone: (619) 557-6400.

THORNTON, Michael B. *(Judge, United States Tax Court)* Appointed by President Bill Clinton.

Office: 400 Second Street N.W., Washington, D.C. 20217-0002.

Telephone: (202) 606-8711.

TIDWELL, Moody R. *(Senior Judge, United States Court of Federal Claims)* Appointed by President Ronald Reagan Feb 15, 1983 to term beginning May 3, 1983. Reappointed by President Bill Clinton 1998. Assumed Senior status, serves by assignment. Born Miami Oklahoma Feb 15, 1939. Educated at Ohio Wesleyan University B.A. 1961, Washington College of Law of American University J.D. 1964 and George Washington University LL.M. 1973. Admitted to practice District of Columbia 1964.

Associate Solicitor 1969-81 and Assistant to the Secretary and Deputy Solicitor 1981-88 U.S. Department of the Interior.

Office: National Courts Building, 717 Madison Place N.W., Washington, D.C. 20005-1086.

Telephone: (202) 219-9942.

TJOFLAT, Gerald Bard *(Judge, United States Court of Appeals Eleventh Circuit)* Appointed to Fifth Circuit for life by President Gerald R. Ford to term beginning Dec 12, 1975. Assigned to Eleventh Circuit Oct 1, 1981. Former Chief Judge. Born Pittsburgh Pennsylvania Dec 6, 1929. Episcopalian. Educated at University of Virginia, University of Cincinnati and Duke University LL.B. 1957. Awarded honorary Doctor of Civil Laws Jacksonville University 1978. Associate Editor Duke Law Journal 1956-57. Admitted to practice Florida 1957. Began legal practice Jacksonville 1957. Judge, Florida Circuit

TJOFLAT, GERALD BARD—*Continued*
Court Fourth Judicial Circuit June 1968 to Oct 1970. Judge, U.S. District Court Middle District of Florida Oct 29, 1970 to Dec 11, 1975.

Author "A Practical Look at the Sentencing Provisions of S. 1722" 72 No. 2 Northwestern University School of Law Journal of Criminal Law and Criminology Summer 1981. Member American Judicature Society, The American Law Institute, The Florida Bar, Jacksonville, Federal and American Bar Associations. Member Advisory Corrections Council of the U.S. Corporal U.S. Army 1953-55. Chairman Committee on the Administration of the Probation System Judicial Conference of the U.S. 1972-87. Member U.S. Delegation Sixth and Seventh United Nations Congresses for the Prevention of Crime and Treatment of Offenders 1980 and 1985.

Mailing address: P.O. Box 960, Jacksonville, Florida 32201-0960.

Telephone: (904) 232-3416.

TORRUELLA, Juan R. *(Judge, United States Court of Appeals First Circuit)* Appointed for life by President Ronald Reagan to term beginning Oct 1984. Chief Judge 1994 to June 15, 2001. Born San Juan Puerto Rico June 7, 1933. Educated at University of Pennsylvania Wharton School of Business B.S. 1954, Boston University School of Law J.D. 1957, University of Virginia School of Law LL.M. 1984 and University of Puerto Rico School of Public Administration M.P.A. 1984. In legal practice San Juan 1959-74. Judge 1974 to Oct 1984 and Chief Judge 1982-84, U.S. District Court District of Puerto Rico, appointed by President Gerald R. Ford.

Office: U.S. Courthouse, Fourth Floor, 300 Recinto Sur Street, San Juan, Puerto Rico 00901.

Telephone: (787) 977-6146.

TRAXLER, William B., Jr. *(Judge, United States Court of Appeals Fourth Circuit)* Appointed for life by President Bill Clinton to term beginning Oct 21, 1998. Born Greenville South Carolina May 1, 1948. Educated at Davidson College B.A. 1970 University of South Carolina School of Law J.D. 1973. Staff member South Carolina Law Review. Member Omicron Delta Kappa. Admitted to practice South Carolina 1973, U.S. District Court District of South Carolina 1974, U.S. Court of Appeals Fourth Circuit 1974 and U.S. Supreme Court 1981. In legal practice Greenville 1973-74. Judge, South Carolina Circuit Court Thirteenth Judicial Circuit 1985-92. Judge, U.S. District Court District of South Carolina 1992-98.

Chief Deputy Solicitor 1975-81 and Solicitor 1981-85 Thirteenth Judicial Circuit South Carolina. Author "An Empirical Examination of the 235 No. 1 Housing Program" 25 South Carolina L. Rev. 93-149, 1973; "The Problem of the Mentally Ill Criminal Defendant" 3 No. 2 *SCLEOA Magazine* 20-21, 1982; "Removal of Bullets from Wounded Defendants" 3 No. 5 *SCLEOA Magazine* 6-8, 1982; "Using Confidential Informants" 1 No. 6 *SCLEOA Update* 13, July 1984; "Allocating Responsibility Among Tortfeasors After the Adoption of Comparative Negligence" 19 No. 3 *The Defense Line* 7-9, Summer 1991; and "Comparative Negligence in South Carolina: Adopted but Unresolved" *South Carolina Lawyer* 32-36, July/Aug 1991. Member South Carolina Bar and Greenville County Bar Association. Recipient Award for untiring efforts to improve the quality of justice in the Thirteenth Judicial Circuit from Bonner R. Kidd Home for Alcoholics, Citation of Appreciation from Greenville Chapter American Legion, Outstanding Service Award from South Carolina Solicitors Association, Award for Outstanding Service to Victims from Southeastern Victim/Witness Conference and Leadership Award from South Carolina Department of Probation, Parole and Pardon Services.

Mailing address: P.O. Box 10127, Greenville, South Carolina 29603-0127.

Telephone: (864) 241-2730.

TROTT, Stephen S. *(Judge, United States Court of Appeals Ninth Circuit)* Appointed for life by President Ronald Reagan to term beginning 1988. Born Glen Ridge New Jersey Dec 12, 1939. Educated at Wesleyan University B.A. 1962 and Harvard Law School LL.B. 1965.

With Los Angeles County District Attorney's Office 1966-81. U.S. Attorney Central District of California 1981-83. Assistant Attorney General Criminal Division U.S. Department of Justice 1983-86. Associate Attorney General 1986-88.

Office: 667 Federal Bldg. & U.S. Courthouse, 550 West Fort Street, Boise, Idaho 83724-0040.

Telephone: (208) 334-1612.

TSOUCALAS, Nicholas *(Senior Judge, United States Court of International Trade)* Appointed for life by President Ronald Reagan Sept 5, 1985 to term beginning June 6, 1986. Assumed Senior status, serves by assignment. Born New York New York Aug 24, 1926. Greek Orthodox. Educated at Kent State University B.S. 1949 and New York Law School LL.B. 1951. Admitted to practice New York 1953. In legal practice New York City 1953-55 and 1959-68. Judge, The Criminal Court of the City of New York 1968-86. Acting Justice, New York Supreme Court 1975-82.

Assistant U.S. Attorney Southern District of New York 1955-59. Instructor in Immigration Law Hunter College 1978-80 and Queens College 1978-81. Founder Eastern Orthodox Lawyers Association. Member New York County Lawyers' Association, Queens County, New York State, Customs and International Trade, Federal and American Bar Associations. Radio Operator Second Class USN 1944-46 and 1951-52. Republican. Enjoys stamp collecting.

Office: One Federal Plaza, New York, New York 10278-0001.

Telephone: (212) 264-2918.

TURNER, James T. *(Judge, United States Court of Federal Claims)* Appointed by President Ronald Reagan to term beginning 1987. Reappointed by President George W. Bush 2002, current term expires Oct 2017. Born Clifton Forge Virginia March 12, 1938. Educated at Wake Forest University B.A. 1960 and University of Virginia LL.B. 1965 replaced by J.D. Member Omicron Delta Kappa. Admitted to practice Virginia, U.S. Courts of Appeals Fourth and Federal Circuits and U.S. Supreme Court. In legal practice Norfolk 1965-79. Magistrate, U.S. District Court Eastern District of Virginia 1979-87.

Inactive Member Norfolk and Portsmouth Bar Association. Judicial Member Virginia State Bar and Virginia Bar Association. Member American Bar Association

TURNER, JAMES T.—*Continued*

(National Conference of Federal Trial Judges Judicial Administration Division).

Office: National Courts Building, 717 Madison Place N.W., Washington, D.C. 20005-1086.

Telephone: (202) 219-9574.

UNPINGCO, John S. *(Chief Judge, United States District Court District of Guam)* Appointed by President George Bush to term beginning Nov 9, 1992. Reappointed by President George W. Bush 2002, current term expires Oct 9, 2012. Born Barrigada Guam July 1, 1950. Roman Catholic. Educated at St. Louis University B.A. magna cum laude 1972, New York University M.B.A. 1976 J.D. 1976 and Georgetown University LL.M. 1983. Law Clerk to Hon. Paul J. Abbate, Superior Court of Guam 1974. Admitted to practice Guam 1977, District of Columbia 1983 and California 1992.

Member State Bar of California and Guam Bar Association. Lieutenant Colonel USAF 1977-92 JAGC 1977-84. Counsel Naval Air Warfare Center, China Lake California 1987-92. Member Knights of Columbus and Boy Scouts of America.

Office: U.S. Courthouse, Fourth Floor, 520 West Soledad Avenue, Hagåtña, Guam 96910.

Telephone: (671) 473-9200.

VAN GRAAFEILAND, Ellsworth A. *(Senior Judge, United States Court of Appeals Second Circuit)* Appointed for life by President Gerald R. Ford to term beginning Jan 14, 1975. Assumed Senior status May 5, 1985, serves by assignment. Born Rochester New York May 11, 1915. Educated at University of Rochester A.B. 1937 and Cornell University Law School LL.B. 1940. Admitted to practice New York 1940, Interstate Commerce Commission 1947, U.S. District Courts Western 1949 and Northern 1953 Districts of New York, U.S. Court of Appeals Second Circuit 1949, U.S. Tax Court 1968 and U.S. Supreme Court 1972. In legal practice Rochester 1940-74.

Fellow American Bar Foundation and American College of Trial Lawyers. Member New York Bar Foundation, Monroe County (Past President), New York State (Past President) and American Bar Associations.

Office: 423 Federal Building, 100 State Street, Rochester, New York 14614-1369.

Telephone: (716) 263-3160.

VASQUEZ, Juan Flores *(Judge, United States Tax Court)* Appointed by President Bill Clinton Sept 14, 1994 to term beginning May 1, 1995. Current term expires May 2010. Born San Antonio Texas June 24, 1948. Catholic. Educated at University of Texas at Austin B.B.A. in Accounting 1972, State University of New York at Buffalo, University of Houston Law Center J.D. 1977 and New York University Law School LL.M. in Taxation 1978. Admitted to practice Texas 1977, U.S. Tax Court 1978, U.S. District Court Southern 1982 and Western 1985 Districts of Texas and U.S. Court of Appeals Fifth Circuit 1982. Board Certified—Tax Law—Texas Board of Legal Specialization. In legal practice San Antonio 1982-95.

Trial Attorney Office of Chief Counsel Internal Revenue Service 1978-82. Member 1990-91 and Chairman 1991 Director's Practitioner Liaison Committee Austin District Internal Revenue Service. Fellow San Antonio Bar Foundation and Texas Bar Foundation. Founding Member San Antonio Chapter National Association of Hispanic Certified Public Accountants. Member Greater Austin Tax Litigation Association, College of State Bar of Texas, National Judicial College, State Bar of Texas (Tax and Probate Sections), Mexican-American Bar Association of San Antonio (Treasurer), Houston Mexican-American, Texas Mexican-American (Treasurer), National Hispanic and American (Section of Taxation) Bar Associations. Accountant Coopers & Lybrand, Los Angeles 1972-74.

Office: 400 Second Street N.W., Washington, D.C. 20217-0002.

Telephone: (202) 606-8986.

VAUGHN, Mark W. *(Judge, Bankruptcy Appellate Panel First Circuit)* Selected by the Judicial Council of the First Circuit. Also Chief Judge, U.S. Bankruptcy Court District of New Hampshire. Appointed by U.S. Court of Appeals First Circuit judges to term beginning Nov 12, 1993. Term expires Nov 12, 2007. Born New York New York July 30, 1941. Educated at Franklin & Marshall College A.B. 1963 and Boston College Law School J.D. 1970. Admitted to practice New Hampshire 1970 and U.S. District Court District of New Hampshire 1970. In legal practice Manchester 1970-93.

Certified in Business Bankruptcy Law by American Board of Bankruptcy Certification. Fellow New Hampshire Bar Foundation and American College of Bankruptcy. Member American Bankruptcy Institute, National Conference of Bankruptcy Judges, Manchester, New Hampshire and American Bar Associations. USN 1963-67.

Office: Federal Building, 275 Chestnut Street, Manchester, New Hampshire 03101-2411.

Telephone: (603) 222-2680.

VOTOLATO, Arthur N. *(Chief Judge, Bankruptcy Appellate Panel First Circuit)* Selected by the Judicial Council of the First Circuit. Also Judge, U.S. Bankruptcy Court District of Rhode Island. Appointed by U.S. District Court judge to term beginning June 25, 1968. Reappointed by U.S. Court of Appeals judges. Born Providence Rhode Island Aug 20, 1930. Educated at University of Rhode Island B.A. 1953 and Boston University School of Law LL.B. 1956. Admitted to practice Rhode Island 1956 and U.S. District Court District of Rhode Island 1957. In legal practice Providence 1956-62. Judge, First Circuit Bankruptcy Appellate Panel (Maine) and Chief Judge, First Circuit Bankruptcy Appellate Panel (Massachusetts) 1981-84.

Chief Special Counsel Rhode Island Department of Public Works 1962-68. Author "Injunctions and Restraining Orders Under the Bankruptcy Act" Rhode Island Bar Annual 1970-71 and "A Review of Recent Equal Protection Challenges to the Dischargeability of Alimony Provisions of Section 17(a)7 of the Bankruptcy Act" 13 Suffolk L. Rev. Rhode Island Survey 1979. Editorial Advisory Board 1975-90 and Digest Editor 1975-84 American Bankruptcy L. Jour. Editor National Conference of Bankruptcy Judges Newsletter 1970-75. Important Decisions: In re Wasserman 3 B.C.D. 467 Bankr. D.R.I. 1977; In re Hagan 41 B.R. 122 Bankr. D.R.I. 1984; In re Cournoyer 43 B.R. 354 Bankr. D.R.I. 1984; In re Gibbons 52 B.R. 861 Bankr. D.R.I. 1985; Monzack v. A.D.B. Investors (In re EMB Assocs., Inc.) 92 B.R. 9 Bankr. D.R.I. 1988, later proceeding In re Max Sugarman Funeral Home, Inc. 94 B.R. 16 Bankr. D.R.I. 1988, later proceeding In re EMB Assocs., Inc. 100 B.R. 629 Bankr. D.R.I. 1989, aff'd in part and

VOTOLATO, ARTHUR N.—*Continued*

rev'd in part, Max Sugarman Funeral Home, Inc. v. A.D.B. Investors 127 B.R. 408 D.R.I. 1989, vacated, in part, remanded Max Sugarman Funeral Home, Inc. v. A.D.B. Investors 926 F.2d 1248 1st Cir. 1991, later proceeding In re Max Sugarman Funeral Home, Inc. 130 B.R. 119 Bankr. D.R.I. 1991, on remand Monzack v. A.D.B. Investors 1992 Bankr. LEXIS 2074 Bankr. D.R.I. 1992; In re Newport Offshore, Ltd. 75 B.R. 919, aff'd 871 F.2d 223 1st Cir. Mass. March 31, 1989, judgment aff'd by U.S. v. Energy Resources Co., Inc. 110 S. Ct. 2139, 1990; In re Cardinale 142 B.R. 42 Bankr. D.R.I. 1992; and In re Flynn 143 B.R. 798 Bankr. D.R.I. 1992.

Adjunct Professor of Bankruptcy Law Roger Williams College 1977-82. Chairman Committee on Consolidation of Clerk's Office. Former Member Rhode Island Trial Lawyers Association and The Association of Trial Lawyers of America. Fellow American College of Bankruptcy. Member Bankruptcy Judges Advisory Committee Administrative Office of the U.S. Courts 1988-91. Member Northeast Bankruptcy Law Institute (Board of Advisors 1991), National Conference of Bankruptcy Judges (Liaison Committee on Special Court Judges 1973, Member Committee on Conference Newsletter 1973, First Circuit Board of Governors 1973-76, Liaison Committee to the Federal Courts Study Committee 1988-90), Rhode Island (Form Book Project 1960-62, Committee on Property Law 1964-66, Committee on Continuing Legal Education Programming 1976-77, Federal Court Bench/Bar Committee 1980-81, Committee on Creditor-Debtor Rights 1986), Federal (Secretary Rhode Island Chapter 1988-90) and American (Committee on Standards of Judicial Conduct 1970-71 and Member 1969-75 National Conference of Special Court Judges) Bar Associations. Speaker/Panelist Continuing Legal Education Speaker's Program Rhode Island Bar Association 1969-80, Eastern Regional Conference of Referees in Bankruptcy 1970, Advanced Seminar on Bankruptcy Practising Law Institute 1985, First Circuit Judicial Conference 1985 and Seminar on Bankruptcy Litigation and New England Cambridge Massachusetts 1989. Judge for mock trials Rhode Island Legal/Education Partnership 1988-90. Airman First Class USAF 1950-51. Republican Candidate for Rhode Island Attorney General 1962. Board of Management Greater Providence YMCA 1973-75. Board of Directors Ocean State Marathon Committee 1979-83. Trustee University of Rhode Island Foundation since 1988. Former Member Urban League of Rhode Island (Board of Directors 1980-81, Member Education Committee 1980-81, Scholarship Committee 1980-81). Member Boston University Alumni Association since 1956, Narragansett Bay Yachting Association 1960-81, Aircraft Owners and Pilots Association since 1981 and Mooney Aircraft Pilots Association since 1988. Enjoys running, sailing, skiing and flying.

Office: The Federal Center, 380 Westminster Street, Providence, Rhode Island 02903-3256.

Telephone: (401) 528-4487.

WALDRON, Thomas F. *(Judge, Bankruptcy Appellate Panel Sixth Circuit)* Selected by the Judicial Council of the Sixth Circuit. Former Chief Judge Appellate Panel. Also Chief Judge, U.S. Bankruptcy Court Southern District of Ohio. Chief Judge Bankruptcy Court since April 30, 1999.

Office: 120 West Third Street, Room 121, Dayton, Ohio 45402.

Telephone: (937) 225-2863.

WALKER, John M., Jr. *(Chief Judge, United States Court of Appeals Second Circuit)* Appointed for life by President George Bush to term beginning Dec 19, 1989. Chief Judge since Oct 1, 2000. Born New York New York Dec 26, 1940. Episcopalian. Educated at Yale University B.A. 1962 and University of Michigan Law School J.D. 1966. Admitted to practice New York 1969, U.S. District Court Southern District of New York 1971, District of Columbia, U.S. Courts of Appeals Second 1972 and District of Columbia 1983 Circuits and U.S. Supreme Court. In legal practice New York City 1969-70 and 1975-81. Judge, U.S. District Court Southern District of New York Sept 9, 1985 to Nov 26, 1989, appointed by President Ronald Reagan.

Assistant U.S. Attorney 1970-75. President Federal Judges Association. Director Institute of Judicial Administration. Member Committee on the Budget Judicial Conference since 1991. Member The American Law Institute, The Association of the Bar of the City of New York, The District of Columbia Bar, New York State and American Bar Associations. Recipient Alexander Hamilton Award 1985 and Secret Service Honor Award 1985 from U.S. Treasury Department. Assistant Secretary of the Treasury 1981-85.

Office: Connecticut Financial Center, 157 Church Street, New Haven, Connecticut 06510.

Telephone: (203) 773-2181.

WALLACE, J. Clifford *(Senior Judge, United States Court of Appeals Ninth Circuit)* Appointed for life by President Richard M. Nixon to term beginning July 14, 1972. Chief Judge Feb 1, 1991 to March 1, 1996. Assumed Senior status April 8, 1996, serves by assignment. Born San Diego California Dec 11, 1928. Church of Jesus Christ of Latter-day Saints. Educated at San Diego State University B.A. with honors and distinction 1952 and University of California at Berkeley LL.B. 1955. Honorary LL.D. Brigham Young University 1987, Western State University College of Law 1987 and California Western School of Law 1990. Board of Editors University of California Law Review. Member Blue Key (Past President), Phi Kappa Delta, Lambda Delta Sigma (Past President) and Sigma Chi (Former Vice President). Recipient "S" Medal and Honor Ring. Listed in *Who's Who in American Universities and Colleges.* Admitted to practice California 1955. Began legal practice San Diego 1955. Judge, U.S. District Court Southern District of California Oct 29, 1970 to July 13, 1972.

Former Member Advisory Panel American Enterprise Institute for Public Policy Research ten year Project to Study the Constitution. Author "Evidence: Right of Opponent to Production of Memoranda Used by Witness to Refresh Recollection Prior to Testifying" 41 California L. Rev. 753, 1953; "Family Law: Appellate Contempt Jurisdiction Pending Custody Appeal: Continuing Jurisdiction of Trial Court Custody Orders Before the Appellate Court—Contempt: Requirement of Notice for Constructive Contempt: Contempt for Violation of a Statutory Stay" 42 California L. Rev. 885, 1954; "Dismissals and Retraxits" Association of Southern California Defense Counsel Report of Third Annual Seminar 1964; "Must We Have the Nunn Bill? The Alternative of Judi-

WALLACE, J. CLIFFORD—*Continued*

cial Councils of the Circuits" 51 Indiana L. Jour. 297, 1976; "Our Judicial System Needs Help: A Few Inside Thoughts" 12 University of San Francisco L. Rev. 3, 1977; "Judicial Administration in a System of Independents: A Tribe with Only Chiefs" Brigham Young University L. Rev. 39, 1978; "The Nunn Bill: An Unneeded Compromise of Judicial Independence" 61 *Judicature* 476, 1978; "Wanted: Advocates Who Can Argue in Writing" 67 Kentucky L. Jour. 375, 1979; "The Jurisprudence of Judicial Restraint: A Return to the Moorings" 50 George Washington L. Rev. 1, 1981, reprinted in *Views from the Bench, the Judiciary and Constitutional Politics* 155-165 Chatham House 1985 and *Judges on Judging View from the Bench* 163-174 Chatham House 1997; "Working Paper—Future of the Judiciary" 94 F.R.D. 225, 1981; "American Inns of Court: A Way to Improve Advocacy" ABA Jour. 282, March 1982; "Judicial Reform and the Pound Conference of 1976" 80 Michigan L. Rev. 592, 1982; "The Nature and Extent of Intercircuit Conflicts: A Solution Needed for a Mountain or a Molehill" 71 California L. Rev. 913, 1983; "A Two Hundred Year Old Constitution in Modern Society" 61 Texas L. Rev. 1575, 1983; book review of C. Wright *The Law of Federal Courts* 4th ed. 1983, 62 Texas L. Rev. 191, 1983; "Before State and Federal Courts Clash" *American Bar Association Judges' Journal* 36 Fall 1985; "Man Does Not Live by Law Alone" Introduction to *Crime and Punishment in Modern America* The Institute for Government and Politics of the Free Congress Research and Education Foundation 1986; "Whose Constitution? An Inquiry into the Limits of Constitutional Interpretation" *Still the Law of the Land? Essays on Changing Interpretations of the Constitution* 1-13 Hillsdale College Press 1987, reprinted in Working Paper Series No. 6 Washington Legal Foundation Sept 1986 reprinted in part 71 *Judicature* 81, 1987 reprinted in *Judicial Politics, Readings from Judicature* 1992; "The Influence of the United States Constitution on Pacific Nations" 16 Korean Journal of Comparative Law 14 Dec 1988, revised 30 South Texas L. Rev. 353 July 1989; "Israeli and American Conceptions of Religious Freedom: A Response to Izhak Englard" *Religion and Law Biblical-Judaic and Islamic Perspectives* 377, 1990; "The Future of the Judiciary: A Proposal" 27 California Western L. Rev. 361, 1990-91; Keynote Address *Proceedings of the Western Regional Conference on State-Federal Judicial Relationships, June 4-5, 1993* State Justice Institute 1993; "Tackling the Caseload Crisis" 88 American Bar Association Journal 1994; "The Case for Large Federal Courts of Appeals" 77 *Judicature* 288, 1994; Proceedings of the Conference on Administrative Courts "How the People are Protected from Their Government's Errant Conduct: The United States Experience" 51 Journal of the Thai Bar Association 219 Ministry of Justice Thailand 1995; "Developing the Mission of the Federal Courts—A Method to Determine the Size of the Federal Judiciary" 27 Connecticut L. Rev. 851, 1995; "An Idea: The American Inns of Court" X No. 1 The Bencher 1995; "The Ninth Circuit Should Not Be Split" 56 Ohio State L. Jour. 941, 1995; "A New Era of Federal-Tribal Court Cooperation" 79 *Judicature* 150, 1995; "Resolving Judicial Corruption While Preserving Judicial Independence: Comparative Perspectives" 28 California Western International L. Jour. 341, 1998; "Inter-Branch Communication: A Time to Heal and Help" 2 No. 1 *Jurist: Books-on-Law* Jan 1, 1999; "Judicial Education and Training in Asia and the Pacific" 21 No. 4 Michigan Journal of International Law Summer 2000; "The Framers' Establishment Clause: How High the Wall?" Brigham Young University L. Rev. 755, 2001; "An Essay on Independence of the Judiciary: Independence from What and Why" 58 No. 2 New York University Annual Survey of American Law Judges' Forum 2001; and "Civil Pretrial Procedures in Asia and the Pacific: A Comparative Analysis" 34 No. 1 George Washington International L. Rev. 2002.

Lecturer or Speaker American Association of Law Librarians, ABA House of Delegates, ABA National Conference of State Bar Presidents, ABA Section of Litigation, ALI-ABA courses, American College of Trial Lawyers, American Enterprise Institute for Public Policy Research, American Inns of Court, American Judicature Society, Appellate Judges Seminar sponsored by the Institute of Continuing Legal Education, Louisiana State University Law School and Appellate Judges Conference of the American Bar Association, Brookings Institute Conference on the Judiciary at Williamsburg 1979, 1981, 1983 and 1985 and at Charlottesville 1987, California Continuing Education of the Bar, Judicial Conference of the U.S. Subcommittee on Judicial Developments, Judicial Conferences of the Second and Ninth Circuits, Los Angeles Trial Lawyers Association, Vinson & Elkins Lectureship at University of Texas School of Law, Bangalore India Bar Association, Bangladesh Institute of Law and International Affairs, Bar Council of Malaysia, Center for Constructive Alternatives Hillsdale College, College of Law St. Louis University Baguio Philippines, Council of Grand Justices Republic of China, Harvard Law School Alumni Association of New York, Institute of American Culture Academia Sinica Taipei Taiwan, International Legal Society Seoul Korea, National Bar Council of India, Annual Conference Philippine Judges Association, Shanghai Legal Society, Sri Lanka Judges Institute, Taipei Bar Associations, Judges Association Tel Aviv Israel, University of Colombo Sri Lanka, American Cultural Centers Damascus Syria and Islamabad Pakistan, Conference of Asian Chief Judicial Administrators Malacca Malaysia, American Cultural Center Dhaka Bangladesh, Bangladesh Supreme Court, Court of Appeals and High Court of Tanzania, Fiji High Court, Fiji Law Society, Hong Kong University, Mongolian Parliament Legal Committee, Papua New Guinea Judicial Conference, Tribhuvan University Law College Nepal and University of the South Pacific. Visiting Professor of Law and Lecturer Brigham Young University School of Law. Adjunct Professor of Law and Lecturer University of San Diego School of Law and California Western School of Law.

Member and Consultant Center for Human Rights American Bar Association since 2002. Member National Committee on United States-China Relations since 2002. Former Chair Conference of Chief Circuit Judges. Originated idea and developed concept for the American Inns of Court. Senior Advisor on Legal Systems and Judicial Administration to The Asia Foundation (working with judiciaries in eighteen Asian countries on judicial administration improvements). Former Member Association of Southern California Defense Counsel (Board of Directors), American Board of Trial Advocates, International Association of Insurance Counsel (Professional Liability and Malpractice Committee), Judicial Conference of the U.S. (Executive Committee), State Bar of California

WALLACE, J. CLIFFORD—*Continued*

(Committee on Legislation, Committee on Rules of Court Procedure), San Diego County (Vice President, Board of Directors, Chairman Committee on Crime Prevention and Control) and American (Special Advisory Committee on International Activities 1997-98) Bar Associations. Member Institute of Judicial Administration. Recipient Distinguished Service Award from California Newspaper Publishers Association 1979, Honorary Alumni Award from Brigham Young University 1979, Significant Sig Award from Sigma Chi 1979, Silver Beaver Award from Boy Scouts of America 1981 and Distinguished Alumnus of the College of Arts and Letters Award from San Diego State University 1985. Corecipient Boalt Hall Alumni Association Citation Award 1989. Honorary Member Phi Alpha Delta and American Inns of Court I. Honorary Chairman Phi Alpha Delta Inns of Court. Aviation Electronic Technician Second Class USN 1946-49. Former Member Board of Visitors Brigham Young University School of Law (Executive Committee, Chairman of Faculty and Curriculum Committee) and Board of Councilors University of Southern California Law Center. Former Member Board of Directors and Executive Committee and Vice President San Diego County Council. Member Boy Scouts of America and San Diego County Nominating Committee Red Cross 1984.

Office: 4192 U.S. Courthouse, 940 Front Street, San Diego, California 92101-8918.

Telephone: (619) 557-6114.

WALLACH, Evan J. *(Judge, United States Court of International Trade)* Appointed for life by President Bill Clinton 1995. Educated at University of Arizona B.A. 1973, University of California at Berkeley J.D. 1976 and Cambridge University, England LL.B. with honors in International Law 1981. Member Phi Beta Kappa, Phi Kappa Phi, Kappa Tau Alpha and Alpha Gamma Sigma. In legal practice Las Vegas 1976-95.

Author "Defense Based Executive Powers of Prior Restraint: The UK & the US" 1983 and "Analysis of Crude Oil as a Munition de Guerre" 1992 International and Comparative Law Quarterly, "Extradition to the Rwandan War Crimes Tribunal: Is Another Treaty Required?" UCLA Journal of International Law and Foreign Affairs 1998 and "Procedural and Evidentiary Rules of the Post-World War II War Crimes Trials: Did They Provide an Outline for International Legal Procedure?" Columbia Journal of Transnational Law 1999. Adjunct Professor of Law New York Law School since 1997. Recipient Liberty Bell Award from American Bar Association 1993. Nevada National Guard JAGC 1989-95. Attorney/Advisor International Affairs Division U.S. Army JAGC Feb 1991 to June 1991. Recipient Bronze Star, Air Medal, Good Conduct Medal, two Meritorious Service Medals, Vietnam Campaign Medal with three battle stars and RVN Cross of Gallantry with Palm. General Counsel and Public Policy Advisor to U.S. Senator Harry Reid 1987-88.

Office: One Federal Plaza, New York, New York, 10278-0001.

Telephone: (212) 264-2237.

WARDLAW, Kim M. *(Judge, United States Court of Appeals Ninth Circuit)* Appointed for life by President Bill Clinton to term beginning Aug 3, 1998. Born San Francisco California July 2, 1954. Educated at University of California at Los Angeles A.B. 1976 J.D. 1979. Law Clerk to Hon. William P. Gray, U.S. District Court Central District of California 1979-80. In legal practice Los Angeles 1980-95. Judge, U.S. District Court Central District of California 1995 to Aug 1998, appointed by President Bill Clinton.

Member Presidential Transition Justice Team I Department of Justice 1992-93. Member Mayoral Transition Committee Los Angeles Mayor-Elect Richard Riordan 1993.

Office: 500 Court of Appeals Building, 125 South Grand Avenue, Pasadena, California 91105-1644.

Telephone: (626) 229-7130.

WEIS, Joseph F., Jr. *(Senior Judge, United States Court of Appeals Third Circuit)* Appointed for life by President Richard M. Nixon to term beginning March 15, 1973. Assumed Senior status April 1, 1988, serves by assignment. Born Pittsburgh Pennsylvania March 12, 1923. Catholic. Educated at Duquesne University B.A. 1947 and University of Pittsburgh J.D. 1950. Awarded honorary LL.D. Dickinson School of Law 1989. Admitted to practice Pennsylvania 1950, U.S. District Court District of Pennsylvania, U.S. Court of Appeals and U.S. Supreme Court. In legal practice Allegheny County 1950-68. Judge, Pennsylvania Court of Common Pleas Fifth Judicial District 1968-70. Judge, U.S. District Court Western District of Pennsylvania 1970-73.

Author "A New Name and a New Financial Policy for the Courts" PBA Quarterly, Vol. XLI Jan 1970; "Electronics Expand Courtrooms' Walls" 63 ABA Journal 1713 Dec 1977; "Austin L. Staley" (in memoriam) 17 Duquesne L. Rev. 239, 1978-79; "Electronic Mail" 22 Judges Journal 14, 1983; "Agency Non-Acquiescence—Respectful Lawlessness or Legitimate Disagreement?" 48 University of Pittsburgh L. Rev. 845, 1987; "The Constitution's Second Century: The Shift in Emphasis from Property Rights to Personal Rights" 26 Duquesne L. Rev. 1, 1987; "A Judicial Perspective on Deference to Administrative Agencies: Some Grenades From the Trenches" 2 Administrative L. Jour. 301, 1988; "The Federal Rules and the Hague Conventions: Concerns of Conformity and Comity" 50 University of Pittsburgh L. Rev. 903, 1989; "The Federal Courts Study Committee Begins Its Work" 21 St. Mary's L. Jour. 15, 1989; "A Tale of Two Systems" 60 University of Cincinnati L. Rev. 429, 1991; "Recommendations of the Federal Courts Study Committee" 26 International Society of Barristers 397, 1991; "The Hague Evidence Convention and United States Civil Procedural Rules" 90 Zeitschrift für Vergleichende Rechts-wissenschaft 411, 1991; "The Federal Sentencing Guidelines—It's Time for a Reappraisal" 29 American Criminal L. Rev. 823, 1992; "Are Courts Obsolete?" 67 Notre Dame L. Rev. 1385, 1992; "Changing the Federal Courts and Avoiding the Mistakes of History" 3 Widener Journal of Public Law 2, 1994; "Service By Mail—Is the Stamp of Approval from the Hague Convention Always Enough?" 57 Law and Contemporary Problems 165, 1994; "Professionalism on the Bench: Wisdom from Job, Dear Abby and Gilbert & Sullivan" 142 Probate L. Jour. 19, Dec 1994; "Disconnecting the Overloaded Circuits—A Plug for a Unified Court of Appeals" 39 St. Louis University L. Jour. 455, 1995; "The Case for Appellate Court Revision" (reviewing Thomas E. Baker "Rationing Justice on Appeal: The Problems of the United States Court of Appeals" 1994) 93 Michigan L. Rev. 401, 1995; and "Nine Divided by Three: A Formula for Unification?" 15 The

WEIS, JOSEPH F., JR.—*Continued*

Journal of Law & Politics 445, 1999. Co-author with G. Bermant "Automation in the Federal Courts: Progress, Prospects and Problems" 26 Judges Journal 14, 1987.

Adjunct Professor University of Pittsburgh School of Law. Former Vice President Allegheny County Bar Association. Honorary Fellow (formerly active) International Academy of Trial Lawyers. Past President Academy of Trial Lawyers of Allegheny County. Former member Federal Judges Conference on Delay in Criminal Cases. Chairman International Judicial Conferences London 1985 and Toronto 1986, Federal Courts Study Commission and Futurist Subcommittee The 1988 Bicentennial Committee Court of Common Pleas Allegheny County. Fellow American Bar Foundation. Member American Canadian Legal Exchange, American Judicature Society, Judicial Conference of the Third Circuit (Chairman Committee on Experiment with Video Conference Arguments and Committee on Experiments of Videotape Trial Proceedings), Judicial Conference of the U.S. (Former Chairman Standing Committee on Rules of Practice and Procedure, Advisory Committee on Civil Rules, Administration of the Bankruptcy System Committee and Subcommittee on Judicial Improvements, Member Committee on International Judicial Relations), Institute of Judicial Administration, Pennsylvania and American (Former member Conference of State Trial Judges, Chairman Committee on Technology and the Courts, member Committee on Design of Courtrooms and Court Facilities, Chairman 1981-83 and member Executive Committee Appellate Judges' Conference Judicial Administration Division) Bar Associations. Lecturer on Impact Decisions of the Supreme Court and Trial Procedures for appellate judges' seminars (nationwide and various legal groups), Appellate Judges Seminar Programs and Federal Judicial Center Programs. Keynote speaker Conference of American Institute of Architects in Chicago (subject of Justice Facilities). Participant in programs of Legal Medicine in Rome and London. Conducted pilot project on video-tape depositions in trials for Federal Judicial Center. Supervised pilot project on word processing and electronic mail in Court of Appeals. Recipient St. Thomas More Award 1971, Phillip Amram Award 1991, Edward J. Devitt Distinguished Service to Justice Award 1993 and History Makers Award for Government and Law from Historical Society of Western Pennsylvania 1996. Captain U.S. Army WWII Patton's Fourth Armored Division 1943-48. Recipient Bronze Star and Purple Heart with oak leaf cluster. Advisory Committee Master of Laws Program University of Virginia School of Law. Former member Board of Administration Diocese of Pittsburgh. Member St. Scholastica Church, Fourth Armored Division Association, American Legion, Disabled American Veterans, Catholic War Veterans, Military Order of the World Wars, Knights of Columbus and Knights of Malta.

Office: 513 U.S. Post Office & Courthouse, 700 Grant Street, Pittsburgh, Pennsylvania 15219.

Telephone: (412) 208-7310.

WELLS, Thomas B. *(Chief Judge, United States Tax Court)* Appointed by President Ronald Reagan to term beginning Oct 13, 1986. Reappointed by President George W. Bush Oct 10, 2001, current term expires Oct 2016. Chief Judge since June 1, 2000. Born Akron Ohio July 2, 1945. Presbyterian. Educated at Miami University B.S. 1967, Emory University J.D. 1973 and New York University LL.M. in Taxation 1978. Admitted to practice Georgia 1973, District of Columbia (honorary), U.S. Tax Court and U.S. Supreme Court. In legal practice Visalia Georgia 1973-77 and Atlanta Georgia 1978-86.

Attorney Toombs County Georgia 1975-77 and City of Visalia Georgia 1975-77. Member J. Edgar Murdock Inns of court (President since 2000), State Bar of Georgia and American Bar Association. Member Metropolitan Club of Washington and Chevy Chase Club.

Office: 400 Second Street N.W., Washington, D.C. 20217-0002.

Telephone: (202) 606-8700.

WHALEN, Laurence J. *(Judge, United States Tax Court)* Appointed by President George Bush.

Office: 400 Second Street N.W., Washington, D.C. 20217-0002.

Telephone: (202) 606-8741.

WIDENER, H. Emory, Jr. *(Judge, United States Court of Appeals Fourth Circuit)* Appointed for life by President Richard M. Nixon to term beginning Oct 1972. Born Abingdon Virginia April 30, 1923. Presbyterian. Educated at Virginia Polytechnic Institute and State University 1940-41, U.S. Naval Academy B.S. 1944 and Washington and Lee University LL.B. 1953. Board of Student Editors Washington and Lee Law Review 1950-53. Member Phi Alpha Delta. Awarded honorary LL.D. Washington and Lee University 1977. Member Phi Alpha Delta and Order of the Coif. Admitted to practice Virginia 1951, U.S. District Court Western District of Virginia 1953, U.S. Court of Appeals Fourth Circuit 1959 and U.S. Supreme Court 1964. In legal practice Bristol 1953-69. U.S. Commissioner, Western District of Virginia 1963-66. Judge 1969-72 and Chief Judge 1971-72, U.S. District Court Western District of Virginia.

Author "A Survey of Election Law Reform in Virginia" William & Mary L. Rev. 1970, "Some Random Thoughts on Judicial Restraint" Washington and Lee L. Rev. 1974, "The Criminal Trial in Virginia" (chapter on opening statements and closing argument) Committee on CLE 1965 and other law review contributions. Instructor Southern Seminary & Junior College 1950-51. Adjunct Instructor University of Texas at Austin School of Law July and Aug 1974, Washington and Lee University School of Law since 1998 and College of William & Mary School of Law since 1999. Member The American Law Institute, Virginia State Bar and Virginia Bar Association. Lieutenant j.g. USN 1944-49. Lieutenant USNR 1951-52. Republican.

Mailing address: P.O. Box 868, Abingdon, Virginia 24212-0868.

Telephone: (540) 628-3138.

WIENER, Jacques L., Jr. *(Judge, United States Court of Appeals Fifth Circuit)* Appointed for life by President George Bush March 12, 1990 to term beginning May 25, 1990. Born Shreveport Louisiana Oct 2, 1934. Religious affiliation: Reform Judaism. Educated at Tulane University B.A. 1956 J.D. 1961. Editor-in-Chief Tulane Law Review 1961. Member Phi Beta Kappa and Order of the Coif. Admitted to practice Louisiana 1961. In legal practice Shreveport 1961-90.

Fellow The American College of Trust and Estate Counsel, International Academy of Estate and Trust Law, Louisiana Bar Foundation and American Bar Foundation. Member Louisiana State Law Institute (Council Member), The American Law Institute, Shreveport (Pres-

WIENER, JACQUES L., JR.—*Continued*

ident), Louisiana State and American Bar Associations. Lieutenant j.g. USNR 1956-58. Enjoys fly fishing, upland game bird and waterfowl hunting, traveling and photography.

Office: 244 U.S. Court of Appeals Bldg., 600 Camp Street, New Orleans, Louisiana 70130.

Telephone: (504) 310-8098.

WIESE, John P. *(Senior Judge, United States Court of Federal Claims)* Appointed by President Ronald Reagan to term beginning Oct 1, 1982. Assumed Senior status Oct 13, 2001, serves by assignment. Born Brooklyn New York April 19, 1934. Educated at Hobart College 1962 and University of Virginia School of Law LL.B. 1965. Law Clerk to U.S. Court of Claims 1965-66 and to Hon. Linton M. Collins, U.S. Court of Claims 1966-67. Member Phi Beta Kappa. Trial Commissioner, U.S. Court of Claims 1974-82.

Member Bar Association of the District of Columbia and American Bar Association. U.S. Army 1957-59.

Office: National Courts Building, 717 Madison Place N.W., Washington, D.C. 20005-1086.

Telephone: (202) 219-9653.

WILKINS, William W., Jr. *(Chief Judge, United States Court of Appeals Fourth Circuit)* Appointed for life by President Ronald Reagan to term beginning 1986. Chief Judge since Feb 15, 2003. Born Anderson South Carolina March 29, 1942. Baptist. Educated at Davidson College B.A. 1964 and University of South Carolina School of Law J.D. 1967. Editor-in-Chief South Carolina Law Review 1967. Captain South Carolina Moot Court Team. Recipient Outstanding Graduate of the Year Award 1967, Samuel L. Prince Moot Court Award and CJS Award for Labor Law. Member Wig and Robe, Sigma Alpha Epsilon and Phi Delta Phi. Admitted to practice South Carolina 1967, U.S. District Court 1967, U.S. Court of Appeals Fourth Circuit 1969 and U.S. Supreme Court 1970. Began legal practice Greenville 1971. Judge, U.S. District Court District of South Carolina 1981-86.

Solicitor Thirteenth Judicial Circuit South Carolina 1978-81. Chair U.S. Sentencing Commission 1985-94. Author "Discovery of Existence and Amount of Defendant's Insurance Policy" 17 South Carolina L. Rev. 750, 1965; "Lockouts: Return to the Common Law Ruling" 18 South Carolina L. Rev. 299, 1966; "The Family Purpose Doctrine" 18 South Carolina L. Rev. 638, 1966 republished in *The Personal Injury Commentator* Callaghan & Company; "Plea Negotiations, Acceptance of Responsibility, Role of Offender, and Departures: Policy Decisions in Promulgation of Federal Sentencing Guidelines" 23 Wake Forest L. Rev. 181, 1988; "Sentencing Reform and Appellate Review" 46 Washington & Lee L. Rev. 429, 1989; and "Relevant Conduct: The Cornerstone of the Federal Sentencing Guidelines" 41 South Carolina L. Rev. 495, 1990. Important Decisions: Woomer v. Aiken (death penalty) 856 F.2d 677, 1988; United States v. Owens (search and seizure) 848 F.2d 462, 57 USLW 2026, 1988; and Plyler v. Evatt (prison capacity) 846 F.2d 208, 1988. Instructor in Law Greenville Technical College 1973-97. Lecturer Taft Seminar Clemson University 1976-80. Member Governor's Committee on Criminal Justice and Delinquency 1975-80, South Carolina Trial Lawyers Association 1976-81. Chair Committee on Criminal Law Judicial Conference of the U.S. since 1999. Member South Carolina Bar since 1967. Recipient Service to Mankind Award from Sertoma International 1975 and from Heritage Club 1976, Distinguished Service Award from Wade Hampton-Taylors Jaycees 1977, Award of Appreciation for Outstanding Public Service from Home Builders Association of Greenville 1979, Citizen of the Year Award from Kiwanis Club 1982 and Justice Award from Foundation for Improvement of Justice 1989. Captain U.S. Army 1967-69. Recipient Commendation Medal for Meritorious Service 1969. Republican. Legal aide to Senator Strom Thurmond 1970-71. State Campaign Director Reelect Strom Thurmond Campaign 1972. Chairman Greenville County Literacy Society 1972-73. Member Rotary Club Greenville 1975-80. Trustee Strom Thurmond Foundation since 1978. Director YMCA Metropolitan Board 1979-81. Enjoys squash, tennis and golf.

Mailing address: P.O. Box 10857, Greenville, South Carolina 29603-0857.

Telephone: (864) 233-7081.

WILKINSON, James Harvie, III *(Judge, United States Court of Appeals Fourth Circuit)* Appointed for life by President Ronald Reagan to term beginning 1984. Former Chief Judge. Born New York New York Sept 29, 1944. Educated at Yale University B.A. 1967 and University of Virginia School of Law J.D. 1972. Law Clerk to Hon. Lewis F. Powell, U.S. Supreme Court 1972-73.

Deputy Assistant U.S. Attorney General Civil Rights Division U.S. Department of Justice 1982-83. Editorial Page Editor *Norfolk Virginian-Pilot* 1978-81. Associate Professor 1973-78 and Professor 1983 University of Virginia School of Law. U.S. Army 1968-69.

Office: 230 U.S. Courthouse, 255 West Main Street, Charlottesville, Virginia 22902.

Telephone: (434) 296-7063.

WILLIAMS, Ann Claire *(Judge, United States Court of Appeals Seventh Circuit)* Appointed for life by President Bill Clinton to term beginning Nov 17, 1999. Born Detroit Michigan Aug 16, 1949. Educated at Wayne State University B.A. 1970, University of Michigan M.A. 1972 and University of Notre Dame Law School J.D. 1975. Honorary LL.D. Lake Forest College May 9, 1987, William Mitchell College of Law and University of Notre Dame. Honorary Doctor of Public Service University of Portland May 2, 1993. Law Clerk to Hon. Robert A. Sprecher, U.S. Court of Appeals Seventh Circuit 1975-76. Admitted to practice Illinois 1975, U.S. Court of Appeals Seventh Circuit, U.S. District Court Northern District of Illinois and U.S. Supreme Court. Judge, U.S. District Court Northern District of Illinois April 4, 1985 to Nov 16, 1999.

Assistant U.S. Attorney 1976-85 and Chief U.S. Attorney Organized Crime Drug Enforcement Task Force North Central Region 1983-85. Chair Committee on Court Administration and Case Management Judicial Conference of the U.S. since 1993. Board of Directors National Institute for Trial Advocacy since 1996. Board Member National Association for Public Interest Law since 2002. Member Illinois Judicial Council, National Association of Women Judges, Federal Judges Association (President 1999, President Elect two years, Treasurer four years), Black Women Lawyers Association of Greater Chicago, Women's Bar Association of Illinois, Cook County, Illinois State, National and Federal (Board Member) Bar Associations. Faculty Member since 1979

WILLIAMS, ANN CLAIRE—*Continued*

and Board Member since 1996 National Institute for Trial Advocacy. Faculty Member Federal Judicial Center. Recipient Edith S. Sampson Memorial Award from Illinois Judicial Council Sept 19, 1986, Thurgood Marshall Award from Chicago-Kent College of Law April 17, 1986, Headliner Award from Women of Wayne State University Alumni Association May 2, 1987, Earl Dickerson Award from Chicago Bar Association 1997 and Women and Vision Award from Women's Bar Association of Illinois 1998. Named Person of the Year by *Chicago Lawyer* Dec 2000. Teacher Detroit Board of Education 1969-72. Secretary and Board of Trustees University of Notre Dame. Enjoys music and reading.

Office: 2612 U.S. Courthouse, 219 South Dearborn Street, Chicago, Illinois 60604.

Telephone: (312) 435-5532.

WILLIAMS, Karen J. *(Judge, United States Court of Appeals Fourth Circuit)* Appointed for life by President George Bush Jan 27, 1992. Born Orangeburg South Carolina Aug 4, 1951. Educated at Columbia College B.A. 1972 and University of South Carolina School of Law J.D. 1980. In legal practice Orangeburg 1980-92.

Office: 1021 Middleton Street, Orangeburg, South Carolina 29115.

Telephone: (803) 533-0711.

WILLIAMS, Stephen F. *(Senior Judge, United States Court of Appeals District of Columbia Circuit)* Appointed for life by President Ronald Reagan to term beginning June 16, 1986. Assumed Senior status, serves by assignment. Born New York New York Sept 23, 1936. Educated at Yale University B.A. magna cum laude 1958 and Harvard Law School J.D. magna cum laude 1961. Board of Editors Harvard Law Review 1959-61. Admitted to practice New York 1962 and Colorado 1977. In legal practice New York City 1962-69.

Assistant U.S. Attorney Southern District of New York 1966-69. Co-author with H. Williams, R. Maxwell and C. Meyers *Cases on Oil & Gas Law* Foundation 1986 and with R. Maxwell, R. Martin and B. Kramer *Cases on Oil & Gas Law* Foundation 1992. Professor University of Colorado 1969-86. Visiting Professor University of California at Los Angeles 1975-76, University of Chicago 1979-80 and Southern Methodist University 1983-84. Member The American Law Institute and American Bar Association. E-2 U.S. Army 1961-62.

Office: 3800 U.S. Courthouse, 333 Constitution Avenue N.W., Washington, D.C. 20001-2866.

Telephone: (202) 216-7210.

WILSON, Charles R. *(Judge, United States Court of Appeals Eleventh Circuit)* Appointed for life by President Bill Clinton to term beginning Sept 13, 1999. Born Pensacola Florida Oct 14, 1954. Educated at University of Notre Dame B.A. 1976 J.D. 1979. Law Clerk to Hon. Joseph Woodrow Hatchett, U.S. Court of Appeals Fifth Circuit 1979-80. In legal practice Tampa 1981-86. Judge, Hillsborough County Court 1986-90. Magistrate Judge, U.S. District Court Middle District of Florida 1990-94.

Assistant County Attorney Hillsborough County 1980-81. U.S. Attorney Middle District of Florida 1994-99.

Office: 16B U.S. Courthouse, 801 North Florida Avenue, Tampa, Florida 33602-3800.

Telephone: (813) 301-5650.

WINTER, Ralph K., Jr. *(Senior Judge, United States Court of Appeals Second Circuit)* Appointed for life by President Ronald Reagan to term beginning Jan 5, 1982. Former Chief Judge. Assumed Senior status Sept 30, 2000, serves by assignment. Born Waterbury Connecticut July 30, 1935. Educated at Yale University B.A. 1957 LL.B. 1960. Law Clerk to Chief Judge Caleb M. Wright, U.S. District Court District of Delaware 1960-61 and Hon. Thurgood Marshall, U.S. Court of Appeals Second Circuit 1961-62.

Consultant to Subcommittee on Separation of Powers U.S. Senate Judiciary Committee 1968-72. William K. Townsend Professor Yale University Law School 1962-81. Senior Fellow The Brookings Institute 1968-70. John Simon Guggenheim Fellow 1971-72 and Adjunct Scholar 1972-81 American Enterprise Institute.

Office: U.S. Courthouse, 141 Church Street, New Haven, Connecticut 06510.

Telephone: (203) 782-3682.

WOLFE, Norman H. *(Special Trial Judge, United States Tax Court)* Appointed by U.S. Tax Court Chief Judge Samuel B. Starrett to term beginning July 1, 1985. Born New York New York Sept 21, 1928. Jewish. Educated at Yale College B.A. 1950 and Columbia University School of Law LL.B. 1953. Member Phi Beta Kappa and Phi Delta Phi. Harlan Fiske Stone Scholar and Kent Scholar. Admitted to practice New York 1953 and Massachusetts 1965. In legal practice New York 1957-59 and Boston Massachusetts 1965-85.

Trial Attorney Appellate Section Tax Division U.S. Department of Justice 1959-65. Co-author Monograph "Negotiated Development and Open Space Preservation" Lincoln Institute Land Policy. Member American Bar Association (Section of Taxation). Participant New England Federal Tax Institute and Massachusetts Continuing Legal Education. Captain JAGC U.S. Army 1954-57.

Office: 400 Second Street N.W., Washington, D.C. 20217-0002.

Telephone: (202) 874-6047.

WOLLMAN, Roger L. *(Judge, United States Court of Appeals Eighth Circuit)* Appointed for life by President Ronald Reagan. Chief Judge April 24, 1999 to Jan 31, 2002. Born Frankfort South Dakota May 29, 1934. Educated at Tabor College B.A. 1957, University of South Dakota LL.B. magna cum laude 1962 and Harvard University LL.M. 1964. In legal practice Aberdeen 1964-71. Former Associate Justice and Chief Justice, South Dakota Supreme Court, elected 1970. State's Attorney Brown County 1967-71. U.S. Army 1957-59.

Office: 315 U.S. Courthouse, 400 South Phillips Avenue, Sioux Falls, South Dakota 57104-6851.

Telephone: (605) 330-4411.

WOOD, Diane P. *(Judge, United States Court of Appeals Seventh Circuit)* Appointed for life by President Bill Clinton to term beginning July 24, 1995. Born Plainfield New Jersey July 4, 1950. Educated at University of Texas at Austin B.A. with highest honors 1971 J.D. with high honors 1975. Member Phi Beta Kappa and Order of the Coif. Law Clerk to Hon. Irving L. Goldberg, U.S. Court of Appeals Fifth Circuit 1975-76 and Hon. Harry A. Blackmun, U.S. Supreme Court 1976-77. Admitted to practice District of Columbia 1978, Illinois 1993, U.S. District Court District of Columbia, U.S. Courts of Appeals Fifth and Seventh Cir-

WOOD, DIANE P.—*Continued*

cuits and U.S. Supreme Court. In legal practice Washington D.C. 1978-80.

Attorney-Advisor Office of the Assistant Legal Adviser for Economic and Business Affairs U.S. Department of State 1977-78. Deputy Assistant Attorney General for International, Appellate and Legal Policy Matters Antitrust Division U.S. Department of Justice Aug 1993 to July 1995. Contributing Editor *Preview of United States Supreme Court Cases* Public Education Division American Bar Association 1984-88. Author "Fine-Tuning Judicial Federalism: A Proposal for the Reform of the Anti-Injunction Act" Brigham Young University L. Rev. 289, 1990; Conference Paper "Allocating Authority in a Federal System" USSR-US Conference on Law and Economic Cooperation American Bar Association 1990; Chapter 5 "International Competition in a Diverse World: Can One Size Fit All?" Fordham Corporate Law Institute 71, 1991; "The Impossible Dream: Real International Antitrust" 277, 1992 and "Sex Discrimination in Life and Law" 1, 1999 University of Chicago Legal Forum; Chapter 2 "User Friendly Competition Law in the U.S.C." *Procedure and Enforcement in EC and US Competition Law: Proceedings of the Leiden Seminar on User-Friendly Competition Law* Sweet & Maxwell 1993; "Justice Blackmun and Individual Rights" 97 Dickinson L. Rev. 421, 1993; "United States Antitrust Law in the Global Market" 1 Indiana Journal of Global Legal Studies 409, 1994; "The Internationalization of Antitrust Law: Options for the Future" 44 DePaul L. Rev. 1289, 1995; "A Cooperative Framework for National Regulators" Symposium on Global Competition and Public Policy in an Era of Technological Integration 72 Chicago-Kent L. Rev. 521, 1996; "Regulation in the Single Global Market: From Anarchy to World Federalism?" 23 Ohio Northern University L. Rev. 297, 1996; Chapter 14 "The WTO Agreement on Government Procurement: An Antitrust Perspective" *Law and Policy in Public Purchasing* 1997; "The Role of the Judge in Competition Enforcement" Robert Schuman Centre Annual on European Competition Law 1996, 359 Kluwer 1997; "Generalist Judges in a Specialized World" 50 Southern Methodist University L. Rev. 1755, 1997; "The Role of Economics and Economists in Competition Cases" 1 OECD Journal of Comp. Law and Policy 82, 1999; "International Law and Federalism: What Is the Reach of Regulation?" 23 Harvard Journal of Law and Public Policy 97, 1999; "Soft Harmonization Among Competition Laws: Track Record and Prospects" Symposium on Global Antitrust Law and Policy Sept 2002; "Diffusion and Focus in International Legal Scholarship" 1 Chicago Journal of International Law 141, 2000; "Commentary on *The Futures Problem* by Geoffrey C. Hazard, Jr." 148 University of Pennsylvania L. Rev. 1933, 2000; "Health, Heart and Mind: The Contributions of Richard A. Posner to Health Law and Policy" 17 Journal of Contemporary Health Law and Politics ix 2000; Chapter 19 "Intellectual Property in the Courts: The Role of Judge" *Expanding the Boundaries of Intellectual Property: Innovation Policy for the Knowledge Society* edited by R. Dreyfuss, D. Zimmerman and H. First 2001; Chapter 1 "The Evolution of Antitrust Law in the United States" *Trade Practices Act: A Twenty-Five Year Stocktake* edited by Frances Hanks and Philip Williams Federation Press 2001; "Techniques of Judicial Federalism" Working Paper X, Panel Three: Courts and Judges, European Competition Law Annual: 2000, The Modernisation of EC Antitrust Policy 2001; and "International Harmonization of Antitrust Law: The Tortoise or the Hare?" 3 Chicago Journal of International Law 391, 2002. Co-author with Professor Richard P. Whish *Merger Cases in the Real World: A Study of Merger Control Procedures* OECD 1994 and with Harvey Goldschmid and Robert Pitofsky *Trade Regulation Casebook* Foundation Press 4th ed. 1997 5th ed. 2003.

Assistant Professor of Law Georgetown University Law Center 1980-81. Professor July 1981 to Aug 1993 and Senior Lecturer on Law since 1995 University of Chicago Law School. Visiting Assistant Professor of Law Cornell Law School 1985-86. Visiting Professor of Law University of San Diego Institute of International and Comparative Law Summer 1990, 1991, 1997, 1999, 2001 and 2003. Member Senior Advisory Group Civil Justice Project Brookings Institution 1989-90. Consultant Antitrust Division U.S. Department of Justice 1986-87 and Committee on Competition Law and Policy Working Party No. 3 on International Cooperation Organisation for Economic Co-operation and Development 1992-93. Former Member American Bar Association (Chair Committee on Bilateral Investment Treaties 1980-82, Co-chair Committee on International Antitrust Law 1987-90 and Council Member 1989-91 Section of International Law and Practice, Chair Subcommittee on International Unfair Competition 1989-91 and Vice Chair 1991-95 Committee on International Antitrust and Foreign Competition Law Section of Antitrust Law). Member U.S. Association of Constitutional Law, American Society of International Law (Executive Council 1997-2000, Vice President 1998-2000) and The American Law Institute. Judge regional competitions Jessup International Moot Court 1979, 1985 and semi-final round 1989. Board Member Hyde Park-Kenwood Community Health Center 1983-85. Member Chicago Bar Association Symphony Orchestra and North Shore Chamber Orchestra. Enjoys music (oboe, English horn, piano and singing), reading and handcrafts.

Office: 2602 U.S. Courthouse, 219 South Dearborn Street, Chicago, Illinois 60604-1803.

Telephone: (312) 435-5521.

Fax: (312) 408-5117

E-mail address: diane_wood@ca7.uscourts.gov

WOOD, Harlington, Jr. *(Senior Judge, United States Court of Appeals Seventh Circuit)* Appointed for life by President Gerald R. Ford to term beginning 1976. Assumed Senior status Jan 15, 1992, serves by assignment. Born Illinois April 17, 1920. Protestant. Educated at University of Illinois B.A. 1942 J.D. 1948. Admitted to practice Illinois 1948. Began legal practice Springfield 1948. Judge, U.S. District Court Southern District of Illinois 1973-76.

U.S. Attorney Southern District of Illinois 1958-61. Associate Deputy Attorney General for U.S. Attorneys 1969-70 and Assistant Attorney General Civil Division 1972-73 U.S. Department of Justice Washington D.C. Distinguished Visiting Professor St. Louis University School of Law 1996-2002. Chairman Administrative Office Oversight Committee 1987-91. Member Long Range

WOOD, HARLINGTON, JR.—*Continued*
Planning Committee 1990-96. Member Abraham Lincoln Association.

Mailing address: P.O. Box 299, Springfield, Illinois 62705-0299.

Telephone: (217) 492-4742.

YOCK, Robert J. *(Senior Judge, United States Court of Federal Claims)* Assumed office 1982. Assumed Senior status, serves by assignment. Born St. James Minnesota Jan 11, 1938. Educated at St. Olaf College B.A. 1959, University of Strasbourg (France) 1961, University of Michigan J.D. 1962, Old Dominion College 1964-65 and University of Minnesota 1966-67. Admitted to practice Minnesota 1962, U.S. Supreme Court 1965 and District of Columbia 1972. In legal practice St. Paul Minnesota 1966-69. Trial Judge, U.S. Court of Claims 1977-82.

Chief Counsel National Archives Office of General Counsel General Services Administration 1969-70. Executive Assistant to Administrator 1970-72 and Assistant General Counsel 1972-77 General Services Administration. Member The District of Columbia Bar and Minnesota State Bar Association. USN JAGC 1962-66.

Office: National Courts Building, 717 Madison Place N.W., Washington, D.C. 20005-1086.

Telephone: (202) 219-9644.

ALABAMA

Capital MONTGOMERY

UNITED STATES DISTRICT COURTS DISTRICTS OF ALABAMA

Within Alabama there are three United States District Courts. For descriptive information refer to the United States Courts section.

MIDDLE DISTRICT consists of three divisions.

Eastern Division includes Chambers, Lee, Macon, Randolph, Russell and Tallapoosa counties. The court sits at Opelika.

Northern Division includes Autauga, Barbour, Bullock, Butler, Chilton, Coosa, Covington, Crenshaw, Elmore, Lowndes, Montgomery and Pike counties. The court sits at Montgomery.

Southern Division includes Coffee, Dale, Geneva, Henry and Houston counties. The court sits at Dothan.

Chief Judge
W. Harold Albritton III

Judges
Myron H. Thompson
Mark E. Fuller

Senior Judges
Truman M. Hobbs
Ira DeMent

Clerk
Debra P. Hackett
P.O. Box 711
Montgomery, Alabama 36101-0711
(334) 954-3600

NORTHERN DISTRICT consists of seven divisions.

Eastern Division includes Calhoun, Clay, Cleburne and Talladega counties. The court sits at Anniston.

Jasper Division includes Fayette, Lamar, Marion, Walker and Winston counties. The court sits at Jasper.

Middle Division includes Cherokee, DeKalb, Etowah, Marshall and St. Clair counties. The court sits at Gadsden.

Northeastern Division includes Cullman, Jackson, Lawrence, Limestone, Madison and Morgan counties. The court sits at Decatur and Huntsville.

Northwestern Division includes Colbert, Franklin and Lauderdale counties. The court sits at Florence.

Southern Division includes Blount, Jefferson and Shelby counties. The court sits at Birmingham.

Western Division includes Bibb, Greene, Pickens, Sumter and Tuscaloosa counties. The court sits at Tuscaloosa.

Chief Judge
U. W. Clemon

Judges
Edwin L. Nelson
Sharon Lovelace Blackburn
Charles Lynwood Smith, Jr.
Inge P. Johnson
Karon O. Bowdre

Senior Judges
James H. Hancock
Junius Foy Guin, Jr.
Robert B. Propst
William M. Acker, Jr.

Clerk
Perry D. Mathis
140 U.S. Courthouse
1729 Fifth Avenue North
Birmingham, Alabama 35203
(205) 278-1700

SOUTHERN DISTRICT consists of two divisions.

Northern Division includes Dallas, Hale, Marengo, Perry and Wilcox counties. The court sits at Selma.

Southern Division includes Baldwin, Choctaw, Clarke, Conecuh, Escambia, Mobile, Monroe and Washington counties. The court sits at Mobile.

Chief Judge
Charles R. Butler, Jr.

Judge
Callie V. Granade

Senior Judges
Virgil Pittman
William Brevard Hand
Richard W. Vollmer, Jr.

Clerk
Charles R. Diard
123 U.S. Courthouse
113 St. Joseph Street
Mobile, Alabama 36602-3621
(251) 690-2371

UNITED STATES MAGISTRATE JUDGES OF ALABAMA

MIDDLE DISTRICT
Charles S. Coody
Vanzetta Penn McPherson
Susan Russ Walker
Delores R. Boyd

NORTHERN DISTRICT
Terry Michael Putnam
Paul W. Greene
Robert R. Armstrong, Jr.
Harwell G. Davis, III
John E. Ott

AL-KS

UNITED STATES DISTRICT COURTS
DISTRICTS OF ALABAMA—*Continued*

SOUTHERN DISTRICT
William E. Cassady
Bert William Milling, Jr.
William H. Steele
Kristi D. Lee

UNITED STATES BANKRUPTCY COURTS OF ALABAMA

MIDDLE DISTRICT

Chief Judge
William R. Sawyer

Judge
Dwight H. Williams, Jr.

Bankruptcy Clerk
Richard S. Oda
P.O. Box 1248
Montgomery, Alabama 36102-0248
(334) 954-3800

NORTHERN DISTRICT

Chief Judge
Tamara O. Mitchell

Judges
James S. Sledge
Benjamin Cohen
Jack Caddell
Thomas B. Bennett
C. Michael Stilson

Acting Bankruptcy Clerk
Richard Mauk
120 Federal Building
1800 Fifth Avenue North
Birmingham, Alabama 35203-2110
(205) 714-4000

SOUTHERN DISTRICT

Chief Judge
William S. Shulman

Judge
Margaret A. Mahoney

Bankruptcy Clerk
Geraldine S. Lester
201 St. Louis Street
Mobile, Alabama 36602-2900
(251) 441-5391

ALABAMA SUPREME COURT

The Supreme Court is Alabama's court of last resort. The court consists of a chief justice and eight associate justices elected in statewide partisan elections for six-year terms. Vacancies are filled by the governor. Retired justices may be asked by the chief justice to serve as the need arises.

The Supreme Court has exclusive appellate jurisdiction in actions involving title to or possession of land, in civil cases when the amount exceeds $50,000 and in all appeals involving utility rates from orders of the Alabama Public Service Commission. The court may review decisions of the Court of Civil Appeals or the Court of Criminal Appeals on a writ of certiorari and has original jurisdiction of writs of quo warranto and mandamus in relation to matters in which no other court has jurisdiction. All capital cases are reviewed by the court. The court may also issue writs of injunction, habeas corpus and other remedial writs necessary to the exercise of proper jurisdiction and has administrative and supervisory control over the lower courts. The court may answer questions of state law certified to it by a federal court and has the authority to give advisory opinions to the governor and the legislature regarding important constitutional questions.

The court sits at Montgomery and may sit at other locations at the discretion of the court.

Chief Justice
Roy S. Moore

Associate Justices

Robert B. Harwood, Jr.	Champ Lyons, Jr.
Harold F. See	Douglas I. Johnstone
Jean Williams Brown	J. Gorman Houston, Jr.
Thomas A. Woodall	Jacquelyn L. Stuart

Active Retired Associate Justice
Hugh Maddox

Clerk
Robert G. Esdale
300 Dexter Avenue
Montgomery, Alabama 36104
(334) 242-4609

Administrative Director of Courts
Rich Hobson
Administrative Office of Courts
300 Dexter Avenue
Montgomery, Alabama 36104-3741
(334) 242-0300

ALABAMA COURT OF CRIMINAL APPEALS

The Court of Criminal Appeals is an intermediate appellate court in Alabama. The court consists of a presiding judge and four judges elected in statewide partisan elections for six-year terms. Vacancies are filled by the governor. A presiding judge is elected by peer vote. Retired judges may be asked by the chief justice to serve as the need arises.

The court has exclusive appellate jurisdiction of all misdemeanors including violations of municipal ordinances, all felonies and all post conviction writs in criminal cases. The court has original jurisdiction in the issuance of remedial writs necessary to the exercise of proper jurisdiction.

The court sits en banc at Montgomery.

Presiding Judge
H. W. "Bucky" McMillan

Judges
Sue Bell Cobb
Pamela Willis Baschab
Greg Shaw
Alisa K. Wise

Active Retired Judge
John Malcolm Patterson

ALABAMA COURT OF CRIMINAL APPEALS—*Continued*

Clerk
Lane W. Mann
300 Dexter Avenue
Montgomery, Alabama 36104-3741
(334) 242-4590

ALABAMA COURT OF CIVIL APPEALS

The Court of Civil Appeals, created in 1969, is a court of intermediate appellate jurisdiction in Alabama. The court consists of a presiding judge and four judges elected in statewide partisan elections for six-year terms. Vacancies are filled by the governor. The presiding judge is selected on the basis of seniority. Retired judges may be asked by the chief justice to serve as the need arises.

The court has exclusive appellate jurisdiction in all civil cases when the amount in controversy does not exceed $50,000, as well as cases deflected from the Supreme Court, and in domestic relations cases. The court hears all appeals regarding workers' compensation as well as all appeals from administrative agencies other than the Alabama Public Service Commission. The court may issue writs necessary to the exercise of proper jurisdiction.

The court sits at Montgomery and at other locations at the discretion of the court.

Presiding Judge
Sharon G. Yates

Judges
Glenn Murdock
William C. Thompson
Craig S. Pittman
John B. Crawley

Clerk
John H. Wilkerson, Jr.
300 Dexter Avenue
Montgomery, Alabama 36104
(334) 242-4093

ALABAMA CIRCUIT COURT

The Circuit Court is Alabama's court of general jurisdiction. The sixty-seven counties are divided into forty-one judicial circuits. Each circuit contains one to five counties. Circuit Court is held in every county by law. Judges are elected in partisan elections from their respective circuits for six-year terms. Vacancies are filled by the governor. A presiding judge is elected by peer vote in each circuit to a three-year term. Retired judges may be asked by the chief justice to serve as the need arises and may also provide on-going assistance to the intermediate courts of appeals.

The court has exclusive original jurisdiction of all civil actions in which the matter in controversy exceeds $10,000 and original jurisdiction concurrent with the District Court in matters exceeding $3,000 but not exceeding $10,000, exclusive of interest and costs. The court has exclusive original criminal jurisdiction of all felony prosecutions and of misdemeanor or ordinance violations which are lesser offenses within a felony charge. The court also has concurrent jurisdiction with the District Court to receive guilty pleas in felony cases not punishable by death. The court exercises appellate jurisdiction of civil, criminal and juvenile cases from the District Court and prosecutions for ordinance violations from Municipal Courts. Appeals to the Circuit Court are tried de novo with or without a jury as provided by law. The court may issue extraordinary writs and exercise superintendence over lower courts.

The court sits at each county seat and as specified.

FIRST JUDICIAL CIRCUIT includes Choctaw, Clarke and Washington counties. The court sits at Butler, Grove Hill and Chatom.

Presiding Judge
Harold L. Crow

Judge
James Thomas Baxter

SECOND JUDICIAL CIRCUIT includes Butler, Crenshaw and Lowndes counties. The court sits at Greenville, Luverne and Hayneville.

Presiding Judge
H. Edward McFerrin

THIRD JUDICIAL CIRCUIT includes Barbour and Bullock counties. The court sits at Clayton, Eufaula and Union Springs.

Presiding Judge
Burt Smithart

FOURTH JUDICIAL CIRCUIT includes Bibb, Dallas, Hale, Perry and Wilcox counties. The court sits at Centreville, Selma, Greensboro, Marion and Camden.

Presiding Judge
Marvin Wayne Wiggins

Judges
Thomas R. Jones
Jack W. Meigs

FIFTH JUDICIAL CIRCUIT includes Chambers, Macon, Randolph and Tallapoosa counties. The court sits at Lafayette, Tuskegee, Wedowee, Dadeville and Alexander City.

Presiding Judge
Howard F. Bryan, IV

Judges
Ray D. Martin
Tom F. Young, Jr.

SIXTH JUDICIAL CIRCUIT includes Tuscaloosa County. The court sits at Tuscaloosa.

Presiding Judge
L. Scott Coogler

Judges
Herschel T. Hamner, Jr.
Philip N. Lisenby
John Henry England, Jr.
Charles R. Malone
Thomas S. Wilson

SEVENTH JUDICIAL CIRCUIT includes Calhoun and Cleburne counties. The court sits at Anniston and Heflin.

Presiding Judge
R. Joel Laird, Jr.

ALABAMA CIRCUIT COURT—*Continued*

Judges
Malcolm B. Street, Jr.
Samuel Holt Monk, II
Jack W. Hughes
Louie H. Turner, Jr.

EIGHTH JUDICIAL CIRCUIT includes Morgan County. The court sits at Decatur.

Presiding Judge
Steven E. Haddock

Judges
Sherrie W. Brown
Glenn E. Thompson

NINTH JUDICIAL CIRCUIT includes Cherokee and DeKalb counties. The court sits at Centre and Fort Payne.

Presiding Judge
Randall L. Cole

Judges
David A. Rains
J. Kevin Grimes

TENTH JUDICIAL CIRCUIT includes Jefferson County. The court sits at Birmingham and Bessemer.

BIRMINGHAM DIVISION

Presiding Judge
J. Scott Vowell

Judges

James H. Hard, IV
Sandra H. Storm
Alfred Bahakel
Edward L. Ramsey
Ralph A. Ferguson, Jr.
G. William Noble
Tommy Nail
Houston L. Brown
Tom King, Jr.
Helen Shores Lee
Caryl P. Privett
Michael W. McCormick
J. Gary Pate
John C. Calhoun
Tennant Smallwood, Jr.
Allwin E. Horn, III
Gloria T. Bahakel
Joseph L. Boohaker
Virginia A. Vinson
Clyde E. Jones
Laura Petro
Robert S. Vance, Jr.

BESSEMER DIVISION

Presiding Judge
Teresa B. Petelos

Judges
Dan C. King, III
Douglas Mac Parsons
Eugene R. Verin

ELEVENTH JUDICIAL CIRCUIT includes Lauderdale County. The court sits at Florence.

Presiding Judge
Ned Michael Suttle

Judges
Larry Mack Smith
Michael T. Jones

TWELFTH JUDICIAL CIRCUIT includes Coffee and Pike counties. The court sits at Elba, Enterprise and Troy.

Presiding Judge
Thomas E. Head, III

Judges
Robert W. Barr
Steven E. Blair

THIRTEENTH JUDICIAL CIRCUIT includes Mobile County. The court sits at Mobile.

Presiding Judge
Robert G. Kendall

Judges

Ferrill D. McRae
Rosemary D. Chambers
William H. McDermott
Herman Thomas
Julian D. Banks
John F. Butler
Joseph S. Johnston
John R. Lockett
James C. Wood
Roderick P. Stout

FOURTEENTH JUDICIAL CIRCUIT includes Walker County. The court sits at Jasper.

Presiding Judge
Hugh Beaird

Judges
James C. Brotherton
Jerry K. Selman

FIFTEENTH JUDICIAL CIRCUIT includes Montgomery County. The court sits at Montgomery.

Presiding Judge
Charles Price

Judges

Richard H. Dorrough
John L. Capell, III
W. Mark Anderson, III
Johnny Hardwick
Eugene W. Reese
William A. Shashy
Tracy S. McCooey
Truman M. Hobbs, Jr.

SIXTEENTH JUDICIAL CIRCUIT includes Etowah County. The court sits at Gadsden.

Presiding Judge
William W. Cardwell

Judges
William H. Rhea, III
Donald W. Stewart
William A. Millican

SEVENTEENTH JUDICIAL CIRCUIT includes Greene, Marengo and Sumter counties. The court sits at Eutaw, Linden and Livingston.

Presiding Judge
Eddie Hardaway, Jr.

EIGHTEENTH JUDICIAL CIRCUIT includes Shelby County. The court sits at Columbiana.

Presiding Judge
D. Al Crowson

Judges
J. Michael Joiner
G. Daniel Reeves
Hub Harrington

NINETEENTH JUDICIAL CIRCUIT includes Autauga, Chilton and Elmore counties. The court sits at Prattville, Clanton and Wetumpka.

ALABAMA CIRCUIT COURT—*Continued*

Presiding Judge
John B. Bush

Judges
Sibley G. Reynolds
Ben A. Fuller

TWENTIETH JUDICIAL CIRCUIT includes Henry and Houston counties. The court sits at Abbeville and Dothan.

Presiding Judge
Larry K. Anderson

Judges
S. Edward Jackson
Denny L. Holloway
C. Lawson Little

TWENTY-FIRST JUDICIAL CIRCUIT includes Escambia County. The court sits at Brewton.

Presiding Judge
Bradley E. Byrne

Judge
Joseph B. Brogden

TWENTY-SECOND JUDICIAL CIRCUIT includes Covington County. The court sits at Andalusia.

Presiding Judge
M. Ashley McKathan

Judge
Charles A. Short

TWENTY-THIRD JUDICIAL CIRCUIT includes Madison County. The court sits at Huntsville.

Presiding Judge
Loyd H. Little, Jr.

Judges
Joseph L. Battle
James P. Smith
Bruce E. Williams
Laura W. Hamilton
William K. Bell

TWENTY-FOURTH JUDICIAL CIRCUIT includes Fayette, Lamar and Pickens counties. The court sits at Fayette, Vernon and Carrollton.

Presiding Judge
James W. Moore, Jr.

TWENTY-FIFTH JUDICIAL CIRCUIT includes Marion and Winston counties. The court sits at Hamilton and Double Springs.

Presiding Judge
Bobby R. Aderholt

Judge
John H. Bentley

TWENTY-SIXTH JUDICIAL CIRCUIT includes Russell County. The court sits at Phenix City.

Presiding Judge
Albert L. Johnson

Judge
George R. Greene

TWENTY-SEVENTH JUDICIAL CIRCUIT includes Marshall County. The court sits at Guntersville and Albertville.

Presiding Judge
Allen T. Jolley

Judge
David Evans

TWENTY-EIGHTH JUDICIAL CIRCUIT includes Baldwin County. The court sits at Bay Minette.

Presiding Judge
James H. Reid

Judges
Charles C. Partin
Robert E. Wilters
Joseph L. "Lang" Floyd

TWENTY-NINTH JUDICIAL CIRCUIT includes Talladega County. The court sits at Talladega and Sylacauga.

Presiding Judge
Jerry L. Fielding

Judge
Julian M. King

THIRTIETH JUDICIAL CIRCUIT includes St. Clair County. The court sits at Ashville and Pell City.

Presiding Judge
William E. Hereford

Judge
Charles E. Robinson

THIRTY-FIRST JUDICIAL CIRCUIT includes Colbert County. The court sits at Tuscumbia.

Presiding Judge
Harold V. Hughston, Jr.

Judge
Jacqueline M. Hatcher

THIRTY-SECOND JUDICIAL CIRCUIT includes Cullman County. The court sits at Cullman.

Presiding Judge
Don L. Hardeman

Judge
H. Frank Brunner

THIRTY-THIRD JUDICIAL CIRCUIT includes Dale and Geneva counties. The court sits at Ozark and Geneva.

Presiding Judge
Philip Ben McLauchlin, Jr.

Judge
Kenneth W. Quattlebaum

THIRTY-FOURTH JUDICIAL CIRCUIT includes Franklin County. The court sits at Russellville.

Presiding Judge
Sharon H. Hester

ALABAMA CIRCUIT COURT—*Continued*

THIRTY-FIFTH JUDICIAL CIRCUIT includes Conecuh and Monroe counties. The court sits at Evergreen and Monroeville.

Presiding Judge
Samuel H. Welch, Jr.

THIRTY-SIXTH JUDICIAL CIRCUIT includes Lawrence County. The court sits at Moulton.

Presiding Judge
A. Philip Reich, II

THIRTY-SEVENTH JUDICIAL CIRCUIT includes Lee County. The court sits at Opelika.

Presiding Judge
Robert M. Harper

Judges
Richard D. Lane
Jacob A. Walker, III

THIRTY-EIGHTH JUDICIAL CIRCUIT includes Jackson County. The court sits at Scottsboro.

Presiding Judge
William W. Haralson

Judge
Jenifer C. Holt

THIRTY-NINTH JUDICIAL CIRCUIT includes Limestone County. The court sits at Athens.

Presiding Judge
George T. Craig

Judge
James W. Woodroof, Jr.

FORTIETH JUDICIAL CIRCUIT includes Clay and Coosa counties. The court sits at Ashland and Rockford.

Presiding Judge
John E. Rochester

FORTY-FIRST JUDICIAL CIRCUIT includes Blount County. The court sits at Oneonta.

Presiding Judge
Robert E. Austin

ALABAMA DISTRICT COURT

The District Court is Alabama's state trial court of limited jurisdiction. It is a non-jury court of record. Each county comprises a single district. Judges are elected by the voters of their respective districts for six-year terms. Vacancies are filled by the governor. Retired judges may be asked by the chief justice to serve as the need arises.

The court has original civil jurisdiction concurrent with the Circuit Court in matters not exceeding $10,000 and in civil actions based on unlawful detainer. The court exercises exclusive small claims jurisdiction in matters not exceeding $3,000 exclusive of interest and costs. The court has exclusive original trial jurisdiction over all misdemeanors including traffic infractions, except prosecutions by municipalities having Municipal Courts and any prosecution which is within the exclusive jurisdiction of the Circuit Court. The court has original jurisdiction over criminal misdemeanors, holds preliminary hearings in felony prosecutions and can receive guilty pleas in felony cases not punishable by death. The court also exercises juvenile jurisdiction concurrent with the Circuit Court as provided by law. The court may issue writs necessary to the exercise of proper jurisdiction.

The court sits at each county seat, in each municipality with a population of 1,000 or more where no municipal court exists and as provided by law.

District	Judge
Autauga	Phillip W. Wood
Baldwin	Jody W. Bishop
	Carmen Bosch
Barbour	Robert L. Bowden
Bibb	James M. White
Blount	John J. Dobson
Bullock	Michael O. Emfinger
Butler	James MacDonald Russell, Jr.
Calhoun	R. Allen Crow
	Larry F. Warren
	Gus W. Colvin, Jr.
Chambers	Joel G. Holley
Cherokee	Sheri Carver
Chilton	Rhonda J. Hardesty
Choctaw	Don P. Scurlock, III
Clarke	William E. Kimbrough
Clay	George C. Simpson
Cleburne	Warren Glea Sarrell, Jr.
Coffee	John C. Dowling
Colbert	George E. Carpenter
Conecuh	Jeffrey T. Brock
Coosa	Robert J. Teel, Jr.
Covington	Frank L. McGuire, III
Crenshaw	William R. King
Cullman	Kim J. Chaney
	Terri W. Thomas
Dale	Fred R. Steagall
	William H. Filmore
Dallas	Nathaniel Walker
DeKalb	Steven L. Whitmire, II
Elmore	Mary E. Culberson
Escambia	J. David Jordan
Etowah	C. Wayne Owen
	William D. Russell, Jr.
Fayette	Jerry L. Clary
Franklin	Paula B. McDowell
Geneva	Charles W. Fleming, Jr.
Greene	Lillie Jones-Osborne
Hale	William A. Ryan
Henry	Charles W. Woodham
Houston	M. John Steensland
	Brady E. Mendheim
Jackson	Ralph H. Grider
Jefferson	
Birmingham Division	John H. Alsbrooks, Jr.
	Orson L. Johnson
	Elise D. Barclay
	Robert G. Cahill
	R. O. Hughes
	S. Phillip Bahakel
	David N. Lichtenstein
	Robert P. Bynon, Jr.
	John G. Lowther

ALABAMA DISTRICT COURT—*Continued*

Bessemer Division	Vincent J. Schilleci, Jr.
	Ralph E. Coleman, Jr.
	Eric M. Fancher
Lamar	Lewis E. Gosa
Lauderdale	Deborah B. Paseur
Lawrence	Randel Hood Mullican
Lee	Michael A. Nix
	Russell Keith Bush
Limestone	Jeanne W. Anderson
	Robert M. Baker
Lowndes	Terri L. Bozeman
Macon	Aubrey Ford, Jr.
Madison	Susan T. Moquin
	Karen Kimbrell Hall
	Martha L. Sherrod
Marengo	Wesley Wade Drinkard
Marion	James C. Cashion
Marshall	Francis Timothy Riley
	Howard G. Hawk
Mobile	Michael E. McMaken
	Judson W. Wells, Sr.
	George A. Brown
	Delano J. Palughi
	Charles N. McKnight
Monroe	William J. Causey, Jr.
Montgomery	Lynn Clardy Bright
	Margaret Givhan
	Lucie U. McLemore
Morgan	David H. Bibb
	David J. Breland
Perry	Richard Moore Avery, Jr.
Pickens	Ira B. Colvin
Pike	William G. Hightower
Randolph	W. Patrick Whaley
Russell	Michael J. Bellamy
	Eric B. Funderburk
St. Clair	James E. Hill, Jr.
Shelby	Patricia M. Smith
	Ronald E. Jackson
Sumter	Tammy J. Montgomery
Talladega	George N. Sims
	Tommy R. Dobson
Tallapoosa	Clayton K. Taylor
Tuscaloosa	James C. Guin, III
	Joel R. Chandler
Walker	Larry E. Lapkovitch
	Jimmy D. Wells
Washington	Jerry L. Turner
Wilcox	Jo Celeste Pettway
Winston	Samuel L. Masdon

ALABAMA PROBATE COURTS

The Probate Courts are courts of limited jurisdiction in Alabama and are located in each county. Judges are elected by the voters of their respective counties for six-year terms.

The courts have original and general jurisdiction over probate of wills, administration of estates, guardianship, adoptions and civil commitment of incompetents. The courts also handle recording of all land partitions and sales within the county as well as maintaining indices of recording information for instruments of conveyance.

The courts sit at the county seats and as prescribed by law.

ALABAMA MUNICIPAL COURTS

The Municipal Courts are courts of limited jurisdiction in Alabama established in each municipal corporation except in those which elected not to have such courts. If a municipality chooses to abolish its court, jurisdiction of the court is transferred to the District Court. Judges are appointed by the governing body of the municipality. Full-time judges are appointed for four-year terms and part-time judges for two-year terms.

The courts have jurisdiction over all ordinance violations within their police jurisdiction. The courts have concurrent jurisdiction with the District Court over all acts constituting violations of state law committed within the police jurisdiction of the municipality which may be prosecuted as breaches of municipal ordinances.

Alabama Counties and County Seats

Autauga
Prattville

Baldwin
Bay Minette

Barbour
Clayton

Bibb
Centreville

Blount
Oneonta

Bullock
Union Springs

Butler
Greenville

Calhoun
Anniston

Chambers
Lafayette

Cherokee
Centre

Chilton
Clanton

Choctaw
Butler

Clarke
Grove Hill

Clay
Ashland

Cleburne
Heflin

Coffee
Elba

Colbert
Tuscumbia

Conecuh
Evergreen

Coosa
Rockford

Covington
Andalusia

Crenshaw
Luverne

Cullman
Cullman

Dale
Ozark

Dallas
Selma

DeKalb
Fort Payne

Elmore
Wetumpka

Escambia
Brewton

Etowah
Gadsden

Fayette
Fayette

Franklin
Russellville

Geneva
Geneva

Greene
Eutaw

COUNTIES AND COUNTY SEATS—*Continued*

Hale
Greensboro

Henry
Abbeville

Houston
Dothan

Jackson
Scottsboro

Jefferson
Birmingham

Lamar
Vernon

Lauderdale
Florence

Lawrence
Moulton

Lee
Opelika

Limestone
Athens

Lowndes
Hayneville

Macon
Tuskegee

Madison
Huntsville

Marengo
Linden

Marion
Hamilton

Marshall
Guntersville

Mobile
Mobile

Monroe
Monroeville

Montgomery
Montgomery

Morgan
Decatur

Perry
Marion

Pickens
Carrollton

Pike
Troy

Randolph
Wedowee

Russell
Phenix City

St. Clair
Ashville

Shelby
Columbiana

Sumter
Livingston

Talladega
Talladega

Tallapoosa
Dadeville

Tuscaloosa
Tuscaloosa

Walker
Jasper

Washington
Chatom

Wilcox
Camden

Winston
Double Springs

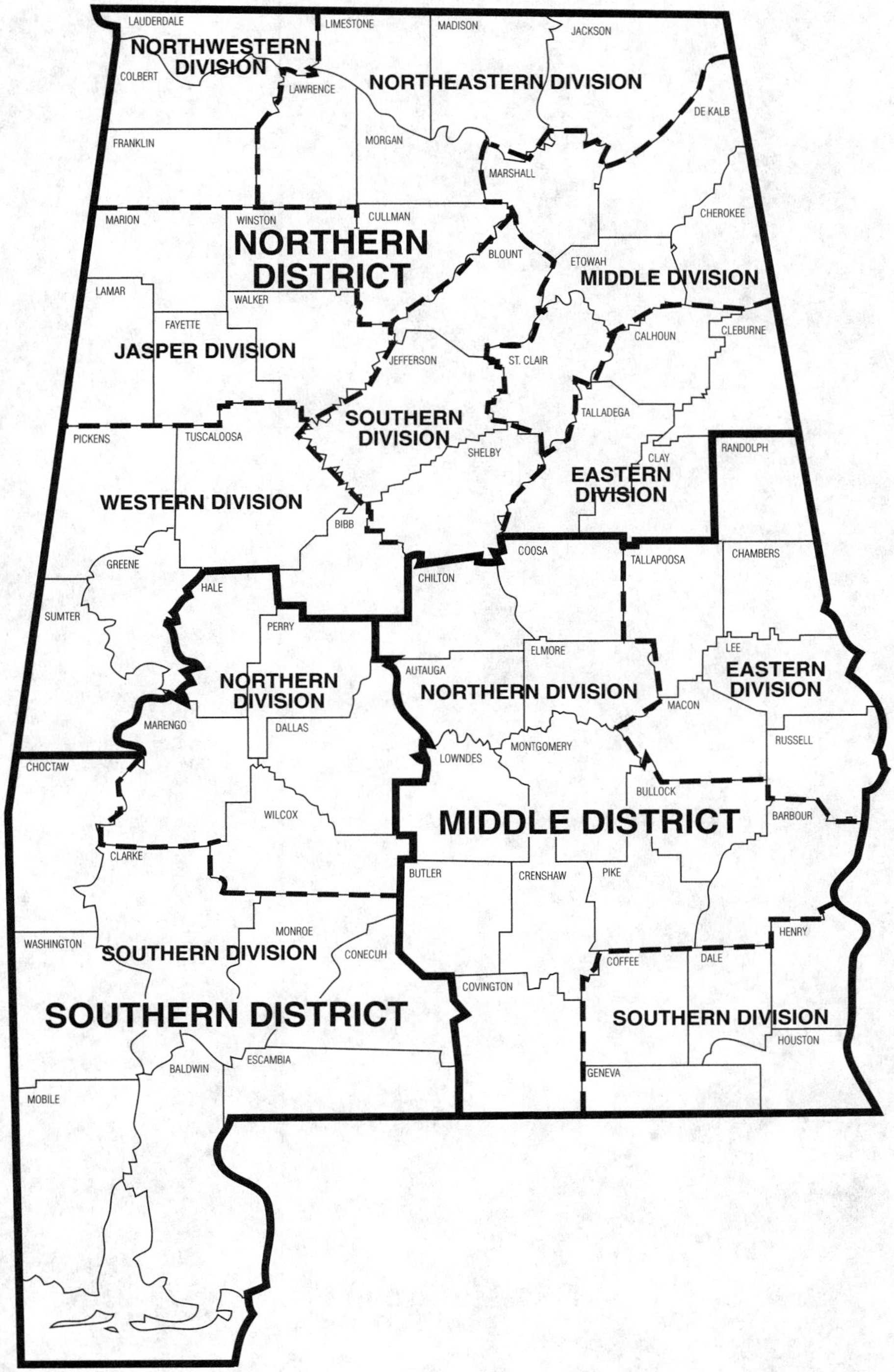
LAUDERDALE
LIMESTONE
MADISON
JACKSON
NORTHWESTERN DIVISION
COLBERT
LAWRENCE
NORTHEASTERN DIVISION
DE KALB
FRANKLIN
MORGAN
MARSHALL
MARION
WINSTON
CULLMAN
CHEROKEE
NORTHERN DISTRICT
BLOUNT
ETOWAH
MIDDLE DIVISION
LAMAR
WALKER
FAYETTE
CALHOUN
CLEBURNE
JASPER DIVISION
JEFFERSON
ST. CLAIR
TALLADEGA
SOUTHERN DIVISION
PICKENS
TUSCALOOSA
SHELBY
RANDOLPH
CLAY
EASTERN DIVISION
WESTERN DIVISION
BIBB
GREENE
COOSA
TALLAPOOSA
CHAMBERS
HALE
CHILTON
SUMTER
PERRY
ELMORE
LEE
EASTERN DIVISION
AUTAUGA
NORTHERN DIVISION
NORTHERN DIVISION
MACON
MARENGO
DALLAS
LOWNDES
MONTGOMERY
RUSSELL
CHOCTAW
BULLOCK
WILCOX
MIDDLE DISTRICT
BARBOUR
CLARKE
BUTLER
CRENSHAW
PIKE
HENRY
MONROE
WASHINGTON
SOUTHERN DIVISION
CONECUH
COFFEE
DALE
COVINGTON
SOUTHERN DISTRICT
SOUTHERN DIVISION
HOUSTON
BALDWIN
ESCAMBIA
GENEVA
MOBILE

UNITED STATES DISTRICT COURTS DISTRICTS OF ALABAMA

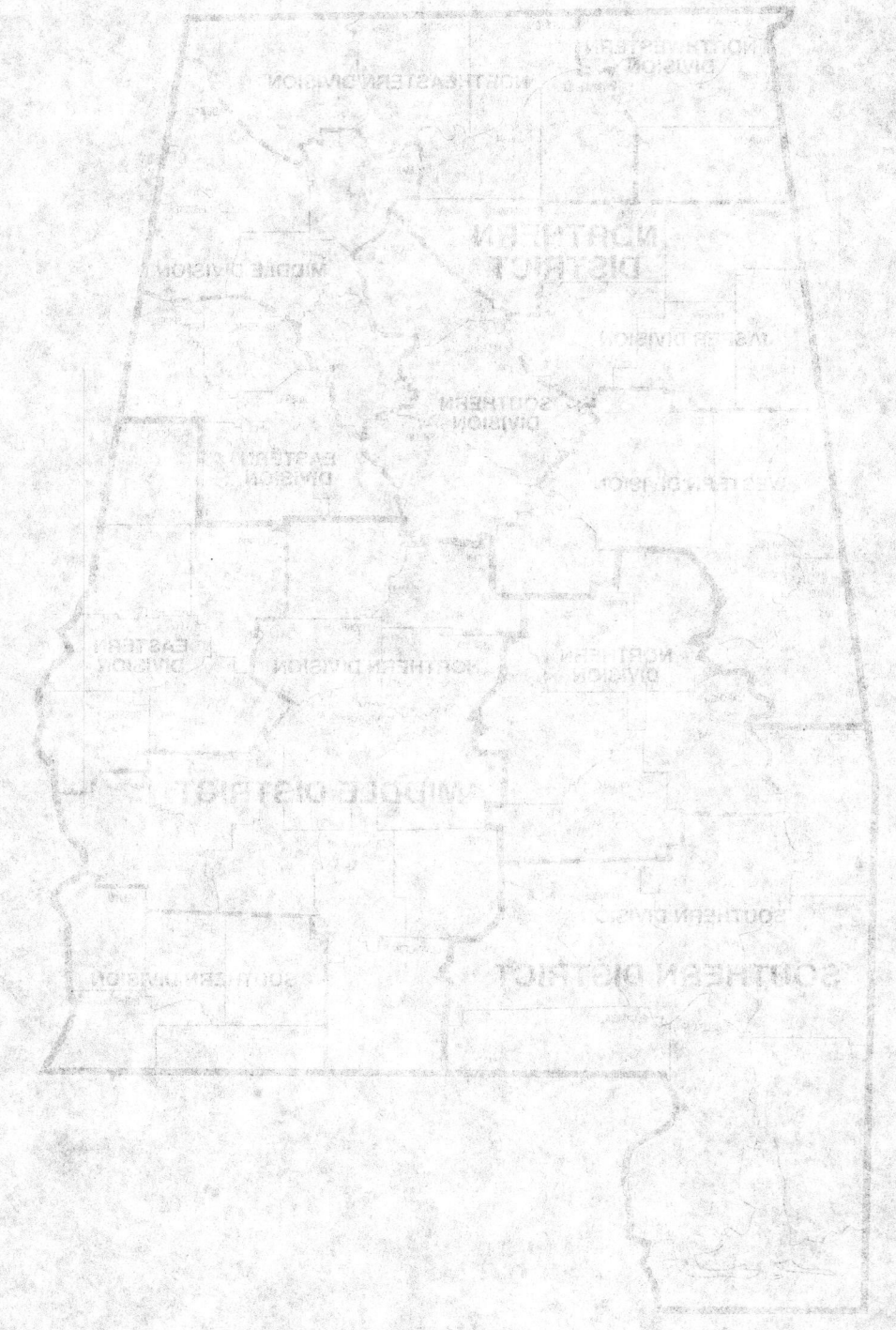

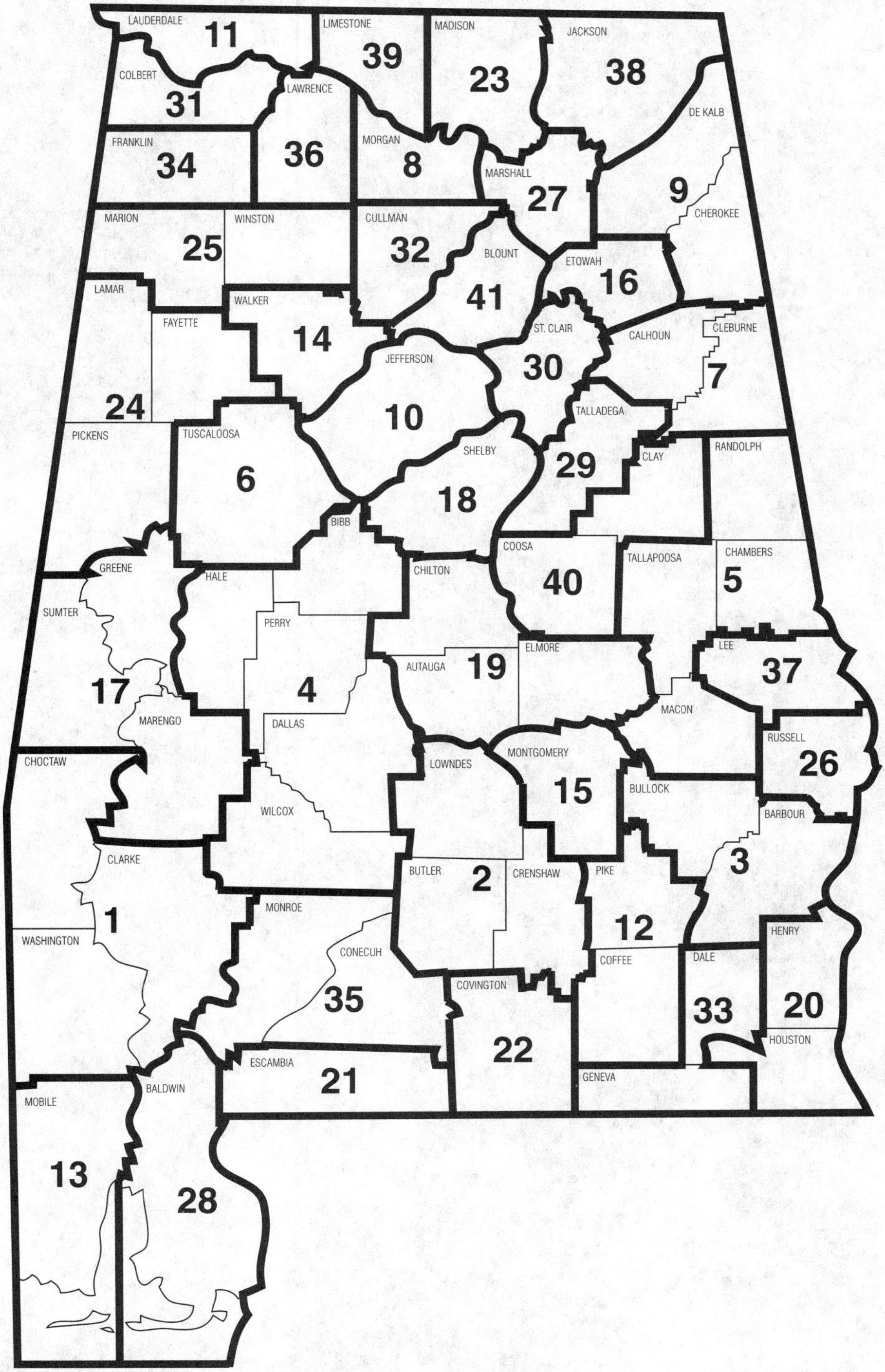
LAUDERDALE
11
LIMESTONE
39
MADISON
23
JACKSON
38
COLBERT
31
LAWRENCE
DE KALB
FRANKLIN
34
36
MORGAN
8
MARSHALL
27
9
CHEROKEE
MARION
25
WINSTON
CULLMAN
32
BLOUNT
41
ETOWAH
16
LAMAR
WALKER
14
FAYETTE
ST. CLAIR
CALHOUN
CLEBURNE
JEFFERSON
30
7
24
10
TALLADEGA
PICKENS
TUSCALOOSA
6
SHELBY
29
CLAY
RANDOLPH
18
BIBB
COOSA
CHAMBERS
GREENE
HALE
CHILTON
40
TALLAPOOSA
5
SUMTER
PERRY
ELMORE
LEE
AUTAUGA
19
37
17
4
MACON
MARENGO
DALLAS
RUSSELL
26
CHOCTAW
LOWNDES
MONTGOMERY
15
BULLOCK
WILCOX
BARBOUR
CLARKE
BUTLER
2
CRENSHAW
PIKE
3
MONROE
12
1
HENRY
WASHINGTON
CONECUH
COFFEE
DALE
COVINGTON
35
33
20
HOUSTON
ESCAMBIA
22
21
GENEVA
BALDWIN
MOBILE
13
28

JUDICIAL CIRCUITS OF ALABAMA CIRCUIT COURT

ALABAMA

ACKER, William M., Jr. *(Senior Judge, United States District Court Northern District of Alabama)* Appointed for life by President Ronald Reagan to term beginning Sept 1982. Assumed Senior status, serves by assignment. Born Birmingham Alabama Oct 25, 1927. United Methodist. Educated at Birmingham-Southern College B.A. magna cum laude 1949 and Yale Law School LL.B. 1952. Member Phi Delta Phi and Thomas Swann Barristers' Union. Admitted to practice Alabama 1952, U.S. District Courts Middle, Northern and Southern Districts of Alabama, U.S. Courts of Appeals Fifth and Eleventh Circuits and U.S. Supreme Court. In legal practice Birmingham 1952-82. Judge, Irondale Municipal Court 1957.

Author "*United States v. Handley:* A New Direction in Fifth Amendment Jurisprudence in the Eleventh Circuit or an Aberration?" 44 Alabama L. Rev. 143, 1992; "Making Sense of Victim Restitution: A Critical Perspective" 6 No. 4 Federal Sentencing Reporter Jan-Feb 1994; and "Can the Courts Rescue ERISA?" 29 Cumberland L. Rev. 285, 1998-99. Adjunct Professor of Constitutional Law Birmingham-Southern College 1992. Member Alabama State Bar and Birmingham Bar Association. Named Outstanding Young Man of Alabama 1958, Alumnus of the Year by Marion Institute 1994 and Alumnus of the Year by Birmingham-Southern College 1996. Private U.S. Army 1946-47. Republican. Member Jefferson County Republican Party and Executive Committee Alabama State Republican Party. Delegate Republican Convention 1972, 1976 and 1980. Enjoys jogging.

Office: 481 U.S. Courthouse, 1729 Fifth Avenue North, Birmingham 35203.

Telephone: (205) 278-1880.

ADERHOLT, Bobby R. *(Presiding Judge, Alabama Circuit Court Twenty-fifth Judicial Circuit)* Elected to term beginning Jan 11, 1977. Reelected 1982, 1988, 1994 and 2000. Current term expires Jan 2007. Born Haleyville Alabama Dec 6, 1935. Congregational Christian. Educated at Birmingham-Southern College A.B. 1958, Cumberland School of Law and University of Alabama LL.B. 1959. President Student Bar Association Cumberland School of Law. Member Omicron Delta Kappa and Delta Theta Phi. Admitted to practice Alabama 1959. In legal practice Haleyville 1959-61. Judge, Winston County Court of Law and Equity 1962-73.

Author "History of a Lawsuit" W. H. Anderson Co. 1963. Associate Professor of Law Cumberland School of Law of Samford University 1961-63. Listed in *Who's Who in Alabama, Outstanding Personalities of the South* and *Who's Who in Law.* Republican. Member Alabama State Republican Executive Committee 1978-1984. Member Masonic Lodge, Northwest Alabama Shrine Club and Zamora Temple of the Shrine.

Mailing address: P.O. Box 639, Haleyville 35565.

Office: Highway 13 South, Haleyville 35565.

Telephone: (205) 921-2200, 486-2257, 489-5029.

E-mail address: aderholt@sonet.net

ALBRITTON, W. Harold, III *(Chief Judge, United States District Court Middle District of Alabama)* Appointed for life by President George Bush to term beginning May 17, 1991. Chief Judge since Feb 8, 1998. Born Andalusia Alabama 1936. Educated at Marion Institute and University of Alabama A.B. 1958 J.D. 1960. Board of Editors Alabama Law Review 1959-60. Member Phi Beta Kappa, Phi Delta Phi and Farrah Order of Jurisprudence (now a chapter of Order of the Coif). Admitted to practice Alabama 1960.

Past President University of Alabama School of Law Foundation. Fellow American College of Trial Lawyers and American Bar Foundation. Member American Judicature Society, Montgomery Chapter American Inns of Court, Federal Judges Association, Alabama State Bar (Disciplinary Commission 1981-84, Board of Commissioners 1981-90, President Elect 1989-90, President 1990-91) and American Bar Association. Captain U.S. Army JAGC 1960-62.

Mailing address: P.O. Box 629, Montgomery 36101-0629.

Telephone: (334) 954-3710.

ALSBROOKS, John H., Jr. *(Judge, Jefferson County District Court Birmingham Division)* Appointed by Governor George C. Wallace to term beginning Jan 6, 1984. Elected to subsequent terms.

Office: 716 Richard Arrington Jr. Blvd. N., Room 570, Birmingham 35203.

Telephone: (205) 325-5336.

ANDERSON, Jeanne W. *(Judge, Limestone County District Court)* Appointed by Governor Harold Guy Hunt to term beginning Oct 1, 1991.

Mailing address: P.O. Box 1102, Athens 35612.

Office: Courthouse Square, Athens 35611.

Telephone: (256) 233-6419.

ANDERSON, Larry K. *(Presiding Judge, Alabama Circuit Court Twentieth Judicial Circuit)* Appointed by Governor Forrest "Fob" James to term beginning April 4, 1996. Elected 1998, current term expires Jan 2005. Born Chicago Illinois April 13, 1954. Presbyterian. Educated at University of Alabama at Birmingham B.A. with honors 1979 and Cumberland School of Law of Samford University J.D. 1983. Member Omicron Delta Kappa. Admitted to practice Alabama 1983, U.S. District Court District of Alabama and U.S. Court of Appeals Eleventh Circuit. In private legal practice Dothan 1993-96.

Assistant District Attorney Twentieth Judicial Circuit 1983-86. City Attorney Dothan 1986-93. Member Circuit Judges Association, Alabama State Bar and Houston County Bar Association. Attended Alabama Judicial Conferences. Republican.

Mailing address: P.O. Drawer 6406, Dothan 36302.

Office: 114 North Oates Street, Dothan 36303.

Telephone: (334) 671-8761.

ANDERSON, W. Mark, III *(Judge, Alabama Circuit Court Fifteenth Judicial Circuit)* Appointed by Governor Forrest "Fob" James to term beginning Feb 1, 1997. Elected Nov 1998, current term expires Jan 2005. Born Montgomery Alabama March 19, 1937. Educated at University of Alabama B.S. 1960 J.D. 1962. Law Clerk

ANDERSON, W. MARK, III—*Continued*

to Hon. James S. Coleman, Alabama Supreme Court 1962-63. Member Phi Alpha Delta and Omicron Delta Kappa. Admitted to practice Alabama 1962, U.S. District Court Middle District of Alabama 1963, U.S. Court of Appeals Fifth Circuit 1964 and U.S. Supreme Court 1967. In legal practice Montgomery 1966-97.

County Attorney Montgomery County 1973-76. Author *The Bankruptcy Court* 1989, *Bankruptcy Ethics* 1989 and *Initiating The Probate Process* 1995 The National Business Institute. Member Federalist Society, Circuit Judges Association, Alabama State Bar and Montgomery County Bar Association (President 1997). Listed in *Who's Who in Alabama, Who's Who in the South and Southwest* and *Personalities of the South.* Colonel USAR (retired). Chairman Montgomery County Republican Executive Committee 1992-96. Elder Trinity Presbyterian Church. Member Lions, Friends of the Library (Past President). Enjoys reading, collecting, writing and sports.

Office: Montgomery County Courthouse Annex, 100 South Lawrence Street, Montgomery 36104-4240.

Telephone: (334) 832-1375.

ARMSTRONG, Robert R., Jr. *(Magistrate Judge, United States District Court Northern District of Alabama)* Appointed by U.S. District Court judges. Former Presiding Judge, Alabama Circuit Court Eighteenth Judicial Circuit.

Office: 274 U.S. Courthouse, 1729 Fifth Avenue North, Birmingham 35203.

Telephone: (205) 278-1910.

AUSTIN, Robert E. *(Presiding Judge, Alabama Circuit Court Forty-first Judicial Circuit)* Appointed by Governor Harold Guy Hunt to term beginning Nov 14, 1988. Elected to subsequent terms. Former Presiding Judge. Former Judge, Blount County District Court.

Mailing address: P.O. Box 638, Oneonta 35121.

Office: 220 Second Avenue East, Oneonta 35121.

Telephone: (205) 625-4145.

AVERY, Richard Moore, Jr. *(Judge, Perry County District Court)* Elected to term beginning Jan 16, 1977. Reelected 1982, 1988, 1994 and 2000. Current term expires 2007. Born Greensboro Alabama Nov 17, 1946. Presbyterian. Educated at University of Alabama B.A. with honors 1971 J.D. 1975. Member Phi Eta Sigma, Farrah Order of Jurisprudence and Sigma Alpha Epsilon. Admitted to practice Alabama 1975. Began legal practice Marion 1975.

Chief Clerk Hale County Probate Office 1971-72. Member Alabama Young Lawyers Association, District Judges Association, Alabama State Bar and American Bar Association. Named to Outstanding Young Men of America 1978. Private USAR 1968. Democrat. Member State of Alabama Live-In-A-Landmark Council, Friends of Perry County Library, Perry County Preservation and Historical Society, American Red Cross and University of Alabama Alumni Association. Advisory Board Smithsonian Institute Historical Tours. Patron Judson College. Interested in historical preservation. Enjoys reading, gardening and horseback riding.

Mailing address: P.O. Box 146, Marion 36756.

Office: Washington Street, Marion 36756.

Telephone: (334) 683-2215.

BAHAKEL, Alfred *(Judge, Alabama Circuit Court Tenth Judicial Circuit Birmingham Division)* Elected to term beginning Jan 19, 1993. Reelected 1998, current term expires Jan 2005.

Office: 801 Richard Arrington Jr. Blvd. N., Room 606, Birmingham 35203.

Telephone: (205) 325-5648.

BAHAKEL, Gloria T. *(Judge, Alabama Circuit Court Tenth Judicial Circuit Birmingham Division)*

Office: 801 Richard Arrington Jr. Blvd. N., Courtroom 405, Birmingham 35203.

Telephone: (205) 325-5323.

BAHAKEL, S. Phillip *(Judge, Jefferson County District Court Birmingham Division)*

Office: 120 Second Court North, Birmingham 35204.

Telephone: (205) 214-8688.

BAKER, Robert M. *(Judge, Limestone County District Court)*

Office: County Courthouse, 200 Washington Street, Athens 35611.

Telephone: (256) 233-8083.

BANKS, Julian D. *(Judge, Alabama Circuit Court Thirteenth Judicial Circuit)*

Office: Mobile Government Plaza, 205 Government Street, Mobile 36644-2217.

Telephone: (251) 574-8488.

BARCLAY, Elise D. *(Judge, Jefferson County District Court Birmingham Division)* Elected to term beginning Jan 17, 1989. Reelected 1994 and 2000. Current term expires Jan 2007.

Office: 120 North Second Court, Birmingham 35204.

Telephone: (205) 325-5489.

BARR, Robert W. *(Judge, Alabama Circuit Court Twelfth Judicial Circuit)* Elected to term beginning Jan 19, 1993. Reelected 1998, current term expires Jan 2005. Former Presiding Judge.

Mailing address: P.O. Box 805, Troy 36081.

Office: One Church Street, Troy 36081.

Telephone: (334) 566-1307, 347-2519.

BASCHAB, Pamela Willis *(Judge, Alabama Court of Criminal Appeals)* Elected Nov 1996 to term beginning Jan 1997. Reelected 2002, current term expires Jan 2009. Born Mobile Alabama July 26, 1947. Educated at University of North Alabama 1965, University of South Alabama 1974 and St. Mary's University School of Law J.D. 1982. Recipient American Jurisprudence Award Constitutional Law. In legal practice Foley and Elberta. Presiding Judge Baldwin County District Court 1988-92. Former Judge, Alabama Circuit Court Twenty-eighth Judicial Circuit, elected Nov 1992.

Former Assistant District Attorney Mobile County. Former Member Circuit Court Judges Association. Member American Judges Association and Alabama State Bar. Former Co-chair Alabama Task Force on Law Enforcement Education in Domestic Violence. Member Optimist Club and Chamber of Commerce. Co-Founder Baldwin County Domestic Violence Shelter.

Office: 300 Dexter Avenue, Montgomery 36104.

Telephone: (334) 353-4241.

BATTLE, Joseph L. *(Judge, Alabama Circuit Court Twenty-third Judicial Circuit)* Elected to term beginning

BATTLE, JOSEPH L.—*Continued*
Jan 17, 1989. Reelected to subsequent terms. Former Presiding Judge.
Office: Madison County Courthouse, 100 Northside Square, Huntsville 35801.
Telephone: (256) 532-3432.

BAXTER, James Thomas *(Judge, Alabama Circuit Court First Judicial Circuit)* Born Chatom Alabama Dec 27, 1953. Religious affiliation: Tibbie Baptist. Educated at University of Southern Mississippi B.A. 1975 and Cumberland School of Law of Samford University J.D. 1979. Member Phi Delta Phi. Admitted to practice Alabama 1979. Began legal practice Chatom 1979. Judge, Chatom Municipal Court 1980-82. Former Judge, Washington County District Court, elected to term beginning Jan 18, 1983.
Member Alabama State Bar, Washington County and First Judicial Circuit Bar Associations. Democrat. President Washington County Heart Association 1980-82. Chairman Washington County Affiliate of Catholic Social Services 1980-83. Member Planning Committee Washington County United Way since 1989. Enjoys hunting, fishing and woodworking.
Mailing address: P.O. Box 1418, Chatom 36518.
Office: 1 Court Street, Chatom 36518.
Telephone: (251) 847-2304.
Fax: (251) 847-6633

BEAIRD, Hugh *(Presiding Judge, Alabama Circuit Court Fourteenth Judicial Circuit)* Elected to term beginning Jan 17, 1995. Reelected 2000, current term expires Jan 2007. Former Judge, Walker County District Court.
Mailing address: P.O. Box 4, Jasper 35502.
Office: Nineteenth Street and Second Avenue, Jasper 35501.
Telephone: (205) 384-7263.

BELL, William K. *(Judge, Alabama Circuit Court Twenty-third Judicial Circuit)*
Office: Madison County Courthouse, 100 Northside Square, Huntsville 35801.
Telephone: (256) 532-3636.

BELLAMY, Michael J. *(Judge, Russell County District Court)* Appointed by Governor Forrest "Fob" James to term beginning Sept 15, 1999. Elected 2000, current term expires Jan 2007. Born Columbus Georgia April 19, 1952. Baptist. Educated at Tuskegee University B.S. with departmental honors 1973 and Southern University J.D. 1976. Member Delta Theta Phi. Admitted to practice Alabama 1979 and U.S. District Court Middle District of Alabama. In legal practice Phenix City 1980-98. Judge, Phenix City Municipal Court 1982-96.
Assistant District Attorney Russell County 1977-79 and Macon County 1979-80. Captain USAR. Trustee and Deacon Franchise Baptist Church. President Phenix-Russell Boys and Girls Club. Member Russell County Chamber of Commerce, Tuskegee Alumni Club and U.S.O., Inc. Enjoys golfing, fishing and walking.
Mailing address: P.O. Box 1770, Phenix City 36868-1770.
Office: Russell County Courthouse, 501 Fourteenth Street, Phenix City 36868.
Telephone: (334) 298-0931.

BENNETT, Thomas B. *(Judge, United States Bankruptcy Court Northern District of Alabama)* Appointed by U.S. Court of Appeals Eleventh Circuit judges.
Office: 128 Federal Building, 1800 Fifth Avenue North, Birmingham 35203-2110.
Telephone: (205) 714-3880.

BENTLEY, John H. *(Judge, Alabama Circuit Court Twenty-fifth Judicial Circuit)*
Mailing address: P.O. Box 297, Hamilton 35570.
Telephone: (205) 921-2200.

BIBB, David H. *(Judge, Morgan County District Court)* Appointed by Governor Forrest "Fob" James July 10, 1981. Elected 1982, 1988, 1994 and 2000. Current term expires Jan 2007. Born Anniston Alabama June 12, 1945. Episcopalian. Educated at Princeton University A.B. 1967 and University of Alabama School of Law J.D. 1970. Law Clerk to Hon. James N. Bloodworth, Alabama Supreme Court 1970. Admitted to practice Alabama 1970. Began legal practice Decatur 1970.
Member Alabama State Bar and Morgan County Bar Association. Democrat.
Mailing address: P.O. Box 668, Decatur 35602.
Office: 302 Lee Street, Decatur 35601.
Telephone: (256) 351-4765.

BISHOP, Jody W. *(Judge, Baldwin County District Court)*
Mailing address: P.O. Box 250, Bay Minette 36507.
Office: Baldwin County Courthouse, Courthouse Square, Bay Minette 36507.
Telephone: (251) 580-1647.

BLACKBURN, Sharon Lovelace *(Judge, United States District Court Northern District of Alabama)* Appointed for life by President George Bush to term beginning 1991. Born Pensacola Florida May 7, 1950. Educated at University of Alabama at Tuscaloosa B.A. 1973 and Cumberland School of Law of Samford University J.D. 1977. Law Clerk to Hon. Robert Edward Varner, U.S. District Court Middle District of Alabama 1977-78.
Assistant U.S. Attorney Civil Division 1979-85 and Criminal Division 1985-91 Northern District of Alabama.
Office: 730 U.S. Courthouse, 1729 Fifth Avenue North, Birmingham 35203.
Telephone: (205) 278-1810.

BLAIR, Steven E. *(Judge, Alabama Circuit Court Twelfth Judicial Circuit)* Former Judge, Coffee County District Court, elected to term beginning Jan 17, 1995.
Mailing address: P.O. Box 310306, Enterprise 36331.
Office: County Courthouse, 104 North Edwards Street, Enterprise 36330.
Telephone: (334) 347-4785.

BOOHAKER, Joseph L. *(Judge, Alabama Circuit Court Tenth Judicial Circuit Birmingham Division)*
Office: 716 Richard Arrington Jr. Blvd. N., Courtroom 360, Birmingham 35203.
Telephone: (205) 325-5753.

BOSCH, Carmen *(Judge, Baldwin County District Court)*
Mailing address: P.O. Box 355, Bay Minette 36507.
Office: Courthouse Square, Bay Minette 36507.
Telephone: (251) 937-0235.

BOWDEN, Robert L. *(Judge, Barbour County District Court)* Appointed by Governor Forrest "Fob" James to term beginning Jan 15, 1997.

Office: 201 Barbour County Courthouse, 303 East Broad Street, Eufaula 36027.

Telephone: (334) 687-1512.

BOWDRE, Karon O. *(Judge, United States District Court Northern District of Alabama)* Appointed for life by President George W. Bush to term beginning Nov 14, 2001. Born Montgomery Alabama 1955. Educated at Samford University B.A. 1977 J.D. 1981. Law Clerk to Hon. Junius Foy Guin, Jr., U.S. District Court Northern District of Alabama 1981-82. In legal practice Alabama 1982-90.

Professor of Law Cumberland School of Law of Samford University 1990-2001.

Office: 140 U.S. Courthouse, 1729 Fifth Avenue North, Birmingham 35203.

Telephone: (205) 278-1800.

BOYD, Delores R. *(Magistrate Judge, United States District Court Middle District of Alabama)* Appointed by U.S. District Court judges to term beginning Sept 14, 2001. Term expires Sept 13, 2009. Educated at University of Alabama 1972 and University of Virginia School of Law J.D. 1975. Law Clerk to Hon. John C. Godbold, U.S. Court of Appeals Fifth Circuit 1975-76. Member Phi Beta Kappa. In legal practice Alabama 1976-2001. Presiding Judge, Montgomery Municipal Court Jan 19, 2000 to Aug 31, 2001.

Bar Examiner Alabama 1979-82. Chairperson Alabama Board of Bar Examiners 1995-98.

Mailing address: P.O. Box 430, Montgomery 36101-0430.

Office: U.S. Courthouse, 1 Church Street, Montgomery 36104-4018.

Telephone: (334) 954-3740.

Fax: (334) 954-3741

E-mail address: Delores_Boyd@almd.uscourts.gov

BOZEMAN, Terri L. *(Judge, Lowndes County District Court)*

Mailing address: P.O. Box 455, Hayneville 36040.

Office: Washington Street, Hayneville 36040.

Telephone: (334) 548-2591.

BRELAND, David J. *(Judge, Morgan County District Court)* Appointed by governor to term beginning Jan 21, 1983. Elected to subsequent terms.

Mailing address: P.O. Box 668, Decatur 35602.

Office: 302 Lee Street, Decatur 35601.

Telephone: (256) 351-4760.

BRIGHT, Lynn Clardy *(Judge, Montgomery County District Court)* Appointed by Governor George C. Wallace April 27, 1983. Elected 1984, 1990, 1996 and 2002. Current term expires Jan 2009. Born Montgomery Alabama July 31, 1953. Baptist. Educated at Alabama Christian College A.A. (Salutatorian) 1973, Auburn University B.S. with highest honors 1975 and Jones Law Institute J.D. 1979. Admitted to practice Alabama 1979. Began legal practice Montgomery 1979.

Former City Attorney Millbrook and Special Assistant Attorney General. Member Alabama District Judges Association, Alabama State Bar, Montgomery County and American Bar Associations. Faculty Member Alabama Judicial College and National Judicial College. Named Woman of the Year by American Business Women's Association 1985, Woman of Distinction by Soroptimist International of Montgomery 1994, Woman of Achievement by *The Montgomery Advertiser* 1995 and Public Citizen of the Year by Montgomery Unit National Association of Social Workers 1996. Family honored as "Family of the Year" 1989 by *The Montgomery Advertiser* and *Alabama Journal.* Inducted into Robert E. Lee High School Hall of Fame 1995. Recipient Howell Heflin Award for contributions to Alabama's Court Referral Program 1996 and Justice for Victims Award from The Family Sunshine Center 1996. Former Member State Task Force Against Child Abuse. Chairman of the Board First Baptist Church Community Ministries. Honorary Chairperson Alabama Dance Theater. Board of Directors Montgomery Ballet, Montgomery Symphony Orchestra, Montgomery Museum of Fine Arts, Montgomery Zoological Society, Jubilee Cityfest, Alabama Shakespeare Festival, Family Guidance Center and American Cancer Society. Member Montgomery County Domestic Violence Task Force and Council Against Drug and Alcohol Abuse. Participant Envision Montgomery 2020.

Office: Montgomery County Courthouse, 251 South Lawrence Street, Montgomery 36104.

Telephone: (334) 832-2559.

BROCK, Jeffrey T. *(Judge, Conecuh County District Court)* Elected to term beginning Jan 17, 1995. Reelected 2000, current term expires Jan 2007.

Mailing address: P.O. Box 227, Evergreen 36401.

Office: Courthouse Square, Evergreen 36401.

Telephone: (251) 578-2421.

BROGDEN, Joseph B. *(Judge, Alabama Circuit Court Twenty-first Judicial Circuit)* Appointed by Governor George C. Wallace to term beginning Jan 1, 1986. Elected to subsequent terms. Former Presiding Judge. Born Gantt Alabama Nov 14, 1939. Methodist. Educated at Auburn University B.S. and Cumberland School of Law J.D. Admitted to practice Alabama 1969, Florida and U.S. District Court Southern District of Alabama. In legal practice Atmore and Monroeville Alabama and Century Florida. Former City Judge.

Former Assistant District Attorney. Member Alabama State Bar, The Florida Bar, Escambia County and American Bar Associations. Attended The National Judicial College and Alabama Judicial College. USN. Previously worked as claims adjuster.

Mailing address: P.O. Box 795, Brewton 36427.

Office: 318 Bellville Avenue, Brewton 36426.

Telephone: (251) 867-0253.

BROTHERTON, James C. *(Judge, Alabama Circuit Court Fourteenth Judicial Circuit)* Assumed office June 22, 1976. Elected to subsequent terms. Former Presiding Judge.

Mailing address: P.O. Box 1603, Jasper 35502.

Office: Nineteenth Street and Second Avenue, Jasper 35501.

Telephone: (205) 384-7234.

BROWN, George A. *(Judge, Mobile County District Court)*

Office: 2315 Costarides Street, Mobile 36617.

Telephone: (251) 574-5245.

BROWN, Houston L. *(Judge, Alabama Circuit Court Tenth Judicial Circuit Birmingham Division)*
Office: 716 Richard Arrington Jr. Blvd. N., Room 650, Birmingham 35263-0035.
Telephone: (205) 325-5367.

BROWN, Jean Williams *(Associate Justice, Alabama Supreme Court)* Elected Nov 1998 to term beginning Jan 18, 1999. Term expires Jan 2005. First woman elected to serve on two Alabama appellate courts. Born Birmingham Alabama. Educated at Samford University with honors 1974 and University of Alabama School of Law J.D. 1977. Member Bench and Bar Legal Honor Society. Admitted to practice Alabama 1977, U.S. Court of Appeals Eleventh Circuit and U.S. Supreme Court. Judge, Alabama Court of Criminal Appeals 1996-99.
Assistant Attorney General Criminal Appeals Division Alabama 19 years. Past President Friends of the Montgomery Ballet. Former docent Montgomery Museum of Fine Arts. Former advisor Boy Scouts Explorer Club. Sustaining Member Montgomery Junior League. Member First Baptist Church.
Office: 300 Dexter Avenue, Montgomery 36104.
Telephone: (334) 353-4244.

BROWN, Sherrie W. *(Judge, Alabama Circuit Court Eighth Judicial Circuit)* Elected to term beginning Jan 17, 1995. Reelected 2000, current term expires Jan 2007. Former Presiding Judge.
Mailing address: P.O. Box 668, Decatur 35602.
Office: 302 Lee Street, Decatur 35601.
Telephone: (256) 351-4700.

BRUNNER, H. Frank *(Judge, Alabama Circuit Court Thirty-second Judicial Circuit)* Appointed by Governor James E. Folsom to term beginning Dec 8, 1993. Elected 1994 and 2000. Current term expires Jan 15, 2007. Former Presiding Judge. Born Cullman Alabama April 17, 1951. United Church of Christ. Educated at St. Bernard College B.S. magna cum laude 1973 and Birmingham School of Law J.D. with third class honors 1981. Admitted to practice Alabama 1981.
Office: 313 Cullman County Courthouse, 500 Second Avenue S.W., Cullman 35055.
Telephone: (256) 775-4653.

BRYAN, Howard F., IV *(Presiding Judge, Alabama Circuit Court Fifth Judicial Circuit)* Elected 1976 to term beginning Jan 16, 1977. Reelected 1982, 1988, 1994 and 2000. Current term expires Jan 2007. Born Birmingham Alabama Aug 18, 1947. Member First Baptist Church of West Point (Deacon). Educated at University of Alabama B.S. 1969 J.D. 1972. Law Clerk to Associate Justice Robert B. Harwood, Alabama Supreme Court 1973-74. Admitted to practice Alabama 1972. Began legal practice Tuscaloosa 1972. In legal practice Lanett 1974-77.
Member Alabama State Bar and American Bar Association. Captain USAR 1969-77. Democrat. Member Alabama Alumni Association and Chambers County Mental Health Association. Board of Directors East Alabama Mental Health Association.
Office: County Courthouse, Two Lafayette Street, Lafayette 36862.
Telephone: (334) 864-4328, (334) 724-2526, (256) 357-4551.

BUSH, John B. *(Presiding Judge, Alabama Circuit Court Nineteenth Judicial Circuit)* Appointed by Governor George C. Wallace Dec 8, 1986. Elected Nov 1988, 1994 and 2000. Current term expires Jan 2007. Born Montgomery Alabama June 15, 1956. Baptist. Educated at Auburn University B.S. 1978 and Cumberland School of Law of Samford University J.D. 1981. Law Clerk to Hon. Joseph D. Phelps, Alabama Circuit Court Fifteenth Judicial Circuit June 1981 to June 1982. Member Phi Delta Phi and Phi Gamma Delta. Admitted to practice Alabama 1981 and U.S. District Courts Middle 1982 and Northern 1986 Districts of Alabama. In legal practice Prattville June 1, 1982 to May 1, 1983 and Montgomery May 1, 1983 to Dec 8, 1986.
Former Member Montgomery County Trial Lawyers Association, Alabama Trial Lawyers Association, The Association of Trial Lawyers of America and Alabama State Bar. Former Faculty Member Alabama Judicial College. Republican. Former Member Millbrook Jaycees and Tri-Community Kiwanis Club. Enjoys hunting.
Office: 8935 U.S. Highway 231, Wetumpka 36092.
Telephone: (334) 567-1148, (334) 361-3766, (205) 755-0311.

BUSH, Russell Keith *(Judge, Lee County District Court)* Elected to term beginning Jan 16, 2001. Term expires Jan 2007. Born Dadeville Alabama Feb 25, 1965. Methodist. Educated at Auburn University B.A. 1987 and University of Alabama School of Law J.D. 1990. Trial Advocacy Team Moot Court Board. Admitted to practice Alabama 1990, U.S. District Court Middle District of Alabama 1990 and U.S. Court of Appeals Eleventh Circuit 1992. In legal practice Opelika Sept 1990 to Jan 2001.
Assistant City Attorney Auburn 1993-96. Member Alabama State Bar and American Bar Association. Republican. Board Member Lee County Red Cross and Museum of East Alabama. Member Opelika Kiwanis Club and Opelika-Auburn Jaycees. Enjoys sports and music.
Office: 2311 Gateway Drive, Suite 106, Opelika 36801-6858.
Telephone: (334) 749-7141.
Fax: (334) 737-3380
E-mail address: russell.bush@alacourt.state.al.us

BUTLER, Charles R., Jr. *(Chief Judge, United States District Court Southern District of Alabama)* Appointed for life by President Ronald Reagan to term beginning Nov 1, 1988. Chief Judge since July 9, 1994. Born New York New York March 28, 1940. Educated at Washington and Lee University B.A. 1962 and University of Alabama School of Law LL.B. 1966. Admitted to practice Alabama 1966. In legal practice Mobile 1975-88.
Assistant Public Defender 1968-70 and District Attorney 1971-75 Mobile County. Author "Chief to Chief: A Guide to Effective Communication" *Federal Probation* March 1996. Past President Eleventh Circuit District Judges Association. Former Liaison Member Space and Facilities Subcommittee Judicial Conference Committee on Court Administration and Management. Former Member Judicial Conference Committee on Criminal Law and Probation and Pretrial Services Automation and Technology Umbrella Group. Member Executive Committee Judicial Conference of the U.S. 2000-02 and Eleventh Circuit Pattern Jury Instruction Committee.

BUTLER, CHARLES R., JR.—*Continued*
Member Judicial Council of the Eleventh Circuit (Executive Committee).
Office: U.S. Courthouse, 113 St. Joseph Street, Mobile 36602-3606.
Telephone: (251) 690-2175.

BUTLER, John F. *(Judge, Alabama Circuit Court Thirteenth Judicial Circuit)* Elected 1982, 1988, 1994 and 2000. Current term expires Jan 2007. Born Andalusia Alabama Dec 22, 1943. Presbyterian. Educated at Troy State University B.A. 1965 and University of Alabama J.D. 1973. Member Pi Kappa Phi and Phi Delta Phi. Admitted to practice Alabama 1973. Began legal practice Mobile 1973.
Colonel USAR since 1965. Worked as radio broadcaster 1959-65.
Office: 2315 Costarides Street, Mobile 36617.
Telephone: (251) 574-8470.

BYNON, Robert P., Jr. *(Judge, Jefferson County District Court Birmingham Division)*
Office: 716 Richard Arrington Jr. Blvd. N., Room 510, Birmingham 35203.
Telephone: (205) 325-5328.

BYRNE, Bradley E. *(Presiding Judge, Alabama Circuit Court Twenty-first Judicial Circuit)* Elected to term beginning Jan 20, 1987. Reelected to subsequent terms. Current term expires Jan 2005. Born Brewton Alabama March 1, 1954. Episcopalian. Educated at University of Southern Mississippi B.S. with honors 1976 and University of Alabama J.D. 1979. Admitted to practice Alabama 1979 and Florida 1980. In legal practice Brewton and Atmore Alabama 1979-86.
City Prosecutor Atmore 1984-86. Attended General Jurisdiction Course The National Judicial College. Member Rotary Club. Enjoys golf, fishing and hunting.
Mailing address: P.O. Box 1211, Brewton 36427.
Office: 318 Bellville Avenue, Brewton 36426.
Telephone: (251) 867-0281.

CADDELL, Jack *(Judge, United States Bankruptcy Court Northern District of Alabama)* Appointed by U.S. Court of Appeals Eleventh Circuit judges.
Mailing address: P.O. Box 2004, Decatur 35602-2004.
Telephone: (256) 353-2817.

CAHILL, Robert G. *(Judge, Jefferson County District Court Birmingham Division)* Elected 1988 to term beginning Jan 1989. Reelected 1994 and 2000. Current term expires Jan 2007. Born Birmingham Alabama Nov 5, 1946. Catholic. Educated at Auburn University B.S. 1968 and Cumberland School of Law J.D. 1973. Admitted to practice Alabama 1973 and U.S. District Court Northern District of Alabama 1979. In legal practice Birmingham 1984-89.
Chief Deputy District Attorney Anniston 1973-78. Deputy District Attorney Birmingham 1978-84. Instructor in Alabama Peace Officer Standards and Training since 1980. Member Alabama District Judges Association, Alabama State Bar and Birmingham Bar Association. Republican. Enjoys fishing and boating.
Office: 801 Richard Arrington Jr. Blvd. N., Room 205, Birmingham 35203.
Telephone: (205) 325-5296.

CALHOUN, John C. *(Judge, Alabama Circuit Court Tenth Judicial Circuit Birmingham Division)* Appointed by Governor James E. Folsom to term beginning Oct 4, 1993. Elected to subsequent term.
Office: 2124 Seventh Avenue North, Room 210, Birmingham 35203.
Telephone: (205) 325-5406.

CAPELL, John L., III *(Judge, Alabama Circuit Court Fifteenth Judicial Circuit)* Appointed by Governor Forrest "Fob" James to term beginning April 4, 1996.
Office: Courthouse Annex, 100 South Lawrence Street, Montgomery 36104-4240.
Telephone: (334) 832-7761.

CARDWELL, William W. *(Presiding Judge, Alabama Circuit Court Sixteenth Judicial Circuit)* Appointed by Governor Forrest "Fob" James to term beginning May 6, 1981. Elected 1982, 1988, 1994 and 2000. Current term expires Jan 2007. Born Birmingham Alabama March 21, 1941. Episcopalian. Educated at University of Alabama B.S. LL.B. Admitted to practice Alabama 1966 and U.S. District Court Northern District of Alabama 1966. In legal practice Gadsden 1966-81.
Member Planning Commission Gadsden 1974-76. Member Alabama State Bar (Former Secretary-Treasurer Young Lawyers Section) and Etowah County Bar Association (Past President). Attended Alabama Judicial College and The National Judicial College. Recipient 500 Hour Continuing Judicial Education Award from Alabama Judicial College. Sergeant USMC 1966. Past President Young Democrats Etowah County. Enjoys sports and gardening.
Office: 307 Judicial Building, 801 Forrest Avenue, Gadsden 35901.
Telephone: (256) 549-5368.

CARPENTER, George E. *(Judge, Colbert County District Court)* Elected to term beginning Dec 1, 1980. Reelected 1986, 1992 and 1998. Current term expires Jan 2005. Born Colbert County Alabama May 8, 1951. Baptist. Educated at University of North Alabama B.S. 1973 and Birmingham School of Law J.D. 1978. Admitted to practice Alabama 1978. Began legal practice Tuscumbia 1978.
Second Lieutenant USAS Military Police 1973. Democrat. Member Breakfast Optimist Club of Muscle Shoals. Enjoys biking, hiking and visiting historic places.
Office: Colbert County Courthouse, 201 North Main Street, Tuscumbia 35674.
Telephone: (256) 386-8524.

CARVER, Sheri *(Judge, Cherokee County District Court)*
Office: Cherokee County Courthouse, 100 Main Street, Centre 35960.
Telephone: (256) 927-3683.

CASHION, James C. *(Judge, Marion County District Court)* Appointed by Governor George C. Wallace to term beginning Sept 8, 1986. Elected to subsequent terms.
Mailing address: P.O. Box 1476, Hamilton 35570.
Office: 132 South Military, Hamilton 35570.
Telephone: (205) 921-3181.

CASSADY, William E. *(Magistrate Judge, United States District Court Southern District of Alabama)* Appointed by U.S. District Court judges.
Office: 306 U.S. Courthouse, 113 St. Joseph Street, Mobile 36602-3624.
Telephone: (251) 690-2345.

CAUSEY, William J., Jr. *(Judge, Monroe County District Court)* Elected to term beginning Jan 17, 1989. Reelected 1994 and 2000. Current term expires Jan 2007.
Office: Monroe County Courthouse, Courthouse Square, Monroeville 36461.
Telephone: (251) 743-4381.

CHAMBERS, Rosemary D. *(Judge, Alabama Circuit Court Thirteenth Judicial Circuit)* Appointed by Governor Harold Guy Hunt to term beginning Jan 4, 1993.
Office: 2600 Mobile Government Plaza, 205 Government Street, Mobile 36644-2217.
Telephone: (251) 574-8463.

CHANDLER, Joel R. *(Judge, Tuscaloosa County District Court)* Elected to term beginning Jan 19, 1993. Reelected 1998, current term expires Jan 2005.
Office: Tuscaloosa County Courthouse, Sixth Floor, 714 Greensboro Avenue, Tuscaloosa 35401.
Telephone: (205) 349-3870.

CHANEY, Kim J. *(Judge, Cullman County District Court)* Elected to term beginning Jan 19, 1993. Reelected 1998, current term expires Jan 2005.
Office: 213 Cullman County Courthouse, 500 Second Avenue S.W., Cullman 35055.
Telephone: (256) 775-4766.

CLARY, Jerry L. *(Judge, Fayette County District Court)* Appointed by Governor Harold Guy Hunt to term beginning Oct 7, 1988. Elected to subsequent term.
Mailing address: P.O. Box 616, Fayette 35555.
Office: Fayette County Courthouse, 103 North Temple Avenue, Fayette 35555.
Telephone: (205) 932-4613.

CLEMON, U. W. *(Chief Judge, United States District Court Northern District of Alabama)* Appointed for life by President Jimmy Carter to term beginning 1980. Chief Judge since Nov 20, 1999. Born Fairfield Alabama April 9, 1943. Educated at Miles College B.A. 1965 and Columbia University School of Law J.D. 1968. In legal practice Birmingham 1969-80.
Member State Senate Alabama 1975-80.
Office: 519 U.S. Courthouse, 1729 Fifth Avenue North, Birmingham 35203.
Telephone: (205) 278-1850.

COBB, Sue Bell *(Judge, Alabama Court of Criminal Appeals)* Elected 1994 and 2000. Current term expires Jan 2007. Alternate Chief Judge Court of the Judiciary 1997-2001. Methodist. Educated at University of Alabama B.A. in History J.D. 1981. Recipient Phi Alpha Theta Scholarship Key. Moot Court Board. Member Bench and Bar Honor Society and Farrah Law Society. Former Judge, Conecuh County District Court (one of Alabama's youngest judges).
Past President Alabama Council of Juvenile and Family Court Judges. Board of Directors Farrah Law Society. Recipient Woman of Achievement Award from *Montgomery Advertiser* 1995, Volunteer of the Year Award, Wes Nowlin Award and St. George Medal from American Cancer Society, Distinguished Service Awards from National Juvenile Detention Association and Alabama Probation Officers Institute and Bishop Barron Public Service Award from Alabama State Employee's Association. Former Chairman of the Board Alabama Division American Cancer Society. Chairman of the Board Children First Foundation. Graduate Leadership Alabama. Member Montgomery Kiwanis Club, First United Methodist Church and Alabama Solution.
Office: 300 Dexter Avenue, Montgomery 36104.
Telephone: (334) 242-4615.

COHEN, Benjamin *(Judge, United States Bankruptcy Court Northern District of Alabama)* Appointed by U.S. Court of Appeals Eleventh Circuit judges.
Office: 311 Federal Building, 1800 Fifth Avenue North, Birmingham 35203-2110.
Telephone: (205) 714-3865.

COLE, Randall L. *(Presiding Judge, Alabama Circuit Court Ninth Judicial Circuit)* Elected to term beginning Nov 1974. Reelected 1976, 1982, 1988, 1994 and 2000. Current term expires Jan 2007. Presiding Judge since 1979. Born Portersville Alabama March 17, 1943. Methodist. Educated at Jacksonville State University B.A. 1965 and University of Alabama J.D. 1968. Staff member Alabama Law Review 1967. Member Order of the Coif. Admitted to practice Alabama 1968. Began legal practice Fort Payne 1969. Clerk U.S. Court of Appeals 1968-69.
Chairman Alabama Judicial Inquiry Commission. Member Alabama Circuit Judges Association (Past President) and Alabama State Bar. Attended National College of the State Judiciary 1975 and American Academy of the Judiciary 1976. Democrat.
Office: 403 County Courthouse, 300 Grand Avenue South, Fort Payne 35967.
Telephone: (256) 845-8540.

COLEMAN, Ralph E., Jr. *(Judge, Jefferson County District Court Bessemer Division)* Appointed by Governor George C. Wallace to term beginning May 8, 1984. Elected Nov 1986, 1992 and 1998. Current term expires Jan 2005. Born Tuscaloosa Alabama May 9, 1957. Southern Baptist. Educated at Samford University A.B. 1979 and Cumberland School of Law J.D. cum laude 1982. Admitted to practice Alabama 1982. In legal practice Birmingham 1982-84.
Member Alabama District Judges Association (Past President), Alabama State Bar, Bessemer and Birmingham Bar Associations. Republican. Interests include travel, history and golf.
Office: 517 Courthouse Annex, 1801 Third Avenue North, Bessemer 35020.
Telephone: (205) 481-4195.
Fax: (205) 481-8097

COLVIN, Gus W., Jr. *(Judge, Calhoun County District Court)* Elected Nov 1988 to term beginning Jan 1989. Reelected 1994 and 2000. Current term expires Jan 2007. Educated at Mississippi State University B.A. 1962 and University of Mississippi J.D. 1965. Member Phi Alpha Delta. Admitted to practice Mississippi 1965 and Alabama 1965. In legal practice Anniston Alabama 1966-89.
Office: Calhoun County Courthouse, 25 West Eleventh Street, Anniston 36201.
Telephone: (256) 231-1870.

COLVIN, Ira B. *(Judge, Pickens County District Court)*
Mailing address: P.O. Box 426, Carrollton 35447.
Office: One Courthouse Square, Carrollton 35447.
Telephone: (205) 367-2076.

COODY, Charles S. *(Magistrate Judge, United States District Court Middle District of Alabama)* Appointed by U.S. District Court judges.
Mailing address: P.O. Box 158, Montgomery 36101-0158.
Telephone: (334) 954-3700.

COOGLER, L. Scott *(Presiding Judge, Alabama Circuit Court Sixth Judicial Circuit)*
Office: 318 Tuscaloosa County Courthouse, 714 Greensboro Avenue, Tuscaloosa 35401.
Telephone: (205) 349-3870.

CRAIG, George T. *(Presiding Judge, Alabama Circuit Court Thirty-ninth Judicial Circuit)* Appointed by Governor Harold Guy Hunt to term beginning Oct 1, 1991. Former Judge, Limestone County District Court.
Mailing address: P.O. Box 1257, Athens 35612.
Office: Courthouse Square, Athens 35611.
Telephone: (256) 233-6440.

CRAWLEY, John B. *(Judge, Alabama Court of Civil Appeals)* Elected to term beginning Jan 1995. Reelected 2000, current term expires Jan 2007. Born Troy Alabama Feb 28, 1940. Baptist. Educated at Auburn University, Troy State University and University of Alabama. Law Clerk to Alabama Court of Appeals. Admitted to practice Alabama 1966, U.S. Court of Appeals Eleventh Circuit and U.S. Supreme Court. In legal practice Dothan 1968-69 and Troy 1969-91 and 1993-94. Judge, Alabama Circuit Court Twelfth Judicial Circuit April 1991 to Jan 1993, appointed by Governor Harold Guy Hunt.
Assistant Attorney General Department of Revenue Alabama. Member Alabama State Bar and American Bar Association. Member Chief Justice Perry Hooper's Task Force on Judicial Elections. Deacon Banks Baptist Church.
Office: 300 Dexter Avenue, Montgomery 36104.
Telephone: (334) 242-4207.

CROW, Harold L. *(Presiding Judge, Alabama Circuit Court First Judicial Circuit)* Elected to term beginning Jan 17, 1995. Reelected 2000, current term expires Jan 2007. Born Thomasville Alabama Dec 4, 1943. Protestant. Educated at University of North Alabama B.S. 1967 and Jones Law School J.D. 1977. Member Sigma Delta Kappa. Admitted to practice Alabama 1977. Began legal practice Montgomery 1978. Former Judge, Clarke County District Court, assumed office June 3, 1980.
Member Alabama District Judges Association (President 1984-85), Alabama Circuit Judges Association and Alabama State Bar. Colonel USAR (retired).
Mailing address: P.O. Box 914, Grove Hill 36451.
Office: 117 Court Street, Grove Hill 36451.
Telephone: (251) 275-8667.

CROW, R. Allen *(Judge, Calhoun County District Court)* Appointed by Governor Forrest "Fob" James to term beginning Dec 1, 1979. Elected to subsequent terms.
Office: Calhoun County Courthouse, 25 West Eleventh Street, Anniston 36201.
Telephone: (256) 231-1830.

CROWSON, D. Al *(Presiding Judge, Alabama Circuit Court Eighteenth Judicial Circuit)* Appointed by Governor Harold Guy Hunt to term beginning Oct 1988. Elected 1990, 1996 and 2002. Current term expires Jan 2009. Born Bessemer Alabama Aug 30, 1945. Educated at University of Alabama B.S. 1967 and Birmingham School of Law J.D. 1973. Member Sigma Delta Kappa. Admitted to practice Alabama 1973. In legal practice Birmingham 1973-88.
Faculty member Birmingham School of Law 1974-79 and Jefferson State Junior College 1975-88. Member Alabama State Bar, Birmingham and Shelby County Bar Associations. Accountant 1967-73. Board of Directors Lions Club and Salvation Army. Member First and Ten Club University of Alabama. Enjoys tennis and fishing.
Office: 112 North Main Street, Columbiana 35051.
Telephone: (205) 669-3760.

CULBERSON, Mary Elizabeth *(Judge, Elmore County District Court)* Elected to term beginning Jan 21, 1997. Reelected Nov 5, 2002, current term expires Jan 20, 2009. Admitted to practice Alabama 1988, U.S. District Courts Middle 1988, Northern 1988 and Southern 1988 Districts of Alabama and U.S. Court of Appeals Eleventh Circuit 1988.
Assistant Attorney General Alabama 1988-97. Member American Judges Association. Attended The National Judicial College 1998 and 2001. USAF 1972-76.
Mailing address: P.O. Box 924, Wetumpka 36092.
Office: 8935 Highway 231 North, Wetumpka 36092.
Telephone: (334) 567-1154.

DAVIS, Harwell G., III *(Magistrate Judge, United States District Court Northern District of Alabama)* Appointed by U.S. District Court judges to term beginning March 19, 1998. Term expires March 2006.
Office: 103 U.S. Courthouse, 101 Holmes Avenue N.E., Huntsville 35801.
Telephone: (256) 539-7705.

DeMENT, Ira *(Senior Judge, United States District Court Middle District of Alabama)* Appointed for life by President George Bush to term beginning March 18, 1992. Chief Judge Wake Island Court of Appeals since 1985. Assumed Senior status, serves by assignment. Born Birmingham Alabama Dec 21, 1931. Methodist. Educated at University of Alabama A.B. 1953 LL.B. 1958 replaced by J.D. 1969. Law Clerk to Hon. Pelham J. Merrill, Alabama Supreme Court 1958-59. Member Phi Alpha Delta and Sigma Chi. Admitted to practice Alabama 1958, U.S. District Courts Middle 1958, Southern 1967 and Northern 1977 Districts of Alabama and District of Columbia 1972, U.S. Courts of Appeals Fifth 1958, District of Columbia 1972 and Eleventh 1981 Circuits, U.S. Supreme Court 1966, U.S. Tax Court 1972, U.S. Court of Federal Claims 1972, U.S. Court of Military Appeals 1972 and U.S. Customs Court 1976. In legal practice Montgomery 1961-69 and 1977-80. Hearing Officer Alabama Environmental Management Commission 1989-92.
Assistant City Attorney and Legal Advisor to Police and Fire Departments Montgomery 1965-69. Special Assistant Attorney General Alabama 1966-69, 1981-82 and 1983-92. U.S. Attorney Middle District of Alabama May 19, 1969 to Aug 31, 1997. General Counsel Commission on Aging 1980-82 and Air War College Foundation 1981-92 Alabama. Special Counsel Department of Youth Services Alabama 1989-92. General Counsel Humane Society and Animal Shelter Montgomery 1990-92. Author "A Plea for the Condemned" 29 No. 4 *The Alabama Lawyer* Oct 1968. Member Editorial Advisory Board *The Alabama Lawyer* 1966-72. Instructor U.S. Army Infantry School 1962-63, Agency, Criminal and

DEMENT, IRA—*Continued*

Constitutional Law Jones Law School 1962-64, Montgomery Police Academy 1964-77 and Law Enforcement University of Alabama Extension Service 1967. Lecturer on Constitutional Law Alabama Police Academy 1971-75 and Woodrow Wilson School of Public and International Affairs Princeton University 1977. Adjunct Faculty The New College University of Alabama 1974-75. Adjunct Professor Department of Psychology University of Alabama 1975-92. Member 1973-75 and Chairman 1976 Subcommittee on Professional Proficiency and Communication Attorney General's Advisory Committee of U.S. Attorneys. Member Judicial Election Participation Committee 1976-77. Attorney General's Task Force on Federal-State Responsibility Alabama 1986-87. Former Member National Panel of Arbitrators American Arbitration Association, National District Attorneys Association, American Judicature Society, The Association of Trial Lawyers of Alabama, Montgomery Trial Lawyers Association, The Association of Trial Lawyers of America, National Association of Former U.S. Attorneys, Alabama Criminal Defense Lawyers Association, National Association of Criminal Defense Lawyers and Air Force Retired Judge Advocates Association. Member American Inns of Court, Alabama State Bar (Committee on Congestion in Appellate Courts 1971-72, Task Force on Minimum Standards for Criminal Justice 1973-75, Judicial Election Participation Committee 1976-77, Co-chairman Military Law Committee 1984-92, Family Law Section), The District of Columbia Bar, Montgomery County (Executive Committee 1967), Federal (Charter Member Montgomery Alabama Chapter) and American (Section of Criminal Law) Bar Associations.

Listed in *Who's Who in the South and Southwest* since 1971, *Who's Who in Government* 1972-77, Contemporary Notables since 1974, Men of Achievement since 1975, *Who's Who in the United States* 1975, *International Who's Who in Community Service* since 1975, Community Leaders and Noteworthy Americans 1976, *Who's Who in American Law* 1977, *Who's Who in Society* since 1980, *Who's Who in the World* since 1987 and *Who's Who in America* since 1993. Recipient Award for Distinguished Service from International Association of Firefighters 1975, Rockefeller Public Service Award in Management of Social Conflict from Woodrow Wilson School of Public and International Affairs Princeton University 1976, Significant Sig Award from Sigma Chi 1998 and Judicial Award of Merit from Alabama State Bar 1998. Republican. Served to First Lieutenant 1953-55 and Lieutenant Colonel 1955-74 USAR. Major General USAFR (retired). Mobilization Assistant to JAG USAF. Distinguished Military Graduate University of Alabama 1953. Recipient Army of Occupational Medal (Germany) 1954, National Service Defense Medal 1954, Armed Forces Reserve Medal with two hourglass devices 1963, 1973 and 1983. Meritorious Service Medal 1976, Legion of Merit 1982, State of Alabama Distinguished Service Medal 1989, Air Force Distinguished Service Medal 1989, Air Force Longevity Service Award Ribbon with Silver and three Bronze Oak Leaf Clusters, Army Expert Marksmanship Badge (Rifle, Carbine and Pistol), Air Force Expert Marksmanship Ribbon with Bronze Star Device (Rifle and Pistol) and Army Service Ribbon. Former Member Fraternal Order of Police, Alabama Peace Officers Association, Reserve Officers Association of the U.S., Air Force Association, Alabama Historical Association, Alabama Association of Chiefs of Police (honorary) and Montgomery Firefighters Association Local 1444 (honorary). Member Advisory Board Law Enforcement Academy University of Alabama 1972-92 and Auburn University at Montgomery 1975-92. Director Alumni Association 1973-75 and Presidential Advisory Council 1977-78. Life Member Air War College Alumni Association since 1981 and Air War College Foundation since 1985. Member The Eleventh Circuit Historical Society 1984-92 and 32° Scottish Rite Mason and Shriner.

Mailing address: P.O. Box 2149, Montgomery 36102-2149.

Telephone: (334) 954-3680.

DOBSON, John J. *(Judge, Blount County District Court)* Appointed by Governor Harold Guy Hunt to term beginning Nov 21, 1988. Elected to subsequent terms.

Office: 209 Blount County Courthouse, 220 Second Avenue East, Oneonta 35121.

Telephone: (205) 625-4147.

DOBSON, Tommy R. *(Judge, Talladega County District Court)* Appointed by Governor Harold Guy Hunt to term beginning Jan 1989. Elected Nov 1990, 1996 and 2002. Current term expires Jan 2009. Born Sylacauga Alabama March 24, 1949. Protestant. Educated at Auburn University I.E. 1971 and Birmingham School of Law J.D. 1980. Admitted to practice Alabama 1980 and U.S. District Courts Northern 1981 and Middle 1984 Districts of Alabama. In legal practice Pelham 1980-83 and Sylacauga 1981-88.

Chairman Talladega County Juvenile Task Force. Member Talladega County Mental Health Committee on Child Abuse, Alabama District Judges Association (Secretary-Treasurer), Juvenile Judges Association, Alabama State Bar, Talladega County and American Bar Associations. Previously worked as Plant Engineer, FMC Corp., Staff Engineer The Commodore Corp. and Caterpillar Sales Representative Thompson Tractor Co. Past Coordinator Alabama Airport Development Project. Commissioner Alabama Department of Aeronautics. Chairman Sylacauga Airport Board. Advisory Member Children's Trust Fund of Alabama. President Sylacauga Flying Club. Member Sylacauga Chamber of Commerce and Administrative Board First United Methodist Church. Enjoys flying and boating.

Mailing address: P.O. Box 1238, Sylacauga 35150.

Office: 400 North Norton, Sylacauga 35150.

Telephone: (256) 249-1003.

DORROUGH, Richard H. *(Judge, Alabama Circuit Court Fifteenth Judicial Circuit)* Appointed by George C. Wallace to term beginning Oct 1, 1984. Elected to subsequent terms.

Office: Courthouse Annex, 100 South Lawrence Street, Montgomery 36104-4240.

Telephone: (334) 832-2556.

DOWLING, John C. *(Judge, Coffee County District Court)*

Mailing address: P.O. Box 311446, Enterprise 36331-1446.

Office: 104 North Edwards Street, Enterprise 36330.

Telephone: (334) 393-2949.

DRINKARD, Wesley Wade *(Judge, Marengo County District Court)* Assumed office Oct 1, 2000. Born Dec

DRINKARD, WESLEY WADE—*Continued*

15, 1944. Educated at Birmingham-Southern College 1963-65 and University of Alabama School of Law J.D. 1969. In legal practice Alabama 1969-89.

Assistant District Attorney Seventeenth Judicial Circuit 1990-2000. Member Alabama State Bar. Named Prosecutor of the Year by Alabama Child Support Enforcement Association 1995. Recipient Silver Beaver Award from Boy Scouts of America. President Alabama Child Support Association 1996-97 and 1999-2000. District Governor District 6880, 2000-2001. Board of Directors Camp ASCCA (Easter Seal Camp for Special children and adults) since 2001. Former Member Board of Directors Harriet's House (domestic abuse shelter). Former Packmaster Cub Scout Post 42. Former Scoutmaster Boy Scout Troop 42. Rotary Paul Harris Fellow. Advisory Board Black Warrior Council. Eagle Scout Boy Scouts of America. Lifetime Member Linden United Methodist Church. Member Linden County Club (Past President and Former Member Board of Directors).

Mailing address: P.O. Box 480445, Linden 36748.
Office: 101 East Coats Avenue, Linden 36748.
Telephone: (334) 295-8774.
E-mail address: wdrinkard@westal.net

EMFINGER, Michael O. *(Judge, Bullock County District Court)* Appointed by Governor Harold Guy Hunt to term beginning March 23, 1990.

Mailing address: P.O. Box 8, Union Springs 36089.
Office: 217 North Prairie, Union Springs 36089.
Telephone: (334) 738-2730.

ENGLAND, John Henry, Jr. *(Judge, Alabama Circuit Court Sixth Judicial Circuit)* Appointed by Governor Don Siegelman. Born Uniontown Alabama June 5, 1947. Educated at Tuskegee University B.A. 1969 and University of Alabama School of Law J.D. 1974. Member Alpha Phi Alpha. In legal practice Tuscaloosa 1974-93. Former Judge and Presiding Judge, Alabama Circuit Court Sixth Judicial Circuit, appointed by Governor James E. Folsom June 21, 1993. Associate Justice, Alabama Supreme Court Sept 1999 to Jan 2001.

Member Alabama Circuit Judges Association, Alabama Lawyers Association (President 1988-89), American Inns of Court, Tuscaloosa County and National Bar Associations. U.S. Army 1970-72. Former Member Tuscaloosa City Council and State Democratic Executive Committee. Graduate Leadership Alabama 1996. Board of Trustees University of Alabama Systems. Trustee and Sunday School teacher Bailey Tabernacle Church. Board Member Boys and Girls Clubs, Barnes Branch YMCA, Community Services Program of West Alabama, Salvation Army, Boy Scouts, Black Warrior Council and 21st Century Youth Leadership. Member Jaycees, Exchange Club, Tuscaloosa Civitan Club and Tuscaloosa Tennis Club.

Office: Tuscaloosa County Courthouse, Second Floor, 714 Greensboro Avenue, Tuscaloosa 35401.
Telephone: (205) 349-3870.

EVANS, David *(Judge, Alabama Circuit Court Twenty-seventh Judicial Circuit)* Born Gadsden Alabama June 20, 1947. Presbyterian. Educated at Georgia State University B.B.A. 1969 and University of Alabama J.D. 1975. Admitted to practice Alabama 1975. In legal practice Albertville 1975-77 and Boaz 1977-91. Former Judge, Marshall County District Court, elected to term beginning Jan 1991.

First Lieutenant U.S. Army 1969-71. Democrat. Enjoys hunting, fishing, biking, running and hiking.

Mailing address: P.O. Box 308, Guntersville 35976.
Office: 425 Gunter Avenue, Guntersville 35976.
Telephone: (256) 571-7776.

FANCHER, Eric M. *(Judge, Jefferson County District Court Bessemer Division)*

Office: 505 Courthouse Annex, 1801 Third Avenue North, Bessemer 35020.
Telephone: (205) 481-4190.

FERGUSON, Ralph A., Jr. *(Judge, Alabama Circuit Court Tenth Judicial Circuit Birmingham Division)* Appointed by Governor Forrest "Fob" James to term beginning Nov 9, 1995.

Office: 2124 Seventh Avenue North, Courtroom 240, Birmingham 35203.
Telephone: (205) 325-5562.

FIELDING, Jerry L. *(Presiding Judge, Alabama Circuit Court Twenty-ninth Judicial Circuit)* Elected to term beginning Jan 18, 1983. Reelected 1988, 1994 and 2000. Current term expires Jan 2007.

Mailing address: P.O. Box 541, Talladega 35161.
Office: 148 East Street North, Talladega 35160.
Telephone: (256) 761-2108, 245-2116.

FILMORE, William H. *(Judge, Dale County District Court)*

Office: Dale County Courthouse, Court Square, Ozark 36361.
Telephone: (334) 774-4431.

FLEMING, Charles W., Jr. *(Judge, Geneva County District Court)* Elected to term beginning Jan 19, 1993. Reelected 1998, current term expires Jan 2005.

Mailing address: P.O. Box 758, Geneva 36340.
Office: 200 North Commerce Street, Geneva 36340.
Telephone: (334) 684-5630.

FLOYD, Joseph L. "Lang" *(Judge, Alabama Circuit Court Twenty-eighth Judicial Circuit)* Appointed by Governor Don Siegelman Jan 16, 2001. Elected 2002, current term expires Jan 2009. Born Dothan Alabama July 17, 1956. Southern Baptist. Educated at Troy State University B.S. 1978 and Cumberland School of Law of Samford University J.D. 1984. Law Clerk to Hon. Floyd C. Enfinger, Jr., Alabama Circuit Court Twenty-eighth Judicial Circuit 1984-85. Admitted to practice Alabama 1984, U.S. District Court Southern District of Alabama 1985, Florida 1986 and U.S. Supreme Court 1988. In legal practice Mobile Alabama 1985-86 and Daphne and Fairhope Alabama 1986-97. Judge, Fairhope Municipal Court 1992-97. Judge, Baldwin County District Court Jan 22, 1997 to Jan 15, 2001.

Member Alabama State Bar. Major USAR since 1988. Republican. Member Baldwin County and Alabama Republican Party. Board Member Boys and Girls Clubs of South Alabama. Member Eastern Shore Sertoma Club. Enjoys golf.

Office: 312 Courthouse Square, Suite 21, Bay Minette 36507.
Telephone: (251) 937-0237.

FORD, Aubrey, Jr. *(Judge, Macon County District Court)* Appointed by Governor George C. Wallace Sept 2, 1977. Elected 1978, 1984, 1990, 1996 and 2002. Current term expires Jan 2009. Born Philadelphia Pennsylvania Dec 14, 1948. Baptist. Educated at Community

FORD, AUBREY, JR.—*Continued*

College of Philadelphia A.A. 1969, Lincoln University B.A. 1970 and Howard University J.D. 1974. Member Alpha Phi Alpha. Admitted to practice Pennsylvania 1974, Alabama 1975, U.S. Court of Appeals Fifth Circuit 1975 and U.S. District Court Middle District of Alabama 1975. In legal practice Tuskegee Alabama 1975-77.

With Alabama Attorney General's Office 1975. Chairman Alabama Unified Judicial System Personnel Appeals Board. Member Alabama District Judges Association (President 1988-89), Alabama Juvenile Judges Association, The Association of Trial Lawyers of America, National Council of Juvenile and Family Court Judges, National and American Bar Associations. Recipient Langston Chapter Phi Alpha Delta Service Award, Miles College School of Law Founder's Day Award and Alabama Child Support Association's Judge of the Year Award 1988. Advisory Board member Judicial Education Project Institute for Court Management 1987-90. Board member Eastern Regional Child Support Association 1988-90. Democrat. Member Tuskegee Chamber of Commerce, Tuskegee Optimist Club and Tuskegee Chapter Howard University Alumni Association. Deacon Greenwood Missionary Baptist Church, Tuskegee. Enjoys reading, traveling and public speaking.

Mailing address: P.O. Box 830703, Tuskegee 36083.
Office: 101 East Northside Street, Tuskegee 36083.
Telephone: (334) 727-6110.

FULLER, Ben A. *(Judge, Alabama Circuit Court Nineteenth Judicial Circuit)* Appointed by Governor Forrest "Fob" James to term beginning Oct 7, 1996.

Mailing address: P.O. Box 680206, Prattville 36068.
Office: 134 North Court Street, Prattville 36067.
Telephone: (334) 361-3766, (205) 755-0311, (334) 567-1148.

FULLER, Mark E. *(Judge, United States District Court Middle District of Alabama)* Appointed for life by President George W. Bush to term beginning Dec 2, 2002. Born Enterprise Alabama 1958. Educated at University of Alabama B.S. 1982 J.D. 1985. In legal practice Alabama 1985-96.

Office: U.S. Courthouse, 15 Lee Street, Montgomery 36104.
Telephone: (334) 954-3640.

FUNDERBURK, Eric B. *(Judge, Russell County District Court)*

Mailing address: P.O. Box 2488, Phenix City 36868.
Office: 501 Fourteenth Street, Phenix City 36868.
Telephone: (334) 297-1347.

GIVHAN, Margaret *(Judge, Montgomery County District Court)* Elected 1994 to term beginning Jan 15, 1995. Reelected 2000, current term expires Jan 2007. Born St. Louis Missouri. Episcopalian. Educated at University of Alabama B.A. 1968 and Jones School of Law J.D. 1982. Admitted to practice Alabama 1983, U.S. District Court Middle District of Alabama 1983, U.S. Court of Appeals Eleventh Circuit 1984 and U.S. Supreme Court 1986. In legal practice Montgomery 1983-90.

Author "Recent Decisions" Montgomery County Bar Association Newsletter 1986-94. Former Member American Bar Association. Member National Association of Women Judges, Alabama State Bar and Montgomery County Bar Association. Attended general jurisdiction course The National Judicial College Reno Nevada 1995. Republican.

Office: Montgomery County Courthouse, 251 South Lawrence Street, Montgomery 36104.
Telephone: (334) 832-1359.

GOSA, Lewis E. *(Judge, Lamar County District Court)* Appointed by Governor Harold Guy Hunt to term beginning Nov 8, 1988. Elected 1990, 1996 and 2002. Current term expires Jan 2009. Born Lamar County Alabama April 9, 1940. Southern Baptist. Educated at University of North Alabama B.S. 1962 and University of Alabama J.D. 1968. Admitted to practice Alabama 1968. In legal practice Vernon 1968-88.

Member Alabama State Bar. First Lieutenant U.S. Army 1962-65. Member Kiwanis Club.

Mailing address: P.O. Box 643, Vernon 35592.
Office: 330 First Street N.E., Vernon 35592.
Telephone: (205) 695-9427.

GRANADE, Callie V. *(Judge, United States District Court Southern District of Alabama)* Appointed for life by President George W. Bush to term beginning Feb 20, 2002. Born Lexington Virginia 1950. Educated at Hollins College B.A. 1972 and University of Texas School of Law J.D. 1975. Law Clerk to Hon. John C. Godbold, U.S. Court of Appeals Fifth Circuit 1975-76.

Office: U.S. Courthouse, 113 St. Joseph Street, Mobile 36602-3606.
Telephone: (251) 690-3133.

GREENE, George R. *(Judge, Alabama Circuit Court Twenty-sixth Judicial Circuit)* Former Judge, Russell County District Court, appointed by Governor George C. Wallace to term beginning Nov 9, 1979.

Mailing address: P.O. Box 820, Phenix City 36868.
Office: Russell County Courthouse, 501 Fourteenth Street, Phenix City 36867.
Telephone: (334) 297-4567.

GREENE, Paul W. *(Magistrate Judge, United States District Court Northern District of Alabama)* Appointed by U.S. District Court judges.

Office: 319 U.S. Courthouse, 1729 Fifth Avenue North, Birmingham 35203.
Telephone: (205) 278-1930.

GRIDER, Ralph H. *(Judge, Jackson County District Court)* Elected June 24, 1986 to term beginning Jan 19, 1987. Reelected 1992 and 1999. Current term expires Jan 2005. Born Scottsboro Alabama March 17, 1954. United Methodist. Educated at University of North Alabama B.A. with honors 1976 and Cumberland School of Law of Samford University J.D. 1980. Member Phi Alpha Delta. Admitted to practice Alabama 1980. In legal practice Scottsboro 1980-86.

Member Alabama State Bar, Jackson County and American Bar Associations. Member Boy Scouts of America, Kiwanis Club and Scottsboro-Jackson County Chamber of Commerce. Enjoys fishing, traveling and antiques.

Office: Jackson County Courthouse, 102 Laurel Street, Scottsboro 35768.
Telephone: (256) 574-9355.

GRIMES, J. Kevin *(Judge, Alabama Circuit Court Ninth Judicial Circuit)* Elected Nov 1998 to term beginning Jan 19, 1999. Term expires Jan 19, 2005. Born East Point Georgia Dec 25, 1966. Baptist. Educated at

GRIMES, J. KEVIN—*Continued*

Jacksonville State University B.S. 1988 and University of Alabama School of Law J.D. 1991. Admitted to practice Alabama 1991 and U.S. District Court Northern District of Alabama 1991. In legal practice Centre 1991-99.

Attended Alabama Judicial College.

Office: 300 County Courthouse Annex, 102 Main Street, Centre 35960.

Telephone: (256) 927-0500.

E-mail address: judge.grimes@alalinc.net

GUIN, James C., III *(Judge, Tuscaloosa County District Court)* Elected to term beginning Jan 20, 1987. Reelected 1992 and 1998. Current term expires Jan 2005.

Office: Tuscaloosa County Courthouse, Sixth Floor, 714 Greensboro Avenue, Tuscaloosa 35401.

Telephone: (205) 349-3870.

GUIN, Junius Foy, Jr. *(Senior Judge, United States District Court Northern District of Alabama)* Appointed for life by President Richard M. Nixon to term beginning April 18, 1973. Assumed Senior status, serves by assignment. Born Russellville Alabama Feb 2, 1924. Member Church of Christ (Elder). Educated at Georgia Institute of Technology 1940-41, University of Alabama A.B. magna cum laude J.D. 1947 and Magic Valley Christian College LL.D. 1963. Member Phi Beta Kappa, Omicron Delta Kappa and Farrah Order of Jurisprudence (now Order of the Coif). Admitted to practice Alabama 1948. In legal practice Russellville 1948-73.

Adjunct Lecturer Cumberland School of Law of Samford University 1974-91 and University of Alabama School of Law 1977-91. Member American Judicature Society, The American Law Institute, Alabama Law Institute (Director 1969-73 and since 1976), World Peace Through Law Center, Alabama Supreme Court Advisory Committee on Rules of Civil Procedure 1971-73, Alabama State Bar (Board of Bar Commissioners 1965-73, Second Vice President 1969-70), Jefferson County and American (Special Committee on Residential Real Estate Transactions 1972-73) Bar Associations. First Chairman Judicial Commission of Alabama 1972-73. Recipient Award of Merit from Alabama State Bar 1973. Named Russellville Citizen of the Year 1973. First Lieutenant U.S. Army Infantry 1943-46. Republican State Finance Chairman 1972-73 and Republican County Chairman 1954-58 and 1971-72. Candidate for U.S. Senate from Alabama 1954. Chairman Alabama Lawyers Finance Committee to Reelect the President 1972. President Abstract Trust Co., Inc. 1958-73. Former Secretary Iuka TV Cable Co., Inc. and Haleyville TV Cable Co., Inc. Former Director First National Bank and Franklin Federal Savings and Loan Association of Russellville. Chairman Russellville City Planning Committee 1954-57. Rotarian. Member American Radio Relay League, Monday Morning Quarterback Club and Inverness Golf and Country Club. Enjoys amateur radio (W4RLS)—licensed since 1950.

Office: 619 U.S. Courthouse, 1729 Fifth Avenue North, Birmingham 35203.

Telephone: (205) 278-1830.

HADDOCK, Steven E. *(Presiding Judge, Alabama Circuit Court Eighth Judicial Circuit)* Elected to term beginning Jan 17, 1995. Reelected 2000, current term expires Jan 2007.

Mailing address: P.O. Box 668, Decatur 35602.

Office: 302 Lee Street, Decatur 35601.

Telephone: (256) 351-4750.

HALL, Karen Kimbrell *(Judge, Madison County District Court)* Appointed by Governor Forrest "Fob" James to term beginning April 5, 1996. Elected Nov 5, 1996 and 2002. Current term expires Jan 2009. Born Michigan Oct 28, 1960. Baptist. Educated at University of Florida B.A. 1981 and Cumberland School of Law of Samford University J.D. 1985. Listed in *Who's Who Among American Law Students.* First Place Southeastern Region and Second Place National Finalist National Mock Trial Competition 1984-85. Articles Editor American Journal of Trial Advocacy. Judicial Clerk to Hon. Robert P. Bradley, Alabama Court of Civil Appeals 1985-86. Admitted to practice Alabama 1986 and Florida 1986.

Assistant District Attorney Madison County 1986-96. Co-author *The Investigation and Prosecution of Child Abuse* National District Attorneys Association 1987 (Editor 2nd ed. 1993), "Alabama Standard Guidelines for Developing Local Community Protocols for Intervention in Child Sexual Abuse" 1988, *Best Practices Manual* National Network of Children's Advocacy Centers 1989 and "Multidisciplinary Teams Improve Services" National Resource Center of Child Sexual Abuse News 1992. Member Attorney General's Child Abuse/Domestic Violence Task Force 1989-90. Member Madison County Domestic Violence Task Force, Alabama Children's Justice Task Force, Alabama State Bar and Madison County Bar Association. Former Board Member Chi-Ho. Former Member Executive Committee Big Brothers/Big Sisters of North Alabama, Inc. Past President National Resource Center of Child Sexual Abuse. Past President and Board of Directors National Children's Advocacy Center. Founding Member Alabama Network of Children's Advocacy Centers and National Network of Children's Advocacy Center (Past President). Founding Steering Committee Member VOICES for Alabama Children. Superintendents Advisory Board Huntsville City Schools. Member Department of Human Resources Multidisciplinary Management Team and Alabama Day Care Association Council.

Office: Madison County Courthouse, 100 Northside Square, Huntsville 35801.

Telephone: (256) 532-3455.

HAMILTON, Laura W. *(Judge, Alabama Circuit Court Twenty-third Judicial Circuit)* Former Judge, Madison County District Court, elected to term beginning Jan 14, 1991.

Office: Madison County Courthouse, 100 Northside Square, Huntsville 35801.

Telephone: (256) 532-3631.

HAMNER, Herschel T., Jr. *(Judge, Alabama Circuit Court Sixth Judicial Circuit)* Elected to term beginning Jan 17, 1995. Reelected 2000, current term expires Jan 2007. Former Presiding Judge.

Office: Tuscaloosa County Courthouse, Fifth Floor, 714 Greensboro Avenue, Tuscaloosa 35401.

Telephone: (205) 349-3870.

HANCOCK, James H. *(Senior Judge, United States District Court Northern District of Alabama)* Appointed for life by President Richard M. Nixon to term begin-

HANCOCK, JAMES H.—*Continued*

ning April 1973. Assumed Senior status May 1, 1996, serves by assignment. Also serves U.S. Court of Appeals Eleventh Circuit. Born Montgomery Alabama April 30, 1931. Educated at University of Alabama at Tuscaloosa B.S. 1953 LL.B. 1957. Law Clerk to Hon. John L. Goodwyn, Alabama Supreme Court. In legal practice Birmingham 1957-73.

Office: 681 U.S. Courthouse, 1729 Fifth Avenue North, Birmingham 35203.

Telephone: (205) 278-1840.

HAND, William Brevard *(Senior Judge, United States District Court Southern District of Alabama)* Appointed for life by President Richard M. Nixon to term beginning Oct 1, 1971. Former Chief Judge. Assumed Senior status, serves by assignment. Born Mobile Alabama Jan 18, 1924. Member Dauphin Way United Methodist Church. Educated at University of Alabama B.S. LL.B. 1949 replaced by J.D. Honorary LL.D. University of Mobile. Admitted to practice Alabama 1949. Began legal practice Mobile 1949.

Author "Affirmative Action: La Mort de la Republique? A Second Cry From the Wilderness" 44 No. 1 Alabama L. Rev. 1, 1997. Member Federal District Judges Association, Alabama State Bar, Mobile and Federal Bar Associations. Former member Federation of Insurance Counsel, National Association of Railroad Trial Counsel, Alabama Defense Lawyers Association, The Defense Research Institute, Inc. and American Judicature Society. Private U.S. Army 1943-46. Member Alabama Republican Executive Committee 1964-71. Chairman Mobile County Republican Executive Committee 1968-71. Member Mystic Societies. Enjoys fishing, golfing and farming.

Office: U.S. Courthouse, 113 St. Joseph Street, Mobile 36602-3606.

Telephone: (251) 690-2821.

HARALSON, William W. *(Presiding Judge, Alabama Circuit Court Thirty-eighth Judicial Circuit)* Appointed by Governor James E. Folsom to term beginning April 1, 1994.

Office: 302 Jackson County Courthouse, 102 Laurel Street, Scottsboro 35768.

Telephone: (256) 574-9345.

HARD, James H., IV *(Judge, Alabama Circuit Court Tenth Judicial Circuit Birmingham Division)* Appointed by Governor Forrest "Fob" James to term beginning May 1, 1982. Elected to subsequent terms.

Office: 801 Richard Arrington Jr. Blvd. N., Room 406, Birmingham 35203.

Telephone: (205) 325-5349.

HARDAWAY, Eddie, Jr. *(Presiding Judge, Alabama Circuit Court Seventeenth Judicial Circuit)* Elected to term beginning Jan 17, 1995. Reelected 2000, current term expires Jan 2007. Former Judge, Sumter County District Court, assumed office Jan 1987.

Mailing address: P.O. Drawer 290, Livingston 35470.

Office: Franklin Street, Livingston 35470.

Telephone: (205) 652-6169.

HARDEMAN, Don L. *(Presiding Judge, Alabama Circuit Court Thirty-second Judicial Circuit)* Elected to term beginning Jan 17, 1995. Reelected 2000, current term expires Jan 2007.

Office: Cullman County Courthouse, 500 Second Avenue S.W., Cullman 35055.

Telephone: (256) 775-4765.

HARDESTY, Rhonda J. *(Judge, Chilton County District Court)*

Mailing address: P.O. Box 1187, Clanton 35046.

Office: Chilton County Courthouse, 500 Second Avenue North, Clanton 35045.

Telephone: (205) 755-1558.

HARDWICK, Johnny *(Judge, Alabama Circuit Court Fifteenth Judicial Circuit)*

Office: County Courthouse, 251 South Lawrence Street, Montgomery 36104-4279.

Telephone: (334) 832-4950.

HARPER, Robert M. *(Presiding Judge, Alabama Circuit Court Thirty-seventh Judicial Circuit)* Appointed by Governor George C. Wallace to term beginning July 16, 1986. Elected to subsequent terms.

Office: Lee County Justice Center, 2311 Gateway Drive, Opelika 36801.

Telephone: (334) 749-7158.

HARRINGTON, Hub *(Judge, Alabama Circuit Court Eighteenth Judicial Circuit)*

Office: County Courthouse, 112 North Main Street, Columbiana 35051.

Telephone: (205) 669-3760.

HARWOOD, Robert B., Jr. *(Associate Justice, Alabama Supreme Court)* Born Oct 17, 1939. Educated at University of the South 1958-59 and University of Alabama B.S. 1962 LL.B. 1963. Member Order of the Coif (President 1980-81). Admitted to practice Alabama 1963, U.S. District Courts Middle, Northern and Southern Districts of Alabama, U.S. Court of Appeals Eleventh Circuit and U.S. Supreme Court. Deputy City Judge, Tuscaloosa 1975-80. Former Judge, Alabama Circuit Court Sixth Judicial Circuit, appointed by Governor Harold Guy Hunt to term beginning Oct 9, 1991.

Special Assistant Attorney General 1969-75. Editor and Principal Author *Handbook on Alabama Appellate Procedures* Alabama Program of Continuing Legal Education Alabama State Bar 1967. Co-author and Co-editor revised edition *Handbook on Alabama Appellate Procedures* Alabama Bar Institute for Continuing Legal Education 1979. Lecturer on Law and Trial Advocacy University of Alabama School of Law 1971-83 and since 1989. Former Member The Defense Research Institute, Inc., Alabama Defense Lawyers Association, Tuscaloosa County Trial Lawyers Association, Alabama Trial Lawyers Association and The Association of Trial Lawyers of America. Fellow American College of Trial Lawyers. Advocate American Board of Trial Advocates. Board of Directors Alabama Association of Circuit Judges. Member Standing Committee on Appellate Procedure 1974-85, Civil Case Management Manual Committee since 1990, Pattern Jury Instructions-Civil Committee since 1991 and Batson Committee since 1994 Alabama Supreme Court. Member Tuscaloosa Inn of Court (President 1991-92), Alabama Law Institute, Alabama State Bar (Chairman Litigation Section 1990-91), Tuscaloosa County (President 1978-79) and American Bar Associations. Recipient Outstanding Alumnus Award from Farrah Law Society 1992 and Silver Beaver Award from

HARWOOD, ROBERT B., JR.—*Continued*

Boy Scouts of America 1994. Member Tuscaloosa County Civil Service Board 1969-73 and Exchange Club of Tuscaloosa (President Exchange Club of Greater Tuscaloosa 1967-68). Executive Board since 1976 and President 1993 The Black Warrior Council Boy Scouts of America. Board of Directors FOCUS On Senior Citizens of Tuscaloosa County since 1993. Member Leadership Association of The United Way of Tuscaloosa County, Inc. Vestry Member and Senior Warden Christ Episcopal Church 1991-94.
Office: 300 Dexter Avenue, Montgomery 36104.
Telephone: (334) 242-4593.

HATCHER, Jacqueline M. *(Judge, Alabama Circuit Court Thirty-first Judicial Circuit)*
Office: Colbert County Courthouse, 201 North Main Street, Tuscumbia 35674.
Telephone: (256) 386-8528.

HAWK, Howard G. *(Judge, Marshall County District Court)* Elected to term beginning Jan 16, 2001. Reelected Nov 2002, current term expires Jan 20, 2009. Born Florence Alabama Nov 4, 1957. Educated at University of Alabama at Birmingham B.A. with honors 1980 and University of Alabama School of Law J.D. 1983. Admitted to practice Alabama 1983. In legal practice Arab 1983-86 and 1993-2000.
FBI Agent 1986-92. Former Member State House of Representatives Alabama (Chair Ways and Means Committee 1994-00).
Mailing address: P.O. Box 608, Guntersville 35976.
Telephone: (256) 571-7779.
Fax: (256) 571-7857
E-mail address: hawkhg@mindspring.com

HEAD, Thomas E., III *(Presiding Judge, Alabama Circuit Court Twelfth Judicial Circuit)* Elected to term beginning Jan 17, 1995. Reelected 2000, current term expires Jan 2007.
Office: 1501 Forest Lake Drive, Elba 36323.
Telephone: (334) 897-5525.

HEREFORD, William E. *(Presiding Judge, Alabama Circuit Court Thirtieth Judicial Circuit)* Appointed by Governor Harold Guy Hunt to term beginning June 1, 1991.
Office: 307 County Courthouse, 1815 Cogswell Avenue, Pell City 35125.
Telephone: (205) 338-9491.

HESTER, Sharon H. *(Presiding Judge, Alabama Circuit Court Thirty-fourth Judicial Circuit)* Former Judge, Franklin County District Court, elected to term beginning Jan 17, 1995.
Mailing address: P.O. Box 148, Russellville 35653.
Office: 510 North Jackson Street, Russellville 35653.
Telephone: (256) 332-8893.

HIGHTOWER, William G. *(Judge, Pike County District Court)* Assumed office Jan 16, 1977. Elected to subsequent terms.
Office: Pike County Courthouse, Church Street, Troy 36081.
Telephone: (334) 566-5222.

HILL, James E., Jr. *(Judge, St. Clair County District Court)* Elected to term beginning Jan 17, 1995. Reelected 2000, current term expires Jan 2007.
Office: 308 St. Clair County Courthouse, 1815 Cogswell Avenue, Pell City 35125.
Telephone: (205) 338-3869.

HOBBS, Truman M. *(Senior Judge, United States District Court Middle District of Alabama)* Appointed for life by President Jimmy Carter to term beginning April 14, 1980. Former Chief Judge. Assumed Senior status Feb 8, 1991, serves by assignment. Born Selma Alabama Feb 8, 1921. Episcopalian. Educated at University of North Carolina A.B. 1942 and Yale Law School LL.B. 1948. Law Clerk to Justice Hugo Black, U.S. Supreme Court 1948-49. Member Phi Beta Kappa, Phi Delta Phi and Delta Kappa Epsilon. Admitted to practice Alabama 1948. Began legal practice Birmingham 1949. In legal practice Montgomery.
Author "Scope of Appellate Review in F.E.L.A. Cases" University of Tennessee L. Rev. 1958 and "Products Liability—Legal Battleground of the 1960's" 23 Alabama Lawyer 14, 1962. Fellow American College of Trial Lawyers and International Academy of Trial Lawyers. Member Alabama State Bar, Montgomery County and American Bar Associations. Lieutenant USN 1942-46.
Office: Federal Building, 15 Lee Street, Montgomery 36104.
Telephone: (334) 954-3750.

HOBBS, Truman M., Jr. *(Judge, Alabama Circuit Court Fifteenth Judicial Circuit)*
Office: Montgomery County Courthouse, 251 South Lawrence Street, Montgomery 36104-4279.
Telephone: (334) 832-4950.

HOLLEY, Joel G. *(Judge, Chambers County District Court)* Appointed by Governor Forrest "Fob" James to term beginning April 24, 1980. Elected to subsequent terms.
Office: Chambers County Courthouse, Two Lafayette Street, Lafayette 36862.
Telephone: (334) 864-4320.

HOLLOWAY, Denny L. *(Judge, Alabama Circuit Court Twentieth Judicial Circuit)* Elected to term beginning Jan 17, 1989. Reelected 1994 and 2000. Current term expires Jan 2007. Former Presiding Judge. Former Judge, Houston County District Court.
Mailing address: P.O. Drawer 6406, Dothan 36302.
Office: 114 North Oates Street, Dothan 36303.
Telephone: (334) 677-4848.

HOLT, Jenifer C. *(Judge, Alabama Circuit Court Thirty-eighth Judicial Circuit)* Appointed by Governor Forrest "Fob" James to term beginning Oct 1, 1996.
Office: 337 Jackson County Courthouse, Market Street, Scottsboro 35768.
Telephone: (256) 574-9350.

HORN, Allwin E., III *(Judge, Alabama Circuit Court Tenth Judicial Circuit Birmingham Division)* Appointed by Governor Forrest "Fob" James to term beginning March 28, 1996.
Office: 716 Richard Arrington Jr. Blvd. N., Courtroom 350, Birmingham 35203.
Telephone: (205) 325-5365.

HOUSTON, J. Gorman, Jr. *(Associate Justice, Alabama Supreme Court)* Appointed by Governor George Wallace to term beginning Sept 16, 1985. Elected 1986, 1992 and 1998. Current term expires 2004. Born Eufaula Alabama March 11, 1933. Methodist. Educated at Auburn University B.S. 1955 and University of Alabama School of Law LL.B. 1956 replaced by J.D. 1969. Law Clerk to Chief Justice Ed Livingston, Alabama Supreme Court 1956-57. Member Sigma Nu, Phi Eta Sigma, Phi Kappa Phi and Squires. Admitted to practice Alabama 1956. In legal practice Eufaula 1960-85.

Author "Punitive Damages: A Historical Perspective" The Alabama Lawyer 1991. Important Decisions: Purvis v. PPG Industries, Inc. 502 So.2d 714, 70 ALR 4th 16, 1987; Entrekin v. Atlantic Richfield Co. 519 So.2d 447, 80 ALR 4th 963, 1987; Green Oil Co. v. Hornsby 539 So.2d 218, 1989; Ex parte Bayliss 550 So.2d 986, 1989; and Ex parte Frazier 562 So.2d 560, 1989. Member Alabama Bar Examiners' Association (Bar Examiner 1979-82), Alabama State Bar (Bar Commissioner 1982-85) and Barbour County Bar Association (President 1975). Attended numerous Continuing Legal Education programs Cumberland School of Law and County Bar Associations and Judicial Conferences for the Alabama Administrative Office of Courts. Named Citizen of the Year Eufaula 1979. Recipient Alumni Achievement in Humanities Award from Auburn University 1993. USAF 1957-60. Mayor pro tem/Alderman City of Eufaula. Past President Eufaula and Barbour County Chamber of Commerce, Heritage Association, Kiwanis Club, Rotary Club, Hospital Association and Water Works and Sewer Board. Chairman Eufaula Sesquicentennial Committee 1973. Trustee Eufaula Library Board. Chairman Administrative Board, Sunday School Teacher and Lay Leader First United Methodist Church of Eufaula. Member Advisory Council R.S.V.P.

Office: 300 Dexter Avenue, Montgomery 36104.

Telephone: (334) 242-4587.

HUGHES, Jack W. *(Judge, Alabama Circuit Court Seventh Judicial Circuit)* Appointed by Governor Harold Guy Hunt to term beginning Feb 4, 1988. Elected 1990, 1996 and 2002. Current term expires Jan 2009. Born Birmingham Alabama Oct 7, 1946. Baptist. Educated at Jacksonville State University B.S. 1973 and Birmingham School of Law J.D. 1982. Admitted to practice Alabama 1984. In legal practice Anniston 1984-88.

Member Alabama Council of Family and Juvenile Court Judges, Alabama Circuit Judges Association, Alabama State Bar and Calhoun County Bar Association. Participant General Jurisdiction 1988 and Sentencing 1988 Courses The National Judicial College. E-4 U.S. Army 1967-69. Chief of Police Valdosta Georgia and Selma Alabama. Police Captain Anniston Alabama. Board of Directors Boy's Club, Children's Trust Fund and Coosa Valley Regional Juvenile Detention Center. Enjoys family, church and fishing.

Office: 210 Calhoun County Courthouse, 25 West Eleventh Street, Anniston 36201.

Telephone: (256) 231-1735, 463-2651.

HUGHES, R. O. *(Judge, Jefferson County District Court Birmingham Division)* Appointed by Governor Harold Guy Hunt to term beginning Feb 1, 1993.

Office: 801 Richard Arrington Jr. Blvd. N., Room 206, Birmingham 35203.

Telephone: (205) 325-5018.

HUGHSTON, Harold V., Jr. *(Presiding Judge, Alabama Circuit Court Thirty-first Judicial Circuit)* Appointed by Governor Forrest "Fob" James to term beginning Dec 30, 1998. Elected 2000, current term expires 2007. Born Sheffield Alabama Jan 9, 1954. Presbyterian. Educated at University of Alabama B.A. 1976 J.D. 1979. Member Bench and Bar Honor Society. Admitted to practice Alabama 1981, Florida 1981 and U.S. District Court 1981. In legal practice Tuscumbia Alabama 1981-98.

Member Alabama Circuit Judges Association, Alabama State Bar and The Florida Bar. Democrat.

Office: Colbert County Courthouse, 201 North Main Street, Tuscumbia 35674.

Telephone: (256) 386-8526.

JACKSON, Ronald E. *(Judge, Shelby County District Court)* Elected Nov 1990 to term beginning Jan 1991. Reelected Nov 1996 and Nov 2002. Current term expires Jan 2009. Born Pensacola Florida Nov 26, 1946. Christian. Educated at Harding University B.A. 1968, Abilene Christian University M.A. 1973 and University of Alabama School of Law J.D. 1980. Admitted to practice Alabama 1981 and U.S. District Court Northern District of Alabama 1981. In legal practice Pelham 1981-91.

Member Alabama State Bar and Birmingham Bar Association. Attended and taught numerous conferences and seminars. Teacher 1968-69 and 1971-72 and Administrative Assistant to the Superintendent 1973-78 Conecuh County Board of Education. Legal Counsel 1984-90 and Executive Committee 1984-98 Shelby County Republican Party. Member Alabama Republican Party. Board of Managers and Former Board Chairman YMCA Shelby County. Board of Directors Family Connection, Inc. (formerly Shelby County Youth Services and Attention Home). Enjoys working with youth, gardening and youth and adult sports.

Mailing address: P.O. Box 1398, Columbiana 35051.

Office: 112 North Main Street, Columbiana 35051.

Telephone: (205) 669-3787.

JACKSON, S. Edward *(Judge, Alabama Circuit Court Twentieth Judicial Circuit)* Appointed by Governor Harold Guy Hunt to term beginning Nov 7, 1987. Elected to subsequent terms. Current term expires Jan 2009. Former Presiding Judge. Born Dothan Alabama March 30, 1948. Baptist. Educated at Samford University B.A. 1970 J.D. 1973. Admitted to practice Alabama 1973 and U.S. District Court District of Alabama 1975. In legal practice Dothan Sept 1973 to Nov 1987.

Assistant District Attorney Twentieth Judicial Circuit April 1974 to Nov 1977. Member Alabama State Bar and Houston County Bar Association. Republican. Member Kiwanis. Enjoys hunting, fishing and tree farming. Personal Statement or Quote: "Honesty is the best policy."

Mailing address: P.O. Box 6406, Dothan 36302.

Office: 100 North Oates Street, Dothan 36303.

Telephone: (334) 677-4854.

JOHNSON, Albert L. *(Presiding Judge, Alabama Circuit Court Twenty-sixth Judicial Circuit)* Elected to term beginning Jan 21, 1997. Born Columbus Georgia June 5, 1950. Baptist. Educated at Huntingdon College B.S. 1972, Georgia State University M.B.A. 1977 and Cumberland School of Law of Samford University J.D. 1980. Listed in *Who's Who in American Colleges and Universities*. Member Phi Alpha Delta. Admitted to

JOHNSON, ALBERT L.—*Continued*

practice Alabama 1980 and Georgia. Former Judge, Russell County District Court, appointed by Governor George C. Wallace to term beginning Oct 1, 1984.

Former Assistant District Attorney. Alabama House of Representatives 1982-83. Adjunct Professor Troy State University 1981-83. Member Alabama State Bar, Russell County and American Bar Associations. Attended The National Judicial College 1985. Democrat. Enjoys farming, hunting and fishing.

Mailing address: P.O. Box 1126, Phenix City 36868-1126.

Office: 501 Fourteenth Street, Phenix City 36867.

Telephone: (334) 297-1366.

JOHNSON, Inge P. *(Judge, United States District Court Northern District of Alabama)* Appointed for life by President Bill Clinton to term beginning Oct 23, 1998. Born Svendborg Denmark Dec 19, 1945. Presbyterian. Educated at City of London College, England Certificate in International Law 1968, University of Copenhagen School of Law, Denmark Candidatus Juris 1969 and University of Alabama School of Law M.C.L. 1970 J.D. 1973. Editorial Board Alabama Law Review 1972-73. Admitted to practice Denmark 1969 and Alabama 1973. Began legal practice Copenhagen Denmark 1970 and Tuscumbia Alabama 1973. Judge Muscle Shoals Municipal Court 1978-79. Judge and Presiding Judge Alabama Circuit Court Thirty-first Judicial Circuit Jan 16, 1979 to Oct 22, 1998.

Co-author "The Echoes of Gideon and Reverberations of Argersinger: Legal Representation of Indigent Criminal Defendants in Alabama" 25 No. 1 Alabama L. Rev. 229 Fall 1972 and "The Law of Trusts in Alabama" 25 No. 2 Alabama L. Rev. Spring 1973. Assistant Professor of Procedure University of Copenhagen School of Law Fall 1970 to Spring 1971. Member The Association of Trial Lawyers of America, Alabama Association of Circuit Judges, National Conference of State Trial Judges (Executive Committee 1982-86 and Chairman Committee on Crisis in the Jails and Prisons in America), Federal Judges Association, U.S. District Judges Association, Alabama State Bar, Colbert County and American (Judicial Administration Division) Bar Associations. Recipient Woman of the Year Award 1979 and Woman of Achievement Award 1979 from Colbert County Business and Professional Women's Club, Boss of the Year Award from Colbert County Legal Secretaries Association 1981-82, Friends of Federally Employed Women's Award from Tennessee Valley Authority 1982 and Daughters of the American Revolution Americanism Medal 2000. Board of Directors Alabama Law School Foundation, Inc. and Helen Keller Birthplace Foundation, Inc. Member Danish-American Heritage Association, Inc. and Danish Immigrant Museum.

Office: 361 U.S. Courthouse, 1729 Fifth Avenue North, Birmingham 35203.

Telephone: (205) 278-1970.

JOHNSON, Orson L. *(Judge, Jefferson County District Court Birmingham Division)* Appointed by Governor George C. Wallace to term beginning Jan 6, 1984. Elected to subsequent terms.

Office: 801 Richard Arrington Jr. Blvd. N., Room 306, Birmingham 35203.

Telephone: (205) 325-5013.

JOHNSTON, Joseph S. *(Judge, Alabama Circuit Court Thirteenth Judicial Circuit)* Appointed by Governor Forrest "Fob" James to term beginning April 18, 1997.

Office: Mobile Government Plaza, 205 Government Street, Mobile 36644-2217.

Telephone: (251) 574-8685.

JOHNSTONE, Douglas I. *(Associate Justice, Alabama Supreme Court)* Born Mobile Alabama Nov 15, 1941. Episcopalian. Educated at Rice University B.A. with honors 1963 and Tulane University J.D. 1966. Moot Court. Member Phi Delta Phi. Admitted to practice Alabama 1966, U.S. District Court Southern District of Alabama, U.S. Court of Appeals and U.S. Supreme Court. Began legal practice Mobile 1966. Judge, Mobile County District Court June 1, 1984 to Aug 28, 1985. Judge, Alabama Circuit Court Thirteenth Judicial Circuit Aug 28, 1985 to Jan 18, 1999.

State Representative 1974-78. Author "History of Provision for Equity in Alabama" Alabama Lawyer July 1966. Member Alabama State Bar and Mobile Bar Association. Named Outstanding Freshman Representative by Capitol Press Corps. Captain U.S. Army Combat Engineer Corps 1963-72. Democrat. Active in conservation and community improvement. Enjoys sailing and flying.

Office: 300 Dexter Avenue, Montgomery 36104.

Telephone: (334) 242-4597.

JOINER, J. Michael *(Judge, Alabama Circuit Court Eighteenth Judicial Circuit)* Elected to term beginning Jan 19, 1993. Reelected 1998, current term expires Jan 2005.

Mailing address: P.O. Box 975, Columbiana 35051.

Office: Shelby County Courthouse, 112 North Main Street, Columbiana 35051.

Telephone: (205) 669-3861.

JOLLEY, Allen T. *(Presiding Judge, Alabama Circuit Court Twenty-seventh Judicial Circuit)*

Mailing address: P.O. Box 546, Albertville 35950.

Office: 200 West Main Street, Albertville 35950.

Telephone: (256) 878-8597, 571-7776.

JONES, Clyde E. *(Judge, Alabama Circuit Court Tenth Judicial Circuit Birmingham Division)*

Office: 716 Richard Arrington Jr. Blvd. N., Room 713, Birmingham 35203-0044.

Telephone: (205) 325-5395.

JONES, Michael T. *(Judge, Alabama Circuit Court Eleventh Judicial Circuit)*

Office: 503 Lauderdale County Courthouse, 200 South Court Street, Florence 35630.

Telephone: (256) 760-5831.

JONES, Thomas R. *(Judge, Alabama Circuit Court Fourth Judicial Circuit)* Elected to term beginning Jan 17, 1995. Reelected 2000, current term expires Jan 2007. Former Presiding Judge.

Mailing address: P.O. Box 1225, Selma 36702.

Office: Courthouse Annex, 102 Church Street, Selma 36701.

Telephone: (205) 926-3103, (334) 874-2510, (334) 624-4334.

JONES-OSBORNE, Lillie *(Judge, Greene County District Court)*
Mailing address: P.O. Box 310, Eutaw 35462.
Office: 400 Morrow Avenue, Eutaw 35462.
Telephone: (205) 372-3143.

JORDAN, J. David *(Judge, Escambia County District Court)*
Mailing address: P.O. Box 1463, Brewton 36427-1463.
Office: 318 Bellville Avenue, Brewton 36426.
Telephone: (251) 867-0252.

KENDALL, Robert G. *(Presiding Judge, Alabama Circuit Court Thirteenth Judicial Circuit)* Appointed by Governor George Wallace to term beginning Oct 1, 1984. Elected Nov 1986, 1992 and 1998. Current term expires Jan 2005. Born Evergreen Alabama Nov 15, 1939. Educated at University of Alabama B.A. 1961 LL.B. 1963. Staff member University of Alabama Law Review 1962-63. Law Clerk to Hon. John L. Goodwyn, Alabama Supreme Court 1965. Admitted to practice Alabama 1963. In legal practice Mobile 1965-84. Magistrate, U.S. District Court Southern District of Alabama 1972-76. First Lieutenant U.S. Army 1963-65.
Office: Mobile Government Plaza, 205 Government Street, Mobile 36644-2217.
Telephone: (251) 574-8457.

KIMBROUGH, William E. *(Judge, Clarke County District Court)* Appointed by Governor Forrest "Fob" James to term beginning May 10, 1995.
Mailing address: P.O. Box 931, Grove Hill 36451.
Office: 114 Court Street, Grove Hill 36451.
Telephone: (251) 275-8296.

KING, Dan C., III *(Judge, Alabama Circuit Court Tenth Judicial Circuit Bessemer Division)*
Office: 615 Courthouse Annex, 1801 Third Avenue North, Bessemer 35020.
Telephone: (205) 481-4175.

KING, Julian M. *(Judge, Alabama Circuit Court Twenty-ninth Judicial Circuit)* Elected to term beginning Jan 17, 1995. Reelected 2000, current term expires Jan 2007.
Mailing address: P.O. Box 697, Talladega 35161.
Office: 148 East Street North, Talladega 35160.
Telephone: (205) 362-2112, (256) 761-2106.

KING, Tom, Jr. *(Judge, Alabama Circuit Court Tenth Judicial Circuit Birmingham Division)* Appointed by Governor Don Siegelman to term beginning March 29, 2001. Elected Nov 5, 2002, current term expires Jan 20, 2009. Born Tuscaloosa Alabama July 29, 1949. Baptist. Educated at University of Alabama B.S. 1971 and Cumberland School of Law J.D. 1976. Admitted to practice Alabama 1976. In legal practice Birmingham 1976-90 and 1996-2001.
Vice President and Corporate Counsel New South Federal Savings Bank Jan 1991 to Aug 1996.
Office: 716 Richard Arrington Jr. Blvd. N., Birmingham 35203.
Telephone: (205) 325-5025.

KING, William R. *(Judge, Crenshaw County District Court)* Assumed office Jan 16, 1977. Elected to subsequent terms.
Office: Crenshaw County Courthouse, 308 South Glennwood Avenue, Luverne 36049.
Telephone: (334) 335-6568.

LAIRD, R. Joel, Jr. *(Presiding Judge, Alabama Circuit Court Seventh Judicial Circuit)* Appointed by Governor Harold Guy Hunt to term beginning Aug 6, 1990. Elected to subsequent terms.
Office: Calhoun County Courthouse, 25 West Eleventh Street, Anniston 36201.
Telephone: (256) 231-1822, 463-2651.

LANE, Richard D. *(Judge, Alabama Circuit Court Thirty-seventh Judicial Circuit)* Elected 1998 to term beginning Jan 1999. Term expires Jan 2005. Born Port Jefferson New York Oct 25, 1941. Southern Baptist. Educated at Auburn University B.A. 1963 and University of Alabama LL.B. 1966. Member Phi Kappa Tau. Admitted to practice Alabama 1966, U.S. Court of Military Appeals 1967, Florida 1970 and U.S. Supreme Court 1974. Former Judge, Auburn Municipal Court and Camp Hill Municipal Court. Former Judge, Lee County District Court, elected to term beginning Jan 14, 1985.
Assistant State Attorney Clearwater Florida 1970-71 and Auburn Alabama. Member Alabama State Bar, The Florida Bar and Lee County Bar Association (Former President). USMC 1967-70 and Major USMCR 1970-80. Democrat. Member Lakeview Baptist Church (Sunday school teacher, lay speaker), Auburn Lions Club, American Legion, VFW, Elks, Masons, Eastern Star, Shriners, Gideon International and Lee County March of Dimes (Former Chairman). Enjoys hunting, family activities and coaching recreation league.
Office: Lee County Justice Center, 2311 Gateway Drive, Opelika 36801.
Telephone: (334) 749-7141.
Fax: (334) 749-2949
E-mail address: richard.lane@alacourt.state.al.us

LAPKOVITCH, Larry E. *(Judge, Walker County District Court)* Appointed by Governor Forrest "Fob" James to term beginning Dec 3, 1980. Elected to subsequent terms.
Mailing address: P.O. Box 150, Jasper 35502.
Office: Walker County Courthouse, Nineteenth Street, Jasper 35501.
Telephone: (205) 384-7240.

LEE, Helen Shores *(Judge, Alabama Circuit Court Tenth Judicial Circuit Birmingham Division)*
Office: 716 Richard Arrington Jr. Blvd. N., Room 330, Birmingham 35203.
Telephone: (205) 325-5635.

LEE, Kristi D. *(Magistrate Judge, United States District Court Southern District of Alabama)* Appointed by U.S. District Court judges to term beginning Jan 5, 2000. Term expires Jan 2008.
Office: U.S. Courthouse, 113 St. Joseph Street, Mobile 36602-3606.
Telephone: (334) 690-2020.

LICHTENSTEIN, David N. *(Judge, Jefferson County District Court Birmingham Division)*
Office: 716 Richard Arrington Jr. Blvd. N., Room 813, Birmingham 35263.
Telephone: (205) 325-5339.

LISENBY, Philip N. *(Judge, Alabama Circuit Court Sixth Judicial Circuit)* Appointed by Governor Forrest "Fob" James to term beginning May 29, 1996.
Office: Tuscaloosa County Courthouse, Fifth Floor, 714 Greensboro Avenue, Tuscaloosa 35401.
Telephone: (205) 349-3870.

LITTLE, C. Lawson *(Judge, Alabama Circuit Court Twentieth Judicial Circuit)* Elected to term beginning Jan 17, 1995. Reelected 2000, current term expires Jan 2007.
Mailing address: P.O. Drawer 6406, Dothan 36302.
Office: 114 North Oates Street, Dothan 36303.
Telephone: (334) 677-4889.

LITTLE, Loyd H., Jr. *(Presiding Judge, Alabama Circuit Court Twenty-third Judicial Circuit)* Elected to term beginning Jan 17, 1995. Reelected 2000, current term expires Jan 2007.
Office: Madison County Courthouse, 100 Northside Square, Huntsville 35801.
Telephone: (256) 532-3440.

LOCKETT, John R. *(Judge, Alabama Circuit Court Thirteenth Judicial Circuit)*
Office: Mobile Government Plaza, 205 Government Street, Mobile 36644.
Telephone: (251) 574-8477.

LOWTHER, John G. *(Judge, Jefferson County District Court Birmingham Division)*
Office: 716 Richard Arrington Jr. Blvd. N., Room 560, Birmingham 35203.
Telephone: (205) 325-5593.

LYONS, Champ, Jr. *(Associate Justice, Alabama Supreme Court)* Appointed by Governor Forrest "Fob" James March 23, 1998. Elected 2000, current term expires Jan 2007. Born Boston Massachusetts Dec 6, 1940. Educated at Harvard University B.A. 1962 and University of Alabama School of Law J.D. 1965. Editor-in-Chief Alabama Law Review. Member Omicron Delta Kappa, Bench and Bar Honor Society and Farrah Law Society (Former Chair). Law Clerk to Hon. Daniel H. Thomas, U.S. District Court Southern District of Alabama. In legal practice Montgomery and Mobile 1976 to Jan 1998.
President Mobile Bar Association 1991. Former Alabama Commissioner National Conference of Commissioners on Uniform State Laws. Member 1971-98 and Former Chair Supreme Court Advisory Committee on Rules of Civil Procedure. Member 1976-95 and Former Chair Supreme Court Advisory Committee on District Courts. Fellow American Bar Foundation. Member Alabama Law Institute and The American Law Institute. Special Counsel 1995-97 and Legal Advisor 1998 to Governor Forrest "Fob" James, Jr. Member Christ Anglican Church.
Office: 300 Dexter Avenue, Montgomery 36104.
Telephone: (334) 242-4351.

MADDOX, Hugh *(Active Retired Associate Justice, Alabama Supreme Court)* Appointed by Governor Albert P. Brewer to term beginning Oct 1969. Elected 1970, 1976, 1982, 1988 and 1994. Retired Jan 15, 2001, serves when called. Born Covington County Alabama April 17, 1930. Southern Baptist. Educated at University of Alabama A.B. 1952 J.D. 1957. Named Distinguished Military Graduate. Law Clerk to Alabama Court of Appeals and U.S. District Court. Member Omicron Delta Kappa, Sigma Delta Chi, Phi Alpha Delta, Jasons and Quadrangle. Admitted to practice Alabama 1957. Judge, Alabama Circuit Court Fifteenth Judicial Circuit 1963.
Former Field Examiner Veterans Administration and Assistant District Attorney Fifteenth Judicial Circuit. Author *Alabama Rules of Criminal Procedure* Michie 1990. Important Decisions: Bagby Elevator and Electric Company v. McBride et al. S.C. 204 and 104-X, 1974, Beck v. State 396 So.2d 645, 1981 and Ex-parte Branch 526 So.2d 609, 1987. Instructor Jones Law Institute 1963-64 and 1976, Troy State University 1976-77 and Auburn University 1977. Board of Trustees American Inn of Court 1999. Member Institute of Judicial Administration, Alabama Law Institute, American Judicature Society, Alabama State Bar and American Bar Association. Member Alabama Judicial Study Commission and Judicial Conference of Alabama. Named Man of the Year by Montgomery County YMCA 1988 and Senior of Achievement by Montgomery Council on Aging 1999. Recipient Judicial Award of Merit from Alabama State Bar 1997. First Lieutenant USAF 1952-54 and Colonel USAF Active Reserve 1982 (retired). Democrat. Legal Advisor to Governors George C. Wallace, Lurleen B. Wallace and Albert P. Brewer. Member Kiwanis Club (Board of Directors), YMCA, YMCA Youth Legislature and Maxwell AFB Officers Club. Enjoys handball, tennis, woodworking and writing.
Office: 300 Dexter Avenue, Montgomery 36104.
Telephone: (334) 242-4931.

MAHONEY, Margaret A. *(Judge, United States Bankruptcy Court Southern District of Alabama)* Appointed by U.S. Court of Appeals Eleventh Circuit judges. Former Chief Judge.
Office: 201 St. Louis Street, Mobile 36602-2900.
Telephone: (251) 441-5628.

MALONE, Charles R. *(Judge, Alabama Circuit Court Sixth Judicial Circuit)*
Office: Tuscaloosa County Courthouse, Second Floor, 714 Greensboro Avenue, Tuscaloosa 35401.
Telephone: (205) 349-3870.

MARTIN, Ray D. *(Judge, Alabama Circuit Court Fifth Judicial Circuit)* Former Judge, Tallapoosa County District Court, elected to term beginning Jan 15, 1991.
Office: 204 Tallapoosa County Courthouse, 125 North Broadnax, Dadeville 36853.
Telephone: (256) 825-1084, 357-2066.

MASDON, Samuel L. *(Judge, Winston County District Court)*
Mailing address: P.O. Box 613, Haleyville 35565.
Office: 2539 Sixth Avenue, Haleyville 35565.
Telephone: (205) 486-9554.

McCOOEY, Tracy S. *(Judge, Alabama Circuit Court Fifteenth Judicial Circuit)*
Office: Montgomery County Courthouse, 251 South Lawrence Street, Montgomery 36104-4279.
Telephone: (334) 832-1365.

McCORMICK, Michael W. *(Judge, Alabama Circuit Court Tenth Judicial Circuit Birmingham Division)* Elected to term beginning Jan 17, 1989. Reelected 1994 and 2000. Current term expires Jan 2007. Former Judge, Jefferson County Court Birmingham Division.
Office: 801 Richard Arrington Jr. Blvd. N., Courtroom 605, Birmingham 35203.
Telephone: (205) 325-5290.

McDERMOTT, William H. *(Judge, Alabama Circuit Court Thirteenth Judicial Circuit)*
Office: Mobile Government Plaza, 205 Government Street, Mobile 36644-2812.
Telephone: (251) 574-5639.

McDOWELL, Paula B. *(Judge, Franklin County District Court)*
Mailing address: P.O. Box 180, Russellville 35653.
Office: 410 North Jackson, Russellville 35653.
Telephone: (256) 332-8886.

McFERRIN, H. Edward *(Presiding Judge, Alabama Circuit Court Second Judicial Circuit)* Appointed by Governor Harold Guy Hunt April 6, 1992 to term beginning June 1, 1992. Elected to subsequent terms. Current term expires Jan 2007. Born Greenville Alabama Sept 25, 1944. Episcopalian. Educated at Samford University B.S. 1966 and University of Alabama J.D. 1969. Admitted to practice Alabama 1969, U.S. Court of Military Appeals 1969 and U.S. District Courts Middle 1973 and Southern 1983 Districts of Alabama and U.S. Courts of Appeals Fifth 1973 and Eleventh 1982 Circuits. In legal practice Greenville 1973-92.
Captain U.S. Army JAGC Oct 1969 to Aug 1973.
Mailing address: P.O. Box 515, Greenville 36037.
Office: 700 Court Square, Greenville 36037.
Telephone: (334) 382-3621, 335-6568, 548-2252.

McGUIRE, Frank L. "Trippy", III *(Judge, Covington County District Court)* Elected to term beginning Jan 19, 1993. Reelected 1998, current term expires Jan 2005.
Office: Covington County Courthouse, Court Square, Andalusia 36420.
Telephone: (334) 428-2570.

McKATHAN, M. Ashley *(Presiding Judge, Alabama Circuit Court Twenty-second Judicial Circuit)* Appointed by Governor Harold Guy Hunt to term beginning March 4, 1991.
Office: Covington County Courthouse, Court Square, Andalusia 36420.
Telephone: (334) 428-2550.

McKNIGHT, Charles N. *(Judge, Mobile County District Court)*
Office: Mobile Government Plaza, 205 Government Street, Mobile 36602.
Telephone: (251) 574-8438.

McLAUCHLIN, Philip Ben, Jr. *(Presiding Judge, Alabama Circuit Court Thirty-third Judicial Circuit)* Appointed by Governor George C. Wallace to term beginning April 19, 1976. Elected 1976, 1982, 1988, 1994 and 2000. Current term expires Jan 2007. Born Dothan Alabama Dec 19, 1940. Methodist. Educated at University of Alabama B.S. in Accounting 1963 LL.B. 1966. Staff member University of Alabama Law Review 1965-66. Member Alpha Tau Omega, Phi Eta Sigma, Phi Delta Phi and Beta Gamma Sigma. Admitted to practice Alabama 1966. U.S. District Court Middle District of Alabama 1968 and U.S. Supreme Court 1973. In legal practice Ozark 1966-76.
Executive Board 1986-2002, Educational Committee 1981-2003, Secretary-Treasurer 1994-95, Second Vice President 1995-96, First Vice President 1996-97, President 1997-98 and Board of Directors Alabama Association of Circuit Judges. Member 1989-95 and Chairman since 1996 Circuit Judges Time Standards Committee, Member Advisory Committee on Impact of Welfare Reform and Centralized Collection of Child Support since 1996 and Advisory Committee to Study Management and Collections of Court Cost, Fines and Restitution Alabama Supreme Court. Member Alabama Judicial Planning Committee 1994-98. Member Courts Legislative Coordinating Council 1995-97 and 2002. Member Alabama Criminal Justice Information Center Commission 1998. Member Committee on Sentencing 1998 and Chairman Special Committee for Indigent Defense Services 2000 Alabama Judicial Study Commission. Member Judicial Inquiry Commission 1999 and Unified Family Court Advisory Commission 1999 Alabama. Member Pro Se Task Force Administrative Office of Courts and Alabama State Bar since 2000. Past President Dale County Bar Association. Member National Conference on Court Related Needs of the Elderly and Persons with Disabilities, American Judicature Society, American Judges Association, Alabama State Bar (Task Force on Intra Bench and Bar Communications 1998) and American Bar Association. Faculty Member Alabama Judicial College. Attended "Children in Court" The National Judicial College. Listed in *Who's Who* and *Who's Who in American Law*. Recipient Continuing Education Award from Alabama State Bar. Specialist Four U.S. Army 1966-72. Democrat. Past President and Vice President Lisenby PTA. Director Boys and Girls Club of Ozark and Flowers Center for the Performing Arts. Administrative Board First United Methodist Church, Ozark. Member American Legion, Ozark Rotary Club and Friends of Ozark. Enjoys fishing, hunting, golf and reading.
Mailing address: P.O. Box 1305, Ozark 36361.
Office: Court Square, Ozark 36360.
Telephone: (334) 774-8011, 684-2494.

McLEMORE, Lucie U. *(Judge, Montgomery County District Court)* Assumed office 2001. Educated at Huntingdon College B.A. 1973 and Jones Law Institute J.D. 1981. Law Clerk to Hon. Perry O. Hooper, Alabama Circuit Court Circuit Fifteen 1981-83. In legal practice Montgomery 1986-2000.
Legal Research Aide to Director of Finance Alabama Department of Finance 1983-86. Former Chair Voter Registration and Absentee Ballot Projects Montgomery County Republican Party. Board of Directors ex officio Montgomery Area Crime Stoppers. Read-aloud volunteer Montgomery Public Schools.
Office: Montgomery County Courthouse, 251 South Lawrence Street, Montgomery 36104.
Telephone: (334) 832-1391.
E-mail address: lucie.mclemore@alacourt.state.al.us

McMAKEN, Michael E. *(Judge, Mobile County District Court)* Elected to term beginning Jan 20, 1987. Reelected Nov 3, 1992 and Nov 1998. Current term expires Jan 2005. Born Lawton Oklahoma May 10, 1947. Methodist. Educated at Purdue University B.A. 1969 and University of Alabama M.B.A. 1976 J.D. 1976. Admitted to practice Alabama 1976. In legal practice Tuscaloosa 1976 to Jan 1977 and Mobile Jan 1977 to Jan 1987.
Assistant District Attorney Tuscaloosa 1976-77 and Mobile Jan 1977 to March 1979. Special Assistant Attorney General 1980 to Jan 1987. Member Attorney General's Task Force Committee on Child Abuse and Domestic Violence. Member Alabama State Bar, Mobile and American Bar Associations. Attended General Jurisdiction Course The National Judicial College Sept 1988.

MCMAKEN, MICHAEL E.—*Continued*
Previously employed by Army & Air Force Exchange Service and ICI America, Inc. Board of Directors Junior Achievement. Member Children's Justice Task Force for Alabama, Mobile Chamber of Commerce Government Feasibility Task Force and Emergency Shelter Care (for Children) Task Force. Enjoys scuba diving, racquetball, basketball, photography, fishing, hunting, softball, tennis and camping.
Office: Mobile Government Plaza, 205 Government Street, Mobile 36602.
Telephone: (251) 574-8681.

McMILLAN, H. W. "Bucky" *(Presiding Judge, Alabama Court of Criminal Appeals)* Elected to term beginning Jan 14, 1985. Reelected 1990, 1996 (highest percentage vote of any judicial candidate) and 2002. Current term expires Jan 2009. Episcopalian. Educated at University of Alabama B.A. 1976 and Samford University Cumberland School of Law J.D. 1980. Admitted to practice Alabama 1980.
Executive Assistant Attorney General and Chief Prosecutor 1980-84 Alabama. Chief Prosecutor Attorney General's Task Force. Alternate Chief Judge of Judiciary. Member Standing Committee on Rules of Appellate Procedure, Standing Committee on Rules of Juvenile Procedure and Legislative Coordinating Council Alabama Court of Criminal Appeals. Member Alabama District Attorneys Association, Alabama State Bar, Birmingham, Montgomery County and American Bar Associations. Listed in Strathmore's *Who's Who* (for demonstrating leadership and achievement in his profession) 2001. Former Member Board of Advisors Jones Law School Faulkner University, Governor's Commission on School Violence and Alabama Anti-Drug Commission. President Mountain Brook Athletics. Board of Directors Parent Partnership. Board Member Alabama "I Can Through Education" Foundation. Coach Dizzy Dean Little League National Champions 1994, eleven-year-old AAU Basketball State Champions 1994, sixteen-year-old State Ice Basketball Team Alabama 2000, winners of Atlanta Adidas National Classic 2000 and Challenge of the South 2000. Member President's Cabinet University of Alabama and Cathedral Church of the Advent.
Office: 300 Dexter Avenue, Montgomery 36104.
Telephone: (334) 242-4573.

McPHERSON, Vanzetta Penn *(Magistrate Judge, United States District Court Middle District of Alabama)* Appointed by U.S. District Court judges.
Mailing address: P.O. Box 1629, Montgomery 36102-1629.
Telephone: (334) 954-3730.

McRAE, Ferrill David *(Judge, Alabama Circuit Court Thirteenth Judicial Circuit)* Appointed by Governor George C. Wallace to term beginning 1965. Elected to subsequent terms. Former Presiding Judge. Born Irvine Kentucky June 12, 1934. Member Dauphin Way Baptist Church. Educated at University of Alabama B.S. 1959 LL.B. 1961. Admitted to practice Alabama 1961. Began legal practice Mobile 1961.
Instructor in Business Law University of South Alabama 1974-75 and 1977. Member Alabama Association of Circuit Judges, American Admiralty Association, Alabama State Bar, Mobile County and American Bar Associations. Attended National College of the State Judiciary 1967. Sergeant U.S. Army 1955-57. Democrat. Executive Board member Boy Scouts of America and T.B. and Health Association. Member Loop Lodge, Scottish Rite Temple, Abba Temple Shrine and VFW. Former member Mobile Jaycees.
Office: 6100 Mobile Government Plaza, 205 Government Street, Mobile 36644-2613.
Telephone: (251) 574-8485.

MEIGS, Jack W. *(Judge, Alabama Circuit Court Fourth Judicial Circuit)* Appointed by Governor Harold Guy Hunt to term beginning March 6, 1991. Former Presiding Judge.
Mailing address: P.O. Box 475, Centreville 35042.
Office: 35 Court Square East, Centreville 35042.
Telephone: (205) 926-3120, (334) 874-2507, (334) 624-4334.

MENDHEIM, Brady E. *(Judge, Houston County District Court)*
Mailing address: P.O. Drawer 6406, Dothan 36302.
Office: 114 North Oates, Dothan 36303.
Telephone: (334) 677-4881.

MILLICAN, William A. *(Judge, Alabama Circuit Court Sixteenth Judicial Circuit)*
Office: 303 Judicial Building, 801 Forrest Avenue, Gadsden 35901.
Telephone: (256) 549-5364.

MILLING, Bert William, Jr. *(Magistrate Judge, United States District Court Southern District of Alabama)* Appointed by U.S. District Court judges to term beginning Nov 21, 1986. Reappointed Nov 21, 1994 and Nov 21, 2002. Current term expires Nov 2010. Born Mobile Alabama March 5, 1946. Religious affiliation: Anglican. Educated at College of William & Mary A.B. 1968 and University of Alabama J.D. 1971. Admitted to practice Alabama 1971 and U.S. District Court Southern District of Alabama 1972. In legal practice Mobile 1975-77. Court Referee, Alabama Circuit Court Thirteenth Judicial Circuit 1978-81.
Special Assistant Attorney General 1974-75, Assistant District Attorney 1977-78, Counsel U.S. Senate Judiciary Committee Subcommittee on Security and Terrorism 1981-83 and Assistant U.S. Attorney 1983-86. Member Christian Legal Society, Federal Magistrate Judges Association, Alabama State Bar and Mobile Bar Association. Captain U.S. Army AGC 1971-74 (Legal Officer 1971-72 and Legal Assistance Officer 1972-74). Alabama National Guard. Served to Major USAR 1975-87 (retired). Enjoys exercising, reading, photography, music and family activities.
Office: 301 U.S. Courthouse, 113 St. Joseph Street, Mobile 36602-3623.
Telephone: (251) 690-3202.

MITCHELL, Tamara O. *(Chief Judge, United States Bankruptcy Court Northern District of Alabama)* Appointed by U.S. Court of Appeals Eleventh Circuit judges.
Office: 112 Federal Building, 1800 Fifth Avenue North, Birmingham 35203-2110.
Telephone: (205) 714-3850.

MONK, Samuel Holt, II *(Judge, Alabama Circuit Court Seventh Judicial Circuit)* Assumed office Dec 1, 1979. Elected 1982, 1988, 1994 and 2000. Current term expires Jan 2007. Former Presiding Judge. Born Anniston Alabama July 14, 1946. Episcopalian. Educated at Jacksonville State University A.B. 1969 and University

MONK, SAMUEL HOLT, II—*Continued*

of Alabama J.D. 1975. One of Founding Editors Law and Psychology Review 1974-75. Member Order of the Coif. Admitted to practice Alabama 1975, U.S. District Court Northern District of Alabama 1975, U.S. Tax Court 1977 and U.S. Supreme Court 1988. Began legal practice Anniston 1975. Judge, Oxford Municipal Court 1976-77. Judge, Calhoun-Cleburne Counties District Court 1978-79.

Assistant City Attorney Anniston 1976-78. Part-time Assistant District Attorney 1976-78. Member Alabama Association of Circuit Judges, Alabama State Bar and American Bar Association. Captain U.S. Army 1969-72. Democrat. Board of Directors Calhoun County Unit American Cancer Society and Choccolocco Council Boy Scouts of America. Member Rotary Club. Enjoys photography and fishing.

Mailing address: P.O. Box 636, Anniston 36202-0636.
Office: County Courthouse, Anniston 36201.
Telephone: (256) 231-1821, 463-2651.

MONTGOMERY, Tammy Jackson *(Judge, Sumter County District Court)* Elected Nov 1996 to term beginning Jan 21, 1997. Reelected 2002, current term expires Jan 2009. Born Demopolis Alabama Aug 10, 1959. Baptist. Educated at University of Alabama B.S. cum laude 1981 J.D. 1984. Law Clerk to Hon. Sally Greenhaw and Hon. Lynn Bright, Montgomery County District Court 1984-85. Moot Court. Admitted to practice Alabama 1984.

Deputy District Attorney Montgomery County 1985-86 and Jefferson County 1986-96. Member Alabama State Bar and Seventeenth Judicial Circuit Bar Association. Named one of Outstanding Young Women in America 1997. Recipient Dr. Martin Luther King Jr. Humanitarian Award from Southern Christian Leadership Conference 1998. Democrat. Member Children of the Village Network. Enjoys travel, dog breeding, reading and sports.

Mailing address: P.O. Box 9, Livingston 35470.
Office: Courthouse Square, Franklin Street, Livingston 35470.
Telephone: (205) 652-7364.

MOORE, James W., Jr. *(Presiding Judge, Alabama Circuit Court Twenty-fourth Judicial Circuit)* Appointed by Governor James E. Folsom to term beginning Dec 16, 1993. Elected to subsequent term.

Mailing address: P.O. Box 778, Fayette 35555.
Office: 103 North Temple Avenue, Fayette 35555.
Telephone: (205) 932-3169, 695-7193, 367-8179.

MOORE, Roy S. *(Chief Justice, Alabama Supreme Court)* Educated at U.S. Military Academy B.S. 1969 and University of Alabama School of Law J.D. 1977. In legal practice Gadsden 1982-92. Former Judge, Alabama Circuit Court Sixteenth Judicial Circuit, appointed by Governor Harold Guy Hunt to term beginning Nov 23, 1992.

Deputy District Attorney Etowah County Alabama 1977-82. Author "Religion in the Public Square" 29 No. 2 Cumberland L. Rev. 1998-99 and "Putting God Back in the Public Square" 28 No. 8 *Imprimis* Aug 1999. Recipient Family, Faith and Freedom Citation from Family Research Council 1999 and National Spirit of Life Award from African-American Family Association 1999.

Office: 300 Dexter Avenue, Montgomery 36104.
Telephone: (334) 242-4599.

MOQUIN, Susan T. *(Judge, Madison County District Court)* Elected to term beginning Jan 17, 1995. Reelected 2000, current term expires Jan 2007.

Office: Madison County Courthouse, 100 Northside Square, Huntsville 35801.
Telephone: (256) 532-3618.

MULLICAN, Randel Hood *(Judge, Lawrence County District Court)* Elected 1982 to term beginning Jan 17, 1983. Reelected 1988, 1994 and 2000. Current term expires Jan 2007. Born Moulton Alabama Aug 14, 1954. Baptist. Educated at University of Alabama A.B. magna cum laude 1976 J.D. 1979. Member Phi Alpha Delta and Phi Beta Kappa. Admitted to practice Alabama 1979. Began legal practice Moulton 1979.

Assistant District Attorney Thirty-sixth Judicial Circuit 1979-82. Member National District Attorneys Association 1979-82, Alabama Association of District Judges, Alabama State Bar and American Bar Association. Democrat. Member United Way and Jesse Owens Run Race Committee. Enjoys running and gardening.

Office: 14330 Court Street, Suite 307, Moulton 35650.
Telephone: (256) 974-2450.

MURDOCK, Glenn *(Judge, Alabama Court of Civil Appeals)* Born Enterprise Alabama June 25, 1956. Educated at University of Alabama B.A. summa cum laude 1978 and University of Virginia School of Law J.D. 1981. Law Clerk to Hon. Clarence W. Allgood, U.S. District Court Northern District of Alabama. National Moot Court Team. Member Phi Beta Kappa.

Member Alabama State Bar and Birmingham Bar Association. Member Rotary Club of Birmingham.

Office: 300 Dexter Avenue, Montgomery 36104.
Telephone: (334) 242-4102.

NAIL, Tommy *(Judge, Alabama Circuit Court Tenth Judicial Circuit Birmingham Division)*

Office: 716 Richard Arrington Jr. Blvd. N., Room 305, Birmingham 35203.
Telephone: (205) 327-8205.

NELSON, Edwin L. *(Judge, United States District Court Northern District of Alabama)* Magistrate 1974-90. Appointed Judge for life by President George Bush to term beginning Feb 9, 1990. Born Brewton Alabama Feb 10, 1940. Episcopalian. Educated at Cumberland School of Law of Samford University LL.B. 1969. Admitted to practice Alabama 1969, U.S. District Court Northern District of Alabama 1969 and U.S. Supreme Court 1973. Began legal practice Fort Payne 1969.

Member Alabama State Bar and Birmingham Bar Association. ET2 USN 1958-62. Republican. Field Representative for Congressman John Buchanan 1965-68. Candidate U.S. Congress 1972. Past member Jefferson County, DeKalb County and Alabama State Republican Committees. Board of Directors and Past President Traveler's Aid Society of Birmingham. Enjoys photography, folk music and computers.

Office: 786 U.S. Courthouse, 1729 Fifth Avenue North, Birmingham 35203.
Telephone: (205) 278-1820.

NIX, Michael A. *(Judge, Lee County District Court)* Elected to term beginning Jan 20, 1987. Reelected 1992 and 1998. Current term expires Jan 2005.

Office: 118 Lee County Justice Center, 2311 Gateway Drive, Opelika 36801.
Telephone: (334) 749-7150.

NOBLE, G. William *(Judge, Alabama Circuit Court Tenth Judicial Circuit Birmingham Division)*
Office: 716 Richard Arrington Jr. Blvd. N., Courtroom 610, Birmingham 35203.
Telephone: (205) 325-5020.

OTT, John E. *(Magistrate Judge, United States District Court Northern District of Alabama)* Appointed by U.S. District Court judges to term beginning April 6, 1998. Term expires April 2006.
Office: 268 U.S. Courthouse, 1729 Fifth Avenue North, Birmingham 35203-2039.
Telephone: (205) 278-1920.

OWEN, C. Wayne *(Judge, Etowah County District Court)* Elected 1982, 1988, 1994 and 2000. Current term expires Jan 2007. Born Birmingham Alabama Sept 27, 1947. Methodist. Educated at University of Alabama B.S. 1970 J.D. 1972. Admitted to practice Alabama 1972. In legal practice Gadsden 1972-82.
Captain USAR 1969-79. Member Kiwanis Club.
Office: 201 Etowah County Courthouse, 801 Forrest Avenue, Gadsden 35901.
Telephone: (256) 549-5321.

PALUGHI, Delano J. *(Judge, Mobile County District Court)*
Office: Mobile Government Plaza, 205 Government Street, Mobile 36602.
Telephone: (251) 574-6615.

PARSONS, Douglas Mac *(Judge, Alabama Circuit Court Tenth Judicial Circuit Bessemer Division)*
Office: 613 Courthouse Annex, 1801 Third Avenue North, Bessemer 35020.
Telephone: (205) 481-4170.

PARTIN, Charles C. *(Judge, Alabama Circuit Court Twenty-eighth Judicial Circuit)* Appointed by Governor George C. Wallace to term beginning Nov 26, 1985. Elected Nov 1988, Nov 1994 and Nov 2000. Current term expires Jan 2007. Former Presiding Judge. Born Montgomery Alabama Jan 9, 1946. Catholic. Educated at University of Alabama A.B. 1968 J.D. 1971. Editorial Board Alabama Law Review 1969-71. Law Clerk to Hon. Dan T. McCall, Alabama Supreme Court 1971-72. Member Phi Delta Phi and Bench and Bar. Admitted to practice Alabama 1971 and U.S. District Courts Middle 1971 and Southern 1972 Districts of Alabama. In legal practice Bay Minette 1972-85.
President Baldwin County Bar Association 1976-77. Associate Member Alabama State Bar. Republican. Member Red Cross, Boy Scouts of America and Kiwanis. Interests include fishing and computers.
Mailing address: P.O. Box 358, Bay Minette 36507.
Office: Courthouse Square, Bay Minette 36507.
Telephone: (251) 937-0273.

PASEUR, Deborah B. *(Judge, Lauderdale County District Court)* Elected to term beginning Jan 20, 1981. Reelected 1986, 1992 and 1998. Current term expires Jan 2005.
Office: Lauderdale County Courthouse, 200 South Court Street, Florence 35630.
Telephone: (256) 760-5815.

PATE, J. Gary *(Judge, Alabama Circuit Court Tenth Judicial Circuit Birmingham Division)* Appointed by Governor Harold Guy Hunt to term beginning June 29, 1992. Elected to subsequent term.
Office: 2124 Seventh Avenue North, Room 230, Birmingham 35203-2728.
Telephone: (205) 325-5022.

PATTERSON, John Malcolm *(Active Retired Judge, Alabama Court of Criminal Appeals)* Appointed by Governor George C. Wallace to term beginning April 9, 1984. Elected Nov 1984 and 1990. Retired, serves when called. Former Presiding Judge. Born Goldville Alabama Sept 27, 1921. Methodist. Educated at University of Alabama J.D. 1949. Board Member Alabama Law Review 1947-49. Member Phi Eta Sigma, Omicron Delta Kappa, Alpha Tau Omega, Phi Alpha Delta and Farrah Order of Jurisprudence. Admitted to practice Alabama 1949. Began legal practice Phenix City 1949. In legal practice Montgomery 1963-84.
Attorney General 1955-59 and Governor (Youngest governor elected in Alabama) 1959-63 State of Alabama. Member Alabama State Bar, Montgomery County and American Bar Associations. Named one of ten Outstanding Young Men in America by U.S. Junior Chamber of Commerce 1956 and one of four Outstanding Young Men in Alabama 1956. Lieutenant Colonel U.S. Army Artillery 1940-46 and 1951-53. Chairman Board of Trustees Lyman Ward Military Academy. Member Alabama Academy of Honor (Former Chairman). Enjoys cattle farming.
Office: 300 Dexter Avenue, Montgomery 36130-1555.
Telephone: (334) 353-3706.
Fax: (334) 353-3172

PETELOS, Teresa B. *(Presiding Judge, Alabama Circuit Court Tenth Judicial Circuit Bessemer Division)* Elected Nov 1994 to term beginning Jan 17, 1995. Reelected 2000, current term expires Jan 2007. Born Jefferson County Alabama Oct 31, 1956. Greek Orthodox. Educated at University of Alabama at Birmingham B.S. 1980 and Birmingham School of Law J.D. 1985. Admitted to practice Alabama 1986.
Member National Association of Women Judges and Bessemer County Bar Association.
Office: 607 Courthouse Annex, 1801 Third Avenue North, Bessemer 35020.
Telephone: (205) 481-4181.

PETRO, Laura *(Judge, Alabama Circuit Court Tenth Judicial Circuit Birmingham Division)*
Office: 801 Richard Arrington Jr. Blvd. N., Room 505, Birmingham 35203.
Telephone: (205) 325-5646.

PETTWAY, Jo Celeste *(Judge, Wilcox County District Court)* Appointed by Governor George C. Wallace July 29, 1984 to term beginning Aug 9, 1984. Elected 1986, 1992 and 1998. Current term expires Jan 2005. Born Consul Alabama March 18, 1952. Baptist. Member National Baptist Convention, Inc. Educated at Auburn University B.A. 1973 and University of Alabama B.S.W. with honors 1976 M.S.W. with honors 1978 J.D. 1982. Member Phi Alpha Delta and Alpha Kappa Alpha. Admitted to practice Alabama 1982, U.S. District Courts Northern 1982, Middle 1984 and Southern 1984 Districts of Alabama and U.S. Court of Appeals Eleventh Circuit 1983. Began legal practice Tuscaloosa 1982.
Member Alabama Lawyers Association, Alabama State Bar, Dallas County, Tuscaloosa County, National and American Bar Associations. Member Order of the

PETTWAY, JO CELESTE—*Continued*

Eastern Star St. Mary's Chapter 367. Enjoys needlepoint, crocheting, reading, creative writing and fishing.
Mailing address: P.O. Box 549, Camden 36726.
Office: 12 Waters Street, Camden 36726.
Telephone: (334) 682-4619.

PITTMAN, Craig S. *(Judge, Alabama Court of Civil Appeals)* Elected to term beginning Jan 2001. Term expires Jan 2007. Born Enterprise Alabama Sept 6, 1956. Episcopalian. Educated at Middlebury College B.A. with honors 1978 and Cumberland School of Law of Samford University J.D. 1981. Law Clerk to Hon. Virgil Pittman, U.S. District Court Southern District of Alabama 1981-83. Admitted to practice Alabama 1981 and Florida 1982. In legal practice Mobile Alabama 1983-2000.

Member Southeastern Admiralty Law Institute, The Maritime Law Association of the U.S., Alabama State Bar and The Florida Bar. Republican.
Office: 300 Dexter Avenue, Montgomery 36104.
Telephone: (334) 353-5169.

PITTMAN, Virgil *(Senior Judge, United States District Court Southern District of Alabama)* Appointed for life by President Lyndon B. Johnson to term beginning June 1966. Chief Judge 1971-81. Assumed Senior status 1981, serves by assignment. Periodically sits on U.S. Court of Appeals Eleventh Circuit. Born Enterprise Alabama March 28, 1916. Baptist. Educated at University of Alabama B.S. 1939 LL.B. 1940. Member Omicron Delta Kappa. Admitted to practice Alabama 1940. In legal practice Gadsden 1946-51. Judge 1951-66 and Presiding Judge 1953-66, Alabama Circuit Court Sixteenth Judicial Circuit.

Special Agent FBI 1940-44. Author "Circuit Court Proceedings in Acquisition of a Tract of Right of Way" University of Alabama 1959, "A Judge Looks at Right of Way Condemnation Proceedings" University of Alabama 1960 and "Technical Pitfalls in Right of Way Proceedings" University of Alabama 1961, papers presented at Right of Way Conference. Lecturer on Business Law, Economics and Political Science University of Alabama Center at Gadsden 1948-66. Member Alabama State Bar and Etowah County Bar Association (President 1949). Lieutenant j.g. USNR 1944-46. Democrat. State Board of Education 1951. Trustee Samford University 1974-90 and since 1992.
Office: U.S. Courthouse, 113 St. Joseph Street, Mobile 36602-3606.
Telephone: (251) 690-2381.

PRICE, Charles *(Presiding Judge, Alabama Circuit Court Fifteenth Judicial Circuit)* Appointed by Governor George C. Wallace to term beginning April 5, 1983. Elected to subsequent terms.
Office: Montgomery County Courthouse, 251 South Lawrence Street, Montgomery 36104-4279.
Telephone: (334) 832-1331.

PRIVETT, Caryl P. *(Judge, Alabama Circuit Court Tenth Judicial Circuit Birmingham Division)*
Office: 716 Richard Arrington Jr. Blvd. N., Courtroom 370, Birmingham 35203.
Telephone: (205) 325-5200.

PROPST, Robert B. *(Senior Judge, United States District Court Northern District of Alabama)* Appointed for life by President Jimmy Carter to term beginning 1980. Assumed Senior status July 15, 1996, serves by assignment. Born Ohatchee Alabama July 13, 1931. Educated at University of Alabama at Tuscaloosa B.S. 1953 J.D. 1957. In legal practice Anniston 1957-80. U.S. Army 1953-55.
Mailing address: P.O. Box 820, Anniston 36202-0820.
Telephone: (256) 236-4170.

PUTNAM, Terry Michael *(Magistrate Judge, United States District Court Northern District of Alabama)* Appointed by U.S. District Court judges to term beginning Feb 9, 1987. Reappointed 1995 and Feb 9, 2003. Current term expires Feb 8, 2011. Born Albany Georgia June 7, 1954. Educated at University of Alabama B.A. magna cum laude 1976 J.D. 1979. Senior Editor Alabama Law Review 1978-79. Member Order of the Coif. Admitted to practice Alabama 1979, U.S. District Court Northern District of Alabama 1979, U.S. Courts of Appeals Fifth 1980 and Eleventh 1981 Circuits and U.S. Supreme Court 1985. In legal practice Florence 1979-87.

Author "Warrantless Seizures: The Plain-View Doctrine in Alabama" Alabama L. Rev. Winter 1979 and "The Utilization of Magistrate Judges in the Federal District Courts of Alabama" 28 No. 3 Cumberland L. Rev. 1997-98. Member Federal Magistrate Judges Association and Alabama State Bar. Lecturer on Survey of Recent Legal Developments May 1986, Overview of Alabama Rules 59 and 60 Sept 1988, The Role and Function of Magistrates in Federal Civil Proceedings Nov 1990, Bond and Detention in Federal Criminal Practice July 1992 and Significant Changes in Federal Civil Procedure Nov 1994 Alabama Law Institute CLE, "Federal Criminal Practice: A Walk-Through" Cumberland School of Law CLE Oct 1993 and Federal Court Practice Young Lawyers Section Birmingham Bar Association Sept 1993 and Sept 1994. Moderator for panel discussion on Gangs Alabama Council on Crime and Delinquency Oct 1992. Enjoys tennis and sailing.
Office: 275 U.S. Courthouse, 1729 Fifth Avenue North, Birmingham 35203.
Telephone: (205) 278-1900.

QUATTLEBAUM, Kenneth W. *(Judge, Alabama Circuit Court Thirty-third Judicial Circuit)*
Mailing address: P.O. Box 908, Ozark 36361.
Office address: Court Square, Ozark 36360.
Telephone: (334) 774-3726, 684-2494.

RAINS, David A. *(Judge, Alabama Circuit Court Ninth Judicial Circuit)* Appointed by Governor Forrest "Fob" James May 25, 1981. Elected to subsequent terms.
Office: 406 County Courthouse, 300 Grand Avenue South, Fort Payne 35967.
Telephone: (256) 927-5452, 845-8545.

RAMSEY, Edward L. *(Judge, Alabama Circuit Court Tenth Judicial Circuit Birmingham Division)* Elected to term beginning Jan 17, 1995. Reelected 2000, current term expires Jan 2007.
Office: 716 Richard Arrington Jr. Blvd. N., Room 670, Birmingham 35203.
Telephone: (205) 325-5280.

REESE, Eugene W. *(Judge, Alabama Circuit Court Fifteenth Judicial Circuit)* Elected to term beginning Jan

REESE, EUGENE W.—*Continued*

15, 1991. Reelected 1996 and 2002. Current term expires Jan 2009.

Office: Montgomery County Courthouse, 251 South Lawrence Street, Montgomery 36104-4279.

Telephone: (334) 832-1360.

REEVES, G. Daniel *(Judge, Alabama Circuit Court Eighteenth Judicial Circuit)*

Mailing address: P.O. Box 1209, Columbiana 35051.

Office: Shelby County Courthouse, 112 North Main Street, Columbiana 35051.

Telephone: (205) 669-8588.

REICH, A. Philip, II *(Presiding Judge, Alabama Circuit Court Thirty-sixth Judicial Circuit)* Elected to term beginning Jan 17, 1989. Reelected 1994 and 2000. Current term expires Jan 2007. Born Gadsden Alabama May 28, 1948. Methodist. Educated at University of Alabama B.S. 1970 J.D. 1974. Admitted to practice Alabama 1974 and U.S. District Court Northern District of Alabama 1977. In legal practice Moulton 1976-88.

Member Alabama Circuit Judges Association and Alabama State Bar. Attended General Jurisdiction Course The National Judicial College Sept 1988.

Mailing address: P.O. Box 395, Moulton 35650.

Office: 14330 Court Street, Moulton 35650.

Telephone: (256) 974-2444.

REID, James H. *(Presiding Judge, Alabama Circuit Court Twenty-eighth Judicial Circuit)* Elected 1988 to term beginning Jan 20, 1989. Reelected 1994 and 2000. Current term expires Jan 2007. Born Greenville Alabama Dec 15, 1944. Methodist. Educated at University of South Alabama B.A. and University of Alabama J.D. Admitted to practice Alabama 1974. Municipal Judge Fairhope 1977-81 and Loxley 1977-87.

City Attorney Fairhope 1981-88. Member Alabama State Bar and Baldwin County Bar Association (Former President). USN 1963-67.

Office: 312 Courthouse Square, Suite 22, Bay Minette 36507.

Telephone: (251) 937-0290.

REYNOLDS, Sibley G. *(Judge, Alabama Circuit Court Nineteenth Judicial Circuit)* Elected to term beginning Jan 20, 1993. Reelected 1998, current term expires Jan 2005. Former Presiding Judge. Born Jefferson County Alabama March 14, 1956. Methodist. Educated at University of Alabama B.S. 1978 LL.B./J.D. 1982. Admitted to practice Alabama 1982 and U.S. District Courts Middle 1985 and Northern 1985 Districts of Alabama. In legal practice Clanton 1982-92.

Member Alabama State Bar. Attended numerous Judicial Conferences. Member National Rifle Association. Enjoys hunting and fishing.

Mailing address: P.O. Box 70, Clanton 35045.

Office: 500 Second Avenue North, Clanton 35045.

Telephone: (334) 361-3766, (205) 755-0311.

RHEA, William H., III *(Judge, Alabama Circuit Court Sixteenth Judicial Circuit)* Appointed by governor to term beginning Jan 13, 1987. Former Presiding Judge.

Office: 305 Judicial Building, 801 Forrest Avenue, Gadsden 35901.

Telephone: (256) 549-5317.

RILEY, Francis Timothy *(Judge, Marshall County District Court)* Elected Nov 1992 to term beginning Jan 7, 1993. Reelected Nov 1998, current term expires Jan 2005. Born Butler Alabama June 27, 1956. Methodist. Educated at University of Alabama B.A. magna cum laude 1980 J.D. 1983. Admitted to practice Alabama 1983, U.S. District Court Northern District of Alabama 1983 and U.S. Court of Appeals Eleventh Circuit 1984. In legal practice Albertville 1983-89 and Guntersville 1990-93.

With U.S. Attorney's Office Birmingham 1981-82.

Mailing address: P.O. Box 388, Albertville 35950.

Office: 200 West Main Street, Albertville 35950.

Telephone: (256) 878-2007.

ROBINSON, Charles E. *(Judge, Alabama Circuit Court Thirtieth Judicial Circuit)*

Office: 217 County Courthouse, 1815 Cogswell Avenue, Pell City 35125.

Telephone: (205) 594-2187.

ROCHESTER, John E. *(Presiding Judge, Alabama Circuit Court Fortieth Judicial Circuit)* Appointed by governor to term beginning Jan 16, 1987. Elected to subsequent terms. Former Judge, Alabama Circuit Court Eighteenth Judicial Circuit. Former Judge, Clay County District Court.

Mailing address: P.O. Box 40, Ashland 36251.

Office: County Courthouse, Court Square, Ashland 36251.

Telephone: (256) 354-2242, 377-4988.

RUSSELL, James MacDonald, Jr. *(Judge, Butler County District Court)*

Office: Butler County Courthouse, 700 Court Square, Greenville 36037.

Telephone: (334) 382-6125.

RUSSELL, William D., Jr. *(Judge, Etowah County District Court)* Appointed by Governor James E. Folsom to term beginning Oct 4, 1993.

Office: 200 Judicial Building, 801 Forrest Avenue, Gadsden 35901.

Telephone: (256) 549-5319.

RYAN, William A. *(Judge, Hale County District Court)* Appointed by Governor Harold Guy Hunt to term beginning Feb 12, 1987. Elected to term beginning Jan 19, 1989. Reelected 1994 and 2000. Current term expires Jan 2007. Born Tuscaloosa Alabama June 11, 1949. United Methodist. Educated at University of Alabama B.S.I.E. 1971 J.D. 1982. Admitted to practice Alabama 1982 and U.S. District Court Southern District of Alabama 1983. In legal practice Moundville 1982-87 and Greensboro 1982-87.

Member Alabama State Bar and American Bar Association. Participant General Jurisdiction course The National Judicial College Reno Nevada 1988. Employed at Bank of Moundville 1971-82. Member Board of Education Hale County 1984-87. Member Jaycees, Lions, Rotary, Masons and Kiwanis Clubs. Enjoys golf, music and woodworking.

Mailing address: P.O. Box 27, Greensboro 36744.

Office: 1001 Main Street, Greensboro 36744.

Telephone: (334) 624-8561.

SARRELL, Warren Glea, Jr. *(Judge, Cleburne County District Court)* Appointed by Governor Harold

SARRELL, WARREN GLEA, JR.—*Continued*
Guy Hunt to term beginning Feb 15, 1989. Elected to subsequent term.
Office: 202 Cleburne County Courthouse, 120 Vickery Street, Heflin 36264.
Telephone: (256) 463-5955.

SAWYER, William R. *(Chief Judge, United States Bankruptcy Court Middle District of Alabama)* Appointed by U.S. Court of Appeals Eleventh Circuit judges to term beginning May 24, 1999. Term expires May 2013. Chief Judge since Oct 18, 1999.
Mailing address: P.O. Box 35, Montgomery 36101-0035.
Telephone: (334) 954-3880.

SCHILLECI, Vincent J., Jr. *(Judge, Jefferson County District Court Bessemer Division)* Appointed by Governor Forrest "Fob" James to term beginning June 23, 1981. Elected to subsequent terms.
Office: 511 Courthouse Annex, 1801 Third Avenue North, Bessemer 35020.
Telephone: (205) 481-4140.

SCURLOCK, Don P., III *(Judge, Choctaw County District Court)* Elected to term beginning Jan 20, 1987. Reelected 1992 and 1999. Current term expires Jan 2005.
Office: Choctaw County Courthouse, 117 South Mulberry, Butler 36904.
Telephone: (205) 459-3828.

SEE, Harold F. *(Associate Justice, Alabama Supreme Court)* Elected Nov 1996 to term beginning Jan 20, 1997. Reelected Nov 2002, current term expires Jan 2009. Born Chicago Illinois Nov 7, 1943. Baptist. Educated at Emporia State University B.A. 1966, Iowa State University M.S. 1969 and University of Iowa College of Law J.D. with honors 1973. Member Order of the Coif. Admitted to practice Illinois 1973 and Alabama 1981. In legal practice Chicago Illinois 1973-76.
Reporter Alabama Trade Secrets Acts. Herbert D. Warner Professor 1976-96 and Director International Study Programs University of Alabama School of Law. Member Association for Conflict Resolution, American Law and Economics Association, Alabama Law Institute, The American Law Institute, Alabama State Bar and American Bar Association. Previously worked as a sheet metal worker and a roofer. Founding President and Member Carroll's Creek Volunteer Fire Department. Member First Baptist Church, Montgomery. Member V.O.C.A.L. (victims' rights advocacy group).
Office: 300 Dexter Avenue, Montgomery 36104.
Telephone: (334) 242-1001.

SELMAN, Jerry K. *(Judge, Alabama Circuit Court Fourteenth Judicial Circuit)*
Mailing address: P.O. Box 2388, Jasper 35502.
Office: 1801 Third Avenue, Room 224, Jasper 35501.
Telephone: (205) 384-7237.

SHASHY, William A. *(Judge, Alabama Circuit Court Fifteenth Judicial Circuit)* Appointed by Governor Forrest "Fob" James to term beginning Sept 11, 1996.
Office: Montgomery County Courthouse, 251 South Lawrence Street, Montgomery 36104-4279.
Telephone: (334) 832-1370.

SHAW, Greg *(Judge, Alabama Court of Criminal Appeals)* Born 1957. Educated at Auburn University B.S. 1979 and Cumberland School of Law of Samford University J.D. 1982. Recipient American Jurisprudence Award in Evidence. Admitted to practice Alabama 1982.
Staff Attorney to Hon. Janie Ledlow Shores 1984-85 and Hon. J. Gorman Houston, Jr. 1985-2000, Alabama Supreme Court.
Office: 300 Dexter Avenue, Montgomery 36104.
Telephone: (334) 353-3596.

SHERROD, Martha L. *(Judge, Madison County District Court)*
Office: Madison County Courthouse, 100 Northside Square, Huntsville 35801.
Telephone: (256) 532-6990.

SHORT, Charles A. *(Judge, Alabama Circuit Court Twenty-second Judicial Circuit)*
Office: Covington County Courthouse, Andalusia 36420.
Telephone: (334) 428-2520.

SHULMAN, William S. *(Chief Judge, United States Bankruptcy Court Southern District of Alabama)* Appointed by U.S. Court of Appeals Eleventh Circuit judges. Chief Judge since Jan 10, 2003.
Office: 201 St. Louis Street, Mobile 36602-2900.
Telephone: (251) 441-5625.

SIMPSON, George C. *(Judge, Clay County District Court)* Appointed by Governor George C. Wallace to term beginning Jan 16, 1987. Reappointed by Governor Guy Hunt Jan 19, 1987. Elected 1988, 1994 and 2000. Current term expires Jan 2007. Born New York New York Dec 29, 1945. Methodist. Educated at University of North Alabama and University of Alabama B.A. 1971 J.D. 1974. Law Clerk to Presiding Judge Aubrey M. Cates, Alabama Court of Criminal Appeals 1974-75. Admitted to practice Alabama 1974. In legal practice Lineville 1976-87. Judge, Lineville Municipal Court 1976-86.
Assistant District Attorney Mobile County 1975-76. Former member Alabama Municipal Judges Association. Member Alabama District Judges Association. Graduate Alcohol and Drug Seminar The National Judicial College 1980. E-4 U.S. Army 1966-68. Previously employed by Delta Airlines 1967-69. Member Lineville Jaycees 1976-82, Lineville Volunteer Fire Department 1976-86, Lineville Industrial Development Board 1976-84 and 1986-87, Clay County Exchange Club since 1982 and Lineville Downtown Development Board 1986-87.
Mailing address: P.O. Box 880, Ashland 36251.
Office: Clay County Courthouse, Court Square, Ashland 36251.
Telephone: (256) 354-7633.

SIMS, George N. *(Judge, Talladega County District Court)* Elected to term beginning Jan 17, 1989. Reelected 1994 and 2000. Current term expires Jan 2007.
Mailing address: P.O. Box 764, Talladega 35161.
Office: 148 E Street North, Talladega 35160.
Telephone: (256) 761-2113.

SLEDGE, James S. *(Judge, United States Bankruptcy Court Northern District of Alabama)* Appointed by U.S. Court of Appeals Eleventh Circuit judges June 1991. Term expires 2005. Born Gadsden Alabama July 1947. Episcopalian. Educated at Auburn University B.A. 1969 and University of Alabama J.D. 1974. Admitted to practice Alabama 1974. In legal practice Gadsden 1974-91.

SLEDGE, JAMES S.—*Continued*

Member Alabama Trial Lawyers Association, National Conference of Bankruptcy Judges, American Bankruptcy Institute, The Association of Trial Lawyers of America, Alabama State Bar and American Bar Association (Chair Publications and Communications Committee Judicial Division, Chair National Conference of Federal Trial Judges and Chair Elect Judicial Division). Recipient Governor's Award on the Arts 1993. Captain U.S. Army Intelligence 1969-71. Founder and Chairman Center for Cultural Arts. Chair Alabama State Council on the Arts.

Office: 117 U.S. Courthouse, 1129 Noble Street, Anniston 36201.

Telephone: (256) 741-1500.

SMALLWOOD, Tennant M., Jr. *(Judge, Alabama Circuit Court Tenth Judicial Circuit Birmingham Division)* Elected Nov 1994 to term beginning Jan 17, 1995. Reelected 2000, current term expires Jan 2007. Born Lanett Alabama July 16, 1934. Southern Baptist. Educated at Samford University A.B. 1957 and Birmingham School of Law J.D. 1962. Admitted to practice Alabama 1963, U.S. District Court 1963 and U.S. Court of Appeals for the Armed Forces. Judge and Presiding Judge, Birmingham Municipal Court 1963-94.

Member American Judges Association, American Judicature Society, Alabama State Bar, Birmingham and American Bar Associations. Attended The National Judicial College, Administrative Office of Courts, American Academy of Judicial Education, Institute for Court Management, Judge Advocate Generals Command and General Staff School, National Issues Seminar U.S. Army War College and lectures on the Law of Land Warfare and the Geneva and Hague Conventions. Recipient Traffic Court Program Award from American Bar Association 1971. Lieutenant Colonel JAGC 1973-87. Member Muscular Dystrophy Association. Enjoys ice hockey, travel and photography.

Office: 716 Richard Arrington Jr. Blvd. N., Courtroom 340, Birmingham 35203-0102.

Telephone: (205) 325-5644.

SMITH, Charles Lynwood, Jr. *(Judge, United States District Court Northern District of Alabama)* Appointed for life by President Bill Clinton. Born Talladega Alabama Feb 25, 1943. Methodist. Educated at University of Alabama B.A. 1966 J.D. 1971 and Rutgers University M.A. 1967. Recipient Henderson M. Somerville Law Prize 1971. Named Outstanding Graduate Phi Delta Phi 1971. Editorial Board Alabama Law Review 1969-71. Law Clerk to Hon. Frank H. McFadden, U.S. District Court Northern District of Alabama 1971-72. Member Pi Sigma Alpha, Omega Delta Kappa, Phi Delta Phi and Sigma Chi. Admitted to practice Alabama 1971, U.S. District Courts Northern District of Alabama 1971 and Northern District of Texas 1974 and U.S. Court of Appeals Fifth Circuit 1974. In legal practice Huntsville 1972-81. Judge, Madison County District Court April 1981 to Aug 1981. Judge, Alabama Circuit Court Twenty-third Judicial Circuit Aug 24, 1981 to Jan 4, 1996, appointed by Governor Forrest "Fob" James.

Author "Strengthening the Florida Legislature" 1970. Member Alabama State Bar (President Young Lawyers Section 1978-79). Board of Directors 1978-81 and Chairman 1980-81 Huntsville Electric Utility. Program Chairman Leadership 2000 Training Program 1988-89 and Board of Directors since 1987 Huntsville-Madison County Chamber of Commerce. Democrat. Member Madison County Democratic Executive Committee 1974-81. President Madison County Young Democrats 1977-78. Chairman Historical Huntsville Foundation 1974-76. District Chairman Chickasaw District Tennessee Valley Council Boy Scouts of America 1981-82. Enjoys farming, gardening and hunting.

Office: 207 U.S. Courthouse, 101 Holmes Avenue N.E., Huntsville 35801.

Telephone: (256) 533-9490.

SMITH, James P. *(Judge, Alabama Circuit Court Twenty-third Judicial Circuit)* Elected to term beginning Jan 1995. Reelected 2000, current term expires Jan 2007. Born Texarkana Arkansas Oct 17, 1950. Methodist. Educated at University of Alabama B.A. with high honors 1973 J.D. with honors 1976. Member Order of the Coif. Admitted to practice Alabama 1976, U.S. District Court Northern District of Alabama 1976 and U.S. Court of Appeals Eleventh Circuit 1988. In legal practice Huntsville 1976-94.

Member Alabama State Bar, Madison County and American Bar Associations. Attended Alabama Judicial College. Recipient five legislative awards from Alabama Law Institute, Outstanding Legislator Award and Alabama PTA Legislative Award. Democrat. Member Alabama House of Representatives 1978-82 and Alabama Senate 1982-94. Enjoys backpack hiking, hunting and target shooting.

Office: Madison County Courthouse, 100 Northside Square, Huntsville 35801.

Telephone: (256) 532-3394.

SMITH, Larry Mack *(Judge, Alabama Circuit Court Eleventh Judicial Circuit)* Elected Nov 1992 to term beginning Jan 19, 1993. Reelected Nov 1998, current term expires Jan 2005. Born Florence Alabama Nov 26, 1940. Religious affiliation: Church of Christ. Educated at University of North Alabama B.S. 1964 and Birmingham School of Law J.D. 1975. Law Clerk to Hon. Joseph J. Jasper, Alabama Circuit Court Tenth Judicial Circuit 1974-75. Admitted to practice Alabama 1975 and U.S. District Court Northern District of Alabama 1979. In legal practice Florence 1979-92. Municipal Judge, City of Killen 1981-92 and City of Florence 1985-92.

Instructor in Business Law University of North Alabama 1984-86. Member Alabama Circuit Judges Association, Alabama State Bar and American Bar Association. Attended Alabama Judicial Conference bi-annually. Alabama National Guard 1965-70. Member Rotary Club. Interests include golf, reading, antique furniture and gardening.

Office: 317 Lauderdale County Courthouse, 200 South Court Street, Florence 35630.

Telephone: (256) 760-5825.

SMITH, Patricia M. *(Judge, Shelby County District Court)* Appointed by Governor Forrest "Fob" James to term beginning Jan 7, 1980. Elected 1980, 1986, 1992 and 1998. Current term expires Jan 2005. Born Urbana Illinois Feb 20, 1952. Roman Catholic. Educated at Troy State University B.S. cum laude 1973 and Jones Law School J.D. 1976. Admitted to practice Alabama 1977. In legal practice Pelham 1978.

Instructor Alabama Judicial College. Member Shelby

SMITH, PATRICIA M.—*Continued*

County Bar Association. Previously employed at Regional Office Veterans Administration Montgomery.
Mailing address: P.O. Box 1115, Columbiana 35051.
Office: Shelby County Courthouse, 112 North Main Street, Columbiana 35051.
Telephone: (205) 669-3730.

SMITHART, Burt *(Presiding Judge, Alabama Circuit Court Third Judicial Circuit)*
Mailing address: P.O. Box 230, Union Springs 36089.
Office: 217 North Prairie Street, Union Springs 36089.
Telephone: (334) 775-3408, 738-3286, 687-1524.

STEAGALL, Fred R. *(Judge, Dale County District Court)* Appointed by Governor George C. Wallace May 1985. Elected Nov 1986, Nov 1992 and Nov 1998. Current term expires Jan 2005. Born Ozark Alabama Aug 21, 1954. Methodist. Educated at Auburn University B.A. 1978, Cumberland School of Law of Samford University J.D. 1981 and Emory University LL.M. 1982. Admitted to practice Alabama 1981. In legal practice Ozark 1982-85.
Member Alabama State Bar and Dale County Bar Association. Democrat. Officer Ozark Rotary Club. Advisor Carroll High School Interact Club. Board of Directors Ozark Area Chamber of Commerce, Retired Senior Volunteer Program, Southeast Alabama Youth Services, Flowers Center for the Performing Arts, Dale County Council for Parenting and Protecting Children, Dale County Auburn Club and Ozark Boys and Girls Club.
Mailing address: P.O. Box 1346, Ozark 36361.
Office: Court Square, Ozark 36360.
Telephone: (334) 774-7008.

STEELE, William H. *(Magistrate Judge, United States District Court Southern District of Alabama)* Appointed by U.S. District Court judges.
Office: U.S. Courthouse, 113 St. Joseph Street, Mobile 36602-3606.
Telephone: (251) 690-3239.

STEENSLAND, M. John *(Judge, Houston County District Court)* Appointed by Governor Harold Guy Hunt to term beginning Jan 26, 1989. Elected to subsequent terms.
Mailing address: P.O. Drawer 6406, Dothan 36302.
Office: 114 North Oates, Dothan 36303.
Telephone: (334) 677-4851.

STEWART, Donald W. *(Judge, Alabama Circuit Court Sixteenth Judicial Circuit)* Elected to term beginning Jan 18, 1983. Reelected 1988, 1994 and 2000. Current term expires Jan 2007. Former Presiding Judge. Born Etowah County Alabama Aug 10, 1943. Presbyterian. Educated at University of Alabama B.S. 1968 J.D. 1971. Member Phi Alpha Delta. Admitted to practice Alabama 1971 and U.S. District Courts Middle 1971, Northern 1971 and Southern 1971 Districts of Alabama 1971. In legal practice Gadsden 1971-83.
Past President and Founding Member Etowah County Chapter American Inns of Court. Joint Incorporator Etowah County Community Correction Authority (alternative sentencing program). Member State Committee on Criminal Procedure, Alabama Circuit Judges Association, Alabama State Bar and Etowah County Bar Association. Attended The National Judicial College. U.S. Army 1961-64. Board of Directors Etowah County Council on Domestic Violence. Advisory Board County Extension Office. Board Member Paralegal Program Gadsden State Community College. Member Gadsden Civitan Club. Enjoys outdoor activities, woodworking, civil war history and genealogy.
Office: Etowah County Courthouse, 801 Forrest Avenue, Gadsden 35901.
Telephone: (256) 549-5372.

STILSON, C. Michael *(Judge, United States Bankruptcy Court Northern District of Alabama)* Appointed by U.S. Court of Appeals Eleventh Circuit judges.
Mailing address: P.O. Box 3226, Tuscaloosa 35403-3226.
Telephone: (205) 758-3718.

STORM, Sandra H. *(Judge, Alabama Circuit Court Tenth Judicial Circuit Birmingham Division)* Elected to term beginning Jan 17, 1989. Reelected 1994 and 2000. Current term expires Jan 2007.
Office: 120 North Second Court, Birmingham 35204.
Telephone: (205) 325-5538.

STOUT, Roderick P. *(Judge, Alabama Circuit Court Thirteenth Judicial Circuit)*
Mailing address: P.O. Box 1038, Mobile 36652-1038.
Office: Mobile Government Plaza, Mobile 36644.
Telephone: (251) 574-8481.

STREET, Malcolm B., Jr. *(Judge, Alabama Circuit Court Seventh Judicial Circuit)* Elected Dec 15, 1976 to term beginning Jan 18, 1977. Reelected 1982, 1988, 1994 and 2000. Current term expires Jan 2007. Presiding Judge 1982-91. Born Anniston Alabama Jan 10, 1942. Christian. Educated at Birmingham-Southern College A.B. 1964 and Duke University J.D. 1967. Member Omicron Delta Kappa and Phi Eta Sigma. Admitted to practice Alabama 1967. Began legal practice Anniston 1967.
Professor and Dean Jacksonville State University School of Law Enforcement 1970-76. Instructor North East Alabama Police Academy 1972-76. Member American Judicature Society, Alabama State Bar, Calhoun County and American Bar Associations. Recipient Anniston Young Man of the Year Award 1970. Finalist White House Fellow 1973. Named Outstanding Educator of America. Recipient Silver Beaver Award from Boy Scouts of America. Democrat. Member Alabama Young Democrats (Vice President 1968-72), Regional Alcoholism Council (President 1974-75), Coosa Valley Youth Services Board (Vice President 1976-78), Choccolocco Council Boy Scouts of America (District Chairman 1977-79, Vice President 1980-82, President 1983 and 1984), Masons, York Bodies, Shriners, Rotary Club (President 1988) and Indian Oaks Christian Church (Elder and Treasurer). Enjoys scouting, broadcasting and sports.
Office: County Courthouse, 25 West Eleventh Street Box 1, Anniston 36201.
Telephone: (256) 231-1820, 463-2651.

STUART, Jacquelyn "Lyn" Lufkin *(Associate Justice, Alabama Supreme Court)* Born Atmore Alabama Sept 23, 1955. United Methodist. Educated at Auburn University B.A. with high honors 1977 and University of Alabama J.D. 1980. Member Phi Alpha Phi. Admitted to practice Alabama 1980, U.S. District Courts Middle 1980, Northern 1980 and Southern 1980 Districts of Alabama and U.S. Court of Appeals Eleventh Circuit

STUART, JACQUELYN "LYN" LUFKIN—*Continued*
1980. Former Judge, Baldwin County District Court, elected to term beginning Jan 18, 1989. Former Judge, Alabama Circuit Court Twenty-eighth Judicial Circuit, appointed by Governor Forrest "Fob" James to term beginning Jan 21, 1997.

Assistant Attorney General and Special Assistant Attorney General Alabama 1980-83. Assistant District Attorney Baldwin County 1985-88. Member Alabama Council of Juvenile and Family Court Judges (Past President) and Alabama Circuit Judges Association. Attended General Jurisdiction course The National Judicial College 1991 and The Family and the Courts course National Symposium on Children 1992. Executive Board Alabama Federation of Women's Clubs. Member Kiwanis, Heritage Junior Women's Club and Jubilee Woman's Club. Enjoys swimming and hand-sewing.

Office: 300 Dexter Avenue, Montgomery 36104.
Telephone: (334) 242-4585.

SUTTLE, Ned Michael *(Presiding Judge, Alabama Circuit Court Eleventh Judicial Circuit)* Appointed by Governor George C. Wallace to term beginning Oct 1, 1984. Elected 1986, 1992 and 1998. Current term expires Jan 2005. Born Beaufort South Carolina May 22, 1951. Educated at Memphis State University B.A. cum laude 1973 and Indiana University School of Law J.D. summa cum laude 1976. Member Order of the Coif. Admitted to practice Tennessee 1976 and Alabama 1979.

Office: Lauderdale County Courthouse, Fourth Floor, 200 South Court Street, Florence 35630.
Telephone: (256) 760-5820.

TAYLOR, Clayton K. *(Judge, Tallapoosa County District Court)*
Office: Tallapoosa County Courthouse, 125 North Broadnax, Dadeville 36853.
Telephone: (256) 825-1086.

TEEL, Robert J., Jr. *(Judge, Coosa County District Court)* Assumed office Jan 16, 1977. Elected to subsequent terms.
Mailing address: P.O. Box 115, Rockford 35136.
Office: Main Street, Rockford 35136.
Telephone: (256) 377-4957.

THOMAS, Herman *(Judge, Alabama Circuit Court Thirteenth Judicial Circuit)* Born Mobile Alabama 1961. Catholic. Admitted to practice Florida 1986 and Alabama 1987. Former Judge, Mobile County District Court, appointed by Governor Harold Guy Hunt to term beginning March 23, 1990.

Former Adjunct Professor Criminal Procedure II University of South Alabama. Board of Directors Mobile Mental Health Center, Mobile United, South Alabama United Way, Alabama Civil Justice Foundation, America's Junior Miss, Boy Scouts of America and Penelope House Shelter. Trustee University of South Alabama and Spring Hill College. Member Success by Six, Challenge 2.0.0.0. and U.S.S. Battleship Commission.

Office: Mobile Government Plaza, 205 Government Street, Mobile 36644-2217.
Telephone: (251) 574-8799.

THOMAS, Terri W. *(Judge, Cullman County District Court)* Elected to term beginning Jan 21, 1997. Reelected 2002, current term expires Jan 2009.
Office: Cullman County Courthouse, 500 Second Avenue S.W., Cullman 35055.
Telephone: (256) 775-4767.

THOMPSON, Glenn E. *(Judge, Alabama Circuit Court Eighth Judicial Circuit)* Elected to term beginning Jan 17, 1995. Reelected 2000, current term expires Jan 2007. Former Presiding Judge. Born Hartselle Alabama April 28, 1952. Christian. Educated at University of Alabama B.A. 1974 and Cumberland School of Law of Samford University J.D. 1978. Admitted to practice Alabama 1978. In legal practice Hartselle Feb 1979 to Dec 1994. Judge, Hartselle Municipal Court 1980 to Dec 1994.

Assistant Attorney General Alabama 1978-79. Member Alabama Circuit Judges Association (Board Member since 1999), Alabama State Bar and Morgan County Bar Association. Democrat.

Mailing address: P.O. Box 668, Decatur 35602.
Office: 302 Lee Street, Fourth Floor, Decatur 35601.
Telephone: (256) 351-4785.
Fax: (256) 351-4789
E-mail address: glenn.thompson@alacourt.state.al.us

THOMPSON, Myron H. *(Judge, United States District Court Middle District of Alabama)* Appointed for life by President Jimmy Carter to term beginning 1980. Chief Judge 1991-98. Born Tuskegee Alabama Jan 7, 1947. Educated at Yale University B.A. 1969 J.D. 1972. In legal practice Montgomery Alabama 1974-80.
Assistant Attorney General Alabama 1972-74.
Mailing address: P.O. Box 235, Montgomery 36101-0235.
Telephone: (334) 954-3650.

THOMPSON, William C. *(Judge, Alabama Court of Civil Appeals)* Elected Nov 1996 to term beginning Jan 1997. Reelected Nov 2002, current term expires Jan 2009. Educated at University of Alabama B.A. 1984 and Samford University Cumberland School of Law J.D. 1988. Admitted to practice Alabama 1988 and U.S. District Courts Middle and Northern Districts of Alabama.

Former Member Judicial Compensation Commission. Chief Judge Alabama Court of the Judiciary. Member Alabama State Bar, Birmingham, Montgomery County and American Bar Associations. Former Assistant Legal Advisor to the Governor of Alabama. Member St. Stephen's Episcopal Church.

Office: 300 Dexter Avenue, Montgomery 36104.
Telephone: (334) 242-4980.

TURNER, Jerry L. *(Judge, Washington County District Court)*
Mailing address: P.O. Box 1025, Chatom 36518.
Office: Washington County Courthouse, Court Street, Chatom 36518.
Telephone: (251) 847-2164.

TURNER, Louie H., Jr. *(Judge, Alabama Circuit Court Seventh Judicial Circuit)*
Office: Calhoun County Courthouse, 25 West Eleventh Street, Anniston 36201.
Telephone: (256) 231-1733.

VANCE, Robert S., Jr. *(Judge, Alabama Circuit Court Tenth Judicial Circuit Birmingham Division)*
Office: 660 Jefferson County Courthouse, 716 Richard Arrington Jr. Blvd. N., Birmingham 35203.
Telephone: (205) 325-5035.

VERIN, Eugene R. *(Judge, Alabama Circuit Court Tenth Judicial Circuit Bessemer Division)*
Office: 708 Courthouse Annex, 1801 Third Avenue North, Bessemer 35020.
Telephone: (205) 481-4198.

VINSON, Virginia A. *(Judge, Alabama Circuit Court Tenth Judicial Circuit Birmingham Division)*
Office: 801 Richard Arrington Jr. Blvd. N., Room 710, Birmingham 35203.
Telephone: (205) 214-8683.

VOLLMER, Richard W., Jr. *(Senior Judge, United States District Court Southern District of Alabama)* Appointed for life by President George Bush March 1990 to term beginning June 18, 1990. Assumed Senior status Dec 31, 2000, serves by assignment. Born St. Louis Missouri March 7, 1926. Catholic. Educated at Spring Hill College Pre-Law 1946-49 and University of Alabama LL.B. 1953. Paul Harris Fellow. Board of Editors Alabama Law Review 1953. Admitted to practice Alabama 1953, U.S. District Court Southern District of Alabama 1956 and U.S. Court of Appeals 1963. In legal practice Mobile 1956-90.
President 1984-85 and Charter Member American Board of Trial Advocates. Member Alabama State Bar, Mobile (President 1990) and American Bar Associations. USN 1944-46 and 1950-52. Senior Member and Paul Harris Fellow Rotary International.
Office: 113 St. Joseph Street, Mobile 36602-3606.
Telephone: (251) 694-4545.
E-mail address: Vollmer@als.uscourts.gov

VOWELL, J. Scott *(Presiding Judge, Alabama Circuit Court Tenth Judicial Circuit Birmingham Division)* Elected to term beginning Jan 17, 1995. Reelected 2000, current term expires Jan 2007.
Office: 716 Richard Arrington Jr. Blvd. N., Courtroom 370, Birmingham 35203.
Telephone: (205) 325-5388.

WALKER, Jacob A., III *(Judge, Alabama Circuit Court Thirty-seventh Judicial Circuit)* Former Presiding Judge.
Office: Lee County Justice Center, 2311 Gateway Drive, Opelika 36801.
Telephone: (334) 749-7156.

WALKER, Nathaniel *(Judge, Dallas County District Court)* Elected to term beginning Jan 20, 1987. Reelected 1992 and 1998. Current term expires Jan 2005.
Mailing address: P.O. Box 23, Selma 36702.
Office: Dallas County Courthouse, 102 Church Street, Selma 36701.
Telephone: (334) 874-2529.

WALKER, Susan Russ *(Magistrate Judge, United States District Court Middle District of Alabama)* Appointed by U.S. District Court judges.
Mailing address: P.O. Box 180, Montgomery 36101-0180.
Telephone: (334) 954-3670.

WARREN, Larry F. *(Judge, Calhoun County District Court)* Elected to term beginning Jan 20, 1987. Reelected 1992 and 1998. Current term expires Jan 2005.
Office: Calhoun County Courthouse, 25 West Eleventh Street Box 8, Anniston 36201.
Telephone: (256) 231-1866.

WELCH, Samuel H., Jr. *(Presiding Judge, Alabama Circuit Court Thirty-fifth Judicial Circuit)* Elected to term beginning Jan 19, 1989. Reelected Jan 17, 1995 and 2000. Current term expires Jan 2007. Born Carrollton Georgia Dec 30, 1950. Religious affiliation: Southern Baptist. Educated at Birmingham Southern College B.A. cum laude 1972 and University of Alabama School of Law J.D. 1976. Editor Law and Psychology Review 1975-76. Admitted to practice Alabama 1976. In legal practice Birmingham 1976-78 and Monroeville 1978-83. Municipal Judge, Monroeville 1980-83. Judge, Monroe County District Court 1983-89.
Major USAR. Member Kiwanis.
Mailing address: P.O. Box 601, Monroeville 36461.
Office: Courthouse Square, Monroeville 36460.
Telephone: (251) 578-7015, 743-3649.

WELLS, Jimmy D. *(Judge, Walker County District Court)*
Mailing address: P.O. Box 3165, Jasper 35502.
Office: Courthouse Annex, Eighteenth and Third Avenue, Jasper 35501.
Telephone: (205) 384-7260.

WELLS, Judson W., Sr. *(Judge, Mobile County District Court)*
Office: Mobile Government Plaza, 205 Government Street, Mobile 36602.
Telephone: (251) 574-8722.

WHALEY, W. Patrick *(Judge, Randolph County District Court)* Elected to term beginning Jan 17, 1989. Reelected 1994 and 2000. Current term expires Jan 2007.
Mailing address: P.O. Box 267, Wedowee 36278.
Office: Highway 431, Wedowee 36278.
Telephone: (256) 357-4921.

WHITE, James M. *(Judge, Bibb County District Court)* Elected 1976 to term beginning Jan 17, 1977. Reelected 1982, 1988, 1994 and 2000. Current term expires Jan 2007. Born Dothan Alabama Jan 31, 1937. Baptist. Educated at Southwest Mississippi Junior College A.A. 1957 and University of Alabama LL.B. 1962. President Morgan Chapter Phi Alpha Delta 1961. Law School Representative Student Legislature 1961. Admitted to practice Alabama 1962. In legal practice Huntsville 1962-70 and Centreville 1970-77. Judge, Brent Municipal Court 1972-76.
President Alabama Association of District Judges 1994-95. Second Vice Chairman Alabama Judicial Inquiry Commission. Member Alabama State Bar (President Young Lawyers Section 1968-69). Democrat. Enjoys hunting, fishing and boating.
Office: Bibb County Courthouse, 35 Court Square East, Centreville 35042.
Telephone: (205) 926-3106.

WHITMIRE, Steven L., II *(Judge, DeKalb County District Court)*
Office: 103 Public Safety Annex, 210 Grand Avenue South, Fort Payne 35967.
Telephone: (256) 845-8574.

ALABAMA

WIGGINS, Marvin Wayne *(Presiding Judge, Alabama Circuit Court Fourth Judicial Circuit)* Elected June 30, 1998 to term beginning Jan 19, 1999. Term expires Jan 16, 2005. First African American Judge in the Fourth Judicial Circuit. Born Greensboro Alabama Sept 9, 1964. Educated at Alabama State University B.A. with honors 1986, Howard University School of Law J.D. 1990 and Emory University School of Law LL.M. 1992. Member Pi Gamma Mu and Alpha Gamma Mu. Recipient Jurisprudence Awards for Federal Jurisdiction, Property II and Appellate Advocacy. Admitted to practice Alabama 1990, U.S. District Courts Middle, Northern and Southern Districts of Alabama and U.S. Court of Appeals Eleventh Circuit. In legal practice Montgomery 1990-95 and Selma 1995-99.

Member Alabama Lawyers Association. Recipient William Moses Kunstler Racial Justice Award 1997. Member Alabama Democratic Conference and New South Coalition. Chairman Hale County Community Enrichment Society, Inc. and Clearinghouse for the Blackbelt Faith Based and Non-Profit Initiative Programs. Deacon, Tutor and Youth Worker Williams Chapel. Certified Basketball Official Alabama High School Athletic Association. Member Saints Conference (Chairperson) and Southern Christian Leadership Conference.

Office: 52 Hale County Courthouse, 1001 Main Street, Greensboro 36744.
Telephone: (334) 624-5620.
Fax: (334) 624-5622
E-mail address: Marvin.Wiggins@alacourt.state.al.us

WILLIAMS, Bruce E. *(Judge, Alabama Circuit Court Twenty-third Judicial Circuit)* Appointed by Governor Forrest "Fob" James to term beginning Feb 16, 1996.

Office: Madison County Courthouse, 100 Northside Square, Huntsville 35801.
Telephone: (256) 532-3754.

WILLIAMS, Dwight H., Jr. *(Judge, United States Bankruptcy Court Middle District of Alabama)* Appointed by U.S. Court of Appeals Eleventh Circuit judges to term beginning October 18, 1999. Term expires Oct 2013.

Mailing address: P.O. Box 1248, Montgomery 36102-0248.
Telephone: (334) 954-3890.

WILSON, Thomas S. *(Judge, Alabama Circuit Court Sixth Judicial Circuit)* Appointed by Governor George C. Wallace to term beginning April 26, 1985. Elected 1986, 1992 and 1998. Current term expires Jan 2005. Former Presiding Judge. Born Alexander City Alabama Nov 4, 1948. United Methodist. Educated at University of Alabama B.A. M.A. and Birmingham School of Law J.D. Member Sigma Delta Kappa. Admitted to practice Alabama 1979. Judge, Tuscaloosa County District Court Jan 23, 1983 to 1985.

Lieutenant Colonel USAR. Democrat. Member Civitan Club, Gideon and American Legion. Enjoys fishing and the stock market.

Office: 205 Tuscaloosa County Courthouse, 714 Greensboro Avenue, Tuscaloosa 35401.
Telephone: (205) 349-3870.

WILTERS, Robert E. *(Judge, Alabama Circuit Court Twenty-eighth Judicial Circuit)* Former Judge, Baldwin County District Court, elected to term beginning Jan 19, 1993.

Mailing address: P.O. Box 835, Bay Minette 36507.
Office: Courthouse Square, Bay Minette 36507.
Telephone: (251) 580-2570.

WISE, Alisa K. *(Judge, Alabama Court of Criminal Appeals)* Born Geneva Alabama Dec 14, 1962. Educated at Auburn University B.S. 1985 M.P.A. and Jones Law Institute J.D. 1994. Admitted to practice Alabama 1994.

Former Program Chairman and Former Public Affairs Officer Montgomery County Bar Association. Member Judicial Task Force Montgomery County Bar Association and Committee on Volunteer Lawyers Program Alabama State Bar. Named National Young Republican of the Year 1999. Member Montgomery Junior League and The Family Sunshine Center Associate Board.

Office: 300 Dexter Avenue, Montgomery 36104.
Telephone: (334) 353-3558.

WOOD, James C. *(Judge, Alabama Circuit Court Thirteenth Judicial Circuit)*

Office: Mobile Government Plaza, 205 Government Street, Mobile 36644-2217.
Telephone: (251) 574-8475.

WOOD, Phillip W. *(Judge, Autauga County District Court)* Appointed by Governor George C. Wallace to term beginning Aug 1, 1983. Elected to subsequent terms. Born Panama City Florida Sept 4, 1951. Baptist. Educated at Auburn University B.A. 1973 and University of Alabama J.D. 1977. Admitted to practice Alabama 1978. Began legal practice Prattville 1978.

Autauga County Commission Jan 1981 to Aug 1983 and Board of Zoning Adjustment Prattville June 1978 to Aug 1983. Instructor Troy State University since 1979. Member Alabama State Bar. Major Alabama Air National Guard. Democrat. Board of Directors Prattville Chamber of Commerce. Member Lions Club. Enjoys jogging and wood carving.

Office: Autauga County Courthouse, 134 North Court Street, Prattville 36067.
Telephone: (334) 361-3733.

WOODALL, Thomas A. *(Associate Justice, Alabama Supreme Court)* Elected to term beginning Jan 2001. Born Meridian Mississippi 1950. Educated at Millsaps College B.A. magna cum laude 1972 and University of Virginia School of Law J.D. 1975. Listed in *Who's Who in American Colleges and Universities.* Member Omicron Delta Kappa, Eta Sigma and Phi Alpha Theta. Judge, Alabama Circuit Court Tenth Judicial Circuit Birmingham Division Feb 15, 1996 to Jan 2001, appointed by Governor Forrest "Fob" James.

Vice Chairman Alabama Pattern Jury Instruction-Civil Committee 1992-2001. Former Member Executive Committee and Past Chair Grievance, Civil Courts Procedures, Membership and Lawyer Referral Service Committees Birmingham Bar Association. Named "Top 40 Under 40" by Birmingham Business Journal 1989.

Office: 300 Dexter Avenue, Montgomery 36104.
Telephone: (334) 242-4579.

WOODHAM, Charles W. *(Judge, Henry County District Court)* Appointed by Governor James E. Folsom to term beginning Oct 6, 1993. Elected 1994 and 2000. Current term expires Jan 2007. Born Dothan Alabama Feb 14, 1942. Baptist. Educated at University of Alabama B.A. 1964 J.D. 1971. Editorial Board Alabama

WOODHAM, CHARLES W.—*Continued*

Law Review 1969-71. Member Order of the Coif. Admitted to practice Alabama 1971, U.S. District Court Middle District of Alabama 1974 and U.S. Court of Appeals Eleventh Circuit 1984. In legal practice Abbeville 1971-76.

Legal Counsel Henry County Hospital Board 1976-93, Henry County Board of Education 1978-93 and City of Abbeville 1983-93. Member Alabama Trial Lawyers Association (Board of Governors 1983-85), The Association of Trial Lawyers of America, American Judicature Society, Alabama State Bar, Henry County and American Bar Associations. Captain U.S. Army 1965-68. Enjoys golf and fishing.

Office: Henry County Courthouse, Suite H, 101 Court Square, Abbeville 36310.

Telephone: (334) 585-5712.

WOODROOF, James W., Jr. *(Judge, Alabama Circuit Court Thirty-ninth Judicial Circuit)* Appointed by Governor Forrest "Fob" James to term beginning Aug 1, 1996.

Mailing address: P.O. Box 486, Athens 35612.
Office: Courthouse Square, Athens 35611.
Telephone: (256) 233-6410.

YATES, Sharon G. *(Presiding Judge, Alabama Court of Civil Appeals)* Elected Nov 1992 to term beginning Jan 19, 1993. Reelected 1998, current term expires Jan 2005. First woman to sit on the Alabama Court of Civil Appeals. Born Alexander City Alabama Nov 21, 1952. Educated at University of Alabama 1975 M.A. in Educational Administration 1976 J.D. 1982. Summer Law Clerk to Chief Justice C. C. Torbert, Jr., Alabama Supreme Court 1980. Member Phi Delta Phi and Farrah Law Society. Admitted to practice Alabama, U.S. District Court Middle District of Alabama and U.S. Court of Appeals Eleventh Circuit. In legal practice 1984-89.

Staff Attorney to Hon. Samuel Alston Beatty, Alabama Supreme Court 1982. Professor of Law in Evidence, Civil Procedure, Legal Ethics, Administrative Law, Contracts and Criminal Law Jones Law School May 1989 to Nov 1992. Vice Chair Alabama Supreme Court's Alternative Dispute Resolution Commission. Board of Directors Alabama Lawyers for Children and Child Protect, Inc. Member The Family Preservation Court Improvement Project. Member Alice M. Meadows Council Bar Participation Committee. Member Alabama Task Force on Judicial Elections. Member Third Citizen's Conference on Alabama State Courts. Planning Staff Office of Education Bureau of Post-Secondary Education 1975-78. Educational Programmer Southeast Regional Resource Center.

Office: 300 Dexter Avenue, Montgomery 36104.

Telephone: (334) 242-4096.

YOUNG, Tom F., Jr. *(Judge, Alabama Circuit Court Fifth Judicial Circuit)*

Office: One Court Square, Room 306, Alexander City 35010-0158.

Telephone: (256) 234-7901.

ALASKA

Capital JUNEAU

UNITED STATES DISTRICT COURT DISTRICT OF ALASKA

The court sits at Anchorage, Fairbanks, Juneau, Ketchikan and Nome. For descriptive information refer to the United States Courts section.

Chief Judge
John W. Sedwick

Judges
James Keith Singleton, Jr.
Ralph R. Beistline

Senior Judges
James A. von der Heydt
James M. Fitzgerald
H. Russel Holland

Clerk
Michael D. Hall
Federal Building and U.S. Courthouse
222 West Seventh Avenue, Box 4
Anchorage, Alaska 99513-7564
(907) 677-6100

UNITED STATES MAGISTRATE JUDGES OF ALASKA

John D. Roberts
Albert H. Branson
Mary E. Guss
Matthew D. Jamin
Philip M. Pallenberg
Joseph W. Miller

UNITED STATES BANKRUPTCY COURT OF ALASKA

Chief Judge
Donald MacDonald IV

Recalled Judge
Herbert A. Ross

Bankruptcy Clerk
Wayne W. Wolfe
138 Old Federal Building
605 West Fourth Avenue
Anchorage, Alaska 99501-2296
(907) 271-2655

ALASKA SUPREME COURT

The Supreme Court is Alaska's court of last resort. The court consists of a chief justice and four associate justices. Justices are appointed by the governor from nominees of the Alaska Judicial Council and are subject to retention vote on a nonpartisan ballot at the first general election held more than three years after the appointment. Subsequent ten-year terms are by retention vote. The chief justice is elected by peer vote to serve a three-year term; terms may not be consecutive.

The court has statewide appellate jurisdiction. The court hears appeals of final judgments entered by the Superior Court in any civil action. In criminal proceedings and certain quasi-criminal matters, such as juvenile delinquency, the court has discretion to review decisions made by the Court of Appeals. The Supreme Court may also take jurisdiction of a case if the Court of Appeals certifies it involves a significant question of constitutional law or an issue of substantial public interest. The court has administrative authority over all courts and the practice of law in the state and may issue writs necessary to the exercise of proper jurisdiction.

The court sits en banc on a monthly basis at Anchorage and Fairbanks, semi-annually at Juneau and occasionally at other court locations.

Chief Justice
Dana Fabe

Associate Justices
Warren W. Matthews, Jr.
Robert L. Eastaugh
Alexander O. Bryner
Walter L. "Bud" Carpeneti

Clerk
Marilyn May
303 K Street
Anchorage, Alaska 99501-2084
(907) 264-0608

Administrative Director
Stephanie J. Cole
820 West Fourth Avenue
Anchorage, Alaska 99501-2005
(907) 264-0548

ALASKA COURT OF APPEALS

The Court of Appeals is the court of intermediate appellate jurisdiction created by the Alaska Legislature in 1980. Judges are appointed by the governor from nominees of the Alaska Judicial Council and are subject to retention vote at the first general election held more than three years after the appointment. Subsequent eight-year terms are by retention vote. A chief judge is appointed by the chief justice for a one-year term and may serve successive terms.

The court has appellate jurisdiction in actions and proceedings commenced in the Superior Court including appeals from judgments in criminal cases, post-conviction relief matters, juvenile delinquency cases, extradition cases, habeus corpus matters and cases involving probation and parole decisions, bail and the excessiveness or leniency of a sentence. The court also has jurisdiction to review sentences imposed by either the Superior Court or District Court and discretionary review of District Court criminal appeals to the Supreme Court. The Court of Appeals may issue injunctions,

ALASKA COURT OF APPEALS—*Continued*

writs and all other process necessary for the complete exercise of its jurisdiction.

The court sits en banc at Anchorage.

Chief Judge
Robert G. Coats

Judges
David Mannheimer
David C. Stewart

ALASKA SUPERIOR COURT

The Superior Court is Alaska's trial court of general jurisdiction. The court consists of four districts defined by geographic boundaries. Judges are appointed by the governor from nominees of the Alaska Judicial Council and are subject to retention vote in their respective judicial districts at the first general election held more than three years after appointment. Subsequent six-year terms are by retention vote. The chief justice designates a presiding judge in each judicial district to serve a one-year term. A presiding judge may serve successive terms. Judges may be temporarily assigned anywhere in the state up to ninety days per year, or for longer periods with the judge's acquiescence. The chief justice may appoint retired judges to serve on the bench under a special appointment pro tempore.

The court has original jurisdiction of all civil and criminal matters and exclusive jurisdiction in all domestic relations matters, children's proceedings, probate, guardianship and civil commitments. The court has concurrent jurisdiction of matters in the District Courts; however, no action within this concurrent jurisdiction except petitions for injunctive relief in domestic violence cases may be filed in the Superior Court except as provided by Supreme Court rules. The court has appellate jurisdiction of cases from the District Courts and may issue writs relevant to that jurisdiction.

FIRST JUDICIAL DISTRICT includes the "Panhandle" area in Southeastern Alaska. The court sits at Juneau, Ketchikan, Sitka and Wrangell/Petersburg.

Presiding Judge
Larry Weeks (Juneau)

Judge	Location
Patricia A. Collins	Juneau
Trevor N. Stephens	Ketchikan
Michael A. Thompson	Ketchikan
Larry C. Zervos	Sitka

SECOND JUDICIAL DISTRICT includes Northwest Alaska and the North Slope region. The court sits at Barrow, Kotzebue and Nome.

Presiding Judge
Michael I. Jeffery (Barrow)

Judge	Location
Richard Erlich	Kotzebue
Ben J. Esch	Nome

THIRD JUDICIAL DISTRICT includes the Aleutian Chain, the Bristol Bay region, the greater Anchorage region, Kenai Peninsula, Kodiak, Matanuska Valley and the Prince William Sound-Copper River region. The court sits at Anchorage, Dillingham, Kenai, Kodiak, Palmer and Valdez.

Presiding Judge
Dan A. Hensley (Anchorage)

Judge	Location
Larry D. Card	Anchorage
Morgan Christen	Anchorage
Sharon Gleason	Anchorage
Stephanie Joannides	Anchorage
Peter A. Michalski	Anchorage
William Morse	Anchorage
John Reese	Anchorage
Mark Rindner	Anchorage
John Suddock	Anchorage
Sen K. Tan	Anchorage
Phillip Volland	Anchorage
Michael Wolverton	Anchorage
vacancy	Anchorage
vacancy	Anchorage
Fred Torrisi	Dillingham
Harold M. Brown	Kenai
Jonathan H. Link	Kenai
Donald D. Hopwood	Kodiak
Beverly Winslow Cutler	Palmer
Eric Smith	Palmer

FOURTH JUDICIAL DISTRICT includes Interior Alaska. The court sits at Bethel and Fairbanks.

Presiding Judge
Niesje J. Steinkruger (Fairbanks)

Judge	Location
Dale O. Curda	Bethel
Leonard Devaney, III	Bethel
Charles Pengilly	Fairbanks
Richard D. Savell	Fairbanks
Mark I. Wood	Fairbanks
vacancy	Fairbanks
vacancy	Fairbanks

ALASKA DISTRICT COURTS

The District Courts are Alaska's courts of limited jurisdiction. Judges are appointed by the governor upon nomination by the Alaska Judicial Council and are subject to retention vote in their respective judicial districts at the first general election held more than one year after appointment. Subsequent four-year terms are by retention vote. The presiding Superior Court judge of each district may designate a deputy presiding judge to serve a one-year term; successive terms are permissible.

The courts have civil jurisdiction in cases involving $50,000 or less. The courts hear small claims up to $7,500. The courts have criminal jurisdiction over all state misdemeanors and local ordinances, may order injunctive relief in domestic violence cases, may issue summonses, arrest warrants and search warrants, hear preliminary hearings in felony cases and handle matters involving children on an emergency basis.

Magistrate posts have been created in many cities and towns to handle routine matters and ease the workload of district judges and also to serve rural areas of the state. Magistrates are appointed by and serve at the pleasure of the presiding Superior Court judge of each judicial district. Magistrates do not have to be law-trained.

FIRST JUDICIAL DISTRICT court sits at Juneau and Ketchikan.

ALASKA DISTRICT COURTS—*Continued*

Judge	Location
Peter Froehlich	Juneau
Kevin Miller	Ketchikan

SECOND JUDICIAL DISTRICT jurisdiction is exercised by magistrates and as provided by Supreme Court rules.

THIRD JUDICIAL DISTRICT court sits at Anchorage, Homer, Palmer and Valdez.

Deputy Presiding Judge
Samuel D. Adams (Anchorage)

Judge	Location
Brian Clark	Anchorage
John R. Lohff	Anchorage
Gregory J. Motyka	Anchorage
Sigurd E. Murphy	Anchorage
Nancy J. Nolan	Anchorage
Stephanie Rhoades	Anchorage
Jack Smith	Anchorage
James Wanamaker	Anchorage
M. Francis Neville	Homer
Suzanne Lombardi	Palmer
Joel H. Bolger	Valdez

FOURTH JUDICIAL DISTRICT court sits at Fairbanks.

Deputy Presiding Judge
Jane F. Kauvar

Judges
Raymond Funk
vacancy

Alaska Boroughs, Cities and Unified Governments

Aleutians East Borough
Sand Point

Municipality of Anchorage
Anchorage

Bristol Bay Borough
Naknek

Denali Borough
Healy

Fairbanks North Star Borough
Fairbanks

Haines Borough
Haines

City and Borough of Juneau
Juneau

Kenai Peninsula Borough
Soldotna

Ketchikan Gateway Borough
Ketchikan

Kodiak Island Borough
Kodiak

Lake and Peninsula Borough
King Salmon

Matanuska-Susitna Borough
Palmer

North Slope Borough
Barrow

Northwest Arctic Borough
Kotzebue

City and Borough of Sitka
Sitka

City and Borough of Yakutat
Yakutat

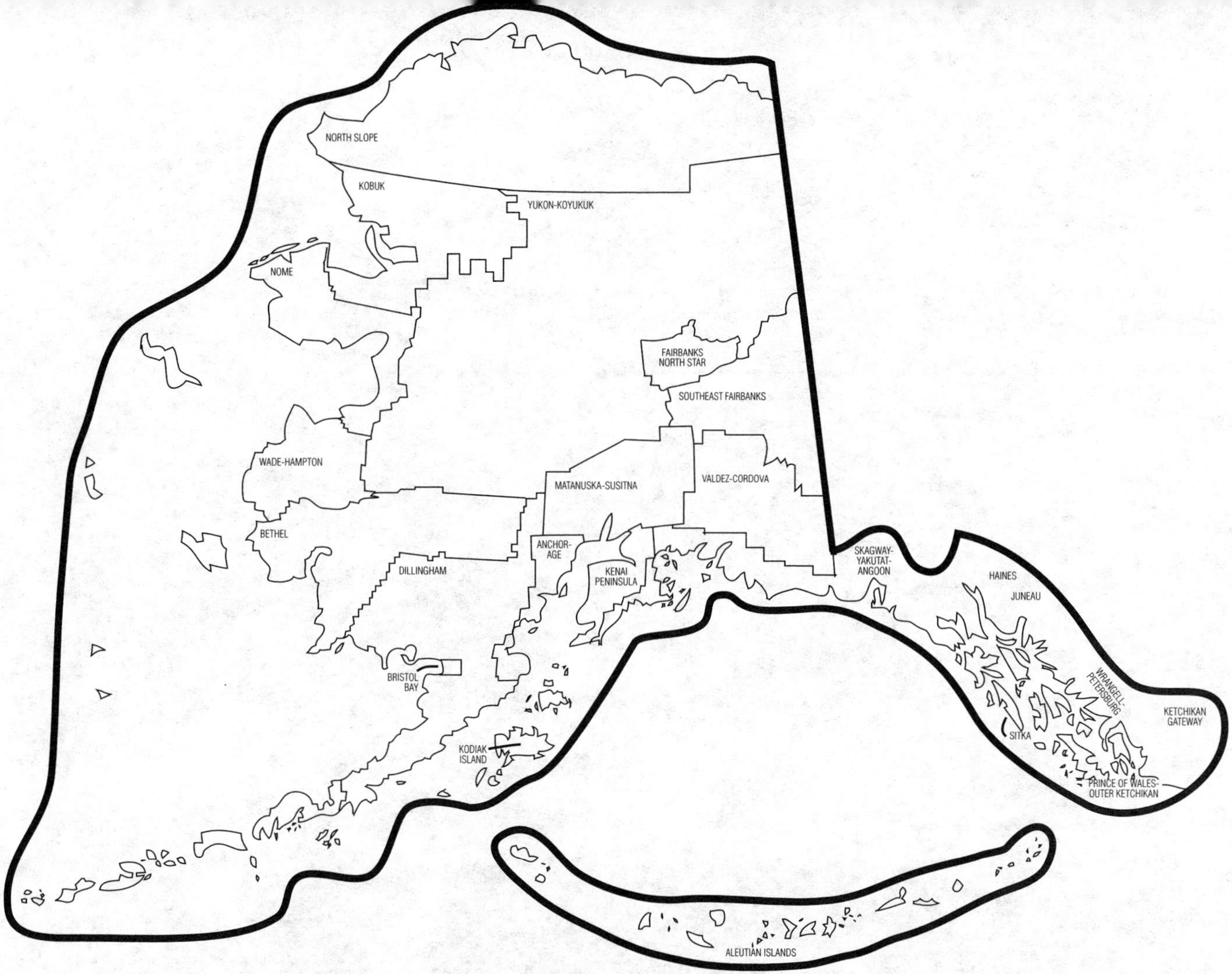
NORTH SLOPE
KOBUK
YUKON-KOYUKUK
NOME
FAIRBANKS NORTH STAR
SOUTHEAST FAIRBANKS
WADE-HAMPTON
MATANUSKA-SUSITNA
VALDEZ-CORDOVA
BETHEL
ANCHOR-AGE
DILLINGHAM
KENAI PENINSULA
SKAGWAY-YAKUTAT-ANGOON
HAINES
JUNEAU
BRISTOL BAY
WRANGELL-PETERSBURG
KETCHIKAN GATEWAY
SITKA
KODIAK ISLAND
PRINCE OF WALES-OUTER KETCHIKAN
ALEUTIAN ISLANDS

UNITED STATES DISTRICT COURT DISTRICT OF ALASKA

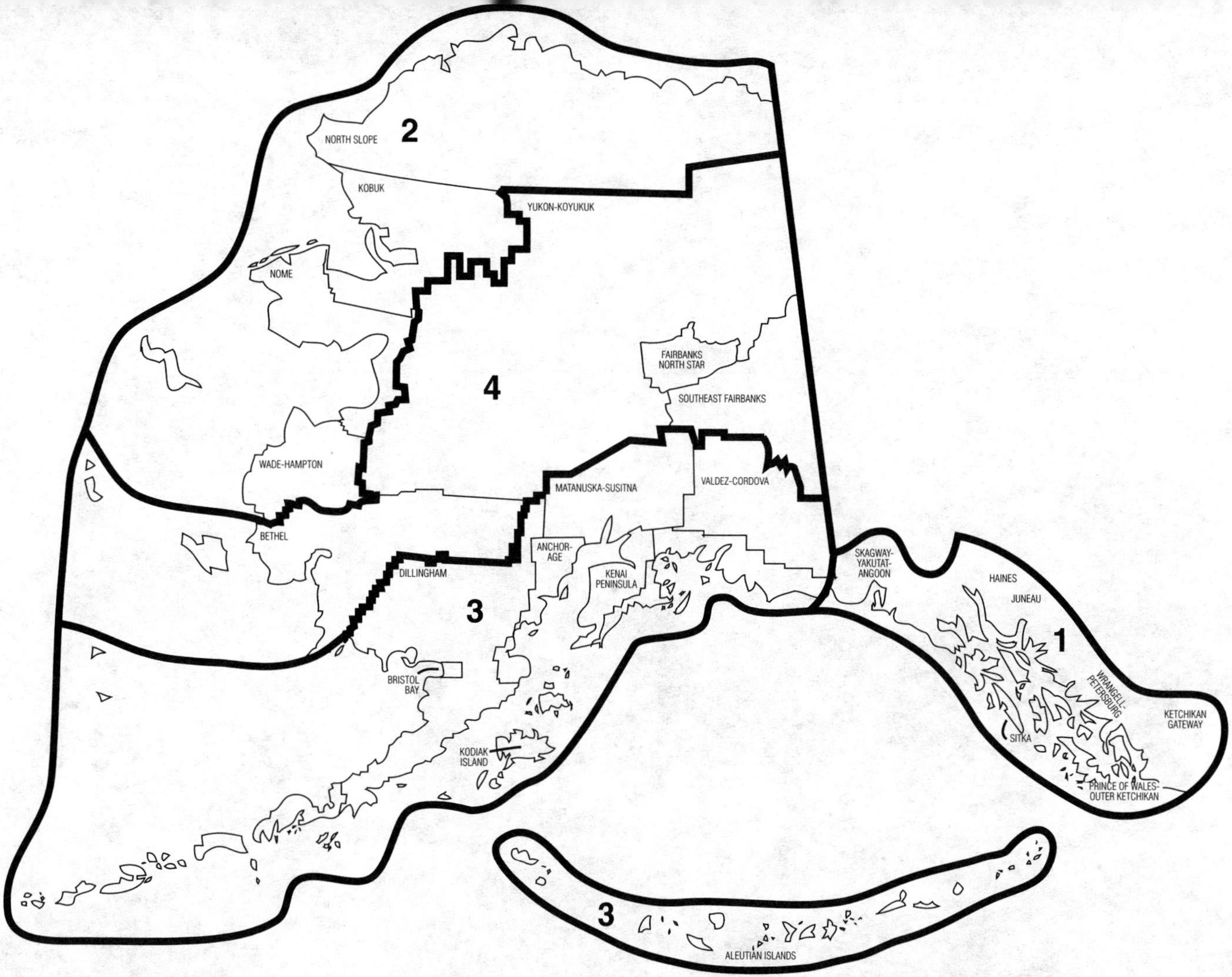
2
NORTH SLOPE
KOBUK
YUKON-KOYUKUK
NOME
4
FAIRBANKS NORTH STAR
SOUTHEAST FAIRBANKS
WADE-HAMPTON
MATANUSKA-SUSITNA
VALDEZ-CORDOVA
BETHEL
ANCHOR-AGE
KENAI PENINSULA
DILLINGHAM
3
BRISTOL BAY
KODIAK ISLAND
SKAGWAY-YAKUTAT-ANGOON
HAINES
JUNEAU
1
WRANGELL-PETERSBURG
SITKA
KETCHIKAN GATEWAY
PRINCE OF WALES-OUTER KETCHIKAN
3
ALEUTIAN ISLANDS

JUDICIAL DISTRICTS OF ALASKA SUPERIOR COURT AND ALASKA DISTRICT COURTS

ALASKA

ADAMS, Samuel D. *(Deputy Presiding Judge, Alaska District Court Third Judicial District)* Appointed by Governor Tony Knowles Sept 2, 1999 to term beginning Dec 1, 1999. Born Anchorage Alaska June 1, 1956. Educated at University of Alaska at Anchorage B.S. 1980 and University of Oregon J.D. 1985. Law Clerk to Hon. Beverly Winslow Cutler, Alaska Superior Court Third Judicial District 1985-86. Admitted to practice Alaska 1985. In legal practice Anchorage 1986-88.

Assistant District Attorney Anchorage 1988-93 and 1995-97. Special Prosecutor State of Alaska 1993-95 and 1997-99.

Office: 825 West Fourth Avenue, Anchorage 99501-2004.

Telephone: (907) 264-0643.

E-mail address: sdadams@courts.state.ak.us

BEISTLINE, Ralph R. *(Judge, United States District Court District of Alaska)* Appointed for life by President George W. Bush to term beginning May 24, 2002. Judge 1992 to May 2002 and Former Presiding Judge, Alaska Superior Court Fourth Judicial District, appointed by Governor Walter J. Hickel.

Office: Federal Building Box 4, 222 West Seventh Avenue, Anchorage 99513-7564.

Telephone: (907) 677-6257.

BOLGER, Joel H. *(Judge, Alaska District Court Third Judicial District)* Appointed by Governor Tony Knowles to term beginning 1997.

Mailing address: Box 127, Valdez 99686-0127.

Telephone: (907) 835-2266.

BRANSON, Albert H. *(Magistrate Judge, United States District Court District of Alaska)* Appointed by U.S. District Court judges.

Office: Federal Building Box 33, 222 West Seventh Avenue, Anchorage 99513-7525.

Telephone: (907) 677-6256.

BROWN, Harold M. *(Judge, Alaska Superior Court Third Judicial District)* Appointed by Governor Tony Knowles to term beginning 1996.

Office: 125 Trading Bay Drive, Suite 100, Kenai 99611-7717.

Telephone: (907) 283-8510.

BRYNER, Alexander O. *(Associate Justice, Alaska Supreme Court)* Appointed by Governor Tony Knowles Jan 24, 1997. Born 1943. Educated at Stanford University B.A. J.D. Law Clerk to Chief Justice George Boney, Alaska Supreme Court 1969-71. In legal practice Anchorage 1974-75. Judge, Alaska District Court Third Judicial District 1975-77. Chief Judge, Alaska Court of Appeals July 30, 1980 to 1997, appointed by Governor Jay S. Hammond.

With Public Defender Agency Anchorage 1972-74. U.S. Attorney Alaska 1977-80.

Office: 303 K Street, Anchorage 99501-2084.

Telephone: (907) 264-0632.

CARD, Larry D. *(Judge, Alaska Superior Court Third Judicial District)* Appointed by Governor Walter J. Hickel to term beginning 1993. Former Presiding Judge.

Office: 825 West Fourth Avenue, Anchorage 99501-2004.

Telephone: (907) 264-0414.

CARPENETI, Walter L. "Bud" *(Associate Justice, Alaska Supreme Court)* Appointed by Governor Tony Knowles to term beginning Nov 1998. Born San Francisco California Dec 1, 1945. Educated at Stanford University A.B. with distinction 1967, University of Columbia 1967-68 and University of California Boalt Hall School of Law J.D. 1970. Managing Editor University of California Law Review 1969-70. Law Clerk to Hon. John H. Dimond 1970-71 and Hon. Jay Rabinowitz 1971 Alaska Supreme Court. Admitted to practice Alaska 1970 and California 1971 Alaska Supreme Court. Began legal practice San Francisco California 1972. In legal practice Juneau Alaska 1974-81. Judge, Alaska Superior Court First Judicial District Oct 15, 1981 to 1998, appointed by Governor Jay S. Hammond.

Public Defender four years. Author "Legislative Apportionment: Multi-Member Districts and Fair Representation" University of Pennsylvania L. Rev. 1972 and book review of *Reapportionment in the 70's* University of California L. Rev. 1972. Member Alaska Judicial Council 1980-81 and Alaska Commission on Judicial Conduct 1991-95.

Mailing address: P.O. Box 114100, Juneau 99811-4100.

Telephone: (907) 463-4771.

CHRISTEN, Morgan *(Judge, Alaska Superior Court Third Judicial District)* Appointed by Governor Tony Knowles.

Office: 825 West Fourth Avenue, Anchorage 99501-2004.

Telephone: (907) 264-0667.

CLARK, Brian *(Judge, Alaska District Court Third Judicial District)* Appointed by governor.

Office: 825 West Fourth Avenue, Anchorage 99501-2004.

Telephone: (907) 264-0665.

COATS, Robert G. *(Chief Judge, Alaska Court of Appeals)* Appointed by Governor Jay S. Hammond July 30, 1980 to term beginning Sept 15, 1980. Retained by election. Chief Judge since 1997. Born Spokane Washington Jan 7, 1943. Protestant. Educated at University of Washington B.A. cum laude 1965 and Harvard University School of Law LL.B. 1968. Law Clerk to Hon. Jay A. Rabinowitz, Alaska Supreme Court 1968-69 and 1971. Admitted to practice Alaska 1971.

Assistant Public Defender Kenai 1972. Assistant Public Defender 1973-78 and Assistant Attorney General 1978-80 Fairbanks. Member Alaska Bar Association. Specialist Five U.S. Army 1969-71. Enjoys tennis and skiing.

Office: 303 K Street, Anchorage 99501-2084.

Telephone: (907) 264-0757.

COLLINS, Patricia A. *(Judge, Alaska Superior Court First Judicial District)* Appointed by Governor Tony Knowles to term beginning 1999. Former part-time Magistrate Judge, U.S. District Court District of Alaska, appointed by U.S. District Court judges. Former Judge, Alaska District Court First Judicial District, appointed by Governor Tony Knowles.

Mailing address: P.O. Box 114100, Juneau 99811-4100.

Telephone: (907) 463-4741.

CURDA, Dale O. *(Judge, Alaska Superior Court Fourth Judicial District)* Appointed by Governor Steve Cowper Dec 20, 1989 to term beginning Feb 9, 1990. Retained by election Nov 8, 1994 and Nov 2000. Current term expires 2006. Born Oak Park Illinois Oct 29, 1942. Educated at Illinois Benedictine College B.A. 1964, Trinity College M.A.T. 1970 and Antioch School of Law J.D. 1980. Admitted to practice Alaska 1983. In legal practice Bethel 1984-87. Magistrate Alaska Court System 1980-83.

District Attorney Bethel 1987-90. Training Judge Alaska Court System since 1990.

Mailing address: Box 130, Bethel 99559-0130.

Telephone: (907) 543-1114.

CUTLER, Beverly Winslow *(Judge, Alaska Superior Court Third Judicial District)* Appointed by Governor Jay S. Hammond to term beginning Oct 28, 1982. Retained by election. First woman to fill a Superior Court judgeship in Alaska. Born Washington D.C. Sept 10, 1949. Educated at Stanford University B.A. 1971 and Yale University J.D. 1974. Admitted to practice Alaska 1975. Judge, Alaska District Court Third Judicial District Sept 26, 1977 to Oct 27, 1982, appointed by Governor Jay S. Hammond.

With Alaska Public Defender Agency at Anchorage 1975-77. Member Anchorage Association of Women Lawyers, National Association of Women Judges, Anchorage, Alaska and American Bar Associations. Enjoys sports, family and farming.

Office: 435 South Denali Street, Palmer 99645-6437.

Telephone: (907) 746-7500.

DEVANEY, Leonard, III *(Judge, Alaska Superior Court Fourth Judicial District)* Appointed by Governor Tony Knowles to term beginning May 1, 2002.

Mailing address: Box 130, Bethel 99559-0130.

Telephone: (907) 543-1114.

EASTAUGH, Robert L. *(Associate Justice, Alaska Supreme Court)* Appointed by Governor Walter J. Hickel April 1994. Born Seattle Washington Nov 11, 1943. Educated at Yale University B.A. and University of Michigan Law School J.D. Admitted to practice Alaska 1968. In legal practice 22 years.

Assistant District Attorney Anchorage. Assistant Attorney General Alaska.

Office: 303 K Street, Anchorage 99501-2084.

Telephone: (907) 264-0624.

ERLICH, Richard *(Judge, Alaska Superior Court Second Judicial District)* Appointed by Governor Walter J. Hickel to term beginning 1991.

Mailing address: Box 317, Kotzebue 99752-0317.

Telephone: (907) 442-3664.

ESCH, Ben J. *(Judge, Alaska Superior Court Second Judicial District)* Appointed by Governor Tony Knowles to term beginning 1996.

Mailing address: Box 1110, Nome 99762-1110.

Telephone: (907) 443-5216.

FABE, Dana *(Chief Justice, Alaska Supreme Court)* Appointed by Governor Tony Knowles Jan 26, 1996 to term beginning March 1996. Retained by election 2000. Current term expires 2010. Chief Justice since July 1, 2000. First woman to serve on Alaska Supreme Court. Born Cincinnati Ohio March 29, 1951. Educated at Cornell University B.A. 1973 and Northeastern University J.D. 1976. Law Clerk to Hon. Edmond W. Burke, Alaska Supreme Court 1976-77. Admitted to practice Alaska 1977. Judge, Alaska Superior Court Third Judicial District 1988-96, appointed by Governor Steve Cowper.

Staff attorney 1977-81 and Chief Public Defender 1981-88 Alaska Public Defender Agency. Chairperson Alaska Criminal Pattern Jury Instructions Committee 1984-88, Supreme Court Committee on Contempt Procedures 1991 and Alaska Civil Rules Committee 1994-2001. Board of Directors Alaska Bar Association 1987-88. Training Judge Third Judicial District 1991-96. Vice Chair Tribal Relations Committee Conference of Chief Justices. Alumna of the Year Northeastern University School of Law 1983. Alumni Public Service Award Northeastern University School of Law 1991. Co-chair Joint State Federal Gender Equality Task Force 1996-2000. Member Soroptimist International of Cook Inlet.

Office: 303 K Street, Anchorage 99501-2084.

Telephone: (907) 264-0622.

FITZGERALD, James M. *(Senior Judge, United States District Court District of Alaska)* Appointed for life by President Gerald R. Ford to term beginning Feb 28, 1975. Former Chief Judge. Assumed Senior status, serves by assignment. Born Portland Oregon Oct 7, 1920. Educated at University of Oregon 1941, Willamette University B.A. 1942 LL.B. 1951 and University of Washington Institute of Public Administration 1951-52. Admitted to practice Oregon 1951, U.S. Court of Appeals Ninth Circuit 1953, Territory of Alaska 1953 and U.S. Supreme Court 1959. Judge, Alaska Superior Court 1959-72. Associate Justice, Alaska Supreme Court 1972-75, appointed by Governor William Allen Egan.

Former Assistant U.S. Attorney and City Attorney Anchorage. Legal Counsel to Governor of Alaska. Commissioner of Public Safety Alaska 1959. Member Oregon State Bar, Alaska and American Bar Associations. Private U.S. Army 1940-41. Technical Sergeant USMC 1942-46. Democrat. Advisory Board Salvation Army. Member Anchorage Hockey Association, U.S. Ski Association and Alyeska Ski Club of Alaska.

Office: Federal Building Box 50, 222 West Seventh Avenue, Anchorage 99513-7579.

Telephone: (907) 677-6253.

FROEHLICH, Peter *(Judge, Alaska District Court First Judicial District)* Appointed by Governor Steve Cowper to term beginning 1989.

Mailing address: Box 114100, Juneau 99811-4100.

Telephone: (907) 463-4730.

FUNK, Raymond *(Judge, Alaska District Court Fourth Judicial District)* Appointed by Governor Tony Knowles to term beginning 1998.

Office: 101 Lacey Street, Fairbanks 99701-4765.

Telephone: (907) 452-9328.

GLEASON, Sharon *(Judge, Alaska Superior Court Third Judicial District)* Appointed by Governor Tony Knowles.

Office: 825 West Fourth Avenue, Anchorage 99501-2004.

Telephone: (907) 264-0772.

GUSS, Mary E. *(Magistrate Judge, United States District Court District of Alaska)* Appointed by U.S. District Court judges to term beginning Dec 14, 2000. Serves part time.

Office: 507 U.S. Courthouse, 648 Mission Street, Ketchikan 99901.

Telephone: (907) 225-0530.

HENSLEY, Dan A. *(Presiding Judge, Alaska Superior Court Third Judicial District)* Appointed by Governor Tony Knowles to term beginning 1996.

Office: 825 West Fourth Avenue, Anchorage 99501-2004.

Telephone: (907) 264-0403.

HOLLAND, H. Russel *(Senior Judge, United States District Court District of Alaska)* Appointed for life by President Ronald Reagan to term beginning July 23, 1984. Former Chief Judge. Assumed Senior status Sept 18, 2001, serves by assignment. Born Pontiac Michigan Sept 18, 1936. Catholic. Educated at University of Michigan B.B.A. 1958 LL.B. 1961. Law Clerk to Chief Justice, Alaska Supreme Court 1961-63. Admitted to practice Alaska 1963. Began legal practice Anchorage 1963.

Assistant U.S. Attorney 1963-65. Member Anchorage, Alaska and American Bar Associations.

Office: Federal Building Box 54, 222 West Seventh Avenue, Anchorage 99513-7545.

Telephone: (907) 677-6252.

HOPWOOD, Donald D. *(Judge, Alaska Superior Court Third Judicial District)* Appointed by Governor Steve Cowper to term beginning 1990. Retained by election 1994 and 2000.

Office: 204 Mission Road, Room 124F, Kodiak 99615-7312.

Telephone: (907) 486-1623.

JAMIN, Matthew D. *(Magistrate Judge, United States District Court District of Alaska)* Appointed by U.S. District Court judges to term beginning Nov 1, 1984. Reappointed Nov 1, 1988, Nov 1, 1992, Nov 1, 1996 and Nov 1, 2000. Current term expires Nov 1, 2004. Serves part time. Born New Brunswick New Jersey Nov 29, 1947. Educated at Colgate University B.S. with honors 1969 and Harvard University J.D. 1974. Admitted to practice Alaska 1974, U.S. District Court District of Alaska 1974 and U.S. Court of Appeals Ninth Circuit 1980. Began legal practice Kodiak 1974.

Member Alaska Bar Association.

Office: 323 Carolyn Street, Kodiak 99615.

Telephone: (907) 486-6061.

JEFFERY, Michael I. *(Presiding Judge, Alaska Superior Court Second Judicial District)* Appointed by Governor Jay S. Hammond Oct 1982 to term beginning Dec 3, 1982. Retained by election 1986, 1992 and 1998. Current term expires 2004. Presiding Judge since 1993. Born Los Angeles California Dec 29, 1944. Presbyterian. Educated at Stanford University A.B. 1966 and Yale Law School J.D. 1969. Board of Editors Yale Law Journal 1968-69. Admitted to practice Massachusetts 1969, U.S. District Courts District of Massachusetts 1969, District of California 1970 and District of Alaska 1977, California 1970 and Alaska 1977.

Attorney for publicly funded legal services organizations Boston Massachusetts 1969-70 and Barrow Alaska 1977-82. Author Note "Foul Buzzards and Obscene Harpies? The FBI's Use of Sec. 1001 in Criminal Investigations" Yale L. Jour. 1969. President Alaska Conference of Judges 1986-87. Member Alaska Juvenile Justice Advisory Committee 1998-2003 and Criminal Justice Assessment Commission 1999. Member Ukpiagvik (Barrow), Alaska and American Bar Associations. Attended NITA of the North, Alaska Bar Association National Institute of Trial Advocacy CLE Aug 1981 and General Jurisdiction, Mediation and other Sessions The National Judicial College May 1983-94. Member Governor's Review Board on Alcoholism 1980-82, Mayor's Blue Ribbon Panel on Alcohol and Drug Abuse 1986-87 and Statewide Steering Committee on Fetal Alcohol Syndrome 2000-03. Past President Silak-Kuagvik Communications (KBRW Community Radio), Barrow Alaska. Advisory Board Seva Foundation, San Rafael California. Member and Past President Rotary Club of Barrow (Nuvuk). Enjoys set net fishing in Bristol Bay and Eskimo drumming. Active in church choir and youth program.

Mailing address: Box 270, Barrow 99723-0270.

Telephone: (907) 852-4800.

JOANNIDES, Stephanie *(Judge, Alaska Superior Court Third Judicial District)* Appointed by Governor Tony Knowles April 10, 2000. Former Judge, Alaska District Court Third Judicial District, appointed by Governor Tony Knowles to term beginning 1995.

Office: 825 West Fourth Avenue, Anchorage 99501-2004.

Telephone: (907) 264-0430.

KAUVAR, Jane F. *(Deputy Presiding Judge, Alaska District Court Fourth Judicial District)* Appointed by Governor Jay S. Hammond to term beginning March 27, 1981. Retained by election. Current term expires 2006. Born Denver Colorado July 21, 1948. Educated at University of Colorado B.A. with honors 1970 and University of California Boalt Hall School of Law J.D. 1973. Staff member Ecology Law Quarterly 1971-73. Law Clerk to Chief Justice Jay A. Rabinowitz, Alaska Supreme Court 1973-74. Admitted to practice Alaska 1973. Began legal practice Fairbanks 1973.

Former Assistant District Attorney and Assistant Public Defender. Member Alaska Bar Association. Attended Search and Seizure Course The National Judicial College May 1982 and Evidence Course American Academy of Judicial Education Aug 1988. Enjoys swimming, bicycling and traveling.

Office: 101 Lacey Street, Fairbanks 99701-4765.

Telephone: (907) 452-9371.

LINK, Jonathan H. *(Judge, Alaska Superior Court Third Judicial District)* Appointed by Governor Steve Cowper to term beginning Oct 1, 1990. Retained by election. Born Washington D.C. Jan 22, 1944. Educated at Whittier College B.A. 1965 and University of California Hastings College of the Law J.D. 1972. Admitted to practice Alaska 1972, U.S. District Court District of Alaska 1972 and U.S. Court of Appeals Ninth Circuit

LINK, JONATHAN H.—*Continued*

1972. In legal practice Anchorage 1972-74 and Fairbanks 1974-90.

Office: 125 Trading Bay Drive, Suite 100, Kenai 99611-7717.

Telephone: (907) 283-8506.

LOHFF, John R. *(Judge, Alaska District Court Third Judicial District)* Appointed by Governor Walter J. Hickel March 8, 1991 to term beginning May 3, 1991. Retained by election 1994, 1998 and 2002. Current term expires 2006. Former Deputy Presiding Judge. Educated at University of Iowa B.A. 1967 and Golden Gate University J.D. 1973. Admitted to practice Iowa 1974 and Alaska 1978. In legal practice Anchorage 1979-91.

Office: 825 West Fourth Avenue, Anchorage 99501-2004.

Telephone: (907) 264-0666.

LOMBARDI, Suzanne *(Judge, Alaska District Court Third Judicial District)* Appointed by Governor Tony Knowles to term beginning 1997.

Office: 435 South Denali, Palmer 99645-6437.

Telephone: (907) 746-7500.

MacDONALD, Donald, IV *(Chief Judge, United States Bankruptcy Court District of Alaska)* Appointed by U.S. Court of Appeals Ninth Circuit judges. Term expires July 2004.

Office: 138 Old Federal Building, 605 West Fourth Avenue, Anchorage 99501-2296.

Telephone: (907) 271-2667.

MANNHEIMER, David *(Judge, Alaska Court of Appeals)* Appointed by governor to term beginning 1990.

Office: 303 K Street, Anchorage 99501-2084.

Telephone: (907) 264-0754.

MATTHEWS, Warren W., Jr. *(Associate Justice, Alaska Supreme Court)* Appointed by Governor Jay S. Hammond to term beginning June 1977. Retained by election. Chief Judge 1987-90 and 1997 to June 30, 2000. Born Santa Cruz California April 5, 1939. Educated at Stanford University B.A. 1961 and Harvard Law School J.D. 1964. Admitted to practice Alaska 1965. In legal practice Anchorage 1964-77.

Member Alaska and American Bar Associations.

Office: 303 K Street, Anchorage 99501-2084.

Telephone: (907) 264-0618.

MICHALSKI, Peter A. *(Judge, Alaska Superior Court Third Judicial District)* Appointed by Governor William Sheffield to term beginning March 11, 1985. Retained by election Nov 1988, 1994 and Nov 7, 2000. Current term expires 2007. Born St. Paul Minnesota 1946. United Methodist. Educated at University of Minnesota B.A. 1968 J.D. 1971.

Assistant Attorney General Juneau 1971-73. Assistant District Attorney Fairbanks 1973-77. Chief Office of Special Prosecutions and Appeals 1977-85. Commissioned Officer U.S. Army ROTC 1970-78 (active duty for training only).

Office: 825 West Fourth Avenue, Anchorage 99501-2004.

Telephone: (907) 264-0510.

MILLER, Joseph W. *(Magistrate Judge, United States District Court District of Alaska)* Appointed by U.S. District Court judges to term beginning June 21, 2002. Serves part time.

Office: U.S. Courthouse, 101 Twelfth Avenue, Fairbanks 99701-6283.

Telephone: (907) 451-5795.

MILLER, Kevin *(Judge, Alaska District Court First Judicial District)* Appointed by Governor Tony Knowles to term beginning 1999.

Office: 415 Main Street, Room 400, Ketchikan 99901-6399.

Telephone: (907) 225-3197.

MORSE, William *(Judge, Alaska Superior Court Third Judicial District)* Appointed by governor.

Office: 825 West Fourth Avenue, Anchorage 99501-2004.

Telephone: (907) 264-0425.

MOTYKA, Gregory J. *(Judge, Alaska District Court Third Judicial District)* Appointed by Governor Walter J. Hickel to term beginning 1991.

Office: 825 West Fourth Avenue, Anchorage 99501-2004.

Telephone: (907) 264-0665.

MURPHY, Sigurd E. *(Judge, Alaska District Court Third Judicial District)* Appointed by Governor Walter J. Hickel to term beginning 1992.

Office: 825 West Fourth Avenue, Anchorage 99501-2004.

Telephone: (907) 264-0666.

NEVILLE, M. Francis *(Judge, Alaska District Court Third Judicial District)* Appointed by governor to term beginning 1990.

Office: 3670 Lake Street, Suite 400, Homer 99603-7647.

Telephone: (907) 235-8171.

NOLAN, Nancy J. *(Judge, Alaska District Court Third Judicial District)* Appointed by Governor Tony Knowles.

Office: 825 West Fourth Avenue, Anchorage 99501-2004.

Telephone: (907) 264-0643.

PALLENBERG, Philip M. *(Magistrate Judge, United States District Court District of Alaska)* Appointed by U.S. District Court judges to term beginning Dec 14, 2000. Serves part time.

Mailing address: P.O. Box 020349, Juneau 99802-0349.

Telephone: (907) 586-7337.

PENGILLY, Charles *(Judge, Alaska Superior Court Fourth Judicial District)* Appointed by Governor Tony Knowles. Born Minneapolis Minnesota May 16, 1948. Educated at University of California at Berkeley B.A. 1970 J.D. 1980. Law Clerk to Chief Justice Jay A. Rabinowitz, Alaska Supreme Court 1980-81. Admitted to practice California 1980 and Alaska 1981. In legal practice Fairbanks. Former Judge, Alaska District Court Fourth Judicial District, appointed by Governor Steve Cowper to term beginning Oct 1990.

Author "Never Cry Anders" 9 Criminal Justice Journal 45, 1986, "Post-Plea Appeal of Dispositive Issues" 5 Alaska L. Rev. 221, 1988 and "Restitution, Retribution, and the Constitution" 7 Alaska L. Rev. 333, 1990.

Office: 101 Lacey Street, Fairbanks 99701-4765.

Telephone: (907) 452-9317.

REESE, John *(Judge, Alaska Superior Court Third Judicial District)* Appointed by Governor Steve Cowper to term beginning Sept 1989. Retained by election Nov 1992 and Nov 1998. Current term expires Nov 2004. Born Shawnee Oklahoma Nov 15, 1943. Educated at Oklahoma State University B.A. 1965 and University of Oklahoma J.D. 1968. Admitted to practice Oklahoma 1968, Alaska 1969, U.S. District Court District of Alaska 1969 and U.S. Court of Appeals Tenth Circuit 1989. In legal practice Anchorage Alaska 1975-89.

Office: 825 West Fourth Avenue, Anchorage 99501-2004.

Telephone: (907) 264-0401.

RHOADES, Stephanie *(Judge, Alaska District Court Third Judicial District)* Appointed by Governor Walter J. Hickel to term beginning Aug 1992. Retained by election 1994, 1998 and 2002. Current term expires 2006. Born Newton Massachusetts Sept 24, 1958. Educated at University of Massachusetts B.A. 1983 and Northeastern University School of Law J.D. 1986. Law clerk to Hon. Allen T. Compton, Alaska Supreme Court 1986-87. Admitted to practice Massachusetts 1986 and Alaska 1987. In legal practice Anchorage 1987-92.

Assistant District Attorney Anchorage 1988-92. Member Alaska and Massachusetts Bar Associations. Attended General Jurisdiction Course May 1993 and Advanced Evidence Course Oct 1998 The National Judicial College. Panelist and Participant Sixth Annual Training Conference National Association of Drug Court Professionals June 2000 and "Future Research on Mental Health Courts and Other Jail Diversion Strategies: Setting an Agenda/Building Partnerships" John D. and Catherine T. MacArthur Foundation and National Institute of Mental Health June 2001. Discussion Leader and Participant "Co-Occurring Mental and Substance Abuse Disorders" The National Judicial College May 2002. Recipient Chuck Melick Memorial Award from Assets, Inc. 1998, Achievement Award from Mental Health Association in Alaska 1999, Award of Recognition from Anchorage Alaska Chapter National Alliance for the Mentally Ill 2000 and Woman of Distinction Award from Soroptimist International of Cook Inlet 2000.

Office: 825 West Fourth Avenue, Anchorage 99501-2004.

Telephone: (907) 264-0666.

RINDNER, Mark *(Judge, Alaska Superior Court Third Judicial District)* Appointed by Governor Tony Knowles 2000.

Office: 825 West Fourth Avenue, Fourth Floor, Anchorage 99501-2004.

Telephone: (907) 264-0412.

ROBERTS, John D. *(Magistrate Judge, United States District Court District of Alaska)* Appointed by U.S. District Court judges to term beginning June 3, 1977. Reappointed to subsequent terms. Born Orlando Florida Nov 1, 1942. Episcopalian. Educated at Hampden-Sydney College B.S. 1964 and Washington and Lee University LL.B. 1968. Law Clerk to Hon. Charles R. Scott, U.S. District Court Middle District of Florida 1968-69. Member Legal Research Association, Phi Alpha Delta, Chi Phi and Psi Chi. Admitted to practice Virginia 1968, Florida 1969, U.S. Courts of Appeals Fifth 1970 and Ninth 1974 Circuits, U.S. Supreme Court 1973 and Alaska 1976. In legal practice Arlington Virginia 1969-70.

Assistant U.S. Attorney Middle District of Florida 1970-74 and District of Alaska 1974-77. Member National Council of U.S. Magistrates (Ninth Circuit Director 1984 and 1985), Ninth Circuit Judicial Conference (Chairperson U.S. Magistrates Liaison Committee 1985), Virginia State Bar, Alaska and American (Executive Board National Conference of Special Court Judges Judicial Administration Division since 1986) Bar Associations. Recipient Special Achievement Award from U.S. Attorney General Levi 1976. Listed in *Who's Who in American Law.* Republican. Board of Directors Teen Challenge of Alaska 1984-93, Alaska Youth For Christ 1993-96 and Governor's Prayer Breakfast since 1994. Chairman Eagle Scout Review Board Boy Scouts of America since 1993.

Office: Federal Building Box 46, 222 West Seventh Avenue, Anchorage 99513-7563.

Telephone: (907) 677-6255.

ROSS, Herbert A. *(Recalled Judge, United States Bankruptcy Court District of Alaska)* Appointed by U.S. Court of Appeals Ninth Circuit judges. Appointed Recalled Judge by the Judicial Council of the Ninth Circuit.

Office: 138 Old Federal Building, 605 West Fourth Avenue, Anchorage 99501-2296.

Telephone: (907) 271-2630.

SAVELL, Richard D. *(Judge, Alaska Superior Court Fourth Judicial District)* Appointed by Governor Steve Cowper to term beginning 1987. Former Presiding Judge.

Office: 101 Lacey Street, Fairbanks 99701-4765.

Telephone: (907) 452-9315.

SEDWICK, John W. *(Chief Judge, United States District Court District of Alaska)* Appointed for life by President George Bush to term beginning 1992. Chief Judge since Sept 2, 2002. Born Kittanning Pennsylvania March 13, 1946. Educated at Dartmouth College B.A. 1968 and Harvard Law School J.D. 1972. In legal practice Anchorage 1972-81 and 1982-92.

Sergeant U.S. Air National Guard 1969-71. Director Division of Land and Water Management Department of Natural Resources Alaska 1981-82.

Office: Federal Building, 222 West Seventh Avenue, #32, Anchorage 99513.

Telephone: (907) 677-6251.

SINGLETON, James Keith, Jr. *(Judge, United States District Court District of Alaska)* Appointed for life by President George Bush to term beginning 1990. Former Chief Judge. Born Oakland California Jan 27, 1939. Roman Catholic. Educated at University of Santa Clara, University of California at Berkeley A.B. in Political Science 1961 and Boalt Hall School of Law LL.B. 1964. Admitted to practice Alaska 1965 and California 1965. In legal practice Anchorage Alaska 1965-70. Judge, Alaska Superior Court Third Judicial District 1970-80, appointed by Governor Keith Miller. Judge, Alaska Court of Appeals 1980-90, appointed by Governor Jay S. Hammond.

Member State Bar of California, Anchorage, Alaska and American Bar Associations. Republican. District Chairman Republican Party 1969-70. Chairman State Local Boundary Commission 1966-70. Member Board of

SINGLETON, JAMES KEITH, JR.—*Continued*

Directors Alaska Children's Service 1970-73 and Breakthrough 1978-80.

Office: Federal Building Box 41, 222 West Seventh Avenue, Anchorage 99513-9987.

Telephone: (907) 677-6250.

SMITH, Eric *(Judge, Alaska Superior Court Third Judicial District)* Appointed by Governor Tony Knowles to term beginning 1996.

Office: 435 South Denali Street, Palmer 99645-6437.

Telephone: (907) 746-7500.

SMITH, Jack *(Judge, Alaska District Court Third Judicial District)* Appointed by governor.

Office: 825 West Fourth Avenue, Anchorage 99501-2004.

Telephone: (907) 264-0665.

STEINKRUGER, Niesje J. *(Presiding Judge, Alaska Superior Court Fourth Judicial District)* Appointed by Governor Steve Cowper to term beginning 1988.

Office: 101 Lacey Street, Fairbanks 99701-4765.

Telephone: (907) 452-9313.

STEPHENS, Trevor N. *(Judge, Alaska Superior Court First Judicial District)* Appointed by Governor Tony Knowles Aug 1, 2000.

Office: 415 Main Street, Room 400, Ketchikan 99901-6399.

Telephone: (907) 225-3141.

STEWART, David C. *(Judge, Alaska Court of Appeals)* Appointed by Governor Tony Knowles to term beginning 1997.

Office: 303 K Street, Anchorage 99501-2084.

Telephone: (907) 264-0751.

SUDDOCK, John *(Judge, Alaska Superior Court Third Judicial District)* Appointed by governor.

Office: 825 West Fourth Avenue, Anchorage 99501-2004.

Telephone: (907) 264-0418.

TAN, Sen K. *(Judge, Alaska Superior Court Third Judicial District)* Appointed by Governor Tony Knowles Dec 3, 1996. Born May 1, 1955. Educated at University of Kent at Canterbury, England B.A. with honors 1978 and Northeastern University School of Law J.D. 1982. Admitted to practice Alaska 1983.

Office: 825 West Fourth Avenue, Anchorage 99501-2004.

Telephone: (907) 264-0408.

THOMPSON, Michael A. *(Judge, Alaska Superior Court First Judicial District)* Appointed by Governor Walter J. Hickel to term beginning 1991.

Office: 415 Main Street, Room 400, Ketchikan 99901-6399.

Telephone: (907) 225-3141.

TORRISI, Fred *(Judge, Alaska Superior Court Third Judicial District)* Appointed by Governor Tony Knowles Nov 28, 1996 to term beginning Jan 2, 1997. Retained by election Nov 2000. Current term expires Nov 2006. Educated at University of Notre Dame B.S. 1970 and University of Maine J.D. 1974. Admitted to practice Alaska 1974.

Mailing address: Box 909, Dillingham 99576-0909.

Telephone: (907) 842-5215.

E-mail address: ftorrisi@courts.state.ak.us

VOLLAND, Phillip *(Judge, Alaska Superior Court Third Judicial District)* Appointed by governor.

Office: 825 West Fourth Avenue, Anchorage 99501-2004.

Telephone: (907) 264-0406.

von der HEYDT, James A. *(Senior Judge, United States District Court District of Alaska)* Appointed for life by President Lyndon B. Johnson to term beginning 1966. Former Chief Judge. Assumed Senior status, serves by assignment. Born Miles City Montana July 15, 1919. Educated at Albion College A.B. 1942 and Northwestern University J.D. 1951. Member Phi Delta Phi and Sigma Nu. Admitted to practice Alaska 1951. In legal practice Nome 1953-59. Judge, Alaska Superior Court First Judicial District 1959-66.

U.S. Commissioner Nome 1951. U.S. Attorney District of Alaska Division Two 1951-53. Member Alaska House of Representatives 1957-59. Member American Judicature Society and Alaska Bar Association (Board of Governors 1955-59 and President 1958-59). Member Wilson Ornithologists Society and 32° Scottish Rite Shriners. President Anchorage Fine Arts Museum Association. Specializes in study of Arctic bird life. Artist and writer.

Office: Federal Building Box 40, 222 West Seventh Avenue, Anchorage 99513-7536.

Telephone: (907) 677-6254.

WANAMAKER, James *(Judge, Alaska District Court Third Judicial District)* Appointed by Governor Walter J. Hickel to term beginning 1993.

Office: 825 West Fourth Avenue, Anchorage 99501-2004.

Telephone: (907) 264-0643.

WEEKS, Larry *(Presiding Judge, Alaska Superior Court First Judicial District)* Appointed by Governor Steve Cowper to term beginning Sept 10, 1990. Born Homberg Illinois March 9, 1943. Educated at University of Illinois B.S. 1969 J.D. 1972. Admitted to practice Illinois 1972, Alaska 1973, U.S. District Court District of Alaska 1973 and U.S. Court of Appeals Ninth Circuit 1973. In legal practice Juneau 1983-88.

District Attorney Juneau 1975-79 and Anchorage 1979-82. Member Juneau, Alaska (Member 1985-90 and President 1988-89 Board of Governors), Illinois State and American Bar Associations. U.S. Army 1961-64. Member local school and municipal advisory committees and Friends of Alaska State Museum. Enjoys the outdoors.

Mailing address: Box 114100, Juneau 99811-4100.

Telephone: (907) 463-4742.

WOLVERTON, Michael *(Judge, Alaska Superior Court Third Judicial District)* Appointed by Governor Tony Knowles. Former Judge and Presiding Judge, Alaska District Court Third Judicial District, appointed by Governor Tony Knowles to term beginning 1996.

Office: 825 West Fourth Avenue, Anchorage 99501-2004.

Telephone: (907) 264-0410.

WOOD, Mark I. *(Judge, Alaska Superior Court Fourth Judicial District)* Appointed by Governor Tony Knowles to term beginning Sept 2002. Born Evanston Illinois May 13, 1948. Church of Jesus Christ of Latter-Day Saints. Educated at Stanford University A.B. with honors 1970 and Cornell Law School J.D. 1975. Re-

WOOD, MARK I.—*Continued*

search Editor Cornell International Law Review 1973-75. Law Clerk to Hon. James M. Fitzgerald, Alaska Supreme Court Summer 1974. Admitted to practice Alaska 1975 and U.S. District Court District of Alaska 1975. In legal practice Fairbanks 1975-79. Judge Jan 1993 to Sept 2002 and Deputy Presiding Judge 2000-01, Alaska District Court Fourth Judicial District, appointed by Governor Walter J. Hickel. Magistrate Training Judge 1999-2001. Former Judge pro tem, Alaska Superior Court Fourth Judicial District.

Assistant District Attorney (Supervisor Sexual Assault Unit 1983-86 and Juvenile Waiver Unit 1983-93) Fairbanks 1979-93. Instructor in Criminal and Constitutional Law State Police Academy Sitka 1988-93. Member Tanana Valley and Alaska Bar Associations. Attended National Institute for Trial Advocacy Seattle Washington Sept 1981 and The National Judicial College Reno Nevada Sept 1993 to Oct 1993, April 1996, Nov 1997, May 1998, May 1999 and July 2001. Republican. Delegate to State Convention 1978, 1980, 1984 and 1990. Precinct Chairman 1976-84. Member Fairbanks Child Sexual Abuse Task Force 1983-85 and Statewide Steering Committee for Law Related Education 1992-93. Executive Board and Committee Member Midnight Sun Council Boy Scouts of America since 1986. Interests include reading (science fiction and historical fiction), basketball, cross country running and skiing and history of the Mormon church.

Office: 101 Lacey Street, Room 463, Fairbanks 99701-4765.

Telephone: (907) 452-9311.

ZERVOS, Larry C. *(Judge, Alaska Superior Court First Judicial District)* Appointed by governor to term beginning 1990. Former Judge, Alaska District Court Fourth Judicial District.

Office: 304 Lake Street, Room 203, Sitka 99835-7759.

Telephone: (907) 747-6271.

ARIZONA

Capital PHOENIX

UNITED STATES DISTRICT COURT DISTRICT OF ARIZONA

The court sits at Globe, Phoenix, Prescott and Tucson. For descriptive information refer to the United States Courts section.

Chief Judge

Stephen M. McNamee

Judges

Paul G. Rosenblatt
Roslyn Olson Silver
Raner C. Collins
Susan Ritchie Bolton
Frederick J. Martone
David C. Bury
John M. Roll
Frank R. Zapata
James A. Teilborg
Mary H. Murguia
Cindy K. Jorgenson

Senior Judges

Charles L. Hardy
Earl H. Carroll
Robert C. Broomfield
Alfredo C. Marquez
William Docker Browning
Roger Gordon Strand

Clerk

Richard H. Weare
130 U.S. Courthouse
401 West Washington Street
Phoenix, Arizona 85003-2118
(602) 322-7100

UNITED STATES MAGISTRATE JUDGES OF ARIZONA

Morton Sitver
Nancy Fiora
Virginia A. Mathis
Glenda E. Edmonds
Bernardo P. Velasco
Charles R. Pyle
Jay R. Irwin
Stephen L. Verkamp
James C. Carruth
Lawrence O. Anderson
David K. Duncan
Jacqueline Marshall

UNITED STATES BANKRUPTCY COURT OF ARIZONA

Chief Judge

Sarah S. Curley

Judges

George B. Nielsen, Jr.
James M. Marlar
Randolph J. Haines
Redfield T. Baum, Sr.
Charles G. Case II
Eileen W. Hollowell

Bankruptcy Clerk

Kevin E. O'Brien
P.O. Box 34151
Phoenix, Arizona 85067-4151
(602) 640-5800

SUPREME COURT OF ARIZONA

The Supreme Court is Arizona's court of last resort. The court consists of five justices appointed by the governor for initial two-year terms. Subsequent terms of six years are by retention vote. The chief justice and vice chief justice are elected by peer vote to five-year terms. Retirement is mandatory at age seventy; however, the chief justice may assign retired justices as needed, usually for a period of six months.

The court has final appellate jurisdiction over all other courts in the state except in some actions arising in Justice and Municipal Courts and exclusive appellate jurisdiction in cases involving the death penalty. Decisions of the Court of Appeals may be reviewed at the discretion of the court. The court also has exclusive jurisdiction in cases between counties. The court exercises original jurisdiction concerning admission to the bar, discipline of judges and supervision of lower courts and may issue writs necessary to the exercise of proper jurisdiction.

The court oversees the "Rule 28" process, which is the rule of procedure that permits any person, association or agency to petition for adoption, amendment or repeal of rules or procedures for the Arizona Courts.

The court sits en banc at Phoenix and usually recesses in July.

Chief Justice

Charles E. Jones

Vice Chief Justice

Ruth V. McGregor

Justices

Rebecca Berch
Michael D. Ryan
Andrew D. Hurwitz

Clerk

Noël K. Dessaint
Arizona State Courts Building
1501 West Washington
Phoenix, Arizona 85007-3231
(602) 542-9396

Administrative Director

David K. Byers
411 Arizona State Courts Building
1501 West Washington
Phoenix, Arizona 85007
(602) 542-9301

ARIZONA COURT OF APPEALS

The Court of Appeals is Arizona's intermediate appellate court. Judges are appointed by the governor for initial two-year terms and are then subject to retention votes every six years. A chief judge and vice chief judge of each division are elected annually by peer vote. Retirement is mandatory at age seventy; however, the chief justice may assign retired judges to serve as needed, usually for a period of six months.

ARIZONA COURT OF APPEALS—*Continued*

The court exercises appellate jurisdiction over all cases appealed from the Superior Court except those cases involving the death penalty, which must be appealed directly to the Supreme Court. In addition, Division One has statewide responsibility to review decisions of the Industrial Commission and unemployment compensation appeals from the Arizona Department of Economic Security. The court may issue writs necessary to the exercise of proper jurisdiction.

The court consists of two divisions. Division One is composed of five departments, each with a panel of three judges who rotate periodically. Each panel consists of two judges elected from Maricopa County and one judge elected from the remaining counties in the division. Division Two is composed of two departments, each with a panel of three judges who rotate periodically. Each panel consists of two judges elected from Pima County and one judge elected from the remaining counties in the division.

DIVISION ONE includes Apache, Coconino, La Paz, Maricopa, Mohave, Navajo, Yavapai and Yuma counties. The court sits at Phoenix, but may sit elsewhere as needed.

Chief Judge
Sheldon H. Weisberg

Vice Chief Judge
John C. Gemmill

Judges

Daniel A. Barker	Susan A. Ehrlich
William F. Garbarino	Philip L. Hall
Patrick G. Irvine	Donn Kessler
Jefferson L. Lankford	Cecil B. Patterson, Jr.
Maurice Portley	Murray G. Snow
James B. Sult	Jon W. Thompson
Ann A. Scott Timmer	Lawrence Winthrop

DIVISION TWO includes Cochise, Gila, Graham, Greenlee, Pima, Pinal and Santa Cruz counties. The court sits at Tucson, but may sit elsewhere as needed.

Chief Judge
Philip G. Espinosa

Vice Chief Judge
John Pelander

Judges
J. William Brammer, Jr.
William E. Druke
M. Jan Flòrez
Joseph W. Howard

SUPERIOR COURT OF ARIZONA

The Superior Court is Arizona's court of general jurisdiction. It is a single court with a division in every county. In counties with populations of less than 250,000, judges are elected for four-year terms; in counties with populations of 250,000 or more judges are appointed by the governor for initial two-year terms and are then subject to retention votes every four years. Counties with less than 250,000 can change from the popular election system to the appointment system at any time by a majority vote of the county's population. There is at least one judge for each county, and the number of additional judges is proportional to the county's population. Presiding judges are appointed in each county by the Supreme Court to serve for the remainder of their four-year terms. An associate presiding judge is appointed by the presiding judge with the approval of the Supreme Court to act during the absence or unavailability of the presiding judge. Retirement is mandatory at age seventy; however, the chief justice may assign retired judges to serve as needed, usually for a period of six months.

In counties having three or more Superior Court judges, the presiding judge may appoint court commissioners to act as full-time judicial officers. Commissioners usually hear matters where a default has been entered against a party and may also preside at the initial appearance of a defendant charged with a crime.

The court has original civil jurisdiction when the amount in question is $5,000 or more and original criminal jurisdiction in all felony cases and misdemeanors not otherwise provided for by law. The court also has civil jurisdiction in cases of equity, title to real property, insolvency proceedings and probate and divorce matters. In Greenlee and Maricopa counties the court also hears water rights cases. The court has concurrent civil jurisdiction with the Justice of the Peace Courts in forcible entry and detainer cases and exclusive jurisdiction in juvenile matters. The court hears appeals de novo and appeals on the record from the lower courts in criminal and civil cases. The court may issue writs necessary to the exercise of proper jurisdiction.

The court ordinarily sits at each county seat, but sessions may be held elsewhere when authorized by county supervisors or when in the judge's opinion public interest so requires.

---

*Presiding Judge
†Associate Presiding Judge

County	Judge
Apache	Michael C. Nelson*
Cochise	Thomas E. Collins*
	Stephen M. Desens
	Wallace R. Hoggatt
	Charles A. Irwin
Coconino	Fred Newton*
	Charles D. Adams
	H. Jeffrey Coker
	Danna Hendrix
Gila	Robert Duber II*
	Peter Cahill
Graham	R. Douglas Holt*
Greenlee	Monica Stauffer*
La Paz	Michael J. Burke*
Maricopa	Colin F. Campbell*
	Barbara Mundell†
	Mark F. Aceto
	Linda A. Akers
	Rebecca A. Albrecht
	Arthur T. Anderson
	Louis A. Araneta
	Silvia R. Arellano
	Mark W. Armstrong
	Anna M. Baca

SUPERIOR COURT OF ARIZONA—*Continued*

Maricopa—Cont.
Eddward Ballinger, Jr.
Janet Barton
Craig A. Blakey, II
Robert Budoff
Edward O. Burke
John A. Buttrick
Jeffrey S. Cates
David R. Cole
Connie Contes
Dennis W. Dairman
Norman J. Davis
John Ditsworth
Gary E. Donahoe
Margaret H. Downie
Thomas Dunevant, III
Alfred M. Fenzel
Kenneth L. Fields
John F. Foreman
Pamela J. Franks
Pendleton Gaines
Frank T. Galati
J. Richard Gama
John M. Gaylord
Stephen A. Gerst
Robert L. Gottsfield
Warren J. Granville
Cari A. Harrison
Brian R. Hauser
Joseph B. Heilman
Bethany G. Hicks
Ruth H. Hilliard
M. Jean Hoag
Cathy M. Holt
Jeffrey A. Hotham
Robert Houser
Carey S. Hyatt
Brian K. Ishikawa
Barbara M. Jarrett
Michael D. Jones
Paul A. Katz
James H. Keppel
Andrew G. Klein
Margaret R. Mahoney
J. Kenneth Mangum
Gregory H. Martin
Crane McClennen
Colleen A. McNally
Michael R. McVey
Linda Miles
Robert H. Oberbillig
Karen L. O'Connor
Michael J. O'Melia
Thomas W. O'Toole
James Padish
Douglas Rayes
Peter C. Reinstein
Ronald S. Reinstein
Emmet J. Ronan
Teresa A. Sanders
Mark Santana
William P. Sargeant, III
Barry C. Schneider
Jonathan H. Schwartz
Linda K. Scott
Steven D. Sheldon
Roland J. Steinle, III
Sherry K. Stephens
David M. Talamante
William L. Topf, III
Dean Trebesch
Richard J. Trujillo
David K. Udall
Maria del Mar Verdin
Michael O. Wilkinson
Eileen Willett
Penny Ladell Willrich
Michael A. Yarnell
vacancy
vacancy

Mohave
Robert R. Moon*
Randolph A. Bartlett†
James Edward Chavez
Steven F. Conn
Richard Weiss
Charlotte Wells

Navajo
Dale Nielson*
Gloria Kindig
Thomas L. Wing

Pima
John S. Leonardo*
Patricia G. Escher†
Edgar B. Acuña
Michael D. Alfred
Deborah Bernini
Ted B. Borek
Christopher C. Browning
Hector E. Campoy
Carmine Cornelio
Michael Cruikshank
John E. Davis
Jane L. Eikleberry
Richard S. Fields
Howard Hantman
Charles V. Harrington
Jan Kearney
John F. Kelly
Virginia Kelly
Kenneth Lee
Leslie Beth Miller
Michael Owen Miller
Clark W. Munger
Richard D. Nichols
Lina S. Rodriguez
Charles S. Sabalos
Paul E. Tang
Stephen C. Villarreal
Nanette Marie Warner

Pinal
William J. O'Neil*
Gilberto V. Figueroa
Boyd T. Johnson
Stephen F. McCarville
Kelly Marie Robertson
Janna L. Vanderpool

Santa Cruz
James A. Soto*
Kimberly A. Corsaro
Anna M. Montoya-Paez

Yavapai
Raymond W. Weaver, Jr.*
William T. Kiger†
Robert Brutinel
Thomas Lindberg
David Mackey
Janis Ann Sterling

SUPERIOR COURT OF ARIZONA—*Continued*

Yuma	Tom C. Cole* Andrew W. Gould Kirby Kongable John N. Nelson Thomas A. Thode

ARIZONA TAX COURT

The Tax Court is a court of special jurisdiction in Arizona. It was created by the legislature in 1988 to hear statewide tax-related issues exclusively. The court is located in and administered by the Superior Court in Maricopa County.

ARIZONA JUSTICE OF THE PEACE COURTS

The Justice of the Peace Courts are courts of limited jurisdiction. Counties are divided into precincts, and each precinct has a judge elected at the general election for a four-year term. Only Maricopa and Pima counties have presiding judges, who are elected by peer vote for two-year terms. Retirement is mandatory at age seventy.

The courts have exclusive jurisdiction over civil actions when the amount involved is $5,000 or less and concurrent jurisdiction with the Superior Court in forcible entry and detainer actions provided the rental value does not exceed $1,000 per month and damages sought are less than $5,000. The courts also have jurisdiction over traffic violations and all other misdemeanors when the penalty does not exceed six months imprisonment and/or a fine of $1,000. The courts may conduct preliminary hearings in felony cases and issue writs necessary to the exercise of proper jurisdiction.

The courts sit at each of the eighty-three precincts.

ARIZONA MUNICIPAL COURTS

The Municipal Courts, also known as Police Courts, are courts of limited jurisdiction and are mandated by state law in each incorporated city or town. Municipal judges are usually appointed by city or town councils and serve such terms as provided by local charter or ordinance, usually two years but may be longer. The position of presiding judge is also established at local discretion. Retirement is mandatory at age seventy; however, retired judges may serve by assignment.

The courts have jurisdiction of all cases involving city or town ordinances and concurrent jurisdiction with the Justice of the Peace Courts over violations of state law committed within the city limits. The courts have no civil jurisdiction except in domestic violence cases. However, the courts may initiate garnishment proceedings to collect outstanding fines, fees and other charges owed to the court.

The courts sit at each incorporated city or town, as well as some unincorporated cities and towns.

Arizona Counties and County Seats

Apache
St. Johns

Cochise
Bisbee

Coconino
Flagstaff

Gila
Globe

Graham
Safford

Greenlee
Clifton

La Paz
Parker

Maricopa
Phoenix

Mohave
Kingman

Navajo
Holbrook

Pima
Tucson

Pinal
Florence

Santa Cruz
Nogales

Yavapai
Prescott

Yuma
Yuma

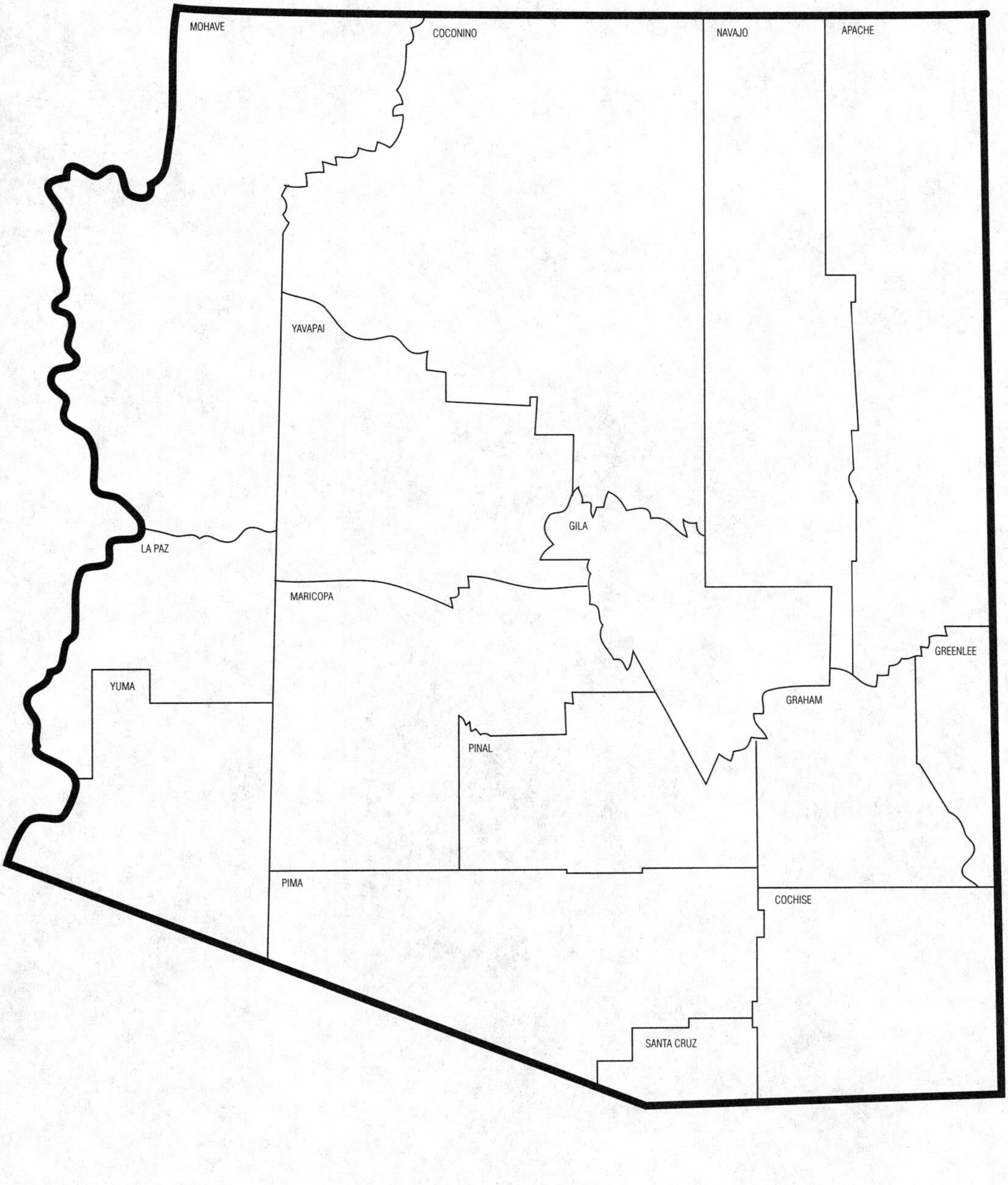
MOHAVE
COCONINO
NAVAJO
APACHE
YAVAPAI
GILA
LA PAZ
MARICOPA
GREENLEE
YUMA
GRAHAM
PINAL
PIMA
COCHISE
SANTA CRUZ

UNITED STATES DISTRICT COURT DISTRICT OF ARIZONA

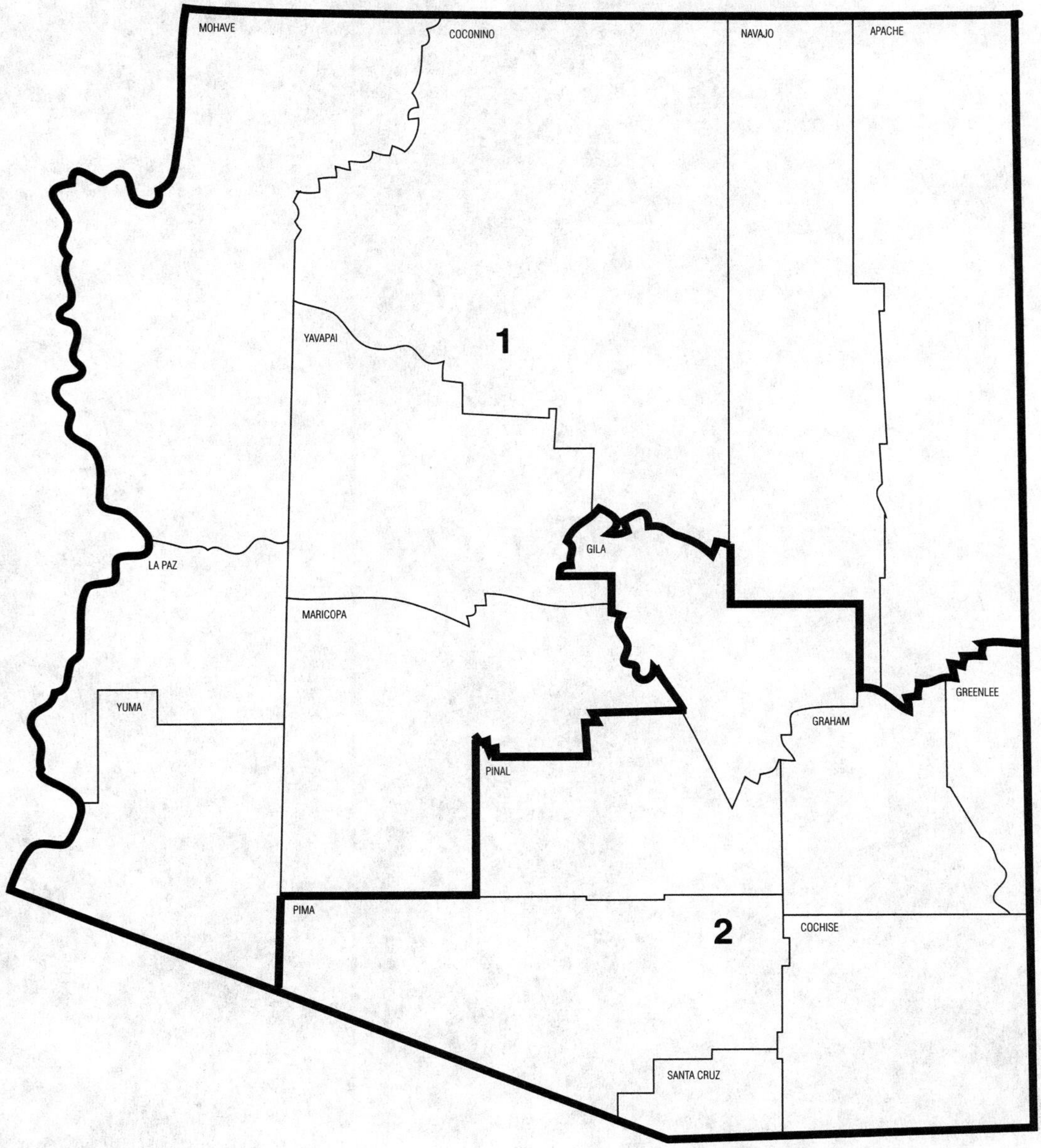
MOHAVE
COCONINO
NAVAJO
APACHE
YAVAPAI
1
GILA
LA PAZ
MARICOPA
GREENLEE
YUMA
GRAHAM
PINAL
PIMA
2
COCHISE
SANTA CRUZ

DIVISIONS OF ARIZONA COURT OF APPEALS

ARIZONA

ACETO, Mark F. *(Judge, Superior Court of Arizona Maricopa County)* Appointed by governor. Currently serves Criminal Court.
Office: 4B Southeast Court, 222 East Javelina Avenue, Mesa 82510.
Telephone: (602) 506-5261.
Fax: (602) 506-2029
E-mail address: maceto@superiorcourt.maricopa.gov

ACUÑA, Edgar B. *(Judge, Superior Court of Arizona Pima County)* Appointed by governor. Currently serves as Presiding Criminal Court Judge.
Office: New Courts Building, 110 West Congress, Tucson 85701.
Telephone: (520) 740-3620.
Fax: (520) 740-3664
E-mail address: eacuna@sc.co.pima.az.us

ADAMS, Charles D. *(Judge, Superior Court of Arizona Coconino County)* Currently serves as Presiding Juvenile Court Judge.
Office: Coconino County Courthouse, 200 North San Francisco, Flagstaff 86001.
Telephone: (928) 779-6784.
Fax: (928) 779-6642
E-mail address: cadams@courts.sp.state.az.us

AKERS, Linda A. *(Judge, Superior Court of Arizona Maricopa County)* Appointed by governor. Currently serves Criminal Court.
Office: 3B Southeast Court, 222 East Javelina Avenue, Mesa 85210.
Telephone: (602) 506-1541.
Fax: (602) 506-2029
E-mail address: lakers@superiorcourt.maricopa.gov

ALBRECHT, Rebecca A. *(Judge, Superior Court of Arizona Maricopa County)* Court Commissioner 1982-85. Appointed Judge by Governor Bruce Babbitt Feb 25, 1985. Retained by election, current term expires Jan 1, 2005. Former Associate Presiding Judge. Currently serves Civil Court. Born Nürnberg Germany Feb 1, 1949. Episcopalian. Educated at Arizona State University B.A. 1971 J.D. 1975. Admitted to practice Arizona 1975 and U.S. District Court District of Arizona 1975. In legal practice Phoenix 1975-82.
Member Maricopa County (President 1990-91) and American Bar Associations. Previously worked as secondary school teacher.
Office: 201 West Jefferson, Phoenix 85003.
Telephone: (602) 506-3727.
Fax: (602) 506-2651
E-mail address: ralbrech@superiorcourt.maricopa.gov

ALFRED, Michael D. *(Judge, Superior Court of Arizona Pima County)* Appointed by governor. Former Presiding Domestic Relations Judge. Currently serves Criminal Court.
Office: New Courts Building, 110 West Congress Street, Tucson 85701.
Telephone: (520) 740-3123.
Fax: (520) 740-3546
E-mail address: malfred@sc.co.pima.az.us

ANDERSON, Arthur T. *(Judge, Superior Court of Arizona Maricopa County)* Appointed by Governor Jane Dee Hull. Currently serves Criminal Court.
Office: 8A Central Court Building, 201 West Jefferson, Phoenix 85003-2205.
Telephone: (602) 506-0341.
Fax: (602) 506-7867
E-mail address: aanderso@superiorcourt.maricopa.gov

ANDERSON, Lawrence O. *(Magistrate Judge, United States District Court District of Arizona)* Appointed by U.S. District Court judges to term beginning Sept 23, 1998. Term expires Sept 2006. Born Phoenix Arizona Sept 7, 1948. Roman Catholic. Educated at University of San Francisco B.S. 1971 and Arizona State University J.D. 1974. Law Clerk to Hon. Paul W. LaPrade, Arizona Superior Court Maricopa County 1972. Admitted to practice Arizona 1975, U.S. District Court District of Arizona 1975, U.S. Court of Appeals Ninth Circuit 1975 and U.S. Supreme Court 1980. In legal practice Phoenix 1975-90. Judge, Superior Court of Arizona Maricopa County July 6, 1990 to Sept 22, 1998, appointed by Governor Rose Mofford.
Member American Judicature Society, State Bar of Arizona and Maricopa County Bar Association. Recipient Outstanding Citizens Award from National Council on Disability 1993. Republican. Little League Coach 1989-93. Member Arizona Easter Seal Society since 1992. Enjoys sports and fishing.
Office: 322 U.S. Courthouse, 401 West Washington Street, Phoenix 85003-2120.
Telephone: (602) 322-7620.

ARANETA, Louis A. *(Judge, Superior Court of Arizona Maricopa County)* Currently serves Criminal Court.
Office: 9A Central Court Building, 201 West Jefferson Street, Phoenix 85003-2205.
Telephone: (602) 506-1179.
Fax: (602) 506-7867
E-mail address: laraneta@superiorcourt.maricopa.gov

ARELLANO, Silvia R. *(Judge, Superior Court of Arizona Maricopa County)* Currently serves Juvenile Court.
Office: 1080 Southeast Court, 222 East Javelina Avenue, Mesa 85210.
Telephone: (602) 506-3649.
Fax: (602) 506-2651
E-mail address: sarellan@superiorcourt.maricopa.gov

ARMSTRONG, Mark W. *(Judge, Superior Court of Arizona Maricopa County)* Appointed by Governor Evan Mecham to term beginning Jan 1, 1988. Retained by election 1990, 1994, 1998 and 2002. Current term expires Dec 31, 2006. Former Associate Presiding Judge. Currently serves as Presiding Family Court Judge. Born Youngstown Ohio Feb 28, 1951. Methodist. Educated at Mount Union College B.S. cum laude 1973, Youngstown State University, University of Arizona J.D. with distinction 1977 and Cleveland-Marshall College of Law. Staff member Cleveland State Law Review 1975. Member Sigma Alpha Epsilon and Phi Alpha Delta (Vice Justice 1975). Admitted to practice Arizona 1977, U.S. Court of Military Appeals 1978, U.S. District Court Dis-

ARMSTRONG, MARK W.—*Continued*

trict of Arizona 1982 and U.S. Court of Appeals Ninth Circuit 1982. In legal practice Flagstaff 1982-84 and Phoenix 1985-87.

Instructor Columbia College 1978-80, Park College 1981 and Northern Arizona University 1984. Board of Trustees Coconino County Legal Aid 1984. Member State Bar of Arizona, Coconino County (Treasurer 1983), Maricopa County and American Bar Associations. Judge General Jurisdiction Session The National Judicial College 1988. Captain JAGC USAF 1977-88 and USAFR since 1986. Recipient Air Force Commendation Medals 1978, 1980 and 1981 and Meritorious Service Medals 1994 and 1998. Member Reserve Officers Association and Air Force Association. Enjoys softball, swimming, tennis and reading.

Office: 4B Central Court Building, 201 West Jefferson Street, Phoenix 85003.

Telephone: (602) 506-7896.

E-mail address: maarmstr@superiorcourt.maricopa.gov

BACA, Anna M. *(Judge, Superior Court of Arizona Maricopa County)* Appointed by governor. Currently serves Civil Court.

Office: 811 East Court Building, 101 West Jefferson, Phoenix 85003-2205.

Telephone: (602) 506-1810.

Fax: (602) 506-7867

E-mail address: abaca@superiorcourt.maricopa.gov

BALLINGER, Eddward, Jr. *(Judge, Superior Court of Arizona Maricopa County)* Appointed by governor. Currently serves as Associate Presiding Criminal Court Judge.

Office: 514 East Court Building, 101 West Jefferson Street, Phoenix 85003.

Telephone: (602) 506-8551.

Fax: (602) 506-1183

E-mail address: eballing@superiorcourt.maricopa.gov

BARKER, Daniel A. *(Judge, Arizona Court of Appeals Division One)* Appointed by Governor Jane Dee Hull to term beginning 2001. Term expires Jan 2005. Educated at Stanford University B.A. with honors 1977 and Brigham Young University J.D. 1981. Rhodes Scholar 1977-78. In legal practice Phoenix 1983-92. Judge and Associate Presiding Judge, Superior Court of Arizona Maricopa County 1992-2001, appointed by Governor Fife Symington.

Member Arizona Commission on Judicial Performance Review, Arizona Judges Association (Legislative Committee), J. Reuben Clark Law Society, Los Abogados Hispanic Bar Association and State Bar of Arizona (Executive Council Appellate Practice Section). Republican. Chair Connecting with the Community Arizona Court of Appeals Division One. Member Society of St. Vincent de Paul.

Office: 1501 West Washington, Phoenix 85007.

Telephone: (602) 542-3492.

BARTLETT, Randolph A. *(Associate Presiding Judge, Superior Court of Arizona Mohave County)*

Office: County Courthouse, 2001 College Drive, Lake Havasu City 86403.

Telephone: (928) 453-0739.

Fax: (928) 453-0713

E-mail address: rbartlet@courts.sp.state.az.us

BARTON, Janet *(Judge, Superior Court of Arizona Maricopa County)* Appointed by Governor Jane Dee Hull. Currently serves Juvenile Court.

Office: 107 Juvenile Court Center, 3125 West Durango, Phoenix 85009.

Telephone: (602) 506-5340.

Fax: (602) 506-1372

E-mail address: jabarton@superiorcourt.maricopa.gov

BAUM, Redfield T., Sr. *(Judge, United States Bankruptcy Court District of Arizona)* Appointed by U.S. Court of Appeals Ninth Circuit judges.

Mailing address: P.O. Box 34151, Phoenix 85067-4151.

Telephone: (602) 640-5850.

BERCH, Rebecca *(Justice, Supreme Court of Arizona)* Appointed by Governor Jane Dee Hull to term beginning March 13, 2002. Educated at Arizona State University B.S. 1976 J.D. 1979 M.A. 1990. Judge, Arizona Court of Appeals Division One 1998 to March 12, 2002, appointed by Governor Jane Dee Hull. In legal practice 1979-85.

Solicitor General Arizona 1991-94. Special Counsel 1995-96 and First Assistant 1996-98 Arizona Attorney General. Member Civil Justice Reform Act Advisory Committee 1992-94 and Civil Practice Committee State Bar of Arizona 1992-95. Co-chair Arizona Appellate Practice Institute. Member Judicial Ethics Advisory Committee, Board of Certified Court Reporters and Committee on Examinations Supreme Court of Arizona. Board of Directors Arizona State University College of Law Alumni Association 1982-85 and Homeless Legal Assistance Project 1990-99.

Office: 1501 West Washington, Phoenix 85007.

Telephone: (602) 542-4531.

E-mail address: rberch@azbar.org

BERNINI, Deborah *(Judge, Superior Court of Arizona Pima County)* Appointed by governor. Former Presiding Juvenile Court Judge. Currently serves Civil Court.

Office: New Courts Building, 110 West Congress, Tucson 85701.

Telephone: (520) 740-2976.

Fax: (520) 628-7104

E-mail address: dbernini@sc.co.pima.az.us

BLAKEY, Craig A., II *(Judge, Superior Court of Arizona Maricopa County)* Appointed by governor. Currently serves Family Court.

Office: 13D Central Court Building, 201 West Jefferson, Phoenix 85003-2205.

Telephone: (602) 506-7806.

Fax: (602) 506-7867

E-mail address: cblakey@superiorcourt.maricopa.gov

BOLTON, Susan Ritchie *(Judge, United States District Court District of Arizona)* Appointed for life by President Bill Clinton to term beginning Oct 20, 2000. Born Pennsylvania 1951. Educated at University of Iowa B.A. 1973 J.D. with honors 1975. Law Clerk to Hon. Laurance T. Wren, Arizona Court of Appeals 1975-77. Admitted to practice Iowa 1975, Arizona 1976 and U.S. District Court District of Arizona 1976. In legal practice Phoenix 1977-88. Judge Oct 1988 to Oct 2000, Former Presiding Civil Judge and Former Presiding Special Assignment Judge, Superior Court of Arizona Maricopa County, appointed by Governor Rose Mofford.

Author "Working with Violent Families" Sage Publi-

BOLTON, SUSAN RITCHIE—*Continued*
cations 1986. Member Arizona Women Lawyers Association (President 1986), National Association of Women Judges, Arizona Judges Association, State Bar of Arizona, Maricopa County and American Bar Associations.
Office: 522 U.S. Courthouse, 401 West Washington Street, Phoenix 85003-2153.
Telephone: (602) 322-7570.

BOREK, Ted B. *(Judge, Superior Court of Arizona Pima County)* Appointed by Governor Jane Dee Hull to term beginning July 10 2000. Retained by election 2002, current term expires 2006. Currently serves Civil Court. Born Pittsburgh Pennsylvania Feb 1944. Protestant. Educated at U.S. Military Academy B.S. 1966 and University of Arizona College of Law J.D. 1972. Writer and Editor Arizona Law Review 1970-72. Law Clerk to Hon. C. A. Muecke, U.S. District Court District of Arizona 1972-73. Admitted to practice Arizona 1972, U.S. Court of Appeals Ninth Circuit, U.S. Court of Appeals for the Armed Forces and U.S. Supreme Court.
Assistant U.S. Attorney District of Arizona 1990-2000. Member State Bar of Arizona (Committees on Continuing Legal Education and Professionalism), Pima County, Federal (First President Tucson Chapter) and American Bar Associations. Recipient Earl M. Kintner Award from Federal Bar Association 1996. U.S. Army JAGC 1972-90. Republican. Mediator and Past Board President Our Town Family Center. Former Member St. Philips' Vestry, West Point Society of Southern Arizona, Tucson Catalina Rotary and College of Law Mentor Program. Enjoys traveling, biking, skiing and reading. Personal Statement or Quote: "Be respectful; be respected."
Office: 110 West Congress, Tucson 85701.
Telephone: (520) 740-3130.
Fax: (520) 740-3665
E-mail address: tborek@sc.co.pima.az.us

BRAMMER, J. William, Jr. *(Judge, Arizona Court of Appeals Division Two)* Appointed by governor to term beginning 1997. Retained by election. Educated at University of Arizona B.S. 1964 J.D. 1967. In legal practice Tucson 1968-97.
Assistant City Attorney Tucson. Past President Pima County Bar Association. Board of Governors State Bar of Arizona. Former Member and Chair Examinations Committee Supreme Court of Arizona. Former Member Commission on Judicial Performance Review. Past President University of Arizona Law College Association. Former Member National Board of Directors University of Arizona's Alumni Association and Board of Directors Council of School Attorneys National School Boards Association.
Office: State Office Building, 400 West Congress Street, Tucson 85701-1374.
Telephone: (520) 628-6945.
E-mail address: brammer@apltwo.ct.state.az.us

BROOMFIELD, Robert C. *(Senior Judge, United States District Court District of Arizona)* Appointed for life by President Ronald Reagan. Chief Judge 1994 to Aug 12, 1999. Assumed Senior status Aug 12, 1999, serves by assignment. Born Detroit Michigan June 18, 1933. Methodist. Educated at Pennsylvania State University B.S.B.A. 1955 and University of Arizona LL.B. 1961. Law Clerk-Bailiff to Hon. Jack D. H. Hays, Superior Court of Arizona Maricopa County 1961-62. Admitted to practice Arizona 1961. Began legal practice Phoenix 1961. Volunteer Referee 1965-70, Judge 1971-72 and Presiding Judge 1972-74 Juvenile Division and Judge 1971-74 and Presiding Judge 1974-85, Superior Court of Arizona Maricopa County.
Member since 1974, President 1978-79 and Chairman Board of Directors 1980-81 National Conference of Metropolitan Courts. Member City of Phoenix Judicial Selection Advisory Board 1975-80, Arizona Judicial Ethics Advisory Committee 1975-81, Criminal Justice Group 1976-85 and Judicial Planning Committee of the Arizona Supreme Court 1977-85. Chairman Court Delay Reduction Committee National Conference of State Trial Judges 1979-81. Board of Directors National Center for State Courts 1980-85. President Arizona Judges Association 1981-82. Member Commission on Trial Court Performance National Center for State Courts 1986-88. Member 1987-95 and Chairman 1989-95 Security, Space and Facilities Committee and Member since 1997 Budget Committee U.S. Judicial Conference. Chairman Task Force on Court Reporting Ninth Circuit Judicial Council 1988. Member State Bar of Arizona, Maricopa County and American (Executive Committee 1977-85 and Chairman 1983-84 National Conference of State Trial Judges and member 1976-80 and Chairman 1978-80 Committee on Court Administration and Council member 1983-84 Judicial Administration Division) Bar Associations. Attended Regular Session 1971 and Court Administration Session 1974, Faculty member Court Administration Session 1975-81 and Faculty Advisor Regular Session 1976 The National Judicial College. First Lieutenant USAF (pilot) 1955-58. Arizona Air National Guard 1958-61. Captain USAFR (inactive 1961-72). Member 1965-70, Clerk 1966-68 and President 1969-70 Paradise Valley School Board. Board of Directors Crisis Nursery 1976-81 and Phoenix Together (Sponsor of Phoenix Town Halls) 1982-83. Advisory Board Theodore Roosevelt Council Boy Scouts of America 1968-75, Arizona Cactus Pine Council Girl Scouts of America 1971-75 and Arizona Association for Children with Learning Disabilities 1972-75. Member Phoenix Chamber of Commerce Respect for Law Committee 1969-70, Rotary International Phoenix-Midtown 1973-76, Comprehensive Data Systems Policy Board 1975-85 and Arizona Academy Training Committee (Sponsor of Arizona Town Halls) since 1980.
Office: 626 U.S. Courthouse, 401 West Washington Street, Phoenix 85003-2158.
Telephone: (602) 322-7540.

BROWNING, Christopher C. *(Judge, Superior Court of Arizona Pima County)* Appointed by Governor Jane Dee Hull Sept 1998 to term beginning Dec 4, 1998. Retained by election. Former Presiding Civil Court Judge. Currently serves Civil Court. Born Orleans France July 17, 1956. Educated at University of Arizona B.A. 1978 J.D. 1981. Admitted to practice Arizona 1981, U.S. District Court District of Arizona 1981, U.S. Court of Appeals Ninth Circuit 1995 and U.S. Supreme Court 1996. Certified Specialist, Injury/Wrongful Death Litigation—Arizona Board of Legal Specialization 1992. In legal practice Tucson Arizona 1981-98.
Member 1981-98 and President 1998 Tucson Defense Bar Association. Member American Board of Trial Advocates (President 1997), State Bar of Arizona and Pima County Bar Association. Former Member Board of Di-

BROWNING, CHRISTOPHER C.—*Continued*
rectors Tucson Conquistadors and Tucson Zoological Society.
Office: New Courts Building, 110 West Congress Street, Tucson 85701.
Telephone: (520) 740-3875.
E-mail address: christopher_browning-@sc.co.pima.az.us

BROWNING, William Docker *(Senior Judge, United States District Court District of Arizona)* Appointed for life by President Ronald Reagan to term beginning May 11, 1984. Assumed Senior status, serves by assignment. Former Chief Judge. Born Tucson Arizona May 19, 1931. Episcopalian. Educated at University of Arizona B.B.A. 1954 LL.B. 1960. Member Sigma Alpha Epsilon, Delta Sigma Pi and Phi Delta Phi. Admitted to practice Arizona 1960, U.S. District Court District of Arizona 1960, U.S. Court of Appeals Ninth Circuit 1965 and U.S. Supreme Court 1967. In legal practice Tucson 1960-84.
Instructor in Common Law Pleading 1965 and Trial Practice and Procedure 1968-73 University of Arizona College of Law. Delegate Ninth Circuit Judicial Conference 1968-77, 1979-82 and 1990-93. Member Arizona Judicial Nominating Commission on Appellate Court Appointments 1975-79. Board of Trustees Institute for Court Management 1978-84. Member Ninth Circuit Judicial Council 1990-93 and Commission on Structural Alternatives for the Federal Courts of Appeals 1997-99. Fellow American College of Trial Lawyers and American Bar Foundation. Member Center for Public Resources CPR Legal Program, American Board of Trial Advocates, Judicial Conference of the U.S. (Member 1987-92 and Chairman 1990-92 Committee on Court and Judicial Security, Representative Ninth Circuit District Court 1990-93), American Judicature Society (Board of Directors 1975-77), Federal Judges Association (Board of Directors 1990-95), State Bar of Arizona (Chairman Uniform Jury Instructions Committee 1962-66 and Merit Selection of Judges Committee 1973-76, member Securities Regulation Committee 1964-66, Board of Governors 1968-74, President Elect 1971-72, President 1972-73), Pima County (Executive Committee 1964-68, Medical Legal Screening Panel 1965-75, President 1967-68) and American (Special Committee on Housing and Urban Development Law 1973-76, Committee on Urban Problems and Human Affairs 1978-80) Bar Associations. Recipient Herbert Lincoln Harley Award from American Judicature Society 1978. Named Outstanding Member by State Bar of Arizona 1980 and Distinguished Citizen by University of Arizona 1995. First Lieutenant USAF 1954-57. Captain Arizona Air National Guard 1958-61. President Tucson Conquistadors 1982-83.
Office: 6160 U.S. Courthouse, 405 West Congress Street, Tucson 85701-5061.
Telephone: (520) 205-4510.

BRUTINEL, Robert *(Judge, Superior Court of Arizona Yavapai County)* Currently serves as Presiding Juvenile Court Judge.
Office: 401 Yavapai County Courthouse, 120 South Cortez, Prescott 86301.
Telephone: (928) 771-3305.
Fax: (928) 771-3495
E-mail address: rbrutine@courts.sp.state.az.us

BUDOFF, Robert *(Judge, Superior Court of Arizona Maricopa County)* Appointed by Governor Jane Dee Hull. Currently serves Family Court.
Office: 7A Central Court Building, 201 West Jefferson, Phoenix 85003-2205.
Telephone: (602) 506-4569.
Fax: (602) 506-7867
E-mail address: rbudoff@superiorcourt.maricopa.gov

BURKE, Edward O. *(Judge, Superior Court of Arizona Maricopa County)* Appointed by Governor Jane Dee Hull. Former Presiding Civil Court Judge. Currently serves Family Court.
Office: 2 Old Courthouse, 125 West Washington, Phoenix 85003.
Telephone: (602) 506-6538.
Fax: (602) 506-7867
E-mail address: eburke@superiorcourt.maricopa.gov

BURKE, Michael J. *(Presiding Judge, Superior Court of Arizona La Paz County)*
Office: 1316 Kofa Avenue, Parker 85344.
Telephone: (928) 669-6134.
Fax: (928) 669-2186
E-mail address: mburke2@courts.sp.state.az.us

BURY, David C. *(Judge, United States District Court District of Arizona)* Appointed for life by President George W. Bush to term beginning March 29, 2002. Educated at Oklahoma State University 1964 and University of Arizona College of Law J.D. 1967. In legal practice Tucson 34 years.
Office: 6170 U.S. Courthouse, 405 West Congress Street, Tucson 85701.
Telephone: (520) 205-4560.

BUTTRICK, John A. *(Judge, Superior Court of Arizona Maricopa County)* Appointed by Governor Jane Dee Hull. Currently serves Civil Court.
Office: 301 Old Courthouse, 125 West Washington, Phoenix 85003.
Telephone: (602) 506-0971.
Fax: (602) 506-7867
E-mail address: jbuttric@superiorcourt.maricopa.gov

CAHILL, Peter *(Judge, Superior Court of Arizona Gila County)*
Office: 1400 East Ash, Globe 85501.
Telephone: (928) 425-3231.
Fax: (928) 425-3605
E-mail address: pcahill@courts.sp.state.az.us

CAMPBELL, Colin F. *(Presiding Judge, Superior Court of Arizona Maricopa County)* Appointed by governor.
Office: 4A Central Court Building, 201 West Jefferson, Phoenix 85003-2205.
Telephone: (602) 506-3837.
Fax: (602) 506-7867
E-mail address: ccampbel@superiorcourt.maricopa.gov

CAMPOY, Hector E. *(Judge, Superior Court of Arizona Pima County)* Appointed by Governor Jane Dee Hull. Currently serves as Presiding Juvenile Court Judge.
Office: Juvenile New Court Center, 2225 East Ajo Way, Tucson 85713.
Telephone: (520) 740-2966.
Fax: (520) 628-7104
E-mail address: hcampoy@sc.co.pima.az.us

CARROLL, Earl H. *(Senior Judge, United States District Court District of Arizona)* Appointed for life by President Jimmy Carter to term beginning 1980. Assumed Senior status Oct 10, 1994, serves by assignment. Born Tucson Arizona March 26, 1925. Educated at University of Arizona B.S. 1948 LL.B. 1951. Law Clerk to Supreme Court of Arizona 1951-52. In legal practice Phoenix 1952-81.

Special Counsel City of Tombstone 1962-65.

Office: 521 U.S. Courthouse, 401 West Washington Street, Phoenix 85003-2151.

Telephone: (602) 322-7530.

CARRUTH, James C. *(Magistrate Judge, United States District Court District of Arizona)* Appointed by U.S. District Court judges.

Office: 3180 U.S. Courthouse, 405 West Congress Street, Tucson 85701-5010.

Telephone: (520) 205-4610.

CASE, Charles G., II *(Judge, United States Bankruptcy Court District of Arizona)* Appointed by U.S. Court of Appeals Ninth Circuit judges.

Mailing address: P.O. Box 34151, Phoenix 85067-4151.

Telephone: (602) 640-5850.

CATES, Jeffrey S. *(Judge, Superior Court of Arizona Maricopa County)* Appointed by Governor Bruce Babbitt to term beginning March 5, 1979. Retained by election. Current term expires 2003. Presiding Civil Judge July 1982 to June 1984. Former Presiding Tax Court Judge. Currently serves Criminal Court. Born Portland Maine March 8, 1943. Jewish. Educated at Boston College B.S. 1964 and Boston University J.D. 1968. Admitted to practice Arizona 1969. Began legal practice Phoenix 1969.

Lecturer and author "How to Handle a Bankruptcy (Chapter XIII Proceedings)" 1976, "Practice and Procedures in Juvenile Court: Criminal & Civil (Adoptions, Severances and Dependency)" 1977, "Judges' Handbook on Juvenile Court Law and Procedures" presented at State Judges Convention 1978 and "Award of Attorney's Fees Under A.R.S. 12-341.01" presented at State Judges Conventions 1981 and 1983 and State Bar Convention 1983. Former member Phoenix Chapter Arizona Trial Lawyers Association (Board of Directors, former Vice President and Treasurer), The Association of Trial Lawyers of America, Arizona Judges Association (Vice President, Past President, Secretary) State Bar of Arizona and Maricopa County Bar Association. Past Trial Court Representative Arizona Supreme Court Council on Judicial Education and Training 1983-87. Recipient Certificate for Outstanding Services to CLE program from State Bar of Arizona 1978 and Award for Outstanding Services from Maricopa County Juvenile Court 1978. Democrat. Member Adopt-Co-op of Arizona, a nonprofit corporation 1975-79 (Board of Directors, past President and Vice President). Board of Trustees Parents Anonymous. Enjoys photography.

Office: 7D Central Court Building, 201 West Jefferson, Phoenix 85003-2205.

Telephone: (602) 506-3551.

Fax: (602) 506-7867

E-mail address: jcates@superiorcourt.maricopa.gov

CHAVEZ, James Edward *(Judge, Superior Court of Arizona Mohave County)* Appointed to term beginning Aug 1, 1990. Elected 1994, 1998 and 2002. Current term expires Dec 31, 2006. Former Presiding Juvenile Court Judge and Associate Presiding Judge. Born Kingman Arizona June 25, 1952. Educated at University of Arizona B.S.N.E. 1974 and Stanford Law School J.D. 1978. Admitted to practice Colorado 1978 and Arizona 1981.

Attorney City of Kingman 1984-90.

Mailing address: P.O. Box 7000, Kingman 86402-7000.

Office: Mohave County Courthouse, 401 East Spring Street, Kingman 86401.

Telephone: (928) 753-0785.

Fax: (928) 718-5506

COKER, H. Jeffrey *(Judge, Superior Court of Arizona Coconino County)* Elected to term beginning Jan 1, 1985. Reelected 1988, 1992, 1996 and 2000. Current term expires Jan 2005. Former Presiding Juvenile Court Judge and Presiding Judge. Born Tucson Arizona June 2, 1948. Educated at Northern Arizona University B.S. 1970 and Arizona State University J.D. 1974. Member Phi Alpha Delta. Admitted to practice Arizona 1974. Began legal practice Phoenix 1974.

Office: Coconino County Courthouse, 200 North San Francisco, Flagstaff 86001.

Telephone: (928) 779-6801.

Fax: (928) 779-2165

E-mail address: jcoker@courts.sp.state.az.us

COLE, David R. *(Judge, Superior Court of Arizona Maricopa County)* Appointed by governor. Currently serves Civil Court and Family Court.

Office: Northwest Regional Center, 14264 West Tierra Buena Law, Surprise 85374.

Telephone: (602) 506-5808.

E-mail address: dcole@superiorcourt.maricopa.gov

COLE, Tom C. *(Presiding Judge, Superior Court of Arizona Yuma County)*

Office: Yuma County Courthouse, 168 South Second Avenue, Yuma 85364-2296.

Telephone: (928) 329-2190.

Fax: (928) 329-2004

E-mail address: toco@court.co.yuma.az.us

COLLINS, Raner C. *(Judge, United States District Court District of Arizona)* Appointed for life by President Bill Clinton to term beginning Aug 19, 1998. Born Malvern Arkansas July 8, 1952. Educated at Arkansas Polytechnic University B.A. 1973 and University of Arizona College of Law J.D. 1975. Former Presiding Juvenile Court Judge. City Magistrate, City of Tucson Court 1981-83Judge pro temp 1985-88 and Judge 1988-98, Superior Court of Arizona Pima County.

Trial Attorney 1976-81 and County Attorney 1983-85 Pima County Attorney's Office.

Office: 5170 U.S. Courthouse, 405 West Congress Street, Tucson 85701-5010.

Telephone: (520) 205-4540.

COLLINS, Thomas E. *(Presiding Judge, Superior Court of Arizona Cochise County)*

Mailing address: P.O. Box Drawer CT, Bisbee 85603.

Telephone: (520) 432-8520.

Fax: (520) 432-8528

E-mail address: tcollins@courts.sp.state.az.us

CONN, Steven F. *(Judge, Superior Court of Arizona Mohave County)* Currently serves as Presiding Criminal Court Judge.
Mailing address: P.O. Box 7000, Kingman 86402.
Office: Mohave County Courthouse, 401 East Spring Street, Kingman 86401.
Telephone: (928) 753-0709.
Fax: (928) 753-8938
E-mail address: sconn@courts.sp.state.az.us

CONTES, Connie *(Judge, Superior Court of Arizona Maricopa County)* Appointed by governor. Currently serves Family Court.
Office: 5C Central Court Building, 201 West Jefferson, Phoenix 85003-2205.
Telephone: (602) 506-7768.
Fax: (602) 506-7867
E-mail address: ccontes@superiorcourt.maricopa.gov

CORNELIO, Carmine *(Judge, Superior Court of Arizona Pima County)* Appointed by governor. Currently serves Civil Court.
Office: New Courts Building, 110 West Congress, Tucson 85701.
Telephone: (520) 740-8301.
Fax: (520) 628-8318
E-mail address: ccornelio@sc.co.pima.az.us

CORSARO, Kimberly A. *(Judge, Superior Court of Arizona Santa Cruz County)* Currently serves as Presiding Juvenile Court Judge.
Mailing address: P.O. Box 1929, Nogales 85628.
Office: Santa Cruz County Complex, Nogales 85621.
Telephone: (520) 375-7720.
Fax: (520) 761-7857

CRUIKSHANK, Michael *(Judge, Superior Court of Arizona Pima County)* Appointed by governor. Currently serves Juvenile Court.
Office: Juvenile Court Center, 2225 East Ajo Way, Tucson 85713.
Telephone: (520) 740-4470.
Fax: (520) 628-7104
E-mail address: mcruikshank@sc.co.pima.az.us

CURLEY, Sarah S. *(Chief Judge, United States Bankruptcy Court District of Arizona)* Chief judge since June 27, 2002.
Mailing address: P.O. Box 34151, Phoenix 85067-4151.
Telephone: (602) 640-5850.

DAIRMAN, Dennis W. *(Judge, Superior Court of Arizona Maricopa County)* Appointed by governor. Currently serves Juvenile Court.
Office: 1094 Southeast Court, 222 East Javelina Avenue, Mesa 85210.
Telephone: (602) 506-1855.
Fax: (602) 506-2651
E-mail address: ddairman@superiorcourt.maricopa.gov

DAVIS, John E. *(Judge, Superior Court of Arizona Pima County)* Appointed by governor. Former Associate Presiding Juvenile Judge. Former Presiding Juvenile Court Judge. Currently serves Criminal Court.
Office: Juvenile New Court Center, 2225 East Ajo Way, Tucson 85713.
Telephone: (520) 740-3129.
Fax: (520) 740-3146
E-mail address: jdavis@sc.co.pima.az.us

DAVIS, Norman J. *(Judge, Superior Court of Arizona Maricopa County)* Appointed by governor. Currently serves as Presiding Northwest Court Judge.
Office: Northwest Regional Center, 14264 West Tierra Buena Lane, Surprise 85374.
Telephone: (602) 506-5262.
Fax: (602) 372-9440
E-mail address: ndavis@superiorcourt.maricopa.gov

DESENS, Stephen M. *(Judge, Superior Court of Arizona Cochise County)*
Mailing address: P.O. Box Drawer W, Bisbee 85603.
Telephone: (520) 432-9340.
Fax: (520) 432-2416
E-mail address: sdesens@courts.sp.state.az.us

DITSWORTH, John *(Judge, Superior Court of Arizona Maricopa County)* Appointed by Governor Jane Dee Hull. Currently serves Family Court.
Office: 6B Central Court Building, 201 West Jefferson, Phoenix 85003-2205.
Telephone: (602) 506-8288.
Fax: (602) 506-3123
E-mail address: jditswor@superiorcourt.maricopa.gov

DONAHOE, Gary E. *(Judge, Superior Court of Arizona Maricopa County)* Appointed by Governor Jane Dee Hull. Currently serves Civil Court.
Office: 412 East Court Building, 101 West Jefferson, Phoenix 85003.
Telephone: (602) 506-3712.
Fax: (602) 506-7867
E-mail address: gdonahoe@superiorcourt.maricopa.gov

DOWNIE, Margaret H. *(Judge, Superior Court of Arizona Maricopa County)* Appointed by Governor Jane Dee Hull. Currently serves as Presiding Civil Court Judge.
Office: 201 Old Courthouse, 125 West Washington, Phoenix 85003.
Telephone: (602) 506-5015.
Fax: (602) 506-7867
E-mail address: mdownie@superiorcourt.maricopa.gov

DRUKE, William E. *(Judge, Arizona Court of Appeals Division Two)* Appointed by Governor Fife Symington to term beginning 1992. Retained by election. Former Vice Chief Judge and Chief Judge. Born Phoenix Arizona Dec 5, 1938. Educated at Arizona State University B.S. 1961 and University of Arizona J.D. 1969. Admitted to practice Arizona 1969. In legal practice 1985-92. City Magistrate, City of Tucson Court 1972-74. Judge, Superior Court of Arizona Pima County 1975-85.
Deputy County Attorney Pima County 1970-72.
Office: State Office Building, 400 West Congress Street, Tucson 85701-1374.
Telephone: (520) 628-6950.
E-mail address: druke@apltwo.ct.state.az.us

DUBER, Robert, II *(Presiding Judge, Superior Court of Arizona Gila County)* Elected to term beginning Jan 4, 1987. Reelected 1990, 1994, 1998 and 2002. Current term expires Jan 2007. Born Globe Arizona July 28, 1951. Lutheran. Educated at Arizona State University B.S. 1973 J.D. 1976. Admitted to practice Arizona 1976, U.S. District Court District of Arizona 1976 and U.S. Court of Appeals Ninth Circuit. In legal practice Globe

DUBER, ROBERT, II—*Continued*

1976-80 and 1985-86. County Attorney Gila County 1981-84.

Office: 1400 East Ash, Globe 85501.
Telephone: (928) 425-3231.
Fax: (928) 425-3605
E-mail address: rduber@courts.sp.state.az.us

DUNCAN, David K. *(Magistrate Judge, United States District Court District of Arizona)* Appointed by U.S. District Court judges to term beginning June 14, 2001. Term expires June 13, 2009. Born Evansville Indiana Oct 3, 1958. Educated at Brown University 1977-79 and University of Arizona B.A. 1984 J.D. with high distinction 1987. Note and Casenote Editor Arizona Law Review 1984-87. Law Clerk to Hon. William D. Browning, U.S. District Court District of Arizona 1987-89. Member Order of the Coif. Admitted to practice Arizona 1987. In legal practice Arizona 1989-97.

Assistant U.S. Attorney District of Arizona 1997-2001. Member Arizona Women Lawyers Association, Maricopa County, Federal and American Bar Associations. Area Chair Brown Alumni Schools Program.

Office: 325 U.S. Courthouse, SPC 14, 401 West Washington Street, Phoenix 85003.
Telephone: (602) 322-7630.
Fax: (602) 322-7639
E-mail address: DAVID_DUNCAN-@AZD.USCOURTS.GOV

DUNEVANT, Thomas, III *(Judge, Superior Court of Arizona Maricopa County)* Former Presiding Civil Judge. Former Court Commissioner. Currently serves Juvenile Court.

Office: 146 Juvenile Court Center, 3125 West Durango, Phoenix 85009.
Telephone: (602) 506-2050.
Fax: (602) 506-4121
E-mail address: tdunevan@superiorcourt.maricopa.gov

EDMONDS, Glenda E. *(Magistrate Judge, United States District Court District of Arizona)* Appointed by U.S. District Court judges to term beginning Feb 19, 1998. Term expires Feb 2006.

Office: 3170 U.S. Courthouse, 405 West Congress Street, Tucson 85701-5010.
Telephone: (520) 205-4620.

EHRLICH, Susan A. *(Judge, Arizona Court of Appeals Division One)* Appointed by Governor Rose Mofford to term beginning Oct 1, 1989. Retained by election Nov 3, 1992 and Nov 1998. Current term expires Jan 2005. Educated at Wellesley College B.A. 1970 and Arizona State University College of Law J.D. 1974. Law Clerk to Chief Justice Jack D. H. Hays, Arizona Supreme Court 1974-76. Admitted to practice Arizona 1974, U.S. District Court District of Arizona 1974, U.S. Courts of Appeals Ninth 1974, First, Second, Fourth, Fifth, Sixth, Seventh, Eighth, Ninth, Tenth and District of Columbia Circuits 1978-79, U.S. Supreme Court 1977 and District of Columbia 1978. In legal practice Phoenix 1976-77.

Attorney Appellate Section Civil Division U.S. Department of Justice 1978-80. Assistant U.S. Attorney and Chief Appellate Section District of Arizona 1981-89. Author *Handbook: Appeals in the Ninth Circuit* State Bar of Arizona 1987 and 1989 and "The Increasing Federalization of Crime" Arizona State L. Jour. Fall 2000. Co-author with Jack D. H. Hays "The Ability of the Mentally Retarded to Plead Guilty" Arizona State L. Jour. Winter 1975 and with William A. Holohan "Tribute to Chief Justice Jack D. H. Hays" 37 Arizona L. Rev. 951, 1995. Instructor U.S. Attorney General's Advocacy Institute 1982-88. Recipient commendations for case work from Drug Enforcement Administration 1985, from Criminal Investigation Division Internal Revenue Service 1986, from Federal Bureau of Investigation 1986 and from Organized Crime Drug Enforcement Task Force 1986. Recipient Director's Award for Superior Performance as Assistant U.S. Attorney 1986 and Special Achievement Award 1989 from Executive Office for U.S. Attorneys Department of Justice, U.S. Attorney's Sustained Superior Performance Award 1987 and 1988, Award for Significant Contributions from Arizona Women Lawyers Association 1996 and Friend of Phoenix Award 1998. Listed in *Who's Who in America, Who's Who of American Women* and *Who's Who in American Law*. President Arizona Women Lawyers' Association 1989 and Lorna E. Lockwood Inn of Court 1994-95. Chairperson Arizona Supreme Court Committee on Judicial Education 1994-96. Member American Judicature Society (Editorial Committee), State Bar of Arizona (Vice Chairman Tribal and Federal Court Forum) and American Bar Association (Committee on Continuing Education Appellate Judges' Conference Continuing). Former Member Board of Directors University of Arizona Law College Association, Phoenix Chamber Music Society, St. Mary's Food Bank and Friendly (Settlement) House. Vice President Board of Directors Phoenix Bach Choir. Member Institutional Biosafety Committee University of Arizona and Maricopa County Association of Governments Domestic Violence Council.

Office: 1501 West Washington Street, Phoenix 85007.
Telephone: (602) 542-5305.
Fax: (602) 542-4833

EIKLEBERRY, Jane L. *(Judge, Superior Court of Arizona Pima County)* Appointed by Governor Jane Dee Hull. Currently serves Civil Court.

Office: New Courts Building, 110 West Congress, Tucson 85701.
Telephone: (520) 740-4236.
Fax: (520) 740-8660
E-mail address: jeikleberry@sc.co.pima.az.us

ESCHER, Patricia G. *(Associate Presiding Judge, Superior Court of Arizona Pima County)* Appointed by governor. Currently serves as Presiding Drug Court Judge.

Office: New Courts Building, 110 West Congress, Tucson 85701.
Telephone: (520) 740-8169.
Fax: (520) 740-0753
E-mail address: pescher@sc.co.pima.az.us

ESPINOSA, Philip G. *(Chief Judge, Arizona Court of Appeals Division Two)* Appointed by Governor Fife Symington to term beginning 1992. Retained by election. Former Vice Chief Judge. Born Tucson Arizona Aug 23, 1952. Educated at University of Arizona B.A. 1978 J.D. 1983.

Assistant U.S. Attorney 1983-92 and Deputy Chief

ESPINOSA, PHILIP G.—*Continued*

Assistant U.S. Attorney Criminal Division 1990-92 Ninth Circuit.

Office: State Office Building, 400 West Congress Street, Tucson 85701-1374.
Telephone: (520) 628-6948.
E-mail address: espinosa@apltwo.ct.state.az.us

FENZEL, Alfred M. *(Judge, Superior Court of Arizona Maricopa County)* Appointed by Governor Jane Dee Hull. Currently serves Criminal Court.

Office: 3A Southeast Court, 222 East Javelina Avenue, Mesa 85210.
Telephone: (602) 506-7080.
Fax: (602) 506-2029
E-mail address: afenzel@superiorcourt.maricopa.gov

FIELDS, Kenneth L. *(Judge, Superior Court of Arizona Maricopa County)* Appointed by governor. Former Presiding Domestic Relations Court Judge. Currently serves Civil Court.

Office: 914 East Court Building, 101 West Jefferson, Phoenix 85003.
Telephone: (602) 506-2060.
Fax: (602) 506-1183
E-mail address: kfields@superiorcourt.maricopa.gov

FIELDS, Richard S. *(Judge, Superior Court of Arizona Pima County)* Appointed by Governor Fife Symington to term beginning May 1997. Retained by election. Term expires Dec 2004. Currently serves Family Court. Born Ravenna Ohio Feb 4, 1953. Protestant. Educated at The Ohio State University B.A. summa cum laude 1975 and University of Arizona College of Law J.D. 1978. Admitted to practice Arizona 1978, U.S. District Court District of Arizona 1980 and U.S. Court of Appeals Ninth Circuit 1982. In legal practice Tucson Oct 1978 to May 1997.

Founder Tucson Chapter National Wild Turkey Federation. Enjoys bowhunting and wildlife conservation.

Office: New Courts Building, 110 West Congress Street, Tucson 85701.
Telephone: (520) 740-8434.
Fax: (520) 740-8136
E-mail address: rfields@sc.co.pima.az.us

FIGUEROA, Gilberto V. *(Judge, Superior Court of Arizona Pinal County)* Appointed by Governor Jane Dee Hull to term beginning Sept 14, 1998. Elected Nov 3, 1998 and 2002. Current term expires Dec 31, 2006. Born Cumpas Sonora Mexico. Catholic. Educated at University of Arizona B.A. 1976 J.D. 1979. Member Phi Delta Phi. Admitted to practice Arizona 1979, U.S. District Court District of Arizona 1980 and U.S. Court of Appeals Ninth Circuit 1991. In legal practice Casa Grande Arizona 1980-92. Judge pro tem, Superior Court of Arizona Pinal County 1996.

County Attorney Pinal County 1993-96. Member Arizona Minority Judges Caucus, Arizona Judges Association, Los Abogados, Hispanic National Bar Association, State Bar of Arizona, Pinal County and American Bar Associations. Attended Arizona Judicial Conference. Member Sunrise Optimist Club of Casa Grande (Past President) and Arizona High School All Stars Steering Committee. Enjoys reading, writing and sports.

Mailing address: P.O. Box 1583, Florence 85232.
Office: Building E, 31 North Pinal Street, Florence 85232.
Telephone: (520) 866-6290.
Fax: (520) 866-6500
E-mail address: gfiguero@courts.sp.state.az.us

FIORA, Nancy *(Magistrate Judge, United States District Court District of Arizona)* Appointed by U.S. District Court judges.

Office: 3160 U.S. Courthouse, 405 West Congress Street, Tucson 85701-5010.
Telephone: (520) 205-4600.

FLÒREZ, M. Jan *(Judge, Arizona Court of Appeals Division Two)* Appointed by Governor Fife Symington to term beginning 1996. Retained by election. Born Jacksonville Texas Aug 26, 1944. Educated at University of Central Arkansas B.A. 1966 and University of Arizona J.D. 1980. Admitted to practice Arizona 1980. In legal practice Nogales 1980-92.

County Attorney Santa Cruz County 1993-96.

Office: State Office Building, 400 West Congress Street, Tucson 85701-1374.
Telephone: (520) 628-6949.
E-mail address: florez@apltwo.ct.state.az.us

FOREMAN, John F. *(Judge, Superior Court of Arizona Maricopa County)* Appointed by governor. Former Presiding Juvenile Court Judge. Currently serves Criminal Court.

Office: 8C Central Court Building, 201 West Jefferson Street, Phoenix 85003-2205.
Telephone: (602) 506-3194.
Fax: (602) 506-7867
E-mail address: jforeman@superiorcourt.maricopa.gov

FRANKS, Pamela J. *(Judge, Superior Court of Arizona Maricopa County)* Appointed by governor. Former Presiding Probate/Mental Health Court Judge. Currently serves Criminal Court.

Office: 13E Central Court Building, 201 West Jefferson, Phoenix 85003-2205.
Telephone: (602) 506-3528.
Fax: (602) 506-7867
E-mail address: pfranks@superiorcourt.maricopa.gov

GAINES, Pendleton *(Judge, Superior Court of Arizona Maricopa County)* Appointed by Governor Jane Dee Hull. Former Associate Presiding Family Court Judge. Currently serves Civil Court.

Office: 814 East Court Building, 101 West Jefferson, Phoenix 85003.
Telephone: (602) 506-3940.
Fax: (602) 506-1183
E-mail address: pgaines@superiorcourt.maricopa.gov

GALATI, Frank T. *(Judge, Superior Court of Arizona Maricopa County)* Court Commissioner May 2, 1984 to Oct 21, 1985. Appointed Judge by Governor Bruce Babbitt to term beginning Oct 22, 1985. Retained by election Nov 1988, Nov 1992, Nov 1996 and 2000. Current term expires Jan 2005. Currently serves Civil Court. Born Bridgeport Connecticut Aug 13, 1948. Educated at University of Arizona B.A. 1970 J.D. 1973. Admitted to practice Arizona 1973. Began legal practice Phoenix 1973.

Assistant Attorney General Arizona 1973-76 and 1981-84. Deputy County Attorney Maricopa County 1976-81. Author "Due Process and Equal Protection Limitations Upon Penal Administration" 10 Arizona B.

GALATI, FRANK T.—*Continued*

Jour. 1974. Member State Bar of Arizona (Chairman Criminal Justice Section 1983-84) and American Bar Association (Criminal Justice Section Liaison to State Bar of Arizona). Winner Roger L. Perry Legal Writing Award 1974. Enjoys sports, reading and family.

Office: 612 East Court Building, 101 West Jefferson Street, Phoenix 85003.
Telephone: (602) 506-3126.
Fax: (602) 506-1183
E-mail address: fgalati@superiorcourt.maricopa.gov

GAMA, J. Richard *(Judge, Superior Court of Arizona Maricopa County)* Appointed by Governor Jane Dee Hull. Currently serves Civil Court.

Office: 611 East Court Building, 101 West Jefferson, Phoenix 85003.
Telephone: (602) 506-1245.
Fax: (602) 506-7867
E-mail address: jgama@superiorcourt.maricopa.gov

GARBARINO, William F. *(Judge, Arizona Court of Appeals Division One)* Appointed by Governor Fife Symington to term beginning 1991. Retained by election. Educated at Northern Arizona University 1963 and University of Arizona J.D. 1967. Judge 1982-91, Presiding Judge 1989-91 and Former Presiding Juvenile Judge, Superior Court of Arizona Coconino County, appointed by Governor Bruce Babbitt.

Office: 1501 West Washington, Phoenix 85007.
Telephone: (602) 542-3491.
Fax: (602) 542-4833

GAYLORD, John M. *(Judge, Superior Court of Arizona Maricopa County)* Appointed by Governor Jane Dee Hull to term beginning Jan 2000. Retained by election 2002, current term expires Nov 2006. Currently serves Criminal Court. Born San Antonio Texas Sept 25, 1956. Roman Catholic. Educated at Northern Arizona University B.S. 1978 and Arizona State University College of Law J.D. 1981. Admitted to practice Arizona 1981, U.S. District Court District of Arizona 1981, U.S. Court of Appeals for the Armed Forces 1982, Colorado 1999 and U.S. Tax Court. In legal practice Phoenix 1987-88 and Chandler 1990-94 Arizona.

Assistant Attorney General Arizona 1989-90. With Attorney General's Office Arizona 1994-99. Member Los Abogados. Lieutenant Colonel USMCR (retired). Republican. Member Knights of Columbus and Boy Scouts of America. Enjoys hiking, camping, motorcycling and most sports. Personal Statement or Quote: "Never miss a good chance to shut up" (Will Rogers).

Office: 222 East Javelina Avenue, Mesa 85210.
Telephone: (602) 506-0424.
Fax: (602) 506-2029
E-mail address: jgaylord@superiorcourt.maricopa.gov

GEMMILL, John C. *(Vice Chief Judge, Arizona Court of Appeals Division One)* Appointed by Governor Jane Dee Hull to term beginning 2001. Vice Chief Judge since 2003. Educated at University of Arizona B.S. with highest distinction 1971 J.D. with highest distinction 1976. Recipient Freeman Medal as an outstanding graduate 1971. Co-winner Joseph S. Jenckes, Jr. Oral Advocacy Contest 1976. Member Order of the Coif. In legal practice Phoenix 25 years.

Office: 1501 West Washington, Phoenix 85007.
Telephone: (602) 542-4828.
Fax: (602) 542-4833

GERST, Stephen A. *(Judge, Superior Court of Arizona Maricopa County)* Appointed by Governor Bruce Babbitt to term beginning Jan 16, 1984. Retained by election. Former Presiding Special Assignment Judge. Former Presiding Domestic Relations Judge. Currently serves Criminal Court. Born Phoenix Arizona April 25, 1942. Jewish. Educated at University of Arizona LL.B. 1966. Began legal practice Phoenix Arizona.

Office: 12E Central Court Building, 201 West Jefferson, Phoenix 85003.
Telephone: (602) 506-5978.
Fax: (602) 506-7867
E-mail address: sgerst@superiorcourt.maricopa.gov

GOTTSFIELD, Robert L. *(Judge, Superior Court of Arizona Maricopa County)* Appointed by Governor Bruce Babbitt to term beginning Feb 1, 1980. Retained by election. Currently serves Civil Court. Born Brooklyn New York March 6, 1935. Catholic. Educated at State University of New York at Binghamton B.A. magna cum laude 1956, Cornell University Law School J.D. 1960 and Arizona State University M.C. 1981. Admitted to practice New York 1960 and Arizona 1964.

Office: 202 Old Courthouse, 125 West Washington, Phoenix 85003.
Telephone: (602) 506-3132.
Fax: (602) 506-7867
E-mail address: rgottsfi@superiorcourt.maricopa.gov

GOULD, Andrew W. *(Judge, Superior Court of Arizona Yuma County)*

Office: County Courthouse, 168 South Second Avenue, Yuma 85364-2296.
Telephone: (928) 329-2200.
Fax: (928) 329-2004
E-mail address: ango@court.co.yuma.az.us

GRANVILLE, Warren J. *(Judge, Superior Court of Arizona Maricopa County)* Appointed by Governor Jane Dee Hull. Currently serves Criminal Court.

Office: 9D Central Court Building, 201 West Jefferson, Phoenix 85003-2205.
Telephone: (602) 506-0434.
Fax: (602) 506-7867
E-mail address: wgranvil@superiorcourt.maricopa.gov

HAINES, Randolph J. *(Judge, United States Bankruptcy Court District of Arizona)* Appointed by U.S. Court of Appeals Ninth Circuit judges to term beginning March 17, 2000. Term expires March 16, 2014. Born Whitewater Wisconsin July 29, 1948. Educated at University of Wisconsin B.A. 1971, Yale University Ph.D. 1975 and Stanford University Law School J.D. 1978. Article Editor Stanford Law Review 1977-78. Member Order of the Coif. Admitted to practice Arizona 1978. In legal practice Phoenix 1978-2000.

Author "The Unwarranted Attack on New Value" 72 American Bankruptcy L. Jour. 387 Summer 1998. Member National Conference of Bankruptcy Judges and The Selden Society. Member Scribes. Political affiliation: Independent.

Mailing address: P.O. Box 34151, Phoenix 85067-4151.
Telephone: (602) 640-5800.
E-mail address: randy_haines@azb.uscourts.gov

HALL, Philip L. *(Judge, Arizona Court of Appeals Division One)* Appointed by Governor Jane Dee Hull to term beginning 2001. Educated at University of Arizona B.S. 1977 and Cornell University Law School J.D. 1981. Judge, Superior Court of Arizona Yuma County 1993-2001.
Office: 1501 West Washington, Phoenix 85007.
Telephone: (602) 542-4826.
Fax: (602) 542-7801

HANTMAN, Howard *(Judge, Superior Court of Arizona Pima County)* Appointed by governor. Currently serves Criminal Court.
Office: New Courts Building, 110 West Congress Street, Tucson 85701.
Telephone: (520) 740-3527.
Fax: (520) 740-3547
E-mail address: hhantman@sc.co.pima.az.us

HARDY, Charles L. *(Senior Judge, United States District Court District of Arizona)* Appointed for life by President Jimmy Carter May 23, 1980. Assumed Senior status, serves by assignment. Born Los Angeles California Jan 24, 1919. Mormon. Educated at University of Arizona B.S. 1947 LL.B. 1949. Member Alpha Kappa Psi. Admitted to practice Arizona 1949. Began legal practice Phoenix 1949. Judge, Superior Court of Arizona Maricopa County 1966-80.
Chairman Committee on Jury Instructions Ninth Circuit since 1987. Member American Judicature Society, Federal Judges Association, State Bar of Arizona, Maricopa County and American Bar Associations. Captain USAS Field Artillery 1941-45. Democrat. Member Arizona Board of Crippled Children Services 1965-66. Enjoys gardening, backpacking, fishing and photography.
Office: 130 U.S. Courthouse, 401 West Washington Street, Phoenix 85003-2118.
Telephone: (602) 322-7100.

HARRINGTON, Charles V. *(Judge, Superior Court of Arizona Pima County)* Appointed by governor. Currently serves Juvenile Court.
Office: New Courts Building, 110 West Congress, Tucson 85701.
Telephone: (520) 740-4471.
Fax: (520) 740-8318
E-mail address: charrington@sc.co.pima.az.us

HARRISON, Cari A. *(Judge, Superior Court of Arizona Maricopa County)* Appointed by Governor Jane Dee Hull. Currently serves Civil Court.
Office: 303 Old Courthouse, 125 West Washington, Phoenix 85003.
Telephone: (602) 506-0967.
Fax: (602) 506-7867
E-mail address: charriso@superiorcourt.maricopa.gov

HAUSER, Brian R. *(Judge, Superior Court of Arizona Maricopa County)* Appointed by Governor Fife Symington to term beginning June 6, 1991. Retained by election Nov 8, 1994, Nov 1998 and 2002. Current term expires Dec 31, 2006. Currently serves Criminal Court. Born New York New York Jan 7, 1953. Educated at Temple University B.A. 1974 J.D. 1977. Admitted to practice Pennsylvania 1977, U.S. District Courts Eastern District of Pennsylvania 1978 and District of Arizona 1980, U.S. Courts of Appeals Third 1978 and Ninth 1981 Circuits, Arizona 1980 and U.S. Supreme Court 1986. In legal practice Philadelphia Pennsylvania 1977-79.
Assistant Attorney General Arizona 1980-84. Deputy County Attorney Maricopa County 1984-91. Former Member American Inn of Court.
Office: 8D Central Court Building, 201 West Jefferson, Phoenix 85003.
Telephone: (602) 506-6086.
Fax: (602) 506-4121
E-mail address: bhauser@superiorcourt.maricopa.gov

HEILMAN, Joseph B. *(Judge, Superior Court of Arizona Maricopa County)* Appointed by Governor Jane Dee Hull. Currently serves Civil Court, Family Court and Probate Court.
Office: B Northwest Regional Center, 14264 West Tierra Buena Lane, Surprise 85374.
Telephone: (602) 506-0292.
E-mail address: jheilman@superiorcourt.maricopa.gov

HENDRIX, Danna *(Judge, Superior Court of Arizona Coconino County)*
Office: Coconino County Courthouse, 200 North San Francisco, Flagstaff 86001.
Telephone: (928) 779-6546.
Fax: (928) 214-0165
E-mail address: dhendrix@courts.sp.state.az.us

HICKS, Bethany G. *(Judge, Superior Court of Arizona Maricopa County)* Appointed by Governor Jane Dee Hull. Former Presiding Family Court Judge. Currently serves Civil Court. Born Elmira New York Sept 8, 1951. Educated at Vassar College A.B. 1973, Boston University M.Ed. 1975 and Arizona State University College of Law J.D. 1984. Admitted to practice Arizona 1984. In legal practice Scottsdale and Paradise Valley.
Member Arizona Women Lawyers Association (Steering Committee since 1998), State Bar of Arizona, Maricopa County (Co-chairman Alternative Dispute Resolution Committee and Chairman Subcommittee on Domestic Relations Alternative Dispute Resolution Committee) and American Bar Associations. Listed in *Who's Who in the World, Who's Who in American Law, Who's Who of American Women, Who's Who in the West* and *Who's Who of Emerging Leaders in America.* Board of Governors All Saints' Episcopal Day School 1993-94. Volunteer Teach for America since 1998. Member All Saints' Episcopal Day School Parent Association (Executive Committee and Secretary 1991-92 and President 1993-94) and National Charity League (Class Advisor and Board of Directors 1996).
Office: Central Court Building, 201 West Jefferson Street, Phoenix 85003.
Telephone: (602) 506-2139.
E-mail address: bhicks@superiorcourt.maricopa.gov

HILLIARD, Ruth H. *(Judge, Superior Court of Arizona Maricopa County)* Former Court Commissioner. Appointed Judge by governor. Currently serves Criminal Court.
Office: 10D Central Court Building, 201 West Jefferson, Phoenix 85003-2205.
Telephone: (602) 506-3145.
Fax: (602) 506-7867
E-mail address: rhilliar@superiorcourt.maricopa.gov

HOAG, M. Jean *(Judge, Superior Court of Arizona Maricopa County)* Currently serves as Presiding Southeast Court Judge.

Office: 2C Southeast Court, 222 East Javelina Avenue, Mesa 85210.
Telephone: (602) 506-3130.
E-mail address: jhoag@superiorcourt.maricopa.gov

HOGGATT, Wallace R. *(Judge, Superior Court of Arizona Cochise County)* Appointed by Governor Fife Symington to term beginning May 2, 1996. Elected Nov 5, 1996, Nov 1998 and 2002. Current term expires Jan 2007. Former Presiding Judge. Currently serves as Presiding Juvenile Court Judge. Born Las Vegas Nevada Oct 29, 1955. Christian. Educated at University of Arizona B.A. with high distinction 1975 J.D. with high distinction 1979. Member Phi Delta Phi and Order of the Coif. Admitted to practice Arizona 1979, U.S. District Court District of Arizona 1979, U.S. Court of Appeals Ninth Circuit 1982 and U.S. Supreme Court 1983. In legal practice Douglas 1979-84 and Sierra Vista 1985-96.

Chief Public Defender Cochise County 1984-85. Instructor in Business Law 1981-83 and 1989-90 and Ethics 1994 Cochise College. Member Arizona Judges Association, American Judges Association, State Bar of Arizona and Cochise County Bar Association.

Office: 202 Superior Court, 100 Colonia De Salud, Sierra Vista 85635.
Telephone: (520) 803-3080.
Fax: (520) 458-4148
E-mail address: whoggatt@courts.sp.state.az.us

HOLLOWELL, Eileen W. *(Judge, United States Bankruptcy Court District of Arizona)* Appointed by U.S. Court of Appeals Ninth Circuit judges to term beginning Sept 19, 2000. Term expires Sept 2014. Educated at University of Massachusetts, University of Michigan and University of Arizona J.D. with high distinction. In legal practice Tucson.

Office: 110 South Church Avenue, Room 8112, Tucson 85701-1608.
Telephone: (520) 620-7500.

HOLT, Cathy M. *(Judge, Superior Court of Arizona Maricopa County)* Appointed by Governor Jane Dee Hull. Currently serves Civil Court.

Office: 309 Old Courthouse, 125 West Washington, Phoenix 85003.
Telephone: (602) 506-3105.
Fax: (602) 506-7867
E-mail address: cholt@superiorcourt.maricopa.gov

HOLT, R. Douglas *(Presiding Judge, Superior Court of Arizona Graham County)*

Office: Graham County Courthouse, 800 Main, Safford 85546.
Telephone: (928) 428-3310.
Fax: (928) 428-1032
E-mail address: dholt@graham.az.gov

HOTHAM, Jeffrey A. *(Judge, Superior Court of Arizona Maricopa County)* Appointed by governor. Currently serves Criminal Court.

Office: 12A Central Court Building, 201 West Jefferson, Phoenix 85003-2205.
Telephone: (602) 506-3963.
Fax: (602) 506-1183
E-mail address: jhotham@superiorcourt.maricopa.gov

HOUSER, Robert *(Judge, Superior Court of Arizona Maricopa County)* Appointed by governor. Currently serves Family Court.

Office: 5G Central Court Building, 201 West Jefferson, Phoenix 85003.
Telephone: (602) 506-5424.
E-mail address: houserr001-@superiorcourt.maricopa.gov

HOWARD, Joseph W. *(Judge, Arizona Court of Appeals Division Two)* Appointed by governor to term beginning 1997. Retained by election. Born Ohio 1950. Educated at Arizona State University B.S.B.A. 1972 J.D. 1976. Certified Specialist, Real Estate Law—Arizona Board of Legal Specialization. In legal practice Casa Grande 1976-1997.

Office: State Office Building, 400 West Congress Street, Tucson 85701-1374.
Telephone: (520) 628-6946.
E-mail address: howard@apltwo.ct.state.az.us

HURWITZ, Andrew D. *(Justice, Supreme Court of Arizona)* Appointed by Governor Janet Napolitano Jan 27, 2003. Educated at Princeton University A.B. cum laude 1968 and Yale Law School J.D. 1972. Law Clerk to U.S. District Court District of Connecticut 1972, Hon. J. Joseph Smith, U.S. Court of Appeals Second Circuit 1972-73 and Hon. Potter Stewart, U.S. Supreme Court 1973-74. Admitted to practice Connecticut 1973, Arizona 1974, U.S. District Courts District of Arizona 1975 and District of Connecticut 1977, U.S. Court of Appeals Ninth 1975, Second 1977 and Seventh 1987 Circuits, U.S. Supreme Court 1976 and U.S. Tax Court 1987. In legal practice 1974-80 and 1983-2003.

Office: 1501 West Washington, Phoenix 85007.
Telephone: (602) 542-4532.
Fax: (602) 542-9481

HYATT, Carey S. *(Judge, Superior Court of Arizona Maricopa County)* Appointed by Governor Jane Dee Hull. Currently serves Criminal Court.

Office: 912 East Court Building, 101 West Jefferson, Phoenix 85003.
Telephone: (602) 506-3566.
Fax: (602) 506-7867
E-mail address: chyatt@superiorcourt.maricopa.gov

IRVINE, Patrick G. *(Judge, Arizona Court of Appeals Division One)* Appointed by governor.

Office: 1501 West Washington, Phoenix 85007.
Telephone: (602) 542-3493.
Fax: (602) 542-4833
E-mail address: pirvine@courts.sp.state.az.us

IRWIN, Charles A. *(Judge, Superior Court of Arizona Cochise County)* Elected to term beginning Nov 22, 1996. Reelected 2000, current term expires Jan 2005. Former Presiding Juvenile Court Judge. Born Albuquerque New Mexico May 12, 1954. Roman Catholic. Educated at University of Arizona B.S. 1976 J.D. with honors 1985 and Boston University M.S.B.A. 1982. Admitted to practice Arizona 1985, U.S. District Court District of Arizona 1985, U.S. Court of Appeals Ninth Circuit 1985 and U.S. Supreme Court 1994. In legal practice Sierra Vista 1985-96.

Member National Council of Juvenile and Family Court Judges, Arizona Judicial Association and State Bar

IRWIN, CHARLES A.—*Continued*

of Arizona. Captain U.S. Army Military Police Corp 1976-82. Enjoys hiking, camping and snow skiing.

Mailing address: P.O. Box CG, Bisbee 85603.

Office: County Court Building, Second Floor, Quality Hill, Bisbee 85603.

Telephone: (520) 432-8540.

E-mail address: cirwin@courts.sp.state.az.us

IRWIN, Jay R. *(Magistrate Judge, United States District Court District of Arizona)* Appointed by U.S. District Court judges to term beginning Aug 16, 2000. Term expires Aug 2008.

Office: 325 West 19th Street, Yuma 85364.

Telephone: (928) 329-4766.

ISHIKAWA, Brian K. *(Judge, Superior Court of Arizona Maricopa County)* Appointed by governor. Currently serves Family Court.

Office: 4C Southeast Court, 222 East Javelina Avenue, Mesa 85210.

Telephone: (602) 506-5225.

Fax: (602) 506-2029

E-mail address: bishikaw@superiorcourt.maricopa.gov

JARRETT, Barbara M. *(Judge, Superior Court of Arizona Maricopa County)* Appointed by Governor Fife Symington 1992. Retained by election, current term expires Dec 31, 2004. Currently serves Criminal Court. Born Smithville Arkansas 1940. Educated at University of Texas at Austin B.S. 1972 and Arizona State University College of Law J.D. with honors 1977. Admitted to practice Arizona 1977, U.S. District Court District of Arizona 1977, U.S. Court of Appeals Ninth Circuit 1979 and U.S. Supreme Court 1989.

Office: 4E Southeast Court, 222 East Javelina Avenue, Mesa 85210.

Telephone: (602) 506-1650.

Fax: (602) 506-2029

E-mail address: bjarrett@superiorcourt.maricopa.gov

JOHNSON, Boyd T. *(Judge, Superior Court of Arizona Pinal County)* Judge pro temp Jan 1995 to March 1996. Appointed by Governor Fife Symington to term beginning March 1996. Retained by election Jan 1997 and Jan 2001. Current term expires Dec 2004. Born Phoenix Arizona Nov 11, 1947. Educated at Arizona State University B.S. with distinction 1973 J.D. 1976. Member Phi Alpha Delta. Admitted to practice Arizona 1976 and U.S. District Court District of Arizona. In legal practice Coolidge July 1976 to July 1984.

Chief Deputy County Attorney July 1984 to Nov 1992 and Public Defender Nov 1992 to Jan 1995 Pinal County. Member American Judges Association and State Bar of Arizona. U.S. Army Dec 1965 to Sept 1968 Vietnam. Member of historic preservation and several veterans organizations. Enjoys numismatics, golf and spending time with family. Personal Statement of Quote: "Be prepared, be on time and be professional."

Mailing address: P.O. Box 2998, Florence 85232.

Office: Building E, 31 North Pinal Street, Florence 85232.

Telephone: (520) 866-6525.

Fax: (520) 866-6500

E-mail address: btjohnson@courts.sp.state.az.us

JONES, Charles E. *(Chief Justice, Supreme Court of Arizona)* Appointed by Governor Fife Symington to term beginning 1996. Retained by election. Vice Chief Justice 1997 to Jan 2002. Chief Justice since Jan 8, 2002. Born June 12, 1935. Educated at Brigham Young University B.A. 1959 and Stanford Law School J.D. 1962. Law Clerk to Chief Judge Richard H. Chambers, U.S. Court of Appeals Ninth Circuit 1962-63. Member Pi Sigma Alpha and Blue Key. Admitted to practice California 1962, U.S. District Court District of Arizona 1963, U.S. Courts of Appeals Ninth 1963 and Tenth 1974 Circuits, Arizona 1964 and U.S. Supreme Court 1979. In legal practice Arizona 1963-96.

Lawyer Delegate Judicial Conference of the Ninth Circuit 1974 and 1975. Member State Bar of Arizona (Board of Legal Specialization 1981-88), Maricopa County and American Bar Associations. Recipient Alumni Distinguished Service Award from Brigham Young University Alumni Association 1982 and Feuerstein Award for ethics in the law of Industrial Relations from University of Arizona 1998. Former Member Board of Visitors Brigham Young University Law School (Chairman 1978-81). Member J. Reuben Clark Law Society (National Chairman 1994-98).

Office: 1501 West Washington, Phoenix 85007.

Telephone: (602) 542-4534.

Fax: (602) 542-4506

E-mail address: cjones@supreme.sp.state.az.us

JONES, Michael D. *(Judge, Superior Court of Arizona Maricopa County)*

Office: 10A Central Court Building, 201 West Jefferson, Phoenix 85003-2205.

Telephone: (602) 506-2030.

Fax: (602) 506-7867

E-mail address: mjones@superiorcourt.maricopa.gov

JORGENSON, Cindy K. *(Judge, United States District Court District of Arizona)* Appointed for life by President George W. Bush to term beginning March 15, 2002. Educated at University of Arizona B.S. 1974 J.D. 1977. Former Judge and Presiding Domestic Relations Court Judge, Superior Court of Arizona Pima County.

Office: 5180 U.S. Courthouse, 405 West Congress Street, Tucson 85701.

Telephone: (520) 205-4550.

KATZ, Paul A. *(Judge, Superior Court of Arizona Maricopa County)* Appointed by governor. Currently serves as Presiding Tax Court Judge.

Office: 101 Old Courthouse, 125 West Washington, Phoenix 85003.

Telephone: (602) 506-5806.

Fax: (602) 506-7867

E-mail address: pkatz@superiorcourt.maricopa.gov

KEARNEY, Jan *(Judge, Superior Court of Arizona Pima County)* Appointed by governor. Currently serves Family Court.

Office: New Courts Building, 110 West Congress, Tucson 85701.

Telephone: (520) 740-8782.

Fax: (520) 740-8020

E-mail address: jkearney@sc.co.pima.az.us

KELLY, John F. *(Judge, Superior Court of Arizona Pima County)* Appointed by governor. Former Presiding Juvenile Judge. Currently serves Civil Court.

Office: New Courts Building, 110 West Congress Street, Tucson 85701.

Telephone: (520) 740-8481.

KELLY, JOHN F.—*Continued*

Fax: (520) 740-2720
E-mail address: jkelly@sc.co.pima.az.us

KELLY, Virginia *(Judge, Superior Court of Arizona Pima County)* Appointed by governor. Currently serves Criminal Court.

Office: New Courts Building, 110 West Congress, Tucson 85701.
Telephone: (520) 740-3125.
Fax: (520) 740-3140
E-mail address: vkelly@sc.co.pima.az.us

KEPPEL, James H. *(Judge, Superior Court of Arizona Maricopa County)* Appointed by governor. Currently serves Criminal Court.

Office: 2D Southeast Court, 222 East Javelina Avenue, Mesa 85210.
Telephone: (602) 506-4251.
Fax: (602) 506-2029
E-mail address: jkeppel@superiorcourt.maricopa.gov

KESSLER, Donn *(Judge, Arizona Court of Appeals Division One)* Appointed by Governor Janet Napolitano May 5, 2003.

Office: 1501 West Wahington, Phoenix 85007.

KIGER, William T. *(Associate Presiding Judge, Superior Court of Arizona Yavapai County)*

Office: 406 Yavapai County Courthouse, 120 South Cortez, Prescott 86301.
Telephone: (928) 771-3307.
Fax: (928) 771-3508
E-mail address: wkiger@courts.sp.state.az.us

KINDIG, Gloria *(Judge, Superior Court of Arizona Navajo County)* Former Presiding Judge.

Mailing address: P.O. Box 668, Holbrook 86025.
Office: Navajo County Courthouse, Holbrook 86025.
Telephone: (928) 524-4220.
Fax: (928) 524-4246
E-mail address: gkindig@courts.sp.state.az.us

KLEIN, Andrew G. *(Judge, Superior Court of Arizona Maricopa County)* Appointed by governor. Currently serves Juvenile Court.

Office: 1067 Southeast Court, 222 East Javelina Avenue, Mesa 85210.
Telephone: (602) 506-4645.
Fax: (602) 506-4132
E-mail address: aklein@superiorcourt.maricopa.gov

KONGABLE, Kirby *(Judge, Superior Court of Arizona Yuma County)* Judge pro tem 1994-97. Appointed Judge by Governor Fife Symington May 1997 to term beginning June 1997. Elected Nov 1998 and Nov 2002. Current term expires Dec 31, 2006. Currently serves as Presiding Juvenile Court Judge. Born Hinsdale Illinois Aug 25, 1951. Presbyterian. Educated at Arizona State University B.S.B.A. 1973 J.D. 1976. Admitted to practice Arizona 1976 and U.S. District Court District of Arizona 1979. Certified Specialist, Criminal Law—Arizona Board of Legal Specialization 1991-94. In legal practice Yuma 1977-94.

Member State Bar of Arizona and Yuma County Bar Association (President 1991). Republican. Enjoys golf and weightlifting.

Office: Yuma County Juvenile Court Center, 2440 West 28th Street, Yuma 85364.
Telephone: (928) 314-1900.
Fax: (928) 726-4720

LANKFORD, Jefferson Lewis *(Judge, Arizona Court of Appeals Division One)* Appointed by Governor Rose Mofford Nov 1989. Retained by election Nov 1992 and Nov 1998. Current term expires Jan 2005. Born Louisville Kentucky Oct 5, 1951. Educated at University of Kentucky B.A. 1973 and University of Virginia J.D. 1978 LL.M. 1992. Law Clerk to Hon. Pierce Lively, U.S. Court of Appeals Sixth Circuit 1978-79. Admitted to practice Arizona 1978, U.S. District Court District of Arizona and U.S. Courts of Appeals Sixth, Ninth, Tenth, District of Columbia and Federal Circuits. In legal practice Phoenix 1979-89.

Editor *Arizona Litigation Guide* Maricopa County Bar Association 1989 and rev. ed. 1993. Co-editor *Arizona Appellate Handbook* 2nd ed. 1, 2 and 3 State Bar of Arizona. Co-author *The Law of Negligence in Arizona* The Michie Company 1992 2nd ed. 1997. Author *Arizona DUI* Lexis Law Publishing 2000. Chair *Arizona Attorney* Editorial Board 1990-94. Board of Directors Arizona Judicial College 1991-94. Vice Chair 1991-95 and Chair 1995-2000 Judicial Ethics Advisory Committee. Recipient Member of the Year Maricopa County Bar Association 1989. Staff assistant U.S. House of Representatives 1973-75.

Office: 1501 West Washington, Phoenix 85007.
Telephone: (602) 542-1432.
Fax: (602) 542-4833
E-mail address: jlankford@courts.sp.state.az.us

LEE, Kenneth *(Judge, Superior Court of Arizona Pima County)* Appointed by governor. Former Presiding Civil Court Judge and Associate Presiding Judge. Currently serves Criminal Court.

Office: Pima County Superior Court Building, 110 West Congress Street, Tucson 85701.
Telephone: (520) 740-8531.
Fax: (520) 740-3254
E-mail address: klee@sc.co.pima.az.us

LEONARDO, John S. *(Presiding Judge, Superior Court of Arizona Pima County)* Appointed by Governor Fife Symington to term beginning Feb 1, 1993. Retained by election 1996 and 2000. Current term expires Jan 1, 2005. Former Presiding Criminal Court Judge. Born Des Moines Iowa Jan 4, 1947. Educated at University of Notre Dame B.A. with honors 1969 and George Washington University J.D. with honors 1972. Staff member George Washington Law Review. Admitted to practice Maryland 1972, Arizona, Indiana, U.S. Courts of Appeals Seventh and Ninth Circuits and U.S. Supreme Court.

Assistant U.S. Attorney Northern District of Indiana 1973-82 and District of Arizona 1982-93.

Office: Superior Court Building, 110 West Congress, Tucson 85701.
Telephone: (520) 740-8005.
Fax: (520) 740-3924

LINDBERG, Thomas *(Judge, Superior Court of Arizona Yavapai County)* Appointed by Governor Jane D. Hull to term beginning Jan 1, 2001. Elected Nov 2002, current term expires Dec 31, 2006. Born Jackson Michigan Aug 24, 1952. Catholic. Educated at University of Arizona B.A. with distinction 1974 J.D. 1977. Admitted to practice Arizona 1977 and U.S. District Court District of Arizona 1977. In legal practice Tucson 1978-79.

LINDBERG, THOMAS—*Continued*

Assistant City Attorney Tucson July 1979 to June 1981. Deputy Attorney July 1981 to Aug 1987 and Chief Criminal Division Aug 1987 to Dec 2000 Yavapai County. Past President and Former Board Member Yavapai Big Brothers/Big Sisters.

Office: Yavapai County Courthouse, 120 South Cortez, Prescott 86301.
Telephone: (928) 771-3580.
Fax: (928) 771-3582
E-mail address: tlindber@courts.sp.state.az.us

MACKEY, David *(Judge, Superior Court of Arizona Yavapai County)*

Office: 3505 West Highway 260, Room 107, Camp Verde 86322.
Telephone: (928) 567-7722.
Fax: (928) 567-7724
E-mail address: randerso@courts.sp.state.az.us

MAHONEY, Margaret R. *(Judge, Superior Court of Arizona Maricopa County)* Appointed by governor. Currently serves Family Court.

Office: 5B Central Court Building, 201 West Jefferson, Mesa 85003-2205.
Telephone: (602) 506-0387.
E-mail address: mmahoney-@superiorcourt.maricopa.gov

MANGUM, J. Kenneth *(Judge, Superior Court of Arizona Maricopa County)* Appointed by Governor Rose Mofford to term beginning Jan 1991. Retained by election 1994, 1998 and 2002. Current term expires Dec 31, 2006. Currently serves Juvenile Court. Born Pasadena California Feb 24, 1945. Church of Jesus Christ of Latter-Day Saints. Educated at Brigham Young University B.A. magna cum laude 1969, University of Chicago J.D. 1972 and George Washington University. Admitted to practice Arizona 1972, U.S. District Court District of Arizona 1972 and U.S. Court of Military Appeals 1973. In legal practice Phoenix 1976-90.

Important decision: State v. Lyle Eugene Keidel (Defendant murdered his wife in 1966. Twenty-eight years later the eyewitness daughter, age five at the time of the crime, reports incident to police. Guilty verdict. Aired on "Dateline" NBC April 1996.) CR 94-08312 March and April 1995. Member Phoenix Association of Defense Counsel 1976-90. Member State Bar of Arizona and Maricopa County Bar Association (Secretary Young Lawyers Division 1981-82). Lieutenant USNR JAGC 1972-76. Republican. Board Member Phoenix Corporate Ministry 1983-86. Member Phoenix Rotary Club. Enjoys backpacking and reading.

Office: 3125 West Durango, Phoenix 85009.
Telephone: (602) 506-4567.
Fax: (602) 506-7867
E-mail address: kmangum@superiorcourt.maricopa.gov

MARLAR, James M. *(Judge, United States Bankruptcy Court District of Arizona)* Appointed by U.S. Court of Appeals Ninth Circuit judges. Also Judge, Bankruptcy Appellate Panel Ninth Circuit. Selected by the Judicial Council of the Ninth Circuit.

Office: 110 South Church Avenue, Suite 8112, Tucson 85701-1608.
Telephone: (520) 620-7500.

MARQUEZ, Alfredo C. *(Senior Judge, United States District Court District of Arizona)* Appointed for life by President Jimmy Carter to term beginning July 25, 1980. Assumed Senior status 1992, serves by assignment. Born Winkelman Arizona June 30, 1922. Educated at University of Arizona B.A. 1948 LL.B. 1950. In legal practice 1958-80.

Assistant State Attorney General 1951-52. Deputy County Attorney Pima County 1953-54. Part-time City Prosecutor. Important Decisions: Planned Parenthood v. Neely (unconstitutionally vague statute) CIV 89-489 TUC-ACM 1992; Planned Parenthood v. Casey (undue burden) 505 U.S. 833, 1992; United States v. Valdez-Gonzalez (socio-economic conditions and the internal politics of the drug trade) 957 F.2d 643 9th Cir. 1992; American Lung Association v. Browner CIV 93-643 TUC-ACM 884 F. Supp. 345 Ariz. 1994; Defenders of Wildlife v. Browner CIV 93-234 TUC-ACM 888 F. Supp. 1003 Ariz. 1995; Grijalva v. Shalala CIV 93-711 TUC-ACM 1997 WL 155392 Ariz. March 3, 1997 aff'd 152 F.3d 1115 9th Cir. 1998 cert. granted judgment vacated and remanded 119 S. Ct. 1573, 1999; Defenders v. Ballard CIV 97-794 TUC-ACM 73 F. Supp. 2d 1094 Ariz. 1999; Planned Parenthood v. LaWall 804 F. Supp 180 F.3d 1022 9th Cir. 1999 aff'd 180 F.3d 1022 9th Cir. amended 193 F.3d 1042 9th Cir. 1999; Southwest Center for Biological Diversity v. Babbitt (environmental protections for the pygmy-owl) CIV 97-704 TUC-ACM; and Flores v. State of Arizona (class-action school case) CIV 92-596 TUC-ACM. Member American Board of Trial Advocates, American Judicature Society and American Bar Association. U.S. Naval Air Corps 1943-45. Administrative Assistant to Congressman Udall 1955.

Office: 405 West Congress Street, Suite 6180, Tucson 85701.
Telephone: (520) 205-4500.

MARSHALL, Jacqueline *(Magistrate Judge, United States District Court District of Arizona)* Appointed by U.S. District Court judges to term beginning July 11, 2001.

Office: 6650 U.S. Courthouse, 405 West Congress Street, Tucson 85701.
Telephone: (520) 205-4640.

MARTIN, Gregory H. *(Judge, Superior Court of Arizona Maricopa County)* Former Associate Presiding Criminal Court Judge.

Office: 11E Central Court Building, 201 West Jefferson Street, Phoenix 85003-2205.
Telephone: (602) 506-3441.
Fax: (602) 506-7867
E-mail address: gmartin@superiorcourt.maricopa.gov

MARTONE, Frederick J. *(Judge, United States District Court District of Arizona)* Appointed for life by President George W. Bush to term beginning Jan 30, 2002. Born Fall River Massachusetts Nov 8, 1943. Educated at College of the Holy Cross B.S. 1965, University of Notre Dame J.D. 1972 and Harvard University LL.M. 1975. Note and Comment Editor Notre Dame Lawyer 1970-72. Law Clerk to Hon. Edward F. Hennessey, Massachusetts Supreme Judicial Court 1972-73. Admitted to practice Massachusetts 1972, Arizona 1974, U.S. District Courts District of Arizona and District of Massachusetts, U.S. Courts of Appeals First and Ninth Circuits and U.S. Supreme Court 1977. In legal practice Phoenix Arizona 1973-85. Judge, Superior Court of Arizona Maricopa County 1985-92, appointed by Governor Bruce Babbitt. Justice, Supreme Court of Arizona Feb

MARTONE, FREDERICK J.—*Continued*

28, 1992 to Feb 2002, appointed by Governor Fife Symington.

Author Comment 46 Notre Dame Lawyer 610, 1971; "Constitutional Rights of the Accused" 60 Massachusetts L. Quar. 19, 1975; "American Indian Tribal Self-Government in the Federal System" 51 Notre Dame Lawyer 600, 1976; "Of Power and Purpose" 54 Notre Dame Lawyer 829, 1979; "Adversary Adjudication on Trial" 21 Arizona State L. Jour. 227, 1989; and book reviews 27 No. 2 *Arizona Attorney* 13, 1990, 30 No. 10 *Arizona Attorney* 49, 1994 and 32 No. 6 *Arizona Attorney* 49, 1996 and *Judges Journal* 43 Summer 1998. Adjunct Professor of Law Arizona State University College of Law. Member Horace Rumpole Inn of Court, Arizona Judges Association, American Judicature Society, State Bar of Arizona, Maricopa County and American Bar Associations. Captain USAF 1965-69.

Office: 526 U.S. Courthouse, 401 West Washington Street, Phoenix 85003-2158.
Telephone: (602) 322-7590.

MATHIS, Virginia A. *(Magistrate Judge, United States District Court District of Arizona)* Appointed by U.S. District Court judges.

Office: 323 U.S. Courthouse, 401 West Washington Street, Phoenix 85003-2120.
Telephone: (602) 322-7610.

McCARVILLE, Stephen F. *(Judge, Superior Court of Arizona Pinal County)*

Mailing address: P.O. Box 828, Florence 85232.
Office: Building E, 31 North Pinal Street, Florence 85232.
Telephone: (520) 866-6319.
Fax: (520) 866-6500
E-mail address: smccarvi@courts.sp.state.az.us

McCLENNEN, Crane *(Judge, Superior Court of Arizona Maricopa County)* Appointed by governor. Currently serves Criminal Court.

Office: 10E Central Court Building, 201 West Jefferson Street, Phoenix 85003-2205.
Telephone: (602) 506-3901.
Fax: (602) 506-7867
E-mail address: cmcclenn@superiorcourt.maricopa.gov

McGREGOR, Ruth V. *(Vice Chief Justice, Supreme Court of Arizona)* Appointed by Governor Jane Dee Hull to term beginning Feb 13, 1998. Vice Chief Justice since Jan 2002. Educated at University of Iowa B.A. summa cum laude 1964 M.A. 1965 and Arizona State University College of Law J.D. summa cum laude. Member Phi Beta Kappa, Alpha Lambda Delta and Mortar Board. In legal practice Phoenix Aug 1974 to Sept 1981 and Aug 1982 to Dec 1989. Judge Dec 1989 to Feb 1998, Vice Chief Judge July 1993 to July 1995 and Chief Judge July 1995 to July 1997, Arizona Court of Appeals Division One.

Law Clerk to Hon. Sandra Day O'Connor, U.S. Supreme Court Sept 1981 to July 1982. Member Supreme Court of Arizona Disciplinary Commission 1984-89. Member 1991-97 and Vice Chair 1993-97 Supreme Court of Arizona Commission on Judicial Conduct. Fellow American Bar Association. Founding Fellow Arizona Bar Foundation. Master of the Bench Arizona Inns of Court since 1988. Member Supreme Court of Arizona Literacy Programs for Probationers (Judicial Liaison 1993-95), Arizona Judges' Association since 1990, National Association of Women Judges since 1990, State Bar of Arizona and Maricopa County Bar Association.

Office: 1501 West Washington, Phoenix 85007.
Telephone: (602) 542-5789.
Fax: (602) 542-9785
E-mail address: rmcgregor@supreme.sp.state.az.us

McNALLY, Colleen A. *(Judge, Superior Court of Arizona Maricopa County)* Appointed by governor. Currently serves Civil Court and Family Court.

Office: Northwest Regional Center, 14264 West Tierra Buena Lane, Surprise 85374.
Telephone: (602) 506-5961.
E-mail address: cmcnally@superiorcourt.maricopa.gov

McNAMEE, Stephen M. *(Chief Judge, United States District Court District of Arizona)* Appointed for life by President George Bush to term beginning June 8, 1990. Chief Judge since Aug 13, 1999. Educated at University of Cincinnati B.S. 1964 and University of Arizona M.A. 1967 J.D. 1969.

U.S. Attorney District of Arizona 1985-90.
Office: 625 U.S. Courthouse, 401 West Washington Street, Phoenix 85003-2158.
Telephone: (602) 322-7500.

McVEY, Michael R. *(Judge, Superior Court of Arizona Maricopa County)* Currently serves Juvenile Court.

Office: 155 Juvenile Court Center, 3125 West Durango, Phoenix 85009.
Telephone: (602) 506-3167.
Fax: (602) 506-7867
E-mail address: mmcvey@superiorcourt.maricopa.gov

MILES, Linda *(Judge, Superior Court of Arizona Maricopa County)* Appointed by governor. Currently serves Juvenile Court.

Office: 157 Juvenile Court Center, 3125 West Durango, Phoenix 85009.
Telephone: (602) 506-6452.
Fax: (602) 506-7867
E-mail address: lmiles@superiorcourt.maricopa.gov

MILLER, Leslie Beth *(Judge, Superior Court of Arizona Pima County)* Appointed by Governor Bruce Babbitt to term beginning Aug 2, 1985. Retained by election. Former Presiding Criminal Judge, Former Presiding Drug Court Judge and Former Associate Presiding Judge. Currently serves Civil Court. Born New York Oct 29, 1951. Educated at Goucher College B.A. 1973 and St. Louis University Law School J.D. 1976. Admitted to practice Arizona 1976. Magistrate, Tucson Municipal Court 1982-85.

Assistant Public Defender Pima County Tucson 1978-82. President Arizona Association of Drug Court Professionals 2000-02. Member Arizona Women Lawyers Association, National Association of Women Judges (Board of Directors since 1995), Arizona Judges Association (President 1992-93), State Bar of Arizona (President Elect 1982-83 and President 1983-84 Young Lawyers Section, Board of Governors 1983-85), Pima County (Chairperson Community Law Week 1982-84, Board of Directors 1982-2002, Chair Continuing Legal Education Committee 1983-85 and Trial Advocacy Program 1986-88, President 1989-90) and American (Executive Council 1995-98, Vice Chair 1998-99, Chair-Elect 1999-2000 and Chair 2000-01 National Conference of State Trial Judges) Bar Associations. Attended National College for

MILLER, LESLIE BETH—*Continued*

Criminal Defense 1979 and The National Judicial College 1983 and 1986. Faculty Arizona Trial Advocacy Program 1987. Board Member Tucson Issues Forum 1983-85 and Women Studies Advisory Board University of Arizona since 1986. Board Member since 1985 and President 1995-96 Boys and Girls Club of Tucson. Board Member Tucson International Mariachi Conference since 1987. Board Member 1988-95 and President 1991-92 La Frontera Center. APEX Mentor Program since 1988. Board of Directors YMCA since 1995. Enjoys traveling and camping.

Office: 110 West Congress Street, Tucson 85701.
Telephone: (520) 740-8215.
Fax: (520) 740-3654
E-mail address: lmiller@sc.co.pima.az.us

MILLER, Michael Owen *(Judge, Superior Court of Arizona Pima County)* Appointed by governor. Currently serves Juvenile Court.

Office: Juvenile New Court Center, 2225 East Ajo Way, Tucson 85713.
Telephone: (520) 740-2966.
Fax: (520) 740-7104
E-mail address: mmiller@sc.co.pima.az.us

MONTOYA-PAEZ, Anna M. *(Judge, Superior Court of Arizona Santa Cruz County)*

Mailing address: P.O. Box 1929, Nogales 85628.
Office: Santa Cruz County Complex, Nogales 85621.
Telephone: (520) 375-7730.
Fax: (520) 761-7934
E-mail address: amontoy2@courts.sp.state.az.us

MOON, Robert R. *(Presiding Judge, Superior Court of Arizona Mohave County)* Assumed office Jan 2, 1994. Elected Nov 5, 1996 and 2000. Current term expires Dec 31, 2004. Born Kewanee Illinois Sept 21, 1953. Protestant. Educated at Arizona State University B.A. with honors 1975 J.D. 1978. Admitted to practice Arizona 1979 and U.S. District Court District of Arizona 1983. In legal practice Kingman 1983-89.

Deputy Attorney Mohave County 1979-83 and 1989-94. Republican.

Mailing address: P.O. Box 7000, Kingman 86402.
Office: Mohave County Courthouse, 401 East Spring Street, Kingman 86401.
Telephone: (928) 753-0762.
Fax: (928) 753-1892
E-mail address: rmoon@courts.sp.state.az.us

MUNDELL, Barbara *(Associate Presiding Judge, Superior Court of Arizona Maricopa County)* Appointed by governor. Former Associate Presiding Juvenile Court Judge. Currently serves as Presiding Probate/Mental Health Court Judge.

Office: 102 Old Courthouse, 125 West Washington, Phoenix 85003.
Telephone: (602) 506-6130.
Fax: (602) 506-7867
E-mail address: bmundell@superiorcourt.maricopa.gov

MUNGER, Clark W. *(Judge, Superior Court of Arizona Pima County)* Appointed by governor. Currently serves as Presiding Probate Court Judge.

Office: New Courts Building, 110 West Congress, Tucson 85701.
Telephone: (520) 740-3072.
Fax: (520) 740-3986
E-mail address: cmunger@sc.co.pima.az.us

MURGUIA, Mary H. *(Judge, United States District Court District of Arizona)* Appointed for life by President Bill Clinton to term beginning Dec 12, 2000. Born Kansas City Kansas Sept 6, 1960. Educated at University of Kansas B.S. 1982 B.A. 1982 J.D. 1985.

Assistant District Attorney Wyandotte County 1985-90. Assistant U.S. Attorney District of Arizona 1990-2000. Counsel to Director's staff 1998-99, Principal Deputy Director 1999 and Director 1999-2000 Executive Office for U.S. Attorneys.

Office: 525 U.S. Courthouse, 401 West Washington Street, Phoenix 85003-2154.
Telephone: (602) 322-7580.

NELSON, John N. *(Judge, Superior Court of Arizona Yuma County)*

Office: Yuma County Courthouse, 168 South Second Avenue, Yuma 85364-2296.
Telephone: (928) 329-2204.
Fax: (928) 783-4590
E-mail address: jono@court.co.yuma.az.us

NELSON, Michael C. *(Presiding Judge, Superior Court of Arizona Apache County)* Appointed by Governor Rose Mofford March 8, 1989. Elected Nov 1990, Nov 1994, Nov 1998 and Nov 2002. Current term expires Dec 31, 2006. Born Denver Colorado Nov 22, 1948. Educated at Stanford University A.B. 1970 and University of Arizona J.D. 1977. Admitted to practice Arizona 1977, Navajo Nation 1977 and New Mexico 1978. In legal practice Window Rock Arizona 1977-89.

Mailing address: P.O. Box 667, St. Johns 85936.
Telephone: (928) 337-7555.
Fax: (928) 337-7586
E-mail address: mnelson@co.apache.az.us

NEWTON, Fred *(Presiding Judge, Superior Court of Arizona Coconino County)*

Office: Coconino County Courthouse, 200 North San Francisco, Flagstaff 86001.
Telephone: (928) 779-6598.
Fax: (928) 214-0164
E-mail address: fnewton@courts.sp.state.az.us

NICHOLS, Richard D. *(Judge, Superior Court of Arizona Pima County)* Appointed by governor. Currently serves Criminal Court.

Office: New Courts Building, 110 West Congress Street, Tucson 85701.
Telephone: (520) 740-3567.
Fax: (520) 740-3111
E-mail address: rnichols@sc.co.pima.az.us

NIELSEN, George B., Jr. *(Judge, United States Bankruptcy Court District of Arizona)* Former Chief Judge.

Mailing address: P.O. Box 34151, Phoenix 85067.
Telephone: (602) 640-5850.

NIELSON, Dale *(Presiding Judge, Superior Court of Arizona Navajo County)* Former Associate Presiding Judge.

Mailing address: P.O. Box 668, Holbrook 86025.
Office: Navajo County Courthouse, Holbrook 86025.
Telephone: (928) 524-4217.
Fax: (928) 524-4246
E-mail address: dnielson@courts.sp.state.az.us

OBERBILLIG, Robert H. *(Judge, Superior Court of Arizona Maricopa County)* Appointed by governor. Currently serves Family Court.

Office: 2F Southeast Court, 222 East Javelina Avenue, Mesa 85210.

Telephone: (602) 506-2194.

Fax: (602) 506-2029

E-mail address: roberbil@superiorcourt.maricopa.gov

O'CONNOR, Karen L. *(Judge, Superior Court of Arizona Maricopa County)* Appointed by governor. Currently serves Family Court.

Office: 6D Central Court Building, 201 West Jefferson, Phoenix 85003-2205.

Telephone: (602) 506-0428.

Fax: (602) 506-7867

E-mail address: kaoconno@superiorcourt.maricopa.gov

O'MELIA, Michael J. *(Judge, Superior Court of Arizona Maricopa County)* Appointed by Governor Bruce Babbitt to term beginning Dec 10, 1984. Retained by election 1992, 1996 and 2000. Current term expires Dec 31, 2004. Currently serves Civil Court. Born Rhinelander Wisconsin April 16, 1942. Catholic. Educated at University of Wisconsin B.S. 1964 and Marquette University J.D. 1968. Staff member Marquette Law Review 1967-68. Member Delta Theta Phi. Admitted to practice Wisconsin 1968, Arizona 1972 and U.S. Supreme Court 1972. In legal practice Rhinelander Wisconsin 1968-72 and Phoenix Arizona 1972-84.

Board of Directors Arizona Bar Foundation 1989-91. Member State Bar of Arizona, State Bar of Wisconsin and Maricopa County Bar Association. Faculty member Arizona Trial Advocacy Course 1986-95. Chairman Arizona College of Trial Advocacy 1990 and 1991. Attended The National Judicial College and numerous judicial conferences. Enjoys jogging, bird hunting, golf, basketball and coaching youth basketball and softball.

Office: 614 East Court Building, 101 West Jefferson, Phoenix 85003.

Telephone: (602) 506-3135.

E-mail address: momelia@superiorcourt.maricopa.gov

O'NEIL, William J. *(Presiding Judge, Superior Court of Arizona Pinal County)* Currently serves as Presiding Juvenile Court Judge.

Mailing address: P.O. Box 847, Florence 85232.

Office: Building E, 31 North Pinal Street, Florence 85232.

Telephone: (520) 866-6319.

Fax: (520) 866-6385

E-mail address: woneil@courts.sp.state.az.us

O'TOOLE, Thomas W. *(Judge, Superior Court of Arizona Maricopa County)* Appointed by Governor Bruce Babbitt to term beginning 1984. Presiding Criminal Court Judge 1988-90 and since 2001. Former Civil, Juvenile and Domestic Relations Judge.

Office: 514 East Court Building, 101 West Jefferson Street, Phoenix 85003.

Telephone: (602) 506-5994.

Fax: (602) 506-1183

E-mail address: totoole@superiorcourt.maricopa.gov

PADISH, James *(Judge, Superior Court of Arizona Maricopa County)* Court Commissioner 1997-99. Appointed by Governor Jane Dee Hull to term beginning 1999. Currently serves Family Court. Born Gary Indiana Jan 26, 1956. Catholic. Educated at Indiana University B.S. 1978 and John Marshall Law School J.D. 1981. Admitted to practice Illinois 1981, Indiana 1982 and Arizona 1987. In legal practice Chicago Illinois 1983-85 and Phoenix Arizona 1989-92.

Executive Director Public Defender Program Phoenix 1992. Public Defender Phoenix 1997. Republican. Board of Directors D.N.A. People's Legal Services, Inc. Parent Advisory Board Our Lady of Perpetual Help School.

Office: 7B Central Court Building, 201 West Jefferson, Phoenix 85003-2205.

Telephone: (602) 506-3652.

Fax: (602) 506-7867

E-mail address: jpadish@superiorcourt.maricopa.gov

PATTERSON, Cecil B., Jr. *(Judge, Arizona Court of Appeals Division One)* Appointed by Governor Fife Symington to term beginning Sept 5, 1995. Retained by election. Presbyterian. Educated at Hampton University B.A. and Arizona State University J.D. In legal Practice 1972-73. Judge, Superior Court of Arizona Maricopa County April 7, 1980 to Jan 31, 1991, appointed by Governor Bruce Babbitt.

Staff Attorney Maricopa County Legal Aid Society 1971-72. Legal Counsel and Housing Discrimination Attorney Phoenix Urban League 1973-75. Trial Deputy Maricopa County Public Defender's Office 1975-80. Chief Counsel Human Services Division Arizona Attorney General Feb 6, 1991 to Aug 31, 1995. Member Committee on Judicial Performance Review Arizona Supreme Court 1992 and since 1999 and Civil Rights Committee National Association of Attorneys General 1994. Fellow Arizona Bar Foundation and American Bar Foundation. Member American Inns of Court, National Council of Juvenile and Family Court Judges, American Judges Association, H. B. Daniels Bar Association, State Bar of Arizona (Board of Governors 1977), Maricopa County (Law/Media Steering Committee 1989), National (Member Executive Committee and Treasurer Judicial Council) and American Bar Associations. Attended Program for Senior Executives in State and Local Government John F. Kennedy School of Government Harvard University June 1993. Recipient Trailblazer Award from Arizona Black Lawyers Association 1992, Distinguished Service Award from The Judicial Council National Bar Association 1992, Martin Luther King, Jr. "Living the Dream" Award from City of Phoenix 1998 and West Field Distinguished Service Award 1999 and Valley of the Sun Metro Board Outstanding Leadership Award 1999 from YMCA. Board of Directors Maricopa County Legal Aid Society 1972, Progress Association for Economic Development 1973, Valley Christian Centers 1976, Maricopa County Chapter NAACP 1977, YMCA 1992 and Samaritan Health Services 1992-95. Member Minority Advisory Committee Arizona State University 1993-95 and Ad Hoc Use of Force/Cultural Awareness Task Force City of Phoenix 1995. Chairman Valley of the Sun United Way 1994-96 and Valley of the Sun YMCA 1998 and 1999. Member Presbyterian Church in the United States of America.

Office: 1501 West Washington, Phoenix 85007.

Telephone: (602) 542-4867.

Fax: (602) 542-4833

E-mail address: cpatterson@courts.sp.state.az.us

PELANDER, John *(Vice Chief Judge, Arizona Court of Appeals Division Two)* Appointed by Governor Fife Symington to term beginning May 1995. Retained by election. Born Cleveland Ohio Jan 26, 1951. Educated at

PELANDER, JOHN—*Continued*

Wittenberg University B.A. 1973, University of Arizona J.D. with high distinction 1976 and University of Virginia School of Law LL.M. in Judicial Process 1998. Member Order of the Coif. Admitted to practice Arizona 1976.

Office: State Office Building, 400 West Congress Street, Tucson 85701-1374.

Telephone: (520) 628-6947.

E-mail address: pelander@apltwo.ct.state.az.us

PORTLEY, Maurice *(Judge, Arizona Court of Appeals Division One)* Appointed by Governor Janet Napolitano. Born San Antonio Texas June 1954. Roman Catholic. Educated at Arizona State University B.S. cum laude 1975 and University of Michigan J.D. 1978. Associate Articles Editor Journal of Law Reform 1977-78. Member Phi Sigma Kappa. Admitted to practice Arizona 1979, U.S. Court of Military Appeals 1979, U.S. Supreme Court 1982, U.S. District Court District of Arizona 1984 and U.S. Court of Appeals Ninth Circuit 1984. In legal practice Phoenix July 1984 to Feb 1991. Former pro tem Judge, Arizona Court of Appeals Division One. Judge Feb 28, 1991 to 2003 and Presiding Judge Southeast Judicial District Oct 1992 to May 1997, Superior Court of Arizona Maricopa County, appointed by Governor Rose Mofford.

Author "State Legislative Responses to the Arab Boycott of Israel" Journal of Law Reform Spring 1977; "Can Military Justice Withstand Critical Scrutiny" *Judicature* Oct 1983; "Rape Trauma Syndrome" *The Army Lawyer* Nov 1984; "The Due Process Clause of the Fifth Amendment" Dec 1991, "The Arizona Court of Military Appeals: A New Challenge for the Arizona Supreme Court" June 1994 and "Indian Child Welfare Act: A Primer" Feb 2000 *Arizona Attorney;* and "Forged Checks: An Analysis of Civil Liability Under the Uniform Commercial Code" 28 Arizona State L. Jour. Fall 1996. Editor *The Judge's Newsletter* June 1993 to March 1994. Member Conference Committee Commission on Judicial Performance since 1994, Commission on Judicial Conduct since 1993, St. Thomas More Society (Board of Directors 1989 and 1992), Sandra Day O'Connor Inn of Court 1991-1993, Lorna Lockwood Inn of Court 1994, The Defense Research Institute, Inc., The Association of Trial Lawyers of America, National Council of Juvenile and Family Court Judges, American Judges Association, American Judicature Society since 1977, Hayzel B. Daniels, State Bar of Arizona (Member Board of Governor's Committee to Reexamine the Bar Examination Process 1989-92, Creditors-Debtors Committee 1989-92, Commission on Women and Minorities 1992-95 and Bench-Bar Committee 1992-96), Maricopa County (Member 1988-95 and Chairperson 1989-92 Minorities in the Law Committee, Member Trial by Jury Program Committee 1991-94, Member Law/Media Steering Committee 1991-94, Board of Directors 1991-94, Member Special Joint Corporate Counsel/Minorities in the Law Committee 1992, Member The Lawyers Cultural Diversity Task Force), National and American Bar Associations. Faculty Professionalism Course 1992-94 and Continuing Legal Education Courses State Bar of Arizona and Continuing Legal Education Courses Maricopa County Bar Association. Member Judicial Conference Planning Committee 1993. Faculty since 1993 and Lecturer "Congeniality and the Bench" New Judge Orientation May 1995 and 1996 Arizona Judicial College. Lecturer "Ethics, the Judicial Canons and Court Employees" Council on Judicial Education and Training Maricopa County Superior Court May and Sept 1995. Recipient Humanitarian Award by Buffalo Soldier's Reenactment Association 1995. U.S. Army Judge Advocate General's Corps July 1979 to July 1984. USAR 1984-93. Military Judge Arizona Army National Guard 1993 to March 1996. Board of Directors Valley Citizens League 1992-93, Friendly House 1992-94, Friends of the Phoenix Public Library 1994-96, Tri-City Community Service Center, Inc. 1994-97, Great Arizona Puppet Theater since 1995 and Cancer Resource Network since 1996. Board of Directors since 1993, Executive Committee since 1995, Member Strategic Planning Task Force and Training Committee, Participant 24th and 40th Town Halls, Panel Chair 60th and 69th Town Halls Arizona Town Hall. Board of Directors since 1991 and President 1995-97 A Stepping Stone Foundation. Nation Chief Indian Guides Program 1992-93 and member Indian Maidens Program Scottsdale YMCA. Board of Directors 1994-97, Historian 1995-96 and member Visionary Awards Committee 1995 and 1997 Class XIII Valley Leadership. Webelos Den Leader Cub Scout Pack 426 Boy Scouts of America 1995-97. Co-chair Arizona Environmental Strategic Alliance Advisory Council 1996-97. Guest Lecturer Department of Political Science Arizona State University. Judge Mock Trial Program and Client Counseling Program and Participant Career Symposium Arizona State University Law School. Member Military Affairs Committee Phoenix Chamber of Commerce 1986-91 and Impact Spending Committee Valley of the Sun United Way 1993-95. Member Black Board of Directors Project, Phoenix Town Hall and Phoenix Urban League.

Office: 1501 West Washington, Phoenix 85007.

PYLE, Charles R. *(Magistrate Judge, United States District Court District of Arizona)* Appointed by U.S. District Court judges to term beginning June 28, 2001.

Office: 5660 U.S. Courthouse, 405 West Congress Street, Tucson 85701.

Telephone: (520) 205-4650.

RAYES, Douglas *(Judge, Superior Court of Arizona Maricopa County)* Appointed by governor. Currently serves Criminal Court.

Office: 11C Central Court Building, 201 West Jefferson, Phoenix 85003-2205.

Telephone: (602) 506-0816.

Fax: (602) 506-7867

E-mail address: drayes@superiorcourt.maricopa.gov

REINSTEIN, Peter C. *(Judge, Superior Court of Arizona Maricopa County)* Appointed by governor. Currently serves Civil Court.

Office: 11A Central Court Building, 201 West Jefferson Street, Phoenix 85003-2205.

Telephone: (602) 506-6368.

Fax: (602) 506-7867

E-mail address: preinste@superiorcourt.maricopa.gov

REINSTEIN, Ronald S. *(Judge, Superior Court of Arizona Maricopa County)* Appointed by Governor Bruce Babbitt Oct 1985 to term beginning Dec 2, 1985. Retained by election Nov 1988, Nov 1992, Nov 1996 and Nov 2000. Current term expires Jan 1, 2005. Presiding Judge Criminal Division 1990-98. Associate Presiding Judge 1998-2000. Born Camden New Jersey April 13, 1948. Educated at Miami University, Ohio 1966-68

REINSTEIN, RONALD S.—*Continued*

and Indiana University B.A. 1970 J.D. 1973. Member Phi Alpha Delta. Admitted to practice Arizona 1974, U.S. District Court District of Arizona 1978 and U.S. Supreme Court 1980.

Trial Unit Supervisor and Head of Sex Crimes Unit Maricopa County Attorney's Office 1974-85. Chair Supreme Court Post-conviction Relief Review Committee. Consultant National Institute of Justice. Member Arizona Supreme Court Community Punishment Advisory Committee, National Commission on the Future of DNA Evidence, National Resource Board of the Center for Sex Offender Management, The Association of Trial Lawyers of America, National Institute for Trial Advocacy, Arizona Judges Association and State Bar of Arizona. Lecturer National College of District Attorneys since 1983. Faculty member National Institute for Trial Advocacy since 1983, Center for Effective Public Policy, National Council of Juvenile and Family Court Judges, American Probation and Parole Association, National Center for the Prosecution of Child Abuse, American Judicature Society National Sentencing Symposium, Arizona Prosecuting Attorneys' Advisory Council, Einstein Institute for Health, Science and the Courts, National Victims Conference and numerous State Judicial and Prosecutor's Conferences on Child Sexual Abuse, Sentencing and DNA Evidence. Named Lecturer of Merit National College of District Attorneys 1988. Recipient Awards of Excellence from Maricopa County Victim-Witness Program, Arizona Sex Crimes Investigators Association, Maricopa County Attorney's Office, National Institute for Trial Advocacy and Arizona State Lottery. Recipient Attorney General Distinguished Service Award 1991, Sunshine Award from Society of Professional Journalists 1993, Outstanding Judge Award from Maricopa County Bar Association 1994 and Outstanding Judge Award 1998 and Judicial Award of Excellence 1999 from State Bar of Arizona. Democrat. Commissioner Arizona State Lottery 1985. Member Governor's Office for Children Task Force on Children's Justice and Academy of Law Alumni Fellows Indiana University School of Law. Enjoys running, travel and all sports.

Office: 201 West Jefferson Street, Phoenix 85003.
Telephone: (602) 506-3921.
Fax: (602) 506-7867
E-mail address: rreinste@superiorcourt.maricopa.gov

ROBERTSON, Kelly Marie *(Judge, Superior Court of Arizona Pinal County)*
Mailing address: P.O. Box 2077, Florence 85232.
Office: Building E, 31 North Pinal Street, Florence 85232.
Telephone: (520) 866-6327.
Fax: (520) 866-6500
E-mail address: juezakelly@hotmail.com

RODRIGUEZ, Lina S. *(Judge, Superior Court of Arizona Pima County)* Appointed by Governor Bruce Babbitt Nov 14, 1983 to term beginning Jan 3, 1984. Retained by election Nov 1986, 1990, Nov 1994, Nov 1998 and Nov 2002. Current term expires Dec 2006. Currently serves as Presiding Arbitration Judge. Born Salt Lake City Utah Sept 27, 1949. Christian. Educated at University of Arizona B.A. with honors 1972 LL.B. 1977. Admitted to practice Arizona 1977. In legal practice Tucson 1977-84.

Associate and Shareholder Bilby, Shoenhair, Warnock & Dolph, P.C. 1977-84. Member Arizona Judges Association, National Association of Women Judges, State Bar of Arizona and Pima County Bar Association. Recognized for High Achievement by National Council of Hispanic Women 1986. Named Hispanic Woman of the Year by Hispanic Professional Action Committee 1988 and Woman on the Move by YWCA 1988. Recipient Outstanding Service Award in adopting and implementing standards relating to juror use and management from American Bar Association and National Center for State Courts 1990-91. Honoree "Trail Blazers and Pioneers: 100 Women and Minority Lawyers" Maricopa County Bar Association Oct 2000. Language Arts Teacher Apollo Junior High School Tucson 1972-74. Enjoys running, hiking, golfing and reading.

Office: New Courts Building, 110 West Congress Street, Tucson 85701.
Telephone: (520) 740-8241.
Fax: (520) 740-3790
E-mail address: lrodriguez@sc.co.pima.az.us

ROLL, John M. *(Judge, United States District Court District of Arizona)* Appointed for life by President George Bush to term beginning Nov 27, 1991. Born Pittsburgh Pennsylvania Feb 8, 1947. Roman Catholic. Educated at University of Arizona B.A. 1969 J.D. 1972 and University of Virginia School of Law LL.M. 1990. Extern to Hon. Ben C. Birdsall, Superior Court of Arizona Pima County 1970. Law Clerk to Hon. Joe Jacobson, Superior Court of Arizona Pima County 1972. Member Alpha Phi Omega. Admitted to practice Arizona 1972, U.S. District Court District of Arizona 1973, U.S. Supreme Court 1977 and U.S. Court of Appeals Ninth Circuit 1980. Former Judge, Arizona Court of Appeals Division Two, appointed by Governor Evan Mecham to term beginning May 28, 1987.

Assistant City Attorney Jan 1973 to May 1973. Deputy County Attorney Pima County May 1973 to July 1980. Assistant U.S. Attorney District of Arizona Aug 1980 to May 1987. Author "Merit Selection: The Arizona Experience" Arizona State L. Jour. Feb 1991, "The Rules Have Changed: Amendments to the Federal Rules of Civil Procedure" 43 Defense L. Jour. 577, 1994, *Ninth Circuit Judges' Benchbook on Pretrial Criminal Proceedings* Ninth Circuit Executive Office 1998, 2000 and 2002 and "Recent Developments in Employment Discrimination Litigation" *The Federal Lawyer* Spring 2003. Member since 1994 and Chair 1998-2001 Committee on Model Jury Instructions U.S. Court of Appeals Ninth Circuit. Member Judicial Conference Committee on Criminal Rules. Member State Bar of Arizona (Criminal Jury Instruction Subcommittee 1977-78, Public Lawyers CLE Subcommittee since 1989), Pima County and American (Mental Health Standards Subcommittee 1981-83) Bar Associations. Participant CEELI Program American Bar Association Fall 1997. Recipient Outstanding Alumnus Award from University of Arizona College of Law 1992.

Office: 5190 U.S. Courthouse, 405 West Congress Street, Tucson 85701-5010.
Telephone: (520) 205-4520.

RONAN, Emmet J. *(Judge, Superior Court of Arizona Maricopa County)* Appointed by governor. Currently serves Juvenile Court.

Office: 1091 Southeast Court, 222 East Javelina Avenue, Mesa 85210.

RONAN, EMMET J.—*Continued*

Telephone: (602) 506-0438.
Fax: (602) 506-2651
E-mail address: eronan@superiorcourt.maricopa.gov

ROSENBLATT, Paul G. *(Judge, United States District Court District of Arizona)* Appointed for life by President Ronald Reagan to term beginning July 6, 1984. Born Prescott Arizona April 4, 1928. Protestant. Educated at Seattle University 1946-47, University of Washington 1947-51 and University of Arizona B.A. in English with honors 1957 J.D. 1963. Law Clerk to Hon. George Sterling, Superior Court of Arizona Maricopa County 1983. Member Sigma Chi and Phi Delta Phi. Admitted to practice Arizona 1963, U.S. District Court District of Arizona 1963, U.S. Court of Appeals Ninth Circuit 1965 and U.S. Supreme Court 1967. In legal practice Prescott 1971-73. Presiding Judge, Superior Court of Arizona Yavapai County 1973-84.

Assistant Attorney General Arizona 1963-67. Administrative Assistant to Congressman 1967-71. Member National Lawyers Club, Arizona Judges Association (Secretary 1980-81, Vice President 1981-82, President 1982-83 and Chairman Executive Committee), State Bar of Arizona, Yavapai County and American (Delegate National Conference of State Trial Judges Judicial Administration Division 1980-84) Bar Associations. Attended The National Judicial College 1974. Congressional Delegate White House Conference on Children 1970. Delegate Arizona Academy 1977. Corporal USAR (Special Category of Army Air Force) 1951-53. Republican. Member Board of Directors West Yavapai Guidance Clinic, University of Arizona Alumni Association, Yavapai Symphony Association, Congressional Staff Club U.S. House of Representatives and Grand Canyon Council Boy Scouts of America. Former District Chairman Old Capitol District Boy Scouts of America. Past President Washington D.C. Chapter Arizona Alumni Club and Arizona State Society. Member The Smoki People, Arizona Academy (Past member and Delegate Arizona Town Hall) and The Bull Elephants of Capitol Hill.

Office: 621 U.S. Courthouse, 401 West Washington Street, Phoenix 85003-2156.
Telephone: (602) 322-7510.

RYAN, Michael D. *(Justice, Supreme Court of Arizona)* Appointed by Governor Jane Dee Hull to term beginning 2002. Educated at St. John's University B.A. 1967 and Arizona State University J.D. 1977. Judge pro tem, Superior Court of Arizona Maricopa County 1985-86. Judge, Superior Court of Arizona Maricopa County 1986-96, appointed by Governor Bruce Babbitt. Judge 1996-2002 and Vice Chief Judge 2001-02, Arizona Court of Appeals Division One, appointed by Governor Fife Symington.

Deputy County Attorney Maricopa County 1977-85. Member Committee on Probation Officer Certification 1995-96 and Chair Committee on the Appointment of Counsel for Indigent Defendants in Capital Cases Arizona Supreme Court. Member Arizona Attorney General's Capital Case Commission and Maricopa County Bar Association. Member Maricopa County Resource Site Team Center for Sex Offender Management since 1995 and X-Tattoo Advisory Committee Parks, Recreation and Library Department At Risk Youth Division since 1996.

Office: 1501 West Washington, Phoenix 85007.
Telephone: (602) 542-4531.
Fax: (602) 542-9017
E-mail address: mryan@courts.sp.state.az.us

SABALOS, Charles S. *(Judge, Superior Court of Arizona Pima County)* Appointed by Governor Fife Symington Jan 20, 1993. Retained by election Nov 5, 1996 and 2000. Current term expires Jan 1, 2005. Currently serves as Presiding Civil Court Judge. Born New York New York March 5, 1950. Greek Orthodox. Educated at University of Arizona B.S. 1971 J.D. 1974. Member Phi Delta Phi. Admitted to practice Arizona 1974, U.S. District Court District of Arizona 1975, U.S. Court of Appeals Ninth Circuit 1979, U.S. Supreme Court 1979 and District of Columbia 1991. In legal practice Tucson 1977-90.

Deputy County Attorney Pima County 1974-77. Assistant U.S. Attorney 1990-93. Master Morris K. Udall Inn of Court since 1999. Member Arizona State Commission on Performance Review since 2003. Co-chair Arizona Judicial Conference. Member Arizona Trial Lawyers Association, Arizona Judges Association and American Bar Association. Attended The National Judicial College 1993. Recipient Special Achievement Award from U.S. Department of Justice 1991. Republican.

Office: New Courts Building, 110 West Congress Street, Tucson 85701.
Telephone: (520) 740-8617.

SANDERS, Teresa A. *(Judge, Superior Court of Arizona Maricopa County)* Appointed by governor. Currently serves Juvenile Court.

Office: 161 Juvenile Court Center, 3125 West Durango, Phoenix 85009.
Telephone: (602) 506-4791.
Fax: (602) 506-7867
E-mail address: tsanders@superiorcourt.maricopa.gov

SANTANA, Mark *(Judge, Superior Court of Arizona Maricopa County)* Appointed by governor. Currently serves Civil Court.

Office: 413 East Court Building, 101 West Jefferson, Phoenix 85003.
Telephone: (602) 506-6849.
Fax: (602) 506-7867
E-mail address: msantana@superiorcourt.maricopa.gov

SARGEANT, William P., III *(Judge, Superior Court of Arizona Maricopa County)* Appointed by Governor Bruce Babbitt to term beginning June 2, 1986. Retained by election 1988, 1992, 1996 and 2000. Current term expires Dec 31, 2004. Currently serves Juvenile Court. Born Denver Colorado Feb 28, 1938. Episcopalian. Educated at University of Arizona B.S. 1960 LL.B. 1963. Member Phi Alpha Delta. Admitted to practice Arizona 1963. In legal practice Phoenix 1964-86.

City Prosecutor Tucson 1963. With Internal Revenue Service 1964-66. Member American Bar Association. Corporal USMC. Director Crossroads. Member Kiwanis. Enjoys photography, genealogy and computers.

Office: 201 West Jefferson, Phoenix 85003.
Telephone: (602) 506-3663.
Fax: (602) 506-4121
E-mail address: wsargean@superiorcourt.maricopa.gov

SCHNEIDER, Barry C. *(Judge, Superior Court of Arizona Maricopa County)* Appointed by Governor Bruce Babbitt to term beginning Dec 1985. Retained by election Nov 1988, Nov 1992, Nov 1996 and 2000. Cur-

SCHNEIDER, BARRY C.—*Continued*

rent term expires Dec 31, 2004. Presiding Civil Court Judge Dec 1988 to June 1991 and Sept 1999 to March 2000. Served Criminal Court 1991-94 and since 2000. Presiding Domestic Relations Judge 1995-98. Born Bronx New York Feb 24, 1943. Jewish. Educated at Harpur College B.A. 1964 and St. John's University J.D. 1968. Associate Editor St. John's Law Review 1967-68. Admitted to practice New York 1968, Arizona 1972 and U.S. District Court District of Arizona. In legal practice New York City 1968-71 and Phoenix 1971-86.

Contributing Author *Litigation Magazine*. Adjunct Faculty Member Arizona State University College of Law. Former Member Dispute Resolution Task Force Commission on the Courts and Civil Jury Instruction Committee State Bar of Arizona. Master Bencher and Past President Horace Rumpole Inn of Court. Judicial Ethics Advisory Board since Jan 1999. Member Arizona Judicial Council, Committee on More Effective Use of Juries, State-Federal Judicial Council and Committee on Criminal Justice and Chair Superior Court Committee Supreme Court of Arizona. Member Maricopa County Bar Association (Former Chair Bench/Bar Committee). Faculty Member Arizona College of Trial Advocacy and National Institute for Trial Advocacy. Instructor New Judge Orientation Arizona Judicial College. Recipient Henry S. Stevens Outstanding Judge Award from Maricopa County Bar Association 1997. Democrat. Former Board member Jewish Community Centers of Greater Phoenix, Jewish Federation of Greater Phoenix and American Civil Liberties Union. Enjoys sports, reading and traveling.

Office: 13A Central Court Building, 201 West Jefferson, Phoenix 85003-2205.
Telephone: (602) 506-3351.
Fax: (602) 506-7867
E-mail address: bschneid@superiorcourt.maricopa.gov

SCHWARTZ, Jonathan H. *(Judge, Superior Court of Arizona Maricopa County)* Appointed by governor. Currently serves Criminal Court.

Office: 12D Central Court Building, 201 West Jefferson, Phoenix 85003-2205.
Telephone: (602) 506-3541.
Fax: (602) 506-7867
E-mail address: jschwart@superiorcourt.maricopa.gov

SCOTT, Linda K. *(Judge, Superior Court of Arizona Maricopa County)* Appointed by governor. Former Associate Presiding Juvenile Judge. Currently serves as Presiding Juvenile Court Judge.

Office: 1077 Southeast Court, 222 East Javelina Avenue, Mesa 85210.
Telephone: (602) 506-2610.
Fax: (602) 506-2651
E-mail address: lscott@superiorcourt.maricopa.gov

SHELDON, Steven D. *(Judge, Superior Court of Arizona Maricopa County)* Appointed by Governor Rose Mofford to term beginning Jan 4, 1990. Retained by election Nov 1992, 1996 and 2000. Current term expires Jan 1, 2005. Currently serves Family Court. Born Santa Monica California Oct 1946. Educated at California State Polytechnic University (Pomona) and Loyola Law School J.D. with honors 1974. Member St. Thomas More Society. Admitted to practice Arizona 1974 and U.S. District Court District of Arizona 1974. In legal practice Phoenix 1974-77 and 1982-89.

Member Tempe Planning and Zoning Commission 1987-89. Author "Arizona Habitual Criminal Statute" 23 Arizona State B. Jour. Oct/Nov 1987, "Waiving the Rights to Appeal; Time for Reconsideration" 10 No. 10 Maricopa Lawyer 1 Oct 1991, "Judge-Conducted Voir Dire in Criminal Cases, Rule 18.5(d)" 12 No. 6 Maricopa Lawyer 1 June 1993 and "Dual Juries—A Useful Trial Management Tool" 5 No. 3 Trial Practice State Bar of Arizona Fall 1994. Member State Bar of Arizona, Maricopa County and American Bar Associations. Petty Officer USN 1965-69. Special Agent FBI 1977-82. Former Member Rotary International.

Office: 912 East Court Building, 101 West Jefferson, Phoenix 85003.
Telephone: (602) 506-3944.
Fax: (602) 506-1183
E-mail address: ssheldon@superiorcourt.maricopa.gov

SILVER, Roslyn Olson *(Judge, United States District Court District of Arizona)* Appointed for life by President Bill Clinton to term beginning Oct 14, 1994. First woman appointed for the Phoenix Division. Born Phoenix Arizona Feb 28, 1946. Educated at University of California at Santa Barbara B.A. 1968 and Arizona State University College of Law J.D. cum laude 1971. Comment Editor Law Review. Law Clerk to Hon. Lorna E. Lockwood, Supreme Court of Arizona 1971-72. In legal practice 1972-73 and 1978-79.

Advisor and Litigator Navajo Nation Native American Rights Fund 1974-76. In-house Labor Counsel Greyhound-Dial Corporation 1976-78. Trial Attorney Equal Employment Opportunity Commission 1979-80. Assistant U.S. Attorney 1980-94, Chief Criminal Division 1986-94 and Acting First Assistant 1986-94 U.S. Attorney's Office District of Arizona. Contributing Editor *Federal Civil Procedure Before Trial, Rutter Group Practice Guide*. Professor American Institute of Paralegal Studies and Arizona State University Center for Executive Development. Chair Article III Judges Education Committee U.S. Court of Appeals Ninth Circuit. Master Lorna E. Lockwood Inn of Court for Maricopa County. Fellow American Bar Foundation. Named Alumnus of the Year by Arizona State University 1996, Outstanding Member of the Legal Community by Arizona Women Lawyers Association 1999 and one of 100 Significant Women and Minorities in Arizona's Legal History 2000. Advisory Board Lodestar Mediation Clinic Arizona State University College of Law. Board of Visitors University of Arizona College of Law.

Office: 624 U.S. Courthouse, SPC 59, 401 West Washington Street, Phoenix 85003-2158.
Telephone: (602) 322-7520.

SITVER, Morton *(Magistrate Judge, United States District Court District of Arizona)* Appointed by U.S. District Court judges.

Office: 324 U.S. Courthouse, 401 West Washington Street, Phoenix 85003-2120.
Telephone: (602) 322-7600.

SNOW, Murray G. *(Judge, Arizona Court of Appeals Division One)* Appointed by governor.

Office: 1501 West Washington, Phoenix 85007.
Telephone: (602) 542-1478.
Fax: (602) 542-4833
E-mail address: gsnow@courts.sp.state.az.us

SOTO, James A. *(Presiding Judge, Superior Court of Arizona Santa Cruz County)*
Mailing address: P.O. Box 1929, Nogales 85628.
Office: Santa Cruz County Complex, Nogales 85621.
Telephone: (520) 375-7730.
Fax: (520) 761-7934
E-mail address: jsoto@courts.sp.state.az.us

STAUFFER, Monica *(Presiding Judge, Superior Court of Arizona Greenlee County)*
Mailing address: P.O. Box 1296, Clifton 85533.
Telephone: (928) 865-3872.
Fax: (928) 865-5358
E-mail address: mstauffe@courts.sp.state.az.us

STEINLE, Roland J., III *(Judge, Superior Court of Arizona Maricopa County)* Appointed by governor. Currently serves Family Court.
Office: 11D Central Court Building, 201 West Jefferson, Phoenix 85003-2205.
Telephone: (602) 506-7893.
Fax: (602) 506-7867
E-mail address: rsteinle@superiorcourt.maricopa.gov

STEPHENS, Sherry K. *(Judge, Superior Court of Arizona Maricopa County)* Appointed by governor. Currently serves Juvenile Court.
Office: 1067 Maricopa Juvenile Court, 1810 South Lewis, Mesa 85210.
Telephone: (602) 506-4818.
Fax: (602) 506-4132
E-mail address: sstephen@superiorcourt.maricopa.gov

STERLING, Janis Ann *(Judge, Superior Court of Arizona Yavapai County)*
Office: 203 Yavapai County Superior Court House, 120 South Cortez Street, Prescott 86301.
Telephone: (928) 771-3303.
Fax: (928) 771-3433
E-mail address: jsterling@courts.sp.state.az.us

STRAND, Roger Gordon *(Senior Judge, United States District Court District of Arizona)* Appointed for life by President Ronald Reagan. Assumed Senior status, serves by assignment. Born Peekskill New York April 28, 1934. Educated at Hamilton College A.B. 1955 and Cornell University LL.B. 1961. Member Phi Delta Phi. Admitted to practice Arizona 1961. In legal practice Phoenix 1961-67. Former Judge and Associate Presiding Judge, Superior Court of Arizona Maricopa County, appointed to term beginning 1967.
Member Committee on Automation and Technology Judicial Conference of the U.S. Member Arizona Judges Association, State Bar of Arizona, Maricopa County and American Bar Associations. Attended National College of State Trial Judges 1968. Member Central Arizona Arthritis Foundation (Board of Directors, Chairman 1964-65) and Aircraft Owners and Pilots Association. Commercial pilot and amateur radio operator.
Office: 622 U.S. Courthouse, 401 West Washington Street, Phoenix 85003-2156.
Telephone: (602) 322-7550.

SULT, James B. *(Judge, Arizona Court of Appeals Division One)* Appointed by Governor Fife Symington to term beginning 1995. Retained by election. Educated at Arizona State University B.A. 1963 and University of Arizona J.D. 1970. In legal practice 1971-72 and 1974-81. Judge, Superior Court of Arizona Yavapai County 1982-95.
Attorney Public Defender's Office Pima County 1972-74. Board of Directors Salvation Army and Wilderness Challenge. Member Advisory Management Committee Prescott Public Library and Friends of the Prescott Public Library.
Office: 1501 West Washington, Phoenix 85007.
Telephone: (602) 542-1480.
Fax: (602) 542-4833
E-mail address: jbsult@courts.sp.state.az.us

TALAMANTE, David M. *(Judge, Superior Court of Arizona Maricopa County)* Appointed by governor. Currently serves Family Court.
Office: 2G Southeast Court, 222 East Javelina Avenue, Mesa 85210.
Telephone: (602) 506-6251.
Fax: (602) 506-3029
E-mail address: dtalaman@superiorcourt.maricopa.gov

TANG, Paul E. *(Judge, Superior Court of Arizona Pima County)* Appointed by governor. Currently serves Criminal Court.
Office: New Courts Building, 110 West Congress, Tucson 85701.
Telephone: (520) 740-8441.
Fax: (520) 740-8140
E-mail address: ptang@sc.co.pima.az.us

TEILBORG, James A. *(Judge, United States District Court District of Arizona)* Appointed for life by President Bill Clinton to term beginning Oct 17, 2000. Born Pueblo Colorado Dec 29, 1942. Educated at University of Arizona College of Law J.D. 1966. In legal practice Phoenix 1967-2000.
Office: 523 U.S. Courthouse, 401 West Washington Street, Phoenix 85003-2154.
Telephone: (602) 322-7560.

THODE, Thomas A. *(Judge, Superior Court of Arizona Yuma County)* Former Presiding Juvenile Court Judge.
Office: Yuma County Courthouse, 168 South Second Avenue, Yuma 85364-2296.
Telephone: (928) 329-2202.
Fax: (928) 329-2004
E-mail address: thth@court.co.yuma.az.us

THOMPSON, Jon W. *(Judge, Arizona Court of Appeals Division One)* Appointed by Governor Fife Symington to term beginning 1995. Retained by election. Educated at Northern Arizona University B.S. 1975 and University of Colorado J.D. 1979. In legal practice Phoenix 1979-80 and 1990-95. Judge pro tem, Superior Court of Arizona Coconino County 1989-90.
Deputy County Attorney Yuma County 1980-83 and Coconino County 1983-88. Member State Bar of Arizona. Elder and Deacon Flagstaff Federated Community Church since 1986. Board Member Coconino County Silent Witness 1992-95 and Coconino County Victim-Witness 1992-95.
Office: 1501 West Washington, Phoenix 85007.
Telephone: (602) 542-5304.
Fax: (602) 542-4833

TIMMER, Ann A. Scott *(Judge, Arizona Court of Appeals Division One)* Appointed by governor. Educated at University of Arizona B.A. 1982 and Arizona State University J.D. 1985. Note and Comment Editor Arizona State Law Journal. National Moot Court Team. Member Order of Barristers and Order of the Coif.

TIMMER, ANN A. SCOTT—*Continued*

President Maricopa Chapter Arizona Women Lawyers Association. Co-President Elect Lorna Lockwood Inn of Court. Member Maricopa County Task Force on Hiring and Retention of Women and Minority Lawyers and State Bar of Arizona. Board of Directors Community Legal Services and New Arizona Family, Inc. Sunday School Teacher. Member Advisory Board Volunteer Lawyers.

Office: 1501 West Washington, Phoenix 85007.
Telephone: (602) 542-1479.
Fax: (602) 542-4833
E-mail address: atimmer@courts.sp.state.az.us

TOPF, William L., III *(Judge, Superior Court of Arizona Maricopa County)* Appointed by governor. Currently serves Family Court.

Office: 6C Central Court Building, 201 West Jefferson, Phoenix 85003-2205.
Telephone: (602) 506-2990.
Fax: (602) 506-1183
E-mail address: wtopf@superiorcourt.maricopa.gov

TREBESCH, Dean *(Judge, Superior Court of Arizona Maricopa County)* Appointed by governor. Currently serves Family Court.

Office: 7C Central Court Building, 201 West Jefferson, Phoenix 85003-2205.
Telephone: (602) 506-8760.
Fax: (602) 506-3123
E-mail address: dtrebesch@superiorcourt.maricopa.gov

TRUJILLO, Richard J. *(Judge, Superior Court of Arizona Maricopa County)* Appointed by governor. Currently serves Family Court.

Office: 6F Central Court Building, 201 West Jefferson, Phoenix 85003-2205.
Telephone: (602) 506-5495.
Fax: (602) 506-7867
E-mail address: rtrujillo@superiorcourt.maricopa.gov

UDALL, David K. *(Judge, Superior Court of Arizona Maricopa County)* Appointed by governor. Currently serves Family Court.

Office: 4D Southeast Court, 222 East Javelina Avenue, Mesa 85210.
Telephone: (602) 506-5514.
Fax: (602) 506-1654
E-mail address: dudall@superiorcourt.maricopa.gov

VANDERPOOL, Janna L. *(Judge, Superior Court of Arizona Pinal County)*

Mailing address: P.O. Box 986, Florence 85232.
Office: Pinal County Courthouse, 31 North Pinal Street, Florence 85232.
Telephone: (520) 866-6993.
Fax: (520) 866-6994
E-mail address: jvanderpool@courts.sp.state.az.us

VELASCO, Bernardo P. *(Magistrate Judge, United States District Court District of Arizona)* Former part-time Magistrate. Appointed Magistrate Judge by U.S. District Court judges to term beginning Sept 29, 2000. Judge April 1, 1985 to Sept 28, 2000 and Former Associate Presiding Judge, Superior Court of Arizona Pima County.

Office: 5133 U.S. Courthouse, 405 West Congress Street, Tucson 85701.
Telephone: (520) 205-4630.

VERDIN, Maria del Mar *(Judge, Superior Court of Arizona Maricopa County)* Appointed by governor. Currently serves Family Court.

Office: 2E Southeast Court, 222 East Javelina Avenue, Mesa 85210.
Telephone: (602) 506-2603.
Fax: (602) 506-2029
E-mail address: mverdin@superiorcourt.maricopa.gov

VERKAMP, Stephen L. *(Magistrate Judge, United States District Court District of Arizona)* Appointed by U.S. District Court judges to term beginning Oct 1, 1976. Reappointed 1984 and 1988. Served part time 1976-91. Appointed full time Feb 1, 1991. Reappointed Feb 1999, current term expires Feb 2007. Born San Diego California March 1, 1943. Catholic. Educated at University of Arizona B.S. with honors in Business Administration 1965 J.D. 1968. Admitted to practice Arizona 1968. Began legal practice Flagstaff 1972.

Member State Bar of Arizona. Captain USAS 1969-71. Republican.

Mailing address: P.O. Box 698, Flagstaff 86002-0698.
Telephone: (928) 774-2566.

VILLARREAL, Stephen C. *(Judge, Superior Court of Arizona Pima County)* Appointed by governor. Currently serves Juvenile Court.

Office: Juvenile New Court Center, 2225 East Ajo Way, Tucson 85713.
Telephone: (520) 740-2054.
Fax: (520) 628-7104
E-mail address: svillarreal@sc.co.pima.az.us

WARNER, Nanette Marie *(Judge, Superior Court of Arizona Pima County)* Appointed by Governor Bruce Babbitt to term beginning March 7, 1986. Retained by election Nov 1988, Nov 1992, Nov 1996 and 2000. Current term expires Jan 2005. Former Associate Presiding Juvenile Court Judge and Presiding Juvenile Court Judge. Currently serves Criminal Court and Domestic Court. Born Phoenix Arizona Oct 19, 1951. Educated at University of Arizona B.A. magna cum laude with honors in Sociology 1973 and Georgetown University Law Center J.D. 1976. Member Phi Beta Kappa. Admitted to practice Arizona 1976, U.S. District Court District of Arizona 1976 and U.S. Court of Appeals Ninth Circuit 1983. In legal practice Tucson 1976-86.

Adjunct Professor University of Arizona Fall 1984. Member Arizona Judges Association, Arizona Women Lawyers Association, National Association of Women Judges, State Bar of Arizona, Pima County and American Bar Associations.

Office: New Courts Building, 110 West Congress, Tucson 85701.
Telephone: (520) 740-8045.
Fax: (520) 740-8313
E-mail address: nwarner@sc.co.pima.az.us

WEAVER, Raymond W., Jr. *(Presiding Judge, Superior Court of Arizona Yavapai County)* Former Presiding Juvenile Court Judge.

Office: Yavapai County Courthouse, 120 South Cortez, Prescott 86301.
Telephone: (928) 771-3316.
Fax: (928) 771-3497
E-mail address: rweaver@courts.sp.state.az.us

WEISBERG, Sheldon H. *(Chief Judge, Arizona Court of Appeals Division One)* Appointed by Governor

WEISBERG, SHELDON H.—*Continued*

Fife Symington Nov 13, 1992 to term beginning Dec 18, 1992. Retained by election 1996 and Nov 2002. Current term expires Dec 31, 2008. Former Vice Chief Judge. Chief Judge since 2003. Born Cleveland Ohio July 20, 1946. Jewish. Educated at Bucknell University and The Ohio State University B.A. 1969 J.D. cum laude 1974. Admitted to practice Arizona 1974, U.S. District Court District of Arizona 1976, U.S. Court of Appeals Ninth Circuit 1976 and U.S. Supreme Court 1979. In legal practice Kingman 1976-92. Judge pro tempore Superior Court of Arizona Mohave County 1977-92.

Important Decisions: Movers v. Waddell (administrative review jurisdiction) 880 P.2d 639, 1987, Evenstad v. Arizona (state immunities) 178 Ariz. 578, 875 P.2d 811, 1993 and Victor v. Victor (lack of jurisdiction over religious divorce) 177 Ariz. 231, 866 P.2d 899, 1993. Member State Bar of Arizona, Mohave County and American Bar Associations. Major USAR (retired). Republican.

Office: 1501 West Washington, Phoenix 85007.
Telephone: (602) 542-1434.
Fax: (602) 542-4833

WEISS, Richard *(Judge, Superior Court of Arizona Mohave County)*

Mailing address: P.O. Box 7000, Kingman 86402.
Office: Mohave County Courthouse, 401 East Spring Street, Kingman 86401.
Telephone: (928) 753-6934.
Fax: (928) 753-8938
E-mail address: rweiss@courts.sp.state.az.us

WELLS, Charlotte *(Judge, Superior Court of Arizona Mohave County)*

Office: Bullhead City Justice Court, 2225 Trane Road, Bullhead City 86442.
Telephone: (928) 758-0726.
Fax: (928) 758-0726
E-mail address: cwells@courts.sp.state.az.us

WILKINSON, Michael O. *(Judge, Superior Court of Arizona Maricopa County)* Appointed by governor. Currently serves Criminal Court.

Office: 613 East Court Building, 101 West Jefferson, Phoenix 85003.
Telephone: (602) 506-3776.
Fax: (602) 506-1183
E-mail address: mwilkins@superiorcourt.maricopa.gov

WILLETT, Eileen *(Judge, Superior Court of Arizona Maricopa County)* Appointed by governor. Currently serves Criminal Court.

Office: 13C Central Court Building, 201 West Jefferson, Phoenix 85003-2205.
Telephone: (602) 506-3343.
Fax: (602) 506-3123
E-mail address: ewillett@superiorcourt.maricopa.gov

WILLRICH, Penny Ladell *(Judge, Superior Court of Arizona Maricopa County)* Court Commissioner 1995-99. Appointed by Governor Jane Dee Hull to term beginning 1999. First African American woman appointed Arizona Superior Court Judge. Currently serves Criminal Court. Born Grand Prairie Texas Aug 12, 1954. Baptist. Educated at University of Texas at Arlington B.A. 1974 B.A. 1976, Antioch School of Law J.D. 1982 and Springfield College M.S. with honors 2001. Admitted to practice Texas 1983, U.S. District Courts Northern District of Texas 1983 and District of Arizona 1988, U.S. Courts of Appeals Fifth 1983 and Ninth 1988 Circuits and Arizona 1988. In legal practice Phoenix 1994-95.

Staff Attorney and Managing Attorney West Texas Legal Services 1982-87. Managing Attorney and Litigation Director Community Legal Services 1987-92. Instructor in Legal Writing and Family Law Paralegal Program University of Texas at Arlington 1985-87; Justice Studies Paralegal Program, Legal Research and Writing and Family Law Phoenix College 1989-99; and Lawyering Practice and Theory Arizona State University College of Law Spring 2001. President Hayzel B. Daniels Bar Association 1990-92 and 1999-2000. Former Member Commission on Minorities Supreme Court of Arizona. Member National Association of Women Judges and State Bar of Arizona (Ethics Committee). Recipient Manager of the Year Award from Community Legal Services, Image Award from NAACP and Outstanding African American Alumni Award from University of Texas at Arlington. Named Community Leader in Law by 100 Black Men of Phoenix, Inc. Assistant Director Division of Children and Family Services Arizona Department of Economic Security 1992-94. Volunteer Jurist Arizona High School Mock Trial Competition since 1995. Children's Church Teacher and Sunday School Teacher First New Life Missionary Baptist Church since 1996. Co-founder Arizona Association of Women for Change. Member NAACP. Interests include sports, music and reading. Personal Statement or Quote: "I can do all things through Christ, that strengthens me."

Office: 3D Southeast Court, 222 East Javelina Avenue, Mesa 85210.
Telephone: (602) 506-2502.
Fax: (602) 506-2651
E-mail address: pwillric@superiorcourt.maricopa.gov

WING, Thomas L. *(Judge, Superior Court of Arizona Navajo County)* Former Presiding Judge. Currently serves as Presiding Juvenile Court Judge.

Mailing address: P.O. Box 668, Holbrook 86025.
Office: Navajo County Courthouse, Holbrook 86025.
Telephone: (928) 524-4213.
Fax: (928) 524-4246
E-mail address: twing@courts.sp.state.az.us

WINTHROP, Lawrence *(Judge, Arizona Court of Appeals Division One)* Appointed by governor.

Office: 1501 West Washington, Phoenix 85007.
Telephone: (602) 542-1430.
Fax: (602) 542-4833
E-mail address: lwinthro@courts.sp.state.az.us

YARNELL, Michael A. *(Judge, Superior Court of Arizona Maricopa County)* Appointed by governor. Currently serves Civil Court.

Office: 512 East Court Building, 101 West Jefferson, Phoenix 85003.
Telephone: (602) 506-3851.
Fax: (602) 506-3123
E-mail address: myarnell@superiorcourt.maricopa.gov

ZAPATA, Frank R. *(Judge, United States District Court District of Arizona)* Magistrate Judge 1994-96. Appointed Judge for life by President Bill Clinton to term beginning 1996. Born Safford Arizona July 23,

ZAPATA, FRANK R.—*Continued*

1944. Educated at Eastern Arizona College A.A. 1964 and University of Arizona B.A. 1966 J.D. 1973.

Staff Attorney Pima County Legal Aid Society 1973-74. Assistant Federal Public Defender 1974-84 and Chief Assistant Federal Public Defender 1984-94 Arizona.

Office: 5160 U.S. Courthouse, 405 West Congress Street, Tucson 85701-5010.

Telephone: (520) 205-4530.

ARKANSAS

Capital LITTLE ROCK

UNITED STATES DISTRICT COURTS DISTRICTS OF ARKANSAS

Within Arkansas there are two United States District Courts. For descriptive information refer to the United States Courts section.

EASTERN DISTRICT consists of five divisions.

Eastern Division includes Cross, Lee, Monroe, Phillips, St. Francis and Woodruff counties. The court sits at Helena.

Jonesboro Division includes Clay, Craighead, Crittenden, Greene, Lawrence, Mississippi, Poinsett and Randolph counties. The court sits at Jonesboro.

Northern Division includes Cleburne, Fulton, Independence, Izard, Jackson, Sharp and Stone counties. The court sits at Batesville.

Pine Bluff Division includes Arkansas, Chicot, Cleveland, Dallas, Desha, Drew, Grant, Jefferson and Lincoln counties. The court sits at Pine Bluff.

Western Division includes Conway, Faulkner, Lonoke, Perry, Pope, Prairie, Pulaski, Saline, Van Buren, White and Yell counties. The court sits at Little Rock.

Chief Judge
Susan Webber Wright

Judges
George Howard, Jr.
William R. Wilson, Jr.
James M. Moody

Senior Judges
Garnett Thomas Eisele
Stephen M. Reasoner

Clerk
James W. McCormack
402 U.S. Courthouse
600 West Capitol Avenue
Little Rock, Arkansas 72201-3325
(501) 604-5351

WESTERN DISTRICT consists of six divisions.

El Dorado Division includes Ashley, Bradley, Calhoun, Columbia, Ouachita and Union counties. The court sits at El Dorado.

Fayetteville Division includes Benton, Madison and Washington counties. The court sits at Fayetteville.

Fort Smith Division includes Crawford, Franklin, Johnson, Logan, Polk, Scott and Sebastian counties. The court sits at Fort Smith.

Harrison Division includes Baxter, Boone, Carroll, Marion, Newton and Searcy counties. The court sits at Harrison.

Hot Springs Division includes Clark, Garland, Hot Spring, Montgomery and Pike counties. The court sits at Hot Springs.

Texarkana Division includes Hempstead, Howard, Lafayette, Little River, Miller, Nevada and Sevier counties. The court sits at Texarkana.

Chief Judge
Jimm Larry Hendren

Judges
Harry F. Barnes
Robert T. Dawson

Clerk
Christopher R. Johnson
P.O. Box 1547
Fort Smith, Arkansas 72902-1547
(479) 783-6833

UNITED STATES MAGISTRATE JUDGES OF ARKANSAS

EASTERN DISTRICT
Henry Louis Jones, Jr.
H. David Young
John F. Forster, Jr.
Jerry W. Cavaneau
J. Thomas Ray

WESTERN DISTRICT
Beverly Stites Jones
Bobby E. Shepherd

UNITED STATES BANKRUPTCY COURTS OF ARKANSAS

EASTERN DISTRICT

Chief Judge
Audrey R. Evans

Judges
James Gordon Mixon
Richard D. Taylor

Bankruptcy Clerk
Jean E. Rolfs
P.O. Drawer 3777
Little Rock, Arkansas 72203-3777
(501) 918-5500

WESTERN DISTRICT

Chief Judge
Audrey R. Evans

Judges
James Gordon Mixon
Richard D. Taylor

UNITED STATES DISTRICT COURTS DISTRICTS OF ARKANSAS—*Continued*

Bankruptcy Clerk
Jean E. Rolfs
P.O. Drawer 3777
Little Rock, Arkansas 72203-3777
(501) 918-5500

ARKANSAS SUPREME COURT

The Supreme Court is Arkansas' court of last resort. The court consists of a chief justice and six associate justices elected for eight-year terms in nonpartisan elections. Vacancies are filled by the governor; however, appointees are not eligible for election to the office. Retirement is mandatory at age seventy.

The court has appellate jurisdiction over cases from the Circuit Court involving interpretation of the state constitution; elections; attorney discipline; products liability; usury; a prior decision by the court; the law of torts; mineral, oil or gas rights; construction of deeds and wills; appeals from the Arkansas Public Service, Transportation and Pollution Control Commissions; and criminal cases in which a cumulative sentence of thirty years or the death penalty is imposed or a post conviction relief petition sought. The court may review decisions from the Court of Appeals, but there is no appeal by right. The court may issue writs necessary to the exercise of proper jurisdiction.

The court sits en banc at Little Rock and recesses during July and August.

Chief Justice
W. H. "Dub" Arnold

Associate Justices

Tom Glaze	Donald L. Corbin
Robert L. Brown	Annabelle Clinton Imber
Ray Thornton	Jim Hannah

Clerk
Leslie Steen
Justice Building
625 Marshall Street
Little Rock, Arkansas 72201
(501) 682-6845

Director
James D. Gingerich
Administrative Office of the Courts
Justice Building
625 Marshall Street
Little Rock, Arkansas 72201-1020
(501) 682-9400

ARKANSAS COURT OF APPEALS

The Court of Appeals, implemented July 1, 1979, is Arkansas' court of intermediate appellate jurisdiction. The court consists of a chief judge and eleven judges elected in nonpartisan elections to eight-year terms from Court of Appeals districts statewide. In accordance with legislation first adopted during the 1993 legislative session, the number of judges in the Court of Appeals increased from six to twelve. The governor appointed a total of six new judges to the Court of Appeals; three began terms on January 1, 1996 and three began terms on January 1, 1997. The six newly appointed judges stood for election at the November 2000 general election to four-year terms from the six existing districts. In 2003 the Eighty-fourth General Assembly redrew boundary lines to create a seventh district, which will schedule its first election in 2008. A chief judge is appointed by the chief justice for a four-year term and may be reappointed for subsequent terms. Retirement is mandatory at age seventy; however, retired judges may serve by assignment of the chief justice.

The court has appellate jurisdiction over the Circuit Court except in those cases appealed directly to the Supreme Court. The court generally hears cases involving contracts, torts, workers' compensation and employment benefits, and criminal cases not involving the death penalty or life imprisonment. There is no appeal by right from the Court of Appeals to the Supreme Court. The court may issue any writs, directives, orders and mandates that are appropriate within the limits established by the Supreme Court.

The court is authorized to sit en banc or in panels of three judges each. The court sits at Little Rock and may, at its discretion, sit at any county seat.

DISTRICT ONE includes Clay, Craighead, Crittenden, Cross, Greene, Lonoke, Mississippi, Monroe, Poinsett, Prairie, White and Woodruff counties.

DISTRICT TWO includes Baxter, Boone, Cleburne, Conway, Faulkner, Fulton, Independence, Izard, Jackson, Lawrence, Marion, Newton, Pope, Randolph, Searcy, Sharp, Stone and Van Buren counties.

DISTRICT THREE includes Benton, Carroll, Crawford, Franklin, Johnson, Madison and Washington counties.

DISTRICT FOUR includes Clark, Garland, Hempstead, Hot Spring, Howard, Little River, Logan, Miller, Montgomery, Pike, Polk, Scott, Sebastian, Sevier and Yell counties.

DISTRICT FIVE includes Ashley, Bradley, Calhoun, Cleveland, Columbia, Dallas, Drew, Grant, Lafayette, Lincoln, Nevada, Ouachita and Union counties.

DISTRICT SIX includes Perry, Pulaski and Saline counties.

DISTRICT SEVEN includes Arkansas, Chicot, Desha, Jefferson, Lee, Phillips and St. Francis counties.

Chief Judge
John F. Stroud, Jr.

Judges

John Mauzy Pittman	Josephine Linker Hart
Robert Gladwin	John B. Robbins
Sam N. Bird	Larry D. Vaught
Olly Neal	Wendell L. Griffen
Terry Crabtree	Karen Baker
Andree Layton Roaf	

ARKANSAS CIRCUIT COURT

The Circuit Court is the court of general trial jurisdiction in Arkansas. Effective July 1, 2001, the Chancery Court was eliminated as a separate court of equity due to Arkansas Constitutional Amendment 80, giving the Circuit Court jurisdiction in that area. Circuit judges are elected in nonpartisan elections to six-year terms by the voters of each judicial circuit. Prior to July 1, 2001, jud-

ARKANSAS CIRCUIT COURT—*Continued*

ges served four-year terms. Retirement is mandatory at age seventy.

The court has original jurisdiction over all civil cases and in criminal cases except where exclusive jurisdiction is conferred upon another court. Effective January 1, 2002, the court consists of five divisions: criminal, civil, probate, domestic relations, and juvenile. The court hears appeals de novo from lower courts and may issue writs necessary to the exercise of proper jurisdiction.

The court sits at each county seat and as indicated.

FIRST JUDICIAL CIRCUIT includes Cross, Lee, Monroe, Phillips, St. Francis and Woodruff counties. The court sits at Wynne, Marianna, Clarendon, Helena, Forrest City and Augusta.

Judges

Kathleen Bell
Baird Kinney
L. T. Simes, II
Bentley E. Story
Harvey Yates

SECOND JUDICIAL CIRCUIT includes Clay, Craighead, Crittenden, Greene, Mississippi and Poinsett counties. The court sits at Corning, Piggott, Jonesboro, Lake City, Marion, Paragould, Osceola, Blytheville and Harrisburg.

Judges

Larry Boling
David Burnett
William Lee Fergus
John N. Fogleman
David Goodson
Victor Hill
Pamela Honeycutt
David N. Laser
Rice Van Ausdall
Ralph Wilson, Jr.

THIRD JUDICIAL CIRCUIT includes Jackson, Lawrence, Randolph and Sharp counties. The court sits at Newport, Walnut Ridge, Pocahontas and Hardy.

Judges

Harold Erwin
Kevin N. King
Phillip Smith

FOURTH JUDICIAL CIRCUIT includes Madison and Washington counties. The court sits at Huntsville and Fayetteville.

Judges

Mary Ann Gunn
Mark Lindsay
Mike Mashburn
Kim M. Smith
William Storey
Stacey Zimmerman

FIFTH JUDICIAL CIRCUIT includes Franklin, Johnson and Pope counties. The court sits at Ozark, Charleston, Clarksville and Russellville.

Judges

Ken Coker, Jr.
Richard Gardner
John S. Patterson
Dennis Sutterfield

SIXTH JUDICIAL CIRCUIT includes Perry and Pulaski counties. The court sits at Perryville and Little Rock.

Judges

Ellen B. Brantley
Wiley Branton
Tim Fox
Alice Sprinkle Gray
Rita Gruber
Marion Humphrey
Collins Kilgore
John W. Langston
Mary McGowan
James Moody
Richard Moore
Chris Piazza
Mackie Pierce
Williard Proctor
Barry Sims
Vann Smith
Joyce Williams Warren

SEVENTH JUDICIAL CIRCUIT includes Grant and Hot Spring counties. The court sits at Sheridan and Malvern.

Judges

Phillip H. Shirron
Chris E. Williams

EIGHTH NORTH JUDICIAL CIRCUIT includes Hempstead and Nevada counties. The court sits at Hope and Prescott.

Judges

Duncan Culpepper
James H. Gunter, Jr.

EIGHTH SOUTH JUDICIAL CIRCUIT includes Lafayette and Miller counties. The court sits at Lewisville and Texarkana.

Judges

Joe E. Griffin
Jim Hudson
Kirk D. Johnson

NINTH EAST JUDICIAL CIRCUIT includes Clark County. The court sits at Arkadelphia.

Judge

John Thomas

NINTH WEST JUDICIAL CIRCUIT includes Howard, Little River, Pike and Sevier counties. The court sits at Nashville, Ashdown, Murfreesboro and DeQueen.

Judges

Ted C. Capeheart
Charles A. Yeargan

TENTH JUDICIAL CIRCUIT includes Ashley, Bradley, Chicot, Desha and Drew counties. The court sits at Hamburg, Warren, Lake Village, Arkansas City, McGehee and Monticello.

Judges

Bynum Gibson
Don E. Glover
Jerry Mazzanti
Samuel B. Pope
Robert C. Vittitow

ELEVENTH EAST JUDICIAL CIRCUIT includes Arkansas County. The courts sits at DeWitt and Stuttgart.

Judge

David Henry

ELEVENTH WEST JUDICIAL CIRCUIT includes Jefferson and Lincoln counties. The court sits at Pine Bluff and Star City.

Judges

William Benton
Thomas E. Brown
Fred D. Davis
Leon Jamison
Berlin Jones
Hendrix Arthur Taylor, Jr.

ARKANSAS CIRCUIT COURT—*Continued*

TWELFTH JUDICIAL CIRCUIT includes Sebastian County. The court sits at Fort Smith and Greenwood.

Judges

J. Michael Fitzhugh
Harry Albers Foltz
Mark Hewett
Jim Marschewski
Jim D. Spears
Norman Wilkinson

THIRTEENTH JUDICIAL CIRCUIT includes Calhoun, Cleveland, Columbia, Dallas, Ouachita and Union counties. The court sits at Hampton, Rison, Magnolia, Fordyce, Camden and El Dorado.

Judges

Carol Crafton Anthony
Larry Chandler
David Guthrie
Edward Jones
Edwin A. Keaton
Hamilton Hobbs Singleton

FOURTEENTH JUDICIAL CIRCUIT includes Baxter, Boone, Marion and Newton counties. The court sits at Mountain Home, Harrison, Yellville and Jasper.

Judges

Gary B. Isbell
Roger V. Logan, Jr.
John Putman
Gordon Webb

FIFTEENTH JUDICIAL CIRCUIT includes Conway, Logan, Scott and Yell counties. The court sits at Morrilton, Booneville, Paris, Waldron, Danville and Dardanelle.

Judges

Paul Danielson
David H. McCormick
Terry Sullivan

SIXTEENTH JUDICIAL CIRCUIT includes Cleburne, Fulton, Independence, Izard and Stone counties. The court sits at Heber Springs, Salem, Batesville, Melbourne and Mountain View.

Judges

Stephen Choate
John Norman Harkey
John Dan Kemp, Jr.
Tim Weaver

SEVENTEENTH JUDICIAL CIRCUIT includes Prairie and White counties. The court sits at De Valls Bluff, Des Arc and Searcy.

Judges

Robert Edwards
Craig Hannah
Bill Mills

EIGHTEENTH EAST JUDICIAL CIRCUIT includes Garland County. The court sits at Hot Springs.

Judges

Vicki Cook
Tom Smitherman
David Switzer
John Homer Wright

EIGHTEENTH WEST JUDICIAL CIRCUIT includes Montgomery and Polk counties. The court sits at Mount Ida and Mena.

Judge

J. W. Looney

NINETEENTH EAST JUDICIAL CIRCUIT includes Carroll County. The court sits at Berryville and Eureka Springs.

Judge

Alan D. Epley

NINETEENTH WEST JUDICIAL CIRCUIT includes Benton County. The court sits at Bentonville.

Judges

David Clinger
Xollie Duncan
Jay Finch
Tom J. Keith
John R. Scott

TWENTIETH JUDICIAL CIRCUIT includes Faulkner, Searcy and Van Buren counties. The court sits at Conway, Marshall and Clinton.

Judges

Charles E. Clawson, Jr.
Linda Collier
Mike Maggio
David Reynolds

TWENTY-FIRST JUDICIAL CIRCUIT includes Crawford County. The court sits at Van Buren.

Judges

Gary Cottrell
Mike Medlock

TWENTY-SECOND JUDICIAL CIRCUIT includes Saline County. The court sits at Benton.

Judges

Gary M. Arnold
Robert Garrett
Grisham Phillips

TWENTY-THIRD JUDICIAL CIRCUIT includes Lonoke County. The court sits at Lonoke.

Judges

Lance Hanshaw
Phillip Whiteaker

ARKANSAS DISTRICT COURTS

District Courts are courts of limited jurisdiction in Arkansas. Effective July 1, 2001, Municipal Courts in Arkansas, which were established in cities with populations of 2,400 or more and in any county seat regardless of population, became District Courts. Jurisdiction is countywide except in those counties having two county seats. Judges are elected for four-year terms. For judges who were in office as of July 1, 2001, terms will expire on Dec 31, 2004. The judges must be attorneys and, except in Little Rock, Hot Springs and Pine Bluff, may practice law.

The courts have exclusive jurisdiction over all city ordinance violations and concurrent jurisdiction with the Circuit Court and Justice of the Peace Courts over misdemeanor criminal cases and civil cases when the amount in controversy does not exceed $5,000, except as provided by law. The courts also have jurisdiction over felony preliminary hearings and small claims cases. The District Courts of Little Rock and North Little Rock

ARKANSAS DISTRICT COURTS—*Continued*

are separated into divisions. Little Rock District Court consists of three divisions for administrative purposes; North Little Rock District Court has both a Civil/Criminal Division and a Traffic Division. Appeals are to the Circuit Court.

District Court	Judge
Arkadelphia	Randy Hill
Ashdown	John C. Finley, III
Ash Flat	Raymond T. Starken
Augusta	John D. Eldridge, III
Batesville	John Gregg
Beebe	Thomas M. Hughes, III
Benton	Mike Robinson
Benton County-West	Jeff Conner
Bentonville	John Arthur Skaggs
Berryville	Kent Coxsey
Biscoe	Gary B. Rogers
Blytheville	Shannon Langston
Booneville	Paul X. Williams
Bradley County	Robert "Bob" Garner
Brinkley	John W. Martin
Bryant	Curtis Rickard
Cabot	Joe O'Bryan
Camden	Phil Foster
Carlisle	Joseph V. Svoboda
Charleston	Joe Ramos
Cherokee Village	Raymond T. Starken
Clarendon	Steve Elledge
Clarksville	Len W. Bradley
Clinton	John Aldworth
Conway	Russell "Jack" Roberts
Corning	Rick Rodery
Cotton Plant	Richard L. Proctor
Crossett	Billy Hubbell
DeQueen	Robert L. Lowery
Dermott	Chuck Gibson
Des Arc	Robert Abney
De Valls Bluff	Gary B. Rogers
DeWitt	Claude Jenkins
Dumas	Howard "Corky" Holthoff
East Camden	Dan Ives
Elkins	Ray A. Reynolds
England	Joseph V. Svoboda
Eudora	Stephen Tisdale
Eureka Springs	Tim S. Parker
Fayetteville	Rudy Moore
Fordyce	Thomas L. Mays
Forrest City	Steve Routon
Fort Smith	David P. Saxon
	Daniel Stewart
Greenwood	Wayland A. Parker, II
Hamburg	Reid Harrod
Hampton	Ron A. Phillips
Harrisburg	Steve Inboden
Harrison	Gail Inman-Campbell
Hazen	Gary B. Rogers
Heber Springs	Michael E. Irwin
Helena	Chalk Mitchell
Hope	Tony Yocum
Hot Springs	Marcia R. Hearnsberger
	Ralph L. Ohm
Hoxie	Wm. Larry Hayes
Huntsville	W. Q. Hall
Jacksonville	Robert Batton
Jasper	Peter L. DeStefano, Jr.
Jonesboro	Ray Spruell
Lake City	Ray Spruell
Lake Village	David F. Gillison, Jr.
Lepanto	Jim Dunlap
Lewisville	Edward Cochran
Lincoln County	Victor Harper
Little Rock	
First Division	Lee Munson
Second Division	Victor A. Fleming
Third Division	David A. Stewart
Lonoke	Kenneth Williams
Magnolia	Rodney Chambers
Malvern	David Mac Glover
Marianna	Dan Felton, III
Marion County	Judith Bearden
Marked Tree	Jim Dunlap
Marshall	Jerry D. Patterson
Maumelle	David L. Pake
McCrory	Richard L. Proctor
McGehee	Gibbs Ferguson
Melbourne	David Miller
Mena	Jerry Ryan
Miller County	Carol Cannedy Dalby
Monticello	Kenneth A. Harper
Morrilton	J. Scott Adams
Mountain Home	Van Gearhart
Mountain View	Adam Harkey
Mount Ida	William McKimm
Murfreesboro	Jim Bob Steel
Nashville	Edwin J. Alford
Newport	Ronald L. Winningham
North Little Rock	
Civil/Criminal Division	Jim Hamilton
Traffic Division	Brent Standridge
Osceola	Mike Gibson
Ozark	Joe Ramos
Paragould	Dan Stidham
Paris	David Cravens
Perry County	Elizabeth Wise
Piggott	Rick Rodery
Pine Bluff	Robert Tolson, Jr.
	Waymond Brown
Pocahontas	John Throesch
Prairie Grove	Jim Boyd
Prescott	Eugene Hale
Pulaski County	Wayne Gruber
Rector	Rick Rodery
Rison	Ron A. Phillips
Rogers	Doug Schrantz
Russellville	Don Bourne
Salem	Jim Short
Searcy	Clarence P. Shoffner
Sheridan	J. Larry Allen
Sherwood	Milas Howard Hale, II
Siloam Springs	Stephen Thomas
Springdale	Stanley W. Ludwig
Star City	Victor Harper
Stuttgart	J. W. Green, Jr.
Texarkana	Carol Cannedy Dalby
Trumann	Steve Inboden
Tyronza	Jim Dunlap
Union County	George Ellis Van Hook, Jr.
Van Buren	Steven Peer
Waldron	Donald Goodner
Walnut Ridge	Wm. Larry Hayes

ARKANSAS DISTRICT COURTS—*Continued*

Ward	Joseph V. Svoboda
West Fork	Casey Jones
West Helena	Jesse E. "Rusty" Porter, Jr.
West Memphis	William P. Rainey
Wrightsville	Dennis Lee James
Wynne	Richard L. Proctor
Yell County	Jerry Don Ramey

ARKANSAS COUNTY COURTS

The County Courts are courts of limited jurisdiction in Arkansas. Judges are elected by the voters of each county for two-year terms.

The courts have exclusive original jurisdiction in matters relating to county taxes, county expenditures and settlement of demands against the county.

ARKANSAS CITY COURTS

The mayor or qualified elector appointed by the mayor of towns or second class cities is vested with the same judicial powers as justices of the peace and has jurisdiction over violations of city ordinances. Formerly called Mayor's Courts, these courts were designated City Courts in 1971. There is no right to a jury trial.

ARKANSAS POLICE COURTS

Police Court judges are elected for four-year terms. The courts serve a similar function and have jurisdiction similar to that of the City Courts. A court is automatically abolished by the creation of a Municipal Court.

Arkansas Counties and County Seats

Arkansas
DeWitt
Stuttgart

Ashley
Hamburg

Baxter
Mountain Home

Benton
Bentonville

Boone
Harrison

Bradley
Warren

Calhoun
Hampton

Carroll
Berryville
Eureka Springs

Chicot
Lake Village

Clark
Arkadelphia

Clay
Piggott
Corning

Cleburne
Heber Springs

Cleveland
Rison

Columbia
Magnolia

Conway
Morrilton

Craighead
Jonesboro
Lake City

Crawford
Van Buren

Crittenden
Marion

Cross
Wynne

Dallas
Fordyce

Desha
Arkansas City

Drew
Monticello

Faulkner
Conway

Franklin
Ozark
Charleston

Fulton
Salem

Garland
Hot Springs

Grant
Sheridan

Greene
Paragould

Hempstead
Hope

Hot Spring
Malvern

Howard
Nashville

Independence
Batesville

Izard
Melbourne

Jackson
Newport

Jefferson
Pine Bluff

Johnson
Clarksville

Lafayette
Lewisville

Lawrence
Walnut Ridge

Lee
Marianna

Lincoln
Star City

Little River
Ashdown

Logan
Paris
Booneville

Lonoke
Lonoke

Madison
Huntsville

Marion
Yellville

Miller
Texarkana

Mississippi
Blytheville
Osceola

Monroe
Clarendon

Montgomery
Mount Ida

Nevada
Prescott

Newton
Jasper

Ouachita
Camden

Perry
Perryville

Phillips
Helena

Pike
Murfreesboro

Poinsett
Harrisburg

Polk
Mena

Pope
Russellville

Prairie
Des Arc
De Valls Bluff

Pulaski
Little Rock

Randolph
Pocahontas

St. Francis
Forrest City

Saline
Benton

Scott
Waldron

Searcy
Marshall

Sebastian
Fort Smith
Greenwood

Sevier
DeQueen

COUNTIES AND COUNTY SEATS—*Continued*

Sharp
Ash Flat

Stone
Mountain View

Union
El Dorado

Van Buren
Clinton

Washington
Fayetteville

White
Searcy

Woodruff
Augusta

Yell
Danville
Dardanelle

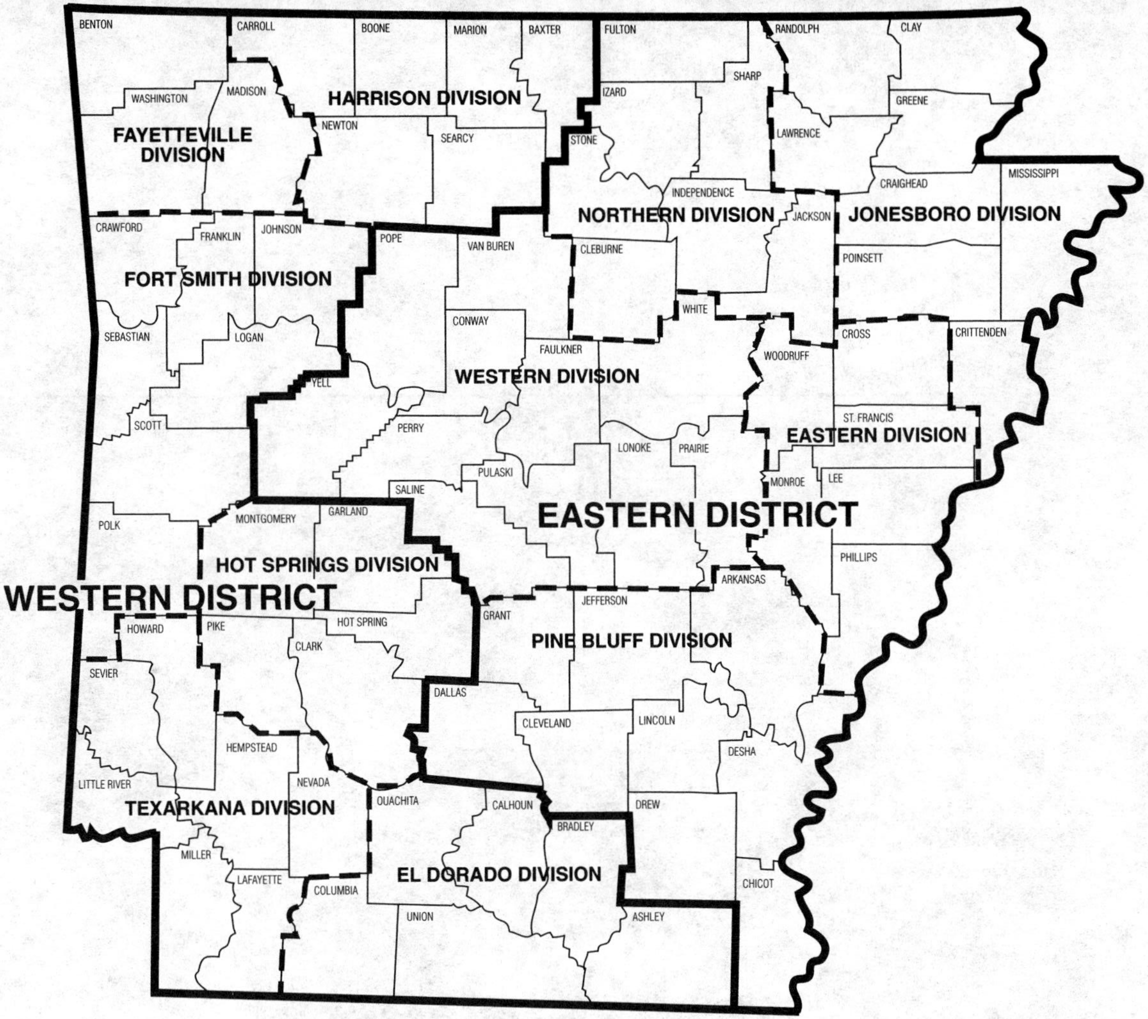
WESTERN DISTRICT
EASTERN DISTRICT
FAYETTEVILLE DIVISION
HARRISON DIVISION
FORT SMITH DIVISION
NORTHERN DIVISION
JONESBORO DIVISION
WESTERN DIVISION
EASTERN DIVISION
HOT SPRINGS DIVISION
PINE BLUFF DIVISION
TEXARKANA DIVISION
EL DORADO DIVISION
BENTON
CARROLL
BOONE
MARION
BAXTER
FULTON
RANDOLPH
CLAY
WASHINGTON
MADISON
NEWTON
SEARCY
STONE
IZARD
SHARP
LAWRENCE
GREENE
CRAIGHEAD
MISSISSIPPI
INDEPENDENCE
JACKSON
CRAWFORD
FRANKLIN
JOHNSON
POPE
VAN BUREN
CLEBURNE
POINSETT
SEBASTIAN
LOGAN
CONWAY
WHITE
CROSS
CRITTENDEN
FAULKNER
WOODRUFF
YELL
SCOTT
PERRY
ST. FRANCIS
LONOKE
PRAIRIE
PULASKI
MONROE
LEE
SALINE
POLK
MONTGOMERY
GARLAND
PHILLIPS
ARKANSAS
JEFFERSON
GRANT
HOWARD
PIKE
HOT SPRING
CLARK
SEVIER
DALLAS
CLEVELAND
LINCOLN
DESHA
HEMPSTEAD
LITTLE RIVER
NEVADA
OUACHITA
CALHOUN
DREW
BRADLEY
MILLER
LAFAYETTE
COLUMBIA
UNION
ASHLEY
CHICOT

UNITED STATES DISTRICT COURTS DISTRICTS OF ARKANSAS

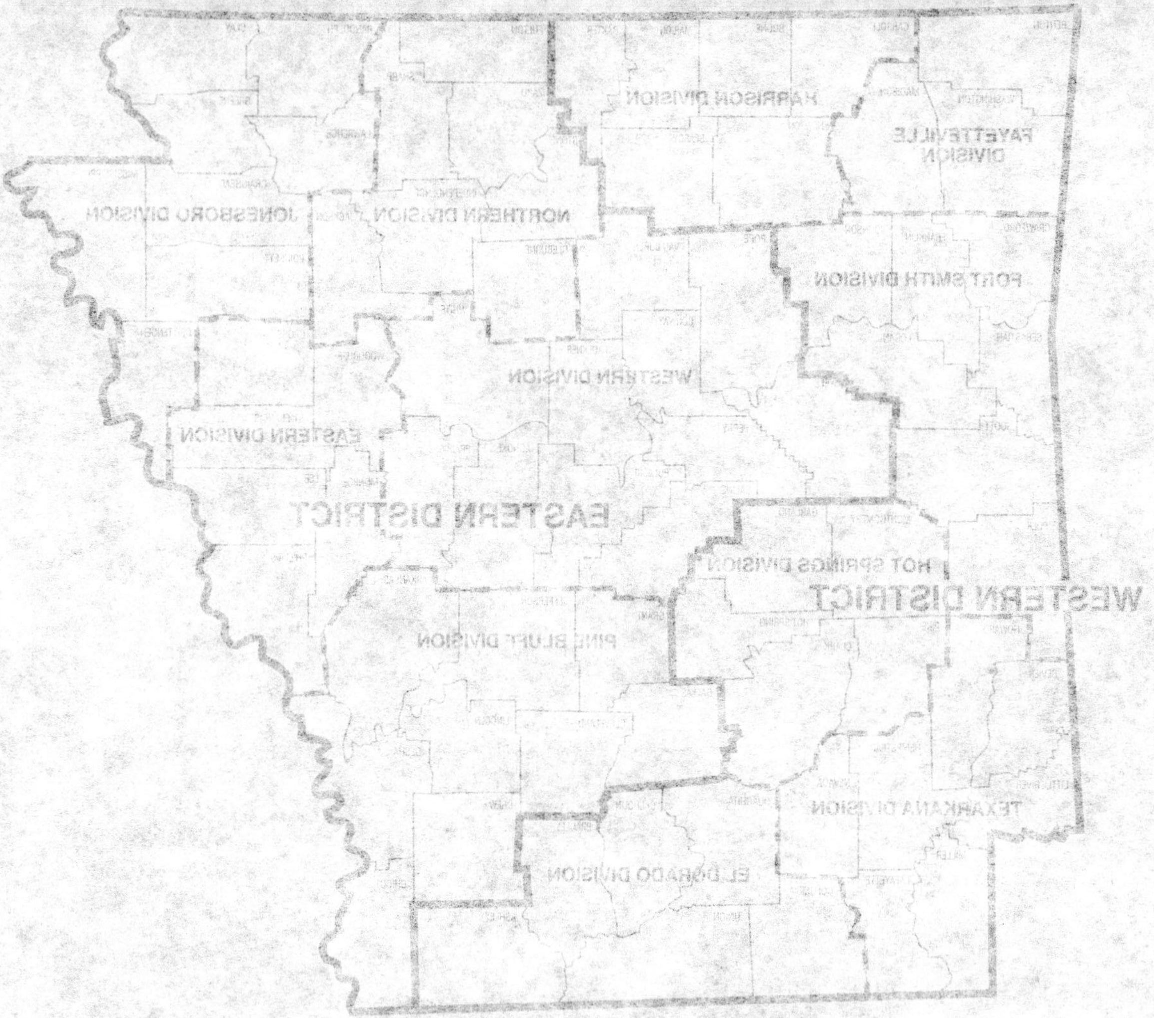
EASTERN DISTRICT
WESTERN DISTRICT
JONESBORO DIVISION
NORTHERN DIVISION
HARRISON DIVISION
FAYETTEVILLE DIVISION
FORT SMITH DIVISION
WESTERN DIVISION
EASTERN DIVISION
HOT SPRINGS DIVISION
PINE BLUFF DIVISION
TEXARKANA DIVISION
EL DORADO DIVISION

UNITED STATES DISTRICT COURTS DISTRICTS OF ARKANSAS

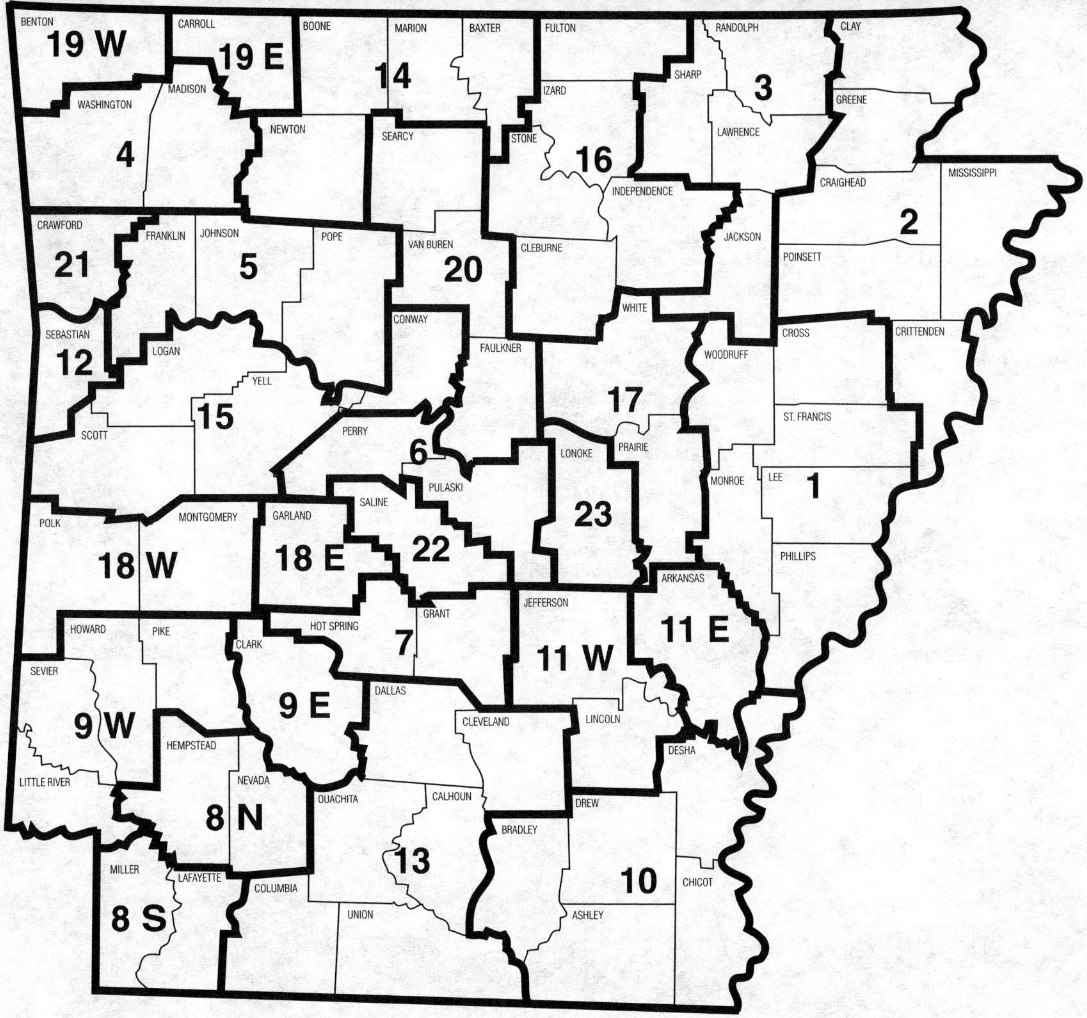
BENTON
19 W
CARROLL
19 E
BOONE
MARION
BAXTER
14
FULTON
RANDOLPH
CLAY
SHARP
3
IZARD
MADISON
WASHINGTON
4
NEWTON
SEARCY
STONE
16
LAWRENCE
GREENE
INDEPENDENCE
CRAIGHEAD
MISSISSIPPI
2
CRAWFORD
FRANKLIN
JOHNSON
5
POPE
VAN BUREN
20
CLEBURNE
JACKSON
POINSETT
21
SEBASTIAN
12
LOGAN
YELL
15
CONWAY
FAULKNER
WHITE
WOODRUFF
CROSS
CRITTENDEN
SCOTT
PERRY
6
17
ST. FRANCIS
LONOKE
PRAIRIE
PULASKI
MONROE
LEE
1
SALINE
POLK
MONTGOMERY
GARLAND
18 W
18 E
22
23
PHILLIPS
ARKANSAS
JEFFERSON
GRANT
HOWARD
PIKE
HOT SPRING
CLARK
7
11 E
11 W
SEVIER
9 W
9 E
DALLAS
CLEVELAND
LINCOLN
HEMPSTEAD
DESHA
LITTLE RIVER
NEVADA
8 N
OUACHITA
CALHOUN
DREW
BRADLEY
13
MILLER
LAFAYETTE
COLUMBIA
10
CHICOT
8 S
UNION
ASHLEY

JUDICIAL CIRCUITS OF ARKANSAS CIRCUIT COURT

ARKANSAS

ABNEY, Robert *(Judge, Des Arc District Court)* Term expires Dec 31, 2004.
Mailing address: P.O. Box 225, Des Arc 72040.
Telephone: (870) 256-4183.
Fax: (870) 256-4184

ADAMS, J. Scott *(Judge, Morrilton District Court)* Term expires Dec 31, 2004.
Office: 207 East Church, Morrilton 72110.
Telephone: (501) 354-1464.

ALDWORTH, John *(Judge, Clinton District Court)* Term expires Dec 31, 2004.
Mailing address: P.O. Box 762, Clinton 72031.
Telephone: (501) 745-8801.

ALFORD, Edwin J. *(Judge, Nashville District Court)* Elected to term beginning Jan 1, 1977. Reelected to subsequent terms. Current term expires Dec 31, 2004. Born Ozan Arkansas Feb 2, 1945. Baptist. Educated at Henderson State Teachers College B.A. 1968 and University of Arkansas J.D. 1971. Admitted to practice Arkansas 1972. Began legal practice Nashville 1972. USMCR 1963-68.
Office: 510 North Second Street, Nashville 71852.
Telephone: (870) 845-1645.

ALLEN, J. Larry *(Judge, Sheridan District Court)* Term expires Dec 31, 2004.
Office: 201 North Oak Street, Sheridan 72150.
Telephone: (870) 942-3195.

ANTHONY, Carol Crafton *(Judge, Arkansas Circuit Court Thirteenth Judicial Circuit)* Appointed by Governor Jim Guy Tucker to term beginning December 3, 1993. Elected 1994, 1996, 1998 and 2002. Current term expires Dec 31, 2008. Born Conway Arkansas Oct 9, 1953. Methodist. Law Clerk to Hon. Marian F. Penix, Arkansas Court of Appeals 1979-80 and Senior Judge Oren Harris, U.S. District Courts Eastern and Western Districts of Arkansas 1981-84. Admitted to practice Arkansas 1979, U.S. District Court District of Arkansas and U.S. Court of Appeals Eighth Circuit. In legal practice El Dorado 1984-91. Magistrate Judge, United States District Court Western District of Arkansas 1987-93, appointed by U.S. District Court judges. Served part time. Former Chancellor, Arkansas Chancery Court Thirteenth Judicial Circuit. Served Juvenile Division.

Member Union City and Arkansas Bar Associations. Board Member United Way. Enjoys tennis.
Office: 101 North Washington, Suite 203, El Dorado 71730.
Telephone: (870) 864-1947.
Fax: (870) 864-1946

ARNOLD, Gary M. *(Judge, Arkansas Circuit Court Twenty-second Judicial Circuit)* Elected to term beginning Jan 1, 1991. Reelected 1994, 1998 and 2002. Current term expires Dec 31, 2008. Serves Juvenile, Criminal and Civil Divisions. Born Tulsa Oklahoma June 17, 1947. Baptist. Educated at Henderson State University B.S. 1970 and University of Arkansas at Little Rock School of Law J.D. 1981. Admitted to practice Arkansas 1982. In legal practice Benton 1982-88. Former Chancellor, Arkansas Chancery Court Twenty-second Judicial Circuit.

Prosecuting Attorney Seventh Judicial Circuit 1989-90. Member Saline County, Arkansas and American Bar Associations. Sergeant E-5 U.S. Army (honorable discharge 1976). Previously employed as laboratory director. Member numerous community and civic organizations. Enjoys snow skiing, reading and jogging.
Office: Saline County Courthouse, 200 North Main, Benton 72015.
Telephone: (501) 303-5664.
Fax: (501) 303-5695

ARNOLD, W. H. "Dub" *(Chief Justice, Arkansas Supreme Court)* Elected Nov 1996 to term beginning Jan 1, 1997. Term expires Dec 31, 2004. Born Arkadelphia Arkansas May 19, 1935. Baptist. Educated at Henderson State University B.A. 1957 and University of Arkansas at Little Rock LL.B. 1962. Admitted to practice Arkansas 1963. Judge, Clark County Municipal Court 1979-80. Judge, Arkansas Circuit Court Ninth East Judicial Circuit 1991-96. Chancellor, Arkansas Chancery Court Ninth East Judicial Circuit 1991-96.

Former Deputy Prosecuting Attorney Clark County. Former Prosecuting Attorney Eighth Judicial District and Ninth East Judicial District. Chair Arkansas Workers' Compensation Commission. Member Arkansas Judicial Council, Clark County, Southwest Arkansas, Arkansas and American Bar Associations.
Office: Justice Building, 625 Marshall Street, Little Rock 72201.
Telephone: (501) 682-6861.

BAKER, Karen *(Judge, Arkansas Court of Appeals)* Elected Nov 2000 to term beginning Jan 1, 2001. Term expires Dec 31, 2008. Educated at Arkansas Tech University B.S. 1983 and University of Arkansas at Little Rock School of Law J.D. 1987. Assistant Editor University of Arkansas at Little Rock Law Journal. Admitted to practice Arkansas 1987. In legal practice Clinton. Judge, Arkansas Circuit Court Twentieth Judicial Circuit 1995-2000. Chancellor, Arkansas Chancery Court Twentieth Judicial Circuit 1995-2000.
Office: Justice Building, 625 Marshall Street, Little Rock 72201.
Telephone: (501) 682-7993.

BARNES, Harry F. *(Judge, United States District Court Western District of Arkansas)* Appointed for life by President Bill Clinton Oct 26, 1993 to term beginning Dec 22, 1993. Born Memphis Tennessee May 14, 1932. Methodist. Educated at Vanderbilt University 1950-52, U.S. Naval Academy B.S. 1956 and University of Arkansas LL.B. 1964. Circulation Manager University of Arkansas Law Review 1963. Admitted to practice Arkansas 1964 and U.S. District Court 1964. Began legal practice Camden 1964. Juvenile Judge, Ouachita County 1972-82. Special Associate Justice, Arkansas Supreme Court Sept 23, 1976 to March 1977. Judge, Camden Municipal Court 1975-82. Judge, Arkansas Circuit Court Thirteenth Judicial Circuit Jan 1, 1983 to Dec 21, 1993.

Important Decision: State of Arkansas v. Porter R.

BARNES, HARRY F.—*Continued*

Rogers, Sr. Cr. 75-156, 1976. Instructor in Criminal Law Arkansas Law Enforcement Training Academy since 1972. Member The Association of Trial Lawyers of America, Arkansas Trial Lawyers Association, Ouachita County, Union County, Arkansas and American Bar Associations. Colonel USMCR since 1956. Democrat. Enjoys tennis, jogging, hunting and fishing.

Mailing address: P.O. Box 1735, El Dorado 71731-1735.
Telephone: (870) 862-1303.

BATTON, Robert *(Judge, Jacksonville District Court)* Term expires Dec 31, 2004.

Office: 1414 West Main, Jacksonville 72076.
Telephone: (501) 982-9531.

BEARDEN, Judith *(Judge, Marion County District Court)* Term expires Dec 31, 2004. Educated at University of Kansas J.D. 1968.

Mailing address: P.O. Box 301, Yellville 72687-1090.
Telephone: (870) 449-4019.
Fax: (870) 449-4078

BELL, Kathleen *(Judge, Arkansas Circuit Court First Judicial Circuit)* Assumed office July 1, 2001. Former Chancellor, Arkansas Chancery Court First Judicial Circuit.

Mailing address: P.O. Box 177, West Helena 72342.
Telephone: (870) 338-5522.
Fax: (870) 338-5595

BENTON, William *(Judge, Arkansas Circuit Court Eleventh West Judicial Circuit)*

Office: 108 East Barraque, Suite 212, Pine Bluff 71601.
Telephone: (870) 541-5381.
Fax: (870) 541-5380

BIRD, Sam N. *(Judge, Arkansas Court of Appeals)* Elected Nov 5, 1996 to term beginning Jan 1, 1997. Term expires Dec 31, 2004. Born El Dorado Arkansas Jan 19, 1940. Baptist. Educated at Florida State University B.S. 1962 and University of Arkansas at Fayetteville J.D. Associate Editor University of Arkansas Law Review. Admitted to practice Arkansas 1970 and U.S. District Court District of Arkansas 1970. In legal practice Monticello 1970-90. Judge, Arkansas Circuit Court Tenth Judicial Circuit 1991-97. Chancellor, Arkansas Chancery Court Tenth Judicial Circuit 1991-97.

Captain USAF 1962-67. Democrat.

Office: Justice Building, 625 Marshall Street, Little Rock 72201.
Telephone: (501) 682-7478.

BOLING, Larry *(Judge, Arkansas Circuit Court Second Judicial Circuit)*

Mailing address: P.O. Box 9046, Jonesboro 72403.
Telephone: (870) 933-4590.
Fax: (870) 933-4596

BOURNE, Don *(Judge, Russellville District Court)* Elected to term beginning Jan 1, 2001. Term expires Dec 31, 2004. Born Vicksburg Mississippi June 10, 1956. Educated at Arkansas Tech University B.S. 1977 and University of Arkansas at Fayetteville J.D. 1980. Admitted to practice Arkansas 1980.

City Attorney 1987-2000. U.S. Army 1980-83.

Office: 205 West Second, Russellville 72801.
Telephone: (479) 968-1393.
Fax: (479) 968-4166

BOYD, Jim *(Judge, Prairie Grove District Court)*

Office: 4264 North Frontage Road, Fayetteville 72703.
Telephone: (479) 442-3612.
Fax: (479) 442-7257

BRADLEY, Len W. *(Judge, Clarksville District Court)* Elected to term beginning June 12, 1984. Reelected to subsequent terms. Current term expires Dec 31, 2004. Born Clarksville Arkansas June 19, 1956. Baptist. Educated at University of Arkansas B.A. 1978 J.D. with honors 1981. Member Phi Beta Kappa. Admitted to practice Arkansas 1981. Began legal practice Clarksville 1981.

Member Arkansas Volunteer Lawyers for the Elderly, Arkansas (Family Law Section) and American Bar Associations. Previously worked as factory worker and farm laborer. Democrat. Board of Directors Forrester-Davis Memorial Center for Exceptional Children. Member Johnson County Historical Society, Clarksville Kiwanis Club, American Cancer Society and Arkansas Municipal League. Enjoys athletics, especially weightlifting, football and basketball.

Office: 210 West Main Street, Clarksville 72830.
Telephone: (479) 754-6000.

BRANTLEY, Ellen B. *(Judge, Arkansas Circuit Court Sixth Judicial Circuit)* Assumed office July 1, 2001. Born Little Rock Arkansas Sept 13, 1948. Presbyterian. Educated at Wellesley College B.A. 1970 and University of Virginia J.D. 1973. Editorial Board University of Virginia Law Review 1971-73. Law Clerk to Hon. Thomas Eisele, U.S. District Court Eastern District of Arkansas 1973-75. Admitted to practice Arkansas 1973. In legal practice Little Rock 1976-78. Chancellor, Arkansas Chancery Court Sixth Judicial Circuit Dec 19, 1986 to June 30, 2001, appointed by Governor Bill Clinton.

Assistant Attorney General Arkansas 1976-78. Author "Probate: The Law in Arkansas" Harrison 1981. Professor University of Arkansas at Fayetteville 1975-76 and University of Arkansas at Little Rock 1978-86. Adjunct Faculty member University of Arkansas at Little Rock since 1989. Member Arkansas Association of Women Lawyers, Pulaski County, Arkansas and American Bar Associations. Named Judge of the Year by National Child Support Enforcement Association 1995 and Top 100 Women—Arkansas 1996, 1997 and 1998.

Office: 401 West Markham, Room 310, Little Rock 72201.
Telephone: (501) 340-8542.
Fax: (501) 340-6034

BRANTON, Wiley *(Judge, Arkansas Circuit Court Sixth Judicial Circuit)* Serves Juvenile Division. Former Chancellor, Arkansas Chancery Court Sixth Judicial Circuit.

Office: 3001 West Roosevelt, Little Rock 72204.
Telephone: (501) 340-6666.
Fax: (501) 340-6928

BROWN, Robert L. *(Associate Justice, Arkansas Supreme Court)* Elected to term beginning Jan 1, 1991. Reelected 1998, current term expires Dec 31, 2006. Born Houston Texas June 30, 1941. Episcopalian. Educated at University of the South B.A. with honors 1963, Columbia University M.A. with honors 1965 and Uni-

BROWN, ROBERT L.—*Continued*

versity of Virginia J.D. 1968. Member Phi Alpha Delta. Admitted to practice Arkansas 1968, U.S. Court of Appeals Eighth Circuit and U.S. Supreme Court. In legal practice Little Rock 1968-71 and 1978-90.

Deputy Prosecuting Attorney 1971-72. Legal Aide to Governor 1972-76 and U.S. Senator 1972-76. Administrative Aide to Congressman 1977-78. Instructor in National Government University of Arkansas at Little Rock 1985. Member Pulaski County, Arkansas and American Bar Associations. Enjoys playing tennis and writing.

Office: Justice Building, 625 Marshall Street, Little Rock 72201.

Telephone: (501) 682-6864.

BROWN, Thomas E. *(Judge, Arkansas Circuit Court Eleventh West Judicial Circuit)* Serves Juvenile Division. Former Chancellor, Arkansas Chancery Court Eleventh Judicial Circuit West.

Mailing address: P.O. Box 9260, Pine Bluff 71611.

Telephone: (870) 541-5461.

Fax: (870) 541-5464

BROWN, Waymond *(Judge, Pine Bluff District Court)* Term expires Dec 31, 2004.

Office: 200 East Eighth Avenue, Pine Bluff 71601.

Telephone: (870) 543-1860.

Fax: (870) 543-1889

BURNETT, David *(Judge, Arkansas Circuit Court Second Judicial Circuit)* Elected to term beginning Jan 1983. Reelected 1986, 1990, 1994, 1998 and 2002. Current term expires 2008. Born Blytheville Arkansas Aug 18, 1941. Christian. Educated at University of Arkansas B.A. in History and Political Science 1963 J.D. 1966. Member Phi Alpha Delta. Admitted to practice Arkansas 1966, U.S. District Courts Eastern and Western Districts of Arkansas, U.S. Court of Appeals Eighth Circuit and U.S. Supreme Court. In legal practice Osceola 1969-75. Former Chancellor, Arkansas Chancery Court Second Judicial Circuit.

Prosecuting Attorney Second Judicial District of Arkansas 1975-82. Guest Faculty member Hastings College of the Law 1981-82. Member Governor's Task Force on DWI, Governor's Task Force on Child Abuse and Criminal Detention Facilities Study Commission. Member Christian Legal Society, Arkansas Prosecuting Attorneys Association (Secretary 1975, Board of Directors since 1976, Vice President 1980-81 and President 1981-82), National District Attorneys Association, The Association of Trial Lawyers of America, Osceola (Past President and Secretary-Treasurer), Northeast Arkansas, Arkansas and American Bar Associations. Attended Prosecuting Attorney Course Northwestern University School of Law 1974, National Homicide Symposium California District Attorneys Association 1977, Trial and Evidence Course National College of District Attorneys 1978 and Criminal Trial Advocacy Course Hastings College of the Law 1979. Graduate The National Judicial College University of Nevada 1983. Named one of Outstanding Young Men of Arkansas 1975. Captain Military Police, Company Commander and Security Officer HAC U.S. Army 1967-69. Recipient Bronze Star, Army Commendation Award, Vietnam Campaign Ribbon Four Stars, Vietnam Service Ribbon and Vietnamese Government Staff Award. Worked in accounting office Agrico Chemical Company 1966. Member State Democratic Central Committee and County Democratic Central Committee. Secretary and Attorney Osceola Riverport Authority. Member Mississippi River Parkway Commission 1972-77. Past President Osceola Kiwanis. Board of Governors Presbyterian Christian Day School. Board member First Christian Church Osceola. Secretary Draft Board 106. Member Gideons, Osceola Boys Club, American Legion, Osceola Chamber of Commerce, Junior Chamber of Commerce and Veterans of Foreign Wars. Works with Boy Scouts in the Northeast Area Council. Enjoys golf, fishing, hunting, tennis, shooting and crafts.

Mailing address: P.O. Box 704, Osceola 72370.

Telephone: (870) 933-4579.

Fax: (870) 933-4596

CAPEHEART, Ted C. *(Judge, Arkansas Circuit Court Ninth West Judicial Circuit)* Elected to term beginning Jan 1, 1983. Reelected 1986, 1990, 1994, 1998 and 2002. Current term expires Dec 31, 2008. Serves Juvenile Division. Born Winthrop Arkansas Dec 17, 1947. Educated at Henderson State College B.A. 1969 and University of Arkansas J.D. 1975. Law Clerk to Hon. Thomas F. Butt, Arkansas Circuit Court Fourth Judicial Circuit 1975. Member Theta Xi. Began legal practice Ashdown 1975. Former Chancellor, Arkansas Chancery Court Ninth Judicial Circuit West.

Chief Deputy Prosecuting Attorney 1981-83. Member Arkansas Lawyers Association, Arkansas and American Bar Associations. First Lieutenant U.S. Army 1969-72. Democrat. Enjoys hunting, fishing, reading, music and travel.

Mailing address: P.O. Box 546, Ashdown 71822.

Telephone: (870) 898-7228.

Fax: (870) 898-7262

CAVANEAU, Jerry W. *(Magistrate Judge, United States District Court Eastern District of Arkansas)* Appointed by U.S. District Court judges.

Office: 360 U.S. Courthouse, 600 West Capitol Avenue, Little Rock 72201-3325.

Telephone: (501) 604-5200.

CHAMBERS, Rodney *(Judge, Magnolia District Court)* Term expires Dec 31, 2004.

Mailing address: P.O. Box 157, Magnolia 71753.

Telephone: (870) 234-1692.

CHANDLER, Larry *(Judge, Arkansas Circuit Court Thirteenth Judicial Circuit)* Former Chancellor, Arkansas Chancery Court Thirteenth Judicial Circuit. Served Juvenile Division.

Mailing address: P.O. Box 785, Magnolia 71753.

Telephone: (870) 235-3781.

Fax: (870) 235-3780

CHOATE, Stephen *(Judge, Arkansas Circuit Court Sixteenth Judicial Circuit)* Elected Nov 1990 to term beginning Jan 1, 1991. Reelected Nov 1994, 1998 and 2002. Current term expires Dec 31, 2008. Born Little Rock Arkansas July 24, 1944. Episcopalian. Educated at Hendrix College B.A. 1966 and University of Arkansas J.D. 1969. Member Delta Theta Phi. Admitted to practice Arkansas 1969, U.S. District Court Eastern District of Arkansas 1969 and Massachusetts 1981. In legal practice Little Rock Arkansas 1969-74 and Heber Springs Arkansas 1974-91. Judge, Heber Springs Municipal Court 1983-85 and 1987-89. Judge, Arkansas Circuit Court Sixteenth Judicial Circuit 1985-87, appointed

CHOATE, STEPHEN—*Continued*

by Governor William Clinton. Former Chancellor, Arkansas Chancery Court Sixteenth Judicial Circuit.
Mailing address: P.O. Box 525, Heber Springs 72543.
Telephone: (501) 362-3125.
Fax: (501) 362-4650

CLAWSON, Charles E., Jr. *(Judge, Arkansas Circuit Court Twentieth Judicial Circuit)* Former Chancellor, Arkansas Chancery Court Twentieth Judicial Circuit.
Office: Faulkner County Courthouse, Conway 72034.
Telephone: (501) 450-4970.
Fax: (501) 450-4972

CLINGER, David *(Judge, Arkansas Circuit Court Nineteenth West Judicial Circuit)*
Office: Courthouse Annex, 201 N.E. Second Street, Bentonville 72712.
Telephone: (479) 271-1063.
Fax: (479) 271-1050

COCHRAN, Edward *(Judge, Lewisville District Court)* Term expires Dec 31, 2004.
Mailing address: P.O. Box 335, Stamps 71860.
Telephone: (870) 921-4347.

COKER, Ken, Jr. *(Judge, Arkansas Circuit Court Fifth Judicial Circuit)* Serves Juvenile Division. Former Chancellor, Arkansas Chancery Court Fifth Judicial Circuit.
Mailing address: P.O. Box 2408, Russellville 72811.
Telephone: (479) 968-3869.
Fax: (479) 880-1810

COLLIER, Linda *(Judge, Arkansas Circuit Court Twentieth Judicial Circuit)* Serves Juvenile Division. Former Chancellor, Arkansas Chancery Court Twentieth Judicial Circuit.
Office: Faulkner County Courthouse, Conway 72034.
Telephone: (501) 450-4931.
Fax: (501) 450-9526

CONNER, Jeff *(Judge, Benton County-West District Court)*
Mailing address: P.O. Box 459, Gentry 72734.
Telephone: (479) 736-8579.

COOK, Vicki *(Judge, Arkansas Circuit Court Eighteenth East Judicial Circuit)* Serves Juvenile Division. Former Chancellor, Arkansas Chancery Court Eighteenth Judicial Circuit East.
Office: 224 Hazel Street, Hot Springs 71901.
Telephone: (501) 622-3770.
Fax: (501) 321-0067

CORBIN, Donald L. *(Associate Justice, Arkansas Supreme Court)* Elected Nov 1990 to term beginning Jan 1, 1991. Reelected 1998, current term expires Dec 31, 2006. Born Hot Springs Arkansas March 29, 1938. Church of Christ. Educated at University of Arkansas B.A. 1964 J.D. 1966. Member Sigma Alpha Epsilon. Admitted to practice Arkansas 1966 and U.S. District Court Western District of Arkansas 1966. In legal practice Lewisville and Stamps 1967-80. Judge 1981-87 and Chief Judge 1987-90, Arkansas Court of Appeals.
Member Southwest Arkansas, Arkansas and American (Council of Chief Judges 1983, 1987, 1989) Bar Associations. USMC 1955-59. Democrat. State Representative Arkansas General Assembly 1971-80. Enjoys duck hunting.
Office: Justice Building, 625 Marshall Street, Little Rock 72201.
Telephone: (501) 682-6838.

COTTRELL, Gary *(Judge, Arkansas Circuit Court Twenty-first Judicial Circuit)* Serves Juvenile Division. Former Judge, Van Buren Municipal Court. Former Chancellor, Arkansas Chancery Court Twenty-first Judicial Circuit.
Office: 25 County Courthouse, 300 Main Street, Van Buren 72956.
Telephone: (479) 474-6332.
Fax: (479) 471-3212

COXSEY, Kent *(Judge, Berryville District Court)* Term expires Dec 31, 2004.
Mailing address: P.O. Box 226, Berryville 72616.
Telephone: (870) 423-3948.
Fax: (870) 423-6411

CRABTREE, Terry *(Judge, Arkansas Court of Appeals)* Appointed by Governor Mike Huckabee to term beginning Jan 1, 1997. Elected Nov 2000 to term beginning Jan 1, 2001, current term expires Dec 31, 2008. Educated at University of Arkansas B.S. J.D. Former Judge, Arkansas Circuit Court Nineteenth Judicial Circuit. Former Chancellor, Arkansas Chancery Court Nineteenth Judicial Circuit.
Former Public Defender and City Attorney.
Office: Justice Building, 625 Marshall Street, Little Rock 72201.
Telephone: (501) 682-7951.

CRAVENS, David *(Judge, Paris District Court)* Term expires Dec 31, 2004.
Office: 24 East Main, Paris 72855.
Telephone: (479) 963-3131.

CULPEPPER, Duncan *(Judge, Arkansas Circuit Court Eighth North Judicial Circuit)* Serves Juvenile Division. Former Chancellor, Arkansas Chancery Court Eighth Judicial Circuit North.
Mailing address: P.O. Box 605, Prescott 71856-0605.
Telephone: (870) 887-8787.
Fax: (870) 887-3208

DALBY, Carol Cannedy *(Judge, Miller County and Texarkana District Courts)*
Mailing address: P.O. Box 3030, Texarkana 71854.
Telephone: (903) 735-4800.

DANIELSON, Paul *(Judge, Arkansas Circuit Court Fifteenth Judicial Circuit)*
Mailing address: P.O. Drawer 80, Booneville 72927.
Telephone: (479) 675-5145.
Fax: (479) 675-0207

DAVIS, Fred D. *(Judge, Arkansas Circuit Court Eleventh West Judicial Circuit)* Elected to term beginning Jan 1, 1989. Reelected 1992, 1996 and 2000. Current term expires Dec 31, 2008. Educated at University of Arkansas B.A. 1967 J.D. 1972. In legal practice 1978-88. Former Chancellor, Arkansas Chancery Court Eleventh Judicial Circuit West.
Chief Deputy Prosecuting Attorney Eleventh Circuit 1975-78.
Mailing address: P.O. Box 9140, Pine Bluff 71611.
Telephone: (870) 541-5465.
Fax: (870) 541-5337

DAWSON, Robert T. *(Judge, United States District Court Western District of Arkansas)* Appointed for life by President Bill Clinton to term beginning 1998. Born El Dorado Arkansas Aug 1, 1938. Educated at University of Arkansas B.A. 1960 LL.B. 1965. In legal practice Fort Smith 1965-98.
Mailing address: P.O. Box 1624, Fort Smith 72902-1624.
Telephone: (479) 783-2898.

DeSTEFANO, Peter L., Jr. *(Judge, Jasper District Court)* Elected Nov 1990 to term beginning Jan 1, 1991. Reelected 1994 and 1998. Current term expires Dec 31, 2004. Born Connecticut June 16, 1951. Educated at Yale University B.A. with honors 1973 and Fordham University J.D. with honors 1977. Admitted to practice New York 1977, Connecticut 1979, Arkansas 1981, U.S. District Courts Southern District of New York and Western District of Arkansas and U.S. Court of Appeals Second Circuit.
Mailing address: P.O. Box 316, Jasper 72641.
Telephone: (870) 741-8977.

DUNCAN, Xollie *(Judge, Arkansas Circuit Court Nineteenth West Judicial Circuit)* Assumed office July 1, 2001. Former Chancellor, Arkansas Chancery Court Nineteenth Judicial Circuit West.
Office: 220 Benton County Courthouse, Bentonville 72712.
Telephone: (479) 271-1024.
Fax: (479) 271-5706

DUNLAP, Jim *(Judge, Lepanto, Marked Tree and Tyronza District Courts)* Term expires Dec 31, 2004.
Mailing address: P.O. Box 386, Marked Tree 72365.
Telephone: (870) 358-4060.

EDWARDS, Robert *(Judge, Arkansas Circuit Court Seventeenth Judicial Circuit)* Former Chancellor, Arkansas Chancery Court Seventeenth Judicial Circuit.
Office: White County Courthouse, Searcy 72143.
Telephone: (501) 279-6212.
Fax: (501) 421-3285

EISELE, Garnett Thomas *(Senior Judge, United States District Court Eastern District of Arkansas)* Appointed for life by President Richard M. Nixon to term beginning Aug 17, 1970. Former Chief Judge. Assumed Senior status, serves by assignment. Born Hot Springs Arkansas Nov 3, 1923. Educated at University of Florida, Indiana University, Washington University A.B. final honors 1947 and Harvard University LL.B. 1950 LL.M. 1951. Admitted to practice Arkansas 1951. In legal practice Hot Springs 1951-53 and Little Rock 1960-70.

Assistant U.S. Attorney 1953-55. Important Decisions: Environmental Defense Fund et al. v. Corps of Engineers of the U.S. Army et al. 1970-72; George Hamilton et al. v. Monroe Love et al. 1971-73; Jim Lendall v. George O. Jernigan Jr. 1976; American Party v. George O. Jernigan 1977; Grigsby et al. v. Mabry et al. (jury impartiality) PB-C-78-32, 1980-83; Cryts et al. v. Lindsey (authority of bankruptcy judge) 1982; U.S.A. v. Brittman PB-C-88-444; Franz et al. v. Lockhart H-C-89-4; and M.C. Jeffers v. Bill Clinton. Member Judicial Conference Committees on Administration of the Federal Magistrates System 1978-87 and Administration of the Bankruptcy System 1983-88. Fellow Arkansas Bar Foundation and American Bar Foundation. Member William R. Overton Inn of Court, The American Law Institute, American Judicature Society, Federal Judges Association (Board of Directors since 1990), Pulaski County, Arkansas and American (Executive Committee National Conference of Federal Trial Judges since 1985) Bar Associations. Named Outstanding Federal Trial Court Judge in the Country by The Association of Trial Lawyers of America 1977, Best District Judge in Arkansas Circuit Court Eighth Judicial Circuit by *American Lawyers* publication 1980 and Outstanding Trial Judge by Arkansas Trial Lawyers Association 1988-89. Delegate Arkansas Constitutional Convention 1969. Private USAS 1942-46. Republican. Trustee University of Arkansas 1969-70. Enjoys jogging, swimming, flying and travel.
Office: 502 U.S. Courthouse, 600 West Capitol Avenue, Little Rock 72201-3325.
Telephone: (501) 604-5160.

ELDRIDGE, John D., III *(Judge, Augusta District Court)* Term expires Dec 31, 2004.
Mailing address: P.O. Box 479, Augusta 72006.
Telephone: (870) 347-2521.
Fax: (870) 347-5084

ELLEDGE, Steve *(Judge, Clarendon District Court)* Term expires Dec 31, 2004.
Office: 114 New York, Box 472, Brinkley 72021.
Telephone: (870) 734-1787.

EPLEY, Alan D. *(Judge, Arkansas Circuit Court Nineteenth East Judicial Circuit)* Assumed office July 1, 2001. Elected 2002, current term expires Dec 31, 2008. Serves Criminal, Civil, Probate, Domestic Relations and Juvenile Divisions. Born Fayetteville Arkansas Aug 31, 1945. Educated at University of Arkansas B.S.B.A. 1968 J.D. 1974. Admitted to practice Arkansas 1974. Began legal practice Eureka Springs 1974. Judge, Eureka Springs Municipal Court 1979-98. Former Chancellor, Arkansas Chancery Court Nineteenth Judicial Circuit East, elected to term beginning Jan 1, 1999.

Member Carroll-Madison County (President 1980-81), Arkansas and American Bar Associations. Staff Sergeant USAF 1969-72. Member Rotary Club of Eureka Springs.
Mailing address: P.O. Drawer 231, Berryville 72616.
Telephone: (870) 423-7131.
Fax: (870) 423-5824

ERWIN, Harold *(Judge, Arkansas Circuit Court Third Judicial Circuit)* Former Chancellor, Arkansas Chancery Court Third Judicial Circuit.
Office: Jackson County Courthouse, Newport 72112.
Telephone: (870) 523-7424.
Fax: (870) 523-7404

EVANS, Audrey R. *(Chief Judge, United States Bankruptcy Courts Eastern and Western Districts of Arkansas)* Appointed by U.S. Court of Appeals Eighth Circuit judges to term beginning Feb 17, 2002. Chief Judge since Jan 1, 2003.
Mailing address: P.O. Box 3274, Little Rock 72203-3274.
Telephone: (501) 918-5660.

FELTON, Dan, III *(Judge, Marianna District Court)* Term expires Dec 31, 2004.
Office: Six West Chestnut Street, Marianna 72360.
Telephone: (870) 295-5275.
Fax: (870) 295-4209

FERGUS, Wiliam Lee *(Judge, Arkansas Circuit Court Second Judicial Circuit)* Assumed office July 1,

FERGUS, WILIAM LEE—*Continued*

2001. Elected to term beginning Nov 5, 2002. Term expires Dec 31, 2008. Born Memphis Tennessee Sept 23, 1948. Christian. Educated at Westminster College B.A. 1970 and University of Arkansas J.D. 1975. Admitted to practice Arkansas 1975, U.S. District Court Eastern District of Arkansas 1975, U.S. Court of Appeals Eighth Circuit 1975, U.S. Tax Court 1980 and U.S. Supreme Court 1981. Judge, Osceola Municipal Court 1991-2000.

Deputy Prosecuting Attorney 1975-78.

Mailing address: P.O. Box 1472, Jonesboro 72403.
Telephone: (870) 933-4548.
Fax: (870) 933-7711
E-mail address: LFergus@craigheadcounty.org

FERGUSON, Gibbs *(Judge, McGehee District Court)* Elected Nov 1988 to term beginning Jan 1, 1989. Reelected Nov 1992, 1996 and 2000. Current term expires Dec 31, 2004. Born Desha County Arkansas July 27, 1943. Methodist. Educated at University of Arkansas at Monticello B.A. 1964 and University of Arkansas at Fayetteville M.A. 1966 J.D. 1971. Case Note Writer Arkansas Law Review 1966-67. Member Phi Alpha Delta. Admitted to practice Arkansas 1971, U.S. District Court Eastern District of Arkansas 1971 and U.S. Court of Appeals Eighth Circuit 1971. In legal practice McGehee since 1971.

City Attorney McGehee 1973-88. Deputy Prosecuting Attorney and Civil Attorney Desha County 1973-88. First Vice President Arkansas Municipal Judges Council 1992-93. Member Arkansas Bar Association. Attended Arkansas Municipal Judges College bi-annually 1988-92. Second Lieutenant USMC 1967-69. Political affiliation: Independent. Board of Directors First National Bank of McGehee since 1976. Member Lions Club and Chamber of Commerce. Interested in nature and conservation.

Office: 209 West Oak, McGehee 71654.
Telephone: (870) 222-6660.

FINCH, Jay *(Judge, Arkansas Circuit Court Nineteenth West Judicial Circuit)* Serves as Juvenile and Drug Court Judge. Former Chancellor, Arkansas Chancery Court Nineteenth Judicial Circuit West.

Office: 203 East Central, Bentonville 72712.
Telephone: (479) 271-1020.
Fax: (479) 271-5752

FINLEY, John C., III *(Judge, Ashdown District Court)* Elected to term beginning Jan 1, 1983. Reelected 1986, 1990, 1994 and 1998. Current term expires Dec 31, 2004. Born Texarkana Arkansas Jan 10, 1949. Member First Baptist Church Ashdown. Educated at Ouachita Baptist University B.A. magna cum laude 1971 and University of Arkansas School of Law J.D. 1974. Member Delta Theta Phi, Phi Theta Kappa and Alpha Chi. Admitted to practice Arkansas 1974, U.S. District Court Western District of Arkansas 1974 and U.S. Supreme Court 1980. Began legal practice Ashdown 1974.

Member American Judges Association, Southwest Arkansas (Vice President 1979-82, President 1982), Arkansas and American Bar Associations. Member Ashdown Rotary Club, Little River County Historical Society, Little River County Chamber of Commerce and Sons of the American Revolution. Church organist.

Mailing address: P.O. Box 405, Ashdown 71822.
Telephone: (870) 898-3147.

FITZHUGH, J. Michael *(Judge, Arkansas Circuit Court Twelfth Judicial Circuit)* Elected Nov 1998 to term beginning Jan 1, 1999. Reelected 2002, current term expires Dec 31, 2008. Born Little Rock Arkansas Aug 5, 1947. Educated at University of Arkansas B.A. 1969 J.D. 1973. Law Clerk to Hon J. Smith Henley, U.S. District Court Eastern District of Arkansas 1973-74 and Hon. Oren Harris, U.S. District Court Western District of Arkansas 1973-74. Member Phi Alpha Delta. Admitted to practice Arkansas 1973 and U.S. Supreme Court 1980. In legal practice Fort Smith 1993-99.

Assistant U.S. Attorney 1974-85 and U.S. Attorney 1985-93 Western District of Arkansas. Member Sebastian County and Arkansas Bar Associations.

Office: 35 South Sixth Street, Room 308, Fort Smith 72901.
Telephone: (479) 782-8667.
Fax: (479) 784-1566

FLEMING, Victor A. "Vic" *(Judge, Little Rock District Court)* Elected Nov 1996 to term beginning Jan 1, 1997. Reelected 2000, current term expires Dec 31, 2004. Serves Second Division. Born Jackson Mississippi Dec 26, 1951. Presbyterian (PCUSA). Educated at Davidson College B.A. 1973 and University of Arkansas at Little Rock J.D. 1978. Executive Editor University of Arkansas at Little Rock Law Journal 1978. Admitted to practice Arkansas 1978, U.S. Tax Court 1979 and U.S. Supreme Court 1982. In legal practice Little Rock 1978-97.

Author "Real Lawyers Do Change Their Briefs" Rose Publishing Company 1989 and "Law, Literature & Laughter" 1992 and "Perry's Dead! (and the 'Juice' is Loose)" 1995 I Swear Enterprises. Fellow Arkansas Bar Foundation (Member 1981-2001 and Chair 1989-2001 Legal Writing Committee). Member William R. Overton Inn of Court, Arkansas (Tenured Member House of Delegates) and American Bar Associations. Presenter "Stress Management" Workshop The National Judicial College 1998 and American Inns of Court Foundation 1999. Faculty Member The National Judicial College since 2000. Named Outstanding District Judge of the Year by Arkansas Bar Association 1999 and 2001 and Lawyer Citizen of the Year by Pulaski County Bar Association 1999. USAR 1970-73. Member 1986-96 and Chair 1991-94 Arkansas Educational Television Commission. Member Rotary Club of Little Rock (Director 1997-2000). Interests include golfing, creative problem solving, crosswords, humor and spirituality. Personal Statement or Quote: "Don't hide your dreams in the sunshine. Take them with you out to greet the dawn."

Office: 600 West Markham, Little Rock 72201.
Telephone: (501) 371-4733.

FOGLEMAN, John N. *(Judge, Arkansas Circuit Court Second Judicial Circuit)* Elected June 1994 to term beginning Jan 1, 1995. Reelected 1998 and 2002. Current term expires Dec 31, 2008. Born Memphis Tennessee Jan 2, 1956. Methodist. Educated at Arkansas State University B.S.E. with honors 1978 and University of Arkansas J.D. with honors 1981. Admitted to practice Arkansas 1981 and U.S. District Court Eastern District of Arkansas 1981. In legal practice West Memphis 1981. Former Chancellor, Arkansas Chancery Court Second Judicial Circuit.

City Attorney Marion 1982-94. Deputy Prosecuting Attorney Crittenden County 1984-94. Member Arkansas Judicial Council (Judicial Resources Assessment Com-

FOGLEMAN, JOHN N.—*Continued*

mittee 1995-2001) and Arkansas Bar Association (Executive Council, House of Delegates). Attended General Jurisdiction Course The National Judicial College July 1995. Member Marion School Board 1985-94. Enjoys running, golfing, gardening and reading.
Office: 206 River Trace Drive, Marion 72364.
Telephone: (870) 739-3156.
Fax: (870) 739-9826

FOLTZ, Harry Albers *(Judge, Arkansas Circuit Court Twelfth Judicial Circuit)* Assumed office July 1, 2001. Born Fort Smith Arkansas April 19, 1939. Episcopalian. Educated at Washington and Lee University A.B. 1962 and University of Arkansas J.D. 1965. Member Phi Delta Theta. Admitted to practice Arkansas 1965. Began legal practice Fort Smith 1965. Judge, Fort Smith Municipal Court 1983-86. Chancellor, Arkansas Chancery Court Twelfth Judicial Circuit Jan 1, 1987 to June 30, 2001.
Social Services Attorney Arkansas 1971-73. Legal Aid Attorney Sebastian County 1973-78. Executive Director Western Arkansas Legal Services 1978-83. Member Sebastian County (President 1980-81), Arkansas and American Bar Associations. Democrat. Former President Crawford Sebastian Community Development Corporation. Former Chairman Fort Smith Day Nursery. Former Board of Directors Fort Smith United Way and Lincoln Day Care Center. Vestry St. John's Episcopal Church. Member Rotary Club. Interests include boating, jogging and current events.
Office: 35 South Sixth Street, Room 309, Fort Smith 72901.
Telephone: (479) 782-0394.
Fax: (479) 784-1539

FORSTER, John F., Jr. *(Magistrate Judge, United States District Court Eastern District of Arkansas)* Appointed by U.S. District Court judges to term beginning March 14, 1986. Reappointed 1994 and March 2002. Current term expires 2010. Born Corsicana Texas Dec 18, 1942. Episcopalian. Educated at North Texas State University B.A. 1965 and University of Arkansas School of Law J.D. 1969. Staff member Arkansas Law Review 1967-68. Member Phi Alpha Delta. Admitted to practice Arkansas 1969, U.S. District Courts Eastern 1969 and Western 1970 Districts of Arkansas, Northern 1980 and Eastern 1982 Districts of Texas, Western District of Tennessee 1983 and Eastern District of Oklahoma 1984, U.S. Court of Appeals Eighth Circuit 1972 and U.S. Supreme Court 1972. In legal practice Little Rock 1969-72 and 1976-78 and North Little Rock 1978-86. Special Commissioner, Arkansas Workers' Compensation Commission 1979, appointed by governor.
Deputy Prosecuting Attorney Sixth Judicial District Arkansas 1972. Assistant U.S. Attorney Eastern District of Arkansas 1972-76. Author "The Police Executive in Arkansas Today" Arkansas Association of Chiefs of Police May 1978 and Chapter III "Grand Jury" *Arkansas Criminal Law Handbook* Arkansas Bar Association Sept 1985. Important Decisions: Hudson v. Lockhart (habeas corpus) 679 F. Supp. 891 E.D. Ark. 1986, Draper v. Red Devil, Inc. (discovery) 114 F.R.D. 46 1987 and Perry v. Chief of Police City of Marianna Arkansas (habeas corpus) 660 F. Supp. 1546 E.D. Ark. 1987. Adjunct Faculty University of Arkansas at Little Rock School of Law since 1973 and Memphis State University School of Law since 1987. Fellow American Board of Criminal Lawyers. Chairman Arkansas Workers' Compensation Revision Commission 1976-78. Certified Criminal Trial Advocate National Board of Trial Advocates since 1980. Member Arkansas Trial Lawyers Association (Board of Directors 1979-80), Pulaski County (Board of Directors 1984-85) and Arkansas (Chairman Workers' Compensation Institute 1978, member House of Delegates 1984-87, Vice Chair Specialization and Advertising Committee since 1986) Bar Associations. Attended U.S. Magistrates National Conference, New Orleans June 1986, Eighth Circuit Judicial Conference, Minneapolis July 1986, Arkansas Trial Lawyers Association Trial Practice Seminar Oct 1986 and National Employment Law Institute, Dallas 1986. Faculty Arkansas Advocacy Institute Spring 1988. Recipient Letter of Commendation for Successful Prosecution of Governments First Felony Jury Conviction, Wounded Knee Special Prosecution Unit 1974. Board of Directors Junior Baseball Program since 1984 and VOCALS (Volunteers of Central Arkansas Legal Services) since 1984. Enjoys hunting, fishing and cross-country running.
Office: 553 U.S. Courthouse, 600 West Capitol Avenue, Little Rock 72201-3325.
Telephone: (501) 604-5190.

FOSTER, Phil *(Judge, Camden District Court)* Term expires Dec 31, 2004.
Office: 213 Madison Street, Camden 71701.
Telephone: (870) 836-2794.

FOX, Tim *(Judge, Arkansas Circuit Court Sixth Judicial Circuit)*
Office: 401 West Markham, Room 210, Little Rock 72201.
Telephone: (501) 340-8416.
Fax: (501) 340-6047

GARDNER, Richard *(Judge, Arkansas Circuit Court Fifth Judicial Circuit)* Assumed office July 1, 2001. Former Chancellor, Arkansas Chancery Court Fifth Judicial Circuit.
Mailing address: P.O. Box 2692, Russellville 72801.
Telephone: (479) 968-2280.
Fax: (479) 968-6091

GARNER, Robert "Bob" *(Judge, Bradley County District Court)* Term expires Dec 31, 2004. Former Judge, Warren Municipal Court.
Mailing address: P.O. Box 352, Warren 71671.
Telephone: (870) 226-5155.

GARRETT, Robert *(Judge, Arkansas Circuit Court Twenty-second Judicial Circuit)* Assumed office July 1, 2001. Born Little Rock Arkansas Aug 12, 1947. Methodist. Educated at University of Arkansas B.S. 1972 J.D. 1975. Admitted to practice Arkansas 1975. Began legal practice Benton 1975. Chancellor, Arkansas Chancery Court Twenty-second Judicial Circuit Jan 1, 1985 to June 30, 2001.
Member Saline County and Arkansas Bar Associations. Specialist Five U.S. Army 1967-69. Democrat. Member VFW. Enjoys water sports.
Office: 200 North Main, Suite 204, Benton 72015.
Telephone: (501) 303-5635.
Fax: (501) 303-5636

GEARHART, Van *(Judge, Mountain Home District Court)* Term expires Dec 31, 2004.
Mailing address: P.O. Box 1823, Mountain Home 72654-1923.
Telephone: (870) 425-2196.

GIBSON, Bynum *(Judge, Arkansas Circuit Court Tenth Judicial Circuit)* Elected to term beginning Jan 1, 1998. Reelected 2002, current term expires Dec 31, 2008. Serves Criminal, Civil, Domestic Relations, Probate and Juvenile Divisions. Born Little Rock Arkansas June 27, 1949. Episcopalian. Educated at Trinity University B.A. 1971 and University of Arkansas School of Law J.D. 1974. Admitted to practice Arkansas and U.S. Court of Appeals Eighth Circuit. In legal practice 1975-98. Judge, Dermott Municipal Court 1982-87. Former Chancellor, Arkansas Chancery Court Tenth Judicial Circuit.
Member Arkansas Bar Association. State Representative 1987-93. Chairman Democratic Party of Arkansas 1993-98.
Office: Drew County Courthouse, 210 South Main, Monticello 71655.
Telephone: (870) 367-7604.
Fax: (870) 367-2092

GIBSON, Chuck *(Judge, Dermott District Court)* Term expires Dec 31, 2004.
Mailing address: P.O. Box 510, Dermott 71638.
Telephone: (870) 538-3288.

GIBSON, Mike *(Judge, Osceola District Court)*
Office: 317 West Hale, Osceola 72370.
Telephone: (870) 563-3700.
Fax: (870) 563-3714

GILLISON, David F., Jr. *(Judge, Lake Village District Court)* Appointed by Lake Village City Council to term beginning Jan 1, 1977. Elected 1978, 1982, 1986, 1990, 1994 and 1998. Current term expires Dec 31, 2004. Born Lake Village Arkansas March 24, 1939. Episcopalian. Educated at Rhodes College and University of Arkansas B.A. 1961 J.D. 1963. Admitted to practice Arkansas 1963. In legal practice Lake Village 1963-94. Judge, Eudora Municipal Court 1978-89.
Member Arkansas Bar Association.
Mailing address: P.O. Box 669, Lake Village 71653.
Telephone: (870) 265-2235.

GLADWIN, Robert *(Judge, Arkansas Court of Appeals)* Elected to term beginning Jan 1, 2003. Term expires Dec 31, 2010. Educated at University of Arkansas B.A. 1978 J.D. 1981. In legal practice Fayetteville 1984-85 and Prairie Grove 1985-2002. Judge, Lincoln City Court 1986-2000. Judge, Prairie Grove District Court 1986-2002. Magistrate, Arkansas Circuit Court Fourth Judicial Circuit 2002.
Office: Justice Building, 625 Marshall Street, Little Rock 72201.
Telephone: (501) 682-7474.

GLAZE, Tom *(Associate Justice, Arkansas Supreme Court)* Elected to term beginning Jan 1, 1987. Reelected 1994 and 2002. Current term expires Dec 31, 2010. Born Jan 14, 1938. Educated at University of Arkansas at Fayetteville B.S.B.A. 1960 LL.B. 1964 replaced by J.D. 1970. Member University of Arkansas Razorback Baseball Team 1957-60. Admitted to practice Arkansas, U.S. District Courts and U.S. Supreme Court. In legal practice 1970-79. Chancellor, Arkansas Chancery Court Sixth Judicial Circuit Jan 1979 to Dec 31, 1980. Judge, Arkansas Court of Appeals Jan 1, 1981 to Dec 31, 1986.
Executive Director Election Research Council, Inc. 1965. Legal Advisor and Office Manager for Winthrop Rockefeller 1965-66. Staff Attorney Pulaski County Legal Aid 1966-67. Assistant Attorney General and Deputy Attorney General (Head of Special Projects Division) 1967-70. Co-author Arkansas Election Code 1969 and Arkansas Consumer Act. Lecturer on Business Law 1971-72 and Adjunct Faculty Member 1979-82, 1985 and 1987 University of Arkansas at Little Rock. Chairman Special Advisory Committee to Arkansas State Board of Election Commissioners 1970-71. Legal Advisor to Pulaski County Board of Election Commissioners 1973-74. Contractual Consultant to Subcommittee on Elections House Administration Committee U.S. House of Representatives 1974. Member Arkansas Supreme Court ad hoc Committee on Foster Care and Adoption Assessment 1995. Initiated the Consumer Protection Division of the Attorney General's Office. Organizer, Past President and Chairman of the Board The Election Laws Institute, Inc. Member Pulaski County and Arkansas Bar Associations. Attended General Jurisdiction Session and Evidence Graduate Session The National Judicial College 1978, Appellate Opinion Writing The American Academy of Judicial Education 1983 and National Council of Juvenile and Family Court Judges Faculty Training Conference 1985 and 1988.
Office: Justice Building, 625 Marshall Street, Little Rock 72201.
Telephone: (501) 682-6870.

GLOVER, David Mac *(Judge, Malvern District Court)*
Mailing address: P.O. Box 454, Malvern 72104.
Telephone: (501) 337-9537.
Fax: (501) 337-9570

GLOVER, Don E. *(Judge, Arkansas Circuit Court Tenth Judicial Circuit)* Elected Nov 3, 1992 to term beginning Jan 4, 1993. Reelected 1996 and 2000. Current term expires Dec 31, 2004. Born Dermott Arkansas April 1, 1944. Baptist. Educated at University of Arkansas at Pine Bluff B.S. 1965 and Howard University J.D. 1973. Admitted to practice Arkansas 1974 and Louisiana 1976. In legal practice Monroe Louisiana 1979-81, Pine Bluff Arkansas 1981-84, Crossett Arkansas 1984-92 and Dermott Arkansas 1984-92. Judge, Dermott Municipal Court 1986-92.
Staff Attorney and Managing Attorney Legal Services 1974-79. Member W. Harold Flowers Law Society, Arkansas and Louisiana State Bar Associations. E-5 U.S. Army 1967-70. Peace Corps Volunteer Venezuela 1965-67. Enjoys tennis, jogging, reading and farming.
Mailing address: P.O. Box 398, McGehee 71654.
Telephone: (870) 222-6885.
Fax: (870) 222-4781

GOODNER, Donald *(Judge, Waldron District Court)* Elected to term beginning Jan 1, 1987. Reelected 1990, 1994 and 1998. Current term expires Dec 31, 2004. Born Fort Smith Arkansas Feb 24, 1942. Methodist. Educated at University of Arkansas B.S. 1965 J.D. 1968. Member Phi Alpha Delta. Admitted to practice Arkansas 1968, U.S. District Courts Western 1968 and Eastern 1971 Districts of Arkansas, U.S. Court of Appeals

GOODNER, DONALD—*Continued*

Eighth Circuit 1972 and U.S. Supreme Court 1972. In legal practice Waldron since 1968.

County Attorney 1975-78. City Attorney 1975-82. Member Arkansas Bar Association (House of Delegates 1976-78, Vice Chairman Real Estate Section 1986-87 and 1990-91 Title Insurance Section). Democrat. Member Waldron Area Chamber of Commerce.

Mailing address: P.O. Box 567, Waldron 72958.

Telephone: (479) 637-3286.

GOODSON, David *(Judge, Arkansas Circuit Court Second Judicial Circuit)* Elected June 12, 1990 to term beginning Jan 1, 1991. Reelected 1994, 1998 and 2002. Current term expires Dec 31, 2008. Born Jonesboro Arkansas May 29, 1951. Baptist. Educated at Arkansas State University B.A. 1973 and University of Arkansas J.D. 1976. Member Phi Delta Alpha. Admitted to practice Arkansas 1976 and U.S. District Court Eastern District of Arkansas 1976. In legal practice Paragould 1976-84. Judge, Greene County Municipal Court 1979-80. Former Chancellor, Arkansas Chancery Court Second Judicial Circuit.

Public Defender Greene County 1985-90.

Office: 320 West Court Street, Room 210, Paragould 72450.

Telephone: (870) 239-6331.

Fax: (870) 236-4185

GRAY, Alice Sprinkle *(Judge, Arkansas Circuit Court Sixth Judicial Circuit)* Assumed office July 1, 2001. Born Rison Arkansas Feb 6, 1954. African Methodist Episcopalian. Educated at Lincoln University B.S. 1976, University of Detroit 1979 and University of Arkansas at Little Rock J.D. 1984. Admitted to practice Arkansas 1984. Chancellor, Arkansas Chancery Court Sixth Judicial Circuit January 1, 1993 to June 30, 2001.

Staff Attorney and Managing Attorney Legal Services of Arkansas 1984-88. With City Attorney's Office Little Rock 1988-89. Important Decision: Bosnick v. Pledger (federal retirees' state income tax litigation) 1994. Member W. Harold Flowers Law Society, Pulaski County and Arkansas Bar Associations. Attended seminars on advanced evidence, constitutional criminal procedure and judicial reasoning and decision-making. Enjoys reading, sports and family activities.

Office: 401 West Markham, Room 350, Little Rock 72201.

Telephone: (501) 340-8530.

Fax: (501) 340-6035

GREEN, J. W., Jr. *(Judge, Stuttgart District Court)* Term expires Dec 31, 2004.

Mailing address: P.O. Box 848, Stuttgart 72160.

Telephone: (870) 673-1673.

GREGG, John *(Judge, Batesville District Court)*

Mailing address: P.O. Box 2496, Batesville 72503.

Telephone: (870) 793-7556.

Fax: (870) 793-6921

GRIFFEN, Wendell L. *(Judge, Arkansas Court of Appeals)* Appointed by Governor Jim Guy Tucker to term beginning Jan 1, 1996. Elected Nov 2000 to term beginning Jan 1, 2001, current term expires Dec 31, 2008. Born Prescott Arkansas. Educated at University of Arkansas B.A. 1973 J.D. 1979. In legal practice Little Rock.

Chairman Arkansas Workers' Compensation Commission April 1985 to Feb 1987.

Office: Justice Building, 625 Marshall Street, Little Rock 72201.

Telephone: (501) 682-7987.

GRIFFIN, Joe E. *(Judge, Arkansas Circuit Court Eighth South Judicial Circuit)* Serves Juvenile Division. Started felony drug court Arkansas Circuit Court Eighth Judicial District South Nov 2001. Born Nashville Arkansas Nov 28, 1949. Missionary Baptist. Deacon Central Baptist Church Texarkana. Educated at University of Arkansas B.S.B.A. 1971 J.D. 1974. Member Sigma Nu. Admitted to practice Arkansas 1974, U.S. District Court Western District of Arkansas 1974 and U.S. Supreme Court. Began legal practice Texarkana 1974. Former Judge, Texarkana Municipal Court, elected 1982 and 1986. Juvenile Court Referee, Miller County Juvenile Court 1983-89. Former Chancellor, Arkansas Chancery Court Eighth Judicial Circuit South.

City Attorney Texarkana April 1975 to Dec 1982. Member Arkansas Judicial Council, Texarkana (Past Secretary), Southwest Arkansas and Arkansas Bar Associations. Served to Captain USAR 1971-79. Democratic delegate to Arkansas State Convention 1982. Member Masons. Enjoys bass fishing, quail and deer hunting.

Office: Miller County Courthouse, Texarkana 71854.

Telephone: (870) 774-2421.

Fax: (870) 772-4680

GRUBER, Rita *(Judge, Arkansas Circuit Court Sixth Judicial Circuit)* Serves Juvenile Division. Former Chancellor, Arkansas Chancery Court Sixth Judicial Circuit.

Office: 3001 West Roosevelt, Little Rock 72204.

Telephone: (501) 340-6723.

Fax: (501) 340-7011

GRUBER, Wayne *(Judge, Pulaski County District Court)*

Office: 3001 West Roosevelt, Little Rock 72204.

Telephone: (501) 340-6832.

Fax: (501) 340-6899

GUNN, Mary Ann *(Judge, Arkansas Circuit Court Fourth Judicial Circuit)* Former Chancellor, Arkansas Chancery Court Fourth Judicial Circuit.

Mailing address: P.O. Box 4640, Fayetteville 72702.

Telephone: (479) 973-8420.

Fax: (479) 973-8426

GUNTER, James H., Jr. *(Judge, Arkansas Circuit Court Eighth North Judicial Circuit)* Elected to term beginning Jan 1, 1983. Reelected 1984, 1990, 1994, 1998 and 2002. Current term expires Dec 31, 2008. Born Atlanta Texas March 8, 1943. Baptist. Educated at Texas A&M University B.B.A. 1965 and University of Houston J.D. 1972. Member Delta Theta Phi. Admitted to practice Texas 1972, Arkansas 1973, U.S. District Court 1973 and U.S. Supreme Court 1980. Began legal practice Houston Texas 1972. In legal practice Hope Arkansas 1973. Former Chancellor, Arkansas Chancery Court Eighth Judicial Circuit North.

Prosecuting Attorney 1976-82. President Elect Arkansas Judicial Council. Member Southwest Arkansas, Arkansas and American Bar Associations. Member Lions Club. Enjoys golf and genealogy.

Mailing address: P.O. Box 621, Hope 71801.

Telephone: (870) 777-4544.

Fax: (870) 777-6568

GUTHRIE, David *(Judge, Arkansas Circuit Court Thirteenth Judicial Circuit)*
Office: 205 Union County Courthouse, 101 North Washington, El Dorado 71730.
Telephone: (870) 864-1968.
Fax: (870) 864-1969

HALE, Eugene *(Judge, Prescott District Court)* Term expires Dec 31, 2004.
Mailing address: P.O. Box 5, Prescott 71857.
Telephone: (870) 887-5634.
Fax: (870) 887-5634

HALE, Milas Howard, II *(Judge, Sherwood District Court)* Elected to term beginning Feb 1, 1971. Reelected to subsequent terms. Current term expires Dec 31, 2004. Born Belleville Arkansas Jan 2, 1935. Episcopalian. Educated at Arkansas Polytechnic College and University of Arkansas B.A. 1960 J.D. 1960 LL.B. 1960. Named Outstanding Debater of Arkansas 1957. Member Phi Alpha Delta. Admitted to practice Arkansas 1960. In legal practice Little Rock and North Little Rock since 1960.
With the Prosecuting Attorney's Office Pulaski County 1960. Deputy Prosecuting Attorney Pulaski County 1960-61. Deputy Attorney General of Arkansas 1961-63. City Attorney Sherwood 1968-71. Author "Arkansas Labor Law Handbook" State of Arkansas 1963 and "Laws and Ordinances of Sherwood" Central Printing 1969. Instructor adult Business Law class since 1971. Member Arkansas Municipal Judges Association (Secretary since 1975), Pulaski County, North Pulaski County, Arkansas and American Bar Associations. Second Lieutenant U.S. Army 1960. Democrat. Enjoys fishing.
Office: 4801 North Hills Boulevard, #1550, North Little Rock 72116.
Telephone: (501) 753-4800.

HALL, W. Q. *(Judge, Huntsville District Court)* Term expires Dec 31, 2004.
Mailing address: P.O. Box 7, Huntsville 72740.
Telephone: (479) 738-2410.

HAMILTON, Jim *(Judge, North Little Rock District Court)* Term expires Dec 31, 2004. Serves Civil/Criminal Division.
Office: 200 West Pershing Boulevard, North Little Rock 72114.
Telephone: (501) 791-8559.

HANNAH, Craig *(Judge, Arkansas Circuit Court Seventeenth Judicial Circuit)*
Office: Courts Building, Searcy 72143.
Telephone: (501) 279-6221.
Fax: (501) 279-6224

HANNAH, Jim *(Associate Justice, Arkansas Supreme Court)* Elected to term beginning Jan 1, 2001. Term expires Dec 31, 2008. Born Long Beach California Dec 26, 1944. Presbyterian. Educated at Drury College 1962-63 and University of Arkansas at Fayetteville B.S.B.A. 1968 J.D. 1968. Admitted to practice Arkansas 1968 and U.S. District Court Eastern District of Arkansas 1968. Began legal practice Searcy 1968. Judge, Kensett City Court 1972-78, Rose Bud City Court 1972-78 and White County Juvenile Court 1974-78. Special Chancellor, Arkansas Chancery Court Oct 1978 to Dec 1978. Chancellor, Arkansas Chancery Court Seventeenth Judicial Circuit Jan 1, 1979 to 2000.
City Attorney Searcy 1969-78, Augusta 1969-71, Bradford 1969-71, Garner 1970-78 and Des Arc 1972-78. Deputy Prosecuting Attorney Woodruff County 1971. Secretary Arkansas State Board of Pardons and Paroles 1971-78. Legislative Aide to Governor Dale Bumpers 1972. Instructor in Business Law Harding College 1978. Chairman Court Reporters Examiners Board since 1992 and Judicial Resources Assessment Committee 1994-95 and President 1995-96 Arkansas Judicial Council. Member White County (Secretary-Treasurer 1969, Vice President 1970, President 1971) and Arkansas Bar Associations. Attended The American Judicial Academy 1979 and 1985 and The National Judicial College 1979-84 and 1986. Faculty Advisor The National Judicial College 1982 and 1986. Democrat. Co-chairman Dale Bumpers for Governor White County 1970 and 1972. Chairman Dale Bumpers for U.S. Senate 1974. Delegate State Democratic Convention 1970, 1972, 1974, 1976 and 1978. Board member Alcoholic Halfway House. Chairman White County Heart Fund 1969 and Searcy Little League Basketball since 1970 (Coach). President University of Arkansas Medical School Parents Club 1992-93. Member Searcy Kiwanis Club (Past Treasurer and Secretary) and Chamber of Commerce. Little League baseball coach and former member Searcy Little League baseball committee. Enjoys tennis, basketball and spectator sports.
Office: Justice Building, 625 Marshall Street, Little Rock 72201.
Telephone: (501) 682-6873.

HANSHAW, Lance *(Judge, Arkansas Circuit Court Twenty-third Judicial Circuit)* Elected to term beginning 1991. Reelected to subsequent terms. Current term expires 2008. Serves Criminal, Civil, Probate, Domestic Relations and Juvenile Divisions. Born Black Oak Arkansas Oct 20, 1938. Protestant. Former Judge, Cabot and Lonoke Municipal Courts. Former Chancellor, Arkansas Chancery Court Twenty-third Judicial Circuit.
Office: 301 North Center, Suite 303, Lonoke 72086-0219.
Telephone: (501) 676-3131.
Fax: (501) 676-3034

HARKEY, Adam *(Judge, Mountain View District Court)* Term expires Dec 31, 2004.
Mailing address: HC 71 Box 4, Mountain View 72560.
Telephone: (870) 269-3465.

HARKEY, John Norman *(Judge, Arkansas Circuit Court Sixteenth Judicial Circuit)* Former Chancellor, Arkansas Chancery Court Sixteenth Judicial Circuit.
Mailing address: P.O. Box 2656, Batesville 72503.
Telephone: (870) 793-8890.
Fax: (870) 793-8888

HARPER, Kenneth A. *(Judge, Monticello District Court)* Elected Nov 4, 1998 to term beginning Jan 1, 1999. Term expires Dec 31, 2004. Born Pine Bluff Arkansas Nov 16, 1960. Catholic. Educated at University of Arkansas at Fayetteville B.S.P.A. 1982 and University of Arkansas at Little Rock J.D. 1989. Admitted to practice Arkansas 1989, Tennessee 1990 and U.S. District Courts Eastern and Western Districts of Arkansas and Western District of Tennessee. In legal practice West Memphis Arkansas and Memphis Tennessee 1989-91 and Monticello Arkansas 1991-2001.
Member Southeast Arkansas Legal Institute, Arkansas Trial Lawyers Association and Arkansas Bar Association. Attended The National Judicial College 2000. Polit-

HARPER, KENNETH A.—*Continued*
ical affiliation: Independent. President Board of Directors Boys and Girls Club of Drew County.
Mailing address: P.O. Drawer 487, Monticello 71657.
Telephone: (870) 367-6102.
Fax: (870) 367-9224
E-mail address: harperlaw@seark.net

HARPER, Victor *(Judge, Lincoln County and Star City District Courts)* Term expires Dec 31, 2004.
Office: 717 South Lincoln, Star City 71667.
Telephone: (870) 628-4118.

HARROD, Reid *(Judge, Hamburg District Court)* Term expires Dec 31, 2004.
Mailing address: P.O. Box 310, Hamburg 71646.
Telephone: (870) 853-5236.

HART, Josephine Linker *(Judge, Arkansas Court of Appeals)* Elected to term beginning Jan 1999. Term expires Dec 31, 2006. Born Russellville Arkansas. Educated at Arkansas Tech University 1965 and University of Arkansas School of Law J.D. 1971. Law Clerk to Hon. Frank Holt, Arkansas Supreme Court Jan 1971 to June 1972. In legal practice Batesville 1972-99. Colonel USAR JAGC 1965-98.
Office: Justice Building, 625 Marshall Street, Little Rock 72201.
Telephone: (501) 682-7470.

HAYES, Wm. Larry *(Judge, Hoxie and Walnut Ridge District Courts)* Term expires Dec 31, 2004.
Mailing address: P.O. Box 404, Walnut Ridge 72476.
Telephone: (870) 886-9797.

HEARNSBERGER, Marcia Renaud *(Judge, Hot Springs District Court)* Elected to term beginning Jan 1, 1999. Term expires Dec 31, 2004. Born Dearborn Michigan Nov 7, 1954. Catholic. Educated at University of Dallas B.A. cum laude 1976 and University of Arkansas at Fayetteville J.D. 1979. Admitted to practice Arkansas. Judge, Arkansas Circuit Court Eighteenth Judicial Circuit East Oct 1997 to Dec 31, 1998, appointed by Governor Mike Huckabee.
Deputy Prosecuting Attorney and Chief Deputy Prosecuting Attorney Garland and Pulaski Counties 1979-97. Board member YMCA. President St. Johns Pastoral Council. Enjoys tennis.
Mailing address: P.O. Box 700, Hot Springs 71902.
Telephone: (501) 321-6761.

HENDREN, Jimm Larry *(Chief Judge, United States District Court Western District of Arkansas)* Appointed for life by President George Bush to term beginning 1992. Chief Judge since 1997. Born Gravette Arkansas June 11, 1940. Educated at University of Arkansas B.A. 1964 LL.B. 1965. In legal practice Bentonville 1968-69, 1970-77 and 1979-92. Chancellor, Arkansas Chancery Court Sixteenth Judicial Circuit 1977-78.
Mailing address: P.O. Box 3487, Fayetteville 72702-3487.
Telephone: (479) 444-7876.

HENRY, David *(Judge, Arkansas Circuit Court Eleventh East Judicial Circuit)*
Mailing address: P.O. Box 1166, Stuttgart 72160.
Telephone: (870) 673-3181.
Fax: (870) 673-1168

HEWETT, Mark *(Judge, Arkansas Circuit Court Twelfth Judicial Circuit)* Serves Juvenile Division. Former Chancellor, Arkansas Chancery Court Twelfth Judicial Circuit.
Office: 35 South Sixth Street, Room 305, Fort Smith 72901.
Telephone: (479) 783-1727.
Fax: (479) 784-1543

HILL, Randy *(Judge, Arkadelphia District Court)* Term expires Dec 31, 2004.
Office: 308A Clay Street, Arkadelphia 71923.
Telephone: (870) 230-8500.
Fax: (870) 230-8501

HILL, Victor *(Judge, Arkansas Circuit Court Second Judicial Circuit)*
Mailing address: P.O. Box 768, West Memphis 72303.
Telephone: (870) 735-0707.
Fax: (870) 735-1567

HOLTHOFF, Howard "Corky" *(Judge, Dumas District Court)* Term expires Dec 31, 2004.
Office: 152 South Main, Dumas 71639.
Telephone: (870) 382-2444.

HONEYCUTT, Pamela *(Judge, Arkansas Circuit Court Second Judicial Circuit)* Elected to term beginning Jan 2003. Term expires Dec 31, 2008. Born Craighead County Arkansas Oct 26, 1960. Educated at Arkansas State University B.S. 1983, University of Arkansas at Fayetteville School of Law J.D. 1985 and Emory University LL.M. in Litigation 1988. Admitted to practice Arkansas 1986, U.S. District Court District of Arkansas 1986, U.S. Court of Appeals Eighth Circuit 1987 and Georgia 1989. Judge, Jonesboro and Lake City District Courts Jan 1997 to Jan 2003.
City Attorney Jonesboro Dec 1989 to Dec 1994. Member Arkansas District Judges Council, American Judges Association, State Bar of Georgia, Craighead County and Arkansas Bar Associations. Completed series of "Campus Court" programs where actual court is conducted in high school auditorium. Member Business and Professional Women, ALTRUSA and Lions Club. Enjoys traveling, riding motorcycles and remodeling old homes.
Mailing address: P.O. Box 1951, Jonesboro 72403-1951.
Telephone: (870) 933-4594.
Fax: 933-7707
E-mail address: phoneycutt@craigheadcty.org

HOWARD, George, Jr. *(Judge, United States District Court Eastern District of Arkansas)* Appointed for life by President Jimmy Carter March 1980 to term beginning Oct 30, 1980. Born Pine Bluff Arkansas May 13, 1924. Southern Baptist. Educated at Lincoln University 1948-50 and University of Arkansas School of Law at Fayetteville B.S. J.D. Awarded honorary LL.D. Morris-Booker Memorial College. Member Alpha Phi Alpha. Admitted to practice Arkansas 1953, U.S. District Court 1953, U.S. Court of Appeals Eighth Circuit 1959 and U.S. Supreme Court 1959. In legal practice Pine Bluff 1953-79. Associate Justice, Arkansas Supreme Court 1977-78. Judge, Arkansas Court of Appeals 1979-80.
Member Arkansas State Claims Commission. Important Decisions: In re State of Missouri 7 B.R. 974, 1980; Boyd v. McGehee School District 612 F. Supp.

HOWARD, GEORGE, JR.—*Continued*

86; Sherpell v. Humnoke School District 619 F. Supp. 670; Lewellen v. Raff 649 F. Supp. 1229; Claiborne v. Beebe School District 687 F. Supp. 1358; Armstrong v. Sims 715 F. Supp. 1440, E.D. Ark. 1989; Allen v. Lincoln County Election Commission 789 F. Supp. 976, E.D. Ark. 1992; Phillips v. Sugrue 800 F. Supp. 879, E.D. Ark. 1992; Breshear v. Butt 863 F. Supp. 913, E.D. Ark. 1994; and McKay, et al. v. County Election Commissioners for Pulaski County Arkansas, et al. W.J., F.R.D. 1994 WL688275, 3 A.D. Cases 1601 E.D. Ark. Nov 29, 1994. Member Arkansas Judicial Council, American Judicature Society, Jefferson County (President 1974-75), Arkansas and American Bar Associations. Recipient Distinguished Jurist Award from National Bar Association 1980, Supreme Court Committee on Professional Conduct Award 1980, Outstanding Trial Judge's Award from Arkansas Trial Lawyers Association 1984-85 and Wiley A. Branton Symposium Award from National Bar Association Nov 3, 1989. Inducted into Arkansas Black Hall of Fame Oct 1, 1994. Petty Officer Third Class (coxswain) USN 1943-46. Member New Town Missionary Baptist Church (Superintendent of Church School, Board of Trustees), Prince Hall Grand Lodge, F&AM of Arkansas (33° Mason) and Arkansas Endowment for the Humanities. Enjoys fishing and hunting.

Office: 276 U.S. Courthouse, 600 West Capitol Avenue, Little Rock 72201-3325.
Telephone: (501) 604-5120.

HUBBELL, Billy *(Judge, Crossett District Court)* Term expires Dec 31, 2004.
Mailing address: P.O. Box 574, Crossett 71635.
Telephone: (870) 364-6114.

HUDSON, Jim *(Judge, Arkansas Circuit Court Eighth South Judicial Circuit)* Serves Juvenile Division. Former Chancellor, Arkansas Chancery Court Eighth Judicial Circuit South.
Office: Miller County Courthouse, Texarkana 71854.
Telephone: (870) 772-9618.
Fax: (870) 773-3354

HUGHES, Thomas M., III *(Judge, Beebe District Court)* Elected Nov 1984 to term beginning Jan 1, 1985. Reelected Nov 1988, 1992, 1996 and 2000. Current term expires Dec 31, 2004. Born Racine Wisconsin June 14, 1949. Presbyterian. Educated at University of Wisconsin-Madison B.B.A. with distinction 1971 and St. Louis University J.D. 1974. Admitted to practice Arkansas 1974. In legal practice Beebe 1974-92 and Searcy since 1992.

Member Arkansas District Judges Association, American Judges Association, White County and Arkansas Bar Associations. Political affiliation: Independent. Member Searcy Country Club. Enjoys golf.
Mailing address: P.O. Box 91, Searcy 72143.
Telephone: (501) 268-0504.

HUMPHREY, Marion *(Judge, Arkansas Circuit Court Sixth Judicial Circuit)* Former Judge, Little Rock Municipal Court.
Office: 401 West Markham, Room 420, Little Rock 72201.
Telephone: (501) 340-8590.
Fax: (501) 340-6039

IMBER, Annabelle Clinton *(Associate Justice, Arkansas Supreme Court)* Elected 1996 to term beginning Jan 1, 1997. Term expires Dec 31, 2006. Educated at Smith College B.A. 1971 and University of Arkansas School of Law J.D. 1977. In legal practice Little Rock 1977-88. Judge, Arkansas Circuit Court Sixth Judicial Circuit 1984. Chancellor, Arkansas Chancery Court Sixth Judicial Circuit 1989-96.
Office: Justice Building, 625 Marshall Street, Little Rock 72201.
Telephone: (501) 682-6867.

INBODEN, Steve *(Judge, Harrisburg and Trumann District Courts)* Term expires Dec 31, 2004.
Mailing address: P.O. Box 22, Trumann 72472.
Telephone: (870) 483-7682.

INMAN-CAMPBELL, Gail *(Judge, Harrison District Court)*
Mailing address: P.O. Box 1940, Harrison 72601.
Telephone: (870) 741-3448.

IRWIN, Michael E. *(Judge, Heber Springs District Court)* Elected to term beginning 1997. Reelected 2000, current term expires Dec 31, 2004. Born Heber Springs Arkansas Aug 11, 1948. Educated at University of Arkansas B.S.B.A. 1970 J.D. 1973. Admitted to practice Arkansas 1973, U.S. District Court District of Arkansas 1873 and U.S. Supreme Court 1975. In legal practice Heber Springs since 1973.

Member Arkansas Municipal Judges Association, American Judges Association, Cleburne County, Arkansas and American Bar Associations.
Mailing address: P.O. Box 368, Heber Springs 72543.
Telephone: (501) 362-5806.
Fax: (501) 362-8715
E-mail address: splash@arkansas.net

ISBELL, Gary B. *(Judge, Arkansas Circuit Court Fourteenth Judicial Circuit)* Elected Nov 4, 1989 to term beginning Jan 9, 1990. Reelected 1994, 1998 and 2002. Current term expires Dec 31, 2008. Serves Juvenile and Probate Divisions. Born Wichita Kansas Dec 12, 1948. Christian. Educated at Harding University B.A. 1971 and University of Arkansas J.D. 1974. Admitted to practice Arkansas 1974, U.S. District Courts Eastern and Western Districts of Arkansas, U.S. Court of Appeals Eighth Circuit and U.S. Supreme Court. In legal practice Yellville 1979-88 and Mountain Home 1988-90. Former Chancellor, Arkansas Chancery Court Fourteenth Judicial Circuit.

Assistant Attorney General 1974-77. Deputy Prosecuting Attorney Fourteenth Judicial Circuit 1977-90. Enjoys fishing, gardening and raising children.
Mailing address: 301 East Sixth Street, Suite 154, Mountain Home 72653-3903.
Office: Baxter County Courthouse, One East Seventh Street, Mountain Home 72653.
Telephone: (870) 425-8625.
Fax: (870) 425-8630
E-mail address: judgeisbell@centurytel.net

IVES, Dan *(Judge, East Camden District Court)* Term expires Dec 31, 2004.
Office: 3060 Roseman, Camden 71701.
Telephone: (870) 836-4166.

JAMES, Dennis Lee *(Judge, Wrightsville District Court)* Appointed by Mayor Lorraine D. Smith Jan 1990. Elected Nov 1990, Nov 1994 and 1998. Current

JAMES, DENNIS LEE—*Continued*

term expires Dec 31, 2004. Born Little Rock Arkansas Sept 22, 1954. Protestant. Educated at University of Arkansas at Little Rock B.A. 1975 J.D. 1978. Member Phi Alpha Delta. Admitted to practice Arkansas 1978, U.S. District Courts Eastern 1978 and Western 1980 Districts of Arkansas, U.S. Court of Appeals Eighth Circuit 1978 and U.S. Supreme Court 1981. In legal practice Little Rock since 1978. Judge, City Court of Wrightsville 1986-89.

Deputy Prosecuting Attorney Sixth Judicial District 1978-79. Member Arkansas Municipal Judges Council (Board Member 1997-98, Secretary/Treasurer 1998-99, Second Vice President 1999-2000, First Vice President 2000-01, President 2001-02, Chairman ad hoc Subcommittee for revision of Arkansas Rules for Inferior Courts), American Judges Association, Pulaski County and Arkansas Bar Associations. Speaker Arkansas Rules of Civil Procedure—Inferior Court Rules National Business Institute Seminar June 21, 1994 and "Defining the Role of Court Clerk" Judicial Ethics Municipal Court Clerk's Association Sept 1999. Committeeman Pulaski County Democratic Party 1974-76. Participated in Feed the Multitudes/Union Rescue Mission. Judge State Citizen Bee Scholarship Contest 1987-91. Member Triumph Marque Leader 1999 and 2000 and British Motoring Club of Arkansas. Interests include vintage British sports cars, historical re-enacting (pioneer, civil war, western and Native American) and music (guitar, banjo and vocals).

Office: 519 East Capitol, 2-West, Little Rock 72202.
Telephone: (501) 376-9654.
Fax: (501) 376-8479

JAMISON, Leon *(Judge, Arkansas Circuit Court Eleventh West Judicial Circuit)* Assumed office July 1, 2001. Former Chancellor, Arkansas Chancery Court Eleventh Judicial Circuit West.

Office: 204 Jefferson County Courthouse, Pine Bluff 71611.
Telephone: (870) 541-5383.
Fax: (870) 541-5385

JENKINS, Claude *(Judge, DeWitt District Court)* Term expires Dec 31, 2004.

Mailing address: P.O. Box 409, DeWitt 72042.
Telephone: (870) 946-3586.

JOHNSON, Kirk D. *(Judge, Arkansas Circuit Court Eighth South Judicial Circuit)* Born Minden Louisiana Sept 27, 1949. Baptist. Educated at University of Arkansas B.S.B.A. 1971 J.D. 1974. Member Phi Alpha Delta. Admitted to practice Arkansas 1974, Texas 1975 and U.S. District Courts Western District of Arkansas 1974 and Eastern District of Texas 1975. In legal practice Texarkana Arkansas 1974-90. Former Judge, Miller County and Texarkana District Courts, elected to term beginning Jan 1, 1991.

Deputy Prosecuting Attorney 1977-82 and Prosecuting Attorney 1983-86 Eighth Judicial District. Member State Bar of Texas and Arkansas Bar Association. Democrat. Enjoys playing golf, snow skiing and water skiing.

Office: 304 Miller County Courthouse, Texarkana 71854.
Telephone: (870) 774-7722.
Fax: (870) 774-0008

JONES, Berlin *(Judge, Arkansas Circuit Court Eleventh West Judicial Circuit)*

Office: Jefferson County Courthouse, Pine Bluff 71611.
Telephone: (870) 541-5368.
Fax: (870) 536-8937

JONES, Beverly Stites *(Magistrate Judge, United States District Court Western District of Arkansas)* Appointed by U.S. District Court judges.

Mailing address: P.O. Box 1525, Fort Smith 72902-1525.
Telephone: (479) 783-7045.

JONES, Casey *(Judge, West Fork District Court)* Term expires Dec 31, 2004.

Mailing address: P.O. Box 339, West Fork 72774.
Telephone: (479) 839-3249.

JONES, Edward *(Judge, Arkansas Circuit Court Thirteenth Judicial Circuit)* Assumed office July 1, 2001. Former Chancellor, Arkansas Chancery Court Thirteenth Judicial Circuit.

Office: Union County Courthouse, El Dorado 71730.
Telephone: (870) 864-1937.
Fax: (870) 864-1937

JONES, Henry Louis, Jr. *(Magistrate Judge, United States District Court Eastern District of Arkansas)* Appointed by U.S. District Court judges to term beginning Dec 1978. Reappointed Dec 1986, Dec 22, 1994 and Dec 2002. Current term expires Dec 2010. Born Little Rock Arkansas March 27, 1945. Baptist. Educated at Yale University B.A. 1967 and University of Michigan Law School J.D. 1972. Law Clerk to Hon. G. Thomas Eisele, U.S. District Court Eastern District of Arkansas June 1972 to July 1973 and Hon. Gerald W. Heaney, U.S. Court of Appeals Eighth Circuit July 1973 to July 1974. Summer Tutor for first year law students. Member Elihu Senior Society, Black Law Students Alliance and Washtenaw County Legal Aid Society. In legal practice Little Rock 1974-78.

Member Arkansas Humanities Council 1987-92. Member Committee on Codes of Conduct Judicial Conference of the U.S. Member Arkansas Council N.C.C.J. Librarian Yale History of Art Library 1964-67 (school terms). Instructor Arkansas Economic Opportunity Agency Study Centers 1967-69. Research Associate Rockefeller Public Relations Little Rock 1967-69. Research Assistant to Ann Arbor City Attorney 1969-71. Attorney for Washtenaw County Legal Aid Society 1970. Instructor in Trial Practice University of Arkansas at Little Rock School of Law 1981. Previously worked for Hoerner Box Company Little Rock 1964, as postal clerk Little Rock Post Office 1965 and in direct mail advertising department Olin Mathieson Corporation 1966. Member Arkansas Human Relations Council 1963. Board of Directors Winthrop Rockefeller Foundation 1975-78, 1979-89 and since 1994, Carver YMCA 1981-90, University of Central Arkansas Foundation Jan 1989-90 and Little Rock Arts and Humanities Promotion Commission 1986-90. Board of Trustees University of Central Arkansas 1975-89. Member, Deacon and Trustee Mount Zion Baptist Church.

Office: 521 U.S. Courthouse, 600 West Capitol Avenue, Little Rock 72201-3325.
Telephone: (501) 604-5170.

ARKANSAS

KEATON, Edwin A. *(Judge, Arkansas Circuit Court Thirteenth Judicial Circuit)* Born Little Rock Arkansas June 13, 1952. Baptist. Educated at University of Arkansas at Fayetteville B.A. 1974 J.D. 1977. Admitted to practice Arkansas 1977, U.S. District Court Western District of Arkansas 1978 and U.S. Court of Appeals Eighth Circuit 1982. In legal practice Camden since 1977. Former Judge, Camden and East Camden Municipal Courts, elected to terms beginning March 8, 1983. Former Chancellor, Arkansas Chancery Court Thirteenth Judicial Circuit.

Member Harold Flowers Law Society, Ouachita County (Vice President 1981-84) and Arkansas Bar Associations. Enjoys tennis, chess and golf.

Office: 145 Jefferson Street, Box 8, Camden 71701.
Telephone: (870) 837-2270.
Fax: (870) 837-2273

KEITH, Tom J. *(Judge, Arkansas Circuit Court Nineteenth West Judicial Circuit)* Assumed office Jan 1, 1987. Born Danville Arkansas Nov 12, 1938. Educated at University of Arkansas B.A. 1970 J.D. 1973. Admitted to practice Arkansas 1973. Former Chancellor, Arkansas Chancery Court Nineteenth Judicial Circuit. Judge, Rogers Municipal Court 1983-86.

Journalist 1960-71. Member Benton County and Arkansas Bar Associations. Private First Class USMC 1957-60. Republican. Member Exchange Club, Youth Baseball and Chamber of Commerce.

Office: 225 Benton County Courthouse, Bentonville 72712.
Telephone: (479) 271-1026.
Fax: (479) 271-5708

KEMP, John Dan, Jr. *(Judge, Arkansas Circuit Court Sixteenth Judicial Circuit)* Elected to term beginning Jan 1, 1987. Reelected 1990, 1994, 1998 and 2002. Current term expires Dec 31, 2008. Born Batesville Arkansas Sept 8, 1951. Church of Christ. Educated at University of Arkansas B.A. 1973 J.D. 1976. Admitted to practice Arkansas 1976. Began legal practice Mountain View 1976. Judge, Mountain View Municipal Court 1977-86, appointed by Governor David Pryor. Judge, Calico Rock City Court 1979-81. Juvenile Court Referee, Stone County Juvenile Court 1980-82. Former Chancellor, Arkansas Chancery Court Sixteenth Judicial Circuit.

City Attorney Mountain View Jan 1, 1977 to Aug 4, 1977. Member Arkansas Municipal Judges Council (President 1984-85), Arkansas and American Bar Associations. Toll Fellow Council of State Governments Kentucky 1986. Previously employed by Arkhola Sand and Gravel Company Engineering Department, Van Buren Arkansas summers 1971-73. Democrat. Delegate Arkansas Constitutional Convention 1979-80 and Democratic State and National Conventions 1984. Democratic State Committeeman for Stone County 1984-86. Member Mountain View Area Chamber of Commerce (Board of Directors 1979-84 and 1985-87, President 1981-82 and 1986-87), Mountain View Lions Club (President 1977-79), Stone County Historical Society (Board of Directors 1985-87), Stone County Tennis Association (President 1986-87) and Blue Mountain Masonic Lodge 202 (Treasurer 1983-95). Enjoys tennis, fishing, golf and softball.

Mailing address: P.O. Box 329, Mountain View 72560.
Telephone: (870) 269-8989.
Fax: (870) 269-8964

KILGORE, Collins *(Judge, Arkansas Circuit Court Sixth Judicial Circuit)* Assumed office July 1, 2001. Former Chancellor, Arkansas Chancery Court Sixth Judicial Circuit.

Office: 401 West Markham, Room 330, Little Rock 72201.
Telephone: (501) 340-8534.
Fax: (501) 340-5625

KING, Kevin N. *(Judge, Arkansas Circuit Court Third Judicial Circuit)* Born Fort Leonard Wood Missouri Jan 20, 1954. Religious affiliation: Church of Christ. Educated at University of Arkansas B.S.B.A. 1976 J.D. 1979. Admitted to practice Arkansas 1979 and U.S. District Court Eastern District of Arkansas. In legal practice Hardy since 1979. Judge, Sharp County Juvenile Court 1979-87. Former Judge, Ash Flat and Cherokee Village Districts Courts, elected to term beginning Jan 1, 1984.

City Attorney Mammoth Spring 1985-96. Member Arkansas Municipal Judge's Association. Recipient E. W. Green Outstanding Citizen Award 1992. Interests include working with youth basketball and baseball programs.

Mailing address: P.O. Box 477, Ash Flat 72513.
Telephone: (870) 994-3515.
Fax: (870) 994-3515

KINNEY, Baird *(Judge, Arkansas Circuit Court First Judicial Circuit)* Serves Juvenile Division. Former Chancellor, Arkansas Chancery Court First Judicial Circuit.

Mailing address: P.O. Box 2, Forrest City 72336.
Telephone: (870) 633-5995.
Fax: (870) 633-5995

LANGSTON, John W. *(Judge, Arkansas Circuit Court Sixth Judicial Circuit)* Elected to term beginning Jan 1, 1983. Reelected 1986, 1990, 1994, 1998 and 2002. Current term expires Dec 31, 2008. Born Little Rock Arkansas June 19, 1941. Religious affiliation: Bible Study Fellowship. Educated at University of Arkansas J.D. 1966. Member Lambda Chi Alpha. Admitted to practice Arkansas 1966. Began legal practice Little Rock 1966.

Board of Directors Little Rock 1978-82. Member Arkansas and American Bar Associations. Sergeant USMC 1960-66. Democrat.

Office: 401 West Markham, Room 440, Little Rock 72201.
Telephone: (501) 340-8593.
Fax: (501) 340-8822

LANGSTON, Shannon *(Judge, Blytheville District Court)*

Office: 115 North Second, Blytheville 72315.
Telephone: (870) 762-0808.

LASER, David N. *(Judge, Arkansas Circuit Court Second Judicial Circuit)* Elected Nov 1998 to term beginning Jan 1, 1999. Reelected 2002, current term expires Dec 31, 2008. Born Forrest City Arkansas Feb 17, 1941. Presbyterian. Educated at University of Arkansas B.A. 1963 J.D. 1966. Admitted to practice Arkansas 1966, U.S. District Courts Eastern 1967 and Western 1967 Districts of Arkansas and U.S. Court of Appeals Eighth Circuit 1967. In legal practice Eudora 1966-67 and Jonesboro 1967-98. Former Chancellor, Arkansas Chancery Court Second Judicial Circuit.

LASER, DAVID N.—*Continued*

Member Craighead County, Arkansas and American Bar Associations.
Mailing address: P.O. Box 420, Jonesboro 72403.
Telephone: (870) 933-4599.
Fax: (870) 933-7707
E-mail address: JudgeLaser@yahoo.com

LINDSAY, Mark *(Judge, Arkansas Circuit Court Fourth Judicial Circuit)* Assumed office January 1, 2001. Born Little Rock Arkansas April 30, 1954. Methodist. Educated at University of Arkansas at Fayetteville B.S.B.A. 1977 J.D. 1979. Admitted to practice Arkansas 1979, U.S. District Courts Eastern 1979 and Western 1979 Districts of Arkansas, U.S. Court of Appeals Eighth Circuit 1979, U.S. Tax Court 1979 and U.S. Supreme Court 1986. In legal practice Fayetteville 1979-2000. Judge, West Fork Municipal Court 1985-2000. Chancellor, Arkansas Chancery Court Fourth Judicial Circuit March 27, 2000 to December 31, 2000, appointed by Governor Mike Huckabee.
Member Arkansas Judicial Council, Arkansas Municipal Judges Council (President 1997-98), Washington County (President 1990-91), Arkansas and American Bar Associations.
Mailing address: P.O. Box 1612, Fayetteville 72702.
Telephone: (479) 444-1548.
Fax: (479) 444-1620

LOGAN, Roger V., Jr. *(Judge, Arkansas Circuit Court Fourteenth Judicial Circuit)* Assumed office July 1, 2001. Former Chancellor, Arkansas Chancery Court Fourteenth Judicial Circuit.
Office: 100 North Main, #302, Harrison 72601.
Telephone: (870) 741-2484.
Fax: (870) 741-5357

LOONEY, J. W. *(Judge, Arkansas Circuit Court Eighteenth West Judicial Circuit)*
Office: 507 Church Street, Room 203, Mena 71953.
Telephone: (479) 394-8107.
Fax: (479) 394-8109

LOWERY, Robert L. *(Judge, DeQueen District Court)* Assumed office Jan 1, 1985. Elected to subsequent terms. Current term expires Dec 31, 2004.
Mailing address: P.O. Box 1147, DeQueen 71832.
Telephone: (870) 642-8740.

LUDWIG, Stanley W. *(Judge, Springdale District Court)* Term expires Dec 31, 2004.
Office: 201 North Spring Street, Springdale 72764.
Telephone: (479) 750-8143.

MAGGIO, Mike *(Judge, Arkansas Circuit Court Twentieth Judicial Circuit)* Appointed by Governor Mike Huckabee to term beginning Jan 1, 2001. Elected May 2001, current term expires Dec 31, 2007. Born New Orleans Louisiana June 16, 1961. Catholic. Educated at Millsaps College B.A. 1983 and University of Arkansas at Little Rock J.D. 1989. Member Phi Alpha Delta. Admitted to practice Arkansas 1990. In legal practice Conway 1990-2000. Former Chancellor, Arkansas Chancery Court Twentieth Judicial Circuit.
Office: Faulkner County Courthouse, 801 Locust Street, Conway 72034.
Telephone: (501) 450-4904.
Fax: (501) 450-4977

MARSCHEWSKI, Jim *(Judge, Arkansas Circuit Court Twelfth Judicial Circuit)*
Office: 35 South Sixth Street, Room 201, Fort Smith 72901.
Telephone: (479) 783-1103.
Fax: (479) 784-1527

MARTIN, John W. *(Judge, Brinkley District Court)* Term expires Dec 31, 2004.
Office: 114 North New York Street, Brinkley 72021.
Telephone: (870) 734-1787.

MASHBURN, Mike *(Judge, Arkansas Circuit Court Fourth Judicial Circuit)* Assumed office July 1, 2001. Former Chancellor, Arkansas Chancery Court Fourth Judicial Circuit.
Mailing address: P.O. Box 1583, Fayetteville 72702.
Telephone: (479) 444-1556.
Fax: (479) 444-1883

MAYS, Thomas L. *(Judge, Fordyce District Court)* Term expires Dec 31, 2004.
Mailing address: P.O. Box 710, Fordyce 71742.
Telephone: (870) 352-5165.

MAZZANTI, Jerry *(Judge, Arkansas Circuit Court Tenth Judicial Circuit)* Assumed office July 1, 2001. Former Judge, Arkansas Circuit Court Tenth Judicial Circuit. Former Chancellor, Arkansas Chancery Court Tenth Judicial Circuit.
Mailing address: P.O. Box 191, Lake Village 71653.
Telephone: (870) 265-8070.
Fax: (870) 265-8069

McCORMICK, David H. *(Judge, Arkansas Circuit Court Fifteenth Judicial Circuit)* Elected May 21, 2002. Term expires Dec 31, 2008. Born Russellville Arkansas Sept 8, 1954. Southern Baptist. Educated at University of Central Arkansas B.B.A. 1976 M.B.A. 1980 and University of Arkansas J.D. 1979. Member Phi Alpha Delta. Admitted to practice Arkansas 1979 and U.S. District Court Eastern District of Arkansas 1979. In legal practice Russellville since 1979. Judge, Yell County District Court 1986 and 1991-2002, appointed by Governor Bill Clinton.
Deputy Prosecuting Attorney Yell County 1987-89. Member Arkansas Trial Lawyers Association, The Association of Trial Lawyers of America, Pope County, Arkansas and American Bar Associations. Enjoys hunting.
Mailing address: P.O. Box 7, Dardanelle 72834.
Telephone: (479) 229-3580.
Fax: (479) 229-1095

McGOWAN, Mary *(Judge, Arkansas Circuit Court Sixth Judicial Circuit)* Former Chancellor, Arkansas Chancery Court Sixth Judicial Circuit.
Office: 401 West Markham, Room 320, Little Rock 72201.
Telephone: (501) 340-5602.
Fax: (501) 340-5640

McKIMM, William *(Judge, Mount Ida District Court)* Term expires Dec 31, 2004.
Mailing address: P.O. Box 667, Mount Ida 71957.
Telephone: (870) 867-2182.

MEDLOCK, Mike *(Judge, Arkansas Circuit Court Twenty-first Judicial Circuit)*
Office: Professional Building, 100 South Fourth Street, Van Buren 72956.

MEDLOCK, MIKE—*Continued*

Telephone: (479) 471-3290.
Fax: (479) 471-3292

MILLER, David *(Judge, Melbourne District Court)* Mailing address: P.O. Box 420, Melbourne 72556.
Telephone: (870) 368-4311.

MILLS, Bill *(Judge, Arkansas Circuit Court Seventeenth Judicial Circuit)*
Office: Wilbur D. Mills Courts Building, Searcy 72143.
Telephone: (501) 279-6219.
Fax: (501) 279-6218

MITCHELL, Chalk *(Judge, Helena District Court)*
Office: 405S Cherry Street, Helena 72342.
Telephone: (870) 817-0377.
Fax: (870) 817-0378

MIXON, James Gordon *(Judge, United States Bankruptcy Courts Eastern and Western Districts of Arkansas)* Appointed by U.S. District Court judges to term beginning March 26, 1984. Reappointed by U.S. Court of Appeals Eighth Circuit judges June 1986 and Dec 9, 2001. Current term expires June 2016. Former Chief Judge. Born Helena Arkansas Aug 27, 1941. Episcopalian. Educated at Arkansas State Teachers College and University of Arkansas 1968. Law Clerk to Hon. John A. Fogleman, Arkansas Supreme Court 1968-69. Admitted to practice Arkansas 1968. In legal practice Little Rock 1969-73 and Bentonville 1973-84.
Assistant U.S. Attorney Eastern District of Arkansas 1969-73. City Attorney Bentonville 1974-77. Member Arkansas Bar Association. Seaman USN 1963-65. Enjoys tennis and fishing.
Mailing address: P.O. Drawer 3777, Little Rock 77203-3777.
Telephone: (501) 918-5640.

MOODY, James *(Judge, Arkansas Circuit Court Sixth Judicial Circuit)*
Office: 401 West Markham, Room 240, Little Rock 72201.
Telephone: (501) 340-8426.
Fax: (501) 340-6038

MOODY, James M. *(Judge, United States District Court Eastern District of Arkansas)* Appointed for life by President Bill Clinton to term beginning Sept 25, 1995. Born El Dorado Arkansas Feb 14, 1940. Methodist. Educated at University of Arkansas B.S.I.M. 1962 J.D. 1964. Staff member University of Arkansas Law Review. Admitted to practice Arkansas 1964. In legal practice Little Rock 1966-93.
Member Pulaski County, Arkansas and American Bar Associations. First Lieutenant U.S. Army. Enjoys golfing, fishing and running.
Office: 381 U.S. Courthouse, 600 West Capitol Avenue, Little Rock 72201-3325.
Telephone: (501) 604-5150.

MOORE, Richard *(Judge, Arkansas Circuit Court Sixth Judicial Circuit)*
Office: 401 West Markham, Room 340, Little Rock 72201.
Telephone: (501) 340-5610.
Fax: (501) 340-6037

MOORE, Rudy *(Judge, Fayetteville District Court)* Term expires Dec 31, 2004.
Office: 100 B West Rock, Fayetteville 72701.
Telephone: (479) 587-3590.

MUNSON, Lee *(Judge, Little Rock District Court)* Term expires Dec 31, 2004. Serves First Division. Former Chancellor, Arkansas Chancery Court Sixth Judicial Circuit.
Office: 600 West Markham, Little Rock 72201.
Telephone: (501) 371-4441.

NEAL, Olly *(Judge, Arkansas Court of Appeals)* Appointed by Governor Jim Guy Tucker to term beginning Jan 1, 1996. Elected Nov 2000 to term beginning Jan 1, 2001, current term expires Dec 31, 2008. Educated at LeMoyne-Owen College B.S. and University of Arkansas at Little Rock School of Law J.D. In legal practice 1979-91. Judge, Arkansas Circuit Court First Judicial Circuit 1993-95.
Prosecuting Attorney First Judicial District 1991-92.
Office: Justice Building, 625 Marshall Street, Little Rock 72201.
Telephone: (501) 682-7983.

O'BRYAN, Joe *(Judge, Cabot District Court)* Elected Nov 1990 to term beginning Jan 1, 1991. Reelected Nov 1994 and 1998. Current term expires Dec 31, 2004. Born Greenville South Carolina July 5, 1949. Presbyterian. Educated at Baylor University B.A. 1972 J.D. 1973. Admitted to practice Arkansas 1974, U.S. District Court Eastern District of Arkansas 1974, U.S. Courts of Appeals Sixth 1980 and Eighth 1988 Circuits and U.S. Supreme Court 1982. In legal practice Cabot since 1974. Referee, Arkansas Chancery Court Seventeenth Judicial Circuit Juvenile Division 1984-89.
Member Arkansas District Judges Council and Lonoke County Bar Association (President 1985).
Mailing address: P.O. Box 687, Cabot 72023.
Telephone: (501) 843-3548.

OHM, Ralph L. *(Judge, Hot Springs District Court)* Elected Nov 1998 to term beginning Jan 1, 1999. Term expires Dec 31, 2004. Born Mulberry Arkansas July 15, 1957. Episcopalian. Educated at Henderson State University B.A. 1979 and University of Arkansas at Little Rock J.D. 1982. Admitted to practice Arkansas 1982, U.S. District Courts Eastern and Western Districts of Arkansas, U.S. Courts of Appeals Fifth and Eighth Circuits and U.S. Supreme Court. In legal practice Hot Springs.
County Attorney Garland County since 1993. Member Arkansas Trial Lawyers Association, The Association of Trial Lawyers of American, Arkansas and American Bar Associations. Enjoys running.
Mailing address: P.O. Box 1558, Hot Springs 71902-1558.
Telephone: (501) 624-7555.
Fax: (501) 939-2020

PAKE, David L. *(Judge, Maumelle District Court)* Elected Nov 6, 1986 to term beginning Jan 1, 1987. Reelected Nov 1990, Nov 1994 and Nov 1998. Current term expires Dec 31, 2004. Born Pine Bluff Arkansas Jan 27, 1948. Religious affiliation: Bible Church. Educated at University of Arkansas at Little Rock B.S. 1969

PAKE, DAVID L.—*Continued*

and University of Arkansas at Fayetteville J.D. 1977. Admitted to practice Arkansas 1977.
Office: 100 Millwood, Maumelle 72118.
Telephone: (501) 851-7800.
Fax: (501) 851-7427

PARKER, Tim S. *(Judge, Eureka Springs District Court)* Elected Nov 3, 1998 to term beginning Jan 1, 1999. Term expires Dec 31, 2004. Born Warren Arkansas Jan 1, 1962. Roman Catholic. Educated at Hendrix College B.A. 1984 and University of Arkansas at Fayetteville J.D. 1991. Admitted to practice Arkansas 1991, U.S. District Courts Eastern 1991 and Western 1991 Districts of Arkansas and Western District of Tennessee 1993, U.S. Courts of Appeals Eighth 1992 and Sixth 1997 Circuits, Tennessee 1993, Missouri 1994 and U.S. Supreme Court 1998. In legal practice Marianna Arkansas 1991-94 and Eureka Springs Arkansas since 1994.
Member Knights of Columbus and Freemasons. Enjoys hunting and fishing.
Mailing address: P.O. Box 470, Eureka Springs 72632.
Telephone: (479) 253-8732.

PARKER, Wayland A., II *(Judge, Greenwood District Court)* Term expires Dec 31, 2004.
Mailing address: P.O. Box 925, Greenwood 72936.
Telephone: (479) 996-4116.

PATTERSON, Jerry D. *(Judge, Marshall District Court)* Elected to term beginning 1981. Reelected 1984, 1988, 1992, 1996 and 2000. Current term expires Dec 31, 2004. Born Albany California March 21, 1943. Baptist. Educated at University of Arkansas B.S. 1966 J.D. 1970. Admitted to practice Arkansas 1970. Began legal practice Marshall 1970. In legal practice Harrison 1976. Judge, Marshall Municipal Court 1971-72. Special Judge, Arkansas Chancery Court and Arkansas Circuit Court 1984.
Deputy Prosecuting Attorney 1970-71. City Attorney Marshall 1970-72. Prosecuting Attorney Fourteenth Judicial Circuit 1976-78. Important Decision: Cannady v. Cannady 1984. Instructor in Agricultural Law 1971-72. Member Searcy County (President 1972-85) and Arkansas Bar Associations. Member Searcy County Industrial Development Commission, Masons and Shriners. Enjoys fishing, photography, hunting, tennis and canoeing.
Mailing address: P.O. Drawer 620, Marshall 72650.
Telephone: (870) 448-5112.

PATTERSON, John S. *(Judge, Arkansas Circuit Court Fifth Judicial Circuit)* Elected to term beginning Jan 1983. Reelected 1986, 1990, 1994, 1998 and 2002. Current term expires Dec 31, 2008. Born Clarksville Arkansas Dec 7, 1945. Presbyterian. Educated at University of Arkansas B.A. 1967 J.D. 1970. Member Phi Alpha Delta. Admitted to practice Arkansas 1970 and U.S. District Court Western District of Arkansas 1970. In legal practice Clarksville 1970-83. Judge, Clarksville Municipal Court 1977-83.
Deputy Prosecuting Attorney 1971-83. Important Decision: Ronald Gene Simmons (defendant allowed to waive right to appeal death sentence) aff'd U.S. Supreme Court 1988. Member Arkansas and American Bar Associations. Attended The National Judicial College four times. Democrat. Enjoys elk hunting, fishing and skiing.
Mailing address: P.O. Box 36, Clarksville 72830.
Telephone: (479) 754-2400.
Fax: (479) 754-2400

PEER, Steven *(Judge, Van Buren District Court)* Term expires Dec 31, 2004.
Office: 1003 Broadway, Van Buren 72956.
Telephone: (479) 474-1671.

PHILLIPS, Grisham *(Judge, Arkansas Circuit Court Twenty-second Judicial Circuit)* Former Chancellor, Arkansas Chancery Court Twenty-second Judicial Circuit.
Office: 200 North Main, Benton 72015.
Telephone: (501) 303-5628.
Fax: (501) 303-5629

PHILLIPS, Ron A. *(Judge, Hampton and Rison District Courts)* Term expires Dec 31, 2004.
Mailing address: P.O. Box 787, Fordyce 71742.
Telephone: (870) 352-7105.

PIAZZA, Chris *(Judge, Arkansas Circuit Court Sixth Judicial Circuit)*
Office: 401 West Markham, Room 230, Little Rock 72201.
Telephone: (501) 340-8424.
Fax: (501) 340-8872

PIERCE, Mackie *(Judge, Arkansas Circuit Court Sixth Judicial Circuit)* Assumed office July 1, 2001. Former Chancellor, Arkansas Chancery Court Sixth Judicial Circuit.
Office: 401 West Markham, Room 360, Little Rock 72201.
Telephone: (501) 340-5620.
Fax: (501) 340-5657

PITTMAN, John Mauzy *(Judge, Arkansas Court of Appeals)* Assumed office 1993. Educated at Vanderbilt University and University of Arkansas at Fayetteville B.S. 1962 LL.B. 1968. In legal practice West Helena 1968-80. Chancellor, Arkansas Chancery Court First Judicial Circuit 1981-92.
Office: Justice Building, 625 Marshall Street, Little Rock 72201.
Telephone: (501) 682-7487.

POPE, Samuel B. *(Judge, Arkansas Circuit Court Tenth Judicial Circuit)* Elected Nov 1994 to term beginning Jan 1, 1995. Reelected 1998 and May 2002. Current term expires Dec 31, 2008. Born Crossett Arkansas Nov 25, 1953. Baptist. Educated at University of Arkansas at Fayetteville B.S.P.A. 1976 J.D. 1979. Staff member Arkansas Law Review 1978-79. Admitted to practice Arkansas 1979 and U.S. District Courts Eastern 1979 and Western 1979 Districts of Arkansas. In legal practice Hamburg 1979-80 and Crossett 1987-90. Judge, Wilmot City Court 1987-90.
Prosecuting Attorney Tenth Judicial District 1983-86 and 1991-94.
Office: Ashley County Courthouse, 215 West Jefferson Street, Hamburg 71646.
Telephone: (870) 853-2032.
Fax: (870) 853-2032

PORTER, Jesse E. "Rusty", Jr. *(Judge, West Helena District Court)* Elected to term beginning Jan 1, 1983. Reelected 1986, 1990, 1994 and 1998. Current term expires Dec 31, 2004. Born Helena Arkansas Nov

PORTER, JESSE E. "RUSTY", JR.—*Continued*

29, 1948. Baptist. Educated at University of Arkansas at Fayetteville B.S.B.A. with honors 1970 J.D. 1973. Staff member Arkansas Law Review. Law Clerk to Chief Justice Carleton Harris, Arkansas Supreme Court. Member Sigma Pi and Phi Alpha Delta. Admitted to practice Arkansas 1973. Began legal practice West Helena 1975.

Member Phillips County (President 1980-82), Arkansas (House of Delegates 1980-83) and American Bar Associations. Reserve Captain USASR 1975-82. President American Cancer Society Phillips County. Member Helena-West Helena United Way, Boy Scouts of America, Rotary Club of Helena, East Arkansas Regional Mental Health Board, West Helena Promotional Association and Great River Road Promotional Association. Interested in railroads.

Mailing address: P.O. Box 2747, West Helena 72390.
Telephone: (870) 572-3751.
Fax: (870) 572-3752

PROCTOR, Richard L. *(Judge, Cotton Plant, McCrory and Wynne District Courts)* Appointed by Governor David Pryor to term beginning Dec 1976. Elected 1978, 1982, 1986, 1990, 1994 and 1998. Current term expires Dec 31, 2004. Born Wynne Arkansas Dec 7, 1944. Southern Baptist. Educated at Arkansas State University and University of Arkansas B.S. 1968 J.D. 1968. Admitted to practice Arkansas 1968. Began legal practice Wynne 1968.

Member Cross County (Past President), Arkansas (House of Delegates) and American Bar Associations. Democrat. Member Rotary Club. Enjoys tennis, golf, fishing and hunting.

Office: 108 Mississippi Street, Wynne 72396.
Telephone: (870) 238-3831.

PROCTOR, Williard *(Judge, Arkansas Circuit Court Sixth Judicial Circuit)*
Office: 401 West Markham, Room 410, Little Rock 72201.
Telephone: (501) 340-8550.
Fax: (501) 340-8465

PUTMAN, John *(Judge, Arkansas Circuit Court Fourteenth Judicial Circuit)*
Office: 305 County Courthouse, 100 North Main, Harrison 72601.
Telephone: (870) 741-3800.
Fax: (870) 741-2563

RAINEY, William P. *(Judge, West Memphis District Court)* Term expires Dec 31, 2004.
Mailing address: P.O. Box 766, West Memphis 72303.
Telephone: (870) 739-4446.

RAMEY, Jerry Don *(Judge, Yell County District Court)*
Mailing address: P.O. Box 389, Dardanelle 72834.
Telephone: (479) 229-3233.

RAMOS, Joe *(Judge, Charleston and Ozark District Courts)* Term expires Dec 31, 2004.
Mailing address: P.O. Box 403, Ozark 72949.
Telephone: (479) 965-7577.
Fax: (479) 965-7577

RAY, J. Thomas *(Magistrate Judge, United States District Court Eastern District of Arkansas)* Appointed by U.S. District Court judges to term beginning June 28, 2000. Term expires June 2008.
Office: 149 U.S. Courthouse, 600 West Capitol Avenue, Little Rock 72201-3325.
Telephone: (501) 604-5230.

REASONER, Stephen M. *(Senior Judge, United States District Court Eastern District of Arkansas)* Appointed for life by President Ronald Reagan to term beginning April 9, 1988. Former Chief Judge. Assumed Senior status Sept 19, 2002, serves by assignment. Born Houston Texas 1944. Episcopalian. Educated at University of Arkansas B.A. 1966 J.D. with honors 1969. Editor-in-Chief Arkansas Law Review 1968-69. Member Phi Alpha Delta. Admitted to practice Arkansas 1969. In legal practice Jonesboro 1969-88.

Member Craighead County and Arkansas Bar Associations.

Office: 560 U.S. Courthouse, 600 West Capitol Avenue, Little Rock 72201-3325.
Telephone: (501) 604-5110.

REYNOLDS, David *(Judge, Arkansas Circuit Court Twentieth Judicial Circuit)* Former Chancellor, Arkansas Chancery Court Twentieth Judicial Circuit.
Office: Faulkner County Courthouse, Second Floor, Conway 72034.
Telephone: (501) 450-4925.
Fax: (501) 450-4966

REYNOLDS, Ray A. *(Judge, Elkins District Court)* Elected to term beginning Jan 1985. Reelected 1988, 1992, 1996 and 2000. Current term expires Dec 31, 2004. Born Concord Massachusetts July 16, 1949. Baptist. Educated at University of Colorado B.A. 1971 and University of Arkansas J.D. 1974. Member Order of Barristers and Phi Alpha Delta. Admitted to practice Arkansas 1977 and U.S. District Court Western District of Arkansas 1978. In legal practice Fayetteville since 1977 and Springdale 1981-82. Substitute Municipal Judge and Small Claims Referee 1981-87.

City Prosecutor since 1982 and City Attorney since 1984 Farmington. Member Arkansas Municipal Judges League, Washington County and Arkansas Bar Associations. Instructor in Arkansas Omnibus DWI Law Washington County Bar Seminar 1983. Attended Arkansas Bar Association meeting (DWI Law) 1984 and Washington County Bar Seminars (Federal and Municipal Practice). Previously employed at Raymond's Drywall Company and Beckwith Drywall Company, Denver Colorado. Democrat. Coached Elkins High School Moot Court Team 1986. Numerous appearances on *Call Your Lawyer* Fayetteville Open Channel Public Service Television. Participant "Lawyers in Schools" programs Washington County Bar Association. Member Fayetteville Elks Club and Paradise Valley Athletic Club. Enjoys golf, hunting, fishing and tennis.

Office: 28 South College Avenue #3, Fayetteville 72701.
Telephone: (479) 521-0503.

RICKARD, Curtis *(Judge, Bryant District Court)* Term expires Dec 31, 2004.
Office: 208 West Third, Bryant 72022.
Telephone: (501) 315-2200.

ROAF, Andree Layton *(Judge, Arkansas Court of Appeals)* Appointed by Governor Mike Huckabee to term beginning Jan 1, 1997. Elected Nov 2000 to term

ROAF, ANDREE LAYTON—*Continued*
beginning Jan 1, 2001, current term expires Dec 31, 2004. Educated at Michigan State University B.S. 1962 and University of Arkansas at Little Rock J.D. 1978. In legal practice 1979-95. Associate Justice, Arkansas Supreme Court 1995-96.
Office: Justice Building, 625 Marshall Street, Little Rock 72201.
Telephone: (501) 682-7989.

ROBBINS, John B. *(Judge, Arkansas Court of Appeals)* Elected to term beginning Jan 1, 1993. Reelected 1996, current term expires Dec 31, 2004. Former Chief Judge. Born Malvern Arkansas Dec 13, 1942. Baptist. Educated at Henderson State University 1960, Southern Methodist University Southwest Graduate School of Banking Graduate in Trust 1967, University of Tennessee 1971-72, Ouachita Baptist University 1972 and Vanderbilt University J.D. 1973. Law Clerk to Chief Judge Pat Mehaffy, U.S. Court of Appeals Eighth Circuit 1973-74. Member Order of the Coif. Admitted to practice Arkansas 1973. Began legal practice Hot Springs 1974. Chancellor, Arkansas Chancery Court Eighteenth Judicial Circuit East 1985-92.
Member Garland County, Arkansas and American Bar Associations. Former Board member Salvation Army, Garland County Council on Aging, Arkansas Jail Ministries and Garland County Chapter American Red Cross. Member Mid-American Lions Club (Past President).
Office: Justice Building, 625 Marshall Street, Little Rock 72201.
Telephone: (501) 682-7482.

ROBERTS, Russell "Jack" *(Judge, Conway District Court)* Term expires Dec 31, 2004.
Office: 1312 Oak Street, Conway 72032.
Telephone: (501) 329-6698.
Fax: (501) 450-9884

ROBINSON, Mike *(Judge, Benton District Court)* Term expires Dec 31, 2004.
Office: 1605 Edison Avenue, Benton 72015.
Telephone: (501) 303-5670.

RODERY, Rick *(Judge, Corning, Piggott and Rector District Courts)* Term expires Dec 31, 2004.
Mailing address: P.O. Box 247, Piggott 72454.
Telephone: (870) 598-2218.
Fax: (870) 598-3272

ROGERS, Gary B. *(Judge, Biscoe, De Valls Bluff and Hazen District Courts)* Term expires Dec 31, 2004.
Mailing address: P.O. Box 436, Hazen 72064.
Telephone: (501) 375-9151.

ROUTON, Steve *(Judge, Forrest City District Court)* Elected Nov 1990 to term beginning Jan 1, 1991. Reelected Nov 1994 and Nov 1998. Current term expires Dec 31, 2004. Born Hope Arkansas 1954. Methodist. Educated at Hendrix College B.A. 1976 and University of Arkansas J.D. 1979. Law Clerk to Hon. O. H. Hargraves, Arkansas Circuit Court First Judicial Circuit 1977. Member Phi Alpha Delta. Admitted to practice Arkansas 1979, U.S. District Court District of Arkansas 1979 and U.S. Court of Appeals Eighth Circuit 1979. In legal practice Forrest City. Juvenile Referee, St. Francis County Court 1981-85. Probate Referee, Arkansas Chancery Court First Judicial Circuit 1981-85.
Member Arkansas and American Bar Associations. Democratic State Executive Committee since 1994.
Office: 615 East Cross, Forrest City 72335.
Telephone: (870) 633-5703.

RYAN, Jerry *(Judge, Mena District Court)* Term expires Dec 31, 2004.
Office: 510 Church Avenue, Mena 71953.
Telephone: (479) 394-3532.

SAXON, David P. *(Judge, Fort Smith District Court)* Term expires Dec 31, 2004.
Office: 35 South Sixth Street, Fort Smith 72901.
Telephone: (479) 784-2429.

SCHRANTZ, Doug *(Judge, Rogers District Court)* Term expires Dec 31, 2004.
Office: 221 North Third Street, Rogers 72756.
Telephone: (479) 636-2500.

SCOTT, John R. *(Judge, Arkansas Circuit Court Nineteenth West Judicial Circuit)* Appointed by Governor Mike Huckabee to term beginning Oct 1, 2001. Elected 2002, current term expires Dec 31, 2008. Born Fayetteville Arkansas July 8, 1951. Episcopalian. Educated at University of Arkansas at Fayetteville B.A. 1973 J.D. 1977. Admitted to practice Arkansas 1978, U.S. District Courts Eastern and Western Districts of Arkansas and Eastern District of Texas, U.S. Court of Appeals Eighth Circuit and U.S. Supreme Court. In legal practice Rogers 1978-2001.
Office: 102 N.E. A, Box 12, Bentonville 72712.
Telephone: (479) 271-1022.
Fax: (479) 271-5750
E-mail address: jscott@co.benton.ar.us

SHEPHERD, Bobby E. *(Magistrate Judge, United States District Court Western District of Arkansas)* Appointed by U.S. District Court judges. Born Arkadelphia Arkansas Nov 18, 1951. Baptist. Educated at Ouachita Baptist University B.A. with honors 1973 and University of Arkansas at Fayetteville J.D. with honors 1976. Articles Editor Arkansas Law Review 1974-76. Admitted to practice Arkansas 1976, U.S. District Court Western District of Arkansas 1976, U.S. Court of Appeals Eighth Circuit 1977 and U.S. Supreme Court 1979. In legal practice El Dorado 1976-90. Magistrate, Union County Municipal Court 1980-90. Former Judge, Arkansas Circuit Court Thirteenth Judicial Circuit, elected to term beginning Jan 1, 1991. Former Chancellor, Arkansas Chancery Court Thirteenth Judicial Circuit, served Juvenile Division.
Member Union County, Arkansas and American Bar Associations. Captain USAR 1973-80.
Mailing address: P.O. Box 1733, El Dorado 71731-1733.
Telephone: (870) 863-3173.

SHIRRON, Phillip H. *(Judge, Arkansas Circuit Court Seventh Judicial Circuit)* Elected Nov 1988 to term beginning Jan 1, 1989. Reelected 1990, 1994, 1998 and 2002. Current term expires Dec 31, 2008. Serves Juvenile Division. Born Little Rock Arkansas Aug 1, 1947. Baptist. Educated at University of Central Arkansas B.B.A. 1970 and University of Arkansas at Little Rock J.D. 1976. Admitted to practice Arkansas 1976 and U.S. District Court Eastern District of Arkansas 1976. In legal practice Sheridan 1976-88. Former Chancellor, Arkansas Chancery Court Seventh Judicial Circuit.

SHIRRON, PHILLIP H.—*Continued*

Deputy Prosecuting Attorney Grant County 1977-84. Member Grant County and Arkansas Bar Associations. E-5 USAR 1968-74. Manager Southwestern Bell Telephone 1970-74. Democrat. Member Sheridan Rotary Club. Enjoys hunting, fishing and outdoor activities.

Office: 109 Grant County Courthouse, 101 West Center Street, Sheridan 72150.
Telephone: (870) 942-7818.
Fax: (870) 942-1622

SHOFFNER, Clarence P. "Phil" *(Judge, Searcy District Court)* Elected to term beginning Jan 1, 2001. Term expires Dec 31, 2004. Also serves McRae City Court since 1977. Born Searcy Arkansas Jan 28, 1943. Presbyterian. Educated at University of Central Arkansas B.S. with honors 1965 and University of Arkansas M.A. 1971 J.D. 1976. Admitted to practice Arkansas 1976, U.S. District Court District of Arkansas 1976, U.S. Court of Appeals Eighth Circuit 1976 and U.S. Supreme Court 1979. In legal practice Searcy Arkansas since 1976.

City Attorney City of McRae 1977-2000 and City of Beebe 1996-2000. Member White County and Arkansas Bar Associations.

Office: 107 East Center, Searcy 72143.
Telephone: (501) 268-2133.
Fax: (501) 268-7773
E-mail address: phil@cablelynx.com

SHORT, Jim *(Judge, Salem District Court)* Term expires Dec 31, 2004.

Mailing address: P.O. Box 988, Salem 72576.
Telephone: (870) 895-2986.

SIMES, L. T., II *(Judge, Arkansas Circuit Court First Judicial Circuit)*

Mailing address: P.O. Box 2775, Helena 72390.
Telephone: (870) 338-5518.
Fax: (870) 338-5591

SIMS, Barry *(Judge, Arkansas Circuit Court Sixth Judicial Circuit)* Former Judge, North Little Rock District Court.

Office: 401 West Markham, Room 220, Little Rock 72201.
Telephone: (501) 340-5630.
Fax: (501) 340-8872

SINGLETON, Hamilton Hobbs *(Judge, Arkansas Circuit Court Thirteenth Judicial Circuit)* Assumed office July 1, 2001. Term expires Dec 31, 2004. Born Winslow Arizona Sept 20, 1948. Presbyterian. Educated at University of Arkansas at Fayetteville B.S.B.A. 1971 J.D. 1975. Admitted to practice Arkansas 1975 and U.S. District Court Western District of Arkansas 1976. In legal practice Camden 1975-94. Chancellor, Arkansas Chancery Court Thirteenth Judicial Circuit Jan 1, 1995 to June 30, 2001.

Chief Deputy Prosecutor Ouachita and Calhoun Counties Arkansas 1981-94. Member Arkansas Judicial Council (Chair Long Range Planning Committee and Domestic Relations and Probate Ad Litem) and Arkansas Bar Association. Enjoys shop and anything outdoors. Personal Statement or Quote: "It is too pretty to play golf."

Mailing address: P.O. Box 763, Camden 71711.
Telephone: (870) 837-2272.
Fax: (870) 837-2271
E-mail address: chancery@cei.net

SKAGGS, John Arthur *(Judge, Bentonville District Court)* Elected to term beginning Jan 1, 1987. Reelected to subsequent terms. Current term expires Dec 31, 2004. Born Vancouver Washington April 12, 1945. Educated at University of Arkansas B.S.E. 1970 J.D. 1976. Admitted to practice Arkansas 1980. In legal practice Bentonville since 1980.

Member Benton County Bar Association.

Mailing address: P.O. Box 327, Bentonville 72712.
Telephone: (501) 273-3422.
E-mail address: lawoffic@nwa.quik.com

SMITH, Kim M. *(Judge, Arkansas Circuit Court Fourth Judicial Circuit)* Elected to term beginning Jan 1, 1987. Reelected 1990, 1994, 1998 and 2002. Current term expires Dec 31, 2008. Born Joplin Missouri Sept 26, 1949. Catholic. Educated at University of Missouri B.S.B.A. 1971 and University of Arkansas J.D. 1975. Admitted to practice Arkansas 1975.

Deputy Prosecuting Attorney 1975-78. Prosecuting Attorney Fourth District 1979-86. President Arkansas Prosecuting Attorneys Association 1983. Member W. B. Putman American Inn of Court (President 1990-92) and Washington County Bar Association. E-5 Missouri Army National Guard 1971-77. Democrat. Member Fayetteville Rotary Club (President 1984-85). Enjoys golf, fishing and camping.

Mailing address: P.O. Drawer 1206, Fayetteville 72702-1206.
Telephone: (479) 444-1552.
Fax: (479) 444-1752
E-mail address: ksmith@co.washington.ar.us

SMITH, Phillip *(Judge, Arkansas Circuit Court Third Judicial Circuit)* Serves Juvenile Division. Former Judge, Pocahontas Municipal Court.

Office: 108 South Marr, Pocahontas 72455.
Telephone: (870) 892-8610.
Fax: (870) 892-9150

SMITH, Vann *(Judge, Arkansas Circuit Court Sixth Judicial Circuit)* Assumed office July 1, 2001. Born Memphis Tennessee Jan 13, 1951. Presbyterian. Educated at University of Virginia and University of Arkansas B.A. 1973 J.D. 1976. Law Clerk to Arkansas Supreme Court 1976-77. Member Phi Alpha Delta. Admitted to practice Arkansas 1976, U.S. District Court Eastern District of Arkansas 1977, U.S. Courts of Appeals Eighth 1978 and Federal 1985 Circuits and U.S. Supreme Court 1980. In legal practice Little Rock 1977-88. Judge, Arkansas Circuit Court Sixth Judicial Circuit 1988-90. Chancellor, Arkansas Chancery Court Sixth Judicial Circuit Jan 1, 1990 to June 30, 2001.

Member William Overton Inn of Court 1988-97. Member Pulaski County (Secretary-Treasurer 1988-90), Arkansas and American Bar Associations. Attended Arkansas Bar Association Annual Conference 1976-96, National Council of Juvenile and Family Court Judges since 1989, The National Judicial College and American Academy of Judicial Education. Instructor in Domestic Issues Arkansas Trial Lawyers Seminar 1991. Former Member Big Brothers/Big Sisters and Advocates for Battered Women. Member Boy Scouts of America.

Office: 401 West Markham, Room 300, Little Rock 72201.
Telephone: (501) 340-8538.
Fax: (501) 340-6036

SMITHERMAN, Tom *(Judge, Arkansas Circuit Court Eighteenth East Judicial Circuit)* Elected to term beginning Jan 1, 1989. Reelected 1992, 1996 and 2000. Current term expires Dec 31, 2004. Former Chancellor, Arkansas Chancery Court Eighteenth Judicial Circuit East.

Office: 201 Garland County Courthouse, Hot Springs 71901.

Telephone: (501) 622-3760.

Fax: (501) 622-3605

SPEARS, Jim D. *(Judge, Arkansas Circuit Court Twelfth Judicial Circuit)* Assumed office July 1, 2001. Born Fayetteville Arkansas March 5, 1946. Methodist. Educated at Arkansas Tech University B.A. 1968 and University of Arkansas School of Law J.D. 1973. Admitted to practice Arkansas 1973, U.S. District Court Western District of Arkansas 1973, U.S. Court of Appeals Eighth Circuit 1977 and U.S. Supreme Court 1978. In legal practice Fort Smith 1973-83. Administrative Law Judge, Arkansas Workers' Compensation Commission 1983-93. Chancellor, Arkansas Chancery Court Twelfth Judicial Circuit Jan 1, 1993 to June 30, 2001.

Assistant Federal Public Defender 1981-82. Member Arkansas Judicial Council, Sebastian County and Arkansas Bar Associations. Recipient Grady Secrest Humanitarian Award from Fort Smith Jaycees 1996, Jack White Community Leadership Award from Leadership Fort Smith Alumni Association 1998 and Silver Beaver Award from Boy Scouts. President Fort Smith Rotary Club 2001-02. Interests include history, Boy Scouts, community development and promotion of the arts.

Office: 523 Garrison Avenue, Fifth Floor, Fort Smith 72901.

Telephone: (479) 784-1560.

Fax: (479) 784-1563

E-mail address: jspears@co.sebastian.ar.us

SPRUELL, Ray *(Judge, Jonesboro and Lake City District Courts)*

Office: 410 West Washington, Jonesboro 72401.

Telephone: (870) 933-4584, 933-4508.

Fax: (870) 933-4582

STANDRIDGE, Brent *(Judge, North Little Rock District Court)* Serves Traffic Division.

Office: 200 West Pershing Boulevard, North Little Rock 72114.

Telephone: (501) 791-8562.

STARKEN, Raymond T. *(Judge, Ash Flat and Cherokee Village District Courts)*

Mailing address: P.O. Box 550, Cherokee Village 72525-0550.

Telephone: (870) 856-3286.

Fax: (870) 856-3309

STEEL, Jim Bob *(Judge, Murfreesboro District Court)* Term expires Dec 31, 2004.

Mailing address: P.O. Box 548, Nashville 71852.

Telephone: (870) 845-4532.

STEWART, Daniel *(Judge, Fort Smith District Court)*

Office: 35 South Sixth Street, Fort Smith 72901.

Telephone: (479) 784-2427.

Fax: (479) 784-2438

STEWART, David A. *(Judge, Little Rock District Court)* Elected Nov 1994 to term beginning Jan 1, 1995. Reelected 1998, current term expires Dec 31, 2004. Serves Third Division. Born Sewickley Pennsylvania July 1, 1941. United Methodist. Educated at University of Arkansas at Fayetteville B.S.B.A. 1963 J.D. 1967. Admitted to practice Arkansas 1966, U.S. District Court District of Arkansas 1966 and U.S. Supreme Court 1971.

Office: 500 West Markham, Room 112, Little Rock 72201.

Telephone: (501) 371-4464.

Fax: (501) 399-3459

STIDHAM, Dan *(Judge, Paragould District Court)* Term expires Dec 31, 2004.

Mailing address: P.O. Box 856, Paragould 72450.

Telephone: (870) 236-7600.

STOREY, William *(Judge, Arkansas Circuit Court Fourth Judicial Circuit)*

Mailing address: P.O. Box 1405, Fayetteville 72702.

Telephone: (479) 444-1560.

Fax: (479) 444-1565

STORY, Bentley E. *(Judge, Arkansas Circuit Court First Judicial Circuit)* Assumed office July 31, 2001. Born Helena Arkansas Aug 20, 1949. Baptist. Educated at Arkansas State University B.A. 1971, Memphis State University J.D. 1974 and University of Virginia Judge Advocate General's School 1974. Admitted to practice Arkansas 1974, Tennessee 1974, U.S. Court of Military Appeals 1974 and U.S. District Court Eastern District of Arkansas 1981. Began legal practice West Memphis Arkansas 1977. In legal practice Forrest City Arkansas 1978. Referee, Bastardy Court St. Francis County 1979-82. Referee, Probate Court St. Francis County 1979-82. Chancellor, Arkansas Chancery Court First Judicial Circuit Jan 1, 1983 to June 30, 2001.

Member St. Francis County, Arkansas and American Bar Associations. Captain U.S. Army JAGC 1974-77 and USAR since 1977 and Lieutenant Colonel USAR.

Mailing address: P.O. Box 249, Forrest City 72336-0249.

Telephone: (870) 261-1740.

Fax: (870) 261-1733

STROUD, John F., Jr. *(Chief Judge, Arkansas Court of Appeals)* Appointed by Governor Jim Guy Tucker to term beginning Jan 1, 1996. Elected Nov 2000 to term beginning Jan 1, 2001, current term expires Dec 31, 2004. Born Hope Arkansas Oct 3, 1931. Methodist. Educated at University of Arkansas B.A. 1959 LL.B. 1960. Comments Editor and Business Manager University of Arkansas Law Review 1958-59. Member Delta Theta Phi. Admitted to practice Arkansas 1959, U.S. Supreme Court 1963 and Texas 1988. In legal practice Texarkana 1959-61, 1963-79 and 1981-95. Associate Justice, Arkansas Supreme Court 1980-81.

City Attorney Texarkana 1960-61. Past Chair Arkansas Bar Foundation. Fellow The American College of Trust and Estate Counsel and American Bar Foundation. Member State Bar of Texas, Texarkana, Pulaski County, Southwest Arkansas, Arkansas (Past President, Former Chairman Executive Council) and American Bar Associations. Recipient Outstanding Alumnus from University of Arkansas Law School and Distinguished Eagle Scout Award from Boy Scouts of America. Lieutenant Colonel USAF (Pilot 1951-56). President Texarkana Chamber of Commerce and Texarkana Rotary Club. Chairman of the Board First United Methodist Church. Chairman Texar-

STROUD, JOHN F., JR.—*Continued*

kana United Way. Enjoys tennis, golf, hunting and fishing.
Office: 625 Marshall Street, Little Rock 72201.
Telephone: (501) 682-7977.
Fax: (501) 682-7972

SULLIVAN, Terry *(Judge, Arkansas Circuit Court Fifteenth Judicial Circuit)*
Mailing address: P.O. Box 400, Danville 72833.
Telephone: (479) 495-7975.
Fax: (479) 495-2607

SUTTERFIELD, Dennis *(Judge, Arkansas Circuit Court Fifth Judicial Circuit)* Former Judge, Russellville Municipal Court. Former Chancellor, Arkansas Chancery Court Fifth Judicial Circuit.
Mailing address: P.O. Box 249, Russellville 72801.
Telephone: (479) 967-5011.
Fax: (479) 967-6070

SVOBODA, Joseph V. *(Judge, Carlisle, England and Ward District Courts)* Term expires Dec 31, 2004. Former Judge, Lonoke Municipal Court.
Mailing address: P.O. Box 554, Carlisle 72024.
Telephone: (870) 552-3436, (501) 842-3911, (501) 843-6351.

SWITZER, David *(Judge, Arkansas Circuit Court Eighteenth East Judicial Circuit)* Assumed office July 1, 2001. Former Judge, Arkansas Circuit Court Eighteenth Judicial Circuit East. Former Chancellor, Arkansas Chancery Court Eighteenth Judicial Circuit East.
Office: 303 Garland County Courthouse, Hot Springs 71901.
Telephone: (501) 622-3755.
Fax: (501) 622-3629

TAYLOR, Hendrix Arthur, Jr. *(Judge, Arkansas Circuit Court Eleventh West Judicial Circuit)* Elected to term beginning Jan 1, 1975. Reelected to subsequent terms. Current term expires Dec 31, 2008. Born Pine Bluff Arkansas Jan 18, 1941. Member St. Joseph Catholic Church. Educated at Kemper Military School A.A. 1960 and University of Arkansas B.S.B.A. 1962 J.D. 1965. Recipient highest score mid-year Arkansas Bar Exam 1965. Member Omicron Delta Kappa. Admitted to practice Arkansas 1965. In legal practice Pine Bluff 1969-72.
Pine Bluff City Attorney 1972-74. Co-chairman Southeast Arkansas Trial Practice Committee since 1986. Member Arkansas Judicial Compensation Committee since 1986, Arkansas Judicial Council (Co-chairman Committee on Continuing Legal Education since 1984), Southeast Arkansas Criminal Justice Planning Council Executive Committee, Jefferson County, Arkansas and American Bar Associations. Board of Directors Arkansas Institute of Continuing Legal Education since 1975. Delegate National Conference of the Judiciary on the Rights of Victims of Crime The National Judicial College Reno Nevada Nov 1983. Named one of the Outstanding Young Men of America 1977. Listed in *Who's Who in American Law* 1983-84. Captain U.S. Army JAGC 1965-69. Recipient Bronze Star 1967 and Army Accommodation Medal 1969. Democrat. Member Arkansas Criminal Detention Facilities Board, Democratic State Committee 1973-75, Jefferson County Young Democrats Club (President 1972-73), Arkansas Young Democrats Club, Pine Bluff Opportunity Industrial Center, Pine Bluff Chamber of Commerce and Jefferson County Farm Bureau. Enjoys fishing and hunting.
Mailing address: P.O. Box 8705, Pine Bluff 71601.
Telephone: (870) 541-5377.
Fax: (870) 536-8937

TAYLOR, Richard D. *(Judge, United States Bankruptcy Courts Eastern and Western Districts of Arkansas)* Appointed by U.S. Court of Appeals Eighth Circuit judges to term beginning Jan 3, 2003. Term expires Jan 2017.
Mailing address: P.O. Box 3097, Fayetteville 72702-3097.
Telephone: (479) 582-9067.

THOMAS, John *(Judge, Arkansas Circuit Court Ninth East Judicial Circuit)* Serves Juvenile Division. Former Judge, Arkadelphia Municipal Court. Former Chancellor, Arkansas Chancery Court Ninth Judicial Circuit East.
Mailing address: P.O. Box 966, Arkadelphia 71923.
Telephone: (870) 246-8218.
Fax: (870) 246-9378

THOMAS, Stephen *(Judge, Siloam Springs District Court)* Term expires Dec 31, 2004.
Office: 114 South Broadway, Siloam Springs 72761.
Telephone: (479) 524-6605.

THORNTON, Ray *(Associate Justice, Arkansas Supreme Court)* Assumed office 1997. Born Conway Arkansas July 16, 1928. Educated at Yale University and University of Arkansas School of Law. In legal practice fourteen years.
Deputy Prosecuting Attorney Pulaski County 1956-57 and Perry County 1956-57. Attorney General Arkansas 1971-73. Chairman State Board of Law Examiners 1969-70. Member U.S. House of Representatives 1973-79 and 1991-97 (Judiciary Committee considering the impeachment of Richard M. Nixon). President Arkansas State University 1980-84 and University of Arkansas 1984-89.
Office: Justice Building, 625 Marshall Street, Little Rock 72201.
Telephone: (501) 682-6876.

THROESCH, John *(Judge, Pocahontas District Court)*
Office: 1510 Pace Road, Pocahontas 72455.
Telephone: (870) 892-4033.
Fax: (870) 892-4392

TISDALE, Stephen *(Judge, Eudora District Court)* Term expires Dec 31, 2004.
Mailing address: P.O. Drawer 610, Eudora 71640.
Telephone: (870) 355-2504.

TOLSON, Robert, Jr. *(Judge, Pine Bluff District Court)* Elected to term beginning Jan 1, 1995. Reelected 1998, current term expires Dec 31, 2004. Born Monticello Arkansas Jan 7, 1944. Methodist. Educated at University of Houston B.B.A. 1967 J.D. 1968. Admitted to practice Arkansas 1968 and U.S. District Court Eastern District of Arkansas 1968.
City Attorney Pine Bluff 1976-94. Member Arkansas City Attorneys Association, Arkansas District Judges Council, Jefferson County, Arkansas and American Bar Associations.
Mailing address: P.O. Box 8221, Pine Bluff 71611.
Office: 200 East Eighth Avenue, Pine Bluff 71601.

TOLSON, ROBERT, JR.—*Continued*

Telephone: (870) 543-1860.
Fax: (870) 543-1889

VAN AUSDALL, Rice *(Judge, Arkansas Circuit Court Second Judicial Circuit)* Assumed office Jan 1, 1987. Elected to subsequent terms. Former Chancellor, Arkansas Chancery Court Second Judicial Circuit.

Mailing address: P.O. Box 500, Harrisburg 72432.
Telephone: (870) 578-2332.
Fax: (870) 578-5791

VAN HOOK, George Ellis, Jr. *(Judge, Union County District Court)* Magistrate Oct 1983 to Dec 1990. Elected Judge Nov 6, 1990 to term beginning Jan 1, 1991. Reelected Nov 8, 1994 and Nov 11, 1998. Current term expires Dec 31, 2004. Born El Dorado Arkansas Aug 27, 1948. Educated at University of Arkansas B.S.B.A. 1970 J.D. 1973. Admitted to practice Arkansas 1973, U.S. District Courts Eastern 1974 and Western 1974 Districts of Arkansas and U.S. Court of Appeals Eighth Circuit 1978. In legal practice Pine Bluff June 1973 to July 1974 and since April 1976. Former Judge, El Dorado Municipal Court.

Staff Attorney Arkansas State Highway and Transportation Department Sept 1974 to April 1976. Contract Attorney Union County Child Support Enforcement Unit Sept 1981 to Dec 1990. Member Union County Bar Association (President 1986). Board Member Arkansas Cost of the Judiciary Study Commission 1986, El Dorado Chamber of Commerce, Boys and Girls Club of El Dorado, Boy Scouts Union District, South Arkansas Arts Center, El Dorado Planning Commission and El Dorado Planning and Zoning Commission. Board of Advisors Salvation Army. Board of Directors Union County United Way. Advisory Board Arkansas Department of Community Punishment. Charter Member Union County Academic Foundation, Inc., Exchange Club of El Dorado and Union County Community Foundation.

Mailing address: P.O. Box 490, El Dorado 71730.
Telephone: (870) 863-5119.

VAUGHT, Larry D. *(Judge, Arkansas Court of Appeals)* Elected Nov 2000 to term beginning Jan 1, 2001. Term expires Dec 31, 2004. Born Booneville Arkansas May 6, 1947. Presbyterian. Educated at Washington University at St. Louis A.B. 1969 and University of Arkansas at Little Rock J.D. with honors 1979. Admitted to practice Arkansas 1979, U.S. District Courts Eastern 1979 and Western 1979 Districts of Arkansas, U.S. Court of Appeals Eighth Circuit 1979 and U.S. Supreme Court 1984. In legal practice Little Rock 1982-89. Judge, Pulaski County Municipal Court Nov 23, 1993 to 2000.

Deputy Prosecuting Attorney Sixth Judicial District 1979-81. County Attorney Pulaski County 1989-93. Member American Association of Criminal Defense Lawyers, The Association of Trial Lawyers of America, Pulaski County, Arkansas (House of Delegates 1992-95) and American Bar Associations. Democrat. Enjoys music.

Office: Justice Building, Second Floor, 625 Marshall Street, Little Rock 72201.
Telephone: (501) 682-7490.

VITTITOW, Robert C. *(Judge, Arkansas Circuit Court Tenth Judicial Circuit)* Assumed office July 1, 2001. Born DeWitt Arkansas Dec 24, 1940. Methodist. Educated at University of Arkansas at Monticello B.S. and Tulane University School of Law LL.B. Admitted to practice Arkansas 1966, U.S. District Court Eastern District of Arkansas 1968 and U.S. Supreme Court 1971. In legal practice DeWitt 1966-67 and Warren 1967-89. Judge, Warren and Bradley County Municipal Court 1970-71. Chancellor, Arkansas Chancery Court Tenth Judicial Circuit Jan 1, 1989 to June 30, 2001.

Member Arkansas Bar Association. Attended "General Jurisdiction" 1989 and "Advanced Evidence" 1990 The National Judicial College. Enjoys golf and reading.

Office: Bradley County Courthouse, 101 East Cedar, Warren 71671.
Telephone: (870) 226-4420.
Fax: (870) 226-4424

WARREN, Joyce Williams *(Judge, Arkansas Circuit Court Sixth Judicial Circuit)* Appointed by Governor Bill Clinton to term beginning Aug 1, 1989. Elected Nov 1990, Nov 1994, Nov 1998 and 2002. Current term expires Dec 31, 2008. Serves Juvenile Division. Born Oct 25, 1949. Baptist. Educated at University of Arkansas B.A. in Sociology and Anthropology 1971 J.D. 1976. Law Clerk to Hon. Darrell L. Hickman, Associate Justice Arkansas Supreme Court Jan 1977 to Sept 1977. Member Sigma Gamma Rho. In legal practice March 1981 to Jan 1982. Juvenile Judge, Pulaski County Jan 1983 to July 1987 (first black female judge in Arkansas). Paternity Judge, Pulaski County July 1987 to Aug 1989. Former Chancellor, Arkansas Chancery Court Sixth Judicial Circuit.

Assistant Attorney General State of Arkansas Oct 1977 to Dec 1978. Staff Attorney Central Arkansas Legal Services Jan 1982 to Dec 1982. Legal Counsel Criminal Justice and Highway Safety Information Center. Liaison to Arkansas Department of Health. Legal Advisor to State Department of Health. Adjunct Faculty Columbia College 1977-82. Member 1986-93 and Chairperson of the Board 1989-90 Arkansas State Board of Law Examiners. Member Foster Care and Adoption Assessment Ad Hoc Committee Arkansas Supreme Court since 1995 and Arkansas Child Support Commission since 1999. Member Arkansas Judicial Council, Arkansas Association of Women Lawyers, Harold Flowers Law Society, National Council of Juvenile and Family Court Judges, Pulaski County, Arkansas, National and American Bar Associations. Attended Summer College for Juvenile and Family Court Judges University of Nevada, Reno 1983. Attended courses American Academy of Judicial Education. Named one of three Worthen Arkansas Professional Women of Distinction 1988 and one of Top 100 Women in Arkansas *Arkansas Business* 1995 and 1996. Recipient Lawyer-Citizen Award from Pulaski County Bar Association 1990. Listed in three editions *Outstanding Young Women in America.* Administrative Assistant to Governor Bill Clinton Jan 1979 to Feb 1981. Board of Directors Arkansas Council on Brotherhood National Conference of Christians and Jews since 1984 and Altrusa Club of Little Rock 1986-88. Board of Directors since 1988 and Chairperson 1992-2000 New Futures for Little Rock Youth. Member Arkansas Youth Suicide Prevention Commission since 1993. Vice President since 1994 and Board of Trustees since 1994 Arkansas Wilderness Institutes. Board of Trustees Arkansas Museum of Science and History since

WARREN, JOYCE WILLIAMS—*Continued*

Sept 1995. Member Altrusa Club of Little Rock and Arkansas Advocates for Children and Families.
Office: 3001 West Roosevelt, Little Rock 72204.
Telephone: (501) 340-6724, 340-6725.
Fax: (501) 340-7016

WEAVER, Tim *(Judge, Arkansas Circuit Court Sixteenth Judicial Circuit)*
Mailing address: P.O. Box 1361, Melbourne 72556.
Telephone: (870) 368-3640.
Fax: (870) 368-7457

WEBB, Gordon *(Judge, Arkansas Circuit Court Fourteenth Judicial Circuit)*
Mailing address: P.O. Box 785, Harrison 72602.
Telephone: (870) 741-2102.
Fax: (870) 741-1874

WHITEAKER, Phillip *(Judge, Arkansas Circuit Court Twenty-third Judicial Circuit)* Serves Juvenile Division. Former Chancellor, Arkansas Chancery Court Twenty-third Judicial Circuit.
Office: 301 North Center, Suite 101, Lonoke 72086.
Telephone: (501) 676-3007.
Fax: (501) 676-3059

WILKINSON, Norman *(Judge, Arkansas Circuit Court Twelfth Judicial Circuit)* Assumed office July 1, 2001. Former Chancellor, Arkansas Chancery Court Twelfth Judicial Circuit.
Office: 35 South Sixth Street, Room 204, Fort Smith 72901.
Telephone: (479) 782-3035.
Fax: (479) 784-1537

WILLIAMS, Chris E. *(Judge, Arkansas Circuit Court Seventh Judicial Circuit)* Born Malvern Arkansas July 13, 1954. Methodist. Educated at Henderson State University B.A. 1978 and University of Arkansas School of Law J.D. 1981. Member Delta Theta Phi. Admitted to practice Arkansas 1981 and U.S. District Court District of Arkansas 1981. In legal practice Malvern 1981-94. Juvenile Judge, Hot Spring County Court 1983-86. Former Judge, Malvern District Court, elected to term beginning Jan 1992.
City Attorney Malvern 1986-91. Board of Governors American Judges Association. Member Lions Club. Enjoys golfing and duck hunting.
Office: Hot Spring County Courthouse, Locust and Second Streets, Malvern 72104.
Telephone: (501) 337-7651.
Fax: (501) 337-7744

WILLIAMS, Kenneth *(Judge, Lonoke District Court)*
Office: 107 West Second, Lonoke 72086.
Telephone: (501) 552-7513.
Fax: (501) 676-7807

WILLIAMS, Paul X. *(Judge, Booneville District Court)* Term expires Dec 31, 2004.
Mailing address: P.O. Box 147, Booneville 72927.
Telephone: (479) 675-2880.
Fax: (479) 675-3512

WILSON, Ralph, Jr. *(Judge, Arkansas Circuit Court Second Judicial Circuit)* Appointed by Governor Bill Clinton to term beginning Aug 1, 1989. Elected Nov 6, 1990 to term beginning Jan 3, 1991. Reelected Nov 8, 1994, 1998 and May 21, 2002. Current term expires Dec 31, 2008. Born Osceola Arkansas Oct 25, 1950. Methodist. Educated at University of Arkansas B.A. 1972 J.D. 1975. Member Phi Alpha Delta. Admitted to practice Arkansas 1975, U.S. District Court Eastern District of Arkansas 1976 and U.S. Supreme Court 1978. In legal practice Osceola 1975-89. Former Chancellor, Arkansas Chancery Court Second Judicial Circuit.
Instructor in Business Law I Mississippi County Community College 1975-93. Member Arkansas Judicial Council, Arkansas and American Bar Associations. Delegate to Arkansas Constitutional Convention 1979-80. Attended "General Jurisdiction I" 1990, "General Jurisdiction II" 1991, "Current Issues in Family Law" 1992, "Advanced Evidence" 1994 and "Probate Courts: Contemporary Issues" 1997 The National Judicial College, "No Reversals/Correct Rulings: Evidence in Action" 1992 and "Advanced Evidence" 1999 American Academy of Judicial Education, "Family Law: The Crucial Issues" 1993, "Fall College: The Role of the Juvenile Court Judge" 1995 and "Child Abuse and Neglect Institute" 1998 National Council of Juvenile and Family Court Judges and "The Judge as Fact Finder and Decision Maker" American College of Judicial Education 1996. Trustee Kiwanis International Foundation since 2001. Member Arkansas Natural Heritage Commission 1985-94. Past President Osceola-South Mississippi County Chamber of Commerce and Riverlawn Country Club. Former Governor Missouri-Arkansas District Kiwanis International. Enjoys travel and sports.
Mailing address: P.O. Box 506, Osceola 72370.
Telephone: (870) 563-6035.
Fax: (870) 563-6035

WILSON, William R., Jr. *(Judge, United States District Court Eastern District of Arkansas)* Appointed for life by President Bill Clinton to term beginning 1993. Born Little Rock Arkansas Dec 18, 1939. Educated at Hendrix College B.A. 1962 and Vanderbilt University School of Law J.D. 1965. In legal practice Texarkana 1965-66 and Little Rock 1969-93.
Deputy Prosecuting Attorney Miller County 1965-66.
Office: 423 U.S. Courthouse, 600 West Capitol Avenue, Little Rock 72201-3325.
Telephone: (501) 604-5140.

WINNINGHAM, Ronald L. *(Judge, Newport District Court)* Term expires Dec 31, 2004.
Mailing address: P.O. Box 741, Newport 72112.
Telephone: (870) 523-6516.

WISE, Elizabeth *(Judge, Perry County District Court)* Term expires Dec 31, 2004.
Mailing address: Courthouse Square, Perryville 72126.
Telephone: (501) 889-2881.

WRIGHT, John Homer *(Judge, Arkansas Circuit Court Eighteenth East Judicial Circuit)* Born Hot Springs Arkansas Nov 13, 1950. Methodist. Educated at Hendrix College B.A. 1972 and University of Arkansas at Fayetteville J.D. 1975. Admitted to practice Arkansas 1975, U.S. District Court Western District of Arkansas 1976, U.S. Court of Appeals Eighth Circuit 1977 and U.S. Supreme Court 1978. In legal practice Hot Springs since 1975. Former Judge, Hot Springs Municipal Court, elected to term beginning Oct 28, 1985.

WRIGHT, JOHN HOMER—*Continued*

Deputy Prosecuting Attorney 1980-81. Member Garland County and Arkansas Bar Associations.
Office: 301 Garland County Courthouse, Hot Springs 71901.
Telephone: (501) 321-1333.
Fax: (501) 623-5149

WRIGHT, Susan Webber *(Chief Judge, United States District Court Eastern District of Arkansas)* Appointed for life by President George Bush to term beginning May 11, 1990. Born Texarkana Arkansas Aug 22, 1948. Educated at Randolph-Macon Woman's College B.A. 1970, University of Arkansas at Fayetteville M.P.A. 1973 and University of Arkansas School of Law J.D. with high honors 1975. Articles Editor 1974 and Editor-in-Chief 1975 Arkansas Law Review. Law Clerk to Hon. J. Smith Henley, U.S. Court of Appeals Eighth Circuit 1975-76. Admitted to practice Arkansas 1975.
Author "Medicolegal Issues in Wound Management" 1 University of Arkansas at Little Rock L. Jour. 455, 1979; "Arkansas Corporate Fiduciary Standards: Interested Directors' Contracts and the Doctrine of Corporate Opportunity" 4 University of Arkansas at Little Rock L. Jour. 39, 1982; "*Texaco v. Short* and Possible Dormant Mineral Legislation for Arkansas" *Arkansas Natural Resources Law Institute Proceedings* 1983; "Damages or Compensation for Unconstitutional Land Use Regulation" 37 Arkansas L. Rev. 612, 1984; "Fiduciary Duties Arising from Ownership of Oil and Gas Interests" *Arkansas Natural Resources Law Institute Proceedings* 1985; "Multiple Interests in Oil and Gas Ownership" *Arkansas Natural Resources Law Institute Proceedings* 1987; "The Arkansas Law of Oil and Gas" Chapters I and II 9 University of Arkansas at Little Rock L. Jour. 223, Chapter III 9 University of Arkansas at Little Rock L. Jour. 467, 1986-87, Chapter IV 10 University of Arkansas at Little Rock L. Jour. 5, 1987-88 and Chapter V 10 University of Arkansas at Little Rock L. Jour. 699, 1987-88; "Uncertainties in the Law of Sexual Harassment" 33 Richmond L. Rev. 11, 1999; "In Defense of Judicial Independence" 25 Oklahoma City L. Rev. 633, 2000; and "High Profile Cases in a Technological Age" 65 Missouri L. Rev. 785, 2000. Co-author with Robert R. Wright *Land Use in a Nutshell* West Publishing Co. 1978 2nd ed. 1985. Assistant Professor and Assistant Dean 1976-78, Associate Professor 1980-83 and Professor July 1983 to May 1990 University of Arkansas at Little Rock School of Law. Visiting Assistant Professor University of Arkansas at Fayetteville School of Law Summer 1980. Visiting Associate Professor The Ohio State University College of Law Jan 1981 to June 1981. Visiting Associate Professor Louisiana State University Law Center 1982-83. Former Member Advisory Committee to the United States Court of Appeals for the Eighth Circuit and Advisory Committee on Reappointment of U.S. Magistrate. Board Member American Judicature Society. Member Volunteer Organization for Central Arkansas Legal Services (VOCALS), Arkansas Association of Women Lawyers (Vice President 1977-78), The American Law Institute, Federal Judges Association, Pulaski County, Arkansas and American Bar Associations. Speaker Arkansas Natural Resources Law Institute Arkansas Bar Association 1983, 1985 and 1987. Participant Law and Economics Institute for Law Professors Law and Economics Center of Emory University Summer 1984. Recipient Faculty Excellence Award for Teaching from University of Arkansas at Little Rock School of Law 1990 and Randolph-Macon Woman's College Alumnae Achievement Award 1993. Member Arkansas Women's Forum and Baptist Women's/Children's Health Advisory Committee.
Office: 522 U.S. Courthouse, 600 West Capitol Avenue, Little Rock 72201-3325.
Telephone: (501) 604-5100.

YATES, Harvey *(Judge, Arkansas Circuit Court First Judicial Circuit)* Former Judge, West Helena Municipal Court.
Mailing address: P.O. Box 2084, West Helena 72390.
Telephone: (870) 338-5520.
Fax: (870) 338-5524

YEARGAN, Charles A. *(Judge, Arkansas Circuit Court Ninth West Judicial Circuit)* Elected Nov 1996 to term beginning Jan 1, 1997. Reelected Nov 1998 and May 2002. Current term expires Dec 31, 2008. Born Nashville Arkansas Sept 19, 1951. Religious affiliation: Church of Christ. Educated at University of Arkansas at Fayetteville B.S.P.A. 1973 J.D. 1976. Member Delta Theta Phi. Admitted to practice Arkansas 1976 and U.S. District Court 1977. In legal practice Glenwood 1977-97. Judge, Murfeesboro Municipal Court 1990-97. Former Chancellor, Arkansas Chancery Court Ninth Judicial Circuit West.
City Attorney Glenwood 1976-91. Deputy Prosecuting Attorney Ninth East Judicial Circuit 1980-90. Member Arkansas and American Bar Associations. Attended "Current Issues in Family Law" Feb 21, 1997, General Jurisdiction Course Aug 1, 1997, Conducting the Trial Nov 20, 1998 and No Reversals-Correct Rulings Oct 2, 1999. Recipient Community Service Award from Glenwood 1991. Named Tourism Person of the Year by Arkansas Department of Parks and Tourism 1993. Democrat. Former Member University of Arkansas Alumni Board and Lion's Club. Enjoys travel and stamps.
Mailing address: P.O. Box 820, Murfreesboro 71958.
Office: 225 South Washington Street, Murfreesboro 71958.
Telephone: (870) 285-2900.
Fax: (870) 285-2950

YOCUM, Tony *(Judge, Hope District Court)* Term expires Dec 31, 2004.
Mailing address: P.O. Box 583, Hope 71802-0583.
Telephone: (870) 777-8871.

YOUNG, H. David *(Magistrate Judge, United States District Court Eastern District of Arkansas)* Appointed by U.S. District Court judges.
Office: 442 U.S. Courthouse, 600 West Capitol Avenue, Little Rock 72201-3325.
Telephone: (501) 604-5180.

ZIMMERMAN, Stacey *(Judge, Arkansas Circuit Court Fourth Judicial Circuit)* Elected Nov 7, 1998 to term beginning Jan 1, 1999. Reelected 2002, current term expires Dec 31, 2008. Serves Juvenile Division. Born Amarillo Texas. Educated at Texas Tech University B.S. magna cum laude 1983 M.S. 1986 J.D. 1986 and University of Arkansas LL.M. 1988. Admitted to practice Texas 1987 and Arkansas 1989. In legal practice Fayetteville Arkansas 1989-98. Former Chancellor, Arkansas Chancery Court Fourth Judicial Circuit.

ZIMMERMAN, STACEY—*Continued*

Deputy Prosecutor 1991-98. Member American Inns of Court, State Bar of Texas and Arkansas Bar Association. Attended various conferences on juvenile justice. Recipient 40 under 40 Award from Northwest Arkansas Business Journal 1999 and Fayetteville's Young Top Five Award 2000.

Office: 885 Clydesdale Drive, Fayetteville 72701.

Telephone: (479) 444-1739.

Fax: (479) 444-1749

CALIFORNIA

Capital SACRAMENTO

UNITED STATES DISTRICT COURTS DISTRICTS OF CALIFORNIA

Within California there are four United States District Courts. For descriptive information refer to the United States Courts section.

CENTRAL DISTRICT consists of three divisions.

Eastern Division includes Riverside and San Bernardino counties. The court sits at Riverside and San Bernardino, and may sit at other locations not more than five miles from either city.

Southern Division includes Orange County. The court sits at Santa Ana.

Western Division includes Los Angeles, San Luis Obispo, Santa Barbara and Ventura counties. The court sits at Los Angeles.

Chief Judge

Consuelo Bland Marshall

Judges

Manuel L. Real
Terry J. Hatter, Jr.
Alicemarie H. Stotler
Stephen V. Wilson
Dickran Tevrizian
Ronald S. W. Lew
Gary L. Taylor
Lourdes G. Baird
Audrey Brodie Collins
Robert James Timlin
George Herbert King
Dean D. Pregerson
Christina A. Snyder
Margaret M. Morrow
A. Howard Matz
Nora Manella
David O. Carter
Gary Feess
Virginia A. Phillips
Florence-Marie Cooper
Percy Anderson
John F. Walter
Robert G. Klausner

Senior Judges

A. Andrew Hauk
Robert J. Kelleher
Wm. Matthew Byrne, Jr.
Robert M. Takasugi
Mariana R. Pfaelzer
Edward Rafeedie
Harry L. Hupp
William J. Rea
William D. Keller
J. Spencer Letts

Clerk

Sherri R. Carter
G-8 U.S. Courthouse
312 North Spring Street
Los Angeles, California 90012
(213) 894-3535

EASTERN DISTRICT includes Alpine, Amador, Butte, Calaveras, Colusa, El Dorado, Fresno, Glenn, Inyo, Kern, Kings, Lassen, Madera, Mariposa, Merced, Modoc, Mono, Nevada, Placer, Plumas, Sacramento, San Joaquin, Shasta, Sierra, Siskiyou, Solano, Stanislaus, Sutter, Tehama, Trinity, Tulare, Tuolumne, Yolo and Yuba counties. The court sits at Fresno, Redding and Sacramento.

Chief Judge

William B. Shubb

Judges

David F. Levi
Oliver W. Wanger
Garland E. Burrell, Jr.
Anthony W. Ishii
Frank C. Damrell, Jr.
Morrison C. England, Jr.

Senior Judges

Lawrence K. Karlton
Robert E. Coyle
Edward J. Garcia

Clerk

Jack L. Wagner
4-200 U.S. Courthouse
501 I Street
Sacramento, California 95814-2322
(916) 930-4000

NORTHERN DISTRICT includes Alameda, Contra Costa, Del Norte, Humboldt, Lake, Marin, Mendocino, Monterey, Napa, San Benito, San Francisco, San Mateo, Santa Clara, Santa Cruz and Sonoma counties. The court sits at Eureka, Oakland, San Francisco and San Jose.

Chief Judge

Marilyn Hall Patel

Judges

Vaughn R. Walker
James Ware
Saundra Brown Armstrong
Ronald M. Whyte
Claudia Wilken
Maxine M. Chesney
Susan Yvonne Illston
Martin J. Jenkins
Charles R. Breyer
Jeremy D. Fogel
William Alsup
Phyllis J. Hamilton
Jeffrey Steven White

Senior Judges

Samuel Conti
William W Schwarzer
Thelton E. Henderson
D. Lowell Jensen

Clerk

Richard W. Wieking
U.S. Courthouse
450 Golden Gate Avenue
P.O. Box 36060
San Francisco, California 94102-3489
(415) 522-2000

SOUTHERN DISTRICT includes Imperial and San Diego counties. The court sits at San Diego.

Chief Judge

Marilyn L. Huff

Judges

Judith N. Keep
Irma E. Gonzalez
Napoleon A. Jones, Jr.
Barry Ted Moskowitz

UNITED STATES DISTRICT COURTS DISTRICTS OF CALIFORNIA—*Continued*

Jeffrey T. Miller
M. James Lorenz
Thomas J. Whelan

Senior Judges

Howard B. Turrentine
Gordon Thompson, Jr.
William B. Enright
Rudi M. Brewster
John S. Rhoades, Sr.

Clerk

W. Samuel Hamrick, Jr.
4290 Federal Building
880 Front Street
San Diego, California 92101-8900
(619) 557-6348

UNITED STATES MAGISTRATE JUDGES OF CALIFORNIA

CENTRAL DISTRICT

Willard W. McEwen, Jr.
Charles F. Eick
Stephen J. Hillman
Andrew J. Wistrich
Rosalyn M. Chapman
Arthur Nakazato
Ralph Zarefsky
Jeffrey W. Johnson
Victor B. Kenton
Patrick J. Walsh
Paul L. Abrams
Marc L. Goldman
Carolyn Turchin
James W. McMahon
Robert N. Block
Carla M. Woehrle
Margaret A. Nagle
Stephen E. Miller
Stephen G. Larson
Jennifer T. Lum
Fernando M. Olguin
Suzanne H. Segal

EASTERN DISTRICT

John F. Moulds
Gregory G. Hollows
Peter A. Nowinski
Hollis G. Best
Lawrence J. O'Neill
Craig M. Kellison
Dennis L. Beck
Sandra Snyder
Dale A. Drozd
Kimberly J. Mueller

NORTHERN DISTRICT

Larry B. Nord
Patricia V. Trumbull
Bernard Zimmerman
Elizabeth D. Laporte
Richard Seeborg
Howard R. Lloyd
Wayne D. Brazil
Maria-Elena James
James L. Larson
Joseph C. Spero
Edward M. Chen

SOUTHERN DISTRICT

Louisa Porter
Ruben Brooks
James F. Stiven
John A. Houston
Roger T. Benitez
Leo S. Papas
Anthony J. Battaglia
Larry A. Burns
Nita L. Stormes

Recalled Magistrate Judges

Edward A. Infante (Northern)
Joseph E. Schmitt (Southern)
Roger C. McKee (Southern)

UNITED STATES BANKRUPTCY COURTS OF CALIFORNIA

CENTRAL DISTRICT

Chief Judge

Barry Russell

Judges

David N. Naugle
Samuel L. Bufford
James N. Barr
Robin L. Riblet
Alan M. Ahart
Mitchel Roy Goldberg
Ernest M. Robles
Erithe A. Smith
Ellen Carroll
Peter H. Carroll
Geraldine Mund
John E. Ryan
Arthur M. Greenwald
Kathleen T. Lax
Vincent P. Zurzolo
Robert W. Alberts
Thomas B. Donovan
Meredith A. Jury
Sheri Bluebond

Bankruptcy Clerk

Jon D. Ceretto
1260 Federal Building
255 East Temple Street
Los Angeles, California 90012
(213) 894-6244

EASTERN DISTRICT

Chief Judge

Michael S. McManus

Judges

Christopher M. Klein
Jane Dickson McKeag
Whitney Rimel
Thomas C. Holman
W. Richard Lee

Recalled Judges

Richard T. Ford
David E. Russell
Brett J. Dorian

Bankruptcy Clerk

Richard G. Heltzel
3-200 U.S. Courthouse
501 I Street
Sacramento, California 95814
(916) 930-4400

NORTHERN DISTRICT

Chief Judge

Edward D. Jellen

Judges

Thomas E. Carlson
Leslie J. Tchaikovsky
Marilyn Morgan
Arthur S. Weissbrodt
Alan Jaroslovsky
Randall J. Newsome
James R. Grube
Dennis Montali

Bankruptcy Clerk

Gloria L. Franklin
P.O. Box 7341
San Francisco, California 94120-7341
(415) 268-2300

SOUTHERN DISTRICT

Chief Judge

John J. Hargrove

Judges

James W. Meyers
Louise DeCarl Adler
Peter W. Bowie

UNITED STATES DISTRICT COURTS DISTRICTS OF CALIFORNIA—*Continued*

Bankruptcy Clerk
Barry K. Lander
U.S. Courthouse
325 West F Street
San Diego, California 92101-6991
(619) 557-5620

CALIFORNIA SUPREME COURT

The Supreme Court is California's court of last resort. The court consists of a chief justice and six associate justices appointed by the governor and confirmed by the Commission on Judicial Appointments. After confirmation, justices serve until the next gubernatorial election and then run unopposed on a nonpartisan ballot for election to twelve-year terms. Retired justices may serve the state courts by assignment of the chief justice.

The court has original jurisdiction in mandamus, certiorari, prohibition and habeas corpus proceedings. The court may review decisions of the Courts of Appeal, but a constitutional amendment enacted in 1985 enables the court to select specific issues for review rather than deciding all the issues in every case appealed to it. The court has final appellate jurisdiction over all cases in which a judgment of death has been pronounced. The court also reviews the recommendations of the Commission on Judicial Performance and the State Bar of California concerning the removal and suspension of judges and attorneys for misconduct.

The court sits en banc and holds session all year. The court sits regularly at San Francisco, Los Angeles and Sacramento, but special sessions may be held elsewhere.

Chief Justice
Ronald M. George

Associate Justices
Joyce Luther Kennard
Kathryn Mickle Werdegar
Carlos R. Moreno
Marvin R. Baxter
Ming W. Chin
Janice R. Brown

Clerk
Fritz Ohlrich
455 Golden Gate Avenue
San Francisco, California 94102-3660
(415) 865-7015

Administrative Director of the Courts
William C. Vickrey
455 Golden Gate Avenue
San Francisco, California 94102-3660
(415) 865-4200

CALIFORNIA COURTS OF APPEAL

The Courts of Appeal are courts of intermediate appellate jurisdiction in California. Justices are appointed by the governor and confirmed by the Commission on Judicial Appointments. After confirmation, justices serve until the next gubernatorial election and then run unopposed on a nonpartisan ballot for election to twelve-year terms. California has six appellate districts, each composed of one or more divisions. The chief justice appoints a presiding justice to each appellate district or division. In districts having only one division, the presiding justice shall act as the administrative presiding justice. In districts having more than one division, the chief justice appoints one presiding justice to serve as administrative head of the entire district. Retired justices may serve the state courts by assignment of the chief justice.

The courts have appellate jurisdiction in all cases on appeal from Superior Courts except when judgment of death has been pronounced, and in other cases as prescribed by statute. The courts have original jurisdiction in writ proceedings.

FIRST DISTRICT includes Alameda, Contra Costa, Del Norte, Humboldt, Lake, Marin, Mendocino, Napa, San Francisco, San Mateo, Solano and Sonoma counties and consists of five divisions. The court sits at San Francisco.

Administrative Presiding Justice
William R. McGuiness

DIVISION ONE

Presiding Justice
James J. Marchiano

Associate Justices
Sandra Lynn Margulies
William D. Stein
Douglas E. Swager

DIVISION TWO

Presiding Justice
John Anthony Kline

Associate Justices
Paul R. Haerle
James R. Lambden
Ignazio "Nace" John Ruvolo

DIVISION THREE

Presiding Justice
William R. McGuiness

Associate Justices
Carol A. Corrigan
Joanne C. Parrilli
Stuart R. Pollak

DIVISION FOUR

Presiding Justice
Laurence Donald Kay

Associate Justices
Timothy A. Reardon
Maria P. Rivera
Patricia K. Sepulveda

DIVISION FIVE

Presiding Justice
Barbara J. R. Jones

Associate Justices
Linda Marino Gemello
Mark B. Simons
Lawrence T. Stevens

SECOND DISTRICT includes Los Angeles, San Luis Obispo, Santa Barbara and Ventura counties and consists of eight divisions. The court sits at Los Angeles and Ventura.

CALIFORNIA COURTS OF APPEAL—*Continued*

Administrative Presiding Justice
Charles S. Vogel

DIVISION ONE

Presiding Justice
Vaino Hassan Spencer

Associate Justices
Robert M. Mallano
Reuben A. Ortega
Miriam A. Vogel

DIVISION TWO

Presiding Justice
Roger W. Boren

Associate Justices
Judith Ashmann-Gerst
Michael Gordon Nott
Kathryn Doi Todd

DIVISION THREE

Presiding Justice
Joan Dempsey Klein

Associate Justices
Richard D. Aldrich
H. Walter Croskey
Patti S. Kitching

DIVISION FOUR

Presiding Justice
Charles S. Vogel

Associate Justices
Daniel A. Curry
Norman L. Epstein
J. Gary Hastings

DIVISION FIVE

Presiding Justice
Paul A. Turner

Associate Justices
Orville A. Armstrong
Margaret M. Grignon
Richard M. Mosk

DIVISION SIX

Presiding Justice
Arthur Gilbert

Associate Justices
Paul H. Coffee
Steven Zalkind Perren
Kenneth R. Yegan

DIVISION SEVEN

Presiding Justice
Dennis M. Perluss

Associate Justices
Earl Johnson, Jr.
Norvell "Fred" Woods, Jr.
vacancy
vacancy

DIVISION EIGHT

Presiding Justice
Candace D. Cooper

Associate Justices
Paul Boland
Laurence D. Rubin
vacancy

THIRD DISTRICT includes Alpine, Amador, Butte, Calaveras, Colusa, El Dorado, Glenn, Lassen, Modoc, Mono, Nevada, Placer, Plumas, Sacramento, San Joaquin, Shasta, Sierra, Siskiyou, Sutter, Tehama, Trinity, Yolo and Yuba counties. The court sits at Sacramento.

Administrative Presiding Justice
Arthur G. Scotland

Presiding Justice
Arthur G. Scotland

Associate Justices

Coleman A. Blease	Connie M. Callahan
Rodney Davis	Harry E. Hull, Jr.
Daniel M. Kolkey	Fred K. Morrison
George Nicholson	Vance W. Raye
Ronald B. Robie	Richard M. Sims, III

FOURTH DISTRICT includes Imperial, Inyo, Orange, Riverside, San Bernardino and San Diego counties and consists of three divisions. Division One sits at San Diego, Division Two sits at San Bernardino and Division Three sits at Santa Ana.

Administrative Presiding Justice
Daniel J. Kremer

DIVISION ONE

Presiding Justice
Daniel J. Kremer

Associate Justices

Cynthia G. Aaron	Patricia D. Benke
Judith Lynnette Haller	Richard D. Huffman
Judith D. McConnell	Alex C. McDonald
James A. McIntyre	Gilbert Nares
Terry O'Rourke	

DIVISION TWO

Presiding Justice
Manuel Angelo Ramirez

Associate Justices

Barton C. Gaut	Thomas E. Hollenhorst
Jeffrey King	Art W. McKinster
Betty Ann Richli	James D. Ward

DIVISION THREE

Presiding Justice
David George Sills

Associate Justices

Richard M. Aronson	William W. Bedsworth
Richard David Fybel	Raymond J. Ikola
Eileen C. Moore	Kathleen E. O'Leary
William F. Rylaarsdam	

FIFTH DISTRICT includes Fresno, Kern, Kings, Madera, Mariposa, Merced, Stanislaus, Tulare and Tuolumne counties. The court sits at Fresno.

CALIFORNIA COURTS OF APPEAL—*Continued*

Administrative Presiding Justice
James A. Ardaiz

Presiding Justice
James A. Ardaiz

Associate Justices
Tim S. Buckley
Nickolas J. Dibiaso
Thomas A. Harris
Steven M. Vartabedian
vacancy
Dennis A. Cornell
Gene M. Gomes
Herbert I. Levy
Rebecca A. Wiseman

SIXTH DISTRICT includes Monterey, San Benito, Santa Clara and Santa Cruz counties. The court sits at San Jose.

Administrative Presiding Justice
Conrad Lee Rushing

Presiding Justice
Conrad Lee Rushing

Associate Justices
Patricia Bamattre-Manoukian
Eugene M. Premo
vacancy
Franklin D. Elia
Nathan D. Mihara
William M. Wunderlich

CALIFORNIA TRIAL COURTS

Prior to June 1998, California's trial courts comprised the Superior Courts and Municipal Courts, each with its own jurisdiction and number of judges fixed by the Legislature. In accordance with the Trial Court Realignment and Efficiency Act of 1991, some Superior Courts consolidated or coordinated their courts with their corresponding Municipal Courts. The Act called for major court administration reforms, including the mandate that all trial courts coordinate administratively and judicially in order to share resources, improve access and reduce operating costs. On June 2, 1998, California voters approved Proposition 220, a constitutional amendment that permits the judges in each county to unify their Superior Courts and Municipal Courts into a single Superior Court with jurisdiction over all types of cases if a majority of Superior Court and Municipal Court judges within the county approve. As of Feb 8, 2001, all fifty-eight counties have unified their trial courts.

SUPERIOR COURTS OF CALIFORNIA

The Superior Courts are courts of general trial jurisdiction in California. Judges serve six-year terms and are elected by voters of the county on a nonpartisan ballot at general elections. Vacancies are filled by appointment of the governor. In counties with more than one judge serving, a presiding judge is chosen by peer vote to serve a term of not less than one year. The number of judges in each of the fifty-eight counties is determined by the state legislature. Retired judges may serve by assignment of the chief justice.

The courts have original trial jurisdiction over all criminal cases including felonies, misdemeanors and traffic matters. The courts also have jurisdiction over all civil cases including family law, probate, juvenile and general civil matters. The courts have exclusive jurisdiction in all cases involving violations of ordinances of cities or towns. The courts have appellate jurisdiction in limited civil cases (where $25,000 or less is at issue) and misdemeanors; these appeals are heard by a three-judge appellate panel in each county. When a small claims case is appealed, a Superior Court judge decides the case. Appeals may also be transferred to the Courts of Appeal.

The courts sit at the county seats and as indicated.

SUPERIOR COURT OF CALIFORNIA COUNTY OF ALAMEDA sits at Hayward, Oakland and Pleasanton.

Judges
Jeffrey S. Allen
Gail Brewster Bereola
Steven A. Brick
Kenneth Mark Burr
Cecilia P. Castellanos
Stephen A. Dombrink
Robert Fairwell
Keith H. Fudenna
Jack Gifford
Dan Grimmer
Roy Hashimoto
George C. Hernandez, Jr.
David E. Hunter
D. Ronald Hyde
Richard B. Iglehart
Richard O. Keller
John F. Kraetzer
Robert K. Kurtz
William A. McKinstry
Barbara J. Miller
Christine K. Moruza
Henry E. Needham, Jr.
Gary M. Picetti
Gloria F. Rhynes
Frank Roesch
Bonnie Lewman Sabraw
Philip V. Sarkisian
Harry R. Sheppard
Julia Spain
Trina Thompson Stanley
Alice Vilardi
Horace Wheatley
Carlos G. Ynostroza
vacancy
vacancy
Gordon S. Baranco
Jacob Blea, III
Carol S. Brosnahan
Joan S. Cartwright
Julie Conger
Leopoldo E. Dorado
Robert B. Freedman
Delbert C. Gee
Larry J. Goodman
Brenda Fay Harbin-Forte
Peggy Fulton Hora
Jeffrey W. Horner
Joseph Hurley
Allan D. Hymer
Ken Martin Kawaichi
Kenneth R. Kingsbury
David M. Krashna
Jo-Lynne Q. Lee
Dennis J. McLaughlin
Carl W. Morris
Vernon K. Nakahara
Yolanda N. Northridge
Thomas M. Reardon
James A. Richman
Jon R. Rolefson
Ronald M. Sabraw
Reginald P. Saunders
Winifred Younge Smith
Donald B. Squires
Jon S. Tigar
Hugh A. Walker
Marshall Ivan Whitley
Patrick J. Zika
vacancy

SUPERIOR COURT OF CALIFORNIA COUNTY OF ALPINE sits at Markleeville.

Judges
Harold Bradford
David L. DeVore

SUPERIOR COURT OF CALIFORNIA COUNTY OF AMADOR sits at Jackson.

Judges
Susan C. Harlan
David Sargent Richmond

SUPERIOR COURT OF CALIFORNIA COUNTY OF BUTTE sits at Oroville.

CALIFORNIA TRIAL COURTS—*Continued*

Judges

Stephen E. Benson
Roger G. Gilbert
Robert A. Glusman
Gerald Hermansen
Steven J. Howell
Thomas W. Kelly
William R. Patrick
James F. Reilley
Barbara L. Roberts
Darrell W. Stevens

SUPERIOR COURT OF CALIFORNIA COUNTY OF CALAVERAS sits at San Andreas.

Judges

John E. Martin
Douglas V. Mewhinney

SUPERIOR COURT OF CALIFORNIA COUNTY OF COLUSA sits at Colusa.

Judges

S. William Abel
John H. Tiernan

SUPERIOR COURT OF CALIFORNIA COUNTY OF CONTRA COSTA sits at Martinez.

Judges

John M. Allen
Steven K. Austin
Barry Baskin
Peter A. Berger
Laurel S. Brady
Terence L. Bruiniers
Theresa J. Canepa
Judith S. Craddick
Joyce M. Cram
Merle R. Eaton
Richard S. Flier
David B. Flinn
Garrett J. Grant
Harlan G. Grossman
Lois Haight
Joni T. Hiramoto
John William Kennedy
William M. Kolin
Thomas M. Maddock
Bruce Clayton Mills
Cheryl Mills
John C. Minney
Mary Ann O'Malley
William O'Malley
Diana Becton Smith
George V. Spanos
Peter L. Spinetta
John Hideki Sugiyama
James R. Trembath
Bruce Van Voorhis
Barbara Ann Zúñiga
vacancy
vacancy

SUPERIOR COURT OF CALIFORNIA COUNTY OF DEL NORTE sits at Crescent City.

Judges

William H. Follett
Robert W. Weir

SUPERIOR COURT OF CALIFORNIA COUNTY OF EL DORADO sits at Placerville and South Lake Tahoe.

Judges

Eddie T. Keller
Suzanne N. Kingsbury
Jerald Lasarow
Douglas C. Phimister
Douglas B. Proud
James R. Wagoner

SUPERIOR COURT OF CALIFORNIA COUNTY OF FRESNO sits at Fresno.

Judges

Gary S. Austin
Donald S. Black
Carlos A. Cabrera
A. Dennis Caeton
Jane Cardoza
Hilary A. Chittick
Fred Dupras
Wayne R. Ellison
Gregory T. Fain
William Kent Hamlin
Brad R. Hill
Gary D. Hoff
Dale Ikeda
Franklin P. Jones
Lawrence Jones
Timothy A. Kams
Stephen Joseph Kane
Jon N. Kapetan
Debra Kazanjian
W. Kent Levis
Ralph Nunez
Robert H. Oliver
James R. Oppliger
Gary R. Orozco
Harry N. Papadakis
Rosendo Pena, Jr.
James Petrucelli
R. L. "Chip" Putnam
Edward Sarkisian, Jr.
Alan M. Simpson
M. Bruce Smith
Mark Wood Snauffer
John F. Vogt
Denise Lee Whitehead
Jane A. York
vacancy

SUPERIOR COURT OF CALIFORNIA COUNTY OF GLENN sits at Willows.

Judges

Donald Cole Byrd
Angus Saint-Evens

SUPERIOR COURT OF CALIFORNIA COUNTY OF HUMBOLDT sits at Eureka.

Judges

J. Michael Brown
Timothy Paul Cissna
John T. Feeney
Marilyn B. Miles
Dale A. Reinholtsen
W. Bruce Watson, Jr.
Christopher G. Wilson

SUPERIOR COURT OF CALIFORNIA COUNTY OF IMPERIAL sits at El Centro.

Judges

Matias R. Contreras
Raymond Cota
Donal B. Donnelly
Annie M. Gutierrez
James H. Harmon
Jeffrey Bruce Jones
Juan Ulloa
Christopher W. Yeager
Joseph Zimmerman

SUPERIOR COURT OF CALIFORNIA COUNTY OF INYO sits at Independence.

Judges

Brian Lamb
Dean Stout

SUPERIOR COURT OF CALIFORNIA COUNTY OF KERN sits at Bakersfield.

Judges

Robert J. Anspach
Michael G. Bush
Sidney P. Chapin
L. Bryce Chase
Lee Phillip Felice
John L. Fielder
Gary T. Friedman
Stephen P. Gildner
Frank Allen Hoover
Colette M. Humphrey
Gary A. Ingle
John I. Kelly
Michael B. Lewis
Robert E. McDaniel
Charles P. McNutt
Sharon Mettler
Romero J. Moench
Richard J. Oberholzer
John D. Oglesby
Charles B. Pfister
Craig Phillips
Catherine D. Purcell
John I. Quinlen
Roger D. Randall
Harry Anthony Staley
James M. Stuart
Jon Edward Stuebbe
Robert S. Tafoya
Jerold L. Turner
Kenneth Twisselman, II
Arthur E. Wallace
Clarence Westra, Jr.
Gary R. Witt

SUPERIOR COURT OF CALIFORNIA COUNTY OF KINGS sits at Hanford.

Judges

Lynn C. Atkinson
Louis F. Bissig
Charles R. Johnson
Ronald Maciel

CALIFORNIA TRIAL COURTS—*Continued*

George Orndoff
John G. O'Rourke
Peter M. Schultz

SUPERIOR COURT OF CALIFORNIA COUNTY OF LAKE sits at Lakeport.

Judges

Robert L. Crone, Jr.
Stephen Owen Hedstrom
David W. Herrick
Arthur H. Mann

SUPERIOR COURT OF CALIFORNIA COUNTY OF LASSEN sits at Susanville.

Judges

Stephen Douglas Bradbury
Ridgely L. Lazard

SUPERIOR COURT OF CALIFORNIA COUNTY OF LOS ANGELES sits at Alhambra, Burbank, Compton, Downey, Glendale, Inglewood, Lancaster, Long Beach, Los Angeles, Monterey Park, Norwalk, Pasadena, Pomona, San Fernando, Santa Monica, Sylmar, Torrance and Van Nuys.

Judges

Judith Abrams
Richard A. Adler
Gregory W. Alarcon
Bradford L. Andrews
Conrad Richard Aragon
Mark S. Arnold
Paul A. Bacigalupo
Henry T. Barela
William P. Barry
Floyd V. Baxter
Helen I. Bendix
Margaret Miller Bernal
William Beverly, Jr.
William J. Birney
Aviva Koenigsberg Bobb
James R. Brandlin
Kevin Clement Brazile
Kevin L. Brown
Nancy Brown
Susan Bryant-Deason
Alan Buckner
J. Michael Byrne
Judith L. Champagne
Victor E. Chávez
John Joseph Cheroske
Judith C. Chirlin
Charles Q. Clay, III
Lisa Hart Cole
Joan Comparet-Cassani
Chris R. Conway
Lawrence W. Crispo
J. Stephen Czuleger
Gary E. Daigh
Richard E. Denner
Joseph F. De Vanon
Joseph E. DiLoreto
John P. Doyle
Maureen Duffy-Lewis
Robert A. Dukes
Leslie A. Dunn
Lee Smalley Edmon
Jacob Adajian
Dennis A. Aichroth
Alice E. Altoon
Deborah B. Andrews
Phillip J. Argento
Monica Bachner
Valerie L. Baker
Antonio Barreto, Jr.
James Allen Bascue
Candace J. Beason
Elihu M. Berle
Lauren Weiss Bernstein
Tricia Ann Bigelow
Kenneth A. Black
Bob S. Bowers, Jr.
Joseph A. Brandolino
Irma Jean Brown
Leslie E. Brown
Soussan G. Bruguera
Daniel J. Buckley
Barbara Lee Burke
James C. Chalfant
Victoria G. Chaney
Victoria Chavez
William Chidsey, Jr.
Deborah L. Christian
Ronald S. Coen
Patricia L. Collins
Jacqueline Ann Connor
Michael A. Cowell
Janice Claire Croft
James R. Dabney
Ralph W. Dau
Ellen Carol Deshazer
Rudolph A. Diaz
David Isumu Doi
John T. Doyle
Michael M. Duggan
James R. Dunn
Anita H. Dymant
Anne Harwood Egerton
Emilie Harris Elias
Carol Williams Elswick
Peter Paul Espinoza
Christopher Estes
Dewey Lawes Falcone
Dean E. Farrar
Michael J. Farrell
Edward A. Ferns
Eudon Ferrell
Kelvin D. Filer
John S. Fisher
Paul G. Flynn
Elden S. Fox
Kenneth R. Freeman
Haley J. Fromholz
Fred J. Fujioka
Brian F. Gasdia
George Genesta
Bert Glennon, Jr.
Allan J. Goodman
Dudley W. Gray, II
Warren G. Greene
Philip S. Gutierrez
Alan B. Haber
John D. Harris
Ray L. Hart
Margaret M. Hay
Patrick J. Hegarty
Margaret Henry
Martin Larry Herscovitz
Philip H. Hickok
William F. Highberger
Joe W. Hilberman
Deirdre H. Hill
Michael R. Hoff
Amy D. Hogue
Charles E. Horan
David Maxwell Horwitz
Mary Thornton House
Jack P. Hunt
Susan E. Isacoff
Frank Y. Jackson
Dzintra I. Janavs
Barbara R. Johnson
Jane L. Johnson
Marion J. Johnson
Ann I. Jones
Mark A. Juhas
Alan S. Kalkin
Leon S. Kaplan
Andrew C. Kauffman
Kathleen Kennedy-Powell
Mark C. Kim
Steven J. Kleifield
Clifford Klein
Larry S. Knupp
Sandy R. Kriegler
John Kronstadt
Ruth Ann Kwan
Marvin M. Lager
Xenophon F. Lang, Jr.
Charles Carter Lee
Linda K. Lefkowitz
Arthur M. Lew
Elizabeth A. Lippitt
Daniel S. Lopez
Laura Ellison
Ruffo Espinosa, Jr.
Ruth Essegian
William F. Fahey
Thomas Falls
John P. Farrell
Irving S. Feffer
Gary J. Ferrari
Larry Paul Fidler
Dale S. Fischer
Madeleine Flier
Rodney G. Forneret
Josh M. Fredricks
Terry Friedman
Richard L. Fruin, Jr.
Hugh C. Gardner, III
Francis A. Gately, Jr.
Harvey Giss
Hank Goldberg
Carol Boas Goodson
Terry A. Green
Elizabeth A. Grimes
Paul Gutman
Gary R. Hahn
Leland B. Harris
Michael Harwin
Marcelita V. Haynes
John L. Henning
Thomas K. Herman
Robert L. Hess
Robert J. Higa
Bob T. Hight
Alice C. Hill
Ernest M. Hiroshige
Marilyn Lois Hoffman
Rose Hom
H. Chester Horn, Jr.
Francis J. Hourigan
Richard C. Hubbell
Maral Injejikian
Lance Allan Ito
Karl W. Jaeger
Arthur H. Jean, Jr.
Frank J. Johnson
Jerry E. Johnson
Michael Johnson
Morris Bruce Jones
James A. Kaddo
Bernard J. Kamins
Craig D. Karlan
Michael K. Kellogg
Gregory Keosian
Abraham Khan
Richard H. Kirschner
Brett Carroll Klein
Michael E. Knight
Richard G. Kolostian
Marlene Kristovich
Carolyn B. Kuhl
Owen Lee Kwong
Dennis J. Landin
Luis A. Lavin
Gibson W. Lee
Lisa B. Lench
Peter D. Lichtman
George R. G. Lomeli
Gilbert M. Lopez

CALIFORNIA TRIAL COURTS—*Continued*

John David Lord
Michael S. Luros
Paula Adele Mabrey
Lyle Michael MacKenzie
Robert D. Mackey
William A. MacLaughlin
Katherine Mader
Stephen A. Marcus
John L. Martinez
Jean E. Matusinka
Philip K. Mautino
Veronica Simmons McBeth
Patti Jo McKay
Peter Joseph Meeka
John Vernon Meigs
Rita J. Miller
Michael S. Mink
R. Bruce Minto
Lawrence J. Mira
Peter J. Mirich
Mark V. Mooney
Jack W. Morgan
Wendell Mortimer, Jr.
Mary Ann Murphy
Richard Naranjo
Michael Nash
Mark G. Nelson, Sr.
Jacqueline H. Nguyen
Karen Joy Nudell
Joanne B. O'Donnell
Steven D. Ogden
Vincent H. Okamoto
Charlaine F. Olmedo
Tomson T. Ong
S. James Otero
Yvette M. Palazuelos
Lorna Parnell
Roy L. Paul
Robert J. Perry
Victor H. Persón
Thomas A. Peterson
James B. Pierce
William R. Pounders
Daniel P. Ramirez
Cynthia Rayvis
Carol H. Rehm, Jr.
Marsha N. Revel
Andria K. Richey
Morton Rochman
Pamela R. Rogers
Richard R. Romero
Michelle R. Rosenblatt
Kevin A. Ross
Frances Rothschild
Rand Steven Rubin
Tammy Chung Ryu
Yvonne T. Sanchez
Jose I. Sandoval
John H. Sandoz
Steven P. Sanora
Michael T. Sauer
David Martin Schacter
Barbara Marie Scheper
Robert Alan Schnider
Ana Maria Luna
Richard W. Lyman, Jr.
Kenji Machida
Malcolm H. Mackey
Ronni B. MacLaren
Patrick T. Madden
Gregg Marcus
Bruce F. Marrs
Robert M. Martinez
Laura A. Matz
Jon M. Mayeda
Charles W. McCoy, Jr.
Chesley McKay, Jr.
Thomas I. McKnew, Jr.
Barbara Ann Meiers
Patrick Timothy Meyers
David Sherman Milton
David L. Minning
David Mintz
Raymond D. Mireles
Anthony J. Mohr
Tracy T. Moreno
Judson W. Morris, Jr.
Aurelio Muñoz
Deanne Smith Myers
Lloyd M. Nash
Richard Neidorf
Rodney E. Nelson
Cary H. Nishimoto
Gregory C. O'Brien, Jr.
Sam Ohta
Dan Thomas Oki
Robert P. O'Neill
Rafael A. Ongkeko
John W. Ouderkirk
Charles F. Palmer
Michael E. Pastor
David W. Perkins
Suzanne E. Person
Stephen D. Petersen
Charles L. Peven
Jan A. Pluim
Daniel S. Pratt
Curtis B. Rappe
Mel Red Recana
John H. Reid
Randy Rhodes
Richard E. Rico
Jesus I. Rodriguez
Randolph Rogers
Gerald Rosenberg
Alan S. Rosenfield
Frederick Rotenberg
Charles G. Rubin
William C. Ryan
Raul Anthony Sahagun
Teresa Sanchez-Gordon
Robert J. Sandoval
Melvin D. Sandvig
Cesar C. Sarmiento
Stephanie Sautner
Darlene E. Schempp
Patricia M. Schnegg
Robert J. Schuit
Howard J. Schwab
Teri Schwartz
John Segal
Charles D. Sheldon
Dorothy L. Shubin
Shari Kreisler Silver
C. Edward Simpson
C. Robert Simpson
Ronald V. Skyers
Terry Lee Smerling
Ronald M. Sohigian
Michael C. Solner
Philip L. Soto
Susan M. Speer
William N. Sterling
Emily A. Stevens
Thomas William Stoever
Kathryne A. Stoltz
Mary Strobel
Steven C. Suzukawa
Coleman A. Swart
Barry A. Taylor
Meredith C. Taylor
Leland H. Tipton
John A. Torribio
Rolf Michael Treu
Michael Anthony Tynan
Carlos A. Uranga
Richard W. Van Dusen
Craig Elliott Veals
Richard F. Walmark
Fumiko Hachiya Wasserman
Stanley Martin Weisberg
David S. Wesley
Diana M. Wheatley
Thomas R. White
L. Jeffrey Wiatt
William G. Willett
Alexander H. Williams, III
James L. Wright
David P. Yaffe
Laurie D. Zelon
vacancy
Keith L. Schwartz
Ramona G. See
Norman J. Shapiro
John P. Shook
Rosemary Shumsky
Jessica Perrin Silvers
Zaven V. Sinanian
Lois Anderson Smaltz
Spurgeon E. Smith
Thomas R. Sokolov
David Sotelo
S. Patricia Spear
Marjorie S. Steinberg
Michael L. Stern
William D. Stewart
Charles W. Stoll
Richard A. Stone
James M. Sutton, Jr.
Leslie A. Swain
Norman Perry Tarle
Eric C. Taylor
Sandra Ann Thompson
Patricia J. Titus
Thomas N. Townsend
Marcus O. Tucker, Jr.
Cynthia L. Ulfig
Judith A. Vander Lans
Steven Van Sicklen
Michael P. Vicencia
Fred N. Wapner
Allen J. Webster, Jr.
Debre Katz Weintraub
William R. Weisman
Carl J. West
Elizabeth Allen White
Gloria L. White-Brown
John Shepard Wiley, Jr.
Thomas J. Willhite, Jr.
Richard B. Wolfe
David A. Workman
George H. Wu
Reginald Yates
vacancy

SUPERIOR COURT OF CALIFORNIA COUNTY OF MADERA sits at Madera.

Judges

Thomas L. Bender
Jennifer R. S. Detjen
Edward P. Moffat, II
Charles A. Wieland
John W. DeGroot
David D. Minier
Roger L. Wayne

SUPERIOR COURT OF CALIFORNIA COUNTY OF MARIN sits at San Rafael.

Judges

Verna A. Adams
Michael B. Dufficy
John Stephen Graham
James R. Ritchie
John A. Sutro, Jr.
Terrence R. Boren
Lynn Duryee
William McGivern, Jr.
Vernon F. Smith
Lynn O'Malley Taylor

SUPERIOR COURT OF CALIFORNIA COUNTY OF MARIPOSA sits at Mariposa.

CALIFORNIA TRIAL COURTS—*Continued*

Judges

Wayne R. Parrish
F. Dana Walton

SUPERIOR COURT OF CALIFORNIA COUNTY OF MENDOCINO sits at Ukiah.

Judges

Ronald Brown
Richard James Henderson
Eric Labowitz
Leonard J. LaCasse
Jonathan M. Lehan
Cindee F. Mayfield
Henry Kent Nelson
vacancy

SUPERIOR COURT OF CALIFORNIA COUNTY OF MERCED sits at Merced.

Judges

Betty L. Dawson
Frank Dougherty
Hugh Flanagan
Ronald W. Hansen
John D. Kirihara
Robert D. Quall

SUPERIOR COURT OF CALIFORNIA COUNTY OF MODOC sits at Alturas.

Judges

Larry L. Dier
vacancy

SUPERIOR COURT OF CALIFORNIA COUNTY OF MONO sits at Bridgeport.

Judges

Stan Eller
Edward Forstenzer

SUPERIOR COURT OF CALIFORNIA COUNTY OF MONTEREY sits at Monterey and Salinas.

Judges

Richard M. Curtis
Susan M. Dauphiné
Wendy Clark Duffy
Terrance R. Duncan
Michael S. Fields
Adrienne M. Grover
Kay T. Kingsley
Albert H. Maldonado
Gary E. Meyer
Robert F. Moody
Robert A. O'Farrell
Marla Osborne-Anderson
John M. Phillips
Jonathan R. Price
Russell D. Scott
Stephen A. Sillman
Jose A. Velasquez
Lydia Villarreal

SUPERIOR COURT OF CALIFORNIA COUNTY OF NAPA sits at Napa.

Judges

Richard A. Bennett
Raymond A. Guadagni
Stephen Thomas Kroyer
W. Scott Snowden
Francisca P. Tisher
Ronald T. L. Young

SUPERIOR COURT OF CALIFORNIA COUNTY OF NEVADA sits at Nevada City.

Judges

Carl F. Bryan, II
M. Kathleen Butz
John H. Darlington
Albert Perry Dover
Ersel L. Edwards
C. Anders Holmer

SUPERIOR COURT OF CALIFORNIA COUNTY OF ORANGE sits at Santa Ana.

Judges

John S. Adams
Frederick P. Aguirre
Margaret R. Anderson
Matthew S. Anderson
Gail A. Andler
Andrew P. Banks
Ronald L. Bauer
Richard E. Behn
Carl Biggs
Thomas James Borris
Hugh Michael Brenner
Francisco P. Briseño
James M. Brooks
Jonathan H. Cannon
Cormac J. Carney
Marjorie Laird Carter
David R. Chaffee
Dennis S. Choate
Thierry Patrick Colaw
John Conley
Corey Scott Cramin
Donna L. Crandall
James J. Di Cesare
Daniel J. Didier
Patrick H. Donahue
Kim Garlin Dunning
Mary Fingal Erickson
William Lee Evans
Frank F. Fasel
Sheila Fell
Francisco F. Firmat
John L. Flynn, III
Richard O. Frazee, Sr.
William R. Froeberg
Robert H. Gallivan
Stephanie George
Geoffrey T. Glass
Thomas M. Goethals
James P. Gray
W. Michael Hayes
Frederick Paul Horn
Derek W. Hunt
Robert Byron Hutson
Pamela Lee Iles
C. Robert Jameson
Lance Jensen
Derek Guy Johnson
Gerald G. Johnston
M. Marc Kelly
Richard M. King
Carolyn Kirkwood
Ronald Patrick Kreber
Caryl A. Lee
Gregory H. Lewis
Wendy Lindley
Brett London
Kellie MacEachen
Glenn A. Mahler
Kazuharu Makino
Charles Margines
James Patrick Marion
Joy W. Markman
Michael McCartin
David Thomas McEachen
Dan McNerney
Kimberly Meninger
Franz E. Miller
Linda Lancet Miller
Jamoa A. Moberly
William M. Monroe
Robert James Moss
Gregory Munoz
Kirk H. Nakamura
Michael J. Naughton
Nho Trong Nguyen
Gary S. Paer
Steven L. Perk
Nancy A. Pollard
Peter J. Polos
James Howard Poole
Gregg L. Prickett
Roger B. Robbins
Craig E. Robison
Luis A. Rodriguez
Glenda Sanders
B. Tam Nomoto Schumann
James V. Selna
H. Warren Siegel
Susanne S. Shaw
Carla M. Singer
Claudia Silbar
Richard Stanford, Jr.
Clay M. Smith
James Allen Stotler
Nancy Wieben Stock
Stephen J. Sundvold
Elaine Streger
Thomas N. Thrasher
David A. Thompson
Josephine Staton Tucker
Richard Toohey
John M. Watson
David C. Velasquez
John C. Woolley
Randell L. Wilkinson
vacancy
vacancy
vacancy

SUPERIOR COURT OF CALIFORNIA COUNTY OF PLACER sits at Auburn.

Judges

John L. Cosgrove
J. Richard Couzens
Larry D. Gaddis
James D. Garbolino
Eugene S. Gini, Jr.
Frances A. Kearney
Joseph O'Flaherty
Alan V. Pineschi
James L. Roeder

SUPERIOR COURT OF CALIFORNIA COUNTY OF PLUMAS sits at Quincy.

Judges

Ira R. Kaufman
Garrett Olney

CALIFORNIA TRIAL COURTS—*Continued*

SUPERIOR COURT OF CALIFORNIA COUNTY OF RIVERSIDE sits at Blythe, Indio, Palm Springs and Riverside.

Judges

B. J. Bjork
Gordon R. Burkhart
Thomas H. Cahraman
Mark Ashton Cope
James A. Cox
Graham Anderson Cribbs
Stephen D. Cunnison
H. Morgan Dougherty
Thomas Douglass, Jr.
L. Becky Dugan
Charles D. Field
Richard Todd Fields
Lawrence W. Fry
J. Thompson Hanks
James S. Hawkins
Timothy J. Heaslet
Helios "Joe" Hernandez
Ronald R. Heumann
Dallas Scott Holmes
Erik Michael Kaiser
Jean Pfeiffer Leonard
Roger A. Luebs
Patrick F. Magers
Dennis A. McConaghy
Janice M. McIntyre
Robert J. McIntyre
Douglas P. Miller
W. Charles Morgan
H. Dennis Myers
Arjuna T. Saraydarian
Christopher J. Sheldon
Vilia Sherman
Elisabeth Sichel
Robert George Spitzer
Charles Stafford, Jr.
Robert Gregory Taylor
Ronald L. Taylor
Christian Thierbach
Gary B. Tranbarger
Gloria Connor Trask
Rodney L. Walker
James T. Warren
Sharon J. Waters
Edward D. Webster
Randall D. White
Albert J. Wojcik
Paul E. Zellerbach
vacancy
vacancy

SUPERIOR COURT OF CALIFORNIA COUNTY OF SACRAMENTO sits at Sacramento.

Judges

David W. Abbott
Gerald S. Bakarich
Jerilyn L. Borack
Trena H. Burger-Plavan
Raymond M. Cadei
Roland L. Candee
Tani G. Cantil-Sakauye
Thomas M. Cecil
Shelleyanne W. L. Chang
Lloyd G. Connelly
David De Alba
Patricia C. Esgro
Greta Fall
Timothy M. Frawley
Michael T. Garcia
Maryanne G. Gilliard
Richard H. Gilmour
Joe S. Gray
Jeffrey L. Gunther
Kenneth L. Hake
Janice Carolyn Hayes
James Paul Henke
Judy Holzer Hersher
Russell L. Hom
Talmadge R. Jones
Michael P. Kenny
Charles C. Kobayashi
James L. Long
Patrick Marlette
Peter J. McBrien
Loren E. McMaster
Cheryl Chun Meegan
John A. Mendez
James M. Mize
James I. Morris
Gary S. Mullen
Troy L. Nunley
Gail D. Ohanesian
Richard Kent Park
Kenneth G. Peterson
Steven H. Rodda
John Van Dyke "Jack" Sapunor
Renard F. Shepard
D. Robert Shuman
Pamela Smith-Steward
Michael S. Ullman
Jane Ure
Brian R. Van Camp
Emily E. Vasquez
Michael G. Virga
John P. Winn
vacancy

SUPERIOR COURT OF CALIFORNIA COUNTY OF SAN BENITO sits at Hollister.

Judges

Steven R. Sanders
Harry J. Tobias

SUPERIOR COURT OF CALIFORNIA COUNTY OF SAN BERNARDINO sits at Barstow, Fontana, Joshua Tree, Rancho Cucamonga, San Bernardino and Victorville.

Judges

Larry W. Allen
Donald R. Alvarez
Stephen H. Ashworth
Kenneth Barr
Walter L. Blackwell, III
Joan Marie Borba
Joseph R. Brisco
Gerard S. Brown
Paul M. Bryant, Jr.
Ronald Christianson
Dennis G. Cole
Keith D. Davis
Michael M. Dest
James M. Dorr
James A. Edwards
Douglas M. Elwell
W. Robert Fawke
Douglas Alan Fettel
Jules E. Fleuret
Mary E. Fuller
Donna G. Garza
Douglas N. Gericke
John B. Gibson
Thomas Daniel Glasser
J. Michael Gunn
Arthur Harrison
Sylvia L. Husing
Craig S. Kamansky
Michael R. Libutti
Cynthia Ann Ludvigsen
Frederick A. Mandabach
John Nevin Martin
Brian S. McCarville
James C. McGuire
Roberta McPeters
Patrick Joseph Morris
Phillip M. Morris
Eric M. Nakata
Peter H. Norell
John M. Pacheco
Barry L. Plotkin
Margaret A. Powers
Tara Reilly
Shahla S. Sabet
Brian David Saunders
Gus James Skropos
Michael A. Smith
Bert L. Swift
John M. Tomberlin
Ingrid Adamson Uhler
John Peter Vander Feer
Raymond P. Van Stockum
A. Rex Victor
John P. Wade
Christopher J. Warner
James Michael Welch
Katrina West
Linda M. Wilde
Rufus L. Yent
Raymond C. Youngquist
vacancy
vacancy
vacancy

SUPERIOR COURT OF CALIFORNIA COUNTY OF SAN DIEGO sits at Chula Vista, El Cajon, San Diego and Vista.

Judges

Eugene Mac Amos, Jr.
Michael M. Anello
Rafael A. Arreola
Jeffrey Barton
Cynthia Ann Bashant
Jay M. Bloom
J. Michael Bollman
Jeffrey Bostwick
Larrie R. Brainard
Frank A. Brown
Desiree Bruce-Lyle
William S. Cannon
Timothy Casserly
Richard G. Cline
Robert Crawford Coates
Patricia K. Cookson
Patricia A. Y. Cowett
David John Danielsen
John L. Davidson
Peter C. Deddeh
Steven R. Denton
Vincent P. DiFiglia
H. Ronald Domnitz
Raymond Edwards, Jr.
John S. Einhorn
Harry M. Elias
Kevin A. Enright
Charles Ervin
Herbert J. Exarhos
Lisa Foster
Jeffrey F. Fraser
Peter Gallagher
Charles Raymond Gill
David M. Gill
Christine K. Goldsmith
Jan Goldsmith
Daniel B. Goldstein
Alvin E. Green, Jr.
Lisa Guy-Schall
J. Richard Haden

CALIFORNIA TRIAL COURTS—*Continued*

Laura Halgren
Laura Palmer Hammes
Louis R. Hanoian
Albert Harutunian, III
Charles R. Hayes
Judith F. Hayes
Thomas C. Hendrix
Esteban Hernandez
Marshall York Hockett
Yuri Hofmann
William J. Howatt, Jr.
Susan D. Huguenor
Edward B. Huntington
Joan K. Irion
Carol Isackson
Gerald C. Jessop
Gale E. Kaneshiro
William H. Kennedy
Janet Ide Kintner
K. Michael Kirkman
Roger W. Krauel
William H. Kronberger
Melinda J. Lasater
Thomas Oliver LaVoy
Joan Marie Lewis
Lantz Lewis
Lillian Y. Lim
Frederic L. Link
Joe O. Littlejohn
Frederick Maguire
Runston G. Maino
Wesley R. Mason, III
Robert E. May
William McGrath, Jr.
John Meyer
Amalia Meza
James R. Milliken
Richard E. Mills
Thomas R. Mitchell
William D. Mudd
William R. Nevitt, Jr.
Thomas P. Nugent
David Oberholtzer
Robert F. O'Neill
Adrienne A. Orfield
Michael B. Orfield
Christine V. Pate
William C. Pate
Wayne L. Peterson
Ronald S. Prager
Allan J. Preckel
Joel M. Pressman
Linda B. Quinn
Sheridan E. Reed
Bernard E. Revak
Charles G. Rogers
David W. Ryan
Dana Makoto Sabraw
DeAnn M. Salcido
Janis L. Sammartino
Terry J. Scott
Philip D. Sharp
Howard H. Shore
Michael Smyth
Kenneth Kai-Young So
Jacqueline Marion Stern
Lawrence W. Stirling
Richard Strauss
Eddie C. Sturgeon
Ronald L. Styn
David M. Szumowski
John M. Thompson
Timothy W. Tower
Robert J. Trentacosta
Leo Valentine, Jr.
Luis Rafael Vargas
Marguerite L. Wagner
Joan P. Weber
Michael D. Wellington
Kerry Wells
Richard Whitney
S. Charles Wickersham
Browder Willis, III
Margie G. Woods
vacancy
vacancy
vacancy

SUPERIOR COURT OF CALIFORNIA CITY AND COUNTY OF SAN FRANCISCO sits at San Francisco.

Judges

Paul H. Alvarado
David Louis Ballati
Carlos Bea
Jerome T. Benson
Anne Bouliane
Susan M. Breall
Peter J. Busch
Ellen Chaitin
John Joseph Conway
Nancy Davis
John E. Dearman
Gail Dekreon
Robert L. Dondero
Wallace Painter Douglass
Katherine A. Feinstein
Ernest H. Goldsmith
David A. Garcia
Donna J. Hitchens
Charles F. Haines
Harold E. Kahn
Teri L. Jackson
Newton J. Lam
Richard A. Kramer
Donna Alyson Little
Cynthia Ming-Mei Lee
Patrick J. Mahoney
Lenard D. Louie
James J. McBride
Tomar Mason
Perker L. Meeks, Jr.
Kevin M. McCarthy
Thomas J. Mellon, Jr.
Charlene P. Mitchell
Donald S. Mitchell
Philip J. Moscone
John E. Munter
Ronald Evans Quidachay
A. James Robertson, II
Alex Saldamando
John Kennedy Stewart
Lillian Kwok Sing
Kay Tsenin
Julie M. Tang
Diane Elan Wick
James L. Warren
Charlotte Walter Woolard
Mary E. Wiss
Carol Yaggy
vacancy
vacancy

SUPERIOR COURT OF CALIFORNIA COUNTY OF SAN JOAQUIN sits at Stockton.

Judges

George Abdallah, Jr.
Robert F. Baysinger
James E. Cadle
Stephen G. Demetras
Bernard J. Garber
Michael N. Garrigan
Richard J. Guiliani
James E. Hammerstone, Jr.
Thomas M. Harrington
Carter P. Holly
Lesley D. Holland
Anthony P. Lucaccini
Elizabeth Humphreys
Rolleen Kent McIlwrath
Richard M. Mallett
William J. Murray, Jr.
Bobby W. McNatt
Michael E. Platt
John W. Parker
Franklin M. Stephenson
K. Peter Saiers
Terrence R. Van Oss
F. Clark Sueyres, Jr.
David P. Warner
Richard Vlavianos
vacancy

SUPERIOR COURT OF CALIFORNIA COUNTY OF SAN LUIS OBISPO sits at San Luis Obispo.

Judges

Earle Jeffrey Burke
Michael L. Duffy
Teresa Estrada-Mullaney
Dodie A. Harman
Douglas Hilton
Barry T. LaBarbera
Christopher G. Money
Roger Picquet
Martin J. Tangeman
John A. Trice
Donald George Umhofer

SUPERIOR COURT OF CALIFORNIA COUNTY OF SAN MATEO sits at Redwood City and South San Francisco.

Judges

Joseph E. Bergeron
Marta S. Diaz
Steven L. Dylina
H. James Ellis
Robert D. Foiles
Mark R. Forcum
Beth Labson Freeman
Norman Joseph Gatzert
Dale A. Hahn
Stephen M. Hall
Carl W. Holm
Jonathan E. Karesh
Margaret J. Kemp
Quentin L. Kopp
Richard C. Livermore
Barbara J. Mallach
George A. Miram
Carol L. Mittlesteadt
Craig L. Parsons
Rosemary Pfeiffer
John W. Runde
John G. Schwartz
Phrasel L. Shelton
Marie S. Weiner
Judith Whitmer
vacancy

SUPERIOR COURT OF CALIFORNIA COUNTY OF SANTA BARBARA sits at Santa Barbara and Santa Maria.

Judges

Thomas R. Adams
Thomas Pearce Anderle
Clifford Anderson, III
Barbara J. Beck
James W. Brown
Rick S. Brown
Zel Canter
Denise de Bellefeuille
Rogelio R. Flores
Diana R. Hall

CALIFORNIA TRIAL COURTS—*Continued*

Brian Hill
James B. Jennings
Joseph Lodge
Rodney S. Melville
Timothy J. Staffel
James F. Iwasko
Harry J. Loberg
J. William McLafferty
Frank J. Ochoa

SUPERIOR COURT OF CALIFORNIA COUNTY OF SANTA CLARA sits at Palo Alto and San Jose.

Judges

Joyce Allegro
Robert A. Baines
Thang Nguyen Barrett
Susan Bernardini
Arthur Bocanegra
Gilbert T. Brown
Neal Anthony Cabrinha
Dolores A. Carr
James H. Chang
Paul C. Cole
Charles J. Cory
Alden E. Danner
Edward J. Davila
Ron M. Del Pozzo
Thomas C. Edwards
James C. Emerson
Robert Michael Foley
John J. Garibaldi
Mary Ann Grilli
Charles Wilson Hayden
Joseph Huber
Jerald A. Infantino
Margaret Johnson
James P. Kleinberg
Edward F. Lee
Ronald T. Lisk
Patricia M. Lucas
Stephen V. Manley
William F. Martin
Hugh F. Mullin, III
Jerome S. Nadler
Leslie C. Nichols
Risë Jones Pichon
Randolf J. Rice
Kenneth L. Shapero
Rodney J. Stafford
Richard C. Turrone
Gregory H. Ward
Erica R. Yew
vacancy
Robert L. Ambrose
Kenneth Paul Barnum
Paul R. Bernal
Joseph F. Biafore, Jr.
Jerome E. Brock
Andrea Y. Bryan
Thomas W. Cain
David A. Cena
Sharon A. Chatman
Linda R. Condron
Ray E. Cunningham
William R. Danser
Raymond Davilla, Jr.
Leonard P. Edwards
William J. Elfving
Alfonso Fernandez
Catherine A. Gallagher
Nazario A. Gonzales
Thomas P. Hansen
John F. Herlihy
Eugene M. Hyman
Jamie A. Jacobs-May
Marliese G. Kim
Jack Komar
Mary Jo Levinger
Richard J. Loftus, Jr.
Katherine Lucero
Socrates P. Manoukian
Kevin E. McKenney
Kevin J. Murphy
Rene Navarro
Diane Northway
Marcel B. Poche
C. Randall Schneider
Douglas K. Southard
Patrick E. Tondreau
Brian Walsh
Jean High Wetenkamp
vacancy

SUPERIOR COURT OF CALIFORNIA COUNTY OF SANTA CRUZ sits at Santa Cruz.

Judges

Kathleen K. Akao
Michael Einum Barton
Thomas E. Kelly
Heather D. Morse
Samuel S. Stevens
Robert B. Atack
Arthur Danner
Richard J. McAdams
John Steven Salazar
Robert B. Yonts, Jr.

SUPERIOR COURT OF CALIFORNIA COUNTY OF SHASTA sits at Redding.

Judges

Anthony A. Anderson
Gregory M. Caskey
William D. Gallagher
Bradley L. Boeckman
Wilson Curle
Steven E. Jahr
Monica Marlow
James Ruggiero
Richard A. McEachen

SUPERIOR COURT OF CALIFORNIA COUNTY OF SIERRA sits at Downieville.

Judges

William W. Pangman
William A. Skillman

SUPERIOR COURT OF CALIFORNIA COUNTY OF SISKIYOU sits at Yreka.

Judges

William J. Davis
Robert F. Kaster
Roger T. Kosel
Chris Stromsness

SUPERIOR COURT OF CALIFORNIA COUNTY OF SOLANO sits at Fairfield.

Judges

Paul Lloyd Beeman
Peter B. Foor
William C. Harrison
Scott L. Kays
James F. Moelk
David Edwin Power
Franklin R. Taft
Luis Mario Villarreal
Allan P. Carter
Ramona Joyce Garrett
Garry T. Ichikawa
Harry S. Kinnicutt
Michael E. Nail
R. Michael Smith
Cynda Riggins Unger
vacancy

SUPERIOR COURT OF CALIFORNIA COUNTY OF SONOMA sits at Santa Rosa.

Judges

Lawrence G. Antolini
James Gordon Bertoli
Rene Auguste Chouteau
Elliot Daum
Allan D. Hardcastle
Knoel L. Owen
Laurence K. Sawyer
Elaine Watters
Raima H. Ballinger
Robert S. Boyd
Robert P. Dale
Raymond J. Giordano
Gary Nadler
Arnold D. Rosenfield
Mark Tansil
Cerena Wong

SUPERIOR COURT OF CALIFORNIA COUNTY OF STANISLAUS sits at Modesto.

Judges

Nancy Ashley
Loretta Murphy Begen
Michael R. Cummins
John E. Griffin, Jr.
Wray F. Ladine
Linda A. McFadden
Susan D. Siefkin
David G. Vander Wall
vacancy
Roger M. Beauchesne
Terry K. Cole
Aldo Girolami
Hurl W. Johnson, III
William A. Mayhew
Donald E. Shaver
Marie Sovey Silveira
John G. Whiteside

SUPERIOR COURT OF CALIFORNIA COUNTY OF SUTTER sits at Yuba City.

Judges

Christopher Chandler
Robert H. Damron
Timothy J. Evans
H. Ted Hansen
Perry Parker

SUPERIOR COURT OF CALIFORNIA COUNTY OF TEHAMA sits at Red Bluff.

CALIFORNIA TRIAL COURTS—*Continued*

Judges

John J. Garaventa
Edward J. King, III
Dennis E. Murray
Richard Scheuler

SUPERIOR COURT OF CALIFORNIA COUNTY OF TRINITY sits at Weaverville.

Judges

Anthony C. Edwards
James Woodward

SUPERIOR COURT OF CALIFORNIA COUNTY OF TULARE sits at Visalia.

Judges

Ronn M. Couillard
Stephen Drew
Darryl B. Ferguson
Walter L. Gorelick
James W. Hollman
Joseph A. Kalashian
Elisabeth B. Krant
John P. Moran
Patrick J. O'Hara
Melinda Myrle Reed
Glade F. Roper
Valeriano Saucedo
Gerald F. Sevier
William Silveira, Jr.
Martin W. Staven
Paul Anthony Vortmann

SUPERIOR COURT OF CALIFORNIA COUNTY OF TUOLUMNE sits at Sonora.

Judges

Douglas C. Boyack
Eric L. Du Temple
William G. Polley
Eleanor Provost

SUPERIOR COURT OF CALIFORNIA COUNTY OF VENTURA sits at Ventura.

Judges

Brian John Back
Edward F. Brodie
Frederick H. Bysshe, Jr.
Charles Campbell, Jr.
Bruce A. Clark
James P. Cloninger
Tari L. Cody
Donald D. Coleman
Manuel J. Covarrubias
Herbert Curtis, III
John E. Dobroth
Arturo F. Gutierrez
Steven Hintz
Thomas J. Hutchins
Kent M. Kellegrew
Barry B. Klopfer
Barbara A. Lane
David W. Long
Kevin J. McGee
Vincent O'Neill, Jr.
Roland N. Purnell
Glen M. Reiser
Kenneth W. Riley
Rebecca S. Riley
John R. Smiley
Henry J. Walsh
Colleen Toy White
vacancy

SUPERIOR COURT OF CALIFORNIA COUNTY OF YOLO sits at Woodland.

Judges

Timothy L. Fall
W. Arvid Johnson
William S. Lebov
Stephen L. Mock
Donna Petre
Doris L. Shockley
Michael W. Sweet
Thomas Edward Warriner
vacancy

SUPERIOR COURT OF CALIFORNIA COUNTY OF YUBA sits at Marysville.

Judges

Dennis J. Buckley
James L. Curry
Kathleen R. O'Connor
David E. Wasilenko
vacancy

California Counties and County Seats

Alameda
Oakland

Alpine
Markleeville

Amador
Jackson

Butte
Oroville

Calaveras
San Andreas

Colusa
Colusa

Contra Costa
Martinez

Del Norte
Crescent City

El Dorado
Placerville

Fresno
Fresno

Glenn
Willows

Humboldt
Eureka

Imperial
El Centro

Inyo
Independence

Kern
Bakersfield

Kings
Hanford

Lake
Lakeport

Lassen
Susanville

Los Angeles
Los Angeles

Madera
Madera

Marin
San Rafael

Mariposa
Mariposa

Mendocino
Ukiah

Merced
Merced

Modoc
Alturas

Mono
Bridgeport

Monterey
Salinas

Napa
Napa

Nevada
Nevada City

Orange
Santa Ana

Placer
Auburn

Plumas
Quincy

Riverside
Riverside

Sacramento
Sacramento

San Benito
Hollister

San Bernardino
San Bernardino

San Diego
San Diego

San Francisco
San Francisco

San Joaquin
Stockton

San Luis Obispo
San Luis Obispo

San Mateo
Redwood City

Santa Barbara
Santa Barbara

Santa Clara
San Jose

Santa Cruz
Santa Cruz

COUNTIES AND COUNTY SEATS—*Continued*

Shasta
Redding

Sierra
Downieville

Siskiyou
Yreka

Solano
Fairfield

Sonoma
Santa Rosa

Stanislaus
Modesto

Sutter
Yuba City

Tehama
Red Bluff

Trinity
Weaverville

Tulare
Visalia

Tuolumne
Sonora

Ventura
Ventura

Yolo
Woodland

Yuba
Marysville

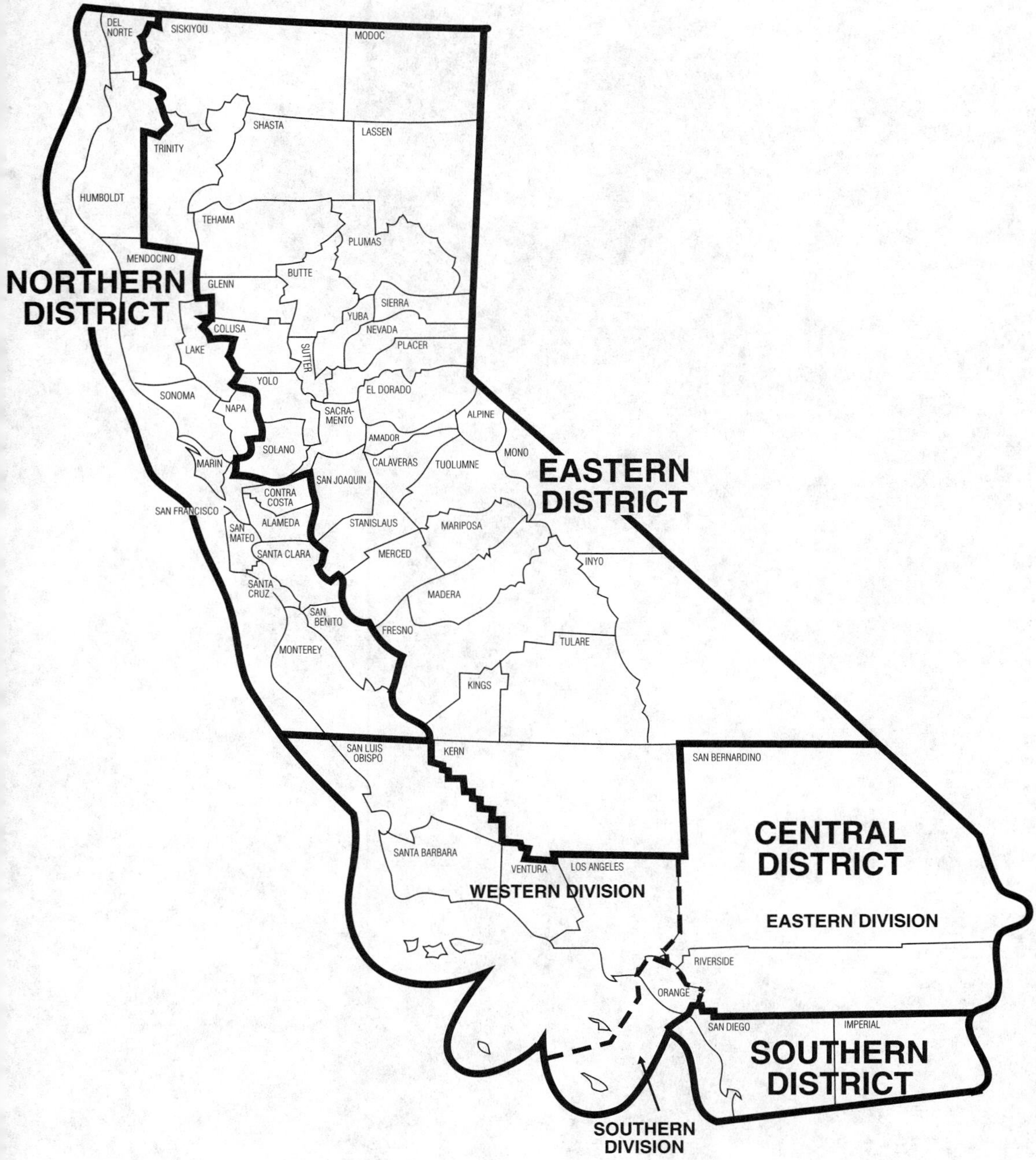
NORTHERN DISTRICT
EASTERN DISTRICT
CENTRAL DISTRICT
SOUTHERN DISTRICT
WESTERN DIVISION
EASTERN DIVISION
SOUTHERN DIVISION
DEL NORTE
SISKIYOU
MODOC
SHASTA
LASSEN
TRINITY
HUMBOLDT
TEHAMA
PLUMAS
MENDOCINO
GLENN
BUTTE
SIERRA
YUBA
NEVADA
COLUSA
PLACER
SUTTER
LAKE
YOLO
EL DORADO
SONOMA
NAPA
SACRA-MENTO
ALPINE
AMADOR
MONO
SOLANO
MARIN
CALAVERAS
TUOLUMNE
SAN JOAQUIN
CONTRA COSTA
SAN FRANCISCO
ALAMEDA
STANISLAUS
MARIPOSA
SAN MATEO
SANTA CLARA
MERCED
INYO
SANTA CRUZ
MADERA
SAN BENITO
FRESNO
MONTEREY
TULARE
KINGS
SAN LUIS OBISPO
KERN
SAN BERNARDINO
SANTA BARBARA
VENTURA
LOS ANGELES
RIVERSIDE
ORANGE
SAN DIEGO
IMPERIAL

UNITED STATES DISTRICT COURTS DISTRICTS OF CALIFORNIA

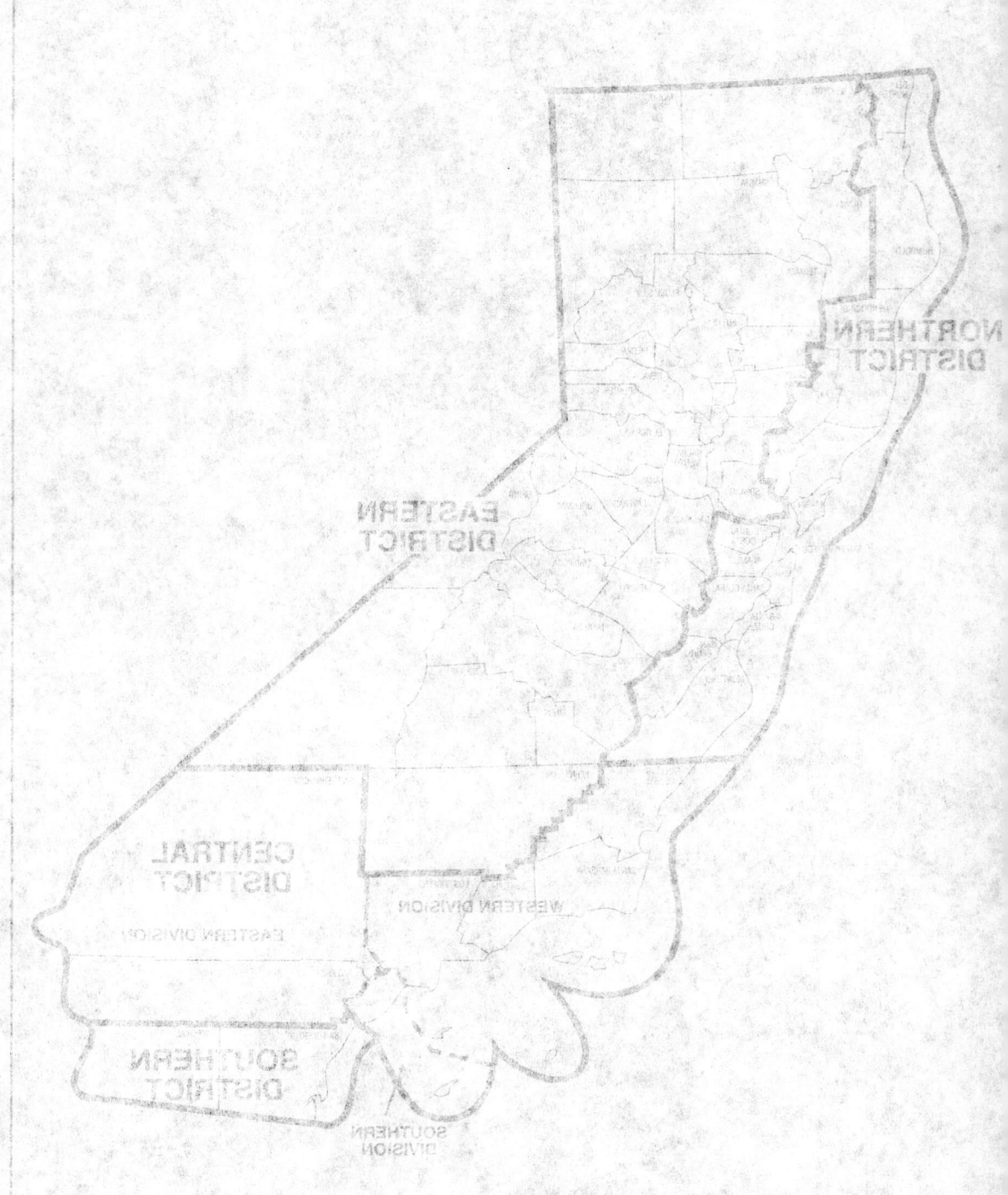

DEL NORTE
SISKIYOU
MODOC
SHASTA
LASSEN
TRINITY
3
HUMBOLDT
TEHAMA
PLUMAS
MENDOCINO
BUTTE
GLENN
SIERRA
1
LAKE
YUBA
COLUSA
NEVADA
PLACER
SUTTER
YOLO
EL DORADO
SONOMA
NAPA
SACRA-MENTO
ALPINE
AMADOR
SOLANO
MONO
MARIN
SAN JOAQUIN
CALAVERAS
TUOLUMNE
CONTRA COSTA
SAN FRANCISCO
ALAMEDA
SAN MATEO
STANISLAUS
MARIPOSA
SANTA CLARA
MERCED
INYO
SANTA CRUZ
MADERA
SAN BENITO
FRESNO
5
TULARE
MONTEREY
6
KINGS
SAN LUIS OBISPO
KERN
SAN BERNARDINO
4
SANTA BARBARA
VENTURA
LOS ANGELES
2
RIVERSIDE
ORANGE
SAN DIEGO
IMPERIAL

DISTRICTS OF CALIFORNIA COURTS OF APPEAL

CALIFORNIA

AARON, Cynthia G. *(Associate Justice, California Court of Appeal Fourth District Division One)* Appointed by Governor Gray Davis. Former Magistrate Judge, U.S. District Court Southern District of California, appointed by U.S. District Court judges.

Office: 750 B Street, Suite 300, San Diego 92101.

Telephone: (619) 645-2760.

ABBOTT, David W. *(Judge, Superior Court of California County of Sacramento)*

Office: Courthouse, 720 Ninth Street, Sacramento 95814.

Telephone: (916) 874-5476.

ABDALLAH, George J., Jr. *(Judge, Superior Court of California County of San Joaquin)* Assumed office June 8, 1998. Presiding Judge since Jan 1, 2002. Presiding Judge Jan 1, 1996 to Dec 31, 1997 and Former Judge, Manteca-Ripon-Escalon-Tracy Municipal Court San Joaquin County.

Office: 222 East Weber Avenue, Room 303, Stockton 95202.

Telephone: (209) 468-2827.

ABEL, S. William *(Judge, Superior Court of California County of Colusa)* Presiding Judge Jan 1, 1999 to Dec 31, 1999 and since Jan 1, 2002. Former Judge, Colusa-Williams Justice Court Colusa County.

Mailing address: 532 Oak Street, Colusa 95932.

Office: 547 Market Street, Colusa 95932.

Telephone: (530) 458-5149.

ABRAMS, Judith *(Judge, Superior Court of California County of Los Angeles)* Assumed office Jan 22, 2000. Former Judge, Los Angeles Municipal Court Los Angeles County.

Office: Los Angeles Airport Courthouse, 11701 South La Cienega Boulevard, Los Angeles 90045.

Telephone: (310) 727-6010.

ABRAMS, Paul L. *(Magistrate Judge, United States District Court Central District of California)* Appointed by U.S. District Court judges to term beginning Jan 14, 2002.

Office: 926 U.S. Courthouse, 312 North Spring Street, Los Angeles 90012.

Telephone: (213) 894-3535.

ADAJIAN, Jacob *(Judge, Superior Court of California County of Los Angeles)* Assumed office Jan 22, 2000. Former Judge, Los Angeles Municipal Court Los Angeles County.

Office: Criminal Courts Building, 210 West Temple Street, Los Angeles 90012-3210.

Telephone: (213) 974-6535.

ADAMS, John S. *(Judge, Superior Court of California County of Orange)*

Mailing address: P.O. Box 1994, Santa Ana 92702-1994.

Office: Central Justice Center, 700 Civic Center Drive West, Santa Ana 92701.

Telephone: (714) 834-3734.

ADAMS, Thomas R. *(Judge, Superior Court of California County of Santa Barbara)* Former Presiding Judge.

Office: 1100 Anacapa Street, Santa Barbara 93101.

Telephone: (805) 568-2220.

ADAMS, Verna A. *(Judge, Superior Court of California County of Marin)*

Mailing address: P.O. Box 4988, San Rafael 94913-4988.

Office: Hall of Justice, 3501 Civic Center Drive, San Rafael 94903.

Telephone: (415) 499-6407.

ADLER, Louise DeCarl *(Judge, United States Bankruptcy Court Southern District of California)* Appointed by U.S. District Court judges to term beginning March 5, 1984. Reappointed by U.S. Court of Appeals Ninth Circuit judges 1987 and 2001. Current term expires 2015. Chief Judge 1996-2001. Born Chicago Illinois May 15, 1945. Educated at Chatham College B.A. 1966 and Loyola University J.D. 1970. Admitted to practice Illinois 1970 and California 1972. In legal practice Chicago Illinois 1970-72 and San Diego California 1972-84.

Founding Member Lawyers Club of San Diego 1972 and San Diego Bankruptcy Forum 1990. Board of Governors 1991-92, Secretary 1992-93, Vice President 1993-94 and President 1994-95 National Conference of Bankruptcy Judges. Member State Bar of California (Vice Chair 1975-77 and Chair 1977 Business Law Section). Instructor at numerous judicial conferences and seminars.

Office: U.S. Courthouse, 325 West F Street, San Diego 92101-6989.

Telephone: (619) 557-5661.

ADLER, Richard A. *(Judge, Superior Court of California County of Los Angeles)* Former Judge, Los Angeles Municipal Court Los Angeles County.

Office: Van Nuys Courthouse East, 6230 Sylmar Avenue, Van Nuys 91401.

Telephone: (818) 374-2265.

AGUIRRE, Frederick P. *(Judge, Superior Court of California County of Orange)*

Mailing address: P.O. Box 5000, Fullerton 92838-0500.

Office: North Justice Center, 1275 North Berkeley Avenue, Fullerton 92832.

Telephone: (714) 773-4000.

AHART, Alan M. *(Judge, United States Bankruptcy Court Central District of California)* Appointed by U.S. Court of Appeals Ninth Circuit judges to term beginning April 1988. Reappointed April 4, 2002, current term expires April 3, 2016. Educated at University of California at Berkeley B.A. honors with great distinction 1970, State University of New York J.D. 1975 and University of Pennsylvania LL.M. 1979. Articles Editor New York Law School Law Review. In legal practice Los Angeles area 1976 to March 1988.

Author *California Practice Guide: Enforcing Judgments and Debts* The Rutter Group. Board of Governors Financial Lawyers Conference. Member National Confer-

AHART, ALAN M.—*Continued*

ence of Bankruptcy Judges, State Bar of California, Federal and American Bar Associations. Interests include history of ancient civilizations, hiking, camping and fishing.

Office: Federal Building, 255 East Temple Street, Los Angeles 90012.

Telephone: (213) 894-3745.

AICHROTH, Dennis A. *(Judge, Superior Court of California County of Los Angeles)* Assumed office Jan 22, 2000. Former Judge, Citrus Municipal Court Los Angeles County.

Office: South Gate Courthouse, 8640 California Avenue, South Gate 90280.

Telephone: (323) 563-4027.

AKAO, Kathleen K. *(Judge, Superior Court of California County of Santa Cruz)*

Office: Main Courthouse, 701 Ocean Street, Santa Cruz 95060.

Telephone: (831) 454-2012.

ALARCON, Gregory Wilson *(Judge, Superior Court of California County of Los Angeles)* Former Judge, Los Angeles Municipal Court Los Angeles County.

Office: Courthouse, 111 North Hill Street, Los Angeles 90012.

Telephone: (213) 974-5411.

ALBERTS, Robert W. *(Judge, United States Bankruptcy Court Central District of California)* Appointed by U.S. Court of Appeals Ninth Circuit judges.

Office: 6135 U.S. Courthouse, 411 West Fourth Street, Santa Ana 92701-4593.

Telephone: (714) 338-5420.

ALDRICH, Richard D. *(Associate Justice, California Court of Appeal Second District Division Three)* Appointed by Governor Pete Wilson to term beginning Aug 29, 1994. Retained by election. Born Los Angeles California June 15, 1938. Educated at Loyola University of Los Angeles B.S. 1960 and University of California at Los Angeles LL.B. 1963. Admitted to practice California 1963, U.S. District Court Central District of California 1963, U.S. Court of Appeals Ninth Circuit 1987 and U.S. Supreme Court 1989. In legal practice Los Angeles 1963-90 and Beverly Hills 1971-91. Judge, Superior Court of California Ventura County Jan 1991 to Aug 1994, appointed by Governor George Deukmejian.

President and General Counsel Casualty Insurance Company of California 1967-68. General Counsel LFC Financial Corporation 1969-70 and Equitable Savings & Loan Association 1969-70. Counsel Great Western Savings & Loan Association 1970-71. President Ventura American Inn of Court 1994-95. Member Superior Court Dependency Court Improvement Project Los Angeles 1985 and Committee on Book of Approved Jury Instructions 1986-90. Chair Select Committee on Trial Court Coordination Implementation 1994, Business Court Study Task Force 1996 and Complex Litigation Task Force 1997. Former Member Los Angeles Trial Lawyers Association and California Trial Lawyers Association. Judicial Fellow American College of Trial Lawyers and International Academy of Trial Lawyers. Member American Board of Trial Advocates (Advocate since 1975, Los Angeles Executive Committee since 1981), California Judicial Council (Civil and Small Claims Standing Advisory Committee 1992-98, Chair Case Management and Delay Reduction Subcommittee 1992-97, ADR Subcommittee 1992-98, Executive and Planning Committee since 1999), International Academy of Trial Judges (President 2000-01), California Judges Association, American Judicature Society, Los Angeles County (Judicial Resources Committee 1985-86, Chair Court Improvements Committee 1986-88) and American Bar Associations. Established Ventura County Multi-Door Courthouse which provides litigants with multiple modalities for early resolution of their disputes without trial 1992. Founder Second District Settlement Conference and Mediation Program which recruits experienced appellate practitioners to act as mediators and settlement conference officers 1995. Faculty Member Bernard E. Witkin California Judicial College since 1991. Lecturer on "Reinventing the Legal System" World Affairs Council Panel World Affairs Council Oct 28, 1993; "Judicial Independence in a Democratic Society" Slovak Judges Association Bratislave Slovakia Nov 15, 1993 and Judges Association of the Czech Republic Brno Czech Republic Nov 17, 1993 American Bar Association; "Access to Lawyering Under the ADA: Surveys and Solutions" Convention San Diego 1993, "Alternative Dispute Resolution: Court and Legislative Developments" Convention San Diego 1993 and "Litigating Under the A.D.A." Convention Anaheim 1994 State Bar of California; "An Overview of the Legal and Judicial Systems in the United States" International Academy of Trial Lawyers Beijing China Oct 1994; "Judicial Survival in Los Angeles" Annual Meeting Conference San Francisco Sept 1995 and "View from the Other Side: Take Two!" Annual Meeting Conference Monterey Oct 1996 California Judges Association; "Access to the Courts for Persons with Disabilities" Public Hearings Chair Draft California Rule of Court Judicial Council of California Los Angeles Oct 1995; "Understanding Contractual Arbitration—The Award" Matthew Bender CLE Los Angeles 1998; and "Business Court Roundtable and the Evolving Role of Complex Litigation Courts" National Center for State Courts Justice Roundtable Washington D.C. 1999. Recipient Trial Lawyer of the Year Award from American Board of Trial Advocates California 1990, Superior Court Trial Judge of the Year Award from Ventura County Trial Lawyers Association 1992, Public Safety Award from Knights of Columbus 1992 and 1993 and Chief Justice Roger J. Traynor Appellate Justice of the Year Award 2000. Named Outstanding Jurist of the Year by Ventura County Bar Association 1992 and 1993. Board of Directors Friends of Child Advocates 1987-90 and Interface Family Services of Ventura County 1991-93. Chair Board of Regents Loyola Marymount University 1999-2001. Former Board of Directors Blind Children's Learning Center. Board Member Mary Health of the Sick Convalescent Home.

Office: 300 South Spring Street, Los Angeles 90013.

Telephone: (213) 830-7000.

E-mail address: Justice.Richard.D.Aldrich@jud.ca.gov

ALLEGRO, Joyce *(Judge, Superior Court of California County of Santa Clara)*

Office: Hall of Justice West Wing, 200 West Hedding Street, San Jose 95110.

Telephone: (408) 808-6600.

ALLEN, Jeffrey S. *(Judge, Superior Court of California County of Alameda)* Assumed office July 31,

ALLEN, JEFFREY S.—*Continued*

1998. Former Judge, Alameda Municipal Court Alameda County.

Office: Hall of Justice, 2233 Shoreline Drive, Alameda 94501.

Telephone: (510) 268-4209.

ALLEN, John M. *(Judge, Superior Court of California County of Contra Costa)* Assumed office June 8, 1998. Former Judge, Delta Municipal Court Contra Costa County.

Office: 45 Civic Avenue, Pittsburg 94565.

Telephone: (925) 427-8173.

ALLEN, Larry W. *(Judge, Superior Court of California County of San Bernardino)* Assumed office Aug 10, 1998. Former Judge, San Bernardino County Municipal Court.

Office: 14455 Civic Drive, Victorville 92392.

Telephone: (760) 243-8684.

ALSUP, William *(Judge, United States District Court Northern District of California)* Appointed for life by President Bill Clinton to term beginning Aug 17, 1999. Born Jackson Mississippi June 27, 1945. Educated at Mississippi State University B.S. 1967 and Harvard University M.P.P. 1971 J.D. 1971. Law Clerk to Hon. William O. Douglas, U.S. Supreme Court 1971-72. In legal practice Oakland 1972-78 and 1980-99.

Assistant to U.S. Solicitor General 1978-80 and Special Counsel Antitrust Division 1998 U.S. Department of Justice.

Office: U.S. Courthouse, Box 36060, 450 Golden Gate Avenue, San Francisco 94102-3489.

Telephone: (415) 522-3684.

ALTOON, Alice E. *(Judge, Superior Court of California County of Los Angeles)* Assumed office Jan 22, 2000. Elected 2002, current term expires Jan 2009. Educated at University of California at Los Angeles B.A. 1968 and University of Southern California J.D. 1980. Member Phi Alpha Delta. Admitted to practice California 1980. Judge, Los Angeles Municipal Court Los Angeles County June 12, 1987 to Jan 21, 2000, appointed by Governor George Deukmejian.

Member California Judges Association, Armenian and American Bar Associations.

Office: Criminal Courts Building, 210 West Temple Street, Los Angeles 90012-3210.

Telephone: (213) 974-6535.

ALVARADO, Paul H. *(Judge, Superior Court of California City and County of San Francisco)* Appointed by Governor George Deukmejian to term beginning Sept 7, 1989. Elected June 10, 1990, Nov 6, 1996 and 2002. Current term expires Jan 2009. Born Honduras July 12, 1939. Roman Catholic. Educated at St. Mary's College B.A. 1961 and University of California Hastings College of the Law J.D. 1964. Member Phi Alpha Delta. Admitted to practice California 1965 and U.S. Court of Appeals Ninth Circuit 1965. In legal practice San Francisco 1970-86. Judge, San Francisco Municipal Court San Francisco County 1986-89.

With District Attorney's Office Alameda County 1965-70. Author "Use a Gun, Possibly Go to Prison" 1982 and "California's New Insanity Test" 1982 California Trial Lawyers Association. Instructor in Legal Writing University of California Hastings College of the Law 1981-83. Member Queen's Bench, La Raza, San Francisco, Italian-American and American Bar Associations. Recipient Certificate of Appreciation from California Trial Lawyers Association. Lieutenant Colonel USAR 1964-94. Member San Francisco Presidio Society. Enjoys golf, handball, photography and traveling.

Office: Civic Center Courthouse, 400 McAllister Street, San Francisco 94102-4514.

Telephone: (415) 551-4020.

ALVAREZ, Donald R. *(Judge, Superior Court of California County of San Bernardino)*

Office: 14455 Civic Drive, Victorville 92392.

Telephone: (760) 243-8684.

AMBROSE, Robert Lawrence *(Judge, Superior Court of California County of Santa Clara)* Assumed office July 30, 1998. Former Judge, Santa Clara County Municipal Court.

Office: 1095 Homestead Road, Santa Clara 95050.

Telephone: (408) 556-3016.

AMOS, Eugene Mac, Jr. *(Judge, Superior Court of California County of San Diego)* Assumed office Dec 1, 1998. Former Judge and Presiding Judge, San Diego Municipal Court San Diego County.

Mailing address: P.O. Box 122724, San Diego 92112-2724.

Office: 330 West Broadway, San Diego 92101.

Telephone: (619) 685-6148.

ANDERLE, Thomas Pearce *(Judge, Superior Court of California County of Santa Barbara)*

Office: 1100 Anacapa Street, Santa Barbara 93101.

Telephone: (805) 568-2220.

ANDERSON, Anthony A. *(Judge, Superior Court of California County of Shasta)* Assumed office June 3, 1998. Educated at San Jose State University B.A. and University of Santa Clara J.D. Judge, Shasta County Municipal Court Jan 8, 1991 to June 2, 1998.

Office: 1500 Court Street, Redding 96001-1685.

Telephone: (530) 225-5714.

ANDERSON, Clifford R., III *(Judge, Superior Court of California County of Santa Barbara)* Presiding Judge since Jan 1, 2003.

Office: 118 East Figueroa Street, Santa Barbara 93101.

Telephone: (805) 568-2735.

ANDERSON, Margaret R. *(Judge, Superior Court of California County of Orange)* Assumed office Aug 10, 1998. Born New Castle Pennsylvania April 12, 1933. Protestant. Educated at Orange Coast College A.A. summa cum laude and Western State University B.S.L. summa cum laude 1975 J.D. summa cum laude 1977. Recipient American Jurisprudence Awards 1975, 1976, 1977 and 1978, Corpus Juris Awards 1975, 1976, 1977 and 1978, Carl Marcks Scholarship 1976, Wall Street Journal Award 1977, Foundation Press Awards 1977 and 1978 and First American TITLE Award 1977 and 1978. Staff member 1976 and Book Review Editor 1977 Western State University Law Review. Admitted to practice California 1978 and U.S. District Court Central District of California 1978. Began legal practice Orange County 1978. Judge, North Orange County Municipal Court Jan 7, 1985 to Jan 3, 1993. Judge, Harbor Municipal Court Orange County Jan 4, 1993 to Aug 9, 1998.

Deputy Public Defender Orange County 1978-85. Author "To Carey and Back, Rights of the Meretricious

ANDERSON, MARGARET R.—*Continued*

Spouse in California" Western State University L. Rev. June 1976. Guest lecturer Western State University College of Law. Member California Attorneys for Criminal Justice, California Judges Association, National Association of Women Judges, Orange County Trial Lawyers Association, Orange County Women Lawyers, State Bar of California, Orange County and American Bar Associations. Board of Directors Orange County Mental Health Association. Instructor California Judicial Education Seminars 1986 and 1997. Inducted into Western State University of Law Hall of Fame June 1986 and Orange Coast College Hall of Fame Sept 1990. Accountant U.S. Marine Corps 1954-56 and Office of Naval Intelligence 1957-61. Republican. Board of Directors H.O.M.E.S. and National Council of Alcohol and Drug. Trustee Southern California College of Law. Enjoys miniature building, reading and travel.

Office: 4601 Jamboree Road, Newport Beach 92260.
Telephone: (949) 476-4608.

ANDERSON, Matthew S. *(Judge, Superior Court of California County of Orange)*

Office: 30143 Crown Valley Parkway, Laguna Niguel 92677-2089.
Telephone: (949) 249-5053.

ANDERSON, Percy *(Judge, United States District Court Central District of California)* Appointed for life by President George W. Bush to term beginning June 12, 2002. Born Long Beach California 1948. Educated at University of California at Los Angeles A.B. 1970 J.D. 1975. In legal practice California 1985-2002.

Office: 163 U.S. Courthouse, 312 North Spring Street, Los Angeles 90012.
Telephone: (213) 894-3535.

ANDLER, Gail A. *(Judge, Superior Court of California County of Orange)* Former Judge, Central Orange County Municipal Court.

Mailing address: P.O. Box 1994, Santa Ana 92702-1994.
Office: Central Justice Center, 700 Civic Center Drive West, Santa Ana 92701.
Telephone: (714) 834-3734.

ANDREWS, Bradford L. *(Judge, Superior Court of California County of Los Angeles)* Assumed office Jan 22, 2000. Elected 2002, current term expires Jan 2009. Born Pasadena California Oct 11, 1944. Educated at California State University at Long Beach B.A. 1967, University of Southern California M.P.A. with honors 1976 and Whittier College School of Law J.D. 1982. Admitted to practice California 1982. In legal practice Long Beach 1982-83. Judge Dec 31, 1987 to Jan 21, 2000 and Former Presiding Judge, Long Beach Municipal Court Los Angeles County, appointed by Governor George Deukmejian.

Deputy City Prosecutor 1983-84 and Deputy City Attorney 1984-87 Long Beach. Former member Los Angeles County Bar Association. Member State Bar of California and Long Beach Bar Association. Attended California Judicial Education and Research The National Judicial College 1988. Police Officer Long Beach 1968-82. Republican. Liaison between Long Beach Bar Association and Long Beach Unified School District. Involved in planning, coordinating and implementing legal education programs and activities for students in grades K-12.

Office: Long Beach Courthouse, 415 West Ocean Boulevard, Long Beach 90802.
Telephone: (562) 491-6130.

ANDREWS, Deborah B. *(Judge, Superior Court of California County of Los Angeles)* Assumed office Jan 22, 2000. Former Judge, Long Beach Municipal Court Los Angeles County.

Office: Long Beach Courthouse, 415 West Ocean Boulevard, Long Beach 90802.
Telephone: (562) 491-6130.

ANELLO, Michael M. *(Judge, Superior Court of California County of San Diego)*

Mailing address: P.O. Box 122724, San Diego 92112-2724.
Office: 325 South Melrose Drive, Vista 92083.
Telephone: (760) 726-9595.

ANSPACH, Robert J. *(Judge, Superior Court of California County of Kern)*

Office: 1415 Truxtun Avenue, Bakersfield 93301.
Telephone: (661) 868-4934.

ANTOLINI, Lawrence G. *(Judge, Superior Court of California County of Sonoma)* Former Judge, Sonoma County Municipal Court.

Office: 3035 Cleveland Avenue, Santa Rosa 95403.
Telephone: (707) 565-1100.

ARAGON, Conrad Richard *(Judge, Superior Court of California County of Los Angeles)* Assumed office Jan 22, 2000. Presiding Judge July 1, 1996 to Dec 31, 1997 and Former Judge, East Los Angeles Municipal Court Los Angeles County.

Office: Pomona Courthouse South, 400 Civic Center Plaza, Pomona 91766.
Telephone: (909) 620-3023.

ARDAIZ, James A. *(Administrative Presiding Justice, California Court of Appeal Fifth District and Presiding Justice, California Court of Appeal Fifth District)* Appointed by Governor George Deukmejian to term beginning 1987. Retained by election. Presiding Justice since 1994. Educated at California State University at Fresno 1970 and University of California Hastings College of the Law J.D. 1974. Judge, Consolidated Fresno Municipal Court Fresno County 1980-83. Judge, Superior Court of California Fresno County 1983-87, appointed by Governor George Deukmejian.

Chief Deputy District Attorney County of Fresno. Coauthor *California Evidence.* Consultant California Judges' Benchguide on Felony Sentencing, California Criminal Pre-trial Proceedings Deskbook, California Criminal Trial Deskbook and California Criminal Posttrial Proceeding Deskbook. Instructor on Criminal Law and Evidence California State University at Fresno. Professor of Evidence San Joaquin College of Law. Chairman Executive Committee Judicial Council of California. Chair Task Force on Trial Court Funding and Employees State of California. Faculty California Judicial College. Lecturer DNA Evidence FBI Academy at Quantico. Named California's Outstanding Jurist by California Judicial Council 1999. Member Pilgrim Congregational Church (Board of Trustees). Enjoys soccer, running and painting.

Office: 2525 Capitol Street, Fresno 93721.
Telephone: (559) 445-5491.

ARGENTO, Phillip J. *(Judge, Superior Court of California County of Los Angeles)* Assumed office Jan 22, 2000. Serves Northeast District. Educated at Pasadena City College 1963-65, Pomona College 1967, University of California at Los Angeles M.J. 1968 and Georgetown University Law Center J.D. 1975. In legal practice 1975-82. Judge Feb 1982 to Jan 21, 2000, Assistant Presiding Judge 1983-85 and Presiding Judge 1985-86 and Jan 1996 to Dec 1997, Pasadena Municipal Court Los Angeles County, appointed by Governor Edmund G. Brown, Jr.

Consultant *California Criminal Law* 2nd and 3rd eds. California Continuing Education of the Bar 1994 and 1995 and Chapter 376 "Municipal Courts" *California Pleading and Practice* Matthew Bender 1995. Adjunct Professor of Law Loyola University Law School 1983-84 and 1999. Adjunct Professor of Criminal Justice Pasadena City College 1990-2002, of Trial Advocacy University of La Verne College of Law 1995-96 and of Criminal Law Glendale University College of Law 2002. Arbitrator American Arbitration Association 1979-82. Member California Judges Association (Executive Board 1988-89), Presiding Judges Association of Los Angeles County (Chair), Los Angeles County Municipal Courts Judges Association, Italian-American Lawyers, State Bar of California, Pasadena (Chairman Speakers Bureau 1979-81), Los Angeles County (Landlord-Tenant Settlement Officer 1978 and member Economic Litigation since 1983) and American Bar Associations. Faculty member Continuing Judicial Studies Program Berkeley 1985-90. Attended College of Trial Advocacy Pepperdine University, "Advanced Strategy and Tactics in Personal Injury Suit" and "Medicine for Trial Lawyers" University of Southern California and California Judicial College 1982 and 1985. USAR active duty 1969. Public Relations Intern Auto Club of Southern California 1967. Researcher-writer Los Angeles Times Student Outlook 1968-69. Press Assistant League of Women Voters National Office 1973-74. Press Aide Tunney Campaign Oct 1969 to Nov 1970. Special Assistant to U.S. Senator John V. Tunney 1971-73. Member Holy Family Church South Pasadena, Foothill Family Service (Board of Directors 1979-85 and President 1982-83), Pasadena Area League of Women Voters (Evening Unit Chairperson 1977-79), Pomona College Alumni Club (President 1979-81) and Pasadena Sierra Club (President 1987-88).

Office: Pasadena Courthouse, 300 East Walnut Avenue, Pasadena 91101.

Telephone: (626) 356-5243.

ARMSTRONG, Orville A. *(Associate Justice, California Court of Appeal Second District Division Five)* Appointed by governor. Former Judge, Superior Court of California Los Angeles County.

Office: 300 South Spring Street, Los Angeles 90013.

Telephone: (213) 830-7000.

ARMSTRONG, Saundra Brown *(Judge, United States District Court Northern District of California)* Appointed for life by President George Bush to term beginning 1991. Born Oakland California March 23, 1947. Educated at Merritt College A.A. 1967, California State University at Fresno B.A. 1969 and University of San Francisco School of Law J.D. 1977. Judicial Extern to California Courts of Appeals 1977. Judge, Superior Court of California Alameda County 1989-91.

Deputy District Attorney Alameda County 1978-79 and 1980-82. Trial Attorney Public Integrity Section U.S. Department of Justice 1982-83. Commissioner Consumer Product Safety Commission 1983-86 and U.S. Parole Commission 1986-89. Senior Consultant Committee on Criminal Justice California Assembly 1979-80.

Office: 400-S Federal Building, 1301 Clay Street, Oakland 94612-5212.

Telephone: (510) 637-3559.

ARNOLD, Mark S. *(Judge, Superior Court of California County of Los Angeles)* Assumed office Jan 22, 2000. Former Judge, South Bay Municipal Court Los Angeles County.

Office: Torrance Courthouse, 825 Maple Avenue, Torrance 90503.

Telephone: (310) 222-8808.

ARONSON, Richard M. *(Associate Justice, California Court of Appeal Fourth District Division Three)* Appointed by Governor Gray Davis. Former Judge, Superior Court of California County of Orange.

Mailing address: P.O. Box 22055, Santa Ana 92702.

Telephone: (714) 558-6777.

ARREOLA, Rafael A. *(Judge, Superior Court of California County of San Diego)* Assumed office Dec 1, 1998. Former Judge, San Diego Municipal Court San Diego County.

Mailing address: P.O. Box 122724, San Diego 92112-2724.

Office: 220 West Broadway, San Diego 92101.

Telephone: (619) 531-3820.

ASHLEY, Nancy *(Judge, Superior Court of California County of Stanislaus)* Assumed office July 31, 1998. Former Judge, Stanislaus County Municipal Court.

Office: 800 Eleventh Street, Modesto 95354.

Telephone: (209) 558-6000.

ASHMANN-GERST, Judith *(Associate Justice, California Court of Appeal Second District Division Two)* Appointed by Governor Gray Davis. Former Judge, Los Angeles Municipal Court Los Angeles County. Former Judge, Superior Court of California County of Los Angeles.

Office: 300 South Spring Street, Los Angeles 90013.

Telephone: (213) 830-7000.

ASHWORTH, Stephen H. *(Judge, Superior Court of California County of San Bernardino)*

Office: 14455 Civic Drive, Victorville 92392.

Telephone: (760) 243-8684.

ATACK, Robert B. *(Judge, Superior Court of California County of Santa Cruz)* Assumed office July 1, 1998. Former Judge and Presiding Judge, Santa Cruz County Municipal Court.

Office: Main Courthouse, 701 Ocean Street, Santa Cruz 95060.

Telephone: (831) 454-2012.

ATKINSON, Lynn C. *(Judge, Superior Court of California County of Kings)* Appointed by Governor Pete Wilson to term beginning Feb 10, 1992. Elected Nov 1992 and 1998. Current term expires Jan 2005. Presiding Judge July 1, 1993 to June 30, 1994; July 1, 1996 to June 30, 1997; and since Jan 1, 2003. Serves Hanford Division. Born Hanford California Jan 20, 1947. Religious affiliation: Church of Christ. Educated at Pepperdine University B.S. 1969 and University of California

ATKINSON, LYNN C.—*Continued*
at Davis J.D. 1972. Admitted to practice California 1973. In legal practice Lemoore 1973-92.
City Attorney Lemoore 1975-82. Republican.
Office: 1426 South Drive, Hanford 93230.
Telephone: (559) 582-3211.

AUSTIN, Gary S. *(Judge, Superior Court of California County of Fresno)* Former Judge, Consolidated Fresno Municipal Court Fresno County.
Office: Courthouse, 1100 Van Ness Avenue, Fresno 93724-0002.
Telephone: (559) 488-1825.

AUSTIN, Steven K. *(Judge, Superior Court of California County of Contra Costa)*
Office: Courthouse, 725 Court Street, Martinez 94553.
Telephone: (925) 646-2950.

BACHNER, Monica *(Judge, Superior Court of California County of Los Angeles)*
Office: West Covina Courthouse, 1427 West Covina Parkway, West Covina 91790.
Telephone: (626) 813-3223.

BACIGALUPO, Paul A. *(Judge, Superior Court of California County of Los Angeles)*
Office: Compton Courthouse, 200 West Compton Boulevard, Compton 90220.
Telephone: (310) 603-7842.

BACK, Brian John *(Judge, Superior Court of California County of Ventura)*
Mailing address: P.O. Box 6489, Ventura 93006-6489.
Office: 800 South Victoria Avenue, Ventura 93009-0001.
Telephone: (805) 654-2965.

BAINES, Robert A. *(Judge, Superior Court of California County of Santa Clara)* Assumed office July 30, 1998. Elected 2002, current term expires Jan 2009. Born Sacramento California 1945. Educated at University of California at Riverside A.B. with honors 1966 and Boalt Hall School of Law J.D. 1969. Member Phi Beta Kappa. Admitted to practice California 1970, U.S. District Court Northern District of California 1970, U.S. Supreme Court 1975 and U.S. Court of Appeals Ninth Circuit 1976. Began legal practice San Jose 1970. Judge, Santa Clara County Municipal Court Jan 2, 1983 to July 29, 1998, appointed by Governor Edmund G. Brown, Jr.
Staff Attorney Legal Aid Society Santa Clara County 1970-75. Directing Attorney Santa Clara County Bar Association Law Foundation, Inc. 1975-80. Assistant City Attorney San Jose 1980-82. Member Justice System Advisory Board Santa Clara County 1979-80. Visiting Lecturer on Law University of Santa Clara 1979-80. Former Member State Bar of California (Commission on Judicial Nominees Evaluation 1978-79) and Santa Clara County Bar Association (Federal Courts Committee, Finance Committee, Fair Judicial Campaign Practices Committee, Secretary 1982). Member California Judges Association. Named Trial Judge of the Year by Santa Clara County Trial Lawyers Association 2000.
Office: 190 West Hedding Street, San Jose 95110.
Telephone: (408) 299-8973.

BAIRD, Lourdes G. *(Judge, United States District Court Central District of California)* Appointed for life by President George Bush to term beginning 1992. Born Ecuador May 12, 1935. Educated at Los Angeles City College A.A. 1971 and University of California at Los Angeles B.A. 1973 J.D. 1976. In legal practice Los Angeles 1983-86. Judge, East Los Angeles Municipal Court 1986-87 and Los Angeles Municipal Court 1987-88 Los Angeles County. Judge, Superior Court of California Los Angeles County 1988-90.
Assistant U.S. Attorney 1977-83 and U.S. Attorney 1990-92 Central District of California.
Office: Federal Building, 255 East Temple Street, Los Angeles 90012.
Telephone: (213) 894-1478.

BAKARICH, Gerald S. "Jerry" *(Judge, Superior Court of California County of Sacramento)* Assumed office June 17, 1998. Elected 2002, current term expires Jan 1, 2009. Born Sacramento California Nov 14, 1941. Catholic. Educated at California State University at Sacramento B.A. 1974 and Lincoln Law School J.D. 1982. Named Outstanding Graduate Lincoln Law School 1982. Admitted to practice California 1982 and U.S. District Court Eastern District of California 1982. Judge, Sacramento Municipal Court Sacramento County Jan 1, 1991 to June 16, 1998, appointed by Governor George Deukmejian.
Deputy District Attorney Sacramento County 1984-90. Member National Association of Drug Court Professionals and California Judges Association. Named Alumni of the Year by Lincoln Law School 1991. U.S. Army 1964-67. California National Guard since 1972. Enjoys traveling and golfing.
Office: Courthouse, 720 Ninth Street, Sacramento 95814.
Telephone: (916) 874-5476.

BAKER, Valerie L. *(Judge, Superior Court of California County of Los Angeles)* Appointed by Governor George Deukmejian to term beginning Feb 1987. Elected June 1988, 1994 and 2000. Current term expires Jan 2007. Serves West District. Born Minneapolis Minnesota June 25, 1949. Educated at University of California at Santa Barbara B.A. in English with highest honors 1971 M.A. in English with honors 1972 and University of California at Los Angeles J.D. 1975. Book Review Editor University of California at Los Angeles Law Review 1974-75. Admitted to practice California 1975 and U.S. District Court Central District of California 1975. In legal practice Los Angeles 1975-77 and 1980-86. Judge, Los Angeles Municipal Court Los Angeles County 1986-87.
With U.S. Attorney's Office Central District of California 1977-80. Author and Lecturer Rutter Group. Instructor Southwestern School of Law 1987. Board Member Association of Business Trial Lawyers 1986-91. Member Los Angeles County Bar Association (Litigation Executive Committee since 1997).
Office: Santa Monica Courthouse, 1725 Main Street, Santa Monica 90401.
Telephone: (310) 260-3762.

BALLATI, David Louis *(Judge, Superior Court of California City and County of San Francisco)* Assumed office Dec 31, 1998. Former Judge, San Francisco Municipal Court San Francisco County.
Office: Civic Center Courthouse, 400 McAllister Street, San Francisco 94102-4514.
Telephone: (415) 551-4020.

BALLINGER, Raima H. *(Judge, Superior Court of California County of Sonoma)*
Office: 600 Administration Drive, Santa Rosa 95403.
Telephone: (707) 565-1100.

BAMATTRE-MANOUKIAN, Patricia *(Associate Justice, California Court of Appeal Sixth District)* Appointed by Governor George Deukmejian Oct 16, 1989. Retained by election Nov 6, 1990 and Nov 2002. Former Administrative Presiding Justice and Presiding Justice. Born Los Angeles California June 11, 1950. Catholic. Educated at University of California at Los Angeles B.A. 1972, University of Southern California M.P.A. 1974 Ph.D. in Public Administration 1989 and Loyola Law School J.D. 1977. Recipient U.S. Public Health Fellowship 1972 and Henry Reining Award in Public Administration. Member Alpha Delta Pi, Phi Alpha Delta and St. Thomas More Society. Admitted to practice California 1977. Began legal practice Santa Ana 1977. Judge, West Orange County Municipal Court Orange County Oct 1983 to June 1985, appointed by Governor George Deukmejian. Judge, Santa Clara County Municipal Court July 1985 to March 1988. Judge March 1988 to Oct 1989 and Supervising Judge Family Law 1989, Superior Court of California Santa Clara County.

Deputy District Attorney Orange County Oct 1977 to Oct 1983 (Writs and Appeals 1977-78, Juvenile Court 1978-79, Misdemeanor Prosecutions and Sex and Child Abuse Deputy for West Court 1979-80, Felony Prosecutions 1980-81, Career Criminal Unit 1981-82 and Homicide Unit 1982-83). Contributor Evidence Training Tape California Center for Judicial Education and Research 1989. Author Book Review *America's First Woman Lawyer, The Biography of Myra Bradwell* 35 No. 3 Santa Clara L. Rev. 1995. Instructor in Trial Techniques Santa Clara University School of Law 1985-88 and in Trial Skills Workshop Stanford Law School 1997. Lecturer San Jose Police Department 1986, Palo Alto Police Department 1987, on Family Law for Attorney's Briefcase 1989 and Foothill Junior College 1996-97. Former Member AOC (Advisory Committee on Local Rules 1989-90, Family Court Services Advisory Committee 1990), Orange County Deputy District Attorneys Association, California District Attorneys Association, Judicial Council of California (Advisory Committee to Implement the Gender Fairness Proposals 1991, Subcommittee to Establish a Complaint Resolution Procedure 1991, Executive Committee 1993), State Bar of California and Orange County Bar Association. Life Member California Women Lawyers. Member Juvenile Justice Diversion Program (Shortstop 1980-83 and Executive Committee 1984-85), Appellate Courts Security Committee since 1993, Blue Ribbon Commission on Jury System Improvement 1996 and Appellate Advisory Committee since 1996. Member California Judges Association (Chair Education Planning and Coordinating Committee 1993, Midyear Chair 1995), California Center for Judicial Education and Research (Member 1994-97 and Chair 1997 Governing Committee), National Association of Women Judges and Santa Clara County Bar Association. Instructor "Jury Selection/Voir Dire" College of Trial Advocates Orange County Bar Association 1982, "Cross-Examination" New Prosecutors Course California District Attorneys Association 1982, "Handling Civil Writs" Continuing Education of the Bar 1991, "Working Together: Gender Bias in the Legal Profession" Santa Clara County Bar Association 1992 and "Civil Procedure Before Trial" The Rutter Group 1992 and 1994. Seminar Leader 1986 and Faculty Member "Advanced Criminal Procedure Before Trial" 1987-90 and "Judicial Leadership" 1991 California Judicial College. Judge Moot Court Competition Santa Clara University School of Law 1990 and 1993 and Heisler Moot Court Competition, Monterey 1992. Named Outstanding Young Women of America 1980 and Judge of the Year by Orange County Narcotics Officers Association 1985. Recipient St. Thomas More Award 1992 and Bernard E. Jefferson Award from California Judges Association 1995. Listed in *Who's Who in American Law* 2nd ed.
Office: 333 West Santa Clara Street, Suite 1060, San Jose 95113.
Telephone: (408) 277-1004.

BANKS, Andrew P. *(Judge, Superior Court of California County of Orange)*
Mailing address: P.O. Box 1994, Santa Ana 92702-1994.
Office: Central Justice Center, 700 Civic Center Drive West, Santa Ana 92701.
Telephone: (714) 834-3734.

BARANCO, Gordon S. *(Judge, Superior Court of California County of Alameda)* Appointed by Governor George Deukmejian to term beginning April 23, 1984. Elected 1988, 1994 and 2000. Current term expires Jan 2007. Born Oakland California Feb 25, 1948. Educated at University of California B.A. 1969 J.D. 1972. Admitted to practice California 1973. Began legal practice San Francisco 1973. In legal practice Oakland 1980. Judge, Oakland-Piedmont-Emeryville Municipal Court Alameda County 1980-84.
Office: Administration Building, 1221 Oak Street, Oakland 94612.
Telephone: (510) 271-5130.

BARELA, Henry T. *(Judge, Superior Court of California County of Los Angeles)* Assumed office Jan 22, 2000. Former Judge and Presiding Judge, East Los Angeles Municipal Court Los Angeles County.
Office: Criminal Courts Building, 210 West Temple Street, Los Angeles 90012-3210.
Telephone: (213) 974-6535.

BARNUM, Kenneth Paul *(Judge, Superior Court of California County of Santa Clara)* Assumed office July 30, 1998. Elected 2002, current term expires Jan 2009. Born Burbank California Aug 21, 1948. Educated at University of California at Los Angeles B.A. 1971, Southern Illinois University M.B.A. 1981 and Southwestern University School of Law J.D. 1980. Admitted to practice California 1980. In legal practice Los Altos 1985-95. Former Judge, Santa Clara County Municipal Court.
District Attorney San Mateo County 1981-85.
Office: 605 West El Camino Real, Sunnyvale 94087.
Telephone: (408) 481-3500.

BARR, James N. *(Judge, United States Bankruptcy Court Central District of California)* Appointed by U.S. Court of Appeals Ninth Circuit judges to term beginning Jan 12, 1987. Reappointed Jan 2001, current term expires Jan 2015. Born Kewanee Illinois Oct 21, 1940. Educated at Illinois Wesleyan University B.S. 1962 and Illinois Institute of Technology, Chicago-Kent College of Law J.D. 1971. Admitted to practice Illinois 1972, U.S. District Courts Northern District of Illinois 1972 and

BARR, JAMES N.—*Continued*

Central 1977 and Southern 1977 Districts of California, U.S. Courts of Appeals Seventh 1972 and Ninth 1977 Circuits and California 1977. In legal practice Chicago 1972-76 and California 1977-86.

Ex Officio Member Board of Directors Orange County Bankruptcy Forum since 1988. Editorial Board California Bankruptcy Journal since 1989. President Peter M. Elliott Inn of Court 1990-91. Founder Warren J. Ferguson American Inn of Court 2000. Lieutenant USN 1962-67.

Office: 6165 Federal Bldg. & U.S. Courthouse, 411 West Fourth Street, Santa Ana 92701-4593.

Telephone: (714) 338-5430.

BARR, Kenneth *(Judge, Superior Court of California County of San Bernardino)* Assumed office Aug 10, 1998. Former Judge, San Bernardino County Municipal Court.

Office: 351 North Arrowhead Avenue, San Bernardino 92415-0240.

Telephone: (909) 387-3922.

BARRETO, Antonio, Jr. *(Judge, Superior Court of California County of Los Angeles)* Assumed office Jan 22, 2000. Elected 2000, current term expires Jan 2007. Born New Bedford Massachusetts Feb 14, 1951. Educated at University of California at Los Angeles B.A. 1974, California State University at Northridge and Southwestern University School of Law J.D. 1977. Admitted to practice California 1977 and U.S. District Court Central District of California 1983. Judge Jan 3, 1990 to Jan 21, 2000 and Presiding Judge 1991, 1993, 1995, 1997 and 1999, Culver Municipal Court Los Angeles County, appointed by Governor George Deukmejian.

Deputy District Attorney Los Angeles County 1978-90. Enjoys golf and guitar.

Office: Los Angeles Airport Courthouse, 11701 South La Cienega Boulevard, Los Angeles 90045.

Telephone: (310) 727-6010.

BARRETT, Thang Nguyen *(Judge, Superior Court of California County of Santa Clara)* Assumed office July 30, 1998. Former Judge, Santa Clara County Municipal Court.

Office: 191 North First Street, San Jose 95113.

Telephone: (408) 882-2100.

BARRY, William P. *(Judge, Superior Court of California County of Los Angeles)*

Office: Compton Courthouse, 200 West Compton Boulevard, Compton 90220.

Telephone: (310) 603-7842.

BARTON, Jeffrey *(Judge, Superior Court of California County of San Diego)*

Mailing address: P.O. Box 122724, San Diego 92112-2724.

Office: 325 South Melrose Drive, Vista 92083.

Telephone: (760) 726-9595.

BARTON, Michael Einum *(Judge, Superior Court of California County of Santa Cruz)* Assumed office July 1, 1998. Presiding Judge since Jan 1, 2003. Presiding Judge Jan 1, 1996 to Dec 31, 1996 and Former Judge, Santa Cruz County Municipal Court.

Office: Main Courthouse, 701 Ocean Street, Santa Cruz 95060.

Telephone: (831) 454-2012.

BASCUE, James Allen *(Judge, Superior Court of California County of Los Angeles)* Presiding Judge Jan 1, 2001 to Dec 31, 2002.

Office: Courthouse, 111 North Hill Street, Los Angeles 90012.

Telephone: (213) 974-5411.

BASHANT, Cynthia Ann *(Judge, Superior Court of California County of San Diego)*

Office: 2851 Meadowlark Drive, San Diego 92123.

Telephone: (858) 694-4601.

BASKIN, Barry *(Judge, Superior Court of California County of Contra Costa)*

Office: 100 37th Street, Richmond 94805-2136.

Telephone: (510) 374-3800.

BATTAGLIA, Anthony J. *(Magistrate Judge, United States District Court Southern District of California)* Appointed by U.S. District Court judges.

Office: 1145 U.S. Courthouse, 940 Front Street, San Diego 92101-8927.

Telephone: (619) 557-3446.

BAUER, Ronald L. *(Judge, Superior Court of California County of Orange)* Commissioner 1984-90. Appointed Judge by Governor George Deukmejian to term beginning Jan 2, 1991. Elected Nov 3, 1992 and 1998. Current term expires Jan 2005. Born Altoona Pennsylvania Aug 22, 1941. United Methodist. Educated at Harvard College A.B. 1962, University of Virginia School of Law LL.B. 1965 and University of Edinburgh, Scotland 1966. Editorial Board Virginia Law Review 1963-65. Member Phi Delta Phi and Order of the Coif. Admitted to practice Virginia 1965, California 1967, U.S. District Court Central District of California 1969 and U.S. Court of Appeals Ninth Circuit 1969. In legal practice Santa Ana California 1967-84.

Author Case Notes 49 Virginia L. Rev. 1025 and 1030, 1964. Editor Orange County Bar Bulletin 1969-71. Editorial Board California State B. Jour. 1971-74. Instructor in Contracts, Conflict of Laws and Trial Practice Western State University School of Law 1968-70 and 1994-2003. Former Member State Bar of California. Member California Judges Association. Lecturer Panels on Injunctive Relief and Discovery California Continuing Education of the Bar 1986-94. Instructor in Civil Practice programs Rutter Group CLE 1986-2002. Faculty Member California Continuing Judicial Studies Programs on Discovery and Civil Law and Procedure 1989-2003. Enjoys sports.

Mailing address: P.O. Box 22028, Santa Ana 92702-2028.

Office: Civil Complex Center, 751 West Santa Ana Boulevard, Santa Ana 92701.

Telephone: (714) 568-4811.

BAXTER, Floyd V. *(Judge, Superior Court of California County of Los Angeles)* Assumed office Jan 22, 2000. Presiding Judge Jan 1, 1996 to Dec 31, 1997 and

BAXTER, FLOYD V.—*Continued*
Former Judge, Newhall Municipal Court Los Angeles County.
Office: Santa Clarita Courthouse, 23747 West Valencia Boulevard, Valencia 91355.
Telephone: (661) 253-7301.

BAXTER, Marvin R. *(Associate Justice, California Supreme Court)* Appointed by governor to term beginning Jan 1991. Retained by election. Born Fowler California Jan 9, 1940. Educated at California State University at Fresno B.S. and University of California Hastings College of the Law J.D. 1966. In legal practice Fresno 1970-83. Associate Justice, California Court of Appeal Fifth District Dec 1988 to Jan 1991.
Deputy District Attorney Fresno County 1967-69. Former Chair California Supreme Court Library Committee. President 1973-74 and Former Member Board of Directors Fresno County Young Lawyers Association. President 1981 and Former Member Board of Directors Fresno County Bar Association. Former Member Board of Directors Fresno County Legal Services, Inc. and California Young Lawyers Association. Chair Building Committee and Official Reports Committee California Supreme Court. Member Judicial Council of California (Chair Policy Coordination and Liaison Committee, Former Chair Appellate Advisory Committee). Recipient Outstanding Service Award from California State University at Fresno Alumni Association 1977, Alumnus of the Year Award from Fresno Chapter Hastings College of the Law Alumni Association 1995, Mentor Award from Fresno County Young Lawyers Association 1996 and Distinguished Alumnus Award from California State University at Fresno 1996 and Hastings College of the Law 1998. Appointments Secretary to Governor George Deukmejian 1983-88. President and Board Member Trust Council, President and Board Member Fresno State Alumni Association. Director Emeritus University of California Hastings College of the Law.
Office: 350 McAllister Street, San Francisco 94102-4783.
Telephone: (415) 865-7080.

BAYSINGER, Robert F. *(Judge, Superior Court of California County of San Joaquin)* Assumed office June 8, 1998. Born Lodi California June 3, 1945. Religious affiliation: Lutheran/Catholic. Educated at California State University at Sacramento B.A. 1968 and La Salle University Law School 1972. Member Alpha Sigma Phi. Admitted to practice California 1973. Began legal practice Stockton 1973. Commissioner and Judge pro tem 1979-84, Judge June 19, 1984 to June 7, 1998 and Presiding Judge Jan 1, 1996 to Dec 31, 1996, Lodi Municipal Court San Joaquin County, appointed by Governor George Deukmejian.
Former Deputy District Attorney San Joaquin County. Guest lecturer San Joaquin Delta College. Member California Court Commissioners (Board of Directors 1981-84) and California Judges Association 1979-82 and since 1984. Inactive member State Bar of California. Participant California Judicial College 1979. Received P.O.S.T. Certificate 1971. Fingerprint Examiner California Department of Justice 1966-68. Investigator California Department of Alcoholic Beverage Control 1968-73. Republican. Member Chamber of Commerce, Boy Scouts of America, Lodi Boys Club, Lodi-Tokay Rotary Club, Friends of the Library, Big Brothers/Big Sisters, United Way Campaign, San Joaquin County Historical Society and San Joaquin County Zoological Society.
Office: 315 West Elm Street, Lodi 95240.
Telephone: (209) 333-6753.

BEA, Carlos *(Judge, Superior Court of California City and County of San Francisco)*
Office: Civic Center Courthouse, 400 McAllister Street, San Francisco 94102-4514.
Telephone: (415) 551-4020.

BEASON, Candace J. *(Judge, Superior Court of California County of Los Angeles)* Former Judge, Los Angeles Municipal Court Los Angeles County.
Office: Alhambra Courthouse, 150 West Commonwealth Avenue, Alhambra 91801.
Telephone: (626) 308-5537.

BEAUCHESNE, Roger M. *(Judge, Superior Court of California County of Stanislaus)* Assumed office July 31, 1998. Presiding Judge July 1, 1995 to June 30, 1997 and Former Judge, Stanislaus County Municipal Court.
Office: 800 Eleventh Street, Modesto 95354.
Telephone: (209) 558-6000.

BECK, Barbara J. *(Judge, Superior Court of California County of Santa Barbara)* Assumed office Aug 3, 1998. Serves Juvenile Division. Born Columbia Mississippi July 16, 1941. Baptist. Educated at Hinds Junior College A.A. 1962, Citrus Belt Law School B.S. 1972 J.D. 1974. Admitted to practice California 1974. Began legal practice Riverside 1975. In legal practice Santa Maria 1979. Associate Justice pro tem, California Court of Appeal Feb 1986 to April 1986. Judge April 19, 1984 to Aug 2, 1998 and Presiding Judge Jan 1, 1995 to Dec 31, 1996, North Santa Barbara County Municipal Court, appointed by Governor George Deukmejian.
Former Attorney Public Defender's Office. Member California Women Lawyers since 1976, California Judges Association since 1984, National Association of Women Judges since 1984, State Bar of California 1975-84 and North Santa Barbara County Bar Association since 1979. Technical Sergeant E-6 (Medical Technician, Urology Surgical Technician) USAF 1964-72. Previously worked in real estate sales and as bookkeeper. Republican. Member Santa Maria Women's Network, American Legion, Rotary Club of Santa Maria, Minerva Club and Disabled American Veterans. Enjoys hunting, fishing and reading Louis L'Amour.
Office: 812-B West Foster Road, Santa Maria 93455.
Telephone: (805) 568-2220.

BECK, Dennis L. *(Magistrate Judge, United States District Court Eastern District of California)* Appointed by U.S. District Court judges to term beginning March 12, 1990. Reappointed March 12, 1998, current term expires 2006. Currently serves as Chief Magistrate Judge. Educated at College of William & Mary B.A. 1969 J.D. 1972. Staff member 1970-71 and Special Projects Editor 1972 William and Mary Law Review. Admitted to practice California 1972. In legal practice Fresno 1978-79 and 1985-87. Judge, Superior Court of California Kings County 1983-85.
With District Attorneys Office Fresno County 1972-78, 1979-82 and 1987-90.
Office: 3489 U.S. Courthouse, 1130 O Street, Fresno 93721.
Telephone: (559) 498-7537.

BEDSWORTH, William W. *(Associate Justice, California Court of Appeal Fourth District Division Three)* Appointed by Governor Pete Wilson to term beginning 1997. Retained by election. Born Long Beach California Nov 21, 1947. Educated at Loyola University of Los Angeles B.A. cum laude 1968 and University of California at Berkeley J.D. 1971. Admitted to practice California 1972. Judge, Superior Court of California Orange County Jan 1987 to 1997.

Deputy District Attorney 1972-87. Adjunct Faculty Western State University College of Law 1987-91. Author *What I Saw and Heard* Syntext Publishing Jan 1995. Works as goal judge for the National Hockey League (Mighty Ducks of Anaheim).

Office: 925 North Spurgeon Street, Santa Ana 92701-3700.

Telephone: (714) 558-6777.

BEEMAN, Paul Lloyd *(Judge, Superior Court of California County of Solano)*

Office: 321 Tuolumne Street, Vallejo 94590.

Telephone: (707) 553-5876.

BEGEN, Loretta Murphy *(Judge, Superior Court of California County of Stanislaus)* Assumed office July 31, 1998. Former Judge, Stanislaus County Municipal Court.

Office: 800 Eleventh Street, Modesto 95354.

Telephone: (209) 558-6000.

BEHN, Richard E. *(Judge, Superior Court of California County of Orange)* Assumed office Aug 10, 1998. Presiding Judge Jan 1, 1996 to Dec 31, 1996 and Former Judge, North Orange County Municipal Court.

Mailing address: P.O. Box 14169, Orange 92863-1569.

Office: Lamoreaux Justice Center, 341 The City Drive, Orange 92868.

Telephone: (714) 935-7236.

BENDER, Thomas L. *(Judge, Superior Court of California County of Madera)* Assumed office July 1, 1998. Former Judge, Madera County Municipal Court.

Office: 209 West Yosemite Avenue, Madera 93637.

Telephone: (559) 675-7907.

BENDIX, Helen I. *(Judge, Superior Court of California County of Los Angeles)* Assumed office Jan 22, 2000. Born New York July 24, 1952. Educated at Cornell University B.A. 1973 and Yale Law School J.D. 1976. Law Clerk to Hon. Shirley M. Hufstedler, U.S. Court of Appeals Ninth Circuit 1976-77. Member Phi Beta Kappa. Admitted to practice California 1976, District of Columbia 1978, U.S. District Courts District of Columbia 1980 and Central 1986 and Southern 1990 Districts of California and U.S. Courts of Appeals District of Columbia 1981 and Ninth 1987 Circuits. In legal practice District of Columbia 1978-85, Century City California 1986-89 and Los Angeles California 1989-96. Judge, Los Angeles Municipal Court Los Angeles County March 6, 1997 to Jan 21, 2000, appointed by Governor Pete Wilson.

General Counsel KCET Sept 1996 to Feb 1997. Author "Interaction of Business and Government in Japan: Lessons for the United States" 15 International Law 571, 1981; "Firms Owe Mothers in Law a Break" *Legal Times* Dec 5, 1988; "An Introduction to ADR" *ADR Newsletter* June 1993; "ADR is Alive and Well in the California District Courts" *ADR Newsletter* Los Angeles County Bar Association Jan 1994; "An ADR Primer" *ADR Sourcebook* Los Angeles County Bar Association June 1994; "Alternative Routes" *Los Angeles and San Francisco Daily Journal* Dec 13, 1995; "How Much Must Experts Disclose?" *Los Angeles and San Francisco Daily Journal* Jan 26, 1996; and "Judicial Muses" *Los Angeles Daily Journal* Nov 29, 1999. Co-author with R. Chernick "Renting the Judge" *Litigation* American Bar Association Fall 1994. Acting Professor of Public International Law and Japanese Law 1980 and Visiting Professor of Law in Civil Procedure and Remedies 1985-86 University of California at Los Angeles School of Law. Adjunct Professor of Law American University 1983. Founding Member and Officer ADR Section 1990-91. Member Commercial Arbitration Panel American Arbitration Association 1989-96, Panel of Mediators Los Angeles County Superior Court 1994-96, Panel of Distinguished Neutral in Los Angeles Center for Public Resources 1996-97. President Dispute Resolution Services since 1997. Vice Chair Alternative Dispute Resolution Committee and Member Media Committee Superior Court of California. Member Judicial Council of California (Access and Fairness Advisory Committee, Ad Hoc Committee on Mediator Ethics, Supreme Court Advisory Committee on Canon 6D), Municipal Court Judges Association (Annual Conference Committee 1997, Legislation Committee 1998, Budget Committee 1999), Municipal Court (Chair Media Subcommittee of the Courts and the Public Committee 1998, Legislation Committee 1998, Speakers Bureau since 1998, Budget Committee 1999), State Bar of California (Chair International Law Section 1990-91, Member Commission on Foreign Legal Practice 1991) and Los Angeles County Bar Association (Board of Trustees 1994-97, Diversity Roundtable 1994-95, Governance Committee 1995, Government Resources Committee 1996-97, Bench, Bar and Media Committee 1999, Founding Member and Officer ADR Section 1994-98, Chairperson Outstanding Trial Jurist Review Committee 1995).

Presenter "Dispute Resolution Alternatives" Practising Law Institute Conference San Francisco June 10 and June 17, 1994; "Strategies for Corporate Counsel: ADR and Your Bottom Line" conference sponsored by the women lawyers of Heller, Ehrman, White & McAuliffe April 11, 1995; "Litigating an International Case" International Law Section Los Angeles County Bar Association April 18, 1995; "Outside Counsel's Perspective on ADR" CPR's Annual Spring Meeting San Francisco June 18, 1995; "Recent Revisions to the Export Control Laws and Recent Developments in ADR" Annual International Law Weekend International Law Section State Bar of California July 29, 1995; "Recent Developments on Federal Rules of Civil Procedure Regarding Expert Discovery" Annual Meeting California Society of Certified Public Accountants Dec 5-6, 1995; "So You Don't Have an ADR Policy?" ADR Section Los Angeles County Bar Association March 7, 1996; "Three Strikes and You're Out: Court Funding Crises" Chancery Club April 11, 1996; "ADR and Litigation Consultants" Advanced Litigation Forum California Society of Certified Public Accountants April 29-30, 1996; and "The Role of the Judge" Optimist Club March 18, 1998. Named one of ten lawyers featured in "Ten Years of Upheaval and Ten Who Made It Happen" by *American Lawyers* 10th Anniversary Edition March 1989 and one of fifty women featured in "The 50 Most Powerful Women in Los Angeles Law" by *Los Angeles Business Journal* Feb 9,

BENDIX, HELEN I.—*Continued*

1998. Immediate Past Chairwoman Twelfth Grade Class Los Angeles Founder Chapter National Charity League. Violinist and Violist Palisades Symphony. Member Chancery Club. Enjoys jogging (former marathon runner) and children's school activities.

Office: Courthouse, 111 North Hill Street, Los Angeles 90012.

Telephone: (213) 974-5411.

BENITEZ, Roger T. *(Magistrate Judge, U.S. District Court Southern District of California)* Appointed by U.S. District Court judges to term beginning Jan 2, 2001. Former Judge, Superior Court of California County of Imperial.

Office: 321 South Waterman Avenue, El Centro 92243-2264.

Telephone: (760) 353-1271.

BENKE, Patricia D. *(Associate Justice, California Court of Appeal Fourth District Division One)* Appointed by Governor George Deukmejian to term beginning June 1988. Retained by election Nov 6, 1990 and Nov 8, 1994. Current term expires Jan 2007. Educated at California State University at San Diego A.B. 1971 and University of San Diego School of Law J.D. 1974. Admitted to practice California 1974, U.S. District Court District of California 1974, U.S. Court of Appeals Ninth Circuit 1974 and U.S. Supreme Court 1979. Judge, San Diego Municipal Court San Diego County 1984-86. Judge, Superior Court of California San Diego County 1986-88.

Deputy Attorney General San Diego 1974-83. Adjunct Professor of Law Thomas Jefferson School of Law. Political Writer and Analyst San Diego public television station KPBS-TV. Member Park and Recreation Board for the City of San Diego.

Office: 750 B Street, Suite 300, San Diego 92101.

Telephone: (619) 645-2760.

BENNETT, Richard A. *(Judge, Superior Court of California County of Napa)* Appointed by Governor Pete Wilson to term beginning Nov 1996. Assistant Presiding Judge 1996-98 and Presiding Judge Jan 1, 2000 to Dec 31, 2001. Presiding Judge Appellate Department 1997. Educated at Golden Gate University B.A. 1970 and University of California Hastings College of the Law J.D. 1973. Admitted to practice California 1973, U.S. Court of Appeals Ninth Circuit 1973 and U.S. Supreme Court 1976. In legal practice Calistoga and St. Helena 1973-82. Judge 1985-96 and Presiding Judge 1987, 1990 and 1993, Napa County Municipal Court, appointed by Governor George Deukmejian. First Presiding Judge 1993 and Assistant Presiding Judge 1994-96, Napa County Municipal and Superior Courts.

Assistant City Attorney Calistoga. Deputy District Attorney, Chief Family Support Division and Acting Chief Deputy Criminal Division Napa County 1982-85. Vice President and Founding Member Inn of Court for Marin, Sonoma and Napa Counties 1997. Member Napa Valley College Administration of Justice Advisory Committee, California Judges Foundation (Court Administration Committee 1991-92), California Judges Association, American Judges Association, American Judges Foundation, State Bar of California and Napa County Bar Association. Attended California Judicial College 1986, "The English Court System" Magdalen College Oxford University 1990 and "The Irish and Scottish Court Systems" Trinity College Dublin Ireland 1997 and University of Edinburgh Scotland 1997 California Judges Foundation Conference and The National Judicial College. Instructor Annual Conference of Georgia Superior Court Judges 1993. Speaker Annual Meeting of California Superior Court Clerks Association 1993, Training Seminar for Attorneys, Family Support Officers and Investigators California District Attorneys Association 1996 and "Technology for Courts and Judges" The National Judicial College 1997. Keynote Graduation Speaker Basic Police Academy Class and Paralegal Program Napa Valley College. Chairman Napa County Family Violence Prevention Council 1993-94 and Napa County Child Abuse Prevention Council 1996-98. Trustee Napa County Law Library (Past President Board of Trustees). Former Member Board of Directors Napa Rotary Club, Board of Trustees Napa County Legal Assistance Agency and Napa Chamber of Commerce. Member Leadership Napa Valley.

Office: Napa County Courthouse, 825 Brown Street, Napa 94559.

Telephone: (707) 299-1100.

BENSON, Jerome T. *(Judge, Superior Court of California City and County of San Francisco)* Assumed office Dec 31, 1998. Former Judge, San Francisco Municipal Court San Francisco County.

Office: Hall of Justice, 850 Bryant Street, San Francisco 94103.

Telephone: (415) 553-1159.

BENSON, Stephen E. *(Judge, Superior Court of California County of Butte)* Elected to term beginning Jan 2001. Term expires Jan 2007. Born San Francisco California Aug 15, 1946. Educated at Pacific Union College B.A. 1968 M.A. 1970, Western State University J.D. 1978 and University of California Hastings College of the Law 1982. Admitted to practice California 1979 and U.S. District Court Eastern District of California. In legal practice Chico 1981-2000.

Member California Judges Association (Elections Committee) and American Judges Association. Board Member Advisory Board Butte County Mental Health 1986-89. Chairman Medical Ethics Committee Feather River Hospital 1999-2000. Enjoys hiking, playing tennis and basketball.

Office: One Court Street, Oroville 95965.

Telephone: (530) 538-7611.

E-mail address: sbenson@buttecourt.ca.gov

BEREOLA, Gail Brewster *(Judge, Superior Court of California County of Alameda)* Assumed office July 31, 1998. Former Judge, Oakland-Piedmont-Emeryville Municipal Court Alameda County.

Office: Courthouse, 661 Washington Street, Oakland 94607.

Telephone: (510) 268-7601.

BERGER, Peter A. *(Judge, Superior Court of California County of Contra Costa)* Assumed office June 8, 1998. Presiding Judge Jan 1, 1997 to Dec 31, 1997 and Former Judge, Bay Municipal Court Contra Costa County.

Office: 100 37th Street, Richmond 94805-2136.

Telephone: (510) 374-3800.

BERGERON, Joseph E. *(Judge, Superior Court of California County of San Mateo)*
Office: Hall of Justice, 400 County Center, Redwood City 94063.
Telephone: (650) 363-4516.

BERLE, Elihu M. *(Judge, Superior Court of California County of Los Angeles)*
Office: Courthouse, 111 North Hill Street, Los Angeles 90012.
Telephone: (213) 974-5411.

BERNAL, Margaret Miller *(Judge, Superior Court of California County of Los Angeles)* Assumed office Jan 22, 2000. Former Judge, Whittier Municipal Court Los Angeles County.
Office: Whittier Courthouse, 7339 South Painter Avenue, Whittier 90602.
Telephone: (562) 907-3046.

BERNAL, Paul R. *(Judge, Superior Court of California County of Santa Clara)*
Office: 270 Grant Avenue, Palo Alto 94306.
Telephone: (650) 462-3800.

BERNARDINI, Susan *(Judge, Superior Court of California County of Santa Clara)*
Office: 115 Terraine Street, San Jose 95113.
Telephone: (408) 491-4700.

BERNSTEIN, Lauren Weiss *(Judge, Superior Court of California County of Los Angeles)*
Office: Courthouse, 111 North Hill Street, Los Angeles 90012.
Telephone: (213) 974-5411.

BERTOLI, James Gordon *(Judge, Superior Court of California County of Sonoma)*
Office: 600 Administration Drive, Santa Rosa 95403.
Telephone: (707) 565-1100.

BEST, Hollis G. *(Magistrate Judge, United States District Court Eastern District of California)* Appointed by U.S. District Court judges to term beginning March 1, 1994. Reappointed 2002, current term expires 2010. Born Curry County New Mexico July 10, 1926. Protestant. Educated at Fresno State College (now California State University at Fresno) B.A. 1948 and Stanford University J.D. 1951. Admitted to practice California 1951. In legal practice Fresno 1953-72. Judge, Superior Court of California Fresno County Dec 1972 to Oct 1984, appointed by Governor Ronald Reagan. Associate Justice Oct 1984 to Sept 1990 and Presiding Justice Sept 17, 1990 to Feb 28, 1994, California Court of Appeal Fifth District, appointed by Governor George Deukmejian.

With Fresno District Attorney's Office 1951-53. Member Executive Committee 1969-71 and Vice Chairman 1971 Conference of State Bar Delegates. Former Member Judicial Council of California. Member California Judges Association (Executive Board) and Fresno County Bar Association (President 1963). Instructor San Joaquin College of Law 1973-84. Lieutenant j.g. USN 1944-46. Republican. Enjoys golf and fishing.

Mailing address: P.O. Box 575, Yosemite National Park 95389-0575.
Telephone: (209) 372-0320.

BEVERLY, William C., Jr. *(Judge, Superior Court of California County of Los Angeles)* Former Judge, Long Beach Municipal Court Los Angeles County.
Office: Courthouse, 111 North Hill Street, Los Angeles 90012.
Telephone: (213) 974-5411.

BIAFORE, Joseph F., Jr. *(Judge, Superior Court of California County of Santa Clara)* Presiding Judge Jan 1, 1995 to Dec 31, 1996. Former Judge, Santa Clara County Municipal Court.
Office: Old Courthouse, 161 North First Street, San Jose 95113.
Telephone: (408) 882-2340.

BIGELOW, Tricia Ann *(Judge, Superior Court of California County of Los Angeles)* Former Judge, Los Angeles Municipal Court Los Angeles County. Served Hollywood Branch.
Office: Criminal Courts Building, 210 West Temple Street, Los Angeles 90012-3210.
Telephone: (213) 974-6535.

BIGGS, Carl *(Judge, Superior Court of California County of Orange)* Assumed office Aug 10, 1998. Former Judge, South Orange County Municipal Court.
Office: 4601 Jamboree Road, Newport Beach 92660.
Telephone: (949) 476-4789.

BIRNEY, William J. *(Judge, Superior Court of California County of Los Angeles)*
Office: Norwalk Courthouse, 12720 Norwalk Boulevard, Norwalk 90650.
Telephone: (562) 807-7266.

BISSIG, Louis F. *(Judge, Superior Court of California County of Kings)* Presiding Judge Jan 1, 2000 to Dec 31, 2002.
Office: 1426 South Drive, Hanford 93230.
Telephone: (559) 582-3211.

BJORK, B. J. *(Judge, Superior Court of California County of Riverside)* Assumed office July 29, 1998. Former Judge, Desert Municipal Court Riverside County.
Office: Larson Justice Center, 46-200 Oasis Street, Indio 92201.
Telephone: (760) 863-8426.

BLACK, Donald S. *(Judge, Superior Court of California County of Fresno)*
Office: Courthouse, 1100 Van Ness Avenue, Fresno 93724-0002.
Telephone: (559) 488-1825.

BLACK, Kenneth A. *(Judge, Superior Court of California County of Los Angeles)*
Office: Courthouse, 111 North Hill Street, Los Angeles 90012.
Telephone: (213) 974-5411.

BLACKWELL, Walter L., III *(Judge, Superior Court of California County of San Bernardino)* Serves Valley Division.
Office: 17780 Arrow Boulevard, Fontana 92335.
Telephone: (909) 350-9322.

BLEA, Jacob, III *(Judge, Superior Court of California County of Alameda)*
Office: Hall of Justice, 5672 Stoneridge Drive, Pleasanton 94588.
Telephone: (925) 551-6886.

BLEASE, Coleman A. *(Associate Justice, California Court of Appeal Third District)* Appointed by governor.
Office: 914 Capitol Mall, Sacramento 95814.
Telephone: (916) 654-0209.

BLOCK, Robert N. *(Magistrate Judge, United States District Court Central District of California)* Appointed by U.S. District Court judges.
Office: U.S. Courthouse, 312 North Spring Street, Los Angeles 90012.
Telephone: (213) 894-6512.

BLOOM, Jay M. *(Judge, Superior Court of California County of San Diego)* Assumed office Dec 1, 1998. Former Judge, San Diego Municipal Court San Diego County.
Mailing address: P.O. Box 122724, San Diego 92112-2724.
Office: 220 West Broadway, San Diego 92101.
Telephone: (619) 531-3820.

BLUEBOND, Sheri *(Judge, United States Bankruptcy Court Central District of California)* Appointed by U.S. Court of Appeals Ninth Circuit judges to term beginning Feb 1, 2001. Term expires Feb 1, 2015. Born Los Angeles California May 15, 1961. Jewish. Educated at University of California at Los Angeles B.A. summa cum laude 1982 J.D. 1985. Staff member UCLA Law Review 1983-85. Member Order of the Coif. Admitted to practice California 1985. In legal practice Los Angeles 1985-2001.

Author "What Every Real Estate Lawyer Should Know About the 1994 Amendments to the Bankruptcy Code" *Practical Real Estate Lawyer* July 1995, "Insulating Purchasers in Bankruptcy from Successor Liability" *The Review of Banking & Financial Services* April 1998 and "To File or Not to File" American Bar Association Journal July 1999. Panel of Mediators Bankruptcy Mediation Program. Member American Bankruptcy Institute, Los Angeles County (Bankruptcy Committee Commercial Law and Bankruptcy Section, Executive Committee) and American Bar Associations. Speaker "A Stranger in Our Midst: Lending to and Enforcing Rights Against Limited Liability Companies" Commercial Law and Bankruptcy Section Los Angeles County Bar Association Nov 1995; "Raiders at the Gate: Using 'Revlon Duty' as a Sword or Shield in Corporate Change Battles in Chapter 11" Subcommittee on Loan Workouts and Bankruptcy Committee on Banking Law March 1996, "The Search for Signs of Intelligent Life in the Universe: Formulating Cost Effective Solutions to Common Business Problems" Committee on Small Business Aug 1998 and "Advising Clients in the Penumbra of Insolvency" Committees on Small Business and Business Bankruptcy August 2001 Section of Business Law American Bar Association; "Strange Bedfellows: Partnerships in Bankruptcy Revisited" Oct 1996 and "Mission Impossible? Preventing Successor Liability and Future Claims in Chapter 11" Nov 1998 Financial Lawyers Conference; "Identifying Investment Opportunities in Workouts & Turnarounds" The Institute for International Research Dec 1997; "Bridging Over Troubled Waters: Communications in the Troubled Company Environment" Turnaround Management Association Sept 1998; and "Is the Next Recession on the Horizon? Things You Should Know Before the Sun Sets on Your Borrower" 34th Annual Bank Counsel Seminar California Bankers' Association April 2001. Board of Trustees Jewish Big Brothers/Camp Max Straus.
Office: 255 East Temple Street, Suite 1482, Los Angeles 90012.
Telephone: (213) 894-8980.
E-mail address: Sheri_Bluebond@cacb.uscourts.gov

BOBB, Aviva Koenigsberg *(Judge, Superior Court of California County of Los Angeles)* Appointed by Governor Pete Wilson to term beginning Aug 31, 1994. Elected 1994 and 2000. Current term expires Jan 2007. Born New York New York Jan 26, 1946. Educated at Wellesley College B.A. 1967 and University of California Boalt Hall School of Law J.D. 1971. Admitted to practice California 1972 and U.S. District Court Central District of California 1972. In legal practice Los Angeles 1972-80. Judge, Los Angeles Municipal Court Los Angeles County 1980-94.
Office: Courthouse, 111 North Hill Street, Los Angeles 90012.
Telephone: (213) 974-5411.

BOCANEGRA, Arthur *(Judge, Superior Court of California County of Santa Clara)*
Office: Hall of Justice West Wing, 200 West Hedding Street, San Jose 95110.
Telephone: (408) 808-6600.

BOECKMAN, Bradley L. *(Judge, Superior Court of California County of Shasta)* Presiding Judge Jan 1, 1999 to Dec 31, 2000.
Office: 1500 Court Street, Redding 96001-1685.
Telephone: (530) 225-5714.

BOLAND, Paul *(Associate Justice, California Court of Appeal Second District Division Eight)* Appointed by Governor Gray Davis to term beginning 2001. Born Los Angeles California Jan 25, 1942. Roman Catholic. Educated at Loyola Marymount University B.A. 1963, University of Southern California J.D. 1966 and Georgetown University LL.M. 1967. Law Clerk to U.S. District Court Central District of California 1967-68. Admitted to practice California 1967. Judge, Superior Court of California County of Los Angeles 1981-2001, appointed by Governor Edmund G. Brown, Jr.

Staff Attorney and Deputy Director of Litigation Western Center on Law and Poverty 1968-70. Associate Dean, Professor of Law and Director of Clinical Legal Education University of California at Los Angeles School of Law 1970-81. Member Judicial Council of California 1995-2000. Member California Judges Association (President 1995-96), American Judicature Society and Los Angeles County Bar Association. Recipient Outstanding Jurist Award from Los Angeles County Bar Association and Alfred McCourtney Trial Jurist Award from Los Angeles Trial Lawyers Association. Named Judge of the Year by Constitutional Rights Foundation and Trial Judge of the Year by California Trial Lawyers Association. Member California Supreme Court Historical Society.
Office: 300 South Spring Street, Los Angeles 90013.
Telephone: (213) 830-7373.
Fax: (213) 830-7017
E-mail address: paul.boland@jud.ca.gov

BOLLMAN, J. Michael *(Judge, Superior Court of California County of San Diego)* Appointed by Governor Pete Wilson to term beginning Jan 16, 1992. Elected 1992 and 1998. Current term expires Jan 2005. Born

BOLLMAN, J. MICHAEL—*Continued*

Rock Island Illinois April 6, 1939. Presbyterian. Educated at Coe College B.A. 1961, State University of Iowa M.A. 1964 and Illinois Institute of Technology Chicago-Kent College of Law J.D. 1965. Admitted to practice Illinois 1965, California 1968 and U.S. District Courts. Certified Family Law Specialist California Board of Legal Specialization. In legal practice Park Ridge Illinois 1965-67 and San Diego California since 1968. Judge, El Cajon Municipal Court San Diego County Dec 10, 1985 to Jan 15, 1992.

Adjunct Professor of Law National University College of Law 1987. Fellow American Academy of Matrimonial Lawyers. Member San Diego County Judges Association (Board of Directors since 1986), State Bar of California, San Diego County and American Bar Associations. Named Outstanding Young Man of San Diego County 1972. Faculty Member California Continuing Judicial Studies Program 1987-88 and 1992, California Center for Judicial Education and Research 1987-92 and "The Family Lawyer: Ethics and Avoiding Malpractice" Continuing Education of the Bar Program 1992. News Director Radio Station KPIG Cedar Rapids Iowa 1960-61. Manager First Capitol Signs Iowa City Iowa 1961-63. Board of Directors Combined Health Agencies Drive 1973-80, San Diego County Chapter American Heart Association 1973-80, United Way 1974-76 and Camp Oliver since 1983. Chairman San Diego County Heart Association Fund Raising Drive 1975. Enjoys jogging, spectator sports, theater and music.

Mailing address: P.O. Box 122724, San Diego 92112-2724.

Office: 220 West Broadway, San Diego 92101.

Telephone: (619) 531-3820.

BORACK, Jerilyn L. *(Judge, Superior Court of California County of Sacramento)*

Office: Courthouse, 720 Ninth Street, Sacramento 95814.

Telephone: (916) 874-5476.

BORBA, Joan Marie *(Judge, Superior Court of California County of San Bernardino)* Assumed office Aug 10, 1998. Serves Rancho District. Former Judge, San Bernardino County Municipal Court. Served West Valley Division.

Office: 8303 North Haven Avenue, Rancho Cucamonga 91730.

Telephone: (909) 945-4131.

BOREN, Roger W. *(Presiding Justice, California Court of Appeal Second District Division Two)* Associate Justice Division Five 1987-93, appointed by Governor George Deukmejian. Presiding Justice Division Two since Jan 12, 1993. Retained by election. Born Bingham Canyon Utah Sept 11, 1941. Church of Jesus Christ of Latter-day Saints. Educated at University of California at Berkeley B.A. 1966, San Jose State University M.A. 1968 and University of California at Los Angeles J.D. 1973. Admitted to practice California 1973. Began legal practice Los Angeles 1973. Former Judge, Newhall Municipal Court Los Angeles County, appointed by Governor George Deukmejian to term beginning Feb 8, 1984. Judge, Superior Court of California Los Angeles County 1985-87.

Member California District Attorneys Association, California Judges Association, State Bar of California and Los Angeles County Bar Association. Captain U.S. Army 1968-70 and USAR. Republican. Enjoys basketball, tennis, running and photography.

Office: 300 South Spring Street, Los Angeles 90013.

Telephone: (213) 830-7000.

BOREN, Terrence R. *(Judge, Superior Court of California County of Marin)*

Mailing address: P.O. Box 4988, San Rafael 94913-4988.

Office: Hall of Justice, 3501 Civic Center Drive, San Rafael 94903.

Telephone: (415) 499-6407.

BORRIS, Thomas James *(Judge, Superior Court of California County of Orange)* Assumed office Aug 10, 1998. Presiding Judge Jan 1, 1997 to Dec 31, 1997 and Former Judge, West Orange County Municipal Court.

Office: West Justice Center, 8141 Thirteenth Street, Westminster 92683.

Telephone: (714) 896-7181.

BOSTWICK, Jeffrey *(Judge, Superior Court of California County of San Diego)*

Mailing address: P.O. Box 122724, San Diego 92112-2724.

Office: 1551-55 Sixth Avenue, San Diego 92101.

BOULIANE, Anne *(Judge, Superior Court of California City and County of San Francisco)*

Office: Civic Center Courthouse, 400 McAllister Street, San Francisco 94102-4514.

Telephone: (415) 551-4020.

BOWERS, Bob S., Jr. *(Judge, Superior Court of California County of Los Angeles)* Assumed office Jan 22, 2000. Presiding Judge Jan 1, 1996 to Dec 31, 1997 and Former Judge, Compton Municipal Court Los Angeles County.

Office: Criminal Courts Building, 210 West Temple Street, Los Angeles 90012-3210.

Telephone: (213) 974-6535.

BOWIE, Peter W. *(Judge, United States Bankruptcy Court Southern District of California)*

Office: U.S. Courthouse, 325 West F Street, San Diego 92101-6989.

Telephone: (619) 557-5158.

BOYACK, Douglas C. *(Judge, Superior Court of California County of Tuolumne)* Assumed office April 23, 1999. Elected 2002, current term expires Jan 2009. Born Albany California Nov 15, 1947. Church of Jesus Christ of Latter-day Saints. Educated at University of California at Santa Barbara B.A. 1972 and University of California Hastings College of the Law J.D. 1975. Admitted to practice California 1975 and U.S. District Court Northern District of California 1975. In legal practice Sonora 1976-77. Judge Jan 7, 1991 to April 22, 1999 and Presiding Judge Jan 1, 1996 to Dec 31, 1997, Tuolumne County Municipal Court.

Deputy District Attorney and Assistant District Attorney Tuolumne County 1977-90. Instructor in law enforcement training classes Columbia Junior College 1977-79. Member California Judges Association. Participant New Judges Orientation Feb 1991 and California Judicial College July 1991 California Center for Judicial Education and Research. Participant in Scouting, youth

BOYACK, DOUGLAS C.—*Continued*

athletics and school fund raising. Enjoys family, friends, outdoors and tennis.

Office: Washington Courthouse, 60 North Washington Street, Sonora 95370.

Telephone: (209) 533-5563.

BOYD, Robert S. *(Judge, Superior Court of California County of Sonoma)* Appointed by Governor Pete Wilson to term beginning Jan 12, 1998. Elected 1998, current term expires Jan 2005. Born San Francisco California 1941. Educated at University of California at Berkeley B.S. 1964 and University of California Hastings College of the Law J.D. 1971. Admitted to practice California 1972 and U.S. District Court District of California 1972. In legal practice San Francisco 1972-77 and Santa Rosa 1977-98.

USN 1964-68. Member Rotary Club.

Office: 600 Administration Drive, Santa Rosa 95403.

Telephone: (707) 565-1100.

BRADBURY, Stephen Douglas *(Judge, Superior Court of California County of Lassen)* Presiding Judge since Jan 1, 1999. Former Judge, Lassen County Municipal Court.

Office: 6 Courthouse, 220 South Lassen Street, Susanville 96130.

Telephone: (530) 251-8228.

BRADFORD, Harold *(Judge, Superior Court of California County of Alpine)* Appointed by Governor Pete Wilson to term beginning Jan 21, 1992. Elected Nov 1992, 1996 and 2002. Current term expires Jan 2009. Presiding Judge since July 1, 1998.

Mailing address: P.O. Box 276, Markleeville 96120.

Office: 99 Water Street, Markleeville 96120.

Telephone: (530) 694-2113.

BRADY, Laurel S. *(Judge, Superior Court of California County of Contra Costa)* Presiding Judge since Jan 1, 2003.

Office: 725 Court Street, Department 1/31, Martinez 94553.

Telephone: (925) 646-2662.

BRAINARD, Larrie R. *(Judge, Superior Court of California County of San Diego)* Assumed office Dec 1, 1998. Born Pasadena California Sept 22, 1942. Methodist. Educated at Citrus College A.A. 1962, University of California at Los Angeles B.A. 1964 and California Western School of Law J.D. with honors 1968. Head Notes and Comments Editor California Western Law Review. Admitted to practice California 1969. Began legal practice San Diego 1969. Judge March 16, 1979 to Nov 30, 1998 and Presiding Judge Jan 1, 1996 to Dec 31, 1996, El Cajon Municipal Court San Diego County, appointed by Governor Edmund G. Brown, Jr.

Member State Bar of California and San Diego Bar Association. E-4 U.S. Army 1960-64. Previously worked as electrician. Enjoys sports, basketball, bridge and reading.

Mailing address: P.O. Box 122724, San Diego 92112-2724.

Office: 250 East Main Street, El Cajon 92020.

Telephone: (619) 441-4336.

BRANDLIN, James R. *(Judge, Superior Court of California County of Los Angeles)* Former Judge, South Bay Municipal Court Los Angeles County.

Office: Los Angeles Airport Courthouse, 11701 South La Cienega Boulevard, Los Angeles 90045.

Telephone: (310) 727-6010.

BRANDOLINO, Joseph A. *(Judge, Superior Court of California County of Los Angeles)*

Office: East Los Angeles Courthouse, 214 South Fetterly Avenue, Los Angeles 90022.

Telephone: (323) 780-2055.

BRAZIL, Wayne D. *(Magistrate Judge, United States District Court Northern District of California)* Appointed by U.S. District Court judges to term beginning June 1984. Reappointed 1992 and 2000. Current term expires 2008. Educated at Stanford University B.A. in History with great distinction 1966, Harvard University M.A. in American History 1967 Ph.D. 1975 and University of California Boalt Hall School of Law J.D. 1975. President Stanford in Germany 1965. Recipient Henry E. Rosen Honors Scholarship 1965-66, Rockefeller Brothers Theological Fellowship (declined) 1966 and Lloyd W. Dinkelspiel Award 1966. Woodrow Wilson National Fellow 1966-67 and NDEA Harvard Fellow 1967-70. Member Phi Beta Kappa, Phi Delta Phi and Order of the Coif. Staff member California Law Review. Extern Law Clerk to Hon. John J. Purchio, Superior Court of California Alameda County 1973-74 and Chief Justice Donald R. Wright, California Supreme Court 1974. In legal practice San Francisco 1975-78.

Author "Emory's First Atlanta Dean: Howard Odum's Brief Tenure" 51 The Emory Magazine 17 Spring 1975, "The Attorney as Victim: Toward More Candor About the Psychological Price Tag of Litigation Practice" 3 Journal Legal Profession 107, 1978, "The Adversary Character of Civil Discovery: A Critique and Proposals for Change" 31 Vanderbilt L. Rev. 1295 Fall 1978 cited in Advisory Committee's Note to support 1983 amendments to Rule 26, "Unanticipated Client Perjury and the Collision of Rules of Ethics, Evidence and Constitutional Law" 44 Missouri L. Rev. 601 Fall 1979, telescoped version published as "Surprise Testimonial Fraud by Clients: How Should Counsel Respond?" The Journal of The Missouri Bar 385, Sept 1979 and revised version "Monograph Series: Problems in Professional Responsibility" ABA Center for Professional Responsibility Fall 1981, "Views from the Front Lines: Observations by Chicago Lawyers About the System of Civil Discovery" American Bar Foundation Res. Journal 217 Spring 1980, "Civil Discovery: Lawyers' Views of Its Effectiveness, Its Principal Problems and Abuses" American Bar Foundation Res. Journal 787 Fall 1980 cited twice in Advisory Committee's Note to support 1983 amendments to Rule 26, "Notes on the Country Life Commission" 1 The Rural Sociologist 92 March 1981, "Civil Discovery: How Bad Are the Problems?" 67 ABA Journal 450 April 1981, "Some Historical Antecedents of Modern Rural Sociology: The Early Work of Howard W. Odum" 1 The Rural Sociologist 198 July 1981, "Improving Judicial Controls over the Pretrial Development of Civil Actions: Model Rules for Case Management and Sanctions" American Bar Foundation Res. Journal 873 Fall 1981, "Reflections on Community, Responsibility and Legal Education" 9 Journal of the Legal Profession 1984, "Ethical Perspective on Discovery Reform" 3 The Rev. of Litigation 51 Winter 1983, "Special Masters in

BRAZIL, WAYNE D.—*Continued*

the Pretrial Development of Big Cases: Potential and Problems" American Bar Foundation Res. Journal 287 Spring 1982, "Referring Discovery Tasks to Special Masters: Is Rule 53 a Source of Authority and Restrictions?" American Bar Foundation Res. Journal 143 Winter 1983, "Social Forces and Sectional Self-Scrutiny" 2 Perspectives on the American South 73, 1984, "Settling Civil Suits: Litigators' Views About Appropriate Roles and Effective Techniques for Federal Judges" ABA Press 1984, "Special Masters in Complex Litigation" 53 Chicago L. Rev. 1986 and *Effective Approaches to Settlement* Prentice Hall 1988. Co-author with Geoffrey C. Hazard and Paul R. Rice "Managing Complex Litigation: A Practical Guide to the Use of Special Masters" American Bar Foundation 1983. Teacher and Counselor Upward Bound University of Massachusetts 1968-69. Visiting Assistant Professor of Law on Litigation Skills University of Kentucky 1978. Associate Professor of Law University of Missouri 1978-80. Professor of Law University of California Hastings College of the Law since 1980 (on leave).

Project Director Studies of Civil Discovery, Case Management Techniques and Pretrial Uses of Special Masters American Bar Foundation 1979-83 and American Bar Association Study of Attorneys' Views About How Federal Judges Can Contribute Most to Settling Civil Actions since 1983. Consultant American Bar Association Special Committee for the Study of Discovery Abuse Section of Litigation 1980-82, Study of Civil Discovery Indiana State Bar Association 1982, Committee to Evaluate Discovery Problems and Recommend Local Rules U.S. District Court Southern District of New York since 1982 and Problems in Civil Discovery State Bar of California 1983-84. Grant Applications Referee Empirical Studies in Judicial Administration National Science Foundation since 1981. Coordinator and Reporter Task Force on Expedition of Civil Actions U.S. District Court Northern District of California since 1982. Advisory Committee on Civil Rules Judicial Conference of the U.S. since March 1988. Member The American Law Institute, State Bar of California (Judicial Council Joint Commission on Discovery since May 1984) and American Bar Association (Lawyers Conference Judicial Administration Division). Seminar Leader and Speaker Fellows of the American Bar Foundation Seminars on Discovery Abuse Kansas City Oct 1979 and Chicago Feb 1980. Visiting Scholar American Bar Foundation 1979 and 1980. Speaker and Panelist Western New England Law Reform Symposium March 1981, Special Masters in Pretrial Development of Civil Actions American Bar Association Section of Litigation and Fellows of the American Bar Foundation Aug 1982, Settlement Symposium U.S. District Court Northern District of California Jan 1984 and "Early Neutral Evaluation: A Tool to Expedite Resolution of Civil Disputes" Center for Public Resources Aspen Colorado Annual Meeting June 1984. Panelist and Contributing Reporter National Conference on Discovery Reform American Bar Association Austin Texas Nov 1982. Featured Speaker Hastings College of the Law Annual Dinner Honoring Judges of the U.S. Court of Appeals Ninth Circuit and California Supreme Court Sept 1983. Panelist/Participant Working Conference on Discovery Abuse Federal Judicial Center Washington D.C. Nov 1983. Speaker on "Judicial Roles in Settlement" Joint Meeting Executive Committees National Conference of Federal Trial Judges and Lawyers Judicial Administration Division American Bar Association Feb 1984. Principal Speaker "Judicial Facilitation of Settlement" Plenary Session Judicial Administration Division American Bar Association Annual Meeting Aug 1984. Principal Speaker and Paper Writer (American side) "Case Management" Plenary Session Judicial Administration Division Joint Meeting American Bar Association and Law Society of England and Wales London 1985. Captain USAR Adjutant General Branch (inactive since 1974). Volunteer Teacher and Community Organizer Volunteers in Asia New Territories Hong Kong 1966.

Office: 400-S Federal Building, 1301 Clay Street, Oakland 94612-5212.

Telephone: (510) 637-3324.

BRAZILE, Kevin Clement *(Judge, Superior Court of California County of Los Angeles)*

Office: Courthouse, 111 North Hill Street, Los Angeles 90012.

Telephone: (213) 974-5411.

BREALL, Susan M. *(Judge, Superior Court of California City and County of San Francisco)*

Office: Civic Center Courthouse, 400 McAllister Street, San Francisco 94102-4514.

Telephone: (415) 551-4020.

BRENNER, Hugh Michael *(Judge, Superior Court of California County of Orange)*

Mailing address: P.O. Box 1994, Santa Ana 92702-1994.

Office: Central Justice Center, 700 Civic Center Drive West, Santa Ana 92701.

Telephone: (714) 834-3734.

BREWSTER, Rudi M. *(Senior Judge, United States District Court Southern District of California)* Appointed for life by President Ronald Reagan to term beginning June 29, 1984. Assumed Senior status, serves by assignment. Born Sioux Falls South Dakota May 18, 1932. Lutheran. Educated at Princeton University A.B. cum laude 1954 and Stanford Law School J.D. 1960. Admitted to practice California 1961, U.S. District Court Southern District of California 1961 and U.S. Supreme Court 1964. Began legal practice San Diego 1961.

Fellow American College of Trial Lawyers. Member American Board of Trial Advocates, State Bar of California and San Diego County Bar Association. Captain USNR JAG 1963-81 (retired). Enjoys skiing, hunting and camping.

Office: 4165 U.S. Courthouse, 940 Front Street, San Diego 92101-8902.

Telephone: (619) 557-6190.

BREYER, Charles R. *(Judge, United States District Court Northern District of California)* Appointed for life by President Bill Clinton Nov 12, 1997 to term beginning Jan 1, 1998. Born San Francisco California Nov 3, 1941. Educated at Harvard College A.B. with honors 1963 and University of California Boalt Hall School of Law J.D. with honors 1966. Law Clerk to Chief Judge Oliver J. Carter, U.S. District Court District of California 1966-67. Admitted to practice California 1966, U.S. Court of Appeals Ninth Circuit 1966 and U.S. Supreme Court 1974. In legal practice San Francisco 1975-78 and 1980-97.

Assistant District Attorney 1967-72 and Chief Assis-

BREYER, CHARLES R.—*Continued*

tant District Attorney 1979. Assistant Special Prosecutor Watergate Special Prosecution Force 1973-74. Instructor University of California Hastings College of the Law since 1999 and University of San Francisco since 1999. Member American College of Trial Lawyers and American Bar Association. Captain JAGC 1965-73.

Office: U.S. Courthouse, Box 36060, 450 Golden Gate Avenue, San Francisco 94102-3489.

Telephone: (415) 522-3660.

BRICK, Steven A. *(Judge, Superior Court of California County of Alameda)*

Office: Hall of Justice, 24405 Amador Street, Hayward 94544.

Telephone: (510) 670-5060.

BRISCO, Joseph R. *(Judge, Superior Court of California County of San Bernardino)* Assumed office Aug 10, 1998. Serves Needles-Calzona Division. Former Judge, San Bernardino County Municipal Court.

Office: 1111 Bailey Avenue, Needles 92363.

Telephone: (760) 326-9250.

BRISEÑO, Francisco Pedro *(Judge, Superior Court of California County of Orange)* Appointed by Governor Edmund G. Brown, Jr. April 6, 1979. Elected to subsequent terms. Born La Puente California May 2, 1939. Catholic. Educated at Long Beach State College B.A. 1961 and Loyola University J.D. 1968. Admitted to practice California 1969. Began legal practice Santa Ana 1969. Judge, Central Orange County Municipal Court 1977-79.

Adjunct Professor Pepperdine University School of Law 1976-78. Member State Bar of California, Orange County and Mexican-American Bar Associations. Major USMC JAGC 1961-69 (Vietnam 1968-69).

Mailing address: P.O. Box 1994, Santa Ana 92702-1994.

Office: Central Justice Center, 700 Civic Center Drive West, Santa Ana 92701.

Telephone: (714) 834-3734.

BROCK, Jerome E. *(Judge, Superior Court of California County of Santa Clara)* Assumed office July 30, 1998. Former Judge, Santa Clara County Municipal Court.

Office: Hall of Justice East Wing, 190 West Hedding Street, San Jose 95110.

Telephone: (408) 808-6600.

BRODIE, Edward F. *(Judge, Superior Court of California County of Ventura)* Assumed office June 10, 1998. Former Judge, Ventura County Municipal Court.

Mailing address: P.O. Box 6489, Ventura 93006-6489.

Office: 800 South Victoria Avenue, Ventura 93009-0001.

Telephone: (805) 654-2965.

BROOKS, James M. *(Judge, Superior Court of California County of Orange)* Assumed office Aug 10, 1998. Former Judge and Presiding Judge, Central Orange County Municipal Court.

Mailing address: P.O. Box 1994, Santa Ana 92702-1994.

Office: Central Justice Center, 700 Civic Center Drive West, Santa Ana 92701.

Telephone: (714) 834-3734.

BROOKS, Ruben *(Magistrate Judge, United States District Court Southern District of California)* Appointed by U.S. District Court judges.

Office: 1171 U.S. Courthouse, 940 Front Street, San Diego 92101-8926.

Telephone: (619) 557-3404.

BROSNAHAN, Carol S. *(Judge, Superior Court of California County of Alameda)* Assumed office July 31, 1998. Former Judge and Presiding Judge, Berkeley-Albany Municipal Court Alameda County.

Office: Berkeley Courthouse, 2120 Martin Luther King Jr. Way, Berkeley 94704.

Telephone: (510) 644-6909.

BROWN, Frank A. *(Judge, Superior Court of California County of San Diego)* Assumed office Dec 1, 1998. Elected to term beginning Jan 3, 2000, current term expires Jan 3, 2006. Born San Diego California Dec 21, 1943. Educated at San Diego State University B.A. 1966, U.S. International University M.A. 1968 and California Western School of Law J.D. 1991. Editor California Western Law Review 1990-91. Admitted to practice California 1992. Judge, San Diego Municipal Court San Diego County Jan 3, 1989 to Nov 30, 1998.

Former Deputy District Attorney San Diego.

Mailing address: P.O. Box 122724, San Diego 92112-2724.

Office: 220 West Broadway, San Diego 92101.

Telephone: (619) 531-3820.

BROWN, Gerard S. *(Judge, Superior Court of California County of San Bernardino)* Serves Rancho District.

Office: 8303 North Haven Avenue, Rancho Cucamonga 91730.

Telephone: (909) 945-4131.

BROWN, Gilbert T. *(Judge, Superior Court of California County of Santa Clara)* Assumed office July 30, 1998. Former Judge, Santa Clara County Municipal Court.

Office: Hall of Justice East Wing, 190 West Hedding Street, San Jose 95110.

Telephone: (408) 808-6600.

BROWN, Irma Jean *(Judge, Superior Court of California County of Los Angeles)* Assumed office Jan 22, 2000. Term expires Jan 2005. Born Los Angeles California May 17, 1948. Educated at Loyola Marymount University B.A. with honors 1970 J.D. 1973. Admitted to practice California 1975 and U.S. District Court Central District of California. In legal practice Los Angeles 1977-82. Court Commissioner 1982-86 and Judge Jan 27, 1986 to Jan 21, 2000, Compton Municipal Court Los Angeles County, appointed by Governor George Deukmejian.

Author "Minor the Juvenile Court" Legal Aid Society of Los Angeles 1976. Important Decision: People v. Pritchard (driving under the influence) 1984. Instructor Peoples College of Law, Los Angeles 1976-78. Board Member California Judges Association 1993-96 and California Center for Judicial Education and Research (Governing Committee). Member Executive Committee Los Angeles County Municipal Court. Member Black Women Lawyers of Los Angeles (President 1976-78), California Association of Black Lawyers, State Bar of California, John M. Langston (Vice President 1979), Minority, Los Angeles County and National Bar Associations.

BROWN, IRMA JEAN—*Continued*

Attended California Judicial College 1982, 1986 and 1987. Faculty Member California Center for Judicial Education and Research. Named Loyola Marymount University Alumnus of the Year and Jordon High School Alumnus of the Year. Recipient Certificate of Commendation from U.S. Congress, Certificate of Commendation from California State Senate, Certificate of Commendation from Los Angeles County Board of Supervisors and Community Service Award from Cities of Compton, Carson and Lynwood. Board of Directors Alumni Association Loyola Marymount University. Board of Regents Loyola Marymount University. Board of Trustees Escuela de Montesori, Cecil L. Murray Education Center and First A.M.E. Church, Los Angeles. Member NAACP, Los Angeles City Links and Jack and Jill of America.

Office: Inglewood Juvenile Courthouse, 110 Regent Street, Inglewood 90301.

Telephone: (310) 419-5281.

BROWN, J. Michael *(Judge, Superior Court of California County of Humboldt)* Former Presiding Judge.

Office: 825 Fifth Street, Eureka 95501.

Telephone: (707) 269-1200.

BROWN, James W. *(Judge, Superior Court of California County of Santa Barbara)*

Office: 1100 Anacapa Street, Santa Barbara 93101.

Telephone: (805) 568-2220.

BROWN, Janice R. *(Associate Justice, California Supreme Court)* Appointed by Governor Pete Wilson to term beginning May 2, 1996. Retained by election. In legal practice 1990-91. Associate Justice, California Court of Appeal Third District Nov 4, 1994 to May 2, 1996, appointed by Governor Pete Wilson.

With Attorney General's Office 1979-87. Deputy Secretary and General Counsel California Business, Transportation and Housing Agency 1987-90. Legal Affairs Secretary to Governor Pete Wilson Jan 7, 1991 to Nov 1994.

Office: 350 McAllister Street, San Francisco 94102-4797.

Telephone: (415) 865-7000.

BROWN, Kevin L. *(Judge, Superior Court of California County of Los Angeles)* Assumed office Jan 22, 2000. Former Judge, Los Angeles Municipal Court Los Angeles County, assumed office Sept 18, 1998.

Office: Criminal Courts Building, 210 West Temple Street, Los Angeles 90012-3210.

Telephone: (213) 974-6535.

BROWN, Leslie E. *(Judge, Superior Court of California County of Los Angeles)*

Office: Pasadena Courthouse, 300 East Walnut Street, Pasadena 91101.

Telephone: (626) 356-5689.

BROWN, Nancy *(Judge, Superior Court of California County of Los Angeles)* Appointed by Governor George Deukmejian to term beginning Dec 16, 1984. Elected 1988, 1992 and 1998. Current term expires Jan 2005. Serves Children's Court. Born Chicago Illinois Nov 1, 1935. Protestant. Educated at Indiana University A.B. with honors 1957 and Stanford University Law School LL.B. 1960. Admitted to practice California 1961. Judge, Los Angeles Municipal Court Los Angeles County, appointed by Governor Edmund G. Brown, Jr. Nov 8, 1976 to Dec 15, 1984.

Office: 201 Centre Plaza Drive, Monterey Park 91754-2158.

Telephone: (323) 526-6330.

BROWN, Rick S. *(Judge, Superior Court of California County of Santa Barbara)* Assumed office Aug 3, 1998. Former Judge, North Santa Barbara County Municipal Court.

Office: 312-H East Cook Street, Santa Maria 93454.

Telephone: (805) 346-7414.

BROWN, Ronald *(Judge, Superior Court of California County of Mendocino)* Presiding Judge since Jan 1, 2002.

Mailing address: P.O. Box 996, Ukiah 95482.

Office: Courthouse, 100 North State Street, Ukiah 95482.

Telephone: (707) 467-6437.

BRUCE-LYLE, Desiree *(Judge, Superior Court of California County of San Diego)*

Mailing address: P.O. Box 122724, San Diego 92112-2724.

Office: 220 West Broadway, San Diego 92101.

Telephone: (619) 531-3820.

BRUGUERA, Soussan G. *(Judge, Superior Court of California County of Los Angeles)* Assumed office Jan 22, 2000. Former Judge, Los Angeles Municipal Court Los Angeles County.

Office: Courthouse, 111 North Hill Street, Los Angeles 90012.

Telephone: (213) 974-5411.

BRUINIERS, Terence L. *(Judge, Superior Court of California County of Contra Costa)* Appointed by Governor Pete Wilson to term beginning Oct 16, 1998. Born Jan 8, 1946. Educated at University of California at Berkeley B.A. 1969 J.D. with honors 1973. Member Order of the Coif. Admitted to practice California 1973. In legal practice San Francisco 1981-98.

Deputy District Attorney Alameda County 1973-80. USMCR 1965-71.

Office: Courthouse, 725 Court Street, Martinez 94553.

Telephone: (925) 646-2950.

E-mail address: TBRUI-@SC.CO.CONTRA-COSTA.CA.US

BRYAN, Andrea Y. *(Judge, Superior Court of California County of Santa Clara)* Assumed office July 30, 1998. Elected 2000, current term expires 2006. Born Budapest Hungary Feb 23, 1951. Educated at University of Santa Clara B.S.C. 1972 and University of the Pacific McGeorge School of Law J.D. 1978. Admitted to practice California 1980, Nevada 1981, U.S. District Courts District of Nevada 1982 and Northern District of California 1985, U.S. Court of Appeals Ninth District 1986 and U.S. Supreme Court 1986. Judge, Santa Clara County Municipal Court Jan 28, 1994 to July 29, 1998, appointed by Governor Pete Wilson.

Deputy District Attorney Washoe County Nevada 1981-84. Senior Deputy City Attorney San Jose 1984-94.

Office: 191 North First Street, San Jose 95113.

Telephone: (408) 299-2074.

E-mail address: abryan@sct.co.scl.ca.us

BRYAN, Carl F., II *(Judge, Superior Court of California County of Nevada)* Presiding Judge Jan 1, 1999 to Dec 31, 2000. Former Judge, Grass Valley Justice Court Nevada County.
Office: 201 Church Street, Nevada City 95959-2504.
Telephone: (530) 265-1311.

BRYANT, Paul M., Jr. *(Judge, Superior Court of California County of San Bernardino)* Appointed by Governor George Deukmejian to term beginning Sept 26, 1989. Elected Nov 6, 1990, 1996 and 2002. Current term expires Jan 2009. Serves Rancho District. Born Fontana California Dec 15, 1947. Catholic. Educated at California State University at San Bernardino B.A. 1970 and Whittier College School of Law J.D. 1975. Admitted to practice California 1975. In legal practice Fontana 1976. Commissioner 1985-88 and Judge 1988-89, San Bernardino County Municipal Court West Valley Division.
Deputy District Attorney San Bernardino County 1976-85. Honorary member San Bernardino County Bar Association. Member California Judges Association, Western San Bernardino County and American (Judicial Administration Division) Bar Associations. Attended California Judicial College 1987 and 1990. Participant "Jurisprudence" 1988, "Fact-Finding and Decision Making" 1989 and "Family Law and Procedure" 1990 and 1991 California Continuing Judicial Studies Program. Republican. Enjoys sailing, racquetball, reading history and philosophy and classical music.
Office: 8303 North Haven Avenue, Rancho Cucamonga 91730.
Telephone: (909) 945-4131.

BRYANT-DEASON, Susan *(Judge, Superior Court of California County of Los Angeles)* Elected Nov 1994 to term beginning Jan 2, 1995. Reelected 2000, current term expires Jan 2007. Former Supervising Judge Eastlake Juvenile Court. Serves on Civil Fast Track since 1999. Born San Antonio Texas June 19, 1946. Educated at University of California at Los Angeles B.A. 1968 and Southwestern University School of Law J.D. 1978. Member Phi Alpha Delta. Admitted to practice California 1980 and U.S. Court of Appeals Ninth Circuit.
Deputy District Attorney Los Angeles County 1981-94. Special Assistant U.S. Attorney 1985-94. Member California Judges Association and National Women Judges Association.
Office: Courthouse, 111 North Hill Street, Los Angeles 90012.
Telephone: (213) 974-5411.

BUCKLEY, Daniel J. *(Judge, Superior Court of California County of Los Angeles)*
Office: West Covina Courthouse, 1427 West Covina Parkway, West Covina 91790.
Telephone: (626) 813-3223.

BUCKLEY, Dennis J. *(Judge, Superior Court of California County of Yuba)* Appointed by Governor George Deukmejian to term beginning Dec 12, 1986. Elected 1988, 1994 and 2000. Current term expires Jan 2007. Presiding Judge Jan 1, 1997 to Dec 31, 1997. Born Johannesburg South Africa Nov 2, 1942. Protestant. Educated at Virginia Polytechnic and State University B.Sc. 1967 and John Marshall Law School J.D. 1972. Admitted to practice Illinois 1972 and California 1974. In legal practice Marysville California 1976-86.
Assistant State's Attorney Illinois 1972-74. Deputy District Attorney California 1975. Public Defender Yuba County 1976-86. Instructor California Northern School of Law 1987-88. Former Member California Trial Lawyers Association, State Bar of California and Illinois State Bar Association.
Office: 215 Fifth Street, Marysville 95901.
Telephone: (530) 749-7600.

BUCKLEY, Tim S. *(Associate Justice, California Court of Appeal Fifth District)* Appointed by Governor George Deukmejian to term beginning Dec 1990. Retained by election. Educated at University of California at Santa Barbara B.A. 1967 and Santa Clara University School of Law J.D. 1973. Staff member Santa Clara Law Review. Judge, Hanford Justice Court Kings County 1978-85. Judge, Superior Court of California Kings County 1985-90.
Office: 2525 Capitol Street, Fresno 93721.
Telephone: (559) 445-5491.

BUCKNER, Alan *(Judge, Superior Court of California County of Los Angeles)*
Office: Courthouse, 111 North Hill Street, Los Angeles 90012.
Telephone: (213) 974-5411.

BUFFORD, Samuel L. *(Judge, United States Bankruptcy Court Central District of California)* Appointed by U.S. Court of Appeals Ninth Circuit judges to term beginning Nov 25, 1985. Reappointed Nov 1999, current term expires Nov 2013. Born Phoenix Arizona Nov 19, 1943. Protestant. Educated at Wheaton College B.A. 1964, University of Texas Ph.D. 1969, University of Michigan J.D. magna cum laude 1973 and University of Geneva. Associate Editor Journal of Law Reform 1971-73 and Michigan Law Review 1972-73. Admitted to practice New York 1975, Ohio 1975 and California 1977. In legal practice San Francisco 1977-79 and Los Angeles 1979-85 California.
Board of Editors California Bankruptcy Journal 1988-90. Editor-in-Chief American Bankruptcy Law Journal 1990-94. Important Decisions: In re Skyler Ridge 80 B.R. 500 Bankr. C.D. Cal. 1987; In re Mortgage and Realty Trust 125 B.R. 575 Bankr. C.D. Cal. 1991; AEG Acquisition Corp. v. Zenith Productions, Ltd. (In re AEG Acquisition Corp.) 127 B.R. 34 Bankr. C.D. Cal. 1991; and Coyne v. Westinghouse Credit Corp. (In re Globe Illumination Co.) 149 B.R. 614 Bankr. C.D. Cal. 1993. Instructor Louisiana State University 1967-68. Assistant Professor of Philosophy Eastern Michigan University 1968-74. Assistant Professor of Law The Ohio State University 1975-77. Lecturer on Law University of Southern California since 1988. Member Los Angeles County Bar Association (Chairman Ethics Committee 1985-86). Board of Directors Financial Lawyers Conference 1987-90.
Office: Federal Building, 225 East Temple Street, Los Angeles 90012.
Telephone: (213) 894-0992.

BURGER-PLAVAN, Trena H. *(Judge, Superior Court of California County of Sacramento)*
Office: Courthouse, 720 Ninth Street, Sacramento 95814.
Telephone: (916) 874-5476.

BURKE, Barbara Lee *(Judge, Superior Court of California County of Los Angeles)* Assumed office Jan 22, 2000. Term expires Jan 2005. Born California Feb

BURKE, BARBARA LEE—*Continued*

1, 1942. Protestant. Educated at University of California at Los Angeles A.B. 1963 J.D. 1966. Judge May 13, 1981 to Jan 21, 2000 and Former Presiding Judge, Glendale Municipal Court Los Angeles County, appointed by Governor Edmund G. Brown, Jr.

Office: Pasadena Courthouse, 300 East Walnut Avenue, Pasadena 91101.

Telephone: (626) 356-5689.

BURKE, Earle Jeffrey *(Judge, Superior Court of California County of San Luis Obispo)* Presiding Judge Jan 1, 2000 to Dec 31, 2001.

Office: County Government Center, 1035 Palm Street, San Luis Obispo 93408-2500.

Telephone: (805) 781-5421.

BURKHART, Gordon R. *(Judge, Superior Court of California County of Riverside)* Appointed by Governor George Deukmejian to term beginning Jan 1986. Elected 1992 and 1998. Current term expires Jan 2005. Born Portland Oregon May 13, 1945. Church of Jesus Christ of Latter-day Saints. Educated at Riverside City College A.A. with honors 1967, Brigham Young University B.A. with honors 1969 and California Western University J.D. with honors 1972. Student Writing Editor International Law Journal 1971-72. Member Phi Alpha Delta (Past President Beaumont Chapter). Admitted to practice California 1972. In legal practice Riverside 1972-86.

Instructor in Conflicts of Law 1979-80 and Trial Practice 1980-85 Citrus Belt Law School. Former member Southern California Defense Council Association, California Trial Advocates Association, State Bar of California and Riverside Bar Association. Member American Board of Trial Advocates, California Judges Association and American Bar Association. Instructor in California Juvenile Law California Center for Judicial Education and Research 1987. Recipient Award of Merit and Silver Beaver from Boy Scouts of America. President California Inland Empire Council of Boy Scouts of America 1998-2000. Numerous administrative positions in church and Boy Scouts of America. Enjoys family, jogging, snow skiing, woodworking, water sports, hiking, camping and ham radio.

Office: Hall of Justice, 4100 Main Street, Riverside 92501.

Telephone: (909) 955-2300.

BURNS, Larry A. *(Magistrate Judge, United States District Court Southern District of California)* Appointed by U.S. District Court judges. Born Pasadena California. Educated at Point Loma College B.A. 1976 and University of San Diego J.D. 1979.

Fellow American College of Trial Lawyers. Republican.

Office: 1165 U.S. Courthouse, 940 Front Street, San Diego 92101-8921.

Telephone: (619) 557-5874.

BURR, Kenneth Mark *(Judge, Superior Court of California County of Alameda)* Appointed by Governor Pete Wilson to term beginning Nov 19, 1997. Elected Nov 3, 1998, current term expires Jan 2005. Born Boston Massachusetts Dec 27, 1944. Protestant. Educated at California State University at Northridge B.A. 1969 and Southwestern University J.D. cum laude 1974. Admitted to practice California 1974 and U.S. District Court Central District of California 1974. In legal practice Beverly Hills 1974-77.

Deputy District Attorney Los Angeles County 1977-79. Senior Deputy District Attorney Alameda County 1979-97. Co-author Chapter 29 "Presentation of Case and Argument" *California Criminal Law Procedure and Practice* 1986 2nd ed. 1994 3rd ed. 1996 and 4th ed. 1998 California Continuing Education of the Bar. Consultant *California Trial Objections* 3rd ed. California Continuing Education of the Bar 1995. Author "In The Way of Justice" *The Family* KQED TV9 Nov 21, 1990, Chapter 5 "Jury Voir Dire" *Trial Tactics* 1993 and 3rd ed. 1998 California District Attorneys Association. Member Earl Warren American Inn of Court, Alameda County Women Lawyers Association, California Judges Association and Alameda County Bar Association. Lecturer "Interrogation: 'I Said What They Wanted to Hear'" Point of View—Law Enforcement Video Training Program 1988 and "Eyewitness Identification and Testimony" Continuing Education of the Bar 1989. Frequent Lecturer on Trial Tactics, Procedures and Techniques Continuing Education of the Bar, California District Attorneys Association, Association of Government Lawyers in Capital Litigation, New York State District Attorneys Association, New York Prosecutors Training Institute, Colorado District Attorneys Council, National Black Prosecutors Association, Federal Bureau of Investigation, International Association of Homicide Investigators, Federal Bar Council of New York, College of Judicial Education and Research and California Judges Association. Named The Outstanding Sexual Assault Prosecutor from 1971-91 by Bay Area Women Against Rape, The California Prosecutor of the Year by Citizens for Law and Order 1986 and Outstanding Trial Prosecutor by California District Attorneys Association 1989. Recipient Outstanding Trial Advocacy Award in Capital Cases from Association of Government Attorneys in Capital Litigation 1995 and Distinguished Lecturer Award from New York Prosecutors Training Institute Statewide Conference on Capital Prosecution 1996. Republican. Enjoys triathlons and competitive swimming with U.S. Masters Swimmers.

Office: Hall of Justice, 24405 Amador Street, Hayward 94544.

Telephone: (510) 670-5060.

E-mail address: kburr@sct.mail.co.alameda.ca.us

BURRELL, Garland E., Jr. *(Judge, United States District Court Eastern District of California)* Appointed for life by President George Bush to term beginning 1992. Born Los Angeles California July 4, 1947. Educated at California State University at Los Angeles B.A. 1972, Washington University M.S.W. and California Western School of Law J.D. 1976.

Deputy District Attorney 1976-78, Deputy City Attorney 1978-79 and Senior Deputy Attorney 1986-90 Sacramento. Deputy Chief 1979-85 and Chief 1990-92 Civil Division U.S. Attorney's Office Eastern District of California.

Office: 13-200 U.S. Courthouse, 501 I Street, Sacramento 95814-2322.

Telephone: (916) 930-4115.

BUSCH, Peter J. *(Judge, Superior Court of California City and County of San Francisco)*

Office: Hall of Justice, 850 Bryant Street, San Francisco 94103.

Telephone: (415) 553-1159.

BUSH, Michael G. *(Judge, Superior Court of California County of Kern)* Assumed office July 1, 2000. Serves Juvenile Branch. Former Judge, Bakersfield Municipal Court Kern County.
Office: 2100 College Avenue, Bakersfield 93305.
Telephone: (661) 868-4270.

BUTZ, M. Kathleen *(Judge, Superior Court of California County of Nevada)* Elected to term beginning Jan 6, 1997. Reelected 2002, current term expires Jan 2009. Presiding Judge Nevada County Grand Juries 1997-1999. Assistant Presiding Judge 1999-2000. Presiding Judge Jan 1, 2001 to Dec 31, 2002. Born Auburn California June 21, 1950. Educated at University of California at Davis B.A. with honors 1972 J.D. 1981. Admitted to practice California 1982 and U.S. District Court Eastern District of California 1982. In legal practice Nevada City 1982-96.
Author "Demurrers" *Civil Procedure Before Trial* Continuing Education of the Bar 1990. Member Civil Law and Procedure Planning Committee 1998-2000, Member 1999-2001 and Vice Chair 2000-01 Planning Committee 2000 Cow County Judges' Institute and Member Rural Courts Education Committee 2000-02 California Center for Judicial Education and Research. Former Member State Bar of California. Member California Judges Association. Faculty Civil Law and Procedure Institute California Center for Judicial Education and Research 1998. Seminar Leader 1998 and Faculty 1998-2001 B. E. Witkin Judicial College of California.
Office: 201 Church Street, Nevada City 95959-2504.
Telephone: (530) 265-1311.

BYRD, Donald Cole *(Judge, Superior Court of California County of Glenn)* Presiding Judge Feb 2, 1998 to June 30, 1999; Jan 1, 2001 to Dec 31, 2001; and since Jan 1, 2003.
Office: 526 West Sycamore Street, Willows 95988-2746.
Telephone: (530) 934-6415.

BYRNE, J. Michael *(Judge, Superior Court of California County of Los Angeles)* Former Judge, Rio Hondo Municipal Court Los Angeles County.
Office: Pasadena Courthouse, 300 East Walnut Street, Pasadena 91101.
Telephone: (626) 356-5689.

BYRNE, Wm. Matthew, Jr. *(Senior Judge, United States District Court Central District of California)* Appointed for life by the President. Former Chief Judge. Assumed Senior status Feb 28, 1998, serves by assignment. Born Los Angeles California Sept 3, 1930. Educated at University of Southern California B.S. 1953 LL.B. 1956. Admitted to practice California.
Former Federal Prosecutor. Member Los Angeles County Bar Association (Vice Chairman Human Rights Section). Executive Director President's Commission on Campus Unrest 1970.
Office: U.S. Courthouse, 312 North Spring Street, Los Angeles 90012.
Telephone: (213) 894-3535.

BYSSHE, Frederick H., Jr. *(Judge, Superior Court of California County of Ventura)*
Mailing address: P.O. Box 6489, Ventura 93006-6489.
Office: 800 South Victoria Avenue, Ventura 93009-0001.
Telephone: (805) 654-2965.

CABRERA, Carlos A. *(Judge, Superior Court of California County of Fresno)* Assumed office July 1, 1998. Former Judge, Central Valley Municipal Court Fresno County.
Mailing address: P.O. Box 400, Fowler 93625-0400.
Office: 106 South Sixth Street, Fowler 93625-2438.
Telephone: (559) 834-3215.

CABRINHA, Neal Anthony *(Judge, Superior Court of California County of Santa Clara)* Assumed office July 30, 1998. Former Judge, Santa Clara County Municipal Court.
Office: 191 North First Street, San Jose 95113.
Telephone: (408) 882-2100.

CADEI, Raymond M. *(Judge, Superior Court of California County of Sacramento)*
Office: Courthouse, 720 Ninth Street, Sacramento 95814.
Telephone: (916) 874-5476.

CADLE, James E. *(Judge, Superior Court of California County of San Joaquin)* Assumed office June 8, 1998. Former Judge and Presiding Judge, Manteca-Ripon-Escalon-Tracy Municipal Court San Joaquin County.
Office: 475 East Tenth Street, Tracy 95376-5007.
Telephone: (209) 831-5909.

CAETON, A. Dennis *(Judge, Superior Court of California County of Fresno)*
Office: 1255 Fulton Mall, Fresno 93721.
Telephone: (559) 488-2626.

CAHRAMAN, Thomas H. *(Judge, Superior Court of California County of Riverside)* Serves Family Law Court.
Office: 4175 Main Street, Riverside 92501.
Telephone: (909) 955-1940.

CAIN, Thomas W. *(Judge, Superior Court of California County of Santa Clara)* Assumed office July 30, 1998. Former Judge, Santa Clara County Municipal Court.
Office: 191 North First Street, San Jose 95113.
Telephone: (408) 882-2100.

CALLAHAN, Connie M. *(Associate Justice, California Court of Appeal Third District)* Appointed by Governor Pete Wilson to term beginning 1996. Retained by election. Educated at Stanford University B.A. 1972 and McGeorge School of Law University of the Pacific J.D. 1975. Moot Court Finalist. Admitted to practice California 1975. Commissioner, Stockton Municipal Court San Joaquin County 1986-92. Judge, Superior Court of California San Joaquin County 1992-96. Justice pro tem, California Supreme Court May 1998.
Deputy City Attorney Stockton 1975-76. Deputy District Attorney and Supervising District Attorney San Joaquin County 1976-86. Author "Women in Law" 1973. Lecturer University of the Pacific, University of California at Davis Law School, Humphreys College of the Law and Delta College. Board of Governors and Treasurer Women Lawyers of San Joaquin County 1980-86. Board of Governors San Joaquin County Bar Association 1983-85. Member Civil Institute Planning Committee 1994-95 and Planning Committee Conference on Children as Victims and Witnesses California Center for Judicial Education and Research. Member Executive Legislative Action Network Judicial Council of Califor-

CALLAHAN, CONNIE M.—*Continued*

nia 1994-96. Master of the Bench Anthony M. Kennedy Inn of Court. Member California Judges Association (Executive Board 1995-96), Sacramento Women Lawyers and California Women Lawyers Association. Chairperson Northern California Civil Law and Procedure Workshop 1994. Instructor California Center for Judicial Education and Research and Delta College Police Academy. Recipient Susan B. Anthony Award for legal services 1987, Peacemaker of the Year Award from San Joaquin County Mediation Center 1997 and Juvenile Justice Commission Award for work in field of child abuse/sexual assault. Recognized by Governor George Deukmejian for work in establishing Victim-Witness Mobile Unit. Co-organizer Government Day for Kids 1998. Former Board Member and President San Joaquin County Child Abuse Prevention Center. Judge Red Ribbon Week Competition (yearly campaign to prevent substance abuse), University of California at Davis Moot Court Orals, Texas Young Lawyers Association Regional Trial Competition and Northern California High School Moot Court finals. Member San Joaquin County Domestic Task Force and Rotary International.

Office: 914 Capitol Mall, Sacramento 95814.

Telephone: (916) 654-0209.

CAMPBELL, Charles W., Jr. *(Judge, Superior Court of California County of Ventura)* Presiding Judge Jan 1, 1998 to Dec 31, 2000. Former Judge, Ventura County Municipal Court.

Mailing address: P.O. Box 6489, Ventura 93006-6489.

Office: 800 South Victoria Avenue, Ventura 93009-0001.

Telephone: (805) 654-2965.

CANDEE, Roland L. *(Judge, Superior Court of California County of Sacramento)* Assumed office June 17, 1998. Former Judge, Sacramento Municipal Court Sacramento County.

Office: Courthouse, 720 Ninth Street, Sacramento 95814.

Telephone: (916) 874-5476.

CANEPA, Theresa J. *(Judge, Superior Court of California County of Contra Costa)*

Mailing address: P.O. Box 911, Martinez 94553.

Office: Court Annex, 1010 Ward Street, Martinez 94553.

Telephone: (925) 646-2950.

CANNON, Jonathan H. *(Judge, Superior Court of California County of Orange)* Former Judge, West Orange County Municipal Court.

Mailing address: P.O. Box 1994, Santa Ana 92702-1994.

Office: Central Justice Center, 700 Civic Center Drive West, Santa Ana 92701.

Telephone: (714) 834-3734.

CANNON, William S. *(Judge, Superior Court of California County of San Diego)* Assumed office Dec 1, 1998. Elected to subsequent term. Current term expires Jan 2007. Born Hollywood California Feb 13, 1946. Educated at California Western University B.A. 1967 J.D. 1973. Writer California Western Law Review 1971-72. Admitted to practice California 1973. In legal practice San Diego 1973-80 and 1990-92 and Chula Vista 1980-90. Presiding Judge 1994 and Judge May 28, 1992 to Nov 30, 1998, South Bay Municipal Court San Diego County, appointed by Governor Pete Wilson.

Adjunct Professor of Law University of San Diego School of Law since 1996. Chairman California Municipal Court Institute 1996. Seminar Leader "Family Violence and the Courts, A Unified Response" Judicial Council of California 1994. Faculty Member CJA Annual Meeting 1994 and 1996, Municipal Court Institute 1994 and 1996, Family Law and Procedure Institute 1995 and New Judge Orientation 1996 California Center for Judicial Education and Research. Speaker "Family Violence and the Courts, A California State Conference" 1997, "Responding to Child Maltreatment" 1997 and California District Attorneys Association 1997. Keynote Speaker South County Domestic Violence Symposium 1995. Named Civic Person of the Year by City of Chula Vista 1995. Recipient Outstanding Achievement Award from South San Diego County Domestic Violence Task Force 1996.

Mailing address: P.O. Box 122724, San Diego 92112-2724.

Office: 500 Third Avenue, Chula Vista 91910.

Telephone: (619) 691-4770.

CANTER, Zel *(Judge, Superior Court of California County of Santa Barbara)* Appointed by Governor Edmund G. Brown, Jr. June 26, 1981. Elected to subsequent terms. Born Portsmouth Ohio 1941. Educated at Northwestern University B.S. 1963 and The Ohio State University College of Law J.D. summa cum laude 1966. Associate Editor Ohio State Law Journal 1965. Member Order of the Coif. In legal practice Solvang 1974-81.

Deputy County Counsel 1968-69, Deputy Public Defender 1969-70 and Deputy District Attorney 1970-74 Santa Barbara. Creator of Historic Trials montages displayed at Pepperdine University School of Law since Oct 1, 2001.

Office: 312-H East Cook Street, Santa Maria 93454.

Telephone: (805) 346-7414.

CANTIL-SAKAUYE, Tani Gorre *(Judge, Superior Court of California County of Sacramento)* Assumed office June 17, 1998. Former Judge, Sacramento Municipal Court Sacramento County.

Office: Courthouse, 720 Ninth Street, Sacramento 95814.

Telephone: (916) 874-5476.

CARDOZA, Jane *(Judge, Superior Court of California County of Fresno)* Assumed office July 1, 1998. Former Judge, Consolidated Fresno Municipal Court Fresno County.

Office: 1600 California Street, Kingsburg 93631-1802.

Telephone: (559) 897-2241.

CARLSON, Thomas E. *(Judge, United States Bankruptcy Court Northern District of California)* Appointed by U.S. Court of Appeals Ninth Circuit judges Sept 23, 1985. Reappointed Sept 23, 1999, current term expires Sept 2013. Chief Judge 1992-96. Educated at Beloit College B.A. 1969, Harvard Law School J.D. 1975 and New York University LL.M. in Taxation 1985. Law Clerk to Chief Justice Donald R. Wright, California Supreme Court 1976-77 and Chief Justice Thomas Roberts Rhode Island Supreme Court 1977-78. Admitted to practice California 1976, U.S. District Courts Northern 1977 and Central 1984 Districts of California and U.S. Court of Appeals Ninth Circuit 1978. In legal practice San Francisco 1977-78.

CARLSON, THOMAS E.—*Continued*

Deputy Staff Director U.S. Court of Appeals Ninth Circuit 1978-84. Principal Drafter of Emergency Bankruptcy Rule 1982. Author "Are the Jurisdictional Provisions of the Bankruptcy Amendments of 1984 Constitutional?" No. 9 Norton Bankruptcy Law Adviser 1984, "Distinguishing Core from Noncore Proceedings" No. 1 Norton Bankruptcy Law Adviser 1985, "The Case for Bankruptcy Appellate Panels" Brigham Young University L. Rev. 545, 1990, "A Primer on Jury Trials in Bankruptcy Proceedings" No. 2 Association of Business Trial Lawyers Report March 1992 and "What You Need to Know About the Commission's Proposal on Single-Asset Real Estate" 31 Bankruptcy Court Decisions Nov 25, 1997. Important Decisions: In re Security Gas & Oil, Inc. 70 B.R. 786, 15 Bankr. Ct. Dec. 762, Bankr. N.D. Cal. Feb 27, 1987; In re Woodridge North Apts., Ltd. 71 B.R. 189, 15 Bankr. Ct. Dec. 799, Bankr. N.D. Cal. Mar 18, 1987; In re California Canners and Growers 74 B.R. 336, Bankr. N.D. Cal. May 27, 1987; In re Beugen 81 B.R. 994, Bankr. N.D. Cal. Jan 26, 1988; In re Visidata Corp. 84 B.R. 673, 18 Collier Bankr. Cas. 2d 1302, Bankr. N.D. Cal. Feb 26, 1988; In re Hammarstrom 95 B.R. 160, 18 Bankr. Ct. Dec. 1093, 51 Ed. Law Rep. 532, Bankr. N.D. Cal. Jan 13, 1989; In re Sukhu 107 B.R. 729, Bankr. N.D. Cal. Nov 29, 1989; In re Van Ness Auto Plaza, Inc. 120 B.R. 545, Bankr. N.D. Cal. Oct 26, 1990; In re Outlook/Century, Ltd. 127 B.R. 650, 21 Bankr. Ct. Dec. 1125, Bankr. N.D. Cal. May 13, 1991; In re Pon 164 B.R. 322, Bankr. N.D. Cal. Mar 7, 1994; In re Dollar Associates 172 B.R. 945, 26 Bankr. Ct. Dec. 93, Bankr. N.D. Cal. Oct 4, 1994; In re Hamilton Taft & Co. 176 B.R. 895, 32 Collier Bankr. Cas. 2d 1727, 26 Bankr. Ct. Dec. 665, Bankr. N.D. Cal. Jan 19, 1995; In re Pacific-Atlantic Trading Co. 1996 WL 426820, 77 A.F.T.R. 2d 96-2321, 96-1 USTC P 50,303, Bankr. N.D. Cal. April 30, 1996; In re Davis 177 B.R. 907, 32 Collier Bankr. Cas. 2d 1940, Bankr. L. Rep. P 76,428, Bankr. 9th Cir. Feb 2, 1995; In re Jenkins 188 B.R. 416, 34 Collier Bankr. Cas. 2d 1028, 28 Bankr. Ct. Dec. 111, Bankr. L. Rep. P 76,845, 95 Cal. Daily Op. Serv. 9407, 95 Daily Journal D.A.R. 15,033, Bankr. 9th Cir. Oct 18, 1995; In re Sale Guar. Corp. 220 B.R. 660 Bankr. 9th Cir. 1998; In re Miller 253 B.R. 455 Bankr. N.D. Cal. 2000; and Bassett v. American General Finance, Inc. (In re Bassett) 255 B.R. 747 9th Cir. BAP 2000. Consultant Judiciary Committee House of Representatives in drafting of 1984 Bankruptcy Amendments. Member Ninth Circuit Committee on Bankruptcy Judges Education 1990-93, Ninth Circuit Judicial Council 1992-93, Ninth Circuit Committee on Appointment of Bankruptcy Judges 1992-93 and Ninth Circuit Committee on Bankruptcy Appeals since 1997. Member National Conference of Bankruptcy Judges (Chair Federal Courts Study Committee 1989-90, Member Board of Governors 1991-94), Conference of Chief Bankruptcy Judges of the Ninth Circuit (Chair 1992-93, Member Executive Committee 1992-95) and Federal Judicial Center (Bankruptcy Education Committee 1994-97).

Mailing address: P.O. Box 7341, San Francisco 94120-7341.

Telephone: (415) 268-2360.

CARNEY, Cormac J. *(Judge, Superior Court of California County of Orange)*

Mailing address: P.O. Box 5000, Fullerton 92838-0500.

Office: North Justice Center, 1275 North Berkeley Avenue, Fullerton 92832.

Telephone: (714) 773-4400.

CARR, Dolores A. *(Judge, Superior Court of California County of Santa Clara)*

Office: 170 Park Plaza, San Jose 95113.

Telephone: (408) 534-5600.

CARROLL, Ellen *(Judge, United States Bankruptcy Court Central District of California)* Appointed by U.S. Court of Appeals Ninth Circuit judges to term beginning Feb 17, 1998.

Office: 1634 Federal Building, 255 East Temple Street, Los Angeles 90012.

Telephone: (213) 894-4033.

CARROLL, Peter H. *(Judge, United States Bankruptcy Court Central District of California)* Appointed by U.S. Court of Appeals Ninth Circuit judges to term beginning Aug 1, 2002. Term expires 2016.

Office: 3420 Twelfth Street, Room 365, Riverside 92501-3819.

Telephone: (909) 774-1031.

CARTER, Allan P. *(Judge, Superior Court of California County of Solano)* Assumed office Aug 3, 1998. Former Judge and Presiding Judge, Vallejo-Benicia Municipal Court Solano County.

Office: 321 Tuolumne Street, Vallejo 94590.

Telephone: (707) 553-5876.

CARTER, David O. *(Judge, United States District Court Central District of California)* Appointed for life by President Bill Clinton to term beginning Jan 5, 1999. Born Providence Rhode Island March 28, 1944. Presbyterian. Educated at University of California at Los Angeles B.A. with honors 1967 J.D. 1972. Admitted to practice California 1972. Judge, West Orange County Municipal Court 1981-82 and South Orange County Municipal Court 1982. Judge, Superior Court of California Orange County Dec 22, 1982 to Jan 4, 1999, appointed by Governor Edmund G. Brown, Jr.

Former Senior Trial Attorney in Homicides District Attorney's Office. Instructor California Judicial Education and Research since 1983, CJSP Judges Program 1983-87 and Traffic Workshops 1987. Named Judge of the Year by Orange County Narcotics Officers Association. First Lieutenant USMC 1966-69. Recipient Bronze Star Medal and Purple Heart Medal. Democrat. Member CASA, Juvenile Connection Project and Victim/Witness Assistance Program. Participates in marathons and triathlons.

Office: 1053 U.S. Courthouse, 411 West Fourth Street, Santa Ana 92701-4516.

Telephone: (714) 338-4545.

CARTER, Marjorie Laird *(Judge, Superior Court of California County of Orange)* Assumed office Aug 10, 1998. Presiding Judge Jan 1, 1996 to Dec 31, 1997 and Former Judge, Central Orange County Municipal Court.

Mailing address: P.O. Box 14169, Orange 92863-1569.

Office: Lamoreaux Justice Center, 341 The City Drive, Orange 92868.

Telephone: (714) 935-7236.

CARTWRIGHT, Joan S. *(Judge, Superior Court of California County of Alameda)* Former Judge and Presiding Judge, Oakland-Piedmont-Emeryville Municipal Court Alameda County.

Office: Courthouse, 1225 Fallon Street, Oakland 94612.

Telephone: (510) 272-6070.

CASKEY, Gregory M. *(Judge, Superior Court of California County of Shasta)* Appointed by Governor Pete Wilson to term beginning March 1997. Born Oakland California Sept 2, 1951. Religious affiliation: Christian and Missionary Alliance. Educated at California State University at Chico B.A. and McGeorge School of Law J.D. Member Phi Delta Phi. Admitted to practice California 1976. Began legal practice Sacramento 1977. In legal practice Redding 1979-82. Judge, Shasta County Municipal Court Dec 1, 1982 to 1997.

Deputy District Attorney Sacramento 1977-79. Member Trial Court Improvement Fund Committee California Judges Association 1988-90. Faculty Continuing Judicial Studies Program California Center for Judicial Education and Research 1987. Vice President Shasta County Chemical People, Inc. 1984-85. President Kids' Turn Shasta Cascade 1997-98. Member Neighborhood Church of Redding. Enjoys fishing and bicycling.

Office: 1500 Court Street, Redding 96001-1685.

Telephone: (530) 225-5714.

CASSERLY, Timothy *(Judge, Superior Court of California County of San Diego)* Assumed office Dec 1, 1998. Former Judge, North County Municipal Court San Diego County.

Mailing address: P.O. Box 122724, San Diego 92112-2724.

Office: 325 South Melrose Drive, Vista 92083.

Telephone: (760) 726-9595.

CASTELLANOS, Cecilia P. *(Judge, Superior Court of California County of Alameda)* Assumed office July 31, 1998. Former Judge, Oakland-Piedmont-Emeryville Municipal Court Alameda County.

Office: Courthouse, 1225 Fallon Street, Oakland 94612.

Telephone: (510) 272-6070.

CECIL, Thomas M. *(Judge, Superior Court of California County of Sacramento)* Presiding Judge Sept 4, 1997 to Dec 31, 1999. Former Judge, Sacramento Municipal Court Sacramento County.

Office: Courthouse, 720 Ninth Street, Sacramento 95814.

Telephone: (916) 874-5476.

CENA, David A. *(Judge, Superior Court of California County of Santa Clara)* Assumed office July 30, 1998. Elected 2002, current term expires Jan 2009. Born Weed California Jan 28, 1953. Educated at University of California at Davis A.B. with honors 1975 and University of California Hastings College of Law J.D. 1978. Member Thurston Society. Admitted to practice California 1978 and U.S. District Courts Northern 1978 and Eastern 1981 Districts of California. In legal practice San Jose 1979-95. Judge, Santa Clara County Municipal Court May 2, 1995 to July 29, 1998, appointed by Governor Pete Wilson.

Member State Bar of California (inactive) and Santa Clara County Bar Association. Republican. Enjoys fishing, hunting and woodworking.

Office: 115 Terraine Street, San Jose 95113.

Telephone: (408) 491-4700.

CHAFFEE, David R. *(Judge, Superior Court of California County of Orange)* Former Judge, Harbor Municipal Court Orange County.

Mailing address: P.O. Box 1994, Santa Ana 92702-1994.

Office: Central Justice Center, 700 Civic Center Drive West, Santa Ana 92701.

Telephone: (714) 834-3734.

CHAITIN, Ellen *(Judge, Superior Court of California City and County of San Francisco)* Assumed office Dec 31, 1998. Former Judge, San Francisco Municipal Court San Francisco County.

Office: Civic Center Courthouse, 400 McAllister Street, San Francisco 94102-4514.

Telephone: (415) 551-4020.

CHALFANT, James C. *(Judge, Superior Court of California County of Los Angeles)* Former Judge, Los Angeles Municipal Court Los Angeles County.

Office: Courthouse, 111 North Hill Street, Los Angeles 90012.

Telephone: (213) 974-5411.

CHAMPAGNE, Judith L. *(Judge, Superior Court of California County of Los Angeles)* Former Judge, Los Angeles Municipal Court Los Angeles County.

Office: Criminal Courts Building, 210 West Temple Street, Los Angeles 90012-3210.

Telephone: (213) 974-6535.

CHANDLER, Christopher R. *(Judge, Superior Court of California County of Sutter)* Assumed office June 3, 1998. Former Judge, Sutter County Municipal Court.

Office: 446 Second Street, Yuba City 95991.

Telephone: (530) 822-7360.

CHANEY, Victoria Gerrard *(Judge, Superior Court of California County of Los Angeles)* Appointed by Governor Pete Wilson to term beginning May 13, 1994. Born Los Angeles California Jan 19, 1946. Episcopalian. Educated at Mount St. Mary's College B.S. 1967 and Loyola Marymount University J.D. 1977. Admitted to practice California 1978, U.S. District Court Central District of California 1978, U.S. Court of Appeals Ninth Circuit 1982 and U.S. Supreme Court 1983. Judge, Los Angeles Municipal Court Los Angeles County 1990-94.

City Attorney Los Angeles 1979-90.

Office: Central Civil West, 600 South Commonwealth, Department 324, Los Angeles 90005.

Telephone: (213) 351-8508.

CHANG, James H. *(Judge, Superior Court of California County of Santa Clara)* Appointed by Governor George Deukmejian to term beginning Dec 13, 1989. Elected 1990, 1996 and 2002. Current term expires Jan 2009. Presiding Judge Appellate Division 1999. Born St. Helena California April 29, 1942. Educated at Pacific Union College 1960-62, San Jose State University 1962-63 and University of Santa Clara J.D. 1966. Admitted to practice California 1967, U.S. Court of Appeals Ninth Circuit 1967, U.S. District Court Northern District of California 1967 and U.S. Supreme Court 1973. Began legal practice San Jose 1967. Associate Justice pro tem, California Court of Appeal Sixth District March 1986 to

CHANG, JAMES H.—*Continued*
April 1986. Judge, Santa Clara County Municipal Court 1983-89.

Deputy District Attorney Santa Clara County 1967-83. Member Asian Pacific and Santa Clara County Bar Associations. Republican. Enjoys windsurfing, water skiing and snow skiing.

Office: 191 North First Street, San Jose 95113.

Telephone: (408) 882-2180.

CHANG, Shelleyanne W. L. *(Judge, Superior Court of California County of Sacramento)*

Office: Courthouse, 720 Ninth Street, Sacramento 95814.

Telephone: (916) 874-5476.

CHAPIN, Sidney P. *(Judge, Superior Court of California County of Kern)*

Office: 1415 Truxtun Avenue, Bakersfield 93301.

Telephone: (661) 868-4934.

CHAPMAN, Rosalyn M. *(Magistrate Judge, United States District Court Central District of California)* Appointed by U.S. District Court judges.

Office: U.S. Courthouse, 312 North Spring Street, Los Angeles 90012.

Telephone: (213) 894-4691.

CHASE, L. Bryce *(Judge, Superior Court of California County of Kern)* Assumed office July 1, 2000. Elected 2002, current term expires Jan 2009. Serves Delano-McFarland Branch. Born Eugene Oregon March 30, 1944. Baptist. Educated at University of Southern California B.A. cum laude 1969, Bakersfield College 1962-65, Linfield College 1963 and Northwestern School of Law of Lewis & Clark College J.D. 1975. Admitted to practice California 1975. Began legal practice Delano 1975. Judge July 13, 1981 to June 30, 2000 and Presiding Judge Jan 1, 1997 to June 30, 2000, North Kern Municipal Court Kern County.

Member California Judges Association. E-4 U.S. Army 1967-69. Democrat. President Greater Delano Area Youth Foundation 1984-85. Member Kiwanis Club and Delano Citizens Advisory Committee. Enjoys tennis, golf, jogging and flying.

Office: 1122 Jefferson Avenue, Delano 93215.

Telephone: (661) 725-8797.

CHATMAN, Sharon A. *(Judge, Superior Court of California County of Santa Clara)*

Office: Hall of Justice West Wing, 200 West Hedding Street, San Jose 95110.

Telephone: (408) 808-6600.

CHÁVEZ, Victor E. *(Judge, Superior Court of California County of Los Angeles)* Appointed by Governor George Deukmejian to term beginning Jan 1990. Assistant Presiding Judge 1997 to Dec 31, 1998. Presiding Judge Jan 1, 1999 to Dec 31, 2000. Born Los Angeles California Aug 28, 1930. Roman Catholic. Educated at Loyola University of Los Angeles B.S. 1953 J.D. 1959.

Past President Los Angeles Chapter American Board of Trial Advocates and Mexican American Bar Association of Los Angeles. Founding Member Cowboy Lawyers Association of Los Angeles.

Office: Los Angeles County Courthouse, 111 North Hill Street, Los Angeles 90012.

Telephone: (213) 893-1021.

CHAVEZ, Victoria *(Judge, Superior Court of California County of Los Angeles)* Former Judge, Los Angeles Municipal Court Los Angeles County.

Office: Compton Courthouse, 200 West Compton Boulevard, Compton 90220.

Telephone: (310) 603-7842.

CHEN, Edward M. *(Magistrate Judge, United States District Court Northern District of California)* Appointed by U.S. District Court judges to term beginning April 23, 2001. Educated at University of California at Berkeley A.B. with great distinction 1975 J.D. 1979. Recipient American Jurisprudence Awards in Contracts and Civil Procedure. Associate Editor California Law Review. Judicial Extern to Hon. Mathew Oscar Tobriner, California Supreme Court Aug 1978 to Jan 1979. Law Clerk to Hon. Charles B. Renfrew, U.S. District Court Northern District of California June 1979 to April 1980 and Hon. James R. Browning, U.S. Court of Appeals Ninth Circuit June 1981 to Aug 1982. Member Phi Beta Kappa and Order of the Coif. In legal practice San Francisco Dec 1982 to Aug 1985.

Volunteer Attorney Asian Law Caucus Aug 1980 to June 1981. Staff Counsel ACLU Foundation of Northern California Sept 1985 to March 2001.

Office: U.S. Courthouse, 450 Golden Gate Avenue, San Francisco 94102.

Telephone: (415) 522-2034.

CHEROSKE, John Joseph *(Judge, Superior Court of California County of Los Angeles)*

Office: Compton Courthouse, 200 West Compton Boulevard, Compton 90220.

Telephone: (310) 603-7842.

CHESNEY, Maxine Mackler *(Judge, United States District Court Northern District of California)* Appointed for life by President Bill Clinton. Born San Francisco California Oct 29, 1942. Educated at University of California at Berkeley B.A. with distinction 1964 and Boalt Hall School of Law J.D. 1967. Admitted to practice California 1967. Began legal practice San Francisco 1968. Judge, San Francisco Municipal Court San Francisco County 1979-83. Former Judge, Superior Court of California City and County of San Francisco, appointed by Governor Edmund G. Brown, Jr. Jan 1, 1983.

Deputy District Attorney 1968-76 and Assistant Chief Deputy District Attorney 1976-79 San Francisco. Member California Women Lawyers, Edward J. McFetridge American Inn of Court, U.S. Association of Constitutional Law, National Association of Women Judges, Queen's Bench and Federal Judges Association.

Office: U.S. Courthouse, Box 36060, 450 Golden Gate Avenue, San Francisco 94102-3489.

Telephone: (415) 522-3650.

CHIDSEY, William R., Jr. *(Judge, Superior Court of California County of Los Angeles)* Assumed office Jan 22, 2000. Former Judge, Los Angeles Municipal Court Los Angeles County.

Office: Los Angeles Airport Courthouse, 11701 South La Cienega Boulevard, Los Angeles 90045.

Telephone: (310) 727-6010.

CHIN, Ming W. *(Associate Justice, California Supreme Court)* Appointed by Governor Pete Wilson Jan 25, 1996 to term beginning March 1, 1996. Retained by election. Born Klamath Falls Oregon Aug 31, 1942.

CHIN, MING W.—*Continued*

Catholic. Educated at Bellarmine College Preparatory School 1960 and University of San Francisco B.A. in Political Science 1964 J.D. 1967. Awarded Honorary Doctor of Laws Southwestern University School of Law 1996, Golden Gate University School of Law 1997, University of San Diego School of Law 1998 and Western State University College of Law 1998. Editor University of San Francisco Yearbook 1964. Member Alpha Sigma Nu. Admitted to practice California 1970, U.S. District Courts Central 1971, Eastern 1971 and Northern 1971 Districts of California and U.S. Tax Court 1985. In legal practice Oakland 1973-88. Judge, Superior Court of California Alameda County Hayward Division Jan 1988 to Aug 1990, appointed by Governor George Deukmejian. Associate Justice Aug 20, 1990 to Feb 29, 1996 and Presiding Justice Jan 2, 1995 to Feb 29, 1996, California Court of Appeal First District Division Three.

Deputy District Attorney Alameda County 1970-72. Important Decisions: People v. Humphrey (evidence of battered woman's syndrome is generally relevant to the reasonableness of a defendant's belief in the need to defend) 13 Cal. 4th 1073, 56 Cal. Rptr. 2d 142; Randi W. v. Muroc Joint Unified School District (upholding complaint against school districts for failing to disclose, in recommendation letters, complaints against school teacher for improper conduct with students) 14 Cal. 4th 1066, 60 Cal. Rptr. 2d 263; People v. Monge (state and federal constitutional protections against double jeopardy do not bar retrial of prior serious felony allegations) 16 Cal. 4th 826, 66 Cal. Rptr. 2d 853, aff'd sub nom. Monge v. California, 524 U.S. 721, 118 S.Ct. 2246, 141 L. Ed. 2d 615; Reno v. Baird (individuals who do not qualify as employers may not be sued under the Fair Employment and Housing Act for alleged discriminatory acts or for wrongful discharge) 18 Cal. 4th 640, 76 Cal. Rptr. 2d 499; Green v. Ralee Engineering Co. (administrative regulations promulgated by a public safety statute may be a source of fundamental public policy) 19 Cal. 4th 66, 78 Cal. Rptr. 2d 16; Cel-Tech Communications, Inc. v. Los Angeles Cellular Telephone Co. (seller of cellular telephones below cost is not liable for damages under the Unfair Practices Act, but seller may be liable for unfair competition) 20 Cal. 4th 163, 83 Cal. Rptr. 2d 548; White v. Ultramar (managing agents who determine corporate policy, may render corporation liable for punitive damages) 21 Cal. 4th 563, 88 Cal. Rptr. 2d 19; People v. Falsetta (upholding Penal Code section 1108, allowing admission in sex offense cases of the defendant's prior sex offenses) 21 Cal. 4th 903, 89 Cal. Rptr. 2d 847; and Carrisales v. Department of Corrections (employees are not liable to co-workers for sexual harassment under the Fair Employment and Housing Act) 21 Cal. 4th 1132, 90 Cal. Rptr. 2d 804. Adjunct Professor of Law University of San Francisco School of Law 1989-93. Lecturer on DNA Evidence University of Santa Clara School of Law March 1994 and Traynor Lecture Witkin Judicial College June 1996. Former Member San Francisco District Attorney's Commission on Hate Crimes, Voluntary Legal Service Corporation (Board of Directors 1983-88), California Trial Lawyers Association, Judicial Council of California (Advisory Committee on Racial and Ethnic Bias 1990-97, Appellate Standing Advisory Committee 1993-96) and Alameda County Bar Association Foundation (Board of Directors 1983-88). Member California Judges Association (Public Information and Education Committee), State Bar of California (Referee 1978-79 and Member Executive Committee 1993-94 State Bar Court, Delegate Conference of Delegates 1983-86), Asian American, Alameda County (Chairman Legal Specialization Committee 1981-82 and Court Consolidation Committee 1983, Board of Directors 1983-88, Member Personnel Committee 1984-88 and Administrative Committee 1984-88, Vice President 1986, Chairman Superior Court Liaison Committee 1986-88, President 1987) and American (National Conference of Bar Presidents, Task Force on Unreported Opinions Appellate Judges Conference) Bar Associations.

Graduate California Judges College 1988. Instructor in "The Judiciary" Bar Association of San Francisco Nov 1988; "Family Law" Alameda County Bar Association March 1989; "Punitive Damages" Oct 1991, "Writs and Appeals" Oct 1992, "Labor and Employment Law" Jan 1996 and "Employment Litigation" Jan 1999 and Jan 2000 The Rutter Group; "Scientific Evidence (DNA)" Aug 1994 and "Jurisprudence and Culture" Feb 1995 Continuing Judicial Studies Program, "Delay Reduction" April 1993, "Environmental and Insurance Law" April 1994 and "DNA Evidence" April 1995 Appellate Courts Institute Faculty; "Scientific Evidence" June 1994 and "Privacy Issues in Law" June 1995 Appellate Research Attorneys Institute and "Courtroom Use of DNA Evidence" Criminal Law and Procedure Institute Feb 1995 California Center for Judicial Education and Research; "Scientific Evidence and DNA" Annual Meeting California Judges Association Sept 1994; "DNA Evidence" Continuing Legal Education Program University of San Francisco School of Law Nov 1994; "DNA Evidence in the Courtroom" Placer County Bar Association April 22, 1995; "Essential Skills for the Appellate Judge" July-Aug 1995 The National Judicial College; "Writs" Annual Meeting State Bar of California Sept 30, 1995; and "DNA in the Courtroom" Kansas Judicial Conference Oct 16, 1995. Team Leader Cultural Diversity Continuing Judicial Studies Program California Center for Judicial Education and Research Jan 1993. Speaker Second International Symposium on the Forensic Aspects of DNA Technology FBI Academy March 1993, Lou Ashe Practical Legal Address McGeorge School of Law University of the Pacific March 1994, National Association of Bar Presidents and National Association of Bar Executives Aug 1997, Bernard E. Witkin Legal Information Symposium May 1998, "Attorneys Contributing to Society" Orange County Bar Association 1999, County Counsels' Association Annual Civil Law Conference April 1999, Law Day Address Nevada County Bar Association May 1999 and Judges' Night Address San Mateo County Bar Association May 1999. Keynote Speaker "Fairness or Bias" Asian Law Journal and Asian American Bar Association Symposium Boalt Hall School of Law Feb 21, 1997, "Asian Americans and the Law in the 21st Century" University of California at Los Angeles School of Law Symposium April 1997, Federal Executive Board Quad Council EEO Training Conference Aug 1999, Ventura and Santa Barbara County Trial Lawyers Joint Meeting Sept 1999 and Shasta and Trinity County Bar Associations Bench Bar Night Jan 2000. Program Coordinator Employment Litigation Program California Judges Association/The Rutter Group Jan 1996.

Recipient McQuade Award for Journalism 1964, Distinguished Service Award Alumni Association April 1985 and Alumnus of the Year Award 1988 from Uni-

CHIN, MING W.—*Continued*
versity of San Francisco, Alumnus of the Year 1993 and St. Thomas More Award 1996 from University of San Francisco School of Law, Learned Hand Award from American Jewish Committee 1997, Citizen of the Year Award from Chinese Americans United for Self Empowerment 1998, Public Service and Government Leadership Award from Asian Business Association 1998 and Trailblazer Award from National Asian Pacific American Bar Association 1999. Named Outstanding Judge of the Year Southern Alameda County Bar Association 1989. Captain U.S. Army 1967-69 and USAR 1969-71. Recipient Bronze Star 1969 and Commendation Medal 1969. Republican. Member Alumni Board of Governors 1978-84, Search Committee Athletic Director 1983, Alumni Association (President 1983-84), Planning Committee Health and Recreation Center 1983-84, Personnel Committee 1985-88, Board of Trustees 1985-97, Executive Committee 1986-88 and 1993-98 and Member 1988-98 and Chairman 1993-98 Academic Affairs Committee University of San Francisco. Board of Counselors 1980-98 and Dean Search Committee 1988 University of San Francisco School of Law. Commencement Speaker College of Professional Studies University of San Francisco May 1985, University of San Francisco School of Law May 1994, Southwestern University School of Law May 1996, Golden Gate University School of Law May 1997, University of San Diego School of Law May 1998, Western State University College of Law May 1998, San Jose/Evergreen Community College June 1998 and University of California at Davis School of Law May 1999. Advisory Board St. Vincent's Day Home 1984-87. Board of Directors First District Agricultural Association 1985-88. Member Commonwealth Club of California (Member since 1992 and Chairman 1995 Program Committee, Board of Governors since 1993, Chairman Executive Committee 1996 and President Elect 1997, President 1998). Enjoys skiing, tennis and running.

Office: 350 McAllister Street, San Francisco 94102-4797.

Telephone: (415) 865-7000.

CHIRLIN, Judith C. *(Judge, Superior Court of California County of Los Angeles)* Appointed by Governor George Deukmejian to term beginning June 14, 1985. Elected June 1986, June 1992 and 1998. Current term expires Jan 2005. Born Kingston New York Nov 25, 1947. Jewish. Educated at George Washington University B.A. with honors 1969, Rutgers University M.A. with honors 1970 and University of Southern California J.D. 1974. Book Review Editor Southern California Law Review 1972-74. Member Phi Alpha Delta. Admitted to practice California 1974, U.S. District Courts Central 1974 and Northern 1981 Districts of California and U.S. Supreme Court 1978. In legal practice Los Angeles 1974-85.

Judicial Fellow U.S. Supreme Court 1977-78. Instructor in Legal Issues in Judicial Administration University of Southern California 1975-97. Member Cowboy Lawyers Association, California Judges Association, National Association of Women Judges and American Judicature Society (Board of Directors since 1984, Member since 1986 and Chair 1997-99 Executive Board). Frequent Speaker on Child Witnesses, How to Become a Judge, Sexual Harassment and Gender Bias in the Courts. Consultant on Judicial Process and Court Reform in *inter alia,* Peru, Chile, El Salvador, Honduras, Russian Federation (in support of the reintroduction of jury trials in criminal cases), Bulgaria, Slovakia, Latvia, Serbia and Czech Republic. Named Outstanding Trial Jurist by Los Angeles County Bar Association 1996-97.

Office: Los Angeles County Courthouse, 111 North Hill Street, Los Angeles 90012.

Telephone: (213) 974-6207.

CHITTICK, Hilary A. *(Judge, Superior Court of California County of Fresno)*

Office: Courthouse, 1100 Van Ness Avenue, Fresno 93724-0002.

Telephone: (559) 488-1825.

CHOATE, Dennis S. *(Judge, Superior Court of California County of Orange)* Appointed by Governor George Deukmejian to term beginning May 4, 1989. Born Los Angeles California Sept 22, 1946. Educated at University of California at Los Angeles B.A. 1968 and Loyola University J.D.S. 1972. Admitted to practice California 1972 and U.S. District Court Central District of California 1972. Judge, West Orange County Municipal Court 1987-89.

Mailing address: P.O. Box 1994, Santa Ana 92702-1994.

Office: Central Justice Center, 700 Civic Center Drive West, Santa Ana 92701.

Telephone: (714) 834-3734.

CHOUTEAU, Rene Auguste *(Judge, Superior Court of California County of Sonoma)*

Office: 600 Administration Drive, Santa Rosa 95403.

Telephone: (707) 565-1100.

CHRISTIAN, Deborah L. *(Judge, Superior Court of California County of Los Angeles)*

Office: Inglewood Courthouse, One Regent Street, Inglewood 90301.

Telephone: (310) 419-5121.

CHRISTIANSON, Ronald M. *(Judge, Superior Court of California County of San Bernardino)* Assumed office Aug 10, 1998. Former Judge, San Bernardino County Municipal Court.

Office: 351 North Arrowhead Avenue, San Bernardino 92415-0240.

Telephone: (909) 387-3922.

CISSNA, Timothy Paul *(Judge, Superior Court of California County of Humboldt)*

Office: 825 Fifth Street, Eureka 95501.

Telephone: (707) 269-1200.

CLARK, Bruce A. *(Judge, Superior Court of California County of Ventura)* Assumed office June 10, 1998. Elected 2002, current term expires Jan 2009. Presiding Judge since Jan 1, 2001. Born Winnipeg Manitoba Sept 14, 1944. Protestant. Educated at University of Redlands B.A. 1966 and University of California Boalt Hall School of Law J.D. 1969. Admitted to practice California 1970. Judge Dec 1, 1978 to June 9, 1998, Assistant Presiding Judge 1983 and Presiding Judge 1984 and 1993, Ventura County Municipal Court, appointed by Governor Edmund G. Brown, Jr.

Deputy District Attorney Ventura 1970-78. Member California Judges Association. Republican. Member Rotary International.

Mailing address: P.O. Box 6489, Ventura 93006-6489.

CLARK, BRUCE A.—*Continued*

Office: 800 South Victoria Avenue, Ventura 93009-0001.
Telephone: (805) 654-2965.

CLAY, Charles Q., III *(Judge, Superior Court of California County of Los Angeles)*
Office: Downey Courthouse, 7500 East Imperial Highway, Downey 90242.
Telephone: (562) 803-7057.

CLINE, Richard G. *(Judge, Superior Court of California County of San Diego)*
Mailing address: P.O. Box 122724, San Diego 92112-2724.
Office: 325 South Melrose Drive, Vista 92083.
Telephone: (760) 726-9595.

CLONINGER, James P. *(Judge, Superior Court of California County of Ventura)* Former Judge, Ventura County Municipal Court.
Mailing address: P.O. Box 6489, Ventura 93006-6489.
Office: 800 South Victoria Avenue, Ventura 93009-0001.
Telephone: (805) 654-2965.

COATES, Robert Crawford *(Judge, Superior Court of California County of San Diego)* Assumed office Dec 1, 1998. Born Torrance California Jan 31, 1937. Educated at San Diego State University B.S. in Engineering Geology 1959 and California Western School of Law J.D. 1970. Chairman Appellate Moot Court Board 1970. Member Phi Alpha Delta (Justice 1969). Admitted to practice California 1970 and U.S. Supreme Court 1974. Began legal practice San Diego 1971. Judge, San Diego Municipal Court San Diego County Aug 6, 1982 to Nov 30, 1998, appointed by Governor Edmund G. Brown, Jr.

Author "*Earhart v. William Low Co.*, California Reassesses the Definition of Contractual Relations" 16 California Western L. Rev. 442, 1980, "Making Crime Victims Whole—From Hammurabi to Deukmejian" Forum Magazine, "Representing the Mentally Ill in Civil Litigation" June 1980, "So Your Client's Been Bitten by a Dog" Nov 1980, "Access to the Courts—From the Common Law to San Diego's Legal Aid" Aug 1981, "Crisis Management for Trial Lawyers" Sept 1982, "Remarks on Becoming a Judge" Dec 1982, "Reflections of a New Judge" March 1983 and "The Portable Job" July 1984 Trial Bar News. Co-author with Grant "Asserting Mineral Rights Against the U.S. Government in Federal Court" 23 California Western L. Rev. 1984. Adjunct Professor of Environmental and Natural Resources Law University of San Diego School of Law since 1981. Member San Diego Trial Lawyers Association 1974-82 (Director 1980-82, Parliamentarian 1982), California Trial Lawyers Association 1974-82, California Judges Association, State Bar of California 1971-82, San Diego County 1971-82 and American 1971-82 Bar Associations. Recipient Red Cross Lifesaving Award 1967, Key to the City of Coronado for public courage 1970, Founder's Recognition Award from The Crime Victim's Fund 1982, First Prize for Poetry from San Diego Writers & Editors Guild 1982, Community Service Award from San Diego Housing Commission 1984, President's Award from San Diego Trial Lawyers Association 1986 and Warren Williams Award from American and California Psychiatric Associations for *A Street Is Not a Home*. Named Volunteer of the Year by San Diego Mental Health Association 1978, Distinguished Graduate by San Diego State Geology Department 1983 and One of Ten Outstanding San Diegans by The City Club 1991. Sonarman Third Class USNR 1955-63. Junior Civil Engineer 1959-61 and Administrative Analyst 1961-63 City of San Diego. President Bob Coates & Associates Investments. Democrat. Vice Chairman County Democratic Central Committee 1962. President Democratic Professional Club 1972-74. Member St. Stephen's Church of God in Christ, Mission Valley Rotary Club, MENSA, Mental Health Association (President 1978, Foundation Board Chair 1982, Board of Advisers Chair 1984), California Mining Association, Sierra Club, Torrey Pines Association, San Diego Association of Geologists, Rocky Mountain Mineral Law Foundation (Law Teachers Committee since 1981), The Theodore Roosevelt Association, Eagle Scout Alumni Association (President 1984, 1985 and 2001) and San Diego State University Geology Department Alumni Association (President 1986-87). Board of Directors Ecology Center. Executive Board San Diego County Council Boy Scouts 1984. Author *Ships Crossing at the Dead of Night* (poetry) 1984, *A Street Is Not a Home* Promethary Books 1990 and *The Guys Who Can't Cooks' Cookbook* 1992. Enjoys writing, swimming, hiking and mining. Interested in natural resources, history and philosophy.
Mailing address: P.O. Box 122724, San Diego 92112-2724.
Office: 220 West Broadway, Department 45, San Diego 92101.
Telephone: (619) 531-3091.

CODY, Tari L. *(Judge, Superior Court of California County of Ventura)*
Mailing address: P.O. Box 6489, Ventura 93006-6489.
Office: 800 South Victoria Avenue, Ventura 93009-0001.
Telephone: (805) 654-2965.

COEN, Ronald S. *(Judge, Superior Court of California County of Los Angeles)* Former Judge, Los Angeles Municipal Court Los Angeles County.
Office: San Fernando Courthouse, 900 Third Street, San Fernando 91340.
Telephone: (818) 898-2655.

COFFEE, Paul H. *(Associate Justice, California Court of Appeal Second District Division Six)* Appointed by Governor Pete Wilson to term beginning 1997. Retained by election Nov 1998, current term expires Jan 2011. Born Madera California July 10, 1932. Roman Catholic. Educated at University of California at Berkeley B.S. 1954 J.D. 1962. Admitted to practice California 1963 and U.S. District Court Central District of California 1990. In legal practice San Jose 1963-75 and San Luis Obispo 1975-92. Judge, Superior Court of California San Luis Obispo County 1992-97.

Past President Association of Defense Counsel of Northern California. Fellow American College of Trial Lawyers. Member American Board of Trial Advocates. Participant California Center for Judicial Education and Research 1992 and California Judges Association 1992. Lieutenant USNR (Naval Aviator 1954-59). With Avila Beach County Water District 1976-82. President Central Coast Council of U.S. Navy League. Interests include planes, cars and boats.
Office: 200 East Santa Clara, Ventura 93001.
Telephone: (805) 641-4700.

COLAW, Thierry Patrick *(Judge, Superior Court of California County of Orange)* Appointed by Governor Pete Wilson Aug 20, 1997 to term beginning Oct 14, 1997. Elected June 1998, current term expires June 2004. Educated at University of California at Los Angeles B.A. with honors 1974 and Santa Clara University J.D. 1977. Admitted to practice California 1977, Arizona 1978 and Colorado 1979. In legal practice Orange County California 1978-97.

Recipient Judicial Civility Award from American Inns of Court 1999. Named Judge of Year by American Board of Trial Advocates 2000. USN 1968-72.

Mailing address: P.O. Box 1994, Santa Ana 92702-1994.

Office: 700 Civic Center Drive West, Santa Ana 92701.

Telephone: (714) 834-3734.

COLE, Dennis G. *(Judge, Superior Court of California County of San Bernardino)* Former Presiding Judge. Serves Rancho District.

Office: 8303 North Haven Avenue, Rancho Cucamonga 91730.

Telephone: (909) 945-4131.

COLE, Lisa Hart *(Judge, Superior Court of California County of Los Angeles)* Assumed office Jan 22, 2000. Former Judge, Los Angeles Municipal Court Los Angeles County.

Office: Beverly Hills Courthouse, 9355 Burton Way, Beverly Hills 90210-3669.

Telephone: (310) 288-1288.

COLE, Paul C. *(Judge, Superior Court of California County of Santa Clara)* Assumed office July 30, 1998. Former Judge, Santa Clara County Municipal Court.

Office: 115 Terraine Street, San Jose 95113.

Telephone: (408) 491-4880.

COLE, Terry K. *(Judge, Superior Court of California County of Stanislaus)* Assumed office July 31, 1998. Former Judge and Presiding Judge, Stanislaus County Municipal Court.

Office: 800 Eleventh Street, Modesto 95354.

Telephone: (209) 558-6000.

COLEMAN, Donald D. *(Judge, Superior Court of California County of Ventura)*

Mailing address: P.O. Box 6489, Ventura 93006-6489.

Office: 800 South Victoria Avenue, Ventura 93009-0001.

Telephone: (805) 654-2965.

COLLINS, Audrey Brodie *(Judge, United States District Court Central District of California)* Appointed for life by President Bill Clinton to term beginning May 11, 1994. Born Chester Pennsylvania. Educated at Howard University B.A. in Political Science 1967, American University M.A. in Government and Public Administration 1969 and University of California at Los Angeles J.D. 1977. Awarded Honorary Doctor of Letters California School of Professional Psychology 1995. Recipient Regents Scholarship 1974-77. Staff member UCLA Law Review. Member Phi Beta Kappa and Order of the Coif. Admitted to practice California 1977.

Staff Attorney Legal Aid Foundation of Los Angeles Oct 1977 to Jan 1978. Deputy District Attorney Jan 1978 to Oct 1988, Assistant Director Oct 1988 to Dec 1992 and Assistant District Attorney Dec 7, 1992 to May 11, 1994 Los Angeles County. President Association of Deputy District Attorneys of Los Angeles Courts 1984. Chair 1987-88 and Advisor 1988-90 Executive Committee Criminal Law Section and Member June 1991 to May 1994 and Chair Subcommittee on Moral Character 1992-93 Committee of Bar Examiners State Bar of California. Deputy General Counsel Office of the Special Advisor to Los Angeles Police Department Board of Commissioners 1992. Member California District Attorneys Association 1980-93. Lifetime Member Women Lawyers Association of Los Angeles and California Women Lawyers Association. Member Black Women Lawyers of Los Angeles County, National Association of Women Judges, Federal Judges Association, Langston (Trustee 1993), Los Angeles County (Judiciary Committee 1985-94, Chair Criminal Justice Section 1986-87, Delegate to State Bar Annual Meeting 1986-89, Judicial Appointments Committee 1988-91, Board of Trustees 1989-91, Inn of Court Litigation Section 1990-91, Member Executive Committee Litigation Section 1995-97), National (Lifetime Member) and American (Judicial Administration Division) Bar Associations. Named Lawyer of the Year by Langston Bar Association 1988. Honored by Howard University Alumni Club of Southern California 1989. Recipient Distinguished Service Award from National Black Prosecutors Association 1994, Professional Achievement Award from University of California at Los Angeles Alumni Association 1997 and Ernestine Stahlhut Award from Women Lawyers Association of Los Angeles 1999.

Office: 680 Federal Building, 255 East Temple Street, Los Angeles 90012.

Telephone: (213) 894-3010.

COLLINS, Patricia L. *(Judge, Superior Court of California County of Los Angeles)* Appointed by Governor Pete Wilson to term beginning 1992. Elected 1998, current term expires 2004. Judge pro tem, California Court of Appeal Oct 1994 to Dec 1994. Serves West District. Born Buffalo New York April 23, 1953. Educated at Canisius College 1971-72, State University of New York at Buffalo B.A. summa cum laude 1975 and Georgetown University Law Center J.D. cum laude 1979. Admitted to practice California, U.S. District Courts Central, Northern and Southern Districts of California and U.S. Court of Appeals Ninth Circuit. In legal practice California 1979-82. Judge, Los Angeles Municipal Court Los Angeles County 1988-92, appointed by Governor George Deukmejian.

Assistant U.S. Attorney 1982-88, Major Frauds Unit 1983-87 and Chief Major Crimes Unit 1987-88 Criminal Division Central District of California. Former Member Civil Trial Manual Advisory Board Bureau of National Affairs, Municipal Court Judges Association, Irish American and American Bar Associations. Member California Judges Association, National Judges Association, Women Lawyers Association of Los Angeles and Los Angeles County Bar Association. Recipient Award for Achievement in Advocacy from International Academy of Trial Lawyers and U.S. Attorney Appreciation Award.

Office: Santa Monica Courthouse, 1725 Main Street, Santa Monica 90401.

Telephone: (310) 260-3762.

COMPARET-CASSANI, Joan *(Judge, Superior Court of California County of Los Angeles)* Assumed office Jan 22, 2000. Serves South District. Educated at University of Miami B.A. 1958, University of Michigan M.A. 1961 and Loyola Law School J.D. 1977. Recipient

COMPARET-CASSANI, JOAN—*Continued*

Dade County Scholarship 1954-58. Former Judge, Long Beach Municipal Court Los Angeles County, assumed office 1995.

Deputy Attorney General 1982-95. Author "Chipping Away at Proposition 115" 30 No. 3 Loyola L. Rev. 1053-1062, 1997; "How the Abolition of Diminished Capacity Has Affected Parity of Sentencing in Murder Cases Under the California Determinate Sentencing Law" 29 Southwestern University L. Rev. 51-108, 1999; "Evidentiary Hearings in California Capital Habeas Corpus Proceedings: What Are the Rules of Discovery" 39 Santa Clara L. Rev. 409-446, 1999; "A Primer on the Civil Trial of a Sexually Violent Predator" 37 No. 4, 1057-1116, 2000 and "Balancing the Anonymity of Threatened Witnesses Versus a Defendant's Right of Confrontation: The Waiver Doctrine After Alvarado" 39 No. 4, 1165-1252, 2002 San Diego L. Rev.; and *Uniform Los Angeles Countywide Rules for Municipal Courts.* Visiting Assistant Professor of Philosophy University of Miami 1960. Assistant Professor of Philosophy California State University 1962-66. Member Municipal Court Judges Association (Legislative Liaison Committee 1996-97, Legislative Analysis Committee 1997, Chair California Rules of Court Committee 1997-98, Gang Violence Committee 1997, California Rules Committee 1999), California Judges Association (Criminal Law and Procedure Committee 1997, Judges' Education Committee 2000), American Judges Association and Long Beach Lawyers Association. Member Planning Committee 1996 and Speaker on "1996 Criminal Case Law Update" 1996 Municipal Court Institute and Seminar Leader College for Judges 1996 California Center for Judicial Education and Research. Speaker on "Courtroom Ethics and Performance: What a Judge Expects of a Deputy District Attorney" March 1997 and "Capital Habeas: Theory and Practice" Second Western Regional Conference on State-Federal Judicial Relationships Oct 11-13, 2000. Recipient Merit Award from Municipal Court Judges Association 1998 and 1999. Board of Governors United Cerebral Palsy since 1990. Board Member St. Mary's Medical Hospital since June 2000. Honored Member Strathmore's "Who's Who" 2001-02. Member The National Italian-American Foundation.

Office: Long Beach Courthouse, 415 West Ocean Boulevard, Long Beach 90802.

Telephone: (562) 491-6245.

CONDRON, Linda R. *(Judge, Superior Court of California County of Santa Clara)*

Office: Hall of Justice West Wing, 200 West Hedding Street, San Jose 95110.

Telephone: (408) 808-6600.

CONGER, Julie *(Judge, Superior Court of California County of Alameda)* Assumed office July 31, 1998. Elected 2000, current term expires Jan 2007. Born New York New York Nov 5, 1942. Educated at Smith College B.S. magna cum laude 1963, Massachusetts Institute of Technology M.S. 1968 and University of California Boalt Hall School of Law J.D. 1974. Admitted to practice California 1974. Began legal practice Oakland 1974. In legal practice Berkeley 1979. Judge Jan 3, 1983 to July 30, 1998 and Presiding Judge Jan 1, 1995 to Dec 31, 1997 Berkeley-Albany Municipal Court Alameda County.

Author chapter "Speedy Trial" *Criminal Law* CEB. Member California Judicial Association, State Bar of California and Alameda County Bar Association. Instructor California Judges College 1984. Board of Directors Berkeley Support Services, Patricia McKinley Memorial Foundation and Jewish Community Center. Enjoys gardening, musical saw playing, knitting, raising pets and family activities.

Office: Courthouse, 1225 Fallon Street, Oakland 94612.

Telephone: (510) 272-6070.

CONLEY, John *(Judge, Superior Court of California County of Orange)*

Mailing address: P.O. Box 1994, Santa Ana 92702-1994.

Office: Central Justice Center, 700 Civic Center Drive West, Santa Ana 92701.

Telephone: (714) 834-3734.

CONNELLY, Lloyd G. *(Judge, Superior Court of California County of Sacramento)*

Office: Courthouse, 720 Ninth Street, Sacramento 95814.

Telephone: (916) 874-5476.

CONNOR, Jacqueline Ann *(Judge, Superior Court of California County of Los Angeles)* Appointed by Governor George Deukmejian to term beginning April 25, 1988. Elected to subsequent terms. Currently assigned to Civil Trials Los Angeles West District. Educated at University of Southern California Law Center J.D. 1976. Admitted to practice California 1976 and U.S. District Court Central District of California 1982. Judge, Los Angeles Municipal Court Los Angeles County Oct 6, 1988 to 1988, appointed by Governor George Deukmejian.

With Los Angeles District Attorney's Office 1977-86 (Head Sexual Assault Unit 1979-83). Author "Jury Reform" Journal of Legal Advocacy and Practice University of La Verne L. Rev. Inaugural Issue 1999, "Jury Innovations" Defense Counsel Journal International Association of Defense Counsel April 2000 and "Jury Service in Los Angeles County" *LA Litigator* Los Angeles County Bar Association Winter 2001. Co-chair/Co-founder Sexual Assault Committee California District Attorney's Association 1981-82. Member since 1989 and Co-chair 1991-2000 Grand and Trial Jury Committee, Member Executive Committee 1990-91 and 2000-01, Chair Pro Per Committee 1991-2001, Member Task Force on Fairness and Equality 1994-95, Ad Hoc Plan Oversight Committee 1996-2000, Chair Committee on Jury Innovations since 1998, Member Media Committee 1998-2001 and Chair Trial Jurors Committee since Jan 2001 Los Angeles Superior Court. Member Ad Hoc Committee on Death Penalty Appeals 1992, Nominating Committee California Judges Association 1995, Jury Deliberation Project American Judicature Society 1997-99, Judicial Council Task Force on Jury System Improvement since 1998 and Hung Jury Advisory Committee National Center for State Courts 1999-2000. Faculty Member Trial Management Conference Los Angeles Superior Court 1993 and National Institute for Trial Advocacy 1993. Panelist on "Domestic Violence" Association of Probation Women 1997, "Sex Crimes Legislation" 1997 and "Media in the Courts" 1997 Women Lawyers Association of Los Angeles and Summit Conference Multi-Disciplinary Approach to Child Sexual Abuse 1998. Guest Speaker One Day One Trial Crime Talk TV 1999. Speaker on "Jury Innovations: Next Steps"

CONNOR, JACQUELINE ANN—*Continued*
Conference of Chief Justices Texas Feb 2000 and "The New Look of Jury Trials" Association of Southern California Defense Counsel Jan 2002. Lecturer Los Angeles Sheriff's Department, Los Angeles Police Department, Los Angeles District Attorney's Office, Santa Monica Hospital Medical Center, California Sexual Assault Investigators Association, Inglewood Police Department, El Segundo Police Department and Hawthorne Police Department. Recipient Awards 1977-86 from Los Angeles County Commission on Women, Santa Monica Rape Treatment Center, California Sexual Assault Investigators Association, Los Angeles Sheriff's Department, Inglewood Police Department, El Segundo Police Department and Los Angeles District Attorney's Association. Named Judge of the Year by Century City Bar Association June 1, 2000 and by Criminal Section Los Angeles County Bar Association June 8, 2000. Board of Directors Carthorp School 1993-98.
Office: 1725 Main Street, Santa Monica 90401.
Telephone: (310) 260-3762.

CONTI, Samuel *(Senior Judge, United States District Court Northern District of California)* Appointed for life by President Richard M. Nixon to term beginning Dec 10, 1970. Assumed Senior status, serves by assignment. Born Los Angeles California July 16, 1922. Catholic. Educated at University of Santa Clara B.S. 1945 and Stanford University J.D. 1948. Member Alpha Sigma Nu. Admitted to practice California 1948. Began legal practice San Francisco 1948. In legal practice Martinez 1948-60 and Concord 1960-67. Judge, Superior Court of California Contra Costa County May 1967 to Dec 1970.
City Attorney Concord 1965-67. Member State Bar of California, Contra Costa County and American Bar Associations. U.S. Army.
Office: U.S. Courthouse, Box 36060, 450 Golden Gate Avenue, San Francisco 94102-3489.
Telephone: (415) 522-4080.

CONTRERAS, Matias R. *(Judge, Superior Court of California County of Imperial)* Elected June 7, 1994 to term beginning Jan 2, 1995. Reelected Nov 2000, current term expires Jan 2007. Presiding Judge Jan 1, 1996 to Dec 31, 1996 and Jan 1, 1999 to Dec 31, 1999. Born Calexico California Jan 14, 1946. Roman Catholic. Educated at University of California at Los Angeles B.A. 1967 and University of Southern California J.D. 1972. Admitted to practice California 1973. In legal practice El Centro 1977-80. Judge, Imperial County Municipal Court 1980-94.
Deputy Public Defender Los Angeles County 1973-75. Deputy County Counsel Imperial County 1975-76. Instructor Paralegal Program Imperial Valley College 1976-80 and on Criminal Procedure 1989 and Ethics in the Criminal Justice System 1998-2000 San Diego State University. Former Member and Officer Imperial County Bar Association. Member California Judges Association. Attended California Judges College July 1980 and June 1994. Faculty Member California Judges College 1998-2000. First Lieutenant Signal Corps U.S. Army 1967-69. Democrat. Member Rotary Club. Enjoys golfing, reading and upland game hunting.
Office: 939 West Main Street, El Centro 92243.
Telephone: (760) 482-4374.

CONWAY, Chris R. *(Judge, Superior Court of California County of Los Angeles)* Former Judge, Long Beach Municipal Court Los Angeles County.
Office: Norwalk Courthouse, 12720 Norwalk Boulevard, Norwalk 90650.
Telephone: (562) 807-7266.

CONWAY, John Joseph *(Judge, Superior Court of California City and County of San Francisco)* Assumed office Dec 31, 1998. Elected 2000, current term expires Jan 2007. Born Minneapolis Minnesota Nov 2, 1939. Educated at DePaul University B.A. 1961 and Lincoln University J.D. 1971. Business Editor Lincoln University Law Review. Member Alpha Delta Gamma and Blue Key. Admitted to practice California 1973, U.S. District Court Northern District of California 1973, U.S. Court of Appeals Ninth Circuit 1974 and U.S. Supreme Court 1978. In legal practice San Francisco 1973-92. Judge, San Francisco Municipal Court San Francisco County Feb 14, 1992 to Nov 30, 1998, appointed by Governor Pete Wilson.
Former Member Association of Defense Counsel, American Arbitration Association, Bar Association of San Francisco and American Bar Association (Former Delegate to Law Student Division). Charter Member since 1993 and President 1999-2000 Lawyers Club of San Francisco American Inns of Court. Member San Francisco Municipal Court Judges Association, California Judges Association (Criminal Law and Procedure Committee since 1992), American Judicature Society and American Judges Association. Participant "Civil Law and Procedure Settlement Conference" California Center for Judicial Education and Research 1990. Recipient Silver Key Award and Ninth Circuit Silver Certificate from Law Student Division American Bar Association and Board of Governors Pro Bono Legal Services Commendation 1988-89 and 1989-90. Named Outstanding Pro Bono Attorney by Volunteer Legal Services Program Bar Association of San Francisco 1986 and Judge of the Year by San Francisco Trial Lawyers Association 1997. Captain USMC 1962-67 (Vietnam 1965-66). Lector St. James Church. Former Member CYO Community Center Fair Oaks Neighborhood Association and St. James Church Finance and Heritage Committee. Enjoys hiking, bicycling, fishing, boating, gardening and reading.
Office: Civic Center Courthouse, 400 McAllister Street, San Francisco 94102-4514.
Telephone: (415) 551-4020.

COOKSON, Patricia K. *(Judge, Superior Court of California County of San Diego)* Assumed office Dec 1, 1998. Former Judge, El Cajon Municipal Court San Diego County.
Mailing address: P.O. Box 122724, San Diego 92112-2724.
Office: 250 East Main Street, El Cajon 92020.
Telephone: (619) 441-4336.

COOPER, Candace D. *(Presiding Justice, California Court of Appeal Second District Division Eight)* Appointed by Governor Gray Davis to term beginning Nov 10, 1999. Retained by election 2002, current term expires 2015. Formerly served Division Two. Born Los Angeles California Nov 23, 1948. Educated at University of Southern California B.A. cum laude 1970 J.D. 1973. Staff member University of Southern California Law Review 1972-73. Member Phi Alpha Delta and Delta Sigma Theta. Admitted to practice California 1974. In legal practice Los Angeles Jan 1974 to March

COOPER, CANDACE D.—*Continued*

1980. Judge, Los Angeles Municipal Court Los Angeles County March 13, 1980 to 1987, appointed by Governor Edmund G. Brown, Jr. Judge Oct 5, 1987 to Nov 1999 and Supervising Judge West District 1997-98, Superior Court of California County of Los Angeles, appointed by Governor George Deukmejian.

President California Judges Association 1988-89. Member Attorney General's Judicial Advisory Committee on Child Victim Witnesses 1987-88; Advisory Committee on Private Judges 1989-90, Advisory Committee on Racial and Ethnic Bias in the Courts 1991-97, Select Committee on Judicial Retirement 1993, Trial Court Budge Commission 1997-98 and Subcommittee on the Quality of Judicial Service Task Force on the Quality of Justice 1998-99 Judicial Council of California; and Commission on the Future of the Legal Profession and the State Bar State Bar of California 1992-95. Member Black Women Lawyers of Los Angeles, Women Lawyers of Los Angeles, California Association of Women Lawyers, California Association of Black Lawyers, National Association of Women Judges, Los Angeles County and National Bar Associations. Recipient Ernestine Stahlhut Award from Women Lawyers of Los Angeles 1989, Silver Achievement Award from Los Angeles YWCA 1991, Bernard Jefferson Award from California Association of Black Lawyers 1991 and Joan Dempsey Klein Distinguished Judge Award from California Women Lawyers 1997. Named Outstanding Trial Jurist by Los Angeles County Bar Association 1992-93. Enjoys skiing, needlework and gourmet cooking.

Office: 300 South Spring Street, Los Angeles 90013.
Telephone: (213) 830-7000.
E-mail address: Candace.d.cooper@jud.ca.gov

COOPER, Florence-Marie *(Judge, United States District Court Central District of California)* Appointed for life by President Bill Clinton to term beginning Nov 28, 1999. Born Vancouver British Columbia Feb 9, 1940. Educated at City College of San Francisco and Whittier College School of Law J.D. magna cum laude 1975. Admitted to practice California 1975. Judge, Los Angeles Municipal Court Los Angeles County 1991-92. Commissioner 1983-91 and Judge Dec 17, 1991 to Nov 1999, Superior Court of California County of Los Angeles.

Research Attorney Appellate Department Superior Court of California County of Los Angeles 1975-76. Deputy City Attorney Los Angeles 1977. Law Clerk to Hon. Arthur L. Alarcon, California Court of Appeal Second District 1978-83. Important Decisions: Has tried over twelve death penalty cases since 1986; Engine Manufacturers Assoc. v. South Coast Air Quality Management District 158 F. Supp. 2d 1107 C.D. CA 2001 aff'd 309 F.3d 550, 9th Cir. 2002; Altmann v. Republic of Austria, the Austrian Gallery 142 F. Supp. 2d 1187 C.D. CA 2001 aff'd 2002 WL 31770999 F.3d 9th Cir. 2002; Lord Simon Cairns et al. v. Franklin Mint et al. 107 F. Supp. 2d 1212 C.D. CA 2000 aff'd 292 F.3d 1139, 9th Cir. 2002; Ellison v. Robertson, America Online et al. 189 F. Supp. 2d 1051 C.D. CA 2002; and United States v. AMC Entertainment F. Supp. 2d 2002 WL 31649984 C.D. CA 2002. Adjunct Professor San Fernando Valley College of Law 1980-85. Board of Directors Los Angeles Chapter Federal Bar Association. Board of Governors Association of Business Trial Lawyers. Member Complex Litigation Inn of Court, California Judicial Council (Advisory Committee), State-Federal Judicial Council, Los Angeles Women Lawyers, California Judges Association (Executive Board) and Los Angeles County Bar Association (Executive Committee Litigation Section). Instructor New Judges Statewide Orientation Judicial College and Criminal Law and Procedure and Capital Trials Seminars The National Judicial College. Named Judge of the Year by Criminal Courts Bar Association 1995. Recipient Ernestine Stahlhut Award from Los Angeles Women Lawyers Association 1998, Outstanding Jurist Award from Los Angeles County Bar Association 1999 and Golden Mike Award from Network Television News Broadcasters Association 2000. Legal Secretary 1958-75. Advisory Board Los Angeles Commission on Assaults Against Women. Member Constitutional Rights Foundation. Enjoys cooking, knitting, theater and music.

Office: 760 Roybal Federal Building, 255 East Temple Street, Los Angeles 90012.
Telephone: (213) 894-2147.

COPE, Mark Ashton *(Judge, Superior Court of California County of Riverside)* Assumed office July 29, 1998. Presiding Judge Jan 1, 1997 to Dec 31, 1997 and Former Judge, Three Lakes Municipal Court Riverside County.

Office: 227 North D Street, Building C, Perris 92570.
Telephone: (909) 940-6877.

CORNELL, Dennis A. *(Associate Justice, California Court of Appeal Fifth District)* Appointed by Governor Gray Davis Dec 2000. Born Merced California. Educated at Stanford University 1969 and George Washington University Law Center with honors 1972. Admitted to practice California 1972, U.S. District Court Eastern District of California 1972, U.S. Court of Appeals Ninth Circuit 1972 and U.S. Supreme Court 1976. In legal practice Merced 1972-92. Part-time Magistrate Judge, U.S. District Court Eastern District of California April 19, 1986 to Feb 1992, appointed by U.S. District Court judges. Judge Feb 1992 to Dec 2000 and Presiding Judge July 1, 1998 to June 30, 1999, Superior Court of California County of Merced.

Member Executive Committee of the Conference of Delegates 1980-83 and Member 1985-88 and Vice President 1987-88 Board of Governors State Bar of California. Member California Commission on Judicial Performance 1989-92 and Trial Court Budget Commission 1995-2000. Fellow American Academy of Matrimonial Lawyers.

Office: 2525 Capitol Street, Fresno 93721.
Telephone: (559) 445-5491.

CORRIGAN, Carol A. *(Associate Justice, California Court of Appeal First District Division Three)* Appointed by Governor Pete Wilson to term beginning 1994. Retained by election. Educated at Holy Names College B.A. magna cum laude 1970, St. Louis University 1970-72 and University of California Hastings College of the Law J.D. 1975. Staff member 1973-74 and Note and Comment Editor 1974-75 Hastings Law Journal. Member Pi Gamma Mu, Psi Chi, Kappa Gamma Pi and Quill and Scroll. Judge, Oakland-Piedmont-Emeryville Municipal Court Alameda County 1987-91. Judge, Superior Court of California Alameda County 1991-94.

Deputy District Attorney 1975-85 and Senior Deputy District Attorney 1985-87 Alameda County. Editor-in-Chief *Point of View* Alameda County District Attorney's

CORRIGAN, CAROL A.—*Continued*

Office 1981-84. Contributing Author and Staff Editor *Final Report of President's Task Force on Victims of Crime* 1982. Author Chapters on Plea Bargaining, Jury Selection, Defendants' Statements, Pretrial Law and Motion Procedure, Evidence, Sentencing, Jury Instructions and Mental Defenses *1981 Developments in Criminal Law* Continuing Education of the Bar University of California 1982; Chapter 17 "Overview of *Miranda* Rules and Taking Statements" *Trial Tactics for Prosecutors* California District Attorneys Association 1984; "Meeting Specific Defenses" *The Practical Prosecutor* National College of District Attorneys 1985; "On Prosecutorial Ethics" 13 Hastings Constitutional Law Quarterly 537, 1986; "Rights of the Accused from Arrest to Arraignment" *California Criminal Procedure* Attorney's Brief Case Legal Research Software 1990; and "Diversity, Civility and the Future of Justice in California" 94 *Docket* Sacramento County Bar Association 1994. Visiting Professor of Criminal Law University of Puget Sound School of Law 1981. Adjunct Professor of Law University of California Hastings College of the Law 1981-87 and 1989, University of California Boalt Hall School of Law 1984-94 and University of San Francisco 1988-90. Special Consultant President's Task Force on Victims of Violent Crime 1972-82. Member President's Commission on Organized Crime 1983-86. Board of Directors California District Attorney's Association 1985-87. Former Member California Judicial Council (Member 1988-89 and Chair 1990-93 Advisory Committee on Voir Dire, Commission on the Future of the Courts in California 1990-94, Governing Board Center for Judicial Education and Research 1995-97, Chair Task Force on Jury Instructions since 1996). Member Earl Warren American Inn of Court.

Faculty Legal Services Corporation Training Seminars 1980; National College for Trial and Appellate Advocacy 1980-92 and Federal Practice Seminars 1981-97 Hastings College of the Law; Hawaiian State Public Defenders' Training Program 1981; Hawaiian State Prosecutor's Training Program 1981-83; Deputy Prosecutors' College 1981-87 and National Homicide Symposium 1987 California District Attorney's Association; Trial Advocacy Training Program State of Alaska Department of Law 1983; Western Regional, Advanced Advocates, Northwest Regional, Southern California Regional, Teacher Training and National Programs since 1982 and Private Law Firm Programs since 1982 National Institute for Trial Advocacy; Trial Strategy and Techniques 1984-85 and Career Prosecutor's Course 1985 National College of District Attorneys; Annual and Mid-year Conferences California Judges Association since 1988; and New Judges' Orientation Program 1988-94, Continuing Judicial Studies Programs since 1988, California Judicial College since 1989 and Appellate Institute since 1995 Center for Judicial Education and Research. Lecturer on Annual Developments in Criminal Law University of California Continuing Education of the Bar 1982-83. Panel Chair and Consultant White House Conference on a Drug Free America 1988. Recipient Alumni Award for Professional Achievement from Holy Names College 1981, Woman of Achievement Award from Soroptimist International 1982, Outstanding Instructor Award 1986 and National Homicide Symposium Faculty Award 1987 from California District Attorney's Association, Children's Choice Award from Saint Vincent's Day Home 1994 and Robert E. Keeton Distinguished Faculty Award from National Institute for Trial Advocacy 1997. Member Executive Board Holy Names College Alumni Association 1976-86, Advisory Board Saint Mary's Community Center for the Elderly 1984-89 and Community Advisory Board Providence Hospital 1989-91. Member since 1982 and Chair since 1991 Board of Directors Saint Vincent's Day Home. Board of Directors Goodwill Industries of the Greater East Bay, Inc. 1985-89. Member since 1988 and Chair since 1990 Board of Directors Holy Names College.

Office: 350 McAllister Street, San Francisco 94102-3600.

Telephone: (415) 865-7300.

CORY, Charles J. *(Judge, Superior Court of California County of Santa Clara)* Assumed office July 30, 1998. Elected 2000, current term expires 2007. Born Coulee Dam Washington Jan 30, 1941. Lutheran. Educated at Gonzaga University A.B. cum laude 1963 and Stanford University J.D. 1966. Member Phi Delta Phi. Admitted to practice California 1970, U.S. District Court Northern District of California 1970 and U.S. Court of Appeals Ninth Circuit 1970. In legal practice San Jose 1970-90. Judge, Santa Clara County Municipal Court Dec 31, 1990 to July 29, 1998, appointed by Governor George Deukmejian.

Attorney U.S. Small Business Association 1966. Member California Trial Lawyers Association, American Arbitration Association, The Association of Trial Lawyers of America, Santa Clara County and American Bar Associations. Attended New Judges Orientation March 1991 and Judges College July 1992 California Judges Association. Captain U.S. Army Artillery 1966-68. Adjuster and Claims Supervisor Allstate Insurance Co. 1969-70. Republican. Planning Commissioner Sunnyvale 1976-78. Member Advisory Committee Los Altos Cable TV 1984-90. Coach Babe Ruth and Little League Baseball, AYSO Soccer and Mid Peninsula Tennis Patrons. Enjoys tennis, travel and family activities.

Office: Palo Alto Facility, 270 Grant Avenue, Palo Alto 94306.

Telephone: (650) 462-3800.

COSGROVE, John L. *(Judge, Superior Court of California County of Placer)* Assumed office June 30, 1998. Serves Civil Division. Presiding Judge Jan 1, 1996 to Dec 31, 1996 and Former Judge, Placer County Municipal Court. Served Auburn Division.

Office: 101 Maple Street, Auburn 95603.

Telephone: (530) 889-6550.

COTA, Raymond *(Judge, Superior Court of California County of Imperial)* Assumed office June 22, 1998. Former Judge, Imperial County Municipal Court.

Office: 939 West Main Street, El Centro 92243.

Telephone: (760) 482-4374.

COUILLARD, Ronn M. *(Judge, Superior Court of California County of Tulare)* Assumed office July 27, 1998. Former Judge and Presiding Judge, Tulare County Municipal Court.

Office: County Civic Center, Visalia 93291-4593.

Telephone: (559) 733-6561.

COUZENS, J. Richard *(Judge, Superior Court of California County of Placer)* Appointed by Governor Edmund G. Brown, Jr. to term beginning April 1980. Elected 1982, 1988, 1994 and 2000. Current term ex-

COUZENS, J. RICHARD—*Continued*

pires Jan 2007. Presiding Judge Jan 1, 1996 to Dec 31, 1996. Serves Civil Division. Born San Francisco California Oct 17, 1944. Educated at Sierra Junior College A.A. 1964, University of Washington B.A. 1966 and University of California at Davis J.D. 1969. Editor-in-Chief UCD Law Review. Recipient American Jurisprudence Awards in Torts, Constitutional Law and Property, Scholarship Award in Corporation Law from West Publishing Company and Honorable Mention Scholastic Award from University of California at Davis Law School. Law Clerk to Chief Justices Roger J. Traynor and Donald Wright, California Supreme Court 1969-70. Admitted to practice California 1970, U.S. District Courts Northern 1970 and Eastern 1971 Districts of California, U.S. Court of Appeals Ninth Circuit 1970 and U.S. Supreme Court 1976. Began legal practice Auburn 1970. Judge, Lincoln Justice Court Placer County 1977-78. Judge, Auburn Justice Court Placer County Nov 7, 1978 to April 1980.

Author "Review of 1965 Code Legislation" CEB, "Review of 1967 Code Legislation" CEB 1967, "State Control of Water Pollution" University of California at Davis L. Rev. 1969, "Legal Problems of Agricultural Labor" University of California at Davis L. Rev. 1970 and "California Three Strikes Sentencing" Barrister Press 2002. Instructor Sierra Junior College 1975-76. Chair Placer County Peer Court Project since 1990. Member California Judicial Council (Task Force on Weighted Caseload System, Task Force on Criminal Delay Reduction, Advisory Committee on Uniform Rules for Civil Delay Reduction for Volunteer Courts), Juvenile Court Judges of California (Executive Board), California Judges Association (Peer Counselor Project), Cow Counties Judges Association (Chair since 1999) and Placer County Bar Association (President 1971-72). Panelist and Moderator "Recent Developments in Criminal Law" California CEB. President Auburn Host Lions Club 1976-77. Former Member Placer County School Attendance Review Board and Placer County DeWitt Development Authority. Enjoys photography, horseback riding and tennis.

Office: 101 Maple Street, Auburn 95603.

Telephone: (530) 889-6550.

COVARRUBIAS, Manuel J. *(Judge, Superior Court of California County of Ventura)* Serves East County Division.

Mailing address: P.O. Box 1200, Simi Valley 93062-1200.

Office: 3855-F Alamo Street, Simi Valley 93063.

Telephone: (805) 582-8086.

COWELL, Michael A. *(Judge, Superior Court of California County of Los Angeles)* Commissioner 1977-93. Appointed Judge by Governor Pete Wilson to term beginning 1993. Elected 1994 and 2000. Current term expires 2006. Born India Jan 17, 1940. Roman Catholic. Educated at University of Montreal B.A. magna cum laude 1963 and University of California at Los Angeles School of Law J.D. 1969. Moot Court Honors Program. Admitted to practice California 1970. In legal practice Sherman Oaks 1973-77.

Deputy Public Defender Los Angeles County 1970-73. Important Decisions: People v. Poggi 45 C 3rd 306, 1988; In re Horton 54 C 3rd 82, 1991; and People v. Horton 11 C 4th 1068, 1995. President Southeast Bar Association 1992-93. Named Superior Court Commissioner of the Year by Southeast Bar Association 1983. Recipient Judicial Excellence Award from Los Angeles Criminal Courts Bar Association 1997. Republican. Public Speaking Coach California Mock Trial Program.

Office: Norwalk Courthouse, 12720 Norwalk Boulevard, Norwalk 90650.

Telephone: (562) 807-7276.

COWETT, Patricia A. Y. *(Judge, Superior Court of California County of San Diego)* Assumed office Dec 1, 1998. Former Judge and Presiding Judge, San Diego Municipal Court San Diego County.

Mailing address: P.O. Box 122724, San Diego 92112-2724.

Office: 330 West Broadway, San Diego 92101.

Telephone: (619) 685-6148.

COX, James A. *(Judge, Superior Court of California County of Riverside)* Assumed office July 29, 1998. Former Judge, Mount San Jacinto Municipal Court Riverside County.

Office: 880 North State Street, Hemet 92543.

Telephone: (909) 766-2325.

COYLE, Robert E. *(Senior Judge, United States District Court Eastern District of California)* Appointed for life by President Ronald Reagan to term beginning May 13, 1982. Former Chief Judge. Assumed Senior status, serves by assignment. Born Fresno California May 6, 1930. Protestant. Educated at Fresno State College B.A. 1953 and University of California Hastings College of the Law LL.B. 1956 replaced by J.D. Comment Writer Hastings Law Journal 1956. Member Delta Sigma Phi and Phi Alpha Delta. Admitted to practice California 1956. In legal practice 1956-82.

With Fresno District Attorney's Office 1956. Former Chair Ninth Circuit Conference of Chief Judges. Chair Ninth Circuit Space and Security Committee. Member Federation of Insurance and Corporate Counsel, Ninth Circuit District Judges Association (President 1995-96), International Society of Barristers, American Board of Trial Advocates, State Bar of California (Executive Committee 1973-77, Board of Governors 1979-82, Vice President 1982) and Fresno County Bar Association (Chairman Legal Services 1969, Vice President 1970, President 1971). Republican. Member Sequoia Council of Boy Scouts and Fresno Junior Soccer League (President 1976-77). Board of Trustees United Givers. Board member and Treasurer Fresno Association for Mentally Retarded.

Office: 5116 U.S. Courthouse, 1130 O Street, Fresno 93721.

Telephone: (559) 498-7318.

CRADDICK, Judith S. *(Judge, Superior Court of California County of Contra Costa)*

Office: Courthouse, 725 Court Street, Martinez 94553.

Telephone: (925) 646-2950.

CRAM, Joyce M. *(Judge, Superior Court of California County of Contra Costa)*

Mailing address: P.O. Box 911, Martinez 94553.

Office: Court Annex, 1010 Ward Street, Martinez 94553.

Telephone: (925) 646-2950.

CRAMIN, Corey Scott *(Judge, Superior Court of California County of Orange)* Assumed office Aug 10,

CRAMIN, COREY SCOTT—*Continued*
1998. Presiding Judge Jan 1, 1996 to Dec 31, 1996 and Former Judge, West Orange County Municipal Court.
Mailing address: P.O. Box 14169, Orange 92863-1569.
Office: Lamoreaux Justice Center, 341 The City Drive, Orange 92868.
Telephone: (714) 935-7236.

CRANDALL, Donna L. *(Judge, Superior Court of California County of Orange)* Assumed office Aug 10, 1998. Former Judge, Central Orange County Municipal Court.
Mailing address: P.O. Box 14169, Orange 92863-1569.
Office: Lamoreaux Justice Center, 341 The City Drive, Orange 92868.
Telephone: (714) 935-7236.

CRIBBS, Graham Anderson *(Judge, Superior Court of California County of Riverside)*
Office: Larson Justice Center, 46-200 Oasis Street, Indio 92201.
Telephone: (760) 863-8426.

CRISPO, Lawrence W. *(Judge, Superior Court of California County of Los Angeles)*
Office: Courthouse, 111 North Hill Street, Los Angeles 90012.
Telephone: (213) 974-5411.

CROFT, Janice Claire *(Judge, Superior Court of California County of Los Angeles)* Former Judge, Glendale Municipal Court Los Angeles County.
Office: Pasadena Courthouse, 300 East Walnut Street, Pasadena 91101.
Telephone: (626) 356-5689.

CRONE, Robert L., Jr. *(Judge, Superior Court of California County of Lake)* Presiding Judge July 1, 1995 to June 30, 1997.
Office: 255 North Forbes Street, Lakeport 95453.
Telephone: (707) 263-2526.

CROSKEY, H. Walter *(Associate Justice, California Court of Appeal Second District Division Three)* Appointed by Governor George Deukmejian to term beginning Nov 20, 1987. Retained by election. Born Los Angeles California Aug 2, 1933. Educated at University of Southern California B.S. magna cum laude 1955 LL.B./J.D. 1958. Admitted to practice California 1959, U.S. Court of Military Appeals 1959, District of Columbia 1960 and U.S. Supreme Court 1962. In legal practice 1962-85. Judge, Superior Court of California Los Angeles County Jan 4, 1985 to Nov 20, 1987.
Author "Litigation Cost Shifting, An Economical Path to Court Reform" 8 No. 6 *Los Angeles Lawyer* Sept 1985, "Bad Faith: The Expansion of Tort Remedies in Non-Insurance Litigation" 19 No. 4 Beverly Hills Bar Association Journal Fall 1985 and "Bad Faith in California—Its History, Development and Current Status" XXVI No. 3 *Tort and Insurance Law Journal* American Bar Association Spring 1991. Co-author "Understanding and Applying the Hearsay Rule" 14 No. 11 *Los Angeles Lawyer* Feb 1992, "Avoiding Evidence Pitfalls" 15 No. 1 *Los Angeles Lawyer* March 1992 and *California Practice Guide* 3 vols. Insurance Litigation The Rutter Group 1995. Chair Ad Hoc Committee on Trial Court Funding 1990-92 and Member Appellate Standing Advisory Committee 1993-95 Judicial Council of California. Member Executive Committee of the Los Angeles Superior Court 1986-87 and State-Federal Judicial Council. Recipient Bernard S. Jefferson Award for distinguished service in judicial education from California Judges Association 1992, Roger J. Traynor Memorial Award—Appellate Justice of the Year from Los Angeles Trial Lawyers Association 1993 and Distinguished Service Award—Jurist of the Year from Judicial Council of California 1994. USN JAG May 1, 1959 to April 30, 1962. Elder Presbyterian Church Pacific Palisades.
Office: 300 South Spring Street, Los Angeles 90013.
Telephone: (213) 830-7000.

CUMMINS, Michael Richard *(Judge, Superior Court of California County of Stanislaus)* Assumed office July 31, 1998. Former Judge, Stanislaus County Municipal Court.
Office: 800 Eleventh Street, Modesto 95354.
Telephone: (209) 558-6000.

CUNNINGHAM, Ray E. *(Judge, Superior Court of California County of Santa Clara)* Assumed office July 30, 1998. Former Judge, Santa Clara County Municipal Court.
Office: 12425 Monterey Road, San Martin 95046.
Telephone: (408) 695-5000.

CUNNISON, Stephen D. *(Judge, Superior Court of California County of Riverside)*
Office: Riverside Historic Courthouse, 4050 Main Street, Riverside 92501.
Telephone: (909) 955-1403.

CURLE, Wilson *(Judge, Superior Court of California County of Shasta)* Assumed office June 3, 1998. Presiding Judge Superior and Municipal Courts Jan 1, 1997 to Dec 31, 1997 and Former Judge, Shasta County Municipal Court.
Office: 1500 Court Street, Redding 96001-1685.
Telephone: (530) 225-5714.

CURRY, Daniel A. *(Associate Justice, California Court of Appeal Second District Division Four)* Appointed by Governor Pete Wilson to term beginning 1998. Born Phoenix Arizona March 28, 1937. Educated at Loyola University of Los Angeles B.S. 1957 LL.B. 1960. Admitted to practice California 1961, Hawaii 1972 and New York 1988. In legal practice 1964-67. Judge, Superior Court of California Los Angeles County 1992-98.
Counsel Technicolor, Inc. 1967-70. Senior Vice President and General Counsel Amfac, Inc. 1970-87. Vice President and General Counsel The Times Mirror Company 1987-92. Member Committee on Corporate Law Departments American Bar Association 1973-92, Institute for Corporate Counsel and Coalition for Justice. Captain USAFR JAG 1961-64. Former Director Palama Settlement and Los Angeles Oncologic Institute. Former Trustee Hawaii Medical Library. Former Regent Chaminade University of Honolulu and Loyola Marymount University.
Office: 300 South Spring Street, Los Angeles 90013.
Telephone: (213) 830-7440.

CURRY, James L. *(Judge, Superior Court of California County of Yuba)* Presiding Judge since Jan 7, 1998.
Office: 215 Fifth Street, Marysville 95901.
Telephone: (530) 749-7600.

CURTIS, Herbert, III *(Judge, Superior Court of California County of Ventura)* Assumed office June 10, 1998. Former Judge and Presiding Judge, Ventura County Municipal Court.

Mailing address: P.O. Box 6489, Ventura 93006-6489.
Office: 800 South Victoria Avenue, Ventura 93009-0001.
Telephone: (805) 654-2965.

CURTIS, Richard M. *(Judge, Superior Court of California County of Monterey)* Assumed office Dec 18, 2000. Former Judge, Monterey County Municipal Court.

Mailing address: P.O. Box 1819, Salinas 93902-1819.
Office: 240 Church Street, Salinas 93901.
Telephone: (831) 755-5060.

CZULEGER, J. Stephen *(Judge, Superior Court of California County of Los Angeles)* Assumed office 1990. Judge pro tem, Superior Court of Orange County 1996. Justice pro tem, California Courts of Appeal Division Four 1998. Assistant Supervising Judge Civil Division 2003. Born Feb 8, 1951. Educated at University of Santa Clara B.S. 1973 and Loyola Law School J.D. 1976. Law Clerk/Crier to Hon. David W. Williams, U.S. District Court Central District of California 1974-76. In legal practice Los Angeles 1979-81. Judge, Los Angeles Municipal Court Los Angeles County 1988-90.

Assistant U.S. Attorney Central District of California 1977-81 and 1984-88. Special Attorney Organized Crime Strike Force U.S. Department of Justice Northern District of California 1982-84. Member Executive Committee Los Angeles Municipal Court 1989 and Los Angeles Superior Court 1993-95 and since 2002. Member Executive Board 1995-98 and Vice President 1997-98 California Judges Association. Member Ethics Planning Committee California Center for Judicial Education and Research 2000-01. Lecturer on American Law International Conference Rome, Italy 1985 and on Comparative Law East Africa Regional Conference Nairobi, Kenya 1990 U.S. Department of Justice and judicial conferences California Center for Judicial Education and Research and California Judges Association 1988-2001.

Office: Los Angeles County Courthouse, 111 North Hill Street, Los Angeles 90012.
Telephone: (213) 974-5673.

DABNEY, James R. *(Judge, Superior Court of California County of Los Angeles)*

Office: Courthouse, 111 North Hill Street, Los Angeles 90012.
Telephone: (213) 974-5411.

DAIGH, Gary E. *(Judge, Superior Court of California County of Los Angeles)* Former Judge, South Bay Municipal Court Los Angeles County.

Office: Compton Courthouse, 200 West Compton Boulevard, Compton 90220.
Telephone: (310) 603-7842.

DALE, Robert P. *(Judge, Superior Court of California County of Sonoma)* Assumed office June 12, 1998. Former Judge and Presiding Judge, Sonoma County Municipal Court.

Office: 600 Administration Drive, Santa Rosa 95403.
Telephone: (707) 565-1100.

DAMRELL, Frank C., Jr. *(Judge, United States District Court Eastern District of California)* Appointed for life by President Bill Clinton to term beginning Nov 28, 1997. Born Modesto California July 6, 1938. Educated at University of California at Berkeley B.A. 1961 and Yale Law School LL.B. 1964. In legal practice Modesto 1968-97.

Deputy Attorney General 1964-66 and Deputy District Attorney 1966-68 California.

Office: 15-200 U.S. Courthouse, 501 I Street, Sacramento 95814-2322.
Telephone: (916) 930-4120.

DAMRON, Robert H. *(Judge, Superior Court of California County of Sutter)* Appointed by Governor Pete Wilson March 24, 1993. Elected June 2, 1994 and 2000. Current term expires Jan 2007. Presiding Judge since Jan 1, 1997. Born Illinois 1944. Educated at Drake University B.S. 1967 and California Western School of Law J.D. 1973. Admitted to practice California 1974. Former Judge and Presiding Judge, Sutter County Municipal Court, appointed by Governor George Deukmejian to term beginning April 3, 1989. First Lieutenant USMC 1967-70.

Office: 446 Second Street, Yuba City 95991.
Telephone: (530) 822-7360.

DANIELSEN, David John *(Judge, Superior Court of California County of San Diego)* Former Judge and Presiding Judge, San Diego Municipal Court San Diego County.

Mailing address: P.O. Box 122724, San Diego 92112-2724.
Office: 220 West Broadway, San Diego 92101.
Telephone: (619) 531-3820.

DANNER, Alden E. *(Judge, Superior Court of California County of Santa Clara)*

Office: Hall of Justice East Wing, 190 West Hedding Street, San Jose 95110.
Telephone: (408) 808-6600.

DANNER, Arthur *(Judge, Superior Court of California County of Santa Cruz)*

Office: Main Courthouse, 701 Ocean Street, Santa Cruz 95060.
Telephone: (831) 454-2012.

DANSER, William R. *(Judge, Superior Court of California County of Santa Clara)* Assumed office July 30, 1998. Former Judge, Santa Clara County Municipal Court.

Office: Hall of Justice West Wing, 200 West Hedding Street, San Jose 95110.
Telephone: (408) 808-6600.

DARLINGTON, John H. *(Judge, Superior Court of California County of Nevada)* Appointed by Governor George Deukmejian to term beginning Oct 18, 1989. Elected 1990, 1996 and 2002. Current term expires Jan 2009. Former Presiding Judge. Born Des Moines Iowa Nov 22, 1944. Protestant. Educated at California State University at Northridge B.A. 1966 and Loyola University of Los Angeles J.D. 1969. Member Phi Alpha Delta and Blue Key. Admitted to practice California 1970, U.S. District Courts Central 1970 and Eastern 1971 Districts of California, U.S. Court of Appeals Ninth Circuit 1971 and U.S. Supreme Court 1985.

District Attorney Nevada County 1979-89. Instructor in Criminal Law, Evidence and Consumer Law Sierra Community College 1973-78. Former Member California District Attorneys Association (Board of Directors 1986-88) and Nevada County Bar Association. Republican.

DARLINGTON, JOHN H.—*Continued*

Enjoys choral music, long distance running and backpacking.

Office: 201 Church Street, Suite 7, Nevada City 95959-2504.

Telephone: (530) 265-1273, 265-1751.

Fax: (530) 478-1938

DAU, Ralph W. *(Judge, Superior Court of California County of Los Angeles)* Appointed by Governor Pete Wilson to term beginning Nov 20, 1995. Elected March 1996 and 2002. Current term expires Jan 2008. Born Milwaukee Wisconsin Feb 27, 1938. Educated at University of Texas B.A. 1959 LL.B. with honors 1966. Comment Editor Texas Law Review 1965-66. Member Phi Delta Phi and Order of the Coif. Admitted to practice Texas 1966 and California 1967. In legal practice Los Angeles 1966-95.

Member Advisory Committee on Aeronautical Law American Bar Association 1981-83 and Committee on Federal Courts State Bar of California 1988-91. Faculty National Institute for Trial Advocacy 1983-93. Lieutenant j.g. USN 1959-63.

Office: Courthouse, 111 North Hill Street, Los Angeles 90012.

Telephone: (213) 974-5411.

DAUM, Elliot *(Judge, Superior Court of California County of Sonoma)*

Office: 600 Administration Drive, Santa Rosa 95403.

Telephone: (707) 565-1100.

DAUPHINÉ, Susan M. *(Judge, Superior Court of California County of Monterey)* Assumed office Dec 18, 2000. Elected 2002, current term expires Jan 2009. Born Los Angeles California March 5, 1944. Catholic. Educated at Stanford University A.B. with distinction 1965 and Columbia University School of Law J.D. 1968. Admitted to practice Massachusetts 1969, California 1976, U.S. District Courts Northern 1976 and Central 1987 Districts of California and U.S. Court of Appeals Ninth Circuit 1981. In legal practice Rochester Minnesota 1973-75 and Monterey California 1975-98. Judge, Monterey County Municipal Court June 23, 1998 to Dec 17, 2000, appointed by Governor Pete Wilson.

Attorney United States Department of Health, Education and Welfare 1968-69. Author weekly column "The Law at Work" *Monterey County Herald* 1996-98. Instructor on Commercial Law Old Dominion University, Guantánamo Cuba 1970-72. Past President Monterey County Bar Association. Former Member State Conference of Delegates and State Bar of California. Member California Judges Association (Annual Planning Committee). Selected for judicial/legal delegation to Russia to review constitution and legal reforms 1993.

Office: 1200 Aguajito Road, Monterey 93940.

Telephone: (831) 647-7730.

Fax: (831) 647-7883

DAVIDSON, John L. *(Judge, Superior Court of California County of San Diego)* Assumed office Dec 1, 1998. Former Judge, San Diego Municipal Court San Diego County.

Mailing address: P.O. Box 122724, San Diego 92112-2724.

Office: 220 West Broadway, San Diego 92101.

Telephone: (619) 531-3820.

DAVILA, Edward J. *(Judge, Superior Court of California County of Santa Clara)*

Office: 840 Guadalupe Parkway, San Jose 95110.

Telephone: (408) 808-6200.

DAVILLA, Raymond J., Jr. *(Judge, Superior Court of California County of Santa Clara)*

Office: 840 Guadalupe Parkway, San Jose 95110.

Telephone: (408) 808-6200.

DAVIS, William J. *(Judge, Superior Court of California County of Siskiyou)* Elected to term beginning Jan 8, 2001. Term expires Jan 2007. Educated at University of California at Irvine B.A. 1976 and University of California at Los Angeles J.D. 1979. Admitted to practice California 1980.

Mailing address: P.O. Box 1026, Yreka 96097.

Office: 311 Fourth Street, Yreka 96097.

Telephone: (530) 842-8330.

DAVIS, Keith D. *(Judge, Superior Court of California County of San Bernardino)*

Office: 351 North Arrowhead Avenue, San Bernardino 92415-0240.

Telephone: (909) 387-3922.

DAVIS, Nancy *(Judge, Superior Court of California City and County of San Francisco)*

Office: Hall of Justice, 850 Bryant Street, San Francisco 94103.

Telephone: (415) 553-1159.

DAVIS, Rodney *(Associate Justice, California Court of Appeal Third District)* Appointed by Governor George Deukmejian to term beginning Feb 27, 1989. Retained by election Nov 1990 and 2002. Current term expires Jan 2015. Born Sacramento California Feb 14, 1949. Episcopalian. Educated at University of California at Davis B.A. 1971, University of California Hastings College of the Law J.D. 1974 and University of Southern California M.A. 1979. Staff member Hastings Constitutional Law Quarterly 1974. Admitted to practice California 1974, U.S. District Court Eastern District of California 1974 and U.S. Court of Appeals Ninth Circuit 1974. Began legal practice Sacramento County 1974. Judge, Sacramento Municipal Court Sacramento County 1983-85. Judge, Superior Court of California Sacramento County 1985-89.

Deputy Attorney General 1974-78 and Supervising Deputy Attorney General 1978-83 California. Chief Medi-Cal Fraud Unit California Justice Department 1983. Special Assistant U.S. Attorney Northern District of California 1984-85. Member California Judges Association. Recipient Citation for Excellence and Jerry W. Fielder Award from University of California at Davis. Past President Alumni Association and Former Chair Health System Leadership Council University of California at Davis. Former Trustee University of California at Davis Foundation. Enjoys climbing and swimming.

Office: 900 N Street, Fourth Floor, Sacramento 95814.

Telephone: (916) 654-0209.

DAWSON, Betty L. *(Judge, Superior Court of California County of Merced)* Presiding Judge since Jan 1, 2003.

Office: County Courts Building, 627 West 21st Street, Merced 95340.

Telephone: (209) 385-7531.

DE ALBA, David *(Judge, Superior Court of California County of Sacramento)*
Office: Courthouse, 720 Ninth Street, Sacramento 95814.
Telephone: (916) 874-5476.

DEARMAN, John E. *(Judge, Superior Court of California City and County of San Francisco)* Appointed by Governor Edmund G. Brown, Jr. to term beginning March 5, 1979. Elected 1980, 1986, 1992 and 1998. Current term expires Jan 2005. Former Presiding Judge. Born Texas March 28, 1931. Educated at Wiley College B.A. 1954 and Wayne State University J.D. 1957. Admitted to practice Michigan 1957. In legal practice San Francisco California 1961. Judge, San Francisco Municipal Court San Francisco County 1977-79.
Director Golden Gate Bridge 1966-70 and Metropolitan Transportation Commission 1970-76. Former member State Bar of California and State Bar of Michigan. Democrat. Member County Central Committee 1966-76. Board member Multiple Sclerosis Society, National Conference of Christians and Jews, Community Street Work Center and YMCA. Enjoys jogging.
Office: Civic Center Courthouse, 400 McAllister Street, San Francisco 94102-4514.
Telephone: (415) 551-4020.

de BELLEFEUILLE, Denise *(Judge, Superior Court of California County of Santa Barbara)* Assumed office Aug 3, 1998. Former Judge, Santa Barbara Municipal Court Santa Barbara County.
Office: 1100 Anacapa Street, Santa Barbara 93101.
Telephone: (805) 568-2220.

DEDDEH, Peter C. *(Judge, Superior Court of California County of San Diego)*
Mailing address: P.O. Box 122724, San Diego 92112-2724.
Office: 220 West Broadway, San Diego 92101.
Telephone: (619) 531-3820.

DeGROOT, John W. *(Judge, Superior Court of California County of Madera)* Presiding Judge Jan 1, 1998 to Dec 31, 2000. Former Judge, Chowchilla Justice Court Madera County.
Office: 209 West Yosemite Avenue, Madera 93637.
Telephone: (559) 675-7907.

DEKREON, Gail *(Judge, Superior Court of California City and County of San Francisco)*
Office: Hall of Justice, 850 Bryant Street, San Francisco 94103.
Telephone: (415) 553-1159.

DEL POZZO, Ron M. *(Judge, Superior Court of California County of Santa Clara)*
Office: Hall of Justice West Wing, 200 West Hedding Street, San Jose 95110.
Telephone: (408) 808-6600.

DEMETRAS, Stephen G. *(Judge, Superior Court of California County of San Joaquin)* Former Presiding Judge.
Office: 222 East Weber Avenue, Room 303, Stockton 95202.
Telephone: (209) 468-2827.

DENNER, Richard E. *(Judge, Superior Court of California County of Los Angeles)*
Office: Courthouse, 111 North Hill Street, Los Angeles 90012.
Telephone: (213) 974-5411.

DENTON, Steven R. *(Judge, Superior Court of California County of San Diego)*
Mailing address: P.O. Box 122724, San Diego 92112-2724.
Office: 1551-55 Sixth Avenue, San Diego 92101.

DESHAZER, Ellen Carol *(Judge, Superior Court of California County of Los Angeles)* Assumed office Jan 22, 2000. Former Judge, Compton Municipal Court Los Angeles County.
Office: Compton Courthouse, 200 West Compton Boulevard, Compton 90220.
Telephone: (310) 603-7842.

DEST, Michael M. *(Judge, Superior Court of California County of San Bernardino)* Assumed office Aug 10, 1998. Serves Crest Forest Division. Former Judge, San Bernardino County Municipal Court.
Mailing address: P.O. Box 394, Twin Peaks 92391.
Office: 26010 State Highway 189, Twin Peaks 92391.
Telephone: (909) 336-0620.

DETJEN, Jennifer R. S. *(Judge, Superior Court of California County of Madera)*
Office: 209 West Yosemite Avenue, Madera 93637.
Telephone: (559) 675-7907.

De VANON, Joseph F. *(Judge, Superior Court of California County of Los Angeles)* Appointed by Governor Pete Wilson. Elected 1998, current term expires 2004. Serves Northeast District. Born Chicago Illinois Aug 17, 1950. Educated at University of Southern California B.A. 1972 and Western State University J.D. 1976. Staff member Western State University Law Review 1975-76. Admitted to practice California 1976 and U.S. District Court Central District of California 1977. Judge and Presiding Judge, Glendale Municipal Court Los Angeles County 1990-98.
Deputy Public Defender 1977-86. Member California Judges Association.
Office: Pasadena Courthouse, 300 East Walnut Street, Pasadena 91101.
Telephone: (626) 356-5689.
E-mail address: JdeVanon@LASC.CO.CA.US

DeVORE, David L. *(Judge, Superior Court of California County of Alpine)*
Mailing address: P.O. Box 276, Markleeville 96120.
Office: 99 Water Street, Markleeville 96120.
Telephone: (530) 694-2113.

DIAZ, Marta S. *(Judge, Superior Court of California County of San Mateo)* Serves Juvenile Court.
Office: 21 Tower Road, San Mateo 94402.
Telephone: (650) 312-5554.

DIAZ, Rudolph A. *(Judge, Superior Court of California County of Los Angeles)* Assumed office Jan 22, 2000. Elected 2000, current term expires Jan 2007. Born Los Angeles California Oct 8, 1942. Roman Catholic. Educated at California State University at Long Beach B.S. 1969 and University of Southern California J.D. 1972. Admitted to practice California 1972, U.S. District Court Central District of California 1972, U.S. Court of Appeals Ninth Circuit 1977 and U.S. Supreme Court

DIAZ, RUDOLPH A.—*Continued*

1980. Began legal practice Los Angeles 1972. Judge, Rio Hondo Municipal Court Los Angeles County July 31, 1980 to Jan 21, 2000, appointed by Governor Edmund G. Brown, Jr.

Instructor Loyola University Law School 1979-80. Board member California Public Defender Association 1979-80. Member California Judges Association, Municipal Court Judges Association and Los Angeles County Bar Association 1975-80. Honorary member Mexican-American Bar Association (Vice President 1979). Specialist Five U.S. Army 1960-63. Worked for Pacific Telephone 1963-69. Member El Centro Associates Support Group University of Southern California (President since 1983). Board member 1975-80 and President 1978-80 Los Angeles Center for Law and Justice. Enjoys tennis, bowling and golf.

Office: 1601 Eastlake Avenue, Los Angeles 90033.

Telephone: (323) 226-8591.

DIBIASO, Nickolas J. *(Associate Justice, California Court of Appeal Fifth District)* Appointed by Governor George Deukmejian to term beginning June 27, 1989. Retained by election Nov 6, 1990 and Nov 2002. Current term expires Jan 2015. Judge, Superior Court of California Fresno County 1985-89. Captain U.S. Army 1968-70.

Office: 2525 Capitol Street, Fresno 93721.

Telephone: (559) 445-5491.

DI CESARE, James J. *(Judge, Superior Court of California County of Orange)*

Office: West Justice Center, 8141 Thirteenth Street, Westminster 92683.

Telephone: (714) 896-7181.

DIDIER, Daniel J. *(Judge, Superior Court of California County of Orange)* Appointed by Governor Pete Wilson to term beginning Jan 25, 1992. Elected 1998, current term expires Jan 2005. Born Stockton California Dec 24, 1945. Roman Catholic. Educated at California State University at Fullerton B.A. 1973, Western State University J.D. 1976 and University of Southern California M.B.T. 1984. Admitted to practice California 1977. Judge, West Orange County Municipal Court Nov 22, 1989 to Jan 24, 1992.

Mailing address: P.O. Box 1994, Santa Ana 92702-1994.

Office: Central Justice Center, 700 Civic Center Drive West, Santa Ana 92701.

Telephone: (714) 834-3734.

DIER, Larry L. *(Judge, Superior Court of California County of Modoc)* Assumed office Sept 20, 1999. Presiding Judge Jan 1, 2000 to Dec 31, 2001 and since Aug 22, 2002. Former Judge, Modoc County Municipal Court.

Office: 205 South East Street, Alturas 96101.

Telephone: (530) 233-6222.

DiFIGLIA, Vincent P. *(Judge, Superior Court of California County of San Diego)* Appointed by Governor George Deukmejian to term beginning July 28, 1987. Elected Nov 1988, 1994 and 2000. Current term expires Jan 2007. Born Brooklyn New York March 31, 1942. Educated at Dartmouth College A.B. 1963 and University of Southern California J.D. 1970. Admitted to practice California 1971, U.S. District Courts Southern 1971 and Central 1974 Districts of California and U.S. Supreme Court 1976. In legal practice San Diego 1983-87.

Deputy City Attorney San Diego 1971-83. Instructor University of San Diego 1977-83. Director San Diego County Inns of Court and Master American Inns of Court. Member California Judges Association and American Board of Trial Advocates. Lieutenant USNR 1964-67. Republican. Enjoys golf.

Mailing address: P.O. Box 122724, San Diego 92112-2724.

Office: 330 West Broadway, San Diego 92101.

Telephone: (619) 685-6148.

DiLORETO, Joseph E. *(Judge, Superior Court of California County of Los Angeles)* Appointed by Governor Pete Wilson Oct 13, 1995. Elected Nov 3, 1996 and 2002. Current term expires Jan 2009. Born Norwich Connecticut Jan 21, 1941. Catholic. Educated at University of Portland B.A. with honors 1963 and Loyola Law School J.D. 1966. Staff Writer 1963-66 and Editor 1965-66 Loyola Law Digest. Member Phi Delta Phi. Admitted to practice California 1967, U.S. District Court Southern District of California 1966, U.S. Court of Appeals for the Armed Forces 1972 and U.S. Supreme Court 1972. In legal practice Downey 1969-95.

Deputy District Attorney Orange County 1967-69. Member Judicial Evaluation Committee Los Angeles County Bar Association, California Judges Association, American Judges Association and American Bar Association. Instructor in Micra Credits local bar association. Named America's Leading Trial Lawyer. Republican. Councilman and Mayor City of Downey 1972-76. Member Lincoln Club and National Italian American Foundation. Enjoys automobile racing and vintage car collecting. Has won over 100 amateur and vintage automobile races over the past 20 years.

Office: Long Beach Courthouse, 415 West Ocean Boulevard, Long Beach 90802.

Telephone: (562) 491-6130.

DOBROTH, John E. *(Judge, Superior Court of California County of Ventura)* Assumed office June 10, 1998. Former Judge, Ventura County Municipal Court.

Mailing address: P.O. Box 6489, Ventura 93006-6489.

Office: 800 South Victoria Avenue, Ventura 93009-0001.

Telephone: (805) 654-2965.

DOI, David Isumu *(Judge, Superior Court of California County of Los Angeles)* Assumed office Jan 22, 2000. Former Judge, Los Angeles Municipal Court Los Angeles County.

Office: Courthouse, 111 North Hill Street, Los Angeles 90012.

Telephone: (213) 974-5411.

DOMBRINK, Stephen Allen *(Judge, Superior Court of California County of Alameda)* Assumed office July 31, 1998. Presiding Judge Jan 1, 1997 to Dec 31, 1997 and Former Judge, Oakland-Piedmont-Emeryville Municipal Court Alameda County.

Office: Administration Building, 1221 Oak Street, Oakland 94612.

Telephone: (510) 271-5130.

DOMNITZ, H. Ronald *(Judge, Superior Court of California County of San Diego)* Assumed office Dec 1,

DOMNITZ, H. RONALD—*Continued*

1998. Former Judge and Presiding Judge, San Diego Municipal Court San Diego County.

Mailing address: P.O. Box 122724, San Diego 92112-2724.

Office: 220 West Broadway, San Diego 92101.

Telephone: (619) 531-3820.

DONAHUE, Patrick H. *(Judge, Superior Court of California County of Orange)*

Mailing address: P.O. Box 5000, Fullerton 92838-0500.

Office: North Justice Center, 1275 North Berkeley Avenue, Fullerton 92832.

Telephone: (714) 773-4400.

DONDERO, Robert L. *(Judge, Superior Court of California City and County of San Francisco)* Appointed by Governor Pete Wilson Jan 24, 1992. Elected Feb 1994 and 2000. Current term expires Jan 2007. Born San Francisco California Oct 9, 1945. Educated at Santa Clara University B.A. 1967 and University of California Boalt Hall School of Law J.D. 1970. Admitted to practice California 1971, U.S. District Court Northern District of California 1971 and U.S. Court of Appeals Ninth Circuit 1978. In legal practice San Francisco 1971-92. Former Judge, San Francisco Municipal Court San Francisco County.

District Attorney San Francisco County 1971-78. U.S. Attorney Northern District of California 1978-92. Professor San Francisco Law School since 1991. Member California Judges Association, American Judicature Society and Italian American Bar Association.

Office: Civic Center Courthouse, 400 McAllister Street, San Francisco 94102-4514.

Telephone: (415) 551-4020.

DONNELLY, Donal B. *(Judge, Superior Court of California County of Imperial)* Assumed office June 22, 1998. Former Judge, Imperial County Municipal Court.

Office: 939 West Main Street, El Centro 92243.

Telephone: (760) 482-4374.

DONOVAN, Thomas B. *(Judge, United States Bankruptcy Court Central District of California)* Appointed by U.S. Court of Appeals Ninth Circuit judges to term beginning March 21, 1994. Term expires March 20, 2008. Born Oakland California 1935. Educated at University of California at Berkeley A.B. 1957 J.D. 1962. Associate Editor California Law Review 1960-62. Admitted to practice California 1963 and District of Columbia 1963. In legal practice Washington D.C. 1962-64 and San Francisco California 1964-94.

Member Los Angeles Bankruptcy Forum, American Bankruptcy Institute, Financial Lawyers Conference, Association of Business Trial Lawyers, National Conference of Bankruptcy Judges and Los Angeles County Bar Association. First Lieutenant U.S. Army Security Agency 1957-59.

Office: 1352 Federal Building, 255 East Temple Street, Los Angeles 90012.

Telephone: (213) 894-3728.

DORADO, Leopoldo Edward *(Judge, Superior Court of California County of Alameda)* Assumed office July 31, 1998. Elected 2002, current term expires Jan 2009. Executive Committee 1999 and Appellate Division 1999. Born Oakland California Oct 15, 1949. Educated at University of California at Berkeley B.A. 1971 J.D. 1974. Admitted to practice California 1978. In legal practice San Francisco 1978-79. Judge Sept 1988 to July 30, 1998, Assistant Presiding Judge 1990 and 1995 and Presiding Judge 1991 and 1996, San Leandro-Hayward Municipal Court Alameda County, appointed by Governor George Deukmejian.

Deputy District Attorney San Mateo County 1979-82 and Alameda County 1982-88. Master since 1997, Membership Chair 1998-2001, President Elect 2001-02 and President 2002-03 Earl Warren American Inn of Court. Member Court Interpreters Advisory Panel Judicial Council of California 1998-2002. Member La Raza Lawyers Association, California Judges Association (Ethics Committee 1993-94), Alameda County (Chair Law Day since 1995) and Hispanic National Bar Associations. Faculty National Institute for Trial Advocacy 1985-88 and 1997, "Expediting Civil Trials" Center for Judicial Education and Research Civil Law Institute San Jose 1992 and Hastings Trial Advocacy University of California at San Francisco. Keynote Speaker "DARE" (Drug Awareness and Resistance Education) Hayward and Castro Valley Schools since 1990. Recipient National Award Sixth Best Program 1997 and Local Award Best Program 1997 Earl Warren American Inn of Court and Judicial Distinguished Service Award from Alameda County Bar Association 2001. Mock Trial Competition Judge Alameda County High School since 1988. Mentor since 1990, Chair Mentor Council 1993-96 and State Honoree 1996 Puente Project Chabot Junior College. Vice Chair 1992-94, Leader and Law Post 1992-97 and Chair 1994-96 Explorers Boy Scouts of America. Board of Directors Hispanic Chamber of Commerce of Alameda County 1994-97 and Hayward Girls and Boys Club since 1996. Advisory Board Hispanic Community Affairs Council since 1998. Member 100 Club of Alameda County. Enjoys sports, traveling and reading.

Office: Courthouse, 1225 Fallon Street, Oakland 94612.

Telephone: (510) 272-6070.

DORIAN, Brett J. *(Recalled Judge, United States Bankruptcy Court Eastern District of California)* Appointed Judge by U.S. Court of Appeals Ninth Circuit judges. Appointed Recalled Judge by the Judicial Council of the Ninth Circuit.

Office: 2656 U.S. Courthouse, 1130 O Street, Fresno 93721.

Telephone: (559) 498-7390.

DORR, James M. *(Judge, Superior Court of California County of San Bernardino)* Assumed office Aug 10, 1998. Former Judge, San Bernardino County Municipal Court.

Office: 235 East Mountain View Avenue, Barstow 92311.

Telephone: (760) 256-4819.

DOUGHERTY, Frank *(Judge, Superior Court of California County of Merced)* Assumed office Aug 3, 1998. Former Presiding Judge. Born St. Paul Minnesota Feb 27, 1945. Protestant. Educated at Ventura College A.A. 1971, University of La Verne B.A. 1973 and Ventura College of Law J.D. 1977. Admitted to practice California 1977. Judge Jan 25, 1990 to Aug 2, 1998 and Presiding Judge Jan 1, 1997 to Dec 31, 1997, Merced County Municipal Court, appointed by Governor George Deukmejian.

DOUGHERTY, FRANK—*Continued*

Deputy District Attorney 1978-86 and District Attorney 1986-90 Merced County.

Office: County Courts Building, 627 West 21st Street, Merced 95340.

Telephone: (209) 385-7531.

DOUGHERTY, H. Morgan *(Judge, Superior Court of California County of Riverside)*

Office: Larson Justice Center, 46-200 Oasis Street, Indio 92201.

Telephone: (760) 863-8426.

DOUGLASS, Thomas N., Jr. *(Judge, Superior Court of California County of Riverside)* Assumed office July 29, 1998. Former Judge and Presiding Judge, Desert Municipal Court Riverside County.

Office: Larson Justice Center, 46-200 Oasis Street, Indio 92201.

Telephone: (760) 863-8426.

DOUGLASS, Wallace Painter *(Judge, Superior Court of California City and County of San Francisco)* Born San Francisco California Dec 3, 1936. Educated at Stanford University B.A. 1961 M.A. 1962 and University of California at Berkeley J.D. 1969. Admitted to practice California 1970 and U.S. District Court Eastern District of California 1982. In legal practice San Francisco 1976-84. Judge, San Francisco Municipal Court San Francisco County Jan 4, 1991 to Dec 30, 1998, appointed by Governor George Deukmejian.

Assistant District Attorney 1970-75. Staff Counsel U.S. Consumer and Product Safety Commission 1975-76. Law Clerk to Hon. John W. Holmdahl, California Court of Appeal First District Division One 1984-90. Member Association of Former San Francisco Assistant District Attorneys (Treasurer 1984-85, Second Vice President 1985-86), San Francisco Municipal Court Judges Association and California Judges Association. Participant Law Clerk Program 1985 and 1988 and New Judges Program March 1991 California Center for Judicial Education and Research and New Judges Program Judicial College July 1992. Criminal Law Panelist California Center for Judicial Education and Research Program 1988. Appellate Proceedings Panelist for District Attorney's Family Support Program Feb 1991. Lead Panelist "Handling Misdemeanor Cases" California Continuing Education of the Bar Autumn 1996. E-4 U.S. Army 1956-59. Guest Lecturer and Moot Court Judge at local law schools. Enjoys year-round backpacking.

Office: Civic Center Courthouse, 400 McAllister Street, San Francisco 94102.

Telephone: (415) 551-4020.

DOVER, Albert Perry *(Judge, Superior Court of California County of Nevada)* Assumed office July 1, 1998. Presiding Judge since Jan 1, 2003. Born Chicago Illinois May 8, 1948. Educated at University of Arizona B.S. 1970 J.D. 1974. Admitted to practice Arizona 1974, California 1982 and U.S. District Courts Southern District of Arizona 1974 and Eastern District of California 1982. In legal practice Tucson Arizona 1979-81 and Nevada City California 1984-87. Judge Feb 1987 to June 30, 1998 and Former Presiding Judge, Nevada County Municipal Court, appointed by Nevada County Board of Supervisors.

Office: 201 Church Street, Nevada City 95959-2504.

Telephone: (530) 265-1311.

DOYLE, John P. *(Judge, Superior Court of California County of Los Angeles)* Assumed office Jan 22, 2000. Serves North District. Born Oakland California April 14, 1949. Episcopalian. Educated at Harvard College A.B. cum laude in Economics 1971 and Hastings College of Law J.D. 1978. Articles Editor Hastings Law Journal 1977-78. Extern to Hon. Wiley W. Manuel, California Supreme Court 1977-78. Admitted to practice California 1978 and New York 1979. In legal practice New York New York 1978-82 and Los Angeles California 1982-96. Judge, Los Angeles Municipal Court Los Angeles County April 20, 1996 to Jan 21, 2000, appointed by Governor Pete Wilson.

Assistant U.S. Attorney Central District of California 1982-87. Adjunct Professor of Law Pepperdine University School of Law since 1993. Former Member State Bar of California. Member California Judges Association and Los Angeles County Bar Association. Ensign USN 1971-72. USNR 1972-78 (inactive).

Office: Palmdale Courthouse, 38256 Sierra Highway, Palmdale 93550.

Telephone: (661) 537-2621.

DOYLE, John T. *(Judge, Superior Court of California County of Los Angeles)*

Office: Compton Courthouse, 200 West Compton Boulevard, Compton 90220.

Telephone: (310) 603-7842.

DREW, Stephen *(Judge, Superior Court of California County of Tulare)* Assumed office July 27, 1998. Elected 2000, current term expires Jan 2007. Born Visalia California Aug 6, 1947. Catholic. Educated at Reedley College A.A. 1967 and University of San Francisco B.A. 1969 J.D. 1972. Admitted to practice California 1972. In legal practice Dinuba 1975. Judge May 1978 to July 26, 1998 and Former Presiding Judge, Tulare County Municipal Court.

With Tulare County District Attorney's Office 1973-75. Member State Bar of California and Tulare County Bar Association.

Office: 640 South Alta Avenue, Dinuba 93618.

Telephone: (559) 591-5815.

DROZD, Dale A. *(Magistrate Judge, United States District Court Eastern District of California)* Appointed by U.S. District Court judges to term beginning 1997. Term expires 2005. Born Long Beach California 1955. Educated at University of Southern California 1973-75, California State University at San Diego B.A. 1977 and University of California at Los Angeles J.D. 1980. Law Clerk to Hon. Lawrence K. Karlton, U.S. District Court Eastern District of California 1980-82. In legal practice San Francisco 1982-85 and Sacramento 1986-97.

Office: 8-200 U.S. Courthouse, 501 I Street, Sacramento 95814-2322.

Telephone: (916) 930-4210.

DUFFICY, Michael B. *(Judge, Superior Court of California County of Marin)* Presiding Judge May 1, 1998 to May 1, 2000. Former Judge, Marin County Municipal Court.

Mailing address: P.O. Box 4988, San Rafael 94913-4988.

Office: Hall of Justice, 3501 Civic Center Drive, San Rafael 94903.

Telephone: (415) 499-6407.

DUFFY, Michael L. *(Judge, Superior Court of California County of San Luis Obispo)* Presiding Judge Dec 4, 1995 to Dec 1, 1996. Former Judge, San Luis Obispo County Municipal Court.
Office: County Government Center, 1035 Palm Street, San Luis Obispo 93408-2500.
Telephone: (805) 781-5421.

DUFFY, Wendy Clark *(Judge, Superior Court of California County of Monterey)* Presiding Judge Jan 1, 1997 to Dec 31, 1997 and Former Judge, Monterey County Municipal Court.
Mailing address: P.O. Box 1819, Salinas 93902-1819.
Office: 240 Church Street, Salinas 93901.
Telephone: (831) 755-5060.

DUFFY-LEWIS, Maureen *(Judge, Superior Court of California County of Los Angeles)* Educated at University of Southern California B.A. 1971 and Loyola University School of Law J.D. 1974. Former Judge, Los Angeles Municipal Court Los Angeles County, appointed by Governor George Deukmejian Aug 1987.
Office: Criminal Courts Building, 210 West Temple Street, Los Angeles 90012-3210.
Telephone: (213) 974-6535.

DUGAN, L. Becky *(Judge, Superior Court of California County of Riverside)* Commissioner 1987-99. Elected Nov 1998 to term beginning Jan 3, 1999. Term expires Jan 3, 2005. Born Columbus Ohio April 22, 1955. Educated at California State University at Los Angeles B.A. M.A. and Western State University College of Law J.D. Admitted to practice California 1980. In legal practice Westminster 1980-85.
Deputy Public Defender 1985-87. In re: Marriage of Moss 1998. Instructor Western State University 1982-84 and University of Southern California School of Law 1988-98. Member California Judges Association and Riverside County Bar Association.
Office: Hall of Justice, 4100 Main Street, Riverside 92501.
Telephone: (909) 955-2300.

DUGGAN, Michael M. *(Judge, Superior Court of California County of Los Angeles)* Assumed office Jan 22, 2000. Presiding Judge Jan 1, 1995 to Dec 31, 1996 and Former Judge, Citrus Municipal Court Los Angeles County.
Office: West Covina Courthouse, 1427 West Covina Parkway, West Covina 91790.
Telephone: (626) 813-3223.

DUKES, Robert A. *(Judge, Superior Court of California County of Los Angeles)* Appointed by Governor George Deukmejian to term beginning March 24, 1989. Elected 1990, 1996 and 2002. Current term expires Jan 2009. Presiding Judge since Jan 1, 2003. Born Pomona California Sept 25, 1948. Educated at University of Redlands B.A. 1970 and Southwestern University School of Law J.D. 1976. Admitted to practice California 1977. In legal practice Pasadena and Covina 1980-87. Judge, Pomona Municipal Court Los Angeles County 1987-89.
Former Member Judicial Council of California.
Office: 111 North Hill Street, Los Angeles 90012.
Telephone: (213) 974-5600.

DUNCAN, Terrance R. *(Judge, Superior Court of California County of Monterey)* Assumed office Dec 18, 2000. Presiding Judge since Jan 1, 2003. Born San Francisco California Aug 17, 1941. Educated at University of San Francisco B.A. 1963 J.D. 1966. Admitted to practice California 1969. In legal practice Seaside 1979-82. Court Commissioner 1982-95. Judge, Monterey County Municipal Court 1995-2000.
Staff Attorney Merced Legal Services Association 1969-71. Assistant Public Defender Monterey County 1971-79. Faculty Member Trial Advocacy Program Stanford Law School since 1996. Member Advisory Committee on Traffic Courts Judicial Council of California 1992-94. Former Member California Court Commissioners Association (Board of Directors 1983-87 and 1989-95, First Vice President 1984-86, President 1987-89). Member California Judges Association (Executive Board 1989-92, Secretary-Treasurer 1991-92). Faculty Member California Judicial College 1992-96. Member New Judge Education Planning Committee 1994-96, Faculty Member New Judge Education Program since 1994 and Co-ordinator Mentor Judge Program California Center for Judicial Education and Research. Peace Corps Volunteer Ecuador 1966-68. Board of Directors 1983-91 and President 1987-89 Beacon House Alcohol Recovery Center Pacific Grove California. Board of Directors Sports Car Racing Association of the Monterey Peninsula 1984-91. Chair Monterey County Alcoholism Advisory Board 1986. Member since 1987 and President 1996 Kiwanis' Club of Monterey. Co-founder and President Monterey County Sober Graduation Program since 1988. President Board of Trustees Monterey College of Law since 2001. Enjoys playing tennis and skiing.
Mailing address: P.O. Box 1819, Salinas 93902-1819.
Office: 240 Church Street, Salinas 93901.
Telephone: (831) 755-5060.

DUNN, James R. *(Judge, Superior Court of California County of Los Angeles)*
Office: Los Angeles County Courthouse, 111 North Hill Street, Los Angeles 90012.
Telephone: (213) 974-5629.

DUNN, Leslie A. *(Judge, Superior Court of California County of Los Angeles)* Assumed office Jan 22, 2000. Former Judge, Los Angeles Municipal Court Los Angeles County.
Office: Van Nuys Courthouse West, 14400 Erwin Street Mall, Van Nuys 91401-2705.
Telephone: (818) 374-2601.

DUNNING, Kim Garlin *(Judge, Superior Court of California County of Orange)*
Mailing address: P.O. Box 1994, Santa Ana 92702-1994.
Office: Central Justice Center, 700 Civic Center Drive West, Santa Ana 92701.
Telephone: (714) 834-3734.

DUPRAS, Fred *(Judge, Superior Court of California County of Fresno)* Assumed office July 1, 1998. Elected 2002, current term expires Jan 2009. Born Detroit Michigan Aug 4, 1939. Catholic. Educated at Humphreys College of Law J.D. Admitted to practice California 1976. Began legal practice Fresno 1976. Judge, Central Valley Municipal Court Fresno County Jan 7, 1985 to June 30, 1998. Served Reedley-Dunlap Division.
Instructor Humphreys College of Law since 1979. First Sergeant U.S. Army 1957-63. Republican. Member Lions Club.
Office: 815 G Street, Reedley 93654.
Telephone: (559) 638-3114.

DURYEE, Lynn *(Judge, Superior Court of California County of Marin)* Assumed office June 11, 1998. Former Judge, Marin County Municipal Court, appointed by Governor Pete Wilson June 7, 1993.
Mailing address: P.O. Box 4988, San Rafael 94913-4988.
Office: Hall of Justice, 3501 Civic Center Drive, San Rafael 94903.
Telephone: (415) 499-6407.

Du TEMPLE, Eric L. *(Judge, Superior Court of California County of Tuolumne)* Presiding Judge since Jan 1, 1999.
Office: Historic Courthouse, 41 West Yaney Avenue, Sonora 95370.
Telephone: (209) 533-6504.

DYLINA, Steven L. *(Judge, Superior Court of California County of San Mateo)*
Office: Hall of Justice, 400 County Center, Redwood City 94063.
Telephone: (650) 363-4516.

DYMANT, Anita H. *(Judge, Superior Court of California County of Los Angeles)* Assumed office Jan 22, 2000. Elected Nov 2000, current term expires Jan 2007. Born New York New York Aug 8, 1949. Educated at Brandeis University B.A. with honors 1971 and University of Illinois J.D. 1974. Admitted to practice Illinois 1974, District of Columbia 1975, California 1976 and U.S. District Court Central District of California 1980. In legal practice Ventura California 1976-78. Judge, Los Angeles Municipal Court Los Angeles County Jan 24, 1992 to Jan 21, 2000, appointed by Governor Pete Wilson.
Assistant U.S. Attorney Los Angeles 1981-92. Member Municipal Court Judges Association (Chair Domestic Violence Committee 1997-2000), California Judges Association, National Association of Women Judges and American Judicature Society. Recipient Commendation from U.S. Department of Justice 1988.
Office: Criminal Courts Building, 210 West Temple Street, Los Angeles 90012-3210.
Telephone: (213) 974-5741.

EATON, Merle R. *(Judge, Superior Court of California County of Contra Costa)* Assumed office June 8, 1998. Presiding Judge Jan 1, 1997 to Dec 31, 1997 and Former Judge, Walnut Creek-Danville Municipal Court Contra Costa County.
Mailing address: P.O. Box 5128, Walnut Creek 94596.
Office: 640 Ygnacio Valley Road, Walnut Creek 94596.
Telephone: (925) 646-6763.

EDMON, Lee Smalley *(Judge, Superior Court of California County of Los Angeles)*
Office: Criminal Courts Building, 210 West Temple Street, Los Angeles 90012-3210.
Telephone: (213) 974-6535.

EDWARDS, Anthony C. *(Judge, Superior Court of California County of Trinity)* Assumed office July 1, 1998. Presiding Judge since Jan 1, 2002. Former Judge, Trinity County Municipal Court.
Mailing address: P.O. Box 1258, Weaverville 96093.
Office: 101 Court Street, Weaverville 96093.
Telephone: (530) 623-1208.

EDWARDS, Ersel L. *(Judge, Superior Court of California County of Nevada)* Presiding Judge Superior and Municipal Courts Jan 1, 1997 to Dec 31, 1997. Former Judge and Presiding Judge, Nevada County Municipal Court.
Office: 201 Church Street, Nevada City 95959-2504.
Telephone: (530) 265-1311.

EDWARDS, James A. *(Judge, Superior Court of California County of San Bernardino)* Former Presiding Judge. Born Long Beach California July 16, 1943. Educated at University of Southern California B.A. 1965 and California Western School of Law J.D. 1968. Staff member California Western Law Review 1967-68. Member Phi Alpha Delta. Admitted to practice California 1969. Began legal practice San Bernardino 1969. Judge, Yucaipa Justice Court 1973-78. Judge, Highland-Yucaipa Justice Court 1978-79. Judge, San Bernardino County Municipal Court East Division 1979-86.
Member California Judges Association (Executive Board 1978-79). Faculty member Continuing Judicial Studies Program California Center for Judicial Education and Research 1983-87.
Office: 351 North Arrowhead Avenue, San Bernardino 92415-0240.
Telephone: (909) 387-3922.

EDWARDS, Leonard P. *(Judge, Superior Court of California County of Santa Clara)*
Office: 115 Terraine Street, San Jose 95113.
Telephone: (408) 491-4700.

EDWARDS, Raymond, Jr. *(Judge, Superior Court of California County of San Diego)* Former Judge, San Diego Municipal Court San Diego County.
Mailing address: P.O. Box 122724, San Diego 92112-2724.
Office: 500 Third Avenue, Chula Vista 91910.
Telephone: (619) 691-4770.

EDWARDS, Thomas C. *(Judge, Superior Court of California County of Santa Clara)* Appointed by Governor George Deukmejian to term beginning Dec 14, 1989. Elected 1990, 1996 and 2002. Current term expires Jan 2009. Supervising Judge Juvenile Delinquency 1992-93 and 1995. Presiding Judge Juvenile Court 1996-97. Judge Community Truancy Court since 1994. Judge Juvenile Treatment Court since 1996. Born Urbana Illinois May 8, 1944. Educated at Harvard University B.A. with honors 1969 and Santa Clara University School of Law J.D. 1975. Admitted to practice California 1975, U.S. District Court Northern District of California 1976, U.S. Court of Appeals Ninth Circuit 1976 and U.S. Supreme Court 1979. In legal practice San Jose 1975-89.
Instructor in Trial Techniques 1992, Juvenile Court Law 1995-96 and Moot Court 1996 Santa Clara University School of Law. Lecturer School of Administration of Justice San Jose State University 1996. Associate Member Santa Clara County Peace Officers Association since 1992. Member Superior Court Executive Committee 1994 and 1997, Santa Clara County Juvenile Justice Coordinating Council, California Juvenile Officers Association, California Judges Association, American Judges Association and Santa Clara County Bar Association. Instructor in Escrow Law California Continuing Education of the Bar 1990. Faculty Hastings College of Advocacy since 1991, Continuing Judicial Studies Program California Center for Judicial Education and Research since 1993, Advocacy Skills Workshop Stanford Law School

EDWARDS, THOMAS C.—*Continued*
since 1996. Lecturer "Corporate Criminal Liability" BOMA 1992, "Fitness Hearings" 1992 and "The California Youth Authority" 1995 Santa Clara County Bar Association and California Crime Prevention Officers Association Convention 1996. Panelist Santa Clara County Juvenile Justice Conference 1992. Recipient Resolution of Commendation from Santa Clara County Board of Supervisors 1996. Republican. Board of Directors 1991-93 and Advisory Council since 1995 San Jose Conservation Corps. Member San Jose Gang Task Force since 1993. Advisory Board Positive Alternatives for Youth since 1997. Enjoys backpacking, skiing, playing tennis and reading.
Office: 191 North First Street, San Jose 95113.
Telephone: (408) 882-2100.

EGERTON, Anne Harwood *(Judge, Superior Court of California County of Los Angeles)*
Office: Courthouse, 111 North Hill Street, Los Angeles 90012.
Telephone: (213) 974-5411.

EICK, Charles F. *(Magistrate Judge, United States District Court Central District of California)* Appointed by U.S. District Court judges.
Office: U.S. Courthouse, 312 North Spring Street, Los Angeles 90012.
Telephone: (213) 894-2964.

EINHORN, John S. *(Judge, Superior Court of California County of San Diego)* Appointed by Governor Pete Wilson Sept 1995 to term beginning Oct 1995. Currently serves as Assistant Presiding Judge.
Mailing address: P.O. Box 122724, San Diego 92112-2724.
Office: 220 West Broadway, San Diego 92101.
Telephone: (619) 531-3590.
E-mail address: John.Einhorn@sdcourt.ca.gov

ELFVING, William J. *(Judge, Superior Court of California County of Santa Clara)*
Office: 191 North First Street, San Jose 95113.
Telephone: (408) 882-2120.

ELIA, Franklin D. *(Associate Justice, California Court of Appeal Sixth District)* Appointed by Governor George Deukmejian to term beginning Oct 1988. Retained by election 1990 and Nov 2002. Current term expires Jan 2015. Born July 7, 1950. Educated at Santa Clara University 1972 J.D. 1975. Admitted to practice California 1975. Judge, Santa Clara County Municipal Court 1983-86, appointed by Governor George Deukmejian. Judge, Superior Court of California Santa Clara County 1986-88.
Deputy Attorney General Sacramento and San Francisco and Deputy District Attorney Sacramento 1975-80. Senior Assistant City Attorney Palo Alto 1980-83. Adjunct Professor of Law Santa Clara University. Chief Counsel Committee on Moral Character State Bar of California. Former Member Santa Clara County Bar Association. Member Appellate Indigent Defense Oversight Committee and Standing Subcommittee on Appellate Courts Judicial Council of California. Participant Trial Training Program Stanford University Law School. Member Appellate Advisory Committee Santa Clara University Law School.
Office: 333 West Santa Clara Street, Suite 1060, San Jose 95113.
Telephone: (408) 494-2507.

ELIAS, Emilie Harris *(Judge, Superior Court of California County of Los Angeles)*
Office: Courthouse, 111 North Hill Street, Los Angeles 90012.
Telephone: (213) 974-5411.

ELIAS, Harry M. *(Judge, Superior Court of California County of San Diego)* Assumed office Dec 1, 1998. Elected 2002, current term expires Jan 1, 2009. Born Detroit Michigan April 29, 1950. Educated at University of Michigan B.A. 1972 and University of San Diego J.D. 1975. Admitted to practice California 1975 and U.S. District Court Southern District of California 1975. In legal practice La Mesa 1975-76 and El Cajon 1976. Judge Jan 4, 1991 to Nov 30, 1998 and Former Presiding Judge, North County Municipal Court San Diego County, appointed by Governor George Deukmejian.
Deputy District Attorney San Diego County 1976-90. Member American Judicature Society, California Judges Association and American Bar Association.
Mailing address: P.O. Box 122724, San Diego 92112-2724.
Office: 325 South Melrose Drive, Vista 92083.
Telephone: (760) 726-9595.

ELLER, Stan *(Judge, Superior Court of California County of Mono)* Appointed by Governor Pete Wilson to term beginning Dec 28, 1999. Elected March 7, 2000, current term expires Jan 1, 2006. Born Reno Nevada Aug 8, 1949. Educated at San Diego State University A.B. in Economics with honors 1971 and University of San Diego School of Law J.D. 1974. Admitted to practice California 1974 and U.S. District Court Southern District of California 1974.
Public Defender San Diego County 1975-81. Deputy District Attorney and District Attorney Mono County 1982-99. Board of Directors California District Attorney's Association 1996-98. Member Mono County Bar Association. Recipient Golden Trout Award from California Trout 1991 and Wildlife Conservation Award from California Department of Fish and Game 1994. Democrat. Member Youth Soccer and Parent Teacher Organization. Enjoys skiing, hiking and mountain biking.
Mailing address: P.O. Box 1037, Mammoth Lakes 93546.
Office: 452 Old Mammoth Road, Mammoth Lakes 93546.
Telephone: (760) 924-5444.

ELLIS, H. James *(Judge, Superior Court of California County of San Mateo)* Presiding Judge Jan 1, 1999 to Dec 31, 1999. Former Judge, San Mateo County Municipal Court.
Office: Hall of Justice, 400 County Center, Redwood City 94063.
Telephone: (650) 363-4516.

ELLISON, Laura *(Judge, Superior Court of California County of Los Angeles)* Assumed office Jan 22,

ELLISON, LAURA—*Continued*
2000. Serves Southwest District. Former Judge, South Bay Municipal Court Los Angeles County.
Office: Torrance Courthouse, 825 Maple Avenue, Torrance 90503.
Telephone: (310) 222-8808.

ELLISON, Wayne R. *(Judge, Superior Court of California County of Fresno)*
Office: Courthouse, 1100 Van Ness Avenue, Fresno 93724-0002.
Telephone: (559) 488-1825.

ELSWICK, Carol Williams *(Judge, Superior Court of California County of Los Angeles)* Assumed office Jan 22, 2000. Former Judge, Citrus Municipal Court Los Angeles County.
Office: West Covina Courthouse, 1427 West Covina Parkway, West Covina 91790.
Telephone: (626) 813-3223.

ELWELL, Douglas M. *(Judge, Superior Court of California County of San Bernardino)* Assumed office Aug 10, 1998. Serves East Division. Former Judge, San Bernardino County Municipal Court.
Office: 216 Brookside Avenue, Redlands 92373.
Telephone: (909) 798-8552.

EMERSON, James C. *(Judge, Superior Court of California County of Santa Clara)* Appointed by Governor Pete Wilson to term beginning March 7, 1993. Elected to subsequent term. Born San Mateo California April 25, 1948. Educated at University of California at Berkeley A.B. 1970 and Santa Clara University J.D. 1973. Admitted to practice California 1973, U.S. District Courts Northern 1973 and Eastern 1976 Districts of California and U.S. Court of Appeals Ninth Circuit 1973. In legal practice San Jose 1974-85. Judge, Santa Clara County Municipal Court Jan 4, 1990 to March 6, 1993, appointed by Governor George Deukmejian.
Deputy County Counsel Santa Clara County 1985-90. Chairman Domestic Violence Council Conference and Public Information Subcommittee since 1994. Member California Judges Association (Election Committee 1991-92). Presenter "Recent Developments in Family Law" Continuing Education of the Bar Dec 1994. Board of Visitors Santa Clara University School of Law since 1993. Enjoys aquatic sports, skiing, golfing, traveling, cooking and music.
Office: Hall of Justice East Wing, 190 West Hedding Street, San Jose 95110.
Telephone: (408) 808-6600.

ENGLAND, Morrison C., Jr. *(Judge, United States District Court Eastern District of California)* Appointed for life by President George W. Bush to term beginning Aug 2, 2002. Born St. Louis Missouri Dec 17, 1954. Educated at University of the Pacific B.A. 1977 J.D. 1983. Admitted to practice California 1983. In legal practice Sacramento 1983-96. Judge, Sacramento Municipal Court Sacramento County Aug 15, 1996 to Aug 20, 1997, appointed by Governor Pete Wilson. USAR JAGC. Judge, Superior Court of California County of Sacramento Aug 21, 1997 to Aug 1, 2002, appointed by Governor Pete Wilson.
Office: U.S. Courthouse, 501 I Street, Sacramento 95814-2322.
Telephone: (916) 930-4000.

ENRIGHT, Kevin A. *(Judge, Superior Court of California County of San Diego)* Appointed by Governor Pete Wilson Aug 21, 1997. Born San Diego California April 23, 1953. Educated at Stanford University B.A. 1975 and McGeorge School of Law University of the Pacific J.D. 1979. Admitted to practice California 1979, U.S. District Courts Northern 1979 and Southern 1985 Districts of California and U.S. Supreme Court 1988. In legal practice San Diego 1985-95. Judge, San Diego Municipal Court San Diego County March 8, 1995 to Aug 20, 1997, appointed by Governor Pete Wilson.
Deputy District Attorney Mendocino County 1979-84. Barrister Louis M. Welsh Chapter American Inns of Court 1985-87. Board of Directors Greater San Diego County Barristers Club 1987-88, California Defense Counsel 1994-95, Association of Southern California Defense Counsel 1994-95 and San Diego Inn of Court since 1995. Member Superior Court Committee 1989-92 and Justice System Funding Committee 1994 San Diego County Bar Association. Delegate State Bar of California Conference of Delegates 1991. Board of Directors 1991-93 and President 1993 San Diego Defense Lawyers. Master William B. Enright Chapter American Inns of Court since 1998. Board of Governors San Diego Association of Business Trial Lawyers since 2000. Member San Diego County Judges Association and California Judges Association. Workshop Leader San Diego Inn of Court 1989-94. Speaker "Fast Track Litigation: Arbitration" Judges Orientation/Bridging-the-Gap Program 1990. Instructor National Institute of Trial Advocacy 1994. Moderator "A View from the Bench" Annual Seminar Association of Southern California Defense Counsel 1995. Seminar Leader B. E. Witkin Judicial College of California 1996. Faculty Municipal Courts Institute 1997 and Retired Judges Institute 1997 California Center for Judicial Education and Research. Member Stanford Club of San Diego and Rotary Club of San Diego.
Mailing address: P.O. Box 122724, San Diego 92112-2724.
Office: 330 West Broadway, San Diego 92101.
Telephone: (619) 685-6148.

ENRIGHT, William B. *(Senior Judge, United States District Court Southern District of California)* Appointed for life by President Richard M. Nixon to term beginning July 14, 1972. Assumed Senior status July 12, 1990, serves by assignment. Born New York New York July 1925. Educated at La Salle Academy, Dartmouth College A.B. 1947 and Loyola University LL.B. 1950. Admitted to practice California 1951. In legal practice San Diego 1954-72.
Deputy District Attorney San Diego County 1951-54. Author "California's Aggravated Kidnapping Statute—A Need for Revision" San Diego L. Rev. June 1967 and "The Much Maligned Criminal Lawyer" 46 State B. Jour. 720 Dec 1971. Fellow American College of Trial Lawyers and American Bar Foundation. Diplomate American Board of Trial Advocates. Member Operation of the Jury System since 1977, Defenders, Incorporated (Board of Directors 1965-72 and President 1972), Advisory Board Joint Legislative Committee for Revision of the Penal Code 1970-72, California Board of Legal Specialization 1970-72, Judicial Council 1972, State Bar of California (Board of Governors 1967-70, Special Committee on Criminal Justice 1970-72 and Executive Committee, Law in a Free Society since 1970) and San Diego County Bar Association (Board of Directors 1963-65 and President 1965). Ensign USN 1943-46. Former

ENRIGHT, WILLIAM B.—*Continued*

member United Crusade, Big Brothers, Little League, Urban Coalition and St. Stephen's Group Home Organization. Member Board of Trustees San Diego County Law Library and Justice Foundation 1965-72 and Rotary Club of San Diego.

Office: 4145 U.S. Courthouse, 940 Front Street, San Diego 92101-8903.

Telephone: (619) 557-5537.

EPSTEIN, Norman L. *(Associate Justice, California Court of Appeal Second District Division Four)* Appointed by Governor George Deukmejian to term beginning April 1990. Retained by election. Born Los Angeles California April 9, 1933. Educated at University of California Los Angeles B.A. 1955 LL.B. 1958. Honorary LL.D. University of West Los Angeles 1992 and California State University 1999. Member Phi Alpha Delta. Admitted to practice California 1959 and U.S. Supreme Court 1970. Began legal practice Los Angeles 1959. Judge, Los Angeles Municipal Court Los Angeles County Jan 1975 to March 1980. Judge, Superior Court of California Los Angeles County 1980-90.

Former Deputy Attorney General California. Former Vice Chancellor and General Counsel California State University and Colleges. Author "Digest of California Criminal Cases" CEB 1976-79 and "Case and Commentary" California Judges Association since 1979. Co-author with B. E. Witkin *California Criminal Law* 3rd ed. Bancroft-Whitney Company 2000 and "Civil Trial and Evidence" The Rutter Group. Important Decisions: Chadwick v. Superior Court 106 Cal. App. 3d 108, 164 CR 864, 1980; People v. Camp 104 Cal. App. 3d 244, 163 CR 510, 1980; Rosenfeld, Meyer & Susman v. Cohen 19 Cal. App. 3d 1035, 1987; Commercial National Bank v. Superior Court 14 Cal. App. 4th 393, 1993; Rifkind v. Superior Court 22 Cal. App. 4th 1255, 1994; Los Angeles Electric v. Superior Court 22 Cal. App. 4th 426, 1994; and Ziello v. Superior Court 36 Cal. App. 4th 321, 1995. Lecturer University of Southern California Law Center. Member Committee on California Jury Instructions—Criminal (CALJIC) and Committee on California Jury Instructions—Civil (BAJI) 1979-90. Member National Association of College and University Attorneys (President 1973-74), The American Law Institute, Los Angeles County (Chair ad hoc Committee on Discovery 1985-86) and American (House of Delegates 1976) Bar Associations. Dean California Judicial College 1981-83. Lecturer CEB, California Judges Association, State Bar of California, Los Angeles County Bar Association and The Rutter Group. Named UCLA Law Alumnus of the Year 1970. Recipient Bernard Jefferson Award for Judicial Education 1982 and 1998, President's Award from California Judges Association and Bernard Witkin Medal from State Bar of California. Member Neighborhood Justice Center and UCLA Law Alumni Association (President 1976-77). Enjoys legal writing and biking.

Office: 300 South Spring Street, Los Angeles 90013.

Telephone: (213) 830-7438.

ERICKSON, Mary Fingal *(Judge, Superior Court of California County of Orange)* Assumed office Aug 10, 1998. Educated at California State University at Fullerton B.A. 1974 and University of California at Davis J.D. 1977. Admitted to practice California 1977, U.S. District Courts Central, Eastern, Northern and Southern Districts of California and U.S. Supreme Court. In legal practice Newport Beach Jan 1984 to Feb 1987 and Santa Ana Feb 1987 to Sept 1997. Judge, Orange County Municipal Court Aug 25, 1997 to Aug 9, 1998, appointed by Governor Pete Wilson.

Deputy District Attorney Orange County March 1978 to Jan 1981. Author "What Does a Municipal Court Judge Do Anyway? or, How I Survived the First 6 Months" *The Gavel* Orange County Trial Lawyers Association Spring 1998. Master Bencher since 1998 and Member Board of Directors since 2000 Banyard Inns of Court. Member Outreach Committee Orange County Superior Court since 1999 and Advisory Council Court Referral Program since 2000. Member St. Thomas More Society (Executive Committee since 1999), California Judges Association, Orange County Asian American, Orange County Hispanic and Orange County Bar Associations. Lecturer on "California Construction Law: What Do You Do When . . . ?" National Business Institute Anaheim Nov 15, 1996 and "Causation: Winning the Battle—Losing the War" Consumers Attorneys Association of Los Angeles Marina del Rey 1997. Lecturer/Panelist on "Voir Dire" Cabo San Lucas May 1999 and "Ethics in the Courtroom" Puerto Vallarta May 2000 Mexico Orange County Hispanic Bar Association Seminar. Participant Orange County Superior Court Judges' Educational Conference San Diego Oct 27-28, 2000 and Oct 25-28, 2001; "Court Management for Presiding Judges and Court Executive Officers" Long Beach Nov 2000; Mid-Year Conference California Judges Association Palm Springs 2000; and Criminal Law and Procedure Institute Continuing Judicial Studies Program Long Beach Feb 15-17, 2001. Panelist on "A Lawyer's Professional Responsibility: The Lawyer of the Millennium's Perspective—Lawyer as Servant" Thomas More Seminar Jan 27, 2001 and "Mock Direct and Cross Examinations" Robert Banyard Inn of Court March 2001. Mock Trial Coach Constitutional Rights Foundation 1999-2000. Chair Commission on Ecumenism and Interreligious Affairs Roman Catholic Diocese of Orange since 2000.

Office: West Justice Center, 8141 Thirteenth Street, Westminster 92683.

Telephone: (714) 896-7181.

E-mail address: merickson@occourts.org

ERVIN, Charles *(Judge, Superior Court of California County of San Diego)*

Mailing address: P.O. Box 122724, San Diego 92112-2724.

Office: 250 East Main Street, El Cajon 92020.

Telephone: (619) 441-4336.

ESGRO, Patricia C. *(Judge, Superior Court of California County of Sacramento)* Assumed office June 17, 1998. Former Judge, Sacramento Municipal Court Sacramento County.

Office: Courthouse, 720 Ninth Street, Sacramento 95814.

Telephone: (916) 874-5476.

ESPINOSA, Ruffo, Jr. *(Judge, Superior Court of California County of Los Angeles)* Assumed office Jan 22, 2000. Former Judge and Presiding Judge, Southeast Municipal Court Los Angeles County.

Office: Criminal Courts Building, 210 West Temple Street, Los Angeles 90012-3210.

Telephone: (213) 974-6535.

ESPINOZA, Peter Paul *(Judge, Superior Court of California County of Los Angeles)* Presiding Judge Jan 1, 1995 to Dec 31, 1996 and Former Judge, Southeast Municipal Court Los Angeles County.
Office: Norwalk Courthouse, 12720 Norwalk Boulevard, Norwalk 90650.
Telephone: (562) 807-7266.

ESSEGIAN, Ruth *(Judge, Superior Court of California County of Los Angeles)* Assumed office Jan 22, 2000. Former Judge, Los Angeles Municipal Court Los Angeles County.
Office: Van Nuys Courthouse East, 6230 Sylmar Avenue, Van Nuys 91401.
Telephone: (818) 374-3108.

ESTES, Christopher *(Judge, Superior Court of California County of Los Angeles).*
Office: Lancaster Courthouse, 1040 West Avenue J, Lancaster 93534.
Telephone: (661) 945-6477.

ESTRADA-MULLANEY, Teresa *(Judge, Superior Court of California County of San Luis Obispo)* Former Judge, San Luis Obispo County Municipal Court.
Office: County Government Center, 1035 Palm Street, San Luis Obispo 93408-2500.
Telephone: (805) 781-5421.

EVANS, Timothy J. *(Judge, Superior Court of California County of Sutter)* Elected to term beginning Jan 3, 1989. Reelected to subsequent terms. Presiding Judge Jan 1, 1996 to Dec 31, 1997. Born Oakland California March 30, 1943. Catholic. Educated at University of California at Davis A.B. 1965 and Hastings College of the Law J.D. with honors 1968. Member Thurston Society and Order of the Coif. Admitted to practice California 1969 and U.S. Supreme Court 1976. Certified Specialist Criminal Law. Began legal practice Marysville 1969. Judge, Sutter County Municipal Court 1979-88.
Member California Trial Lawyers Association 1974-78 and Board of Trustees CRLA 1972-78. Active in Little League. Enjoys skiing, jogging and swimming.
Office: 446 Second Street, Yuba City 95991.
Telephone: (530) 822-7360.

EVANS, William Lee *(Judge, Superior Court of California County of Orange)* Assumed office Aug 10, 1998. Former Judge, Central Orange County Municipal Court.
Mailing address: P.O. Box 1994, Santa Ana 92702-1994.
Office: Central Justice Center, 700 Civic Center Drive West, Santa Ana 92701.
Telephone: (714) 834-3734.

EXARHOS, Herbert J. *(Judge, Superior Court of California County of San Diego)* Appointed by Governor George Deukmejian to term beginning Sept 29, 1987. Elected 1988, 1994 and 2000. Current term expires Jan 2007. Born Kansas City Missouri Dec 26, 1942. Episcopalian. Educated at California Western University B.S. 1962 J.D. 1965. Member Phi Alpha Delta. Admitted to practice California 1966. Began legal practice San Diego 1970. Judge, San Diego Municipal Court San Diego County Sept 6, 1983 to Sept 28, 1987, appointed by Governor George Deukmejian.
Instructor Western State University College of Law since 1976. Captain USAR JAGC 1966-70.
Mailing address: P.O. Box 122724, San Diego 92112-2724.
Office: 250 East Main Street, El Cajon 92020.
Telephone: (619) 441-4336.

FAHEY, William F. *(Judge, Superior Court of California County of Los Angeles)*
Office: Criminal Courts Building, 210 West Temple Street, Los Angeles 90012-3210.
Telephone: (213) 974-6535.

FAIN, Gregory T. *(Judge, Superior Court of California County of Fresno)* Serves Juvenile Delinquency Court.
Office: 742 South Tenth Street, Fresno 93702.
Telephone: (559) 455-5195.

FAIRWELL, Robert *(Judge, Superior Court of California County of Alameda)* Assumed office July 31, 1998. Former Judge, San Leandro-Hayward Municipal Court Alameda County.
Office: Hayward Hall of Justice, 24405 Amador Street, Hayward 94544.
Telephone: (510) 670-5060.

FALCONE, Dewey Lawes *(Judge, Superior Court of California County of Los Angeles)*
Office: Norwalk Courthouse, 12720 Norwalk Boulevard, Norwalk 90650.
Telephone: (562) 807-7266.

FALL, Greta *(Judge, Superior Court of California County of Sacramento)*
Office: Courthouse, 720 Ninth Street, Sacramento 95814.
Telephone: (916) 874-5476.

FALL, Timothy L. *(Judge, Superior Court of California County of Yolo)* Assumed office June 3, 1998. Assistant Presiding Judge 1998. Presiding Judge Jan 1, 1999 to Dec 31, 1999. Serves Family Law Department. Educated at Skyline College A.A. 1981, Sussex University, England 1983-84, University of California at Santa Barbara B.A. with honors 1984 and University of California at Davis School of Law J.D. 1987. In legal practice Sacramento 1987-95. Former Judge, Yolo County Municipal Court.
Member Yolo County Criminal Justice Cabinet 1998 and Subcommittee on Quality of Judicial Service Judicial Task Force on Quality of Justice 1998-99 and Task Force on Judicial Service since 2001 Judicial Council of California. Former Member Sacramento County, Yolo County (Treasurer 1994, Executive Committee 1994-95, Secretary 1995, Chair Bench/Bar Committee 1995) and American Bar Associations. Member California Judges Association (Discipline Committee 1997-99, Ethics Committee since 2001). Lecturer on U.S. Constitution to international lawyers University of California at Davis Extension School of Law USA Law Program since 1993. Attended National Symposium on Drug Courts American University 1995, Workplace Sexual Harassment Awareness and Prevention Shasta County Superior Court Pilot Program 1997 and Leading Organizational Change 1998 California Center for Judicial Education and Research/JAIC; Symposium on Judicial Independence and Accountability University of Southern California 1998, Death Penalty Trials 1998 and Literature and Judicial Reasoning 1999 Continuing Judicial Studies Program;

FALL, TIMOTHY L.—*Continued*

California Conference of Presiding Judges 1999, Probate and Mental Health Institute 1999 and Family Law and Procedure Institute 1999 California Center for Judicial Education and Research; and California Judicial Administration Conference 1999. Participant Jurisprudence and Contemporary Issues 2000, Crime and Punishment 2001, Curriculum Committee on Judicial Decision-Making 2001 and Family Law Overview 2002 and Faculty Court Management 2000 Continuing Judicial Studies Program California Center for Judicial Education and Research. Speaker on the court and judiciary City of Winters, Winters High School Youth Day Program, Davis Rotary and Woodland Kiwanis. Sunday School Teacher, Past Elder and Worship Leader First Baptist Church. Assistant Coach in-line hockey, soccer, T-Ball and Little League.

Office: 725 Court Street, Woodland 95695.
Telephone: (530) 666-8598.
Fax: (530) 666-8576
E-mail address: tfall@yolocourts.com

FALLS, Thomas *(Judge, Superior Court of California County of Los Angeles)* Assumed office Jan 22, 2000. Former Judge, Citrus Municipal Court Los Angeles County.

Office: West Covina Courthouse, 1427 West Covina Parkway, West Covina 91790.
Telephone: (626) 813-3223.

FARRAR, Dean E. *(Judge, Superior Court of California County of Los Angeles)* Assumed office Jan 22, 2000. Former Judge, Compton Municipal Court Los Angeles County.

Office: Lynwood Regional Justice Center, 11701 Alameda Street, Lynwood 90262.
Telephone: (323) 357-5000.

FARRELL, John P. *(Judge, Superior Court of California County of Los Angeles)* Appointed by Governor George Deukmejian Oct 4, 1987. Elected Nov 1988, 1994 and 2000. Current term expires Jan 2007. Born New York New York March 16, 1941. Catholic. Educated at Loyola University of Los Angeles B.A. magna cum laude 1962, University of California at Los Angeles M.A. 1965 and Yale Law School J.D. 1966. Admitted to practice California 1967. In legal practice Century City and Los Angeles 1980-86.

Deputy County Counsel Los Angeles County 1970-80 and 1986-87.

Office: San Fernando Courthouse, 900 Third Street, San Fernando 91340.
Telephone: (818) 898-2655.

FARRELL, Michael J. *(Judge, Superior Court of California County of Los Angeles)* Appointed by Governor George Deukmejian to term beginning Jan 1989. Elected June 1990, 1996 and 2002. Current term expires Jan 2009. Supervising Judge Northwest District 1999-2000. Serves North Valley District. Born New York New York March 9, 1938. Catholic. Educated at University of California at Los Angeles B.A. 1962 and Loyola University School of Law J.D. 1965. Admitted to practice California 1966, U.S. District Court Southern District of California 1966 and U.S. Supreme Court 1980. Began legal practice Los Angeles. Judge, Los Angeles Municipal Court Los Angeles County 1986-89.

United States Trustee for the Central District of California U.S. Department of Justice 1985-86. Member California Judges Association (Executive Board 1995-97), The Maritime Law Association of the U.S. and Irish American Bar Association (President 1985-86). Recipient Daniel O'Connell Award from Irish American Bar Association 1990. Named Superior Court Judge of the Year by San Fernando Valley Criminal Bar Association 1993-94 and Judge of the Year by San Fernando Valley Bar Association 2000. U.S. Army 1957-63. Republican. Enjoys travel and gardening.

Office: 900 Third Street, San Fernando 91340.
Telephone: (818) 898-2426.

FASEL, Frank F. *(Judge, Superior Court of California County of Orange)*

Mailing address: P.O. Box 1994, Santa Ana 92702-1994.
Office: Central Justice Center, 700 Civic Center Drive West, Santa Ana 92701.
Telephone: (714) 834-3734.

FAWKE, W. Robert *(Judge, Superior Court of California County of San Bernardino)* Assumed office Aug 10, 1998. Elected 2002, current term expires Jan 2009. Born Oakland California Jan 2, 1945. Protestant. Educated at Loma Linda University B.A. 1966 and Golden Gate University J.D. 1969. Admitted to practice California 1970, U.S. District Court Northern 1970 and Central 1973 Districts of California and U.S. Court of Appeals Ninth Circuit 1970. Judge, San Bernardino County Municipal Court July 17, 1987 to Aug 9, 1998, appointed by Governor George Deukmejian.

District Attorney San Bernardino County 1970-87. Republican. Member San Bernardino County 1978-87 and California State 1980-87 Republican Central Committee. Board member YMCA 1980-86 and San Bernardino Chamber of Commerce 1985-87. Enjoys racquetball and swimming.

Office: 351 North Arrowhead Avenue, San Bernardino 92415-0240.
Telephone: (909) 387-3922.

FEENEY, John T. *(Judge, Superior Court of California County of Humboldt)*

Office: 825 Fifth Street, Eureka 95501.
Telephone: (707) 269-1200.

FEESS, Gary *(Judge, United States District Court Central District of California)* Appointed for life by President Bill Clinton to term beginning Sept 3, 1999. Born Alliance Ohio March 13, 1948. Educated at The Ohio State University B.A. 1970 and University of California at Los Angeles J.D. 1974. In legal practice Los Angeles 1974-79 and 1987-96. Judge, Superior Court of California County of Los Angeles 1996-99.

Assistant U.S. Attorney 1979-87 and Chief Assistant U.S. Attorney 1988-89 U.S. District Court Central District of California.

Office: 740 Federal Building, 255 East Temple Street, Los Angeles 90012.
Telephone: (213) 894-3535.

FEFFER, Irving S. *(Judge, Superior Court of California County of Los Angeles)* Born Los Angeles California April 11, 1931. Educated at University of Southern California B.A. 1953 LL.B. 1957. In legal practice Culver City 1958-64 and Beverly Hills 1964-89 (sole practitioner).

City Attorney Montebello 1979-89, Bell 1980-89,

FEFFER, IRVING S.—*Continued*

South El Monte 1980-89, Whittier 1980-89, Azusa 1984-89 and Baldwin Park 1984-89. Special Attorney Manhattan Beach Police Department 1985-89. Co-author "Presentation of Case" and "Preparation for Trial" *Criminal Law* Cal CEB 1986, 1992, 1996 and 1998. Instructor Los Angeles City College 1964-65 and in Real Estate Law School of Commerce University of Southern California 1964-65. Member Executive Committee Los Angeles Superior Court 1992, 1997 and 1998. Member Inns of Court University of Southern California, California Judges Association, Beverly Hills and Los Angeles County Bar Associations. Lieutenant Colonel USAS 1981-96. Court of Military Appeals 1984. President Law Alumni University of Southern California 1981. Board of Directors Legion Lex 1992 and 1997. Enjoys running and photography.
Office: Courthouse, 111 North Hill Street, Los Angeles 90012.
Telephone: (213) 974-5411.

FEINSTEIN, Katherine A. *(Judge, Superior Court of California City and County of San Francisco)*
Office: Civic Center Courthouse, 400 McAllister Street, San Francisco 94102-4514.
Telephone: (415) 551-4020.

FELICE, Lee Phillip *(Judge, Superior Court of California County of Kern)* Former Judge, Bakersfield Municipal Court Kern County.
Office: 1415 Truxtun Avenue, Bakersfield 93301.
Telephone: (661) 868-4934.

FELL, Sheila *(Judge, Superior Court of California County of Orange)*
Mailing address: P.O. Box 14169, Orange 92863-1569.
Office: Lamoreaux Justice Center, 341 The City Drive, Orange 92868.
Telephone: (714) 935-7236.

FERGUSON, Darryl B. *(Judge, Superior Court of California County of Tulare)* Assumed office July 27, 1998. Presiding Judge since July 1, 2001. Former Judge, Tulare County Municipal Court.
Office: County Civic Center, Visalia 93291-4593.
Telephone: (559) 733-6561.

FERNANDEZ, Alfonso *(Judge, Superior Court of California County of Santa Clara)* Assumed office July 30, 1998. Elected 2000, current term expires Jan 2007. Born Honolulu Hawaii April 12, 1951. Educated at University of San Francisco B.A. 1972 and Golden Gate University J.D. 1975. Admitted to practice California 1976 and U.S. District Court Northern District of California 1976. Judge Feb 15, 1985 to July 29, 1998 and Presiding Judge 1991-92, Santa Clara County Municipal Court, appointed by Governor George Deukmejian.

Member Court Interpretation Advisory Committee National Center for State Courts, Metropolitan Municipal Courts Association and California Judges Association. Honorary Member La Raza Lawyers Association and Santa Clara County Bar Association. Named Alumnus of the Year by El Camino High School 1985 and Outstanding Civic Leader by California Security Bank and Hispanic Development Corporation 1988. Recipient Portrait of Success Award from Hispanic Development Corporation 1988. Participated in Sober Graduation Program 1990 and 1992. Member Hispanic Elected Officials of Santa Clara County.
Office: Hall of Justice East Wing, 190 West Hedding Street, San Jose 95110.
Telephone: (408) 808-6600.

FERNS, Edward A. *(Judge, Superior Court of California County of Los Angeles)* Former Judge, Los Angeles Municipal Court Los Angeles County.
Office: Courthouse, 111 North Hill Street, Los Angeles 90012.
Telephone: (213) 974-5411.

FERRARI, Gary J. *(Judge, Superior Court of California County of Los Angeles)* Supervising Judge Jan 1, 1999 to Dec 31, 2002. Presiding Judge Jan 1, 1997 to Dec 31, 1997 and Former Judge, Long Beach Municipal Court Los Angeles County.
Office: Long Beach Courthouse, 415 West Ocean Boulevard, Long Beach 90802.
Telephone: (562) 491-6153.

FERRELL, Eudon *(Judge, Superior Court of California County of Los Angeles)* Assumed office Jan 22, 2000. Former Judge and Presiding Judge, Inglewood Municipal Court Los Angeles County.
Office: Inglewood Courthouse, One Regent Street, Inglewood 90301.
Telephone: (310) 419-5121.

FETTEL, Douglas Alan *(Judge, Superior Court of California County of San Bernardino)* Assumed office Aug 10, 1998. Serves Valley Division. Former Judge, San Bernardino County Municipal Court.
Office: 17780 Arrow Boulevard, Fontana 92335.
Telephone: (909) 350-9322.

FIDLER, Larry Paul *(Judge, Superior Court of California County of Los Angeles)* Appointed by Governor Pete Wilson Dec 9, 1992. Elected 1992 and 1998. Current term expires Jan 2005. Supervising Judge Criminal Division 1999-2000. Born Los Angeles California Feb 5, 1947. Educated at California State University at Northridge B.A. 1969 and Loyola Marymount University Law School J.D. with special honors 1974. Admitted to practice California 1974. Certified Specialist Criminal Law California Board of Legal Specialization. In legal practice Los Angeles 1974-82. Judge 1983-92, Assistant Presiding Judge 1988 and Presiding Judge 1989, Los Angeles Municipal Court Los Angeles County, appointed by Governor Edmund G. Brown, Jr.

Lecturer Pepperdine University School of Law 1980-81, Los Angeles College of Trial Advocacy 1980-81, Los Angeles Police Academy 1983-92 and Los Angeles Sheriffs Academy 1983-92. Member Los Angeles County Probation Task Force 1982-83, Los Angeles Municipal Court Executive Committee 1984, 1986, 1988, 1989 and 1990, Municipal Court Judges Association (Committees on Legislation and DUI 1984-85, Chair Planning and Research Committee 1990 and 1991), Los Angeles County Criminal Courts (President 1983) and Los Angeles County (Chair Criminal Justice Section 1982-83, Judicial Procedures Commission 1989, Countywide Criminal Justice Coordination Committee 1989, State Trial Courts Committee 1989) Bar Associations. Moderator "Cross-Examination of the Expert Witness Seminar" 1977 and "Search and Seizure Seminar" 1980 Criminal Courts Bar Association, "Criminal Law Symposium" 1979 and "Felony Sentencing Seminar" 1982 Los Ange-

FIDLER, LARRY PAUL—*Continued*

les County Bar Association and "The Good Faith Exception to the Exclusionary Rule" Whittier College of Law 1984. Author syllabus for Los Angeles County Bar Association Criminal Law Symposium 1979 and monthly column "Voir Dire, Jury Instructions and Closing Argument" Criminal Courts Bar Association Newsletter until 1983. Lecturer "Search and Seizure" Municipal and Justice Court Judges Institute 1983-92, "DUI Cases" Municipal and Justice Court Judges Workshop 1983, "Criminal Law and Motion" and "Search and Seizure" California Center for Judicial Education and Research Continuing Judicial Studies Program since 1984, "Criminal Evidence," "Criminal Law and Procedure" and "California Criminal Law, Procedure and Practice" 1986-89 CEB, "Diversion on Drug Offenses" CCBA, "Search and Seizure" New California Appellate Research Attorney Orientation Program 1985-86 and 1993 and Superior Court Criminal Law Institute 1985-94, "Voir Dire" Los Angeles College of Trial Advocacy and Los Angeles County Municipal Courts Planning and Research Legislative Seminar 1989. Faculty Member Continuing Judicial Studies Program 1984-90 and California Judicial College since 1988 (Planning Committee 1990-91). Named Municipal Court Judge of the Year by Criminal Justice Section Los Angeles County Bar Association 1992.

Office: Criminal Courts Building, 210 West Temple Street, Los Angeles 90012-3210.

Telephone: (213) 974-6535.

FIELD, Charles D. *(Judge, Superior Court of California County of Riverside)* Appointed by Governor George Deukmejian to term beginning Jan 26, 1990. Elected Nov 1990, 1996 and 2002. Current term expires Jan 2009. Born San Francisco California Aug 2, 1936. Protestant. Educated at University of California at Riverside B.A. 1958 and University of California at Los Angeles J.D. 1963. Member Phi Alpha Delta. Admitted to practice California 1964 and U.S. District Court Southern District of California 1964. In legal practice Riverside 1964-90.

Author article series on labor relations and employment law Best, Best & Krieger 1984-90. Important Decision: Riverside Citizens v. City of Riverside (mandamus to compel city to put anti-gay and anti-HIV infected ordinance on ballot, ruled unconstitutional by Court of Appeal, hearing denied by Supreme Court) 1 Cal. 4th 1013, 1991. Instructor in Labor and Human Resources Law in Construction Industry University of California at Riverside Graduate School of Management 1988-90. Member California Judges Association, State Bar of California and American Bar Association. Attended programs on Juvenile Law, Trial Management and Judicial Administration California Judicial College California Center for Judicial Education and Research summer 1991. Recipient Alumni Public Service Award from University of California at Riverside 1988 and Arts Contributions Award from Riverside Opera Association 1991. California Air National Guard 1958-64. Claims Examiner Allstate Insurance Company 1959-60. Board of Regents University of California 1975-77. Member Riverside Arts Foundation (Board 1975-86, President 1983-84) and Riverside Art Museum 1984-88. Enjoys golf, travel and tennis.

Office: Riverside Historic Courthouse, 4050 Main Street, Riverside 92501.

Telephone: (909) 955-1960.

FIELDER, John L. *(Judge, Superior Court of California County of Kern)* Assumed office July 1, 2000. Former Judge, West Kern Municipal Court Kern County. Former Judge, Bakersfield Municipal Court Kern County.

Office: 1215 Truxtun Avenue, Bakersfield 93301.

Telephone: (661) 868-2450.

FIELDS, Michael S. *(Judge, Superior Court of California County of Monterey)* Former Judge, Monterey County Municipal Court.

Mailing address: P.O. Box 1819, Salinas 93902-1819.

Office: 240 Church Street, Salinas 93901.

Telephone: (831) 755-5060.

FIELDS, Richard Todd *(Judge, Superior Court of California County of Riverside)*

Office: Hall of Justice, 4100 Main Street, Riverside 92501.

Telephone: (909) 955-2300.

FILER, Kelvin D. *(Judge, Superior Court of California County of Los Angeles)*

Office: Compton Courthouse, 200 West Compton Boulevard, Compton 90220.

Telephone: (310) 603-7842.

FIRMAT, Francisco F. *(Judge, Superior Court of California County of Orange)* Former Judge and Presiding Judge, North Orange County Municipal Court.

Mailing address: P.O. Box 14169, Orange 92863-1569.

Office: Lamoreaux Justice Center, 341 The City Drive, Orange 92868.

Telephone: (714) 935-7236.

FISCHER, Dale S. *(Judge, Superior Court of California County Los Angeles)* Assumed office Jan 22, 2000. Born East Orange New Jersey Oct 17, 1951. Educated at University of South Florida B.A. 1977 and Harvard Law School J.D. 1980. Notes and Comments Editor Harvard Women's Law Journal 1979-80. Member Phi Kappa Phi. Admitted to practice California 1980, U.S. District Courts Central, Eastern, Northern and Southern Districts of California, U.S. Court of Appeals Ninth Circuit and U.S. Supreme Court. In legal practice Los Angeles 1980-97. Judge March 17, 1997 to Jan 21, 2000 and Former Judge pro tem, Los Angeles Municipal Court Los Angeles County, appointed by Governor Pete Wilson.

Former Arbitrator American Arbitration Association. President George McBurney Business Litigation Inn of Court. Member Women Lawyers of Los Angeles, National Association of Women Judges, American Judicature Society, Los Angeles County, Federal and American Bar Associations. Speaker Legislative Seminar Municipal Court Judges' Association 1998 and California Criminal Law and Procedure Institute California Center for Judicial Education and Research 1998. Faculty Southern California Regional Programs on Trial Advocacy and Depositions National Institute for Trial Advocacy. Moderator "How to Win Your Case With Depositions." Recipient Lawyer in the Classroom Award from Constitutional Rights Foundation. Pro Bono City Attorney Los Ange-

FISCHER, DALE S.—*Continued*

les. Member Organization of Women Executives. Enjoys theater and reading.

Office: Criminal Courts Building, 210 West Temple Street, Los Angeles 90012-3210.

Telephone: (213) 974-5755.

FISHER, John S. *(Judge, Superior Court of California County of Los Angeles)* Former Judge, Los Angeles Municipal Court Los Angeles County.

Office: Van Nuys Courthouse West, 14400 Erwin Street Mall, Van Nuys 91401-2705.

Telephone: (818) 374-2601.

FLANAGAN, Hugh *(Judge, Superior Court of California County of Merced)*

Office: County Courts Building, 627 West 21st Street, Merced 95340.

Telephone: (209) 385-7531.

FLEURET, Jules E. *(Judge, Superior Court of California County of San Bernardino)*

Office: 14455 Civic Drive, Victorville 92392.

Telephone: (760) 243-8684.

FLIER, Madeleine *(Judge, Superior Court of California County of Los Angeles)* Former Judge, Los Angeles Municipal Court Los Angeles County.

Office: Courthouse, 111 North Hill Street, Los Angeles 90012.

Telephone: (213) 974-5411.

FLIER, Richard S. *(Judge, Superior Court of California County of Contra Costa)*

Office: Courthouse, 725 Court Street, Martinez 94553.

Telephone: (925) 646-2950.

FLINN, David B. *(Judge, Superior Court of California County of Contra Costa)* Appointed by Governor Pete Wilson to term beginning March 1997. Elected March 1998, current term expires Jan 2005. Born San Francisco California Nov 1, 1938. Jewish. Educated at University of California at Berkeley B.S. 1960 J.D. 1963. Admitted to practice California 1964 and U.S. District Courts Central, Eastern, Northern and Southern Districts of California. In legal practice San Francisco 1964-97.

Office: Courthouse, 725 Court Street, Martinez 94553.

Telephone: (925) 646-4006.

FLORES, Rogelio R. *(Judge, Superior Court of California County of Santa Barbara)*

Office: 312-H East Cook Street, Santa Maria 93454.

Telephone: (805) 346-7414.

FLYNN, John L., III *(Judge, Superior Court of California County of Orange)*

Mailing address: P.O. Box 14169, Orange 92863-1569.

Office: Lamoreaux Justice Center, 341 The City Drive, Orange 92868.

Telephone: (714) 935-7236.

FLYNN, Paul G. *(Judge, Superior Court of California County of Los Angeles)*

Office: Santa Monica Courthouse, 1725 Main Street, Santa Monica 90401.

Telephone: (310) 260-3762.

FOGEL, Jeremy D. *(Judge, United States District Court Northern District of California)* Appointed for life by President Bill Clinton to term beginning March 31, 1998. Born San Francisco California Sept 17, 1949. Jewish. Educated at Stanford University A.B. with honors 1971 and Harvard Law School J.D. with honors 1974. Admitted to practice California 1974 and U.S. District Court Northern District of California 1974. In legal practice San Jose 1974-81. Judge, Santa Clara County Municipal Court 1981-86. Judge, Superior Court of California Santa Clara County June 25, 1986 to March 30, 1998, appointed by Governor George Deukmejian.

Important Decisions: Leatherman Tool Group v. Cooper Industries (standard for trade dress infringement) 98-35147 9th Cir. 1999; Yahoo, Inc. v. La Ligue Contre le Racisme et l'Antisemitisme (international internet jurisdiction) 169 F. Supp. 1181, 2001; PMG International Division v. Cohen (sale of sexually explicit media at military exchanges) 57 F. Supp. 2d; Cybermedia v. Symantec Corp (copyright infringement) 19 F. Supp. 2d 1070; and appellate opinions on assignment to California Court of Appeal Sixth District. Member California Judges Association (Judicial Ethics Committee 1987-88, Executive Board 1988-91, Vice President 1990-91) and State Bar of California (Chair Committee on the Legal Rights of the Handicapped 1979-80, Member Executive Committee Legal Services Section 1980-81). Lecturer Department of Human Development California State University at Hayward 1977-78. Instructor Family Law Institute California Judicial Education and Research 1988-90, Judicial Conduct New Judges' Orientation 1988-89 and Family Law California Continuing Judicial Studies Program 1988-91. Recipient Service Award Mental Health Association of Santa Clara County 1981, President Award from California Judges Association 1997 and LACY Honors Award from Legal Advocates for Children and Youth 1997. Named Judge of the Year by Consumer Attorneys of Santa Clara County 1997. Executive Director Santa Clara County Bar Association Law Foundation, Inc. 1980-81. Member Charter Review Committee City of San Jose 1976-79 and Commission on the Developmentally Disabled County of Santa Clara 1980-81.

Office: U.S. Courthouse, 280 South First Street, San Jose 95113.

Telephone: (408) 535-5426.

FOILES, Robert D. *(Judge, Superior Court of California County of San Mateo)* Assumed office June 12, 1998. Former Judge, San Mateo County Municipal Court.

Office: Hall of Justice, 400 County Center, Redwood City 94063.

Telephone: (650) 363-4516.

FOLEY, Robert Michael *(Judge, Superior Court of California County of Santa Clara)* Former Presiding Judge. Former Judge, Santa Clara County Municipal Court.

Office: Old Courthouse, 161 North First Street, San Jose 95113.

Telephone: (408) 882-2340.

FOLLETT, William H. *(Judge, Superior Court of California County of Del Norte)* Appointed by Governor Gray Davis to term beginning July 17, 2000. Elected 2000, current term expires Jan 1, 2007. Born Hanford California May 8, 1950. Educated at California State University at Fresno B.A. magna cum laude 1973 and McGeorge School of Law University of the Pacific J.D.

FOLLETT, WILLIAM H.—*Continued*

1976. Legislation Editor Pacific Law Journal 1974-76. Member Traynor Honor Society. Admitted to practice California 1979 and U.S. District Courts Eastern 1979 and Northern 1980 Districts of California. In legal practice California 1980-2000.

Office: 450 H Street, Crescent City 95531.
Telephone: (707) 464-7217.
Fax: (707) 465-4005
E-mail address: WmFollett@aol.com

FOOR, Peter B. *(Judge, Superior Court of California County of Solano)*

Mailing address: P.O. Box 2463, Fairfield 94533-0246.
Office: 530 Union Avenue, Suite 200, Fairfield 94533.
Telephone: (707) 421-7827.

FORCUM, Mark R. *(Judge, Superior Court of California County of San Mateo)* Presiding Judge since Jan 1, 2003. Presiding Judge Superior and Municipal Courts Jan 1, 1997 to Dec 31, 1997. Former Judge, San Mateo County Municipal Court.

Office: Hall of Justice, 400 County Center, Redwood City 94063.
Telephone: (650) 363-4516.

FORD, Richard T. *(Recalled Judge, United States Bankruptcy Court Eastern District of California)* Retired Feb 3, 1998. Appointed Recalled Judge by the Judicial Council of the Ninth Circuit.

Mailing address: P.O. Box 1357, Nipomo 93444-1357.
Telephone: (805) 929-8146.

FORNERET, Rodney G. *(Judge, Superior Court of California County of Los Angeles)* Assumed office Jan 22, 2000. Presiding Judge Jan 1, 1997 to Dec 31, 1997 and Former Judge, Inglewood Municipal Court Los Angeles County.

Office: Inglewood Courthouse, One Regent Street, Inglewood 90301.
Telephone: (310) 419-5121.

FORSTENZER, Edward *(Judge, Superior Court of California County of Mono)* Assumed office Dec 28, 1998. Term expires Jan 2005. Presiding Judge since Dec 28, 1998. Born Austria May 6, 1946. Educated at University of Michigan B.A. 1968 and University of California Hastings College of Law J.D. 1971. Admitted to practice California 1972, U.S. District Courts Northern 1972 and Eastern 1974 Districts of California and U.S. Court of Appeals Ninth Circuit 1972. In legal practice Bishop 1976-88. Former Magistrate Judge, U.S. District Court Eastern District of California. Judge, Mono County Municipal Court 1988 to Dec 28, 1998.

Public Defender Mono County 1979-88. Former Member Judicial Council of California. Member California Judges Association and American Judges Association. Member Rotary Club.

Mailing address: P.O. Box 1037, Mammoth Lakes 93546.
Office: Courthouse, Highway 395N, Bridgeport 93517.
Telephone: (760) 924-5444.

FOSTER, Lisa *(Judge, Superior Court of California County of San Diego)*

Mailing address: P.O. Box 122724, San Diego 92112-2724.
Office: 220 West Broadway, San Diego 92101.
Telephone: (619) 531-3820.

FOX, Elden S. *(Judge, Superior Court of California County of Los Angeles)* Assumed office Jan 22, 2000. Former Judge and Presiding Judge, Beverly Hills Municipal Court Los Angeles County.

Office: Beverly Hills Courthouse, 9355 Burton Way, Beverly Hills 90210-3669.
Telephone: (310) 288-1288.

FRASER, Jeffrey F. *(Judge, Superior Court of California County of San Diego)* Assumed office Dec 1, 1998. Born San Francisco California July 15, 1961. Catholic. Educated at University of California at Santa Barbara B.A. with high honors 1984 and Santa Clara University School of Law J.D. 1987. Judge, South Bay Municipal Court San Diego County Sept 9, 1998 to Nov 30, 1998, appointed by Governor Pete Wilson.

Deputy District Attorney San Diego County 1988-98. Board Member San Diego Environmental Health Advisory Board 1995-98, San Diego Criminal Justice Council since 1996 and California Council on Criminal Justice since 1996. Barrister Louis Welsh Inn of Court 1996-98. Former Member San Diego County District Attorney's Association, California District Attorney's Association, State Bar of California and San Diego County Bar Association. Member San Diego Judges Association and California Judges Association. Lecturer on Beginning Trial Advocacy, Advanced Trial Advocacy and Gangs California District Attorney's Association and Evidence San Diego District Attorney's Office. Republican. Board Member The Lincoln Club of San Diego 1991-98, Doris Tate Crime Victim's Bureau 1994-98, Copley Family YMCA 1995-98 and San Diego Partnership for Children since 1999. Enjoys golf.

Mailing address: P.O. Box 122724, San Diego 92112-2724.
Office: 500 Third Avenue, Chula Vista 91910.
Telephone: (619) 691-4770.
E-mail address: jfrasems@co.san-diego.ca.us

FRAWLEY, Timothy M. *(Judge, Superior Court of California County of Sacramento)*

Office: Courthouse, 720 Ninth Street, Sacramento 95814.
Telephone: (916) 874-5476.

FRAZEE, Richard O., Sr. *(Judge, Superior Court of California County of Orange)* Appointed by Governor George Deukmejian to term beginning Dec 4, 1987. Elected June 1988, 1994 and 2000. Current term expires Jan 2007. Born Newark New Jersey March 19, 1938. Protestant. Educated at University of California at Los Angeles B.S. 1961 and University of California Hastings College of the Law J.D. 1966. Admitted to practice California 1967 and U.S. District Court Central District of California 1967. In legal practice Pomona 1967-70, Santa Ana 1970-80 and Laguna Niguel 1980-87.

Adjunct Professor Pepperdine University School of Law 1970-78. Former member California Trial Lawyers Association, State Bar of California, Pomona Valley and Orange County Bar Associations. First Lieutenant U.S. Army 1961-63. Republican. Past President Rotary Club South Laguna Niguel. Charter Director Chamber of

FRAZEE, RICHARD O., SR.—*Continued*

Commerce and Business Club Laguna Niguel. Enjoys scuba diving, sailing, snow skiing, golf and tennis.

Mailing address: P.O. Box 14169, Orange 92863-1569.

Office: Lamoreaux Justice Center, 341 The City Drive, Orange 92868.

Telephone: (714) 935-7274.

FREDRICKS, Josh M. *(Judge, Superior Court of California County of Los Angeles)* Assumed office Jan 22, 2000. Elected 2002, current term expires Jan 2009. Born La Jolla California Sept 12, 1949. Roman Catholic. Educated at University of Southern California A.B. 1972 and Loyola University of Los Angeles J.D. 1976. Admitted to practice California 1976 and U.S. District Court Central District of California 1976. In legal practice Redondo Beach 1976-85 and Hermosa Beach 1985-86. Judge Aug 21, 1986 to Jan 21, 2000 and Former Presiding Judge, South Bay Municipal Court Los Angeles County, appointed by Governor George Deukmejian.

Former Member South Bay Bar Association. Member California Judges Association. Policeman Manhattan Beach 1972-76. Teacher El Camino College 1976-79. Enjoys hunting, gardening, tennis, spectator sports and reading.

Office: Criminal Courts Building, 210 West Temple Street, Los Angeles 90012-3210.

Telephone: (213) 974-6535.

FREEDMAN, Robert Brandeis *(Judge, Superior Court of California County of Alameda)* Assumed office July 31, 1998. Born Los Angeles California Dec 12, 1943. Jewish. Educated at University of California at Los Angeles B.A. 1965 and University of California Boalt Hall School of Law J.D. 1968. Admitted to practice California 1969, U.S. District Courts Northern 1969 and Eastern 1975 Districts of California, U.S. Supreme Court 1975 and U.S. Court of Appeals Ninth Circuit 1983. In legal practice Oakland 1969-96. Judge, Oakland-Piedmont-Emeryville Municipal Court Alameda County Feb 29, 1996 to July 30, 1998, appointed by Governor Pete Wilson.

Member Civil and Small Claims Advisory Committee California Judicial Council. Former Member State Bar of California. Member California Judges Association and Alameda County Bar Association (President 1988). Former lecturer for California Continuing Education of the Bar and local CLE programs. Faculty B. E. Witkin Judicial College since 1998.

Office: Administration Building, 1221 Oak Street, Oakland 94612.

Telephone: (510) 271-5130.

FREEMAN, Beth Labson *(Judge, Superior Court of California County of San Mateo)* Appointed by Governor Gray Davis to term beginning Feb 2, 2001. Born Washington D.C. Nov 21, 1953. Educated at University of California at Berkeley A.B. 1976 and Harvard Law School J.D. 1979. Member Phi Beta Kappa. Admitted to practice District of Columbia 1979, U.S. District Courts Eastern 1980 and Northern 1980 Districts of California, U.S. Courts of Appeals District of Columbia 1980 and Ninth 1980 Circuits and California 1981. In legal practice San Francisco California Sept 1981 to May 1983. Deputy County Counsel San Mateo County May 1983 to Jan 2001.

Office: 400 County Center, Redwood City 94063.

Telephone: (650) 363-4766.

FREEMAN, Kenneth R. *(Judge, Superior Court of California County of Los Angeles)* Former Judge, Los Angeles Municipal Court Los Angeles County.

Office: Courthouse, 111 North Hill Street, Los Angeles 90012.

Telephone: (213) 974-5411.

FRIEDMAN, Gary T. *(Judge, Superior Court of California County of Kern)* Appointed by Governor George Deukmejian Sept 1983. Elected to subsequent terms. Born Bakersfield California April 7, 1943. Educated at Bakersfield College A.A. 1963, University of California at Santa Barbara B.A. 1965 and Boalt Hall School of Law J.D. 1968. James Patterson McBaine Moot Court Board. Admitted to practice California. In legal practice 1969-83. Judge pro tem, West Kern Municipal Court Kern County 1981. Arbitrator, Superior Court of California Kern County 1981-83. Magistrate, U.S. District Court Eastern District of California March 25, 1983 to Sept 16, 1983.

Investigator, Deputy District Attorney and Special Prosecutor Kern County District Attorney's Office 1968-69. Former member Southern California Defense Counsel, Association of Northern California Defense Counsel, California Trial Lawyers Association and State Bar of California. Member California Judges Association and Kern County Bar Association (Director 1975-78 and 1981-82, President 1981). President Bakersfield Downtown Rotary Club 1984-85.

Office: 1415 Truxtun Avenue, Bakersfield 93301.

Telephone: (661) 868-4934.

FRIEDMAN, Terry *(Judge, Superior Court of California County of Los Angeles)*

Office: Santa Monica Courthouse, 1725 Main Street, Santa Monica 90401.

Telephone: (310) 260-3762.

FROEBERG, William R. *(Judge, Superior Court of California County of Orange)* Appointed by Governor George Deukmejian May 11, 1989. Judge, Central Orange County Municipal Court Jan 1986 to May 1989.

Mailing address: P.O. Box 1994, Santa Ana 92702-1994.

Office: Central Justice Center, 700 Civic Center Drive West, Santa Ana 92701.

Telephone: (714) 834-3734.

FROMHOLZ, Haley J. *(Judge, Superior Court of California County of Los Angeles)*

Office: Courthouse, 111 North Hill Street, Los Angeles 90012.

Telephone: (213) 974-5411.

FRUIN, Richard L., Jr. *(Judge, Superior Court of California County of Los Angeles)* Appointed by Governor Pete Wilson to term beginning Nov 15, 1995. Elected to subsequent terms. Current term expires Jan 2009. Born San Francisco California March 22, 1939. Catholic. Educated at University of Pennsylvania B.A. with honors 1961 and University of California at Berkeley J.D. with honors 1965. Admitted to practice California 1966. In legal practice Los Angeles 1966-95.

Author "Inherent Power Sanctions" 1982, "Judicial Outreach in State Courts" 2001, "The Next Society and

FRUIN, RICHARD L., JR.—*Continued*

the Public Courts" 2002, "Judicial Outreach in State Courts" and "Integrating Mediation into the Resolution of Civil Disputes" The Judge's Journal and *Judicial Outreach on a Shoestring: A Working Manual* 1999 American Bar Association, "Protecting Confidential Information" Corporate Counsel Newsletter Los Angeles County Bar Association 1989 and "Defining Internet Jurisdiction" Report Association of Business Trial Lawyers 2002. Chair Court/Community Outreach Committee Los Angeles County Superior Court. Fellow American College of Trial Lawyers. Member Los Angeles County (Chair Antitrust Section) and American (Chair Judicial Division) Bar Associations. USMCR 1962-70. Director Beach Cities Health District 1980-84 and 1992-95, Oceanographic Teaching Stations, Inc. since 1978 and Scope Industries 1992-95. Enjoys scuba diving and traveling.

Office: Courthouse, 111 North Hill Street, Los Angeles 90012.

Telephone: (213) 974-5411.

FRY, Lawrence W. *(Judge, Superior Court of California County of Riverside)* Appointed by Governor Pete Wilson July 8, 1997. Elected 1998, current term expires Jan 2005. Serves Indio Branch. Born Burbank California Nov 23, 1946. Protestant. Educated at University of California at Santa Barbara B.A. 1968 and California Western School of Law J.D. 1975. Admitted to practice California 1976. Judge April 20, 1989 to July 7, 1997 and Former Presiding Judge Desert Municipal Court Riverside County, appointed by Governor George Deukmejian.

Deputy District Attorney Riverside County 1976-80. Founding Member Warren Slaughter American Inns of Court since 1997. Ex-officio Member Desert Bar Association. Member California Judges Association and Riverside Bar Association. Faculty California Center for Judicial Education and Research since 1996. USNR 1968-74.

Office: 46-200 Oasis Street, Indio 92201.

Telephone: (760) 863-8426.

FUDENNA, Keith H. *(Judge, Superior Court of California County of Alameda)*

Office: Fremont Hall of Justice, 39439 Paseo Padre Parkway, Fremont 94538.

Telephone: (510) 795-2329.

FUJIOKA, Fred J. *(Judge, Superior Court of California County of Los Angeles)*

Office: Mental Health Courthouse, 1150 North San Fernando Road, Los Angeles 90065.

Telephone: (323) 226-2908.

FULLER, Mary E. *(Judge, Superior Court of California County of San Bernardino)* Assumed office Aug 10, 1998. Serves Rancho District. Former Judge, San Bernardino County Municipal Court.

Office: 8303 North Haven Avenue, Rancho Cucamonga 91730.

Telephone: (909) 945-4131.

FYBEL, Richard David *(Associate Justice, California Court of Appeal Fourth District Division Three)* Appointed by Governor Gray Davis Feb, 8 2002. Educated at University of California at Los Angeles A.B. 1968 J.D. 1971. Staff member UCLA Law Review. Member Order of the Coif. Judge, Superior Court of California County of Orange March 7, 2000 to 2002.

Mailing address: P.O. Box 22055, Santa Ana 92702.

Telephone: (714) 558-6777.

GADDIS, Larry D. *(Judge, Superior Court of California County of Placer)* Presiding Judge Aug 5, 1998 to June 30, 2000. Serves Juvenile Division. Former Judge, Placer County Municipal Court.

Office: 11270 B Avenue, Auburn 95603.

Telephone: (530) 886-4811.

GALLAGHER, Catherine A. *(Judge, Superior Court of California County of Santa Clara)* Former Judge, Santa Clara County Municipal Court.

Office: 191 North First Street, San Jose 95113.

Telephone: (408) 882-2100.

GALLAGHER, Peter *(Judge, Superior Court of California County of San Diego)*

Mailing address: P.O. Box 122724, San Diego 92112-2724.

Office: 220 West Broadway, San Diego 92101.

Telephone: (619) 531-3820.

GALLAGHER, William D. *(Judge, Superior Court of California County of Shasta)*

Office: 1500 Court Street, Redding 96001-1685.

Telephone: (530) 225-5714.

GALLIVAN, Robert H. *(Judge, Superior Court of California County of Orange)* Assumed office Aug 10, 1998. Former Judge and Presiding Judge, West Orange County Municipal Court.

Mailing address: P.O. Box 1994, Santa Ana 92702-1994.

Office: Central Justice Center, 700 Civic Center Drive West, Santa Ana 92701.

Telephone: (714) 834-3734.

GARAVENTA, John J. *(Judge, Superior Court of California County of Tehama)*

Mailing address: P.O. Box 1170, Red Bluff 96080.

Office: Red Bluff Courthouse, First Floor, 445 Pine Street, Red Bluff 96080.

Telephone: (530) 527-3563.

GARBER, Bernard J. *(Judge, Superior Court of California County of San Joaquin)* Assumed office June 8, 1998. Elected 2002, current term expires Jan 2009. Born Berkeley California June 6, 1946. Educated at University of California at Berkeley A.B. 1967 and Golden Gate University J.D. 1970. Supervising Editor Golden Gate Law Survey. Admitted to practice California 1971. Began legal practice Stockton 1971. Judge Dec 26, 1982 to June 7, 1998 and Former Presiding Judge, Stockton Municipal Court San Joaquin County, appointed by Governor George Deukmejian.

With San Joaquin District Attorney's Office 1972-82. Instructor Humphreys Law School 1975-76. Member California Judges Association (Criminal Law and Procedure Committee). Captain U.S. Army Field Artillery 1971-78 (inactive reserve).

Office: 222 East Weber Avenue, Room 303, Stockton 95202.

Telephone: (209) 468-2827.

GARBOLINO, James Daley *(Judge, Superior Court of California County of Placer)* Appointed by Governor George Deukmejian to term beginning Dec 7, 1984. Elected 1986, 1992 and 1998. Current term expires Jan

GARBOLINO, JAMES DALEY—*Continued*

2005. Presiding Judge July 1, 2000 to June 30, 2002. Born Sacramento California Jan 22, 1943. Catholic. Educated at University of San Francisco B.A. 1966 J.D. 1969. Admitted to practice California 1970 and U.S. Supreme Court 1975. In legal practice Roseville 1974-84.

Deputy Attorney General California Department of Justice 1969-72. Member Capitol City Trial Lawyers, California Judges Association, Judges, Marshals and Constables Association and Placer County Bar Association (President 1975). Corporal USMCR 1961-65. Republican. Assistant Legal Affairs Secretary to Governor Ronald Reagan 1972-74. President Roseville Lodge Sons of Italy. Member Roseville Rotary Club.

Office: 300 Taylor Street, Roseville 95678.
Telephone: (916) 783-1600.

GARCIA, David A. *(Judge, Superior Court of California City and County of San Francisco)* Former Judge, San Francisco Municipal Court San Francisco County.

Office: Civic Center Courthouse, 400 McAllister Street, San Francisco 94102-4514.
Telephone: (415) 551-4020.

GARCIA, Edward J. *(Senior Judge, United States District Court Eastern District of California)* Appointed for life by President Ronald Reagan to term beginning March 23, 1984. Assumed Senior status, serves by assignment. Born Sacramento California Nov 24, 1928. Educated at Sacramento City College A.A. with distinction 1951 and McGeorge School of Law LL.B. with distinction 1958. Admitted to practice California 1959. Judge March 10, 1972 to March 23, 1984 and Presiding Judge 1976-78 and 1982-83, Sacramento Municipal Court Sacramento County, appointed by Governor Ronald Reagan.

Deputy District Attorney 1959-69 and Chief Deputy District Attorney 1969-72 Sacramento County. Member California Judges Association (Executive Board 1977-80, Vice President 1980) and Sacramento County Bar Association 1959-72. Faculty member California Judicial College 1979, 1981 and 1983. Lecturer on Search Warrants New Judges Orientation Seminars 1976-79. Panelist CEB program "How to Handle a Criminal Proceeding" California Center for Judicial Education and Research 1972. Member Governing Committee (Vice Chairman 1983-84) and Journal Planning Committee 1979-82 California Center for Judicial Education and Research. Corporal USAF 1946-49. Republican. Member Mexican-American Educational Association 1962-63 (Board of Directors 1963), University of the Pacific Alumni Association and Elks Lodge 6. Executive Board Golden Empire Council Boy Scouts of America 1975.

Office: 13-200 U.S. Courthouse, 501 I Street, Sacramento 95814-2322.
Telephone: (916) 930-4225.

GARCIA, Michael T. *(Judge, Superior Court of California County of Sacramento)* Presiding Judge since Jan 1, 2002. Former Judge, Sacramento Municipal Court Sacramento County.

Office: Courthouse, 720 Ninth Street, Sacramento 95814.
Telephone: (916) 874-5476.

GARDNER, Hugh C., III *(Judge, Superior Court of California County of Los Angeles)*

Office: Courthouse, 111 North Hill Street, Los Angeles 90012.
Telephone: (213) 974-5411.

GARIBALDI, John J. *(Judge, Superior Court of California County of Santa Clara)* Former Judge, Santa Clara County Municipal Court.

Office: 605 West El Camino Real, Sunnyvale 94087.
Telephone: (408) 481-3500.

GARRETT, Ramona Joyce *(Judge, Superior Court of California County of Solano)* Assumed office Aug 3, 1998. Former Judge, Northern Solano County Municipal Court, appointed by Governor Pete Wilson.

Mailing address: P.O. Box 2463, Fairfield 94533-0246.
Office: 530 Union Avenue, Suite 200, Fairfield 94533.
Telephone: (707) 421-7827.

GARRIGAN, Michael N. *(Judge, Superior Court of California County of San Joaquin)* Former Presiding Judge.

Office: 222 East Weber Avenue, Room 303, Stockton 95202.
Telephone: (209) 468-2827.

GARZA, Donna G. *(Judge, Superior Court of California County of San Bernardino)* Serves Juvenile Court.

Office: 900 East Gilbert Street, San Bernardino 92415-0942.
Telephone: (909) 387-7538.

GASDIA, Brian F. *(Judge, Superior Court of California County of Los Angeles)* Assumed office Jan 22, 2000. Elected 2000, current term expires Jan 1, 2007. Born Los Angeles California. Educated at University of Southern California B.S. 1979 and Loyola Marymount University J.D. 1981. Admitted to practice California 1982 and U.S. Court of Appeals Ninth Circuit 1988. In legal practice Downey 1982-97. Judge, Downey Municipal Court Los Angeles County Aug 6, 1997 to Jan 21, 2000, appointed by Governor Pete Wilson.

Member Southeast District and Los Angeles County Bar Associations. Member Planning Commission City of Downey 1992-97.

Office: Norwalk Courthouse, 12720 Norwalk Boulevard, Norwalk 90650.
Telephone: (562) 807-7266.

GATELY, Francis A., Jr. *(Judge, Superior Court of California County of Los Angeles)* Assumed office Jan 22, 2000. Born New York 1941. Educated at Loyola Marymount University B.A. 1963 J.D. 1971. Admitted to practice California 1972. In legal practice El Monte 1971-87. Judge Nov 9, 1989 to Jan 21, 2000 and Presiding Judge Jan 1, 1997 to Dec 31, 1997, Rio Hondo Municipal Court Los Angeles County, appointed by Governor George Deukmejian.

USN 1963-68.
Office: 350 West Mission Boulevard, Pomona 91766.
Telephone: (909) 620-3152.
Fax: (626) 398-7293
E-mail address: FGATELY@AOL.COM

GATZERT, Norman Joseph *(Judge, Superior Court of California County of San Mateo)* Assumed office June 12, 1998. Serves Northern Branch. Born San Francisco California Oct 3, 1944. Educated at University of

GATZERT, NORMAN JOSEPH—*Continued*

California at Los Angeles B.A. in Political Science cum laude 1965 and Hastings College of the Law J.D. 1968. Admitted to practice California 1969, U.S. District Court Northern District of California 1969, U.S. Court of Appeals Ninth Circuit 1969 and U.S. Supreme Court 1972. In legal practice San Mateo Feb 1969 to May 1972. Traffic Referee June 1, 1972 to Dec 15, 1977, Commissioner Dec 15, 1977 to Jan 2, 1977 and Judge Jan 3, 1994 to June 11, 1998, San Mateo County Municipal Court, appointed by Governor Pete Wilson.

Former Member California Commissioners Association and Association of Municipal Court Clerks of California. Member California Judges Association. USAR JAGC 1968-74 (active duty 1969). Interests include local history, hiking and spectator sports.

Office: 1050 Mission Road, South San Francisco 94080.

Telephone: (650) 877-5435.

GAUT, Barton C. *(Associate Justice, California Court of Appeal Fourth District Division Two)* Appointed by Governor Pete Wilson to term beginning May 30, 1997. Retained by election Nov 1998. Born Gilman Colorado Oct 2, 1935. Educated at University of California at Los Angeles B.A. 1957 and University of California Boalt Hall School of Law LL.B. 1962. Member Phi Beta Kappa and Order of the Coif. Admitted to practice California 1962, U.S. District Courts Central 1962 and Southern Districts of California and U.S. Court of Appeals Ninth Circuit. In legal practice Riverside 1962-95. Judge, Superior Court of California Riverside County 1995-97.

Author Chapter "Jury Instructions" Matthew Bender. Member Committee on Court Congestion and Committee to Rewrite Jury Instructions State Bar of California, Riverside County Barristers (President), California Judges Association and Riverside County Bar Association (President). Panel Member "Jury Voir Dire" Seminar of Business Trial Attorneys. Recipient Award for Excellence in Litigation from Leo A. Deegan Inn of Court. First Lieutenant U.S. Army 1957-1959.

Office: 3389 Twelfth Street, Riverside 92501.

Telephone: (909) 248-0200.

GEE, Delbert C. *(Judge, Superior Court of California County of Alameda)*

Office: Courthouse, 661 Washington Street, Oakland 94607.

Telephone: (510) 268-7601.

GEMELLO, Linda Marino *(Associate Justice, California Court of Appeal First District Division Five)* Appointed by Governor Gray Davis. Former Judge, Superior Court of California County of San Mateo.

Office: 350 McAllister Street, San Francisco 94102-3600.

Telephone: (415) 865-7300.

GENESTA, George *(Judge, Superior Court of California County of Los Angeles)* Assumed office Jan 22, 2000. Former Judge, East Los Angeles Municipal Court Los Angeles County.

Office: Pomona Courthouse South, 400 Civic Center Plaza, Pomona 91766.

Telephone: (909) 620-3023.

GEORGE, Ronald M. *(Chief Justice, California Supreme Court)* Appointed Associate Justice by Governor Pete Wilson to term beginning Sept 3, 1991. Retained by election Nov 8, 1994. Appointed Chief Justice by Governor Pete Wilson to term beginning May 1, 1996. Retained by election Nov 3, 1998, current term expires Jan 2011. Born Los Angeles California March 11, 1940. Educated at Princeton University A.B. 1961 and Stanford University Law School J.D. 1964. Admitted to practice California 1965. Began legal practice Los Angeles 1965. Judge, Los Angeles Municipal Court Los Angeles County 1972-77, appointed by Governor Ronald Reagan. Judge 1977-87 and Supervising Judge Criminal Division 1983-84, Superior Court of California Los Angeles County, appointed by Governor Edmund G. Brown, Jr. Associate Justice, California Court of Appeal Second District Division Four 1987-91, appointed by Governor George Deukmejian.

Deputy Attorney General California Department of Justice 1965-72. Author *California Criminal Trial Judges Benchbook and Deskbook* 1985-88 and *California Judicial Retirement Handbook* 1989. Presiding Judge in Hillside Strangler Trial 1981-83. Chair Judicial Council of California since 1996 and Commission on Judicial Appointments since 1996. Member Governor's Commission on Building for the 21st Century since 1999 and State-Federal Jurisdiction Committee Judicial Conference of the U.S. since 1999. President Elect Conference of Chief Judges. Member California Judges Association (President 1982-83), California State-Federal Judicial Council, Anglo-American Legal Exchange, American Judicature Society and American Bar Association. Instructor California Institute for Trial Advocacy Skills 1979, California Continuing Judicial Studies Program 1981-82, California Judicial College 1982, Criminal Justice Legal Foundation 1992, Capital Case Symposium California State-Federal Judicial Council 1992 and Appellate Judges Seminar American Bar Association 1992. Named Trial Judge of the Year by Los Angeles Metropolitan News 1983, Appellate Justice of the Year by Los Angeles Trial Lawyers Association 1991 and Justice of the Year by Consumer Attorneys of California 1997. Recipient President's Award from California State Association of Counties 1997, Medallion Award (for outstanding moral, intellectual and professional contributions to the law and society) from St. Thomas More Law Honor Society 1997, Special Recognition from Los Angeles County Barristers 1998, Herbert Harley Award (for services in promoting the effective administration of justice) from American Judicature Society 1998, Judge Learned Hand Award 2000, Justice Award from Foundation of the State Bar of California 2000, Maynard Toll Award for Distinguished Public Service 2001 and Rehnquist Award 2002. Republican. Numerous civic and social activities. Enjoys hiking, skiing and marathon running.

Office: 350 McAllister Street, San Francisco 94102.

Telephone: (415) 865-7060.

GEORGE, Stephanie *(Judge, Superior Court of California County of Orange)*

Office: West Justice Center, 8141 Thirteenth Street, Westminster 92683.

Telephone: (714) 896-7181.

GERICKE, Douglas N. *(Judge, Superior Court of California County of San Bernardino)* Assumed office

GERICKE, DOUGLAS N.—*Continued*

Aug 10, 1998. Serves Juvenile Court. Former Judge, San Bernardino County Municipal Court.

Office: 900 East Gilbert Street, San Bernardino 92415-0942.

Telephone: (909) 387-7538.

GIBSON, John B. *(Judge, Superior Court of California County of San Bernardino)* Assumed office Aug 10, 1998. Former Judge, San Bernardino County Municipal Court.

Office: 235 East Mountain View Avenue, Barstow 92311.

Telephone: (760) 256-4819.

GIFFORD, Jack *(Judge, Superior Court of California County of Alameda)* Assumed office July 31, 1998. Former Judge and Presiding Judge, Oakland-Piedmont-Emeryville Municipal Court Alameda County.

Office: Courthouse, 661 Washington Street, Oakland 94607.

Telephone: (510) 268-7601.

GILBERT, Arthur *(Presiding Justice, California Court of Appeal Second District Division Six)* Appointed by Governor Edmund G. Brown, Jr. to term beginning Dec 1982. Retained by election. Former Acting Presiding Judge. Born Los Angeles California Dec 29, 1937. Educated at University of California at Los Angeles B.A. in English Literature 1960 and Boalt Hall School of Law LL.B. 1963. Admitted to practice California 1964. In legal practice Los Angeles 1964-75. Judge, Los Angeles Municipal Court Los Angeles County Sept 1975 to March 1980. Judge, Superior Court of California Los Angeles County March 1980 to Dec 1982.

Deputy City Attorney Criminal Division Los Angeles 1964-65. Author "Juror Perceptions and How They Judge the Judges" The Judges Journal Spring 1979, "Practicing in Juvenile Court—A Delicate Balance" Los Angeles Lawyer Dec 1981, "The Choice to Die—A Private Matter" Student Lawyer May 1982, article on Judicial Discretion *Los Angeles Times* Opinion Section Aug 1982, "The Constitution Should Protect Everyone—Even Lawyers" Pepperdine L. Rev. Dec 1984, Book Review "Intellects and Egos" *Brandeis and Frankfurter—A Dual Biography* Los Angeles Lawyer Feb 1985, Monthly Column "Under Submission" *The Daily Journal* 1991, "Civility—It's Worth the Effort" *Trial Magazine* April 1991 and Book Review "A Beacon of Justice—The Life and Times of Oliver Wendell Holmes" California Lawyer Sept 1991. Important Decision: Cunningham v. Superior Court (denial of equal protection to require attorneys to represent indigents in civil cases without compensation) Cal. App. 177 3d 336, 1986. Instructor Los Angeles Valley Community College 1974-75. Former member Los Angeles County Bar Association and State Bar of California. Member Women Lawyers Association of Los Angeles, Ventura Trial Lawyers Association and Los Angeles Trial Lawyers Association. Chairperson Judicial Council Advisory Committee on Legal Forms 1978-79. Member Governing Committee California Center for Judicial Education and Research 1978-79 and Chief Justice Committee on Court Congestion and Related Problems 1978-79. Faculty Member California Judicial College. Guest Speaker Symposium for Hungarian Judges in American Jurisprudence, Budapest Hungary 1991. Panelist "What Is a Fair Trial?" Program for Russian Judges Central and Eastern European Law Initiative (CEELI) and American Bar Association Moscow Russia 1995. Named Appellate Justice of the Year by California Trial Lawyers Association (now known as Consumer Attorneys of California) 1984 and 1993. Recipient Bernard S. Jefferson Award for contributions to judicial education from California Judges Association 1987, Distinguished Jurist Award from Beverly Hills Bar Association 1992 and Judicial Excellence Award from Criminal Courts Bar Association 1994.

Office: 200 East Santa Clara Street, Ventura 93001.

Telephone: (805) 641-4700.

GILBERT, Roger G. *(Judge, Superior Court of California County of Butte)* Former Presiding Judge.

Office: One Court Street, Oroville 95965.

Telephone: (530) 538-7611.

GILDNER, Stephen P. *(Judge, Superior Court of California County of Kern)* Presiding Judge since Jan 1, 2003.

Office: 1415 Truxtun Avenue, Bakersfield 93301.

Telephone: (661) 868-4934.

GILL, Charles Raymond *(Judge, Superior Court of California County of San Diego)*

Office: 2851 Meadowlark Drive, San Diego 92123.

Telephone: (858) 694-4601.

GILL, David M. *(Judge, Superior Court of California County of San Diego)* Elected to term beginning Jan 8, 1979. Reelected 1984, 1990, 1996 and 2002. Current term expires Jan 2009. Born Indianapolis Indiana Dec 13, 1934. Roman Catholic. Educated at Stanford University A.B. with distinction 1956 J.D. 1959 and Georgetown University LL.M. 1962. Member Sigma Alpha Epsilon. Admitted to practice California 1960, U.S. District Court Southern District of California 1960, U.S. Court of Military Appeals 1960 and U.S. Supreme Court 1963. Certified Specialist Criminal Law California Board of Legal Specialization. Began legal practice Washington D.C. 1960. In legal practice San Diego 1963-74. Judge, San Diego Municipal Court San Diego County 1974-79.

Deputy City Attorney 1963 and Deputy District Attorney 1963-67 San Diego. Instructor University of San Diego School of Law 1968. Adjunct Professor of Law California Western School of Law since 1981. Director and President 1969-74 and Director Emeritus since 1974 San Diego Inn of Court. Master Louis Welsh Chapter #9 American Inns of Court since 1993. Member American Judicature Society, American Judges Association, San Diego County 1972-74 (Director, Secretary and Vice President), Federal and American Bar Associations. Colonel USAR JAGC 1960-90 (retired). Democrat. Commissioner San Diego County Human Relations Commission 1975-79. Vice President (Exploring) San Diego County Council Boy Scouts of America 1977-79. Director and President Boys & Girls Aid Society of San Diego 1969-75 and since 1983. Director and Treasurer Girls Club of San Diego 1966-67. Secretary, Vice President and President San Diego Chapter 57 Reserve Officers Association 1977-80. Member since 1980 and Chairman 1992-93 Board of Management San Diego Armed Services YMCA. Board of Directors Goodwill Industries of San Diego since 1994. Vice Chairman Salvation Army Central Advisory Board since 1979. Host since 1971 and Director since 2000 San Diego Lions Club. Member Bio-Ethics Committee Donald Sharp

GILL, DAVID M.—*Continued*

Community Hospital. Enjoys music, cycling, walking and jogging.

Mailing address: P.O. Box 122724, San Diego 92112-2724.

Office: Courthouse, 220 West Broadway Street, San Diego 92101.

Telephone: (619) 531-3806.

GILLIARD, Maryanne G. *(Judge, Superior Court of California County of Sacramento)*

Office: 3341 Power Inn Road, Sacramento 95826.

Telephone: (916) 875-3400.

GILMOUR, Richard H. *(Judge, Superior Court of California County of Sacramento)* Former Judge, Sacramento Municipal Court Sacramento County.

Office: Courthouse, 720 Ninth Street, Sacramento 95814.

Telephone: (916) 874-5476.

GINI, Eugene S., Jr. *(Judge, Superior Court of California County of Placer)* Serves Family Support Division.

Office: 11546 B Avenue, Auburn 95603.

Telephone: (530) 886-1212.

GIORDANO, Raymond J. *(Judge, Superior Court of California County of Sonoma)* Appointed by Governor George Deukmejian 1985. Elected to subsequent terms. Current term expires 2005. Former Presiding Judge. Educated at University of San Francisco J.D. 1970. Judge, Sonoma County Municipal Court Jan 1981 to Sept 1985.

Office: 3035 Cleveland Avenue, Santa Rosa 95403.

Telephone: (707) 565-1100.

GIROLAMI, Aldo *(Judge, Superior Court of California County of Stanislaus)* Appointed by Governor George Deukmejian to term beginning Sept 1, 1988. Elected June 1988 to term beginning Jan 1989. Reelected 1994 and 2000. Current term expires Jan 2007. Former Presiding Judge. Born Santa Cruz California July 24, 1939. Catholic. Educated at University of Santa Clara B.Sc. 1961 J.D. 1970. Admitted to practice California 1971. Judge, Stanislaus County Municipal Court 1984-88.

Deputy District Attorney June 1971 to Jan 1974 and Chief Assistant District Attorney Jan 1974 to Dec 1984 Stanislaus County. Co-author two chapters *California Criminal Law—Procedures and Practice* CEB 1986. Instructor in Criminal Law Modesto Junior College 1973-75. Former member California District Attorney Association, State Bar of California and Stanislaus County Bar Association. Member California Judges Association. Captain U.S. Army 1962-64. Insurance Claims Adjustor Mutual Services Insurance Company 1964-71.

Office: 800 Eleventh Street, Room 222, Modesto 95354.

Telephone: (209) 525-6371.

GISS, Harvey *(Judge, Superior Court of California County of Los Angeles)*

Office: San Fernando Courthouse, 900 Third Street, San Fernando 91340.

Telephone: (818) 898-2655.

GLASS, Geoffrey T. *(Judge, Superior Court of California County of Orange)* Assumed office Aug 10, 1998. Elected March 7, 2000, current term expires 2006. Born Washington D.C. June 17, 1954. Methodist. Educated at Amherst College B.A. cum laude 1976 J.D. 1980. Admitted to practice Minnesota 1980, California 1982 and U.S. District Courts District of Minnesota 1981 and Central 1985, Eastern 1985, Northern 1985 and Southern 1985 Districts of California. In legal practice Minneapolis Minnesota 1980-82 and Newport Beach California 1982-97. Judge, Harbor Municipal Court Orange County April 7, 1997 to Aug 9, 1998, appointed by Governor Pete Wilson.

Member California Judges Association, State Bar of California (Member 1993-96 and Chair 1996 Rules and Procedures Committee, Committee on Administration of Justice 1997) and Orange County Bar Association (Chair Insurance Law Section 1992). Speaker at miscellaneous seminars on legal topics.

Office: 4601 Jamboree Road, Newport Beach 92660.

Telephone: (949) 476-4789.

GLASSER, Thomas Daniel *(Judge, Superior Court of California County of San Bernardino)* Assumed office Aug 10, 1998. Born Pennsylvania Nov 25, 1946. Catholic. Educated at Long Beach State University B.A. cum laude 1969 and University of California Hastings College of the Law J.D. 1974. Recipient Constitutional Law Award 1973. Member Kappa Sigma. Admitted to practice California 1974. Judge, San Bernardino County Municipal Court Nov 5, 1985 to Aug 9, 1998, appointed by Governor George Deukmejian.

With District Attorney's Office San Bernardino County 1974-85. Former member San Bernardino County and American Bar Associations. E-4 USN 1966-72. Previously employed as furniture mover and steel worker. Republican. Member Boy Scouts of America. Enjoys water and snow skiing, wind surfing, racquetball and camping.

Office: 235 East Mountain View Avenue, Barstow 92311.

Telephone: (760) 256-4819.

GLENNON, Bert, Jr. *(Judge, Superior Court of California County of Los Angeles)* Former Judge, Culver Municipal Court Los Angeles County.

Office: Van Nuys Courthouse East, 6230 Sylmar Avenue, Van Nuys 91401.

Telephone: (818) 374-2265.

GLUSMAN, Robert A. *(Judge, Superior Court of California County of Butte)*

Office: One Court Street, Oroville 95965.

Telephone: (530) 538-7611.

GOETHALS, Thomas M. *(Judge, Superior Court of California County of Orange)*

Mailing address: P.O. Box 1994, Santa Ana 92702-1994.

Office: Central Justice Center, 700 Civic Center Drive West, Santa Ana 92701.

Telephone: (714) 834-3734.

GOLDBERG, Hank *(Judge, Superior Court of California County of Los Angeles)*

Office: Courthouse, 111 North Hill Street, Los Angeles 90012.

Telephone: (213) 974-5411.

GOLDBERG, Mitchel Roy *(Judge, United States Bankruptcy Court Central District of California)* Appointed by U.S. Court of Appeals Ninth Circuit judges to term beginning June 1, 1988. Reappointed June 1, 2002, current term expires May 31, 2016. Born Denver

GOLDBERG, MITCHEL ROY—*Continued*

Colorado March 12, 1943. Educated at University of Colorado at Boulder 1965 J.D. 1968. Recipient Outstanding Oral Speaker Award from CJS 1966. Staff member 1966-68 and Articles Editor 1967-68 Colorado Law Review. Admitted to practice Colorado 1968 and California 1969. In legal practice Santa Ana California 1971-88.

Co-author "Investigative Procedures of Colorado Civil Rights Commission" 40 University of Colorado L. Rev. 97, 1967. Member and Presenter Orange County Legal Education (for minors) Committee 1981-88. Member State Bar of California (Commission on Legal Technicians 1989-90). Captain U.S. Army 1969-71. Recipient Bronze Star and Bronze Star with oak leaf cluster. Enjoys travel and golf.

Office: 3420 Twelfth Street, Room 325, Riverside 92501-3819.

Telephone: (909) 774-1026.

GOLDMAN, Marc L. *(Magistrate Judge, United States District Court Central District of California)* Magistrate Judge Eastern District of Michigan Nov 14, 1983 to 2001. Appointed by U.S. District Court judges to Central District of California to term beginning July 3, 2001. Term expires July 2, 2009. Born Detroit Michigan March 31, 1948. Educated at University of Michigan B.A. 1969 and Wayne State University J.D. with honors 1973. Admitted to practice Michigan 1973 and U.S. District Court Eastern District of Michigan 1976.

Deputy Public Defender Ann Arbor 1974-76. Assistant U.S. Attorney Eastern District of Michigan 1980-83. Assistant Professor 1976-79 and Former Adjunct Professor Wayne State University Law School. Visiting Professor University of Michigan Law School 1979-80.

Office: U.S. Courthouse, 411 West Fourth Street, Santa Ana 92701-4516.

Telephone: (714) 338-4701.

GOLDSMITH, Christine K. *(Judge, Superior Court of California County of San Diego)* Assumed office Dec 1, 1998. Former Judge, El Cajon Municipal Court San Diego County.

Mailing address: P.O. Box 122724, San Diego 92112-2724.

Office: 250 East Main Street, El Cajon 92020.

Telephone: (619) 441-4336.

GOLDSMITH, Ernest H. *(Judge, Superior Court of California City and County of San Francisco)* Appointed by Governor Pete Wilson 1996. Born Oakland California Sept 2, 1936. Educated at University of California at Berkeley B.A. 1957 M.A. 1961 and Stanford Law School LL.B. 1965. Admitted to practice California 1967. In legal practice San Francisco 1973-96.

Assistant District Attorney 1967 and Senior Trial Attorney 1973 San Francisco. Chair Nonprofit Organizations Committee State Bar of California 1994-95.

Office: 400 McAllister Street, San Francisco 94102.

Telephone: (415) 551-4020.

GOLDSMITH, Jan *(Judge, Superior Court of California County of San Diego)*

Mailing address: P.O. Box 122724, San Diego 92112-2724.

Office: 250 East Main Street, El Cajon 92020.

Telephone: (619) 441-4336.

GOLDSTEIN, Daniel B. *(Judge, Superior Court of California County of San Diego)*

Mailing address: P.O. Box 122724, San Diego 92112-2724.

Office: 220 West Broadway, San Diego 92101.

Telephone: (619) 531-3820.

GOMES, Gene M. *(Associate Justice, California Court of Appeal Fifth District)* Appointed by Governor Gray Davis to term beginning May 31, 2002. Born Fresno California 1946. Educated at Fresno State College 1969 and McGeorge School of Law University of the Pacific J.D. 1972. Admitted to practice California 1972 and U.S. Court of Appeals Ninth Circuit. Judge, Consolidated Fresno Municipal Court Fresno County Oct 31, 1980 to Dec 1982, appointed by Governor Edmund G. Brown, Jr. Judge Dec 14, 1982 to 2002 and Presiding Judge Criminal Department for 11 years, Superior Court of California County of Fresno, appointed by Governor Edmund G. Brown, Jr.

Deputy District Attorney 1972-75 and Chief Trial Deputy District Attorney 1975-77 Fresno County. Cofounder and Past President Fresno County Prosecutors Association. Former Chair Criminal Law and Procedures Committee Fresno Trial Lawyers Association. Former Member Criminal Law Committee Fresno County Bar Association. Member California Judges Association (Former Member New Judge Education Planning Committee, Former Chair Criminal Law and Procedure Committee and Former Program Chair Criminal Law Institute). Former Faculty Member California Judicial College.

Office: 2525 Capitol Street, Fresno 93721.

Telephone: (559) 445-6522.

Fax: (559) 445-5769

GONZALES, Nazario A. "Tito" *(Judge, Superior Court of California County of Santa Clara)* Assumed office July 30, 1998. Born Tucson Arizona July 25, 1938. Roman Catholic. Educated at University of Arizona B.A. 1961 J.D. 1966. Law Clerk to Justice John F. Molloy, Arizona Court of Appeals Division Two June 1966 to June 1967. Member Phi Alpha Delta (Secretary 1964-65, Vice Justice 1965-66). Admitted to practice Arizona 1966 (inactive) and California 1970. In legal practice Tucson Arizona 1967-68 and San Jose California 1972. Judge, Santa Clara County Municipal Court Dec 31, 1990 to July 29, 1998, appointed by Governor George Deukmejian.

Deputy Regional Counsel Department of Housing and Urban Development July 1968 to Feb 1970. Deputy Public Defender Feb 1970 to Jan 1972 and Nov 1972 to Nov 1990 and Homicide Team Trial Attorney 1978-90 Santa Clara County. Deputy District Attorney Santa Clara County Nov 1990 to Dec 1990. Co-author Chapter 27 "Trial By Court or Jury" *California Criminal Law, Procedure and Practice* 1st and 2nd eds. Continuing Education of the Bar 1986 and 1994. Instructor Criminal Procedure Lincoln University Law School 1978-82. Board of Directors California Public Defender's Association 1982-90 (Secretary-Treasurer 1987-88, Second Vice President 1988-89, President 1989-90). Former Member West Valley Bar Association (Treasurer 1986 and 1987, Vice President 1988 and 1989). Board of Directors Conflicts Administration Program, Inc. 1995-97. Member California Judges Association. Recipient Visionaries 87 Award for Distinguished Service in the Area of Youth from East Side Youth Center San Jose 1987 and Outstanding Professor Award from Lincoln University Law

GONZALES, NAZARIO A. "TITO"—*Continued*

School 1981-82. USAR 1956-63. Previously worked as Field Epidemiologist U.S. Public Health Service. Republican. Board of Directors and Community Council Catholic Charities Archdiocese of San Francisco and Diocese of San Jose 1980-87. Board of Directors San Jose Museum of Art 1995-2000. Member St. Thomas More Society of Santa Clara County (President 1978-90 Secretary 1988-90) and Committee for Community Involvement San Jose Museum of Art 1994-2000. Advisory Board California Conservation Corp 1991-97. Enjoys reading, working out, listening to classical music and opera and watching old movies.

Office: 115 Terraine Street, San Jose 95113.

Telephone: (408) 491-4700.

GONZALEZ, Irma E. *(Judge, United States District Court Southern District of California)* Former Magistrate Judge. Appointed Judge for life by the President. Former Judge, Superior Court of California San Diego County.

Office: 5135 U.S. Courthouse, 940 Front Street, San Diego 92101-8913.

Telephone: (619) 557-7107.

GOODMAN, Allan J. *(Judge, Superior Court of California County of Los Angeles)* Assumed office Jan 22, 2000. Serves West District. Presiding Judge Jan 1, 1996 to Dec 31, 1996 and Jan 1, 1998 to Dec 31, 1998 and Former Judge, Culver Municipal Court Los Angeles County.

Office: West Los Angeles Courthouse, 1633 Purdue Avenue, Culver City 90025.

Telephone: (310) 312-6593.

GOODMAN, Larry J. *(Judge, Superior Court of California County of Alameda)* Former Judge, San Leandro-Hayward Municipal Court Alameda County.

Office: Courthouse, 1225 Fallon Street, Oakland 94612.

Telephone: (510) 272-6070.

GOODSON, Carol Boas *(Judge, Superior Court of California County of Los Angeles)* Assumed office Jan 22, 2000. Former Judge, Los Angeles Municipal Court Los Angeles County.

Office: Courthouse, 111 North Hill Street, Los Angeles 90012.

Telephone: (213) 974-5411.

GORELICK, Walter L. *(Judge, Superior Court of California County of Tulare)* Assumed office July 27, 1998. Serves Tulare-Pixley Division. Former Judge, Tulare County Municipal Court.

Mailing address: P.O. Box 1136, Tulare 93275.

Office: 425 East Kern Avenue, Tulare 93274.

Telephone: (559) 685-2550.

GRAHAM, John Stephen *(Judge, Superior Court of California County of Marin)* Assumed office June 11, 1998. Educated at Yale University B.A. 1967 and University of California Hastings College of the Law J.D. 1974. Admitted to practice California 1974, U.S. District Courts Northern 1974 and Eastern 1982 Districts of California and U.S. Court of Appeals Ninth Circuit 1974. Judge Jan 3, 1989 to June 10, 1998 and Former Presiding Judge, Marin County Municipal Court.

Member Advisory Committee on Coordination Standards 1991 and Presiding Judges Standing Advisory Committee 1992-93 Judicial Council of California and California Trial Court Budget Commission 1992-98. Lieutenant USN 1967-70.

Mailing address: P.O. Box 4988, San Rafael 94913-4988.

Office: Hall of Justice, 3501 Civic Center Drive, San Rafael 94903.

Telephone: (415) 499-6263.

GRANT, Garrett J. *(Judge, Superior Court of California County of Contra Costa)* Appointed by Governor Pete Wilson Oct 31, 1995. Presiding Judge Jan 1, 2001 to Dec 31, 2002. Born San Francisco California Nov 16, 1942. Educated at University of California at Berkeley B.A. 1964 and Golden Gate University Law School J.D. 1970. Admitted to practice California 1970, U.S. District Court Northern District of California 1970 and U.S. Court of Appeals Ninth Circuit 1970. Former Judge, Bay Municipal Court Contra Costa County, appointed by Governor George Deukmejian to term beginning May 1, 1987.

Chief Homicide Division Contra Costa County District Attorney's Office Martinez 1972-87. Instructor in Courtroom Demeanor, Search and Seizure and Evidence Criminal Justice Training Center Los Medanos College 1982-86. Lecturer on Criminal Advocacy University of California Boalt Hall School of Law 1985-86. Member California Judges Association. Attended California Judicial College 1987 and Seminar on Court Management: Role of the Presiding Judge 1988, Seminar on Trial Court Reduction 1989 and Legal Update in the Civil Law 1989-90 California Center for Judicial Education and Research. Specialist Four USAR 347th General Hospital 1964-70. Judge for Mock Trial Center of Trial and Appellate Advocacy University of California Hastings College of the Law 1987-90. Member St. Mary's Scholarship Steering Committee since 1981 and Rotary Club since 1989. Volunteer CAL Performances since 1985. Enjoys golf, fly fishing, opera and football.

Mailing address: P.O. Box 911, Martinez 94553.

Office: 649 Main Street, Martinez 94553.

Telephone: (925) 646-1542.

GRAY, Dudley W., II *(Judge, Superior Court of California County of Los Angeles)* Assumed office Jan 22, 2000. Former Judge, South Bay Municipal Court Los Angeles County.

Office: Torrance Courthouse, 825 Maple Avenue, Torrance 90503.

Telephone: (310) 222-8808.

GRAY, James P. *(Judge, Superior Court of California County of Orange)* Appointed by Governor George Deukmejian to term beginning July 27, 1989. Elected June 5, 1990, 1996 and 2002. Current term expires Jan 1, 2009. Born Washington D.C. Feb 14, 1945. Protestant. Educated at University of California at Los Angeles B.A. 1966 and University of Southern California J.D. 1971. Member Delta Tau Delta and Blue Key. Admitted to practice California 1972, U.S. District Courts Central 1972 and Southern 1973 Districts of California and U.S. Court of Appeals Ninth Circuit 1975. In legal practice Century City 1978-80 and Newport Beach 1980-83. Judge, Central Orange County Municipal Court 1983-89.

Assistant U.S. Attorney Criminal Division Central District of California 1975-78. Author "Drunk Driving Cases—Non-Traditional Sanctions" Section of Criminal Justice American Bar Association Feb 1986, "Our Drug Laws Have Failed" *Los Angeles Daily Journal* April 22, 1992 and *Why Our Drug Laws Have Failed and What*

GRAY, JAMES P.—*Continued*

We Can Do About It—A Judicial Indictment of the War on Drugs Temple University Press 2001. Instructor in "Criminal Justice System" Chapman College 1990. Member 1988-89 and Member Advisory Committee on Juvenile Court Law 1991-93 California Judicial Council. Former Member Los Angeles and Orange County Bar Associations. Co-founder Association of Former Assistant U.S. Attorneys. President William P. Gray Chapter American Inns of Court. Participant Seminars on Depositions 1983 and Civil Litigation Before Trial 1988 and 1990 CEB. Recipient Resolutions on volunteer service Santa Ana City Council Aug 1990 and combating alcohol abuse Orange County Board of Supervisors Sept 1990. Named Judge of the Year by Orange County Bar Association Business Litigation Section 1992. Lieutenant USNR JAGC 1972-75. Peace Corps volunteer Costa Rica 1966-68. Republican. Member Republican Finance Committee of Orange County 1981-83 and Alcohol Advisory Board Orange County Board of Supervisors 1985-88. Board of Trustees Legion Lex and Orange County Law Library. Advisory Board Pros for Kids. Cub Scout Master 1981-83. Member United Methodist Church Irvine 1979-83 (Board of Trustees and choir member) and Garden Grove since 1990. Composer of song "We Call Ourselves Americans." Enjoys tennis, basketball, travel and singing.

Mailing address: P.O. Box 14169, Orange 92613.

Office: Central Justice Center, 700 Civic Center Drive West, Santa Ana 92701.

Telephone: (714) 834-4680.

GRAY, Joe S. *(Judge, Superior Court of California County of Sacramento)*

Office: Courthouse, 720 Ninth Street, Sacramento 95814.

Telephone: (916) 874-5476.

GREEN, Alvin E., Jr. *(Judge, Superior Court of California County of San Diego)* Assumed office Dec 1, 1998. Judge, San Diego Municipal Court San Diego County.

Mailing address: P.O. Box 122724, San Diego 92112-2724.

Office: 500 Third Avenue, Chula Vista 91910.

Telephone: (619) 691-4770.

GREEN, Terry A. *(Judge, Superior Court of California County of Los Angeles)* Former Judge and Presiding Judge, Pasadena Municipal Court Los Angeles County.

Office: Criminal Courts Building, 210 West Temple Street, Los Angeles 90012-3210.

Telephone: (213) 974-6535.

GREENE, Warren G. *(Judge, Superior Court of California County of Los Angeles)* Appointed by Governor Pete Wilson to term beginning Jan 10, 1997. Elected 1998, current term expires Jan 2005. Born Mexico Missouri June 13, 1949. Methodist. Educated at Stanford University B.A. with honors 1971 and University of Southern California J.D. 1974. Admitted to practice California 1974, U.S. District Courts Central, Eastern, Northern and Southern Districts of California and U.S. Supreme Court. In legal practice Los Angeles 1974-97.

Member Association of Business Trial Lawyers, Los Angeles County and American Bar Associations.

Office: 900 Third Street, San Fernando 91340.

Telephone: (818) 898-2628.

GREENWALD, Arthur M. *(Judge, United States Bankruptcy Court Central District of California)* Appointed by U.S. Court of Appeals Ninth Circuit judges to term beginning March 9, 1988. Reappointed March 9, 2002, current term expires March 8, 2016. Educated at University of California at Los Angeles B.S.B.A. and Southwestern University School of Law. Admitted to practice California 1964 and U.S. Court of Appeals Ninth Circuit 1964. Judge pro tem, Los Angeles Municipal Court Los Angeles County 1980-87.

Assistant U.S. Attorney Central District of California Oct 1964 to March 9, 1987. Judge Panelist Moot Court Program Pepperdine University School of Law. Member National Conference of Bankruptcy Judges, American Bankruptcy Institute, American Judicature Society, Los Angeles County and Federal Bar Associations. Faculty Member Attorney General's Advocacy Institute Aug 1984 and June 1986. Recipient Sustained Superior Performance Award Dec 1967, Special Achievement Award July 1981 and Special Commendation Award Nov 1983 from U.S. Department of Justice. First Lieutenant U.S. Army Quartermaster Corps 1953-55. Recipient U.S. Army Commendation with Medal Pendant Aug 1954. CPA California since 1955. Member Los Angeles County Museum and KCET Public Broadcasting Systems.

Office: 21041 Burbank Boulevard, Woodland Hills 91367.

Telephone: (818) 587-2806.

GRIFFIN, John E., Jr. *(Judge, Superior Court of California County of Stanislaus)*

Office: 800 Eleventh Street, Modesto 95354.

Telephone: (209) 558-6000.

GRIGNON, Margaret M. *(Associate Justice, California Court of Appeal Second District Division Five)* Born Plainfield New Jersey Oct 17, 1950. Educated at University of California at Los Angeles B.A. cum laude 1972 and Loyola University of Los Angeles J.D. summa cum laude 1977. Staff member Loyola Law Review 1975-76. Law Clerk to California Court of Appeal Second District 1977-78. Admitted to practice California 1977. Certified Specialist Tax Law California Board of Legal Specialization. Began legal practice Los Angeles 1978. In legal practice Newport Beach, San Diego, La Jolla, Beverly Hills, Palmdale and Lancaster. Judge, Antelope Municipal Court Los Angeles County Nov 15, 1984 to Dec 1987, appointed by Governor George Deukmejian. Former Judge, Superior Court of California Los Angeles County, appointed by Governor George Deukmejian to term beginning Dec 1987.

Republican. Enjoys skiing, running and reading.

Office: 300 South Spring Street, Los Angeles 90013.

Telephone: (213) 830-7000.

GRILLI, Mary Ann *(Judge, Superior Court of California County of Santa Clara)*

Office: 170 Park Plaza, San Jose 95113.

Telephone: (408) 534-5600.

GRIMES, Elizabeth A. *(Judge, Superior Court of California County of Los Angeles)*

Office: Criminal Courts Building, 210 West Temple Street, Los Angeles 90012-3210.

Telephone: (213) 974-6535.

GRIMMER, Dan *(Judge, Superior Court of California County of Alameda)*
Office: Hayward Hall of Justice, 24405 Amador Street, Hayward 94544.
Telephone: (510) 670-5060.

GROSSMAN, Harlan G. *(Judge, Superior Court of California County of Contra Costa)* Assumed office June 8, 1998. Former Judge, Bay Municipal Court Contra Costa County.
Office: Courts Building, 1020 Ward Street, Martinez 94553.
Telephone: (925) 646-2950.

GROVER, Adrienne M. *(Judge, Superior Court of California County of Monterey)*
Mailing address: P.O. Box 1819, Salinas 93902-1819.
Office: 240 Church Street, Salinas 93901.
Telephone: (831) 755-5060.

GRUBE, James R. *(Judge, United States Bankruptcy Court Northern District of California)* Appointed by U.S. Court of Appeals Ninth Circuit judges to term beginning 1988. Reappointed Aug 12, 2002, current term expires Aug 11, 2016. Educated at University of California at Berkeley 1967 and Santa Clara University J.D. In legal practice 1975-88.
Office: 3035 U.S. Courthouse, 280 South First Street, San Jose 95113.
Telephone: (408) 535-5122.

GUADAGNI, Raymond A. *(Judge, Superior Court of California County of Napa)*
Office: Napa County Criminal Courts Building, 1111 Third Street, Napa 94559.
Telephone: (707) 299-1100.

GUILIANI, Richard J. *(Judge, Superior Court of California County of San Joaquin)*
Office: 222 East Weber Avenue, Room 303, Stockton 95202.
Telephone: (209) 468-2827.

GUNN, J. Michael *(Judge, Superior Court of California County of San Bernardino)* Assumed office Aug 10, 1998. Serves Rancho District. Former Judge, San Bernardino County Municipal Court.
Office: 8303 North Haven Avenue, Rancho Cucamonga 91730.
Telephone: (909) 945-4131.

GUNTHER, Jeffrey L. *(Judge, Superior Court of California County of Sacramento)* Appointed by Governor George Deukmejian to term beginning March 27, 1989. Elected June 6, 1990, Nov 6, 1996 and 2002. Current term expires Jan 2009. Born Los Angeles California Nov 15, 1946. Educated at California State University at Northridge B.A. 1968 and Loyola University of Los Angeles J.D. 1971. Member St. Thomas More Law Honor Society and Phi Alpha Delta (Clerk 1969-70, President 1970-71). Feature Editor *The Loyola Brief.* Admitted to practice California 1971, U.S. District Courts Northern 1971 and Eastern 1971 Districts of California, U.S. Court of Appeals Ninth Circuit 1974 and U.S. Supreme Court 1974. In legal practice Sacramento 1971-72. Judge, Sacramento Municipal Court Sacramento County Dec 1984 to March 1989.

Legal Counsel California Department of Social Services 1971-72. Deputy Attorney General IV California Department of Justice 1972-83. Chief Counsel California Department of Personnel Administration 1983-84. Contributing Author *Administrative Law* CEB 1984. Author "Discipline in California State Service" Jan 1985 and "State Employee Disciplinary Process" California Bar Labor L. Jour., "California Administrative Hearing Practice" revision CEB 1984 and Treatise Chapter *California Public Sector Labor Relations* Matthew Bender 1989. Board of Directors Organization of State Deputy Attorneys General 1978-79. Chair Sacramento Bench-Bar-Media Committee since 1994. Member Bench/Bar Review Committee since 1986, Anthony Kennedy Chapter American Inns of Court, California Judges Foundation, California Judges Association (Court Administration Committee 1985, Civil Committee 1987, Public Information and Education Committee since 1995), State Bar of California and Sacramento County Bar Association (Board of Directors Barristers 1974-77, Organizer and Chairman "Bridging the Gap" 1975-76). Graduate Municipal Court 1985 and Superior Court 1989 California Judges College University of California Boalt Hall School of Law. Lecturer on Law and Motion Nov 1986 and Trial Skills Workshop May 1987 California Continuing Education of the Bar Program and California Judges Association Municipal and Justice Court Institute Dec 1986 (Program Chair on Sentencing Alternatives Dec 1987). Chair Program on Fallacies of Eyewitness Testimony Litigation Section State Bar of California 1996. Instructor in Jurisprudence and Film Continuing Judicial Studies Program 2002. Recipient Resolution commending service to the State of California from California State Assembly Jan 1985, Mothers Against Drunk Drivers Award for sentencing program involving young persons convicted of driving under the influence Jan 1987, Resolution from the Sacramento City Council commending DUI sentencing program of young persons, Community Service Award from Sacramento County Bar Association 1990, Freedom of Information Award from Society of Professional Journalists 1996, Second Place Award in National Competition for Teaching Programs from American Inn of Court 1997 and Distinguished Alumni Award from Loyola Law School Law 2001. District Justice and Alumni Advisor Phi Alpha Delta 1973-76. Board of Directors Make-a-Wish Foundation 1984-96 (grants wishes of seriously ill children), Volunteer Center of Sacramento 1987 (United Way agency that places and trains volunteers in health, welfare, cultural, educational, recreational and civic agencies) and Albert Einstein Home for the Aged. Board of Trustees Sacramento County Law Library (Municipal Court Representative 1985-89, Vice President 1986-87 and since 1995, Superior Court Representative since 1990). Board of Directors and Participant Volunteers in Parole 1985-90 (Big Brother/Sister program sponsored by State Bar of California for California Youth Authority Parolees). Member Advisory Board Legal Center for the Elderly and Disabled, Advisory Committee Drinking Driver Program California Department of Alcohol and Drug Programs and National Safety Council. Enjoys tennis, golf, softball, fishing and bicycle touring.
Office: Courthouse, 720 Ninth Street, Sacramento 95814.
Telephone: (916) 874-5476.

GUTIERREZ, Annie M. *(Judge, Superior Court of California County of Imperial)*
Office: 939 West Main Street, El Centro 92243.
Telephone: (760) 482-4374.

GUTIERREZ, Arturo F. *(Judge, Superior Court of California County of Ventura)* Assumed office June 10, 1998. Former Judge, Ventura County Municipal Court.

Mailing address: P.O. Box 6489, Ventura 93006-6489.

Office: 800 South Victoria Avenue, Ventura 93009-0001.

Telephone: (805) 654-2965.

GUTIERREZ, Philip S. *(Judge, Superior Court of California County of Los Angeles)* Assumed office Jan 22, 2000. Former Judge, Whittier Municipal Court Los Angeles County.

Office: Pomona Courthouse South, 400 Civic Center Plaza, Pomona 91766.

Telephone: (909) 620-3023.

GUTMAN, Paul *(Judge, Superior Court of California County of Los Angeles)*

Office: Van Nuys Courthouse East, 6230 Sylmar Avenue, Van Nuys 91401.

Telephone: (818) 374-2265.

GUY-SCHALL, Lisa *(Judge, Superior Court of California County of San Diego)* Former Judge, San Diego Municipal Court San Diego County.

Mailing address: P.O. Box 122724, San Diego 92112-2724.

Office: 325 South Melrose Drive, Vista 92083.

Telephone: (760) 726-9595.

HABER, Alan B. *(Judge, Superior Court of California County of Los Angeles)* Former Presiding Judge, Santa Monica Municipal Court Los Angeles County.

Office: Santa Monica Courthouse, 1725 Main Street, Santa Monica 90401.

Telephone: (310) 260-3762.

HADEN, J. Richard *(Judge, Superior Court of California County of San Diego)* Appointed by Governor George Deukmejian to term beginning 1985. Elected to subsequent terms. Born Los Angeles California 1944. Educated at California State University at Long Beach B.A. 1967 and University of San Diego J.D. 1974. Member Phi Delta Phi and Kappa Sigma. Judge, San Diego Municipal Court San Diego County 1983-85.

Deputy Attorney General San Diego 1975-83. Instructor Thomas Jefferson College of Law since 1993. President Association of Deputy Attorney Generals 1977-78, San Diego County Judges Association 1987-88 and Louis M. Welsh American Inns of Court. Board of Directors San Diego Inn of Court, Association of Business Trial Lawyers and San Diego County Judges Association. Faculty California Judicial College 1988-92. Frequent Lecturer Continuing Judicial Studies and Rutter Group programs. Captain USNR (retired).

Mailing address: P.O. Box 122724, San Diego 92112-2724.

Office: 330 West Broadway, San Diego 92101.

Telephone: (619) 685-6148.

HAERLE, Paul R. *(Associate Justice, California Court of Appeal First District Division Two)* Appointed by Governor Pete Wilson to term beginning Aug 8, 1994. Retained by election Nov 8, 1994, current term expires Jan 2007. Born Portland Oregon Jan 10, 1932. Educated at Yale University A.B. 1953 and University of Michigan Law School J.D. 1956. Editor-in-Chief Michigan Law Review. Member Barristers and Order of the Coif. In legal practice San Francisco 1956-67 and 1969-94.

Fellow American College of Trial Lawyers. Lawyer Representative Judicial Conference of the Ninth Circuit 1983-88. Member State Bar of California (inactive), Bar Association of San Francisco (inactive) and American Bar Association (Section of Antitrust Law, inactive). Appointments Secretary to Governor Ronald Reagan 1967-69. Chair California Republican Party 1975-77. Member Republican National Committee 1975-77. Trustee World Affairs Council of Northern California. Member Yale Club of Northern California. Enjoys travel, tennis, international affairs and hiking.

Office: 350 McAllister Street, San Francisco 94102-3600.

Telephone: (415) 865-7300.

HAHN, Dale A. *(Judge, Superior Court of California County of San Mateo)* Presiding Judge Superior and Municipal Courts Jan 1, 1996 to Dec 31, 1996. Former Judge, San Mateo County Municipal Court.

Office: Hall of Justice, 400 County Center, Redwood City 94063.

Telephone: (650) 363-4516.

HAHN, Gary R. *(Judge, Superior Court of California County of Los Angeles)* Appointed by Governor George Deukmejian Dec 1989. Elected 1990, 1996 and 2002. Current term expires Jan 2009. Born Pasadena California 1949. Educated at University of California at Los Angeles B.A. 1970 and Loyola Law School J.D. with honors 1973. Admitted to practice California 1973, U.S. District Court District of California 1974, U.S. Court of Appeals Ninth Circuit 1974 and U.S. Supreme Court 1974. Judge, Long Beach Municipal Court Los Angeles County Sept 1988 to Dec 1989.

Deputy Attorney General California Attorney General's Office 1974-88. Member California District Attorneys Association, Long Beach Women's Bar Association, State Bar of California, Long Beach and Los Angeles County Bar Associations.

Office: Compton Courthouse, 200 West Compton Boulevard, Compton 90220.

Telephone: (310) 603-7842.

HAIGHT, Lois *(Judge, Superior Court of California County of Contra Costa)*

Office: Courts Building, 1020 Ward Street, Martinez 94553.

Telephone: (925) 646-2950.

HAINES, Charles F. *(Judge, Superior Court of California City and County of San Francisco)*

Office: Hall of Justice, 850 Bryant Street, San Francisco 94103.

Telephone: (415) 553-1159.

HAKE, Kenneth L. *(Judge, Superior Court of California County of Sacramento)* Former Judge, Sacramento Municipal Court Sacramento County.

Office: Courthouse, 720 Ninth Street, Sacramento 95814.

Telephone: (916) 874-5476.

HALGREN, Laura *(Judge, Superior Court of California County of San Diego)*

Mailing address: P.O. Box 122724, San Diego 92112-2724.

Office: 220 West Broadway, San Diego 92101.

Telephone: (619) 531-3434.

HALL, Diana R. *(Judge, Superior Court of California County of Santa Barbara)* Assumed office Aug 3, 1998. Former Judge and Presiding Judge, North Santa Barbara County Municipal Court.
Office: 312-H East Cook Street, Santa Maria 93454.
Telephone: (805) 346-7414.

HALL, Stephen M. *(Judge, Superior Court of California County of San Mateo)* Assumed office June 12, 1998. Former Judge, San Mateo County Municipal Court.
Office: Hall of Justice, 400 County Center, Redwood City 94063.
Telephone: (650) 363-4516.

HALLER, Judith Lynnette *(Associate Justice, California Court of Appeal Fourth District Division One)* Appointed by Governor Pete Wilson to term beginning 1994. Retained by election. Born Los Angeles California 1946. Educated at University of California at Los Angeles summa cum laude, California Western School of Law J.D. and San Diego State University M.A. Member Phi Beta Kappa. In legal practice 1979-89. Judge, Superior Court of California San Diego County Nov 22, 1989 to Aug 8, 1994, appointed by Governor George Deukmejian.
Deputy District Attorney San Diego 1976-79. Chair Judicial Ethics Committee California Judges Association 2002-03. Former Vice President San Diego County Bar Association. Former Director San Diego Chapter Association of Business Trial Lawyers and San Diego Inn of Court. Former Secretary/Treasurer San Diego Defense Lawyers. Master Enright Chapter American Inns of Court. Lecturer CLE. Former Member Board of Trustees California Western School of Law.
Office: 750 B Street, Suite 300, San Diego 92101-8196.
Telephone: (619) 645-2761.

HAMILTON, Phyllis J. *(Judge, United States District Court Northern District of California)* Magistrate Judge 1991-2000. Appointed Judge for life by President Bill Clinton to term beginning July 6, 2000. Born Jacksonville Illinois June 12, 1952. Educated at Stanford University B.A. 1974 and Santa Clara University School of Law J.D. 1976. Commissioner, Oakland-Piedmont-Emeryville Municipal Court Alameda County 1985-91.
Deputy Public Defender California 1976-80.
Office: U.S. Courthouse, Box 36060, 450 Golden Gate Avenue, San Francisco 94102-3489.
Telephone: (415) 522-4100.

HAMLIN, William Kent *(Judge, Superior Court of California County of Fresno)* Elected June 2, 1998 to term beginning Jan 4, 1999. Term expires Jan 2005. Born Fresno California July 8, 1955. Protestant. Educated at Stanford University B.A. 1981 and University of California Hastings College of the Law J.D. 1987. Chief Managing Editor International and Comparative Law Review 1986-87. Admitted to practice California 1987 and U.S. District Court Eastern District of California 1987. In legal practice Fresno 1987-91.
Deputy District Attorney Fresno County 1991-98. Former Member Fresno County Young Lawyers Association and Fresno County Bar Association. Attended Juvenile Law and Procedure Institute California Center for Judicial Education and Research April 1999 and B. E. Witkin College June 1999. City Council Member Clovis 1994-98. President Downtown Association of Fresno 1991-92. Member Volunteers in Parole Steering Committee (Chair 1995). Enjoys golfing, running, hiking and swimming.
Office: 1100 Van Ness Avenue, Fresno 93724-0002.
Telephone: (559) 488-1825.

HAMMERSTONE, James E., Jr. *(Judge, Superior Court of California County of San Joaquin)* Assumed office June 8, 1998. Former Judge, Stockton Municipal Court San Joaquin County.
Office: 222 East Weber Avenue, Room 303, Stockton 95202.
Telephone: (209) 468-2827.

HAMMES, Laura Palmer *(Judge, Superior Court of California County of San Diego)* Born Vista California June 11, 1946. Educated at Pomona College B.A. cum laude 1968 and Stanford University J.D. 1971. Admitted to practice California 1972. Began legal practice San Diego 1972. Former Judge, San Diego Municipal Court San Diego County, appointed by Governor George Deukmejian to term beginning June 14, 1984.
Former Deputy District Attorney San Diego. Co-author and Editor "Proposition 8: The Victims' Bill of Rights" California District Attorneys Association Dec 1982. Teaching Fellow University of San Diego School of Law 1982. Member California Judges Association. TWIN honoree YWCA Honor for Women in Industry. Republican.
Mailing address: P.O. Box 122724, San Diego 92112-2724.
Office: 220 West Broadway, San Diego 92101.
Telephone: (619) 531-3820.

HANKS, J. Thompson *(Judge, Superior Court of California County of Riverside)* Elected June 6, 1990 to term beginning Aug 7, 1990. Reelected 1996 and 2002. Current term expires Jan 2009. Born Beardstown Illinois May 7, 1944. Lutheran. Educated at University of California at Riverside B.A. 1969 and Pepperdine University School of Law J.D. 1974. Admitted to practice California 1974. Judge, Riverside Municipal Court Riverside County 1988-90.
Assistant District Attorney Riverside County 1974-88. Member California Judges Association since 1988. Attended course on Fact Finding and Decision Making American Academy of Judicial Education July 1990. E-4 USNR 1967-69. Teacher Riverside Unified Schools 1970-71. Enjoys scuba diving, racquetball and running.
Office: Hall of Justice, 4100 Main Street, Riverside 92501.
Telephone: (909) 955-2300.

HANOIAN, Louis R. *(Judge, Superior Court of California County of San Diego)* Assumed office Dec 1, 1998. Former Judge and Presiding Judge, El Cajon Municipal Court San Diego County.
Mailing address: P.O. Box 122724, San Diego 92112-2724.
Office: 250 East Main Street, El Cajon 92020.
Telephone: (619) 441-4336.

HANSEN, H. Ted *(Judge, Superior Court of California County of Sutter)*
Office: 446 Second Street, Yuba City 95991.
Telephone: (530) 822-7360.

HANSEN, Ronald W. *(Judge, Superior Court of California County of Merced)*
Office: 670 West 22nd Street, Merced 95340.
Telephone: (209) 385-7471.

HANSEN, Thomas P. *(Judge, Superior Court of California County of Santa Clara)* Presiding Judge since Jan 1, 2003.
Office: 191 North First Street, San Jose 95113.
Telephone: (408) 882-2100.

HARBIN-FORTE, Brenda Fay *(Judge, Superior Court of California County of Alameda)* Assumed office July 31, 1998. Former Judge, Oakland-Piedmont-Emeryville Municipal Court Alameda County.
Office: Probation Center, 400 Broadway, Oakland 94607.
Telephone: (510) 268-4104.

HARDCASTLE, Allan D. *(Judge, Superior Court of California County of Sonoma)* Presiding Judge since Jan 1, 2003.
Office: 600 Administration Drive, Santa Rosa 95403.
Telephone: (707) 565-1100.

HARGROVE, John J. *(Chief Judge, United States Bankruptcy Court Southern District of California)* Appointed by U.S. Court of Appeals Ninth Circuit judges to term beginning Sept 30, 1985. Reappointed Sept 1999, current term expires Sept 2013. Chief Judge since Jan 2, 2001. Born Babylon New York May 4, 1942. Roman Catholic. Educated at University of Notre Dame B.A. 1964 J.D. 1967. Admitted to practice New York 1968 and California 1971. In legal practice San Diego 1972-85.

Adjunct Professor California Western School of Law Fall 1986. Member Bankruptcy Law Consulting Group California Board of Legal Specialization. Member State Bar of California. Panelist California Continuing Education of the Bar Aug 1989. USMC 1968-72. USMCR 1972-90. Enjoys basketball and coaching youth girls basketball and softball teams.
Office: U.S. Courthouse, 325 West F Street, San Diego 92101-6989.
Telephone: (619) 557-6580.

HARLAN, Susan C. *(Judge, Superior Court of California County of Amador)* Appointed by Governor Pete Wilson to term beginning Oct 31, 1991. Elected 1992 and 1998. Current term expires Jan 2005. Presiding Judge Jan 1, 1999 to Dec 31, 2001. Educated at University of the Pacific B.A. cum laude 1974, Lincoln University Law School J.D. 1979 and McGeorge School of Law LL.M. 1986. Recipient Best Prosecutor Award 1979. Admitted to practice California 1980. In legal practice Sacramento and Sutter Creek 1980-91.

Member California Judges Association. Instructor in Fundamentals of Civil Procedure California CLE. Named Outstanding Alumni by Lincoln University Law School 1992 and Woman of Distinction by Soroptimists 1995. Recipient Distinguished Professional Service Award by University of the Pacific 1996. Republican. Enjoys fishing, vegetable gardening, canning and cooking and making home repairs.
Office: 108 Court Street, Jackson 95642.
Telephone: (209) 223-6463.

HARMAN, Dodie A. *(Judge, Superior Court of California County of San Luis Obispo)*
Office: County Government Center, 1035 Palm Street, San Luis Obispo 93408-2500.
Telephone: (805) 781-5421.

HARMON, James H. *(Judge, Superior Court of California County of Imperial)* Former Presiding Judge.
Office: 939 West Main Street, El Centro 92243.
Telephone: (760) 482-4374.

HARRINGTON, Thomas M. *(Judge, Superior Court of California County of San Joaquin)* Former Judge and Presiding Judge, Manteca-Ripon-Escalon-Tracy Municipal Court San Joaquin County.
Office: 222 East Weber Avenue, Room 303, Stockton 95202.
Telephone: (209) 468-2827.

HARRIS, John D. *(Judge, Superior Court of California County of Los Angeles)* Elected June 2, 1998 to term beginning Jan 3, 1999. Term expires Jan 2005. Born Los Angeles California June 19, 1934. Jewish. Educated at University of California at Berkeley B.A. 1956 and Boalt Hall School of Law J.D. 1959. Member Phi Alpha Delta and Phi Beta Kappa. Admitted to practice California 1959. Began legal practice Los Angeles 1960. Commissioner, Los Angeles Municipal Court 1973-84. Judge, Los Angeles Municipal Court Los Angeles County June 1984 to Dec 31, 1998.

Trial Attorney Los Angeles City Attorney's Office 1960-73. President California Court Commissioners Association 1981-84. Member California Judges Association (Executive Board 1989-92), Los Angeles Municipal Court Judges Association (Chair Education and Historical Events Committee, Executive Committee), Criminal Courts and Los Angeles County Bar Associations. Democrat. Board of Directors Temple Israel of Hollywood. Member Professional Club of Los Angeles (President), Jewish Big Brothers, Los Angeles High School Alumni Association (Past President) and Boalt Hall Alumni Association. Enjoys sports, travel, theater and U.S. history and politics.
Office: Criminal Courts Building, Division 45, 210 West Temple Street, Los Angeles 90012.
Telephone: (213) 974-6015.
Fax: (213) 680-1745.

HARRIS, Leland B. *(Judge, Superior Court of California County of Los Angeles)* Assumed office Jan 22, 2000. Former Judge, Los Angeles Municipal Court Los Angeles County.
Office: Van Nuys Courthouse West, 14400 Erwin Street Mall, Van Nuys 91401-2705.
Telephone: (818) 374-2601.

HARRIS, Thomas A. *(Associate Justice, California Court of Appeal Fifth District)* Appointed by Governor George Deukmejian to term beginning Jan 7, 1991. Retained by election Nov 8, 1994, current term expires Jan 2007. Born Fresno California Sept 21, 1939. Educated at University of Southern California B.A. 1961 and Stanford University J.D. 1964. Admitted to practice California 1965. In legal practice 1967-85. Judge, Consolidated Fresno Municipal Court Fresno County June 14, 1985 to March 19, 1987, appointed by Governor George Deukmejian. Judge, Superior Court of California Fresno

HARRIS, THOMAS A.—*Continued*

County, March 20, 1987 to Jan 6, 1991, appointed by Governor George Deukmejian.

Deputy District Attorney Fresno County 1965-67.

Office: 2525 Capitol Street, Fresno 93721.

Telephone: (559) 445-5491.

HARRISON, Arthur *(Judge, Superior Court of California County of San Bernardino)*

Office: 351 North Arrowhead Avenue, San Bernardino 92415-0940.

Telephone: (909) 387-3922.

HARRISON, William C. *(Judge, Superior Court of California County of Solano)* Appointed by Governor George Deukmejian to term beginning Jan 3, 1991. Elected June 1992 and 1998. Current term expires Jan 2005. Assistant Presiding Judge 1992, 1998 and 1999. Presiding Judge 1993 and Jan 1, 2000 to Dec 31, 2001. Presiding Judge Juvenile Court 1994 and 1997. Born Vallejo California Aug 2, 1941. Presbyterian. Educated at University of California at Berkeley B.S. 1963 and University of California Hastings College of the Law J.D. 1966. Member Phi Delta Phi. Admitted to practice California 1966, U.S. District Courts Northern 1967 and Eastern 1968 Districts of California and U.S. Court of Appeals Ninth Circuit 1967. In legal practice Vallejo 1966-91.

Instructor in Business Law Solano Junior College 1967-70. Former Member The Association of Trial Lawyers of America and California Trial Lawyers Association. President California Judges Association 2000-01. Advisory Member California Judicial Council. Republican. Former Member Rotary Club and Navy League. Enjoys golf, snow skiing and racquetball.

Office: 600 Union Avenue, Fairfield 94533-5000.

Telephone: (707) 421-7827.

E-mail address: wharrison@solanocounty.com

HART, Ray L. *(Judge, Superior Court of California County of Los Angeles)* Assumed office Jan 22, 2000. Former Judge and Supervising Judge, Los Angeles Municipal Court Los Angeles County.

Office: Courthouse, 111 North Hill Street, Los Angeles 90012.

Telephone: (213) 974-5411.

HARUTUNIAN, Albert T., III *(Judge, Superior Court of California County of San Diego)* Assumed office Dec 1, 1998. Former Judge, San Diego Municipal Court San Diego County.

Mailing address: P.O. Box 122724, San Diego 92112-2724.

Office: 220 West Broadway, San Diego 92101.

Telephone: (619) 531-3820.

HARWIN, Michael *(Judge, Superior Court of California County of Los Angeles)* Serves Northwest District. Former Judge, Los Angeles Municipal Court Los Angeles County.

Office: Van Nuys Courthouse East, 6230 Sylmar Avenue, Van Nuys 91401.

Telephone: (818) 374-2265.

HASHIMOTO, Roy *(Judge, Superior Court of California County of Alameda)* Former Judge, San Leandro-Hayward Municipal Court Alameda County.

Office: Hayward Hall of Justice, 24405 Amador Street, Hayward 94544.

Telephone: (510) 670-5060.

HASTINGS, J. Gary *(Associate Justice, California Court of Appeal Second District Division Four)* Appointed by Governor Pete Wilson to term beginning Sept 21, 1993. Retained by election Nov 8, 1994 and Nov 2002. Born Los Angeles California Feb 19, 1943. Presbyterian. Educated at University of Southern California B.S. 1968 and Southwestern University School of Law J.D. magna cum laude 1972. Editor-in-Chief Southwestern University Law Review 1971-72. Admitted to practice California 1972 and U.S. District Court Central District of California 1972. In legal practice Los Angeles 1972-85. Judge, Superior Court of California Los Angeles County 1985-93.

Instructor Civil Procedure Mid Valley College of Law 1976-77 and Southwestern University School of Law 1977-78. Former Member Association of Southern California Defense Counsel, The Defense Research Institute, Inc., State Bar of California and Los Angeles County Bar Association (Law Schools Committee). Member California Judges Association (Civil Law and Procedure Committee, Appellate Courts Committee). Attended Judicial Orientation 1985, California Judicial College 1986, Civil Law and Procedure Institute 1987 and 1989, Family Law Workshop 1991, one week course on Jurisprudence 1993, Appellate Courts Institute since 1994 and three day course on Juvenile Dependency 2000 California Judicial Education and Research Center; Supervising Judges Conference 1988 and 1989 and Criminal Law Seminar 1990 Los Angeles County Superior Court; "Judicial Ethics in Elections" 1994 and "Privacy Issues in Computerized Data Collection" 1994 The National Judicial College; and "Strategic Computing and Telecommunications in the Public Sector" 1994 and "Security and Privacy Issues in Data Collection" 1994 John F. Kennedy School of Government Harvard University. Lecturer "Bad Faith" Stanford Bar Institute and The Lawyers' Club of Los Angeles County 1988 and "Law and Motion Discovery" Los Angeles Trial Lawyers Association Seminar Las Vegas Nevada 1990. Member 1996 and 2002 and Chairman 1997 Planning Committee California Appellate Courts Institute. Presenter Civil Law and Procedure Updates Appellate Courts Institute 1999, California Judges Association Annual Meeting 2000 and Continuing Judicial Studies Program Civil Law and Procedure Institutes 2001-02. Member Organizing Committee Southern California and Northern California Civil Law and Procedure Workshops 1994. Named Alfred J. McCourtney Trial Judge of the Year by Los Angeles Trial Lawyers Association 1993 and Outstanding Judicial Officer by Southwestern University Alumni Association Board of Directors 1995. Recipient Hon. William E. MacFaden Award for dedicated and distinguished service from South Bay Bar Association 1999. Coach and Umpire Sunset Youth Baseball 1981-89. Coach and Referee American Youth Soccer Organization 1981-91. Enjoys running, surfing, golfing, camping and reading.

Office: 300 South Spring Street, Los Angeles 90013.

Telephone: (213) 830-7000.

HATTER, Terry J., Jr. *(Judge, United States District Court Central District of California)* Appointed for

HATTER, TERRY J., JR.—*Continued*

life by the President. Chief Judge March 1, 1998 to Sept 24, 2001. Born Chicago Illinois March 11, 1933. Educated at Wesleyan University A.B. in Government 1954 and University of Chicago J.D. 1960. Member Order of the Coif and Phi Delta Phi. Admitted to practice Illinois 1960, California 1965, U.S. District Courts Northern District of Illinois 1960 and Northern 1962, Eastern 1965 and Central 1970 Districts of California and U.S. Courts of Appeals Seventh 1960 and Ninth 1962 Circuits. In legal practice Chicago Illinois 1961-62. Former Judge, Superior Court of California Los Angeles County, appointed by Governor Edmund G. Brown, Jr. to term beginning May 26, 1977.

Adjudicator U.S. Veterans Administration 1960-61. Assistant Public Defender Cook County 1961-62. Assistant U.S. Attorney Northern District of California 1962-66 (Chief Complaint Section Criminal Division). Chief Counsel San Francisco Neighborhood Legal Assistance Foundation 1966-67. Regional Legal Services Director Office of Economic Opportunity Executive Office of the President 1967-70. Executive Director Western Center on Law and Poverty 1970-73. Executive Assistant to the Mayor, Los Angeles Director of Criminal Justice Planning 1974-75. Special Assistant to the Mayor, Los Angeles Director of Urban Development 1975-77. Author "Regional Criminal Justice Planning: Spur to Action" Los Angeles Bar Bulletin Nov 1974. Lecturer on Constitutional Law University of California San Diego 1970-71. Associate Clinical Professor of Law University of Southern California 1970-74. Professor of Law Loyola University of Los Angeles 1973-75. Former lecturer San Francisco Police Academy. Member Langston Law Club and Los Angeles County Bar Association (Executive Committee Human Rights Section). Former member Charles Houston Law Club and American Judicature Society. Lecturer Colorado State Judicial Conference 1973. Faculty member National College of the State Judiciary 1974. NCO-in-charge Battalion Information and Education USAF 1955-56. Former Vice Chairman Young Democrats of Cook County. Member Project Safer California (Court Caseload Committee). Chairman California State Advisory Council to Legal Services Corporation. Board of Directors National Legal Aid and Defender Association (Former Vice Chairman), Los Angeles Regional Criminal Justice Planning Board (Former Vice Chairman), California Law Center, National Senior Citizens Law Center, National Health Law Program, Mexican American Legal Defense and Education Fund, National Federation of Settlements and Neighborhood Centers and Education Finance and Governance Reform Project. Former Chairman Los Angeles Housing and Community Development Committee, Los Angeles Housing and Community Development Technical Committee, Los Angeles Housing, Economic and Community Development Committee and Real Estate Cooperative Board. Former member Executive Committee Board of Directors Constitutional Rights Foundation, Richmond NAACP and North Richmond Neighborhood House. Former member Mayor's Policy Committee, Mayor's Cabinet Committee on Economic Development, Board of Directors Black Law Center of Los Angeles and Bay Area Social Planning Council Board. Former Vice President Northbay Halfway House. Former Trustee Board of Education Richmond Unified School District. Board of Trustees Wesleyan University. Former member Faculty Senate, Faculty Minority Admissions Committee (Chairman), Faculty Admissions Committee and Administrative Board University of Southern California Law Center. Former member Torch Club and Commonwealth Club of California.

Office: U.S. Courthouse, 312 North Spring Street, Los Angeles 90012.

Telephone: (213) 894-5746.

HAUK, A. Andrew *(Senior Judge, United States District Court Central District of California)* Appointed for life by President Lyndon B. Johnson to term beginning 1966. Chief Judge 1980-82 and Chief Judge Emeritus since 1982. Assumed Senior status 1982, serves by assignment. Born Denver Colorado Dec 29, 1912. Educated at Regis College A.B. 1935, Catholic University of America LL.B. 1938 and Yale University J.S.D. 1942. Sterling Fellow Yale University. Admitted to practice California, Colorado, District of Columbia and U.S. Supreme Court. In legal practice Los Angeles 1946-64. Judge, Superior Court of California Los Angeles County 1964-66.

Former Special Assistant to Attorney General. Counsel Government Antitrust Division U.S. Department of Justice 1939-41. Assistant U.S. District Attorney at Los Angeles 1941-42. Instructor Southwestern University Law School 1940-42. Lecturer University of Southern California Law School 1947-56. Former Member State Bar of California. Member American Judicature Society, Lawyers Club of Los Angeles, Los Angeles County, Federal and American Bar Associations. Lieutenant Commander USNR 1942-46. Vice Chairman California Olympic Committee 1958-62. Official VIII Olympic Winter Games Squaw Valley 1960. Delegate IX Olympic Games Austria 1964. Board of Directors Southern California Committee for Olympic Games. Member Los Angeles Town Hall, World Affairs Council, American Legion, Navy League, U.S. Lawn Tennis Association, Southern California Tennis Patrons Association, Far West Ski Association, Newman Club, Yale University Club of Southern California, Pasadena Valley Hunt Club, Los Angeles Jonathan Club, National Ski Hall of Fame and Yale Law School Association of Southern California (Past President).

Office: U.S. Courthouse, 312 North Spring Street, Los Angeles 90012.

Telephone: (213) 894-5272.

HAWKINS, James S. *(Judge, Superior Court of California County of Riverside)*

Office: Larson Justice Center, 46-200 Oasis Street, Indio 92201.

Telephone: (760) 863-8426.

HAY, Margaret M. *(Judge, Superior Court of California County of Los Angeles)* Former Judge, Long Beach Municipal Court Los Angeles County.

Office: Long Beach Courthouse, 415 West Ocean Boulevard, Long Beach 90802.

Telephone: (562) 491-6130.

HAYDEN, Charles Wilson *(Judge, Superior Court of California County of Santa Clara)* Assumed office Aug 1998. Elected 2002, current term expires Jan 1, 2009. Born Jackson Michigan Feb 15, 1937. Educated at University of Michigan B.S. 1962 and University of California Boalt Hall School of Law J.D. 1965. Admitted to practice California 1966. In legal practice Los Altos 1966-70, San Jose 1970-77 and Mountain View 1977-

HAYDEN, CHARLES WILSON—*Continued*

89. Judge, Santa Clara County Municipal Court Sept 11, 1989 to July 29, 1998, appointed by Governor George Deukmejian.

USAF 1955-58. Political affiliation: Republican/Independent. President Mountain View Kiwanis Club, Mountain View Chamber of Commerce and Mountain View/Los Altos High School Board. Enjoys photography, motorcycles and writing. Personal Statement or Quote: "See your job and do it."

Office: 200 West Hedding Street, San Jose 95110.
Telephone: (408) 299-2332.
Fax: (650) 961-0688
E-mail address: chayden500@aol.com

HAYES, Charles R. *(Judge, Superior Court of California County of San Diego)* Former Judge, San Diego Municipal Court San Diego County.

Mailing address: P.O. Box 122724, San Diego 92112-2724.
Office: 330 West Broadway, San Diego 92101.
Telephone: (619) 685-6148.

HAYES, Janice Carolyn *(Judge, Superior Court of California County of Sacramento)*

Office: Courthouse, 720 Ninth Street, Sacramento 95814.
Telephone: (916) 874-5476.

HAYES, Judith F. *(Judge, Superior Court of California County of San Diego)* Former Judge, San Diego Municipal Court San Diego County.

Mailing address: P.O. Box 122724, San Diego 92112-2724.
Office: 220 West Broadway, San Diego 92101.
Telephone: (619) 531-3820.

HAYES, W. Michael *(Judge, Superior Court of California County of Orange)* Assumed office Aug 10, 1998. Former Judge, North Orange County Municipal Court.

Mailing address: P.O. Box 14169, Orange 92863-1569.
Office: Lamoreaux Justice Center, 341 The City Drive, Orange 92868.
Telephone: (714) 935-7236.

HAYNES, Marcelita V. *(Judge, Superior Court of California County of Los Angeles)* Assumed office Jan 22, 2000. Born Los Angeles California April 5, 1951. Religious affiliation: Nondenominational Christian. Educated at California State University at Los Angeles B.A. 1973 and University of California at Los Angeles J.D. 1976. Admitted to practice California 1977 and U.S. Court of Appeals Ninth Circuit 1977. In legal practice Santa Ana 1979-81 and Los Angeles 1981-83. Judge Jan 22, 1993 to Jan 21, 2000, Presiding Judge 1994-95 and Supervising Judge Civil Division 1995-96, Compton Municipal Court Los Angeles County, appointed by Governor Pete Wilson.

Field Attorney National Labor Relations Board 1977-79. Deputy District Attorney Los Angeles County 1983-93. Member California State Board of Control Restitution Committee since 1996, Black Women Lawyers, California Black Lawyers (Judicial Section), Presiding Judges Association of Los Angeles County (Treasurer 1995-96, Secretary 1996-97, Vice Chair since 1996), Los Angeles County Municipal Court Judges Association (Legislative Committee since 1994), California Judges Association (Legislative Committee since 1994), American Judges Association (Legislative Committee 1995-96), Langston and National (Judicial Section) Bar Associations. Instructor Continuing Judicial Studies Program 1997-98 and New Judges Orientation since 1997 California Judges Association. Recipient Outstanding and Dedicated Service Award from Los Angeles County District Attorney Association 1993, Certification of Appreciation from Los Angeles County Bench and Bar Affiliate 1993, 1994, 1995, 1996 and 1997, Special Achievement Award from Dare to Dream Scholarship Board 1994, Outstanding Service Award for Volunteer Contribution from Audubon Middle School 1995, Excellence Award from City of Compton 1995 and Outstanding Contribution to the Courts and Justice System Award from Western State University College of Law 1996. Named Judge of the Year by Women of Color Breast Cancer Survivors Support Project 1997.

Office: Criminal Courts Building, 210 West Temple Street, Los Angeles 90012-3210.
Telephone: (213) 974-6535.

HEASLET, Timothy J. *(Judge, Superior Court of California County of Riverside)* Assumed office July 29, 1998. Former Judge and Presiding Judge, Western Riverside County Municipal Court.

Office: 505 South Buena Vista Avenue, Corona 92882.
Telephone: (909) 272-5642.

HEDSTROM, Stephen Owen *(Judge, Superior Court of California County of Lake)* Serves Southlake Division.

Office: 7000 A South Center Drive, Clearlake 95422.
Telephone: (707) 994-4589.

HEGARTY, Patrick J. *(Judge, Superior Court of California County of Los Angeles)* Assumed office Jan 22, 2000. Former Judge, Santa Anita Municipal Court Los Angeles County.

Office: Monrovia Courthouse, 300 West Maple Avenue, Monrovia 91016-3390.
Telephone: (626) 301-4056.

HENDERSON, Richard James *(Judge, Superior Court of California County of Mendocino)*

Mailing address: P.O. Box 996, Ukiah 95482.
Office: Courthouse, 100 North State Street, Ukiah 95482.
Telephone: (707) 467-6437.

HENDERSON, Thelton E. *(Senior Judge, United States District Court Northern District of California)* Appointed for life by President Jimmy Carter to term beginning 1980. Chief Judge 1990-97. Assumed Senior status Nov 28, 1998, serves by assignment. Born Shreveport Louisiana Nov 28, 1933. Educated at University of California at Berkeley B.A. 1956 J.D. 1962. In legal practice Oakland 1964-66 and San Francisco 1977-80.

Attorney Civil Rights Division U.S. Department of Justice 1962-63. Directing Attorney East Bayshore Neighborhood Legal Center 1966-69.

Office: U.S. Courthouse, Box 36060, 450 Golden Gate Avenue, San Francisco 94102-3489.
Telephone: (415) 522-3630.

HENDRIX, Thomas C. *(Judge, Superior Court of California County of San Diego)* Assumed office Dec 1, 1998. Presiding Judge Jan 1, 1996 to Dec 31, 1996 and

HENDRIX, THOMAS C.—*Continued*
Former Judge, South Bay Municipal Court San Diego County.

Mailing address: P.O. Box 122724, San Diego 92112-2724.

Office: 220 West Broadway, San Diego 92101.

Telephone: (619) 531-3820.

HENKE, James Paul *(Judge, Superior Court of California County of Sacramento)* Assumed office June 17, 1998. Elected 2000, current term expires Jan 2007. Born Guymon Oklahoma May 27, 1947. Baptist. Educated at San Joaquin Delta Junior College A.A. 1968, California State University at Sacramento B.S. 1970 and McGeorge School of Law University of the Pacific J.D. 1974. Admitted to practice California 1974. Began legal practice Sacramento and Galt 1974. Administrative Hearing Officer, California Department of Benefit Payments 1972-76. Judge, South Sacramento Municipal Court Sacramento County Jan 1, 1977 to June 16, 1998.

Instructor McGeorge School of Law University of the Pacific (assisting in training of hearing officers) 1973-76. Member State Bar of California and Sacramento County Bar Association. Enjoys hunting, fishing, snow skiing and water skiing.

Office: 8978 Elk Grove Boulevard, Elk Grove 95624.

Telephone: (916) 685-9825.

HENNING, John L. *(Judge, Superior Court of California County of Los Angeles)* Serves Children's Court.

Office: 201 Centre Plaza Drive, Monterey Park 91754-2158.

Telephone: (323) 526-6330.

HENRY, Margaret *(Judge, Superior Court of California County of Los Angeles)* Serves Children's Court.

Office: 201 Centre Plaza Drive, Monterey Park 91754-2158.

Telephone: (323) 526-6330.

HERLIHY, John F. *(Judge, Superior Court of California County of Santa Clara)* Appointed by Governor George Deukmejian to term beginning Jan 22, 1990. Elected Nov 1990, 1996 and 2002. Current term expires Jan 2009. Presiding Judge Appellate Division since 2002. Born Atlanta Georgia Dec 17, 1949. Educated at San Jose State University B.A. with distinction 1971 and University of California Hastings College of the Law J.D. 1974. Editorial Associate Hastings Constitutional Law Quarterly 1973-74. Member Phi Delta Phi (President) and St. Thomas More Society (Vice President 1987-88, President 1990-91). Admitted to practice California 1974 and U.S. District Court Northern District of California 1974. In legal practice Los Altos 1974-76 and San Jose 1976-80. Commissioner 1980-83, Judge 1983-90 and Presiding Judge 1986-87, Santa Clara County Municipal Court.

Deputy District Attorney 1976-80. Author "*United States v. Fuller:* Just Compensation Under Attack" Hastings Constitutional L. Quar. 1974 and newspaper articles on real estate NorCal Learning Consortium 1979. Instructor in Real Estate Law Foothill College 1975-81 and Trial Techniques Santa Clara University School of Law since 1984. Faculty Hastings Trial Advocacy College 1979 and 1981 and Stanford University Trial Advocacy Program 1995, 1998, 1999, 2000 and 2002. Adjunct Faculty Santa Clara University School of Law 1999. Member California Court Commissioners Association (Board of Directors 1980-82) and California Judges Association (Criminal Law Committee 1984-85, Civil Law Committee 2001-02). Instructor Paralegal Program on Real Estate Canada College and De Anza College 1991 and since 1996. Board of Directors 1991-92 and Advisory Board since 1996 San Jose Conservation Corporation 1991-92. Member DeAnza Paralegal Advisory Board since 1998. Member Sentencing Alternative Programs (First President of Board 1985-86, Advisory Board 1986-87, Board of Directors 1985-90), California League of Alternative Sentencing Programs (Advisory Board 1986-88), Child Abuse Council Santa Clara County and San Jose Historical Museum Association (Board of Directors 1987-92). Enjoys skiing, tennis, jogging and swimming.

Office: 191 North First Street, San Jose 95113.

Telephone: (408) 299-3412.

HERMAN, Thomas K. *(Judge, Superior Court of California County of Los Angeles)* Assumed office Jan 22, 2000. Former Judge, Los Angeles Municipal Court Los Angeles County.

Office: Los Angeles Airport Courthouse, 11701 South La Cienega Boulevard, Los Angeles 90045.

Telephone: (310) 727-6060.

HERMANSEN, Gerald *(Judge, Superior Court of California County of Butte)* Assumed office June 3, 1998. Presiding Judge Jan 1, 1999 to Dec 31, 2000. Judge, South Butte County Municipal Court Nov 13, 1997 to June 2, 1998.

Office: One Court Street, Oroville 95965.

Telephone: (530) 538-7612.

HERNANDEZ, Esteban *(Judge, Superior Court of California County of San Diego)* Appointed by Governor Gray Davis to term beginning Nov 27, 2000. Born Oxnard California Nov 26, 1955. Educated at University of California at Santa Barbara B.A. with high honors 1977 and University of California Boalt Hall School of Law J.D. 1980.

Staff Attorney Department of Social Services California 1981-83. Deputy Attorney General 1983-2000 and Supervising Deputy Attorney General Appeals, Writs and Trials Section Criminal Division 1992-2000 California. Former Member La Raza Lawyers Association and Association of California State Attorneys. Member San Diego County Judges Association and California Judges Association. Recipient California Attorney General's Award for Excellence 1993 and 1995. Democrat. Interests include music and literature.

Mailing address: P.O. Box 122724, San Diego 92112-2724.

Office: 500 Third Avenue, Chula Vista 91910.

Telephone: (619) 691-4770.

Fax: (619) 691-4438

HERNANDEZ, George C., Jr. *(Judge, Superior Court of California County of Alameda)* Former Judge and Presiding Judge, Fremont-Newark-Union City Municipal Court Alameda County.

Office: Administration Building, 1221 Oak Street, Oakland 94612.

Telephone: (510) 271-5130.

HERNANDEZ, Helios "Joe" *(Judge, Superior Court of California County of Riverside)*
Office: Hall of Justice, 4100 Main Street, Riverside 92501.
Telephone: (909) 955-2300.

HERRICK, David W. *(Judge, Superior Court of California County of Lake)* Presiding Judge since Jan 1, 2002.
Office: 255 North Forbes Street, Lakeport 95453.
Telephone: (707) 263-2526.

HERSCOVITZ, Martin Larry *(Judge, Superior Court of California County of Los Angeles)*
Office: Lancaster Courthouse, 1040 West Avenue J, Lancaster 93534.
Telephone: (661) 945-6477.

HERSHER, Judy Holzer *(Judge, Superior Court of California County of Sacramento)*
Office: Courthouse, 720 Ninth Street, Sacramento 95814.
Telephone: (916) 874-5476.

HESS, Robert L. *(Judge, Superior Court of California County of Los Angeles)* Assumed office Jan 22, 2000. Elected 2002, current term expires Jan 2009. Born Los Angeles California May 21, 1948. Educated at Pomona College B.A. 1970 and University of Southern California J.D. 1976. Executive Editor Southern California Law Review 1975-76. Law Clerk to Chief Judge Albert Lee Stephens, Jr., U.S. District Court Central District of California 1976-68. Admitted to practice California 1976, U.S. Court of Appeals Ninth Circuit 1977, District of Columbia 1979 and U.S. Supreme Court 1985. In legal practice Los Angeles 1978-93. Judge, Los Angeles Municipal Court Los Angeles County Feb 18, 1993 to Jan 22, 2000, appointed by Governor Pete Wilson.
Member California Judges Association (Civil Law and Procedure Committee 1993-97 and since 2000). Recipient Distinguished Judge Award from Los Angeles Municipal Courts Presiding Judges Association 1999. First Lieutenant U.S. Army 1970-73.
Office: Los Angeles County Courthouse, 111 North Hill Street, Los Angeles 90012.
Telephone: (213) 974-5625.

HEUMANN, Ronald R. *(Judge, Superior Court of California County of Riverside)* Appointed by Governor George Deukmejian to term beginning Dec 27, 1989. Elected June 1990, March 1996 and 2002. Current term expires Jan 2009. Born Bell Gardens California March 6, 1937. Religious affiliation: Nondenominational Christian. Educated at Los Angeles State College B.A. 1962 and University of California Hastings College of the Law LL.B. replaced by J.D. 1965. Law Clerk to Superior Court of California Los Angeles County Appellate Division Sept 1965 to Sept 1966. Admitted to practice California 1966 and U.S. District Court Southern District of California 1966. In legal practice Riverside 1966-89.
Former Member Riverside County Bar Association. President Barristers of Riverside County 1969. Member California Judges Association. Attended New Judges Orientation March 1990, Judges College July 1990, Death Penalty Trials seminars, Court Security Seminar, Criminal Trial seminars and Criminal Law study course for judges. Chairman Governing Board Continuing Education of the Bar 1975-76. Police Officer Montebello Jan 2, 1959 to Feb 11, 1962. Republican. Enjoys gardening, traveling, woodworking, golf, sports and walking.
Office: 41002 County Center Drive, Temecula 92590.
Telephone: (909) 600-6400.

HICKOK, Philip H. *(Judge, Superior Court of California County of Los Angeles)*
Office: Norwalk Courthouse, 12720 Norwalk Boulevard, Norwalk 90650.
Telephone: (562) 807-7266.

HIGA, Robert J. *(Judge, Superior Court of California County of Los Angeles)*
Office: Norwalk Courthouse, 12720 Norwalk Boulevard, Norwalk 90650.
Telephone: (562) 807-7266.

HIGHBERGER, William Foster *(Judge, Superior Court of California County of Los Angeles)*
Office: Courthouse, 111 North Hill Street, Los Angeles 90012.
Telephone: (213) 974-5411.

HIGHT, Bob T. *(Judge, Superior Court of California County of Los Angeles)*
Office: Torrance Courthouse, 825 Maple Avenue, Torrance 90503.
Telephone: (310) 222-8808.

HILBERMAN, Joe W. *(Judge, Superior Court of California County of Los Angeles)*
Office: Metropolitan Courthouse, 1945 South Hill Street, Los Angeles 90007-1466.
Telephone: (213) 744-4001.

HILL, Alice C. *(Judge, Superior Court of California County of Los Angeles)* Assumed office Jan 22, 2000. Judge, Los Angeles Municipal Court Los Angeles County Nov 17, 1995 to Jan 21, 2000, appointed by Governor Pete Wilson.
Office: San Fernando Courthouse, 900 Third Street, San Fernando 91340.
Telephone: (818) 898-2655.

HILL, Brad R. *(Judge, Superior Court of California County of Fresno)* Assumed office July 1, 1998. Presiding Judge since Jan 1, 2003. Former Judge, Consolidated Fresno Municipal Court Fresno County.
Office: Courthouse, 1100 Van Ness Avenue, Fresno 93724-0002.
Telephone: (559) 488-1825.

HILL, Brian *(Judge, Superior Court of California County of Santa Barbara)*
Office: 1100 Anacapa Street, Santa Barbara 93101.
Telephone: (805) 568-2220.

HILL, Deirdre H. *(Judge, Superior Court of California County of Los Angeles)* Assumed office Jan 22, 2000. Former Judge, Los Angeles Municipal Court Los Angeles County.
Office: Inglewood Courthouse, One Regent Street, Inglewood 90301.
Telephone: (310) 419-5121.

HILLMAN, Stephen J. *(Magistrate Judge, United States District Court Central District of California)* Appointed by U.S. District Court judges.
Office: 550 U.S. Courthouse, 255 East Temple Street, Los Angeles 90012.
Telephone: (213) 894-6487.

HILTON, Douglas *(Judge, Superior Court of California County of San Luis Obispo)*
Office: County Government Center, 1035 Palm Street, San Luis Obispo 93408-2500.
Telephone: (805) 781-5421.

HINTZ, Steven *(Judge, Superior Court of California County of Ventura)* Assumed office June 10, 1998. Elected 2002, current term expires Jan 2009. Serves Ventura Division. Born Minneapolis Minnesota April 20, 1947. Educated at San Diego State College B.S. 1968 and University of California Boalt Hall School of Law J.D. 1971. Member Sigma Pi. Admitted to practice California 1971 and U.S. Court of Military Appeals 1972. In legal practice Ventura 1975. Judge May 25, 1982 to June 9, 1998, Assistant Presiding Judge 1987 and Presiding Judge 1988, Ventura County Municipal Court, appointed by Governor Edmund G. Brown, Jr.

Deputy District Attorney Ventura County 1975-82. Editor "Arson Investigation" 1980 and "Arson Prosecution" 1980 California District Attorneys Association. Lecturer in Law Ventura College of Law since 1985. Past President Ventura County Deputy District Attorneys Association. Former Vice President Peace Officers Association of Ventura County. Former Vice President and Secretary Public Employees Association of Ventura County. Former Member Juvenile Justice Committee State Bar of California. Named Judge of the Year by Trial Lawyers Association of Ventura County 1984 and 1988 and Teacher of the Year by Ventura College of Law 1987, 1988 and 1998. Lieutenant USNR JAGC 1971-75. Board of Directors Easter Seals Society 1982-88 (President 1985-88). Board of Directors California State Railroad Museum Foundation since 1999. Member Boy Scouts of America (Order of the Arrow 1997, Board of Directors and District Chairman Ventura Council 1999-2000).
Mailing address: P.O. Box 6489, Ventura 93006-6489.
Office: 800 South Victoria Avenue, Ventura 93009-0001.
Telephone: (805) 654-2976.
E-mail address: steven.hintz@mail.co.ventura.ca.us

HIRAMOTO, Joni T. *(Judge, Superior Court of California County of Contra Costa)*
Office: 100 37th Street, Richmond 94805-2136.
Telephone: (510) 374-3800.

HIROSHIGE, Ernest M. *(Judge, Superior Court of California County of Los Angeles)*
Office: Courthouse, 111 North Hill Street, Los Angeles 90012.
Telephone: (213) 974-5411.

HITCHENS, Donna J. *(Judge, Superior Court of California City and County of San Francisco)* Elected June 5, 1990 to term beginning Jan 7, 1991. Reelected 1996 and 2002. Current term expires Jan 2009. Presiding Judge since Jan 1, 2003. Born Washington D.C. Nov 10, 1947. Educated at Springfield College B.S. with honors 1969 M.Ed. with honors 1970 and University of California Boalt Hall School of Law J.D. 1977. Admitted to practice California 1977, U.S. District Courts Northern 1977 and Central 1984 Districts of California and U.S. Court of Appeals Ninth Circuit 1984. In legal practice San Francisco 1985-90.

Staff Attorney Equal Rights Advocates 1978-84. Staff Counsel American Civil Liberties Union of Northern California 1984-85. Author "Family Law" *Sexual Orientation and the Law* Clark-Boardman 1985 and "Feminism in the Nineties: Coalition Strategies" 4 Yale Journal of Law and Feminism 57, 1991. Co-author "Civil Rights Litigation" *California Civil Practice* Bancroft-Whitney 1993. Former Associate Dean University of Maine. Instructor in Sex Discrimination and Gay Rights New College Law School 1981-85 and Individual Human Rights and Judicial Process Seminar University of California Hastings College of the Law 1988 and since 1996. Adjunct Professor of Judicial Process University of California Hastings College of the Law since 1994. Member San Francisco Women Lawyers Alliance, Bay Area Lawyers for Individual Freedom (Board of Directors 1980-84), California Women Lawyers Association, California Judges Association, National Association of Women Judges, Bar Association of San Francisco and State Bar of California. Faculty Member seminars California Judges College California Center for Judicial Education and Research 1992 and 1993, "Depositions" Litigation Section State Bar of California 1991 and 1992 and "Voir Dire" CEB 1992. Recipient Social Action Award from Equal Rights Advocates 1989, Community Service Award from Bay Area Physicians for Human Rights 1990, Legal Services Award from BALIF 1991 and Judge Award from National Council of Juvenile and Family Court Judges 1995. Named Judge of the Year by San Francisco Women Lawyers Alliance Jan 1993. Interests include children's issues, camping, fishing, swimming and horseback riding.
Office: Civic Center Courthouse, 400 McAllister Street, San Francisco 94102-4514.
Telephone: (415) 551-4020.

HOCKETT, Marshall York *(Judge, Superior Court of California County of San Diego)*
Mailing address: P.O. Box 122724, San Diego 92112-2724.
Office: 325 South Melrose Drive, Vista 92083.
Telephone: (760) 726-9595.

HOFF, Gary D. *(Judge, Superior Court of California County of Fresno)* Appointed by Governor Pete Wilson to term beginning Jan 31, 1994. Elected Nov 1994 and Nov 2000. Current term expires Jan 2007. Presiding Judge Juvenile Court Sept 1994 to July 1997. Assistant Presiding Judge Jan 1997 to Dec 31, 1999. Presiding Judge Jan 1, 2000 to Dec 31, 2002. Born Los Angeles California Oct 20, 1948. Catholic. Educated at California State University at Northridge B.A. 1971 and San Fernando Valley College of Law J.D. 1975. Admitted to practice California 1976. In legal practice Van Nuys 1976-77.

Deputy District Attorney 1977-87 and Chief Deputy District Attorney Homicide Unit 1987-94 Fresno County. Former Member State Bar of California (Juvenile Justice Committee 1983-85). Member California Judges Association and Fresno County Bar Association. Named one of California's Most Effective Prosecutors by *California Lawyer* 1990 and Judicial Officer of the Year by Chief Probation Officers of California 1996. Recipient Excellence in Public Service Award from Fresno Business Council 1996. Republican. Enjoys golf and snow skiing.
Office: Courthouse, 1100 Van Ness Avenue, Fresno 93724-0002.
Telephone: (559) 488-1825.

HOFF, Michael R. *(Judge, Superior Court of California County of Los Angeles)* Former Judge, Los Angeles Municipal Court Los Angeles County.

HOFF, MICHAEL R.—*Continued*

Office: Van Nuys Courthouse West, 14400 Erwin Street Mall, Van Nuys 91401-2705.
Telephone: (818) 374-2601.

HOFFMAN, Marilyn Lois *(Judge, Superior Court of California County of Los Angeles)* Assumed office Jan 22, 2000. Former Judge, Los Angeles Municipal Court Los Angeles County.
Office: Courthouse, 111 North Hill Street, Los Angeles 90012.
Telephone: (213) 974-5411.

HOFMANN, Yuri *(Judge, Superior Court of California County of San Diego)* Assumed office Dec 1, 1998. Former Judge, El Cajon Municipal Court San Diego County.
Mailing address: P.O. Box 122724, San Diego 92112-2724.
Office: 325 South Melrose Drive, Vista 92083.
Telephone: (760) 726-9595.

HOGUE, Amy D. *(Judge, Superior Court of California County of Los Angeles)*
Office: Huntington Park Courthouse, 6548 Miles Avenue, Huntington Park 90255-2419.
Telephone: (323) 586-6351.

HOLLAND, Lesley D. *(Judge, Superior Court of California County of San Joaquin)* Appointed by Governor Pete Wilson Nov 5, 1996 to term beginning Dec 10, 1996. Elected 1998, current term expires Jan 2005. Born Paso Robles California March 20, 1954. Presbyterian. Educated at Occidental College A.B. cum laude 1976 and University of California Hastings College of the Law J.D. 1979. Review Editor Hastings Constitutional Law Quarterly 1978-79. Admitted to practice California 1979, U.S. District Courts Eastern 1979, Northern 1979 and Central 1982 Districts of California. In legal practice Stockton 1979-96.
Member California Judges Association.
Office: 315 East Center Street, Manteca 95336.
Telephone: (209) 239-6427.

HOLLENHORST, Thomas E. *(Associate Justice, California Court of Appeal Fourth District Division Two)* Appointed by Governor George Deukmejian to term beginning 1988. Retained by election. Educated at San Jose State University B.A. 1968, University of California Hastings College of the Law J.D. 1971 and University of Virginia School of Law LL.M. 1995. Former Judge, Riverside Municipal Court Riverside County. Former Judge, Superior Court of California Riverside County.
Acting District Attorney, Assistant District Attorney and Deputy District Attorney Riverside County. Chair Governing Committee California Center for Judicial Education and Research. Member California Judges Association (Appellate Indigent Defense Oversight Committee, Ethics Committee, Former Member Executive Board, Former Vice President). Faculty Member California Center for Judicial Education and Research programs and institutes. Member Advisory Board University of Kansas Law and Organizational Economics Center.
Office: 3389 Twelfth Street, Riverside 92501.
Telephone: (909) 248-0200.

HOLLMAN, James W. *(Judge, Superior Court of California County of Tulare)*
Office: 87 East Morton Avenue, Porterville 93257.
Telephone: (559) 782-4710.

HOLLOWS, Gregory G. *(Magistrate Judge, United States District Court Eastern District of California)* Appointed by U.S. District Court judges to term beginning March 7, 1990. Chief Magistrate Judge 1997-2002. Born Brooklyn New York 1947. Educated at Muskingum College B.A. 1969 and Loyola Law School J.D. magna cum laude 1979. In legal practice Los Angeles and San Jose 1979-82.
Office: 8-200 U.S. Courthouse, 501 I Street, Sacramento 95814-2322.
Telephone: (916) 930-4195.

HOLLY, Carter P. *(Judge, Superior Court of California County of San Joaquin)*
Office: 222 East Weber Avenue, Room 303, Stockton 95202.
Telephone: (209) 468-2827.

HOLM, Carl W. *(Judge, Superior Court of California County of San Mateo)* Assumed office June 12, 1998. Former Judge, San Mateo County Municipal Court.
Office: Hall of Justice, 400 County Center, Redwood City 94063.
Telephone: (650) 363-4516.

HOLMAN, Thomas C. *(Judge, United States Bankruptcy Court Eastern District of California)* Appointed by U.S. Court of Appeals Ninth Circuit judges to term beginning Dec 16, 2000. Term expires Dec 2014.
Mailing address: P.O. Box 5276, Modesto 95352.
Telephone: (209) 521-5160.

HOLMER, C. Anders *(Judge, Superior Court of California County of Nevada)* Assumed office July 1, 1998. Elected 2000, current term expires 2006. Born Oakland California Oct 27, 1947. Educated at University of California at Santa Barbara A.B. 1969 and University of California at Davis School of Law J.D. 1972. Admitted to practice California 1972. In legal practice Tahoe City and Truckee 1979-90. Judge and Presiding Judge, Nevada County Municipal Court, appointed by Governor George Deukmejian 1990-98.
Deputy District Attorney Santa Clara County 1973-74 and Nevada County 1974-79. Member Tahoe-Truckee Bar Association (President 1982).
Office: 10075 Levone Avenue, Suite 301, Truckee 96161.
Telephone: (530) 582-7835.
Fax: (530) 582-7875
E-mail address: aholmer@co.nevada.ca.us

HOLMES, Dallas Scott *(Judge, Superior Court of California County of Riverside)* Appointed by Governor Pete Wilson to term beginning 1996. Elected Nov 1998, current term expires Jan 2005. Born Los Angeles California Dec 1940. Presbyterian. Educated at Pomona College A.B. cum laude 1962, London School of Economics and Political Science, England M.Sc. 1964 and University of California Boalt Hall School of Law J.D. 1967. Associate Editor California Law Review 1965-67. Marshall Scholar. Member Phi Beta Kappa and Order of the Coif. Admitted to practice California 1968. In legal practice 1968-96.
Author articles on public transit and agricultural land

HOLMES, DALLAS SCOTT—*Continued*

preservation California L. Rev. 1967 and article on senior zoning Loyola L. Rev. Instructor on Legal Environment of Business Graduate School of Management University of California at Riverside 1977-86. Adjunct Professor of Land Use University of California Hastings College of the Law 1990. President Riverside County Bar Association 1982-83. Vice President and Member Board of Governors State Bar of California 1990-93. Member California Judges Association and American Judges Association. Chair Jury Committee Riverside Superior Court since 1997. Chair Task Force on Jury System Improvements since 1998 and Member Task Force on Retention of Judges 1998-99 and Member 1995-96 Judicial Council of California. Candidate California State Legislature 1972. Member Riverside County Republican Central Committee 1976-78. Board Member University of California Riverside Foundation. Member Rotary Club of Riverside. Enjoys walking and the theatre.

Office: 4050 Main Street, Riverside 92501.

Telephone: (909) 955-1482.

E-mail address: dholmes1@co.riverside.ca.us

HOM, Rose *(Judge, Superior Court of California County of Los Angeles)* Former Judge, Los Angeles Municipal Court Los Angeles County.

Office: Compton Courthouse, 200 West Compton Boulevard, Compton 90220.

Telephone: (310) 603-7842.

HOM, Russell L. *(Judge, Superior Court of California County of Sacramento)*

Office: Courthouse, 720 Ninth Street, Sacramento 95814.

Telephone: (916) 874-5476.

HOOVER, Frank Allen *(Judge, Superior Court of California County of Kern)* Assumed office July 1, 2000. Elected 2002, current term expires Jan 2009. Born Santa Monica California Dec 11, 1947. Protestant. Educated at University of California at Santa Barbara B.A. 1969 and University of California at Los Angeles J.D. 1972. Admitted to practice California 1972. In legal practice Bakersfield 1978-82. Former Associate Justice pro tem, California Court of Appeal Fifth District. Judge Aug 19, 1982 to June 30, 2000 and Presiding Judge Jan 1, 2000 to June 30, 2000, Bakersfield Municipal Court Kern County, appointed by Governor Edmund G. Brown, Jr.

Deputy District Attorney Kern County 1972-78. Important Decisions: Pu Epps (criminal) 182 Cal. App. 3d 1102 and Adoption of Lenn E. (adoption) 182 Cal. App. 3d 210.

Office: 1415 Truxtun Avenue, Bakersfield 93301.

Telephone: (661) 868-4934.

HORA, Peggy Fulton *(Judge, Superior Court of California County of Alameda)* Assumed office July 31, 1998. Term expires Jan 2009. Born Oakland California Jan 20, 1946. Educated at Chabot College A.A. with highest honors 1972, California State University at Hayward B.A. magna cum laude 1975 and University of San Francisco J.D. 1978. Admitted to practice California 1978. Began legal practice Hayward 1978. Judge pro tem, Fremont-Newark-Union City Municipal Court Alameda County 1980-84. Judge pro tem 1980-84, Judge Jan 7, 1985 to July 30, 1998 and Presiding Judge 1989, San Leandro-Hayward Municipal Court Alameda County (first woman elected judge of court).

Legislative Intern to Senator Nicholas Petris 1974-75. Staff Attorney 1978-81 and Managing Attorney 1981-84 Legal Aid Society of Alameda County. Author review of Preble Stolz *Judging Judges* 22 No. 2 Santa Clara L. Rev. 1982. Member Planning Committee and Consultant *Small Claims Benchbook* California Center for Judicial Education and Research 4th ed. 1992, 5th ed. 1993 and 6th ed. 1994. Co-author with Becker "The Legal Community's Response to Drug Use During Pregnancy in the Criminal Sentencing and Dependency Contexts: A Survey of Judges, Prosecuting Attorneys and Defense Attorneys in Ten California Counties" 2 Southern California Review of Law and Women's Studies 527, 1993. Member Senate Select Committee on State Court Reform (Chair Subcommittee on Civil Trial Courts 1983). Director San Francisco Public Interest Law Foundation 1982-84. President Alameda County Democratic Lawyers Club 1983. Member Advisory Committees on Legal Forms 1988-92 and Small Claims 1990-92 California Judicial Council. Chair Civil Law Institute Planning Committee 1992. Board of Directors Women Judges' Fund for Justice 1992-94 (Chair Projects Committee 1992-93). Member Women Lawyers of Alameda County (Board of Directors 1984), California-Nevada Women Judges Association (President 1987-89), National Association of Women Judges (Board of Directors 1987-89), California Judges Association (Chair Elections Committee 1990), State Bar of California (Conference of Delegates 1980-81, Landlord-Tenant Committee 1981-84, Representative to Western Center on Law and Poverty Board of Directors 1983-84), Southern Alameda County (President 1983) and Alameda County Bar Associations.

Faculty Member and Member Planning Committee Municipal and Justice Courts Institute 1987 and National Pre-Bench Training Program American Judicature Society 1990. Faculty Member since 1987 and Associate Dean 1995 California Judicial College. Faculty Member Consumer Law and Civil Procedure 1988-91, AIDS and the Courts 1991 and Domestic Violence 1991 and Member Planning Committee since 1992 Continuing Judicial Studies Program; Landlord/Tenant and Small Claims Procedure and Substantive Law 1988-92 and Trials and Evidence 1992 New Judges Orientation; DUI Clinic 1990 and Real Property Litigation Seminar 1991 California Judges Association; Voir Dire Proposition 115 Workshops 1990; and Fairness in the Courts 1993, Small Claims 1994 and Alcohol and Other Drugs and the Courts 1994 The National Judicial College. Lecturer Commissioners Orientation Administrative Office of the Courts 1988 and Drug Conference National Center for State Courts 1991. Member Planning Committee Judicial College and New Judge Orientation 1988-91. Faculty Member and Seminar Leader Municipal and Justice Courts Institute 1990. Moderator Panel on Pregnant Substance Abusers Human Rights Committee State Bar of California 1990. Faculty Member, Seminar Leader and Member Planning Committee Civil Law Institute 1991. Presenter "Managing Trials" Administrative Office of the Courts Delay Reduction Workshop 1992 and "How to Handle an 11550 Case" Alameda County Bar Association 1992. Conference Chair "What's a Judge to Do? Pregnant Substance Users and the Role of the Court" ABA Convention 1992. Conference Co-chair "Meeting the Challenge: A Judicial Perspective on Substance Abuse and the Role of the Courts" 1992. Panel Chair

HORA, PEGGY FULTON—*Continued*

"Pregnant Substance Users" Conference National Association of Women Judges 1992. Review Panel Member Policy on Perinatal Substance Use National Institute on Drug Abuse 1992. Panel Member "Criminalization of Pregnant Women: The Ethics of Criminal and Civil Sanctions Against Pregnant, Substance-Dependent Women" Education Institute State Bar of California 1993 and "Women Caught in the Crossfire" Seventh International Conference on Drug Policy Reform 1993. Moderator "Extending the Drug Court Rationale to Other Populations/Applications" Drug Courts: The Next Steps Conference National Institute of Justice Miami Florida 1993.

Guest Judge Moot Court Competition Boalt Hall School of Law, University of San Francisco and University of Santa Clara 1980-92. Named Outstanding Woman Graduate by Women's Studies Committee California State University at Hayward 1975, one of Outstanding Young Women of America 1981, Woman of the Year by San Leandro Business and Professional Women's Club 1984 and Outstanding Bay Area Businesswoman by American Business Women's Association 1986. Recipient Woman Helping Women Award from Soroptimist International San Leandro Branch 1978 and 1988 and Castro Valley Branch 1986, Valuable Service Award from Legal Services National Clients' Council 1982, Reed L. Buffington Outstanding Alumnus Award from Chabot College 1984, Woman of Achievement Award from Emeryville Business and Professional Women's Club 1985, Castro Valley Community Leader Award from Toastmasters International 1986, Alumnus of the Year Award 1989 and Outstanding Alumna Award Political Science Department 1994 from California State College at Hayward and Community Service Award from Delta Kappa Gamma Alpha Omega Chapter 1994. Associated Students Chabot College Endowment of Judge Peggy Hora Scholarship 1990. Listed in *World Who's Who of Women* 1986. Previously worked as bookstore clerk, teaching assistant, research assistant and freelance writer. Alternate Low-income Representative Southern Alameda County Economic Opportunity Agency 1972-73. Founder ad hoc Committee to form Commission on the Status of Women Alameda County 1975. Director Volunteer Centers of Alameda County, Inc. 1984, Eden Hospital Foundation 1985-92 and Hispanic Community Affairs Council 1991-94. Member California Elected Women's Association for Education and Research (Board of Directors 1990), Emergency Shelter Program, National Women's Political Caucus (Chair Southern Alameda County Chapter 1980), National Organization for Women (Coordinator East Bay Chapter 1973), 100 Club of Alameda County and Older Women's League.

Office: Hayward Hall of Justice, 24405 Amador Street, Hayward 94544.

Telephone: (510) 670-5060.

HORAN, Charles E. *(Judge, Superior Court of California County of Los Angeles)* Former Judge, Glendale Municipal Court Los Angeles County.

Office: Pomona Courthouse South, 400 Civic Center Plaza, Pomona 91766.

Telephone: (909) 620-3023.

HORN, Frederick Paul *(Judge, Superior Court of California County of Orange)* Assumed office 1993. Assistant Presiding Judge 2000-01. Presiding Judge since Jan 1, 2002. Educated at University of West Los Angeles J.D. 1974. Admitted to practice California 1974. Judge, Harbor Municipal Court Orange County 1991 to May 1993, appointed by Governor George Deukmejian.

Deputy District Attorney Los Angeles County 1974-91. Member 1994-2001 and Chair 1998-2001 Advisory Committee on Access and Fairness and Chair Trial Court Presiding Judges Advisory Committee 2001-03 Judicial Council of California. Former Member New Judge Orientation Planning Committee. Member Planning Committee California Continuing Judicial Studies Program. Faculty Member California Continuing Judicial Studies Program since 1995, B. E. Witkin Judicial College of California since 1997 and New Judges Education Program since 1998.

Mailing address: P.O. Box 1994, Santa Ana 92702-1994.

Office: 700 Civic Center Drive West, Santa Ana 92701.

Telephone: (714) 834-3729.

HORN, H. Chester, Jr. *(Judge, Superior Court of California County of Los Angeles)*

Office: Criminal Courts Building, 210 West Temple Street, Los Angeles 90012-3210.

Telephone: (213) 974-6535.

HORNER, Jeffrey W. *(Judge, Superior Court of California County of Alameda)* Former Judge, Oakland-Piedmont-Emeryville Municipal Court Alameda County.

Office: Courthouse, 1225 Fallon Street, Oakland 94612.

Telephone: (510) 272-6070.

HORWITZ, David Maxwell *(Judge, Superior Court of California County of Los Angeles)* Assumed office Jan 22, 2000. Elected 2000, current term expires Jan 2007. Born Los Angeles California April 25, 1943. Jewish. Educated at University of California at Berkeley B.A. with honors 1964 and University of California at Los Angeles J.D. with honors 1967. Member Kappa Nu and Phi Delta Phi. Winner Moot Court Honors Competition 1967. Admitted to practice California 1968. Began legal practice Santa Monica 1972. Judge, Los Angeles Municipal Court Los Angeles County Feb 1, 1981 to Jan 21, 2000, appointed by Governor Edmund G. Brown, Jr.

Author "Representing Juveniles in Delinquency Proceedings" California Continuing Education of the Bar 1979. Member Juvenile Courts (President 1977-80), Santa Monica and Los Angeles County Bar Associations. Enjoys European travel and cooking.

Office: Criminal Courts Building, 210 West Temple Street, Los Angeles 90012-3210.

Telephone: (213) 974-0080.

HOURIGAN, Francis J., III *(Judge, Superior Court of California County of Los Angeles)* Former Judge, South Bay Municipal Court Los Angeles County.

Office: Torrance Courthouse, 825 Maple Avenue, Torrance 90503.

Telephone: (310) 222-8808.

HOUSE, Mary Thornton *(Judge, Superior Court of California County of Los Angeles)* Assumed office Jan

HOUSE, MARY THORNTON—*Continued*
22, 2000. Former Judge, Pasadena Municipal Court Los Angeles County.
Office: Pasadena Courthouse, 300 East Walnut Avenue, Pasadena 91101.
Telephone: (626) 356-5689.

HOUSTON, John A. *(Magistrate Judge, United States District Court Southern District of California)* Appointed by U.S. District Court judges.
Office: 1118 U.S. Courthouse, 940 Front Street, San Diego 92101-8923.
Telephone: (619) 557-5716.

HOWATT, William J., Jr. *(Judge, Superior Court of California County of San Diego)* Presiding Judge Jan 1, 1996 to Dec 31, 1997. Born San Diego California Dec 30, 1942. Educated at University of California at Berkeley A.B. 1965 and University of San Diego J.D. 1968. Member Theta Xi and Phi Delta Phi. Admitted to practice California 1969 and U.S. District Court Southern District of California 1969. Began legal practice San Diego County 1969. Former Judge, El Cajon Municipal Court San Diego County, appointed by Governor Edmund G. Brown, Jr. to term beginning March 16, 1979.
Former Deputy District Attorney. Member California Judges Association. 4-H leader. Enjoys tennis and woodworking.
Mailing address: P.O. Box 122724, San Diego 92112-2724.
Office: 250 East Main Street, El Cajon 92020.
Telephone: (619) 441-4336.

HOWELL, Steven J. *(Judge, Superior Court of California County of Butte)* Presiding Judge Butte County Consolidated Courts Jan 1, 1997 to Dec 31, 1998. Born Greenville South Carolina Feb 12, 1952. Catholic. Educated at University of California at Davis B.A. 1974 and University of Santa Clara School of Law J.D. magna cum laude 1977. Admitted to practice California 1977, U.S. District Courts Northern 1977, Eastern 1979 and Southern 1983 Districts of California, U.S. Court of Appeals Ninth Circuit 1977 and U.S. Supreme Court 1983. In legal practice San Jose 1977-78 and Oroville 1978-87. Former Judge, South Butte County Municipal Court, appointed by Governor George Deukmejian to term beginning Sept 8, 1987.
Consultant *California Criminal Law* 2nd ed. Continuing Education of the Bar. Former Member Judicial Council. Member California Judges Association (Chairperson Rural Municipal Courts Forum 1992-93) and American Judicature Society. Faculty Court Management 1993-97 and Municipal and Justice Court Institute 1993 Continuing Judicial Studies Program.
Office: One Court Street, Oroville 95965.
Telephone: (530) 538-7612.

HUBBELL, Richard C. *(Judge, Superior Court of California County of Los Angeles)* Appointed by Governor George Deukmejian May 15, 1985. Elected 1986, 1992 and 1998. Current term expires Jan 2005. Born Mineola New York July 10, 1931. Episcopalian. Educated at University of California at Los Angeles A.B. 1954 LL.B. 1958. Member Phi Delta Phi and Phi Kappa Psi. Admitted to practice California 1959, U.S. District Court Southern District of California 1959, U.S. Court of Claims 1962 and U.S. Supreme Court 1963. In legal practice Beverly Hills 1959-64 and Los Angeles 1964-70. Traffic Referee 1970-72, Commissioner 1972-79 and Judge 1979-85, Los Angeles Municipal Court Los Angeles County.
Member St. Nicholas Episcopal Church and UCLA Alumni Association. Enjoys UCLA football, golf and skiing.
Office: Courthouse, 111 North Hill Street, Los Angeles 90012.
Telephone: (213) 974-5411.

HUBER, Joseph *(Judge, Superior Court of California County of Santa Clara)*
Office: Hall of Justice West Wing, 200 West Hedding Street, San Jose 95110.
Telephone: (408) 808-6600.

HUFF, Marilyn L. *(Chief Judge, United States District Court Southern District of California)* Appointed for life by President George Bush to term beginning 1991. Chief Judge since Jan 24, 1998. Born Ann Arbor Michigan March 6, 1951. Educated at Calvin College B.A. 1972 and University of Michigan Law School J.D. 1976. In legal practice San Diego 1976-1991.
Office: U.S. Courthouse, Fourth Floor, 940 Front Street, San Diego 92101-8908.
Telephone: (619) 557-6016.

HUFFMAN, Richard D. *(Associate Justice, California Court of Appeal Fourth District Division One)* Appointed by Governor George Deukmejian to term beginning Oct 13, 1988. Retained by election. Born Los Angeles California Jan 10, 1939. Educated at California State University at Long Beach A.B. with distinction 1961 and University of Southern California J.D. 1965. Admitted to practice California 1966, U.S. District Courts Central 1966 and Southern 1966 Districts of California and U.S. Supreme Court 1975. Judge, Superior Court of California San Diego County 1985-88.
Deputy Attorney General California March 1966 to Feb 1971. Chief Deputy District Attorney Feb 1971 to Nov 1981 and Assistant District Attorney Nov 1981 to May 1985 San Diego County. Adjunct Professor University of San Diego Law School since 1972, San Diego State University 1976-83 and Cal Western Law School since 1987. Fellow American College of Trial Lawyers. Member California Judges Association, Judicial Council of California and American Inns of Court (Senior member). President San Diego Museum of Man 1988. Enjoys sailing.
Office: 750 B Street, Suite 300, San Diego 92101.
Telephone: (619) 645-2760.

HUGUENOR, Susan D. *(Judge, Superior Court of California County of San Diego)* Former Judge, El Cajon Municipal Court San Diego County.
Office: 2851 Meadowlark Drive, San Diego 92123.
Telephone: (858) 694-4601.

HULL, Harry E., Jr. *(Associate Justice, California Court of Appeal Third District)* Appointed by Governor Pete Wilson to term beginning Feb 1998. Retained by election Nov 1998, current term expires Jan 2011. Educated at University of Illinois B.S. 1969 J.D. 1972. Admitted to practice Illinois 1972 and California 1976. In legal practice Sacramento California 1979-95. Judge, Superior Court of California Sacramento County March 1995 to 1997.
Assistant U.S. Attorney Eastern District of California 1976-79. Author "Insurance Coverage in Toxics and

HULL, HARRY E., JR.—*Continued*

Hazardous Waste Matters" McDonough, Holland & Allen Quarterly Newsletter. Adjunct Professor University of California at Davis School of Law. Lecturer American River College. Master of the Bench Milton L. Schwartz American Inn of Court 1995-98 and Anthony M. Kennedy American Inn of Court since 1998. Member Task Force on Jury Instructions Judicial Council of California since 1997. Lecturer Sacramento Barrister's Club and Sacramento Area Legal Assistants. Captain USAF JAGC 1972-76. President and Board Member Greenhaven Youth Soccer Club 1989-93. Judge high school and law school moot court competitions.

Office: 914 Capitol Mall, Sacramento 95814.

Telephone: (916) 654-0209.

HUMPHREY, Colette M. *(Judge, Superior Court of California County of Kern)* Assumed office July 1, 2000. Former Judge, Bakersfield Municipal Court Kern County.

Office: 1215 Truxtun Avenue, Bakersfield 93301.

Telephone: (661) 868-2450.

HUMPHREYS, Elizabeth *(Judge, Superior Court of California County of San Joaquin)*

Office: 222 East Weber Avenue, Room 303, Stockton 95202.

Telephone: (209) 468-2827.

HUNT, Derek W. *(Judge, Superior Court of California County of Orange)*

Mailing address: P.O. Box 1994, Santa Ana 92702-1994.

Office: Central Justice Center, 700 Civic Center Drive West, Santa Ana 92701.

Telephone: (714) 834-3734.

HUNT, Jack P. *(Judge, Superior Court of California County of Los Angeles)* Assumed office Jan 22, 2000. Presiding Judge Jan 1, 1997 to Dec 31, 1997 and Former Judge, Pomona Municipal Court Los Angeles County.

Office: Pomona Courthouse South, 400 Civic Center Plaza, Pomona 91766.

Telephone: (909) 620-3023.

HUNTER, David E. *(Judge, Superior Court of California County of Alameda)* Assumed office July 31, 1998. Elected 2000, current term expires Jan 2007. Educated at Brigham Young University B.A. 1964 and University of California Hastings College of the Law J.D. 1967. Admitted to practice California 1967 and U.S. District Court Northern District of California 1967. Judge, San Leandro-Hayward Municipal Court Alameda County Sept 1, 1978 to July 30, 1998, appointed by Governor Edmund G. Brown, Jr.

President South Alameda County Bar Association 1975 and Association of Municipal Court Judges of Alameda County 1981-82. Chairperson Alameda County Judicial Coordinating Committee 1982-85. Seminar Leader California Center for Judicial Education and Research 1985. Named Municipal Court Judge of the Year by South Alameda County Bar Association 1984 and 1989. USAR 1956-64.

Office: Hayward Hall of Justice, 24405 Amador Street, Hayward 94544.

Telephone: (510) 670-5060.

HUNTINGTON, Edward B. *(Judge, Superior Court of California County of San Diego)* Appointed by Governor Pete Wilson to term beginning Oct 1995. Elected 1996 and 2002. Current term expires Jan 2009. Serves Family Law Court. Born San Diego California 1938. Educated at San Diego State University B.S. 1962, University of California Hastings College of the Law J.D. and University of San Diego LL.M. 1982. Member Phi Delta Phi. Admitted to practice California 1967 and U.S. Tax Court 1982. In legal practice San Diego 1969-95.

Mailing address: P.O. Box 122724, San Diego 92112-2724.

Office: 220 West Broadway, San Diego 92101.

Telephone: (619) 557-2012.

HUPP, Harry L. *(Senior Judge, United States District Court Central District of California)* Appointed for life by President Ronald Reagan to term beginning March 23, 1984. Assumed Senior status, serves by assignment. Born Los Angeles California April 5, 1929. Protestant. Educated at Pomona College and Stanford University A.B. 1953 LL.B. 1955. Board of Editors Stanford Law Review 1954-55. Member Phi Alpha Delta and Order of the Coif. Admitted to practice California 1956, U.S. District Court Central District of California 1956 and U.S. Supreme Court. In legal practice Los Angeles 1956-72. Judge, Superior Court of California Los Angeles County 1972-84.

Office: U.S. Courthouse, 312 North Spring Street, Los Angeles 90012.

Telephone: (213) 894-6730.

HURLEY, Joseph *(Judge, Superior Court of California County of Alameda)* Appointed by Governor Pete Wilson to term beginning Jan 1994. Elected March 1996 and 2002. Current term expires Jan 2009. Born Chicago Illinois Oct 31, 1951. Church of Jesus Christ of Latter-Day Saints. Educated at University of California at Berkeley B.A. with honors 1972 J.D. 1975. Member Phi Beta Kappa. Admitted to practice California 1975. Judge, Pleasanton Livermore Dublin Municipal Court March 1993 to Jan 1994, appointed by Governor Pete Wilson.

Attorney Alameda County District Attorney's Office Jan 1976 to March 1993.

Office: 1225 Fallon Street, Oakland 94612.

Telephone: (510) 208-4928.

HUSING, Sylvia L. *(Judge, Superior Court of California County of San Bernardino)* Serves Rancho District.

Office: 8303 North Haven Avenue, Rancho Cucamonga 91730.

Telephone: (909) 945-4131.

HUTCHINS, Thomas J. *(Judge, Superior Court of California County of Ventura)* Assumed office June 10, 1998. Serves East County Division. Former Judge, Ventura County Municipal Court.

Mailing address: P.O. Box 1200, Simi Valley 93062-1200.

Office: 3855-F Alamo Street, Simi Valley 93063.

Telephone: (805) 582-8086.

HUTSON, Robert Byron *(Judge, Superior Court of California County of Orange)* Former Judge, North Orange County Municipal Court.

Mailing address: P.O. Box 14169, Orange 92863-1569.

Office: Lamoreaux Justice Center, 341 The City Drive, Orange 92868.

Telephone: (714) 935-7236.

HYDE, D. Ronald *(Judge, Superior Court of California County of Alameda)* Assumed office July 31, 1998. Presiding Judge Jan 1, 1996 to Dec 31, 1996 and Former Judge, Livermore-Pleasanton-Dublin Municipal Court Alameda County.

Office: Hall of Justice, 5672 Stoneridge Drive, Pleasanton 94588.

Telephone: (925) 551-6886.

HYMAN, Eugene M. *(Judge, Superior Court of California County of Santa Clara)* Elected Nov 1996 to term beginning 1997. Elected Nov 2002, current term expires Jan 2009. Born Perth Amboy New Jersey May 14, 1950. Jewish. Educated at Cornell College 1968-70, Claremont Men's College B.A. cum laude 1972 and Santa Clara University School of Law J.D. 1977. Admitted to practice California 1979. In legal practice San Jose 1979-90. Judge, Santa Clara County Municipal Court Dec 28, 1990 to 1996, appointed by Governor George Deukmejian.

Author "In Pursuit of a More Workable Exclusionary Rule: A Police Officer's Perspective" 10 Pacific L. Jour. 33, 1979; "What You Can Do When Someone That You Care About Is Being Abused or Battered at Home" 3 Aug/Sept 1996, "Judges Now Have More Sentencing Discretion Under 'Three Strikes' Law" 18 Oct/Nov 1996 and "Teenage Dating Violence Affects 36 Percent of High School Students" 6 Dec/Jan 1997 *The Woman's Voice Magazine*; "No One Wins When Parent Is Pitted Against Child" 1C Sunday Feb 1, 1998 and "Don't Overlook Gender in Jonesboro" 5C Sunday April 12, 1998 Perspective Commentary *San Jose Mercury News*; and "Counselors for Assaultive Men: Part of a Collaborative Approach to Stopping the Violence" 1 No. 1 Newsletter BC (Canada) Association of Counselors of Abusive Men 5, April 2002. Co-author with Jonathan Ng, J.D., M.D. "Who Pays the Bill?" Aug/Sept 1984 and "The Doctor and Medical Malpractice" Aug/Sept 1986 *The Bulletin* Santa Clara County Medical Society; with Hon. Peggy F. Hora Program Materials "California Drug Courts" The Rutter Group 1994; and with Sherry Simmons Comment "Firms Need to Be Aware: Violence Reaches from the Home into the Workplace" *San Jose and Silicon Valley Business Journal* 23A Sept 23-29, 1996. Instructor in Courtroom Demeanor and Evidence Santa Clara County Peace Officers Academy Dec 1979 to May 1991. Lecturer on Workers' Compensation Law 1984, 1985, 1986, 1988, 1990, 1992, 1994 and 1997, Law Office Management 1987, Community Property 1998 and 1999, Juvenile Law 2000 and 2002 and Domestic Violence Law 2001 Santa Clara University School of Law and "Alcohol and Other Drugs and California Courts: A Continuing Challenge" Graduate Program in Psychology Simon Fraser University, Burnaby British Columbia 1995. Board Member California Young Lawyers Association 1980-83. Advisory Board Santa Clara County Criminal Justice System 1982-84. Trustee Santa Clara County Bar Association 1982-84 and 1990. Advisory Board for Research into the Jury System, Grant from the Law Foundation, British Columbia 1995-97. Chair Ethics Advisory Committee Division of Workers' Compensation Department of Industrial Relations 1996-98. Member National Advisory Committee Family Violence Prevention Fund and the National Council of Juvenile and Family Court Judges 2001-02.

Panel Member "Serious and Willful Cases and Discrimination Cases: How to Use the Labor Commissioner and CAL OSHA to Your Advantage in Third-Party Cases" California Trial Lawyers Association 1993. Speaker Workshop on Domestic Violence Cases Criminal Law and Procedure Institute California Center for Judicial Education and Research 1996, "Preparing a Curriculum for Hebrew School Students on Domestic Violence" Community Alternatives on Jewish Education 1997 and "Creating a Legacy of Hope" International Conference on Children Exposed to Domestic Violence Vancouver Oct 1999. Faculty "Understanding Sexual Violence" Continuing Judicial Studies Program 1997 and "Restitution in Criminal Cases" Criminal Law and Procedure Institute 1997 California Center for Judicial Education and Research and "Judicial Accountability Panel: Strategies for Getting the Court to the Table" and "Don't Stop Until the Violence Stops" Tenth Annual National Conference on Domestic Violence National College of District Attorneys Oct 2000. Moderator "Substance Abuse, Treatment and Monitoring in Relation to Child Custody Cases" Palo Alto Area Bar Association 1998. Presenter "Probation: Preventing Violence Against Women" Second Annual Conference Chief Probation Officers of California April 2000, "Teen Dating Violence: Advocates, the Courts, and Probation Working Together for Change" Family Violence and the Courts: A Coordinated Community Response Conference Judicial Council Center for Families, Children and the Courts May 2000, "Justice Workshop" Tenth International Nursing Conference Ending Violence Against Women: Setting the Agenda for the Next Millennium Vancouver June 2000, "Specialized Courts, Principles of Working Cooperatively and Collaboratively" Bridging the Gap Across Canada: A Conference on Working with Abusive Men Victoria Oct 2000, "Our Children Our Future: A Call to Action" International Conference on Children Exposed to Domestic Violence Centre for Children & Families in the Justice System London Family Court Clinic June 2001, "Juvenile and Family Courts: Challenges & Opportunities" National Council of Juvenile and Family Court Judges 64th Annual Conference July 2001 and "Dilemmas in Educational Programming for Judges: Challenges in Community Collaboration" and "Specialized Courts on Violence Against Women" Violence Against Women Symposium 2002: The Work Continues . . .. Co-presenter "Domestic Violence in Juvenile Court" National Council of Juvenile and Family Court Judges 29th National Conference on Juvenile Justice March 2002. Named Man of the Year (for efforts in domestic violence prevention) by Women's Fund 1998. Recipient Seventh Annual Honors for the Improvement of Legal Representation for Minors from Legal Advocates for Children & Youth 2000. Police Officer Santa Clara Police Department 1972-77. Eagle Scout Boy Scouts of America 1964. Member 1983-89 and President 1987-88 University of Santa Clara Law Alumni Association Board. Member Board of Visitors Santa Clara University School of Law 1990-99. Member 1992-94 and Vice President 1994 Board of Directors Santa Clara Val-

HYMAN, EUGENE M.—*Continued*

ley Leadership Project. Board Member Santa Clara County Domestic Violence Council 2000-03.
Office: 191 North First Street, San Jose 95113.
Telephone: (408) 882-2100.

HYMER, Allan D. *(Judge, Superior Court of California County of Alameda)* Assumed office July 31, 1998. Former Judge, Oakland-Piedmont-Emeryville Municipal Court Alameda County.
Office: Courthouse, 661 Washington Street, Oakland 94607.
Telephone: (510) 268-7601.

ICHIKAWA, Garry T. *(Judge, Superior Court of California County of Solano)*
Office: 600 Union Avenue, Fairfield 94533-5000.
Telephone: (707) 421-7827.

IGLEHART, Richard B. *(Judge, Superior Court of California County of Alameda)*
Office: Courthouse, 661 Washington Street, Oakland 94607.
Telephone: (510) 268-7601.

IKEDA, Dale *(Judge, Superior Court of California County of Fresno)*
Office: Courthouse, 1100 Van Ness Avenue, Fresno 93724-0002.
Telephone: (559) 488-1825.

IKOLA, Raymond J. *(Associate Justice, California Court of Appeal Fourth District Division Three)* Appointed by Governor Gray Davis. Former Judge, Superior Court of California County of Orange.
Mailing address: P.O. Box 22055, Santa Ana 92702.
Telephone: (714) 558-6777.

ILES, Pamela Lee *(Judge, Superior Court of California County of Orange)* Assumed office Aug 10, 1998. Elected 2000, current term expires Jan 2007. Supervising Judge 1998, 1999 and 2000. Born California Nov 10, 1944. Educated at California State University at Fullerton B.A. 1965 and Western State University College of Law J.D. 1975. Admitted to practice California 1975 and U.S. District Court District of California 1975. Judge Jan 1983 to Aug 9, 1998 and Presiding Judge 1985-86, 1988, 1991 and 1994, South Orange County Municipal Court, appointed by Governor George Deukmejian.

Volunteer Attorney Jan 1976 to June 1976 and Attorney June 1976 to Dec 1976 Orange County Public Defender's Office. Deputy District Attorney Jan 1977 to Dec 1982 and Child Abuse Coordinator District Attorney IV 1979-82 Orange County District Attorney's Office. Member Orange County Judges Personnel Committee 1985. Member Family Violence Project Advisory Board 1987-89 and Criminal Justice Advocacy Unit Advisory Board 1988 District Attorney's Office San Francisco. Member California Attorney General's Commission (Child Abuse 1986, Criminal Information 1987), Juvenile Officers Association, Orange County District Attorneys Association, California District Attorneys Association, California Women Lawyers, California Judicial Council (Court Profiles Project Committee), California Judges Association (Public Information and Education Committee), State Bar of California (Committee on Crime Victims and Corrections Legal Service Section), Orange County and South Orange County Bar Associations. Drafted legislation to seize vehicles of repeat drunk drivers for sale or destruction (Vehicle Code 23198). Participant Child Witness and the Law Conference 1984, Violent Crime Against the Aging Symposium 1986 and Sexual Assault Awareness Conference 1988 Federal Bureau of Investigation; Municipal and Justice Courts Institute 1986, Child Victim Witness Project 1987, Education of the Judiciary on Child Abuse 1987, Superior Courts Institute/Juvenile Law and Procedure 1989, Judicial Fact Finding and Decision Making 1990, Continuing Judicial Studies Program Winter 1991, Child Witness Continuing Judicial Studies Program Winter 1992 and Judicial Planning Committee Municipal and Justice Courts Institute Summer 1993 California Center for Judicial Education and Research; National Conference of the Judiciary on Victims and Courts 1986 and State of the Art Conference "Presiding in Criminal Court" 1987 U.S. Department of Justice; Elderly Abuse seminar 1986 and Sixth Annual Governor's Conference Workshop on Restitution Collection 1989 Training Conference on Crime Victims; Victim-Witness Committee Peace Officer Standards and Training (POST) 1993-94; and Fourth National Conference on Sexual Victimization of Children Children's Hospital National Medical Center. Faculty Domestic Violence Workshop and Municipal/Justice Courts Delay Reduction Workshop California Judicial Council.

Honorary Consultant California Youth Authority 1984. Recipient Outstanding Service Award from Child Sexual Abuse Network 1983, Distinguished Service Award from Sexual Assault Investigators Association 1983, Orange County Women Lawyers Judge of the Year Award 1984, Outstanding Achievement in the Professions from North Orange County YWCA 1984, California Governor's Victim Service Award 1986, Women of Achievement Award for Excellence in Law from YWCA 1987, Child Advocate of the Year Award from Orange County Child Abuse Task Force 1988, Orange County Board of Supervisors Resolution Commendation for outstanding contribution to Child Abuse Services Team (CAST) 1989, U.S. Justice Department/FBI/GFWC Certificate of Achievement in the New Sexual Assault Awareness Program 1988-90, Lee Steelman Award for dedication to eradicating family violence 1997, Public Commendation for dedicated service to the community from Supervisor Thomas W. Wilson 1997, CASA-CAST Judicial Honoree 1998, Childhelp USA Award for dedication to children March 25, 1999, Colleen Lau Pearson Award from Stop-Gap 1999, Morton Bard Award for Outstanding Contribution to the Victims' Movement from National Association for Victim Assistance 2000, Model of Unity Award from Bahia's of Aliso Viejo, CA May 2001, Fifth Annual Ambassador of Peace Award from Violence Prevention Coalition of Orange County June 2001 and Ralph N. Kleps Award 2001. Inducted into Western State University College of Law Hall of Fame 1999. Republican. Member National Women's Political Caucus. Member Lt. Governor Leo McCarthy's Commission on the Task Force for the Seriously Mentally Ill 1986-88. Member California Sexual Assault Association, National Organization of Victim Assistance (Victim Assistance Programs 1986-88, Child Witness Conference 1987, Advisory Board for State Justice Institute Project 1988, Restorative Community Justice Think Tank), California Department of Youth Authority (Victim Services Project 1986, Victim Programming Advisory Task Force 1987-88), Victims Services Agency New York (Advisory

ILES, PAMELA LEE—*Continued*
Board member Law Enforcement Executive Training and Technical Assistance Project on Domestic Violence 1987, Law Enforcement Response to Domestic Violence 1988-89), Sexual Victimization of Children Committee Federal Bureau of Investigation 1984, Athletes Against Drug Abuse 1987-88, Child Abuse Services Task Force (CAST) 1987-92 and Committee Member Family Advocacy Program Marine Corps 1989-94. Enjoys gourmet cooking and gardening.

Office: 30142 Crown Valley Parkway, Laguna Niguel 92677.

Telephone: (949) 249-5000.

ILLSTON, Susan Yvonne *(Judge, United States District Court Northern District of California)* Appointed for life by President Bill Clinton to term beginning 1995. Born Tokyo Japan June 24, 1948. Educated at Duke University B.A. 1970 and Stanford University J.D. 1973. In legal practice Burlingame 1973-95.

Office: U.S. Courthouse, Box 36060, 450 Golden Gate Avenue, San Francisco 94102-3489.

Telephone: (415) 522-4070.

INFANTE, Edward A. *(Recalled Magistrate Judge, United States District Court Northern District of California)* Appointed Magistrate Judge by U.S. District Court judges to term beginning March 31, 1990. Reappointed March 1998. Appointed Recalled Magistrate Judge by the Judicial Council of the Ninth Circuit June 18, 2001. Serves part time. Born Providence Rhode Island May 22, 1940. Educated at Boston College A.B. 1962 and Boston University School of Law J.D. 1965. Law Clerk to Hon. Edward McEntee, U.S. Court of Appeals First Circuit 1965-66. Admitted to practice Rhode Island 1965, U.S. Courts of Appeals First 1966 and Ninth 1970 Circuits, California 1970 and U.S. District Court Southern District of California 1970. In legal practice San Diego 1969-72. Magistrate, U.S. District Court Southern District of California 1972-86 and U.S. District Court Northern District of California 1986-88.

Important Decisions: Patel v. U.S.A. (interprets discretionary function exception to the Federal Tort Claims Act 28 U.S.C. Section 2680(a) and dismisses plaintiff's claim for negligent infliction of emotional distress under California law) 806 F. Supp. 873 N.D. Cal. 1992; Miller v. County of Santa Cruz (summary judgment granted in favor of defendant where plaintiff failed to appeal administrative affirmance of employment termination) 796 F. Supp. 1316 N.D. Cal. 1992; James v. Equicor (applies de novo standard of review to a denial benefits challenged under Section 1132(a)(1)(B) The Employee Retirement and Income Security Act "ERISA") F. Supp. 804 N.D. Cal. 1992; Williams v. Leybold (interprets several provisions of the Emergency Planning and Community Right to Know Act 42 U.S.C.A. Section 11001 et seq. aka EPCRA) 784 F. Supp. 765 N.D. Cal. 1992; Conner Peripherals, Inc. v. Western Digital Corp. 31 U.S.P.Q.2d 1042 N.D. Cal. 1993; Samuels v. Mitchell 155 F.R.D. 195, 28 Fed. R. Serv. 3d 1434 N.D. Cal. 1994; Economou v. Little 850 F. Supp. 849 N.D. Cal. 1994; and Starsight Telecast, Inc. v. Gemstar Development Corp. F.R.D. 1994 WL 705233 N.D. Cal. Dec 12, 1994. Instructor California Western School of Law 1972-84 and Santa Clara University School of Law since 1990. Member 1972-88 and 1990-92, Treasurer 1979, Vice President 1980 and President 1981 Federal Magistrate Judges Association. U.S. Trustee, Southern District of California 1988-90 and District of Hawaii 1988-90 Department of Justice. Lieutenant USN 1966-69. Captain USNR.

Office: 2112 U.S. Courthouse, 280 South First Street, San Jose 95113.

Telephone: (408) 535-5340.

INFANTINO, Jerald A. *(Judge, Superior Court of California County of Santa Clara)* Assumed office July 30, 1998. Former Judge, Santa Clara County Municipal Court.

Office: 605 West El Camino Real, Sunnyvale 94087.

Telephone: (408) 481-3500.

INGLE, Gary A. *(Judge, Superior Court of California County of Kern)* Assumed office July 1, 2000. Presiding Judge Jan 1, 1996 to Dec 31, 1996 and Former Judge, North Kern Municipal Court Kern County.

Office: 325 Central Valley Highway, Shafter 93263.

Telephone: (661) 746-3312.

INJEJIKIAN, Maral *(Judge, Superior Court of California County of Los Angeles)* Assumed office Jan 22, 2000. Former Judge, Los Angeles Municipal Court Los Angeles County.

Office: Criminal Courts Building, 210 West Temple Street, Los Angeles 90012-3210.

Telephone: (213) 974-6535.

IRION, Joan K. *(Judge, Superior Court of California County of San Diego)*

Mailing address: P.O. Box 122724, San Diego 92112-2724.

Office: 325 South Melrose Drive, Vista 92083.

Telephone: (760) 726-9595.

ISACKSON, Carol *(Judge, Superior Court of California County of San Diego)*

Office: 2851 Meadowlark Drive, San Diego 92123.

Telephone: (858) 694-4601.

ISACOFF, Susan Elizabeth *(Judge, Superior Court of California County of Los Angeles)* Assumed office Jan 22, 2000. Former Judge, Los Angeles Municipal Court Los Angeles County.

Office: Courthouse, 111 North Hill Street, Los Angeles 90012.

Telephone: (213) 974-5411.

ISHII, Anthony W. *(Judge, United States District Court Eastern District of California)* Appointed for life by President Bill Clinton to term beginning Oct 31, 1997. Born Santa Ana California Sept 19, 1946. Educated at Reedley Junior College A.S. 1966, University of the Pacific Pharm.D. 1970 and University of California Boalt Hall School of Law J.D. 1973. In legal practice Fresno 1979-83. Judge, Central Valley Municipal Court Fresno County May 2, 1983 to Oct 30, 1997.

Deputy City Attorney Sacramento 1975. Deputy Public Defender Fresno County 1979.

Office: 5554 U.S. Courthouse, 1130 O Street, Fresno 93721.

Telephone: (559) 498-7341.

ITO, Lance Allan *(Judge, Superior Court of California County of Los Angeles)* Appointed by Governor George Deukmejian to term beginning July 15, 1989. Elected 1990, 1996 and 2002. Current term expires Jan 2009. Born Los Angeles California Aug 2, 1950. Educated at University of California at Los Angeles B.A.

ITO, LANCE ALLAN—*Continued*

cum laude 1972 and University of California at Berkeley J.D. 1975. Admitted to practice California 1975 and U.S. District Court Central District of California 1976. In legal practice Los Angeles 1975-77. Judge, Los Angeles Municipal Court Los Angeles County Dec 18, 1987 to July 14, 1989, appointed by Governor George Deukmejian.

Deputy District Attorney Los Angeles County 1977-87 (Hard Core Gang and Organized Crime Units). Former Member Los Angeles County Association of Deputy District Attorneys (Board of Directors 1984-87) and California District Attorneys Association. Board of Directors California Judges Foundation since 1990. Member California Council on Criminal Justice, California Judges Association, Los Angeles County and Japanese-American Bar Associations. Democrat. Vice Chair California Task Force on Youth Gang Violence 1986 and 1989 and California Task Force on Victims Rights 1988.

Office: Criminal Courts Building, 210 West Temple Street, Los Angeles 90012-3210.

Telephone: (213) 974-6535.

IWASKO, James F. *(Judge, Superior Court of California County of Santa Barbara)*

Office: 115 Civic Center Plaza, Lompoc 93436-6967.

Telephone: (805) 737-7790.

JACKSON, Frank Y. *(Judge, Superior Court of California County of Los Angeles)* Appointed by Governor Pete Wilson to term beginning Feb 1993. Elected 1994 and 2000. Current term expires Jan 2007. Serves North District. Born Alhambra California June 10, 1948. Protestant. Educated at University of Nevada B.A. 1970 and McGeorge School of Law University of the Pacific J.D. with honors 1973. Admitted to practice California 1973 and U.S. District Court Central District of California 1973. In legal practice Lancaster 1973-90. Judge, Antelope Municipal Court Los Angeles County Jan 25, 1990 to Feb 1993.

Instructor in Business Law Golden Gate University 1974-92, Antelope Valley College since 1974 and La Verne University since 1997. Director United Way. Enjoys tennis and basketball.

Office: Palmdale Courthouse, 38256 Sierra Highway, Palmdale 93550.

Telephone: (661) 537-2610.

JACKSON, Teri L. *(Judge, Superior Court of California City and County of San Francisco)*

Office: Hall of Justice, 850 Bryant Street, San Francisco 94103.

Telephone: (415) 553-1159.

JACOBS-MAY, Jamie A. *(Judge, Superior Court of California County of Santa Clara)* Assumed office July 30, 1998. Presiding Judge Jan 1, 1997 to Dec 31, 1997 and Former Judge, Santa Clara County Municipal Court.

Office: 191 North First Street, San Jose 95113.

Telephone: (408) 882-2100.

JAEGER, Karl W. *(Judge, Superior Court of California County of Los Angeles)* Educated at University of Southern California A.B. 1958 and Southwestern University J.D. 1965. Former Judge, Assistant Presiding Judge and Presiding Judge, Los Angeles Municipal Court Los Angeles County, appointed by Governor George Deukmejian to term beginning Jan 1987.

Member Executive Committee Municipal Court Judges Association and Small Claims Committee Administrative Office of the Courts. Attended California Judicial Education and Research Center Judicial College 1987, Advanced Judicial Studies at Northstar 1987 and Team Building, Leadership and Management, Alternative Sentencing and Court Security Institute of Court Management. City Council 1976-82 and Mayor 1979-80 Covina. Director Los Angeles County Sanitation District and Los Angeles County Division League of Cities (Member Revenue and Taxation Committee). President San Gabriel Valley Association of Cities.

Office: Pomona Courthouse South, 400 Civic Center Plaza, Pomona 91766.

Telephone: (909) 620-3023.

JAHR, Steven E. *(Judge, Superior Court of California County of Shasta)* Presiding Judge Jan 1, 1993 to Dec 31, 1996. Former Judge and Presiding Judge, Shasta County Municipal Court.

Executive Board 1991-93 and Vice President 1993 California Judges Association. Member 1993-98 and Chair 1997-98 California Trial Court Budget Commission. Former Member Judicial Council of California. Instructor in Civil Law and Procedure at various institutes California Center for Judicial Education and Research. Recipient Distinguished Service Award as Jurist of the Year from State Judicial Council 1997.

Office: 1500 Court Street, Room 205, Redding 96001-1685.

Telephone: (530) 245-6761.

Fax: (530) 225-5339

JAMES, Maria-Elena *(Magistrate Judge, United States District Court Northern District of California)* Appointed by U.S. District Court judges to term beginning Oct 11, 1994. Reappointed Oct 2002, current term expires Oct 2010. Born Ann Arbor Michigan Aug 22, 1953. Educated at University of California at Irvine B.A. 1975 and University of San Francisco J.D. 1978. Admitted to practice California 1979.

Office: U.S. Courthouse, 450 Golden Gate Avenue, San Francisco 94102.

Telephone: (415) 522-4698.

JAMESON, C. Robert *(Judge, Superior Court of California County of Orange)* Appointed by Governor George Deukmejian May 1, 1987. Elected June 7, 1988, June 1994 and 2000. Current term expires Jan 2007. Presiding Judge Orange County Juvenile Court July 1, 1988 to Dec 31, 1990. Supervising Judge Civil Litigation Panel 1998-99. Presiding Judge Appellate Division 1998-99. Assistant Presiding Judge 2000. Presiding Judge Jan 24, 2000 to Dec 31, 2001. Born Woodland California Jan 8, 1940. Protestant. Educated at University of California at Davis B.A. 1963 and University of California Hastings College of the Law J.D. 1966. Admitted to practice California 1966. In legal practice Santa Ana 1979-84. Judge, Central Orange County Municipal Court 1984-87, appointed by Governor George Deukmejian.

Deputy District Attorney 1967-70 and District Attorney 1970-78 Yolo County. Adjunct Professor of Law Whittier Law School 1998. Named Judge of the Year by Constitutional Rights Foundation 1987 and 1998, Chief Probation Officers Association of California 1990, Consumer Attorneys of California 1997, Business Litigation Section Orange County Bar Association 1998 and Orange County Chapter American Board of Trial Advocates 1999 and Alumnus of the Year by Orange County

JAMESON, C. ROBERT—*Continued*
Chapter Hastings College of the Law Alumni Association 1992. Recipient Commendation Dedication to the Bench, Children and Citizens of Orange County from Orange County Board of Supervisors Feb 1991. Deputy Legislative Counsel California Legislature 1966-67. Enjoys card collecting and cacti.

Mailing address: P.O. Box 1994, Santa Ana 92702-1994.

Office: Central Justice Center, 700 Civic Center Drive West, Santa Ana 92701.

Telephone: (714) 834-3734.

JANAVS, Dzintra I. *(Judge, Superior Court of California County of Los Angeles)*

Office: Courthouse, 111 North Hill Street, Los Angeles 90012.

Telephone: (213) 974-5411.

JAROSLOVSKY, Alan *(Judge, United States Bankruptcy Court Northern District of California)* Appointed by U.S. Court of Appeals Ninth Circuit judges to term beginning Jan 1987. Reappointed Jan 2001, current term expires Jan 2015. Educated at University of California at Los Angeles B.A. and Golden Gate University J.D.

Office: 99 South E Street, Santa Rosa 95404.

Telephone: (707) 525-0386.

JEAN, Arthur H., Jr. *(Judge, Superior Court of California County of Los Angeles)* Born Nashua New Hampshire Sept 22, 1943. Educated at Dartmouth College A.B. 1968 and Harvard University J.D. 1971. Admitted to practice California 1972. Former Judge, Long Beach Municipal Court Los Angeles County, appointed by Governor George Deukmejian to term beginning March 12, 1985.

Former Prosecutor Los Angeles County District Attorney's Office. U.S. Army 1964-67.

Office: Long Beach Courthouse, 415 West Ocean Boulevard, Long Beach 90802.

Telephone: (562) 491-6130.

JELLEN, Edward D. *(Chief Judge, United States Bankruptcy Court Northern District of California)* Appointed by U.S. Court of Appeals Ninth Circuit judges to term beginning Jan 1987. Reappointed Jan 2001, current term expires Jan 2015. Chief Judge since Jan 1997. Educated at University of California at Berkeley A.B. 1967 J.D. 1971. In legal practice San Francisco 1978-86.

Mailing address: P.O. Box 2070, Oakland 94604-2070.

Telephone: (510) 879-3525.

JENKINS, Martin J. *(Judge, United States District Court Northern District of California)* Appointed for life by President Bill Clinton to term beginning 1997. Born San Francisco California Nov 12, 1953. Educated at City College of San Francisco A.A. 1973, Santa Clara University B.A. 1976 and University of San Francisco School of Law J.D. 1980. Judge, Oakland-Piedmont-Emeryville Municipal Court Alameda County 1989-92. Judge, Superior Court of California Alameda County 1992-97.

Deputy District Attorney Alameda County 1981-83. Trial Attorney Civil Rights Division U.S. Department of Justice 1983-85.

Office: U.S. Courthouse, Box 36060, 450 Golden Gate Avenue, San Francisco 94102-3489.

Telephone: (415) 522-4141.

JENNINGS, James B. *(Judge, Superior Court of California County of Santa Barbara)*

Office: 312-H East Cook Street, Santa Maria 93454.

Telephone: (805) 346-7414.

JENSEN, D. Lowell *(Senior Judge, United States District Court Northern District of California)* Appointed for life by President Ronald Reagan to term beginning June 27, 1986. Assumed Senior status, serves by assignment. Born Brigham City Utah June 3, 1928. Church of Jesus Christ of Latter-Day Saints. Educated at University of California at Berkeley A.B. 1949 and University of California Boalt Hall School of Law LL.B. 1952. Member Phi Alpha Delta. Admitted to practice California 1953, U.S. District Court Northern District of California 1968 and U.S. Supreme Court 1982. Certified Specialist Criminal Law California Board of Legal Specialization.

Deputy District Attorney 1955-69 and District Attorney 1969-81 Alameda County. U.S. Assistant Attorney General 1981-83, U.S. Associate Attorney General 1983-85 and U.S. Deputy Attorney General 1985-86 U.S. Department of Justice Washington D.C. Author "Diminished Capacity, Tying the Hands of Justice" *Brief Case* Bar Association of San Francisco 1979 and "The Good Faith Restatement of the Exclusionary Rule" Journal of Criminal Law and Criminology 1982. Vice Chairman Joint Legislative Committee for Revision of the California Penal Code 1970-74. Member Comparative Study of American Bar Association Standards on Criminal Justice 1972 and Sentencing Practices Advisory Committee 1977-81 Judicial Council of California, California Council on Criminal Justice 1974-81, Advisory Board National Crime Information Council 1979-81, Task Force on Incarcerated Minorities California Health and Welfare Department 1980-81 and Advisory Committee on Criminal Rules Judicial Conference of the U.S. 1981-83. Former member California District Attorneys Association (Chairman Law and Legislative Committee 1969-77, President 1979-80), National District Attorneys Association (Commission on Victim/Witness Assistance 1974-81, Assistant Treasurer 1980), Criminal Courts Bar Association of Alameda County (Co-founder 1965, member Advisory Board), Alameda County (Bench-Bar Liaison Committee, Bench-Bar-Media Committee), Federal and American (Mental Health Standards Task Force 1981-83, Vice Chairman Prosecution Function Committee Section of Criminal Justice 1981-86) Bar Associations. Fellow American College of Trial Lawyers. Member California Peace Officers Association (Chairman Law and Legislative Committee 1969-77) and State Bar of California (Commission on Law and Mental Health Problems 1976-78). Lecturer Criminal Law Institute California Center for Judicial Education and Research 1973 and 1978, "Effective Criminal Trial Techniques" American Bar Association 1975, National College of District Attorneys 1977, 1978 and 1981, Short Course for Prosecutors Northwestern School of Law 1979-82 and CEB State Bar of California. Recipient Paul Harris Fellow Honorary Award from Rotary International 1980 and Distinguished Alumnus of the Year Award from University of California Boalt Hall School of Law 1983. Corporal U.S. Army 1952-54. Advisory Board California Technological Research Foundation 1970-74 and Hastings Law School College of Advocacy 1977-86. Mem-

JENSEN, D. LOWELL—*Continued*

ber Boalt Hall Alumni Association (President 1978-79). Enjoys golf and gardening.

Office: 400-S Federal Building, 1301 Clay Street, Oakland 94612-5212.

Telephone: (415) 522-2000.

JENSEN, Lance *(Judge, Superior Court of California County of Orange)*

Mailing address: P.O. Box 1994, Santa Ana 92702-1994.

Office: Central Justice Center, 700 Civic Center Drive West, Santa Ana 92701.

Telephone: (714) 834-3734.

JESSOP, Gerald C. *(Judge, Superior Court of California County of San Diego)*

Mailing address: P.O. Box 122724, San Diego 92112-2724.

Office: 220 West Broadway, San Diego 92101.

Telephone: (619) 531-3820.

JOHNSON, Barbara R. *(Judge, Superior Court of California County of Los Angeles)* Assumed office Jan 22, 2000. Former Judge, Los Angeles Municipal Court Los Angeles County.

Office: Criminal Courts Building, 210 West Temple Street, Los Angeles 90012-3210.

Telephone: (213) 974-6535.

JOHNSON, Charles R. *(Judge, Superior Court of California County of Kings)* Assumed office Feb 8, 2001. Former Judge, Kings County Municipal Court.

Mailing address: 1426 South Drive, Hanford 93230.

Office: 1001 Chittenden Avenue, Corcoran 93212.

Telephone: (559) 992-5193.

JOHNSON, Derek Guy *(Judge, Superior Court of California County of Orange)*

Mailing address: P.O. Box 5000, Fullerton 92838-0500.

Office: North Justice Center, 1275 North Berkeley Avenue, Fullerton 92832.

Telephone: (714) 773-4400.

JOHNSON, Earl, Jr. *(Associate Justice, California Court of Appeal Second District Division Seven)* Appointed by Governor Edmund G. Brown, Jr. to term beginning Dec 1982. Retained by election Nov 1986 and 1998. Current term expires Jan 2011. Born Watertown South Dakota June 10, 1933. Educated at Northwestern University B.A. with departmental honors in Economics 1955 LL.M. in Criminal Law 1961 and University of Chicago Law School J.D. 1960. Ford Foundation Fellow in Criminal Law 1960-61. Book Review Editor University of Chicago Law Review. Member Delta Sigma Rho, Deru and Order of the Coif. Admitted to practice Illinois 1960, U.S. Court of Appeals Ninth Circuit 1964, District of Columbia 1965, U.S. Supreme Court 1966 and California 1972.

Trial Attorney Organized Crime Section U.S. Department of Justice 1961-64. Deputy Director Neighborhood Legal Services Project 1964-65. Deputy Director 1965-66 and Director 1966-68 Legal Services Program Office of Economic Opportunity. Consultant Science Application, Inc. 1979-82. Author Comment "Liability for Violation of State Labor Injunction Where Power to Enjoin Is Subsequently Held to Have Been Pre-empted" 27 U. of Chicago L. Rev. 738-51, 1960, "Organized Crime: Challenge to the American Legal System" Journal of Criminal Law, Criminology and Police Science Vol. 53, 399-425, 1962 and Vol. 54, 1-29 and 127-45, 1963; "A Conservative Rationale for the Legal Services Program" 70 West Virginia L. Rev. 250-63, 1968; "The OEO Legal Services Program" 14 The Catholic Lawyer 99-111, 1968; "Professional Responsibility Aspects of Legal Services Programs" 41 University of Colorado L. Rev. 319-27, 1969; "The Theory and Practice of Legislative Advocacy" 1970 and "The Science, Art and 'Lawyer-lore' of Criminal Trial Advocacy" 1971 University of Southern California; *Justice and Reform: The Formative Years of the American Legal Services Program* Russell Sage Foundation 1974; "Legal Aid's Next Decade: Government-Subsidized Legal Assistance in a Broader Perspective" First International Colloquium on Legal Aid and Legal Services 1977; "Toward Equal Justice Revisited: Two Responses to a Review" American Bar Foundation Research Jour. 943-65, 1977; "Thrown to the Lions: A Plea for a Constitutional Right to Counsel for Low Income Litigants" 4 ABA Bar Leader 16-19 and 29, 1978; *Preliminary Analysis of Alternative Strategies for Processing Civil Disputes* Government Printing Office 1978; "Access to Justice: A New and Wider Focus" 13 Japanese Comparative L. Rev. 87-107, 1979; "Lawyers' Choice: A Theoretical Appraisal of Litigation Investment Decisions" 15 Law and Society Rev. 567-610, 1981; *Dispute Resolution in America: Processes in Evolution* Corporate Press 1984; "The Right to Counsel in Civil Cases: An International Perspective" 19 Loyola of Los Angeles L. Rev. 1985 and *California Trial Guide* 5 Vols. Matthew Bender & Co. 1986. Co-author with William Hobbs and Karen Birlie *Basic Criminal Trial Handbook* University of Southern California 1972; with Mauro Cappelletti and James Gordley *Toward Equal Justice: A Comparative Study of Legal Aid in Modern Societies* Giuffre and Oceana 1975; with Valerie Kantor and Elizabeth Schwartz *Outside the Courts: A Survey of Diversion Alternatives in Civil Cases* National Center for State Courts 1977; with Felstiner " 'New Courts' and Neighborhood Justice in the United States" 5 Melanesian L. Jour. 301-04, 1977; with Schwartz "Beyond Payne: The Case for a Constitutional Right to Representation in Civil Cases for California's Indigent Litigants" 11 Loyola of Los Angeles L. Rev. 249-96, 1978; with Drew "This Nation Has Money for Everything—Except Courts" 17 Judges Jour. 8-11 and 54-56, 1978 and with Dorsaneo *Texas Trial Guide* 5 Vols. Matthew Bender & Co. 1988.

Important Decisions: April Enterprises, Inc. v. KTTV 147 Cal. App. 3d 805, 1983; Ponder v. Blue Cross of Southern California 145 Cal. App. 3d 709, 1983; Collier v. City of Pasadena 142 Cal. App. 3d 917-936, 1983; People v. Dickson 144 Cal. App. 3d 1046, 1983; People v. Javier A. 159 Cal. App. 3d 913, 1984; Motown Record Corp. v. Brockert 160 Cal. App. 3d 123, 1984; In re Cheryl H. 153 Cal. App. 3d 1098-1134, 1984; Spiritual Psychic Science Church v. Azusa 201 Cal. Rptr. 852, 1984; Heckmann v. Ahmanson 168 Cal. App. 3d 119, 1985; In re Marriage of Fricke 181 Cal. App. 3d 997, 1986; Covenant Mutual v. Young 179 Cal. App. 3d 917, 1986; Gardner v. Downtown Porsche 180 Cal. App. 713, 1986; Friends of Westwood v. City of Los Angeles 191 Cal. App. 3d 259, 1987; and Nally v. Grace Community Church 240 Cal. Rptr. 215, 1987. Senior Research Associate and Professor of Law University of Southern California 1969-82. Co-director Access to Jus-

JOHNSON, EARL, JR.—*Continued*
tice Project University of Florence, Italy 1974-79. Member Advisory Panel on Delivery Systems Study Legal Services Corporation 1976-80 and Panel on Predicting Judicial Impact of New Legislation National Academy of Sciences 1977-79. Reporter The Courts and Community Task Force National Conference on State Courts 1977-78. Member American Academy of Political and Social Science, Law and Society Association, California Judges Association (Appellate Courts Committee 1983-86, Judicial Ethics Committee since 1985), State Bar of California (Special Committee on Practical Training of New Lawyers 1975-78, Special Committee on Pro Bono Practice 1977-78 and Standing Committee on Legal Services to the Poor 1976-81 Legal Services Section, Voluntary Legal Services Committee 1979-86), Los Angeles County (Special Committee on Neighborhood Justice Center 1977-81), American (Chairman Right to Legal Services Committee Section of Individual Rights and Responsibilities 1972-75, Advisory Panel Special Committee on Housing and Urban Development 1978-79, Associate and Advisory Committee of Standing Committee on Legal Aid and Indigent Defendants 1969-73, Organized Crime Committee Section of Criminal Law 1970-73, Special Committee on Resolution of Minor Disputes 1976-83) and International Bar Associations.

Visiting Scholar Center for the Study of Law and Society July 1968 to Sept 1969 and Institute of Comparative Law University of Florence Italy 1973 and 1975. Justice Robert H. Jackson Lecturer The National Judicial College July 1980. Faculty member Asian Workshop on Legal Services to the Poor Summer 1974. State Department Lecturer on legal aid and related problems of disputes resolution policy Africa 1975. Visiting Lecturer European University Institute Florence Italy June 1978. Board of Directors Administrative Law College 1978-79. Speaker National Conference on the Causes of Popular Dissatisfaction with the Administration of Justice April 1976, First International Colloquium on Legal Aid London England Oct 25-28, 1976, Conference on Social Science Research and the Courts National Center for State Courts Jan 20-22, 1977, Conference on Resolution of Minor Disputes May 29, 1977 and Conference on Delivery of Legal Services Dec 17, 1977 American Bar Association, Plenary Session Association of American Law Schools Annual Meeting Dec 28, 1977, National Conference on State Courts March 19-22, 1978, Access to Justice Seminar European University Institute Florence Italy June 1978, National Conference of Bar Presidents American Bar Association Annual Meeting Aug 5, 1978, Japan Public Law Association Tokyo Japan Sept 27, 1978, International Access to Justice Colloquium European University Institute Florence Italy Oct 15-19, 1979 and Blackstone Bicentennial Conference Sydney Australia Aug 11-15, 1980. Recipient Justin Dart Award for Academic Innovation 1971 and first annual Loren Miller Legal Services Award 1977. Named Southern California Citizen of the Week by KNX Newsradio April 1978 and Appellate Justice of the Year by Los Angeles Trial Lawyers Association 1988. Listed in *Who's Who in America, Who's Who in American Law* 2nd ed., *Who's Who in the World, Who's Who in the West* and *Contemporary Authors*. USN 1955-58. Member National Advisory Committee on OEO Legal Services Program 1965-73, Association of American Law Schools (Executive Committee Section of Clinical Legal Education 1971-73, Special Committee on Legal Assistants 1972-75), California Rural Legal Assistance (Vice President and Chairman Executive Committee Board of Trustees 1972-75), International Legal Center's Committee on Legal Services in the Developing Countries 1972-75, Executive Committee National Senior Citizens Law Center 1972-74, Western Center on Law and Poverty (President and Board of Trustees 1971-73, Executive Committee 1976-78, California State Bar Representative to Board 1978-80) and Los Angeles County Regional Planning Commission 1980-81. Board of Directors National Legal Aid and Defender Association 1969-77. Cofounder and Board member Action for Legal Rights 1971-75. Secretary Board of Directors National Resource Center for Consumers of Legal Services 1974-79.

Office: 300 South Spring Street, Los Angeles 90013.
Telephone: (213) 830-7000.

JOHNSON, Frank J. *(Judge, Superior Court of California County of Los Angeles)* Assumed office Jan 22, 2000. Former Judge, Los Angeles Municipal Court Los Angeles County.

Office: Van Nuys Courthouse West, 14400 Erwin Street Mall, Van Nuys 91401-2705.
Telephone: (818) 374-2601.

JOHNSON, Hurl William, III *(Judge, Superior Court of California County of Stanislaus)* Former Judge, Stanislaus County Municipal Court.

Office: 800 Eleventh Street, Modesto 95354.
Telephone: (209) 558-6000.

JOHNSON, Jane L. *(Judge, Superior Court of California County of Los Angeles)*

Office: Courthouse, 111 North Hill Street, Los Angeles 90012.
Telephone: (213) 974-5411.

JOHNSON, Jeffrey W. *(Magistrate Judge, United States District Court Central District of California)* Appointed by U.S. District Court judges to term beginning April 20, 1999. Term expires April 2007.

Office: 833 U.S. Courthouse, 312 North Spring Street, Los Angeles 90012.
Telephone: (213) 894-3535.

JOHNSON, Jerry E. *(Judge, Superior Court of California County of Los Angeles)* Assumed office Jan 22, 2000. Former Judge and Presiding Judge, Compton Municipal Court Los Angeles County.

Office: Compton Courthouse, 200 West Compton Boulevard, Compton 90220.
Telephone: (310) 603-7842.

JOHNSON, Margaret *(Judge, Superior Court of California County of Santa Clara)*

Office: 170 Park Plaza, San Jose 95113.
Telephone: (408) 534-5600.

JOHNSON, Marion J. *(Judge, Superior Court of California County of Los Angeles)* Assumed office Jan 22, 2000. Former Judge, Los Angeles Municipal Court Los Angeles County.

Office: Courthouse, 111 North Hill Street, Los Angeles 90012.
Telephone: (213) 974-5411.

JOHNSON, Michael *(Judge, Superior Court of California County of Los Angeles)* Appointed by Governor Pete Wilson to term beginning Dec 15, 1997. Elected June 1998, current term expires Jan 2005. Born Long

JOHNSON, MICHAEL—*Continued*

Beach California Feb 12, 1951. Educated at University of California at Los Angeles B.A. 1973 and University of California Hastings College of the Law J.D. with honors 1976. Member Phi Beta Kappa. Admitted to practice California 1976, U.S. District Courts Central 1977, Eastern 1982, Southern 1983 and Northern 1989 Districts of California and U.S. Courts of Appeals Ninth 1979 and Third 1990 Circuits. In legal practice Los Angeles 1976-97.

Author of various articles California Labor and Employment Law Quarterly 1991-97. Chair Labor and Employment Section State Bar of California 1995-96. Member California Judges Association, Los Angeles County and American Bar Associations. Commissioner California Fair Employment and Housing Commission 1987-97. Established educational partnership program and scholarship fund at Woodrow Wilson High School.

Office: 111 North Hill Street, Los Angeles 90012.
Telephone: (213) 974-5769.

JOHNSON, W. Arvid *(Judge, Superior Court of California County of Yolo)* Assumed office June 3, 1998. Former Judge, Yolo County Municipal Court.

Office: 725 Court Street, Woodland 95695.
Telephone: (530) 666-8598.

JOHNSTON, Gerald G. *(Judge, Superior Court of California County of Orange)*

Mailing address: P.O. Box 1994, Santa Ana 92702-1994.
Office: Central Justice Center, 700 Civic Center Drive West, Santa Ana 92701.
Telephone: (714) 834-3734.

JONES, Ann I. *(Judge, Superior Court of California County of Los Angeles)* Former Magistrate Judge, United States District Court Central District of California, appointed by U.S. District Court judges.

Office: Pomona Courthouse South, 400 Civic Center Plaza, Pomona 91766.
Telephone: (909) 620-3023.

JONES, Barbara J. R. *(Presiding Justice, California Court of Appeal First District Division Five)* Appointed by Governor Pete Wilson to term beginning 1996. Retained by election. Presiding Justice since 1998. Born Plainfield New Jersey March 20, 1943. Educated at Duke University B.A. 1965 and University of San Francisco J.D. 1974. Staff member University of San Francisco Law Review. Member McAuliffe Society. Judge, Superior Court of California City and County of San Francisco 1992-96, appointed by Governor Pete Wilson.

Lifetime Member Queen's Bench (President 1983). Member Advisory Committee on Judicial Ethics 1995-96 and Advisory Committee for the Revision of Canon 6D 1998 California Supreme Court and Advisory Committee on Civil and Small Claims 1995-96, Task Force on Complex Civil Litigation since 1997 and Appellate Mediation Task Force since 1997 Judicial Council of California. Member California Judges Association, National Judges Association, Women Lawyers of Alameda County and California Women Lawyers Association. Faculty Civil Law and Procedure Institutes 1992 and 1995 and Chair Planning Committee 1996 California Center for Judicial Education and Research. Member 1975-85 and President 1984 Board of Governors University of San Francisco School of Law Alumni Association. Member 1989-92 and Board of Directors of Creativity Explored 1990-92 San Francisco Chamber of Commerce Business Volunteers for the Arts. Member Advisory Committee for City College of San Francisco Legal Assisting Program.

Office: 350 McAllister Street, San Francisco 94102-3600.
Telephone: (415) 865-7300.

JONES, Franklin P. *(Judge, Superior Court of California County of Fresno)*

Office: Courthouse, 1100 Van Ness Avenue, Fresno 93724-0002.
Telephone: (559) 488-1825.

JONES, Jeffrey Bruce *(Judge, Superior Court of California County of Imperial)*

Office: 939 West Main Street, El Centro 92243.
Telephone: (760) 482-4374.

JONES, Lawrence *(Judge, Superior Court of California County of Fresno)* Former Judge, Consolidated Fresno Municipal Court Fresno County.

Office: Courthouse, 1100 Van Ness Avenue, Fresno 93724-0002.
Telephone: (559) 488-1825.

JONES, Morris Bruce *(Judge, Superior Court of California County of Los Angeles)* Former Judge, Compton Municipal Court Los Angeles County.

Office: Courthouse, 111 North Hill Street, Los Angeles 90012.
Telephone: (213) 974-5411.

JONES, Napoleon A., Jr. *(Judge, United States District Court Southern District of California)* Appointed for life by President Bill Clinton to term beginning Sept 19, 1994. Born Hodge Louisiana Aug 25, 1940. Protestant. Educated at San Diego State University A.B. 1962 M.S.W. 1967 and University of San Diego School of Law J.D. 1971. Awarded honorary LL.D. California Western School of Law 1994. Associate Editor San Diego Law Review 1970-71. Listed in *Who's Who in American Colleges and Universities* 1970-71. Member Kappa Alpha Psi and Sigma Pi Phi. Admitted to practice California 1972. Judge, San Diego Municipal Court San Diego County July 7, 1977 to June 30, 1982. Judge, Superior Court of California San Diego County July 1, 1982 to Sept 18, 1994.

Staff Attorney California Rural Legal Assistance Jan 1972 to March 1973 and Defenders, Inc. March 1973 to May 1975. Author "To Plea or Not to Plea: The Question Posed by Federal Rule II" 7 No. 1 San Diego L. Rev. 90, 1970, book review *Women's Liberation in China* by Claudie Broyelle California Western International L. Jour. 1978 and "601 Status Offender: The Sin of Omission" 5 No. 6 *California Peace Officers Magazine* 1985. Co-author Chapter 17 "Disqualification of Judges" *California Criminal Procedure Handbook.* Chairman Jail Subcommittee San Diego County Bar Association 1975 and Association of Black Attorneys 1976. Former Board Member Southeast Criminal Justice Coalition and San Diego County Bar Foundation. Ex officio Member Juvenile Justice Commission. Former Member Criminal Defense Lawyers Club, Criminal Justice Committee, Judicial Council Advisory Committee to study Legislative Proposals on Trial Court Unification, California Judges Association (Criminal Law and Procedures Committee, Chair Juvenile Law Committee), Executive Committee

JONES, NAPOLEON A., JR.—*Continued*

San Diego County Superior Court, Juvenile and Family Court Committee on Alcohol and Substance Abuse, Juvenile Court Committee Metropolitan Court Judges and Executive Committee Juvenile Court Judges. Chair Working Group on America's Children at Risk American Bar Association. Member California Black Attorneys Association, National Association of Women Judges, Earl B. Gilliam (Past President) and National Bar Associations. Faculty Member Continuing Judicial Studies Program California Judges Association. Board Member Graduate School for Community Development.

Recipient Distinguished Alumni Award from School of Social Work San Diego State University 1975 and from University of San Diego 1981; Achievement Award from Association of Small Businesses 1977 and from Kappa Alpha Psi Alumni Chapter 1980; Public Service Award from Stepping Stone and Pathfinders United 1984; Frederick Douglas Award from National Association of Negro Business and Professional Women's Club 1984; Distinguished Service Award for Legal Redress from NAACP 1984; Thurgood Marshall Award from Earl B. Gilliam Bar Association 1984 and 1994; Appreciation Award from North County Foster Parents Feb 1986, from San Diego County Juvenile Justice Commission Feb 1986, from San Diego Community Child Abuse Coordinating Council 1986 and from California Continuing Education of the Bar Oct 1986; Distinguished Service Award from California Court of Appeal Fourth Appellate District June 1986 and from Executive Committee Juvenile Court Judges of California 1992 and 1993; Certificate of Appreciation Award from National Association of Social Workers, Inc. May 1990; Hall of Fame Award from San Diego Boys Club Feb 1991; and Plaque of Appreciation for Service from San Diego County Bar Foundation April 4, 1993. Named Outstanding Municipal Court Judge of the Year by San Diego Trial Lawyers Association 1981 and Judge of the Year by California Association of Black Lawyers April 24, 1993. Inducted into San Diego High School Wall of Honor Oct 16, 1993. Selected Member of 100 Black Role Models of San Diego County "Song of My People" Feb 26, 1994.

E-5 U.S. Army 1972-75. Formerly employed by Santa Clara County Welfare Department Foster Home Placement 1966-67 and San Diego Welfare Department Child Protective and Placement Services 1967-78. Democrat. Former Board Member Tradition One Alcohol Treatment Program, San Diego State Alumni Association, San Diego Urban League, San Diego Leukemia Society, California Consortium of Child Abuse Council, California Professional Society on the Abuse of Children, June Burnett Institute, Center for Civic Education—Law in a Free Society and The Salvation Army. Past Chairperson Citizens Advisory Committee Fourth Councilmatic District and San Diego County Commission on Children and Youth. Former member San Diego Integration Task Force, Indigent Defense Policy Board, Conservation Corps, Sankofa Bird Project Advisory Board, ADAPT Advisory Board, Board of Directors Black Communication Center, San Diego-Imperial Girl Scout Council, San Diego Historical Society and Child Welfare Strategic Planning Commission Department of Social Services California. Mentor Nia-UMOIA Valencia Park Elementary School. Board of Visitors San Diego State University School of Social Work. Board Member Project Restore—Women's Drug Treatment Program. Board of Directors San Diego City College Foundation. Member Advisory Board Friend to Friend and Family Literacy Foundation. Director University of San Diego Law Alumni Association Board 1994-95. Interests include civic affairs and organizations and sports.

Office: 2125 U.S. Courthouse, 940 Front Street, San Diego 92101-8912.

Telephone: (619) 557-2993.

JONES, Talmadge R. *(Judge, Superior Court of California County of Sacramento)*

Office: Courthouse, 720 Ninth Street, Sacramento 95814.

Telephone: (916) 874-5476.

JUHAS, Mark A. *(Judge, Superior Court of California County of Los Angeles)*

Office: Palmdale Courthouse, 38256 Sierra Highway, Palmdale 93550.

JURY, Meredith A. *(Judge, United States Bankruptcy Court Central District of California)* Appointed by U.S. Court of Appeals Ninth Circuit judges to term beginning Nov 24, 1997. Term expires Nov 2011. Born Kansas City Missouri April 11, 1947. Educated at University of Colorado B.A. cum laude 1969, University of Wisconsin M.A. 1971 M.S. 1972 and University of California at Los Angeles J.D. 1976. Admitted to practice California 1976, U.S. District Courts Central 1976 and Southern 1982 Districts of California and U.S. Court of Appeals Ninth Circuit 1979. In legal practice Riverside 1976-97.

Member National Conference of Bankruptcy Judges, State Bar of California, Federal (President Inland Empire Chapter 2003) and American Bar Associations.

Office: 3420 Twelfth Street, Room 345, Riverside 92501-3819.

Telephone: (909) 774-1043.

E-mail address: Meredith_Jury@cacb.uscourts.gov

KADDO, James A. *(Judge, Superior Court of California County of Los Angeles)* Former Judge, Los Angeles Municipal Court Los Angeles County.

Office: Van Nuys Courthouse East, 6230 Sylmar Avenue, Van Nuys 91401.

Telephone: (818) 374-2265.

KAHN, Harold E. *(Judge, Superior Court of California City and County of San Francisco)*

Office: Hall of Justice, 850 Bryant Street, San Francisco 94103.

Telephone: (415) 553-1159.

KAISER, Erik Michael *(Judge, Superior Court of California County of Riverside)* Former Presiding Judge.

Office: Riverside Historic Courthouse, 4050 Main Street, Riverside 92501.

Telephone: (909) 955-1960.

KALASHIAN, Joseph A. *(Judge, Superior Court of California County of Tulare)* Former Judge, Tulare County Municipal Court.

Office: County Civic Center, Visalia 93291-4593.

Telephone: (559) 733-6561.

KALKIN, Alan S. *(Judge, Superior Court of California County of Los Angeles)* Assumed office Jan 22, 2000. Presiding Judge Jan 1, 1997 to Dec 31, 1997 and

KALKIN, ALAN S.—*Continued*

Former Judge, Burbank Municipal Court Los Angeles County.

Office: Burbank Courthouse, 300 East Olive, Burbank 91502.

Telephone: (818) 356-3482.

KAMANSKY, Craig S. *(Judge, Superior Court of California County of San Bernardino)* Appointed by Governor George Deukmejian Jan 12, 1988. Elected to term beginning Jan 1, 1989. Reelected 1994 and 2000. Current term expires Jan 2007. Formerly served Central District. Serves East Division. Born Upland California May 12, 1948. Jewish. Educated at University of California at Berkeley A.B. with honors 1970 and University of California at Los Angeles J.D. 1973. Projects and Comment Editor UCLA Law Review 1972-73. Member Chi Psi. Admitted to practice California 1973 and U.S. District Court Central District of California 1973. In legal practice San Bernardino 1976-77. Former Judge, San Bernardino County Municipal Court, appointed by Governor George Deukmejian to term beginning April 28, 1986.

Deputy District Attorney 1973-76 and 1977-81 and Chief Deputy District Attorney 1982-86 San Bernardino County. Republican. Interests include collecting baseball cards, jogging, racquetball, baseball, softball and basketball. Enjoys UCLA football.

Office: 216 Brookside Avenue, Redlands 92373.

Telephone: (909) 798-8552.

KAMINS, Bernard J. *(Judge, Superior Court of California County of Los Angeles)* Appointed by Governor George Deukmejian to term beginning Oct 7, 1986. Elected to subsequent terms. Born Los Angeles California Sept 9, 1942. Educated at University of California B.A. 1965 and University of Southern California J.D. 1968. Admitted to practice California 1970. Judge, Los Angeles Municipal Court Los Angeles County 1985-86.

Deputy Public Defender 1969-85. Author "Creative Sentencing" CEB 1980 and "Cases and Materials Public Defender Law" Pepperdine University Press 1980. Adjunct Professor of Law Pepperdine University since 1978. Member Los Angeles County and American Bar Associations. Board of Directors Westside YMCA. Enjoys jogging, fitness and crossword puzzles.

Office: Santa Monica Courthouse, 1725 Main Street, Santa Monica 90401.

Telephone: (310) 260-3762.

KAMS, Timothy A. *(Judge, Superior Court of California County of Fresno)* Serves Juvenile Delinquency Court.

Office: 742 South Tenth Street, Fresno 93702.

Telephone: (559) 455-5195.

KANE, Stephen Joseph *(Judge, Superior Court of California County of Fresno)* Presiding Judge July 1, 1996 to June 30, 1997.

Office: 1255 Fulton Mall, Fresno 93721.

Telephone: (559) 488-2626.

KANESHIRO, Gale E. *(Judge, Superior Court of California County of San Diego)* Assumed office Dec 1, 1998. Elected 2000, current term expires Jan 2007. Born Hilo Hawaii Oct 4, 1951. Buddhist. Educated at Boston University A.B. with honors 1973 and Washington University School of Law J.D. 1976. Admitted to practice California 1977, U.S. District Court Southern District of California 1977 and U.S. Supreme Court 1981. Judge, San Diego Municipal Court San Diego County March 8, 1989 to Nov 30, 1998, appointed by Governor George Deukmejian.

Member Pan Asian Lawyers of San Diego, California Asian Judges Association, California Judges Association, National Association of Women Judges and San Diego County Bar Association. Member State Advisory Committee on Child Abuse Prevention 1983-84. Chair Committee on Child Abuse Prevention State Social Services Advisory Board 1985-88.

Mailing address: P.O. Box 122724, San Diego 92112-2724.

Office: 220 West Broadway, San Diego 92101.

Telephone: (619) 531-3820.

KAPETAN, Jon N. *(Judge, Superior Court of California County of Fresno)*

Office: Courthouse, 1100 Van Ness Avenue, Fresno 93724-0002.

Telephone: (559) 488-1825.

KAPLAN, Leon S. *(Judge, Superior Court of California County of Los Angeles)*

Office: Van Nuys Courthouse East, 6230 Sylmar Avenue, Van Nuys 91401.

Telephone: (818) 374-2265.

KARESH, Jonathan E. *(Judge, Superior Court of California County of San Mateo)* Appointed by Governor Gray Davis to term beginning Jan 26, 2001. Term expires Jan 2007. Born San Francisco California 1960. Jewish. Educated at University of California at Berkeley A.B. with high honors 1982 J.D. 1985. Admitted to practice California 1985 and U.S. District Court Northern District of California 1985. In legal practice San Francisco 1985-87 and 1989-90.

Deputy District Attorney San Mateo County 1987-89 and 1990-2001. Member California Judges Association. Member California Democratic State Central Committee 1991-2001. Chair 1993-95 and Member 1993-2001 21st Assembly District Democratic Committee. Member Peninsula Temple Beth El. Enjoys baseball, reading and traveling.

Office: 1050 Mission Road, South San Francisco 94080.

Telephone: (650) 877-5440.

Fax: (650) 877-5703

KARLAN, Craig D. *(Judge, Superior Court of California County of Los Angeles)*

Office: Courthouse, 111 North Hill Street, Los Angeles 90012.

Telephone: (213) 974-5411.

KARLTON, Lawrence K. *(Senior Judge, United States District Court Eastern District of California)* Appointed for life by President Jimmy Carter to term beginning 1979. Chief Judge 1983-90. Assumed Senior status May 28, 2000, serves by assignment and continues to carry full case-load. Born Brooklyn New York May 28, 1935. Educated at Columbia University School of Law J.D. 1958. In legal practice Sacramento 1962-76. Judge, Superior Court of California County of Sacramento 1976-79.

KARLTON, LAWRENCE K.—*Continued*

Civilian Legal Officer Sacramento Army Depot 1960-62.

Office: 15-200 U.S. Courthouse, 501 I Street, Sacramento 95814-2322.

Telephone: (916) 930-4130.

KASTER, Robert F. *(Judge, Superior Court of California County of Siskiyou)* Presiding Judge Jan 1, 1999 to June 30, 1999.

Mailing address: P.O. Box 1026, Yreka 96097-1026.

Office: 311 Fourth Street, Yreka 96097.

Telephone: (530) 842-8330.

KAUFFMAN, Andrew C. *(Judge, Superior Court of California County of Los Angeles)* Former Judge and Supervising Judge, Los Angeles Municipal Court Los Angeles County.

Office: Torrance Courthouse, 825 Maple Avenue, Torrance 90503.

Telephone: (310) 222-8808.

KAUFMAN, Ira R. *(Judge, Superior Court of California County of Plumas)* Presiding Judge Jan 1, 2001 to Dec 31, 2002.

Office: 104 Courthouse, 520 Main Street, Quincy 95971.

Telephone: (530) 283-6232.

KAWAICHI, Ken Martin *(Judge, Superior Court of California County of Alameda)* Born Los Angeles California Oct 23, 1941. Methodist. Educated at Pomona College B.A. 1963 and Boalt Hall School of Law LL.B. 1966. Admitted to practice California 1966, U.S. District Court Northern District of California 1967, U.S. Court of Appeals Ninth Circuit 1967 and U.S. Supreme Court 1972. In legal practice Oakland 1967-75. Former Judge, Oakland-Piedmont Municipal Court Alameda County, appointed by Governor Edmund G. Brown, Jr. to term beginning Nov 10, 1975.

Assistant Professor of Ethnic Studies University of California at Berkeley 1970-73. Former member California Trial Lawyers Association, The Association of Trial Lawyers of America, Democratic Lawyers of Alameda County, Asian Law Caucus, National Lawyers Guild of San Francisco (Board of Directors 1970-72), Consumers Group Legal Services of Berkeley (Board of Directors 1974-75), Alameda County and American Bar Associations. Member Judicial Council of California (Advisory Committee on Civil and Social Claims, Advisory Committee on Access and Fairness, Advisory Committee on Race and Ethnic Bias) and American Judicature Society. Democrat. Board of Directors Alameda County Legal Aid Society since 1977. Member Asian Political Caucus, American Civil Liberties Union of Northern California (Board of Directors 1971-72), Japanese-American Citizens League and Sierra Club. Board of Directors Lyon Project East Bay since 1974. Member International Institute East Bay since 1971, Alameda County Easter Seal Society since 1974, Board of Visitors New College School of Law since 1977 and Board of Governors East Bay Community Foundation since 1977. Enjoys backpacking, tennis, ski-touring, music and fishing.

Office: Courthouse, 1225 Fallon Street, Oakland 94612.

Telephone: (510) 272-6070.

KAY, Laurence Donald *(Presiding Justice, California Court of Appeal First District Division Four)* Appointed by Governor Gray Davis 2000. Born San Francisco California Jan 18, 1937. Jewish. Educated at University of California at Berkeley B.S. 1958 J.D. 1963. Associate Editor California Law Review 1962-63. Admitted to practice California 1963. In legal practice San Francisco 1963-81. Judge, San Francisco Municipal Court San Francisco County 1981-83. Judge Jan 2, 1983 to 2000, Presiding Judge Criminal Division 1986-88 and Presiding Judge July 1, 1996 to June 30, 1997, Superior Court of California City and County of San Francisco.

Former Member State Bar of California and San Francisco Bar Association. Honorary President Inns of Court Society of California.

Office: 350 McAllister Street, San Francisco 94102-3600.

Telephone: (415) 865-7300.

KAYS, Scott L. *(Judge, Superior Court of California County of Solano)* Appointed by Governor Pete Wilson April 25, 1997 to term beginning May 29, 1997. Elected June 1998, current term expires Jan 1, 2005. Presiding Judge since Jan 1, 2002. Born Denver Colorado March 31, 1951. Educated at University of California at Irvine B.A. 1973 and Hastings College of the Law J.D. 1976. Admitted to practice California 1976. In legal practice Vallejo 1976-97.

Member California Judges Association, American Judges Association and Solano County Bar Association (President 1995).

Office: 600 Union Avenue, Fairfield 94533-5000.

Telephone: (707) 421-6137.

Fax: (707) 421-7962

E-mail address: skays@solanocounty.com

KAZANJIAN, Debra *(Judge, Superior Court of California County of Fresno)*

Office: Courthouse, 1100 Van Ness Avenue, Fresno 93724-0002.

Telephone: (559) 488-1825.

KEARNEY, Frances A. *(Judge, Superior Court of California County of Placer)*

Office: 101 Maple Street, Department 3, Auburn 95603.

Telephone: (530) 889-6585.

KEEP, Judith N. *(Judge, United States District Court Southern District of California)* Appointed for life by President Jimmy Carter to term beginning 1980. Chief Judge 1991 to Jan 23, 1998. Born Omaha Nebraska March 24, 1944. Educated at Scripps College B.A. 1966 and University of San Diego School of Law J.D. 1970. In legal practice San Diego 1973-76. Judge, San Diego Municipal Court San Diego County 1976-80.

Assistant U.S. Attorney Southern District of California 1976.

Office: 5190 U.S. Courthouse, 940 Front Street, San Diego 92101-8906.

Telephone: (619) 557-5542.

KELLEGREW, Kent M. *(Judge, Superior Court of California County of Ventura)* Serves East County Division.

Mailing address: P.O. Box 1200, Simi Valley 93062-1200.

Office: 3855-F Alamo Street, Simi Valley 93063.

Telephone: (805) 582-8086.

KELLEHER, Robert J. *(Senior Judge, United States District Court Central District of California)* Appointed

KELLEHER, ROBERT J.—*Continued*
for life by President Richard M. Nixon to term beginning Dec 21, 1970. Assumed Senior status, serves by assignment. Born New York New York March 5, 1913. Educated at Williams College A.B. 1935 and Harvard University J.D. 1938. Admitted to practice New York 1939 and California 1942.

Important Decisions: U.S. v. NBC, CBS and ABC 19 FR Serv 2d 737, 1974; Mobil Oil Corporation v. Filtrol and Texaco 391 F. Supp. 337, 1974; Andrews v. Knowlton 509 F. 2d 898, 1975; Manor Drug Stores v. Blue Chip Stamps 339 F. Supp. 35, 1971, aff'd 421 U.S. 723, 1975; Rancho Palos Verdes Corporation v. City of Laguna Beach 390 F. Supp. 1004, 1975; Impler v. Pachtman CU-71-123-RJK, aff'd 424 U.S. 409, 1976; U.S. v. CBS 459 F. Supp. 832, 1978; and American Petroleum Institute v. Knecht 456 F. Supp. 889, 1978. Member American Judicature Society, State Bar of California, Los Angeles County, Federal and American Bar Associations. Lieutenant USN 1943-45. Enjoys tennis. Captain U.S. Davis Cup Team 1962-63. President U.S. Lawn Tennis Association 1967-68.

Office: Federal Building, 255 East Temple Street, Los Angeles 90012.

Telephone: (213) 894-5255.

KELLER, Eddie T. *(Judge, Superior Court of California County of El Dorado)* Appointed by Governor George Deukmejian to term beginning July 28, 1989. Elected June 1990, 1996 and 2002. Current term expires Jan 2009. Former Presiding Judge. Born Sacramento California June 6, 1941. Methodist. Educated at University of California at Berkeley A.B. 1962 and University of California Hastings College of the Law LL.B. 1965. Member Phi Alpha Delta. Recipient Moot Court Award for Best Written Brief 1963. Judge Moot Court Board 1964. Admitted to practice California 1966, U.S. Court of Appeals Ninth Circuit and U.S. Supreme Court. In legal practice Sacramento 1968-89.

Deputy Attorney General State of California. Former Member State Bar of California. Recipient Distinguished Citizen Award 1991 and 1995. Served Peace Corps in Chile 1966-68. Democrat. Trustee Black Oak Mine Unified School District El Dorado County 1977-89. Chairman Children's Network El Dorado County. Founder Teen Court Program El Dorado County. Umpire Little League. Leader 4-H. Enjoys fishing, tennis, reading and community service.

Office: 495 Main Street, Placerville 95667.

Telephone: (530) 621-6426.

KELLER, Richard O. *(Judge, Superior Court of California County of Alameda)* Assumed office July 31, 1998. Born Washington D.C. Dec 10, 1942. Educated at Emory University A.B. 1964 J.D. 1967. Staff member Emory University Law Review 1966-67. Member Bryan Honor Society. Admitted to practice California 1967, Georgia 1967, U.S. District Courts Districts of California 1967 and Georgia 1967, U.S. Courts of Appeal Ninth 1967 and Eleventh 1967 Circuits and U.S. Supreme Court 1971. In legal practice Fremont California 1972-96. Judge, Fremont-Newark-Union City Municipal Court Alameda County Jan 5, 1996 to July 30, 1998, appointed by Governor Pete Wilson.

Author "Torts—Teachers' Liability for Injury to Pupils" Georgia State B. Jour. 1966. Instructor in Criminal Procedure Ohlone College since 1997. Member Trial Courts Budget Commission, California Judicial Council and California Judges Association. USAF JAGC 1967-72. Board of Trustees Fremont-Newark Community College District 1976-96. Member Accrediting Commission for Community and Junior Colleges Western Association of Schools and Colleges 1986-92, School Commission 1992-96 and Niles (Fremont) Rotary. Enjoys skiing, swimming and traveling.

Office: Fremont Hall of Justice, 39439 Paseo Padre Parkway, Fremont 94538.

Telephone: (510) 795-2329.

KELLER, William D. *(Senior Judge, United States District Court Central District of California)* Appointed for life by President Ronald Reagan to term beginning 1984. Assumed Senior status Oct 29, 1999, serves by assignment. Born Los Angeles California Oct 29, 1934. Educated at University of California at Berkeley B.S. 1956 and University of California at Los Angeles School of Law LL.B. 1960. In legal practice California 1964-72 and 1977-84.

Assistant U.S. Attorney Southern District of California 1961-64. U.S. Attorney Central District of California 1972-77.

Office: U.S. Courthouse, 312 North Spring Street, Los Angeles 90012.

Telephone: (213) 894-2659.

KELLISON, Craig M. *(Magistrate Judge, United States District Court Eastern District of California)* Appointed by U.S. District Court judges to term beginning 1988. Reappointed to subsequent terms. Serves part time. Born Reno Nevada May 8, 1950. Educated at University of Nevada B.S. 1962 and Gonzaga University J.D. 1976. Associate Editor Gonzaga Law Review 1975-76. Member Omicron Delta Epsilon and Phi Alpha Delta. Admitted to practice Nevada 1976, California 1977, U.S. District Courts District of Nevada 1976 and Eastern 1977 and Northern 1981 Districts of California, U.S Court of Appeals Ninth Circuit 1977, U.S. Tax Court 1977, U.S. Supreme Court 1981 and Oregon 1988.

Author "Minors Right of Privacy" 10 Gonzaga L. Rev. 907, 1974 and "Accumulated Earnings Tax-Public Versus Close Corporations" 11 Gonzaga L. Rev. 271. Lawyer Delegate to Ninth Circuit Judicial Conference 1983-86. Member Oregon State Bar, State Bar of California, Lassen County (Secretary-Treasurer 1979-80, Vice President 1980-81, President 1983-85), Washoe County and American Bar Associations. Director Lassen College Foundation since 1979 and Lassen Training and Employment Center, Inc. 1987-90. Chairperson Lassen Community Hospital Board of Trustees 1982-86. Board of Trustees 1991-96 and President since 1992 Richmond School Board. Enjoys skiing, backpacking, jogging and traveling.

Office: 60 South Lassen Street, Susanville 96130.

Telephone: (530) 257-5555.

KELLOGG, Michael K. *(Judge, Superior Court of California County of Los Angeles)* Assumed office Jan 22, 2000. Former Judge, Los Angeles Municipal Court Los Angeles County.

Office: Criminal Courts Building, 210 West Temple Street, Los Angeles 90012-3210.

Telephone: (213) 974-6535.

KELLY, John I. *(Judge, Superior Court of California County of Kern)* Appointed by Governor George De-

KELLY, JOHN I.—*Continued*

ukmejian to term beginning Jan 31, 1988. Elected 1988, 1994 and 2000. Current term expires Jan 2007. Presiding Judge Jan 1, 1996 to Dec 31, 1997. Born San Francisco California June 23, 1932. Episcopalian. Educated at University of California at Berkeley, U.S. Naval Academy B.S.E.E. 1955 and Stanford University LL.B. 1962. Admitted to practice California 1963. In legal practice Bakersfield 1963-88.

Instructor California State University at Bakersfield 1973-76. Former member State Bar of California and Kern County Bar Association. Captain USMC 1955-59. President Kern County YMCA, Kern County Taxpayers Association, Bakersfield Rotary Club and Stockdale Country Club. Advisory Board Boy Scout Council and Kern County Youth for Christ. Senior Warden St. Paul's Episcopal Church. Enjoys golf, bridge and travel.

Office: 1415 Truxtun Avenue, Bakersfield 93301.

Telephone: (661) 868-4934.

KELLY, M. Marc *(Judge, Superior Court of California County of Orange)*

Mailing address: P.O. Box 1994, Santa Ana 92702-1994.

Office: Central Justice Center, 700 Civic Center Drive West, Santa Ana 92701.

Telephone: (714) 834-3734.

KELLY, Thomas E. *(Judge, Superior Court of California County of Santa Cruz)* Assumed office July 1, 1998. Former Judge and Presiding Judge, Santa Cruz County Municipal Court.

Office: Main Courthouse, 701 Ocean Street, Santa Cruz 95060.

Telephone: (831) 454-2012.

KELLY, Thomas W. *(Judge, Superior Court of California County of Butte)* Assumed office June 3, 1998. Presiding Judge since Jan 1, 2001. Former Judge, North Butte County Municipal Court.

Office: One Court Street, Oroville 95965.

Telephone: (530) 538-7611.

KEMP, Margaret J. *(Judge, Superior Court of California County of San Mateo)* Appointed by Governor George Deukmejian to term beginning July 3, 1987. Elected Nov 1988, 1994 and 2000. Current term expires Jan 2007. Presiding Judge Criminal Court 1989 and 1996, Juvenile Court 1990-92 and since 1997 and Civil Law and Motion 1994. Civil Settlement Judge since Jan 1, 2001. Born Chicago Illinois Sept 3, 1944. Protestant. Educated at University of Illinois B.S. 1965 and University of California at Berkeley M.A. 1966 J.D. 1971. Admitted to practice California 1972, U.S. District Court Northern District of California 1972, U.S. Court of Appeals Ninth Circuit 1972 and U.S. Supreme Court 1980. Began legal practice Redwood City 1972. In legal practice San Mateo 1976. Judge, San Mateo County Municipal Court June 26, 1978 to July 2, 1987, appointed by Governor Edmund G. Brown, Jr.

Formerly with District Attorney's Office. Member Juvenile Justice Commission San Mateo County 1990-92, San Mateo County District Attorneys Association (President), California Women Lawyers, California Judges Association (Member 1980-81 and Chair 1981-82 Municipal Court Committee, Executive Board 1981-83, Secretary-Treasurer 1982-83, member Ethics Committee 1983-87 and Criminal Law Committee 1987-89), National Association of Women Judges, American Judges Association and San Mateo County Bar Association (Director and Committee Chairman). Seminar leader California Judicial College Faculty 1983. Lecturer California Judicial Education and Research 1990 and California Judges Association Annual Meeting 1990. Frequent lecturer on Criminal Justice and Juvenile Justice matters to local civic groups. Recipient Elinor Falvey Award for outstanding contribution to women from San Mateo County Bar Association. Advisory Board San Mateo County Drug and Alcohol Abuse 1985-96. Teacher 1966-68.

Office: Hall of Justice, 400 County Center, Redwood City 94063.

Telephone: (650) 363-4516.

KENNARD, Joyce Luther *(Associate Justice, California Supreme Court)* Appointed by Governor George Deukmejian to term beginning April 1989. Retained by election. Born Bandung Indonesia May 6, 1941. Became naturalized citizen 1967. Educated at Pasadena City College A.A. 1970 and University of Southern California B.A. magna cum laude 1971 M.P.A. 1974 J.D. 1974. Honorary J.D. Pepperdine University School of Law May 1989. Honorary Doctor of Laws California Western School of Law Dec 1990, Southwestern University School of Law May 1991, Whittier College School of Law May 1994, Lewis & Clark College Northwestern School of Law May 1997 and Lincoln University Law School May 1997. Recipient American Jurisprudence Award in Torts. Member Phi Beta Kappa and Phi Kappa Phi. Judge, Los Angeles Municipal Court Los Angeles County Feb 1986 to Feb 1987. Judge, Superior Court of California Los Angeles County Feb 1987 to March 1988. Associate Justice pro tem California Court of Appeal Second District Division Three Sept 1987 to Nov 1987. Associate Justice, California Court of Appeal Second District Division Five April 1988 to April 1989.

Deputy Attorney General Los Angeles 1975-79. Chair Appellate Advisory Committee Judicial Council of California since May 1996. Recipient Alumni Merit Award from University of Southern California March 1990, Award for Contributing to the Progress of Dignity and Self-Esteem Among Amputees from Sacramento Women Amputees Group March 1990, Ernestine Stahlhut Award from Women Lawyers Association of Los Angeles Oct 1990, People With Disabilities Award from Governor's Hall of Fame Nov 1990, Justice of the Year 1991 Award from California Trial Lawyers Association Nov 1991, Chinese-American Pioneers from Southern California in the Judiciary Award from Chinese Historical Society of Southern California Nov 1992 and 1996, The Trailblazer Award Nov 1994 and Public Service Award Dec 2001 from National Asian Pacific American Bar Association, Spirit of Excellence Award from Commission on Opportunities for Minorities in the Profession Feb 1996 and Margaret Brent Women Lawyers of Achievement Award Aug 1993 from American Bar Association, Legal Impact Award 2000 from Asian Law Alliance March 2000 and First Justice Rose Bird Memorial Award from California Women Lawyers March 2001.

Office: 350 McAllister Street, San Francisco 94102-4783.

Telephone: (415) 865-7100.

KENNEDY, John William *(Judge, Superior Court of California County of Contra Costa)* Appointed by Governor Gray Davis May 7, 2001 to term beginning June

KENNEDY, JOHN WILLIAM—*Continued*

22, 2001. Term expires 2004. Born Lakewood Ohio July 12, 1955. Catholic. Educated at Georgetown University B.S.B.A. 1977 J.D. 1980. Dean's List. Staff member American Criminal Law Review 1979-80. Law Clerk to Hon. James R. Browning, U.S. Court of Appeals Ninth Circuit 1980-82. Admitted to practice California 1981, U.S. District Courts Northern 1981 and Eastern 1982 Districts of California and U.S. Court of Appeals Ninth Circuit 1981.

Deputy District Attorney Contra Costa County 1982-83. Assistant U.S. Attorney Eastern District of California 1983-86 and Northern District of California 1986-2001. Member since 2001 and Board of Directors since 2002 Robert G. McGrath American Inn of Court. Member Reserve One Foundation since 1994. Enjoys coaching soccer, baseball and basketball, skiing, sailing, music and woodworking. Personal Statement or Quote: "Attorneys must be prepared to be effective."

Office: 725 Court Street, Department 8, Martinez 94553.

Telephone: (925) 646-4008.

Fax: (925) 646-9111

E-mail address: JKENN@sc.co.contra-costa.ca.us

KENNEDY, William H. *(Judge, Superior Court of California County of San Diego)*

Mailing address: P.O. Box 122724, San Diego 92112-2724.

Office: 220 West Broadway, San Diego 92101.

Telephone: (619) 531-3820.

KENNEDY-POWELL, Kathleen *(Judge, Superior Court of California County of Los Angeles)* Assumed office Jan 22, 2000. Former Judge, Los Angeles Municipal Court Los Angeles County.

Office: Criminal Courts Building, 210 West Temple Street, Los Angeles 90012-3210.

Telephone: (213) 974-6535.

KENNY, Michael P. *(Judge, Superior Court of California County of Sacramento)*

Office: Courthouse, 720 Ninth Street, Sacramento 95814.

Telephone: (916) 874-5476.

KENTON, Victor B. *(Magistrate Judge, United States District Court Central District of California)* Appointed by U.S. District Court judges to term beginning July 2, 2001. Born New York New York Nov 5, 1947. Educated at University of Connecticut B.A. 1969 and University of California at Los Angeles J.D. 1974. Member Phi Beta Kappa. Admitted to practice California 1974.

Office: 930H U.S. Courthouse, 312 North Spring Street, Los Angeles 90012.

Telephone: (213) 894-0741.

KEOSIAN, Gregory *(Judge, Superior Court of California County of Los Angeles)*

Office: Van Nuys Courthouse East, 6230 Sylmar Avenue, Van Nuys 91401.

Telephone: (818) 374-2265.

KHAN, Abraham *(Judge, Superior Court of California County of Los Angeles)* Assumed office Jan 22, 2000. Former Judge, Los Angeles Municipal Court Los Angeles County.

Office: El Monte Courthouse, 11234 East Valley Boulevard, El Monte 91731.

Telephone: (626) 575-4101.

KIM, Mark C. *(Judge, Superior Court of California County of Los Angeles)* Assumed office Jan 22, 2000. Former Judge, Los Angeles Municipal Court Los Angeles County.

Office: Long Beach Courthouse, 415 West Ocean Boulevard, Long Beach 90802.

Telephone: (562) 491-6130.

KIM, Marliese G. *(Judge, Superior Court of California County of Santa Clara)* Assumed office July 30, 1998. Former Judge, Santa Clara County Municipal Court.

Office: Hall of Justice East Wing, 190 West Hedding Street, San Jose 95110.

Telephone: (408) 808-6600.

KING, Edward J., III *(Judge, Superior Court of California County of Tehama)* Appointed by Governor Pete Wilson to term beginning 1997. Educated at Park College 1969-70, Rollins College B.G.S. 1973 and Western State University College of Law J.D. 1977. Judge, Tehama County Justice Court 1990-93. Judge, Tehama County Municipal Court 1993-97.

Deputy District Attorney 1979-80, Assistant District Attorney 1980-88 and District Attorney 1988-90 Tehama County. Honorary Member Tehama County Bar Association. President 1993 and Former Member Board of Directors Wilcox Oaks Golf Club. Former Member Tehama County Rotary Club and Tehama County Elks Lodge. Enjoys golfing.

Mailing address: P.O. Box 278, Red Bluff 96080.

Office: 633 Washington Street, Red Bluff 96080.

Telephone: (530) 527-0901.

KING, George Herbert *(Judge, United States District Court Central District of California)* Former Magistrate Judge and Chief Magistrate Judge. Appointed Judge for life by President Bill Clinton. Born Oct 12, 1951. Educated at University of California at Los Angeles A.B. magna cum laude 1971 and University of Southern California Law Center J.D. with honors 1974. Senior Staff member Southern California Law Review 1973-74. Member Pi Gamma Mu and Order of the Coif. Co-chair Executive Board Hale Moot Court. Admitted to practice California 1974, U.S. District Court Central District of California 1974, U.S. Court of Appeals Ninth Circuit 1975 and U.S. Supreme Court 1982. In legal practice Los Angeles 1974-75 and 1979-87.

Assistant U.S. Attorney Fraud and Special Prosecutions Section U.S. Attorney's Office 1975-79. Business Litigation Arbitrator Superior Court of California Los Angeles County 1981-87. Lawyer Representative Ninth Circuit Judicial Conference 1985-87. Author "Discovery Motions in Federal Court" Federal Bar Association Journal 1991. Important Decisions: Brown v. Rison (constitutional law) 673 F. Supp. 1505 C.D. Cal. 1987, Lewis v. Bowen (administrative law) 675 F. Supp. 1205 C.D. Cal. 1987, California Irrigation v. Bartron (patent law) 9 U.S.P.Q.2d 1859 C.D. Cal. 1988, Sueyres v. Bowen (administrative law) 1989 U.S. Dist. LEXIS 729 C.D. Cal. 1989 and Stilwell v. Chen (trade secrets/attorneys' fees) 11 U.S.P.Q.2d 1328 U.S. Dist. LEXIS 5971 C.D. Cal. 1989. Adjunct Professor of Trial Advocacy Law South-

KING, GEORGE HERBERT—*Continued*

western University School of Law 1982-83. Board of Directors 1983-87 and Barrister Inn of Court 1984-87 Legion Lex. Member Southern California Chinese Lawyers Association (Board of Governors 1980, President 1984-85, Chair 1986-87), State Bar of California (Commissioner Judicial Nominees Evaluation Commission 1986) and Los Angeles County Bar Association (Federal Courts and Practices Committee, Judicial Evaluation Committee, Delegate State Bar Conference of Delegates 1985-86).

Faculty member U.S. Attorney General's Advocacy Institute 1978-79; Patent Trial Advocacy Program American Bar Association 1982; Civil and Criminal Advocacy Program, Criminal Advocacy Program for the Office of the Prosecuting Attorney and the Office of the Public Defender Honolulu Hawaii Hastings Center for Trial and Appellate Advocacy 1982-85; and Northwest Regionals 1983 and Western Regionals 1983-84 National Institute for Trial Advocacy. Faculty member Trial Advocacy Program 1987-89 and Speaker and Panelist 1989 and 1990 California Continuing Education of the Bar. Speaker and Panelist on Federal Practice Legion Lex American Inns of Court 1988; Pre-trial Tactics in Wrongful Termination Cases Labor Law Section 1988, Practice Before Federal Magistrates Litigation Section 1989, Discovery and Pre-Trial Management Barrister Section 1989 and 1990, Attachment Proceedings in Federal Court Prejudgment Remedies Section 1989 and Appeals of Final Decisions of the Secretary of Health and Human Services Social Security Law Section 1989 Los Angeles County Bar Association; and Federal Criminal Practice 1989 and Federal Civil Practice 1990 Federal Bar Association. Instructor in Civil Procedure Judicial Administration Program University of Southern California 1982-84. President 1982-83 and Chair Oratorical Contest 1984-86 and Zone Oratorical Contest 1987 Los Angeles Chinatown Optimist Club. Enjoys karate, snow skiing and racquetball.

Office: 670 Federal Building, 255 East Temple Street, Los Angeles 90012.

Telephone: (213) 894-5766.

KING, Jeffrey *(Associate Justice, California Court of Appeal Fourth District Division Two)* Appointed by Governor Gray Davis. Former Judge, Superior Court of California County of San Bernardino.

Office: 3389 Twelfth Street, Riverside 92501.

Telephone: (909) 248-0200.

KING, Richard M. *(Judge, Superior Court of California County of Orange)*

Mailing address: P.O. Box 5000, Fullerton 92838-0500.

Office: North Justice Center, 1275 North Berkeley Avenue, Fullerton 92832.

Telephone: (714) 773-4400.

KINGSBURY, Kenneth R. *(Judge, Superior Court of California County of Alameda)* Assumed office 1995. Born Santa Cruz California Nov 3, 1939. Educated at San Jose State University B.S. 1965 and San Francisco Law School 1976. Admitted to practice California 1976 and U.S. District Court Northern District of California 1976. Judge, Oakland-Piedmont-Emeryville Municipal Court Alameda County June 2, 1992 to 1995, appointed by Governor Pete Wilson.

Deputy Probation Officer 1965-77 and Deputy/Senior Deputy District Attorney 1977-92 Alameda County. Member Administration of Justice California Community Colleges, California Judges Association and Alameda County Bar Association (Drug Task Force Advisory Committee). Republican. Interests include vintage automobiles.

Office: 1225 Fallon Street, Room 209, Oakland 94612.

Telephone: (510) 272-6082.

KINGSBURY, Suzanne N. *(Judge, Superior Court of California County of El Dorado)* Elected Nov 5, 1996 to term beginning Jan 6, 1997. Reelected 2002, current term expires Jan 5, 2009. Presiding Judge since June 1999. Born Dayton Ohio 1956. Educated at California State University at Sacramento B.A. 1981 and University of the Pacific McGeorge School of Law J.D. 1982. Admitted to practice California 1982 and U.S. District Court Eastern District of California 1982. In legal practice Sacramento 1982-85 and South Lake Tahoe 1985-96.

Deputy District Attorney 1985-90 and Deputy Public Defender 1990-96 El Dorado County. Adjunct Faculty Evidence and Criminal Law, Criminal Procedure and Juvenile Law Lake Tahoe Community College since 1988. Member Planning Committee California Judicial Administration Conference 2001 and 2003, Planning Committee Rural Courts Institute 2001, 2002 and 2003, Presiding Judges Advisory Committee since 1999 and Task Force on Self Represented Litigants since 2001 Judicial Council. Member Cow County Program Planning Committee California Center for Judicial Education and Research since 2001, Working Group on Dependency Counsel Caseload Standards since 2001, Joint Working Group on Intra-County Venue Issues since 2002, Task Force on Judicial Ethics Issues since 2002 and Presiding Judge and Court Executive Office Education Committee since 2002. Member California Rural Judges Association, California Judges Association (Committee on Criminal Law and Procedure), American Judges Association and American Judicature Society. Attended Faculty Development Workshop California Judicial Center for Education and Research Jan 2002, California Judicial Administration Conference, Judicial College and courses on civil law and procedure, rural courts education, juvenile law and procedure, family law and procedure, CEQA and death penalty cases. Facilitator/Lecturer "Managing Your Court" CJSP Oct 2001. Recipient Distinguished Service Award from California State University at Sacramento Alumni Association March 14, 2002. Board Member Lake Tahoe Educational Foundation.

Office: 1354 Johnson Boulevard, Suite 2, South Lake Tahoe 96150.

Telephone: (530) 573-3064.

Fax: (530) 544-6532

KINGSLEY, Kay T. *(Judge, Superior Court of California County of Monterey)* Assumed office Dec 18, 2000. Former Judge, Monterey County Municipal Court.

Mailing address: P.O. Box 1819, Salinas 93902-1819.

Office: 240 Church Street, Salinas 93901.

Telephone: (831) 755-5060.

KINNICUTT, Harry S. *(Judge, Superior Court of California County of Solano)* Presiding Judge Jan 1, 1998 to Dec 31, 1999.

Office: 600 Union Avenue, Fairfield 94533-5000.

Telephone: (707) 421-7827.

KINTNER, Janet Ide *(Judge, Superior Court of California County of San Diego)* Assumed Dec 1, 1998. Elected 2002, current term expires Jan 2009. Born Dayton Ohio 1944. Educated at University of Arizona B.A. 1966 J.D. 1968. Admitted to practice Arizona 1968 and California 1969. In legal practice San Diego 1968-76. Judge, San Diego Municipal Court San Diego County Feb 1976 to Nov 30, 1998, appointed by Governor Edmund G. Brown, Jr. Enjoys music.
Mailing address: P.O. Box 122724, San Diego 92112-2724.
Office: 220 West Broadway, San Diego 92101.
Telephone: (619) 531-3008.

KIRIHARA, John D. *(Judge, Superior Court of California County of Merced)*
Office: County Courts Building, 627 West 21st Street, Merced 95340.
Telephone: (209) 385-7531.

KIRKMAN, K. Michael *(Judge, Superior Court of California County of San Diego)*
Mailing address: P.O. Box 122724, San Diego 92112-2724.
Office: 325 South Melrose Drive, Vista 92083.
Telephone: (760) 726-9595.

KIRKWOOD, Carolyn *(Judge, Superior Court of California County of Orange)*
Mailing address: P.O. Box 5000, Fullerton 92838-0500.
Office: North Justice Center, 1275 North Berkeley Avenue, Fullerton 92832.
Telephone: (714) 773-4400.

KIRSCHNER, Richard H. *(Judge, Superior Court of California County of Los Angeles)*
Office: Van Nuys Courthouse West, 14400 Erwin Street Mall, Van Nuys 91401-2705.
Telephone: (818) 374-2601.

KITCHING, Patti S. *(Associate Justice, California Court of Appeal Second District Division Three)* Appointed by Governor Pete Wilson to term beginning Jan 1993. Retained by election. Born Los Angeles California Oct 7, 1941. Educated at University of California at Los Angeles 1963 and Loyola Marymount University J.D. cum laude 1974. Member St. Thomas More Society. Judge, Los Angeles Municipal Court Los Angeles County 1988-90. Judge, Superior Court of California Los Angeles County 1990-93.
Deputy Attorney General California 1975-86. Senior Counsel Bank of America 1986-88. Contributing Editor Pretrial Disposition *California Practice Handbook* Matthew Bender 1993. Member Los Angeles Women Lawyers, California Women Lawyers, California Judges Association and National Association of Women Judges. Named Appellate Justice of the Year 1995.
Office: 300 South Spring Street, Los Angeles 90013.
Telephone: (213) 830-7000.

KLAUSNER, Robert G. *(Judge, United States District Court Central District of California)* Appointed for life by President George W. Bush to term beginning Dec 4, 2002. Born Los Angeles California 1941. Educated at University of Notre Dame B.A. 1963 B.S. 1964 and Loyola Law School J.D. 1967. Commissioner 1974-80 and Judge 1980-85, Pasadena Municipal Court Los Angeles County. Judge 1985-2002 and Presiding Judge Jan 1, 1995 to Dec 31, 1996, Superior Court of California County of Los Angeles.
Office: 860 Federal Building, 255 East Temple Street, Los Angeles 90012.
Telephone: (213) 894-3535.

KLEIFIELD, Steven J. *(Judge, Superior Court of California County of Los Angeles)*
Office: Los Angeles Airport Courthouse, 11701 South La Cienega Boulevard, Los Angeles 90045.
Telephone: (310) 727-6010.

KLEIN, Brett Carroll *(Judge, Superior Court of California County of Los Angeles)* Assumed office Jan 22, 2000. Former Judge, Los Angeles Municipal Court Los Angeles County.
Office: Courthouse, 111 North Hill Street, Los Angeles 90012.
Telephone: (213) 974-5411.

KLEIN, Christopher M. *(Judge, United States Bankruptcy Court Eastern District of California)* Also Judge, Bankruptcy Appellate Panel Ninth Circuit. Selected by the Judicial Council of the Ninth Circuit.
Office: 3-200 U.S. Courthouse, 501 I Street, Sacramento 95814-2322.
Telephone: (916) 930-4510.

KLEIN, Clifford *(Judge, Superior Court of California County of Los Angeles)*
Office: Eastlake Juvenile Court, 1601 Eastlake Avenue, Los Angeles 90033.
Telephone: (323) 226-8591.

KLEIN, Joan Dempsey *(Presiding Justice, California Court of Appeal Second District Division Three)* Appointed by Governor Edmund G. Brown Jr. April 1978. Retained by election. Born San Jose California Aug 18, 1924. Educated at San Diego State College (now California State University at San Diego) A.B. 1947 and University of California at Los Angeles LL.B. 1955. Admitted to practice California 1955. Judge 1963-74 and Presiding Judge 1974, Los Angeles County Municipal Court. Judge, Superior Court of California Los Angeles County 1974-78.
Deputy Attorney General 1955-63. Lecturer University of California at Los Angeles, University of Southern California and Loyola University. Member California Council on Criminal Justice 1970-74, Conference of California Judges (Vice Chairperson Committee on Economy and Efficiency), International Federation of Women Lawyers, California Women Lawyers (President 1975), Women Lawyers Association, National Association of Women Judges (Founding President 1979-80) and Los Angeles County Bar Association. Lecturer Conference of California Judges and Continuing Education of the Bar program. Delegate to National Advisory Commission on Criminal Justice Standards and Goals 1973. Chairperson Advisory Committee California Highway Patrol Project for women officers 1976. Recipient Municipal Court Judge of the Year Award from California Trial Lawyers Association 1973, Ernestine Stahlhut Award from Women Lawyers Association 1973, Professional Achievement Award from UCLA Alumni Association 1975 and Myrtle Wreath Award for Contributions to Justice from Hadassah 1977. Selected "Woman of Tomorrow" in the field of law by Welfare Federation of Los Angeles, Alumna of the Year by UCLA Law School 1963, Angel of Distinction by Los Angeles Central City Association

KLEIN, JOAN DEMPSEY—*Continued*

1969, Woman of Achievement by Los Angeles Sunset District California Federation of Business and Professional Women's Clubs, Woman of the Year by *Los Angeles Times* 1975 and one of Ten Most Outstanding Women by Sherman Oaks Chamber of Commerce 1984. Member Business and Professional Women's Club, Legion Lex of USC, UCLA Law School Alumni Association (Past President) and The Dean's Counsel of UCLA Law School. Participant National Conference on Alcoholism Washington D.C. 1965. Advisory Board for Girl's Week Los Angeles City Schools, Gifted Children's Association of San Fernando Valley and Volunteer League of San Fernando Valley. Enjoys travel, tennis, swimming and volleyball.

Office: 300 South Spring Street, Los Angeles 90013.

Telephone: (213) 830-7000.

KLEINBERG, James P. *(Judge, Superior Court of California County of Santa Clara)*

Office: 170 Park Plaza, San Jose 95113.

Telephone: (408) 534-5600.

KLINE, John Anthony *(Presiding Justice, California Court of Appeal First District Division Two)* Appointed by Governor Edmund G. Brown, Jr. to term beginning Dec 24, 1982. Retained by election 1986, 1990 and 2002. Current term expires Jan 2015. Born New York New York Aug 17, 1938. Jewish. Educated at Johns Hopkins University B.A. with honors 1960, Cornell University M.P.A. 1962 and Yale University J.D. 1965. Alfred P. Sloan Fellow Cornell University 1960-62. Recipient Ambrose Gherini Prize and Sutherland Cup Yale University 1965. Law Clerk to Hon. Raymond E. Peters, California Supreme Court 1965-66. Member Phi Alpha Delta. Admitted to practice California 1966, New York 1967, U.S. District Courts Northern District of California 1966 and Southern District of New York 1967 and U.S. Court of Appeals Ninth 1966 and Second 1967 Circuits. In legal practice New York City 1966-70 and San Francisco 1970-75 and Sacramento 1975-80 California. Judge, Superior Court of California San Francisco County 1980-82.

Legal Affairs Secretary to Governor Edmund G. Brown, Jr. 1975-80. Author "An Examination of the Competence of National Courts to Prescribe and Apply International Law: The Sabbatino Case Revisited" 1 University of San Francisco L. Rev. 49, 1966, "Displacement of the Poor from Housing by the Federal-Aid Highway Program: Remedies Under the Highway Relocation Assistance Act of 1968" 4 Clearinghouse Rev. 408, 1970, "Law Reform and the Courts: More Power to the People or to the Profession?" 53 California State B. Jour. 14 Jan/Feb 1978, "Curbing California's Legal Appetite" Opinion Section *Los Angeles Times* Feb 12, 1978, "The Media and the Courts" *Los Angeles Daily Journal* 90th Anniversary Issue Sept 11, 1978, "Is Time Running Out on the Legal Profession?" ABA Bar Leader Nov/Dec 1978 and "Merit Selection: The Pursuit of an Illusion" 55 California State B. Jour. 421, 1980. Coauthor with LeGates "Citizen Participation in the Model Cities Program: Toward a Theory of Collective Bargaining for the Poor" 1 Black L. Jour. 44 Spring 1971, with Sitkin "Financing the Private Practice of Public Interest Law" 13 Arizona L. Rev. 823, 1972 and with Hufstedler, Zolin et al. "Our Congested Courts" 1 Los Angeles Lawyer 14, April 1978 (symposium). Important Decisions: In re marriage of Mentry 142 Cal. Ct. App. 3d 260, 1983, Easton v. Strassburger 152 Cal. Ct. App. 3d 90, 1984 and Prudential Reinsurance Co. v. Superior Court (dissent) 3 Cal. 4th 1118, 1992. Member Lawyers Committee for Urban Affairs 1971-74, California Judges Association, Institute of Judicial Administration, The Association of the Bar of the City of New York 1967-69 and San Francisco Bar Association 1970-75. Recipient Judge Learned Hand Human Relations Award 2002. Democrat. Chairman Board of Directors San Francisco Conservation Corps since 1983 and Golden Gate Kindergarten Association. Board of Directors San Francisco Private Industry Council 1982-88, American Jewish Congress Northern California Division 1982-90 and Youth Service America 1986-90. President Youth Guidance Center Improvement Committee (juvenile detention facility). Enjoys reading and fishing.

Office: 350 McAllister Street, San Francisco 94102-3600.

Telephone: (415) 865-7370.

KLOPFER, Barry B. *(Judge, Superior Court of California County of Ventura)* Assumed office June 10, 1998. Presiding Judge Jan 1, 1996 to Dec 31, 1997 and Former Judge, Ventura County Municipal Court.

Mailing address: P.O. Box 6489, Ventura 93006-6489.

Office: 800 South Victoria Avenue, Ventura 93009-0001.

Telephone: (805) 654-2965.

KNIGHT, Michael E. *(Judge, Superior Court of California County of Los Angeles)* Assumed office Jan 22, 2000. Former Judge, Los Angeles Municipal Court Los Angeles County.

Office: Van Nuys Courthouse East, 6230 Sylmar Avenue, Van Nuys 91401.

Telephone: (818) 374-2265.

KNUPP, Larry S. *(Judge, Superior Court of California County of Los Angeles)* Assumed office Jan 22, 2000. Term expires Jan 2007. Serves Southeast District. Born Whittier California April 7, 1940. Religious affiliation: Disciples of Christ. Educated at Pomona College B.A. 1961 and University of California at Berkeley J.D. 1964. Admitted to practice California 1965 and U.S. District Court Southern District of California 1965. In legal practice Whittier 1965-75. Commissioner 1975-89, Judge Jan 1989 to Jan 21, 2000 and Presiding Judge Jan 1, 1995 to Dec 31, 1997, Whittier Municipal Court Los Angeles County.

Member Whittier Bar Association (President 1974). Member East Whittier Lions Club and Izaak Walton League. Enjoys fishing, philately and travel.

Office: Norwalk Courthouse, 12720 Norwalk Boulevard, Norwalk 90650.

Telephone: (562) 807-7249.

KOBAYASHI, Charles C. *(Judge, Superior Court of California County of Sacramento)* Former Judge, Sacramento Municipal Court Sacramento County.

Office: Courthouse, 720 Ninth Street, Sacramento 95814.

Telephone: (916) 874-5476.

KOLIN, William M. *(Judge, Superior Court of California County of Contra Costa)* Assumed office June 8, 1998. Presiding Judge Jan 1, 1996 to Dec 31, 1997 and

KOLIN, WILLIAM M.—*Continued*

Former Judge, Mount Diablo Municipal Court Contra Costa County.

Office: Courthouse, 725 Court Street, Martinez 94553.

Telephone: (925) 646-2950.

KOLKEY, Daniel M. *(Associate Justice, California Court of Appeal Third District)* Appointed by Governor Pete Wilson to term beginning Dec 31, 1998. Retained by election Nov 2002, current term expires Jan 2015. Born Chicago Illinois April 21, 1952. Educated at Stanford University B.A. with distinction and departmental honors 1974 and Harvard Law School J.D. magna cum laude 1977. Law Clerk to Hon. Dudley B. Bonsal, U.S. District Court Southern District of New York 1977-78. Member Phi Beta Kappa. Admitted to practice California 1977, U.S. District Courts Central 1978, Eastern 1979, Northern 1980 and Southern 1994 Districts of California and District of Arizona 1992, U.S. Court of Appeals Ninth Circuit 1979 and U.S. Supreme Court 1983. In legal practice Los Angeles 1978-94.

Author "California's Adoption of a Code for International Commercial Arbitration and Conciliation" 10 Loyola of Los Angeles International and Comparative L. Jour. 583, 1988; "Fora for the Resolution of International Business Disputes When Doing Business with the People's Republic of China" 12 Loyola of Los Angeles International and Comparative L. Jour. 102, 1989; "Attacking Arbitral Awards: Rights of Appeal and Review in International Arbitrations" 22 International Lawyer 693, 1988; "Reflections on the U.S. Statutory Framework for International Commercial Arbitrations: Its Scope, Shortcomings, and the Advantages of the U.S. Adoption of the UNCITRAL Model Law" 1 The American Review of International Arbitration 491, 1990; "Dispute Resolution and International Commercial Agreements" 1992 and "Dispute Resolution and International Commercial Agreements" 1993 Practising Law Institute; "The Constitutional Cycles of Federalism" 32 Idaho L. Rev. 495, 1996; and "It's Time to Adopt the UNCITRAL Model Law on International Commercial Arbitration" 8 Transnational Law and Contemporary Problems 3, 1998. Co-author with Albert Golbert "California's New International Arbitration and Conciliation Code" 11 *Los Angeles Lawyer* 46 Nov 1988 and with Willard Carr "Labor Relations for Multinational Corporations Doing Business in Europe" 7 Loyola of Los Angeles International and Comparative L. Jour. 1, 1984. Co-editor with Rhoades and Chernick *Practitioner's Handbook on International Arbitration and Mediation* Juris Publishing 2002. Important Decisions: Sacramento Brewing Co. v. Desmond, Miller & Desmond 75 Cal. App. 4th 1082, 1999 and People v. Benjamin 77 Cal. App. 4th 264, 1999. Associate Chartered Institute of Arbitrators 1986-94. President Los Angeles Center for International Commercial Arbitration 1990-94. Arbitrator U.S.-Canada Free Trade Agreement Panel 1990-94. Chair International Law Section Los Angeles County Bar Association 1991-92. Member 1992-94 and Chair 1994 California Law Revision Commission. Member Blue Ribbon Commission on Jury System Improvement 1996. Former Member Anthony Kennedy Inns of Court. Member Pacific Council on International Policy. Legal Affairs Secretary and Counsel to the Governor Governor's Office 1995-98. General Counsel Citizens Research Foundation 1991-94. Member Law and Justice Committee Los Angeles Area Chamber of Commerce 1993-94. Enjoys theater, music and foreign affairs.

Office: Library and Courts Building, 914 Capitol Mall, Sacramento 95814.

Telephone: (916) 654-0209.

Fax: (916) 653-5043

KOLOSTIAN, Richard G. *(Judge, Superior Court of California County of Los Angeles)* Appointed by Governor Edmund G. Brown, Jr. to term beginning Feb 5, 1980. Elected 1982, 1988, 1994 and 2000. Current term expires Jan 2007. Supervising Judge Northwest District 1989-90. Born Los Angeles California Dec 2, 1931. Armenian Orthodox. Educated at Loyola University of Los Angeles B.B.A. 1954 LL.B. 1963. Member Phi Alpha Delta. Admitted to practice California 1964. In legal practice Los Angeles March 1968 to April 1974. Commissioner, Los Angeles Municipal Court Los Angeles County April 1974 to Feb 5, 1980.

Deputy City Attorney and Attorney Police Board of Commissioners Los Angeles 1964-68. Former Member Personnel and Budget Committee, Alternative Dispute Resolution Committee, Bench-Bar Committee and BAJI Committee Superior Court. Member San Fernando Valley Criminal, San Fernando Valley and Los Angeles County (Former Member Bench-Media Committee) Bar Associations. Named Judge of the Year by Constitutional Rights Foundation and San Fernando Valley Criminal Bar Association. USAF Oct 1955 to Oct 1957 and Captain USAFR. Enjoys woodworking, gardening, skiing, backpacking, basketball, golfing and reading.

Office: Van Nuys Courthouse East, 6230 Sylmar Avenue, Van Nuys 91401.

Telephone: (818) 374-2220.

KOMAR, Jack *(Judge, Superior Court of California County of Santa Clara)* Presiding Judge Jan 1, 1999 to Dec 31, 2000.

Office: Old Courthouse, 161 North First Street, San Jose 95113.

Telephone: (408) 882-2340.

KOPP, Quentin L. *(Judge, Superior Court of California County of San Mateo)* Appointed by Governor Pete Wilson Jan 1, 1999 to term beginning Feb 1, 1999. Elected Nov 7, 2000, current term expires Jan 2007. Born Syracuse New York Aug 11, 1928. Jewish. Educated at Dartmouth College A.B. 1949 and Harvard University Law School LL.B. 1952. Rufus Choate Scholar. Admitted to practice District of Columbia 1952, California 1954, U.S. District Court Northern District of California 1954, U.S. Court of Appeals Ninth Circuit 1954, New York 1955 and U.S. Supreme Court 1962. In legal practice New York New York 1954-55 and San Francisco California 1955-98.

Deputy Counsel Waterfront Commission of New York Harbor Nov 1954 to Nov 1955. President Barristers Club of San Francisco 1961 and State Junior Bar 1964. Member House of Delegates American Bar Association 1962-65. Former Member Bar Association of San Francisco (Board of Directors 1960-62) and State Bar of California. Chairman "How to Build a Law Practice" Convention Panel State Bar of California 1985-95. USAF Aug 1952 to Aug 1954. Political affiliation: Independent. Member 1972-86 and President 1976-78 and 1982 San Francisco Board of Supervisors. Member California State Senate 1986-98. Member Lions Club, Order of the Moose, B'nai B'rith, American Legion and Amer-

KOPP, QUENTIN L.—*Continued*

ican Jewish Committee. Enjoys sports, history and travel.
Office: Hall of Justice and Records, 400 County Center, Redwood City 94063.
Telephone: (650) 363-4817.
Fax: (650) 363-4698
E-mail address: qkopp@co.sanmateo.ca.us

KOSEL, Roger T. *(Judge, Superior Court of California County of Siskiyou)* Assumed office June 4, 1998. Elected 2000, current term expires Jan 2007. Presiding Judge since July 1, 1999. Born Oakland California Jan 29, 1943. Educated at University of California at Davis B.A. 1965, University of California at Berkeley M.B.A. 1966 and University of San Francisco J.D. 1973. Admitted to practice California 1974. Judge Jan 7, 1991 to June 3, 1998 and Former Presiding Judge, Siskiyou County Municipal Court, appointed by Siskiyou County Board of Supervisors.
Deputy District Attorney Alameda County 1974-78. Assistant District Attorney 1978-81 and Deputy Public Defender 1988-91 Siskiyou County. Member California Judges Association, American Judges Association and Siskiyou County Bar Association. Lieutenant Commander USNR 1966-70. Member Advisory Board Mercy Medical Center Mount Shasta, Rotary Club of Yreka and Pals Mentoring Program. Enjoys rafting, kayaking, golfing, skiing, sailing, bicycling, jogging, racquet ball, gardening, reading and writing poetry.
Mailing address: P.O. Box 1026, Yreka 96097.
Office: 311 Fourth Street, Yreka 96097.
Telephone: (530) 842-8184.

KRAETZER, John Frederick *(Judge, Superior Court of California County of Alameda)*
Office: Administration Building, 1221 Oak Street, Oakland 94612.
Telephone: (510) 271-5130.

KRAMER, Richard A. *(Judge, Superior Court of California City and County of San Francisco)*
Office: Civic Center Courthouse, 400 McAllister Street, San Francisco 94102-4514.
Telephone: (415) 551-4020.

KRANT, Elisabeth B. *(Judge, Superior Court of California County of Tulare)* Assumed office July 27, 1998. Serves Tulare-Pixley Division. Former Judge, Tulare County Municipal Court.
Office: 425 East Kern Avenue, Tulare 93274.
Telephone: (559) 685-2550.

KRASHNA, David M. *(Judge, Superior Court of California County of Alameda)*
Office: Courthouse, 661 Washington Street, Oakland 94607.
Telephone: (510) 268-7601.

KRAUEL, Roger W. *(Judge, Superior Court of California County of San Diego)*
Mailing address: P.O. Box 122724, San Diego 92112-2724.
Office: 220 West Broadway, San Diego 92101.
Telephone: (619) 531-3820.

KREBER, Ronald Patrick *(Judge, Superior Court of California County of Orange)* Assumed office Aug 10, 1998. Born Yankton South Dakota March 18, 1937. Catholic. Educated at West Los Angeles School of Law 1971. Member West Los Angeles School of Law Law Review. Admitted to practice California 1972 and U.S. District Courts Central 1972, Southern 1981, Eastern 1986 and Northern 1986 Districts of California. In legal practice Newport Beach 1979-88. Judge pro tem, Harbor Municipal Court Orange County 1979-88. Judge, North Orange County Municipal Court Sept 21, 1988 to Nov 7, 1990, appointed by Governor George Deukmejian. Judge Nov 8, 1990 to Aug 9, 1998 and Presiding Judge Jan 1, 1996 to Dec 31, 1996, South Orange County Municipal Court, appointed by Governor George Deukmejian.
Deputy District Attorney Orange County 1972-79 (Trial Deputy Feb 1972 to May 1973, Felony Panel May 1973 to July 1974, Narcotics Task Force July 1974 to Sept 1978, Grand Jury Advisor Sept 1978 to May 1979). Former Member Orange County Trial Lawyers Association (Board of Directors 1982 and 1984), Orange County Narcotics Officers Association and Association of Specialized Criminal Defense. Member California Judges Association, Newport Harbor (Treasurer 1984-85, President 1986), South Orange County (Treasurer 1988), Orange County (Member Founder's Circle, Activities Chairman 1979-87, Co-chairman 1986-88) and Orange County Federal (Founding Member, Board of Directors 1987, Co-chairman Criminal Law Seminar 1987) Bar Associations. Instructor Orange County Sheriff's Academy 1974-78, Federal Drug Enforcement Agency 1975-79 and in Trial Advocacy New Lawyers Training Program Orange County Bar Association 1981-88. Recipient Leadership Award from Los Angeles Police Department 1967 and six meritorious accommodations during and after Watts riots from citizens 1965-67. Named Prosecutor of the Year by Orange County Narcotic Task Force 1974. USMC 1956-59. Patrol Officer 1963-66, Police Officer 1963-72 and Detective Sergeant Homicide Division June 1969 to Feb 1972 Los Angeles Police Department. Instructor Los Angeles Police Academy April 1968 to June 1969. Attended specialist classes University of Southern California School of Law 1975 and 1976, Loyola Marymount University and Arizona State University. Volunteer Community Speaker District Attorney's Office 1973-79. Speaker on Drug Awareness at local high schools 1987-89. Participant court sponsored program which sends youthful former drug users to speak at local high schools 1985-88. Police Explorer Scout Leader 1967-69. Football Booster Laguna Beach High School and Mater Dei High School 1984. Patron American Paralysis Association Orange County Guild 1987-88.
Mailing address: P.O. Box 1994, Santa Ana 92702-1994.
Office: Central Justice Center, 700 Civic Center Drive West, Santa Ana 92701.
Telephone: (714) 834-3734.

KREMER, Daniel J. *(Administrative Presiding Justice, California Court of Appeal Fourth District and Presiding Justice, California Court of Appeal Fourth District Division One)* Appointed by Governor George Deukmejian to term beginning July 1985. Retained by election Nov 1986 and Nov 1998. Current term expires Jan 2011. Educated at Stanford University B.S. 1960 J.D. 1963. Admitted to practice California 1964, U.S. Court of Appeals Ninth Circuit 1964 and U.S. Supreme Court 1969. Judge, Superior Court of California San Diego County 1983 to July 1985, appointed by Governor George Deukmejian.
Deputy Attorney General Sacramento 1964-72. Chief

KREMER, DANIEL J.—*Continued*

Assistant Attorney General Criminal Division California 1983. Former Chair Committee on Criminal Trial Delay Reduction, Library Technology Committee and Rules and Forms Committee and Co-chair Court Technology Committee Judicial Council of California. Chair Task Force on Court Facilities.

Office: 750 B Street, Suite 300, San Diego 92101.

Telephone: (619) 645-2760.

KRIEGLER, Sandy R. *(Judge, Superior Court of California County of Los Angeles)* Appointed by Governor George Deukmejian to term beginning Oct 1989. Elected to subsequent terms. Educated at California State University at Northridge B.A. 1972 and Loyola University School of Law J.D. 1975. Former Judge, Los Angeles Municipal Court Los Angeles County.

Office: Courthouse, 111 North Hill Street, Los Angeles 90012.

Telephone: (213) 974-5411.

KRISTOVICH, Marlene *(Judge, Superior Court of California County of Los Angeles)* Elected June 7, 1994 to term beginning Jan 3, 1995. Served Family Law Division 1996-98 and Civil Fastrack 1998. Educated at University of Southern California B.S. in Accounting and Loyola Law School J.D. Member Phi Alpha Delta. Admitted to practice California 1978. Judge, Los Angeles Municipal Court Los Angeles County Dec 21, 1990 to Jan 2, 1995, appointed by Governor George Deukmejian.

Office: Criminal Courts Building, 210 West Temple Street, Los Angeles 90012-3210.

Telephone: (213) 974-6535.

KRONBERGER, William H. *(Judge, Superior Court of California County of San Diego)* Assumed office Dec 1, 1998. Former Judge, San Diego Municipal Court San Diego County.

Mailing address: P.O. Box 122724, San Diego 92112-2724.

Office: 220 West Broadway, San Diego 92101.

Telephone: (619) 531-3820.

KRONSTADT, John *(Judge, Superior Court of California County of Los Angeles)*

Office: Metropolitan Courthouse, 1945 South Hill Street, Los Angeles 90007-1466.

Telephone: (213) 744-4001.

KROYER, Stephen Thomas *(Judge, Superior Court of California County of Napa)*

Office: Napa County Criminal Courts Building, 1111 Third Street, Napa 94559.

Telephone: (707) 299-1100.

KUHL, Carolyn B. *(Judge, Superior Court of California County of Los Angeles)* Appointed by Governor Pete Wilson to term beginning Oct 24, 1995. Elected 1996 and 2002. Current term expires Jan 2009. Born St. Louis Missouri July 24, 1952. Roman Catholic. Educated at Princeton University A.B. cum laude 1974 and Duke University School of Law J.D. with distinction 1977. Editor Duke Law Journal 1975-77. Law Clerk to Hon. Anthony M. Kennedy, U.S. Court of Appeals Ninth Circuit 1977-78. Member Order of the Coif. Admitted to practice Missouri 1977, California 1979, District of Columbia 1986, U.S. Courts of Appeals First, Eighth, Ninth and District of Columbia Circuits and U.S. Supreme Court. In legal practice Los Angeles 1978-81 and 1986-95.

Special Assistant to U.S. Attorney General 1981-82. Deputy Assistant Attorney General U.S. Department of Justice 1982-85. Principal Deputy U.S. Solicitor General 1985-86. Member The American Law Institute.

Office: Central Civil West, 600 South Commonwealth, Los Angeles 90005.

Telephone: (213) 351-8739.

KURTZ, Robert K. *(Judge, Superior Court of California County of Alameda)* Assumed office 1995. Born San Diego California July 5, 1948. Congregationalist. Educated at University of California at Berkeley A.B. 1970 and Hastings College of the Law J.D. 1973. Admitted to practice California 1973. In legal practice Hayward 1978-81. Judge Oct 24, 1986 to 1995 and Former Presiding Judge, San Leandro-Hayward Municipal Court Alameda County, appointed by Governor George Deukmejian.

Deputy District Attorney Riverside County 1973-76, Del Norte County 1976-77 and Stanislaus County 1977. Assistant Public Defender Alameda County 1981-86.

Office: Hayward Hall of Justice, 24405 Amador Street, Hayward 94544.

Telephone: (510) 670-5060.

KWAN, Ruth Ann *(Judge, Superior Court of California County of Los Angeles)* Former Judge, East Los Angeles Municipal Court Los Angeles County.

Office: Criminal Courts Building, 210 West Temple Street, Los Angeles 90012-3210.

Telephone: (213) 974-6535.

KWONG, Owen Lee *(Judge, Superior Court of California County of Los Angeles)* Appointed by Governor Pete Wilson to term beginning Feb 5, 1993. Elected to subsequent term. Born Sacramento California. Educated University of Utah School of Pharmacy B.S. with honors 1968 and University of California at Los Angeles School of Law J.D. 1973. Member Phi Delta Chi and Rho Chi. Admitted to practice California 1974, U.S. District Courts Central 1974, Eastern 1981 and Northern 1987 Districts of California, U.S. Courts of Appeals Ninth 1974 and Seventh 1982 Circuits and U.S. Supreme Court 1980. Judge, Los Angeles Municipal Court Los Angeles County April 21, 1989 to Feb 5, 1993, appointed by Governor George Deukmejian.

Deputy Attorney General (Supervising Deputy Antitrust Law Section) 1974-89. Special Assistant U.S. Attorney General 1985-89. Member Liaison Subcommittee on Statistical Reporting Judicial Council Court Administration Advisory Committee California Judges Association since 1989. Member Los Angeles Superior Court Executive Committee 1995-96. President California Asian Judges Association 1998-2000. Member Southern California Chinese Lawyers Association (Board of Governors 1986-88), Judicial Council of California (Civil and Small Claims Advisory Committee since 1993) and Asian Judges Association. Former Member Association of California Deputy Attorneys General, Association of California State Attorneys and Municipal Court Judges Association of Los Angeles. President Planning Committee Civic Law and Procedure Institute California Center for Judicial Education and Research 1997. Recipient Public Service Award for pro bono legal services from State Bar of California 1983. Member Asian Business League since 1983. Member California State Advisory Committee United States Commission on Civil Rights

KWONG, OWEN LEE—*Continued*
2002-03. Enjoys skiing, playing tennis, bowling, traveling, rollerblading, bicycling and reading.
Office: Courthouse, 111 North Hill Street, Los Angeles 90012.
Telephone: (213) 974-5411.

LaBARBERA, Barry T. *(Judge, Superior Court of California County of San Luis Obispo)* Presiding Judge since Jan 1, 2002.
Office: County Government Center, 1035 Palm Street, San Luis Obispo 93408-2500.
Telephone: (805) 781-5421.

LABOWITZ, Eric *(Judge, Superior Court of California County of Mendocino)* Assumed office Aug 1, 1998. Serves Ten Mile Branch. Presiding Judge Jan 1, 1998 to Dec 31, 2001. Former Judge, Mendocino County Municipal Court.
Office: 700 South Franklin Street, Fort Bragg 95437.
Telephone: (707) 964-3192.

LaCASSE, Leonard J. *(Judge, Superior Court of California County of Mendocino)*
Mailing address: P.O. Box 996, Ukiah 95482.
Office: Courthouse, 100 North State Street, Ukiah 95482.
Telephone: (707) 467-6437.

LADINE, Wray F. *(Judge, Superior Court of California County of Stanislaus)*
Office: 800 Eleventh Street, Modesto 95354.
Telephone: (209) 558-6000.

LAGER, Marvin M. *(Judge, Superior Court of California County of Los Angeles)* Former Judge, Los Angeles Municipal Court Los Angeles County.
Office: Courthouse, 111 North Hill Street, Los Angeles 90012.
Telephone: (213) 974-5411.

LAM, Newton J. *(Judge, Superior Court of California City and County of San Francisco)*
Office: Hall of Justice, 850 Bryant Street, San Francisco 94103.
Telephone: (415) 553-1159.

LAMB, Brian *(Judge, Superior Court of California County of Inyo)*
Mailing address: P.O. Drawer U, Independence 93526.
Office: 168 North Edwards Street, Independence 93526.
Telephone: (760) 878-0298.

LAMBDEN, James R. *(Associate Justice, California Court of Appeal First District Division Two)* Appointed by Governor Pete Wilson to term beginning 1996. Retained by election. Born Oakland California May 4, 1950. Educated at University of California at Berkeley B.A. with honors 1972 and University of California Hastings College of the Law J.D. 1975. Admitted to practice California 1975. In legal practice 1975-89. Judge, Superior Court of California Alameda County July 1989 to 1996, appointed by Governor George Deukmejian.
Instructor in Law Peralta Community College District 1980. Executive Chairman Alameda County Bar Association Foundation 1986-89. Board of Directors Alameda County Bar Association 1988-89. Member Joint Advisory Committee for Continuing Education 1988-89 and Access to Justice Commission 1997 State Bar of California. Chairman Committee for Certification of Interpreters for the Deaf Judicial Council of California 1992-96. Executive Board California Judges Association 1995-96. Faculty and Planning Committee California Center for Judicial Education and Research 1992-94. Cofounder and Counsel Bay Area Center for Law and the Deaf (BACLAD) 1979-82.
Office: 350 McAllister Street, San Francisco 94102-3600.
Telephone: (415) 865-7300.

LANDIN, Dennis J. *(Judge, Superior Court of California County of Los Angeles)*
Office: Courthouse, 111 North Hill Street, Los Angeles 90012.
Telephone: (213) 974-5411.

LANE, Barbara A. *(Judge, Superior Court of California County of Ventura)* Former Judge, Ventura County Municipal Court.
Mailing address: P.O. Box 6489, Ventura 93006-6489.
Office: 800 South Victoria Avenue, Ventura 93009-0001.
Telephone: (805) 654-2965.

LANG, Xenophon F., Jr. *(Judge, Superior Court of California County of Los Angeles)* Assumed office Jan 22, 2000. Former Judge, Compton Municipal Court Los Angeles County.
Office: Lynwood Regional Justice Center, 11701 Alameda Street, Lynwood 90262.
Telephone: (323) 357-5000.

LAPORTE, Elizabeth D. *(Magistrate Judge, United States District Court Northern District of California)* Appointed by U.S. District Court judges to term beginning April 4, 1998. Term expires April 2006. Born New York New York July 10, 1953. Educated at Princeton University B.A. 1975, St. Anne's College, Oxford England M.A. 1977 and Yale Law School J.D. 1982. Marshall Scholar. Law Clerk to Hon. Marilyn Hall Patel, U.S. District Court Northern District of California 1982-83. Admitted to practice California 1982.
Chair Ninth Circuit Executive Board of Magistrate Judges. Board of Governors Northern California Chapter Association of Business Trial Lawyers. Member Association of Marshall Scholars, Federal Magistrate Judges Association, State Bar of California and San Francisco Bar Association (Executive Committee Section of Litigation). Named Lawyer of the Year by *California Lawyer* 1996.
Office: U.S. Courthouse, Box 36060, 450 Golden Gate Avenue, San Francisco 94102-3489.
Telephone: (415) 522-4135.

LARSON, James L. *(Magistrate Judge, United States District Court Northern District of California)* Appointed by U.S. District Court judges.
Office: U.S. Courthouse, Box 36060, 450 Golden Gate Avenue, San Francisco 94102-3489.
Telephone: (415) 522-2112.

LARSON, Stephen G. *(Magistrate Judge, United States District Court Central District of California)* Appointed by U.S. District Court judges to term beginning Oct 2, 2000.
Office: 260 U.S. Courthouse, 3470 Twelfth Street, Riverside 92501.
Telephone: (213) 894-3535.

LASAROW, Jerald *(Judge, Superior Court of California County of El Dorado)* Assumed office Aug 1, 1998. Serves South Lake Tahoe Branch. Former Judge and Presiding Judge, El Dorado County Municipal Court.

Office: 1354 Johnson Boulevard, Suite 2, South Lake Tahoe 96150.

Telephone: (530) 573-3060.

LASATER, Melinda J. *(Judge, Superior Court of California County of San Diego)* Born Washington D.C. Dec 11, 1948. Educated at University of Wisconsin-Madison B.A. 1970 and University of San Diego J.D. cum laude 1973. Member Phi Alpha Delta. Admitted to practice California 1973, U.S. District Courts Northern and Southern Districts of California and U.S. Court of Appeals Ninth Circuit. Former Judge, San Diego Municipal Court San Diego County, appointed by Governor George Deukmejian to term beginning Jan 28, 1987.

Deputy District Attorney April 1974 to Feb 1987. Instructor in Business Law San Diego State University 1975-76. Member Lawyers Club of San Diego, California Judges Association, National Association of Women Judges and San Diego County Bar Association (Treasurer 1983, Vice President 1984 and President 1985).

Mailing address: P.O. Box 122724, San Diego 92112-2724.

Office: 220 West Broadway, San Diego 92101.

Telephone: (619) 531-3820.

LAVIN, Luis A. *(Judge, Superior Court of California County of Los Angeles)*

Office: Courthouse, 111 North Hill Street, Los Angeles 90012.

Telephone: (213) 974-5411.

LaVOY, Thomas Oliver *(Judge, Superior Court of California County of San Diego)*

Mailing address: P.O. Box 122724, San Diego 92112-2724.

Office: 220 West Broadway, San Diego 92101.

Telephone: (619) 531-3820.

LAX, Kathleen T. *(Judge, United States Bankruptcy Court Central District of California)* Appointed by U.S. Court of Appeals Ninth Circuit judges to term beginning April 4, 1988. Reappointed April 4, 2002, current term expires April 3, 2016. Born Kansas 1945. Educated at University of Kansas B.A. with honors 1967 and University of California at Los Angeles J.D. 1980. Law Clerk to Hon. Calvin K. Ashland, U.S. Bankruptcy Court Central District of California 1980-82. Admitted to practice California 1980. In legal practice Los Angeles 1982-88.

Board of Directors since 1989 and Board of Editors since 1989 California Bankruptcy Journal. Board of Governors Los Angeles Bankruptcy Forum since 1991.

Office: 21041 Burbank Boulevard, Woodland Hills 91367.

Telephone: (818) 587-2823.

LAZARD, Ridgely L. *(Judge, Superior Court of California County of Lassen)*

Office: 6 Courthouse, 220 South Lassen Street, Susanville 96130.

Telephone: (530) 251-8228.

LEBOV, William S. *(Judge, Superior Court of California County of Yolo)* Assumed office June 3, 1998. Term expires Jan 2005. Born Bridgeport Connecticut April 27, 1945. Educated at Bucknell University B.A. 1966 and Willamette University College of Law J.D. 1969. Admitted to practice Connecticut 1969, District of Columbia 1970 and California 1973. Judge Dec 31, 1982 to June 2, 1998 and Presiding Judge Jan 1, 1997 to Dec 31, 1997, appointed by Governor Edmund G. Brown, Jr.

Instructor New Judges Orientation Course.

Office: 725 Court Street, Woodland 95695.

Telephone: (530) 666-8598.

LEE, Caryl A. *(Judge, Superior Court of California County of Orange)* Assumed office Aug 10, 1998. Former Judge, West Orange County Municipal Court.

Mailing address: P.O. Box 14169, Orange 92863-1569.

Office: Lamoreaux Justice Center, 341 The City Drive, Orange 92868.

Telephone: (714) 935-7236.

LEE, Charles Carter *(Judge, Superior Court of California County of Los Angeles)*

Office: Courthouse, 111 North Hill Street, Los Angeles 90012.

Telephone: (213) 974-5411.

LEE, Cynthia Ming-Mei *(Judge, Superior Court of California City and County of San Francisco)*

Office: Hall of Justice, 850 Bryant Street, San Francisco 94103.

Telephone: (415) 553-1159.

LEE, Edward F. *(Judge, Superior Court of California County of Santa Clara)* Elected Nov 5, 1996 to term beginning Dec 6, 1996. Reelected 2002, current term expires Jan 2009. Educated at University of California at Irvine B.A. 1978 and University of California Hastings College of the Law J.D. 1983. Admitted to practice California 1983 and U.S. District Court Northern District of California 1983. Judge, Santa Clara County Municipal Court 1992-96.

Deputy District Attorney 1984-92. Author Chapter on Argument *Trial Tactics* 2nd ed. California District Attorney's Association 1993. Instructor in Trial Practice Santa Clara University School of Law 1989-90 and Business Law, Litigation and Economics National University 1986-94. Member California Judges Association. Instructor in Demonstrative Evidence National Homicide Symposium since 1990. Named Instructor of the Year by California District Attorney's Association 1990-91. Major California National Guard Infantry since 1980. Police Officer 1978-83. Youth Leadership Program Volunteer. Enjoys beekeeping and winemaking.

Office: 12425 Monterey Road, San Martin 95046.

Telephone: (408) 695-5000.

LEE, Gibson W. *(Judge, Superior Court of California County of Los Angeles)* Former Judge, Long Beach Municipal Court Los Angeles County.

Office: Long Beach Courthouse, 415 West Ocean Boulevard, Long Beach 90802.

Telephone: (562) 491-6130.

LEE, Jo-Lynne Q. *(Judge, Superior Court of California County of Alameda)*

Office: Hayward Hall of Justice, 24405 Amador Street, Hayward 94544.

Telephone: (510) 670-5060.

LEE, W. Richard *(Judge, United States Bankruptcy Court Eastern District of California)* Appointed by U.S. Court of Appeals Ninth Circuit judges to term beginning Jan 17, 2001. Term expires Jan 2015.

Office: 2656 U.S. Courthouse, 1130 O Street, Fresno 93711.

Telephone: (559) 498-7390.

LEFKOWITZ, Linda K. *(Judge, Superior Court of California County of Los Angeles)* Former Judge, Los Angeles Municipal Court Los Angeles County.

Office: Santa Monica Courthouse, 1725 Main Street, Santa Monica 90401.

Telephone: (310) 260-3762.

LEHAN, Jonathan M. *(Judge, Superior Court of California County of Mendocino)* Assumed office Aug 1, 1998. Serves Ten Mile Branch. Born Los Angeles California April 25, 1947. Jewish. Educated at California State University at Fullerton B.A. 1968 and California Western School of Law J.D. 1971. Editor California Western Law Review 1970-71. Law Clerk to Hon. M. Kaufman and Hon. R. Gardner, California Court of Appeal Fourth District. Member Phi Delta Phi. Admitted to practice California 1972, U.S. District Court Northern District of California 1974 and U.S. Supreme Court 1975. In legal practice Fort Bragg 1983-90. Judge, Mendocino County Municipal Court Nov 30, 1990 to July 31, 1998, appointed by Mendocino County Board of Supervisors.

Deputy District Attorney Mendocino County 1973-83. Author "Hypnotism as a Criminal Defense" California Western L. Rev. 1970. Contributor *California Drunk Driving Law.* Instructor Barstow Community College 1971-72, Mendocino Community College 1974-75 and College of the Redwoods 1979-80. Referee State Bar Court 1980-84. Member California Judges Association, Mendocino County (President 1989) and American Bar Associations. Faculty California Judicial College University of California at Berkeley 1993 and California Judges Association Conferences 1998 and 1999. Democrat. Director Chamber of Commerce. Member Salmon Restoration Association, Regional Center and Mendocino String Quartet. Enjoys playing viola.

Office: 700 South Franklin Street, Fort Bragg 95437.

Telephone: (707) 964-3192.

LENCH, Lisa B. *(Judge, Superior Court of California County of Los Angeles)*

Office: Whittier Courthouse, 7339 South Painter Avenue, Whittier 90602.

Telephone: (562) 907-3046.

LEONARD, Jean Pfeiffer *(Judge, Superior Court of California County of Riverside)* Assumed office July 29, 1998. Serves Juvenile Court. Former Judge, Western Riverside County Municipal Court.

Office: 9991 County Farm Road, Riverside 92503.

Telephone: (909) 358-4137.

LETTS, J. Spencer *(Senior Judge, United States District Court Central District of California)* Appointed for life by President Ronald Reagan to term beginning Jan 24, 1986. Assumed Senior status Dec 19, 2000, serves by assignment. Born St. Louis Missouri Dec 19, 1934. Educated at Yale University B.A. 1956 and Harvard Law School LL.B. 1960. Admitted to practice Texas 1960, California 1966 and U.S. District Court Central District of California 1966. In legal practice Houston Texas 1960-66 and Los Angeles 1966-86.

Vice President and General Counsel Teledyne, Inc. 1966-74 and 1976-79. Author "Rights of Dissenting Shareholders in Delaware" 1963, "Sales of Control Stock and the Rights of Minority Shareholders" Jan 1971 and "Corporate Governance: A Different Slant" July 1980 The Business Lawyer, "Is There Really a Model Board?" The Changing Boardroom Gulf Publishing Company 1982 and "Cox—An Attempt to Clarify Wrongful Termination Under California Law" Industrial Relations L. Jour. 1989. Bulletin Editor Corporation, Banking and Business Law Section State Bar of Texas 1965. Important Opinions: United States v. Davis (holding sentencing guidelines unconstitutional) 715 F. Supp. 1473, 1989; United States v. Patillo (criticizing mandatory minimum sentences) 817 F. Supp. 839, 1993; DMI Furniture v. Brown, Kraft & Co. (securities) 644 F. Supp. 1517, 1986; Matex v. Murat 638 F. Supp. 775 (securities); and Cox v. Resilient Flooring Division of Congoleum Corp. (wrongful discharge) 638 F. Supp. 726, 1986. Guest Lecturer on Corporate Governance Rice University 1980 and Legal Management University of California at Los Angeles Business School 1994. Adjunct Professor of Professional Ethics University of Southern California Law School 1988. Member Committee on Law and Accounting American Bar Association. Outside Commentator Study of Corporate Directors Arthur Young & Company 1981 and Federal Practice Institute CEB 1986. Captain U.S. Army 1957 USAR 1957-65. Member Blue Ribbon California Insurance Holding Company Act of 1974 Drafting Committee 1973 and Merger Accounting Task Force Financial Accounting Standards Board 1975. Director Black, Sivalls & Bryson, Inc. 1969-74. Director 1981-85 and Chairman of the Board and CEO 1985 Semtech Corporation (Amex). Enjoys tournament tennis and guitar.

Office: U.S. Courthouse, 312 North Spring Street, Los Angeles 90012.

Telephone: (213) 894-2600.

LEVI, David F. *(Judge, United States District Court Eastern District of California)* Appointed for life by President George Bush Nov 5, 1990. Born Chicago Illinois Aug 29, 1951. Jewish. Educated at Harvard University A.B. 1972 M.A. 1974 and Stanford University J.D. 1980. Awarded honorary LL.D. Lincoln University Law School. Former Editor-in-Chief Stanford Law Review. Law Clerk to Hon. Ben Cushing Duniway, U.S. Court of Appeals Ninth Circuit 1980-81 and Hon. Lewis F. Powell, Jr., U.S. Supreme Court 1981-82. Member Order of the Coif. Admitted to practice California 1983.

U.S. Attorney Eastern District of California 1986-90. Author "Equal Treatment of Aliens: Equal Protection or Preemption?" 32 Stanford L. Rev. 1979. Member Attorney General's Advisory Committee for U.S. Attorneys 1988-90 (Chair Public Corruption Subcommittee 1988-90). President Inn of Court University of California at Davis 1992-95. Chair Ninth Circuit Task Force on Racial, Ethnic and Religious Fairness 1994-97. Member since 1994 and Chair since 2000 Advisory Committee on the Federal Rules of Civil Procedure (Chair Subcommittee on Discovery 1996-2000). Member The American Law Institute (Advisor Federal Jurisdiction Project since

LEVI, DAVID F.—*Continued*

1996). Member Visiting Committee Stanford Law School 1988-94 and University of Chicago 1995-98.

Office: 501 I Street, Room 14-230, Sacramento 95814.

Telephone: (916) 930-4090.

Fax: (916) 930-4106

LEVINGER, Mary Jo *(Judge, Superior Court of California County of Santa Clara)*

Office: 191 North First Street, San Jose 95113.

Telephone: (408) 882-2150.

LEVIS, W. Kent *(Judge, Superior Court of California County of Fresno)* Assumed office July 1, 1998. Elected 2001, current term expires Jan 2008. Born Selma California April 25, 1941. Protestant. Educated at California State University at Fresno B.A. 1964 and University of San Diego School of Law J.D. 1969. Law Clerk to California Court of Appeal Fifth District 1969-70. Member Phi Alpha Delta. Admitted to practice California 1970. In legal practice Fresno. Traffic Referee 1977-80, Commissioner 1980-90 and Judge Jan 1990 to June 30, 1998, Consolidated Fresno Municipal Court Fresno County.

Deputy District Attorney County of Fresno 1971-72. Deputy City Attorney and Police Legal Advisor City of Fresno 1973-77. Instructor in Evidence and Trial Techniques Humphreys College of Law 1972-73 and State Center Community College Police Academy 1975-97. Member Criminal Law Education Committee since 2002 and Former Member Planning Committee California Center for Judicial Education and Research. Staff Sergeant E-5 USAF National Guard and Reserve 1963-69.

Office: 1100 Van Ness Avenue, Department 62, Fresno 93724-0002.

Telephone: (559) 488-3578.

LEVY, Herbert I. *(Associate Justice, California Court of Appeal Fifth District)* Appointed by Governor Pete Wilson Aug 5, 1997. Retained by election Nov 1998. Born Fresno California April 12, 1952. Educated at University of California at Davis B.A. magna cum laude 1974 and McGeorge School of Law University of the Pacific J.D. 1977. Life member Traynor Society. Member Phi Delta Phi. Admitted to practice California 1977 and U.S. District Court Eastern District of California 1977. In legal practice Fresno 1977-88. Judge, Consolidated Fresno Municipal Court Fresno County 1988-89. Judge Oct 27, 1989 to 1997 and Presiding Judge Family Law Department 1990-96, Superior Court of California Fresno County.

Member Appellate Standing Advisory Committee since 1998 and Former Member Family Court Services Advisory Committee and Family and Juvenile Law Standing Advisory Committee California Judicial Council. Member Appellate Indigent Defense Oversight Committee since 1998. Member California Judges Association. Group Leader New Judges Orientation Feb 1991, Chairperson Family Law and Procedure Institute Planning Committee 1993 and Member Domestic Violence Curriculum Advisory Committee 1996-2002 California Center for Judicial Education and Research. Group Leader California Judicial College June 1993. Chairperson and original organizer Fresno County Domestic Violence Roundtable 1990-2001. Co-chairperson "Count to Ten" (community-wide campaign in Fresno County to create public awareness of domestic violence and its effect on children) 1997-2001. Member Rotary Club of Fresno and University of California at Davis Alumni Association. Active with public broadcasting station KVPT Channel 18. Collects baseball cards, sports memorabilia and art.

Office: 2525 Capitol Street, Fresno 93721.

Telephone: (559) 445-5523.

LEW, Arthur M. *(Judge, Superior Court of California County of Los Angeles)* Former Judge, Long Beach Municipal Court Los Angeles County.

Office: Compton Courthouse, 200 West Compton Boulevard, Compton 90220.

Telephone: (310) 603-7842.

LEW, Ronald S. W. *(Judge, United States District Court Central District of California)* Appointed for life by President Ronald Reagan to term beginning May 29, 1987. First Chinese-American appointed as a U.S. District Judge in the continental United States. Born Los Angeles California 1941. Educated at Loyola University B.A. 1964 and Southwestern University School of Law J.D. 1971. Member Delta Theta Phi. Admitted to practice California 1971. In legal practice Los Angeles 1974-81. Judge 1982-84 and Supervising Judge 1983, Los Angeles Municipal Court Los Angeles County 1982-84, appointed by Governor Edmund G. Brown, Jr. Justice pro tem, California Court of Appeal Second District 1984. Judge, Superior Court of California Los Angeles County 1984-87, appointed by Governor George Deukmejian. Justice pro tem, California Supreme Court 1985.

Deputy City Attorney Criminal and Civil Liability Divisions Los Angeles City Attorney's Office 1972-74. Member Los Angeles Court Improvement Commission California State Assembly, California Center for Judicial Education and Research, California Asian Judges Association, Southern California Chinese Lawyers Association (Founder), California Judges Association (Historical Committee), Minority Bar Association of Southern California, State Bar of California (Delegate Conference of Delegates 1978-79) and Los Angeles County Bar Association. First Lieutenant U.S. Army 1967-69. Commissioner Los Angeles Fire and Police Pension Commission 1976-82. Member Chinatown Service Center (Founder) and Chinese American Citizenship Alliance.

Office: U.S. Courthouse, 312 North Spring Street, Los Angeles 90012.

Telephone: (213) 894-3508.

LEWIS, Gregory H. *(Judge, Superior Court of California County of Orange)* Assumed office Aug 10, 1998. Former Judge and Presiding Judge, Central Orange County Municipal Court.

Mailing address: P.O. Box 1994, Santa Ana 92702-1994.

Office: Central Justice Center, 700 Civic Center Drive West, Santa Ana 92701.

Telephone: (714) 834-3734.

LEWIS, Joan Marie *(Judge, Superior Court of California County of San Diego)*

Mailing address: P.O. Box 122724, San Diego 92112-2724.

Office: 1551-55 Sixth Avenue, San Diego 92101.

LEWIS, Lantz *(Judge, Superior Court of California County of San Diego)* Assumed office Dec 1, 1998. For-

LEWIS, LANTZ—*Continued*

mer Judge, El Cajon Municipal Court San Diego County.

Mailing address: P.O. Box 122724, San Diego 92112-2724.

Office: 250 East Main Street, El Cajon 92020.

Telephone: (619) 441-4336.

LEWIS, Michael B. *(Judge, Superior Court of California County of Kern)* Assumed office July 1, 2000. Presiding Judge July 1, 1996 to June 30, 1997 and Former Judge, Bakersfield Municipal Court Kern County.

Office: 1215 Truxtun Avenue, Bakersfield 93301.

Telephone: (661) 868-2450.

LIBUTTI, Michael R. *(Judge, Superior Court of California County of San Bernardino)* Serves Valley Division.

Office: 17780 Arrow Boulevard, Fontana 92335.

Telephone: (909) 350-9322.

LICHTMAN, Peter D. *(Judge, Superior Court of California County of Los Angeles)* Former Judge, Los Angeles Municipal Court Los Angeles County.

Office: Central Civil West, 600 South Commonwealth, Los Angeles 90005.

Telephone: (213) 351-8739.

LIM, Lillian Y. *(Judge, Superior Court of California County of San Diego)* Assumed office Dec 1, 1998. Born Berkeley California Sept 16, 1951. Educated at Brown University B.A. with honors 1973 and Western State University J.D. cum laude 1977. Notes Editor Criminal Law Journal. Admitted to practice California 1977. Judge, San Diego Municipal Court San Diego County Jan 1986 to Nov 30, 1998, appointed by Governor George Deukmejian.

Deputy Attorney General 1977-86. Author "Determinate Sentence Law" Criminal Justice Journal 1976. Adjunct Faculty Member Thomas Jefferson School of Law. Member Access and Fairness Committee Judicial Council of California 1998-2000 and Annual Conference Program Committee California Judges Association 2002. Member California Asian Judges Association (President 1993), Pan Asian Lawyers Association (Past President), Filipino American Lawyers Association and San Diego County Bar Association (Delegate to Conference of Delegates). Seminar Leader California Judges College 1991. Instructor Civil Law Institute 1992. Member United Way, Boy Scouts of America and City College Foundation. Enjoys skiing, jogging, soccer and snowboarding.

Mailing address: P.O. Box 122724, San Diego 92112-2724.

Office: 500 Third Avenue, Chula Vista 91910.

Telephone: (619) 691-4770.

LINDLEY, Wendy *(Judge, Superior Court of California County of Orange)* Assumed office Aug 10, 1998. Former Judge, Central Orange County Municipal Court. Presiding Judge Jan 1, 1997 to Dec 31, 1997 and Former Judge, South Orange County Municipal Court.

Mailing address: P.O. Box 1994, Santa Ana 92702-1994.

Office: Central Justice Center, 700 Civic Center Drive West, Santa Ana 92701.

Telephone: (714) 834-3734.

LINK, Frederic L. *(Judge, Superior Court of California County of San Diego)* Former Judge, San Diego Municipal Court San Diego County.

Mailing address: P.O. Box 122724, San Diego 92112-2724.

Office: 220 West Broadway, San Diego 92101.

Telephone: (619) 531-3820.

LIPPITT, Elizabeth A. *(Judge, Superior Court of California County of Los Angeles)* Assumed office Jan 22, 2000. Elected 2002, current term expires Jan 2009. Educated at Colorado College 1981 and University of Denver College of Law J.D. 1986. Co-editor International Law Review 1985. Admitted to practice California 1984 and Colorado 1989. Judge, Los Angeles Municipal Court Los Angeles County May 13, 1996 to Jan 21, 2000, appointed by Governor Pete Wilson.

Deputy District Attorney Los Angeles 1986-96. Instructor Criminal Institute University of California Hastings College of the Law since 1995. Member National Association of Women Judges, California Judges Association and Los Angeles County Bar Association.

Office: San Fernando Courthouse, 900 Third Street, San Fernando 91340.

Telephone: (818) 898-2655.

LISK, Ronald T. *(Judge, Superior Court of California County of Santa Clara)* Former Judge, Santa Clara County Municipal Court.

Office: Hall of Justice East Wing, 190 West Hedding Street, San Jose 95110.

Telephone: (408) 299-3817.

LITTLE, Donna Alyson *(Judge, Superior Court of California City and County of San Francisco)* Assumed office Dec 31, 1998. Born New York New York Aug 31, 1952. Educated at Brown University B.A. magna cum laude 1974 and University of California at Los Angeles J.D. 1978. Law Clerk to Hon. Macklin Fleming and Hon. Edwin Fernando Beach, California Court of Appeal Second District Division Two 1978-81 and 1986-87. Admitted to practice California 1978, U.S. District Court Central District of California 1979 and U.S. Supreme Court 1981. In legal practice Los Angeles 1981-86. Commissioner 1987-90 and Chairperson 1990-91, California Workers' Compensation Appeals Board. Judge Jan 2, 1991 to Dec 30, 1998 and Presiding Judge June 1997 to Dec 1998, San Francisco Municipal Court San Francisco County, appointed by Governor George Deukmejian.

Former Member Supreme Court Advisory Committee on Judicial Ethics, Queen's Bench, San Francisco Women Lawyers Alliance and Santa Monica Bar Association (Board of Directors). Member California Judges Association (Past Chair Judicial Elections Committee). Lecturer Appellate Justice Seminar on Workers' Compensation California Center for Judicial Education and Research 1988. Recipient Commendations from California Commission on the Status of Women 1991 and 1992, San Francisco Commission on the Status of Women 1997 and San Francisco Board of Supervisors 1998. Past President Ivy League Association of Southern California. Former Member and Vice Chair California Commission on the Status of Women. Former member and Chair California State Advisory Committee on Sexual Assault Victim Services. Former Member Santa

LITTLE, DONNA ALYSON—*Continued*

Monica Mountains Conservancy Advisory Committee. Chair San Francisco Family Violence Council.

Office: Hall of Justice, 850 Bryant Street, San Francisco 94103.

Telephone: (415) 553-9435.

LITTLEJOHN, Joe O. *(Judge, Superior Court of California County of San Diego)* Former Judge, San Diego Municipal Court San Diego County.

Mailing address: P.O. Box 122724, San Diego 92112-2724.

Office: 325 South Melrose Drive, Vista 92083.

Telephone: (760) 726-9595.

LIVERMORE, Richard Clifton *(Judge, Superior Court of California County of San Mateo)* Assumed office June 12, 1998. Former Judge, San Mateo County Municipal Court.

Office: Hall of Justice, 400 County Center, Redwood City 94063.

Telephone: (650) 363-4516.

LLOYD, Howard R. *(Magistrate Judge, United States District Court Northern District of California)* Appointed by U.S. District Court judges to term beginning June 4, 2002.

Office: U.S. Courthouse, 280 South First Street, San Jose 95113.

Telephone: (415) 522-2000.

LOBERG, Harry J. *(Judge, Superior Court of California County of Santa Barbara)* Assumed office Aug 3, 1998. Elected 2002, current term expires Jan 2009. Born Ithaca New York Sept 9, 1935. Educated at Cornell University B.A. in Psychology 1959 and University of California at Los Angeles J.D. 1966. Admitted to practice California 1967. In legal practice Santa Barbara 1967-76. Hearing Officer, Santa Barbara Housing Authority 1970-74. Commissioner March 28, 1983 to May 7, 1987, Judge May 7, 1987 to Aug 2, 1998 and Presiding Judge Jan 1, 1996 to Dec 31, 1996, Santa Barbara Municipal Court Santa Barbara County.

Deputy District Attorney Santa Barbara County 1976-83. President Barristers Club of Santa Barbara 1974. Former Member Santa Barbara County Bar Association (President 1982) and California Court Commissioners Association. Member California Judges Association. Recipient Judicial Service Award from Santa Barbara County Bar Association 1992. Personnel Analyst University of California at Santa Barbara 1960-63. Interests include bicycling, sailing, reading and music.

Office: 118 East Figueroa Street, Santa Barbara 93101.

Telephone: (805) 568-2735.

LODGE, Joseph *(Judge, Superior Court of California County of Santa Barbara)* Assumed office Aug 3, 1998. Presiding Judge Jan 1, 1997 to Dec 31, 1997 and Former Judge, Santa Barbara Municipal Court Santa Barbara County.

Office: 118 East Figueroa Street, Santa Barbara 93101.

Telephone: (805) 568-2735.

LOFTUS, Richard J., Jr. *(Judge, Superior Court of California County of Santa Clara)*

Mailing address: 191 North First Street, San Jose 95113.

Office: Hall of Justice East Wing, 190 West Hedding Street, San Jose 95110.

Telephone: (408) 808-6600.

LOMELI, George R. G. *(Judge, Superior Court of California County of Los Angeles)* Assumed office Jan 22, 2000. Elected 2002, current term expires Jan 2009. Born Los Angeles California June 11, 1958. Catholic. Educated at University of Southern California B.S. magna cum laude 1980 Masters 1982 and Whittier College School of Law J.D. 1987. Admitted to practice California 1988 and U.S. Court of Appeals Ninth Circuit 1990. Judge, East Los Angeles Municipal Court Los Angeles County June 17, 1998 to Jan 21, 2000, appointed by Governor Pete Wilson.

Deputy City Attorney Los Angeles 1983-98. Member Los Angeles Latino City Attorneys Association, Mexican-American and American Bar Associations. Recipient Commendation of Merit from Los Angeles Police Department, Los Angeles City Attorney and Los Angeles City Council. Republican. Member California Masons and Optimist Club. Interests include racquetball, stained glass and antiques.

Office: Criminal Courts Building, 210 West Temple Street, Los Angeles 90012-3210.

Telephone: (213) 974-6535.

LONDON, Brett *(Judge, Superior Court of California County of Orange)* Assumed office Aug 10, 1998. Elected 2000, current term expires Jan 2007. Born Ogden Utah Aug 19, 1951. Educated at California State University at Fullerton B.A. with high honors 1976 and Brigham Young University Law School J.D. cum laude 1979. Admitted to practice California 1979, U.S. District Court Central District of California, U.S. Court of Appeals Ninth Circuit and U.S. Supreme Court. Judge Jan 1989 to Aug 9, 1998 and Former Presiding Judge, West Orange County Municipal Court.

Author "The Soviet Union Through Its Laws" 12 No. 1 Western State University L. Rev. 358 Fall 1984 and Casebook *Religion and the Law: Cases and Materials* 1994. Adjunct Professor of Criminal Law, Religion and the Law and Professional Responsibility Western State University College of Law since 1984. Member California Judges Association and Orange County Bar Association. Attended Presiding Judges Seminar Civil Law and Procedure Institute. Recipient Certificate of Excellence in Teaching from Western State University College of Law 1994 and Patrick McCray Award from West Orange County Bar Association 1994. Republican.

Office: Harbor Justice Center, 4601 Jamboree Road, Newport Beach 92660-2595.

Telephone: (949) 476-4699.

LONG, David W. *(Judge, Superior Court of California County of Ventura)* Assumed office Nov 19, 1997. Former Judge, Ventura County Municipal Court.

Mailing address: P.O. Box 6489, Ventura 93006-6489.

Office: 800 South Victoria Avenue, Ventura 93009-0001.

Telephone: (805) 654-2965.

LONG, James L. *(Judge, Superior Court of California County of Sacramento)* Appointed by Governor Edmund G. Brown, Jr. Feb 1982. Elected to subsequent

LONG, JAMES L.—*Continued*

terms. Educated at San Jose State College B.A. in Psychology 1960 and Howard University Law School J.D. 1967. Admitted to practice California, U.S. District Court Eastern District of California and U.S. Supreme Court.

Former Graduate Legal Assistant Legal Aid Society of Sacramento County and Legislative Counsel Bureau California State Legislature. Former Juvenile Hall Counselor and Deputy Probation Officer Sacramento County. Former Assistant Clerk California State Assembly. Former Special Counsel NAACP. Co-author *American Minorities: The Justice Issue* Prentice-Hall, Inc. 1975. Former Assistant Professor Criminal Justice Department California State University at Sacramento. Former member Sacramento Association of Black Attorneys, California Association of Black Lawyers, California Trial Lawyers Association, State Bar of California, Charles Houston, Sacramento County (Bar Council, Attorney-Client Relations Committee, Chairman Liaison Committee with Sacramento Municipal Court Judges), National, Federal and American Bar Associations. Attended California College of the Trial Judge March 1982. Listed in *Who's Who Among Black Americans* 1975 and 1981, *Who's Who in California* 1981 and *Who's Who in Sacramento* 1982. Recipient resolution from Assembly Rules Committee California State Legislature 1970, award from McGeorge School of Law for efforts to increase minority representation in legal field and award for outstanding contributions in the field of civil rights from Riverside Branch NAACP. Second Lieutenant USAR. Member Sacramento County Constituents Council to U.S. Senator S. I. Hayakawa. Former member Board of Directors Oak Park Project Area Committee, Sacramento Chapter NAACP, Observer Foundation and Sacramento Legal Aid Society. Former Oral Panel member Sacramento County Civil Service Commission.

Office: Courthouse, 720 Ninth Street, Sacramento 95814.

Telephone: (916) 874-5476.

LOPEZ, Daniel S. *(Judge, Superior Court of California County of Los Angeles)* Former Judge and Presiding Judge, East Los Angeles Municipal Court Los Angeles County.

Office: Pomona Courthouse South, 400 Civic Center Plaza, Pomona 91766.

Telephone: (909) 620-3023.

LOPEZ, Gilbert M. *(Judge, Superior Court of California County of Los Angeles)*

Office: Huntington Park Courthouse, 6548 Miles Avenue, Huntington Park 90255-2419.

Telephone: (323) 586-6351.

LORD, John David *(Judge, Superior Court of California County of Los Angeles)* Assumed office Jan 22, 2000. Former Judge and Presiding Judge, Downey Municipal Court Los Angeles County.

Office: Long Beach Courthouse, 415 West Ocean Boulevard, Long Beach 90802.

Telephone: (562) 491-6130.

LORENZ, M. James *(Judge, United States District Court Southern District of California)* Appointed for life by President Bill Clinton to term beginning Oct 25, 1999. Born Pasadena California Oct 13, 1935. Educated at University of California at Berkeley B.A. 1957 and California Western School of Law J.D. 1965. Admitted to practice California 1966, U.S. District Courts Southern 1978 and Central 1985 Districts of California and District of Hawaii 1997, U.S. Supreme Court 1980 and U.S. Court of Appeals Ninth Circuit 1981. In legal practice 1982-99.

Deputy District Attorney San Diego County 1966-78. First Assistant U.S. Attorney 1978-79 and U.S. Attorney 1980-81 Southern District of California. Author "Municipal Attorney's Conflict of Interest" San Francisco Barrister L. Jour. Dec 1986 and "Tribute to Those Who Died in the Line of Duty" May 17, 1988 and Opinion Page "Is the Concept of Local Control Over Utilities a Myth?" June 4, 1989 *San Diego Union.* Former Member State Consumer Protection Counsel, California State District Attorneys' Association and National District Attorneys Association. Honorary Member San Diego County Bar Association and State Bar of California. Member Committee to Study and Recommend Changes to Indigent Defense Services of San Diego County, Kutak Report Subcommittee Legal Ethics and Unauthorized Practice Committee, San Diego Crime Commission, Association of Business Trial Lawyers, San Diego County Judges Association and Ninth Circuit District Judges Association. Ad Hoc Lecturer National College of District Attorneys 1976-81. Guest Lecturer on White-Collar Crime FBI Academy 1976-81. First Lieutenant USMC Sept 1957 to Dec 1960, USMCR-R 1961-62 and USMCR 1962-69. Former Member Board of Advisors University of San Diego Paralegal Program. Board of Trustees California Western School of Law. Board of Advisors Marine Corps Recruit Depot Museum and Historical Society. Member University of California Alumni Association.

Office: 2140 U.S. Courthouse, 940 Front Street, San Diego 92101-8911.

Telephone: (619) 557-7669.

Fax: (619) 702-9944

LOUIE, Lenard D. *(Judge, Superior Court of California City and County of San Francisco)* Former Judge, San Francisco Municipal Court San Francisco County.

Office: Hall of Justice, 850 Bryant Street, San Francisco 94103.

Telephone: (415) 553-1159.

LUCACCINI, Anthony P. *(Judge, Superior Court of California County of San Joaquin)* Assumed office June 8, 1998. Former Judge and Presiding Judge, Stockton Municipal Court San Joaquin County.

Office: 222 East Weber Avenue, Room 303, Stockton 95202.

Telephone: (209) 468-2827.

LUCAS, Patricia M. *(Judge, Superior Court of California County of Santa Clara)*

Office: 191 North First Street, San Jose 95113.

Telephone: (408) 882-2100.

LUCERO, Katherine *(Judge, Superior Court of California County of Santa Clara)* Serves Family Court.

Office: 170 Park Plaza, San Jose 95113.

Telephone: (408) 534-5600.

LUDVIGSEN, Cynthia Ann *(Judge, Superior Court of California County of San Bernardino)*

Office: 351 North Arrowhead Avenue, San Bernardino 92415-0240.

Telephone: (909) 387-3922.

LUEBS, Roger A. *(Judge, Superior Court of California County of Riverside)*
Office: 310 Court Executive Office, 4075 Main Street, Riverside 92501.
Telephone: (909) 955-5536.

LUM, Jennifer T. *(Magistrate Judge, United States District Court Central District of California)* Appointed by U.S. District Court judges to term beginning July 2, 2001.
Office: 931 U.S. Courthouse, 312 North Spring Street, Los Angeles 90012.
Telephone: (213) 894-3535.

LUNA, Ana Maria *(Judge, Superior Court of California County of Los Angeles)* Assumed office Jan 22, 2000. Former Judge, Southeast Municipal Court Los Angeles County.
Office: Downey Courthouse, 7500 East Imperial Highway, Downey 90242.
Telephone: (562) 803-7057.

LUROS, Michael S. *(Judge, Superior Court of California County of Los Angeles)* Former Judge, Los Angeles Municipal Court Los Angeles County.
Office: Mental Health Courthouse, 1150 North San Fernando Road, Los Angeles 90065.
Telephone: (323) 226-2908.

LYMAN, Richard W., Jr. *(Judge, Superior Court of California County of Los Angeles)* Assumed office Jan 25, 2000. Former Judge, Long Beach Municipal Court Los Angeles County.
Office: Long Beach Courthouse, 415 West Ocean Boulevard, Long Beach 90802.
Telephone: (562) 491-6130.

MABREY, Paula Adele *(Judge, Superior Court of California County of Los Angeles)* Assumed office Jan 22, 2000. Former Judge, Los Angeles Municipal Court Los Angeles County.
Office: Los Angeles Airport Courthouse, 11701 South La Cienega Boulevard, Los Angeles 90045.
Telephone: (310) 727-6010.

MacEACHEN, Kellie *(Judge, Superior Court of California County of Orange)*
Mailing address: P.O. Box 1994, Santa Ana 92702-1994.
Office: Central Justice Center, 700 Civic Center Drive West, Santa Ana 92701.
Telephone: (714) 834-3734.

MACHIDA, Kenji *(Judge, Superior Court of California County of Los Angeles)*
Office: Inglewood Courthouse, One Regent Street, Inglewood 90301.
Telephone: (310) 419-5121.

MACIEL, Ronald *(Judge, Superior Court of California County of Kings)* Assumed office Feb 8, 2001. Former Judge and Presiding Judge, Kings County Municipal Court.
Office: 1426 South Drive, Hanford 93230.
Telephone: (559) 582-3211.

MacKENZIE, Lyle Michael *(Judge, Superior Court of California County of Los Angeles)* Assumed office Jan 22, 2000. Former Judge, Los Cerritos Municipal Court Los Angeles County.
Office: Bellflower Courthouse, 10025 East Flower Street, Bellflower 90706.
Telephone: (562) 804-8005.

MACKEY, Malcolm H. *(Judge, Superior Court of California County of Los Angeles)* Elected June 1988, 1994 and 2000. Current term expires Jan 2007. Born Hoboken New Jersey July 20, 1929. Protestant. Educated at New York University B.A. 1951 and Southwestern University LL.B. 1958. Member Sigma Lambda Sigma and Court of St. Ives. Admitted to practice California 1959, U.S. District Court 1959 and U.S. Supreme Court 1972. Certified Specialist Criminal Law California Board of Legal Specialization 1976. Began legal practice Los Angeles 1959. Judge 1979-88, Assistant Presiding Judge 1984-85 and Presiding Judge 1985-86, Los Angeles Municipal Court Los Angeles County.
Author *Small Claims Manual* Los Angeles Municipal Court 1979. Member California Judges Association, Lawyers Club of Los Angeles County (President 1977-78), Los Angeles County (Trustee 1978-79) and American Bar Associations. Corporal USMC 1946-48 and USMCR 1948-49. Sales representative Tidewater Oil Company 1951-54. Democrat. Member South Pasadena Masonic Lodge 290, Footprinters and American Federation of Television and Radio Artists. Enjoys tennis, swimming and hiking.
Office: County Courthouse, 111 North Hill Street, Los Angeles 90012.
Telephone: (213) 974-5683.

MACKEY, Robert D. *(Judge, Superior Court of California County of Los Angeles)* Appointed by Governor George Deukmejian to term beginning Sept 20, 1990. Elected 1992 and 1998. Current term expires Jan 2005. Born Dallas Texas Jan 9, 1937. Educated at University of California at Los Angeles B.A. 1962 J.D. 1976 and San Diego State University 1968-70. Managing Editor Black Law Journal 1975-76. Associate Editor UCLA-Alaska Law Journal 1975-76. Member Kappa Alpha Psi. Admitted to practice California 1976. Began legal practice Santa Ana 1976. In legal practice Los Angeles 1980. Judge, Compton Municipal Court Los Angeles County 1984-90.
Former Prosecutor Orange County and Los Angeles County. Author "Adoptions" UCLA-Alaska L. Jour. 1977. Former Member Langston Bar Club, California District Attorneys Association, Los Angeles District Attorneys Association and Orange County Bar Association. Member California Judges Association. Colonel U.S. Army Cavalry since 1962 (active duty 1962-73, reserves 1973-1992). Probation Officer Los Angeles County 1973-76. Republican. Enjoys golf, skiing, model railroading, parachuting, mountain bicycling and reading.
Office: Inglewood Juvenile Courthouse, 110 Regent Street, Inglewood 90301.
Telephone: (310) 419-5281.

MacLAREN, Ronni B. *(Judge, Superior Court of California County of Los Angeles)* Assumed office Jan 22, 2000. Elected 2000, current term expires Jan 2007. Born Los Angeles California May 11, 1955. Episcopalian. Educated at Smith College B.A. magna cum laude 1977 and University of Virginia School of Law J.D. 1980. Admitted to practice California 1980, U.S. District Courts Central 1980, Southern 1981 and Northern 1983 Districts of California and U.S. Court of Appeals Ninth

MACLAREN, RONNI B.—*Continued*

Circuit 1986. In legal practice Los Angeles 1980-85. Judge, Los Angeles Municipal Court Los Angeles County March 6, 1997 to Jan 21, 2000, appointed by Governor Pete Wilson.

Assistant U.S. Attorney Criminal Division Central District of California 1985-97. Author "Limitations on the Power to Terminate Employment" California Continuing Education of the Bar 1982 and "American Samoa White Collar Crime Assessment" Report to U.S. Department of Justice, U.S. Department of the Interior and American Samoa Government 1994. Adjunct Professor of White Collar Crime and Evidence Seminar Loyola Law School since 1996. Member Advisory Committee on Collaborative Justice Courts Judicial Council, Criminal Law Education Committee California Judicial Education and Research, Ethics Committee California Judges Association, National Association of Women Judges and Los Angeles County Bar Association. Lecturer on judicial independence and criminal law to lawyers and judges in the Republic of Georgia. Legal Specialist ABA/CEELI 1997. Faculty California Judicial College since 2000. Recipient Special Achievement Award from U.S. Department of Justice 1991 and Integrity Award from Office of Inspector General U.S. Department of Health and Human Services 1995. Republican. Board of Directors California Literacy. Enjoys mountaineering, swimming and adventure travel.

Office: Criminal Justice Center, 210 West Temple Street, Los Angeles 90012-3210.

Telephone: (213) 974-6961.

MacLAUGHLIN, William A. *(Judge, Superior Court of California County of Los Angeles)*

Office: Courthouse, 111 North Hill Street, Los Angeles 90012.

Telephone: (213) 974-5411.

MADDEN, Patrick T. *(Judge, Superior Court of California County of Los Angeles)* Assumed office Jan 22, 2000. Term expires 2006. Born Long Beach California. Educated at University of California at Los Angeles A.B. 1967 and University of Southern California J.D. 1972. Law Clerk to Hon. Malcolm M. Lucas, U.S. District Court Central District of California 1972-73. Admitted to practice California 1972 and U.S. District Courts Central, Eastern, Northern and Southern Districts of California. In legal practice Long Beach and Los Angeles. Judge, Long Beach Municipal Court Los Angeles County June 1998 to Jan 21, 2000, appointed by Governor Pete Wilson.

Life Member California Women Lawyers. USNR.

Office: 415 West Ocean Boulevard, Long Beach 90802.

Telephone: (562) 491-6131.

Fax: (562) 432-4397

MADDOCK, Thomas M. *(Judge, Superior Court of California County of Contra Costa)* Appointed by Governor Pete Wilson to term beginning Dec 31, 1998. Elected March 7, 2000, current term expires Jan 8, 2007. Born San Francisco California. Catholic. Educated at University of California at Davis B.A. 1968 and University of California Hastings College of the Law J.D. 1977. Admitted to practice California 1977, U.S. District Courts Northern 1977 and Eastern 1983 Districts of California and U.S. Court of Appeals Ninth Circuit 1983. In legal practice Walnut Creek 1981-84.

Deputy District Attorney Contra Costa County 1978-81 and El Dorado County 1984-86. Author *Legal Practice Guide* California Energy Commission 1989. Member California Judges Association. Instructor California Judicial Education and Research 2000. Captain USCGR 1969-94 (retired). Republican. Public Advisor California Energy Commission 1988-91. Deputy Director Department of Consumer Affairs 1991-93. Chief Deputy Director Department of Veterans Affairs 1993-95. Undersecretary Correctional Agency 1995-98. Enjoys golfing, fishing and camping.

Mailing address: P.O. Box 911, Martinez 94553.

Office: 725 Court Street, Martinez 94553.

Telephone: (925) 646-4016.

E-mail address: tmadd@sc.co.contra-costa.ca.us

MADER, Katherine *(Judge, Superior Court of California County of Los Angeles)*

Office: Metropolitan Courthouse, 1945 South Hill Street, Los Angeles 90007-1466.

Telephone: (213) 744-4001.

MAGERS, Patrick F. *(Judge, Superior Court of California County of Riverside)* Former Judge, Riverside Municipal Court Riverside County.

Office: Hall of Justice, 4100 Main Street, Riverside 92501.

Telephone: (909) 955-2300.

MAGUIRE, Frederick *(Judge, Superior Court of California County of San Diego)*

Mailing address: P.O. Box 122724, San Diego 92112-2724.

Office: 325 South Melrose Drive, Vista 92083.

Telephone: (760) 726-9595.

MAHLER, Glenn A. *(Judge, Superior Court of California County of Orange)* Assumed office Aug 10, 1998. Elected 2000, current term expires Jan 2007. Supervising Judge Harbor Justice Center 2000 and 2003. Born Los Angeles California July 5, 1947. Educated at California State University at Northridge B.S.B.A. 1969 and University of Southern California J.D. 1972. Admitted to practice California 1972. Referee 1977-79, Commissioner 1979-86 and Judge Feb 18, 1986 to Aug 9, 1998 and Presiding Judge 1988 and 1994, Harbor Municipal Court Orange County, appointed by Governor George Deukmejian.

Deputy District Attorney Orange County 1972-75 and San Luis Obispo County 1975. Author "Penal Code 1000—Drug Diversion Program" Orange County B. Jour. Spring 1976. Chair Orange County Municipal Court Systems (MCS) Automation Committee 1993 and 1994, Orange County Municipal Court Presiding Judges Committee 1994 and Municipal Court Judges Personnel Committee 1994-97. Member Oct 1995 to Dec 1996 and Chair 1997-2002 Traffic Advisory Committee and Member Trial Court Coordination Advisory Committee March 1996 to Oct 1997 Judicial Council of California. Attended "Civil Law and Procedure" Feb 1977, Oct 1990 and Jan 1991, "Criminal Law and Procedure" Sept 1988 and Feb 2002 and "Court Management: Presiding Judge" Nov 1988 and 1994 California Center for Judicial Education and Research. Instructor in Judicial Ethics and Contempt New Judges College California Center for Judicial Education and Research Dec 1990.

Office: 4601 Jamboree Road, Newport Beach 92660.

Telephone: (949) 476-4699.

MAHONEY, Patrick J. *(Judge, Superior Court of California City and County of San Francisco)* Appointed by Governor Gray Davis to term beginning March 14, 2000. Born San Francisco California Jan 28, 1943. Catholic Educated at Stanford University A.B. 1965 and Hastings College of the Law J.D. 1969. Admitted to practice California 1970, U.S. District Courts District of Columbia 1970 and Northern 1973, Eastern 1978 and Central 1983 Districts of California, U.S. Courts of Appeals District of Columbia 1970 and Ninth 1973 Circuits and U.S. Supreme Court 1975. In legal practice Washington D.C. 1969-72 and San Francisco California 1972-92.

Chief Trial Deputy City and County of San Francisco 1992-2000. Author "Privileged Entry onto Farm Property" 19 Hastings L. Jour. 413, 1968, Class Action Newsletter American Bar Association 1990-92, "Education of Clients" California Law Business Sept 1991 and "The Pyramid" California Lawyer July 2000. Fellow Coro Foundation 1966. Democrat. Board member Legal Aid Society and Legal Community Against Violence. Coached grammar school and middle school baseball, basketball and soccer. Enjoys running and photography.

Office: 400 McAllister Street, San Francisco 94102.

Telephone: (415) 551-4020.

MAINO, Runston G. *(Judge, Superior Court of California County of San Diego)* Term expires Jan 2007. Born Rochester Minnesota Dec 11, 1939. Educated at University of California at Berkeley B.A. 1961 and University of San Francisco J.D. 1968. Admitted to practice California 1968 and U.S. Supreme Court 1974. Former Judge, North County Municipal Court San Diego County, appointed by Governor Edmund G. Brown, Jr. to term beginning Jan 28, 1982.

With District Attorney's Office San Diego 1969-82. President South Bay Bar Association 1980. Captain USMC 1958-64. Republican. Board of Directors San Diego Humane Society 1981.

Mailing address: P.O. Box 122724, San Diego 92112-2724.

Office: 325 South Melrose Drive, Vista 92083.

Telephone: (760) 726-9595.

MAKINO, Kazuharu *(Judge, Superior Court of California County of Orange)* Appointed by Governor George Deukmejian to term beginning Oct 4, 1989. Elected 1990, 1996 and 2002. Current term expires Jan 2009. Born Numazu Japan Sept 23, 1951. Educated at Beloit College B.A. 1973 and McGeorge School of Law J.D. 1976. Admitted to practice California 1977-86. Judge, North Orange County Municipal Court 1986-90.

Deputy District Attorney Orange County 1977-86.

Mailing address: P.O. Box 1994, Santa Ana 92702-1994.

Office: Central Justice Center, 700 Civic Center Drive West, Santa Ana 92701.

Telephone: (714) 834-3734.

MALDONADO, Albert H. *(Judge, Superior Court of California County of Monterey)* Assumed office Dec 18, 2000. Former Judge, Monterey County Municipal Court.

Mailing address: P.O. Box 1819, Salinas 93902-1819.

Office: 240 Church Street, Salinas 93901.

Telephone: (831) 755-5060.

MALLACH, Barbara J. *(Judge, Superior Court of California County of San Mateo)* Assumed office June 12, 1998. Former Judge and Presiding Judge, San Mateo County Municipal Court.

Office: Hall of Justice, 400 County Center, Redwood City 94063.

Telephone: (650) 363-4516.

MALLANO, Robert M. *(Associate Justice, California Court of Appeal Second District Division One)* Appointed by Governor Gray Davis. Born Los Angeles California Oct 7, 1938. Catholic. Educated at Yale University B.A. 1960 and Boalt Hall School of Law LL.B. 1963. Member Order of the Coif. Associate Editor California Law Review. Recipient Fellowship from International Legal Studies Committee to study canon law and comparative law in Rome, Italy 1963-64. Admitted to practice California 1964. Began legal practice Los Angeles 1964. In legal practice Torrance 1969. Former Judge, South Bay Municipal Court Los Angeles County, appointed by Governor Edmund G. Brown, Jr. to term beginning July 3, 1978. Former Judge and Presiding Judge, Superior Court of California County of Los Angeles.

Deputy District Attorney Los Angeles County 1966-69. Member Italian-American Lawyers of California, South Bay (Former Chairman Legal Aid Foundation), Los Angeles County and American Bar Associations. Democrat. Los Angeles Orphanage Advisory Board. Former Procurator-Advocate Marriage Tribunal Los Angeles Archdiocese. Enjoys gardening, bird watching and reading.

Office: 300 South Spring Street, Los Angeles 90013.

Telephone: (213) 830-7510.

MALLETT, Richard M. *(Judge, Superior Court of California County of San Joaquin)* Assumed office June 8, 1998. Former Judge, Stockton Municipal Court San Joaquin County.

Office: 222 East Weber Avenue, Room 303, Stockton 95202.

Telephone: (209) 468-2827.

MANDABACH, Frederick A. *(Judge, Superior Court of California County of San Bernardino)* Assumed office. Elected to subsequent terms. Serves West District. Educated at Golden Gate University B.B.A., Claremont University M.A., Loyola Marymount University Law School J.D. and New York University LL.M. Member St. Thomas More Law Honor Society. Admitted to practice California 1972, U.S. Tax Court 1973 and U.S. Court of Federal Claims 1973. Commissioner, Superior Court of California San Bernardino County Nov 1979 to Feb 1985. Former Judge, San Bernardino County Municipal Court, appointed by Governor George Deukmejian to term beginning Feb 1985.

Co-author with Shirley Brice Heath "Language Status Decisions and the Law in the United States" *Progress in Language Planning, International Perspectives* Berlin, Mouton 1983. Contributing Editor *Practice Under the California Family Law Act* CEB since 1992. Adjunct Professor of Family Law University of La Verne since 2000. Member Judicial Council Advisory Committee on Legal Forms 1987-94, Family Law Committee California Judges Association 1993-94 and Family Law Support Committee and Legislation Committee 1982-85 State Bar of California. Member Arrowhead Chapter Inns of Court, San Bernardino County (Chair Continuing Education 1976-77) and Western San Bernardino County Bar Associations. Established SupportMaster© first spreadsheet-metaphor computer program for child and spousal

MANDABACH, FREDERICK A.—*Continued*
support used in family law courts and law offices 1985-86. Presenter "Criminal Law Legislative Changes Affecting 1990" California Center for Judicial Education and Research March 1990, "Advanced Techniques in Support Calculations: Maximizing Results for Your Clients" East-West Family Law Symposium Claremont Colleges July 29, 1995 and "Tracing: What It Is, When It Is Used, Why It Is Used, How It Is Used" Nov 1999 and "Recent Developments in Family Law" March 2000 IVAMS Family Law Seminar University of La Verne and "Bridging the Gap" San Bernardino County Bar Association. Recipient Family Law Judicial Officer of the Year Award from State Bar of California 1993 and Kaufman-Campbell Outstanding Judge Award from San Bernardino County Bar Association 2000. USCG. Board member San Bernardino County Law Library 1987-89 and since 1993. Member Child Abuse Prevention Committee San Antonio Community Hospital 1982-85. Member Rotary Club of Ontario California 1982-2001.

Office: 8303 North Haven Avenue, Department 19, Rancho Cucamonga 91730.

Telephone: (909) 945-4412.

MANELLA, Nora *(Judge, United States District Court Central District of California)* Appointed for life by President Bill Clinton 1998. Educated at Wellesley College and University of Southern California Law Center. Note and Articles Editor Southern California Law Review. Law Clerk to Hon. John Minor Wisdom, U.S. Court of Appeals Fifth Circuit. In legal practice Washington D.C. and Los Angeles California. Judge, Los Angeles Municipal Court 1990-92, appointed by Governor George Deukmejian. Judge, Superior Court of California County of Los Angeles 1992-93, appointed by Governor Pete Wilson. Judge, U.S. Court of Appeals Ninth Circuit 1999.

Assistant U.S. Attorney Los Angeles 1982-90 and U.S. Attorney Central District of California 1993-98 U.S. Attorney's Office. Important Decision: People v. Robinson (30-year-old murder case profiled on CBS' "Sixty Minutes"). Recipient Ernestine Stahlhut Award from Women Lawyers of Los Angeles 1995 and Alumna Achievement Award from Wellesley College 2000. Named one of 50 Most Influential Women Lawyers in the United States by National Law Journal.

Office: U.S. Courthouse, 312 North Spring Street, Los Angeles 90012.

Telephone: (213) 894-0413.

MANLEY, Stephen V. *(Judge, Superior Court of California County of Santa Clara)* Assumed office July 7, 1998. Presiding Judge Jan 1, 1996 to Dec 31, 1996 and Former Judge, Santa Clara County Municipal Court.

Office: 115 Terraine Street, San Jose 95113.

Telephone: (408) 491-4700.

MANN, Arthur H. *(Judge, Superior Court of California County of Lake)* Assumed office June 30, 1998. Elected 2000, current term expires Jan 2007. Presiding Judge July 1, 1999 to Dec 31, 2001. Born Lakeport California. Presbyterian. Educated at Sonoma State University B.A. 1969 and University of San Diego J.D. 1973. Admitted to practice California 1974. Judge July 15, 1979 to June 29, 1998 and Former Presiding Judge, Lake County Municipal Court, appointed by Lake County Board of Supervisors.

Office: 255 North Forbes Street, Lakeport 95453.

Telephone: (707) 263-2526.

MANOUKIAN, Socrates Peter *(Judge, Superior Court of California County of Santa Clara)* Appointed by Governor Pete Wilson to term beginning March 25, 1993. Elected June 1994 and June 2000. Current term expires Jan 2007. Born Beirut Lebanon April 20, 1950. Educated at Foothill College A.A. 1970, University of California at Los Angeles B.A. 1972, California State University at Long Beach 1973-74 and 1979-80 and Southwestern University School of Law J.D. 1977. Member Theta Delta Chi. Admitted to practice California. In legal practice Los Angeles 1978-82 and San Jose 1983-93.

Former Member Association of Northern California Defense Counsel and State Bar of California. Member American Board of Trial Advocates and California Judges Association. Member Region 43 American Youth Soccer Organization since 1989, Los Altos Pony League Baseball since 1990, Stanford Area Council Cub Scout Pack 35 since 1990, St. Nicholas School Men's Club since 1990, El Camino YMCA Basketball 1993-94 and Los Altos Hills Little League since 1994. Assistant Coach Boys' Fourth Grade Basketball Team St. Nicholas School 1994-95.

Office: 191 North First Street, San Jose 95113.

Telephone: (408) 882-2100.

MARCHIANO, James J. *(Presiding Justice, California Court of Appeal First District Division One)* Appointed by Governor Pete Wilson to term beginning 1998. Presiding Justice since Jan 2002. Born Detroit Michigan June 5, 1943. Roman Catholic. Educated at St. Patrick's College A.B. 1965 and University of California Boalt Hall School of Law J.D. 1969. Admitted to practice California 1970, U.S. District Court Northern District of California 1970 and U.S. Court of Appeals Ninth Circuit 1970. In legal practice San Francisco 1970-78 and Oakland 1978-88. Judge, Superior Court of California Contra Costa County Sept 30, 1988 to 1998, appointed by Governor George Deukmejian.

Author "*State Farm v. Partridge:* Expanding Insurance Liability" 7 Pacific L. Jour. 57, 1976 and Chapter 16 "Misconduct of Counsel and Court" and Chapter 17 "Jury Management" 2 *Civil Procedure During Trial* 1995. Consultant 1 *Civil Procedure During Trial* 1982. Co-author "Handling Depositions" *Action Guide* California Continuing Education of the Bar 2001. Lecturer on Law Trial Practice Course John F. Kennedy Law School 1974-75. Adjunct Professor of Litigation Advocacy Hastings College of the Law 1976-82. Faculty Member Civil College of Advocacy University of California Hastings College of the Law 1977, 1979, 1981 and 1984. Member Robert McGrath American Inn of Court, Jury System Improvement Task Force, California State-Federal Judicial Council, California Judges Association and American Judicature Society. Instructor in Insurance Litigation California Judges Association 1990. Panelist on Trial Practice California Continuing Education of the Bar. Named Trial Judge of the Year Alameda-Contra Costa Trial Lawyers Association 1990. Named Superior Court Judge of the Year by California Trial Lawyers

MARCHIANO, JAMES J.—*Continued*

Association 1992. Enjoys reading history and playing racquetball.

Office: 350 McAllister Street, San Francisco 94102-4712.

Telephone: (415) 865-7270.

MARCUS, Gregg *(Judge, Superior Court of California County of Los Angeles)* Assumed office Jan 22, 2000. Former Judge, Los Angeles Municipal Court Los Angeles County.

Office: Van Nuys Courthouse West, 14400 Erwin Street Mall, Van Nuys 91401-2705.

Telephone: (818) 374-2295.

MARCUS, Stephen A. *(Judge, Superior Court of California County of Los Angeles)* Assumed office Jan 22, 2000. Elected 2000, current term expires Jan 2007. Born Atlanta Georgia Aug 17, 1950. Educated at State University of New York at Stony Brook B.A. magna cum laude 1972, Boston University J.D. 1975 and New York University 1976-79. Admitted to practice New York 1974, Florida 1977, Massachusetts 1977, U.S. Court of Appeals Second Circuit 1978, U.S. Supreme Court 1979, California 1981 and U.S. District Court Central District of California 1982. Commissioner April 1, 1989 to May 18, 1989 and Judge May 19, 1989 to Jan 21, 2000, Los Angeles Municipal Court Los Angeles County.

With Office of State Special Prosecutor New York Aug 1975 to May 1977. Deputy District Attorney Suffolk County New York 1977-78 and Los Angeles County California Oct 1982 to April 1989. Deputy Attorney General New York May 1978 to March 1981. Deputy City Attorney Los Angeles California March 1981 to Oct 1982. Author "Diary of a Drug Court Judge" American University 1994 and "The Singular Importance of Drug Court Graduations." Adjunct Professor of Evidence and Juvenile Law Whittier Law School and University of La Verne Law School 1991-94 and "Drugs and Crime," "Children and the Law" and "Criminal Procedure" California State University at Long Beach 1996-2001. Chair Juvenile Facilities Reform Commission 1985, California Drug Court Symposium Planning Committee 1997 and Statewide Drug Education Committee since 2000. Member Judicial Council Oversight Committee California Drug Court Project 1996-99 and National Task Force on Court Automation and Integration 1997-2001. Former Member Municipal Court Judges Association of Los Angeles County (Chair Legislation Committee), California Deputy District Attorneys Association and California Narcotics Officers Association. Member Information Management System Committee Los Angeles County Drug Court, Countywide Criminal Justice Coordination Committee Los Angeles Superior Court, California Association of Drug Court Professionals (First President 1995), California Judges Association (Board of Directors Executive Board 1996-98, Treasurer/Secretary 1998-99, Access to Justice Committee since 1998, Judicial Ethics Committee), Hellenic-American Bar Association, State Bar of California (Committee on Juvenile Justice 1984-86, Member since 1988 and Chair 1990 Commission on Corrections, Member 1992-96, Secretary and Chair Elect Executive Committee Legal Services Section) and Los Angeles County Bar Association. Planned first Drug Court in Los Angeles. Guest Speaker Drug Court Conferences National Association of Drug Court Professionals 1995-2000. Faculty Member National Prosecutor's Training Program 1998 and 2001, California Judges College and National Prosecutors Conference National Drug Court Institute. Instructor "Drug Court" California Judges College 1999-2000. Guest Speaker "Ethics and Excellence in Addiction Treatment" Betty Ford Center. Recipient Lifetime Achievement Award from Volunteers in Parole 1996, Partnership Award from National Association of Drug Court Professionals 1997 and Freedom Human Rights Award 1998. Former Member Board of Directors Northeast Youth Athletic Center. Member Volunteers in Parole (Statewide Steering Committee since 1993, Board of Governors 1990-98). Involved with theater. Enjoys photography and sports.

Office: Criminal Courts Building, 210 West Temple Street, Los Angeles 90012-3210.

Telephone: (213) 974-6535.

E-mail address: SMARCUS@CO.LA.CA.US

MARGINES, Charles *(Judge, Superior Court of California County of Orange)* Assumed office Aug 10, 1998. Former Judge, Central Orange County Municipal Court.

Office: 700 Civic Center Drive West, Santa Ana 92702-1994.

Telephone: (714) 834-3734.

MARGULIES, Sandra Lynn *(Associate Justice, California Court of Appeal First District Division One)* Appointed by Governor Gray Davis to term beginning Jan 2002. Born Oakland California March 16, 1952. Educated at University of California at Los Angeles B.A. magna cum laude 1974 and Southwestern University School of Law J.D. 1977. Judge, San Leandro-Hayward Municipal Court Alameda County 1985-88. Judge, Superior Court of California County of Alameda 1988-2002.

Office: 350 McAllister Street, San Francisco 94102-3600.

Telephone: (415) 865-7300.

MARION, James Patrick *(Judge, Superior Court of California County of Orange)*

Mailing address: P.O. Box 5000, Fullerton 92838-0500.

Office: North Justice Center, 1275 North Berkeley Avenue, Fullerton 92832.

Telephone: (714) 773-4400.

MARKMAN, Joy W. *(Judge, Superior Court of California County of Orange)* Assumed office Aug 10, 1998. Former Judge, West Orange County Municipal Court.

Mailing address: P.O. Box 14169, Orange 92863-1569.

Office: Lamoreaux Justice Center, 341 The City Drive, Orange 92868.

Telephone: (714) 935-7236.

MARLETTE, Patrick *(Judge, Superior Court of California County of Sacramento)*

Office: Courthouse, 720 Ninth Street, Sacramento 95814.

Telephone: (916) 874-5476.

MARLOW, Monica *(Judge, Superior Court of California County of Shasta)* Assumed office June 3, 1998. Presiding Judge since Jan 1, 2003. Former Judge, Shasta County Municipal Court.

Office: 1500 Court Street, Redding 96001-1685.

Telephone: (530) 225-5714.

MARRS, Bruce F. *(Judge, Superior Court of California County of Los Angeles)* Assumed office Jan 22, 2000. Born Pasadena California. Educated at Pacific University B.A. 1965. Admitted to practice California 1976. Commissioner, Santa Anita Municipal Court 1986-91. Judge, Los Angeles Municipal Court Los Angeles County Jan 3, 1991 to Jan 21, 2000, appointed by Governor George Deukmejian.

Deputy City Attorney San Diego 1976-77. Deputy District Attorney Los Angeles County 1977-86. Captain USMC 1961-76.

Office: Central Courthouse, 111 North Hill Street, Los Angeles 90012.

Telephone: (213) 974-5411.

MARSHALL, Consuelo Bland *(Chief Judge, United States District Court Central District of California)* Appointed for life by President Jimmy Carter Sept 30, 1980. Chief Judge since Sept 25, 2001. Born Knoxville Tennessee Sept 28, 1936. Educated at Howard University Law School LL.B. 1961. Recipient Outstanding Scholastic Achievement Awards for Administrative Law, Corporations Law and Civil Procedure 1960-61. Notes Editor Howard University Law Journal 1960-61. Member Alpha Phi Alpha. Admitted to practice California. In legal practice Los Angeles, California 1968-70. Judge in Juvenile Court 1971-76 and Criminal Division 1977-80, Superior Court of California Los Angeles County. Judge, Inglewood Municipal Court Los Angeles County 1976-77.

Deputy City Attorney Los Angeles 1962-67. Author "Presumption of Payment from Lapse of Time" 6 Howard L. Jour. 95, Jan 1960, "Liquidation for Acquisition of Assets Not Distributed in Complete Liquidation Within the Meaning of 112(b) 6, Internal Revenue Code" 6 Howard L. Jour. 233, June 1960, "The Valuation of 'Property Received' in a Marital Settlement Which Includes a Release of Marital Obligations" 7 Howard L. Jour. 64, Winter 1961 and Syllabus "Juvenile Law and Procedure" Los Angeles Trial Lawyers Association 1977. Appointed by Juvenile Court Presiding Judge to Project Heavy, a Community Resource Board on criminal justice planning 1976. Member Black Women Lawyers Association, Association of Black Lawyers, Los Angeles Women Lawyers Association, California Women Lawyers Association, National Association of Women Judges, California Judges Association and State Bar of California. Attended courses on Probate Law Feb 1970 and Criminal Law and Procedures Sept 1971 University of Southern California. Participant Orientation for Municipal Court Judges 1977, Seminar for Newly Appointed District Court Judges Washington D.C. 1981, Antitrust Seminar for Federal Judges University of Michigan Law School 1981, Evidence & Federal Jurisdiction Seminar Harvard Law School 1982 and "Problems Judges Face in Litigation of Economic Issues" Seminar University of Wisconsin 1984. Lecturer New Family Law Act 1970 and Pretrial Conference and Mandate Status Conference in Federal Court 1983 Continuing Education of the Bar, Los Angeles Student Trial Lawyers Association 1977 and Los Angeles Trial Lawyers Association 1977. Panel Participant Institute for Trial Advocacy Skills University of Southern California Law School 1979. Faculty member Trial Advocacy Seminar and Trial Advocacy Workshop Harvard University 1984. Recipient Recognition for Community Services from Urban League Guild 1963, Community Service from Our Authors Study Club (Negro History Week) 1964 and Community Services from Beta Phi Sigma 1966. Honored by Black Women Lawyers Association 1976 and National Business and Professional Women's Club of Los Angeles 1978. Recipient Certificate of Appreciation for Summer Program for Economically Disadvantaged Youth from City of Los Angeles 1978 and Honorary Teaching Certificate from Los Angeles Unified School District 1980. Cited for Outstanding Service in the "Lawyer-in-the-Classroom Program" by The Constitutional Rights Foundation and Los Angeles County Bar Association. Named Graduate of the Year by Howard University 1981 and Woman of the Year for Contributions to the Improvement of Society by *The Los Angeles Sentinel* 1983. Recipient Presidential Award in Recognition for Services and Contributions in Improving the Quality of Life for Mankind 1984, Certificate of Honor from Black American Law Students Association University of California at Los Angeles 1985, Trophy from Verbum Dei Catholic Boys High School Los Angeles 1986 and Ernestine Stahlhut Award from Women Lawyers Association of Los Angeles 1986. Member Sea-Vu, Howard University Law Alumni Association, Urban League, YMCA and NAACP. Board member Legal Aid Foundation.

Office: U.S. Courthouse, 312 North Spring Street, Los Angeles 90012.

Telephone: (213) 894-6314.

MARTIN, John E. *(Judge, Superior Court of California County of Calaveras)* Presiding Judge Jan 1, 2001 to Dec 31, 2002.

Office: 891 Mountain Ranch Road, San Andreas 95249.

Telephone: (209) 754-6311.

MARTIN, John Nevin *(Judge, Superior Court of California County of San Bernardino)* Assumed office Aug 10, 1998. Elected 2002, current term expires Jan 2009. Born Lexington Mississippi April 21, 1947. Catholic. Educated at University of Mississippi B.A. 1973 and Western State University J.D. 1976. Admitted to practice California 1976, U.S. Court of Appeals Ninth Circuit 1990 and U.S. Supreme Court 1991. In legal practice San Bernardino County 1978-94. Judge, San Bernardino County Municipal Court April 28, 1994 to Aug 9, 1998, appointed by Governor Pete Wilson.

Office: 351 North Arrowhead Avenue, San Bernardino 92415-0240.

Telephone: (909) 387-3922.

MARTIN, William F. *(Judge, Superior Court of California County of Santa Clara)* Former Judge, Santa Clara County Municipal Court.

Office: 191 North First Street, San Jose 95113.

Telephone: (408) 882-2100.

MARTINEZ, John L. *(Judge, Superior Court of California County of Los Angeles)* Assumed office Jan 22, 2000. Presiding Judge July 1, 1996 to June 30, 1997 and Former Judge, Alhambra Municipal Court Los Angeles County.

Office: Alhambra Courthouse, 150 West Commonwealth Avenue, Alhambra 91801.

Telephone: (626) 308-5537.

MARTINEZ, Robert M. *(Judge, Superior Court of California County of Los Angeles)*

Office: Pomona Courthouse South, 400 Civic Center Plaza, Pomona 91766.

Telephone: (909) 620-3023.

MASON, Tomar *(Judge, Superior Court of California City and County of San Francisco)* Assumed office Dec 31, 1998. Presiding Judge June 1, 1996 to May 31, 1997 and Former Judge, San Francisco Municipal Court San Francisco County.

Office: Civic Center Courthouse, 400 McAllister Street, San Francisco 94102-4514.

Telephone: (415) 551-4020.

MASON, Wesley R., III *(Judge, Superior Court of California County of San Diego)*

Mailing address: P.O. Box 122724, San Diego 92112-2724.

Office: 500 Third Avenue, Chula Vista 91910.

Telephone: (619) 691-4770.

MATUSINKA, Jean E. *(Judge, Superior Court of California County of Los Angeles)* Appointed by Governor George Deukmejian to term beginning May 10, 1985. Elected 1986, 1992 and 1998. Current term expires Jan 2005. Serves Southwest District. Born New York New York March 15, 1939. Educated at University of Edinburgh 1961, Hunter College B.A. 1962, Brooklyn Law School J.D. 1966 and University of California at Los Angeles Professional International Business Management 1981-83. Admitted to practice New York 1966, Florida 1967, California 1970, U.S. District Court Central District of California 1970 and U.S. Supreme Court 1970.

Deputy District Attorney Los Angeles County 1970-85. Author "Equality" Second International Congress on Child Abuse and Neglect Abstracts London Pergamon Press, Ltd. 1978; "Child Victims of Homicide" California District Attorneys Association Center for Criminal Justice Policy and Management University of San Diego 1979; "Domestic Violence" Directions, Child Abuse and Neglect Project, Health, Education and Welfare Region IX 1979; "Sexual Abuse—Fact or Fantasy" V No. 5 Newsjournal of the California District Attorneys Association 1980; "Special Considerations in the Prosecution of Spousal Violence" and "Special Considerations in the Prosecution of Child Sexual Assault" 1981 and "Special Considerations in the Prosecution of Spousal Violence" 1982 Los Angeles County Protocol on the Treatment of Problems of Rape and Other Sexual Assaults; "Sexual Abuse of Children" National District Attorneys Association 1982; "Prosecution of the Violent Juvenile Offender" 1983; "Domestic Violence Litigation" 1983 and "The Child Witness" 1983 National College of District Attorneys; and "Prosecution and Defense of Child Abuse" 1985, "Prosecution and Defense of Domestic Violence Cases" 1986 and "Prosecution and Defense of Spouse Abuse and Marital Rape" 1986 Matthew Bender. Co-author and Editor *Child Abuse and Domestic Violence Manual* Los Angeles District Attorney 1980. Clinical Associate Professor since 1985 and Clinical Professor July 2001 of Psychiatry and Behavioral Sciences University of Southern California.

Commission for the Enforcement of Child Abuse Laws California Attorney General's Office 1984-86. Chair Probation Department Committee Los Angeles County Superior Court since 1988. Member Association of Deputy District Attorneys Los Angeles County, Foreign Law Association of Southern California, Judicial Council of California (Child Victim Witness Judicial Advisory Committee 1987-88, Advisory Committee on Sentencing 1988-89), California Judges Association (Court Administration Committee since 1988), California District Attorneys Association, California Sexual Assault Investigators Association, The Florida Bar, State Bar of California (Juvenile Justice Committee 1979-82), Los Angeles County (International Law Section 1981) and American (Section of International Law 1981) Bar Associations. Faculty member Delinquency Control Institute School of Public Administration University of Southern California 1974-85. Attended National Center for the Prevention and Treatment of Child Abuse and Neglect University of Colorado Medical Center 1974 and Executive Training Program in Advanced Criminal Justice Practices "Rape and Its Victims" San Francisco 1977 and California Judicial College 1986. Faculty member National College of District Attorneys 1983-85. Member Child Victim Witness Project Planning Committee California Center for Judicial Education and Research since 1988. Consultant Continuing Education of the Bar 1977-79. Program Coordinator Sexual Assault Prosecution Seminars California District Attorneys Association 1983.

Recipient Certificate of Appreciation from National Organization for Victim Assistance 1983 and Helen Boardman Child Protection Award 1986. Member National Women's Political Caucus 1976-79, Los Angeles County Board of Supervisors 1985-86, State of California Senate Rules Committee 1986 and Public Health Service Advisory Committee for the Development of a National Medical Protocol on Child Sexual Abuse The United States Surgeon General 1987. Chairperson Operations Committee Inter-Agency Council on Child Abuse and Neglect 1979-81 and Deputy in Charge Child Abuse and Domestic Violence Section District Attorney's Office 1983 Los Angeles County Board of Supervisors. President National Board of Directors Parents Anonymous 1973-76. Board member Richstone Family Center 1973-83. Member Research Project on Rape University of California at Los Angeles 1979 and Brooklyn Law School Alumni Association since 1985. Enjoys writing, reading, gardening and traveling.

Office: Torrance Courthouse, 825 Maple Avenue, Torrance 90503.

Telephone: (310) 222-8808.

MATZ, A. Howard *(Judge, United States District Court Central District of California)* Appointed for life by President Bill Clinton to term beginning 1998. Born Brooklyn New York Aug 3, 1943. Educated at Columbia University A.B. 1965 and Harvard University Law School J.D. 1968. Law Clerk to Hon. Morris E. Lasker, U.S. District Court Southern District of New York 1969-70. In legal practice New York City 1970-72 and Los Angeles California 1972-74 and 1979-98.

Assistant U.S. Attorney 1974-78 and Chief Special Prosecutions Unit 1977-78 Central District of California.

Office: 170 U.S. Courthouse, 312 North Spring Street, Los Angeles 90012.

Telephone: (213) 894-5290.

MATZ, Laura A. *(Judge, Superior Court of California County of Los Angeles)* Assumed office Jan 22,

MATZ, LAURA A.—*Continued*
2000. Former Judge, Glendale Municipal Court Los Angeles County.
Office: Glendale Courthouse, 600 East Broadway, Glendale 91206.
Telephone: (818) 500-3524.

MAUTINO, Philip K. *(Judge, Superior Court of California County of Los Angeles)* Assumed office Jan 22, 2000. Supervising Judge, Los Padrinos Juvenile Court since 2001. Born Los Angeles California Nov 6, 1939. Protestant. Educated at University of California at Los Angeles B.S. 1962 M.B.A. 1963 and University of Southern California J.D. 1966. Member Phi Delta Phi. Admitted to practice California 1967 and U.S. District Court Central District of California 1967. In legal practice Whittier 1967-93. Judge Jan 23, 1993 to Jan 21, 2000 and Presiding Judge Jan 1, 1995 to Dec 31, 1997, Los Cerritos Municipal Court Los Angeles County, appointed by Governor Pete Wilson.
Author "Anonymous Juries" California State Bar Journal 1995. Chairman Los Angeles County Municipal Court Presiding Judges Association 1997-2000. Republican.
Office: Los Padrinos Juvenile Courthouse, 7281 East Quill, Downey 90242.
Telephone: (562) 940-8841.

MAY, Robert E. *(Judge, Superior Court of California County of San Diego)* Appointed by Governor George Deukmejian to term beginning Dec 23, 1987. Elected Nov 8, 1988, Nov 8, 1994 and 2000. Current term expires Jan 2007. Born Mobile Alabama Nov 9, 1940. Educated at Pensacola Junior College A.A. 1960, University of Florida B.A. 1962 and University of San Diego J.D. 1970. Admitted to practice California 1970. In legal practice San Diego 1974-77 and El Cajon 1977-83. Judge, El Cajon Municipal Court San Diego County 1986-87.
Deputy District Attorney San Diego County 1970-74. Assistant U.S. Attorney Southern District of California 1983-86. Former member Barrister's Club of San Diego (President 1978) and San Diego County Bar Association (Board of Directors 1979-81, Vice President 1981). Member California Judges Association. Lieutenant USN 1962-66.
Mailing address: P.O. Box 122724, San Diego 92112-2724.
Office: 330 West Broadway, San Diego 92101.
Telephone: (619) 685-6148.

MAYEDA, Jon M. *(Judge, Superior Court of California County of Los Angeles)* Former Judge, Los Angeles Municipal Court Los Angeles County.
Office: Courthouse, 111 North Hill Street, Los Angeles 90012.
Telephone: (213) 974-5411.

MAYFIELD, Cindee F. *(Judge, Superior Court of California County of Mendocino)* Appointed by Governor Pete Wilson to term beginning Nov 17, 1997. Elected 1998, current term expires Jan 2005. Serves Juvenile Court. Born Arcata California Oct 31, 1959. Educated at University of California at Davis B.A. with highest honors 1981 and University of California Hastings College of the Law J.D. magna cum laude 1984. Staff member Hastings Law Review 1983. Member Thurston Society and Order of the Coif. Admitted to practice California 1984 and U.S. District Court Northern District of California. In legal practice 1984-97.
Member Juvenile Judges of California and Mendocino County Bar Association. Member Ukiah City Planning Committee 1994-95. Volunteer CASA 1995-97.
Mailing address: P.O. Box 996, Ukiah 95482.
Office: Courthouse, 100 North State Street, Ukiah 95482.
Telephone: (707) 467-6437.
E-mail address: mayfielc@co.mendocino.ca.us

MAYHEW, William A. *(Judge, Superior Court of California County of Stanislaus)* Assumed office Nov 12, 1995. Assistant Presiding Judge 1997-2000. Presiding Judge Appellate Department 1998-99. Presiding Judge July 1, 2000 to Dec 31, 2002. Educated at Modesto Junior College A.A. 1959, University of California at Los Angeles B.S. 1961 J.D. 1964. Board of Editors UCLA Law Review. Member Order of the Coif. Admitted to practice California 1965, U.S. District Courts Eastern 1965 and Northern 1965 Districts of California, U.S. Court of Appeals Ninth Circuit 1965 and U.S. Tax Court 1968. In legal practice Sacramento 1968-82, Turlock 1986-88 and Modesto 1988-94. Judge, Stanislaus County Municipal Court Sept 2, 1994 to Nov 13, 1995.
Deputy Attorney General California 1964-67. Author "The Abrogation of Sovereign Immunity in Mississippi: The Legislative Problem" 3 Mississippi College L. Rev. 209, 1983; "Bad Faith and the Uninsured Motorist Claims" 19 Forum 168, 1984 reprinted in National Insurance L. Rev. 185, 1984; Chapter 29 "Litigation of Uninsured Motorist Claims" *No-Fault and Uninsured Motorist Automobile Insurance* 1984; "Insurance Contracts: An Overview with Emphasis on Personal Automobile and Homeowner Insurance Policies" 39 Mississippi Law Institute 1, 1984; and "Reasonable Expectations: Seeking a Principled Application" 13 Pepperdine L. Rev. 267, 1986. Associate Professor University of Toledo College of Law 1975-76. Professor of Law Mississippi College School of Law 1982-86. Arbitrator American Arbitration Association 1969-94. Advocate since 1977 American Board of Trial Advocates (Charter Member and Secretary-Treasurer 1985 Mississippi Chapter, Member National Board of Directors 1986-87 and Chair Western Regional Conference 1987). Member California Judges Association (Civil Procedure Committee 1996-98), State Bar of California and American Bar Association. Speaker "Experts: Their Use and Misuse" Legal Skills Program 1982, "Recent Developments in Evidence" Annual Spring Convention American Board of Trial Advocates 1984, "Medical-Legal Problems of Nursing" Mississippi Nurses Association 1985 and "An Overview of the Standard Insurance Policies" Mississippi Law Institute 1985. Chair Panel on Creative Use of Experts Bakersfield Personal Injury Seminar 1990. Major California Army National Guard JAGC 1966-77. Vice Chancellor Episcopal Diocese of San Joaquin 1989-94. Board of Trustees 1989-94 and President 1992 Turlock High School.
Mailing address: P.O. Box 3488, Modesto 95353.
Office: 800 11th Street, Room 100, Modesto 95354.
Telephone: (209) 525-7846.

McADAMS, Richard J. *(Judge, Superior Court of California County of Santa Cruz)* Assumed office July 1, 1998. Born Albany California Feb 27, 1944. Catholic. Educated at University of Oregon 1961-63, University of California at Berkeley A.B. 1965 and Hastings College

MCADAMS, RICHARD J.—*Continued*

of the Law J.D. 1968. Admitted to practice California 1969. Began legal practice San Francisco 1969. In legal practice Santa Cruz 1973-77. Judge, Santa Cruz County Municipal Court June 3, 1977 to June 30, 1998, appointed by Governor Edmund G. Brown, Jr.

With Legal Aid Society of Santa Cruz County 1970-73. Member California Judges Association, State Bar of California and Santa Cruz Bar Association.

Office: Main Courthouse, 701 Ocean Street, Santa Cruz 95060.

Telephone: (831) 454-2012.

McBETH, Veronica Simmons *(Judge, Superior Court of California County of Los Angeles)* Assumed office Jan 22, 2000. Term expires Jan 2005. Educated at Whittier College 1965-67, California State College at San Jose 1968-69, California State University at Los Angeles B.A. 1972 and University of California at Los Angeles J.D. 1975. Staff member UCLA Law Review. Editor-in-Chief Black Law Journal. Admitted to practice California 1975. Judge July 1981 to Jan 22, 2000, Supervising Judge Central Criminal Court 1994-95 and Presiding Judge Jan 1, 1998 to Dec 31, 1999, Los Angeles Municipal Court Los Angeles County.

Deputy City Attorney 1975-81 City of Los Angeles (Trial Deputy 1975-76, Assistant Supervising Attorney Van Nuys Branch 1976-77, Special Counsel to City Attorney 1977-78, Domestic Violence Coordinator/Trials 1978-79 and Supervising Attorney West Los Angeles Branch 1979-81). President Black Women Lawyers Association of Los Angeles 1979-80. Member Executive Committee 1982-87 and since 1988, Chair Personnel Committee 1984-88 and 1994, Judges Orientation Committee 1983-84, House Arrest Committee 1986-87, "Meet Your Judges" Community Forum Committee 1989-91 and P.L. 987.2 Committee Los Angeles Municipal Court. Board of Directors John M. Langston Bar Association 1985-88. Member Executive Board since 1985 and Chair National Bar Association Judicial Council 1990-91 and Commission on Racial and Ethnic Bias in the Courts 1992-93 National Bar Association. Secretary 1986-87, Vice President South 1987-88 and Chair Judicial Section 1988-89 California Association of Black Lawyers. Chair Los Angeles County Municipal Court Judges Association 1988-89. Chair Planning Committee National Conference on Racial and Ethnic Bias in the Courts, National Center for State Courts National Consortium of Task Forces and Commission on Racial Bias in the Courts 1993 and 1994. Member Women Lawyers of Los Angeles, California Judges Association and National Association of Women Judges. Member Planning Committee and Presenter Municipal and Justice Courts Institute California Center for Judicial Education and Research. Lecturer The National Judicial College, Reno Nevada; Pennsylvania Trial Judges Winter Conference, Philadelphia; Conference of Appellate Court Justice American Bar Association, Seattle Washington; Greater Cleveland Trial Judges Seminar, Ohio; and Annual Judges Conference, Minnesota. Recipient Presidential Award from National Bar Association 1987, Raymond Pace Alexander Award from Judicial Council National Bar Association 1989, Judge Thomas Griffith Award from Los Angeles Chapter NAACP 1992, Public Law Award from Public Law Section State Bar of California 1992, Thurgood Marshall Award from Watts Chapter NAACP 1993, Distinguished Service Award from National Center for State Courts 1996 and Municipal Criminal Judge of the Year Award from Century City Bar Association 1996. Named Bernard Jefferson Jurist of the Year by John M. Langston Bar Association 1991 and Judge of the Year by California Association of Black Lawyers 1992. Member Executive Committee UCLA Law School Alumni Association 1982-85. Board of Directors 1986-93, Chair Charities Committee 1987-90 and Services to Youth 1990-93 Los Angeles Chapter Link, Inc. Board of Directors Jack and Jill of America Los Angeles Chapter since 1986 and Operation Field Trip Los Angeles City Schools 1994. Program Chair 1986-87 and Secretary 1987-89 Coalition of 100 Black Women. Member Advisory Board Black Peace Officers Association of Los Angeles County since 1993 and Los Angeles NAACP.

Office: Courthouse, 111 North Hill Street, Los Angeles 90012.

Telephone: (213) 974-5411.

McBRIDE, James J. *(Judge, Superior Court of California City and County of San Francisco)* Assumed office Dec 31, 1998. Former Judge, San Francisco Municipal Court San Francisco County.

Office: Civic Center Courthouse, 400 McAllister Street, San Francisco 94102-4514.

Telephone: (415) 551-4020.

McBRIEN, Peter J. *(Judge, Superior Court of California County of Sacramento)* Former Judge, Sacramento Municipal Court Sacramento County.

Office: 3341 Power Inn Road, Sacramento 95826.

Telephone: (916) 875-3400.

McCARTHY, Kevin M. *(Judge, Superior Court of California City and County of San Francisco)* Elected March 1996 to term beginning Jan 1997. Reelected 2002, current term expires Jan 2009. Born Los Angeles California. Catholic. Educated at University of California at Santa Barbara B.A. with honors 1980 and University of California Hastings College of the Law J.D. 1985. Staff member Constitutional Law Quarterly. Admitted to practice California 1985. In legal practice Alameda County 1985-96.

Adjunct Professor University of California Hastings College of the Law since 1990. Member Judicial Ethics Committee California Judges Association, Criminal Law Advisory Committee California Judicial Council, California Probation Services Task Force, Bay Area Lawyers for Individual Freedom and Bar Association of San Francisco. Seminar Leader New Judge Orientation 1998, 1999, 2000 and 2001, Instructor in Voir Dire and Search and Seizure and Faculty Member of Ongoing Ethics Training California Judicial Education and Research. Member San Francisco Citizens Advisory Committee on Transportation 1990-92.

Office: Civic Center Courthouse, 400 McAllister Street, San Francisco 94102-4514.

Telephone: (415) 551-4020.

McCARTIN, Michael *(Judge, Superior Court of California County of Orange)* Assumed office Aug 10, 1998. Former Judge, West Orange County Municipal Court.

Office: West Justice Center, 8141 Thirteenth Street, Westminster 92683.

Telephone: (714) 896-7181.

McCARVILLE, Brian S. *(Judge, Superior Court of California County of San Bernardino)* Former Judge, San Bernardino County Municipal Court.

Office: 351 North Arrowhead Avenue, San Bernardino 92415-0240.

Telephone: (909) 387-3922.

McCONAGHY, Dennis A. *(Judge, Superior Court of California County of Riverside)* Assumed office July 29, 1998. Elected March 2002, current term expires Jan 2009. Born Benton Harbor Michigan Feb 26, 1941. Christian. Educated at Miami University B.A. 1969, University of Maine M.S. 1973, University of Kansas J.D. 1976 and National University M.B.A. 1980. Admitted to practice Kansas 1976, California 1979, U.S. District Courts District of Kansas 1976 and District of California 1979 and U.S. Supreme Court 1980. Judge, Western Riverside County Municipal Court 1987 to July 28, 1998, appointed by Governor George Deukmejian.

Public Defender 1981-82. District Attorney 1982-84. Major USMC 1960-80.

Office: Hall of Justice, 4100 Main Street, Riverside 92501.

Telephone: (909) 955-2300.

McCONNELL, Judith D. *(Associate Justice, California Court of Appeal Fourth District Division One)* Appointed by Governor Gray Davis to term beginning Oct 3, 2001. Educated at University of California at Berkeley 1966 J.D. 1969. Member Phi Beta Kappa. Judge, San Diego Municipal Court San Diego County 1977-80. Judge April 1, 1980 to Oct 2, 2001 and Presiding Judge 1990-91, Superior Court of California County of San Diego, appointed by Governor Edmund G. Brown, Jr.

With Legal Division Department of Transportation 1969-76. Adjunct Professor of Law University of San Diego Law School 1973-76. Elected Member The American Law Institute 1997. Founder and First President Lawyers Club. Former member Board of Directors California Women Lawyers. Former Member California Judicial Council (Chair Superior Court Committee and Planning Committee, member Advisory Committee on Gender Bias in the Courts and The Future and the Courts). Member California Judges Association (Chairperson Annual Meeting Seminars and Education Planning and Coordinating Committees), National Association of Women Judges (Board of Directors and President) and Foundation for Women Judges (Board of Directors, President). Lecturer 1983 and Chair 1987 Juvenile Law Institute. Chair Task Force on Family Equity.

Office: 750 B Street, Suite 300, San Diego 92101.

Telephone: (619) 645-2760.

McCOY, Charles W., Jr. *(Judge, Superior Court of California County of Los Angeles)* Appointed by Governor Pete Wilson to term beginning Dec 1992. Elected Nov 8, 1994 and 2000. Current term expires Jan 2007. Born Washington D.C. Nov 3, 1946. Protestant. Educated at Purdue University B.S. 1968 and University of Texas J.D. with honors 1975. Member Phi Delta Phi. Admitted to practice California 1975, U.S. District Court Central District of California 1976, U.S. Court of Appeals Ninth Circuit 1976 and U.S. Supreme Court 1980. In legal practice Los Angeles 1975-92.

Contributor *Fundamentals of Legal Research* 6th ed. 1978 and *Model Criminal Antitrust Jury Instructions* 1984. Author "The Paramount Decrees: A Golden Anniversary" American Bar Association Section of Antitrust Journal 1988 and "Why Didn't I think of That?—Think the Unthinkable and Achieve Creative Greatness" Prentice Hall 2002. Adjunct Professor of Law Pepperdine University School of Law 1995. Captain USMC 1968-72.

Office: Central Civil West, 600 South Commonwealth, Los Angeles 90005.

Telephone: (213) 351-8739.

McDANIEL, Robert E. *(Judge, Superior Court of California County of Kern)* Assumed office July 1, 2000. Serves Delano-McFarland Branch. Former Judge, North Kern Municipal Court Kern County.

Office: 1122 Jefferson Avenue, Delano 93215.

Telephone: (661) 725-8797.

McDONALD, Alex C. *(Associate Justice, California Court of Appeal Fourth District Division One)* Appointed by Governor Pete Wilson to term beginning June 1995. Retained by election Nov 2002, current term expires Jan 2015. Born Butte Montana Nov 22, 1936. Educated at Stanford University B.S. 1958, University of California Boalt Hall School of Law LL.B. 1961 and University of Virginia School of Law LL.M. 2001. Revising Editor California Law Review. Law Clerk to Hon Raymond E. Peters, California Supreme Court. Member Order of the Coif. In legal practice California 1963-95.

Office: 750 B Street, Suite 300, San Diego 92101.

Telephone: (619) 645-2757.

McEACHEN, David Thomas *(Judge, Superior Court of California County of Orange)* Appointed by Governor Pete Wilson to term beginning Nov 29, 1993. Elected 1994 and 2000. Current term expires Jan 2007. Serves Criminal Panel since 1993 and Civil Panel since 1998. Started Orange County Drug Court March 1995. Supervising Judge Civil Panel since 2001. Assistant Presiding Judge 2002. Born Los Angeles California July 4, 1942. Roman Catholic. Educated at Oregon State University B.S. 1964 and Southwestern University School of Law J.D. 1974. Member Phi Kappa Phi. Admitted to practice California 1975, U.S. District Court Central District of California 1975 and U.S. Supreme Court 1985. In legal practice Long Beach 1975-79. Judge Jan 24, 1990 to Nov 29, 1993 and Presiding Judge 1993, North Orange County Municipal Court, appointed by Governor George Deukmejian.

Attorney Community Bank 1979-90. Board of Governors Association of Business Trial Lawyers of Orange County 2001. Former Member Long Beach and Los Angeles County Bar Associations. Fellow and Board Trustee since 1994 Orange County Bar Foundation. Member Robert A. Banyard American Inns of Court (President 2000-01), California Judges Association, Orange County and American Bar Associations. Participant Judicial Orientation 1990, Judicial College (Attended 1990, Seminar Leader 1993), Presiding Judges Roles—Management of the Courts 1992 and Civil Law and Procedure 1993 California Center for Judicial Education and Research and Mid-year Conference 1990-93 and Annual Conference 1991-93 California Judges Association. Named Man of the Year by Long Beach Junior Chamber of Commerce 1990, Outstanding Judicial Officer by Southwestern University School of Law 1997 and Judge of the Year by Business Litigation Section Orange County Bar Association 1999, by Orange County Trial Lawyers Association 2000 and by Hispanic Bar Association of Orange County. Recipient Judge George Francis Civility Award from American Board of Trial Advocates 2001 and Judicial

MCEACHEN, DAVID THOMAS—*Continued*
Civility Award from Robert A. Banyard American Inns of Court 2002. Lieutenant USN Vietnam 1964-69. Recipient National Defense Ribbon and Vietnam Service Ribbon. Insurance Agent Hamman, Miller & Beauchamp 1969-71. Republican. Director 1969-70 and Member 1969-71 Long Beach Junior Chamber of Commerce. Member St. Hedwig Church Parish Council 1975-78. Member 1975-79 and Vice President 1976-77 Long Beach Kiwanis. Director Rossmoor Homeowners Association 1988-89. Director since 1995 and Member Community Service Programs, Inc. Governing Board since 1994 and Member Victim/Witness Assistance Program. Enjoys golf, bicycling, backpacking, playing basketball and racquetball.

Mailing address: P.O. Box 1994, Santa Ana 92702-1994.

Office: Central Justice Center, 700 Civic Center Drive West, Santa Ana 92701.

Telephone: (714) 834-3734.

McEACHEN, Richard A. *(Judge, Superior Court of California County of Shasta)* Appointed by Governor George Deukmejian to term beginning July 1, 1986. Elected Nov 1988, Nov 1994 and 2000. Current term expires Jan 2007. Former Presiding Judge. Educated at University of California at Santa Barbara B.A. 1970 and Loyola University of Los Angeles J.D. 1973. Admitted to practice California 1973. Judge, Anderson Justice Court Shasta County Jan 1979 to July 1986.

Deputy District Attorney San Bernardino County 1973-75 and Shasta County 1975-78. Instructor Shasta College 1975-79.

Office: 1500 Court Street, Redding 96001-1685.

Telephone: (530) 225-5714.

McEWEN, Willard W., Jr. *(Magistrate Judge, United States District Court Central District of California)* Appointed by U.S. District Court judges to term beginning June 25, 1973. Reappointed June 1977, 1981, 1985, 1989, 1994 and 2001. Current term expires 2006. Serves part time. Born Dec 26, 1934. Catholic. Educated at Claremont Men's College B.S. 1956 and Hastings College of the Law LL.B. 1960. Admitted to practice California 1960. In legal practice Santa Barbara 1962. Judge pro tem, Santa Barbara Juvenile Court and Superior Court 1970-72.

Deputy Legislative Counsel Sacramento 1960-61. Assistant City Attorney Santa Barbara 1961-62. Member Santa Barbara County 1961-76 and American 1969-76 Bar Associations. Lecturer for the Santa Barbara Adult Education Program on Landlord-Tenant Problems, Real Estate Syndicates, Truth-in-Lending, Estate Planning and Trial Practice. Former Santa Barbara Young Man of the Year. Recipient Distinguished Service Award from Junior Chamber of Commerce 1965. U.S. Army Infantry 1957-58 and Captain USAR 1958-64. Republican. Member Santa Barbara Kiwanis Club (President 1967) and Santa Barbara City Landmarks Advisory Committee 1963-67. Vice President Santa Barbara Harbor Pageants and Exhibits 1964. Chairman Citizens "Save Our Shoreline" Committee 1964, Citizens Community Master Plan Committee 1964, YMCA Membership Drive 1964 and Citizens Advisory Committee on School District Tax Needs 1965. Commissioner Santa Barbara City Water Commission 1965 and Recreation Commission City of Santa Barbara 1970-73. Advisory Board Southern California Auto Club since 1991. Member Santa Barbara Chamber of Commerce (Vice President Board of Directors 1971-73, Chairman Committee on Local Government State Legislation Committee 1965-70 and President 1976), Santa Barbara Heart Association and Santa Barbara Council for the Retarded (Formed Corporation in 1964, Board of Directors for eight years).

Office: 8 East Figueroa Street, Suite 210, Santa Barbara 93101-2720.

Telephone: (805) 963-4325.

McFADDEN, Linda A. *(Judge, Superior Court of California County of Stanislaus)*

Office: 800 11th Street, Modesto 95354.

Telephone: (209) 558-6000.

McGEE, Kevin J. *(Judge, Superior Court of California County of Ventura)* Elected to term beginning Jan 1999. Term expires Jan 2005. Born Brawley California May 25, 1953. Educated at Loyola Marymount University B.A. magna cum laude 1976 and Loyola Law School J.D. cum laude 1979. Admitted to practice California 1979. In legal practice Los Angeles 1979-82.

Deputy District Attorney Ventura County 1982-98. Former Member Board of Directors Ventura County Bar Association. Member California Judges Association. Personal Statement or Quote: "Be ready."

Mailing address: P.O. Box 6489, Ventura 93006-6489.

Office: 800 South Victoria Avenue, Ventura 93009-0001.

Telephone: (805) 654-2983.

E-mail address: Kevin.McGee@mail.co.ventura.ca.us

McGIVERN, William T., Jr. *(Judge, Superior Court of California County of Marin)* Appointed by Governor Pete Wilson to term beginning Oct 31, 1997. Elected 1998, current term expires Jan 1, 2005. Born Evanston Illinois June 20, 1939. Roman Catholic. Educated at University of Notre Dame B.B.A. 1961, University of San Francisco School of Law J.D. 1970 and Georgetown University Law Center LL.M. 1971. Recipient University of San Francisco Award for Scholastic Achievement. Law Clerk to Hon. Samuel Conti, U.S. District Court Northern District of California 1971-73. Member McAuliffe Law Honor Society. Admitted to practice California 1971 and U.S. District Court Northern District of California 1973. In legal practice San Francisco Sept 1992 to Oct 1997.

Assistant U.S. Attorney Nov 1973 to March 1990 and U.S. Attorney March 1990 to Aug 1992 Northern District of California. Member California Judges Association. Republican. Lieutenant Senior Grade USN March 1962 to Aug 1965. Member California Tennis Club (Past President) and Lagunitas Country Club (Past President). Enjoys reading, traveling and playing tennis. Personal Statement or Quote: "Nothing is often a good thing to do, and always a brilliant thing to say" (Edward Bennett Williams, from his autobiography *The Man to See*).

Mailing address: P.O. Box 4988, San Rafael 94913-4988.

Office: 3501 Civic Center Drive, San Rafael 94903.

Telephone: (415) 499-3786.

Fax: (415) 499-7897

E-mail address: wmcgivern@marin.org

McGRATH, William J., Jr. *(Judge, Superior Court of California County of San Diego)* Assumed office Dec

MCGRATH, WILLIAM J., JR.—*Continued*

1, 1998. Former Judge and Presiding Judge, El Cajon Municipal Court San Diego County.
Mailing address: P.O. Box 122724, San Diego 92112-2724.
Office: 250 East Main Street, El Cajon 92020.
Telephone: (619) 441-4294.

McGUINESS, William R. *(Administrative Presiding Justice, California Court of Appeal First District and Presiding Justice, California Court of Appeal First District Division Three)* Appointed Associate Justice Division Four by Governor Pete Wilson to term beginning 1997. Retained by election. Presiding Justice Division Three since Dec 21, 1998. Administrative Presiding Justice First District since Jan 2002. Educated at Santa Clara University 1968 and University of San Francisco J.D. 1972. Judge 1986-97 and Presiding Judge 1994-95, Superior Court of California Alameda County.
Deputy District Attorney 1973-80 and Senior Deputy District Attorney 1980-83 Alameda County. Consultant U.S. Department of Justice 1982. Deputy Associate Attorney General and Associate Deputy Attorney General U.S. Department of Justice 1983-86. Member Appellate Indigent Defense Oversight Advisory Committee 1998-2002, Chair Subordinate Judicial Officer Working Group 2001-02, Member Administrative Presiding Justice Advisory Committee since 2002 and Former Member Trial Court Presiding Judges Standing Advisory Committee Judicial Council of California. Former Chair Alameda County Superior Court Executive Committee. Member Earl Warren American Inn of Court. Counsel to President's Task Force on Victims of Crime 1982.
Office: 350 McAllister Street, San Francisco 94102-3600.
Telephone: (415) 865-7300.

McGUIRE, James C. *(Judge, Superior Court of California County of San Bernardino)* Serves East Desert District.
Office: 6527 White Feather Road, Joshua Tree 92252.
Telephone: (760) 366-4112.

McILWRATH, Rolleen Kent *(Judge, Superior Court of California County of San Joaquin)* Assumed office June 8, 1998. Judge and Presiding Judge, Stockton Municipal Court San Joaquin County Jan 3, 1983 to June 7, 1998.
Office: 222 East Weber Avenue, Room 303, Stockton 95202.
Telephone: (209) 468-2827.

McINTYRE, James A. *(Associate Justice, California Court of Appeal Fourth District Division One)* Appointed by Governor Pete Wilson to term beginning June 1996. Retained by election Nov 1998 and Nov 2002. Current term expires Jan 2015. Educated at Brown University A.B. 1960 and Stanford University J.D. 1963. Admitted to practice California 1963 and U.S. Court of Appeals Ninth Circuit 1963. In legal practice San Diego 1963-93. Judge, Superior Court of California San Diego County 1993-96.
Adjunct Professor of Law University of San Diego School of Law. Fellow American College of Trial Lawyers. Master Enright Chapter American Inns of Court. Diplomate American Board of Trial Advocates. Listed in *The Best Lawyers in America* and *Who's Who Among Practicing Attorneys.* Little League Manager. Soccer Coach.
Office: 750 B Street, Suite 300, San Diego 92101-8196.
Telephone: (619) 645-2803.
Fax: (619) 645-2921

McINTYRE, Janice M. *(Judge, Superior Court of California County of Riverside)* Assumed office July 29, 1998. Elected 2002, current term expires Jan 2009. Born Jamaica New York Aug 23, 1948. Roman Catholic. Educated at Mount St. Mary's College B.A. magna cum laude 1971 and Loyola University School of Law J.D. cum laude 1975. Admitted to practice California 1975 and U.S. District Court Central District of California 1982. Began legal practice Riverside 1975. Judge April 1, 1981 to July 28, 1998 and Former Presiding Judge, Western Riverside County Municipal Court, appointed by Governor Edmund G. Brown, Jr.
Member Inland Counties Women at Law (Vice President 1980-81), California Women Lawyers, National Association of Women Judges and California Judges Association.
Office: Corona Court, 505 South Buena Vista Avenue, Corona 92882.
Telephone: (909) 272-5642.

McINTYRE, Robert J. *(Judge, Superior Court of California County of Riverside)* Former Judge, Desert Municipal Court Riverside County.
Office: Hall of Justice, 4100 Main Street, Riverside 92501.
Telephone: (909) 955-2300.

McKAY, Chesley, Jr. *(Judge, Superior Court of California County of Los Angeles)* Former Judge, Antelope Municipal Court Los Angeles County.
Office: Burbank Courthouse, 300 East Olive, Burbank 91502.
Telephone: (818) 356-3482.

McKAY, Patti Jo *(Judge, Superior Court of California County of Los Angeles)* Assumed office Jan 22, 2000. Former Judge, Los Angeles Municipal Court Los Angeles County.
Office: Courthouse, 111 North Hill Street, Los Angeles 90012.
Telephone: (213) 974-5411.

McKEAG, Jane Dickson *(Judge, United States Bankruptcy Court Eastern District of California)* Appointed by U.S. Court of Appeals Ninth Circuit judges.
Office: 3-200 U.S. Courthouse, 501 I Street, Sacramento 95814-2322.
Telephone: (916) 930-4521.

McKEE, Roger Curtis *(Recalled Magistrate Judge, United States District Court Southern District of California)* Appointed Magistrate Judge by U.S. District Court judges March 30, 1983. Appointed Recalled Magistrate Judge by the Judicial Council of the Ninth Circuit. Born Waterloo Iowa Feb 11, 1931. United Presbyterian (Former Moderator San Diego Presbytery). Educated at University of Northern Iowa B.A. 1955, University of Illinois M.A. 1959 and University of San Diego J.D. 1968. Admitted to practice California 1970. Began legal practice San Diego 1970.
Instructor National University 1972. Member State Bar of California and San Diego County Bar Association. In Industrial Relations 1960-69 and Division Staff

MCKEE, ROGER CURTIS—*Continued*

Attorney 1969-70 General Dynamics Corporation. Captain USNR since 1948 (active duty 1955-58). Member U.S. Navy League, Naval Reserve Association and Reserve Officers Association. Enjoys amateur radio, sailing, hiking, camping and foreign travel.

Office: 321 South Waterman Avenue, Suite 100, El Centro 92243-2264.

Telephone: (760) 353-1271.

McKENNEY, Kevin E. *(Judge, Superior Court of California County of Santa Clara)* Assumed office July 30, 1998. Former Judge, Santa Clara County Municipal Court.

Office: 191 North First Street, San Jose 95113.

Telephone: (408) 882-2100.

McKINSTER, Art W. *(Associate Justice, California Court of Appeal Fourth District Division Two)* Appointed by Governor George Deukmejian to term beginning Dec 27, 1990. Retained by election Nov 8, 1994, current term expires Jan 2007. Born Okmulgee Oklahoma. Educated at University of Southern California B.S. with honors 1968 and University of California Hastings College of the Law J.D. 1971. Judge, San Bernardino County Municipal Court Central Division 1984-85. Judge, Superior Court of California San Bernardino County 1985-90.

Trial Deputy District Attorney 1972-78, Supervising Deputy District Attorney 1977-78 and Chief Deputy District Attorney 1978-84 San Bernardino County. Member Library Technology Committee and Appellate Process Task Force Judicial Council of California. Member California Judges Association. Second Lieutenant USAR JAGC. Former Member Ontario Rotary Club (Vice President 1984) and Bureau of Franchises and Animal Advisory Commission City of San Bernardino. Former Board Member Home of Neighborly Service and San Bernardino Valley Community Concert Association (Vice President 1990). Interests include sports, the theater and working out at the gym.

Office: 3389 12th Street, Riverside 92501.

Telephone: (909) 248-0200.

McKINSTRY, William A. *(Judge, Superior Court of California County of Alameda)* Appointed by Governor George Deukmejian Oct 4, 1989. Elected 1990, 1996 and 2002. Current term expires Jan 2009. Presiding Judge Jan 1, 2000 to Dec 31, 2001. Born San Francisco California April 5, 1944. Roman Catholic. Educated at St. Mary's College of California B.S. 1965 and Hastings College of the Law J.D. 1968. Admitted to practice California 1969 and U.S. Supreme Court 1972. Judge, Oakland-Piedmont-Emeryville Municipal Court Alameda County 1985-89.

Deputy District Attorney 1969. Deputy Attorney General 1974. Senior Deputy District Attorney 1976. Chair Probate and Mental Health Advisory Committee 2000-01 and Member Executive Committee 2000-01 and Trial Court Presiding Judges Advisory Committee Judicial Council of California. Member State Bar of California (Governing Committee of Continuing Education of the Bar 1985-87, Chairman 1987) and Alameda County Bar Association (President 1982). Panelist and Moderator CEB since 1978. Chair Probate Institute California Center for Judicial Education and Research 1997. County Central Committee 1982-84. Advisor Explorer Post Boy Scouts of America 1983-87.

Office: 1225 Fallon Street, Room 209, Oakland 94612.

Telephone: (510) 272-6070, 272-6151.

McKNEW, Thomas I., Jr. *(Judge, Superior Court of California County of Los Angeles)* Appointed by Governor Pete Wilson to term beginning May 9, 1995. Elected Nov 1996 and 2002. Current term expires Jan 2009. Serves Southeast District. Born Washington D.C. June 8, 1936. Catholic. Educated at Benedictine College A.B. 1958 and University of Maryland J.D. 1960. University of Maryland Law Review 1958-59. Member Delta Theta Phi. Admitted to practice Maryland 1960, District of Columbia 1961, California 1966 and U.S. Supreme Court 1966. In legal practice Los Angeles California 1971-83 and 1989-95.

Attorney 1971-83 and Vice President 1983-88 Santa Fe Southern Pacific Corporation. Instructor in Business Law Los Angeles Southwest College 1971-83. Member Ball-Hunt Inn of Court, California Judges Association, The District of Columbia Bar, State Bar of California, Los Angeles County, Irish-American and American Bar Associations. Colonel USAFR JAG 1960-90. Councilman and Mayor Seal Beach 1970-76. Board member Benedictine College. Commodore of Yacht Club. Member Jonathan Club. Enjoys skiing, boating, golfing, fishing and reading.

Office: 12720 Norwalk Boulevard, Norwalk 90650.

Telephone: (562) 807-7326.

McLAFFERTY, J. William *(Judge, Superior Court of California County of Santa Barbara)*

Office: 1100 Anacapa Street, Santa Barbara 93101.

Telephone: (805) 568-2220.

McLAUGHLIN, Dennis J. *(Judge, Superior Court of California County of Alameda)* Assumed office July 31, 1998. Born San Jose California March 22, 1955. Roman Catholic. Educated at Santa Clara University B.S. with honors 1977 J.D. 1980. Member Phi Beta Kappa and Alpha Sigma Nu. Admitted to practice California 1980 and U.S. District Court Northern District of California 1980. Judge, Fremont-Newark-Union City Municipal Court Alameda County Dec 26, 1996 to July 30, 1998, appointed by Governor Pete Wilson.

Deputy District Attorney Alameda County 1980-96. Member California Judges Association and Alameda County Bar Association. Republican.

Office: Fremont Hall of Justice, 39439 Paseo Padre Parkway, Fremont 94538.

Telephone: (510) 795-2329.

McMAHON, James W. *(Magistrate Judge, United States District Court Central District of California)* Appointed by U.S. District Court judges.

Office: U.S. Courthouse, 312 North Spring Street, Los Angeles 90012.

Telephone: (213) 894-3598.

McMANUS, Michael S. *(Chief Judge, United States Bankruptcy Court Eastern District of California)* Appointed by U.S Court of Appeals Ninth Circuit judges to term beginning Jan 11, 1994. Term expires Jan 11, 2008. Chief Judge since Nov 1, 2000. Born Tampa Florida Aug 7, 1953. Educated at University of California at Berkeley with highest honors 1975 and University of California at Los Angeles J.D. 1978. Member Phi Beta

MCMANUS, MICHAEL S.—*Continued*

Kappa and Order of the Coif. Admitted to practice California 1978, U.S. District Court Eastern District of California 1980, U.S. Court of Appeals Ninth Circuit 1987 and U.S. Supreme Court 1992. In legal practice Tustin 1978-79 and Sacramento 1979-94.

Important Decisions: In re Rollins (trustee liability) 175 B.R. 69, 1994; In re Shandrew (treatment of mortgage claims in chapter 13) 210 B.R. 829, 1997; and In re Sargent Walnut Ranches (agricultural producer's liens) 219 B.R. 880, 1998.

Office: 3-200 U.S. Courthouse, 501 I Street, Sacramento 95814.

Telephone: (916) 930-4540.

Fax: (916) 930-4552

McMASTER, Loren E. *(Judge, Superior Court of California County of Sacramento)* Arbitrator 1980-88 and Judge pro tem 1988-99. Appointed by Governor Gray Davis to term beginning Nov 1999. Elected 2002, current term expires Jan 2009. Educated at University of California at Davis A.B. 1966 J.D. 1969. California State Scholar. Staff member University of California at Davis Law Review. Admitted to practice California, U.S. District Courts Central, Eastern, Northern and Southern Districts of California, U.S. Court of Appeals Ninth Circuit and U.S. Supreme Court. Certified Appellate Law Specialist State Bar of California Board of Legal Specialization. In legal practice 1980-99.

Deputy Attorney General California 1969-72. Attorney 1972-73 and Chief Counsel 1973-80 California State Employees Association. Author "Workmen's Compensation, Minimum Wage, and the Farm Worker" 2 University of California at Davis L. Rev. 113, 1969 and "Defending Civil Service Employees from Discharge" 24 American Journal of Trial Advocacy 421-553, 1977. Instructor Sacramento City College 1970-72. Member Appellate Court Committee State Bar of California 1979-81. Judicial Master The Anthony M. Kennedy American Inn of Court.

Office: Courthouse, 720 Ninth Street, Sacramento 95814.

Telephone: (916) 874-5476.

E-mail address: mcmastl@saccourt.com

McNATT, Bobby W. *(Judge, Superior Court of California County of San Joaquin)*

Office: 222 East Weber Avenue, Room 303, Stockton 95202.

Telephone: (209) 468-2827.

McNERNEY, Dan *(Judge, Superior Court of California County of Orange)*

Mailing address: P.O. Box 5000, Fullerton 92838-0500.

Office: North Justice Center, 1275 North Berkeley Avenue, Fullerton 92832.

Telephone: (714) 773-4400.

McNUTT, Charles P. *(Judge, Superior Court of California County of Kern)* Assumed office July 1, 2000. Born Delano California Sept 9, 1947. Educated at Bakersfield Junior College 1965-67, University of California at Davis B.A. 1969 J.D. 1972. Admitted to practice California 1972, U.S. Court of Appeals Ninth Circuit 1972 and U.S. District Court Eastern District of California 1972. In legal practice Delano 1974. Commissioner June 29, 1981 to Oct 15, 1982, Judge Oct 15, 1982 to June 30, 2000 and Presiding Judge July 1, 1998 to June 30, 1999, Bakersfield Municipal Court Kern County.

Deputy District Attorney Kern County 1972-81. Member California Judges Association. Republican. Former member Christian Reformed Church (Deacon 1973-76, Elder 1977-80). Member University Baptist Church (Vice Moderator 1989-90). Enjoys woodworking, camping and fishing.

Office: 1415 Truxtun Avenue, Bakersfield 93301.

Telephone: (661) 868-4934.

McPETERS, Roberta *(Judge, Superior Court of California County of San Bernardino)* Presiding Judge Jan 1, 2000 to Dec 31, 2001. Former Judge, San Bernardino County Municipal Court.

Office: 351 North Arrowhead Avenue, San Bernardino 92415-0240.

Telephone: (909) 387-3922.

MEEGAN, Cheryl Chun *(Judge, Superior Court of California County of Sacramento)* Assumed office June 17, 1998. Former Judge, Sacramento Municipal Court Sacramento County.

Office: Courthouse, 720 Ninth Street, Sacramento 95814.

Telephone: (916) 874-5476.

MEEKA, Peter Joseph *(Judge, Superior Court of California County of Los Angeles)* Assumed office Jan 22, 2000. Former Judge and Presiding Judge, Rio Hondo Municipal Court Los Angeles County.

Office: Pomona Courthouse South, 400 Civic Center Plaza, Pomona 91766.

Telephone: (909) 620-3023.

MEEKS, Perker L., Jr. *(Judge, Superior Court of California City and County of San Francisco)* Assumed office Dec 31, 1998. Former Judge, San Francisco Municipal Court San Francisco County.

Office: Civic Center Courthouse, 400 McAllister Street, San Francisco 94102-4514.

Telephone: (415) 551-4020.

MEIERS, Barbara Ann *(Judge, Superior Court of California County of Los Angeles)* Assumed office Jan 22, 2000. Former Judge, Los Angeles Municipal Court Los Angeles County.

Office: Courthouse, 111 North Hill Street, Los Angeles 90012.

Telephone: (213) 974-5411.

MEIGS, John Vernon *(Judge, Superior Court of California County of Los Angeles)* Assumed office Jan 22, 2000. Presiding Judge Jan 1, 1994 to Dec 31, 1996 and Former Judge, Inglewood Municipal Court Los Angeles County.

Office: Inglewood Courthouse, One Regent Street, Inglewood 90301.

Telephone: (310) 419-5121.

MELLON, Thomas J., Jr. *(Judge, Superior Court of California City and County of San Francisco)*

Office: Civic Center Courthouse, 400 McAllister Street, San Francisco 94102-4514.

Telephone: (415) 551-4020.

MELVILLE, Rodney S. *(Judge, Superior Court of California County of Santa Barbara)* Appointed by Governor George Deukmejian to term beginning Nov 26, 1990. Elected 1992 and 1998. Current term expires Jan 2005. Presiding Judge Jan 1, 2001 to Dec 31, 2002.

MELVILLE, RODNEY S.—*Continued*

Born Douglas Arizona June 7, 1941. Protestant. Educated at San Diego State University B.A. 1965 and University of California Hastings College of the Law J.D. 1968. Member Phi Alpha Delta. Admitted to practice California 1969, U.S. District Court Central District of California 1972 and U.S. Supreme Court 1983. In legal practice Santa Maria 1972-87. Judge, Santa Maria Municipal Court Santa Barbara County 1987-90.

Deputy District Attorney San Bernardino 1969-71 and Santa Barbara County 1971-72. Member Santa Maria-Lompoc Bar Association (President 1987) and Santa Barbara County Bar Association. Graduate California Judges College 1988. USNR 1959-61. Republican. Member Republican Central Committee Santa Barbara County. Trustee Orcutt Union School District 1973-77. Enjoys horses and photography.

Office: 312-H East Cook Street, Santa Maria 93454.
Telephone: (805) 346-7414.

MENDEZ, John A. *(Judge, Superior Court of California County of Sacramento)*

Office: Courthouse, 720 Ninth Street, Sacramento 95814.
Telephone: (916) 874-5476.

MENINGER, Kimberly *(Judge, Superior Court of California County of Orange)*

Mailing address: P.O. Box 1994, Santa Ana 92702-1994.
Office: Central Justice Center, 700 Civic Center Drive West, Santa Ana 92701.
Telephone: (714) 834-3734.

METTLER, Sharon *(Judge, Superior Court of California County of Kern)* Assumed office July 1, 2000. Born Bakersfield California June 29, 1948. United Methodist. Educated at University of California Hastings College of the Law J.D. 1973. Member Order of the Coif. Judge, Bakersfield Municipal Court Kern County July 10, 1981 to June 30, 2000, appointed by Governor Edmund G. Brown, Jr.

President Santa Barbara County Barristers 1976 and Kern County Women Lawyers Association 1981.

Office: 1215 Truxtun Avenue, Bakersfield 93301.
Telephone: (661) 868-2450.

MEWHINNEY, Douglas V. *(Judge, Superior Court of California County of Calaveras)* Assumed office June 3, 1998. Presiding Judge Jan 1, 1999 to Dec 31, 2000 and since Jan 1, 2003. Former Judge, Calaveras County Municipal Court.

Office: 891 Mountain Ranch Road, San Andreas 95249.
Telephone: (209) 754-6311.

MEYER, Gary E. *(Judge, Superior Court of California County of Monterey)* Assumed office Dec 18, 2000. Former Judge, Monterey County Municipal Court.

Mailing address: P.O. Box 1819, Salinas 93902-1819.
Office: 240 Church Street, Salinas 93901.
Telephone: (831) 755-5060.

MEYER, John *(Judge, Superior Court of California County of San Diego)*

Mailing address: P.O. Box 122724, San Diego 92112-2724.
Office: 330 West Broadway, San Diego 92101.
Telephone: (619) 685-6148.

MEYERS, James W. *(Judge, United States Bankruptcy Court Southern District of California)* Former Chief Judge. Former Chief Judge, Bankruptcy Appellate Panel Ninth Circuit.

Office: U.S. Courthouse, 325 West F Street, San Diego 92101-6989.
Telephone: (619) 557-7642.

MEYERS, Patrick Timothy *(Judge, Superior Court of California County of Los Angeles)*

Office: Norwalk Courthouse, 12720 Norwalk Boulevard, Norwalk 90650.
Telephone: (562) 807-7266.

MEZA, Amalia *(Judge, Superior Court of California County of San Diego)*

Mailing address: P.O. Box 122724, San Diego 92112-2724.
Office: 325 South Melrose Drive, Vista 92083.
Telephone: (760) 726-9595.

MIHARA, Nathan D. *(Associate Justice, California Court of Appeal Sixth District)* Appointed by Governor Pete Wilson to term beginning 1993. Retained by election. Educated at University of Washington B.A. 1972 and University of California Hastings College of the Law J.D. 1975. Admitted to practice California 1976, U.S. Court of Appeals Ninth Circuit 1976 and U.S. Supreme Court 1980. In legal practice Menlo Park. Judge, Santa Clara County Municipal Court 1985-88, appointed by Governor George Deukmejian. Judge, Superior Court of California Santa Clara County 1988-93, appointed by Governor George Deukmejian.

Deputy Attorney General California. Member Appellate Process Task Force, California Judges Association, Asian Pacific Bar Association of Silicon Valley and Santa Clara County Bar Association (Law Related Education Committee, Minority Access Committee). Board of Directors Sentencing Alternatives Program since 1995. Active with Little League Baseball, American Youth Soccer Association and Mount Hermon Association.

Office: 333 West Santa Clara Street, Suite 1060, San Jose 95113.
Telephone: (408) 277-1004.

MILES, Marilyn B. *(Judge, Superior Court of California County of Humboldt)* Elected to term beginning Jan 6, 1997. Reelected 2002, current term expires Jan 2009. Presiding Judge since July 1, 2002. Educated at San Jose State University B.A. with honors 1968, Humboldt State University M.A. 1971 and University of California at Davis J.D. 1980. Staff Member University of California at Davis Law Review 1978-79. Law Clerk to Hon. Cruz Reynoso, California Court of Appeal Third District 1979-80. Member Phi Kappa Phi. Admitted to practice California 1980, U.S. District Courts Northern 1980 and Eastern 1981 Districts of California, U.S. Court of Appeals Ninth Circuit 1982, U.S. Court of Claims 1985 and U.S. Supreme Court 1987. In legal practice Eureka 1980-96. Former Judge, Humboldt County Municipal Court.

Former Directing Attorney California Indian Legal Services. Author "Symposium on Children and the Law" University of California at Davis L. Rev. 1997. Member California Judges Association. Attended B. E. Witkin Judicial College California Center for Judicial Education and Research 1997. Recipient President's Pro Bono

MILES, MARILYN B.—*Continued*

Service Award from Board of Governors State Bar of California.
Office: 825 Fifth Street, Eureka 95501.
Telephone: (707) 269-1294.

MILLER, Barbara J. *(Judge, Superior Court of California County of Alameda)*
Office: Hayward Hall of Justice, 24405 Amador Street, Hayward 94544.
Telephone: (510) 670-5060.

MILLER, Douglas P. *(Judge, Superior Court of California County of Riverside)* Assumed office July 29, 1998. Presiding Judge since Jan 1, 2003. Former Judge, Desert Municipal Court Riverside County.
Office: 310 Court Executive Office, 4075 Main Street, Riverside 92501.
Telephone: (909) 955-5536.

MILLER, Franz E. *(Judge, Superior Court of California County of Orange)*
Mailing address: P.O. Box 14169, Orange 92863-1569.
Office: Lamoreaux Justice Center, 341 The City Drive, Orange 92868.
Telephone: (714) 935-7236.

MILLER, Jeffrey T. *(Judge, United States District Court Southern District of California)* Appointed for life by President Bill Clinton. Educated at University of California at Los Angeles B.A. 1964 J.D. 1967. Admitted to practice California 1968. Former Judge, Superior Court of California San Diego County, appointed by Governor George Deukmejian to term beginning Feb 7, 1987.
Office: 3142 U.S. Courthouse, 940 Front Street, San Diego 92101.
Telephone: (619) 557-6627.

MILLER, Linda Lancet *(Judge, Superior Court of California County of Orange)* Assumed office Aug 10, 1998. Former Judge, North Orange County Municipal Court.
Mailing address: P.O. Box 14169, Orange 92863-1569.
Office: Lamoreaux Justice Center, 341 The City Drive, Orange 92868.
Telephone: (714) 935-7236.

MILLER, Rita J. *(Judge, Superior Court of California County of Los Angeles)*
Office: Criminal Courts Building, 210 West Temple Street, Los Angeles 90012-3210.
Telephone: (213) 974-6535.

MILLER, Stephen E. *(Magistrate Judge, United States District Court Central District of California)* Appointed by U.S. District Court judges to term beginning Jan 12, 1998. Reappointed Jan 2002, current term expires Jan 2006. Serves part time.
Mailing address: P.O. Box 6425, San Bernardino 92412.
Telephone: (909) 884-6254.

MILLIKEN, James R. *(Judge, Superior Court of California County of San Diego)* Former Presiding Judge.
Office: 2851 Meadowlark Drive, San Diego 92123.
Telephone: (858) 694-4601.

MILLS, Bruce Clayton *(Judge, Superior Court of California County of Contra Costa)* Assumed office June 8, 1998. Presiding Judge Jan 1, 1996 to Dec 31, 1996 and Former Judge, Walnut Creek-Danville Municipal Court Contra Costa County.
Mailing address: P.O. Box 5128, Walnut Creek 94596.
Office: 640 Ygnacio Valley Road, Walnut Creek 94596.
Telephone: (925) 646-6763.

MILLS, Cheryl *(Judge, Superior Court of California County of Contra Costa)*
Office: Courts Building, 1020 Ward Street, Martinez 94553.
Telephone: (925) 646-2950.

MILLS, Richard E. *(Judge, Superior Court of California County of San Diego)*ailing address: P.O. Box 122724, San Diego 92112-2724.
Office: 325 South Melrose Drive, Vista 92083.
Telephone: (760) 726-9595.

MILTON, David Sherman *(Judge, Superior Court of California County of Los Angeles)*
Office: Courthouse, 111 North Hill Street, Los Angeles 90012.
Telephone: (213) 974-5411.

MINIER, David D. *(Judge, Superior Court of California County of Madera)* Assumed office July 1, 1998. Former Judge, Madera County Municipal Court.
Office: 209 West Yosemite Avenue, Madera 93637.
Telephone: (559) 675-7907.

MINK, Michael S. *(Judge, Superior Court of California County of Los Angeles)* Assumed office Jan 22, 2000. Former Judge, Los Angeles Municipal Court Los Angeles County.
Office: Burbank Courthouse, 300 East Olive, Burbank 91502.
Telephone: (818) 356-3482.

MINNEY, John C. *(Judge, Superior Court of California County of Contra Costa)* Presiding Judge Jan 1, 1995 to Dec 31, 1996. Born Berkeley California Oct 3, 1933. Presbyterian. Educated at Yale University B.A. 1955 and Boalt Hall School of Law J.D. 1958. Admitted to practice California 1959. Former Judge, Walnut Creek-Danville Municipal Court Contra Costa County, appointed by Governor Ronald Reagan to term beginning Jan 3, 1975.
Member California Judges Association (Executive Board 1982-84, Secretary-Treasurer 1984-85). Republican. Board of Directors Alcoholism Council of Contra Costa County 1976-79, Alcohol and Drug Abuse Council of Contra Costa County 1979-87 and Friends Outside of Contra Costa County since 1990.
Office: A. F. Bray Courts Building, 1020 Ward Street, Martinez 94553.
Telephone: (925) 646-4012.

MINNING, David L. *(Judge, Superior Court of California County of Los Angeles)* Assumed office Jan 22, 2000. Former Judge, Los Angeles Municipal Court Los Angeles County.
Office: Courthouse, 111 North Hill Street, Los Angeles 90012.
Telephone: (213) 974-5411.

MINTO, R. Bruce *(Judge, Superior Court of California County of Los Angeles)* Assumed office Jan 22, 2000. Former Judge and Presiding Judge, Citrus Municipal Court Los Angeles County.
Office: Pomona Courthouse South, 400 Civic Center Plaza, Pomona 91766.
Telephone: (909) 620-3023.

MINTZ, David *(Judge, Superior Court of California County of Los Angeles)*
Office: Criminal Courts Building, 210 West Temple Street, Los Angeles 90012-3210.
Telephone: (213) 974-6535.

MIRA, Lawrence J. *(Judge, Superior Court of California County of Los Angeles)* Assumed office Jan 22, 2000. Former Judge, Malibu Municipal Court Los Angeles County.
Office: Malibu Courthouse, 23525 West Civic Center Way, Malibu 90265.
Telephone: (310) 317-1310.

MIRAM, George A. *(Judge, Superior Court of California County of San Mateo)* Assumed office June 12, 1998. Former Judge, San Mateo County Municipal Court.
Office: Hall of Justice, 400 County Center, Redwood City 94063.
Telephone: (650) 363-4516.

MIRELES, Raymond D. *(Judge, Superior Court of California County of Los Angeles)* Former Judge, East Los Angeles Municipal Court Los Angeles County.
Office: Pasadena Courthouse, 300 East Walnut Street, Pasadena 91101.
Telephone: (626) 356-5689.

MIRICH, Peter J. *(Judge, Superior Court of California County of Los Angeles)* Assumed office Jan 22, 2000. Former Judge, Los Angeles Municipal Court Los Angeles County.
Office: San Pedro Courthouse, 505 South Centre Street, San Pedro 90731-3332.
Telephone: (310) 519-6013.

MITCHELL, Charlene P. *(Judge, Superior Court of California City and County of San Francisco)* Assumed office Dec 31, 1998. Former Judge, San Francisco Municipal Court San Francisco County.
Office: Civic Center Courthouse, 400 McAllister Street, San Francisco 94102-4514.
Telephone: (415) 551-4020.

MITCHELL, Donald S. *(Judge, Superior Court of California City and County of San Francisco)*
Office: Civic Center Courthouse, 400 McAllister Street, San Francisco 94102-4514.
Telephone: (415) 551-4020.

MITCHELL, Thomas R. *(Judge, Superior Court of California County of San Diego)*
Mailing address: P.O. Box 122724, San Diego 92112-2724.
Office: 1409 Fourth Avenue, San Diego 92101.
Telephone: (619) 687-2292.

MITTLESTEADT, Carol L. *(Judge, Superior Court of California County of San Mateo)*
Office: Hall of Justice, 400 County Center, Redwood City 94063.
Telephone: (650) 363-4516.

MIZE, James M. *(Judge, Superior Court of California County of Sacramento)*
Office: 3341 Power Inn Road, Sacramento 95826.
Telephone: (916) 875-3400.

MOBERLY, Jamoa A. *(Judge, Superior Court of California County of Orange)* Assumed office Aug 10, 1998. Former Judge, Harbor Municipal Court Orange County.
Office: Harbor Justice Center, 4601 Jamboree Road, Newport Beach 92660-2595.
Telephone: (949) 476-4699.

MOCK, Stephen L. *(Judge, Superior Court of California County of Yolo)* Elected to term beginning Jan 7, 1991. Reelected 1996 and 2002. Current term expires Jan 2009. Born San Francisco California March 27, 1946. Educated at University of California at Davis B.A. 1968 and University of California Boalt Hall School of Law J.D. 1971. Admitted to practice California 1971 and Alaska 1972. Enjoys long distance running, backpacking and biking.
Office: 725 Court Street, Woodland 95695.
Telephone: (530) 666-8598.

MOELK, James F. *(Judge, Superior Court of California County of Solano)* Presiding Judge Jan 1, 1996 to Dec 31, 1996.
Office: 600 Union Avenue, Fairfield 94533-5000.
Telephone: (707) 421-7827.

MOENCH, Romero J. *(Judge, Superior Court of California County of Kern)* Assumed office July 1, 2000. Serves Maricopa-Taft Branch. Presiding Judge Jan 1, 1996 to Dec 31, 1996 and Jan 1, 2000 to June 30, 2000 and Former Judge, South Kern Municipal Court Kern County.
Office: 311 North Lincoln Street, Taft 93268.
Telephone: (661) 763-8566.
Fax: (661) 763-2439

MOFFAT, Edward P., II *(Judge, Superior Court of California County of Madera)* Appointed by Governor George Deukmejian to term beginning Dec 22, 1986. Elected Nov 4, 1986 to term beginning Jan 1, 1987. Reelected 1992 and 1998. Current term expires Jan 2005. Presiding Judge 1989, 1991, 1996, 1997 and since Jan 1, 2002. Judge 1986-2003 and Presiding Judge 1989-2002 Appellate Division Madera Courts. Judge Appellate Department Mariposa County since 1989. Born Denver Colorado Dec 20, 1946. Roman Catholic. Educated at St. Mary's College of California B.S. 1969 and Golden Gate University J.D. 1972. Staff member Golden Gate Law Review 1972. Admitted to practice California 1972, U.S. District Courts Northern 1972 and Eastern 1979 Districts of California, U.S. Court of Appeals Ninth Circuit 1972 and U.S. Supreme Court 1980. In legal practice Sanger and Kingsburg 1974. Justice pro tem, California Court of Appeal Fifth District 1993-95 and 2000.
Deputy District Attorney Madera County 1973-74 and 1975-77. Deputy Public Defender Madera County 1975 and Tulare County 1977-79. Assistant Federal Defender 1979-83. Assistant U.S. Attorney 1983-85. Deputy Chief, Criminal Division U.S. Attorney's Office 1985-86. Instructor Armstrong College of Law Fresno 1974-75. Graduate California Judicial College 1988 and Special Training in Family Law California Center for Judicial Education and Research 1989. Seminar Leader Cow County Judges Conference 1990. Recipient Catholic Man

MOFFAT, EDWARD P., II—*Continued*

of the Year Award from Young Men's Institute 1979. Democrat. First Vice President Madera Chapter Italian Catholic Federation. Judge Mock Trial Competition Madera County Department of Education Program. Member Madera Elks, Madera Trade Club, St. Joachim's Parish Council and School Board, Knights of Columbus, Young Men's Institute (Grand Council), Little League, Italo-American Club, Pan American Club and Italian Catholic Federation. Enjoys sports, travel and cooking.

Office: 209 West Yosemite Avenue, Madera 93637.

Telephone: (559) 675-7907.

MOHR, Anthony J. *(Judge, Superior Court of California County of Los Angeles)* Appointed by Governor Pete Wilson Dec 23, 1997. Serves Central District. Born Los Angeles California May 11, 1947. Jewish. Educated at Wesleyan University B.A. cum laude with Honors in Government 1969, Faculté Internationale pour l'Enseignement du Droit Comparé, Mondovi Italy, Diploma with Honors in comparative law 1975 and Columbia University School of Law J.D. 1972. Associate Editor Columbia Journal of Transnational Law. Law Clerk to Hon. A. Andrew Hauk, U.S. District Court Central District of California 1972-73. Member Phi Beta Kappa and Phi Delta Phi. Admitted to practice California 1972, District of Columbia 1976 and U.S. Supreme Court 1981. In legal practice Los Angeles and Beverly Hills 1973-94. Former Judge, Los Angeles Municipal Court Los Angeles County, appointed by Governor Pete Wilson.

Editorial Board Los Angeles County Bar Journal 1973-74, California State Bar Journal 1979-80 and Los Angeles Lawyer 1990-94. Co-author "Legal Education: Some Student Reflections" 25 Journal of Legal Education 403, 1973, "Constitutional and Procedural Aspects of Employee Access to the Federal Courts: Promotion and Termination" 8 Valparaiso L. Rev. 303, 1974, "The Unruh Civil Rights Act: Just How Far Does It Reach?" 11 Beverly Hills B. Jour. 32, 1977 and "The Child Neglect and Abuse Annual Review in California" 3 Journal of Juvenile Law 31, 1979. Co-editor "Symposium on Juvenile Justice" Los Angeles Bar Bulletin Feb 1975. Author "Litigating Finder's Fee Disputes" 14 Southwestern University L. Rev. 65, 1984, "Liability of Political Candidates and Their Staffs for Campaign Committee Obligations" 15 Pepperdine L. Rev. 33, 1987 and "Suits Against Remote Business Entities" Los Angeles Lawyer March 1993. Faculty Member Attorney Assistant Training Program University of California at Los Angeles 1982-97. Chairperson Committee on Judicial Selection, Compensation and Tenure Young Lawyers Division American Bar Association 1980-83. Board of Directors American Judicature Society 1982-83. Member California Judges Association (Ethics Committee since 2001), Beverly Hills (Board of Governors 1975-80, President Barristers 1979-80, Chair Section on Litigation 1983-86 and Delegation to State Bar Conference of Delegates 1992) and Los Angeles County (Vice Chair Committee on Mandatory Fee Arbitration 1991-94) Bar Associations. Attended California Judicial College June 1995, The Hague Academy of International Law 2000 and Academy of European Law 2002. Panelist on 1986 Discovery Act, Malicious Prosecution, "Hard Depositions" and Settlements Beverly Hills Bar Association and Colorado Conference of World Affairs 2002. Instructor in Ethics and Evidence California Center for Judicial Education and Research. Recipient Distinguished Service Award from Beverly Hills Bar Association 1992. Member Republican State Central Committee 1975-76. Delegate White House Conference on Youth 1971. Member 1974-99 and Panelist on Alcohol, Drugs and the Criminal Courts Annual Student Symposium on the Presidency March 17, 1996 Center for the Study of the Presidency National Advisory Council. Participant National Security Seminar of U.S. Army War College 1976 and National Security Forum of the U.S. Air War College 1984. Board of Directors Mental Health Advisory Services 1982-94, Technion 2000, 1984-97, UCLA International Student Center since 1986 and Performing Tree since 1996. Board of Liaison Citizenship Program 1993-2000. Enjoys sailing, hiking, reading and traveling.

Office: 600 South Commonwealth, Los Angeles 90005.

Telephone: (213) 351-8590.

MONEY, Christopher G. *(Judge, Superior Court of California County of San Luis Obispo)* Former Presiding Judge. Former Judge, San Luis Obispo County Municipal Court.

Office: County Government Center, 1035 Palm Street, San Luis Obispo 93408-2500.

Telephone: (805) 781-5421.

MONROE, William M. *(Judge, Superior Court of California County of Orange)*

Mailing address: P.O. Box 1994, Santa Ana 92702-1994.

Office: Central Justice Center, 700 Civic Center Drive West, Santa Ana 92701.

Telephone: (714) 834-3734.

MONTALI, Dennis *(Judge, United States Bankruptcy Court Northern District of California)* Appointed by U.S. Court of Appeals Ninth Circuit judges to term beginning April 23, 1993. Also Judge, Bankruptcy Appellate Panel Ninth Circuit. Selected by the Judicial Council of the Ninth Circuit. Educated at University of Notre Dame B.A. 1961 and University of California at Berkeley J.D. 1968.

Mailing address: P.O. Box 7341, San Francisco 94120-7341.

Telephone: (415) 268-2320.

MOODY, Robert F. *(Judge, Superior Court of California County of Monterey)* Former Judge and Presiding Judge, Monterey County Municipal Court.

Mailing address: P.O. Box 1819, Salinas 93902-1819.

Office: 240 Church Street, Salinas 93901.

Telephone: (831) 755-5060.

MOONEY, Mark V. *(Judge, Superior Court of California County of Los Angeles)* Former Judge, Los Angeles Municipal Court Los Angeles County.

Office: Criminal Courts Building, 210 West Temple Street, Los Angeles 90012-3210.

Telephone: (213) 974-6535.

MOORE, Eileen C. *(Associate Justice, California Court of Appeal Fourth District Division Three)* Appointed by Governor Gray Davis to term beginning 2000. Educated at University of California at Irvine B.A. cum laude 1975 and Pepperdine University J.D. 1978. Recipient American Jurisprudence Award for Civil Procedure 1978. In legal practice 1978-89. Judge, Superior Court of California County of Orange 1989-2000.

MOORE, EILEEN C.—*Continued*

Assigned Judge, California Court of Appeal Fourth District Four Division Three 1993.

Contributing Editor *California Civil Practice Series* Bancroft Whitney. Author "Courtroom Procedures to Accommodate the Deaf" *Los Angeles Daily Journal* Dec 1990, "Experts Shouldn't Be Advocates" *Los Angeles Times* Opinion-Editorial Section Oct 25, 1995, "Restraining Orders: The E.R. of the Courthouse" California Lawyer Sept 1996, "Domestic Violence and Stalking" *Litigation Magazine* Spring/Summer 1998, "Family Violence Solutions Can Be Adaptable" *Los Angeles Times* Aug 1998, "Different Practices for Different Practices" *ABTL Newsletter* March 2000 and "Judicial Voir Dire More Important Than Ever" *Litigation Magazine* Spring/Summer 2000. Lecturer School of Management University of California at Irvine. Member Advisory Committee on Interpreters for the Deaf and Advisory Committee on Civil and Small Claims California Judicial Council. Member Trial Practice Inn of Court Los Angeles County Bar Association, Robert A. Banyard Inn of Court (President 1992-94) and California Judges Association (Chair Civil Law and Procedures Committee 1991-92). Faculty member Center for Judicial Education and Research. Recipient Distinguished Alumna Award from University of California at Irvine 1992, Alumnus of the Year Award from Pepperdine University School of Law 1993, Judge of the Year Award from Orange County Women Lawyers 1993, Award for work in preventing domestic violence from Laura's House 1999, George Francis Civility Award from Orange County Chapter American Board of Trial Advocates 1999 and Trial Judge of the Year Award from Consumer Attorneys Association of Los Angeles 2000. Second Lieutenant U.S. Army Nurse Corps. Recipient Vietnam Service Medal and National Defense Service Medal. Registered Nurse since 1965. Volunteer Stay-in-School Program 1990-95 and Operation Jumpstart 1995-96. Member Task Force on Violence to Women 1995. Chair Orange County Family Violence Council since 1995. Member Board of Visitors Pepperdine University and Vietnam Veterans of America.

Mailing address: P.O. Box 22055, Santa Ana 92702.
Telephone: (714) 558-6777.
E-mail address: eileen.moore@jud.ca.gov

MORAN, John P. *(Judge, Superior Court of California County of Tulare)* Appointed by Governor George Deukmejian to term beginning Nov 3, 1986. Elected to subsequent terms. Born Los Angeles California Dec 26, 1931. Educated at Stanford University A.B. 1954 LL.B. 1958. Admitted to practice California 1959. In legal practice Porterville 1959-86.

Member State Bar of California and Tulare County Bar Association. First Lieutenant U.S. Army 1954-56.

Office: Tulare County Civic Center, Visalia 93291-4593.

Telephone: (559) 733-6561.

MORENO, Carlos R. *(Associate Justice, California Supreme Court)* Appointed by Governor Gray Davis. Born Los Angeles California Nov 1948. Catholic. Educated at Yale University B.A. 1970 and Stanford University J.D. 1975. Admitted to practice California 1975. In legal practice Los Angeles 1975-86. Judge 1986-93 and Former Presiding Judge, Compton Municipal Court Los Angeles County. Judge, Superior Court of California Los Angeles County 1993-98. Judge, U.S. District Court Central District of California Feb 6, 1998 to Oct 18, 2001, appointed by President Bill Clinton.

Deputy City Attorney Los Angeles 1975-79. Adjunct Professor of Administrative Law California State University at Dominguez Hills 1990 and 1992. Named Criminal Justice Judge of the Year from Los Angeles County Bar Association 1997. Democrat.

Office: 350 McAllister Street, San Francisco 94102-4797.

Telephone: (415) 865-7000.

MORENO, Tracy T. *(Judge, Superior Court of California County of Los Angeles)* Assumed office Jan 22, 2000. Former Judge, Long Beach Municipal Court Los Angeles County.

Office: Long Beach Courthouse, 415 West Ocean Boulevard, Long Beach 90802.

Telephone: (562) 491-6130.

MORGAN, Jack W. *(Judge, Superior Court of California County of Los Angeles)* Appointed by Governor Pete Wilson to term beginning Jan 24, 1994. Elected 1994 and 2000. Current term expires Jan 2007. Born Inglewood California May 4, 1937. Baptist. Educated at University of Southern California B.A. in Political Science cum laude 1959 J.D. 1962 M.A. 1964. Member Phi Delta Phi. Admitted to practice California 1963, U.S. District Court Southern District of California 1963 and U.S. Supreme Court 1972. In legal practice Los Angeles, Inglewood, Marina Del Rey and Torrance.

Office: Compton Courthouse, 200 West Compton Boulevard, Compton 90220.

Telephone: (310) 603-7842.

MORGAN, Marilyn *(Judge, United States Bankruptcy Court Northern District of California)* Appointed by U.S. Court of Appeals Ninth Circuit judges to term beginning June 16, 1988. Reappointed June 16, 2002, current term expires June 15, 2016. Educated at Emory University B.A. 1969 J.D. 1976.

Office: 3035 U.S. Courthouse, 280 South First Street, San Jose 95113.

Telephone: (408) 535-5100.

MORGAN, W. Charles *(Judge, Superior Court of California County of Riverside)* Former Judge and Presiding Judge, Riverside Municipal Court Riverside County.

Office: Hall of Justice, 4100 Main Street, Riverside 92501.

Telephone: (909) 955-2300.

MORRIS, Carl W. *(Judge, Superior Court of California County of Alameda)* Former Judge, Oakland-Piedmont-Emeryville Municipal Court Alameda County.

Office: Administration Building, 1221 Oak Street, Oakland 94612.

Telephone: (510) 271-5130.

MORRIS, James I. *(Judge, Superior Court of California County of Sacramento)*

Office: Courthouse, 720 Ninth Street, Sacramento 95814.

Telephone: (916) 874-5476.

MORRIS, Judson W., Jr. *(Judge, Superior Court of California County of Los Angeles)* Assumed office Jan

MORRIS, JUDSON W., JR.—*Continued*

22, 2000. Former Judge and Presiding Judge, Pasadena Municipal Court Los Angeles County.

Office: Pasadena Courthouse, 300 East Walnut Avenue, Pasadena 91101.

Telephone: (626) 356-5689.

MORRIS, Patrick Joseph *(Judge, Superior Court of California County of San Bernardino)* Appointed by Governor Edmund G. Brown, Jr. to term beginning March 1976. Elected to subsequent terms. Supervising Judge Family Court 1978-81. Presiding Judge Superior Court 1981-84 and Juvenile Court 1984-89. Criminal Law Judge 1989-90. Currently serves as Supervising Criminal Law Judge. Born Needles California Jan 14, 1938. Presbyterian. Educated at University of Redlands B.A. cum laude in Political Science 1959 and Stanford University J.D. 1962. Member Phi Beta Kappa. Admitted to practice California 1963 and U.S. District Court Southern District of California 1963. In legal practice Palo Alto 1963-64 and San Bernardino 1967-76.

Deputy District Attorney San Bernardino County 1964-67. Member California Judges Association (Executive Committee since 1990, President 1992-93), National Council of Juvenile and Family Court Judges, State Bar of California (Chairman Local Administrative Committee 1971-72), San Bernardino County (Chairman Speakers Bureau 1970-76, Law Day Committee 1973-76 and Public Relations Committee 1974) and American Bar Associations. Board of Directors California Trial Lawyers Association, Pomona, San Bernardino and Riverside Chapter 1969-74. Co-chair Advisory Committee on Juvenile Court Law California Judicial Council since 1988. Headed up San Bernardino's first Drug Court. Faculty member Continuing Judicial Studies Program (Member 1978-85 and Chairman 1984-85 Planning Committee), New Judges Orientation Program 1979-80 and Judicial College 1982 and 1989 California Center for Judicial Education and Research. Recipient Distinguished Service Award 1968, San Bernardino Jaycees Outstanding Young Man of the Year Award 1968, Layman's Award for services rendered to San Bernardino Valley in the field of recreation and leisure time pursuits presented by District 11 California Parks and Recreation Society 1971, Golden Man and Boy Award presented by Boys' Club of San Bernardino 1973, Outstanding Citizens Award presented by Los Padrinos (a community service organization serving Chicano youth of San Bernardino and Colton) 1974, Medallion Award for Unusually Devoted Service to Boys presented by Boys' Clubs of America 1975, Distinguished Service Award 1977 and 75th Anniversary Distinguished Alumni Award 1982 University of Redlands Alumni Association, Robert Presley Judicial Award for Leadership in Service to Youth 1989, Meritorious Service Award to the Juvenile Courts of America from National Council of Juvenile and Family Law July 1991 and Voice of the Decade Award from San Bernardino Child Advocacy July 1994. Listed in *Who's Who in the West* 1973-79 and *Outstanding Young Men of America* 1968 and 1969. Named Judge of the Year by California Trial Lawyers Association 1981 and Jurist of the Year by Judicial Council of California 1994.

Private First Class USAR 1962-68. Board of Directors Legal Aid Society of San Bernardino County 1967-73. Board of Education San Bernardino City Unified School District 1971-76 (Board Vice President 1972, Board President 1975-76). Board of Trustees University of Redlands 1971-84 and since 1986. Member 1970-73 and President 1972-73 University of Redlands Alumni Association. Founder and Charter President 1966-68 and Board of Directors 1968-76 Boys' Club of San Bernardino. Chairman Parks and Recreation Commission of San Bernardino 1970-71. Member Recreation and Juvenile Commissions of San Bernardino 1966-70. Chairman Professional Division Arrowhead United Fund Campaign 1968-69, Board of Directors 1968-72 and Chairman Committee to Coordinate Emergency Relief 1982-84 Arrowhead United Way. Member 1967-86, member Board of Directors 1970-72 and 1975-80 and President 1978-79 Kiwanis Club of San Bernardino. Board of Directors San Bernardino YMCA since 1976. Member since 1971, Church School Teacher and Senior High Youth Fellowship Advisor 1972-85, Chairman Church and Society Commission 1979-80, Ruling Editor 1979-82 and Chairman Assistant Pastor Selection Committee 1982 First United Presbyterian Church. Founding Board member 1977, Board of Directors 1977-85 and President 1978-79 Community Arts Production. Board of Directors 1980-85 and member 1982-84 and Chairman 1983-84 Admissions and Allocations Subcommittee Cultural League Advocating Support of the Arts in Society. Juvenile Affairs Advisor and Ex-officio Director The Family Center since 1986.

Office: 351 North Arrowhead Avenue, San Bernardino 92415-0240.

Telephone: (909) 387-3922.

MORRIS, Phillip M. *(Judge, Superior Court of California County of San Bernardino)* Assumed office Aug 10, 1998. Former Judge, San Bernardino County Municipal Court.

Office: 351 North Arrowhead Avenue, San Bernardino 92415-0240.

Telephone: (909) 387-3922.

MORRISON, Fred K. *(Associate Justice, California Court of Appeal Third District)* Appointed by Governor Pete Wilson July 15, 1994. Retained by election Nov 8, 1994, current term expires Jan 2007. Born Honolulu Hawaii June 22, 1941. Educated at Purdue University B.S. in Psychology 1963 and College of William & Mary J.D. with honors 1971. Admitted to practice Virginia 1971 and California 1976. Judge, Sacramento Municipal Court Sacramento County 1985-89. Judge, Superior Court of California Sacramento County March 27, 1989 to 1994, appointed by Governor George Deukmejian.

Assistant U.S. Attorney Eastern District of California 1982-85 (specializing in the prosecution of white collar crime). Professor 1975-82 and Adjunct Professor since 1982 McGeorge School of Law. Major U.S. Army Transportation Corps and JAGC 1963-75 (Vietnam 1966-67). Brigadier General California Army National Guard (retired 1993).

Office: 914 Capitol Mall, Sacramento 95814.

Telephone: (916) 654-0209.

MORROW, Margaret M. *(Judge, United States District Court Central District of California)* Appointed for life by President Bill Clinton to term beginning March 9, 1998. Born Columbus Nebraska Oct 29, 1950. Educated at Bryn Mawr College B.A. magna cum laude 1971 and Harvard University J.D. cum laude 1974. Admitted to practice California 1974. In legal practice Los Angeles 1974-98.

Board of Trustees 1981-83 and 1984-89, President

MORROW, MARGARET M.—*Continued*

Barristers 1982-83 and President 1988-89 Los Angeles County Bar Association. Director Young Lawyers Division 1984-85 and Member House of Delegates 1990-92 American Bar Association. Conference of Delegates Executive Committee 1985-88, Board of Governors 1990-94, Vice President 1992-93 and President 1993-94 State Bar of California. Member Board of Councilors University of Southern California Law Center 1985-91. Member Commission to Draft an Ethics Code for Los Angeles City Government 1989-90. Fellow American Bar Foundation. Recipient Maynard Toll Award from Legal Aid Foundation of Los Angeles 1990, Ernestine Stahlhut Award from Women Lawyers Association of Los Angeles 1994 and Bernard E. Witkin Amicus Curiae Award from Judicial Council of California 1995.

Office: 7100 Federal Building, 255 East Temple Street, Los Angeles 90012.

Telephone: (213) 894-2949.

MORSE, Heather D. *(Judge, Superior Court of California County of Santa Cruz)* Assumed office July 1, 1998. Presiding Judge Jan 1, 1999 to Dec 31, 1999. Former Judge, Santa Cruz County Municipal Court.

Office: 1430 Freedom Boulevard, Watsonville 95076.

Telephone: (831) 763-8060.

MORTIMER, Wendell, Jr. *(Judge, Superior Court of California County of Los Angeles)* Appointed by Governor Pete Wilson Sept 10, 1995. Elected Nov 5, 1996 and 2002. Current term expires Jan 2009. Born Alhambra California April 7, 1937. Presbyterian. Educated at Occidental College B.A. 1958 and University of Southern California Law Center J.D. 1965. Admitted to practice California 1966. In legal practice Los Angeles 1971-95.

Attorney Caltrans State of California 1966-71. Chair Bench-Bar Committee and Member Executive Committee and Complex Litigation Panel Los Angeles Superior Court. Member American Board of Trial Advocates, American Judicature Society, California Judges Association, American Judges Association, International Academy of Trial Judges, State Bar of California, Pasadena, Los Angeles County and American Bar Associations. Panelist Association of Business Trial Lawyers 2000. U.S. Army 1960-62. Republican. Member San Marino City Club and Balboa Yacht Club. Enjoys travel, photography, reading and boating.

Office: Central Civil West, 300 South Commonwealth Avenue, Los Angeles 90005.

Telephone: (213) 351-8739.

MORUZA, Christine K. *(Judge, Superior Court of California County of Alameda)* Assumed office July 31, 1998. Former Judge, Livermore-Pleasanton-Dublin Municipal Court Alameda County.

Office: Hall of Justice, 5672 Stoneridge Drive, Pleasanton 94588.

Telephone: (925) 551-6886.

MOSCONE, Philip J. *(Judge, Superior Court of California City and County of San Francisco)* Assumed office Dec 31, 1998. Born San Francisco California April 16, 1943. Educated at St. Mary's College of California B.S. 1965 and San Francisco Law School J.D. 1970. Judge, San Francisco Municipal Court San Francisco County 1981 to Dec 30, 1998.

Deputy City Attorney San Francisco Jan 1971 to April 1981.

Office: Hall of Justice, 850 Bryant Street, San Francisco 94103.

Telephone: (415) 551-4020.

MOSK, Richard M. *(Associate Justice, California Court of Appeal Second District Division Five)* Appointed by Governor Gray Davis to term beginning 2001. Educated at Stanford University A.B. with great distinction and Harvard Law School J.D. cum laude. Law Clerk to Hon. Mathew Oscar Tobriner, California Supreme Court 1964-65. Member Phi Beta Kappa. Admitted to practice California 1964. In legal practice Los Angeles 1965-2000.

Office: 300 South Spring Street, Los Angeles 90013.

Telephone: (213) 830-7000.

MOSKOWITZ, Barry Ted *(Judge, United States District Court Southern District of California)* Former Magistrate Judge, appointed to term beginning 1986. Appointed Judge for life by President Bill Clinton. Born Paterson New Jersey Aug 17, 1950. Jewish. Educated at Rutgers University B.A. with highest honors 1972 J.D. with high honors 1975. Law Clerk to Hon. Leonard I. Garth, U.S. Court of Appeals Third Circuit 1975-76. Admitted to practice New Jersey 1975, U.S. District Court District of New Jersey 1975, U.S. Courts of Appeals Second 1975, Third 1976 and Ninth 1986 Circuits, U.S. Supreme Court 1979 and California 1986. In legal practice Wayne New Jersey 1982-85.

Assistant U.S. Attorney District of New Jersey 1976-82 and Southern District of California 1985-86. Adjunct Professor of Law Seton Hall University School of Law 1980-81 and Rutgers University School of Law 1981-84. Enjoys sailing and coaching soccer.

Office: 5160 U.S. Courthouse, 940 Front Street, San Diego 92101-8915.

Telephone: (619) 557-5583.

MOSS, Robert James *(Judge, Superior Court of California County of Orange)*

Mailing address: P.O. Box 1994, Santa Ana 92702-1994.

Office: Central Justice Center, 700 Civic Center Drive West, Santa Ana 92701.

Telephone: (714) 834-3734.

MOULDS, John F. *(Magistrate Judge, United States District Court Eastern District of California)* Part-time Magistrate 1983-85. Appointed full time by U.S. District Court judges to term beginning Jan 6, 1986. Reappointed 1994 and 2002. Current term expires Jan 2010. Born Kansas City Missouri March 22, 1938. Educated at Stanford University 1955-58, Sacramento State College A.B. with honors 1960 and University of California Boalt Hall School of Law J.D. 1966. Recipient Earl Warren Award. Legal Editor California Continuing Education of the Bar 1963-66. Admitted to practice California 1967, U.S. District Courts Northern 1967 and Eastern 1968 Districts of California, U.S. Court of Appeals Ninth Circuit 1967, U.S. Claims Court 1982 and U.S. Supreme Court 1985. In legal practice Sacramento 1969-85.

Attorney Sept 1966 to Jan 1968 and Directing Attorney Sacramento Valley Aug 1968 to Sept 1969 California Rural Legal Assistance. Attorney Sacramento County Legal Aid Jan 1968 to Aug 1968. Instructor in Public Law Graduate Seminar Sacramento State College Jan

MOULDS, JOHN F.—*Continued*

1969 to June 1969. Director National Council of Magistrates since 1986. Member State Bar of California, Sacramento County, Federal and American Bar Associations. Attends various legal education conferences and seminars annually. Research Analyst Senate Fact Finding Committee on Education Aug 1960 to Jan 1961. Administrative Assistant to Senator Albert S. Rodda Jan 1961 to Sept 1963. Counsel Sacramento Singlemen's Self-Help Center 1969-74. Member Sacramento Human Relations Commission 1969-75 (Chair 1974) and Sacramento Community Coalition for Media Change 1972-75 (Counsel 1972-75). Member Community Support Organization since 1971 and Moot Court Judge since 1975 University of California at Davis School of Law. Director Sacramento Country Day School since 1982. Board member Sacramento Public Library Foundation since 1985. Enjoys tennis, fly fishing and reading.

Office: 8-240 U.S. Courthouse, 501 I Street, Sacramento 95814-2322.

Telephone: (916) 930-4180.

MUDD, William D. *(Judge, Superior Court of California County of San Diego)* Appointed by Governor George Deukmejian to term beginning Feb 9, 1988. Born Baltimore Maryland Aug 9, 1944. Educated at United States International University B.A. 1966 and University of California Hastings College of the Law J.D. 1969. Admitted to practice California 1970. In legal practice San Diego 1971-83. Commissioner, County Municipal Court Jan 1983 to Jan 6, 1985. Judge, San Diego Municipal Court San Diego County Nov 6, 1984 to Feb 8, 1988.

Deputy City Attorney San Diego 1970-71.

Mailing address: P.O. Box 122724, San Diego 92112-2724.

Office: 220 West Broadway, San Diego 92101.

Telephone: (619) 531-3820.

MUELLER, Kimberly J. *(Magistrate Judge, United States District Court Eastern District of California)* Appointed by U.S. District Court judges to term beginning March 28, 2003.

Office: 501 I Street, Sacramento 95814.

Telephone: (916) 930-4260.

MULLEN, Gary S. *(Judge, Superior Court of California County of Sacramento)* Assumed office June 17, 1998. Former Judge, Sacramento Municipal Court Sacramento County.

Office: Courthouse, 720 Ninth Street, Sacramento 95814.

Telephone: (916) 874-5476.

MULLIN, Hugh F., III *(Judge, Superior Court of California County of Santa Clara)* Appointed by Governor George Deukmejian to term beginning March 31, 1989. Elected 1990, 1996 and 2002. Current term expires Jan 2009. Born San Francisco California July 25, 1942. Roman Catholic. Educated at Santa Clara University B.A in History 1964 and Lincoln University Law School J.D. 1969. Admitted to practice California 1970, U.S. District Court Northern District of California 1970 and U.S. Court of Appeals Ninth Circuit 1970. In legal practice San Mateo 1970-72. Judge, Santa Clara County Municipal Court 1986-89.

Santa Clara County District Attorney's Office 1972-86. Instructor in Criminal Law and Legal Research and Writing Paralegal Program Santa Clara University since 1987. Member California Judges Association. Attended California Judges College and numerous seminars on Criminal Law, Civil Law, Juvenile Law and the Death Penalty California Center for Judicial Education and Research. Democrat.

Office: Hall of Justice East Wing, 190 West Hedding Street, San Jose 95110.

Telephone: (408) 808-6600.

MUND, Geraldine *(Judge, United States Bankruptcy Court Central District of California)* Appointed by U.S. District Court judges Feb 9, 1984. Reappointed by U.S. Court of Appeals Ninth Circuit judges Aug 27, 1986 and Aug 2000. Current term expires Aug 2014. Chief Judge 1997-2002. Born Los Angeles California July 7, 1943. Jewish. Educated at Brandeis University B.A. 1965, Smith College M.S. 1967 and Loyola University J.D. 1977. Admitted to practice California 1977. Began legal practice Beverly Hills 1977.

Member Los Angeles County and American Bar Associations. Past President Temple Israel of Hollywood.

Office: 21041 Burbank Boulevard, Woodland Hills 91367.

Telephone: (818) 587-2840.

MUÑOZ, Aurelio *(Judge, Superior Court of California County of Los Angeles)* Appointed by Governor Edmund G. Brown, Jr. to term beginning April 14, 1980. Elected 1982, 1988, 1994 and 2000. Current term expires Jan 2007. Supervising Judge Criminal Division 1986-87. Born Dinuba California July 23, 1938. Catholic. Educated at University of California at Berkeley 1959-60, Foothill Junior College 1960-62, San Jose State University 1962-63 and University of Santa Clara School of Law J.D. 1966. Research and Copy Editor Santa Clara Lawyer 1965-66. Law Clerk to Hon. Murray Draper, California Court of Appeal First District Division Three 1966-67. Ford Foundation Fellow University of Pennsylvania Law School 1967-69. Member Phi Beta Tau and Tau Delta Phi. Admitted to practice California 1966 and U.S. Courts of Appeals Ninth 1966 and Third 1968 Circuits. Began legal practice Philadelphia Pennsylvania 1967. In legal practice Fresno 1969-72 and Los Angeles 1972-79 California. Judge, Los Angeles Municipal Court Los Angeles County 1979-80.

Assistant Volunteer Defender Philadelphia Pennsylvania 1967. Deputy Public Defender Fresno California 1969-72. Senior Staff Attorney Joint Legislative Committee for revision of Penal Code 1972-73. Supervisor Office of the State Public Defender Los Angeles California 1976-79. Author Casenote "State Encouraged Discrimination" Santa Clara Lawyer 1966 and "Successful Appeal & Writ Practice" Los Angeles Bar Association May 1979. Adjunct Professor of Law Humphreys College of Law 1970-72 and Southwestern College of Law 1985-87. Former member State Bar of California. Member California Judges Association, Los Angeles and Mexican-American Bar Associations. Lecturer on "Criminal Appellate Practice" Criminal Law Seminar California Attorneys for Criminal Justice April 1975, "Felony Sentencing Practices" Judicial College summer 1985, "Death Penalty" Criminal Law and Procedures Institute 1985-86 and California Judicial College 1986 and New Trial Judges Orientation Program Berkeley Jan 1987. Electrical Technician Second Class USN 1956-59. Previously worked as electronics technician for Hewlett-

MUÑOZ, AURELIO—*Continued*

Packard. Democrat. Enjoys reading, gardening and wood refinishing.

Office: Courthouse, 111 North Hill Street, Los Angeles 90012.

Telephone: (213) 974-5411.

MUNOZ, Gregory *(Judge, Superior Court of California County of Orange)*

Mailing address: P.O. Box 1994, Santa Ana 92702-1994.

Office: Central Justice Center, 700 Civic Center Drive West, Santa Ana 92701.

Telephone: (714) 834-3734.

MUNTER, John E. *(Judge, Superior Court of California City and County of San Francisco)* Appointed by Governor Pete Wilson to term beginning Jan 27, 1994. Elected 1996 and 2002. Current term expires Jan 2009. Presiding Judge Appellate Department Jan 1, 1996 to Jan 1, 1998. Born San Francisco California July 27, 1942. Educated at University of California at Berkeley B.A. 1963 and Harvard University J.D. cum laude 1966. Member Phi Beta Kappa. Admitted to practice California 1966, U.S. District Courts Northern 1967, Central 1968, Eastern 1980 and Southern 1985 Districts of California, U.S. Court of Appeals Ninth Circuit 1967 and U.S. Supreme Court 1979. In legal practice San Francisco 1966-93.

Author "Section 16(b) of the Securities Exchange Act of 1934: An Alternative to 'Burning Down the Barn in Order to Kill the Rats'" 52 No. 1 Cornell Law Quarterly Fall 1966. Co-author "Higgins v. Aerojet Corporation: Successfully Defending a Toxic Tort Case" Jan 14, 1987 and "The Aerojet Case: Implications for the Future" June 7, 1989 Toxics Law Reporter. Former Member San Francisco Regional Selection Panel White House Fellowship, Discovery Reform Working Group, Judicial Council Task Force on Complex Litigation, State Bar of California, San Francisco (Judiciary Committee 1985-87) and American Bar Associations. Member Edward J. McFetridge American Inn of Court (Membership Chairperson), California Judges Association, Queen's Bench and Italian-American Bar Association. Panelist program on toxic tort lawsuits Practicing Law Institute 1987, program on employment law Labor Law Section San Francisco Bar Association 1996, programs on employment law 1996 and scientific evidence 1997 California Judges Association and Rutter Group and Annual Trial Symposium Litigation Section State Bar of California 1997. Speaker American Bar Association Annual Convention 1987, California Association of Realtors 1989 and California Center for Judicial Education and Research. Board of Trustees San Francisco Law Library 1995-97. Enjoys tennis, reading, traveling and hiking.

Office: Civic Center Courthouse, 400 McAllister Street, San Francisco 94102-4514.

Telephone: (415) 551-4020.

MURPHY, Kevin J. *(Judge, Superior Court of California County of Santa Clara)* Former Judge, Santa Clara County Municipal Court.

Office: Hall of Justice East Wing, 190 West Hedding Street, San Jose 95110.

Telephone: (408) 808-6600.

MURPHY, Mary Ann *(Judge, Superior Court of California County of Los Angeles)*

Office: Courthouse, 111 North Hill Street, Los Angeles 90012.

Telephone: (213) 974-5411.

MURRAY, Dennis E. *(Judge, Superior Court of California County of Tehama)* Presiding Judge since Jan 1, 1997. Born Upland California Sept 6, 1950. Methodist. Educated at California State University at Long Beach B.S. cum laude 1972 and University of La Verne J.D. 1976. Admitted to practice California 1976. In legal practice Ontario 1976 and Red Bluff 1978. Judge, Red Bluff Justice Court Tehama County 1980-90.

Deputy District Attorney San Bernardino County 1976-78. Assistant District Attorney Tehama County 1978-80. Former member California District Attorneys Association. Member California Judges Association. Republican. Enjoys tennis, skiing and music.

Mailing address: P.O. Box 278, Red Bluff 96080.

Office: Red Bluff Courthouse, Second Floor, 445 Pine Street, Red Bluff 96080.

Telephone: (530) 527-8116.

MURRAY, William J., Jr. *(Judge, Superior Court of California County of San Joaquin)*

Office: 222 East Weber Avenue, Room 303, Stockton 95202.

Telephone: (209) 468-2827.

MYERS, Deanne Smith *(Judge, Superior Court of California County of Los Angeles)* Assumed office Jan 22, 2000. Former Judge and Presiding Judge, South Bay Municipal Court Los Angeles County.

Office: Torrance Courthouse, 825 Maple Avenue, Torrance 90503.

Telephone: (310) 222-8808.

MYERS, H. Dennis *(Judge, Superior Court of California County of Riverside)* Serves Juvenile Court. Former Judge, Mount San Jacinto Municipal Court Riverside County.

Office: 9991 County Farm Road, Riverside 92503.

Telephone: (909) 358-4137.

NADLER, Gary *(Judge, Superior Court of California County of Sonoma)*

Office: 600 Administration Drive, Santa Rosa 95403.

Telephone: (707) 565-1100.

NADLER, Jerome S. *(Judge, Superior Court of California County of Santa Clara)* Assumed office July 30, 1998. Former Judge, Santa Clara County Municipal Court.

Office: Hall of Justice East Wing, 190 West Hedding Street, San Jose 95110.

Telephone: (408) 808-6600.

NAGLE, Margaret A. *(Magistrate Judge, United States District Court Central District of California)* Appointed by U.S. District Court judges.

Office: 826 U.S. Courthouse, 312 Spring Street, Los Angeles 90012.

Telephone: (213) 894-8540.

NAIL, Michael E. *(Judge, Superior Court of California County of Solano)* Former Presiding Judge.

Office: 321 Tuolumne Street, Vallejo 94590.

Telephone: (707) 553-5917.

NAKAHARA, Vernon K. *(Judge, Superior Court of California County of Alameda)* Former Judge, Oakland-Piedmont-Emeryville Municipal Court Alameda County.
Office: Courthouse, 1225 Fallon Street, Oakland 94612.
Telephone: (510) 272-6070.

NAKAMURA, Kirk H. *(Judge, Superior Court of California County of Orange)*
Office: West Justice Center, 8141 Thirteenth Street, Westminster 92683.
Telephone: (714) 896-7181.

NAKATA, Eric M. *(Judge, Superior Court of California County of San Bernardino)* Assumed office Aug 10, 1998. Former Judge, San Bernardino County Municipal Court.
Office: 14455 Civic Drive, Victorville 92392.
Telephone: (760) 243-8684.

NAKAZATO, Arthur *(Magistrate Judge, United States District Court Central District of California)* Appointed by U.S. District Court judges.
Office: U.S. Courthouse, 411 West Fourth Street, Santa Ana 92701-4516.
Telephone: (213) 894-3535.

NARANJO, Richard *(Judge, Superior Court of California County of Los Angeles)*
Office: Courthouse, 111 North Hill Street, Los Angeles 90012.
Telephone: (213) 974-5411.

NARES, Gilbert *(Associate Justice, California Court of Appeal Fourth District Division One)* Appointed by Governor George Deukmejian to term beginning 1988. Retained by election. Born Oceanside California Feb 28, 1943. Educated at University of San Diego B.A. 1964 J.D. 1967. Admitted to practice California 1968 and U.S. Supreme Court 1971. In legal practice Oceanside 1968-76. Judge 1976-78 and Presiding Judge 1977, North County Municipal Court San Diego County. Judge 1978-88, Supervising Judge North County Branch 1981 and 1982 and Judge Appellate Department 1986 and 1987, Superior Court of California San Diego County.
President Bar Association of Northern San Diego County 1974. Named Distinguished Alumnus University of San Diego 1984. Board of Trustees Oceanside Public Library 1974-76 and San Diego County Law Library 1976-86.
Office: 750 B Street, Suite 300, San Diego 92101.
Telephone: (619) 645-2760.

NASH, Lloyd M. *(Judge, Superior Court of California County of Los Angeles)* Assumed office Jan 22, 2000. Former Judge, Los Angeles Municipal Court Los Angeles County.
Office: Santa Clarita Courthouse, 23747 West Valencia Boulevard, Valencia 91355.
Telephone: (661) 253-7301.

NASH, Michael *(Judge, Superior Court of California County of Los Angeles)* Appointed by Governor George Deukmejian Dec 11, 1989. Elected 1990, 1996 and 2002. Current term expires Jan 2009. Serves Children's Court. Born New York New York Aug 6, 1948. Jewish. Educated at University of California at Los Angeles B.A. cum laude 1970 and Loyola University of Los Angeles J.D. 1974. Admitted to practice California 1974, U.S. District Court Central District of California 1974 and U.S. Court of Appeals Ninth Circuit 1981. Began legal practice Los Angeles 1974. Judge, Los Angeles Municipal Court Los Angeles County 1985-89.
Criminal Prosecutor Office of California Attorney General 1974-85. Instructor San Fernando Valley College of Law 1977 and University of West Los Angeles School of Law 1978-81. Member California Judges Association, Juvenile Court Judges of California and National Council of Juvenile and Family Court Judges. Specialist Four USAR 1968-74.
Office: 201 Centre Plaza Drive, Monterey Park 91754-2158.
Telephone: (323) 526-6377.

NAUGHTON, Michael J. *(Judge, Superior Court of California County of Orange)*
Mailing address: P.O. Box 14169, Orange 92863-1569.
Office: Lamoreaux Justice Center, 341 The City Drive, Orange 92868.
Telephone: (714) 935-7236.

NAUGLE, David N. *(Judge, United States Bankruptcy Court Central District of California)*
Office: 3420 12th Street, Room 385, Riverside 92501-3819.
Telephone: (909) 774-1021.

NAVARRO, Rene *(Judge, Superior Court of California County of Santa Clara)* Former Judge, Santa Clara County Municipal Court.
Office: Hall of Justice East Wing, 190 West Hedding Street, San Jose 95110.
Telephone: (408) 808-6600.

NEEDHAM, Henry E., Jr. *(Judge, Superior Court of California County of Alameda)*
Office: Courthouse, 1225 Fallon Street, Oakland 94612.
Telephone: (510) 272-6070.

NEIDORF, Richard *(Judge, Superior Court of California County of Los Angeles)* Appointed by Governor George Deukmejian to term beginning March 24, 1989. Elected 1990, 1996 and 2002. Current term expires Jan 2009. Born Covina California March 12, 1945. Jewish. Educated at California State University at Los Angeles B.S. 1967, California Military Academy 1967 and Southwestern University 1972. Admitted to practice California 1972. In legal practice Los Angeles 1972-87. Judge, Los Angeles Municipal Court Los Angeles County 1987-89.
Instructor Center for Criminal Justice California State University at Long Beach 1985-87. Lieutenant National Guard 1963-68. Former Narcotic Agent Department of Justice. Republican. Enjoys mountain biking, trout fishing and taking long walks.
Office: Santa Monica Courthouse, 1725 Main Street, Santa Monica 90401.
Telephone: (310) 260-3723.

NELSON, Henry Kent *(Judge, Superior Court of California County of Mendocino)* Presiding Judge Mendocino County Coordinated Courts Jan 1, 1997 to Dec 31, 1997. Born Glendale California Sept 30, 1946. Episcopalian. Educated at Bard College B.A. 1968 and Western State University College of Law J.D. 1975. Admitted to practice California 1976 and U.S. District Court Central District of California 1976. In legal practice Newport Beach 1976-79 and Ukiah 1981-83. Former

NELSON, HENRY KENT—*Continued*
Judge, Mendocino County Municipal Court, elected to term beginning Jan 7, 1985.

Member California Judges Association and State Bar of California (inactive). Attended California Judges Orientation College Jan 1985, Conference Dec 1986, California Judicial College July 1990 and Post Graduate Seminar in Advanced Criminal Law March 1991 California Judges Association. Corporal U.S. Army 1968-71. Vice President Nelson Technical Coatings Corporation 1971-76. Republican. Interests include fishing, biking and developing a ranch.

Mailing address: P.O. Box 996, Ukiah 95482.

Office: Courthouse, 100 North State Street, Ukiah 95482.

Telephone: (707) 467-6437.

NELSON, Mark G., Sr. *(Judge, Superior Court of California County of Los Angeles)* Assumed office Jan 22, 2000. Former Judge, Citrus Municipal Court Los Angeles County.

Office: Pomona Courthouse South, 400 Civic Center Plaza, Pomona 91766.

Telephone: (909) 620-3023.

NELSON, Rodney E. *(Judge, Superior Court of California County of Los Angeles)* Appointed by Governor Pete Wilson to term beginning March 1995. Elected Nov 1996 and Nov 2002. Current term expires Dec 31, 2008. Born Minneapolis Minnesota July 4, 1934. Presbyterian. Educated at University of Minnesota B.A. 1956 and Columbia University LL.B. 1960. Board of Editors Columbia Law Review 1958-60. Admitted to practice California 1961. In legal practice Los Angeles. Republican.

Office: Los Angeles County Courthouse, 111 North Hill Street 90012.

Telephone: (213) 974-5665.

NEVITT, William R., Jr. *(Judge, Superior Court of California County of San Diego)*

Mailing address: P.O. Box 122724, San Diego 92112-2724.

Office: 330 West Broadway, San Diego 92101.

Telephone: (619) 685-6148.

NEWSOME, Randall J. *(Judge, United States Bankruptcy Court Northern District of California)* Appointed by U.S. District Court judges to U.S. Bankruptcy Court Southern District of Ohio to term beginning Oct 15, 1982. Reappointed by U.S. Court of Appeals Sixth Circuit judges Oct 1986. Appointed by U.S. Court of Appeals Ninth Circuit judges to U.S. Bankruptcy Court Northern District of California June 1988. Reappointed June 1, 2002, current term expires May 31, 2016. Born Dayton Ohio July 13, 1950. Protestant. Educated at Boston University B.A. summa cum laude 1972 and University of Cincinnati J.D. 1975. Law Clerk to Hon. Carl E. Rubin, U.S. District Court Southern District of Ohio 1975-77. Member Phi Beta Kappa. Admitted to practice Ohio 1975, U.S. District Court Southern District of Ohio 1977, U.S. Court of Appeals Sixth Circuit 1978 and U.S. Supreme Court 1981. Began legal practice Cincinnati 1978.

Mailing address: P.O. Box 2070, Oakland 94604-2070.

Telephone: (510) 879-3530.

NGUYEN, Jacqueline H. *(Judge, Superior Court of California County of Los Angeles)*

Office: Alhambra Courthouse, 150 West Commonwealth Avenue, Alhambra 91801.

Telephone: (626) 308-5537.

NGUYEN, Nho Trong *(Judge, Superior Court of California County of Orange)*

Office: West Justice Center, 8141 Thirteenth Street, Westminster 92683.

Telephone: (714) 896-7181.

NICHOLS, Leslie C. *(Judge, Superior Court of California County of Santa Clara)* Appointed by Governor George Deukmejian to term beginning Feb 24, 1984. Presiding Judge Jan 1, 1997 to Dec 31, 1997. Born Oak Park Illinois May 18, 1941. Educated at Stanford University B.A. in Political Science 1963 and University of California Hastings College of the Law LL.B. 1966. Admitted to practice California 1967, U.S. District Court Northern District of California 1967, U.S. Court of Appeals Ninth Circuit 1967 and U.S. Supreme Court 1973. In legal practice Menlo Park 1969, Los Gatos 1969-70 and Palo Alto 1970-84.

Author "Accusatory Pleadings Framed in Statutory Language—Requirement of Notice to Defendant" 7 Lincoln L. Rev. 64, 1971 and chapter in *Youth and the Law.* Instructor Lincoln University Law School 1971-76. Member San Mateo County Trial Lawyers Association, Santa Clara Trial Lawyers Association, California Attorneys for Criminal Justice (Founding member), California Trial Lawyers Association, The Association of Trial Lawyers of America, American Judicature Society, California Judges Association, State Bar of California (Corrections Commission 1974), Palo Alto Area (Chairman Lawyers Reference Service 1971-72, Delegate State Bar of California Convention 1972-75, Legislation Committee 1975, Fee Arbitration Committee since 1978), San Mateo County, Santa Clara County (Board of Trustees 1974-77, Correctional Reform and Criminal Justice Committee 1974-75, Executive Committee 1975-77, Delegate State Bar of California Convention 1972-75) and American Bar Associations. Instructor Santa Clara County Bar Association Trial Advocacy College Summer 1975 and 1976. Panelist "Attorneys' Fees: Practical, Procedural and Ethical Considerations" CEB 1976 and 1979. Lecturer "Law for the Layman" Palo Alto Area Bar Association, Foothill College 1980. Moderator "Recent Developments in Family Law" CEB 1984. Former lecturer on landlord-tenant law California Human Relations Commission. Board of Directors 1970-78 and President 1976 Santa Clara Legal Aid Society. Member Santa Clara County Alcoholism Advisory Board 1974-75, Santa Clara County Transportation Commission 1977-79 and "Future Cities in the 80's" Task Force 1980. Board of Directors Community Health Abuse Council 1977-79 and Santa Clara County El Camino Hospital Joint Hospital Facilities District 1978-84. Member City Council 1977-82 and former Vice Mayor and Mayor Mountain View. Member and Chair Santa Clara County Intergovernmental Council 1979-81. Board of Directors and Secretary Palo Alto YMCA 1980-82.

Office: 191 North First Street, San Jose 95113.

Telephone: (408) 882-2100.

NICHOLSON, George *(Associate Justice, California Court of Appeal Third District)* Appointed by Governor George Deukmejian to term beginning Aug 23, 1990. Retained by election Nov 8, 1994 and Nov 4, 1998.

NICHOLSON, GEORGE—*Continued*

Current term expires Jan 2011. Born Dallas Texas Feb 15, 1941. Educated at Oakland City College A.A. 1962, California State University at Hayward B.A. 1964 and University of California Hastings College of the Law J.D. 1967. Admitted to practice California 1968, U.S. District Court Eastern District of California 1968, U.S. Court of Appeals Ninth Circuit 1968 and U.S. Supreme Court 1975. Former Judge, Sacramento Municipal Court Sacramento County, appointed by Governor George Deukmejian to term beginning May 1987. Former Judge, Superior Court of California Sacramento County, appointed by Governor George Deukmejian to term beginning 1989. Served by special assignment California Supreme Court 1992.

Deputy District Attorney 1968-74 and Senior Trial Deputy District Attorney 1974-75 Alameda County. Senior Assistant Attorney General 1979-83 and Special Assistant Attorney General California. Deputy Director-Special Projects for the Governor California Office of Planning and Research. Director and Chief Counsel National School Safety Center Pepperdine University 1984-86.

Author "Campus Safety and the California Supreme Court" *Thrust for Educational Leadership* 33 Association of California School Administrators Feb/March 1986; "Campus Drug Dealers: Look Out" *California Peace Officer* 41 California Peace Officers Association March 1986; "A New Era in Campus Safety" *The San Francisco Lawyer* 16 San Francisco Bar Association June/July 1986; "Why School Employees Need Insurance and Where and How to Get It" Jan 1987 and "School Safety: A Continuing Challenge" June 1987 *The Schools' Advocate* 1 Kinghorn Press; "Judges, Technology and the Courthouse of the Future" 44 July 1989 and "Technology and the Future of Justice in California" Judicial Automation Section 3 June 1993 *Government and Technology;* Chapter 9 "The Courthouse of the Future" *Law, Decision-Making and Microcomputers: Cross-National Perspectives* Quorum Books 1990; "Reading, 'Riting or Doing Time" 66 American B. Jour. June 1990; Foreword "Computers and the Law: An Idea Whose Time Has Come" *Computer Technology in Civil Litigation* Bancroft-Whitney Publishing Company 1990; "Judges, Technology and the Future" *Court Review* 5 American Judges Association 1990; "Victims' Rights, Remedies, and Resources: A Maturing Presence in American Jurisprudence" 23 Pacific L. Jour. 815, 1992; and "Administrative and Judicial Duties in the Trial Court After a Guilty or No Contest Plea" 45 Hastings L. Jour. 573, 1994. Principal author Proposition 8 The Victims' Bill of Rights adopted by voters 1982. Coauthor with Hanelt and Washburn "Of Inalienable Rights and Exclusive Remedies" 30 *Education Law Reporter* 11, 1986; with McAlister "Insurance and the Schools" *Independent Agent* 75 Independent Insurance Agents of America July 1986; with Rapp and Carrington "Campus Safety: A Legal Imperative" 33 *Education Law Reporter* 981, 1986 and "Immunity from Liability—Who? When? How?" *The Schools' Advocate* Kinghorn Press Dec 1986; with McAlister "Courts, Risk Management, Safe and Drug-Free Schools" *Thrust for Educational Leadership* 12 Association of California School Administrators Nov/Dec 1986; with Carrington "The Victims' Rights Movement: An Idea Whose Time Has Come—Five Years Later: The Maturing of an Idea" 17 Pepperdine L. Rev. 1, 1989; *School Crime and Violence: Victims' Rights* Pepperdine University Press 1992; with Kolodney "Technology, Access to Justice and the Future: Contributing to Stewardship of the Judiciary in the Public Interest" *Docket* 17 Sacramento County Bar Association Oct 1993; with Kolodney and Kelso "Using Technology to Improve the Justice System" *California County* 10 California State Association of Counties May/June 1994; and "Citizens Urged to Collaborate, Act Against Violence" 4 *School Safety* National School Safety Center Spring 1998.

Important Decision: California State Board of Education v. Honig 13 Cal. App. 4th 720, 1993. Adjunct Professor of Education Pepperdine University Graduate School of Education and Psychology. Former member Victims' Assistance Legal Organization, McGeorge School of Law Crime Victims' Advisory Committee, Commission on the Future of the California Courts (Chair Appellate Courts Committee and Technology Committee 1991-93), National District Attorneys Association, National Association of Prosecutor Coordinators, California District Attorneys Association (Executive Director 1975-79), National School Board Association Council of School Attorneys, National Association of College and University Attorneys, National Organization on Legal Problems of Education, National Education Writers Association, American Judicature Society and American Bar Association (Judicial Administration Division, Victims of Crime Committee Section of Criminal Justice). Master of the Bench Anthony M. Kennedy American Inn of Court. Member Technology Committee Sacramento Municipal Court, Executive/Legislative Action Network Judicial Council of California and Advisory Committee Justice and Technology Forum and National Center for the Courts and the Media. Member California Judges Association (Appellate Committee on Criminal Law and Procedure) and American Judges Association.

Planner "The Rights of Victims of Crime" National Conference of the Judiciary The National Judicial College 1983. Attended National Judicial Conference on Victims and Juvenile Offenders conducted by National Conference of Special Court Judges, National Council of Juvenile and Family Court Judges and The National Judicial College 1985. Facilitator and Participant in four programs on Technology and the Future of the Courts Commission on the Future of the California Courts, San Francisco Dec 1992. Organizer "Technology and the Future of Justice in California: Stewardship of the Judiciary in the Public Interest" Technology Committee of the Commission on the Future of the California Courts in cooperation with McGeorge School of Law and Stanford University Law School and California State Library, Sacramento March 1993. Organizer and Participant "Justice, Journalism and the Future" and Collaborator panel discussion with Steve Kolodney Director of Information Technology State of California and Philip Hager Senior Editor California Lawyer and San Francisco Daily Journal "Telepresence, Virtual Reality and the Law" Bench, Bar, Media Committee Sacramento County Bar Association in cooperation with Federalist Society and Commission on the Future of the California Courts Oct 1993. Presenter to Appellate Court Institute California Center for Judicial Education and Research and California Judges Association 1993 and Planning Committee Appellate Courts Institute 1994. Panelist "Privacy and the National Information Infrastructure" Information Infrastructure

NICHOLSON, GEORGE—*Continued*

Task Force Office of Information and Regulatory Affairs Office of Management and Budget, Executive Office of the President, Sacramento Jan 1994 and "Did the Law Cause Columbine?" National Press Club Washington D.C. Aug 1999. Advisory Board "Justice and Technology Forum" cosponsored by The National Judicial College, National Center for State Courts and California Center for Judicial Education and Research 1994. Instructor The National Judicial College 1986 and 1990. Attended California Judicial College California Center for Judicial Education and Research. Named Honorary Member American Association of Law Libraries 1997. Recipient Award for ten years of support and friendship for the goals and purposes of UNITY Oct 1997, Leadership Award from Government Technology May 1998 and Award of Merit for outstanding contributions to the judiciary from American Judges Association Aug 1998. Previously worked for a steel company. Former member of an iron workers union. Republican. Nominee for Attorney General State of California 1982. Legal/Education Advisor to Governor George Deukmejian 1983-84. Member Republican Central Committee (Executive Committee) 1983-86 and Select Board of Advisors Pacific Law Journal. Expanded Victims of Crime Resource Center McGeorge School of Law. Worked extensively on literacy programs. Community Advisor Chinese American Council of Sacramento and Council of Asian Pacific Islanders Together for Active Leadership (CAPITAL). Enjoys skiing, regular exercise, racquetball, reading and writing.

Office: 914 Capitol Mall, Sacramento 95814.

Telephone: (916) 654-0209.

NISHIMOTO, Cary H. *(Judge, Superior Court of California County of Los Angeles)* Former Judge, Los Angeles Municipal Court Los Angeles County.

Office: Torrance Courthouse, 825 Maple Avenue, Torrance 90503.

Telephone: (310) 222-8808.

NORD, Larry B. *(Magistrate Judge, United States District Court Northern District of California)* Appointed by U.S. District Court judges 1971. Reappointed to subsequent terms. Serves part time. Born Medford Oregon Jan 1, 1941. Catholic. Educated at San Jose State College (now California State University at San Jose) B.A. 1963 and Hastings College of the Law LL.B. 1966. Admitted to practice California 1966. Certified Specialist Family Law California Board of Legal Specialization.

With Legislative Counsel's Office at Sacramento 1966. With Humboldt County District Attorney's Office at Eureka 1968-70. Instructor Humboldt State University 1972. Member California Trial Lawyers Association and Humboldt County Bar Association. Republican.

Office: 518 West Clark Street, Eureka 95501.

Telephone: (707) 443-1432.

NORELL, Peter H. *(Judge, Superior Court of California County of San Bernardino)* Assumed office Aug 10, 1998. Serves Rancho District. Former Judge and Presiding Judge, San Bernardino County Municipal Court.

Office: 8303 North Haven Avenue, Rancho Cucamonga 91730.

Telephone: (909) 945-4131.

NORTHRIDGE, Yolanda N. *(Judge, Superior Court of California County of Alameda)*

Office: Hayward Hall of Justice, 24405 Amador Street, Hayward 94544.

Telephone: (510) 670-5060.

NORTHWAY, Diane *(Judge, Superior Court of California County of Santa Clara)*

Office: 270 Grant Avenue, Palo Alto 94306.

Telephone: (650) 462-3800.

NOTT, Michael Gordon *(Associate Justice, California Court of Appeal Second District Division Two)* Appointed by Governor George Deukmejian to term beginning Dec 27, 1990. Retained by election Nov 1994, current term expires Jan 2007. Born Long Beach California May 1, 1940. Educated at Occidental College B.A. 1962 and University of Southern California LL.B. 1965. Member Phi Delta Phi. Admitted to practice California 1966 and U.S. District Court District of California 1966. In legal practice Long Beach 1966-85. Judge, Long Beach Municipal Court Los Angeles County 1985-87. Judge, Superior Court of California Los Angeles County 1987-90.

Member Long Beach Barristers (President 1974), State Bar of California, Long Beach (Board of Governors 1974-75) and Los Angeles County Bar Associations. Participant California Center for Judicial Education and Research 1986 and 1988. USAR 1965-71.

Office: 300 South Spring Street, Los Angeles 90013.

Telephone: (213) 830-7000.

NOWINSKI, Peter A. *(Magistrate Judge, United States District Court Eastern District of California)* Appointed by U.S. District Court judges Feb 14, 1991. Born Philadelphia Pennsylvania Sept 1942. Educated at San Jose State University B.A. 1966 and University of California Hastings College of the Law J.D. 1969. In legal practice Palo Alto 1969-78 and Sacramento 1987-91.

Office: 8-200 U.S. Courthouse, 501 I Street, Sacramento 95814-2322.

Telephone: (916) 930-4170.

NUDELL, Karen Joy *(Judge, Superior Court of California County of Los Angeles)* Assumed office Jan 22, 2000. Former Judge, Los Angeles Municipal Court Los Angeles County.

Office: Van Nuys Courthouse West, 14400 Erwin Street Mall, Van Nuys 91401-2705.

Telephone: (818) 374-2601.

NUGENT, Thomas P. *(Judge, Superior Court of California County of San Diego)*

Mailing address: P.O. Box 122724, San Diego 92112-2724.

Office: 325 South Melrose Drive, Vista 92083.

Telephone: (760) 726-9595.

NUNEZ, Ralph *(Judge, Superior Court of California County of Fresno)*

Office: 1100 Van Ness Avenue, Fresno 93724-0002.

Telephone: (559) 488-1825.

NUNLEY, Troy L. *(Judge, Superior Court of California County of Sacramento)*

Office: Courthouse, 720 Ninth Street, Sacramento 95814.

Telephone: (916) 874-5476.

OBERHOLTZER, David *(Judge, Superior Court of California County of San Diego)*
Mailing address: P.O. Box 122724, San Diego 92112-2724.
Office: 220 West Broadway, San Diego 92101.
Telephone: (619) 531-3820.

OBERHOLZER, Richard J. *(Judge, Superior Court of California County of Kern)* Former Presiding Judge.
Adjunct Professor California State University at Bakersfield.
Office: 1415 Truxtun Avenue, Bakersfield 93301.
Telephone: (661) 868-4934.

O'BRIEN, Gregory C., Jr. *(Judge, Superior Court of California County of Los Angeles)* Born Alhambra California June 22, 1945. Roman Catholic. Educated at University of Southern California A.B. 1968 and Whittier College J.D. 1972. Member Delta Chi. Admitted to practice California 1972, U.S. District Court District of California 1972 and U.S. Supreme Court 1980. Began legal practice Los Angeles 1972. In legal practice Rosemead 1978. Former Judge, Citrus Municipal Court Los Angeles County, appointed by Governor George Deukmejian to term beginning Jan 8, 1985.
With Los Angeles City Attorney's Office 1972. Attorney Southern California Edison Co. 1978. Author *Lenin Lives!* Stein & Day 1984 and "Speech May Be Free and Talk Cheap, But Judges Can Pay a Heavy Price for Unguarded Expression." 28 Loyola of Los Angeles L. Rev. 815 April 1995 and monthly column "Bench Press" *Los Angeles Daily Journal*. Editor California Courts Commentary California Judges Association 1992-96. Board of Directors California Judges Association since 2000. Lieutenant Colonel Judge Advocate California State Military Reserve 1990-96. Republican. Past member Los Angeles County Republican Executive Committee and Republican State Central Committee. President West Covina Rotary Club 1988-89.
Office: Courthouse, 111 North Hill Street, Los Angeles 90012.
Telephone: (213) 974-5411.

OCHOA, Frank J. *(Judge, Superior Court of California County of Santa Barbara)* Elected Nov 5, 1996 to term beginning Jan 6, 1997. Reelected 2002, current term expires Jan 2009. Presiding Judge Jan 1, 1998 to Dec 31, 2000. Born Long Beach California April 10, 1950. Educated at Long Beach City College 1968-70, University of California at Santa Barbara B.A. in English and History 1972 and University of California at Davis J.D. 1975. Admitted to practice California 1975, U.S. District Courts Eastern 1976 and Central 1979 Districts of California and U.S. Court of Appeals Ninth Circuit 1980. Justice pro tem, California Court of Appeal Second Appellate District Division Six 1985-86. Judge Jan 1, 1983 to 1997 and Presiding Judge 1987-89 and 1993-94, Santa Barbara Municipal Court Santa Barbara County, appointed by Governor Edmund G. Brown, Jr.
Staff Attorney 1976 and Directing Attorney 1976-80 Legal Aid Society of Sacramento County, Inc. (now Legal Services of Northern California, Inc.). Executive Director Legal Aid Foundation of Santa Barbara County, Inc. 1980-83. Faculty Member Santa Barbara College of Law. Member California Judges Association (Member Court Personnel Subcommittee, Chairman Municipal Justice Court Subcommittee, Member 1984-88 and Chairman 1988-90 Court Administration Committee and Executive Board since 1992). Recipient Distinguished Graduate Award from Long Beach Unified School District 1983. Former President Board of Directors Ventura and Santa Barbara Colleges of Law. Former Member Board of Directors University of California at Santa Barbara Alumni Association. Member Santa Barbara Hispanic Achievement Council and Santa Barbara School District Community Outreach Program. Speaker Santa Barbara School District GATE Program. Judicial Coordinator Santa Barbara County High Schools Constitutional Rights Foundation Mock Trial Competition.
Office: 1100 Anacapa Street, Santa Barbara 93101.
Telephone: (805) 568-2220.

O'CONNOR, Kathleen R. *(Judge, Superior Court of California County of Yuba)*
Office: 215 Fifth Street, Marysville 95901.
Telephone: (530) 749-7600.

O'DONNELL, Joanne B. *(Judge, Superior Court of California County of Los Angeles)* Assumed office Jan 22, 2000. Former Judge, Los Angeles Municipal Court Los Angeles County.
Office: Courthouse, 111 North Hill Street, Los Angeles 90012.
Telephone: (213) 974-5411.

O'FARRELL, Robert A. *(Judge, Superior Court of California County of Monterey)* Appointed by Governor Edmund G. Brown, Jr. Sept 1981. Elected 1982, 1988, 1994 and 2000. Current term expires Jan 2007. Presiding Judge Dec 1, 2000 to Dec 31, 2002. Serves Monterey Branch. Born New York New York July 2, 1941. Educated at Ventura College A.A. 1961, California State University at Fresno B.A. 1963 and Hastings College of the Law J.D. 1967. Member Moot Court. Admitted to practice California 1968. Judge, Castroville Justice Court 1974. Judge, Salinas Municipal Court Monterey County 1975-81.
With Ventura County Public Defender's Office 1968 and Monterey County Public Defender's Office Salinas 1969. Instructor in Administration of Justice and Criminal Evidence Monterey Peninsula College 1973. Democrat.
Office: 1200 Aguajito Road, Second Floor, Monterey 93940.
Telephone: (831) 755-5060.

O'FLAHERTY, Joseph *(Judge, Superior Court of California County of Placer)* Assumed office June 30, 1998. Former Judge and Presiding Judge, Placer County Municipal Court.
Office: 10 Culver Street, Department 15, Colfax 95713.
Telephone: (530) 346-8721.

OGDEN, Steven D. *(Judge, Superior Court of California County of Los Angeles)* Assumed office Jan 22, 2000. Term expires Jan 2005. Born Los Angeles California Nov 4, 1943. Religious affiliation: Disciples of Christ. Educated at Occidental College B.A. 1965 and University of California at Los Angeles J.D. 1968. Admitted to practice California 1969. Judge, Antelope Municipal Court Los Angeles County Jan 4, 1999 to Jan 21, 2000.
District Attorney Los Angeles County 1969-99. Member Association of Deputy District Attorneys, Antelope

OGDEN, STEVEN D.—*Continued*

Valley and Los Angeles County Bar Associations. Enjoys golfing, model railroading and computer science.

Office: Lancaster Courthouse, 1040 West Avenue J, Lancaster 93534.

Telephone: (661) 945-6477.

OGLESBY, John D. *(Judge, Superior Court of California County of Kern)* Assumed office July 1, 2000. Presiding Judge Jan 1, 1998 to Dec 31, 1999 and Former Judge, East Kern Municipal Court Kern County.

Office: 1773 Highway 58, Mojave 93501.

Telephone: (661) 824-2436.

OHANESIAN, Gail D. *(Judge, Superior Court of California County of Sacramento)* Assumed office June 17, 1998. Former Judge, Sacramento Municipal Court Sacramento County.

Office: Courthouse, 720 Ninth Street, Sacramento 95814.

Telephone: (916) 874-5476.

O'HARA, Patrick J. *(Judge, Superior Court of California County of Tulare)* Presiding Judge Dec 4, 1998 to June 30, 2001. Former Judge and Presiding Judge, Tulare County Municipal Court.

Office: Tulare County Civic Center, Visalia 93291-4593.

Telephone: (559) 733-6561.

OHTA, Sam *(Judge, Superior Court of California County of Los Angeles)* Assumed office Jan 22, 2000. Former Judge, Los Angeles Municipal Court Los Angeles County.

Office: Metropolitan Courthouse, 1945 South Hill Street, Los Angeles 90007-1466.

Telephone: (213) 744-4001.

OKAMOTO, Vincent H. *(Judge, Superior Court of California County of Los Angeles)*

Office: Inglewood Courthouse, One Regent Street, Inglewood 90301.

Telephone: (310) 419-5121.

OKI, Dan Thomas *(Judge, Superior Court of California County of Los Angeles)* Former Judge and Former Presiding Judge, Citrus Municipal Court Los Angeles County.

Office: Criminal Courts Building, 210 West Temple Street, Los Angeles 90012-3210.

Telephone: (213) 974-6535.

O'LEARY, Kathleen E. *(Associate Justice, California Court of Appeal Fourth District Division Three)* Appointed by Governor Gray Davis Jan 21, 2000. Judge and Presiding Judge, West Orange County Municipal Court 1981 to June 30 1986, appointed by Governor Edmund G. Brown, Jr. Judge and Presiding Judge, Superior Court of California County of Orange July 1, 1986 to Jan 20, 2000, appointed by Governor George Deukmejian.

Mailing address: P.O. Box 22055, Santa Ana 92702.

Telephone: (714) 558-6777.

OLGUIN, Fernando M. *(Magistrate Judge, United States District Court Central District of California)* Appointed by U.S. District Court judges July 23, 2001.

Office: 901 U.S. Courthouse, 312 North Spring Street, Los Angeles 90012.

Telephone: (213) 894-3535.

OLIVER, Robert H. *(Judge, Superior Court of California County of Fresno)* Assumed office July 1, 1998. Educated at California State University at Fresno B.S. and Golden Gate University J.D. Member Beta Gamma Sigma and Golden Key National Honor Society. Certified Estate Planning, Trust and Probate Law Specialist State Bar of California Board of Legal Specialization. Judge April 1995 to June 30, 1998 and Presiding Judge Juvenile Department July 1997 to Aug 1998, Consolidated Fresno Municipal Court Fresno County, appointed by Governor Pete Wilson.

Adjunct Faculty Member Secured Real Property Transactions and Corporate Law San Joaquin College of Law. President Fresno County Young Lawyers, Foundation of the State Bar of California, National Conference of Bar Foundations and Fresno County Bar Association. Member Judicial Nominees Evaluation Commission and State Bar of California (Vice President Board of Governors, Executive Committee Conference of Delegates). Recipient Outstanding Alumnus and Friends Award from California State University at Fresno School of Business 1992, Outstanding Alumnus of Craig School of Business Award from California State University at Fresno Alumni Association 1997, Outstanding Alumnus Award from Golden Gate University School of Law 1999, Award of Recognition from Beverly Hills Bar Foundation and Foundation of the State Bar of California, Public School Advocate Award from Association of California School Administrators and Recognition Award from Fresno Leadership Council. Served to Lieutenant Colonel USAF/California Air National Guard. Chair Board of Governors California State University Fresno Foundation. Board Member Fresno Regional Foundation and San Joaquin College of Law.

Office: 1100 Van Ness Avenue, Fresno 93724-0002.

Telephone: (559) 488-1825.

OLMEDO, Charlaine F. *(Judge, Superior Court of California County of Los Angeles)*

Office: Metropolitan Courthouse, 1945 South Hill Street, Los Angeles 90007-1466.

Telephone: (213) 744-4001.

OLNEY, Garrett *(Judge, Superior Court of California County of Plumas)* Assumed office July 1, 1998. Presiding Judge Jan 1, 1999 to Dec 31, 2000 and since Jan 1, 2003. Former Judge, Plumas County Municipal Court.

Office: 520 Main Street, Room 104, Quincy 95971.

Telephone: (530) 283-6232.

O'MALLEY, Mary Ann *(Judge, Superior Court of California County of Contra Costa)*

Office: A. F. Bray Courts Building, 1020 Ward Street, Martinez 94553.

Telephone: (925) 646-2950.

O'MALLEY, William *(Judge, Superior Court of California County of Contra Costa)*

Office: 45 Civic Avenue, Pittsburgh 94565.

Telephone: (925) 427-8173.

O'NEILL, Lawrence J. *(Magistrate Judge, United States District Court Eastern District of California)* Appointed by U.S. District Court judges to term beginning Jan 26, 1999. Term expires Jan 2007. Serves Fresno Di-

O'NEILL, LAWRENCE J.—*Continued*

vision. Judge and Presiding Judge, Superior Court of California Fresno County 1990-99.

Office: 1116 U.S. Courthouse, 1130 O Street, Fresno 93721.

Telephone: (559) 498-7322.

O'NEILL, Robert F. *(Judge, Superior Court of California County of San Diego)*

Mailing address: P.O. Box 122724, San Diego 92112-2724.

Office: 220 West Broadway, San Diego 92101.

Telephone: (619) 531-3820.

O'NEILL, Robert P. *(Judge, Superior Court of California County of Los Angeles)* Former Judge, Los Angeles Municipal Court Los Angeles County.

Office: Los Angeles Airport Courthouse, 11701 South La Cienega Boulevard, Los Angeles 90045.

Telephone: (310) 727-6010.

O'NEILL, Vincent J., Jr. *(Judge, Superior Court of California County of Ventura)* Former Judge, Ventura County Municipal Court.

Mailing address: P.O. Box 6489, Ventura 93006-6489.

Office: 800 South Victoria Avenue, Ventura 93009-0001.

Telephone: (805) 654-2965.

ONG, Tomson T. *(Judge, Superior Court of California County of Los Angeles)* Assumed office Jan 22, 2000. Former Judge, Long Beach Municipal Court Los Angeles County.

Office: Long Beach Courthouse, 415 West Ocean Boulevard, Long Beach 90802.

Telephone: (562) 491-6130.

ONGKEKO, Rafael A. *(Judge, Superior Court of California County of Los Angeles)*

Office: Lancaster Courthouse, 1040 West Avenue J, Lancaster 93534.

Telephone: (661) 945-6477.

OPPLIGER, James R. *(Judge, Superior Court of California County of Fresno)*

Office: Courthouse, 1100 Van Ness Avenue, Fresno 93724-0002.

Telephone: (559) 488-1825.

ORFIELD, Adrienne A. *(Judge, Superior Court of California County of San Diego)* Assumed office Dec 1, 1998. Term expires Jan 2007. Born Memphis Tennessee June 14, 1953. Catholic. Educated at California State University at San Bernardino B.A. with honors 1975 and University of San Diego School of Law J.D. 1979. Admitted to practice California 1979. In legal practice San Diego 1979-95. Judge, San Diego Municipal Court San Diego County Sept 1995 to Nov 30, 1998, appointed by Governor Pete Wilson.

Adjunct Professor of Lawyering Skills II University of San Diego School of Law 1990-91. Former Member San Diego County Bar Foundation, California Women Lawyers and State Bar of California. Master Louis M. Welsh Inn of Court since 1995. Member Lawyers Club, San Diego County Judges Association (President 1999) and San Diego County Bar Association (President 1994). Named Outstanding Alumna of the Year from University of San Diego School of Law Women in Law 1993. Member 1986-90 and Advisory Board 1990-95 Crime Victims Fund. Enjoys travel and reading.

Mailing address: P.O. Box 122724, San Diego 92112.

Office: 325 South Melrose Drive, Vista 92083.

Telephone: (760) 940-4376.

Fax: (760) 940-4794

ORFIELD, Michael Bennett *(Judge, Superior Court of California County of San Diego)* Assumed office Dec 1, 1998. Born San Diego California May 29, 1949. Educated at University of California at San Diego B.A. 1972, Duke University 1973-74 and California Western School of Law J.D. 1977. Recipient American Jurisprudence Awards in Criminal Law and Wills and Bancroft-Whitney Award Trial Moot Court. Student Article Editor International Law Journal 1976-77. Admitted to practice California 1977 and U.S. District Court Southern District of California 1977. In legal practice San Diego 1977-89. Former Judge pro tem, Superior Court of California. Judge Aug 21, 1989 to Nov 30, 1998 and Presiding Judge Jan 1, 1996 to Dec 31, 1997, San Diego Municipal Court San Diego County, appointed by Governor George Deukmejian.

Assistant District Attorney San Diego 1978-79. Author "Weather Genesis and Weather Neutralization: A New Approach to Weather Modification" California Western International L. Jour. 412, 1976, "They're Here!" *Dicta*, "It's the Law" local newspapers and clean-up provisions of California Code of Civil Procedure 877.6, Assembly Bill 2993. Important Decisions: People v. Cindy Fendell, et al. (a nine defendant trespass and failure to disperse jury trial involving anti-abortion activists blocking entry to a doctor's office), People v. Cabray Scott (child molestation), Evans v. Mercy Hospital Medical Center, George Baehr, M.D. and Murry Reicher, M.D. (medical malpractice), Garro v. Afshani (fraud and delivery), Vincellette v. Coopers & Lybrand (wrongful termination), Curry v. The Vons Companies (wrongful termination, racial discrimination and harassment), Jamul Highland Properties, et al. v. Hewette Stone, et al. (fraud and conspiracy in the foreclosure of land), Bleich v. Conant (personal injury), Zuniga v. County of San Diego, et al. (personal injury) and Jones v. Sweeney (personal injury). Former Member San Diego Defense Lawyers (Founding Member/Steering Committee 1983, Board of Directors, Secretary/Treasurer 1984-86), National Panel of Arbitrators American Arbitration Association, Judicial Council of California, State Bar of California (Special Advisor Committee on the Administration of Justice Economic Litigation Act Subcommittee 1989) and San Diego County Bar Association (Attorney/Client Relations Committee, Fee Dispute Arbitration Committee 1983-89, Conference of Delegates 1985, 1986, 1987, 1988, Bar/Superior Court Bench Committee on Case Control 1986-89, Co-chair Torts and Workers Compensation Subcommittee 1986 and Chair Superior Court Committee 1989). Member ad hoc Committee on Local Rules 1991-92, Criminal Matters Committee 1992-93, Budget and Finance Committee 1994-95, Commissioners Committee 1994-95 and Computer Technology Committee 1994-95 and Chair Legislative Committee 1991-92, Security Committee 1993-94, Retreat Committee 1993-94 and Civil Committee 1994-95 San Diego Municipal Court San Diego County. Master Louis M. Welsch American Inns of Court 1994. Member Jury Instruction Task Force since 1998, San Diego County Judges Association (Board of Directors since 1990, Secretary 1991-92, Vice President 1992-93 and President 1993-94), Judicial

ORFIELD, MICHAEL BENNETT—*Continued*

Council of California, California Judges Association (Civil Law and Procedure Committee 1991-93, Prevailing Party/Attorney Fees as Costs Subcommittee 1991-92, Municipal Court Matters Subcommittee 1991-92, A.O.C. Uniform Local Rules Subcommittee 1991-92 and Member since 1993 and Chair 1994 Court Administration Committee), Lawyers Club of San Diego (Legislation/ Conference of Delegates Committee since 1990 and Joint Committee with San Diego County Bar Association for Uniform Rule Establishment 1993), American Judicature Society and American Bar Association (Committee on Court Delay Reduction National Conference of Special Court Judges 1991-92, Model Court Programs Subcommittee 1991-94, Courts and the Community Committee 1991-94 Judicial Administration Division).

Speaker "Superior Court Fast Track" 1987 and 1988 and "Superior Court Fast Track/Arbitration" 1989, 1990 and 1991 Judges Orientation Program/Bridging the Gap and "Civil Case and Legislation Update" California Civil Law and Procedure Institute for All Trial Court Judges 1991. Panelist "Fast Track Rules for 1991 Superior and Municipal Courts" Law Office Economics and Management Section Seminar 1991, Second Annual Legal Seminar Institute of Real Estate Management 1991, Continuing Legal Education Course on Fast Track programs for the San Diego Superior and Municipal Courts Dec 1991 and June 1992 and "Meet Your Judges Public Forum" San Diego Municipal Court 1992. Member Planning Committee 1994, Speaker "Civil Case and Legislation Update" 1993 and 1994 and Group Leader "Urban Judges Roundtable" 1994 Municipal and Justice Court Institute California Center for Judicial Education and Research. Court Representative and Moderator "Bridging the Gap" Judges Orientation Program since 1996. Faculty Member "Leading Organizational Change" since 1998. Recipient Service Award from San Diego Defense Lawyers 1986 and Barristers Club of San Diego 1986, Citation of Appreciation from American Business Women's Association 1987, Certificate of Appreciation from Commission on the Bicentennial of the United States Constitution 1987 and 1988 and Clinical Education Program University of San Diego School of Law 1990 and 1991 and Exceptional Service Award from San Diego County Judges Association. Vice President Custom Reagent Labs Inc. 1972-73. Republican. Member San Diego Volunteer Lawyers Program 1985-89. Board of Directors 1985-89, Vice Chairman 1985 and 1986, Executive Committee 1986-88, Chairman 1987 and 1988 and Member Advisory Board The Crime Victims Fund. Board of Directors Kiwanis Club of San Diego 1986-89, San Diego County Humane Society since 1990 and First San Diego Courthouse, Inc. Advisor Legal Nurse Consultant Certification Program University of California at San Diego. Member Gensia and St. William Catholic Church. Train enthusiast and amateur astronomer. Enjoys golf.

Mailing address: P.O. Box 122724, San Diego 92112-2724.

Office: 325 South Melrose Drive, Vista 92083.

Telephone: (760) 726-9595.

ORNDOFF, George *(Judge, Superior Court of California County of Kings)* Assumed office Feb 8, 2001. Presiding Judge May 1, 1995 to June 30, 1997 and Former Judge, Kings County Municipal Court.

Mailing address: 1426 South Drive, Hanford 93230.

Office: 501 East Kings Street, Avenal 93204.

Telephone: (559) 386-5225.

O'ROURKE, John G. *(Judge, Superior Court of California County of Kings)* Assumed office Feb 8, 2001. Former Judge, Kings County Municipal Court.

Mailing address: 1426 South Drive, Hanford 93230.

Office: 449 C Street, Lemoore 93245.

Telephone: (559) 924-7757.

O'ROURKE, Terry *(Associate Justice, California Court of Appeal Fourth District Division One)* Appointed by Governor Pete Wilson to term beginning 1998. Born 1947. Educated at Claremont McKenna College B.A. 1969 and Harvard Law School J.D. 1972. In legal practice Los Angeles and San Diego 1973-84. Judge, Superior Court of California Los Angeles County 1984-87, appointed by Governor George Deukmejian. Judge, Superior Court of California San Diego County 1987-98, appointed by Governor George Deukmejian.

Office: 750 B Street, Suite 300, San Diego 92101.

Telephone: (619) 645-2760.

OROZCO, Gary R. *(Judge, Superior Court of California County of Fresno)*

Office: 1100 Van Ness Avenue, Fresno 93724-0002.

Telephone: (559) 488-1825.

ORTEGA, Reuben A. *(Associate Justice, California Court of Appeal Second District Division One)* Appointed by Governor George Deukmejian to term beginning June 10, 1988. Retained by election Nov 1990 and Nov 1994. Current term expires Jan 2007. Born Albuquerque New Mexico Dec 22, 1941. Roman Catholic. Educated at University of New Mexico B.A. 1963 and Georgetown University J.D. 1967. Admitted to practice California 1967 and U.S. District Court Central District of California 1974. In legal practice Long Beach 1973-77. Commissioner 1977-83 and Judge 1984-88, Superior Court of California Los Angeles County.

Deputy District Attorney 1967-73 and Assistant District Attorney 1983-84 Los Angeles. Republican.

Office: 300 South Spring Street, Los Angeles 90013.

Telephone: (213) 830-7533.

OSBORNE-ANDERSON, Marla *(Judge, Superior Court of California County of Monterey)* Assumed office Dec 18, 2000. Born Washington D.C. April 30, 1959. Seventh-Day Adventist. Educated at Loma Linda University B.A. 1981 and University of California at Davis School of Law J.D. 1986. Moot Court Board 1986. Intern to Hon. Terry Hatter, U.S. District Court Central District of California 1984. Admitted to practice California 1986 and U.S. District Court Eastern District of California 1986. In legal practice Sacramento 1985-86. Judge, Monterey County Municipal Court Jan 16, 1995 to Dec 17, 2000, appointed by Governor Pete Wilson.

Deputy District Attorney Monterey County 1987-95. Instructor in Criminal Law Hartnell College 1989. Member California Judges Association, National Association of Women Judges and American Judges Association. Attended June 1996, Teacher/Seminar Leader June 1997 and Faculty Member 1998, 2001 and 2002 Judicial College California Center for Judicial Education and Research. Former Board Member Monterey County Legal Services, Monterey Rape Crisis Center and Hartnell Col-

OSBORNE-ANDERSON, MARLA—*Continued*
lege Foundation. Board Member Community Foundation of Monterey. Member Rotary Club of King City and NAACP. Enjoys golfing, being outdoors and traveling.
Office: 240 Church Street, Rooms 320 and 121, Salinas 93901.
Telephone: (831) 755-5060.

OTERO, S. James *(Judge, Superior Court of California County of Los Angeles)* Former Judge, Los Angeles Municipal Court Los Angeles County.
Office: Courthouse, 111 North Hill Street, Los Angeles 90012.
Telephone: (213) 974-5411.

OUDERKIRK, John W. *(Judge, Superior Court of California County of Los Angeles)* Appointed by Governor George Deukmejian Feb 1989. Elected Nov 1998, current term expires Jan 2004. Serves Family Law Trial Department since 2000. Served Civil Trial Court 1997-2000 and Long Cause Felony Trials Criminal Courts 1992-97. Born New York New York Nov 1942. Educated at California State University, Los Angeles B.S. with honors 1972 and Loyola Law School J.D. 1977. Admitted to practice California 1977. Supervising Judge, Los Angeles County Municipal Court 1990.
Deputy District Attorney Los Angeles County 1978-89. Important Decision: People v. Damian Williams (Reginald Denny beating case) 1993. Board of Directors Association of Deputy District Attorneys 1984. Member Executive Committee Los Angeles Superior Court 2000-01. Attended California Judges College 1989 and 1991, Seminar on Land Use The National Judicial College 1994 and 1997, Seminar on Basic Civil Law 1997, Advanced Civil Law 1998 and Family Law 2000 California Center for Judicial Education and Seminar on Mediation Pepperdine Strauss Institute 2001. Named Criminal Court Judge of the Year by Century City Bar Association 1994. USMCR 1961-66. Board of Directors Devil Pups Inc. since 1994. Enjoys travel, reading, fishing and kayaking.
Office: 111 North Hill Street, Los Angeles 90012.
Telephone: (213) 974-4331.

OWEN, Knoel L. *(Judge, Superior Court of California County of Sonoma)* Assumed office June 12, 1998. Former Judge and Presiding Judge, Sonoma County Municipal Court.
Office: 1450 Guerneville Road, Santa Rosa 95403.
Telephone: (707) 565-1100.

PACHECO, John M. *(Judge, Superior Court of California County of San Bernardino)* Serves East Desert District.
Office: 6527 White Feather Road, Joshua Tree 92252.
Telephone: (760) 366-4112.

PAER, Gary S. *(Judge, Superior Court of California County of Orange)* Commissioner Feb 28, 1997 to Aug 11, 2000. Appointed Judge by Governor Gray Davis to term beginning Aug 11, 2000. Elected 2000, current term expires Jan 1, 2007. Born New York New York Dec 25, 1957. Educated at American University B.S. 1979 and California Western School of Law J.D. 1982. Admitted to practice New Jersey 1983, New York 1983, U.S. District Courts District of New Jersey 1983 and Eastern 1984 and Southern 1984 Districts of New York, California 1984 and U.S. Supreme Court 1991.
Assistant District Attorney Bronx Feb 1984 to July 1985. Senior Deputy District Attorney Orange County July 1985 to Oct 1986 and April 1987 to March 1997. Special Agent FBI 1986-87. Guest Instructor in Criminal Justice Programs Whittier College School of Law, Chapman College and Goldenwest College. Member California Judges Association and Orange County Bar Association. Graduate B. E. Witkin Judicial College of California 1997. Reserve Police Officer Los Angeles Police Department 1991-97. Republican. Member South Orange County Gang Steering Committee, Governing Board of Victim-Witness Programs and Constitutional Rights Foundation (Member Community Focused Planning Committee and Judicial Council, Peer Court Judge and Mock Trial Judge). Enjoys being ice hockey goalie, jogging, reading and traveling.
Office: 700 Civic Center Drive West, Santa Ana 92701.
Telephone: (714) 834-2351.
Fax: (714) 834-6171
E-mail address: gpaer@occourts.org

PALAZUELOS, Yvette M. *(Judge, Superior Court of California County of Los Angeles)*
Office: East Los Angeles Courthouse, 214 South Fetterly Avenue, Los Angeles 90022.
Telephone: (323) 780-2055.

PALMER, Charles F. *(Judge, Superior Court of California County of Los Angeles)*
Office: Courthouse, 111 North Hill Street, Los Angeles 90012.
Telephone: (213) 974-5411.

PANGMAN, William W. *(Judge, Superior Court of California County of Sierra)* Presiding Judge Jan 1, 1999 to Dec 31, 2000 and since Jan 1, 2002.
Mailing address: P.O. Box 476, Downieville 95936.
Office: 100 Courthouse Square, Downieville 95936.
Telephone: (530) 289-3698.

PAPADAKIS, Harry N. *(Judge, Superior Court of California County of Fresno)* Assumed office July 1, 1998. Born California Feb 8, 1944. Admitted to practice California. Began legal practice Santa Clara County. Judge, Central Valley Municipal Court Fresno County April 2, 1984 to June 30, 1998.
Member California Judges Association, State Bar of California, West Valley, Fresno County and Santa Clara County Bar Associations. Sergeant U.S. Army 1967-69. Cattle rancher.
Office: 1100 Van Ness Avenue, Fresno 93724-0002.
Telephone: (559) 488-1825.

PAPAS, Leo S. *(Magistrate Judge, United States District Court Southern District of California)* Appointed by U.S. District Court judges.
Office: 1101 U.S. Courthouse, 940 Front Street, San Diego 92101-8923.
Telephone: (619) 557-6384.

PARK, Richard Kent *(Judge, Superior Court of California County of Sacramento)* Presiding Judge Jan 1, 2000 to Dec 31, 2001.
Office: Courthouse, 720 Ninth Street, Sacramento 95814.
Telephone: (916) 874-5476.

PARKER, John W. *(Judge, Superior Court of California County of San Joaquin)* Assumed office June 8,

PARKER, JOHN W.—*Continued*
1998. Former Judge, Manteca-Ripon-Escalon-Tracy Municipal Court San Joaquin County.
Office: 222 East Weber Avenue, Room 303, Stockton 95202.
Telephone: (209) 468-2827.

PARKER, Perry *(Judge, Superior Court of California County of Sutter)* Assumed office June 3, 1998. Former Judge and Presiding Judge, Sutter County Municipal Court.
Office: 446 Second Street, Yuba City 95991.
Telephone: (530) 822-7360.

PARNELL, Lorna *(Judge, Superior Court of California County of Los Angeles)* Former Judge, Los Angeles Municipal Court Los Angeles County.
Office: Santa Monica Courthouse, 1725 Main Street, Santa Monica 90401.
Telephone: (310) 260-3762.

PARRILLI, Joanne C. *(Associate Justice, California Court of Appeal First District Division Three)* Appointed by Governor Pete Wilson March 15, 1995. Retained by election, current term expires Jan 2, 2015. Born Chicago Illinois Sept 15, 1947. Catholic. Educated at San Francisco State University B.A. magna cum laude 1971, Loyola University and University of San Francisco J.D. 1974. Admitted to practice California 1974. In legal practice Tahoe City 1980-83. Judge, Oakland-Piedmont-Emeryville Municipal Court Alameda County Nov 1, 1985 to Sept 1988. Former Judge, Superior Court of California Alameda County, appointed by Governor George Deukmejian to term beginning Sept 1988.
Deputy District Attorney Alameda County 1974-79 and 1983-85. Special Prosecutor Marin County Nov 1981 to May 1982. Co-author Chapter 22 *California Criminal Law, Procedure and Practice* CEB 1986. Visiting Lecturer Evidence Advocacy Boalt Hall School of Law 1984. Adjunct Professor of Law in Trial Practice University of San Francisco since 1991. Co-chair Bench Bar Liaison Committee Alameda County 1990-91. Member California Judicial Council (Advisory Committee Trial Court Improvement Fund 1988-89, California Court Technology Committee since 1997), California Women Lawyers, American Judicature Society, California Judges Association (Chairperson Courts and Technology Committee 1987, Chairperson Educational Planning and Coordinating Committee 1991-92), National Association of Women Judges, State Bar of California, Alameda County and American (Delegate 1991-92 and Executive Committee since 1992 National Conference of State Trial Judges) Bar Associations. Faculty member Trial and Appellate Advocacy Hastings College of the Law since 1978, National Institute of Trial Advocacy since 1984, Pretrial Motions in Criminal Cases Continuing Judicial Studies Program 1987-88, Orientation Course in Evidence for New Judges Center for Judicial Education and Research 1987-88, Trials Course 1988 and Computer Literacy 1991 California Judges College and Managing Trials Effectively Institute for Court Management of the National Center for State Courts Nov 1990. Lecturer Statewide Traffic Hearing Officers Oct 1986. Guest Speaker Computer Evidence Mid-Year Conference 1988 and New Admitees Program on Civil Law and Motion Alameda County Bar Association Jan 1991 and Jan 1992. Guest Lecturer Personal Injury Update Programs March 1992 and Dec 1992 and Lecturer on Privilege, Privacy and Work Product The Rutter Group. Recipient Outstanding Service Award as Volunteer and Advisory Board Member from Volunteers in Parole April 17, 1986 and President's Award from California Judges Association 1995. Enjoys photography, travel and computer technology.
Office: 350 McAllister Street, San Francisco 94102-3600.
Telephone: (415) 865-7377.

PARRISH, Wayne R. *(Judge, Superior Court of California County of Mariposa)*
Mailing address: P.O. Box 28, Mariposa 95338.
Office: 5088 Bullion Street, Mariposa 95338.
Telephone: (209) 966-2005.

PARSONS, Craig L. *(Judge, Superior Court of California County of San Mateo)* Serves Northern Branch. Former Judge, San Mateo County Municipal Court.
Office: 1050 Mission Road, South San Francisco 94080.
Telephone: (650) 877-5772.

PASTOR, Michael E. *(Judge, Superior Court of California County of Los Angeles)* Assumed office Jan 22, 2000. Former Judge, Los Angeles Municipal Court Los Angeles County.
Office: Criminal Courts Building, 210 West Temple Street, Los Angeles 90012-3210.
Telephone: (213) 974-6535.

PATE, Christine V. *(Judge, Superior Court of California County of San Diego)* Appointed by Governor George Deukmejian Feb 9, 1988. Elected to subsequent terms. Current term expires Jan 2009. Born San Diego California 1943. Catholic. Educated at University of California at Berkeley B.A. 1965 and University of San Diego J.D. cum laude 1969. Admitted to practice California 1970 and U.S. District Court Southern District of California 1970. In legal practice San Diego 1970-88.
President Lawyers Club of San Diego 1982-83. District Nine Representative to Conference of Delegates State Bar of California 1983-86. Director and Secretary San Diego County Bar Association 1986-88.
Mailing address: P.O. Box 128, San Diego 92112.
Office: 220 West Broadway, D-51, San Diego 92101.
Telephone: (619) 531-3848.

PATE, William C. *(Judge, Superior Court of California County of San Diego)* Appointed by Governor George Deukmejian to term beginning Sept 1986. Elected to subsequent terms. Current term expires 2006. Born Coronado California Nov 17, 1943. Methodist. Educated at Whittier College B.A. 1965 and University of San Diego J.D. cum laude 1971. Executive Editor San Diego Law Review 1970-71. Law Clerk to Hon. James M. Carter, U.S. Court of Appeals Ninth Circuit 1971-72. Admitted to practice California 1972. In legal practice San Diego 1972-86.
Former member State Bar of California, San Diego and American Bar Associations. Member California Judges Association. Captain USMC 1966-69.
Mailing address: P.O. Box 122724, San Diego 92112-2724.
Office: 330 West Broadway, San Diego 92101.
Telephone: (619) 685-6148.

PATEL, Marilyn Hall *(Chief Judge, United States District Court Northern District of California)* Appointed for life by the President. Chief Judge since Nov

PATEL, MARILYN HALL—*Continued*

15, 1997. Former Judge, Oakland-Piedmont-Emeryville Municipal Court Alameda County.

Office: U.S. Courthouse, Box 36060, 450 Golden Gate Avenue, San Francisco 94102-3489.

Telephone: (415) 522-3600.

PATRICK, William R. *(Judge, Superior Court of California County of Butte)* Presiding Judge Jan 1, 1995 to Dec 31, 1996.

Office: One Court Street, Oroville 95965.

Telephone: (530) 538-7611.

PAUL, Roy L. *(Judge, Superior Court of California County of Los Angeles)* Assumed office Jan 22, 2000. Presiding Judge Jan 1, 1996 to Dec 31, 1996 and Former Judge, Downey Municipal Court Los Angeles County.

Office: Courthouse, 111 North Hill Street, Los Angeles 90012.

Telephone: (213) 974-5411.

PENA, Rosendo, Jr. *(Judge, Superior Court of California County of Fresno)*

Office: Courthouse, 1100 Van Ness Avenue, Fresno 93724-0002.

Telephone: (559) 488-1825.

PERK, Steven L. *(Judge, Superior Court of California County of Orange)* Assumed office Aug 10, 1998. Former Judge, Central Orange County Municipal Court.

Mailing address: P.O. Box 1994, Santa Ana 92702-1994.

Office: Central Justice Center, 700 Civic Center Drive West, Santa Ana 92701.

Telephone: (714) 834-3734.

PERKINS, David W. *(Judge, Superior Court of California County of Los Angeles)* Assumed office Jan 22, 2000. Elected 2002, current term expires Jan 2009. Serves Southeast District. Born Pampa Texas March 28, 1935. Protestant. Educated at University of Southern California B.S. 1970 and Western State University College of Law J.D. 1976. Admitted to practice California 1977, U.S. District Court of California 1977 and U.S. Supreme Court 1985. In legal practice Downey 1977-90. Judge Jan 8, 1991 to Jan 21, 2000 and Presiding Judge Jan 1, 1997 to Dec 31, 1997, Downey Municipal Court Los Angeles County.

Member American Judicature Society, Presiding Judges Association, Municipal Court Judges Association (Member Gang Violence Committee 1992 and Data Processing Committee 1992-93, Chair Jail Overcrowding Committee 1995), California Judges Association and Southeast District Bar Association (Board of Trustees 1987-89, Vice President 1990). Attended California Judges College 1991 and numerous California Judges Association, Municipal Court Judges Association and California Judicial Education and Research conferences and seminars since 1991. Named Judge of the Year by Southeast District Bar Association 2003. Specialist 4 U.S. Army 1958-60. Previously worked as Captain, Administrative Assistant Chief and Acting Fire Chief Vernon Fire Department 1957-85. Republican. Board of Directors 1992-93 and President 1996 Kiwanis Club of Downey. Enjoys golf, bowling, spectator sports, travel and dogs.

Office: Downey Courthouse, 7500 East Imperial Highway, Downey 90242.

Telephone: (562) 803-7018.

PERLUSS, Dennis M. *(Presiding Justice, California Court of Appeal Second District Division Seven)* Appointed by Governor Gray Davis to term beginning Oct 22, 2001. Presiding Justice since Jan 9, 2003. Born Sacramento California May 12, 1948. Educated at Stanford University B.A. with great distinction 1970 and Harvard Law School J.D. magna cum laude 1973. Editor Harvard Law Review. Law Clerk to Hon. Shirley Hufstedler, U.S. Court of Appeals Ninth Circuit 1973-74 and Hon. Potter Stewart, U.S. Supreme Court 1974-75. Member Phi Beta Kappa. In legal practice 1975-99. Judge, Superior Court of California County of Los Angeles Oct 1999 to Oct 2001.

Office: 300 South Spring Street, Los Angeles 90013.

Telephone: (213) 830-7000.

PERREN, Steven Zalkind *(Associate Justice, California Court of Appeal Second District Division Six)* Appointed by Governor Gray Davis to term beginning Nov 9, 1999. Born Los Angeles California March 9, 1942. Educated at University of California at Los Angeles B.A. 1964 J.D. 1967. Member Pi Lambda Phi. Admitted to practice California 1967, U.S. District Court Central District of California 1973 and U.S. Supreme Court 1979. Began legal practice Ventura 1969. Judge Jan 2, 1983 to Nov 8, 1999, Assistant Presiding Judge 1990-91 and Presiding Judge 1992-93, Superior Court of California County of Ventura.

Instructor in Criminal Law Ventura College of Law 1975-77. Chair Advisory Committee on Trial Court Staffing Administrative Office of the Courts 1992. Chair Criminal Law Advisory Committee since 2001 and Member Task Force on Jury Instructions Judicial Council of California. Member California Judges Association (Committee on Criminal Law and Procedure 1983-2001, Executive Committee 1992-94, Vice President 1994) and California Judges Foundation (Chair since 2002). Instructor in Criminal Law and Procedure 1985 and Sentencing 1986-96 Continuing Judicial Studies Program and California Judges College 1986-97. Participant Juvenile Justice Institute Center for Judicial Education and Research (determining if the juvenile offender shall be transferred to adult court) California Center for Judicial Education and Research 1995-97. Named Ventura County Trial Judge of the Year by Ventura County Trial Lawyers Association 1984 and 1999. Captain U.S. Army Signal Corps 1967-69. Democrat. Board of Directors Ventura Boys and Girls Club 1978-85, C.A.A.N., Temple Beth Torah 1986-88, Casa Pacifica 1995-2001, United Way 1996-2001, Cabrillo Music Theatre since 1999 and University of California at Los Angeles Law Alumni Association. Member Plaza Players Theatre Group 1969-82. Enjoys acting and singing.

Office: 200 East Santa Clara Street, Ventura 93001.

Telephone: (805) 641-4700.

PERRY, Robert J. *(Judge, Superior Court of California County of Los Angeles)*

Office: Criminal Courts Building, 210 West Temple Street, Los Angeles 90012-3210.

Telephone: (213) 974-6535.

PERSON, Suzanne E. *(Judge, Superior Court of California County of Los Angeles)* Assumed office Jan 22, 2000. Former Judge, Los Angeles Municipal Court Los Angeles County.

Office: Criminal Courts Building, 210 West Temple Street, Los Angeles 90012-3210.

Telephone: (213) 974-6535.

PERSÓN, Victor H. *(Judge, Superior Court of California County of Los Angeles)* Appointed by Governor Pete Wilson to term beginning Jan 25, 1992. Elected Nov 1992 and 1998. Current term expires Jan 2005. Born Glendale California June 1, 1946. Episcopalian. Educated at University of Southern California B.S. 1968 and Loyola University of Los Angeles J.D. 1971. Member Phi Alpha Delta. Admitted to practice California 1972, U.S. District Court Central District of California 1972, U.S. Court of Appeals Ninth Circuit 1972 and U.S. Supreme Court 1976. In legal practice Los Angeles 1972-85. Judge, Pasadena Municipal Court Los Angeles County 1985-92.

Deputy District Attorney Los Angeles County 1973-85. Former member State Bar of California, Glendale and Los Angeles County Bar Associations. Member Municipal Court Judges Association of Los Angeles County (Member 1985-91 and Chair 1988-91 Marshal Committee), California Judges Association and Criminal Courts Bar Association. Graduate California Judicial College summer 1986. Attended California Judges Orientation Seminar Jan 1986, California Judges Advanced Criminal Law Seminar Feb 1987, California Continuing Judicial Studies Program Aug 1990, Orientation Program for New Superior Court Judges and Commissioners March 1992 and "Hearing Criminal Cases" Case Management Techniques Seminar for Los Angeles County Superior Judges Jan 7-9, 1993. Member Pasadena Tournament of Roses Association and Pasadena Optimists Club. Enjoys physical fitness and golf.

Office: Courthouse, 111 North Hill Street, Los Angeles 90012.

Telephone: (213) 974-5411.

PETERSEN, Stephen D. *(Judge, Superior Court of California County of Los Angeles)* Appointed by Governor George Deukmejian to term beginning Jan 29, 1988. Elected 1988, 1994 and 2000. Current term expires 2006. Serves Northwest District. Born Spencer Iowa Dec 26, 1943. Educated at University of Iowa B.B.A. 1966 J.D. 1969. Admitted to practice Iowa 1969 and California 1972.

Assistant U.S. Attorney and First Assistant Chief Civil Division Los Angeles 1973-88. Captain U.S. Army active duty 1969-73. Lieutenant Colonel USAR JAGC (retired).

Office: Van Nuys Courthouse East, 6230 Sylmar Avenue, Van Nuys 91401.

Telephone: (818) 374-3112.

PETERSON, Kenneth G. *(Judge, Superior Court of California County of Sacramento)* Former Judge, Sacramento Municipal Court Sacramento County.

Office: Juvenile Center, 9601 Kiefer Boulevard, Sacramento 95827.

Telephone: (916) 875-5009.

PETERSON, Thomas A. *(Judge, Superior Court of California County of Los Angeles)* Assumed office Jan 22, 2000. Former Judge and Presiding Judge, Pomona Municipal Court Los Angeles County.

Office: Pomona Courthouse North, 350 West Mission Boulevard, Pomona 91766.

Telephone: (909) 802-9944.

PETERSON, Wayne L. *(Judge, Superior Court of California County of San Diego)* Presiding Judge Nov 5, 1998 to Dec 31, 2001. Former Judge, San Diego Municipal Court San Diego County.

Mailing address: P.O. Box 122724, San Diego 92112-2724.

Office: 330 West Broadway, San Diego 92101.

Telephone: (619) 685-6148.

PETRE, Donna *(Judge, Superior Court of California County of Yolo)* Appointed by Governor George Deukmejian 1986. Elected 1988, 1994 and 2000. Current term expires Jan 2007. Former Presiding Judge. Born Joliet Illinois April 21, 1947. Educated at Clarke College B.A. 1969, Northwestern University M.A. 1971 and University of California Hastings College of the Law J.D. 1976. Recipient American Jurisprudence Award 1972. Managing Editor Constitutional Law Quarterly 1975-76. Law Clerk to Hon. Thomas W. Caldecott, California Court of Appeal First District 1976-77. Admitted to practice California 1976. Former Judge, Yolo County Municipal Court.

With Criminal Appeals Section 1977-80, Consumer Law Section 1980-83 and Medi-Cal Fraud Division 1983-86 Attorney General's Office. Author "*Worth v. Seldin:* The Substantial Probability Test" Hastings Constitutional Law Quarterly 1976. Adjunct Instructor in Trial Practice University of California at Davis 1989. Member Committee on Administration of Justice in Rural Counties 1988 and Presiding Judges Standing Advisory Committee 1993. Member California Judges Association, Women Lawyers of California, California Women Lawyers and Yolo Bar Association. Seminar leader California Judges Association 1988. Named Woman of Achievement by Business and Professional Women 1989. History editor *Encyclopædia Britannica* 1970-71. Government teacher San Diego 1971-72. Republican. Member Davis Chamber of Commerce, Woodland Chamber of Commerce, Yolo Chamber of Commerce, Association of American University Women, League of Women Voters, Business and Professional Women and Literacy Council. Enjoys opera.

Office: 725 Court Street, Woodland 95695.

Telephone: (530) 666-8598.

PETRUCELLI, James *(Judge, Superior Court of California County of Fresno)*

Office: 1100 Van Ness Avenue, Fresno 93724-0002.

Telephone: (559) 488-1825.

PEVEN, Charles L. *(Judge, Superior Court of California County of Los Angeles)* Serves North Valley District. Born Chicago Illinois March 18, 1934. Educated at Michigan State University B.A. 1955 and University of Michigan J.D. 1958. Admitted to practice California 1959. Commissioner May 1980 to Dec 1987 and Former Judge, Los Angeles Municipal Court Los Angeles County, appointed Judge by Governor George Deukmejian to term beginning Dec 16, 1987.

PEVEN, CHARLES L.—*Continued*

Deputy District Attorney Los Angeles County Nov 1959 to Aug 1971.

Office: San Fernando Courthouse, 900 Third Street, San Fernando 91340.

Telephone: (818) 898-2620.

PFAELZER, Mariana R. *(Senior Judge, United States District Court Central District of California)* Appointed for life by President Jimmy Carter to term beginning 1978. Assumed Senior status Dec 31, 1997, serves by assignment. Born Los Angeles California Feb 4, 1926. Educated at University of California at Santa Barbara A.B. 1949 and University of California at Los Angeles J.D. 1957. In legal practice Los Angeles 1957-78.

Office: U.S. Courthouse, 312 North Spring Street, Los Angeles 90012.

Telephone: (213) 894-7284.

PFEIFFER, Rosemary *(Judge, Superior Court of California County of San Mateo)* Serves Central Branch. Presiding Judge Jan 1, 2000 to Dec 31, 2000.

Office: 800 North Humboldt Street, San Mateo 94401.

Telephone: (650) 573-2617.

PFISTER, Charles B. *(Judge, Superior Court of California County of Kern)* Assumed office July 1, 2000. Former Judge, Bakersfield Municipal Court Kern County.

Office: 1215 Truxtun Avenue, Bakersfield 93301.

Telephone: (661) 868-2450.

PHILLIPS, Craig *(Judge, Superior Court of California County of Kern)* Serves Arvin-Lamont Branch.

Office: 12022 Main Street, Lamont 93241.

Telephone: (661) 845-3741.

PHILLIPS, John M. *(Judge, Superior Court of California County of Monterey)* Presiding Judge Jan 1, 1996 to Dec 31, 1996. Presiding Judge Superior and Municipal Courts since July 1, 1998.

Mailing address: P.O. Box 1819, Salinas 93902-1819.

Office: 240 Church Street, Salinas 93901.

Telephone: (831) 755-5060.

PHILLIPS, Virginia A. *(Judge, United States District Court Central District of California)* Magistrate Judge 1995-99. Appointed Judge for life by President Bill Clinton to term beginning Dec 27, 1999. Born Orange California Feb 14, 1957. Educated at University of California at Riverside B.A. magna cum laude 1979 and University of California Boalt Hall School of Law J.D. 1982. In legal practice Riverside 1982-91. Commissioner, Superior Court of California County of Riverside 1991-95.

Office: U.S. Courthouse, 3470 Twelfth Street, Riverside 92501.

Telephone: (909) 328-4461.

PHIMISTER, Douglas C. *(Judge, Superior Court of California County of El Dorado)*

Office: Administration Office, 2850 Fairlane Court, Placerville 95667.

Telephone: (530) 621-7454.

PICETTI, Gary M. *(Judge, Superior Court of California County of Alameda)* Assumed office July 31, 1998. Elected 2000, current term expires Jan 2007. Born Lodi California March 7, 1947. Educated at Harvard University B.A. 1969 and University of San Francisco J.D. 1972. Admitted to practice California 1972. Began legal practice Oakland 1972. Judge May 16, 1984 to July 30, 1998 and Former Presiding Judge, San Leandro-Hayward Municipal Court Alameda County, appointed by Governor George Deukmejian.

Former Deputy District Attorney. Former Faculty Member California Judges College and California Center for Judicial Education and Research. Democrat. Enjoys family, various sports activities and public speaking.

Office: Hayward Hall of Justice, 24405 Amador Street, Hayward 94544.

Telephone: (510) 670-5060.

PICHON, Risë Jones *(Judge, Superior Court of California County of Santa Clara)* Assumed office July 30, 1998. Born Fort Lewis Washington Oct 3, 1951. Catholic. Educated at Xavier University 1969-71 and University of Santa Clara B.S. cum laude 1973 J.D. 1976. Admitted to practice California 1976 and U.S. District Court Northern District of California 1976. Commissioner 1983-84, Judge July 24, 1984 to July 29, 1998 and Presiding Judge 1990-91, Santa Clara County Municipal Court, appointed by Governor George Deukmejian.

Attorney Public Defender's Office 1976-79 and County Counsel's Office 1979-83 Santa Clara County. Instructor University of Santa Clara Paralegal Institute 1981. Former Member Judicial Council of California. Member Task Force on Professionalism Santa Clara County Bar Association since 1992 and California Commission on Judicial Performance (Chair 2002-03) since 1999. Member California Judges Association (Education Planning and Coordinating Committee since 1991), National Association of Women Judges, National (Judicial Division) and American (Judicial Administration Division) Bar Associations. Instructor Traffic Adjudication Workshop Judicial Council of California 1984 and 1985, California Judicial College 1989-90, The National Judicial College 1991-92 and Voir Dire and Trial Management Skills Workshop California Center for Judicial Education and Research 1992. Member 1988-92 and Chairperson 1991-92 Governing Committee, Judicial Education Subcommittee 1988 and Judicial Skills Committee since 1992 California Center for Judicial Education and Research. Advisory Committee on Trial Court Coordination Plan Standards 1991 and Advisory Committee on Trial Court Coordination Plan Review 1992 California Judicial Council. Alumni Board of Directors (President 1990-91), Board of Visitors 1989-97 and Financial Aid Task Force 1991-92 University of Santa Clara School of Law. Member Strategic Visions Steering Committee Santa Clara County 1991-92, Santa Clara County Board of Law Library Trustees 1991-93 and Charles Lampkin Awards Committee Santa Clara University 1991-95. Enjoys ballroom dancing and piano.

Office: Hall of Justice East Wing, 190 West Hedding Street, San Jose 95110.

Telephone: (408) 808-6600.

PICQUET, Roger *(Judge, Superior Court of California County of San Luis Obispo)* Assumed office July 1, 1998. Elected 2000, current term expires Jan 2007. Presiding Judge Jan 1, 1999 to Dec 31, 1999. Born St. Louis Missouri Sept 18, 1947. Catholic. Educated at University of California at Berkeley B.A. 1969 and University of California Hastings College of the Law J.D. 1977. Admitted to practice California 1977. Judge Dec 3, 1993 to June 30, 1998 and Presiding Judge Nov 1,

PICQUET, ROGER—*Continued*

1995 to Oct 31, 1996, San Luis Obispo County Municipal Court, appointed by Governor Pete Wilson.

Deputy City Attorney and Assistant City Attorney Modesto 1978-83. City Attorney San Luis Obispo 1983-89 and Grover Beach and Paso Robles 1989-93. USN 1969-74 (active duty). USNR 1974-92. Political affiliation: Independent.

Office: 385 County Government Center, 1035 Palm Street, San Luis Obispo 93408-2500.

Telephone: (805) 781-5936.

PIERCE, James B. *(Judge, Superior Court of California County of Los Angeles)* Appointed by Governor George Deukmejian to term beginning Aug 9, 1989. Elected 1990, 1996 and 2002. Current term expires Jan 2009. Serves South District. Born Beatrice Nebraska July 29, 1951. Educated at Loma Linda University B.A. 1971 and University of the Pacific J.D. 1974. Member Phi Delta Phi. In legal practice Los Angeles County 1980-86. Judge pro tem and Juvenile Court Referee 1983-86. Commissioner, Superior Court of California Los Angeles County 1986-88. Judge, Long Beach Municipal Court Los Angeles County April 12, 1988 to Aug 8, 1989, appointed by Governor George Deukmejian.

Deputy District Attorney Sacramento County 1974-80. Adjunct Professor Northrop University 1988-89 and Pacific Coast University 1990-2000. Member California Judges Association. Graduate California Judicial College 1988 and 1990.

Office: Long Beach Courthouse, 415 West Ocean Boulevard, Long Beach 90802.

Telephone: (562) 491-6130.

PINESCHI, Alan V. *(Judge, Superior Court of California County of Placer)* Assumed office June 30, 1998. Presiding Judge since Jan 1, 2003. Serves Family Support Division. Former Judge, Placer County Municipal Court.

Office: 11546 B Avenue, Auburn 95603.

Telephone: (530) 886-1212.

PLATT, Michael E. *(Judge, Superior Court of California County of San Joaquin)*

Office: 222 East Weber Avenue, Room 303, Stockton 95202.

Telephone: (209) 468-2827.

PLOTKIN, Barry L. *(Judge, Superior Court of California County of San Bernardino)* Serves Rancho District.

Office: 8303 North Haven Avenue, Rancho Cucamonga 91730.

Telephone: (909) 945-4131.

PLUIM, Jan A. *(Judge, Superior Court of California County of Los Angeles)*

Office: Pasadena Courthouse, 300 East Walnut Street, Pasadena 91101.

Telephone: (626) 356-5689.

POCHE, Marcel B. *(Judge, Superior Court of California County of Santa Clara)*

Office: Hall of Justice East Wing, 190 West Hedding Street, San Jose 95110.

Telephone: (408) 808-6600.

POLLAK, Stuart R. *(Associate Justice, California Court of Appeal First District Division Three)* Appointed by Governor Gray Davis. Born San Pedro California Aug 24, 1937. Jewish. Educated at Stanford University B.A. with great distinction 1959 and Harvard Law School LL.B. with distinction 1962. Book Review and Legislation Editor Harvard Law Review. Law Clerk to Chief Justice Earl Warren, Associate Justice Stanley Reed and Associate Justice Harold Burton, U.S. Supreme Court 1962-63. Admitted to practice California 1963, U.S. District Courts Central 1965 and Northern 1967 Districts of California, U.S. Court of Appeals Ninth Circuit 1973 and U.S. Supreme Court 1980. In legal practice San Francisco 1965-82. Former Judge, Superior Court of California City and County of San Francisco, appointed by Governor Edmund G. Brown, Jr. to term beginning Aug 12, 1982.

Special Assistant to Assistant Attorney General U.S. Department of Justice Washington D.C. 1963-65. Staff member Commission to Investigate Assassination of President John F. Kennedy 1964. Co-author "Tribute to Earl Warren" 2 Hastings Constitutional L. Quar. 1975, "Political Interference with Publicly Funded Lawyers: The CRLA Controversy and the Future of Legal Services" 24 Hastings L. Jour. 599, 1973, "What's Wrong with Attacks on the Legal Services Program" 58 ABA Jour. 1287, 1972 and "The Antiparalleling Statute: A New Dimension in Public Utility Regulation" 60 California L. Rev. 1116, 1972. Author "Liberalizing Summary Adjudication: A Proposal" 36 Hastings L. Jour. 419, 1985, "Sliding Scale Agreements After Tech-Bilt" VIII Civil Litigation Reporter California Continuing Education of the Bar 121 June 1986 and "Telephone Appearances: No Longer 'If You Please"' II *California Litigation* No. 2 Winter 1989. Member California State Board of Accountancy 1979-82 and U.S. Court of Military Appeals Nominating Commission 1979-81. Former member California Attorneys for Criminal Justice, San Francisco (Chair Federal Courts Committee, member Committee on Fee Arbitration and Criminal Justice Advisory Committee) and American (Sections: Litigation, Antitrust and Corporation, Banking and Business Law) Bar Associations. Member California Judges Association. Democrat. Member San Francisco Crime Committee and Jewish Community Relations Council. Director Hebrew Free Loan Association. Enjoys tennis and skiing.

Office: 350 McAllister Street, San Francisco 94102-3600.

Telephone: (415) 865-7300.

POLLARD, Nancy A. *(Judge, Superior Court of California County of Orange)*

Mailing address: P.O. Box 14169, Orange 92863-1569.

Office: Lamoreaux Justice Center, 341 The City Drive, Orange 92868.

Telephone: (714) 935-7236.

POLLEY, William G. *(Judge, Superior Court of California County of Tuolumne)* Presiding Judge Jan 1, 1996 to Dec 31, 1997.

Office: Historic Courthouse, 41 West Yaney Avenue, Sonora 95370.

Telephone: (209) 533-6504.

POLOS, Peter J. *(Judge, Superior Court of California County of Orange)*

Office: West Justice Center, 8141 Thirteenth Street, Westminster 92683.

Telephone: (714) 896-7181.

POOLE, James Howard *(Judge, Superior Court of California County of Orange)* Former Judge, West Orange County Municipal Court.
Mailing address: P.O. Box 1994, Santa Ana 92702-1994.
Office: Central Justice Center, 700 Civic Center Drive West, Santa Ana 92701.
Telephone: (714) 834-3734.

PORTER, Louisa *(Magistrate Judge, United States District Court Southern District of California)* Appointed by U.S. District Court judges.
Office: 1140 U.S. Courthouse, 940 Front Street, San Diego 92101-8925.
Telephone: (619) 557-5383.

POUNDERS, William R. *(Judge, Superior Court of California County of Los Angeles)* Born Cleveland Ohio June 9, 1939. Educated at Occidental College B.A. 1961 and Loyola University of Los Angeles J.D. 1969. Distinguished military graduate 1961. Managing Editor Loyola of Los Angeles Law Review 1969. Admitted to practice California 1970, U.S. District Court Central District of California 1970, U.S. Court of Appeals Ninth Circuit 1970 and U.S. Supreme Court 1978. Began legal practice Los Angeles 1970. Former Judge, Los Angeles Municipal Court Los Angeles County, appointed by Governor George Deukmejian to term beginning Aug 31, 1983. Supervising Judge Traffic Court 1985.
Former Deputy Attorney General. Author "California Weapon Laws" 1975 and "Prosecutor's Guide to Trial Preparation" 1980 Office of California Attorney General. Member Los Angeles Municipal Court Judges Association and California Judges Association. Lecturer on Criminal Law Annual Recent Developments Program Continuing Education of the Bar since 1992. First Lieutenant USAF 1961-64. Previously worked as survey analyst for Occidental Life Insurance Company. Republican. Enjoys woodworking, auto mechanics, gardening, jogging and swimming.
Office: Criminal Courts Building, 210 West Temple Street, Los Angeles 90012-3210.
Telephone: (213) 974-6535.

POWER, David Edwin *(Judge, Superior Court of California County of Solano)* Assumed office Aug 3, 1998. Former Judge and Presiding Judge, Northern Solano County Municipal Court.
Office: 600 Union Avenue, Fairfield 94533-5000.
Telephone: (707) 421-7827.

POWERS, Margaret A. *(Judge, Superior Court of California County of San Bernardino)* Appointed by Governor Pete Wilson July 5, 1995. Elected Nov 5, 1996 and Nov 5, 2002. Current term expires Jan 4, 2009. Presiding Judge, Victor Valley Drug Court since March 2000. Born Pasadena California Aug 25, 1945. Catholic. Educated at Western State University B.S.L. 1981 J.D. 1983. Recipient Scholastic Merit Award. Editor Western State University Law Review 1981-82. Admitted to practice California 1983, U.S. District Court Central District of California 1984 and U.S. Court of Appeals Ninth Circuit 1984. In legal practice Upland 1983-84. Judge, San Bernardino County Municipal Court Jan 21, 1992 to July 4, 1995, appointed by Governor Pete Wilson.
Deputy District Attorney Orange County 1984-90 and San Bernardino County 1990-92. Member California Judges Association, California Women Lawyers, National Association of Women Judges, High Desert and San Bernardino County Bar Associations. Attended numerous courses in Civil, Criminal and Family Law California Center for Judicial Education and Research 1992-99, California Judicial College 1996 and National Drug Court Institute U.S. Department of Justice March 1999. Named Woman of Distinction by Soroptimists International of the Americas 1999. Republican. Member International Footprint Association, Rotary and Soroptimist. Enjoys motorcycle touring, reading, gardening and sewing.
Office: 14455 Civic Drive, Victorville 92392.
Telephone: (760) 243-8684.

PRAGER, Ronald S. *(Judge, Superior Court of California County of San Diego)* Appointed by Governor George Deukmejian to term beginning Aug 9, 1989. Elected Nov 6, 1990, 1996 and 2002. Current term expires Jan 2009. Born Hartford Connecticut Aug 9, 1943. Educated at Pomona College B.A. 1965 and University of Southern California J.D. 1969. Member Delta Theta Phi. Admitted to practice California 1970 and U.S. District Court Southern District of California 1970. Judge, El Cajon Municipal Court San Diego County 1988-89.
Deputy District Attorney San Diego County 1970-79. Counsel Fair Political Practices Commission 1979-80. Deputy Attorney General California 1980-88. Chief Prosecutor Attorney General's Bureau of Medi-Cal Fraud 1987-88. Instructor in Civil Procedure National University School of Law 1989. Board of Directors Todd Inn of Court and American Business Trial Lawyers of San Diego. Member San Diego Judges Association and California Judges Association. Republican. Enjoys family activities and aerobic exercise.
Office: Hall of Justice, 330 West Broadway, San Diego 92101.
Telephone: (619) 685-6146.

PRATT, Daniel S. *(Judge, Superior Court of California County of Los Angeles)* Former Judge, East Los Angeles Municipal Court Los Angeles County.
Office: Norwalk Courthouse, 12720 Norwalk Boulevard, Norwalk 90650.
Telephone: (562) 807-7266.

PRECKEL, Allan J. *(Judge, Superior Court of California County of San Diego)* Appointed by Governor George Deukmejian to term beginning Sept 21, 1990. Elected June 2, 1992 and 1998. Current term expires Jan 2005. Born Grand Forks North Dakota Nov 12, 1946. Catholic. Educated at Santa Clara University B.S. with honors 1968 and University of Chicago J.D. 1971. Member Phi Delta Phi. Admitted to practice California 1972 and U.S. District Court Southern District of California 1972. Judge, San Diego Municipal Court San Diego County 1989-90.
Deputy District Attorney San Diego County 1972-89. Member San Diego County Judges Association and California Judges Association. Named Judge of the Year by San Diego County Probation Officers Association 1994. Enjoys horses and photography.
Mailing address: P.O. Box 122724, San Diego 92112-2724.
Office: 250 East Main Street, El Cajon 92020.
Telephone: (619) 441-4627.

PREGERSON, Dean D. *(Judge, United States District Court Central District of California)* Appointed for life by President Bill Clinton to term beginning 1996.

PREGERSON, DEAN D.—*Continued*

Born Los Angeles California Jan 28, 1951. Educated at University of California at Los Angeles B.A. 1972 and University of California at Davis School of Law J.D. 1976. In legal practice Ventura California 1978, Agana Guam 1982, Napa California 1982 and Los Angeles California 1983-85 and 1986-96.

Parole Hearing Officer California Department of Corrections 1977. Assistant Public Defender Public Defender Service Corporation Agana Guam 1978-81. Vice President and General Counsel The Torrance Company 1985.

Office: 524 U.S. Courthouse, 312 North Spring Street, Los Angeles 90012.

Telephone: (213) 894-6746.

PREMO, Eugene M. *(Associate Justice, California Court of Appeal Sixth District)* Appointed by Governor George Deukmejian to term beginning Oct 1988. Retained by election. Born San Jose California Aug 28, 1936. Educated at Santa Clara University degree with honors 1957 J.D. with honors 1962. Editor-in-Chief Santa Clara Law Review. Member Alpha Sigma Nu. Began legal practice Santa Clara. In legal practice San Jose. Judge, Santa Clara County Municipal Court Sept 1969 to Dec 1974 Judge, Superior Court of California Santa Clara County Dec 1974 to Oct 1988.

Adjunct Professor of Law Santa Clara University. Member Commission on Judicial Performance 1988-95. Past President Barristers Club and Municipal Court Judges Association. Former Board Member and Vice President Barristers Club of California and California Judges Association. Instructor Continuing Education classes Judges' College and University of California CEB programs. Participant Education Panels Rutter Group. First Lieutenant U.S. Army 1957-59. Board of Visitors Santa Clara University School of Law. Member Athletic Advisory Board Santa Clara University and Kiwanis Club.

Office: 333 West Santa Clara Street, Suite 1060, San Jose 95113.

Telephone: (408) 277-1004.

PRESSMAN, Joel M. *(Judge, Superior Court of California County of San Diego)*

Mailing address: P.O. Box 122724, San Diego 92112-2724.

Office: 325 South Melrose Drive, Vista 92083.

Telephone: (760) 726-9595.

PRICE, Jonathan R. *(Judge, Superior Court of California County of Monterey)* Presiding Judge Jan 1, 1997 to Dec 31, 1997. Former Judge, Monterey County Municipal Court.

Mailing address: P.O. Box 1819, Salinas 93902-1819.

Office: 240 Church Street, Salinas 93901.

Telephone: (831) 755-5060.

PRICKETT, Gregg L. *(Judge, Superior Court of California County of Orange)* Assumed office Aug 10, 1998. Former Judge, North Orange County Municipal Court.

Mailing address: P.O. Box 5000, Fullerton 92838-0500.

Office: North Justice Center, 1275 North Berkeley Avenue, Fullerton 92832.

Telephone: (714) 773-4400.

PROUD, Douglas B. *(Judge, Superior Court of California County of El Dorado)*

Office: Administration Office, 2850 Fairlane Court, Placerville 95667.

Telephone: (530) 621-7454.

PROVOST, Eleanor *(Judge, Superior Court of California County of Tuolumne)* Assumed office April 23, 1999. Elected 2000, current term expires Jan 2007. Born Schenectady New York Aug 22, 1947. Educated at University of California at Berkeley B.A. 1969 and New England School of Law J.D. 1975. Admitted to practice California 1976. Judge, Fourth Justice Court Tuolumne County 1982-88. Judge, Tuolumne County Municipal Court Jan 3, 1995 to April 22, 1999.

Deputy District Attorney Tuolumne County 1977-82. Democrat.

Office: Washington Street Courthouse, 60 North Washington Street, Sonora 95370.

Telephone: (209) 533-5563.

PURCELL, Catherine D. *(Judge, Superior Court of California County of Kern)*

Office: 132 East Coso Street, Ridgecrest 93555.

Telephone: (760) 375-1396.

PURNELL, Roland N. *(Judge, Superior Court of California County of Ventura)* Assumed office June 10, 1998. Former Judge, Ventura County Municipal Court.

Mailing address: P.O. Box 6489, Ventura 93006-6489.

Office: 800 South Victoria Avenue, Ventura 93009-0001.

Telephone: (805) 654-2965.

PUTNAM, R. L. "Chip" *(Judge, Superior Court of California County of Fresno)* Assumed office July 1, 1998. Presiding Judge Juvenile Court Delinquency Division Aug 1998 to Aug 2001. Born Phoenix Arizona Oct 21, 1946. Educated at California State University at Fresno 1969 and San Joaquin College of Law J.D. 1975. Admitted to practice California 1975 and U.S. District Court Eastern District of California 1975. In legal practice Fresno 1975-77 and 1981-83. Judge Dec 15, 1986 to June 30, 1998 and Presiding Judge 1994-95, Consolidated Fresno Municipal Court Fresno County.

Deputy Public Defender 1977-81. Senior Deputy District Attorney Fresno County 1983-86. Member California Judges Association, California District Attorneys Association, State Bar of California and Fresno County Bar Association. Attends Recent Developments in California Law Judges College and Juvenile Law updates. Past President Board of Trustees Fresno County Law Library. Member Rotary. Enjoys sailing, skiing, volleyball and softball.

Office: Courthouse, 1100 Van Ness Avenue, Fresno 93724-0002.

Telephone: (559) 488-1825.

QUALL, Robert D. *(Judge, Superior Court of California County of Merced)* Assumed office Aug 3, 1998. Elected 2002, current term expires Jan 2009. Presiding Judge Jan 1, 2001 to Dec 31, 2002. Born Yakima Washington Aug 15, 1939. Began legal practice Santa Barbara 1966. In legal practice Oakland 1968-70 and Merced 1970-79. Chief Deputy District Attorney 1970-78. Judge Jan 8, 1979 to Aug 2, 1998 and Former Presiding Judge, Merced County Municipal Court.

Office: 670 West 22nd Street, Merced 95340.

Telephone: (209) 385-7471.

QUIDACHAY, Ronald Evans *(Judge, Superior Court of California City and County of San Francisco)* Assumed office Dec 31, 1998. Presiding Judge Jan 1, 2001 to Dec 31, 2002. Born San Francisco California March 8, 1947. Catholic. Educated at San Francisco State University B.A. 1970 and University of California at Berkeley J.D. 1973. Admitted to practice California 1974. Began legal practice San Francisco 1974. Referee 1981-83 and Judge Jan 2, 1983 to Nov 30, 1998, San Francisco Municipal Court San Francisco County, appointed by Governor Edmund G. Brown, Jr.

Former Assistant District Attorney. Former Legal Aid Lawyer. Member California Judges Executive Board 1991-94, Filipino Bar Association of Northern California (Board of Directors 1984-86) and Asian American Bar Association. Faculty California Continuing Judicial Studies Program 1993 and 1994. Vice President National Filipino American Council since 1994.

Office: Civic Center Courthouse, 400 McAllister Street, San Francisco 94102-4514.

Telephone: (415) 551-4020.

QUINLEN, John I. *(Judge, Superior Court of California County of Kern)* Assumed office July 1, 2000. Presiding Judge Jan 1, 1996 to Dec 31, 1997 and Jan 1, 2000 to June 30, 2000 and Former Judge, East Kern Municipal Court Kern County.

Office: 132 East Coso Street, Ridgecrest 93555.

Telephone: (760) 375-1396.

QUINN, Linda B. *(Judge, Superior Court of California County of San Diego)* Former Judge, San Diego Municipal Court San Diego County.

Mailing address: P.O. Box 122724, San Diego 92112-2724.

Office: 330 West Broadway, San Diego 92101.

Telephone: (619) 685-6148.

RAFEEDIE, Edward *(Senior Judge, United States District Court Central District of California)* Appointed for life by the President. Assumed Senior status, serves by assignment. Born Orange New Jersey Jan 6, 1929. Educated at University of Southern California B.S. 1957 J.D. 1959. Member Delta Theta Phi (President 1958-59) and Alpha Gamma Sigma. Legal Assistant State Division of Highways 1958-59. Admitted to practice California 1960 and U.S. District Courts Districts of California 1960. In legal practice Santa Monica 1960-69. Judge, Santa Monica Municipal Court Los Angeles County 1969-71 (Presiding Judge 1971). Former Judge and Supervising Judge West District 1977-78 and 1981-82, Superior Court of California Los Angeles County, appointed by Governor Ronald Reagan Aug 5, 1971.

Member Affiliated Bar Presidents of Los Angeles County 1968, Bench and Bar Committee of Los Angeles County Superior Court 1969, Municipal Court Judges Association of Los Angeles County (Chairman Bail Committee 1971), State Bar of California (Convention Delegate 1963-69, Resolutions Committee 1965) and Santa Monica Bay District Bar Association (Legislative Committee 1965-69, Chairman Judiciary Committee 1969, Chairman Indigent Defense Committee 1962-65, Trustee 1961-69, Treasurer 1966, Vice President 1967, President 1968). Vice President 1974-75 and President 1977-78 Santa Monica Rotary Club. Former Member Executive Board Great Western Council Boy Scouts of America (Vice President 1975, 1976 and 1977, Chairman Scout-O-Rama). Former Coach Pacific Palisades YMCA Basketball four years and Malibu Boys Football and Pacific Palisades Football Associations. Team Manager and Past President Malibu Little League.

Office: U.S. Courthouse, 312 North Spring Street, Los Angeles 90012.

Telephone: (213) 894-6927.

RAMIREZ, Daniel P. *(Judge, Superior Court of California County of Los Angeles)* Assumed office Jan 22, 2000. Presiding Judge Jan 1, 1997 to Dec 31, 1997 and Former Judge, Southeast Municipal Court Los Angeles County.

Office: Huntington Park Courthouse, 6548 Miles Avenue, Huntington Park 90255-2419.

Telephone: (323) 586-6351.

RAMIREZ, Manuel Angelo *(Presiding Justice, California Court of Appeal Fourth District Division Two)* Appointed by Governor George Deukmejian to term beginning Dec 27, 1990. Retained by election 1994, current term expires Jan 2007. Former Associate Justice pro tem California Supreme Court. Born Los Angeles California Jan 11, 1948. Catholic. Educated at East Los Angeles City College A.A. 1968, Whittier College B.A. 1970 and Loyola University of Los Angeles J.D. Admitted to practice California 1976 and U.S. District Court Central District of California 1976. Judge, Central Orange County Municipal Court Orange County 1983-86. Judge, Superior Court of California Orange County 1986-90.

Senior Trial Deputy District Attorney 1976-83 Orange County. Author "Focus on Mediation: Facts and Tips on How to Make it Work for You and Your Client" *Riverside County Lawyer* and "Volunteer Attorney-Mediators Settle Appeals" *California Business Litigation Journal.* Instructor Paralegal Studies Extension Program University of California at Irvine 1981-96. Former member Orange County Juvenile Justice Subcommittee, California District Attorneys Association and State Bar of California. Chair Task Force Appellate Court Subcommittee on Appellate Courthouse Construction Guidelines. Honorary Member Orange County and Riverside County Bar Associations. Member California Judges Association. Seminar Leader California Center for Judicial Education and Research 1986 and California Judicial College Berkeley 1986. Panelist Superintendents' Legal Seminar Office of Education Riverside County since 1992. Recipient Outstanding Hispanic Alumni Award from Whittier College 1987, Commendations from Senator John Seymour and Senator Ed Royce 1990 and James H. Krieger Community Service Award from Riverside County Bar Association 1999. Named Judge of the Year by Constitutional Rights Foundation 1989, Developmental Disabilities Center Orange County 1989 and Serafines de Orange County 1990. Mentor and Volunteer "Adopt-a-Class" Santa Ana Unified School District 1981-97. Founding member Efren Hererra Scholarship Foundation. Co-founder and Inaugural Member Casita de San Jose Home for Abused Children and Latino Peace Officers Association of Orange County. Coach Little League, soccer and National Junior Basketball. Volunteer Cook Southwest Community Center Santa Ana. Member Finance Committee St. Juliana's Church and Orange County Uniform Bail Procedure Committee. Enjoys golfing, cycling, taking long walks and reading.

Office: 3389 12th Street, Riverside 92501.

Telephone: (909) 248-0200.

RANDALL, Roger D. *(Judge, Superior Court of California County of Kern)* Appointed by Governor George

RANDALL, ROGER D.—*Continued*

Deukmejian to term beginning July 7, 1986. Elected to subsequent terms. Former Presiding Judge. Born Thief River Falls Minnesota Nov 16, 1941. Lutheran. Educated at University of the Pacific B.A. cum laude 1963 and Yale University LL.B. 1966. Admitted to practice California 1967, U.S. Court of Appeals Ninth Circuit 1967 and U.S. District Courts Northern, Eastern and Central Districts of California. In legal practice Bakersfield 1973-83. Former Judge, West Kern Municipal Court Kern County, appointed by Governor George Deukmejian to term beginning Nov 4, 1983.

Deputy District Attorney Kern County 1969-73. Member State Bar of California 1967-83. Captain U.S. Army 1966-69. Republican. Member Rotary Club. Enjoys bowling, hiking and reading.

Office: 1415 Truxtun Avenue, Bakersfield 93301.
Telephone: (661) 861-2437.

RAPPE, Curtis B. *(Judge, Superior Court of California County of Los Angeles)*
Office: Criminal Courts Building, 210 West Temple Street, Los Angeles 90012-3210.
Telephone: (213) 974-6535.

RAYE, Vance W. *(Associate Justice, California Court of Appeal Third District)* Appointed by Governor George Deukmejian to term beginning Aug 1990. Retained by election Nov 1990. Educated at University of Oklahoma B.A. 1967 J.D. 1970. Began legal practice Oklahoma City. Former Judge, Superior Court of California Sacramento County, appointed by Governor George Deukmejian.

Deputy Attorney General 1974-80 and Senior Assistant Attorney General 1980-83. Co-author *Family Litigation Practice* California Public Contract Law 1978. Professor of Law Lincoln Law School. Member Judicial Council Committee on the Future of the Courts, Appellate Courts Advisory Committee, Family Law Advisory Committee, Criminal Justice Standards Committee American Bar Association, University of California at Davis Inn of Court and California Judges Association. USAF. Legal Counsel to the Governor 1983-90.

Office: 914 Capitol Mall, Sacramento 95814.
Telephone: (916) 654-0209.

RAYVIS, Cynthia *(Judge, Superior Court of California County of Los Angeles)*
Office: Courthouse, 111 North Hill Street, Los Angeles 90012.
Telephone: (213) 974-5411.

REA, William J. *(Senior Judge, United States District Court Central District of California)* Appointed for life by President Ronald Reagan to term beginning June 15, 1984. Assumed Senior status March 31, 1998, serves by assignment. Born Los Angeles California Feb 21, 1920. Catholic. Educated at Loyola University of Los Angeles B.S. 1942 and University of Colorado LL.B. 1949. Member Phi Delta Phi. Admitted to practice California 1951 and U.S. District Court Southern District of California 1951. In legal practice Los Angeles 1951-68 and Orange County 1964-68. Judge, Superior Court of California Los Angeles County 1968-84.

Co-author *Personal Injury Guide—California Practice Guide* The Rutter Group 1984. Member Southern California Defense Counsel, California Judges Association, American Board of Trial Advocates (President Los Angeles Chapter 1968-69 and National Chapter 1969), Orange County, Los Angeles County and American Bar Associations. Named Trial Judge of the Year by Los Angeles Trial Lawyers Association 1981 and Los Angeles County Bar Association 1986. Recipient Outstanding Judicial Service Award from San Fernando Bar Association 1984. Lieutenant Commander USN 1941-46. Enjoys golf and sports of all kinds.

Office: U.S. Courthouse, 312 North Spring Street, Los Angeles 90012.
Telephone: (213) 894-0466.

REAL, Manuel L. *(Judge, United States District Court Central District of California)* Appointed for life by President Lyndon B. Johnson to term beginning Nov 14, 1966. Former Chief Judge. Born San Pedro California Jan 27, 1924. Catholic. Educated at University of Southern California B.S. 1948 and Loyola University LL.B. 1951. Member Alpha Sigma Nu. Admitted to practice California 1952.

Member American Judicature Society. Lieutenant j.g. USN 1943-46.

Office: U.S. Courthouse, 312 North Spring Street, Los Angeles 90012.
Telephone: (213) 894-5267.

REARDON, Thomas Matthew *(Judge, Superior Court of California County of Alameda)*
Office: Courthouse, 661 Washington Street, Oakland 94607.
Telephone: (510) 268-7601.

REARDON, Timothy A. *(Associate Justice, California Court of Appeal First District Division Four)* Appointed by Governor George Deukmejian to term beginning Aug 20, 1990. Retained by election Nov 8, 1994 and 1998. Current term expires Jan 2011. Born San Francisco California Aug 21, 1941. Catholic. Educated at University of Notre Dame B.A. 1963 and University of California Hastings College of the Law J.D. 1966. Admitted to practice California 1966. Began legal practice San Francisco 1966. Former Judge, San Francisco Municipal Court San Francisco County, appointed by Governor George Deukmejian to term beginning Sept 8, 1983. Judge, Superior Court of California City and County of San Francisco May 16, 1985 to Aug 19, 1990, appointed by Governor George Deukmejian.

Formerly with Office of California Attorney General Criminal Division. President Lawyers Club of San Francisco American Inns of Court. Executive Board St. Thomas More Society. Democrat. Board of Governors Hastings College of the Law Alumni Association.

Office: 350 McAllister Street, San Francisco 94102-3600.
Telephone: (415) 865-7300.

RECANA, Mel Red *(Judge, Superior Court of California County of Los Angeles)* Assumed office Jan 22, 2000. Elected 2000, current term expires Jan 2007. Judge June 12, 1981 to Jan 21, 2000 and Presiding Judge Jan 1, 1996 to Dec 31, 1997, Los Angeles Municipal Court Los Angeles County appointed by Governor Edmund G. Brown, Jr.

Office: Courthouse, 111 North Hill Street, Los Angeles 90012.
Telephone: (213) 974-5411.

REED, Melinda Myrle *(Judge, Superior Court of California County of Tulare)* Assumed office July 27, 1998. Former Judge, Tulare County Municipal Court.
Office: County Civic Center, Visalia 93291-4593.
Telephone: (559) 733-6561.

REED, Sheridan E. *(Judge, Superior Court of California County of San Diego)* Appointed by Governor Edmund G. Brown, Jr. Feb 1981. Elected to subsequent terms. Educated at Scripps College B.A. 1965 and University of San Diego School of Law J.D. with honors 1970. Staff member San Diego Law Review 1968-70. Member Phi Alpha Delta. Admitted to practice California 1971. In legal practice San Bernardino 1971-72 and San Diego 1972-79. Judge, San Diego Municipal Court San Diego County April 10, 1979 to Feb 1981, appointed by Edmund G. Brown, Jr.
Mailing address: P.O. Box 122724, San Diego 92112-2724.
Office: 330 West Broadway, San Diego 92101.
Telephone: (619) 685-6148.

REHM, Carol H., Jr. *(Judge, Superior Court of California County of Los Angeles)* Assumed office Jan 22, 2000. Born Los Angeles California March 30, 1943. Roman Catholic. Educated at University of Southern California B.A. 1966, Southwestern University School of Law J.D. 1974 and London School of Economics and Political Science LL.M. in International Business Law 1988. Admitted to practice California, U.S. District Courts Central and Southern Districts of California, U.S. Court of Appeals Ninth Circuit, U.S. Court of International Trade and U.S. Supreme Court. Judge, Los Angeles Municipal Court Los Angeles County March 17, 1997 to Jan 21, 2000, appointed by Governor Pete.
Special Assistant District Attorney Los Angeles 1984. Deputy Attorney General 1980-83, 1985-87 and 1988-94 and Supervising Deputy Attorney General 1994-97 Civil Division California. Listed in Seventeenth Edition *Who's Who in the West.* First Lieutenant U.S. Army Vietnam. USAR. Served to Major California National Guard. Recipient Bronze Star, Army Commendation Medal and Combat Infantry Badge. Press Officer and Community Relations Officer U.S. Army South Vietnam and U.S. 1967-69. Public Relations Counselor 1969-71. Assistant Director California Field Operations President Ford Committee 1976. Political Director Evelle J. Younger Campaign Committee 1977-79. Member Los Angeles World Affairs Council and American Mensa Society.
Office: Criminal Courts Building, 210 West Temple Street, Los Angeles 90012-3210.
Telephone: (213) 974-6535.

REID, John H. *(Judge, Superior Court of California County of Los Angeles)* Appointed by Governor George Deukmejian to term beginning Oct 7, 1987. Elected to term beginning Jan 3, 1995. Reelected 2000, current term expires Jan 2007. Former Supervising Judge Criminal Courts. Born Los Angeles California Feb 1948. Educated at University of Southern California B.S. 1969 and Southwestern University J.D. 1972. Admitted to practice California 1972. Judge, Los Angeles Municipal Court Los Angeles County 1986-87.
Adjunct Professor of Trial Practice Pepperdine Law School since 1992.
Office: Santa Monica Courthouse, 1725 Main Street, Santa Monica 90401.
Telephone: (310) 260-3762.

REILLEY, James F. *(Judge, Superior Court of California County of Butte)*
Office: One Court Street, Oroville 95965.
Telephone: (530) 538-7611.

REILLY, Tara *(Judge, Superior Court of California County of San Bernardino)* Assumed office Aug 10, 1998. Serves Juvenile Court. Former Judge, San Bernardino County Municipal Court.
Office: 900 East Gilbert Street, San Bernardino 92415-0942.
Telephone: (909) 387-7538.

REINHOLTSEN, Dale A. *(Judge, Superior Court of California County of Humboldt)* Assumed office June 10, 1998. Presiding Judge July 1, 2000 to June 31, 2002. Former Judge, Humboldt County Municipal Court.
Office: 825 Fifth Street, Eureka 95501.
Telephone: (707) 269-1200.

REISER, Glen M. *(Judge, Superior Court of California County of Ventura)*
Mailing address: P.O. Box 6489, Ventura 93006-6489.
Office: 800 South Victoria Avenue, Ventura 93009-0001.
Telephone: (805) 654-2965.

REVAK, Bernard E. *(Judge, Superior Court of California County of San Diego)* Appointed by Governor George Deukmejian to term beginning Sept 1987. Elected 1988, 1994 and 2000. Current term expires Jan 2007. Born New Castle Pennsylvania Oct 7, 1934. Protestant. Educated at San Diego State University B.A. 1961 and University of California Hastings College of the Law J.D. 1964. Admitted to practice California 1965, U.S. District Court Southern District of California 1985 and U.S. Court of Appeals Ninth Circuit 1985.
Instructor in Trial Practice California Western School of Law since 1991. Named Prosecutor of the Year by California District Attorneys Association 1983. Sergeant USMC 1953-57. Interested in studying Winston Churchill and WWII. Enjoys walking and gardening.
Mailing address: P.O. Box 122724, San Diego 92112-2724.
Office: 220 West Broadway, San Diego 92101.
Telephone: (619) 531-3820.

REVEL, Marsha N. *(Judge, Superior Court of California County of Los Angeles)*
Office: Criminal Courts Building, 210 West Temple Street, Los Angeles 90012-3210.
Telephone: (213) 974-5773.

RHOADES, John S., Sr. *(Senior Judge, United States District Court Southern District of California)* Appointed for life by President Ronald Reagan to term beginning 1985. Assumed Senior status Nov 4, 1995, serves by assignment. Born Havre Montana March 18, 1925. Educated at Stanford University A.B. 1948 and University of California Hastings College of the Law J.D. 1951. In legal practice San Diego 1957-85.
Prosecuting Attorney 1955-56 and Deputy City Attorney 1956-57 San Diego.
Office: 3130 U.S. Courthouse, 940 Front Street, San Diego 92101-8905.
Telephone: (619) 557-5960.

RHODES, Randy *(Judge, Superior Court of California County of Los Angeles)* Assumed office Jan 22,

RHODES, RANDY—*Continued*

2000. Former Judge, Los Angeles Municipal Court Los Angeles County.

Office: Glendale Courthouse, 600 East Broadway, Glendale 91206.

Telephone: (818) 500-3524.

RHYNES, Gloria F. *(Judge, Superior Court of California County of Alameda)* Assumed office July 31, 1998. Former Judge, Oakland-Piedmont-Emeryville Municipal Court Alameda County.

Office: Courthouse, 661 Washington Street, Oakland 94607.

Telephone: (510) 268-7601.

RIBLET, Robin L. *(Judge, United States Bankruptcy Court Central District of California)* Appointed by U.S. Court of Appeals Ninth Circuit judges to term beginning 1988. Reappointed March 30, 2002, current term expires March 29, 2016.

Office: Federal Building, 1415 State Street, Santa Barbara 93101-2511.

Telephone: (805) 884-4860.

RICE, Randolf J. *(Judge, Superior Court of California County of Santa Clara)*

Office: Hall of Justice West Wing, 200 West Hedding Street, San Jose 95110.

Telephone: (408) 808-6600.

RICHEY, Andria K. *(Judge, Superior Court of California County of Los Angeles)* Assumed office Jan 22, 2000. Former Judge, Los Angeles Municipal Court Los Angeles County.

Office: Courthouse, 111 North Hill Street, Los Angeles 90012.

Telephone: (213) 974-5411.

RICHLI, Betty Ann *(Associate Justice, California Court of Appeal Fourth District Division Two)* Appointed by Governor Pete Wilson to term beginning 1994. Retained by election. Born Trenton Michigan 1945. Educated at Columbia Union College B.A. 1967, Pepperdine University J.D. 1977, University of Maryland and Loma Linda University. Admitted to practice California 1977. Judge, San Bernardino County Municipal Court 1985-90, appointed by Governor George Deukmejian. Judge 1990-93 and Presiding Judge Juvenile Court 1993-94, Superior Court of California San Bernardino County, appointed by Governor George Deukmejian.

In-House Counsel Redlands City Attorney's Office 1977-78. Deputy District Attorney San Bernardino County 1978-85. Member California District Attorneys Association, California Judicial College, California Judges Association (Appellate Courts Committee, Public Relations, Information and Education Committee), State Bar of California and San Bernardino County Bar Association. Participant National Judicial College, California Judges Association, California Center for Judicial Education and Research and Appellate Courts Institute. Instructor California Peace Officer's Training and Standards courses San Bernardino County Sheriff's Academy and California Highway Patrol. High School English and History teacher 1967-73. Board of Directors Inland Empire Symphony. Board of Visitors Pepperdine University School of Law. Advisor Historical Keyboard Society of Wisconsin. Advisory Board Salvation Army and Juvenile Justice Delinquency Prevention Committee.

Office: 3389 12th Street, Riverside 92501.

Telephone: (909) 248-0200.

RICHMAN, James A. *(Judge, Superior Court of California County of Alameda)*

Office: U.S. Post Office Building, 201 Thirteenth Street, Oakland 94612.

Telephone: (510) 268-2984.

RICHMOND, David Sargent *(Judge, Superior Court of California County of Amador)* Appointed by Governor Pete Wilson to term beginning March 1, 1998. Elected Nov 2000, current term expires Jan 2007. Presiding Judge since Jan 1, 2002. Serves Criminal Division. Born Las Vegas Nevada Oct 16, 1944. Methodist. Educated at California State University at Sacramento B.A. 1970 and McGeorge School of Law University of the Pacific J.D. 1975. Admitted to practice California 1976 and Montana. In legal practice Jackson California 1976 and 1982-83.

Deputy District Attorney 1976-79, Senior Deputy District Attorney 1979-82 and District Attorney and Public Administrator 1983-91 Amador County. Deputy District Attorney IV Sacramento Jan 1991 to May 1995. Chief Assistant District Attorney Placerville May 1995 to March 1998. Instructor in Civil and Criminal Law San Joaquin Delta College 1977-91. President Amador County Bar Association 1982. Legal Technical Advisor Small County Training Conferences and Board of Directors 1984-89 and Member Family Support Curriculum Committee 1995-98 California District Attorneys Association. Member JRS II Oversight Subcommittee California Judges Association since 1999 and Rural Courts Forum since Jan 2002. Instructor in Procedural and Substantive Criminal Law P.O.S.T. Academy California Department of Forestry since 1983. Member Rural Courts Education Committee California Center for Judicial Education and Research since June 2002. Served to Sergeant (E-5) U.S. Army 1967-68 and USAR 1969-70. Republican. Group Supervisor Preston School of Industry California Youth Authority 1971-77. Interests include cattle ranching and writing and reciting cowboy poetry.

Office: 108 Court Street, Jackson 95642.

Telephone: (209) 223-6466.

Fax: (209) 223-6498

RICO, Richard E. *(Judge, Superior Court of California County of Los Angeles)* Assumed office Jan 22, 2000. Educated at Yale University B.A. 1976 and Stanford Law School J.D. 1984. Admitted to practice California 1984. Former Judge, Los Angeles Municipal Court Los Angeles County.

Office: East Los Angeles Courthouse, 214 South Fetterly Avenue, Los Angeles 90022.

Telephone: (323) 780-2015.

RILEY, Kenneth W. *(Judge, Superior Court of California County of Ventura)* Former Judge, Ventura County Municipal Court.

Mailing address: P.O. Box 6489, Ventura 93006-6489.

Office: 800 South Victoria Avenue, Ventura 93009-0001.

Telephone: (805) 654-2965.

RILEY, Rebecca S. *(Judge, Superior Court of California County of Ventura)* Assumed office June 10, 1998. Former Judge, Ventura County Municipal Court.
Mailing address: P.O. Box 6489, Ventura 93006-6489.
Office: 800 South Victoria Avenue, Ventura 93009-0001.
Telephone: (805) 654-2965.

RIMEL, Whitney *(Judge, United States Bankruptcy Court Eastern District of California)* Appointed by U.S. Court of Appeals Ninth Circuit judges to term beginning Feb 4, 1998. Term expires 2012.
Office: 2656 U.S. Courthouse, 1130 O Street, Fresno 93721.
Telephone: (559) 498-7512.

RITCHIE, James R. *(Judge, Superior Court of California County of Marin)* Appointed by Governor Gray Davis to term beginning Feb 2000. Born Chicago Illinois Sept 16, 1941. Educated at Purdue University B.S. 1963 and Hastings College of the Law J.D. 1972. In legal practice San Francisco 1973-2000. USN 1963-69.
Mailing address: P.O. Box 4988, San Rafael 94913-4988.
Office: Hall of Justice, 3501 Civic Center Drive, San Rafael 94913.
Telephone: (415) 473-7051.

RIVERA, Maria P. *(Associate Justice, California Court of Appeal First District Division Four)* Appointed by Governor Gray Davis. Former Judge, Superior Court of California County of Contra Costa.
Office: 350 McAllister Street, San Francisco 94102-3600.
Telephone: (415) 865-7300.

ROBBINS, Roger B. *(Judge, Superior Court of California County of Orange)* Assumed office Aug 10, 1998. Former Judge and Presiding Judge, North Orange County Municipal Court.
Mailing address: P.O. Box 5000, Fullerton 92838-0500.
Office: North Justice Center, 1275 North Berkeley Avenue, Fullerton 92832.
Telephone: (714) 773-4400.

ROBERTS, Barbara L. *(Judge, Superior Court of California County of Butte)*
Office: One Court Street, Oroville 95965.
Telephone: (530) 538-7611.

ROBERTSON, A. James, II *(Judge, Superior Court of California City and County of San Francisco)*
Office: Civic Center Courthouse, 400 McAllister Street, San Francisco 94102-4514.
Telephone: (415) 551-4020.

ROBIE, Ronald B. *(Associate Justice, California Court of Appeal Third District)* Appointed by Governor Gray Davis. Born Oakland California March 13, 1937. Presbyterian. Educated at University of California at Berkeley A.B. with honors 1958 M.J. 1960 and McGeorge School of Law University of the Pacific J.D. with honors 1967. Admitted to practice California 1967 and U.S. Supreme Court 1981. Judge, Sacramento Municipal Court Sacramento County Jan 2, 1983 to June 23, 1986, appointed by Governor Edmund G. Brown, Jr. Former Judge, Superior Court of California County of Sacramento, appointed by Governor George Deukmejian to term beginning June 23, 1986. Presiding Judge Sacramento County Superior and Municipal Courts 1994-95.
State Water Resources Control Board 1969-75. Director of California Department of Water Resources 1975-83. Author "Long-Term Implementation of Water Policies to Enhance the Environment in the Face of Population Pressures" Proceedings, Water Quality Management Symposium, University of California Water Resources Center Report No. 16, 110-116 Dec 1969; "Relationships Between Water Quality and Water Rights" Contemporary Developments in Water Law, University of Texas Center for Research in Water Resources 72-82, 1970; "Water Pollution: An Affirmative Response by the California Legislature" 1 Pacific L. Jour. 2, 1970; "Regional Control of Water Pollution: The California Model" 6 Water Research 1419, 1972; "Some Reflections on Environmental Considerations in Water Rights Administration" 2 Ecology L. Quar. 695, 1972; "State Viewpoint: The Federal Water Pollution Control Act and the States: Love in Bloom or Marriage on the Rocks" 7 Natural Resources Lawyer 231, 1974; "Recognition of Substantive Rights Under NEPA" VII Natural Resources Lawyer 387, 1974; "Modernizing State Water Rights Law: Some Suggestions for New Directions" Utah L. Rev. 760, 1974; "The Penguin Is Esthetically Pleasing" Sept 1976, "California's Program for Dealing with the Drought" Feb 1978 and "Federal Water Policy Impedes California Planning" Annual Conference Proceedings 229 June 29, 1979 American Water Works Association Jour.; "The Public Interest in Water Rights Administration" Rocky Mountain Mineral L. Rev. 1977; "Pressures Created by a Severe Drought on Water Institutions" American Journal of Agricultural Economics Dec 1977; "Water Issues Facing California" Institute of Governmental Studies, University of California at Berkeley 1978; "Area of Origin Statutes—The California Experience" 15 Idaho L. Rev. 419, 1979; "Water Management of the Future—A Ground Water Storage Program for the State Water Project" 11 Pacific L. Jour. 41, 1979; "Irrigation Development in California—Construction or Water Management" Irrigation, Challenges of the 80's American Society of Agricultural Engineers 1 Oct 1980; and "A Water Manager's Commentary on the Public Trust Doctrine" The Public Trust Doctrine in Natural Resources Law and Management, University of California at Davis 132, 1981; and "The Delta Decisions: The Quiet Resolution in Water Rights" 19 Pacific L. Jour. 1113 July 1988.
Co-author with Norman B. Hume "Practice Under California's New Porter-Cologne Water Quality Control Act" 45 Los Angeles Bar Bulletin 177, 1970; with Jerome B. Gilbert "Control of Estuarine Pollution" 11 Natural Resources Jour. 256, 1971; with William R. Attwater "Water Pollution Control: Institutions and Their Financing in California" Water Pollution Research Proceedings of the 7th International Conference, Paris 1974; with Marcia J. Steinberg "Existing Water Laws and Industry Practices: Their Contribution to the Waste of Water" 3 Los Angeles B. Jour. 53 Sept 1977; with Robin R. Reynolds "The California Water Plan—Past, Present and Future" 3 No. 4 Progress and Water Technology 69, 1978; and *California Practice Guide, Environmental Law Module* Bancroft Whitney 1993. Adjunct Professor McGeorge School of Law since 1970 and University of California at Davis 1973-74. Member Executive Board California Judges Association 1990-93, State Bar of California 1967-83, Sacramento County 1967-83 and Ameri-

ROBIE, RONALD B.—*Continued*

can Bar Associations. Member Judicial Council of California 1999-2002. Consultant California Legislature 1960-69. Board of Trustees Mountain Valley Chapter National Multiple Sclerosis Society since 1984. Enjoys collecting old cars.
Office: 914 Capitol Mall, Sacramento 95814.
Telephone: (916) 654-0209.

ROBISON, Craig E. *(Judge, Superior Court of California County of Orange)* Assumed office Aug 10, 1998. Presiding Judge Jan 1, 1996 to Dec 31, 1996 and Former Judge, Harbor Municipal Court Orange County.
Office: Harbor Justice Center, 4601 Jamboree Road, Newport Beach 92660-2595.
Telephone: (949) 476-4699.

ROBLES, Ernest M. *(Judge, United States Bankruptcy Court Central District of California)* Appointed by U.S. Court of Appeals Ninth Circuit judges. Born Mexico Sept 24, 1956. Educated at University of California at Berkeley B.S. 1978 and University of Michigan Law School J.D. 1981. Admitted to practice California 1981.
Board of Directors Los Angeles Bankruptcy Forum 1996-2000. Republican. Enjoys classical music and theatre.
Office: Federal Building, 255 East Temple Street, Los Angeles 90012.
Telephone: (213) 894-1522.

ROCHMAN, Morton *(Judge, Superior Court of California County of Los Angeles)* Serves San Fernando Valley District.
Office: Sylmar Juvenile Courthouse, 16350 Filbert Street, Sylmar 91342.
Telephone: (818) 364-2111.

RODDA, Steven H. *(Judge, Superior Court of California County of Sacramento)*
Office: Courthouse, 720 Ninth Street, Sacramento 95814.
Telephone: (916) 874-5476.

RODRIGUEZ, Jesus I. *(Judge, Superior Court of California County of Los Angeles)*
Office: Torrance Courthouse, 825 Maple Avenue, Torrance 90503.
Telephone: (310) 222-8808.

RODRIGUEZ, Luis A. *(Judge, Superior Court of California Court of Orange)* Assumed office Aug 10, 1998. Elected Nov 7, 2000, current term expires Jan 2007. Born San Jose Costa Rica July 3, 1954. Educated at University of California at San Diego cum laude 1977 and University of California at Berkeley J.D. 1980. In legal practice San Diego and Los Angeles 1980-83. Judge, North Orange County Municipal Court Jan 4, 1994 to Aug 9, 1998.
Deputy City Attorney Santa Ana 1983-89. Senior Assistant City Attorney Orange 1989-94. Advisory and Former Trustee Orange County Bar Foundation. Alternate Executive Committee Orange County Superior Court 1999. Member Criminal Advisory Committee Judicial Council of California, Grand Jury Selection Committee and Community Outreach Committee Orange County Superior Court, Orange County Peer Court Council, Latino Peace Officers Association, National Association of Hispanic Appointed and Elected Officials, California City Attorneys Association, California Judges Association, American Judges Association, Juvenile and Family Law Judges Association and Judicial Council National Hispanic Bar Association. Faculty California Judicial Education and Research since 1995. Instructor in CEB Landlord-Tenant Law 1997-98. Presenter Hispanic Bar Association Conferences. Former Director Crittenton Foundation for Children and Families. Advisory Director Hispanic Education Endowment Fund. Director Orange County Multi-Cultural Institute. Board of Managers Orange County YMCA. Member Rotary International and Santa Ana Santiago Club.
Mailing address: P.O. Box 14169, Orange 92863-1569.
Office: Lamoreaux Justice Center, 341 The City Drive, Orange 92868.
Telephone: (714) 935-7236.

ROEDER, James L. *(Judge, Superior Court of California County of Placer)* Elected June 1988, June 1994 and 2000. Current term expires Jan 2007. Former Presiding Judge. Serves Civil Division. Born Seymour Indiana April 23, 1944. Lutheran. Educated at Wabash College B.A. 1966, Indiana University 1967 and McGeorge School of Law University of the Pacific J.D. 1976. Member Beta Theta Pi. Admitted to practice California 1976. Began legal practice Auburn 1976. Judge, Placer County Municipal Court 1985-88, appointed by Governor George Deukmejian.
Instructor in Business Law Sierra College 1978-84. Member State Bar of California and Placer County Bar Association. Republican. Member Auburn Chamber of Commerce, Forty-niner Business Association and Rotary Club of Auburn. Enjoys jogging, snow skiing and racquetball.
Office: 101 Maple Street, Auburn 95603.
Telephone: (530) 889-6592.
Fax: (530) 889-6533

ROESCH, Frank *(Judge, Superior Court of California County of Alameda)*
Office: Fremont Hall of Justice, 39439 Paseo Padre Parkway, Fremont 94538.
Telephone: (510) 795-2329.

ROGERS, Charles G. *(Judge, Superior Court of California County of San Diego)*
Mailing address: P.O. Box 122724, San Diego 92112-2724.
Office: 325 South Melrose Drive, Vista 92083.
Telephone: (760) 726-9595.

ROGERS, Pamela R. *(Judge, Superior Court of California County of Los Angeles)* Assumed office Jan 22, 2000. Presiding Judge Jan 1, 1997 to Dec 31, 1997 and Former Judge, Antelope Municipal Court Los Angeles County.
Office: Lancaster Courthouse, 1040 West Avenue J, Lancaster 93534.
Telephone: (661) 945-6477.

ROGERS, Randolph *(Judge, Superior Court of California County of Los Angeles)* Assumed office Jan 22, 2000. Former Judge, Antelope Municipal Court Los Angeles County.
Office: Palmdale Courthouse, 38256 Sierra Highway, Palmdale 93550.

ROLEFSON, Jon R. *(Judge, Superior Court of California County of Alameda)* Assumed office July 31, 1998. Term expires Jan 2007. Born Modesto California

ROLEFSON, JON R.—*Continued*

Sept 23, 1948. Educated at University of California at Berkeley A.B. 1970 and University of California Hastings College of the Law J.D. with honors 1973. Member Order of the Coif. Admitted to practice California 1973, U.S. District Court Northern District of California 1973 and U.S. Court of Appeals Ninth Circuit 1973. In legal practice Oakland 1980-91 and Pleasanton 1991-96. Judge, Oakland-Piedmont-Emeryville Municipal Court Alameda County Nov 22, 1996 to July 30, 1998, appointed by Governor Pete Wilson.

Deputy District Attorney Alameda County 1973-80.

Office: Courthouse, 1225 Fallon Street, Oakland 94612.

Telephone: (510) 272-6070.

ROMERO, Richard R. *(Judge, Superior Court of California County of Los Angeles)* Appointed by Governor George Deukmejian to term beginning Dec 11, 1989. Elected 1990, 1996 and 2002. Current term expires Jan 2009. Born Cleveland New Mexico Oct 17, 1949. Roman Catholic. Educated at University of California at Berkeley B.A. 1971 and University of California Hastings College of the Law J.D. 1974. Staff member Hastings Law Journal 1973. Admitted to practice California 1975, U.S. Courts of Appeals Second 1975, Sixth 1975 and Ninth 1978 Circuits and U.S. District Court Central District of California 1977. Judge, East Los Angeles Municipal Court Los Angeles County 1987-89.

Appellate Attorney Criminal Division U.S. Department of Justice 1974-75. Staff Attorney National Labor Relations Board 1976. Assistant U.S. Attorney Los Angeles County 1977-87. Author "Saving the Seashore—Management Planning for the Coastal Zone" Hastings L. Jour. Nov 1973. Member California Judges Association, American Judicature Society, Los Angeles County, Mexican American and American Bar Associations. Member California Alumni Association, Hastings Alumni Association and Los Angeles County Chicano Employees Association. Enjoys running and Latin art and music.

Office: Long Beach Courthouse, 415 West Ocean Boulevard, Long Beach 90802.

Telephone: (562) 491-6130.

ROPER, Glade F. *(Judge, Superior Court of California County of Tulare)* Assumed office July 27, 1998. Elected 2002, current term expires Jan 6, 2009. Serves Porterville Division. Born Boulder Colorado March 23, 1953. Church of Jesus Christ of Latter-Day Saints. Educated at Brigham Young University B.S. 1977 J.D. 1980. Admitted to practice California 1980 and U.S. District Court Eastern District of California 1980. In legal practice Porterville 1981-89. Former Judge and Presiding Judge, Tulare County Municipal Court, appointed by Governor George Deukmejian.

Author "Drug Courts: A Primer for the Family Physician" 15 No. 4 Journal of the American Board of Family Practice Medicine July-Aug 2002. Instructor in Business Law Brigham Young University 1980-81 and Alcohol and Drug Abuse National Rural Institute University of Wisconsin-Stout since 1999. Adjunct Faculty Criminology Department Porterville College. Board of Directors California Association of Drug Court Professionals. Member California Judges Association and National Association of Drug Court Professionals. Named Judge of the Year by Tulare County Trial Lawyers Association 1997 and Man of the Year by Porterville Chamber of Commerce 1997. Board of Directors Porterville Sheltered Workshop and Porterville Chamber of Commerce.

Office: 87 East Morton Avenue, Porterville 93257.

Telephone: (559) 782-4710.

ROSENBERG, Gerald *(Judge, Superior Court of California County of Los Angeles)*

Office: Santa Monica Courthouse, 1725 Main Street, Santa Monica 90401.

Telephone: (310) 260-3762.

ROSENBLATT, Michelle R. *(Judge, Superior Court of California County of Los Angeles)* Former Judge, Los Angeles Municipal Court Los Angeles County.

Office: Pasadena Courthouse, 300 East Walnut Street, Pasadena 91101.

Telephone: (626) 356-5689.

ROSENFIELD, Alan S. *(Judge, Superior Court of California County of Los Angeles)* Assumed office Jan 22, 2000. Former Judge and Presiding Judge, Newhall Municipal Court Los Angeles County.

Office: Santa Clarita Courthouse, 23747 West Valencia Boulevard, Valencia 91355.

Telephone: (661) 253-7301.

ROSENFIELD, Arnold D. *(Judge, Superior Court of California County of Sonoma)* Commissioner 1983-84. Elected Judge to term beginning Jan 7, 1985. Reelected June 1990, 1996 and 2002. Current term expires Jan 2009. Presiding Judge Sonoma County Superior and Municipal Courts Jan 1, 1997 to Dec 31, 1997. Born New Haven Connecticut Aug 8, 1946. Jewish. Educated at Vanderbilt University B.A. 1967 J.D. 1971. Admitted to practice California 1972 and U.S. District Court Northern District of California 1980. Began legal practice San Luis Obispo 1972. In legal practice Petaluma 1980-82.

Deputy District Attorney San Luis Obispo 1972-77 and Santa Rosa 1977-80. Instructor in Consumer Law Sonoma State University 1978-81. Professor of Law Empire College 1978-86. Member Senate Task Force on Family Relations Court 1990. Chairperson Judicial Council Advisory Committee on Juvenile Law. Member California Judges Association and National Council of Juvenile and Family Court Judges. Instructor California Center for Judicial Education and Research since 1987 and California Judicial College since 1988. Board of Directors Social Advocates for Youth (President 1989). Advisory Committees to Jewish Children's and Family Services and Sonoma County Parenting Project. Member Democratic Club of Sonoma County and Lions Club. Enjoys sports, reading and bridge.

Office: 133 Pythian Road, Santa Rosa 95409.

Telephone: (707) 537-6305.

ROSS, Kevin A. *(Judge, Superior Court of California County of Los Angeles)* Assumed office Jan 22, 2000. Former Judge, Inglewood Municipal Court Los Angeles County.

Office: Central Arraignment Courts, 429 Bauchet Street, Los Angeles 90012-2995.

Telephone: (213) 974-6531.

ROTENBERG, Frederick *(Judge, Superior Court of California County of Los Angeles)* Assumed office Jan

ROTENBERG, FREDERICK—*Continued*
22, 2000. Former Judge, Pasadena Municipal Court Los Angeles County.
Office: Alhambra Courthouse, 150 West Commonwealth Avenue, Alhambra 91801.
Telephone: (626) 308-5537.

ROTHSCHILD, Frances *(Judge, Superior Court of California County of Los Angeles)* Educated at Douglass College of Rutgers University 1959-62 and University of California at Los Angeles B.A. 1963 LL.B. 1966. Member Order of the Coif. Admitted to practice California 1967. Began legal practice Los Angeles 1967. Judge, Los Angeles Municipal Court Los Angeles County 1976-78.
Member State Bar of California 1967-75 and Los Angeles County Bar Association.
Office: Courthouse, 111 North Hill Street, Los Angeles 90012.
Telephone: (213) 974-5411.

RUBIN, Charles G. *(Judge, Superior Court of California County of Los Angeles)* Assumed office Jan 22, 2000. Term expires Jan 2006. Born Los Angeles California. Educated at California State University at Los Angeles B.A. 1962 and University of California at Los Angeles J.D. 1965. Member Phi Alpha Delta. Admitted to practice California 1966 and U.S. District Courts Central 1974 and Southern 1974 Districts of California. In legal practice Los Angeles 1970-82. Presiding Judge 1984, 1987, 1990 and 1996 and Judge Jan 3, 1983 to Jan 21, 2000, Beverly Hills Municipal Court Los Angeles County.
Deputy District Attorney Los Angeles County 1966-70. Important Decisions: People v. Zsa Zsa Gabor and People v. Eric and Lyle Menendez. Chairperson Committee on Drinking and Driving and Former Executive Officer Municipal Court Judges Association. Co-chair Jail Study Committee Los Angeles County Bar Association. Board of Governors Beverly Hills Bar Association. Member Ad Hoc Committee to Revise California Driving Under the Influence Laws Los Angeles County and Alternative Dispute Resolution Committee, Mental Health Committee and Drinking Driver Committee Superior Court of California County of Los Angeles. Speaker Colorado Judges Association and Midyear Conference on High Publicity Trials California Judges Association. Instructor The National Judicial College 1988. Former Trustee B'nai B'rith Beverly Hills. Former Member Board of Directors Beverly Hills YMCA. Former Member Advisory Group State Department Motor Vehicle Traffic School. Chairperson Committee on Handling of Mentally Disabled Persons and Commission on Alcoholism Los Angeles County. Board of Directors Californians for a Drug Free Youth and The Maple Counseling Center. Board of Advisors Steps for Recovery. Member Task Force on Drug Abuse Los Angeles County, Southern California Strategic Initiative for a Drug and Gang Free America, Rotary International, Guardians Home for Aging, Beverly Hills Chamber of Commerce and West Hollywood Chamber of Commerce.
Office: Metropolitan Courthouse, 1945 South Hill Street, Los Angeles 90007-1466.
Telephone: (213) 744-4001.

RUBIN, Laurence D. *(Associate Justice, California Court of Appeal Second District Division Eight)* Appointed by Governor Gray Davis. Born Pasadena California Sept 8, 1946. Jewish. Educated at University of California at Los Angeles B.A. 1968 J.D. with honors 1971. Recipient UCLA Alumni Association Award for Academic Achievement 1971. Chief Note and Comment Editor UCLA Law Review 1970-71. Law Clerk to Hon. Stanley Mosk, California Supreme Court 1971-72. Member Order of the Coif. Admitted to practice California 1972, U.S. District Court Central District of California 1973 and U.S. Court of Appeals Ninth Circuit 1974. In legal practice Beverly Hills 1973-81 and Century City 1982. Judge pro tem, Beverly Hills Municipal Court Los Angeles County 1977-82. Judge pro tem, Los Angeles Municipal Court Los Angeles County 1981-82. Assigned Judge, California Court of Appeal Second District Division Five July 1985 to Sept 1985. Assigned Judge, California Court of Appeal Second District Division Two May 1992 to June 1992. Assigned Judge, California Court of Appeal Dec 1995 to May 1996. Judge June 1, 1982 to Jan 21, 2000 and Former Presiding Judge, Santa Monica Municipal Court Los Angeles County, appointed by Governor Edmund G. Brown, Jr. Former Judge, Superior Court of California County of Los Angeles, assumed office Jan 22, 2000.
Author "Punitive Damages in Implied Security Fraud Actions: The Need for Flexibility" 17 UCLA L. Rev. 1280, 1970. Co-author "Premenstrual Syndrome and Criminal Responsibility" 19 UCLA L. Rev. 209, 1971. Editor "Community Service as an Alternative Sentence in Los Angeles County Municipal Courts" 55 pp. Aug 8, 1990. Important Opinions: People v. Mayorga (circumstances under which defendant may raise at a motion for new trial the police's alleged failure to preserve evidence) 171 Cal. App. 3d 929, 1985; People v. Randle (when jury instructions must be given on lesser included or related offenses that are factually distinguishable from charged crimes) 8 Cal. App. 4th 1023, 1992; People v. Butler 43 Cal. App. 4th 1224, 1996; Kim v. JF Enterprises 42 Cal. App. 4th 849, 1996; People v. McClelland 42 Cal. App. 4th 144, 1996; and People v. Nelson 42 Cal. App. 4th 131, 1996. Lecturer Attorney Assistant Program University of California Extension 1974-76. Former Member Presiding Judges Association. Board of Directors California Young Lawyers Association 1979-81 and Managing Committee Bet Tzedek Legal Services 1980-82. Member Westside Courts Executive Committee 1992, Trial Court Coordination Evaluation Advisory Committee since 1993 and SCA 4 Working Group 1997-99 Judicial Council of California. Member Municipal Court Judges Association (Drinking Drivers Committee 1985-87, Chair Jail Overcrowding Committee 1988-92), California Judges Association (Criminal Law and Procedure Committee 1987-91, Member 1991-94 and Chair 1993-94 Committee on Judicial Ethics, Executive Board 1994-97, Vice President 1996-97, Member Disciplinary Committee 1997-98), California Judges Foundation (Board of Directors since 1999), State Bar of California (Delegate 1975), Beverly Hills (Member 1974-81 and President 1980-81 Board of Directors Barristers, Member Board of Governors 1976-77, 1980-81 and 1987-88), Santa Monica (Board of Trustees 1992-94) and Los Angeles County (Member 1983-89 and Chair 1985-87 Neighborhood Justice Center Committee) Bar Associations.
Judge UCLA Trial Advocacy Program 1984-94. Speaker 1989 and Panel Moderator 1990 Jail Overcrowding Municipal Court Judges Association Annual Conference. Member Planning Committee and Panelist

RUBIN, LAURENCE D.—*Continued*

"Meet Your Judges Forum" California Judges Association 1990. Participant Panel Discussion on Proposition 115 KPCC Radio Station 1990 and Alternative Dispute Resolution Programs MCJA Cable Television 1991 Municipal Court Judges Association. Instructor in Ethics California Center for Judicial Education and Research, California Judges Association and Administrative Law Judges since 1993. Recipient Community Service Award from Ocean Park Lodge of the Masons May 7, 1987 and Emil Gumpert Judicial ADR Award from Los Angeles County Bar Association June 11, 1992. Democrat. Volunteer Attorney Public Counsel 1980-82. Volunteer California Special Olympics 1986-93. Board of Directors National Conference of Christians and Jews 1984-88 and Girls Club of Santa Monica since 1984. Chair Neighborhood Justice Center Santa Monica 1985-86. Member General Advisory Board Santa Monica College since 1985. Member 1987-90 and Chair 1990 UCLA Athletic Hall of Fame Selection Committee. Member ad hoc Committee on Jail and Prison Population County Supervisors Association of California 1990. Assistant Coach Marina Cities Hockey Association 1990-94. Witness City of Santa Monica Homeless Task Force 1991 and County of Los Angeles Incarcerated Mentally Ill Task Force 1992. Board of Directors UCLA Law Alumni Association 1991-95 (President since 1995). Member UCLA Law Founders and Bruin Bench. Enjoys tennis, travel, music, spectator sports and sports collectables.

Office: 300 South Spring Street, Los Angeles 90013.

Telephone: (213) 830-7000.

RUBIN, Rand Steven *(Judge, Superior Court of California County of Los Angeles)* Assumed office Jan 22, 2000. Presiding Judge Jan 1, 1996 to Dec 31, 1996 and Former Judge, Burbank Municipal Court Los Angeles County.

Office: Criminal Courts Building, 210 West Temple Street, Los Angeles 90012-3210.

Telephone: (213) 974-6535.

RUGGIERO, James *(Judge, Superior Court of California County of Shasta)* Presiding Judge Jan 1, 2001 to Dec 31, 2002. Former Judge, Shasta County Municipal Court.

Office: 1500 Court Street, Room 205, Redding 96001-1685.

Telephone: (530) 245-6761.

RUNDE, John W. *(Judge, Superior Court of California County of San Mateo)* Assumed office 1997. Presiding Judge Jan 1, 2001 to Dec 31, 2002. Born Milwaukee Wisconsin April 3, 1948. Presbyterian. Educated at University of California at Berkeley A.B. 1970 and University of California Boalt Hall School of Law J.D. 1973. Member Delta Sigma Phi. Admitted to practice California 1973, U.S. District Court Northern District of California 1973 and U.S. Court of Appeals Ninth Circuit 1974. Judge July 1, 1987 to 1997 and Presiding Judge 1992-93 San Mateo County Municipal Court.

Deputy Attorney General Criminal Division San Francisco Aug 1973 to June 1987. Member California Judges Association. Attended California Judicial College California Center for Judicial Education and Research July 1987. Faculty Litigation Advocacy Program Center for Trial and Appellate Advocacy 1988. E-4 California National Guard 1970-76. Republican. Enjoys reading, gardening and jogging.

Office: Hall of Justice, 400 County Center, Redwood City 94063.

Telephone: (650) 363-4516.

RUSHING, Conrad Lee *(Administrative Presiding Justice, California Court of Appeal Sixth District and Presiding Justice, California Court of Appeal Sixth District)* Appointed by Governor Gray Davis. Administrative Presiding Justice and Presiding Justice since Jan 20, 2003. Born Keota Oklahoma Jan 7, 1937. Episcopalian. Educated at San Jose State College (now University of California at San Jose) B.A. 1960 and Boalt Hall School of Law LL.B. 1963. Admitted to practice California 1964. In legal practice Los Angeles 1964-65 and San Jose 1965. Former Judge and Presiding Judge, Superior Court of California County of Santa Clara, appointed by Governor Edmund G. Brown, Jr. to term beginning June 2, 1978.

Author "California Mechanics Liens" 51 California L. Rev. 2, 1963. President Santa Clara County Bar Association 1974. Member 1975-77 and Vice Chairman 1977-78 Executive Committee Conference of Delegates State Bar of California. Democrat. Chairman Fine Arts Commission 1975-78 and City of San Jose Charter Review Commission 1976 and 1978.

Office: 333 West Santa Clara Street, Suite 1060, San Jose 95113.

Telephone: (408) 277-1004.

RUSSELL, Barry *(Chief Judge, United States Bankruptcy Court Central District of California)* Chief Judge since Jan 2, 2003. Former Chief Judge, Bankruptcy Appellate Panel Ninth Circuit.

Office: Federal Building & Courthouse, 255 East Temple Street, Los Angeles 90012.

Telephone: (213) 894-6091.

RUSSELL, David E. *(Recalled Judge, United States Bankruptcy Court Eastern District of California)* Appointed Judge by U.S. Court of Appeals Ninth Circuit judges to term beginning Nov 3, 1986. Retired Dec 15, 2000. Appointed Recalled Judge by the Judicial Council of the Ninth Circuit. Chief Judge Feb 6, 1994 to Nov 1, 2000. Born Chicago Heights Illinois March 19, 1935. Educated at University of California at Berkeley B.S. 1957 and Boalt Hall School of Law LL.B. 1960. Admitted to practice California 1961 and U.S. Tax Court 1967. In legal practice Oakland 1964-65 and Sacramento 1965-86.

Accountant San Francisco 1960-63. CPA California 1965.

Office: 3-200 U.S. Courthouse, 501 I Street, Sacramento 95814-2322.

Telephone: (916) 930-4502.

RUVOLO, Ignazio "Nace" John *(Associate Justice, California Court of Appeal First District Division Two)* Appointed by Governor Pete Wilson to term beginning Dec 2, 1996. Retained by election Nov 1998. Educated at Rutgers College A.B. 1969 and University of San Diego J.D. magna cum laude 1972. Editor-in-Chief San Diego Law Review 1972. In legal practice San Francisco and Walnut Creek 1977-94. Judge, Superior Court of California Contra Costa County Jan 6, 1994 to Dec 1, 1996, appointed by Governor Pete Wilson.

Trial Attorney U.S. Department of Justice 1972-77. Chair First District Mediation Task Force since 1998.

RUVOLO, IGNAZIO "NACE" JOHN—*Continued*

Member Education Planning Committee California Center for Judicial Education and Research since 1996, Appellate Advisory Committee since 1998 and Task Force on Jury Instructions since 1999 Judicial Council of California, Robert G. McGrath American Inns of Court, California Judges Association (Member Judicial Elections Committee 1994-95, Member 1994-97 and since 1998, Vice Chair 1999 and Chair since 2000 Judicial Ethics Committee), National Association of Women Judges, Italian-American Bar Association, Bar Association of San Francisco (Member since 1979 and Chair 1983-84 Ethics Committee, Chair Elections Committee 1984), State Bar of California (Member 1984-89, Chair 1988 and Special Advisor 1989 Committee on Professional Responsibility and Conduct), Contra Costa County (President Section on Professional Responsibility and Practice 1991-94, Member Delegation to State Bar Conference of Delegates 1992-94) and American (Committee on Professional Responsibility, Forum on Construction Industry, Forum on Franchising) Bar Associations. Faculty Member and Seminar Leader California Judicial College 1995-96. Named Trial Judge of the Year by Alameda Contra Costa Trial Lawyers Association 1996. Enjoys fly fishing, jogging and cycling.

Office: 350 McAllister Street, San Francisco 94102-3600.

Telephone: (415) 865-7300.

RYAN, David W. *(Judge, Superior Court of California County of San Diego)* Assumed office Dec 1, 1998. Born Dorchester Massachusetts May 3, 1942. Roman Catholic. Educated at Northeastern University B.S. 1965, City College of the City University of New York M.B.A. and University of San Diego J.D. 1973. Moot Court Board 1972-73. Admitted to practice California 1973 and U.S. Supreme Court 1976. In legal practice Escondido 1980-86. Judge June 6, 1986 to Nov 30, 1998 and Former Presiding Judge, North County Municipal Court San Diego County, appointed by Governor George Deukmejian.

Deputy City Attorney San Diego 1973-80. Author numerous articles in law related publications. Instructor University of San Diego 1986-87. Officer and Director San Diego County Bar Foundation 1986-91. President San Diego County Judges Association 1991. Member Escondido Mayor's Advisory Panel (Chairman Drugs and Crime Committee since 1987), Northern San Diego County (Treasurer and Director 1982-85) and San Diego County Bar Associations. Recipient Boss of the Year Award from Northern San Diego County Legal Secretaries Association 1985 and Lawyer of the Year Award from Northern San Diego County Bar Association 1986. First Lieutenant U.S. Army 1966-69. Financial Analyst Burroughs Corporation 1969-70. With Avco Community Developers Law Department 1971-73. Republican. Interests include gardening, writing legal articles and computer usage in legal applications.

Mailing address: P.O. Box 122724, San Diego 92112-2724.

Office: 325 South Melrose Drive, Suite 120, Vista 92083-6693.

Telephone: (760) 940-4633.

RYAN, John E. *(Judge, United States Bankruptcy Court Central District of California)* Appointed by U.S. Court of Appeals Ninth Circuit judges to term beginning 1986. Reappointed 2000, current term expires 2014. Also Chief Judge, Bankruptcy Appellate Panel Ninth Circuit. Selected by the Judicial Council of the Ninth Circuit. Born Boston Massachusetts Jan 22, 1941. Catholic. Educated at U.S. Naval Academy B.S. 1963 and Georgetown University LL.B. 1972. Articles Editor Georgetown Law Journal 1971-72. Admitted to practice Massachusetts 1972 and California 1976. In legal practice Boston Massachusetts 1972-75 and San Diego California 1984-86.

Attorney CF Braun 1976-78. Senior Attorney Oak Industries 1979-83. Fellow American College of Bankruptcy. Member National Conference of Bankruptcy Judges, State Bar of California and Massachusetts Bar Association. USN 1963-72. Enjoys camping and kayaking. Personal Statement or Quote: "When you come to court, be prepared, be cordial, and be honest."

Office: 411 West Fourth Street, Santa Ana 92701.

Telephone: (714) 338-5450.

Fax: (714) 338-5459

E-mail address: john_ryan@cacb.uscourts.gov

RYAN, William C. *(Judge, Superior Court of California County of Los Angeles)* Assumed office Jan 22, 2000. Term expires 2004. Born Rochester New York March 31, 1951. Educated at State University of New York at Albany B.S. 1982 and Southwestern University School of Law J.D. magna cum laude 1986. Admitted to practice California 1986, U.S. Court of Appeals Ninth 1986 and District of Columbia 1987 Circuits, District of Columbia 1987 and U.S. District Courts Central 1987, Eastern 1987, Northern 1987 and Southern 1987 Districts of California. In legal practice Los Angeles 1986-94. Judge, Los Angeles Municipal Court Los Angeles County Feb 10, 1994 to Jan 21, 2000, appointed by Governor Pete Wilson.

Office: Los Angeles Airport Courthouse, 11701 South La Cienega Boulevard, Los Angeles 90045.

Telephone: (310) 727-6010.

RYLAARSDAM, William F. *(Associate Justice, California Court of Appeal Fourth District Division Three)* Appointed by Governor Pete Wilson. Retained by election. Born Netherlands Feb 13, 1937. Protestant. Educated at University of California at Berkeley B.S. 1957, Loyola University of Los Angeles J.D. cum laude 1964 and University of Virginia School of Law LL.M. 1998. Admitted to practice California 1964. In legal practice Los Angeles 1964-74 and 1978-81, Pasadena 1974-78 and Newport Beach 1981-85. Judge, Superior Court of California Los Angeles County 1985-86. Former Judge, Superior Court of California Orange County, appointed by Governor George Deukmejian to term beginning July 1, 1986.

Author "Discovery and Use of Lay and Expert Witness Reports" Proceedings Association of Southern California Defense Counsel June 1967, "Executive Aviation Revisited—The Duty to Defend vs. The Duty to Pay Attorneys Fees" Verdict Third Quarter 1984, "Russia's Legal System" Verdict Spring 1984, "Judicial Opinion" Spring 1984 and "Common Mistakes in Jury Trials" Winter 1991 California Litigation, "Motions to Be Relieved as Counsel—The Most Difficult Motion to Win?" No. 2 Feb 1990, "The Statement of Undisputed Facts" No. 7 July 1990, "Minute Orders, Attorney Orders, Formal Orders and Similar Subjects of Disorder" No. 10 Oct 1990 and "How Distressing Can a Cause of Action Be?" No. 12 Dec 1990 Orange County Lawyer, "Kill

RYLAARSDAM, WILLIAM F.—*Continued*

the Procedural Dinosaur—A Judge's Modest Proposal to Eliminate the Demurrer" 10 No. 4 California Lawyer April 1990, "Politics and Justice are a Poor Mix" *Los Angeles Times* May 2, 1990, "Courts Under Siege" *Los Angeles Daily Journal* May 8, 1992, Chapter 17 "Tips From a Trial Judge on Courtroom Procedure" *California Trial Handbook* Bancroft-Whitney 1992, "Farewell to Hired Guns" *Los Angeles Daily Journal* and *San Francisco Daily Journal* Aug 26, 1992, "It's Not Just What You Do, It's How You Do It" 14 Civil Litigation Reporter 5 Continuing Education of the Bar Aug 1992, "Judicial Opinion, Preparing for Trial" 6 California Litigation 1 Fall 1992, "Judicial Independence—A Value Worth Protecting" 66 Southern California L. Rev. 1653 May 1993, "A Primer on Complex Litigation" 16 Civil Litigation Reporter 9 Continuing Education of the Bar Feb 1994, "Settlement Between Counsel" 7 California Litigation 3 Litigation Section State Bar of California Spring 1994 and "Statement of Undisputed Facts: Its Role in Summary Judgement" *Los Angeles Daily Journal* and *San Francisco Daily Journal* Dec 5, 1994. Contributing Editor *Civil Procedure Before Trial* California Practice Guide The Rutter Group since 1993. Adjunct Professor of Law Loyola University of Los Angeles 1973-78. President Robert A. Banyard Chapter American Inns of Court 1990-92. Member California Judges Association (Chairman 1990-91 and 1994-95 and member Civil Procedure Committee), Orange County Women Lawyers Association, American Board of Trial Advocates (Orange County Chapter), State Bar of California (Litigation Section, Disciplinary Committee 1973-76, member 1976-81 and Chairman 1977-81 Committee on the Maintenance of Professional Competence, Board of Legal Specialization 1979-81), Orange County (Committee on Professionalism) and American (Former member Section of Tort and Insurance Practice) Bar Associations. Panelist "Discovery in Family Law" CEB Spring 1987 and Moderator New Superior Court Judges Orientation Continuing Legal Education Fall 1987. Lecturer and Panelist Litigation Procedures, Civil Procedures, Insurance Law, Tort Law and Civil Discovery CEB, CJER, The Rutter Group and Orange County Bar Association. Member 1970-73 and Chairman 1971-73 Human Relations Committee, member Planning Commission 1973-78, Redevelopment Agency 1980 and Economic Development Committee 1980-81 City of Pasadena. Board of Governors Loyola Law School Alumni Association 1984-90. Member Pasadena Tournament of Roses Association since 1976 and Newport-Balboa Rotary Club 1983-85. Enjoys reading, swimming and bridge.

Mailing address: P.O. Box 22055, Santa Ana 92702.

Telephone: (714) 558-6777.

RYU, Tammy Chung *(Judge, Superior Court of California County of Los Angeles)*

Office: Los Padrinos Juvenile Courthouse, 7281 East Quill Drive, Downey 90242.

Telephone: (562) 940-8813.

SABET, Shahla S. *(Judge, Superior Court of California County of San Bernardino)* Assumed office Aug 10, 1998. Serves Rancho District. Former Judge, San Bernardino County Municipal Court.

Office: 8303 North Haven Avenue, Rancho Cucamonga 91730.

Telephone: (909) 945-4131.

SABRAW, Bonnie Lewman *(Judge, Superior Court of California County of Alameda)* Former Judge, San Leandro-Hayward Municipal Court Alameda County.

Office: Hayward Hall of Justice, 24405 Amador Street, Hayward 94544.

Telephone: (510) 670-5060.

SABRAW, Dana Makoto *(Judge, Superior Court of California County of San Diego)* Appointed by Governor Pete Wilson to term beginning Nov 12, 1998. Serves North County Division. Born July 3, 1958. Educated at San Diego State University B.S. with distinction and McGeorge School of Law University of the Pacific J.D. with distinction 1985. Traynor Society. Comment and Legislative Review Staff member Pacific Law Journal. Judicial Intern to Hon. Raul A. Ramirez, U.S. District Court Eastern District of California 1984-85. Admitted to practice California 1985. In legal practice Santa Barbara Sept 1985 to Dec 1988 and San Diego Jan 1989 to Sept 29, 1995. Judge Sept 29, 1995 to Nov 12, 1998 and Presiding Judge 1998, North County Municipal Court San Diego County, appointed by Governor Pete Wilson.

Author "Ex Parte Interviews with Present and Former Employees of a Corporate Adversary: The Ethical Parameters" 1 California Litigation Fall 1992. Board of Directors Barristers Club of San Diego 1986-88. Former Member Asian Pacific Bar of California, State Bar of California, San Diego County (Ethnic Minority Relations Committee 1993-95, Arbitration Committee 1993-95, Vice-Chair and MCLE Program Coordinator Insurance Bad Faith Section 1993-95) and Santa Barbara County Bar Associations. Member San Diego Chapter Association of Business Trial Lawyers, Pan Asian Lawyers of San Diego (Board of Directors 1995), St. Thomas More Society (Board of Directors 1994-95), American Inns of Court (Louis M. Welch Chapter since 1991, Founding Member 1997 and President 2000-01 Oliver Wendell Holmes, Jr. Chapter), San Diego County Judges Association and California Judges Association. Instructor Pacific Regional Trial Advocacy Program 1995 and Pacific Regional Deposition Skills Program 1995 National Institute for Trial Advocacy and Judge Trial and Appellate Courts Trial Advocacy Program University of San Diego 1995. Instructor in Trial Advocacy San Diego Inn of Court since 1995. Grand Marshall Camellia Festival Annual Parade Sacramento California 1976. Board of Directors Asian Business Association 1995. President San Diego Chapter Ducks Unlimited 1993-94. Founder The Positive Impact Program since 1998. Little League Manager and Coach since 1998. General Manager 2001 and Board member 2001 Scripps Ranch Falcons Baseball. Member San Diego Chapter McGeorge Alumni Association.

Office: 325 South Melrose Drive, Vista 92083.

Telephone: (760) 940-4371.

SABRAW, Ronald M. *(Judge, Superior Court of California County of Alameda)* Presiding Judge Jan 1, 1997 to Dec 31, 1997. Former Judge, Fremont-Newark-Union City Municipal Court Alameda County.

Office: Administration Building, 1221 Oak Street, Oakland 94612.

Telephone: (510) 271-5130.

SAHAGUN, Raul Anthony *(Judge, Superior Court of California County of Los Angeles)* Assumed office

SAHAGUN, RAUL ANTHONY—*Continued*
Jan 22, 2000. Former Judge, Southeast Municipal Court Los Angeles County.
Office: Whittier Courthouse, 7339 South Painter Avenue, Whittier 90602.
Telephone: (562) 907-3046.

SAIERS, K. Peter *(Judge, Superior Court of California County of San Joaquin)* Former Presiding Judge.
Office: 222 East Weber Avenue, Room 303, Stockton 95202.
Telephone: (209) 468-2827.

SAINT-EVENS, Angus *(Judge, Superior Court of California County of Glenn)* Assumed office July 31, 1998. Presiding Judge July 1, 1999 to June 30, 2000 and Jan 1, 2002 to Dec 31, 2002. Former Judge, Glenn County Municipal Court.
Office: 526 West Sycamore Street, Willows 95988-2746.
Telephone: (530) 934-6415.

SALAZAR, John Steven *(Judge, Superior Court of California County of Santa Cruz)* Serves Juvenile Court.
Mailing address: P.O. Box 1812, Santa Cruz 95061.
Office: 3650 Graham Hill Road, Santa Cruz 95061.
Telephone: (831) 454-2020.

SALCIDO, DeAnn M. *(Judge, Superior Court of California County of San Diego)*
Mailing address: P.O. Box 122724, San Diego 92112-2724.
Office: 220 West Broadway, San Diego 92101.
Telephone: (619) 531-3820.

SALDAMANDO, Alex *(Judge, Superior Court of California City and County of San Francisco)* Former Judge, San Francisco Municipal Court San Francisco County.
Office: Civic Center Courthouse, 400 McAllister Street, San Francisco 94102-4514.
Telephone: (415) 551-4020.

SAMMARTINO, Janis L. *(Judge, Superior Court of California County of San Diego)* Former Judge, San Diego Municipal Court San Diego County.
Mailing address: P.O. Box 122724, San Diego 92112-2724.
Office: 330 West Broadway, San Diego 92101.
Telephone: (619) 685-6148.

SANCHEZ, Yvonne T. *(Judge, Superior Court of California County of Los Angeles)* Assumed office Jan 22, 2000. Former Judge and Presiding Judge, Whittier Municipal Court Los Angeles County.
Office: Whittier Courthouse, 7339 South Painter Avenue, Whittier 90602.
Telephone: (562) 907-3046.

SANCHEZ-GORDON, Teresa *(Judge, Superior Court of California County of Los Angeles)* Assumed office Jan 22, 2000. Former Judge and Presiding Judge, East Los Angeles Municipal Court Los Angeles County.
Office: Courthouse, 111 North Hill Street, Los Angeles 90012.
Telephone: (213) 974-5411.

SANDERS, Glenda *(Judge, Superior Court of California County of Orange)*
Mailing address: P.O. Box 1994, Santa Ana 92702-1994.
Office: Central Justice Center, 700 Civic Center Drive West, Santa Ana 92701.
Telephone: (714) 834-3734.

SANDERS, Steven R. *(Judge, Superior Court of California County of San Benito)*
Office: 205 San Benito Courthouse, 440 Fifth Street, Hollister 95023.
Telephone: (831) 636-4057.

SANDOVAL, Jose I. *(Judge, Superior Court of California County of Los Angeles)*
Office: East Los Angeles Courthouse, 214 South Fetterly Avenue, Los Angeles 90022.
Telephone: (323) 780-2055.

SANDOVAL, Robert J. *(Judge, Superior Court of California County of Los Angeles)*
Office: Burbank Courthouse, 300 East Olive, Burbank 91502.
Telephone: (818) 356-3482.

SANDOZ, John H. *(Judge, Superior Court of California County of Los Angeles)* Commissioner 1981-95. Appointed Judge by Governor Pete Wilson Oct 1995. Elected Nov 1996 and Nov 2002. Current term expires Jan 2009. Born Houston Texas Aug 6, 1933. Educated at University of California at Los Angeles B.A. 1955 and University of Southern California J.D. 1970. Admitted to practice California 1971. In legal practice Los Angeles 1971-81.
Former State Bar of California. Member California Judges Association.
Office: 111 North Hill Street, Department 60, Los Angeles 90012.
Telephone: (213) 974-5705.
Fax: (213) 617-7176.

SANDVIG, Melvin D. *(Judge, Superior Court of California County of Los Angeles)* Assumed office Jan 22, 2000. Former Judge, Los Angeles Municipal Court Los Angeles County.
Office: San Fernando Courthouse Annex, 919 First Street, San Fernando 91340-2928.
Telephone: (818) 898-2401.

SANORA, Steven P. *(Judge, Superior Court of California County of Los Angeles)*
Office: El Monte Courthouse, 11234 East Valley Boulevard, El Monte 91731.
Telephone: (626) 575-4101.

SAPUNOR, John Van Dyke "Jack" *(Judge, Superior Court of California County of Sacramento)* Appointed by Governor George Deukmejian to term beginning Oct 1988. Elected to subsequent terms. Current term expires Jan 2007. Born Sacramento California Feb 6, 1948. Catholic. Educated at University of California at Santa Clara B.A. 1970 J.D. 1973. Admitted to practice California 1974. In legal practice Sacramento 1974. Judge, Sacramento Municipal Court Sacramento County 1985-88.
Deputy District Attorney Sacramento County 1974-85. Member California Judges Association. Republican. Ac-

SAPUNOR, JOHN VAN DYKE "JACK"—*Continued*
tive in Special Olympics. Enjoys downhill skiing, running and softball.

Office: Courthouse, 720 Ninth Street, Sacramento 95814.

Telephone: (916) 874-5476.

SARAYDARIAN, Arjuna T. *(Judge, Superior Court of California County of Riverside)* Assumed office July 29, 1998. Born Amman Jordan Aug 6, 1943. Religious affiliation: Armenian Apostolic. Educated at University of California at Los Angeles, California State University B.A. in Political Science 1968 and McGeorge School of Law J.D. 1971. Recipient American Jurisprudence Awards in Legal Bibliography and Criminal Procedure 1971. Staff member Pacific Law Journal 1969-71. Law Clerk to Superior Court of California Sacramento County 1971-72. Admitted to practice California 1972 and U.S. Supreme Court 1982. Began legal practice Sacramento. In legal practice Los Angeles 1977-81. Judge Jan 7, 1985 to July 28, 1998 and Presiding Judge Jan 1, 1995 to Dec 31, 1996, Three Lakes Municipal Court Riverside County.

Deputy District Attorney 1972-76 and Supervising Deputy District Attorney 1976-77 Sacramento. Branch Court Supervising Deputy District Attorney Perris Riverside County 1983-84. Columnist "Judicially Speaking" for local newspapers. Instructor California State University at Sacramento 1974-76 and Park College. Former member Riverside and Los Angeles Bar Associations. Member California District Attorneys Association 1981-84, Armenian Lawyers Association (Past President) and California Judges Association (Court Administration Committee). Graduate California Judicial College 1985. Attended The National Judicial College. Named Citizen of the Year by Rancho-Temecula Kiwanis 1985, Man of the Year Rancho-Temecula Optimist Club 1989 and Outstanding Rotarian 1990. Recipient U.S. Attorney's Law Enforcement Coordinating Committee Drug Prevention Award 1986 and Drug Prevention Award City of Lake Elsinore 1987. YMCA Parent-Child Leader. District Chairman Boy Scouts of America 1985-87. Chairman U.S. Constitution Bicentennial Essay high school contest Three Lakes area 1987. Past President Temecula Sunrise Rotary Club and Vail Elementary PTA. Former Board Member Menifee Valley Medical Center Foundation. President Temecula Valley PTA Council, Southwest Riverside County Substance Abuse Council and Mount San Jacinto Community Symphony Association. Chairman Riverside County Advisory Committee on Substance Abuse Programs and Mount San Jacinto Community College Foundation. Fourth Vice President Twenty-third District PTA. Board member Palo Verde Community College Foundation. Lecturer on drug abuse, child abuse and molestation. Member Blythe Rotary Club and Blythe Chamber of Commerce. Enjoys reading and jazz.

Office: 265 North Broadway Street, Blythe 92225.

Telephone: (760) 921-7934.

SARKISIAN, Edward, Jr. *(Judge, Superior Court of California County of Fresno)* Assumed office July 1, 1998. Former Judge, Consolidated Fresno Municipal Court Fresno County.

Office: Courthouse, 1100 Van Ness Avenue, Fresno 93724-0002.

Telephone: (559) 488-1825.

SARKISIAN, Philip V. *(Judge, Superior Court of California County of Alameda)* Appointed by Governor George Deukmejian Jan 24, 1986. Elected 1988, 1994 and 2000. Current term expires Jan 2007. Presiding Judge Jan 1, 1998 to Dec 31, 1999. Born Sacramento California Dec 2, 1939. Educated at Stanford University A.B. 1961 and University of California Boalt Hall School of Law LL.B. 1964. Member Phi Delta Phi. Admitted to practice California 1965. Began legal practice Sacramento 1965. In legal practice Los Angeles 1974-77 and San Francisco 1977-84. Administrative Law Judge, California Office of Administrative Hearings 1974-84. Former Judge, Oakland-Piedmont-Emeryville Municipal Court Alameda County, appointed by Governor George Deukmejian to term beginning July 2, 1984.

Member California Judges Association and Alameda County Bar Association.

Office: Courthouse, 1225 Fallon Street, Oakland 94612.

Telephone: (510) 272-6070.

SARMIENTO, Cesar C. *(Judge, Superior Court of California County of Los Angeles)* Former Judge, Los Angeles Municipal Court Los Angeles County.

Office: Criminal Courts Building, 210 West Temple Street, Los Angeles 90012-3210.

Telephone: (213) 974-6535.

SAUCEDO, Valeriano *(Judge, Superior Court of California County of Tulare)*

Office: County Civic Center, Visalia 93291-4593.

Telephone: (559) 733-6561.

SAUER, Michael T. *(Judge, Superior Court of California County of Los Angeles)* Assumed office Jan 22, 2000. Former Judge, Los Angeles Municipal Court Los Angeles County.

Office: Criminal Courts Building, 210 West Temple Street, Los Angeles 90012-3210.

Telephone: (213) 974-6535.

SAUNDERS, Brian David *(Judge, Superior Court of California County of San Bernardino)*

Office: 351 North Arrowhead Avenue, San Bernardino 92415-0240.

Telephone: (909) 387-3922.

SAUNDERS, Reginald P. *(Judge, Superior Court of California County of Alameda)* Assumed office July 31, 1998. Presiding Judge Jan 2, 1997 to Dec 31, 1997 and Former Judge, San Leandro-Hayward Municipal Court Alameda County.

Office: Hayward Hall of Justice, 24405 Amador Street, Hayward 94544.

Telephone: (510) 670-5060.

SAUTNER, Stephanie *(Judge, Superior Court of California County of Los Angeles)* Assumed office Jan 22, 2000. Former Judge, Los Angeles Municipal Court Los Angeles County.

Office: Los Angeles Airport Courthouse, 11701 South La Cienega Boulevard, Los Angeles 90045.

Telephone: (310) 727-6010.

SAWYER, Laurence K. *(Judge, Superior Court of California County of Sonoma)* Appointed by Governor George Deukmejian to term beginning April 3, 1985. Elected 1986, 1992 and 1998. Current term expires April 2005. Presiding Judge Jan 1, 1998 to Dec 31, 2000. Born Napa California Aug 3, 1942. Educated at

SAWYER, LAURENCE K.—*Continued*

Whittier College A.B. with honors 1964 and Hastings College of the Law J.D. with honors 1967. Issue Editor Hastings Law Journal 1966-67. Member Thurston Society and Order of the Coif. Admitted to practice California 1967, U.S. District Court Northern District of California 1967 and U.S. Court of Military Appeals 1968. In legal practice Santa Rosa 1972-85.

Member California Judges Association. Captain U.S. Army JAGC 1968-72.

Office: 1450 Guerneville Road, Santa Rosa 95403.

Telephone: (707) 565-1100.

SCHACTER, David Martin *(Judge, Superior Court of California County of Los Angeles)* Appointed by Governor George Deukmejian Oct 1985. Elected to subsequent terms. Supervising Judge North Valley District 1990-92. Born Toronto Ontario Sept 14, 1941. Became Naturalized Citizen. Educated at Los Angeles Valley College A.A. 1961, California State University at Northridge B.A. 1963, California Western University School of Law 1965 and University of San Fernando Valley School of Law J.D. 1968. Recipient Bancroft-Whitney Award for Outstanding Scholarship in Criminal Law and Real Property from California Western University and National Merit Award from Zeta Beta Tau 1968. Staff member San Fernando Valley Law Review. Member Zeta Beta Tau (President), Gamma Beta and Blue Key (Vice President). Admitted to practice California 1968, U.S. District Court Central District of California 1968, U.S. Court of Appeals Ninth Circuit 1969, U.S. Court of Claims 1969, U.S. Customs Court 1969, U.S. Tax Court 1969 and U.S. Supreme Court 1971. Commissioner, Santa Monica Municipal Court Los Angeles County 1981-85.

Deputy City Attorney Los Angeles 1968-73 (Chief Appellate Department and Special Prosecutions 1972). Senior Research Attorney California Court of Appeals 1973-75. Deputy City Attorney Long Beach 1975-81. Update Author *California Probate Workflow Manual Revised* California Continuing Education of the Bar 1999. Author articles on computers "Interact" Hewlett Packard Communicator. Guest Lecturer Pierce College Sociology Department Los Angeles since 1988. Guest Lecturer 1971 and Speaker 1975 California State University at Northridge. Former Member Federal Maritime Bar. Member California Judges Association (Courts and Technology Committee 1987). Lecturer California Environmental Health Association State of California for the benefit of Health Inspectors of Los Angeles, Orange, San Bernardino, Riverside and various northern counties 1973-74, Administration of Justice Seminar California Lutheran College 1974, California Department of Justice 1977-78 and Third Annual Western Vice Conference 1978. Guest Speaker Beverly Hills Legal Secretaries Association 1971. Speaker Basic Car Plan Hollywood Division 1971, North Area Police Association 1972, Pasadena Legal Secretaries Association 1972, Occidental College 1973, American Institute of Plant Engineers 1975, California Fraud Investigators 1978, Appellate Practice Beverly Hills Bar Association 1978, Third California Jurisdictional Seminar Traveler's Insurance 1988, Business Law Section San Fernando Valley Bar Association 1990, Business Litigation Section Century City Bar Association 1990, Arbitration Tenth Annual Las Vegas Convention of Los Angeles Trial Lawyers Association 1992, Voir Dire Association of Southern California Defense Counsel 32nd Annual Seminar 1993 and Employment for Attorneys University of La Verne MCLE 1996. Graduate California Judicial College 1983 and 1985.

Recipient Commendation Award for Legal Counseling from R. J. Williams Superintendent of Building City of Los Angeles 1969, Award for Legal Counseling from Los Angeles Police Department and Police Commission 1973, Resolution for Outstanding Service while in City Attorney's Office from Los Angeles City Council 1973, Award of Special Recognition from Long Beach Police Department 1981 and Award of Commendation from Santa Monica Police Officers Association 1985. Named Man of the Year by West Side Commissioner's Association 1985 and Alumnus of the Year by University of La Verne 1993. Listed in *Outstanding Young Men of America* 1972 and *Who's Who in American Law.* Member Attorney General's Advisory Board on Obscenity 1972, Special Committee to Coordinate and Investigate Polluters in County of Los Angeles 1976 and Mayor's ad hoc Technical Advisory Committee on Crime Problems in Long Beach 1977. Alternate Co-chairman Legislation Committee National Conference on the Blight of Obscenity 1977. President University of La Verne Law School Alumni Association 1995-99. Scout Master for a trainable mentally retarded boy scout troop in the San Fernando Valley. Member Shomrim Society and PORTOVEC (Hewlett Packard computer users group). Coholder U.S. Patent (5,566,033) for method and apparatus for determining the location of information on magnetic tape Oct 10, 1996. Holder Copyright on board game "Worgit." Interests include photography, auto repair, computer program designing and applications, woodworking and collecting antique cameras and Britain's Ltd. lead toy figures.

Office: Burbank Courthouse, 300 East Olive, Burbank 91502.

Telephone: (818) 356-3482.

SCHEMPP, Darlene E. *(Judge, Superior Court of California County of Los Angeles)*

Office: Van Nuys Courthouse West, 14400 Erwin Street Mall, Van Nuys 91401-2705.

Telephone: (818) 374-2719.

SCHEPER, Barbara Marie *(Judge, Superior Court of California County of Los Angeles)*

Office: San Fernando Courthouse, 900 Third Street, San Fernando 91340.

Telephone: (818) 898-2655.

SCHEULER, Richard *(Judge, Superior Court of California County of Tehama)*

Office: 720 Hoag Street, Corning 96021.

Telephone: (530) 824-4601.

SCHMITT, Joseph E. *(Recalled Magistrate Judge, United States District Court Southern District of California)* Appointed Magistrate Judge by U.S. District Court judges. Appointed Recalled Magistrate Judge by the Judicial Council of the Ninth Circuit.

Office: 321 South Waterman Avenue, Suite 100, El Centro 92243.

Telephone: (760) 353-1271.

SCHNEGG, Patricia M. *(Judge, Superior Court of California County of Los Angeles)*

Office: Criminal Courts Building, 210 West Temple Street, Los Angeles 90012-3210.

Telephone: (213) 974-6535.

SCHNEIDER, C. Randall *(Judge, Superior Court of California County of Santa Clara)* Assumed office July 30, 1998. Former Judge, Santa Clara County Municipal Court.

Office: 191 North First Street, San Jose 95113.

Telephone: (408) 882-2700.

SCHNIDER, Robert Alan *(Judge, Superior Court of California County of Los Angeles)*

Office: Courthouse, 111 North Hill Street, Los Angeles 90012.

Telephone: (213) 974-5411.

SCHUIT, Robert J. *(Judge, Superior Court of California County of Los Angeles)* Assumed office Jan 22, 2000. Former Judge, Los Angeles Municipal Court Los Angeles County.

Office: Chatsworth Courthouse, 9425 Penfield Avenue, Chatsworth 91311.

Telephone: (661) 253-7301.

SCHULTZ, Peter M. *(Judge, Superior Court of California County of Kings)* Appointed by Governor George Deukmejian to term beginning March 1985. Elected 1986, 1992 and 1998. Current term expires Jan 2005. Serves Hanford Division. Presiding Judge Superior and Municipal Courts July 1, 1997 to Dec 31, 1999. Born Honolulu Hawaii May 11, 1949. Educated at Stanford University A.B. 1971 and University of California Hastings College of the Law J.D. 1974. Admitted to practice California 1974 and U.S. District Court Eastern District of California 1977. Judge, Hanford Justice Court Kings County Jan 1985 to Feb 1985.

Former Deputy District Attorney and Assistant District Attorney Kings County. Former Assistant U.S. Attorney Eastern District of California.

Office: 1426 South Drive, Hanford 93230.

Telephone: (559) 582-3211.

SCHUMANN, B. Tam Nomoto *(Judge, Superior Court of California County of Orange)* Former Judge, Central Orange County Municipal Court.

Mailing address: P.O. Box 14169, Orange 92863-1569.

Office: Lamoreaux Justice Center, 341 The City Drive, Orange 92868.

Telephone: (714) 935-7236.

SCHWAB, Howard J. *(Judge, Superior Court of California County of Los Angeles)* Appointed by Governor George Deukmejian May 1985. Elected Nov 1986, Nov 1992 and 1998. Current term expires Jan 2005. Serves North Valley District. Born Charleston West Virginia Feb 13, 1943. Jewish. Educated at University of California at Los Angeles B.A. in History with honors 1964 J.D. 1967. Recipient Bancroft-Whitney Award in Torts 1965. Member Phi Alpha Delta. Admitted to practice California 1968 and U.S. Supreme Court 1972. Began legal practice Los Angeles 1968. Associate Justice pro tem, California Court of Appeal Second District June 1985 to August 1985. Judge, Los Angeles Municipal Court Los Angeles County April 13, 1984 to May 1985, appointed by Governor George Deukmejian.

Legal-Administrative Clerk Litton Industries Oct 1967 to April 1968. Deputy City Attorney Los Angeles April 1968 to Feb 1969. California Deputy Attorney General Feb 1969 to April 1984 (handled Charles Manson and Symbionese Liberation Army cases). Author "Obscene But Not Heard: Recent Developments in the Very Unsettled California Law of Obscenity" 46 No. 12 Oct 1971 and "The Unanimous Jury Requirement in California Criminal Cases" 50 No. 8 June 1975 The Los Angeles Bar Bulletin; "Loose Ends in the Defense of Diminished Capacity" 6 No. 7 Criminal Courts Bulletin July 1972; "Have Crime, Will Travel: Borderlines and California Criminal Jurisdiction" 50 No. 1 California State B. Jour. Jan/Feb 1975; "The California Death Penalty in Light of Recent United States Supreme Court Decisions" Annual Advance Criminal Justice Seminar 1976; "How Far Faretta: Creating Implied Constitutional Rights" 6 No. 1 San Fernando Valley L. Rev. Fall 1977; "Legislating a Death Penalty" The Council of State Governments 1977; Chapters "Murder and the Higher Courts: Appeals in Homicide Cases" and "Murder the Crime—Law of Homicide" *Homicide Investigation and Prosecution* CDAA 1979; "Diminished Capacity—A Guide" Practising Law Institute 1979; "Cause Celebre—Dealing With Problems of Publicity in the Internationally Notorious Criminal Case" 2 No. 2 Whittier L. Rev. 1980; "Your Side of the Story—Final Arguments in Criminal Cases" Effective Criminal Trial Tactics CEB 1980; "Of Gangs and Guilt" 3 No. 9 Dec 1980 and "The History of the Death Penalty in California" 4 No. 6 Sept 1981 Los Angeles Lawyer; "As Little as Possible: The Role of the Trial Judge in Discovery Matters" Discovery Seminar CAALA June 1995; and Chapter "Major Cases Involving Capital Punishment Litigation" *Death Penalty Trials* California Judicial Education and Research 1997. Co-author "Argument in Support of the Constitutionality of the Death Penalty in California" The Attorney General's L. Jour. Oct 1978.

Important Decisions: Meadows v. Lee (opinion discussing nature of third party back up offers in real estate transactions) 175 Cal. App. 3d 475, 1985; Pacific National Ins. Co. v. Webster (opinion relating to strict enforcement of insurance cancellation contractual provisions) 174 Cal. App. 3d 779, 1985; Thrifty Oil Co. v. Batarse (decision requiring lessee to request permission to sublease from landlord before entering into a commercial sublease, factors to be considered in the seeking of equitable relief from forfeiture of a lease) 174 Cal. App. 3d 770, 1985; Bisetti v. United Refrigeration Corp. (decision precluding liability against a landlord arising out of an accident wherein a trespasser fell into an acid vat belonging to the lessee on leased property) 174 Cal. App. 3d 643, 1985; Greenfield v. Spectrum Investment Corp. (opinion discussing liability of an employer for punitive damages arising out of the intentional tort of an employee) 174 Cal. App. 3d 111, 1985; and People v. Villarreal (opinion holding that a bone fracture qualifies as a great bodily injury enhancement as a matter of law, medical testimony need not be limited to that by a licensed physician) 173 Cal. App. 3d 1136, 1985. Adjunct Assistant Professor of Psychiatry and Behavioral Sciences University of Southern California Institute of Psychiatry and Law since 1985. Former Member California District Attorneys Association, Association of Deputy Attorneys General and Council of State Governments Committee on Suggested State Legislation. Founding Member San Fernando Valley Bar Association Inn of Court 1987-90. Member Committees on Criminal Law Jury Instructions since 1987, Bench and Bar since 1987 and Historical since 1987 Superior Court of California Los Angeles County. Chair Committee on Book of Approved Jury Instructions (Civil) since 1999. Member Judicial Council Task Force on Jury Instructions, Munici-

SCHWAB, HOWARD J.—*Continued*
pal Court Judges Association (Committee on Drinking Drivers 1984-85), California Judges Association (Criminal Law and Procedure Committee 1986-93), State Bar of California (Committees on History of Law in California 1975-77, Appellate Courts 1978-80 and Jury Instructions 1980-82, member Criminal Law Section 1982-84), Italian-American and Los Angeles County (Appellate Courts Committee 1982-84, Chair Executive Steering Committee Criminal Justice Section 1983-84) Bar Associations.

Lecturer on "The Supreme Court Death Penalty Decisions and State Legislative Guidelines" The Council of State Governments Annual Meeting Lake Tahoe 1976, "The Charles Manson Legacy: An International Cause Celebre Revisited" The Second Annual National Homicide Symposium Los Angeles 1977, "Higher Courts: Appeals in Homicide Cases" The Third National Homicide Symposium San Diego 1979 and "Brave New World or Recent Developments Which Dramatically Change the Practice of Criminal Law in California" San Fernando Valley Criminal Bar Association 1991. Faculty Lecturer California Center for Judicial Education and Research since 1986 and "Advanced Criminal Procedure Before Trial" Judicial College Berkeley 1987-1990. Panelist "Law and Motion in the San Fernando Valley" Business and Real Property Section San Fernando Valley Bar Association 1994. Lecturer/Panelist on Role of Trial Judge Regarding Civil Discovery Consumer Attorneys Association of Los Angeles 1995. Recipient Certificates of Achievement for participation in National Homicide Symposiums 1977 and 1979 and First Annual William E. James Award 1981 from California District Attorneys Association. Listed in *Who's Who in California* 1988, *Who's Who in American Law* 1992-93, *Who's Who in the West* 1994-95 and *Who's Who in America* 1997. Named Judge of the Year by San Fernando Valley Bar Association 2002. Presided over criminal trial as a Superior Court Judge that became the subject of a book by Anthony Flacco, *A Checklist for Murder: The True Story of Robert John Peernock* Dell Publishing 1995. Enjoys history and book collecting.

Office: San Fernando Courthouse, 900 Third Street, San Fernando 91340.

Telephone: (818) 898-2616.

SCHWARTZ, John G. *(Judge, Superior Court of California County of San Mateo)* Appointed by Governor George Deukmejian to term beginning July 3, 1986. Elected Nov 1988, Nov 1994 and Nov 2000. Current term expires Jan 2007. Presiding Judge 1990. Criminal Presiding Judge 1995. Born Modesto California Aug 17, 1943. Episcopalian. Educated at Willamette University B.A. 1965 and Boalt Hall School of Law J.D. 1968. Law Clerk to Superior Court of California San Mateo County 1969-70. Member Sigma Chi. Admitted to practice California 1969, U.S. District Court Northern District of California 1969, U.S. Court of Appeals Ninth Circuit 1969 and U.S. Supreme Court 1974. In legal practice San Mateo 1970-86.

Member California Judges Association, State Bar of California and San Mateo County Bar Association (President Elect 1986). Republican.

Office: Hall of Justice, 400 County Center, Redwood City 94063.

Telephone: (650) 363-4516.

SCHWARTZ, Keith L. *(Judge, Superior Court of California County of Los Angeles)* Assumed office Jan 24, 2000. Former Judge, Los Angeles Municipal Court Los Angeles County.

Office: Los Angeles Airport Courthouse, 11701 South La Cienega Boulevard, Los Angeles 90045.

Telephone: (310) 727-6010.

SCHWARTZ, Teri *(Judge, Superior Court of California County of Los Angeles)*

Office: Pasadena Courthouse, 300 East Walnut Street, Pasadena 91101.

Telephone: (626) 356-5689.

SCHWARZER, William W *(Senior Judge, United States District Court Northern District of California)* Appointed for life by President Gerald R. Ford to term beginning Aug 4, 1976. Assumed Senior status April 30, 1991, serves by assignment. Born Germany April 30, 1925. Educated at University of Southern California A.B. cum laude 1948 and Harvard University LL.B. cum laude 1951. Teaching Fellow Harvard Law School 1951-52. Admitted to practice California 1953. Began legal practice San Francisco 1953.

Author "Managing Antitrust and Other Complex Litigation" Michie 1982, "Civil Discovery" Prentice-Hall 1994 and *Federal Practice Guide* The Rutter Group 1994. Distinguished Professor University of California Hastings College of the Law. Judicial Fellow American College of Trial Lawyers. Former Chairman Federal-State Jurisdiction Committee Judicial Conference of the U.S. Director Federal Judicial Center 1990-95. Member State Bar of California and American Bar Association (Former Judicial Representative Council Section of Antitrust Law). U.S. Army 1943-46. Senior Counsel President's Commission to Investigate CIA Activities Within the U.S. 1975. Former Board Member Marin Country Day School (President 1967-70) and World Affairs Council of Northern California (Trustee 1960-88). Former member Marin County Aviation Commission (Chairman 1970-76).

Office: U.S. Courthouse, Box 36060, 450 Golden Gate Avenue, San Francisco 94102-3489.

Telephone: (415) 522-4660.

SCOTLAND, Arthur G. *(Administrative Presiding Justice, California Court of Appeal Third District and Presiding Justice, California Court of Appeal Third District)* Appointed by Governor George Deukmejian to term beginning Feb 26, 1989. Presiding Justice since Dec 21, 1998. Born Sacramento California Oct 19, 1946. Educated at University of California at Davis B.A. 1968 and University of the Pacific McGeorge School of Law J.D. with distinction 1974. Recipient American Jurisprudence Award 1971 and Outstanding Achievement Award for Trial Advocacy 1974. Life member Traynor Honor Society. Associate Managing Editor Pacific Law Journal 1972-74. Member Delta Upsilon and Phi Delta Phi. Admitted to practice California 1974, U.S. District Court Eastern District of California 1974 and U.S. Court of Appeals Ninth Circuit 1979. Judge, Superior Court of California Sacramento County April 10, 1987 to Feb 26, 1989.

Deputy District Attorney Sacramento County Dec 1974 to Dec 1976. Deputy Attorney General Dec 1976 to July 1982. Author "The Landmark Abortion Decisions: Justifiable Termination or Miscarriage of Justice?—Proposals for Legislative Response" Pacific L. Jour. 1973. Former member Organization of State Depu-

SCOTLAND, ARTHUR G.—*Continued*

ty Attorneys General (Vice President 1978), California District Attorneys Association and California-Federal Judicial Council. Member California Judicial Council 1994-97. Narcotic Agent California Bureau of Narcotic Enforcement March 1969 to Aug 1971. Republican. Deputy Policy Director Deukmejian Campaign Committee July 1982 to Nov 1982. Assistant Chief of Staff for Governor-Elect George Deukmejian Nov 1982 to Jan 1983. Cabinet Secretary to Governor George Deukmejian Jan 1983 to April 1987. Member Sacramento Children's Home, Los Ninos Service League, Society for the Prevention of Cruelty to Animals and Crocker Art Museum. Manager Land Park Youth Soccer 1979-82 and 1985 and Land Park Little League 1981-84. Assistant Coach Sacramento United Youth Soccer 1983-84. Commissioner Justice League Co-ed Softball since 1978. Enjoys running, skiing, softball and making stained glass lamps and windows.

Office: 914 Capitol Mall, Sacramento 95814.
Telephone: (916) 654-0209.

SCOTT, Russell D. *(Judge, Superior Court of California County of Monterey)* Assumed office Dec 18, 2000. Former Judge, Monterey County Municipal Court.
Mailing address: P.O. Box 1819, Salinas 93902-1819.
Office: 240 Church Street, Salinas 93901.
Telephone: (831) 755-5060.

SCOTT, Terry J. *(Judge, Superior Court of California County of San Diego)* Assumed office Dec 1, 1998. Former Judge, South Bay Municipal Court San Diego County.
Mailing address: P.O. Box 122724, San Diego 92112-2724.
Office: 500 Third Avenue, Chula Vista 91910.
Telephone: (619) 691-4770.

SEE, Ramona G. *(Judge, Superior Court of California County of Los Angeles)* Assumed office Jan 22, 2000. Former Judge, Los Angeles Municipal Court Los Angeles County.
Office: Redondo Beach Courthouse, 117 West Torrance Boulevard, Redondo Beach 90277-3638.
Telephone: (310) 798-6875.

SEEBORG, Richard *(Magistrate Judge, United States District Court Northern District of California)* Appointed by U.S. District Court judges to term beginning Feb 9, 2001.
Office: 5150 U.S. Courthouse, 280 South First Street, San Jose 95113.
Telephone: (408) 535-5357.

SEGAL, John *(Judge, Superior Court of California County of Los Angeles)*
Office: West Los Angeles Courthouse, 1633 Purdue Avenue, Los Angeles 90025-3117.
Telephone: (310) 312-6545.

SEGAL, Suzanne H. *(Magistrate Judge, United States District Court Central District of California)* Appointed by U.S. District Court judges to term beginning July 31, 2002.
Office: 324 U.S. Courthouse, 312 North Spring Street, Los Angeles 90012.
Telephone: (213) 894-3535.

SELNA, James V. *(Judge, Superior Court of California County of Orange)*
Mailing address: P.O. Box 1994, Santa Ana 92702-1994.
Office: Central Justice Center, 700 Civic Center Drive West, Santa Ana 92701.
Telephone: (714) 834-3734.

SEPULVEDA, Patricia K. *(Associate Justice, California Court of Appeal First District Division Four)* Appointed by Governor Pete Wilson to term beginning Dec 21, 1998. Educated at University of California at Berkeley B.A. summa cum laude 1974 and University of California Hastings College of the Law J.D. 1977. Note and Comment Editor Constitutional Law Quarterly. Judge, Superior Court of California Contra Costa County Oct 13, 1989 to Dec 20, 1998, appointed by Governor George Deukmejian.

Deputy District Attorney Contra Costa County 1978-89. Former Judicial Representative Restitution Committee. Former Chair Court Security Oversight Committee and Criminal Trials Committee. Former Member Sentencing Committee Judicial Council of California and Budget Committee. Member; Former Vice Chair; Member Executive Committee since 1995; and Member since 1995 and Former Chair Budget Evaluation and Appeals Committee Trial Court Budget Commission. Member California Judges Association. Enjoys hiking, camping, fishing and gardening.

Office: 350 McAllister Street, San Francisco 94102-3600.
Telephone: (415) 865-7300.

SEVIER, Gerald F. *(Judge, Superior Court of California County of Tulare)*
Office: Tulare County Civic Center, Visalia 93291-4593.
Telephone: (559) 733-6561.

SHAPERO, Kenneth L. *(Judge, Superior Court of California County of Santa Clara)* Assumed office July 30, 1998. Former Judge, Santa Clara County Municipal Court.
Office: 12425 Monterey Road, San Martin 95046.
Telephone: (408) 695-5000.

SHAPIRO, Norman J. *(Judge, Superior Court of California County of Los Angeles)*
Office: Criminal Courts Building, 210 West Temple Street, Los Angeles 90012-3210.
Telephone: (213) 974-5747.

SHARP, Philip D. *(Judge, Superior Court of California County of San Diego)* Appointed by Governor George Deukmejian Aug 7, 1990. Elected Nov 6, 1990, 1996 and 2002. Current term expires Jan 2009. Born Richmond Virginia Aug 7, 1940. Episcopalian. Educated at Washington and Lee University B.A. cum laude 1962 J.D. cum laude 1964. Associate Editor Washington and Lee Law Review 1963-64. Member Omicron Delta Kappa. Admitted to practice Virginia 1964 and California 1969. In legal practice Richmond Virginia 1967-68 and San Diego 1968-89.

President San Diego Defense Lawyers 1988-89. Master American Inns of Court. Fellow American College of Trial Lawyers. Member American Board of Trial Advocates. Instructor Continuing Legal Education Program State Bar of California and American Inns of Court. Captain USMC 1964-67. Recipient Navy Commendation

SHARP, PHILIP D.—*Continued*

Award for service in Vietnam. Enjoys playing golf and racquetball.

Mailing address: P.O. Box 122724, San Diego 92112-2724.

Office: 220 West Broadway, San Diego 92101.

Telephone: (619) 531-3820.

SHAVER, Donald E. *(Judge, Superior Court of California County of Stanislaus)* Assumed office July 31, 1998. Former Judge and Presiding Judge, Stanislaus County Municipal Court.

Office: 800 11th Street, Modesto 95354.

Telephone: (209) 558-6000.

SHAW, Susanne S. *(Judge, Superior Court of California County of Orange)* Assumed office Aug 10, 1998. Former Judge, Harbor Municipal Court Orange County.

Office: Harbor Justice Center, 4601 Jamboree Road, Newport Beach 92660-2595.

Telephone: (949) 476-4699.

SHELDON, Charles D. *(Judge, Superior Court of California County of Los Angeles)* Appointed by Governor George Deukmejian to term beginning Oct 24, 1983. Elected 1984, 1990, 1996 and 2002. Current term expires Jan 2009. Born New York New York. Episcopalian. Educated at Williams College B.A. 1954 and University of Virginia Law School LL.B. 1957. Member Delta Kappa Epsilon. Admitted to practice California 1961. Began legal practice Long Beach 1961.

Deputy District Attorney and Head Deputy District Attorney Los Angeles County 1961-83. Former member California District Attorneys Association. Former member Executive Committee, Legislative Committee, Criminal Procedure Committee and Grand and Trial Jurors Committee Superior Court of California Los Angeles County. Member Clarence Hunt and Joe Ball Inns of Court, Constitutional Rights Foundation, Law in a Free Society Association, Long Beach Legal Aid Association, Long Beach 1961-83 and Los Angeles County 1981-82 Bar Associations. Lieutenant USNR (active duty 1957-60). Vestry All Saints Church. Board of Managers Los Altos YMCA. Member Rotary Club of Long Beach and Long Beach High Schools Advisory Councils. Enjoys biking, running, skiing, swimming and stained glass.

Office: Long Beach Courthouse, 415 West Ocean Boulevard, Long Beach 90802.

Telephone: (562) 491-6130.

SHELDON, Christopher J. *(Judge, Superior Court of California County of Riverside)* Former Judge, Desert Municipal Court Riverside County.

Office: Larson Justice Center, 46-200 Oasis Street, Indio 92201.

Telephone: (760) 863-8426.

SHELTON, Phrasel L. *(Judge, Superior Court of California County of San Mateo)* Former Presiding Judge. Born Colfax Louisiana May 1, 1938. Educated at San Francisco City College 1960-61, Utah State University 1961, University of San Francisco B.A. 1964, California State University at San Jose 1965 and Creighton University School of Law J.D. 1968. Admitted to practice Nebraska 1968 and California 1969. In legal practice San Mateo since 1970. Judge pro tem, San Mateo County Municipal Court Southern Branch 1974. Former Judge, San Mateo County Municipal Court, appointed by Governor Edmund G. Brown, Jr. to term beginning Feb 2, 1976.

Trial Attorney U.S. Department of Justice Anti-Trust Division at Los Angeles 1968-69. Deputy Public Defender Monterey County at Salinas 1969-70. Member American Judges Association, Conference of California Judges, State Bar of California (Administrative Committee Panel 1973-76), San Mateo County (Board member 1974-76) and Charles Houston Bar Associations. Board member San Mateo County Trial Lawyers Association 1973-76. Airman First Class USAF 1965-69. Democrat. Member The Commonwealth Club of California since 1976 and Democratic State Central Committee of California 1974-76. Former Board member San Mateo County Legal Aid Society. Chairman Governing Committee San Mateo County Release on Own Recognizance Program 1970-74. Board member San Mateo County Service League 1974-76. Former Legal Advisor Northern San Mateo County Black Unity Council. Legal Consultant to Samaritan House. Former Board member YMCA, San Mateo County Family Service Agency, Peninsula Red Cross and San Mateo County Suicide Prevention. Former member Committee of 31 San Mateo High School District and Northern Central Neighborhood Council. Former Chairman Congressman Leo Ryan Advisory Committee for selection of candidates to various U.S. military academies. Former member Visiting Nurses Association of San Mateo and Advisory Committee College of San Mateo Radio and Television. Former Associate member San Mateo County Police Chiefs. Enjoys track and field and martial arts.

Office: Hall of Justice, 400 County Center, Redwood City 94063.

Telephone: (650) 363-4516.

SHEPARD, Renard F. *(Judge, Superior Court of California County of Sacramento)* Assumed office June 17, 1998. Former Judge, Sacramento Municipal Court Sacramento County.

Office: Juvenile Center, 9601 Kiefer Boulevard, Sacramento 95827.

Telephone: (916) 875-5009.

SHEPPARD, Harry R. *(Judge, Superior Court of California County of Alameda)* Appointed by Governor Pete Wilson to term beginning Nov 17, 1995. Elected to subsequent terms. Current term expires Jan 2009. Presiding Judge since Jan 1, 2002. Born Schenectady New York Nov 5, 1936. Educated at Colgate University B.A. and University of California Hastings College of the Law J.D. 1966. Admitted to practice California 1966. In legal practice Fremont 1968-95.

Deputy District Attorney 1966-68. Lieutenant Commander USN 1958-62. Enjoys golf.

Office: Courthouse, 1225 Fallon Street, Oakland 94612.

Telephone: (510) 272-6070.

SHERMAN, Vilia *(Judge, Superior Court of California County of Riverside)* Assumed office July 29, 1998. Elected 2002, current term expires Jan 2009. Born St. Ives Huntingdon England July 20, 1941. Educated at University of Leicester, England B.Sc. with honors 1962, University of California at Los Angeles M.A. in Zoology 1966 and Western State University College of Law J.D. summa cum laude 1983. Executive Editor Western State University Law Review 1981-83. Admitted to practice California 1983 and U.S. District Court Central District of California 1983. Judge, Western Riv-

SHERMAN, VILIA—*Continued*

erside County Municipal Court Aug 27, 1994 to July 28, 1998, appointed by Governor Pete Wilson.

Deputy District Attorney Riverside County Sept 1984 to July 1994. Author *The Invertebrates: Function and Form* The McMillan Company 1st ed. 1970 and 2nd ed. 1976 and *Biology: A Human Approach* Oxford University Press 1st ed. 1975, 2nd ed. 1979, 3rd ed. 1983 and 4th ed. 1989. Member Mock Trial Committee 1986, Public Relations Committee 1986 and Judicial Nomination and Evaluation Committee 1986-87 Riverside County Bar Association. Member Executive Committee Riverside County District Attorneys Association 1986, 1987 and 1988. Faculty Member 1997 and Instructor in Advanced Criminal Law and other courses California Judicial College. Named Misdemeanor Deputy of the Year by Riverside County District Attorney's Office 1985 and Felony Trial Deputy of the Year by Western Riverside County District Attorney's Office 1989. Recipient Women of Achievement Certificate of Recognition by Y.W.C.A. 1986, 1991 and 1994 and Child Abuse and Neglect (CAN) Team Certification of Appreciation from Riverside General Hospital 1988. Member Housing Committee and Blue Ribbon Sewer Task Force Riverside Chamber of Commerce 1978-79 and Stringfellow Acid Pits Advisory Committee. Chairman Transportation Committee 1978-79 and Arlington Heights Citizen's Advisory Committee 1978-79 City of Riverside and Santa Ana River Regional Water Quality Board 1979-84. Mentor Judge Corona High School 1994-2002.

Office: Hall of Justice, 4100 Main Street, Riverside 92501.

Telephone: (909) 955-2300.

SHOCKLEY, Doris L. *(Judge, Superior Court of California County of Yolo)* Presiding Judge Jan 1, 1996 to Dec 31, 1996. Former Judge, Yolo County Municipal Court.

Office: 725 Court Street, Woodland 95695.

Telephone: (530) 666-8598.

SHOOK, John P. *(Judge, Superior Court of California County of Los Angeles)* Appointed by Governor George Deukmejian to term beginning May 15, 1985. Elected to subsequent terms. Born Decatur Illinois Oct 30, 1938. Catholic. Educated at Loyola University of Los Angeles B.B.A. in Industrial Relations 1962 and Southwestern University School of Law J.D. 1968. Admitted to practice California 1969, U.S. District Court Central District of California 1969, U.S. Court of Appeals Ninth Circuit 1972 and U.S. Supreme Court 1972. In legal practice Torrance 1974-83. Judge Jan 2, 1983 to May 14, 1985 and Presiding Judge 1985, Compton Municipal Court Los Angeles County, appointed by Governor Edmund G. Brown, Jr.

General Trial Counsel United California Bank 1969-74. Instructor Golden West School of Law 1973-77, Loyola Marymount University 1976-77 and Southwestern University School of Law since 1983-86. Criminal Panel South Bay Legal Aid Office 1974-83. Member California Judges Association and South Bay Bar Association. Republican. Parents Advisory Board Loyola Marymount University since 1980. Member San Pedro Peninsula YMCA. Enjoys reading, swimming and bicycling.

Office: Los Angeles County Courthouse, 111 North Hill Street, Los Angeles 90012.

Telephone: (213) 974-5679.

SHORE, Howard H. *(Judge, Superior Court of California County of San Diego)* Assumed office Dec 1, 1998. Former Judge, San Diego Municipal Court San Diego County.

Mailing address: P.O. Box 122724, San Diego 92112-2724.

Office: 220 West Broadway, San Diego 92101.

Telephone: (619) 531-3820.

SHUBB, William B. *(Chief Judge, United States District Court Eastern District of California)* Appointed for life by President George Bush to term beginning 1990. Chief Judge since 1996. Born Oakland California May 28, 1938. Educated at University of California at Berkeley A.B. 1960 J.D. 1963. Law Clerk to Hon. Sherrill Halbert, U.S. District Court Eastern District of California 1963-65. In legal practice Sacramento 1974-80 and 1981-90.

Assistant U.S. Attorney 1965-71, Chief Assistant U.S. Attorney 1971-74 and U.S. Attorney 1980-81 Eastern District of California.

Office: 14-200 U.S. Courthouse, 501 I Street, Sacramento 95814-2322.

Telephone: (916) 930-4230.

SHUBIN, Dorothy L. *(Judge, Superior Court of California County of Los Angeles)*

Office: West Covina Courthouse, 1427 West Covina Parkway, West Covina 91790.

Telephone: (626) 813-3223.

SHUMAN, D. Robert *(Judge, Superior Court of California County of Sacramento)* Appointed by Governor Gray Davis to term beginning March 1, 2001. Educated at California State University at Sacramento and McGeorge School of Law University of the Pacific J.D. 1970. Admitted to practice California 1971, U.S. District Courts Central, Eastern, Northern and Southern Districts of California, U.S. Court of Appeals Ninth Circuit and U.S. Supreme Court. In legal practice Modesto Feb 1971 to July 1971 and March 1996 to Dec 15, 1998.

Managing Attorney Domestic Relations Unit Legal Aid Society of Sacramento County July 19, 1971 to Aug 31 1972. Staff Counsel and Senior Staff Counsel Sept 1, 1972 to May 1987, Commissioner California Commission on State Mandates Jan 1988 to April 1995, Chief Counsel May 1, 1987 to Dec 27, 1991 and Deputy State Controller Legal Affairs Dec 27, 1991 to May 1, 1995 Office of the Controller California. Senior Staff Counsel Special Taxes and Administration State Board of Equalization May 2, 1995 to March 1, 1996. Coauthor *Guide to Unclaimed Property and Escheat Laws* Commonwealth Publishing Company, Inc. 1st ed. 1982 2nd ed. 1985 3rd ed. 1988. Adjunct Professor of Family Law McGeorge School of Law University of the Pacific March 1972 to June 1972. Panelist Alternative Dispute Resolution Program Conference of California Joint Powers Authorities 1996. Chief Deputy Legal Affairs Secretary to Governor Gray Davis Jan 4, 1999 to Feb 28, 2001.

Office: Courthouse, 720 Ninth Street, Sacramento 95814.

Telephone: (916) 874-5476.

SHUMSKY, Rosemary *(Judge, Superior Court of California County of Los Angeles)* Assumed office Jan

SHUMSKY, ROSEMARY—*Continued*

22, 2000. Former Judge, Los Angeles Municipal Court Los Angeles County.

Office: West Los Angeles Courthouse, 1633 Purdue Avenue, Los Angeles 90025-3117.

Telephone: (310) 312-6545.

SICHEL, Elisabeth *(Judge, Superior Court of California County of Riverside)* Serves Family Law Court.

Office: 4175 Main Street, Riverside 92501.

Telephone: (909) 955-1940.

SIEFKIN, Susan D. *(Judge, Superior Court of California County of Stanislaus)* Assumed office July 31, 1998. Born Long Beach California June 12, 1943. Educated at University of California at Santa Barbara B.A. 1965, Rutgers University M.A. 1966 and Humphreys College J.D. 1983. Admitted to practice California 1983 and U.S. District Court Eastern District of California 1983. In legal practice Modesto 1983-95. Judge, Stanislaus County Municipal Court Dec 1, 1995 to July 30, 1998, appointed by Governor Pete Wilson.

Stanislaus County Women Lawyers (Vice President 1994-95), California Women Lawyers Association (Board of Governors 1993-95), California Judges Association and Stanislaus County Bar Association (President 1989-90). Named Outstanding Woman of Stanislaus County 1982. Member 1975-83 and Vice Mayor Modesto City Council. Board of Directors Parent Resource Center. Member Rotary Club of Modesto and Stanislaus County Commission for Women. Interests include quilting and antiques.

Office: 800 Eleventh Street, Room 100, Modesto 95354.

Telephone: (209) 558-6000.

E-mail address: siefkins@mail.co.stanislaus.ca.us

SIEGEL, H. Warren *(Judge, Superior Court of California County of Orange)*

Office: Harbor Justice Center, 4601 Jamboree Road, Newport Beach 92660-2595.

Telephone: (949) 476-4699.

SILBAR, Claudia *(Judge, Superior Court of California County of Orange)*

Mailing address: P.O. Box 14169, Orange 92863-1569.

Office: Lamoreaux Justice Center, 341 The City Drive, Orange 92868.

Telephone: (714) 935-7236.

SILLMAN, Stephen A. *(Judge, Superior Court of California County of Monterey)* Assumed office Dec 18, 2000. Presiding Judge Jan 1, 1996 to Dec 31, 1996 and Former Judge, Monterey County Municipal Court.

Mailing address: P.O. Box 1819, Salinas 93902-1819.

Office: 240 Church Street, Salinas 93901.

Telephone: (831) 755-5060.

SILLS, David George *(Presiding Justice, California Court of Appeal Fourth District Division Three)* Appointed by Governor George Deukmejian to term beginning Aug 28, 1990. Retained by election Nov 1990 and 1998. Current term expires Jan 2011. Born Peoria Illinois March 21, 1938. Educated at Bradley University B.S. 1959 and University of Illinois LL.B. 1961. Member Phi Delta Phi. Admitted to practice California 1965. In legal practice Santa Ana 1965-77 and Newport Beach 1977-85. Judge, Superior Court of California Orange County 1985-90.

Important Decisions: City of Santa Ana v. Santa Ana Police Benevolent Association 207 Cal. App. 3d 1568, 1988; City of Stanton v. Cox 207 Cal. App. 3d 1557, 1988; Gates v. County of Orange 9 Cal. App. 4th 45, 1992; Wilson v. Laguna Beach 6 Cal. App. 4th 543, 1992; A.C.L. Technologies, Inc. v. Northbrook Property and Casualty Insurance Company 17 Cal. App. 4th 1773 and People v. Soto 30 Cal. App. 4th 340. Instructor School of Business University of California at Irvine 1981. Former member State Bar of California and Orange County Bar Association. Graduate California Judicial College 1986. Faculty member Trial Practice Course Orange County Bar Association 1987-90. Panelist "Law of Bad Faith" and "Civil Procedure Before Trial" The Rutter Group. Captain USMC 1962-65. Republican. Member City Council 1976-85 and Mayor 1976-77, 1979-82 and 1984-85 Irvine. Member Republican State Central Committee of California 1966-68 and Executive Committee Southern California Association of Government 1984-85. Chairman Republican Associates of Orange County 1968-69 and Irvine Health Foundation since 1985. Enjoys jogging, woodworking, travel and reading history.

Office: 925 North Spurgeon Street, Santa Ana 92701-3700.

Telephone: (714) 558-4561.

SILVEIRA, Marie Sovey *(Judge, Superior Court of California County of Stanislaus)*

Office: 800 11th Street, Modesto 95354.

Telephone: (209) 558-6000.

SILVEIRA, William, Jr. *(Judge, Superior Court of California County of Tulare)* Appointed by Governor Edmund G. Brown, Jr. to term beginning March 11, 1980. Elected June 1982, 1988, 1994 and 2000. Current term expires Jan 2007. Former Presiding Judge. Born Hanford California April 7, 1942. Educated at University of California at Berkeley B.A. in History 1964 and University of California at Los Angeles J.D. 1967. Admitted to practice California 1968 and U.S. District Court Central District of California 1968. In legal practice Tulare since 1967. Former Judge, Tulare-Pixley Municipal Court Tulare County, appointed by Governor Edmund G. Brown, Jr. to term beginning Dec 16, 1976.

Member Tulare County Trial Lawyers Association since 1970 (Board of Directors 1970-74, Secretary 1972-73 and Vice President 1973-75) and Tulare County Bar Association (Member Legislative and Resolutions Committee 1975-76, Special Committee on Medical-Legal Cooperation 1973, Volunteers for Representation of Indigents 1974 and Chairman Legislative and Resolutions Committee 1974-75). Attended Continuing Judicial Studies Program 2001 and "Mediation: A Skills Based Program" California Center for Judicial Education and Research 2001. Director Tulare County Legal Services Corporation 1969-73. Member Tulare City Library Board 1972-75, Tulare Citizens Advisory Committee 1972-76, Tulare Planning Commission since 1976. Member Roma Lodge Sons of Italy, Tulare Sewer Bond Committee (Chairman 1972) and Tulare-Angra do Heroismo Sister City Foundation (Board of Directors). Director Pro Youth Visalia 1994-95.

Office: Tulare County Civic Center, Visalia 93291-4593.

Telephone: (559) 733-6561.

SILVER, Shari Kreisler *(Judge, Superior Court of California County of Los Angeles)* Former Judge, Los Angeles Municipal Court Los Angeles County.
Office: San Fernando Courthouse, 900 Third Street, San Fernando 91340.
Telephone: (818) 898-2655.

SILVERS, Jessica Perrin *(Judge, Superior Court of California County of Los Angeles)* Assumed office Jan 22, 2000. Serves Northwest District. Former Judge, Los Angeles Municipal Court Los Angeles County.
Office: Van Nuys Courthouse West, 14400 Erwin Street Mall, Van Nuys 91401-2705.
Telephone: (818) 374-2601.

SIMONS, Mark B. *(Associate Justice, California Court of Appeal First District Division Five)* Appointed by governor. Former Judge and Presiding Judge, Mount Diablo Municipal Court Contra Costa County. Former Judge and Presiding Judge, Superior Court of California County of Contra Costa.
Office: 350 McAllister Street, San Francisco 94102-3600.
Telephone: (415) 865-7300.

SIMPSON, Alan M. *(Judge, Superior Court of California County of Fresno)*
Office: Courthouse, 1100 Van Ness Avenue, Fresno 93724-0002.
Telephone: (559) 448-1825.

SIMPSON, C. Edward *(Judge, Superior Court of California County of Los Angeles)*
Office: Pasadena Courthouse, 300 East Walnut Street, Pasadena 91101.
Telephone: (626) 356-5689.

SIMPSON, C. Robert *(Judge, Superior Court of California County of Los Angeles)* Serves Southeast District.
Office: Norwalk Courthouse, 12720 Norwalk Boulevard, Norwalk 90650.
Telephone: (562) 807-7266.

SIMS, Richard M., III *(Associate Justice, California Court of Appeal Third District)* Appointed by Governor Edmund G. Brown, Jr. to term beginning Dec 29, 1982. Retained by election. Current term expires Jan 2015. Born Oakland California Dec 3, 1943. Educated at Amherst College B.A. cum laude 1965 and Harvard Law School J.D. 1968. Member Alpha Delta Phi. Admitted to California 1969. In legal practice San Francisco 1971-80. Judge, Superior Court of California Placer County May 1980 to Dec 1982.
Volunteer Attorney VISTA 1968-70. Associate Executive Director San Francisco Committee on Crime 1970-71. General Counsel San Francisco Sheriff's Department 1972. Adjunct Professor of Law University of San Francisco School of Law 1972-75. President San Francisco Barristers Club 1974. Board of Directors San Francisco Bar Association 1979-80. Chairman Committee on Judicial Ethics California Judges Association 1986-87. Governing Committee Center for Judicial Education and Research 1990-92. Member State/Federal Judicial Council. Member Rotary International. Enjoys gardening, hiking and skiing.
Office: 914 Capitol Mall, Sacramento 98514.
Telephone: (916) 654-0209.

SINANIAN, Zaven V. *(Judge, Superior Court of California County of Los Angeles)*
Office: West Covina Courthouse, 1427 West Covina Parkway, West Covina 91790.
Telephone: (626) 813-3223.

SING, Lillian Kwok *(Judge, Superior Court of California City and County of San Francisco)* Former Judge and Presiding Judge, San Francisco Municipal Court San Francisco County.
Office: Civic Center Courthouse, 400 McAllister Street, San Francisco 94102-4514.
Telephone: (415) 551-4020.

SINGER, Carla M. *(Judge, Superior Court of California County of Orange)* Elected Nov 5, 1996 to term beginning Jan 6, 1997. Reelected 2002, current term expires Jan 2009. Born St. Paul Minnesota March 31, 1947. Educated at University of California B.A. 1968 and University of West Los Angeles J.D. 1978. Editor University of West Los Angeles Law Review 1975. Admitted to practice California 1979. Judge, North Orange County Municipal Court 1991-97.
Deputy Attorney General 1979-86. Deputy District Attorney 1986-89. Research Attorney Court of Appeal 1989-91. Member California Judges Association, National Association of Women Judges, Orange County Women Lawyers, State Bar of California and Orange County Bar Association.
Mailing address: P.O. Box 1994, Santa Ana 92702-1994.
Office: Central Justice Center, 700 Civic Center Drive West, Santa Ana 92701.
Telephone: (714) 834-3734.

SKILLMAN, William A. *(Judge, Superior Court of California County of Sierra)* Assumed office July 1, 1998. Presiding Judge Jan 1, 2001 to Dec 31, 2001. Former Judge, Sierra County Municipal Court.
Mailing address: P.O. Box 476, Downieville 95936.
Office: 100 Courthouse Square, Downieville 95936.
Telephone: (530) 289-3698.

SKROPOS, Gus James *(Judge, Superior Court of California County of San Bernardino)* Serves Valley Division.
Office: 17780 Arrow Boulevard, Fontana 92335.
Telephone: (909) 350-9322.

SKYERS, Ronald V. *(Judge, Superior Court of California County of Los Angeles)* Assumed office Jan 22, 2000. Former Judge and Presiding Judge, Compton Municipal Court Los Angeles County.
Office: Compton Courthouse, 200 West Compton Boulevard, Compton 90220.
Telephone: (310) 603-7842.

SMALTZ, Lois Anderson *(Judge, Superior Court of California County of Los Angeles)*
Office: Torrance Courthouse, 825 Maple Avenue, Torrance 90503.
Telephone: (310) 222-8808.

SMERLING, Terry Lee *(Judge, Superior Court of California County of Los Angeles)* Elected to term beginning Jan 2, 1989. Reelected 1994 and 2000. Current term expires Jan 2007. Born California May 31, 1945. Educated at University of California at Berkeley B.A. with honors 1967 and Columbia University School of Law J.D. with honors 1970. Admitted to practice Cali-

SMERLING, TERRY LEE—*Continued*

fornia 1971, U.S. District Court Central District of California 1971 and U.S. Court of Appeals Ninth Circuit 1971. Began legal practice Los Angeles 1971. Judge, Los Angeles Municipal Court Los Angeles County 1982-88.

Office: Pasadena Courthouse, 300 East Walnut Street, Pasadena 91101.

Telephone: (626) 356-5689.

SMILEY, John R. *(Judge, Superior Court of California County of Ventura)* Assumed office June 10, 1998. Elected 2000, current term expires Jan 2007. Born Pennsylvania May 4, 1947. Educated at Princeton University A.B. 1970 and Southwestern University J.D. 1973. Admitted to practice California 1973. In legal practice Ventura 1973-86. Judge Aug 1, 1986 to June 9, 1998, Assistant Presiding Judge 1992 and 1993, Presiding Judge 1994 and 1995 and Former Judge, Ventura County Municipal Court, appointed by Governor George Deukmejian.

Instructor Ventura College of Law since 1986 and The National Judicial College 1992-99. Captain USAFR 1970-79.

Mailing address: P.O. Box 6489, Ventura 93006-6489.

Office: 800 South Victoria Avenue, Ventura 93009.

Telephone: (805) 654-2218.

SMITH, Clay M. *(Judge, Superior Court of California County of Orange)* Assumed office Aug 10, 1998. Born Lynwood California 1950. Church of Jesus Christ of Latter-Day Saints. Educated at Brigham Young University B.A. with honors 1974 and University of Utah J.D. 1977. Articles Editor Utah Law Review 1975-77. Law Clerk to Hon. J. Clifford Wallace, U.S. Court of Appeals Ninth Circuit 1977-78. Admitted to practice California 1977, U.S. District Courts Central 1978, Northern 1978 and Southern 1978 Districts of California, U.S. Court of Appeals Ninth Circuit 1978 and U.S. Tax Court 1981. In legal practice Los Angeles 1978-80 and Orange County 1980-97. Judge, North Orange County Municipal Court March 17, 1997 to Aug 9, 1998, appointed by Governor Pete Wilson.

Author of numerous published articles and essays.

Mailing address: P.O. Box 1994, Santa Ana 92702.

Office: 700 Civic Center Drive West, Santa Ana 92702.

Telephone: (714) 834-3734.

SMITH, Diana Becton *(Judge, Superior Court of California County of Contra Costa)*

Office: 100 37th Street, Richmond 94805-2136.

Telephone: (510) 374-3800.

SMITH, Erithe A. *(Judge, United States Bankruptcy Court Central District of California)* Appointed by U.S. Court of Appeals Ninth Circuit judges.

Office: Federal Building, 255 East Temple Street, Los Angeles 90012.

Telephone: (213) 894-4080.

SMITH, M. Bruce *(Judge, Superior Court of California County of Fresno)* Serves Juvenile Delinquincy Court.

Office: 742 South Tenth Street, Fresno 93702.

Telephone: (559) 455-5195.

SMITH, Michael A. *(Judge, Superior Court of California County of San Bernardino)* Elected to term beginning Jan 1, 1987. Reelected June 4, 1992 and 1998. Current term expires Jan 2005. Born Los Angeles California 1950. Educated at California State University at Los Angeles B.A. 1971 and University of San Diego J.D. 1974. Admitted to practice California 1974.

Deputy District Attorney San Bernardino County 1975-86.

Office: 351 North Arrowhead Avenue, San Bernardino 92415-0240.

Telephone: (909) 387-3922.

SMITH, R. Michael *(Judge, Superior Court of California County of Solano)* Former Judge, Northern Solano Municipal Court Solano County.

Office: 600 Union Avenue, Fairfield 94533-5000.

Telephone: (707) 421-7827.

SMITH, Spurgeon E. *(Judge, Superior Court of California County of Los Angeles)* Assumed office Jan 22, 2000. Former Judge, Los Angeles Municipal Court Los Angeles County.

Office: Metropolitan Courthouse, 1945 South Hill Street, Los Angeles 90007-1466.

Telephone: (213) 744-4001.

SMITH, Vernon F. *(Judge, Superior Court of California County of Marin)* Presiding Judge May 1, 1996 to May 1, 1998. Former Judge, Marin County Municipal Court.

Mailing address: P.O. Box 4988, San Rafael 94913-4988.

Office: Hall of Justice, 3501 Civic Center Drive, San Rafael 94903.

Telephone: (415) 499-6407.

SMITH, Winifred Younge *(Judge, Superior Court of California County of Alameda)*

Office: Hayward Hall of Justice, 24405 Amador Street, Hayward 94544.

Telephone: (510) 670-5060.

SMITH-STEWARD, Pamela *(Judge, Superior Court of California County of Sacramento)*

Office: Courthouse, 720 Ninth Street, Sacramento 95814.

Telephone: (916) 874-5476.

SMYTH, Michael *(Judge, Superior Court of California County of San Diego)*

Mailing address: P.O. Box 122724, San Diego 92112-2724.

Office: 220 West Broadway, San Diego 92101.

Telephone: (619) 531-3820.

SNAUFFER, Mark Wood *(Judge, Superior Court of California County of Fresno)*

Office: Courthouse, 1100 Van Ness Avenue, Fresno 93724-0002.

Telephone: (559) 448-1825.

SNOWDEN, W. Scott *(Judge, Superior Court of California County of Napa)* Elected to term beginning Jan 7, 1985. Reelected 1990, 1996 and 2002. Current term expires Jan 2009. Presiding Judge Superior and Municipal Consolidated Courts, Jan 1, 1996 to Dec 31, 1997. Presiding Judge Jan 1, 1997 to Dec 31, 1999 and since Jan 1, 2002. Born San Francisco California April 6, 1946. Episcopalian. Educated at Washington and Lee University B.A. with honors 1968 and University of California Boalt Hall School of Law J.D. 1971. Admitted to practice California 1972. Began legal practice Na-

SNOWDEN, W. SCOTT—*Continued*

pa 1972. In legal practice St. Helena 1977-79. Judge, Napa Municipal Court Napa County Feb 1, 1980 to Jan 6, 1985, appointed by Governor Edmund G. Brown, Jr.

Deputy City Attorney Napa 1972-80. City Attorney Yountville 1978-80. Member California Judges Association (Judicial Elections Committee 1985-86, Chair Courts and Automation Committee 1990-91) and State Bar of California 1972-80 (Member and Chair Committee on Adoptions). Captain USAR 1968-76. Member and Chair St. Helena Planning Commission 1972-75 and Napa County Planning Commission 1976-80.

Office: Napa County Courthouse, 825 Brown Street, Napa 94559.

Telephone: (707) 299-1100.

SNYDER, Christina A. *(Judge, United States District Court Central District of California)* Appointed for life by President Bill Clinton to term beginning Nov 24, 1997. Born Los Angeles California May 27, 1947. Educated at Pomona College B.A. 1969 and Stanford University J.D. 1972. In legal practice California 1972-97.

Office: U.S. Courthouse, 312 North Spring Street, Los Angeles 90012.

Telephone: (213) 894-8551.

SNYDER, Sandra *(Magistrate Judge, United States District Court Eastern District of California)* Appointed by U.S. District Court judges to term beginning May 3, 1993. Reappointed May 3, 2001, current term expires May 2, 2009. Educated at California State University at Fresno B.A. 1968 and Golden Gate University J.D. 1976. Admitted to practice California 1977 and U.S. District Court Eastern District of California 1982. Judge, Fresno Consolidated Municipal Court Fresno County 1989-91. Judge, Superior Court of California Fresno County 1991-93.

Instructor in Civil Trial Practice San Joaquin College of Law 1993. Former Member California Judges Association. Member Fresno County Women Lawyers, California Women Lawyers, National Association of Women Judges and Fresno County Bar Association (Board of Directors 1987-89). Attended 1989 and 1990, Seminar Leader 1991 and Instructor Gender Bias Seminars 1989-96, Update on California Family Law 1992 and Civil Practice in Federal Courts Continuing Legal Education 1994 California Judges College. Named Alumni of the Year by Golden Gate University School of Law 1994 and Mentor of the Year by Fresno County Young Lawyers 1994.

Office: 3419 U.S. Courthouse, 1130 O Street, Fresno 93721.

Telephone: (559) 498-7325.

SO, Kenneth Kai-Young *(Judge, Superior Court of California County of San Diego)*

Mailing address: P.O. Box 122724, San Diego 92112-2724.

Office: 220 West Broadway, San Diego 92101.

Telephone: (619) 531-3820.

SOHIGIAN, Ronald M. *(Judge, Superior Court of California County of Los Angeles)* Appointed by Governor George Deukmejian to term beginning Oct 13, 1988. Elected Nov 1990, 1996 and 2002. Current term expires Jan 2009. Born Fresno California Sept 8, 1937. Religious affiliation: Armenian Orthodox Apostolic. Educated at Yale University B.A. 1958 and Harvard Law School J.D. 1961. Admitted to practice California 1962, U.S. District Courts Central, Eastern, Northern and Southern Districts of California, U.S. Court of Appeals Ninth Circuit and U.S. Supreme Court. In legal practice San Francisco 1962-65, Beverly Hills 1965-70 and Los Angeles 1970-88.

Member California Judges Association. Participant California Judicial College. USAFR 1961-65. USNR JAG 1965-67.

Office: Courthouse, 111 North Hill Street, Los Angeles 90012.

Telephone: (213) 974-5411.

SOKOLOV, Thomas R. *(Judge, Superior Court of California County of Los Angeles)* Assumed office Jan 22, 2000. Former Judge and Presiding Judge, South Bay Municipal Court Los Angeles County.

Office: Torrance Courthouse, 825 Maple Avenue, Torrance 90503.

Telephone: (310) 222-8808.

SOLNER, Michael C. *(Judge, Superior Court of California County of Los Angeles)* Assumed office Jan 22, 2000. Former Judge, Los Angeles Municipal Court Los Angeles County.

Office: Courthouse, 111 North Hill Street, Los Angeles 90012.

Telephone: (213) 974-5411.

SOTELO, David *(Judge, Superior Court of California County of Los Angeles)*

Office: East Los Angeles Courthouse, 214 South Fetterly Avenue, Los Angeles 90022.

Telephone: (323) 780-2055.

SOTO, Philip L. *(Judge, Superior Court of California County of Los Angeles)* Assumed office Jan 24, 2000. Former Judge, Southeast Municipal Court Los Angeles County.

Office: El Monte Courthouse, 11234 East Valley Boulevard, El Monte 91731.

Telephone: (626) 575-4101.

SOUTHARD, Douglas K. *(Judge, Superior Court of California County of Santa Clara)* Assumed office July 30, 1998. Elected 2000, current term expires Jan 2007. Born Los Angeles California July 6, 1948. Lutheran. Educated at Stanford University B.A. in Philosophy 1970 and University of California Hastings College of the Law J.D. 1975. Admitted to practice California 1975, U.S. District Court Northern District of California 1975 and Idaho 1982. In legal practice Mountain View California 1976-77. Judge, Santa Clara County Municipal Court Jan 8, 1988 to July 29, 1998, appointed by Governor George Deukmejian.

Deputy District Attorney Santa Clara County Oct 1977 to Jan 1988. Member California Judges Association and Santa Clara County Bar Association. Republican. Governing Board Stanford Area Council Boy Scouts of America. Regional referee AYSO soccer. Coach/Umpire Los Altos Pony League Baseball. Member Bethel Lutheran Church. Interested in personal computers, cub scouts, little league, youth soccer and home improvement. Enjoys running, mountain biking, softball, surfing, skiing, racquetball, swimming and gardening.

Office: 270 Grant Avenue, Palo Alto 94306.

Telephone: (650) 462-3830.

SPAIN, Julia *(Judge, Superior Court of California County of Alameda)* Assumed office July 31, 1998. For-

SPAIN, JULIA—*Continued*

mer Judge, San Leandro-Hayward Municipal Court Alameda County.

Office: Hayward Hall of Justice, 24405 Amador Street, Hayward 94544.

Telephone: (510) 670-5060.

SPANOS, George V. *(Judge, Superior Court of California County of Contra Costa)*

Office: Courts Building, 1020 Ward Street, Martinez 94553.

Telephone: (925) 646-2950.

SPEAR, S. Patricia *(Judge, Superior Court of California County of Los Angeles)* Assumed office Jan 22, 2000. Elected 2000, current term expires Jan 2007. Serves Children's Court. Born Los Angeles California Sept 1947. Educated at University of California at Los Angeles B.A. 1969 and University of Pittsburgh J.D. 1974. Admitted to practice California 1974 and U.S. District Courts Southern 1974 and Central 1986 Districts of California. In legal practice San Diego 1974-88. Judge, North County Municipal Court San Diego County May 1988 to Dec 1990. Judge, Los Angeles Municipal Court Los Angeles County Dec 1990 to Jan 21, 2000, appointed by Governor George Deukmejian.

Deputy City Attorney San Diego 1976-81. Associate Counsel San Diego Trust and Savings Bank 1983-88. Chair Publications Subcommittee 1981-84 and Membership Committee 1986 San Diego County Bar Association. Chair Courts and the Public Committee Los Angeles Municipal Court 1993-94. Chair Program Committee George McBurney Business Litigation Inn of Court 1999. Member Lawyers Club of San Diego, San Diego Financial Lawyers Association, McBurney Inn of Court, Municipal Court Judges Association (Chair Legislative Lunch Committee 1999) and California Judges Association (Chair Public Information and Education Committee 1996). Chair Annual Meeting Municipal Court Judges Association 1992-93. Coordinator Annual Meeting Driving Under the Influence Programs California Judges Association 1992-93. Member and Presenter Steering Committee Ignition Interlock Workshop Administrative Office of the Courts 1993. Member Affirmative Action Advisory Board San Diego County 1985-88.

Office: 201 Centre Plaza Drive, Monterey Park 91754-2158.

Telephone: (323) 526-6330.

SPEER, Susan M. *(Judge, Superior Court of California County of Los Angeles)* Assumed office Jan 22, 2000. Elected 2002, current term expires Jan 2009. Born Salt Lake City Utah Feb 9, 1953. Methodist. Educated at Mount St. Mary's College B.S.R.N. with honors 1975 and Southwestern University J.D. with honors 1980. Recipient Bancroft-Whitney Jurisprudence Awards in Corporate Law and Civil Procedure. Admitted to practice California 1980. In legal practice Los Angeles 1980-81. Judge, Los Angeles Municipal Court Los Angeles County March 17, 1998 to Jan 21, 2000, appointed by Governor Pete Wilson.

Head Deputy District Attorney Los Angeles County 1981-98. Member California Judges Association (Ethics Committee). Registered Nurse. Republican. Board of Trustees United Methodist Church. Head Coach Chaminade Mock Trial Team. Interests include skiing, cooking and dog shows.

Office: Van Nuys Courthouse East, 6230 Sylmar Avenue, Van Nuys 91401.

Telephone: (818) 374-2265.

SPENCER, Vaino Hassan *(Presiding Justice, California Court of Appeal Second District Division One)* Appointed by Governor Edmund G. Brown, Jr. Aug 18, 1980. Retained by election. Born Los Angeles California July 22, 1920. Educated at Los Angeles City College summa cum laude 1949 and Southwestern University School of Law LL.B. 1952. Admitted to practice California 1952. In legal practice Los Angeles 1952-61. Judge, Los Angeles Municipal Court Los Angeles County 1961-76. Judge, Superior Court of California Los Angeles County 1976-80.

Member California Law Revision Commission 1960-63, Attorney General's Advisory Committee on Constitutional Rights 1959-61, California Judges Association, California Women Lawyers Association, Langston Law Club, Black Women Lawyers Association, National Judicial Council, Judicial Council of California, California Association of Elected Women Officials, Los Angeles County (Human Rights Section) and National Bar Associations. President National Association of Women Judges 1981. Recipient Woman of the Year Award from Los Angeles Sentinel 1952, 1957 and 1962 and Pittsburgh Courier 1946 and 1953 and Trailblazer Award from National Association of Business and Professional Women 1962. Honoree Urban League Equal Opportunities 1961. Recipient Coca Cola Company's Distinguished Citizen Award in Field of Civil Rights 1962, Most Distinguished Alumna Award from Los Angeles City College 1966, Women Powerful Award from Hadassah Los Angeles Chapter 1975, Mary Church Terrell Award (Women for Good Government) 1975, Ernestine Stahlhut Award from Los Angeles Women Lawyers Association 1976 and Award of Appreciation from Black Women Lawyers Association 1976. Member Democratic State Central Committee 1958-60 and 1960-61. Executive Board Democratic County Central Committee 1958-60. President Democratic Minority Conference 1957-60 (Civil Rights Service Award 1960). Executive Board Community Groups for Political Action 1960-62. Director-at-large California Mental Health Association 1962-66. Advisory Committee Bank of Finance 1963-67. Member National Committee Against Discrimination in Housing 1968. Director Model Neighborhood Economic Development Corporation 1970-76. Officer and Director Los Angeles County Commission on Justice 1971-74. Advisory Committee on Legal Equality 1973-76. Member NAACP (Executive Board 1955-56). Board of Trustees Immaculate Heart College 1975-77. Board of Directors Southwestern Alumni Association 1970-76, Themis Society and Salute to Women Leaders.

Office: 300 South Spring Street, Los Angeles 90013.

Telephone: (213) 830-7000.

SPERO, Joseph C. *(Magistrate Judge, United States District Court Northern District of California)* Appointed by U.S. District Court judges to term beginning March 13, 1999. Term expires 2007.

Office: U.S. Courthouse, 450 Golden Gate Avenue, Box 36060, San Francisco 94102-3489.

Telephone: (415) 522-3691.

SPINETTA, Peter L. *(Judge, Superior Court of California County of Contra Costa)* Appointed by Governor

SPINETTA, PETER L.—*Continued*

George Deukmejian to term beginning 1989. Elected 1990, 1996 and 2002. Current term expires Jan 2009. Presiding Judge 1996-98. Born Oakland California 1941. Educated at St Mary's College 1963 and Yale University M.S. J.D. In legal practice 20 years.

Named Trial Judge of the Year by Alameda and Contra Costa County Trial Lawyers Association.

Office: A. F. Bray Courts Building, 1020 Ward Street, Martinez 94553.

Telephone: (925) 646-2950.

SPITZER, Robert George *(Judge, Superior Court of California County of Riverside)* Assumed office July 29, 1998. Elected 2002, current term expires Jan 2009. Born Columbus Ohio Jan 17, 1949. Presbyterian. Educated at University of California at Los Angeles B.A. summa cum laude 1971 and University of Southern California J.D. 1975. Member Phi Alpha Delta. Admitted to practice California 1975 and U.S. District Court Central District of California 1976. In legal practice Beverly Hills 1975-76 and Los Angeles 1976-77. Judge, Western Riverside County Municipal Court Jan 23, 1990 to July 28, 1998, appointed by Governor George Deukmejian.

Supervising Deputy District Attorney Riverside County 1977-90. Member California Judges Association and Leo A. Deegan Inn of Court. Graduate California Judicial College 1990.

Office: Riverside Historic Courthouse, 4050 Main Street, Riverside 92501.

Telephone: (909) 955-1960.

SQUIRES, Donald B. *(Judge, Superior Court of California County of Alameda)* Assumed office July 31, 1998. Elected 2000, current term expires Jan 2007. Born San Francisco California Jan 7, 1947. Episcopalian. Educated at University of California at Berkeley B.A. 1968 and McGeorge School of Law J.D. 1977. Admitted to practice California 1977 and U.S. District Court District of California 1977. Began legal practice Fresno 1978. In legal practice Alameda County 1980-83. Commissioner 1983-84, Judge June 1, 1984 to July 30, 1998 and Presiding Judge Aug 5, 1995 to Jan 12, 1998, Fremont-Newark-Union City Municipal Court Alameda County, appointed by Governor George Deukmejian.

Former Prosecutor. Former member State Bar of California. Member Planning Committee SMASH Conference of Bay Area Judges on DUI Issues 1986. Chair DUI Sentencing Institute for Northern California Judges ("Increasing Judicial Impact"). Member 1983-89 and Chair 1987-89 Judicial Coordinating Committee of Alameda County (Member 1984-87 and Chair 1985-89 DUI Subcommittee). Judicial member Washington Township and Alameda County Bar Associations. Member California Judges Association (Ethics Committee 1986-90, Subcommittee on the American Bar Association 1990 Code since 1991). Attended "DUI" and "DUI Case Management" The National Judicial College 1985 and 1986, "Impact of reproductive technology on the law" Woman Judge's Fund for Justice 1989, AJS Western Judicial Ethics Forum 1989 and Second Northern California Conference on Protecting Children 1990. Lieutenant s.g. USN Vietnam and Ethiopia 1968-72. Enjoys travel, photography and history.

Office: Fremont Hall of Justice, 39439 Paseo Padre Parkway, Fremont 94538.

Telephone: (510) 795-2329.

STAFFEL, Timothy J. *(Judge, Superior Court of California County of Santa Barbara)* Appointed by Governor Pete Wilson Aug 1, 1998. Elected March 2000, current term expires Jan 2007. Born Dec 1, 1956. Educated at San Diego State University B.A. 1978 and McGeorge School of Law University of the Pacific J.D. 1985. Admitted to practice California 1985, Washington 1986 and U.S. Court of Appeals Ninth Circuit 1986. In legal practice Santa Maria California 1987-98.

Supervisor Fourth District Board of Supervisors Santa Barbara County 1993-98. Commissioner California Coastal Commission 1995-98. Member Santa Maria Breakfast Rotary Club. Personal Statement or Quote: "Be on time. Court starts promptly at 8:30 a.m. Be prepared."

Office: 312-H East Cook Street, Santa Maria 93454.

Telephone: (805) 346-7473.

STAFFORD, Charles E., Jr. *(Judge, Superior Court of California County of Riverside)* Assumed office July 29, 1998. Former Judge, Desert Municipal Court Riverside County.

Office: Larson Justice Center, 46-200 Oasis Street, Indio 92201.

Telephone: (760) 863-8426.

STAFFORD, Rodney J. *(Judge, Superior Court of California County of Santa Clara)* Assumed office July 30, 1998. Former Judge and Presiding Judge, Santa Clara County Municipal Court.

Office: Hall of Justice West Wing, 200 West Hedding Street, San Jose 95110.

Telephone: (408) 808-6600.

STALEY, Harry Anthony *(Judge, Superior Court of California County of Kern)* Assumed office July 1, 2000. Born Canton Ohio Jan 22, 1949. Educated at New York University B.S. 1971 and University of San Diego J.D. 1976. Admitted to practice California 1976. Judge, Bakersfield Municipal Court Kern County Nov 3, 1982 to June 30, 2000.

Office: 1215 Truxtun Avenue, Bakersfield 93301.

Telephone: (661) 868-2450.

STANFORD, Richard W., Jr. *(Judge, Superior Court of California County of Orange)* Assumed office Aug 10, 1998. Born Orange California March 15, 1947. Educated at California State University at Fullerton B.A. 1970 and University of Southern California J.D. 1973. Admitted to practice California 1973. Judge March 26, 1985 to Aug 9, 1998 and Presiding Judge 1990-91, Central Orange County Municipal Court, appointed by Governor George Deukmejian.

Deputy District Attorney Orange County 1973-85. Former member California District Attorneys Association, Orange County Deputy District Attorneys Association (Board of Directors 1976-85 and President 1982 and 1983), State Bar of California and Orange County Bar Association. Member California Judges Association.

Mailing address: P.O. Box 5000, Fullerton 92838.

Office: 1275 North Berkeley Avenue, Fullerton 92832.

Telephone: (714) 773-4400.

STANLEY, Trina Thompson *(Judge, Superior Court of California County of Alameda)*

Office: Courthouse, 1225 Fallon Street, Oakland 94612.

Telephone: (510) 272-6070.

STAVEN, Martin W. *(Judge, Superior Court of California County of Tulare)* Assumed office July 27, 1998. Term expires Jan 2009. Currently serves as Presiding Judge Juvenile Court. Born Vermillion South Dakota June 7, 1938. Educated at Golden Gate College of Law J.D. 1967. Admitted to practice California 1967. In legal practice Pasadena and Beverly Hills 1977-80 and Tulare County May 1985 to Feb 1990. Judge, Tulare County Municipal Court Feb 13, 1990 to July 26, 1998, appointed by Governor George Deukmejian.

With Los Angeles County Public Defender's Office Jan 1968 to April 1977 and Tulare County Public Defender's Office March 1980 to May 1985. Corporal U.S. Army 1958-60. Previously employed as title officer. Republican. Board of Directors Tulare County Council on Alcoholism and NCADD. Enjoys reading and watching sports.

Office: 11200 Avenue 368, Visalia 93291.
Telephone: (559) 713-3157.

STEIN, William Douglas *(Associate Justice, California Court of Appeal First District Division One)* Appointed by Governor George Deukmejian to term beginning Aug 21, 1988. Retained by election Nov 1990 and Nov 2002. Current term expires Jan 2015. Born San Francisco California Oct 22, 1940. Roman Catholic. Educated at San Francisco State College B.A. 1962 and Hastings College of the Law J.D. 1965. Staff member Hastings Law Journal 1964-65. Admitted to practice California 1966, U.S. District Court Northern District of California 1966, U.S. Supreme Court 1970 and U.S. Court of Military Appeals 1978. Judge, San Francisco Municipal Court San Francisco County 1984-85. Judge, Superior Court of California City and County of San Francisco June 1985 to Aug 1988, appointed by Governor George Deukmejian.

Deputy Attorney General 1966-78, Assistant Attorney General 1978-84 and Senior Assistant Attorney General 1984 California Department of Justice. Commander USNR JAGC 1969-88.

Office: 350 McAllister Street, San Francisco 94102-3600.
Telephone: (415) 865-7250.

STEINBERG, Marjorie S. *(Judge, Superior Court of California County of Los Angeles)*
Office: Courthouse, 111 North Hill Street, Los Angeles 90012.
Telephone: (213) 974-5411.

STEPHENSON, Franklin M. *(Judge, Superior Court of California County of San Joaquin)*
Office: 315 East Center Street, Manteca 95336.
Telephone: (209) 239-6427.

STERLING, William N. *(Judge, Superior Court of California County of Los Angeles)*
Office: Courthouse, 111 North Hill Street, Los Angeles 90012.
Telephone: (213) 974-5411.

STERN, Jacqueline Marion *(Judge, Superior Court of California County of San Diego)*
Mailing address: P.O. Box 122724, San Diego 92112-2724.
Office: 1551-55 Sixth Avenue, San Diego 92101.

STERN, Michael L. *(Judge, Superior Court of California County of Los Angeles)* Appointed by Governor Gray Davis to term beginning Dec 27, 2001. Educated at Stanford University A.B. 1967, Harvard University J.D. 1971 and University of California at Berkeley LL.M. 1972. Admitted to practice California and District of Columbia.

Office: 400 Civic Center Plaza, Department L, Pomona 91766.
Telephone: (909) 620-3023.

STEVENS, Darrell W. *(Judge, Superior Court of California County of Butte)* Assumed office June 3, 1998. Former Judge and Presiding Judge, North Butte County Municipal Court.

Office: Chico Courthouse, 655 Oleander Avenue, Chico 95926.
Telephone: (530) 895-6502.

STEVENS, Emily A. *(Judge, Superior Court of California County of Los Angeles)* Serves Children's Court. Former Judge, Los Angeles Municipal Court Los Angeles County.

Office: 201 Centre Plaza Drive, Monterey Park 91754-2158.
Telephone: (323) 526-6330.

STEVENS, Lawrence T. *(Associate Justice, California Court of Appeal First District Division Five)* Appointed by governor. Former Judge and Presiding Judge, Superior Court of California San Mateo County. Former Judge, San Mateo County Municipal Court.

Office: 350 McAllister Street, San Francisco 94102-3600.
Telephone: (415) 865-7300.

STEVENS, Samuel S. *(Judge, Superior Court of California County of Santa Cruz)* Appointed by Governor George Deukmejian to term beginning Feb 1989. Elected June 1990, 1996 and 2002. Current term expires Jan 2009. Presiding Judge Jan 1, 2000 to Dec 31, 2000. Born Oakland California May 11, 1945. Educated at University of California at Berkeley B.A. 1966 and University of California Hastings College of the Law J.D. 1969. Admitted to practice California 1969. In legal practice Santa Cruz 1969-89.

Office: Main Courthouse, 701 Ocean Street, Santa Cruz 95060.
Telephone: (831) 454-2012.

STEWART, John Kennedy *(Judge, Superior Court of California City and County of San Francisco)*
Office: Hall of Justice, 850 Bryant Street, San Francisco 94103.
Telephone: (415) 553-1159.

STEWART, William D. *(Judge, Superior Court of California County of Los Angeles)*
Office: Courthouse, 111 North Hill Street, Los Angeles 90012.
Telephone: (213) 974-5411.

STIRLING, Lawrence W. *(Judge, Superior Court of California County of San Diego)* Assumed office Dec 1, 1998. Former Judge, San Diego Municipal Court San Diego County.

Mailing address: P.O. Box 122724, San Diego 92112-2724.
Office: 220 West Broadway, San Diego 92101.
Telephone: (619) 531-3820.

STIVEN, James F. *(Magistrate Judge, United States District Court Southern District of California)* Appointed by U.S. District Court judges to term beginning Aug 5,

STIVEN, JAMES F.—*Continued*

1996. Term expires Aug 5, 2004. Born Highland Illinois Oct 3, 1940. Episcopalian. Educated at University of California at Los Angeles B.S. with honors 1962 J.D. with honors 1969. Senior Editor UCLA Law Review 1967-69. Admitted to practice California 1970, U.S. District Court Southern District of California 1970, U.S. Court of Appeals Ninth Circuit 1976 and U.S. Supreme Court 1992. In legal practice San Diego 1969-96.

Author "Privacy in the Computer Age" UCLA L. Rev. 1968 and "Recent Developments" Journal of Air Law & Commerce 1991. Board of Directors San Diego County Bar Foundation. Board of Governors Association of Business Trial Lawyers. Master American Inns of Court. Member American Board of Trial Advocates, State Bar of California, San Diego County and American (House of Delegates 1982-96) Bar Associations. USMC 1962-66. Democrat. Board of Trustees California Western School of Law. Board of Directors UCLA Alumni Association and UCLA Law School Alumni Association.

Office: 1131 U.S. Courthouse, 940 Front Street, San Diego 92101-8929.

Telephone: (619) 557-7688.

Fax: (619) 702-9991

E-mail address: James_F_Stiven@casd.uscourts.gov

STOCK, Nancy Wieben *(Judge, Superior Court of California County of Orange)* Appointed by Governor George Deukmejian to term beginning Jan 26, 1990. Elected June 1990, 1996 and 2002. Current term expires Jan 2009. Born Oakland California Aug 10, 1951. Episcopalian. Educated at University of California at Davis B.A. 1973 J.D. 1976. Recipient First Place Oral Argument Team and Final Round Outstanding Individual Oral Argument National Moot Court 1975 and Excellence in Advocacy Award from American College of Trial Lawyers 1975. Member Phi Delta Phi. Admitted to practice California 1976, U.S. District Court Central District of California 1979 and U.S. Court of Appeals Ninth Circuit 1980. In legal practice Orange 1976-78.

Assistant U.S. Attorney Los Angeles 1978-80. Member California Judges Association, National Association of Women Judges, California Women Lawyers, Orange County and Federal (Board of Directors 1988-90) Bar Associations. Instructor California Center for Judicial Education and Research since 1990, "Family Law Update" The Rutter Group 1992, Criminal Issues National College of District Attorneys and Trial Skills Attorney General's Advocacy Institute. Recipient Special Achievement Award from U.S. Department of Justice 1980, Appreciation Award from National Association for Missing and Exploited Children 1987, Special Award from U.S. Postal Inspection Service 1989, Award for Judicial Integrity from Consumer Lawyers of California 1997 and Jerrold Oliver Award for Judicial Integrity, Compassion and Courage from Orange County Trial Lawyers Association 1997. Named Judge of the Year by Constitutional Rights Foundation Orange County Chapter 1992 and American Board of Trial Advocates Orange County 1997 and Distinguished Alumnus by King Hall Law School. Republican. Member Bobby Sox Softball Association. Supports Women's Transitional Living Center and Orange County Performing Arts Center. Enjoys youth sports, reading and aerobics.

Mailing address: P.O. Box 14169, Orange 92863-1569.

Office: Lamoreaux Justice Center, 341 The City Drive, Orange 92868.

Telephone: (714) 935-7236.

STOEVER, Thomas William *(Judge, Superior Court of California County of Los Angeles)*

Office: Courthouse, 111 North Hill Street, Los Angeles 90012.

Telephone: (213) 974-5411.

STOLL, Charles W. *(Judge, Superior Court of California County of Los Angeles)*

Office: Glendale Courthouse, 600 East Broadway, Glendale 91206.

Telephone: (818) 500-3524.

STOLTZ, Kathryne A. *(Judge, Superior Court of California County of Los Angeles)* Former Judge, Los Angeles Municipal Court Los Angeles County.

Office: Van Nuys Courthouse West, 14400 Erwin Street Mall, Van Nuys 91401-2705.

Telephone: (818) 374-2601.

STONE, Richard A. *(Judge, Superior Court of California County of Los Angeles)*

Office: Los Angeles Airport Courthouse, 11701 South La Cienega Boulevard, Los Angeles 90045.

Telephone: (310) 727-6010.

STORMES, Nita L. *(Magistrate Judge, United States District Court Southern District of California)* Appointed by U.S. District Court judges to term beginning Jan 3, 2000. Term expires 2008.

Office: U.S. Courthouse, 940 Front Street, San Diego 92101-8900.

Telephone: (619) 557-5391.

STOTLER, Alicemarie H. *(Judge, United States District Court Central District of California)* Appointed for life by President Ronald Reagan to term beginning June 15, 1984. Born Alhambra California May 29, 1942. Protestant. Educated at University of Southern California B.A. 1964 J.D. 1967. Winner Statewide Moot Court Competition 1967. Recipient American Jurisprudence Award in Civil Procedure 1967. Member Kappa Alpha Theta. Admitted to practice California 1967, U.S. District Courts Northern 1967 and Central 1973 Districts of California and U.S. Supreme Court 1976. Certified Specialist Criminal Law California Board of Legal Specialization 1973. In legal practice Orange County 1973-84. Judge, Orange County Harbor Municipal Court Orange County 1976-78. Associate Justice pro tem, California Court of Appeal Fourth District 1977. Judge, Superior Court of California Orange County 1978-83.

Deputy District Attorney Orange County 1967-73. Instructor Orange County Sheriff's Department Academy 1982. Member Rules Committee 1979-80, Chair Family Conciliation Court Committee 1980-82, member Committee for Public Information and Judicial Education 1980-82 and Executive Committee 1981 and Co-chair Judicial Conference 1981 Orange County Superior Court. Advisory Board Women's Law Institute Western State University College of Law 1979-82. Victim/Witness Advisory Committee Office of Criminal Justice Planning 1980-83 and Advisory Group on Juvenile Justice and Delinquency Prevention 1983-84 State of California.

STOTLER, ALICEMARIE H.—*Continued*

Member Criminal Law Advisory Commission Board of Legal Specialization State Bar of California 1983-84. Chairman District Court Symposium 1985, Jury Utilization Committee 1985, U.S. Constitution Bicentennial Committee since 1986, Continuing Education Committee 1990 and Attorney Liaison Committee 1990 Central District of California. Member Orange County Trial Lawyers Association (Board of Directors 1975), California Judges' Foundation (Secretary-Treasurer 1979-80, President 1980-82), California Judges Association since 1976, Ninth Circuit District Judges Association (Executive Committee Ninth Circuit Judicial Conference since 1989, Committee on Jury Instructions since 1990, Committee on Uniform Local Rules), Federal Judges Association (Board of Directors 1989-91), The American Law Institute since 1987, National Association of Women Judges since 1980, Orange County (Committees on Client Relations 1973-76, Judiciary 1975-76, Administration of Justice 1976, member Criminal Law Section 1974-76, Secretary 1984) and American (Sections: Judicial Administration Division, Litigation, Committee on Legislative Affairs since 1990) Bar Associations. Lecturer on Evidence 1982 and Federal Jurisdiction 1985-90 The Rutter Group. Lecturer on Employment Discrimination 1986, 1988, 1989 and 1990 and Sentencing Guidelines 1988 ALI-ABA. Lecturer "Overview of Sentencing Guidelines" Sixth, Seventh, Eighth, Ninth and Tenth Circuit Magistrates Conference 1988, "Criminal Case Pre-Trial Management" and "Relevant Conduct Under the Sentencing Guidelines" New Judges Orientation 1990 and "Criminal Case Management" Seminar for Judges of 3-5 Years' Experience 1990 Federal Judicial Center. Recipient Judge of the Year Award from Orange County Trial Lawyers Association 1978 and Orange County Trial Lawyers' Secretaries Association 1978. Recipient Franklin G. West Award 1985 and Most Outstanding Judge Award Business Litigation Section 1990 Orange County Bar Association. Republican. Board of Trustees George A. Parker Law Foundation 1979-82. Member Planned Giving Committee Orange County Branch Arthritis Foundation 1976-81 and California Elected Women's Association for Education and Research 1979-83. Board of Directors Legion Lex 1981-83. Enjoys traveling with husband, reading and walking.

Office: U.S. Courthouse, 411 West Fourth Street, Santa Ana 92701-4516.

Telephone: (714) 338-4730.

STOTLER, James Allen *(Judge, Superior Court of California County of Orange)* Assumed office Aug 10, 1998. Elected 2001, current term expires Jan 1, 2008. Born Akron Ohio Sept 10, 1941. Catholic. Educated at California State University Long Beach B.S. with honors 1963 and University of California at Los Angeles J.D. 1966. Moot Court. Admitted to practice California 1967 and U.S. District Court Central District of California 1967. In legal practice Tustin 1973-83 and Newport Beach 1983-95. Judge, Central Orange County Municipal Court Oct 12, 1995 to Aug 9, 1998, appointed by Governor Pete Wilson.

Deputy District Attorney Orange County 1967-73. Fellow American College of Trial Lawyers. Member Orange County and American Bar Associations. Republican. Enjoys walking and running. Participant in Los Angeles Marathons 1994-95.

Office: West Justice Center, 8141 Thirteenth Street, Westminster 92683.

Telephone: (714) 896-7181.

STOUT, Dean *(Judge, Superior Court of California County of Inyo)* Presiding Judge since Jan 1, 2003.

Office: 301 West Line Street, Bishop 93514.

Telephone: (760) 872-2597.

STRAUSS, Richard *(Judge, Superior Court of California County of San Diego)* Assistant Presiding Judge Nov 1998 to Dec 31, 2001. Presiding Judge since Jan 1, 2002.

Mailing address: P.O. Box 122724, San Diego 92112-2724.

Office: 220 West Broadway, San Diego 92101.

Telephone: (619) 531-3820.

STREGER, Elaine *(Judge, Superior Court of California County of Orange)* Assumed office Aug 10, 1998. Former Judge, Central Orange County Municipal Court.

Mailing address: P.O. Box 1994, Santa Ana 92702-1994.

Office: Central Justice Center, 700 Civic Center Drive West, Santa Ana 92701.

Telephone: (714) 834-3734.

STROBEL, Mary *(Judge, Superior Court of California County of Los Angeles)*

Office: Huntington Park Courthouse, 6548 Miles Avenue, Huntington Park 90255-2419.

Telephone: (323) 586-6351.

STROMSNESS, Chris *(Judge, Superior Court of California County of Siskiyou)* Assumed office June 4, 1998. Elected 2000, current term expires Jan 2007. Serves Weed Branch. Born Auburn Washington April 30, 1942. Episcopalian. Educated at University of California at Berkeley A.B. 1964 and University of California Hastings College of the Law J.D. 1967. Admitted to practice California 1967 and U.S. District Courts Northern 1967 and Eastern 1968 Districts of California. In legal practice Dunsmuir 1968-92. Judge, McCloud Justice Court Siskiyou County 1977-88. Judge, Siskiyou County Municipal Court June 30, 1992 to June 3, 1998.

City Attorney Dunsmuir 1977-92 and Weed 1990-92. Member California Judges Association, State Bar of California and Siskiyou County Bar Association. Attended California Judicial College 1985. Democrat. Board Member Mount Shasta Hospital 1971-92, Mount Shasta Area Audubon since 1972, Dunsmuir High School 1973-85 and Dunsmuir Scholarship Fund since 1981. Member Dunsmuir Rotary, College of the Siskiyous Foundation and Upper Sacramento River Exchange. Enjoys birding, steelhead, trout and shad fly-fishing, reading and following Dunsmuir High School, Cal, 49ers, Giants and Warriors teams.

Office: 510 North Main Street, Yreka 96097.

Telephone: (530) 842-0180.

STUART, James M. *(Judge, Superior Court of California County of Kern)*

Office: 1415 Truxtun Avenue, Bakersfield 93301.

Telephone: (661) 868-4934.

STUEBBE, Jon Edward *(Judge, Superior Court of California County of Kern)* Former Judge, Bakersfield Municipal Court Kern County.
Office: 1415 Truxtun Avenue, Bakersfield 93301.
Telephone: (661) 868-4934.

STURGEON, Eddie C. *(Judge, Superior Court of California County of San Diego)* Assumed office Dec 1, 1998. Former Judge, El Cajon Municipal Court San Diego County.
Mailing address: P.O. Box 122724, San Diego 92112-2724.
Office: 250 East Main Street, El Cajon 92020.
Telephone: (619) 441-4336.

STYN, Ronald L. *(Judge, Superior Court of California County of San Diego)*
Mailing address: P.O. Box 122724, San Diego 92112-2724.
Office: 220 West Broadway, San Diego 92101.
Telephone: (619) 531-3820.

SUEYRES, F. Clark, Jr. *(Judge, Superior Court of California County of San Joaquin)*
Office: 222 East Weber Avenue, Room 303, Stockton 95202.
Telephone: (209) 468-2827.

SUGIYAMA, John Hideki *(Judge, Superior Court of California County of Contra Costa)*
Office: Courthouse, 725 Court Street, Martinez 94553.
Telephone: (925) 646-2950.

SUNDVOLD, Stephen J. *(Judge, Superior Court of California County of Orange)* Assumed office Aug 10, 1998. Former Judge and Presiding Judge, North Orange County Municipal Court.
Mailing address: P.O. Box 1994, Santa Ana 92702-1994.
Office: Central Justice Center, 700 Civic Center Drive West, Santa Ana 92701.
Telephone: (714) 834-3734.

SUTRO, John A., Jr. *(Judge, Superior Court of California County of Marin)* Assumed office June 11, 1998. Presiding Judge July 1, 2000 to Dec 31, 2001. Former Judge and Presiding Judge, Marin County Municipal Court.
Mailing address: P.O. Box 4988, San Rafael 94913-4988.
Office: Hall of Justice, 3501 Civic Center Drive, San Rafael 94903.
Telephone: (415) 499-6407.

SUTTON, James M., Jr. *(Judge, Superior Court of California County of Los Angeles)* Appointed by Governor George Deukmejian June 8, 1984. Elected 1986, 1992 and 1998. Current term expires Jan 2005. Former Supervising Judge. Serves Southeast District. Born Ponca City Oklahoma April 27, 1932. Protestant. Educated at University of Southern California A.B. cum laude 1954 LL.B. 1960. Member Phi Delta Phi. Admitted to practice California 1961. In legal practice Long Beach 1964-84.
Member California Judges Association. U.S. Army 1954-56.
Office: Norwalk Courthouse, 12720 Norwalk Boulevard, Norwalk 90650.
Telephone: (562) 807-7266.

SUZUKAWA, Steven C. *(Judge, Superior Court of California County of Los Angeles)* Former Judge and Presiding Judge, Compton Municipal Court Los Angeles County.
Office: Compton Courthouse, 200 West Compton Boulevard, Compton 90220.
Telephone: (310) 603-7842.

SWAGER, Douglas E. *(Associate Justice, California Court of Appeal First District Division One)* Appointed by Governor Pete Wilson to term beginning Oct 24, 1995. Retained by election Nov 1998. Born Richmond California Feb 27, 1945. Educated at University of California at Berkeley 1966 and University of California Hastings College of the Law J.D. 1969. In legal practice Contra Costa County. Judge, Bay Municipal Court Contra Costa County Oct 16, 1985 to Nov 4, 1987, appointed by Governor George Deukmejian. Judge Nov 5, 1987 to Oct 23, 1995 and Presiding Judge 1993 and 1994, Superior Court of California Contra Costa County, appointed by Governor George Deukmejian.
Deputy District Attorney Contra Costa County. Consultant *California Judges Benchguide.* Former Member State Trial Court Budget Commission (Executive Committee), Alameda-Contra Costa Trial Lawyers Association and Contra Costa County Bar Association. Member California Judges Association and Italian-American Bar Association. Recipient Distinguished Service Award from YMCA of the USA West Field Committee and Volunteer of the Year Award and Humanitarian of the Year Award from YMCA. Board of Managers West Contra Costa County YMCA (Chief Volunteer Officer 1991-92).
Office: 350 McAllister Street, San Francisco 94102-3600.
Telephone: (415) 865-7300.

SWAIN, Leslie A. *(Judge, Superior Court of California County of Los Angeles)* Assumed office Jan 22, 2000. Former Judge, Los Angeles Municipal Court Los Angeles County.
Office: Hollywood Courthouse, 5925 Hollywood Boulevard, Los Angeles 90028-5434.
Telephone: (323) 856-5751.

SWART, Coleman A. *(Judge, Superior Court of California County of Los Angeles)* Elected to term beginning Jan 3, 1983. Reelected 1988, 1994 and 2000. Current term expires Jan 2007. Born Los Angeles California June 29, 1939. Roman Catholic. Educated at Occidental College B.A. 1961 and Golden Gate University J.D. 1967. Member Alpha Tau Omega. Admitted to practice California 1968. Began legal practice Los Angeles 1968.
Former Deputy District Attorney. Examiner State Bar of California 1975. Instructor Pasadena Community College 1974-76. Member Association of Deputy District Attorneys 1968-82 and Pasadena Bar Association (Legislative Committee 1969-82 and Delegation Chairman State Bar Conference of Delegates 1981 and 1982). Commander USNR 1961-63. Los Angeles County President California Republican Assembly 1980. Board of Directors Metropolitan YMCA.
Office: Pasadena Courthouse, 300 East Walnut Street, Pasadena 91101.
Telephone: (626) 356-5689.

SWEET, Michael W. *(Judge, Superior Court of California County of Yolo)* Presiding Judge since Jan 1, 2002.
Office: 725 Court Street, Woodland 95695.
Telephone: (530) 666-8598.

SWIFT, Bert L. *(Judge, Superior Court of California County of San Bernardino)* Assumed office Aug 10, 1998. Serves East Desert District. Former Judge, San Bernardino County Municipal Court.
Office: 6527 White Feather Road, Joshua Tree 92252.
Telephone: (760) 366-4112.

SZUMOWSKI, David M. *(Judge, Superior Court of California County of San Diego)*
Mailing address: P.O. Box 122724, San Diego 92112-2724.
Office: 220 West Broadway, San Diego 92101.
Telephone: (619) 531-3434.

TAFOYA, Robert S. *(Judge, Superior Court of California County of Kern)*
Office: 1215 Truxtun Avenue, Bakersfield 93301.
Telephone: (661) 868-2450.

TAFT, Franklin R. *(Judge, Superior Court of California County of Solano)* Assumed office Aug 3, 1998. Born San Francisco California Oct 10, 1933. Episcopalian. Educated at San Jose State University B.S. 1960 and University of California Hastings College of the Law J.D. 1963. Admitted to practice California 1964. In legal practice Vallejo 1964-85. Judge July 1985 to Aug 2, 1998 and Former Presiding Judge, Vallejo-Benicia Municipal Court Solano County, appointed by Governor George Deukmejian.
Former member California Trial Lawyers Association and State Bar of California. Private First Class U.S. Army 1956-58. Previously worked as General Contractor. Republican. Member Lions, Navy League and Easter Seal Society. Enjoys skiing and sport cars.
Office: 321 Tuolumne Street, Vallejo 94590.
Telephone: (707) 553-5876.

TAKASUGI, Robert M. *(Senior Judge, United States District Court Central District of California)* Appointed for life by President Gerald R. Ford to term beginning July 6, 1976. Assumed Senior status, serves by assignment. Born Tacoma Washington Sept 12, 1930. Educated at University of California at Los Angeles B.S. 1953 and University of Southern California LL.B. 1959. Recipient Harry J. Bauer Scholarship. Staff member University of Southern California Law Review. Admitted to practice California 1960. In legal practice 1960-73. Judge, Los Angeles Municipal Court Los Angeles County 1973-75 (Administrative Judge 1974 and Presiding Judge 1975). Judge, Superior Court of California Los Angeles County 1976.
Author articles on California mechanics' liens, California criminal discovery, constitutionality of prior convictions, right of the criminal defendant to a speedy trial, constitutional rights during probation and parole violations, contempt procedures and hearing, California insanity laws and legal analyses of landmark decisions. Former Member Code of Conduct Committee Judicial Conference. Member Criminal Justice Standards Review Committee and State Bar of California (Hearing Officer 1973). Guest Lecturer University of California at Los Angeles School of Law, Loyola School of Law and University of Southern California Law Center. Recipient several awards for judicial excellence. U.S. Army Criminal Investigator for Provost Marshal Investigations 1953-55. Recipient U.S. Military Man of the Year Award for the Far East Theater 1954. Hearing Examiner Los Angeles Police Commission 1962-65. Commissioner Los Angeles County Human Relations Commission 1972. Commissioner Senate Committee on Judiciary 1971 and Senate-Assembly Joint Committee on Judicial Reform 1975. Board Member UCLA Council of Presidents. Member Japanese American Citizens League (National Legal Counsel), Selective Service Board (Chairman 1968-70), Alcoholism Council of Greater East Los Angeles Board, East Los Angeles Health System, Inc. Board, East Los Angeles Health Task Force Board, East Los Angeles-Montebello Optimist Club (Honorary Board member), East Los Angeles-Montebello YMCA Board, Daniel Valdez Youth Foundation Board, Salesian Boys' Club Board, East Los Angeles Skills Center Board, Ethnic Concern Committee Board, Asian-American Society for the Blind (Legal counsel) and East Los Angeles College Foundation Board.
Office: U.S. Courthouse, 312 North Spring Street, Los Angeles 90012.
Telephone: (213) 894-2370.

TANG, Julie M. *(Judge, Superior Court of California City and County of San Francisco)* Assumed office Dec 31, 1998. Elected 2002, current term expires Jan 2009. Born Hong Kong Oct 22, 1949. Catholic. Educated at University of San Francisco B.A., Stanford University M.A. and University of California Hastings College of the Law J.D. Admitted to practice California 1982. Judge, San Francisco Municipal Court San Francisco County Jan 1991 to Dec 30, 1998.
Member California Judges Association and Asian American Bar Association. Attended New Judges Orientation Jan 1991, Judicial College June 1991, Annual Conference California Judicial Association June 1992 and "Meeting the Challenge—A Drug Workshop" Nov 1992. Board Member 1977-89 and Chairperson 1978 Chinese American Democratic Club. Member Chinese American Voters Education. Board Member KQED 1979 and San Francisco Community College 1981-90. Member AIDS Literature Review Board 1986-90. Enjoys skiing, reading and dancing.
Office: Hall of Justice, 850 Bryant Street, San Francisco 94103.
Telephone: (415) 553-1159.

TANGEMAN, Martin J. *(Judge, Superior Court of California County of San Luis Obispo)*
Office: County Government Center, 1035 Palm Street, San Luis Obispo 93408-2500.
Telephone: (805) 781-5421.

TANSIL, Mark *(Judge, Superior Court of California County of Sonoma)* Presiding Judge Jan 1, 2001 to Dec 31, 2002.
Office: 600 Administration Drive, Santa Rosa 95403.
Telephone: (707) 565-1100.

TARLE, Norman Perry *(Judge, Superior Court of California County of Los Angeles)*
Office: Criminal Courts Building, 210 West Temple Street, Los Angeles 90012-3210.
Telephone: (213) 974-6535.

TAYLOR, Barry A. *(Judge, Superior Court of California County of Los Angeles)* Assumed office Jan 22,

TAYLOR, BARRY A.—*Continued*

2000. Term expires Jan 2005. Born Los Angeles California Sept 13, 1942. Educated at California State University Northridge A.B. 1964 and University of California Los Angeles J.D. 1967. Admitted to practice California 1969. Commissioner, Superior Court of California Los Angeles County 1991-94. Judge, Los Angeles Municipal Court Los Angeles County Feb 1994 to Jan 21, 2000, appointed by Governor Pete Wilson.

Public Defender Los Angeles 1969-91.

Office: Van Nuys Courthouse West, 14400 Erwin Street Mall, Van Nuys 91401-2705.

Telephone: (818) 374-2601.

TAYLOR, Eric C. *(Judge, Superior Court of California County of Los Angeles)* Assumed office Jan 22, 2000. Former Judge, Inglewood Municipal Court Los Angeles County.

Office: Torrance Courthouse, 825 Maple Avenue, Torrance 90503.

Telephone: (310) 222-8808.

TAYLOR, Gary L. *(Judge, United States District Court Central District of California)* Appointed for life by President George Bush to term beginning 1990. Born Los Angeles California Dec 8, 1938. Educated at University of California at Los Angeles A.B. 1960 J.D. 1963. In legal practice 1966-86. Judge, Superior Court of California County of Orange 1986-90.

Office: 1053 U.S. Courthouse, 411 West Fourth Street, Santa Ana 92701-4516.

Telephone: (714) 338-4710.

TAYLOR, Lynn O'Malley *(Judge, Superior Court of California County of Marin)* Elected to term beginning Jan 7, 1991. Reelected 1996 and 2002. Current term expires Jan 2009. Presiding Judge since Jan 1, 2002. Born Los Angeles California Nov 6, 1943. Episcopalian. Educated at Colorado College 1961-63, University of Arizona B.A. with honors 1964 and San Francisco Law School J.D. 1972. Member Kappa Kappa Gamma and Pi Lambda Theta. Admitted to practice California 1972. In legal practice San Rafael 1973-83. Judge 1983-90 and Presiding Judge 1986 and 1990, Marin County Municipal Court.

Member Jury Instruction Task Force Judicial Council of California since 1997. Member California Judges Association (Annual Meeting Seminar Committee 1985, Chairperson Judicial Elections Committee 1987-88). Faculty Member Elections Workshops California Judges Association 1987-88 and 1993; California Judicial College 1987-88 and 1993; "Sharpening Your Basic Trial Skills" Continuing Education of the Bar 1989 and 1991; "Orientation for New and Returning Judges" 1994 and "Mediation: A Skills Based Program" 2001-02 California Center for Judicial Education and Research; Advocacy Skills Workshop Stanford University 1994-97 and 1999-2002 and University of San Francisco 1994-2002; and Rutter Group Employment Law 2002. Member Terra Linda Rotary Club since 1987 and Marin Forum (President 1990-91). Board of Directors Marin Symphony since 1995 and Marin Council Boy Scouts of America. Enjoys travel and photography.

Mailing address: P.O. Box 4988, San Rafael 94913-4988.

Office: Hall of Justice, 3501 Civic Center Drive, San Rafael 94903.

Telephone: (415) 499-6407.

TAYLOR, Meredith C. *(Judge, Superior Court of California County of Los Angeles)* Former Judge, Los Angeles Municipal Court Los Angeles County.

Office: San Fernando Courthouse, 900 Third Street, San Fernando 91340.

Telephone: (818) 898-2655.

TAYLOR, Robert Gregory *(Judge, Superior Court of California County of Riverside)* Presiding Judge Jan 1, 1999 to Dec 31, 2000.

Office: Palm Springs Court, 3255 East Tahquitz-Canyon Way, Palm Springs 92262.

Telephone: (760) 778-2175.

TAYLOR, Ronald L. *(Judge, Superior Court of California County of Riverside)* Assumed office July 29, 1998. Educated at Cerritos College A.A. 1966, University of California at Riverside A.B. 1968 and University of California at Davis J.D. 1971. Admitted to practice California 1972, U.S. District Courts Central 1974 and Southern 1975 Districts of California, U.S. Court of Appeals Ninth Circuit 1974 and U.S. Supreme Court 1977. Presiding Judge 1985 and 1989-90 and Former Judge, Western Riverside County Municipal Court. Associate Justice pro tem California Court of Appeal Fourth District Division Two Feb 1986 to April 1986. Assistant Presiding Judge 1995-96 and Presiding Judge 1997-98 Consolidated Superior and Municipal Courts Riverside County.

Staff Attorney Merced Legal Services Association 1971-73. Director of Litigation Community Legal Services of Riverside 1973-76. Executive Director Inland Counties Legal Services 1976-82. Co-chairperson Riverside County Court Construction and Site Acquisition Committee since 1985. President Riverside County Municipal Court Judge's Association 1991-92. Advisory Board Access to the Courts Through Technology since 1999. Former Member California Trial Lawyers Association, The Association of Trial Lawyers of America, Metropolitan Superior Courts Association, American Judges Association, State Bar of California (Chairperson The Standing Committee on Legal Services for the Poor 1978-79), Merced County, Riverside County (Founding Member 1993 and Executive Committee 1995-97 Women's Law Section, Judicial Liaison Committee 1992-98), San Bernardino County and American Bar Associations. Member California Commission on Access to Justice (Chair Pro Bono Subcommittee 1997-98), California Center for Judicial Education and Research (Judicial Council Liaison Governing Committee 1998-99), Judicial Council of California (Executive and Planning Committee since 1998) and California Judges Association. Trial Tactics Trainer National Legal Services Corporation 1975-82. Lead Character "Meeting the Challenge of Equal Access to Justice" (a videotape produced by the Office of Legal Services) State Bar of California 1983. Recipient Certificate of Appreciation from Developmental Disabilities Area Board No. 12, 1982, Certificate "for outstanding contributions in the delivery of pro bono and low fee legal services" from Board of Governors State Bar of California 1982, Certificate recognizing outstanding contributions to the courts and justice system from Western State University College of Law 1996 and Communication and Leadership Award from Toastmasters International (District 12-Inland Empire) 1998. U.S. Army 1960-63. Board of Directors Western Center on Law and Poverty 1978-79. Member Legal Services Trust

TAYLOR, RONALD L.—*Continued*
Fund Commission. Interests include long distance running, fishing and American history.
Office: Hall of Justice, 4100 Main Street, Riverside 92501.
Telephone: (909) 955-2300.
E-mail address: RTAYLOR@co.riverside.ca.us

TCHAIKOVSKY, Leslie J. *(Judge, United States Bankruptcy Court Northern District of California)* Appointed by U.S. Court of Appeals Ninth Circuit judges to term beginning 1988. Reappointed April 18, 2002, current term expires April 17, 2016. Educated at University of California Boalt Hall School of Law J.D. 1971.
Mailing address: P.O. Box 2070, Oakland 94604-2070.
Telephone: (510) 879-3540.

TEVRIZIAN, Dickran *(Judge, United States District Court Central District of California)* Appointed for life by President Ronald Reagan 1985. Born Los Angeles California Aug 4, 1940. Educated at University of Southern California B.S. 1962 J.D. 1965. Member Beta Theta Pi and Phi Delta Phi. Admitted to practice California 1966. Judge Los Angeles County Municipal Court 1972-78 and Superior Court of California County of Los Angeles 1978-82.
Member Federal Judges Association. Recipient Trial Judge of the Year Award from California Trial Lawyers Association 1987, Trial Jurist of the Year Award from Los Angeles County Bar Association 1994 and 1995, Peter the Great Gold Medal of Honor from Russian Academy of Natural Sciences 1998, Ellis Island Medal of Honor Award 1999 and Maynard Toll Award 2002.
Office: Federal Building, 255 East Temple Street, Suite 870, Los Angeles 90012.
Telephone: (213) 894-4047.
Fax: (213) 894-0293

THIERBACH, Christian F. "Rick" *(Judge, Superior Court of California County of Riverside)* Assumed office July 29, 1998. Elected Nov 2000, current term expires Jan 2007. Supervising Judge Criminal Division Jan 1997 to 1999. Assistant Presiding Judge 1999-2000. Presiding Judge Jan 1, 2001 to Dec 31, 2002. Educated at University of California at Los Angeles B.A. 1971 and Western State University J.D. 1975. Judge, Western Riverside County Municipal Court 1994 to July 28, 1998.
Deputy District Attorney Riverside County for eighteen years. Named one of the Outstanding Young Men of America by U.S. Junior Chamber of Commerce 1982. Inducted into Western State University Hall of Fame 1996. Member and Past President Board of Education Anaheim Union High School District and Board of Trustees North Orange County Regional Occupational Program.
Office: Hall of Justice, 4100 Main Street, Riverside 92501.
Telephone: (909) 955-2300.

THOMPSON, David A. *(Judge, Superior Court of California County of Orange)*
Mailing address: P.O. Box 1994, Santa Ana 92702-1994.
Office: Central Justice Center, 700 Civic Center Drive West, Santa Ana 92701.
Telephone: (714) 834-3734.

THOMPSON, Gordon, Jr. *(Senior Judge, United States District Court Southern District of California)* Appointed for life by President Richard M. Nixon to term beginning 1970. Former Chief Judge. Assumed Senior status, serves by assignment. Born San Diego California Dec 28, 1929. Educated at University of Southern California and Southwestern University Law School. Admitted to practice California 1956. In legal practice San Diego 1960-70.
With District Attorney's Office San Diego County 1957-60. Member American Board of Trial Advocates (Treasurer), San Diego County (Vice President 1970) and American Bar Associations.
Office: 4194 U.S. Courthouse, 940 Front Street, San Diego 92101-8901.
Telephone: (619) 557-6480.

THOMPSON, John M. *(Judge, Superior Court of California County of San Diego)* Former Judge, San Diego Municipal Court San Diego County.
Mailing address: P.O. Box 122724, San Diego 92112-2724.
Office: 220 West Broadway, San Diego 92101.
Telephone: (619) 531-3820.

THOMPSON, Sandra Ann *(Judge, Superior Court of California County of Los Angeles)* Assumed office Jan 22, 2000. Term expires Jan 2005. Born Hawkins Texas. Protestant. Educated at Linfield College, University of Southern California B.A. in Political Science 1969 and University of Michigan J.D. 1972. Recipient Joseph A. McCarthy and NSSFNS Scholarships. Admitted to practice California 1976. Began legal practice Inglewood 1977. Commissioner Sept 1983 to June 1984 and Judge June 13, 1984 to Jan 21, 2000, South Bay Municipal Court Los Angeles County, appointed by Governor George Deukmejian.
Deputy City Attorney Inglewood 1977-81. Deputy District Attorney Los Angeles County 1981-83. Honorary member South Bay Women Lawyers Association and South Bay Bar Association. Member California Court Commissioners Association, California Judges Association, Municipal Court Judges Association (Chair 1991-93), National Association of Women Judges, Presiding Judges Association, Black Women Lawyers Association of Los Angeles (Job Bank Chair 1984-85), California Association of Black Lawyers, California Women Lawyers, State Bar of California (inactive), John M. Langston, Minority and National Bar Associations. Worked as crisis telephone counselor for Suicide Prevention Center 1979-81. Board of Directors Torrance YWCA 1984-85. Former member Soroptimist International of Torrance (Financial Vice President 1985-86, Board member 1985-86 and Corresponding Secretary 1986). Board of Trustees Casa Colina Foundation of the South Bay. Board of Directors Southern California Youth and Family Center 1988-95. Member American Association of University Women since 1988, Pacific Bell Consumer Advisory Council IX on Plain Language and Advisory Panel on Telecommunications, Steering Committee Casa Colina Wheelchair Tennis Classic and Torrance League of Women Voters.
Office: Torrance Courthouse, 825 Maple Avenue, Torrance 90503.
Telephone: (310) 222-8808.

THRASHER, Thomas N. *(Judge, Superior Court of California County of Orange)* Appointed by Governor George Deukmejian to term beginning Oct 24, 1988.

THRASHER, THOMAS N.—*Continued*

Elected 1990, 1996 and 2002. Current term expires Jan 2009. Born Dallas Texas Oct 29, 1936. Educated at University of California at Los Angeles B.S. 1958 and University of California Hastings College of the Law J.D. 1964. Law Clerk to Hon. Hulls, Superior Court of California Los Angeles County 1964-65. Admitted to practice California 1965. In legal practice Santa Ana 1965-88.

Author "How to Handle the Typical No Asset Bankruptcy" Jan 1973, "Positive Misconduct Excusing an Attorney's Inexcusable Neglect" Spring 1988 and "How to Negotiate the Fast Track Without Running Out of Breath" Sept 1992. Professor of Real Property Western State College of Law 1967-87. President Orange County Barristers 1970-71. Former Member Orange County Criminal Courts Bar Association. Member California Judges Association and Orange County Bar Association (Board of Directors 1979-80). Named Judge of the Year by Business Litigation Section Orange County Bar Association 1994. Lieutenant j.g. USN 1958-61. Enjoys golf and UCLA sports.

Mailing address: P.O. Box 1994, Santa Ana 92702.

Office: 700 Civic Center Drive West, Room B-100, Santa Ana 92701.

Telephone: (714) 834-4694.

TIERNAN, John H. *(Judge, Superior Court of California County of Colusa)* Assumed office Sept 1, 1998. Elected 2000, current term expires Jan 2007. Presiding Judge Jan 1, 2000 to Dec 31, 2001. Born Jersey City New Jersey Nov 6, 1943. Christian. Educated at California State University at Chico B.A. cum laude 1973 and McGeorge School of Law University of the Pacific J.D. 1981. Member Phi Delta Phi. Admitted to practice California 1981. Judge, Colusa County Municipal Court June 9, 1992 to Aug 31, 1998.

Deputy District Attorney Yreka 1981-82, Oroville 1982-86 and Colusa 1986-92. Member California Judges Foundation and California Judges Association. Attended numerous seminars California Center for Judicial Education and Research. Yeoman First Class USN 1961-70. First Sergeant California Army National Guard (retired). Board of Directors Colusa Hospital Foundation. Member Colusa Redskins Athletic Foundation.

Office: 532 Oak Street, Colusa 95932.

Telephone: (530) 458-5149.

TIGAR, Jon S. *(Judge, Superior Court of California County of Alameda)*

Office: Courthouse, 661 Washington Street, Oakland 94607.

Telephone: (510) 268-7601.

TIMLIN, Robert James *(Judge, United States District Court Central District of California)* Appointed for life by the President. Born Buffalo New York July 26, 1932. Roman Catholic. Educated at Georgetown University B.A. cum laude 1954 J.D. 1959 LL.M. 1964. Member Phi Alpha Delta. Admitted to practice Illinois 1959, District of Columbia 1960, U.S. Supreme Court 1962 and California 1965. In legal practice Illinois 1959-60, District of Columbia 1960-64, Los Angeles 1964-66 and Riverside and Corona 1966-76 California. Magistrate, U.S. District Court Central District of California 1971-75. Former Judge, Corona Municipal Court Riverside County. Former Judge, Superior Court of California Riverside County. Former Associate Justice, California Court of Appeal Fourth District Division Two.

Special Attorney Criminal Division U.S. Department of Justice Washington D.C. 1961-64. Assistant U.S. Attorney Central District of California 1964-66. City Attorney Corona 1967-70 and 1971-76 and Norco 1970-72 and 1974-76. Instructor in Real Estate Law Chaffey Junior College District 1969-70 and in Torts California Southern Law School at Riverside 1976-77. Member California Judges Association since 1976 (Executive Board 1986-87). Participant Continuing Education of the Bar program "One Day Non Jury Trial" Riverside 1976 and Judicial Educational Seminars conducted by California Judges Association and California Center for Judicial Education and Research 1976-87. Private First Class U.S. Army in Europe 1955-57. Democrat. Board of Directors Corona Red Cross 1967-70. Board of Trustees Riverside County Law Library 1978-90. Member Riverside County Democratic Central Committee 1968-71 (Vice Chairman 1969-70), State Democratic Central Committee 1970, Comprehensive Health Planning Association for Riverside County 1969-71, Southern California Comprehensive Health Planning Council 1971 and Corona-Norco Family YMCA 1968-78 (President 1976).

Office: U.S. Courthouse, 3470 Twelfth Street, Riverside 92501.

Telephone: (909) 328-4440.

TIPTON, Leland H. *(Judge, Superior Court of California County of Los Angeles)* Assumed office Jan 22, 2000. Elected 2002, current term expires Jan 2009. Born Los Angeles California Jan 28, 1942. Educated at University of Redlands A.B. cum laude 1963 and University of California at Los Angeles School of Law J.D. 1966. Admitted to practice California 1967. Commissioner 1987-97, Judge Jan 7, 1997 to Jan 21, 2000 and Former Presiding Judge, Los Cerritos Municipal Court Los Angeles County.

Deputy Public Defender Los Angeles County 1971-87. Member Cerritos Optimist Club.

Office: Bellflower Courthouse, 10025 East Flower Street, Bellflower 90706.

Telephone: (562) 804-8005.

E-mail address: ltipton@co.la.ca.us

TISHER, Francisca P. *(Judge, Superior Court of California County of Napa)* Assumed office June 3, 1998. Former Judge, Napa County Municipal Court.

Office: Napa County Criminal Courts Building, 1111 Third Street, Napa 94559.

Telephone: (707) 299-1100.

TITUS, Patricia J. *(Judge, Superior Court of California County of Los Angeles)* Elected to term beginning Jan 8, 2001. Term expires Jan 7, 2007. Born Los Angeles. Christian. Educated at Stanford University A.B. 1981 and University of California at Los Angeles School of Law J.D. 1984. Articles Editor Black Law Journal 1983-84. Member Phi Alpha Delta and Delta Sigma Theta. Admitted to practice California 1985 and U.S. District Court District of California 1995. In legal practice Los Angeles July 1985 to Dec 1985.

Deputy District Attorney Los Angeles County Jan 1986 to Dec 2000. Member Judicial Council of California, California Judges Association, American Judges Association, Black Women Lawyers Association of Los Angeles, Inc. (President 1992-93), John M. Langston Bar Association (Board member 1993), Los Angeles County (Trustee 1994-98) and National Bar Associa-

TITUS, PATRICIA J.—*Continued*

tions. Democrat. Member Power Christian Center and Great Beginnings for Black Babies. Enjoys Gospel music, tennis, art and step aerobics. Personal Statement or Quote: "Be prompt, be polite, be prepared."

Office: Criminal Courts Building, 210 West Temple Street, Los Angeles 90012-3210.

Telephone: (213) 974-6535.

E-mail address: PTitus@lasc.co.la.ca.us

TOBIAS, Harry J. *(Judge, Superior Court of California County of San Benito)* Assumed office Sept 1, 1998. Presiding Judge since Jan 1, 2000. Former Judge, San Benito County Municipal Court.

Office: 205 San Benito Courthouse, 440 Fifth Street, Hollister 95023.

Telephone: (831) 636-4057.

TODD, Kathryn Doi *(Associate Justice, California Court of Appeal Second District Division Two)* Appointed by Governor Gray Davis to term beginning Aug 2000. Born Los Angeles California Jan 14, 1942. Educated at Stanford University A.B. 1963 and Loyola University of Los Angeles J.D. 1970. Executive Editor Loyola of Los Angeles Law Review 1969-70. Admitted to practice California 1971. In legal practice Los Angeles 1971-77. Judge, Los Angeles Municipal Court Los Angeles County 1977-81, appointed by Governor Edmund G. Brown, Jr. Judge, Superior Court of California County of Los Angeles 1981-2000, appointed by Governor Edmund G. Brown, Jr.

Member California Judicial Council, California Women Lawyers, California Asian Judges Association, California Judges Association and Japanese American Bar Association. Chair Board of Directors Japanese American Cultural and Community Center. Board of Trustees Los Angeles County Law Library.

Office: 300 South Spring Street, Los Angeles 90013.

Telephone: (213) 830-7000.

TOMBERLIN, John M. *(Judge, Superior Court of California County of San Bernardino)*

Office: 14455 Civic Drive, Victorville 92392.

Telephone: (760) 243-8684.

TONDREAU, Patrick E. *(Judge, Superior Court of California County of Santa Clara)*

Office: Hall of Justice West Wing, 200 West Hedding Street, San Jose 95110.

Telephone: (408) 808-6600.

TOOHEY, Richard *(Judge, Superior Court of California County of Orange)* Former Judge, Harbor Municipal Court Orange County.

Mailing address: P.O. Box 1994, Santa Ana 92702-1994.

Office: Central Justice Center, 700 Civic Center Drive West, Santa Ana 92701.

Telephone: (714) 834-3734.

TORRIBIO, John A. *(Judge, Superior Court of California County of Los Angeles)*

Office: Norwalk Courthouse, 12720 Norwalk Boulevard, Norwalk 90650.

Telephone: (562) 807-7266.

TOWER, Timothy W. *(Judge, Superior Court of California County of San Diego)* Assumed office Dec 1, 1998. Elected 2002, current term expires Jan 2009. Born July 29, 1945. Educated at Sonoma State College 1964-65, University of California at Davis B.A. with honors 1967 and University of California Boalt Hall School of Law J.D. 1970. Staff member California Law Review. Admitted to practice California, U.S. District Courts Central, Northern and Southern Districts of California, U.S. Court of Appeals Ninth Circuit and U.S. Supreme Court. In legal practice San Diego 1971-79. Judge, San Diego Municipal Court San Diego County March 1989 to Nov 30, 1998, appointed by Governor George Deukmejian.

Senior Litigation Counsel San Diego Gas and Electric Co. 1979-89. Former Member San Diego Defense Bar Association, State Bar of California, San Diego County (Client Relations Committee 1975-76, Ethics Committee 1977-82, Superior Court Committee 1983-85) and American Bar Associations. Member San Diego County Judges Association and California Judges Association. Recipient Order of Merit Award from Boy Scouts of America 1989. Youth Sports Coach (basketball since 1973, soccer 1976-94). Former Member San Diego Junior Chamber of Commerce and Harbor Lions Club. Member Boy Scouts of America (Scoutmaster 1982-88 and 1994-99, Member Scout Unit Committee since 1982, Eagle Board since 1985) and Church of Jesus Christ of Latter-Day Saints (Bishop 1988-94, First Counselor in Stake Presidency since Jan 1999). Enjoys playing basketball, surfing, tennis, hunting and fishing; reading scriptures, science fiction, fantasy and historical novels; and playing with children and grandchildren.

Mailing address: P.O. Box 122724, San Diego 92112-2724.

Office: 220 West Broadway, San Diego 92101-2724.

Telephone: (619) 531-3434.

TOWNSEND, Thomas N. *(Judge, Superior Court of California County of Los Angeles)* Assumed office Jan 22, 2000. Former Judge, Compton Municipal Court Los Angeles County.

Office: Compton Courthouse, 200 West Compton Boulevard, Compton 90220.

Telephone: (310) 603-7842.

TRANBARGER, Gary B. *(Judge, Superior Court of California County of Riverside)* Assumed office July 29, 1998. Former Judge, Western Riverside County Municipal Court.

Office: Riverside Historic Courthouse, 4050 Main Street, Riverside 92501.

Telephone: (909) 955-1960.

TRASK, Gloria Connor *(Judge, Superior Court of California County of Riverside)*

Office: Riverside Historic Courthouse, 4050 Main Street, Riverside 92501.

Telephone: (909) 955-1960.

TREMBATH, James R. *(Judge, Superior Court of California County of Contra Costa)*

Office: Courthouse, 725 Court Street, Martinez 94553.

Telephone: (925) 646-2950.

TRENTACOSTA, Robert J. *(Judge, Superior Court of California County of San Diego)* Appointed by Governor Gray Davis. Educated at University of San Diego School of Law J.D. 1979. Board of Directors Moot

TRENTACOSTA, ROBERT J.—*Continued*

Court. National Moot Court Team. Admitted to practice California 1980.

Mailing address: P.O. Box 122724, San Diego 92112-2724.

Office: 220 West Broadway, San Diego 92101.

Telephone: (619) 531-3820.

TREU, Rolf Michael *(Judge, Superior Court of California County of Los Angeles)* Assumed office Jan 22, 2000. Former Judge and Presiding Judge, Citrus Municipal Court Los Angeles County.

Office: Courthouse, 111 North Hill Street, Los Angeles 90012.

Telephone: (213) 974-5411.

TRICE, John A. *(Judge, Superior Court of California County of San Luis Obispo)*

Office: 1050 Monterey Street, San Luis Obispo 93408.

Telephone: (805) 781-5936.

TRUMBULL, Patricia V. *(Magistrate Judge, United States District Court Northern District of California)* Appointed by U.S. District Court judges.

Office: 2112 U.S. Courthouse, 280 South First Street, San Jose 95113.

Telephone: (408) 535-5438.

TSENIN, Kay *(Judge, Superior Court of California City and County of San Francisco)* Assumed office Dec 31, 1998. Former Judge, San Francisco Municipal Court San Francisco County.

Office: Hall of Justice, 850 Bryant Street, San Francisco 94103.

Telephone: (415) 553-1159.

TUCKER, Josephine Staton *(Judge, Superior Court of California County of Orange)*

Mailing address: P.O. Box 1994, Santa Ana 92702-1994.

Office: Central Justice Center, 700 Civic Center Drive West, Santa Ana 92701.

Telephone: (714) 834-3734.

TUCKER, Marcus O., Jr. *(Judge, Superior Court of California County of Los Angeles)* Appointed by Governor George Deukmejian to term beginning May 1, 1985. Elected 1986, 1992 and 1998. Current term expires Jan 2005. Born Santa Monica California Nov 12, 1934. Baptist. Educated at University of Southern California B.A. 1956 and Howard University J.D. 1960. Staff member Howard Law Journal 1959-60. Admitted to practice California 1962. In legal practice Santa Monica 1962-63 and 1967-74. Commissioner, Superior Court of California Los Angeles County 1974-76. Judge, Long Beach Municipal Court Los Angeles County 1976-85.

Deputy City Attorney Santa Monica 1963-65. Assistant U.S. Attorney 1965-67. Assistant Professor of Law Pacific Coast University Law School 1986. Member California Judges Association (President 1972-73), California Black Lawyers Association, John M. Langston and American Bar Associations. Attended "Anglo-American Jurisprudence" Wadham College and Oxford University, England July 1986. Named Judge of the Year by Juvenile Department Superior Court of California Los Angeles County 1986. Private First Class and E-5 U.S. Army 1960. Democrat. President Legal Aid Foundation of Los Angeles 1977-78 and Community Rehabilitation Industries Foundation 1984-86. Board of Directors Long Beach Council Boy Scouts of America since 1977, Long Beach Community Hospital Foundation since 1978 and Volunteers of America since 1986. Interests include comparative law and travel.

Office: Long Beach Courthouse, 415 West Ocean Boulevard, Long Beach 90802.

Telephone: (562) 491-6130.

TURCHIN, Carolyn *(Magistrate Judge, United States District Court Central District of California)* Appointed by U.S. District Court judges.

Office: U.S. Courthouse, 312 North Spring Street, Los Angeles 90012.

Telephone: (213) 894-3589.

TURNER, Jerold L. *(Judge, Superior Court of California County of Kern)* Serves Juvenile Branch.

Office: 2100 College Avenue, Bakersfield 93305.

Telephone: (661) 868-4270.

TURNER, Paul A. *(Presiding Justice, California Court of Appeal Second District Division Five)* Appointed by Governor George Deukmejian to term beginning Nov 2, 1989. Retained by election Nov 1990. Presiding Justice since Jan 6, 1991. Born Shawnee Oklahoma Oct 1947. Educated at California State University at Long Beach B.A. magna cum laude 1969 and University of California at Los Angeles J.D. 1972. Honorary LL.D. University of West Los Angeles School of Law. Admitted to practice California 1973, U.S. District Court Central District of California, U.S. Court of Appeals Ninth Circuit and U.S. Supreme Court. Judge, Los Angeles Municipal Court Los Angeles County Oct 4, 1983 to Feb 28, 1985. Judge, Superior Court of California Los Angeles County March 1, 1985 to Nov 1, 1989, appointed by Governor George Deukmejian.

Office: 300 South Spring Street, Los Angeles 90013.

Telephone: (213) 830-7000.

TURRENTINE, Howard B. *(Senior Judge, United States District Court Southern District of California)* Appointed for life by President Richard M. Nixon to term beginning 1970. Assumed Senior status, serves by assignment. Born Escondido California Jan 22, 1914. Educated at San Diego State College (now California State University at San Diego) A.B. 1936 and University of Southern California LL.B. 1939. Admitted to practice California 1939. In legal practice San Diego 1939-68. Judge, Superior Court of California San Diego County 1968-70. USNR 1941-45.

Office: 2190 U.S. Courthouse, 940 Front Street, San Diego 92101-8909.

Telephone: (619) 557-6630.

TURRONE, Richard Charles *(Judge, Superior Court of California County of Santa Clara)* Assumed office Dec 1985. Presiding Judge Jan 1, 2001 to Dec 31, 2002. Born New York New York Sept 17, 1936. Catholic. Educated at University of Vermont B.A. 1958 and University of California Hastings College of the Law J.D. 1965. Recipient American Jurisprudence Award in Property and Federal Taxation 1964 and Alfred Sutro and Sidney Ehran Scholarships. Research Editor Hastings Law Journal 1963-65. Member Order of the Coif and Thurston Society. Admitted to practice California 1966. Began legal practice Ventura 1966. In legal practice San Francisco 1967-68 and San Jose 1968-83. Commissioner 1983-84 and Judge May 1984 to Dec 1985 Santa Clara

TURRONE, RICHARD CHARLES—*Continued*
County Municipal Court, appointed by Governor George Deukmejian.

Deputy District Attorney Ventura County 1965-67. Director Voluntary Action Center 1970-73. Author "Quo Warranto" 15 Hastings L. Jour. 222, 1963. Professor of Law Lincoln University Law School 1967-82. Member Santa Clara County Bar Association. Named Outstanding Law School Professor by students of Lincoln Law School 1981. Recipient Judge of the Year Award from Consumer Lawyers of Santa Clara County 1996. First Lieutenant USAF 1958-62. Enjoys oenology and gardening.

Office: Old Courthouse, 161 North First Street, San Jose 95113.

Telephone: (408) 882-2340.

TWISSELMAN, Kenneth C., II *(Judge, Superior Court of California County of Kern)*

Office: 1415 Truxtun Avenue, Bakersfield 93301.

Telephone: (661) 868-4934.

TYNAN, Michael Anthony *(Judge, Superior Court of California County of Los Angeles)* Former Judge, Los Angeles Municipal Court Los Angeles County.

Office: Criminal Courts Building, 210 West Temple Street, Los Angeles 90012-3210.

Telephone: (213) 974-6535.

UHLER, Ingrid Adamson *(Judge, Superior Court of California County of San Bernardino)* Assumed office Aug 10, 1998. Serves Rancho District. Former Judge, San Bernardino County Municipal Court.

Office: 8303 North Haven Avenue, Rancho Cucamonga 91730.

Telephone: (909) 945-4131.

ULFIG, Cynthia L. *(Judge, Superior Court of California County of Los Angeles)* Assumed office Jan 22, 2000. Former Judge, Newhall Municipal Court Los Angeles County.

Office: Santa Clarita Courthouse, 23747 West Valencia Boulevard, Valencia 91355.

Telephone: (661) 253-7301.

ULLMAN, Michael S. *(Judge, Superior Court of California County of Sacramento)* Assumed office June 17, 1998. Elected 2000, current term expires Jan 2007. Born Los Angeles California June 30, 1943. Jewish. Educated at University of California at Berkeley B.S. 1964 and University of California at Los Angeles School of Law J.D. 1967. Member Phi Epsilon Pi. Admitted to practice California 1967. Began legal practice Los Angeles 1968-74. In legal practice Sacramento 1976-82. Judge Jan 2, 1983 to June 16, 1998 and Presiding Judge July 1986 to July 1988, Sacramento Municipal Court Sacramento County, appointed by Governor Edmund G. Brown, Jr.

Deputy Public Defender Los Angeles County 1968-74. Member Obledo Commission on Determinate Sentencing 1977, Task Force on Mentally Disordered Offenders 1978, Advisory Committee California Justice System Subvention Program 1979, Advisory Committee California Career Criminal Prosecution 1979 and Advisory Committee on Trial Court Improvement Fund 1989. Advisory Member Judicial Council of California 1991-92. Member Judicial Planning Committee for *California Judges Benchguides: Municipal and Justice Courts* and Governing Committee 1993-97 California Center for Judicial Education and Research. Member Women Lawyers Association of Sacramento, La Raza Lawyers Association, California Judges Association (Executive Board 1989-92, President 1991-92, Former Member Compensation and Retirement Committee, Member and Chair 1995-96 Family Law Committee), State Bar of California (Commission on Corrections 1978-82, Executive Committee Criminal Law Section 1982), Asian Bar Association of Sacramento, Wiley Manuel Bar Association and Sacramento County Bar Association. Lecturer on "Mastering the Art of Determinate Sentencing" 1977, "How to Handle a Marital Dissolution" 1996 and "Irreconcilable Differences? When Bankruptcy and Family Law Collide" 1996 CEB; and "New Legislation" Superior Court Workshop on Criminal Law 1986, "New Legislation" and Municipal and Justice Courts Institute 1987-94 and Family Law Institute 1995-96 California Center for Judicial Education and Research. Faculty Member "Felony Preliminary Hearings" 1986-92 and "Family Law" and "Family Law Trials" 1996 California Judicial College; and New Judges Orientation Program 1990-92, "Municipal Court Management" 1988 and 1989 and "Advanced Family Law" 1995 California Judicial Studies Program. Discussion Leader New Judges Orientation Program May 1989. Seminar Leader California Judicial College 1990. Senior Consultant 1976 and Chief Counsel 1977-83 Assembly Committee on Criminal Justice. Peace Corps volunteer in Guatemala 1967-68. Board of Directors La Familia Counseling Center 1978-83. Board of Trustees Sacramento County Law Library 1983-84. Enjoys skiing and rafting.

Office: 3341 Power Inn Road, Sacramento 95826.

Telephone: (916) 875-3400.

ULLOA, Juan *(Judge, Superior Court of California County of Imperial)* Presiding Judge Jan 1, 1997 to Dec 31, 1997 and since Jan 1, 2002.

Office: 939 West Main Street, El Centro 92243.

Telephone: (760) 482-4374.

UMHOFER, Donald George *(Judge, Superior Court of California County of San Luis Obispo)* Assumed office July 1, 1998. Born St. Louis Missouri March 5, 1944. Roman Catholic. Educated at University of Notre Dame B.A. magna cum laude 1966 and Golden Gate University J.D. 1971. Admitted to practice California 1972. In legal practice Eureka 1972-78 and San Luis Obispo 1978-83. Judge, San Luis Obispo County Municipal Court Jan 2, 1983 to June 30, 1998, appointed by Governor Edmund G. Brown, Jr. Presiding Judge San Luis Obispo County Coordinated Courts Nov 1, 1996 to Oct 31, 1997.

Former Public Defender and District Attorney. Member various nominating committees and public information committees. Member California Judges Association. Faculty member Presiding Judges Course California Center for Judicial Education and Research. Democrat.

Office: County Government Center, 1035 Palm Street, San Luis Obispo 93408-2500.

Telephone: (805) 781-5421.

UNGER, Cynda Riggins *(Judge, Superior Court of California County of Solano)*

Office: 600 Union Avenue, Fairfield 94533-5000.

Telephone: (707) 421-7827.

URANGA, Carlos A. *(Judge, Superior Court of California County of Los Angeles)* Assumed office Jan 22, 2000. Presiding Judge July 1, 1998 to June 30, 1999

URANGA, CARLOS A.—*Continued*
and Former Judge, Alhambra Municipal Court Los Angeles County.
Office: Alhambra Courthouse, 150 West Commonwealth Avenue, Alhambra 91801.
Telephone: (626) 308-5537.

URE, Jane *(Judge, Superior Court of California County of Sacramento)* Assumed office June 17, 1998. Former Judge, Sacramento Municipal Court Sacramento County.
Office: Courthouse, 720 Ninth Street, Sacramento 95814.
Telephone: (916) 874-5476.

VALENTINE, Leo, Jr. *(Judge, Superior Court of California County of San Diego)* Assumed office Dec 1, 1998. Former Judge, San Diego Municipal Court San Diego County.
Office: 2851 Meadowlark Drive, San Diego 92123.
Telephone: (858) 694-4601.

VAN CAMP, Brian R. *(Judge, Superior Court of California County of Sacramento)* Appointed by Governor Pete Wilson to term beginning Jan 31, 1997. Elected 1998, current term expires Jan 2005. Born Halstead Kansas Aug 23, 1940. Presbyterian. Educated at University of California at Berkeley A.B. 1962 LL.B. 1965. Member Phi Delta Phi. Admitted to practice California 1966, U.S. District Courts Northern 1966 and Eastern 1978 Districts of California and U.S. Court of Appeals Ninth Circuit 1966. In legal practice Sacramento 1974-97 and Los Angeles 1978-89.

Deputy Attorney General California 1966-67. Agency Attorney Redevelopment Agency City of Sacramento 1967-70. Commissioner of Corporations California 1971-74. Author Part II, Chapter 8: "The Treasurer's Function as Viewed by the Government Regulator" *The Treasurer's Handbook* Dow Jones-Irwin 1976, "Compliance with New California Nonprofit Corporation Law" 1 No. 1 California Business Law Reporter 1980, "Securities Law: A Legislative Response to Overregulation?" 82 No. 1 *Docket* Sacramento County Bar Association Jan 1982, Chapter 3 "Forming the Corporation and Beginning Operations" *Advising California Nonprofit Corporations* California Continuing Education of the Bar 1984, "Corporate Raiders: Darwin's Helpers or Capital Saboteurs?" *The Business Journal* July 25, 1985 and "Capital Formation in the 1990's" *The Sacramento Venture* (Newsletter of the Sacramento Valley Forum) Spring 1993. Former Member North American Securities Administrators Association (Executive Committee 1972-74) and Midwest Securities Commissioners' Association (President 1973-74). Member Task Force on the Quality of Justice Judicial Council of California 1997-99. Member State Bar of California (Committee on Corporations 1975-78, Committee on Partnerships and Unincorporated Associations 1977-80, Committee on Financial Institutions 1983-86), Sacramento County (Business Law Section) and American (Committee on State Regulation of Securities Section of Business Law 1980-88, Committee on Partnerships 1983-90) Bar Associations. Lecturer California Continuing Education of the Bar, Practising Law Institute and California Certified Public Accountants Society 1972-93. Named Outstanding Young Man of the Year by Sacramento Jaycees 1970, International Young Man of the Year by Active 20-30 Club International 1973 and Paul Harris Fellow by Rotary Club of Sacramento. Listed in *Who's Who in America* since 1982, *Who's Who in American Law* since 1983 and *Who's Who in California* since 1984. Recipient Thomas Jefferson Award from American Institute of Public Service 1994 and Excellence in Achievement Award from The California Alumni Association 1997. Member Republican State Central Committee of California 1974-78. Honorary Delegate Republican National Convention 1992. Board Member The Comstock Club, Inc. 1973-78 (President 1976-77), Sacramento Symphony Association 1973-85 and 1990-93 (Vice President 1975-77, Executive Committee 1978-79 and 1984-85), Lincoln Club of Sacramento Valley 1975-88 (President 1984-86), Sacramento Area Commerce and Trade Organization (SACTO) 1981-92 (President 1986-87), California Chamber of Commerce 1982-97 (Chairman Statewide Energy Task Force 1979-85, Chairman Education Committee 1987-89), Rotary Club of Sacramento 1982-84 and 1989-91 (President 1993-94), California Health Facilities Finance Authority 1985-89, Sacramento Metropolitan Chamber of Commerce 1986-87, Sacramento Valley Venture Capital Forum 1986-90, League to Save Lake Tahoe, Inc. 1988-95 (Executive Committee 1990-91 and 1994-95), Capitol Area Development Authority 1988-97 (Chairman 1991-97), Boalt Hall Alumni Association 1991-94 and Sacramento Symphony Foundation since 1991 (Vice Chairman 1992-94). Enjoys skiing, sailing and playing saxophone in a small jazz band.
Office: Courthouse, 720 Ninth Street, Sacramento 95814.
Telephone: (916) 874-5476.
E-mail address: vancamp@saccourt.com

VANDER FEER, John Peter *(Judge, Superior Court of California County of San Bernardino)* Serves North Desert District.
Office: 235 East Mountain View Avenue, Barstow 92311.
Telephone: (760) 256-4972.

VANDER LANS, Judith A. *(Judge, Superior Court of California County of Los Angeles)*
Office: Long Beach Courthouse, 415 West Ocean Boulevard, Long Beach 90802.
Telephone: (562) 491-6138.

VANDER WALL, David G. *(Judge, Superior Court of California County of Stanislaus)* Presiding Judge since Jan 1, 2003. Former Judge, Stanislaus County Municipal Court.
Office: 800 11th Street, Modesto 95354.
Telephone: (209) 558-6000.

VAN DUSEN, Richard William *(Judge, Superior Court of California County of Los Angeles)* Assumed office Jan 22, 2000. Term expires 2004. Born Visalia California 1945. Lutheran. Educated at Chapman College B.A. with honors 1967, University of Southern California M.A. with honors 1970 and Southwestern University School of Law J.D. 1976. Admitted to practice California 1976. In legal practice West Covina and El Monte 1981-86. Presiding Judge Jan 1, 1996 to Dec 31, 1996 and Judge Jan 1987 to Jan 21, 2000, Rio Hondo Municipal Court Los Angeles County.

Deputy District Attorney 1976-81. Member California Judges Association, Eastern Bar Association and State Bar of California. Republican. Member California Central Committee. Founder and President Irwindale Rotary

VAN DUSEN, RICHARD WILLIAM—*Continued*

Club. President South El Monte Coordinating Committee. Enjoys shooting, skiing, swimming and golf.

Office: El Monte Courthouse, 11234 East Valley Boulevard, El Monte 91731.

Telephone: (626) 575-4101.

VAN OSS, Terrence R. *(Judge, Superior Court of California County of San Joaquin)* Appointed by Governor George Deukmejian to term beginning Dec 27, 1989. Elected 1990, 1996 and 2002. Current term expires Jan 2009. Presiding Judge Jan 1, 2000 to Dec 31, 2001. Born Ohio 1939. Catholic. Educated at San Diego State College A.B. 1962 and Lincoln University Law School J.D. 1970. Admitted to practice California 1971.

Office: 222 East Weber Avenue, Room 303, Stockton 95202.

Telephone: (209) 468-2827.

VAN SICKLEN, Steven *(Judge, Superior Court of California County of Los Angeles)* Serves West District.

Office: Los Angeles Airport Courthouse, 11701 South La Cienega Boulevard, Los Angeles 90045.

Telephone: (310) 727-6010.

VAN STOCKUM, Raymond P. *(Judge, Superior Court of California County of San Bernardino)* Assumed office Aug 10, 1998. Serves Rancho District. Judge May 10, 1990 to Aug 9, 1998 and Presiding Judge July 1, 1995 to June 30, 1997, San Bernardino County Municipal Court.

Office: 8303 North Haven Avenue, Rancho Cucamonga 91730.

Telephone: (909) 945-4131.

VAN VOORHIS, Bruce *(Judge, Superior Court of California County of Contra Costa)* Assumed office June 8, 1998. Born California 1948. Educated at University of California at Berkeley A.B. 1970 and University of California Hastings College of the Law J.D. 1974. Judge Jan 5, 1987 to June 7, 1998 and Former Presiding Judge, Walnut Creek-Danville Municipal Court Contra Costa County.

Mailing address: P.O. Box 5128, Walnut Creek 94596.

Office: 640 Ygnacio Valley Road, Walnut Creek 94596.

Telephone: (925) 646-6763.

VARGAS, Luis Rafael *(Judge, Superior Court of California County of San Diego)* Assumed office Dec 1, 1998. Former Judge and Presiding Judge, South Bay Municipal Court San Diego County.

Mailing address: P.O. Box 122724, San Diego 92112-2724.

Office: 500 Third Avenue, Chula Vista 91910.

Telephone: (619) 691-4770.

VARTABEDIAN, Steven M. *(Associate Justice, California Court of Appeal Fifth District)* Appointed by Governor George Deukmejian to term beginning Oct 19, 1989. Retained by election Nov 1990 and 1998. Current term expires Jan 2011. Born Fresno California May 8, 1950. Presbyterian. Educated at California State University at Fresno B.A. summa cum laude 1972 and University of Santa Clara School of Law J.D. magna cum laude 1975. Member Delta Upsilon and Phi Kappa Phi. Admitted to practice California 1975. Began legal practice Fresno 1975. Judge, Sanger Justice Court Fresno County 1981-83. Judge, Consolidated Fresno Municipal Court Fresno County 1983-87. Judge, Superior Court of California Fresno County 1987-89.

Author "Striking a Delicate Balance in Sex Abuse Cases" 24 No. 4 Judges Journal 16, 1985 and "Enhancing Sentences with Prior Felony Convictions: The Limits of 'Without Limitation'" 23 Pacific L. Jour. 1051, 1992. Important Decisions: People v. Griggs (ADW may have a group of victims rather than one named victim) 216 Cal. App. 3d 734, 1989 and People v. Patten (presence of support persons during sexual assault testimony) 9 Cal. App. 4th 1718, 1992.

Office: 2525 Capitol Street, Fresno 93721.

Telephone: (559) 445-5670.

VASQUEZ, Emily Elizabeth *(Judge, Superior Court of California County of Sacramento)*

Office: Courthouse, 720 Ninth Street, Sacramento 95814.

Telephone: (916) 874-5476.

VEALS, Craig Elliott *(Judge, Superior Court of California County of Los Angeles)* Former Judge, Los Angeles Municipal Court Los Angeles County.

Office: Criminal Courts Building, 210 West Temple Street, Los Angeles 90012-3210.

Telephone: (213) 974-6535.

VELASQUEZ, David Charles *(Judge, Superior Court of California County of Orange)* Appointed by Governor George Deukmejian Sept 24, 1990. Elected 1992 and 1998. Current term expires 2005. Serves Appellate Division since Jan 1998 and Civil Trials Division since Jan 2000. Born Los Angeles California Feb 18, 1951. Educated at California State University at Los Angeles B.A. 1973 and Loyola University School of Law J.D. 1978. Admitted to practice California 1978. Judge, South Orange County Municipal Court 1988-90.

Member Rules and Forms Committee, Grand Jury Selection Committee, California Judges Association, Orange County Hispanic and Orange County Bar Associations.

Mailing address: P.O. Box 1994, Santa Ana 92702-1994.

Office: Central Justice Center, 700 Civic Center Drive West, Santa Ana 92701.

Telephone: (714) 834-3734.

VELASQUEZ, Jose A. *(Judge, Superior Court of California County of Monterey)* Assumed office Dec 18, 2000. Former Judge, Monterey County Municipal Court.

Mailing address: P.O. Box 1819, Salinas 93902-1819.

Office: 240 Church Street, Salinas 93901.

Telephone: (831) 755-5060.

VICENCIA, Michael P. *(Judge, Superior Court of California County of Los Angeles)*

Office: Courthouse, 111 North Hill Street, Los Angeles 90012.

Telephone: (213) 974-5411.

VICTOR, A. Rex *(Judge, Superior Court of California County of San Bernardino)* Serves Juvenile Court.

Office: 900 East Gilbert Street, San Bernardino 92415-0942.

Telephone: (909) 387-7538.

VILARDI, Alice *(Judge, Superior Court of California County of Alameda)*
Office: Courthouse, 661 Washington Street, Oakland 94607.
Telephone: (510) 268-7601.

VILLARREAL, Luis Mario *(Judge, Superior Court of California County of Solano)* Assumed office Aug 3, 1998. Born El Paso Texas Oct 13, 1949. Educated at University of Texas B.A. with honors 1972 and University of San Francisco J.D. 1975. Admitted to practice California 1975. Began legal practice Vallejo 1975. In legal practice Fairfield 1976. Judge, Northern Solano County Municipal Court Dec 1, 1982 to Aug 2, 1998, appointed by Governor Edmund G. Brown, Jr.
Formerly with Public Defender's Office. Instructor Solano Community College 1975-80. Former member California Trial Lawyers Association. Member California Judges Association. Democrat.
Mailing address: P.O. Box 2463, Fairfield 94533-0246.
Office: 530 Union Avenue, Suite 200, Fairfield 94533.
Telephone: (707) 421-7827.

VILLARREAL, Lydia *(Judge, Superior Court of California County of Monterey)*
Mailing address: P.O. Box 1819, Salinas 93902-1819.
Office: 240 Church Street, Salinas 93901.
Telephone: (831) 755-5060.

VIRGA, Michael G. *(Judge, Superior Court of California County of Sacramento)* Elected June 7, 1994 to term beginning Oct 3, 1994. Reelected 2000, current term expires Jan 2007. Born Santa Clara California March 26, 1956. Catholic. Educated at Santa Clara University B.Sc. 1978 J.D. 1981. Admitted to practice California 1981. Judge, Sacramento Municipal Court Sacramento County Jan 4, 1993 to Oct 2, 1994.
Deputy District Attorney Sacramento County 1981-92. Member California Judges Association and Italian-American Bar Association. Attended Orientation for New Judicial Officers 1993, California Judicial College 1993 and Advanced Criminal Law Seminar 1995 California Center for Judicial Education and Research. Adviser Mexican American Sports Association Hall of Fame. Coach and Referee Greenhaven Youth Soccer League. Active Parishioner St. Anthony's Catholic Church Sacramento. Member Italian Cultural Society.
Office: Courthouse, 720 Ninth Street, Sacramento 95814.
Telephone: (916) 874-5476.

VLAVIANOS, Richard *(Judge, Superior Court of California County of San Joaquin)*
Office: 535 West Matthews Road, French Camp 95231.
Telephone: (209) 468-4280.

VOGEL, Charles S. *(Administrative Presiding Justice, California Court of Appeal Second District and Presiding Justice, California Court of Appeal Second District Division Four)* Appointed by Governor Pete Wilson to term beginning 1993. Retained by election Nov 1994. Presiding Justice since 1996. Administrative Presiding Justice since 1997. Educated at Pomona College 1955 and University of California at Los Angeles School of Law J.D. 1959. Admitted to practice California 1959. In legal practice 1959-69 and 1977-93. Judge, Pomona Municipal Court Los Angeles County 1969-70. Judge, Superior Court of California County of Los Angeles 1970-77. Judge Pro Tempore, California Court of Appeal Second District Division Five 1974 and Division One 1976.
Important Decisions: People v. Smith & Powell (the Onion Field Murder) 1974 and People v. Charles Manson et al. 1976. Board of Trustees 1980-82 and President 1985-86 Los Angeles County Bar Association. President Association of Business Trial Lawyers 1984-85. Board of Governors Institute for Corporate Counsel 1986-92. Board of Governors 1987-89 and President 1990-91 State Bar of California. Chair Supreme Court Advisory Committee on Judicial Ethics since 1995. Fellow American College of Trial Lawyers. Named Alumnus of the Year by University of California at Los Angeles School of Law 1986 and Person of the Year by Metropolitan News Enterprise 1992. Recipient Distinguished Pro Bono Award from Western Center on Law & Poverty 1986 and Shattuck-Price Award from Los Angeles County Bar Association 1998. USN 1955-56. President University of California School of Law Alumni Association 1977-78.
Office: 300 South Spring Street, Los Angeles 90013.
Telephone: (213) 830-7000.

VOGEL, Miriam A. *(Associate Justice, California Court of Appeal Second District Division One)* Appointed by governor. Born New York New York May 11, 1940. Educated at Santa Monica City College and Beverly College of Law J.D. magna cum laude 1975. Law Clerk to Hon. Robert S. Thompson, California Court of Appeal Second District Division One Oct 1975 to June 1977. Admitted to practice California 1975 and U.S. District Court Central District of California 1975. In legal practice Los Angeles. Former Judge, Superior Court of California Los Angeles County, appointed by Governor George Deukmejian to term beginning Jan 3, 1986.
Member Business Trial Lawyers, Women Lawyers of Los Angeles Association, California Women Lawyers Association, Los Angeles County and American Bar Associations.
Office: 300 South Spring Street, Los Angeles 90013.
Telephone: (213) 830-7000.

VOGT, John F. *(Judge, Superior Court of California County of Fresno)*
Office: Courthouse, 1100 Van Ness Avenue, Fresno 93724-0002.
Telephone: (559) 448-1825.

VORTMANN, Paul Anthony *(Judge, Superior Court of California County of Tulare)* Appointed by Governor Pete Wilson Jan 1, 1999. Elected 2000, current term expires Jan 1, 2007. Assistant Presiding Judge since 2001. Born July 21, 1944. Educated at Reedley College A.A. 1964, San Francisco State University B.A. 1966 and Golden Gate University J.D. 1969. Admitted to practice California Jan 1970, U.S. District Court Eastern District of California 1974 and U.S. Court of Appeals Ninth Circuit 1976. In legal practice 1973 to Dec 31, 1998.
Deputy Public Defender 1970-71 and Assistant Public Defender 1971-72 County of Tulare. Member American Board of Trial Advocates and California Judges Association (Executive Board since 2001).
Office: Tulare County Civic Center, Visalia 93291-4593.

VORTMANN, PAUL ANTHONY—*Continued*
Telephone: (559) 733-6561.
Fax: (559) 737-4920

WADE, John P. *(Judge, Superior Court of California County of San Bernardino)* Assumed office Aug 10, 1998. Former Judge, San Bernardino County Municipal Court.
Office: 351 North Arrowhead Avenue, San Bernardino 92415-0240.
Telephone: (909) 387-3922.

WAGNER, Marguerite L. *(Judge, Superior Court of California County of San Diego)* Former Judge, North County Municipal Court San Diego County.
Mailing address: P.O. Box 122724, San Diego 92112-2724.
Office: 325 South Melrose Drive, Vista 92083.
Telephone: (760) 726-9595.

WAGONER, James R. *(Judge, Superior Court of California County of El Dorado)*
Office: Administration Office, 2850 Fairlane Court, Placerville 95667.
Telephone: (530) 621-7454.

WALKER, Hugh A. *(Judge, Superior Court of California County of Alameda)* Assumed office July 31, 1998. Presiding Judge Jan 1, 1997 to Dec 31, 1997 and Former Judge, Livermore-Pleasanton-Dublin Municipal Court Alameda County.
Office: Hall of Justice, 5672 Stoneridge Drive, Pleasanton 94588.
Telephone: (925) 551-6886.

WALKER, Rodney L. *(Judge, Superior Court of California County of Riverside)* Assumed office July 29, 1998. Former Judge, Three Lakes Municipal Court Riverside County. Former Judge and Presiding Judge, Mount San Jacinto Municipal Court Riverside County.
Office: Hemet Court, 880 North State Street, Hemet 92543.
Telephone: (909) 766-2325.

WALKER, Vaughn R. *(Judge, United States District Court Northern District of California)* Appointed for life by President George Bush Nov 27, 1989 to term beginning Feb 5, 1990. Born Watseka Illinois Feb 27, 1944. Educated at University of Michigan A.B. with honors 1966 and Stanford University J.D. 1970. Law Clerk to Hon. Robert J. Kelleher, U.S. District Court Central District of California 1971-72. Admitted to practice California 1972. In legal practice 1972-89.
Member California Law Revision Commission 1986-89. Member Lawyers Club of San Francisco (President 1985-86), The American Law Institute and American Bar Association (Judicial Representative Section of Antitrust Law). Director St. Francis Hospital Foundation 1991-97.
Mailing address: P.O. Box 36060, San Francisco 94102.
Office: U.S. Courthouse, 450 Golden Gate Avenue, San Francisco 94102-3489.
Telephone: (415) 522-3620.

WALLACE, Arthur E. *(Judge, Superior Court of California County of Kern)* Former Arbitrator and Judge pro tem. Appointed Judge by Governor George Deukmejian to term beginning June 1986. Presiding Judge 1990-92 and Jan 1, 2000 to Dec 31, 2002. Assistant Presiding Judge 1999. Educated at Bakersfield College, University of California B.S.B.A. 1960 and Hastings College of the Law J.D. with honors 1963. Member Thurston Society and Order of the Coif. In legal practice Bakersfield 1963 to June 1986.
Member State Trial Court Budget Commission 1993-99, Trial Court Presiding Judges Advisory Committee since 2000 and Trial Court Presiding Judges Executive Committee 2001. Member Judicial Council of California (Civil and Small Claims Advisory Committee, Chair Case management Subcommittee 2001).
Office: 1415 Truxtun Avenue, Bakersfield 93301.
Telephone: (661) 868-4934.

WALMARK, Richard F. *(Judge, Superior Court of California County of Los Angeles)*
Office: Courthouse, 111 North Hill Street, Los Angeles 90012.
Telephone: (213) 974-5411.

WALSH, Brian *(Judge, Superior Court of California County of Santa Clara)*
Office: Hall of Justice West Wing, 200 West Hedding Street, San Jose 95110.
Telephone: (408) 808-6600.

WALSH, Henry J. *(Judge, Superior Court of California County of Ventura)* Appointed by Governor Pete Wilson to term beginning July 13, 1998. Elected 2000, current term expires Jan 8, 2007. Born Brooklyn New York Nov 12, 1943. Roman Catholic. Educated at Stanford University B.A. 1965 and Loyola Marymount University J.D. 1970. Admitted to practice California 1971, U.S. District Courts Central 1971, Eastern 1984 and Southern 1984 Districts of California, U.S. Court of Appeals Ninth Circuit 1973 and U.S. Supreme Court 1983. In legal practice Oxnard 1971-78 and 1989-98 and Ventura 1978-89.
Former Member State Bar of California. Member American Inns of Court, American Board of Trial Advocates and California Judges Association. Democrat. Member Buenaventura Caregivers and Catholic Charities. Enjoys gardening, reading and skiing.
Mailing address: P.O. Box 6489, Ventura 93006-6489.
Office: 800 South Victoria Avenue, Ventura 93009-0001.
Telephone: (805) 654-2985.

WALSH, Patrick J. *(Magistrate Judge, United States District Court Central District of California)* Appointed by U.S. District Court judges to term beginning July 18, 2001.
Office: 831 U.S. Courthouse, 312 North Spring Street, Los Angeles 90012.
Telephone: (213) 894-3535.

WALTER, John F. *(Judge, United States District Court Central District of California)* Appointed for life by President George W. Bush to term beginning June 7, 2002. Born Buffalo New York 1944. Educated at Loyola University of Los Angeles B.A. 1966 J.D. 1969. In legal practice California 1969-70 and 1972-2002.
Office: 176 U.S. Courthouse, 312 North Spring Street, Los Angeles 90012.
Telephone: (213) 894-3535.

WALTON, F. Dana *(Judge, Superior Court of California County of Mariposa)* Presiding Judge since Jan 1, 2002.
Mailing address: P.O. Box 28, Mariposa 95338.
Office: 5088 Bullion Street, Mariposa 95338.
Telephone: (209) 966-2005.

WANGER, Oliver W. *(Judge, United States District Court Eastern District of California)* Appointed for life by President George Bush to term beginning 1991. Born Los Angeles California Nov 27, 1940. Educated at University of Southern California B.S. 1963 and University of California Boalt Hall School of Law LL.B. 1966. In legal practice Fresno 1969-91. Temporary Judge 1988 and Judge pro tem 1989, Superior Court of California County of Fresno.
Deputy District Attorney Fresno County 1967-69. City Attorney City of Mendota 1975-80. Adjunct Professor San Joaquin College of Law 1970-94. National Director 1988-90 and Advocate since 1988 American Board of Trial Advocates. Fellow American College of Trial Lawyers and International Academy of Trial Lawyers. Dean 1980-82 and President and Chair Board of Trustees 1984-94 San Joaquin College of Law.
Office: 5104 U.S. Courthouse, 1130 O Street, Fresno 93721.
Telephone: (559) 498-7493.
Fax: (559) 498-7410

WAPNER, Fred N. *(Judge, Superior Court of California County of Los Angeles)* Former Judge, Los Angeles Municipal Court Los Angeles County.
Office: Criminal Courts Building, 210 West Temple Street, Los Angeles 90012-3210.
Telephone: (213) 974-6535.

WARD, Gregory H. *(Judge, Superior Court of California County of Santa Clara)*
Office: 191 North First Street, San Jose 95113.
Telephone: (408) 882-2100.

WARD, James D. *(Associate Justice, California Court of Appeal Fourth District Division Two)* Appointed by Governor Pete Wilson to term beginning June 1996. Retained by election 1998, current term expires Jan 2006. Born Sioux Falls South Dakota Sept 8, 1935. Protestant. Educated at University of South Dakota B.S. 1957 and University of San Francisco J.D. 1959. Admitted to practice California 1960, U.S. District Court Districts of California and U.S. Supreme Court. In legal practice Riverside 1960-93. Judge, Superior Court of California Riverside County 1993-96.
Deputy District Attorney 1960-61. Author chapter in *Discovery* California Continuing Education of Bar 1986 and miscellaneous articles in *Riverside County Lawyer.* Instructor in "Legal Research and Writing" University of California Riverside 1984-2000 and "Remedies" University of La Verne College of Law 1988-89. Past President Riverside County Bar Association. Former Member Board of Governors and Executive Committee Conference of Delegates State Bar of California. Member California Judges Association and American Board of Trial Advocates. Lecturer in "Discovery" California Continuing Education of the Bar 1986-87. Seminar Leader 1995 and Instructor New Judges Training 1996 California Center for Judicial Education and Research. Attended Appellate Justices School The National Judicial College 1996. Recipient Krieger Meritorious Service Award from Riverside County Bar Association 1986. Sergeant USAR 1959-65. Republican. Member Riverside County Central Committee 1962-65. Board of Directors Riverside Community Hospital. President Riverside Opera Association. Lieutenant Governor Kiwanis. Founder and Chair UCRLAW. Member University of California Riverside Foundations and Riverside County Historical Commission. Enjoys skiing, hiking and sailing.
Office: 3389 12th Street, Riverside 92501.
Telephone: (951) 248-0325.
E-mail address: jim_ward@jud.ca.gov

WARE, James *(Judge, United States District Court Northern District of California)* Appointed for life by President George Bush to term beginning 1990. Born Birmingham Alabama Nov 2, 1946. Educated at California Lutheran University B.A. 1969 and Stanford University J.D. 1972. In legal practice Palo Alto 1972-88. Judge, Superior Court of California Santa Clara County 1988-90.
Office: 4050 U.S. Courthouse, 280 South First Street, San Jose 95113.
Telephone: (408) 535-5454.

WARNER, Christopher J. *(Judge, Superior Court of California County of San Bernardino)* Assumed office Aug 10, 1998. Former Judge, San Bernardino County Municipal Court.
Office: 351 North Arrowhead Avenue, San Bernardino 92415-0240.
Telephone: (909) 387-3922.

WARNER, David P. *(Judge, Superior Court of California County of San Joaquin)*
Office: 315 West Elm Street, Lodi 95240.
Telephone: (209) 333-6753.

WARREN, James L. *(Judge, Superior Court of California City and County of San Francisco)*
Office: Hall of Justice, 850 Bryant Street, San Francisco 94103.
Telephone: (415) 553-1159.

WARREN, James T. *(Judge, Superior Court of California County of Riverside)* Former Presiding Judge. Former Judge, Mount San Jacinto Municipal Court Riverside County.
Office: Perris Court, 227 North D Street, Building C, Perris 92570.
Telephone: (909) 940-6877.

WARRINER, Thomas Edward *(Judge, Superior Court of California County of Yolo)* Assumed office June 3, 1998. Presiding Judge Jan 1, 2000 to Dec 31, 2001. Former Judge and Presiding Judge, Yolo County Municipal Court.
Office: 725 Court Street, Woodland 95695.
Telephone: (530) 666-8067.

WASILENKO, David E. *(Judge, Superior Court of California County of Yuba)* Assumed office April 16, 1999. Presiding Judge Jan 1, 1996 to Dec 31, 1996 and Former Judge, Yuba County Municipal Court.
Office: 215 Fifth Street, Marysville 95901.
Telephone: (530) 749-7600.

WASSERMAN, Fumiko Hachiya *(Judge, Superior Court of California County of Los Angeles)* Appointed by Governor George Deukmejian to term beginning Aug 1989. Elected 1990, 1996 and 2002. Current term expires Jan 2009. Judge, Los Angeles Municipal Court Los

WASSERMAN, FUMIKO HACHIYA—*Continued*

Angeles County 1982-87. Judge, South Bay Municipal Court Los Angeles County 1987-89.

Office: Courthouse, 111 North Hill Street, Los Angeles 90012.

Telephone: (213) 974-5411.

WATERS, Sharon J. *(Judge, Superior Court of California County of Riverside)*

Office: Riverside Historic Courthouse, 4050 Main Street, Riverside 92501.

Telephone: (909) 955-1960.

WATSON, John M. *(Judge, Superior Court of California County of Orange)*

Mailing address: P.O. Box 1994, Santa Ana 92702-1994.

Office: Central Justice Center, 700 Civic Center Drive West, Santa Ana 92701.

Telephone: (714) 834-3734.

WATSON, W. Bruce, Jr. *(Judge, Superior Court of California County of Humboldt)* Assumed office June 10, 1998. Presiding Judge July 1, 1998 to June 30, 2000. Born Berkeley California Jan 27, 1947. Protestant. Educated at Sacramento State University B.A. with honors 1972 and McGeorge School of Law University of the Pacific J.D. 1979. Admitted to practice California 1979 and U.S. District Court Northern District of California 1979. In legal practice Eureka 1985-88. Judge, Humboldt County Municipal Court Jan 1993 to June 9, 1998.

Deputy Public Defender Humboldt County 1980-85 and 1988-92. Former Member State Bar of California and Humboldt County Bar Association. Member California Judges Association. Lieutenant U.S. Army 1965-69. Recipient Bronze Star and Ribbon for Vietnam Service. Vice Chairman The United Way Humboldt County 1985-86. Community Speaker Humboldt Connections for Youth. Enjoys family, exercise, reading and recreation.

Office: 825 Fifth Street, Eureka 95501.

Telephone: (707) 269-1200.

WATTERS, Elaine *(Judge, Superior Court of California County of Sonoma)* Appointed by Governor Pete Wilson to term beginning Jan 24, 1992. Elected 1992 and 1998. Current term expires Jan 2005. Presiding Judge Jan 1, 1995 to Dec 31, 1996. Born Canada April 10, 1948. Educated at Syracuse University B.A. magna cum laude 1969 and University of California Hastings College of the Law J.D. 1979. Research Editor Hastings Law Journal 1977-79. Member Order of the Coif. Admitted to practice California 1979 and U.S. District Court Northern District of California 1979. In legal practice Santa Rosa 1979-92.

Office: 600 Administration Drive, Santa Rosa 95403.

Telephone: (707) 565-2927.

WAYNE, Roger L. *(Judge, Superior Court of California County of Madera)* Assumed office July 1, 1998. Former Judge, Madera County Municipal Court.

Office: 141 South Second Street, Chowchilla 93610.

Telephone: (559) 665-4861.

WEBER, Joan P. *(Judge, Superior Court of California County of San Diego)* Former Judge, San Diego Municipal Court San Diego County.

Mailing address: P.O. Box 122724, San Diego 92112-2724.

Office: 325 South Melrose Drive, Vista 92083.

Telephone: (760) 726-9595.

WEBSTER, Allen Joseph, Jr. *(Judge, Superior Court of California County of Los Angeles)*

Office: Compton Courthouse, 200 West Compton Boulevard, Compton 90220.

Telephone: (310) 603-7842.

WEBSTER, Edward D. *(Judge, Superior Court of California County of Riverside)* Presiding Judge Jan 1, 1996 to Dec 31, 1996. Serves Family Law Court.

Office: 4175 Main Street, Riverside 92501.

Telephone: (909) 955-1940.

WEINER, Marie S. *(Judge, Superior Court of California County of San Mateo)* Serves Northern Branch.

Office: 1050 Mission Road, South San Francisco 94080.

Telephone: (650) 877-5772.

WEINTRAUB, Debre Katz *(Judge, Superior Court of California County of Los Angeles)* Assumed office Jan 22, 2000. Former Judge, Los Angeles Municipal Court Los Angeles County.

Office: Van Nuys Courthouse West, 14400 Erwin Street Mall, Van Nuys 91401-2705.

Telephone: (818) 374-2601.

WEIR, Robert W. *(Judge, Superior Court of California County of Del Norte)* Presiding Judge since Jan 1, 2000. Former Judge, Del Norte County Justice Court.

Office: 450 H Street, Crescent City 95531.

Telephone: (707) 464-7217.

WEISBERG, Stanley Martin *(Judge, Superior Court of California County of Los Angeles)* Former Judge, Los Angeles Municipal Court Los Angeles County.

Office: Van Nuys Courthouse East, 6230 Sylmar Avenue, Van Nuys 91401.

Telephone: (818) 374-2265.

WEISMAN, William R. *(Judge, Superior Court of California County of Los Angeles)* Assumed office Jan 22, 2000. Former Judge, Los Angeles Municipal Court Los Angeles County.

Office: San Pedro Courthouse, 505 South Centre Street, San Pedro 90731-3332.

Telephone: (310) 519-6013.

WEISSBRODT, Arthur S. *(Judge, United States Bankruptcy Court Northern District of California)*

Office: 3035 U.S. Courthouse, 280 South First Street, San Jose 95113.

Telephone: (408) 535-5116.

WELCH, James Michael *(Judge, Superior Court of California County of San Bernardino)* Presiding Judge since Jan 1, 2002.

Office: 172 West Third Street, Second Floor, San Bernardino 92415-0302.

Telephone: (909) 387-6500.

WELLINGTON, Michael D. *(Judge, Superior Court of California County of San Diego)* Appointed by Governor George Deukmejian to term beginning March 6, 1989. Elected 1990, 1996 and 2002. Current term ex-

WELLINGTON, MICHAEL D.—*Continued*

pires Jan 2009. Born San Diego California March 12, 1945. Educated at University of New Mexico, San Diego State College B.A. 1968 and University of San Diego School of Law J.D. cum laude 1971. Articles Editor San Diego Law Review 1970-71. Admitted to practice California 1971, U.S. Court of Appeals Ninth Circuit and U.S. Supreme Court.

Deputy Attorney General California 1971-89. Lecturer California Center for Judicial Education and Research, California Continuing Education of the Bar, National Association of Attorneys General, California District Attorneys Association, Association of Government Attorneys in Capital Litigation and Practising Law Institute. President San Diego Psych-Law Society.

Mailing address: P.O. Box 122724, San Diego 92112-2724.

Office: 220 West Broadway, San Diego 92101.

Telephone: (619) 531-3860.

WELLS, Kerry *(Judge, Superior Court of California County of San Diego)*

Mailing address: P.O. Box 122724, San Diego 92112-2724.

Office: 220 West Broadway, San Diego 92101.

Telephone: (619) 531-3820.

WERDEGAR, Kathryn Mickle *(Associate Justice, California Supreme Court)* Appointed by Governor Pete Wilson May 3, 1994. Retained by election 1994 and 2002. Current term expires Jan 2015. Educated at Wellesley College 1954-55, University of California at Berkeley B.A. with honors 1957, University of California Boalt Hall School of Law 1959-61, George Washington University School of Law J.D. with highest distinction 1962 and University of California Boalt Hall School of Law J.D. 1990. Staff member George Washington Law Review. Editor-in-Chief (first woman) University of California Law Review. Recipient five American Jurisprudence Awards. Member Order of the Coif. Admitted to practice California 1964, U.S. District Court Northern District of California 1964 and U.S. Court of Appeals Ninth Circuit 1964. Associate Justice, California Court of Appeal First District Division Three 1991-94, appointed by Governor Pete Wilson.

Legal Assistant Civil Rights Division U.S. Department of Justice 1962-63. Research Attorney California State Study Commission on Mental Retardation 1963-64. Associate University of California at Berkeley Center for Study of Law and Society 1965-67. Special Consultant State Department of Mental Health 1967-68. Consultant California Center for Judicial Education and Research 1968-71. Director Criminal Law Division California Continuing Education of the Bar 1971-78. Senior Staff Attorney to California Court of Appeal First District 1981-85 and to Hon. Edward Panelli, California Supreme Court 1985-91. Author *Mental Retardation and the Law: A Survey of California Laws Affecting the Mentally Retarded* State of California Sacramento 1964, "The Courts and Private ADR: Partners in Serving Justice" 51 No. 2-3 Dispute Resolution Journal 52 1966, "The Solicitor General and Administrative Due Process: A Quarter Century of Advocacy" 36 George Washington L. Rev. 481, 1968, *Benchbook: Misdemeanor Procedure* California College of Trial Judges 1971 revised 1975 California Continuing Education of the Bar Supp. 1983, Chapter 6 "Depositions on Written Interrogatories" *California Civil Discovery Practice* California Continuing Education of the Bar 1975 and "Why a Women on the Bench?" 16 Wisconsin L. Rev. 31 Spring 2001. Editor *California Uninsured Motorist Practice* 1973, *Discovery* California Criminal Law Practice Series 1975 and *California Civil Procedure Before Trial* 1977 California Continuing Education of the Bar. Associate Dean for Academic and Student Affairs and Associate Professor University of San Francisco School of Law 1978-81. Regents' Lecturer University of California at Berkeley 2000. Former Member Committee on Criminal Law and Procedure State Bar of California. Former Member Judicial Council Standing Appellate Advisory Committee (Chair Rules Subcommittee) and Planning Committee Appellate Judges Institute California Center for Judicial Education and Research. Chair Appellate Education Committee California Center for Judicial Education and Research. Member The American Law Institute, California/Nevada Women Judges Association, National Association of Women Judges and California Judges Association (Former Chair Subcommittee on Education Appellate Courts Committee). Recipient Roger J. Traynor Appellate Justice of the Year Award 1996, Justice of the Year Award from Consumer Attorneys of California 1998, Citation Award from University of California Boalt Hall School of Law 2002, Charles Glover Award for Highest Achievement in the Field of Law from George Washington University, Excellence in Achievement Award from California Alumni Association and J. William Fulbright Distinguished Public Service Award from George Washington Law Alumni Association. Listed in *Who's Who in America, Who's Who in American Law, Who's Who of American Women* and *Who's Who in the West.* Board of Directors California Supreme Court Historical Society.

Office: 350 McAllister Street, San Francisco 94102-4797.

Telephone: (415) 865-7032.

Fax: (415) 355-5428

WESLEY, David S. *(Judge, Superior Court of California County of Los Angeles)*

Office: Criminal Courts Building, 210 West Temple Street, Los Angeles 90012-3210.

Telephone: (213) 974-6535.

WEST, Carl J. *(Judge, Superior Court of California County of Los Angeles)* Appointed by Governor Pete Wilson to term beginning April 8, 1996. Elected to subsequent term. Current term expires Jan 2005. Born Pasadena California April 7, 1951. Educated at Occidental College B.A. 1973 and Loyola Marymount University J.D. 1977. Admitted to practice California 1978. In legal practice Pasadena 1980-94 and Los Angeles 1978-80. Judge, Los Angeles Municipal Court Los Angeles County Jan 1994 to April 7, 1996.

Office: Central Civil West, 600 South Commonwealth, Los Angeles 90005.

Telephone: (213) 351-8739.

WEST, Katrina *(Judge, Superior Court of California County of San Bernardino)*

Office: 14455 Civic Drive, Victorville 92392.

Telephone: (760) 243-8684.

WESTRA, Clarence, Jr. *(Judge, Superior Court of California County of Kern)* Presiding Judge Jan 1, 1998 to Dec 31, 1999.
Office: 1415 Truxtun Avenue, Bakersfield 93301.
Telephone: (661) 868-4934.

WETENKAMP, Jean High *(Judge, Superior Court of California County of Santa Clara)* Assumed office July 30, 1998. Former Judge and Presiding Judge, Santa Clara County Municipal Court.
Office: 605 West El Camino Real, Sunnyvale 94087.
Telephone: (408) 481-3500.

WHEATLEY, Diana M. *(Judge, Superior Court of California County of Los Angeles)*
Office: Santa Monica Courthouse, 1725 Main Street, Santa Monica 90401.
Telephone: (310) 260-3762.

WHEATLEY, Horace *(Judge, Superior Court of California County of Alameda)* Assumed office July 31, 1998. Born Lake Charles Louisiana Feb 9, 1939. Baptist. Educated at University of the Pacific B.A. 1961 and Willamette University College of Law J.D. 1964. Admitted to practice California 1965, U.S. Court of Appeals Ninth Circuit 1965 and U.S. Supreme Court 1968. In legal practice San Francisco and Oakland 1965-72 and Los Angeles and Burlingame 1972-79. Former Judge and Presiding Judge, Oakland-Piedmont-Emeryville Municipal Court Alameda County, appointed by Governor Edmund G. Brown, Jr.
Deputy Attorney General California 1965-70.
Office: Justice Center, 600 Washington Street, Oakland 94607.
Telephone: (510) 268-7601.

WHELAN, Thomas J. *(Judge, United States District Court Southern District of California)* Appointed for life by President Bill Clinton to term beginning Nov 5, 1998. Born San Diego California Feb 21, 1940. Educated at University of San Diego B.A. 1961 J.D. 1965. Judge, Superior Court of California San Diego County 1990-98.
Deputy District Attorney San Diego 1969-89.
Office: 3155 U.S. Courthouse, 940 Front Street, San Diego 92101.
Telephone: (619) 557-6625.

WHITE, Colleen Toy *(Judge, Superior Court of California County of Ventura)*
Mailing address: P.O. Box 6489, Ventura 93006-6489.
Office: 800 South Victoria Avenue, Ventura 93009-0001.
Telephone: (805) 654-2965.

WHITE, Elizabeth Allen *(Judge, Superior Court of California County of Los Angeles)* Assumed office Jan 22, 2000. Former Judge, Los Angeles Municipal Court Los Angeles County.
Office: San Pedro Courthouse, 505 South Centre Street, San Pedro 90731-3332.
Telephone: (310) 519-6013.

WHITE, Jeffrey Steven *(Judge, United States District Court Northern District of California)* Appointed for life by President George W. Bush to term beginning Jan 2, 2003. Born New York New York 1945. Educated at Queens College of the City University of New York B.A. 1967 and State University of New York J.D. 1970. In legal practice San Francisco 1978-2002.
Office: U.S. Courthouse, 450 Golden Gate Avenue, San Francisco 94102.
Telephone: (415) 522-2000.

WHITE, Randall D. *(Judge, Superior Court of California County of Riverside)* Assumed office July 29, 1998. Elected 2002, current term expires Jan 1, 2009. Serves Indio Branch. Born California Jan 21, 1952. Methodist. Educated at University of California at Santa Barbara B.A. 1974 and Loyola Law School J.D. 1977. California State Scholar 1970-72. Member Phi Alpha Delta. Admitted to practice California 1978 and U.S. District Court Central District of California 1978. In legal practice Los Angeles 1978-79 and Indio 1979-92. Judge Dec 30, 1992 to July 28, 1998 and Former Presiding Judge, Desert Municipal Court Riverside County, appointed by Governor Pete Wilson.
Senior Deputy Riverside County District Attorney 1979-92. Secretary Loyola Law School Student Bar 1977. Member Budget Committee 1994, Executive Committee 1994 and 1995, Court Construction Oversight Committee 1994-96, Court Services Committee 1995-2000, Grand Jury Committee 1995-2000 and Information Systems Committee 1995-2001 Superior Court of Riverside County. Member California Judges Association (Criminal Law and Procedure Committee 1994-98) and Desert Bar Association (Board of Trustees 1985-92 and President Elect 1992-93). Faculty Member New Judges Orientation 1997-2002 and Advanced Criminal Law Seminars Continuing Judicial Studies Program 1998-2000 California Center for Judicial Education and Research. Member Program Planning Committee Continuing Judicial Studies 1999-2002. Seminar Leader Bernard E. Witken Judicial College 2001. Named Felony Deputy of the Year 1987 with Honorable Mention 1985, 1986 and 1988 by Riverside District Attorney's Office and Attorney of the Year 1988.
Office: Larsen Justice Center, 46-200 Oasis Street, Indio 92201.
Telephone: (760) 863-8426.

WHITE, Thomas R. *(Judge, Superior Court of California County of Los Angeles)*
Office: Santa Clarita Courthouse, 23747 West Valencia Boulevard, Valencia 91355.
Telephone: (661) 253-7301.

WHITE-BROWN, Gloria L. *(Judge, Superior Court of California County of Los Angeles)*
Office: Courthouse, 111 North Hill Street, Los Angeles 90012.
Telephone: (213) 974-5411.

WHITEHEAD, Denise Lee *(Judge, Superior Court of California County of Fresno)*
Office: Courthouse, 1100 Van Ness Avenue, Fresno 93724-0002.
Telephone: (559) 488-1825.

WHITESIDE, John G. *(Judge, Superior Court of California County of Stanislaus)* Presiding Judge July 1, 1998 to June 30, 2000. Former Judge and Presiding Judge, Stanislaus County Municipal Court.
Office: 800 11th Street, Modesto 95354.
Telephone: (209) 558-6000.

WHITLEY, Marshall Ivan *(Judge, Superior Court of California County of Alameda)* Assumed office July 31,

WHITLEY, MARSHALL IVAN—*Continued*

1998. Former Judge, Oakland-Piedmont-Emeryville Municipal Court Alameda County.
Office: Courthouse, 661 Washington Street, Oakland 94607.
Telephone: (510) 268-7601.

WHITMER, Judith *(Judge, Superior Court of California County of San Mateo)* Appointed by Governor George Deukmejian Nov 14, 1988. Elected to subsequent terms. Born Coshocton Ohio March 15, 1944. Educated at Michigan State University B.A. 1965 and University of Michigan J.D. 1971. Admitted to practice California 1972. Judge, San Mateo County Municipal Court 1984-88.
Prosecutor San Francisco District Attorney's Office 1972-84.
Office: Hall of Justice and Records, 400 County Center, Redwood City 94063.
Telephone: (650) 363-4766.

WHITNEY, Richard *(Judge, Superior Court of California County of San Diego)*
Mailing address: P.O. Box 122724, San Diego 92112-2724.
Office: 220 West Broadway, San Diego 92101.
Telephone: (619) 531-3820.

WHYTE, Ronald M. *(Judge, United States District Court Northern District of California)* Appointed for life by President George Bush to term beginning 1992. Born Pomona California Oct 25, 1942. Educated at Wesleyan University A.B. 1964 and University of Southern California J.D. 1967. In legal practice Claremont 1967-68 and San Jose 1971-89. Judge, Superior Court of California Santa Clara County 1989-92.
Office: 2112 U.S. Courthouse, 280 South First Street, San Jose 95113.
Telephone: (408) 535-5331.

WIATT, L. Jeffrey *(Judge, Superior Court of California County of Los Angeles)* Appointed by Governor Pete Wilson to term beginning Sept 12, 1995. Serves North Valley District. Born New York Nov 6, 1943. Educated at University of Southern California B.S. 1966 and Whittier College School of Law J.D. 1974. Admitted to practice California 1974, U.S. District Court Central District of California and U.S. Court of Appeals Fifth and Ninth Circuits. In legal practice Los Angeles 1978-88. Referee Superior Court of California County of Los Angeles 1984-93. Judge, Los Angeles Municipal Court Los Angeles County 1993-95.
Deputy District Attorney Los Angeles 1975-78. Member California Judges Association. Faculty Member California Center for Judicial Education and Research since 1996. USN 1966-70. Republican.
Office: San Fernando Courthouse, 900 Third Street, San Fernando 91340.
Telephone: (818) 898-2634.

WICK, Diane Elan *(Judge, Superior Court of California City and County of San Francisco)* Assumed office Dec 31, 1998. Former Judge and Presiding Judge, San Francisco Municipal Court San Francisco County.
Office: Civic Center Courthouse, 400 McAllister Street, San Francisco 94102-4514.
Telephone: (415) 551-4020.

WICKERSHAM, S. Charles *(Judge, Superior Court of California County of San Diego)*
Mailing address: P.O. Box 122724, San Diego 92112-2724.
Office: 330 West Broadway, San Diego 92101.
Telephone: (619) 685-6148.

WIELAND, Charles A. *(Judge, Superior Court of California County of Madera)* Presiding Judge Jan 1, 2001 to Dec 31, 2001.
Office: 209 West Yosemite Avenue, Madera 93637.
Telephone: (559) 675-7907.

WILDE, Linda M. *(Judge, Superior Court of California County of San Bernardino)*
Office: 13260 Central Avenue, Chino 91710.
Telephone: (909) 465-5269.

WILEY, John Shepard, Jr. *(Judge, Superior Court of California County of Los Angeles)*
Office: Mental Health Courthouse, 1150 North San Fernando Road, Los Angeles 90065.
Telephone: (323) 226-2908.

WILKEN, Claudia *(Judge, United States District Court Northern District of California)* Appointed Part-time Magistrate Judge by U.S. District Court judges to term beginning July 26, 1983. Appointed Full-time Magistrate Judge by U.S. District Court judges to term beginning May 1984. Appointed Judge for life by President Bill Clinton. Born Minnesota Aug 17, 1949. Educated at Stanford University B.A. with honors 1971 and University of California Boalt Hall School of Law J.D. 1975. Admitted to practice California 1975, U.S. District Court Northern District of California 1975, U.S. Court of Appeals Ninth Circuit 1976 and U.S. Supreme Court 1981. In legal practice Berkeley 1978-84.
Staff Attorney Federal Public Defender's Office 1975-78. Important Decisions: Jane Doe, By and Through John Doe v. Petaluma School District F. Supp. 1996, WL 478973 N.D. Cal. 1996; Armstrong v. Wilson 842 F. Supp. 1252 N.D. Cal. 1996; and Sega Enterprises Ltd. v. MAPHIA 948 F. Supp. 923 N.D. Cal 1996. Lecturer University of California Boalt Hall School of Law 1978-84. Professor New College School of Law 1980-85. Member Women Lawyers of Alameda County, National Association of Women Judges, Alameda County and American (Judicial Administration Division) Bar Associations.
Office: 400-S Federal Building, 1301 Clay Street, Oakland 94612-5212.
Telephone: (510) 522-2000.

WILKINSON, Randell L. *(Judge, Superior Court of California County of Orange)* Appointed by Governor George Deukmejian to term beginning Sept 24, 1990. Elected June 1992 and 1998. Current term expires Jan 2005. Born San Bernardino California Nov 3, 1950. Church of Jesus Christ of Latter-Day Saints. Educated at Occidental College 1968-69 and Brigham Young University B.A. magna cum laude 1974 J.D. 1976. Admitted to practice California 1977 and U.S. District Court Central District of California 1985. Judge, Central Orange County Municipal Court 1986-90.
Deputy District Attorney Orange County 1977-86. Special Assistant U.S. Attorney 1984-85. Editor Case Digest California District Attorneys Association 1983-86. Author California Vehicle Code §23182 (increases penalty for drunk drivers who injure more than one person),

WILKINSON, RANDELL L.—*Continued*

passed by California Legislature 1985. Former member California District Attorneys Association and Orange County Bar Association. Member California Judges Association. Guest Lecturer to Bar and Judiciary Brazil 1998, 2001 and 2002. Republican. Enjoys camping, skiing, hiking and snorkeling.
Mailing address: P.O. Box 1994, Santa Ana 92702-1994.
Office: 700 Civic Center Drive West, Santa Ana 92701.
Telephone: (714) 834-3734.

WILLETT, William G. *(Judge, Superior Court of California County of Los Angeles)* Assumed office Jan 22, 2000. Elected 2000, current term expires Jan 2007. Born Torrance California Aug 27, 1944. Educated at Occidental College B.A. 1966 and Southwestern University J.D. cum laude 1973. Special Projects Editor Southwestern University Law Review 1972-73. Law Clerk to Hon. A. Andrew Hauk, U.S. District Court Central District of California 1973-74. Admitted to practice California 1973 and U.S. District Court Central District of California 1973. Judge Nov 1, 1980 to Jan 21, 2000, South Bay Municipal Court Los Angeles County, appointed by Governor Edmund G. Brown, Jr.
City Prosecutor Torrance 1975-80. Lieutenant j.g. USN 1966-69. Enjoys running, biking, weight training, skiing and hunting.
Office: Redondo Beach Courthouse, 117 West Torrance Boulevard, Redondo Beach 90277-3638.
Telephone: (310) 318-8710.

WILLHITE, Thomas Lyle, Jr. *(Judge, Superior Court of California County of Los Angeles)* Former Judge, Los Angeles Municipal Court Los Angeles County.
Office: Criminal Courts Building, 210 West Temple Street, Los Angeles 90012-3210.
Telephone: (213) 974-6535.

WILLIAMS, Alexander H., III *(Judge, Superior Court of California County of Los Angeles)*
Office: Courthouse, 111 North Hill Street, Los Angeles 90012.
Telephone: (213) 974-5411.

WILLIS, Browder, III *(Judge, Superior Court of California County of San Diego)*
Mailing address: P.O. Box 122724, San Diego 92112-2724.
Office: 220 West Broadway, San Diego 92101.
Telephone: (619) 531-3820.

WILSON, Christopher G. *(Judge, Superior Court of California County of Humboldt)*
Office: 825 Fifth Street, Eureka 95501.
Telephone: (707) 269-1200.

WILSON, Stephen V. *(Judge, United States District Court Central District of California)* Appointed for life by President Ronald Reagan to term beginning 1985. Born New York New York March 26, 1941. Educated at Lehigh University B.A. 1963, Brooklyn Law School J.D. 1967 and George Washington University LL.M. 1973. In legal practice Beverly Hills 1977-85.
Trial Attorney Tax Division U.S. Department of Justice 1968-71. Assistant U.S. Attorney Los Angeles 1971-77.
Office: U.S. Courthouse, 312 North Spring Street, Los Angeles 90012.
Telephone: (213) 894-4327.

WINN, John P. *(Judge, Superior Court of California County of Sacramento)*
Office: Courthouse, 720 Ninth Street, Sacramento 95814.
Telephone: (916) 874-5476.

WISEMAN, Rebecca A. *(Associate Justice, California Court of Appeal Fifth District)* Appointed by Governor Pete Wilson. Retained by election. Born Sanger California Sept 6, 1953. Episcopalian. Educated at California State University at Fresno B.A. summa cum laude 1975, University of California at Davis Law School J.D. 1980 and University of Virginia School of Law LL.M. 2001. Admitted to practice California 1980. In legal practice Bakersfield 1980-86. Former Judge, Bakersfield Municipal Court Kern County, appointed by Governor George Deukmejian to term beginning Sept 4, 1986. Former Judge, Superior Court of California Kern County.
With District Attorney's Office Kern County 1981-86. Co-author *Employment Litigation Practice Guide* The Rutter Group. Former member State Bar of California and Kern County Bar Association. Member Kern County Women Lawyers and California Judges Association. Attended California Judicial College University of California at Berkeley July 1988.
Office: 2525 Capitol Street, Fresno 93721.
Telephone: (559) 445-5491.

WISS, Mary E. *(Judge, Superior Court of California City and County of San Francisco)*
Office: Hall of Justice, 850 Bryant Street, San Francisco 94103.
Telephone: (415) 553-1159.

WISTRICH, Andrew J. *(Magistrate Judge, United States District Court Central District of California)* Appointed by U.S. District Court judges to term beginning 1994. Reappointed 2002, current term expires 2010. Educated at University of California at Berkeley A.B. 1972 and University of Chicago J.D. 1976. Member University of Chicago Law Review 1974-76. Law Clerk to Hon. Charles Clark, U.S. Court of Appeals Fifth Circuit 1976-77. In legal practice San Francisco 1978-83 and Palo Alto 1983-94. Judge pro tem, Superior Court of California County of Santa Clara 1993-94.
Contributing Editor *Proof in Competitive Business Practice Litigation* California Continuing Education of the Bar 1993. Co-author with James N. Penrod Chapter "Handling Trials Efficiently" *California Civil Procedure During Trial* California Continuing Education of the Bar 3rd ed. 1995 and with Tyler T. Ochoa "The Puzzling Purposes of Statutes of Limitation" 28 Pacific L. Jour. 453, 1997. Author "How Cognitive Illusions Can Affect Legal Decision Making" 16 No. 2 *Civil Trial Lawyer* Los Angeles County Bar Association Fall 1999. Member Federal Magistrate Judges Association (Committee on Civil and Criminal Rules since 1995), American Psychology-Law Society, The American Law Institute, American Judicature Society, State Bar of California,

WISTRICH, ANDREW J.—*Continued*

Los Angeles County (Executive Committee Litigation Section since 1999) and Federal Bar Associations.
Office: 100 U.S. Courthouse, 312 North Spring Street, Los Angeles 90012.
Telephone: (213) 894-2523.

WITT, Gary R. *(Judge, Superior Court of California County of Kern)* Assumed office July 1, 2000. Serves Arvin-Lamont Branch. Presiding Judge Jan 1, 1999 to Dec 31, 1999 and Former Judge, South Kern Municipal Court Kern County.
Office: 12022 Main Street, Lamont 93241.
Telephone: (661) 845-3741.

WOEHRLE, Carla M. *(Magistrate Judge, United States District Court Central District of California)*
Office: U.S. Courthouse, 312 North Spring Street, Los Angeles 90012.
Telephone: (213) 894-4904.

WOJCIK, Albert J. *(Judge, Superior Court of California County of Riverside)* Assumed office July 29, 1998. Former Judge, Mount San Jacinto Municipal Court Riverside County.
Office: Hemet Court, 880 North State Street, Hemet 92543.
Telephone: (909) 766-2325.

WOLFE, Richard B. *(Judge, Superior Court of California County of Los Angeles)*
Office: Van Nuys Courthouse East, 6230 Sylmar Avenue, Van Nuys 91401.
Telephone: (818) 374-2265.

WONG, Cerena *(Judge, Superior Court of California County of Sonoma)* Assumed office June 12, 1998. Presiding Judge Jan 1, 1996 to Dec 31, 1996 and Former Judge, Sonoma County Municipal Court.
Office: 600 Administration Drive, Santa Rosa 95403.
Telephone: (707) 565-1100.

WOODS, Margie G. *(Judge, Superior Court of California County of San Diego)*
Mailing address: P.O. Box 122724, San Diego 92112-2724.
Office: 500 Third Avenue, Chula Vista 91910.
Telephone: (619) 691-4770.

WOODS, Norvell "Fred", Jr. *(Associate Justice, California Court of Appeal Second District Division Seven)* Appointed by Governor George Deukmejian to term beginning Aug 22, 1988. Retained by election. Current term expires 2006. Born Corpus Christi Texas March 31, 1935. Episcopalian. Educated at Rice University B.A. 1958 and Loyola University of Los Angeles J.D. 1963. Member Phi Delta Phi. Admitted to practice California 1964, U.S. District Court Southern District of California 1964 and U.S. Supreme Court 1971. In legal practice Long Beach 1964-84. Judge, Superior Court of California Los Angeles County 1984-88.
Important Decisions: Milla v. Tamayo (civil) Dec 1986, Dwyer v. Crocker National Bank (civil) March 1987 and Fisher v. San Pedro Peninsula Hospital 1989. Lecturer on Business Law Long Beach City College 1969. Member Long Beach Bar Association (Board of Governors). Lecturer "Trial Tactics" Continuing Education of the Bar 1974, "Civil Law and Motion" The Rutter Group 1987 and "Sanctions" California Center for Judicial Education and Research 1987. Lieutenant Commander USNR 1958-72. Previously worked as grocery store clerk and package boy, section gang Santa Fe Railway, City Maintenance Department, lifeguard and chain dragger for surveyor. Republican. President YMCA (physical fitness instructor), Jaycees and Optimist Club. Judge Advocate and Board of Directors Long Beach Yacht Club. Vice President Long Beach Rotary Club. Enjoys sailing, running and gardening.
Office: 300 South Spring Street, Los Angeles 90013.
Telephone: (213) 830-7405.

WOODWARD, James *(Judge, Superior Court of California County of Trinity)*
Mailing address: P.O. Box 1258, Weaverville 96093.
Office: 101 Court Street, Weaverville 96093.
Telephone: (530) 623-1208.

WOOLARD, Charlotte Walter *(Judge, Superior Court of California City and County of San Francisco)* Former Judge, San Francisco Municipal Court San Francisco County.
Office: Civic Center Courthouse, 400 McAllister Street, San Francisco 94102-4514.
Telephone: (415) 551-4020.

WOOLLEY, John C. *(Judge, Superior Court of California County of Orange)* Appointed by Governor Edmund G. Brown, Jr. Dec 22, 1982. Elected 1984, 1990, 1996 and 2002. Current term expires Jan 2009. Born Indiana Nov 6, 1936. Baptist. Educated at California State University at Long Beach B.S. 1959 and University of Southern California J.D. 1962. Admitted to practice California 1963 and U.S. District Court Central District of California 1963. In legal practice Garden Grove 1963-82.
Deputy City Prosecutor 1963-64 and Assistant City Attorney 1965-70 Garden Grove. Author Editorial "Party Endorsements Will Leave Judges Dangling by Political Threads" *Los Angeles Daily Journal* Oct 11, 1990, "Family Law Update" The Rutter Group 1993 and Editorial "If It Is Violence, Don't Call It 'Domestic'" *Orange County Register* Jan 1995. Instructor in Business Law Golden West Junior College 1965-70. Member Warren J. Ferguson Inn of Court (Charter President 2000-01), American Judicature Society, California Judges Association (Chairman Committee on Family Law 1985-87, Executive Board 1987-90, Secretary Treasurer 1988-89, President 1989-90), West Orange County (President 1979-80), Orange County (President Elect 1982) and American (Judicial Administration Division) Bar Associations. Lecturer on Construction Defect Litigation, Family Law, Law and Motion, Civil Procedure, Complex Litigation, Class Actions and Trial Court Delay Reduction California Center for Judicial Education and Research, Continuing Education of the Bar, The Rutter Group and Mealey Publications 1984-99. Attended Economics Institute for State Judges University of Kansas 1999. Recipient Hon. W. Patrick McCray Award for outstanding contribution to the legal profession from West Orange County Bar Association 1984. Named Judge of the Year by Orange County Bar Association Family Law Section 1985 and Constitutional Rights Foundation of Orange County 1997. Board of Trustees 1987-97 and President 1991-92 Orange County Law Library. President California Conference of County Law Library Trustees and Librarians 1994-96. Member Legion Lex Orange County and Kiwanis (Club President 1972-73, Lieutenant Governor Division Four California-Nevada-Hawaii District Kiwanis International 1976-77). Air War College National

WOOLLEY, JOHN C.—*Continued*

Security Forum 1991. Runs 30 to 50 miles a week and has completed 29 marathons since 1993.

Mailing address: P.O. Box 1994, Santa Ana 92702-1994.

Office: B-100 Orange County Courthouse, 700 Civic Center Drive West, Santa Ana 92701.

Telephone: (714) 834-4656.

WORKMAN, David A. *(Judge, Superior Court of California County of Los Angeles)* Elected to term beginning Jan 3, 1983. Reelected 1988, 1994 and 2000. Current term expires Jan 2007. Born Los Angeles California March 30, 1930. Educated at Stanford University A.B. with distinction 1952 LL.B. 1955. Member Phi Beta Kappa. Admitted to practice California 1958. Began legal practice Los Angeles 1958. Judge, Los Angeles Municipal Court Los Angeles County 1981-83.

Member California Judges Association. Colonel USMCR (retired).

Office: Courthouse, 111 North Hill Street, Los Angeles 90012.

Telephone: (213) 974-5411.

WRIGHT, James L. *(Judge, Superior Court of California County of Los Angeles)* Assumed office Jan 22, 2000. Term expires Jan 1, 2005. Born Seminole Oklahoma Sept 24, 1937. Church of Jesus Christ of Latter-Day Saints. Educated at Long Beach City College A.A. 1956, Yale University 1957 and Pacific Coast University J.D. with distinction 1971. Admitted to practice California 1972 and U.S. District Court Central District of California 1972. In legal practice Long Beach 1972-87. Former Court Clerk and Chief Court Clerk, Superior Court of California. Judge July 13, 1987 to Jan 21, 2000 and Former Presiding Judge, Long Beach Municipal Court Los Angeles County, appointed by Governor George Deukmejian.

Author "Ratification of Bill of Rights" Long Beach USO 1988. Former member State Bar of California, Long Beach and American Bar Associations. Member Los Angeles County Presiding Judges Association and California Judges Association. Member Data Processing Committee 1988 and Lecturer "Civil Law Update" MCJA 1989. E-4 USAF 1956-60. Former Deputy Marshall Los Angeles County. Republican. Member County and State Central Committees. Treasurer Sister City Committee (Qingdao, China/Long Beach, California). Chair Boy Scouts of America. Enjoys computers, photography and book collecting.

Office: Long Beach Courthouse, 415 West Ocean Boulevard, Long Beach 90802.

Telephone: (562) 491-6130.

WU, George H. *(Judge, Superior Court of California County of Los Angeles)*

Office: Courthouse, 111 North Hill Street, Los Angeles 90012.

Telephone: (213) 974-5411.

WUNDERLICH, William M. *(Associate Justice, California Court of Appeal Sixth District)* Appointed by Governor Pete Wilson to term beginning Feb 4, 1993. Retained by election. Born Lincoln Nebraska Nov 2, 1946. Educated at University of Nebraska at Lincoln 1968 and McGeorge School of Law University of the Pacific J.D. 1972. Admitted to practice California 1972. In legal practice Monterey 1980-82. Judge Jan 7, 1985 to Feb 3, 1993 and Presiding Judge 1991 and 1992, Superior Court of California Monterey County.

Prosecutor Monterey County District Attorney's Office 1973-80 and 1982-84. Board of Directors Monterey County Bar Foundation. Member California Judges Association (Executive Board, President Sept 1998 to Sept 1999). Instructor California Judicial College. First Recipient Young Alumnus of the Year Award from University of Nebraska 1987. Former Member Board of Directors American Red Cross (Board of Directors), Monterey College of Law and Children's Services Center. Founding Member Child Abuse Prevention Counsel of Monterey County. Governing Board University of Nebraska Alumni Association (Bay Area Chapter).

Office: 333 West Santa Clara Street, Suite 1060, San Jose 95113.

Telephone: (408) 277-1004.

YAFFE, David P. *(Judge, Superior Court of California County of Los Angeles)*

Office: Courthouse, 111 North Hill Street, Los Angeles 90012.

Telephone: (213) 974-5411.

YAGGY, Carol *(Judge, Superior Court of California City and County of San Francisco)*

Office: Hall of Justice, 850 Bryant Street, San Francisco 94103.

Telephone: (415) 553-1159.

YATES, Reginald *(Judge, Superior Court of California County of Los Angeles)* Assumed office Jan 22, 2000. Presiding Judge Jan 1, 1996 to Dec 31, 1996 and Former Judge, Pomona Municipal Court Los Angeles County.

Office: Pomona Courthouse North, 350 West Mission Boulevard, Pomona 91766.

Telephone: (909) 802-9944.

YEAGER, Christopher W. *(Judge, Superior Court of California County of Imperial)* Assumed office June 22, 1998. Elected 2002, current term expires Jan 2009. Presiding Judge Jan 1, 2000 to Dec 31, 2001. Serves El Centro Branch. Born Fort Pierce Florida Aug 10, 1945. Methodist. Educated at University of California at Berkeley B.A. 1968, California State University at San Bernardino and Citrus Belt Law School J.D. Admitted to practice California 1981, U.S. District Court Southern District of California 1981 and U.S. Supreme Court 1990. Judge Jan 7, 1991 to June 21, 1998 and Presiding Judge Jan 1, 1995 to Dec 31, 1996, Imperial County Municipal Court.

Deputy District Attorney Imperial County 1981-90. Member American Judicature Society, California Judges Association, California Trial Lawyers Association, American Trial Lawyers Association, State Bar of California, Imperial County and American Bar Associations. Attended California Judicial College, New Trial Court Judge Orientation Program, California Civil Law and Procedure Institute and Judicial Perspective on Substance Abuse and the Courts. Sergeant USAR 1970-76. Previously employed as teacher Hesperia School District 1970-77. Democrat. Member Rotary Club of El Centro, Symphony Association, Library Board, Hospital Bioethics Committee and Church Finance Committee. Enjoys active athletics, reading and music.

Office: 939 Main Street, El Centro 92243.

Telephone: (760) 482-4257.

YEGAN, Kenneth R. *(Associate Justice, California Court of Appeal Second District Division Six)* Appointed by Governor George Deukmejian to term beginning 1990. Retained by election. Educated at University of California at Santa Barbara B.A. 1969 and McGeorge School of Law University of the Pacific J.D. 1972. Admitted to practice California 1972, U.S. District Court Eastern District of California 1972, U.S. Court of Appeals Ninth Circuit 1972 and U.S. Supreme Court 1976. In legal practice Thousand Oaks 1982-83. Judge, Ventura County Municipal Court 1983-86. Pro Tem Justice, California Court of Appeal Second District Division Six 1986. Judge, Superior Court of California Ventura County 1986-90.

Deputy Public Defender Ventura County 1972-75. Author "Faretta—The California Experience" 53 No. 6 California State B. Jour. 1978 and "Depublication, The Missing Determinate Sentence Law Opinions" *L.A. Lawyer Magazine* April 1982. Graduate California Judicial College 1983 and Institution of Judicial Administration New York University School of Law 1991.

Office: 200 East Santa Clara Street, Ventura 93001.

Telephone: (805) 641-4740.

YENT, Rufus L. *(Judge, Superior Court of California County of San Bernardino)* Former Judge, San Bernardino County Municipal Court.

Office: 14455 Civic Drive, Victorville 92392.

Telephone: (760) 243-8684.

YEW, Erica R. *(Judge, Superior Court of California County of Santa Clara)*

Office: Hall of Justice West Wing, 200 West Hedding Street, San Jose 95110.

Telephone: (408) 808-6600.

YNOSTROZA, Carlos G. *(Judge, Superior Court of California County of Alameda)* Assumed office July 31, 1998. Born Upland California Jan 23, 1943. Educated at Chaffey Junior College 1960-61, University of California at Berkeley B.A. 1964 and University of California Hastings College of the Law J.D. 1968. Admitted to practice California 1969. Began legal practice Madera 1969. In legal practice San Francisco and Oakland. Judge Sept 11, 1980 to July 30, 1998 and Presiding Judge Jan 1, 1996 to Dec 31, 1996, Oakland-Piedmont-Emeryville Municipal Court Alameda County, appointed by Governor Edmund G. Brown, Jr.

Author "The Farmworker—The Beginning of a New Awareness" 20 American University L. Rev. 39, 1970. Editorial Board California Lawyer Magazine State Bar of California 1985-87. Legal Consultant *The Drugging of the Americas* University of California Press 1976. Adjunct Professor John F. Kennedy University School of Law since Aug 1997. Member La Raza National Lawyers Association (California State President 1977-78), California Judges Association, Hispanic National (Regional Vice President 1977-78, Secretary 1979-80), Criminal Courts and Alameda County Bar Associations. Legal Consultant Social Welfare Course Fresno State College 1970. Faculty Seminar Leader California Judicial College 1984. Faculty member Hastings Litigation Advocacy Program 1984-85 and New Judges Orientation California Center for Judicial Education and Research 1984-92. Recipient special recognition awards from La Familia (Marin County) 1977, Latino Peace Officers Association (Alameda County) 1983, Chicana Foundation of Northern California 1984, Hispanic Leaders Forum of Alameda/Santa Clara County 1986 and United Way of the Bay Area and Hispanic Community Fund of the Bay Area 1993. Named Professor of the Year by John F. Kennedy University School of Law 1998. Board of Directors United Way of the Bay Area 1981-85, Holy Names College 1982-99, Spanish Speaking Unity Council (Alameda County) 1984-91, Easter Seals Society of Alameda County 1985-91, Piedmont Boy Scout Council 1986-90, Hispanic Community Affairs Council 1986-89, Piedmont Unified School District Adult Education since 1986, Puente Project Advisory Board since 1986 and University/Oakland Metropolitan Forum 1987-98. Member since 1981 and President 1986 Board of Directors New Oakland Committee. Board of Directors 1989-99 and Vice President 1995-99 Mental Health Association of Alameda County. Member Latino Advisory Committee on Crime to the Oakland Police Department since 1994.

Office: Courthouse, 661 Washington Street, Oakland 94607.

Telephone: (510) 268-7601.

YONTS, Robert B., Jr. *(Judge, Superior Court of California County of Santa Cruz)* Judge pro tem 1976-94. Appointed Judge by Governor Pete Wilson to term beginning Feb 4, 1994. Elected June 7, 1994 to term beginning Jan 3, 1995. Reelected 2000, current term expires Jan 2007. Presiding Judge Jan 1, 2001 to Dec 31, 2002. Born Seattle Washington Jan 24, 1942. Catholic. Educated at University of Santa Clara B.A. 1963 J.D. 1968. Research Attorney to Associate Justice Joseph Rattigan, California Court of Appeal First District 1968-69. Admitted to practice California 1969, U.S. Court of Appeals Ninth Circuit 1969 and U.S. Supreme Court 1982.

Contributing Editor Chapters 1-6 *California Products Liability* by Cotchett & Cartwright, Matthew Bender & Co. 1970-71. Instructor in Insurance and Corporate Law Monterey College of Law 1986-94 and Introductory Law Courses for Paralegals University of California at Santa Cruz 1987-94. Former Member Santa Cruz Trial Lawyers Association (President 1989-90), California Trial Lawyers Association (Founding President Santa Cruz Chapter) and Santa Cruz County Bar Association. Member Cow County Judges Association and California Judges Association. Instructor in Dental Negligence and Civil Litigation California Trial Lawyers Association 1980. Recipient International Service Award from Rotary International 1991. Served from Second Lieutenant to First Lieutenant U.S. Army 1963-65. USAR 1965-69. Republican since 1982 (before that, a Democrat). Member Santa Cruz Acquatechs 1976-85. Member since 1986 and Board of Directors Santa Cruz Chapter since 1992 Rotary International. Rotary Group Study Exchange Chairman May 1993 to June 1993. Enjoys art, music, photography, scuba diving, sport fishing, travel and playing golf.

Office: Main Courthouse, 701 Ocean Street, Santa Cruz 95060.

Telephone: (831) 454-2012.

YORK, Jane A. *(Judge, Superior Court of California County of Fresno)* Assumed office July 1, 1998. Born St. Helena California July 17, 1944. Episcopalian. Educated at Occidental College 1962-64, University of California at Berkeley A.B. with honors 1966, Georgetown University M.A. 1971 and University of California Hastings College of the Law J.D. 1976. Admitted to practice California 1976 and U.S. District Court Northern

YORK, JANE A.—*Continued*

District of California 1976. In legal practice Napa 1976-83. Referee, Consolidated Fresno Municipal Court Fresno County 1983. Judge, Central Valley Municipal Court Fresno County Jan 20, 1984 to June 30, 1998.

Instructor in Real Estate Law Napa Valley College 1978-82. Member Napa County (1976-82) and Fresno County Bar Associations.

Office: Courthouse, 1100 Van Ness Avenue, Fresno 93724-0002.

Telephone: (559) 488-1825.

YOUNG, Ronald T. L. *(Judge, Superior Court of California County of Napa)* Appointed by Governor Pete Wilson Jan 7, 1997. Born Minneapolis Minnesota June 22, 1948. Episcopalian. Educated at University of Northern Iowa B.A. 1970 and Arizona State University J.D. magna cum laude 1973. Comment Editor Arizona State University Law Review 1972-73. Law Clerk to U.S. District Court District of Arizona 1973-75. Member Delta Upsilon. Admitted to practice California 1973, Arizona 1974, U.S. District Courts District of Arizona 1974 and Northern 1979 and Eastern 1981 Districts of California, U.S. Court of Appeals Ninth Circuit 1975 and U.S. Supreme Court 1983. In legal practice San Diego 1975-76 and Napa 1977-85. Judge Jan 1985 to Jan 1997 and Presiding Judge 1986 and 1989, Napa County Municipal Court.

Former Deputy District Attorney Napa and San Diego. Former Deputy City Attorney Napa. Author "Interagency Conflict of Interests: The Peril to Indian Water Rights" Arizona State University 1972. Member California Judges Association. Trustee Napa County School Board 1979-84. Former President Boys and Girls Club of Napa. Member Rotary Club and Napa Chamber of Commerce. Enjoys tennis, snow skiing and swimming.

Office: 825 Brown Street, Napa 94559.

Telephone: (707) 253-4481.

YOUNGQUIST, Raymond C. *(Judge, Superior Court of California County of San Bernardino)* Former Judge, San Bernardino County Municipal Court.

Office: 13260 Central Avenue, Chino 91710.

Telephone: (909) 465-5269.

ZAREFSKY, Ralph *(Magistrate Judge, United States District Court Central District of California)* Appointed by U.S. District Court judges July 30, 1997. Term expires 2005. Born Houston Texas April 9, 1950. Educated at Northwestern University B.A. 1972 and Stanford Law School J.D. 1976. Law Clerk to Hon. Lawrence T. Lydick, U.S. District Court Central District of California 1976-78. Admitted to practice California 1976, U.S. District Courts Central 1978, Northern 1979, Southern 1982 and Eastern 1988 Districts of California, U.S. Court of Appeals Ninth Circuit 1980, U.S. Supreme Court 1988 and District of Columbia 1993. In legal practice Los Angeles 1978-97.

Office: 931 U.S. Courthouse, 312 North Spring Street, Los Angeles 90012.

Telephone: (213) 894-8526.

ZELLERBACH, Paul E. *(Judge, Superior Court of California County of Riverside)* Elected to term beginning 2000. Term expires 2005. Born San Francisco California May 9, 1953. Presbyterian. Educated at University of California B.A. 1975 and California Western School of Law J.D. magna cum laude 1978. Notes and Comments Editor California Western Law Review. Member Order of the Coif. Admitted to practice California 1978.

Supervising Deputy District Attorney Riverside County 1978-2000.

Office: 4100 Main Street, Riverside 92501.

Telephone: (909) 955-4074.

Fax: (909) 955-4058

E-mail address: pzellerb@co.riverside.ca.us

ZELON, Laurie D. *(Judge, Superior Court of California County of Los Angeles)* Serves Central District.

Office: Criminal Courts Building, 210 West Temple Street, Los Angeles 90012-3210.

Telephone: (213) 974-6535.

ZIKA, Patrick J. *(Judge, Superior Court of California County of Alameda)* Assumed office July 31, 1998. Former Judge, Oakland-Piedmont-Emeryville Municipal Court Alameda County.

Office: Courthouse, 661 Washington Street, Oakland 94607.

Telephone: (510) 268-7601.

ZIMMERMAN, Bernard *(Magistrate Judge, United States District Court Northern District of California)* Appointed by U.S. District Court judges.

Office: U.S. Courthouse, 450 Golden Gate Avenue, San Francisco 94102.

Telephone: (415) 522-4093.

ZIMMERMAN, Joseph *(Judge, Superior Court of California County of Imperial)* Assumed office June 22, 1998. Elected 2002, current term expires Jan 2009. Serves Brawley Branch. Born Watsonville California Dec 26, 1943. Educated at San Diego State University A.B. and University of San Diego J.D. Admitted to practice California 1974 and U.S. District Court Southern District of California 1974. In legal practice Brawley 1975-90. Judge Jan 7, 1991 to June 21, 1998 and Presiding Judge Jan 1, 1997 to Dec 31, 1997, Imperial County Municipal Court.

E-5 USN 1962-66. Board Member Brawley Senior Housing and Physically Disabled, Inc. Member Rotary Club. Enjoys boating, fishing and hiking.

Office: 383 Main Street, Brawley 92227.

Telephone: (760) 344-0710.

ZÚÑIGA, Barbara Ann *(Judge, Superior Court of California County of Contra Costa)* Former Judge and Presiding Judge, Walnut Creek-Danville Municipal Court Contra Costa County.

Office: A. F. Bray Courts Building, 1020 Ward Street, Martinez 94553.

Telephone: (925) 646-2950.

ZURZOLO, Vincent P. *(Judge, United States Bankruptcy Court Central District of California)* Appointed by U.S. Court of Appeals Ninth Circuit judges to term beginning 1988. Reappointed April 18, 2002, current term expires April 17, 2016.

Office: Federal Building, 255 East Temple Street, Los Angeles 90012.

Telephone: (213) 894-3755.

COLORADO

Capital DENVER

UNITED STATES DISTRICT COURT DISTRICT OF COLORADO

The court sits at Boulder, Denver, Durango, Grand Junction, Montrose, Pueblo and Sterling. For descriptive information refer to the United States Courts section.

Chief Judge
Lewis T. Babcock

Judges

Richard P. Matsch
Wiley Y. Daniel
Marcia S. Krieger
Edward W. Nottingham
Walker D. Miller
Robert E. Blackburn

Senior Judges
John Lawrence Kane, Jr.
Zita Leeson Weinshienk
Daniel B. Sparr

Clerk
Gregory C. Langham
A105 U.S. Courthouse
901 Nineteenth Street
Denver, Colorado 80294-3589
(303) 335-2076

UNITED STATES MAGISTRATE JUDGES OF COLORADO

O. Edward Schlatter
Michael J. Watanabe
Craig B. Shaffer
Patricia A. Coan
Boyd N. Boland
Gudrun J. Rice

Recalled Magistrate Judge
James M. Robb

UNITED STATES BANKRUPTCY COURT OF COLORADO

Chief Judge
Sidney B. Brooks

Judges
A. Bruce Campbell
Elizabeth E. Brown
Howard R. Tallman

Bankruptcy Clerk
Bradford L. Bolton
U.S. Custom House
721 Nineteenth Street
Denver, Colorado 80202-2508
(303) 844-4045

COLORADO SUPREME COURT

The Supreme Court is Colorado's court of last resort. The court consists of seven justices but may be increased to nine upon request of the court and with the concurrence of two-thirds of each house of the General Assembly. Justices are appointed by the governor from a list of candidates submitted by the Supreme Court Nominating Commission. Justices serve initial two-year terms and thereafter stand for retention at general elections for ten-year terms. The chief justice, who is elected by peer vote for a nonspecific term, is the executive head of the judicial system. Retirement is mandatory at age seventy-two; however, retired justices may serve as senior justices by assignment of the state court administrator.

The court has initial appellate jurisdiction over cases involving constitutionality, decisions or actions of the Public Utilities Commission, habeas corpus, water priorities and the election code. The court also has certiorari review over appeals initiated in the Court of Appeals and the District Courts. The court has original jurisdiction in the issuance of original and remedial writs and administrative authority over the lower courts.

The court may sit in departments but must sit en banc to hear any case involving constitutions of the United States or Colorado. The court sits at Denver and holds session all year.

Chief Justice
Mary J. Mullarkey

Justices

Gregory J. Hobbs, Jr.
Alex Joseph Martinez
Nancy E. Rice
Michael L. Bender
Rebecca Love Kourlis
Nathan B. Coats

Clerk
Mac V. Danford
Colorado State Judicial Building
Two East 14th Avenue
Denver, Colorado 80203
(303) 861-1111

State Court Administrator
Gerald A. Marroney
1301 Pennsylvania Street, Suite 300
Denver, Colorado 80203
(303) 837-3668

COLORADO COURT OF APPEALS

The Court of Appeals is Colorado's intermediate appellate court. The court consists of a chief judge and fifteen judges appointed by the governor from a list of candidates submitted by the Supreme Court Nominating Commission. Judges serve initial two-year terms and thereafter stand for retention at general elections for eight-year terms. The chief judge is appointed by the chief justice to serve a nonspecified term. Retirement is mandatory at age seventy-two; however, retired judges may serve as senior judges by assignment of the state court administrator.

The court has initial appellate jurisdiction over appeals from final judgments of the District Courts and Denver Probate and Juvenile Courts, except for those

COLORADO COURT OF APPEALS—*Continued*

matters which lie directly to the Supreme Court. It also reviews the decisions of several state administrative agencies. The court has the authority to issue writs, directives and mandates necessary to the determination of cases within its jurisdiction.

The court sits in divisions of three judges each on a rotating basis as assigned by the chief judge. The court sits at Denver but may occasionally sit at Colorado Springs and Grand Junction.

Chief Judge
Janice B. Davidson

Judges

Peter H. Ney
Sandra I. Rothenberg
Robert J. Kapelke
Arthur P. Roy
Henry E. Nieto
John R. Webb
Russell Carparelli
Marsha Piccone
Jose D. L. Marquez
Daniel Marc Taubman
James S. Casebolt
JoAnn L. Vogt
John Daniel Dailey
Dennis A. Graham
Alan Loeb

COLORADO DISTRICT COURTS

The District Courts are Colorado's trial courts of general jurisdiction. Judges are appointed by the governor from a list of candidates submitted by the nominating commission of the judicial district in which a vacancy occurs. Judges serve initial two-year terms and thereafter stand for retention at general elections for six-year terms. The chief judge of each district is appointed by the chief justice to serve a nonspecific term. Judges serve in any or all of the counties within their respective districts as assigned by the chief judge. Retirement is mandatory at age seventy-two; however, retired judges may serve as senior judges by assignment of the state court administrator.

The courts have original jurisdiction over all civil, criminal, juvenile, domestic relations, probate and mental health matters, except in the city and county of Denver, where probate and mental health matters are heard by the Denver Probate Court and juvenile matters by the Denver Juvenile Court. The courts have appellate jurisdiction of final decisions of the County Courts. If a Municipal Court is a court of record, its appeals also lie to the District Court in its county.

The courts sit at the county seats.

---

*Also serves Water Court

FIRST JUDICIAL DISTRICT includes Gilpin and Jefferson counties. The court sits at Central City and Golden.

Chief Judge
L. Thomas Woodford

Judges

Leland P. Anderson
Brian Boatright
Christopher J. Munch
Frank Plaut
Jane A. Tidball
Jack W. Berryhill
R. Brooke Jackson
Stephen M. Munsinger
Ruthanne N. Polidori
James D. Zimmerman

SECOND JUDICIAL DISTRICT includes the city and county of Denver. The court sits at Denver.

Chief Judge
H. Jeffrey Bayless

Judges

John W. Coughlin
Shelley I. Gilman
Robert S. Hyatt
Paul A. Markson, Jr.
Michael A. Martinez
John N. McMullen
R. Michael Mullins
J. Stephen Phillips
Gloria A. Rivera
Herbert L. Stern III
Martin F. Egelhoff
Morris B. Hoffman
Lawrence A. Manzanares
Frank Martinez
Robert L. McGahey, Jr.
Joseph E. Meyer III
Larry J. Naves
Sheila A. Rappaport
William D. Robbins

THIRD JUDICIAL DISTRICT includes Huerfano and Las Animas counties. The court sits at Walsenburg and Trinidad.

Chief Judge
Claude W. Appel

Judge
George A. Newnam

FOURTH JUDICIAL DISTRICT includes El Paso and Teller counties. The court sits at Colorado Springs and Cripple Creek.

Chief Judge
Gilbert A. Martinez

Judges

Peter W. Booth
Theresa M. Cisneros
David A. Gilbert
Thomas Kelly Kane
Thomas L. Kennedy
Steven T. Pelican
Larry E. Schwartz
D. Richard Toth
Rebecca S. Bromley
Edward S. Colt, II
Richard V. Hall
James P. Kelly
G. David Miller
Kirk S. Samelson*
Timothy Simmons

FIFTH JUDICIAL DISTRICT includes Clear Creek, Eagle, Lake and Summit counties. The court sits at Georgetown, Eagle, Leadville and Breckenridge.

Chief Judge
W. Terry Ruckriegle

Judges
Richard H. Hart
David Richard Lass
R. Thomas Moorhead

SIXTH JUDICIAL DISTRICT includes Archuleta, La Plata and San Juan counties. The court sits at Pagosa Springs, Durango and Silverton.

Chief Judge
Gregory G. Lyman*

Judges
David L. Dickinson*
Jeffrey R. Wilson

SEVENTH JUDICIAL DISTRICT includes Delta, Gunnison, Hinsdale, Montrose, Ouray and San Miguel counties. The court sits at Delta, Gunnison, Lake City, Montrose, Ouray and Telluride.

Chief Judge
J. Steven Patrick*

COLORADO DISTRICT COURTS—*Continued*

Judges
Dennis P. Friedrich
Charles R. Greenacre*

EIGHTH JUDICIAL DISTRICT includes Jackson and Larimer counties. The court sits at Walden and Fort Collins.

Chief Judge
James H. Hiatt

Judges
Jolene C. Blair
Terence Gilmore
Daniel J. Kaup*
Arnaud Newton

NINTH JUDICIAL DISTRICT includes Garfield, Pitkin and Rio Blanco counties. The court sits at Glenwood Springs, Aspen and Meeker.

Chief Judge
Thomas W. Ossola*

Judges
James Berkley Boyd
T. Peter Craven*

TENTH JUDICIAL DISTRICT includes Pueblo County. The court sits at Pueblo.

Chief Judge
Dennis Maes*

Judges
David A. Cole
Scott B. Epstein
James H. Frasher, Jr.
Victor I. Reyes
Rosalie Vigna

ELEVENTH JUDICIAL DISTRICT includes Chaffee, Custer, Fremont and Park counties. The court sits at Salida, Westcliffe, Canon City and Fairplay.

Chief Judge
Kenneth M. Plotz

Judges
Charles M. Barton
Julie G. Marshall

TWELFTH JUDICIAL DISTRICT includes Alamosa, Conejos, Costilla, Mineral, Rio Grande and Saguache counties. The court sits at Alamosa, Conejos, San Luis, Creede, Del Norte and Saguache.

Chief Judge
O. John Kuenhold*

Judge
Pattie P. Swift

THIRTEENTH JUDICIAL DISTRICT includes Kit Carson, Logan, Morgan, Phillips, Sedgwick, Washington and Yuma counties. The court sits at Burlington, Sterling, Fort Morgan, Holyoke, Julesburg, Akron and Wray.

Chief Judge
Steven E. Shinn

Judges
James R. Leh
Douglas R. Vannoy
Joseph J. Weatherby

FOURTEENTH JUDICIAL DISTRICT includes Grand, Moffat and Routt counties. The court sits at Hot Sulphur Springs, Craig and Steamboat Springs.

Chief Judge
Michael A. O'Hara*

Judge
Paul R. McLimans

FIFTEENTH JUDICIAL DISTRICT includes Baca, Cheyenne, Kiowa and Prowers counties. The court sits at Springfield, Cheyenne Wells, Eads and Lamar.

Chief Judge
Stanley A. Brinkley

Judge
Paul D. Tallman

SIXTEENTH JUDICIAL DISTRICT includes Bent, Crowley and Otero counties. The court sits at Las Animas, Ordway and La Junta.

Chief Judge
M. Jon Kolomitz

Judge
Michael A. Schiferl

SEVENTEENTH JUDICIAL DISTRICT includes Adams and Broomfield counties. The court sits at Brighton and Broomfield.

Chief Judge
Harlan R. Bockman

Judges

C. Scott Crabtree	Katherine R. Delgado
Thomas Richard Ensor	Donald W. Marshall, Jr.
Chris Melonakis	John E. Popovich, Jr.
C. Vincent Phelps, Jr.	
John J. Vigil	

EIGHTEENTH JUDICIAL DISTRICT includes Arapahoe, Douglas, Elbert and Lincoln counties. The court sits at Englewood, Castle Rock, Kiowa and Hugo.

Chief Judge
John P. Leopold

Judges

Angela Arkin	Thomas J. Curry
Timothy L. Fasing	Nancy A. Hopf
Paul A. King	James F. Macrum, Jr.
Cheryl L. Post	Gerald Rafferty
Juanita Rice	Robert H. Russell, II
William B. Sylvester	vacancy
vacancy	vacancy

NINETEENTH JUDICIAL DISTRICT includes Weld County. The court sits at Greeley.

Chief Judge
Roger A. Klein*

Judges
Gilbert A. Gutierrez
James Hartmann, Jr.

COLORADO DISTRICT COURTS—*Continued*

J. Robert Lowenbach
Daniel S. Maus

TWENTIETH JUDICIAL DISTRICT includes Boulder County. The court sits at Boulder.

Chief Judge
Roxanne Bailin

Judges
Frank Dubofsky
Carol Glowinsky
Daniel C. Hale
Lael E. Montgomery
Morris W. Sandstead, Jr.

TWENTY-FIRST JUDICIAL DISTRICT includes Mesa County. The court sits at Grand Junction.

Chief Judge
Charles A. Buss

Judges
Amanda Bailey
David A. Bottger
Nicholas R. Massaro, Jr.

TWENTY-SECOND JUDICIAL DISTRICT includes Dolores and Montezuma counties. The court sits at Dove Creek and Cortez.

Chief Judge
Sharon L. Hansen

DENVER COURTS OF SPECIAL AND LIMITED JURISDICTION

Judges of the two special and limited jurisdiction courts of Denver are appointed by the governor from a list of candidates submitted by a nominating commission. Initial appointments are for two-year terms, after which judges stand for retention at general elections for six-year terms. Retirement is mandatory at age seventy-two. The Denver Juvenile and Probate Courts are state courts and their jurisdiction covers the city and county of Denver. The Denver Superior Court was abolished November 14, 1986, and its jurisdiction transferred to the District Court of the Second Judicial District.

DENVER JUVENILE COURT

The Denver Juvenile Court has exclusive jurisdiction of all juvenile matters, including delinquency, supervision, dependency and neglect, relinquishment, adoption, paternity and support matters.

Presiding Judge
Karen Ashby

Judges
Dana U. Wakefield
Orrelle R. Weeks

DENVER PROBATE COURT

The Denver Probate Court has exclusive jurisdiction over probate matters and adjudication of the mentally ill.

Presiding Judge
C. Jean Stewart

COLORADO WATER COURTS

The Water Courts are courts of special jurisdiction in Colorado. Judges are selected by the Supreme Court from among the District Court judges, who serve in addition to their District Court duties.

The courts have jurisdiction in the determination of water rights, uses and administration of water resources and all other water matters within the jurisdiction. All appeals are filed directly with the Supreme Court.

Colorado has seven Water Courts, one in each of the major river basins: the South Platte, Arkansas, Rio Grande, Gunnison, Colorado, White and San Juan rivers.

DIVISION ONE consists of the northeastern portion of the state. The court sits at Greeley in Weld County.

Judges
Roger A. Klein
vacancy

DIVISION TWO consists of the southeastern portion of the state. The court sits at Pueblo in Pueblo County.

Judges
Dennis Maes
Kirk S. Samelson

DIVISION THREE consists of the south-central portion of the state. The court sits at Alamosa in Alamosa County.

Judges
O. John Kuenhold
vacancy

DIVISION FOUR consists of the southwest-central portion of the state. The court sits at Montrose in Montrose County.

Judges
J. Steven Patrick
Charles R. Greenacre

DIVISION FIVE consists of the northwest-central portion of the state. The court sits at Glenwood Springs in Garfield County.

Judges
Thomas W. Ossola
T. Peter Craven

DIVISION SIX consists of the northwestern portion of the state. The court sits at Steamboat Springs in Routt County.

Judges
Michael A. O'Hara
Daniel J. Kaup

DIVISION SEVEN consists of the southwestern portion of the state. The court sits at Durango in La Plata County.

Judges
Gregory G. Lyman
David L. Dickinson

COLORADO COUNTY COURTS

The County Courts are courts of limited jurisdiction in Colorado. Judges are appointed by the governor from a list of names submitted by the nominating commission of the judicial district in which a vacancy occurs; in

COLORADO COUNTY COURTS—*Continued*

Denver, judges are appointed by the mayor. After initial two-year appointments, judges stand for retention at the next general election for four-year terms. In the metropolitan counties or counties with large caseloads, judges are required to be attorneys licensed to practice in Colorado; they serve full time. These counties include Adams, Arapahoe, Boulder, Clear Creek, Denver (city and county), Douglas, El Paso, Jefferson, La Plata, Larimer, Mesa, Pueblo and Weld. In all other counties, judges need not be attorneys. Retirement is mandatory at age seventy-two; however, retired judges may serve as senior judges by assignment of the state court administrator. Associate and assistant county judges also serve the court, usually outside the county seat. These judges are appointed in the same manner as county judges.

The courts have original jurisdiction, concurrent with the District Courts, in civil cases involving $10,000 or less. The courts have original criminal jurisdiction over misdemeanors and preliminary felony hearings and may issue writs as prescribed by law. The courts hear appeals de novo from those Municipal Courts which are not courts of record.

The courts sit at the county seats or anywhere in the county as needed.

County	Judge
Adams	Ovid R. Beldock
	Cindy Hull Bruner
	Michael A. Cox
	Emil A. Rinaldi
	Sabino E. Romano
	Jeffrey L. Romeo
Alamosa	Martin A. Gonzales
Arapahoe	Alex R. Bencze
	Christopher C. Cross
	Ethan D. Feldman
	Richard Morgan Jauch
	Dana Elizabeth Murray
	Steven R. Ruddick
	Robert C. Tobias
Archuleta	James E. Denvir
Baca	W. Michael Porter
Bent	Mark A. MacDonnell
Boulder	David A. Archuleta
	Carolyn Hoye Enichen
	Diane R. MacDonald
	Thomas J. B. Reed
	John F. Staveley
Broomfield	Randall J. Davis
Chaffee	William P. Alderton
Cheyenne	vacancy
Clear Creek	Russell H. Granger
Conejos	Gordon J. Bosa
Costilla	Kimberly L. Wood
Crowley	Carl W. Ross
Custer	Harold D. Taylor
Delta	Sandra K. Miller
Denver	Andrew S. Armatas
	Johnny C. Barajas
	Larry L. Bohning
	Kathleen M. Bowers
	James B. Breese
	Doris E. Burd
	Brian T. Campbell
	Mary Celeste
	Robert B. Crew, Jr.
Denver—Cont.	Herbert H. Galchinsky
	Alfred C. Harrell
	Claudia J. Jordan
	John M. Marcucci
	Melvin Okamoto
	Aleene Ortiz-White
	Robert L. Patterson
	Raymond Nathan Satter
Dolores	Susan Whicher
Douglas	Susanna Meissner-Cutler
	James S. Miller
Eagle	Terri Sue Diem
Elbert	Kevin Sidel
El Paso	Karla J. Hansen
	Barney Iuppa
	Sylvia A. Manzanares
	Lawrence D. Martin
	James S. Patterson
	Stephen J. Sletta
	Daniel S. Wilson
	vacancy
Fremont	William Gobin Fox
Garfield	Stephen L. Carter
	Victor M. Zerbi, Jr.
Gilpin	Frederic B. Rodgers
Grand	Mary C. Hoak
Gunnison	Ben F. Eden
Hinsdale	Larry E. Vickers
Huerfano	Robert E. Haeger
Jackson	Rex A. Shaw
Jefferson	Judy L. Archuleta
	James C. Demlow
	Kim H. Goldberger
	Charles T. Hoppin
	Tina Olsen
	Roy G. Olson, Jr.
Kiowa	Gary W. Davis
Kit Carson	J. Curt Penny, Jr.
Lake	Wayne Patton
La Plata	Martha T. Minot
Larimer	Christine A. Carney
	John E. Kochenburger
	Ronald L. Schultz
	C. Edward Stirman
Las Animas	Bruce Billings
Lincoln	Truston Lee Fisher
Logan	Robert B. Smith
Mesa	Thomas M. Deister
	Arthur R. Smith
Mineral	Robert M. Wardell
Moffat	Mary Lynne James
Montezuma	Todd J. Plewe
Montrose	John J. Michel
	Bette R. Nickell
Morgan	Michael J. Schingle
Otero	Ralph N. Wadleigh
Ouray	David S. Westfall
Park	Stanley J. Mayhew
Phillips	David O. Colver
Pitkin	Erin Fernandez-Ely
Prowers	Larry E. Stutler
Pueblo	Adele K. Anderson
	Kathleen K. Hearn
	Ernest J. Ruybalid
Rio Blanco	Laurie A. Noble
	Gerard C. Viscardi
Rio Grande	Michael H. Trujillo

COLORADO COUNTY COURTS—*Continued*

Routt	James H. Garrecht
Saguache	Amanda K. Pearson
San Juan	Todd P. Risberg
San Miguel	Sharon Elaine Shuteran
Sedgwick	Max E. Carlson
Summit	Edward J. Casias
Teller	Jackson L. Peters, Jr.
Washington	Kevin L. Hoyer
Weld	Carol M. Haller
	Lynn J. Karowsky
	Charles Unfug
Yuma	Thomas J. Callahan

COLORADO MUNICIPAL COURTS

Municipal Courts are authorized in home rule cities and in statutory towns and cities. Judges are appointed by the governing body of the municipality for a term of not less than two years.

The courts have jurisdiction over municipal ordinance violations. Appeals from Municipal Courts are handled in two ways: if the Municipal Court is a court of record, the appeal is to the District Court in that county; if the Municipal Court is not a court of record, the appeal is by trial de novo to the County Court.

There are approximately 215 Municipal Courts in Colorado with an estimated 230 judges. The judges are to be attorneys where possible.

Colorado Counties and County Seats

Adams
Brighton

Alamosa
Alamosa

Arapahoe
Littleton

Archuleta
Pagosa Springs

Baca
Springfield

Bent
Las Animas

Boulder
Boulder

Broomfield
Broomfield

Chaffee
Salida

Cheyenne
Cheyenne Wells

Clear Creek
Georgetown

Conejos
Conejos

Costilla
San Luis

Crowley
Ordway

Custer
Westcliffe

Delta
Delta

Denver
Denver

Dolores
Dove Creek

Douglas
Castle Rock

Eagle
Eagle

Elbert
Kiowa

El Paso
Colorado Springs

Fremont
Canon City

Garfield
Glenwood Springs

Gilpin
Central City

Grand
Hot Sulphur Springs

Gunnison
Gunnison

Hinsdale
Lake City

Huerfano
Walsenburg

Jackson
Walden

Jefferson
Golden

Kiowa
Eads

Kit Carson
Burlington

Lake
Leadville

La Plata
Durango

Larimer
Fort Collins

Las Animas
Trinidad

Lincoln
Hugo

Logan
Sterling

Mesa
Grand Junction

Mineral
Creede

Moffat
Craig

Montezuma
Cortez

Montrose
Montrose

Morgan
Fort Morgan

Otero
La Junta

Ouray
Ouray

Park
Fairplay

Phillips
Holyoke

Pitkin
Aspen

Prowers
Lamar

Pueblo
Pueblo

Rio Blanco
Meeker

Rio Grande
Del Norte

Routt
Steamboat Springs

Saguache
Saguache

San Juan
Silverton

San Miguel
Telluride

Sedgwick
Julesburg

Summit
Breckenridge

Teller
Cripple Creek

Washington
Akron

Weld
Greeley

Yuma
Wray

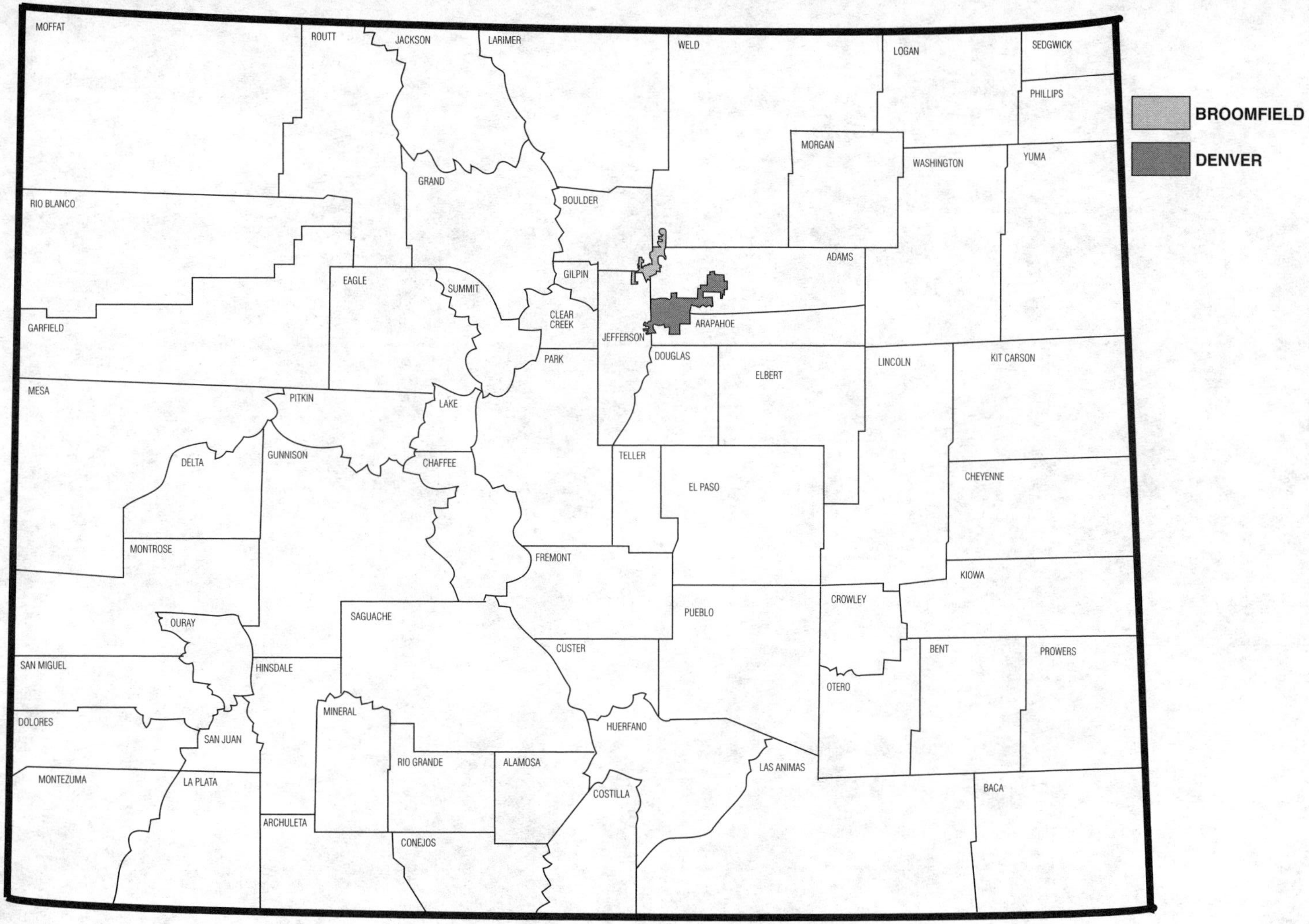
MOFFAT
ROUTT
JACKSON
LARIMER
WELD
LOGAN
SEDGWICK
PHILLIPS
BROOMFIELD
DENVER
MORGAN
WASHINGTON
YUMA
GRAND
BOULDER
RIO BLANCO
ADAMS
GILPIN
EAGLE
SUMMIT
CLEAR CREEK
ARAPAHOE
GARFIELD
JEFFERSON
DOUGLAS
PARK
ELBERT
LINCOLN
KIT CARSON
MESA
PITKIN
LAKE
GUNNISON
CHAFFEE
DELTA
TELLER
EL PASO
CHEYENNE
MONTROSE
FREMONT
KIOWA
CROWLEY
SAGUACHE
PUEBLO
OURAY
CUSTER
BENT
PROWERS
SAN MIGUEL
HINSDALE
OTERO
DOLORES
MINERAL
HUERFANO
SAN JUAN
RIO GRANDE
ALAMOSA
LAS ANIMAS
MONTEZUMA
LA PLATA
COSTILLA
BACA
ARCHULETA
CONEJOS

UNITED STATES DISTRICT COURT DISTRICT OF COLORADO

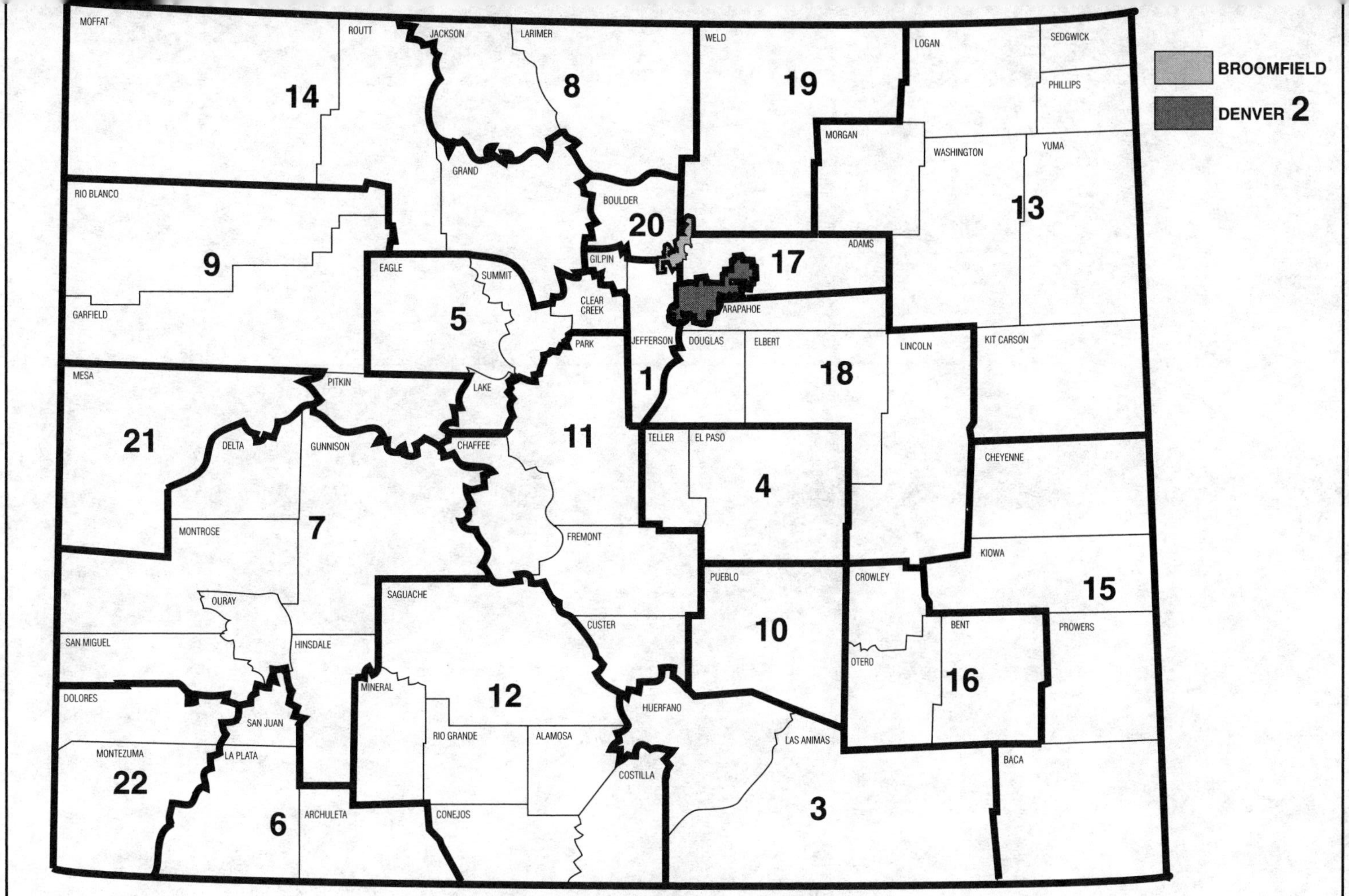
MOFFAT
ROUTT
JACKSON
LARIMER
WELD
LOGAN
SEDGWICK
PHILLIPS
BROOMFIELD
DENVER 2
14
8
19
MORGAN
WASHINGTON
YUMA
GRAND
RIO BLANCO
BOULDER
20
13
9
EAGLE
SUMMIT
GILPIN
17
ADAMS
CLEAR CREEK
ARAPAHOE
GARFIELD
5
PARK
JEFFERSON
DOUGLAS
ELBERT
LINCOLN
KIT CARSON
MESA
PITKIN
LAKE
1
18
21
DELTA
GUNNISON
CHAFFEE
11
TELLER
EL PASO
CHEYENNE
4
MONTROSE
7
FREMONT
KIOWA
PUEBLO
CROWLEY
15
SAGUACHE
OURAY
CUSTER
10
BENT
PROWERS
SAN MIGUEL
HINSDALE
OTERO
16
MINERAL
12
DOLORES
HUERFANO
SAN JUAN
RIO GRANDE
ALAMOSA
LAS ANIMAS
MONTEZUMA
LA PLATA
BACA
22
COSTILLA
3
6
ARCHULETA
CONEJOS

JUDICIAL DISTRICTS OF COLORADO DISTRICT COURTS

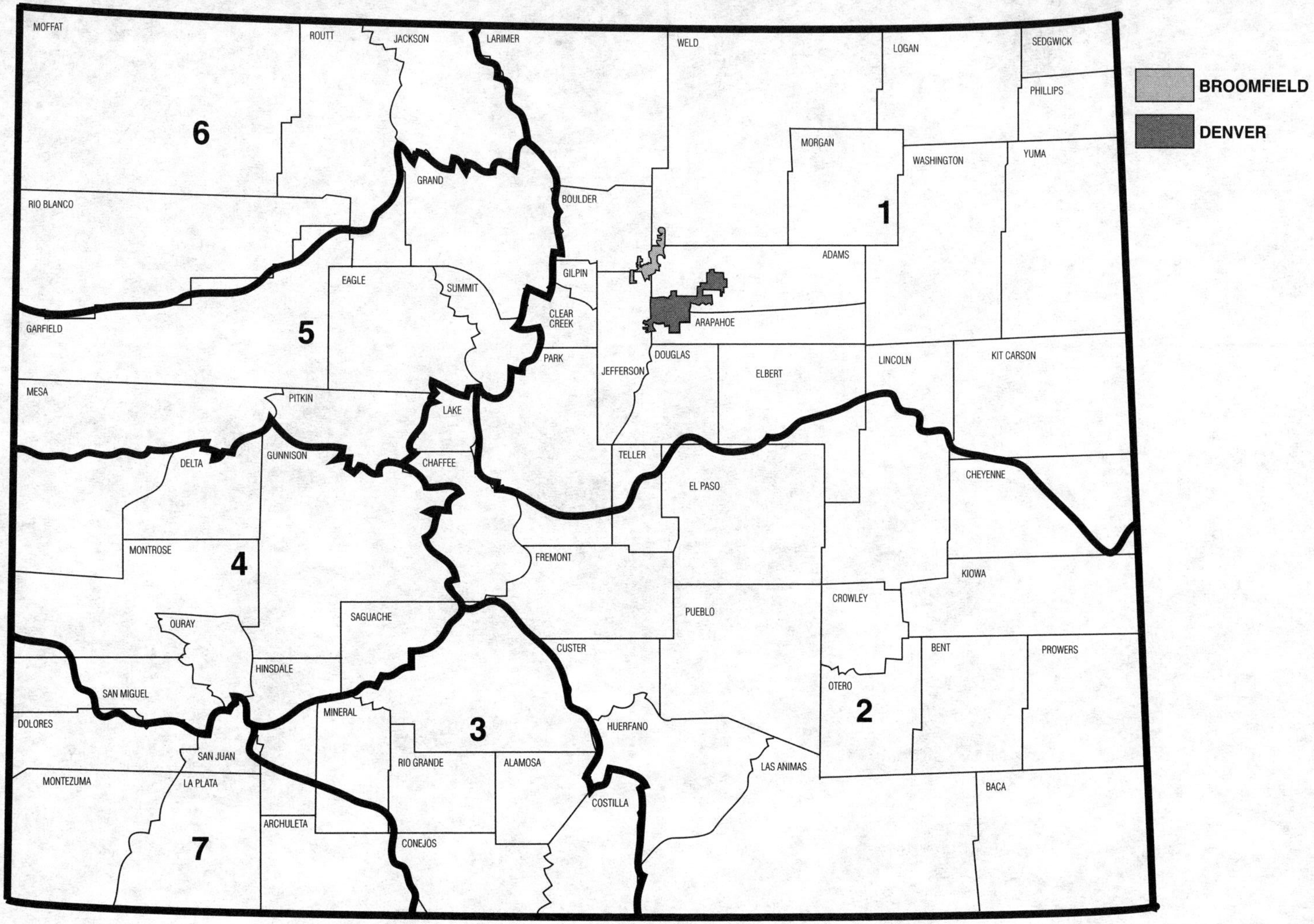
BROOMFIELD
DENVER
MOFFAT
ROUTT
JACKSON
LARIMER
WELD
LOGAN
SEDGWICK
PHILLIPS
6
MORGAN
WASHINGTON
YUMA
GRAND
BOULDER
RIO BLANCO
1
ADAMS
GILPIN
EAGLE
SUMMIT
CLEAR CREEK
ARAPAHOE
GARFIELD
5
PARK
DOUGLAS
JEFFERSON
ELBERT
LINCOLN
KIT CARSON
MESA
PITKIN
LAKE
GUNNISON
DELTA
CHAFFEE
TELLER
EL PASO
CHEYENNE
MONTROSE
4
FREMONT
KIOWA
CROWLEY
SAGUACHE
OURAY
PUEBLO
CUSTER
BENT
PROWERS
HINSDALE
SAN MIGUEL
OTERO
MINERAL
2
DOLORES
3
HUERFANO
SAN JUAN
RIO GRANDE
ALAMOSA
LAS ANIMAS
MONTEZUMA
LA PLATA
BACA
COSTILLA
ARCHULETA
7
CONEJOS

DIVISIONS OF COLORADO WATER COURTS

COLORADO

ALDERTON, William P. *(Judge, Chaffee County Court)* Appointed by Governor Roy Romer to term beginning July 1, 1990. Retained by election Nov 3, 1992, 1996 and 2000. Current term expires Jan 2005. Born Oakland California Sept 3, 1949. Educated at Whitman College B.A. 1971 and Creighton University School of Law J.D. 1974. Admitted to practice Colorado 1975 and U.S. District Court District of Colorado 1975. In legal practice Colorado Springs 1975-79, Cortez 1979-80 and Salida since 1981.

Mailing address: P.O. Box 279, Salida 81201.

Office: Chaffee County Judicial Building, 142 Crestone, Salida 81201.

Telephone: (719) 539-6031.

ANDERSON, Adele K. *(Judge, Pueblo County Court)* Appointed by Governor Roy Romer to term beginning Sept 11, 1989. Retained by election 1992, 1996 and 2000. Current term expires Jan 9, 2005. Born Winona Minnesota Jan 25, 1949. Roman Catholic. Educated at St. Mary College B.A. magna cum laude 1971 and Washington University at St. Louis J.D. 1981. Olin Fellowship. Admitted to practice Colorado 1981 and U.S. District Court District of Colorado 1981. In legal practice Pueblo 1981-89. District Magistrate, Kansas District Court District Fifteen 1975-78.

President Colorado County Court Judges Association 1997-98. Member Pueblo County and Colorado Bar Associations. Attended The National Judicial College 1991. Enjoys wildflowers and computers.

Office: Pueblo County Judicial Building, 320 West Tenth Street, Pueblo 81003.

Telephone: (719) 583-7041.

ANDERSON, Leland P. *(Judge, Colorado District Court First Judicial District)* Appointed by Governor Roy Romer Dec 1996 to term beginning Feb 3, 1997. Retained by election 2000, current term expires Jan 2007. Born Denver Colorado Aug 14, 1948. Educated at North Park College B.A. summa cum laude 1970 and University of Denver College of Law J.D. 1975. Associate Editor Denver Law Review 1974-75. Law Clerk to Hon. William Erickson, Colorado Supreme Court 1975-76. Admitted to practice Colorado 1975, U.S. Court of Appeals Tenth Circuit and U.S. Supreme Court. In legal practice Denver.

Deputy District Attorney Denver 1976-79. Columnist "Off The Record" *The Colorado Lawyer*. Fellow American Bar Foundation. Member Colorado (Board of Governors) and American Bar Associations. Recipient Trial Lawyer of the Year Award from Trial Lawyers for Public Justice 1993. Recognized for legal services by Colorado Senate and for legal services to the poor by Colorado Bar Association. Corporal USMCR 1970-73 and USAR 1973-76. Enjoys astronomy, mythology, writing and mountaineering.

Office: 100 Jefferson County Parkway, Golden 80401-6002.

Telephone: (303) 271-6120.

Fax: (303) 271-6270

APPEL, Claude W. *(Chief Judge, Colorado District Court Third Judicial District)* Appointed by governor. Former Judge, Huerfano County Court, assumed office Jan 8, 1985.

Office: 304 Huerfano County Courthouse, 401 Main Street, Walsenburg 81089.

Telephone: (719) 738-1040.

ARCHULETA, David Anthony *(Judge, Boulder County Court)* Appointed by Governor Bill Owens to term beginning Aug 2, 1999. Retained by election 2002, current term expires Dec 2006. Born Denver Colorado Feb 21, 1963. Educated at University of Colorado B.A. 1985 J.D. 1989. Admitted to practice Colorado 1989.

Deputy District Attorney Boulder County 1990-99. Member Penfield Tate II American Inn of Court, Colorado Hispanic and Boulder County Bar Associations. Enjoys hiking, squash and rollerblading. Interested in history, computers, music of all kinds and movies.

Office: 1035 Kimbark, Longmont 80501.

Telephone: (303) 682-6880.

Fax: (303) 682-6707

E-mail address: david.archuleta@judicial.state.co.us

ARCHULETA, Judy L. *(Judge, Jefferson County Court)* Appointed by Governor Bill Owens.

Office: 100 Jefferson County Parkway, Golden 80401-6002.

Telephone: (303) 271-6220.

Fax: (303) 271-6272

ARKIN, Angela *(Judge, Colorado District Court Eighteenth Judicial District)* Appointed by Governor Bill Owens.

Office: 2009 Douglas County Justice Center, 4000 Justice Way, Castle Rock 80104.

Telephone: (303) 663-7200.

ARMATAS, Andrew S. *(Judge, Denver County Court)* Former Presiding Judge.

Office: 108 City and County Building, 1437 Bannock Street, Denver 80202.

Telephone: (720) 865-8010.

ASHBY, Karen *(Presiding Judge, Denver Juvenile Court)* Appointed by governor.

Office: 157 City and County Building, 1437 Bannock, Denver 80202.

Telephone: (720) 865-8286.

BABCOCK, Lewis T. *(Chief Judge, United States District Court District of Colorado)* Appointed for life by President Ronald Reagan to term beginning Nov 21, 1988. Chief Judge since June 8, 2000. Born Rocky Ford Colorado April 4, 1943. Presbyterian. Educated at University of Denver B.A. cum laude 1965 J.D. 1968 and University of Virginia School of Law LL.M. 1988. Member Phi Beta Kappa and Order of St. Ives. Admitted to practice Colorado 1968. Began legal practice Rocky Ford 1968. Judge, Colorado District Court Sixteenth Judicial District June 23, 1976 to May 20, 1983, appointed by Governor Richard D. Lamm. Judge, Colorado Court of Appeals May 23, 1983 to Nov 21, 1988, appointed by Governor Richard D. Lamm.

BABCOCK, LEWIS T.—*Continued*

Las Animas City Attorney 1969-72. Rocky Ford City Attorney 1970-76. Assistant District Attorney Sixteenth Judicial District 1973-76. Author "Rippey v. Denver U.S. National Bank—Trustee's Duty of Loyalty" Denver L. Jour. 1968 and "Musings on Establishing the Rural Practice" Colorado Lawyer April 1972. Member Sixteenth Judicial District (President 1971), Colorado and American Bar Associations. Colorado National Guard 1968-74. Member Rotary International. Enjoys golf, photography, reading and Indian art of American Southwest.

Office: U.S. Courthouse, 901 Nineteenth Street, Denver 80294-3589.

Telephone: (303) 844-2527.

BAILEY, Amanda *(Judge, Colorado District Court Twenty-first Judicial District)* Appointed by governor.

Mailing address: P.O. Box 20000, Grand Junction 81502-5030.

Office: Mesa County Justice Center, 125 North Spruce, Grand Junction 81501.

Telephone: (970) 257-3666.

BAILIN, Roxanne *(Chief Judge, Colorado District Court Twentieth Judicial District)* Appointed by Governor Roy Romer Sept 1, 1987. Retained by election. Born Sioux Falls South Dakota May 11, 1949. Educated at University of Chicago A.B. 1971 and New York University School of Law J.D. 1974. Admitted to practice Colorado 1975. Began legal practice Trinidad Colorado 1974. Former Judge, Boulder County Court, appointed by Governor Richard D. Lamm Jan 10, 1983.

Clinical Professor University of Colorado School of Law 1977-82.

Mailing address: P.O. Box 4249, Boulder 80306-4249.

Office: Boulder Justice Center, 1777 Sixth Street, Boulder 80302.

Telephone: (303) 441-3744.

BARAJAS, Johnny C. *(Judge, Denver County Court)*

Office: 108 City and County Building, 1437 Bannock Street, Denver 80202.

Telephone: (720) 865-8281.

BARTON, Charles M. *(Judge, Colorado District Court Eleventh Judicial District)* Appointed by Governor Bill Owens.

Office: 136 Justice Center Road, Room 103, Canon City 81212.

Telephone: (719) 269-0113.

BAYLESS, H. Jeffrey *(Chief Judge, Colorado District Court Second Judicial District)* Appointed by Governor Richard D. Lamm Sept 1986 to term beginning Jan 13, 1987. Retained by election Nov 1990, 1996 and 2002. Current term expires Jan 2009. Born Galesburg Illinois Dec 20, 1945. Educated at Cornell College B.A. 1967 and University of Denver J.D. cum laude 1971. Law Clerk to Hon. Sherman Finesilver, U.S. District Court District of Colorado 1971-73. Admitted to practice Colorado 1971, U.S. District Court District of Colorado 1971 and U.S. Court of Appeals Tenth Circuit 1980. In legal practice Denver 1979-82.

Deputy District Attorney 1973-79 and Chief Deputy District Attorney 1982-86 Denver. Author "Grand Jury Reform: The Colorado Experience" ABA Journal May 1981. Member Denver, Colorado and American Bar Associations. Enjoys golf.

Office: 256 City and County Building, 1437 Bannock, Denver 80202.

Telephone: (720) 865-9064.

BELDOCK, Ovid R. *(Judge, Adams County Court)* Appointed by governor.

Office: Adams County Justice Center, 1100 Judicial Center Drive, Brighton 80601.

Telephone: (303) 654-3380.

BENCZE, Alex R. *(Judge, Arapahoe County Court)* Appointed by governor.

Office: Arapahoe County Justice Center, 7325 South Potomac Street, Englewood 80112.

Telephone: (303) 649-6262.

BENDER, Michael L. *(Justice, Colorado Supreme Court)* Appointed by Governor Roy Romer Jan 2, 1997 to term beginning Feb 5, 1997. Retained by election. Educated at Dartmouth College B.A. 1964, University of Colorado School of Law J.D. 1967 and Institute of Criminal Law and Procedure Georgetown University Law Center 1967. In legal practice Los Angeles 1979-80 and Denver 1983-97.

Deputy State Public Defender 1968-71. Associate Regional Attorney Denver Regional Litigation Center Equal Employment Opportunity Commission 1974-75. Supervising Attorney Jefferson County Public Defender's Office 1975-77. Division Chief Denver Public Defender's Office 1977-78. Member Committee for Criminal Justice Act U.S. District Court District of Colorado 1991-93. Liaison Member Attorney Regulation Advisory Committee (assisted in reorganization of attorney discipline system for state) 1998-99, Court Services since 1998 and Colorado Public Education Committee; Co-chair Civil Justice Committee since 1998; Chair District Court Need since 1999 and Magistrate Need since 1999 and Member Office of Dispute Resolution Advisory Committee since 2000 and Domestic Relations Reform Committee Colorado Supreme Court. Member Governor's Task Force on Civil Justice Reform since 1999. Member Colorado Trial Lawyer's Association (Board of Directors 1985-87), Colorado (Board of Governors 1980-82 and 1989-91) and American (Chair 1990-91 and Member Committee on Criminal Justice Standards 1997-2000 Section of Criminal Justice) Bar Associations. Member Law Alumni Board University of Colorado School of Law since 1999.

Office: Colorado State Judicial Building, Two East 14th Avenue, Denver 80203.

Telephone: (303) 861-1111.

BERRYHILL, Jack W. *(Judge, Colorado District Court First Judicial District)* Appointed by governor.

Office: 100 Jefferson County Parkway, Golden 80401-6002.

Telephone: (303) 271-6190.

Fax: (303) 271-6114

BILLINGS, Bruce *(Judge, Las Animas County Court)* Appointed by Governor Bill Owens.

Office: 304 Las Animas County Courthouse, 200 East First Street, Trinidad 81082.

Telephone: (719) 846-3316.

BLACKBURN, Robert E. *(Judge, United States District Court District of Colorado)* Appointed for life by President George W. Bush to term beginning March 8,

BLACKBURN, ROBERT E.—*Continued*

2002. Former Judge, Colorado District Court Sixteenth Judicial District.

Office: A741 U.S. Courthouse, 901 Nineteenth Street, Denver 80294.

Telephone: (303) 335-2350.

BLAIR, Jolene C. *(Judge, Colorado District Court Eighth Judicial District)* Appointed by Governor Bill Owens.

Office: 100 Larimer County Justice Center, 201 La Porte Avenue, Fort Collins 80521-2761.

Telephone: (970) 498-6244.

BOATRIGHT, Brian *(Judge, Colorado District Court First Judicial District)* Appointed by governor.

Office: 100 Jefferson County Parkway, Golden 80401-6002.

Telephone: (303) 271-6434.

Fax: (303) 271-6124

BOCKMAN, Harlan R. *(Chief Judge, Colorado District Court Seventeenth Judicial District)* Appointed by governor.

Office: Adams County Justice Center, 1100 Judicial Center Drive, Brighton 80601.

Telephone: (303) 654-3260.

BOHNING, Larry L. *(Judge, Denver County Court)* Appointed by Mayor William McNichols to term beginning Jan 8, 1980. Retained by election 1982, 1986, 1990, 1994, 1998 and 2002. Current term expires Jan 2007. Born Harrold South Dakota Aug 20, 1942. Unitarian-Universalist. Educated at Dakota Wesleyan University B.A. 1965 and University of South Dakota J.D. 1968. Member Phi Delta Phi. Admitted to practice South Dakota 1968 and Colorado 1970. Began legal practice Pierre South Dakota 1968. In legal practice Denver Colorado since 1970.

Staff Attorney South Dakota Legislative Research Council 1968-70 and Colorado Legislative Drafting Office 1970-72. Assistant City Attorney Denver 1973-80. Author "Liquor Licensing in Colorado" Colorado Lawyer Feb 1980. Instructor in Government Regis College 1972-74 and Business Law American Institute of Banking 1972-82. Member Colorado Trial Judges Council, American Judicature Society, The State Bar of South Dakota, Denver, Colorado (Board of Governors 1996-97) and American Bar Associations. Named Alumnus of the Year Dakota Wesleyan University 1984 (Commencement Speaker May 1984). Recipient Judicial Excellence Award Denver Bar Association 1990. Board member Support Systems Consolidated and Rocky Mountain Memorial Society. Member President's Council Iliff School of Theology. Member YMCA Moot Court, Denver Rotary Club, Rocky Mountain Women's Institute and Colorado Historical Society. Enjoys photography, drama and the study of Western U.S. history.

Office: 108 City and County Building, 1437 Bannock Street, Denver 80202.

Telephone: (720) 640-4715.

BOLAND, Boyd N. *(Magistrate Judge, United States District Court District of Colorado)* Appointed by U.S. District Court judges to term beginning Feb 9, 2000. Term expires 2008. Born Grand Junction Colorado Nov 29, 1954. Educated at University of Denver B.A. summa cum laude 1977 and Columbia University J.D. 1980. Law Clerk to Hon. Paul Vincent Hodges, Jr., Colorado Supreme Court 1980-81. Admitted to practice Colorado 1980, U.S. District Court District of Colorado 1980, U.S. Supreme Court 1988 and U.S. Court of Appeals Tenth Circuit. In legal practice Denver 1981-2000.

Office: 901 Nineteenth Street, Denver 80294.

Telephone: (303) 844-6408.

Fax: (303) 335-2267

BOOTH, Peter W. *(Judge, Colorado District Court Fourth Judicial District)* Appointed by governor. Former Judge, El Paso County Court.

Mailing address: P.O. Box 2980, Colorado Springs 80901-2980.

Office: 20 East Vermijo, Colorado Springs 80903.

Telephone: (719) 448-7545.

BOSA, Gordon J. *(Judge, Conejos County Court)* Appointed by Governor Richard D. Lamm to term beginning Sept 1, 1980. Retained by election. Born Cleveland Ohio March 31, 1947. Educated at University of Maryland A.A. 1973, Ohio University B.S.C. summa cum laude 1975 and The Ohio State University J.D. 1978. Member Phi Delta Phi. Admitted to practice Colorado 1978. In legal practice Alamosa and La Jara 1980.

Conejos Deputy District Attorney 1979. Member San Luis Valley and Colorado Bar Associations. Staff Sergeant USAF 1970-74. Democrat.

Mailing address: P.O. Box 128, Conejos 81129.

Office: Conejos County Courthouse, Main Street, Conejos 81129.

Telephone: (719) 376-5466.

BOTTGER, David A. *(Judge, Colorado District Court Twenty-first Judicial District)* Referee Oct 21, 1983 to April 9, 1987. Appointed Judge by Governor Roy Romer March 31, 1987. Retained by election. Born Painesville Ohio Jan 27, 1951. Educated at Ohio Northern University B.A. summa cum laude 1973 and University of Notre Dame School of Law J.D. magna cum laude 1976. Admitted to practice Colorado 1976. Law Clerk to Justice Robert B. Lee, Colorado Supreme Court 1976-77. In legal practice Denver 1977-83 and Grand Junction 1983.

Mailing address: P.O. Box 20000, Grand Junction 81502-5030.

Office: Mesa County Justice Center, 125 North Spruce, Grand Junction 81501.

Telephone: (970) 257-3630.

BOWERS, Kathleen M. *(Judge, Denver County Court)*

Office: 108 City and County Building, 1437 Bannock Street, Denver 80202.

Telephone: (720) 640-2366.

BOYD, James Berkley *(Judge, Colorado District Court Ninth Judicial District)* Appointed by Governor Bill Owens.

Office: 300 Pitkin County Courthouse, 506 East Main, Aspen 81611.

Telephone: (970) 925-7635.

BREESE, James B. *(Judge, Denver County Court)* Appointed by Mayor Federico Peña to term beginning April 1, 1987. Retained by election Nov 1990, Nov 1994, Nov 1998 and Nov 2002. Current term expires Jan 2007. Born Chicago Illinois April 5, 1947. Educated at Harvard College A.B. with honors 1969 and Northeastern University School of Law J.D. 1973. Admitted to practice Colorado 1973, U.S. District Court District

BREESE, JAMES B.—*Continued*
of Colorado 1974, U.S. Court of Appeals Tenth Circuit 1977 and U.S. Supreme Court 1978.

Associate Clinical Professor University of Denver School of Law 1978-79 and University of Colorado School of Law 1979-82. President Thompson Marsh Inns of Court. Member American Inns of Court, American Judicature Society, Denver and Colorado Bar Associations. Attended Advanced Trial Advocacy course National Institute of Trial Advocacy 1981. Recipient Faculty Humanist Award from University of Colorado School of Law 1981.

Office: 108 City and County Building, 1437 Bannock Street, Denver 80202.

Telephone: (720) 865-7880.

BRINKLEY, Stanley A. *(Chief Judge, Colorado District Court Fifteenth Judicial District)* Appointed by Governor Bill Owens.

Office: 300 Prowers County Courthouse, 301 South Main, Lamar 81052.

Telephone: (719) 336-7424.

BROMLEY, Rebecca S. *(Judge, Colorado District Court Fourth Judicial District)* Appointed by Governor Bill Owens to term beginning June 2001. Term expires Jan 2004. Born Morgantown West Virginia. Protestant. Educated at Smith College A.B. 1967, University of Virginia J.D. 1971 and University of Nevada at Reno M.J.S. 1995. Admitted to practice Virginia 1971 and Colorado 1972. Began legal practice Colorado Springs 1972. Referee, Colorado District Court Fourth Judicial District 1981-84. Judge, El Paso County Court Jan 7, 1985 to June 2001, appointed by Governor Richard D. Lamm. Acting District Judge for Probate 1989 to June 2001.

Member Law Committee Colorado Board of Law Examiners 1981-87, El Paso County (President 1985-86) and Colorado (Board of Governors 1984-86, Executive Council 1985-86, Trustee 1989-92) Bar Associations. Recipient Recognition Award from Colorado Woman's Bar Association 1986 and Judicial Excellence Award from County Court Judges Association 1995. Named Outstanding Woman Lawyer El Paso County 1986.

Mailing address: P.O. Box 2980, Colorado Springs 80901-2980.

Office: 20 East Vermijo, Colorado Springs 80903.

Telephone: (719) 448-7540.

BROOKS, Sidney B. *(Chief Judge, United States Bankruptcy Court District of Colorado)* Appointed by U.S. Court of Appeals Tenth Circuit judges 1988. Reappointed 2002, current term expires Jan 4, 2016. Chief Judge since Feb 19, 2003. Born Denver Colorado Feb 14, 1945. Educated at University of Colorado B.A. 1967 and University of Denver J.D. 1971. Admitted to practice Colorado 1971 and U.S. Court of Appeals Tenth Circuit. In legal practice Denver 1971-88.

Speaker on matters pertaining to bankruptcy, judicial management and care administration and international insolvency issues American Bankruptcy Institute, National Conference of Bankruptcy Judges, The American Law Institute, Federal Judicial Center, International Bar Association, U.S. Agency for International Development, World Bank and Organization for Economic Cooperation and Development.

Office: U.S. Customs House, 721 19th Street, Denver 80202-2508.

Telephone: (303) 844-5997.

BROWN, Elizabeth E. *(Judge, United States Bankruptcy Court District of Colorado)* Appointed by U.S. Court of Appeals Tenth Circuit judges to term beginning April 16, 2001. Term expires 2015.

Office: U.S. Customs House, 721 19th Street, Denver 80202-2508.

Telephone: (303) 844-4978.

BRUNER, Cindy Hull *(Judge, Adams County Court)* Appointed by Governor Roy Romer. Retained by election Nov 8, 1994, Nov 1998 and Nov 2002. Current term expires Jan 2007. Presiding Judge Jan 1, 1996 to Dec 31, 1997 and Jan 1, 2001 to Dec 31, 2002. Born Waterbury Connecticut April 26, 1949. Educated at University of Vermont B.S. 1979 and University of Colorado J.D. 1984. Law Clerk to Hon. Donald Abram, U.S. District Court District of Colorado 1984-85. Member Phi Delta Phi. Admitted to practice Colorado 1984 and U.S. District Court District of Colorado 1985.

Deputy District Attorney Adams County 1985-91. Member Committee on Rules of Criminal Procedure Colorado Supreme Court since Jan 1995. Member Adams County and Colorado (Executive Council Criminal Law Section since 1994) Bar Associations. Attended Nov 1992 and Faculty Advisor June 1994 to July 1994 Advanced Special Court Jurisdiction The National Judicial College. Volunteer Scripter Local Public TV Art Auction since 1992 and Ecumenical Refugee Services since 1997. Enjoys exercising, gardening, cooking and traveling, children and grandchildren.

Office: Adams County Justice Center, 1100 Judicial Center Drive, Brighton 80601.

Telephone: (303) 654-3340.

BURD, Doris E. *(Judge, Denver County Court)* Appointed by Mayor Federico Peña to term beginning Jan 23, 1989. Retained by election 1992, 1996 and 2000. Current term expires Jan 2005. Born Lock Haven Pennsylvania June 6, 1945. Educated at Lock Haven State University B.A. summa cum laude 1966 and Temple University School of Law J.D. 1975. Admitted to practice Colorado 1975. In legal practice Denver 1980-88.

Member Colorado Women's and Denver Bar Associations. Recipient Judicial Excellence Award from Denver Bar Association June 1996. Enjoys hiking and reading.

Office: 108 City and County Building, 1437 Bannock Street, Denver 80202.

Telephone: (720) 865-7900.

BUSS, Charles A. *(Chief Judge, Colorado District Court Twenty-first Judicial District)* Appointed by Governor Richard D. Lamm to term beginning Sept 1, 1977. Retained by election. Chief Judge since April 10, 1987. Born Madison Wisconsin Feb 3, 1943. Educated at University of Wisconsin-Madison B.S. with honors 1965 J.D. with honors 1968. Staff member Wisconsin Law Review. Admitted to practice Wisconsin 1968 and Colorado 1968.

Author three articles/comments University of Wisconsin Law Review. Member The Association of Trial Lawyers of America, Colorado Bar Association and State Bar of Wisconsin. Former member Colorado Criminal Justice Council (LEAA state governing body).

BUSS, CHARLES A.—*Continued*

Member American Civil Liberties Union. Enjoys biking, climbing, hiking, skiing, photography, wood carving, tennis and reading.
Mailing address: P.O. Box 20000, Grand Junction 81502-5030.
Office: Mesa County Justice Center, 125 North Spruce, Grand Junction 81501.
Telephone: (970) 257-3635.

CALLAHAN, Thomas J. *(Judge, Yuma County Court)* Appointed by governor.
Mailing address: P.O. Box 347, Wray 80758.
Office: Yuma County Courthouse, 200 East Third, Wray 80758.
Telephone: (970) 332-4118.
Fax: (970) 332-4119

CAMPBELL, A. Bruce *(Judge, United States Bankruptcy Court District of Colorado)* Appointed by U.S. Court of Appeals Tenth Circuit judges to term beginning March 22, 2001. Term expires 2015.
Office: U.S. Customs House, 721 19th Street, Denver 80202-2508.
Telephone: (303) 844-2294.

CAMPBELL, Brian T. *(Judge, Denver County Court)*
Office: 108 City and County Building, 1437 Bannock Street, Denver 80202.
Telephone: (720) 865-8070.

CARLSON, Max E. *(Judge, Sedgwick County Court)* Appointed by governor.
Office: Sedgwick County Courthouse, Third and Pine, Julesburg 80737.
Telephone: (970) 474-3627.
Fax: (970) 474-2026

CARNEY, Christine A. *(Judge, Larimer County Court)* Appointed by governor.
Office: 100 Larimer County Justice Center, 201 La Porte Avenue, Fort Collins 80521-2761.
Telephone: (970) 498-6213.

CARPARELLI, Russell *(Judge, Colorado Court of Appeals)* Appointed by Governor Bill Owens Aug 28, 2002 to term beginning Jan 14, 2003. Term expires Jan 2005. Educated at University of Denver College of Law J.D. and University of Virginia School of Law LL.M. In legal practice for 28 years.
Office: Colorado State Judicial Building, Two East Fourteenth Avenue, Denver 80203.
Telephone: (303) 861-1111.

CARTER, Stephen L. *(Judge, Garfield County Court)* Appointed by Governor John A. Love to term beginning July 1972. Retained by election. Currently serves as Special Associate Judge. Born New York New York May 23, 1945. Methodist. Educated at University of Colorado B.S. 1967 J.D. 1971. Admitted to practice Colorado 1971. Judge, Rifle Municipal Court 1972-76.
With Garfield County District Attorney's Office at Glenwood Springs 1971. City Attorney for Rifle. Member Ninth Judicial District, Colorado and American Bar Associations. Democrat. Peace Corps Volunteer in Colombia 1967. Enjoys amateur radio, hiking and skiing.
Office: Rifle County Courthouse, 110 East 18th Street, Rifle 81650.
Telephone: (970) 625-5100.

CASEBOLT, James S. *(Judge, Colorado Court of Appeals)* Appointed by Governor Roy Romer to term beginning Feb 14, 1994. Retained by election 1996, current term expires 2004. Born Denver Colorado 1950. Educated at Colorado College B.A. magna cum laude 1972 and University of Colorado J.D. 1975. Member Phi Beta Kappa. Admitted to practice Colorado 1975, U.S. District Court District of Colorado 1975, U.S. Court of Appeals Tenth Circuit 1981 and U.S. Court of Federal Claims 1988. In legal practice Grand Junction 1975-94.
Member Denver, Mesa County and Colorado Bar Associations.
Office: Colorado State Judicial Building, Two East Fourteenth Avenue, Denver 80203.
Telephone: (303) 837-3793.

CASIAS, Edward J. *(Judge, Summit County Court)* Appointed by Governor Bill Owens.
Mailing address: P.O. Box 185, Breckenridge 80424.
Office: Summit County Justice Center, 501 North Park Avenue, Breckenridge 80424.
Telephone: (970) 453-2272.

CELESTE, Mary *(Judge, Denver County Court)*
Office: 108 City and County Building, 1437 Bannock Street, Denver 80202.
Telephone: (720) 865-7880.

CISNEROS, Theresa M. *(Judge, Colorado District Court Fourth Judicial District)* Appointed by Governor Roy Romer to term beginning Jan 1, 1997. Retained by election. Educated at University of Colorado B.A. and University of Denver J.D.
Former Public Defender. Member Colorado Women's, Colorado Hispanic, Colorado Criminal Defense and Colorado Bar Associations. Recipient Professional of the Year Award from Association of Retarded Citizens 1995.
Mailing address: P.O. Box 2980, Colorado Springs 80901-2980.
Office: 20 East Vermijo, Colorado Springs 80903.
Telephone: (719) 448-7528.

COAN, Patricia A. *(Magistrate Judge, United States District Court District of Colorado)* Appointed by U.S. District Court judges.
Office: U.S. Courthouse, 901 Nineteenth Street, Denver 80294-3589.
Telephone: (303) 844-4892.

COATS, Nathan B. *(Justice, Colorado Supreme Court)* Appointed by Governor Bill Owens April 24, 2000 to term beginning May 25, 2000. Educated at University of Colorado B.A. 1971 J.D. 1975.
Assistant Attorney General 1978-83 and Deputy Attorney General 1983-86 Appellate Section. Chief Appellate Deputy District Attorney Second Judicial District Denver County 1986 to May 2000.
Office: Colorado State Judicial Building, Two East Fourteenth Avenue, Denver 80203.
Telephone: (303) 861-1111.

COLE, David A. *(Judge, Colorado District Court Tenth Judicial District)* Appointed by Governor Roy Romer to term beginning Jan 14, 1997. Retained by election 2000, current term expires Jan 2007. Born Forest Hills New York March 29, 1948. Methodist. Educated at University of Colorado B.S. 1970 and University of Denver College of Law J.D. 1973. Law Clerk to

COLE, DAVID A.—*Continued*
Hon. David Brofman, Denver Probate Court 1972-73. Admitted to practice Colorado 1973 and U.S. District Court District of Colorado 1973. In legal practice Pueblo 1974-88. Former Judge, Pueblo County Court, appointed by Governor Roy Romer 1988.

Past President Pueblo County Young Lawyers Association. Member Personnel Committee Tenth Judicial District. Member Colorado County Judges Association, Pueblo (Former Treasurer) and Colorado (Member Clients and Media Rights Committee, Law Career Committee, Entertainment Committee) Bar Associations. Attended The National Judicial College Nov 1991 and numerous Colorado Judicial Seminars. Started Mothers Against Drunk Driving Victims Impact Seminar Program for Convicted Drunk Drivers Pueblo 1989. Democrat. Former Precinct Committee Chairman. Member Pueblo Domestic Violence Task Force, Pueblo County Developmental Disabilities—M/H Consortium, Making the Grade Juvenile Justice Reform Committee, Centennial High School Booster Club and Runyon Field Baseball Coaching Staff. Board Member and Former Coach Pueblo Rangers Soccer, Inc. Enjoys sports and coaching youth.

Office: Pueblo County Judicial Building, 320 West Tenth Street, Pueblo 81003.

Telephone: (719) 583-7016.

COLT, Edward S., II *(Judge, Colorado District Court Fourth Judicial District)* Appointed by Governor Bill Owens to term beginning Sept 1, 1999. Retained by election 2002, current term expires Jan 2009. Born Colorado Springs Colorado Nov 13, 1955. Educated at Colorado University B.S. in Journalism 1978 and California Western School of Law J.D. 1986. Admitted to practice Colorado 1986. Judge, Colorado Springs Municipal Court 1993-99.

Deputy District Attorney 1986-93. Member El Paso County Bar and Colorado Bar Association. Board Member Teen Court.

Office: 101 West Bennett Avenue, Cripple Creek 80813.

Telephone: (719) 689-0450.

COLVER, David O. *(Judge, Phillips County Court)* Appointed by governor.

Office: Phillips County Courthouse, 221 South Interocean, Holyoke 80734.

Telephone: (970) 854-3279.

Fax: (970) 854-3179

COUGHLIN, John W. *(Judge, Colorado District Court Second Judicial District)* Appointed by governor. Former Judge, Denver County Court.

Office: 256 City and County Building, 1437 Bannock, Denver 80202.

Telephone: (720) 865-8611.

COX, Michael A. *(Judge, Adams County Court)* Appointed by governor.

Office: Adams County Justice Center, 1100 Judicial Center Drive, Brighton 80601.

Telephone: (303) 654-3320.

CRABTREE, C. Scott *(Judge, Colorado District Court Seventeenth Judicial District)* Appointed by Governor Bill Owens.

Office: Adams County Justice Center, 1100 Judicial Center Drive, Brighton 80601.

Telephone: (303) 654-3233.

CRAVEN, T. Peter *(Judge, Colorado District Court Ninth Judicial District and Judge, Colorado Water Court Division Five)* Appointed to District Court by Governor Roy Romer to term beginning Jan 1991. Retained by election. Appointed to Water Court by Chief Justice. Born Denver Colorado Dec 23, 1940. Educated at Georgetown University A.B. 1962 and University of Michigan LL.B. 1965. Admitted to practice Colorado 1965, U.S. District Court District of Colorado 1965 and U.S. Court of Appeals Tenth Circuit 1965. In legal practice Denver 1965-69 and Glenwood Springs 1970-90.

City Attorney Carbondale 1973-90, Glenwood Springs 1976-80 and Basalt 1977-80.

Office: 104 Garfield County Courthouse, 109 Eighth Street, Glenwood Springs 81601-3303.

Telephone: (970) 947-3850.

CREW, Robert B., Jr. *(Judge, Denver County Court)* Appointed to term beginning Sept 6, 1977. Retained by election. Born Dayton Ohio May 11, 1941. Educated at Northwestern University B.S.B.A. 1963, University of Michigan 1967 and University of Cincinnati J.D. 1968. Admitted to practice Ohio 1968 and Colorado 1969.

Member Denver and Colorado Bar Associations.

Office: 108 City and County Building, 1437 Bannock Street, Denver 80202.

Telephone: (720) 865-8090.

CROSS, Christopher C. *(Judge, Arapahoe County Court)* Appointed by Governor Roy Romer. Retained by election.

Office: 15400 East Fourteenth Place, #201, Aurora 80011.

Telephone: (303) 363-7005.

CURRY, Thomas J. *(Judge, Colorado District Court Eighteenth Judicial District)* Appointed by Governor Richard D. Lamm to term beginning Nov 14, 1986. Retained by election. Born Washington D.C. April 22, 1948. Episcopalian. Educated at Western State College of Colorado 1966-67, Colorado State University B.A. with distinction 1970, St. Mary's University of San Antonio 1970-71 and University of Denver College of Law J.D. 1973. Member Order of St. Ives. Admitted to practice Colorado 1973 and U.S. Supreme Court 1978. Began legal practice Denver 1973. Judge, Douglas County Court Aug 4, 1981 to Nov 13, 1986, appointed by Governor Richard D. Lamm.

With District Attorney's Office Eighteenth Judicial District 1980-81. Member Douglas-Elbert County and Colorado Bar Associations. Enjoys golf, fishing and skiing.

Office: 2009 Douglas County Justice Center, 4000 Justice Way, Castle Rock 80104.

Telephone: (303) 663-7210.

DAILEY, John Daniel *(Judge, Colorado Court of Appeals)* Appointed by Governor Bill Owens Nov 23, 1999 to term beginning Jan 7, 2000. Born Hornell New York Feb 16, 1952. Educated at Bucknell University B.A. cum laude 1974 and Syracuse University College of Law J.D. summa cum laude 1977. Recipient Award for Scholastic Excellence from Justinian Honorary Law Society and American Jurisprudence Awards in Criminal Law, Evidence and Future Interests. Law Clerk to Hon. David W. Enoch, Colorado Court of Appeals 1977-78. Member Order of the Coif. Admitted to practice Colorado, New York, U.S. District Court District of Colo-

DAILEY, JOHN DANIEL—*Continued*
rado, U.S. Court of Appeals Tenth Circuit and U.S. Supreme Court.

Assistant Attorney General Litigation Section; First Assistant Attorney General Appellate and Human Resources Sections; Deputy Attorney General Appellate, Criminal Enforcement and Consumer Protection Sections and Assistant Solicitor General Attorney General's Office 1978-2000. Member Colorado Criminal Justice Commission 1989-90 and 1993-94. Member Colorado Bar Association.

Office: Colorado State Judicial Building, Two East Fourteenth Avenue, Denver 80203.

Telephone: (303) 837-3789.

DANIEL, Wiley Y. *(Judge, United States District Court District of Colorado)* Appointed for life by President Bill Clinton to term beginning Sept 1, 1995. Educated at Howard University B.A. 1968 J.D. 1971. Staff member and Managing Editor Howard Law Journal 1969-71. In legal practice Denver.

Author "Whistle-Blowing Is a Last Resort When Counsel Discovers Business Noncompliance" 7 No. 3 *Preventive Law Reporter* Sept 1988, "Colorado Law Update 1993, Commercial Law" Colorado Trial Lawyers Association Sept 1993 and monthly Presidential column July 1992 to June 1993 and "Observations from the Bench" Sept 1999 *The Colorado Lawyer.* Adjunct Faculty Member University of Denver College of Law and in "Trial Tactics" University of Colorado School of Law. Past President Western States Bar Conference and Thompson G. Marsh Inn of Court. Trustee American Inns of Court Foundation. Fellow Colorado Bar Foundation and American Bar Foundation. Member Grievance Committee Colorado Supreme Court 1981-1987, Planning Committee Tenth Circuit Judicial Conference June 1998 and Civil Justice Reform Act Advisory Group U.S. District Court District of Colorado 1991-94. Member Sam Cary Bar Association (Past President), Denver (Former First Vice President, Former Member Board of Trustees), Colorado (President 1992-93, Former Vice President, Former President Elect), National and American Bar Associations. Speaker American/Russian Criminal Law and Procedure Workshop Central and Eastern European Law Initiative Project American Bar Association Sochi Russia Sept 1997. Former Member Colorado State Board of Agriculture. Former Board Member Bonfils Blood Center. Member and Chair Board of Trustees Iliff School of Theology. Board Member and Mentor The Bridge Project. Member The Just the Beginning Foundation.

Office: U.S. Courthouse, 901 Nineteenth Street, Denver 80294-3589.

Telephone: (303) 844-2170.

DAVIDSON, Janice B. *(Chief Judge, Colorado Court of Appeals)* Appointed by Governor Roy Romer to term beginning July 1988. Retained by election. Chief Judge since May 1, 2003. Born Nov 21, 1945. Educated at Skidmore College B.S. in Government 1966 and University of Pennsylvania Law School J.D. 1969. Admitted to practice New York 1970 and Colorado 1971. In legal practice 1984-85. Judge, Denver County Court 1985-88.

Appellate Section New York Legal Aid Society 1969-71. Public Defender Denver 1971-73. With Denver Litigation Center Equal Employment Opportunity Commission 1973-74. With Attorney General's Office Colorado 1975-84.

Office: Colorado State Judicial Building, Two East Fourteenth Avenue, Denver 80203.

Telephone: (303) 837-3797.

DAVIS, Gary W. *(Judge, Kiowa County Court)* Appointed by governor.

Mailing address: P.O. Box 353, Eads 81036.

Office: Kiowa County Courthouse, 200 East 13th Street, Eads 81036.

Telephone: (719) 438-5531.

DAVIS, Randall J. *(Judge, Broomfield County Court)* Appointed by Governor Bill Owens.

Office: Broomfield County Court, 17 Des Combes Drive, Broomfield 80020.

Telephone: (720) 887-2139.

DEISTER, Thomas M. *(Judge, Mesa County Court)* Appointed by Governor Roy Romer to term beginning Oct 17, 1994. Retained by election 1996 and 2000. Current term expires 2005. Born Oakland California Dec 10, 1948. Church of Christ. Educated at University of Denver B.A. 1971 J.D. 1974. Admitted to practice Colorado 1974. In legal practice Grand Junction May 1978 to Jan 1987.

Assistant District Attorney Mesa County Jan 1987 to Oct 17, 1994. USNR JAGC 1971-78.

Mailing address: P.O. Box 20000, Grand Junction 81502-5030.

Office: Mesa County Justice Center, 125 North Spruce, Grand Junction 81501.

Telephone: (970) 257-3651.

E-mail address: Tom.Deister@judicial.state.co.us

DELGADO, Katherine R. *(Judge, Colorado District Court Seventeenth Judicial District)* Appointed by Governor Bill Owens to term beginning July 2002. Educated at Colorado College B.A. 1979 and University of Denver College of Law J.D. 1983. Admitted to practice Colorado 1984.

Office: Adams County Justice Center, 1100 Judicial Center Drive, Brighton 80601.

Telephone: (303) 654-3257.

DEMLOW, James C. *(Judge, Jefferson County Court)* Appointed by Governor Richard D. Lamm to term beginning April 30, 1982. Retained by election 1984, 1988, 1992, 1996 and 2000. Current term expires Jan 2005. Born Fort Collins Colorado Aug 7, 1945. Lutheran. Educated at Colorado State University B.S.M.E. 1967 and University of Denver J.D. 1973. Member Pi Tau Sigma, Sigma Tau, Kappa Mu Epsilon, Omicron Delta Kappa and Phi Delta Theta. Admitted to Colorado 1973, U.S. District Court District of Colorado 1973 and U.S. Supreme Court 1977. Began legal practice Denver 1973. In legal practice Lakewood and Golden 1974-82. Judge, Morrison Municipal Court 1979-82.

Senior Engineer Martin Marietta Corporation 1967-73. Member First Judicial District and Colorado Bar Associations. Member Lakewood Optimist Club and Lakewood Swim Club. Licensed Soccer Referee.

Office: 100 Jefferson County Parkway, Golden 80401-6002.

Telephone: (303) 271-6250.

Fax: (303) 271-6272

DENVIR, James E. *(Judge, Archuleta County Court)* Appointed by Governor Roy Romer.
Mailing address: P.O. Box 148, Pagosa Springs 81147.
Office: Archuleta County Courthouse, 449 San Juan Street, Pagosa Springs 81147.
Telephone: (970) 264-2400.

DICKINSON, David L. *(Judge, Colorado District Court Sixth Judicial District and Judge, Colorado Water Court Division Seven)* Appointed to District Court by Governor Roy Romer to term beginning Dec 4, 1998. Retained by election, current term expires Jan 2009. Appointed to Water Court by Chief Justice. Born San Diego California Oct 14, 1945. Lutheran. Educated at Colorado School of Mines Prof.Engr. 1968 and University of Denver J.D. 1976. Admitted to practice Colorado 1977, U.S. District Court District of Colorado 1977 and U.S. Court of Appeals Tenth Circuit 1994. In legal practice Durango 1985-98.
Assistant City Attorney Denver 1977-81. County Attorney La Plata County 1981-85. Member Southwest Colorado and Colorado (Past President, Former Member Board of Governors) Bar Associations. Recipient Donald W. Hoagland Award 1986 and Professionalism Award 1998 from Colorado Bar Association. Member Boy Scouts of America. Enjoys sailing and travel.
Mailing address: P.O. Box 3340, Durango 81302-3340.
Office: La Plata County Courthouse, 1060 Second Avenue 81301.
Telephone: (970) 247-2304.
E-mail address: david.dickinson@judicial.state.co.us

DIEM, Terri Sue *(Judge, Eagle County Court)* Appointed by governor.
Mailing address: P.O. Box 597, Eagle 81631.
Office: Eagle County Justice Center, 885 Chambers Avenue, Eagle 81631.
Telephone: (970) 328-6373.

DUBOFSKY, Frank *(Judge, Colorado District Court Twentieth Judicial District)* Appointed by governor.
Mailing address: P.O. Box 4249, Boulder 80306-4249.
Office: Boulder Justice Center, 1777 Sixth Street, Boulder 80302.
Telephone: (303) 441-3748.

EDEN, Ben F. *(Judge, Gunnison County Court)* Appointed by Governor Roy Romer. Retained by election.
Office: Gunnison County Courthouse, 200 East Virginia Avenue, Gunnison 81230.
Telephone: (970) 641-3500.

EGELHOFF, Martin F. *(Judge, Colorado District Court Second Judicial District)* Appointed by governor.
Office: 256 City and County Building, 1437 Bannock, Denver 80202.
Telephone: (720) 865-9065.

ENICHEN, Carolyn Hoye *(Judge, Boulder County Court)* Appointed by governor.
Mailing address: P.O. Box 4249, Boulder 80306-4249.
Office: Boulder Justice Center, 1777 Sixth Street, Boulder 80302.
Telephone: (303) 441-3732.

ENSOR, Thomas Richard *(Judge, Colorado District Court Seventeenth Judicial District)* Appointed by governor. Born Evanston Illinois Sept 28, 1946. Christian. Educated at Indiana University B.A. 1968 J.D. 1971. Admitted to practice Illinois 1971 and Colorado 1972. Judge, Adams County Court March 6, 1978 to Jan 20, 1981, appointed by Governor Richard D. Lamm.
With Adams County Legal Aid Brighton 1971 and Brighton District Attorney's Office 1973. Instructor Community College of Denver 1972-77. Member Adams County and Colorado Bar Associations. Former member National District Attorneys Association. Democrat. Board member Denver Regional Council of Governments Criminal Justice Advisory Committee and Adams County Task Force on Alcoholism. Enjoys singing, sports and playing guitar.
Office: Adams County Justice Center, 1100 Judicial Center Drive, Brighton 80601.
Telephone: (303) 654-3240.

EPSTEIN, Scott B. *(Judge, Colorado District Court Tenth Judicial District)* Appointed by Governor Bill Owens to term beginning March 27, 2000.
Office: Pueblo County Judicial Building, 320 West Tenth Street, Pueblo 81003.
Telephone: (719) 583-7013.

FASING, Timothy L. *(Judge, Colorado District Court Eighteenth Judicial District)* Appointed by Governor Roy Romer. Retained by election. Former Judge, Arapahoe County Court.
Office: Arapahoe County Justice Center, 7325 South Potomac Street, Englewood 80112.
Telephone: (303) 649-6242.

FELDMAN, Ethan D. *(Judge, Arapahoe County Court)* Appointed by Governor Roy Romer Dec 31, 1991 to term beginning Feb 17, 1992. Retained by election Nov 1994, Nov 1998 and 2002. Current term expires Jan 2007. Born Altadena California June 26, 1948. Educated at Northwestern University B.A. 1970 and University of Denver J.D. 1974. Admitted to practice Colorado 1974 and U.S. District Court District of Colorado 1974. In legal practice Littleton 1980-86 and Greenwood Village 1986-92. Associate Judge, Glendale Municipal Court 1980-92.
Deputy District Attorney and Chief Deputy District Attorney Eighteenth Judicial District 1974-80. Member Arapahoe County (President 1990-91) and Colorado (Board of Governors 1989-91, Executive Council Criminal Law Section since 1993) Bar Associations.
Office: 1790 West Littleton Boulevard, Littleton 80120.
Telephone: (303) 798-0541.

FERNANDEZ-ELY, Erin *(Judge, Pitkin County Court)* Appointed by governor.
Office: 300 Pitkin County Courthouse, 506 East Main, Aspen 81611.
Telephone: (970) 925-7635.

FISHER, Truston Lee *(Judge, Lincoln County Court)* Appointed by governor.
Mailing address: P.O. Box 128, Hugo 80821.
Office: Lincoln County Courthouse, 103 Third Avenue, Hugo 80821.
Telephone: (719) 743-2455.

FOX, William Gobin *(Judge, Fremont County Court)* Appointed by governor.
Office: 136 Justice Center Road, Room 103, Canon City 81212.
Telephone: (719) 269-0106.

FRASHER, James H., Jr. *(Judge, Colorado District Court Tenth Judicial District)* Appointed by Governor Roy Romer. Retained by election. Former Judge, Pueblo County Court.
Office: Pueblo County Judicial Building, 320 West Tenth Street, Pueblo 81003.
Telephone: (719) 583-7008.

FRIEDRICH, Dennis P. *(Judge, Colorado District Court Seventh Judicial District)* Appointed by Governor Bill Owens.
Office: Montrose County Justice Center, 1200 North Grand Avenue Bin A, Montrose 81401-3146.
Telephone: (970) 252-4300.

GALCHINSKY, Herbert H. *(Judge, Denver County Court)*
Office: 108 City and County Building, 1437 Bannock Street, Denver 80202.
Telephone: (720) 913-7540.

GARRECHT, James H. *(Judge, Routt County Court)* Appointed by governor.
Mailing address: P.O. Box 773117, Steamboat Springs 80477.
Office: Routt County Courthouse, 522 Lincoln Avenue, Steamboat Springs 80477.
Telephone: (970) 879-5020.

GILBERT, David A. *(Judge, Colorado District Court Fourth Judicial District)* Appointed by Governor Bill Owens.
Mailing address: P.O. Box 997, Cripple Creek 80813.
Office: Teller County Courthouse, 101 West Bennett Avenue, Cripple Creek 80813.
Telephone: (719) 689-2543.
El Paso County telephone: (719) 448-7540.

GILMAN, Shelley I. *(Judge, Colorado District Court Second Judicial District)* Appointed by Governor Roy Romer. Retained by election.
Office: 256 City and County Building, 1437 Bannock, Denver 80202.
Telephone: (720) 865-9063.

GILMORE, Terence *(Judge, Colorado District Court Eighth Judicial District)* Appointed by Governor Bill Owens.
Office: 100 Larimer County Justice Center, 201 La Porte Avenue, Fort Collins 80521-2761.
Telephone: (970) 498-6229.

GLOWINSKY, Carol *(Judge, Colorado District Court Twentieth Judicial District)* Appointed by Governor Roy Romer to term beginning Jan 14, 1997. Retained by election. Educated at State University of New York at Albany B.A. and University of Denver J.D. Former Judge, Boulder County Court.
Former Instructor City of Boulder Mediation Project. Clinical Professor of Law University of Colorado School of Law 1983-94. Member Boulder and Colorado Bar Associations.
Mailing address: P.O. Box 4249, Boulder 80306-4249.
Office: Boulder Justice Center, 1777 Sixth Street, Boulder 80302.
Telephone: (303) 441-3771.

GOLDBERGER, Kim H. *(Judge, Jefferson County Court)* Appointed by Governor Richard D. Lamm Oct 9, 1975 to term beginning Nov 3, 1975. Retained by election 1978, 1982, 1986, 1990, 1994, 1998 and 2002. Current term expires Jan 2007. Presiding Judge 1978-82. Born Highland Park Michigan July 16, 1947. Jewish. Educated at Western Michigan University B.A. 1965 and University of Toledo J.D. 1972. Admitted to practice Colorado 1972, U.S. District Court for Colorado 1972, U.S. Court of Appeals Tenth Circuit 1972 and U.S. Supreme Court 1977. Began legal practice Evergreen 1972.
Instructor Denver Community College 1977-78. President Colorado Association of County Judges 1982. Member Supreme Court Standing Committee on Rules of Civil Procedure Colorado State Judicial Conference 1978-85. Finisher New York City Marathon 1984, 1985, 1986, 1989, 1993 and 1996 and Boston Marathon 1992, 1993 and 1996.
Office: 100 Jefferson County Parkway, Golden 80401-6002.
Telephone: (303) 271-6240.
Fax: (303) 271-6272

GONZALES, Martin A. *(Judge, Alamosa County Court)* Appointed by Governor Bill Owens.
Office: Alamosa County Courthouse, 702 Fourth Street, Alamosa 81101.
Telephone: (719) 589-4998.

GRAHAM, Dennis A. *(Judge, Colorado Court of Appeals)* Appointed by Governor Bill Owens.
Office: Colorado State Judicial Building, Two East Fourteenth Avenue, Denver 80203.
Telephone: (303) 837-3708.

GRANGER, Russell H. *(Judge, Clear Creek County Court)* Appointed by Governor Roy Romer.
Mailing address: P.O. Box 367, Georgetown 80444.
Office: Clear Creek County Courthouse, 5th and Argentine, Georgetown 80444.
Telephone: (303) 569-3273.

GREENACRE, Charles R. *(Judge, Colorado District Court Seventh Judicial District and Judge, Colorado Water Court Division Four)* Appointed to District Court by Governor Bill F. Owens. Appointed to Water Court by Chief Justice. Former Judge, Montrose County Court.
Office: 338 Delta County Courthouse, 501 Palmer Street, Delta 81401.
District Court telephone: (970) 874-6296.
Water Court telephone: (970) 874-4416.

GUTIERREZ, Gilbert A. *(Judge, Colorado District Court Nineteenth Judicial District)* Appointed by Governor Bill Owens. Educated at New Mexico Highlands University B.A. and University of New Mexico J.D. Former Judge, Weld County Court, appointed by Governor Roy Romer to term beginning Jan 14, 1997.
Assistant District Attorney Clovis New Mexico 1980-84. Former Member National Association of District Attorneys. Member National Association of Criminal Defense Lawyers, The Association of Trial Lawyers of America, State Bar of New Mexico, Weld County, Colorado and American Bar Associations. Member Board of Trustees Clovis Community College.
Mailing address: P.O. Box 2038, Greeley 80632.
Office: Weld County Courthouse, 901 Ninth Avenue, Greeley 80631.
Telephone: (970) 351-7300.

HAEGER, Robert E. *(Judge, Huerfano County Court)* Appointed by Governor Roy Romer to term beginning Nov 8, 1987. Retained by election 1990, 1994, 1998 and 2002. Current term expires Jan 2007. Born El-

HAEGER, ROBERT E.—*Continued*
gin Illinois Nov 30, 1939. Methodist. Educated at Iowa Wesleyan College B.A. and Chicago-Kent College of Law J.D. Member Sigma Phi Epsilon. Admitted to practice Illinois 1966, U.S. District Court Northern District of Illinois 1967, U.S. Supreme Court 1973 and Colorado 1988. In legal practice Dundee Illinois 1966-85.

Assistant State Attorney Illinois 1968-74. Member Southern Colorado and Colorado Bar Associations. Enjoys fishing, flying, reading and woodwork. Licensed pilot.

Office: 304 Huerfano County Courthouse, 401 Main Street, Walsenburg 81089.

Telephone: (719) 738-1040.

HALE, Daniel C. *(Judge, Colorado District Court Twentieth Judicial District)* Appointed by Governor Roy Romer to term beginning June 1, 1996. Retained by election. Educated at University of Colorado B.A. J.D.

Member Boulder County (Former Treasurer and President), Colorado and American Bar Associations. Recipient Optimist Club Award for Distinguished Service for Advancing Respect for Law 1984 and Certificate of Professionalism from Colorado Bar Association 1991. President and Board Member Developmental Disabilities Center.

Mailing address: P.O. Box 4249, Boulder 80306-4249.

Office: Boulder Justice Center, 1777 Sixth Street, Boulder 80302.

Telephone: (303) 441-3744.

HALL, Richard V. *(Judge, Colorado District Court Fourth Judicial District)* Appointed by governor. Former Judge, El Paso County Court.

Mailing address: P.O. Box 2980, Colorado Springs 80901-2980.

Office: 20 East Vermijo, Colorado Springs 80903.

Telephone: (719) 448-7504.

HALLER, Carol M. *(Judge, Weld County Court)* Appointed by Governor Roy Romer to term beginning Dec 6, 1996. Retained by election. Educated at Indiana University B.A. and University of Colorado School of Law J.D.

Former Member National Association of Criminal Defense Lawyers. Member Weld County, Colorado Criminal Defense, Colorado Women's and Colorado Bar Associations. Named Employee of the Year Adams County Public Defender's Office.

Mailing address: P.O. Box 2038, Greeley 80632.

Office: Weld County Courthouse, 901 Ninth Avenue, Greeley 80631.

Telephone: (970) 351-7300.

HANSEN, Karla J. *(Judge, El Paso County Court)* Appointed by Governor Bill Owens.

Mailing address: P.O. Box 2980, Colorado Springs 80901-2980.

Office: 20 East Vermijo, Colorado Springs 80903.

Telephone: (719) 448-7612.

HANSEN, Sharon L. *(Chief Judge, Colorado District Court Twenty-second Judicial District)* Appointed by Governor Roy Romer. Retained by election. Former Judge, Montezuma County Court.

Office: 210 Montezuma District Court, 109 West Main, Cortez 81321-3190.

Telephone: (970) 565-1111.

HARRELL, Alfred C. *(Judge, Denver County Court)*
Office: 108 City and County Building, 1437 Bannock Street, Denver 80202.

Telephone: (720) 865-8610.

HART, Richard H. *(Judge, Colorado District Court Fifth Judicial District)* Appointed by Governor Richard D. Lamm to term beginning March 3, 1980. Retained by election 1982, 1988, 1994 and 2000. Current term expires Jan 2007. Born Denver Colorado Sept 7, 1939. Episcopalian. Educated at Yale University B.A. 1962 and University of Colorado LL.B. 1965. Admitted to practice Colorado 1965. In legal practice Colorado Springs 1965-66, Denver 1966-71 and Vail 1971-80.

Member Continental Divide (President 1979-80), Colorado (Board of Governors 1980-82 and 1998-2002) and American Bar Associations.

Mailing address: P.O. Box 597, Eagle 81631.

Office: Eagle County Justice Center, 885 Chambers Avenue, Eagle 81631.

Telephone: (970) 328-6373.

HARTMANN, James, Jr. *(Judge, Colorado District Court Nineteenth Judicial District)* Appointed by Governor Bill Owens.

Mailing address: P.O. Box 2038, Greeley 80632.

Office: Weld County Courthouse, 901 Ninth Avenue, Greeley 80631.

Telephone: (970) 351-7300.

HEARN, Kathleen K. *(Judge, Pueblo County Court)* Appointed by Governor Roy Romer. Retained by election.

Office: Pueblo County Judicial Building, 320 West Tenth Street, Pueblo 81003.

Telephone: (719) 583-7038.

HIATT, James H. *(Chief Judge, Colorado District Court Eighth Judicial District)* Appointed by Governor Richard D. Lamm to term beginning May 1986. Retained by election 1988, 1994 and 2000. Current term expires Jan 2007. Born Tulsa Oklahoma Dec 2, 1946. Educated at College of William & Mary B.A. 1969 and University of Oklahoma Law Center J.D. 1972. Admitted to practice Oklahoma 1973 and Colorado 1977. In legal practice northern Colorado 1981-84.

Administrator legal services programs 1973-81. Instructor Oklahoma City University School of Law 1975. Member Larimer County and Colorado Bar Associations. Second Lieutenant U.S. Army infantry 1972.

Office: 100 Larimer County Justice Center, 201 La Porte Avenue, Fort Collins 80521-2761.

Telephone: (970) 498-6235.

HOAK, Mary C. *(Judge, Grand County Court)* Appointed by Governor Bill Owens to term beginning 2002. Educated at University of Chicago Law School J.D. In legal practice Grand County for eight years.

Mailing address: P.O. Box 192, Hot Sulphur Springs 80451.

Office: Grand County Courthouse, 308 Byers Street, Hot Sulphur Springs 80451.

Telephone: (970) 725-3357.

HOBBS, Gregory J., Jr. *(Justice, Colorado Supreme Court)* Appointed by Governor Roy Romer to term beginning May 1, 1996. Retained by election Nov 1998, current term expires Jan 2009. Born Gainesville Florida Dec 15, 1944. Catholic. Educated at University of Notre Dame B.A. magna cum laude 1966 and University of

HOBBS, GREGORY J., JR.—*Continued*

California Boalt Hall School of Law J.D. 1971. Supreme Court Editor California Law Review 1970-71. Law Clerk to Hon. William E. Doyle, U.S. Court of Appeals Tenth Circuit 1971-72. Member Order of the Coif. Admitted to practice Colorado 1971, U.S. District Courts District of Colorado 1971 and Northern District of California 1972, U.S. Courts of Appeals Tenth 1971 and Ninth 1972 Circuits and California 1972. In legal practice Denver Colorado 1979-96.

Enforcement Attorney Region Eight U.S. Environmental Protection Agency 1973-75. First Assistant Attorney General Natural Resources Section and Special Prosecutor and Acting Director Medicaid Fraud Control Unit Attorney General's Office Colorado 1975-79. Co-author with Bennett W. Raley "Water Quality Versus Water Quantity: A Delicate Balance" 34 Rocky Mountain Mineral Law Institute 24 No. 1, 1988 and "Water Rights Protection in Water Quality Law" 60 University of Colorado L. Rev. 841, 1989. Author "Legislative and Judicial Oversight of Rulemaking" 18 *Colorado Lawyer* 245, 1989; "Ripeness, Exhaustion and Administrative Practice" *The Environmental Law Manual* 1992 and "Ecological Integrity and Water Rights Takings in the Post-Lucas Era" *Water Law Trends, Policy and Practice* 1995 ABA SONREEL; and "Interpreting the Ecological Integrity Myth" 24 *Environmental Law* 1185, 1994. Important Decisions: Bennett Bear Creek Farm Water and Sanitation District v. City and County of Denver 928 P.2d 1254, 1996; Simpson v. Highland Irrigation Company 917 P.2d 1242, 1996; and People v. Schafer 946 P.2d 938, 1997. Adjunct Professor Masters Degree Program in Environmental Law and Management University of Denver 1991-93. Member Denver (Public Legal Education Committee), Colorado (Public Legal Education Committee) and American Bar Associations. Attended Appellate Judges Conference New York University 1997 and Western Water Law Judges Conference 1997. Recipient President's Award from National Water Resources Association. Eagle Scout. Previously worked as a sixth grade teacher New York City. Former Peace Corps Volunteer Colombia. Former Vice Chair Metropolitan Air Quality Council and Colorado Air Quality Commission. Co-chair Denver Metropolitan Area Eating Disorder Family Support Group. Member Denver Area Council and Philmont Ranch Committee National Council Boy Scouts of America, National Water Resource Association, Metropolitan Transportation Development Commission and Environmental 2000 Citizens Advisory Committee. Enjoys hiking, camping, fishing and poetry.

Office: Colorado State Judicial Building, Two East Fourteenth Avenue, Denver 80203.

Telephone: (303) 861-1111.

HOFFMAN, Morris B. *(Judge, Colorado District Court Second Judicial District)* Appointed by governor.

Office: 256 City and County Building, 1437 Bannock, Denver 80202.

Telephone: (720) 865-8612.

HOPF, Nancy A. *(Judge, Colorado District Court Eighteenth Judicial District)* Appointed by Governor Bill Owens.

Office: Arapahoe County Justice Center, 7325 South Potomac Street, Englewood 80112.

Telephone: (303) 649-6332.

HOPPIN, Charles T. *(Judge, Jefferson County Court)* Appointed by Governor Roy Romer to term beginning May 1, 1996. Retained by election. Educated at Duke University B.A. and University of Colorado J.D.

Member First Judicial District (Former President) and Colorado (Family Law Section) Bar Associations. Volunteer Foothills Parks and Recreation Preschool Program.

Office: 100 Jefferson County Parkway, Golden 80401-6002.

Telephone: (303) 271-6210.

Fax: (303) 271-6272

HOYER, Kevin L. *(Judge, Washington County Court)* Appointed by governor.

Mailing address: P.O. Box 455, Akron 80720.

Office: Washington County Courthouse, First and Ash, Akron 80720.

Telephone: (970) 345-2756.

Fax: (970) 345-2829

HYATT, Robert S. *(Judge, Colorado District Court Second Judicial District)* Appointed by governor. Former Judge, Denver County Court.

Office: 256 City and County Building, 1437 Bannock, Denver 80202.

Telephone: (720) 865-8305.

IUPPA, Barney *(Judge, El Paso County Court)* Appointed by Governor Roy Romer to term beginning 1995. Retained by election 1998 and 2002. Current term expires 2007. Born Trinidad Colorado Nov 28, 1948. Catholic. Educated at University of Denver B.A. 1970 J.D. 1973. Staff member Denver University Law Review 1973. Member Order of St. Ives. Admitted to practice Colorado 1973, U.S. District Court District of Colorado 1973, U.S. Supreme Court 1977 and U.S. Court of Appeals Tenth Circuit 1994. In legal practice Colorado Springs 1977-85 and 1989-95.

District Attorney Fourth Judicial District Jan 1985 to Jan 1989.

Mailing address: P.O. Box 2980, Colorado Springs 80901-2980.

Office: 20 East Vermijo, Colorado Springs 80903.

Telephone: (719) 448-7624.

JACKSON, R. Brooke *(Judge, Colorado District Court First Judicial District)* Appointed by Governor Roy Romer June 1998 to term beginning Oct 19, 1998. Retained by election Nov 2000, current term expires Jan 2007. Born Bozeman Montana March 5, 1947. Educated at Dartmouth College A.B. magna cum laude 1969 and Harvard Law School J.D. cum laude 1972. First Place Ames Moot Court Competition. Member Phi Beta Kappa and Alpha Theta. Admitted to practice Colorado 1972 and District of Columbia. In legal practice Denver 1972-98.

Author "Environmental Cleanups and Insurance: Isn't There a Better Way?" 21 Environmental Reporter 767 The Bureau of National Affairs, Inc. 1990; "Liability Insurance for Pollution Claims: Avoiding a Litigation Wasteland" 26 Tulsa L. Jour. 209 Winter 1990; "A Practical Guide to Prosecuting Pollution Claims" 38 Risk Management 40 Aug 1991; "Environmental Damage Claims: Colorado Favors Insureds" 41 Trial Talk 6, Jan 1992 and "Environmental Insurance Litigation Revisited: A Kinder, Gentler (Cheaper, Better) Approach" 41 Trial Talk 330 Dec 1992. Co-author "ABA Manual for Complex Insurance Coverage Litigation: A Prescrip-

JACKSON, R. BROOKE—*Continued*
tion for Efficient, Cost Effective and Management Litigation—A Reply" VIII Fordham Environmental L. Jour. 59 Fall 1996. Instructor in Trial Advocacy University of Colorado School of Law Jan 1984, Jan 1985, Jan 1987, May 1989, Jan 1991 and Jan 1998. Board of Directors Colorado Trial Lawyers Association 1992-96. Fellow, American College of Trial Lawyers. Member Denver, Jefferson County, Colorado and American (Co-chair Committee on Insurance Coverage Section of Litigation 1994-97) Bar Associations.

Instructor in Advanced Program 1986, Basic Program 1987 and Motions Program 1990-91 National Institute for Trial Advocacy. Presenter "Insurance Coverage Issues in Environmental Litigation" Dartmouth Lawyers Association March 31, 1990; "Comprehensive General Liability Insurance Litigation in the 1990's" Mid-Year Meeting Section of Litigation April 7, 1990, "Handling Environmental Insurance Coverage Issues" Spring Meeting Section of Business Law April 10, 1992, "Sunscreen for Trial Lawyers: Mock Try Your Case and Don't Get Burned" Annual Mid-Year Meeting Section of Litigation Feb 1998 and "The Mock Trial as a Settlement Mechanism and Trial Preparation Tool—A Live Demonstration and Soup-to-Nuts Guide" Annual Convention Section of Litigation April 1998 American Bar Association; "Rebuttal Summation on Damages Issues in Commercial and Business Tort Litigation" Advanced Seminar The Association of Trial Lawyers of America Aug 16, 1990; "Insurance Coverage for Environmental Damage: The Law and the Practice" Convention Wyoming State Bar Sept 6, 1990; "Practical Aspects of 'Insurance Coverage' Cases in Environmental Law/Toxic Tort Litigation" Environmental and Toxic Torts Seminar Feb 8, 1991 and "The Basics of Insurance Claims for Environmental Losses" Seminar Nov 20, 1992 Colorado Trial Lawyers Association; "Insurance Coverage for Environmental Claims—Legal and Practical Issues" Annual Meeting Idaho State Bar July 23, 1992; "Insurance Coverage Litigation Update" Annual Convention Colorado Trial Lawyers Association and Kansas Trial Lawyers Association Aug 12, 1994; and "Taming the Dragon: Management of the Legal Team in Complex Cases" Annual Convention Colorado Bar Association Aug 9, 1997. Listed in *The Best Lawyers in America* and *Who's Who in American Law.*

Office: 100 Jefferson County Parkway, Golden 80401-6002.
Telephone: (303) 271-6160.
Fax: (303) 271-6114
E-mail address: rbrooke.jackson@judicial.state.co.us

JAMES, Mary Lynne *(Judge, Moffat County Court)* Appointed by Governor Richard D. Lamm to term beginning Oct 1, 1984. Retained by election 1986, 1990, 1994, 1998 and 2002. Current term expires Jan 2007. Born Cambridge Nebraska 1948. Protestant. Educated at University of Nebraska B.A. 1970 M.A. 1972 J.D. cum laude 1976. Assistant Editor University of Nebraska Law Review 1975-76. Law Clerk to Hon. Hale McCown, Nebraska Supreme Court 1976-77. Member Phi Beta Kappa. Admitted to practice Nebraska 1976, Colorado 1977 and U.S. District Courts District of Nebraska 1976 and District of Colorado 1977. In legal practice Craig Colorado 1977-84.

Author "Taxation: Disclaimer or Renunciation Under Nebraska Statutes" 55 No. 3 Nebraska L. Rev. 1976. Member Colorado County Judges Association, Colorado and Nebraska State Bar Associations.

Office: Moffat County Courthouse, 221 West Victory Way, Craig 81625.
Telephone: (970) 824-8254.

JAUCH, Richard Morgan *(Judge, Arapahoe County Court)* Court Referee 1982-85. Appointed Judge by Governor Richard D. Lamm to term beginning Oct 1, 1985. Retained by election. Current term expires Jan 2005. Born Indianapolis Indiana Oct 2, 1942. Educated at Lake Forest College B.A. 1966 and University of Denver J.D. 1975. Admitted to practice Colorado 1976. In legal practice Littleton 1979-81.

District Attorney Arapahoe County 1981-82. Instructor Arapahoe Community College 1985-86 and 1993. Attended The National Judicial College July 1986, Oct 1988, Nov 1992 and March 1999. E-4 U.S. Army 1963-64. Employed by U.S. Gypsum Company 1966-67. Teacher Englewood High School 1969-79. Involved with Colorado Special Olympics.

Office: 1790 West Littleton Boulevard, Littleton 80120.
Telephone: (303) 798-0270.
E-mail address: richard.jauch@judicial.state.co.us

JORDAN, Claudia J. *(Judge, Denver County Court)* Office: 108 City and County Building, 1437 Bannock Street, Denver 80202.
Telephone: (720) 640-3478.

KANE, John Lawrence, Jr. *(Senior Judge, United States District Court District of Colorado)* Appointed for life by President Jimmy Carter to term beginning Jan 3, 1978. Assumed Senior status April 8, 1988, serves by assignment. Born Tucumcari New Mexico Feb 14, 1937. Catholic. Educated at University of Colorado B.A. 1958 and University of Denver J.D. 1960. Honorary LL.D. University of Denver 1997. Editor-in-Chief University of Denver Law Journal 1959. First place Kingsley All-University Oratorical Contest 1959 and Pattison Law Oratorical Contest 1960. Member Phi Delta Phi. Admitted to practice Colorado 1961, U.S. District Court District of Colorado 1961, U.S. Court of Appeals Tenth Circuit 1962, U.S. Supreme Court 1966 and U.S. Tax Court 1974. Began legal practice Brighton 1961. In legal practice Denver 1964 and 1969-77.

Deputy District Attorney Adams County 1961-62. Public Defender Adams County 1964-67. Deputy Director Peace Corps Calcutta India 1967-69. Author "Legal Ethics and Competence in Trial Practice" ABA Jour. Aug 1976, reprinted in Catholic Mind Jan 1977, "Peeling the English Onion" Colorado Lawyer Sept 1975, reprinted in 10 International Society of Barristers Quarterly 4, Oct 1975, "The Risk of Non-Persuasion" Litigation Fall 1978 and "Small Cases" Litigation Spring 1984. Important Decisions: Trujillo v. Heckler (social security) 569 F.Supp. 631, Ramos v. Lamm (prison conditions) 539 F.Supp. 730, Williams v. Burns (defamation) 540 F.Supp. 1243 and De La Llana Castellon v. INS (immigration) 16 F.3d 1093, 10th Cir. 1994. Adjunct Professor of Law 1978-88, Miller Distinguished Visiting Professor of Law 1991 and Silverstein Distinguished Adjunct Professor of Law 1994 University of Denver. Visiting Lecturer on Law Trinity College, Dublin Ireland 1989. Adjunct Professor University of Colorado School of Law 1996-97. Fellow International Society of Barristers 1974-78 and International Academy of Trial Lawyers since 1975. Honorary Life Member American Board of Trial

KANE, JOHN LAWRENCE, JR.—*Continued*

Advocates 1988. Member Tenth Circuit Judicial Council 1986-87, American Judicature Society since 1978, Catholic Lawyers Guild (Vice President 1977), Colorado (Chairman Legal Education and Admissions to Bar 1974-76, Long Range Planning Committee 1977) and American (Council Section of Criminal Law 1967, Chairman Long Range Planning Committee Section of Litigation 1974-77) Bar Associations. Recipient St. Thomas More Award for Outstanding Contributions to the Law, Religion and Country from Catholic Lawyers Guild of Colorado 1983, Award of Merit from U.S. Information Agency 1985, Evans Award for Distinguished Service from University of Denver 1986, Lifetime Judicial Achievement Award National Association of Criminal Defense Attorneys 1987, B'nai B'rith Annual Civil Rights Award 1988. Enjoys vocal music (choir, opera, study), hiking, cooking, theatre, poetry and sports.

Office: U.S. Courthouse, 901 Nineteenth Street, Denver 80294-3589.

Telephone: (303) 844-6118.

KANE, Thomas Kelly *(Judge, Colorado District Court Fourth Judicial District)* Appointed by Governor Roy Romer to term beginning Sept 9, 1994. Retained by election Nov 1996 and 2002. Current term expires Jan 2009. Born Colorado Springs Colorado Jan 9, 1952. Catholic. Educated at University of Colorado B.A. with honors 1974 J.D. 1977. Admitted to practice Colorado 1977 and U.S. Court of Appeals Tenth Circuit 1977. In legal practice Colorado Springs 1977-94.

Member El Paso County Bar Association.

Mailing address: P.O. Box 2980, Colorado Springs 80901-2980.

Office: 20 East Vermijo, Colorado Springs 80903.

Telephone: (719) 448-7508.

KAPELKE, Robert J. *(Judge, Colorado Court of Appeals)* Appointed by Governor Roy Romer to term beginning Jan 4, 1994. Retained by election. Born Aug 26, 1941. Educated at University of Colorado B.A. 1963 J.D. 1966 and University of Chicago M.C.L. 1969. Law Clerk to Hon. Alfred A. Arraj, U.S. District Court District of Colorado 1966-67. Admitted to practice Colorado 1966. In legal practice 1969-93.

Office: Colorado State Judicial Building, Two East Fourteenth Avenue, Denver 80203.

Telephone: (303) 837-3715.

KAROWSKY, Lynn J. *(Judge, Weld County Court)* Magistrate 1981-96. Appointed Judge by Governor Roy Romer to term beginning Aug 1, 1996. Retained by election. Born Greeley Colorado 1949. Jewish. Educated at Stanford University B.A. and University of Colorado J.D. 1974. Admitted to practice Colorado 1974 and U.S. District Court District of Colorado 1974. In legal practice Greeley 1974-80.

Assistant Professor of Law College of Business Administration University of Northern Colorado 1981-96. President Weld County Bar Association 1997-98. Treasurer Greeley Philharmonic Orchestra.

Mailing address: P.O. Box 2038, Greeley 80632.

Office: Weld County Courthouse, 901 Ninth Avenue, Greeley 80631.

Telephone: (970) 351-7300.

KAUP, Daniel J. *(Judge, Colorado District Court Eighth Judicial District and Judge, Colorado Water Court Division Six)* Appointed to District Court by Governor Bill Owens. Appointed to Water Court by Chief Justice.

District Court office: 100 Larimer County Justice Center, 201 La Porte Avenue, Fort Collins 80521-2761.

Telephone: (970) 498-6239.

Water Court mailing address: P.O. Box 773117, Steamboat Springs 80477.

Office: Routt County Courthouse, 522 Lincoln Avenue, Steamboat Springs 80477.

Telephone: (970) 879-5020.

KELLY, James P. *(Judge, Colorado District Court Fourth Judicial District)* Appointed by Governor Bill Owens.

Mailing address: P.O. Box 2980, Colorado Springs 80901-2980.

Office: 20 East Vermijo, Colorado Springs 80903.

Telephone: (719) 448-7599.

KENNEDY, Thomas L. *(Judge, Colorado District Court Fourth Judicial District)* Appointed by governor.

Mailing address: P.O. Box 2980, Colorado Springs 80901-2980.

Office: 20 East Vermijo, Colorado Springs 80903.

Telephone: (719) 227-5192.

KING, Paul A. *(Judge, Colorado District Court Eighteenth Judicial District)* Appointed by Governor Bill Owens.

Office: 2009 Douglas County Justice Center, 4000 Justice Way, Castle Rock 80104.

Telephone: (303) 663-7215.

KLEIN, Roger A. *(Chief Judge, Colorado District Court Nineteenth Judicial District and Judge, Colorado Water Court Division One)* Appointed to District Court by Governor Roy Romer June 29, 1995 to term beginning Aug 21, 1995. Retained by election Nov 1998, current term expires Jan 2005. Appointed to Water Court by Chief Justice. Born Cleveland Ohio Dec 5, 1941. Educated at Allegheny College B.A. 1964 and University of Colorado School of Law J.D. 1967. Admitted to practice Colorado 1967 and U.S. District Court District of Colorado 1976. In legal practice Greeley 1974-95.

Deputy Public Defender State of Colorado 1970-74. Member Weld County and Colorado Bar Associations.

Mailing address: P.O. Box 2038, Greeley 80632.

Office: Weld County Courthouse, 901 Ninth Avenue, Greeley 80631.

Telephone: (970) 351-7300.

KOCHENBURGER, John E. *(Judge, Larimer County Court)* Appointed by Governor Richard D. Lamm to term beginning June 1984. Retained by election Nov 1986, Nov 1990, Nov 1994, Nov 1998 and 2002. Current term expires Jan 2007. Born Greeley Colorado Feb 14, 1931. Protestant. Educated at University of Colorado B.S. 1955 LL.B. 1955. Admitted to practice Colorado 1955 and U.S. District Court District of Colorado 1955. In legal practice Fort Morgan 1957-58 and Fort Collins 1958-83. Assistant Judge, Fort Collins Municipal Court 1969-80.

Member Colorado and American Bar Associations. Corporal U.S. Army. Member Lions Club.

Office: 110 Loveland Police and Courts Building, 810 East Tenth Street, Loveland 80537-4942.

Telephone: (970) 679-4418.

KOLOMITZ, M. Jon *(Chief Judge, Colorado District Court Sixteenth Judicial District)* Appointed by Governor Richard D. Lamm to term beginning Feb 1985. Retained by election Nov 1988, Nov 1994 and Nov 2000. Current term expires Jan 2007. Born La Junta Colorado February 3, 1941. Catholic. Educated at University of Colorado B.S. 1963 J.D. 1966. Member Phi Delta Phi. Admitted to practice Colorado 1966 and U.S. District Court District of Colorado 1966. In legal practice La Junta 1969-85. Judge, La Junta Municipal Court 1974-85.

Member and President La Junta School Board 1976-85. Member Colorado Bar Association. F.B.I. 1966-69. Member Boy Scouts. Enjoys railroads, gardening and collecting.

Office: 207 Otero County Courthouse, 13 West Third Street, La Junta 81050.

Telephone: (719) 384-4981.

KOURLIS, Rebecca Love *(Justice, Colorado Supreme Court)* Appointed by Governor Roy Romer to term beginning July 17, 1995. Retained by election Nov 1998, current term expires Jan 2009. Born Nov 11, 1952. Educated at Stanford University B.A. with distinction 1973 J.D. 1976. Honorary LL.D. University of Denver College of Law 1997. Admitted to practice Colorado, U.S. Court of Federal Claims, U.S. District Court District of Colorado, U.S. Courts of Appeal Tenth and District of Columbia Circuits and U.S. Supreme Court. In legal practice Craig 1978-87. Judge 1987-94 and Chief Judge 1991-94 Colorado District Court Fourteenth Judicial District. Judge, Colorado Water Court Division Six 1987-94.

Editorial Board Public Land Law Review 1990-94. Board of Trustees Rocky Mountain Mineral Law Foundation 1990-92. Member Committee on Civil Jury Instructions 1990-95, Gender Bias Task Force and Standing Committee on Gender and Justice 1990-97 and Committee on Administrative Restructure 1992, Chair Standing Committee on Jury Reform since 1996, Judicial Advisory Council 1997-2002 and Standing Committee on Families in the Courts since 2002 and Co-chair Advisory Committee on Attorney Regulation 1997-2002 Colorado Supreme Court. Member State Court Administrator Selection Committee 1992 and Colorado Judicial Institute Alternative Dispute Resolution Committee 1994. President District Court Judges Association 1993-94. Arbiter Judicial Arbiter Group, Inc. Aug 1994 to July 1995. Former Member The American Law Institute. Fellow Colorado Bar Foundation and American Bar Foundation. Member Colorado Bar Association (Board of Governors 1983-85, Board of Directors Mineral Law Section 1985, Senior Vice President 1987-88). Named Woman of the Year by Northwest Colorado Daily Press 1993. Recipient President's Awards for Community Service Teen Court 1993 and Domestic Procedures Revisions 1994 from Northwestern Colorado Bar Association, Trailblazer Award from American Association of University Women 1998, Mary Lathrop Award from Colorado Women's Bar Association 2001 and Judicial Excellence Award from Academy of Matrimonial Lawyers 2002. Member Colorado Commission on Higher Education 1980-81 and Long Range Planning Committee Moffat County School District 1990. Advisory Board Northwest Colorado Community College 1986-88 and Education for the Gifted and Talented State of Colorado 1992-93. Board Member Moffat County Learning Resource Center 1987 and Moffat County Teen Court 1992-94. Board of Visitors Stanford University Law School 1989-94 and University of Denver College of Law 1995-2002. Board of Trustees Kent Denver School 1996-2002.

Office: Colorado State Judicial Building, Two East Fourteenth Avenue, Denver 80203.

Telephone: (303) 861-1111.

KRIEGER, Marcia S. *(Judge, United States District Court District of Colorado)* Appointed for life by President George W. Bush to term beginning March 1, 2002. Judge 1994-2000 and Chief Judge Jan 5, 2000 to 2002, U.S. Bankruptcy Court District of Colorado, appointed by U.S. Court of Appeals Tenth Circuit judges.

Office: U.S. Courthouse, 901 Nineteenth Street, Denver 80294-3589.

Telephone: (303) 335-2289.

KUENHOLD, O. John *(Chief Judge, Colorado District Court Twelfth Judicial District and Judge, Colorado Water Court Division Three)* Appointed to District Court by Governor Richard D. Lamm to term beginning Feb 3, 1981. Retained by election. Current term expires Jan 2007. Appointed to Water Court by Chief Justice. Born Cleveland Ohio June 26, 1944. Protestant. Educated at Colgate University B.A. 1966 and University of Michigan J.D. 1969. Admitted to practice Colorado 1969, U.S. District Court District of Colorado and U.S. Court of Appeals Tenth Circuit. Began legal practice Alamosa 1969.

Member San Luis Valley and Colorado Bar Associations. Enjoys skiing, cycling and flying.

Office: Alamosa County Courthouse, 702 Fourth Street, Alamosa 81101.

Telephone: (719) 589-4996.

LASS, David Richard *(Judge, Colorado District Court Fifth Judicial District)* Appointed by Governor Roy Romer to term beginning Oct 31, 1996. Retained by election Nov 1998, current term expires Jan 2005. Born Evanston Illinois June 26, 1943. Lutheran. Educated at Valparaiso University B.A. 1965 and Wayne State University J.D. 1968. Admitted to practice Colorado 1968. In legal practice Breckenridge 1973-86. Judge, Frisco Municipal Court 1984-96. Judge, Summit County Court, Jan 3, 1986 to Oct 30, 1996, appointed by Governor Richard D. Lamm.

Attorney Denver Legal Aid Society 1968-73. Town Attorney Blue River 1976-77. Deputy District Attorney 1977. Prosecuting Attorney Frisco 1977-84. Co-author *D.U.I. Benchbook* for Colorado judges Sept 1990. Officer Colorado County Judges Association (Secretary 1991-92, Treasurer 1992-93, Vice President 1993-94, President 1994-95). Member Continental Divide (former Secretary-Treasurer, Vice President and President) and Colorado (Board of Governors 1981-82) Bar Associations. Enjoys travel, photography and outdoor sports.

Mailing address: P.O. Box 269, Breckenridge 80424.

Office: Summit County Justice Center, 501 North Park Avenue, Breckenridge 80424.

Telephone: (970) 453-2241.

Eagle telephone: (970) 328-6373.

LEH, James R. *(Judge, Colorado District Court Thirteenth Judicial District)* Appointed by Governor Richard D. Lamm to term beginning Jan 3, 1978. Retained by election, current term expires Jan 2005. Former Chief Judge. Born Sterling Colorado Oct 12, 1935. Presbyterian. Educated at Princeton University A.B. cum

LEH, JAMES R.—*Continued*

laude 1957 and Yale University LL.B. 1960. Admitted to practice Colorado 1961. Began legal practice Sterling 1961.

Attorney 1963-68 and Commissioner 1973-78 Logan County. Member Thirteenth Judicial District and Colorado (Board of Governors 1974-77) Bar Associations. Recipient Sterling Citizen of the Year Award 1972 and Jacob V. Schaetzel Award honoring outstanding dedication in the delivery of legal services to the poor from Colorado Bar Association 1999. E-5 Class U.S. Army and Colorado National Guard 1960-66. Enjoys reading, writing and long-distance running.

Mailing address: P.O. Box 71, Sterling 80751.

Office: Logan County Courthouse, Third and Ash, Sterling 80751.

Telephone: (970) 522-6565.

Fax: (970) 522-6566

LEOPOLD, John P. *(Chief Judge, Colorado District Court Eighteenth Judicial District)* Appointed by Governor Roy Romer to term beginning Sept 18, 1987. Retained by election 1990, 1996 and 2002. Current term expires Jan 2009. Born New York New York Sept 14, 1946. Congregationalist. Educated at Colby College B.A. 1968 and University of Denver J.D. 1974. Law Clerk to Hon. Saul Pinchick, Colorado District Court Second Judicial District 1973-74. Admitted to practice Colorado 1974, U.S. District Court District of Colorado 1974 and U.S. Court of Appeals Tenth Circuit 1976. In legal practice Littleton 1974-87. Associate Municipal Judge Littleton and Sheridan 1984-87.

Member Arapahoe County (President 1985-86) and Colorado (Board of Governors 1986-87) Bar Associations. Attended Advanced Evidence Course The National Judicial College July 1991. Panelist "Dealing with Hardball Trial Tactics and Difficult Judges" Professional Education Seminars, Inc. Dec 1992 and "Colorado's New Rules of Civil Procedure" Nov 1994. Attended National Mass Tort Conference, Cincinnati Ohio Nov 1994. Recipient Tommy D. Drinkwine Outstanding Young Lawyer Award from Arapahoe County Bar Association 1985. Sergeant USAF 1968-72. Recipient Air Medal with four oak leaf clusters. Member First Plymouth Congregational Church (Ministry of Christian Outreach 1992-93, Ministry of Worship and the Arts since 1995). Interests include symphony, opera, Major League Baseball and travel.

Office: Arapahoe County Justice Center, 7325 South Potomac Street, Englewood 80112.

Telephone: (303) 649-6302.

LOEB, Alan *(Judge, Colorado Court of Appeals)* Appointed by Governor Bill Owens May 7, 2003.

Office: Colorado State Judicial Building, Two East Fourteenth Avenue, Denver 80203.

Telephone: (303) 837-3785.

LOWENBACH, J. Robert *(Judge, Colorado District Court Nineteenth Judicial District)* Appointed by Governor Roy Romer.

Mailing address: P.O. Box 2038, Greeley 80632.

Office: Weld County Courthouse, 901 Ninth Avenue, Greeley 80631.

Telephone: (970) 351-7300.

LYMAN, Gregory G. *(Chief Judge, Colorado District Court Sixth Judicial District and Judge, Colorado Water Court Division Seven)* Appointed to District Court by Governor Roy Romer 1996. Retained by election. Appointed to Water Court by Chief Justice. Educated at University of Illinois and University of Colorado School of Law.

Mailing address: P.O. Box 3340, Durango 81302-3340.

Office: La Plata County Courthouse, 1060 Second Avenue, Durango 81301.

Telephone: (970) 247-2304.

MacDONALD, Diane R. *(Judge, Boulder County Court)* Appointed by governor.

Mailing address: P.O. Box 4249, Boulder 80306-4249.

Office: Boulder Justice Center, 1777 Sixth Street, Boulder 80302.

Telephone: (303) 441-3767.

MacDONNELL, Mark A. *(Judge, Bent County Court)* Appointed by governor.

Office: Bent County Courthouse, 725 Bent, Las Animas 81054.

Telephone: (719) 456-1353.

MACRUM, James F., Jr. *(Judge, Colorado District Court Eighteenth Judicial District)* Appointed by governor. Former Judge, Arapahoe County Court.

Office: Arapahoe County Justice Center, 7325 South Potomac Street, Englewood 80112.

Telephone: (303) 649-6292.

MAES, Dennis *(Chief Judge, Colorado District Court Tenth Judicial District and Judge, Colorado Water Court Division Two)* Appointed to District Court by Governor Roy Romer to term beginning April 15, 1988. Retained by election Nov 1990, Nov 1996 and 2002. Current term expires Jan 2009. Appointed to Water Court by Chief Justice. Educated at Southern Colorado State College B.S. 1967 and University of Colorado J.D. 1972. Admitted to practice Colorado 1972.

Office: Pueblo County Judicial Building, 320 West Tenth Street, Pueblo 81003.

Telephone: (719) 583-7011.

MANZANARES, Lawrence A. *(Judge, Colorado District Court Second Judicial District)* Appointed by Governor Roy Romer to term beginning Nov 1998. Retained by election Nov 2002, current term expires 2009. Born Colorado. Educated at University of Denver B.A. in Psychology magna cum laude 1979 and Harvard Law School J.D. 1982. Judge, Denver County Court 1991-98.

Office: 256 City and County Building, 1437 Bannock, Denver 80202.

Telephone: (720) 865-8306.

Fax: (720) 865-8582

MANZANARES, Sylvia A. *(Judge, El Paso County Court)* Appointed by Governor Roy Romer.

Mailing address: P.O. Box 2980, Colorado Springs 80901-2980.

Office: 20 East Vermijo, Colorado Springs 80903.

Telephone: (719) 448-7628.

MARCUCCI, John M. *(Judge, Denver County Court)*

Office: 108 City and County Building, 1437 Bannock Street, Denver 80202.

Telephone: (720) 865-9062.

MARKSON, Paul A., Jr. *(Judge, Colorado District Court Second Judicial District)* Appointed by governor.
Office: 256 City and County Building, 1437 Bannock, Denver 80202.
Telephone: (720) 865-9070.

MARQUEZ, Jose D. L. *(Judge, Colorado Court of Appeals)* Appointed by Governor Roy Romer to term beginning July 15, 1988. Retained by election 1990 and 1998. Current term expires Jan 2007. Born Las Mesitas Colorado Sept 24, 1941. Catholic. Educated at St. John's University B.A. cum laude 1964, University of Texas J.D. 1970 and University of Virginia School of Law LL.M. 2001. Admitted to practice Texas 1971, Colorado 1972 and U.S. District Courts Western District of Texas 1971 and District of Colorado 1972. In legal practice Grand Junction 1978-84. Judge, Colorado District Court Twenty-first Judicial District 1984-88.
Attorney Colorado Rural Legal Services, Inc. 1972-75. Regional Assistant Attorney General Department of Law Colorado 1975-77. Fellow Colorado Bar Foundation. Member Denver (Board of Trustees 1998-2001), Colorado Hispanic, Colorado (Board of Governors 1995-97) and American Bar Associations. Member Board of Continuing Legal Education. Captain USAF JAG 1966-72. Enjoys bicycling, golfing, fishing, hiking, camping, music and reading.
Office: Colorado State Judicial Building, Two East Fourteenth Avenue, Denver 80203.
Telephone: (303) 837-3786.

MARSHALL, Donald W., Jr. *(Judge, Colorado District Court Seventeenth Judicial District)* Appointed by Governor Richard D. Lamm to term beginning Nov 1, 1986. Retained by election 1988, 1994 and 2000. Current term expires Jan 2007. Born Denver Colorado Sept 22, 1941. Methodist. Educated at University of Denver B.A. 1966 J.D. with honors 1972. Admitted to practice Colorado 1972, U.S. District Court District of Colorado 1972 and U.S. Court of Appeals Tenth Circuit 1982. In legal practice Brighton and Westminster 1973-86. Part-time Judge, Thornton Municipal Court 1976-86.
Office: Adams County Justice Center, 1100 Judicial Center Drive, Brighton 80601.
Telephone: (303) 654-3250.

MARSHALL, Julie G. *(Judge, Colorado District Court Eleventh Judicial District)* Appointed by governor.
Office: 136 Justice Center Road, Room 103, Canon City 81212.
Telephone: (719) 269-0116.

MARTIN, Lawrence D. *(Judge, El Paso County Court)* Appointed by Governor Roy Romer to term beginning Sept 16, 1996. Retained by election.
Mailing address: P.O. Box 2980, Colorado Springs 80901-2980.
Office: 20 East Vermijo, Colorado Springs 80903.
Telephone: (719) 448-7616.

MARTINEZ, Alex Joseph *(Justice, Colorado Supreme Court)* Appointed by Governor Roy Romer to term beginning Jan 14, 1997. Retained by election 1998, current term expires Jan 2009. First Native Colorado Hispanic to serve on Colorado Supreme Court. Born Denver Colorado April 19, 1951. Educated at Reed College 1969-72 and University of Colorado B.A. 1973 J.D. 1976. Danielson Scholar for High Promise of Effective Community Service University of Colorado School of Law. Admitted to practice Colorado 1976. Judge, Pueblo County Court Feb 3, 1983 to Aug 25, 1988, appointed by Governor Richard D. Lamm. Judge, Colorado District Court Tenth Judicial District Aug 26, 1988 to Jan 13, 1997, appointed by Governor Roy Romer.
Public Defender Denver 1976-79. Chief Public Defender Pueblo 1979-83. Member Colorado Criminal Justice Commission 1985-88. Member Colorado District Judges Association, Juvenile Court Judges Association, Pueblo Hispanic, Pueblo, Colorado Hispanic and Colorado Bar Associations. Attended The National Judicial College 1984 and 1990.
Office: Colorado State Judicial Building, Two East Fourteenth Avenue, Denver 80203.
Telephone: (303) 861-1111.

MARTINEZ, Frank *(Judge, Colorado District Court Second Judicial District)* Appointed by governor.
Office: 256 City and County Building, 1437 Bannock, Denver 80202.
Telephone: (720) 865-8614.

MARTINEZ, Gilbert A. *(Chief Judge, Colorado District Court Fourth Judicial District)* Appointed by Governor Roy Romer to term beginning Dec 14, 1989. Retained by election Nov 1992 and Nov 1998. Current term expires Jan 2005. Born Trinidad Colorado May 19, 1951. Catholic. Educated at University of Colorado B.A. 1973 J.D. 1977. Admitted to practice Colorado 1978 and U.S. District Court District of Colorado 1978.
Public Defender Colorado Springs 1986-89. Member Colorado Hispanic (Board of Directors since 1989) and Colorado Bar Associations.
Mailing address: P.O. Box 2980, Colorado Springs 80901-2980.
Office: 20 East Vermijo, Colorado Springs 80903.
Telephone: (719) 448-7536.

MARTINEZ, Michael A. *(Judge, Colorado District Court Second Judicial District)* Magistrate Seventeenth Judicial District April 1996 to Sept 2000. Appointed Judge by Governor Bill Owens Sept 15, 2000 to term beginning Nov 2000. Term expires Jan 2005. Educated at University of Colorado B.A. 1983 and University of Denver College of Law J.D. 1986. Admitted to practice Colorado 1987, U.S. District Court District of Colorado 1987, U.S. Court of Appeals Tenth Circuit 1987 and District of Columbia 1989. In legal practice Denver 1987 and 1991-92.
Assistant City Attorney Denver 1987-91. Associate General Counsel Regional Transportation District Denver 1992-96. Faculty National Institute for Trial Advocacy since 1992. Instructor "Training Advocates to Represent Whole Child" American Bar Association-National Institute for Trial Advocacy Oct 2002. Member Rocky Mountain Children's Advocacy Clinic since 1999.
Office: 256 City and County Building, 1437 Bannock, Denver 80202.
Telephone: (720) 865-8308.
Fax: (720) 865-8582
E-mail address: michaela.martinez@judicial.state.co.us

MASSARO, Nicholas R., Jr. *(Judge, Colorado District Court Twenty-first Judicial District)* Appointed by governor.
Mailing address: P.O. Box 20000, Grand Junction 81502-5030.

MASSARO, NICHOLAS R., JR.—*Continued*
Office: Mesa County Justice Center, 125 North Spruce, Grand Junction 81501.
Telephone: (970) 257-3637.

MATSCH, Richard P. *(Judge, United States District Court District of Colorado)* Appointed for life by President Richard M. Nixon to term beginning 1974. Chief Judge 1994-2000. Born Burlington Iowa June 8, 1930. Educated at University of Michigan A.B. 1951 J.D. 1953. Judge, United States Bankruptcy Court District of Colorado 1965-74.
Assistant U.S. Attorney District of Colorado 1959-61. Deputy City Attorney City and County of Denver 1961-63.
Office: 207 U.S. Courthouse, 1823 Stout Street, Denver 80257.
Telephone: (303) 844-4627.

MAUS, Daniel S. *(Judge, Colorado District Court Nineteenth Judicial District)* Appointed by Governor Bill Owens October 1, 2002.
Mailing address: P.O. Box 2038, Greeley 80632.
Office: Weld County Courthouse, 901 Ninth Avenue, Greeley 80631.
Telephone: (970) 351-7300.

MAYHEW, Stanley J. *(Judge, Park County Court)* Appointed by governor.
Mailing address: P.O. Box 190, Fairplay 80440.
Office: Park County Courthouse, 300 Fourth Street, Fairplay 80440.
Telephone: (719) 836-2940.

McGAHEY, Robert L., Jr. *(Judge, Colorado District Court Second Judicial District)* Appointed by governor.
Office: 256 City and County Building, 1437 Bannock, Denver 80202.
Telephone: (720) 865-8302.

McLIMANS, Paul R. *(Judge, Colorado District Court Fourteenth Judicial District)* Appointed by Governor Bill Owens to term beginning Jan 3, 2003. Educated at University of Wisconsin.
Office: 300 Moffat County Courthouse, 221 West Victory Way, Craig 81625.
Telephone: (970) 448-7532.

McMULLEN, John N. *(Judge, Colorado District Court Second Judicial District)* Appointed by governor. Former Chief Judge.
Office: 256 City and County Building, 1437 Bannock, Denver 80202.
Telephone: (720) 865-8303.

MEISSNER-CUTLER, Susanna *(Judge, Douglas County Court)* Appointed by Governor Roy Romer. Retained by election.
Office: 2009 Douglas County Justice Center, 4000 Justice Way, Castle Rock 80104.
Telephone: (303) 663-7234.

MELONAKIS, Chris *(Judge, Colorado District Court Seventeenth Judicial District)* Appointed by governor.
Office: Adams County Justice Center, 1100 Judicial Center Drive, Brighton 80601.
Telephone: (303) 654-3290.

MEYER, Joseph E., III *(Judge, Colorado District Court Second Judicial District)* Appointed by Governor Roy Romer to term beginning Jan 15, 1997. Retained by election. Educated at Williams College B.A. and Harvard Law School J.D.
Member Denver, Colorado and American Bar Associations.
Office: 256 City and County Building, 1437 Bannock, Denver 80202.
Telephone: (720) 865-8743.

MICHEL, John J. *(Judge, Montrose County Court)* Appointed by Governor Bill Owens.
Office: Montrose County Justice Center, 1200 North Grand Avenue Bin A, Montrose 81401-3146.
Telephone: (970) 252-4310.

MILLER, G. David *(Judge, Colorado District Court Fourth Judicial District)* Appointed by Governor Bill Owens.
Mailing address: P.O. Box 2980, Colorado Springs 80901-2980.
Office: 20 East Vermijo, Colorado Springs 80903.
Telephone: (719) 448-7532.

MILLER, James S. *(Judge, Douglas County Court)* Appointed by governor.
Office: 2009 Douglas County Justice Center, 4000 Justice Way, Castle Rock 80104.
Telephone: (303) 663-7230.

MILLER, Sandra K. *(Judge, Delta County Court)* Appointed by Governor Bill Owens.
Office: 338 Delta County Courthouse, 501 Palmer Street, Delta 81416.
Telephone: (970) 874-6289.

MILLER, Walker D. *(Judge, United States District Court District of Colorado)* Appointed for life by President Bill Clinton April 1996 to term beginning October 1996. Educated at University of Colorado LL.B. 1963, University of Freiburg, Germany 1964-65 and University of Chicago M.C.L. 1965. Ford Foundation Fellow. Case Note Editor University of Colorado Law Review. Member Order of the Coif. In legal practice Greeley 1965-66 and 1969-96.
Assistant Professor of Law University of Kansas School of Law 1966-69. Member Colorado Rural Electric Attorneys, Colorado Bar Foundation, American Judicature Society, Weld County (Vice President 1978-79, President 1979-80), Colorado (Board of Governors 1988-92, Vice President 1993-94, Executive Committee 1993-94) and American Bar Associations. Recipient Award for Outstanding Practitioner from University of Colorado School of Law 1996. Member Law School Dean Selection Committee University of Kansas 1968 and University of Colorado 1973-74. Member 1977-81 and 1990-95 and President 1994 University of Colorado Alumni Board.
Office: 938 U.S. Courthouse, 901 Nineteenth Street, Denver 80294.
Telephone: (303) 844-2468.

MINOT, Martha T. *(Judge, La Plata County Court)* Appointed by Governor Roy Romer to term beginning 1995. Retained by election.
Mailing address: P.O. Box 759, Durango 81302.
Office: La Plata County Courthouse, 1060 Second Avenue, Durango 81301.
Telephone: (970) 247-2004.

MONTGOMERY, Lael E. *(Judge, Colorado District Court Twentieth Judicial District)* Appointed by Governor Bill Owens. Educated at University of Colorado B.A. J.D. Former Judge, Boulder County Court, appointed by Governor Roy Romer to term beginning Jan 14, 1997.

Deputy District Attorney Twentieth Judicial District. Member Committee on Gender and Justice Supreme Court. Member Boulder Women's, Colorado Women's, Boulder and Colorado Bar Associations.

Mailing address: P.O. Box 4249, Boulder 80306-4249.

Office: Boulder Justice Center, 1777 Sixth Street, Boulder 80302.

Telephone: (303) 441-1776.

MOORHEAD, R. Thomas *(Judge, Colorado District Court Fifth Judicial District)* Appointed by Governor Bill Owens.

Mailing address: P.O. Box 597, Eagle 81631.

Office: Eagle County Justice Center, 885 Chambers Avenue, Eagle 81631.

Telephone: (970) 328-6373.

MULLARKEY, Mary J. *(Chief Justice, Colorado Supreme Court)* Appointed by Governor Roy Romer to term beginning June 29, 1987. Retained by election 1990 and 2000. Current term expires Jan 2011. Chief Justice since Aug 1, 1998. Born New London Wisconsin Sept 28, 1943. Catholic. Educated at St. Norbert College B.A. cum laude 1965 and Harvard Law School LL.B. 1968. Awarded Honorary Doctor of Laws Degree St. Norbert College 1989. Admitted to practice Wisconsin 1968, U.S. Supreme Court 1972, Colorado 1974, U.S. District Courts Eastern District of Wisconsin 1974 and District of Colorado 1974 and U.S. Court of Appeals Tenth Circuit 1975. In legal practice Denver 1985-87.

Attorney-Advisor Office of the Solicitor U.S. Department of the Interior 1968-73. Assistant Regional Attorney Equal Employment Opportunity Commission 1973-75. First Assistant Attorney General Appellate Section 1975-79 and Solicitor General 1979-82 Department of Law Colorado. Legal Advisor to Governor Richard D. Lamm 1982-85. Member Colorado Bar Foundation, American Bar Foundation, Thompson G. Marsh Inn of Court, Colorado Women's, Denver, Colorado and American Bar Associations. Recipient Alumni Award for Distinguished Achievement in the Humanities from St. Norbert College 1980 and Recognition Award from Colorado Women's Bar Association 1986.

Office: Colorado State Judicial Building, Two East Fourteenth Avenue, Denver 80203.

Telephone: (303) 861-1111.

MULLINS, R. Michael *(Judge, Colorado District Court Second Judicial District)* Appointed by governor.

Office: 256 City and County Building, 1437 Bannock, Denver 80202.

Telephone: (720) 865-8615.

MUNCH, Christopher J. *(Judge, Colorado District Court First Judicial District)* Appointed by governor.

Office: 100 Jefferson County Parkway, Golden 80401-6002.

Telephone: (303) 271-6170.

Fax: (303) 271-6124

MUNSINGER, Stephen M. *(Judge, Colorado District Court First Judicial District)* Appointed by Governor Bill Owens.

Office: 100 Jefferson County Parkway, Golden 80401-6002.

Telephone: (303) 271-6460.

MURRAY, Dana Elizabeth *(Judge, Arapahoe County Court)* County Court Magistrate 1989-92. Appointed Judge by Governor Roy Romer to term beginning Oct 16, 1992. Retained by election Nov 6, 1994, Nov 1998 and Nov 2002. Current term expires Jan 2007. Born Denver Colorado Dec 6, 1958. Catholic. Educated at Colorado College B.A. 1981 and University of Denver J.D. 1986. Admitted to practice Colorado 1986 and U.S. District Court District of Colorado 1988.

Deputy District Attorney Eighteenth Judicial District 1986-89. Member Arapahoe County and Colorado Bar Associations. Recipient Tommy Drinkwine Outstanding Young Lawyer Award 1996. Enjoys outdoor sports, gardening and race walking.

Office: 15400 East 14th Place, #201, Aurora 80011.

Telephone: (303) 360-7854.

NAVES, Larry J. *(Judge, Colorado District Court Second Judicial District)* Appointed by governor.

Office: 256 City and County Building, 1437 Bannock, Denver 80202.

Telephone: (720) 865-8613.

NEWNAM, George A. *(Judge, Colorado District Court Third Judicial District)* Appointed by Governor Bill Owens. Former Judge, Las Animas County Court.

Office: 304 Las Animas County Courthouse, 200 East First Street, Trinidad 81082.

Telephone: (719) 846-3316.

NEWTON, Arnaud *(Judge, Colorado District Court Eighth Judicial District)* Appointed by Governor Richard D. Lamm Sept 8, 1982 to term beginning Jan 3, 1983. Retained by election, current term expires Jan 2005. Born Brush Colorado July 22, 1934. Episcopalian. Educated at Colorado State University B.S. 1956 and University of Denver J.D. 1964. Admitted to practice Colorado 1964. Began legal practice Fort Collins 1964.

Member Larimer County (President 1976) and Colorado Bar Associations. First Lieutenant U.S. Army 1957-59.

Office: 100 Larimer County Justice Center, 201 La Porte Avenue, Fort Collins 80521-2761.

Telephone: (970) 498-6218.

NEY, Peter H. *(Judge, Colorado Court of Appeals)* Appointed by Governor Roy Romer to term beginning April 20, 1988. Retained by election Nov 1990 and Nov 1998. Current term expires Jan 2007. Born Nuremberg Germany Nov 11, 1931. Educated at Philadelphia College of Art B.F.A. 1953 and University of Denver College of Law J.D. 1966. Member Order of St. Ives. Admitted to practice Colorado 1966, U.S. District Court District of Colorado 1966, U.S. Court of Appeals Tenth Circuit 1966 and U.S. Supreme Court. In legal practice Englewood 1966-78 and Littleton 1978-88.

Deputy District Attorney Arapahoe County 1967. City Attorney Sheridan 1968. Member Grievance Committee Colorado Supreme Court 1982-88. U.S. Army 1953-55. Board of Directors 1969-81 and Chairman 1972 Ameri-

NEY, PETER H.—*Continued*

can Civil Liberties Union Colorado. Board of Directors Town Hall Arts Center 1982-88 Littleton.
Office: Colorado State Judicial Building, Two East Fourteenth Avenue, Denver 80203.
Telephone: (303) 837-3725.

NICKELL, Bette R. *(Judge, Montrose County Court)* Appointed by governor. Currently serves as Associate Judge.
Mailing address: P.O. Box 78, Nucla 81424.
Office: Nucla County Courthouse, 320 Main, Nucla 81424.
Telephone: (970) 864-7373.

NIETO, Henry E. *(Judge, Colorado Court of Appeals)* Appointed by Governor Bill Owens Nov 23, 1999. Born July 13, 1939. Educated at St. Mary of the Plains College B.A. 1961 and University of Denver J.D. 1967. Judge, Jefferson County Court 1978-85. Judge 1985 to Dec 1999 and Chief Judge 1995-99, Colorado District Court First Judicial District.
Office: Colorado State Judicial Building, Two East Fourteenth Avenue, Denver 80203.
Telephone: (303) 837-3711.

NOBLE, Laurie A. *(Judge, Rio Blanco County Court)* Appointed by governor. Currently serves as Associate Judge.
Office: City and County Municipal Building, 209 East Main, Rangely 81648.
Telephone: (970) 675-2342.

NOTTINGHAM, Edward W. *(Judge, United States District Court District of Colorado)* Appointed for life by President George Bush to term beginning 1989. Born Denver Colorado Jan 9, 1948. Educated at Cornell University A.B. 1969 and University of Colorado School of Law J.D. 1972. Law Clerk to U.S. District Court District of Colorado 1972-73. In legal practice Denver 1973-76 and 1978-87 and Grand Junction 1987-89.
Assistant U.S. Attorney District of Colorado 1976-78.
Office: U.S. Courthouse, 901 Nineteenth Street, Denver 80294-3589.
Telephone: (303) 844-5018.

O'HARA, Michael A. *(Chief Judge, Colorado District Court Fourteenth Judicial District and Judge, Colorado Water Court Division Six)* Appointed to District Court by Governor Bill Owens. Appointed to Water Court by Chief Justice.
Mailing address: P.O. Box 773117, Steamboat Springs 80477.
Office: Routt County Courthouse, 522 Lincoln Avenue, Steamboat Springs 80477.
Telephone: (970) 879-5020.

OKAMOTO, Melvin *(Judge, Denver County Court)* Appointed by Mayor Wellington Webb. Educated at University of Wyoming B.S. 1969 J.D. 1975. Admitted to practice Colorado 1976 and California 1976. Magistrate, Denver Juvenile Court 1981-99.
Deputy District Attorney Weld County 1976-81.
Office: 108 City and County Building, 1437 Bannock Street, Denver 80202.
Telephone: (720) 865-7870.

OLSEN, Tina *(Judge, Jefferson County Court)* Appointed by Governor Roy Romer.
Office: 100 Jefferson County Parkway, Golden 80401-6002.
Telephone: (303) 271-6230.
Fax: (303) 271-6272

OLSON, Roy G., Jr. *(Judge, Jefferson County Court)* Appointed by governor.
Office: 100 Jefferson County Parkway, Golden 80401-6002.
Telephone: (303) 271-6104.
Fax: (303) 271-6272

ORTIZ-WHITE, Aleene *(Judge, Denver County Court)*
Office: 108 City and County Building, 1437 Bannock Street, Denver 80202.
Telephone: (720) 865-7930.

OSSOLA, Thomas W. *(Chief Judge, Colorado District Court Ninth Judicial District and Judge, Colorado Water Court Division Five)* Appointed to District Court by governor. Appointed to Water Court by Chief Justice. Former Judge, Garfield County Court.
Office: 104 Garfield County Courthouse, 109 Eighth Street, Glenwood Springs 81601-3303.
Telephone: (970) 947-3840.

PATRICK, J. Steven *(Chief Judge, Colorado District Court Seventh Judicial District and Judge, Colorado Water Court Division Four)* Appointed to District Court by Governor Roy Romer to term beginning Jan 1993. Retained by election Nov 1996 and 2002. Current term expires Jan 2009. Appointed to Water Court by Chief Justice. Born Des Moines Iowa Sept 15, 1953. Protestant. Educated at Simpson College B.A. summa cum laude 1974 and Yale Law School J.D. 1977. Admitted to practice Colorado 1977 and U.S. District Court District of Colorado 1977. In legal practice Denver 1977-79 and Gunnison 1981-91. Judge, Gunnison County Court 1991-93. Judge, Gunnison, Crested Butte and Mt. Crested Butte Municipal Courts 1991-93.
Deputy District Attorney Seventh Judicial District 1979-81. Fellow Colorado Bar Foundation. Member Seventh Judicial District and Colorado Bar Associations.
Office: Gunnison County Courthouse, 200 East Virginia Avenue, Gunnison 81230.
Telephone: (970) 641-3500.

PATTERSON, James S. *(Judge, El Paso County Court)* Appointed by Governor Roy Romer to term beginning Oct 11, 1991. Retained by election 1994, 1998 and 2002. Current term expires 2007. Born Dallas Texas July 14, 1949. Educated at University of Colorado B.A. 1971 and University of Arkansas J.D. 1974. Admitted to practice Colorado 1974 and U.S. District Court District of Colorado 1974. In legal practice Colorado Springs 1981-91. Former Judge, Colorado Springs Municipal Court.
Assistant District Attorney Fourth Judicial District 1974-81. Member El Paso County Bar and Colorado Bar Association.
Office: 20 East Vermijo, Colorado Springs 80903.
Telephone: (719) 448-7620.
E-mail address: James.Patterson@judicial.state.co.us

PATTERSON, Robert L. *(Judge, Denver County Court)* Appointed by Mayor Federico Peña to term beginning Aug 15, 1985. Retained by election Nov 1988,

PATTERSON, ROBERT L.—*Continued*

1992, 1996 and 2000. Current term expires Jan 2005. Born Detroit Michigan Aug 2, 1945. Baptist. Educated at Colorado State University B.S. 1968 and University of Colorado J.D. 1974. Recipient Martin Luther King, Jr. Graduate Fellowship 1969. Admitted to practice Colorado 1975, U.S. District Courts District of Colorado 1980 and Western District of Washington 1980 and U.S. Courts of Appeals Ninth 1981 and Tenth 1981 Circuits.

Staff Attorney Denver Legal Aid Society 1974-76. Deputy Public Defender Colorado 1976-80. Federal Assistant Public Defender Seattle Washington 1980-81. Assistant Attorney General Colorado 1981-85. Former Part-time Instructor Community College of Denver. Member Sam Cary, Loren Miller, Denver, Colorado and National (Judicial Council since 1986) Bar Associations. Attended National Conference of National Bar Association 1983, 1984, 1986 and 1990-2002 and Annual Colorado Judicial Conferences since 1985. Recipient Colorado Public Defender Achievement Award 1980, Certificate of Appreciation from Denver Bar Association 1986, Distinguished Service Award from Judicial Council National Bar Association 2001 and CTM from Toastmasters International 2002. Inducted into Clyburn Village Living Senior Hall of Fame 2001. Participant Adopt-a-School Law Day 1986. Coach youth soccer team Montbello Soccer Association for 13 seasons. Founding Director Black Education Program University of Colorado at Boulder. Former Assistant Director Project for Generating Opportunities Colorado State University. Member Manual High School Booster Club and Toastmasters International. Resource Person for Gifted and Talented Program Pomona High School. Interested in skiing, golf, Denver Broncos and Tai Chi Chuan martial arts.

Office: 108 City and County Building, 1437 Bannock Street, Denver 80202.

Telephone: (720) 865-8013.

PATTON, Wayne *(Judge, Lake County Court)* Appointed by Governor Bill Owens.

Mailing address: P.O. Box 55, Leadville 80461.

Office: Lake County Courthouse, Fifth and Harrison Avenue, Leadville 80461.

Telephone: (719) 486-0334.

PEARSON, Amanda K. *(Judge, Saguache County Court)* Appointed by Governor Roy Romer. Retained by election.

Office: Saguache County Courthouse, 4th and Christy, Saguache 81149.

Telephone: (719) 655-2522.

PELICAN, Steven T. *(Judge, Colorado District Court Fourth Judicial District)* Appointed by Governor Richard D. Lamm to term beginning Jan 1, 1986. Retained by election Nov 1988, 1994 and 2000. Current term expires Jan 2007. Born Los Angeles California Nov 20, 1945. Episcopalian. Educated at University of California at Santa Barbara B.A. 1967 and University of Colorado J.D. 1971. Law Clerk to Hon. Robert B. Lee, Colorado Supreme Court 1971-72. Admitted to practice Colorado 1972 and U.S. District Court District of Colorado 1972. In legal practice Colorado Springs 1972-85.

Deputy District Attorney Fourth Judicial District 1972-75. Member Colorado State Trial Judges Association, El Paso County and Colorado Bar Associations. Attended course on General Jurisdiction The National Judicial College 1988. Vice President Pikes Peak Branch Cystic Fibrosis Foundation.

Mailing address: P.O. Box 2980, Colorado Springs 80901-2980.

Office: 20 East Vermijo, Colorado Springs 80903.

Telephone: (719) 448-7520.

PENNY, J. Curt, Jr. *(Judge, Kit Carson County Court)* Appointed by governor.

Office: 301 Kit Carson County Courthouse, 251 Sixteenth Street, Burlington 80807.

Telephone: (719) 346-5524.

Fax: (719) 346-7805

PETERS, Jackson L., Jr. *(Judge, Teller County Court)* Appointed by governor.

Mailing address: P.O. Box 997, Cripple Creek 80813.

Office: Teller County Courthouse, 101 West Bennett Avenue, Cripple Creek 80813.

Telephone: (719) 689-2543.

PHELPS, C. Vincent, Jr. *(Judge, Colorado District Court Seventeenth Judicial District)* Appointed by Governor Roy Romer to term beginning Feb 15, 1996. Retained by election. Educated at Nebraska State University B.A. and University of Nebraska J.D. Admitted to practice Colorado, Nebraska, U.S. Court of Appeals Tenth Circuit and U.S. Supreme Court. Former Judge, Brighton Municipal Court.

Board of Directors Colorado Municipal Judges Association. Former President Brighton Economic Development Corporation. Former Vice President Bright Education Foundation.

Office: Adams County Justice Center, 1100 Judicial Center Drive, Brighton 80601.

Telephone: (303) 654-3249.

PHILLIPS, J. Stephen *(Judge, Colorado District Court Second Judicial District)* Appointed by Governor Richard D. Lamm to term beginning April 27, 1983. Retained by election. Former Chief Judge. Born Peoria Illinois Dec 4, 1942. Educated at University of Wyoming B.A. 1965 and University of Colorado J.D. 1968. Admitted to practice Colorado 1968, U.S. Court of Military Appeals 1969 and U.S. Supreme Court 1975. In legal practice Denver 1974-83.

Colorado Attorney General Denver 1974-82. U.S. Attorney General Denver 1982-83. Co-authored as committee member *Colorado Jury Instructions* West Publishing Co. 1983. Captain U.S. Army JAGC 1969-74.

Office: 256 City and County Building, 1437 Bannock, Denver 80202.

Telephone: (720) 865-8307.

PICCONE, Marsha *(Judge, Colorado Court of Appeals)* Appointed by Governor Bill Owens May 7, 2003.

Office: Colorado State Judicial Building, Two East Fourteenth Avenue, Denver 80203.

Telephone: (303) 837-3785.

PLAUT, Frank *(Judge, Colorado District Court First Judicial District)* Appointed by Governor Roy Romer to term beginning Jan 14, 1997. Retained by election. Educated at Northwestern University B.A. cum laude and Harvard Law School J.D. Member Phi Beta Kappa.

Fellow American College of Trial Lawyers. Member

PLAUT, FRANK—*Continued*

First Judicial District, Denver and Colorado (President 1987-88, Director Lend-a-Lawyer Inc.) Bar Associations.
Office: 100 Jefferson County Parkway, Golden 80401-6002.
Telephone: (303) 271-6150.
Fax: (303) 271-6114

PLEWE, Todd J. *(Judge, Montezuma County Court)* Appointed by Governor Bill Owens to term beginning 2002. Educated at University of Colorado School of Law J.D.
Office: Justice Building, 601 North Mildred Road, Cortez 81321-2995.
Telephone: (970) 565-7580.

PLOTZ, Kenneth M. *(Chief Judge, Colorado District Court Eleventh Judicial District)* Appointed by Governor Roy Romer Feb 1, 1989. Retained by election Nov 1992 and Nov 1998. Current term expires Jan 2005. Born Newark New Jersey April 13, 1948. Educated at University of Denver B.A. 1970 J.D. 1973. Admitted to practice Colorado 1973. In legal practice Leadville 1974-79.
Public Defender Salida 1979-89. Regional Director Colorado State Public Defender's Office 1979-89. Member Heart of the Rockies and Colorado Bar Associations. Enjoys triathlons and skiing.
Mailing address: P.O. Box 279, Salida 81201.
Office: Chaffee County Judicial Building, 142 Crestone Avenue, Salida 81201.
Telephone: (719) 539-2561.

POLIDORI, Ruthanne N. *(Judge, Colorado District Court First Judicial District)* Appointed by governor.
Office: 100 Jefferson County Parkway, Golden 80401-6002.
Telephone: (303) 271-6180.
Fax: (303) 271-6114

POPOVICH, John E., Jr. *(Judge, Colorado District Court Seventeenth Judicial District)* Appointed by governor.
Office: Adams County Justice Center, 1100 Judicial Center Drive, Brighton 80601.
Telephone: (303) 654-3280.

PORTER, W. Michael *(Judge, Baca County Court)* Appointed by governor.
Office: Baca County Courthouse, 741 Main Street, Springfield 81073.
Telephone: (719) 523-4555.

POST, Cheryl L. *(Judge, Colorado District Court Eighteenth Judicial District)* Appointed by Governor Roy Romer.
Office: Arapahoe County Justice Center, 7325 South Potomac Street, Englewood 80112.
Telephone: (303) 649-6282.

RAFFERTY, Gerald *(Judge, Colorado District Court Eighteenth Judicial District)* Appointed by Governor Bill Owens to term beginning 1999. Retained by election Nov 2002, current term expires Jan 13, 2009. Educated at U.S. Air Force Academy B.S. 1967 and John Marshall Law School J.D. with honors 1978. Admitted to practice Illinois 1978 and Colorado 1981.
Former Special Agent FBI. Assistant U.S. Attorney Chicago 1978-88 and Denver 1989-95. Former Deputy District Attorney Denver. Adjunct Professor University of Denver School of Law. USAF.
Office: Arapahoe County Justice Center, 7325 South Potomac Street, Englewood 80112.
Telephone: (303) 649-6252.
E-mail address: Gerald.Rafferty@judicial.state.co.us

RAPPAPORT, Sheila A. *(Judge, Colorado District Court Second Judicial District)* Appointed by Governor Bill Owens to term beginning July 17, 2000.
Office: 256 City and County Building, 1437 Bannock, Denver 80202.
Telephone: (720) 865-8602.

REED, Thomas Jefferson Boyd *(Judge, Boulder County Court)* Appointed by Governor Richard D. Lamm to term beginning June 10, 1985. Retained by election Nov 1988, 1992, 1996 and 2000. Current term expires Jan 2005. Born Mayfield Kentucky Feb 27, 1947. Educated at Vanderbilt University B.A. 1969 and University of Colorado J.D. 1972. Admitted to practice Colorado 1972. In legal practice Denver 1979-81 and Boulder 1981-85.
Graduate course on Limited Jurisdiction Courts The National Judicial College 1986. Democrat.
Mailing address: P.O. Box 4249, Boulder 80306-4249.
Office: Boulder Justice Center, 1777 Sixth Street, Boulder 80302.
Telephone: (303) 441-3768.

REYES, Victor I. *(Judge, Colorado District Court Tenth Judicial District)* Appointed by Governor Roy Romer Aug 26, 1998 to term beginning Jan 12, 1999. Born Athens Greece July 14, 1959. Catholic. Educated at Emory University B.A. 1981 and Georgetown University Law Center J.D. 1984. Admitted to practice Colorado 1984, U.S. District Court District of Colorado 1984, U.S. Court of Appeals Tenth Circuit 1990 and U.S. Supreme Court 1990. In legal practice Pueblo.
Deputy Public Defender. Instructor in Criminal Law University of Southern Colorado 1994-95 and Paralegal Courses Pueblo Community College since 1996. Member Colorado Judicial Conference Committee 1999-2001 and Criminal Rules Committee Colorado since 1999. Member National Council of Juvenile and Family Court Judges, Pueblo County Hispanic (President), Pueblo County and Colorado Bar Associations. Attended Fourth Judicial Conference Mexico City 1999 and Domestic Violence Conference Albuquerque New Mexico 1999. Faculty Member on Immigration Issues in Domestic Violence Cases The National Judicial College. Named Colorado Public Defender of the Year 1997. Board of Directors St. Therese Catholic School since 1999. Member Pueblo County Domestic Violence Task Force. Enjoys golf and racquetball.
Office: Pueblo County Judicial Building, 320 West Tenth Street, Pueblo 81003.
Telephone: (719) 583-7001.

RICE, Gudrun J. *(Magistrate Judge, United States District Court District of Colorado)* Appointed by U.S. District Court judges to term beginning Feb 7, 2001. Term expires Feb 6, 2005. Born 1943. Educated at Smith College B.A. 1965 and University of Denver J.D. cum laude 1973. In legal practice Grand Junction since 1984. District Court Referee and Juvenile Commissioner, Seventh Judicial District 1982-84.
Deputy District Attorney Seventh Judicial District 1977-81. Member Federal Magistrate Judges Association,

RICE, GUDRUN J.—*Continued*

Mesa County, Colorado Women's and Colorado Bar Associations. Volunteer Peace Corps Venezuela 1973-75. Trustee Mesa County Public Library District.
Mailing address: P.O. Box 3208, Grand Junction 81502.
Office: Federal Building & Courthouse, Room 310, 402 Rood Avenue, Grand Junction 81501.
Telephone: (970) 241-8932.
Fax: (970) 241-6214
E-mail address: Gudrun_J_Rice@cod.uscourts.gov

RICE, Juanita *(Judge, Colorado District Court Eighteenth Judicial District)* Appointed by Governor Bill Owens.
Office: Arapahoe County Justice Center, 7325 South Potomac Street, Englewood 80112.
Telephone: (303) 649-6212.

RICE, Nancy E. *(Justice, Colorado Supreme Court)* Appointed by Governor Roy Romer to term beginning Aug 31, 1998. Retained by election. Born Boulder Colorado June 2, 1950. Educated at Tufts University B.A. cum laude 1972 and University of Utah College of Law J.D. 1975. Editor-in-Chief University of Utah Journal of Contemporary Law. Law Clerk to Hon. Fred Winner, U.S. District Court District of Colorado 1975-76. Judge, Colorado District Court Second Judicial District 1987-98.
Deputy State Public Defender Appellate Division 1976-77. Assistant U.S. Attorney 1977-87 and Deputy Chief Civil Division 1985-87 U.S. Attorney's Office. Member Supreme Court Ad Hoc Committee on the Revision of the Colorado Civil Rules 1994 and Supreme Court Civil Rules Committee 1998. Master Rhone-Brackett Inn of Court 1993-97. Member Denver, Colorado Women's and Colorado Bar Associations. Co-chair Women's Judges Association National Conference Denver 1990.
Office: Colorado State Judicial Building, Two East Fourteenth Avenue, Denver 80203.
Telephone: (303) 861-1111.

RINALDI, Emil A. *(Judge, Adams County Court)* Appointed by governor.
Office: Adams County Justice Center, 1100 Judicial Center Drive, Brighton 80601.
Telephone: (303) 654-3360.

RISBERG, Todd P. *(Judge, San Juan County Court)* Appointed by Governor Bill Owens Dec 3, 2001. Educated at University of Colorado School of Law J.D.
Mailing address: P.O. Box 900, Silverton 81433.
Office: San Juan County Courthouse, 1447 Greene Street, Silverton 81433.
Telephone: (970) 387-5790.

RIVERA, Gloria A. *(Judge, Colorado District Court Second Judicial District)* Appointed by Governor Bill Owens to term beginning 1999. Retained by election. Educated at University of Colorado B.S. 1983 and University of Denver J.D. 1988.
Former Deputy District Attorney Denver. Previously employed with Braniff International Airlines.
Office: 256 City and County Building, 1437 Bannock, Denver 80202.
Telephone: (720) 865-8306.

ROBB, James M. *(Recalled Magistrate Judge, United States District Court District of Colorado)* Appointed Magistrate Judge by U.S. District Court judges. Appointed Recalled Magistrate Judge by the Judicial Council of the Tenth Circuit to term beginning Jan 12, 2001.
Mailing address: P.O. Box 3208, Grand Junction 81502-3208.
Telephone: (970) 241-8932.

ROBBINS, William D. *(Judge, Colorado District Court Second Judicial District)* Appointed by Governor Bill Owens.
Office: 256 City and County Building, 1437 Bannock, Denver 80202.
Telephone: (720) 865-8308.

RODGERS, Frederic B. *(Judge, Gilpin County Court)* Appointed by Governor Richard D. Lamm Oct 31, 1986 to term beginning Feb 4, 1987. Retained by election Nov 1990, Nov 1994, Nov 1998 and Nov 2002. Current term expires Jan 2007. Born Albany New York Sept 29, 1940. Episcopalian. Educated at Amherst College A.B. 1963 and Albany Law School J.D. 1966. Member Psi Upsilon. Admitted to practice New York 1966, U.S. Court of Military Appeals 1968, Colorado 1972, U.S. Supreme Court 1974, U.S. Court of Appeals Tenth Circuit 1983 and U.S. Court of Federal Claims 2002. In legal practice Denver and Breckenridge Colorado 1979-91. Magistrate, Denver Juvenile Court 1973-79. Presiding Judge, Breckenridge Municipal Court 1978-88, Westminster Municipal Court 1979-96, Central City Municipal Court 1980, Edgewater Municipal Court 1980-86, Empire Municipal Court 1980-98, Blue River Municipal Court 1982-96, Idaho Spring Municipal Court 1983-96 and Black Hawk Municipal Court 1984-94.
Chief Deputy District Attorney Denver 1972-73. Author articles in *The Judges Journal*, *The Colorado Lawyer* and other legal periodicals. Co-author *Modern Judicial Ethics* 1992 and *The Improvement of the Administration of Justice* 7th ed. 2001 American Bar Association Press. Board of Editors *The Judges Journal* since 1996. Former Member Editorial Board *Courts Health Science and the Law* Georgetown University. President Denver Law Club 1981-92, Colorado Municipal Judges Association 1985-86 and Colorado County Judges Association 1995-96. Member Colorado Trial Judges Council 1994-97. President Rhone-Brackett American Inn of Court since 2002. Trustee First Judicial District Bar Association. Life Fellow Colorado Bar Foundation. Fellow American Bar Foundation. Member Denver (Board of Trustees 1979-82), Colorado (Board of Governors 1986-88, 1990-92, 1993-99 and since 2002) and American (Chair National Conference of Special Court Judges 1989-90, Member House of Delegates since 1994, Chair Judicial Division 1998-99, Member Board of Governors since 2001, Nominating Committee) Bar Associations. Member since 1993 and Chair 1999 Faculty Council The National Judicial College Reno Nevada. Alumnus National College of Juvenile Justice. Speaker at state and national legal education seminars. Listed in *Who's Who in American Law* since 1983, *Who's Who in the West* since 1987 and *Who's Who in America* since 1992. Named "Outstanding County Judge" by a state victim rights organization 1991. Major USAR JAGC 1967-72. Military Judge USAR. Recipient two Bronze Stars with oak leaf clusters, Air Medal and Army Commendation Medal with three oak leaf clusters. Fellow Paul Harris

RODGERS, FREDERIC B.—*Continued*

Rotary. Enjoys skiing, bicycling, music and playing the banjo.

Office: 200 Gilpin County Justice Center, 2960 Dory Hill Road, Golden 80403-8780.

Telephone: (303) 582-5323.

Fax: (303) 582-3112

E-mail address: rodgers@abanet.org

ROMANO, Sabino E. *(Judge, Adams County Court)* Appointed by governor.

Office: Adams County Justice Center, 1100 Judicial Center Drive, Brighton 80601.

Telephone: (303) 654-3340.

ROMEO, Jeffrey L. *(Judge, Adams County Court)* Appointed by governor.

Office: Adams County Justice Center, 1100 Judicial Center Drive, Brighton 80601.

Telephone: (303) 654-3330.

ROSS, Carl W. *(Judge, Crowley County Court)* Appointed by governor.

Office: Crowley County Courthouse, 110 East Sixth, Ordway 81063.

Telephone: (719) 267-4468.

ROTHENBERG, Sandra Iris *(Judge, Colorado Court of Appeals)* Appointed by Governor Roy Romer to term beginning Aug 14, 1990. Retained by election. Born March 8, 1943. Educated at University of Miami B.A. 1965 J.D. 1968 and Georgetown University LL.M. 1973. Admitted to practice Florida 1968, Colorado 1970 and District of Columbia 1970. In legal practice 1975-79. Judge, Colorado District Court Second Judicial District 1979-90.

Office: Colorado State Judicial Building, Two East Fourteenth Avenue, Denver 80203.

Telephone: (303) 837-3723.

ROY, Arthur P. *(Judge, Colorado Court of Appeals)* Appointed by Governor Roy Romer to term beginning March 4, 1994. Retained by election Nov 5, 1996, current term expires Jan 11, 2005. Born Baton Rouge Louisiana Nov 23, 1940. Presbyterian. Educated at Iowa State University B.S. 1962 and University of Colorado J.D. 1969. Associate Editor Colorado Law Review 1968-69. Admitted to practice Colorado 1969, U.S. District Court District of Colorado 1969, U.S. Court of Appeals Tenth Circuit 1972 and U.S. Supreme Court 1973. In legal practice Greeley 1974-94.

Assistant City Attorney Fort Collins 1969-70 and Greeley 1975-77. Assistant Attorney General Assistant Legal Counsel to State Board of Agriculture Colorado 1971-72. Deputy District Attorney Nineteenth Judicial District 1973-74. Special Counsel to Insurance Commissioner Colorado 1980-83. Member American Academy of Hospital Attorneys 1986-94. Member Weld County (Board of Governors Representative 1980-82, President Elect 1984-85, President 1985-86), Colorado (Board of Governors 1980-83 and 1984-85, Executive Committee 1982-83 and 1984-85, Vice President 1984-85) and American Bar Associations. Served to Captain USAR April 1963 to Aug 1973. Republican.

Office: Colorado State Judicial Building, Two East Fourteenth Avenue, Denver 80203.

Telephone: (303) 837-3768.

RUCKRIEGLE, W. Terry *(Chief Judge, Colorado District Court Fifth Judicial District)* Appointed by Governor Richard D. Lamm to term beginning Aug 31, 1984. Retained by election Nov 1986, Nov 1992 and Nov 1998. Current term expires Jan 2005. Chief Judge since Jan 1994. Born Kokomo Indiana Aug 26, 1947. Catholic. Educated at Indiana University B.S. 1969 J.D. 1973. Admitted to practice Indiana 1973, U.S. Courts of Appeals Seventh 1973 and Tenth 1974 Circuits, Colorado 1974 and U.S. District Court District of Colorado 1974. In legal practice Denver and Idaho Springs Colorado 1974-76.

Assistant District Attorney 1975-84. Instructor in Economics and Political Science Pahlavi University, Shiraz Iran 1971-72. Instructor Legal Intern Program University of Denver 1974-75. Member Colorado Bar Association (Board of Governors 1980-82 and 1988-95). Attended The National Judicial College 1985, 1990, 1992 and 1995.

Mailing address: P.O. Box 269, Breckenridge 80424.

Office: Summit County Justice Center, 501 North Park Avenue, Breckenridge 80424.

Telephone: (970) 453-2241.

Georgetown telephone: (303) 569-3272.

RUDDICK, Steven R. *(Judge, Arapahoe County Court)* Appointed by Governor Roy Romer to term beginning Nov 21, 1994. Retained by election Nov 1998 and 2002. Current term expires Jan 2007. Born Denver Colorado Nov 6, 1954. Roman Catholic. Educated at Metropolitan State College B.A. summa cum laude 1977 and University of Denver College of Law J.D. 1980. Winner President's Award. Member Phi Alpha Delta and Order of St. Ives. Admitted to practice Colorado 1980 and U.S. Court of Appeals Tenth Circuit 1980. In legal practice Aurora 1979-81.

Assistant City Attorney Aurora 1981-94. Special Prosecutor Denver City and Denver County 1992. Legal Counsel Local Liquor Licensing Authority Board. Legal Advisor Finance and Tax Administration Divisions. Coauthor "1993 Special Session Summary" *Colorado Lawyer* Oct 1993. Faculty Member University of Colorado Graduate School of Public Affairs 1993-95. Law Lecturer Arapahoe and Front Range Community Colleges and Denver Business College. President Colorado Trial Judges Council 1996-97. Chairman PRIDE Committee Eighteenth Judicial District 1996-97. Master Thompson G. Marsh Inn of Court. Chairman Colorado Municipal Bond Supervision Advisory Board. Member Chief Justice and County Judges' Legislative Advisory Committees. Member Judiciary Finance, Legal Services, Criminal Justice Commission, Juvenile Justice Subcommittee, Western Legislative States Council Education Committee, Joint Interim Committee on Juvenile Violence, Judiciary, Transportation and Energy, Colorado Commission on the Aging and Joint Interim Committees on Criminal Justice. Member Arapahoe, Aurora (Secretary-Treasurer 1983-84 and 1996-97, Vice President 1984-85, President 1985-86) and Colorado Bar Associations. Moot Court Judge Daniel S. Hoffman Student Trial Competition University of Denver and Thomas Tang National Appellate Competition Asian American Bar Association. Recipient Legislator of the Year Awards from Colorado Counties Inc 1989, Colorado Social Legislation Committee 1991, Colorado Sierra Club 1992, CoPIRG 1994, Aurora Business and Professional Women Association and Colorado Environmental Health Association. Recipient Education Legislator of the Year Award from Auro-

RUDDICK, STEVEN R.—*Continued*

ra P.S.E. 1993. Previously worked as package handler, clerk, furniture maker, driver's helper, warehouseman, janitor, theatre manager and actor. County Part Vice Chairman, House District Chair and Captain Precinct Committee Person Arapahoe County Democratic Part 1976-94. National Delegate Democratic National Conventions 1984 and 1988. Chairman Democratic Central Committee Eighteenth Judicial District 1985-94. Lead Democrat House Judiciary Committee 1987-92. Member House of Representatives District 36, 1987-92 and State Senate District 29, 1993-94 Colorado. Former Board member Arapahoe County Child P.A.C., Eighteenth Judicial District Reorganizational Committee, Aurora Gang Task Force, Aurora P.A.L., East Gate Lions and Eleanor Roosevelt Club. Lector and Eucharistic Minister St. Pius X since 1988. Executive Member Denver/Aurora Lowry Air Force Base Economic Recovery Project Reuse Committee 1991-94. Civilian Appointee National Security Forum U.S. Air War College 1992. Board Director Aurora History Museum Foundation since 1992 and Downtown Aurora Visual Arts since 1994. Grand Marshall 1991 and Parade Judge 1995-96 Aurora Gateway to the Rockies Parade. Member Catholic Lawyers' Guild, Downtown Aurora Business Association, Aurora Chamber of Commerce, Leadership Aurora Alumni, Aurora Civitan Club, Aurora Knights of Columbus, Columbine Masonic Lodge, Aurora Sister Cities and Denver Broncos Quarterback Club. Interests include reading, computers, golf, nature hiking, biking and the Denver Broncos.

Office: 15400 East 14th Place, #201, Aurora 80011.

Telephone: (303) 363-7105.

RUSSELL, Robert H., II *(Judge, Colorado District Court Eighteenth Judicial District)* Appointed by governor. Former Judge, Arapahoe County Court.

Office: Arapahoe County Justice Center, 7325 South Potomac Street, Englewood 80112.

Telephone: (303) 649-6202.

RUYBALID, Ernest J. *(Judge, Pueblo County Court)* Appointed by Governor Roy Romer to term beginning Jan 16, 1997. Retained by election. Educated at Southern Colorado State College and University of Colorado School of Law J.D.

Member Pueblo County Hispanic, Colorado Hispanic, Pueblo County (Chairman Continuing Legal Education Committee) and Colorado Bar Associations. Member Community Advisory Board Greenway Nature Center Pueblo. Member Highland Park Elementary School Parent Teacher Association.

Office: Pueblo County Judicial Building, 320 West Tenth Street, Pueblo 81003.

Telephone: (719) 583-7044.

SAMELSON, Kirk S. *(Judge, Colorado District Court Fourth Judicial District and Judge, Colorado Water Court Division Two)* Appointed to District Court by Governor Bill Owens 2000. Retained by election Nov 2002, current term expires Jan 2009. Appointed to Water Court by Chief Justice. Educated at U.S. Air Force Academy B.S. 1973 and University of Denver J.D. 1977. Admitted to practice Colorado 1978.

Visiting Professor Colorado College 1993-2000. USAF JAGC 1978-83.

Mailing address: P.O. Box 2980, Colorado Springs 80901-2980.

Office: 20 East Vermijo, Colorado Springs 80903.

Telephone: (719) 227-5193.

SANDSTEAD, Morris W., Jr. *(Judge, Colorado District Court Twentieth Judicial District)* Appointed by Governor Richard D. Lamm to term beginning Jan 11, 1983. Retained by election 1986, 1992 and 1998. Current term expires Jan 2005. Born Sterling Colorado Oct 30, 1942. Methodist. Educated at Duke University B.A. 1964 and University of Colorado J.D. 1967. Law Clerk to Hon. Alfred A. Arraj, U.S. District Court District of Colorado 1967-68. Admitted to practice Colorado 1967, U.S. District Court District of Colorado 1967 and U.S. Supreme Court 1974. In legal practice Boulder 1968-82.

Instructor National Institute of Trial Advocacy 1983. Member Boulder County and Colorado Bar Associations. Enjoys bicycling, classical music, opera, tap dancing, basketball and cooking. Interested in the French Revolution.

Mailing address: P.O. Box 4249, Boulder 80306-4249.

Office: Boulder Justice Center, 1777 Sixth Street, Boulder 80302.

Telephone: (303) 441-3764.

SATTER, Raymond Nathan *(Judge, Denver County Court)* Appointed by Mayor Federico Peña to term beginning Oct 30, 1987. Retained by election 1990, 1994, 1998 and 2002. Current term expires Jan 2007. Currently serves as Presiding Judge. Born Denver Colorado Oct 19, 1948. Educated at University of Denver B.A. 1970 and Catholic University of America J.D. 1973. Admitted to practice Colorado 1973 and U.S. Supreme Court 1976. In legal practice Denver 1973-87. Associate Judge, Englewood Municipal Court 1985-86.

Important Decision: Order denying choice of evils in homeless activists trespass trial Dec 21, 1988. Member Colorado Bar Association (Ethics Committee). Former Board member and officer Denver Symphony Association. Former Board member and Past President Denver Young Artists Orchestra. Enjoys sailing, bicycling, playing bridge, music, hiking, camping and motorcycling.

Office: 108 City and County Building, 1437 Bannock Street, Denver 80202.

Telephone: (720) 865-7870.

SCHIFERL, Michael A. *(Judge, Colorado District Court Sixteenth Judicial District)* Appointed by Governor Bill Owens.

Office: 207 Otero County Courthouse, 13 West Third Street, La Junta 81050.

Telephone: (719) 384-4951.

SCHINGLE, Michael J. *(Judge, Morgan County Court)* Appointed by Governor Bill Owens.

Mailing address: P.O. Box 695, Fort Morgan 80701.

Office: Morgan County Justice Center, 400 Warner, Fort Morgan 80701.

Telephone: (970) 542-3414.

Fax: (970) 542-3416

SCHLATTER, O. Edward *(Magistrate Judge, United States District Court District of Colorado)* Appointed by U.S. District Court judges. Former Chief Judge, Colorado District Court Eleventh Judicial District.

Office: U.S. Courthouse, 901 Nineteenth Street, Denver 80294-3589.

Telephone: (303) 844-4507.

SCHULTZ, Ronald L. *(Judge, Larimer County Court)* Appointed by Governor John D. Vanderhoof to

SCHULTZ, RONALD L.—*Continued*

term beginning Sept 1974. Retained by election. Current term expires Jan 2005. Born Batesland South Dakota 1941. Lutheran. Educated at Colorado State University B.S. with honors 1964 and University of Denver J.D. 1967. Member Phi Alpha Delta. Admitted to practice Colorado 1967 and South Dakota 1968. Began legal practice Denver Colorado 1967. In legal practice Batesland South Dakota 1968.

With Denver City Attorney's Office 1967-70. Chief Deputy District Attorney Colorado Eighth Judicial District 1971-74. Important Decisions: Criminal prosecution of nuclear train blockade cases 1984. Member The State Bar of South Dakota and Colorado Bar Association. Guest Speaker on the judiciary. Interests include auto restoration, flying, boating and instilling community interest in the jury system through speaking efforts.

Office: 100 Larimer County Justice Center, 201 La Porte Avenue, Fort Collins 80521-2761.

Telephone: (970) 498-6207.

SCHWARTZ, Larry E. *(Judge, Colorado District Court Fourth Judicial District)* Appointed by Governor Roy Romer to term beginning Jan 1, 1997. Retained by election. Educated at University of Colorado B.A. J.D.

Former Deputy District Attorney Fourth Judicial District. Member El Paso County (Trustee, Member Criminal Law Committee) and Colorado Bar Associations.

Mailing address: P.O. Box 2980, Colorado Springs 80901-2980.

Office: Judicial Building, 20 East Vermijo, Colorado Springs 80903.

Telephone: (719) 448-7632.

SHAFFER, Craig B. *(Magistrate Judge, United States District Court District of Colorado)* Appointed by U.S. District Court judges to term beginning Jan 18, 2001.

Office: A432 U.S. Courthouse, 901 Nineteenth Street, Denver 80294-3589.

Telephone: (303) 844-2117.

SHAW, Rex A. *(Judge, Jackson County Court)* Appointed by governor.

Mailing address: P.O. Box 308, Walden 80480.

Office: Jackson County Courthouse, 396 Lafever Street, Walden 80480.

Telephone: (970) 723-4363.

SHINN, Steven E. *(Chief Judge, Colorado District Court Thirteenth Judicial District)* Appointed by Governor Richard D. Lamm May 31, 1986 to term beginning July 7, 1986. Retained by election Nov 1988, Nov 1994 and Nov 2000. Current term expires Jan 10, 2007. Born St. Francis Kansas June 27, 1949. Educated at University of Northern Colorado B.A. 1971 and University of Denver College of Law J.D. 1974. Law Clerk to Hon. George G. Priest, Colorado District Court First Judicial District 1972-74. Member Phi Alpha Delta. Admitted to practice Colorado 1974, U.S. District Court District of Colorado 1974 and U.S. Court of Appeals Tenth Circuit 1978. In legal practice Lakewood 1974-77 and Yuma 1977-85. Judge, Wray Municipal Judge 1978-85.

City Attorney Yuma 1977-85. Author *Comparative Analysis of Federal Rules of Evidence* 1974. Part-time Professor of Criminal Justice Northeastern Junior College since 1995. Member Thirteenth Judicial District and Colorado Bar Associations. Attended Law of Search and Seizure The National Judicial College Reno Nevada. Named Parent of the Year by Colorado FCCLA 1996. Member Sterling Baseball Organization. 4-H Leader. Enjoys raising registered cattle, training therapy dogs and golfing.

Mailing address: P.O. Box 71, Sterling 80751.

Office: Logan County Courthouse, Third and Ash, Sterling 80751.

Telephone: (970) 522-6565.

Fax: (970) 522-6566

SHUTERAN, Sharon Elaine *(Judge, San Miguel County Court)* Appointed by Governor Richard D. Lamm to term beginning Aug 29, 1984. Retained by election, current term expires Jan 2007. Born Denver Colorado Sept 15, 1953. Jewish. Educated at Reed College 1970-71 and 1973 and University of Denver B.A. 1975 J.D. 1978. Admitted to practice Colorado 1978. Began legal practice Denver 1978. In legal practice Telluride since 1979. Judge, Telluride Municipal Court Jan 1981 to Dec 1981.

Attorney Legal Aid Society of Denver Prison Law Project and Adams County Legal Services 1978-79 VISTA. Deputy District Attorney Seventh Judicial District 1981-83. Member Colorado Judicial Advisory Council, Colorado County Judges Association, Colorado Women's and Colorado Bar Associations. Speaker and Trainer on the legal system, mediation and domestic violence in schools and the community. Democrat. Owner, manager, pastry chef and bookkeeper Excelsior Cafe July 1979-92. Private Mediator JAMS/Endispute Denver. Former Member Telluride Planning and Zoning Commission, Street and Parking Task Force, Downtown Planning Task Force and Anti-Defamation League Civil Rights Commission. Volunteer Telluride Film Festival, Telluride AIDS Benefit, Telluride Council for Arts and Humanities, Telluride Mountain School, San Miguel Resource Center and Telluride Ski and Snowboard Club. Conductor empowerment workshops for mediators and personal growth workshops. Enjoys reading, hiking, skiing, backpacking, traveling, cooking and computers.

Mailing address: P.O. Box 919, Telluride 81435.

Office: San Miguel County Courthouse, 305 South Colorado, Telluride 81435.

Telephone: (970) 728-3891.

SIDEL, Kevin *(Judge, Elbert County Court)* Appointed by Governor Roy Romer to term beginning Jan 1995. Retained by election 1998 and Nov 2002. Current term expires Jan 2007. Admitted to practice Colorado 1988. In legal practice Denver 1988-89.

Deputy District Attorney Eighteenth Judicial District 1989-94.

Mailing address: P.O. Box 232, Kiowa 80117.

Office: Elbert County Courthouse, 751 Ute Street, Kiowa 80117.

Telephone: (303) 621-2131.

SIMMONS, Timothy *(Judge, Colorado District Court Fourth Judicial District)* Appointed by governor.

Mailing address: P.O. Box 2980, Colorado Springs 80901-2980.

Office: 20 East Vermijo, Colorado Springs 80903.

Telephone: (719) 227-5129.

SLETTA, Stephen J. *(Judge, El Paso County Court)* Appointed by governor.
Mailing address: P.O. Box 2980, Colorado Springs 80901-2980.
Office: 20 East Vermijo, Colorado Springs 80903.
Telephone: (719) 448-7600.

SMITH, Arthur R. *(Judge, Mesa County Court)* Appointed by governor.
Mailing address: P.O. Box 20000, Grand Junction 81502-5030.
Office: Mesa County Justice Center, 125 North Spruce, Grand Junction 81501.
Telephone: (970) 257-3652.

SMITH, Robert B. *(Judge, Logan County Court)* Appointed by Governor Bill Owens.
Mailing address: P.O. Box 1907, Sterling 80751.
Office: Logan County Courthouse Annex, Third and Ash, Sterling 80751.
Telephone: (970) 522-1572.
Fax: (970) 522-2875

SPARR, Daniel B. *(Senior Judge, United States District Court District of Colorado)* Appointed for life by President George Bush. Assumed Senior status May 1, 2001, serves by assignment. Born Denver Colorado June 8, 1931. Episcopalian. Educated at University of Denver B.S.B.A. 1952 J.D. 1966. Admitted to practice Colorado 1966. Began legal practice Denver 1966. Former Judge, Colorado District Court Second Judicial District, appointed by Governor Richard D. Lamm to term beginning March 1, 1978.
Instructor Arapahoe Community College 1973-76 and Metropolitan State College 1979. Member Denver (Chairman Topical Luncheons Committee, Board of Trustees 1976-79), Colorado (Chairman Legal Assistants Committee 1974-76) and American Bar Associations. CLE Instructor 1973-75. Captain USAF 1952-55. Paralegal Advisory Boards Arapahoe Community College, Metropolitan State College and Denver Paralegal Institute. Enjoys snow and water skiing, boating and fishing.
Office: U.S. Courthouse, 901 Nineteenth Street, Denver 80294-3589.
Telephone: (303) 844-4694.

STAVELEY, John F. *(Judge, Boulder County Court)* Appointed by Governor Bill Owens.
Mailing address: P.O. Box 4249, Boulder 80306-4249.
Office: Boulder Justice Center, 1777 Sixth Street, Boulder 80302.
Telephone: (303) 441-3735.

STERN, Herbert L., III *(Judge, Colorado District Court Second Judicial District)* Appointed by governor. Educated at University of California at Berkeley B.A. 1970, Goddard College M.A. 1973 and University of Denver J.D. 1977.
Office: 256 City and County Building, 1437 Bannock, Denver 80202.
Telephone: (720) 865-8304.

STEWART, C. Jean *(Presiding Judge, Denver Probate Court)* Appointed by Governor Roy Romer to term beginning May 1995. Retained by election.
Office: 230 City and County Building, 1437 Bannock Street, Denver 80202.
Telephone: (720) 865-8311.

STIRMAN, C. Edward *(Judge, Larimer County Court)* Appointed by governor.
Office: 100 Larimer County Justice Center, 201 La Porte Avenue, Fort Collins 80521-2761.
Telephone: (970) 498-6210.

STUTLER, Larry E. *(Judge, Prowers County Court)* Appointed by Governor Roy Romer. Retained by election.
Office: 100 Prowers County Courthouse, 301 South Main, Lamar 81052.
Telephone: (719) 336-7416.

SWIFT, Pattie P. *(Judge, Colorado District Court Twelfth Judicial District)* Appointed by Governor Bill Owens to term beginning Feb 28, 2003. Born Columbus Ohio Sept 14, 1959. Educated at St. John's College B.A. 1982 and University of New Mexico School of Law J.D. with honors 1989. Survey Editor New Mexico Law Review 1988-89. Admitted to practice New Mexico 1989 and Colorado 1990. In legal practice Alamosa Colorado 1990-92. Judge, Costilla County Court Jan 10, 1989 to Feb 27, 2003.
Member State Bar of New Mexico, San Luis Valley and Colorado Bar Associations.
Office: County Courthouse, Sixth and Cherry, Drawer W, Del Norte 81132.
Telephone: (719) 657-3395.

SYLVESTER, William B. *(Judge, Colorado District Court Eighteenth Judicial District)* Appointed by Governor Bill Owens.
Office: Arapahoe County Justice Center, 7325 South Potomac Street, Englewood 80112.
Telephone: (303) 649-6232.

TALLMAN, Howard R. *(Judge, United States Bankruptcy Court District of Colorado)* Appointed by U.S. Court of Appeals Tenth Circuit judges.
Office: U.S. Customs House, 721 19th Street, Denver 80202-2508.
Telephone: (303) 844-8309.

TALLMAN, Paul D. *(Judge, Colorado District Court Fifteenth Judicial District)* Appointed by Governor Bill Owens to term beginning Jan 2003. Educated at University of Denver J.D. 1973. Former Judge, Cheyenne County Court, appointed by Governor Roy Romer to term beginning April 1987.
Office: 300 Prowers County Courthouse, 301 South Main, Lamar 81052.
Telephone: (719) 336-7424.

TAUBMAN, Daniel Marc *(Judge, Colorado Court of Appeals)* Appointed by Governor Roy Romer Nov 11, 1992 to term beginning March 1, 1993. Retained by election Nov 1996, current term expires Dec 2004. Born Brooklyn New York Feb 25, 1948. Jewish. Educated at Cornell University A.B. magna cum laude 1969 and Harvard Law School J.D. 1974. Articles Editor Harvard Civil Rights-Civil Liberties Law Review Jan 1974 to June 1974. Editor, Editorial Manager and News Editor Harvard Law Record. Law Clerk to Hon. Charles E. Stewart, Jr., U.S. District Court Southern District of New York 1974-75. Member Pi Delta Epsilon. Admitted to practice Colorado 1975, New York 1975, U.S. District Courts District of Colorado 1975 and Eastern 1975 and Southern 1975 Districts of New York, U.S. Court of Appeals Tenth Circuit 1975, California 1978 and U.S. Supreme Court 1988.

TAUBMAN, DANIEL MARC—*Continued*

Staff Attorney Center on Social Welfare Policy and Law New York City Sept 1980 to April 1982. Director Colorado Coalition of Legal Services Programs April 1982 to Feb 1993. Author "Picketers at the Doorstep" 9 Harvard Civil Rights-Civil Liberties L. Rev. 96, 1974; "The Clerkship Experience" 27 Harvard Law School Bulletin 26 Fall 1975; "The County Poor Laws—Cowboys and Indigents" 9 Colorado Lawyer 1555 Aug 1980; "Providing Effective Representation in Welfare Fraud Cases" 15 Clearinghouse Review 53 May 1981; "New Disability Law Provides Continuing Benefits Pending Appeal" 12 Colorado Lawyer 774 May 1983; "Winning Social Security Termination Cases" 13 Colorado Lawyer 449 March 1984; "Social Security Begins Implementation of New Reform Law" Colorado Lawyer 813 May 1985; Chapter on public benefits *The AIDS Issue—Your Legal Rights* Colorado Lawyers Committee 1989 and 1993; Tenth Circuit Update of Social Security Disability Cases *Social Security Reporting Service* West 1990, 1991 and 1994; "Expanded Eligibility for SSI Children's Disability Benefits" 20 Colorado Lawyer 709 April 1991; "The Role of the State Support Centers in the 1990s and Beyond" 26 Clearinghouse Review 75 Special Issue 1992; Chapter on evaluation of pain *An Advocate's Guide to Surviving the SSI System* 1992; Chapter on *in forma pauperis* practice *Colorado Appellate Handbook* 1994; and "The Depth and Breadth of Pro Bono Work in Colorado" 26 *Colorado Lawyer* 53 Sept 1997. Managing Editor *Colorado Public Benefits Desk Manual* 1984 and *Colorado Consumer Desk Manual* 1987 Colorado Coalition of Legal Service Programs. Column Editor Disability Law Committee *Colorado Lawyer* 1988-2001. Board of Trustees Legal Aid Foundation of Colorado 1983-93. Member Legal Services Corporation National Training Task Force 1986-87. Board of Directors Lend a Lawyer, Inc. 1990-95. Member Public Education Committee since 1995 and Legal Services/Pro Bono Subcommittee Judicial Advisory Council 1997-99 Colorado Supreme Court. Former Member El Paso County (Library Committee 1976-77), Eleventh Judicial District and American Bar Associations. Fellow Colorado Bar Foundation. Member Denver (Legal Services Committee 1982-87, Public Legal Education Committee 1988) and Colorado (Member 1982-2001 and Chair 1985-88 Disability Law Committee, Member Ethics Committee since 1989 and Appellate Practice Subcommittee since 1991, Member since 1995 and Chair 1995-97 Availability of Legal Services Committee, Board of Governors 1996-98) Bar Associations. Recipient Jacob V. Schaetzel Award from Colorado Bar Association 2000. Volunteer Peace Corps Cuzco Peru July 1969 to Aug 1971. Board of Directors 1983-87 and Secretary 1984-86 Peace Corps/VISTA Alumni of Colorado. Treasurer National Organization of State Support Units 1986-93. Den Leader Cub Scouts 1987-89. Coach Odyssey of the Mind 1991-97. Hobbies and interests include puns, cooking and cross country skiing.

Office: Colorado State Judicial Building, Two East Fourteenth Avenue, Denver 80203.

Telephone: (303) 837-3719.

E-mail address: daniel.taubman@judicial.state.co.us

TAYLOR, Harold D. *(Judge, Custer County Court)* Appointed by Governor Roy Romer to term beginning Feb 1, 1992. Retained by election Nov 1994, Nov 1998 and Nov 2002. Current term expires Jan 2007. Born Albany Oklahoma May 26, 1934. Protestant. Education at Southeastern Oklahoma State University B.S. 1958 and University of Northern Colorado M.S. 1960 Ph.D. 1971. Member Lambda Sigma Tau.

Chair Education Committee 1992-96 and Conference Planning Committee 1994 and Executive Director 1996-2001 National Judges Association. Attended National Judges Association Education Conferences Colorado Springs Colorado 1994, Oklahoma City Oklahoma 1995, Baker City Oregon 1996, Kalispell Montana 1997, Jackson Mississippi 1998 and St. Johnsbury Vermont 1999. Named California Teacher of the Year in Mathematics 1989 and Outstanding Non-attorney Judge in the U.S. by National Judges Association. Recipient Presidential Award for Excellence in Teaching Mathematics 1989 presented by President George Bush in Rose Garden Ceremony and Kenneth L. MacEachern Memorial Award Reno Nevada 2000. Staff Sergeant U.S. Army 1953-56. President local school board, county board of zoning adjustment and county planning commission. Board Member health clinic foundation. Enjoys writing, photography and classifying wild flowers.

Mailing address: P.O. Box 60, Westcliffe 81252.

Office: Custer County Courthouse, 205 South Sixth Street, Westcliffe 81252.

Telephone: (719) 783-2274.

Fax: (719) 783-2995

TIDBALL, Jane A. *(Judge, Colorado District Court First Judicial District)* Appointed by Governor Roy Romer Sept 1998 to term beginning Jan 12, 1999. Retained by election Nov 2002, current term expires Jan 12, 2009. Born Helena Montana Feb 23, 1959. Educated at University of Colorado B.A. 1980 J.D. with distinction 1984. Law Clerk to Hon. Murray Richtel, Colorado District Court Twentieth Judicial District 1983-84 and Hon. Aurel M. Kelly, Colorado Court of Appeals 1984-85. Member Phi Beta Kappa. Admitted to practice Colorado 1984 and U.S. District Courts District of Colorado 1986 and District of Arizona 1991. In legal practice Denver and Boulder 1985-91. Magistrate, Colorado District Court Twentieth Judicial District 1995-98.

Member First Judicial District, Women's and Colorado Bar Associations. Enjoys spending time with sons.

Office: 100 Jefferson County Parkway, Golden 80401-6002.

Telephone: (303) 271-6130.

Fax: (303) 271-6124

TOBIAS, Robert C. *(Judge, Arapahoe County Court)* Appointed by Governor Roy Romer to term beginning 1995. Retained by election.

Office: 1790 West Littleton Boulevard, Littleton 80120.

Telephone: (303) 795-0303.

TOTH, D. Richard *(Judge, Colorado District Court Fourth Judicial District)* Appointed by Governor Roy Romer July 1987. Retained by election. Born Colorado Springs Colorado Nov 7, 1946. Educated at Colorado College B.A. 1968 and Drake University J.D. 1975. Member Phi Delta Theta. Admitted to practice Colorado 1975. Began legal practice Colorado Springs 1975. Juvenile Commissioner July 1979 to Feb 1981. Former Judge, El Paso County Court, appointed by Governor Richard D. Lamm to term beginning Feb 23, 1981.

TOTH, D. RICHARD—*Continued*

Member El Paso County and Colorado Bar Associations. Enjoys backpacking and fly fishing.

Mailing address: P.O. Box 2980, Colorado Springs 80901-2980.

Office: Judicial Building, 20 East Vermijo, Colorado Springs 80903.

Telephone: (719) 448-7512.

TRUJILLO, Michael H. *(Judge, Rio Grande County Court)* Appointed by governor. Former Judge, Saguache County Court.

Mailing address: P.O. Box 427, Del Norte 81132.

Office: Sixth and Cherry, Del Norte 81132.

Telephone: (719) 657-3394.

UNFUG, Charles *(Judge, Weld County Court)* Appointed by Governor Bill Owens.

Mailing address: P.O. Box 2038, Greeley 80632.

Office: Weld County Courthouse, 901 Ninth Avenue, Greeley 80631.

Telephone: (970) 351-7300.

VANNOY, Douglas R. *(Judge, Colorado District Court Thirteenth Judicial District)* Appointed by governor.

Mailing address: P.O. Box 130, Fort Morgan 80701.

Office: Morgan County Justice Center, 400 Warner, Fort Morgan 80701.

Telephone: (970) 542-3435.

Fax: (970) 542-3436

VICKERS, Larry Everett *(Judge, Hinsdale County Court)* Appointed by governor.

Mailing address: P.O. Box 245, Lake City 81235.

Office: Hinsdale County Courthouse, 317 Henson, Lake City 81235.

Telephone: (970) 944-2227.

VIGIL, John J. *(Judge, Colorado District Court Seventeenth Judicial District)* Appointed by governor. Former Judge, Adams County Court.

Office: Adams County Justice Center, 1100 Judicial Center Drive, Brighton 80601.

Telephone: (303) 654-3270.

VIGNA, Rosalie *(Judge, Colorado District Court Tenth Judicial District)* Appointed by Governor Roy Romer.

Office: Pueblo County Judicial Building, 320 West Tenth Street, Pueblo 81003.

Telephone: (719) 583-7005.

VISCARDI, Gerard C. *(Judge, Rio Blanco County Court)* Appointed by Governor Roy Romer to term beginning Jan 14, 1997. Retained by election Nov 1998 and 2002. Current term expires Jan 2007. Educated at Baldwin-Wallace College and Ohio Northern University College of Law J.D.

Former Assistant Attorney Department of Social Services Rio Blanco County. Member Rio Blanco Drug/Alcohol Council 1978-82. Member Mental Health Community Advisory Council 1979-81. Member Colorado Bar Association.

Mailing address: P.O. Box 1150, Meeker 81641.

Office: Rio Blanco County Courthouse, 555 Main Street, Meeker 81641.

Telephone: (970) 878-5622.

VOGT, JoAnn L. *(Judge, Colorado Court of Appeals)* Appointed by Governor Roy Romer to term beginning Dec 31, 1997. Retained by election. Born Aug 31, 1943. Educated at University of Nebraska B.A. 1965, University of Chicago M.S. 1967 Ph.D. 1972 and University of Denver College of Law J.D. 1986. Fulbright Scholar Universität Hamburg, Germany 1965-66. Law Clerk to Chief Justice Joseph R. Quinn, Colorado Supreme Court 1986-87. In legal practice 1987-98.

Member Denver, Colorado Women's and Colorado Bar Associations. Board of Directors Legal Aid Society of Metropolitan Denver.

Office: Colorado State Judicial Building, Two East Fourteenth Avenue, Denver 80203.

Telephone: (303) 837-3726.

WADLEIGH, Ralph N. *(Judge, Otero County Court)* Appointed by Governor Roy Romer to term beginning Jan 11, 1988. Retained by election Nov 1990, 1994, 1998 and 2002. Current term expires Jan 2007. Born Cheraw Colorado June 14, 1932. Methodist. Educated at Otero Junior College A.A. 1952 and University of Colorado LL.B. 1958. Admitted to practice Colorado 1958, U.S District Court District of Colorado 1958, U.S. Court of Appeals Tenth Circuit 1971 and U.S. Supreme Court 1972. In legal practice La Junta 1958-88.

Deputy District Attorney Sixteenth Judicial District 1959-72. City Attorney La Junta 1966-88. Member Sixteenth Judicial District (Past President) and Colorado (Past Vice President) Bar Associations. Corporal U.S. Army 1953-55.

Office: 105 Otero County Courthouse, 13 West Third Street, La Junta 81050.

Telephone: (719) 384-4721.

WAKEFIELD, Dana U. *(Judge, Denver Juvenile Court)* Appointed by governor. Former Presiding Judge.

Office: 157 City and County Building, 1437 Bannock Street, Denver 80202.

Telephone: (720) 865-8288.

WARDELL, Robert M. *(Judge, Mineral County Court)* Appointed by governor.

Office: Mineral County Courthouse, North First Street, Creede 81130.

Telephone: (719) 658-2575, 658-2440.

WATANABE, Michael Jiro *(Magistrate Judge, United States District Court District of Colorado)* Appointed by U.S. District Court judges to term beginning Feb 12, 1999. Term expires Feb 2007. Born Huntington Park California June 5, 1953. Educated at LaVerne College B.A. cum laude 1975 and California Western School of Law J.D. 1979. Recipient Ahmanson Scholarship for Business Administration and Economics and CSF Leadership Scholarship. Lead Articles Editor Comparative Labor Law Journal. Listed in *Who's Who in American Colleges and Universities* 1975. Member Phi Alpha Delta and Pi Gamma Mu. Admitted to practice Colorado 1979, U.S. Court of International Trade 1995, U.S. District Court District of Colorado, U.S. Courts of Appeals Ninth and Tenth Circuits and U.S. Supreme Court. In legal practice Englewood Feb 1986 to Nov 1987. Judge Nov 16, 1987 to Feb 11, 1999 and Grand Jury Judge 1989 and 1990, Colorado District Court Eighteenth Judicial District, appointed by Governor Roy Romer.

Deputy Legislative Counsel Nevada Nov 1979 to Dec 1980. Deputy District Attorney Eighteenth Judicial District Colorado Jan 1981 to Jan 1986. Instructor in Crimi-

WATANABE, MICHAEL JIRO—*Continued*

nal Law Paralegal and Police Science Program Arapahoe Community College since 1985. Master of the Bench since 1993, President, Vice President, Treasurer and Secretary Judge Alfred A. Arraj American Inn of Court. Member Domestic Relations Rules Subcommittee Concerning Rules 16.2 and 26.2, 1994 and 1995. Former Member Colorado Trial Lawyers Association, Colorado District Attorneys Association, Colorado Defense Lawyers Association, National District Attorneys Association, The Association of Trial Lawyers of America and Douglas/Elbert County Bar Association. Member Colorado District Judges Association, Asia-Pacific Lawyers Association, American Judicature Society, Asian American Bar Association of Colorado, Arapahoe County (Board of Directors 1990-92), Colorado (Judiciary Section Council since 1996) and American Bar Associations. Alumni Member General Jurisdiction Sept 1989 and Oct 1991, Faculty Advisor April 1994 and May 1994 and Instructor in Evidentiary Issues in Understanding Financial Statements May 1995 The National Judicial College. Presenter Fourth Annual Guardian Ad Litem Training Program May 1994, Eighteenth Annual Child Custody Conference Oct 1994 and Nineteenth Annual Child Custody Conference Sept 1995. Trainer in Judging Trials National Institute for Trial Advocacy. Listed in *Who's Who in Practicing Attorneys* since 1989 and *Who's Who in American Law*. Previously worked as high school teacher and football coach. Board of Directors Arapahoe County Community Corrections 1992 and 1993. Active with Boy Scouts of America. Enjoys fishing, softball, golf, traveling, teaching, reading and performing community service.

Office: U.S. Courthouse, 901 Nineteenth Street, Denver 80294.

Telephone: (303) 844-2403.

Fax: (303) 335-2199

WEATHERBY, Joseph J. *(Judge, Colorado District Court Thirteenth Judicial District)* Appointed by governor. Former Chief Judge.

Mailing address: P.O. Box 130, Fort Morgan 80701.

Office: Morgan County Justice Center, 400 Warner, Fort Morgan 80701.

Telephone: (970) 542-3435.

Fax: (970) 542-3436

WEBB, John R. *(Judge, Colorado Court of Appeals)* Appointed by Governor Bill Owens.

Office: Colorado State Judicial Building, Two East Fourteenth Avenue, Denver 80203.

Telephone: (303) 837-3731.

WEEKS, Orrelle R. *(Judge, Denver Juvenile Court)* Appointed by Governor John A. Love to term beginning May 18, 1973. Retained by election 1976, 1982, 1988, 1994 and 2000. Current term expires Jan 2007. Former Presiding Judge. Born Pueblo Colorado Sept 21, 1935. Episcopalian. Educated at University of Colorado B.A. 1957 LL.B. 1962. Admitted to practice Colorado 1962.

With Denver District Attorney's Office 1963. Member Denver, Colorado and American Bar Associations.

Office: 157 City and County Building, 1437 Bannock Street, Denver 80202.

Telephone: (720) 865-8287.

WEINSHIENK, Zita Leeson *(Senior Judge, United States District Court District of Colorado)* Appointed for life by President Jimmy Carter to term beginning Oct 10, 1979. Assumed Senior status April 3, 1998, serves by assignment. Born St. Paul Minnesota April 3, 1933. Jewish. Educated at University of Arizona B.A. magna cum laude 1955, University of Colorado 1952-54, Harvard Law School J.D. cum laude 1958 and University of Copenhagen 1958-59. Awarded honorary L.H.D. Loretto Heights College May 1985 and Honorary LL.D. University of Denver Aug 1990. Fulbright Scholar. Member Phi Beta Kappa and Phi Kappa Phi. Honorary member Order of the Coif 1972 and Phi Alpha Delta 1979. Admitted to practice Colorado 1959. Judge, Denver Municipal Court 1964-65 (Denver's first woman judge). Judge, Denver County Court 1965-71. Judge, Colorado District Court Second Judicial District 1972-79, appointed by Governor John A. Love.

Probation Counselor, Legal Advisor and Referee Denver Juvenile Court 1959-64. Author "The Danish Child Welfare Committee System" Fulbright paper 1959. Lecturer University of Denver Bar Refresher on Legal Ethics 1960-71 and University of Denver Law School Evening Division 1969. Fellow Colorado Bar Foundation and American Bar Foundation. Former member Colorado District Judges Association. Member District Judges Association of the Tenth Judicial Circuit (President 1986-88), Judicial Conference of the U.S. (Committee on Orientation of Newly Appointed District Judges), Federal Judges Association, Denver (Second Vice President 1970-71), Colorado Women's, Colorado and American (Former Member National Conference of State Trial Judges, Member Executive Committee and Vice Chair 1992-93 National Conference of Federal Trial Judges) Bar Associations. Invited Speaker National Conference on the Judiciary 1971. Discussion Leader National Conference of Special Court Judges 1970. Special Court Faculty National College of the State Judiciary 1973. Lecturer at University of Iowa Law School 1974, National College of District Attorneys 1974, University of Denver School of Social Work Seminars 1974 and 1975, University of Colorado Denver Center 1975 and 1976, St. Louis University 1975 and 1976 and Regis College 1976. Named Denver Business and Professional Women's Woman of the Year 1969 and one of *Harper's Bazaar* "100 Women in Touch With Our Time" 1971. Recipient "Women Helping Women" Award from Soroptimist International of Denver 1983 and Hanna G. Solomon Award from National Council of Jewish Women 1986. Democrat. Board of Directors Denver Crime Stoppers, Inc. Member Harvard Law School Association, Denver League of Women Voters and Women's Forum of Colorado (Vice President 1977-78).

Office: U.S. Courthouse, 901 Nineteenth Street, Denver 80294-3589.

Telephone: (303) 335-2784.

WESTFALL, David S. *(Judge, Ouray County Court)* Appointed by governor.

Mailing address: P.O. Box 643, Ouray 81427.

Office: Ouray County Courthouse, 541 Fourth, Ouray 81427.

Telephone: (970) 325-4405.

WHICHER, Susan *(Judge, Dolores County Court)* Appointed by Governor Bill Owens.

Mailing address: P.O. Box 511, Dove Creek 81324-0511.

WHICHER, SUSAN—*Continued*

Office: Dolores County Courthouse, 409 North Main, Dove Creek 81324.

Telephone: (970) 677-2258.

WILSON, Daniel S. *(Judge, El Paso County Court)* Appointed by Governor Bill Owens May 30, 2002 to term beginning July 1, 2002. Educated at University of Nebraska J.D. In legal practice 1989-94.

Mailing address: P.O. Box 2980, Colorado Springs 80901-2980.

Office: 20 East Vermijo, Colorado Springs 80903.

Telephone: (719) 448-7608.

WILSON, Jeffrey R. *(Judge, Colorado District Court Sixth Judicial District)* Appointed by Governor Bill Owens.

Mailing address: P.O. Box 3340, Durango 81302-3340.

Office: La Plata County Courthouse, 1060 Second Avenue, Durango 81301.

Telephone: (970) 259-2304.

WOOD, Kimberly L. *(Judge, Costilla County Court)* Appointed by Governor Bill Owens to term beginning Feb 28, 2003. Educated at Baylor University and Washington and Lee University School of Law J.D. Former Juvenile Magistrate, Twelfth Judicial District.

Office: Costilla County Courthouse, Main Street, San Luis 81151.

Telephone: (719) 672-3681.

WOODFORD, L. Thomas *(Chief Judge, Colorado District Court First Judicial District)* Appointed by Governor Roy Romer. Retained by election.

Office: 100 Jefferson County Parkway, Golden 80401-6002.

Telephone: (303) 271-6110.

Fax: (303) 271-6124

ZERBI, Victor M., Jr. *(Judge, Garfield County Court)* Appointed by governor.

Office: 104 Garfield County Courthouse, 109 Eighth Street, Glenwood Springs 81601.

Telephone: (970) 947-3870.

ZIMMERMAN, James D. *(Judge, Colorado District Court First Judicial District)* Appointed by Governor Richard D. Lamm to term beginning 1982. Retained by election 1985, 1991 and 1997. Current term expires Jan 2004. Born Tulsa Oklahoma 1943. Educated at University of Colorado B.A. 1966 and University of Denver J.D. 1969. Admitted to practice Colorado 1969. Judge, Jefferson County Court 1975-82.

Office: 100 Jefferson County Parkway, Golden 80401-6002.

Telephone: (303) 271-6140.

Fax: (303) 271-6124

CONNECTICUT

Capital HARTFORD

UNITED STATES DISTRICT COURT DISTRICT OF CONNECTICUT

The court sits at Bridgeport, Hartford, New Haven, New London and Waterbury. For descriptive information refer to the United States Courts section.

Chief Judge

Robert N. Chatigny

Judges

Dominic J. Squatrito	Alvin W. Thompson
Janet Bond Arterton	Christopher F. Droney
Janet C. Hall	Stefan R. Underhill

Senior Judges

Ellen Bree Burns
Warren W. Eginton
Peter C. Dorsey
Alan H. Nevas
Alfred V. Covello

Clerk

Kevin F. Rowe
U.S. Courthouse
141 Church Street
New Haven, Connecticut 06510
(203) 773-2140

UNITED STATES MAGISTRATE JUDGES OF CONNECTICUT

Thomas P. Smith
Joan G. Margolis
Holly B. Fitzsimmons
Donna F. Martinez
William I. Garfinkel

UNITED STATES BANKRUPTCY COURT OF CONNECTICUT

Chief Judge

Alan H. W. Shiff

Judges

Albert S. Dabrowski
Lorraine Murphy Weil

Recalled Judge

Robert L. Krechevsky

Bankruptcy Clerk

Deborah S. Hunt
Federal Building
450 Main Street
Hartford, Connecticut 06103
(860) 240-3675

CONNECTICUT SUPREME COURT

The Supreme Court is Connecticut's court of last resort. The court consists of a chief justice and six associate justices appointed to eight-year terms by the General Assembly upon nomination of the governor from a list compiled by the Judicial Selection Commission. Justices also serve as judges of the Superior Court. A chief justice is appointed to serve an eight-year term by the General Assembly upon nomination of the governor from a list compiled by the Judicial Selection Commission. A judge of the Appellate Court or the Superior Court may be designated by the chief justice to sit as a member of the court to hear a particular case. Retirement is mandatory at age seventy; however, justices who voluntarily retire before that time may continue to serve the court part time as senior associate justices. Fully retired justices may be appointed by the chief justice to serve as judge trial referees.

The court has exclusive appellate jurisdiction over certain cases from the Superior Court. These cases include appeals involving the validity of a state statute or state constitutional provision, conviction for a felony when the maximum sentence exceeds twenty years, review of a death sentence, a dispute over an election or primary, reprimand or censure of a probate judge, judicial removal or suspension of a judge, decisions of the Judicial Review Council, writs of error and matters of substantial public interest. The court has appellate jurisdiction over the Appellate Court only if certification is granted upon petition.

The court may sit en banc or in panels of five justices. The court sits at Hartford and recesses during July, August and September.

Chief Justice

William J. Sullivan

Associate Justices

David M. Borden	Flemming L.
Joette Katz	Norcott, Jr.
Richard N. Palmer	Christine Vertefeuille
Peter T. Zarella	

Acting Chief Clerk

Michele Angers, Esq.
Supreme Court Building
231 Capitol Avenue
Hartford, Connecticut 06106
(860) 757-2200

Chief Court Administrator

Hon. Joseph H. Pellegrino
Supreme Court Building
231 Capitol Avenue
Hartford, Connecticut 06106
(860) 757-2100

CONNECTICUT APPELLATE COURT

The Appellate Court, Connecticut's court of intermediate appellate jurisdiction, was established July 1, 1983. The court consists of a chief judge and eight judges appointed to eight-year terms by the General Assembly upon nomination of the governor from a list compiled by the Judicial Selection Commission. In the event an appellate judge is appointed to Chief Court Administrator, the judge is released from appellate duties unless the Chief Justice deems otherwise. A tenth appellate judge may be appointed to serve for the remainder of the newly designated administrator's term or retirement, whichever occurs earlier. A chief judge is appointed by and serves at the pleasure of the chief justice. Retirement is mandatory at age seventy; however, judges who voluntarily retire before that time may continue to serve the court part time as senior judges. Fully retired judges may be appointed by the chief justice to serve as judge trial referees.

The court has appellate jurisdiction over the Superior Court and Probate Court except when the Supreme Court has exclusive jurisdiction.

The court may sit en banc or in panels of three judges at Hartford.

Chief Judge

William J. Lavery

Judges

Paul M. Foti
Joseph H. Pellegrino
Joseph P. Flynn
Thomas G. West
C. Ian McLachlan
Barry R. Schaller
Anne C. Dranginis
Thomas A. Bishop
Alexandra D. DiPentima

Senior Judge

Sidney S. Landau

CONNECTICUT SUPERIOR COURT

The Superior Court became Connecticut's sole court of general jurisdiction effective July 1, 1978. Jurisdiction which was previously exercised by the Court of Common Pleas and the Juvenile Court has been transferred to the Superior Court. Judges are appointed to eight-year terms by the General Assembly upon nomination of the governor from a list compiled by the Judicial Selection Commission. Retirement is mandatory at age seventy; however, judges who voluntarily retire before that time may continue to serve the court part time as senior judges. Fully retired judges may serve as judge referees. From these judge referees, the chief justice may designate judge trial referees, to whom cases of an adversary nature may be referred. Such designations may not exceed one year.

The court consists of five divisions. The Criminal Division has jurisdiction of cases involving felonies, misdemeanors, motor vehicle infractions and other infractions. The Civil Division's jurisdiction includes administrative appeals, landlord-tenant relations and small claims. The Family Division exercises jurisdiction over support and paternity actions and all other family relations matters including dissolution of marriage cases. Juvenile Matters exercises jurisdiction over juvenile matters, including delinquency, neglect, abuse, dependency and termination of parental rights. Administrative Appeals handles appeals from municipal and state administrative actions.

The state is divided into thirteen judicial districts: Ansonia-Milford, Danbury, Fairfield, Hartford, Litchfield, Middlesex, New Britain, New Haven, New London, Stamford-Norwalk, Tolland, Waterbury and Windham. Each district is divided into Criminal, Civil, Family and Housing Divisions. Judges may be assigned to any one of the four divisions. The chief court administrator appoints an administrative judge to serve in each judicial district and a chief administrative judge to serve in each of the Criminal, Civil and Family Divisions, and for Juvenile Matters, Administrative Appeals, Judicial Marshals and Judge Trial Referees. Both types of administrative judges serve at the pleasure of the chief court administrator.

Judges

Holly Abery-Wetstone
Salvatore C. Agati
Joan K. Alexander
Richard E. Arnold
Thayer Baldwin, Jr.
James M. Bentivegna
Marylouise S. Black
Kevin E. Booth
Daniel Brennan, Jr.
Vanessa L. Bryant
Patrick Carroll, III
Patrick J. Clifford
Henry S. Cohn
Thomas J. Corradino
Juliett L. Crawford
Lloyd Cutsumpas
Richard A. Damiani
Maureen D. Dennis
Robert J. Devlin, Jr.
Joseph W. Doherty
John Redmond Downey
Kevin G. Dubay
Richard W. Dyer
Gerard F. Esposito
Roland D. Fasano
Jack W. Fischer
G. Sarsfield Ford
Stephen F. Frazzini
Stanley T. Fuger, Jr.
Richard P. Gilardi
David P. Gold
James T. Graham
F. Herbert Gruendel
Susan B. Handy
Lubbie Harper, Jr.
Michael Hartmere
Arthur A. Hiller
William Holden
Bruce P. Hudock
Clarance J. Jones
Burton A. Kaplan
Jonathan J. Kaplan
John F. Kavanewsky, Jr.
James G. Kenefick, Jr.
Joseph Q. Koletsky
John J. Langenbach
Edward J. Leavitt
Bruce L. Levin
Joseph A. Licari, Jr.
Michael A. Mack
Paul Matasavage
Taggart D. Adams
Jon M. Alander
Bethany J. Alvord
Julia L. Aurigemma
Robert E. Beach, Jr.
Marshall Berger, Jr.
Jon C. Blue
Elizabeth A. Bozzuto
Robert C. Brunetti
Richard E. Burke
John R. Caruso
E. Curtissa R. Cofield
Richard Comerford, Jr.
Emmet L. Cosgrove
William T. Cremins
Frank D'Addabbo, Jr.
Michael R. Dannehy
James J. Devine
Julia DiCocco Dewey
Edward S. Domnarski
John C. Driscoll
Christina G. Dunnell
Carmen Elisa Espinosa
Dennis G. Eveleigh
Brian T. Fischer
Francis J. Foley, III
Deborah Kochiss Frankel
Elizabeth Gallagher
James P. Ginocchio
Elaine Gordon
Edward C. Graziani
Arthur Hadden
Patricia Lilly Harleston
Lawrence L. Hauser
Beverly J. Hodgson
Robert L. Holzberg
Frank A. Iannotti
Barbara Bailey Jongbloed
Edward R. Karazin, Jr.
Christine E. Keller
Andre M. Kocay
Linda K. Lager
Douglas S. Lavine
Sandra Vilardi Leheny
George Levine
Carmen L. Lopez
Robert A. Martin
Kevin P. McMahon

CONNECTICUT SUPERIOR COURT—*Continued*

Robert F. McWeeny
Douglas C. Mintz
John W. Moran
John F. Mulcahy, Jr.
Lynda B. Munro
Thomas L. Nadeau
Thomas V. O'Keefe, Jr.
Thomas F. Parker
John W. Pickard
Sheila M. Prats
Linda Pearce Prestley
Dale W. Radcliffe
Susan S. Reynolds
Antonio C. Robaina
Angela C. Robinson-Thomas
Nicola E. Rubinow
Angelo L. dos Santos
Philip A. Scarpellino
Stuart M. Schimelman
Carl J. Schuman
Samuel J. Sferrazza
Robert B. Shapiro
Barbara J. Sheedy
Joseph M. Shortall
Jorgé A. Simon
Elliot N. Solomon
Barry Keith Stevens
Wendy W. Susco
Patricia A. Swords
Carl E. Taylor
Bruce W. Thompson
David R. Tobin
Wilson J. Trombley
Thomas F. Upson
Gary J. White
Heidi G. Winslow
Thomas P. Miano
Sheridan L. Moore
A. William Mottolese
Edward J. Mullarkey
William P. Murray
Raymond R. Norko
Howard T. Owens, Jr.
A. Susan Peck
Patty Jenkins Pittman
Barbara M. Quinn
Robert T. Resha
Earl B. Richards
Richard A. Robinson
Eddie Rodriguez, Jr.
Chase T. Rogers
William B. Rush
Thelma A. Santos
Howard Scheinblum
Jane S. Scholl
Karen Skromme Nash Sequino
Michael E. Shay
Michael R. Sheldon
Jonathan E. Silbert
David W. Skolnick
Robert F. Stengel
Terence A. Sullivan
Cynthia K. Swienton
Lois Tanzer
George N. Thim
Kevin Tierney
Richard J. Tobin
John Turner
Bradford J. Ward
Peter E. Wiese
Carol A. Wolven

Senior Judges

Salvatore F. Arena
Barbara A. Coppeto
L. Scott Melville
Russell F. Potter, Jr.
Richard A. Walsh
Leonard M. Cocco
Charles D. Gill
Aaron Ment
Samuel H. Teller

---

*Does not serve as Judge Trial Referee

Judge Referees

Arnold W. Aronson
Sidney Axelrod
Herbert Barall
Edgar W. Bassick, III
William C. Bieluch
John D. Brennan
Walter R. Budney
John M. Byrne
Donald W. Celotto
Bernadette Conway
Thomas H. Corrigan
Hugh C. Curran
Joseph F. Dannehy
John T. Downey
Antoinette L. Dupont
Ronald J. Fracasse
Frederick A. Freedman
Hadley W. Austin
Myron R. Ballen
David M. Barry
Robert I. Berdon
James F. Bingham
Frederica S. Brenneman
Robert P. Burns
Robert J. Callahan
Simon S. Cohen
Michael P. Conway
Albert Cretella, Jr.
Frank H. D'Andrea, Jr.
Anthony V. DeMayo
Philip R. Dunn
John C. Flanagan
Samuel Freed
Samuel S. Freedman
Bernard D. Gaffney
Samuel S. Goldstein
Jack L. Grogins
Robert J. Hale
Dennis F. Harrigan
Seymour L. Hendel
Francis X. Hennessy
D. Michael Hurley
Julius J. Kremski
William B. Lewis
John P. Maiocco, Jr.
Francis M. McDonald, Jr.
Socrates H. Mihalakos
Martin L. Nigro
Francis J. O'Brien*
Norris L. O'Neill
Ellen Ash Peters
Joseph J. Purtill
John N. Reynolds
George W. Ripley, II
John J. Ronan
John J. P. Ryan
Robert Satter
David M. Shea
Daniel F. Spallone
Edward F. Stodolink
Joseph H. Sylvester
Jerry Wagner
Howard F. Zoarski
Joseph H. Goldberg
Joseph Gormley
William L. Hadden, Jr.
Harry Hammer
Arthur H. Healey
Mary R. Hennessey
William F. Hickey, Jr.
Lawrence C. Klaczak
Robert C. Leuba
Alva P. Loiselle*
John P. Maloney
Frank S. Meadow
Howard J. Moraghan
Stanley Novack
Edward Y. O'Connell*
John Ottaviano, Jr.
Romeo G. Petroni
Max H. Reicher
Morton I. Riefberg
Richard M. Rittenband
Jay E. Rubinow*
Angelo G. Santaniello
William Shaughnessy
Allen W. Smith
Joseph L. Steinberg
George D. Stoughton
Paul M. Vasington
William L. Wollenberg

CONNECTICUT PROBATE COURTS

Probate Courts are courts of limited jurisdiction in Connecticut. Judges are elected to four-year terms by the voters in each probate district, which may consist of one or more towns. Probate judges need not be attorneys. Retirement is mandatory at age seventy.

The courts have jurisdiction over the estates of deceased persons and matters involving adoptions, testamentary trusts, conservators, commitment of the mentally ill and guardians of the persons and estates of minors. Appeals may be taken to the Superior Court in the judicial district in which the Probate Court is located.

District	Judge
Andover	Elaine N. Camposeo
Ansonia	See Derby
Ashford	Dennis R. Poitras
Avon	Cynthia C. Becker
Barkhamsted	See New Hartford
Beacon Falls	See Naugatuck
Berlin	Walter A. Clebowicz
Bethany	Guy D. Yale
Bethel	Daniel W. O'Grady
Bethlehem	See Woodbury
Bloomfield	Steven M. Zelman
Bolton	See Andover
Bozrah	Stanley A. Mokrzewski
Branford	John E. Donegan
Bridgeport	Paul J. Ganim
Bridgewater	See New Milford
Bristol	Andre D. Dorval
Brookfield	Joseph P. Secola
Brooklyn	James K. Kelley
Burlington	Charles W. Bauer
Canaan	Barbara G. Seamans
Canterbury	See Plainfield
Canton	Marygale Bouldin

CONNECTICUT PROBATE COURTS—*Continued*

Chaplin	See Eastford
Cheshire	Raymond F. Voelker
Chester	See Saybrook
Clinton	Raymond J. Rigat
Colchester	Kevin Kennedy
Colebrook	See Winchester
Columbia	See Andover
Cornwall	Margaret D. Cooley
Coventry	See Mansfield
Cromwell	See Middletown
Danbury	Dianne E. Yamin
Darien	John B. Rearden, Jr.
Deep River	Patricia L. Damon
Derby	Clifford D. Hoyle
Durham	See Middletown
Eastford	Michael H. Ellsworth
East Granby	Paul A. Ridgeway
East Haddam	Paul D. Buhl
East Hampton	Anne C. McKinney
East Hartford	Allan T. Driscoll
East Haven	Michael A. Albis
East Lyme	Jeffrey A. McNamara
Easton	See Trumbull
East Windsor	Marilyn Lassman Fisher
Ellington	O. James Purnell, III
Enfield	Susan L. Warner
Essex	Deborah M. Pearl
Fairfield	Daniel F. Caruso
Farmington	J. David Morrissey
Franklin	See Norwich
Glastonbury	Donald L. Hamer
Goshen	See Torrington
Granby	Philip D. Main
Greenwich	David W. Hopper
Griswold	George L. Kennedy
Groton	Frederick W. Palm, Jr.
Guilford	Joel E. Helander
Haddam	Sharon G. Kapitulik
Hamden	Salvatore L. Diglio
Hampton	Stuart Case
Hartford	Robert K. Killian, Jr.
Hartland	See New Hartford
Harwinton	Patrick J. Wall
Hebron	Kevin C. Connors
Kent	Barbara L. Miller
Killingly	Thomas E. Dupont, Sr.
Killingworth	Judith P. Lentz
Lebanon	See Colchester
Ledyard	Pamela M. Rowe
Lisbon	See Norwich
Litchfield	Helen Ruwet Bunnell
Lyme	Richard Lightfoot
Madison	Carol B. Lougee
Manchester	John W. Cooney
Mansfield	Claire C. Twerdy
Marlborough	Frank J. Corbo, Jr.
Meriden	John F. Papandrea
Middlebury	See Waterbury
Middlefield	See Middletown
Middletown	Joseph D. Marino
Milford	Beverly Streit-Kefalas
Monroe	See Trumbull
Montville	Ronald K. McDaniel, Jr.
Morris	See Litchfield
Mystic	See Groton or Stonington
Naugatuck	Peter E. Mariano
New Britain	See Berlin
New Canaan	Russell A. Kimes, Jr.
New Fairfield	William P. DeFeo
New Hartford	Norman E. Rogers, Jr.
New Haven	John A. Keyes
Newington	Sheila M. Hennessey
New London	Mathew H. Greene
New Milford	Martin F. Landgrebe
Newtown	Margot S. Hall
Niantic	See East Lyme
Norfolk	Linda F. Riiska
North Branford	Frank J. Forgione
North Canaan	See Canaan
North Haven	Michael R. Brandt
North Stonington	Teresa A. Pensis
Norwalk	Anthony DePanfilis
Norwich	Linda M. Salafia
Old Lyme	Sylvia L. Peterson
Old Saybrook	Roger W. Goodnow
Orange	John J. Carangelo
Oxford	John W. Fertig, Jr.
Plainfield	Kathleen Sendley Barry
Plainville	Heidi Famiglietti
Plymouth	Nancy S. Henderson
Pomfret	Cecile D. Stoddard
Portland	Richard J. Guliani
Preston	See Norwich
Prospect	See Cheshire
Putnam	Ernest J. Cotnoir
Redding	Richard L. Emerson
Ridgefield	Joseph A. Egan, Jr.
Rocky Hill	See Newington
Roxbury	Jeannette M. Puglio
Salem	John W. Butts
Salisbury	Richard T. Fitzgerald
Saybrook	Helen B. Bennet
Scotland	See Windham
Seymour	See Derby
Sharon	Suzanne J. Xanthos
Shelton	Fred J. Anthony
Sherman	See New Fairfield
Simsbury	Paul J. Knierim
Somers	See Stafford
Southbury	Thomas Michael Sutnik
Southington	Bryan F. Meccariello
South Windsor	See East Windsor
Sprague	See Norwich
Stafford	Thomas J. Fiore
Stamford	Gerald M. Fox, Jr.
Sterling	See Plainfield
Stonington	Paul E. Cravinho
Stratford	F. Paul Kurmay
Suffield	Edward G. McAnaney
Thomaston	Joseph J. Fairchild
Thompson	Aileen A. Witkowski
Tolland	Cheryl H. Brown
Torrington	Michael F. Magistrali
Trumbull	John P. Chiota
Union	See Stafford
Vernon	See Ellington
Voluntown	See Norwich
Wallingford	Philip A. Wright, Jr.
Warren	See Litchfield
Washington	Victoria M. Cherniske
Waterbury	Thomas P. Brunnock
Waterford	See New London

CONNECTICUT PROBATE COURTS—*Continued*

Watertown	See Woodbury
Westbrook	Constance J. Vogell
West Hartford	Sydney W. Elkin
West Haven	E. Michael Heffernan
Weston	See Westport
Westport	Kevin M. O'Grady
Wethersfield	See Newington
Willington	See Tolland
Wilton	See Norwalk
Winchester	Alan M. Barber
Windham	Dennis O'Brien
Windsor	Brian T. Griffin
Windsor Locks	William C. Leary
Winsted	See Winchester
Wolcott	See Waterbury
Woodbridge	Robert H. Horowitz
Woodbury	Domenick Calabrese
Woodstock	Nancy M. Gale

Connecticut Counties

Fairfield
Hartford
Litchfield
Middlesex
New Haven
New London
Tolland
Windham

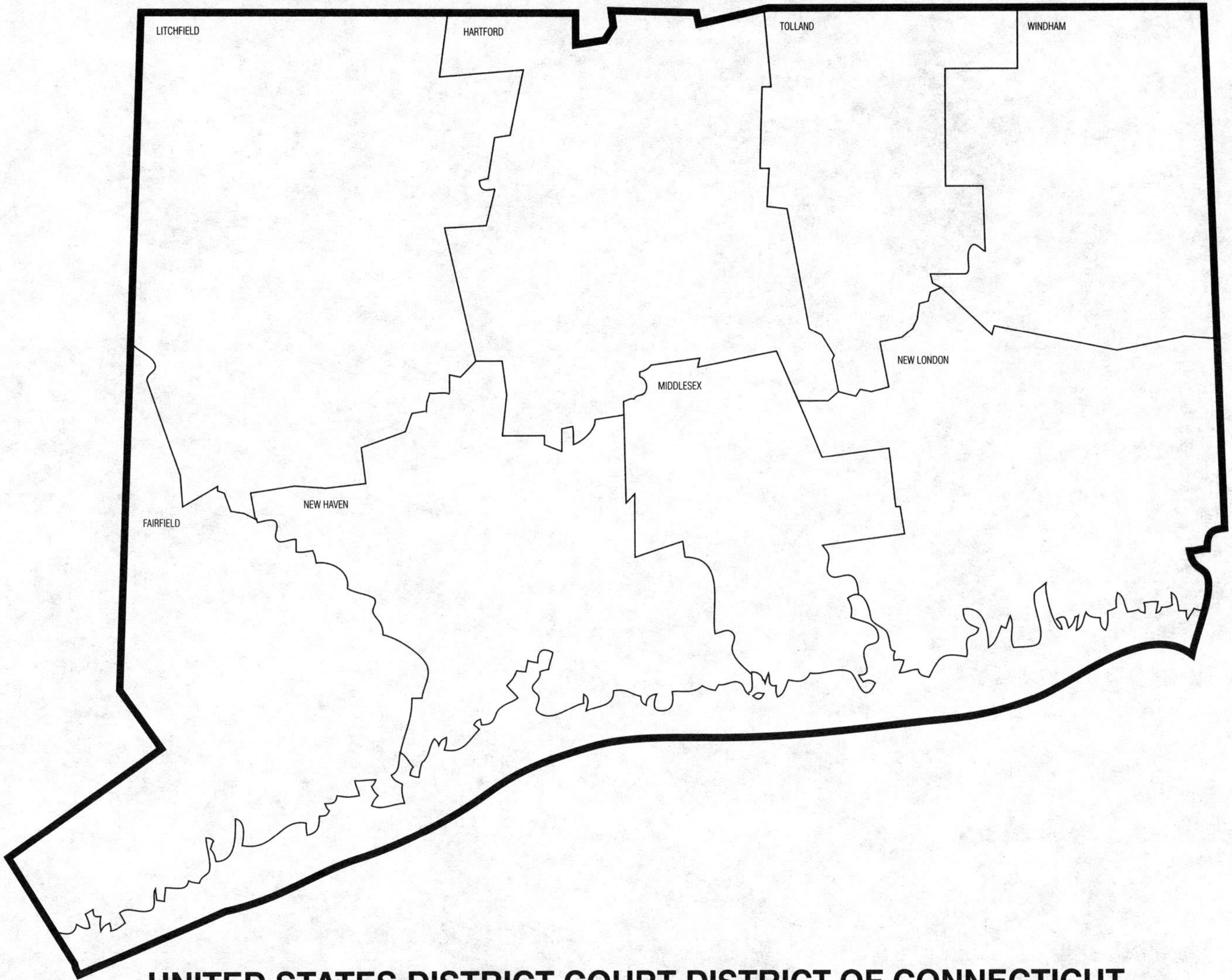
LITCHFIELD
HARTFORD
TOLLAND
WINDHAM
NEW LONDON
MIDDLESEX
NEW HAVEN
FAIRFIELD

UNITED STATES DISTRICT COURT DISTRICT OF CONNECTICUT

CONNECTICUT

ABERY-WETSTONE, Holly *(Judge, Connecticut Superior Court)* Appointed to term beginning April 2001. Term expires April 2009. Born Hartford Connecticut July 8, 1954. Jewish. Educated at St. Joseph College B.A. 1976 and Western New England College School of Law J.D. cum laude 1980. Admitted to practice Connecticut 1980, U.S. District Court District of Connecticut 1985 and U.S. Tax Court 1986. In legal practice Farmington 1991-2000.

Past President Hartford Association of Women Attorneys. Member Hartford County, Connecticut (Former Chair and Co-founder Franchise Law Section) and American (Section of Family Law) Bar Associations. Member West Hartford Democratic Town Committee 1991-97. Member 1997-99 and Minority Leader 1999-2001 West Hartford Town Council. Past President and Member Board of Trustees Montessori School of Greater Hartford.

Office: One Court Street, Middletown 06457.
Telephone: (860) 343-6417.
Fax: (860) 343-6326
E-mail address: Holly.Aberywetstone@jud.state.ct.us

ADAMS, Taggart D. *(Judge, Connecticut Superior Court)* Appointed.

Office: Judicial District Courthouse, 123 Hoyt Street, Stamford 06905.
Telephone: (203) 965-5315.
Fax: (203) 965-5389

AGATI, Salvatore C. *(Judge, Connecticut Superior Court)* Appointed.

Office: 172 Golden Hill Street, Bridgeport 06604.
Telephone: (203) 579-6568.
Fax: (203) 382-8408

ALANDER, Jon M. *(Judge, Connecticut Superior Court)* Appointed to term beginning Aug 1993. Reappointed 2001, current term expires Aug 2009. Former Presiding Judge. Educated at Boston College B.A. with honors 1975 and Yale Law School J.D. 1978. Member Inns of Court. Admitted to practice Connecticut 1978.

Mailing address: P.O. Box 210, Milford 06460.
Office: 14 West River Street, Milford 06460.
Telephone: (203) 878-5791.
Fax: (203) 876-8072

ALBIS, Michael A. *(Judge, East Haven District Probate Court)*

Office: Town Hall, 250 Main Street, East Haven 06512.
Telephone: (203) 468-3895.
Fax: (203) 468-5155

ALEXANDER, Joan K. *(Judge, Connecticut Superior Court)* Appointed.

Office: 121 Elm Street, New Haven 06510.
Telephone: (203) 789-7491.
Fax: (203) 789-7492

ALVORD, Bethany J. *(Judge, Connecticut Superior Court)* Appointed.

Office: 20 Park Street, Rockville 06066.
Telephone: (860) 896-4930.
Fax: (860) 870-3295

ANTHONY, Fred J. *(Judge, Shelton District Probate Court)* Elected Nov 8, 1994 to term beginning Jan 4, 1995. Reelected 1998 and 2002. Current term expires Jan 2007. Born Derby Connecticut Aug 29, 1964. Educated at Providence College B.A. 1986 and Villanova University School of Law J.D. 1989. Admitted to practice Connecticut 1989, U.S. District Court District of Connecticut 1990 and U.S. Supreme Court 2000. Began legal practice Shelton.

Assistant Corporation Counsel Shelton 1991-94. Member Connecticut Trial Lawyers Association, The Association of Trial Lawyers of America, Valley (President 1994-95), Connecticut and American Bar Associations. Commencement Speaker Villanova University School of Law 1989. Member Shelton Republican Town Committee since 1990.

Mailing address: P.O. Box 127, Shelton 06484.
Office: 40 White Street, Shelton 06484.
Telephone: (203) 924-8462.
Fax: (203) 924-8943

ARENA, Salvatore F. *(Senior Judge, Connecticut Superior Court)* Appointed. Former Administrative Judge Middlesex Judicial District. Retired.

Office: Judicial District Courthouse, One Court Street, Middletown 06457.
Telephone: (860) 343-6570.
Fax: (860) 343-6589

ARNOLD, Richard E. *(Judge, Connecticut Superior Court)* Appointed.

Office: Judicial District Courthouse, 235 Church Street, New Haven 06510.
Telephone: (203) 503-6830.
Fax: (203) 789-6826

ARONSON, Arnold W. *(Judge Referee, Connecticut Superior Court)* Appointed Judge to term beginning May 30, 1982. Reappointed May 30, 1990. Former Presiding Judge Tax Session Connecticut. Former Assistant Administrative Judge and Presiding Judge Civil Division Hartford-New Britain Judicial District. Retired. Became Judge Referee Dec 10, 1996. Currently serves as Judge Trial Referee. Born Hartford Connecticut Dec 10, 1926. Educated at University of Connecticut B.A. 1951 J.D. 1954 and University of Hartford M.S.T. Admitted to practice Connecticut 1954.

Former Town Attorney. Member Connecticut and American (Judicial Immunity Committee National Conference of State Trial Judges Judicial Administration Division) Bar Associations. Major U.S. Army (retired). Alumni Advisory Board Barney Graduate School of Business University of Hartford.

Office: 20 Franklin Square, New Britain 06051.
Telephone: (860) 515-5050.
Fax: (860) 515-5051

ARTERTON, Janet Bond *(Judge, United States District Court District of Connecticut)* Appointed for life by President Bill Clinton Jan 23, 1995 to term beginning

ARTERTON, JANET BOND—*Continued*

May 15, 1995. Born Philadelphia Pennsylvania Feb 8, 1944. Educated at Mount Holyoke College B.S. 1966 and Northeastern University School of Law J.D. 1977. In legal practice New Haven 1978-95. Former Attorney Trial Referee Connecticut Superior Court and Special Master U.S. District Court District of Connecticut.

Author "Employment Discrimination Claims in State Court: A Laboratory for Experimentation" New York L. Rev. 1984 and 1995 and "Jury Trials Under Title VII of the Civil Rights Act of 1964" K. Spriggs *Representing Plaintiffs in Title VII Actions* John Wiley & Sons 1994. Co-author with Phelan "Disability Discrimination in the Workplace" Clark Boardman Callaghan 1992. Instructor in Trial Practice Yale Law School. Former Member Federal Civil Justice Reform Act Advisory Committee, U.S. Magistrate Judge Selection Committee, State Court Rules Advisory Committee and U.S. District Court Local Rules Advisory Committee, Board of Governors Connecticut Trial Lawyers Association and Chairperson Federal Practice Section Connecticut Bar Association. Fellow Connecticut Bar Foundation and American Bar Association. Frequent Lecturer on matters of judicial administration and litigation practice in the federal courts. Recipient Maria Miller Stewart Recognition Award from Connecticut Women's Education and Legal Fund 1996. Listed in *The Best Lawyers in America.*

Office: U.S. Courthouse, 141 Church Street, New Haven 06510.

Telephone: (203) 773-2456.

AURIGEMMA, Julia L. *(Judge, Connecticut Superior Court)* Appointed.

Office: Courthouse, One Court Street, Middletown 06457.

Telephone: (860) 343-6570.

Fax: (860) 343-6589

AUSTIN, Hadley W. *(Judge Referee, Connecticut Superior Court)* Appointed Judge. Retired. Currently serves as Judge Trial Referee.

Office: One Courthouse Square, Norwich 06360.

Telephone: (860) 886-0144.

Fax: (860) 823-1019

AXELROD, Sidney *(Judge Referee, Connecticut Superior Court)* Appointed Judge. Former Presiding Judge Family Division Parts S & D. Retired. Currently serves as Judge Trial Referee.

Office: Judicial District Courthouse, 300 Grand Street, Waterbury 06702.

Telephone: (203) 596-4033.

Fax: (203) 596-4488

BALDWIN, Thayer, Jr. *(Judge, Connecticut Superior Court)* Appointed to term beginning April 11, 2001. Term expires April 11, 2009. Born Waterbury Connecticut Nov 20, 1940. Christian. Educated at Yale University A.B. 1962 and Georgetown University Law Center LL.B. 1965. Admitted to practice Connecticut 1965, U.S. District Court District of Connecticut 1965 and U.S. Court of Appeals Second Circuit 1966. In legal practice New Haven 1965-2001.

Corporation Counsel New Haven Jan 1, 1976 to Sept 1, 1978 and June 22, 1998 to March 31, 2001. Chief Health System Regulation Connecticut Jan 1, 1980 to Feb 26, 1982. Former Member American Arbitration Association and Connecticut Bar Association.

Office: 230 Main Street Extension, Middletown 06457.

Telephone: (860) 344-2986.

Fax: (860) 344-3038

E-mail address: thayer.baldwin@jud.state.ct.us

BALLEN, Myron R. *(Judge Referee, Connecticut Superior Court)* Appointed Judge. Former Assistant Administrative Judge and Administrative Judge Fairfield Judicial District. Retired. Became Judge Referee March 29, 1999. Currently serves as Judge Trial Referee.

Office: Judicial District Courthouse, 1061 Main Street, Bridgeport 06604.

Telephone: (203) 579-6540.

Fax: (203) 579-6928

BARALL, Herbert *(Judge Referee, Connecticut Superior Court)* Appointed Judge to term beginning Feb 22, 1979. Reappointed 1987 and 1995. Former Chief Administrative Judge Juvenile Court and Presiding Judge Family, Civil and Criminal Divisions Hartford Judicial District. Former Senior Judge. Became Judge Referee Aug 17, 2002. Currently serves as Judge Trial Referee. Born New York New York Aug 17, 1932. Educated at New York University B.S. 1953 and Harvard University LL.D. cum laude 1956. Member Beta Gamma Sigma. Admitted to practice Connecticut 1956, U.S. District Court District of Connecticut 1959 and U.S. Supreme Court 1963. Began legal practice East Hartford 1959.

Member Hartford County, Connecticut and American Bar Associations. Instructor Connecticut Judicial Institute Summer 1983 and 1984. First Lieutenant USAF Staff Judge Advocate 1957-59. Councilman East Hartford 1959-63. Member East Hartford Board of Education 1963-67. Chairman Governor's Advisory Council on Mental Retardation 1982-92. Founder Connecticut League for Autistic Children. Advisory Council Connecticut Special Education. Enjoys tennis, ballroom dancing and reading.

Office: 100 Washington Street, Hartford 06106.

Telephone: (860) 566-3468.

Fax: (860) 566-3449

BARBER, Alan M. *(Judge, Winchester District Probate Court)*

Mailing address: P.O. Box 625, Winsted 06098-0625.

Office: 338 Main Street, Winsted 06098.

Telephone: (860) 379-5576.

BARRY, David M. *(Judge Referee, Connecticut Superior Court)* Appointed Judge. Former Presiding Judge. Retired. Currently serves as Judge Trial Referee.

Office: 20 Park Street, Rockville 06066.

Telephone: (860) 896-4930.

Fax: (860) 870-3295

BARRY, Kathleen Sendley *(Judge, Plainfield District Probate Court)* Elected Nov 1975. Reelected 1978, 1982, 1986, 1990, 1994, 1998 and 2002. Current term expires 2007. Born Providence Rhode Island July 22, 1947. Roman Catholic. Educated at Amherst College B.A. with honors 1969 and Providence College M.E. 1976.

Member Connecticut Probate Assembly, Connecticut Council on Adoptions and National College of Probate Judges. Also employed as teacher. Member Democratic Town Committee since 1973 and Board of Tax Review

BARRY, KATHLEEN SENDLEY—*Continued*

1974-75. Enjoys family activities, travel and stamp collecting.
Office: Town Hall, Eight Community Avenue, Plainfield 06374.
Telephone: (860) 230-3031.

BASSICK, Edgar W., III *(Judge Referee, Connecticut Superior Court)* Appointed Judge to term beginning Feb 5, 1986. Reappointed 1994. Former Presiding Judge Family Division Fairfield Judicial District. Former Senior Judge. Became Judge Referee Sept 26, 1997. Currently serves as Judge Trial Referee. Born Bridgeport Connecticut Sept 26, 1927. Episcopalian. Educated at Yale College B.A. 1950 and Harvard Law School J.D. 1955. Admitted to practice Connecticut 1955, U.S. District Court District of Connecticut 1956, U.S. Court of Appeals Second Circuit 1957 and U.S. Supreme Court 1959. In legal practice Bridgeport 1955-86.
Member Connecticut Chapter American Academy of Matrimonial Lawyers, American Judicature Society, Bridgeport, Connecticut and American Bar Associations. Second Lieutenant 1946-48 and First Lieutenant 1950-52 U.S. Army Infantry. Board of Directors Mt. Grove Cemetery Association. Member Barnum Festival, Inc. (Ringmaster 1966, President 1972), Exchange Club of Bridgeport (President 1967), Algonquin Club (President 1980-81) and P. T. Barnum Foundation.
Office: Judicial District Courthouse, 1061 Main Street, Bridgeport 06604.
Telephone: (203) 579-6540.
Fax: (203) 579-6928

BAUER, Charles W. *(Judge, Burlington District Probate Court)* Elected to term beginning Jan 1, 1979. Reelected to subsequent terms. Born Hartford Connecticut Nov 26, 1943. Educated at Hamilton College B.A. 1965 and University of Connecticut J.D. 1968. Admitted to practice Connecticut 1971, Kentucky, Pennsylvania, U.S. District Court District of Connecticut, U.S. Court of Appeals Second Circuit and U.S. Supreme Court. In legal practice New Britain Connecticut.
Town Counsel Burlington since 1982. Served in Peace Corps Botswana Africa 1968-71. Chairman Board of Directors New Britain Foundation for Public Giving.
Office: 200 Spielman Highway, Burlington 06013.
Telephone: (860) 673-2108.

BEACH, Robert E., Jr. *(Judge, Connecticut Superior Court)* Appointed.
Office: Judicial District Courthouse, 95 Washington Street, Hartford 06106.
Telephone: (860) 548-2850.
Fax: (860) 548-2887

BECKER, Cynthia C. *(Judge, Avon District Probate Court)*
Office: 60 West Main Street, Avon 06001.
Telephone: (860) 409-4348.

BENNET, Helen B. *(Judge, Saybrook District Probate Court)*
Mailing address: P.O. Box 628, Chester 06412.
Office: 65 Main Street, Chester 06412.
Telephone: (860) 526-0007.

BENTIVEGNA, James M. *(Judge, Connecticut Superior Court)* Appointed.
Office: Courthouse, 131 North Main Street, Bristol 06010.
Telephone: (860) 582-8111.
Fax: (860) 585-8799

BERDON, Robert I. *(Judge Referee, Connecticut Superior Court)* Retired. Became Judge Referee Dec 24, 1999. Currently serves as Judge Trial Referee. Born New Haven Connecticut Dec 24, 1929. Educated at University of Connecticut B.S. 1951 J.D. 1957 and University of Virginia LL.M. in Judicial Process 1988. In legal practice New Haven 1957-73. Judge, Connecticut Superior Court 1973-91. Associate Justice, Connecticut Supreme Court 1991-99.
Author "A Child's Right to Counsel in a Contested Custody Proceeding Resulting from a Termination of the Marriage" 50 Connecticut B. Jour. 150, 1976; "Protecting Individual Liberties Under the State Constitution" 56 Connecticut B. Jour. 236, 1982; "Abolish the Grand Jury" New Haven Register Feb 25, 1985; "Connecticut Equal Protection Clause: Requirement of Strict Scrutiny when Classifications are Based upon Sex, Physical Disability or Mental Disability" 29 Connecticut History 130, 1988 and 64 Connecticut B. Jour. 386, 1990; "An Analytical Framework for Raising State Constitutional Claims in Connecticut" 14 Quinnipiac L. Rev. 191, 1994; and "Freedom of the Press and the Connecticut Constitution" 26 Connecticut L. Rev. 659, 1994. Adjunct Professor of State Constitutional Law University of Bridgeport 1986-91. Member American Judicature Society, Connecticut Bar Foundation, New Haven County, Connecticut (Executive Committee Litigation Section 1982-85 and 1988-92, Former Member Executive Committee Human Rights and Responsibilities Section) and American (Jury Management Committee National Conference of State Trial Judges Judicial Division 1982-85) Bar Associations. Named Outstanding State Trial Judge in the United States by The Association of Trial Lawyers of America 1982. Recipient Judiciary Award from Connecticut Bar Association 1991, RisCassi-Koskoff Civil Justice Award from Connecticut Trial Lawyers Association 1999 and Judicial Recognition Award from Connecticut Defense Lawyers Association 1999. Celebrated for judicial career and accomplishments by Quinnipiac College School of Law 1999. First Lieutenant U.S. Army 1951-53. With Bank of Manhattan 1953-54. Treasurer State of Connecticut 1971-73. Member Connecticut Board of Pardons 1991-92. Member U.S. Supreme Court Historical Society.
Office: Judicial District Courthouse, 235 Church Street, New Haven 06510.
Telephone: (203) 789-7922.

BERGER, Marshall K., Jr. *(Judge, Connecticut Superior Court)* Appointed.
Office: Judicial District Courthouse, 95 Washington Street, Hartford 06106.
Telephone: (860) 548-2850.
Fax: (860) 548-2887

BIELUCH, William C. *(Judge Referee, Connecticut Superior Court)* Retired. Became Judge Referee Nov 12, 1988. Currently serves as Judge Trial Referee. Born Hartford Connecticut Nov 12, 1918. Roman Catholic. Educated at Brown University A.B. magna cum laude 1939 and Yale University J.D. 1942. Member Phi Beta Kappa. Admitted to practice Connecticut 1942. Began

BIELUCH, WILLIAM C.—*Continued*

legal practice Washington D.C. 1942. In legal practice Hartford 1945-68. Judge, Connecticut Circuit Court Aug 8, 1968 to July 31, 1973. Judge, Connecticut Court of Common Pleas Aug 1, 1973 to Dec 30, 1976. Judge, Connecticut Superior Court Dec 31, 1976 to Sept 23, 1985. Judge, Connecticut Appellate Court Sept 24, 1985 to Nov 11, 1988.

Important Decisions: Commission on Human Rights and Opportunities v. Carbone 1970; Groton v. Medbery et al. 1972; Hilton of San Juan, Inc. v. Lateano et al. 1972; LeClair v. Woodward 1970; Richards v. Greyhound Lines, Inc. 1972; State v. Anonymous 1971; Hartford v. Public Utilities Comm. 1973; Lance v. Welfare Commr. 1975; Lauricella v. Planning & Zoning Board of Appeals 1974; Mangene Sr. v. Aetna Life Ins. Co. 1974; Old Lyme Associates Corp. v. Zoning Comm. of Old Lyme 1974; Oliver v. Zoning Commission 1974; President and Fellows of Harvard College v. Ledyard 1975; Venditto v. Auletta Jr. et al. 1974; Hartford v. Public Utilities Commission 1976; Simon v. Mullin 1977; Hartford v. Associated Construction Co. 1978; and Cologne v. Westfarms Associates 1982. Member Hartford County and Connecticut Bar Associations. Instructor in Administrative Law Connecticut Bar Association CLE 1984-85. Recipient Archdiocesan Medal of Appreciation 1970. Lieutenant j.g. USCGR 1943-45. Named Knight of St. Gregory 1973. Republican.

Office: Judicial District Courthouse, 95 Washington Street, Hartford 06106.
Telephone: (860) 548-2850.
Fax: (860) 548-2887

BINGHAM, James F. *(Judge Referee, Connecticut Superior Court)* Appointed Judge. Former Administrative Judge Stamford-Norwalk Judicial District. Former Assistant Administrative Judge and Presiding Judge for Criminal Division. Former Senior Judge. Currently serves as Judge Trial Referee.

Office: 123 Hoyt Street, Stamford 06905.
Telephone: (203) 965-5315.
Fax: (203) 965-5389

BISHOP, Thomas A. *(Judge, Connecticut Appellate Court)* Appointed to term beginning Dec 2001. Born New Rochelle New York 1941. Educated at University of Notre Dame B.A. 1963 and Georgetown University Law Center J.D. 1969. Admitted to practice Connecticut 1969 and U.S. District Court District of Connecticut 1970. Judge Sept 1994 to Dec 2001, Assistant Administrative Judge Tolland Judicial District Sept 1994 to Sept 1996 and Presiding Judge Family Division Parts S and D Sept 1996 to April 1999, Connecticut Superior Court.

Office: 95 Washington Street, Hartford 06106.
Telephone: (860) 548-2828.

BLACK, Marylouise S. *(Judge, Connecticut Superior Court)* Appointed.

Office: 80 Doyle Road, Bantam 06750.
Telephone: (860) 567-3942.
Fax: (860) 567-3934

BLUE, Jon C. *(Judge, Connecticut Superior Court)* Appointed to term beginning April 25, 1989. Reappointed 1997, current term expires 2005. Born Springfield Minnesota Sept 30, 1948. Educated at Carleton College B.A. with honors 1970 and Stanford Law School J.D. 1973. Admitted to practice California 1974 and Connecticut 1974. In legal practice New Haven Connecticut 1973-76.

Staff Attorney Connecticut Prison Association 1976-81. Assistant Public Defender New Haven 1982-89. Author "Defining Extreme Emotional Disturbance" 64 Connecticut B. Jour. 473, 1990; "High Noon Revisited" 101 Yale L. Jour. 1475, 1992; "The Government of the Living—The Legacy of the Dead" 33 University of Richmond L. Rev. 325, 1999; and "Judicial Tenure in Connecticut: How it Was Gained and How it Was Lost—1818-1863" 20 Quinnipiac L. Rev. 125, 2000. Important Decisions: Burritt Interfinancial Bancorporation v. Brooker Pointe Associates 625 A.2d 851, 1992; Bradford v. Brennan 631 A.2d 1165, 1992; JLM Inc. v. Meehan 649 A.2d 1, 1993; Pechiney Corp. v. Crystal 643 A.2d 319, 1994; Stanton v. Carlson Sales, Inc. 728 A.2d 534, 1998; Janicki v. Hospital of St. Raphael 744 A.2d 963, 1999; and Privee v. Burns 749 A.2d 689, 1999. Interests include history and travel.

Office: Judicial District Courthouse, 235 Church Street, New Haven 06510.
Telephone: (203) 503-6830.
Fax: (203) 789-6826

BOOTH, Kevin E. *(Judge, Connecticut Superior Court)* Appointed.

Office: Judicial District Courthouse, 95 Washington Street, Hartford 06106.
Telephone: (860) 548-2850.
Fax: (860) 548-2887

BORDEN, David M. *(Associate Justice, Connecticut Supreme Court)* Appointed. Born Hartford Connecticut Aug 4, 1937. Jewish. Educated at Amherst College B.A. magna cum laude 1959 and Harvard University LL.B. cum laude 1962. Member Phi Beta Kappa. Admitted to practice Connecticut 1962, U.S. District Court District of Connecticut 1962, U.S. Court of Appeals Second Circuit 1965 and U.S. Supreme Court 1969. Began legal practice Hartford 1962. Judge, Connecticut Court of Common Pleas 1977-78. Judge, Connecticut Superior Court July 1, 1978 to Aug 14, 1983. Former Judge, Connecticut Appellate Court, appointed by Governor William A. O'Neill to term beginning Aug 15, 1983.

Chief Counsel to Joint Committee on the Judiciary, Connecticut General Assembly 1975-76. Lecturer on Law University of Connecticut School of Law 1970-73. Executive Director Connecticut Commission to Revise the Criminal Statutes 1963-71. Member Hartford County and Connecticut Bar Associations. Democrat. Enjoys skiing, jogging and reading.

Office: 231 Capitol Avenue, Hartford 06106.
Telephone: (860) 757-2200.

BOULDIN, Marygale *(Judge, Canton District Probate Court)*

Mailing address: P.O. Box 175, Collinsville 06022-0175.
Office: Town Hall, Four Market Street, Collinsville 06019.
Telephone: (860) 693-7851.
Fax: (860) 693-7889

BOZZUTO, Elizabeth A. *(Judge, Connecticut Superior Court)* Appointed.

Office: Courthouse, 146 White Street, Danbury 06810.
Telephone: (203) 207-8690.
Fax: (203) 207-8689

BRANDT, Michael R. *(Judge, North Haven District Probate Court)*
Mailing address: P.O. Box 175, North Haven 06473-0175.
Office: 18 Church Street, North Haven 06473-2503.
Telephone: (203) 239-5321.
Fax: (203) 239-1874

BRENNAN, Daniel E., Jr. *(Judge, Connecticut Superior Court)* Appointed to term beginning March 3, 1999. Term expires March 11, 2007. Born Houston Texas Oct 21, 1942. Jewish. Educated at University of the State of New York B.S. with honors 1975 and University of Bridgeport J.D. 1981. Admitted to practice Connecticut 1981, U.S. District Court District of Connecticut 1991 and U.S. Supreme Court 1994. In legal practice Bridgeport and Trumbull 1981-99.

Chief Legal Counsel City of Bridgeport Police 1981-85. Chief Labor Counsel Bridgeport 1981-85. Founder and Faculty Member Connecticut Trial Advocacy Institute. Member National Council of Juvenile and Family Court Judges, American Judges Association (Co-chair Court Security Committee) and Connecticut Bar Association (Former Chair Litigation Section).
Office: Judicial District Courthouse, 1061 Main Street, Bridgeport 06604.
Telephone: (203) 579-6540.
Fax: (203) 579-6928
E-mail address: Daniel.Brennan@jud.state.ct.us

BRENNAN, John D. *(Judge Referee, Connecticut Superior Court)* Appointed Judge to term beginning July 1, 1978. Former Administrative Judge Hartford-New Britain Judicial District. Retired. Currently serves as Judge Trial Referee. Former Judge, Connecticut Court of Common Pleas.
Office: Judicial District Courthouse, 95 Washington Street, Hartford 06106.
Telephone: (860) 548-2850.
Fax: (860) 548-2887

BRENNEMAN, Frederica S. *(Judge Referee, Connecticut Superior Court)* Appointed Judge to term beginning July 1, 1978. Reappointed 1986 and 1994. Former Senior Judge. Became Judge Referee July 10, 1996. Currently serves as Judge Trial Referee. Born Ann Arbor Michigan July 10, 1926. Congregationalist. Educated at Radcliffe College B.A. magna cum laude 1947 and Harvard Law School LL.B. 1953. Honorary D.H.L. St. Joseph College 2000. Member Phi Beta Kappa. Admitted to practice District of Columbia 1953, Massachusetts 1954 and Connecticut 1956. In legal practice Torrington Connecticut 1956-61 and Essex Connecticut 1961-67. Judge, Connecticut Juvenile Court District Three 1967-78.

Attorney Antitrust Division Appellate Section U.S. Department of Justice 1955-56. Law Clerk to Connecticut General Assembly 1967. Member Connecticut Judges Association, National Association of Counsel for Children, National CASA Association, National Council of Juvenile and Family Court Judges and Connecticut Bar Association. Democrat. Interested in theatre and traveling. "Mother of Amy Brenneman, creator and star of hit TV dramatic series *Judging Amy* based on her impressions of my life as a Juvenile Court Judge with young children at home."

BROWN, Cheryl H. *(Judge, Tolland District Probate Court)* Elected Nov 1998 to term beginning Jan 1999. Reelected 2002, current term expires Jan 2007. Born Hartford Connecticut Oct 13, 1952. Protestant. Educated at Eastern Connecticut State University B.S. 1974.

Republican. Member Friends of the Library. Enjoys traveling and raising a family.
Office: Hicks Memorial Municipal Center, 21 Tolland Green, Tolland 06084.
Telephone: (860) 871-3640.
Fax: (860) 871-3641
E-mail address: cbrown@tolland.org

BRUNETTI, Robert C. *(Judge, Connecticut Superior Court)* Appointed.
Office: 121 Elm Street, New Haven 06510.
Telephone: (203) 789-7491.
Fax: (203) 789-7492

BRUNNOCK, Thomas P. *(Judge, Waterbury District Probate Court)*
Office: 236 Grand Street, Waterbury 06702.
Telephone: (203) 755-1127.
Fax: (203) 597-0824

BRYANT, Vanessa L. *(Judge, Connecticut Superior Court)* Appointed.
Office: Courthouse, 20 Franklin Square, New Britain 06051.
Telephone: (860) 515-5050.
Fax: (860) 515-5051

BUDNEY, Walter R. *(Judge Referee, Connecticut Superior Court)* Appointed Judge. Former Administrative Judge and Presiding Judge Middlesex Judicial District. Former Senior Judge. Currently serves as Judge Trial Referee.
Office: One Court Street, Middletown 06457.
Telephone: (860) 343-6570.
Fax: (860) 343-6589

BUHL, Paul D. *(Judge, East Haddam District Probate Court)* Elected Nov 8, 1994. Reelected 1998 and 2002. Current term expires Jan 2007.
Mailing address: P.O. Box 217, East Haddam 06423.
Office: Goodspeed Plaza, East Haddam 06423.
Telephone: (860) 873-5028.

BUNNELL, Helen Ruwet *(Judge, Litchfield District Probate Court)*
Mailing address: P.O. Box 505, Litchfield 06759.
Office: 74 West Street, Litchfield 06759.
Telephone: (860) 567-8065.
Fax: (860) 567-2538

BURKE, Richard E. *(Judge, Connecticut Superior Court)* Appointed. Born New York New York July 6, 1946. Roman Catholic. Educated at Marquette University A.B. 1969, Tulane University School of Law J.D. 1973 and University of Miami School of Law LL.M. 1979. Admitted to practice New York 1974, Connecticut 1976, Florida 1976, California 1988, Illinois 1988, New Jersey 1988, Texas 1988, Massachusetts 1989 and Pennsylvania 1989. In legal practice New Canaan Connecticut since 1980. Former Judge, New Canaan District Probate Court, elected to term beginning Jan 7, 1987.

Editor and Co-author *Connecticut Real Property Law* Atlantic Law Books 1984. Board of Editors Probate L. Jour. University of Bridgeport School of Law since 1989. Adjunct Professor of Trust and Estate Law University of Bridgeport School of Law 1979, 1989 and 1991. Member Probate Reorganization Committee State

BURKE, RICHARD E.—*Continued*

of Connecticut 1989-91. Member Connecticut Probate Judges Assembly (Executive Committee since 1993), National College of Probate Judges, The Florida Bar, State Bar of California, New Canaan (President 1987), Connecticut, New York State and American Bar Associations. Attended Probate Course The National Judicial College Feb 1988, National College of Probate Judges Seminars 1987-92 and Mediation Course Harvard Law School 1991. Instructor "Evidence for Probate Judges" seminar Connecticut Assembly of Probate Judge Nov 1990. Recipient Certificate of Commendation from Judicial Department State of Connecticut 1987 and 1990. Member New Canaan Exchange Club.

Office: 920 Broad Street, Hartford 06106.
Telephone: (860) 566-8290.
Fax: (860) 566-1658

BURNS, Ellen Bree *(Senior Judge, United States District Court District of Connecticut)* Appointed for life by President Jimmy Carter. Chief Judge 1988-92. Assumed Senior status 1992, serves by assignment. First woman to serve U.S. District Court District of Connecticut. Born New Haven Connecticut Dec 13, 1923. Roman Catholic. Educated at Albertus Magnus College B.A. summa cum laude 1944 and Yale University LL.B. 1947. Awarded honorary LL.D. Albertus Magnus College 1974, University of New Haven 1981, Sacred Heart University 1986 and Fairfield University 1991. Honorary member Phi Delta Phi and Burns Inn, University of Bridgeport 1980. Admitted to practice Connecticut 1947. Judge, Connecticut Circuit Court Oct 1973 to Dec 1974. Judge, Connecticut Court of Common Pleas Jan 1975 to May 1976. Judge, Connecticut Superior Court 1976-78 (first woman to serve Superior Court).

Guggenheim Fellow Yale Law School 1974-75. Fellow American Bar Foundation. Member Commission to Reorganize Judicial Department 1975 and Commission on Parole Evaluation and Rehabilitation 1975-76. Distinguished Achievement Award Winner Connecticut Federation of Business and Professional Women's Clubs 1976. Recipient Distinguished Alumna Award from Albertus Magnus College 1971, Charles Carroll of Carrolton Award from John Barry Assembly Knights of Columbus 1974, Judiciary Award from Connecticut Trial Lawyers Association 1978, Cross Pro Ecclesia et Pontifice 1981, Judiciary Award from Connecticut Bar Association 1987, Connecticut Law Review Award 1987 and Raymond E. Baldwin Public Service Award from Bridgeport School of Law 1992. Member School Board Archdiocese of Hartford 1971-76 and State Law Library Advisory Board 1977-78. Trustee Albertus Magnus College since 1985.

Office: U.S. Courthouse, 141 Church Street, New Haven 06510.
Telephone: (203) 773-2105.

BURNS, Robert P. *(Judge Referee, Connecticut Superior Court)* Appointed Judge. Former Senior Judge. Currently serves as Judge Trial Referee.

Office: Judicial District Courthouse, 235 Church Street, New Haven 06510.
Telephone: (203) 503-6830.
Fax: (203) 789-6826

BUTTS, John W. *(Judge, Salem District Probate Court)*

Office: 270 Hartford Road, Salem 06420.
Telephone: (860) 859-3873.
Fax: (860) 443-5160

BYRNE, John M. *(Judge Referee, Connecticut Superior Court)* Appointed Judge. Former Senior Judge. Currently serves as Judge Trial Referee.

Office: 20 Franklin Square, New Britain 06051.
Telephone: (860) 515-5050.
Fax: (860) 515-5051

CALABRESE, Domenick *(Judge, Woodbury District Probate Court)*

Mailing address: P.O. Box 84, Woodbury 06798.
Office: 281 Main Street South, Woodbury 06798.
Telephone: (203) 263-2417.
Fax: (203) 263-2748

CALLAHAN, Robert J. *(Judge Referee, Connecticut Superior Court)* Retired. Currently serves a Judge Trial Referee. Former Associate Justice and Chief Justice, Connecticut Supreme Court.

Office: Judicial District Courthouse, 123 Hoyt Street, Stamford 06905.
Telephone: (203) 965-5315.
Fax: (203) 965-5389

CAMPOSEO, Elaine N. *(Judge, Andover District Probate Court)* Elected Nov 6, 1990 to term beginning Jan 9, 1991. Reelected 1994, 1998 and 2002. Current term expires Jan 2007. Born Hartford Connecticut. Educated at Hartford College for Women A.A. 1969, Eastern Connecticut State University B.S. with honors 1983 and Western New England College School of Law J.D. 1988. Admitted to practice Connecticut 1989. In legal practice Manchester since 1989.

Member Manchester, Connecticut and American Bar Associations.

Office: 222 Bolton Center Road, Bolton 06043.
Telephone: (860) 647-7979.
Fax: (860) 649-3187

CARANGELO, John J. *(Judge, Orange District Probate Court)*

Office: 525 Orange Center Road, Orange 06477.
Telephone: (203) 891-2160.
Fax: (203) 891-2161

CARROLL, Patrick L., III *(Judge, Connecticut Superior Court)* Appointed.

Office: 146 White Street, Danbury 06810.
Telephone: (203) 207-8690.
Fax: (203) 207-8689

CARUSO, Daniel F. *(Judge, Fairfield District Probate Court)* Elected Nov 5, 1994 to term beginning Jan 4, 1995. Reelected Nov 1998 and Nov 2002. Current term expires Jan 2007. Interim Judge New Canaan District 2001 and Greenwich District 2002. Born Greenwich Connecticut Dec 12, 1957. Roman Catholic. Educated at University of Connecticut B.A. 1980 and University of Vermont J.D. 1983. Admitted to practice Connecticut 1983 and U.S. District Court District of Connecticut. Began legal practice Fairfield 1984.

Member Connecticut General Assembly 1989-95 (Judiciary Committee 1989-95, Assistant House Minority Leader 1992-95). Member Connecticut Bar Association (Executive Committee Estates and Trusts Section). Dele-

CARUSO, DANIEL F.—*Continued*

gate Republican National Convention 1992. Treasurer Town of Fairfield 1993-95. Eagle Scout. Member Red Cross and Kiwanis.

Office: Sullivan Independence Hall, 725 Old Post Road, Fairfield 06430.
Telephone: (203) 256-3041.
Fax: (203) 256-3044

CARUSO, John R. *(Judge, Connecticut Superior Court)* Appointed.

Office: Judicial District Courthouse, 95 Washington Street, Hartford 06106.
Telephone: (860) 548-2850.
Fax: (860) 548-2887

CASE, Stuart *(Judge, Hampton District Probate Court)* Elected Nov 6, 2001. Reelected Nov 5, 2002, current term expires Jan 2007. Born New York New York Nov 12, 1941. Educated at Columbia University B.A. 1962, New School for Social Research M.A. 1966 and Western New England College School of Law J.D. cum laude 1991. Staff member Western New England College Law Review 1990. Admitted to practice Connecticut 1991, U.S. District Court District of Connecticut 1992, Mashautucket Pequot Tribal Court 1995 and Mohegan Tribal Court 1995. In legal practice Mansfield Center 1992-2001.

Former Member National Employment Lawyers Association, Windham County and Connecticut Bar Associations. Secretary Hampton Zoning Board of Appeals 1980-88. Personal Statement or Quote: "Even in a small-town court such as this, where the atmosphere is informal, civility is demanded and expected. We also expect attorneys to be prepared."

Mailing address: P.O. Box 143, Hampton 06247.
Office: 164 Main Street, Hampton 06247.
Telephone: (860) 455-9132.
Fax: (860) 455-0517
E-mail address: law@case.tm

CELOTTO, Donald W. *(Judge Referee, Connecticut Superior Court)* Appointed Judge to term beginning July 1, 1978. Reappointed to subsequent term. Former Assistant Administrative Judge, Presiding Judge and Administrative Judge New Haven Judicial District. Retired. Became Judge Referee Oct 19, 1994. Currently serves as Judge Trial Referee. Born New Haven Connecticut Oct 19, 1924. Roman Catholic. Educated at Yale University B.A. 1948 and University of Connecticut LL.B. 1954. Admitted to practice Connecticut 1954 and U.S. District Court District of Connecticut 1956. Began legal practice New Haven 1954. Judge, Connecticut Court of Common Pleas Feb 7, 1974 to June 30, 1978.

Lecturer Quinnipiac College since 1961. Member New Haven County Bar Association (President since 1972). Sergeant 1943-46 and First Lieutenant 1950-52 U.S. Army Infantry. Republican. Former State Central Republican Committeeman.

Office: Judicial District Courthouse, 235 Church Street, New Haven 06510.
Telephone: (203) 503-6830.
Fax: (203) 789-6826

CHATIGNY, Robert N. *(Chief Judge, United States District Court District of Connecticut)* Appointed for life by President Bill Clinton Sept 29, 1994. Chief Judge since Feb 4, 2003. Born Oct 17, 1951. Educated at Brown University A.B. 1973 and Georgetown University Law Center J.D. 1978. Law Clerk to Hon. Samuel Conti, U.S. District Court Northern District of California 1979-80, Hon. Jose A. Cabranes, U.S. District Court District of Connecticut 1980 and Hon. Jon O. Newman, U.S. Court of Appeals Second Circuit 1980-81. In legal practice Washington, D.C. 1981-83 and Hartford 1984-94.

Member Connecticut Judicial Selection Commission, Connecticut Commission on Prison and Jail Overcrowding, Committee on Rules and Internal Operating Procedures U.S. Court of Appeals Second Circuit and Civil Justice Advisory Group U.S. District Court District of Connecticut. Advisor to Federal Courts Study Committee Judicial Conference of the United States. Bencher Oliver Ellsworth Inn of Court. Member Hartford County, Connecticut (House of Delegates, Executive Committee Federal Practice Section) and American (Committee on White Collar Crime Section of Criminal Justice, Section of Litigation) Bar Associations.

Office: Federal Bldg. & U.S. Courthouse, 450 Main Street, Hartford 06103.
Telephone: (860) 240-3659.

CHERNISKE, Victoria M. *(Judge, Washington District Probate Court)* Elected Nov 1991 to term beginning Jan 1992. Reelected Nov 1994, Nov 1998 and 2002. Current term expires Jan 2007. Born New Milford Connecticut Feb 21, 1954. Episcopalian. Educated at Eastern Wyoming College B.A. 1974.

Republican. Member Washington Parks and Recreation Commission, Steep Rock Association and First Congregational Church of Washington. Enjoys horseback riding, camping, skating and hiking.

Mailing address: P.O. Box 295, Washington Depot 06794-0295.
Office: Town Hall, Two Bryan Memorial Plaza, Washington Depot 06794.
Telephone: (860) 868-7974.
Fax: (860) 868-0512

CHIOTA, John P. *(Judge, Trumbull District Probate Court)*

Office: Town Hall, 5866 Main Street, Trumbull 06611-5416.
Telephone: (203) 452-5068.
Fax: (203) 452-5092

CLEBOWICZ, Walter A. *(Judge, Berlin District Probate Court)*

Mailing address: P.O. Box 400, New Britain 06050-0400.
Office: One Liberty Square, New Britain 06051.
Telephone: (860) 826-2696.
Fax: (860) 826-2695

CLIFFORD, Patrick J. *(Judge, Connecticut Superior Court)* Appointed. Former Assistant Administrative Judge Middlesex Judicial District.

Office: One Court Street, Middletown 06457.
Telephone: (860) 343-6570.
Fax: (860) 343-6589

COCCO, Leonard M. *(Senior Judge, Connecticut Superior Court)* Appointed. Retired.

Office: 1061 Main Street, Bridgeport 06604.
Telephone: (203) 579-6540.
Fax: (860) 579-6928

COFIELD, E. Curtissa R. *(Judge, Connecticut Superior Court)* Appointed. Former Presiding Judge.
Office: 111 Phoenix Avenue, Enfield 06082.
Telephone: (860) 741-3727.
Fax: (860) 741-3474

COHEN, Simon S. *(Judge Referee, Connecticut Superior Court)* Appointed Judge 1960. Retired. Currently serves as Judge Trial Referee.
Office: Judicial District Courthouse, 95 Washington Street, Hartford 06106.
Telephone: (860) 548-2850.
Fax: (860) 548-2887

COHN, Henry S. *(Judge, Connecticut Superior Court)* Appointed to term beginning July 22, 1997. Term expires July 23, 2005. Born Hartford Connecticut 1945. Jewish. Educated at Johns Hopkins University B.A. with honors 1967 and University of Connecticut J.D. with honors 1970. Notes Editor Connecticut Law Review 1967-70. Law Clerk to Hon. T. Emmet Clarie, U.S. District Court District of Connecticut 1970-71. Admitted to practice Connecticut 1970, U.S. District Court District of Connecticut 1970, U.S. Court of Appeals Second Circuit 1973 and U.S. Supreme Court 1974. In legal practice Hartford 1979-83.
Assistant Attorney General Connecticut 1983-97. Author "Great Hartford Circus Fire" Yale University Press 1991. Instructor University of Connecticut Administrative Law Clinic 1975-97. Member Hartford City, Connecticut, Federal and American Bar Associations. Secretary of State Connecticut 1979.
Office: 95 Washington Street, Hartford 06106.
Telephone: (860) 548-2820.

COMERFORD, Richard F., Jr. *(Judge, Connecticut Superior Court)* Appointed. Former Presiding Judge Criminal Division.
Office: 123 Hoyt Street, Stamford 06905.
Telephone: (203) 965-5315.
Fax: (203) 965-5389

CONNORS, Kevin C. *(Judge, Hebron District Probate Court)*
Office: 15 Gilead Road, Hebron 06248.
Telephone: (860) 228-5971.

CONWAY, Bernadette *(Judge Referee, Connecticut Superior Court)* Appointed Judge. Retired. Currently serves as Judge Trial Referee.
Office: 121 Elm Street, New Haven 06510.
Telephone: (203) 789-7491.
Fax: (203) 789-7492

CONWAY, Michael P. *(Judge Referee, Connecticut Superior Court)* Appointed Judge to term beginning July 1, 1978. Reappointed 1986. Former Senior Judge. Became Judge Referee Jan 29, 1997. Currently serves as Judge Trial Referee. Born Norwich Connecticut Jan 29, 1927. Roman Catholic. Educated at Georgetown University A.B. 1950 and University of Connecticut LL.D. 1953. Admitted to practice Connecticut 1953 and U.S. District Court District of Connecticut 1954. Began legal practice Norwich 1953. Judge, Sprague Municipal Court 1964-67. Judge, Connecticut Juvenile Court 1967-78.
Member New London County, Connecticut and American Bar Associations. State Representative Connecticut 1959-62. Seaman USN 1945-46.
Office: One Courthouse Square, Norwich 06360.
Telephone: (860) 886-0144.
Fax: (860) 823-1019

COOLEY, Margaret D. *(Judge, Cornwall District Probate Court)* Elected Nov 1986 to term beginning Jan 1987. Reelected Nov 1990, Nov 1994, Nov 1998 and 2002. Current term expires Jan 2007. Born New York New York Oct 27, 1939. Educated at Radcliffe College A.B. magna cum laude 1961 and University of California Hastings College of the Law J.D. 1973.
Mailing address: P.O. Box 157, Cornwall 06753-0157.
Office: Town Office Building, Pine Street, Cornwall 06753.
Telephone: (860) 672-2677.

COONEY, John W. *(Judge, Manchester District Probate Court)*
Office: 66 Center Street, Manchester 06040.
Telephone: (860) 647-3227.
Fax: (860) 647-3236

COPPETO, Barbara A. *(Senior Judge, Connecticut Superior Court)* Appointed. Former Administrative Judge Ansonia-Milford Judicial District. Retired.
Mailing address: P.O. Box 210, Milford 06460.
Office: 14 West River Street, Milford 06460.
Telephone: (203) 878-5791.
Fax: (203) 876-8072

CORBO, Frank J., Jr. *(Judge, Marlborough District Probate Court)*
Mailing address: P.O. Box 29, Marlborough 06447.
Office: 26 North Main Street, Marlborough 06447.
Telephone: (860) 295-6239.

CORRADINO, Thomas J. *(Judge, Connecticut Superior Court)* Appointed.
Office: Judicial District Courthouse, 70 Huntington Street, New London 06320.
Telephone: (860) 442-2977.
Fax: (860) 447-8701

CORRIGAN, Thomas H. *(Judge Referee, Connecticut Superior Court)* Appointed Judge to term beginning July 1, 1978. Reappointed 1986. Former Senior Judge. Became Judge Referee Jan 4, 1997. Currently serves as Judge Trial Referee. Born Hartford Connecticut Jan 4, 1927. Catholic. Educated at College of the Holy Cross B.A. 1950 and Boston College J.D. 1952. Admitted to practice Connecticut 1952. Began legal practice Hartford 1952. Judge, Connecticut Court of Common Pleas Nov 1968 to June 30, 1978.
City Counselor Hartford 1955-68. Member Hartford County, Connecticut and American Bar Associations. Staff Sergeant USAS 1945-46. Democrat.
Office: Judicial District Courthouse, 95 Washington Street, Hartford 06106.
Telephone: (860) 548-2850.
Fax: (860) 548-2887

COSGROVE, Emmet L. *(Judge, Connecticut Superior Court)* Appointed.
Office: Judicial District Courthouse, 155 Church Street, Putnam 06260.
Telephone: (860) 963-9466.
Fax: (860) 963-8918

COTNOIR, Ernest J. *(Judge, Putnam District Probate Court)*
Office: Town Hall, 126 Church Street, Putnam 06260.

COTNOIR, ERNEST J.—*Continued*

Telephone: (860) 963-6868.
Fax: (860) 963-6814

COVELLO, Alfred V. *(Senior Judge, United States District Court District of Connecticut)* Appointed for life by President George Bush Sept 1992. Former Chief Judge. Assumed Senior status Feb 4, 2003, serves by assignment. Born Hartford Connecticut Feb 4, 1933. Roman Catholic. Educated at Harvard University A.B. 1954 and University of Connecticut School of Law J.D. 1960. Admitted to practice Connecticut 1960 and U.S. District Court District of Connecticut 1960. In legal practice Hartford 1960-74. Judge, Connecticut Circuit Court 1974-75. Judge, Connecticut Court of Common Pleas 1975-78. Judge, Connecticut Superior Court 1978-87. Associate Justice, Connecticut Supreme Court June 1987 to 1992.

Author *Connecticut Civil Procedure* Stephenson 2nd ed. revision to Vol. II, 1981 and revision to Vol. I, 1982. Fellow American Bar Association. Member Federal Judges Association, Hartford County, Connecticut and American Bar Associations. Attended Intermediate Appellate Judges Seminar 1981 and Appellate Judges Seminar 1987 Institute of Judicial Administration. Attended National Council of Juvenile and Family Court Judges 1984. U.S. Army Infantry 1955-57. Connective National Guard (active reserve) 1957-59. Trustee Loomis-Chaffee School since 1984 and The Bushnell Memorial. Airline Transport Pilot and Flight Instructor.

Office: Federal Bldg. & U.S. Courthouse, 450 Main Street, Hartford 06103.
Telephone: (860) 240-3218.

CRAVINHO, Paul E. *(Judge, Stonington District Probate Court)*
Mailing address: P.O. Box 312, Stonington 06378-0312.
Office: 152 Elm Street, Stonington 06378.
Telephone: (860) 535-5090.
Fax: (860) 535-0520

CRAWFORD, Juliett L. *(Judge, Connecticut Superior Court)* Appointed.
Office: 101 Lafayette Street, Hartford 06106.
Telephone: (860) 566-3861.
Fax: (860) 566-6977

CREMINS, William T. *(Judge, Connecticut Superior Court)* Appointed.
Mailing address: P.O. Box 210, Milford 06460.
Office: 14 West River Street, Milford 06460.
Telephone: (203) 878-5791.
Fax: (203) 876-8072

CRETELLA, Albert W., Jr. *(Judge Referee, Connecticut Superior Court)* Retired. Became Judge Referee May 18, 1995. Currently serves as Judge Trial Referee. Former Senior Judge, Connecticut Appellate Court.
Office: Judicial District Courthouse, 235 Church Street, New Haven 06510.
Telephone: (203) 503-6830.
Fax: (203) 789-6826

CURRAN, Hugh C. *(Judge Referee, Connecticut Superior Court)* Appointed Judge to term beginning July 1, 1978. Former Administrative Judge Ansonia-Milford Judicial District. Retired. Currently serves as Judge Trial Referee. Former Judge, Connecticut Court of Common Pleas.
Mailing address: P.O. Box 210, Milford 06460.
Office: 14 West River Street, Milford 06460.
Telephone: (203) 878-5791.
Fax: (203) 876-8072

CUTSUMPAS, Lloyd *(Judge, Connecticut Superior Court)* Appointed.
Office: Judicial District Courthouse, 300 Grand Street, Waterbury 06702.
Telephone: (203) 596-4033.
Fax: (203) 596-4488

DABROWSKI, Albert S. *(Judge, United States Bankruptcy Court District of Connecticut)* Appointed by U.S. Court of Appeals Second Circuit judges to term beginning Nov 1, 1993. Term expires Oct 31, 2007. Born Manchester Connecticut July 10, 1944. Educated at University of Connecticut B.S. 1967 and Suffolk University Law School J.D. 1970. Technical Editor Suffolk University Law Review 1968-70. Admitted to practice District of Columbia 1971, Connecticut, Massachusetts, U.S. District Courts District of Connecticut, District of Columbia and District of Massachusetts, U.S. Courts of Appeals Second and District of Columbia Circuits and U.S. Supreme Court.

With U.S. Department of Justice, Washington D.C. 1970-73. Assistant U.S. Attorney 1973-91 and U.S. Attorney 1991-93 Connecticut. Member Bar Association of the District of Columbia, Connecticut, Massachusetts and American Bar Associations. Recipient The John Marshall Award for Outstanding Legal Achievement 1990.

Office: Connecticut Financial Center, 18th Floor, 157 Church Street, New Haven 06510.
Telephone: (203) 773-2132.

D'ADDABBO, Frank M., Jr. *(Judge, Connecticut Superior Court)* Appointed.
Office: 400 Grand Street, Waterbury 06702.
Telephone: (203) 236-8200.
Fax: (203) 236-8205

DAMIANI, Richard A. *(Judge, Connecticut Superior Court)* Appointed.
Office: Judicial District Courthouse, 1061 Main Street, Bridgeport 06604.
Telephone: (203) 579-6540.
Fax: (203) 579-6928

DAMON, Patricia L. *(Judge, Deep River District Probate Court)* Elected Nov 8, 1994. Reelected Nov 1998 and 2002. Current term expires Jan 2007.
Mailing address: P.O. Box 391, Deep River 06417.
Office: Town Hall, 174 Main Street, Deep River 06417.
Telephone: (860) 526-6026.
Fax: (860) 526-6094

D'ANDREA, Frank H., Jr. *(Judge Referee, Connecticut Superior Court)* Appointed Judge. Retired. Currently serves as Judge Trial Referee.
Office: Judicial District Courthouse, 123 Hoyt Street, Stamford 06905.
Telephone: (203) 965-5315.
Fax: (203) 965-5389

DANNEHY, Joseph F. *(Judge Referee, Connecticut Superior Court)* Retired. Currently serves as Judge Trial Referee. Judge, Connecticut Circuit Court 1961-65.

DANNEHY, JOSEPH F.—*Continued*

Chief Judge, Connecticut Court of Common Pleas 1965-68. Judge, Connecticut Superior Court Sept 24, 1968 to March 14, 1984. Chief Presiding Judge, Connecticut Appellate Court 1984-85. Associate Justice, Connecticut Supreme Court 1985-87.

Office: Judicial District Courthouse, 108 Valley Street, Willimantic 06226.
Telephone: (860) 423-8491.
Fax: (860) 423-9115

DANNEHY, Michael R. *(Judge, Connecticut Superior Court)* Appointed.
Office: 920 Broad Street, Hartford 06106.
Telephone: (860) 566-8290.
Fax: (860) 566-1658

DeFEO, William P. *(Judge, New Fairfield District Probate Court)*
Office: Four Brush Hill Road, New Fairfield 06812.
Telephone: (203) 312-5627.
Fax: (203) 312-5612

DeMAYO, Anthony V. *(Judge Referee, Connecticut Superior Court)* Appointed Judge to term beginning Oct 19, 1981. Reappointed March 1990. Former Presiding Judge Housing Division New Haven Judicial District. Senior Judge Jan 22, 1993 to March 1994. Became Judge Referee April 27, 1994. Currently serves as Judge Trial Referee. Born New Haven Connecticut April 27, 1924. Roman Catholic. Educated at Yale University B.A. 1948 and University of Connecticut School of Law J.D. 1951. Admitted to practice Connecticut 1951, U.S. District Court District of Connecticut 1953, U.S. Court of Appeals Second Circuit 1969 and U.S. Supreme Court 1969. In legal practice New Haven 1951-77.

Public Defender New Haven County 1966-81. Author "Ten Years of Homicides in New Haven County" Connecticut B. Jour. Dec 1979. Important Decisions: Hilton v. New Haven (right to shelter) Superior Court 1989 and Savage v. Comm. Aaronson 214 Conn. 256, 1990. Instructor in Criminal Law University of New Haven 1976-81 and in Trial Practice Yale University Law School 1988-93. President Connecticut Bar Association 1969-70. Fellow American Bar Foundation. Board of Directors Connecticut Bar Foundation 1968-70 and since 1988. Member New Haven County and American Bar Associations. Attended National Institute for Trial Advocacy 1976. Lecturer Connecticut Bar Association CLE on three occasions. Instructor and Attendee Connecticut Judges Institute. Recipient Outstanding Citizen Award from Hagaman Library 1979, Professional Service Award 1986 and Charles J. Parker Legal Aid Award 1992 Connecticut Bar Association, Lifetime Achievement Award from New Haven County Bar Association 1999 and Pro Bono Award from Connecticut Law Tribune 2000. Named Man of the Year by Foxon Recreation League, East Haven 1985. Staff Sergeant U.S. Army 1943-46. Past President New Haven Philatelic Society, University of Connecticut Alumni Association and Foxon-Deer Run School PTA. Hobbies include philately, opera, civil war and forest management.

Office: Judicial District Courthouse, 235 Church Street, New Haven 06510.
Telephone: (203) 503-6830.

DENNIS, Maureen D. *(Judge, Connecticut Superior Court)* Appointed.
Office: 172 Golden Hill Street, Bridgeport 06604.
Telephone: (203) 579-6568.
Fax: (203) 382-8430

DePANFILIS, Anthony *(Judge, Norwalk District Probate Court)*
Mailing address: P.O. Box 2009, Norwalk 06852-2009.
Office: 125 East Avenue, Norwalk 06851.
Telephone: (203) 854-7737.
Fax: (203) 854-7825

DEVINE, James J. *(Judge, Connecticut Superior Court)* Appointed.
Office: One Courthouse Square, Norwich 06360.
Telephone: (860) 886-0144.
Fax: (860) 823-1019

DEVLIN, Robert J., Jr. *(Judge, Connecticut Superior Court)* Appointed.
Office: One Courthouse Square, Norwich 06360.
Telephone: (860) 886-0144.
Fax: (860) 823-1019

DEWEY, Julia DiCocco *(Judge, Connecticut Superior Court)* Appointed.
Office: Judicial District Courthouse, 1061 Main Street, Bridgeport 06604.
Telephone: (203) 579-6540.
Fax: (203) 579-6928

DIGLIO, Salvatore L. *(Judge, Hamden District Probate Court)* Elected at special election to term beginning May 24, 1983. Reelected 1986, 1990, 1994, 1998 and 2002. Current term expires Jan 2007. Born New Haven Connecticut Aug 20, 1943. Catholic. Educated at Providence College B.A. 1966 and University of Connecticut School of Law J.D. 1970. Admitted to practice Connecticut 1972. Began legal practice New Haven 1972. In legal practice Hamden 1972.

Deputy Coroner 1973-76 and Coroner 1976-79 New Haven County. Democrat.

Office: Memorial Town Hall, 2372 Whitney Avenue, Hamden 06518.
Telephone: (203) 287-2570.
Fax: (203) 287-2571

DiPENTIMA, Alexandra D. *(Judge, Connecticut Appellate Court)* Appointed. Former Judge, Connecticut Superior Court.
Office: 95 Washington Street, Hartford 06106.
Telephone: (860) 548-2828.

DOHERTY, Joseph W. *(Judge, Connecticut Superior Court)* Appointed.
Office: Judicial District Courthouse, 1061 Main Street, Bridgeport 06604.
Telephone: (203) 579-6540.
Fax: (203) 579-6928

DOMNARSKI, Edward S. *(Judge, Connecticut Superior Court)* Appointed.
Office: One Courthouse Square, Norwich 06360.
Telephone: (860) 886-0144.
Fax: (860) 823-1019

DONEGAN, John E. *(Judge, Branford District Probate Court)*
Mailing address: P.O. Box 638, Branford 06405-0638.
Office: 1019 Main Street, Branford 06405.
Telephone: (203) 488-0318.
Fax: (203) 315-4715

DORSEY, Peter C. *(Senior Judge, United States District Court District of Connecticut)* Appointed for life by President Ronald Reagan July 29, 1983. Former Chief Judge. Assumed Senior status Jan 2, 1998, serves by assignment. Born New London Connecticut March 24, 1931. Catholic. Educated at Yale University B.A. 1953 and Harvard Law School LL.B. 1959. Admitted to practice Connecticut 1959, U.S. District Court District of Connecticut 1960, U.S. Court of Appeals Second Circuit 1962 and U.S. Supreme Court 1975. Began legal practice New Haven 1959.
U.S. Attorney District of Connecticut 1974-77. Adjunct Professor of Law Quinnipiac University School of Law. Fellow American College of Trial Lawyers. Member American Bar Endowment, American Judicature Society, Connecticut (Board of Governors 1966-69 and 1974-78, President 1978) and American (House of Delegates 1974-78) Bar Associations. Recipient Judiciary Award from Connecticut Trial Lawyers Association and Judiciary Award from Connecticut Bar Association. Lieutenant Commander USNR 1953-63.
Office: U.S. Courthouse, 141 Church Street, New Haven 06510.
Telephone: (203) 773-2427.

DORVAL, Andre D. *(Judge, Bristol District Probate Court)* Elected Nov 8, 1994. Reelected 1998 and 2002. Current term expires Jan 2007.
Office: City Hall, 111 North Main Street, Bristol 06010.
Telephone: (860) 584-6230.
Fax: (860) 584-3818

DOWNEY, John Redmond *(Judge, Connecticut Superior Court)* Appointed.
Office: 146 White Street, Danbury 06810.
Telephone: (203) 207-8690.
Fax: (203) 207-8689

DOWNEY, John T. *(Judge Referee, Connecticut Superior Court)* Appointed Judge. Former Administrative Judge Family Division Part J and Chief Administrative Judge Juvenile Matters. Former Senior Judge. Currently serves as Judge Trial Referee.
Office: Judicial District Courthouse, 235 Church Street, New Haven 06510.
Telephone: (203) 503-6830.
Fax: (203) 789-6826

DRANGINIS, Anne C. *(Judge, Connecticut Appellate Court)* Appointed to term beginning Nov 2000. Term expires Nov 2008. Catholic. Educated at Manhattanville College A.B. in Philosophy 1969 and University of Connecticut School of Law J.D. 1972. In legal practice Bloomfield 1972-78. Judge, Connecticut Superior Court 1985-2000. Former Administrative Judge, Litchfield Judicial District. Former Chief Administrative Judge, Family Division Parts S and D and Presiding Judge, Family Division New Britain Judicial District.
Assistant State's Attorney Litchfield Judicial District 1978-85. Member Law Revision Commission 1976-80, Bar Examining Committee Connecticut since 1979, Sentence Review Division Connecticut Superior Court 1987-89 and Executive Committee Connecticut Judicial Department. Member Connecticut Judges Association and Connecticut Bar Association. Attended National Institute for Trial Advocacy Cornell University July 1976 and Jan 1977, National District Attorneys Association: "Short Course for Prosecutors" Northwestern University School of Law July 1978, "The Prosecution of Violent Crimes" Boston Massachusetts Feb 15-16, 1979 and "Trial Advocacy for Prosecutors" Singer Island Florida Nov 1-5, 1981; National Conference of the Judiciary on Bioethics The National Judicial College Sept 7-10, 1989; and "Women, Families and Reproduction" Judicial Decision Making Women Judges' Fund for Justice Washington D.C. April 5-7, 1991. Faculty Member "Preparation of a Child Witness in a Sexual Assault Case" Training Session for Connecticut Prosecutors, Office of Chief State's Attorney June 22, 1979; "Plea Bargaining" Advanced Criminal Trial Advocacy Seminar, Connecticut Bar Association Nov 9, 1979; "Depositions of, Preparation of and Handling of Medical Experts" Fall Seminar on Civil Litigation, Connecticut Trial Lawyers Association Dec 8, 1979; "Pathology Section" Seminar on the Use of Forensic Science, Yale Law Women's Association April 7, 1980; Seminar in Forensic Science Master's Program, University of New Haven April 13, 1981; Seminar on Forensic Evidence for Connecticut Prosecutors, Office of Chief State's Attorney, U.S. Navy Submarine Base Groton Connecticut Summer 1983; "The Child As A Witness In Sexual Assault Cases" Annual Meeting National Association of Forensic Social Workers, Mystic Connecticut April 1988; "The Child As Witness" Federal Crimes Against Children, U.S. Department of Justice, Alexandria Virginia, Feb 16-17, 1989; "Complex Issues in Law & Medicine" State Justice Institute, The National Judicial College, Princeton New Jersey Oct 4-6, 1990; "Dog Tracking Evidence in Criminal Prosecution" 19th Annual Meeting National Police Bloodhound Association, Mystic Connecticut; and Rape Crisis Seminar, Torrington Police Department.
Office: 95 Washington Street, Hartford 06106.
Telephone: (860) 548-2828.

DRISCOLL, Allan T. *(Judge, East Hartford District Probate Court)*
Office: Town Hall, 740 Main Street, East Hartford 06108.
Telephone: (860) 291-7278.

DRISCOLL, John C. *(Judge, Connecticut Superior Court)* Appointed.
Office: One Court Street, Middletown 06457.
Telephone: (860) 343-6570.
Fax: (860) 343-6589

DRONEY, Christopher F. *(Judge, United States District Court District of Connecticut)* Appointed for life by President Bill Clinton to term beginning Sept 22, 1997. Born Hartford Connecticut June 22, 1954. Roman Catholic. Educated at College of the Holy Cross B.A. magna cum laude 1976 and University of Connecticut School of Law J.D. 1979. Notes and Comments Editor Connecticut Law Review 1978-79. Admitted to practice Connecticut 1979. In legal practice Hartford 1979-93.
U.S. Attorney District of Connecticut 1993-97.
Office: Federal Bldg. & U.S. Courthouse, 450 Main Street, Hartford 06103.
Telephone: (860) 240-2635.

DUBAY, Kevin G. *(Judge, Connecticut Superior Court)* Appointed.
Office: Judicial District Courthouse, 300 Grand Street, Waterbury 06702.
Telephone: (203) 596-4033.
Fax: (203) 596-4488

DUNN, Philip R. *(Judge Referee, Connecticut Superior Court)* Appointed Judge. Retired. Currently serves as Judge Trial Referee.
Office: 20 Franklin Square, New Britain 06051.
Telephone: (860) 515-5050.
Fax: (860) 515-5051

DUNNELL, Christina G. *(Judge, Connecticut Superior Court)* Appointed.
Office: 20 Franklin Square, New Britain 06051.
Telephone: (860) 515-5050.
Fax: (860) 515-5051

DUPONT, Antoinette L. *(Judge Referee, Connecticut Superior Court)* Retired. Became Judge Referee Jan 10, 1999. Currently serves as Judge Trial Referee. Born New York New York Jan 10, 1929. Educated at Brown University B.A. 1950 and Harvard Law School J.D. 1954. In legal practice 1954-77. Judge, Connecticut Court of Common Pleas 1977. Judge 1978-83 and Chief Administrative Judge Civil Division 1983, Connecticut Superior Court. Judge 1983-84, Chief Judge 1984-97 and Senior Judge 1997-99, Connecticut Appellate Court.
Special Counsel City of New London 1960-61. Past President Connecticut Judges Association. Fellow James Cooper Connecticut Bar Association and American Bar Association. Member The American Law Institute.
Office: Appellate Court, 95 Washington Street, Hartford 06106.
Telephone: (860) 548-2828.
Fax: (860) 548-2870

DUPONT, Thomas E., Sr. *(Judge, Killingly District Probate Court)*
Office: 172 Main Street, Killingly 06239.
Telephone: (860) 779-5319.

DYER, Richard W. *(Judge, Connecticut Superior Court)* Appointed to term beginning Sept 1994. Reappointed 2002, current term expires 2010. Former Acting Presiding Judge. Born Manchester Connecticut July 24, 1950. Educated at College of the Holy Cross B.A. cum laude 1972 and University of Connecticut School of Law J.D. 1977. In legal practice Manchester. Admitted to practice Connecticut and District of Columbia.
Former Chairman Connecticut Juvenile Justice Advisory Committee. Member Connecticut Judges Association, The District of Columbia Bar and Connecticut Bar Association. Lieutenant Colonel USAFR (retired). Former Chairman Manchester Board of Education.
Office: One Court Street, Middletown 06457.
Telephone: (860) 343-6570.
Fax: (860) 343-6589
E-mail address: Richard.Dyer@jud.state.ct.us

EGAN, Joseph A., Jr. *(Judge, Ridgefield District Probate Court)*
Office: Town Hall, 400 Main Street, Ridgefield 06877.
Telephone: (203) 431-2776.
Fax: (203) 431-2722

EGINTON, Warren W. *(Senior Judge, United States District Court District of Connecticut)* Appointed for life by President Jimmy Carter to term beginning Aug 1, 1979. Assumed Senior status, serves by assignment. Born Brooklyn New York Feb 16, 1924. Episcopalian. Educated at Princeton University B.A. with honors 1948 and Yale Law School J.D. 1951. Admitted to practice New York 1952 and Connecticut 1954. Began legal practice New York 1952. In legal practice Connecticut 1953-79.
Editor-in-Chief Products Liability L. Jour. Butterworth 1988-93. Adjunct Teaching Fellow New York University School of Law Evening Division 1952-60. Adjunct Professor of Law Fordham University School of Law 1992. Founding President Raymond E. Baldwin American Inns of Court. Fellow American Bar Foundation. Member Advisory Council Judicial Leadership Development Council, Institute for Judicial Administration, American Judicature Society, Connecticut and American Bar Associations. First Lieutenant U.S. Army 1943-46. Lieutenant Colonel USAR 1946-72 (retired). Trustee Loomis Chaffee School.
Office: Federal Bldg. & U.S. Courthouse, 915 Lafayette Boulevard, Bridgeport 06604-4765.
Telephone: (203) 579-5819.

ELKIN, Sydney W. *(Judge, West Hartford District Probate Court)*
Office: 50 South Main Street, West Hartford 06107.
Telephone: (860) 523-3174.
Fax: (860) 236-8352

ELLSWORTH, Michael H. *(Judge, Eastford District Probate Court)*
Mailing address: P.O. Box 207, Eastford 06242-0207.
Telephone: (860) 974-3024.
Fax: (860) 974-0624

EMERSON, Richard L. *(Judge, Redding District Probate Court)*
Mailing address: P.O. Box 1125, Redding 06875.
Office: Town Hall, 100 Hill Road, Redding 06896.
Telephone: (203) 938-2326.
Fax: (203) 938-8816

ESPINOSA, Carmen Elisa *(Judge, Connecticut Superior Court)* Appointed to term beginning Jan 10, 1992. Reappointed March 2000, current term expires March 2008. Born Puerto Rico Feb 27, 1949. Catholic. Educated at Central Connecticut State University B.S. with honors 1971, Brown University M.A. 1973 and George Washington University J.D. 1976. Admitted to practice District of Columbia 1976, U.S. Court of Appeals Second Circuit 1982, Connecticut 1986 and U.S. District Court District of Connecticut 1986.
Assistant U.S. Attorney District of Connecticut 1980-92.
Office: 20 Franklin Square, New Britain 06051.
Telephone: (860) 515-5050.
Fax: (860) 515-5051

ESPOSITO, Gerard F. *(Judge, Connecticut Superior Court)* Appointed.
Office: 239 Whalley Avenue, New Haven 06511.
Telephone: (203) 786-0337.
Fax: (203) 786-0327

EVELEIGH, Dennis G. *(Judge, Connecticut Superior Court)* Appointed.
Office: 71 Main Street, Danbury 06810.
Telephone: (203) 797-4407.
Fax: (203) 731-2813

FAIRCHILD, Joseph J. *(Judge, Thomaston District Probate Court)*
Mailing address: P.O. Box 136, Thomaston 06787.
Office: 158 Main Street, Thomaston 06787.
Telephone: (860) 283-4874.

FAMIGLIETTI, Heidi *(Judge, Plainville District Probate Court)* Elected Nov 8, 1994. Reelected 1998 and 2002. Current term expires Jan 2007.
Office: One Central Square, Plainville 06062.
Telephone: (860) 793-0221.
Fax: (860) 793-2424

FASANO, Roland D. *(Judge, Connecticut Superior Court)* Appointed.
Office: Judicial District Courthouse, 235 Church Street, New Haven 06510.
Telephone: (203) 503-6830.
Fax: (203) 789-6826

FERTIG, John W., Jr. *(Judge, Oxford District Probate Court)* Elected to term beginning Nov 1979. Reelected 1982, 1986, 1990, 1994, 1998 and 2002. Current term expires Jan 2007. Born New York New York Oct 29, 1945. Educated at Ursinus College B.A. 1967 and University of Tennessee J.D. 1970. Member Phi Alpha Delta. Admitted to practice Connecticut 1970. Began legal practice Waterbury 1971. In legal practice Prospect and Oxford since 1977.

Member Lower Naugatuck Valley, Waterbury and Connecticut Bar Associations. Captain U.S. Army 1970-78. Democrat. Member Oxford Historical Society. Interested in antiques. Enjoys gardening, road racing, ice hockey, tennis and antique cars.
Office: Town Hall, Route 67, Oxford 06478.
Telephone: (203) 888-2543.

FIORE, Thomas J. *(Judge, Stafford District Probate Court)*
Mailing address: P.O. Box 63, Stafford Springs 06076-0063.
Office: Town Hall, Main Street, Stafford Springs 06076.
Telephone: (860) 684-1783.
Fax: (860) 684-7173

FISCHER, Brian T. *(Judge, Connecticut Superior Court)* Appointed.
Office: 54 West Main Street, Meriden 06451.
Telephone: (203) 238-6137.
Fax: (203) 238-6423

FISCHER, Jack W. *(Judge, Connecticut Superior Court)* Appointed.
Office: 146 White Street, Danbury 06810.
Telephone: (203) 207-8690.
Fax: (203) 207-8689

FISHER, Marilyn Lassman *(Judge, East Windsor District Probate Court)*
Office: Town Hall, 1540 Sullivan Avenue, South Windsor 06074-2786.
Telephone: (860) 644-2511.
Fax: (860) 648-5047

FITZGERALD, Richard T. *(Judge, Salisbury District Probate Court)*
Mailing address: P.O. Box 525, Salisbury 06068.
Office: Town Hall, 27 Main Street, Salisbury 06068.
Telephone: (860) 435-5183.
Fax: (860) 435-6125

FITZSIMMONS, Holly B. *(Magistrate Judge, United States District Court District of Connecticut)* Appointed by U.S. District Court judges.
Office: Federal Bldg. & U.S. Courthouse, 915 Lafayette Boulevard, Bridgeport 06604-4768.
Telephone: (203) 579-5640.

FLANAGAN, John C. *(Judge Referee, Connecticut Superior Court)* Appointed Judge. Retired. Became Judge Referee March 24, 1991. Currently serves as Judge Trial Referee. Educated at Yale Law School LL.B. 1948.
Office: Judicial District Courthouse, 235 Church Street, New Haven 06510.
Telephone: (203) 789-7922.
Fax: (203) 789-6826

FLYNN, Joseph P. *(Judge, Connecticut Appellate Court)* Appointed to term beginning 2001. Term expires 2009. Educated at Fairfield University 1962 and Georgetown University 1965. Admitted to practice Connecticut. In legal practice Ansonia 1965-85. Judge, Connecticut Superior Court 1985-2001. Former Deputy Chief Court Administrator. Former Administrative Judge and Presiding Judge, Ansonia-Milford Judicial District. Former Assistant Administrative Judge and Presiding Judge Civil Division, Waterbury Judicial District.

Corporation Counsel Town of Seymour 1967-71. Adjunct Instructor Fairfield University 1985. Member Connecticut Judges Association (Past President), Valley (Past President) and Connecticut Bar Associations. Served to Lieutenant Commander USNR JAGC. Counsel to State Senate Majority Leader 1971-72 and State Senator 1975-79.
Office: 95 Washington Street, Hartford 06106.
Telephone: (860) 548-2828.

FOLEY, Francis J., III *(Judge, Connecticut Superior Court)* Appointed to term beginning 1993. Reappointed May 2001. Current term expires 2009. Former Presiding Judge. Currently serves as Administrative Judge Windham Judicial District. Educated at Boston College B.Sc. 1963 and Boston University School of Law LL.B. 1968.
Office: Superior Court, 120 School Street, Danielson 06239.
Telephone: (860) 779-8500.
Fax: (860) 779-8492
E-mail address: francis.foley@jud.state.ct.us

FORD, G. Sarsfield *(Judge, Connecticut Superior Court)* Appointed to term beginning July 1, 1978. Reappointed 1986, 1994 and 2002. Current term expires 2010. Former Administrative Judge Fairfield Judicial District. Born Bridgeport Connecticut Sept 6, 1933. Roman Catholic. Educated at University of Notre Dame A.B. 1955 and Georgetown University LL.B. 1958. Admitted to practice Connecticut 1958. Began legal practice Bridgeport 1958. Judge, Connecticut Court of Common Pleas May 15, 1973 to June 30, 1978.

FORD, G. SARSFIELD—*Continued*

Member Bridgeport and Connecticut Bar Associations. USMC 1952-58 and U.S. Army 1959-60.
Office: Judicial District Courthouse, 1061 Main Street, Bridgeport 06604.
Telephone: (203) 579-6540.
Fax: (203) 579-6928

FORGIONE, Frank J. *(Judge, North Branford District Probate Court)*
Mailing address: P.O. Box 214, North Branford 06471.
Office: 1599 Foxon Road, North Branford 06471.
Telephone: (203) 315-6007.

FOTI, Paul M. *(Judge, Connecticut Appellate Court)* Appointed 1988. Reappointed 1996, current term expires 2004. Born New Haven Connecticut Jan 25, 1935. Educated at Fordham University B.S. 1956 and University of Connecticut School of Law J.D. 1959. In legal practice New Haven 1959-65. Judge, Connecticut Court of Common Pleas 1978 and Connecticut Superior Court 1978-88.
Part time Clerk and Assistant Prosecuting Attorney Circuit Court 1961-65. Prosecuting Attorney Connecticut Court of Common Pleas and Circuit Court 1965-78.
Office: 95 Washington Street, Hartford 06106.
Telephone: (860) 548-2828.

FOX, Gerald M., Jr. *(Judge, Stamford District Probate Court)*
Mailing address: P.O. Box 10152, Stamford 06904-2152.
Office: 888 Washington Boulevard, Stamford 06901.
Telephone: (203) 323-2149.
Fax: (203) 964-1830

FRACASSE, Ronald J. *(Judge Referee, Connecticut Superior Court)* Appointed Judge. Former Administrative Judge New Haven Judicial District. Retired. Currently serves as Judge Trial Referee.
Office: Judicial District Courthouse, 235 Church Street, New Haven 06510.
Telephone: (203) 503-6830.
Fax: (203) 789-6826

FRANKEL, Deborah Kochiss *(Judge, Connecticut Superior Court)* Appointed. Former Presiding Judge Family Division Parts S and D.
Office: Judicial District Courthouse, 235 Church Street, New Haven 06510.
Telephone: (203) 503-6830.
Fax: (203) 789-6826

FRAZZINI, Stephen F. *(Judge, Connecticut Superior Court)* Appointed.
Office: Judicial District Courthouse, 15 West Street, Litchfield 06759.
Telephone: (860) 567-5438.
Fax: (860) 567-4642

FREED, Samuel *(Judge Referee, Connecticut Superior Court)* Appointed Judge. Former Chief Administrative Judge Civil Division. Retired. Became Judge Referee May 8, 1997. Currently serves as Judge Trial Referee.
Office: Judicial District Courthouse, 95 Washington Street, Hartford 06106.
Telephone: (860) 548-2850.
Fax: (860) 548-2887

FREEDMAN, Frederick A. *(Judge Referee, Connecticut Superior Court)* Retired. Became Judge Referee April 3, 1999. Currently serves as Judge Trial Referee. Born Bridgeport Connecticut April 3, 1929. Educated at University of Connecticut B.A. 1951 and Yale Law School LL.B. 1954. In legal practice Bridgeport 1957-81. Judge 1981-92 and Chief Administrative Judge Family Division 1986-92, Connecticut Superior Court. Judge 1992-94, Administrative Judge Appellate System 1993-94 and Senior Judge 1994-99, Connecticut Appellate Court.
Town Attorney Monroe 1961-65. Board of Directors Association of Family and Conciliation Courts 1984-86. Member Connecticut Task Force on Gender, Justice and the Courts and Connecticut Bar Association. Member Commission on Compensation for Elected State Officials and Judges and Governor's Policy Advisory Council for the Annie E. Casey Foundation Child Welfare Reform Initiative. Member Board of Finance Monroe 1960-63.
Office: 17 Belden Avenue, Norwalk 06850.
Telephone: (203) 846-3237.
Fax: (203) 847-8710

FREEDMAN, Samuel S. *(Judge Referee, Connecticut Superior Court)* Appointed Judge to term beginning July 1, 1978. Reappointed Feb 7, 1979, Feb 1987 and 1995. Retired. Became Judge Referee July 5, 1997. Currently serves as Judge Trial Referee. Born Bridgeport Connecticut July 5, 1927. Jewish. Educated at University of Connecticut 1948, George Washington University A.B. in Government 1950 and Yale University J.D. 1954. Member Phi Beta Kappa and Pi Gamma Mu. Admitted to practice Connecticut 1954, U.S. District Court District of Connecticut 1959 and U.S. Supreme Court. Began legal practice Bridgeport 1954. In legal practice Westport 1964.
Co-author "ERA: May a State Change Its Vote?" Wayne State University Press 1978. Lecturer on "Government: The Legislative Process" Sacred Heart University 1974. Guest Lecturer Fairfield University and Connecticut College. Visiting Lecturer in Law Yale Law School 1976-78 and Yale School of Organization and Management 1980. Adjunct Professor of Law Quinnipiac College School of Law since 1983. Honorary Life member National Association of Criminal Defense Lawyers. Chairman Advisory Committee on State's Deinstitutionalization of the Handicapped Study 1987-88. Appointed Public Defender Services Commission 1988, 1991 and 1994. Member Chief Justice's Committee to Review Court Rules 1985, Connecticut Task Force on Court Reform 1986, The American Law Institute (Advisory Committee on Complex Litigation 1988-93), Executive Committee Superior Court, Connecticut Judges Association, Bridgeport, Westport and Connecticut (Former member Criminal Law Committee, Criminal Justice Section, Civil Justice Section Executive Committee and Committee on International Law) Bar Associations. Associate Commissioner National Conference of Commissioners on Uniform State Laws 1977-78. Named Outstanding Freshman Legislator 1973. Yeoman Third Class USNR 1945-51. State Representative 135th District Connecticut 1973-75 (Member Judiciary Committee, Chairman Criminal Justice and Public Defender Subcommittees 1973-75). Legislative Commissioner Connecticut (Chief Legal Counsel) 1975-78. Former member Republican Town Committee Westport. State Republican Party Parliamentarian 1976 and 1977. Member Nationalities Service Center (Executive Board and Vice President), Yale Law School Fund

FREEDMAN, SAMUEL S.—*Continued*

Drive and United Fund Drive. Former member Yale Clubs of New York and Fairfield County, Algonquin Club and Torch Club International. Member Executive Board and President Western Connecticut Association of Phi Beta Kappa. Author newspaper column on government and the arts Westport News and Lakeville Journal. Enjoys sailing and writing.
Office: 17 Belden Avenue, Norwalk 06850.
Telephone: (203) 846-3237.

FUGER, Stanley T., Jr. *(Judge, Connecticut Superior Court)* Appointed.
Office: 20 Park Street, Rockville 06066.
Telephone: (860) 896-4930.
Fax: (860) 870-3295

GAFFNEY, Bernard D. *(Judge Referee, Connecticut Superior Court)* Appointed Judge 1982. Former Administrative Judge New Britain Judicial District. Currently serves as Judge Trial Referee.
Office: 20 Franklin Square, New Britain 06051.
Telephone: (860) 515-5050.

GALE, Nancy M. *(Judge, Woodstock District Probate Court)*
Office: 415 Route 169, Woodstock 06281.
Telephone: (860) 928-2223.

GALLAGHER, Elizabeth A. *(Judge, Connecticut Superior Court)* Appointed.
Office: Judicial District Courthouse, 300 Grand Street, Waterbury 06702.
Telephone: (203) 596-4033.
Fax: (203) 596-4488

GANIM, Paul J. *(Judge, Bridgeport District Probate Court)*
Office: 202 State Street, Bridgeport 06604.
Telephone: (203) 576-3945.
Fax: (203) 576-7898

GARFINKEL, William I. *(Magistrate Judge, United States District Court District of Connecticut)* Appointed by U.S. District Court judges.
Office: Federal Bldg. & U.S. Courthouse, 915 Lafayette Boulevard, Bridgeport 06604.
Telephone: (203) 579-5593.

GILARDI, Richard P. *(Judge, Connecticut Superior Court)* Appointed.
Office: Judicial District Courthouse, 235 Church Street, New Haven 06510.
Telephone: (203) 503-6830.
Fax: (203) 789-6826

GILL, Charles D. *(Senior Judge, Connecticut Superior Court)* Appointed to term beginning Sept 12, 1983. Reappointed 1992 and 2000. Former Assistant Administrative Judge Litchfield Judicial District. Former Presiding Judge Civil Division. Retired. Born New Haven Connecticut July 21, 1938. Roman Catholic. Educated at Southern Connecticut State College B.S. 1961 and Catholic University of America J.D. 1964. Contributor Catholic University Law Review 1962-64. Admitted to practice Connecticut 1964, District of Columbia 1964, U.S. District Court District of Connecticut 1964 and U.S. Court of Appeals Second Circuit 1965. In legal practice New Haven 1964-70.
Author "A Neighborhood Law Office" Cleveland-Marshall L. Rev. 1965 and "The American Child—Chattel or Child Citizen" Ohio Northern University L. Rev. 1991. Member American Judges Association. Conducted numerous seminars on Children's Rights. Recipient Annual Crime Victims Award from Attorney General Richard Thornburgh and President George Bush and Paul Harris Fuller Award from Rotary International. Private U.S. Army 1958-64. Alderman New Haven 1966-70. Enjoys bridge, drama and music.
Office: Judicial District Courthouse, 15 West Street, Litchfield 06759.
Telephone: (860) 567-5438.
Fax: (860) 567-4642

GINOCCHIO, James P. *(Judge, Connecticut Superior Court)* Appointed.
Office: 400 Grand Street, Waterbury 06702.
Telephone: (203) 236-8200.
Fax: (203) 236-8205

GOLD, David P. *(Judge, Connecticut Superior Court)* Appointed.
Office: 172 Golden Hill Street, Bridgeport 06604.
Telephone: (203) 579-6568.
Fax: (203) 382-8408

GOLDBERG, Joseph H. *(Judge Referee, Connecticut Superior Court)* Appointed Judge to term beginning Feb 11, 1978. Senior Judge Feb 14, 1984 to Jan 19, 1996. Became Judge Referee Jan 20, 1996. Currently serves as Judge Trial Referee. Born Norwich Connecticut Jan 20, 1926. Jewish. Educated at Yale University B.S. 1948 and Harvard University LL.B. 1951. Admitted to practice Connecticut 1951. Began legal practice Norwich 1951. Judge, Connecticut Circuit Court 1973-74. Judge, Connecticut Court of Common Pleas 1974-78.
City Assistant Prosecutor Norwich 1953-55. Corporal USMC 1943-46. City Council Norwich 1955-56. State Senator Nineteenth District Connecticut 1957-58. State Claims Commissioner 1959-67. State Legislative Commissioner 1967-73.
Office: Judicial District Courthouse, 70 Huntington Street, New London 06320.
Telephone: (860) 442-2977.
Fax: (860) 447-8701

GOLDSTEIN, Samuel S. *(Judge Referee, Connecticut Superior Court)* Appointed Judge to term beginning Jan 4, 1983. Reappointed 1991. Retired. Became Judge Referee July 4, 1995. Currently serves as Judge Trial Referee. Born Hartford Connecticut July 4, 1925. Educated at Trinity College B.A. 1948 and Yale University LL.D. 1951. Member Phi Beta Kappa. Admitted to practice Connecticut 1951. Began legal practice Hartford 1951.
Corporation Counsel West Hartford 1967-69. Member Connecticut and American Bar Associations. Corporal USAAC 1944-46. Member Emanuel Synagogue.
Office: Superior Court for Juvenile Matters, 81 Kirkwood Road, West Hartford 06117.
Telephone: (860) 236-1398.

GOODNOW, Roger W. *(Judge, Old Saybrook District Probate Court)*
Office: 263 Main Street, Suite 105, Old Saybrook 06475.
Telephone: (860) 395-3128.
Fax: (860) 395-3125

GORDON, Elaine *(Judge, Connecticut Superior Court)* Appointed to term beginning 1988. Currently serves as Administrative Judge Middlesex Judicial District.
Office: One Court Street, Middletown 06457.
Telephone: (860) 343-6570.
Fax: (860) 343-6589

GORMLEY, Joseph *(Judge Referee, Connecticut Superior Court)* Appointed Judge. Former Presiding Judge Bridgeport Geographical Area Two. Former Senior Judge. Currently serves as Judge Trial Referee.
Office: Judicial District Courthouse, 1061 Main Street, Bridgeport 06604.
Telephone: (203) 579-6540.
Fax: (203) 579-6928

GRAHAM, James T. *(Judge, Connecticut Superior Court)* Appointed.
Office: 54 West Main Street, Meriden 06451.
Telephone: (203) 238-6137.
Fax: (203) 238-6423

GRAZIANI, Edward C. *(Judge, Connecticut Superior Court)* Appointed.
Office: Judicial District Courthouse, 69 Brooklyn Street, Rockville 06066.
Telephone: (860) 896-4930.
Fax: (860) 870-0394

GREENE, Mathew H. *(Judge, New London District Probate Court)*
Mailing address: P.O. Box 148, New London 06320.
Office: 181 Captain's Walk, New London 06320.
Telephone: (860) 443-7121.
Fax: (860) 437-8155

GRIFFIN, Brian T. *(Judge, Windsor District Probate Court)* Elected Nov 7, 1994 to term beginning Jan 1, 1995. Reelected Nov 4, 1998 and Nov 5, 2002. Current term expires Dec 31, 2006. Born Holyoke Massachusetts Aug 31, 1955. Catholic. Educated at St. Francis Xavier University, Canada B.A. 1977 and Loyola University of New Orleans School of Law J.D. 1980. Admitted to practice Connecticut 1980. In legal practice Windsor Locks since 1984.
Attorney Advisor Benefits Review Board U.S. Department of Labor 1980-84. Member Connecticut Probate Assembly, National College of Probate Judges and Connecticut Bar Association. Democrat. Member Windsor Town Council 1987-95. Mayor Windsor 1991-95. Member Lions Club and Police Athletic League. Enjoys sports, politics and travel.
Mailing address: P.O. Box 342, Windsor 06095-2994.
Office: 75 Broad Street, Windsor 06095.
Telephone: (860) 285-1976.
Fax: (860) 285-1909

GROGINS, Jack L. *(Judge Referee, Connecticut Superior Court)* Appointed Judge to term beginning Dec 2, 1994. Retired. Became Judge Referee Feb 27, 2001. Currently serves as Judge Trial Referee. Born Norwalk Connecticut Feb 27, 1931. Jewish. Educated at University of Connecticut B.A. J.D. 1955. Board of Student Editors Connecticut Law Review 1953-55. Admitted to practice Connecticut 1955, U.S. District Court District of Connecticut 1958 and U.S. Supreme Court 1961. In legal practice Bridgeport 1957-61 and Fairfield 1961-94.
Assistant Prosecuting Attorney Connecticut 1963-74. Author "Chemical Tests of Drunk Driving, Their Reliability and Admissibility" 29 Connecticut Bar Journal 1955. Former President Fairfield Bar Association. Member Connecticut Judges Association, Bridgeport and Connecticut Bar Associations. Attended Connecticut judicial schooling Dec 1994 to Jan 1995. Seaman First Class USN 1956-57. Former Member Fairfield Democratic Town Committee. Alternate Delegate Democratic State Convention Connecticut. Founding Member Fairfield County Booksellers Association. Enjoys tennis, travel, autograph collecting and literary events.
Mailing address: P.O. Box 210, Milford 06460.
Office: Judicial District Courthouse, 14 West River Street, Milford 06460.
Telephone: (203) 878-5791.
Fax: (203) 876-8072

GRUENDEL, F. Herbert *(Judge, Connecticut Superior Court)* Appointed.
Office: Judicial District Courthouse, 235 Church Street, New Haven 06510.
Telephone: (203) 503-6830.
Fax: (203) 789-6826

GULIANI, Richard J. *(Judge, Portland District Probate Court)*
Mailing address: P.O. Box 71, Portland 06480-0071.
Office: 33 East Main Street, Portland 06480.
Telephone: (860) 342-6739.

HADDEN, Arthur *(Judge, Connecticut Superior Court)* Appointed.
Office: One Courthouse Square, Norwich 06360.
Telephone: (860) 886-0144.
Fax: (860) 823-1019

HADDEN, William L., Jr. *(Judge Referee, Connecticut Superior Court)* Appointed Judge to term beginning Oct 8, 1974. Reappointed to subsequent terms. Retired. Became Judge Referee Dec 23, 1995. Currently serves as Judge Trial Referee. Born New Haven Connecticut Dec 23, 1925. Roman Catholic. Educated at University of Connecticut B.A. 1950 J.D. 1953. Admitted to practice Connecticut 1953. Began legal practice New Haven 1953.
Member Connecticut Bar Association. USAS 1944-46. Unemployment Compensation Commissioner for Connecticut 1974. Vice Chairman Connecticut Public Utilities Commission 1972-74. Republican. State Representative from Hamden 1960-62. Hamden Republican Town Chairman 1970-72. Enjoys golfing, fishing, skiing, gardening and playing tennis.
Office: Judicial District Courthouse, 235 Church Street, New Haven 06510.
Telephone: (203) 503-6830.
Fax: (203) 789-6826

HALE, Robert J. *(Judge Referee, Connecticut Superior Court)* Appointed Judge. Retired. Became Judge Referee April 28, 1991. Currently serves as Judge Trial Referee.
Office: 100 Washington Street, Hartford 06106.
Telephone: (860) 566-3468.
Fax: (860) 566-3449

HALL, Janet C. *(Judge, United States District Court District of Connecticut)* Appointed for life by President Bill Clinton to term beginning Oct 14, 1997. Born Lowell Massachusetts Sept 15, 1948. Educated at Mount Holyoke A.B. magna cum laude 1970 and New York University J.D. 1973. Articles Editor Annual Survey of

HALL, JANET C.—*Continued*

American Law 1972-73. Admitted to practice Massachusetts 1973, District of Columbia 1976, U.S. District Courts District of Massachusetts 1974 and District of Connecticut 1980, U.S. Courts of Appeals Fourth 1979, Second 1987 and District of Columbia 1993 Circuits, Connecticut 1980 and U.S. Supreme Court 1991. In legal practice Boston Massachusetts Sept 1973 to Sept 1975, District of Columbia Oct 1975 to Dec 1979 and Hartford Connecticut Jan 1980 to Oct 1997.

Special Assistant U.S. Attorney Eastern District of Virginia Sept 1979 to Dec 1979. Author "Securities Litigation" 65 Connecticut B. Jour. S.I. 50 May 1990. Member Merit Selection Committee for Bankruptcy Judges 1992-93 and Chair 1993 and Member 1996 Merit Selection Committee for Magistrate Judges U.S. District Court District of Connecticut. Member Planning Committee Judicial Conference of the Second Circuit 1992-97. Fellow Connecticut Bar Foundation (Director 1992-97, Member Investment Committee 1993-97 and Grantmaking Committee 1995-97) and American Bar Foundation. Member Federal Bar Council (Trustee 1990-92, Chair 1992 and Member Planning Committee 1993 Winter Bench-Bar Conference, Vice President 1992-95, Chair of the Board 1995-97), Connecticut (Executive Committee 1988-97 and Vice Chair 1995-97 Federal Practice Section, House of Delegates 1990-97, Nominating Committee 1993, Clients' Security Fund Committee 1994-97) and American Bar Associations.

Office: Federal Bldg. & U.S. Courthouse, 915 Lafayette Boulevard, Bridgeport 06604.
Telephone: (203) 579-5554.

HALL, Margot S. *(Judge, Newtown District Probate Court)*
Office: Edmond Town Hall, 45 Main Street, Newtown 06470-2157.
Telephone: (203) 270-4280.

HAMER, Donald L. *(Judge, Glastonbury District Probate Court)*
Mailing address: P.O. Box 6523, Glastonbury 06033-6523.
Office: 2155 Main Street, Glastonbury 06033.
Telephone: (860) 652-7629.
Fax: (860) 368-2520

HAMMER, Harry *(Judge Referee, Connecticut Superior Court)* Appointed Judge to term beginning July 1, 1978. Reappointed 1986 and 1994. Retired. Became Judge Referee Dec 20, 1996. Currently serves as Judge Trial Referee. Born Allentown Pennsylvania Dec 20, 1926. Jewish. Educated at City College of the City University of New York, University of Connecticut A.B. 1949 and Columbia University LL.B. 1954. Admitted to practice Connecticut 1955. Began legal practice Hartford 1955. In legal practice Rockville 1956-75. Judge, Connecticut Court of Common Pleas May 5, 1975 to June 30, 1978.

Corporation Counsel Rockville 1956-58. Rules Committee Connecticut Superior Court 1984-90. Member Tolland County (President 1965-66) and Connecticut Bar Associations. First Lieutenant USAR 1945-47 and 1950-52. General Assembly Connecticut 1959-61. Deputy Secretary of State 1970-75. Democrat. Chairman Tolland County March of Dimes, Vernon-Rockville Charter Consolidation Committee 1958 and Committee for New Tolland County Courthouse 1965-66. Presiding Justice Rockville Elks 1970-75. Director Congregation B'nai Israel.

Mailing address: P.O. Box 325, Rockville 06066.
Office: Judicial District Courthouse, 69 Brooklyn Street, Rockville 06066.
Telephone: (860) 896-4938.
Fax: (860) 870-0394
E-mail address: harry.hammer@jud.state.ct.us

HANDY, Susan B. *(Judge, Connecticut Superior Court)* Appointed.
Office: 20 Franklin Square, New Britain 06051.
Telephone: (860) 515-5050.
Fax: (860) 515-5051

HARLESTON, Patricia Lilly *(Judge, Connecticut Superior Court)* Appointed.
Office: 20 Park Street, Rockville 06066.
Telephone: (860) 872-7536.
Fax: (860) 871-1802

HARPER, Lubbie, Jr. *(Judge, Connecticut Superior Court)* Appointed.
Office: Judicial District Courthouse, 235 Church Street, New Haven 06510.
Telephone: (203) 503-6830.
Fax: (203) 789-6826

HARRIGAN, Dennis F. *(Judge Referee, Connecticut Superior Court)* Appointed Judge to term beginning March 17, 1982. Reappointed March 17, 1990 and 1998. Former Presiding Judge Family Division Part D and Administrative Judge Waterbury Judicial District. Retired. Became Judge Referee Jan 19, 2000. Currently serves as Judge Trial. Referee. Born Ossining New York Jan 19, 1930. Roman Catholic. Educated at Fordham University B.S. 1951 J.D. 1955. Admitted to practice Connecticut 1955. In legal practice Milford 1957-82. Judge, Town Court 1959-60.

Office: Judicial District Courthouse, 123 Hoyt Street, Stamford 06905.
Telephone: (203) 965-5315.
Fax: (203) 965-5389

HARTMERE, Michael *(Judge, Connecticut Superior Court)* Appointed. Former Assistant Administrative Judge Ansonia-Milford Judicial District.
Office: 400 Grand Street, Waterbury 06702.
Telephone: (203) 236-8200.
Fax: (203) 236-8205

HAUSER, Lawrence L. *(Judge, Connecticut Superior Court)* Appointed. Former Presiding Judge.
Office: Judicial District Courthouse, 1061 Main Street, Bridgeport 06604.
Telephone: (203) 579-6540.
Fax: (203) 579-6928

HEALEY, Arthur H. *(Judge Referee, Connecticut Superior Court)* Retired. Currently serves as Judge Trial Referee. Former Judge and Chief Judge, Connecticut Superior Court, appointed to term beginning 1965. Former Associate Justice, Connecticut Supreme Court.
Office: Judicial District Courthouse, 70 Huntington Street, New London 06320.
Telephone: (860) 442-2977.
Fax: (860) 447-8701

HEFFERNAN, E. Michael *(Judge, West Haven District Probate Court)*
Mailing address: P.O. Box 127, West Haven 06516.
Office: 355 Main Street, West Haven 06516.
Telephone: (203) 937-3552.
Fax: (203) 937-3556

HELANDER, Joel E. *(Judge, Guilford District Probate Court)*
Office: Town Hall, 31 Park Street, Guilford 06437.
Telephone: (203) 453-8006.

HENDEL, Seymour L. *(Judge Referee, Connecticut Superior Court)* Appointed Judge to term beginning Feb 17, 1978. Reappointed 1986, 1994 and 2002. Administrative Judge 1985-90 and Presiding Judge Civil Division 1991-97 New London Judicial District. Senior Judge Nov 1, 1996 to Sept 30, 2001. Became Judge Referee Oct 1, 2001. Judge Trial Referee since Oct 1, 2001. Born New London Connecticut Oct 1, 1931. Jewish. Educated at Columbia College A.B. in Economics with highest honors and distinction 1953, Oxford University, Oxford England 1954 and Harvard University LL.B. 1956. Awarded Henry Evans Traveling Fellowship 1954. Member Phi Beta Kappa. Admitted to practice Connecticut 1956, Massachusetts 1956, U.S. District Courts District of Massachusetts 1956 and District of Connecticut 1956, U.S. Court of Appeals Second Circuit 1960 and U.S. Supreme Court 1967. Began legal practice Boston Massachusetts 1956. In legal practice New London Connecticut 1958-78. Judge, Connecticut Court of Common Pleas Feb 17, 1978 to June 30, 1978.

Author "Materials on Business Organizations and Bankruptcy" Course Manual for Basic Law for Legal Assistants Mitchell College 1978. Lecturer in Basic Law for Legal Assistants Mitchell College 1974-78. Chairman Connecticut Court Visitation Program Committee since 1980. Alternate member Connecticut Superior Court Sentence Review Division 1983-88. Vice Chairman Executive Committee Connecticut Center for Judicial Education 1986-90. Chairman Task Force on Judicial Department Security 1988-90, Judicial Branch Statewide Security Committee 1990-96 and Judicial Branch Civil Task Force Trial Subgroup 1993-94. Member Connecticut Judges Association (Chairman General Welfare Committee 1979-80), Connecticut Superior Court Judges Institute (Member 1983-84 and Chairman 1984-92 Curriculum Committee), New London County (Chairman Public Relations Committee 1974-78, Law Day Committee 1974-75, Law Day Chairman 1975, Executive Committee 1975-78), Connecticut (Law Day Committee 1975-76, Law Day Chairman 1976, Delegate to House of Delegates 1975-77, Member since 1976 and Chairman 1977-78 Special Committee on Lawyers and the Community, Chairman Law Line Program 1977, Member Commission on the Legal Profession 1978-80, Section on Litigation since 1978, Special Committee on Liaison with the State Courts 1978-82, Bicentennial Committee on U.S. Constitution 1986) and American (Judicial Administration Division since 1978) Bar Associations.

Recipient United Jewish Appeal Gold Medal Award 1967 and United Jewish Appeal Leadership Award 1974. Member Executive Committee and Counsel to New London Democratic Town Committee 1974-78. Member National Leaders Training Fellowship Committee National Federation of Jewish Men's Clubs 1964-70 (Chairman Leaders Training Fellowship Committee Connecticut Valley Region 1964-70), Community Development Action Plan Committee on Education, Recreation and Culture 1968-69, Council of Jewish Federations National Small Cities Committee 1970-74, American Committee for Celebration of Twenty-fifth Anniversary of State of Israel 1973, Columbia College Alumni Assembly 1973-76, National Jewish Community Relations Advisory Council Commission on International Community Relations Concerns 1975-76 and Columbia College Bicentennial Committee 1986. Co-leader Interfaith Study Mission to Israel 1974. Vice President Connecticut Jewish Community Relations Council 1977-78. President Beth El Men's Club 1962-63 and New London Junior High School PTA 1969-70. Director Eastern Connecticut Symphony 1958-89 (President 1961-62), Jewish Community Council of Greater New London since 1970 (President 1970-74) and Beth El Synagogue 1968-71. Chairman Columbia College Alumni Representative Committee of Southeastern Connecticut since 1962, Israel Emergency Fund Campaign 1967, MacDowell Festival of American Music 1967 and 1968, Eastern Connecticut Symphony Maintenance Fund Campaign 1968 and Federated Jewish Appeal of Greater New London 1976-77. Enjoys music, cross-country skiing and bicycling.
Office: Judicial District Courthouse, 70 Huntington Street, New London 06320.
Telephone: (860) 442-2977.

HENDERSON, Nancy S. *(Judge, Plymouth District Probate Court)*
Office: 80 Main Street, Terryville 06786.
Telephone: (860) 585-4014.

HENNESSEY, Mary R. *(Judge Referee, Connecticut Superior Court)* Appointed Judge. Former Administrative Judge Hartford-New Britain Judicial District. Retired. Currently serves as Judge Trial Referee.
Office: Judicial District Courthouse, 95 Washington Street, Hartford 06106.
Telephone: (860) 548-2850.
Fax: (860) 548-2887

HENNESSEY, Sheila M. *(Judge, Newington District Probate Court)*
Office: 66 Cedar Street, Newington 06111.
Telephone: (860) 665-1285.
Fax: (860) 665-1331

HENNESSY, Francis X. *(Judge Referee, Connecticut Superior Court)* Retired. Became Judge Referee Sept 11, 2000. Currently serves as Judge Trial Referee. Born New York New York Sept 11, 1930. Educated at Fordham University B.S. 1957 and University of Connecticut J.D. 1961. Admitted to practice Connecticut 1961. In legal practice Hartford 1962-63 and Windsor 1963-76. Judge, Connecticut Juvenile Court 1976-78. Judge, Connecticut Superior Court July 1, 1978 to 1994. Chief Administrative Judge Family Division 1979-86. Deputy Chief Court Administrator 1986-94. Judge, Connecticut Appellate Court 1994-2000.

Commissioner of Special Revenue Connecticut 1971-76. Author article on jurisdiction Connecticut B. Jour. 1985 and chapter in *AIDS and the Courts* 1990. Instructor in working with children in the Courts Center for Child Welfare Studies Saint Joseph College 1985-90. Member Hartford, Windsor (President 1972-73) and Connecticut Bar Associations. Presenter on AIDS and the courts 1988 and Conservatorships and Guardianships 1991 Conference of Chief Justices. Speaker National Conference on AIDS and the Courts National Institute

HENNESSY, FRANCIS X.—*Continued*

of Justice and State Justice Institute 1989. Named Democrat of the Year by Windsor Democratic Town Commission 1974. Recipient Distinguished Service Award from Family Law Section Hartford and Connecticut Bar Associations 1986 and Warren E. Burger Award for Outstanding Service for Children 1989. Corporal U.S. Army 1951-53. Awarded the Purple Heart and Combat Infantryman Badge. Chairman Democratic Town Committee Windsor 1964-74.

Office: Appellate Court, 95 Washington Street, Hartford 06106.

Telephone: (860) 548-2828.

HICKEY, William F., Jr. *(Judge Referee, Connecticut Superior Court)* Appointed Judge. Former Assistant Administrative Judge and Administrative Judge Stamford-Norwalk Judicial District. Former Senior Judge. Became Judge Referee May 28, 1999. Currently serves as Judge Trial Referee.

Office: Judicial District Courthouse, 123 Hoyt Street, Stamford 06905.

Telephone: (203) 965-5315.

Fax: (203) 965-5389

HILLER, Arthur A. *(Judge, Connecticut Superior Court)* Appointed 1999.

Office: Judicial District Courthouse, 1601 Main Street, Bridgeport 06604.

Telephone: (203) 579-6540.

Fax: (203) 579-6928

HODGSON, Beverly J. *(Judge, Connecticut Superior Court)* Appointed Nov 2, 1987. Reappointed 1995, current term expires 2003. Born May 20, 1948. Educated at Brown University B.A. magna cum laude 1970, Harvard University Graduate School of Education M.A.T. 1971 and Yale Law School J.D. 1976. Member Phi Beta Kappa. Admitted to practice Connecticut 1976, U.S. District Court District of Connecticut 1976, U.S. Court of Appeals Second Circuit and U.S. Supreme Court. In legal practice Bridgeport 1976-87.

Author *Alternative Dispute Resolution in Connecticut's Courts* 1998 updated 2001. Member The American Law Institute.

Office: 400 Grand Street, Waterbury 06702.

Telephone: (203) 236-8200.

Fax: (203) 236-8205

HOLDEN, William *(Judge, Connecticut Superior Court)* Appointed.

Mailing address: P.O. Box 210, Milford 06460.

Office: 14 West River Street, Milford 06460.

Telephone: (203) 878-5791.

Fax: (203) 876-8072

HOLZBERG, Robert L. *(Judge, Connecticut Superior Court)* Appointed. Former Assistant Administrative Judge Hartford-New Britain Judicial District.

Office: Judicial District Courthouse, 300 Grand Street, Waterbury 06702.

Telephone: (203) 596-4033.

Fax: (203) 596-4488

HOPPER, David W. *(Judge, Greenwich District Probate Court)*

Mailing address: P.O. Box 2540, Greenwich 06836-2540.

Office: Town Hall, 101 Field Point Road, Greenwich 06830-6463.

Telephone: (203) 622-3766.

Fax: (203) 622-6451

HOROWITZ, Robert H. *(Judge, Woodbridge District Probate Court)* Elected Nov 8, 1994. Reelected 1998 and 2002. Current term expires Jan 2007.

Office: Town Hall, 11 Meetinghouse Lane, Woodbridge 06525.

Telephone: (203) 389-3410.

Fax: (203) 389-3480

HOYLE, Clifford D. *(Judge, Derby District Probate Court)*

Office: City Hall, Second Floor, 253 Main Street, Ansonia 06401.

Telephone: (203) 734-1277.

Fax: (203) 734-0922

HUDOCK, Bruce P. *(Judge, Connecticut Superior Court)* Appointed.

Office: 172 Golden Hill Street, Bridgeport 06604.

Telephone: (203) 579-6568.

Fax: (203) 382-8430

HURLEY, D. Michael *(Judge Referee, Connecticut Superior Court)* Appointed Judge to term beginning Oct 22, 1982. Reappointed 1991. Former Administrative Judge New London Judicial District and Presiding Judge Civil Division. Retired. Became Judge Referee Oct 18, 1996. Currently serves as Judge Trial Referee. Born Brooklyn New York Oct 18, 1926. Educated at Catholic University of America 1945-49, Manhattan College B.A. 1952 and New York Law School LL.B. 1959. Admitted to practice New York 1959 and Connecticut 1966. Began legal practice Hartford Connecticut 1966.

Assistant State's Attorney Connecticut 1975. Instructor in Evidence University of New Haven at New London 1980. Member Connecticut Trial Lawyers Association, Hartford, New London and Connecticut Bar Associations. Named Outstanding Civic Leader of America 1967. Recipient Farmington Valley Herald Award for Service to Youth 1970 and Chamber of Commerce Award for Community Service 1971. USAF 1952-54. Member Democratic Town Committee. Vice Chairman Simsbury Cultural & Recreation Committee. President and Director Simsbury Theater Guild. Director Simsbury Summer Theater for Youth. Interested in theater. Enjoys playing tennis, golfing and sailing.

Office: Judicial District Courthouse, 70 Huntington Street, New London 06320.

Telephone: (860) 442-2977.

Fax: (860) 447-8701

IANNOTTI, Frank A. *(Judge, Connecticut Superior Court)* Appointed.

Office: 400 Grand Street, Waterbury 06702.

Telephone: (203) 236-8200.

Fax: (203) 236-8205

JONES, Clarance J. *(Judge, Connecticut Superior Court)* Appointed.

Office: One Court Street, Middletown 06457.

Telephone: (860) 343-6570.

Fax: (860) 343-6589

JONGBLOED, Barbara Bailey *(Judge, Connecticut Superior Court)* Appointed.
Office: 978 Hartford Turnpike, Waterford 06385.
Telephone: (860) 440-5880.
Fax: (860) 440-5885

KAPITULIK, Sharon G. *(Judge, Haddam District Probate Court)*
Office: 30 Field Park Drive, Haddam 06438.
Telephone: (860) 345-8531.

KAPLAN, Burton A. *(Judge, Connecticut Superior Court)* Appointed.
Office: 121 Elm Street, New Haven 06510.
Telephone: (203) 789-7491.
Fax: (203) 789-7492

KAPLAN, Jonathan J. *(Judge, Connecticut Superior Court)* Appointed to term beginning 1985. Reappointed to subsequent terms. Current term expires 2010. Former Assistant Administrative Judge Tolland Judicial District. Born Bridgeport Connecticut March 5, 1946. Educated at Bryant College B.S. 1968 and University of Connecticut School of Law J.D. cum laude 1971. Admitted to practice Connecticut 1971, U.S. District Court District of Connecticut, U.S. Court of Appeals Second Circuit and U.S. Supreme Court. In legal practice Rockville 1971-85.
Office: 20 Park Street, Rockville 06066.
Telephone: (860) 896-4930.
Fax: (860) 870-3295

KARAZIN, Edward R., Jr. *(Judge, Connecticut Superior Court)* Appointed to term beginning June 29, 1990. Reappointed 1998, current term expires 2006. Born New York New York Feb 24, 1940. Educated at Boston College A.B. 1961 and Fordham University School of Law J.D. 1964. Admitted to practice Connecticut 1964. In legal practice Westport 1964-90.
Vice Chairman Board of Finance Westport 1983-90. Adjunct Professor Western Connecticut State University since 1990. Former Member American Inns of Court. Captain U.S. Army Vietnam 1965-67. Recipient Bronze Star.
Office: 123 Hoyt Street, Stamford 06905.
Telephone: (203) 965-5315.
Fax: (203) 965-5389

KATZ, Joette *(Associate Justice, Connecticut Supreme Court)* Appointed to term beginning 1992. Administrative Judge Aug 1, 1994 to June 1, 2000. Educated at Brandeis University B.A. 1974 and University of Connecticut J.D. 1977. In legal practice 1977-78. Former Judge, Connecticut Superior Court.
Assistant Public Defender 1981-83. Chief of Legal Services Public Defender Services 1983-89. Instructor in Ethics and Criminal Law Quinnipiac College. Past President Fairfield County Branch American Inns of Court. Former Member Public Defender Commission and Law Revision Commission. Member The American Law Institute.
Office: 231 Capitol Avenue, Hartford 06106.
Telephone: (860) 757-2200.

KAVANEWSKY, John F., Jr. *(Judge, Connecticut Superior Court)* Appointed.
Office: 123 Hoyt Street, Stamford 06905.
Telephone: (203) 965-5315.
Fax: (203) 965-5389

KELLER, Christine E. *(Judge, Connecticut Superior Court)* Appointed.
Office: 101 Lafayette Street, Hartford 06106.
Telephone: (860) 566-3861.
Fax: (860) 566-6977

KELLEY, James K. *(Judge, Brooklyn District Probate Court)* Elected to term beginning Jan 7, 1987. Reelected to subsequent terms. Current term expires Jan 2007. Born Putnam Connecticut Aug 23, 1950. Catholic. Educated at Assumption College A.B. with honors 1972 and Western New England College School of Law J.D. 1976. Admitted to practice Connecticut 1976 and U.S. District Court District of Connecticut 1976. In legal practice Brooklyn and Danielson since 1976.
Member Windham County, Connecticut and American Bar Associations. Instructor American Banking Institute 1985-87. Commissioner Brooking Housing Authority.
Mailing address: P.O. Box 356, Brooklyn 06234-0356.
Office: Town Hall, Four Wolf Den Road, Brooklyn 06234.
Telephone: (860) 774-5973.
Fax: (860) 779-3744

KENEFICK, James G., Jr. *(Judge, Connecticut Superior Court)* Appointed.
Office: Judicial District Courthouse, 235 Church Street, New Haven 06510.
Telephone: (203) 503-6830.
Fax: (203) 789-6826

KENNEDY, George L. *(Judge, Griswold District Probate Court)*
Mailing address: P.O. Box 369, Jewett City 06351.
Office: Town Hall, 32 School Street, Jewett City 06351.
Telephone: (860) 376-0216.
Fax: (860) 376-0216

KENNEDY, Kevin *(Judge, Colchester District Probate Court)*
Office: Town Hall, 127 Norwich Avenue, Colchester 06415.
Telephone: (860) 537-7290.
Fax: (860) 537-0547

KEYES, John A. *(Judge, New Haven District Probate Court)*
Mailing address: P.O. Box 905, New Haven 06504-0905.
Office: 200 Orange Street, First Floor, New Haven 06504.
Telephone: (203) 946-4880.
Fax: (203) 946-5962

KILLIAN, Robert K., Jr. *(Judge, Hartford District Probate Court)* Elected 1984, 1986, 1990, 1994, 1998 and 2002. Current term expires Jan 2007. Born Hartford Connecticut Jan 29, 1947. Roman Catholic. Educated at Union College and University B.A. 1969 and Georgetown University J.D. 1972. Admitted to practice Connecticut 1972, District of Columbia 1974, U.S. District Court District of Connecticut 1972 and U.S. Court of Appeals Second Circuit 1973. In legal practice Hartford since 1972.
Author *Basic Probate in Connecticut* National Business Institute 2002. Member Investment Advisory Council State of Connecticut 1995-2000. Member National College of Probate Judges, National College of Juvenile and Family Court Judges, Connecticut Probate Assembly

KILLIAN, ROBERT K., JR.—*Continued*
(Executive Committee since 1988, President-Judge 1997-1999), The Association of Trial Lawyers of America, Hartford County, Connecticut and American Bar Associations. Frequent lecturer on issues relating to estates, mental health, children's law, elder law and rights of the disabled. Named Connecticut's Outstanding Probate Judge by Connecticut Probate Assembly 1990. Previously employed as Washington Bureau Chief WTIC AM-FM-TV3 1969-72. Democrat. Counsel to U.S. Senator Abraham A. Ribicoff 1972-74 and to Lieutenant Governor of Connecticut 1974-78. Chairman March of Dimes Birth Defects Foundation (Connecticut Chapter). Board of Advisors Hartford Police Athletic League and Intensive Education Center for Learning Disabled. Regent University of Hartford. Trustee Hartt School of Music. Director Yeats Drama Foundation. Interests include magic, golf and UCONN basketball.
Office: 250 Constitution Plaza, Third Floor, Hartford 06103-2800.
Telephone: (860) 757-9150.
Fax: (860) 724-1503

KIMES, Russell A., Jr. *(Judge, New Canaan District Probate Court)*
Office: Town Hall, 77 Main Street, New Canaan 06840.
Telephone: (203) 594-3050.
Fax: (203) 594-3128

KLACZAK, Lawrence C. *(Judge Referee, Connecticut Superior Court)* Appointed Judge. Former Administrative Judge Tolland Judicial District. Retired. Currently serves as Judge Trial Referee.
Office: Judicial District Courthouse, 69 Brooklyn Street, Rockville 06066.
Telephone: (860) 896-4930.
Fax: (860) 870-0394

KNIERIM, Paul J. *(Judge, Simsbury District Probate Court)*
Mailing address: P.O. Box 495, Simsbury 06070-0495.
Office: 933 Hopmeadow Street, Simsbury 06070.
Telephone: (860) 658-3277.

KOCAY, Andre M. *(Judge, Connecticut Superior Court)* Appointed. Former Assistant Administrative Judge Litchfield Judicial District.
Office: 20 Franklin Square, New Britain 06051.
Telephone: (860) 515-5050.
Fax: (860) 515-5051

KOLETSKY, Joseph Q. *(Judge, Connecticut Superior Court)* Appointed to term beginning Nov 6, 1985. Reappointed March 12, 1986, March 12, 1994 and March 12, 2002. Current term expires March 11, 2010. Born New Haven Connecticut Feb 28, 1938. Educated at Yale University B.A. 1959 J.D. 1962. Member Phi Delta Phi. Admitted to practice Connecticut 1962, U.S. Court of Military Appeals 1966 and U.S. Supreme Court 1966. In legal practice New London, Hartford and Essex 1966-85.
Former member Connecticut Trial Lawyers Association. Member New London County Bar Association. Captain JAGC USNR (retired). Former Member Executive Committee Yale Law School Association.
Office: 70 Huntington Street, New London 06320.
Telephone: (860) 442-2977.

KRECHEVSKY, Robert L. *(Recalled Judge, United States Bankruptcy Court District of Connecticut)* Appointed Judge by U.S. District Court Judges to term beginning Nov 1, 1978. Appointed Recalled Judge by the Judicial Council of the Second Circuit. Term expires March 15, 2004. Former Chief Judge Bankruptcy Court. Former Judge, Bankruptcy Appellate Panel Second Circuit, selected by the Judicial Council of the Second Circuit. Born Hartford Connecticut Aug 11, 1922. Educated at Yale University 1943 and University of Connecticut School of Law LL.B. with honors 1948. Admitted to practice Connecticut 1948. In legal practice Hartford 1948-78.
Office: Federal Bldg. & U.S. Courthouse, 450 Main Street, Hartford 06103.
Telephone: (860) 240-3679.

KREMSKI, Julius J. *(Judge Referee, Connecticut Superior Court)* Appointed Judge to term beginning July 1, 1978. Retired. Became Judge Referee April 12, 1989. Currently serves as Judge Trial Referee. Former Judge, Connecticut Court of Common Pleas.
Office: 20 Franklin Square, New Britain 06051.
Telephone: (860) 515-5050.
Fax: (860) 515-5051

KURMAY, F. Paul *(Judge, Stratford District Probate Court)* Elected 1978 to term beginning Jan 3, 1979. Re-elected 1982, 1986, 1990, 1994, 1998 and 2002. Current term expires Jan 2007. Born Bridgeport Connecticut Oct 22, 1944. Roman Catholic. Educated at University of Virginia B.A. 1966 and Georgetown University J.D. 1969. Member Phi Beta Kappa and Pi Kappa Phi. Admitted to practice Connecticut 1969. Began legal practice Stratford 1969.
Assistant Town Attorney 1978-79. Member Executive Committee since 1986 and Second Vice President 1991-93 Connecticut Probate Assembly. Member Bridgeport Bar Association. Named Outstanding Probate Judge of the Year 1990. City Councilman Stratford 1973-77. Deacon Roman Catholic Church, ordained May 25, 1985.
Office: 468 Birdseye Street, Second Floor, Stratford 06615.
Telephone: (203) 385-4023.
Fax: (203) 375-6253

LAGER, Linda K. *(Judge, Connecticut Superior Court)* Appointed to term beginning Jan 10, 1992. Reappointed March 2000, current term expires March 2008. Born Brooklyn New York April 26, 1951. Educated at State University of New York at Buffalo B.A. summa cum laude 1972 and Boston University J.D. 1975. Staff member Boston University Law Review 1973-75. Law Clerk to Presiding Justice John A. Speziale, Connecticut Appellate Court 1975-77. Admitted to practice Connecticut 1975, U.S. District Court District of Connecticut 1976, U.S. Court of Appeals Second Circuit 1979 and U.S. Supreme Court 1979.
Assistant State's Attorney New Haven Connecticut 1979-82. Assistant U.S. Attorney District of Connecticut 1982-92. Lecturer on Law University of Connecticut 1977-81. Lecturer Landmarks Seminar Yale University School of Medicine since 1995. Member Connecticut Bar Association.
Office: 106 Elizabeth Street, Derry 06418.
Telephone: (203) 735-8695.
Fax: (203) 734-6294
E-mail address: linda.lager@jud.state.ct.us

LANDAU, Sidney S. *(Senior Judge, Connecticut Appellate Court)* Appointed. Reappointed 1998. Retired. Born New York New York April 19, 1935. Jewish. Educated at Alfred University B.A. 1956 and New York University LL.B. 1959. Admitted to practice New York 1960, Connecticut 1961 and U.S. District Courts Eastern, Northern and Southern Districts of New York. In legal practice Stamford Connecticut 1961-76. Judge, Connecticut Court of Common Pleas 1976-78. Former Judge, Connecticut Superior Court, appointed to term beginning July 1, 1978.

Assistant Prosecuting Attorney Connecticut 1968-72. Adjunct Professor of Law Quinnipiac College since 1980.

Office: 95 Washington Street, Hartford 06106.
Telephone: (860) 548-2828.
Fax: (860) 548-2870

LANDGREBE, Martin F. *(Judge, New Milford District Probate Court)*

Office: 10 Main Street, New Milford 06776.
Telephone: (860) 355-6029.

LANGENBACH, John J. *(Judge, Connecticut Superior Court)* Appointed to term beginning Jan 8, 1988. Reappointed 1996, current term expires 2004. Former Assistant Administrative Judge Hartford-New Britain Judicial District. Born Lincoln Park New Jersey. Educated at Yale University B.A. with honors 1960 and University of Pennsylvania LL.B. 1963. Law Clerk to Hon. John M. Comley, Connecticut Supreme Court 1963-64. Admitted to practice Connecticut 1963, U.S. District Court District of Connecticut, U.S. Court of Appeals Second Circuit and U.S. Supreme Court. In legal practice Hartford 1964-88.

Corporation Counsel West Hartford 1975-77. Member Connecticut Judges Association, American Judges Association, Hartford County, Connecticut and American Bar Associations.

Office: Judicial District Courthouse, 95 Washington Street, Hartford 06106.
Telephone: (860) 548-2850.
Fax: (860) 548-2887

LAVERY, William J. *(Chief Judge, Connecticut Appellate Court)* Appointed Judge Sept 1989. Reappointed March 1990 and 1998. Current term expires 2006. Chief Judge since March 12, 2000. Born New Haven Connecticut March 26, 1938. Roman Catholic. Educated at Fairfield University A.B. 1959 and Fordham University LL.B. 1964. Admitted to practice Connecticut 1964 and U.S. District Court District of Connecticut 1964. Judge, Connecticut Superior Court Sept 1981 to Sept 1989.

Housing Attorney City of Bridgeport 1969-72. Town and Borough Attorney Newtown 1976-81. Graduate The National Judicial College 1984. E-4 USAR 1961-64. Member Connecticut State Legislature 1967-71. General Counsel to Speaker of the House Connecticut State Legislature 1971-73. Vice Chairman Connecticut Commission on Hospital and Health Care 1976-81.

Office: Judicial District Courthouse, 95 Washington Street, Hartford 06106.
Telephone: (860) 548-2828.

LAVINE, Douglas S. *(Judge, Connecticut Superior Court)* Appointed.

Office: 101 Lafayette Street, Hartford 06106.
Telephone: (860) 566-3861.
Fax: (860) 566-6977

LEARY, William C. *(Judge, Windsor Locks District Probate Court)* Elected to term beginning Nov 1971. Reelected to subsequent terms. Current term expires Jan 2007. Born Hartford Connecticut Aug 4, 1938. Roman Catholic. Educated at Providence College A.B. 1960 and University of Connecticut LL.B. 1965. Admitted to practice Connecticut 1965. Began legal practice Hartford 1965. In legal practice Windsor Locks 1973.

Member Greater Enfield (President 1980-81), Hartford County and Connecticut Bar Associations. Airman Connecticut National Guard 1960-66. Worked for *Hartford Courant* 1960-65. Member Charter Revision Commission 1964 and 1980 and Windsor Locks Police Commission 1966-68. Industrial Development Commission since 1970. Democrat. Connecticut General Assembly 1967-71. Member Windsor Locks Lions Club (President 1970-71) and Riverside Council Knights of Columbus.

Office: Town Office Building, 50 Church Street, Windsor Locks 06096.
Telephone: (860) 627-1450.
Fax: (860) 627-1451

LEAVITT, Edward J. *(Judge, Connecticut Superior Court)* Appointed.

Office: 121 Elm Street, New Haven 06510.
Telephone: (203) 789-7937.
Fax: (203) 789-7539

LEHENY, Sandra Vilardi *(Judge, Connecticut Superior Court)* Appointed. Former Assistant Administrative Judge Danbury Judicial District.

Office: Judicial District Courthouse, 300 Grand Street, Waterbury 06702.
Telephone: (203) 596-4033.
Fax: (203) 596-4488

LENTZ, Judith P. *(Judge, Killingworth District Probate Court)*

Office: Town Office Building, 323 Route 81, Killingworth 06419.
Telephone: (860) 663-2304.

LEUBA, Robert C. *(Judge Referee, Connecticut Superior Court)* Appointed Judge. Former Assistant Administrative Judge New London Judicial District. Former Deputy Chief Court Administrator. Chief Court Administrator Jan 4, 1999 to Nov 27, 2000. Former Senior Judge. Currently serves as Judge Trial Referee.

Office: Judicial District Courthouse, 70 Huntington Street, New London 06320.
Telephone: (860) 442-2977.
Fax: (860) 447-8701

LEVIN, Bruce L. *(Judge, Connecticut Superior Court)* Appointed.

Office: Judicial District Courthouse, 1061 Main Street, Bridgeport 06604.
Telephone: (203) 579-6540.
Fax: (203) 579-6928

LEVINE, George *(Judge, Connecticut Superior Court)* Appointed to term beginning Sept 30, 1994. Reappointed 2002, current term expires Nov 2010. Born Hartford Connecticut May 12, 1938. Jewish. Educated at Yale University A.B. 1960 and Columbia University LL.B. 1963. Admitted to practice Connecticut 1963, U.S. District Court District of Connecticut 1964, U.S.

LEVINE, GEORGE—*Continued*

Court of Appeals Second Circuit 1966 and U.S. Supreme Court 1974.

Mailing address: 20 Franklin Square, New Britain 06051.

Telephone: (860) 515-5050.

Fax: (860) 515-5051

LEWIS, William B. *(Judge Referee, Connecticut Superior Court)* Appointed Judge. Former Presiding Judge Civil Division, Assistant Administrative Judge and Administrative Judge Stamford-Norwalk Judicial District. Former Senior Judge. Currently serves as Judge Trial Referee.

Office: Judicial District Courthouse, 123 Hoyt Street, Stamford 06905.

Telephone: (203) 965-5315.

Fax: (203) 965-5389

LICARI, Joseph A., Jr. *(Judge, Connecticut Superior Court)* Appointed. Former Assistant Administrative Judge and Administrative Judge New Haven Judicial District.

Office: Judicial District Courthouse, 235 Church Street, New Haven 06510.

Telephone: (203) 503-6830.

Fax: (203) 789-6826

LIGHTFOOT, Richard *(Judge, Lyme District Probate Court)* Elected to term beginning Jan 2002. Reelected 2002, current term expires Jan 2007. Educated at Yale University B.A. 1959 and Harvard Law School J.D. 1963. Admitted to practice Connecticut 1963 and New York 1968. In legal practice Connecticut 1963-69 and New York 1968-73.

Office: Town Hall, 480 Hamburg Road, Lyme 06371.

Telephone: (860) 434-7733.

LOISELLE, Alva P. *(Judge Referee, Connecticut Superior Court)* Retired. Became Judge Referee July 4, 1980. Former Judge Trial Referee. Born Willimantic Connecticut July 4, 1910. Roman Catholic. Educated at University of Connecticut B.S. 1934 LL.D. 1943. Admitted to practice Connecticut 1943. Judge, Connecticut Court of Common Pleas 1952-57. Judge, Connecticut Superior Court 1957-71. Justice, Connecticut Supreme Court, May 14, 1971 to July 3, 1980.

Corporation Counsel Willimantic City 1945-47. Instructor University of Connecticut 1946-52. Member Connecticut and American Bar Associations. Recipient Outstanding Alumni Award from University of Connecticut 1966 and from University of Connecticut Law School 1974. Alderman Willimantic City 1939-43. Enjoys bowling and boating.

LOPEZ, Carmen L. *(Judge, Connecticut Superior Court)* Appointed.

Office: One Court Street, Middletown 06457.

Telephone: (860) 343-6570.

Fax: (860) 343-6589

LOUGEE, Carol B. *(Judge, Madison District Probate Court)*

Mailing address: P.O. Box 205, Madison 06443.

Office: Eight Campus Drive, Madison 06443.

Telephone: (203) 245-5661.

Fax: (203) 245-5653

MACK, Michael A. *(Judge, Connecticut Superior Court)* Appointed.

Office: 81 Columbia Avenue, Willimantic 06226.

Telephone: (860) 456-5700.

Fax: (860) 456-5702

MAGISTRALI, Michael F. *(Judge, Torrington District Probate Court)* Elected to term beginning Jan 1999. Reelected 2002, current term expires Dec 2006. Born Torrington Connecticut Nov 19, 1953. Educated at University of Connecticut 1971-72, Marlboro College 1973-74 and Boston College B.A. magna cum laude 1976 J.D. 1980. Admitted to practice Massachusetts 1980, Connecticut 1981, U.S. District Courts District of Massachusetts 1980 and District of Connecticut 1985, U.S. Court of Appeals First Circuit 1980 and U.S. Supreme Court 2001. In legal practice Winsted Connecticut Nov 1985 to Sept 1999 and Torrington Connecticut since 1999.

Assistant Corporation Counsel City of Boston Oct 1980 to Oct 1984. Assistant Attorney General Massachusetts Oct 1984 to Nov 1985. Contributing Editor Annual Survey of Massachusetts Law 1982 and 1983. Member Connecticut Trial Lawyers Association, National College of Probate Judges, Litchfield County and Connecticut Bar Associations. Member Torrington Republican Town Committee. Past President and Former Member Board of Directors Westside School Community Association and Friendship Plus, Inc. Former Vice President/Director Housatonic Center for Mental Health. Former Chairman Ethics Commission City of Torrington. Former Director Northwest Connecticut AIDS Project. Former Moderator Center Congregational Church. Former Coach Varsity Alumni Girl's Basketball League. Board of Directors and Treasurer Torrington Historic Preservation Trust. Member United Way of Greater Torrington Area (Chairman General Campaign 1997, Second Vice President, Board of Directors), Torrington Rotary Club (Past President) and Northwest Connecticut Girl Scouts.

Office: 140 Main Street, Torrington 06790.

Telephone: (860) 489-2215, 626-0777.

MAIN, Philip D. *(Judge, Granby District Probate Court)*

Mailing address: P.O. Box 240, Granby 06035-0240.

Office: Town Hall, 15 North Granby Road, Granby 06035.

Telephone: (860) 653-8944.

MAIOCCO, John P., Jr. *(Judge Referee, Connecticut Superior Court)* Appointed Judge. Former Senior Judge. Currently serves as Judge Trial Referee.

Office: Judicial District Courthouse, 1061 Main Street, Bridgeport 06604.

Telephone: (203) 579-6540.

Fax: (203) 579-6928

MALONEY, John P. *(Judge Referee, Connecticut Superior Court)* Appointed Judge. Former Administrative Judge Civil Division Part A. Former Chief Administrative Judge Administrative Appeals. Former Senior Judge. Currently serves as Judge Trial Referee.

Office: 101 Lafayette Street, Hartford 06106.

Telephone: (860) 566-3861.

Fax: (860) 566-6977

MARGOLIS, Joan G. *(Magistrate Judge, United States District Court District of Connecticut)* Appointed by U.S. District Court judges.
Office: U.S. Courthouse, 141 Church Street, New Haven 06510.
Telephone: (203) 773-2350.

MARIANO, Peter E. *(Judge, Naugatuck District Probate Court)*
Office: Town Hall, 229 Church Street, Naugatuck 06770.
Telephone: (203) 720-7046.
Fax: (203) 729-9452

MARINO, Joseph D. *(Judge, Middletown District Probate Court)*
Office: 94 Court Street, Middletown 06457.
Telephone: (860) 347-7424.
Fax: (860) 346-1520

MARTIN, Robert A. *(Judge, Connecticut Superior Court)* Appointed.
Office: Judicial District Courthouse, 70 Huntington Street, New London 06320.
Telephone: (860) 442-2977.
Fax: (860) 447-8701

MARTINEZ, Donna F. *(Magistrate Judge, United States District Court District of Connecticut)* Appointed by U.S. District Court judges Feb 8, 1994. Educated at University of Connecticut B.S. 1973 M.S. 1975 J.D. 1978.
Assistant Corporation Counsel Hartford 1978-80. Assistant U.S. Attorney and Chief Organized Crime/Drug Enforcement Task Force District of Connecticut 1980-94. Instructor Yale Law School. Member Olliver Ellsworth Chapter American Inns of Court (Past President, Former Vice President), Federal Magistrate Judges' Association, Hispanic Bar Association, Connecticut and Federal Bar Associations. Instructor U.S. Department of Justice Advocacy Institute. Board of Directors American Leadership Forum.
Office: Federal Bldg. & U.S. Courthouse, 450 Main Street, Hartford 06103.
Telephone: (860) 240-3605.

MATASAVAGE, Paul *(Judge, Connecticut Superior Court)* Appointed.
Office: 83 Prospect Street, Waterbury 06702.
Telephone: (203) 596-4202.
Fax: (203) 596-4431

McANANEY, Edward G. *(Judge, Suffield District Probate Court)* Elected to term beginning April 10, 2000. Reelected 2002, current term expires Jan 2, 2007. Born Yonkers New York. Educated at College of the Holy Cross A.B. 1979 and Boston College Law School J.D. 1986. Managing Editor Boston College International and Comparative Law Review 1985-86. Admitted to practice Connecticut 1986 and New York 1995. In legal practice Suffield Connecticut since 1991 and Yonkers New York since 1995.
Town Attorney Suffield 1992. Member Connecticut and New York State Bar Associations. Captain USNR since 1979.
Office: Town Hall, 83 Mountain Road, Suffield 06078.
Telephone: (860) 668-3835.
Fax: (860) 668-3029

McDANIEL, Ronald K., Jr. *(Judge, Montville District Probate Court)*
Office: 310 Norwich-New London Turnpike, Uncasville 06382.
Telephone: (860) 848-9847.
Fax: (860) 848-2116

McDONALD, Francis M., Jr. *(Judge Referee, Connecticut Superior Court)* Retired. Became Judge Referee Jan 22, 2001. Currently serves as Judge Trial Referee. Born Waterbury Connecticut Jan 22, 1931. Educated at College of the Holy Cross B.A. 1953 and Yale Law School LL.B. 1956. Former Judge, Connecticut Superior Court. Associate Justice and Chief Justice, Connecticut Supreme Court 1996-2001.
Special Agent Federal Bureau of Investigation 1956-58. Assistant U.S. Attorney Connecticut 1958-60. Assistant Prosecuting Attorney Waterbury Circuit Court 1961-65. Deputy Chief Prosecuting Attorney Connecticut Circuit Courts 1965-68. State's Attorney Waterbury Judicial District 1968-84. Judge, Connecticut Superior Court 1984-96.
Office: 400 Grand Street, Waterbury 06702.
Telephone: (203) 236-8200.
Fax: (203) 236-8205

McKINNEY, Anne C. *(Judge, East Hampton District Probate Court)* Elected Nov 8, 1994. Reelected 1998 and 2002. Current term expires Jan 2007.
Office: Town Hall Annex, 20 East High Street, East Hampton 06424.
Telephone: (860) 267-9262.
Fax: (860) 267-6453

McLACHLAN, C. Ian *(Judge, Connecticut Appellate Court)* Appointed. Former Judge, Connecticut Superior Court, appointed 1996.
Office: 95 Washington Street, Hartford 06106.
Telephone: (860) 548-2828.

McMAHON, Kevin P. *(Judge, Connecticut Superior Court)* Appointed.
Office: 112 Broad Street, New London 06320.
Telephone: (860) 443-8343.
Fax: (860) 437-1168

McNAMARA, Jeffrey A. *(Judge, East Lyme District Probate Court)*
Mailing address: P.O. Box 519, Niantic 06357.
Office: 108 Pennsylvania Avenue, Niantic 06357.
Telephone: (860) 739-6931.
Fax: (860) 739-6930

McWEENY, Robert F. *(Judge, Connecticut Superior Court)* Appointed to term beginning Feb 1989. Reappointed 1997, current term expires 2005. Former Chief Administrative Judge Tax and Administrative Appeal Division. Born New York New York July 18, 1946. Educated at Boston University B.A. 1968 and University of Connecticut J.D. with honors 1973. Admitted to practice Connecticut 1973, U.S. District Court District of Connecticut 1975, U.S. Court of Appeals Second Circuit 1975 and U.S. Supreme Court 1984. In legal practice Hartford 1975-89.
Attorney General Electric Company 1973-75. Adjunct Instructor in Employment Discrimination Western New England College School of Law 1990-93. Chairman Labor and Employment Law Section Connecticut Bar Association 1981-82. Instructor at numerous employment law seminars Connecticut Bar Association 1980-91. Fac-

MCWEENY, ROBERT F.—*Continued*

ulty Member on Employment Discrimination American Bar Association Las Vegas Nevada 1990. Recipient Law Day Speaker Award 1990. U.S. Army Dec 1968 to Sept 1970.

Office: 400 Grand Street, Waterbury 06702.
Telephone: (203) 236-8200.

MEADOW, Frank S. *(Judge Referee, Connecticut Superior Court)* Appointed Judge to term beginning Jan 4, 1983. Reappointed Feb 9, 1991. Retired. Became Judge Referee Oct 3, 1992. Currently serves as Judge Trial Referee. Born New Haven Connecticut Oct 3, 1922. Jewish. Educated at Tufts University B.S. with honors 1947 and University of Miami LL.B. 1951. Admitted to practice Florida 1951 and Connecticut 1952. Began legal practice Miami Florida 1951. In legal practice New Haven Connecticut 1952.

Assistant Corporation Counsel New Haven 1961-75. Important Decision: Mediation of L'Ambiance Plaza Construction Disaster with Judge Robert C. Zampano, U.S. District Court District of Connecticut 1988. Member The Florida Bar, New Haven County and Connecticut Bar Associations. Recipient Distinguished Service Award from Greater Bridgeport Bar Association 1990. Lieutenant j.g. USN 1944-46. Democrat. Member Woodbridge Country Club. Enjoys golf.

Office: Judicial District Courthouse, 235 Church Street, New Haven 06510.
Telephone: (203) 503-6830.
Fax: (203) 789-6826

MECCARIELLO, Bryan F. *(Judge, Southington District Probate Court)*
Mailing address: P.O. Box 165, Southington 06489-0165.
Office: 75 Main Street, Southington 06489.
Telephone: (860) 276-6253.
Fax: (860) 276-6255

MELVILLE, L. Scott *(Senior Judge, Connecticut Superior Court)* Appointed. Retired.
Office: Judicial District Courthouse, 1061 Main Street, Bridgeport 06604.
Telephone: (203) 579-6540.
Fax: (203) 579-6928

MENT, Aaron *(Senior Judge, Connecticut Superior Court)* Appointed to term beginning July 1, 1978. Reappointed. Former Chief Administrative Judge Criminal Division. Former Deputy Chief Court Administrator and Chief Court Administrator. Retired. Became Senior Judge Jan 4, 1999. Educated at University of Connecticut B.A. and Boston University School of Law LL.B. In legal practice 1961-76. Judge, Connecticut Court of Common Pleas 1976-78.

Former Chief Legislative Liaison and Counsel to Governor Ella T. Grasso. Former Aide and Counsel to Speaker House of Representatives General Assembly Connecticut. Former Member Board of Aldermen Bridgeport. Recipient Bice Clemow Award in recognition of his work on the cause of open and accountable government in Connecticut from Connecticut Council on Freedom of Information 1992. USAS.

Office: 231 Capitol Avenue, Hartford 06106.
Telephone: (860) 757-2100.
Fax: (860) 757-2130

MIANO, Thomas P. *(Judge, Connecticut Superior Court)* Appointed. Former Assistant Administrative Judge Hartford-New Britain Judicial District.
Office: 101 Lafayette Street, Hartford 06106.
Telephone: (860) 566-3861.
Fax: (860) 566-6977

MIHALAKOS, Socrates H. *(Judge Referee, Connecticut Superior Court)* Former Senior Judge. Became Judge Referee June 2003. Currently serves as Judge Trial Referee. Born June 1933. Former Judge, Connecticut Superior Court. Former Judge, Connecticut Appellate Court.
Office: Judicial District Courthouse, 300 Grand Street, Waterbury 06702.
Telephone: (203) 596-4033.
Fax: (203) 596-4488

MILLER, Barbara L. *(Judge, Kent District Probate Court)*
Mailing address: P.O. Box 185, Kent 06757-0185.
Office: Town Hall, 41 Kent Green Boulevard, Kent 06757.
Telephone: (860) 927-3729.

MINTZ, Douglas C. *(Judge, Connecticut Superior Court)* Appointed.
Office: Judicial District Courthouse, 123 Hoyt Street, Stamford 06905.
Telephone: (203) 965-5315.
Fax: (203) 965-5389

MOKRZEWSKI, Stanley A. *(Judge, Bozrah District Probate Court)* Elected Nov 8, 1994. Reelected 1998 and 2002. Current term expires Jan 2007.
Office: Bozrah Town Hall, One River Road, Bozrah 06334.
Telephone: (860) 889-2958.
Fax: (860) 887-7571

MOORE, Sheridan L. *(Judge, Connecticut Superior Court)* Appointed.
Office: 172 Golden Hill Street, Bridgeport 06604.
Telephone: (203) 579-6568.
Fax: (203) 382-8408

MORAGHAN, Howard J. *(Judge Referee, Connecticut Superior Court)* Appointed Judge to term beginning July 1, 1978. Reappointed to subsequent terms. Former Administrative Judge Danbury Judicial District. Retired. Became Judge Referee Aug 28, 2000. Currently serves as Judge Trial Referee. Judge, Connecticut Circuit Court 1970-75. Judge, Connecticut Court of Common Pleas Jan 1, 1975 to June 30, 1978.
Office: 146 White Street, Danbury 06810.
Telephone: (203) 207-8690.
Fax: (203) 207-8689

MORAN, John W. *(Judge, Connecticut Superior Court)* Appointed.
Mailing address: P.O. Box 210, Milford 06460.
Office: 14 West River Street, Milford 06460.
Telephone: (203) 878-5791.
Fax: (203) 876-8072

MORRISSEY, J. David *(Judge, Farmington District Probate Court)*
Office: One Monteith Drive, Farmington 06032.
Telephone: (860) 675-2360.
Fax: (860) 673-8262

MOTTOLESE, A. William *(Judge, Connecticut Superior Court)* Appointed Sept 28, 1988. Reappointed 1997, current term expires 2005. Former Presiding Judge Civil Division Fairfield Judicial District. Born Greenwich Connecticut Feb 19, 1935. Roman Catholic. Educated at Holy Cross College A.B. with honors 1956 and Georgetown University Law Center J.D. 1959. Admitted to practice District of Columbia 1959 and Connecticut 1961. In legal practice Greenwich Connecticut 1961-88.

Town Attorney Greenwich 1974-81. Member Connecticut Criminal Justice Commission 1991-95. Member Connecticut Judges Association (Former Vice President, President 1996-97). Faculty Connecticut Judges Institute 1994, 1996, 1997, 2000 and 2002. Recipient Columbus Day Award from St. Lawrence Society 1990 and Professional Civic and Community Award from Police Anchor Club Branch No. 25, 1991. Enjoys reading, fishing, canoeing, hiking and art.

Office: 11 Commerce Street, Norwalk 06850.
Telephone: (203) 866-9275.
Fax: (203) 838-5883

MULCAHY, John F., Jr. *(Judge, Connecticut Superior Court)* Appointed.
Office: 101 Lafayette Street, Hartford 06106.
Telephone: (860) 566-3861.
Fax: (860) 566-6977

MULLARKEY, Edward J. *(Judge, Connecticut Superior Court)* Appointed.
Office: 101 Lafayette Street, Hartford 06106.
Telephone: (860) 566-3861.
Fax: (860) 566-6977

MUNRO, Lynda B. *(Judge, Connecticut Superior Court)* Appointed.
Office: Judicial District Courthouse, 235 Church Street, New Haven 06510.
Telephone: (203) 503-6830.
Fax: (203) 789-6826

MURRAY, William P. *(Judge, Connecticut Superior Court)* Appointed.
Office: 20 Franklin Square, New Britain 06051.
Telephone: (860) 515-5050.
Fax: (860) 515-5051

NADEAU, Thomas L. *(Judge, Connecticut Superior Court)* Appointed.
Office: 106 Elizabeth Street, Derby 06418.
Telephone: (203) 735-8695.
Fax: (203) 735-2047

NEVAS, Alan H. *(Senior Judge, United States District Court District of Connecticut)* Appointed for life by President Ronald Reagan to term beginning Oct 26, 1985. Assumed Senior status, serves by assignment. Born Norwalk Connecticut March 27, 1928. Educated at Syracuse University A.B. 1949 and New York University LL.B. 1951. Admitted to practice Connecticut 1951, U.S. District Court District of Connecticut 1955, U.S. Supreme Court 1964 and U.S. Court of Appeals Second Circuit 1967. In legal practice Westport 1954-81.

U.S. Attorney Connecticut 1981-85. Member Connecticut Bar Association. Sergeant First Class U.S. Army 1952-54. Republican. State Representative Connecticut General Assembly 1971-77 (Deputy House Majority Leader 1973-75, Deputy House Minority Leader 1975-77).

Office: Federal Bldg. & U.S. Courthouse, 915 Lafayette Boulevard, Bridgeport 06604-4768.
Telephone: (203) 579-5983.

NIGRO, Martin L. *(Judge Referee, Connecticut Superior Court)* Appointed Judge. Former Senior Judge. Became Judge Referee May 4, 1999. Currently serves as Judge Trial Referee.
Office: Judicial District Courthouse, 123 Hoyt Street, Stamford 06905.
Telephone: (203) 965-5315.
Fax: (203) 965-5389

NORCOTT, Flemming L., Jr. *(Associate Justice, Connecticut Supreme Court)* Appointed 1992. Born New Haven Connecticut Oct 11, 1943. Educated at Columbia University B.A. 1965 J.D. 1968. Honorary LL.D. University of New Haven 1993. Judge, Connecticut Superior Court 1979-87. Judge, Connecticut Appellate Court 1987-92.

Assistant Attorney General U.S. Virgin Islands. Lecturer Yale Law School. Peace Corps Volunteer Nairobi Kenya.

Office: 231 Capitol Avenue, Hartford 06106.
Telephone: (860) 757-2200.

NORKO, Raymond R. *(Judge, Connecticut Superior Court)* Appointed to term beginning Nov 5, 1985. Reappointed 1993 and 2001. Current term expires 2009. Born Jamaica New York Oct 19, 1942. Educated at University of Connecticut B.S. 1967 and University of Toledo J.D. 1970. Admitted to practice Connecticut 1971, U.S. District Court District of Connecticut 1971, U.S. Court of Appeals Second Circuit 1971 and U.S. Supreme Court 1977. Former Small Claims Commissioner. Former Motor Vehicle Magistrate.

Instructor Eastern Connecticut State University 1976-84. Fellow American Bar Association. President Connecticut Bar Foundation. Chairman Connecticut Prison Association. Former member Federal Bar Association. Member Hartford County and Connecticut Bar Associations. Recipient Charles Parker Legal Service Award from Connecticut Bar Association Nov 1985 and Distinguished Service Award from Hartford County Bar Association May 1986. Sergeant First Class USAF 1960-64. Enjoys squash and scuba diving.

Office: 410 Center Street, Manchester 06040.
Telephone: (860) 646-5874.
Fax: (860) 645-7540

NOVACK, Stanley *(Judge Referee, Connecticut Superior Court)* Appointed Judge to term beginning July 1, 1978. Reappointed to subsequent terms. Former Administrative Judge Stamford-Norwalk Judicial District and Administrative Judge Family Division Parts S and D. Former Senior Judge. Became Judge Referee July 11, 2000. Currently serves as Judge Trial Referee. Judge, Connecticut Court of Common Pleas 1975-78.
Office: Judicial District Courthouse, 123 Hoyt Street, Stamford 06905.
Telephone: (203) 965-5315.
Fax: (203) 965-5389

O'BRIEN, Dennis *(Judge, Windham District Probate Court)*
Mailing address: P.O. Box 34, Willimantic 06226.

O'BRIEN, DENNIS—*Continued*

Office: 979 Main Street, Willimantic 06226.
Telephone: (860) 465-3049.
Fax: (860) 465-3012

O'BRIEN, Francis J. *(Judge Referee, Connecticut Superior Court)* Appointed Judge to term beginning Jan 1, 1976. Senior Judge April 1, 1983 to June 13, 1989. Became Judge Referee June 14, 1989. Former Judge Trial Referee. Born Cleveland Ohio June 14, 1919. Roman Catholic. Educated at Fordham University B.A. 1941 and University of Connecticut 1948. Judge, Meriden City Court 1957. Judge, Connecticut Circuit Court 1961. Judge, Connecticut Court of Common Pleas 1965.

Member New Haven, Connecticut and American Bar Associations. First Lieutenant USAS 1946. Democrat.

O'CONNELL, Edward Y. *(Judge Referee, Connecticut Superior Court)* Retired. Became Judge Referee March 12, 2000. Former Judge Trial Referee. Born Stafford Connecticut March 12, 1930. Roman Catholic. Educated at University of Connecticut B.A. 1951 J.D. with honors 1954. Admitted to practice Connecticut 1954, U.S. District Court District of Connecticut 1956, U.S. Supreme Court 1963 and U.S. Court of Appeals Second Circuit 1971. Began legal practice Stafford Springs 1954. Judge, Borough Court of Stafford Springs 1955-60. Judge, Stafford District Probate Court 1960-78. Judge, Connecticut Court of Common Pleas 1978. Judge, Connecticut Superior Court July 1, 1978 to Oct 1, 1987. Judge and Chief Judge, Connecticut Appellate Court Oct 1, 1987 to March 11, 2000.

Assistant Prosecuting Attorney Borough Court of Stafford Springs 1954-55. Borough Counsel Stafford Springs 1958-77. Town Counsel Stafford 1960-77. Author "Statutory Liability of a Dog's Keeper" 26 Conn. B. Jour. 417, 1952 and "Recrimination in Connecticut" 27 Conn. B. Jour. 376, 1953. Member Commercial Law League of America, National College of Probate Judges, International College of Probate Judges, American Judicature Society, Tolland County (President 1958-59), Hartford County, Connecticut (House of Delegates 1975-76) and American Bar Associations. U.S. Army 1947-48. Lieutenant Colonel USAFR 1948-77 (retired). County Chairman March of Dimes 1955-58. Chairman Civil Defense Advisory Council 1955-65. President Stafford Public Library Association 1962-64 and Johnson Memorial Hospital 1974-77. Director Asnuntuck Community College Foundation 1975-77. Member Stafford Rotary Club, Connecticut Prison Association and Stafford Public Health Nursing Association.

O'GRADY, Daniel W. *(Judge, Bethel District Probate Court)*
Mailing address: P.O. Box 144, Bethel 06801.
Office: One School Street, Bethel 06801.
Telephone: (203) 794-8508.

O'GRADY, Kevin M. *(Judge, Westport District Probate Court)*
Office: 100 Town Hall, 110 Myrtle Avenue, Westport 06880.
Telephone: (203) 341-1100.
Fax: (203) 341-1102

O'KEEFE, Thomas V., Jr. *(Judge, Connecticut Superior Court)* Appointed.
Office: One Court Street, Middletown 06457.
Telephone: (860) 343-6570.
Fax: (860) 343-6589

O'NEILL, Norris L. *(Judge Referee, Connecticut Superior Court)* Appointed Judge to term beginning May 22, 1978. Reappointed 1986 and 1994. Retired. Became Judge Referee May 26, 1996. Currently serves as Judge Trial Referee. Born Newark New Jersey May 26, 1926. Roman Catholic. Educated at Brown University 1946-48 and Rutgers University LL.B. 1951. Admitted to practice Connecticut 1952, New Jersey 1952 and U.S. District Courts District of Connecticut 1952 and District of New Jersey 1952. In legal practice Hartford Connecticut 1952-78.

Co-author "Recent History of the Connecticut Antitrust Act" 50 Conn. B. Jour. 274 Sept 1976. Member Hartford County and Connecticut Bar Associations. Private First Class U.S. Army 1944-46. Representative General Assembly Connecticut 1967-71. Democrat. President Urban League of Greater Hartford 1961-63. President Community Council of Greater Hartford. Enjoys tennis.

Office: Judicial District Courthouse, 95 Washington Street, Hartford 06106.
Telephone: (860) 548-2861.
Fax: (860) 548-2887

OTTAVIANO, John, Jr. *(Judge Referee, Connecticut Superior Court)* Appointed Judge to term beginning July 1, 1978. Retired. Became Judge Referee Oct 2, 1987. Currently serves as Judge Trial Referee. Born New Haven Connecticut Oct 2, 1917. Roman Catholic. Educated at Yale University B.A. 1938 and Harvard Law School LL.B. 1941. Admitted to practice Connecticut 1941. Began legal practice New Haven 1946. Judge, Connecticut Circuit Court 1969-75. Judge, Connecticut Court of Common Pleas 1975-78.

Author "Supervening Negligence in Connecticut" Connecticut B. Jour. 1941. Instructor in Business Law Junior College of Commerce at New Haven 1946-51. Member New Haven County, Connecticut and American Bar Associations. Recipient Star of Solidarity and Order of Merit from the President of the Republic of Italy. Captain USAS AGD active duty 1942-46 USASR 1946-51. Special Assistant to Legislative Commissioner 1953. State Treasurer 1955-59. Republican. Member since 1935 Order Sons of Italy in America (The Supreme Venerable in America and Canada 1951-55). Lector since 1983 and Core Member and Facilitator of the Renew Process 1984-86 Church of the Epiphany. Master 4° Knights of Columbus Southern District Connecticut 1962-66. Member ABC Sanctioned Bowling Leagues since 1950. Enjoys ten-pin bowling.

Office: Judicial District Courthouse, 235 Church Street, New Haven 06510.
Telephone: (203) 503-6830.
Fax: (203) 789-6826

OWENS, Howard T., Jr. *(Judge, Connecticut Superior Court)* Appointed.
Office: Judicial District Courthouse, 1061 Main Street, Bridgeport 06604.
Telephone: (203) 579-6540.
Fax: (203) 579-6928

PALM, Frederick W., Jr. *(Judge, Groton District Probate Court)*
Office: Town Hall, 45 Fort Hill Road, Groton 06340.

PALM, FREDERICK W., JR.—*Continued*

Telephone: (860) 441-6655.
Fax: (860) 441-6657

PALMER, Richard N. *(Associate Justice, Connecticut Supreme Court)* Appointed to term beginning March 18, 1993. Reappointed March 18, 2001, current term expires March 18, 2009. Born Hartford Connecticut May 27, 1950. Educated at Trinity College B.A. 1972 and University of Connecticut School of Law J.D. with high honors 1977. Honorary J.D. Quinnipiac University 1999. Associate Editor University of Connecticut Law Review. Law Clerk to Hon. Jon O. Newman, U.S. District Court District of Connecticut 1977-78. Member Phi Beta Kappa. Admitted to practice Connecticut 1977, U.S. District Court District of Connecticut 1978, District of Columbia 1980 and U.S. Court of Appeals Second Circuit 1981. In legal practice 1978-80 and 1984-86.

Assistant U.S. Attorney 1980-83 and 1987-90 and U.S. Attorney 1991 District of Connecticut. Chief State's Attorney Connecticut 1991-93. Board of Directors Justice Education Center. Recipient Award for Community Service from Trinity Club of Hartford 1993 and Distinguished Graduate Award from University of Connecticut Law School Alumni Association 1997. Board of Managers Hartford YMCA.

Mailing address: Drawer N, Station A, Hartford 06106.
Office: 231 Capitol Avenue, Hartford 06106.
Telephone: (860) 757-2115.

PAPANDREA, John F. *(Judge, Meriden District Probate Court)* Elected Nov 8, 1994. Reelected Nov 1998 and 2002. Current term expires Jan 2007.

Office: 113 City Hall, 142 East Main Street, Meriden 06450.
Telephone: (203) 630-4150.
Fax: (203) 630-4043

PARKER, Thomas F. *(Judge, Connecticut Superior Court)* Appointed. Former Assistant Administrative Judge New London Judicial District.

Office: 231 Capitol Avenue, Hartford 06106.
Telephone: (860) 757-2100.
Fax: (860) 757-2130

PEARL, Deborah M. *(Judge, Essex District Probate Court)*

Office: Town Hall, 29 West Avenue, Essex 06426.
Telephone: (860) 767-4347.

PECK, A. Susan *(Judge, Connecticut Superior Court)* Appointed to term beginning March 1996. Term expires March 2004. Born Boston Massachusetts April 19, 1946. Educated at University of Massachusetts B.A. 1967, Boston University M.S. 1971 and University of Connecticut School of Law J.D. with honors 1976. Staff member Urban Law Journal 1973-75. Law Clerk to Hon. Robert C. Zampano, U.S. District Court District of Connecticut 1976-77. Member Phi Delta Phi. Admitted to practice Connecticut 1976, U.S. District Court District of Connecticut 1977, U.S. Court of Appeals Second Circuit 1979 and U.S. Supreme Court 1980. In legal practice Hartford 1977-96.

Instructor University of Connecticut School of Law 1976-78. Member Connecticut Bar Foundation (Chair Oral History Subcommittee) Hartford County, Connecticut and American (Judicial Division) Bar Associations.

Office: 20 Franklin Square, New Britain 06051.
Telephone: (860) 515-5050.
Fax: (860) 515-5051
E-mail address: susan.peck@jud.state.ct.us

PELLEGRINO, Joseph H. *(Judge, Connecticut Appellate Court)* Appointed to term beginning March 2000. Chief Court Administrator since Dec 27, 2000. Educated at University of Notre Dame B.A. 1958, Fairfield University M.A. 1962 and Boston College J.D. 1963. Admitted to practice Connecticut 1963. In legal practice New Haven 1963-90. Judge 1990 to March 2000 and Chief Administrative Judge May 1997 to March 2000, Connecticut Superior Court.

Fellow Connecticut Bar Foundation.
Office: 231 Capitol Avenue, Hartford 06106.
Telephone: (860) 757-2100.

PENSIS, Teresa A. *(Judge, North Stonington District Probate Court)* Elected Nov 8, 1994. Reelected Nov 1998 and 2002. Current term expires Jan 2007.

Mailing address: P.O. Box 204, North Stonington 06359-0204.
Office: 391 Norwich Westerly Road, No. 2, North Stonington 06359.
Telephone: (860) 535-8441.

PETERS, Ellen Ash *(Judge Referee, Connecticut Superior Court)* Retired 1996. Became Judge Referee March 21, 2000. Currently serves as Judge Trial Referee. Born Berlin Germany March 21, 1930. Educated at Swarthmore College B.A. with honors 1951 and Yale University LL.B. cum laude 1954. Awarded honorary M.A. Yale University 1964, honorary LL.D. University of Hartford 1983, Swarthmore College 1983, Georgetown University 1984, Yale University 1985, Connecticut College 1985, New York Law School 1985 and Colgate University 1986, Trinity College 1987, Bates College 1987, Wesleyan University 1987, DePaul University 1988, University of Connecticut 1992 and University of Rochester 1994 and honorary HL.D. St. Joseph College 1986 and Albertus Magnus College 1990. Law Clerk to Hon. Charles E. Clark, U.S. Court of Appeals Second Circuit 1954-55. Member Phi Beta Kappa and Order of the Coif. Admitted to practice Connecticut 1957 and U.S. District Court District of Connecticut 1965. Associate Justice May 10, 1978 to 1984, Chief Justice 1984-96 and Senior Associate Justice 1996 to March 20, 2000, Connecticut Supreme Court.

Author "Commercial Transactions: Cases, Texts and Problems" Bobbs-Merrill 1971 and "Negotiable Instruments Primer" Bobbs-Merrill 1974. Important Decisions: State v. Stoddard (state constitutional right to know counsel is at hand) 206 Conn. 157, 537 A.2d 446, 1988; Sheff v. O'Neill (state constitution and Hartford schools racial segregation) 238 Conn. 1, 678 A.2d 1267, 1996; In re Baby Girl B. (termination of parental rights; time to open) 224 Conn. 263, 618 A.2d 1, 1992; Doe v. Stamford (AIDS exposure and workers' compensation) 241 Conn. 692, 699 A.2d 52, 1997; Michaud v. Wawruck (open adoption agreement) 209 Conn. 407, 551 A.2d 738, 1988; State v. Hammond (NDA exculpatory evidence) 221 Conn. 264, 604 A.2d 793, 1992; Kaufman v. Danbury Zoning Comm. (affordable housing, zoning, presumptions) 232 Conn. 122, 653 A.2d 798, 1995; Fonfara v. Reapportionment Comm. (prima facie showing to overturn legislative reapportionment) 222 Conn. 166,

PETERS, ELLEN ASH—*Continued*

610 A.2d 153, 1992; State v. Jarzbeck (sexual assault of child; state evidence of compelling need to videotape) 210 Conn. 396, 554 A.2d 1094, 1989; and Mahoney v. Lensink (suicide at state mental hospital, scope of statutory duties) 213 Conn. 548, 569 A.2d 518, 1990. Tutor in Law University of California at Berkeley 1955-56. Professor of Law 1956-78, Adjunct Professor of Law 1978-84 and Professorial Lecturer since 1998 Yale Law School. Board of Directors 1992-96 and Chairman 1994 National Center for State Courts. Member Conference of Chief Justices (President 1994), The American Law Institute (Council member since 1984), Connecticut and American Bar Associations. Member Connecticut Board of Pardons 1978-80, Connecticut Law Revision Commission 1978-84. Recipient Connecticut Trial Lawyers Association Award 1982, Ella Grasso Distinguished Service Medal 1982, Yale Law School Distinguished Service Medal 1983, Pioneer Woman Award from Hartford College for Women 1988, Judicial Award 1992 and Special Award 1996 from Connecticut Bar Association, Distinguishing Service Award from University of Connecticut Law School Alumni Association 1993, Raymond E. Baldwin Public Service Award from Quinnipiac College Law School 1995, Distinguishing Service Award from Connecticut Law Tribune 1996 and National Center of State Courts 1996. Named Laura A. Johnson Woman of the Year by Hartford College 1996. Member Connecticut Permanent Commission on the Status of Women 1973-74. Trustee Yale New Haven Hospital 1981-85 and Yale Corporation 1986-92. Board of Managers Swarthmore College 1970-81. Honorary Chairman U.S. Constitutional Bicentennial Committee 1986-91. Member Hartford Foundation, American Academy of Arts and Sciences and American Philosophy Society. Interested in music. Enjoys reading and walking.

Office: Judicial District Courthouse, 95 Washington Street, Hartford 06106.
Telephone: (860) 548-2850.
Fax: (860) 548-2887

PETERSON, Sylvia L. *(Judge, Old Lyme District Probate Court)* Elected Nov 8, 1994. Reelected Nov 1998 and 2002. Current term expires Jan 2007.

Office: Town Hall, 52 Lyme Street, Old Lyme 06371.
Telephone: (860) 434-1605.

PETRONI, Romeo G. *(Judge Referee, Connecticut Superior Court)* Appointed Judge. Retired. Became Judge Referee Jan 17, 1999. Currently serves as Judge Trial Referee. Born Ridgefield Connecticut Jan 17, 1929. Roman Catholic. Educated at Syracuse University B.A. 1950 and Fordham University School of Law LL.B. 1953. Member Kappa Sigma. Admitted to practice District of Columbia 1953, Connecticut 1955 and New York 1956. Began legal practice Ridgefield Connecticut. Former Judge, Ridgefield District Probate Court, elected to term beginning Jan 1, 1973.

Town Counsel Ridgefield 1959-65. Member Connecticut Bar Association. Private First Class U.S. Army 1953-55. State Representative Connecticut 1961-67. State Senator Connecticut 1971-74. Republican. Director several civic and charitable organizations. Interested in history.

Office: 146 White Street, Danbury 06810.
Telephone: (203) 207-8690.
Fax: (203) 207-8689

PICKARD, John W. *(Judge, Connecticut Superior Court)* Appointed.

Office: Judicial District Courthouse, 15 West Street, Litchfield 06759.
Telephone: (860) 567-5438.
Fax: (860) 567-4642

PITTMAN, Patty Jenkins *(Judge, Connecticut Superior Court)* Appointed.

Office: Judicial District Courthouse, 300 Grand Street, Waterbury 06702.
Telephone: (203) 596-4033.
Fax: (203) 596-4488

POITRAS, Dennis R. *(Judge, Ashford District Probate Court)*

Mailing address: P.O. Box 61, Ashford 06278.
Office: 20 Pompey Hollow Road, Ashford 06278.
Telephone: (860) 429-4986.
Fax: (860) 487-2027

POTTER, Russell F., Jr. *(Senior Judge, Connecticut Superior Court)* Appointed to term beginning Jan 8, 1988. Reappointed 1996. Former Administrative Judge Windham Judicial District. Retired. Born Windham Connecticut April 13, 1936. Congregationalist. Educated at University of Connecticut B.A. 1958 LL.B. 1961. Admitted to practice Connecticut 1961. In legal practice Willimantic 1965-88.

Member Windham County and Connecticut Bar Associations. Major USAFR 1961-81 (retired).

Office: Judicial District Courthouse, 108 Valley Street, Willimantic 06226.
Telephone: (860) 423-8491.
Fax: (860) 423-9115

PRATS, Sheila M. *(Judge, Connecticut Superior Court)* Appointed.

Office: 20 Franklin Square, New Britain 06051.
Telephone: (860) 515-5050.
Fax: (860) 515-5051

PRESTLEY, Linda Pearce *(Judge, Connecticut Superior Court)* Appointed.

Office: Judicial District Courthouse, 95 Washington Street, Hartford 06106.
Telephone: (860) 548-2850.
Fax: (860) 548-2887

PUGLIO, Jeannette M. *(Judge, Roxbury District Probate Court)* Elected Nov 8, 1994. Reelected 1998 and 2002. Current term expires Jan 2007.

Mailing address: P.O. Box 203, Roxbury 06783.
Office: Town Hall, 29 North Street, Roxbury 06783.
Telephone: (860) 354-1184.
Fax: (860) 355-3091

PURNELL, O. James, III *(Judge, Ellington District Probate Court)* Elected to term beginning Nov 17, 1999. Reelected 2002, current term expires Jan 10, 2007. Born Richmond Virginia Jan 18, 1949. Congregationalist. Educated at University of Hartford A.A. 1969, Middlebury College A.B. 1972, Case Western Reserve University M.S.L.S. 1976 and Western New England College J.D. 1981. Member Phi Delta Phi. Admitted to practice Connecticut 1982 and U.S. District Court District of Connecticut 1982. In legal practice Rockville Sept 1981 to Sept 1987 and Feb 1989 to Sept 1992, Hartford Sept 1987 to Jan 1989 and Vernon since Oct 1992.

Author "The Next Decade of Lawyering" 5 No. 8

PURNELL, O. JAMES, III—*Continued*

Trends in Law Library Management and Technology 6 April 1993, "U.S. State & Local Tax Bibliography" 5 No. 5 *State Tax Notes* 267 Aug 2, 1993, "The Internet, A Step in the Right Direction" 8 No. 2 *Connecticut Lawyer* 12 Oct 1997 and "The Full Fabric of the Web; Useful Sites for the Legal Community" 23 No. 49 *The Connecticut Law Tribune* 8A Dec 8, 1997. Co-instructor in Advanced Legal Research 1994-95 and "Teaching the TA's to Teach" 1994-95, Instructor "Teaching the TA's to Teach" 1996 and Guest Instructor in Internet Research Techniques and Connecticut Law Research Spring 1998 University of Connecticut School of Law. Reference Services Liaison and Computer Services Liaison to New England Law Library Consortium 1994-98. Member Committee to choose delegates National Conference on Legal Information Issues Law Librarians of New England Spring 1995. Member Hartford Area Law Librarians, Southern New England Law Librarians Association (Internet Committee 1994-97, President 1998-99), American Association of Law Libraries, The Associations of Trial Lawyers of America, National College of Probate Judges, Tolland County (President 1995-96, Chairman Library Committee since 1998), Connecticut (Council of Bar Presidents 1995-96) and American Bar Associations. Member Panel "Net Gain: Learning to Bank on the Internet" 88th Annual Meeting July 16, 1995, Panel "Around the World in Eighty Minutes: Foreign and International Law Sources on the Internet" 90th Annual Meeting July 21, 1997, "Teaching Research in Academic Law Libraries" 91st Annual Meeting July 9-10, 1998 and Teaching Team "The Importance of Legal Research in the Practice of Law" 1999 AALL Workshop *Basic Legal Reference* 92nd Annual Meeting July 15-17, 1999 American Association of Law Libraries. Participant "Judicial Decisions on the Internet, Storage, Retrieval, Copyright and Vendor-neutral Citations" Annual Meeting Association of Reporters of Judicial Decisions Aug 4, 1995 and "Cool Sites for Lawyers (and Other Cool Sites)" Legal Tech Expo/Midyear Meeting Connecticut Bar Association Nov 18, 1997. Listed in *Who's Who in American Law* 2000/2001, *Who's Who in the World* 2001 and *Who's Who in America* 2002. Medical Reference Librarian Boston University School of Medicine Sept 1976 to Aug 1977. Director Information Services School of Pharmacy Aug 1977 to Sept 1981 and Reference Librarian Law School Library Oct 1992 to May 1998 University of Connecticut. Regional Information Manager Lexis-Nexis May 1998 to July 1999. Eagle Scout 1964. Reader Read Across America 2001 and 2002. Past Master Fayette Lodge #69 AF & AM. Scoutmaster Troop 92 Boy Scouts of America. Member Choir and Bell Choir First Congregational Church. Board of Trustees Rockville Public Library. Corporator Eastern Connecticut Health Network. Member University of Hartford Alumni Council. Enjoys camping, skiing, organ playing, singing, bell ringing and reading.

Mailing address: P.O. Box 268, Rockville 06066-0268.
Office: 14 Park Place, Rockville 06066.
Telephone: (860) 872-0519.
Fax: (860) 870-5140
E-mail address: jpurnell3@att.net

PURTILL, Joseph J. *(Judge Referee, Connecticut Superior Court)* Appointed Judge. Former Assistant Administrative Judge and Administrative Judge New London Judicial District. Retired. Became Judge Referee Aug 13, 1997. Currently serves as Judge Trial Referee.
Office: Judicial District Courthouse, 70 Huntington Street, New London 06320.
Telephone: (860) 442-2977.
Fax: (860) 447-8701

QUINN, Barbara M. *(Judge, Connecticut Superior Court)* Appointed.
Office: 20 Franklin Square, New Britain 06051.
Telephone: (860) 515-5050.
Fax: (860) 515-5051

RADCLIFFE, Dale W. *(Judge, Connecticut Superior Court)* Appointed.
Office: Judicial District Courthouse, 235 Church Street, New Haven 06510.
Telephone: (203) 503-6830.
Fax: (203) 789-6826

REARDEN, John B., Jr. *(Judge, Darien District Probate Court)*
Office: Town Hall, Two Renshaw Road, Darien 06820.
Telephone: (203) 656-7342.
Fax: (203) 656-0774

REICHER, Max H. *(Judge Referee, Connecticut Superior Court)* Appointed Judge. Retired. Currently serves as Judge Trial Referee.
Office: 20 Franklin Square, New Britain 06051.
Telephone: (860) 515-5050.
Fax: (860) 515-5051

RESHA, Robert T. *(Judge, Connecticut Superior Court)* Appointed. Former Presiding Judge.
Office: 20 Franklin Square, New Britain 06051.
Telephone: (860) 515-5050.
Fax: (860) 515-5051

REYNOLDS, John N. *(Judge Referee, Connecticut Superior Court)* Appointed Judge Oct 4, 1977. Retired. Became Judge Referee July 15, 1989. Currently serves as Judge Trial Referee. Born New Haven Connecticut July 15, 1919. Roman Catholic. Educated at Providence College B.S.B.A. 1941, Georgetown University LL.B. 1950 and New York University LL.M. in Taxation 1951. Admitted to practice Connecticut 1950 and District of Columbia 1950. Began legal practice New Haven 1950. Judge, Connecticut Circuit Court 1961-74. Judge, Connecticut Court of Common Pleas 1974-77.

Member The District of Columbia Bar, New Haven County and Connecticut Bar Associations. Lieutenant USNR 1942-46. Board of Aldermen New Haven 1952-59.
Office: Judicial District Courthouse, 235 Church Street, New Haven 06510.
Telephone: (203) 503-6830.
Fax: (203) 789-6826

REYNOLDS, Susan S. *(Judge, Connecticut Superior Court)* Appointed.
Office: 17 Belden Avenue, Norwalk 06850.
Telephone: (203) 846-3237.
Fax: (203) 847-8710

RICHARDS, Earl B. *(Judge, Connecticut Superior Court)* Appointed.
Office: 54 West Main Street, Meriden 06451.
Telephone: (203) 238-6137.
Fax: (203) 238-6423

RIDGEWAY, Paul A. *(Judge, East Granby District Probate Court)* Elected to term beginning Jan 7, 1987. Reelected 1990, 1994, 1998 and 2002. Current term expires Jan 2007. Born Springfield Massachusetts Sept 30, 1941. Congregationalist. Educated at Western New England College B.M.E. 1974 M.B.A. 1978 J.D. 1981. Admitted to practice Connecticut 1982.

Previously worked as engineer for Space Heating and Cooling Systems. Republican. Mason.

Mailing address: P.O. Box 542, East Granby 06026-0542.

Office: Town Hall, Nine Center Street, East Granby 06026.

Telephone: (860) 653-3434.

Fax: (860) 653-7085

RIEFBERG, Morton I. *(Judge Referee, Connecticut Superior Court)* Appointed Judge Nov 6, 1985. Former Assistant Administrative Judge Danbury Judicial District. Retired. Became Judge Referee March 31, 1997. Currently serves as Judge Trial Referee.

Office: 146 White Street, Danbury 06810.

Telephone: (203) 207-8690.

Fax: (203) 207-8689

RIGAT, Raymond J. *(Judge, Clinton District Probate Court)*

Mailing address: P.O. Box 130, Clinton 06413-0130.

Office: Eliot House, 50 East Main Street, Clinton 06413.

Telephone: (860) 669-6447.

RIISKA, Linda F. *(Judge, Norfolk District Probate Court)* Elected Nov 8, 1994. Reelected Nov 1998 and 2002. Current term expires Jan 2007.

Mailing address: P.O. Box 648, Norfolk 06058-0648.

Office: 19 Maple Avenue, Norfolk 06058.

Telephone: (860) 542-5134.

RIPLEY, George W., II *(Judge Referee, Connecticut Superior Court)* Appointed Judge. Retired. Currently serves as Judge Trial Referee.

Office: 106 Elizabeth Street, Derby 06418.

Telephone: (203) 735-8695.

Fax: (203) 735-2047

RITTENBAND, Richard M. *(Judge Referee, Connecticut Superior Court)* Appointed Judge. Retired. Currently serves as Judge Trial Referee.

Office: 100 Washington Street, Hartford 06106.

Telephone: (860) 566-3468.

Fax: (860) 566-3449

ROBAINA, Antonio C. *(Judge, Connecticut Superior Court)* Appointed.

Office: Judicial District Courthouse, 95 Washington Street, Hartford 06106.

Telephone: (860) 548-2850.

Fax: (860) 548-2887

ROBINSON, Richard A. *(Judge, Connecticut Superior Court)* Appointed.

Office: One Court Street, Middletown 06457.

Telephone: (860) 343-6570.

Fax: (860) 343-6589

ROBINSON-THOMAS, Angela C. *(Judge, Connecticut Superior Court)* Appointed.

Office: Judicial District Courthouse, 235 Church Street, New Haven 06510.

Telephone: (203) 503-6830.

Fax: (203) 789-6826

RODRIGUEZ, Eddie, Jr. *(Judge, Connecticut Superior Court)* Appointed.

Office: 101 Lafayette Street, Hartford 06106.

Telephone: (203) 566-3861.

Fax: (203) 566-6977

ROGERS, Chase T. *(Judge, Connecticut Superior Court)* Appointed. Former Presiding Judge.

Office: 123 Hoyt Street, Stamford 06905.

Telephone: (203) 965-5315.

Fax: (203) 965-5389

ROGERS, Norman E., Jr. *(Judge, New Hartford District Probate Court)* Elected Nov 1990 to term beginning Jan 9, 1991. Reelected 1994, 1998 and 2002. Current term expires Jan 2008. Born Winsted Connecticut Feb 10, 1951. Roman Catholic. Educated at Hartwick College B.A. in History 1972, Western New England College School of Law J.D. cum laude 1979 and Boston University School of Law LL.M. in Taxation 1997. Admitted to practice Connecticut 1979 and U.S. District Court District of Connecticut 1979.

Executive Secretary Connecticut Probate Assembly since 1993. Member Connecticut and American Bar Associations. U.S. Navy 1972-75. Senior Vice President Barclays Business Credit, Inc. 1984-94. Selectman Town of New Hartford 1984-88. Member Republican Town Committee New Hartford 1979-91. Chairman Farmington River National Wild and Scenic River Committee 1988-94. Board Member New Hartford Historical Society and Connecticut Farmland Trust.

Mailing address: P.O. Box 308, New Hartford 06057.

Office: Town Hall, 530 Main Street, New Hartford 06057.

Telephone: (860) 379-3254.

Fax: (860) 379-8560

RONAN, John J. *(Judge Referee, Connecticut Superior Court)* Appointed Judge to term beginning May 1, 1984. Reappointed May 1, 1992 and May 2000. Former Presiding Judge and Chief Administrative Judge Criminal Division Fairfield Judicial District. Former Deputy Chief Court Administrator. Retired. Currently serves as Judge Trial Referee. Born Bridgeport Connecticut Nov 3, 1932. Roman Catholic. Educated at Fairfield University B.S.S. 1954 and University of Connecticut (evening division) J.D. 1963. Admitted to practice Connecticut 1963, U.S. District Court District of Connecticut 1964 and U.S. Supreme Court 1965. In legal practice Milford 1963-84.

Assistant State's Attorney (part-time) Connecticut Court of Common Pleas, Circuit Court and Superior Court July 1967 to May 1984. Author "Criminal Courts on the Cutting Edge" Connecticut Law Tribune April 8, 1996. Chair Criminal Division Task Force and Former Member Superior Court Rules Committee and Executive Committee Connecticut Superior Court. Former Chair Criminal Technology Enhancement Committee. Member Milford, New Haven County, Connecticut and American Bar Associations. Attended American Academy of Judicial Education 1986. Former Captain USMC. Previously employed at Southern New England Telephone Company. Former Chairman Milford Red Cross Blood Program and United Way (Professional Division). Past President St. Mary's Holy Name Society. Former Director Milford Human Resources Development Agency, Fairfield Uni-

RONAN, JOHN J.—*Continued*

versity Fellows and Milford Club. Former member Milford City Wide Drug Committee. Member Marine Corps League.

Mailing address: P.O. Box 210, Milford 06460.
Office: 14 West River Street, Milford 06460.
Telephone: (203) 878-5791.
Fax: (203) 876-8072

ROWE, Pamela M. *(Judge, Ledyard District Probate Court)*
Office: 741 Col. Ledyard Highway, Route 117, Ledyard 06339.
Telephone: (860) 464-3219.
Fax: (860) 464-8531

RUBINOW, Jay E. *(Judge Referee, Connecticut Superior Court)* Appointed Judge to term beginning 1967. Senior Judge March 1977 to Feb 26, 1982. Became Judge Referee Feb 27, 1982. Former Judge Trial Referee. Born Hartford Connecticut Feb 27, 1912. Member Temple Beth Sholom. Educated at Harvard University A.B. magna cum laude 1933 LL.B. 1937. Admitted to practice Connecticut 1938. Began legal practice Manchester 1938. Chief Judge, Connecticut Circuit Court 1960-67.

RUBINOW, Nicola E. *(Judge, Connecticut Superior Court)* Appointed.
Office: One Court Street, Middletown 06457.
Telephone: (860) 343-6570.
Fax: (860) 343-6589

RUSH, William B. *(Judge, Connecticut Superior Court)* Appointed. Former Assistant Administrative Judge Fairfield Judicial District.
Office: Judicial District Courthouse, 1061 Main Street, Bridgeport 06604.
Telephone: (203) 579-6540.
Fax: (203) 579-6928

RYAN, John J. P. *(Judge Referee, Connecticut Superior Court)* Appointed Judge. Former Senior Judge. Currently serves as Judge Trial Referee.
Office: Judicial District Courthouse, 123 Hoyt Street, Stamford 06905.
Telephone: (203) 965-5315.
Fax: (203) 965-5389

SALAFIA, Linda M. *(Judge, Norwich District Probate Court)* Clerk 1974-81. Elected Judge to term beginning Nov 11, 1981. Reelected 1982, 1986, 1990, 1994, 1998 and 2002. Current term expires Jan 2007. Born Norwich Connecticut Oct 16, 1946. Roman Catholic.

Member Editorial Board Connecticut Probate Law Journal 1985-91. Member Connecticut Probate Assembly (Recording Secretary 1990-94, Second Vice President 1995, First Vice President 1997-98, President Judge since 1999), Connecticut Council on Adoption and National College of Probate Judges. Named Woman of the Year by Norwich Business and Professional Women's Club 1985. Previously employed as a legal secretary. Member Norwich Federated Democratic Women 1981-84. Corporator Norwich Free Academy 1982-99. Director Dime Savings Bank since 1984, Voluntary Action Center 1984-89, Widowed Persons Service 1985-88, American Cancer Society 1986-89 and Backus Foundation 1987-90. Member Norwich Rotary Club since 1987 (President 1995-96). Advisory Board March of Dimes 1990-95. Enjoys public speaking, reading, music and computers.

Mailing address: P.O. Box 38, Norwich 06360-0038.
Office: 100 Broadway, Norwich 06360.
Telephone: (860) 887-2160.
Fax: (860) 887-2401

SANTANIELLO, Angelo G. *(Judge Referee, Connecticut Superior Court)* Retired. Became Judge Referee May 28, 1994. Currently serves as Judge Trial Referee. Born New London Connecticut May 28, 1924. Roman Catholic. Educated at College of the Holy Cross B.A. 1945 and Georgetown University LL.B. 1950 replaced by J.D. Admitted to practice Connecticut 1950 and U.S. District Court District of Connecticut. In legal practice New London 1950-65. Judge, Connecticut Circuit Court Jan 1, 1966 to Sept 30, 1971. Judge, Connecticut Court of Common Pleas Oct 1, 1971 to July 30, 1973. Judge 1973-85, Administrative Judge 1978-85 and Chief Administrative Judge 1979-85, Connecticut Superior Court. Associate Justice 1985-87 and Senior Associate Justice 1987-94, Connecticut Supreme Court.

Assistant Prosecuting Attorney New London Police Court 1951-55. Director Pre-argument Conference Settlement Program since 1987. Chairman Judges Settlement Education Training Process 1991-95. Chief Mediator Sta-Fed ADR, Inc. 1993-95. Mediator Connecticut Superior Court Annexed Mediation Program since 1996. Member American Justinian Society, North American Conference of Judges, New London County and Connecticut Bar Associations. Recipient Columbus Award (outstanding Italian-American citizen in New London, Waterford and Groton area) 1964, In Hoc Signo Award (highest award given to alumnus for dedication and service to alma mater) from College of the Holy Cross 1976, Citizen of the Year Award from New London B.P.O.E. #360, 1993, Judicial Award from Connecticut Trial Lawyers Association 1997, Law Day Award from Connecticut Supreme Court 1999 and Henry J. Naruk Award from Connecticut Bar Association. Lieutenant j.g. USNR 1942-46. Republican. College of the Holy Cross Athletic Council 1971-77. Member Order Sons of Italy in America and Tusana-Columbus Lodge 464. Board of Trustees New London Public Library, Mitchell College and Lawrence & Memorial Hospital (Board of Incorporators). Board of Directors Holy Cross Alumni, American Cancer Society and New London Federal Savings and Loan.

Office: Judicial District Courthouse, 70 Huntington Street, New London 06320.
Telephone: (860) 442-2977.
Fax: (860) 447-8701

SANTOS, Angelo L. dos *(Judge, Connecticut Superior Court)* Appointed.
Office: 80 Washington Street, Hartford 06106.
Telephone: (860) 756-7920.
Fax: (860) 756-7925

SANTOS, Thelma A. *(Judge, Connecticut Superior Court)* Appointed.
Office: 20 Franklin Square, New Britain 06051.
Telephone: (860) 515-5050.
Fax: (860) 515-5051

SATTER, Robert *(Judge Referee, Connecticut Superior Court)* Appointed Judge to term beginning July 1, 1975. Reappointed to subsequent term. Former Senior Judge. Became Judge Referee Aug 19, 1989. Currently

SATTER, ROBERT—*Continued*

serves as Judge Trial Referee. Born Chicago Illinois Aug 19, 1919. Educated at Rutgers University B.A. 1941 and Columbia Law School LL.B. 1947. Member Phi Beta Kappa. Admitted to practice New York 1947 and Connecticut 1952. Judge, Connecticut Court of Common Pleas July 1, 1975 to June 30, 1978.

Author "Not By Law Alone" Connecticut B. Jour. 1947, "Lawyers and Legislative Lobbying" Connecticut B. Jour. 1960, "False Arrest: Compensation or Deterrence" Connecticut B. Jour. 1969, "Changing Roles of Courts and Legislatures" Connecticut L. Rev. Spring 1979, "The Quality of a Trial Judges Experience" ABA Jour. Spring 1979, "Litigation Under the Connecticut Constitution—Developing a Sound Jurisprudence" Connecticut L. Rev. Fall 1982, *Doing Justice: A Trial Judge at Work* Simon and Schuster 1990; *A Path in the Law* Connecticut Law Book Co. 1996; and *The Furniture of My Mind* Carriage House Press 1999. Important Decisions: La Fontaine v. Family Drug Stores Inc. 33 Conn. Supp. 66, 1976; State Management Association of Connecticut, Inc. v. O'Neil 40 Conn. Supp. 381, 1986; and Connecticut Light and Power Company v. Department of Public Utility Control 40 Conn. Supp. 521, 1986. Adjunct Professor of Legislative Process University of Connecticut Law School since 1976. Member Hartford chapter American Inns of Court, Hartford County and Connecticut Bar Associations. Lieutenant USNR 1942-46. Representative General Assembly Connecticut 1959-66. Democrat. General Counsel to Democratic Legislators 1967-75. Board of Finance of Newington. President Greater Hartford Community Council 1962-64. Chairman Board of Trustees Westledge School 1974-75. Member Connecticut Humanities Council 1979-85. Tennis doubles champion of Newington 1958-68.

Office: Judicial District Courthouse, 95 Washington Street, Hartford 06106.
Telephone: (860) 548-2850.
Fax: (860) 548-2887

SCARPELLINO, Philip A. *(Judge, Connecticut Superior Court)* Appointed.
Office: 400 Grand Street, Waterbury 06702.
Telephone: (203) 236-8200.
Fax: (203) 236-8205

SCHALLER, Barry R. *(Judge, Connecticut Appellate Court)* Appointed. Born Hartford Connecticut Nov 23, 1938. Episcopalian. Educated at Yale University B.A. 1960 J.D. 1963. Member Phi Delta Phi. Admitted to practice Connecticut 1963, U.S. District Court District of Connecticut 1963, U.S. Court of Appeals Second Circuit and U.S. Supreme Court. In legal practice New Haven 1963-74. Former Judge, Connecticut Superior Court, appointed to term beginning Feb 1974.

Author "Faulkner's Law" 12 No. 3 Bridgeport L. Rev. Oct 1992; "Literature, Law, and the Art of Judging" *Court Review* American Judges Association Dec 1992; "Law and Literature: At the Heart of American Society" Connecticut Law Tribune Oct 1993; "Managerial Judging" National L. Jour. Nov 1, 1993; "Managerial Judging: A Principled Approach to Complex Cases in State Court" 68 No. 2 Connecticut B. Jour. April 1994; "Getting the Stories Right" 26 No. 2 Connecticut L. Rev. Winter 1994; "Culturally Speaking: Equality, Responsibility and the Social Compact" 14 No. 3 Quinnipiac L. Rev. Fall 1994; "Perspectives on Family Violence: Problems and Solutions" Connecticut Law Tribune Jan 12, 1995 and Jan 19, 1995; "Violence in American Culture is Deeply Rooted" National L. Jour. Oct 14, 1996; "Stories in the Courtroom: Narrative Authority of Judges" 33 No. 3 *Court Review* American Judges Association Fall 1996; and *A Vision of American Law: Judging Law, Literature, and the Stories We Tell* Greenword Press 1997. Visiting Lecturer Yale University 1986 and 1988. Guggenheim Fellow Yale Law School 1975-76, 1984 and 1985-86. Charter Life Fellow Connecticut Bar Foundation. Member American Judicature Society, Connecticut Judges Association, American Judges Association, The American Law Institute, Connecticut and American Bar Associations. Attended The National Judicial College. Instructor for Orientation of Judges Connecticut. Faculty Connecticut Judges Institute and American Academy of Judicial Education. Executive Committee Connecticut Center for Judicial Education. Recipient Book Award for A Vision of American Law from Quinnipiac Law School 1997. Member Board of Pardons Connecticut (Chairman 1973-74), Connecticut Planning Committee on Criminal Administration, Superior Court Deskbook Committee (Chairperson 1985-91) and Superior Court Jury Instruction Committee. Associate Fellow Branford College Yale University. Co-secretary and Council Member Yale Class of 1960.

Office: 95 Washington Street, Hartford 06106.
Telephone: (860) 548-2828.

SCHEINBLUM, Howard *(Judge, Connecticut Superior Court)* Appointed.
Office: 111 Phoenix Avenue, Enfield 06082.
Telephone: (860) 741-3727.
Fax: (860) 741-3474

SCHIMELMAN, Stuart M. *(Judge, Connecticut Superior Court)* Appointed.
Office: Judicial District Courthouse, 70 Huntington Street, New London 06320.
Telephone: (860) 442-2977.
Fax: (860) 447-8701

SCHOLL, Jane S. *(Judge, Connecticut Superior Court)* Appointed.
Office: 20 Park Street, Rockville 06066.
Telephone: (860) 896-4930.
Fax: (860) 870-3295

SCHUMAN, Carl J. *(Judge, Connecticut Superior Court)* Appointed to term beginning Jan 3, 1998. Term expires March 2006. Born New London Connecticut Jan 27, 1954. Jewish. Educated at Harvard University B.A. magna cum laude 1976 and Duke University J.D. 1979. Editor Duke Law Journal 1978. Law Clerk to Connecticut Superior Court 1979-80. Admitted to practice Connecticut 1979, U.S. District Court District of Connecticut 1980, U.S. Court of Appeals Second Circuit 1981 and U.S. Supreme Court 1982.

Assistant State's Attorney 1980-86. Assistant Attorney General 1987-89. Assistant U.S. Attorney 1989-97. Contributing author Connecticut B. Jour. 1980-89. Important Decisions: State v. Carlson (admissibility of HGN test in DUI case) 45 Conn. Supp. 461 Sup. Ct. 1998 and Beach v. Jean (summary judgment in case of alleged sexual abuse by member of clergy) 46 Conn. Supp. 252, 2000. Instructor in Law University of Connecticut School of Law 1981-91. Member Connecticut Bar Association. En-

SCHUMAN, CARL J.—*Continued*

joys skiing, cycling, running, swimming and playing saxophone, guitar and piano.
Office: 400 Grand Street, Waterbury 06702.
Telephone: (203) 236-8200.
Fax: (203) 236-8205
E-mail address: carl.schuman@jud.state.ct.us

SEAMANS, Barbara G. *(Judge, Canaan District Probate Court)*
Mailing address: P.O. Box 905, Canaan 06018-0905.
Office: Town Hall, 100 Pease Street, Canaan 06018.
Telephone: (860) 824-7114.

SECOLA, Joseph P. *(Judge, Brookfield District Probate Court)*
Mailing address: P.O. Box 5192, Brookfield 06804.
Office: Town Hall, 100 Pocono Road, Brookfield 06804.
Telephone: (203) 775-3700.
Fax: (203) 775-5316

SEQUINO, Karen Skromme Nash *(Judge, Connecticut Superior Court)* Appointed to term beginning Nov 1985. Reappointed to subsequent term. Former Assistant Administrative Judge Ansonia-Milford Judicial District. Born Detroit Michigan Aug 23, 1947. Educated at University of Michigan B.A. with high honors 1968 and Yale University Law School J.D. 1972. Admitted to practice Connecticut 1972, U.S. District Court District of Connecticut, U.S. Court of Appeals Second Circuit and U.S. Supreme Court. In legal practice New Haven 1972-82.
Deputy Corporation Counsel New Haven 1982-85. Treasurer Connecticut Bar Association 1981-84.
Office: 121 Elm Street, New Haven 06510.
Telephone: (203) 789-7491.
Fax: (203) 789-7492

SFERRAZZA, Samuel J. *(Judge, Connecticut Superior Court)* Appointed.
Office: 20 Park Street, Rockville 06066.
Telephone: (860) 896-4930.
Fax: (860) 870-3295

SHAPIRO, Robert B. *(Judge, Connecticut Superior Court)* Appointed.
Office: Judicial District Courthouse, 95 Washington Street, Hartford 06106.
Telephone: (860) 548-2850.
Fax: (860) 548-2887

SHAUGHNESSY, William *(Judge Referee, Connecticut Superior Court)* Appointed Judge to term beginning Jan 21, 1980. Reappointed Feb 1, 1988. Retired. Became Judge Referee July 17, 1999. Currently serves as Judge Trial Referee. Born Hartford Connecticut July 17, 1929. Roman Catholic. Educated at Trinity College B.S. 1951, Boston College M.S.S.W. 1953 and University of Connecticut LL.B. 1960. Member Sigma Phi Sigma and Phi Beta Kappa. Admitted to practice Connecticut 1960 and U.S. District Court District of Connecticut 1962. Began legal practice Hartford 1960.
Public Defender Middlesex County 1973-80. Instructor Wethsfield School of Law (now University of Bridgeport) 1970-72. First Lieutenant U.S. Army. Member Board of Education Hartford 1965-69. Enjoys gardening.
Office: 20 Franklin Square, New Britain 06051.
Telephone: (860) 515-5050.
Fax: (860) 515-5051

SHAY, Michael E. *(Judge, Connecticut Superior Court)* Appointed.
Office: Judicial District Courthouse, 123 Hoyt Street, Stamford 06905.
Telephone: (203) 965-5315.
Fax: (203) 965-5389

SHEA, David M. *(Judge Referee, Connecticut Superior Court)* Retired. Became Judge Referee July 1, 1992. Judge Trial Referee since Oct 1, 1996. Born Hartford Connecticut July 1, 1922. Roman Catholic. Educated at Wesleyan University B.A. cum laude 1944 and Yale University LL.B. 1948. Admitted to practice Connecticut 1948, U.S. District Court District of Connecticut 1949 and U.S. Supreme Court 1957. In legal practice Greenwich 1948-49 and Hartford 1949-66. Judge, Connecticut Superior Court Jan 1, 1966 to Nov 12, 1981. Associate Justice, Connecticut Supreme Court Nov 12, 1981 to July 1, 1992.
Author "The Limits of the Judiciary: Some Thoughts on Original Intent Theory" 24 Connecticut L. Rev. 147, Fall 1991. Adjunct Professor University of Connecticut School of Law 1992-93. Member Hartford County and Connecticut Bar Associations. Recipient citation from Connecticut Bar Association Jan 1, 1992. Technician Fifth Class U.S. Army 1943-46. Democrat.
Office: Judicial District Courthouse, 95 Washington Street, Hartford 06106.
Telephone: (860) 548-2850.

SHEEDY, Barbara J. *(Judge, Connecticut Superior Court)* Appointed.
Office: Judicial District Courthouse, 1061 Main Street, Bridgeport 06604.
Telephone: (203) 579-6540.
Fax: (203) 579-6928

SHELDON, Michael R. *(Judge, Connecticut Superior Court)* Appointed to term beginning June 7, 1991. Reappointed 1999, current term expires June 7, 2007. Born Schenectady New York April 6, 1949. Educated at Princeton University A.B. 1971 and Yale University J.D. 1974. Admitted to practice District of Columbia 1975, U.S. District Courts District of Columbia 1975, District of Connecticut 1976 and Northern District of New York 1976, U.S. Courts of Appeals District of Columbia 1975 and Second 1988 Circuits, Connecticut 1976 and U.S. Supreme Court 1978.
Professor of Law University of Connecticut 1976-91. Member Oliver Ellsworth Inn of Court and Connecticut Bar Association.
Office: 95 Washington Street, Hartford 06106.
Telephone: (860) 548-2850.
Fax: (860) 548-2887
E-mail address: michael.sheldon@jud.state.ct.us

SHIFF, Alan H. W. *(Chief Judge, United States Bankruptcy Court District of Connecticut)* Appointed by U.S. District Court judges to term beginning March 30, 1981. Reappointed by U.S. Court of Appeals Second Circuit judges. Born New Haven Connecticut June 2, 1934. Educated at Yale University B.A. 1957 and University of Virginia School of Law LL.B. 1960. Admitted to practice Connecticut 1960, U.S. District Court District of Connecticut 1960 and U.S. Court of Appeals Second Circuit 1969. Began legal practice New Haven 1960.

SHIFF, ALAN H. W.—*Continued*

Former Judge, Bankruptcy Appellate Panel Second Circuit, selected by the Judicial Council of the Second Circuit.

Member Federal Criminal Justice Act Panel to represent indigent defendants. Special Counsel Energy and Public Utilities Committee Connecticut General Assembly. Member National Panel of Arbitrators American Arbitration Association and Connecticut Bar Association.

Office: Federal Bldg. & U.S. Courthouse, 915 Lafayette Boulevard, Bridgeport 06604-4771.
Telephone: (203) 579-5806.

SHORTALL, Joseph M. *(Judge, Connecticut Superior Court)* Appointed.
Office: 20 Franklin Square, New Britain 06051.
Telephone: (860) 515-5050.
Fax: (860) 515-5051

SILBERT, Jonathan E. *(Judge, Connecticut Superior Court)* Appointed. Former Assistant Administrative Judge New Haven Judicial District.
Office: Judicial District Courthouse, 235 Church Street, New Haven 06510.
Telephone: (203) 503-6830.
Fax: (203) 789-6826

SIMON, Jorgé A. *(Judge, Connecticut Superior Court)* Appointed.
Office: 80 Washington Street, Hartford 06106.
Telephone: (860) 756-7010.
Fax: (860) 756-7025

SKOLNICK, David W. *(Judge, Connecticut Superior Court)* Appointed.
Office: Judicial District Courthouse, 235 Church Street, New Haven 06510.
Telephone: (203) 503-6830.
Fax: (203) 789-6826

SMITH, Allen W. *(Judge Referee, Connecticut Superior Court)* Appointed Judge Nov 1979. Reappointed March 1988. Former Senior Judge. Currently serves as Judge Trial Referee. Born Boston Massachusetts March 3, 1931. Jewish. Educated at University of Connecticut A.B. with honors 1953 and The Ohio State University J.D. 1953-54. Admitted to practice Connecticut 1960 and U.S. District Court District of Connecticut 1960. In legal practice Hartford 1960-72.

Assistant Prosecutor 1964-79. Previously employed as physical chemist by Pratt & Whitney Aircraft 1954-60. Democrat. Enjoys family, grandchildren and sports.
Office: 410 Center Street, Manchester 06040.
Telephone: (860) 646-5874.
Fax: (860) 645-7540

SMITH, Thomas P. *(Magistrate Judge, United States District Court District of Connecticut)* Appointed by U.S. District Court judges.
Office: Federal Bldg. & U.S. Courthouse, 450 Main Street, Hartford 06103.
Telephone: (860) 240-3640.

SOLOMON, Elliot N. *(Judge, Connecticut Superior Court)* Appointed. Former Presiding Judge Family Division.
Office: 101 Lafayette Street, Hartford 06106.
Telephone: (860) 566-3861.
Fax: (860) 566-6977

SPALLONE, Daniel F. *(Judge Referee, Connecticut Superior Court)* Retired. Currently serves as Judge Trial Referee. Former Judge and Administrative Judge, Connecticut Superior Court Middlesex Judicial District. Judge, Connecticut Court of Common Pleas 1974-78. Former Judge, Connecticut Appellate Court.
Office: One Court Street, Middletown 06457.
Telephone: (860) 343-6570.
Fax: (860) 343-6589

SQUATRITO, Dominic J. *(Judge, United States District Court District of Connecticut)* Appointed for life by President Bill Clinton to term beginning 1994. Born Hartford Connecticut April 9, 1939. Educated at Wesleyan University B.A. 1961 and Yale University LL.B. 1965. Fulbright Scholar. In legal practice Manchester 1966-94.

Counsel Housing Authority Town of Manchester 1972-79 and Connecticut State Legislature Judiciary Committee 1974-75. Chief Counsel Connecticut State Senate 1976-80.
Office: Federal Bldg. & U.S. Courthouse, 450 Main Street, Hartford 06103.
Telephone: (860) 240-3873.

STEINBERG, Joseph L. *(Judge Referee, Connecticut Superior Court)* Appointed Judge. Retired. Became Judge Referee Oct 6, 1998. Currently serves as Judge Trial Referee.
Office: 100 Washington Street, Hartford 06106.
Telephone: (860) 566-3468.
Fax: (860) 566-3449

STENGEL, Robert F. *(Judge, Connecticut Superior Court)* Appointed.
Office: Judicial District Courthouse, 95 Washington Street, Hartford 06106.
Telephone: (860) 548-2850.
Fax: (860) 548-2887

STEVENS, Barry Keith *(Judge, Connecticut Superior Court)* Appointed to term beginning Nov 27, 1994. Reappointed 2002, current term expires Nov 2010. Born Norwalk Connecticut Feb 12, 1953. Baptist. Educated at Harvard College B.A. magna cum laude 1975 and New York University School of Law J.D. 1978. Admitted to practice Connecticut 1978, U.S. District Court District of Connecticut and U.S. Court of Appeals Second Circuit. In legal practice Hartford 1978-81, Bridgeport 1981-88, Stratford 1989, Milford 1990-92 and Fairfield 1992-94.

Assistant U.S. Attorney 1981-89. Important Decisions: Bourke v. Stamford Hospital 44 Conn. Sup. 544, 1997, Zeldes, Needle & Cooper v. Shrader 45 Conn. Sup. 130, 1997 and State of Connecticut v. 1,014.00 U.S. Currency et al., D.N. CV95-00509 judicial district of Fairfield at G.A. 2. Instructor in Legal History of Race Relations and Current Issues in Civil Rights Trinity College 1980-98 and American Legal History Quinnipiac College School of Law 1996-98.
Office: Judicial District Courthouse, 1061 Main Street, Bridgeport 06604.
Telephone: (203) 579-6540.
Fax: (203) 579-6928

STODDARD, Cecile D. *(Judge, Pomfret District Probate Court)*
Office: Five Haven Road, Route 44, Pomfret Center 06259.
Telephone: (860) 974-0186.

STODOLINK, Edward F. *(Judge Referee, Connecticut Superior Court)* Appointed Judge to term beginning July 1, 1978. Reappointed to subsequent terms. Former Assistant Administrative Judge Danbury Judicial District. Retired. Became Judge Referee Nov 15, 1998. Currently serves as Judge Trial Referee. Judge, Connecticut Court of Common Pleas 1974-78.
Office: Judicial District Courthouse, 1061 Main Street, Bridgeport 06604.
Telephone: (203) 579-6540.
Fax: (203) 579-6928

STOUGHTON, George D. *(Judge Referee, Connecticut Superior Court)* Retired. Became Judge Referee Nov 27, 1989. Currently serves as Judge Trial Referee. Born New York New York Nov 27, 1919. Episcopalian. Educated at Trinity College B.Sc. 1942 and Dalhousie University, Halifax, Nova Scotia LL.B. 1949. Admitted to practice Connecticut 1950, U.S. District Court District of Connecticut, U.S. Court of Appeals Second Circuit and U.S. Supreme Court. In legal practice Hartford. Judge, Connecticut Superior Court Sept 24, 1979 to March 8, 1988. Judge, Connecticut Appellate Court March 9, 1988 to Nov 26, 1989.
Assistant State's Attorney 1959-75 and State's Attorney 1975-79 Hartford County. Fellow American College of Trial Lawyers. Captain U.S. Army 1942-46.
Office: Judicial District Courthouse, 95 Washington Street, Hartford 06106.
Telephone: (860) 548-2850.
Fax: (860) 548-2887

STREIT-KEFALAS, Beverly *(Judge, Milford District Probate Court)*
Mailing address: P.O. Box 414, Milford 06460.
Office: 70 West River Street, Milford 06460.
Telephone: (203) 783-3205.
Fax: (203) 783-3364

SULLIVAN, Terence A. *(Judge, Connecticut Superior Court)* Appointed.
Office: Judicial District Courthouse, 69 Brooklyn Street, Rockville 06066.
Telephone: (860) 896-4930.
Fax: (860) 870-0394

SULLIVAN, William J. *(Chief Justice, Connecticut Supreme Court)* Appointed 1999. Term expires 2007. Born March 12, 1939. Educated at Providence College 1962 and College of William and Mary School of Law J.D. 1965. Judge, Connecticut Superior Court 1978-97. Judge, Connecticut Appellate Court 1997-99.
Civil Service Commissioner March 1974 to July 1975 and Corporation Counsel Jan 1976 to Sept 1978 City of Waterbury. Member since Sept 1995 and Chairman since Sept 1999 Connecticut Criminal Justice Commission. Member Judges Executive Committee Oct 1, 1997 to Sept 30, 1999. Chairman Judicial Department's Civil/Family Working Committee. Member Connecticut Judges Association (Executive Board 1996-99), Waterbury, Connecticut and Virginia Bar Associations. Captain U.S. Army 1965-66. Director Connecticut Vietnam Veterans Bonus Division 1967-70. Member Society of the First Division, Veterans of Foreign Wars and Providence College Alumni Association.
Office: 231 Capitol Avenue, Hartford 06106.
Telephone: (860) 757-2116.

SUSCO, Wendy W. *(Judge, Connecticut Superior Court)* Appointed.
Office: 101 Lafayette Street, Hartford 06106.
Telephone: (860) 566-3861.
Fax: (860) 566-6977

SUTNIK, Thomas Michael *(Judge, Southbury District Probate Court)*
Mailing address: P.O. Box 674, Southbury 06488-0674.
Office: 421 Main Street South, Southbury 06488.
Telephone: (203) 262-0641.
Fax: (203) 264-9310

SWIENTON, Cynthia K. *(Judge, Connecticut Superior Court)* Appointed.
Office: 120 School Street, Danielson 06239.
Telephone: (860) 779-8500.
Fax: (860) 779-8492

SWORDS, Patricia A. *(Judge, Connecticut Superior Court)* Appointed.
Office: 410 Center Street, Manchester 06040.
Telephone: (860) 646-5874.
Fax: (860) 645-7540

SYLVESTER, Joseph H. *(Judge Referee, Connecticut Superior Court)* Appointed Judge to term beginning Jan 19, 1990. Retired. Became Judge Referee Feb 21, 1999. Currently serves as Judge Trial Referee and Chief Administrative Judge. Born Derby Connecticut Feb 21, 1929. Roman Catholic. Educated at Northeastern University and Boston College J.D. Admitted to practice Massachusetts 1953, Connecticut 1955, U.S. District Court District of Connecticut 1958 and U.S. Supreme Court 1973. In legal practice Shelton Connecticut 1955-76 and Derby Connecticut 1976-90. Judge, Shelton City Court 1958-60.
Prosecutor Connecticut Circuit Court 1960-70 and Connecticut Court of Common Pleas 1970-78. Assistant State's Attorney Connecticut Superior Court 1978-80. Past President Oronoque Village Tax District. Member Valley (Secretary 1958, Treasurer 1959, Vice President 1960, President 1961) and Connecticut (Ethics and Grievance Committee 1970-80) Bar Associations. Recipient Distinguished Service Award from Junior Chamber of Commerce 1962, Book of Golden Deeds Award from Exchange Club 1970 and Outstanding Service Award from Connecticut Superior Court Family Relations Department 1980. YN3 USN June 1946 to April 1948. Founder Exchange Club of Huntington-Shelton. Interests include autos, travel and gardening.
Office: 106 Elizabeth Street, Derby 06418.
Telephone: (203) 735-8695.

TANZER, Lois *(Judge, Connecticut Superior Court)* Appointed.
Office: 20 Franklin Square, New Britain 06051.
Telephone: (860) 515-5050.
Fax: (860) 515-5051

TAYLOR, Carl E. *(Judge, Connecticut Superior Court)* Appointed.
Office: 83 Prospect Street, Waterbury 06702.
Telephone: (203) 596-4202.
Fax: (203) 596-4431

TELLER, Samuel H. *(Senior Judge, Connecticut Superior Court)* Appointed. Retired. Became Senior Judge Oct 11, 1999.

Office: Judicial District Courthouse, 69 Brooklyn Street, Rockville 06066.
Telephone: (860) 896-4930.
Fax: (860) 870-0394

THIM, George N. *(Judge, Connecticut Superior Court)* Appointed. Former Administrative Judge Fairfield Judicial District.

Office: Judicial District Courthouse, 1061 Main Street, Bridgeport 06604.
Telephone: (203) 579-6540.
Fax: (203) 579-6928

THOMPSON, Alvin W. *(Judge, United States District Court District of Connecticut)* Appointed for life by President Bill Clinton to term beginning 1994. Born Baltimore Maryland March 2, 1953. Educated at Princeton University B.A. 1975 and Yale University J.D. 1978. In legal practice Hartford 1978-94.

Office: Federal Bldg. & U.S. Courthouse, 450 Main Street, Hartford 06103.
Telephone: (860) 240-3224.

THOMPSON, Bruce W. *(Judge, Connecticut Superior Court)* Appointed. Former Assistant Administrative Judge Ansonia-Milford Judicial District.

Office: Judicial District Courthouse, 235 Church Street, New Haven 06510.
Telephone: (203) 503-6830.
Fax: (203) 789-6826

TIERNEY, Kevin *(Judge, Connecticut Superior Court)* Appointed to term beginning Jan 3, 1994. Reappointed 2002, current term expires 2010. Born Greenwich Connecticut Oct 8, 1938. Roman Catholic. Educated at Williams College B.A. 1960 and Fordham University School of Law J.D. 1963. Member Gamma Eta Gamma. Admitted to practice Connecticut 1963. In legal practice Greenwich 1963-93.

James W. Cooper Fellow. Recipient Charles J. Parker Legal Services Award from Connecticut Bar Association 1996. U.S. Army. Member Kiwanis Club.

Office: 123 Hoyt Street, Stamford 06905.
Telephone: (203) 965-5315.
Fax: (203) 965-5389

TOBIN, David R. *(Judge, Connecticut Superior Court)* Appointed. Born Greenwich Connecticut June 21, 1942. Roman Catholic. Educated at University of Notre Dame B.B.A. in Accounting 1964 and New York University School of Law J.D. 1967. Admitted to practice Connecticut 1967 and New York 1980. Began legal practice Greenwich Connecticut. Former Judge, Greenwich District Probate Court, elected Nov 6, 1990 to term beginning Jan 7, 1991.

Member Greenwich, Connecticut and American Bar Associations. Named Outstanding Government Citizen of the Year Greenwich Chamber of Commerce June 1992. Lieutenant USN JAGC 1967-71. Republican. Moderator of Representative Town Meeting of Greenwich 1971-95. Enjoys golf.

Office: 172 Golden Hill Street, Bridgeport 06604.
Telephone: (203) 579-6568.
Fax: (203) 382-8408

TOBIN, Richard J. *(Judge, Connecticut Superior Court)* Appointed.

Office: 123 Hoyt Street, Stamford 06905.
Telephone: (203) 965-5315.
Fax: (203) 965-5389

TROMBLEY, Wilson J. *(Judge, Connecticut Superior Court)* Appointed to term beginning Sept 1, 1998. Reappointed Feb 10, 1999, current term expires Feb 10, 2007. Born Waterbury Connecticut Nov 30, 1944. Roman Catholic. Educated at Fairfield University B.A. 1966 and George Washington University National Law Center J.D. 1969. Admitted to practice Connecticut 1970 and U.S. District Court District of Connecticut 1972. In legal practice Waterbury 1970-72 and Wolcott 1972-96. Family Support Magistrate 1996-98.

Town Attorney Wolcott 1978-82 and 1994-96. Former Member American Bar Association. Member Connecticut Bar Association. Member and Chairman Wolcott Town Council. Member Wolcott Exchange Club and Wolcott Chamber of Commerce. Enjoys travel and golf.

Office: One Court Street, Middletown 06457.
Telephone: (860) 343-6570.
Fax: (860) 343-6589
E-mail address: wilson.trombley@jud.state.ct.us

TURNER, John *(Judge, Connecticut Superior Court)* Appointed.

Office: 239 Whalley Avenue, New Haven 06511.
Telephone: (203) 786-0337.
Fax: (203) 786-0327

TWERDY, Claire C. *(Judge, Mansfield District Probate Court)*

Office: Municipal Building, Four South Eagleville Road, Storrs 06268.
Telephone: (860) 429-3313.
Fax: (860) 429-4088

UNDERHILL, Stefan R. *(Judge, United States District Court District of Connecticut)* Appointed by President Bill Clinton to term beginning Sept 1, 1999. Born Battle Creek Michigan June 9, 1956. Educated at University of Virginia B.A. 1978, Oxford University B.A. 1981 and Yale University J.D. 1984. Law Clerk to Hon. Jon O. Newman, U.S. Court of Appeals Second Circuit 1984-85. In legal practice Stamford 1985-99.

Office: Federal Bldg. & U.S. Courthouse, 915 Lafayette Boulevard, Bridgeport 06604-4768.
Telephone: (203) 579-5714.

UPSON, Thomas F. *(Judge, Connecticut Superior Court)* Appointed to term beginning April 10, 2001. Term expires April 10, 2009. Born Waterbury Connecticut Sept 30, 1941. Protestant. Educated at Washington & Jefferson College B.A. 1963, Trinity College and University of Connecticut School of Law LL.B. 1968. Admitted to practice Connecticut 1969, U.S. District Court District of Connecticut 1969 and U.S. Supreme Court 1973. In legal practice Waterbury 1969-2001.

Member Waterbury, Connecticut and American Bar Associations. Member State Senate Connecticut (Fifteenth District) 1985-2001.

Office: 146 White Street, Danbury 06810.
Telephone: (203) 207-8690.
Fax: (203) 207-8689

VASINGTON, Paul M. *(Judge Referee, Connecticut Superior Court)* Appointed Judge to term beginning Nov 12, 1981. Reappointed. Retired. Became Judge Referee

VASINGTON, PAUL M.—*Continued*

Dec 1, 1994. Currently serves as Judge Trial Referee. Born Norwich Connecticut Dec 7, 1924. Roman Catholic. Educated at University of Connecticut B.S. 1949 J.D. 1952. Student Board of Editors University of Connecticut Law Review 1950-51. Member Sigma Nu. Admitted to practice Connecticut 1952. Began legal practice Hartford 1952. In legal practice Norwich 1953. Judge, Norwich District Probate Court 1971-81. Former Judge, Norwich City Court.

Former Assistant Prosecutor Connecticut Circuit Court. Instructor of Law University of Connecticut 1952-55. Member Connecticut Probate Assembly (President 1979-81), New London County and Connecticut Bar Associations. Staff Sergeant USAS Infantry 1943-46. Democrat. Member Norwich Elks Lodge (Past Exalted Ruler), Knights of Columbus, VFW and American Legion. Enjoys golf and chess.

Office: One Courthouse Square, Norwich 06360.
Telephone: (860) 886-0144.
Fax: (860) 823-1019

VERTEFEUILLE, Christine S. *(Associate Justice, Connecticut Supreme Court)* Appointed to term beginning Jan 3, 2000. Term expires Jan 2008. Born New Britain Connecticut Dec 10, 1950. Educated at Trinity College B.A. 1972 and University of Connecticut School of Law J.D. 1975. In legal practice 1975-89. Judge 1989 to Sept 12, 1999, Administrative Judge Waterbury Judicial District 1994-99 and Complex Litigation Judge 1999, Connecticut Superior Court. Judge, Connecticut Appellate Court Sept 13, 1999 to Jan 2, 2000.

Former Alternate Member Waterbury Grievance Panel and New Haven Grievance Panel 1985-89. Member Executive Committee Real Property Section Connecticut Bar Association 1988-89. Member Commission to Study the Attorney Grievance Process. Faculty Member Connecticut Judges Institute. Recipient Judicial Award from Connecticut Trial Lawyers Association 1995. Member Cheshire Commission on Handicapped and Disabled 1988-89.

Office: 231 Capitol Avenue, Hartford 06106.
Telephone: (860) 757-2200.

VOELKER, Raymond F. *(Judge, Cheshire District Probate Court)* Elected to term beginning Jan 1983. Reelected 1986, 1990, 1994, 1998 and 2002. Current term expires Jan 2007. Born Plainfield New Jersey May 4, 1945. Episcopalian. Educated at Marietta College B.A. 1967 and Case Western Reserve University J.D. 1970. Admitted to practice Ohio 1970 and Connecticut 1973. Began legal practice Cleveland Ohio 1970. In legal practice Waterbury Connecticut 1973-93 and Cheshire Connecticut since 1994.

Attorney Federal Reserve Bank Cleveland Ohio 1970. Member Waterbury and Connecticut Bar Associations. Republican. Mayor and Chairman Town Council Cheshire Connecticut 1981-82. Member Mattatuck Fife and Drum Band and Cheshire Chamber of Commerce. Hobbies include antique refinishing and scuba diving.

Office: 84 South Main Street, Cheshire 06410.
Telephone: (203) 271-6608.
Fax: (203) 271-6628

VOGELL, Constance J. *(Judge, Westbrook District Probate Court)* Elected Nov 8, 1994. Reelected 1998 and 2002. Current term expires Jan 2007.

Mailing address: P.O. Box 676, Westbrook 06498.
Office: 1163 Boston Post Road, Westbrook 06498.
Telephone: (860) 399-5661.
Fax: (860) 399-9568

WAGNER, Jerry *(Judge Referee, Connecticut Superior Court)* Appointed Judge to term beginning Sept 12, 1979. Reappointed to subsequent terms. Former Senior Judge. Became Judge Referee Aug 2, 1996. Judge Trial Referee since Aug 2, 1996. Born New Haven Connecticut Aug 2, 1926. Jewish. Educated at Yale University B.S. 1946 and Harvard Law School LL.B. 1949. Admitted to practice Connecticut 1949, Massachusetts 1949, District of Columbia 1950 and U.S. Supreme Court 1960. In legal practice New Haven Connecticut 1949-50, Washington D.C. 1950-53, Hartford Connecticut 1953-57 and Bloomfield Connecticut 1957-79.

Part-time Instructor University of Connecticut School of Law 1974-75. Member American Judicature Society and Hartford County Bar Association. Named Outstanding Young Man by Connecticut Jaycees 1961. Recipient Isaiah Award from Hartford Jewish Federation 1973, Americanism Award 1976 and Humanitarian Award 1984 from B'nai B'rith, Human Rights Award from NAACP 1994 and Religious Freedom Award from Touro Synagogue 2001. USAAC 1944-45. General Assembly Connecticut 1958-59. Counsel to State Senate Majority 1966-67. Special Assistant Humphrey Presidential Campaign 1968. Volunteer Bloomfield Fire Department 1956-86. Past President Jewish Historical Society of Greater Hartford. Past Vice President United Synagogue for Conservative Judaism. President Wintonbury Historical Society. Board Member World Council of Synagogues, Hartford Jewish Federation (Past President, Chairman Education Commission, Honorary Chairman Hartford Jewish Community Relations Committee), American Jewish Congress, Hartford Jewish Community Center, Connecticut Historical Society, National Hillel Commission (Executive Committee), Yale Club of Hartford and Harvard Law School Association of Connecticut. Interests include restoring and binding books and collecting fire-fighting memorabilia. Personal Statement or Quote: "An ill agreement is better than a good judgment."

Office: 100 Washington Street, Hartford 06106.
Telephone: (860) 566-3468.
Fax: (860) 566-3449

WALL, Patrick J. *(Judge, Harwinton District Probate Court)*

Office: Town Hall, 100 Bentley Drive, Harwinton 06791.
Telephone: (860) 485-1403.

WALSH, Richard A. *(Senior Judge, Connecticut Superior Court)* Appointed. Former Administrative Judge Litchfield Judicial District. Retired. Became Senior Judge Dec 31, 1998.

Office: Judicial District Courthouse, 15 West Street, Litchfield 06759.
Telephone: (860) 567-5438.
Fax: (860) 567-4642

WARD, Bradford J. *(Judge, Connecticut Superior Court)* Appointed.
Office: 101 Lafayette Street, Hartford 06106.
Telephone: (860) 566-3861.
Fax: (860) 566-6977

WARNER, Susan L. *(Judge, Enfield District Probate Court)* Elected Nov 8, 1994. Reelected Nov 1998 and 2002. Current term expires Jan 2007.
Office: 820 Enfield Street, Enfield 06082.
Telephone: (860) 253-6305.
Fax: (860) 253-6388

WEIL, Lorraine Murphy *(Judge, United States Bankruptcy Court District of Connecticut)* Appointed by U.S. Court of Appeals Second Circuit judges to term beginning April 23, 1999. Term expires April 2013. Born Queens New York Sept 8, 1946. Educated at New York University, Eastern Connecticut State University B.A. 1979 and University of Connecticut School of Law J.D. with high honors 1983. Law Clerk to Hon Robert L. Krechevsky, U.S. Bankruptcy Court District of Connecticut Sept 1983 to Aug 1984. In legal practice Hartford Sept 1984 to April 22, 1999.
Office: Connecticut Financial Center, 18th Floor, 157 Church Street, New Haven 06510.
Telephone: (203) 773-2717.

WEST, Thomas G. *(Judge, Connecticut Appellate Court)* Appointed. Former Judge, Connecticut Superior Court. Former Administrative Judge Danbury Judicial District.
Office: 95 Washington Street, Hartford 06106.
Telephone: (860) 548-2828.

WHITE, Gary J. *(Judge, Connecticut Superior Court)* Appointed. Former Presiding Judge.
Office: 146 White Street, Danbury 06810.
Telephone: (203) 207-8690.
Fax: (203) 207-8689

WIESE, Peter E. *(Judge, Connecticut Superior Court)* Appointed. Former Assistant Administrative Judge Litchfield Judicial District.
Office: 54 West Main Street, Meriden 06451.
Telephone: (203) 238-6137.
Fax: (203) 238-6423

WINSLOW, Heidi G. *(Judge, Connecticut Superior Court)* Appointed.
Mailing address: P.O. Box 210, Milford 06460.
Office: 14 West River Street, Milford 06451.
Telephone: (203) 878-5791.
Fax: (203) 876-8072

WITKOWSKI, Aileen A. *(Judge, Thompson District Probate Court)*
Mailing address: P.O. Box 74, North Grosvenordale 06255.
Office: 815 Riverside Drive, North Grosvenordale 06255.
Telephone: (860) 923-2203.

WOLLENBERG, William L. *(Judge Referee, Connecticut Superior Court)* Appointed Judge. Retired. Currently serves as Judge Trial Referee.
Office: 920 Broad Street, Hartford 06106.
Telephone: (860) 566-8290.
Fax: (860) 566-1658

WOLVEN, Carol A. *(Judge, Connecticut Superior Court)* Appointed.
Office: Judicial District Courthouse, 1061 Main Street, Bridgeport 06604.
Telephone: (203) 579-6540.
Fax: (203) 579-6928

WRIGHT, Philip A., Jr. *(Judge, Wallingford District Probate Court)*
Office: Town Hall, 45 South Main Street, Wallingford 06492.
Telephone: (203) 294-2100.
Fax (203) 294-2109

XANTHOS, Suzanne J. *(Judge, Sharon District Probate Court)*
Mailing address: P.O. Box 1177, Sharon 06069.
Office: 63 Main Street, Sharon 06069.
Telephone: (860) 364-5514.
Fax: (860) 364-5789

YALE, Guy D. *(Judge, Bethany District Probate Court)*
Office: Town Hall, 40 Peck Road, Bethany 06524.
Telephone: (203) 393-3744.

YAMIN, Dianne E. *(Judge, Danbury District Probate Court)* Elected Nov 5, 1990 to term beginning Jan 20, 1991. Reelected Nov 8, 1994, Nov 1998 and Nov 2002. Current term expires Jan 2007. Born Danbury Connecticut June 4, 1961. Roman Catholic. Educated at Lehigh University A.B. with high honors 1983 and Mercer University School of Law J.D. 1986. Member Phi Delta Phi. Admitted to practice Connecticut 1986 and U.S. District Court District of Connecticut 1989. In legal practice Greater Danbury since 1986.
Author "Living Wills in Connecticut" The Source General Practice Magazine 1990 and chapter "Adoption" *Connecticut Lawyers Datebook* Connecticut Bar Association. Chairman Judicial Ethics Committee. Member Connecticut Probate Assembly, National College of Probate Judges, Danbury, Connecticut and American Bar Associations. Attended National Seminar National College of Probate Judges annually 1992-2001. Speaker over 150 probate seminars since 1990. Recipient Connecticut Outstanding Young Citizen Award from Connecticut Jaycees 1994 and Pro Bono Award from Connecticut Legal Services. Profiled in *Barrister* Magazine Summer 1995. Republican. Member Commission on Aging and President's Council of Women at Lehigh University. Board of Directors Danbury Music Centre, Hispanic Center of Greater Danbury and Connecticut Brass Society. Enjoys ballet and travel.
Office: City Hall Building, 155 Deer Hill Avenue, Danbury 06810.
Telephone: (203) 797-4521.

ZARELLA, Peter T. *(Associate Justice, Connecticut Supreme Court)* Appointed to term beginning Jan 22, 2001. Educated at Northeastern University B.S. 1972 and Suffolk University J.D. 1975. Admitted to practice Massachusetts 1975, Connecticut 1977, U.S. District Courts District of Massachusetts 1976, District of Connecticut 1977 and Southern District of New York 1990, U.S. Court of Appeals Second Circuit 1985 and U.S. Supreme Court 1985. In legal practice Hartford 1977-96. Judge and Presiding Judge Family Division, Connecticut

ZARELLA, PETER T.—*Continued*

Superior Court 1996 to Dec 1999. Judge, Connecticut Appellate Court Dec 1999 to Jan 2001.

Office: 231 Capitol Avenue, Hartford 06106.

Telephone: (860) 757-2119.

ZELMAN, Steven M. *(Judge, Bloomfield District Probate Court)* Elected to term beginning 1991. Born Bronx New York Aug 17, 1947. Educated at University of Connecticut B.A. 1969 and Suffolk University J.D. 1972. Admitted to practice Massachusetts 1973, Connecticut 1974, U.S. District Court District of Connecticut 1975 and U.S. Supreme Court 1978. In legal practice Hartford Connecticut 1975 to April 1986 and Bloomfield Connecticut May 1986 to Jan 1991.

Member Continuing Legal Education Committee since 1993 and Executive Board since April 1999 Connecticut Probate Assembly. Former Member Hartford County Bar and American Bar Association. Member Commercial Law League of America, The Association of Trial Lawyers of America, National College of Probate Judges and Connecticut Bar Association (Executive Committee 1988-89 Commercial Law and Bankruptcy Section, Member Estate and Probate Section). Lecturer "Connecticut Creditors Remedies & Bankruptcy" Professional Education Systems 1991, "Conservatorships" Connecticut Probate Assembly 1992 and "Collecting Judgments in Connecticut" National Business Institute 1993. Member Bloomfield Board of Selectman 1977-78, Bloomfield Inland-Wetland and Watercourses Commission 1978-81, Bloomfield Town Plan and Zoning Commission 1978-86 and Bloomfield Rotary 1986-96. President Congregation Teferes Israel Synagogue 1989-91. Board of Directors Federation Homes 1992-97, Beth David Synagogue 1993-97, University of Connecticut Alumni Association 1993-98 and Beth Hillel Synagogue since Sept 2000.

Office: Bloomfield Town Hall, 800 Bloomfield Avenue, Bloomfield 06002.

Telephone: (860) 769-3548.

Fax: (860) 769-3598

ZOARSKI, Howard F. *(Judge Referee, Connecticut Superior Court)* Appointed Judge. Former Senior Judge. Currently serves as Judge Trial Referee.

Office: Judicial District Courthouse, 235 Church Street, New Haven 06510.

Telephone: (203) 503-6830.

Fax: (203) 789-6826

DELAWARE

Capital DOVER

UNITED STATES DISTRICT COURT DISTRICT OF DELAWARE

The court sits at Wilmington. For descriptive information refer to the United States Courts section.

Chief Judge
Sue L. Robinson

Judges
Joseph J. Farnan, Jr.
Gregory M. Sleet
Kent A. Jordan

Senior Judges
James L. Latchum
Murray M. Schwartz
Joseph J. Longobardi

Clerk
Peter T. Dalleo
Federal Building
Lockbox 18, 844 North King Street
Wilmington, Delaware 19801-3570
(302) 573-6170

UNITED STATES MAGISTRATE JUDGE OF DELAWARE

Mary Pat Thynge

UNITED STATES BANKRUPTCY COURT OF DELAWARE

Chief Judge
Peter J. Walsh

Judge
Mary F. Walrath

Bankruptcy Clerk
David Bird
Marine Midland Building
Fifth Floor, 824 Market Street
Wilmington, Delaware 19801
(302) 252-2900

DELAWARE SUPREME COURT

The Supreme Court is Delaware's court of last resort. The court consists of a chief justice and four justices appointed for twelve-year terms by the governor with consent of the Senate from a list of candidates provided by the Judicial Nominating Commission. Retired justices may serve by assignment.

The court has final appellate jurisdiction over all civil cases from Chancery, Superior and Family Courts and over criminal cases in which the penalty is death, imprisonment over one month or a fine exceeding $100. The court may issue extraordinary writs and other writs necessary to the exercise of proper jurisdiction.

The court sits en banc or in three-member panels at Dover and holds session all year.

Chief Justice
E. Norman Veasey

Justices
Joseph T. Walsh
Randy J. Holland
Carolyn Berger
Myron T. Steele

Clerk
Cathy L. Howard
Supreme Court Building
55 The Green
Dover, Delaware 19901
(302) 739-4155

Administrative Office of the Courts
State Court Administrator
Dennis B. Jones
11600 New Castle County Courthouse
500 North King Street
Wilmington, Delaware 19801-3734
(302) 255-0088

DELAWARE COURT OF CHANCERY

The Court of Chancery is Delaware's court of statewide general equity jurisdiction. The court consists of one chancellor and four vice chancellors who are appointed for twelve-year terms by the governor with consent of the Senate from a list of candidates provided by the Judicial Nominating Commission.

The court has jurisdiction over all equity matters including corporate matters, petitions concerning trusts, estates and other fiduciary matters, disputes involving real property such as boundary and title disputes and commercial and contractual matters. The court also has jurisdiction over guardianship of minors, trustees for the mentally ill and other matters. Trials by jury are heard in the Superior Court. Appeals are to the Supreme Court.

The court sits at Dover, Georgetown and Wilmington.

Chancellor
William B. Chandler, III

Vice Chancellors
Jack B. Jacobs
Stephen P. Lamb
Leo E. Strine, Jr.
John W. Noble

DELAWARE SUPERIOR COURT

The Superior Court is Delaware's court of general jurisdiction. Nineteen judges are appointed for twelve-year terms by the governor with consent of the Senate from

DELAWARE SUPERIOR COURT—*Continued*

a list of candidates provided by the Judicial Nominating Commission. The president judge has administrative responsibility for the Court. Three judges serve as resident judges and must reside in the counties from which they are appointed. The remaining judges serve as associate judges.

The court has statewide original jurisdiction over criminal and civil cases, except equity cases. The court has exclusive jurisdiction over felonies and drug offenses with the exception of possession of marijuana and most felonies and drug offenses involving minors. The court hears appeals on the law from the Court of Common Pleas, the Industrial Accident Board, Unemployment Insurance Appeal Board, Alcohol Beverage Control Commission, Tax Appeal Board, Zoning and Adjustment Boards and other quasi-judicial bodies, as well as on adult criminal cases from the Family Court. The court also conducts trials de novo from Alderman's Courts and Justice of the Peace Courts. Appeals are to the Supreme Court.

The court sits at each county seat.

President Judge
Henry duPont Ridgely

County	Resident Judge
Kent	James T. Vaughn, Jr.
New Castle	Richard R. Cooch
Sussex	T. Henley Graves

County	Associate Judge
Kent	William L. Witham, Jr.
New Castle	Richard S. Gebelein
	Charles H. Toliver, IV
	Haile L. Alford
	Fred S. Silverman
	John E. Babiarz, Jr.
	Susan C. Del Pesco
	Jerome O. Herlihy
	Carl Goldstein
	William C. Carpenter
	Peggy L. Ableman
	Joseph R. Slights, III
	Jan R. Jurden
Sussex	Richard F. Stokes
	E. Scott Bradley

DELAWARE FAMILY COURT

The Family Court is a court of special statewide jurisdiction in Delaware. Fifteen judges are appointed for twelve-year terms by the governor with Senate approval from a list of candidates provided by the Judicial Nominating Commission. The chief judge has statewide administrative responsibilities. The remaining judges are assigned to the three counties as associate judges.

The court has jurisdiction over juvenile delinquency, child neglect, dependency, child abuse, adult misdemeanor crimes against juveniles, child and spouse support, paternity of children, custody and visitation of children, divorces and annulments, terminations of parental rights, adoptions, property divisions, specific enforcement of separation agreements, guardianship over minors, peril to the family relationship and intra-family misdemeanor crimes. The court does not have jurisdiction over adults charged with felonies or over juveniles charged with first degree murder, rape or kidnapping. Appeals are to the Supreme Court with the exception of adult criminal cases, which are appealed to the Superior Court.

The court sits at Dover, Georgetown and Wilmington.

Chief Judge
Vincent James Poppiti

County	Associate Judge
Kent	William N. Nicholas
	William J. Walls, Jr.
	Mardi F. Pyott
New Castle	Mark D. Buckworth
	Aida Waserstein
	Jay H. Conner
	Alison Whitmer Tumas
	William L. Chapman, Jr.
	Barbara D. Crowell
	Chandlee Johnson Kuhn
	Robert B. Coonin
Sussex	Kenneth M. Millman
	Peter B. Jones
	John E. Henriksen

DELAWARE COURT OF COMMON PLEAS

The Court of Common Pleas is a court of limited jurisdiction in Delaware. Judges are appointed for twelve-year terms by the governor with consent of the Senate from a list of candidates provided by the Judicial Nominating Commission. The judge with the most seniority serves as chief judge; the remaining judges serve as associate judges. As of May 1, 1998, the Wilmington Municipal Court merged with the Delaware Court of Common Pleas. Terms for judges who were serving the Wilmington Municipal Court have been carried over.

The court has concurrent jurisdiction with the Superior Court in civil cases when the amount in controversy does not exceed $50,000 but has unlimited jurisdiction of counterclaims. The court has criminal jurisdiction of all misdemeanors except drug-related offenses other than possession of marijuana. Jury trials are available to all defendants except in New Castle County, where jury trials are referred to the Superior Court. Appeals are to the Superior Court.

The court sits at each county seat.

Chief Judge
Alex Jerome Smalls

County	Associate Judge
Kent	Merrill C. Trader
	Charles W. Welch, III
New Castle	William C. Bradley, Jr.
	Jay Paul James
	John K. Welch
	Joseph F. Flickinger, III
Sussex	Rosemary B. Beauregard
	Kenneth S. Clark, Jr.

DELAWARE JUSTICE OF THE PEACE COURTS

Justice of the Peace Courts are courts of limited jurisdiction in Delaware. Magistrates are appointed for four-year terms by the governor with Senate approval from a list provided by the Magistrates Screening Committee.

DELAWARE JUSTICE OF THE PEACE COURTS—*Continued*

Deputy chief magistrates are designated by the chief magistrate from among the magistrates in each county to serve four-year terms.

The courts exercise jurisdiction over civil cases not exceeding $15,000. The courts, except two in Sussex County, one in Kent County and two in New Castle County, have criminal jurisdiction over minor misdemeanors and motor vehicle cases, excluding felonies, and may act as committing magistrates for all crimes. Jurisdiction is concurrent with the Court of Common Pleas. Appeals are de novo to the Superior Court.

There are nineteen courts in operation, and sessions are held throughout the state.

DELAWARE ALDERMAN'S COURTS

The Alderman's Courts are courts of limited jurisdiction established in Delaware municipalities as authorized by city or town charters. Individual municipal charters prescribe the qualifications and methods of selection of aldermen, but most are appointed by the mayor or the city governing body. In New Castle and Elsmere, the mayor serves as judge of the court. Some municipalities require that judges be qualified as attorneys.

Generally, the courts have jurisdiction over violations of municipal ordinances including minor misdemeanors, traffic offenses and parking violations and over minor civil matters, but the specific jurisdiction varies according to each city charter. Appeals are heard de novo by the Superior Court.

Delaware Counties and County Seats

Kent
Dover

New Castle
Wilmington

Sussex
Georgetown

NEW CASTLE
KENT
SUSSEX

UNITED STATES DISTRICT COURT DISTRICT OF DELAWARE

DELAWARE

ABLEMAN, Peggy L. *(Associate Judge, Delaware Superior Court New Castle County)* Appointed by Governor Thomas R. Carper to term beginning Oct 30, 2000. Born July 1950. Former Associate Judge, Delaware Family Court New Castle County, appointed by Governor Pierre S. du Pont IV Sept 30, 1983.

Office: 10400 New Castle County Courthouse, 500 North King Street, Wilmington 19801-3733.

Telephone: (302) 255-0660.

ALFORD, Haile L. *(Associate Judge, Delaware Superior Court New Castle County)* Appointed by Governor Michael N. Castle to term beginning July 17, 1992. Term expires July 17, 2004. Born July 1949.

Office: 10400 New Castle County Courthouse, 500 North King Street, Wilmington 19801-3733.

Telephone: (302) 255-0668.

BABIARZ, John E., Jr. *(Associate Judge, Delaware Superior Court New Castle County)* Appointed by Governor Michael N. Castle to term beginning Oct 24, 1985. Reappointed 1997, current term expires Oct 2009. Born Nov 1941.

Office: 10400 New Castle County Courthouse, 500 North King Street, Wilmington 19801-3733.

Telephone: (302) 255-0658.

BEAUREGARD, Rosemary B. *(Associate Judge, Delaware Court of Common Pleas Sussex County)* Appointed by Governor Thomas R. Carper.

Office: Sussex County Courthouse, One The Circle, Georgetown 19947.

Telephone: (302) 856-5977.

BERGER, Carolyn *(Justice, Delaware Supreme Court)* Appointed by Governor Tom Carper to term beginning July 22, 1994. Term expires July 22, 2006. Educated at University of Rochester B.A. 1969 and Boston University Masters in Elementary Education 1971 J.D. 1976. Honorary LL.D. Widener University School of Law 1996. In legal practice 1979-84. Vice Chancellor, Delaware Court of Chancery March 27, 1984 to 1994, appointed by Governor Pierre S. du Pont IV.

Deputy Attorney General Delaware Department of Justice 1976-79. Former Associate Member Board of Bar Examiners. Member The American Law Institute, Rodney Inn of Court and American Bar Foundation. Former Member Board of Directors Jewish Federation and Delaware Region National Conference of Christians and Jews. Past President and Former Vice President Milton & Hattie Kutz Home. Former Member Community Advisory Council Junior League of Wilmington.

Office: Carvel State Office Building, 11th Floor, 820 North French Street, Wilmington 19801.

Telephone: (302) 577-8730.

BRADLEY, E. Scott *(Associate Judge, Delaware Superior Court Sussex County)* Appointed by Governor Thomas R. Carper to term beginning April 7, 2000.

Office: Sussex County Courthouse, Race and Market Streets, Georgetown 19947.

Telephone: (302) 856-5256.

BRADLEY, William C., Jr. *(Associate Judge, Delaware Court of Common Pleas New Castle County)* Appointed by Governor Sherman W. Tribbitt to term beginning Dec 17, 1976. Reappointed 1988 and 2000. Current term expires 2012. Born St. Louis Missouri Nov 24, 1937. Educated at University of Notre Dame B.S.Ch.E. 1959 and New York Law School 1966. Admitted to practice District of Columbia 1966 and Delaware 1967. In legal practice Wilmington 1973.

Assistant Public Defender 1967. Deputy Attorney General Delaware 1969-72. Legal Counsel to Governor Sherman W. Tribbitt 1974-76. Democrat.

Office: 11800 New Castle County Courthouse, 500 North King Street, Wilmington 19801-3734.

Telephone: (302) 255-0854.

BUCKWORTH, Mark D. *(Associate Judge, Delaware Family Court New Castle County)* Appointed by Governor Tom Carper to term beginning July 13, 1994. Term expires July 13, 2006. Born May 1956.

Office: 9400 New Castle County Courthouse, 500 North King Street, Wilmington 19801-3732.

Telephone: (302) 255-0323.

CARPENTER, William C., Jr. *(Associate Judge, Delaware Superior Court New Castle County)* Appointed by Governor Thomas R. Carper to term beginning Oct 18, 1993. Term expires Oct 18, 2005. Born June 1951.

Office: 10400 New Castle County Courthouse, 500 North King Street, Wilmington 19801-3733.

Telephone: (302) 255-0670.

CHANDLER, William B., III *(Chancellor, Delaware Court of Chancery)* Appointed Vice Chancellor by Governor Michael N. Castle to term beginning March 29, 1989. Appointed Chancellor by Governor Thomas R. Carper to term beginning June 30, 1997, current term expires June 30, 2009. Born Dagsboro Delaware Jan 3, 1951. Methodist. Educated at University of Delaware B.A. cum laude 1973, University of South Carolina J.D. cum laude 1976 and Yale Law School LL.M. 1979. Executive Editor South Carolina Law Review 1975-76. Law Clerk to Hon. James L. Latchum, U.S. District Court District of Delaware 1976-78. Member Order of the Coif and Order of the Wig and Robe. Admitted to practice Delaware 1976. In legal practice Delaware 1983-85. Associate Judge Sept 30, 1985 to June 30, 1986 and Resident Associate Judge June 30, 1986 to March 29, 1989, Delaware Superior Court Sussex County, appointed by Governor Michael N. Castle.

Author Comment "Invoking the Spousal Immunity Rule" 24 South Carolina L. Rev. 610, 1975 and Note "The New Rules of Federal Evidence" 25 South Carolina L. Rev. 440, 1976. Co-author chapter 7 *The Delaware Constitution of 1897,* 1997. Assistant Professor of Law University of Alabama 1979-81. Adjunct Professor of Law Delaware Law School of Widener University 1982-83. Member The American Law Institute and The Delaware State Bar Association. Legal Counsel to Gov-

CHANDLER, WILLIAM B., III—*Continued*

ernor Pierre S. du Pont IV 1981-83. Enjoys reading, tennis and surf fishing.
Office: The Circle, Georgetown 19947.
Telephone: (302) 856-5424.

CHAPMAN, William L., Jr. *(Associate Judge, Delaware Family Court New Castle County)* Appointed by Governor Tom Carper to term beginning April 11, 1995. Term expires April 11, 2007. Born Jan 1961. Associate Judge, Wilmington Municipal Court April 22, 1994 to April 11, 1995.
Office: 9400 New Castle County Courthouse, 500 North King Street, Wilmington 19801-3732.
Telephone: (302) 255-0312.

CLARK, Kenneth S., Jr. *(Associate Judge, Delaware Court of Common Pleas Sussex County)* Appointed by Governor Thomas R. Carper to term beginning April 28, 2000. Term expires April 28, 2012. Born 1954. Educated at Swarthmore College B.A. 1976 and University of California Hastings College of the Law J.D. cum laude 1982. Staff member 1980-81 and Note and Comment Editor 1981-82 Hastings Law Journal. Member Thurston Society. Admitted to practice California 1982 and Delaware 1985. In legal practice Los Angeles California 1982-85 and Georgetown Delaware 1985-2000.
Member American Judges Association and The Delaware State Bar Association.
Office: Sussex County Courthouse, One The Circle, Georgetown 19957.
Telephone: (302) 856-5963.
E-mail address: kenclark@state.de.us

CONNER, Jay H. *(Associate Judge, Delaware Family Court New Castle County)* Appointed by Governor Pierre S. du Pont IV Dec 17, 1981. Reappointed by Governor Thomas R. Carper July 13, 1994, current term expires July 13, 2006. Born July 1938.
Office: 9400 New Castle County Courthouse, 500 North King Street, Wilmington 19801-3732.
Telephone: (302) 255-0292.

COOCH, Richard R. *(Resident Judge, Delaware Superior Court New Castle County)* Appointed Associate Judge by Governor Michael N. Castle June 15, 1992 to term beginning Aug 31, 1992. Appointed Resident Judge by Governor Thomas R. Carper to term beginning May 11, 2000. Term expires May 10, 2012. Born Wilmington Delaware June 7, 1948. Episcopalian. Educated at Williams College B.A. 1970 and University of North Carolina School of Law J.D. 1973. Admitted to practice Delaware 1973, U.S. District Court District of Delaware 1973 and U.S. Court of Appeals Third Circuit 1989. In legal practice Wilmington 1973-74 and 1977-92.
Deputy Attorney General Delaware Department of Justice 1975-77. Attorney Delaware House of Representatives 1979-81. Former Member and Former Chair Supreme Court Advisory Committee on Litigation Ethical Problems and Judicial Ethics Advisory Committee. Former Chair Superior Court Advisory Committee on Criminal Jury Instructions. Member The Delaware State Bar Association (Assistant Treasurer 1985-87, Treasurer 1987-89). Judicial Member Commission on Continuing Legal Education. President New Castle Historical Society since 1989.
Office: 500 North King Street, Wilmington 19801.
Telephone: (302) 255-0664.

COONIN, Robert B. *(Associate Judge, Delaware Family Court New Castle County)* Appointed by Governor Ruth Ann Minner.
Office: 9400 New Castle County Courthouse, 500 North King Street, Wilmington 19801-3732.
Telephone: (302) 255-0301.

CROWELL, Barbara D. *(Associate Judge, Delaware Family Court New Castle County)* Appointed by Governor Tom Carper to term beginning March 1, 1996. Term expires March 1, 2008. Born Oct 1943.
Office: 9400 New Castle County Courthouse, 500 North King Street, Wilmington 19801-3732.
Telephone: (302) 255-0309.

DEL PESCO, Susan C. *(Associate Judge, Delaware Superior Court New Castle County)* Appointed by Governor Michael N. Castle to term beginning May 20, 1988. Reappointed 2000, current term expires 2012. Born Long Beach California May 20, 1946. Educated at University of California at Santa Barbara B.A. 1967, Widener University J.D. 1975 and University of Virginia LL.M. 2001. Admitted to practice Delaware 1975. In legal practice Wilmington 1976-88.
Recipient Women's Leadership Award The Delaware State Bar Association 1966, She Knows Where She's Going Award Girls Clubs of Delaware, Inc. 1989 and The Delaware Law School of Widener University Alumni Association Outstanding Achievement Award Widener University 1987. Republican.
Office: New Castle County Courthouse, 500 North King Street, Wilmington 19801.
Telephone: (302) 255-0659.

FARNAN, Joseph J., Jr. *(Judge, United States District Court District of Delaware)* Appointed for life by President Ronald Reagan July 18, 1985. Former Chief Judge. Born Philadelphia Pennsylvania. Roman Catholic. Educated at King's College A.B. 1967 and University of Toledo J.D. 1970. Case Note Editor University of Toledo Law Review 1969-70. Admitted to practice New Jersey 1970 and Delaware 1972. In legal practice Wilmington 1972-76.
Office: Federal Building, Lockbox 27, 844 North King Street, Wilmington 19801-3529.
Telephone: (302) 573-6155.

FLICKINGER, Joseph F., III *(Associate Judge, Delaware Court of Common Pleas New Castle County)* Appointed by governor.
Office: 11800 New Castle County Courthouse, 500 North King Street, Wilmington 19801-3734.
Telephone: (302) 255-0860.

GEBELEIN, Richard S. *(Associate Judge, Delaware Superior Court New Castle County)* Appointed by Governor Pierre S. du Pont IV to term beginning Oct 5, 1984. Reappointed Dec 5, 1996, current term expires Dec 5, 2008. Born Darby Pennsylvania June 8, 1946. Catholic. Educated at University of Pittsburgh B.S. 1967 and Villanova University J.D. 1970. Law Clerk to Chancellor William Duffy, Delaware Court of Chancery 1970-71. Admitted to practice Delaware 1971, Pennsylvania 1971 and U.S. Supreme Court 1974. Began legal practice Wilmington Delaware 1971.
Deputy Attorney General 1971-74, State Solicitor 1974-75, Chief Deputy Public Defender 1975-76 and Attorney General 1979-83 State of Delaware. Instructor Delaware Law School of Widener University since 1973

GEBELEIN, RICHARD S.—*Continued*

and University of Delaware since 1982. Executive Working Group U.S. Department of Justice 1979-83. Commissioner since 1985 and Chairman since 1988 Sentencing Accountability Commission. Member Legislative Subcommittee 1980-83 and Chairman Institutions and Corrections Subcommittee 1980-83 National Association of Attorneys General. Member The Delaware State and American Bar Associations. Lieutenant Colonel Delaware Army National Guard since 1979. Republican.

Office: 10400 New Castle County Courthouse, 500 North King Street, Wilmington 19801-3733.

Telephone: (302) 255-0661.

GOLDSTEIN, Carl *(Associate Judge, Delaware Superior Court New Castle County)* Appointed by Governor Michael N. Castle to term beginning Nov 29, 1990. Reappointed by Governor Ruth Ann Minner 2002, current term expires 2014. Born Chester Pennsylvania Sept 23, 1938. Jewish. Educated at University of Pennsylvania B.A. with honors 1960 LL.B. 1963. Admitted to practice Delaware and District of Columbia 1964. Began legal practice Wilmington 1964. Associate Judge, Wilmington Municipal Court June 1, 1970 to Nov 29, 1990, appointed by Governor Russell W. Peterson.

Assistant City Solicitor Wilmington 1968-70. Member American Judicature Society, The Delaware State and American Bar Associations. Republican. Member Brandywine Friends of Old Time Music (President since 1972).

Office: 10400 New Castle County Courthouse, 500 North King Street, Wilmington 19801-3733.

Telephone: (302) 255-0662.

GRAVES, T. Henley *(Resident Judge, Delaware Superior Court Sussex County)* Appointed Associate Judge by Governor Michael N. Castle to term beginning June 1, 1989. Appointed Resident Judge by Governor Thomas R. Carper to term beginning Jan 19, 2000. Term expires Jan 19, 2012. Born Aug 1948.

Office: Sussex County Courthouse, Race and Market Streets, Georgetown 19947.

Telephone: (302) 856-5257.

HENRIKSEN, John E. *(Associate Judge, Delaware Family Court Sussex County)* Appointed by governor.

Office: 10 The Circle, Georgetown 19947.

Telephone: (302) 856-4645.

HERLIHY, Jerome O. *(Associate Judge, Delaware Superior Court New Castle County)* Appointed by Governor Michael N. Castle Jan 1989 to term beginning Feb 21, 1989. Reappointed 2001, current term expires April 19, 2013. Born Wilmington Delaware April 24, 1941. Lutheran. Educated at Dartmouth College A.B. 1963 and University of Pennsylvania LL.B. 1966. Admitted to practice Delaware 1966, U.S. District Court District of Delaware, U.S. Court of Appeals Third Circuit and U.S. Supreme Court. In legal practice Wilmington 1974-89.

Deputy Attorney General Delaware Department of Justice 1966-69. Counsel to Governor Russell Wilbur Peterson 1969-71. Chief Deputy Attorney General 1971-74. Member The Delaware State and American Bar Associations.

Office: 10400 New Castle County Courthouse, 500 North King Street, Wilmington 19801-3733.

Telephone: (302) 255-0663.

HOLLAND, Randy J. *(Justice, Delaware Supreme Court)* Appointed by Governor Michael N. Castle to term beginning Dec 12, 1986. Reappointed 1999, current term expires Feb 7, 2011. Born Elizabeth New Jersey Jan 27, 1947. Methodist. Educated at Swarthmore College B.A. 1969 and University of Pennsylvania J.D. cum laude 1972. Admitted to practice Delaware 1972 and U.S. Supreme Court 1976. In legal practice Georgetown 1972-86.

Author Chapter 12 *Delaware Appellate Handbook* since 1986, "Ethical Considerations in Dealing with the Media" Federal Lawyer 1996 and "State Constitutions, Purpose and Function" Temple L. Rev. 1996. Editor-in-Chief *Delaware Constitution of 1897—The First 100 Years* 1997. Co-editor *Delaware Supreme Court Golden Anniversary* 2001 and *Delaware Constitution: A Reference Guide* Greenwood Press 2002. Adjunct Professor Widener University School of Law since 1991 and University of Pennsylvania School of Law 1993-94. Visiting Adjunct Professor University of Iowa College of Law since 1997 and Vanderbilt University School of Law since 2000. Co-chair National Judicial Advisory Committee Federal Office of Child Support Enforcement 1991-93. President Terry-Carey Inn of Court 1991-94. Chair Delaware Code of Judicial Conduct Revision Committee 1991-94. Trustee since 1992 and President since 2000 American Inns of Court Foundation. Co-chair Task Force on Racial and Ethnic Fairness in the Courts since 1994. Co-chair Delaware Courts Planning Committee 1995-96. Member Liaison Justice to Delaware Supreme Court (Board on Professional Responsibility 1987-94, Board of Bar Examiners since 1994, Supreme Court Rules Committee since 1994). Member Advisory Committees (Certified Question Project 1994-95, Judicial Conduct Organizations 1994-97, Courts and Media since 1996). Member American Judicature Society (Trustee since 1992) and American Bar Association (Standing Committee on Lawyer Competence since 1995). Participant Delaware Bar, Bench, Media Conference 1990-96. Advisory Committee American Bar Association Model Rules of Judicial Disciplinary Enforcement Videotape and Teaching Guide The National Judicial College 1996. Recipient Henry C. Loughlin Prize for Legal Ethics 1972, Outstanding Young Man Award Milford Jaycees 1974, Milford High School Alumni Association Award 1985, Distinguished Milford High School Alumnus Award 1987, National Golden Heart Award to a Jurist by ACES 1991, Judge of the Year National Child Support Enforcement Association 1992 and City of Milford Award 1992. Founding Director Milford Senior Center 1972-75. Director Sussex County Arts Council 1973-75. President Milford High Alumni Association 1975. Chairman Administrative Board since 1976, Trustee since 1976, Lay Leader since 1979, Former Sunday School Teacher and Former Youth Fellowship Leader Avenue United Methodist Church. Member Swarthmore College Alumni Council 1979-80. Coach Little League Baseball 1983-86 and Little League Basketball 1985-86. Trustee Peninsula Conference United Methodist Church 1985-86.

Mailing address: P.O. Box 369, Georgetown 19947.

Office: Family Court Building, First Floor, Georgetown 19947.

Telephone: (302) 856-5363.

JACOBS, Jack B. *(Vice Chancellor, Delaware Court of Chancery)* Appointed by Governor Michael N. Castle Sept 30, 1985. Reappointed 1997, current term expires 2009. Born Houston Texas July 23, 1942. Jewish. Edu-

JACOBS, JACK B.—*Continued*
cated at University of Chicago B.A. 1964 and Harvard Law School LL.B. 1967. Member Phi Beta Kappa. Law Clerk to Delaware Superior Court and Delaware Court of Chancery 1967-68. Admitted to practice Delaware 1968, U.S. District Court District of Delaware 1968, U.S. Court of Appeals Third Circuit 1968 and U.S. Supreme Court 1975. In legal practice Wilmington 1968-85.

Author "The New Delaware Consent to Service Statute" 33 Business Lawyer 701, 1978; "Delaware Receivers and Trustees: Unsung Ministers of Corporate Last Rites" 7 Del. Journal of Corp. Law 251, 1982; "State Claims in Federal Securities Litigation" 15 The Review of Securities Regulation No. 18, Oct 27, 1982; "How to Win an Injunction" 10 No. 1 Litigation 20, 1983; and various articles and program course materials "New Dimensions in Securities Litigation: Planning and Strategies" ALI-ABA CLE. Adjunct Professor Widener University School of Law. Member The American Law Institute, The Delaware State (member Corporate Law Section since 1973, Chairman Program Committee 1980-81 and Subcommittee to Revise Delaware Securities Act 1980-82) and American (Sections: Business Law, Litigation) Bar Associations. Faculty Participant and Panelist in various state and national Continuing Legal Education programs. Democrat. Board of Directors Mental Health Association of Delaware 1971-73 and Delaware Symphony Association. Board of Directors 1978-88, Assistant Treasurer 1980-81, Treasurer 1981-82 and Secretary 1982-83 Jewish Federation of Delaware. Executive Committee 1982-89 and Vice Chairman 1985-1988 National Jewish Community Relations Advisory Council. President Harvard Law School Association of Delaware 1984-86. President The Milton & Hattie Kutz Home, Inc. 1990-92. Member Governmental Relations Committee United Way of Delaware 1982-85. Enjoys classical music, biking and skiing.

Office: 11400 New Castle County Courthouse, 500 North King Street, Wilmington 19801-3734.

Telephone: (302) 255-0509.

JAMES, Jay Paul *(Associate Judge, Delaware Court of Common Pleas New Castle County)* Appointed by Governor Thomas R. Carper. Born March 1941. Former Associate Judge, Delaware Family Court New Castle County, appointed by Governor Pierre S. du Pont IV to term beginning June 30, 1978.

Office: 11800 New Castle County Courthouse, 500 North King Street, Wilmington 19801-3734.

Telephone: (302) 255-0856.

JONES, Peter B. *(Associate Judge, Delaware Family Court Sussex County)* Appointed by Governor Thomas R. Carper.

Office: 10 The Circle, Georgetown 19947.

Telephone: (302) 845-5540.

JORDAN, Kent A. *(Judge, United States District Court District of Delaware)* Appointed for life by President George W. Bush to term beginning Nov 27, 2002.

Office: 6325 Federal Building, Lockbox 10, 844 North King Street, Wilmington 19801.

Telephone: (302) 573-6001.

JURDEN, Jan R. *(Associate Judge, Delaware Superior Court New Castle County)* Appointed by Governor Ruth Ann Minner to term beginning May 29, 2001.

Office: 10400 New Castle County Courthouse, 500 North King Street, Wilmington 19801-3733.

Telephone: (302) 255-0665.

KUHN, Chandlee Johnson *(Associate Judge, Delaware Family Court New Castle County)* Appointed by Governor Thomas R. Carper.

Office: 9400 New Castle County Courthouse, 500 North King Street, Wilmington 19801-3732.

Telephone: (302) 255-0305.

LAMB, Stephen P. *(Vice Chancellor, Delaware Court of Chancery)* Appointed by Governor Thomas R. Carper.

Office: 11400 New Castle County Courthouse, 500 North King Street, Wilmington 19801-3734.

Telephone: (302) 255-0510.

LATCHUM, James L. *(Senior Judge, United States District Court District of Delaware)* Appointed for life by President Lyndon B. Johnson to term beginning Aug 22, 1968. Chief Judge Oct 9, 1973 to Dec 23, 1983. Assumed Senior status Dec 23, 1983, serves by assignment. Born Milford Delaware Dec 23, 1918. Presbyterian. Educated at Princeton University A.B. cum laude 1940 and University of Virginia LL.B. 1946. Graduated second in law school class. Virginia Law Review Editorial Board 1941-43 and 1946 (Decisions Editor 1942) and Law School Advisory Council 1942. Member Raven Society, Sigma Nu Phi, Pi Delta Epsilon and Order of the Coif. Admitted to practice Virginia 1942, Delaware 1947, U.S. District Courts District of Delaware 1947 and District of Maryland 1958, U.S. Tax Court 1947, U.S. Court of Appeals Third Circuit 1948 and U.S. Supreme Court 1949.

Attorney Delaware State Highway Department 1949-51, Delaware Interstate Highway Division 1955-63 and Delaware River and Bay Authority 1963-68. Assistant U.S. Attorney 1951-53. Member court-appointed Committee to draft Rules of Criminal Procedure for Delaware Superior Court 1950-52, court-appointed Committee to draft Rules of Orphans' Court 1957-58, Delaware Supreme Court Censor Committee 1960-68 (Chairman 1962-68), American Bridge, Tunnel and Turnpike Association Law Committee 1956-68, National Conference Federal Trial Judges Executive Committee 1976, Delaware Constitutional Revision Commission (Chairman 1968), Judge Advocates Association, American Judicature Society, Virginia State Bar, The Delaware State (Continuing Legal Education Committee 1949-52, Administration of Justice Committee 1955-59, Federal Judicial Appointments Committee 1957-58, Adoption of Uniform Commercial Code Committee 1957-59) and American (Advisory Committee of the Standing Committee on American Citizenship 1954-68, Third Circuit Grievance Committee 1967-68) Bar Associations. Lieutenant Colonel U.S. Army JAGC active duty 1942-46 USAR 1946-61 (retired). Member Committee for Revising Rules of Baltimore Synod 1958-60 and New Castle Presbytery Committee on Bills and Overtures 1959-68. Member Wilmington Park Trust Fund Commission 1963-67, First and Central Presbyterian Church (Elder 1956-59 and 1967-69; member 1950-56 and President 1955-56 and 1967-69 Board of Trustees; Superintendent Church School), Wilmington Charter Revision Committee

LATCHUM, JAMES L.—*Continued*

(Chairman 1961-62), Historical Society of Delaware and University Club.

Office: Federal Building, Lockbox 20, 844 North King Street, Wilmington 19801-3583.

Telephone: (302) 573-6167.

LONGOBARDI, Joseph J. *(Senior Judge, United States District Court District of Delaware)* Appointed for life by President Ronald Reagan to term beginning May 3, 1984. Chief Judge 1989-96. Assumed Senior status June 15, 1997, serves by assignment. Born Wilmington Delaware 1930. Educated at Washington College B.A. 1952 and Temple University School of Law LL.B. 1957. In legal practice Delaware 1957-59 and Wilmington Delaware 1964-74. Associate Judge, Delaware Superior Court 1974-82. Vice Chancellor, Delaware Court of Chancery 1982-84.

Office: Federal Building, Lockbox 40, 844 North King Street, Wilmington 19801-3572.

Telephone: (302) 573-6151.

MILLMAN, Kenneth M. *(Associate Judge, Delaware Family Court Sussex County)* Appointed by Governor Michael N. Castle to term beginning Oct 31, 1986. Reappointed 1998, current term expires Oct 31, 2010. Born Milford Delaware May 19, 1948. Methodist. Educated at High Point College B.A. 1970 and Wake Forest University J.D. 1973. Member Phi Alpha Delta. Admitted to practice Delaware 1973 and U.S. District Court District of Delaware 1976. In legal practice Georgetown 1973-86.

Member Sussex County, The Delaware State and American Bar Associations. Chairman Sussex County Republican Party 1981-85. Member Kiwanis.

Office: 10 The Circle, Georgetown 19947.

Telephone: (302) 856-5417.

NICHOLAS, William N. *(Associate Judge, Delaware Family Court Kent County)* Appointed by Governor Michael N. Castle to term beginning May 14, 1992. Term expires May 14, 2004. Born April 1950.

Office: 400 Court Street, Dover 19901.

Telephone: (302) 739-6565.

NOBLE, John W. *(Vice Chancellor, Delaware Court of Chancery)* Appointed by governor.

Office: Kent County Courthouse, 38 The Green, Dover 19901.

Telephone: (302) 739-4397.

POPPITI, Vincent James *(Chief Judge, Delaware Family Court)* Appointed by Governor Michael N. Castle to term beginning Jan 31, 1992. Term expires Jan 31, 2004. Chief Judge since Jan 31, 1992. Born Wilmington Delaware Nov 1, 1945. Catholic. Educated at Fordham University A.B. summa cum laude 1967, University of Virginia School of Law J.D. 1970 and Temple University School of Law 1977-79. Law Clerk to Delaware Superior Court New Castle County and Delaware Court of Chancery 1970-71. Member Order of the Coif. In legal practice Wilmington June 1975 to Feb 1977. Associate Judge, Delaware Family Court Feb 14, 1979 to June 17, 1983. Associate Judge June 17, 1983 to Jan 18, 1990 and Resident Associate Judge Jan 18, 1990 to Jan 31, 1992 Delaware Superior Court, appointed by Pierre S. du Pont IV.

Chief of Civil Division Department of Justice Feb 14, 1977 to Feb 14, 1979. Founding Board of Editors Delaware Lawyer 1983-96. Author "Support in Behalf of Children" Delaware Lawyer Summer 1993 and "May It Please The Court" *The Brief* Winter 1993, republished in Coverage Jan/Feb 1997. Adjunct Faculty Member on Domestic Violence Wilmington College Fall 1995 and Fall 1997. Chair Domestic Violence Coordinating Council since Dec 1993. Member Child Support Task Force Oversight Committee, Conflict Resolution Committee, Chief Justice's Conference (Long Range Goals for Reducing Violence and Short Term Goals Committee), DPI (Code of Conduct Committee, Crime Reporting Committee), Delaware Judicial Conference Executive Committee, Dispositional Guidelines Committee for Juveniles, Juvenile Justice Advisory Group, White House Advisory Council on Violence Against Women and Rodney Inns of Court. Panel Moderator "A Study of Jury Attitudes" 1987 and Participant Superior Court Civil Practice 1988 Delaware Bench and Bar Conference. Panelist "Sticks and Stones May Break My Bones. . ." Section of Litigation American Bar Association Fall Meeting Oct 1990. Co-presenter "Cry Out for Justice" Delaware United Prevention of Child Abuse March 31, 1993, American Justinian Society of Jurists Summer Convention June 12, 1993, Rotary Club June 24, 1993 and Kiwanis Club of Wilmington; and "Domestic Violence: Let's Get Civil" People's Law School April 6, 1994 and Wilmington Women in Business April 20, 1994. Presenter Infant Mortality Symposium Consumer Workshop Jan 30, 1995; "Complex Insurance Coverage Litigation: The View From the Bench" Insurance Coverage Litigation Annual Mid-Year Meeting March 4, 1995; "Is the Family a Corporate Stakeholder?" March 21, 1996 and Family Re-union V June 24, 1996 Work and Family Conference; Seventh Annual Child Care Conference General Services Administration Aug 7, 1996; and "Adapting to Different Learning Styles" Family Re-Union VI: Families and Learning June 24, 1997. Recipient J. Thompson Brown Award for Outstanding Contributions to Family Life in Delaware from Family and Children Services of Delaware, Inc. Nov 4, 1994; Award for Excellence for Committee Health Betterment in Preventing Youth and Family Violence from Delaware Public Health Association Nov 15, 1994; Community Award in Recognition of Contribution to the Infant Mortality Symposium and Town Meetings from Perinatal Association of Delaware Oct 5, 1995; and William H. Rehnquist Award for Judicial Excellence from National Center of State Courts Nov 18, 1996. Captain USAF JAGC May 1971 to May 1975. Colonel Delaware Air National Guard since Aug 1975.

Past President and Board Member Catholic Youth Organization 1979-84 and Children's Repertory Theatre, Inc. 1982-84. Ad Hoc Member Community Advisor Board Bureau of Juvenile Correction 1979-83. Board of Directors SODAT-Delaware, Inc. 1980-84 and 1989-95 and Blue Cross Blue Shield of Delaware, Inc. 1981-97. Member Advisory Committee on Para-Legal Education University of Delaware 1979-81, Delaware Guidance for Children and Youth 1980-83, Advisory Council 70001 Program 1981-84, Advisory Committee Center for Pastoral Care 1984-86, Boy Scouts of America 1988 and United Way Youth Violence Initiative Feb 1994 to 1996. Former Chairperson Audit Committee and Member Executive Committee Blue Cross Blue Shield of Delaware, Inc. V.A. Volunteer since 1982. Board Member Delaware Perinatal since Oct 1995. Trustee Children's Advocacy Center of Delaware, Inc. since Nov

POPPITI, VINCENT JAMES—*Continued*

1995. Member Committee on Drug Free Schools and Communities, Healthy Children's Committee Delaware Health Care Commission, Interagency Council for Children and Families, Interagency Council on Adoptions and Steering Committee Police Athletic League. Enjoys singing, acting and cooking.

Office: 9450 New Castle County Courthouse, 500 North King Street, Wilmington 19801-3736.

Telephone: (302) 255-0296.

PYOTT, Mardi F. *(Associate Judge, Delaware Family Court Kent County)* Appointed by governor.

Office: 400 Court Street, Dover 19901.

Telephone: (302) 739-5755.

RIDGELY, Henry duPont *(President Judge, Delaware Superior Court)* Appointed Associate Judge Kent County by Governor Pierre S. du Pont IV to term beginning Sept 14, 1984. Appointed Resident Associate Judge Kent County by Governor Michael N. Castle May 4, 1988. Appointed President Judge by Governor Michael N. Castle to term beginning Sept 25, 1990. Reappointed by Governor Ruth Ann Minner 2002, current term expires 2014. Born Dover Delaware May 31, 1949. Episcopalian. Educated at Syracuse University B.S. 1971, Catholic University of America J.D. 1973 and George Washington University LL.M. 1974. Admitted to practice Delaware 1974 and District of Columbia 1978. Began legal practice Dover 1974.

State Senate Attorney Delaware 1981-84. Member The Delaware State (Vice President 1976-77) and American Bar Associations. Republican.

Office: 38 The Green, Dover 19901.

Telephone: (302) 739-5331.

ROBINSON, Sue L. *(Chief Judge, United States District Court District of Delaware)* Magistrate Judge 1988-91. Appointed Judge for life by President George Bush to term beginning Nov 18, 1991. Chief Judge since July 1, 2000. Born Mount Carmel Illinois Feb 3, 1952. Educated at University of Delaware B.A. 1974 and University of Pennsylvania Law School J.D. 1978. In legal practice Wilmington 1978-83.

Assistant U.S. Attorney District of Delaware 1983-88.

Office: Federal Building, Lockbox 31, 844 North King Street, Wilmington 19801-3568.

Telephone: (302) 573-6310.

SCHWARTZ, Murray M. *(Senior Judge, United States District Court District of Delaware)* Part-time Bankruptcy Referee 1969-74. Appointed Judge for life by President Richard M. Nixon to term beginning 1974. Chief Judge 1985-89. Assumed Senior status July 24, 1989, serves by assignment. Born Ephrata Pennsylvania March 23, 1931. Educated at University of Pennsylvania B.S. 1952 LL.B. 1955 and University of Virginia School of Law LL.M. 1982. Law Clerk to Hon. Caleb Merrill Wright, U.S. District Court District of Delaware 1955-57. In legal practice Wilmington 1958-74.

Office: Federal Building, Lockbox 44, 844 North King Street, Wilmington 19801-3578.

Telephone: (302) 573-6355.

SILVERMAN, Fred S. *(Associate Judge, Delaware Superior Court New Castle County)* Appointed by Governor Thomas R. Carper to term beginning Oct 12, 1993. Term expires Oct 12, 2005. Born Nov 1950.

Office: 10400 New Castle County Courthouse, 500 North King Street, Wilmington 19801-3733.

Telephone: (302) 255-0669.

SLEET, Gregory M. *(Judge, United States District Court District of Delaware)* Appointed for life by President Bill Clinton Jan 27, 1998 to term beginning April 30, 1998. Born New York New York March 5, 1951. Educated at Hampton University B.A. 1973 and Rutgers University School of Law J.D. 1976. In legal practice Philadelphia Pennsylvania 1983-90.

Assistant Public Defender Defender Association of Philadelphia 1976-83. Deputy Attorney General Delaware Department of Justice 1990-92. Counsel Hercules, Inc. 1992-94. U.S. District Attorney District of Delaware 1994-98.

Office: Federal Building, Lockbox 19, 844 North King Street, Wilmington 19801.

Telephone: (302) 573-6470.

SLIGHTS, Joseph R., III *(Associate Judge, Delaware Superior Court New Castle County)* Appointed by Governor Thomas R. Carper to term beginning Nov 2, 2000.

Office: 10400 New Castle County Courthouse, 500 North King Street, Wilmington 19801-3733.

Telephone: (302) 255-0656.

SMALLS, Alex Jerome *(Chief Judge, Delaware Court of Common Pleas)* Appointed by Governor Tom Carper to term beginning Oct 8, 1993. Term expires Oct 8, 2005. Born Georgetown South Carolina Aug 18, 1950. United Methodist. Educated at Morgan State College B.A. 1972 and Rutgers University School of Law J.D. 1976. Admitted to practice Delaware 1978. Associate Judge, Wilmington Municipal Court Feb 15, 1991 to Nov 8, 1993.

Deputy Attorney General Delaware 1981-85. Member American Bar Association (National Conference of Special Court Judges).

Office: Courthouse, Fifth and King Streets, Wilmington 19801.

Telephone: (302) 577-2430.

STEELE, Myron T. *(Justice, Delaware Supreme Court)* Appointed by Governor Thomas R. Carper to term beginning July 28, 2000. Born Taunton Massachusetts July 28, 1945. Episcopalian. Educated at University of Virginia B.A. 1967 J.D. 1970. Articles Editor Virginia Journal of International Law 1968-70. Member Phi Alpha Delta. Admitted to practice Delaware 1970, Virginia 1970, U.S. District Court District of Delaware 1970 and U.S. Court of Appeals Third Circuit 1974. In legal practice Wilmington 1970-71 and Dover 1971-88. Associate Judge May 31, 1988 to Nov 1, 1990 and Resident Associate Judge Nov 1, 1990 to May 12, 1994, Delaware Superior Court Kent County, appointed by Governor Michael N. Castle. Former Vice Chancellor, Delaware Court of Chancery, appointed by Governor Tom Carper to term beginning May 12, 1994.

Deputy Attorney General Delaware 1971-72. Senate Attorney Delaware General Assembly 1974. Chairman Delaware Consumer Affairs Board 1976-88. Counselor 1992-93 and President 1994-95 Terry-Carey American Inn of Court. Member American Board of Trial Attorneys, Virginia State Bar, Kent County (President 1979), The Delaware State (Vice President Executive Commit-

STEELE, MYRON T.—*Continued*

tee 1980 and 1997) and American Bar Associations. First Lieutenant U.S. Army 1971. Served to Colonel Delaware Army National Guard (retired). Democrat. Member Democratic State Executive Committee 1983-87. Democratic County Chairman 1985-86. Chairman Central Delaware Health Care Corporation (Kent General Hospital) 1991-96. Board Member Delaware Community Foundation and Delaware Historical Society. Member Kiwanis (Past President). Enjoys racquetball, water fowling and horseback riding.

Mailing address: P.O. Box 476, Dover 19903.
Office: 57 The Green, Dover 19901.
Telephone: (302) 739-4214.

STOKES, Richard F. *(Associate Judge, Delaware Superior Court Sussex County)* Appointed by Governor Thomas R. Carper to term beginning April 22, 1999. Born Jan 1946. Associate Judge, Delaware Court of Common Pleas Sussex County July 26, 1996 to April 21, 1999, appointed by Governor Thomas R. Carper.

Office: Sussex County Courthouse, Race and Market Streets, Georgetown 19947.
Telephone: (302) 856-5264.

STRINE, Leo E., Jr. *(Vice Chancellor, Delaware Court of Chancery)* Appointed by Governor Thomas R. Carper.

Office: 11400 New Castle County Courthouse, 500 North King Street, Wilmington 19801-3734.
Telephone: (302) 255-0511.

THYNGE, Mary Pat *(Magistrate Judge, United States District Court District of Delaware)* Appointed by U.S. District Court judges.

Office: Federal Building, Lockbox 8, 844 North King Street, Wilmington 19801-3555.
Telephone: (302) 573-6173.

TOLIVER, Charles H., IV *(Associate Judge, Delaware Superior Court New Castle County)* Appointed by Governor Michael N. Castle to term beginning Feb 9, 1990. Reappointed by Governor Ruth Ann Minner 2002. Current term expires 2014. Born Jan 1951.

Office: 10400 New Castle County Courthouse, 500 North King Street, Wilmington 19801-3733.
Telephone: (302) 255-0657.

TRADER, Merrill C. *(Associate Judge, Delaware Court of Common Pleas Kent County)* Appointed by Governor Russell W. Peterson to term beginning Sept 14, 1972. Reappointed Sept 14, 1984 and Feb 7, 1997. Current term expires Feb 7, 2009. Born Cherrydale Virginia Jan 14, 1932. Educated at Western Maryland College B.A. 1954 and Washington and Lee University LL.B. 1958. Contributing Writer Washington & Lee Law Review 1957-58. Law Clerk to Hon. William Storey, Delaware Superior Court 1957-60. Admitted to practice Virginia 1958, Delaware 1958 and U.S. District Court District of Delaware 1961. Began legal practice Dover Delaware. Master, Delaware Family Court 1970-72.

Assistant Deputy Attorney General 1963-64 and Deputy Attorney General 1965-69 Kent County. Member American Judicature Society, The Delaware State and American Bar Associations. Republican. Member Holy Cross Roman Catholic Church. Enjoys swimming, gardening and reading historical and political books.

Mailing address: 20 Sherwood Court, Dover 19901.
Office: Kent County Courthouse, Dover 19901.
Telephone: (302) 739-4617.

TUMAS, Alison Whitmer *(Associate Judge, Delaware Family Court New Castle County)* Appointed by Governor Michael N. Castle June 1992 to term beginning Sept 15, 1992. Term expires Sept 15, 2004. Born Aug 1959.

Office: 9400 New Castle County Courthouse, 500 North King Street, Wilmington 19801-3732.
Telephone: (302) 255-0321.
Fax: (302) 255-2237

VAUGHN, James T., Jr. *(Resident Judge, Delaware Superior Court Kent County)* Appointed by Governor Thomas R. Carper to term beginning Oct 28, 1998.

Office: 38 The Green, Dover 19901.
Telephone: (302) 739-5333.

VEASEY, E. Norman *(Chief Justice, Delaware Supreme Court)* Appointed by Governor Michael N. Castle to term beginning April 7, 1992. Current term expires April 7, 2004. Chief Justice since April 7, 1992. Born Wilmington Delaware Jan 9, 1933. Episcopalian. Educated at Dartmouth College A.B. 1954 and University of Pennsylvania LL.B. 1957. Awarded honorary LL.D. Widener University 1993 and University of Delaware 2003. Board of Editors 1955-56 and Senior Editor 1956-57 University of Pennsylvania Law Review. Admitted to practice Delaware 1958, U.S. District Court District of Delaware 1958, U.S. Courts of Appeals Third 1962 and Federal 1984 Circuits and U.S. Supreme Court 1963. In legal practice Wilmington 1957-92.

Deputy Attorney General 1961-62 and Chief Deputy Attorney General 1963 Delaware. Author "Fiduciary Problems of Directors of Target Company" No. 371 PLI No. B4-6591 *Corporate Law and Practice Course Handbook Series* 1981; "New Insights into Judicial Deference to Directors' Business Decisions: Should We Trust the Courts?" 39 *Business Lawyer* 1461 Aug 1984; "The New Incarnation of the Business Judgement Rule in Takeover Defenses" 11 Delaware Journal of Corporate Law 503, 1986; and "A Statute Was Needed to Stop Abuses" *New York Times* Feb 8, 1988. Co-author with Jesse A. Finkelstein *Appraisal Rights and Fairness of Price in Mergers and Consolidations* The Bureau of National Affairs, Inc. 1984 supplement 1987; with R. Balotti and J. Finkelstein *The Delaware Law of Corporations and Business Organizations* Law and Business 1985 supplements 1988 and 1990; with Jesse A. Finkelstein and Robert J. Shaughnessy "The Delaware Takeover Law: Some Issues, Strategies and Comparisons" 43 *Business Lawyer* 865 May 1988, reprinted Bowne Digest for Corporate and Securities Lawyers 2 No. 9 Sept 1988 and Journal of the Japanese Institute of International Law 17 No. 3 March 1989 and 17 No. 4 April 1989; and with Gregory V. Varallo, Kevin G. Abrams and Frederick L. Cottrell, III "Counseling Directors on the Business Judgement Rule and the Duty of Loyalty" 361 No. 731 *Corporate Law and Practice Course Handbook Series* 1991. Editor *The Business Lawyer* 1992-93. Director Institute of Law and Economics University of Pennsylvania 1988-89. Member Judicial Ethics Advisory Committee University of Pennsylvania Law School Center on Professionalism. Member 1970-80 and Chair 1973-80 Delaware Board of Bar Examiners. Co-chair

VEASEY, E. NORMAN—*Continued*

Governor's Franchise Tax Study Committee 1974. Chair Special Committee on Supreme Court Rules Revision 1977-78. Co-chair Delaware Intergovernmental Task Force 1977-80. Chair Permanent Advisory Committee on Supreme Court Rules Delaware Supreme Court 1978-87. Member 1980 and Chair 1987 Magistrate Merit Selection Panel U.S. District Court District of Delaware. Member Long Range Courts Planning Committee 1983-85. Board of Directors 1994-96, President 1999-2000 and Chair Committee on Professionalism and Lawyer Competence Conference of Chief Justices. Permanent Lawyer Member Judicial Conference of the Third Circuit (Lawyers Advisory Committee 1986-88). Chair Board of Directors National Center for State Courts 1999-2000. Member Standing Committee on Rules of Practice and Procedure United States Judicial Conference. Co-chair National Conference of Lawyers and Representatives of the Media. Judicial Fellow American College of Trial Lawyers (Alternatives for Dispute Resolution Committee 1985-91). Life Fellow American Bar Foundation. Member American Intellectual Property Law Association, The American Law Institute, American Judicature Society, American Arbitration Association, Delaware State (Chair General Corporation Law Committee 1969-74; President 1982-83; Alternate Dispute Resolution Committee; General Corporation Law Section; Intellectual Property Law Section; Litigation Section; Lawyer Conduct Committee) and American (Chair Program Committee 1984-87, Officer since 1991, Chair 1994-95 and Council Member Section of Business Law; Chair Commission on Ethics 2000 since 1997; Standing Committee on Professional Discipline; Section of Litigation) Bar Associations. Recipient Dartmouth College Class of 1954 Award Dec 1995, Lewis F. Powell, Jr. Award for Professionalism and Ethics American Inns of Court Foundation Oct 1996, St. Thomas More Society Award and ACCA Award. Legal Officer and Captain Air Force Reserves 1957-63 and Inactive Reserve 1963-68 Delaware Air National Guard. Director Beneficial Corporation 1979-92. Co-chair Governor's Committee on Criminal Law Revision 1965-68. Chair Governor's Task Force on Reorganization of Executive Branch Delaware State Government 1969-71. Director Wilmington Rotary Club 1975-77. Trustee University of Delaware 1976-92. Vice Chair Presidential Search Committee University of Delaware 1988-89. Former Senior Warden and Vestry Member Cathedral Church of St. John. Member U.S. Supreme Court Historical Society. Enjoys golfing, tennis, fly fishing, skiing, hiking, music, reading, horseback riding and writing.

Office: Carvel State Building, 11th Floor, 820 North French Street, Wilmington 19801.

Telephone: (302) 577-8700.

WALLS, William J., Jr. *(Associate Judge, Delaware Family Court Kent County)* Appointed by Governor Michael N. Castle to term beginning Sept 1, 1992. Term expires Sept 1, 2004. Born July 1957.

Office: 400 Court Street, Dover 19901.

Telephone: (302) 739-6560.

WALRATH, Mary F. *(Judge, United States Bankruptcy Court District of Delaware)* Appointed by U.S. Court of Appeals Third Circuit judges to term beginning Sept 9, 1998. Term expires Sept 2012.

Office: Marine Midland Building, 824 North Market Street, Wilmington 19801.

Telephone: (302) 252-2929.

WALSH, Joseph T. *(Justice, Delaware Supreme Court)* Appointed by Governor Michael N. Castle Sept 30, 1985. Reappointed 1997, current term expires Nov 21, 2009. Born May 1930. Educated at La Salle College B.A. with honors 1952 and Georgetown University Law Center LL.B. 1954. Admitted to practice District of Columbia 1954 and Delaware 1955. In legal practice Wilmington 1958-72. Associate Judge, Delaware Superior Court New Castle County 1972-84. Vice Chancellor, Delaware Court of Chancery 1984-85.

Office: Carvel State Office Building, 11th Floor, 820 North French Street, Wilmington 19801.

Telephone: (302) 577-8690.

WALSH, Peter J. *(Chief Judge, United States Bankruptcy Court District of Delaware)* Appointed by U.S. Court of Appeals Third Circuit judges. Chief Judge since Sept 9, 1998.

Office: Marine Midland Building, 824 North Market Street, Wilmington 19801.

Telephone: (302) 252-2925.

WASERSTEIN, Aida *(Associate Judge, Delaware Family Court New Castle County)* Appointed by Governor Thomas R. Carper to term beginning Oct 20, 1995. Term expires Oct 20, 2007. Born Feb 1948. Educated at Bryn Mawr College B.A. 1971 and University of Pennsylvania Law School J.D. 1973. Admitted to practice District of Columbia 1973, Pennsylvania 1973, Delaware 1976, U.S. District Court District of Delaware 1977 and U.S. Supreme Court 1980.

Member The Delaware State Bar Association (Former Secretary, Women and the Law, Family Law, Labor Law Sections). Recipient New Lawyer Award for Distinguished Service from The Delaware State Bar Association 1985 and award from Delaware Region National Conference of Christians and Jews April 1995. Democrat. Chair Delaware Human Relations Commission 1994-95.

Office: 500 North King Street, Suite 9510, Wilmington 19801.

Telephone: (302) 255-0316.

WELCH, Charles W., III *(Associate Judge, Delaware Court of Common Pleas Kent County)* Appointed by governor. Born Wilmington Delaware Jan 22, 1959. Educated at University of Delaware B.S.A.C. 1981 and Villanova University J.D. 1984. Admitted to practice Delaware 1985 and Pennsylvania 1985.

Republican. State Representative 1994-2000 and House Majority Whip 1996-2000. Personal Statement or Quote: "Make sure to have an understanding so that there are no misunderstandings."

Office: 38 The Green, Dover 19901.

Telephone: (302) 739-4618.

WELCH, John K. *(Associate Judge, Delaware Court of Common Pleas New Castle County)* Assumed office May 1, 1998. Term expires June 17, 2008. Born Columbus Ohio May 1953. Roman Catholic. Educated at George Washington University B.B.A. 1975 and Widener University School of Law J.D. 1979. Law Clerk to Delaware State Department of Justice. Admitted to prac-

WELCH, JOHN K.—*Continued*

tice Delaware 1982, Pennsylvania 1982, U.S. District Court District of Delaware 1982 and U.S. Court of Appeals Third Circuit 1987. Associate Judge, Wilmington Municipal Court June 17, 1996 to April 30, 1998, appointed by Governor Thomas R. Carper.

Deputy Attorney General State of Delaware 1983-96. Member Delaware Judicial Conference, American Judges Association and American Bar Association. Speaker on Freedom of Information Act, Administrative Law and Civil Litigation The Delaware State Bar Association. Attended Special Court Jurisdiction The National Judicial College. Democrat. Former Staff Assistant Senator Joseph R. Biden, Jr. Enjoys racquetball and golf.

Office: 11800 New Castle County Courthouse, 500 North King Street, Wilmington 19801-3734.

Telephone: (302) 255-0858.

WITHAM, William L., Jr. *(Associate Judge, Delaware Superior Court Kent County)* Appointed by Governor Thomas R. Carper to term beginning Feb 18, 1999. Term expires 2011. Born Dayton Ohio Aug 10, 1947. Protestant. Educated at University of Delaware B.A. 1970 and University of Maryland J.D. 1973. Member Omicron Delta Kappa. Admitted to practice Pennsylvania 1975 and Delaware 1976. In legal practice Dover Delaware 1975-1999.

Member Board of Bar Examiners 1992-96, U.S. Third Circuit Merit Selection Screening Committee 1993 and Governor's Magistrate Screening Committee 1993-98. Member The Delaware State (Bankruptcy Subcommittee 1992-98, Professional Guidance Committee 1995-98, Commercial Law Subcommittee 1998), Pennsylvania and American (Committee on Business Bankruptcy 1993-98, Committee on Credit Union 1993-98) Bar Associations. Recipient Outstanding Citizen Award from Central Delaware Branch YMCA 1987. U.S. Army 1973-74. Colonel Delaware National Guard. Board of Managers Central Delaware Branch YMCA 1978-95. President Central Delaware Committee on Alcohol and Drug Abuse, Inc. 1980-99. Member 1992-93 and Chairman 1993-99 Dover Parking Authority. Director 1992-95 and Legal Advisor 1995-99 Delaware Regional Ballet Company. Member Downtown Dover Development Corporation 1993-99. Trustee Delaware Technical and Community College 1996-99. Member Presbyterian Church of Dover (Elder since 1992) and Dover Kiwanis Club (Past President).

Office: 38 The Green, Dover 19901.

Telephone: (302) 739-5332.

E-mail address: wwitham-jr@state.de.us

DISTRICT OF COLUMBIA

UNITED STATES DISTRICT COURT OF THE DISTRICT OF COLUMBIA

The United States District Court of the District of Columbia has the same jurisdiction as the other U.S. District Courts plus jurisdiction of all laws applicable exclusively to the District of Columbia which are joined in the same indictment or information with a federal offense. For further descriptive information refer to the United States Courts section.

Chief Judge
Thomas F. Hogan

Judges

Royce C. Lamberth	Gladys Kessler
Ricardo Manuel Urbina	Paul L. Friedman
Emmet G. Sullivan	James Robertson
Colleen Kollar-Kotelly	Henry H. Kennedy, Jr.
Richard W. Roberts	Ellen Segal Huvelle
Reggie B. Walton	John D. Bates
Richard J. Leon	Rosemary M. Collyer

Senior Judges

William Benson Bryant	Thomas A. Flannery
Louis F. Oberdorfer	John Garrett Penn
Norma Holloway Johnson	Thomas P. Jackson

Clerk
Nancy Mayer-Whittington
1834 U.S. Courthouse
333 Constitution Avenue N.W.
Washington, D.C. 20001-2802
(202) 354-3510

UNITED STATES MAGISTRATE JUDGES OF THE DISTRICT OF COLUMBIA

Deborah A. Robinson
Alan Kay
John M. Facciola

UNITED STATES BANKRUPTCY COURT OF THE DISTRICT OF COLUMBIA

Judge
S. Martin Teel, Jr.

Bankruptcy Clerk
Denise H. Curtis
4411 U.S. Courthouse
333 Constitution Avenue N.W.
Washington, D.C. 20001-2802
(202) 273-0042

DISTRICT OF COLUMBIA COURT OF APPEALS

The Court of Appeals is the District of Columbia's court of last resort. The court consists of a chief judge and eight associate judges appointed for fifteen-year terms by the President of the United States with approval of the U.S. Senate. Judges are initially appointed based on the recommendations of the District of Columbia Judicial Nominating Commission; reappointments are based on the recommendations of the District of Columbia Commission on Judicial Disabilities and Tenure. The chief judge is designated by the Judicial Nominating Commission from among the active judges for a four-year term. Retirement is usually at age seventy-four; however, senior judges may serve by assignment.

The court has jurisdiction over appeals from the Superior Court and, to the extent provided by law, jurisdiction to review orders and decisions of administrative agencies of the district. The court has the authority to manage admissions and grievances associated with membership in The District of Columbia Bar. The court's decisions are final regarding nonstatutory common law; however, all decisions concerning statutes of the United States relevant to the District of Columbia may be appealed to the U.S. Supreme Court.

The court sits in three-judge panels rotating within three divisions unless a hearing or rehearing before the court en banc is ordered.

Chief Judge
Annice M. Wagner

Associate Judges

John A. Terry	John M. Steadman
Frank E. Schwelb	Michael W. Farrell
Vanessa Ruiz	Inez Smith Reid
Eric T. Washington	Stephen Glickman

Senior Judges

John W. Kern, III	Warren M. King
Frank Q. Nebeker	Theodore R. Newman, Jr.
William C. Pryor	
James A. Belson	John M. Ferren

Clerk
Garland Pinkston, Jr., Esq.
500 Indiana Avenue N.W.
Washington, D.C. 20001
(202) 879-2725

District of Columbia Court System Executive Officer
Anne B. Wicks
500 Indiana Avenue N.W., Room 1500
Washington, D.C. 20001
(202) 879-1700

SUPERIOR COURT OF THE DISTRICT OF COLUMBIA

The Superior Court is the District of Columbia's court of general jurisdiction. Judges are appointed for fifteen-year terms by the President of the United States with approval of the U.S. Senate. Judges are initially appointed based on the recommendations of the District of Columbia Judicial Nominating Commission; subsequent reappointments are based on the recommendations of the

SUPERIOR COURT OF THE DISTRICT OF COLUMBIA—*Continued*

District of Columbia Commission on Judicial Disabilities and Tenure. The chief judge is designated by the Judicial Nominating Commission from among the active judges to serve a four-year term. Retirement is usually at age seventy-four; however, senior judges may serve by assignment of the chief judge.

The court consists of the following statutory divisions: Civil, Criminal and Probate. The divisions may be further divided into branches as prescribed by Superior Court rule. In 2001, the Family Division was renamed the Family Court.

The court's Civil Division has unlimited jurisdiction of all matters at law or in equity which are not reserved for another court or division. The small claims and conciliation branch has jurisdiction of all claims not exceeding $5,000. The court's Criminal Division has jurisdiction of all criminal cases (including traffic) involving laws applicable to the District of Columbia. The Probate Division has jurisdiction of cases involving the probate of wills and estates. The court also has a Tax Office which has exclusive jurisdiction of appeals for review of tax assessments and hears cases brought by the District of Columbia for imposition of criminal penalties under the statutes relating to taxes. The Family Court has exclusive jurisdiction of cases involving juveniles, child abuse, divorce, custody and support, paternity, adoption, commitment of the mentally ill and other cases as defined by law.

Judges of the court are assigned to the various divisions by the chief judge.

Chief Judge

Rufus G. King, III

Associate Judges

Mary Ellen Abrecht
Geoffrey M. Alprin
Judith Bartnoff
John H. Bayly, Jr.
Ronna L. Beck
Anna Blackburne-Rigsby
James E. Boasberg
Shellie F. Bowers
Patricia A. Broderick
A. Franklin Burgess, Jr.
Zoe Bush
John M. Campbell
Russell F. Canan
Erik Christian
Kaye K. Christian
Jeanette Clark
Natalia Combs Greene
Harold Cushenberry, Jr.
Linda Kay Davis
Rafael Diaz
Herbert B. Dixon, Jr.
Frederick D. Dorsey
Stephanie Duncan-Peters
Mildred M. Edwards
Gerald I. Fisher
Wendell P. Gardner, Jr.
Steffen W. Graae
Brook Hedge
William M. Jackson
J. Ramsey Johnson
Anita Josey-Herring
Ann O'Regan Keary
Noel Anketell Kramer
Neal E. Kravitz
Lynn Leibovitz
Cheryl M. Long
José M. López
Zinora Mitchell-Rankin
Robert E. Morin
Thomas J. Motley
John M. Mott
Hiram E. Puig-Lugo
Michael Lee Rankin
Judith E. Retchin
Robert Isaac Richter
Robert R. Rigsby
Maurice Ross
Lee F. Satterfield
Nan R. Shuker
Mary A. Gooden Terrell
Linda D. Turner
Odessa F. Vincent
Frederick H. Weisberg
Susan R. Winfield
Rhonda Reid Winston
Melvin R. Wright
Joan Zeldon

Senior Judges

Arthur L. Burnett, Sr.
Robert S. Tignor
Fred B. Ugast
Paul R. Webber, III
Henry F. Greene
John R. Hess
Leonard Braman
Stephen F. Eilperin
Tim Murphy
Peter H. Wolf
Eugene N. Hamilton
Stephen G. Milliken
Truman Morrison, III
Bruce D. Beaudin
Margaret A. Haywood
Bruce Stephan Mencher
Gregory E. Mize
George H. Goodrich
Ronald P. Wertheim
Patricia A. Wynn

Clerk

Duane B. Delaney
500 Indiana Avenue N.W.
Room 2500
Washington, D.C. 20001
(202) 879-1400

DISTRICT OF COLUMBIA

ABRECHT, Mary Ellen *(Associate Judge, Superior Court of the District of Columbia)* Appointed by President George Bush to term beginning Sept 14, 1990. Term expires 2005. Born Massachusetts Dec 18, 1945. Episcopalian. Educated at Mount Holyoke College B.A. 1967 and Georgetown University J.D. 1974. Admitted to practice District of Columbia 1975, U.S. Court of Appeals District of Columbia Circuit 1975 and U.S. Supreme Court 1980.

Assistant U.S. Attorney District of Columbia 1975-90. Special Counsel U.S. Sentencing Commission 1986-87. Member American Inns of Court (President Bryant Inn 1997-98), National Association of Women Judges and The District of Columbia Bar (Legal Ethics Committee 1988-90). Police officer Washington D.C. 1968-75.

Office: 500 Indiana Avenue N.W., Washington, D.C. 20001.

Telephone: (202) 879-7834.

ALPRIN, Geoffrey M. *(Associate Judge, Superior Court of the District of Columbia)* Appointed by President Ronald Reagan Nov 24, 1982 to term beginning Jan 7, 1983. Reappointed by President Bill Clinton 1998, current term expires Jan 2013. Currently serves as Presiding Judge Family Court. Born Providence Rhode Island Oct 12, 1939. Educated at University of Pennsylvania A.B. 1961 and Georgetown University Law Center J.D. 1964. Managing Editor Georgetown Law Journal 1962-64. Law Clerk at Large U.S. Court of Appeals District of Columbia Circuit 1964-65. Member Phi Delta Phi. Admitted to practice District of Columbia 1965.

Assistant U.S. Attorney District of Columbia 1965-68. General Counsel District of Columbia Metropolitan Police Department 1971-73. Assistant Director National Institute of Justice 1973-77. Deputy Corporation Counsel in Charge of Criminal Division Washington D.C. 1977-83. Important Decisions: In the matter of Brooks (mental retardation) C.R. 253-81, 111 Daily Washington Law Reporter 1301 July 7, 1983 and U.S. v. Brown (First Amendment) C.R. 10901-83, 112 Daily Washington Law Reporter 441 March 6, 1984. Member The District of Columbia Bar.

Office: 500 Indiana Avenue N.W., Room 3600, Washington, D.C. 20001.

Telephone: (202) 879-1577.

Fax: (202) 879-0116

BARTNOFF, Judith *(Associate Judge, Superior Court of the District of Columbia)* Appointed by President Bill Clinton.

Office: 500 Indiana Avenue N.W., Room 1540, Washington, D.C. 20001.

Telephone: (202) 879-1988.

Fax: (202) 879-0171

BATES, John D. *(Judge, United States District Court District of Columbia)* Appointed for life by President George W. Bush to term beginning Dec 20, 2001. Educated at Wesleyan University 1968 and University of Maryland School of Law J.D. 1976. Law Clerk to Senior Judge Roszel C. Thomsen, U.S. District Court District of Maryland 1976-77.

Office: U.S. Courthouse, 333 Constitution Avenue N.W., Washington, D.C. 20001-2802.

Telephone: (202) 354-3430.

BAYLY, John H., Jr. *(Associate Judge, Superior Court of the District of Columbia)* Appointed by President George Bush to term beginning Sept 10, 1990. Term expires Aug 6, 2005. Born Washington D.C. Jan 26, 1944. Roman Catholic. Educated at Fordham University B.A. with honors 1966 and Harvard Law School J.D. 1969. Phi Beta Kappa. Admitted to practice District of Columbia 1969, U.S. District Court District of Columbia 1969, U.S. Court of Appeals District of Columbia Circuit 1969 and U.S. Supreme Court 1974. In legal practice Washington D.C.

Assistant U.S. Attorney 1971-75 and 1978-85. Counsel U.S. Senate 1975-76. Author "Some Reflections on Legal Services" 21 No. 8 Clearinghouse Review 1988. Honorary member Bar Association of the District of Columbia. Member The Counselors, Lawyers' Club, Bryant American Inns of Court and The District of Columbia Bar. Instructor CLE 1988, 1990 and 1994. Recipient Commendation for representation in litigation from the U.S. Army 1980 and Commendation for representation in litigation from the U.S. Park Service 1983. Former member Legal Services Corporation (President 1989-90). Member John Carroll Society Washington D.C.

Office: 500 Indiana Avenue N.W., Room 1520, Washington, D.C. 20001.

Telephone: (202) 879-7874.

E-mail address: baylyjh@dcsc.gov

BEAUDIN, Bruce D. *(Senior Judge, Superior Court of the District of Columbia)* Appointed by President Ronald Reagan to term beginning Oct 15, 1984. Assumed Senior status, serves by assignment. Born Hartford Connecticut Sept 28, 1939. Roman Catholic. Educated at Holy Cross Seminary A.A. 1959, Fairfield University A.B. with honors 1961 and Georgetown University Law Center J.D. 1964. Admitted to practice Virginia 1964, District of Columbia 1965 and U.S. Supreme Court 1968. Began legal practice Washington D.C. 1965.

Staff Attorney 1964-67 and Director 1968 Public Defender Service. Director Pretrial Services Agency 1968-84.

Office: 500 Indiana Avenue N.W., Room 5520, Washington, D.C. 20001.

Telephone: (202) 879-1575.

Fax: (202) 879-0178

BECK, Ronna L. *(Associate Judge, Superior Court of the District of Columbia)* Appointed by President Bill Clinton to term beginning June 16, 1995. Term expires 2010. Born Pittsburgh Pennsylvania. Educated at University of Michigan B.A. and Yale Law School J.D. 1972. Judicial Clerk to Hon. Theodore R. Newman, Jr., Superior Court of the District of Columbia. In legal practice 1977-95.

Former Court-appointed Mediator Superior Court of

BECK, RONNA L.—*Continued*

the District of Columbia. Staff Attorney Public Defender Service District of Columbia. Deputy Special Counsel to Civil Service Commission. Member The District of Columbia Bar. Volunteer Attorney Neighborhood Legal Services Program. Child-Life Volunteer Children's Hospital.
Office: 500 Indiana Avenue N.W., Room JM-640, Washington, D.C. 20001.
Telephone: (202) 879-1162.
Fax: (202) 879-0175

BELSON, James A. *(Senior Judge, District of Columbia Court of Appeals)* Appointed by President Ronald Reagan to term beginning June 30, 1981. Assumed Senior status, serves by assignment. Born Milwaukee Wisconsin Sept 23, 1931. Catholic. Educated at Georgetown University A.B. cum laude 1953 J.D. 1956 LL.M. 1962. Board of Editors Georgetown Law Journal. Law Clerk to Hon. E. Barrett Prettyman, U.S. Court of Appeals District of Columbia Circuit 1956-57. Member Phi Alpha Delta. Admitted to practice District of Columbia 1956, U.S. Court of Military Appeals 1957, Maryland 1962 and U.S. Supreme Court 1967. In legal practice Washington D.C. 1960-68. Associate Judge, Superior Court of the District of Columbia April 8, 1968 to June 29, 1981, appointed by President Lyndon B. Johnson.
Fellow American Bar Foundation. Member Executive Committee 1982-91 and Director since 1982 Council for Court Excellence. Bencher since 1983 and Bencher Emeritus American Inn of Court VI. First Vice President John Carroll Society 1989-91. Member American Judicature Society (Director 1980-85), Bar Association of the District of Columbia (Chairman Junior Bar 1965-66, Director 1966-67, Chairman Legal Aid Committee 1967-68) and American Bar Association. Member Advisory Committee National Conference on Bail and Criminal Justice 1962-65 and Standing Committee on Civil Legal Aid Judicial Conference of the District of Columbia Circuit 1967-70. Faculty member The National Judicial College 1973-80. Chairman Arbitration Committee District of Columbia Judicial Conference 1979-80. Officer U.S. Army JAGC 1957-60. Member since 1990 and Chairman 1997-99 Board of Directors SHARE D.C. Inc. food program. Member Order of Malta Federal Association since 1980 (Board of Directors since 1988, President 1991-94, Chairman Task Force on Cuba 1994-2000).
Office: 500 Indiana Avenue N.W., Room 5510, Washington, D.C. 20001.
Telephone: (202) 879-2760.

BLACKBURNE-RIGSBY, Anna *(Associate Judge, Superior Court of the District of Columbia)* Appointed by the President.
Office: 500 Indiana Avenue N.W., Room 3540, Washington, D.C. 20001.
Telephone: (202) 879-0055.
Fax: (202) 879-0041

BOASBERG, James E. *(Associate Judge, Superior Court of the District of Columbia)* Appointed by President George W. Bush.
Office: 500 Indiana Avenue N.W., Room JM-430, Washington, D.C. 20001.
Telephone: (202) 879-4886.
Fax: (202) 879-7823

BOWERS, Shellie F. *(Associate Judge, Superior Court of the District of Columbia)* Appointed by the President.
Office: 500 Indiana Avenue N.W., Room 3000, Washington, D.C. 20001.
Telephone: (202) 879-1288.
Fax: (202) 879-0109

BRAMAN, Leonard *(Senior Judge, Superior Court of the District of Columbia)* Appointed by President Richard M. Nixon Nov 1970. Assumed Senior status, serves by assignment. Born Philadelphia Pennsylvania Aug 21, 1925. Jewish. Educated at Temple University B.A. 1949 and University of Virginia LL.B. 1952. Admitted to practice District of Columbia 1953, U.S. District Court District of Columbia 1953, U.S. Court of Appeals District of Columbia Circuit 1954 and U.S. Supreme Court 1959.
Important Decisions: United States v. William Christian et al. (mass murders of the Hanafi Muslims) and The Washington Post Company v. International Printing and Graphic Communications Union, Local No. 6, et al. Member American Judicature Society, State Trial Judges Association, The District of Columbia Bar and American Bar Association. Recipient Bigelow Teaching Fellowship University of Chicago Law School 1954-55. Flight Officer USAS 1943-45.
Office: 500 Indiana Avenue N.W., Room 3440, Washington, D.C. 20001.
Telephone: (202) 879-1440.
Fax: (202) 879-0177

BRODERICK, Patricia A. *(Associate Judge, Superior Court of the District of Columbia)* Appointed by President Bill Clinton.
Office: 500 Indiana Avenue N.W., Room 1410, Washington, D.C. 20001.
Telephone: (202) 879-8345.
Fax: (202) 879-8348

BRYANT, William Benson *(Senior Judge, United States District Court District of Columbia)* Appointed for life by President Lyndon B. Johnson July 1965. Chief Judge April 1977 to Sept 1981. Assumed Senior status, serves by assignment. Born Wetumpka Alabama Sept 18, 1911. Educated at Howard University A.B. 1932 LL.B. 1936. In legal practice Washington D.C. 1954-65. Former Judge, Special Court on Regional Rail Reorganization.
Assistant U.S. Attorney District of Columbia 1951-54. Member Committee on Admissions and Grievances of U.S. District Court District of Columbia 1959-65, District of Columbia Board of Appeals and Review, District of Columbia Special Police Trial Board and American Bar Association. Honorary member National Lawyers Club. U.S. Army 1943-47.
Office: 6309 U.S. Courthouse, 333 Constitution Avenue N.W., Washington, D.C. 20001-2802.
Telephone: (202) 354-3480.

BURGESS, A. Franklin, Jr. *(Associate Judge, Superior Court of the District of Columbia)* Appointed by President Ronald Reagan June 28, 1983 to term beginning Sept 23, 1983. Reappointed by President Bill Clinton 1998, current term expires 2013. Born Greenville South Carolina March 15. Episcopalian. Educated at Princeton University A.B. in History 1965 and Harvard Law School J.D. cum laude 1971. Law Clerk to Hon. Levin Hicks Campbell, U.S. District Court District of

BURGESS, A. FRANKLIN, JR.—*Continued*
Massachusetts 1972 and U.S. Court of Appeals First Circuit 1972-73. Admitted to practice Massachusetts 1973 and District of Columbia 1977. In legal practice 1973-83.

Public Defender 1977-83. Important Decisions: U.S. v. Barber M1535-84, Nov 26, 1984; U.S. v. Phillip Roy, Dec 24, 1985; Jones v. U.S. Dissent 516 A.2d 513, 1986; Donnelly Associates v. D.C. Historic Preservation Review Board No. 84-1594 D.C., Jan 14, 1987; Tenley & Cleveland Park Emergency Committee v. D.C. CA4475-86, June 8, 1987; U.S. v. Williams, etc. M15407-87 and M15516-87, March 31, 1988; Murdock v. Huguley RS1262-85R, Jan 17, 1989; In the Matters of D. H., D.H. N097-89 and N098-89, Aug 1, 1989; U.S. v. Kennedy M15643-89 and M15642-89, Jan 12, 1990; and U.S. v. Smith M772-89, Sept 14, 1990. Member The District of Columbia Bar, Boston and American Bar Associations. Attended Judicial Conference of the District of Columbia. Employed by U.S. Peace Corps 1965-67, Charlotte Country Day School 1968-69 and Time, Inc. 1970-71. Member New England Conservatory of Music and Grace Episcopal Church (Rector Search Committee, Interim Rector Search Committee, Vestry Committee).

Office: 500 Indiana Avenue N.W., Room 5640, Washington, D.C. 20001.
Telephone: (202) 879-1164.
Fax: (202) 879-0118

BURNETT, Arthur L., Sr. *(Senior Judge, Superior Court of the District of Columbia)* Appointed by President Ronald Reagan Nov 30, 1987. Assumed Senior status 1998, serves by assignment. Born 1935. Educated at Howard University B.A. summa cum laude and New York University LL.B. 1958. Associate Research Editor New York University Law Review. Admitted to practice District of Columbia 1958. Magistrate, U.S. District Court District of Columbia June 1969 to Nov 1975 and Jan 1980 to Nov 30, 1987.

Attorney General's Honors Program U.S. Department of Justice 1958-65. Assistant U.S. Attorney 1965-68. Legal Advisor District of Columbia Metropolitan Police Department Dec 1968 to June 1969. Assistant General Counsel Legal Advisory Division U.S. Civil Service Commission 1975-78. Associate General Counsel Office of Personnel Management 1978-80. Author numerous legal articles in law reviews, law journals and other legal publications. Adjunct Professor of Law Catholic University since 1997 and Howard University School of Law since 1998. President National Council of U.S. Magistrates 1983-84 and Prettyman-Leventhal American Inn of Court 1994-95. Member Bar Association of the District of Columbia, National, Federal (Chairman Standing Committee on U.S. Magistrates 1983, Council on the Administration of Justice 1983, Deputy Chairman Council on Federal Litigation 1983, President District of Columbia Chapter 1984) and American (Chairman National Conference of Special Court Judges Judicial Administration Division 1974-75, Secretary Section of Administrative Law and Regulatory Practice 1993-95, Chair Committee on Rules of Criminal Procedure and Evidence Section of Criminal Justice 1993-97, Member Sections: Individual Rights and Responsibilities, Litigation, Tort and Insurance Practice) Bar Associations. Past Lecturer Federal Judicial Center, The National Judicial College and bar association CLE programs on criminal and civil law.

Office: 500 Indiana Avenue N.W., Room JM-680, Washington, D.C. 20001.
Telephone: (202) 879-4883, 879-4627.

BUSH, Zoe *(Associate Judge, Superior Court of the District of Columbia)* Appointed by President Bill Clinton.

Office: 500 Indiana Avenue N.W., Room 2520, Washington, D.C. 20001.
Telephone: (202) 879-0023.
Fax: (202) 879-0173

CAMPBELL, John MacLaughlin *(Associate Judge, Superior Court of the District of Columbia)* Appointed by President Bill Clinton to term beginning Dec 1, 1997. Term expires Nov 12, 2012. Born Wooster Ohio Aug 5, 1953. Educated at Yale University B.A. 1975 J.D. 1981. Editor-in-Chief Yale Law Journal 1980-81. Law Clerk to Hon. Jon O. Newman, U.S. Court of Appeals Second Circuit 1981-82. Admitted to practice District of Columbia 1983 and U.S. Courts of Appeals Fourth 1985, First 1987 and District of Columbia 1995 Circuits. In legal practice Washington D.C. 1982-84.

Trial Attorney Public Integrity Section U.S. Department of Justice 1985-91. Chief Public Corruption Section U.S. Attorney's Office 1991-97. Member The District of Columbia Bar and American Bar Association.

Office: 500 Indiana Avenue N.W., Room 3610, Washington, D.C. 20001.
Telephone: (202) 879-1430.
Fax: (202) 879-0101

CANAN, Russell F. *(Associate Judge, Superior Court of the District of Columbia)* Appointed by President Bill Clinton.

Office: 500 Indiana Avenue N.W., Room 3420, Washington, D.C. 20001.
Telephone: (202) 879-1952.
Fax: (202) 879-0160

CHRISTIAN, Erik *(Associate Judge, Superior Court of the District of Columbia)* Appointed by President George W. Bush.

Office: 500 Indiana Avenue N.W., Room 1020, Washington, D.C. 20001.
Telephone: (202) 879-1760.
Fax: (202) 879-1764

CHRISTIAN, Kaye K. *(Associate Judge, Superior Court of the District of Columbia)* Appointed by President George Bush.

Office: 500 Indiana Avenue N.W., Room 2510, Washington, D.C. 20001.
Telephone: (202) 879-1668.
Fax: (202) 879-0092

CLARK, Jeanette *(Associate Judge, Superior Court of the District of Columbia)* Appointed by President George W. Bush.

Office: 500 Indiana Avenue N.W., Room 2620, Washington, D.C. 20001.
Telephone: (202) 879-0417.
Fax: (202) 879-0430

COLLYER, Rosemary M. *(Judge, United States District Court District of Columbia)* Appointed for life by President George W. Bush to term beginning Jan 2, 2003. Born Port Chester New York 1945. Educated at

COLLYER, ROSEMARY M.—*Continued*

Trinity College B.A. 1968 and University of Denver J.D. 1977. Admitted to practice Colorado 1977 and District of Columbia 1990. In legal practice District of Columbia 1989-2003.

Office: U.S. Courthouse, 333 Constitution Avenue N.W., Washington, D.C. 20001-2802.
Telephone: (202) 354-3560.

COMBS GREENE, Natalia *(Associate Judge, Superior Court of the District of Columbia)* Appointed by President Bill Clinton.

Office: 500 Indiana Avenue N.W., Room JM-660, Washington, D.C. 20001.
Telephone: (202) 879-8350.
Fax: (202) 879-8363

CUSHENBERRY, Harold, Jr. *(Associate Judge, Superior Court of the District of Columbia)* Appointed by President Ronald Reagan.

Office: 500 Indiana Avenue N.W., Room 5610, Washington, D.C. 20001.
Telephone: (202) 879-4866.
Fax: (202) 879-0130

DAVIS, Linda Kay *(Associate Judge, Superior Court of the District of Columbia)* Appointed by President Bill Clinton to term beginning June 19, 1995. Term expires 2010. Educated at Oberlin College 1962-64, University of California at Berkeley B.A. 1968 and Harvard Law School J.D. 1972.

Staff Attorney Public Defender Service Family and Criminal Divisions Superior Court of the District of Columbia 1973-76. Trial Attorney 1976-79, Deputy Chief 1979-84 and Chief 1984-95 Criminal Section Civil Rights Division U.S. Department of Justice. Recipient John Doar Award for exceptional accomplishments and high standards of excellence and dedication in the enforcement of civil rights laws Civil Rights Division U.S. Department of Justice 1993. Recipient Attorney General's Distinguished Service Award June 22, 1995.

Office: 500 Indiana Avenue N.W., Washington, D.C. 20001.
Telephone: (202) 879-0050.

DIAZ, Rafael *(Associate Judge, Superior Court of the District of Columbia)* Appointed by President Bill Clinton.

Office: 500 Indiana Avenue N.W., Room 1600, Washington, D.C. 20001.
Telephone: (202) 879-1125.
Fax: (202) 879-0170

DIXON, Herbert B., Jr. *(Associate Judge, Superior Court of the District of Columbia)* Appointed by President Ronald Reagan to term beginning June 7, 1985. Reappointed by President Bill Clinton to term beginning April 2000, current term expires 2015.

Office: 500 Indiana Avenue N.W., Room 2530, Washington, D.C. 20001.
Telephone: (202) 879-4808.
Fax: (202) 879-0127

DORSEY, Frederick D. *(Associate Judge, Superior Court of the District of Columbia)* Appointed by President George Bush.

Office: 500 Indiana Avenue N.W., Room 1440, Washington, D.C. 20001.
Telephone: (202) 879-7837.
Fax: (202) 879-0138

DUNCAN-PETERS, Stephanie *(Associate Judge, Superior Court of the District of Columbia)* Appointed by President George Bush.

Office: 500 Indiana Avenue N.W., Room 1000, Washington, D.C. 20001.
Telephone: (202) 879-1882.
Fax: (202) 879-0156

EDWARDS, Mildred M. *(Associate Judge, Superior Court of the District of Columbia)* Appointed by the President.

Office: 500 Indiana Avenue N.W., Room 3630, Washington, D.C. 20001.
Telephone: (202) 879-7840.
Fax: (202) 879-0135

EILPERIN, Stephen Francis *(Senior Judge, Superior Court of the District of Columbia)* Appointed by President Ronald Reagan to term beginning June 30, 1983. Reappointed to subsequent term. Assumed Senior status 1998, serves by assignment. Born Brooklyn New York 1937. Educated at Columbia College B.A. and Columbia Law School LL.B. 1963. Editor Columbia Law Review. Law Clerk to Hon. Charles M. Metzner, U.S. District Court Southern District of New York. Kent Scholar. Admitted to practice District of Columbia 1963. In legal practice Washington D.C. 1966-72.

Civil Rights Division 1964-65 and Assistant Section Chief Appellate Section Civil Division 1973-75 U.S. Department of Justice. Assistant General Counsel 1975, Solicitor in Charge of all litigation in Federal Court System 1976-82 and Administrative Judge 1982-83 Nuclear Regulatory Commission. Recipient Presidential Pen for Work on Voting Rights Act of 1965 under Hon. Harold H. Greene, U.S. Department of Justice Outstanding Performance Award and Nuclear Regulatory Commission Distinguished Service Award.

Office: 500 Indiana Avenue N.W., Washington, D.C. 20001.
Telephone: (202) 879-1010.

FACCIOLA, John M. *(Magistrate Judge, United States District Court District of Columbia)* Appointed by U.S. District Court judges to term beginning 1997. Term expires 2005. Educated at College of the Holy Cross A.B. cum laude and Georgetown University Law Center J.D.. In legal practice 1973-82.

Assistant District Attorney New York County 1969-73. Assistant U.S. Attorney District of Columbia 1982-97. Board of Editors Federal Courts Law Review. Adjunct Professor of Law Georgetown University Law Center and Catholic University of America School of Law since 1982. Master and President William B. Bryant Inn of Court. Fellow American Bar Foundation. Past President Indigent Civil Litigation Fund. Board of Directors John Carroll Society. Chair Red Mass Committee.

Office: 1426 U.S. Courthouse, 333 Constitution Avenue N.W., Washington, D.C. 20001-2802.
Telephone: (202) 354-3130.

FARRELL, Michael W. *(Associate Judge, District of Columbia Court of Appeals)* Appointed by President George Bush.

Office: 500 Indiana Avenue N.W., Sixth Floor, Washington, D.C. 20001.
Telephone: (202) 879-2790.

FERREN, John M. *(Senior Judge, District of Columbia Court of Appeals)* Appointed by President Jimmy Carter to term beginning Sept 6, 1977. Reappointed 1992. Assumed Senior status 1999, serves by assignment. Born Kansas City Missouri July 21, 1937. Presbyterian (Elder). Educated at Harvard University A.B. magna cum laude 1959 LL.B. 1962. Member Phi Beta Kappa. Admitted to practice Illinois 1962, Massachusetts 1967 and District of Columbia 1970. Began legal practice Chicago Illinois 1962. In legal practice Washington D.C. 1970-77.

Corporation Counsel District of Columbia 1997-99. Director Legal Service Program, Teaching Fellow and Lecturer on Law Harvard Law School 1966-70. Former Member Chicago Commission on Human Relations (Legislative Subcommittee on Consumer Credit, Committee on New Residents), Washington Lawyer's Committee for Civil Rights Under Law (Executive Committee), Council on Legal Education for Professional Responsibility Inc. (Executive Committee and Board of Directors) and Massachusetts Bar Association (Co-chairman Committee on Legal Services and the Poor). Fellow American Bar Foundation. Member The American Law Institute, The District of Columbia Bar (Disciplinary Board 1972-76) and American Bar Association (Commission on a National Institute of Justice 1972-75, Consortium on Legal Services and the Public 1972-73 and 1976-82, Chairman Special Committee on Public Interest Practice 1976-78). Treasurer and Board of Directors Firman Neighborhood House Chicago 1964-66. Originator and Chairman Church Federation of Greater Chicago Neighborhood Legal Advice Clinics 1964-66. Board of Directors Peoples Development Corporation Washington D.C. 1970-74, The National Resource Center for Consumers of Legal Services 1973-77 and The George A. Wiley Memorial Fund 1974-84. Member National Committee Against Discrimination in Housing 1974-77 (Executive Committee of Legal Advisory Committee) and Steering Committee National Prison Project of the ACLU Foundation 1975-77.

Office: 500 Indiana Avenue N.W., Sixth Floor, Washington, D.C. 20001.

Telephone: (202) 879-2772.

FISHER, Gerald I. *(Associate Judge, Superior Court of the District of Columbia)* Appointed by the President.

Office: 500 Indiana Avenue N.W., Room JM-420, Washington, D.C. 20001.

Telephone: (202) 879-8388.

Fax: (202) 879-8327

FLANNERY, Thomas A. *(Senior Judge, United States District Court District of Columbia)* Appointed for life by President Richard M. Nixon Nov 1971. Assumed Senior status, serves by assignment. Born Washington D.C. May 10, 1918. Educated at Columbus University (now Catholic University of America) LL.B. 1940. Admitted to practice District of Columbia 1940. In legal practice 1962-69. Special Hearing Officer Department of Justice 1964-68.

Assistant U.S. Attorney District of Columbia 1950-62. Nominated by President Nixon as U.S. Attorney District of Columbia 1969. Lecturer Northwestern University School of Law. Fellow American College of Trial Lawyers. Member Judicial Conference of the District of Columbia Circuit, Committee on the Administration of Justice of the Judicial Council and The District of Columbia Bar (Board of Directors). Board of Trustees Legal Aid Agency of District of Columbia. Combat Intelligence Officer USAF 1942-45.

Office: U.S. Courthouse, 333 Constitution Avenue N.W., Washington, D.C. 20001-2802.

Telephone: (202) 354-3300.

FRIEDMAN, Paul L. *(Judge, United States District Court District of Columbia)* Appointed for life by President Bill Clinton to term beginning Aug 1994. Educated at Cornell University 1965 and State University of New York at Buffalo School of Law J.D. 1968. Law Clerk to Hon. Aubrey E. Robinson, Jr., U.S. District Court District of Columbia and Hon. Roger Robb U.S. Court of Appeals District of Columbia Circuit.

Assistant U.S. Attorney District of Columbia 1970-74. Assistant to Solicitor General of the U.S. 1974-76. President The District of Columbia Bar 1986-87. Member Council The American Law Institute. Associate Independent Counsel Iran-Contra Investigation 1987-88.

Office: 6321 U.S. Courthouse, 333 Constitution Avenue N.W., Washington, D.C. 20001-2802.

Telephone: (202) 354-3490.

GARDNER, Wendell P., Jr. *(Associate Judge, Superior Court of the District of Columbia)* Appointed by President George Bush.

Office: 500 Indiana Avenue N.W., Room 1420, Washington, D.C. 20001.

Telephone: (202) 879-1810.

Fax: (202) 879-0418

GLICKMAN, Stephen *(Associate Judge, District of Columbia Court of Appeals)* Appointed by President Bill Clinton to term beginning July 1999. Term expires 2014. Educated at Cornell University A.B. 1969 and Yale Law School J.D. 1973.

Office: 500 Indiana Avenue N.W., Sixth Floor, Washington, D.C. 20001.

Telephone: (202) 879-2740.

GOODRICH, George Herbert *(Senior Judge, Superior Court of the District of Columbia)* Appointed by President Richard M. Nixon to term beginning July 1969. Reappointed by President Jimmy Carter July 1979. Assumed Senior status, serves by assignment. Born Charleston West Virginia June 19, 1925. Presbyterian. Educated at Williams College B.A. 1949 and University of Virginia LL.B. 1952 J.D. 1977. Admitted to practice District of Columbia 1952 and Maryland 1958. Began legal practice Washington D.C. 1952.

Author "Eyewitness Testimony in Criminal Cases" Judges Journal 1975. Important Decisions: U.S. v. Charles Pender (directed government to choose between voluntary and involuntary charges in a single count) Cr. No. 69071-73, 1974; U.S. v. Jerome Burnett (procedure by which defendant can obtain prosecution evidence) Cr. No. 73588-73, 1974; U.S. v. Jackson (held that expert testimony on human visual perception and eyewitness testimony is not a recognized subfield of psychology) Cr. No. 16158-74, 1975; U.S. v. Lawrence Stewart (upholding conviction of aiding and abetting in murder case) Cr. No. 45659-75, 1976; McIntosh v. Washington (upheld constitutionality of handgun law) C.A. 11262-76, 1977; Zane v. Perper (held innkeeper to higher duty of care to guest than landlord to tenant) C.A. No. 3405-76, 1977; U.S. v. Stevens (upheld constitutionality of the sodomy statute) Cr. No. 47571-72; and Board of Directors v. 2029 Connecticut Avenue (interpretation of D.C. condominium statute) C.A. 16996-80. Instructor Ameri-

GOODRICH, GEORGE HERBERT—*Continued*

can Institute of Banking 1964-68, American University 1968-72 and St. Albans School 1974-84. Member Bar Association of the District of Columbia (Secretary 1962-69), The District of Columbia Bar and Unified Bar of the District of Columbia. Participant and faculty member National College of the State Judiciary. Recipient Superior Court Award for Service as Presiding Judge of Family Division 1981 and Juvenile Restitution Program Award for Outstanding Service to Youth 1981. USN 1943-46. Republican. Enjoys photography, tennis, swimming, ice skating, Civil War history and teaching law courses.

Office: 500 Indiana Avenue N.W., Room 5520, Washington, D.C. 20001.

Telephone: (202) 879-1055.

GRAAE, Steffen W. *(Associate Judge, Superior Court of the District of Columbia)* Appointed by President Ronald Reagan July 2, 1982 to term beginning Aug 31, 1982. Reappointed 1997, current term expires 2012. Born Copenhagen Denmark Sept 25, 1940. Educated at Yale University B.A. 1962, Oxford University, England M.A. 1969 and Georgetown University J.D. 1973. Law Clerk to Hon. John Garrett Penn, Superior Court of the District of Columbia 1974. Admitted to practice District of Columbia 1973.

Author "Disorderly Conduct & Related Minor Offenses" 1975 and "District of Columbia Statutory & Case Law Annotated to the Federal Rules of Evidence" Lexis Nexis Matthew Bender 2002. Adjunct Professor Georgetown University Law Center 1975-76. Member Bar Association of the District of Columbia, The District of Columbia Bar and American Bar Association.

Office: 500 Indiana Avenue N.W., Washington, D.C. 20001.

Telephone: (202) 879-1244.

GREENE, Henry F. *(Senior Judge, Superior Court of the District of Columbia)* Appointed by President Ronald Reagan to term beginning April 14, 1981. Reappointed 1996. Assumed Senior status 2001, serves by assignment. Born New York New York June 17, 1941. Educated at Harvard University A.B. cum laude 1963 and Columbia University LL.B. 1966. Law Clerk to Hon. William B. Bryant, U.S. District Court District of Columbia 1966-68. Admitted to practice District of Columbia 1967 and U.S. Supreme Court 1970. Began legal practice Washington D.C. 1967.

Assistant U.S. Attorney District of Columbia 1968-81. Editor "Criminal Jury Instructions for the District of Columbia" Bar Association of the District of Columbia 2nd ed. 1972, 3rd ed. 1978. Faculty member The National Judicial College 1987-93. Member American Bar Association 1974-80. Recipient Younger Lawyer Award from Federal Bar Association 1975, Assistant U.S. Attorneys Association Harold J. Sullivan Award 1978 and Marvin E. Preis Award from Bar Association of the District of Columbia Young Lawyers Section 1978.

Office: 500 Indiana Avenue N.W., Room 2440, Washington, D.C. 20001.

Telephone: (202) 879-1455.

HAMILTON, Eugene N. *(Senior Judge, Superior Court of the District of Columbia)* Appointed by President Richard M. Nixon 1970. Reappointed to subsequent terms. Former Chief Judge. Assumed Senior status, serves by assignment. Born 1932. Educated at University of Illinois B.A. LL.B. 1959.

Former Senior Trial Attorney U.S. Department of Justice. Program Chairman Georgetown University Law Center CLE Division. Active in community programs for children and senior citizens. Foster parent.

Office: 500 Indiana Avenue N.W., Room 5520, Washington, D.C. 20001.

Telephone: (202) 879-1727.

Fax: (202) 879-0410

HAYWOOD, Margaret Austin *(Senior Judge, Superior Court of the District of Columbia)* Appointed by President Richard M. Nixon April 1972 to term beginning July 20, 1972. Assumed Senior status 1985, serves by assignment. Born Knoxville Tennessee Oct 8, 1912. Protestant. Educated at Robert H. Terrell Law School LL.B. with honors 1940. Awarded honorary Doctor of Humanics Elmhurst College May 1974, honorary Doctor of Humane Letters Carleton College June 1975 and honorary LL.D. Catawba College Dec 1976 and Doane College May 1979. Member Gamma Delta Epsilon and Lambda Kappa Mu. Admitted to practice District of Columbia 1942, U.S. District Court District of Columbia 1942, U.S. Court of Appeals District of Columbia Circuit 1942 and U.S. Supreme Court 1945. In legal practice Washington D.C. 1942-72.

Consultant U.S. Department of Education. Member American Judicature Society, Women's Bar Association, Bar Association of the District of Columbia, Washington and American Bar Associations. Named one of America's Outstanding Women by National Council of Negro Women, Inc. June 1951, Woman of the Year by The Barristers' Wives, Inc. April 1954 and Woman Lawyer of the Year by Women's Bar Association April 1972. Listed in *Who's Who of American Women* since 1958, *The International Two Thousand Women of Achievement* 1972, *Who's Who in Government* 1972-73, *Who's Who in Religion* 1975, *Who's Whom Among Black Americans* 1977-78 and *Who's Who in the South and Southeast.* Recipient citation for effective contribution to the legal field and to good government from National Bar Association July 1968, Certificate of Appreciation for contributions to the administration of justice from Bar Association of the District of Columbia Dec 1978, Certificate of Appreciation for Advancement of Human Rights and Fundamental Freedoms from Capital Area Division United Nations Association Dec 1979, citation for distinction as jurist, civil rights leader, educator and humanitarian from Washington and Vicinity Federation of Women's Clubs May 1980, award for outstanding leadership and service as an attorney and jurist from Women Lawyers Division Greater Washington Area Chapter National Bar Association April 1982 and Martin Luther King, Jr. Service Award commending legal and humanitarian services from The Student Bar Association Howard University School of Law March 1983. Elected to D.C. Women's Commission Hall of Fame March 1992. Licensed Real Estate Broker. Republican. Charter Member District of Columbia Council 1967-72 (Former Chairman Manpower, Economic Development and Labor Committee). Alternate Member Board of Directors Washington Metropolitan Area Transit Authority Jan 1970 to July 1972. Former Board of Directors United Givers Fund, Health and Welfare Council, Washington Urban League, Inc., Southeast Neighborhood House, Family & Child Services of Washington D.C., Girl Scouts of the Nation's Capital and Council of Churches of Greater

HAYWOOD, MARGARET AUSTIN—*Continued*

Washington. Former Member Executive Council United Church of Christ, Inc. and National Board of Congregational Christian Churches. Moderator (First Woman) United Church of Christ 1973-75. Former Member Mayor's Economic Development Committee, Mayor's Manpower Advisory Committee and District of Columbia Commission on the Status of Women. Board Member D.C. Women's Commission for Crime Prevention (Past Treasurer). Charter Member and Former Parliamentarian Executive Women in Government. Member Zonta Club of Washington D.C., Transit Officials Emeritus and People's Congregational Church. Enjoys collecting owl figurines and working crossword puzzles.

Office: 500 Indiana Avenue N.W., Room 5520, Washington, D.C. 20001.

Telephone: (202) 879-4633.

Fax: (202) 879-0178

HEDGE, Brook *(Associate Judge, Superior Court of the District of Columbia)* Appointed by President George Bush.

Office: 500 Indiana Avenue N.W., Room 2020, Washington, D.C. 20001.

Telephone: (202) 879-1886.

Fax: (202) 879-0158

HESS, John R. *(Senior Judge, Superior Court of the District of Columbia)* Appointed by the President. Assumed Senior status, serves by assignment.

Office: 500 Indiana Avenue N.W., Room 2440, Washington, D.C. 20001.

Telephone: (202) 879-1420.

Fax: (202) 879-0179

HOGAN, Thomas F. *(Chief Judge, United States District Court District of Columbia)* Appointed for life by President Ronald Reagan to term beginning Aug 1982. Chief Judge since June 19, 2001. Educated at Georgetown University A.B. 1960 J.D. 1966 and George Washington University Masters Program 1960-62. St. Thomas More Fellow. Law Clerk to Hon. William B. Jones, U.S. District Court District of Columbia 1966-67.

Adjunct Professor of Law Georgetown University Law Center. Member since 2000 and Executive Committee since 2001 Judicial Conference of the U.S. Member Executive Committee U.S. District Court District of Columbia. Chair Courtroom Technology Subcommittee. Master Prettyman-Leventhal Inn of Court. Board Member Federal Judicial Center. Counsel National Commission for the Reform of Federal Criminal Laws 1967-68.

Office: 4435 U.S. Courthouse, 333 Constitution Avenue N.W., Washington, D.C. 20001-2802.

Telephone: (202) 354-3420.

HUVELLE, Ellen Segal *(Judge, United States District Court District of Columbia)* Appointed for life by President Bill Clinton to term beginning Jan 12, 2000. Educated at Wellesley College B.A. 1970, Yale University M.C.P. 1972 and Boston College Law School J.D. 1975. Law Clerk to Chief Justice Edward F. Hennessey, Massachusetts Supreme Judicial Court. Associate Judge, Superior Court of the District of Columbia Sept 1990 to 1999, appointed by President George Bush.

Former Instructor in Trial Practice Trial Advocacy Workshop Harvard Law School and University of Virginia School of Law. Fellow American Bar Association. Member Edward Bennett Williams Inn of Court.

Office: U.S. Courthouse, 333 Constitution Avenue N.W., Washington, D.C. 20001-2802.

Telephone: (202) 354-3230.

JACKSON, Thomas P. *(Senior Judge, United States District Court District of Columbia)* Appointed for life by President Ronald Reagan to term beginning June 1982. Assumed Senior status Jan 31, 2002, serves by assignment. Educated at Dartmouth College 1958 and Harvard Law School 1964.

Past President The District of Columbia Bar. USN.

Office: 2429 U.S. Courthouse, 333 Constitution Avenue N.W., Washington, D.C. 20001-2802.

Telephone: (202) 354-3310.

JACKSON, William M. *(Associate Judge, Superior Court of the District of Columbia)* Appointed by President George Bush.

Office: 500 Indiana Avenue N.W., Room 2630, Washington, D.C. 20001.

Telephone: (202) 879-1909.

Fax: (202) 879-0191

JOHNSON, J. Ramsey *(Associate Judge, Superior Court of the District of Columbia)* Appointed by the President.

Office: 500 Indiana Avenue N.W., Room 3020, Washington, D.C. 20001.

Telephone: (202) 879-8306.

Fax: (202) 879-8342

JOHNSON, Norma Holloway *(Senior Judge, United States District Court District of Columbia)* Appointed for life by President Jimmy Carter May 12, 1980 to term beginning July 8, 1980. Former Chief Judge. Assumed Senior status June 18, 2001, serves by assignment. Born Lake Charles Louisiana. Protestant. Educated at District of Columbia Teachers College B.S. magna cum laude 1955 and Georgetown University J.D. 1962. Admitted to practice District of Columbia 1962. Associate Judge, Superior Court of the District of Columbia 1970-80, appointed by President Richard M. Nixon.

With U.S. Department of Justice Washington D.C. 1963-67. Assistant Corporation Counsel Washington D.C. 1967-70. Member National Association of Women Judges, The District of Columbia Bar, Washington, Women's, National and American Bar Associations.

Office: U.S. Courthouse, 333 Constitution Avenue N.W., Washington, D.C. 20001-2802.

Telephone: (202) 354-3500.

JOSEY-HERRING, Anita *(Associate Judge, Superior Court of the District of Columbia)* Appointed by President Bill Clinton to term beginning 1998. Term expires 2013.

Office: 500 Indiana Avenue N.W., Room 2640, Washington, D.C. 20001.

Telephone: (202) 879-1574.

Fax: (202) 879-0107

KAY, Alan *(Magistrate Judge, United States District Court District of Columbia)* Appointed by U.S. District Court judges to term beginning Sept 1991. Reappointed Sept 1999, current term expires Sept 2007. Educated at George Washington University B.A. 1957 J.D. 1959. Law Clerk to Hon. Alexander Holtzoff and Hon. William B. Jones, U.S. District Court District of Columbia. In legal practice District of Columbia 1967-1991.

KAY, ALAN—*Continued*

Attorney Public Defender Service. With U.S. Attorneys Office.

Office: 1130 U.S. Courthouse, 333 Constitution Avenue N.W., Washington, D.C. 20001-2802.

Telephone: (202) 354-3030.

KEARY, Ann O'Regan *(Associate Judge, Superior Court of the District of Columbia)* Appointed by President George Bush.

Office: 500 Indiana Avenue N.W., Room 2430, Washington, D.C. 20001.

Telephone: (202) 879-1863.

Fax: (202) 879-0149

KENNEDY, Henry H., Jr. *(Judge, United States District Court District of Columbia)* Appointed for life by President Bill Clinton. Born Columbia South Carolina Feb 22, 1948. Methodist. Educated at Princeton University A.B. 1970 and Harvard University J.D. 1973. Admitted to practice District of Columbia 1973. Member Sigma Pi Phi, Epsilon Boule and Barristers. Former Magistrate, U.S. District Court District of Columbia, appointed by U.S. District Court judges to term beginning April 22, 1976. Former Associate Judge, Superior Court of the District of Columbia, appointed by the President.

With U.S. Attorney's Office at Washington D.C. 1973-76. Important Decisions: University of the District of Columbia Faculty Assn. v. Board of Trustees 994 F. Supp. 1 D.D.C. 1998, Joo v. Japan 172 F. Supp. 2d 52 D.D.C. 2001 and National Coalition to Save Our Mall v. Babbitt 161 F. Supp. 2d 14 D.D.C. 2001. Fellow American Bar Foundation. Member The American Law Institute, Bar Association of the District of Columbia, The District of Columbia Bar, Washington and Federal Bar Associations. Trustee Princeton University. Enjoys tennis.

Office: 4317 U.S. Courthouse, 333 Constitution Avenue N.W., Washington, D.C. 20001-2802.

Telephone: (202) 354-3350.

KERN, John W., III *(Senior Judge, District of Columbia Court of Appeals)* Appointed by President Lyndon B. Johnson 1968. Assumed Senior status 1984, serves by assignment. Educated at Princeton University and Harvard Law School. Law Clerk to Chief Judge, U.S. Court of Appeals District of Columbia Circuit.

Former Assistant U.S. Attorney. Former Assistant to Assistant Attorney General Fred M. Vinson, Jr., Criminal Division U.S. Department of Justice.

Office: 500 Indiana Avenue N.W., Sixth Floor, Washington, D.C. 20001.

Telephone: (202) 879-2754.

KESSLER, Gladys *(Judge, United States District Court District of Columbia)* Appointed for life by President Bill Clinton June 18, 1994. Educated at Cornell University B.A. and Harvard University LL.B. Former Associate Judge, Superior Court of the District of Columbia, appointed by President Jimmy Carter to term beginning June 3, 1977.

Former Appellate Attorney National Labor Relations Board. Co-author with Edward Berlin and Anthony A. Roisman "Public Interest Law" George Washington L. Rev. May 1970 and "Consumers of the World Unite" chapter in *With Justice for Some* 1970. Author "The Economics of Public Interest Litigation" Litigation Magazine 1976, "The Value of Sisterhood on the Bench" Trial Magazine Aug 1983, "Affirmative Action Can Mean the Best Person for the Job" Judges' Journal Fall 1983, "Crisis in Child Support" Trial Magazine Dec 1984 and Forward on National Association of Women Judges Symposium Issue Golden Gate Law Review Feb 1984. Assistant Professorial Lecturer George Washington University Law School 1971-73. Vice President 1979-81 and President 1982-83 National Association of Women Judges. Board of Directors National Center for State Courts. Member American Judicature Society and The District of Columbia Bar (Chairperson Subcommittee on Procedures and Subcommittee on the Code, member Ethics Committee 1974-77 and Nominating Committee 1976). Appointed member Advisory Committee on Procedures of the U.S. Court of Appeals District of Columbia Circuit 1976-77. Guest Lecturer Civil Rights Commission, Brookings Institution, American University Law School and Harvard Law School. Member Committee on Arrangements "Racism, Sexism and Sexual Preference in the Practice of Law" Thirteenth Judicial Conference of the District of Columbia June 16-17, 1988. Recipient Woman Lawyer of the Year Award from Women's Bar Association May 23, 1983 and Judicial Excellence Award from Trial Lawyers of Washington May 20, 1987. Founding President Women's Legal Defense Fund 1971 (Vice President 1976, Board of Directors 1972-73 and 1975). Member American Civil Liberties Union Screening Committee 1973-77, Women Judges' Fund for Justice, Committee for Public Advocacy Executive Committee and League of Women Voters Education Fund Legal Advisory Panel.

Office: U.S. Courthouse, 333 Constitution Avenue N.W., Washington, D.C. 20001-2802.

Telephone: (202) 354-3440.

KING, Rufus G., III *(Chief Judge, Superior Court of the District of Columbia)* Appointed by President Ronald Reagan July 17, 1984 to term beginning Nov 2, 1984. Reappointed Nov 2, 1999, current term expires Nov 2014. Deputy Presiding Judge 1994-97 and Presiding Judge 1998-99 Civil Division. Born New Haven Connecticut June 16, 1942. Episcopalian. Educated at Princeton University A.B. 1966 and Georgetown University Law Center J.D. 1971. Law Clerk to Hon. William C. Pryor, Superior Court of the District of Columbia 1968-71. Member Phi Alpha Delta and Barristers. Admitted to practice District of Columbia 1971, U.S. Supreme Court 1975 and Maryland 1984. In legal practice Washington D.C. 1971-84.

Chair Superior Court Judges Committee on Technology 1987-2000, Superior Court Committee on Child Support Guidelines 1988-89 and District of Columbia Domestic Violence Coordinating Council 1995-97. Former Member The Association of Trial Lawyers of America, Superior Court Trial Lawyers Association and NASD Arbitration Panel. National Panel of Arbitrators American Arbitration Association. Member American Inns of Court (Emeritus), The American Law Institute, American Judges Association, SPIDR, Bar Association of District of Columbia, The District of Columbia Bar (Member 1977-84 and Chair 1980-82 Fee Arbitration Board, Chair Election Committee 1979, member Court System Study Committee 1981-83, Chair ad hoc Committee on Court Annexed Arbitration), Maryland State Bar Association, Inc. and American Bar Association. Instructor "Introduction to Computers" The National Judicial College Nov 1987. Panelist "Mediation" National Conference on Dis-

KING, RUFUS G., III—*Continued*
pute Resolution and State Courts Nov 1988. Enjoys reading, music, running and traveling.
Office: 500 Indiana Avenue N.W., Washington, D.C. 20001.
Telephone: (202) 879-1600.
E-mail address: arking3@aol.com

KING, Warren M. *(Senior Judge, District of Columbia Court of Appeals)* Appointed by President George Bush. Assumed Senior status Nov 1998, serves by assignment. Former Associate Judge, Superior Court of the District of Columbia.
Office: 500 Indiana Avenue N.W., Sixth Floor, Washington, D.C. 20001.
Telephone: (202) 626-8871.

KOLLAR-KOTELLY, Colleen C. *(Judge, United States District Court District of Columbia)* Appointed for life by President Bill Clinton. Born New York New York. Educated at Catholic University of America B.A. in English 1965 J.D. 1968. Law Clerk to Hon. Catherine B. Kelly, District of Columbia Court of Appeals. Former Associate Judge, Superior Court of the District of Columbia, appointed by President Ronald Reagan Oct 23, 1984.
Staff Attorney Department of Justice Criminal Division three years. Former Chief Legal Counsel St. Elizabeth's Hospital (currently an agency of Department of Health and Human Services). Member Bar Association of the District of Columbia. Guest speaker for American Psychiatric Association, American Academy of Psychiatry and the Law, Washington Psychiatric Society and the District of Columbia Mental Health Association. Recipient Certificate of Appreciation from St. Elizabeth's Hospital 1981 and Award for Meritorious Achievement from the Alcohol, Drug Abuse and Mental Health Administration Department of Health and Human Services 1984.
Office: 4323 U.S. Courthouse, 333 Constitution Avenue N.W., Washington, D.C. 20001-2802.
Telephone: (202) 354-3340.

KRAMER, Noel Anketell *(Associate Judge, Superior Court of the District of Columbia)* Appointed by President Ronald Reagan to term beginning Oct 18, 1984. Reappointed by President Bill Clinton Oct 1999, current term expires Oct 2014. Born Bay City Michigan Nov 22, 1945. Episcopalian. Educated at Vassar College B.A. cum laude 1967 and University of Michigan J.D. cum laude 1971. Note and Comment Editor Michigan Law Review 1970-71. Admitted to practice District of Columbia 1971 and U.S. Supreme Court 1976. In legal practice Washington D.C. 1971-76.
Assistant U.S. Attorney District of Columbia 1976-84. Member District of Columbia Courts Judicial Ethics Committee 1992-97. Delegate National Conference of State Trial Judges American Bar Association. Fellow American Bar Foundation. Member The American Law Institute, National Association of Women Judges (Treasurer 1995-96, President 2000-01, Secretary), Women's Bar Association of the District of Columbia and The District of Columbia Bar (Committee on Civility in the Profession). Member Medical Ethics Committee Episcopal Diocese of Washington D.C.
Office: 500 Indiana Avenue N.W., Room 3530, Washington, D.C. 20001.
Telephone: (202) 879-1446.
Fax: (202) 879-0124

KRAVITZ, Neal E. *(Associate Judge, Superior Court of the District of Columbia)* Appointed by President Bill Clinton.
Office: 500 Indiana Avenue N.W., Room 3620, Washington, D.C. 20001.
Telephone: (202) 879-8353.
Fax: (202) 879-4775

LAMBERTH, Royce C. *(Judge, United States District Court District of Columbia)* Appointed for life by President Ronald Reagan to term beginning Nov 1987. Educated at University of Texas School of Law LL.B. 1967.
Assistant U.S. Attorney and Chief Civil Division 1978-87 District of Columbia. Captain U.S. Army JAGC 1968-74.
Office: 4434 U.S. Courthouse, 333 Constitution Avenue N.W., Washington, D.C. 20001-2802.
Telephone: (202) 354-3380.

LEIBOVITZ, Lynn *(Associate Judge, Superior Court of the District of Columbia)* Appointed by President George W. Bush.
Office: 500 Indiana Avenue N.W., Room JM-610, Washington, D.C. 20001.
Telephone: (202) 879-0441.
Fax: (202) 879-0444

LEON, Richard J. *(Judge, United States District Court District of Columbia)* Appointed for life by President George W. Bush to term beginning March 20, 2002. Educated at College of the Holy Cross A.B. 1971, Suffolk University Law School J.D. cum laude 1974 and Harvard Law School LL.M. 1981. In legal practice District of Columbia 1989-2002.
Office: U.S. Courthouse, 333 Constitution Avenue N.W., Washington D.C. 20001-2802.
Telephone: (202) 354-3580.

LONG, Cheryl M. *(Associate Judge, Superior Court of the District of Columbia)* Appointed by the President.
Office: 500 Indiana Avenue N.W., Room 1630, Washington, D.C. 20001.
Telephone: (202) 879-1200.
Fax: (202) 879-0134

LÓPEZ, José M. *(Associate Judge, Superior Court of the District of Columbia)* Appointed by President George Bush April 17, 1990. Term expires 2005. Born Dominican Republic. Educated at Middlebury College B.A. 1973 and Suffolk University Law School J.D. 1977. Associate Editor Suffolk University Law Review. Admitted to practice District of Columbia, New York and U.S. District Court District of Columbia. In legal practice Washington D.C. 1980-90.
Attorney-Advisor Benefits Review Board U.S. Department of Labor 1977-79. Member District of Columbia Traffic Adjudications Appeals Board 1982-90. Attorney Member District of Columbia Board of Appeals and Review (Chair Hearing Panel) 1987-90. Member Advisory Committee on Probate and Fiduciary Rules Superior Court of the District of Columbia and Mayor's Commission on Latino Community Development. Chair Judicial Education Committee since 1994. Public Speaker The District of Columbia Bar Community Law Program.

LÓPEZ, JOSÉ M.—*Continued*

Member Hispanic Bar Association (Steering Committee). Counsel Anthony Houses, Inc. 1979-80.

Office: 500 Indiana Avenue N.W., Room 3410, Washington, D.C. 20001.

Telephone: (202) 879-7877.

MENCHER, Bruce Stephan *(Senior Judge, Superior Court of the District of Columbia)* Appointed by President Gerald R. Ford to term beginning Oct 14, 1975. Presiding Judge Family Division 1988-90. Assumed Senior status Oct 1, 1991, serves by assignment. Born Washington D.C. May 21, 1935. Educated at George Washington University B.A. 1957 J.D. with honors 1960. Assistant Research Editor George Washington Law Review 1959-60. Member Phi Delta Phi. Admitted to practice District of Columbia 1960 and U.S. Supreme Court 1964. In legal practice Washington D.C. 1969-75.

General Attorney Honors Program Office of the General Counsel Department of Agriculture 1960-61. Assistant Corporation Counsel District of Columbia 1961-67. Attorney-Advisor Office of the General Counsel Bureau for Africa, Agency for International Development 1967-69. Author "Constitutional Law—Court Martial Jurisdiction Over Civilians in Foreign Countries During Peacetime" 28 George Washington L. Rev. 913, 1960; "A Plea to Save the Draft" (humorous) 35 Nos. 8-10 District of Columbia B. Jour. 35 Aug-Oct 1968; "Whenever You're Ready, Miss Hershey" (humorous) 36-37 Nos. 11, 12, 1, 2 District of Columbia B. Jour. 60 Nov-Feb 1969; "Condemnation Enters the Twentieth Century" 38 Nos. 7-10 District of Columbia B. Jour. 48 July-Oct 1971; "Every Lawyer Is Entitled to One Excuse" (humorous) 6 No. 5 District Lawyer May-June 1982; "Jury Instructions—A Weak Link" 7 No. 4 *The Washington Lawyer* March-April 1993; "Civility—A Casualty of Modern Litigation, An Alert to the Bench and Bar" 8 No. 1 *The Washington Lawyer* Sept-Oct 1993; and "Return to Civility" 9 No. 5 *The Washington Lawyer* May-June 1995. Professorial Lecturer on Law George Washington University National Law Center 1982-83. Lecturer on Criminal Justice National Cathedral School/St. Alban's School 1985. Faculty Advisor The National Judicial College 1995. Member George Washington American Inn of Court (President 1999-2000), George Washington Law Association (Executive Committee 1972-77 and Treasurer 1974, Second Vice President 1975, Executive Committee 1976-88 District of Columbia Chapter), Barristers (Executive Committee 1981-82, 1984-85), Bar Association of the District of Columbia (Director 1975 and 1998-2000), The District of Columbia Bar and American Bar Association. President Barrister Inn Phi Delta Phi 1974-75. Recipient Alumni Service Award 1975 and Distinguished Alumni Achievement Award 1987 George Washington University, Judge of the Year Award from the Association of Plaintiffs Trial Attorneys 1983, Samuel Green Award for Distinguished Service to the Washington D.C. Legal Community and Phi Delta Phi Legal Fraternity 1985 and appreciation and recognition awards for work in Family Law and Child Support Enforcement from local bar associations, District of Columbia government and Federal government. General Alumni Governing Board George Washington University 1972-80.

Office: 500 Indiana Avenue N.W., Room 5520, Washington, D.C. 20001.

Telephone: (202) 879-1358.

Fax: (202) 879-0178

MILLIKEN, Stephen G. *(Senior Judge, Superior Court of the District of Columbia)* Appointed by President George Bush. Assumed Senior status, serves by assignment.

Office: 500 Indiana Avenue N.W., Room 5520, Washington, D.C. 20001.

Telephone: (202) 879-1823.

Fax: (202) 879-0410

MITCHELL-RANKIN, Zinora *(Associate Judge, Superior Court of the District of Columbia)* Appointed by President George Bush.

Office: 500 Indiana Avenue N.W., Room 2420, Washington, D.C. 20001.

Telephone: (202) 879-7846.

Fax: (202) 879-0136

MIZE, Gregory E. *(Senior Judge, Superior Court of the District of Columbia)* Appointed by President George Bush to term beginning Sept 7, 1990. Assumed Senior status, serves by assignment. Born Chicago Illinois Aug 9, 1946. Roman Catholic. Educated at Loyola University of Chicago A.B. with honors 1968, St. Mary of the Lake Seminary S.T.B. with honors 1970 and Georgetown University Law Center J.D. 1973. Admitted to practice District of Columbia 1974, U.S. Court of Appeals District of Columbia Circuit 1974 and U.S. Supreme Court 1980. In legal practice Washington D.C. 1974-75.

General Counsel District of Columbia City Counsel 1983-90. Author "A Guide to Deciphering the Laws of a Unique City-State Legislature—The Council of the District of Columbia" 2 Potomac L. Rev. 1, 1979, "On Better Jury Selection—Spotting UFO Jurors Before They Enter the Jury Room" 31 No. 1 *Court Review Magazine* Spring 1999 and "A Legal Discrimination" *The Washington Post* Oct 8, 2000. Important Decisions: United States v. Dobkin (constitutionality of Congress' antiloitering statute) 119 Daily Washington Law Reporter 2213 Oct 16, 1991 and In the matter of A.J. (evidence in child neglect case) 120 Daily Washington Law Reporter 725 April 9, 1992. Adjunct Professor of Legislation Antioch School of Law 1982-86 and Administrative Law Georgetown University Law Center 1985-87. Director Council for Court Excellence, Inc. 1982-99 (Executive Committee). Lecturer at numerous CLE courses sponsored by The District of Columbia Bar or Georgetown University Law Center 1977-87. Speaker "Trial Trends and Innovations in Presenting the Case to the Jury" Judicial Conference of the District of Columbia Circuit June 14, 1996; "The Jury Pool: A Window on the Jury System" Midyear Meeting American Judicature Society March 13, 1998; "Planning for Reform in Your Jurisdiction" Jury Reform Workshop Phoenix Arizona Dec 6 to Dec 9, 1998; "Revitalizing American Juries: Learning from the Reforms in Arizona, Washington, D.C. and New York" National Conference of Metropolitan Courts Oct 6, 1999; "A Community Dialogue: Jurors Speak, Judges Listen" New York Avenue Presbyterian Church Oct 13, 1999; "Peremptory Challenges—Should We Use Them or Lose Them?" A Presidential Showcase Program 2000 Winter Convention The District of Columbia Bar March 3, 2000; "Jury Service and the Costs of Peremptory Challenges" Morning Edition with Bob Edwards National Public Radio Dec 6, 2000; and "Creating a Democratic Jury System," "Reducing Juror Hardship

MIZE, GREGORY E.—*Continued*

and Increasing the Opportunity to Serve" and "Implementing State Jury Programs" Jury Summit 2001 Jan 31 to Feb 3, 2001. Recipient Award for Merit for exceptional performance on a bar project 1979 and Award for sustained contributions to mandatory course on District of Columbia rules of professional responsibility and District of Columbia practice Sept 2001 from The District of Columbia Bar and Charles A. Horsky Award for jury reform efforts from Council for Court Excellence, Inc. May 2000. President Lt. Joseph P. Kennedy Institute, Inc. 1985-86. Board of Governors District of Columbia School of Law 1993-96. Director District of Columbia Central Kitchen. Member Military District of Washington Officer's Club.

Office: 500 Indiana Avenue N.W., Room 5520, Washington, D.C. 20001.
Telephone: (202) 879-1395.
Fax: (202) 879-0178
E-mail address: mizege@dcsc.gov

MORIN, Robert E. *(Associate Judge, Superior Court of the District of Columbia)* Appointed by President Bill Clinton to term beginning 1996. Term expires 2011.
Office: 500 Indiana Avenue N.W., Room JM-630, Washington, D.C. 20001.
Telephone: (202) 879-1550.
Fax: (202) 879-4811

MORRISON, Truman A., III *(Senior Judge, Superior Court of the District of Columbia)* Appointed by the President. Assumed Senior status, serves by assignment.
Office: 500 Indiana Avenue N.W., Room 5520, Washington, D.C. 20001.
Telephone: (202) 879-1060.
Fax: (202) 879-0410

MOTLEY, Thomas J. *(Associate Judge, Superior Court of the District of Columbia)* Appointed by the President.
Office: 500 Indiana Avenue N.W., Room 1510, Washington, D.C. 20001.
Telephone: (202) 879-8377.
Fax: (202) 879-8357

MOTT, John M. *(Associate Judge, Superior Court of the District of Columbia)* Appointed by the President.
Office: 500 Indiana Avenue N.W., Room 2600, Washington, D.C. 20001.
Telephone: (202) 879-8393.
Fax: (202) 879-8396

MURPHY, Tim *(Senior Judge, Superior Court of the District of Columbia)* Appointed by President Lyndon B. Johnson to term beginning Nov 10, 1966. Reappointed by President Gerald R. Ford 1975. Assumed Senior status, serves by assignment. Born Glens Falls New York July 21, 1929. Catholic. Educated at St. Michael's College B.S. cum laude 1951 and Georgetown University LL.B. 1954 LL.M. 1959. Admitted to practice District of Columbia 1954 and New York 1955. Began legal practice Glens Falls New York 1958.

Staff attorney National Labor Relations Board Aug 1958. Assistant U.S. Attorney District of Columbia 1960-66. Special Assistant, Deputy Assistant and Associate Deputy U.S. Attorney General 1990-94. Author "His Honor Has Problems Too" Center for Study of Democratic Institution 1971 and "Trial Court Use of the Standards" American Criminal L. Rev. 1974. Important Decisions: J. H. Marshall & Associates v. Wm. A. Burleson C.A. 9611-71, 1971; In re N.M.S. 51-806-J, 1974; H. G. Smithy Co. v. Washington Medical Center Inc. C.A. 10474-73, 1975; United States v. Clinton Mims 41788-75, 1976; and United States v. Fred Bailey 56148-72, 1976. Instructor Catholic University of America. Former Member American Judicature Society, Federal and American (Council Member Judicial Administration Division and Section of Criminal Justice) Bar Associations. Member The District of Columbia Bar and New York State Bar Association. Faculty The National Judicial College, District Attorneys College, National College of Criminal Defense Lawyers and Public Defenders at Houston and F.B.I. Academy, Quantico Virginia. USMC 1954-58. Colonel USMCR (retired).

Office: 500 Indiana Avenue N.W., Washington, D.C. 20001.
Telephone: (202) 879-1099.

NEBEKER, Frank Q. *(Senior Judge, District of Columbia Court of Appeals)* Appointed by President Richard M. Nixon to term beginning May 13, 1969. Assumed Senior status, serves by assignment. Born Salt Lake City Utah April 23, 1930. Educated at Weber State College A.A., 1950, University of Utah B.S. 1953 and American University J.D. 1955. Admitted to practice District of Columbia 1956. Chief Judge, U.S. Court of Appeals for Veteran Claims, appointed by President George Bush to term beginning Oct 16, 1989.

Trial Attorney Internal Security Division U.S. Department of Justice 1956-58. Assistant U.S. Attorney 1958-69 and Chief Appellate Division 1962-69 District of Columbia. Instructor American University Law School 1965. Member Appellate Judges Conference and American Bar Association (Judicial Administration Division). Correspondence Secretary The White House 1954-55. Former Director Office of Government Ethics.

Office: 500 Indiana Avenue N.W., Sixth Floor, Washington, D.C. 20001.
Telephone: (202) 879-2778.

NEWMAN, Theodore R., Jr. *(Senior Judge, District of Columbia Court of Appeals)* Appointed by President Gerald R. Ford to term beginning Oct 1976. Chief Judge 1978-84. Assumed Senior status, serves by assignment. Born July 5, 1934. Educated at Brown University A.B. 1955 LL.D. 1980 and Harvard Law School 1958. In legal practice Washington D.C. 1962-70. Associate Judge, Superior Court of the District of Columbia Nov 1970-76.

With U.S. Department of Justice Civil Rights Division 1961-62. USAF Judge Advocate.

Office: 500 Indiana Avenue N.W., Sixth Floor, Washington, D.C. 20001.
Telephone: (202) 879-2739.

OBERDORFER, Louis F. *(Senior Judge, United States District Court District of Columbia)* Appointed for life by the President to term beginning 1977. Assumed Senior status, serves by assignment. Born Birmingham Alabama Feb 21, 1919. Educated at Dartmouth College A.B. 1939 and Yale University LL.B. 1946. Editor-in-Chief Yale Law Journal 1941. Admitted to practice Alabama 1946 and District of Columbia 1949. Law Clerk to Hon. Hugo L. Black, U.S. Supreme Court 1946-47. In legal practice Washington D.C. 1947-77.

Assistant Attorney General Tax Division Department of Justice 1961-65. Visiting Lecturer Yale Law School 1966 and 1971. Co-chairman Lawyers Committee on

OBERDORFER, LOUIS F.—*Continued*

Civil Rights Under Law 1967-69. Member Advisory Committee Federal Rules of Civil Procedure 1962-84, Alabama State Bar, The District of Columbia Bar (Board of Governors 1972-77 and President 1977), Federal and American Bar Associations. Served to Captain U.S. Army 1941-46. Member Yale Law School Association (President 1971-73).

Office: 2309 U.S. Courthouse, 333 Constitution Avenue N.W., Washington, D.C. 20001-2802.

Telephone: (202) 354-3270.

PENN, John Garrett *(Senior Judge, United States District Court District of Columbia)* Appointed for life by President Richard M. Nixon to term beginning Nov 20, 1970. Former Chief Judge. Assumed Senior status March 31, 1998, serves by assignment. Born Pittsfield Massachusetts March 19, 1932. Episcopalian. Educated at University of Massachusetts B.A. 1954 and Boston University LL.B. 1957. Admitted to practice Massachusetts 1957, U.S. Court of Military Appeals 1958, U.S. Court of Claims 1967, U.S. Supreme Court 1967, U.S. Court of Appeals District of Columbia Circuit 1970 and District of Columbia 1970.

Trial Attorney, Reviewer and Assistant Chief U.S. Department of Justice Tax Division 1961-70. Important Decisions: Kelly v. District of Columbia 1974, Stolhman v. District of Columbia 1976 and Ball v. District of Columbia 1976. Fellow National Institute of Public Affairs Woodrow Wilson School of Public and International Affairs Princeton University 1967-68. Member American Judicature Society, The District of Columbia Bar, Massachusetts, Federal and American Bar Associations. First Lieutenant U.S. Army JAGC 1958-61.

Office: 6600 U.S. Courthouse, 333 Constitution Avenue N.W., Washington, D.C. 20001-2802.

Telephone: (202) 354-3450.

PRYOR, William C. *(Senior Judge, District of Columbia Court of Appeals)* Appointed by President Lyndon B. Johnson to term beginning April 4, 1968. Reappointed by President Jimmy Carter April 1978. Former Chief Judge. Assumed Senior status, serves by assignment. Born Washington D.C. May 29, 1932. Protestant. Educated at Dartmouth College B.A. 1954 and Georgetown University LL.B. with honors 1959. Admitted to practice District of Columbia 1959, Ohio 1964 and U.S. Supreme Court 1965.

With U.S. Department of Justice Washington D.C. 1959. Instructor Georgetown University Law Center 1969 and 1971 and Potomac Law School since 1976. Member The District of Columbia Bar, Washington and American Bar Associations. Attended National College of the State Judiciary 1973. Lieutenant USAS 1955-56. Democrat. Board of Directors YMCA, St. Albans School, Opportunities Industrialization Center, American Cancer Society and Washington Athletic Club. Enjoys sports.

Office: 500 Indiana Avenue N.W., Sixth Floor, Washington, D.C. 20001.

Telephone: (202) 879-2745.

PUIG-LUGO, Hiram E. *(Associate Judge, Superior Court of the District of Columbia)* Appointed by President Bill Clinton to term beginning July 6, 1999. Term expires July 6, 2014. Born San German Puerto Rico 1961. Educated at University of Wisconsin B.S. 1984 J.D. 1988. Note and Comment Editor Wisconsin Law Review 1987-88. Admitted to practice District of Columbia 1988, Wisconsin 1988 and Puerto Rico 1990.

Staff Attorney Appellate Division 1989-90 and Trial Division 1990-94 Public Defender Service. Deputy Chief Trial Division Public Defender Service 1994-96. Trial Attorney Civil Rights Division U.S. Department of Justice 1996-99. Contributor *Criminal Practice Institute Training Manual* 1989-94 and *D.C. Practice Manual* 1997. Co-editor *Criminal Practice Institute Trial Manual* 1995-96. Instructor Proyecto de Reforma Judicial de El Salvador June 1996 and in Trial Advocacy Instituto of Estudios Avanzados de Venezuela April 1999 and Ministerio Publico de Argentina June 2000. Board Member Neighborhood Legal Services Program 1998-1999. Member Hispanic Bar Association of District of Columbia (Board Member 1992-93, 1997-98 and 1999-2000). Attended General Jurisdiction The National Judicial College July 2000. Recipient W. Eugene Clingan Memorial Scholarship Award 1984, Wisconsin Law Alumni Award 1987, Public Service Award from Posner Foundation 1988 and Legal Community Award from District of Columbia Courts Hispanic Heritage Celebration 1996. Board Member Latin American Youth Center 1990-92.

Office: 500 Indiana Avenue N.W., Washington, D.C. 20001.

Telephone: (202) 879-8370.

Fax: (202) 879-8374

E-mail address: PUIGLUHE@DCSC.GOV

RANKIN, Michael Lee *(Associate Judge, Superior Court of the District of Columbia)* Appointed by President Ronald Reagan Dec 17, 1985 to term beginning Jan 27, 1986. Reappointed by President Bill Clinton, current term expires Dec 16, 2015. Presiding Judge Criminal and Special Operations Divisions 1998-2001. Born Holly Springs Mississippi Aug 7, 1946. Educated at Lincoln University B.A. 1967 and Howard University School of Law J.D. 1970. Member Omega Psi Phi. Admitted to practice District of Columbia 1970, U.S. Courts of Appeals District of Columbia 1975 and Third 1976 Circuits and U.S. Supreme Court 1976. In legal practice Washington D.C. 1978-80.

Attorney Advisor Office of General Counsel Office of Economic Opportunity March 1972 to May 1972. Staff Attorney Public Defender Service of the District of Columbia 1972-76. Assistant Public Defender District of the Virgin Islands 1976-78. Assistant U.S. Attorney June 1980 to Jan 1986 and Deputy Chief Felony Trial Division Dec 1984 to Jan 1986 U.S. Attorney's Office District of Columbia. Special Assistant to U.S. Attorney District of the Virgin Islands 1981. President Charlotte E. Ray American Inns of Court 1994-95. Member The District of Columbia Bar and Washington Bar Association. Faculty Board member The Association of Trial Lawyers of America 1985. Attended Judicial Management and Training Conference, Cockeysville Maryland May 1, 1986 to May 4, 1986; Judicial Conference June 14, 1986 to June 20, 1986, In-Service Judicial Training Program Oct 1986, 23rd Annual Criminal Practice Institute Oct 31, 1986 to Nov 1, 1986 District of Columbia; Judicial Sentencing Institute Conference, Reston Virginia Nov 6, 1986 to Nov 8, 1986; and National Conference of Federal Judges, District of Columbia. First Lieutenant U.S. Army 1966-72. Employed by Civil Rights Division U.S. Department of Justice 1968-70.

Office: 500 Indiana Avenue N.W., Room 5630, Washington, D.C. 20001.

RANKIN, MICHAEL LEE—*Continued*
Telephone: (202) 879-1220.
Fax: (202) 879-0129

REID, Inez Smith *(Associate Judge, District of Columbia Court of Appeals)* Appointed by President Bill Clinton Feb 22, 1995 to term beginning June 23, 1995. Term expires 2010. Educated at Tufts University magna cum laude, Yale Law School J.D., University of California at Los Angeles M.A. and Columbia University Ph.D. in Public Law and Government. In legal practice Washington D.C. 1985-95.

Former Corporation Counsel for the District of Columbia, Inspector General of the U.S. Environmental Protection Agency, Deputy General Counsel for Regulation Review U.S. Department of Health and Human Services and General Counsel to the New York State Division for Youth. Adjunct Professor and Constitutional Scholar American University. Former Instructor West Virginia University College of Law, Barnard College, City University of New York and State University of New York.

Office: 500 Indiana Avenue N.W., Sixth Floor, Washington, D.C. 20001.
Telephone: (202) 879-2726.

RETCHIN, Judith E. *(Associate Judge, Superior Court of the District of Columbia)* Appointed by President George Bush.

Office: 500 Indiana Avenue N.W., Room 3520, Washington, D.C. 20001.
Telephone: (202) 879-1866.
Fax: (202) 879-0150

RICHTER, Robert Isaac *(Associate Judge, Superior Court of the District of Columbia)* Appointed by President Ronald Reagan to term beginning Oct 24, 1984. Reappointed by President Bill Clinton Oct 1999, current term expires Oct 24, 2014. Born New York New York June 26, 1947. Jewish. Educated at University of Vermont B.A. magna cum laude 1969 and University of Chicago J.D. cum laude 1972. Comment Editor University of Chicago Law Review 1970-72. Law Clerk to Hon. Irving L. Goldberg, U.S. Court of Appeals Fifth Circuit 1972-73 and Hon. Harry A. Blackmun, U.S. Supreme Court 1973-74. Admitted to practice New York 1973 and District of Columbia 1974. In legal practice Washington D.C. 1974-75.

Assistant U.S. Attorney District of Columbia 1975-78. Assistant Chief of Operations Public Integrity Section Criminal Division U.S. Department of Justice 1978-84.

Office: 500 Indiana Avenue N.W., Room 2410, Washington, D.C. 20001.
Telephone: (202) 879-1422.
Fax: (202) 879-0125

RIGSBY, Robert R. *(Associate Judge, Superior Court of the District of Columbia)* Appointed by President George W. Bush.

Office: 500 Indiana Avenue N.W., Room JM-620, Washington, D.C. 20001.
Telephone: (202) 879-4344.
Fax: (202) 879-4348

ROBERTS, Richard W. *(Judge, United States District Court District of Columbia)* Appointed for life by President Bill Clinton to term beginning July 31, 1998. Educated at Vassar College A.B. cum laude 1974, School for International Training M.I.A. 1978 and Columbia University J.D. 1978.

Trial Attorney and Chief Criminal Section Civil Rights Division U.S. Department of Justice. Principal Assistant U.S. Attorney District of Columbia. Assistant U.S. Attorney Southern District of New York.

Office: U.S. Courthouse, 333 Constitution Avenue N.W., Washington, D.C. 20001-2802.
Telephone: (202) 354-3400.

ROBERTSON, James *(Judge, United States District Court District of Columbia)* Appointed for life by President Bill Clinton to term beginning Dec 1994. Educated at Princeton University 1959 and George Washington University National Law Center LL.B. 1965.

With Lawyers' Committee for Civil Rights Under the Law 1969-72. Past President The District of Columbia Bar and Southern Africa Legal Services and Legal Education, Inc.

Office: 6315 U.S. Courthouse, 333 Constitution Avenue N.W., Washington, D.C. 20001-2802.
Telephone: (202) 354-3460.

ROBINSON, Deborah A. *(Magistrate Judge, United States District Court District of Columbia)* Appointed by U.S. District Court judges to term beginning July 18, 1988. Reappointed July 1996, current term expires July 2004. Educated at Morgan State University and Emory University School of Law. Law Clerk to Hon. H. Carl Moultrie, I, Superior Court of the District of Columbia 1978-79.

With U.S. Attorney's Office District of Columbia.

Office: 1114 U.S. Courthouse, 333 Constitution Avenue N.W., Washington, D.C. 20001-2802.
Telephone: (202) 354-3070.

ROSS, Maurice *(Associate Judge, Superior Court of the District of Columbia)* Appointed by President George W. Bush.

Office: 500 Indiana Avenue N.W., Room 3640, Washington, D.C. 20001.
Telephone: (202) 879-1765.
Fax: (202) 879-1769

RUIZ, Vanessa *(Associate Judge, District of Columbia Court of Appeals)* Appointed by President Bill Clinton to term beginning 1994. Term expires 2009. Born San Juan Puerto Rico March 22, 1950. Educated at Wellesley College 1972 and Georgetown University Law Center 1975. In legal practice 1975-83 and 1987-91.

Senior Counsel Sears World Trade, Inc. 1983-87. Corporation Counsel District of Columbia 1991-94. Coauthor *Europe Without Frontiers: A Lawyer's Guide* Bureau of National Affairs 1989. Adjunct Professor of European Community Law Georgetown University Law Center. Chair District of Columbia Judicial Conference 1999. Former Co-chair Committee on Race & Ethnicity District of Columbia Circuit Task Force on Gender, Race & Ethnic Bias. Former Chair Task Force on Families and Violence District of Columbia Court of Appeals. Member Advisory Committee on Judicial Conduct District of Columbia Court of Appeals. Member Executive Committee and Chair Public Service Committee Council for Court Excellence. Member The American Law Institute, National Association of Women Judges, Hispanic Bar Association of the District of Columbia and The District of Columbia Bar (Pro Bono Programs Committee, Former Member New Rules Committee). Speaker Civitas International Conference Dec 1999, Or-

RUIZ, VANESSA—*Continued*

ganization of American States Washington D.C. and numerous conferences on judicial reform and the role of women in legal reform Rio de Janeiro and Sao Paulo Brazil. Participant Biennial Conference International Association of Women Judges 2000. Mentor to Latino law students. Participant in programs to educate the Latino community and young Latinos about the law and the courts.

Office: 500 Indiana Avenue N.W., Sixth Floor, Washington, D.C. 20001.
Telephone: (202) 879-2761.
E-mail address: vruiz@dcca.state.dc.us

SATTERFIELD, Lee F. *(Associate Judge, Superior Court of the District of Columbia)* Appointed by President George Bush.

Office: 500 Indiana Avenue N.W., Room 1530, Washington, D.C. 20001.
Telephone: (202) 879-1918.
Fax: (202) 879-0159

SCHWELB, Frank E. *(Associate Judge, District of Columbia Court of Appeals)* Appointed by President Ronald Reagan Nov 10, 1987 to term beginning May 5, 1988. Reappointed 2003, current term expires 2018. Born Prague Czechoslovakia June 24, 1932. Educated at Yale University B.A. 1953 and Harvard Law School LL.B. 1958. Member Phi Beta Kappa. Admitted to practice New York 1958 and District of Columbia 1972. Began legal practice New York 1958. Associate Judge, Superior Court of the District of Columbia Dec 20, 1979 to May 5, 1988, appointed by President Jimmy Carter.

Chief Eastern Section 1969 and Housing Section 1969-79 Civil Rights Division Department of Justice. Special Counsel Health, Education and Welfare Secretary's Review Panel on New Drug Regulation 1976-77. Author "The Sit-In Demonstration: Criminal Trespass or Constitutional Right?" 36 New York University L. Rev. 799, April 1961, "Obtaining Affirmative Relief Under the American Civil Rights Laws" IV Human Rights Jour. 555, Strasbourg France 1971, "From Illusion to Reality: Relief in Civil Rights Cases" Notre Dame Lawyer 49, Oct 1972 and "Outline of Law Relating to Discrimination in Housing" Prentice Hall Equal Opportunity in Housing Reporter 2351, Sept 1977. Important Judicial Opinions written include Criminal, Civil, Family, Juvenile and other areas. Important Appellate Opinions: United States v. Porter (admissibility of DNA evidence) 618 A.2d 629 D.C. 1992; In re Abrams 689 A.2d 6 D.C. 1997 (applicability of presidential pardon authority to disciplinary proceeding against attorney); and District of Columbia v. Sierra Club 670 A.2d 354 D.C. 1996 (right to judicial review, separation of powers). Lecturer on Equal Housing Opportunity at various law schools and bar associations 1969-79. Member World Association of Judges and The District of Columbia Bar. Instructor on Landlord and Tenant Law, Civil Practice and Small Claims CLE Courses 1980-83. Member U.S. Judicial Delegation to training session of Slovak and Czech judges Slovakia 1992. Frequently briefs visiting Czech judges and attorneys regarding U.S. legal system as well as judges and attorneys from other ex-communist states. Participant programs on Human Rights and Justice Delayed is Justice Denied televised to Asia, Africa and Latin America U.S. Information Agency and Worldnet. Recipient several Department of Justice Awards for Sustained Superior Performance and named Younger Federal Lawyer of the Year by Federal Bar Association Selection Committee 1967. Specialist Third Class U.S. Army 1955-57. Former member American Civil Liberties Union, Amnesty International and NAACP. Member Czechoslovak Society of Arts and Sciences and U.S. People to People Delegation to Asia (Japan, People's Republic of China, Hong Kong and Taiwan) 1984. Participant Voice of America One Broadcast in Czech to Czechoslovakia. Enjoys travel and sports, especially soccer, tennis and table tennis. Interested in Gilbert and Sullivan, Shakespeare and Czech activities.

Office: 500 Indiana Avenue N.W., Sixth Floor, Washington, D.C. 20001.
Telephone: (202) 879-2730.

SHUKER, Nan R. *(Associate Judge, Superior Court of the District of Columbia)* Appointed by President Ronald Reagan Oct 28, 1983 to term beginning Dec 2, 1983. Reappointed by President Bill Clinton to term beginning Dec 2, 1998, current term expires Dec 2, 2013. Currently serves as Deputy Presiding Judge Civil Division. Born Gulfport Mississippi April 13, 1945. Educated at State University of New York at Binghamton B.A. in Economics 1966 and American University Washington College of Law J.D. 1969. Attended St. Elizabeth's Hospital Psychodrama Training 1970 and Seminar in Group Dynamics American University 1970-71.

Staff member Center for the Administration of Justice 1969-72, Assistant Director for Community and Clinical Programs 1970-71, Director Law Enforcement Programs 1971-72, Lecturer 1971-73 and Adjunct Professor 1974-79 American University. Staff Attorney 1972-74, Assistant Chief 1974-81 and Chief 1981-83 Juvenile Section Office of the Corporation Counsel. Member District of Columbia Mayor's Commission on Crime, National Advisory Committee for the Child Abuse and Neglect Model Law Department of Health, Education and Welfare, Advisory Committee Psychiatric Institute on Minority Employment and Treatment, Law Enforcement and Community Crime Control Committee and Juvenile Justice Committee District of Columbia Criminal Justice Coordinating Board, District of Columbia's Juvenile Justice Advisory Group (Vice Chairman Steering Committee), District of Columbia's Inter-Agency Committee on Child Abuse and Neglect (Chairman Subcommittee on Legislation), The District of Columbia Bar, Women's and American Bar Associations. Testified on Child Abuse and Neglect and the Juvenile Justice System before the District of Columbia City Council and U.S. Congressional Committees. Attended Juvenile Justice Institute 1976 and Major Juvenile Offenders Workshop 1979.

Office: 500 Indiana Avenue N.W., Room 3430, Washington, D.C. 20001.
Telephone: (202) 879-1207.
Fax: (202) 879-0120

STEADMAN, John M. *(Associate Judge, District of Columbia Court of Appeals)* Appointed by President Ronald Reagan to term beginning June 27, 1985. Reappointed by President Bill Clinton June 2000, current term expires June 2015. Born Honolulu Hawaii Aug 8, 1930. Educated at Yale University B.A. 1952 and Harvard University LL.B. 1955. Treasurer Harvard Law Review 1953-55. Recipient Sinclair-Kennedy Traveling Fellowship Award 1955-56. Admitted to practice District of

STEADMAN, JOHN M.—*Continued*
Columbia 1955, California 1956 and Hawaii 1977. In legal practice San Francisco California 1956-63 and Washington D.C. 1979-85.
Attorney U.S. Department of Justice 1963-64. General Counsel USAF 1968-70. Co-author with D. Schwartz and S. B. Jacoby "Litigation with the Federal Government" 2nd edition ALI/ABA 1983. Visiting Professor University of Pennsylvania Law School 1970-72. Professor 1972-85 and Associate Dean 1979-84 Georgetown University Law Center. Member American Bar Association. Deputy Undersecretary for International Affairs U.S. Department of the Army 1964-65. Special Assistant to Deputy Secretary and Secretary U.S. Department of Defense 1965-68.
Office: 500 Indiana Avenue N.W., Sixth Floor, Washington, D.C. 20001.
Telephone: (202) 879-2785.

SULLIVAN, Emmet G. *(Judge, United States District Court District of Columbia)* Appointed for life by President Bill Clinton March 22, 1994 to term beginning Nov 18, 1994. Born Washington D.C. Educated at Howard University B.A. in Political Science 1968 J.D. 1971. Law Clerk to Hon. James A. Washington, Jr., Superior Court of the District of Columbia. In legal practice 1973-84. Associate Judge, Superior Court of the District of Columbia Oct 3, 1984 to Nov 24, 1991, appointed by President Ronald Reagan. Served as Deputy Presiding Judge and Presiding Judge Probate and Tax Divisions. Associate Judge, District of Columbia Court of Appeals Nov 25, 1991 to Nov 17, 1994, appointed by President George Bush.
Visiting Faculty Member Trial Advocacy Workshop Harvard Law School 1996. Adjunct Professor Howard University School of Law. Chair Task Force on Families and Violence for the District of Columbia Courts since 1994. Commissioner District of Columbia Judicial Disabilities and Tenure Commission 1996-2001. Former Chairperson Rules Committee Probate and Tax Divisions Superior Court of the District of Columbia. Former Member Court Rules Committee and Jury Plan Committee. Former Member Board of Directors D.C. Law Students in Court Program, Voluntary Arbitration Committee D.C. Judicial Conference and Committee on Grievances U.S. District Court. Board of Directors Council for Court Excellence. Commissioner District of Columbia Judicial Nomination Commission. Chair Legislative Subcommittee Committee on Criminal Law Judicial Conference of the United States. Member Bar Association of the District of Columbia (Former Member Nominating Committee), Washington and National Bar Associations. Chairperson "Rejuvenating Juvenile Justice—Responses to the Problems of Juvenile Violence in the District of Columbia" Nineteenth Annual Judicial Conference of the District of Columbia June 1994. Recipient Thurgood Marshall Award of Excellence from Howard University Alumni Association. Member Frederick Abramson Memorial Foundation.
Office: 2327 U.S. Courthouse, 333 Constitution Avenue N.W., Washington, D.C. 20001-2802.
Telephone: (202) 354-3260.

TEEL, S. Martin, Jr. *(Judge, United States Bankruptcy Court District of Columbia)* Appointed by U.S. Court of Appeals District of Columbia Circuit judges to term beginning Feb 8, 1988. Reappointed Feb 8, 2002, current term expires Feb 8, 2016. Born Pensacola Florida 1945. Educated at University of Virginia College of Arts and Sciences B.A. with honors 1967 J.D. 1970. Law Clerk to Hon. Roger Robb, U.S. Court of Appeals District of Columbia Circuit 1970-71. Admitted to practice Virginia 1970, District of Columbia 1971, U.S. District Court District of Columbia 1971, U.S. Court of Appeals District of Columbia Circuit 1971 and U.S. Supreme Court 1980.
Attorney 1971-82 and Assistant Section Chief 1982-88 Tax Division U.S. Department of Justice.
Office: 2106 U.S. Courthouse, 333 Constitution Avenue N.W., Washington, D.C. 20001-2802.
Telephone: (202) 273-0708.

TERRELL, Mary A. Gooden *(Associate Judge, Superior Court of the District of Columbia)* Appointed by President Bill Clinton to term beginning 1997. Term expires 2012.
Office: 500 Indiana Avenue N.W., Room JM-670, Washington, D.C. 20001.
Telephone: (202) 879-1639.
Fax: (202) 879-1642

TERRY, John A. *(Associate Judge, District of Columbia Court of Appeals)* Appointed by President Ronald Reagan July 2, 1982 to term beginning Sept 1, 1982. Reappointed by President Bill Clinton 1997, current term expires 2012. Born Utica New York May 6, 1933. Educated at Yale University B.A. magna cum laude 1954 and Georgetown University J.D. 1960. Board of Editors Georgetown Law Journal 1959-60. Admitted to practice District of Columbia 1960, U.S. Court of Appeals District of Columbia Circuit 1960 and U.S. Supreme Court 1965. In legal practice Washington D.C. 1968-69.
Assistant U.S. Attorney District of Columbia 1962-67. Attorney National Commission on Reform of Federal Criminal Laws 1967-68. Chief Appellate Division U.S. Attorney's Office District of Columbia 1969-82. Member The District of Columbia Bar (Board of Governors 1977-82) and American Bar Association.
Office: 500 Indiana Avenue N.W., Sixth Floor, Washington, D.C. 20001.
Telephone: (202) 879-2780.

TIGNOR, Robert S. *(Senior Judge, Superior Court of the District of Columbia)* Appointed by President Ronald Reagan to term beginning Oct 24, 1984. Assumed Senior status, serves by assignment. Born Washington D.C. Educated at Howard University B.A. 1965 and George Washington University National Law Center J.D. 1968. Staff member George Washington Law Review 1966-68.
Senior Trial Attorney U.S. Department of Justice Feb 1979 to Oct 1984.
Office: 500 Indiana Avenue N.W., Suite JM-680, Washington, D.C. 20001.
Telephone: (202) 879-1252.

TURNER, Linda D. *(Associate Judge, Superior Court of the District of Columbia)* Appointed by President George Bush.
Office: 500 Indiana Avenue N.W., Room 2000, Washington, D.C. 20001.
Telephone: (202) 879-1819.
Fax: (202) 879-0147

UGAST, Fred B. *(Senior Judge, Superior Court of the District of Columbia)* Appointed by President Richard M. Nixon to term beginning Dec 10, 1973. Reappointed by President Ronald Reagan Nov 26, 1988. Former Chief Judge. Assumed Senior status, serves by assignment. Born Washington D.C. Sept 18, 1923. Catholic. Educated at St. Charles summa cum laude 1944, Catholic University of America B.A. in Philosophy 1945 M.A. 1946 and Harvard University LL.B. 1950. Awarded honorary D.H.L. Catholic University of America 1994. Recipient Basselin Foundation Scholarship. Admitted to practice District of Columbia 1950, U.S. District Court District of Columbia 1950, U.S. Court of Claims 1950, U.S. Court of Appeals District of Columbia Circuit 1950 and U.S. Supreme Court 1954.

With the Department of Justice 1950. Acting Assistant Attorney General Tax Division Department of Justice Aug to Nov 1971. Important Decisions: Wensel et al. v. Washington (acupuncture) Civ. Nos. 11004-74 and 11005-74, 1975; U.S. v. Paula Frendak (bifurcated trial, insanity defense imposed by court) Cr. No. 38208-74, 1976; U.S. v. Charles Reavis (murder-felony) Cr. No. 28501-75, 1975; and National Graduate University v. District of Columbia (tax) No. 2251, Jan 1975. Judge in Residence Columbus School of Law Catholic University of America since 1994. Former member Federal Bar Association. Member Bar Association of the District of Columbia and American Bar Association. Recipient Department of Justice Sustained Superior Performance Award 1961, Attorney General's Award for Exceptional Service (Highest Justice Department award) 1971, Annual Recognition Award for distinguished service in area of mental health from Washington Psychiatric Society 1981, Distinguished Fellow Award from Superior Court Trial Lawyers Association, Professional Service Award from Middle Atlantic States Correctional Association, Alumni Award from Catholic University of America, James C. Eastman Award and Judicial Honoree Award from Bar Association of the District of Columbia, Justice Tom C. Clark Award from National Conference of Metropolitan Courts, H. Carl Moultrie Award of Judicial Excellence, Chairman's Special Award from National Bar Association, Sadie T. M. Alexander Award from National Association of Black Women Attorneys, Distinguished Service Award from National Center for State Courts and Award of Merit from Joint Committee on Judicial Administration of the District of Columbia. Honored by designation of Judge Fred B. Ugast Forensic Psychiatric Center for thirty-bed psychiatric center and Chief Judge Fred B. Ugast Forensic Evaluation Branch for section of Saint Elizabeth's Hospital as recognition of exceptional work in mental health legal field. Republican. Member John Carroll Society and Columbia Country Club. Enjoys tennis and swimming.

Office: 500 Indiana Avenue N.W., Room 2440, Washington, D.C. 20001.

Telephone: (202) 879-1890.

URBINA, Ricardo Manuel *(Judge, United States District Court District of Columbia)* Appointed for life by President Bill Clinton to term beginning July 1994. Born New York New York Jan 31, 1946. Catholic. Educated at Georgetown University B.A. with honors 1967 J.D. 1970. Member Phi Delta Phi. Admitted to practice District of Columbia 1970, U.S. District Court District of Columbia 1970, U.S. Court of Appeals District of Columbia Circuit 1970, U.S. Court of Military Appeals 1970 and U.S. Supreme Court 1980. In legal practice Washington D.C. 1974-81. Former Associate Judge, Superior Court of the District of Columbia, appointed by President Ronald Reagan to term beginning April 20, 1981.

Former Staff Attorney Public Defender Service, District of Columbia. General Counsel Atlantic Real Title Corporation 1976-80. Author "Rules For Self Help: Avoiding and Encountering the Disciplinary Process" Hispanic Bar Association of D.C. April 1984. Co-author with Dr. Margaret Beyer, Ph.D. "Practice Paper Series" American Bar Association Aug 1986. Important Decisions: Abbey v. Jackson et al. 483 A.2d 330 (D.C. 1984); Group Hospitalization et al. v. Blue Cross-Blue Shield et al. C.A. 4630-84, 112 Wash. D.L. Rptr. 1729 (Aug 30, 1984); Habib v. Thurston, L&T 77391-83; Bradford Brown v. District of Columbia; and Jerry M., et al v. District of Columbia, et al. Professor of Law Howard University School of Law 1974-81 and Georgetown University Law Center 1983. Adjunct Professor of Law George Washington University National Law Center since 1995. Executive Board Member American Inn of Court. Member Hispanic Bar Association of the District of Columbia, The District of Columbia Bar, Bar Association of the District of Columbia, Hispanic National, National and American Bar Associations. Voted Professor of the Year by Howard University law students 1979. Recipient Recognition of Merit Award from Congressional Hispanic Caucus 1981, Juarez-Lincoln Award 1983, Hispanic of the Year Award 1984, Appreciation Award from AYUDA, Commissioner's Award for Outstanding Leadership and Service in the Prevention of Child Abuse and Neglect from Federal Department of Health and Human Services 1988 and Exceptional Commitment to D.C. Youth Award from Multi-Cultural Bilingual High School 1989. Named Washingtonian of the Year 1987. Executive Board Member Concerned Citizens on Alcohol Abuse. Board Member National Council of La Raza and National Home Library Foundation. Instrumental in establishing interpreter services in Superior Court of District of Columbia through Hispanic Bar Association (Judicial Liaison Project). Assisted in formation of proposed legislation for establishment of permanent in-house interpreter services for the foreign-born and hearing-impaired. Involved with After School Kids (assists juveniles in correction system). Marathon runner. Practices martial arts. Enjoys playing guitar. Personal Statement or Quote: "You make a living from what you get. You make a life from what you give".

Office: 4311 U.S. Courthouse, 333 Constitution Avenue N.W., Washington, D.C. 20001-2802.

Telephone: (202) 354-3390.

VINCENT, Odessa F. *(Associate Judge, Superior Court of the District of Columbia)* Appointed by President George W. Bush.

Office: 500 Indiana Avenue N.W., Room 1430, Washington, D.C. 20001.

Telephone: (202) 879-0447.

Fax: (202) 879-0450

WAGNER, Annice M. *(Chief Judge, District of Columbia Court of Appeals)* Appointed by President George Bush. Former Associate Judge, Superior Court of the District of Columbia.

Office: 500 Indiana Avenue N.W., Sixth Floor, Washington, D.C. 20001.

Telephone: (202) 879-2770.

WALTON, Reggie B. *(Judge, United States District Judge District of Columbia)* Appointed for life by President George W. Bush to term beginning Oct 29, 2001. Born North Charleroi Pennsylvania Feb 8, 1949. Baptist. Educated at West Virginia State College B.A. 1971 and Washington College of Law of American University J.D. 1974. Admitted to practice Pennsylvania 1974, District of Columbia 1976, U.S. District Courts Eastern District of Pennsylvania 1975 and District of Columbia 1981, U.S. Court of Appeals District of Columbia Circuit 1977 and U.S. Supreme Court 1980. Associate Judge July 12, 1981 to May 1989 and Deputy Presiding Judge Criminal Division July 1986 to May 1989, Superior Court of the District of Columbia, appointed by President Ronald Reagan. Associate Judge Dec 6, 1991 to Oct 26, 2001, Presiding Judge Domestic Violence Unit 2000 and Presiding Judge Family Division 2001, Superior Court of the District of Columbia, appointed by President George Bush.

Staff Attorney Defender Association of Philadelphia Aug 1974 to Feb 1976. Assistant U.S. Attorney March 1976 to July 1980 and Executive Assistant U.S. Attorney July 1980 to July 1981 District of Columbia (Chief Career Criminal Unit July 1979 to July 1980). Associate Director Office of National Drug Control Policy Executive Office of the President June 1989 to May 17, 1991. Senior White House Advisor for Crime The White House May 20, 1991 to Dec 5, 1991. Co-author "Pretrial Drug Testing—An Essential Component of the National Drug Control Strategy" Journal of Public Law Brigham Young University J. Reuben Clark Law School 1991. Important Opinions: Shaw v. District of Columbia F. Supp. 2d 2002 WL 31769445 D.D.C. Nov 22, 2002; National R.R. Passenger Corp. v. Expresstrak L.L.C. F. Supp. 2d 2002 WL 31730866 D.D.C. Dec 5, 2002; Hopkins v. Women's Div. General Bd. of Global Ministries F. Supp. 2d 2002 WL 31886673 D.D.C. Dec 12, 2002; U.S. ex rel. Corbett Technology Solutions, Inc. v. Safeco Ins. Co. of America F. Supp. 2d 2002 WL 31886645 D.D.C. Dec 12, 2002; and VoteHemp, Inc. v. Drug Enforcement Admin. F. Supp. 2d 2002 WL 31886647 D.D.C. Dec 23, 2002. Faculty Member College of Trial Advocacy George Washington University National Law Center since 1983. Distinguished Scholar Lecturer Albany State College April 30, 1991. Distinguished Guest Lecturer Lincoln University May 1, 1991. Adjunct Faculty Member Trial Advocacy Workshop Harvard University Law School since 1994. Member Lawyer Competency Committee 1984-87 and Delegate National Conference of State Trial Judges 1986 American Bar Association. Member Joint Committee on Judicial Administration for the District of Columbia Courts 1985-89. Consultant (Peer Reviewer) Office of Justice Programs National Institute of Justice 1986-89. Member National Advisory Committee National Institute for Citizen Education in the Law 1987-90. Master Edward Bennett Williams American Inns of Court 1989-99. Member Advocates Association National Institute for Trial Advocacy, Bar Association of the District of Columbia (Criminal Instructions Committee 1984-86), and Washington Bar Association.

Instructor "Trial of a Homicide Case" 1980 and 1997 and "Voir Dire, Opening Statement and Closing Argument" 1981 Criminal Practice Institute Bar Association of the District of Columbia, National Institute for Trial Advocacy Georgetown University Law Center 1983-89 and since 1991, Traffic Court Seminar American Bar Association Oct 1984 and Oct 1987, Advocacy Institute U.S. Department of Justice July 1993, Annual Expert Witness and Litigation Seminar SEAK, Inc. 1993 and 1997 and Judicial Training Workshop (Russia) Central East European Law Institute American Bar Association 1996. Faculty Member The National Judicial College since 1999. Listed in *Who's Who Among Students in American Universities and Colleges* 1970-71, *Who's Who Among Black Americans* 1980-81, *Who's Who in American Law* 1985, *Who's Who in Society* 1986, *Who's Who in Law Enforcement* 1990, *Black Judges on Justice: Prospectives from the Bench* 1995, *Who's Who in the World* 2000 and *Who's Who in America* 2001. Named one of Outstanding Young Men in America U.S. Jaycees 1984, one of Men of Achievement International Biographical Centre 1987 and 75th Anniversary Paul Harris Fellow The Rotary Foundation of Rotary International 1992. Recipient Dean's Award for Distinguished Service from Washington College of Law of American University 1989, Award for Distinguished Service to the Community and the Nation from Young Lawyers Section Bar Association of the District of Columbia 1989, H. Carl Moultrie Award from District of Columbia Branch NAACP 1989, Secretary's Award from Department of Veterans Affairs 1990, Distinguished Service Award from Cook County State's Attorney, National Center for the Prosecution of Child Abuse and Blue Cross-Blue Shield of Illinois 1990, William H. Hastie Award from Judicial Council National Bar Association 1993, Outstanding Community Service Award Washington Area Council on Alcoholism and Drug Abuse, Inc. 1994, Special Achievement Award from Black Law Students Association Washington College of Law of American University 1997, North Star Award from Washington College of Law of American University 2000 and Judge Hart T. Mankin Memorial Award from The Federal American Inn of Court 2001. Republican. Instructor Inmate Law Clinic Graterford State Prison Pennsylvania 1974-76. Member Panel on Research of Criminal Careers National Academy of Sciences 1983-86, Task Force on Interscholastic Programs District of Columbia Public Schools 1987, White House Conference for a Drug Free America 1987-88, Dean's Advisory Council Washington College of Law of American University 1987-89 and since 1995, Big Brothers of America 1987-96 and D.C. Cares, Inc. 1990. Honorary Member Capital Ballet Guild, Inc. 1989. Board of Directors Big Brothers of the National Capital Area 1990, National Center for Missing and Exploited Children 1990-91, The Robert A. Shuker Scholarship Fund since 1993 and Hillcrest Children's Center 1994-96. Member Advisory Board Jump Start for Young Children, Inc. since 2001. Enjoys cooking, traveling and weight-lifting.

Office: 1834 U.S Courthouse, 333 Constitution Avenue N.W., Washington, D.C. 20001.

Telephone: (202) 354-3290.

WASHINGTON, Eric T. *(Associate Judge, District of Columbia Court of Appeals)* Appointed by President Bill Clinton to term beginning June 7, 1999. Term expires 2014. Born Jersey City New Jersey December 2, 1953. Educated at Tufts University B.A. 1976 and Columbia University J.D. 1979. Admitted to practice Texas 1979, District of Columbia 1985, U.S. District Court District of Columbia, U.S. Court of Appeals Fifth, Eleventh and District of Columbia Circuits and U.S. Supreme Court. In legal practice Houston Texas 1979-82 and Washington D.C. 1983-95. Associate Judge, Superi-

WASHINGTON, ERIC T.—*Continued*
or Court of the District of Columbia July 14, 1995 to June 6, 1999, appointed by President Bill Clinton.

Special Counsel to the Corporation Counsel and Principal Deputy Counsel for the District of Columbia 1987-89. Member District of Columbia Bar (Former Member CJA/CCAN Committee, Standing Committee on the Federal Judiciary, Nominating Committee, Steering Committee District of Columbia Affairs Section). Former Legislative Director and Counsel to Congressman Michael A. Andrews. Former Chairman District of Columbia Democratic Party. Member Metropolitan Board of Directors Boys and Girls Clubs of Greater Washington. Member Board of Directors Boys and Girls Clubs Foundation.

Office: 500 Indiana Avenue N.W., Sixth Floor, Washington, D.C. 20001.

Telephone: (202) 879-2750.

WEBBER, Paul R., III *(Senior Judge, Superior Court of the District of Columbia)* Appointed by President Jimmy Carter to term beginning May 5, 1977. Reappointed to subsequent term. Assumed Senior status Jan 1998, serves by assignment. Born Gadsden South Carolina Jan 24, 1934. Educated at South Carolina State University B.A. 1955 J.D. magna cum laude 1957. Listed in *Who's Who in American Colleges and Universities.* Member Alpha Phi Alpha and Sigma Pi Phi. Admitted to practice District of Columbia, South Carolina, California and U.S. Supreme Court. In legal practice Columbia South Carolina 1958-59, Los Angeles California 1960-64 and Washington D.C. 1969-77.

Trial Attorney Antitrust Division U.S. Department of Justice 1964-67. Managing Attorney Washington D.C. Neighborhood Legal Services Program 1967-69. Counsel Media Committee Congressional Black Caucus 1971-74. Instructor on Business Law Allen University 1958-59. Assistant Law Librarian UCLA Law School 1959-60. Lecturer on Communications Law Howard University 1972-76. Adjunct Professor of Law George Washington University 1973. Board of Judges Third Party Custody Committee, Appointment of Counsel Committee, Judicial Conference Planning Committee, Legislation and Instructions Committee and Civil Rules Advisory Committee. Member American Arbitration Association 1972-77, Bar Association of the District of Columbia, The District of Columbia Bar, South Carolina Bar, State Bar of California, Washington, National (Judicial Council, Chairman Civil Practice and Family Law Section 1972-73) and American Bar Associations. Listed in *Who's Who Among Black Americans.* Named Outstanding Trial Judge of the Year by The Trial Lawyers Association of Metropolitan Washington D.C. 1985-86. Board of Directors National Association of Hearing and Speech Action 1972-76, National Child Day Care Association 1973-76, Family & Child Services 1975-81 and Columbia Hospital for Women 1979-82. Advisory Board United Negro College Fund since 1983. Member NAACP, Urban League and The Guardsmen, Inc. (National President 1989).

Office: 500 Indiana Avenue N.W., Room 2440, Washington, D.C. 20001.

Telephone: (202) 879-1426.

Fax: (202) 879-0179

WEISBERG, Frederick H. *(Associate Judge, Superior Court of the District of Columbia)* Appointed by President Jimmy Carter to term beginning Jan 13, 1978. Reappointed by President George Bush. Current term expires Jan 13, 2008. Currently serves as Presiding Judge Criminal Division. Born Buffalo New York March 22, 1944. Educated at Cornell University B.A. 1965, University of Michigan J.D. cum laude 1968 and New York University LL.M. 1970. Member Order of the Coif. Notes and Comments Editor University of Michigan Law Review. Recipient Jason L. Honigman Award for most substantial contribution by Law Review Editor and Fiorello LaGuardia Award for graduating first in class in New York University LL.M. program. Admitted to practice New York 1968 and District of Columbia 1970.

With Public Defender Service Washington D.C. 1970-77 (Chief of Appellate Division 1974-77). Associate Professorial Lecturer in Law George Washington University 1976-83.

Office: 500 Indiana Avenue N.W., Room 5600, Washington, D.C. 20001.

Telephone: (202) 879-1066.

Fax: (202) 879-0108

WERTHEIM, Ronald P. *(Senior Judge, Superior Court of the District of Columbia)* Appointed by President Ronald Reagan to term beginning Jan 6, 1982. Assumed Senior status, serves by assignment. Born Philadelphia Pennsylvania Sept 7, 1933. Educated at University of Pennsylvania B.S. with honors 1954 LL.B. with honors 1957 and Hague Academy of International Law Dipl. with honors 1962. Editor-in-Chief University of Pennsylvania Law Review 1956-57. Member Alpha Sigma Phi, Pi Gamma Mu and Beta Gamma Sigma. Admitted to practice Pennsylvania 1958 and District of Columbia 1969. In legal practice Philadelphia Pennsylvania 1957-59.

Assistant Defender Philadelphia 1959-61. Deputy General Counsel 1964-66 and Associate Director Northeast Brazil 1966-68 Peace Corps. Advisor to Secretary of Defense for Law of the Sea Negotiations 1977. Alternate U.S. Representative Sixth United Nations Conference on the Law of the Sea 1977. Member U.S. Merit System Protection Board 1979-82. Author "An Inquiry into Criminal Guilt & Law, Liberty & Psychiatry" 64 Columbia L. Rev. Associate Professor of Law University of Virginia School of Law 1961-64. Private Arbitrator JAMS since 1995. Member The American Law Institute and American Bar Association (National Conference of State Trial Judges). Attended General Jurisdiction Course The National Judicial College 1982. Member Cosmos Club of Washington D.C.

Office: 500 Indiana Avenue N.W., Room 5520, Washington, D.C. 20001.

Telephone: (202) 879-1170.

WINFIELD, Susan R. *(Associate Judge, Superior Court of the District of Columbia)* Appointed by the President. Currently serves as Deputy Presiding Judge Family Court.

Office: 500 Indiana Avenue N.W., Room 3510, Washington, D.C. 20001.

Telephone: (202) 879-1272.

Fax: (202) 879-0126

WINSTON, Rhonda Reid *(Associate Judge, Superior Court of the District of Columbia)* Appointed by President Bill Clinton.

Office: 500 Indiana Avenue N.W., Room 1620, Washington, D.C. 20001.

WINSTON, RHONDA REID—*Continued*

Telephone: (202) 879-4750.
Fax: (202) 879-0172

WOLF, Peter H. *(Senior Judge, Superior Court of the District of Columbia)* Appointed by President Jimmy Carter Sept 18, 1978 to term beginning April 11, 1979. Deputy Presiding Judge Jan 1, 1992 to Oct 31, 1993 and Presiding Judge Nov 1, 1993 to July 1994 Probate Division. Assumed Senior status Sept 1994, serves by assignment. Born Glen Ridge New Jersey May 5, 1935. Presbyterian. Educated at Cornell University B.E.E. 1958 M.E.E. 1959 and Harvard Law School LL.B. 1962. Law Clerk to Hon. George L. Hart, Jr., U.S. District Court District of Columbia 1962-63. Admitted to practice District of Columbia 1962, U.S. Tax Court 1965 and U.S. Supreme Court 1966. In legal practice 1970-79.

Assistant Corporation Counsel District of Columbia 1963-65. Staff attorney President's Commission on Crime in the District of Columbia 1965-66. Senior Research Attorney Georgetown University Law Center Institute of Criminal Law and Procedure 1966-69. Author "A Survey of the Expanded Exclusionary Rule" 32 George Washington L. Rev. 193, 1963; "An Antireapportionment Amendment: Can It Be Legally Ratified?" 52 ABA Jour. 326, 1966; BASIC computer program *Child Support Guidelines* Superior Court of the District of Columbia 1987; and "So What's It Like Being a Judge?" 1987 and "Humor in the Court" 2000 *The Washington Lawyer*. Important Decisions: In re Dixon (denied authority for so-called "ministers" of the Universal Life Church to perform marriages in the District of Columbia) 1981; Ceco Corp. v. Coleman (did away with "*Murray* credit" in personal injury cases where the plaintiff has also received workers' compensation benefits) 441 A.2d 940 D.C. 1982; anticipated Cutchember v. Payne (allowed HLA test results in evidence over respondent's objection in paternity cases) 466 A.2d 1240 D.C. 1983; anticipated Corbin v. U.S. (defendant may be prosecuted both for possession of marijuana and PCP where substance seized was PCP-laced marijuana) 481 A.2d 1301 D.C. 1984; first judge to order summary jury trial in District of Columbia 1987; and U.S. v. Vaughn (explaining decision to incarcerate pregnant cocaine addict) 1988. Member Bar Association of the District of Columbia (Board of Directors 1971-74) and The District of Columbia Bar (Board of Governors 1971-76). Personal Statement or Quote: "Be Concise."

Office: 500 Indiana Avenue N.W., Room 3440, Washington, D.C. 20001.
Telephone: (202) 879-1088.
Fax: (202) 879-0177
E-mail address: p-wolf@pop.net

WRIGHT, Melvin R. *(Associate Judge, Superior Court of the District of Columbia)* Appointed by the President.

Office: 500 Indiana Avenue N.W., Room JM-650, Washington, D.C. 20001.
Telephone: (202) 879-8336.
Fax: (202) 879-8339

WYNN, Patricia A. *(Senior Judge, Superior Court of the District of Columbia)* Appointed by President George Bush. Assumed Senior status, serves by assignment.

Office: 500 Indiana Avenue N.W., Room 5520, Washington, D.C. 20001.
Telephone: (202) 879-4630.
Fax: (202) 879-0178

ZELDON, Joan *(Associate Judge, Superior Court of the District of Columbia)* Appointed by President George Bush.

Office: 500 Indiana Avenue N.W., Room 1640, Washington, D.C. 20001.
Telephone: (202) 879-1590.
Fax: (202) 879-0137

FLORIDA

Capital TALLAHASSEE

UNITED STATES DISTRICT COURTS DISTRICTS OF FLORIDA

Within Florida there are three United States District Courts. For descriptive information refer to the United States Courts section.

MIDDLE DISTRICT includes Baker, Bradford, Brevard, Charlotte, Citrus, Clay, Collier, Columbia, De Soto, Duval, Flagler, Glades, Hamilton, Hardee, Hendry, Hernando, Hillsborough, Lake, Lee, Manatee, Marion, Nassau, Orange, Osceola, Pasco, Pinellas, Polk, Putnam, St. Johns, Sarasota, Seminole, Sumter, Suwannee, Union and Volusia counties. The court sits at Fernandina, Fort Myers, Jacksonville, Live Oak, Ocala, Orlando, St. Petersburg and Tampa.

Chief Judge

Patricia C. Fawsett

Judges

Elizabeth A. Kovachevich
Harvey E. Schlesinger
Ralph W. Nimmons, Jr.
Anne C. Conway
Steven D. Merryday
Henry Lee Adams, Jr.
Susan C. Bucklew
Richard A. Lazzara
James D. Whittemore
John Antoon, II
John E. Steele
James S. Moody, Jr.
Gregory A. Presnell
Timothy J. Corrigan

Senior Judges

George C. Young
William Terrell Hodges
Howell W. Melton
William John Castagna
John H. Moore, II
George Kendall Sharp

Clerk

Sheryl L. Loesch
300 U.S. Courthouse
80 North Hughey Avenue
Orlando, Florida 32801
(407) 835-4222

NORTHERN DISTRICT includes Alachua, Bay, Calhoun, Dixie, Escambia, Franklin, Gadsden, Gilchrist, Gulf, Holmes, Jackson, Jefferson, Lafayette, Leon, Levy, Liberty, Madison, Okaloosa, Santa Rosa, Taylor, Wakulla, Walton and Washington counties. The court sits at Gainesville, Marianna, Panama City, Pensacola and Tallahassee.

Chief Judge

Roger Vinson

Judges

Lacey A. Collier
Robert L. Hinkle
Stephan P. Mickle

Senior Judges

William Henry Stafford, Jr.
Maurice M. Paul

Clerk

William M. McCool
U.S. Courthouse
111 North Adams Street
Tallahassee, Florida 32301-7717
(850) 521-3501

SOUTHERN DISTRICT includes Broward, Dade, Highlands, Indian River, Martin, Monroe, Okeechobee, Palm Beach and St. Lucie counties. The court sits at Fort Lauderdale, Fort Pierce, Key West, Miami and West Palm Beach.

Chief Judge

William J. Zloch

Judges

Federico A. Moreno
Donald L. Graham
K. Michael Moore
Ursula M. Ungaro-Benages
Daniel T. K. Hurley
Joan A. Lenard
Donald M. Middlebrooks
Alan S. Gold
William P. Dimitrouleas
Patricia A. Seitz
Adalberto J. Jordan
Paul C. Huck
Kenneth A. Marra
Jose E. Martinez

Senior Judges

James Lawrence King
Norman C. Roettger, Jr.
William M. Hoeveler
Jose A. Gonzalez, Jr.
James C. Paine
Kenneth L. Ryskamp
Shelby Highsmith

Court Administrator/Clerk

Clarence Maddox
Federal Courthouse Square
301 North Miami Avenue
Miami, Florida 33128-7788
(305) 523-5100

UNITED STATES MAGISTRATE JUDGES OF FLORIDA

MIDDLE DISTRICT

Thomas G. Wilson
Howard T. Snyder
Elizabeth A. Jenkins
David A. Baker
Thomas B. McCoun III
Mark A. Pizzo
James G. Glazebrook
Mary S. Scriven
Karla R. Spaulding
Douglas N. Frazier
Gary R. Jones
Thomas E. Morris
Sheri Polster Chappell

NORTHERN DISTRICT

Larry A. Bodiford
William C. Sherrill, Jr.
Gordon Miles Davis
Margaret C. Rodgers

SOUTHERN DISTRICT

Hugh J. Morgan
William C. Turnoff
Lurana S. Snow
Linnea R. Johnson
Ann E. Vitunac
Ted E. Bandstra

UNITED STATES DISTRICT COURTS DISTRICTS OF FLORIDA—*Continued*

Barry S. Seltzer	Stephen T. Brown
Barry L. Garber	Frank J. Lynch, Jr.
Robert L. Dube	Andrea M. Simonton
John J. O'Sullivan	Patrick A. White

Recalled Magistrate Judge
Peter R. Palermo (Southern)

UNITED STATES BANKRUPTCY COURTS OF FLORIDA

MIDDLE DISTRICT

Chief Judge
Thomas E. Baynes

Judges

George L. Proctor	C. Timothy Corcoran, III
Jerry A. Funk	Arthur B. Briskman
Karen S. Jennemann	Michael G. Williamson
Paul M. Glenn	

Recalled Judge
Alexander L. Paskay

Bankruptcy Clerk
David K. Oliveria
727 U.S. Courthouse
801 North Florida Avenue
Tampa, Florida 33602-3899
(813) 301-5050, 301-5027

NORTHERN DISTRICT

Judge
Lewis M. Killian, Jr.

Bankruptcy Clerk
William Blevins
3120 City Center Building
227 North Bronough Street
Tallahassee, Florida 32301
(850) 942-8933

SOUTHERN DISTRICT

Chief Judge
Robert A. Mark

Judges
A. Jay Cristol
Paul G. Hyman, Jr.
Steven H. Friedman
Raymond B. Ray

Bankruptcy Clerk
Karen Eddy
1401 Federal Building
51 S.W. First Avenue
Miami, Florida 33130
(305) 714-1800

FLORIDA SUPREME COURT

The Supreme Court is Florida's court of last resort. The court consists of a chief justice and six justices elected on a statewide nonpartisan ballot for six-year terms. Vacancies are filled by the governor from a list of names submitted by a judicial nominating commission. Justices must stand for retention on a nonpartisan ballot at the next general election occurring at least one year after appointment. Retention elections are held every six years thereafter. A chief justice is elected by a majority vote of the justices to serve a two-year term. Retirement is mandatory at age seventy; however, justices who turn seventy while in office may finish their current term. Retired justices may serve as senior justices upon assignment of the court.

The court has exclusive jurisdiction over civil and criminal appeals involving constitutional questions, the death penalty, bond validation and certificates of indebtedness and shall review actions of statewide agencies relating to rates or service of utilities. The court has discretionary review of any decision that affects a class of constitutional or state officers, that is certified as possessing great public interest or that is in direct conflict with a decision made by a District Court of Appeal or the Supreme Court on the same question of law. The court may answer questions certified to it by a federal court and issue writs necessary to the exercise of its complete jurisdiction.

Five justices constitute a quorum, with the concurrence of four justices necessary for a decision. The court must sit en banc for appeals involving capital cases, the validity of a state or federal statute or provisions of the Florida or federal constitution. The court sits at Tallahassee.

Chief Justice
Harry L. Anstead

Justices

Charles Talley Wells	Barbara J. Pariente
R. Fred Lewis	Peggy A. Quince
Raoul G. Cantero, III	Kenneth B. Bell

Senior Justices
Ben F. Overton
James E. Alderman
Leander J. Shaw, Jr.
Major B. Harding

Clerk
Tom Hall
Supreme Court Building
500 South Duval Street
Tallahassee, Florida 32399-1927
(850) 488-0125

State Court Administrator
Robin L. Lubitz
Supreme Court Building
500 South Duval Street
Tallahassee, Florida 32399-1900
(850) 922-5081

FLORIDA DISTRICT COURTS OF APPEAL

The District Courts of Appeal are Florida's courts of intermediate appellate jurisdiction. Judges are elected at general elections on nonpartisan ballots for six-year terms. Vacancies are filled by the governor from a list of names submitted by a judicial nominating commission. Judges must stand for retention on a nonpartisan ballot at the next general election occurring at least one year after appointment. Retention elections are held every six years thereafter. A chief judge is elected by

FLORIDA DISTRICT COURTS OF APPEAL—*Continued*

peer vote in each district for a two-year term. Retirement is mandatory at age seventy; however, judges who turn seventy while in office may finish their current term. Retired judges may serve as senior judges upon assignment of the Supreme Court.

The courts have jurisdiction over civil and criminal appeals including those taken as a matter of right from final judgments of trial courts, review of administrative action not directly appealable to another court or as prescribed by law and interlocutory orders as provided by Supreme Court rules. The courts may issue writs necessary to the exercise of their complete jurisdiction.

The state is divided into five districts with one court in each district. The court sits in panels of three judges and the concurrence of two judges is necessary for a decision.

FIRST DISTRICT includes Alachua, Baker, Bay, Bradford, Calhoun, Clay, Columbia, Dixie, Duval, Escambia, Franklin, Gadsden, Gilchrist, Gulf, Hamilton, Holmes, Jackson, Jefferson, Lafayette, Leon, Levy, Liberty, Madison, Nassau, Okaloosa, Santa Rosa, Suwannee, Taylor, Union, Wakulla, Walton and Washington counties. The court sits at Tallahassee.

Chief Judge
Michael E. Allen

Judges

Edward T. Barfield
Anne Cawthon Booth
Marguerite Davis
Paul Hawkes
Joseph Lewis, Jr.
Ricky Polston
Peter Webster
James R. Wolf
Robert T. Benton II
Edwin B. Browning, Jr.
Richard W. Ervin, III
Charles J. Kahn, Jr.
Philip J. Padovano
William A. Van Nortwick, Jr.

SECOND DISTRICT includes Charlotte, Collier, De Soto, Glades, Hardee, Hendry, Highlands, Hillsborough, Lee, Manatee, Pasco, Pinellas, Polk and Sarasota counties. The court sits at Lakeland.

Chief Judge
Chris W. Altenbernd

Judges

Charles T. Canady
Virginia M. Hernandez Covington
Patricia Kelly
E. J. Salcines
Thomas E. Stringer, Sr.
Darryl C. Casanueva
Charles A. Davis, Jr.
Carolyn K. Fulmer
Stevan T. Northcutt
Morris Silberman
James W. Whatley

THIRD DISTRICT includes Dade and Monroe counties. The court sits at Miami.

Chief Judge
Alan R. Schwartz

Judges

Gerald B. Cope, Jr.
David M. Gersten
Melvia B. Green
David L. Levy
Robert L. Shevin
John Fletcher
Mario P. Goderich
James R. Jorgenson
Juan Ramirez, Jr.
Linda Ann Wells

FOURTH DISTRICT includes Broward, Indian River, Martin, Okeechobee, Palm Beach and St. Lucie counties. The court sits at West Palm Beach.

Chief Judge
Mark E. Polen

Judges

Gary M. Farmer
Bobby W. Gunther
Larry Klein
George A. Shahood
Barry J. Stone
Martha C. Warner
Robert M. Gross
Frederick A. Hazouri
Melanie G. May
W. Matthew Stevenson
Carole Y. Taylor

FIFTH DISTRICT includes Brevard, Citrus, Flagler, Hernando, Lake, Marion, Orange, Osceola, Putnam, St. Johns, Seminole, Sumter and Volusia counties. The court sits at Daytona Beach.

Chief Judge
Emerson R. Thompson, Jr.

Judges

Jacqueline R. Griffin
Richard B. Orfinger
Earle W. Peterson, Jr.
Thomas D. Sawaya
Vincent G. Torpy, Jr.
David A. Monaco
William D. Palmer
Robert J. Pleus, Jr.
Winifred J. Sharp

SENIOR DISTRICT COURTS OF APPEAL JUDGES

Warren H. Cobb
James C. Dauksch, Jr.
Oliver L. Green, Jr.
Charles M. Harris
Gerald Mager
Melvin Orfinger
Herboth S. Ryder
Jack R. Schoonover
Edward F. Threadgill
Paul W. Danahy, Jr.
John W. Dell
Vincent T. Hall
L. Arthur Lawrence, Jr.
Joseph Nesbitt
William C. Owen, Jr.
John M. Scheb
Larry G. Smith

FLORIDA CIRCUIT COURTS

The Circuit Courts are Florida's courts of general jurisdiction. Judges are elected on a nonpartisan ballot for six-year terms. Vacancies are filled by the governor from a list of names submitted by a judicial nominating commission. A chief judge is elected by peer vote in each circuit for a two-year term. Retirement is mandatory at age seventy; however, judges who turn seventy while in office may finish their current term. Retired judges may serve as senior judges upon assignment of the Supreme Court.

The courts have original jurisdiction of all felonies and of all misdemeanors which are lesser offenses included within a felony charge. The courts have exclusive original jurisdiction in all actions at law which do not fall under the County Courts' jurisdiction; proceedings relating to settlement of estates of decedents and minors, guardianship and other probate matters; juvenile matters excluding traffic offenses; and all cases involving the legality of tax assessment, title to and boundaries or possession of real estate. The courts have appellate jurisdiction over cases from County Courts except when appealable directly to the Supreme Court or accepted for appeal by the District Courts of Appeal. The courts may review administrative action as prescribed by law and may issue writs or injunctions necessary or proper to the exercise of their complete jurisdiction.

The state is divided into twenty judicial circuits, and the courts sit at each county seat in the circuits.

FLORIDA CIRCUIT COURTS—*Continued*

FIRST JUDICIAL CIRCUIT includes Escambia, Okaloosa, Santa Rosa and Walton counties. The court sits at Pensacola, Crestview, Milton and DeFuniak Springs.

Chief Judge
John P. Kuder

Judges
Michael G. Allen
G. Robert Barron
Frank L. Bell
Nickolas P. Geeker
Marci L. Goodman
Jack R. Heflin
T. Michael Jones
Lewis R. "Bob" Lindsey
Edward Nickinson, III
Linda Lee Nobles
John T. Parnham
Paul D. Rasmussen
Thomas T. Remington
Jan Shackelford
Kim A. Skievaski
William F. Stone
Terry D. Terrell
William J. Tolton, Jr.
Kenneth L. Williams

Senior Judges
Erwin Fleet
Laura Melvin
Joseph Q. Tarbuck

SECOND JUDICIAL CIRCUIT includes Franklin, Gadsden, Jefferson, Leon, Liberty and Wakulla counties. The court sits at Apalachicola, Quincy, Monticello, Tallahassee, Bristol and Crawfordville.

Chief Judge
William L. Gary

Judges
Thomas H. Bateman, III
Nikki Ann Clark
John C. Cooper
John E. Crusoe
P. Kevin Davey
Kathleen F. Dekker
Janet E. Ferris
Charles A. Francis
James C. Hankinson
Terry P. Lewis
George S. Reynolds, III
N. Sanders Sauls
Jonathan Sjostrom
L. Ralph Smith, Jr.

Senior Judges
J. Lewis Hall, Jr.
F. E. Steinmeyer, III

THIRD JUDICIAL CIRCUIT includes Columbia, Dixie, Hamilton, Lafayette, Madison, Suwannee and Taylor counties. The court sits at Lake City, Cross City, Jasper, Mayo, Madison, Live Oak and Perry.

Chief Judge
James Roy Bean

Judges
Paul S. Bryan
Julian E. Collins
E. Vernon Douglas
Thomas J. Kennon, Jr.
John Weston Peach

Senior Judges
John R. Agner
Wallace M. Jopling

FOURTH JUDICIAL CIRCUIT includes Clay, Duval and Nassau counties. The court sits at Green Cove Springs, Jacksonville and Fernandina Beach.

Chief Judge
Donald R. Moran, Jr.

Judges
Charles W. Arnold, Jr.
Aaron K. Bowden
Frederic A. Buttner
Hugh Carithers, Jr.
Karen K. Cole
McCarthy Crenshaw, Jr.
Brian Jordan Davis
Henry E. Davis
Lance M. Day
Peter L. Dearing
Robert M. Foster
Peter Fryefield
David M. Gooding
Lawrence P. Haddock
Jean M. Johnson
E. McRae Mathis
Linda F. McCallum
William G. McCaulie
Charles Mitchell, Jr.
Bernard Nachman
Jack M. Schemer
John H. Skinner
A. C. Soud, Jr.
Brad Stetson
L. Haldane Taylor
Frederick B. Tygart
Waddell Wallace, III
Michael Weatherby
David C. Wiggins
William A. Wilkes

Senior Judges
Virginia Q. Beverly
Alban E. Brooke
Ellis T. Fernandez, Jr.
Sam Goodfriend
Mattox S. Hair
James L. Harrison
Thomas D. Oakley
R. Hudson Olliff
Dorothy Harris Pate
Clifford B. Shepard, Jr.
John D. Southwood

FIFTH JUDICIAL CIRCUIT includes Citrus, Hernando, Lake, Marion and Sumter counties. The court sits at Inverness, Brooksville, Tavares, Ocala and Bushnell.

Chief Judge
Victor J. Musleh

Judges
Carven D. Angel
Don F. Briggs
David B. Eddy
Sandra Edwards-Stephens
Barbara Gurrola
Mark J. Hill
Richard Howard
T. Michael Johnson
Brian Lambert
William G. Law, Jr.
Raymond T. McNeal
Daniel B. Merritt, Sr.
Curtis J. Neal
Sandra Sue Robbins
Lawrence J. Semento
William Singbush
G. Richard Singletary
Jack Springstead
Hale R. Stancil
William T. Swigert, Sr.
Patricia V. Thomas
Richard Tombrink, Jr.

Senior Judge
John W. Booth

SIXTH JUDICIAL CIRCUIT includes Pasco and Pinellas counties. The court sits at Dade City, Clearwater and St. Petersburg.

Chief Judge
David A. Demers

Judges
Linda H. Allan
Linda H. Babb
W. Douglas Baird
Bruce Boyer
W. Lowell Bray, Jr.
James R. Case
Wayne L. Cobb
Charles W. Cope
Daniel D. Diskey
Brandt C. Downey III
Crockett Farnell
Dee Anna Farnell
Philip J. Federico
Marion Lucas Fleming
George W. Greer
Raymond O. Gross
Nelly N. Khouzam
Lauren Laughlin
John C. Lenderman
Nancy Moate Ley
Walter D. Logan
Richard A. Luce
J. Thomas McGrady
Stanley R. Mills
Robert J. Morris, Jr.
Thomas E. Penick, Jr.
R. Timothy Peters
Frank Quesada

FLORIDA CIRCUIT COURTS—*Continued*

Peter R. Ramsberger
John K. Renke
Anthony Rondolino
Jack A. St. Arnold
John A. Schaefer
Susan F. Schaeffer
Mark I. Shames
Irene Sullivan
Lynn Tepper
Ray E. Ulmer, Jr.
Craig C. Villanti
William R. Webb

Senior Judges

Owen S. Allbritton
Horace A. Andrews
Robert E. Beach
Fred L. Bryson
Helen S. Hansel
Robert F. Michael, Jr.
Gerard J. O'Brien, Jr.
Howard P. Rives, Jr.
David Seth Walker

SEVENTH JUDICIAL CIRCUIT includes Flagler, Putnam, St. Johns and Volusia counties. The court sits at Bunnell, Palatka, St. Augustine and De Land.

Chief Judge

Robert K. Rouse, Jr.

Judges

John M. Alexander
Shawn L. Briese
James R. Clayton
John V. Doyle
S. James Foxman
Richard S. Graham
Hubert L. Grimes
Kim C. Hammond
Edward Hedstrom
R. Michael Hutcheson
Patrick Gene Kennedy
Terrill J. Larue
Robert K. Mathis
A. W. Nichols, III
William A. Parsons
Julianne Piggotte
Edwin P.B. Sanders
C. McFerrin Smith, III
J. Michael Traynor
J. David Walsh
John W. Watson, III
Joseph G. Will

Senior Judges

Stephen L. Boyles
E. L. "Gene" Eastmoore
William C. Johnson, Jr.
Robert E. Lee, Jr.
James T. Nelson
Richard O. Watson
Richard G. Weinberg

EIGHTH JUDICIAL CIRCUIT includes Alachua, Baker, Bradford, Gilchrist, Levy and Union counties. The court sits at Gainesville, Macclenny, Starke, Trenton, Bronson and Lake Butler.

Chief Judge

Stan R. Morris

Judges

Robert P. Cates
Chester B. Chance
Maurice V. Giunta
David A. Glant
Martha Ann Lott
Toby S. Monaco
Robert E. Roundtree Jr.
Elzie Stanford Sanders
Peter K. Sieg
Frederick D. Smith
Larry Gibbs Turner

Senior Judges

Nath C. Doughtie
R. A. Green, Jr.
Benjamin M. Tench
Theron A. Yawn, Jr.

NINTH JUDICIAL CIRCUIT includes Orange and Osceola counties. The court sits at Orlando and Kissimmee.

Chief Judge

Belvin Perry

Judges

Gail Adams
John H. Adams, Sr.
Alan S. Apte
Theotis Bronson
Jay P. Cohen
Richard F. Conrad
Daniel P. Dawson
Robert M. Evans
William C. Gridley
Donald E. Grincewicz
James Charles Hauser
James E. Henson
Anthony H. Johnson
John Marshall Kest
Lawrence R. Kirkwood
Walter Komanski
Frederick Lauten, Jr.
C. Alan Lawson
Cynthia Z. MacKinnon
Roger J. McDonald
A. Thomas Mihok
Jeffords D. Miller
Renee A. Roche
Jose R. Rodriguez
Dorothy J. Russell
Maura T. Smith
Thomas B. Smith
George A. Sprinkel, IV
Stan Strickland
R. James Stroker
Janet C. Thorpe
Thomas W. Turner
Margaret T. Waller
Bob Wattles
Alice Blackwell White
Reginald D. Whitehead

Senior Judges

Cecil H. Brown
Ted P. Coleman
Lon S. Cornelius, Jr.
Frank N. Kaney
Frederick T. Pfeiffer
Rom W. Powell
Charles N. Prather

TENTH JUDICIAL CIRCUIT includes Hardee, Highlands and Polk counties. The court sits at Wauchula, Sebring and Bartow.

Chief Judge

Charles B. Curry

Judges

Roger A. Alcott
Ralph Artigliere
Charles Lee Brown
Robert L. Doyel
Julian Dale Durrance
Judith J. Flanders
Ronald A. Herring
J. Michael Hunter
Donald G. Jacobsen
Harvey Kornstein
J. David Langford
John F. Laurent
Dennis Paul Maloney
Ellen Sly Masters
J. Michael McCarthy
Randall G. McDonald
Richard G. Prince
Susan Wadsworth Roberts
Olin W. Shinholser
W. Bruce Smith

Senior Judges

Daniel True Andrews
Edward R. Bentley
Cecelia M. Moore
William A. Norris, Jr.
J. Tim Strickland

ELEVENTH JUDICIAL CIRCUIT includes Dade County. The court sits at Miami.

Chief Judge

Joseph P. Farina

Judges

Cecilia Maria Altonaga
Jerald Bagley
Jennifer D. Bailey
Mary R. Barzee
Scott Bernstein
Stanford Blake
Joel H. Brown
Gisela Cardonne Ely
Thomas M. Carney
Michael B. Chavies
Jeri B. Cohen
Manuel A. Crespo
Maria E. Dennis
Amy Steele Donner
Ronald C. Dresnick
Pedro P. Echarte, Jr.
Kevin M. Emas
Margarita G. Esquiroz
Ivan F. Fernandez
Alex E. Ferrer

FLORIDA CIRCUIT COURTS—*Continued*

Eugene J. Fierro
Leon M. Firtel
Gill S. Freeman
Ronald M. Friedman
Michael A. Genden
Norman S. Gerstein
Mindy S. Glazer
Leonard E. Glick
Jon I. Gordon
Maynard "Skip" Gross
Henry Howell Harnage
Gerald D. Hubbart
William Johnson
Sandy Karlan
Maria M. Korvick
Judith L. Kreeger
Maxine Cohen Lando
Lester Langer
Cindy S. Lederman
Ellen Leesfield
Barbara S. Levenson
D. Bruce Levy
Henry Leyte-Vidal
Peter R. Lopez
David C. Miller
Celeste Hardee Muir
Dennis J. Murphy
Robert M. Pineiro
Victoria Platzer
Jose Manuel Rodriguez
Rosa Rodriguez
Jeffrey Rosinek
Arthur L. Rothenberg
Leslie B. Rothenberg
Marc Schumacher
Lawrence A. Schwartz
Jacqueline H. Scola
Robert N. Scola, Jr.
Bernard S. Shapiro
Sidney B. Shapiro
Paul Siegel
Victoria S. Sigler
Scott J. Silverman
Stuart M. Simons
Fredricka G. Smith
Bertila Soto
Daryl E. Trawick
Diane V. Ward
Thomas S. Wilson, Jr.
David H. Young
Sarah Zabel

Senior Judges

Amy N. Dean
Adele Segall Faske
Richard Yale Feder
Seymour Gelber
Carol R. Gersten
William E. Gladstone
Murray Goldman
James C. Henderson
Rosemary Usher Jones
Robert Paul Kaye
Edward S. Klein
Francis X. Knuck
Allen Kornblum
Richard V. Margolius
Edmund W. Newbold
Robert H. Newman
Thomas K. Peterson
Leonard Rivkind
Steven D. Robinson
Michael H. Salmon
Arthur I. Snyder
Harold Solomon
W. Thomas Spencer
Herbert Stettin
Arthur Howard Taylor
David L. Tobin

TWELFTH JUDICIAL CIRCUIT includes De Soto, Manatee and Sarasota counties. The court sits at Arcadia, Bradenton and Sarasota.

Chief Judge

Robert B. Bennett, Jr.

Judges

Durand J. Adams
Scott M. Brownell
Frederick A. DeFuria
Nancy K. Donnellan
Peter A. Dubensky
Janette C. Dunnigan
Deno G. Economou
Marc Gilner
Lee E. Haworth
Paul E. Logan
Robert W. McDonald, Jr.
Edward Nicholas
Andrew D. Owens, Jr.
James S. Parker
Harry M. Rapkin
Charles E. Roberts
Becky A. Titus
Charles E. Williams

Senior Judges

Robert J. Boylston
Stephen L. Dakan
Thomas M. Gallen
Robert E. Hensley
Lynn N. Silvertooth
Gilbert A. Smith

THIRTEENTH JUDICIAL CIRCUIT includes Hillsborough County. The court sits at Tampa.

Chief Judge

Manuel Menendez, Jr.

Judges

James D. Arnold
Rex Barbas
James Barton, III
Emmett Lamar Battles
Herbert Baumann, Jr.
Debra Behnke
Charles E. Bergmann
Anthony K. Black
John K. Carey
Martha J. Cook
Marva L. Crenshaw
Jack Espinosa, Jr.
Katherine G. Essrig
Ronald N. Ficarrotta
Barbara Fleischer
Robert A. Foster
William Fuente
Frank A. Gomez
Gregory P. Holder
Charlene Edwards Honeywell
Claudia Rickert Isom
Perry A. Little
William P. Levens
Richard A. Nielsen
Vivian C. Maye
Sam Pendino
J. Rogers Padgett, Sr.
Denise A. Pomponio
Daniel L. Perry
Monica L. Sierra
Susan Sexton
Ralph C. Stoddard
Robert J. Simms
Wayne S. Timmerman
Chet A. Tharpe

Senior Judges

Daniel E. Gallagher
John M. Gilbert
Roland Gonzalez
Robert W. Rawlins, Jr.
Ralph Steinberg

FOURTEENTH JUDICIAL CIRCUIT includes Bay, Calhoun, Gulf, Holmes, Jackson and Washington counties. The court sits at Panama City, Blountstown, Port St. Joe, Bonifay, Marianna and Chipley.

Chief Judge

Judy Markham Pittman

Judges

Richard Albritton
Dedee S. Costello
Glenn L. Hess
Harry H. McClellan
Michael C. Overstreet
Allen L. Register
Don T. Sirmons
William Leon Wright

Senior Judges

N. Russell Bower
Russell A. Cole, Jr.
Clinton E. Foster

FIFTEENTH JUDICIAL CIRCUIT includes Palm Beach County. The court sits at West Palm Beach.

Chief Judge

Edward H. Fine

Judges

Ronald V. Alvarez
Moses Baker, Jr.
Thomas Barkdull, III
William J. Berger
Peter D. Blanc
Lucy Chernow Brown
Catherine M. Brunson
Harold J. Cohen
Jeffrey J. Colbath
Roger B. Colton
Jack H. Cook
David F. Crow
Edward A. Garrison
John J. Hoy
Kathleen J. Kroll
Jorge LaBarga
Diana Lewis
Hubert R. Lindsey
Mary Elisabeth Lupo
Elizabeth T. Maass
Karen L. Martin
Timothy P. McCarthy
Sandra K. McSorley
Karen M. Miller
Richard L. Oftedal
John L. Phillips
Stephen A. Rapp
Kenneth D. Stern
Gary L. Vonhof
Richard I. Wennet
John D. Wessel
Jeffrey Winikoff
Arthur G. Wroble

FLORIDA CIRCUIT COURTS—*Continued*

Senior Judges

Richard B. Burk
Walter N. Colbath, Jr.
Michael D. Miller
Marvin U. Mounts, Jr.
Edward Rodgers

SIXTEENTH JUDICIAL CIRCUIT includes Monroe County. The court sits at Key West.

Chief Judge

Richard Gale Payne

Judges

Luis M. Garcia
Mark H. Jones
Sandra F. Taylor

SEVENTEENTH JUDICIAL CIRCUIT includes Broward County. The court sits at Fort Lauderdale.

Chief Judge

Dale Ross

Judges

Cheryl J. Aleman
Robert Lance Andrews
Susan Aramony
Paul L. Backman
Marcia Beach
Arthur M. Birken
John B. Bowman
George Angen Brescher
Miette K. Burnstein
Robert B. Carney
Patricia W. Cocalis
Geoffrey D. Cohen
James I. Cohn
Dorian Damoorgian
Richard D. Eade
J. Leonard Fleet
John A. Frusciante
Ana Isabel Gardiner
Michael L. Gates
Marc H. Gold
Renee Goldenberg
Barry E. Goldstein
Charles M. Greene
Mel Grossman
Patti Englander Henning
Ilona M. Holmes
Alfred Horowitz
Michael G. Kaplan
Stanton S. Kaplan
Julie Koenig
Lawrence L. Korda
David H. Krathen
Susan L. Lebow
John T. Luzzo
Thomas M. Lynch, IV
Leroy H. Moe
John J. Murphy
Michael J. Orlando
Robert A. Rosenberg
Ronald Rothschild
Sheldon M. Schapiro
Larry S. Seidlin
Andrew L. Siegel
Mark A. Speiser
Jeffrey E. Streitfeld
Victor Tobin
Linda Vitale
Peter M. Weinstein
Elijah H. Williams
Howard M. Zeidwig

Senior Judges

Robert A. Butterworth
Robert O. Collins
Robert J. Fogan
M. Daniel Futch, Jr.
Raymond J. Hare
Harry G. Hinckley, Jr.
William C. Johnson
James A. McCauley
James M. Reasbeck
Robert C. Scott
Leonard L. Stafford
O. Edgar Williams, Jr.

EIGHTEENTH JUDICIAL CIRCUIT includes Brevard and Seminole counties. The court sits at Titusville and Sanford.

Chief Judge

Bruce W. Jacobus

Judges

Meryl Lee Allawas
Nancy F. Alley
T. Mitchell Barlow
Warren Burk
Lisa Davidson
Alan A. Dickey
W. David Dugan
O. H. "Bill" Eaton, Jr.
Kerry I. Evander
Thomas Freeman
John M. Griesbaum
Charles M. Holcomb
Kenneth Lester
George Maxwell, III
Donna L. McIntosh
John Dean Moxley, Jr.
Debra Steinberg Nelson
James E.C. Perry
Tonya Baccus Rainwater
J. Preston Silvernail
Gene R. Stephenson

Senior Judges

Martin Budnick
S. Joseph Davis, Jr.
Wallace Haile Hall
Lawrence V. Johnston
Jere E. Lober
Robert B. McGregor
C. Vernon Mize, Jr.
Edward J. Richardson
Harry Stein
J. William Woodson

NINETEENTH JUDICIAL CIRCUIT includes Indian River, Martin, Okeechobee and St. Lucie counties. The court sits at Vero Beach, Stuart, Okeechobee and Fort Pierce.

Chief Judge

Marc A. Cianca

Judges

Cynthia G. Angelos
Ben L. Bryan, Jr.
Burton C. Conner
Cynthia L. Cox
John E. Fennelly
Dwight Luther Geiger
Robert A. Hawley
Paul B. Kanarek
Scott M. Kenney
Steven Levin
Robert R. Makemson
William Roby
Larry Schack
Dan L. Vaughn

Senior Judges

William L. Hendry
Charles E. Smith
Rupert Jasen Smith
C. Pfeiffer Trowbridge

TWENTIETH JUDICIAL CIRCUIT includes Charlotte, Collier, Glades, Hendry and Lee counties. The court sits at Punta Gorda, East Naples, Moore Haven, La Belle and Fort Myers.

Chief Judge

William Blackwell

Judges

Isaac Anderson, Jr.
Franklin G. Baker
Theodore H. Brousseau
John S. Carlin
G. Keith Cary
R. Thomas Corbin
Cynthia A. Ellis
Lynn F. Gerald, Jr.
Hugh D. Hayes, Jr.
William C. McIver
Lauren Levy Miller
Daniel R. Monaco
William John Nelson
Donald E. Pellecchia
Thomas S. Reese
Jay B. Rosman
James H. Seals
Hugh E. Starnes
Margaret Ogilvie Steinbeck
James R. Thompson
Sherra Winesett

Senior Judges

Charles T. Carlton
R. Wallace Pack
Robert T. Shafer, Jr.

FLORIDA COUNTY COURTS

The County Courts are courts of limited jurisdiction located in every county in Florida. Judges are elected at nonpartisan elections for six-year terms. Prior to the No-

FLORIDA COUNTY COURTS—*Continued*

vember 1998 election, judges served four-year terms. Vacancies are filled by the governor from a list of names submitted by a judicial nominating commission. Retirement is mandatory at age seventy; however, judges who turn seventy while in office may finish their current term. Retired judges may serve as senior judges upon assignment of the Supreme Court.

The courts have original jurisdiction over all misdemeanors except those which are lesser offenses included within a felony charge and over all violations of municipal and county ordinances. In civil matters, the courts have jurisdiction of all actions at law in which the matter in controversy does not exceed $15,000 and is not within the exclusive jurisdiction of the Circuit Courts. The courts may hear certain domestic relations matters involving dissolution of marriage and may issue final order for dissolution in uncontested cases.

The courts sit at each county seat and other places as may be specified.

County	Judge
Alachua	Jeanne D. Crenshaw
	Aymer L. Curtin
	Phyllis D. Kotey
	Ysleta McDonald
	James P. Nilon
Baker	Joseph M. Williams
Bay	John D. O'Brien
	Elijah Smiley
	Thomas F. Welch
Bradford	Johnny R. Hobbs
Brevard	Rhonda E. Babb
	Cathleen B. Clarke
	Kenneth Friedland
	John M. Harris
	A. B. Majeed
	William T. McCluan
	David E. Silverman
	George B. Turner
Broward	Fred Berman
	Gary R. Cowart
	Steven P. DeLuca
	Robert F. Diaz
	Martin R. Dishowitz
	Leonard Feiner
	Jane D. Fishman
	Peggy Gehl
	William W. Herring
	Kathleen D. Ireland
	Joel Lazarus
	Robert W. Lee
	Ginger Lerner-Wren
	Joseph A. Murphy
	Jerry Pollock
	Linda Raspolich Pratt
	Mary Rudd Robinson
	Louis H. Schiff
	Lee Jay Seidman
	Steven G. Shutter
	Peter Skolnik
	Jay S. Spechler
	Lisa G. Trachman
	Zebedee W. Wright
	Robert S. Zack
	Sharon L. Zeller
Calhoun	Kevin Grover
Charlotte	Peter A. Bell
	W. Wayne Woodard
Citrus	Mark J. Yerman
Clay	Richard R. Townsend
Collier	Lawrence D. Martin
	Vincent Murphy
	Eugene C. Turner
Columbia	Thomas B. Coleman
Dade	A. Leo Adderly
	Mercedes A. Bach
	Beth Bloom
	Linda N. Dakis
	Rosa C. Figarola
	Mary Jo Francis
	Wendell M. Graham
	Andrew S. Hague
	Ivan Hernandez
	Amy B. Karan
	Carroll J. Kelly
	Lawrence D. King
	Shelley J. Kravitz
	Mark King Leban
	Myriam Lehr
	Steven Leifman
	Luise Krieger Martin
	Karen Mills-Francis
	Edward K. Newman
	Ana Maria Pando
	Cristina Pereyra-Shuminer
	Catherine M. Pooler
	Orlando A. Prescott
	Israel U. Reyes
	Bonnie L. Rippingille
	Michael J. Samuels
	Caryn Canner Schwartz
	Jacqueline Schwartz
	Sheldon R. Schwartz
	Fred Seraphin
	Martin Shapiro
	Roger A. Silver
	Samuel J. Slom
	Linda S. Stein
	Raphael Steinhardt
	Richard J. Suarez
	Jeffrey D. Swartz
	Teretha L. Thomas
	Dava J. Tunis
	Ellen Sue Venzer
	Deborah White-Labora
DeSoto	Don T. Hall
Dixie	Marshall M. Clements
Duval	Roberto A. Arias
	Harold C. Arnold
	Tyrie W. Boyer
	Charles G. Cofer
	Mallory D. Cooper
	Eleni Elia Derke
	Pauline Drayton-Harris
	Emmet F. Ferguson, III
	Gary Flower
	Russell L. Healey
	Ronald P. Higbee
	John A. Moran
	James A. Ruth
	Brent D. Shore
	Sharon Howard Tanner
Escambia	David B. Ackerman

FLORIDA COUNTY COURTS—*Continued*

Escambia—Cont.	Thomas E. Johnson
	Patricia A. Kinsey
	George J. Roark, III
	William P. White, Jr.
Flagler	Sharon Atack
Franklin	Van P. Russell
Gadsden	Stewart E. Parsons
Gilchrist	Edward Philman
Glades	Jack E. Lundy
Gulf	Fred N. Witten
Hamilton	David Edgar Bembry
Hardee	Marcus Ezelle
Hendry	James D. Sloan
Hernando	Peyton B. Hyslop
Highlands	Peter F. Estrada
Hillsborough	Charlotte W. Anderson
	James V. Dominguez
	Gaston J. Fernandez
	Walter R. Heinrich
	Paul L. Huey
	Manuel A. Lopez
	Elvin L. Martinez
	Eric Renard Myers
	Nick Nazaretian
	Joelle Ann Ober
	Raul C. Palomino, Jr.
	Michelle Peden
	Cheryl K. Thomas
	Christine K. Vogel
	Mark Wolfe
Holmes	Robert E. Brown
Indian River	David C. Morgan
	Joe A. Wild
Jackson	Woodrow W. Hatcher
Jefferson	Robert Plaines
Lafayette	Harlow H. Land, Jr.
Lake	Richard Boylston
	Donna F. Miller
Lee	James R. Adams
	John W. Dommerich
	Leigh Frizzell Hayes
	J. Frank Porter
	Radford R. Sturgis
	Edward J. Volz, Jr.
Leon	Augustus D. Aikens, Jr.
	Timothy D. Harley
	Judith W. Hawkins
	Donald Modesitt
	James O. Shelfer
Levy	Joseph E. Smith
Liberty	Kenneth Hosford
Madison	H. Wetzel Blair
Manatee	George K. Brown, Jr.
	Robert A. Farrance
	Doug Henderson
Marion	John E. Futch
	Frances S. King
	Robert James McCune
Martin	David Harper
	Stewart R. Hershey
Monroe	Ruth Becker-Painter
	Wayne M. Miller
	William R. Ptomey, Jr.
	Susan Vernon
Nassau	Robert E. Williams
Okaloosa	A. Keith Brace
	T. Patterson Maney
	Kelvin C. Wells
Okeechobee	Shirley M. Brennan
Orange	C. Jeffery Arnold
	Deb S. Blechman
	Jerry L. Brewer
	Leon B. Cheek, III
	Nancy Lynn Clark
	Jeffrey M. Fleming
	Carolyn B. Freeman
	James Glatt, Jr.
	Janis Halker
	Thomas R. Kirkland
	Wilfredo Martinez
	W. Michael Miller
	Antoinette Plogstedt
	Wayne Shoemaker
	Alan C. Todd
Osceola	Carol E. Draper
	Ronald A. Legendre
	Jon B. Morgan
Palm Beach	Nelson Bailey
	William A. Bollinger
	Charles Burton
	Cory J. Ciklin
	Barry M. Cohen
	Sheree Cunningham
	Paul A. Damico
	Peter M. Evans
	Jonathan D. Gerber
	Donald Hafele
	Laura S. Johnson
	Susan R. Lubitz
	Krista Marx
	Paul O. Moyle
	Nancy Perez
	Robert Steven Schwartz
	Debra Moses Stephens
Pasco	Robert P. Cole
	Debra Roberts
	Marc H. Salton
	William G. Sestak
Pinellas	Michael F. Andrews
	Henry J. Andringa
	William B. Blackwood, Jr.
	Patrick K. Caddell
	Shawn Crane
	Thomas B. Freeman
	Walt Fullerton
	Karl B. Grube
	Seung Woo Im
	Paul A. Levine
	Myra Scott McNary
	William H. Overton
	Dorothy L. Vaccaro
	Amy M. Williams
Polk	Mark F. Carpanini
	Timothy Coon
	Mary Catherine Green
	Anne Kaylor
	Michael E. Raiden
	Steven Selph
	Keith P. Spoto
	Karla Foreman Wright
	James Alan Yancey

FLORIDA COUNTY COURTS—*Continued*

Putnam	Peter T. Miller
	Elizabeth A. Morris
St. Johns	Patti Ann Christensen
	Charles J. Tinlin
St. Lucie	James W. Midelis
	Thomas J. Walsh, Jr.
	Philip J. Yacucci
Santa Rosa	Colie Nichols, Jr.
	Ronald Swanson
Sarasota	Kimberly C. Bonner
	Barbara B. Briggs
	David L. Denkin
	Judith M. Goldman
	Emanuel LoGalbo
Seminole	Carmine M. Bravo
	Ralph E. Eriksson
	Mark Edward Herr
	Donald Marblestone
	John R. Sloop
Sumter	Thomas D. Skidmore
Suwannee	William Slaughter, II
Taylor	Stephen Murphy
Union	David Leroy Reiman
Volusia	Thomas E. Bevis
	Steven deLaroche
	H. Pope Hamrick, Jr.
	Mary Jane Henderson
	Frank Marriott, Jr.
	Peter Marshall
	John Roger Smith
	Stasia Warren
	Freddie J. Worthen
Wakulla	Jill C. Walker
Walton	David Walker Green
Washington	Colby Peel

Senior Judge	County Served
John C. Adkins	Brevard County
Jesse C. Barber	Polk County
Jack Block	Dade County
Eli Breger	Dade County
David C. Clark	Palm Beach County
Philip Cook	Dade County
Robert M. Deehl	Dade County
Burton C. Easton	Pinellas County
Charles D. Edelstein	Dade County
Thomas R. Ellinor	Bay County
Loree S. Feiler	Dade County
Marvin H. Gillman	Dade County
Howard Harrison, Jr.	Palm Beach County
William W. Henderson, Jr.	Escambia County
Fredric M. Hitt	Seminole County
Richard L. Hood	Gadsden County
Bernard R. Jaffe	Dade County
Gerald J. Klein	Dade County
Murray Z. Klein	Dade County
Calvin R. Mapp	Dade County
Morton Lee Perry	Dade County
George H. Pierce	Bradford County
William J. Piquette	Dade County
Deborah Dale Pucillo	Palm Beach County
William H. Seaver	Pasco County
Raymond L. Simpson	Duval County
Radford W. Smith	Pinellas County
Kirby Sullivan	Glades County

Florida Counties and County Seats

Alachua
Gainesville

Baker
Macclenny

Bay
Panama City

Bradford
Starke

Brevard
Titusville

Broward
Fort Lauderdale

Calhoun
Blountstown

Charlotte
Punta Gorda

Citrus
Inverness

Clay
Green Cove Springs

Collier
Naples

Columbia
Lake City

Dade
Miami

DeSoto
Arcadia

Dixie
Cross City

Duval
Jacksonville

Escambia
Pensacola

Flagler
Bunnell

Franklin
Apalachicola

Gadsden
Quincy

Gilchrist
Trenton

Glades
Moore Haven

Gulf
Port St. Joe

Hamilton
Jasper

Hardee
Wauchula

Hendry
La Belle

Hernando
Brooksville

Highlands
Sebring

Hillsborough
Tampa

Holmes
Bonifay

Indian River
Vero Beach

Jackson
Marianna

Jefferson
Monticello

Lafayette
Mayo

Lake
Tavares

Lee
Fort Myers

Leon
Tallahassee

Levy
Bronson

Liberty
Bristol

Madison
Madison

Manatee
Bradenton

Marion
Ocala

Martin
Stuart

Monroe
Key West

COUNTIES AND COUNTY SEATS—*Continued*

Nassau
Fernandina Beach

Okaloosa
Crestview

Okeechobee
Okeechobee

Orange
Orlando

Osceola
Kissimmee

Palm Beach
West Palm Beach

Pasco
Dade City

Pinellas
Clearwater

Polk
Bartow

Putnam
Palatka

St. Johns
St. Augustine

St. Lucie
Fort Pierce

Santa Rosa
Milton

Sarasota
Sarasota

Seminole
Sanford

Sumter
Bushnell

Suwannee
Live Oak

Taylor
Perry

Union
Lake Butler

Volusia
De Land

Wakulla
Crawfordville

Walton
DeFuniak Springs

Washington
Chipley

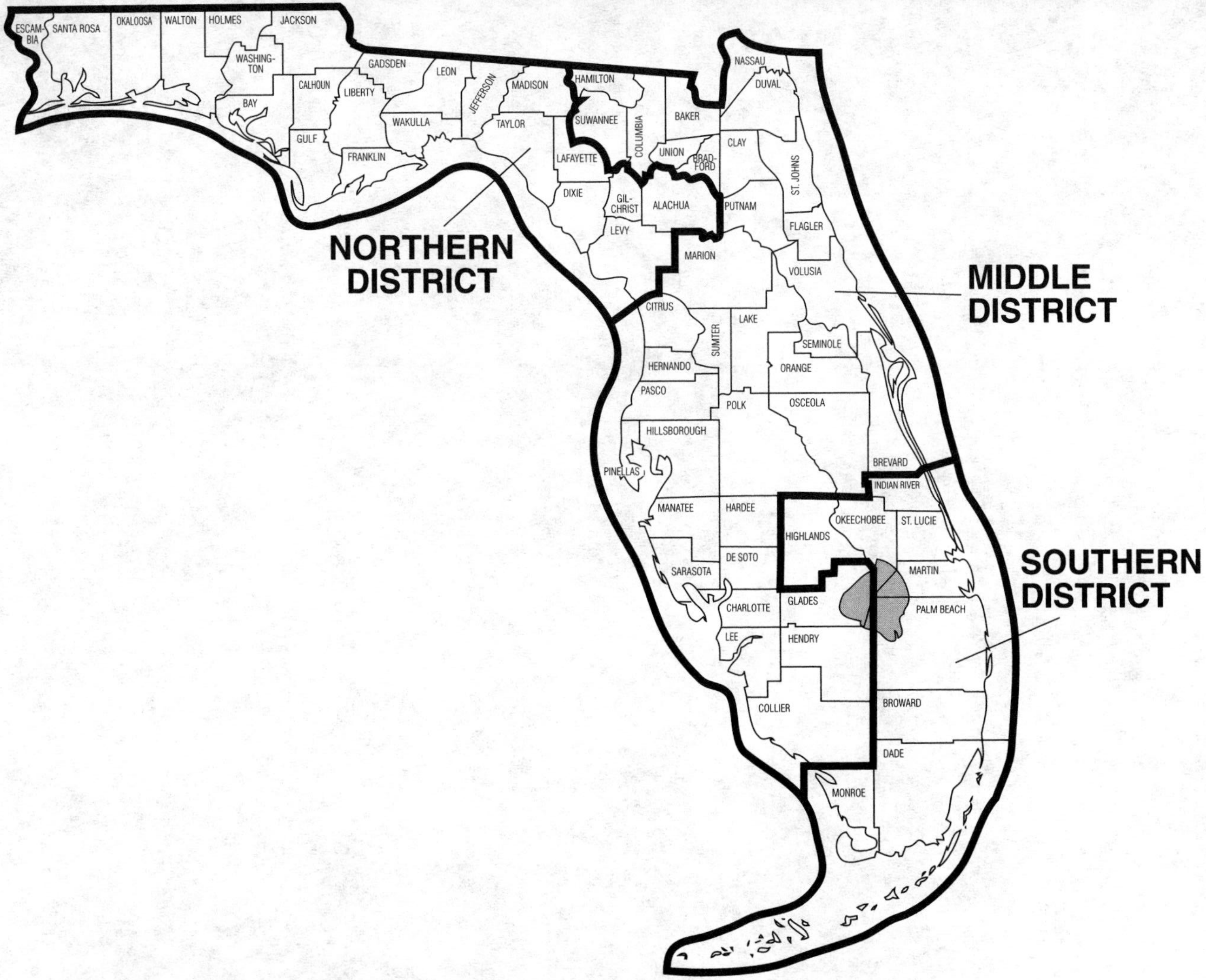

ESCAM-BIA
SANTA ROSA
OKALOOSA
WALTON
HOLMES
JACKSON
WASHING-TON
BAY
CALHOUN
GULF
GADSDEN
LIBERTY
FRANKLIN
WAKULLA
LEON
JEFFERSON
MADISON
TAYLOR
HAMILTON
SUWANNEE
COLUMBIA
LAFAYETTE
DIXIE
GIL-CHRIST
LEVY
ALACHUA
UNION
BRAD-FORD
BAKER
NASSAU
DUVAL
CLAY
ST. JOHNS
PUTNAM
FLAGLER
MARION
VOLUSIA
CITRUS
SUMTER
LAKE
SEMINOLE
ORANGE
HERNANDO
PASCO
POLK
OSCEOLA
HILLSBOROUGH
PINELLAS
BREVARD
INDIAN RIVER
MANATEE
HARDEE
OKEECHOBEE
ST. LUCIE
HIGHLANDS
DE SOTO
SARASOTA
MARTIN
CHARLOTTE
GLADES
PALM BEACH
LEE
HENDRY
COLLIER
BROWARD
DADE
MONROE
NORTHERN DISTRICT
MIDDLE DISTRICT
SOUTHERN DISTRICT

UNITED STATES DISTRICT COURTS DISTRICTS OF FLORIDA

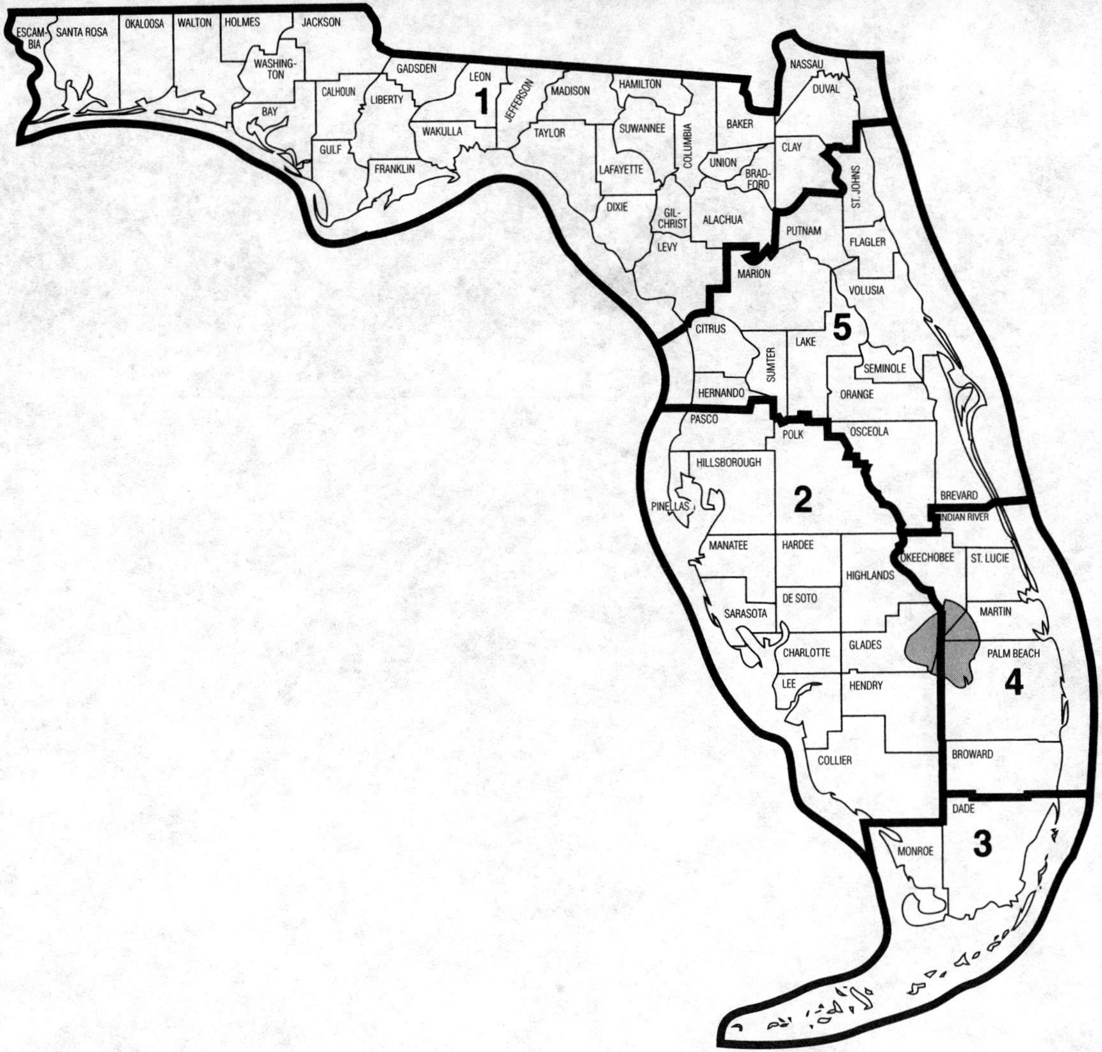
ESCAM-BIA
SANTA ROSA
OKALOOSA
WALTON
HOLMES
JACKSON
WASHING-TON
BAY
CALHOUN
GULF
GADSDEN
LIBERTY
FRANKLIN
LEON
1
WAKULLA
JEFFERSON
MADISON
TAYLOR
HAMILTON
SUWANNEE
LAFAYETTE
DIXIE
COLUMBIA
GIL-CHRIST
LEVY
BAKER
UNION
BRAD-FORD
ALACHUA
NASSAU
DUVAL
CLAY
ST. JOHNS
PUTNAM
FLAGLER
MARION
VOLUSIA
CITRUS
5
LAKE
SUMTER
SEMINOLE
ORANGE
HERNANDO
PASCO
POLK
OSCEOLA
HILLSBOROUGH
PINELLAS
2
BREVARD
INDIAN RIVER
MANATEE
HARDEE
HIGHLANDS
OKEECHOBEE
ST. LUCIE
DE SOTO
SARASOTA
MARTIN
CHARLOTTE
GLADES
PALM BEACH
LEE
HENDRY
4
COLLIER
BROWARD
DADE
MONROE
3

DISTRICTS OF FLORIDA DISTRICT COURTS OF APPEAL

1
2
3
4
5

DISTRICTS OF FLORIDA DISTRICT COURTS OF APPEAL

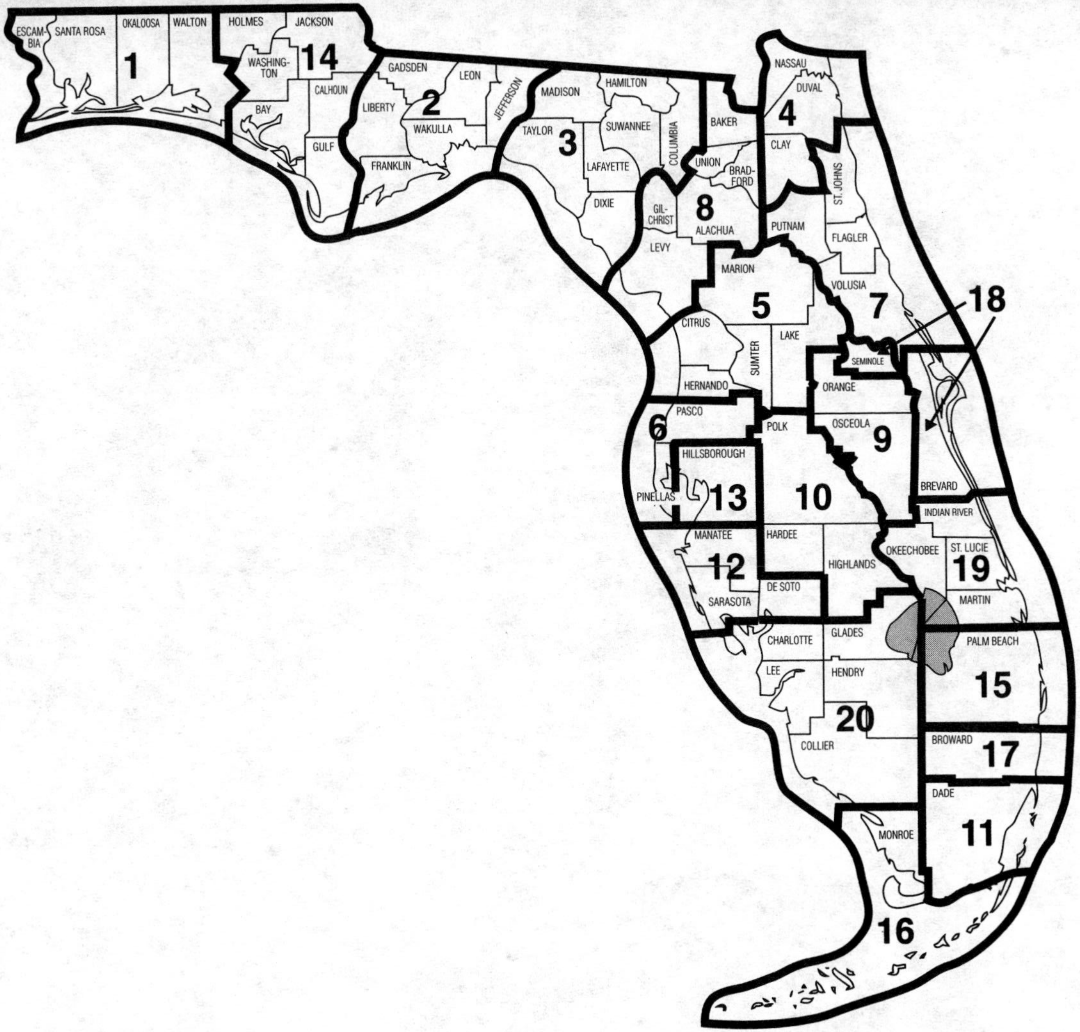
ESCAMBIA
SANTA ROSA
OKALOOSA
WALTON
1
HOLMES
JACKSON
WASHINGTON
14
CALHOUN
BAY
GULF
GADSDEN
LEON
LIBERTY
2
WAKULLA
FRANKLIN
JEFFERSON
MADISON
HAMILTON
TAYLOR
3
SUWANNEE
COLUMBIA
LAFAYETTE
DIXIE
BAKER
UNION
BRADFORD
GILCHRIST
8
ALACHUA
LEVY
NASSAU
DUVAL
4
CLAY
ST. JOHNS
PUTNAM
FLAGLER
MARION
VOLUSIA
5
7
18
CITRUS
SUMTER
LAKE
SEMINOLE
ORANGE
HERNANDO
PASCO
6
POLK
OSCEOLA
9
HILLSBOROUGH
PINELLAS
13
10
BREVARD
INDIAN RIVER
MANATEE
HARDEE
OKEECHOBEE
ST. LUCIE
19
12
HIGHLANDS
DE SOTO
SARASOTA
MARTIN
CHARLOTTE
GLADES
PALM BEACH
LEE
HENDRY
15
20
COLLIER
BROWARD
17
DADE
MONROE
11
16

JUDICIAL CIRCUITS OF FLORIDA CIRCUIT COURTS

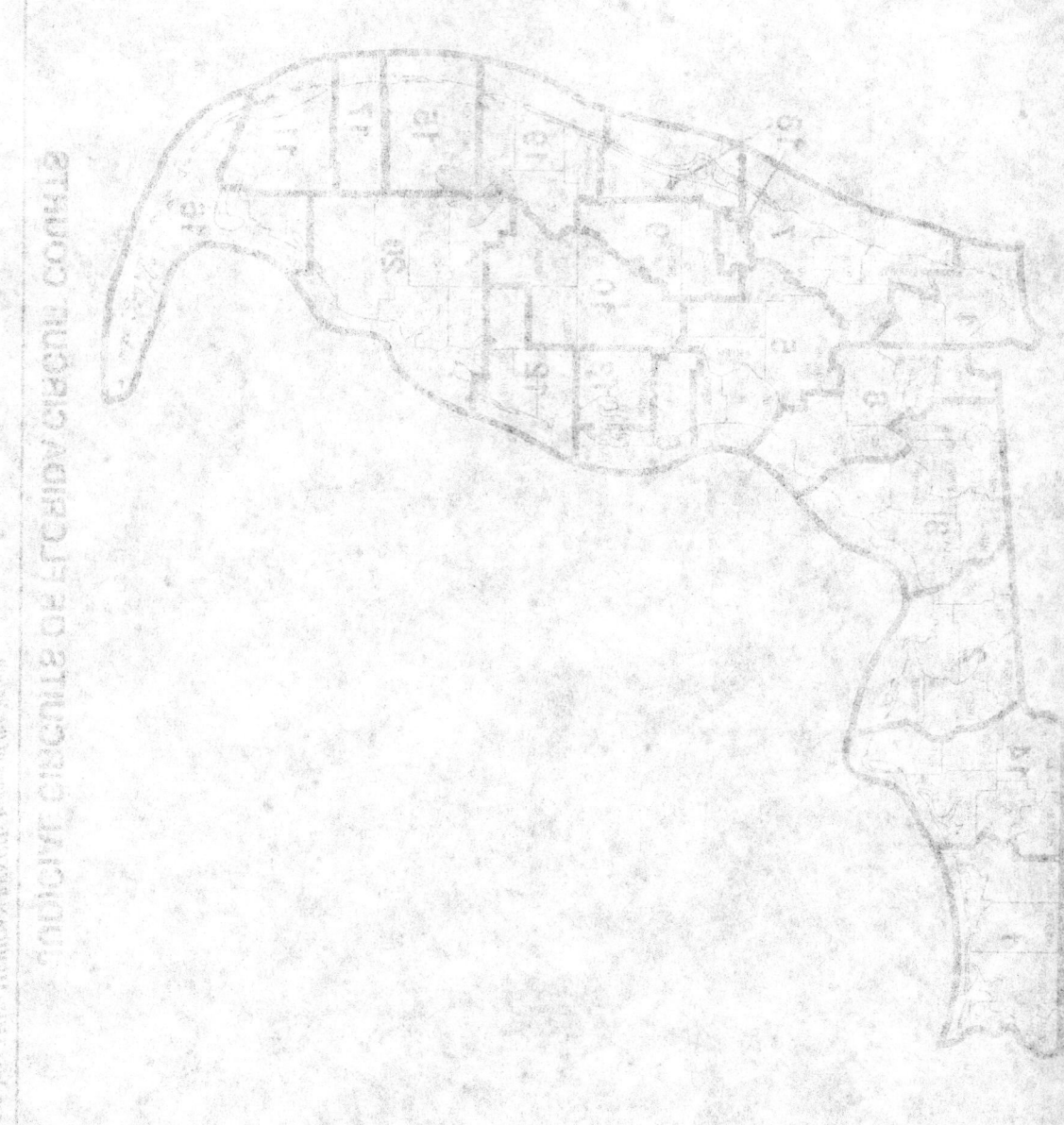

FLORIDA

ACKERMAN, David B. *(Judge, Escambia County Court)* Elected to term beginning Jan 1991. Reelected 1994 and 1998. Current term expires Jan 2005.
Office: Judicial Building, 190 Governmental Center, Pensacola 32501.
Telephone: (850) 595-4420.
Fax: (850) 595-4404

ADAMS, Durand J. *(Judge, Florida Circuit Court Twelfth Judicial Circuit)*
Mailing address: P.O. Box 1000, Bradenton 34206.
Office: 1115 Manatee Avenue West, Bradenton 32305.
Telephone: (941) 749-7156.
Fax: (941) 742-5964

ADAMS, Gail *(Judge, Florida Circuit Court Ninth Judicial Circuit)*
Office: 1740 Orange County Courthouse, 425 North Orange Avenue, Orlando 32801.
Telephone: (407) 836-2224.

ADAMS, Henry Lee, Jr. *(Judge, United States District Court Middle District of Florida)* Appointed for life by President Bill Clinton to term beginning 1993. Born Jacksonville Florida April 8, 1945. Educated at Florida Agricultural and Mechanical University B.S. 1966 and Howard University School of Law J.D. 1969. In legal practice Jacksonville 1972-79. Judge, Florida Circuit Court Fourth Judicial Circuit 1979-93.
Assistant Public Defender Duval County 1970-72. Fellow Duval County Legal Aid Association 1969-70.
Mailing address: P.O. Box 52567, Jacksonville 32201-2567.
Telephone: (904) 549-1930.

ADAMS, James R. *(Judge, Lee County Court)*
Office: Lee County Justice Center, 1700 Monroe Street, Fort Myers 33901.
Telephone: (239) 335-2954.
Fax: (239) 335-2586

ADAMS, John H., Sr. *(Judge, Florida Circuit Court Ninth Judicial Circuit)* Former Judge, Orange County Court.
Office: Osceola County Courthouse, 12 South Vernon Avenue, Kissimmee 34741.
Telephone: (407) 343-2491.

ADDERLY, A. Leo *(Judge, Dade County Court)*
Office: 1017 Dade County Courthouse, 73 West Flagler Street, Miami 33130.
Telephone: (305) 349-7012.

ADKINS, John C. *(Senior Judge, Brevard County Court)* Assumed office Jan 3, 1989. Assumed Senior Judge status, serves by assignment.
Office: Moore Justice Center, 2825 Judge Fran Jamieson Way, Viera 32940-8006.
Telephone: (321) 637-5555.

AGNER, John R. *(Senior Judge, Florida Circuit Court Third Judicial Circuit)* Former Chief Judge. Assumed Senior Judge status, serves by assignment.
Mailing address: P.O. Box 1000, Perry 32347.
Telephone: (386) 758-2163.

AIKENS, Augustus D., Jr. *(Judge, Leon County Court)*
Office: 265-E Leon County Courthouse, 301 South Monroe Street, Tallahassee 32301.
Telephone: (850) 577-4314.
Fax: (850) 922-0070

ALBRITTON, Richard *(Judge, Florida Circuit Court Fourteenth Judicial Circuit)*
Mailing address: P.O. Box 2237, Panama City 32402.
Telephone: (850) 747-5318.
Fax: (850) 747-5159

ALCOTT, Roger A. *(Judge, Florida Circuit Court Tenth Judicial Circuit)*
Mailing address: P.O. Box 9000, Box J-108, Bartow 33831-9000.
Telephone: (863) 534-4625.
Fax: (863) 534-7723

ALDERMAN, James E. *(Senior Justice, Florida Supreme Court)* Appointed by Governor Reubin Askew to term beginning April 11, 1978. Retained by election 1980. Chief Justice July 1982 to June 1984. Assumed Senior Justice status, serves by assignment. Born Fort Pierce Florida Nov 1, 1936. Episcopalian. Educated at University of Florida B.A. 1958 LL.B. 1961. Admitted to practice Florida 1961. Began legal practice Fort Pierce 1961. U.S. Commissioner and Magistrate, U.S. District Court Southern District of Florida 1962-71. Judge, St. Lucie County Court 1971-72. Judge, Florida Circuit Court Nineteenth Judicial Circuit 1973-76. Judge, Florida District Court of Appeal Fourth District 1976-78.
Member The Florida Bar.
Office: 500 South Duval Street, Tallahassee 32399.

ALEMAN, Cheryl J. *(Judge, Florida Circuit Court Seventeenth Judicial Circuit)*
Office: Broward County Courthouse, 201 S.E. Sixth Street, Fort Lauderdale 33301.
Telephone: (954) 831-6341.
Fax: (954) 831-5572

ALEXANDER, John M. *(Judge, Florida Circuit Court Seventh Judicial Circuit)*
Office: Judicial Center, 4010 Lewis Speedway, St. Augustine 32095.
Telephone: (904) 823-2380.
Fax: (904) 823-2392

ALLAN, Linda H. *(Judge, Florida Circuit Court Sixth Judicial Circuit)*
Office: Criminal Justice Center, 14250 49th Street North, Clearwater 33762.
Telephone: (727) 464-7115.
Fax: (727) 464-7684

ALLAWAS, Meryl Lee *(Judge, Florida Circuit Court Eighteenth Judicial Circuit)*
Office: Moore Justice Center, Second Floor, 2825 Judge Fran Jamieson Way, Viera 32940-8006.
Telephone: (321) 617-7285.

ALLBRITTON, Owen S. *(Senior Judge, Florida Circuit Court Sixth Judicial Circuit)* Elected to term beginning Jan 1985. Reelected 1990. Assumed Senior Judge status, serves by assignment. Born Clearwater Florida July 25, 1926. Admitted to practice Florida 1951.
Office: Judicial Building, 545 First Avenue North, St. Petersburg 33701.
Telephone: (727) 464-4470.

ALLEN, Michael E. *(Chief Judge, Florida District Court of Appeal First District)* Appointed by Governor Bob Martinez to term beginning Jan 2, 1990. Retained by election. Chief Judge since July 1, 2001. Born Quincy Florida Dec 16, 1949. Educated at Florida State University B.S. 1971 and Stetson University College of Law J.D. 1975. In legal practice Florida Oct 1975 to Dec 1980.
Assistant State Attorney Oct 1978 to March 1980. Public Defender Second Judicial Circuit Jan 1981 to Jan 1990. Past President Gadsen County Bar Association. Former Member Judicial Council of Florida and The Florida Bar. Honorary Life Member Florida Public Defender Association and Florida Association of Criminal Defense Lawyers.
Office: 301 Martin Luther King Jr. Boulevard, Tallahassee 32399-1850.
Telephone: (850) 487-1000.
Fax: (850) 921-4768

ALLEN, Michael G. *(Judge, Florida Circuit Court First Judicial Circuit)* Appointed by Governor Jeb Bush to term beginning Feb 7, 2000. Term expires Jan 6, 2003. Born Pensacola Florida Oct 13, 1956. Educated at Florida State University B.S. 1978 J.D. 1981. Admitted to practice Florida 1981 and U.S. District Court Northern District of Florida 1983. In legal practice Pensacola 1982-94. Judge, Santa Rosa County Court Jan 3, 1995 to 2000.
Office: 6865 S.W. Caroline Street, Box S, Milton 32570.
Telephone: (850) 623-0135.
Fax: (850) 623-2802

ALLEY, Nancy F. *(Judge, Florida Circuit Court Eighteenth Judicial Circuit)* Elected Sept 1996 to term beginning Jan 1, 1997. Reelected 2002, current term expires Jan 2009. Born Mississippi. Educated at University of Mississippi B.A. 1974 and Villanova University J.D. 1983. Admitted to practice Florida 1983, U.S. Court of Federal Claims 1987, Mississippi 1988 and District of Columbia 1991. In legal practice Altamonte Springs Florida 1983-96. General Master, Florida Circuit Court Eighteenth Judicial Circuit 1987-88.
With Department of Welfare 1988 and Office of General Counsel Jackson Mississippi 1988-91. Department of Welfare since 1988. Instructor in Wills, Trusts and Estates Barry University School of Law since 1999. Member FCPBP, Central Florida Association of Women Lawyers, Broward County Florida Association of Women Lawyers, The Florida Bar, The Mississippi Bar, Brevard County and Seminole County Bar Associations. Recipient Outstanding Achievement Award from JROTC Lake Howell High School, Special Appreciation Award from DCFS and Thomas Wigham Award. Member Tiger Bay, Rotary Club, PBAS and Chamber of Commerce. Interests include reading.
Office: Seminole County Courthouse, 301 North Park Avenue, Sanford 32771-1292.
Telephone: (407) 665-4262.
Fax: (407) 665-5349

ALTENBERND, Chris W. *(Chief Judge, Florida District Court of Appeal Second District)* Appointed by Governor Bob Martinez to term beginning Jan 3, 1989. Retained by election 1990, 1996 and 2002. Current term expires Jan 2009. Born Muscatine Iowa Jan 18, 1949. Educated at University of Missouri B.A. with honors 1972, Harvard Law School J.D. 1975 and University of Virginia LL.M. in Judicial Process 1998. Member Phi Beta Kappa.
Office: 600 Tampa Branch Headquarters, 801 East Twiggs Street, Tampa 33602-3547.
Telephone: (813) 272-3430.
Fax: (813) 229-6534

ALTONAGA, Cecilia Maria *(Judge, Florida Circuit Court Eleventh Judicial Circuit)* Appointed by Governor Jeb Bush to term beginning Sept 1999. Elected 2002, current term expires Jan 2009. Serves Juvenile Division. Born Baltimore Maryland Dec 26, 1962. Roman Catholic. Educated at Florida International University B.A. with highest honors 1983 and Yale Law School J.D. 1986. Articles Editor Yale Journal of International Law. Law Clerk to Chief Judge Edward B. Davis, U.S. District Court Southern District of Florida 1987-88. Director Yale Moot Court Board. Member Phi Eta Sigma. Admitted to practice Florida 1986, U.S. District Court Southern District of Florida 1987 and U.S. Court of Appeals Eleventh Circuit 1988. In legal practice Miami 1988-96. Judge, Dade County Court May 1996 to 1999, appointed by Governor Lawton Chiles.
Assistant County Attorney Dade County 1988-96. Member Eleventh Judicial Circuit Professionalism Committee, Florida Association of Women Lawyers, First Family Law American Inn of Court, Cuban American Bar Association, Hialeah-Miami Lakes and Dade County (Schools Committee) Bar Associations. Instructor "Competitive Bidding and Bid Disputes in Local Government Purchases of Goods and Services" 18th Annual Local Government Law in Florida Seminar May 1995, "Small Claims and the *Pro Se* Litigant" Annual Business Meeting Florida Conference of County Court Judges 1997 and "Economic Loss Rule in Florida" Florida Advanced Judicial College Orlando May 1999. Guest Speaker "Domestic Violence and Issues in the Workplace" Spring Educational Institute International Association of Personnel in Employment Security Deerfield Beach April 3, 1998 and Florida Coalition Against Domestic Violence Clearinghouse Project May 1999. Recipient "Mujeres y Poder" Lifetime Achievement Award from Diario de la Mujer and Alumni Award for College of Arts and Sciences from Florida International University. Pro Bono Attorney Guardian Ad Litem Project 1995-96. Member Junior League of Dade County. Charter Member Advisory Board Honors College Florida International University.
Office: 624 Gerstein Justice Building, 1351 N.W. Twelfth Street, Miami 33125.
Telephone: (305) 548-5769.
Fax: (305) 548-5553

ALVAREZ, Ronald V. *(Judge, Florida Circuit Court Fifteenth Judicial Circuit)* Assumed office April 2, 1993.
Office: South County Courthouse, 200 West Atlantic Avenue, Delray Beach 33444.
Telephone: (561) 274-1415.
Fax: (561) 274-1406

ANDERSON, Charlotte W. *(Judge, Hillsborough County Court)* Elected to term beginning Jan 3, 1995. Reelected 1998, current term expires Jan 2005.
Office: 200 Annex, 800 East Kennedy Boulevard, Tampa 33602-4146.
Telephone: (813) 272-6562.
Fax: (813) 276-2329

ANDERSON, Isaac, Jr. *(Judge, Florida Circuit Court Twentieth Judicial Circuit)* Elected July 1990. Reelected 1996 and 2002. Current term expires Jan 2009. Born Fort Myers Florida July 11, 1946. United Methodist. Educated at Miami University, Ohio B.A. and Washington College of Law of American University J.D. Member Kappa Alpha Psi. Admitted to practice Florida 1977, U.S. District Court Middle District of Florida, U.S. Court of Appeals Eleventh Circuit and U.S. Supreme Court. In legal practice Fort Myers and Naples 1977-81. Judge, Lee County Court 1981-90.
Member The Florida Bar, Lee County, National and American Bar Associations. Attended courses on Special Courts Jurisdiction Nov 6-18, 1983, Evidence July 14-19, 1985, Great Issues in American Law July 21-26, 1985, Judicial Writing in Trial Courts Specialty July 26 to Aug 2, 1986 and Conducting the Civil Trial Oct 25-30, 1987 The National Judicial College and Juvenile Law Specialty Course State Court Administrator's Office Florida Feb 26-28, 1990. Sergeant USAF 1965-68. Hobbies include reading, fishing and old home restoration.
Office: Lee County Justice Center Complex, 1700 Monroe Street, Fort Myers 33901.
Telephone: (239) 335-2412.
Fax: (239) 335-2588

ANDREWS, Daniel True *(Senior Judge, Florida Circuit Court Tenth Judicial Circuit)* Elected to term beginning Jan 8, 1991. Reelected 1996. Assumed Senior Judge status, serves by assignment. Born St. Joseph Missouri Aug 18, 1950. Presbyterian. Educated at University of North Florida B.B.A. with honors 1974 and Ohio Northern University J.D. 1980. Admitted to practice Florida 1980. Began legal practice Bartow 1980. In legal practice Lakeland 1982. Judge, Polk County Court Jan 8, 1985 to Jan 7, 1991.
Former Assistant State Attorney. Member The Florida Bar and Lakeland Bar Association. Specialist Five U.S. Army 1970-73 (Vietnam). Operations Manager Mutual Companies 1974-77. Enjoys horses and muscle cars.
Mailing address: P.O. Box 9000, Drawer J-133, Bartow 33831-9000.
Office: 255 North Broadway, Bartow 33830.
Telephone: (863) 534-4690.

ANDREWS, Horace A. *(Senior Judge, Florida Circuit Court Sixth Judicial Circuit)* Elected to term beginning Jan 1, 1991. Assumed Senior Judge status Jan 1, 1997, serves by assignment. Born Plant City Florida Oct 2, 1932. Baptist. Educated at University of Florida B.S.B.A. 1954 and Stetson College of Law J.D. 1970. Member Phi Alpha Delta. Admitted to practice Florida 1970. Judge, Pinellas County Court 1980-91.
Mailing address: P.O. Box 15835, St. Petersburg 33731.
Telephone: (727) 381-9260.

ANDREWS, Michael F. *(Judge, Pinellas County Court)*
Office: Criminal Justice Center, 14250 49th Street North, Clearwater 33762.
Telephone: (727) 464-6470.
Fax: (727) 464-6484

ANDREWS, Robert Lance *(Judge, Florida Circuit Court Seventeenth Judicial Circuit)* Appointed by Governor Robert Graham to term beginning 1982. Elected to subsequent terms. Born Hollywood Florida Feb 6, 1941. Methodist. Educated at Broward Community College A.S. 1964, Florida Atlantic University B.S. 1968 and University of Georgia J.D. 1972. Admitted to practice Florida 1972, U.S. District Court Southern District of Florida 1972, U.S. Court of Appeals Fifth Circuit 1972, U.S. Supreme Court 1975 and U.S. Court of Military Appeals 1977. Began legal practice Hollywood 1972. In legal practice Miami 1974-77. Judge, Broward County Court 1978-82, appointed by Governor Reubin Askew.
Assistant U.S. Attorney 1974-77. Commander USN since 1975 (retired). Member Masonic Lodge 209.
Office: 1020 Broward County Courthouse, 201 S.E. Sixth Street, Fort Lauderdale 33301.
Telephone: (954) 831-7717.
Fax: (954) 831-5572

ANDRINGA, Henry J. *(Judge, Pinellas County Court)*
Office: 501 First Avenue North, Room A218, St. Petersburg 33701.
Telephone: (727) 582-7788.
Fax: (727) 582-7422

ANGEL, Carven D. *(Judge, Florida Circuit Court Fifth Judicial Circuit)* Elected 1978 to term beginning Jan 2, 1979. Reelected 1984, 1990, 1996 and 2002. Current term expires Jan 2009. Born Raleigh North Carolina Jan 20, 1943. Member First Presbyterian Church. Educated at University of North Carolina B.A. 1965 and University of Florida J.D. 1968. Member Phi Beta Kappa. Admitted to practice Florida 1968. Began legal practice Ocala 1970. Judge, Marion County Court 1974-79.
Member The Florida Bar and American Bar Association.
Office: 110 N.W. First Avenue, Ocala 34475.
Telephone: (352) 401-6735.
Fax: (352) 401-6760

ANGELOS, Cynthia G. *(Judge, Florida Circuit Court Nineteenth Judicial Circuit)* Appointed by Governor Lawton Chiles Sept 8, 1993.
Office: 320 Courthouse Addition, 218 South Second Street, Fort Pierce 34950.
Telephone: (772) 462-1469.

ANSTEAD, Harry Lee *(Chief Justice, Florida Supreme Court)* Appointed by Governor Lawton Chiles to term beginning Aug 29, 1994. Retained by election. Born Jacksonville Florida Nov 4, 1937. Educated at University of Florida B.A. J.D. and University of Virginia LL.M. Judge and Chief Judge, Florida District Court of Appeal Fourth District 1976-94. Also served as Acting Judge County Court and Circuit Court.

ANSTEAD, HARRY LEE—*Continued*

Former Member Commission on the Structure of Florida's Courts. Former Member and Vice Chair Committee on Civil Jury Instructions Florida Supreme Court. Chair Commission on Professionalism Florida Supreme Court. Founder American Inn of Court. Member The Florida Bar and American Bar Association. Attended Trial Judges Education Program National College of the State Judiciary. Former Member Board of Governors Shepard Broad Law Center Nova Southeastern University and St. Thomas University Law School. Member Holy Name of Jesus Catholic Church. Founder Urban League of Palm Beach County and Beautiful Palm Beaches, Inc. Enjoys travel and marathon running.

Office: Supreme Court Building, 500 South Duval Street, Tallahassee 32399-1925.

Telephone: (850) 488-2281.

Fax: (850) 487-4696.

ANTOON, John, II *(Judge, United States District Court Middle District of Florida)* Appointed for life by President Bill Clinton to term beginning June 2, 2000. Born Bakersfield California May 16, 1946. Educated at Florida Southern College B.A. 1968, Florida State University College of Law J.D. 1971 and Florida Institute of Technology M.S. 1993. In legal practice 1971-84. Judge 1985-95 and Former Chief Judge, Florida Circuit Court Eighteenth Judicial Circuit. Judge 1995-2000 and Former Chief Judge, Florida District Court of Appeal Fifth District.

Prosecutor City of Cocoa 1971-72. Assistant Public Defender Eighteenth Judicial Circuit 1972-76.

Office: U.S. Courthouse, 80 North Hughey Avenue, Orlando 32801.

Telephone: (407) 835-4200.

APTE, Alan S. *(Judge, Florida Circuit Court Ninth Judicial Circuit)*

Office: 2000 East Michigan, Orlando 32806.

Telephone: (407) 836-2324.

ARAMONY, Susan *(Judge, Florida Circuit Court Seventeenth Judicial Circuit)*

Office: 358 Broward County Courthouse, 201 S.E. Sixth Street, Fort Lauderdale 33301.

Telephone: (954) 831-6916.

Fax: (954) 831-7997

ARIAS, Roberto A. *(Judge, Duval County Court)* Appointed by Governor Lawton Chiles to term beginning July 1, 1995. Elected Sept 1996 and 2000. Current term expires Jan 2007. Born Camaguey Cuba Oct 20, 1954. Episcopalian. Educated at Florida International University B.A. 1976 and The Ohio State University College of Law J.D. 1980. Admitted to practice Florida 1980, U.S. District Court Middle District of Florida 1986 and U.S. Court of Appeals Eleventh Circuit 1986. In legal practice Jacksonville 1985-95.

Assistant Public Defender 1981-85. Member Center for State Courts (Board Member since 1999) and Judicial Pro Bono Task Force. County Court Mentor Judge Florida Conference of County Judges since 1996. Past President Arlington Rotary Club. Board Member Hospice of Northeast Florida. Vestry Christ Episcopal Church. Membership Committee Girl Scouts. Active in Boy Scouts. Enjoys fishing.

Office: Duval County Courthouse, 330 East Bay Street, Jacksonville 32202.

Telephone: (904) 630-2580.

Fax: (904) 630-2979

ARNOLD, C. Jeffery *(Judge, Orange County Court)* Appointed by Governor Lawton Chiles to term beginning May 1994. Educated at College of William & Mary B.A. 1966 and Florida State University College of Law J.D. 1969. Admitted to practice Florida 1969, U.S. District Courts Middle 1969, Northern 1981 and Southern 1981 Districts of Florida and U.S. Court of Appeals Eleventh Circuit 1969. In legal practice Orlando 1969-94.

Former Member Florida Council of Bar Association Presidents, Inc. (Board of Directors 1986-91, President 1989-90) and Florida Academy of Trial Lawyers. Member Conference of County Court Judges of Florida (Member since 1995 and Chairman 1999 Education Committee, Member since 1995 and Vice Chairman 1999 and 2001 Criminal Law Committee, Circuit Representative Ninth Judicial Circuit since 1998, Board of Directors since 1998, President Elect 2002-03), The Florida Bar (Vice Chairman Ninth Judicial Circuit Grievance Committee 1979-82, Chairman Voluntary Bar Liaison Committee 1991-92) and The Orange County Bar Association, Inc. (Board of Directors/Executive Council 1981-86, President 1984-85, Chairman Judicial Relations Committee 2001-03). Presentation Coordinator "Mental Health" Summer 1999 Conference of County Court Judges of Florida. Lecturer "Ethical Considerations in Mortgage Foreclosures" The Florida Bar, "Trial Tactics," Collecting on a Final Judgment" and "Advanced Real Estate" National Business Institute, "Eminent Domain in Florida" and "Current Developments in Domestic Relations Law" Florida Academy of Trial Lawyers and "Ethics in Real Estate Transactions" Attorney's Title Insurance Fund, Inc. Recipient Distinguished Leadership Award from Conference of County Court Judges of Florida 1999 and 2000, Outstanding Jurist of the Year Award from Young Lawyers Division The Florida Bar 2000, "Personal Commitment to Victims of Crime" Award from Victim Services Coalition of Central Florida 2001 and Jurist of the Year Award from Florida Conference of County Court Judges 2002. Captain U.S. Army 1970-72. Recipient Army Commendation Medal 1972. Assistant Coach Winter Park Little League 1975-76. Board of Directors 1984-88 and President 1986-87 Brookshire Elementary School PTA. Board of Directors 1984-98 and President 1993-94 Winter Park High School Foundation, Inc. Participant Ninth Judicial Circuit Teen Court since 1996 and Habitat for Humanity since 1996. Former Member Florida Supreme Court Historical Society. Member Orange County Legal Aid Society (Board of Trustees 1984-86, Teen Court since 1995, Night Court since 1996), Central Florida Chapter College of William & Mary Alumni Association (Board of Directors since 1990, Vice President 1992-93), Council of 100 Orlando Florida (Board of Directors since 1998), Florida Citrus Sports Association (Founder 1969, Team Selection Committee since 1972, Tournament of Champions Committee since 1990), Downtown Orlando

ARNOLD, C. JEFFERY—*Continued*

Branch Rotary Club and National Safety Council (DUI Advisory Committee since 1996).

Office: 375 Orange County Courthouse, 425 North Orange Avenue, Orlando 32801.

Telephone: (407) 836-2324.

Fax: (407) 835-5145

ARNOLD, Charles W., Jr. *(Judge, Florida Circuit Court Fourth Judicial Circuit)* Appointed by Governor Lawton Chiles Sept 18, 1997 to term beginning Jan 1, 1998. Elected Nov 7, 2000, current term expires Jan 2007. Born Jacksonville Florida Jan 3, 1944. Presbyterian. Educated at University of Florida B.S.B.A. 1966 J.D. 1968. Attorney General University of Florida Honor Court. Member Florida Blue Key. Admitted to practice Florida 1968, U.S. District Courts Middle, Northern and Southern Districts of Florida, U.S. Courts of Appeals Fifth and Eleventh Circuits, U.S. Tax Court and U.S. Supreme Court. In legal practice Jacksonville 1973-92 and 1994-97.

Assistant General Counsel 1968-69 and General Counsel 1992-94 Jacksonville. Assistant State Attorney Florida 1969-73. Member Professionalism Committee since 2001 and Courthouse Design Committee Florida Circuit Court Fourth Judicial Circuit. Fellow American College of Trial Lawyers. Member Chester Bedell Inn of Court, The Florida Bar, Jacksonville (Former Chairman Criminal Law Section) and American Bar Associations. Past President San Jose Athletic Association. Former Director Jacksonville Sports Development Authority. Member Rotary Club Mandarin (Former Director). Enjoys baseball.

Office: 201 Duval County Courthouse, 330 East Bay Street, Jacksonville 32202.

Telephone: (904) 630-2567.

Fax: (904) 630-2979

ARNOLD, Harold C. *(Judge, Duval County Court)*

Office: Duval County Courthouse, 330 East Bay Street, Jacksonville 32202.

Telephone: (904) 630-2535.

Fax: (904) 630-2979

ARNOLD, James D. *(Judge, Florida Circuit Court Thirteenth Judicial Circuit)* Assumed office Dec 24, 1989. Elected to subsequent terms. Former Judge, Hillsborough County Court.

Office: 311 Hillsborough County Courthouse, 419 Pierce Street, Tampa 33602-4022.

Telephone: (813) 272-6993.

ARTIGLIERE, Ralph *(Judge, Florida Circuit Court Tenth Judicial Circuit)*

Mailing address: P.O. Box 9000, Drawer J-154, Bartow 33831-9000.

Telephone: (863) 534-5860.

Fax: (863) 534-4094

ATACK, Sharon *(Judge, Flagler County Court)* Appointed by Governor Lawton Chiles to term beginning Feb 13, 1995.

Mailing address: P.O. Box 921, Bunnell 32110.

Telephone: (386) 437-7438.

Fax: (386) 437-7438

BABB, Linda H. *(Judge, Florida Circuit Court Sixth Judicial Circuit)*

Office: Dade City Courthouse, 38053 Live Oak Avenue, Dade City 33525.

Telephone: (352) 521-4404.

Fax: (352) 521-4107

BABB, Rhonda E. *(Judge, Brevard County Court)*

Office: 160 Melbourne Courthouse, 51 South Nieman Avenue, Melbourne 32901-1261.

Telephone: (321) 952-4702.

Fax: (321) 952-4705

BACH, Mercedes A. *(Judge, Dade County Court)* Elected to term beginning Jan 3, 1995. Reelected 1998, current term expires Jan 2005.

Office: 1-6 Coral Gables Courthouse, 3100 Ponce de Leon Boulevard, Coral Gables 33134.

Telephone: (305) 569-2502.

Fax: (305) 529-2733

BACKMAN, Paul L. *(Judge, Florida Circuit Court Seventeenth Judicial Circuit)* Appointed to term beginning April 1, 1993. Reelected 1994 and 2000. Current term expires Jan 2007. Born Jamaica New York Jan 28, 1949. Jewish. Educated at Southampton College of Long Island University B.A. 1971 and John Marshall Law School J.D. 1975. Member Phi Alpha Delta and The Gavel Society. Admitted to practice Florida 1975 and U.S. District Court Southern District of Florida. In legal practice Hollywood 1975-84. Former Judge, Broward County Court, Jan 8, 1985 to 1993.

Associate Professor of Advanced Litigation for Paralegals Nova University. Former Member Florida Conference of County Court Judges. Member Florida Conference of Circuit Court Judges, The Florida Bar and Broward County Bar Association. Attended Florida Advanced Judicial College and The National Judicial College. Enjoys jigsaw puzzles, golf, basketball and travel.

Office: 5790 Broward County Courthouse, 201 S.E. Sixth Street, Fort Lauderdale 33301.

Telephone: (954) 831-7566.

Fax: (954) 831-7387

BAGLEY, Jerald *(Judge, Florida Circuit Court Eleventh Judicial Circuit)* Appointed by Governor Lawton Chiles Jan 30, 1995 to term beginning March 1, 1995.

Office: 407 Gerstein Justice Building, 1351 N.W. Twelfth Street, Miami 33125-1632.

Telephone: (305) 548-5166.

BAILEY, Jennifer D. *(Judge, Florida Circuit Court Eleventh Judicial Circuit)*

Office: 1001 Dade County Courthouse, 73 West Flagler Street, Miami 33130.

Telephone: (305) 349-7016.

Fax: (305) 349-7011

BAILEY, Nelson *(Judge, Palm Beach County Court)*

Office: Criminal Justice Complex, 3228 Gun Club Road, West Palm Beach 33406.

Telephone: (561) 688-4599.

Fax: (561) 688-4597

BAIRD, William Douglas *(Judge, Florida Circuit Court Sixth Judicial Circuit)* Appointed by Governor Bob Martinez May 1988. Elected Nov 1988, 1994 and 2000. Current term expires Jan 2007. Born Knoxville Tennessee April 29, 1943. Protestant. Educated at University of Colorado B.A. 1965 and Stetson University

BAIRD, WILLIAM DOUGLAS—*Continued*

College of Law J.D. 1968. Member Sigma Alpha Epsilon. Admitted to practice Florida 1968 and U.S. District Court District of Florida 1969. In legal practice St. Petersburg 1968-86. Judge, Pinellas Park Municipal Court 1972-73. Judge, Pinellas County Court 1986-88.

City Attorney Treasure Island 1972-86. Chairman Sixth Judicial Circuit Grievance Committee. Member National Institute of Municipal Law Officers, Sixth Circuit Judicial Nominating Commission, Pinellas Inns of Court, The Florida Bar, St. Petersburg and American Bar Associations. Attended Florida Bar Trial Seminar Florida Judicial College. Enjoys classical music, reading, sports and bicycling.

Office: 315 Court Street, Clearwater 33756.
Telephone: (727) 464-3232.

BAKER, David A. *(Magistrate Judge, United States District Court Middle District of Florida)* Appointed by U.S. District Court judges.

Office: 501 U.S. Courthouse, 80 North Hughey Avenue, Orlando 32801.
Telephone: (407) 835-4290.

BAKER, Franklin G. *(Judge, Florida Circuit Court Twentieth Judicial Circuit)* Appointed by Governor Lawton Chiles Dec 15, 1993.

Office: Collier County Government Complex, 3301 Tamiami Trail East, Naples 34112.
Telephone: (239) 774-8126.
Fax: (239) 774-9654

BAKER, Moses, Jr. *(Judge, Florida Circuit Court Fifteenth Judicial Circuit)*

Office: Palm Beach County Courthouse, 205 North Dixie Highway, West Palm Beach 33401.
Telephone: (561) 355-4622.
Fax: (561) 355-6048

BANDSTRA, Ted E. *(Magistrate Judge, United States District Court Southern District of Florida)* Appointed by U.S. District Court judges.

Office: U.S. Courthouse, 300 N.E. First Avenue, Miami 33132.
Telephone: (305) 523-5700.

BARBAS, Rex *(Judge, Florida Circuit Court Thirteenth Judicial Circuit)*

Office: 340 Hillsborough County Courthouse, 419 Pierce Street, Tampa 33602-4022.
Telephone: (813) 272-5777.
Fax: (813) 276-8015

BARBER, Jesse C. *(Senior Judge, Polk County Court)* Assumed Senior Judge status, serves by assignment.

Mailing address: P.O. Box 9000, Drawer J-133, Bartow 33831-9000.
Office: 255 North Broadway, Bartow 33830.
Telephone: (863) 534-4690.

BARFIELD, Edward T. *(Judge, Florida District Court of Appeal First District)* Assumed office Feb 1984. Retained by election. Former Chief Judge. Born Pensacola Florida Jan 15, 1943. Educated at Pensacola Junior College A.A. 1961, Davidson College A.B. 1963 and Tulane University LL.B. 1966 replaced by J.D. In legal practice Pensacola 1969-80. Judge, Florida Circuit Court First Judicial Circuit May 1980 to Feb 1984.

Member Committee on Standard Jury Instructions in Civil Cases Florida Supreme Court, Workers' Compensation Rules Committee and Legislative Task Force on Administrative Procedures Act. Attorney Escambia County School Board.

Office: 301 Martin Luther King Jr. Boulevard, Tallahassee 32399-1850.
Telephone: (850) 487-0451.
Fax: (850) 488-7989

BARKDULL, Thomas H., III *(Judge, Florida Circuit Court Fifteenth Judicial Circuit)*

Office: Palm Beach County Courthouse, 205 North Dixie Highway, West Palm Beach 33401.
Telephone: (561) 355-1523.

BARLOW, T. Mitchell *(Judge, Florida Circuit Court Eighteenth Judicial Circuit)* Former Judge, Brevard County Court.

Office: Moore Justice Center, Third Floor, 2825 Judge Fran Jamieson Way, Viera 32940-8006.
Telephone: (321) 617-7274.
Fax: (321) 617-7277

BARRON, G. Robert *(Judge, Florida Circuit Court First Judicial Circuit)*

Office: C125 Okaloosa County Courthouse Annex, 1250 North Eglin Parkway, Shalimar 32579.
Telephone: (850) 651-7470.
Fax: (850) 609-3073

BARTON, James, III *(Judge, Florida Circuit Court Thirteenth Judicial Circuit)* Former Judge, Hillsborough County Court, elected to term beginning Jan 1991.

Office: 419 Pierce Street, Room 314-B, Tampa 33602.
Telephone: (813) 272-6995.

BARZEE, Mary R. *(Judge, Florida Circuit Court Eleventh Judicial Circuit)*

Office: 2127 Gerstein Justice Building, 1351 N.W. Twelfth Street, Miami 33125.
Telephone: (305) 548-5730.

BATEMAN, Thomas H., III *(Judge, Florida Circuit Court Second Judicial Circuit)* Former Judge, Leon County Court, appointed by Governor Bob Martinez to term beginning Feb 7, 1990.

Office: 365-C Leon County Courthouse, 301 South Monroe Street, Tallahassee 32301-1853.
Telephone: (850) 577-4315.
Fax: (850) 922-0327

BATTLES, Emmett Lamar *(Judge, Florida Circuit Court Thirteenth Judicial Circuit)*

Office: 415 Tower, 801 East Twiggs Street, Tampa 33602.
Telephone: (813) 272-5819.
Fax: (813) 276-2079

BAUMANN, Herbert, Jr. *(Judge, Florida Circuit Court Thirteenth Judicial Circuit)*

Office: 419 Pierce Street, Room 204, Tampa 33602-4022.
Telephone: (813) 272-5894.

BAYNES, Thomas E. *(Chief Judge, United States Bankruptcy Court Middle District of Florida)* Appointed by U.S. Court of Appeals Eleventh Circuit judges to term beginning Oct 1987. Reappointed Oct 6, 2001, current term expires 2015. Chief Judge since Aug 2, 2000. Born New York New York 1940. Presbyterian. Educated at University of Georgia B.B.A. 1962, Emory University

BAYNES, THOMAS E.—*Continued*

J.D. 1967 LL.M. 1972 and Yale University LL.M. 1973. Sterling Fellow Yale University 1972-73. Member Phi Alpha Delta. Admitted to practice Georgia 1968, U.S. Supreme Court 1971 and Florida 1981. In legal practice Lake Wales Florida 1981-87.

Author *Eminent Domain Law in Florida* 1980 and *Florida Mortgage Law* 1999 Harrison Co. Professor of Law and Public Administration Nova University Center for the Study of Law 1972-81. Judicial Fellow U.S. Supreme Court 1976-77. Member Supreme Court Historical Society and The American Law Institute. Commander USNR JAGL 1960-80 (retired). Board of Directors H. Lee Moffitt Cancer Center.

Office: U.S. Courthouse, 801 North Florida Avenue, Tampa 33602-3899.

Telephone: (813) 301-5082.

BEACH, Marcia *(Judge, Florida Circuit Court Seventeenth Judicial Circuit)* Elected Nov 7, 2000 to term beginning Jan 2001. Term expires Jan 2007.

Office: 6790 Broward County Courthouse, 201 S.E. Sixth Street, Fort Lauderdale 33301.

Telephone: (954) 831-7871.

BEACH, Robert E. *(Senior Judge, Florida Circuit Court Sixth Judicial Circuit)* Appointed by Governor Claude R. Kirk, Jr. to term beginning Jan 1968. Elected 1968, 1972, 1978, 1984 and 1990. Assumed Senior Judge status, serves by assignment. Born Hollywood California July 26, 1930. Educated at University of Tampa B.A. 1955 and Stetson University LL.B. 1958. Member Sigma Phi Epsilon and Phi Alpha Delta. Admitted to practice Florida 1958. Began legal practice St. Petersburg 1959.

Author pamphlet "So You're Going To Be a Witness" The Florida Bar 1976. Adjunct Instructor Stetson University College of Law since 1974, University of South Florida since 1978 and St. Petersburg Junior College since 1978. Member Pinellas Trial Lawyers Association (President 1966), Stetson Lawyers Association (President 1968), St. Petersburg Bar Association (Chairman Liberty Bell Award since 1965) and The Florida Bar (Chairman Public Relations Committee 1966-68 and 1975-77). Recipient Outstanding Alumnus Award 1970 and Distinguished Public Service Award 1973 from University of Tampa. Republican. Assistant Campaign Chairman 1960 and 1966 and Campaign Chairman 1964 Pinellas County. President Interprofessional Family Council, Inc. 1971-72 and South Side Jr. High School PTA 1971-72. Board of Directors Futures Unlimited (workshop for the retarded) and National Foundation for Infantile Paralysis since 1962. Member Board of Overseers Stetson University College of Law, Legal Assistants Advisory Committee St. Petersburg Junior College since 1977, Fundraising Committee for Museum of Fine Arts, Suncoasters and Dragon Club. Enjoys competitive swimming, backpacking, canoe racing and photography.

Office: Judicial Building, 545 First Avenue North, St. Petersburg 33701.

Telephone: (727) 464-4470.

BEAN, James Roy *(Chief Judge, Florida Circuit Court Third Judicial Circuit)* Appointed by Governor Lawton Chiles to term beginning June 8, 1992. Reappointed Feb 14, 1994. Elected 1994 and 2000. Current term expires Jan 2007. Chief Judge since July 1, 2001. Born Saginaw Michigan Jan 16, 1948. Presbyterian. Educated at Michigan State University B.A. with honors 1970 and Wayne State University J.D. 1973. Recipient award for Best Moot Court Brief from Wayne State University Law School 1971. Admitted to practice Florida 1974 and U.S. District Courts Southern 1976, Northern 1980 and Middle 1983 Districts of Florida. In legal practice West Palm Beach 1974-77.

Assistant State Attorney and Chief Branch Office Third Judicial Circuit 1977-92. Instructor in Business Law Valdosta State University 1974. Member Florida Conference of Circuit Court Judges, The Florida Bar, Taylor County Bar Association and Foundation (Past President) and Third Circuit Bar Association. ROTC Michigan State University 1966-68. Member First Presbyterian Church, Rotary and Elks. Enjoys fishing, golf, college football and classic films.

Mailing address: P.O. Drawer 1000, Perry 32347.

Telephone: (850) 838-3520.

Fax: (850) 838-3521

BECKER-PAINTER, Ruth *(Judge, Monroe County Court)* Elected to term beginning Jan 1991. Reelected 1994 and 1998. Current term expires Jan 2005.

Office: Marathon Branch Courthouse, 3117 Overseas Highway, Marathon 33050.

Telephone: (305) 289-6029.

Fax: (305) 289-6089

BEHNKE, Debra *(Judge, Florida Circuit Court Thirteenth Judicial Circuit)* Former Judge, Hillsborough County Court, assumed office Jan 3, 1989.

Office: 462 Tower, 801 East Twiggs Street, Tampa 33602-3554.

Telephone: (813) 307-4750.

Fax: (813) 276-2079

BELL, Frank L. *(Judge, Florida Circuit Court First Judicial Circuit)* Term expires Jan 2005. Born Pensacola Florida Sept 9, 1939. Catholic. Educated at University of Southern Mississippi B.S. 1963 and Cumberland School of Law of Samford University J.D. 1966. Admitted to practice Florida 1966 and Alabama 1966. Former Judge Escambia County Court, elected to term beginning Jan 2, 1973.

Member Society of the Bar of the First Judicial Circuit of Florida, The Florida Bar, Alabama State Bar and American Bar Association. Private First Class U.S. Army 1959. Enjoys golf.

Office: Judicial Building, 190 Governmental Center, Pensacola 32501.

Telephone: (850) 595-4436.

Fax: (850) 595-4404

BELL, Kenneth B. *(Justice, Florida Supreme Court)* Former Judge, Florida Circuit Court First Judicial Circuit, elected to term beginning Jan 1991.

Office: Supreme Court Building, 500 South Duval Street, Tallahassee 32399.

Telephone: (850) 488-2361.

BELL, Peter A. *(Judge, Charlotte County Court)*

Office: Charlotte County Justice Center, 350 East Marion Avenue, Punta Gorda 33950.

Telephone: (941) 637-2291.

Fax: (941) 637-2283

BEMBRY, David Edgar *(Judge, Hamilton County Court)* Elected Nov 11, 1978 to term beginning Jan 2, 1979. Reelected 1982, 1986, 1990, 1994 and 1998. Current term expires Jan 2005. Born Jasper Florida Dec 11,

BEMBRY, DAVID EDGAR—*Continued*

1946. Baptist. Educated at Florida State University B.S. 1970 J.D. 1973. Admitted to practice Florida 1973. In legal practice West Palm Beach 1973-75, Madison 1975-78 and Jasper 1978-79.

Member Third Judicial Circuit Bar Association. Former member The Association of Trial Lawyers of America. Ensign Third Class USMC 1963-65. Member Jasper Lions Club. Former Director and Treasurer Madison Rotary Club. Enjoys canoeing, biking and hiking.

Office: 207 N.E. First Street, Room 103, Jasper 32052.

Telephone: (386) 792-1220.

Fax: (386) 792-0556

BENNETT, Robert B., Jr. *(Chief Judge, Florida Circuit Court Twelfth Judicial Circuit)*

Mailing address: P.O. Box 48927, Sarasota 34230.

Office: 2002 Ringling Boulevard, Sarasota 34237.

Telephone: (941) 861-7942.

Fax: (941) 861-7913

BENTLEY, Edward R. *(Senior Judge, Florida Circuit Court Tenth Judicial Circuit)* Assumed Senior Judge status, serves by assignment.

Mailing address: P.O. Box 9000, Drawer J-133, Bartow 33831-9000.

Office: 255 North Broadway, Bartow 33830.

Telephone: (863) 534-4690.

BENTON, Robert T., II *(Judge, Florida District Court of Appeal First District)* Appointed by Governor Lawton Chiles to term beginning Jan 4, 1994. Retained by election Nov 1996 and 2002. Current term expires Jan 2009. Born Indianapolis Indiana Jan 16, 1946. Educated at Johns Hopkins University B.A. 1967, University of Florida J.D. with honors 1970 and Harvard Law School LL.M. 1971. Law Clerk to Chief Judge William A. McRae, Jr., U.S. District Court Middle District of Florida 1972. Recipient honorary scholarship from University of Florida Law Center, Birch Award and American Jurisprudence Awards in Jurisprudence, Law and Medicine, Commercial Paper, Evidence, Constitutional Law and State and Local Taxation. Member Phi Kappa Phi and Order of the Coif. Hearing Officer Florida Division of Administrative Hearings 1977-94.

Staff Attorney Florida Rural Legal Services 1971. Assistant Public Defender Twelfth Judicial Circuit Florida 1974-75. Law Clerk to Hon. Joseph W. Hatchett, Florida Supreme Court 1975-77. Co-author "Administrative Adjudication" *Florida Administrative Practice* 1981, 1990 and 1993. Author "Retroactivity in Licensing Cases" June 1985 and "Formal Hearings Under Florida's Human Rights Act" Oct 1989 Florida B. Jour., "Administrative Proceedings" *Getting Paid for Doing Good: Recovering and Defending Statutory Attorneys' Fees* 1992, "Fees, Costs and the APA" *Practicing Before the Division of Administrative Hearings* 1992, "The Rule Challenge Challenge" Administrative Law Section Newsletter The Florida Bar Jan 1993 and "Attorneys' Fees and Costs Awards" Florida Administrative Practice 1993. Editor Administrative Law column Florida Bar Journal 1987-89. Instructor Boston University School of Law 1970-71. Interim Assistant Professor University of Florida College of Law 1972-73. Member The Florida Bar (Chair 1984-86 and Member Rules Committee, Member Executive Committee 1995-96 and Committee on Designation Administrative Law Section, Member Committee on Appellate Rules 1987-88 and since 1996 and Code and Rules of Evidence Committee since 1995) and Tallahassee Bar Association. Faculty Advisor The National Judicial College. Paul Harris Fellow. Board Member Holy Comforter Episcopal Day School 1984-86. Member Habitat for Humanity (Tallahassee Construction, Design and Site Selection Committee 1984 and 1992), St. John's Episcopal Church (Member Vestry 1996-99), Florida Committee Hurricane Island Outward Bound School and Rotary Club of Tallahassee.

Office: 301 Martin Luther King Jr. Boulevard, Tallahassee 32399-1850.

Telephone: (850) 487-1000.

Fax: (850) 921-4768

BERGER, William J. *(Judge, Florida Circuit Court Fifteenth Judicial Circuit)*

Office: Palm Beach County Courthouse, 201 North Dixie Highway, West Palm Beach 33401.

BERGMANN, Charles E. *(Judge, Florida Circuit Court Thirteenth Judicial Circuit)*

Office: Hillsborough County Courthouse, 419 Pierce Street, Tampa 33602-4022.

Telephone: (813) 272-6913.

Fax: (813) 276-8015.

BERMAN, Fred *(Judge, Broward County Court)* Appointed by Governor Lawton Chiles April 18, 1995.

Office: 359 Broward County Courthouse, 201 S.E. Sixth Street, Fort Lauderdale 33301.

Telephone: (954) 831-7567.

BERNSTEIN, Scott *(Judge, Florida Circuit Court Eleventh Judicial Circuit)*

Office: 212 Juvenile Justice Center, 3300 N.W. 27th Avenue, Miami 33142.

Telephone: (305) 638-6238.

Fax: (305) 638-6064

BEVERLY, Virginia Q. *(Senior Judge, Florida Circuit Court Fourth Judicial Circuit)* Appointed by Governor Reubin Askew to term beginning Jan 10, 1977. Elected 1978, 1984 and 1990. Assumed Senior Judge status, serves by assignment. Born Wilmington North Carolina Oct 20, 1926. Roman Catholic. Educated at St. Joseph's College B.S. 1948 and University of North Carolina LL.B. 1953. Admitted to practice North Carolina 1953, Georgia 1960 and Florida 1965. Began legal practice Wilmington North Carolina 1953.

Member The Florida Bar and State Bar of Georgia.

Office: Duval County Courthouse, 330 East Bay Street, Jacksonville 32202.

Telephone: (904) 630-1693.

BEVIS, Thomas E. *(Judge, Volusia County Court)* Elected Sept 1, 1992 to term beginning Jan 5, 1993. Reelected 1996 and 2000. Current term expires Jan 1, 2007. Born Jacksonville Florida Sept 17, 1942. Episcopalian. Educated at Florida State University B.S. in Accounting 1969 J.D. with honors 1972. Admitted to practice Florida 1972 and U.S. District Court Middle District of Florida 1982. In legal practice DeLand 1976-89.

Assistant State Attorney Seventh Judicial Circuit 1972-76 and 1989-93. Circuit Representative Seventh Circuit 1996-97 and District Vice President Fifth District 1997-99 Florida Conference of County Court Judges.

BEVIS, THOMAS E.—*Continued*

Member The Florida Bar and Volusia County Bar Association. Enjoys fishing, golf and reading.

Office: Volusia County Courthouse, 101 North Alabama Avenue, Deland 32724.

Telephone: (386) 736-5947.

Fax: (386) 740-5114

BIRKEN, Arthur M. *(Judge, Florida Circuit Court Seventeenth Judicial Circuit)* Appointed by Governor Bob Martinez to term beginning 1988. Elected March 29, 1988. Reelected 1994 and 2000. Current term expires Jan 2007. Born Newburgh New York Nov 23, 1948. Jewish. Educated at New York University B.A. 1970 and Washington College of Law of American University J.D. 1973. Admitted to practice District of Columbia 1974, Florida 1974 and Pennsylvania 1974. Began legal practice Washington D.C. 1974. In legal practice Fort Lauderdale Florida 1975. Judge, Broward County Court 1982-88, appointed by Governor Robert Graham.

Assistant General Counsel Broward County 1975-76. Assistant City Attorney Hallandale 1976-78. City Attorney Tamarac 1978-82. Author "Gulf of Venezuela: Border Dispute" Lawyer of the Americas University of Miami School of Law Feb 1974 and Chapter "Other Criminal Traffic Offenses" *DUI and Other Traffic Offenses in Florida* The Florida Bar CLE 1986. Board of Directors Broward County Area Agency on Aging, Florida Ocean Sciences Institute, Fort Lauderdale Try Center, B'nai B'rith Justice Unit 3126 and Jewish Community Center of Fort Lauderdale 1984-86. Enjoys films and bicycling.

Office: 822 Broward County Courthouse, 201 S.E. Sixth Street, Fort Lauderdale 33301.

Telephone: (954) 831-7819.

Fax: (954) 831-5572

BLACK, Anthony K. *(Judge, Florida Circuit Court Thirteenth Judicial Circuit)*

Office: 801 East Twiggs Street, Room 414, Tampa 33602.

Telephone: (813) 276-2478.

Fax: (813) 276-2079

BLACKWELL, William *(Chief Judge, Florida Circuit Court Twentieth Judicial Circuit)* Appointed by Governor Bob Martinez Dec 10, 1987 to term beginning Jan 1, 1988. Elected Nov 8, 1988, 1994 and 2000. Current term expires Jan 2007. Born Bushnell Florida March 18, 1936. Roman Catholic. Educated at University of Florida B.S. 1960 and South Texas College of Law J.D. 1976. Member Phi Alpha Delta. Admitted to practice Texas 1976 and U.S. District Courts Southern District of Texas 1976 and Southern 1977 and Middle 1977 Districts of Florida and Florida 1977. In legal practice Port Lavaca Texas 1976-77 and Naples Florida 1977-87.

Author "Leasing Oil and Gas Rights, Landowner's Perspective" Florida B. Jour. Nov 1983. Member Calhoun County (Texas) and Collier County (President 1986-87) Bar Associations. U.S. Navy 1955-56. Republican. Campaign Manager Collier County John Connolly for President 1978. Enjoys collecting guns, hunting and shooting sports.

Office: Charlotte County Justice Center, 350 East Marion Avenue, Punta Gorda 33950.

Telephone: (941) 637-2375.

Fax: (941) 637-2358

BLACKWOOD, William B., Jr. *(Judge, Pinellas County Court)* Appointed by Governor Reubin Askew to term beginning April 5, 1977. Elected to subsequent terms. Born Anniston Alabama Sept 28, 1941. Educated at Louisiana State University B.S. 1967 and University of Florida J.D. 1971. Member Phi Alpha Delta. Admitted to practice Florida 1971. In legal practice Clearwater 1974.

State's Attorney Clearwater 1971. Former member Pinellas County Criminal Defense Lawyers, Florida Academy of Trial Lawyers, Pinellas County Trial Lawyers and Clearwater Bar Association. Attended National College of the State Judiciary at Reno 1977. E-5 U.S. Army 1961-64. Board of Directors St. Petersburg YMCA. Former member Pinellas Advisory Council for Medical Planning and Optimist Club.

Office: Historic Old Courthouse, 324 South Fort Harrison Avenue, Clearwater 33756.

Telephone: (727) 464-3545.

BLAIR, H. Wetzel *(Judge, Madison County Court)*

Office: Madison County Courthouse, Madison 32340.

Telephone: (850) 973-6221.

Fax: (850) 973-2059

BLAKE, Stanford *(Judge, Florida Circuit Court Eleventh Judicial Circuit)* Elected to term beginning Jan 3, 1995. Reelected 2000, current term expires Jan 2007.

Office: 212 Gerstein Justice Building, 1351 N.W. 12th Street, Miami 33125.

Telephone: (305) 548-5721.

Fax: (305) 548-7320

BLANC, Peter D. *(Judge, Florida Circuit Court Fifteenth Judicial Circuit)* Former Judge, Palm Beach County Court, appointed by Governor Bob Martinez to term beginning March 12, 1990.

Office: South County Courthouse, 200 West Atlantic Avenue, Delray Beach 33444.

Telephone: (561) 274-1415.

Fax: (561) 274-1406

BLECHMAN, Deb S. *(Judge, Orange County Court)* Elected to term beginning Jan 3, 1995. Reelected 1998, current term expires Jan 2005.

Office: 825 Orange County Courthouse, 425 North Orange Avenue, Orlando 32801.

Telephone: (407) 836-2354.

BLOCK, Jack *(Senior Judge, Dade County Court)* Elected to term beginning Jan 8, 1985. Reelected Sept 1988 and Sept 1992. Assumed Senior Judge status, serves by assignment. Born Newark New Jersey Sept 2, 1926. Jewish. Educated at University of Miami J.D. 1949. Recipient football scholarship. Admitted to practice Florida 1949. In legal practice Miami since 1949. Municipal Judge and Associate Municipal Judge City of South Miami 1962-68. While Municipal Judge attempted to create a probation department for Municipal Court. In connection established a non-profit corporation for this purpose known as South Miami Project Misdemeanant, Inc.

Councilman City of South Miami 1958-60. Responsible for creation of City Public Library. Elected Mayor City of South Miami 1968, subsequently reelected for eight terms. Appointed Lieutenant Colonel Aide de Camp Georgia Governor's Staff Jan 14, 1975 and Kentucky Colonel to Governor Julian M. Carroll Aug 16, 1978. Member National Panel of Arbitrators American

BLOCK, JACK—*Continued*

Arbitration Association, Lawyers' Title Guaranty Fund, American Judicature Society, North American Judges Association and The Florida Bar (Florida Bar Committee on Landlord and Tenants). Volunteer instructor South Miami Community School. Named honorary citizen of Jackson Mississippi, San Salvador April 23, 1976 and Tucson Arizona June 11, 1977. Honorary Member South Miami Senior High School Cobra Band Feb 19, 1974 and Honorary Crew Member McDonald's Corp. April 27, 1980. Member of Honor Interamerica Chamber of Commerce of Greater Miami Sept 1976. Ecology Honor Roll Ecology Strategies, Inc. Member Order of Orchid Gulfstream March 1, 1980. Recipient Awards of Merit from National Federation of Music Clubs 1975, City of Hialeah April 12, 1977, Boy Scouts of America Jan 27, 1980 and South Miami Chamber of Commerce Jan 1985. Named Boss of Year by American Business Women's Association Miami-Kachina Chapter 1980. Recipient Honorary Plaque from Latin Chamber of Commerce Aug 29, 1968, Award of Appreciation El Concejo Provincial de Maynas Iquitos Peru Sept 19, 1968, Distinguished Visitor Award La Corporation Municipalde Guatemala June 30, 1970, JESCA James E. Scott Community Association Community Service Award 1972-73, Award of Community Service United Way of Dade County 1974 and 1975, Distinguished Service Award Dade County League of Cities June 27, 1975, Salute Award Progress for Dade County, Inc. July 30, 1975, Distinguished Service Award J. R. E. Lee Center Community School Aug 2, 1977, Landscape Award Marshall Williamson Park Dade Chapter State Winner 1977, Certificate of Participation Metrorail Metropolitan Dade County June 7, 1979. Certificate of Achievement J. R. E. Lee Center June 12, 1979, Certificate of Appreciation from Dade County Jan 24, 1984 and Resolution naming Jack Block Mayor Emeritus City of South Miami Jan 17, 1984. Listed in *Who's Who in Government* Third Edition Marquis Who's Who Publication Board. Recipient Certificate of Grateful Recognition from President's Council on Youth Opportunity 1968. Recipient Certificates of Appreciation from South Miami Lions Club Feb 6, 1969, Central Baptist Church of Miami Florida and Crusade of the Americas March 27, 1969, Dade County Youth Fair Feb 28, 1970, City of Miami Beach July 8, 1971, Justice of the Peace and Constables Association of Florida 1971-72, South Miami Chamber of Commerce March 16, 1974, South Miami High School Cobra Band June 1974, Metropolitan Dade County Sept 22, 1975, Metropolitan Miami Flower Show 1975, Reubin Askew 1974 Gubernatorial Campaign Oct 10, 1975, South Miami Chamber of Commerce Bicentennial Parade March 13, 1976, Shriners June 7, 1976, Bicentennial Commission of Florida Nov 16, 1976, Lawton Chiles 1976 Senatorial Campaign Thank You, Kiwanis Club of South Miami April 21, 1977, South Miami International Mardi Gras and Festival Outstanding Participant Dec 1979, University of Miami Alumni Association April 13, 1980, American Cancer Society, North Dade-North Miami Rotary Club, Volunteer in Sight TV Dade County Public Schools and Speak Up to America Essay Contest Certified Plumbers of South Florida.

Technician Four U.S. Army Infantry and Medical Corps 1944-45. Previously worked as shoe salesman and waiter. Chairman Danny Thomas South Miami Youth Drive for Leukemia. Neighborhood Commissioner Boy Scouts of America. Football coach South Miami Youth Recreation Program. Past Chancellor Knights of Pythias. Former President Civic Association of South Miami. Former Member Elks and Moose, South Miami Chamber of Commerce and University of Miami Alumni Gridders Association. Former Member South Miami Homeowners and Southwest Realtors Associations. Organizer and active participant in Friends of South Miami Public Library. Member Keep Florida Beautiful, Inc. (Past President), Citizens Advisory Board South Miami Hospital Jan 15, 1960 and The Italians, Inc.

Office: 511 Dade County Courthouse, 73 West Flagler Street, Miami 33130.

Telephone: (305) 349-7001.

BLOOM, Beth *(Judge, Dade County Court)* Elected to term beginning Jan 3, 1995. Reelected 1998, current term expires Jan 2005. Born Bronx New York June 24, 1962. Jewish. Educated at University of Florida B.S. 1984 and University of Miami J.D. with honors 1988. Admitted to practice Florida 1988. In legal practice Miami 1988-94.

Adjunct Faculty University of Miami School of Law. Member Florida Conference of County Court Judges, Miami Beach, Dade County and American Bar Associations. Faculty College of Advanced Judicial Studies Florida Judicial College. Recipient Florida Blue Key 1984, Iron Arrow 1988 and President's Award from The Florida Bar 1993. Board of Directors South Florida Inner City Games. Enjoys jogging.

Office: 609 Gerstein Justice Building, 1351 N.W. Twelfth Street, Miami 33125.

Telephone: (305) 548-5400.

Fax: (305) 548-5557

BODIFORD, Larry A. *(Magistrate Judge, United States District Court Northern District of Florida)* Appointed by U.S. District Court judges. Serves part time.

Mailing address: P.O. Box 2528, Panama City 32402-2528.

Telephone: (850) 763-0723.

BOLLINGER, William A. *(Judge, Palm Beach County Court)*

Office: Palm Beach County Courthouse, 205 North Dixie Highway, West Palm Beach 33401.

Telephone: (561) 355-2330.

BONNER, Kimberly C. *(Judge, Sarasota County Court)* Appointed by Governor Jeb Bush to term beginning Jan 2002. Educated at Stetson University B.A. 1986, University of West Florida M.A. 1987 and Pepperdine University J.D. 1990.

Mailing address: P.O. Box 48927, Sarasota 34237.

Telephone: (941) 861-7967.

BOOTH, Anne Cawthon *(Judge, Florida District Court of Appeal First District)* Appointed by Governor Reubin O'Donovan Askew to term beginning Jan 3, 1978. Retained by election 1980, 1986, 1992 and 1998. Current term expires Jan 2005. Chief Judge 1985-87. Born Gainesville Florida March 2, 1934. Episcopalian. Educated at University of Florida B.S. with high honors 1956 J.D. with high honors 1961. Recipient Kroger Scholarship for Outstanding Agricultural Student 1954, Phi Sigma Award for Individual Research 1956, Brick Award for Research and Writing and American Jurisprudence Awards in Mortgages, Municipal Corporations, Contracts, Equity and Pleading. Member Phi Beta Kap-

BOOTH, ANNE CAWTHON—*Continued*

pa, Phi Kappa Phi, Alpha Lambda Delta, Sigma Delta Pi, Phi Sigma, Lambda Sigma Delta, Phi Delta Delta, Chi Omega and Order of the Coif. Admitted to practice Florida 1961. In legal practice Tallahassee 1973-78.

Legal Aide Florida Supreme Court 1962-73. Author Comments, Notes and Articles Fall 1958 and Summer and Fall 1961 U. of Florida L. Rev. Co-author "Jurisdiction" CLE Vol. on Appellate Practice The Florida Bar 1966 and "Florida's En Banc Rule" University of Florida L. Rev. Fall 1984. Member Committee to Draft Workers' Compensation Rules of Procedure 1978. Secretary Florida Conference of District Court of Appeal Judges 1980. Member Tallahassee Association of Women Lawyers, Committee on Standards of Conduct Governing Judges (Vice Chairman 1979-83, Chairman 1984-85), Florida Courts' Restructure Commission 1985-86, The Florida Bar and Tallahassee Bar Association.

Office: 301 Martin Luther King Jr. Boulevard, Tallahassee 32399-1850.

Telephone: (850) 487-1000.

Fax: (850) 921-4768

BOOTH, John W. *(Senior Judge, Florida Circuit Court Fifth Judicial Circuit)* Elected to term beginning Jan 1, 1969. Reelected to subsequent terms. Former Chief Judge. Assumed Senior Judge status, serves by assignment. Born Gainesville Florida Jan 13, 1924. Member St. James Episcopal Church. Educated at University of Florida B.S.B.A. 1949 and Stetson University LL.B. 1951. Admitted to practice Florida 1951. In legal practice Florida 1951-66. Judge, Lake County Court 1966-68.

Honorary and Charter Member Citrus-Hernando Inn of Court. Member Florida Conference of Circuit Judges, American Judicature Society and The Florida Bar. Judicial Leader The National Judicial College Assembly 2001. USAAC 1943-46. Republican. Enjoys hunting and fishing.

Office: Marion County Judicial Center, 110 N.W. First Avenue, Ocala 34475.

Telephone: (352) 742-4139.

BOWDEN, Aaron K. *(Judge, Florida Circuit Court Fourth Judicial Circuit)* Appointed by Governor Bob Martinez to term beginning Oct 6, 1989. Elected to subsequent terms.

Office: Duval County Courthouse, 330 East Bay Street, Jacksonville 32202.

Telephone: (904) 630-2591.

Fax: (904) 630-2979

BOWER, N. Russell *(Senior Judge, Florida Circuit Court Fourteenth Judicial Circuit)* Appointed by Governor Reubin Askew to term beginning Jan 1, 1977. Elected 1978, 1984, 1990 and 1996. Former Chief Judge. Assumed Senior Judge status, serves by assignment. Born Miami Florida Jan 1, 1939. Southern Baptist. Educated at Gulf Coast Community College, Troy State University B.S. in Business Administration 1963 and University of Florida J.D. 1967. Admitted to practice Florida 1968. Began legal practice Sarasota 1968. In legal practice Panama City 1968.

Assistant State Attorney Oct 1970 to Dec 1976. Member The Florida Bar, Bay County and American Bar Associations. Enjoys hunting and fishing.

Mailing address: P.O. Box 27, Panama City 32402.

Office: 300 East Fourth Street, Panama City 32401.

Telephone: (850) 747-5327.

BOWMAN, John B. *(Judge, Florida Circuit Court Seventeenth Judicial Circuit)*

Office: Broward County Courthouse, 201 S.E. Sixth Street, Fort Lauderdale 33301.

BOYER, Bruce *(Judge, Florida Circuit Court Sixth Judicial Circuit)* Elected Nov 6, 1990 to term beginning Jan 8, 1991. Reelected Nov 5, 1996 and 2002. Current term expires Jan 2009. Born Indianapolis Indiana Nov 29, 1946. Educated at Eastern Kentucky University B.A. 1969, Morehead State University M.A. 1971 and University of Kentucky J.D. 1977.

Office: 410 Criminal Justice Center, 14250 49th Street North, Clearwater 33762.

Telephone: (727) 464-3263.

BOYER, Tyrie W. *(Judge, Duval County Court)* Elected 2000 to term beginning Jan 1, 2001. Term expires Jan 2, 2007. Born Jacksonville Florida Aug 2, 1948. Episcopalian. Educated at University of Florida M.S.B.A. 1972 J.D. 1976. Admitted to practice Florida 1976, U.S. District Court Middle District of Florida 1977, U.S. Supreme Court 1977 and U.S. Courts of Appeals Fifth 1981 and Eleventh 1981 Circuits. Board Certified as a Specialist in Civil Trial Law by The Florida Bar 1983. In legal practice Jacksonville 1978-2001.

Assistant Public Defender Fourth Judicial Circuit of Florida 1976-77. Author "Accidents Caused by Defective Autos" *Trying the Automobile Injury Case in Florida* July 1991 and Aug 1992, "Initial Considerations" *Personal Injury Litigation Practice in Florida* Dec 1991, "Screening the Case—Why It Is Such a Critical Step" July 1993 and "Preparing and Examining Witnesses—How You Do It Is Critical to Your Case" July 1993 *Strategies for Success in Personal Injury Cases in Florida*, "Ethics—It's Legal but Is It Right?" *Bad Faith Litigation in Florida* April 1994, "Trial of the Case" *Trying the Soft Tissue Injury Case in Florida* Oct 1995 and "Overview and Update of the Law Regarding the Wrongful Death Act" *Trying the Wrongful Death Case in Florida* Jan 1998 National Business Institute, Inc. Adjunct Professor Florida Coastal School of Law. Member Academy of Florida Trial Lawyers, The Association of Trial Lawyers of America, American Board of Trial Advocates, National Board of Trial Advocacy, The Florida Bar (Chairman Professional Ethics Committee and Rules of Civil Procedure Committee), Jacksonville, Clay County, Federal and American Bar Associations. Captain USAR. Former Member Board of Directors Jacksonville Chapter University of Florida Alumni Association. Former Board Member Riverside Facility YMCA and Gainesville Board United Way. Former Member Jacksonville Community Council, Inc. Board of Directors Orange Park Facility Salvation Army and Jacksonville Historical Society. Paul Harris Fellow Rotary International. Member Jacksonville Jaycees, Gator Club of Jacksonville and Jacksonville Chamber of Commerce. Enjoys hunting, fishing, bridge, reading, outdoor recreation and sports. Personal Statement or Quote: "Come to court prepared and with law even if you think the legal matter is mundane."

Office: 330 East Bay Street, Suite 324, Jacksonville 32202.

Telephone: (904) 630-2579.

Fax: (904) 630-8358

BOYLES, Stephen L. *(Senior Judge, Florida Circuit Court Seventh Judicial Circuit)* Elected to term beginning Jan 1991. Reelected 1996. Assumed Senior Judge status, serves by assignment.
Office: 101 North Alabama Avenue, De Land 32724.
Telephone: (386) 257-6097.

BOYLSTON, Richard *(Judge, Lake County Court)* Appointed by Governor Bob Martinez to term beginning Jan 2, 1990. Elected to subsequent terms.
Mailing address: P.O. Box 7800, Tavares 32778-7800.
Office: Lake County Judicial Center, Tavares 32778.
Telephone: (352) 742-4203.
Fax: (352) 742-4229

BOYLSTON, Robert J. *(Senior Judge, Florida Circuit Court Twelfth Judicial Circuit)* Assumed Senior Judge status, serves by assignment.
Mailing address: P.O. Box 48927, Sarasota 34230.
Office: 2002 Ringling Blvd., Sarasota 34237.
Telephone: (941) 861-7800.

BRACE, A. Keith *(Judge, Okaloosa County Court)*
Office: Okaloosa County Courthouse, 101 James Lee Boulevard, Crestview 32536.
Telephone: (850) 689-5730.
Fax: (850) 689-5749

BRAVO, Carmine M. *(Judge, Seminole County Court)* Elected Sept 1996 to term beginning Jan 1997. Reelected 2000, current term expires Jan 2007. Born Rome New York Feb 4, 1942. Catholic. Educated at University of Miami B.B.A. 1966 and Suffolk University Law School J.D. 1969. Member Williams Inns of Court. Admitted to practice Florida 1969 and U.S. District Court Middle District of Florida 1976. In legal practice Longwood 1972-96.

Member The Florida Bar, Orange County and Seminole County Bar Associations. Attended Florida College of Advanced Judicial Studies. Honor Club President and Distinguished District Governor Sertoma International. Past President Chamber of Commerce. Member Coalition for Community Justice and Knights of Columbus. Active as youth sports coach.
Office: Seminole County Courthouse, 301 North Park Avenue, Sanford 32771-1292.
Telephone: (407) 665-4108.

BRAY, W. Lowell, Jr. *(Judge, Florida Circuit Court Sixth Judicial Circuit)* Assumed office July 1, 1983. Elected to subsequent terms. Born Mansfield Louisiana Sept 13, 1945. Member Seven Springs Baptist Chapel. Educated at Louisiana Polytechnic Institute (now Louisiana Tech University) B.S.M.E. cum laude 1967 M.A. in English 1969 and University of Florida J.D. with high honors 1973. Recipient Law Center Scholarship and American Jurisprudence Awards in Criminal Law and Procedure II and Estates and Trusts I. Staff member University of Florida Law Review. Judicial Intern to Florida Circuit Court. Member Order of the Coif, Tau Beta Pi and Pi Tau Sigma. In legal practice New Port Richey 1973-83.

Teacher Ebarb High School 1968-69. Instructor in English Florida Junior College 1969-71. Member West Pasco Bar Association (President Elect 1983). Past President Rotary Club of New Port Richey.
Office: 111 West Pasco Government Center, 7530 Little Road, New Port Richey 34654.
Telephone: (727) 847-8128.
Fax: (727) 847-8164

BREGER, Eli *(Senior Judge, Dade County Court)* Elected to term beginning Jan 6, 1987. Assumed Senior Judge status, serves by assignment. Born New York New York Nov 28, 1926. Religious affiliation: Hebrew. Educated at Oklahoma A & M College, Southern Methodist University, University of Texas and University of Miami J.D. 1949. Admitted to practice Florida 1949, U.S. District Court Southern District of Florida 1949, U.S. Courts of Appeals Fifth 1951 and Eleventh 1981 Circuits and U.S. Supreme Court 1971. In legal practice Miami Beach 1949-62 and Miami 1962-86. Judge, North Miami Beach Municipal Court 1954.

Hearing Examiner Florida Department of Pollution Control 1972-74. Instructor in Real Property and Wills Miami Dade Community College 1987-88. Seaman First Class USN Sept 1944 to Dec 1945.
Office: 511 Dade County Courthouse, 73 West Flagler Street, Miami 33130.
Telephone: (305) 349-7001.

BRENNAN, Shirley M. *(Judge, Okeechobee County Court)*
Office: 304 N.W. Second Street, Okeechobee 34972.
Telephone: (863) 763-3193.
Fax: (863) 763-7260

BRESCHER, George Angen *(Judge, Florida Circuit Court Seventeenth Judicial Circuit)* Appointed by Governor Bob Martinez to term beginning Jan 1991. Elected 1996 and 2002. Current term expires Jan 2009. Born Elizabeth New Jersey March 24, 1943. Educated at Stetson University 1961-63, Monmouth College B.S. 1966 and University of Miami School of Law J.D. 1969. Member Delta Theta Phi. Admitted to practice Florida 1969, U.S. Court of Military Appeals 1969, U.S. Supreme Court 1972 and U.S. District Court Southern District of Florida 1977. In legal practice Fort Lauderdale 1977 and 1985-86. Judge, Broward County Court 1977-82 and July 1986 to Jan 1991.

Assistant State Attorney Broward County 1973-77. Adjunct Professor of Business Law St. Thomas University since 1985. Member The Florida Bar and Broward County Bar Association. Attended Florida Judicial College and The National Judicial College. Captain U.S. Army JAGC 1969-73. Military Judge, Special Court Martial 1972-73. Sheriff Broward County 1982-84. Member Broward County Commission on Alcoholism, Inc., Broward County Crime Commission and Broward Chapter National Safety Council.
Office: 930 Broward County Courthouse, 201 S.E. Sixth Street, Fort Lauderdale 33301.
Telephone: (954) 831-7850

BREWER, Jerry L. *(Judge, Orange County Court)* Elected to term beginning Jan 3, 1995. Reelected 1998, current term expires Jan 2005.
Office: 840 Orange County Courthouse, 425 North Orange Avenue, Orlando 32801.
Telephone: (407) 836-2352.

BRIESE, Shawn L. *(Judge, Florida Circuit Court Seventh Judicial Circuit)* Former Judge, Volusia County Court.
Office: Volusia County Justice Center, 251 North Ridgewood Avenue, Daytona Beach 32114.

BRIESE, SHAWN L.—*Continued*

Telephone: (386) 239-7790
Fax: (386) 239-7833

BRIGGS, Barbara B. *(Judge, Sarasota County Court)*
Office: 4000 South Tamiami Trail, Venice 34293.
Telephone: (941) 861-3292.
Fax: (941) 861-3050

BRIGGS, Don F. *(Judge, Florida Circuit Court Fifth Judicial Circuit)* Appointed by Governor Bob Martinez to term beginning Feb 19, 1990. Elected to subsequent terms.
Mailing address: P.O. Box 7800, Tavares 32778-7800.
Office: Lake County Courthouse, Tavares 32778.
Telephone: (352) 742-4224.
Fax: (352) 742-4370

BRISKMAN, Arthur B. *(Judge, United States Bankruptcy Court Middle District of Florida)* Appointed by U.S. Court of Appeals Eleventh Circuit judges.
Office: 950 South Trust Bank Building, 135 West Central Boulevard, Orlando 32801.
Telephone: (407) 648-6225.

BRONSON, Theotis *(Judge, Florida Circuit Court Ninth Judicial Circuit)* Former Judge, Orange County Court.
Office: 1125 Orange County Courthouse, 425 North Orange Avenue, Orlando 32801.
Telephone: (407) 836-2229.

BROOKE, Alban E. *(Senior Judge, Florida Circuit Court Fourth Judicial Circuit)* Assumed Senior Judge status, serves by assignment.
Office: Duval County Courthouse, 330 East Bay Street, Jacksonville 32202.
Telephone: (904) 630-1693.

BROUSSEAU, Theodore H. *(Judge, Florida Circuit Court Twentieth Judicial Circuit)* Elected 1978 to term beginning Jan 2, 1979. Reelected 1984, 1990, 1996 and 2002. Current term expires Jan 2009. Born Colorado Springs Colorado April 13, 1944. Educated at U.S. Air Force Academy 1965-66 and Stetson University B.A. 1968 J.D. 1971. Admitted to practice Florida 1971. Began legal practice Naples 1971.

Author Chapter 2a "Criminal Pretrial" and Chapter 5 "Criminal Trial" *Florida Judges Manual.* Faculty member Florida Judicial College since 1985 and The National Judicial College since 1988. Republican. Past President Collier County Republican Club. Chairman Ronald Reagan's Campaign Collier County 1976. Interests include horticulture, computer programming, beekeeping, wine and beer making, tennis and soccer.

Office: Collier County Government Complex, Bldg. L, 3301 Tamiami Trail East, Naples 34112.
Telephone: (239) 774-8121.
Fax: (239) 774-9654

BROWN, Cecil H. *(Senior Judge, Florida Circuit Court Ninth Judicial Circuit)* Elected 1972 to term beginning Jan 1, 1973. Reelected 1978 and 1984. Assumed Senior Judge status, serves by assignment. Born Darlington Florida March 11, 1923. Protestant. Educated at Florida State University B.S. in Public Administration 1951 and University of Florida LL.B. 1952. Admitted to practice Florida 1952.

General Counsel Orlando Civil Service Board 1957-72. Attended National College of the State Judiciary 1975. USNR PTO 1942-46.

Office: Orange County Courthouse, 425 North Orange Avenue, Orlando 32801.
Telephone: (407) 836-2050.

BROWN, Charles Lee *(Judge, Florida Circuit Court Tenth Judicial Circuit)* Former Judge, Polk County Court.
Mailing address: P.O. Box 9000, Drawer J141, Bartow 33831-9000.
Telephone: (863) 534-7761.

BROWN, George K., Jr. *(Judge, Manatee County Court)*
Mailing address: P.O. Box 1000, Bradenton 34206.
Office: 1115 Manatee Avenue West, Bradenton 34206.
Telephone: (941) 749-7136.
Fax: (941) 742-5971

BROWN, Joel H. *(Judge, Florida Circuit Court Eleventh Judicial Circuit)* Assumed office Jan 7, 1994. Former Judge, Dade County Court, appointed by Governor Bob Martinez to term beginning July 30, 1990.
Office: 2214 Courthouse Center, 175 N.W. First Avenue, Miami 33128.
Telephone: (305) 349-5720.

BROWN, Lucy Chernow *(Judge, Florida Circuit Court Fifteenth Judicial Circuit)* Elected to term beginning Jan 1991. Reelected 1996 and 2002. Current term expires Jan 2009.
Office: Palm Beach County Courthouse, 205 North Dixie Highway, West Palm Beach 33401.
Telephone: (561) 355-4866.

BROWN, Robert E. *(Judge, Holmes County Court)* Elected 1982 to term beginning Jan 4, 1983. Reelected 1986, 1990, 1994 and 1998. Current term expires Jan 2005. Born Washington County Florida May 16, 1932. Baptist. Educated at Holland Law School University of Florida. Judge, Holmes County Court 1973.

Associate member American Bar Association. Member Florida Conference of County Court Judges and Panhandle Bar Association of Florida. Member Masonic Lodge, Scottish Rite, Kiwanis and American Legion.

Office: 201 North Oklahoma Street, Suite 201, Bonifay 32425.
Telephone: (850) 547-1104.

BROWN, Stephen T. *(Magistrate Judge, United States District Court Southern District of Florida)* Appointed by U.S. District Court judges March 1991. Reappointed March 1999, current term expires March 2007. Born New York New York Feb 1, 1947. Educated at Florida State University B.S. 1968 and University of Miami J.D. 1972. Staff member University of Miami Law Review 1969-72. Member Delta Theta Phi, Bar and Gavel and Order of Wig and Robe. Admitted to practice Florida 1972, U.S. District Court Southern District of Florida 1973, U.S. Court of Appeals Eleventh Circuit 1973 and U.S. Supreme Court 1976. In legal practice Miami 1972-91.

Instructor Trial Advocacy Program University of Miami 1982-84. Member Advisory Committee on Local Rules and Procedures U.S. District Court Southern District of Florida. Member Federal Magistrate Judges Association, The Florida Bar, Dade County and American Bar Associations. Vice President University of Miami

BROWN, STEPHEN T.—*Continued*

Law School Alumni Association. Board of Directors Leadership Council College of Arts and Sciences Florida State University. Enjoys snow skiing, fishing and golf.

Office: U.S. Courthouse, 300 N.E. First Avenue, Miami 33132.

Telephone: (305) 523-5740.

BROWNELL, Scott MacKenzie *(Judge, Florida Circuit Court Twelfth Judicial Circuit)* Elected to term beginning Jan 1987. Reelected 1992 and 1998. Current term expires Jan 2005. Born Willmar Minnesota Nov 7, 1949. Religious affiliation: United Church of Christ. Educated at Eckerd College B.A. 1971 and University of Florida J.D. 1974. Admitted to practice Florida 1974, U.S. District Court 1975 and U.S. Supreme Court 1981. In legal practice Bradenton 1974-86.

Instructor Legal Assistant Program Manatee Community College 1978-86. Member Academy of Florida Trial Lawyers, Florida Conference of Circuit Court Judges, The Florida Bar, Manatee (President 1984) and Sarasota County Bar Associations. Recipient MacArthur Distinguished Alumni Award from Eckerd College 1987. Political affiliation: Independent. Past President Faith United Church of Christ of Manatee County. Former Director Manatee Chamber of Commerce. Enjoys sailing.

Mailing address: P.O. Box 1000, Bradenton 34206.

Office: 1115 Manatee Avenue West, Bradenton 34205.

Telephone: (941) 749-7138.

Fax: (941) 742-5956

BROWNING, Edwin B., Jr. *(Judge, Florida District Court of Appeal First District)* Assumed office Dec 1998. Retained by election Nov 7, 2000, current term expires Jan 2007. Born Madison Florida Oct 8, 1939. Educated at Florida State University B.S. 1961 and University of Florida LL.B. 1964 replaced by J.D. In legal practice Madison 1964-98.

Former Prosecuting Attorney Madison County. Past President Third Circuit Bar Association. Former Member Academy of Florida Trial Lawyers, The Association of Trial Lawyers of America and The Florida Bar. Member American Board of Trial Advocates. Former Chairman Board of Directors Bank of Madison County. Former Trustee North Florida Community College. Former Member Environmental Regulation Commission Florida. Deacon Madison First Baptist Church.

Office: 301 South Martin Luther King Jr. Boulevard, Tallahassee 32399-1850.

BRUNSON, Catherine M. *(Judge, Florida Circuit Court Fifteenth Judicial Circuit)* Appointed by Governor Lawton Chiles Aug 3, 1994.

Office: Palm Beach County Courthouse, 205 North Dixie Highway, West Palm Beach 33401.

Telephone: (561) 355-2595.

Fax: (561) 355-1616

BRYAN, Ben L., Jr. *(Judge, Florida Circuit Court Nineteenth Judicial Circuit)*

Office: 100 S.E. Ocean Boulevard, Suite A263, Stuart 34994.

Telephone: (772) 288-5575.

Fax: (772) 223-7901

BRYAN, Paul S. *(Judge, Florida Circuit Court Third Judicial Circuit)* Elected Nov 1992 to term beginning Jan 5, 1993. Reelected 1998, current term expires Jan 2005. Former Chief Judge. Born Florida Oct 1, 1953. Baptist. Educated at LaGrange College B.A. 1974 and University of Florida School of Law J.D. with honors 1977. Admitted to practice Florida 1977 and U.S. District Court Middle District of Florida 1979. In legal practice Lake City 1990-93.

Author two chapters *Florida Prosecutor's Manual* F.P.A.A. Certified Legal Instructor Lake City Community College since 1978. Faculty Member Florida College of Advanced Legal Studies. Interests include kids, classic cars and cattle.

Mailing address: P.O. Box 2083, Lake City 32056-2083.

Telephone: (386) 758-2147.

Fax: (386) 758-2151

BRYSON, Fred L. *(Senior Judge, Florida Circuit Court Sixth Judicial Circuit)* Assumed Senior Judge status, serves by assignment.

Office: Judicial Building, 545 First Avenue North, St. Petersburg 33701.

Telephone: (727) 464-4470.

BUCKLEW, Susan C. *(Judge, United States District Court Middle District of Florida)* Appointed for life by President Bill Clinton to term beginning 1993. Born Tampa Florida May 12, 1942. Educated at Florida State University B.A. 1964, University of South Florida M.A. 1968 and Stetson University College of Law J.D. 1977. Judge, Hillsborough County Court 1982-86. Judge, Florida Circuit Court Thirteenth Judicial Circuit 1986-93.

Corporate Legal Counsel Jim Walter Corporation 1978-82.

Office: U.S. Courthouse, 801 North Florida Avenue, Tampa 33602-3800.

Telephone: (813) 301-5858.

BUDNICK, Martin *(Senior Judge, Florida Circuit Court Eighteenth Judicial Circuit)* Assumed office Jan 24, 1989. Elected 1990. Assumed Senior Judge status, serves by assignment. Born New York New York 1930. Educated at University of Florida B.S.B.A. 1953 and University of Miami J.D. 1958. Admitted to practice Florida 1958. E-6 U.S. Army 1953-55. Judge, Brevard County Court Jan 1973 to Jan 24, 1989.

Office: Moore Justice Center, 2825 Judge Fran Jamieson Way, Viera 32940-8006.

Telephone: (321) 637-5555.

BURK, Richard B. *(Senior Judge, Florida Circuit Court Fifteenth Judicial Circuit)* Appointed by Governor Robert Graham Jan 15, 1982. Elected to term beginning Jan 5, 1983. Reelected Nov 1988 and 1994. Assumed Senior Judge status, serves by assignment. Born Tampa Florida March 26, 1932. Episcopalian. Educated at University of Florida B.A. 1954 J.D. 1959. Member Phi Alpha Delta. Admitted to practice Florida 1959. Began legal practice Palm Beach County.

Member The Florida Bar and Palm Beach County Bar Association. Attended The National Judicial College. Captain USAR 1954-63. Member Kiwanis, Forum Club, Palm Beach County Charter Commission, West Palm Beach Charter Revision Committee, and West Palm Beach Code Revision Committee.

Office: Palm Beach County Courthouse, 205 North Dixie Highway, West Palm Beach 33401.

Telephone: (561) 355-2431.

BURK, Warren *(Judge, Florida Circuit Court Eighteenth Judicial Circuit)* Elected Nov 8, 1994 to term beginning Jan 1, 1995. Reelected 2000, current term expires Dec 31, 2006. Born Detroit Michigan April 8, 1935. Catholic. Educated at Northwestern University B.S. 1957 and University of Detroit LL.B. with honors 1959 replaced by J.D. Business Editor University of Detroit Law Review 1958-59. Member Phi Delta Phi and Gamma Eta Gamma. Admitted to practice Michigan 1970, Florida 1971 and California 1975. In legal practice Detroit Michigan, Oceanside California and Cocoa Beach and Melbourne Florida.

Assistant State Attorney 1977-89. Author "Peaceful Picketing" 1958-59 and "Punishment of Direct Cr. Cont." 1958-59 University of Detroit Law Review. Member The Florida Bar, State Bar of California, Brevard County and Federal Bar Associations. Recipient Copyright Law Prize American Society of Composers, Authors and Publishers 1958 and American Juris Prizes in Corporations, Common Law, Pleadings. USAF and Michigan Air Guard. Political affiliation: Nonpartisan. Twelve-Gallon Blood Donor. Member Knights of Columbus and Brevard Cultural Alliance, Inc.

Office: Justice Center, Fourth Floor, 2825 Judge Fran Jamieson Way, Viera 32940-8006.

Telephone: (321) 617-7258.

Fax: (321) 617-7292

BURNSTEIN, Miette K. *(Judge, Florida Circuit Court Seventeenth Judicial Circuit)* Elected 1976 to term beginning Jan 4, 1977. Reelected 1982, 1988, 1994 and 2000. Current term expires Jan 2007. Former Chief Judge. Born Budapest Hungary Dec 23, 1936. Jewish. Educated at Syracuse University B.S. 1958 and University of Miami J.D. 1961. Admitted to practice Florida 1961 and U.S. Supreme Court 1967. Began legal practice Hollywood Florida 1961.

Member South Broward, Broward County and American Bar Associations.

Office: 1030 Broward County Courthouse, 201 S.E. Sixth Street, Fort Lauderdale 33301.

Telephone: (954) 831-7833

BURTON, Charles *(Judge, Palm Beach County Court)*

Office: Palm Beach County Courthouse, 205 North Dixie Highway, West Palm Beach 33401.

Telephone: (561) 355-2172.

BUTTERWORTH, Robert A. *(Senior Judge, Florida Circuit Court Seventeenth Judicial Circuit)* Assumed Senior Judge status, serves by assignment.

Office: Broward County Courthouse, 201 S.E. Sixth Street, Fort Lauderdale 33301.

Telephone: (954) 831-7740.

BUTTNER, Frederic A. *(Judge, Florida Circuit Court Fourth Judicial Circuit)* Appointed by Governor Bob Martinez to term beginning April 30, 1990. Elected to subsequent terms.

Mailing address: P.O. Drawer 1867, Green Cove Springs 32043.

Office: Clay County Courthouse, Green Cove Springs 32043.

Telephone: (904) 269-6323.

Fax: (904) 278-4728

CADDELL, Patrick K. *(Judge, Pinellas County Court)*

Office: Criminal Justice Center, 14250 49th Street North, Clearwater 33762.

Telephone: (727) 464-6219.

Fax: (727) 464-6484

CANADY, Charles T. *(Judge, Florida District Court of Appeal Second District)*

Mailing address: P.O. Box 327, Lakeland 33802-0327.

Office: 1005 East Memorial Boulevard, Lakeland 33801.

CANTERO, Raoul G., III *(Justice, Florida Supreme Court)*

Office: Supreme Court Building, 500 South Duval Street, Tallahassee 32399-1925.

Telephone: (850) 410-8092.

Fax: (850) 487-2823.

CARDONNE ELY, Gisela *(Judge, Florida Circuit Court Eleventh Judicial Circuit)* Appointed by Governor Bob Martinez to term beginning July 1988. Elected 1988, 1994 and 2000. Current term expires 2007. Served Criminal Division July 1988 to Dec 1990. Assistant Administrative Judge Juvenile Division Jan 1991 to June 1993. Serves General Jurisdiction Division since 1993. Educated at Barry University B.A. cum laude 1971 M.A. 1979 and University of Miami J.D. 1976. Listed in *Who's Who in American Colleges and Universities* 1972. Member Lambda Iota Tau, Delta Epsilon Sigma, Alpha Mu Gamma, Kappa Gamma Pi and Lambda Sigma. Admitted to practice Florida 1976, U.S. District Court Southern District of Florida 1983, U.S. Court of Appeals 1983 and U.S. Supreme Court 1983. In legal practice Miami. Judge, Dade County Court May 1982 to Jan 1993 and June 1986 to June 1988.

Former Assistant City Attorney and Deputy City Attorney Miami. Member Legislative Committee on Equal Education for Women U.S. Department of Health, Education and Welfare Washington D.C. Oct 1979. Member National Conference on Law Enforcement and Criminal Justice Washington D.C. Oct 1980. Member 21st Century Justice Committee Florida Supreme Court 1993-94. Member Court Reporting Review Committee 1994-95, Criminal Court Appointment Review Specially Appointed Public Defenders Committee, Space Committee and Court Emergency Committee Eleventh Judicial Circuit. Former Member Peter T. Fay American Inn of Court, American Arbitration Association and American Bar Association. Member Florida Association of Women Lawyers, The Florida Bar Foundation (Access for Middle Class to Legal Services 1995), Florida Conference of Circuit Court Judges (Chair Civil Section since 1992, Chair 1997-98, Member Education Section), National Association of Women Judges, American Judges Association, Cuban American Bar Association (Board of Directors 1981-83, Treasurer 1984), National Hispanic Bar Association, The Florida Bar (Unauthorized Practice Law Committee 1981-86, Chair Civil Section since 1992, Member Joint Committee Trial Lawyers Section on Professionalism since 1994), Miami Beach and Dade County (Co-Chair Bar Liaison Committee 1983-84 and Member Judicial Relations Committee 1984 Young Lawyers Section, Coordinator Writing Competition Local Government Section) Bar Associations. Speaker Fourth Conference Lawyer of the Americas 1984. Lecturer on Ethics National Hispanic Bar Association 1987. Recipient Certificate of Appreciation from City of Miami June

CARDONNE ELY, GISELA—*Continued*

1988. Previously worked as Hearing Examiner Dade County School Board. Board of Directors 1977-78 and President 1978-79 Miami Beach Community Mental Health, Inc. Board of Directors Spanish American League Against Discrimination 1982-83. Board Member Dade County Traffic Safety Council 1985-89 and Metro Traffic Safety Institute 1991. Participant Ronald McDonald House programs 1982 and Miami Beach Jaycee Women 1983. Member Public Law Interest Bank 1982-86, Miami Commission on Status of Women 1984-86, Coalition of Hispanic American Women, Women in Government Service, Greater Miami Jewish Federation, Latin Business Professional Women, Hadassah and Pioneer Women.

Office: 1500 Dade County Courthouse, 73 West Flagler Street, Miami 33130.
Telephone: (305) 349-7024.
Fax: (305) 375-4118

CAREY, John K. *(Judge, Florida Circuit Court Thirteenth Judicial Circuit)*
Office: Hillsborough County Courthouse, 419 Pierce Street, Tampa 33604-4022.

CARITHERS, Hugh, Jr. *(Judge, Florida Circuit Court Fourth Judicial Circuit)* Appointed by Governor Lawton Chiles Jan 21, 1993.
Office: 206 Duval County Courthouse, 330 East Bay Street, Jacksonville 32202.
Telephone: (904) 630-2111.
Fax: (904) 630-8484

CARLIN, John S. *(Judge, Florida Circuit Court Twentieth Judicial Circuit)* Former Judge, Lee County Court, elected to term beginning Jan 1991.
Office: Lee County Justice Center, 1700 Monroe Street, Fort Myers 33901.
Telephone: (239) 335-2871.

CARLTON, Charles T. *(Senior Judge, Florida Circuit Court Twentieth Judicial Circuit)* Appointed by Governor Claude R. Kirk, Jr. 1970. Elected 1972, 1978, 1984 and 1990. Deputy Chief Judge 1976-78. Chief Judge 1978-80. Assumed Senior Judge status, serves by assignment. Born Fort Pierce Florida Nov 7, 1935. Educated at University of Florida A.B. 1957 and Stetson University J.D. 1963. Recipient Delta Theta Phi Key for Excellence in Scholarship. Honor Court Attorney. Secretary Student Body. Member Pi Kappa Phi. Admitted to practice Florida 1963. In legal practice Fort Pierce 1963-70. Administrative Judge, Charlotte County Court 1971-72. Administrative Judge, Glades and Hendry County Courts 1971-75.

Assistant City Attorney and Special Prosecutor Fort Pierce 1965-67. State Attorney Nineteenth Judicial Circuit 1968-70. Member Florida Conference of Circuit Court Judges, The Florida Bar, Collier County and American Bar Associations. Recipient Good Government Award 1968 and Distinguished Service Award 1970 from Jaycees. Florida National Guard 1953-56. Captain USMC 1957-60. Republican. Former member Board of Directors Stetson Lawyers Association, YMCA and Pelican Yacht Club. Former Vice President and President St. Lucie County Chapter University of Florida Alumni Association. Past President Legal Services, Inc. Former First Vice President United Fund. Former Director Florida Bank of Fort Pierce. Board of Directors Big Brothers. Member Marine Corps Reserve Officers Association, Marine Corps League, Elks and Cattlemen's Association. Enjoys skiing, bicycling, running, swimming and triathlons.

Office: Charlotte County Justice Center, 350 East Marion Avenue, Punta Gorda 33950.
Telephone: (239) 335-2299.

CARNEY, Robert B. *(Judge, Florida Circuit Court Seventeenth Judicial Circuit)*
Office: 1010A Broward County Courthouse, 201 S.E. Sixth Street, Fort Lauderdale 33301.
Telephone: (954) 831-7642.

CARNEY, Thomas M. *(Judge, Florida Circuit Court Eleventh Judicial Circuit)* Former Judge, Dade County Court.
Office: 304 Gerstein Justice Building, 1351 N.W. Twelfth Street, Miami 33125.
Telephone: (305) 548-5771.

CARPANINI, Mark F. *(Judge, Polk County Court)*
Office: 225 North Broadway, Bartow 33830.

CARY, G. Keith *(Judge, Florida Circuit Court Twentieth Judicial Circuit)* Former Judge, Lee County Court.
Mailing address: P.O. Box 567, LaBelle 33975-0567.
Office: Hendry County Courthouse, LaBelle 33935.
Telephone: (863) 675-5225.
Fax: (863) 675-5361

CASANUEVA, Darryl C. *(Judge, Florida District Court of Appeal Second District)* Appointed by Governor Lawton Chiles to term beginning Feb 14, 1998. Retained by election 2000, current term expires Jan 2007. Born Tampa Florida Aug 7, 1951. Roman Catholic. Educated at University of South Florida B.A. 1973, Loyola University School of Law J.D. 1976 and University of Virginia School of Law LL.M. in Judicial Process 2001. Admitted to practice Florida 1976. In legal practice Port Charlotte and Punta Gorda 1978-90. Judge, Florida Circuit Court Twentieth Judicial Circuit Jan 1991 to 1998.

Assistant State Attorney Twentieth Judicial Circuit 1976-78. Recipient Liberty Bell Award from Lee County Bar Association 2000.

Office: 801 Twiggs Street, Suite 600, Tampa 33602.
Telephone: (813) 272-3430.

CASE, James R. *(Judge, Florida Circuit Court Sixth Judicial Circuit)* Former Chief Judge.
Office: 417 Pinellas County Courthouse, 315 Court Street, Clearwater 33756.
Telephone: (727) 464-3548.
Fax: (727) 464-3610

CASTAGNA, William John *(Senior Judge, United States District Court Middle District of Florida)* Appointed for life by President Jimmy Carter. Assumed Senior status, serves by assignment. Born Philadelphia Pennsylvania June 25, 1924. Educated at University of Pennsylvania 1941-42 and University of Florida LL.B. 1949 replaced by J.D. Admitted to practice Florida 1949. In legal practice 1949-1979.

Member The Florida Bar (Board of Governors 1966-70) and Clearwater Bar Association (Former Vice President and President). Democrat.

Office: 14B U.S. Courthouse, 801 North Florida Avenue, Tampa 33602-4511.
Telephone: (813) 301-5935.

CATES, Robert P. *(Judge, Florida Circuit Court Eighth Judicial Circuit)* Former Chief Judge.
Office: 303 Alachua County Courthouse, 201 East University Avenue, Gainesville 32601.
Telephone: (352) 374-3653.
Fax: (352) 374-5238

CHANCE, Chester B. *(Judge, Florida Circuit Court Eighth Judicial Circuit)* Born New York Oct 3, 1940. Educated at University of Florida B.S. in Finance 1962 law degree 1964. Admitted to practice Florida 1965, U.S. District Courts for Middle 1965 and Northern 1966 Districts of Florida and U.S. Supreme Court 1973. In legal practice Tampa 1965 and Gainesville 1965-73. Judge, Alachua County Court, appointed by Governor Reubin Askew to term beginning 1973.
Assistant Public Defender 1966-68. Co-author *Bench Book Guide to the Implementation of American Bar Standards of Criminal Justice* American Bar Association 1975 and Misdemeanor Section of *Florida Trial Judges Bench Book*. Former Instructor in Business Law University of Florida and in Law Enforcement Santa Fe Community College. Vice Chairman National Conference of Special Court Judges (State Chairman Committee for the Implementation of American Bar Association Standards of Criminal Justice, Chairman Education Committee, past member Legislative Committee, past Chairman Manuals Committee). President Elect Florida Conference of County Court Judges (Chairman Education Committee and former member Board of Directors). Member Statewide Courts Task Force of Governor's Council on Criminal Justice, Court-News Media Committee of the Florida Supreme Court, Judicial Training Advisory Committee of the Florida Supreme Court, Trial Judges Bench Book Committee of the Circuit Judges Conference, The Florida Bar, Eighth Judicial Circuit and American (Criminal Justice Section) Bar Associations.
Co-chairman Education Committee Florida Conference of County Court Judges 1975. Former Chairman Eighth Judicial Circuit Supreme Court Bicentennial Committee. Past member Governor's Committee on Effective Highway Safety Adjudication and Special Advisory Committee to the Florida Supreme Court on rules of procedure for Traffic Courts. Participant American Society of Newspaper Editors Workshop on Legal and Ethical Issues as They Relate to the Press Dec 1976 and LEAA Conference of Improved Lower Court Case Handling at Atlanta Georgia Sept 1976. Speaker Implementation Conferences on New Traffic Court Rules of Procedure at Tampa and Gainesville Nov and Dec 1974 and at National Conference for Improvement of Criminal Justice at National College of the State Judiciary April 1975. Guest speaker on Criminal Justice Standards at Annual Convention of Florida Council of Crime and Delinquency 1974 and Florida League of Women Voters Conference on the Judiciary 1976. Instructor College of New Florida Judges at University of Florida 1975 and 1976 and County Judges Mid-Year Educational Conference University of Florida 1975. Recognized by resolution passed by National Conference of Special Court Judges for "Tremendous contribution to the improvement of the administration of justice in the Courts of Special Jurisdiction" 1975. Recipient Distinguished Leadership Award for Contribution to Judicial Education from Florida Conference of County Court Judges 1976. Chairman Alachua County Democratic Executive Committee 1968-72. Past Chairman Alachua County Citizens for Tax Reform, Gainesville Citizens Advisory Committee and State Government Committee of Gainesville Area Chamber of Commerce. Past Executive Director Alachua County Housing Authority. Past member Board of Directors Alachua County Democratic Club. Board of Directors Gator City Kiwanis Club, Gainesville Neighborhood Development, Inc. and Gainesville Boys Club.
Office: 301 Alachua County Courthouse, 201 East University Avenue, Gainesville 32601.
Telephone: (352) 374-3642.
Fax: (352) 374-5238

CHAPPELL, Sheri Polster *(Magistrate Judge, United States District Court Middle District of Florida)* Appointed by U.S. District Court judges to term beginning April 21, 2003. Former Judge, Lee County Court.
Office: 2110 First Street, Fort Myers 33901.
Telephone: (239) 461-2060.

CHAVIES, Michael B. *(Judge, Florida Circuit Court Eleventh Judicial Circuit)* Appointed by Governor Lawton Chiles Jan 28, 1993.
Office: 1307 Courthouse Center, 175 N.W. First Avenue, Miami 33128.
Telephone: (305) 349-7020.
Fax: (305) 349-5543

CHEEK, Leon B., III *(Judge, Orange County Court)* Appointed by Governor Lawton Chiles to term beginning Jan 30, 1998. Elected 2000, current term expires Jan 2007. Born Orlando Florida Sept 12, 1947. Methodist. Educated at University of Florida B.A. 1969 J.D. 1972. Member Phi Alpha Delta and Tau Kappa Epsilon. Admitted to practice Florida 1972, U.S. District Court Middle District of Florida, U.S. Courts of Appeals Fifth and Eleventh Circuits and U.S. Supreme Court. In legal practice Orlando 1972-76 and Fern Park 1990-98.
Recipient Pro Bono Service Award from Florida Supreme Court 1995. Enjoys mountain climbing.
Office: 830 Orange County Courthouse, 425 North Orange Avenue, Orlando 32801.
Telephone: (407) 836-0524.
Fax: (407) 836-2315

CHRISTENSEN, Patti Ann *(Judge, St. Johns County Court)*
Office: Judicial Center, 4010 Lewis Speedway, St. Augustine 32084.
Telephone: (904) 823-2376.
Fax: (904) 823-2391

CIANCA, Marc A. *(Chief Judge, Florida Circuit Court Nineteenth Judicial Circuit)* Chief Judge since July 1, 2001. Former Judge, Martin County Court.
Office: 315 Courthouse Addition, 218 South Second Street, Fort Pierce 34950.
Telephone: (772) 462-1461.
Fax: (772) 462-2783

CIKLIN, Cory J. *(Judge, Palm Beach County Court)* Elected to term beginning Jan 3, 1995. Reelected 1998, current term expires Jan 2005.
Office: 3188 PGA Boulevard, Palm Beach Gardens 33410.
Telephone: (561) 624-6551.
Fax: (561) 624-6549

CLARK, David C. *(Senior Judge, Palm Beach County Court)* Assumed Senior Judge status, serves by assignment.
Office: Palm Beach County Courthouse, 205 North Dixie Highway, West Palm Beach 33401.
Telephone: (561) 355-2431.

CLARK, Nancy Lynn *(Judge, Orange County Court)*
Office: 440 Orange County Courthouse, 425 North Orange Avenue, Orlando 32801.
Telephone: (407) 836-0570.

CLARK, Nikki Ann *(Judge, Florida Circuit Court Second Judicial Circuit)* Appointed by Governor Lawton Chiles Aug 30, 1993.
Office: Leon County Courthouse, 301 South Monroe Street, Tallahassee 32301.
Telephone: (850) 577-4301.
Fax: (850) 577-4475

CLARKE, Cathleen B. *(Judge, Brevard County Court)*
Office: 130 Melbourne Courthouse, 50 South Nieman Avenue, Melbourne 32901-1261.
Telephone: (321) 952-4702.
Fax: (321) 952-4704

CLAYTON, James R. *(Judge, Florida Circuit Court Seventh Judicial Circuit)*
Office: 110 Courthouse Annex, 125 East Orange Avenue, Daytona Beach 32114.
Telephone: (386) 257-6072.
Fax: (386) 248-8122

CLEMENTS, Marshall M. *(Judge, Dixie County Court)*
Mailing address: P.O. Box 1995, Cross City 32628-1995.
Office: Dixie County Courthouse, Cross City 32628.
Telephone: (352) 498-1234.
Fax: (352) 498-1477

COBB, Warren H. *(Senior Judge, Florida District Court of Appeal)* Appointed by Governor Robert Graham to term beginning Nov 1, 1979. Retained by election Nov 1980, Nov 1986, Nov 1992 and Nov 1998. Chief Judge 1984-86. Assumed Senior Judge status, serves by assignment. Born Pensacola Florida Aug 5, 1932. Methodist. Educated at Florida State University B.S. cum laude 1955 and University of Florida LL.B. 1958. Member Phi Beta Kappa and Phi Kappa Phi. Admitted to practice Florida 1959. In legal practice DeLand 1959-61 and Daytona Beach and Ormond Beach 1961-72. Judge 1973-79 and Chief Judge 1977-79, Florida Circuit Court Seventh Judicial Circuit.
President State Conference of District Court of Appeal Judges 1984-85. Supreme Court Committee on Standard Jury Instructions (Civil) 1980-84. State Judicial Council 1984-85. Member Humane Society.
Office: 300 South Beach Street, Daytona Beach 32114.
Telephone: (386) 947-1500.

COBB, Wayne L. *(Judge, Florida Circuit Court Sixth Judicial Circuit)* Appointed by Governor Reubin Askew to term beginning Feb 1, 1977. Elected 1978, 1984, 1990, 1996 and 2002. Current term expires Jan 2009. Born Clearwater Florida March 25, 1936. Educated at University of Florida B.A. 1961 LL.B. 1964 replaced by J.D. 1967. Admitted to practice Florida 1964 and U.S. District Court Middle District of Florida 1966. Began legal practice New Port Richey 1964. Judge, New Port Richey Municipal Court 1966-67.
Member The Florida Bar. Recipient Distinguished Service Award from New Port Richey Jaycees 1966. Corporal USMC 1954-57. President New Port Richey Chamber of Commerce 1967-69. Board of Trustees Pasco-Hernando Community College 1972-77.
Office: Dade City Courthouse, 38053 Live Oak Avenue, Dade City 33523.
Telephone: (352) 521-4414.

COCALIS, Patricia W. *(Judge, Florida Circuit Court Seventeenth Judicial Circuit)* Former Judge, Broward County Court.
Office: 1010B Broward County Courthouse, 201 S.E. Sixth Street, Fort Lauderdale 33301.
Telephone: (954) 831-7749.
Fax: (954) 831-5572

COFER, Charles G. *(Judge, Duval County Court)* Appointed by Governor Lawton Chiles July 1998. Retained by election 2000, current term expires Jan 2007. Born Radford Virginia June 27, 1952. United Methodist. Educated at Duke University B.A. magna cum laude 1974 and University of Virginia J.D. 1977. Admitted to practice Florida 1977. In legal practice Jacksonville June 1977 to Jan 1980.
Assistant Public Defender Jacksonville Jan 1980 to July 1998. Member The Florida Bar and Jacksonville Bar Association.
Office: 332 Duval County Courthouse, 300 East Bay Street, Jacksonville 32202.
Telephone: (904) 630-2576.
Fax: (904) 630-8359

COHEN, Barry M. *(Judge, Palm Beach County Court)* Elected to term beginning Jan 1991. Reelected 1994 and 1998. Current term expires Jan 2005.
Office: South County Courthouse, 200 West Atlantic Avenue, Delray Beach 33444.
Telephone: (561) 274-1425.
Fax: (561) 274-1467

COHEN, Geoffrey D. *(Judge, Florida Circuit Court Seventeenth Judicial Circuit)* Former Judge, Broward County Court.
Office: Broward County Courthouse, 201 S.E. Sixth Street, Fort Lauderdale 33301.
Telephone: (954) 831-7823.
Fax: (954) 831-5572

COHEN, Harold J. *(Judge, Florida Circuit Court Fifteenth Judicial Circuit)* Born New York New York Jan 17, 1947. Jewish. Educated at State University of New York at Binghamton (Harpur College) B.A. 1967, Brooklyn College of the City University of New York teaching certificate 1968 and George Washington University J.D. with honors 1971. Member ARISTA National Honor Society. Admitted to practice Florida 1971, U.S. District Court Southern District of Florida 1971 and U.S. Supreme Court 1975. Judge, Palm Beach County Court 1977-84.
With State Attorney's Office West Palm Beach 1971-76. Instructor in Criminal Justice Palm Beach Junior College 1971-76 and Courts and Society Florida Atlantic University 1972. Former member National District Attorneys Association, Florida Prosecuting Attorneys Association, Florida Conference of County Court Judges and

COHEN, HAROLD J.—*Continued*

American Bar Association. Member The Florida Bar and Palm Beach County Bar Association. Attended National Institute for Trial Advocacy 1973 and The National Judicial College 1977, 1978 and 1996. Democrat. Former member Board of Trustees Jewish Community Day School of Palm Beach County, Board of Directors Hospice of Palm Beach County Inc., West Palm Beach Jaycees, B'nai B'rith and Jewish Federation of Palm Beach County. Board of Directors Health and Human Services Planning Association Palm Beach County.

Office: West County Complex Courthouse, 38844 State Road 80, Belle Glade 33430.

Telephone: (561) 996-4841.

COHEN, Jay P. *(Judge, Florida Circuit Court Ninth Judicial Circuit)* Assumed office Dec 22, 1993. Judge, Orange County Court April 12, 1990 to Dec 21, 1993, appointed by Governor Bob Martinez.

Office: 835 Orange County Courthouse, 425 North Orange Avenue, Orlando 32801.

Telephone: (407) 836-2276.

COHEN, Jeri B. *(Judge, Florida Circuit Court Eleventh Judicial Circuit)* Former Judge, Dade County Court.

Office: 205 Juvenile Justice Center, 3300 N.W. 27th Avenue, Miami 33142.

Telephone: (305) 638-6879.

Fax: (305) 638-6354

COHN, James I. *(Judge, Florida Circuit Court Seventeenth Judicial Circuit)* Appointed by Governor Lawton Chiles June 13, 1995.

Office: 5760 Broward County Courthouse, 201 S.E. Sixth Street, Fort Lauderdale 33301.

Telephone: (954) 831-7091.

COLBATH, Jeffrey J. *(Judge, Florida Circuit Court Fifteenth Judicial Circuit)* Former Judge, Palm Beach County Court.

Office: South County Courthouse, 200 West Atlantic Avenue, Delray Beach 33444.

Telephone: (561) 274-1487.

COLBATH, Walter N., Jr. *(Senior Judge, Florida Circuit Court Fifteenth Judicial Circuit)* Former Chief Judge. Assumed Senior Judge status, serves by assignment.

Office: Palm Beach County Courthouse, 205 North Dixie Highway, West Palm Beach 33401.

Telephone: (561) 355-2431.

COLE, Karen K. *(Judge, Florida Circuit Court Fourth Judicial Circuit)* Appointed by Governor Lawton Chiles Nov 5, 1993 to term beginning Jan 4, 1994.

Office: Duval County Courthouse, 330 East Bay Street, Jacksonville 32202.

Telephone: (904) 630-2111.

Fax: (904) 630-2979

COLE, Robert P. *(Judge, Pasco County Court)*

Office: 109 Dade City Courthouse, 38053 Live Oak Avenue, Dade City 33523.

Telephone: (352) 521-4424.

COLE, Russell A., Jr. *(Senior Judge, Florida Circuit Court Fourteenth Judicial Circuit)* Appointed by Governor Bob Martinez to term beginning Jan 2, 1990. Elected to subsequent terms. Assumed Senior Judge status, serves by assignment.

Mailing address: P.O. Box 27, Panama City 32402.

Office: 300 East Fourth Street, Panama City 32401.

Telephone: (850) 747-5327.

COLEMAN, Ted P. *(Senior Judge, Florida Circuit Court Ninth Judicial Circuit)* Former Chief Judge. Assumed Senior Judge status, serves by assignment.

Office: Orange County Courthouse, 425 North Orange Avenue, Orlando 32801.

Telephone: (407) 836-2050.

COLEMAN, Thomas B. *(Judge, Columbia County Court)*

Mailing address: P.O. Box 2065, Lake City 32056.

Telephone: (386) 758-1000.

COLLIER, Lacey A. *(Judge, United States District Court Northern District of Florida)* Appointed for life by President George Bush Nov 20, 1991. Born Demopolis Alabama June 23, 1935. Educated at University of Alabama 1953-55, U.S. Naval Postgraduate School B.A. in Government 1970, University of West Florida M.A. in Political Science 1972 B.A. in Accounting 1975 and Florida State University College of Law J.D. with honors 1977. Member Phi Alpha Delta. Judge, Florida Circuit Court First Judicial Circuit 1984-91.

Assistant State Attorney Office of the State Attorney First Judicial Circuit of Florida 1977-84. Author Continuances Section *Prosecutors Manual* 1982. Adjunct Professor of Political Science University of West Florida 1973. Lecturer Robert A. Taft Institute of Government 1989-91. Advisor Grand Juries First Judicial Circuit 1978-84. Former Member Florida Prosecuting Attorney's Association (Chairman Oversight Subcommittee for Periodical "The Prosecutor" and Member Education Committee), Florida Conference of Circuit Judges and American Bar Association. Founding Member and Executive Board Pensacola Chapter American Inns of Court since 1991. Member The Florida Bar (Standard Jury Instructions Committee 1989-91), Okaloosa-Walton and Escambia-Santa Rosa Bar Associations. Lecturer Louisiana Judges Conference 1986. Chairman Education Conference Subcommittee Florida Conference of Circuit Judges 1987-89. Faculty Florida New Judges' College 1989-91. Recipient Distinguished Alumni Award from University of West Florida 1988, God In Government Award from Cantonment-Ensley Ministerial Association 1991 and Distinguished Service Award from Florida Council on Crime and Delinquency 1991. Named Professional Leader of the Year by Pensacola BIP 1989. Lieutenant Commander USN April 1955 to Sept 1975 (retired). Member Pensacola Jaycees 1971-72, Public Safety Task Force Action '76 1974, City-County Drug Abuse Commission 1980-83 (President 1982-83), Presidential Search Committee University of West Florida 1987, Northwest Florida Fellowship of Christian Athletes 1992-93 and Commissioning Committee USS Mitscher (DD-57) 1994. President Men's Club St. Paul's Catholic Church 1972. Division Leader C.F.C./United Way 1973. Vice Chairman Escambia County Charter Committee 1978-79. Board of Directors Alumni Association Florida State University College of Law 1980-81. Charter Member National Museum of Naval Aviation Foundation 1985. Chairman Revenue Study Committee City of Pensacola 1985-86, Task Force on Port/Airport Development 1987-89 and Building and Sites Task Force 1989-91 Committee of 100 Chamber of Commerce and The Pensacola

COLLIER, LACEY A.—*Continued*

Committee National Museum of Naval Aviation Foundation 1990-91. Official Advisor Escambia Governmental Study Commission 1986-87. Trustee University of West Florida Foundation since 1988 (President 1993-94) and Pensacola Little Theater/Cultural Center 1989-94. Advisory Board Students in Free Enterprise University of West Florida 1989-91, The African-American Heritage Society since 1990 and Sacred Heart Hospital 1991-93. President Advisory Board—Nativity since 1990 and Lector/Liturgical Assistant Catholic Church. Secretary Board of Directors Big Brother/Big Sister of Northwest Florida 1990-91. Member Executive Club, Pensacola Ski Club, Irish Politicians Club, Association of Naval Aviation, American Legion, Tiger Point Country Club and Navy League.

Office: U.S. Courthouse, One North Palafox Street, Pensacola 32501-5625.

Telephone: (850) 444-0174.

COLLINS, Julian E. *(Judge, Florida Circuit Court Third Judicial Circuit)* Former Judge, Columbia County Court.

Mailing address: P.O. Box 2077, Lake City 32056-2077.

Office: Columbia County Courthouse, Lake City 32056.

Telephone: (386) 719-7546.

Fax: (386) 839-7546

COLLINS, Robert O. *(Senior Judge, Florida Circuit Court Seventeenth Judicial Circuit)* Elected to term beginning Jan 1991. Reelected 1996. Assumed Senior Judge status, serves by assignment.

Office: Broward County Courthouse, 201 S.E. Sixth Street, Fort Lauderdale 33301.

Telephone: (954) 831-7740.

COLTON, Roger B. *(Judge, Florida Circuit Court Fifteenth Judicial Circuit)* Appointed by Governor Lawton Chiles to term beginning March 1, 1994. Elected July 1994 and July 2000. Current term expires Jan 2007. Born Bloomington Illinois Aug 5, 1937. Methodist. Educated at Illinois Wesleyan University B.S. 1959 and Northwestern University J.D. 1962. Member Phi Alpha Delta. Admitted to practice Florida 1970, U.S. District Court Southern District of Florida, U.S. Courts of Appeals Fifth and Eleventh Circuits and U.S. Supreme Court. In legal practice West Palm Beach 1971-94.

Office: Palm Beach County Courthouse, 205 North Dixie Highway, West Palm Beach 33401.

Telephone: (561) 355-4156.

CONNER, Burton Cornell *(Judge, Florida Circuit Court Nineteenth Judicial Circuit)* Appointed by Governor Lawton Chiles 1997. Elected 1998, current term expires Jan 2005. Born Dec 9. 1952. Catholic. Educated at Duke University with honors 1975 and University of Florida J.D. with honors 1977. Admitted to practice Florida 1978.

Office: 213 Courthouse Addition, 218 South Second Street, Fort Pierce 34950.

Telephone: (772) 462-2545.

Fax: (772) 462-2546

CONRAD, Richard F. *(Judge, Florida Circuit Court Ninth Judicial Circuit)* Former Judge, Orange County Court.

Office: 2015 Orange County Courthouse, 425 North Orange Avenue, Orlando 32801.

Telephone: (407) 836-2223.

CONWAY, Anne C. *(Judge, United States District Court Middle District of Florida)* Appointed for life by President George Bush to term beginning 1991. Born Cleveland Ohio July 30, 1950. Educated at John Carroll University B.A. 1972 and University of Florida College of Law J.D. 1975. Law Clerk to Hon. John A. Reed, Jr., U.S. District Court Middle District of Florida 1975-77. In legal practice Orlando 1978-91.

Office: 646 U.S. Courthouse, 80 North Hughey Avenue, Orlando 32801.

Telephone: (407) 835-4270.

COOK, Jack H. *(Judge, Florida Circuit Court Fifteenth Judicial Circuit)* Appointed by Governor Robert Graham to term beginning Oct 1, 1981. Elected 1982, 1988, 1994 and 2000. Current term expires Jan 2007. Former Chief Judge. Born Cleveland Ohio Nov 30, 1943. Protestant. Educated at Hope College B.A. 1965 and The Ohio State University J.D. 1968. Member Emersonians. Admitted to practice Ohio 1972 and Florida 1975. Began legal practice Columbus Ohio 1972. In legal practice West Palm Beach Florida 1975.

Member Supreme Court Committee on Standard Jury Instructions (Civil). Member Academy of Florida Trial Lawyers, The Association of Trial Lawyers of America, American Inns of Court, The Florida Bar, Palm Beach County and American Bar Associations. First Lieutenant U.S. Army 1968-71. Enjoys running, swimming and boating.

Office: Palm Beach County Courthouse, 205 North Dixie Highway, West Palm Beach 33401.

Telephone: (561) 355-3730.

Fax: (561) 355-3922

COOK, Martha J. *(Judge, Florida Circuit Court Thirteenth Judicial Circuit)*

Office: Hillsborough County Courthouse, 419 Pierce Street, Tampa 33602.

COOK, Philip *(Senior Judge, Dade County Court)* Appointed by Governor Robert Graham Feb 1982. Elected to term beginning Jan 1983. Reelected 1986 and 1990. Assumed Senior Judge status, serves by assignment. Born New York New York Jan 18, 1925. Religious affiliation: Hebrew. Educated at Champlain College 1948 and University of Miami B.S. 1950 J.D. 1952. Admitted to practice Florida 1952. In legal practice Miami 1952-82.

Member The Florida Bar and Dade County Bar Association. Sergeant U.S. Army 1943-46.

Office: 511 Dade County Courthouse, 73 West Flagler Street, Miami 33130.

Telephone: (305) 349-7001.

COON, Timothy *(Judge, Polk County Court)* Assumed office Nov 1995. Born Lynn Haven Florida March 3, 1949. Educated at Gulf Coast Community College A.A. 1972, University of South Florida B.A. 1975 and Florida State University J.D. 1978. Admitted to practice Florida 1979. In legal practice Lakeland Nov 1983 to June 1984 and Jan 1985 to Nov 1995.

Assistant State Attorney Sept 1978 to March 1979

COON, TIMOTHY—*Continued*
and Chief Consumer Fraud Section June 1984 to Jan 1985 State Attorney's Office Polk County Florida. USAF Aug 1968 to May 1972 and USAF JAG Sept 1979 to Sept 1983. Lieutenant Colonel USAFR JAG Dec 1983 to Jan 2001 (retired). Interests include reading, golfing, bowling and music.
Mailing address: P.O. Box 9000, Drawer J-140, Bartow 33831-9000.
Telephone: (863) 534-7780.
Fax: (863) 534-7723

COOPER, John C. *(Judge, Florida Circuit Court Second Judicial Circuit)*
Office: Leon County Courthouse, 301 South Monroe Street, Tallahassee 32301.
Telephone: (850) 577-4313.
Fax: (850) 922-0327

COOPER, Mallory D. *(Judge, Duval County Court)* Elected Sept 1996 to term beginning Jan 1997. Reelected Sept 2000, current term expires Jan 2007. Educated at Winthrop College and Florida State University College of Law J.D. cum laude 1986. Member Phi Delta Phi. Admitted to practice Florida 1987.
Assistant State Attorney Fourth Judicial Circuit 1987-96. Member The Florida Bar, Jacksonville and American Bar Associations.
Office: Duval County Courthouse, 330 East Bay Street, Jacksonville 32202.
Telephone: (904) 630-7009.
Fax: (904) 630-2979

COPE, Charles W. *(Judge, Florida Circuit Court Sixth Judicial Circuit)*
Office: 423 Pinellas County Courthouse, 315 Court Street, Clearwater 33756.
Telephone: (727) 464-3594.

COPE, Gerald B., Jr. *(Judge, Florida District Court of Appeal Third District)* Appointed by Governor Bob Martinez to term beginning Dec 19, 1988. Retained by election Nov 6, 1990, Nov 5, 1996 and Nov 5, 2002. Current term expires Jan 1, 2009. Born Orangeburg South Carolina Aug 2, 1946. Educated at Yale University B.A. cum laude 1968, Harvard Law School 1968-69, Florida State University College of Law J.D. with highest honors 1977 and University of Virginia LL.M. 1992. Editor-in-Chief Florida State University Law Review 1977. Member Order of the Coif. Admitted to practice Florida 1978, U.S. District Courts Southern 1978, Middle 1981 and Northern 1981 Districts of Florida, U.S. Courts of Appeals Fifth 1978 and Eleventh 1981 Circuits, U.S. Supreme Court 1982 and U.S. Tax Court 1985. In legal practice Miami 1978-88.
Author "Toward a Right of Privacy as a Matter of State Constitutional Law" 5 Florida State University L. Rev. 631, 1977, "To Be Let Alone: Florida's Proposed Right of Privacy" 6 Florida State University L. Rev. 671, 1978, "A Quick Look at Florida's New Right of Privacy" 55 Florida B. Jour. 12, 1981 and "Discretionary Review of the Decisions of Intermediate Appellate Courts: A Comparison of Florida's System with those of Other States and the Federal System" 45 Florida L. Rev. 21, 1993. Member The American Law Institute and The Florida Bar (Appellate Court Rules Committee 1988-2000).
Office: 2001 S.W. 117th Avenue, Miami 33175-1716.
Telephone: (305) 229-3200.

CORBIN, R. Thomas *(Judge, Florida Circuit Court Twentieth Judicial Circuit)* Appointed by Governor Lawton Chiles Dec 10, 1993.
Office: Lee County Justice Center, 1700 Monroe Street, Fort Myers 33901.
Telephone: (239) 335-2500.
Fax: (239) 335-2589

CORCORAN, C. Timothy, III *(Judge, United States Bankruptcy Court Middle District of Florida)* Appointed by U.S. Court of Appeals Eleventh Circuit judges.
Office: 727 U.S. Courthouse, 801 North Florida Avenue, Tampa 33602-3899.
Telephone: (813) 301-5200.

CORNELIUS, Lon S., Jr. *(Senior Judge, Florida Circuit Court Ninth Judicial Circuit)* Assumed Senior Judge status, serves by assignment.
Office: Orange County Courthouse, 425 North Orange Avenue, Orlando 32801.
Telephone: (407) 836-2050.

CORRIGAN, Timothy J. *(Judge, United States District Court Middle District of Florida)* Magistrate Judge 1996-2002. Appointed Judge for life by President George W. Bush to term beginning Sept 14, 2002. Born Jacksonville Florida 1956. Educated at University of Notre Dame B.A. 1978 and Duke University School of Law J.D. 1981. Law Clerk to Hon. Gerald Bard Tjoflat, U.S. Court of Appeals Eleventh Circuit 1981-82. In legal practice Florida 1982-96.
Mailing address: P.O. Box 52029, Jacksonville 32201-2029.
Telephone: (904) 549-1300.

COSTELLO, Dedee S. *(Judge, Florida Circuit Court Fourteenth Judicial Circuit)* Appointed by Governor Robert Graham to term beginning Jan 1986. Elected 1986, 1992 and 1998. Current term expires Jan 2005. Born Richmond Virginia March 31, 1947. Educated at American University B.A. 1969 and Emory University School of Law J.D. 1972. Member Phi Alpha Delta. Admitted to practice Florida 1972, Georgia 1972 and District of Columbia 1975. In legal practice Panama City Florida 1974-85.
Chair Standard Jury Instruction in Criminal Cases Committee since 2003. Member The Florida Bar, State Bar of Georgia, Bay County and American Bar Associations.
Mailing address: P.O. Box 1089, Panama City 32402.
Telephone: (850) 747-5341.

COVINGTON, Virginia M. Hernandez *(Judge, Florida District Court of Appeal Second District)* Appointed by Governor Jeb Bush to term beginning Sept 25, 2001. Retained by election Nov 5, 2002, current term expires Jan 5, 2009. Born Tampa Florida July 12, 1955. Educated at University of Tampa B.S. cum laude 1976 M.B.A. 1977 and Georgetown University Law Center J.D. 1980. Recipient Outstanding Female Graduate Award Class of 1976-77. Editor The Tax Lawyer 1978-80. Admitted to practice Florida 1980, U.S. District Court Middle District of Florida 1983 and U.S. Court of Appeals Eleventh Circuit 1983.
Trial Attorney Federal Trade Commission 1980-81.

COVINGTON, VIRGINIA M. HERNANDEZ—*Continued*

Assistant State Attorney Hillsborough County 1982-83. Assistant U.S. Attorney 1983-2001 and Chief Asset Forfeiture Section Jan 1989 to Sept 24, 2001 Middle District of Florida. Former Chair Government Law Section Hillsborough County Bar Association. Executive Board and Founding Member Herbert G. Goldburg Criminal Law Inn of Court. Lecturer on Trial Advocacy Practices and Procedures Chile, Argentina, Mexico, Venezuela, Colombia and Honduras. Recipient Director's Award 1990 and 1996 and Award for Outstanding Contribution to the Asset Forfeiture Program 1993 from Executive Office for Asset Forfeiture and Raymond E. Fernandez Award from Hillsborough County Sheriff's Hispanic Advisory Council 1999. Past President Tampa Hispanic Heritage. Former Chair Board of Counselors University of Tampa. Former Member Hispanic Needs and Services Council.

Mailing address: P.O. Box 327, Lakeland 33802-0327.
Office: 1005 East Memorial Boulevard, Lakeland 33801.
Telephone: (863) 499-2290.
Fax: (863) 413-2649

COWART, Gary R. *(Judge, Broward County Court)*
Office: 201 S.E. Sixth Street, Fort Lauderdale 33301.
Telephone: (954) 831-7568.
Fax: (954) 831-5572

COX, Cynthia L. *(Judge, Florida Circuit Court Nineteenth Judicial Circuit)* Elected Nov 3, 1996 to term beginning Jan 7, 1997. Reelected 2002, current term expires Dec 31, 2008. Administrative Judge Family Division Jan 1999 to 2002. Serves Criminal Felony Division and Drug Court Indian River County since 2002. Born Vero Beach Florida Dec 13, 1960. Methodist. Educated at Florida State University B.S. 1982 J.D. 1986, University of South Florida and University of Tampa. Production Assistant Florida State University Law Review 1984-86. Law Clerk to Hon. Larry G. Smith, Florida District Court of Appeal First District 1985-86. Admitted to practice Florida 1986 and U.S. District Court Middle District of Florida 1988. In legal practice Sarasota and Venice 1986-88, Vero Beach 1988-97.

Author "Domestic Violence and Children" Nov 2000 and "The Guardian Ad Litem Program, A Powerful Voice for Children" May 2001 Florida Parenting News, "So, You've Been Called to Testify . . ." Supervised Visitation Networker Spring 2001, "A View from the Bench" Bench and Bar Visitation Report Spring 2001 and "What Family Judges Really Want to Hear" Family Law Commentator Fall 2002. Adjunct Professor Indian River Community College 1990. Supreme Court Certified Arbitrator 1991-97 and Family Mediator 1995-97. Judicial Chairperson Domestic Violence Task Force since Jan 1997. Former Member Florida Association of Women Lawyers, Academy of Florida Trial Lawyers, The Association of Trial Lawyers of America, The Florida Bar, Sarasota/Venice, Indian River County and American Bar Associations. Chairperson Supervised Visitation Project, Chair Family Law Advisory Committee, Judicial Co-Chair Pro Bono Committee, Member Budget and Oversight Committee and Professionalism and Bench/Bar Committee Nineteenth Judicial Circuit. Member Committee on Trial Court Performance and Accountability Judicial Management Council and Supervised Visitation Workgroup Model Courts Subcommittee Family Court Steering Committee. Team Leader Statewide Conference on Pro Se Litigation and Member Access to Justice Task Force Florida Supreme Court. Team Member Summit on Redefining Florida's Family Courts. Member Florida Conference of Circuit Judges, American Judges Association, St. Lucie and Indian River County Bar Associations. Recipient President's Pro Bono Award from The Florida Bar 1996. Former Board Member and Chairperson Visiting Nurse Association/Hospice. Former Member Chamber of Commerce, Downtown Vero Beach Association, Exchange Club of Indian River, March of Dimes Walkamerica Steering Committee, DOVES for Safespace, Exchange Club of Sarasota/Bradenton and Florida Coalition Against Domestic Violence. Board Member Visiting Nurse Association of the Treasure Coast. Committee Member Character Counts Coalition of Indian River County. Member Seminole Boosters Indian River. Enjoys travel, boating and the beach. Personal Statement or Quote: "It's easier to prevent a problem than it is to resolve one!"

Office: 2000 Sixteenth Avenue, Suite 384, Vero Beach 32960.
Telephone: (772) 770-5050.
Fax: (772) 770-5335

CRANE, Shawn *(Judge, Pinellas County Court)*
Office: 29582 U.S. Highway 19 North, Clearwater 33761.
Telephone: (727) 464-8740.
Fax: (727) 464-8749

CRENSHAW, Jeanne Dawes *(Judge, Alachua County Court)*
Office: Alachua County Courthouse, 201 East University Avenue, Gainesville 32601.

CRENSHAW, Marva L. *(Judge, Florida Circuit Court Thirteenth Judicial Circuit)* Former Judge, Hillsborough County Court, appointed by Governor Bob Martinez to term beginning Feb 8, 1989.
Office: Hillsborough County Courthouse, 419 Pierce Street, Tampa 33602.
Telephone: (813) 272-5777.
Fax: (813) 276-8015

CRENSHAW, McCarthy, Jr. *(Judge, Florida Circuit Court Fourth Judicial Circuit)* Appointed by Governor Lawton Chiles to term beginning Sept 1992. Elected to terms beginning Jan 1993 and Jan 1999. Current term expires Jan 2005. Born Sherman Texas. Christian. Educated at University of Georgia A.B. 1964 J.D. 1972 and Dallas Theological Seminary Th.M. 1989. Admitted to practice Florida 1972. In legal practice Jacksonville 1972-92.

City Council Jacksonville 1975-79.
Office: Clay County Courthouse, 825 North Orange Avenue, Green Cove Springs 32043.
Telephone: (904) 278-4760.
Fax: (904) 278-4726

CRESPO, Manuel A. *(Judge, Florida Circuit Court Eleventh Judicial Circuit)*
Office: 625 Gerstein Justice Building, 1351 N.W. Twelfth Street, Miami 33125.
Telephone: (305) 548-5536.

CRISTOL, A. Jay *(Judge, United States Bankruptcy Court Southern District of Florida)* Appointed by U.S. Court of Appeals Eleventh Circuit judges Dec 17, 1984 to term beginning April 18, 1985. Reappointed 1999,

CRISTOL, A. JAY—*Continued*
current term expires April 16, 2013. Chief Judge Oct 1, 1993 to Sept 25, 1999. Born Fountain Hill Pennsylvania Sept 25, 1929. Jewish. Educated at University of Miami B.A. 1958 LL.B. cum laude 1959 replaced by J.D. Ph.D. 1997. Staff member and Research Editor University of Miami Law Review 1957-59. Member Phi Alpha Delta, Omicron Delta Kappa, Iron Arrow and Order of Wig and Robe. Admitted to practice Florida 1959, U.S. District Court Southern 1959 and Northern 1963 Districts of Florida, U.S. Court of Appeals Fifth Circuit 1959, U.S. Supreme Court 1965, U.S. Court of Military Appeals 1967 and U.S. Court of Claims 1971. In legal practice Miami 1959-85.

Special Assistant Attorney General Florida 1959, 1961, 1963 and 1965 Legislative sessions. Author "Noise and People: Making Your AICUZ Work" *Student Guide for Air Installations Compatible Use Zones* Naval School Civil Engineer Corps Officer ed. 1981; "A Terrorist Is a Terrorist Is a Terrorist" 33 Naval Reserve Association News 5, 1986; "Bankruptcy Comes to the People's Republic of China" Conference News National Conference of Bankruptcy Judges Aug 1986; "The Reorganization and Litigation Strategies for the Non-Specialist in Florida" National Business Institute 1987; "Bankruptcy Update" Annual Legal Assistance Symposium The Florida Bar 1988; "Basic Bankruptcy in Florida" National Business Institute 1989; "The Day I Flew the Goodyear Blimp" 9 No. 1 Florida Aviation Historical Society News Jan 1988; "Blue Thunder Patrol: Drug Interdiction Off Cape Florida" Customs Today Winter 1988; "The Non-Lawyer Provider of Bankruptcy Legal Services: Angel or Vulture?" 2 American Bankruptcy Institute L. Rev. 353 Winter 1994; "The Liberty Incident" Program on Information Resources Policy 105, *Seminar on Intelligence, Command and Control* Guest Presentations Harvard College Spring 1995; "Theoretical Legal Problems in Converting the Central and Eastern European Military Industrial Complex to a Free Market Economy" No. 27 *Foundation Notes* Naval War College Foundation Spring 1996; "Slovenia's Efforts to Further Westernize" No. 28 *Foundation Notes* Naval War College Foundation Winter 1996; and "Notwithstanding Unartful Draftspersonship, Congress Intended The Automatic Stay To Become Operative Upon Entry Of An Order For Relief" 4 No. 2 American Bankruptcy Institute L. Rev. 505, Winter 1996. Honorary Professor of Law U.S. Naval Justice Law School 1983. Lecturer International Institute of Humanitarian Law San Remo Italy 1984-88. Adjunct Professor University of Miami School of Law since 1988. Fellow American College of Bankruptcy. Member Advisory Committee on Bankruptcy Rules Judicial Conference of the U.S. 1996. Board of Governors and Member International Law Committee National Conference of Bankruptcy Judges. Member Bankruptcy Bar Association of Southern Florida, The Florida Bar, Dade County, Lawyer-Pilots and American Bar Associations. Instructor in Bankruptcy Law to Russian judges Atlanta 1994 and to Hong Kong, Malaysian, Indian, Thai and South African judges New Orleans Oct 1995 National Conference of Bankruptcy Judges. Instructor in Bankruptcy Law to Czech judges Czech Republic Feb 1996 and Slovenian judges Slovenia March 1996 Judicial Development Program U.S. Department of State. Instructor in Bankruptcy Reorganization Law to Thai judges, lawyers and receivers Thailand Ministry of Justice Nov 1997 and Nov 1999. Captain USNR 1951-88 (retired). Recipient Meritorious Service Medal, Navy Commendation Medal, Navy Achievement Medal, China Service Medal, National Defense Medal, Navy and Marine Corps Overseas Service Medal, Naval Reserve Medal and Vietnam Service Medal. Previously employed as a pilot for Eastern Airlines. Board of Trustees University of Miami. Director Miami Chapter American Red Cross. Enjoys flying, water skiing, wind surfing and history.

Office: 1412 Federal Building, 51 S.W. First Avenue, Miami 33130.

Telephone: (305) 536-4121.

CROW, David F. *(Judge, Florida Circuit Court Fifteenth Judicial Circuit)*

Office: Palm Beach County Courthouse, 205 North Dixie Highway, West Palm Beach 33401.

CRUSOE, John E. *(Judge, Florida Circuit Court Second Judicial Circuit)* Assumed office Jan 2, 1990. Elected to subsequent terms. Born Sebring Florida May 12, 1944. Episcopalian. Educated at Florida State University B.A. 1966 and Cumberland School of Law of Samford University J.D. 1970. Member Kappa Alpha and Sigma Delta Kappa. Admitted to practice Florida 1970. Began legal practice Tallahassee 1970. Judge, Small Claims Court 1971-72. Judge, Leon County Court Jan 2, 1981 to Jan 1990.

President and Director Legal Aid Society 1973-77. Member The Florida Bar and Tallahassee Bar Association (Director 1978). Named one of Outstanding Young Men of America 1981. E-5 USAR 1966-72. Democrat. Director Tallahassee Teen Center. Enjoys golf, fishing, hunting and watching his son play baseball.

Office: Leon County Courthouse, 301 South Monroe Street, Tallahassee 32301.

Telephone: (850) 577-4302.

Fax: (850) 577-4476

CUNNINGHAM, Sheree *(Judge, Palm Beach County Court)* Appointed by Governor Lawton Chiles Nov 15, 1993.

Office: Criminal Justice Complex, 3228 Gun Club Road, West Palm Beach 33406.

Telephone: (561) 688-4600.

Fax: (561) 688-4597

CURRY, Charles B. *(Chief Judge, Florida Circuit Court Tenth Judicial Circuit)* Elected Nov 1988 to term beginning Jan 3, 1989. Reelected Nov 1994 and Nov 2000. Current term expires Jan 4, 2007. Born Haines City Florida May 13, 1952. Presbyterian. Educated at Saint Leo College B.A. with honors 1975 and Florida State University J.D. 1978. Member Phi Delta Phi. Admitted to practice Florida 1979, U.S. District Court Middle District of Florida 1979, U.S. Court of Appeals Eleventh Circuit 1982 and U.S. Supreme Court 1982. Began legal practice Bartow 1979. In legal practice Fort Meade and Lakeland 1980-83. Judge, Polk County Court Jan 4, 1983 to Jan 2, 1989.

Assistant State Attorney Tenth Judicial Circuit 1979-80. Important Decision: Roe v. Amica Mutual Insurance Co. (contracts to enter non-binding arbitration held not contrary to state Arbitration Code or public policy) 533 So.2d 279, Fla. 1988. Instructor Police Academy Polk Community College 1979-80. Member Florida Council on Crime and Delinquency, Conference of County Court Judges of Florida (Board member 1984), Florida Confer-

CURRY, CHARLES B.—*Continued*
ence of Circuit Judges, The Florida Bar (Health Law Committee 1982) and Tenth Judicial Circuit Bar Association. Attended County Judges Course University of Florida 1983, General Jurisdiction Course The National Judicial College University of Nevada-Reno 1985 and Circuit Judges Course Florida State University 1989. Named Club Rotarian of the Year 1982. Recipient Judicial Service Award from Program to Aid Drug Abusers 1983, Dedicated Service Award from Rotary Club 1984 and Judicial Service Award from Justice for Children 1987. Staff Sergeant USAF 1971-76. Department of Commerce Florida 1977-79. Board of Directors Sunshine Council of Campfire. Member Polk County Overall Advisory Council on Agriculture, Bartow Chamber of Commerce, Rotary International, American Legion Post 72 and National Rifle Association. Enjoys fishing, golf and music.

Mailing address: P.O. Box 9000, Drawer J-133, Bartow 33831-9000.
Office: 255 North Broadway, Bartow 33830.
Telephone: (863) 534-4666.
Fax: (863) 534-4626

CURTIN, Aymer L. *(Judge, Alachua County Court)* Appointed by Governor Robert Martinez to term beginning Feb 8, 1989. Elected to subsequent terms.

Office: 201 Alachua County Courthouse, 201 East University Avenue, Gainesville 32601.
Telephone: (352) 374-3650.
Fax: (352) 374-5238

DAKAN, Stephen L. *(Senior Judge, Florida Circuit Court Twelfth Judicial Circuit)* Former Chief Judge. Assumed Senior Judge status, serves by assignment.

Mailing address: P.O. Box 48927, Sarasota 34230.
Office: 2002 Ringling Boulevard, Sarasota 34237.
Telephone: (941) 861-7800.

DAKIS, Linda N. *(Judge, Dade County Court)* Appointed by Governor Bob Martinez to term beginning Dec 19, 1989. Elected to subsequent terms.

Office: 418 Dade County Courthouse, 73 West Flagler Street, Miami 33130.
Telephone: (305) 349-7034.

DAMICO, Paul Anthony *(Judge, Palm Beach County Court)* Appointed by Governor Jeb Bush to term beginning Nov 19, 2002. Term expires Jan 1, 2005. Serves Criminal Division. Born New York July 3, 1960. Christian. Educated at Florida State University B.S. cum laude 1983 J.D. 1986. Admitted to practice Florida 1986, District of Columbia 1986, U.S. Supreme Court 1999, U.S. District Court Southern District of Florida and U.S. Court of Appeals Eleventh Circuit. Board Certified as a Specialist in Criminal Law—Trial by The Florida Bar since 1992.

Assistant State Attorney Palm Beach County 1986-96. First Assistant Public Defender Fifteenth Judicial Circuit 1996-2002. Author "Making of a Wiretap" F.S. Chapter 934 Criminal Law Newsletter The Florida Bar April 1995. Adjunct Professor of Criminal Law Practice Barry University since 1992. Former Member National Board of Trial Advocacy, National District Attorneys Association and American Bar Association. Member Executive Committee Weed and Seed Program since 1998. Organizer Public Defender/State Attorney Professional Responsibility Workshop The Florida Bar Oct 1999. Instructor Citizen's Academy Criminal Justice Commission 1999-2000. Presenter Criminal Justice Leadership Palm Beach County 1999-2000. Lecturer Palm Beach County Justice Teaching Institute 2000. Recipient Awards for Electronic Surveillance Legal Advisor Role from West Palm Beach Police Department 1995 and Drug Enforcement Agency 1996, Outstanding Leadership Award from Weed and Seed Program Criminal Justice Commission 1997, President's Award 1999 and 2000 and Distinguished Past President's Award 2001 from Kiwanis of Central Palm Beach County, Kiwanis Fellow Award from Florida Kiwanis Foundation 2000 and Adjunct Professor Award from Barry University 2000. Listed in *Who's Who in America* and *Who's Who in American Law.* Republican Executive Committeeman District Six since 1997. Member Candidate Endorsement Review Committee 2000. Co-founder and Vice President Republican Charities of Palm Beach County 2000-01. Certified Firearm Instructor since 1997. Volunteer Triumphant Trotter Program (for disabled children) 1998-2000, Holiday Food Outreach Project 1998-2000, Shots for Tots Immunization Program 1999-2000, Action Club Program (for mentally disabled children) 1999-2000 and Bringing Up Grades Awards Program Palm Beach County Primary Schools 1999-2000. Board Member Victim Advocacy Advisory Counsel 1999 and Safe Schools Advisory Council 2000. Advisory Board Barry University. Member Kiwanis (Past President). Enjoys scuba diving, golf and marksmanship. Personal Statement or Quote: "Our purpose is to dispense justice efficiently and economically with an emphasis on justice."

Office: Palm Beach County Courthouse, 205 North Dixie Highway, West Palm Beach 33401.
Telephone: (561) 355-6892.

DAMOORGIAN, Dorian *(Judge, Florida Circuit Court Seventeenth Judicial Circuit)*

Office: 446 Broward County Courthouse, 201 S.E. Sixth Street, Fort Lauderdale 33301.
Telephone: (954) 831-6974.

DANAHY, Paul W., Jr. *(Senior Judge, Florida District Court of Appeal)* Appointed by Governor Reubin Askew 1977. Retained by election 1978, 1984, 1990 and 1996. Former Chief Judge. Assumed Senior Judge status, serves by assignment. Born Hopkinton Massachusetts April 19, 1928. Educated at University of Tampa B.A. 1951 and University of Florida J.D. 1957. In legal practice Tampa 1957-75. Judge, Florida Circuit Court Thirteenth Judicial Circuit 1975-77, appointed by Governor Reubin Askew.

Former Assistant Attorney General Florida. U.S. Commissioner Southern District of Florida 1963. Member Florida House of Representatives 1966-74. Adjunct Professor of Law Stetson University College of Law 1974-75. Former member Thirteenth Judicial Circuit Grievance Committee. Member American Judicature Society and Hillsborough County Bar Association (Former member Board of Directors). U.S. Army.

Office: 1005 East Memorial Boulevard, Lakeland 33801.
Telephone: (863) 499-2290.

DAUKSCH, James C., Jr. *(Senior Judge, Florida District Court of Appeal)* Assumed Senior Judge status, serves by assignment.
Office: 300 South Beach Street, Daytona Beach 32114.
Telephone: (386) 947-1500.

DAVEY, P. Kevin *(Judge, Florida Circuit Court Second Judicial Circuit)*
Office: 365-B Leon County Courthouse, Tallahassee 32301.
Telephone: (850) 577-4303.
Fax: (850) 922-0327

DAVIDSON, Lisa *(Judge, Florida Circuit Court Eighteenth Judicial Circuit)*
Office: Moore Justice Center, Fourth Floor, 2825 Judge Fran Jamieson Way, Viera 32940-8006.
Telephone: (321) 617-7281.
Fax: (321) 617-7292

DAVIS, Brian Jordan *(Judge, Florida Circuit Court Fourth Judicial Circuit)* Assumed office Feb 1994. Served Family Law Division Feb 1994 to Dec 1995 and Civil Division Jan 1996 to Dec 1998. Serves Juvenile Division since Jan 1999. Born Jacksonville Florida Jan 28, 1953. Educated at Princeton University B.A. 1974 and University of Florida J.D. 1980. Staff member University of Florida Law Review 1979-80. Admitted to practice Florida 1981, U.S. District Court Middle District of Florida 1981 and U.S. Courts of Appeals Fifth 1981 and Eleventh 1981 Circuits. In legal practice Sept 1980 to March 1982 and May 1988 to July 1991.

Assistant State Attorney March 1982 to April 1988 and Chief Assistant State Attorney July 1991 to Feb 1994 Fourth Judicial Circuit. Advisory Board Pre-Law Studies Program University of North Florida 1997-99. Former Member Judicial Nominating Commission Florida District Court of Appeal First District (Vice Chairman 1993), Academy of Florida Trial Lawyers, D. W. Perkins (President 1985, Founder Annual Scholarship Banquet), Jacksonville (Law Week Committee 1981, Pro Bono/Legal Aid Committee 1991 and 1994), National and American Bar Associations. Member Civil Jury Instruction Committee Florida Supreme Court since 1996, Committee on Trial Court Performance and Accountability Judicial Management Council 1999-2001, The Chester Bedell Inn of Court and The Florida Bar (Grievance Committee 1989-91, Legal Needs of Children Commission 2000-01). Faculty National College of Trial Advocacy The Association of Trial Lawyers of America 1989-93. Recipient African American Achievers Award from J. M. Family Enterprises, Inc. 1995, Martin Luther King, Jr. Humanitarian Award from Jewish Federation 1997 and Domestic Peace Award from Hubbard House, Inc. 1999. Employee Relations Coordinator Oct 1974 to Aug 1977 American Can Company. Assistant Scoutmaster Troop 51, 1982-84, District Commission Member 1992, Council Executive Board 1994-97, Urban Scouting District Commissioner 1994-99 and Urban Scouting District Chair 1999-2001 Boy Scouts of America. Volunteer American Cancer Society 1985-95 and Jacksonville Community Council, Inc. 1987-95. Participant Leadership Jacksonville 1987. Chairman Council of Ministries Ebenezer United Methodist Church 1988-90. Board of Directors Help Center, Inc. 1991-92 (Chairman 1993), Hubbard House, Inc. 1991-94, Cathedral Foundation 1997 and Pace Center for Girls 1999. Youth Facilitator Operation Streets 1992-93. Board Member National Council of Jewish Women/Hippy 1992-99. Board of Directors 1996-2001 and Member Executive Committee 1997 National Conference of Christians and Jews. Member Community Advisory Board Jaguars Foundation since 1995. Chairman Mayor's Domestic Violence Task Force 1998-99. Life Member NAACP.
Office: 416 Centre Street, Fernandina Beach 32034.
Telephone: (904) 491-7275.
Fax: (904) 491-2051

DAVIS, Charles A., Jr. *(Judge, Florida District Court of Appeal Second District)* Appointed by Governor Jeb Bush to term beginning 1999. Term expires Jan 2007. Born Winter Haven Florida March 7, 1948. Educated at Trevecca Nazarene College B.A. with high honors 1970, University of Cincinnati M.A. 1971 and University of Florida J.D. with honors 1975. Judge, Polk County Court 1983-85. Judge 1985-99 and Chief Judge 1995-99, Florida Circuit Court Tenth Judicial Circuit.
Mailing address: P.O. Box 327, Lakeland 33802-0327.
Office: 1005 East Memorial Boulevard, Lakeland 33801-2019.
Telephone: (863) 499-2290.
Fax: (863) 413-2649

DAVIS, Gordon Miles *(Magistrate Judge, United States District Court Northern District of Florida)* Appointed by U.S. District Court judges.
Office: U.S. Courthouse, One North Palafox Street, Pensacola 32501-5625.
Telephone: (850) 470-8145.

DAVIS, Henry E. *(Judge, Florida Circuit Court Fourth Judicial Circuit)*
Office: Duval County Courthouse, 330 East Bay Street, Jacksonville 32202.
Telephone: (904) 630-2534.
Fax: (904) 630-2979

DAVIS, Marguerite "Ditti" *(Judge, Florida District Court of Appeal First District)* Appointed by Governor Lawton Chiles Sept 16, 1993. Retained by election. Born Washington D.C. Nov 12, 1947. Educated at University of South Florida B.A. with honors 1968 and Florida State University J.D. with honors 1971. Recipient American Jurisprudence Awards in Remedies, Land Finance, Family Law, Creditors' Rights and Debtors' Remedies, Trial Practice, Labor Law and Mass Communications Law. Member Phi Alpha Delta, Phi Theta Kappa and Gold Key. Admitted to practice Florida 1971, U.S. District Courts Middle 1971 and Northern 1971 Districts of Florida and U.S. Supreme Court. In legal practice 1985-93.

Senior Legal Aide 1971-85 and Executive Assistant to Chief Justice 1982-84 Florida Supreme Court. Co-author with Fred Karl "Impeachment in Florida" 6 Florida State University L. Rev. 2, 1978. Author "Attorney's Fees: Draft Your Contract Cautiously" LXIII No. 5 May 1989 and "A Plea for Uniformity" LXIV No. 4 April 1990 The Florida Bar Journal; *Court Awarded Attorney Fees* (three-volume federal treatise) revise and supplement every six months Matthew Bender 1989-94; and "Attorney's Fees and Costs in Administrative Proceedings" XIII No. 3 *Administrative Law Section Newsletter* March 1991. Member Special Disciplinary Rule Committee Florida Supreme Court 1977-78. Chair Local Rules Advisory Committee Florida Supreme Court since 1988. Member American Arbitration Association, Judicial Management Council (Member Committee on Appellate

DAVIS, MARGUERITE "DITTI"—*Continued*
Court Workload and Jurisdiction 1996-98, Chair Appellate Rules Liaison Committee Appellate Practice and Advocacy Section 1996-98, Chairperson Arts in the Court Committee since 1999), The Florida Bar (Disciplinary Rule Committee 1985-87, Member since 1988 and Chairperson 1995-97 Appellate Rules Committee, Member Second Judicial Circuit Grievance Committee 1990-92, Member Standards for Appellate Practice Certification Ad Hoc Committee 1992-93, Member Advertising Committee since 1992, Member since 1995 and Chairperson 1997-98 Rules of Judicial Administration, Member since 1995 and Chairperson 1999-2000 and 2001-02 Judicial Evaluation Committee, Member Executive Council Appellate Advocacy Section) and American Bar Association. Board of Directors Florida Supreme Court Historical Society since 1985 and University of South Florida Alumni Association 1999-2001. Member Trinity Methodist Church, Florida State University Law School Alumni Association and Florida Economics Club.

Office: 301 Martin Luther King Jr. Boulevard, Tallahassee 32399-1850.

Telephone: (850) 487-1000.

Fax: (850) 921-4768

DAVIS, S. Joseph, Jr. *(Senior Judge, Florida Circuit Court Eighteenth Judicial Circuit)* Appointed by Governor Robert Graham to term beginning Dec 14, 1979. Elected 1980 and 1986. Assumed Senior Judge status, serves by assignment. Certified Mediator and Arbitrator. Born Leesburg Georgia May 19, 1923. Baptist. Educated at John B. Stetson University B.A. and Stetson College of Law LL.B. Member Phi Alpha Delta and Phi Kappa Alpha. Admitted to practice Florida 1957 and U.S. District Court Middle District of Florida 1965. Began legal practice Sanford 1957.

City Attorney Altamonte Springs 1958-79, Longwood 1967-77 and Oviedo 1968-79. Member Constitutional Revision Commission 1965-67, Florida Mediation Qualification Advisory Panel, The Florida Bar, Seminole County (President 1964) and American Bar Associations. First Lieutenant USAR 1952-58. Member Florida House of Representatives 1962-66. Member and Chairman Board of Trustees Seminole Community College 1965-70. Member Salvation Army Advisory Board and Greater Sanford Chamber of Commerce. Enjoys fishing, golf and reading.

Office: Moore Justice Center, 2825 Judge Fran Jamieson Way, Viera 32940-8006.

Telephone: (321) 637-5555.

DAWSON, Daniel P. *(Judge, Florida Circuit Court Ninth Judicial Circuit)* Elected to term beginning Jan 1991. Reelected 1996 and 2002. Current term expires Jan 2009.

Office: Osceola County Courthouse, 2 Courthouse Square, Kissimmee 34741.

Telephone: (407) 343-2506.

Fax: (407) 835-5067

DAY, Lance M. *(Judge, Florida Circuit Court Fourth Judicial Circuit)*

Office: Duval County Courthouse, 330 East Bay Street, Jacksonville 32202.

Telephone: (904) 630-2349.

Fax: (904) 630-2979

DEAN, Amy N. *(Senior Judge, Florida Circuit Court Eleventh Judicial Circuit)* Elected to term beginning Jan 1991. Reelected 1996. Assumed Senior Judge status, serves by assignment.

Office: 511 Dade County Courthouse, 73 West Flagler Street, Miami 33130.

Telephone: (305) 349-7001.

DEARING, Peter L. *(Judge, Florida Circuit Court Fourth Judicial Circuit)* Appointed by Governor Bob Martinez to term beginning March 1988. Elected Sept 1988, 1994 and 2000. Current term expires Jan 2007. Born Jacksonville Florida Aug 26, 1946. Episcopalian. Educated at University of the South B.A. with honors 1968 and University of Florida J.D. with honors 1970. Editor University of Florida Law Review 1969-70. Law Clerk to Hon. Gerald Bard Tjoflat, U.S. District Court Middle District of Florida 1970-71. Member Phi Delta Phi, Order of the Coif and Florida Blue Key. Admitted to practice Florida 1971, U.S. District Courts Middle 1971, Northern 1975 and Southern 1979 Districts of Florida, U.S. Courts of Appeals Fifth 1972 and Eleventh 1972 Circuits, U.S. Tax Court 1974, U.S. Claims Court 1974 and U.S. Supreme Court 1976. In legal practice Jacksonville 1975-88 and Miami 1978-80.

Author Comment 22 University of Florida L. Rev. 168, 1969 and Article 23 University of Florida L. Rev. 549, 1971. Member Christian Legal Society, The Florida Bar (Chairman Law Enforcement Programs Committee 1982 and Grievance Committee 1983-84), Jacksonville (Chairman Legal Ethics Committee, Co-Chairman Judicial Relations Committee) Federal (President Northeast Florida Chapter 1977-78) and American Bar Associations. Instructor in Arbitration and Mediation at several Florida conferences and seminars. Listed in *Who's Who in American Law* First Edition. Recipient award from U.S. Justice Department 1975 and Community Service Award from Jacksonville Sheriff's Office 1983. Republican. Participates in church and ministry-related activities, Boy Scouts and several charitable organizations. Interests include stamp collecting, fishing, golf and spending time with family.

Office: 219 Duval County Courthouse, 330 East Bay Street, Jacksonville 32202.

Telephone: (904) 630-2540.

Fax: (904) 630-2979

DEEHL, Robert M. *(Senior Judge, Dade County Court)* Assumed office 1972. Elected to subsequent terms. Former Administrative Judge Civil Division. Assumed Senior Judge status, serves by assignment. Born Mount Freedom New Jersey June 30, 1925. Educated at University of Florida A.A. 1947 J.D. 1949. Admitted to practice Florida 1949. Began legal practice Miami 1949. Judge, Metropolitan Court 1964-72.

Member American Judges Association, The Florida Bar, Dade County and American Bar Associations. Lecturer and Faculty Advisor National College of the State Judiciary 1975-76. USMC 1943-46 and USAR 1946-49. President Advocate, Inc. (non-profit organization for rehabilitation of Dade County first offenders). Member Coral Gables Chamber of Commerce, Elks, Kiwanis, Shriners, Masons and American Legion. Enjoys fishing and photography.

Office: 511 Dade County Courthouse, 73 West Flagler Street, Miami 33130.

Telephone: (305) 349-7001.

DeFURIA, Frederick A. *(Judge, Florida Circuit Court Twelfth Judicial Circuit)* Elected 2002 to term beginning Jan 2003. Term expires Jan 2009. Educated at Ithaca College B.A. 1968 and Stetson University J.D. 1973. Former Judge and Senior Judge, Sarasota County Court.

Mailing address: P.O. Box 1000, Bradenton 34205.

Office: Manatee County Courthouse, 1115 Manatee Avenue West, Bradenton 34206.

Telephone: (941) 742-5942.

Fax: (941) 742-5989

DEKKER, Kathleen F. *(Judge, Florida Circuit Court Second Judicial Circuit)* Former Judge, Leon County Court.

Office: Leon County Courthouse, 301 South Monroe Street, Tallahassee 32301.

Telephone: (850) 577-4304.

Fax: (850) 577-4478

deLAROCHE, Steven *(Judge, Volusia County Court)*

Office: Courthouse Annex, 125 East Orange Avenue, Daytona Beach 32114.

Telephone: (386) 257-6058.

Fax: (386) 257-6094

DELL, John W. *(Senior Judge, Florida District Court of Appeal)* Assumed Senior Judge status, serves by assignment.

Office: 1525 Palm Beach Lakes Boulevard, West Palm Beach 33402.

Telephone: (561) 242-2000.

DeLUCA, Steven P. *(Judge, Broward County Court)*

Office: 216 Broward County Courthouse, 201 S.E. Sixth Street, Fort Lauderdale 33301.

Telephone: (954) 831-0322.

DEMERS, David A. *(Chief Judge, Florida Circuit Court Sixth Judicial Circuit)* Appointed by Governor Lawton Chiles to term beginning March 22, 1994. Elected 1994 and 2000. Current term expires Jan 2007. Chief Judge since July 1, 2001. Born Nashua New Hampshire Oct 30, 1946. Catholic. Educated at Florida State University 1969-70 and Stetson University B.A. J.D. Admitted to practice Florida 1972, U.S. District Court Middle District of Florida 1973, U.S. Court of Appeals Fifth Circuit 1974 and U.S. Supreme Court 1977. In legal practice Gainesville 1974-75 and St. Petersburg 1972 and 1977-81. Judge, Pinellas County Court July 26, 1981 to March 21, 1994, appointed by Governor Robert Graham.

Member Committee for *Florida Judges' Manual* since 1988. Author of extensive materials on criminal law. Instructor in Business Law Hillsborough Community College 1977-79 and Research and Writing St. Petersburg Junior College since 1983. Adjunct Professor of Trial Practice Stetson College of Law. Former Member Florida Judicial Council and American Bar Association. Master Bencher Pinellas Inns of Court since 1988. Member Florida Conference of County Court Judges (Past President) and Florida Court Educational Council. Presenter Traffic Adjudication Seminar since 1987. Associate Dean 1987-94 and Faculty Member Florida Judicial College since 1987. Faculty Member Advanced Judicial Studies Program The National Judicial College. Board of Directors Family Resources.

Office: 400 Judicial Building, 545 First Avenue North, St. Petersburg 33701.

Telephone: (727) 582-7882.

Fax: (727) 582-7210

DENKIN, David L. *(Judge, Sarasota County Court)*

Mailing address: P.O. Box 48927, Sarasota 34230.

Office: Judicial Center, 2002 Ringling Boulevard, Sarasota 34237.

Telephone: (941) 861-7895.

Fax: (941) 861-7919

DENNIS, Maria E. *(Judge, Florida Circuit Court Eleventh Judicial Circuit)*

Office: 410 Gerstein Justice Building, 1351 N.W. Twelfth Street, Miami 33125.

Telephone: (305) 548-5167.

DERKE, Eleni Elia *(Judge, Duval County Court)* Elected to term beginning Jan 3, 1995. Reelected 1998, current term expires Jan 2005.

Office: Duval County Courthouse, 330 East Bay Street, Jacksonville 32202.

Telephone: (904) 630-2582.

Fax: (904) 630-2979

DIAZ, Robert F. *(Judge, Broward County Court)* Appointed by Governor Lawton Chiles July 6, 1992.

Office: 423 Broward County Courthouse, 201 S.E. Sixth Street, Fort Lauderdale 33301.

Telephone: (954) 831-7783.

Fax: (954) 831-6058

DICKEY, Alan A. *(Judge, Florida Circuit Court Eighteenth Judicial Circuit)* Elected 1990 to term beginning 1991. Reelected 1996 and 2002. Current term expires Jan 2009. Administrative Judge Criminal Division 1993-95. Jury Management Judge since 1991. Born Hutchinson Kansas July 16, 1943. Educated at Stetson University B.A. 1965 and University of Florida College of Law J.D. 1968. Member Lambda Chi Alpha, Beta Alpha Sigma and Phi Delta Phi. Admitted to practice Florida 1968. In legal practice De Land 1968-71 and Sanford 1973-76. Judge 1976-91, Administrative Judge 1978-80 and Supervising Judge Probation Department 1988-91, Seminole County Court.

Assistant State Attorney 1971 and Assistant Public Defender 1973 Eighteenth Judicial Circuit. Member Florida Conference of County Court Judges (Former Member Board of Directors) and Seminole County Bar Association (Former Treasurer, Former Secretary, Former Vice President). Recipient Distinguished Service Award for Judicial Service from Florida Council on Crime and Delinquency Chapter VII 1989. Named Rotarian of the Year 1991-92. Paul Harris Fellow. Member Sanford Rotary Club, De Land Elks Club and Greater Sanford Chamber of Commerce.

Office: Seminole County Courthouse, 301 North Park Avenue, Sanford 32771-1292.

Telephone: (407) 665-4250.

DIMITROULEAS, William P. *(Judge, United States District Court Southern District of Florida)* Appointed for life by President Bill Clinton to term beginning June 1, 1998. Born Lynn Massachusetts March 28, 1951. Educated at Furman University B.A. magna cum laude 1973 and University of Florida J.D. with honors 1975. Admitted to practice Florida 1976. Judge, Florida Circuit

DIMITROULEAS, WILLIAM P.—*Continued*

Court Seventeenth Judicial Circuit March 27, 1989 to May 31, 1998, appointed by Governor Bob Martinez.

Assistant Public Defender March 20, 1976 to Oct 30, 1977 and Assistant State Attorney Nov 1, 1977 to March 26, 1989 Seventeenth Judicial Circuit.

Office: 203 U.S. Courthouse, 299 East Broward Boulevard, Fort Lauderdale 33301.

Telephone: (954) 769-5650.

DISHOWITZ, Martin R. *(Judge, Broward County Court)* Appointed by Governor Lawton Chiles Nov 4, 1993.

Office: 410 Broward County Courthouse, 201 S.E. Sixth Street, Fort Lauderdale 33301.

Telephone: (954) 831-5601.

Fax: (954) 831-5572

DISKEY, Daniel D. *(Judge, Florida Circuit Court Sixth Judicial Circuit)*

Office: 104 West Pasco Government Center, 7530 Little Road, New Port Richey 34654.

Telephone: (727) 847-8059.

DOMINGUEZ, James V. *(Judge, Hillsborough County Court)* Appointed by Governor Bob Martinez to term beginning Jan 3, 1990. Elected to subsequent terms.

Office: 253 Tower, 801 East Twiggs Street, Tampa 33602-3554.

Telephone: (813) 272-5228.

DOMMERICH, John W. *(Judge, Lee County Court)* Appointed by Governor Bob Martinez to term beginning Nov 13, 1989. Elected to subsequent terms.

Office: Lee County Justice Center, 1700 Monroe Street, Fort Myers 33901.

Telephone: (239) 335-2913.

Fax: (239) 335-2587

DONNELLAN, Nancy K. *(Judge, Florida Circuit Court Twelfth Judicial Circuit)* Elected to term beginning Jan 3, 1995. Reelected 2000, current term expires Jan 2007.

Mailing address: P.O. Box 48927, Sarasota 34230.

Office: 2002 Ringling Boulevard, Sarasota 34237.

Telephone: (941) 861-7934.

Fax: (941) 861-7912

DONNER, Amy Steele *(Judge, Florida Circuit Court Eleventh Judicial Circuit)* Appointed by Governor Robert Graham to term beginning Dec 7, 1984. Elected 1990, Nov 5, 1996 and 2002. Current term expires Jan 2009. Born New York New York. Jewish. Educated at University of Miami A.B. 1963 J.D. 1974 LL.M. 1987. Law Clerk to Hon. Milton A. Friedman, Florida Circuit Court Eleventh Judicial Circuit 1972-73. Member Alpha Lambda Delta and Kappa Delta Pi. Admitted to practice Florida 1974, U.S. District Court Southern District of Florida 1975, U.S. Tax Court 1979 and U.S. Supreme Court 1979. In legal practice Miami 1974-84.

Important Decisions: Stern v. Stern 636 So. 2d 735, Fla. App. 4 Dist. 1993; Romano v. Romano 632 So. 2d 207, Fla. App. 4 Dist. 1994; and Traina v. State of Florida. Member Florida Association of Women Lawyers, National Association of Women Judges, American Judges Association, Cuban American Bar Association and Dade County Bar Association. Lecturer Advanced Judicial College. Named Woman of the Year by Na' Amat USA and Leading Lady of Miami by the March of Dimes. Listed in *Who's Who in Law* and *International Who's Who of Professional and Business Women.*

Office: 243 Dade County Courthouse, 73 West Flagler Street, Miami 33130.

Telephone: (305) 349-7044.

DOUGHTIE, Nath C. *(Senior Judge, Florida Circuit Court Eighth Judicial Circuit)* Elected 1986 to term beginning Jan 6, 1987. Reelected 1992 and 1998. Assumed Senior Judge status, serves by assignment. Born Aug 1937. Educated at Auburn University B.S. 1959 and University of Florida J.D. 1966. In legal practice 1968-78. Judge, Alachua County Court Jan 1, 1979 to Jan 1, 1987.

Assistant Counsel Florida Department of Agriculture 1966. House Counsel Science & Engineering 1967-72. Instructor Legal Assistant Program Santa Fe Community College and Trial Advocacy Program University of Florida School of Law. Member Florida Sentencing Guidelines Commission since 1983, Florida Conference of County Court Judges (Circuit Representative, Chairman Sentencing Committee, Chairman Florida Bar Liaison Committee, Chairman Criminal Rules & Law Reform Committee and Delegate and Alternate to ABA Convention 1983 and 1984) and The Florida Bar (Consumer Protection Law Committee 1975, Jurisprudence & Law Reform Committee 1975, Delinquency and Crime Prevention Committee 1975, Summary Rules Committee 1975, Integration and By-Laws Committee 1975, Designated Reviewer for Eighth Circuit Grievance Committee 1975-79, Board of Governors 1975-79, Labor Relations Law Committee 1976, Budget Committee 1977, Disciplinary Procedure Committee 1977-78, General Practice Section 1978-79, Long-Range Planning Committee 1979, Civil Rules Committee 1982-85 and Chairman Summary Procedure Rules Committee 1981-84). Graduate Florida Judicial College 1979, The National Judicial College 1980 and National Academy of Correction 1984. Instructor Florida New Judges College and Alabama Judicial College. Delegation leader People-to-People International 1981. Lieutenant USMC 1959-62. Public school teacher Duval County 1962. Director Friends of Five (Public TV), YMCA and Gainesville Community Theater. Life member University of Florida Law Center Association. Member Rotary Club of Greater Gainesville (President 1983-84), University of Florida Law Center Council and Santa Fe Community College Legal Assistant Advisory Committee.

Office: Alachua County Courthouse, 201 East University Avenue, Gainesville 32601.

Telephone: (352) 374-3648.

DOUGLAS, E. Vernon *(Judge, Florida Circuit Court Third Judicial Circuit)* Elected Nov 1988 to term beginning Jan 3, 1989. Reelected 1994 and 2000. Current term expires Jan 2007. Former Chief Judge. Born Lake City Florida April 17, 1947. Church of Jesus Christ of Latter-day Saints. Educated at Lake City Community College 1967, University of Florida B.A. 1969 and Stetson University J.D. 1973. Staff member Stetson Law Review. Admitted to practice Florida 1973. In legal practice Lake City 1973-75. Judge, Columbia County Court 1977-89.

Assistant State's Attorney Third Judicial Circuit 1975-76. Instructor in Business Law Lake City Community College 1978-79. Member The Florida Bar, Third Judicial Circuit and Columbia County Bar Associations.

DOUGLAS, E. VERNON—*Continued*

Named Citizen of the Year of Columbia County by Rotary 1981-82 and North Florida Judicial Officer of the Year by North Florida Correctional Officers 1989. Recipient Distinguished Service Award from Jaycees of Florida 1982. Green Beret U.S. Army Special Forces 1969-70. Democrat. Founder 1980 and Aerial Events Producer since 1980 North Florida Air Show. Director 1987 and President 1990-91 International Council of Air Shows. President Kindergarten Parent-Teacher-Student Association 1987-88 and Parent-Teacher Lay Advisory Niblack Middle School 1990-91. Former Chairman Lake City Community College Foundation. Keynote Speaker State Conference of Cooperative Education Students of Florida 1989 and opening session Convention of International Council of Air Shows 1990. Annual Speaker Student Leadership Conference Lake City Community College. Master of Ceremonies John H. Whitehead Appreciation Banquet. Member Rotary, American Heart Association (Former Columbia County Chairman), Boy Scouts (Suwannee River District Commissioner), Ducks Unlimited, Annual Lake City Fun Run Committee, Columbia County United Way Committee, Lake City Chamber of Commerce and Citizens Advisory Council Lake City Community Correctional Center. Private pilot. Enjoys family, golf, tennis, photography, jogging, reading philosophy and studying human behavior.

Mailing address: P.O. Drawer 2075, Lake City 32056-2075.

Telephone: (386) 758-1010.

Fax: (386) 758-1188

DOWNEY, Brandt C., III *(Judge, Florida Circuit Court Sixth Judicial Circuit)* Elected to term beginning Jan 3, 1989. Reelected 1994 and 2000. Current term expires Jan 2007. Born Indianapolis Indiana Feb 25, 1945. Presbyterian. Educated at Indiana University B.S. 1968 and Stetson University J.D. 1971. Member Beta Theta Pi and Phi Delta Phi. Admitted to practice Florida 1971. Began legal practice Clearwater 1971. Judge, Pinellas County Court 1985-89.

Member The Florida Bar, Clearwater and American Bar Associations. Colonel USAR since 1968. 143rd Transportation Command Orlando Florida. Past President Big Brothers/Big Sisters and Mental Health Association. Past President Upper Pinellas Association of Retarded Citizens. President Foundation for Mental Health. Former Secretary District Mental Health Board. Member American Legion, Masons and Scottish Rite. Enjoys swimming, yard work, basketball and volleyball.

Office: Criminal Justice Center, 14250 49th Street North, Clearwater 33762.

Telephone: (727) 464-6475.

DOYEL, Robert L. *(Judge, Florida Circuit Court Tenth Judicial Circuit)*

Mailing address: P.O. Box 9000, Drawer J-119, Bartow 33831.

Office: 255 North Broadway, Seventh Floor, Bartow 33830-3912.

Telephone: (863) 534-4668.

Fax: (863) 534-7783

DOYLE, John V. *(Judge, Florida Circuit Court Seventh Judicial Circuit)* Elected to term beginning Jan 1991. Reelected 1996 and 2002. Current term expires Jan 2009.

Office: 120 West Indiana Avenue, Room 206, De Land 32720.

Telephone: (386) 943-7060.

Fax: (386) 822-5021

DRAPER, Carol E. *(Judge, Osceola County Court)*

Office: Osceola County Courthouse, 12 South Vernon Avenue, Kissimmee 34741.

Telephone: (407) 343-2513.

DRAYTON-HARRIS, Pauline M. *(Judge, Duval County Court)*

Office: 340 Duval County Courthouse, 330 East Bay Street, Jacksonville 32202.

Telephone: (904) 630-2581.

Fax: (904) 630-2979

DRESNICK, Ronald Charles *(Judge, Florida Circuit Court Eleventh Judicial Circuit)* Appointed by Governor Lawton Chiles March 1, 1996. Served Family Division 1996 and Criminal Division 1996 to Jan 2003. Born Hollywood Florida July 18, 1944. Educated at American University B.A. 1966, University of Miami School of Law J.D. cum laude 1970 and Harvard Law School LL.M. 1971. Associate Editor University of Miami Law Review. Member Society of Bar and Gavel and Order of Wig and Robe. Admitted to practice Florida 1970, U.S. District Courts Middle, Northern and Southern Districts of Florida, Eastern District of Michigan and District of Washington, U.S. Courts of Appeals Fifth and Eleventh Circuits and U.S. Tax Court. In legal practice Hollywood June 1971 to Nov 1971 and Miami 1974 to Feb 1996.

Assistant Dade County Public Defender 1971-74. Author "Casenote on Proximate Cause" 23 University of Miami L. Rev. 848, 1969 and "Uses of the Video-Tape Recorder in Legal Education" 25 University of Miami L. Rev. 543, 1971. Co-author with Clifford C. Alloway and Susan L. Dresnick *Florida Evidence* D & S Publishers 1971 and with Hugh L. Sowards and James Mofsky "Survey of Florida Corporate and Securities Law" 24 University of Miami L. Rev. Former Instructor in Constitutional Law and Trial Advocacy and Adjunct Professor of Litigation Skills since 1996 University of Miami School of Law. Member Grievance Committee and Bar Counsel The Florida Bar. Member Academy of Florida Trial Lawyers (Former Member Board of Directors Criminal Law Section), Florida Association of Criminal Defense Lawyers (Past President), National Association of Criminal Defense Lawyers, Inc., Dade County and American Bar Associations. Former Lecturer on Criminal Law and Ethics The Florida Bar and Academy of Florida Trial Lawyers. Lecturer "View from the Bench: Legal Ethics" Dade County Bar Association Pro Bono Program April 1996. Recipient "Pro Bono Service Award Put Something Back" from Dade County Bar Association. Member since 1987 and Chairman 1994-96 Board of Directors Easter Seal Society of Dade County. Hearing Examiner Dade County School Board 18 years. Former Member Metropolitan Dade County Independent Commission of Inquiry "Hurricane Andrew." Member B'nai B'rith Bench and Bar.

Office: 524 Dade County Courthouse, 73 West Flagler Street, Miami 33130.

Telephone: (305) 349-7140.

Fax: (305) 349-7011

DUBE, Robert L. *(Magistrate Judge, United States District Court Southern District of Florida)* Appointed by U.S. District Court judges.
Office: 236 U.S. Courthouse, 300 N.E. First Avenue, Miami 33132.
Telephone: (305) 523-5770.

DUBENSKY, Peter A. *(Judge, Florida Circuit Court Twelfth Judicial Circuit)* Appointed by Governor Bob Martinez Jan 2, 1990. Elected to subsequent terms.
Mailing address: P.O. Box 1000, Bradenton 34206.
Office: 1115 Manatee Avenue West, Bradenton 34205.
Telephone: (941) 749-7140.
Fax: (941) 742-5964

DUGAN, W. David *(Judge, Florida Circuit Court Eighteenth Judicial Circuit)*
Office: Moore Justice Center, Fourth Floor, 2825 Judge Fran Jamieson Way, Viera 32940-8006.
Telephone: (321) 617-7279.

DUNNIGAN, Janette C. *(Judge, Florida Circuit Court Twelfth Judicial Circuit)* Appointed by Governor Lawton Chiles Dec 17, 1993.
Mailing address: P.O. Box 1000, Bradenton 34206.
Office: 1115 Manatee Avenue West, Bradenton 34205.
Telephone: (941) 749-7170.
Fax: (941) 742-5957

DURRANCE, Julian Dale *(Judge, Florida Circuit Court Tenth Judicial Circuit)* Elected Sept 4, 1984 to term beginning Jan 6, 1985. Reelected 1990, 1996 and 2002. Current term expires Jan 2009. Born Bartow Florida July 25, 1946. Baptist. Educated at Edison Junior College A.A. and Florida State University B.A. J.D. Member Phi Delta Phi. Admitted to practice Florida 1976 and U.S. District Court Middle District of Florida. Began legal practice Tampa 1976. In legal practice Bartow 1978. Judge, Polk County Court Jan 6, 1981 to Jan 5, 1985.

Former Assistant State Attorney, Deputy Tax Assessor Polk County and Assistant Sergeant-at-Arms and Senate Bill Drafter Florida State Senate. Instructor Hillsborough Community College, Polk Community College, Tampa Police Academy and Polk Police Academy. Member The Florida Bar. Graduate National College of District Attorneys. Member Bartow Rotary, Bartow Chamber of Commerce, Fort Meade Masonic Lodge, Polk County Historical Commission and First Baptist Church of Bartow. Enjoys hunting and fishing.
Mailing address: P.O. Box 9000, Drawer J111, Bartow 33830-9000.
Telephone: (863) 534-4648.

EADE, Richard D. *(Judge, Florida Circuit Court Seventeenth Judicial Circuit)*
Office: 910A Broward County Courthouse, 201 S.E. Sixth Street, Fort Lauderdale 33301.
Telephone: (954) 831-7660.
Fax: (954) 831-5572

EASTMOORE, E. L. "Gene" *(Senior Judge, Florida Circuit Court Seventh Judicial Circuit)* Elected 1972 to term beginning Jan 2, 1973. Reelected 1978 and 1984. Chief Judge July 1, 1975 to 1977. Assumed Senior Judge status, serves by assignment. Born Jacksonville Florida 1929. Educated at University of Florida B.A. 1950 J.D. 1952. Member Phi Delta Phi. Admitted to practice Florida 1952, U.S. District Court Middle District of Florida and U.S. Court of Appeals Fifth Circuit. In legal practice Palatka June 1954 to Jan 1, 1973.

Former Attorney Cities of Palatka, Welaka, Pomona Park and Interlachen. Member National Institute of Municipal Law Officers, Florida Conference of Circuit Court Judges (Executive Board 1973-83, Secretary-Treasurer 1977-78, Chairman Elect 1978-79, Chairman 1979-80), The Florida Bar, Putnam County (President 1959-60) and American Bar Associations. Graduate The National Judicial College. Recipient Distinguished Service Award as Outstanding Young Man of the Year from Palatka Junior Chamber of Commerce 1955. U.S. Army Artillery 1951-54 (Counsel for General Courts Martial 1952-54) and Florida National Guard 1954. Retired as Colonel Air Defense Artillery 1982. Director Putnam County Alcohol and Drug Council and Rodeheaver Boys' Ranch. President Palatka Skeet Club 1966 and Putnam County Blood Bank 1967-71. Lieutenant Governor Division 18 Florida Kiwanis 1967. Charter Director Putnam County United Fund. Chairman March of Dimes and Boy Scouts Charity Drives. Charter member Putnam County Development Authority 1961-64. Member Florida State Chamber of Commerce (Military Affairs Committee), Putnam County Chamber of Commerce (Past Director), Florida State and National Skeet Shooting Associations, Palatka Jaycees 1954-65 (Former Director), American Legion, VFW, Palatka Elks Lodge 1232, Palatka Kiwanis (Secretary 1962 and President 1963) and St. Mark's Episcopal Church at Palatka (President Layman's League 1955-56, Vestryman and Senior Warden 1969).
Office: 101 North Alabama Avenue, De Land 32724.
Telephone: (386) 257-6097.

EASTON, Burton C. *(Senior Judge, Pinellas County Court)* Assumed Senior Judge status, serves by assignment.
Office: Judicial Building, 545 First Avenue North, St. Petersburg 33701.
Telephone: (727) 464-4470.

EATON, O. H. "Bill", Jr. *(Judge, Florida Circuit Court Eighteenth Judicial Circuit)* Elected 1986 to term beginning Jan 6, 1987. Reelected 1992 and 1998. Current term expires Jan 2005. Chief Judge 1989-91. Born Fort Meyers Florida May 7, 1943. Educated at University of Florida B.S.B.A. 1965 J.D. 1968. Member Phi Delta Phi and Pi Kappa Alpha. Admitted to practice Florida 1968, U.S. District Court Middle District of Florida 1971, U.S. Supreme Court 1972 and U.S. Court of Appeals Fifth Circuit 1975. In legal practice Seminole County 1973-86. General Master, Florida Circuit Court Eighteenth Judicial Circuit 1981.

Assistant State Attorney 1971-73. Author "Developing a Rational Sentencing Policy in Florida" Dec 1995, "Frustrated by a Deadbeat Parent? Try Invoking the Dog Law" April 2002 and "Discovery of Public Records in Capital Cases" April 2002 Florida B. Jour.; "The Florida Punishment Code, A Return to Law Without Order" *Florida Defender* Winter 1997; and "Dealing with the Courts" *In Brief* Jan 1999. Member Florida Sentencing Commission 1991-98. Chair Criminal Justice Section Florida Conference of Circuit Court Judges 1993-96. Member since 1997, Member Electronic Filing Subcommittee since 1997, Member since 1997 and Chair 2000 Trial Court Technology Subcommittee and Chair Automated Sentencing Committee since 2002 Florida Court

EATON, O. H. "BILL", JR.—*Continued*
Technology Commission. Member Legislative Review Committee since 1997, The Morris Committee on Capital Case Post Conviction Procedures 1998-2002, Criminal Appeals Reform Act Committee 1999-2002 and Criminal Court Steering Committee since 2002 Florida Supreme Court. Member The Florida Bar (Member since 1994, Vice Chair 1999-2000 and Chair 2000-01, Chair Special Subcommittee on Pretrial Discovery 1995, Chair Subcommittee III 1998-99, Criminal Rules of Procedure Committee, Member Judicial Administration Committee 2000-01, Court Technology Committee since 2001, Executive Council Criminal Law Section since 2002), Brevard County and Seminole County (President 1980) Bar Associations.

Faculty Member Florida College of Advanced Judicial Studies since 1991 and The National Judicial College since 2000. Recipient Distinguished Service Award from Florida Council on Crime and Delinquency 1987-88, Thomas E. Whigham Pro Bono Service Award 1990, Award of Distinction from Seminole County Bar Association 1994, Williams/Johnson Outstanding Jurist Award from Brevard County and Seminole County Bar Associations 1998 and Steven M. Goldstein Criminal Justice Award for Lifelong Commitment to the Causes of Liberty and Justice 1999. Named Man of the Year by Central Florida Vietnam Legal Memorial Association 2002. Captain U.S. Army 1968-70. Recipient Bronze Star, Joint Service Commendation Medal, Army Commendation Medal, Vietnam Campaign Medal, Vietnam Service Medal and National Defense Service Medal. Board of Advisors Barry University College of Law since 1994. President Alumni Association and Member Board of Trustees St. Andrews Sewanee School 1996-99.

Office: Seminole County Courthouse, 301 North Park Avenue, Sanford 32771-1292.
Telephone: (407) 665-4239.
Fax: (407) 665-4292

ECHARTE, Pedro P., Jr. *(Judge, Florida Circuit Court Eleventh Judicial Circuit)*
Office: 602 Gerstein Justice Building, 1351 N.W. Twelfth Street, Miami 33125.
Telephone: (305) 548-5403.

ECONOMOU, Deno G. *(Judge, Florida Circuit Court Twelfth Judicial Circuit)*
Mailing address: P.O. Box 1000, Bradenton 34206.
Office: 1115 Manatee Avenue West, Bradenton 34205.
Telephone: (941) 742-5942.
Fax: (941) 742-5957

EDDY, David B. *(Judge, Florida Circuit Court Fifth Judicial Circuit)*
Office: Marion County Judicial Center, 110 N.W. First Avenue, Ocala 34475.
Telephone: (352) 401-7868.
Fax: (352) 401-7881

EDELSTEIN, Charles D. *(Senior Judge, Dade County Court)* Appointed by Governor Robert Graham to term beginning Aug 17, 1979. Elected to subsequent terms. Assumed Senior Judge status, serves by assignment. Born Asbury Park New Jersey Oct 2, 1938. Jewish. Educated at University of Florida B.A. 1960 LL.B. 1963. Board of Editors University of Florida Law Review 1963. Law Clerk to Hon. Charles A. Carroll, Florida District Court of Appeal Third District 1963-64. Member Phi Alpha Delta. Admitted to practice Florida 1963 and New Jersey 1965. Began legal practice Asbury Park New Jersey 1964. In legal practice Miami Florida 1965.

Editorial Board Justice System Journal since 1975. Instructor National Sheriffs Association and Delinquency Control Institute. Adjunct Professor Florida International University 1973-74 and University of Miami. Professor Miami-Dade Community College 1970-75, University of Southern California 1975-77 and Florida Atlantic University 1977-79. Member Dade-Miami Criminal Justice Council. Chairman Victims Assistance Council. Member American Judicature Society, Florida Conference of County Judges, The Florida Bar, Dade County and New Jersey State Bar Associations. Instructor The National Judicial College 1982-83, Florida Judicial College 1984, Alabama Judicial College and Florida Juvenile Justice Institute. Ford Fellow Institute for Court Management 1972. Previously worked as court consultant for Koba Associates, American University, Public Systems Management, Florida Supreme Court and Institute for Court Management. Member American Heart Association, Hispanic Affairs Committee, Spanish-American League Against Discrimination and B'nai B'rith. Enjoys reading, writing, traveling, fishing and cooking.

Office: 511 Dade County Courthouse, 73 West Flagler Street, Miami 33130.
Telephone: (305) 349-7001.

EDWARDS-STEPHENS, Sandra *(Judge, Florida Circuit Court Fifth Judicial Circuit)* Former Judge, Marion County Court, elected to term beginning Jan 1991.
Office: Marion County Judicial Center, 110 N.W. First Avenue, Ocala 34475.
Telephone: (352) 401-6740.
Fax: (352) 401-6760

ELLINOR, Thomas R. *(Senior Judge, Bay County Court)* Assumed Senior Judge status, serves by assignment.
Mailing address: P.O. Box 27, Panama City 32402.
Office: 300 East Fourth Street, Panama City 32401.
Telephone: (850) 747-5327.

ELLIS, Cynthia A. *(Judge, Florida Circuit Court Twentieth Judicial Circuit)* Appointed by Governor Lawton Chiles to term beginning 1998. Elected 2000, current term expires Jan 2007. Born Fort Myers Florida Oct 9, 1955. Catholic. Educated at University of Florida B.A. with honors 1976 J.D. 1978. Admitted to practice Florida 1979. Judge, Collier County Court Jan 1990 to 1998.

Assistant State Attorney Gainesville 1979-86 and Naples 1986-90. Member National Association of Women Judges and The Florida Bar. Attended "Fundamentals of Family Law," "Domestic Violence" and "Civil Service" Advanced Judicial College 1993 and "Opinion Writing and Logic for Judges" The National Judicial College 1994. Recipient "She Knows Where She Is Going" Award from Girls' Inc. of Collier County 1991 and Outstanding Victim Advocacy Award from Crime Victim's Rights Coalition 1994. Member Substance Abuse Advisory Board David Lawrence Center 1990. Chairperson Naples Alliance for Children 1990-92. Council Member Collier County Extension Advisory Board 1990-94. Board of Directors YMCA of Collier County 1991-97.

ELLIS, CYNTHIA A.—*Continued*
Enjoys school activities with children, activities for the University of Florida, camping and fishing.

Office: Collier County Government Complex, Building L, 3301 Tamiami Trail East, Naples 34112.

Telephone: (239) 732-2783.

Fax: (239) 774-9654

EMAS, Kevin M. *(Judge, Florida Circuit Court Eleventh Judicial Circuit)* Former Judge, Dade County Court.

Office: 424 Gerstein Justice Building, 1351 N.W. Twelfth Street, Miami 33125.

Telephone: (305) 548-5478.

Fax: (305) 548-5348

ERIKSSON, Ralph E. *(Judge, Seminole County Court)* Elected to term beginning Jan 3, 1995. Reelected 1998, current term expires Jan 2005. Administrative Judge 1997-98. Born June 3, 1947. Educated at University of Florida B.S.B.A. 1969 and Florida State University College of Law J.D. 1972. Member Delta Tau Delta and Phi Delta Phi. Admitted to practice Florida 1972 and U.S. District Court Middle District of Florida 1973. In legal practice Orlando 1972-73.

Assistant State Attorney Eighteenth Judicial Circuit 1974-94. Author "The Courts Should Let Some Sunshine In" Florida B. Jour. July/Aug 1991. Chairperson Seminole County Juvenile Justice Council 1993-95. Member The Florida Bar (Juvenile Court Rules Committee 1991-95, Rules of Judicial Administration Committee 1993-95) and Seminole County Bar Association (President 1981). Eighteenth Judicial Circuit Representative Florida Conference of County Court Judges 1998-2000.

Office: Seminole County Courthouse, 301 North Park Avenue, Sanford 32771-1292.

Telephone: (407) 665-4121.

ERVIN, Richard W., III *(Judge, Florida District Court of Appeal First District)* Elected 1976 to term beginning Jan 4, 1977. Retained by election 1982, 1988, 1994 and Nov 7, 2000. Current term expires Jan 1, 2007. Former Chief Judge. Born Putnam County Florida Oct 16, 1934. Educated at Florida State University B.A. 1957 and University of Florida LL.B. 1960. Member Phi Beta Kappa. Admitted to practice Florida 1960. In legal practice Tallahassee 1963-69.

Assistant U.S. Attorney 1960-63. Tallahassee Public Defender 1963-76. Member Governor's Advisory Council of Criminal Justice, Tallahassee Bar Association and The Florida Bar. Member Church of the Advent.

Office: 301 Martin Luther King Jr. Boulevard, Tallahassee 32399-1850.

Telephone: (850) 487-1000.

Fax: (850) 921-4768

ESPINOSA, Jack, Jr. *(Judge, Florida Circuit Court Thirteenth Judicial Circuit)*

Office: 109 Annex, 800 East Kennedy Boulevard, Tampa 33602-4146.

Telephone: (813) 301-7288.

Fax: (813) 276-8448

ESQUIROZ, Margarita G. *(Judge, Florida Circuit Court Eleventh Judicial Circuit)* Appointed by Governor Robert Graham to term beginning Feb 21, 1984. Elected to subsequent terms. First Hispanic woman appointed judge in Florida. Born Havana Cuba Feb 7, 1945. Educated at Miami-Dade Junior College A.A. with honors 1969 and University of Miami B.B.A. in Accounting cum laude 1971 J.D. cum laude 1974. Recipient local honor and Irwin Scholarships and American Jurisprudence Awards in Florida Civil Procedure and Administrative Law. Articles and Comments Editor University of Miami Law Review. Finalist Freshman Moot Court Competition and member Moot Court Board. Member Beta Gamma Sigma, Beta Alpha Psi and Society of Wig and Robe. Admitted to practice Florida. Judge, Industrial Claims Court June 4, 1979 to Feb 20, 1984, appointed by Governor Bob Graham.

Assistant Attorney General Florida 1974-79. Author Casenote "Implied Warranties in the Sale of Real Estate" 26 U. of Miami L. Rev. 838 Summer 1972. Co-author with Walter H. Beckham "Eleventh Survey of Florida Law" 28 U. of Miami L. Rev. 662 Spring 1974. Member Florida Association of Women Lawyers (State Association and Dade County Chapter), The Florida Bar, Dade County (associate) and Cuban American (Honorary President) Bar Associations. "Margarita Esquiroz Day" proclaimed by City of Miami Mayor and Commission Aug 26, 1979. Recipient "Floridana" Award as one of Ten Most Outstanding Women by Cuban Women's Club 1982. Hispanic Heritage Award for Leadership from Host Committee of Hispanic Organizations at Organization of American States Building Washington D.C. 1991 and LeRoy Collins Distinguished Alumni Award from Florida Association of Community Colleges 1991. Featured in "Prominent People in Florida Government" Sept 1980 edition and "100 Influentials" by Hispanic Business May 1983. Named Outstanding Woman of 1984 by Miami Ballet Society May 1984 and Alumni of the Year by the American Association of Community and Junior Colleges, Kansas City Missouri 1991. Previously worked as legal secretary, law library assistant and student instructor. Member Cuban Women's Club and Concerned Citizens of Northeast Dade.

Office: 635 Dade County Courthouse, 73 West Flagler Street, Miami 33130.

Telephone: (305) 349-7049.

ESSRIG, Katherine G. *(Judge, Florida Circuit Court Thirteenth Judicial Circuit)* Former Judge, Hillsborough County Court, elected to term beginning Jan 1991.

Office: 801 East Twiggs Street, Room 462, Tampa 33602.

Telephone: (813) 272-7137.

Fax: (813) 276-2079

ESTRADA, Peter F. *(Judge, Highlands County Court)*

Office: Highlands County Courthouse, 430 South Commerce Avenue, Sebring 33870.

Telephone: (863) 402-6614.

Fax: (863) 402-6575

EVANDER, Kerry I. *(Judge, Florida Circuit Court Eighteenth Judicial Circuit)* Former Judge, Brevard County Court, appointed by Governor Bob Martinez to term beginning April 19, 1989.

Office: Moore Justice Center, Fourth Floor, 2825 Judge Fran Jamieson Way, Viera 32940-8006.

Telephone: (321) 617-7287.

Fax: (321) 617-7293

EVANS, Peter M. *(Judge, Palm Beach County Court)* Assumed office Jan 3, 1989. Elected to subsequent terms.
Office: Palm Beach County Courthouse, 205 North Dixie Highway, West Palm Beach 33401.
Telephone: (561) 355-1500.
Fax: (561) 355-1516

EVANS, Robert M. *(Judge, Florida Circuit Court Ninth Judicial Circuit)* Elected to term beginning Jan 3, 1995. Reelected 2000, current term expires Jan 2007. Currently serves as Administrative Judge Domestic Division.
Office: 425 North Orange Avenue, Orlando 32801.
Telephone: (407) 836-2336.

EZELLE, Marcus *(Judge, Hardee County Court)*
Office: 412 West Orange Street, Room A-104, Wauchula 33873.
Telephone: (863) 773-3174.

FARINA, Joseph P. *(Chief Judge, Florida Circuit Court Eleventh Judicial Circuit)* Appointed by Governor Bob Martinez March 7, 1989. Elected to subsequent terms.
Office: 511 Dade County Courthouse, 73 West Flagler Street, Miami 33130.
Telephone: (305) 349-7054.
Fax: (305) 349-7059

FARMER, Gary M. *(Judge, Florida District Court of Appeal Fourth District)* Assumed office 1991. Educated at Florida Atlantic University B.A. 1970 and University of Toledo College of Law J.D. 1973. Recipient American Jurisprudence Award in Contracts. Managing Editor University of Toledo Law Review. Law Clerk to Hon. Nicholas J. Walinski, U.S. District Court Northern District of Ohio 1973-75. Member Phi Alpha Theta. Admitted to practice Florida, U.S. District Court Southern District of Florida, U.S. Court of Appeals Eleventh Circuit and U.S. Supreme Court.
Member The Florida Bar.
Mailing address: P.O. Box 3315, West Palm Beach 33402-3315.
Office: 1525 Palm Beach Lakes Boulevard, West Palm Beach 33401.
Telephone: (561) 242-2048.
Fax: (561) 242-2100

FARNELL, Crockett *(Judge, Florida Circuit Court Sixth Judicial Circuit)*
Office: 421 Pinellas County Courthouse, 315 Court Street, Clearwater 33756.
Telephone: (727) 464-3233.

FARNELL, Dee Anna *(Judge, Florida Circuit Court Sixth Judicial Circuit)* Elected to term beginning Jan 3, 1995. Reelected 2000, current term expires Jan 2007.
Office: Criminal Justice Center, 14250 49th Street North, Clearwater 33762.
Telephone: (727) 464-7350.

FARRANCE, Robert A. *(Judge, Manatee County Court)*
Mailing address: P.O. Box 1000, Bradenton 34206.
Office: 1115 Manatee Avenue West, Bradenton 34205.
Telephone: (941) 742-5928.
Fax: (941) 742-5964

FASKE, Adele Segall *(Senior Judge, Florida Circuit Court Eleventh Judicial Circuit)* Assumed Senior Judge status, serves by assignment.
Office: 511 Dade County Courthouse, 73 West Flagler Street, Miami 33130.
Telephone: (305) 349-7001.

FAWSETT, Patricia C. *(Chief Judge, United States District Court Middle District of Florida)* Appointed for life by President Ronald Reagan to term beginning 1986. Chief Judge since Jan 1, 2003. Born Montreal Canada Aug 21, 1943. Educated at University of Florida B.A. 1965, M.A.T. 1966 J.D. 1973. In legal practice Orlando 1973-86.
Office: 611 U.S. Courthouse, 80 North Hughey Avenue, Orlando 32801.
Telephone: (407) 835-4250.

FEDER, Richard Yale *(Senior Judge, Florida Circuit Court Eleventh Judicial Circuit)* Appointed by Governor Robert Graham to term beginning Sept 3, 1981. Elected 1982, 1988 and 1994. Former Administrative Judge Family Law. Assumed Senior Judge status, serves by assignment. Born Passaic New Jersey March 9, 1928. Jewish. Educated at Duke University A.B. 1948 and New York University School of Law J.D. 1951. Member Zeta Beta Tau. Admitted to practice New Jersey 1952 and Florida 1959. Began legal practice Passaic and Closter New Jersey 1952. In legal practice Miami and Miami Beach Florida 1959-81.
Author "Doctor, Your Slip Is Showing" Passaic County Bar Reporter 1955, "Religion and the Law" Florida B. Jour. 1970, "Everything You Always Wanted to Know About Being a Witness" B.O.L.O. 1982 and Chapter "Expert Witnesses" *Florida Family Law* Matthew Bender 1986. Important Decision: Ernst v. Ernst 1984. Visiting Lecturer on Trial Advocacy University of Miami School of Law 1984 and Nova University School of Law 1984. Adjunct Professor University of Miami School of Law since 1984. Adjunct Professor of Family Law St. Thomas School of Law. Member American Judicature Society, The Florida Bar (CLE Committee 1978-87, Steering Committee Trial Lawyers Section since 1983, and Executive Committee Family Law Section since 1983, First Chair Family Rules Committee 1992-94, Judicial Administration Rules Committee since 1992), Passaic County 1952-59, Dade County and American Bar Associations. Instructor in Trial Advocacy for The Florida Bar since 1982 (Chairperson Family Law Trial Advocacy Annual Workshop). Recipient Nelson Poynter Award for Civil Liberties 1981, Jurist of the Year Award from Academy of Florida Trial Lawyers 1987-88, Second Annual Chief Justice Warren Burger Healer Award from National Council of Children's Rights 1988, Outstanding Jurist Award from Young Lawyers Section The Florida Bar 1988, Outstanding Jurist Award from Florida Chapter Matrimonial Lawyers of America 1989, First Annual Judge of the Year Award from South Florida Hospital Risk Management Association and First Lifetime Achievement Award from Florida Chapter American Academy of Matrimonial Lawyers. Staff Sergeant New Jersey National Guard 1948-54. Previously worked as camp counselor and director, shoe salesman, theater manager, reporter and actor. National Board member 1968-81 and Florida Chairman 1976-78

FEDER, RICHARD YALE—*Continued*
American Civil Liberties Union. Enjoys French, Italian, Jewish and Chinese cooking.
Office: 511 Dade County Courthouse, 73 West Flagler Street, Miami 33130.
Telephone: (305) 349-7001.

FEDERICO, Philip J. *(Judge, Florida Circuit Court Sixth Judicial Circuit)* Elected to term beginning Jan 3, 1995. Reelected 2000, current term expires Jan 2007.
Office: Criminal Justice Center, 14250 49th Street North, Clearwater 33762.
Telephone: (727) 464-7457.

FEILER, Loree S. *(Senior Judge, Dade County Court)* Elected to term beginning Jan 1991. Assumed Senior Judge status, serves by assignment.
Office: 511 Dade County Courthouse, 73 West Flagler Street, Miami 33130.
Telephone: (305) 349-7001.

FEINER, Leonard *(Judge, Broward County Court)* Elected to term beginning Jan 3, 1989. Reelected to subsequent terms. Current term expires Jan 1, 2007. Born Brooklyn New York Oct 19, 1947. Educated at Bernard M. Baruch College of the City University of New York B.B.A. 1970 and St. John's University School of Law J.D. 1973. Admitted to practice New York 1974 and Florida 1975. In legal practice New York New York 1974-75 and Fort Lauderdale Florida 1975-88.
Member The Florida Bar and New York State Bar Association.
Office: 427 Broward County Courthouse, 201 S.E. Sixth Street, Fort Lauderdale 33301.
Telephone: (954) 831-7821.
Fax: (954) 831-7260

FENNELLY, John E. *(Judge, Florida Circuit Court Nineteenth Judicial Circuit)*
Office: 384 Indian River County Courthouse, 2000 Sixteenth Avenue, Vero Beach 32960.
Telephone: (772) 770-5050.
Fax: (772) 770-5335

FERGUSON, Emmet F., III *(Judge, Duval County Court)*
Office: Duval County Courthouse, 330 East Bay Street, Jacksonville 32202.
Telephone: (904) 630-2577.
Fax: (904) 630-2979

FERNANDEZ, Ellis T., Jr. *(Senior Judge, Florida Circuit Court Fourth Judicial Circuit)* Assumed Senior Judge status, serves by assignment.
Office: Duval County Courthouse, 330 East Bay Street, Jacksonville 32202.
Telephone: (904) 630-1693.

FERNANDEZ, Gaston J. *(Judge, Hillsborough County Court)* Appointed by Governor Lawton Chiles to term beginning Jan 18, 1999. Elected to term beginning Jan 2, 2001, current term expires Jan 1, 2007. Catholic. Educated at University of South Florida B.A. and South Texas College of Law J.D. 1978. Admitted to practice Florida 1978. In legal practice Tampa March 1984 to Dec 2000.
Assistant State Attorney Sept 1978 to Feb 1984. USAR. Member Boys and Girls Club of Tampa Bay. Enjoys golf.
Office: 204A Annex, 800 East Kennedy Boulevard, Tampa 33602-4146.
Telephone: (813) 272-5809.
Fax: (813) 276-2329

FERNANDEZ, Ivan F. *(Judge, Florida Circuit Court Eleventh Judicial Circuit)*
Office: Juvenile Justice Center, 3300 N.W. 27th Avenue, Miami 33132.
Telephone: (305) 638-6879.

FERRER, Alex E. *(Judge, Florida Circuit Court Eleventh Judicial Circuit)* Elected to term beginning Jan 3, 1995. Reelected 2000, current term expires Jan 2007.
Office: 1915 Courthouse Center, 175 N.W. First Avenue, Miami 33128.
Telephone: (305) 349-5735.
Fax: (305) 349-6171

FERRIS, Janet E. *(Judge, Florida Circuit Court Second Judicial Circuit)* Assumed office Jan 4, 1999. Administrative Judge Criminal Division since Aug 1999. Educated at Boston University B.A. summa cum laude with distinction 1973 and Florida State University J.D. 1976. In legal practice Tallahassee 1989-91.
Assistant State Attorney Seventeenth Judicial Circuit 1976-77. Assistant Attorney General Florida Office of the Attorney General 1977-80. General Counsel Florida Department of Law Enforcement 1980-88 and Florida Department of Juvenile Justice 1994-98. Author "Civil Actions Under Florida's Racketeer Influenced and Corrupt Organizations Act" *RICO Investigators' and Prosecutors' Manual* Office of the Governor State of Florida March 1981, "Present and Potential Legal Job Protections Available to Heads of Police Agencies" 14 No. 5 *The Florida Police Chief* May 1988 and *Civil RICO Pleading Manual* National Association of Attorneys General April 1990. Member Family Court Steering Committee Florida Supreme Court 1995-98. Member 1995-99 and Chair 1998-99 Juvenile Court Rules Committee. Member Juvenile Fairness Subcommittee Fairness Commission and Kayla McKean Implementation Ad Hoc Committee Florida Supreme Court. Member Criminal Workgroup Committee on Trial Court Performance and Accountability Judicial Management Council. Member Tallahassee Women Lawyers (Treasurer 1989-90), The Florida Association of Police Attorneys (Secretary 1982-83, Vice President 1984-85, President 1986-87), The Florida Bar (Unauthorized Practice of Law Committee Second Judicial Circuit 1984-91, Federal Court Practice Committee 1990-91) and Tallahassee Bar Association. Instructor Organized Crime Institute and Florida Department of Law Enforcement Academy 1979-89. Panelist Women in Government Workshop North Florida Chapter American Society for Public Administration 1985. Participant 21st Century Justice Project 1993-94, Participant and Facilitator Long Range Planning Workshop 1996 and Speaker Family Courts Conference May 1996 Florida Supreme Court. Presenter Florida Conference of Circuit Court Judges 1996, 1997 and 1999 and International Conference on Restorative Justice 1998. Senior Research Associate Institute for Intergovernmental Research 1989. Secretary Florida Department of Business Regulation 1991-93. Chief Inspector General Florida Executive Office of the Governor 1993-94. Moot Court Judge Florida State University College of Law 1984-90. Board Member 1987-99, Vice President 1990 and President 1992-94

FERRIS, JANET E.—*Continued*

Leon Association for Retarded Citizens. Commentator Florida Public Radio 1988-91. Board of Directors North Florida Legal Services 1989-91. Member LeMoyne Art Foundation.

Office: 365-D Leon County Courthouse, 301 South Monroe Street, Tallahassee 32301.

Telephone: (850) 577-4305.

Fax: (850) 922-0327

FICARROTTA, Ronald N. *(Judge, Florida Circuit Court Thirteenth Judicial Circuit)* Appointed by Governor Jeb Bush to term beginning May 1999. Elected Sept 2000, current term expires Jan 2007. Born Tampa Florida Dec 30, 1958. Educated at University of Florida B.S. 1979 and South Texas College of Law J.D. 1982. Member Phi Alpha Delta. Admitted to practice Florida 1983 and U.S. District Court Middle District of Florida. Judge, Hillsborough County Court March 10, 1994 to May 1999, appointed by Governor Lawton Chiles.

Assistant State Attorney 1983-94. Member Family Law Inns of Court, Tampa Bay Inns of Court, Florida Conference of County Court Judges, Florida Conference of Circuit Court Judges and Hillsborough County Bar Association.

Office: 122 Courthouse Annex, 800 East Kennedy Boulevard, Tampa 33602.

Telephone: (813) 276-8961.

Fax: (813) 276-2339

FIERRO, Eugene J. *(Judge, Florida Circuit Court Eleventh Judicial Circuit)* Elected to term beginning Jan 1991. Reelected 1996 and 2002. Current term expires Jan 2009. Former Associate Administrative Judge Family Division. Currently serves Circuit Court Appellate Panel Civil, Family and Criminal Divisions. Born New York New York Sept 3, 1941. Educated at University of Miami B.Ed. 1962 J.D. 1967. Guest Editorialist Miami Law Review. Member Phi Delta Phi, Bar and Gavel Legal Society and University of Miami Tax Law Society. Admitted to practice Florida 1967, U.S. District Court Southern District of Florida 1967, U.S. Courts of Appeals Fifth 1968 and Eleventh 1981 Circuits and U.S. Supreme Court 1972. In legal practice Miami 1967-90.

Administrator Dade County Comprehensive Pro Bono Plan ("Put Something Back") since 1991. Author "It's Here—Now What? A Primer on Attorney Pro Bono Services" 1992 and "The Lawyers Trial Book: A Guide to the 1997 Amendment to the Rules of Florida Civil Procedure" 1997 Florida B. Jour., "Child Support Collection" Florida Bar News Oct 1992, "Hand Your License to the Bailiff: Florida's Effort to Collect Delinquent Child Support" American Journal of Family Law 1993 and Chapter "Organization and Development of the Case" *Civil Practice Before Trial* The Florida Bar CLE. Member Standing Committee on Pro Bono Florida Supreme Court. Member American Judicature Society, National Council of Juvenile and Family Court Judges, National Conference of Bar Presidents, American Judges Association, The Florida Bar (Civil Procedure Rules Committee since 1992) and Coral Gables Bar Association (President 1988). Lecturer on Judicial Ethics including the ethics of lawyers dealing with judges CLE Coral Gables Bar Association 1991 and "Closing Argument" and "Trial Techniques" numerous Bar Associations. Faculty Member Florida Conference of Circuit Court Judges 1992 and Florida College of Advanced Judicial Studies 1994. Recipient Man of the Year Award from Coral Gables Bar Association 1989, Certificate of Appreciation from Metropolitan Dade County Commission 1991, 1993 and 1996, Judicial Award of Merit 1992, Bench and Bar Award from Young Lawyers Section 1992, Judicial Award for Pro Bono Service 1992 and Pro Bono Honor Roll 1992 Dade County Bar Association, Service Award from Concerned Matrimonial Lawyers 1992, Davis Productivity Award from Florida Tax Watch 1996, Alumnus of Distinction Award from University of Miami School of Law 1999 and Pro Bono Award from American Bar Association 1999. Inducted into Miami Beach Senior High Hall of Fame 2002. Nominated for The Miami Herald Spirit of Excellence Award. Previously worked as school teacher 1962-67. Member Iron Arrow Honor Society University of Miami, Boy Scouts of America, Indian Guides and PTA. Involved with youth sports 1982-85 and Dade Day in Tallahassee 1989. Enjoys college and professional sports, travel, antiques, antique automobiles, reading and music.

Office: 2015 Courthouse Center, 175 N.W. First Avenue, Miami 33128.

Telephone: (305) 349-5723.

Fax: (305) 349-6172

FIGAROLA, Rosa C. *(Judge, Dade County Court)*

Office: 402 Gerstein Justice Building, 1351 N.W. Twelfth Street, Miami 33125.

Telephone: (305) 548-5120.

FINE, Edward H. *(Chief Judge, Florida Circuit Court Fifteenth Judicial Circuit)* Appointed by Governor Robert Graham 1986. Elected 1986, 1992 and 1998. Current term expires Jan 2005. Chief Judge since July 1, 2001. Educated at Vanderbilt University B.A. 1968 and University of Florida J.D. 1971. Member Phi Alpha Delta. Admitted to practice Florida 1971. In legal practice West Palm Beach 1973-78. Judge, Palm Beach County Court 1978-86, appointed by Governor Reubin Askew.

Member The Florida Bar. Attended Circuit Judges Conference.

Office: Palm Beach County Courthouse, 205 North Dixie Highway, West Palm Beach 33401.

Telephone: (561) 355-6386.

Fax: (561) 355-1622

FIRTEL, Leon M. *(Judge, Florida Circuit Court Eleventh Judicial Circuit)*

Office: 415 Gerstein Justice Building, 1351 N.W. Twelfth Street, Miami 33125.

Telephone: (305) 548-5168.

Fax: (305) 548-5610

FISHMAN, Jane D. *(Judge, Broward County Court)*

Office: 210 West Regional Courthouse, 100 North Pine Island Road, Plantation 33324.

Telephone: (954) 831-2314.

Fax: (954) 831-5572

FLANDERS, Judith J. *(Judge, Florida Circuit Court Tenth Judicial Circuit)*

Mailing address: P.O. Box 9000, Drawer J-109, Bartow 33831-9000.

Telephone: (863) 534-4627.

FLEET, Erwin *(Senior Judge, Florida Circuit Court First Judicial Circuit)* Elected 1972 to term beginning Jan 2, 1973. Reelected 1978 and 1984. Assumed Senior Judge status Dec 31, 1990, serves by assignment. Born

FLEET, ERWIN—*Continued*

Boston Massachusetts Sept 25, 1927. Jewish. Educated at University of Florida B.S.B.A. 1949 J.D. 1950. Admitted to practice Florida 1950, U.S. District Court Northern District of Florida and U.S. Supreme Court. Began legal practice Fort Walton Beach 1950. Judge, Florida Circuit Court First Judicial Circuit 1957-59. U.S. Commissioner, 1959-71 and U.S. Magistrate, 1971-73 Eglin Air Force Base.

Assistant State Attorney First Judicial Circuit 1955-57. School Board Attorney Okaloosa County 1962-73. Member Florida Conference of Circuit Court Judges (Past Chairman), The Florida Bar, Society of the Bar of the First Judicial Circuit (Past President), Okaloosa-Walton (Past President) and American (Judicial Administration Division) Bar Associations. U.S. Army Korean War. Past Commodore Fort Walton Beach Yacht Club. Member Boy Scouts of America (Past District Chairman, Cubmaster, Scoutmaster and Sea Explorer Advisor), Fort Walton Beach Lions Club (Past President), Fort Walton Beach Chamber of Commerce (Past President) and Fort Walton Beach Elks Lodge (Past Exalted Ruler).

Office: Okaloosa County Courthouse Annex, Shalimar 32579.

Telephone: (850) 609-0834.

FLEET, J. Leonard *(Judge, Florida Circuit Court Seventeenth Judicial Circuit)* Elected to term beginning Jan 1983. Reelected 1988, 1994 and 2000. Current term expires Jan 2007. Born Live Oak Florida Feb 19, 1934. Jewish. Educated at University of Florida B.S.B.A. 1956 J.D. 1959 and University of Nevada Reno M.J.S. 1994. Business Manager University of Florida Law Review 1958. Member Phi Alpha Delta. Admitted to practice Florida 1960, District of Columbia (inactive), U.S. District Court Southern District of Florida, U.S. Courts of Appeal Fifth and Eleventh Circuits and U.S. Supreme Court. In legal practice Hollywood 1960-82. Judge, Cooper City Municipal Court 1965.

Assistant City Prosecutor Hollywood 1964-66. Author "Bench View of a Child Victim Trial" *Champion Magazine* National Association of Criminal Defense Lawyers 1987 and "Confrontation: Hearsay and Child Abuse" Wisconsin Association of Criminal Defense Lawyers May 1988. Compiler of materials on Disability, Trial, Death Penalty Cases and Pretrial Procedures *Florida Judges' Trial Manual.* Adjunct Professor of Legal Ethics Nova University 1983 and Graduate and Undergraduate Programs Lynn University since 1997. Lecturer Southeast Symposium on Sexual Abuse Trials Huntsville Alabama Feb 1986, on "Use of Hearsay and Videotaped Testimony as an Alternative to Requiring a Child Witness to Personally Appear at Trial" Florida Conference of Circuit Court Judges 1986, on "Televised Testimony as an Alternative Means of Presenting Testimony of Children" Florida Department of Law Enforcement 1986, on "Videotaped Interviews" Court Appointed Special Advocates, Austin Texas 1987 and on "Judicial Discretion in the Use of Videotaped Testimony" National Conference on Missing and Exploited Children 1987, Broward County Forensic Association 1987, Broward County Police Academy 1987 and Children's Medical Services Child Protection Team Florida Department of Health and Rehabilitation 1987. Member Broward County Criminal Defense Attorneys Association (Founder and Charter President 1970-71, President 1981-82), National Association of Criminal Defense Attorneys (Honorary), The Florida Bar (Committee on the Legal Needs of Children), Broward County and American Bar Associations. Recipient Distinguished Service Awards from Broward County Chapter American Red Cross 1985, Broward County Hearing and Speech Association Deaf Center 1985 and Women in Distress 1986, Judicial Award from National Center for Missing and Exploited Children 1987, Award from Chapter IV Florida Council on Crime and Delinquency 1990 and Service Award from Retired Detectives Association of the City of New York. Board of Directors Broward County Chapter American Red Cross 1985-88. Member B'nai B'rith (Past President Hollywood Sunshine Lodge, Vice President Programming 1987, President 1988, Chaplain and Board of Directors 1989 Justice Unit 5207). Interests include flying single-engine airplanes, camping, dancing, family activities and listening to operatic, classical, contemporary and country and western music.

Office: 920 Broward County Courthouse, 201 S.E. Sixth Street, Fort Lauderdale 33301.

Telephone: (954) 831-7714

FLEISCHER, Barbara *(Judge, Florida Circuit Court Thirteenth Judicial Circuit)* Former Judge, Hillsborough County Court.

Office: 125 Annex, 800 East Kennedy Boulevard, Tampa 33602-4146.

Telephone: (813) 272-7139.

FLEMING, Jeffrey M. *(Judge, Orange County Court)*

Office: 425 Orange County Courthouse, 425 North Orange Avenue, Orlando 32801.

Telephone: (836) 407-2312.

Fax: (836) 835-5234

FLEMING, Marion Lucas *(Judge, Florida Circuit Court Sixth Judicial Circuit)* Elected Nov 1996 to term beginning Jan 7, 1997. Reelected 2002, current term expires Jan 7, 2009. Admitted to practice Florida 1983.

Assistant State Attorney Sixth Judicial Circuit Florida 1983-87.

Office: Criminal Justice Center, 14250 49th Street North, Clearwater 33762.

Telephone: (727) 464-7333.

FLETCHER, John *(Judge, Florida District Court of Appeal Third District)* Appointed by Governor Lawton Chiles to term beginning 1996. Born Philadelphia Pennsylvania 1937. Educated at University of Miami B.A. 1959 and University of Florida J.D. 1962. Admitted to practice Florida 1962, U.S. District Courts Middle 1967 and Southern Districts of Florida, U.S. Court of Appeals Fifth Circuit and U.S. Supreme Court. In legal practice 1973-96.

Assistant County Attorney and Chief Assistant Pinellas County 1962 to Aug 1967. Assistant County Attorney Dade County Aug 1967 to Aug 1973. General Counsel Sanibel-Captiva Island Water Association 1978-85.

Office: 2001 S.W. 117th Avenue, Miami 33175-1716.

Telephone: (305) 229-3200.

Fax: (305) 229-3206

FLOWER, Gary *(Judge, Duval County Court)*

Office: Duval County Courthouse, 330 East Bay Street, Jacksonville 32202.

Telephone: (904) 630-7136.

Fax: (904) 630-2979

FOGAN, Robert J. *(Senior Judge, Florida Circuit Court Seventeenth Judicial Circuit)* Assumed Senior Judge status, serves by assignment.
Office: Broward County Courthouse, 201 S.E. Sixth Street, Fort Lauderdale 33301.
Telephone: (954) 831-7740.

FOSTER, Clinton E. *(Senior Judge, Florida Circuit Court Fourteenth Judicial Circuit)* Assumed Senior Judge status, serves by assignment.
Mailing address: P.O. Box 27, Panama City 32402.
Office: 300 East Fourth Street, Panama City 32401.
Telephone: (850) 747-5327.

FOSTER, Robert A. *(Judge, Florida Circuit Court Thirteenth Judicial Circuit)* Elected Nov 7, 2000 to term beginning Jan 2001. Term expires Jan 2007.
Office: 332A Hillsborough County Courthouse, 419 Pierce Street, Tampa 33602.
Telephone: (813) 272-6997.

FOSTER, Robert M. *(Judge, Florida Circuit Court Fourth Judicial Circuit)*
Mailing address: P.O. Box 456, Fernandina Beach 32035-0456.
Office: Nassau County Courthouse, Fernandina Beach 32034.
Telephone: (800) 895-3143.
Fax: (904) 321-5901

FOXMAN, S. James *(Judge, Florida Circuit Court Seventh Judicial Circuit)* Former Chief Judge.
Office: Volusia County Courthouse, 101 North Alabama Avenue, De Land 32724.
Telephone: (386) 257-6071.
Fax: (386) 248-8132

FRANCIS, Charles A. *(Judge, Florida Circuit Court Second Judicial Circuit)*
Office: 365-A Leon County Courthouse, Tallahassee 32301.
Telephone: (850) 577-4306.
Fax: (850) 922-0327

FRANCIS, Mary Jo *(Judge, Dade County Court)*
Office: 205 North Dade Justice Center, 15555 Biscayne Boulevard, Miami 33160.
Telephone: (305) 354-8770.

FRAZIER, Douglas N. *(Magistrate Judge, United States District Court Middle District of Florida)* Appointed by U.S. District Court judges to term beginning January 8, 2000.
Office: U.S. Courthouse, 2110 First Street, Fort Myers 33901.
Telephone: (239) 461-2120.

FREEMAN, Carolyn B. *(Judge, Orange County Court)* Elected to term beginning Jan 1991. Reelected 1994 and 1998. Current term expires Jan 2005.
Office: 430 Orange County Courthouse, 425 North Orange Avenue, Orlando 32801.
Telephone: (407) 836-2093.
Fax: (407) 836-0492

FREEMAN, Gill S. *(Judge, Florida Circuit Court Eleventh Judicial Circuit)* Appointed by Governor Lawton Chiles Aug 4, 1997. Born New York New York June 24, 1949. Educated at Temple University B.A. cum laude 1970 and University of Miami M.A. 1973 J.D. cum laude 1977. Staff member University of Miami Law Review. In legal practice Miami Nov 1977 to July 1997.

Chair Political Endorsement Committee Dade County Chapter 1982-84, President Elect 1983-84 and President 1984-85 Florida Association for Women Lawyers. Vice President 1983, Chair Board of Directors 1985-86 and Member Foundation Board of Directors 1987 National Association of Women's Bar Associations. Member Grievance Committee 1984-86, Unlicensed Practice of Law Committee 1984-92 and Continuing Legal Education Committee 1986-89 The Florida Bar. Vice Chairman Gender Bias Study Commission 1987-90 and Chair Gender Bias Implementation Commission 1991-94 Florida Supreme Court. Member All Bar Conference Committee 1996. Fellow American Bar Association. Master Bencher Family Law Inns of Court since 1993. Member 1996-99 and Chair since June 1999 Supreme Court Commission on Fairness. Instructor Florida Bar Trial Advocacy Seminar 1989 and 1996. Recipient "In the Company of Women" Award from Metro Dade County 1989, Mattie Belle Davis Award (for outstanding contributions to women and the law) from Dade County Chapter Florida Association for Women Lawyers 1990-91, Legal Services Pro Bono Award 1992 and Athena Award from Coral Gables Chamber of Commerce 1998. Listed in *Who's Who of American Women* 1992 and *Who's Who International* 1992. Teacher Dade County public schools 1970-76. President Zonta Club of Downtown Miami 1996-97. Chair Board of Directors Spectrum Programs 1996-98. Chair Board of Directors Journey Institute 1996-2001. Trustee since 1996 and Chair Trustees Committee 2002 Dade County Law Library.
Office: Dade County Courthouse, 73 West Flagler Street, Miami 33130.
Telephone: (305) 349-7109.

FREEMAN, Thomas *(Judge, Florida Circuit Court Eighteenth Judicial Circuit)*
Office: 301 North Park Avenue, Sanford 32771.
Telephone: (407) 665-4241.
Fax: (407) 665-4226

FREEMAN, Thomas B. *(Judge, Pinellas County Court)* Appointed by Governor Robert Graham June 1981. Elected to subsequent terms. Current term expires Jan 2005. Born Pontiac Michigan Oct 13, 1944. Educated at St. Petersburg Junior College A.A. 1964 and Stetson University B.A. 1966 J.D. 1969. Member Phi Delta Phi. Admitted to practice Florida 1969. Began legal practice St. Petersburg 1969.

Legislative Assistant to State Senator John T. Ware 1971. Attorney City of Seminole 1973-81. Member Florida Judicial Qualifications Commission since 1987, Legal Aid Society of St. Petersburg, The Florida Bar (Board of Governors Young Lawyers Section 1978-80, Small Claims Rules Committee, Rules of Judicial Administration Committee, Vice Chair Simplified Forms Committee) and St. Petersburg Bar Association. Attended Florida Judicial College 1982. Sixth Judicial Circuit Representative County Judges Conference Orlando 1987. Former member Board of Directors Seminole Chamber of Commerce.
Office: Pinellas County Criminal Justice Ctr., 14250 49th Street North, Clearwater 33762.
Telephone: (727) 464-6902.

FRIEDLAND, Kenneth *(Judge, Brevard County Court)*
Office: Titusville Courthouse, 506 South Palm Avenue, Titusville 32796-3592.
Telephone: (321) 264-6777.
Fax: (321) 264-6760

FRIEDMAN, Ronald M. *(Judge, Florida Circuit Court Eleventh Judicial Circuit)* Elected to term beginning Jan 8, 1985. Reelected 1990, 1996 and 2002. Current term expires Jan 2009. Administrative Judge Appellate Division 2000-02. Born Miami Florida June 11, 1942. Jewish. Educated at University of North Carolina B.S.B.A. 1964, University of Miami School of Law J.D. 1967 and New York University School of Law LL.M. in Taxation 1968. Admitted to practice Florida 1967 and California 1969. In legal practice Beverly Hills and Los Angeles California 1968-76 and Miami Florida 1976-84.
Author *How to Prove a Profit Motive in Horse Breeding* Prentice-Hall, Inc. 1976. Instructor Northrop University School of Law 1975-76. Chairman Tax Committee Beverly Hills Bar Association 1965. Former Chairman Tax Committee Los Angeles Bar Association and ad hoc Trial Practices and Procedures Committee. Former Arbitrator American Arbitration Association. Member The Florida Bar (Board of Governors Circuit Committee) and State Bar of California. Listed in *Who's Who in American Law* 1983-2002. Recipient B'nai B'rith Youth Organization International Gold Key Award 1992 and Thomas Davison III Service Award from University of Miami Law Alumni Association 1993. Past President South Dade Council of B'nai B'rith Lodges and Koach Lodge B'nai B'rith. Past President and Current Board Member B'nai B'rith Bench and Bar Unit. Past President and Current Board Member Adult Board Greater Miami B'nai B'rith Youth Organization. Former Vice President Adult Board Florida B'nai B'rith Youth Organization. Former Honorary Member Board of Directors Epilepsy Foundation of South Florida. Former Member Board of Directors Jewish Family and Children's Services. Former Member Board of Directors, Former Committee Member Youth Services and Member Leadership Council Greater Miami Jewish Foundation. Former Trustee and Judicial Director University of Miami Alumni Association. Former Youth Commissioner National B'nai B'rith. Former Chairman Dade County Outstanding Citizens Award Committee. Member and Leadership Council Greater Miami Jewish Federation.
Office: 1304 Dade County Courthouse, 73 West Flagler Street, Miami 33130.
Telephone: (305) 349-7065.

FRIEDMAN, Steven H. *(Judge, United States Bankruptcy Court Southern District of Florida)* Appointed by U.S. Court of Appeals Eleventh Circuit judges.
Office: 335 Federal Building, 701 Clematis Street, West Palm Beach 33401.
Telephone: (561) 655-6872.

FRUSCIANTE, John A. *(Judge, Florida Circuit Court Seventeenth Judicial Circuit)* Elected to term beginning Jan 1991. Reelected 1996 and 2002. Current term expires Jan 2009.
Office: 910B Broward County Courthouse, 201 S.E. Sixth Street, Fort Lauderdale 33301.
Telephone: (954) 831-7704.
Fax: (954) 831-5572

FRYEFIELD, Peter *(Judge, Florida Circuit Court Fourth Judicial Circuit)*
Office: 107 Duval County Courthouse, 330 East Bay Street, Jacksonville 32202.
Telephone: (904) 630-2527.
Fax: (904) 630-1974

FUENTE, William *(Judge, Florida Circuit Court Thirteenth Judicial Circuit)* Former Judge, Hillsborough County Court, appointed by Governor Lawton Chiles June 14, 1994.
Office: 124 Annex Tower, 801 East Twiggs Street, Tampa 33602.
Telephone: (813) 272-6851.
Fax: (813) 276-8015

FULLERTON, Walt *(Judge, Pinellas County Court)* Appointed by Governor Bob Martinez to term beginning Jan 1, 1988. Elected Nov 8, 1988, 1992, 1996 and 2000. Current term expires Jan 1, 2007. Born Schenectady New York. Educated at Williams College B.A. with honors 1972 and Emory University J.D. 1978. Admitted to practice Florida, Colorado, Georgia, U.S. District Court Middle District of Florida, U.S. Courts of Appeals Fifth and Eleventh Circuits and U.S. Supreme Court.
Instructor in Criminal Justice Institute St. Petersburg Junior College 1988-99 and in Advanced Judicial Studies Program New Judges College. Lieutenant USNR (Vietnam veteran 1972-75).
Office: 501 First Avenue North, Room A223, St. Petersburg 33701.
Telephone: (727) 582-7822.
Fax: (727) 582-7737

FULMER, Carolyn K. *(Judge, Florida District Court of Appeal Second District)* Assumed office Nov 10, 1993. Retained by election. Born Jacksonville Florida Aug 24, 1947. Presbyterian. Educated at University of South Florida B.A. with honors 1969 and Florida State University M.S. with honors 1970 J.D. with honors 1975. Staff member and Indexer Florida State University Law Review 1974-75. Law Clerk Florida State University Attorney's Office 1973-75. Member Kappa Alpha Theta. Admitted to practice Florida 1976. Judge, Polk County Court 1981-83. Judge, Florida Circuit Court Tenth Judicial Circuit June 1, 1983 to Nov 9, 1993, appointed by Governor Robert Graham.
Assistant Attorney Polk County Board of Commissioners 1976. Member Construction Industry Licensing Board 1978 and The Florida Bar. Member League of Women Voters. Board member Peace River Center for Personal Development. Enjoys tennis, running, swimming and reading.
Mailing address: P.O. Box 327, Lakeland 33802-0327.
Office: 1005 East Memorial Boulevard, Lakeland 33801-2019.
Telephone: (863) 499-2290.
Fax: (863) 413-2649

FUNK, Jerry A. *(Judge, United States Bankruptcy Court Middle District of Florida)* Appointed by U.S. Court of Appeals Eleventh Circuit judges.
Mailing address: P.O. Box 559, Jacksonville 32201-0559.
Telephone: (904) 232-3862.

FUTCH, John E. *(Judge, Marion County Court)*
Office: Marion County Judicial Center, 110 N.W. First Avenue, Ocala 34475.
Telephone: (352) 401-6745.
Fax: (352) 401-6776

FUTCH, M. Daniel, Jr. *(Senior Judge, Florida Circuit Court Seventeenth Judicial Circuit)* Assumed Senior Judge status, serves by assignment.
Office: Broward County Courthouse, 201 S.E. Sixth Street, Fort Lauderdale 33301.
Telephone: (954) 831-7740.

GALLAGHER, Daniel E. *(Senior Judge, Florida Circuit Court Thirteenth Judicial Circuit)* Appointed by Governor Reubin Askew to term beginning July 15, 1978. Elected to subsequent terms. Assumed Senior Judge status, serves by assignment. Born Cleveland Ohio Oct 7, 1929. Roman Catholic. Educated at John Carroll University B.S. 1951 and Case Western Reserve University LL.B. 1954 LL.M. 1962. Member Phi Delta Phi. Admitted to practice Ohio 1954, U.S. District Courts Northern District of Ohio 1962 and Middle District of Florida 1964, Florida 1964, U.S. Courts of Appeals Fifth 1965, Sixth 1984 and Eleventh 1984 Circuits, U.S. Supreme Court 1971, District of Columbia 1976, Texas 1989, Oklahoma 1992 and Colorado 1993. In legal practice Tampa Florida 1964-68. Judge of Industrial Claims 1968-78.
U.S. Attorney Cleveland Ohio 1956. Assistant to Vice President Great Lakes Towing Company 1956-58. Instructor in Business Law University of California Extension Overseas Division 1955-56. Certified Mediator Florida and U.S. District Court Middle District of Florida. Member American Judicature Society, The Maritime Law Association of the U.S., The District of Columbia Bar, The Florida Bar (Admiralty, Workmen's Compensation and International Law Sections, Secretary Workmen's Compensation Section 1974-76), State Bar of Texas, Colorado, Ohio State, Oklahoma, Federal and American (Insurance, Negligence and Compensation Law Committees) Bar Associations. Secretary Conference of Industrial Claims Judges. Member Hillsborough County Bar Association Speakers Bureau 1974-76 and Law Day Speakers Bureau 1974-75. Attended The National Judicial College 1979. Recipient Citation of Achievement from Conference of Judges of Industrial Claims. Sergeant U.S. Army Infantry First Cavalry Division 1954-56. President Catholic Lawyers Guild 1996-98. Vice President Sacred Heart Men's Club. Member Palma Ceia Golf and Country Club and University Club.
Office: Hillsborough County Courthouse, 419 Pierce Street, Tampa 33602-4022.
Telephone: (813) 272-5894.

GALLEN, Thomas M. *(Senior Judge, Florida Circuit Court Twelfth Judicial Circuit)* Elected Sept 1984 to term beginning Jan 1, 1985. Reelected Sept 1, 1990 and 1996. Former Chief Judge. Assumed Senior Judge status, serves by assignment. Born Tampa Florida Dec 28, 1932. Catholic. Educated at Florida State University B.S. 1957 and University of Florida J.D. 1960. Member Phi Delta Psi. Admitted to practice Florida 1960 and U.S. Supreme Court 1965. Began legal practice Bradenton.
Member House of Representatives 1968-72 and Senate 1972-78 Florida. Sergeant U.S. Army Special Forces Airborne 1952-55. Member Kiwanis.
Mailing address: P.O. Box 48927, Sarasota 34230.
Office: 2002 Ringling Boulevard, Sarasota 34237.
Telephone: (941) 861-7800.

GARBER, Barry L. *(Magistrate Judge, United States District Court Southern District of Florida)* Appointed by U.S. District Court judges.
Office: U.S. Courthouse, 300 N.E. First Avenue, Miami 33132.
Telephone: (305) 523-5730.

GARCIA, Luis M. *(Judge, Florida Circuit Court Sixteenth Judicial Circuit)*
Office: Upper Keys Government, 88820 Overseas Highway, Tavernier 33070.
Telephone: (305) 852-7165.
Fax: (305) 852-7113

GARDINER, Ana Isabel *(Judge, Florida Circuit Court Seventeenth Judicial Circuit)*
Office: 4910 Broward County Courthouse, 201 S.E. Sixth Street, Fort Lauderdale 33301.
Telephone: (954) 831-6767.

GARRISON, Edward A. *(Judge, Florida Circuit Court Fifteenth Judicial Circuit)* Born Pensacola Florida Sept 30, 1952. Educated at University of South Florida B.A. 1973 and Florida State University J.D. 1975. Admitted to practice Florida 1975 and U.S. District Courts Southern 1976 and Middle 1978 Districts of Florida. Began legal practice West Palm Beach 1975. In legal practice Palm Beach 1977-80. Former Judge, Palm Beach County Court, elected to term beginning Jan 6, 1981.
Member The Association of Trial Lawyers of America and Palm Beach County Bar Association. Member Palm Beach County Rotary Club. Enjoys golf, tennis and flying.
Office: Palm Beach County Courthouse, 205 North Dixie Highway, West Palm Beach 33401.
Telephone: (561) 355-2698.
Fax: (561) 355-3922

GARY, William L. *(Chief Judge, Florida Circuit Court Second Judicial Circuit)* Chief Judge since July 1, 2001.
Office: 365-I Leon County Courthouse, Tallahassee 32301.
Telephone: (850) 577-4307.
Fax: (850) 922-0327

GATES, Michael L. *(Judge, Florida Circuit Court Seventeenth Judicial Circuit)*
Office: 201 S.E. Sixth Street, Room 822-B, Fort Lauderdale 33301.
Telephone: (954) 831-7112.
Fax: (954) 831-5572

GEEKER, Nickolas P. *(Judge, Florida Circuit Court First Judicial Circuit)* Elected Sept 1984 to term beginning Jan 1985. Reelected Sept 1990, Sept 1996 and 2002. Current term expires Jan 2009. Born Pensacola Florida Dec 15, 1944. Greek Orthodox. Educated at Louisiana Tech University B.A. 1966 and Florida State University J.D. 1969. Law Clerk to Hon. David L. Middlebrooks, U.S. District Court Northern District of Florida 1970-73. Member Phi Delta Phi. Admitted to practice Florida 1969, U.S. District Court Northern District of Florida 1970, U.S. Courts of Appeals Fifth 1973 and

GEEKER, NICKOLAS P.—*Continued*

Eleventh 1981 Circuits and U.S. Supreme Court 1980. In legal practice Pensacola 1982-84.

Assistant U.S. Attorney 1973-75 and U.S. Attorney 1976-82 Northern District of Florida.

Office: Judicial Building, Sixth Floor, 190 Governmental Center, Pensacola 32501.

Telephone: (850) 595-4439.

Fax: (850) 595-4404

GEHL, Peggy *(Judge, Broward County Court)* General Master 1989-95. Appointed Judge by Governor Lawton Chiles to term beginning Sept 12, 1995. Elected Sept 1996 and Sept 2000. Current term expires Jan 1, 2007. Born Lebanon Indiana Nov 14, 1947. Educated at University of Florida B.S. 1969 and University of Denver J.D. 1976. Staff member Denver Law Journal 1974-76. Admitted to practice Colorado 1976 and Florida 1977. In legal practice Fort Lauderdale Florida 1976-89.

Editor *County Court Courier* since 1999. Member Judicial Qualifications Commission since 2001. Executive Board Conference of County Court Judges since 1999.

Office: 335 Broward County Courthouse, 201 S.E. Sixth Street, Fort Lauderdale 33301.

Telephone: (954) 831-7675.

Fax: (954) 831-8546

GEIGER, Dwight Luther *(Judge, Florida Circuit Court Nineteenth Judicial Circuit)* Elected to term beginning June 24, 1976. Reelected to subsequent terms. Current term expires Jan 2007. Former Chief Judge. Born New Kensington Pennsylvania May 24, 1943. Educated at Stetson University B.S. 1965 and University of Florida J.D. 1970. Admitted to practice Florida 1968. Began legal practice Stuart 1971. Judge, Martin County Court 1973-76.

Adjunct Professor Florida Institute of Technology 1975-82. Member The Florida Bar, Martin County and American Bar Associations. First Lieutenant U.S. Army 1968-70. Currently Colonel USAR. Past President Stuart Civitan and Fort Pierce Alcohol and Substance Abuse Council. Charter member Martin County Taping Studio for Visually and Physically Handicapped. Former Board member Tri-County Rehabilitation Center. Board Member Children's Home Society of Florida. Member St. Mary's Episcopal Church. Enjoys racquetball, sailing and jogging.

Office: 213 Courthouse Addition, 218 South Second Street, Fort Pierce 34950.

Telephone: (772) 462-2382.

Fax: (772) 462-1952

GELBER, Seymour *(Senior Judge, Florida Circuit Court Eleventh Judicial Circuit)* Appointed by Governor Reubin O'Donovan Askew to term beginning July 11, 1974. Elected to subsequent terms. Assumed Senior Judge status, serves by assignment. Born Bronx New York Sept 1, 1919. Jewish. Educated at University of Miami J.D. 1953 and Florida State University M.A. 1968 Ph.D. 1970. Admitted to practice Florida 1953.

Office: 511 Dade County Courthouse, 73 West Flagler Street, Miami 33130.

Telephone: (305) 349-7001.

GENDEN, Michael A. *(Judge, Florida Circuit Court Eleventh Judicial Circuit)*

Office: 817 Dade County Courthouse, 73 West Flagler Street, Miami 33130.

Telephone: (305) 349-7069.

Fax: (305) 349-7071

GERALD, Lynn F., Jr. *(Judge, Florida Circuit Court Twentieth Judicial Circuit)* Appointed by Governor Bob Martinez Aug 2, 1989. Elected to subsequent terms.

Office: Lee County Justice Center, 1700 Monroe Street, Fort Myers 33901.

Telephone: (239) 335-2228.

Fax: (239) 335-2589

GERBER, Jonathan D. *(Judge, Palm Beach County Court)*

Office: Palm Beach County Courthouse, 205 North Dixie Highway, West Palm Beach 33401.

Telephone: (561) 355-3500.

Fax: (561) 355-3841

GERSTEIN, Norman S. *(Judge, Florida Circuit Court Eleventh Judicial Circuit)* Former Judge, Dade County Court.

Office: 1201 Dade County Courthouse, 73 West Flagler Street, Miami 33130.

Telephone: (305) 349-7074.

Fax: (305) 375-4211

GERSTEN, Carol R. *(Senior Judge, Florida Circuit Court Eleventh Judicial Circuit)* Elected to term beginning Jan 1991. Reelected 1996. Assumed Senior Judge status, serves by assignment.

Office: 511 Dade County Courthouse, 73 West Flagler Street, Miami 33130.

Telephone: (305) 349-7001.

GERSTEN, David M. *(Judge, Florida District Court of Appeal Third District)* Assumed office April 19, 1989. Retained by election. Born Dade County Florida. Educated at University of Florida B.A. in History 1973 J.D. 1975. Member Florida Blue Key 1972. Judge, Dade County Court 1980-82. Judge, Florida Circuit Court Eleventh Judicial Circuit Jan 1983 to April 18, 1989.

Member Florida Association of Trial Lawyers, The Association of Trial Lawyers of America and American Bar Association. Appointed Secretary of State Representative on Cultural Affairs 1980 and member District 11 Advisory Council Department of Health & Rehabilitative Services 1980. Board of Trustees Coconut Grove Cares, Inc. since 1980. Member Miami Beach Jaycees.

Office: 2001 S.W. 117th Avenue, Miami 33175-1716.

Telephone: (305) 229-3200.

Fax: (305) 229-3206

GILBERT, John M. *(Senior Judge, Florida Circuit Court Thirteenth Judicial Circuit)* Assumed Senior Judge status, serves by assignment.

Office: Hillsborough County Courthouse, 419 Pierce Street, Tampa 33602-4022.

Telephone: (813) 272-5894.

GILLMAN, Marvin H. *(Senior Judge, Dade County Court)* Assumed Senior Judge status, serves by assignment.

Office: 511 Dade County Courthouse, 73 West Flagler Street, Miami 33130.

Telephone: (305) 349-7001.

GILNER, Marc *(Judge, Florida Circuit Court Twelfth Judicial Circuit)* Former Judge, Manatee County Court, appointed by Governor Bob Martinez to term beginning Jan 2, 1989.

Mailing address: P.O. Box 1000, Bradenton 34206.

Office: 1115 Manatee Avenue West, Bradenton 34205.

Telephone: (941) 749-7169.

Fax: (941) 742-5957

GIUNTA, Maurice V. *(Judge, Florida Circuit Court Eighth Judicial Circuit)* Assumed office March 15, 1993. Born Passaic New Jersey Aug 4, 1942. Educated at Monmouth College B.A. 1966 and University of Florida J.D. 1974. Admitted to practice Florida 1974. Judge, Alachua County Court Jan 1987 to March 14, 1993. Assistant State Attorney 1974-86.

Office: 408 Alachua County Courthouse, 201 East University Avenue, Gainesville 32601.

Telephone: (352) 374-3645.

Fax: (352) 374-5238

GLADSTONE, William E. *(Senior Judge, Florida Circuit Court Eleventh Judicial Circuit)* Assumed Senior Judge status, serves by assignment.

Office: 511 Dade County Courthouse, 73 West Flagler Street, Miami 33130.

Telephone: (305) 349-7001.

GLANT, David A. *(Judge, Florida Circuit Court Eighth Judicial Circuit)*

Office: 410 Alachua County Courthouse, 201 East University Avenue, Gainesville 32601.

Telephone: (352) 384-3021.

Fax: (352) 381-0186

GLATT, James, Jr. *(Judge, Orange County Court)*

Office: 470 Orange County Courthouse, 425 North Orange Avenue, Orlando 32801.

Telephone: (407) 836-2024.

Fax: (407) 836-2315

GLAZEBROOK, James G. *(Magistrate Judge, United States District Court Middle District of Florida)* Appointed by U.S. District Court judges to term beginning Feb 1, 1996. Term expires Jan 31, 2004. Born New York New York Feb 22, 1955. Episcopalian. Educated at Harvard University Jan-May 1976, Middlebury College A.B. cum laude with departmental honors 1977 and Case Western Reserve University School of Law J.D. 1980. Editorial Staff Case Western Reserve Law Review 1978-79 and Editor Journal of International Law 1979-80 and Canada-United States Law Journal 1979-80. Law Clerk to Hon. John A. Reed, Jr., U.S. District Court Middle District of Florida June 1980 to Jan 1983. Admitted to practice Florida 1980, District of Columbia 1984, New York 1984, U.S. Courts of Appeals Second, Third, Tenth and Eleventh Circuits and U.S. Supreme Court. In legal practice New York 1983-90.

Assistant U.S. Attorney Middle District of Florida Sept 17, 1990 to Jan 31, 1996. Chairman Federal State Health Care Fraud Task Force Orlando Division Middle District of Florida Dec 1992 to April 1994. Member American Bar Association (Immediate Past Chair National Conference of Federal Trial Judges Judicial Division). Chancellor and Vestryman St. Bartholomew's Episcopal Church 1987-90.

Office: U.S. Courthouse, 80 North Hughey Avenue, Orlando 32801.

Telephone: (407) 835-4310.

GLAZER, Mindy S. *(Judge, Florida Circuit Court Eleventh Judicial Circuit)* Elected to term beginning Jan 2001. Educated at University of Miami B.A. 1988 LL.M. 1992 and St. Thomas University School of Law J.D. 1991.

Office: 208 Juvenile Justice Center, 3300 N.W. 27th Avenue, Miami 33142.

Telephone: (305) 638-6873.

Fax: (305) 638-5788

GLENN, Paul M. *(Judge, United States Bankruptcy Court Middle District of Florida)* Appointed by U.S. Court of Appeals Eleventh Circuit judges to term beginning Nov 24, 1993. Term expires Nov 24, 2007. Serves Tampa Division. Born Thomasville Georgia Feb 25, 1945. Methodist. Educated at Florida State University B.A. cum laude 1967 and Duke University School of Law J.D. 1970. Member Phi Beta Kappa, Phi Kappa Phi and Omicron Delta Kappa. Admitted to practice Florida 1970, U.S. District Court Middle District of Florida 1971, U.S. Supreme Court 1987 and U.S. Court of Appeals Eleventh Circuit 1989. In legal practice Jacksonville 1970-76 and 1989-93 and Miami 1976-81.

Member American Bankruptcy Institute, Tampa Bay Bankruptcy Bar Association, The Florida Bar, Jacksonville, Hillsborough County and American Bar Associations. Speaker at CLE seminars The Florida Bar and American Bar Association since 1994 and Pre-Seminar Workshop American Bankruptcy Law and Practice Seminar Stetson University 1995-2001.

Office: U.S. Courthouse, 801 North Florida Avenue, Tampa 33602-3899.

Telephone: (813) 301-5052.

GLICK, Leonard E. *(Judge, Florida Circuit Court Eleventh Judicial Circuit)* Elected to term beginning Jan 1991. Reelected 1996 and 2002. Current term expires Jan 2009.

Office: 300 Gerstein Justice Building, 1351 N.W. Twelfth Street, Miami 33125.

Telephone: (305) 548-5761.

GODERICH, Mario P. *(Judge, Florida District Court of Appeal Third District)* Assumed office 1990. Retained by election. Born Oriente Cuba Nov 5, 1932. Educated at Instituto del Vedado, Cuba B.A. 1952, University of Havana, Cuba D.C.L. 1957 and University of Miami J.D. 1966. Member Phi Delta Phi and Society of Wig and Robe. Admitted to practice Florida 1969. In legal practice Havana Cuba 1957-61. Judge, Industrial Claims Court 1975-78, appointed by Governor Reubin Askew. Judge, Florida Circuit Court Eleventh Judicial Circuit 1978-90, appointed by Governor Reubin Askew.

Professor of English Literature Havana Normal School, Cuba 1952-60. Legal Research Assistant Miami 1965-66. Circulation Supervisor 1966-67, Assistant Law Librarian 1967-70, Law Librarian 1970-75, Assistant Professor of Law 1970-73 and Professor of Law 1973-75 University of Miami School of Law. Editor American Association of Law Libraries Newsletter 1969-74. Former member Florida Conference of Industrial Claims Judges (Executive Board 1976-77, Representative of Dade County judges 1976-78, Treasurer 1978, Associate

GODERICH, MARIO P.—*Continued*

Commissioner Industrial Relations Commission 1978). Member Cuban-American Lawyers Association (Board), The Florida Bar, Havana and American Bar Associations. Lecturer Workmen's Compensation Workshop University of Miami 1976-79 and Nova University Law Center 1977-78. Participant 1979 and Instructor 1983 The National Judicial College. Elected Outstanding Judge of the Criminal Division by Florida Council on Crime and Delinquency 1981. Member Professionales de Cuba, Lions International, Metro Dade County Community Relations Board (Vice Chairman 1978-79), Health Planning System Review Committee, Metro Dade County Citizens Advisory Council 1975-76, International YMCA (Board of Directors 1978-79), Board of Directors Hope School, Board of Directors United Way of Dade County, Big Brothers/Big Sisters of Greater Miami (Board of Directors 1980), Boy Scouts of America (Board of Directors 1980), Dade County Public School System Advisory Committee of School/Mental Health Co-operative 1980, Cuban National Planning Council and Spanish-American League Against Discrimination.

Office: 2001 S.W. 117th Avenue, Miami 33175-1716.
Telephone: (305) 229-3200.
Fax: (305) 229-3206

GOLD, Alan S. *(Judge, United States District Court Southern District of Florida)* Appointed for life by President Bill Clinton to term beginning July 1997. Educated at University of Florida B.A. with high honors 1966, Duke University School of Law J.D. 1969 and University of Miami School of Law LL.M. in Taxation 1974. Law Clerk to Chief Judge Charles Carroll, Florida District Court of Appeal District Three 1969-71. In legal practice 1975-92. Judge, Florida Circuit Court Eleventh Judicial Circuit 1992 to July 1997, appointed by Governor Lawton Chiles.

Assistant Attorney Dade County 1971-75. Adjunct Professor of Environmental, Land Use and Administrative Law University of Miami. Former Executive Council Environmental and Land Use Section The Florida Bar. Member American College of Real Estate Lawyers. Lecturer The Florida Bar and national planning associations. Listed in *The Best Lawyers in America* 1989-90 and 1991-92, *Who's Who in America* and *Who's Who in American Law* seventh ed. 1992-93. Named Distinguished Scholar/Lecturer by Journal of Environmental and Land Use Law Florida State University College of Law.

Office: Federal Courthouse Square, 10th Floor, 301 North Miami Avenue, Miami 33128.
Telephone: (305) 523-5580.

GOLD, Marc H. *(Judge, Florida Circuit Court Seventeenth Judicial Circuit)* Elected Sept 1996 to term beginning Jan 7, 1997. Reelected 2002, current term expires Jan 2009. Born Detroit Michigan May 5, 1947. Educated at Wayne State University B.S. 1969 Ph.D. 1976 and Nova University J.D. 1981. Law Clerk to Chief Judge Burton R. Lifland, U.S. Bankruptcy Court Southern District of New York 1982-83. Admitted to practice Florida 1982, U.S. District Courts Middle 1982, Northern 1982 and Southern 1982 Districts of Florida, New York 1984 and U.S. Court of Appeals Eleventh Circuit 1985. In legal practice 1983-96.

Instructor Nova University Center for the Study of Law 1983.

Office: 6910 Broward County Courthouse, 201 S.E. Sixth Street, Fort Lauderdale 33301.
Telephone: (954) 831-7807.
Fax: (954) 831-5572

GOLDENBERG, Renee *(Judge, Florida Circuit Court Seventeenth Judicial Circuit)*

Office: 742 Broward County Courthouse, 201 S.E. Sixth Street, Fort Lauderdale 33301.
Telephone: (954) 831-7395.

GOLDMAN, Judith M. *(Judge, Sarasota County Court)* Assumed office Jan 3, 1989. Elected to subsequent terms.

Mailing address: P.O. Box 48927, Sarasota 34230.
Office: 2002 Ringling Boulevard, Sarasota 34237.
Telephone: (941) 861-7962.
Fax: (941) 861-7916

GOLDMAN, Murray *(Senior Judge, Florida Circuit Court Eleventh Judicial Circuit)* Assumed Senior Judge status, serves by assignment.

Office: 511 Dade County Courthouse, 73 West Flagler Street, Miami 33130.
Telephone: (305) 349-7001.

GOLDSTEIN, Barry E. *(Judge, Florida Circuit Court Seventeenth Judicial Circuit)* Elected Nov 6, 1990 to term beginning Jan 8, 1991. Reelected 1996 and 2002. Current term expires Jan 2009.

Office: 1005B Broward County Courthouse, 201 S.E. Sixth Street, Fort Lauderdale 33301.
Telephone: (954) 831-7755.
Fax: (954) 831-5533

GOMEZ, Frank A. *(Judge, Florida Circuit Court Thirteenth Judicial Circuit)* Former Judge, Hillsborough County Court, elected to term beginning Jan 3, 1995.

Office: Office 429, 801 East Twiggs Street, Tampa 33602.
Telephone: (813) 307-4750.
Fax: (813) 276-2079

GONZALEZ, Jose A., Jr. *(Senior Judge, United States District Court Southern District of Florida)* Appointed for life by President Jimmy Carter to term beginning July 28, 1978. Assumed Senior status, serves by assignment. Born Tampa Florida Nov 26, 1931. Methodist. Educated at University of Florida B.A. 1952 J.D. 1957. Honorary LL.D. Nova Southeastern University 1998. Member Florida Blue Key, Hall of Fame, Phi Alpha Delta and Phi Eta Sigma. Admitted to practice Florida 1958, U.S. District Court Southern District of Florida 1959, U.S. Courts of Appeals Fifth 1959 and Eleventh 1982 Circuits and U.S. Supreme Court 1963. In legal practice Fort Lauderdale 1958-64. Judge 1964-78 and Chief Judge 1969-70, Florida Circuit Court Seventeenth Judicial Circuit.

Assistant State Attorney Fifteenth Judicial Circuit 1961-64. Author "Jury Instructions" Florida Civil Trial Practice Second Edition The Florida Bar 1970. Important Decisions: Skywalker Records, Inc. v. Navarro 739 F. Supp. 578 S.D. Fla. 1990 and James Stanley v. United States 574 F. Supp. 474 S.D. Fla. 1983. Member American Judicature Society, The Florida Bar, Broward County and American Bar Associations. Attended National College of the State Judiciary 1977 and Program of Instruction for Lawyers Harvard Law School 1983 and

GONZALEZ, JOSE A., JR.—*Continued*

1989. Named one of Florida's Five Outstanding Young Men by Florida Jaycees 1967, one of Five Outstanding Young Men Broward County by Hollywood Jaycees 1967 and Broward Legal Executive of the Year 1978. Recipient Theodore R. Kupferman Award from Laymen's National Bible Association 1990. First Lieutenant U.S. Army 1952-54. Claims Representative State Farm Insurance 1957-58. Democrat. Former member Young Democratic Club of Broward County. Past President Fort Lauderdale-Southside Kiwanis Club. Past Director Broward Chapter Arthritis Foundation of America. Former Vice President Henderson Clinic. Director Fort Lauderdale Jaycees. Member Florida Alumni Association, Fort Lauderdale Touchdown Club, Fort Lauderdale Yacht Club and Pittsfield Country Club. Avid football fan (formerly published a weekly Gator football newsletter each fall). Enjoys music (Mozart and opera).

Office: 205D U.S. Courthouse, 299 East Broward Boulevard, Fort Lauderdale 33301.

Telephone: (954) 769-5560.

GONZALEZ, Roland *(Senior Judge, Florida Circuit Court Thirteenth Judicial Circuit)* Assumed Senior Judge status, serves by assignment. Born Tampa Florida Jan 23, 1929. Baptist. Educated at University of Florida B.S.B.A. 1951 LL.B. with honors 1953. Admitted to practice Florida 1953 and U.S. District Court Southern District of Florida 1953. Began legal practice Tampa 1953. Judge, Hillsborough County Court 1978-83.

Assistant County Attorney Hillsborough County 1973-77. Captain USAF 1954-56 and USAFR 1956-65.

Office: Hillsborough County Courthouse, 419 Pierce Street, Tampa 33602-4022.

Telephone: (813) 272-5894.

GOODFRIEND, Sam *(Senior Judge, Florida Circuit Court Fourth Judicial Circuit)* Assumed Senior Judge status, serves by assignment.

Office: Duval County Courthouse, 330 East Bay Street, Jacksonville 32202.

Telephone: (904) 630-1693.

GOODING, David M. *(Judge, Florida Circuit Court Fourth Judicial District)*

Office: Duval County Courthouse, 330 East Bay Street, Jacksonville 32202.

Telephone: (904) 630-2322.

GOODMAN, Marci L. *(Judge, Florida Circuit Court First Judicial Circuit)*

Office: Santa Rosa County Courthouse, Box K, 6865 S.W. Caroline Street, Milton 32570.

Telephone: (850) 623-0135.

Fax: (850) 626-4268

GORDON, Jon I. *(Judge, Florida Circuit Court Eleventh Judicial Circuit)* Appointed by Governor Reubin O'Donovan Askew Nov 1, 1977. Elected to subsequent terms. Educated at Vanderbilt University B.A. 1967 and University of Florida J.D. with honors 1970. Staff member University of Florida Law Review. Member Phi Kappa Phi and Order of the Coif. Admitted to practice Florida, U.S. District Court Southern District of Florida, U.S. Court of Appeals Fifth Circuit and U.S. Supreme Court.

Author Note "Aircraft Hijacking: Civil and Criminal Aspects" 22 University of Florida L. Rev. 72, 1969. Coauthor with B. Young "Creative Lawyering: Remedies for Custodial Abuses and Willful Breaches of Matrimonial Judgments" Part One LXVI No. 3 March 1992 and Part Two LXVI No. 4 April 1992 The Florida Bar. Instructor in Trial Practice Legal Assistant Program Miami-Dade Community College Fall Quarter 1975. Former Instructor Cuban-American Program University of Florida. Former Member Grievance Committee "C" Eleventh Judicial Circuit. Member Dade County Bar Association (Speaker Chairman Naturalization Committee). Former Member Board of Directors Miami Jewish Home and Hospital for the Aged. Former Member Dade County Water and Sewer Board.

Office: 400 Dade County Courthouse, 73 West Flagler Street, Miami 33130.

Telephone: (305) 349-7078.

GRAHAM, Donald L. *(Judge, United States District Court Southern District of Florida)* Appointed for life by President George Bush Oct 4, 1991. Born Salisbury North Carolina Dec 15, 1948. Educated at West Virginia State College B.A. magna cum laude 1971 and The Ohio State University College of Law J.D. 1974. Recipient Moot Court Best Oralist Award and Judge Harter Memorial Hooding Award as Outstanding Trial Practice Student. Member Alpha Kappa Mu. Admitted to practice Ohio 1974, Florida 1980, New York 1985, U.S. Court of International Trade, U.S Court of Appeals for the Armed Forces and U.S. Supreme Court. In legal practice Miami Florida 1984-91.

Assistant U.S. Attorney Southern District of Florida 1979-84 (Chief Special Prosecutions, Chief Major Narcotics Traffickers Section, Chief Intake Unit, Special Assignment Miami Strike Force Organized Crime and Racketeering Section U.S. Department of Justice). Adjunct Instructor in Business Law University of Maryland 1975-77. Member Grievance Committee 1988-91 and Chairman 11-I 1991 The Florida Bar. U.S. Advisory Board on the Investigative Capacity of the Department of Defense 1994. Former Member National Association of Criminal Defense Lawyers, Inc. (Chairman Military Law Committee 1991). Member Black Lawyers Association (Miami), Council of Florida Bar Presidents, The Association of Trial Lawyers of America, Dade County, National, Federal (President 1985 and Executive Board 1985-91 South Florida Chapter) and American Bar Associations. Recipient Arthur S. Fleming Award presented to One of Ten Outstanding Young Men and Women in Federal Service 1981, Certificate of Merit from Dade County Bar Association 1989, Special Achievement Award from U.S. Department of Justice, Award for Exceptional Service as a Member of the Advisory Board on the Investigative Capacity from U.S. Department of Defense and JURIS Award for Judicial Efficiency. U.S. Army JAGC 1974-79. Lieutenant Colonel USAR. Recipient Commendation Medal with five oak leaf clusters and Achievement Medal.

Office: Federal Justice Building, 99 N.E. Fourth Street, Miami 33132.

Telephone: (305) 523-5130.

GRAHAM, Richard S. *(Judge, Florida Circuit Court Seventh Judicial Circuit)*

Office: Volusia County Courthouse, 125 East Orange Avenue, Daytona Beach 32114.

Telephone: (386) 257-6071.

Fax: (386) 248-8132

GRAHAM, Wendell M. *(Judge, Dade County Court)* Office: 1-5 Coral Gables Branch Court, 3100 Ponce De Leon Boulevard, Coral Gables 33134.
Telephone: (305) 569-2518.
Fax: (305) 569-2558

GREEN, David Walker *(Judge, Walton County Court)*
Office: Walton County Courthouse, 571 Highway 90 East, Defuniak Springs 32433.
Telephone: (850) 892-8131.
Fax: (850) 892-8377

GREEN, Mary Catherine *(Judge, Polk County Court)*
Mailing address: P.O. Box 9000, J-131, Bartow 33831-9000.
Telephone: (863) 534-4667.
Fax: (863) 534-7783

GREEN, Melvia B. *(Judge, Florida District Court of Appeal Third District)* Assumed office April 13, 1994. Retained by election. Born Miami Florida Nov 13, 1953. Baptist. Educated at Northwestern University B.S. with honors 1975 and University of Miami J.D. 1978. Admitted to practice Florida 1979 and U.S. District Courts Middle 1979 and Southern 1980 Districts of Florida. In legal practice Miami 1983-87. Judge, Dade County Court 1987-89. Former Judge, Florida Circuit Court Eleventh Judicial Circuit, appointed by Governor Bob Martinez to term beginning Oct 1989.
Member Qualifications Committee Florida Parole Commission since 1990. Member Florida Association of Women Lawyers, American Judges Association, Dade County and National (Women Lawyers Division) Bar Associations. Attended The National Judicial College and Florida Judicial College. Recipient Achievement Award from South Florida Chapter National Federation of Business and Professional Women 1989. Named Government Role Model of the Year by South Florida Transplant Foundation 1990. Volunteer Dade County public schools. Judge Miami Herald Silver Knights Award. Enjoys reading and travel.
Office: 2001 S.W. 117th Avenue, Miami 33175-1716.
Telephone: (305) 229-3200.
Fax: (305) 229-3206

GREEN, Oliver L., Jr. *(Senior Judge, Florida District Court of Appeal)* Assumed Senior Judge status, serves by assignment. Born South Carolina Nov 19, 1932. Episcopalian. Educated at University of Alabama B.S. 1957 and Stetson University J.D. 1958. Admitted to practice Florida 1958. Began legal practice Lakeland 1958. Judge, Lakeland Municipal Court 1970-71. Judge, Polk County Magistrate Court 1971-72. Former Judge and Chief Judge, Florida Circuit Court Tenth Judicial Circuit, elected to term beginning Jan 2, 1973.
Office: 1005 East Memorial Boulevard, Lakeland 33801-2019.
Telephone: (863) 499-2290.

GREEN, R. A., Jr. *(Senior Judge, Florida Circuit Court Eighth Judicial Circuit)* Assumed Senior Judge status, serves by assignment.
Office: Alachua County Courthouse, 201 East University Avenue, Gainesville 32601.
Telephone: (352) 374-3648.

GREENE, Charles M. *(Judge, Florida Circuit Court Seventeenth Judicial Circuit)* Elected to term beginning Jan 1991. Reelected 1996 and 2002. Current term expires Jan 2009. Formerly served Criminal and Family Divisions. Currently serves Civil Division. Educated at Union College B.A. and Nova Southeastern University J.D.
Assistant State Attorney Seventeenth Judicial Circuit. Member The Florida Bar and New York State Bar Association.
Office: Broward County Courthouse, 201 S.E. Sixth Street, Fort Lauderdale 33301.
Telephone: (954) 831-7700.

GREER, George W. *(Judge, Florida Circuit Court Sixth Judicial Circuit)*
Office: 484 Pinellas County Courthouse, 315 Court Street, Clearwater 33756.
Telephone: (727) 464-3933.
Fax: (727) 464-5471

GRIDLEY, William C. *(Judge, Florida Circuit Court Ninth Judicial Circuit)* Elected to term beginning Jan 1, 1973. Reelected 1978, 1984, 1990, 1996 and 2002. Current term expires Jan 2009. Former Chief Judge. Born Orlando Florida Nov 26, 1941. Episcopalian. Educated at University of Florida B.A. 1963 J.D. 1965. Member Phi Delta Phi. Admitted to practice Florida 1966. Began legal practice Orlando 1966. Judge, Orange County Juvenile Court 1972, appointed by Governor Reubin Askew.
Author "On Making Right Decisions" Christian Legal Society 1976 and "Jurisdiction, Venue and Service of Process in Modification Proceedings" Chapter 5 *Support, Custody and Marital Property in Florida* The Florida Bar 1978. Member The Florida Bar and American Bar Association. Enjoys tennis and chess.
Office: 1710 Orange County Courthouse, 425 North Orange Avenue, Orlando 32801.
Telephone: (407) 836-2014.
Fax: (407) 836-0452

GRIESBAUM, John M. *(Judge, Florida Circuit Court Eighteenth Judicial Circuit)*
Office: Moore Justice Center, Third Floor, 2825 Judge Fran Jamieson Way, Viera 32940-8006.
Telephone: (321) 617-7289.

GRIFFIN, Jacqueline R. *(Judge, Florida District Court of Appeal Fifth District)* Appointed by Governor Bob Martinez to term beginning Nov 14, 1989. Retained by election. Chief Judge 1997-99. Born Chelsea Massachusetts Dec 15, 1946. Educated at University of North Carolina at Greensboro B.A. 1968 and University of Florida M.A.T. 1970 J.D. with high honors 1975. Named Outstanding Senior Law Student 1975. Editor-in-Chief University of Florida Law Review 1975. Member Phi Kappa Phi and Order of the Coif. Admitted to practice Florida 1975. In legal practice Orlando 1975-90.
Committee Chair Florida Conference of District Court of Appeal Judges since 1991. Master of the Bench American Inns of Court 1992-93. Fellow American Bar Foundation since 1993. Chair State Courts' Civil Litigation Task Force 1997. Member Judicial Management Council since 1999. Member The American Law Institute, The Florida Bar, U.S. Supreme Court Bar, Orange County and American Bar Associations. Graduate New York University Program for Intermediate Appellate Judges 1990. Faculty Member Advanced Judicial College and Florida Judicial College since 1992. Organizer and Interim Dean Appellate Judicial College 1994. Board of

GRIFFIN, JACQUELINE R.—*Continued*

Directors Kathleen Anderson Work Opportunity Center Seminole County 1983-86 and RESPOND (Orlando Rape Crisis Center) 1988. Member University of Florida Law Center Council 1985-88. Volunteer Orange County Guardian Ad Litem Program 1989 and West Volusia Humane Society. Judge Moot Court/Trial Competition since 1990.

Office: 300 South Beach Street, Daytona Beach 32114.

Telephone: (386) 947-1583.

Fax: (386) 947-1563

GRIMES, Hubert L. *(Judge, Florida Circuit Court Seventh Judicial Circuit)* Appointed by Governor Jeb Bush to term beginning Jan 2000. Elected Nov 2002, current term expires Jan 2009. Currently serves Family Court Division. Born Bartow Florida Dec 17, 1953. Religious affiliation: African Methodist Episcopalian. Educated at Kentucky State University B.S. with honors 1975 and University of Georgia J.D. 1980. Member Sigma Pi Phi and Alpha Phi Alpha. Admitted to practice Georgia 1980, Florida 1981 and U.S. District Court Middle District of Florida 1981. In legal practice Daytona Beach Florida 1985-88. Judge, Volusia County Court 1988-99.

Staff Attorney Central Florida Legal Services 1980-83. Adjunct Instructor in Criminal Law Bethune-Cookman College 1981-84 and in Business Law University of Central Florida 1985. Co-chair County Court Caseload Management 1992, Member Court Technology Committee since 1995 and Chairman County/Circuit Court Liaison Committee Seventh Judicial Circuit. President Elect 1994-96 and President 1996-98 Florida Conference of County Court Judges. Member DUI Programs Review Board 1994-98, Commission on Professionalism 1998-2001 and Family Court Steering Committee 1998-2000 Florida Supreme Court. President Virgil Hawkins Chapter The National Judicial Council since 2002. Member National Bar Association. Faculty Member Dealing with Pro Se Litigants 1991, 1992 and 1995, Landlord-Tenant Update for New Judges 1992-98, Racial, Gender and Ethnic Bias in the Court System 1993, Ethical Considerations for Judicial Assistants 1994, Juveniles in Traffic Court 1995, Juvenile Dispositions 2002 and Juvenile Delinquency 2002 Florida Judicial College and Traffic Court 1995-2000, Domestic Violence 1995-2000 and Courts and the Media 1996 The National Judicial College. Attended Florida Judicial College, Florida College of Advanced Judicial Studies Institute and The National Judicial College. Founder and Executive Director Central Florida Community Development Corporation 1983-88. Board of Counselors Bethune-Cookman College. Member Allen Chapel A.M.E. Church (Men's Sunday School Teacher, Men's Ministry), Calvary Christian Center of Ormond Beach and Richard V. Moore Community Center. Enjoys reading and traveling.

Office: 101 North Alabama Avenue, Suite D432, Deland 32724.

Telephone: (386) 822-5744.

Fax: (386) 740-5128

GRINCEWICZ, Donald E. *(Judge, Florida Circuit Court Ninth Judicial Circuit)* Former Judge, Orange County Court, appointed by Governor Lawton Chiles April 14, 1994.

Office: 1130 Orange County Courthouse, 425 North Orange Avenue, Orlando 32801.

Telephone: (407) 836-0560.

GROSS, Maynard "Skip" *(Judge, Florida Circuit Court Eleventh Judicial Circuit)* Elected Nov 1994 to term beginning Jan 1, 1995. Reelected 2000, current term expires Jan 2007. Born Queens New York. Educated at Georgetown University A.B. and University of Miami J.D. with honors 1967. Member Phi Alpha Delta (President 1965-66). Admitted to practice Florida 1967, U.S. District Courts Middle 1985 and Southern Districts of Florida, Trial Bar of U.S. District Court Southern District of Florida and U.S. Courts of Appeals Eleventh 1981 and Fifth Circuits. In legal practice Miami 1967-94.

Assistant State Attorney Florida 1967-69. Assistant Public Defender Dade County 1969-71. Member First Family Inns of Court, Eugene P. Spellman American Inn of Court, American Judges Association, Cuban American, South Miami-Kendall, Miami Beach and Dade County Bar Associations. Recipient Certificate of Meritorious Service from City of Hialeah Gardens 1989, Pro Bono Service Award from Dade County Bar Association 1994, Pro Bono Service Award from South Miami-Kendall Bar Association 1994 and Outstanding Membership Recognition Award from Academy of Florida Trial Lawyers. Named Jurist of the Year 2000-2001 by First Family Law Inns of Court. Member Concerned Citizens of Northeast Dade and Northeast Dade Coalition. Enjoys playing golf and fishing.

Office: 1925 Courthouse Center, 175 N.W. First Avenue, Miami 33128.

Telephone: (305) 349-5680.

GROSS, Raymond O. *(Judge, Florida Circuit Court Sixth Judicial Circuit)* Appointed by Governor Lawton Chiles April 6, 1994.

Office: 473 Pinellas County Courthouse, 315 Court Street, Clearwater 33756.

Telephone: (727) 464-3239.

Fax: (727) 464-3082

GROSS, Robert M. *(Judge, Florida District Court of Appeal Fourth District)* Born Washington D.C. Dec 4, 1951. Educated at Williams College B.A. magna cum laude 1973 and Cornell University J.D. 1976. Admitted to practice Florida 1976, New York 1977 and District of Columbia 1977. Began legal practice New York City 1976. In legal practice West Palm Beach Florida 1977. Judge, Palm Beach County Court Dec 1984 to March 1991, appointed by Governor Bob Graham. Judge, Florida Circuit Court Fifteenth Judicial Circuit March 1991 to Nov 1995, appointed by Governor Lawton Chiles.

Assistant District Attorney New York County 1976-77. Assistant State Attorney Palm Beach County 1977-81. Member Palm Beach County and American Bar Associations.

Mailing address: P.O. Box 3315, West Palm Beach 33402-3315.

Office: 1525 Palm Beach Lakes Boulevard, West Palm Beach 33401.

Telephone: (561) 242-2068.

Fax: (561) 242-2100

GROSSMAN, Mel *(Judge, Florida Circuit Court Seventeenth Judicial Circuit)*
Office: 790 Broward County Courthouse, 201 S.E. Sixth Street, Fort Lauderdale 33301.
Telephone: (954) 831-7759.
Fax: (954) 831-5572

GROVER, Kevin *(Judge, Calhoun County Court)*
Office: 117 Calhoun County Courthouse, 20859 East Central Avenue, Blountstown 32424.
Telephone: (850) 674-5061.
Fax: (850) 674-9791

GRUBE, Karl B. *(Judge, Pinellas County Court)* Elected 1976 to term beginning Jan 3, 1977. Reelected 1980, 1984, 1988, 1992, 1996 and 2000. Current term expires Jan 2007. Born Elmhurst Illinois Jan 13, 1946. Protestant. Educated at Elmhurst College B.S.B.A. 1967, Stetson University J.D. 1970 and University of Nevada Reno Master of Judicial Studies 1992. Admitted to practice Florida 1970 and Colorado 1993. In legal practice St. Petersburg Florida 1973-75 and Seminole Florida 1975-77.

Assistant Public Defender Sixth Judicial Circuit 1970-73 (Senior Assistant Pasco County 1972). City Attorney Redington Beach 1975-77. Author "The Intoxicated Confessor" 4 No. 3 Criminal Law Section Newsletter The Florida Bar May 1980; "Radar Speed Measurement: The Controversy Continues" 54 No. 6 The Florida B. Jour. June 1980; "Traffic Restitution Program Gets Green Light From Victims and Offenders" 6 No. 2 *State Court Journal* National Center for State Courts Spring 1982; Pamphlet "Collecting the Judgment" Pinellas County Court System 1983; "Search and Seizure of Automobiles: Their Occupants and Contents," "Problems Related to Plea Taking in Traffic Court Criminal Cases," "The Feasibility of Collectively Arraigning Criminal Defendants in Traffic Court," "Using Alternative Means to Collect Fines and Costs: One Traffic Court Judge's Approach" and "When the Fine Isn't Paid" The National Judicial College; Chapter 3 "Civil Traffic Infractions" *DUI and Other Traffic Offenses in Florida* The Florida Bar Oct 1986; and "1986 Legislature Gives Green Light to Changes in Florida's Motor Vehicle Laws" *Res Ipsa Loquitur* Clearwater Bar Association Sept 1986. Important Opinion: Terranova v. State of Florida 474 So. 2d 1206 Fla. Dist. Ct. App. 1985. Guest Lecturer 1976-86 and Moot Court Competition Judge 1981-83 Stetson University College of Law. Guest Lecturer Pinellas County Police Academy.

Member Committee on Standards of Conduct Governing Judges since 1983, Traffic Court Review Committee since 1983 and Education Council since 1983 Florida Supreme Court. Member Florida Judicial Council (formerly Florida Court Efficiency Council), Florida Conference of County Court Judges (District Representative 1980, Vice President 1981, Chairman Audit Committee 1981 and Education Committee 1983-84, President Elect 1984, President 1985-86), American Judges Association (Committee on Highway Safety since 1984), The Florida Bar (Vice Chairman Traffic Rules Committee 1984-86, member Rules of Judicial Administration Committee since 1985), Clearwater and American (Delegate National Conference of Special Court Judges 1984-85, Member Committee on Judicial Compensation, Chairperson Committee on Education 1986-87, Chair Annual Meeting Program Committee 1993-94 and Liaison to Section of Family Law 1995 Judicial Administration Division) Bar Associations. Attended courses "Constitutional Criminal Procedure Evidence" and "Traffic Court Law and Procedure" American Academy of Judicial Education and "Criminal Defense Law" Northwestern University College of Law 1971. Faculty Advisor since 1981, Faculty Council since 1997 and Participant "Special Court Jurisdiction," "Sentencing Misdemeanants," "Traffic Court Specialty Course," "Criminal Law," "Evidence" and "Judicial Writing in Trial Courts" The National Judicial College. Faculty Member Traffic Adjudication Seminars Florida Courts Continuing Education since 1982. Seminar Coordinator and Faculty Member CLE Programs on Florida DUI Law Clearwater Bar Association 1983-84. Board member and Special Counsel Society for Prevention of Cruelty to Animals 1975-76. Member St. Petersburg Citizens Council on Crime Prevention since 1975. Citizens Advisory Board Largo Correctional Facility since 1978. Board member Pinellas Comprehensive Alcohol Services since 1983. Enjoys photography, swimming and collecting special interest automobiles.
Office: 501 First Avenue North, Room A212, St. Petersburg 33701.
Telephone: (727) 582-7880.
Fax: (727) 582-7209

GUNTHER, Bobby W. *(Judge, Florida District Court of Appeal Fourth District)* Assumed office 1986. Retained by election. Current term expires Jan 2007. Chief Judge 1995-97. Educated at University of Florida B.A. 1963 J.D. 1965. In legal practice 1966-73. Judge, Broward County Court 1973-81. Judge, Florida Circuit Court Seventeenth Judicial Circuit 1981-86.

Member 1977-86 and Secretary 1982 Broward Commission on the Status of Women. Member The Florida Bar and Broward County Bar Association. Member Governor's Task Force on Criminal Justice System Reform 1980-82.
Mailing address: P.O. Box 3315, West Palm Beach 33402-3315.
Office: 1525 Palm Beach Lakes Boulevard, West Palm Beach 33401.
Telephone: (561) 242-7229.
Fax: (561) 242-2100

GURROLA, Barbara *(Judge, Florida Circuit Court Fifth Judicial Circuit)*
Office: Citrus County Courthouse, 110 North Apopka Avenue, Inverness 34450.
Telephone: (352) 341-6709.
Fax: (352) 341-6738

HADDOCK, Lawrence Page *(Judge, Florida Circuit Court Fourth Judicial Circuit)* Born Jacksonville Florida Nov 1, 1945. Methodist. Educated at Harvard University in History 1967 and University of Florida J.D. 1970. Began legal practice Jacksonville 1970. Former Judge, Duval County Court, assumed office Oct 7, 1974.
Office: Duval County Courthouse, 330 East Bay Street, Jacksonville 32202.
Telephone: (904) 630-2526.
Fax: (904) 630-2979

HAFELE, Donald *(Judge, Palm Beach County Court)*
Office: Palm Beach County Courthouse, 205 North Dixie Highway, West Palm Beach 33401.
Telephone: (561) 355-2439.

HAGUE, Andrew S. *(Judge, Dade County Court)*
Office: 510 Gerstein Justice Building, 1351 N.W. 12th Street, Miami 33125.
Telephone: (305) 548-5185.
Fax: (305) 545-3534

HAIR, Mattox S. *(Senior Judge, Florida Circuit Court Fourth Judicial Circuit)* Assumed Senior Judge status, serves by assignment.
Office: Duval County Courthouse, 330 East Bay Street, Jacksonville 32202.
Telephone: (904) 630-1693.

HALKER, Janis *(Judge, Orange County Court)*
Office: 820 Orange County Courthouse, 425 North Orange Avenue, Orlando 32801.
Telephone: (407) 836-2034.

HALL, Don T. *(Judge, DeSoto County Court)* Elected Sept 5, 1994 to term beginning Jan 1, 1995. Re-elected 1998, current term expires Jan 2005. Born Miami Florida Sept 4, 1955. Methodist. Educated at University of Miami B.B.A. 1983 and St. Thomas University M.B.A. J.D. 1990. Law Clerk to Chief Judge James Lawrence King, U.S. District Court Southern District of Florida 1990-91. Admitted to practice Florida 1990 and U.S. District Courts Middle and Southern Districts of Florida. In legal practice Miami, Sarasota and Arcadia.
Mailing address: P.O. Box 590, Arcadia 34265.
Office: 115 Oak Street, Arcadia 34266.
Telephone: (863) 993-4644.
Fax: (863) 494-5809

HALL, J. Lewis, Jr. *(Senior Judge, Florida Circuit Court Second Judicial Circuit)* Former Chief Judge. Assumed Senior Judge status, serves by assignment.
Office: Leon County Courthouse, 301 South Monroe Street, Tallahassee 32301.
Telephone: (850) 577-4420.

HALL, Vincent T. *(Senior Judge, Florida District Court of Appeal)* Appointed by Governor Robert Graham to term beginning March 8, 1985. Retained by election Nov 1986 and Nov 1992. Assumed Senior Judge status, serves by assignment. Born Fort Lauderdale Florida Aug 2, 1932. Religious affiliation: First Christian Church. Educated at Duke University B.A. 1954 and University of Miami LL.B. 1958. Admitted to practice Florida 1958. In legal practice Miami 1958-64 and Arcadia 1964-69. Judge, DeSoto County Court 1969-75. Judge, Florida Circuit Court Twelfth Judicial Circuit 1975-85.
Member 1965-68 and Chairman 1967-68 DeSoto County Hospital Board. Member The Florida Bar. Attended Appellate Judges Seminar Lake Tahoe Nevada Aug 1986 and Portland Maine Sept 1988 American Bar Association. First Lieutenant USAF 1955-57.
Office: 1005 East Memorial Boulevard, Lakeland 33801.
Telephone: (863) 499-2290.

HALL, Wallace Haile *(Senior Judge, Florida Circuit Court Eighteenth Judicial Circuit)* Elected to term beginning Jan 1993. Assumed Senior Judge status, serves by assignment. Born Okahumpka Florida Jan 18, 1937. Educated at Carson-Newman College B.A. 1958 and University of Florida J.D. 1965. Admitted to practice Florida 1966. Judge, Seminole County Court May 1968 to Jan 1993.
Commander USNR 1959-63 (retired). Member Markham Woods Presbyterian Church.
Office: Moore Justice Center, 2825 Judge Fran Jamieson Way, Viera 32940-8006.
Telephone: (321) 637-5555.

HAMMOND, Kim C. *(Judge, Florida Circuit Court Seventh Judicial Circuit)* Former Chief Judge.
Mailing address: P.O. Box 896, Bunnell 32110.
Office: Flagler County Courthouse, Bunnell 32110.
Telephone: (386) 437-7402.
Fax: (386) 437-7403

HAMRICK, H. Pope, Jr. *(Judge, Volusia County Court)* Assumed office Jan 3, 1989. Elected to subsequent terms.
Office: Courthouse Annex, 125 East Orange Avenue, Daytona Beach 32114.
Telephone: (386) 257-6060.

HANKINSON, James C. *(Judge, Florida Circuit Court Second Judicial Circuit)*
Office: 365-F Leon County Courthouse, 301 South Monroe Street, Tallahassee 32301.
Telephone: (850) 577-4320.
Fax: (850) 922-0327

HANSEL, Helen S. *(Senior Judge, Florida Circuit Court Sixth Judicial Circuit)* Assumed Senior Judge status, serves by assignment.
Office: Judicial Building, 545 First Avenue North, St. Petersburg 33701.
Telephone: (727) 464-4470.

HARDING, Major B. *(Senior Justice, Florida Supreme Court)* Appointed by Governor Lawton Chiles Jan 22, 1991. Retained by election 1992 and 1998. Chief Justice July 1998 to June 2000. Assumed Senior Justice status, serves by assignment. Born Charlotte North Carolina Oct 13, 1935. Episcopalian. Educated at Wake Forest University B.S. 1957 LL.B. 1959 and University of Virginia School of Law LL.M. in Judicial Process 1995. Honorary LL.D. Stetson University 1991 and Florida Coastal School of Law 1999. Member Phi Delta Phi, Sigma Chi and Scabbard & Blade Honorary Military Fraternity. Admitted to practice North Carolina 1959 and Florida 1960. Began legal practice 1964. Judge, Juvenile Court 1968-70. Judge, Florida Circuit Court Fourth Judicial Circuit 1970-91.
Assistant County Solicitor Duval County Criminal Court of Record 1962-63. President Tallahassee American Inn of Court 1997-98. Founding Member Chester Bedell Inn of Court. Ex-officio Board Member American Inns of Court. Member Matrimonial Law Commission, Gender Bias Study Commission, Bench Bar Commission, Florida Court Education Council (Chair since 1996), Judicial Council and Committee on Law Related Education Florida Supreme Court (Chair), The Florida Bar, The North Carolina State Bar and American Bar Association (Member Admission Committee). Attended Juvenile Judges College 1969 and National College of State Trial Judges 1971. Dean 1984-92 and Faculty Member since 1984 Florida New Judges College. Dean Florida Judicial College since 1984. Chairman elect Florida Conference of Circuit Judges. Nominated Outstanding Circuit Judge by Young Lawyers Section Jacksonville Bar Association 1980. Recipient American Academy of Matrimonial Lawyers Award 1986, Significant Sig Award from Sigma Chi 1997, Justice Harry Lee An-

HARDING, MAJOR B.—*Continued*

stead Professionalism Award from Dade County Trial Lawyers Association Sept 1998, Jurist of the Year Award from Jacksonville Chapter American Board of Trial Advocates 2000, Distinguished Service Award from National Center for State Courts 2001, Jurist of the Year Award from American Board of Trial Advocates in Florida 2001, William A. Dugger Professional Integrity Award from Capital Rotary Club and Judicial Recognition Award from Commission on Lawyer Assistance Program American Bar Association. First Lieutenant U.S. Army JAGC 1960-62. Attended Judge Advocate Generals School. President Tallahassee Rotary Club 1995-96. Past President Riverside Rotary Club. Board member Daniel Memorial (hospital for emotionally disturbed youth). Board of Visitors Wake Forest School of Law and Reformed Theological Seminary. Chairman United States Constitution Bicentennial Commission of Jacksonville. Member St. Johns Episcopal Church. Enjoys tennis.

Office: Supreme Court Building, 500 South Duval Street, Tallahassee 32399-1925.

HARE, Raymond J. *(Senior Judge, Florida Circuit Court Seventeenth Judicial Circuit)* Elected to term beginning Jan 1973. Reelected 1978 and 1984. Assumed Senior Judge status, serves by assignment. Born New York New York Sept 27, 1925. Catholic. Educated at Wagner College 1946-48 and University of Miami J.D. 1951. Admitted to practice Florida 1951. Began legal practice Fort Lauderdale 1951. Judge, Court of Record Broward County 1960-69.

Member The Florida Bar, Broward County and American Bar Associations. U.S. Army 1943-46.

Office: Broward County Courthouse, 201 S.E. Sixth Street, Fort Lauderdale 33301.

Telephone: (954) 831-7740.

HARLEY, Timothy D. *(Judge, Leon County Court)*

Office: 265-B Leon County Courthouse, 301 South Monroe Street, Tallahassee 32301.

Telephone: (850) 577-4316.

Fax: (850) 922-0070

HARNAGE, Henry Howell *(Judge, Florida Circuit Court Eleventh Judicial Circuit)*

Office: 2019 Courthouse Center, 175 N.W. First Avenue, Miami 33128.

Telephone: (305) 349-5726.

HARPER, David *(Judge, Martin County Court)*

Mailing address: P.O. Box 1410, Stuart 34995.

Telephone: (772) 288-5561.

HARRIS, Charles M. *(Senior Judge, Florida District Court of Appeal)* Assumed office Nov 15, 1989. Retained by election. Chief Judge 1993-95. Assumed Senior Judge status, serves by assignment. Educated at College of the Ozarks B.A. with honors and University of Florida J.D. In legal practice Titusville 1964-84. Judge, Florida Circuit Court Eighteenth Judicial Circuit 1984-89.

President Florida Conference of District Court of Appeal Judges 1995-96. Former Member Board of Directors Brevard County Bar Association. Former Director Central Florida Legal Services, Inc. Director and President North Brevard YMCA. Member Florida Theater Restoration Committee.

Office: 300 South Beach Street, Daytona Beach 32114.

Telephone: (386) 947-1500.

HARRIS, John M. *(Judge, Brevard County Court)*

Office: Titusville Courthouse, 506 South Palm Avenue, Titusville 32796.

Telephone: (321) 952-4702.

Fax: (321) 952-4704

HARRISON, Howard H., Jr. *(Senior Judge, Palm Beach County Court)* Assumed Senior Judge status, serves by assignment.

Office: Palm Beach County Courthouse, 205 North Dixie Highway, West Palm Beach 33401.

Telephone: (561) 355-2431.

HARRISON, James L. *(Senior Judge, Florida Circuit Court Fourth Judicial Circuit)* Assumed Senior Judge status, serves by assignment.

Office: Duval County Courthouse, 330 East Bay Street, Jacksonville 32202.

Telephone: (904) 630-1693.

HATCHER, Woodrow Wilson *(Judge, Jackson County Court)* Elected 1976 to term beginning Jan 4, 1977. Reelected 1980, 1984, 1988, 1992, 1996 and 2000. Current term expires Jan 2007. Born Florida March 26, 1943. Baptist. Educated at Florida State University B.S. 1964 and Troy State University M.S. 1972. Interested in athletics and youth recreational programs.

Mailing address: P.O. Drawer 957, Marianna 32447.

Office: 4445 Lafayette Street, Marianna 32446.

Telephone: (850) 482-9656.

Fax: (850) 482-9642

HAUSER, James Charles *(Judge, Florida Circuit Court Ninth Judicial Circuit)* Appointed by Governor Robert Graham to term beginning April 28, 1990. Elected 1990, 1996 and 2002. Current term expires Jan 2009. Born Niagara Falls New York Jan 21, 1948. Jewish. Educated at Wharton School of Finance and Commerce University of Pennsylvania B.A. 1970 and Boston University J.D. 1973. Admitted to practice Florida 1973. Began legal practice Orlando 1973. Judge, Orange County Court 1980-90, appointed by Governor Robert Graham.

Author "Florida Residential Landlord & Tenant" D&S Publishing 1983, "Is Refusal to Take a Breathalyzer Test Admissible?" 6 Nova L. Rev. 151 Spring 1983, "Direct Appeal from County Court to the District Court of Appeal" Florida B. Jour. April 1984 and "Texas Residential Landlord Tenant" 1986 and "Attorney's Fees in Florida" 1989 Butterworths. Important Decision: State v. Roche (breathalyzer case) 1 Fla. Supp. 2d 50, 1980. Instructor University of Central Florida since 1984. Member The Florida Bar. Instructor Florida Conference of County Court Judges 1982-84, Florida Judicial College 1983-84 and The National Judicial College. Lecturer Florida New Judges College since 1982. Named Jurist of the Year by the Young Lawyers Division of the Florida Bar. National Guard. Enjoys tennis, baseball, history, reading and classical music.

Office: 1730 Orange County Courthouse, 425 North Orange Avenue, Orlando 32801.

Telephone: (407) 836-2036.

Fax: (407) 836-0452

HAWKES, Paul *(Judge, Florida District Court of Appeal First District)*
Office: 301 Martin Luther King Jr. Boulevard, Tallahassee 32399-1850.
Telephone: (850) 488-3949.
Fax: (850) 488-7989

HAWKINS, Judith W. *(Judge, Leon County Court)* Elected Nov 1996 and 2000. Term expires Jan 1, 2007. Born Greensboro North Carolina Jan 29, 1951. Seventh-Day Adventist. Educated at Andrews University B.A. 1973, The Ohio State University M.S. 1977 and Florida State University J.D. 1984. Admitted to practice Florida 1985. Board Certified as a Specialist in Marital and Family Law by the Florida Bar 1995. In legal practice Tallahassee 1985-96.

Adjunct Professor Florida A. & M. University. Certified as a Specialist in Family Mediation by the Florida Supreme Court 1993. Member Trial Court Work Performance Standards Advisory Committee 1993-94, Grievance Committee Second Judicial Circuit The Florida Bar 1993-95, Family Courts Steering Committee Florida Supreme Court 1996-98 and Florida Courts Technology Commission 1999. Circuit Representative 1997 and Member Committee for Review and Notification of Criminal and Juvenile Legislation 2001 and President's Ad Hoc Committee on Community Service 2001 Florida Conference of County Court Judges. Member Tallahassee Women Lawyers (Board Member), Tallahassee Barristers (Treasurer 1987 and 1994-96), Tallahassee Section American Inns of Court, Southern Union Society of Adventist Attorneys, Legal Aid Foundation Board and Tallahassee Bar Association (Board Member 1993). Participant Justice Teaching Institute 1998-1999. Recipient Barristers' Outstanding Involvement Award 1987, Guardian Ad Litem Outstanding Attorney Award 1989-90, Parents Anonymous Volunteer Recognition Award 1990, Achievement Award from 100 Black Men of America, Inc. 1999, FAWL 50th Anniversary Golden Star Award 2001 and Award from Operation Reachback, Inc. 2001. Condominium Specialist Department of Business Regulation Florida 1980-84. Former Member Legal Services of North Florida (President 1992-93). Member Lincoln High School Partners for Excellence 1992-93, Executive Committee Southern Union of Seventh-Day Adventists 1992-96, Capital City Planning Commission 1993-96 and Florida High School Mock Trial Competition 1998-99. Board of Directors Adventist Health System Sunbelt and American Marine Institute. Member Marathana Seventh-Day Adventist Church and ZONTA. Enjoys traveling, quiet time, presenting seminars, mentoring, shopping, reading and anonymously helping others.
Office: 265-A Leon County Courthouse, 301 South Monroe Street, Tallahassee 32301.
Telephone: (850) 577-4317.
Fax: (850) 922-0070

HAWLEY, Robert A. *(Judge, Florida Circuit Court Nineteenth Judicial Circuit)* Elected to term beginning Jan 3, 1995. Reelected 2000, current term expires Jan 2007.
Office: 324 Courthouse Addition, 218 South Second Street, Fort Pierce 34950.
Telephone: (772) 462-1470.
Fax: (772) 462-1849

HAWORTH, Lee E. *(Judge, Florida Circuit Court Twelfth Judicial Circuit)*
Mailing address: P.O. Box 48927, Sarasota 34230.
Office: 2002 Ringling Boulevard, Sarasota 34237.
Telephone: (941) 861-7950.
Fax: (941) 861-7914

HAYES, Hugh D., Jr. *(Judge, Florida Circuit Court Twentieth Judicial Circuit)* Former Judge, Collier County Court.
Office: Collier County Government Complex, Bldg. L, 3301 Tamiami Trail East, Naples 34112.
Telephone: (239) 774-8116.
Fax: (239) 774-9654

HAYES, Leigh Frizzell *(Judge, Lee County Court)*
Office: Lee County Justice Center, 1700 Monroe Street, Fort Myers 33901.
Telephone: (239) 335-2338.
Fax: (239) 335-2587

HAZOURI, Frederick A. *(Judge, Florida District Court of Appeal Fourth District)* Assumed office 1998. Retained by election 2000, current term expires Jan 2007. Educated at University of Florida B.A. 1965 J.D. cum laude 1967. Law Clerk to Florida District Court of Appeal Fourth District 1967-68. In legal practice 1968-95. Judge, Florida Circuit Court Fifteenth Judicial Circuit 1995-98.

Diplomat American College of Trial Lawyers. Member Academy of Florida Trial Lawyers (President 1980-81), National Board of Trial Advocacy and The Florida Bar. Mentor Palm Beach County Schools.
Mailing address: P.O. Box 3315, West Palm Beach 33402-3315.
Office: 1525 Palm Beach Lakes Boulevard, West Palm Beach 33401.
Telephone: (561) 242-7218.
Fax: (561) 242-2100

HEALEY, Russell L. *(Judge, Duval County Court)*
Office: 324 Duval County Courthouse, 330 East Bay Street, Jacksonville 32202.
Telephone: (904) 630-2565.
Fax: (904) 630-2979

HEDSTROM, Edward *(Judge, Florida Circuit Court Seventh Judicial Circuit)*
Mailing address: P.O. Box 1317, Palatka 32178.
Telephone: (386) 329-0263.
Fax: (386) 329-0896

HEFLIN, Jack R. *(Judge, Florida Circuit Court First Judicial Circuit)*
Office: B121 Okaloosa County Courthouse Annex, 1250 North Eglin Parkway, Shalimar 32579.
Telephone: (850) 651-7478.
Fax: (850) 651-7725

HEINRICH, Walter R. *(Judge, Hillsborough County Court)* Elected Nov 1988. Reelected 1992, 1996 and 2000. Served Civil Division Jan 1989 to July 1989. Acting Circuit Judge Thirteenth Judicial Circuit since Jan 1989. Educated at University of South Florida B.A. and South Texas College of Law J.D.
Office: 123 Annex, 800 East Kennedy Boulevard, Tampa 33602-4146.
Telephone: (813) 272-5883.
Fax: (813) 276-2339

HENDERSON, Doug *(Judge, Manatee County Court)* Elected to term beginning Jan 3, 1995. Reelected 1998, current term expires Jan 2005.
Mailing address: P.O. Box 1000, Bradenton 34206.
Telephone: (941) 749-7135.
Fax: (941) 742-5964

HENDERSON, James C. *(Senior Judge, Florida Circuit Court Eleventh Judicial Circuit)* Assumed Senior Judge status, serves by assignment.
Office: 511 Dade County Courthouse, 73 West Flagler Street, Miami 33130.
Telephone: (305) 349-7001.

HENDERSON, Mary Jane Nettles *(Judge, Volusia County Court)* Elected Nov 1990 to term beginning Jan 1991. Reelected 1994 and 1998. Current term expires Jan 2005. Born Mobile Alabama Sept 28 1954. Methodist. Educated at University of Alabama B.S. 1976 and Cumberland School of Law J.D. 1980. Editorial Board American Journal of Trial Advocacy 1978-80. Admitted to practice Florida 1980 and Alabama 1980. In legal practice New Smyrna Beach 1981-90.
Member Rotary. Enjoys sailing.
Office: 124 Courthouse Annex, 124 Riverside Drive, New Smyrna Beach 32069.
Telephone: (386) 423-3313.
Fax: (386) 423-3313

HENDERSON, William W., Jr. *(Senior Judge, Escambia County Court)* Elected to term beginning Jan 3, 1973. Reelected 1976, 1980 and 1984. Former Administrative Judge. Assumed Senior Judge status 1988, serves by assignment. Born Bogalusa Louisiana March 12, 1918. Roman Catholic. Educated at University of North Carolina B.A. 1948 LL.B. 1950. Admitted to practice North Carolina 1950, U.S. Supreme Court 1955, U.S. Court of Military Appeals 1955, Florida 1959 and U.S. District Court 1960. Began legal practice at Lenoir North Carolina 1950. Judge, Small Claims Court Escambia County Florida 1969. Judge, Juvenile Division Court of Record Escambia County 1969-71.
Member Executive Committee National Conference of Special Court Judges 1974-77, Society of Bar of First Judicial Circuit (Executive Committee 1962), The Florida Bar and American Bar Association. Former Vice President, Director and President 1982-83 Florida Conference of County Court Judges. Recipient Escambia County Action '76 Bicentennial Award, Governmental Area. Lieutenant Colonel USAFR 1941-78. Director Crippled Children's Association. Vice President and Director Gulf Coast Council Boy Scouts of America.
Mailing address: Judicial Building, 190 Governmental Center, Pensacola 32501.
Telephone: (850) 595-4400.

HENDRY, William L. *(Senior Judge, Florida Circuit Court Nineteenth Judicial Circuit)* Former Chief Judge. Assumed Senior Judge status, serves by assignment.
Office: 218 South Second Street, Fort Pierce 34950.
Telephone: (772) 462-1472.

HENNING, Patti Englander *(Judge, Florida Circuit Court Seventeenth Judicial Circuit)* Elected 1984 to term beginning Jan 8, 1985. Reelected 1990, 1996 and 2002. Current term expires Jan 2009. Born Miami Beach Florida Nov 9, 1952. Jewish. Educated at Cornell University B.A. 1974 and University of Florida College of Law J.D. 1976. Admitted to practice Florida 1976 and U.S. Court of Appeals District of Columbia Circuit 1979. Began legal practice Tallahassee 1976. In legal practice Fort Lauderdale 1977. Judge, Broward County Court 1981-85.
Chief Appeals Division State Attorney's Office 1977-80. Assistant Attorney General State of Florida 1976-77. Member American Judges Association, National Association of Women Judges, Florida Conference of Circuit Court Judges, The Florida Bar, Broward County and American Bar Associations. Named one of Outstanding Young Women of America 1981 and Outstanding Young Leader by Florida Jaycees 1984. Recipient Woman of Achievement Award 1981. Listed in *Who's Who of Florida* 1982-83 and *Who's Who in the South and Southwest* 19th ed. Member B'nai B'rith Justice Unit.
Office: 996 Broward County Courthouse, 201 S.E. Sixth Street, Fort Lauderdale 33301.
Telephone: (954) 831-7787.

HENSLEY, Robert E. *(Senior Judge, Florida Circuit Court Twelfth Judicial Circuit)* Assumed Senior Judge status, serves by assignment.
Mailing address: P.O. Box 48927, Sarasota 34230.
Office: 2002 Ringling Boulevard, Sarasota 34237.
Telephone: (941) 861-7800.

HENSON, James E. *(Judge, Florida Circuit Court Ninth Judicial Circuit)*
Office: 2000 East Michigan, Orlando 32806.
Telephone: (407) 836-7590.

HERNANDEZ, Ivan *(Judge, Dade County Court)*
Office: 500 Gerstein Justice Building, 1351 N.W. Twelfth Street, Miami 33125.
Telephone: (305) 548-5237.

HERR, Mark Edward *(Judge, Seminole County Court)*
Office: Seminole County Courthouse, 301 North Park Avenue, Sanford 32771-1292.
Telephone: (407) 665-4110.

HERRING, Ronald A. *(Judge, Florida Circuit Court Tenth Judicial Circuit)* Elected Nov 8, 1994 to term beginning Jan 3, 1995. Reelected 2000, current term expires Jan 2007. Born Lakeland Florida Jan 27, 1944. Southern Baptist. Educated at Rollins College B.S. 1976 M.S.C. 1978 and University of South Carolina J.D. 1982. Staff member South Carolina Law Review 1981-82. Member Order of the Wig and Robe and Order of the Coif. Admitted to practice Florida 1983, U.S. District Court Middle District of Florida 1984, U.S. Court of Appeals Eleventh Circuit 1984 and U.S. Supreme Court 1989. In legal practice Lakeland 1985. Judge, Polk County Court Jan 3, 1989 to Jan 1995.
Assistant State Attorney Tenth Judicial Circuit 1982-85. Assistant Attorney General Department of Legal Affairs 1987. Note 34 South Carolina L. Rev. 595, 1982. Member Polk County Trial Lawyers Association, The Association of Trial Lawyers of America, Lakeland and Winter Haven Bar Associations. U.S. Army 1966-68.
Mailing address: P.O. Box 9000, Drawer J-110, Bartow 33831.
Telephone: (863) 534-4650.
Fax: (863) 534-7721

HERRING, William W. *(Judge, Broward County Court)* Appointed by Governor Reubin Askew to term beginning Oct 1, 1977. Elected 1978, 1982, 1986, 1990, 1994 and 1998. Current term expires Jan 2005. Born

HERRING, WILLIAM W.—*Continued*

Miami Florida May 23, 1943. Protestant. Educated at University of Florida B.A. with honors 1965 J.D. 1968. Member Phi Beta Kappa and Phi Kappa Phi. Admitted to practice Florida 1968 and U.S. District Courts Middle 1969 and Southern 1973 Districts of Florida. Began legal practice Punta Gorda 1968.

Research Aide Florida District Court of Appeal First District 1970. With State Attorney General's office Criminal Appeals Division at Tallahassee and West Palm Beach 1971-72. Chief of Appeals Division Broward County Public Defender's Office 1973-76. Head of Civil and Appeals Divisions Broward County State Attorney's Office 1977. Member Florida Conference of County Court Judges, The Florida Bar, Broward County, Charlotte County (Secretary-Treasurer 1969) and Florida Governmental (1970-71) Bar Associations. Democrat. Enjoys dancing, tennis, bowling and reading science fiction and fantasy.

Office: 785 Broward County Courthouse, 201 S.E. Sixth Street, Fort Lauderdale 33301.
Telephone: (954) 831-7825.

HERSHEY, Stewart R. *(Judge, Martin County Court)*
Mailing address: P.O. Box 1289, Stuart 34995-1289.
Telephone: (772) 288-5556.
Fax: (772) 221-1305

HESS, Glenn L. *(Judge, Florida Circuit Court Fourteenth Judicial Circuit)* Elected to term beginning Jan 3, 1995. Reelected 2000, current term expires Jan 2007.
Mailing address: P.O. Box 2237, Panama City 32402.
Telephone: (850) 747-5653.
Fax: (850) 747-5159

HIGBEE, Ronald P. *(Judge, Duval County Court)*
Office: 340 Duval County Courthouse, 330 East Bay Street, Jacksonville 32202.
Telephone: (904) 630-2937.
Fax: (904) 630-2979

HIGHSMITH, Shelby *(Senior Judge, United States District Court Southern District of Florida)* Appointed for life by President George Bush to term beginning 1991. Assumed Senior status March 15, 2002, serves by assignment. Born Jacksonville Florida Jan 31, 1929. Educated at Georgia Military College A.A. 1949 and University of Kansas B.A. 1958 LL.B. 1958. In legal practice Kansas City Missouri 1958-59 and Miami Florida 1959-70 and 1975-91. Judge, Florida Circuit Court Eleventh Judicial Circuit 1970-75.

Chief Legal Advisor Governor's War on Crime Program 1967-68. Special Counsel Florida Racing Commission 1969-70. Member Law Enforcement Planning Counsel of Florida 1969-70.

Office: Federal Justice Building, 99 N.E. Fourth Street, Miami 33132.
Telephone: (305) 523-5170.

HILL, Mark J. *(Judge, Florida Circuit Court Fifth Judicial Circuit)* Assumed office Sept 27, 1989. Elected to subsequent terms. Born Orlando Florida Dec 21, 1951. Educated at University of South Florida B.A. with honors 1974 and South Texas College of Law J.D. 1977. Admitted to practice Florida 1978 and Texas 1978. Began legal practice Tavares Florida 1978. Judge, Lake County Court Jan 3, 1985 to Sept 26, 1989.

With State Attorney's Office Tavares 1978-82. Former member West Central Florida Driver Improvement Program. Member State Bar of Texas and Lake County Bar Association. Member Civitan Club of Leesburg and Eustis Elks Club.

Mailing address: P.O. Box 7800, Tavares 32778-7800.
Office: Lake County Courthouse, Tavares 32778.
Telephone: (352) 742-4218.
Fax: (352) 742-4229

HINCKLEY, Harry G., Jr. *(Senior Judge, Florida Circuit Court Seventeenth Judicial Circuit)* Assumed office Feb 15, 1980. Elected Nov 1980, 1986 and 1992. Assumed Senior Judge status, serves by assignment. Born Miami Florida Jan 14, 1928. Catholic. Educated at Stetson University A.B. 1950 and University of Miami LL.B. 1955. Chief Justice Honor Court. Assistant Manager University of Miami Law Review 1954. Member Phi Alpha Delta and Pi Kappa Alpha. Admitted to practice Florida 1955. In legal practice Miami 1955-63 and Fort Lauderdale 1963-80.

Former member International Association of Insurance Counsel. Member Florida Conference of Circuit Court Judges (Criminal Section), Broward County and Dade County (Director 1961-62) Bar Associations. USNR 1945-46 and U.S. Army 1951-52. Past President Rio Vista Property Owners Association. Member University of Miami Alumni Association, Stetson University Alumni Association, Lauderdale Yacht Club and University Club. Enjoys fishing, photography and travel.

Office: Broward County Courthouse, 201 S.E. Sixth Street, Fort Lauderdale 33301.
Telephone: (954) 831-7740.

HINKLE, Robert L. *(Judge, United States District Court Northern District of Florida)* Appointed for life by President Bill Clinton to term beginning Aug 6, 1996. Born Apalachicola Florida Nov 7, 1951. Educated at Florida State University B.A. magna cum laude 1972 and Harvard Law School J.D. magna cum laude 1976. Law Clerk to Hon. Irving L. Goldberg, U.S. Court of Appeals Fifth Circuit 1976-77. Member Phi Beta Kappa. Admitted to practice Florida 1976. In legal practice Atlanta Georgia 1977-78 and Tallahassee Florida 1978-96.

Office: U.S. Courthouse, 111 North Adams Street, Tallahassee 32301-7717.
Telephone: (850) 521-3601.

HITT, Fredric M. *(Senior Judge, Seminole County Court)* Assumed Senior Judge status, serves by assignment.
Office: Moore Justice Center, 2825 Judge Fran Jamieson Way, Viera 32940-8006.
Telephone: (321) 637-5555.

HOBBS, Johnny R. *(Judge, Bradford County Court)* Elected to term beginning Jan 3, 1995. Reelected 1998, current term expires Jan 2005.
Mailing address: P.O. Drawer 340, Starke 32091.
Office: Bradford County Courthouse, Starke 32091.
Telephone: (904) 966-6221.
Fax: (904) 966-6166

HODGES, William Terrell *(Senior Judge, United States District Court Middle District of Florida)* Appointed for life by President Richard M. Nixon to term beginning 1971. Former Chief Judge. Assumed Senior status May 2, 1999, serves by assignment. Born Lake Wales Florida April 28, 1934. Educated at University of Florida B.S.B.A. 1956 LL.B. 1958 J.D. 1967. Executive

HODGES, WILLIAM TERRELL—*Continued*

Editor University of Florida Law Review 1957-58. Admitted to practice Florida 1959. In legal practice Tampa 1958-71.

Instructor in Business Law University of South Florida 1961-66. Member American Judicature Society, The Florida Bar (Chairman Grievance Committee 1967-70 and Uniform Commercial Code Committee 1970-71), Tampa-Hillsborough County and American Bar Associations.

Office: Federal Building and U.S. Courthouse, 207 N.W. Second Street, Ocala 34475-6666.

Telephone: (352) 690-6907.

HOEVELER, William M. *(Senior Judge, United States District Court Southern District of Florida)* Appointed for life by President Jimmy Carter to term beginning May 26, 1977. Assumed Senior status, serves by assignment. Born Paris France Aug 23, 1922. Educated at Temple University 1941-43, Bucknell University B.A. 1947 and Harvard Law School LL.B. 1950. Member Omicron Delta Kappa and Phi Alpha Delta (Honorary member). Admitted to practice Pennsylvania 1951, Florida 1951, U.S. District Court Southern District of Florida and U.S. Courts of Appeals Fifth and Third Circuits. In legal practice Miami since 1951.

Author "Liability of Insurance Agents, Architects and Engineers" American Bar Association INCL Section 1966, "Lawyers Liability" New York Law Journal Trial Magazine, "Liability of Architects, Engineers and Contractors" The Forum 1973, "The Professional in Court, The Lawyer" American Bar Association INCL Section 1976, "Products Liability" American Bar Association National Institute 1977, "How Can a Lawyer Engaged in the Litigation Process Avoid Being Sued for Malpractice" American Bar Association National Institute 1977, "In Defense of the Jury" 11 Brief 2 Feb 1981, "View From the Bench" 11 Brief 2 Nov 1981, "What Will the Changes Bring?" 12 *Tort and Insurance Practice Section Publication* Brief 28 May 1983, "The Uncertain Future of Liberal Discovery" 3 *Trial Advocate Quarterly* 54 April 1984 and "Cures for the Litigation Ills" 11 Brief 2 Aug. Contributor with William Hicks and James Rineman *Florida Practice Guide: Personal Injury* Callaghan & Co. 1988. Guest Lecturer University of Miami School of Law. Judicial Fellow American College of Trial Lawyers. Honorary Fellow American College of Construction Lawyers. Honorary Diplomate American Board of Trial Advocates. Member U.S. District Court Committee for Review of Local Rules, The American Law Institute, American Judicature Society, The Florida Bar (Personal Injury and Wrongful Death Advisory Committee 1976, Tort Litigation Review Commission 1985-86, Chairman Standing Committee on Professionalism 1992-93 and 1993-94), Philadelphia, Dade County (Chairman Charity Drives Committee 1966) and American (Chairman Committee on Products, Professional and General Liability Law 1972-73; Program Chairman 1975 and member Governing Council 1975-78 Section of Insurance, Negligence and Compensation Law; Governing Committee of Forum Committee on Construction Industry; Chairman Executive Committee National Conference of Federal Trial Judges Judicial Administration Division 1989-90) Bar Associations. Lecturer on Damages 1976 and at Civil Trial Advocacy Seminar 1975-77 and frequent Contributor on closing argument practice Trial Advocacy Seminar The Florida Bar CLE Program. Speaker on Federal Rules, cross examination, trial techniques (aviation), discovery and abuse, damages, professionalism, ethics and constitutional law (First Amendment) The Florida Bar and Dade County Bar Association. Named Best District Judge in Eleventh Circuit by *The American Lawyer* 1983. Recipient Award of Merit from Miami Beach Bar Association 1983-84, Judicial Distinction Award from Florida Association of Criminal Defense Attorneys 1986-87, Law Enforcement Award from Sons of the American Revolution Sept 1990, Silver Medallion Award for Brotherhood from National Conference of Christians and Jews Feb 1991, Lifetime Achievement Award from Greater Miami Jewish Federation Nov 1991 and Distinction in Chosen Profession Alumni Award from Bucknell University 1992. Listed in *Who's Who in America.* Lieutenant USMC 1942-46. Incorporator and member Board of Directors Youth Industries, Inc. Vestry Member 1986-89 and 1990-91, Senior Warden 1990-91, Lay Reader and Chalice Bearer St. Stephens Episcopal Church. Board of Trustees Transition, Inc. and South Florida Jail Ministries. Reader and Board of Trustees Recording for the Blind. Board of Directors Metro YMCA. Member Kiwanis Club (Chairman Support of Churches Committee).

Office: Federal Courthouse Square, 301 North Miami Avenue, Miami 33128-7797.

Telephone: (305) 523-5570.

HOLCOMB, Charles M. *(Judge, Florida Circuit Court Eighteenth Judicial Circuit)* Elected Nov 6, 1990 to term beginning Jan 8, 1991. Reelected Nov 5, 1996 and Nov 5, 2002. Current term expires Jan 5, 2009. Born Live Oak Florida June 18, 1936. Protestant. Educated at Stetson University B.A. 1954 and University of Florida J.D. 1966. Member Phi Alpha Delta. Admitted to practice Florida 1966 and U.S. District Court Middle District of Florida 1969. In legal practice Merritt Island 1966-70 and 1979-82 and Cocoa 1970-79 and 1982-90. Judge, Cocoa Municipal Court 1969-71.

Author *Florida Real Estate Contracts* Revere Publishers 1987 and *Florida Mortgage Foreclosure Practice Guide* Revere Publishers 1996. Member Vassar B. Carlton Inns of Court. USMCR 1952-66. Enjoys flying, gun collecting, knife and sword collecting, target shooting and skeet.

Office: 506 Palm Avenue, Titusville 32796.

Telephone: (321) 264-6756.

Fax: (321) 264-6904

HOLDER, Gregory P. *(Judge, Florida Circuit Court Thirteenth Judicial Circuit)* Assumed office 1996. Serves Civil Division since Jan 2001. Educated at U.S. Military Academy B.S. 1975, University of West Florida M.B.A. 1978 and Stetson University College of Law J.D. 1981. Associate Editor Stetson Law Review. Admitted to practice Florida, U.S. District Courts Middle District of Florida and District of Utah, U.S. Court of Appeals Eleventh Circuit, U.S. Court of Appeals for the Armed Forces and U.S. Supreme Court. In legal practice 1988-95. Judge, Hillsborough County Court Jan 3, 1995 to 1996.

Assistant City Attorney Temple Terrace 1988-91. Author "Implied Warranty of Habitability: Does It Exist in Florida Leaseholds?" 10 Stetson L. Rev. 563, 1981. Co-author "The Implied Warranty of Habitability Applicable to Florida Leaseholds" X No. 2 The Florida Bar Real Property, Probate and Trust Law Section Review 11 Feb 1982 and "Damages Are Not Automatic in a Map of Reservation Case" 3 The Florida Bar Eminent Domain

HOLDER, GREGORY P.—*Continued*

Committee Newsletter 7 June 1993. Adjunct Assistant Professor Embry-Riddle Aeronautical University. Adjunct Professor University of Phoenix. Member Florida Dependency Court Improvement Committee 1997. Chairperson Civil Justice Section 1999 and Member Education Committee Florida Conference of Circuit Court Judges. Chairperson Military Affairs Committee 1999 and Member Eminent Domain Committee The Florida Bar. President and Director Ferguson-White Inns of Court. Recipient Robert W. Patton Outstanding Jurist Award from Young Lawyers Division Hillsborough County Bar Association 1999-2000. Colonel USAFR. Military Judge, Eastern Circuit of the U.S. Board of Directors 1987-95 and Chairman 1990-94 MacDill Federal Credit Union. Board Member Downtown Tampa Metropolitan YMCA 1991-95. Advisory Board Gasparilla Distance Classic Association, Inc. since 1991. Member Tampa Chamber of Commerce, Sun City and Tampa Retired Officers Associations, Florida Conservation Association, Florida West Coast West Point Society, Westshore Evening BPW, American Legion Post 139, Fellowship Lodge 265 and Free & Accepted Masons.

Office: 370 Hillsborough County Courthouse, 419 Pierce Street, Tampa 33602-4022.

Telephone: (813) 272-6873.

Fax: (813) 276-8015

HOLMES, Ilona M. *(Judge, Florida Circuit Court Seventeenth Judicial Circuit)* Former Judge, Broward County Court, appointed by Governor Lawton Chiles to term beginning May 3, 1995.

Office: 4820 Broward County Courthouse, 201 S.E. Sixth Street, Fort Lauderdale 33301.

Telephone: (954) 831-7797.

Fax: (954) 831-5533

HONEYWELL, Charlene Edwards *(Judge, Florida Circuit Court Thirteenth Judicial Circuit)*

Office: 340 Hillsborough County Courthouse, 419 Pierce Street, Tampa 33602.

Telephone: (813) 272-6999.

HOOD, Richard L. *(Senior Judge, Gadsden County Court)* Assumed Senior Judge status, serves by assignment.

Office: Leon County Courthouse, 301 South Monroe Street, Tallahassee 32301.

Telephone: (850) 577-4420.

HOROWITZ, Alfred *(Judge, Florida Circuit Court Seventeenth Judicial Circuit)* Former Judge, Broward County Court.

Office: 6850 Broward County Courthouse, 201 S.E. Sixth Street, Fort Lauderdale 33301.

Telephone: (954) 831-7765.

HOSFORD, Kenneth *(Judge, Liberty County Court)*

Office: Liberty County Courthouse, Bristol 32321.

Telephone: (850) 643-2272.

Fax: (850) 643-5035

HOWARD, Richard *(Judge, Florida Circuit Court Fifth Judicial Circuit)*

Office: Citrus County Courthouse, 110 North Apopka Avenue, Inverness 34450.

Telephone: (352) 341-6705.

Fax: (352) 341-6738

HOY, John J. *(Judge, Florida Circuit Court Fifteenth Judicial Circuit)* Elected to term beginning Jan 1991. Reelected 1996 and 2002. Current term expires Jan 2009.

Office: Palm Beach County Courthouse, 205 North Dixie Highway, West Palm Beach 33401.

Telephone: (561) 355-6385.

HUBBART, Gerald D. *(Judge, Florida Circuit Court Eleventh Judicial Circuit)* Elected 1992 to term beginning Jan 3, 1993. Reelected 1998, current term expires Jan 2005. Born Kankakee Illinois. Educated at Augustana College A.B. 1984 and University of Illinois J.D. 1971. Admitted to practice Florida 1972 and U.S. Supreme Court 1982. Began legal practice Miami. Judge, Dade County Court Jan 3, 1989 to 1993.

Assistant Public Defender 1972-79. Assistant State Attorney 1984-88. Instructor University of Miami School of Law 1995-96 and St. Thomas University Law School 1996. U.S. Army 1967-69.

Office: 414 Dade County Courthouse, 73 West Flagler Street, Miami 33130.

Telephone: (305) 349-7082.

HUCK, Paul C. *(Judge, United States District Court Southern District of Florida)* Appointed for life by President Bill Clinton to term beginning Aug 5, 2000. Born Covington Kentucky July 22, 1940. Educated at University of Florida B.A. 1962 J.D. 1965. In legal practice Florida 1965-2000.

Office: 1067 Federal Justice Building, 99 N.E. Fourth Street, Miami 33132.

Telephone: (305) 523-5520.

HUEY, Paul L. *(Judge, Hillsborough County Court)*

Office: 202 Annex, 800 East Kennedy Boulevard, Tampa 33602.

Telephone: (813) 272-5809.

Fax: (813) 276-2329

HUNTER, J. Michael *(Judge, Florida Circuit Court Tenth Judicial Circuit)* Former Judge, Polk County Court, elected to term beginning Jan 3, 1995.

Mailing address: P.O. Box 9000, Drawer J-101, Bartow 33831.

Office: 255 North Broadway, Bartow 33830.

Telephone: (863) 402-6902.

HURLEY, Daniel T. K. *(Judge, United States District Court Southern District of Florida)* Appointed for life by President Bill Clinton to term beginning March 1994. Born Fitchburg Massachusetts Feb 24, 1943. Educated at St. Anselm College A.B. cum laude 1964 and George Washington University J.D. 1968. Law Clerk to Hon. John H. Pratt, U.S. District Court District of Columbia and Hon. Roger Robb, U.S. Court of Appeals District of Columbia Circuit. Admitted to practice District of Columbia 1969, Florida 1969 and California 1979. Judge, Palm Beach County Court Dec 2, 1975 to Aug 31, 1977. Judge, Florida Circuit Court Fifteenth Judicial Circuit 1977-79. Judge, Florida District Court of Appeal Fourth District 1979-86. Judge 1986-94 and Chief Judge 1988-93, Florida Circuit Court Fifteenth Judicial Circuit.

Assistant County Solicitor Palm Beach County 1970-

HURLEY, DANIEL T. K.—*Continued*

73. Executive Assistant State Attorney Fifteenth Judicial Circuit 1973-75.

Office: 352 Federal Building, 701 Clematis Street, West Palm Beach 33401-5196.

Telephone: (561) 803-3450.

HUTCHESON, R. Michael *(Judge, Florida Circuit Court Seventh Judicial Circuit)* Former Judge, Volusia County Court.

Office: Justice Center, 251 North Ridgewood Avenue, Daytona Beach 32114.

Telephone: (386) 239-7792.

Fax: (386) 239-7833

HYMAN, Paul G., Jr. *(Judge, United States Bankruptcy Court Southern District of Florida)* Appointed by U.S. Court of Appeals Eleventh Circuit judges. Born Miami Florida Sept 17, 1952. Educated at Vanderbilt University B.A. in Economics 1974 and University of Miami J.D. 1977. Admitted to practice Florida 1977, U.S. District Courts Southern 1977 and Middle 1982 Districts of Florida and District of Colorado 1984, U.S. Courts of Appeals Fifth 1977, Eleventh 1981 and Tenth 1982 Circuits and Colorado 1984. In legal practice Florida 1977-83 and Colorado 1984-94.

U.S. Attorneys Office Southern District of Florida 1979-81. Member The Florida Bar, Colorado (Chairman Bankruptcy Committee 1991-93) and American Bar Associations. Director Great Plains Bankruptcy Conference.

Office: 404 U.S. Courthouse, 299 East Broward Boulevard, Fort Lauderdale 33301.

Telephone: (954) 769-5770.

HYSLOP, Peyton B. *(Judge, Hernando County Court)* Appointed by Governor Bob Martinez to term beginning Jan 1, 1990. Elected 1990, 1994 and 1998. Current term expires Jan 2005. Born Indianapolis Indiana Sept 24, 1952. Presbyterian. Educated at University of South Florida B.A. 1973 and Cumberland School of Law J.D. cum laude 1983. Law Clerk to Hon. William Acker, U.S. District Court Northern District of Alabama 1984. Member Phi Alpha Delta. Admitted to practice Florida 1983, Alabama 1984 and U.S. District Courts Northern District of Alabama 1984 and Middle District of Florida 1984. In legal practice Birmingham Alabama 1983-84 and Brooksville Florida 1984-90.

Chief Assistant County Attorney Hernando County Florida 1985-90. Member American Judicature Society, Alabama State Bar, The Florida Bar, Hernando County and American Bar Associations. Previously employed as package car driver for UPS 1973-80. Member Kiwanis Club of Brooksville.

Office: 20 North Main Street, Room 340, Brooksville 34601.

Telephone: (352) 754-4295.

Fax: (352) 754-4267

IM, Seung Woo *(Judge, Pinellas County Court)*

Office: Criminal Justice Center, 14250 49th Street North, Clearwater 33762.

Telephone: (727) 464-6193.

IRELAND, Kathleen D. *(Judge, Broward County Court)*

Office: Broward County Courthouse, 201 S.E. Sixth Street, Fort Lauderdale 33301.

Telephone: (954) 831-7671.

ISOM, Claudia Rickert *(Judge, Florida Circuit Court Thirteenth Judicial Circuit)* Elected to term beginning Jan 1991. Reelected 1996 and 2002. Current term expires Jan 2009. Born Waterloo Iowa Nov 13, 1951. Admitted to practice Florida 1975, U.S. District Courts Middle 1975 and Northern 1981 Districts of Florida, U.S. Courts of Appeals Fifth 1981 and Eleventh 1981 Circuits and U.S. Supreme Court 1989. In legal practice 1986-90.

Assistant State Attorney Thirteenth Judicial Circuit 1979-82. Legal Counsel Florida Department of Health and Rehabilitative Services 1984-86. Vice Chair 1998-2001 and Chair 1999-2000 Standing Committee on Professionalism The Florida Bar. President 1999-2000 and Master/Judge Tampa Bay Inn of Court. Director and Member Hillsborough Association of Women Lawyers. Member Florida Conference of Circuit Court Judges and Hillsborough County Bar Association. Presenter/Moderator "The Perception of Justice" National Conference on the American Inns of Court 1996, "Practicing Beyond the Rules" 1998, "Lying, Cheating and Stealing" May 1999 and "Motions for Disqualification" Feb 2001 Brown Bag CLE Series Hillsborough County Bar Association, "Winning Professionalism Strategies" Hillsborough County Bar Association/George Edgecomb Bar Association/Hillsborough Association of Women Lawyers Seminar Jan 1999 and "Liability in the Workplace, Sexual Harassment, Discrimination and Fairness" Florida Conference of Circuit Court Judges June 1999. Panelist Bench/Bar Conference Hillsborough County Bar Association 1997 and "Diversity & Professionalism Seminar" Hillsborough County Bar Association/George Edgecomb Bar Association/Hillsborough Association of Women Lawyers Seminar Jan 1999. Moderator and Panelist "Practicing with Professionalism" Seminar Young Lawyers Division The Florida Bar Summer 1998. Faculty Member "Professionalism—Walking the Line Between Control and Recusal" Florida College of Advanced Judicial Studies May 2000. Co-presenter "Diversity and Professionalism" Trial Advocacy Seminar The Florida Bar Feb 2001. Member League of Women Voters.

Office: 419 Pierce Street, Room 314, Tampa 33602-3549.

Telephone: (813) 272-6972.

Fax: (813) 276-2725

Website address: www.fljud13.org

JACOBSEN, Donald G. *(Judge, Florida Circuit Court Tenth Judicial Circuit)*

Mailing address: P.O. Box 9000, Drawer J107, Bartow 33831.

Telephone: (863) 534-4649.

JACOBUS, Bruce W. *(Chief Judge, Florida Circuit Court Eighteenth Judicial Circuit)* Chief Judge since July 1, 2001.

Office: Moore Justice Center, Second Floor, 2825 Judge Fran Jamieson Way, Viera 32940-8006.

Telephone: (321) 617-7260.

Fax: (321) 617-7264

JAFFE, Bernard R. *(Senior Judge, Dade County Court)* Assumed Senior Judge status, serves by assignment.

Office: 511 Dade County Courthouse, 73 West Flagler Street, Miami 33130.

Telephone: (305) 349-7001.

JENKINS, Elizabeth A. *(Magistrate Judge, United States District Court Middle District of Florida)* Appointed by U.S. District Court judges Dec 16, 1985. Reappointed Dec 16, 1993 and Dec 16, 2001. Current term expires Dec 2009.
Office: U.S. Courthouse, 801 North Florida Avenue, Tampa 33602-3800.
Telephone: (813) 301-5774.

JENNEMANN, Karen S. *(Judge, United States Bankruptcy Court Middle District of Florida)* Appointed by U.S. Court of Appeals Eleventh Circuit judges.
Office: 900 South Trust Bank Building, 135 West Central Boulevard, Orlando 32801.
Telephone: (407) 648-6832.

JOHNSON, Anthony H. *(Judge, Florida Circuit Court Ninth Judicial Circuit)* Elected to term beginning Jan 7, 1997. Reelected 2002, current term expires 2009. Born Pensacola Florida Nov 11, 1948. Religious affiliation: Assembly of God. Educated at American University B.S. in Administration of Justice 1974, University of South Florida Masters program and Stetson University College of Law J.D. 1980. Law Clerk 1979-81. Vice President Society of Trial Advocacy. Listed in *Who's Who in American Colleges and Universities* 1980. Member Alpha Phi Sigma and Delta Theta Phi (Dean). Admitted to practice Florida 1981. Former Senior Judge, Orange County Court, elected to term beginning Jan 8, 1985.
Assistant State Attorney Ninth Judicial Circuit 1981-85. Co-author 1982 Pocket Part Supplement to *Florida Criminal Trial Practice Forms* Masterson, Harrison Company 1980. Member Florida Conference of Circuit Court Judges and The Florida Bar. USMC Vietnam 1966-69. Commander (Reserve Naval Intelligence Officer) USNR since 1978. Detective Metropolitan Police Department Washington D.C. 1970-75. Deputy Sheriff Pinellas County 1975. Special Agent U.S. Secret Service Tampa Field Office 1976-78. Licensed private pilot. Master mariner. Enjoys sailing, diving, flying, soaring, kayaking and mountain climbing.
Office: 1110 Orange County Courthouse, 425 North Orange Avenue, Orlando 32801.
Telephone: (407) 836-0565.

JOHNSON, Jean M. *(Judge, Florida Circuit Court Fourth Judicial Circuit)* Former Judge, Duval County Court.
Office: Duval County Courthouse, 330 East Bay Street, Jacksonville 32202.
Telephone: (904) 630-2530.
Fax: (904) 630-2979

JOHNSON, Laura S. *(Judge, Palm Beach County Court)*
Office: Palm Beach County Courthouse, 205 North Dixie Highway, West Palm Beach 33401.

JOHNSON, Linnea R. *(Magistrate Judge, United States District Court Southern District of Florida)* Appointed by U.S. District Court judges. Currently serves as Chief Magistrate Judge.
Office: 316 Federal Building, 701 Clematis Street, West Palm Beach 33401.
Telephone: (561) 803-3470.

JOHNSON, T. Michael *(Judge, Florida Circuit Court Fifth Judicial Circuit)*
Mailing address: P.O. Box 7800, Tavares 32778-7800.
Telephone: (352) 742-4215.
Fax: (352) 742-4370

JOHNSON, Thomas E. *(Judge, Escambia County Court)* Assumed office Jan 3, 1989. Elected to subsequent terms.
Office: Judicial Building, 190 Governmental Center, Pensacola 32501.
Telephone: (850) 595-4427.
Fax: (850) 595-4404

JOHNSON, William *(Judge, Florida Circuit Court Eleventh Judicial Circuit)*
Office: 210 Juvenile Justice Center, 3300 N.W. 27th Avenue, Miami 33142.
Telephone: (305) 638-6229.
Fax: (305) 638-6355

JOHNSON, William C., Jr. *(Senior Judge, Florida Circuit Court Seventh Judicial Circuit)* Elected to term beginning Jan 1985. Reelected Nov 6, 1990 and 1996. Assumed Senior Judge status, serves by assignment. Born Providence Rhode Island Mar 25, 1930. Educated at Brown University A.B. and University of Virginia J.D. Admitted to practice Virginia 1958 and Florida 1959. In legal practice Daytona Beach Florida 1962-84.
Member The Florida Bar and Virginia State Bar. Commander USNR 1959-84 (retired). Enjoys sports, reading and swimming.
Office: 101 North Alabama Avenue, De Land 32724.
Telephone: (386) 257-6097.

JOHNSON, William Clayton *(Senior Judge, Florida Circuit Court Seventeenth Judicial Circuit)* Elected 1972 to term beginning Jan 1, 1973. Reelected to subsequent terms. Assumed Senior Judge status, serves by assignment. Born Duluth Minnesota Sept 25, 1924. Educated at University of Miami B.B.A. 1950 and New York Law School LL.B. 1956. Member Sigma Chi and Delta Theta Phi. Admitted to practice Minnesota 1957 and Florida 1958. In legal practice Fort Lauderdale and Deerfield Beach Florida 1964-68. Judge, Broward County Court of Record March 1968 to Dec 1972.
Assistant County Attorney Duluth Minnesota 1958-64. City Prosecutor Fort Lauderdale 1964. Assistant Public Defender Broward County 1967-68. Appointed by Governor Claude R. Kirk, Jr. to Broward County Narcotics Guidance Council 1970-72. Member The Florida Bar and Minnesota State Bar Association. Attended National College of State Trial Judges 1969 and 1971. USAAC 1943-45. Special Agent FBI 1951-58. Republican. Chairman Society of Former Special Agents FBI Gold Coast Chapter 1970. Justice of Subordinate Forum Pompano Beach Elks Lodge. Elder and Trustee Community Presbyterian Church of Deerfield Beach 1969-72. Member Judicial and Policy Committee South Florida Presbytery 1970-74. 32° Mason.
Office: Broward County Courthouse, 201 S.E. Sixth Street, Fort Lauderdale 33301.
Telephone: (954) 831-7740.

JOHNSTON, Lawrence V. *(Senior Judge, Florida Circuit Court Eighteenth Judicial Circuit)* Elected 1986 to term beginning Jan 6, 1987. Reelected 1992. Assumed Senior Judge status, serves by assignment. Born

JOHNSTON, LAWRENCE V.—*Continued*

Virginia June 12, 1947. Former Judge, Brevard County Court.

Office: Moore Justice Center, 2825 Judge Fran Jamieson Way, Viera 32940-8006.
Telephone: (321) 637-5555.

JONES, Gary R. *(Magistrate Judge, United States District Court Middle District of Florida)* Part-time Magistrate Judge Northern District of Florida April 2, 1998 to April 30, 2000. Appointed to Middle District of Florida by U.S. District Court judges to term beginning May 1, 2000.

Office: 337 U.S. Courthouse, 207 N.W. Second Street, Ocala 34475-6666.
Telephone: (352) 369-4869.

JONES, Mark H. *(Judge, Florida Circuit Court Sixteenth Judicial Circuit)* Former Chief Judge.

Office: Monroe County Courthouse Annex, Third Floor, 500 Whitehead Street, Key West 33040.
Telephone: (305) 292-3422.
Fax: (305) 295-3625

JONES, Rosemary Usher *(Senior Judge, Florida Circuit Court Eleventh Judicial Circuit)* Assumed Senior Judge status, serves by assignment.

Office: 511 Dade County Courthouse, 73 West Flagler Street, Miami 33130.
Telephone: (305) 349-7001.

JONES, T. Michael *(Judge, Florida Circuit Court First Judicial Circuit)* Former Judge, Okaloosa County Court.

Office: Judicial Building, 190 Governmental Center, Pensacola 32501.
Telephone: (850) 595-4445.
Fax: (850) 595-4404

JOPLING, Wallace M. *(Senior Judge, Florida Circuit Court Third Judicial Circuit)* Elected to term beginning Jan 4, 1977. Reelected 1982. Assumed Senior Judge status 1989, serves by assignment. Born Cordele Georgia Jan 15, 1917. Methodist. Educated at University of Florida A.B. with honors 1938 LL.B. 1940 replaced by J.D. Member Phi Kappa Phi, Phi Delta Phi, Phi Eta Sigma, Kappa Alpha and Florida Blue Key. Admitted to practice Florida 1940, U.S. District Courts Southern 1940 and Middle 1950 Districts of Florida, U.S. Supreme Court 1957 and U.S. Court of Appeals Fifth Circuit 1974. Began legal practice Jacksonville 1940. In legal practice Lake City 1946-77. Judge, Lake City Municipal Court 1947-51.

Deputy Commissioner Florida Industrial Commission 1953-55 and 1961-63. Fellow American College of Trial Lawyers. Member The Florida Bar (Board of Governors), Lake City (President 1955) and Third Judicial Circuit (President) Bar Associations. Colonel USAR Field Artillery 1940-65 (active duty 1941-46). Instructor Judge Advocate General Reserve School 1950-60. Democrat. President Lake City Rotary Club 1955 and Lake City Chamber of Commerce 1956. Attorney Columbia County School Board 1962-75. Enjoys hunting, fishing and football.

Mailing address: P.O. Drawer 1000, Perry 32347.
Telephone: (386) 758-2163.

JORDAN, Adalberto J. *(Judge, United States District Court Southern District of Florida)* Appointed for life by President Bill Clinton to term beginning Oct 1, 1999. Born Havana Cuba Dec 7, 1961. Educated at University of Miami B.A. magna cum laude 1984 J.D. summa cum laude 1987. Law Clerk Hon. Sandra Day O'Connor, U.S. Supreme Court 1988-89. Admitted to practice Florida 1987. In legal practice Miami 1989-94.

Assistant U.S. Attorney Southern District of Florida 1994-99. Member The Florida Bar, Dade County and American Bar Associations.

Office: Federal Courthouse Square, Eighth Floor, 301 North Miami Avenue, Miami 33128.
Telephone: (305) 523-5560.
Fax: (305) 523-5569

JORGENSON, James R. *(Judge, Florida District Court of Appeal Third District)* Appointed by Governor Robert Graham 1981. Retained by election 1982, 1988, 1994 and Nov 7, 2000. Current term expires Jan 2007. Born Kansas City Missouri June 29, 1937. Protestant. Educated at Miami-Dade Junior College A.S. in Criminology 1964, Florida State University B.S. in Criminology 1966 J.D. 1968 and University of Virginia School of Law LL.M. 1984. Ford Foundation Fellow Northwestern University School of Law 1969. Member Delta Theta Phi. Admitted to practice Florida 1969. Began legal practice Miami 1969. Judge, Dade County Court 1977-79, appointed by Governor Reubin Askew. Judge, Florida Circuit Court Eleventh Judicial Circuit 1979-81, appointed by Governor Robert Graham.

Police Legal Advisor 1969-72 and Court Services Division Chief 1972-76 Dade County Public Safety Department. Assistant Attorney Dade County 1977. Author "When Are 'Miranda' Warnings Required" National Sheriff's Magazine April-May 1970. Co-author "Municipal Police Departments in Florida: Problems and Prospects" Florida State University 1969; "Police Selection and Training in the United States" 7 American Criminal L. Quar. 4, 1969; "Organized Crime—A Civil Approach" Police Chief Magazine April 1970 and 116 Congressional Record 67, April 29, 1970; and "The Police Legal Advisor" Florida B. Jour. Feb 1971. Member Florida Law Revision Commission 1970-72, Governor's Commission on Statewide Prosecution Function, Advisory Committee on ABA Standards for Criminal Justice and ABA Task Force to Update Standards for Criminal Justice. Board of Directors and General Counsel National Association of Police Attorneys. Associate member National District Attorneys Association. Member Southeast Institute for Criminal Justice (Advisory Board 1978-80), The American Law Institute, American Judicature Society, The Florida Bar (Chairman Law Enforcement Programs Committee 1975-77), Dade County (Criminal Court Subcommittee and Fair Trial-Free Press Committee) and American (Committee on News Reporting and Fair Trial Judicial Administration Division and Committee on White Collar Crime Section of Criminal Justice) Bar Associations. Airman Second Class USAF Air Police 1957-60. Police Officer Dade County Public Safety Department 1960-64. Member Coconut Grove Sailing Club and Boy Scouts of America. Enjoys sailing.

Office: 2001 S.W. 117th Avenue, Miami 33175-1716.
Telephone: (305) 229-3200.
Fax: (305) 229-3206

KAHN, Charles J., Jr. *(Judge, Florida District Court of Appeal First District)* Appointed by Governor Lawton Chiles April 9, 1991 to term beginning June 1991. Retained by election. Born Antonio Texas Sept 14, 1951.

KAHN, CHARLES J., JR.—*Continued*
Educated at Vanderbilt University B.A. cum laude 1973 and University of Florida J.D. with honors 1977. In legal practice Pensacola 1979-91.
Assistant State Attorney Twelfth Judicial Circuit 1977-78. Assistant Public Defender Second Judicial Circuit 1978. Litigation Attorney Florida Department of Transportation 1978-79. Master Lawyer Tallahassee American Inn of Court. Member Gender Bias Study Implementation Commission Florida Supreme Court, Academy of Florida Trial Lawyers, The Association of Trial Lawyers of America and The Florida Bar. President Northeast Pensacola Sertoma Club 1988-89. President Temple Beth El 1989-91. Trustee Temple Israel.
Office: 301 Martin Luther King Jr. Boulevard, Tallahassee 32399-1850.
Telephone: (850) 487-2323.
Fax: (850) 488-7989

KANAREK, Paul B. *(Judge, Florida Circuit Court Nineteenth Judicial Circuit)* Appointed by Governor Bob Martinez to term beginning Jan 1, 1988. Elected Nov 1988, 1994 and 2000. Current term expires Jan 2007. Former Chief Judge. Born West Palm Beach Florida April 26, 1950. Jewish. Educated at University of Florida B.A. 1972 J.D. 1975. Admitted to practice Florida 1975. In legal practice Vero Beach 1980-87.
Assistant Public Defender 1975-78 and Chief Assistant Public Defender 1978-80 Nineteenth Circuit.
Office: Indian River Courthouse, 2000 Sixteenth Avenue, Suite 375, Vero Beach 32960.
Telephone: (772) 770-5052.
Fax: (772) 770-5133

KANEY, Frank N. *(Senior Judge, Florida Circuit Court Ninth Judicial Circuit)* Elected 1976 to term beginning Jan 4, 1977. Reelected 1982, 1988 and 1994. Assumed Senior Judge status, serves by assignment. Born Tampa Florida Feb 4, 1937. Educated at Florida State University B.S. in Speech 1958 and University of Miami LL.B. 1965. Admitted to practice Florida 1965, U.S. District Court Middle District of Florida and U.S. Court of Appeals Fifth Circuit. Judge, Orange County Court 1973-77.
Adjunct Professor of Constitutional Law Florida Technological University 1970-72. Member The Florida Bar, Orange County and American Bar Associations. Faculty Member Florida College of Advanced Judicial Studies. Dean The Florida Judges College. First Lieutenant U.S. Army 1958-62. Political affiliation: Independent. Member Park Lake Presbyterian Church of Orlando (Session). Member Kiwanis Club of North Orlando and Orlando Touchdown Club.
Office: Orange County Courthouse, 425 North Orange Avenue, Orlando 32801.
Telephone: (407) 836-2050.

KAPLAN, Michael G. *(Judge, Florida Circuit Court Seventeenth Judicial Circuit)*
Office: Broward County Courthouse, 201 S.E. Sixth Street, Fort Lauderdale 33301.

KAPLAN, Stanton S. *(Judge, Florida Circuit Court Seventeenth Judicial Circuit)* Elected 2002. Term expires Jan 2009. Born New York New York March 4, 1936. Educated at University of Miami B.B.A. with honors 1959 J.D. with honors 1961. Enjoys Bonsai.
Office: 308 Broward County Courthouse, 201 S.E. Sixth Street, Fort Lauderdale 33301.
Telephone: (954) 831-7791.

KARAN, Amy B. *(Judge, Dade County Court)* Elected to term beginning Jan 3, 1995. Reelected 1998, current term expires Jan 2005.
Office: 1919 Courthouse Center, 175 N.W. First Avenue, Miami 33128.
Telephone: (305) 349-5674.

KARLAN, Sandy *(Judge, Florida Circuit Court Eleventh Judicial Circuit)*
Office: 2327 Courthouse Center, 175 N.W. First Avenue, Miami 33128.
Telephone: (305) 349-5753.
Fax: (305) 349-6179

KAYE, Robert Paul *(Senior Judge, Florida Circuit Court Eleventh Judicial Circuit)* Appointed by Governor Robert Graham Sept 1981. Elected 1981. Reelected 1987 and 1993. Assumed Senior Judge status, serves by assignment. Born Rockville Centre New York March 4, 1924. Religious affiliation: Hebrew. Educated at University of Florida B.A. 1950 and University of Miami LL.B. 1957. Admitted to practice Florida 1957. Began legal practice Miami 1957.
Member Florida Conference of Circuit Court Judges, The Florida Bar and Dade County Bar Association. U.S. Army 1951-53.
Office: 511 Dade County Courthouse, 73 West Flagler Street, Miami 33130.
Telephone: (305) 349-7001.

KAYLOR, Anne *(Judge, Polk County Court)* Elected to term beginning Jan 1991. Reelected 1994 and 1998. Current term expires Jan 2005.
Mailing address: P.O. Box 9000, Drawer J-129, Bartow 33831-9000.
Office: Polk County Courthouse, Bartow 33830.
Telephone: (863) 534-4088.
Fax: (863) 534-4108

KELLY, Carroll J. *(Judge, Dade County Court)*
Office: 247 Courthouse Center, 175 N.W. First Avenue, Miami 33128.
Telephone: (305) 349-5703.
Fax: (305) 349-5676

KELLY, Patricia *(Judge, Florida District Court of Appeal Second District)* Appointed by Governor Jeb Bush to term beginning Dec 2001. Born New Orleans Louisiana Dec 25, 1956. Educated at University of South Florida B.A. cum laude and University of Florida College of Law J.D. cum laude 1986. Board Certified as a Specialist in Appellate Practice by The Florida Bar. In legal practice West Palm Beach and Tampa 1986-89.
Mailing address: P.O. Box 327, Lakeland 33802.
Telephone: (863) 499-2290.
Fax: (863) 413-2649

KENNEDY, Patrick Gene *(Judge, Florida Circuit Court Seventh Judicial Circuit)* Born Minneapolis Minnesota June 24, 1943. Episcopalian. Educated at Stetson University B.A. 1965 J.D. 1968. Member Pi Kappa Alpha and Phi Alpha Delta. Admitted to practice Florida 1969. In legal practice Daytona Beach and De Land 1971-85. Former Judge, Volusia County Court, ap-

KENNEDY, PATRICK GENE—*Continued*
pointed by Governor Robert Graham to term beginning Jan 2, 1986.

Member The Florida Bar and Volusia County Bar Association. E-5 U.S. Army 1969-71. Democrat. Delegate State Convention 1979. Member Volusia County Democratic Executive Committee 1983. Former Vice Chairman Port Orange Planning and Zoning Board. Past President South Daytona Chamber of Commerce. Member Port Orange Rotary. Enjoys scuba diving and fishing.

Office: Courthouse Annex, 125 East Orange Avenue, Daytona Beach 32114.

Telephone: (386) 257-6051.

Fax: (386) 248-8130

KENNEY, Scott M. *(Judge, Florida Circuit Court Nineteenth Judicial Circuit)*

Office: P. P. Cobb Building, Drawer 2C, 100 Avenue A, Fort Pierce 34950.

Telephone: (772) 462-1465

Fax: (772) 462-1190

KENNON, Thomas J., Jr. *(Judge, Florida Circuit Court Third Judicial Circuit)* Assumed office Oct 11, 1993. Former Chief Judge. Born Quitman Georgia March 11, 1939. Methodist. Educated at University of Florida B.S.B.A. 1962 J.D. 1966. Member Phi Delta Phi. Began legal practice Live Oak 1966. Judge, Suwannee County Court Jan 3, 1973 to Oct 10, 1993.

Member The Florida Bar and Third Judicial Circuit Bar Association. Sergeant Florida National Guard 1962-68. Democrat. Past President Live Oak Jaycees and Suwannee County Bassmasters. Past President and Secretary Rotary Club of Live Oak. Enjoys bass fishing.

Office: Suwannee County Courthouse, 200 South Ohio Avenue, Live Oak 32060.

Telephone: (386) 362-6353.

Fax: (386) 362-7685

KEST, John Marshall *(Judge, Florida Circuit Court Ninth Judicial Circuit)*

Office: 2000 East Michigan, Orlando 32806.

Telephone: (407) 836-7590.

KHOUZAM, Nelly N. *(Judge, Florida Circuit Court Sixth Judicial Circuit)* Appointed by Governor Lawton Chiles to term beginning June 1994. Served Civil Division June 1994 to Dec 1994, Criminal Division Jan 1995 to Dec 1996, Career Criminal/Habitual Offender Division Jan 1997 to Dec 1997 and Family Division Jan 1999 to 2001. Criminal Administrative Judge Jan 1998 to Dec 1998. Currently serves Criminal Division. Educated at University of Florida B.A. 1979 J.D. with honors 1981 and University of Oxford, England 1980. Staff Attorney to Hon. Jack R. Schoonover, Florida District Court of Appeal Second District Feb 1982 to Feb 1984. Admitted to practice Florida, U.S. District Court Middle District of Florida, U.S. Court of Appeals Eleventh Circuit and U.S. Supreme Court. In legal practice St. Petersburg April 1984 to Jan 1990 and Clearwater Jan 1990 to May 1994.

Author "A Review of the Pre-Suit Screening Provisions of the Comprehensive Medical Malpractice Reform Act and Its Interpretation and Application by Florida Courts" Trial Advocate Quarterly July 1989, "A Review of the Pre-Suit Screening Provisions of the Comprehensive Medical Malpractice Reform Act" Florida B. Jour. April 1990, "An Update of the Medical Malpractice Reform Act" Trial Advocate Quarterly July 1990, "D.P.R., Friend or Foe?" 31 No. 6 PICOMESO April 1992, "Medical Malpractice: A Review of the Presuit Screening Provisions of the Florida Medical Malpractice Act" Nova L. Rev. 1995 and "From the Bench: Do's and Don't's of Talking to the Jury" 23 No. 4 *Litigation Magazine* Summer 1997 and *Best of ABA Sections* Spring 1998. Editor "Ethical Considerations in Representing a Land Trust and Its Principals" The Florida Bar Real Property, Probate and Trust Law Section Seminar 1993. Co-author Chapter "Pretrial Stipulations and Orders" *Business Litigation in Florida CLE Manual* 1997 and 2000.

Barrister 1987-94, Chronicler/Reporter 1991-92 and Member Executive Committee 1991-93 Pinellas Inn of Court. President Barney Masterson Inn of Court 1996-98. Member Pinellas County Court Security Committee 1998. Former Member Florida Defense Lawyers Association, American Judges Association, Clearwater, St. Petersburg, and American Bar Associations. Member Education Committee for Educational Programs for Circuit Judges Conferences since 1995. Member Professionalism Committee 1998 and Chairman Pro Bono Committee since 1995 and Pro Se Advisory Committee since 1996 Sixth Judicial Circuit. Member Canakaris Family Law Inn of Court, American Board of Trial Advocates, Florida Conference of Circuit Court Judges (Chairman Criminal Section 1997-99, Member Executive Committee since 1997, Chair Family Law Section 1999-2000, Secretary/Treasurer 2002) and The Florida Bar (Vice Chairman Malpractice Negligence Division 1989-90 and Risk Management Committee 1993-94 Health Law Section, Member Grievance Committee for the Sixth Judicial Circuit 1990-93, Appellate Court Rules Committee 1992-95, Criminal Procedure Rules Committee 1995-98, Rules of Judicial Administration Committee since 1998).

Lecturer "What Physicians Can Do to Reduce Risks" Pinellas County Medical Society June 1989, "What Health and Home Care Providers Can Do to Reduce Risks-Viewpoint of the Defense Attorney" American Institute of Medical Law, Inc. Feb 1989, Sept 1989, Nov 1990 and Jan 1991, "Reducing the Risk of Medical Malpractice" Humana Hospital St. Petersburg March 1992 and "Women in Untraditional Fields; Women in the Judiciary" University of South Florida Feb 1997. Mentor for New Judges, Florida Circuit Court Sixth Judicial Circuit since 1996. Speaker "Professionalism, Ethics and the Pro Bono Aspirational Goal of Florida Attorneys" St. Petersburg Bar Association Pro Bono Committee March 1997, "Professionalism and the Trial Lawyer" Joint Seminar of the St. Petersburg, Clearwater and Hillsborough Bar Associations May 15, 1998 and "Preserving Errors During Jury Selection" The Florida Bar Appellate Section Oct 1999. Panel Member "Decision Making, Ethics and Civility in Appellate Practice" Stetson University College of Law April 4, 1997, "Professionalism and the Criminal Prosecutor" Stetson University College of Law April 11, 1997 and "Legal Ethics and the Media, a Delicate Balance" St. Petersburg Junior College Nov 6, 1998. Instructor in Criminal Law "Factors to Consider in Sentencing" Florida College of Advanced Judicial Studies May 18, 1999 and Family Law "Kayla McLean Act, Attorney Misconduct" Jan 2000. Faculty Member Florida College of Advanced Judicial Studies and Florida New Judges College.

Listed in *Who's Who in American Law* 1991-99, *Who's Who in America* since 1993, *International Who's*

KHOUZAM, NELLY N.—*Continued*

Who 1995 and *Who's Who in American Women* 1998. Nominated Woman of the Year by American Biographical Institute 1992. Board of Directors Florida Bay Chapter March of Dimes Birth Defects Foundation 1991-94. Member Nominating Committee and Board of Directors Florida Legal Services 1997. Former Member Clearwater Branch American Association of University Women. Member Tampa Bay YWCA 75th Anniversary Leadership Committee, Advisory Council Personal Enrichment through Mental Health Services, Inc. (PEMHS) and Holy Family Catholic Church.

Office: Criminal Justice Center, 14250 49th Street North, Clearwater 33762.

Telephone: (727) 464-6425.

Fax: (727) 464-7384

KILLIAN, Lewis M., Jr. *(Judge, United States Bankruptcy Court Northern District of Florida)* Appointed by U.S. Court of Appeals Eleventh Circuit judges to term beginning Sept 22, 1986. Educated at U.S. Military Academy 1969 and Florida State University J.D. with honors 1976.

Member National Conference of Bankruptcy Judges, Bankruptcy Bar Association for the Northern District of Florida and Tallahassee Bar Association. Member Rotary International.

Office: 3120 City Center Building, 227 North Bronough Street, Tallahassee 32301-1378.

Telephone: (850) 942-8943.

KING, Frances S. *(Judge, Marion County Court)* Elected to term beginning Jan 3, 1995. Reelected 1998, current term expires Jan 2005.

Office: Marion County Judicial Center, 110 N.W. First Avenue, Ocala 34475.

Telephone: (352) 401-7824.

Fax: (352) 401-6744

KING, James Lawrence *(Senior Judge, United States District Court Southern District of Florida)* Appointed for life by President Richard M. Nixon to term beginning 1970. Former Chief Judge. Assumed Senior status, serves by assignment. Born Miami Florida Dec 20, 1927. Educated at University of Florida B.A. 1949 LL.B. 1953. Member Blue Key, Pi Kappa Tau and Phi Delta Phi. Admitted to practice Florida 1953. In legal practice Miami 1953-64. Judge, Florida Circuit Court Eleventh Judicial Circuit 1964-70. Justice pro tem, Florida Supreme Court 1965. Judge pro tem, Florida District Courts of Appeal Second, Third and Fourth Districts 1965-68. Judge pro tem, U.S. Court of Appeals Fifth Circuit 1977 and 1978. Chief Judge, U.S. District Court District of the Canal Zone 1978.

Member U.S. Team studying English Civil Procedures, London England 1974 and Joint Commission on Code of Judicial Conduct 1974-76. President Fifth Circuit U.S. District Judges Association 1977-78. Member The American Law Institute, Institute of Judicial Administration, Judicial Conference of the U.S. (Advisory Committee on Judicial Activities since 1973, Commission to Consider Standards for Admission to Practice in Federal Courts 1976-79, Committee on Bankruptcy Legislation 1977-78, Chairman Implementation Committee on Admission of Attorneys to Federal Practice since 1979), The Florida Bar (Board of Governors 1958-63, President Junior Bar Section 1963-64) and American Bar Association. Recipient Award of Merit from Young Lawyers Section The Florida Bar 1967 and Outstanding Alumnus Award from University of Florida 1981. Inducted into University of Florida Hall of Fame. First Lieutenant USAF 1953-55. Democrat. State Executive Council 1956-69 and Board of Regents 1963 University of Florida. Florida Control Board Governing State Universities and Colleges 1964.

Office: 1127 Federal Justice Building, 99 N.E. Fourth Street, Miami 33132.

Telephone: (305) 523-5000.

KING, Lawrence D. *(Judge, Dade County Court)*

Office: 2301 South Dade Justice Center, 10710 S.W. 211th Street, Miami 33189.

Telephone: (305) 252-5840.

KINSEY, Patricia A. *(Judge, Escambia County Court)*

Office: Judicial Building, 190 Governmental Center, Pensacola 32501.

Telephone: (850) 595-4424.

Fax: (850) 595-4404

KIRKLAND, Thomas R. *(Judge, Orange County Court)*

Office: 385-B Orange County Courthouse, 425 North Orange Avenue, Orlando 32801.

Telephone: (407) 836-2272.

Fax: (407) 836-0492

KIRKWOOD, Lawrence R. *(Judge, Florida Circuit Court Ninth Judicial Circuit)* Elected 1980 to term beginning Jan 6, 1981. Reelected 1986, 1992 and 1998. Current term expires Jan 2005. Born Chicago Illinois June 29, 1941. Presbyterian. Educated at Florida Southern College B.A. 1969 and University of Florida College of Law J.D. 1971. Member Tau Kappa Epsilon, Phi Delta Phi and Pi Gamma Mu. Admitted to practice Florida 1972. Began legal practice Winter Park 1972.

Author Chapter 5 "Sentencing" Criminal Volume of *The Florida Judge's Manual* Florida Conference of Circuit Court Judges 1985. Important Decision: Riesen v. State 1985. Member Judicial Relations Committee, Media and Public Relations Committee, The Florida Bar and Orange County Bar Association. Recipient Able Toastmaster Award 1978 and Alumni Achievement Award from Florida Southern College 1979. Corporal USMC 1961-65. Florida State Representative 1976-80. Republican. Named Orange County Young Republican of the Year 1976. Member Winter Park Toastmasters, Winter Park Chamber of Commerce, Leukemia Society of America, Rotary International and Greenhouse Family Counseling Center. Enjoys photography, wood furniture refinishing and running.

Office: 2045 Orange County Courthouse, 425 North Orange Avenue, Orlando 32801.

Telephone: (407) 836-2018.

Fax: (407) 835-5134

KLEIN, Edward S. *(Senior Judge, Florida Circuit Court Eleventh Judicial Circuit)* Assumed Senior Judge status, serves by assignment.

Office: 511 Dade County Courthouse, 73 West Flagler Street, Miami 33130.

Telephone: (305) 349-7001.

KLEIN, Gerald J. *(Senior Judge, Dade County Court)* Assumed Senior Judge status, serves by assignment.

Office: 511 Dade County Courthouse, 73 West Flagler Street, Miami 33130.
Telephone: (305) 349-7001.

KLEIN, Larry *(Judge, Florida District Court of Appeal Fourth District)* Appointed by Governor Lawton Chiles to term beginning Jan 21, 1993. Retained by election, current term expires Jan 2007. Educated at University of Michigan B.A. 1962, University of Florida College of Law J.D. 1964 and University of Virginia LL.M. in Judicial Process 1998. Member Editorial Board University of Florida Law Review 1963-64.

Board of Directors Florida Rural Legal Services 1970-72. Board of Directors 1970-74 and President 1974 Palm Beach County Legal Aid Society. Fellow American College of Trial Lawyers, American Bar Foundation and American Academy of Appellate Lawyers. Member The Florida Bar and Palm Beach County Bar Association (President 1975-76). Board of Directors Palm Beach County United Way 1968-70.

Mailing address: P.O. Box 3315, West Palm Beach 33402-3315.
Office: 1525 Palm Beach Lakes Boulevard, West Palm Beach 33401.
Telephone: (561) 242-2000.
Fax: (561) 242-2906

KLEIN, Murray Z. *(Senior Judge, Dade County Court)* Assumed Senior Judge status, serves by assignment. Born Orlando Florida.

Office: 511 Dade County Courthouse, 73 West Flagler Street, Miami 33130.
Telephone: (305) 349-7001.

KNUCK, Francis X. *(Senior Judge, Florida Circuit Court Eleventh Judicial Circuit)* Assumed Senior Judge status, serves by assignment.

Office: 511 Dade County Courthouse, 73 West Flagler Street, Miami 33130.
Telephone: (305) 349-7001.

KOENIG, Julie *(Judge, Florida Circuit Court Seventeenth Judicial Circuit)* Elected to term beginning Jan 3, 1995. Reelected 2000, current term expires Jan 2007. Born Hackensack New Jersey Dec 27, 1941. Roman Catholic. Educated at Northwestern University B.A. 1963, Michigan State University M.A. 1966 and Nova Southeastern University J.D. 1981. Law Clerk to U.S. District Court Southern District of Florida 1981-82. Admitted to practice Florida 1981, U.S. District Courts Middle 1982 and Southern 1982 Districts of Florida and U.S. Court of Appeals Eleventh Circuit 1982. In legal practice Fort Lauderdale 1982-96.

Member American Judicature Society, The Florida Bar, Broward County (President 1983) and American Bar Associations. Counsel Broward County Children's Services. Enjoys children, reading, skiing and horses. Personal Statement or Quote: "Be prepared. Please bring case law."

Office: 201 S.E. Sixth Street, #997, Fort Lauderdale 33301.
Telephone: (954) 831-7554

KOMANSKI, Walter *(Judge, Florida Circuit Court Ninth Judicial Circuit)* Former Judge, Orange County Court.

Office: 2020 Orange County Courthouse, 425 North Orange Avenue, Orlando 32801.
Telephone: (407) 836-2039.

KORDA, Lawrence L. *(Judge, Florida Circuit Court Seventeenth Judicial Circuit)* Elected to term beginning Jan 1979. Reelected 1984, 1990, 1996 and 2002. Current term expires Jan 2009. Born Hollywood Florida June 27, 1947. Jewish. Educated at The Citadel B.A. 1968 and Mercer University J.D. 1973. Dean Delta Theta Phi. Admitted to practice Florida 1973 and U.S. District Court District of Florida 1981.

Assistant Public Defender 1973-77. General Master Broward County Courts 1978-79. Juvenile Services Board Military Academy Nomination Review Committee. Member Hollywood Beach Kiwanis.

Office: 801 Broward County Courthouse, 201 S.E. Sixth Street, Fort Lauderdale 33301.
Telephone: (954) 831-7708.

KORNBLUM, Allen *(Senior Judge, Florida Circuit Court Eleventh Judicial Circuit)* Assumed Senior Judge status, serves by assignment. Born New York New York Jan 16, 1929. Religious affiliation: Hebrew. Educated at University of Miami LL.B. 1954. Member Zeta Beta Tau. Admitted to practice Florida 1954. Began legal practice Miami 1954. Former Judge, Dade County Court, appointed to term beginning May 13, 1981.

Instructor Miami-Dade Community College since 1978. Member American Judges Association, The Florida Bar and Dade County Bar Association. Staff Sergeant USAF 1946-49 and 1951-52. Past President PTA and Optimists.

Office: 511 Dade County Courthouse, 73 West Flagler Street, Miami 33130.
Telephone: (305) 349-7001.

KORNSTEIN, Harvey *(Judge, Florida Circuit Court Tenth Judicial Circuit)* Elected 1998 to term beginning Jan 1999. Term expires Jan 2005. Educated at University of Florida B.A. with honors 1973 J.D. 1976. Judge, Polk County Court Aug 1984 to Jan 1985 and Jan 3, 1989 to Jan 1999.

Assistant State Attorney Tenth Judicial Circuit 1980-84. Field Counsel Medicaid Fraud Control Unit 1985-88. Special Assistant State Attorney Sixth, Thirteenth and Nineteenth Circuits. Vice Chair Sentencing Committee and Member Civil Rules Committee Florida Conference of County Court Judges. Member Military Affairs Committee The Florida Bar. Member The Association of Trial Lawyers of America and American Judges Association. Attended Florida Judicial College 1989 and The National Judicial College 1990. USNR 1974-81. USAFR since 1981. Enjoys jogging, family activities and church.

Mailing address: P.O. Box 9000, Drawer J-134, Bartow 33831-9000.
Telephone: (863) 534-4652.

KORVICK, Maria Marinello *(Judge, Florida Circuit Court Eleventh Judicial Circuit)* Appointed by Governor Robert Graham Dec 1979 to term beginning 1980. Elected to subsequent terms. Current term expires 2006. Born Cuba Feb 23, 1946. Roman Catholic. Educated at Miami-Dade Community College and University of Miami J.D. Admitted to practice Florida and U.S. District Court Southern District of Florida.

KORVICK, MARIA MARINELLO—*Continued*

Assistant State Attorney Dade County 1973-79. Member Florida Association of Women Lawyers, The Florida Bar (Executive Council), Dade County and Cuban-American Bar Associations. Panel Family Division Seminars The Florida Bar March 1987 and April 1988. Previously employed as junior high school teacher Dade County Schools.

Office: 310 Dade County Courthouse, 73 West Flagler Street, Miami 33130.

Telephone: (305) 349-7086.

Fax: (305) 349-7090

KOTEY, Phyllis D. *(Judge, Alachua County Court)*

Office: 205 Alachua County Courthouse, 201 East University Avenue, Gainesville 32601.

Telephone: (352) 337-6130.

Fax: (352) 381-0171

KOVACHEVICH, Elizabeth Anne *(Judge, United States District Court Middle District of Florida)* Appointed for life by the President. Former Chief Judge. Born Canton Illinois Dec 14, 1936. Educated at St. Petersburg Junior College A.A. 1956, University of Miami B.B.A. magna cum laude in Finance 1958 and Stetson University J.D. 1961. Member Phi Delta Delta, Beta Gamma Sigma, Phi Theta Kappa, Phi Kappa Phi and Alpha Sigma Epsilon. Listed in *Who's Who in American Colleges and Universities* 1958 and 1961. Admitted to practice Florida 1961, U.S. District Courts Middle 1961 and Southern 1961 Districts of Florida, U.S. Court of Appeals Fifth Circuit 1961 and U.S. Supreme Court 1968. In legal practice St. Petersburg 1961-73. Nominated by President Gerald R. Ford to U.S. District Court Middle District of Florida 1976. Former Judge, Florida Circuit Court Sixth Judicial Circuit, elected to term beginning Jan 2, 1973. First woman judge elected in Sixth Judicial Circuit.

Research and Administrative Aide to Pinellas County Legislative Delegation 1961. Member Pinellas County Trial Lawyers, The Association of Trial Lawyers of America, American Judicature Society, Florida Association of Women Lawyers, The Florida Bar, St. Petersburg (Chairman Legislative Committee 1963-64, Secretary 1969) and American Bar Associations. Chairman St. Petersburg Professional Legal project "Days in Court" 1967. Producer/Coordinator television production "A Race to Judgment." Appointed by Chief Justice Florida Supreme Court as Chairman Supreme Court Bicentennial Committee for Sixth Judicial Circuit 1975-76 (conceived and coordinated three-part television program *Layman and the Law*). Recipient St. Petersburg Panhellenic Appreciation Award 1964, Mrs. Charles Ulrick Bay Award, Associated Women's Students Woman of the Year Award, Diploma for distinguished achievement from The Two Thousand Women of Achievement of London England, St. Petersburg Rotary Award, St. Petersburg Quarterback Club Award, Pinellas United Fund Award in Recognition of Concern and Meritorious Effort on behalf of the people of Pinellas County 1968, Beta Sigma Phi Woman of the Year Award 1970, Stetson University Distinguished Alumni Award 1970, American Legion Auxiliary Unit 14 President's Award for Community Service 1970, Outstanding Young Women of America Award 1970 and 1972, Dedication to Christian Ideals Award and Man of the Year Award from Knights of Columbus Districts 20-21 in 1972, U.S. Department of Defense Certificate of Appreciation 1975, U.S. Navy Recruiting Command Appreciation Award 1975 and Royal Order of the Pedageese from University of West Florida (with exalted rank of Chief Black Feather Ultimate Guide).

Listed in *Who's Who in American Women, Who's Who in The South and Southwest, Who's Who in Commerce and Industry* and *Dictionary of International Biography*. Member Florida Governor's Commission on Status of Women 1968-70 (compiled booklet "Florida Family Rights and Duties"), Board of Regents State of Florida 1970-72, Defense Advisory Committee on Women in the Service U.S. Department of Defense 1973-76 and President's Commission on White House Fellowships since 1973 (originally appointed by Richard M. Nixon and later Gerald R. Ford). Honorary member St. Petersburg Legal Secretaries Association 1966. Legal Advisor and Board of Directors Young Women's Residence, Inc. 1968. Legal Advisor and original member Council for Continuing Education of Women of Pinellas County, Inc. 1968. Vice Chairman and Chairman Seminar "Today's Woman in Tomorrow's World." Chairman Good Neighbors Division of Pinellas County United Fund 1968. Attended 20th Annual National Security Forum, Air War College Maxwell Air Force Base 1973. Life member Children's Hospital and St. Petersburg YWCA. Member St. Mary's Roman Catholic Church at St. Petersburg.

Office: 1730 U.S. Courthouse, 801 North Florida Avenue, Tampa 33602-3800.

Telephone: (813) 301-5730.

KRATHEN, David H. *(Judge, Florida Circuit Court Seventeenth Judicial Circuit)*

Office: Broward County Courthouse, 201 S.E. Sixth Street, Fort Lauderdale 33301.

KRAVITZ, Shelley J. *(Judge, Dade County Court)*

Office: 615 Dade County Courthouse, 73 West Flagler Street, Miami 33130.

Telephone: (305) 349-7091.

Fax: (305) 349-7093

KREEGER, Judith L. *(Judge, Florida Circuit Court Eleventh Judicial Circuit)*

Office: 2114 Courthouse Center, 175 N.W. First Avenue, Miami 33128.

Telephone: (305) 349-5729.

Fax: (305) 349-6177

KROLL, Kathleen J. *(Judge, Florida Circuit Court Fifteenth Judicial Circuit)* Assumed office Feb 8, 1994. Born Chicago Illinois May 7, 1954. Educated at Tufts University B.A. magna cum laude 1975, Antioch School of Law J.D. 1978 and Harvard University M.P.A. 1984. Admitted to practice Florida 1979, U.S. District Court Southern District of Florida 1979, U.S. Court of Appeals Eleventh Circuit 1981, U.S. Supreme Court 1982 and District of Columbia 1986. Judge, Palm Beach County Court Jan 8, 1985 to Feb 7, 1994.

Instructor in Law Palm Beach Junior College. Member Association of Women Judges, Palm Beach County Association of Women Lawyers (Co-founder), Florida Association of Women Lawyers, The Association of Trial Lawyers of America, Judicial Conference of the U.S., The Florida Bar, Palm Beach County, South Palm Beach County and American Bar Associations. Member American Red Cross (Director 1986), Executive Women of the Palm Beaches, Inc., Forum Club of the Palm

KROLL, KATHLEEN J.—*Continued*

Beaches, Girl Scouts, League of Women Voters, Norton Art Gallery and Dreher Park Zoo.

Office: Palm Beach County Courthouse, 205 North Dixie Highway, West Palm Beach 33401.
Telephone: (561) 355-4378.
Fax: (561) 355-1699

KUDER, John P. *(Chief Judge, Florida Circuit Court First Judicial Circuit)* Former Judge, Escambia County Court.

Office: Judicial Building, 190 Governmental Center, Pensacola 32501.
Telephone: (850) 595-4448.
Fax: (850) 595-4552

LaBARGA, Jorge *(Judge, Florida Circuit Court Fifteenth Judicial Circuit)*

Office: Palm Beach County Courthouse, 205 North Dixie Highway, West Palm Beach 33401.
Telephone: (561) 355-3964.
Fax: (561) 355-1616

LAMBERT, Brian *(Judge, Florida Circuit Court Fifth Judicial Circuit)*

Office: Marion County Judicial Center, 110 N.W. First Avenue, Ocala 34475.
Telephone: (352) 401-6785.
Fax: (352) 401-7881

LAND, Harlow H., Jr. *(Judge, Lafayette County Court)* Elected to term beginning Jan 7, 1985. Reelected 1988, 1992, 1996 and 2000. Current term expires Jan 2007. Born Gainesville Florida July 23, 1943. Episcopalian. Educated at University of Florida B.S.B.A. 1965 and Florida State University J.D. 1971. Member Sigma Phi Epsilon and Phi Delta Phi. Admitted to practice Florida 1971 and U.S. Court of Military Appeals 1972. In legal practice Mayo 1977-84.

State Attorney Third Judicial Circuit 1976-77 Florida. With Third Circuit Public Defenders Office 1977-82. Attorney Town of Mayo 1977-84. Member Florida Conference of County Court Judges (Executive Committee 1985, 1986, 1988, 1990), The Florida Bar and Third Circuit Bar Association (Chairman Grievance Committee 1980 and Unauthorized Practice of Law Committee 1983). Attended General Jurisdiction Course The National Judicial College 1986. Captain U.S. Army Transportation Officer 1965-67 and JAGC 1971-75. Awarded Bronze Star 1968, Meritorious Service Medal 1974 and Army Commendation Medal 1975. Worked as Traffic Manager St. Joe Paper Company 1967-68. Worked for Lafayette County Development Authority 1977-84 and Lafayette County Chamber of Commerce 1981-84. Member Mayo Rotary Club (Past President) and Lafayette Chamber of Commerce. Assistant Scout Master Boy Scouts of America. Enjoys travel, camping and history.

Mailing address: P.O. Box 197, Mayo 32066.
Telephone: (386) 294-1555.
Fax: (386) 294-4233

LANDO, Maxine Cohen *(Judge, Florida Circuit Court Eleventh Judicial Circuit)* Elected to term beginning Jan 2, 1995. Reelected 2000, current term expires Jan 2007. Served Criminal Division 1995-99. Serves Family Division since 1999. Educated at University of Michigan B.A. 1971 and University of Miami School of Law J.D. 1974. Admitted to practice Florida 1974 and Trial Bar of U.S. District Court Southern District of Florida 1979. In legal practice Miami 1985-91. Judge, Dade County Court Jan 1991 to Jan 1, 1995. Acting Circuit Court Judge for Felony, Drug Court and Juvenile Matters 1991-94.

Assistant Public Defender Dade County 1974-85. Lecturer "Winning the Trial: Understanding Psychology of Juries" University of Miami School of Continuing Studies 1988. Member 1985-90 and Board of Directors 1989-90 Florida Association of Criminal Defense Lawyers. Former Member Coral Gables, South Miami-Kendall, Federal and American Bar Associations. Member Florida Association of Women Lawyers, First American Family Inns of Court, American Judges Association, The Florida Bar (Grievance Committee 1982-85, Ethics Subcommittee 1988-89, DUI and Traffic Committee 1989-90, Criminal Section Jury Instructions Committee 1989-90), Dade County (Juvenile Court Committee 1986-87, Criminal Court Committee 1987-90) and Cuban American Bar Associations. Lecturer at seminars County Court Judges Association. Instructor New Judges Trial Skills College since 1991 and in Criminal Law Florida College of Advanced Judicial Studies since 1991. Mentor Coordinator for New Judges Florida Eleventh Judicial Circuit since 1996. Recipient Distinguished Service Award from Florida Council on Crime and Delinquency District VIII 1997. Former Member South Dade Branch Jewish Federation (Chairperson South Dade Consortium), Urban League, NAACP and Coalition of Hispanic American Women. Life Member Aliyah Hadassah, Opera Guild and Young Patroness of the Opera. Board of Directors Bench and Bar Unit of B'nai B'rith and Bet Shira Congregation of Greater Miami. Member Biscayne Bay Kiwanis and University of Miami Alumni Association.

Office: 412 Dade County Courthouse, 73 West Flagler Street, Miami 33130.
Telephone: (305) 349-7144.
Fax: (305) 349-7011

LANGER, Lester *(Judge, Florida Circuit Court Eleventh Judicial Circuit)* Former Judge, Dade County Court.

Office: 206 Juvenile Justice Center, 3300 N.W. 27th Avenue, Miami 33142.
Telephone: (305) 638-6106.
Fax: (305) 638-6347

LANGFORD, J. David *(Judge, Florida Circuit Court Tenth Judicial Circuit)* Assumed office Nov 28, 1989. Elected to subsequent terms. Born Frostproof Florida Dec 26, 1950. Southern Baptist. Educated at Polk Junior College A.A. 1970 and University of Florida B.A. 1972 J.D. 1975. Admitted to practice Florida 1975. In legal practice Avon Park Feb 1978 to Jan 1987. Assistant State Attorney Sebring June 1975 to Jan 1978. Judge, Highlands County Court Jan 6, 1987 to Nov 27, 1989.

Office: 430 South Commerce Avenue, Sebring 33870.
Telephone: (863) 402-6617.

LARUE, Terrill J. *(Judge, Florida Circuit Court Seventh Judicial Circuit)*

Mailing address: P.O. Box 758, Palatka 32178.
Office: Putnam County Courthouse, Palatka 32178.
Telephone: (386) 329-0266.
Fax: (386) 329-1275

LAUGHLIN, Lauren *(Judge, Florida Circuit Court Sixth Judicial Circuit)*
Office: Criminal Justice Center, 14250 49th Street North, Clearwater 33762.
Telephone: (727) 464-8101.
Fax: (727) 464-6204

LAURENT, John F. *(Judge, Florida Circuit Court Tenth Judicial Circuit)*
Mailing address: P.O. Box 9000, Drawer J-118, Bartow 33831-9000.
Telephone: (863) 534-4651.
Fax: (863) 534-4094

LAUTEN, Frederick, Jr. *(Judge, Florida Circuit Court Ninth Judicial Circuit)* Appointed by Governor Jeb Bush Nov 1999 to term beginning 2000. Elected 2002, current term expires Jan 2009. Born Chicago Illinois 1952. Catholic. Educated at Rollins College B.A. with honors 1975 M.B.A. with honors 1976 and Villanova University School of Law J.D. 1979. Admitted to practice Florida 1979 and District of Columbia 1982. Judge, Orange County Court Sept 24, 1993 to 2000, appointed by Governor Lawton Chiles.
Assistant State Attorney 1982-93.
Office: 815 Orange County Courthouse, 425 North Orange Avenue, Orlando 32801.
Telephone: (407) 836-2009.
Fax: (407) 836-0450

LAW, William G., Jr. *(Judge, Florida Circuit Court Fifth Judicial Circuit)* Elected Nov 1994 to term beginning Jan 3, 1995. Reelected Nov 2000, current term expires Jan 2007. Born Upper Darby Pennsylvania Oct 21, 1955. Methodist. Educated at Juniata College B.S. 1977 and Stetson University J.D. 1979. Staff member Stetson Law Review 1978-79. Admitted to practice Florida 1980 and U.S. District Court District of Florida 1980. Judge, Lake County Court Jan 2, 1990 to Jan 2, 1995, appointed by Governor Bob Martinez.
Author "Proper Cause and Reappointment of Non-Tenured Teachers" Florida B. Jour. Feb 1980.
Mailing address: P.O. Box 7800, Tavares 32778-7800.
Office: Lake County Judicial Center, Tavares 32778.
Telephone: (352) 742-4390.
Fax: (352) 742-4370

LAWRENCE, L. Arthur, Jr. *(Senior Judge, Florida District Court of Appeal)* Assumed Senior Judge status, serves by assignment. Born Chattahoochee Florida March 24, 1939. Educated at Emory University B.A. 1960 and University of Florida LL.B. 1963 replaced by J.D. Admitted to practice Florida 1963. Began legal practice Live Oak 1963. Former Judge, Live Oak Municipal Court. Former Judge and Chief Judge, Florida Circuit Court Third Judicial Circuit, elected to term beginning Jan 2, 1979.
Public Defender Feb 1, 1964 to Jan 3, 1969 and State Attorney Feb 1, 1974 to Jan 2, 1979 Third Judicial Circuit. Member The Florida Bar and Third Judicial Circuit Bar Association. Member First Baptist Church of Live Oak. Enjoys hunting.
Office: 301 South Martin Luther King Boulevard Jr., Tallahassee 32399.
Telephone: (850) 486-8136.

LAWSON, C. Alan *(Judge, Florida Circuit Court Ninth Judicial Circuit)* Appointed by Governor Jeb Bush to term beginning Jan 1, 2002. Term expires Jan 3, 2005. Born Lakeland Florida May 12, 1961. Educated at Clemson University with highest honors 1983 and Florida State University with highest honors 1987. Member Order of the Coif. Admitted to practice Florida 1987.
Office: 2025 Orange County Courthouse, 425 North Orange Avenue, Orlando 32801.
Telephone: (407) 836-0577.
Fax: (407) 835-5086

LAZARUS, Joel *(Judge, Broward County Court)*
Office: 460 Broward County Courthouse, 201 S.E. Sixth Street, Fort Lauderdale 33301.
Telephone: (954) 831-5842.
Fax: (954) 831-5572

LAZZARA, Richard A. *(Judge, United States District Court Middle District of Florida)* Appointed for life by President Bill Clinton to term beginning 1997. Born Tampa Florida Dec 17, 1945. Educated at Loyola University B.A. 1967 and University of Florida College of Law J.D. 1970. In legal practice Tampa 1974-86. Judge, Hillsborough County Court 1987. Judge, Florida Circuit Court Thirteenth Judicial Circuit 1988-93. Judge, Florida District Court of Appeal Second District Nov 10, 1993 to 1997.
Assistant County Solicitor Hillsborough County 1970-72. Assistant State Attorney Hillsborough County 1973.
Office: U.S. Courthouse, 801 North Florida Avenue, Tampa 33602-3800.
Telephone: (813) 301-5350.

LEBAN, Mark King *(Judge, Dade County Court)*
Office: 2322 Courthouse Center, 175 N.W. First Avenue, Miami 33128.
Telephone: (305) 349-5756.
Fax: (305) 349-5755

LEBOW, Susan L. *(Judge, Florida Circuit Court Seventeenth Judicial Circuit)* Former Judge, Broward County Court.
Office: 4790 Broward County Courthouse, 201 S.E. Sixth Street, Fort Lauderdale 33301.
Telephone: (954) 831-7853.

LEDERMAN, Cindy S. *(Judge, Florida Circuit Court Eleventh Judicial Circuit)* Assumed office July 18, 1994. Former Judge, Dade County Court.
Office: 201 Juvenile Justice Center, 3300 N.W. 27th Avenue, Miami 33142.
Telephone: (305) 638-6087.
Fax: (305) 634-9921

LEE, Robert E., Jr. *(Senior Judge, Florida Circuit Court Seventh Judicial Circuit)* Assumed Senior Judge status, serves by assignment.
Office: 101 North Alabama Avenue, De Land 32724.
Telephone: (386) 257-6097.

LEE, Robert W. *(Judge, Broward County Court)*
Office: 6760 Broward County Courthouse, 201 S.E. Sixth Street, Fort Lauderdale 33301.
Telephone: (954) 831-5509.
Fax: (954) 831-5572

LEESFIELD, Ellen *(Judge, Florida Circuit Court Eleventh Judicial Circuit)* Appointed by Governor Lawton Chiles Sept 8, 1993.
Office: 413 Gerstein Justice Building, 1351 N.W. Twelfth Street, Miami 33125.
Telephone: (305) 349-7101.

LEGENDRE, Ronald A. *(Judge, Osceola County Court)* Elected 1980 to term beginning Jan 6, 1981. Reelected 1984, 1988, 1992, 1996 and 2000. Current term expires Jan 2007. Born Manchester New Hampshire Feb 12, 1948. Catholic. Educated at Loyola University A.B. 1970 and Florida State University J.D. 1973. Admitted to practice Florida 1973. Began legal practice Kissimmee 1973.

Member Florida Conference of County Court Judges, The Association of Trial Lawyers of America, The Florida Bar and Osceola County Bar Association (President 1979). Past President, former Zone Chairman and former Chief YMCA Parent-Child Program of Indian Guides and Princesses. Started Boys Club Soccer League 1978 and Osceola Youth Soccer Club 1982. Soccer Coach since 1978 and Little League baseball manager since 1982. Member Kissimmee Lions Club, St. Cloud-Kissimmee Knights of Columbus, Osceola County Council on Youth and Adam Walsh Center (Member Advisory Board).

Office: Osceola County Courthouse, 12 South Vernon Avenue, Kissimmee 34741.
Telephone: (407) 343-2509.

LEHR, Myriam *(Judge, Dade County Court)*
Office: 206 North Dade Justice Center, 15555 Biscayne Boulevard, Miami 33160.
Telephone: (305) 354-8722.

LEIFMAN, Steven *(Judge, Dade County Court)*
Office: 617 Gerstein Justice Building, 1351 N.W. Twelfth Street, Miami 33125.
Telephone: (305) 548-5394.
Fax: (305) 548-5552

LENARD, Joan A. *(Judge, United States District Court Southern District of Florida)* Appointed for life by President Bill Clinton to term beginning 1995. Born Amityville New York Jan 7, 1952. Educated at Rockland Community College A.A. 1972, Roger Williams College B.A. 1973 and Antioch School of Law J.D. 1976. Judge, Dade County Court 1982-93. Judge, Florida Circuit Court Eleventh Judicial Circuit 1993-95.

Assistant State Attorney 1976-78, Chief Consumer Fraud Division 1978-80 and Chief Consumer and Economic Crime Division 1980-92 Dade County.

Office: Federal Courthouse Square, 301 North Miami Avenue, Miami 33128-7788.
Telephone: (305) 523-5500.

LENDERMAN, John C. *(Judge, Florida Circuit Court Sixth Judicial Circuit)* Appointed by Governor Lawton Chiles to term beginning Feb 17, 1992. Elected Nov 1992 and 1998. Current term expires Jan 2005. Administrative Judge Pinellas County Family Division 1995-96. Born Miami Florida Nov 9, 1943. Catholic. Educated at Florida State University B.A. 1966 and Stetson University College of Law J.D. 1969. Admitted to practice Florida 1969 and U.S. Supreme Court 1972. Board Certified as a Specialist in Marital and Family Law by The Florida Bar. In legal practice St. Petersburg 1969-92.

Adjunct Professor of Family Law and Domestic Relations Aug 1993 to Nov 1993 and Family Law Litigation 1995-97 Stetson University College of Law. Adjunct Professor Nova University. Member Florida Supreme Court Family Court Steering Committee 1996-2002. Member The Florida Bar (Member 1975-78 and Chairman 1977-78 Grievance Committee, Member Circuit Arbitration Committee 1989-91, Unauthorized Practice of Law Committee) and St. Petersburg Bar Association. Lecturer on Family Law CLE and Coordinator and Local Representative for Bar CLE Programs The Florida Bar. Lecturer, Presenter and Department Head Florida College of Advanced Judicial Studies and Florida Conference of Circuit Court Judges. Mentor Judge since 1995. Attended Judicial Writing course The National Judicial College Reno Nevada Oct 26-31, 1996. Recipient Jurist of the Year Award for most significant contribution to Florida Family Law from American Academy of Matrimonial Lawyers Florida Chapter 1997. Vice Chair and Organizer Pinellas County Domestic Violence Task Force 1993-97.

Office: Judicial Building, 545 First Avenue North, St. Petersburg 33701.
Telephone: (727) 582-7792.
Fax: (727) 582-7242

LERNER-WREN, Ginger *(Judge, Broward County Court)*
Office: 429 Broward County Courthouse, 201 S.E. Sixth Street, Fort Lauderdale 33301.
Telephone: (954) 831-7240.

LESTER, Kenneth *(Judge, Florida Circuit Court Eighteenth Judicial Circuit)*
Office: Seminole County Courthouse, 301 North Park Avenue, Sanford 32771-1292.
Telephone: (407) 665-4224.
Fax: (407) 665-4241

LEVENS, William P. *(Judge, Florida Circuit Court Thirteenth Judicial Circuit)* Appointed by Governor Jeb Bush. Born Mount Vernon Illinois May 11, 1947. Educated at University of Florida B.A. 1969 J.D. 1972. Admitted to practice Florida 1972. In legal practice Tampa 1972-2000.

Office: 332B Hillsborough County Courthouse, 419 Pierce Street, Tampa 33602-4022.
Telephone: (813) 272-6992.
Fax: (813) 276-2232

LEVENSON, Barbara S. *(Judge, Florida Circuit Court Eleventh Judicial Circuit)*
Office: 505 Dade County Courthouse, 73 West Flagler Street, Miami 33130.
Telephone: (305) 349-7096.

LEVIN, Steven *(Judge, Florida Circuit Court Nineteenth Judicial Circuit)*
Office: 100 S.E. Ocean Boulevard, Suite A35, Stuart 34994.
Telephone: (772) 288-5570.
Fax: (772) 288-5572

LEVINE, Paul A. *(Judge, Pinellas County Court)* Appointed by Governor Lawton Chiles June 10, 1994.
Office: Criminal Justice Center, 14250 49th Street North, Clearwater 33762.
Telephone: (727) 464-6059.

LEVY, D. Bruce *(Judge, Florida Circuit Court Eleventh Judicial Circuit)*
Office: 311 Dade County Courthouse, 73 West Flagler Street, Miami 33130.
Telephone: (305) 349-7117.
Fax: (305) 634-9921

LEVY, David L. *(Judge, Florida District Court of Appeal Third District)* Appointed by Governor Bob Mar-

LEVY, DAVID L.—*Continued*

tinez to term beginning Jan 3, 1989. Retained by election Nov 6, 1990, 1996 and 2002. Current term expires Jan 2009. Born Miami Florida Dec 25, 1943. Educated at University of Miami B.A. in Government 1965 and University of Tulsa J.D. 1968. Admitted to practice Florida, U.S. District Court Southern District of Florida, U.S. Court of Appeals Fifth Circuit and U.S. Tax Court. Judge, Florida Circuit Court Eleventh Judicial Circuit Jan 9, 1978 to Jan 2, 1989.

Appointed Assistant State Attorney Eleventh Judicial Circuit by State Attorney Richard E. Gerstein April 15, 1970 (assigned to Felony Division Sept 1970 to Sept 1971). Chief Prosecutor Criminal Division Sept 1971 to May 1973 and Chief Prosecutor Organized Crime and Public Corruption Prosecution Unit May 1973 to Jan 1978 Dade County State Attorney's Office. Executive Assistant to State Attorney Richard E. Gerstein June 1976 to Jan 1978. Legal Advisor to Dade County Grand Jury May 1977 to Jan 1978. Participant Governor's Challenge Program 1982. Member Committee on Standards of Conduct Governing Judges Jan 1988 to Jan 1989 and Dec 1991 to March 1993 and Judicial Ethics Advisory Committee since Oct 1998. Adjunct Lecturer Institute on Organized Crime June 1974 to Jan 1978. Adjunct Professor of Criminal Justice Nova University 1977-79, St. Thomas University (formerly Biscayne College) since 1982, St. Thomas University School of Law 1984-87 and since 1995, Florida International University since 1986, University of Miami since 1987 and Miami-Dade Community College since 1990. Member Florida Conference of Circuit Court Judges (Criminal Justice and Law School Liaison Committees), Florida Conference of District Court of Appeal Judges, The Florida Bar, Dade County and American Bar Associations. Attended "Career Prosecutors Course," "Organized Crime Seminar" and "Advanced Organized Crime Seminar" National College of District Attorneys. Listed in *Who's Who in Florida* 1982. Junior high school teacher 1968-70. Member Juvenile Diabetes Research Foundation and Criminal Justice Craft Advisory Committee Dade County Public School System.

Office: 2001 S.W. 117th Avenue, Miami 33175-1716.
Telephone: (305) 229-3200.
Fax: (305) 229-3206

LEWIS, Diana *(Judge, Florida Circuit Court Fifteenth Judicial Circuit)*

Office: Palm Beach County Courthouse, 205 North Dixie Highway, West Palm Beach 33401.

LEWIS, Joseph, Jr. *(Judge, Florida District Court of Appeal First District)* Assumed office 2001. Born Tallahassee Florida Jan 6, 1953. Educated at University of Montana B.S. 1974 and Florida State University College of Law J.D. 1977. Admitted to practice U.S. District Courts Middle, Northern and Southern Districts of Florida and District of Arizona, Trial Bar of U.S. District Court Southern District of Florida, U.S. Courts of Appeals Fourth, Ninth and Eleventh Circuits and U.S. Supreme Court.

Judicial Research Aide Florida Industrial Relations Commission 1977-78. Assistant Public Defender Second Judicial Circuit 1978-81. Senior Attorney General Civil Litigation Section 1981-95 and Bureau Chief Employment Litigation Section 1995-2000 Office of the Attorney General. President 1995-96 and Member Executive Board 1997 Government Bar Association. Master Tallahassee Chapter American Inns of Court since 2002. Member The Florida Bar (At-large Representative 1997-2001, Member Executive Council 1998-2001, Secretary 2001-02 and Treasurer since 2002 Government Law Section, Vice Chair Second Circuit Fee Arbitration Committee 1999-2000 and Federal Court Practice Committee 2000-01, Member Appellate Court Rules Committee since 2001, Executive Council Criminal Law Section since 2002), Tallahassee (Board of Directors 1999-2001) and National Bar Associations. Recipient Claude Pepper Outstanding Government Lawyer Award 1995 and Award for Meritorious Public Service 2000 from The Florida Bar, Award for Complete Dedication to the Advancement of the Organization from Government Bar Association 1996 and Community Service Award from Neighborhood Justice Center and Legal Services of North Florida, Inc. 1997. Board of Directors Boys and Girls Club of the Big Bend 1994-95. Member Tallahassee Urban League since 1995.Mentor Leon County Public Schools since 2001. Charter Member C. K. Steele Memorial Jaycees. Former Member Lincoln High School Quarterback Club.

Office: 301 Martin Luther King Jr. Boulevard, Tallahassee 32399-1850.
Telephone: (850) 487-1000.
Fax: (850) 921-4768

LEWIS, R. Fred *(Justice, Florida Supreme Court)* Appointed by Governor Lawton Chiles Dec 8, 1998 to term beginning Jan 1, 1999. Retained by election Nov 7, 2000, current term expires Jan 2007. Born Beckley West Virginia Dec 14, 1947. Educated at Florida Southern College B.A. cum laude 1969 and University of Miami School of Law J.D. cum laude 1972. Staff member University of Miami Law Review. Member Appellate Moot Court team. Member Omicron Delta Kappa, Bar and Gavel and Order of Barristers. Began legal practice Miami.

Member The Florida Bar. U.S. Army. Board of Directors Miami Children's Hospital.

Office: Supreme Court Building, 500 South Duval Street, Tallahassee 32399-1925.
Telephone: (850) 488-0007.
Fax: (850) 487-4696

LEWIS, Terry P. *(Judge, Florida Circuit Court Second Judicial Circuit)* Former Judge, Leon County Court.

Office: Gadsden County Courthouse Annex, 24 North Adams Street, Quincy 32351.
Telephone: (850) 875-3626.
Fax: (850) 875-7265

LEY, Nancy Moate *(Judge, Florida Circuit Court Sixth Judicial Circuit)*

Office: Criminal Justice Center, 14250 49th Street North, Clearwater 33762.
Telephone: (727) 464-6222.
Fax: (727) 464-3573

LEYTE-VIDAL, Henry *(Judge, Florida Circuit Court Eleventh Judicial Circuit)* Former Judge, Dade County Court.

Office: 203 Juvenile Justice Center, 3300 N.W. 27th Avenue, Miami 33142.
Telephone: (305) 638-6521.

LINDSEY, Hubert R. *(Judge, Florida Circuit Court Fifteenth Judicial Circuit)*
Office: Palm Beach County Courthouse, 205 North Dixie Highway, West Palm Beach 33401.
Telephone: (561) 355-3832.

LINDSEY, Lewis R. "Bob" *(Judge, Florida Circuit Court First Judicial Circuit)* Born Pensacola Florida Aug 19, 1944. Christian. Educated at University of Florida A.A. 1965 B.S. 1969 and Cumberland School of Law of Samford University J.D. 1974. Member Alpha Tau Omega. Admitted to practice Florida 1974. Began legal practice DeFuniak Springs 1974. Former Judge, Walton County Court, appointed by Governor Robert Graham to term beginning Aug 1, 1984.
Assistant State Attorney 1976-82. Member The Florida Bar. Attended General Jurisdiction Seminar The National Judicial College 1986. Previously employed with Farmers Home Administration 1968-70. Enjoys family life, hunting, fishing and horses.
Office: Walton County Courthouse, 571 Highway 90 East, DeFuniak Springs 32433.
Telephone: (850) 892-8134.
Fax: (850) 892-8377

LITTLE, Perry A. *(Judge, Florida Circuit Court Thirteenth Judicial Circuit)* Assumed office Dec 8, 1993. Former Judge, Hillsborough County Court.
Office: 437 Tower, 801 East Twiggs Street, Tampa 33602-3554.
Telephone: (813) 272-5775.
Fax: (813) 276-2079

LOBER, Jere E. *(Senior Judge, Florida Circuit Court Eighteenth Judicial Circuit)* Appointed by Governor Bob Martinez to term beginning Jan 2, 1989. Elected to subsequent terms. Former Chief Judge. Assumed Senior Judge status, serves by assignment.
Office: Moore Justice Center, 2825 Judge Fran Jamieson Way, Viera 32940-8006.
Telephone: (321) 637-5555.

LoGALBO, Emanuel *(Judge, Sarasota County Court)* Appointed by Governor Robert Graham to term beginning Jan 2, 1986. Elected Nov 1986, 1990, 1994 and 1998. Current term expires Jan 2005. Born Chicago Illinois June 15, 1943. Roman Catholic. Educated at St. Mary of the Lakes Seminary B.A. 1966 and John Marshall Law School J.D. 1972. Admitted to practice Illinois 1972, U.S. District Court Northern District of Illinois 1972 and Florida 1974.
Assistant Public Defender Cook County Illinois Nov 9, 1972 to Jan 31, 1977. Assistant State Attorney Feb 1977 to Dec 1985 and Assistant Public Defender Jan 1985 to Dec 1986 Twelfth Judicial Circuit, Sarasota Florida. Author "Motion to Disqualify Judge" pp. 526-529, "Motion to Disqualify Defense Attorney" pp. 529-532 and "Motion to Disqualify Prosecution" pp. 532-535 *Florida Prosecutor's Manual* 1982. Member Florida Prosecuting Attorneys Association, American Judicature Society, The Florida Bar and Illinois State Bar Association. Attended Traffic Adjudication Seminar Dec 1985, Annual Education Meeting Jan 1986 and Specialty Courses on Evidence and Judicial Writing June 1986 Florida Conference of County Court Judges and Florida Judicial College Florida State Conference Center March 1986. With Peace Corps, Brazil 1966. Junior high school teacher in Chicago's ghetto community 1967-69. Psychiatric aide Illinois State Psychiatric Institute, Chicago 1968-69. Member Knights of Columbus. Enjoys reading, singing in church choir, children's bible studies, classical music and family activities.
Mailing address: P.O. Box 48927, Sarasota 34230.
Office: 2002 Ringling Boulevard, Sarasota 34237.
Telephone: (941) 861-7956.
Fax: (941) 861-7915

LOGAN, Paul E. *(Judge, Florida Circuit Court Twelfth Judicial Circuit)*
Mailing address: P.O. Box 1000, Bradenton 34206.
Office: 1115 Manatee Avenue West, Bradenton 34205.
Telephone: (941) 742-5957.
Fax: (941) 742-5983

LOGAN, Walter D. *(Judge, Florida Circuit Court Sixth Judicial Circuit)*
Office: 211 Judicial Building, 545 First Avenue North, St. Petersburg 33701.
Telephone: (727) 582-7288.

LOPEZ, Manuel A. *(Judge, Hillsborough County Court)*
Office: 225 Tower, 801 East Twiggs Street, Tampa 33602-3554.
Telephone: (813) 757-3949.
Fax: (813) 757-3956

LOPEZ, Peter R. *(Judge, Florida Circuit Court Eleventh Judicial Circuit)*
Office: 229 Gerstein Justice Building, 1351 N.W. Twelfth Street, Miami 33125.
Telephone: (305) 548-5733.
Fax: (305) 548-5610

LOTT, Martha Ann *(Judge, Florida Circuit Court Eighth Judicial Circuit)* Former Judge, Alachua County Court, elected to term beginning Jan 1991.
Office: 305 Alachua County Courthouse, 201 East University Avenue, Gainesville 32601.
Telephone: (352) 374-3646.
Fax: (352) 381-0121

LUBITZ, Susan R. *(Judge, Palm Beach County Court)* Appointed by Governor Bob Martinez to term beginning Jan 2, 1990. Elected to subsequent terms.
Office: South County Courthouse, 200 West Atlantic Avenue, Delray Beach 33444.
Telephone: (561) 274-1420.

LUCE, Richard A. *(Judge, Florida Circuit Court Sixth Judicial Circuit)* Former Judge, Pinellas County Court.
Office: Criminal Justice Center, 14250 49th Street North, Clearwater 33762.
Telephone: (727) 464-6430.

LUNDY, Jack E. *(Judge, Glades County Court)*
Mailing address: P.O. Box 579, Moore Haven 33471.
Office: Glades County Courthouse, Moore Haven 33471.
Telephone: (863) 946-6031.
Fax: (863) 946-2917

LUPO, Mary Elisabeth *(Judge, Florida Circuit Court Fifteenth Judicial Circuit)* Former Judge, Palm Beach County Court.
Office: Palm Beach County Courthouse, 205 North Dixie Highway, West Palm Beach 33401.

LUPO, MARY ELISABETH—*Continued*

Telephone: (561) 355-2256.
Fax: (561) 355-2410

LUZZO, John T. *(Judge, Florida Circuit Court Seventeenth Judicial Circuit)* Appointed by Governor Robert Graham to term beginning 1985. Elected 1986, 1992 and 1998. Current term expires Jan 2005. Born Chicago Illinois Aug 21, 1946. Catholic. Educated at University of Florida B.S.J. with honors 1968 J.D. with honors 1973, Florida Atlantic University and University of South Florida. Member Phi Delta Phi. Admitted to practice Florida 1973, U.S. District Court Southern District of Florida 1973 and U.S. Tax Court 1981. In legal practice Davie, Hollywood and Fort Lauderdale 1973-81. Judge, Broward County Court 1981-85. Associate Judge, Florida District Court of Appeal Fourth District June 1987.

Adjunct Professor of Law Nova University 1980-81. Legislative Chairman Florida Conference of County Court Judges 1983-85. Member since 1986 and Vice Chairman since 1990 Legislative Committee and Representative Florida District Court of Appeal Fourth District since 1989 Florida Conference of Circuit Court Judges. Member Broward County Estate Planning Council, The Florida Bar (Member since 1986, Co-chairman 1988-90 and Chairman 1991 Code and Rules of Civil Evidence Committee, Member Committee on Professionalism since 1989), Broward County (Law Day USA Committee 1985, Young Lawyers Section, Broward Lawyers Care Program since 1988) and American Bar Associations. Co-chairman Statewide Practice of Law Economics Seminar 1978. Attended "General Jurisdiction" The National Judicial College 1982, "Evidence" Seminar American Judges Association 1984 and "Appellate Writing for Trial Judges and Civil Jurisdiction" Seminar Harvard University 1986. Faculty Advisor The National Judicial College summer 1987. Previously employed as a sports writer and sales representative. Board of Directors Columbus Civic Club since 1982 and American Red Cross since 1983. Honorary Director Broward County Crime Commission 1985. Enjoys reading, sports and art.

Office: 1020A Broward County Courthouse, 201 S.E. Sixth Street, Fort Lauderdale 33301.
Telephone: (954) 831-7829.
Fax: (954) 831-5572

LYNCH, Frank J., Jr. *(Magistrate Judge, United States District Court Southern District of Florida)* Appointed by U.S. District Court judges.

Office: 300 South Sixth Street, Second Floor, Fort Pierce 34950.
Telephone: (772) 595-9312.

LYNCH, Thomas M., IV *(Judge, Florida Circuit Court Seventeenth Judicial Circuit)* Assumed office April 6, 1995. Former Judge, Broward County Court.

Office: 999 Broward County Courthouse, 201 S.E. Sixth Street, Fort Lauderdale 33301.
Telephone: (954) 831-7831.

MAASS, Elizabeth T. *(Judge, Florida Circuit Court Fifteenth Judicial Circuit)* Former Judge, Palm Beach County Court, appointed by Governor Bob Martinez to term beginning Dec 22, 1989.

Office: Palm Beach County Courthouse, 205 North Dixie Highway, West Palm Beach 33401.
Telephone: (561) 355-6050.
Fax: (561) 355-1652

MacKINNON, Cynthia Z. *(Judge, Florida Circuit Court Ninth Judicial Circuit)* Appointed by Governor Lawton Chiles Dec 22, 1993.

Office: Juvenile Justice Center, 2000 East Michigan Street, Orlando 32806.
Telephone: (407) 836-7590.
Fax: (407) 836-7599

MAGER, Gerald *(Senior Judge, Florida District Court of Appeal)* Former Chief Judge. Assumed Senior Judge status, serves by assignment.

Office: 1525 Palm Beach Lakes Boulevard, West Palm Beach 33402.
Telephone: (561) 242-2000.

MAJEED, A. B. *(Judge, Brevard County Court)* Appointed by Governor Lawton Chiles to term beginning 1993. Elected to term beginning 1999, current term expires 2005. Educated at Howard University magna cum laude and Catholic University of America School of Law J.D. Member Phi Beta Kappa. Admitted to practice Florida, District of Columbia, New York, Pennsylvania and U.S. Supreme Court.

Former Instructor in Law B.C.C. Criminal Justice Center. Member Brevard County Bar Association. Guest Speaker on American Pride and Patriotism Temple Israel, Democratic Executive Committee, Democratic Women's Committee, Daughters of the American Revolution, Annual Banquet Sons of the American Revolution, Knights of Columbus, South Brevard Scottish Rite Club, National Association of Retired Federal Employees, Law Day Brevard County Bar Association, Annual Banquet NAACP, Martin Luther King Memorial March, Annual Banquet Palm Bay Area Chamber of Commerce, Melbourne Area Chamber of Commerce, STOP (Stop Turning Out Prisoners), Leadership Brevard, Keep Brevard Beautiful, Elks Club, Lions Club, Sertoma Club and Rotary Club. Graduate Florida Judges School. Course Instructor New County Judges Program. Judicial Representative and Chairman Brevard County Elections Canvassing Board.

Office: Moore Justice Center, Third Floor, 2825 Judge Fran Jamieson Way, Viera 32940-8006.
Telephone: (321) 617-7270.
Fax: (321) 617-7277

MAKEMSON, Robert R. *(Judge, Florida Circuit Court Nineteenth Judicial Circuit)* Appointed by Governor Bob Martinez Feb 8, 1989. Elected to subsequent terms.

Office: 327 Courthouse Addition, 218 South Second Street, Fort Pierce 34950.
Telephone: (772) 462-1200.
Fax: (772) 462-1203

MALONEY, Dennis Paul *(Judge, Florida Circuit Court Tenth Judicial Circuit)* Born Washington D.C. Feb 9, 1946. Catholic. Educated at Wheeling College B.S. 1969 and University of Florida J.D. 1974. Admitted to practice Florida 1974. Judge, Polk County Court 1973-81.

With Office of the Public Defender Tenth Judicial Circuit at Bartow 1974. E-3 USMCR 1965-71.

Mailing address: P.O. Box 9000, Drawer J115, Bartow 33831-9000.
Telephone: (863) 534-4624.
Fax: (863) 534-7721

MANEY, T. Patterson *(Judge, Okaloosa County Court)* Appointed by Governor Bob Martinez to term beginning May 19, 1989. Elected to subsequent terms.
Office: County Courthouse Annex, Box 4, 1250 North Eglin Parkway, Shalimar 32579.
Telephone: (850) 651-7486.
Fax: (850) 651-7725

MAPP, Calvin R. *(Senior Judge, Dade County Court)* Appointed by Governor Reubin O'Donovan Askew July 1973. Elected to subsequent terms. Assumed Senior Judge status, serves by assignment. Born Miami Florida Sept 10, 1924. Educated at Morris Brown College A.B. and Howard University LL.B. Awarded honorary LL.D. Morris Brown College 1974. Life member Kappa Alpha Psi. Admitted to practice Florida 1965, U.S. District Court Southern District of Florida and U.S. Supreme Court. Began legal practice Miami 1965.
Former Assistant State Attorney Dade County. Member Miami Police Department eight years. Author "Traffic (A Compilation of Florida's Traffic Laws)" Calvin R. Mapp 1980, 1983, 1985 and 1987. Member American Judicature Society, Governor's Commission on Criminal Justice Standards and Goals, Governor's Commission Task Force on Courts, Cocoanut Grove Cares, Inc. (Mayor's Joint Committee for Retraining of Ex-Offenders), Dade County Criminal Justice Advisory Council, The Florida Bar (Former Member Crime and Delinquency Committee), National and American Bar Associations. Former Member Florida Criminal Defense Attorneys Association. Attended National College of the State Judiciary. Recipient Housing Corporation of America Award 1971, Certificate of Appreciation from Florida State Conference NAACP 1974, Kappa League Award from Kappa Alpha Psi 1974 and Mt. Zion Baptist Church Award 1974. Named Community Lawyer of the Year 1972 and Judge of Distinction by Charmettes, Inc. 1976. Listed in *Personalities of the South* 1974 and *Who's Who in Black America* 1975-76. Staff Sergeant U.S. Army 1944-46. Democrat. Treasurer Heritage Cub Scouts Troop 254. Former Vice Chairman Dade County Housing and Urban Development and Assistant Executive Director Dade County Relations Board. Member Mt. Zion Baptist Church, Miami Jai Lites, Lions Club Advisory Board Florida Licensed Practical Nurses Association and Miami Varsity Club. Former member Dade County Selective Service Board, Family and Children Services, Gold Coast Democratic Club, North Miami Beach Voters and Layman Leagues, Florida Supreme Court Committee on the Bicentennial and Dade County Planning Advisory Board on Implementation of Land Use Master Plan. Received patent for Disposable Syringe July 5, 1977 and Electra Toy Hoop April 25, 1978. Enjoys gardening.
Office: 511 Dade County Courthouse, 73 West Flagler Street, Miami 33130.
Telephone: (305) 349-7001.

MARBLESTONE, Donald *(Judge, Seminole County Court)*
Office: Seminole County Courthouse, 301 North Park Avenue, Sanford 32771-1292.
Telephone: (407) 665-4105.

MARGOLIUS, Richard V. *(Senior Judge, Florida Circuit Court Eleventh Judicial Circuit)* Assumed Senior Judge status, serves by assignment. Former Judge, Dade County Court.
Office: 511 Dade County Courthouse, 73 West Flagler Street, Miami 33130.
Telephone: (305) 349-7001.

MARK, Robert A. *(Chief Judge, United States Bankruptcy Court Southern District of Florida)* Appointed by U.S. Court of Appeals Eleventh Circuit judges. Chief Judge since Sept 25, 1999.
Office: 1401 Federal Building, 51 S.W. First Avenue, Miami 33130.
Telephone: (305) 714-1760.

MARRA, Kenneth A. *(Judge, United States District Court Southern District of Florida)* Appointed for life by President George W. Bush to term beginning Sept 16, 2002. Former Judge, Florida Circuit Court Fifteenth Judicial Circuit.
Office: 205E U.S. Courthouse, 299 East Broward Boulevard, Fort Lauderdale 33301.
Telephone: (954) 769-5680.

MARRIOTT, Frank, Jr. *(Judge, Volusia County Court)*
Office: 203 Courthouse Annex, 125 East Orange Avenue, Daytona Beach 32114.
Telephone: (386) 257-6074.
Fax: (386) 257-6094

MARSHALL, Peter *(Judge, Volusia County Court)*
Office: Courthouse Annex, 125 East Orange Avenue, Daytona Beach 32114.
Telephone: (386) 257-6042.
Fax: (386) 257-6094

MARTIN, Karen L. *(Judge, Florida Circuit Court Fifteenth Judicial Circuit)* Former Judge, Palm Beach County Court.
Office: Palm Beach County Courthouse, 205 North Dixie Highway, West Palm Beach 33401.
Telephone: (561) 355-3842.
Fax: (561) 355-2389

MARTIN, Lawrence D. *(Judge, Collier County Court)*
Office: 3301 Tamiami Trail East, Bldg. L, Naples 34112.
Telephone: (239) 774-8747.
Fax: (239) 774-9654

MARTIN, Luise Krieger *(Judge, Dade County Court)*
Office: 502 Gerstein Justice Building, 1351 N.W. Twelfth Street, Miami 33125.
Telephone: (305) 548-5122.

MARTINEZ, Elvin L. *(Judge, Hillsborough County Court)*
Office: 232 Tower, 801 East Twiggs Street, Tampa 33602-3554.
Telephone: (813) 272-6853.

MARTINEZ, Jose E. *(Judge, United States District Court Southern District of Florida)* Appointed for life by President George W. Bush to term beginning Sept 17, 2002.
Office: Federal Courthouse Square, Third Floor, 301 North Miami Avenue, Miami 33128.
Telephone: (305) 523-5590.

MARTINEZ, Wilfredo *(Judge, Orange County Court)*

Office: 380-A Orange County Courthouse, 425 North Orange Avenue, Orlando 32801.

Telephone: (407) 836-0521.

MARX, Krista *(Judge, Palm Beach County Court)* Elected Nov 3, 1998 to term beginning Jan 6, 1999. Term expires Jan 4, 2005. Born Fort Lauderdale Florida May 20, 1960. Catholic. Educated at Florida State University B.A. 1982 J.D. 1985. Vice President Phi Delta Phi. Admitted to practice Florida 1985.

Assistant State Attorney Palm Beach County Florida 1985-98. Board of Directors Palm Beach County Bar Association 1989-99. Member Florida Association of Women Lawyers, American Inns of Court, Florida Conference of County Court Judges, The Florida Bar and American Bar Association. Enjoys traveling, running and skiing.

Office: 205 North Dixie Highway, West Palm Beach 33401.

Telephone: (561) 355-1520.

Fax: (561) 355-1652

MASTERS, Ellen Sly *(Judge, Florida Circuit Court Tenth Judicial Circuit)* Former Judge, Polk County Court.

Mailing address: P.O. Box 9000, Drawer J-102, Bartow 33831-9000.

Office: Polk County Courthouse, Bartow 33830.

Telephone: (863) 534-4149

MATHIS, E. McRae *(Judge, Florida Circuit Court Fourth Judicial Circuit)*

Office: Duval County Courthouse, 330 East Bay Street, Jacksonville 32202.

Telephone: (904) 630-2111.

Fax: (904) 630-2979

MATHIS, Robert K. *(Judge, Florida Circuit Court Seventh Judicial Circuit)* Elected Nov 1990 to term beginning Jan 8, 1991. Reelected 1996 and 2002. Current term expires Jan 2009. Born St. Augustine Florida April 9, 1949. Presbyterian. Educated at University of North Carolina at Chapel Hill B.S.B.A. 1971 and Florida State University College of Law J.D. 1973. Member Kappa Sigma. Admitted to practice Florida 1974 and U.S. District Court Middle District of Florida. In legal practice St. Augustine 1974-77. Judge, St. Johns County Court Jan 7, 1983 to Jan 7, 1991.

Assistant State Attorney 1974-83 (Division Chief 1977-83). Important Decision: State v. Howard Reed (no right to jury trial for misdemeanor cases) 1983. President Florida Conference of County Court Judges 1989-90. Member National District Attorneys Association, National College of District Attorneys, Florida Prosecuting Attorneys Association, The Florida Bar and St. Johns County Bar Association. Instructor Florida Judicial College. USMCR 1969-70. Member Rotary, Elks, USO and Boy Scouts. Enjoys hunting, fishing and scuba diving.

Office: 365 St. Johns County Judicial Center, 4010 Lewis Speedway, St. Augustine 32095.

Telephone: (904) 823-2565.

Fax: (904) 823-2683

MAXWELL, George W., III *(Judge, Florida Circuit Court Eighteenth Judicial Circuit)*

Office: Moore Justice Center, Second Floor, 2825 Judge Fran Jamieson Way, Viera 32940-8006.

Telephone: (321) 617-7256.

MAY, Melanie G. *(Judge, Florida District Court of Appeal Fourth District)* Born Lake Worth Florida Jan 13, 1952. Episcopalian. Educated at Broward Community College A.A. with honors 1971, Florida Atlantic University B.S. with honors 1973 and Nova University Center for the Study of Law J.D. summa cum laude 1981. Executive Editor Nova Law Journal. Law Clerk to Hon. Peter T. Fay, U.S. Court of Appeals Eleventh Circuit 1981-82. Member Phi Kappa Phi and Phi Theta Kappa. Admitted to practice Florida 1981, U.S. District Courts Middle 1981 and Southern 1981 Districts of Florida and U.S. Courts of Appeals Fifth 1981 and Eleventh 1981 Circuits. In legal practice Fort Lauderdale 1982-91. Former Judge, Florida District Court of Appeal Fourth District. Judge, Florida Circuit Court Seventeenth Judicial Circuit, appointed by Governor Lawton Chiles to term beginning April 15, 1991.

Author "Trial of a Treasure Hunter" 4 Nova L. Jour. 237, 1980 and "Legal Malpractice: Walking the Conflict Tightrope" 4 *Trial Advocate Quarterly* 35 April 1985. Instructor in Legal Research and Writing Nova University Center for the Study of Law 1982-84. Member 1989 and 1991, Chairman Northern Division 1990 and since 1992 and Chairman 1993 Federal Magistrate Selection Panel. Member Juvenile Justice Board since 1991. President Stephen R. Booher Inn of Court 1992-93. Former Member Broward Lawyers Care and Broward County Women Lawyers' Association. Member The Florida Bar (Admiralty Law Committee 1983-84, Unauthorized Practice of Law Committee 1984-90, Appellate Rules Committee 1987-93, Grievance Committee 1990), Broward County (Chairman Social Committee and Judicial Reception 1984-85, Secretary-Treasurer 1986, President Elect 1987 and President 1988 Young Lawyers Section, Member CLE Committee 1988, Judicial Selection and Tenure Committee 1989, Board of Directors 1990, Law Day Subcommittee 1992, Chairman Legal Ethics Subcommittee 1993-94) and Federal (Secretary 1986, President Elect 1987, President 1988 and Representative to Joint Judicial Conference of the Fifth and Eleventh Circuits 1989 Broward County Chapter) Bar Associations. Speaker on Appellate Practice Federal Bar Association 1982 and Bridge the Gap Seminar The Florida Bar 1988-90. Listed in *Who's Who of American Women* 1985. Recipient Outstanding Service Award from Young Lawyers Section Broward County Bar Association 1985, President's Award from Broward County Chapter Federal Bar Association 1986, Up and Comers Award from Government Division Price Waterhouse 1992, Special Recognition Award from Family Life Institution 1993, Recognition Award for Hurricane Andrew from Broward County Bar Association 1993, Outstanding Community Service Award from Junior League 1994, Woman of Distinction Award from Women's Political Caucus 1994, Commitment In Service Award from D10 ADM Planning Council 1994 and Outstanding Jurist Award from Young Lawyers Section The Florida Bar 1994. Finalist Business Profit Category Woman of the Year Award 1986. Named Woman of Achievement by Sunrise Lakes Phase III Women's Club 1993. Business Teacher St. Thomas Aquinas High School 1973. Officer Alumni Association 1982 and Board of Governors 1990 Nova University

MAY, MELANIE G.—*Continued*

Center for the Study of Law. Former Member American Cancer Society (Action 100), Junior League (Board Member, Chair Advisory Planning) and Alcohol, Drug Abuse & Mental Health Council. Board Member CHARLEE 1992-93. Advisory Board Juvenile Detention Center since 1992. Co-Chair Board PACE since 1992.

Mailing address: P.O. Box 3315, West Palm Beach 33402-3315.

Office: 1525 Palm Beach Lakes Boulevard, West Palm Beach 33401.

Telephone: (561) 242-2028.

Fax: (561) 242-2100

MAYE, Vivian C. *(Judge, Florida Circuit Court Thirteenth Judicial Circuit)*

Office: 393 Hillsborough County Courthouse, 419 Pierce Street, Tampa 33602-4022.

Telephone: (813) 272-5496.

McCALLUM, Linda F. *(Judge, Florida Circuit Court Fourth Judicial Circuit)* Appointed by Governor Jeb Bush to term beginning 2001. Term expires 2004. Born Tehran Iran Nov 3, 1962. Educated at Florida State University B.S. 1983 and Cumberland School of Law of Samford University J.D. 1986. Staff member American Journal of Trial Advocacy 1984-86. Honor Court Justice 1984-86. Admitted to practice Florida 1986, U.S. District Court Middle District of Florida 1986 and U.S. Court of Appeals Eleventh Circuit 1987. Judge, Duval County Court Jan 1995 to Jan 1998, appointed by Governor Lawton Chiles.

Assistant State Attorney Fourth Judicial Circuit 1986-94. Vice Chair Jacksonville Women Lawyers Association. Member Criminal Rules Committee The Florida Bar and Professionalism, Judicial Relations and Special Needs of Children 1999-2002 and Long Range Planning Committee 2000 Jacksonville Bar Association. Member Governor's Statewide Advocacy Council, Mayor's Commission on the Status of Women and Mayor's Victim's Assistance Advisory Council. Member Leadership Jacksonville, Jacksonville Women's Network and Leadership Florida. Enjoys sports, reading and writing.

Office: Duval County Courthouse, 330 East Bay Street, Jacksonville 32202.

Telephone: (904) 630-2688.

Fax: (904) 630-2979

McCARTHY, J. Michael *(Judge, Florida Circuit Court Tenth Judicial Circuit)*

Mailing address: P.O. Box 9000, Drawer J-136, Bartow 33831-9000.

Telephone: (863) 534-4646.

Fax: (863) 534-7722

McCARTHY, Timothy P. *(Judge, Florida Circuit Court Fifteenth Judicial Circuit)* Appointed by Governor Lawton Chiles to term beginning Feb 23, 1998. Elected 2000, current term expires Jan 1, 2007. Family Court Judge 1998-2000. Currently serves as Civil Court Judge. Born Buffalo New York Sept 9, 1945. Educated at Indiana State University B.A. 1968 and Notre Dame Law School J.D. 1971. Admitted to practice Florida 1971, Indiana 1971, U.S. District Courts Northern District of Indiana 1971 and Southern District of Florida 1976, U.S. Courts of Appeals Seventh 1971, Fifth 1980 and Eleventh 1982 Circuits and U.S. Supreme Court 1980. Board Certified as a Specialist in Business Litigation and Civil Trial Law by The Florida Bar. In legal practice West Palm Beach 1975-98. Hearing Officer, Civil Traffic Infractions Palm Beach County 1996-98. Temporary Associate Judge, Florida District Court of Appeal Fourth District Sept 1999.

Assistant U.S. Attorney South Bend Indiana 1971-73. Assistant State Attorney West Palm Beach 1973-75. Arbitrator and Mediator American Arbitration Association 1980-1998. Chairman and Member Fifteenth Judicial Circuit Grievance Committee 1989-91. Scoring Judge National Student Trial Advocacy Competition Southeastern Region Association of Trial Lawyers of America 1994-2000. Co-chair Palm Beach County Civil Practice Committee 1996-97. Former Member Academy of Florida Trial Lawyers. Florida Certified Circuit Mediator. Member Palm Beach County Bar Association. Seminar Lecturer on Construction Law, Arbitration, Mediation and Family Law CLE since 1980. Recipient Jurist of the Year Award from South Palm Beach County Bar Association 1999. Mayor 1987, 1988 and 1990 and Town Council Lake Clarke Shores 1989-91. Member Palm Beach County Charter Advisory Council 1987 and Lake Clarke Shores Code Enforcement Board 1993. Member Notre Dame Club of the Palm Beaches and Kiwanis Club of West Palm Beach.

Office: 205 North Dixie Highway, West Palm Beach 33401.

Telephone: (561) 355-2147.

Fax: (561) 355-6079

McCAULEY, James A. *(Senior Judge, Florida Circuit Court Seventeenth Judicial Circuit)* Assumed Senior Judge status, serves by assignment.

Office: Broward County Courthouse, 201 S.E. Sixth Street, Fort Lauderdale 33301.

Telephone: (954) 831-7740.

McCAULIE, William Gregg *(Judge, Florida Circuit Court Fourth Judicial Circuit)*

Office: Duval County Courthouse, 330 East Bay Street, Jacksonville 32202.

Telephone: (904) 630-2592.

Fax: (904) 630-2979

McCLELLAN, Harry H. *(Judge, Florida Circuit Court Fourteenth Judicial Circuit)*

Office: Gulf County Courthouse, 1000 Cecil Costin Senior Boulevard, Port St. Joe 32456.

Telephone: (850) 227-1117.

Fax: (850) 227-1142

McCLUAN, William T. *(Judge, Brevard County Court)*

Office: Moore Justice Center, Third Floor, 2825 Judge Fran Jamieson Way, Viera 32940-8006.

Telephone: (321) 617-7268.

Fax: (321) 617-7277

McCOUN, Thomas B., III *(Magistrate Judge, United States District Court Middle District of Florida)* Appointed by U.S. District Court judges.

Office: 1254 U.S. Courthouse, 801 North Florida Avenue, Tampa 33602-3800.

Telephone: (813) 301-5550.

McCUNE, Robert James *(Judge, Marion County Court)*

Office: Marion County Judicial Center, 110 N.W. First Avenue, Ocala 34475.

MCCUNE, ROBERT JAMES—*Continued*
Telephone: (352) 401-7824.
Fax: (352) 401-7840

McDONALD, Randall G. *(Judge, Florida Circuit Court Tenth Judicial Circuit)* Former Chief Judge. Born Pottstown Pennsylvania Dec 12, 1947. Lutheran. Educated at University of Richmond B.A. 1969 and Stetson University J.D. 1973. Admitted to practice Florida 1973. Began legal practice Florida 1973. Judge, Polk County Court 1977-81.
Instructor in Business Law Lakeland College 1974-76. Warrant Officer U.S. Army 1969-75.
Mailing address: P.O. Box 9000, Drawer J-116, Bartow 33831-9000.
Telephone: (863) 534-4622.
Fax: (863) 534-4023

McDONALD, Robert W., Jr. *(Judge, Florida Circuit Court Twelfth Judicial Circuit)* Appointed by Governor Lawton Chiles March 13, 1995.
Mailing address: P.O. Box 48927, Sarasota 34230.
Office: 2002 Ringling Boulevard, Sarasota 34237.
Telephone: (941) 861-7935.
Fax: (941) 861-7920

McDONALD, Roger J. *(Judge, Florida Circuit Court Ninth Judicial Circuit)* Elected to term beginning Jan 1997. Served Criminal Division 1997-98. Serves Domestic Relations Division since 1999. Educated at Florida State University B.S. in Finance 1965 and University of Florida School of Law J.D. 1971.
Member The Florida Bar (Former Member Unauthorized Practice of Law Committee) and Orange County Bar Association (Liaison with Orange County Public Television and Member Historical Preservation Committee and Speaker's Committee). Speaker "Florida Collection Law and Foreclosure" National Business Institute, Inc. Participant Seminar on Foreclosures Orange County Bar Association. Career Participant Legal Aid Society Services. Former Chairperson Courthouse Committee and Law Library Committee.
Office: Two Courthouse Square, Suite 6410, Kissimmee 34741.
Telephone: (407) 343-2503.
Fax: (407) 835-5068

McDONALD, Ysleta *(Judge, Alachua County Court)*
Office: 206 Alachua County Courthouse, 201 East University Avenue, Gainesville 32601.
Telephone: (352) 374-3607.
Fax: (352) 381-0177

McGRADY, J. Thomas *(Judge, Florida Circuit Court Sixth Judicial Circuit)* Appointed by Governor Jeb Bush to term beginning Jan 1, 2002. Term expires Jan 1, 2004. Educated at University of Florida B.A. 1971 J.D. 1974. Admitted to practice Florida 1974, U.S. District Court Middle District of Florida, U.S. Court of Appeals Eleventh Circuit and U.S. Supreme Court. In legal practice St. Petersburg 1974-99. Judge, Pinellas County Court Aug 1999 to Dec 31, 2001.
Office: 545 First Avenue North, St. Petersburg 33701.
Telephone: (727) 582-7436.
Fax: (727) 582-7413

McGREGOR, Robert B. *(Senior Judge, Florida Circuit Court Eighteenth Judicial Circuit)* Elected to term beginning Jan 1973. Reelected to subsequent terms. Former Chief Judge. Assumed Senior Judge status, serves by assignment. Born Flint Michigan Feb 9, 1930. Methodist. Educated at University of Chicago B.A. 1950 and University of Miami B.B.A. 1954 J.D. 1954. Named Outstanding First, Second, Third and Fourth Year U.S. Army ROTC Cadet, Distinguished Military Student and Distinguished Military Graduate University of Miami. Admitted to practice Florida 1954. Began legal practice Merritt Island 1958. Judge, Cocoa Beach Municipal Court 1960-65. Judge, Brevard County Small Claims Court 1964-67. Judge, Brevard County Magistrate Court 1967-72.
President Florida Small Claims Court Judges Association 1970-71. Member Seminole County and Brevard County Bar Associations (Secretary 1961 and President 1962). Attended National College of State Trial Judges 1969 and National College of Juvenile Justice 1974. First Lieutenant U.S. Army 1954-58. Democrat. President Cocoa Beach Jaycees 1963 and Cocoa Beach Kiwanis 1966. Enjoys home workshop.
Office: Moore Justice Center, 2825 Judge Fran Jamieson Way, Viera 32940-8006.
Telephone: (321) 637-5555.

McINTOSH, Donna L. *(Judge, Florida Circuit Court Eighteenth Judicial Circuit)* Former Judge, Seminole County Court.
Office: Seminole County Courthouse, 301 North Park Avenue, Sanford 32771.
Telephone: (407) 665-4245.
Fax: (407) 665-4289

McIVER, William C. *(Judge, Florida Circuit Court Twentieth Judicial Circuit)* Elected Sept 1984 to term beginning Jan 3, 1985. Reelected Sept 1990, Sept 1996 and 2002. Current term expires Jan 2009. Born Baltimore Maryland Jan 3, 1946. Educated at Edison Community College A.A. 1965, University of Maryland B.A. with honors 1970 and University of Florida J.D. 1973. Member Phi Kappa Phi and Phi Delta Phi. Admitted to practice Florida 1974. In legal practice Fort Meyers 1974-77. Judge, Lee County Court 1977-85.
Adjunct Professor University of South Florida 1978-84. Member The Florida Bar, Lee County and American Bar Associations. Sergeant USAF Security Service 1967-71.
Office: Lee County Justice Center, 1700 Monroe Street, Fort Myers 33901.
Telephone: (239) 335-2388.
Fax: (239) 335-2588

McNARY, Myra Scott *(Judge, Pinellas County Court)*
Office: 29582 U.S. Highway 19 North, Clearwater 33761.
Telephone: (727) 464-3034.
Fax: (727) 464-5484

McNEAL, Raymond T. *(Judge, Florida Circuit Court Fifth Judicial Circuit)* Elected Sept 12, 1982 to term beginning Jan 1, 1983. Reelected 1988, 1994 and 2000. Current term expires Jan 2007. Born Ocala Florida April 9, 1946. Educated at University of Florida B.A. 1969 J.D. 1973. Staff member University of Florida Law Review. Member Phi Delta Phi. Admitted to practice Florida 1973. In legal practice Ocala 1973-76. Judge, Marion County Court 1979-82.
Assistant State Attorney 1974-76 and Chief Assistant State Attorney 1976-78 Fifth Circuit. Author "It's The

MCNEAL, RAYMOND T.—*Continued*

Law, Domestic Violence" March 1994 and "Are You Being Stalked?" May 1994 *Women's Self Defense* and "A Simple Approach to Interstate Child Custody Jurisdiction" *The Family Law Commentator* Dec 1995. Member D. R. Smith Inn American Inn of Court, Florida Conference of Circuit Court Judges (Education Committee), American Judicature Society, The Florida Bar (Longterm Advisory Committee Family Law Section) and Marion County Bar Association (Family Law Committee, Probate, Guardianship and Elder Law Committee). Faculty Member on Search and Seizure, Mental Health Issues (Criminal), Managing Pro Se Litigants (Family), Interstate Child Custody Jurisdiction, Garnishment and Income Deduction Orders and Contempt of Court Issues for Family Judges Florida College of Advanced Judicial Studies. Recipient Award of Merit from Marion District 1985 and Silver Beaver Award from North Florida Council 1986 Boy Scouts of America, Ocala Jaycees Distinguished Service Award 1980, Distinguished Service Award from Florida Council on Crime and Delinquency 1982, Pro Bono Awards from Withlacoochee Area Legal Services 1992, 1993 and 1994, Recognition for assistance to women and children from Marion County Rape Crisis-Spouse Abuse Center 1993, citation for Dedicated Service to the Family Law Section and Families in Marion County from Marion County Bar Association 1995 and Outstanding Service award from Marion-Citrus Mental Health Centers, Inc. 1996. Democrat. Board of Directors Boys and Girls Club of Marion County, Inc. Member at Large North Florida Council Boy Scouts of America. Member First Methodist Church, Ocala Lions Club (President 1979-80), Florida Council on Crime and Delinquency, Elks Lodge 286, Citizens Advisory Board Child Abuse Prevention Project 1984-86 and Marion County School Board (Drug and Alcohol Task Force 1985-86 and School Advisory Committee 1986-87). Enjoys hunting, fishing, camping and country western dancing.

Office: Marion County Judicial Center, 110 N.W. First Avenue, Ocala 34475.

Telephone: (352) 401-6755.

Fax: (352) 401-6776

McSORLEY, Sandra K. *(Judge, Florida Circuit Court Fifteenth Judicial Circuit)* Former Judge, Palm Beach County Court, appointed by Governor Bob Martinez to term beginning Dec 22, 1989.

Office: Palm Beach County Courthouse, 205 North Dixie Highway, West Palm Beach 33401.

Telephone: (561) 355-3625.

MELTON, Howell W. *(Senior Judge, United States District Court Middle District of Florida)* Appointed for life by President Jimmy Carter to term beginning May 12, 1977. Assumed Senior status Feb 1, 1991. Born Atlanta Georgia Dec 15, 1923. Educated at University of Florida LL.B. 1948 replaced by J.D. 1967. Member Phi Delta Phi, Phi Delta Theta and Florida Blue Key. Admitted to practice Florida 1948, U.S. District Court Southern District of Florida 1948 and U.S. Supreme Court 1960. Judge, Florida Circuit Court Seventh Judicial Circuit 1961-77.

Member The Florida Bar (Former Chairman Council of Bar Presidents and Director Junior Bar Section), St. Johns County (Past President), Jacksonville, Federal and American Bar Associations. Former member Florida Conference of Circuit Court Judges (Secretary-Treasurer 1972, Chairman Elect 1973, Chairman 1974, Executive Committee 1975-76). Recipient St. Augustine's Jaycee Distinguished Service Award 1953. First Lieutenant U.S. Army JAGC 1943-46. Former member Board of Social Welfare District Five St. Johns County 1955-56, Board of Directors St. Johns County Mental Health Association, St. Augustine Junior Chamber of Commerce, St. Augustine and St. Johns County Chamber of Commerce (Director 1957-68 and Vice President 1958), St. Augustine YMCA (Director and Vice President), Community Chest United Fund of St. Augustine (Vice President and Director, General Chairman of 1957 fund raising campaign), Flagler Hospital of St. Augustine (President Board of Directors, Chairman Board of Trustees), Third Army Advisory Committee, Health Planning Council of the Jacksonville Area Inc., St. Johns County Blood Bank (Past Secretary) and St. Johns County Welfare Federation (Past President). Member First United Methodist Church at St. Augustine (President Board of Trustees 1976-79 and former Chairman Administrative Board), Masons, Officers' Club of St. Augustine (Past Vice President) and Board of Trustees Flagler College.

Office: 300 North Hogan Street, Room 11-300, Jacksonville 32202.

Telephone: (904) 549-1940.

MELVIN, Laura *(Senior Judge, Florida Circuit Court First Judicial Circuit)* Appointed by Governor Bob Martinez April 12, 1990. Assumed Senior Judge status, serves by assignment.

Office: Judicial Building, 190 Governmental Center, Pensacola 32501.

Telephone: (850) 595-4400.

MENENDEZ, Manuel, Jr. *(Chief Judge, Florida Circuit Court Thirteenth Judicial Circuit)* Appointed by Governor Robert Graham to term beginning Feb 1, 1984. Elected 1984, 1990, 1996 and 2002. Current term expires Jan 2009. Chief Judge since July 1, 2001. Born Tampa Florida Aug 2, 1947. Educated at University of Florida A.A. 1967 B.A. 1969 J.D. with honors 1972. Executive Editor University of Florida Law Review 1971-72. Law Clerk to Hon. T. Frank Hobson, Jr., Florida District Court of Appeal Second District 1972. Member Phi Delta Phi and Pi Kappa Phi. Admitted to practice Florida 1972 and U.S. Supreme Court 1976. Began legal practice Jacksonville 1973. Judge, Hillsborough County Court 1983-84. Associate Judge, Florida District Court of Appeal Second District 1984, 1987, 1996 and 1999.

Assistant U.S. Attorney 1973-77 and Chief Assistant U.S. Attorney 1978-83 Middle District of Florida. Past President William Glenn Terrell Inn American Inns of Court. Former Member Southeastern Admiralty Law Institute, National District Attorneys Association and Florida Conference of County Court Judges. Member American Judicature Society, Florida Conference of Circuit Court Judges, The Florida Bar (Former Chair Criminal Rules Procedure Committee and Rules of Judicial Administration Committee, Member Judicial Administration, Selection and Tenure Committee), Jacksonville, Hillsborough County, Federal (Jacksonville and Tampa Bay Chapters) and American Bar Associations. Attended The National Judicial College 1983 and 1995, The Florida Judicial College 1983 and 1984 and American Academy of Judicial Education 1984 1994. Faculty member Florida Judicial College and The Florida Bar State Attorney-

MENENDEZ, MANUEL, JR.—*Continued*

Public Defender Clinic University of Florida. Recipient Service Award from Eighth Judicial Circuit Bar Association 1972, Award for Meritorious Achievement in Public Service from West Tampa Civic Clubs Association 1983, letters of recommendation from Duval County Sheriff and Director FBI and Outstanding Jurist Award from Hillsborough County Bar Association 1999. Captain USAR 1969-83. Advisory Board Salvation Army 1987-91. Member Gator Boosters, Tampa Gator Club, University of Florida Law Center Association, University of Florida Alumni Association, University of Florida Law Review Alumni Association, Propeller Club of the U.S. (Ports of Jacksonville and Tampa), Tiger Bay Club of Tampa Bay and Rough Riders. Enjoys golf, fishing, travel, reading and Florida football.

Office: 214F Hillsborough County Courthouse, 419 Pierce Street, Tampa 33602-4022.

Telephone: (813) 272-5022.

Fax: (813) 272-5522

MERRITT, Daniel B., Sr. *(Judge, Florida Circuit Court Fifth Judicial Circuit)* Assumed office 1998. Presiding Judge Appellate Division 2001. Born Eustis Florida March 11, 1942. Educated at McNeese State University B.S. 1965 and University of Florida J.D. 1967. Board Certified as a Specialist in Marital and Family Law by The Florida Bar. In legal practice 1968-98. Judge, Brooksville Municipal Court 1968-73.

President Tri-County Bar Association 1976. Master of the Bench Citrus-Hernando Inn of Court. Supreme Court Certified Arbitrator. Member Florida Conference of Circuit Court Judges, Association of Professional Family Mediators, The Florida Bar, Fifth Circuit (Member 1973, 1978-81 and 1986-89 and Chairman 1981 Grievance Committee), Hernando County (President 1976), and American Bar Associations. Recipient Distinguished Judicial Service Award from Chapter 31 Florida Council on Crime and Delinquency. Eagle Scout 1957 and Assistant Scout Master and Scout Master 1969-72 Boy Scout Troop #71, District Director Gulf Ridge Council 1994-95 and District Vice Chairman Withlacoochee District 1995-96 Boy Scouts of America. Board of Directors Hernando County Law Library Board 1968-98. President Brooksville Golf & Country Club 1975 and 1987 and Brooksville Kiwanis Club 1976. Coach Hernando High School Tennis Team 1981. Volunteer Judge and Advisor Teen Court. Member State of Florida's Commission on Responsible Fatherhood, Hernando County Chamber of Commerce, Hernando County Lodge 97 Free and Accepted Masons and Hernando County Cattlemen's Association.

Office: 432 Hernando County Courthouse, 20 North Main Street, Brooksville 34601.

Telephone: (352) 754-4221.

MERRYDAY, Steven D. *(Judge, United States District Court Middle District of Florida)* Appointed for life by President George Bush to term beginning 1992. Born Palatka Florida Nov 2, 1950. Educated at University of Florida B.A. 1972 J.D. 1975. In legal practice Tampa 1975-92.

Office: U.S. Courthouse, 801 North Florida Avenue, Tampa 33602-3800.

Telephone: (813) 301-5001.

MICHAEL, Robert F., Jr. *(Senior Judge, Florida Circuit Court Sixth Judicial Circuit)* Assumed office 1972. Elected 1974, 1980 and 1986. Assumed Senior Judge status, serves by assignment. Born Greensboro North Carolina Dec 16, 1930. Educated at Duke University A.B. 1953 and Stetson University J.D. 1964. Admitted to practice Florida 1964. Began legal practice St. Petersburg 1964. Judge, Civil and Criminal Court of Record 1970-72.

Vice Chairman Juvenile Judges Conference of Circuit Court. Captain USAF 1953-55. Member First Presbyterian Church (Elder), Sertoma, Child Guidance Clinic, Jaycees, Pinellas County Youth Symphony, Science Center, Eckerd College President's Round Table and Pinellas County Mental Health Board (Youth Advisor). Enjoys tennis.

Office: Judicial Building, 545 First Avenue North, St. Petersburg 33701.

Telephone: (727) 464-4470.

MICKLE, Stephan P. *(Judge, United States District Court Northern District of Florida)* Appointed for life by President Bill Clinton to term beginning 1998. Born New York New York June 18, 1944. Educated at University of Florida B.A. 1965 M.Ed. 1966 J.D. 1970. In legal practice Fort Lauderdale 1971 and Gainesville 1972-79. Judge, Alachua County Court 1979-84. Judge, Florida Circuit Court Eighth Judicial Circuit 1984-92. Judge, Florida District Court of Appeal First District 1993-98.

Attorney Office of Legal Services U.S. Office of Equal Opportunity 1970. Special Assistant Public Defender Eighth Judicial Circuit 1974.

Office: Federal Building, 401 S.E. First Avenue, Gainesville 32601.

Telephone: (352) 380-2742.

MIDDLEBROOKS, Donald M. *(Judge, United States District Court Southern District of Florida)* Appointed for life by President Bill Clinton to term beginning 1997. Born Orlando Florida Dec 31, 1946. Educated at University of Florida B.S.B.A. 1968 J.D. 1972. In legal practice Orlando 1973-74 and West Palm Beach 1977-97.

General Counsel, Governmental Assistant to Governor and Assistant General Counsel Office of the State Governor 1974-77.

Office: U.S. Courthouse, 701 Clematis Street, West Palm Beach 33401.

Telephone: (561) 514-3720.

MIDELIS, James W. *(Judge, St. Lucie County Court)* Appointed by Governor Robert Graham to term beginning Jan 1, 1986. Elected 1986, 1990, 1994 and 1998. Current term expires Jan 2005. Born Paterson New Jersey Dec 27, 1935. Greek Orthodox. Educated at University of Florida B.S. 1967 and Florida State University College of Law J.D. 1970. Admitted to practice Florida 1970.

Assistant State Attorney 1972-85. Instructor Indian River Community College 1982-85. Member American Judges Association and The Florida Bar. Attended Florida Judiciary Conference 1986, 1987, 1988, 1989, 1990, 1991 and 1992. Recipient St. Lucie Bar Association Award 1989. USAF. Enjoys fishing, skiing and racquetball.

Office: 226 Courthouse Addition, 218 South Second Street, Fort Pierce 34950.

Telephone: (772) 462-1474.

MIHOK, A. Thomas *(Judge, Florida Circuit Court Ninth Judicial Circuit)*
Office: 1120 Orange County Courthouse, 425 North Orange Avenue, Orlando 32801.
Telephone: (407) 836-2350.
Fax: (407) 836-0451

MILLER, David C. *(Judge, Florida Circuit Court Eleventh Judicial Circuit)* Elected to term beginning Jan 2, 2001. Born Miami Florida Dec 1, 1953. Educated at University of Florida 1975 and Nova Southeastern University Shepard Broad Law Center J.D. 1978. Admitted to practice Florida 1979, U.S. District Courts Middle and Southern Districts of Florida and Trial Bar of U.S. District Court Southern District of Florida. In legal practice Fort Lauderdale 1979, Hialeah 1980 and Miami 1981.
Personal Statement or Quote: "Be prepared, be professional or be sorry."
Office: 217 Gerstein Justice Building, 1351 N.W. Twelfth Street, Miami 33125.
Telephone: (305) 548-5728.

MILLER, Donna F. *(Judge, Lake County Court)* Elected to term beginning Jan 3, 1995. Reelected 1998, current term expires Jan 2005.
Mailing address: P.O. Box 7800, Tavares 32778-7800.
Office: Lake County Judicial Center, Tavares 32778.
Telephone: (352) 742-4206.
Fax: (352) 742-4229

MILLER, Jeffords D. *(Judge, Florida Circuit Court Ninth Judicial Circuit)* Appointed by Governor Bob Martinez to term beginning Nov 23, 1987. Elected Nov 5, 1988, 1994 and 2000. Current term expires Jan 2007. Formerly served Felony Criminal Division, Domestic Relations Division, Family Court Division and General Civil Division. Currently serves as Administrative Judge Civil Division. Born Kissimmee Florida Jan 13, 1936. Baptist. Educated at Rollins College B.A. 1959 M.A.T. 1963 and Cumberland School of Law of Samford University J.D. 1967. Law Clerk to Hon. Harlan Hobart Grooms, U.S. District Court Northern District of Alabama 1967-68. Member Phi Delta Phi and Sigma Chi. Admitted to practice Florida 1967 and Alabama 1967. In legal practice Birmingham Alabama 1967-68 and Kissimmee Florida 1968-69.
Chief Assistant State Attorney Osceola County Florida 1969-87. Former Instructor in Criminal Law Valencia Community College and Graduate Program Rollins College. Member Alabama State Bar, The Florida Bar, Orange County and Osceola County Bar Associations. Previously worked as school teacher and U.S. Postal Service employee. Past Master Orange Blossom Lodge 80 Masons. 33° Scottish Rite Mason. Member Elks, Moose and Shriners.
Office: 6300 Osceola County Courthouse, Two Courthouse Square, Kissimmee 34741.
Telephone: (407) 343-2491.
Fax: (407) 835-5121

MILLER, Karen M. *(Judge, Florida Circuit Court Fifteenth Judicial Circuit)*
Office: Palm Beach County Courthouse, 205 North Dixie Highway, West Palm Beach 33401.

MILLER, Lauren Levy *(Judge, Florida Circuit Court Twentieth Judicial Circuit)* Judge Eleventh Judicial Circuit Jan 3, 1995 to 1998. Senior Judge Twentieth Judicial Circuit Jan 1999 to 2001. Appointed Judge by Governor Jeb Bush Oct 25, 2001 to term beginning Jan 2002. Educated at Brandeis University B.A. cum laude 1980 and University of Miami School of Law J.D. 1983. Admitted to practice Florida 1983 and U.S. District Court Southern District of Florida 1983. Judge, Dade County Court Jan 1991 to 1994.
Assistant City Attorney North Miami Beach 1983-90. Instructor in Civil Litigation University of Miami 1987. Member Florida Association for Women Lawyers, National Association for Women Judges and The Florida Bar. Attended Trial Skills Workshop. Lecturer on County Court practice "Bridge the Gap" program The Florida Bar 1991-94. Faculty Member Florida Judicial College 1992-98.
Office: Collier County Government Complex, Building L, 3301 Tamiami Trail East, Naples 34112.
Telephone: (239) 774-8909.
Fax: (239) 774-9654

MILLER, Michael D. *(Senior Judge, Florida Circuit Court Fifteenth Judicial Circuit)* Assumed Senior Judge status, serves by assignment. Former Judge, Palm Beach County Court.
Office: Palm Beach County Courthouse, 205 North Dixie Highway, West Palm Beach 33401.
Telephone: (561) 355-2431.

MILLER, Peter T. *(Judge, Putnam County Court)* Elected to term beginning Jan 8, 1985. Reelected 1988, 1992, 1996 and 2000. Current term expires Jan 2007.
Mailing address: P.O. Box 398, Palatka 32178-0398.
Telephone: (386) 329-0269.
Fax: (386) 329-0896

MILLER, W. Michael *(Judge, Orange County Court)* Elected to term beginning Jan 1991. Reelected 1994 and 1998. Current term expires Jan 2005.
Office: 380B Orange County Courthouse, 425 North Orange Avenue, Orlando 32801.
Telephone: (407) 836-2091.

MILLER, Wayne M. *(Judge, Monroe County Court)* Assumed office Jan 3, 1989. Elected to subsequent terms.
Office: Monroe County Courthouse Annex, 500 Whitehead Street, First Floor, Key West 33040.
Telephone: (305) 292-3424.
Fax: (305) 295-3603

MILLS, Stanley R. *(Judge, Florida Circuit Court Sixth Judicial Circuit)* Appointed by Governor Bob Martinez to term beginning Feb 1, 1989. Elected to subsequent terms.
Office: West Pasco Government Center, 7530 Little Road, New Port Richey 34654.
Telephone: (727) 847-8092.

MILLS-FRANCIS, Karen *(Judge, Dade County Court)*
Office: 207 North Dade Justice Center, 15555 Biscayne Boulevard, Miami 33160.
Telephone: (305) 354-8771.

MITCHELL, Charles O., Jr. *(Judge, Florida Circuit Court Fourth Judicial Circuit)*
Office: Duval County Courthouse, 330 East Bay Street, Jacksonville 32202.
Telephone: (904) 630-2395.
Fax: (904) 630-2979

MIZE, C. Vernon, Jr. *(Senior Judge, Florida Circuit Court Eighteenth Judicial Circuit)* Assumed Senior Judge status, serves by assignment.

Office: Moore Justice Center, 2825 Judge Fran Jamieson Way, Viera 32940-8006.

Telephone: (321) 637-5555.

MODESITT, Donald *(Judge, Leon County Court)*

Office: 265-G Leon County Courthouse, 301 South Monroe Street, Tallahassee 32301.

Telephone: (850) 577-4318.

Fax: (850) 922-0070

MOE, Leroy H. *(Judge, Florida Circuit Court Seventeenth Judicial Circuit)* Appointed by Governor Reubin O'Donovan Askew 1971. Elected to subsequent terms. Current term expires Jan 2009. Acting Chief Judge and Chief Judge Probate Division. Born Pittsburgh Pennsylvania July 7, 1941. Lutheran. Educated at University of Florida B.A. 1963 J.D. 1965. Member Phi Alpha Delta and Theta Chi. Admitted to practice Florida 1966 and U.S. District Court District of Florida 1966. Began legal practice Fort Lauderdale 1966. In legal practice Hollywood 1967-71. Judge, Pembroke Park Municipal Court 1967-69. Judge, Broward County Court 1971-72. Special appointment to Florida District Court of Appeal 1975-76.

Author "Florida's New Mental Health Act" Broward County Bar Association 1972. Important Decision: Eleanor Ritchie Estate (she left approximately $11,000,000 to her 83 stray dog "pets") 1972. Guest Lecturer Nova University Law School since 1974. Member The Florida Bar and Broward County Bar Association. Recipient Liberty Bell Award, American Institute of Bankers Award, Kiwanis Awards and Rotary Club Award. President Areawide Council on Aging 1976-77. Member Kiwanis, Optimist Club, Prospect Hall College Board, Mental Health Board, Task Force on Aging, Task Force on Shoplifting and Bar/Bench Liaison Committee. Enjoys carpentry, boating, swimming, kayaking and camping.

Office: 930 Broward County Courthouse, 201 S.E. Sixth Street, Fort Lauderdale 33301.

Telephone: (954) 831-7793.

MONACO, Daniel R. *(Judge, Florida Circuit Court Twentieth Judicial Circuit)*

Office: Collier County Government Complex, Bldg. L, 3301 Tamiami Trail East, Naples 34112.

Telephone: (239) 774-8118.

Fax: (239) 774-9654

MONACO, David A. *(Judge, Florida District Court of Appeal Fifth District)* Former Judge, Florida Circuit Court Seventh Judicial Circuit.

Office: 300 South Beach Street, Daytona Beach 32114.

Telephone: (386) 947-1513.

Fax: (386) 947-1565

MONACO, Toby S. *(Judge, Florida Circuit Court Eighth Judicial Circuit)*

Office: 416 Alachua County Courthouse, 201 East University Avenue, Gainesville 32601.

Telephone: (352) 374-3641.

Fax: (352) 374-5238

MOODY, James S., Jr. *(Judge, United States District Court Middle District of Florida)* Appointed for life by President Bill Clinton to term beginning July 29, 2000. Born Plant City Florida March 31, 1947. Educated at University of Florida B.S. with high honors 1969 J.D. with honors 1972. Listed in *Who's Who Among American College and University Students.* Member Phi Kappa Phi, Omicron Delta Kappa, Beta Gamma Sigma, Blue Key and Order of the Coif. In legal practice 1972-94 Judge, Florida Circuit Court Thirteenth Judicial Circuit Jan 3, 1995 to July 28, 2000.

Author "The Birth of a Legal Presumption" Florida B. Jour. Nov 1996. Member The Florida Bar (Member 1974-77, Vice Chairman 1976 and Chairman 1977 Jurisprudence Committee, Member 1978-81, Vice Chairman 1979 and Chairman 1980 Attorneys Fee Committee, Member Annual Meeting Committee 1982) and Hillsborough County Bar Association (Chairman Law Library Committee 1980-83, Member Medical/Legal Committee 1982, Vice President 1986, President 1987, Board of Directors). Recipient Golden Chain Award from Plant City Lions Club 1980, 1981 and 1982. Named Outstanding Young Man of America by U.S. Jaycees 1982. Listed in *Who's Who of Emerging Leaders in America* Second ed. 1988, *Community Leaders of America* 14th ed. 1990 and *Who's Who in American Law* Fifth, Sixth and Ninth editions. CPA. Judge Mock Trial Competition American Bar Association University of Florida at Gainesville 1993. Member and First Chairman Plant City Historic Resources Board. Board of Directors Sun Bank of Tampa Bay. Chancellor St. Peter's Episcopal Church. Member Plant City Arts Council, East Hillsborough Historical Society, United Way (Member Merger Task Force 1993, Co-Chair 1994 Campaign and Founder Anchor Club East Hillsborough County Chapter, Board of Directors Hillsborough County Chapter and East Hillsborough County Chapter, Member Economic Development Council) and Plant City Lions Club (Member since 1973, Program Chairman, Tail Twister, Director, Third Vice President, Second Vice President, First Vice President, President).

Office: U.S. Courthouse, 801 North Florida Avenue, Tampa 33602.

Telephone: (813) 301-5680.

MOORE, Cecelia M. *(Senior Judge, Florida Circuit Court Tenth Judicial Circuit)* Appointed by Governor Lawton Chiles Feb 8, 1994. Assumed Senior Judge status, serves by assignment.

Mailing address: P.O. Box 9000, Drawer J-133, Bartow 33831-9000.

Office: 255 North Broadway, Bartow 33830.

Telephone: (863) 534-4690.

MOORE, John H., II *(Senior Judge, United States District Court Middle District of Florida)* Appointed for life by President Ronald Reagan to term beginning Dec 15, 1981. Former Chief Judge. Assumed Senior status, serves by assignment. Born Atlantic City New Jersey Aug 5, 1929. Protestant. Educated at Syracuse University B.S. 1952 and University of Florida J.D. 1961. Executive Editor University of Florida Law Review 1960. Member Phi Alpha Delta and Beta Theta Pi. Admitted to practice Florida 1961 and U.S. Supreme Court 1968. Began legal practice Atlanta Georgia 1961. In legal practice Fort Lauderdale 1961-67. Judge, Florida Circuit Court Seventeenth Judicial Circuit 1967-77. Judge, Florida District Court of Appeal Fourth District Sept 12, 1977 to Dec 1981, appointed by Governor Reubin Askew.

Member Florida Constitution Revision Committee

MOORE, JOHN H., II—*Continued*

1977-78 and Chairman Florida Judicial Qualifications Commission 1980-81. Member American Judicature Society, Florida Conference of Circuit Court Judges (Secretary-Treasurer 1975-76 and Chairman Elect 1976-77), The Florida Bar, Jacksonville, Broward County and American Bar Associations. Commander USNR 1948-71 (active duty 1952-56). Member U.S. Navy League, Timuquana Country Club, U.S. Tennis Association and Rotary Club. Honorary Trustee Broward Community College. Honorary Alumnus Nova University. Enjoys boating, golf and tennis.

Mailing address: P.O. Box 53137, Jacksonville 32201-3137.

Telephone: (904) 549-1980.

MOORE, K. Michael *(Judge, United States District Court Southern District of Florida)* Appointed for life by President George Bush to term beginning 1992. Born Coral Gables Florida July 17, 1951. Educated at Florida State University B.A. 1972 and Fordham University School of Law J.D. 1976.

Assistant U.S. Attorney Southern District of Florida 1976-81. Supervisory Assistant U.S. Attorney 1981-82, Chief Assistant U.S. Attorney 1983-87 and U.S. Attorney 1987-89 Northern District of Florida. Director U.S. Marshals Service U.S. Department of Justice 1989-92.

Office: 1168 Federal Justice Building, 99 N.E. Fourth Street, Miami 33132.

Telephone: (305) 523-5160.

MORAN, Donald R., Jr. *(Chief Judge, Florida Circuit Court Fourth Judicial Circuit)* Former Judge, Duval County Court.

Office: 220 Duval County Courthouse, 330 East Bay Street, Jacksonville 32202.

Telephone: (904) 630-2541.

Fax: (904) 630-2477

MORAN, John A. *(Judge, Duval County Court)* Elected to term beginning Jan 1991. Reelected 1994 and 1998. Current term expires Jan 2005.

Office: Duval County Courthouse, 330 East Bay Street, Jacksonville 32202.

Telephone: (904) 630-2578.

Fax: (904) 630-2979

MORENO, Federico A. *(Judge, United States District Court Southern District of Florida)* Appointed for life by President George Bush. Born Venezuela April 10, 1952. Roman Catholic. Educated at University of Notre Dame A.B. cum laude 1974 and University of Miami J.D. 1978. Admitted to practice Florida 1978, U.S. District Courts Southern 1978 and Middle 1986 Districts of Florida, U.S. Courts of Appeals Fifth 1981 and Eleventh 1981 Circuits and U.S. Supreme Court 1983. Judge, Dade County Court 1986-87. Former Judge, Florida Circuit Court Eleventh Judicial Circuit, appointed by Governor Bob Martinez to term beginning 1987.

Former Instructor University of Notre Dame, Stockton State College and Atlantic Community College. Member The Association of Trial Lawyers of America and American Bar Association. Attended Florida Judicial College.

Office: 1061 Federal Justice Building, 99 N.E. Fourth Street, Miami 33132.

Telephone: (305) 523-5110.

MORGAN, David C. *(Judge, Indian River County Court)* Elected Sept 7, 1996 to term beginning Jan 7, 1997. Reelected 2000, current term expires Jan 2007. Born Vero Beach Florida April 16, 1957. Church of God. Educated at Mercer University B.A. 1978 J.D. 1981. Admitted to practice Florida 1981.

Chief Assistant State Attorney Nineteenth Judicial Circuit 1981-97. Author "Attacking Mental Health Defenses" 1994 and "The Sentencing Phase of a Capital Trial" 1995 FPAA. Member The Florida Bar and Indian River Bar Association. Recipient Eugene Berry Memorial Award 1994. Member Kiwanis Club. Enjoys golf and officiating high school sports.

Office: 263 Indian River County Courthouse, 2000 16th Avenue, Vero Beach 32960.

Telephone: (772) 770-5070.

Fax: (772) 770-5477

MORGAN, Hugh J. *(Magistrate Judge, United States District Court Southern District of Florida)* Appointed by U.S. District Court judges Oct 1981. Reappointed 1985, 1989, 1993, 1997 and 2001. Current term expires Oct 2005. Serves part time. Born Key West Florida June 1, 1941. Catholic. Educated at University of Florida B.A. 1964 J.D. 1968. Member Sigma Nu, Phi Kappa Phi and Florida Blue Key. Admitted to practice Florida 1968, Trial Bar of U.S. District Court Southern District of Florida 1972, U.S. District Court Middle District of Florida 1982 and U.S. Court of Appeals Eleventh Circuit 1986. In legal practice Key West since 1968.

Member Academy of Florida Trial Lawyers (Board of Directors), The Association of Trial Lawyers of America, The Florida Bar (Board of Governors Young Lawyers Section 1972-77, Executive Council Trial Lawyers Section 1980-83) and Monroe County Bar Association (President 1975-77). Instructor 1977-86, Chairman 1980 and Lecturer 1981-82 Trial Advocacy Program The Florida Bar. Lecturer Academy of Florida Trial Lawyers Spring 1986. Member Rotary Club (Past President) and Jaycees (Former member Board of Directors). Enjoys diving, fishing and antique bottle collecting.

Office: 203 Federal Building, 301 Simonton Street, Key West 33040.

Telephone: (305) 296-5676.

MORGAN, Jon B. *(Judge, Osceola County Court)*

Office: Osceola County Courthouse, 12 South Vernon Avenue, Kissimmee 34741.

Telephone: (407) 343-2516.

MORRIS, Elizabeth A. *(Judge, Putnam County Court)*

Mailing address: P.O. Box 147, Palatka 32178.

Telephone: (386) 326-2736.

Fax: (386) 329-2736

MORRIS, Robert J., Jr. *(Judge, Florida Circuit Court Sixth Judicial Circuit)* Appointed by Governor Jeb Bush 2001. Educated at University of Florida B.S. and DePaul University J.D. Admitted to practice Florida 1980. In legal practice Tampa and Tarpon Springs seventeen years. Former Judge, Pinellas County Court, appointed by Governor Lawton Chiles 1997.

Assistant State Attorney Sixth Judicial Circuit.

Office: 14250 49th Street North, Clearwater 33762.

Telephone: (727) 464-6137.

Fax: (727) 464-3807

MORRIS, Stan R. *(Chief Judge, Florida Circuit Court Eighth Judicial Circuit)* Former Judge, Alachua County Court.
Office: 302 Alachua County Courthouse, 201 East University Avenue, Gainesville 32601.
Telephone: (352) 374-3640.
Fax: (352) 381-0127

MORRIS, Thomas E. *(Magistrate Judge, United States District Court Middle District of Florida)* Appointed by U.S. District Court judges to term beginning March 8, 2001. Term expires 2009.
Office: U.S. Courthouse, 311 West Monroe Street, Jacksonville 32202.
Telephone: (904) 549-1953.

MOUNTS, Marvin U., Jr. *(Senior Judge, Florida Circuit Court Fifteenth Judicial Circuit)* Assumed Senior Judge status, serves by assignment.
Office: Palm Beach County Courthouse, 205 North Dixie Highway, West Palm Beach 33401.
Telephone: (561) 355-2431.

MOXLEY, John Dean, Jr. *(Judge, Florida Circuit Court Eighteenth Judicial Circuit)* Former Chief Judge.
Office: Titusville Courthouse, 506 South Palm Avenue, Titusville 32796-3592.
Telephone: (321) 264-6759.
Fax: (321) 264-6772

MOYLE, Paul O. *(Judge, Palm Beach County Court)* Appointed by Governor Lawton Chiles May 25, 1994.
Office: Palm Beach County Courthouse, 205 North Dixie Highway, West Palm Beach 33401.
Telephone: (561) 355-6302.

MUIR, Celeste Hardee *(Judge, Florida Circuit Court Eleventh Judicial Circuit)* Appointed by Governor Bob Martinez to term beginning June 25, 1990. Elected 1990, 1996 and 2002. Current term expires Jan 2009. Born Fernandina Beach Florida Aug 1, 1949. Episcopalian. Educated at University of Florida B.A. 1970 and Florida State University J.D. 1973. Law Clerk to Hon. William O. Mehrtens, U.S. District Court Southern District of Florida Aug 1973 to June 1975. Admitted to practice Florida 1973. In legal practice Miami June 1975 to Dec 1985. Judge, Dade County Court Nov 11, 1985 to June 25, 1990, appointed by Governor Robert Graham.
Editor *Court Handbook for Dade County Lawyers* Dade County Bar Association Young Lawyers Section 1976. Author "*Breakstone v. MacKenzie,* A Keystone Case for Judicial Reform" The Florida B. Jour. 1990. Editorial Board The Florida B. Jour. 1992-95. Member Procedures Committee Judicial Nominating Commission The Florida Bar 1989-92. Former Member Florida Conference of County Court Judges and Florida Conference of Circuit Court Judges. Member American Inns of Court, Dade County (President Elect 1981-82 and President 1982-83 Young Lawyers Section, Board of Directors 1983-85) and American (Ethics Committee, Law Week Committee) Bar Associations. Attended General Jurisdiction Course The National Judicial College Oct 1986. Named Outstanding Director by Dade County Bar Association Young Lawyers Section 1983. Board of Directors 1986-95 and 1998-2002 (Secretary 1999-2000) YMCA. Member Executive Committee YMCA of Greater Miami, Inc. 1993-95. Delegate Diocesan Convention 1994-98. Chapter Member Trinity Episcopal Cathedral 1999-2001. Principal for a day Carver Middle School 2000. Chair Committee on Constitution Canons. Enjoys reading, music, antiques and sailing.
Office: 303 Dade County Courthouse, 73 West Flagler Street, Miami 33130.
Telephone: (305) 349-7109.

MURPHY, Dennis J. *(Judge, Florida Circuit Court Eleventh Judicial Circuit)*
Office: 204 Gerstein Justice Building, 1351 N.W. Twelfth Street, Miami 33125.
Telephone: (305) 548-5715.

MURPHY, John J. *(Judge, Florida Circuit Court Seventeenth Judicial Circuit)*
Office: Broward County Courthouse, 201 S.E. Sixth Street, Fort Lauderdale 33301.

MURPHY, Joseph A. *(Judge, Broward County Court)*
Office: 421 Broward County Courthouse, 201 S.E. Sixth Street, Fort Lauderdale 33301.
Telephone: (954) 831-7706.

MURPHY, Stephen *(Judge, Taylor County Court)*
Mailing address: P.O. Box 914, Perry 32348.
Telephone: (850) 838-3510.
Fax: (850) 838-3548

MURPHY, Vincent *(Judge, Collier County Court)*
Office: Collier County Government Complex, Bldg. L, 3301 Tamiami Trail East, Naples 34112.
Telephone: (239) 774-8114.
Fax: (239) 774-9654

MUSLEH, Victor J. *(Chief Judge, Florida Circuit Court Fifth Judicial Circuit)* Appointed Nov 1987 by Governor Bob Martinez to term beginning Jan 1, 1988. Elected 1993 and 1999. Current term expires Jan 2006. Chief Judge since July 1, 2001. Born Ocala Florida Jan 8, 1934. Roman Catholic. Educated at University of Florida B.S. 1957 LL.B. 1960. Member Phi Alpha Delta. Admitted to practice Florida 1960. In legal practice Ocala 1960-1984. Judge, Marion County Court 1984-87.
Second Lieutenant U.S. Army 1957. Member Elks, Rotary Club, Knights of Columbus and Ocala High School/Forest High School Foundation. Interested in all sports.
Office: 4030 Marion County Judicial Center, 110 N.W. First Avenue, Ocala 34475.
Telephone: (352) 401-6770.
Fax: (352) 401-6789

MYERS, Eric Renard *(Judge, Hillsborough County Court)*
Office: 800 East Kennedy Boulevard, Room 201, Tampa 33602-4146.
Telephone: (813) 272-7138.
Fax: (813) 276-8015

NACHMAN, Bernard *(Judge, Florida Circuit Court Fourth Judicial Circuit)* Elected to term beginning Jan 1991. Reelected 1996 and 2002. Current term expires Jan 2009.
Office: Duval County Courthouse, 330 East Bay Street, Jacksonville 32202.
Telephone: (904) 630-2532.
Fax: (904) 630-2979

NAZARETIAN, Nick *(Judge, Hillsborough County Court)*
Office: 203 Annex, 800 East Kennedy Boulevard, Tampa 33602.
Telephone: (813) 276-2781.
Fax: (813) 276-2329

NEAL, Curtis J. *(Judge, Florida Circuit Court Fifth Judicial Circuit)*
Office: Hernando County Courthouse, 20 North Main Street, Brooksville 34601.
Telephone: (352) 754-4287.
Fax: (352) 754-4266

NELSON, Debra Steinberg *(Judge, Florida Circuit Court Eighteenth Judicial Circuit)*
Office: Seminole County Courthouse, 301 North Park Avenue, Sanford 32771-1292.
Telephone: (407) 665-4220.
Fax: (407) 665-4241

NELSON, James T. *(Senior Judge, Florida Circuit Court Seventh Judicial Circuit)* Elected 1963 to term beginning Jan 1964. Reelected to subsequent terms. Assumed Senior Judge status, serves by assignment. Born Daytona Beach Florida May 29, 1917. Catholic. Educated at University of Alabama and Stetson University LL.B. Admitted to practice Florida 1941. Began legal practice Fort Lauderdale 1941. In legal practice Daytona Beach 1946-51. Judge, Volusia County Small Claims Court 1951-64.
Member The Florida Bar and American Bar Association. Recipient Outstanding Young Man of the Year Award 1951 and Good Government Award 1953 from Daytona Beach Jaycees. Lieutenant Commander USAS 1941-44. Democrat. Past President Daytona Beach Jaycees and Daytona Beach Lions Club. Enjoys golf and fishing.
Office: 101 North Alabama Avenue, De Land 32724.
Telephone: (386) 257-6097.

NELSON, William John *(Judge, Florida Circuit Court Twentieth Judicial Circuit)* Appointed by Governor Robert Graham 1982. Elected to subsequent terms. Born Orangeburg South Carolina Oct 24, 1939. Presbyterian. Educated at Pennsylvania Military College (now Widener University) B.S.B.A. 1963 and Stetson University J.D. 1968. Admitted to practice Florida 1968. Began legal practice Fort Myers 1968. Judge, Lee County Court 1973-82.
Member The Florida Bar, Lee County and American Bar Associations. Enjoys flying and hunting.
Office: Lee County Justice Center, 1700 Monroe Street, Fort Myers 33901.
Telephone: (239) 335-2478.
Fax: (239) 335-2589

NESBITT, Joseph *(Senior Judge, Florida District Court of Appeal)* Appointed by governor 1979. Assumed Senior Judge status, serves by assignment. Born Leesburg Florida January 16, 1930. Educated at University of Florida B.A. 1951 and University of Miami LL.B. 1957. Former Judge, Florida Circuit Court Eleventh Judicial Circuit.
Office: 2001 S.W. 117th Avenue, Miami 33175-1716.
Telephone: (305) 229-3200.

NEWBOLD, Edmund W. *(Senior Judge, Florida Circuit Court Eleventh Judicial Circuit)* Assumed Senior Judge status, serves by assignment. Born Miami Florida Sept 3, 1923. Christian. Educated at University of Miami B.S.B.A. 1944 J.D. 1948. Member Phi Alpha Delta. Admitted to practice Florida 1948. Judge, Dade County Court 1972-81.
Board of Directors 1974 and Vice President 1975-76 Florida Conference of County Court Judges. Member The Florida Bar. Lieutenant j.g. USNR. Former Government Appeal Agent local draft board. Member Miami Civil Service Board 1953-60 (Chairman 1955-60 and Legal Advisor 1960-72). President Kenwood Elementary PTA 1963-64 and Miami Killian Senior High School Booster Club 1970-71. Past President Coconut Grove Exchange Club and Coconut Grove Chamber of Commerce.
Office: 511 Dade County Courthouse, 73 West Flagler Street, Miami 33130.
Telephone: (305) 349-7001.

NEWMAN, Edward K. *(Judge, Dade County Court)* Elected to term beginning Jan 3, 1995. Reelected 1998, current term expires Jan 2005.
Office: 616 Gerstein Justice Building, 1351 N.W. Twelfth Street, Miami 33125.
Telephone: (305) 548-5397.

NEWMAN, Robert H. *(Senior Judge, Florida Circuit Court Eleventh Judicial Circuit)* Elected to term beginning Jan 3, 1983. Reelected 1988 and 1994. Assumed Senior Judge status, serves by assignment. Born New York New York Sept 28, 1927. Educated at University of Miami B.B.A. 1950 J.D. 1952. Admitted to practice Florida 1952, U.S. Supreme Court 1961 and U.S. Court of Appeals Fifth Circuit 1961. Began legal practice Miami 1952. Judge, Dade County Court 1978-82.
Assistant State Attorney 1959-61. Assistant U.S. Attorney 1961-63. Member American Judicature Society and The Florida Bar. Named Man of the Year by Temple Beth Am Bonds for Israel. Past President Dade County Association of Voluntary Health Agencies, Scopus Lodge, B'nai B'rith Lodge and Temple Beth Am. Member Union of America Hebrew Congregations (Former Trustee National Board, Past President Southeast Florida Federation), Leukemia Society of America (National Officer) and Health Systems Agency of South Florida. Enjoys tennis.
Office: 511 Dade County Courthouse, 73 West Flagler Street, Miami 33130.
Telephone: (305) 349-7001.

NICHOLAS, Edward *(Judge, Florida Circuit Court Twelfth Judicial Circuit)*
Mailing address: P.O. Box 48927, Sarasota 34230.
Office: 2002 Ringling Boulevard, Sarasota 34237.

NICHOLS, A. W., III *(Judge, Florida Circuit Court Seventh Judicial Circuit)*
Mailing address: P.O. Box 26, Palatka 32178.
Telephone: (386) 329-0471.
Fax: (386) 329-1276

NICHOLS, Colie, Jr. *(Judge, Santa Rosa County Court)* Appointed by Governor Reubin Askew to term beginning Jan 14, 1974. Elected to subsequent terms. Current term expires Jan 4, 2005. Born Graceville Florida Feb 5, 1935. Baptist. Educated at Florida State University B.S. 1959. Member Sigma Phi Epsilon.
Probation and Parole Supervisor 1960-68. Member Governor's Advisory Committee on Criminal Justice 1974-76, Alcoholism Rehabilitation Advisory Subcouncil

NICHOLS, COLIE, JR.—*Continued*

1976-81 and Florida Conference of County Judges (Co-chairman Legislative Committee 1978-79, Director and Treasurer 1978-79, First Vice President 1986-87). Past President West Florida Council on Crime and Delinquency, Milton Lions Club, United Way of Santa Rosa County, Santa Rosa County Mental Health Association, Santa Rosa County Health Council, Oakhurst School PTA and Mentors Toastmasters. Member Santa Rosa Historical Society, Milton Quarterback Club and First Baptist Church (Trustee Chairman, Deacon).

Office: 6865 Caroline Street, Suite S, Milton 32570.
Telephone: (850) 623-0135.
Fax: (850) 623-1696

NICKINSON, Edward P., III *(Judge, Florida Circuit Court First Judicial Circuit)* Appointed by Governor Bob Martinez Oct 6, 1989. Elected to subsequent terms.

Office: Juvenile Justice Center, 2251 North Palafox Street, Pensacola 32501.
Telephone: (850) 595-3710.
Fax: (850) 595-3711

NIELSEN, Richard A. *(Judge, Florida Circuit Court Thirteenth Judicial Circuit)*

Office: 800 East Kennedy Boulevard, Tampa 33602-4146.
Telephone: (813) 272-5819.
Fax: (813) 276-2329

NILON, James P. *(Judge, Alachua County Court)*

Office: Alachua County Courthouse, 201 East University Avenue, Gainesville 32601.
Telephone: (352) 384-3081.
Fax: (352) 374-5238

NIMMONS, Ralph W., Jr. *(Judge, United States District Court Middle District of Florida)* Appointed for life by the President. Born Dallas Texas Sept 14, 1938. Educated at University of Texas 1956-58 and University of Florida B.A. 1960 J.D. 1963. Admitted to practice Florida 1963 and U.S. Supreme Court 1970. In legal practice Jacksonville 1963-77. Judge, Florida Circuit Court Fourth Judicial Circuit 1977-83, appointed by Governor Reubin Askew. Former Judge, Florida District Court of Appeal First District, assumed office Jan 1983.

Assistant Public Defender Fourth Judicial Circuit 1965-69. First Assistant State Attorney Fourth Judicial Circuit 1969-71. Chief Assistant General Counsel City of Jacksonville 1971-83. Member Metropolitan Criminal Justice Advisory Council 1977-79 and Task Force on Prison Overcrowding 1982-83. Member Trial Court Study Commission 1987-88. Former member National Institute of Municipal Law Officers, National District Attorneys Association, Florida State Prosecuting Attorneys Association and Florida State Public Defenders Association. Member Florida Conference of Circuit Court Judges 1977-83 (Chairman Committee on Criminal Legislation 1979-80, Chairman Criminal Justice Section 1980-83, Executive Committee 1980-83), The Florida Bar (Vice Chairman Grievance Committee 1973-76), Jacksonville (Ethics Committee 1972-73, Chairman Criminal Law Committee 1972-73, member 1973-75 and Chairman 1974-75 Judicial Candidates Committee) and American Bar Associations. Speaker and lecturer seminars of Florida Conference of Circuit Court Judges. Recipient Donald K. Carroll Award as Outstanding Member of the Judiciary from Jacksonville Junior Chamber of Commerce 1980 and State of Florida Distinguished Service Award-Judiciary from the Florida Council on Crime and Delinquency 1981. Named Outstanding Judge in Duval County by county chapter Florida Council on Crime and Delinquency 1981 and Outstanding Circuit Judge by Jacksonville Bar Association Young Lawyers Section 1981. Board of Trustees Jacksonville Children's Hospital 1972-83. Member Riverside Baptist Church Jacksonville (President Corporate Board 1976, Chairman Board of Deacons 1982, Board of Trustees Day School). Member First Baptist Church Tallahassee (Chairman Board of Deacons 1988-89).

Mailing address: P.O. Box 1110, Jacksonville 32201-1110.
Telephone: (904) 232-1490.

NOBLES, Linda Lee *(Judge, Florida Circuit Court First Judicial Circuit)* Former Judge, Escambia County Court.

Office: 190 Governmental Center, Pensacola 32501.
Telephone: (850) 595-4459.
Fax: (850) 595-4461

NORRIS, William A., Jr. *(Senior Judge, Florida Circuit Court Tenth Judicial Circuit)* Former Chief Judge. Assumed Senior Judge status, serves by assignment.

Mailing address: P.O. Box 9000, Drawer J-133, Bartow 33831-9000.
Office: 255 North Broadway, Bartow 33830.
Telephone: (863) 534-4690.

NORTHCUTT, Stevan T. *(Judge, Florida District Court of Appeal Second District)* Appointed by Governor Lawton Chiles to term beginning Jan 6, 1997. Born Tallahassee Florida Aug 1, 1954. Educated at University of South Florida B.A. 1975 and Florida State University College of Law J.D. 1978. In legal practice Tampa 1978-97.

Office: 600 Tampa Branch Headquarters, 801 East Twiggs Street, Tampa 33602-3547.
Telephone: (813) 272-3430.
Fax: (813) 229-6534

OAKLEY, Thomas D. *(Senior Judge, Florida Circuit Court Fourth Judicial Circuit)* Appointed by Governor Reubin Askew to term beginning Feb 1974. Elected 1974, 1980 and 1986. Assumed Senior Judge status, serves by assignment. Born Jacksonville Florida Nov 18, 1919. Episcopalian. Educated at University of Florida J.D. 1949. Admitted to practice Florida 1949. Began legal practice Jacksonville 1949.

Assistant County Attorney 1953-68. Assistant General Counsel 1958-74. Member The Florida Bar and Jacksonville Bar Association. First Lieutenant USAAC 1941-45.

Office: Duval County Courthouse, 330 East Bay Street, Jacksonville 32202.
Telephone: (904) 630-1693.

OBER, Joelle Ann *(Judge, Hillsborough County Court)* Elected to term beginning Jan 7, 1997. Reelected 2000, current term expires Jan 2007. Born Staten Island New York March 16, 1957. Catholic. Educated at University of South Florida B.A. 1979 and South Texas College of Law J.D. 1983. Member Phi Alpha Delta. Admitted to practice Florida 1984 and U.S. District Court Middle District of Florida 1985. In legal practice 1984-96.

OBER, JOELLE ANN—*Continued*

Prosecutor and Assistant State Attorney 1984-86 and 1993. Member Hillsborough Association of Women Lawyers, Florida Association of Women Lawyers, National Association of Women Judges and Hillsborough County Bar Association. Member Leadership Hillsborough, Florida Conservation Association, League of Women Voters and Tiger Bay Club. Enjoys music, travel and boating.

Office: 235 Tower, 801 East Twiggs Street, Tampa 33602-3554.

Telephone: (813) 272-6749.

O'BRIEN, Gerard J., Jr. *(Senior Judge, Florida Circuit Court Sixth Judicial Circuit)* Elected 1980 to term beginning Jan 5, 1981. Reelected 1986 and 1992. Chief Judge Pasco County 1982-83. Assumed Senior Judge status, serves by assignment. Born San Diego California May 8, 1924. Roman Catholic. Educated at University of Notre Dame B.S. cum laude 1945 LL.B. cum laude 1949 replaced by J.D. and Catholic University of America LL.M. 1952. Admitted to practice District of Columbia 1949, Indiana 1958 and Florida 1965. In legal practice Washington D.C. 1949-50, Indianapolis Indiana 1958 and St. Petersburg Florida 1965. Judge, South Pasadena Municipal Court 1970-72.

Attorney Office of General Counsel U.S. Department of Agriculture Washington D.C.1950-53. Assistant U.S. Attorney Trial and Appellate Division District of Columbia 1953-56. Attorney Tax Division U.S. Department of Justice Washington D.C. 1956-58. City Attorney and Prosecutor South Pasadena 1967-70. Author "Insanity Under Durham Case" Catholic University L. Rev. 1957 and "Insanity Plea as a Defense" American-Catholic Psychiatric Association 1958. Important Decisions: Chris Rusaw v. State of Florida (sexual battery case) 63 So. 2d 628, 1984 and State of Florida v. Tom Franklin Sawyer (first degree murder confession suppressed for psychological coercion) 15 LLW 135, Jan 12, 1990. Adjunct Faculty Member Stetson College of Law 1967-69. Guest Lecturer George Washington University 1957, Catholic University of America 1957 and University of South Florida 1984. Former Member The District of Columbia Bar and Indiana State Bar Association. Member Rico-Bono Roman Law Society, American Judicature Society, The Florida Bar, St. Petersburg, Indianapolis and American Bar Associations. Lecturer Conference of Florida Circuit Court Judges 1984. Graduate The National Judicial College, Reno Nevada 1986. Recipient Exemplar Award from University of Notre Dame 1997. Lieutenant j.g. USN PTO 1943-46. Executive Director Great Books Society Library of Congress 1956-58. Republican. Active in Governors' races of Senator Skip Bafallis and Jack Eckerd and Presidential race of Ronald Reagan. Delegate Republican Convention of Florida. Member Mental Health Planning Commission of Indiana 1962 and Pinellas County Charter Commission of Florida 1976. Director American National Bank of South Pasadena 1966-69 and American National Bank of Clearwater 1970-73. Member St. Petersburg Elks Club, Judge of Forum 1997-98.

Office: Judicial Building, 545 First Avenue North, St. Petersburg 33701.

Telephone: (727) 464-4470.

O'BRIEN, John D. *(Judge, Bay County Court)*

Mailing address: P.O. Box 2269, Panama City 32402.

Office: Bay County Courthouse, Panama City 32401.

Telephone: (850) 747-5211.

Fax: (850) 747-5629

OFTEDAL, Richard L. *(Judge, Florida Circuit Court Fifteenth Judicial Circuit)* Former Chief Judge.

Office: Palm Beach County Courthouse, 205 North Dixie Highway, West Palm Beach 33401.

Telephone: (561) 355-4897.

Fax: (561) 355-1616

OLLIFF, R. Hudson *(Senior Judge, Florida Circuit Court Fourth Judicial Circuit)* Elected 1974 to term beginning Jan 1, 1975. Reelected 1980, 1986 and 1992. Assumed Senior Judge status, serves by assignment. Born Daytona Beach Florida Aug 24, 1925. Baptist. Educated at University of Florida J.D. 1952. Admitted to practice Florida 1952 and U.S. Supreme Court 1964. Began legal practice Jacksonville 1952. Judge, Criminal Court of Record 1971-74.

Chief Assistant County Solicitor 1957-64. Chief Assistant State Attorney 1964-65. Important Decisions: Dobbert v. State of Florida, Florida Supreme Court 1976; Barclay v. State of Florida, Florida Supreme Court 1977; and Dobbert v. Florida, U.S. Supreme Court 1977. Member Florida Circuit Court Judges Conference, The Florida Bar and Jacksonville Bar Association. Recipient Prosecuting Attorney Certificate of Merit from Governor of Florida 1965. Private U.S. Army Paratroops 1943-46 (WWII European combat with 17th and 101st Airborne Divisions). Recipient Bronze Star Medal, three battle stars, Invasion Arrowhead, Combat Infantry Medal and parachute jump wings. Board of Directors University Christian School, Jacksonville. 32° Mason and Shriner.

Office: Duval County Courthouse, 330 East Bay Street, Jacksonville 32202.

Telephone: (904) 630-1693.

ORFINGER, Melvin *(Senior Judge, Florida District Court of Appeal)* Chief Judge July 1, 1982 to June 30, 1984. Assumed Senior Judge status, serves by assignment. Former Judge, Florida Circuit Court Seventh Judicial Circuit.

Office: 300 South Beach Street, Daytona Beach 32114.

Telephone: (386) 947-1500.

ORFINGER, Richard B. *(Judge, Florida District Court of Appeal Fifth District)* Assumed office 2000. Born Daytona Beach Florida May 19, 1952. Educated at Tulane University B.A. 1974 and University of Florida J.D. with honors 1976. Admitted to practice Florida, U.S. District Court Middle District of Florida, U.S. Court of Appeals Eleventh Circuit and U.S. Supreme Court. In legal practice 1979-91. Judge 1991-2000 and Chief Judge 1996-99, Florida Circuit Court Seventh Judicial Circuit.

Assistant State Attorney Seventh Judicial Circuit 1976-78. Member Weighted Caseload System Committee 1998 and Chair Equal Opportunity Employment Committee 1998-99 State Court System. Former Member Volusia County Civil Trial Attorneys Association (Board of Directors and Treasurer 1990-91), Florida Prosecuting Attorneys Association, American Hospital Attorneys Association, National Health Lawyers Association and Florida Conference of Circuit Judges. Member Volusia Flagler Association of Women Lawyers, The Florida

ORFINGER, RICHARD B.—*Continued*

Bar, Volusia County (Board of Directors 1984-86, Treasurer 1990-91) and American Bar Associations. Speaker and Presenter Florida College of Advanced Judicial Studies 1999. Lecturer Approved CLE The Florida Bar. Recipient Judicial Leadership Award from Florida Council on Crime and Delinquency 1999. Board of Directors 1980-81 and Volunteer Pro Bono Attorney Central Florida Legal Services. Board of Directors 1980-84 and Vice President 1983 ACT, Inc. Board of Directors 1982-98, Vice President 1987-88 and President 1993-95 Temple Beth-El. Board of Directors YMCA 1984-86 and Museum of Arts and Sciences 1986-88. Member Volusia County Drug Abuse Task Force 1994-99. Member Tiger Bay Club, Daytona Beach Rotary Club and Florida Blue Key.

Office: 300 South Beach Street, Daytona Beach 32114.

Telephone: (386) 947-1510.

Fax: (386) 947-1562

ORLANDO, Michael J. *(Judge, Florida Circuit Court Seventeenth Judicial Circuit)*

Office: Broward County Courthouse, 201 S.E. Sixth Street, Fort Lauderdale 33301.

O'SULLIVAN, John J. *(Magistrate Judge, United States District Court Southern District of Florida)* Appointed by U.S. District Court judges to term beginning April 1, 1999. Term expires 2007.

Office: Federal Courthouse Square, 301 North Miami Avenue, Miami 33128.

Telephone: (305) 523-5920.

OVERSTREET, Michael C. *(Judge, Florida Circuit Court Fourteenth Judicial Circuit)*

Mailing address: P.O. Box 2237, Panama City 32402.

Telephone: (850) 747-5653.

Fax: (850) 747-5159

OVERTON, Ben F. *(Senior Justice, Florida Supreme Court)* Assumed office March 27, 1974. Retained by election. Chief Justice March 1976 to July 1978. Assumed Senior Justice status, serves by assignment. Born Green Bay Wisconsin Dec 15, 1926. Episcopalian. Educated at University of Florida B.S. 1951 J.D. 1952 and University of Virginia LL.M. 1984. Awarded honorary LL.D. Stetson University 1975 and Nova University 1977. Admitted to practice Florida 1952. In legal practice St. Petersburg Beach 1952-56 and St. Petersburg 1956-64. Judge, Florida Circuit Court Sixth Judicial Circuit 1964-74.

With Office of State Attorney General at Tallahassee 1952. Part-time faculty member Stetson University 1971-74. Member American Judicature Society (Board of Directors 1977-78, Secretary 1980-83), The Florida Bar and American Bar Association. Executive Council 1977-78 and Chairman Judicial Education Committee Conference of Chief Justices. Executive Committee Appellate Judges Conference 1977-84. Chairman subcommittee for Enforcement of Judicial Discipline 1978. Chairman Judicial Council of Florida since 1985. Instructor in Condemnation Proceedings Florida Bar CLE 1966 and 1970; Judicial Discretion National College of the State Judiciary 1969, 1970, 1972, 1974 and 1977; Dialogue of Civil and Criminal Jury Trials 1967; and Chairman Florida Bar CLE 1971-74. Faculty member National College of the State Judiciary 1968-76. Board of Directors The National Judicial College 1976-87 (Chairman Academic Committee). USAS JAGC (retired 1974). Enjoys tennis.

Office: 500 South Duval Street, Tallahassee 32399.

OVERTON, William H. *(Judge, Pinellas County Court)*

Office: 1800 66th Street North, St. Petersburg 33701.

Telephone: (727) 582-7620.

OWEN, William C., Jr. *(Senior Judge, Florida District Court of Appeal)* Assumed Senior Judge status 1987, serves by assignment. Born Memphis Tennessee Dec 24, 1922. Educated at Tulane University B.A. 1944 and University of Florida LL.B. 1948. Member Phi Delta Phi, Omicron Delta Kappa and Pi Kappa Alpha. Admitted to practice Florida 1948, U.S. District Court Southern District of Florida 1948 and U.S. Court of Appeals Fifth Circuit 1960. In legal practice Clewiston 1948-58 and West Palm Beach 1958-67 and 1976-80. Judge 1967-76 and Chief Judge 1973-75, Florida District Court of Appeal Fourth District. Judge, Florida Circuit Court Nov 16, 1982 to 1987, appointed by Governor Robert Graham.

Member The Florida Bar, Palm Beach County and American Bar Associations. Lieutenant j.g. USN 1943-46. Elder Memorial Presbyterian Church since 1962. Member Kiwanis Club (Past President) and American Legion Post 93 (Past Commander). Enjoys golf.

Mailing address: 7128 Deer Point Lane, West Palm Beach 33411.

OWENS, Andrew D., Jr. *(Judge, Florida Circuit Court Twelfth Judicial Circuit)* Former Chief Judge.

Mailing address: P.O. Box 48927, Sarasota 34230.

Office: 2002 Ringling Boulevard, Sarasota 34237.

Telephone: (941) 861-7946.

Fax: (941) 861-7913

PACK, R. Wallace *(Senior Judge, Florida Circuit Court Twentieth Judicial Circuit)* Elected 1972 to term beginning Jan 2, 1973. Reelected 1978, 1984, 1990 and 1996. Former Chief Judge. Assumed Senior Judge status, serves by assignment. Born Beaumont Texas Dec 25, 1928. Presbyterian. Educated at Davidson College B.S. 1950 and Southern Methodist University J.D. with honors 1953. Editor Southwestern Law Journal 1952-53. Member Order of Barristers and Order of the Woolsack. Admitted to practice Texas 1953 and Florida 1967. Began legal practice Dallas Texas 1953. In legal practice Fort Myers Florida 1967. Judge, Lee County Court 1971-73.

Member The Florida Bar, State Bar of Texas, Lee County and American Bar Associations. Republican. Director Canterbury School 1965-74 (President 1968-70) and Lee County Mental Health Clinic 1971-73. Past Commodore Royal Palm Yacht Club. Member Masonic Lodge, York Rite, Shriners and Kiwanis Club. Enjoys sailing, photography, skeet shooting and soaring.

Office: Charlotte County Justice Center, 350 East Marion Avenue, Punta Gorda 33950.

Telephone: (239) 335-2299.

PADGETT, J. Rogers, Sr. *(Judge, Florida Circuit Court Thirteenth Judicial Circuit)* Appointed by Governor Reubin O'Donovan Askew Nov 1977. Elected to subsequent terms. Current term expires Jan 2009. Born

PADGETT, J. ROGERS, SR.—*Continued*

Clearwater Florida May 8, 1938. Judge, Hillsborough County Court 1975-77.

Office: 334 Annex Tower, 801 East Twiggs Street, Tampa 33602-3549.

Telephone: (813) 272-6870.

PADOVANO, Philip J. *(Judge, Florida District Court of Appeal First District)* Assumed office 1996. Born Hackensack New Jersey Jan 28, 1947. Educated at Florida State University B.S. 1969 and Stetson University College of Law J.D. 1973. Staff member Stetson Law Review 1973. In legal practice Florida 1973-88. Judge 1988-96 and Chief Judge 1993-96, Florida Circuit Court Second Judicial Circuit.

Chair Committee on Florida Standard Jury Instructions in Criminal Cases since 1997 and Committee to Recommend Minimum Standards for Lawyers in Capital Cases since 1997.

Office: 301 Martin Luther King Jr. Boulevard, Tallahassee 32399-1850.

Telephone: (850) 487-1000.

Fax: (850) 488-7989

PAINE, James C. *(Senior Judge, United States District Court Southern District of Florida)* Appointed for life by President Jimmy Carter to term beginning Nov 2, 1979. Assumed Senior status, serves by assignment. Born Valdosta Georgia May 20, 1924. Episcopalian. Educated at University of Florida A.A. 1943, Columbia University B.S. 1947 and University of Virginia LL.B. 1950 replaced by J.D. Business Manager Virginia Law Review 1949-50. Member Phi Alpha Delta. Admitted to practice Florida 1950, U.S. District Court Southern District of Florida 1951, U.S. Court of Appeals Fifth Circuit 1952 and U.S. Supreme Court 1959. In legal practice West Palm Beach 1950-79.

Member American Judicature Society, The Florida Bar, Palm Beach County, Federal and American Bar Associations. Lieutenant USNR 1943-46. Democrat. Member Greater West Palm Beach Chamber of Commerce (Past President) and Children's Home Society of Florida (Past President). Enjoys boating and reading.

Office: 453 Federal Building, 701 Clematis Street, West Palm Beach 33401.

Telephone: (561) 803-3430.

PALERMO, Peter R. *(Recalled Magistrate Judge, United States District Court Southern District of Florida)* Appointed Magistrate Judge by U.S. District Court judges to term beginning Jan 15, 1971. Reappointed to subsequent terms. Appointed Recalled Magistrate Judge by the Judicial Council of the Eleventh Circuit. Born Pittsburgh Pennsylvania June 15, 1918. Catholic. Educated at Pennsylvania State University B.A. 1941 and University of Miami J.D. 1950. Member Phi Alpha Delta and Justinian Society. Admitted to practice Florida 1950. Began legal practice Miami 1950. Judge, City of West Miami 1953-58.

Florida State Prosecutor 1950-53. Vice President League of Municipal Judges 1956. Member American Judicature Society, Florida Association for Women Lawyers, The Florida Bar, Dade County and Federal Bar Associations. Captain USAAC 1941-45. Mayor West Miami 1947-53. Former member Lions, Knights of Columbus and Woodmen of the World.

Office: U.S. Courthouse, 300 N.E. First Avenue, Miami 33132.

Telephone: (305) 523-5760.

PALMER, William D. *(Judge, Florida District Court of Appeal Fifth District)* Assumed office Oct 2000. Born Adrian Michigan Aug 22, 1952. Educated at Rensselaer Polytechnic Institute B.S. with honors 1973 and Boston College Law School J.D. cum laude 1976. Recipient Award for Outstanding Management Student from *The Wall Street Journal.* Editor-in-Chief Environmental Affairs Law Review.

Member The Florida Bar and Orange County Bar Association. Board of Directors Boys and Girls Clubs of Central Florida.

Office: 300 South Beach Street, Daytona Beach 32114.

Telephone: (386) 947-1502.

Fax: (386) 947-1562

PALOMINO, Raul C., Jr. *(Judge, Hillsborough County Court)* Appointed by Governor Lawton Chiles Dec 8, 1993.

Office: 203B Annex, 800 East Kennedy Boulevard, Tampa 33602-4146.

Telephone: (813) 272-5122.

Fax: (813) 276-2329

PANDO, Ana Maria *(Judge, Dade County Court)*

Office: 507 Gerstein Justice Building, 1351 N.W. Twelfth Street, Miami 33125.

Telephone: (305) 548-5193.

PARIENTE, Barbara J. *(Justice, Florida Supreme Court)* Appointed by Governor Lawton Chiles to term beginning Dec 10, 1997. Retained by election Nov 7, 2000, current term expires Jan 2007. Born New York New York Dec 24, 1948. Educated at Boston University with highest honors 1970 and George Washington University J.D. with highest honors 1973. Member Order of the Coif. Law Clerk to Hon. Norman C. Roettger, Jr., U.S. District Court Southern District of Florida 1973-75. Admitted to practice Florida 1973. Board Certified as a Specialist in Civil Trial Law by The Florida Bar. In legal practice Florida 1975-93. Judge, Florida District Court of Appeal Fourth District Sept 1993 to Dec 1997, appointed by Governor Lawton Chiles.

Author "A Profession for the New Millenium: Restoring Public Trust and Confidence in Our System of Justice" 74 Florida Bar Jour 50 Jan 2000.Certified by the National Board of Trial Advocacy 1986. Former Board of Directors Florida Bar Foundation. Former Member Grievance Committee and Nominating Commission Fifteenth Judicial Circuit. Chair Steering Committee on Families and Children in the Courts and Liaison to Task Force on Treatment-Based Drug Courts Florida Supreme Court. Member National Judges' Advisory Committee for the Balanced and Restorative Justice Project Department of Justice. Founding Member and Master Palm Beach County Chapter American Inns of Court. Member Florida Association for Women Lawyers, National Association for Women Judges, The Florida Bar (Commission on the Legal Needs of Children 2000-02) and American Bar Association (Committee on Coalition for Justice). Faculty Member Justice Teaching Institute Florida Supreme Court. Recipient Law Day Speech Award from American Bar Association 1998, Lifetime Achieve-

PARIENTE, BARBARA J.—*Continued*
ment Award from Palm Beach County Jewish Federation 1998, Distinguished Judicial Service Award from Florida Council on Crime and Delinquency 2000 and Breaking the Glass Ceiling Award from Jewish Museum of Florida 2002. Former Board of Directors Legal Aid Society of Palm Beach County. Former Mentor Take Stock in Children and Communities in Schools Mentoring Program. Former Volunteer Judge, Palm Beach County Youth Court program.

Office: Supreme Court Building, 500 South Duval Street, Tallahassee 32399-1925.
Telephone: (850) 488-8421.

PARKER, James S. *(Judge, Florida Circuit Court Twelfth Judicial Circuit)* Born Arcadia Florida Jan 27, 1944. Methodist. Educated at University of Florida B.A. 1966 J.D. 1969. Former Judge, DeSoto County Court, appointed by Governor Reubin O'Donovan Askew to term beginning Oct 1, 1975.

Mailing address: P.O. Box 48927, Sarasota 34230.
Office: 2002 Ringling Boulevard, Sarasota 34237.
Telephone: (941) 861-4866.
Fax: (941) 861-4865

PARNHAM, John T. *(Judge, Florida Circuit Court First Judicial Circuit)* Former Chief Judge.

Office: Juvenile Justice Center, 2251 North Palafox Street, Pensacola 32501.
Telephone: (850) 595-3715.
Fax: (850) 595-4451

PARSONS, Stewart E. *(Judge, Gadsden County Court)*

Mailing address: P.O. Box 469, Quincy 32351.
Telephone: (850) 627-6452.
Fax: (850) 627-2333

PARSONS, William A. *(Judge, Florida Circuit Court Seventh Judicial Circuit)*

Mailing address: P.O. Box 388, Palatka 32178.
Telephone: (386) 329-0266.
Fax: (386) 329-1275

PASKAY, Alexander L. *(Recalled Judge, United States Bankruptcy Court Middle District of Florida)* Appointed Judge by U.S. Court of Appeals Eleventh Circuit judges. Appointed Recalled Judge by the Judicial Council of the Eleventh Circuit.

Office: U.S. Courthouse, 801 North Florida Avenue, Tampa 33602-3899.
Telephone: (813) 301-5146.

PATE, Dorothy Harris *(Senior Judge, Florida Circuit Court Fourth Judicial Circuit)* Elected 1976 to term beginning Jan 1977. Reelected 1982 and 1988. Assumed Senior Judge status, serves by assignment. Born Eureka Kansas Feb 26, 1933. Presbyterian. Educated at Southwestern at Memphis B.A. 1955 and University of Florida J.D. 1970. Admitted to practice Florida 1971.

With State Attorney's Office Jacksonville 1971. Member The Florida Bar (Vice Chairman State Crime and Delinquency 1976-77), Jacksonville and American Bar Associations. Democrat. Active in juvenile delinquency and youth programs. Enjoys golf, bridge and reading.

Office: Duval County Courthouse, 330 East Bay Street, Jacksonville 32202.
Telephone: (904) 630-1693.

PAUL, Maurice M. *(Senior Judge, United States District Court Northern District of Florida)* Appointed for life by President Ronald Reagan to term beginning 1982. Chief Judge 1993-97. Assumed Senior status July 31, 1997, serves by assignment. Born Jacksonville Florida May 16, 1932. Educated at University of Florida B.S. 1954 B.A. 1954 LL.B. 1960. In legal practice 1960-72. Judge, Florida Circuit Court Ninth Judicial Circuit 1973-82.

Office: 307 Federal Building, 401 S.E. First Avenue, Gainesville 32601-6805.
Telephone: (352) 380-2415.

PAYNE, Richard Gale *(Chief Judge, Florida Circuit Court Sixteenth Judicial Circuit)* Elected Sept 1988 to term beginning 1989. Reelected 1994 and 2000. Current term expires Jan 2007. Chief Judge 1995-97 and since July 1, 2001. Chief Administrative Juvenile Court Judge since 1998. Born Girard Pennsylvania July 13, 1942. Educated at Youngstown University 1961-63, Edinboro State College B.S. 1966 and Florida State University J.D. 1970. Recipient International Law Fellowship 1967. Public Defender Trial Intern. Member Delta Theta Phi. Admitted to practice Florida 1971, U.S. District Courts Northern 1971 and Southern 1973 Districts of Florida, U.S. Courts of Appeals Fifth 1981 and Eleventh 1981 Circuits and U.S. Supreme Court 1981. In legal practice Key West 1971-75. Judge, Monroe County Court 1980-88.

Legal Advisor Florida Legislative Reference Bureau 1971. Assistant County Solicitor 1971-72 and Assistant County Attorney 1975-80 Monroe County. Assistant Public Defender Sixteenth Judicial Circuit 1972-73.

Office: Monroe County Courthouse Annex, Fourth Floor, 502 Whitehead Street, Key West 33040.
Telephone: (305) 292-3433.
Fax: (305) 295-3611

PEACH, John Weston *(Judge, Florida Circuit Court Third Judicial Circuit)* Appointed by Governor Reubin O'Donovan Askew to term beginning May 1978. Elected 1978, 1984, 1990, 1996 and 2002. Current term expires Jan 2009. Former Chief Judge. Born Gainesville Florida Feb 15, 1938. Methodist. Educated at University of Florida A.A. 1958, Jacksonville University B.A. 1962 and Mercer University LL.B. 1965. Staff member Mercer Law Review 1964-65. Member Delta Theta Phi and Alpha Gamma Rho. Admitted to practice Florida 1966. Began legal practice Jasper 1967. Judge, Hamilton County Court 1973-78.

Member The Florida Bar and Third Judicial Circuit Bar Association. USAR 1959-67.

Office: 207 N.E. First Street, Jasper 32052.
Telephone: (386) 792-1719.
Fax: (386) 792-1937

PEDEN, Michelle *(Judge, Hillsborough County Court)*

Office: 204 B Annex, 800 East Kennedy Boulevard, Tampa 33602.
Telephone: (813) 272-6854.
Fax: (813) 276-2329

PEEL, Colby *(Judge, Washington County Court)*

Mailing address: P.O. Box 561, Chipley 32428.
Telephone: (850) 638-6268.
Fax: (850) 415-5014

PELLECCHIA, Donald E. *(Judge, Florida Circuit Court Twentieth Judicial Circuit)* Appointed by Governor Bob Martinez Jan 2, 1990. Elected to subsequent terms.
Office: Charlotte County Justice Center, 350 East Marion Avenue, Punta Gorda 33950.
Telephone: (941) 637-2170.
Fax: (941) 637-2283

PENDINO, Sam *(Judge, Florida Circuit Court Thirteenth Judicial Circuit)* Former Judge, Hillsborough County Court.
Office: 390 Hillsborough County Courthouse, 419 Pierce Street, Tampa 33602-4022.
Telephone: (813) 272-6994.

PENICK, Thomas E., Jr. *(Judge, Florida Circuit Court Sixth Judicial Circuit)* Former Judge, Pinellas County Court.
Office: 300 Judicial Building, 545 First Avenue North, St. Petersburg 33701.
Telephone: (727) 582-7820.
Fax: (727) 582-7470

PEREYRA-SHUMINER, Cristina *(Judge, Dade County Court)*
Office: 2701 South Dade Justice Center, 10710 S.W. 211th Street, Miami 33189.
Telephone: (305) 252-5848.
Fax: (305) 234-1521

PEREZ, Nancy *(Judge, Palm Beach County Court)*
Office: Palm Beach County Courthouse, 205 North Dixie Highway, West Palm Beach 33401.
Telephone: (561) 624-6551.
Fax: (561) 355-1652

PERRY, Belvin *(Chief Judge, Florida Circuit Court Ninth Judicial Circuit)* Elected Sept 1988, 1994 and 2000. Current term expires Jan 2007. Chief Judge since July 1, 2001. First elected Black judge in Orange County.
Office: Orange County Courthouse, 425 North Orange Avenue, Orlando 32801.
Telephone: (407) 836-2008.
Fax: (407) 836-2006

PERRY, Daniel L. *(Judge, Florida Circuit Court Thirteenth Judicial Circuit)* Former Judge and Senior Judge, Hillsborough County Court, elected to term beginning Jan 1991.
Office: 129 Annex, 800 East Kennedy Boulevard, Tampa 33602-4146.
Telephone: (813) 272-6874.

PERRY, James E.C. *(Judge, Florida Circuit Court Eighteenth Judicial Circuit)* Assumed office 2000. Administrative Judge Civil Division since 2000. Educated at St. Augustine's College B.A. 1966 and Columbia University School of Law J.D. 1972. In legal practice Augusta Georgia 1973, Sanford Florida 1976-82 and Orlando Florida 1976-82 and 1984-93.
Staff Attorney Augusta Legal Aid Society 1972. Vice President and General Counsel Seminole Employment Economic Development Council 1974. Chapter 7 Bankruptcy Trustee U.S. Bankruptcy Court 1993. Former Member National Association of Bond Lawyers. Member Williams Inns of Court, Florida Conference of Circuit Court Judges, The Paul C. Perkins Bar Association, The Florida Bar (Former Member Grievance Committee), State Bar of Georgia, Orange County and National (Florida Chapter) Bar Associations. Recipient Humanitarian Award from Seminole County NAACP and Paul C. Perkins Award from Orange County NAACP. First Lieutenant U.S. Army 1967-69. Board of Trustees St. Augustine's College 2000. Former Chairman Minority Advisory Council to the President University of Central Florida. Former Member Metro Orlando Economic Development Committee and Executive Committee of Director Great Orlando YMCA. President Jackie Robinson Sports Association. Board of Directors NCCJ. Trustee and Choir Member Carter Tabernacle Church. Captain Heart of Florida United Way Campaign. Life Member St. Augustine Alumni Association. Member Leadership Florida XI and Civilian/Military Community Relations Council.
Mailing address: P.O. Box 2514, Sanford 32772-2514.
Office: Seminole County Courthouse, 301 North Park Avenue, Sanford 32771-1292.
Telephone: (407) 665-4218.
Fax: (407) 665-5349

PERRY, Morton Lee *(Senior Judge, Dade County Court)* Assumed Senior Judge status, serves by assignment.
Office: 511 Dade County Courthouse, 73 West Flagler Street, Miami 33130.
Telephone: (305) 349-7001.

PETERS, R. Timothy *(Judge, Florida Circuit Court Sixth Judicial Circuit)* Appointed by Governor Lawton Chiles to term beginning 1995. Elected 1996 and 2002. Current term expires Jan 2009. Served Criminal Division 1995-99. Serves Family Division since 2000. Educated at University of Florida B.A. 1971 J.D. 1973. Board Certified as a Specialist in Real Estate Law by The Florida Bar. In legal practice 1973-95.
Columnist "The Law Says" *Clearwater Sun* 1985-89. Author *Florida Deficiency Judgments, A Practitioner's Manual with Forms* Lindsay Press 1994. Editor "Res Ispa Loquitur" Clearwater Bar Association 1995. Chairman Real Property Law Committee 1987-88 and Pro Bono Committee 1988-89 Clearwater Bar Association. Member 1993-95 and Chairman 1995 Grievance Committee C Sixth Judicial Circuit and Member Condominium and Planned Development Committee The Florida Bar. Listed in *Who's Who in American Law* and *Who's Who in South and Southwest.* First Lieutenant U.S. Army Infantry 1966-68. Recipient Silver Star, Bronze Star with "V" device, Bronze Star, Purple Heart and Army Commendation Medal. Director and Officer 1976-78 and President 1978 Legal Aide Society of Clearwater. Founding Director and Officer Gulf Coast Legal Services 1979-81. Member Condominium Study Commission 1990-91. Former Director Suncoast Chapter Community Associations Institute and Girls Softball Clearwater for Youth. Former Team Manager junior and senior baseball team Clearwater National Little League.
Office: 489 Pinellas County Courthouse, 315 Court Street, Clearwater 33756.
Telephone: (727) 464-3635.
Fax: (727) 464-6204

PETERSON, Earle W., Jr. *(Judge, Florida District Court of Appeal Fifth District)* Appointed by Governor Bob Martinez to term beginning Jan 2, 1990. Retained by election Jan 1, 1993 and 1998. Current term expires 2005. Former Chief Judge. Educated at Florida State University B.S. 1957 and University of Florida J.D. with

PETERSON, EARLE W., JR.—*Continued*

high honors 1964. Editor-in-Chief Symposium Edition University of Florida Law Review 1964. Member Order of the Coif. Admitted to practice Florida 1965. In legal practice 1965-88. Judge, Florida Circuit Court Fifth Judicial Circuit 1988-90.

Member The Florida Bar and American Bar Association. Airman Basic USAF 1953-57 and First Lieutenant U.S. Army 1957-58.

Office: 300 South Beach Street, Daytona Beach 32114.

PETERSON, Thomas K. *(Senior Judge, Florida Circuit Court Eleventh Judicial Circuit)* Appointed by Governor Bob Martinez March 7, 1989. Assumed Senior Judge status, serves by assignment.

Office: 511 Dade County Courthouse, 73 West Flagler Street, Miami 33130.

Telephone: (305) 349-7001.

PFEIFFER, Frederick T. *(Senior Judge, Florida Circuit Court Ninth Judicial Circuit)* Elected 1972 to term beginning Jan 1, 1973. Reelected 1978, 1984 and 1990. Former Chief Judge. Assumed Senior Judge status, serves by assignment. Born Cleveland Ohio July 26, 1925. Educated at University of North Carolina A.B. 1947 and George Washington University LL.B. 1950.

Lieutenant j.g. USN 1943-46. Member Emmanuel Episcopal Church (Senior Warden, Treasurer Executive Committee and Chairman Finance, Dioceses of South and Central Florida since 1956).

Office: Orange County Courthouse, 425 North Orange Avenue, Orlando 32801.

Telephone: (407) 836-2050.

PHILLIPS, John L. *(Judge, Florida Circuit Court Fifteenth Judicial Circuit)* Former Judge, Palm Beach County Court.

Office: Palm Beach County Courthouse, 205 North Dixie Highway, West Palm Beach 33401.

Telephone: (561) 355-1565.

PHILMAN, Edward *(Judge, Gilchrist County Court)* Assumed office Jan 3, 1989. Elected to subsequent terms.

Mailing address: P.O. Box 262, Trenton 32693.

Telephone: (352) 463-3400.

Fax: (352) 463-3472

PIERCE, George H. *(Senior Judge, Bradford County Court)* Assumed Senior Judge status, serves by assignment. Currently serves Eighth Judicial Circuit.

Office: Alachua County Courthouse, 201 East University Avenue, Gainesville 32601.

Telephone: (352) 337-6277.

PIGGOTTE, Julianne *(Judge, Florida Circuit Court Seventh Judicial Circuit)* Appointed by Governor Bob Martinez to term beginning Jan 2, 1989. Elected to subsequent terms.

Office: 251 North Ridgeway Avenue, Suite 297, Daytona Beach 32114.

Telephone: (386) 239-7793.

Fax: (386) 239-7879

PINEIRO, Robert M. *(Judge, Florida Circuit Court Eleventh Judicial Circuit)* Former Judge, Dade County Court, appointed by Governor Bob Martinez to term beginning Jan 3, 1990.

Office: 603 Gerstein Justice Building, 1351 N.W. Twelfth Street, Miami 33125.

Telephone: (305) 548-5405.

PIQUETTE, William J. *(Senior Judge, Dade County Court)* Assumed Senior Judge status, serves by assignment.

Office: 511 Dade County Courthouse, 73 West Flagler Street, Miami 33130.

Telephone: (305) 349-7001.

PITTMAN, Judy Markham *(Chief Judge, Florida Circuit Court Fourteenth Judicial Circuit)* Former Judge, Bay County Court.

Mailing address: P.O. Box 27, Panama City 32402.

Office: 300 East Fourth Street, Panama City 32401.

Telephone: (850) 747-5320.

Fax: (850) 747-5159

PIZZO, Mark A. *(Magistrate Judge, United States District Court Middle District of Florida)* Appointed by U.S. District Court judges.

Office: 1154 U.S. Courthouse, 801 North Florida Avenue, Tampa 33602-3800.

Telephone: (813) 301-5011.

PLAINES, Robert *(Judge, Jefferson County Court)*

Office: Jefferson County Courthouse, Monticello 32344.

Telephone: (850) 342-0191.

Fax: (850) 342-0222

PLATZER, Victoria *(Judge, Florida Circuit Court Eleventh Judicial Circuit)* Elected Sept 4, 1994 to term beginning Jan 3, 1995. Reelected 2000, current term expires Jan 2007. Born Miami Florida. Jewish. Educated at Florida Atlantic University B.A. 1970 and University of Miami J.D. 1982. Law Clerk to Hon. Matt M. Railey, Colorado District Court Fourth Judicial District. Member Phi Sigma Tau. Admitted to practice Florida 1983 and Colorado 1984. In legal practice Miami 1984-94.

Office: 2227 Courthouse Center, 175 N.W. First Avenue, Miami 33128.

Telephone: (305) 349-5738.

Fax: (305) 349-6178

PLEUS, Robert J., Jr. *(Judge, Florida District Court of Appeal Fifth District)* Appointed by Governor Jeb Bush April 2, 2000. Born Orlando Florida Jan 9, 1936. Educated at University of Notre Dame B.A. 1957, University of Florida College of Law J.D. 1962 and Loyola University M.A. 1999. Board Certified as a Specialist in Real Estate Law by The Florida Bar. In legal practice 1962-2000.

Certified Circuit Court Civil Mediator. Board of Governors 1970-72 and 1976-81 and President Young Lawyers Division 1972 The Florida Bar. President Orange County Bar Association 1976. Member Windermere Town Council 1972-74. Mayor Town of Windermere 1988-94. President Windermere Rotary Club 1976, Orange County Historical Society 1995 and Tiger Bay Club of Orlando 1996. Past Grand Knight and District Deputy Knights of Columbus. Permanent Deacon Catholic Church.

Office: 300 South Beach Street, Daytona Beach 32114.

Telephone: (386) 947-1550.

Fax: (386) 947-1562

PLOGSTEDT, Antoinette *(Judge, Orange County Court)*
Office: 420 Orange County Courthouse, 425 North Orange Avenue, Orlando 32801.
Telephone: (407) 836-2246.

POLEN, Mark E. *(Chief Judge, Florida District Court of Appeal Fourth District)* Appointed by Governor Bob Martinez to term beginning 1989. Retained by election. Chief Judge since July 1, 2001. Born Aurora Illinois March 29, 1945. Jewish. Educated at University of Iowa B.B.A. 1966 and University of Miami J.D. 1969. Member Alpha Epsilon Pi, Phi Kappa Psi and Phi Delta Phi. Admitted to practice Florida 1969 and U.S. District Court Southern District of Florida 1969. Began legal practice Miami 1969, in legal practice Fort Lauderdale 1974. Judge, Industrial Claims Court 1977-79. Deputy Commissioner 1977-79. Associate Judge, Florida Industrial Commission Nov 1978. Judge, Florida Circuit Court Seventeenth Judicial Circuit 1979-89, appointed by Governor Robert Graham.
Member Florida Conference of Appellate Judges and The Florida Bar (Chair Family Law Section 1994-95, Co-Chair Bench/Bar Committee, Judicial Administration, Selection and Tenure Committee, Family Law Rules Committee 1992-95). Member B'nai B'rith Justice Unit (President 1986) and Fort Lauderdale Dog Club. Enjoys reading and collecting baseball cards.
Mailing address: P.O. Box 3315, West Palm Beach 33402-3315.
Office: 1525 Palm Beach Lakes Boulevard, West Palm Beach 33401.
Telephone: (561) 242-2043.
Fax: (561) 242-2100

POLLOCK, Jerry *(Judge, Broward County Court)* Elected to term beginning Jan 1991. Reelected 1994 and 1998. Current term expires Jan 2005.
Office: 331 Broward County Courthouse, 201 S.E. Sixth Street, Fort Lauderdale 33301.
Telephone: (954) 831-6722.
Fax: (954) 831-5572

POLSTON, Ricky *(Judge, Florida District Court of Appeal First District)* Assumed office Jan 2, 2001. Term expires Jan 2007. Born Graceville Florida Nov 20, 1955. Educated at Chipola Junior College A.A. 1975 and Florida State University B.S. summa cum laude 1977 J.D. with high honors 1986. Staff member Florida State University Law Review 1985-86. Member Order of the Coif. Admitted to practice U.S. District Court Middle, Northern and Southern Districts of Florida, U.S. Courts of Appeals Eleventh and Federal Circuits, U.S. Court of Federal Claims, U.S. Tax Court and U.S. Supreme Court. In legal practice 1987-2000.
CPA 1978. Certified Circuit Court Mediator since 1997. Member Tallahassee Inn of Court (Former Treasurer), Tallahassee and American Bar Associations. Member Florida Institute of CPAs, American Institute of Certified Public Accountants, Celebration Baptist Church and Christian Heritage Church.
Office: 301 Martin Luther King Jr. Boulevard, Tallahassee 32399-1850.
Telephone: (850) 487-1000.
Fax: (850) 921-4768

POMPONIO, Denise Almeida *(Judge, Florida Circuit Court Thirteenth Judicial Circuit)* Appointed by Governor Jeb Bush to term beginning Sept 1999. Reappointed to term beginning April 25, 2002, current term expires Jan 6, 2004. Born Tampa Florida April 7, 1958. Presbyterian. Educated at University of South Florida Criminal Justice 1979 and South Texas College of Law J.D. 1982. Admitted to practice Florida 1983. In legal practice Tampa 1990-93. Former Judge, Hillsborough County Court.
Assistant State Attorney 1983-90 and Chief of Arson and Explosives 1993-99 Hills County. Personal Statement or Quote: "Be punctual and polite!"
Office: 800 East Kennedy Boulevard, Room 109, Tampa 33602.
Telephone: (813) 272-7225.
Fax: (813) 276-8015

POOLER, Catherine M. *(Judge, Dade County Court)* Appointed by Governor Bob Martinez April 1, 1987. Elected Sept 1988, 1992, 1996 and 2000. Current term expires Jan 2007. Born Springfield Massachusetts Oct 7, 1954. Educated at Princeton University A.B. 1976 and University of Miami School of Law J.D. 1979. Admitted to practice Florida 1979 and U.S. District Court Southern District of Florida 1979.
Assistant State Attorney Dade County 1977-87. Hobbies include reading, sewing and doing needlepoint.
Office: 73 West Flagler Street, #1015, Miami 33130.
Telephone: (305) 349-7113.

PORTER, J. Frank *(Judge, Lee County Court)*
Office: Lee County Justice Center, 1700 Monroe Street, Fort Myers 33901.
Telephone: (239) 335-2618.
Fax: (239) 335-2264

POWELL, Rom W. *(Senior Judge, Florida Circuit Court Ninth Judicial Circuit)* Elected Nov 12, 1978 to term beginning Jan 2, 1979. Reelected 1984 and 1990. Assumed Senior Judge status 1997, serves by assignment. Born Atlanta Georgia May 31, 1935. Methodist. Educated at Dartmouth College A.B. 1957 and Stetson University College of Law LL.B. 1963. Member Delta Tau Delta and Delta Theta Phi. Admitted to practice Florida 1963, U.S. District Court Middle District of Florida 1965 and U.S. Court of Appeals Fifth Circuit 1974. Began legal practice Tampa 1963. In legal practice Winter Park 1965-68.
Assistant State Attorney Hillsborough County 1963-65. Assistant Solicitor 1965-66 and Solicitor 1968-72 Orange County. Chief Assistant State Attorney Orange County 1972-78. Author chapter "Jury Instructions" *Criminal Trial Practice in Florida* Florida Bar CLE 1984. Important Decision: State of Florida v. Andrews (first DNA fingerprint criminal trial in U.S.) 533 So. 2d 841, Fla. 5th DCA, 1988. Instructor in Criminal Justice University of Central Florida 1971 and Rollins College 1977-78. Former member Florida Prosecuting Attorneys Association (Director 1970-72), Orange County Criminal Justice Council (President 1971) and National District Attorneys Association (Associate Director 1976-78). Member Florida Supreme Court Committee on Standard Criminal Jury Instructions 1986-87, Florida Conference of Circuit Court Judges, The Florida Bar and Orange County Bar Association. Instructor Florida Judicial College 1983-87. Recipient Distinguished Service Award from Florida Council on Crime and Delinquency 1982-

POWELL, ROM W.—*Continued*
83. First Lieutenant USMC 1957-61. Enjoys dove hunting, fishing, canoeing and camping.
Office: Orange County Courthouse, 425 North Orange Avenue, Orlando 32801.
Telephone: (407) 836-2050.

PRATHER, Charles N. *(Senior Judge, Florida Circuit Court Ninth Judicial Circuit)* Assumed office Feb 7, 1990. Elected 1996. Assumed Senior Judge status, serves by assignment. Born Orlando Florida May 2, 1935. Episcopalian. Educated at Stetson University B.A. 1957 LL.B. 1963. Member Delta Theta Phi. Admitted to practice Florida 1963 and U.S. District Court Middle District of Florida 1964. In legal practice Orlando 1963-83. Judge, Orange County Court 1983-90.
Member The Florida Bar and Orange County Bar Association. Retired as Colonel USAR 1987. Enjoys carpentry and boating.
Office: Orange County Courthouse, 425 North Orange Avenue, Orlando 32801.
Telephone: (407) 836-2050.

PRATT, Linda Raspolich *(Judge, Broward County Court)* Elected to term beginning Jan 6, 1987. Reelected 1990, 1994 and 1998. Current term expires Jan 2005. Born Pensacola Florida Dec 4, 1951. Catholic. Educated at Newcomb College B.A. magna cum laude 1973 and Tulane University School of Law J.D. with honors 1976. Law Clerk to Hon. Norman C. Roettger, Jr., U.S. District Court Southern District of Florida 1976-78. Member Phi Beta Kappa and Phi Alpha Delta. Admitted to practice Florida 1976, U.S. District Court Southern District of Florida and U.S. Courts of Appeals Fifth and Eleventh Circuits. In legal practice Hollywood Florida 1978-86.
Member Florida Conference of County Court Judges, Broward County Women Lawyers Association, National Association of Women Lawyers, American Judges Association, Broward County, Federal and American Bar Associations. Enjoys music, choral singing and travel.
Office: 455 Broward County Courthouse, 201 S.E. Sixth Street, Fort Lauderdale 33301.
Telephone: (954) 831-7776.

PRESCOTT, Orlando Alberto *(Judge, Dade County Court)*
Office: 508 Gerstein Justice Building, 1351 N.W. Twelfth Street, Miami 33125.
Telephone: (305) 548-5194.
Fax: (305) 545-2246

PRESNELL, Gregory A. *(Judge, United States District Court Middle District of Florida)* Appointed for life by President Bill Clinton to term beginning Aug 2, 2000. Born 1942. Educated at College of William & Mary B.A. 1964 and University of Florida J.D. with high honors 1966. Member Order of the Coif.
Chairman Ninth Judicial Circuit Nominating Committee 1982-83. Board of Directors Florida Bar Foundation 1984-88. Fellow American College of Trial Lawyers. Member The Florida Bar (Board of Governors 1989-93, Member Business Litigation Certification Committee) and Orange County Bar Association (President 1975). President Florida Legal Services 1977-79.
Office: 300 U.S. Courthouse, 80 North Hughey Avenue, Orlando 32801.
Telephone: (407) 835-4301.
Fax: (407) 835-4317

PRINCE, Richard G. *(Judge, Florida Circuit Court Tenth Judicial Circuit)* Former Acting Judge. Born Aug 14, 1951. Roman Catholic. Educated at Stetson University B.A. cum laude 1973 J.D. 1976. Florida Board of Regents Scholar 1969-70 and International Honors Scholar 1971-72. Member Phi Alpha Theta and Phi Delta Phi. Admitted to practice Florida 1976, U.S. District Courts Middle 1980, Southern 1980 and Northern 1980 Districts of Florida, U.S. Courts of Appeals Fifth 1980 and Eleventh 1981 Circuits and Trial Bars of U.S. District Courts Southern 1983 and Northern 1984 Districts of Florida. Began legal practice Bartow 1976. In legal practice Winter Haven 1980. Former Judge, Polk County Court, elected to term beginning Jan 8, 1985.
Author "Commentary on *Borras v. State*" Cupola Magazine 1975. Instructor Polk Community College 1976-84, South Florida Junior College 1982-84 and Florida Southern College 1984. Member Florida Prosecuting Attorneys Association 1976-78 and 1982-84, Stetson Society of Trial Advocacy, Conference of County Court Judges of Florida and The Florida Bar. Recipient Public Defender Certificate of Merit 1976. Named Outstanding Young Man of America 1980. Listed in *Who's Who of Florida* 1982-83. Previously worked as heavy equipment operator and truck driver. Adult Sunday School teacher. Member Board of Directors Big Brothers/Big Sisters of Polk County. Women's Firearm Training instructor. Enjoys hunting and fishing.
Mailing address: P.O. Box 9000, Drawer J135, Bartow 33831.
Telephone: (863) 534-4647.
Fax: (863) 534-7722

PROCTOR, George L. *(Judge, United States Bankruptcy Court Middle District of Florida)* Chief Judge Sept 13, 1999 to Aug 1, 2000.
Mailing address: P.O. Box 559, Jacksonville 32201-0559.
Telephone: (904) 232-2154.

PTOMEY, William R., Jr. *(Judge, Monroe County Court)* Assumed office 1987. Elected to subsequent terms. Administrative Judge 1988-94 and since 1998. Educated at University of Alabama B.A. 1971 and Cumberland School of Law J.D. 1974. Admitted to practice Florida 1974. In legal practice 1976-81.
Assistant Public Defender Florida First Judicial Circuit 1974-76. Assistant State Attorney 1981-87 and Chief Assistant State Attorney Florida Sixteenth Judicial Circuit. Instructor in Criminal Law Florida Keys Community College since 1995. Faculty Member Florida Judicial College since 1996.
Office: Upper Keys Government Center, 88820 Overseas Highway, Tavernier 33070.
Telephone: (305) 852-7155.
Fax: (305) 585-7123

PUCILLO, Deborah Dale *(Senior Judge, Palm Beach County Court)* Assumed Senior Judge status, serves by assignment.
Office: Palm Beach County Courthouse, 205 North Dixie Highway, West Palm Beach 33401.
Telephone: (561) 355-2431.

QUESADA, Frank *(Judge, Florida Circuit Court Sixth Judicial Circuit)* Appointed by Governor Lawton Chiles Nov 18, 1993.

Office: Criminal Justice Center, 14250 49th Street North, St. Petersburg 33762.

Telephone: (727) 464-7276.

Fax: (727) 464-6910

QUINCE, Peggy A. *(Justice, Florida Supreme Court)* Appointed by Governor Lawton Chiles and Governor Elect Jeb Bush Dec 8, 1998. Retained by election Nov 7, 2000, current term expires Jan 2007. Born Norfolk Virginia Jan 3, 1948. Educated at Howard University B.S. 1970 and Catholic University of America J.D. 1975. Honorary Doctor of Laws Stetson University College of Law 1999. Member Phi Alpha Delta, Alpha Kappa Alpha and Black American Law Students Association. Began legal practice Norfolk Virginia 1977. In legal practice Bradenton Florida 1978-80. Judge, Florida District Court of Appeal Second District Jan 4, 1994 to Dec 7, 1998, appointed by Governor Lawton Chiles (first African-American woman appointed to Florida District Court of Appeal). Hearing Officer, Rental Accommodations Office.

Former Assistant Attorney General and Tampa Bureau Chief Criminal Division Attorney General's Office Feb 1980 to 1993. Former Member Tampa Bay Inn of Court, Hillsborough Association of Women Lawyers, George Edgecomb Bar Association and Hillsborough County Bar Association. Supreme Court Liaison to Workers' Compensation Committee, Judicial Ethics Advisory Committee and Supreme Court's Commission on Fairness. Member Tallahassee Association of Women Lawyers, The Florida Bar (Former Member Gender Equality Committee, Criminal Law Certification Committee, Executive Councils of the Government Lawyers and Criminal Law Section; Member Executive Council Appellate Section, Government Lawyers Section, Criminal Law Section, Equal Opportunity Section), Virginia State Bar, and National Bar Association. Recipient William H. Hastie Award from Judicial Council National Bar Association 2001, Woman of Distinction Award from Girl Scouts 2001, Presidential Achievement Award from National Bar Association, Jurist Award for outstanding leadership achievements and dedicated service to the community at large from Women Lawyers Division National Bar Association, award for community service and advancement of equal justice under law from Virgil Hawkins Bar Association, Appreciation Award for inspiration and devotion to our youth from Broward County School Board, award for distinguished service and continuing commitment to the people of Florida from Fort Lauderdale B'nai B'rith and award for contribution to civil rights from Lakeland NAACP. Former Assistant Sunday School Teacher New Hope Missionary Baptist Church. Member NAACP, Urban League and Jack and Jill of America, Inc.

Office: Supreme Court Building, 500 South Duval Street, Tallahassee 32399-1925.

Telephone: (850) 922-5624.

RAIDEN, Michael E. *(Judge, Polk County Court)* Appointed by Governor Lawton Chiles Feb 8, 1994.

Mailing address: P.O. Box 9000, Drawer J-137, Bartow 33831-9000.

Telephone: (863) 534-4366.

Fax: (863) 534-4108

RAINWATER, Tonya Baccus *(Judge, Florida Circuit Court Eighteenth Judicial Circuit)* Elected Nov 1990 to term beginning Jan 1991. Reelected 1996 and 2002. Current term expires Jan 2009. Born Granite City Illinois April 13, 1956. Methodist. Educated at Florida State University B.S. 1976, University of Florida J.D. 1978 and Florida Institute of Technology M.B.A. 1988. Moot Court. Admitted to practice Florida 1979, U.S. District Court Middle District of Florida and U.S. Courts of Appeal Fifth and Eleventh Circuits. In legal practice Indian Harbour Beach 1981-86. Judge, Brevard County Court 1987-91.

Adjunct Professor Florida Institute of Technology 1985-86. Attended General Jurisdiction Course The National Judicial College Spring and Fall 1989. Faculty Advisor The National Judicial College Summer 1995.

Office: Moore Justice Center, 2825 Judge Fran Jamieson Way, Viera 32940-8006.

Telephone: (321) 617-7283.

RAMIREZ, Juan, Jr. *(Judge, Florida District Court of Appeal Third District)* Born Havana Cuba Sept 11, 1945. Educated at Vanderbilt University B.A. 1968 M.A. 1969, University of Connecticut 1975 and University of Florida. Admitted to practice Florida 1975. In legal practice Miami 1975-88. Judge, Dade County Court March 7, 1988 to April 1990, appointed by Governor Bob Martinez. Former Judge, Florida Circuit Court Eleventh Judicial Circuit, appointed by Governor Bob Martinez to term beginning April 1990.

Adjunct Professor St. Thomas University School of Law since 1992.

Office: 2001 S.W. 117th Street, Miami 33175-1716.

Telephone: (305) 229-3200.

Fax: (305) 229-3206

RAMSBERGER, Peter R. *(Judge, Florida Circuit Court Sixth Judicial Circuit)* Former Judge, Pinellas County Court, elected to term beginning Jan 1991.

Office: 217 Judicial Building, 545 First Avenue North, St. Petersburg 33701.

Telephone: (727) 582-7224.

Fax: (727) 582-7273

RAPKIN, Harry M. *(Judge, Florida Circuit Court Twelfth Judicial Circuit)*

Office: South County Courthouse, 4000 South Tamiami Trail, Venice 34293.

Telephone: (941) 861-3240.

Fax: (941) 861-3730

RAPP, Stephen A. *(Judge, Florida Circuit Court Fifteenth Judicial Circuit)*

Office: Palm Beach County Courthouse, 205 North Dixie Highway, West Palm Beach 33401.

Telephone: (561) 355-3838.

RASMUSSEN, Paul D. *(Judge, Florida Circuit Court First Judicial Circuit)* Elected to term beginning Jan 1991. Reelected 1996 and 2002. Current term expires Jan 2009.

Office: Santa Rosa County Courthouse, Box K, 6865 South Caroline Street, Milton 32570.

Telephone: (850) 623-0135.

Fax: (850) 626-4268

RAWLINS, Robert W., Jr. *(Senior Judge, Florida Circuit Court Thirteenth Judicial Circuit)* Assumed Senior Judge status, serves by assignment.
Office: Hillsborough County Courthouse, 419 Pierce Street, Tampa 33602-4022.
Telephone: (813) 272-5894.

RAY, Raymond B. *(Judge, United States Bankruptcy Court Southern District of Florida)* Appointed by U.S. Court of Appeals Eleventh Circuit judges.
Office: U.S. Courthouse, 299 East Broward Boulevard, Fort Lauderdale 33301.
Telephone: (954) 769-5760.

REASBECK, James Milton *(Senior Judge, Florida Circuit Court Seventeenth Judicial Circuit)* Elected 1972 to term beginning Jan 3, 1973. Reelected 1978, 1984 and 1990. Assumed Senior Judge status, serves by assignment. Born Meadville Pennsylvania Nov 25, 1926. Educated at Allegheny College and University of Miami J.D. 1957. Admitted to practice Florida 1960. Began legal practice Hollywood 1960. Judge, Florida Industrial Claims Court Oct 9, 1967 to Nov 4, 1968. Judge, Broward County Court of Record Nov 5, 1968 to Jan 2, 1973.
Member The Florida Bar and South Broward County Bar Association. Ensign U.S. Merchant Marines 1944-48 and Corporal U.S. Army 1950-52. Republican. Enjoys fishing and golf. Interested in orchids and gardening.
Office: Broward County Courthouse, 201 S.E. Sixth Street, Fort Lauderdale 33301.
Telephone: (954) 831-7740.

REESE, Thomas S. *(Judge, Florida Circuit Court Twentieth Judicial Circuit)* Appointed by Governor Robert Graham to term beginning Oct 1, 1979. Elected 1980, 1986, 1992 and 1998. Current term expires Jan 2005. Former Chief Judge.
Office: Lee County Justice Center, 1700 Monroe Street, Fort Myers 33901.
Telephone: (239) 335-2472.
Fax: (239) 335-2586

REGISTER, Allen L. *(Judge, Florida Circuit Court Fourteenth Judicial Circuit)* Former Judge, Washington County Court, assumed office Oct 1, 1992.
Mailing address: P.O. Box 2237, Panama City 32402.
Telephone: (850) 747-5338.
Fax: (850) 747-5159

REIMAN, David Leroy *(Judge, Union County Court)*
Office: 104 Union County Courthouse, Lake Butler 32054.
Telephone: (352) 496-2621.
Fax: (352) 496-1718

REMINGTON, Thomas T. *(Judge, Florida Circuit Court First Judicial Circuit)* Appointed by Governor Lawton Chiles Jan 27, 1993 to term beginning March 3, 1993. Elected Nov 1994 and 2000. Current term expires Jan 2007. Born Keyser West Virginia Sept 16, 1943. Episcopalian. Educated at Florida Southern College B.S. 1966 and Florida State University J.D. 1970. Admitted to practice Florida 1971, U.S. District Court Northern District of Florida 1971, U.S. Supreme Court 1974, U.S. Court of Appeals Fifth 1977 and Eleventh 1983 Circuits. Board Certified as a Specialist in Civil Trial Law by The Florida Bar. In legal practice Fort Walton Beach 1971-93.
Assistant Public Defender 1971 and Assistant State Attorney 1972-75 First Judicial Circuit. Certified by the National Board of Trial Advocacy as a Specialist in Civil Trial Practice 1993. Former Member Academy of Florida Trial Lawyers, Association of Trial Lawyers of America, Okaloosa-Walton Bar Association (President 1973 and 1992). First Lieutenant U.S. Army Infantry 1967. Political affiliation: Nonpartisan.
Office: C121 Okaloosa County Courthouse Annex, 1250 North Eglin Parkway, Shalimar 32579.
Telephone: (850) 651-7474.
Fax: (850) 651-7333

RENKE, John K. *(Judge, Florida Circuit Court Sixth Judicial Circuit)*
Office: Government Center, 7530 Little Road, New Port Richey 34654.
Telephone: (727) 847-8180.
Fax: (727) 847-8046

REYES, Israel U. *(Judge, Dade County Court)*
Office: Gerstein Justice Building, 1351 N.W. Twelfth Street, Miami 33125.
Telephone: (305) 548-5201.

REYNOLDS, George S., III *(Judge, Florida Circuit Court Second Judicial Circuit)* Elected to term beginning Jan 1989. Reelected 1994 and 2000. Current term expires Jan 2007. Administrative Judge Family Law Division July 1992 to June 1997. Former Chief Judge. Born Albany Georgia Aug 30, 1949. Presbyterian. Educated at Florida State University B.S. 1971 J.D. 1974. Admitted to practice Florida 1975, U.S. District Courts Middle 1980, Northern 1980 and Southern 1980 Districts of Florida, U.S. Court of Appeals Eleventh Circuit 1980 and U.S. Supreme Court 1980. Began legal practice Tallahassee 1975. Judge, Leon County Court 1985-89.
Member Executive Committee Florida Conference of Circuit Judges 1996-98. Member Florida Government Bar Association (President 1981), The Florida Bar (Family Law Rules Committee since 1993) and Tallahassee Bar Association. Named Jurist of the Year by Florida Chapter American Academy of Matrimonial Lawyers 1996.
Office: 365-K Leon County Courthouse, 301 South Monroe Street, Tallahassee 32301.
Telephone: (850) 577-4310.
Fax: (850) 922-0327

RICHARDSON, Edward J. *(Senior Judge, Florida Circuit Court Eighteenth Judicial Circuit)* Assumed Senior Judge status, serves by assignment.
Office: Moore Justice Center, 2825 Judge Fran Jamieson Way, Viera 32940-8006.
Telephone: (321) 637-5555.

RIPPINGILLE, Bonnie L. *(Judge, Dade County Court)*
Office: 235 Courthouse Center, 175 N.W. First Avenue, Miami 33128.
Telephone: (305) 349-5701.

RIVES, Howard P., Jr. *(Senior Judge, Florida Circuit Court Sixth Judicial Circuit)* Appointed by Governor Robert Graham to term beginning Dec 2, 1985. Elected 1986. Assumed Senior Judge status, serves by assignment. Born Sept 20, 1923. Presbyterian. Educated at The Citadel 1941-42, University of Florida 1942 LL.B. 1949 and University of Kentucky 1946-47. Member Phi Kappa Tau and Phi Delta Phi. Admitted to practice Florida 1949, U.S. District Courts Middle 1949,

RIVES, HOWARD P., JR.—*Continued*

Northern 1949 and Southern 1949 Districts of Florida, U.S. Courts of Appeals Fifth 1949 and Eleventh 1981 Circuits and U.S. Supreme Court 1955. In legal practice Florida 1949-85.

Assistant State Attorney Sixth Judicial Circuit 1963-64. Former City Attorney eight years. Author Chapter 20 *Florida Bar Probate Practice Manual* The Florida Bar 1968 rev. 1969-76. Member Florida Bar Foundation (President 1983-84), Academy of Florida Trial Lawyers, American Judicature Society, The Association of Trial Lawyers of America, The Florida Bar (Board of Governors 1970-74, Officer and Director 1976-84), Clearwater (President 1951) and American Bar Associations. Attended Florida Judicial College 1985, The National Judicial College 1987 and numerous CLE seminars. Major U.S. Army ETO WWII 1943-46. Member Rotary Club of Clearwater since 1950, Masons Lodge 127, Belleview Biltmore Country Club and American Seniors Golf. Interests include historical societies, hunting, fishing, boating and golf.

Office: Judicial Building, 545 First Avenue North, St. Petersburg 33701.
Telephone: (727) 464-4470.

RIVKIND, Leonard *(Senior Judge, Florida Circuit Court Eleventh Judicial Circuit)* Elected to term beginning Jan 1975. Reelected to subsequent terms. Former Chief Judge. Assumed Senior Judge status, serves by assignment. Born Philadelphia Pennsylvania Sept 24, 1926. Jewish. Educated at University of Miami B.B.A. 1949 J.D. magna cum laude 1954 LL.M. 1967. Editor-in-Chief Miami Law Review. Honorable mention Outstanding Law Graduate. Member Iron Arrow and Omicron Delta Kappa. Admitted to practice Florida 1954. Began legal practice Miami Beach 1954.

Former Special Assistant State Attorney Dade County and Special Florida Assistant Attorney General. Author "Usury, Inc.—Incorporation to Avoid Usury Law" U. of Miami L. Rev. 1955, "Paralegals—A Storm Petrel?" Florida B. Jour. 1975 and "Obscenity Laws" North American Judges Association Journal. Member Supreme Court Committee on Standard Jury Instructions (civil) 1981-88, The Florida Bar (Chairman Unauthorized Practice Committee 1970-75 and Grievance Committee 1976) and Miami Beach Bar Association (President 1965). Sergeant USAS 1945-47.

Office: 511 Dade County Courthouse, 73 West Flagler Street, Miami 33130.
Telephone: (305) 349-7001.

ROARK, George J., III *(Judge, Escambia County Court)*
Office: Judicial Building, 190 Governmental Center, Pensacola 32501.
Telephone: (850) 595-4430.
Fax: (850) 595-4404

ROBBINS, Sandra Sue *(Judge, Florida Circuit Court Fifth Judicial Circuit)* Former Judge, Marion County Court.
Office: Marion County Judicial Center, 110 N.W. First Avenue, Ocala 34475.
Telephone: (352) 401-7820.
Fax: (352) 401-7875

ROBERTS, Charles E. *(Judge, Florida Circuit Court Twelfth Judicial Circuit)*
Mailing address: P.O. Box 48927, Sarasota 34230.
Office: 2002 Ringling Boulevard, Sarasota 34237.

ROBERTS, Debra *(Judge, Pasco County Court)*
Office: West Pasco Government Center, 7350 Little Road, New Port Richey 34654.
Telephone: (727) 815-7025.
Fax: (727) 847-8164

ROBERTS, Susan Wadsworth *(Judge, Florida Circuit Court Tenth Judicial Circuit)* Appointed by Governor Robert Graham to term beginning May 30, 1984. Elected 1984, 1990, 1996 and 2002. Current term expires Jan 2009. Born Daytona Beach Florida June 16, 1944. Baptist. Educated at Daytona Beach Junior College A.A. 1964 and Florida State University B.A. 1966 J.D. 1969. Law Clerk to Hon. Woodie A. Liles, Florida District Court of Appeal Second District. Member Phi Delta Delta. Admitted to practice Florida 1970 and U.S. District Court Middle District of Florida. In legal practice Lakeland 1970-76. Judge, Lakeland Municipal Court 1976-77. Judge, Polk County Court Jan 4, 1977 to May 29, 1984.

Former Public Defender and Prosecutor Lakeland Municipal Court. Former Member Technology Committee Supreme Court. Member Florida Association of Women Lawyers (Tenth Judicial Circuit Chapter), The Florida Bar (Former Member Technology Committee), Lakeland and Tenth Judicial Circuit Bar Associations. Recipient Award for Distinguished Service from Domestic Violence Task Force 1997 and Humanitarian Award from Polk County Chapter Bethune Cookman College Alumni 1999. Chairman Leadership Lakeland Judicial/Law Enforcement Day 1996-2000. Board of Governors Center for Florida History. Chairman Polk County Domestic Violence Task Force. Member Criminal Justice Advisory Board University of South Florida, Lakeland Christina Rotary, Order of Eastern Star, Bartow Chamber of Commerce, Lakeland Chamber of Commerce, Polk County Historic Society, St. Augustine Genealogy Society, Flagler County Historic Society and Imperial Polk Geneological Society. Enjoys gardening, bicycling, baseball and opera.

Mailing address: P.O. Box 9000, Drawer J117, Bartow 33831-9000.
Telephone: (863) 534-4623.

ROBINSON, Mary Rudd *(Judge, Broward County Court)* Appointed by Governor Bob Martinez to term beginning June 14, 1989. Elected to subsequent terms.
Office: 329 Broward County Courthouse, 201 S.E. Sixth Street, Fort Lauderdale 33301.
Telephone: (954) 831-7039.
Fax: (954) 831-5572

ROBINSON, Steven D. *(Senior Judge, Florida Circuit Court Eleventh Judicial Circuit)* Elected 1984 to term beginning Jan 8, 1985. Reelected 1990 and 1996. Assumed Senior Judge status, serves by assignment. Born Miami Florida Sept 3, 1943. Educated at University of Pennsylvania B.S. in Economics 1965, University of Miami School of Law J.D. cum laude 1968 and University of Nevada Reno M.J.S. 1993. Admitted to practice Florida 1968. In legal practice Miami 1970-72 and 1974-76 and Homestead 1972-74. Judge, Dade County Court Jan 5, 1977 to Jan 7, 1985.

Author "Tortious Water and Land Use in the Big Cy-

ROBINSON, STEVEN D.—*Continued*

press Swamp" 25 U. of Miami L. Rev. 690, 1970 and "Community Control: 'In Lieu of Incarceration'" 49 Florida B. Jour. 45, 1985. Member Florida Council on Criminal Justice 1979-83. Member National Council of Juvenile and Family Court Judges (Lead Judge Miami Model Court) and Dade County Bar Association. Member Visiting Committee Department of the Ancient Near East, Metropolitan Museum New York.

Office: 511 Dade County Courthouse, 73 West Flagler Street, Miami 33130.

Telephone: (305) 349-7001.

ROBY, William *(Judge, Florida Circuit Court Nineteenth Judicial Circuit)*

Office: Martin County Courthouse, 100 East Ocean Boulevard, Stuart 34994.

Telephone: (772) 463-3281.

Fax: (772) 463-3283

ROCHE, Renee A. *(Judge, Florida Circuit Court Ninth Judicial Circuit)* Former Judge, Orange County Court.

Office: Juvenile Justice Center, 2000 East Michigan Street, Orlando 32801.

Telephone: (407) 836-7590.

RODGERS, Edward *(Senior Judge, Florida Circuit Court Fifteenth Judicial Circuit)* Assumed office 1977. Elected to subsequent terms. Former Chief Judge. Assumed Senior Judge status, serves by assignment. Born Pittsburgh Pennsylvania Aug 12, 1927. Episcopalian. Educated at Howard University B.A. 1949 and Florida A. & M. University LL.B 1963. In legal practice West Palm Beach 1963-73. Judge ad litem, West Palm Beach Municipal Court 1965-68. Judge, Riviera Beach Municipal Court (part time) 1966-69. Judge, Palm Beach County Court 1973-77.

Assistant State Attorney Palm Beach County 1965-66. Member The Florida Bar and National Bar Association. Recipient Jefferson Award Washington D.C. July 1992. Seaman Third Class USN as Photographer's Mate 1944-46. Democrat. Member Lions Club. Enjoys swimming, golf and tennis.

Office: Palm Beach County Courthouse, 205 North Dixie Highway, West Palm Beach 33401.

Telephone: (561) 355-2431.

RODGERS, Margaret C. *(Magistrate Judge, United States District Court Northern District of Florida)* Appointed by U.S. District Court judges to term beginning May 9, 2002.

Office: U.S. Courthouse, One North Palafox Street, Pensacola 32501.

Telephone: (850) 435-8448.

RODRIGUEZ, Jose Manuel *(Judge, Florida Circuit Court Eleventh Judicial Circuit)* Former Judge, Dade County Court, appointed by Governor Lawton Chiles Jan 7, 1994.

Office: 209 Gerstein Justice Building, 1351 N.W. Twelfth Street, Miami 33125.

Telephone: (305) 548-5718.

Fax: (305) 548-5610

RODRIGUEZ, Jose R. *(Judge, Florida Circuit Court Ninth Judicial Circuit)* Assumed office Dec 22, 1993. Former Judge, Orange County Court.

Office: Juvenile Justice Center, 2000 East Michigan Street, Orlando 32806.

Telephone: (407) 836-7590.

Fax: (407) 836-7599

RODRIGUEZ, Rosa *(Judge, Florida Circuit Court Eleventh Judicial Circuit)*

Office: 2222 Courthouse Center, 175 N.W. First Avenue, Miami 33128.

Telephone: (305) 349-5681.

ROETTGER, Norman Charles, Jr. *(Senior Judge, United States District Court Southern District of Florida)* Appointed for life by President Richard M. Nixon to term beginning June 2, 1972. Former Chief Judge. Assumed Senior status, serves by assignment. Born Lucasville Ohio Nov 3, 1930. Methodist. Educated at The Ohio State University B.A. 1952 and Washington and Lee University LL.B. magna cum laude 1958. Member Order of the Coif. Admitted to practice Ohio 1958 and Florida 1958. Began legal practice Cincinnati Ohio 1958. In legal practice Fort Lauderdale Florida 1959-69 and 1971-72.

Deputy General Counsel U.S. Department of Housing and Urban Development Feb 1969 to March 1971 (Acting General Counsel July to Nov 1970). Member Broward County, Federal and American Bar Associations. USN 1952-55, presently Captain USNR. Republican. Member African Safari Club of Florida, Reserve Officers Association, Masons and Boone and Crockett Club. Enjoys art and big game hunting.

Office: U.S. Courthouse, 299 East Broward Boulevard, Fort Lauderdale 33301.

Telephone: (954) 769-5550.

RONDOLINO, Anthony *(Judge, Florida Circuit Court Sixth Judicial Circuit)* Appointed by Governor Bob Martinez Jan 2, 1990. Elected to subsequent terms.

Office: 317 Judicial Building, 545 First Avenue North, St. Petersburg 33701.

Telephone: (727) 582-7702.

Fax: (727) 582-7278

ROSENBERG, Robert A. *(Judge, Florida Circuit Court Seventeenth Judicial Circuit)*

Office: 822 Broward County Courthouse, 201 S.E. Sixth Street, Fort Lauderdale 33301.

Telephone: (954) 831-6021.

Fax: (954) 831-5572

ROSINEK, Jeffrey *(Judge, Florida Circuit Court Eleventh Judicial Circuit)* Appointed by Governor Bob Martinez to term beginning Jan 2, 1990. Elected Sept 1990, 1996 and 2002. Current term expires Jan 2009. Born Brooklyn New York Sept 13, 1941. Jewish. Educated at University of Miami A.B. 1963 J.D. 1974. Recipient Outstanding Evening Student Award from University of Miami School of Law. Member Order of the Wig and Robe (Chancellor 1972-74). Admitted to practice Florida 1974, U.S. District Court Southern District of Florida 1974, U.S. Courts of Appeals Fifth 1980 and Eleventh 1981 Circuits and U.S. Supreme Court 1980. In legal practice Miami 1977-86. Judge, Dade County Court March 17, 1986 to Dec 1989, appointed by Governor Robert Graham.

Author "Pro Bono" Florida B. Jour. April 1986. For-

ROSINEK, JEFFREY—*Continued*

mer Instructor Boston University. Member American Judges Association (Secretary 1992-93, Second Vice President 1993-94, First Vice President 1994-95, President 1996-97), The Florida Bar (Judicial Nominating Procedures Committee), South Miami-Kendall (Founder Pro Bono Project, President 1982-83) and American Bar Associations. Chairman Annual Education Conference American Judges Association 1992. Convention Honoree and Recipient Key of Honor from Florida District of Key Club International. Former teacher Coral Gables High School. Chairman Selection Committee for Military Academies Nineteenth Congressional District. Florida Chairman Project Concern International-WFM. Chairman US-Israel Exchange Program. Board of Trustees Haven Center for Mentally Retarded. Member Kiwanis (Steering Committee Florida District, Distinguished President and Lieutenant Governor with honors). Enjoys tennis and karate.

Office: 405 Gerstein Justice Building, 1351 N.W. Twelfth Street, Miami 33125.

Telephone: (305) 548-5103.

ROSMAN, Jay B. *(Judge, Florida Circuit Court Twentieth Judicial Circuit)* Former Judge, Lee County Court.

Office: Lee County Justice Center, 1700 Monroe Street, Fort Myers 33901.

Telephone: (239) 335-2274.

Fax: (239) 335-2589

ROSS, Dale *(Chief Judge, Florida Circuit Court Seventeenth Judicial Circuit)* Former Judge, Broward County Court.

Office: 881 Broward County Courthouse, 201 S.E. Sixth Street, Fort Lauderdale 33301.

Telephone: (954) 831-7837.

Fax: (954) 831-5572

ROTHENBERG, Arthur L. *(Judge, Florida Circuit Court Eleventh Judicial Circuit)* Former Judge, Dade County Court.

Office: 311 Dade County Courthouse, 73 West Flagler Street, Miami 33130.

Telephone: (305) 349-7117.

ROTHENBERG, Leslie B. *(Judge, Florida Circuit Court Eleventh Judicial Circuit)*

Office: 400 Gerstein Justice Building, 1351 N.W. Twelfth Street, Miami 33125.

Telephone: (305) 548-5102.

ROTHSCHILD, Ronald *(Judge, Florida Circuit Court Seventeenth Judicial Circuit)* Born Cleveland Ohio Dec 9, 1945. Jewish. Educated at The Ohio State University B.A. 1969 and Cleveland State University J.D. 1974. Admitted to practice Florida 1974, Ohio 1974, U.S. District Court Southern District of Florida 1975 and U.S. Supreme Court 1981. In legal practice Hollywood 1974-91. Former Judge, Broward County Court, elected to term beginning Jan 1991.

Member The Florida Bar and Broward County Bar Association (Bar Grievance Committee 1982-85, Bar/Bench Committee 1988-91, Public and Client Information Committee 1988-91, Professional Ethics Committee since 1992). Attended Florida Judicial College 1991, Florida Conference of County Court Judges 1991-98 and Florida Conference of Circuit Judges since 1999. Lieutenant U.S. Army 1969-71. Enjoys outdoor activities and avocational volunteering for social service organizations.

Office: Broward County Courthouse, 201 S.E. Sixth Street, Fort Lauderdale 33301.

Telephone: (954) 831-7795.

Fax: (954) 831-5544

ROUNDTREE, Robert E., Jr. *(Judge, Florida Circuit Court Eighth Judicial Circuit)*

Office: Alachua County Courthouse, 201 East University Avenue, Gainesville 32601.

Telephone: (352) 374-3644.

Fax: (352) 337-6126

ROUSE, Robert K., Jr. *(Chief Judge, Florida Circuit Court Seventh Judicial Circuit)* Appointed by Governor Lawton Chiles Sept 21, 1995 to term beginning Oct 23, 1995. Elected Nov 5, 1996 and 2002. Current term expires Jan 5, 2009. Born Lexington Kentucky Jan 15, 1946. Educated at Florida State University B.S. 1968 and University of Florida J.D. 1974. Member Phi Alpha Delta. Admitted to practice Florida 1975, U.S. Supreme Court 1979 and U.S. Court of Appeals Eleventh Circuit 1981. In legal practice Daytona Beach 1975-95.

Member Volusia Civil Trial Attorneys Association, American Board of Trial Advocates, The Florida Bar and Volusia County Bar Association. USAR 1969-75.

Office: Volusia County Courthouse, 101 North Alabama Avenue, DeLand 32724.

Telephone: (386) 626-6590.

Fax: (386) 943-7076

RUSSELL, Dorothy J. *(Judge, Florida Circuit Court Ninth Judicial Circuit)* Appointed by Governor Bob Martinez Nov 7, 1989 to term beginning Jan 4, 1990. Elected 1990, 1996 and 2002. Current term expires Jan 2009. Born Richmond Virginia March 21, 1944. Presbyterian. Educated at Olympic College A.A. 1966, State University of New York at Buffalo B.Ed. 1968, Rollins College M.Ed. 1970 and Stetson University J.D. 1978. Member Phi Delta Phi. Admitted to practice Florida 1979, U.S. District Court Middle District of Florida 1981 and U.S. Court of Appeals Eleventh Circuit 1981. Began legal practice Orlando 1979. Judge, Orange County Court 1983-89.

Important Decisions: State v. Jeffrey Morin (right to jury trial) TO82-99690, 1983; State v. Ronald Lee Young (right to counsel on DUI arrest) TO83-6795, 1983; State v. Thomas Fritsch (search and seizure on traffic arrest) MO84-635; State v. Charles Bernard Caudle (order denying defense motion to vacate sentence and to issue writ of error coram nobis); State v. Blue (right to Counsel prior to taking breathalyzer) 9 Fla. Supp. 2d 3, 1984; State v. Smith (requirement of APA Judicial Review to challenge admission of breathalyzer certifications) F.S. 120.57; State v. Caudle (use of prior DUI convictions to enhance subsequent DUI penalties) TO83-26909; The Wise Co., Inc. v. Dwyler Marine, Inc. (attorney fee entitlement) SO86-5885; State v. Rivers et al (racketeering wire tap) 84,610; and State v. Spaziano CR75-1305 (3.850 Motions) Sept 1996. Instructor Valencia Community College 1973-76. Member Central Florida Criminal Justice Council (President 1985), Florida Conference of Circuit Court Judges, Orange County Association of Women Lawyers, Florida Association of Women Lawyers, National Association of Women Judges, The Florida Bar and Orange County Bar Association. Recipient Distinguished Judicial Service Award from FCCD 1985-86 and 1994-95 and Award for Out-

RUSSELL, DOROTHY J.—*Continued*

standing Contributions for Guardian ad litem from Ninth Judicial Circuit 1991. Teacher Boone High School 1968-76. Previously worked as secretary for U.S. Navy Publication and Printing Service Office. Director Fluery Foundation 1984-86 and Orlando Women's Executive Council since 1982. Board of Directors Metropolitan Alcohol Council of Orlando 1985-89 and Central Florida Safety Council 1987-89. Director Florida Safety Association since 1992. Enjoys tennis, bridge and golf.

Office: 1135 Orange County Courthouse, 425 North Orange Avenue, Orlando 32801.

Telephone: (407) 836-2282.

RUSSELL, Van P. *(Judge, Franklin County Court)*

Office: Franklin County Courthouse, 33 Market Street, Apalachicola 32320.

Telephone: (850) 653-9505.

Fax: (850) 653-2261

RUTH, James A. *(Judge, Duval County Court)*

Office: Duval County Courthouse, 330 East Bay Street, Jacksonville 32202.

Telephone: (904) 630-2568.

Fax: (904) 630-2979

RYDER, Herboth S. *(Senior Judge, Florida District Court of Appeal)* Appointed by Governor Reubin Askew to term beginning Sept 16, 1977. Retained by election 1978, 1984 and 1990. Chief Judge 1984-86. Assumed Senior Judge status, serves by assignment. Born Tallahassee Florida June 8, 1928. Roman Catholic. Educated at University of Miami, Florida State University B.S. 1950 and University of Florida LL.B. 1959. Admitted to practice Florida 1959. Began legal practice Tampa 1959. Judge, Hillsborough County Court of Record Oct 1, 1971 to Jan 1, 1973. Judge, Florida Circuit Court Thirteenth Judicial Circuit Jan 1, 1973 to Sept 15, 1977.

Former Assistant Attorney General Florida. Former Field Attorney NLRB. Assistant State Attorney Thirteenth Judicial Circuit 1962-63. Member Governor's Commission on Criminal Justice Standards and Goals 1974-75 and Florida Supreme Court Committee on Standard Jury Instructions in Civil Cases. Member Department of Offender Rehabilitation 1976-78. President Florida Conference of District Court of Appeal Judges 1990-91. Former member American Judicature Society, The Association of Trial Lawyers of America, Florida Trial Lawyers Association, Bay Area Trial Lawyers Association, American Arbitration Association, Federal and American Bar Associations. Member The Florida Bar and Hillsborough County Bar Association (President 1969 and Board of Directors since 1960). Faculty member Florida Judicial College and Terrell Inn The American Inns of Court Foundation. Recipient Betterment of Administration of Criminal Justice Award from Law Enforcement Agencies of Hillsborough County 1970, Distinguished Service Award for Impartial Administration of Justice from Frontiers of America 1973 and Award from Fraternal Order of Police Associate Lodge 27, 1975. Named Most Outstanding Jurist of 1988 by Hillsborough Bar Association 1988. First Lieutenant USAF 1951-56. Democrat. Chairman Florida Drug Abuse Advisory Council Region V 1973-78. Advisory Council Florida Department of Offender Rehabilitation 1976-78. Member Timuquanian Society (President 1970) and Sertoma Club.

Office: 1005 East Memorial Boulevard, Lakeland 33801.

Telephone: (863) 499-2290.

RYSKAMP, Kenneth L. *(Senior Judge, United States District Court Southern District of Florida)* Appointed for life by President Ronald Reagan to term beginning May 2, 1986. Assumed Senior status Jan 1, 2000. Born Grand Rapids Michigan Aug 10, 1932. Presbyterian. Educated at Calvin College A.B. 1955 and University of Miami LL.B. 1956 replaced by J.D. 1967. Law Clerk to Hon. Mallory Horton, Florida District Court of Appeal Third District 1957-59. Member Delta Theta Phi. Admitted to practice Florida 1956, Michigan 1957, U.S. District Court Southern District of Florida 1957, U.S. Courts of Appeals Fifth 1957 and Eleventh 1981 Circuits and U.S. Supreme Court 1970. In legal practice Miami 1959-86.

Member Federal Judges Association, The Florida Bar, State Bar of Michigan and American Bar Association.

Office: 416 Federal Building, 701 Clematis Street, West Palm Beach 33401.

Telephone: (561) 803-3420.

ST. ARNOLD, Jack A. *(Judge, Florida Circuit Court Sixth Judicial Circuit)*

Office: Criminal Justice Center, 14250 49th Street North, Clearwater 33762.

Telephone: (727) 464-6435.

Fax: (727) 464-8109

SALCINES, E. J. *(Judge, Florida District Court of Appeal Second District)* Appointed by Governor Lawton Chiles to term beginning 1998. Retained by election 2000, current term expires Jan 2007. Born Tampa Florida July 18, 1938. Educated at Florida Southern College B.A. 1959 and South Texas College of Law J.D. 1963. Honorary LL.D. Florida Southern College 2002. Admitted to practice Florida 1963, Texas 1963 and U.S. Supreme Court 1967.

Office: 600 Tampa Branch Headquarters, 801 East Twiggs Street, Tampa 33602-3547.

Telephone: (813) 272-3430.

Fax: (813) 229-6534

SALMON, Michael H. *(Senior Judge, Florida Circuit Court Eleventh Judicial Circuit)* Assumed Senior Judge status, serves by assignment.

Office: 511 Dade County Courthouse, 73 West Flagler Street, Miami 33130.

Telephone: (305) 349-7001.

SALTON, Marc H. *(Judge, Pasco County Court)*

Office: 109 West Pasco Government Center, 7530 Little Road, New Port Richey 34654.

Telephone: (727) 847-8173.

SAMUELS, Michael J. *(Judge, Dade County Court)*

Office: 231 Courthouse Center, 175 N.W. First Avenue, Miami 33128.

Telephone: (305) 349-5700.

SANDERS, Edwin P.B. *(Judge, Florida Circuit Court Seventh Judicial Circuit)* Appointed by Governor Robert Graham to term beginning June 10, 1983. Elected 1984, 1990, 1996 and 2002. Current term expires Jan 2009. Born Madisonville Kentucky July 12, 1940. Episcopalian. Educated at Stetson University B.S.

SANDERS, EDWIN P.B.—*Continued*

1965 J.D. 1968. Member Pi Kappa Alpha and Delta Theta Phi. Admitted to practice Florida 1968. In legal practice De Land 1968-83.

Member The Florida Bar, Volusia County and American Bar Associations. Private First Class U.S. Army 1960-62 and Staff Sergeant Florida National Guard 1962-66. Member De Land Airport Advisory Board 1983. Board of Management Duvall Home for Retarded Children and West Volusia YMCA. Member De Land Rotary Club and Lake Beresford Yacht Club. Enjoys hunting and fishing.

Office: 130 West New York Avenue, Room 207, De-Land 32720.

Telephone: (386) 736-5946.

Fax: (386) 943-7076

SANDERS, Elzie Stanford *(Judge, Florida Circuit Court Eighth Judicial Circuit)* Assumed office 1981. Elected to subsequent terms. Chief Judge July 1, 1991 to June 30, 1995. Born Nashville Georgia Aug 20, 1939. Educated at Jacksonville University B.A. 1961 and University of Florida J.D. 1968. Admitted to practice Florida 1968. In legal practice Starke 1968-72. Judge, Bradford County Court 1973-80.

Bradford County Zoning Board Attorney 1970-72. Hampton City Attorney 1971-72. Bradford County Prosecuting Attorney 1971-72. Instructor in Police Standards Course 1974 and 1976. Member Eighth Judicial Circuit Bar Association and The Florida Bar. Aviation Machinist Mate Two (turbojet engine mechanic) USNR 1961-68. Democrat. President Bradford County Bicentennial Committee 1975-76. Member St. Mark's Episcopal Church (Vestry 1972-75, Senior Warden 1974 and 1975 and representative Diocesan Convention 1972, 1973 and 1974), Board of Trustees Bradford County Historical Society 1970-77, Board of Governors Bradford County Chamber of Commerce 1973-77, Bradford Community Mental Health Advisory Committee (Chairman 1974-75), Bradford County Fair Association 1974-75, Starke Jaycees (President 1970-71 and Board of Directors 1971-72), Starke Rotary Club (Board of Directors 1976-77) and Starke Golf and Country Club. Enjoys gardening.

Office: 303 Alachua County Courthouse, 201 East University Avenue, Gainesville 32601.

Telephone: (352) 374-3606.

Fax: (352) 374-5238

SAULS, N. Sanders *(Judge, Florida Circuit Court Second Judicial Circuit)* Appointed by Governor Bob Martinez Oct 2, 1989. Elected to subsequent terms. Former Chief Judge.

Office: 330-A Leon County Courthouse, Tallahassee 32301.

Telephone: (850) 577-4311.

Fax: (850) 410-3381

SAWAYA, Thomas D. *(Judge, Florida District Court of Appeal Fifth District)* Appointed by Governor Jeb Bush to term beginning Feb 21, 2000. Born Ocala Florida July 10, 1952. Educated at University of South Florida B.A. 1974 and Stetson University College of Law J.D. 1977. Member Kappa Sigma. Admitted to practice Florida 1978, U.S. District Court Middle District of Florida 1978 and U.S. Court of Appeals Fifth Circuit 1978. In legal practice Ocala 1978-86. Judge, Marion County Court 1986-90. Judge 1991 to Feb 20, 2000 and Presiding Judge Appellate Division 1993-97, Florida Circuit Court Fifth Judicial Circuit. Associate Judge, Florida District Court of Appeal Fifth District April 1991.

Assistant State Attorney Fifth Judicial Circuit 1985-86. Author "The Accident Report Privilege After *Brackin*: A Step in the Right Direction" May 1986, "Use of Criminal Convictions in Civil Proceedings: Statutory Collateral Estoppel Under Florida and Federal Law" Nov 1988, "Attorney's Right to Compensation When Prematurely Discharged Without Cause" Feb 1989, "Denying Coverage Under Liability Insurance Policies in Florida: The Claims Administration Statute" Jan 1990 and "The Work Product Privilege in a Nutshell" July/Aug 1993 The Florida B. Jour.; "Coverage Under the CGL: A Gordian Knot of Interpretation" May 1988 and "Coverage Under the New Commercial Policies: Loosening the Gordian Knot of Interpretation" June 1988 *For the Defense*; "Use of Criminal Convictions in Subsequent Civil Proceedings: Statutory Collateral Estoppel Under Florida and Federal Law and the Intentional Act Exclusion Clause" 40 No. 3 University of Florida L. Rev. Summer 1988; "From the Bench: Hypnotic Testimony (Admissibility of Hypnotically Enhanced or Retrieved Testimony in Criminal Proceedings" 15 No. 4 *Litigation* Summer 1989; "Willie Loman Joins the Bar: Death of a Profession" American Bar Association Journal Oct 1990; and *Florida Personal Injury and Wrongful Death Actions* West Group 2001-02 ed. 2001. President D. R. Smith Inn of Court. Member Florida Conference of County Court Judges, The Florida Bar and Marion County Bar Association. Faculty Member Florida Conference of Circuit Court Judges and College of Advanced Judicial Studies. Mentor for New Judges Florida Judicial College Mentor Program 1993-94 and since 1997. Recipient Barbara Sanders Memorial Award from Florida Bar Journal 1989, Erskine Mayo Ross Award from American Bar Association Journal 1990, Distinguished Service Award from Florida Council on Crime and Delinquency 1993 and Distinguished Graduate Award from Department of Elementary Schools National Catholic Educational Association 1997. Former Member Board of Directors West Central Florida Driver Improvement School. Vice Chairman Marion District of the North Florida Council, Inc. Boy Scouts of America since 1987. Enjoys legal research and writing and fishing.

Office: 300 South Beach Street, Daytona Beach 32114.

Telephone: (386) 947-1555.

Fax: (386) 947-1562

SCHACK, Larry *(Judge, Florida Circuit Court Nineteenth Judicial Circuit)* Elected to term beginning Jan 1991. Reelected 1996 and 2002. Current term expires Jan 2009. Born New York 1953. Educated at Case Western Reserve University B.A. cum laude 1976 and Boston University School of Law J.D. 1980. Admitted to practice Florida 1980, U.S. Courts of Appeals Fifth 1981 and Eleventh 1981 Circuits, Trial Bar of U.S. District Court Southern District of Florida 1984, District of Columbia 1985, U.S. Supreme Court 1986 and New York 1992. In legal practice Palm Beach County 1984-88.

Assistant State's Attorney Eleventh Circuit 1980-81 and Fifteenth Circuit 1981-82 and Chief Felony Division Fifteenth Circuit 1982-84 and Supervisor Felony Division Nineteenth Circuit 1988-90 Office of the State Attorney. Important Opinions: SuarezBurgos v. Morhaim So. 2d 368 Fla. Dist. Ct. App. dissenting opinion 1999;

SCHACK, LARRY—*Continued*

Mosley v. State 739 So. 2d 672 Fla. Dist. Ct. App. majority opinion 1999; State v. Luders 731 So. 2d 163 Fla. Dist. Ct. App. concurring opinion 1999; State v. Gosier 737 So. 2d 1121 Fla. Dist. Ct. App. majority opinion 1999; RHS Corp. v. City of Boynton Beach 736 So. 2d 1211 Fla. Dist. Ct. App. majority opinion 1999; and Wilson v. State 734 So. 2d 1107 Fla. Dist. Ct. App. concurring opinion 1999. Member Committee on the Rules of Criminal Procedure The Florida Bar May 1993 to Jan 1994 and Committee on Rules to Implement the Criminal Punishment Code Florida Supreme Court since 1998. Recipient Award for Excellence from Chapter XI Florida Council on Crime and Delinquency 1996, Community Service Award from St. Lucie County School Board for Character Counts 1997 and Leadership Award from United Way of Martin County for Character Counts 2000. Member Advisory Board Character Counts Martin County since 1995 and Indian River County.

Office: 263 Martin County Courthouse, 100 Southeast Ocean Boulevard, Stuart 34994.

Telephone: (772) 288-5575.

SCHAEFER, John A. *(Judge, Florida Circuit Court Sixth Judicial Circuit)*

Office: 417 Criminal Justice Center, 14250 49th Street North, Clearwater 33762.

Telephone: (727) 464-7115.

Fax: (727) 464-6204

SCHAEFFER, Susan F. *(Judge, Florida Circuit Court Sixth Judicial Circuit)* Appointed by Governor Robert Graham to term beginning June 1, 1982. Elected 1982, 1988, 1994 and 2000. Current term expires Jan 2007. Former Chief Judge. Born Kittanning Pennsylvania June 29, 1942. Protestant. Educated at St. Petersburg Junior College A.A. 1962, Florida State University B.S. 1964 and Stetson University J.D. with honors 1971. Recipient The Florida Bar Award as Outstanding Graduate Stetson University. State Moot Court Team 1970. Listed in *Who's Who in American Colleges and Universities.* Admitted to practice Florida 1971, U.S. District Court Middle District of Florida 1973, U.S. Court of Appeals Fifth Circuit 1975 and U.S. Supreme Court 1975. In legal practice St. Petersburg 1973-82.

Public Defender 1975-78. Assistant Professor Stetson University 1971-73. Member Criminal Defense Lawyers of Pinellas County (President 1982), National Association of Criminal Defense Lawyers, Inc., Pinellas County Trial Lawyers Association, Academy of Florida Trial Lawyers (Vice Chairman Criminal Law Section 1979-80 and Board of Directors 1980-82), The Association of Trial Lawyers of America, The Florida Bar (Criminal Rules Committee Criminal Law Section), St. Petersburg and American Bar Associations. Named one of Ten Outstanding Trial Advocates in State of Florida by Stetson Society of Trial Advocacy 1980. Recipient highest rating in poll of judges by Pinellas County Bar Association 1984, 1986 and 1988. IRS Agent Jacksonville 1964-68. Member Pinellas Emergency Mental Services Leadership. Enjoys reading, racquetball, bridge, music and golf.

Office: 417 Judicial Building, 545 First Avenue North, St. Petersburg 33701.

Telephone: (727) 582-7743.

Fax: (727) 582-7806

SCHAPIRO, Sheldon M. *(Judge, Florida Circuit Court Seventeenth Judicial Circuit)*

Office: 5820 Broward County Courthouse, 201 S.E. Sixth Street, Fort Lauderdale 33301.

Telephone: (954) 831-7785.

Fax: (954) 831-5572

SCHEB, John M. *(Senior Judge, Florida District Court of Appeal)* Appointed by Governor Reubin Askew to term beginning Jan 1, 1975. Retained by election 1976, 1982 and 1988. Chief Judge 1980-82. Assumed Senior Judge status Jan 31, 1992, serves by assignment. Born Orlando Florida April 25, 1926. Catholic. Educated at St. Petersburg Junior College 1946-47, University of Florida 1947-48 J.D. 1950, Florida Southern College B.A. 1980 and University of Virginia LL.M. 1984. Awarded honorary LL.D. Stetson University College of Law 1983 and honorary D.H.L. Florida Southern College 1991. Member Lambda Chi Alpha and Phi Alpha Delta. Admitted to practice Florida 1950, U.S. District Court Southern District of Florida 1952, U.S. Courts of Appeals Fifth 1956 and Eleventh 1982 Circuits, U.S. Supreme Court 1966 and U.S. Court of Appeals for the Armed Forces 1980. Began legal practice Sarasota 1950. Associate Judge, Sarasota Municipal Court 1957-59.

City Attorney Sarasota 1959-70. Author "Florida's Courts of Appeal: Intermediate Courts Become Final" Stetson L. Rev. 1984, "Making Intermediate Courts Final" *Judicature* 1984 and "Termination of Life Support Systems for Minor Children: Evolving Legal Responses" Tennessee L. Rev. 1986. Co-author *Criminal Law and Procedure* West Publishing Co. 1989, 1994 and 1999. Important Decisions: Hesson v. Walmsley Construction Company (implied warranty of habitability applies to both house and lot) Fla. Dist. Ct. App. 422 So. 2d 943, 1982 and In re guardianship of Barry (parents right to cause removal of life supports from comatose child) Fla. Dist. Ct. App. 445 So. 2d 365, 1984. Adjunct Professor of Criminal Justice Florida Southern College 1981-91. Adjunct Professor 1992-94 and Distinguished Professorial Lecturer since 1995 Stetson University College of Law. Member Judge John M. Scheb American Inn of Court (President 1991-93), Florida Conference of District Court of Appeal Judges (President 1985-86), American Judicature Society, The Florida Bar, Sarasota County (President 1966-67) and American Bar Associations. Chairman Steering Committee "Florida Bar Manual on Appellate Practice" 1978 and 1986 editions. Recipient Silver Beaver Award from Boy Scouts of America 1973, Honor Awards for Public Addresses from Freedoms Foundation 1977 and 1991, A. Sherman Christensen Award from American Inns of Court 1995 and James C. Adkins Appellate Award 1997. USAAC 1944-46 and Colonel USAFR JAG (retired). Member Sarasota Kiwanis Club (President 1963) and Sunnyland Council Boy Scouts of America (President 1972-73). Enjoys travel, reading, writing and gardening.

Mailing address: 1616 North Drive, Sarasota 34239.

SCHEMER, Jack M. *(Judge, Florida Circuit Court Fourth Judicial Circuit)*

Office: Duval County Courthouse, 330 East Bay Street, Jacksonville 32202.

Telephone: (904) 630-2528.

Fax: (904) 630-2979

SCHIFF, Louis H. *(Judge, Broward County Court)* Office: 142 North Regional Courthouse, 1600 West Hillsborough Boulevard, Deerfield Beach 33442.
Telephone: (954) 831-7839.
Fax: (954) 831-1249

SCHLESINGER, Harvey Erwin *(Judge, United States District Court Middle District of Florida)* Magistrate Judge Aug 29, 1975 to July 1, 1991. Appointed Judge for life by President George Bush to term beginning July 2, 1991. Born New York New York June 4, 1940. Jewish. Educated at The Citadel B.A. with departmental honors 1962 and University of Richmond J.D. 1965. Recipient Gold Stars, Williams Scholarship Award, American Jurisprudence Awards and Phi Alpha Delta Scholarship Award. Member Omicron Delta Kappa, Pi Sigma Alpha, Phi Alpha Delta and McNeill Law Society. Admitted to practice Florida 1965 and Virginia 1965. In legal practice Jacksonville Florida 1968-70.

Chief Assistant U.S. Attorney Middle District of Florida 1970-75. Editor Conference Newsletter National Conference of Special Court Judges Judicial Administration Division American Bar Association 1987-89. Instructor John Marshall Law School 1967-68. Adjunct Professor University of North Florida 1983-91. Chairman U.S. District Court Forms Task Force since 1983. Member Supreme Court Advisory Committee on Federal Rules of Criminal Procedure 1986-93. Member since 1996 and Chairman since 1998 Judicial Conference Committee on Administration of Federal Magistrate Judges System. Master of the Bench Chester Bedell Inn of Court (President 1992-96). Former Member National Council of U.S. Magistrate Judges (President 1987-88). Member Eleventh Circuit District Judges Association (Secretary/Treasurer 1998-2000, Vice President 2000-01, President 2001-02), The Florida Bar, Jacksonville (Chairman Naturalization Committee 1970-75), Virginia, Federal (Chapter President 1974-75, Vice President 1978-79 and President 1981-82) and American (Rules of Criminal Procedure and Evidence Committee Section of Criminal Justice since 1979, National Conference of Special Court Judges 1975-90, National Conference of Federal Trial Judges since 1990 Judicial Administration Division, Co-chair Federal Membership Committee) Bar Associations. Instructor Federal Judicial Center. Recipient Silver Beaver Award from Boy Scouts of America, Special Commendation from U.S. Attorney General 1974, Franklin Flashner Judicial Award as Outstanding Limited Jurisdiction Trial Judge in U.S. from American Bar Association 1989, Silver Medallion Humanitarian Award from National Conference of Christians and Jews 1992, Founders Award from Federal Magistrate Judges Association 1999 and William Green Award for Professional Excellence 2000. Named Paul Harris Fellow by Rotary International 1992 and Jurist of the Year by American Board of Trial Advocates 2001. Captain U.S. Army JAGC 1965-68. Trustee Jacksonville Community Foundation. Member Shriners, Rotary International, North Florida Council Boy Scouts of America, Inc. (Executive Committee, Chairman Exploring Division 1989-91) and National Conference of Christians and Jews (Chairman Regional Board Jacksonville 1984-89, Member National Board 1986-95). 33° Mason.

Mailing address: P.O. Box 1740, Jacksonville 32201-1740.
Office: 311 West Monroe Street, Jacksonville 32202.
Telephone: (904) 549-1990.

SCHOONOVER, Jack R. *(Senior Judge, Florida District Court of Appeal)* Appointed by Governor Robert Graham to term beginning Oct 16, 1981. Retained by election 1982, 1988 and 1994. Former Chief Judge. Assumed Senior Judge status, serves by assignment. Born Winona Minnesota July 23, 1934. Methodist. Educated at Winona State College and University of Florida J.D. 1962. Associate Editor University of Florida Law Review 1962. Member Phi Alpha Delta. Admitted to practice Florida 1962. In legal practice Punta Gorda 1962-69 and Port Charlotte 1969-75. Judge, Punta Gorda City Court 1973-74. Judge, Florida Circuit Court Twentieth Judicial Circuit 1975-81.

Assistant State Attorney 1969-72. Former member Charlotte County Bar Association (President 1966-68). Member The Florida Bar. Staff Sergeant USAF 1952-56.
Office: 1005 East Memorial Boulevard, Lakeland 33801.
Telephone: (863) 499-2290.

SCHUMACHER, Marc *(Judge, Florida Circuit Court Eleventh Judicial Circuit)* Former Judge, Dade County Court, elected to term beginning Jan 1991.
Office: 2128 Courthouse Center, 175 N.W. First Avenue, Miami 33128.
Telephone: (305) 349-5732.

SCHWARTZ, Alan R. *(Chief Judge, Florida District Court of Appeal Third District)* Appointed by Governor Reubin O'Donovan Askew Nov 1978. Elected 1980, 1986, 1992 and 1998. Chief Judge since Jan 1983. Born Pittsburgh Pennsylvania July 14, 1934. Educated at Harvard College A.B. magna cum laude 1955 LL.B. cum laude 1958. Member Phi Beta Kappa. Judge, Florida Circuit Court Eleventh Judicial Circuit 1973-78, appointed by Governor Reubin O'Donovan Askew.

Board of Directors 1965-68 and 1969-72 Dade County Bar Association. President Florida Conference of District Court of Appeal Judges 1982. Member Florida Commission on Matrimonial Law 1982-85. Member The American Law Institute, Judges Consultative Group on Principles of the Law of Family Dissolution and The Florida Bar. President Harvard Law School Association of Florida 1981-82. Member Visiting Committee University of Miami School of Law 1982-93.
Office: 2001 S.W. 117th Avenue, Miami 33175-1716.
Telephone: (305) 229-3200.
Fax: (305) 229-3206

SCHWARTZ, Caryn Canner *(Judge, Dade County Court)* Elected Nov 1992 to term beginning Jan 5, 1993. Reelected Nov 1996 and 2000. Current term expires Jan 2007. Born Miami Beach Florida May 21, 1950. Educated at University of Maryland B.A. 1972, McGeorge School of Law University of the Pacific J.D. with distinction 1984 and New York University School of Law LL.M. in Taxation 1985. Member Traynor Honor Society. Admitted to practice Florida 1985, California 1985, U.S. District Court Eastern District of California 1985, U.S. Tax Court 1989, Colorado 1996 and U.S. Supreme Court 1996. In legal practice Sacramento California 1985-87 and Miami Florida 1987-93.

Contributing Author "How to Protect Our Children in School." Adjunct Professor St. Thomas University Summer 1996. Field Instructor University of Florida School of Law Summer and Fall 2002. Former Faculty Advisor Faculty Advisory Committee Graduate Program in Estate Planning University of Miami School of Law. Member Florida Conference of County Court Judges (Civil Rules,

SCHWARTZ, CARYN CANNER—*Continued*

Small Claims and Conference Committees), Florida Association for Women Lawyers, American Judges Association, The Florida Bar, State Bar of California, Miami Beach, North Dade, Colorado and Cuban American Bar Associations. Attended General Jurisdiction course The National Judicial College Oct 1994; Evidence, DUI, Criminal Procedure courses Advanced Judicial College May 1995; and Advanced Evidence course American Academy of Judicial Education April 1996. Former Lecturer "Estate and Income Tax Planning Benefits from Qualified Retirement Plans and IRAs" The Florida Bar. Participant Judicial Internship Program University of Miami, Advance Academic Internship Program Miami-Dade Public School System and Justice Teaching Institute Eleventh Judicial Circuit. Recipient Outstanding Judge Award from Mothers Against Drunk Driving 2000. Board of Directors and Member Nominating and Program/Operations Committees Community Partnership for Homeless, Inc. Member Criminal Justice Committee Miami-Dade Homeless Trust. Board of Governors and High School Volunteer Program Organizer Samuel Scheck Hillel Community Day School. Volunteer Hands in Action. Horizon's Mentor PACE Center for Girls, Inc. Dade County Bar Association. Member American Association of University Women and Greater Miami Jewish Federation (Women's Division, Lawyers' Division and Former Member Professional Advisory Committee Foundation of Jewish Philanthropies). Enjoys spending time with family and friends, snorkeling, snow skiing, bicycling, traveling, attending sporting events, music concerts and art festivals and collecting sports memorabilia and antiques.

Office: 1104 Dade County Courthouse, 73 West Flagler Street, Miami 33130.

Telephone: (305) 349-7127.

SCHWARTZ, Jacqueline *(Judge, Dade County Court)*

Office: Dade County Courthouse, 73 West Flagler Street, Miami 33130.

Telephone: (305) 354-5877.

SCHWARTZ, Lawrence A. *(Judge, Florida Circuit Court Eleventh Judicial Circuit)* Assumed office 1997. Elected 2000, current term expires 2007. Born Miami Beach Florida Aug 23, 1944. Educated at University of Oklahoma B.A. 1967, Florida Atlantic University M.E.D. 1970 and McGeorge School of Law University of the Pacific J.D. 1978. Admitted to practice Florida 1978, California 1978 and Colorado 1995. Judge, Dade County Court 1991-1997.

Deputy District Attorney District Attorney's Office Sacramento California 1979-87. Assistant State Attorney State Attorney's Office Miami Florida 1987-91. Instructor Paralegal Program Miami Dade Community College since 1991. Member The Florida Bar, State Bar of California, Miami Beach, Dade County and Colorado Bar Associations.

Office: 215 Gerstein Justice Building, 1351 N.W. Twelfth Street, Miami 33125.

Telephone: (305) 548-5727.

Fax: (305) 548-7320

SCHWARTZ, Robert Steven *(Judge, Palm Beach County Court)* Elected Sept 4, 1986 to term beginning Jan 6, 1987. Reelected Sept 4, 1990, 1994 and 1998. Current term expires Jan 2005. Born Baltimore Maryland June 7, 1950. Episcopal. Educated at University of Maryland B.S. 1974 and University of Baltimore J.D. cum laude 1980. Member Heuisler Honor Society. Admitted to practice Florida 1981.

Assistant State Attorney Fifteenth Judicial Circuit 1980-86. Author "A Practical View of Chapter 85-53" Florida B. Jour. Oct 1985, "The Use of Williams Rule Evidence in Sexual Crimes Against Children or Who's Afraid of the Williams Rule" Criminal Law Section Newsletter The Florida Bar May 1986, "New Trial Lawyers Need to Court More than Judges" Florida Bar News March 15, 1990 and *Landlord-Tenant Rights & Obligations for Non-Lawyers* 1991. Important Decision: State v. Carbone (upheld order defining serious bodily injury) 564 So. 2d 1253, 4th DCA, 1990. Member The Florida Bar and Palm Beach County Bar Association. Probation Officer 1975-80 and Teacher 1974-75 Baltimore. Member Charter Review Committee Town of Jupiter 1986. Enjoys sailing, fishing and boating.

Office: Palm Beach County Courthouse, 205 North Dixie Highway, West Palm Beach 33401.

Telephone: (561) 355-2598.

SCHWARTZ, Sheldon Ronald *(Judge, Dade County Court)* Elected Sept 1996 to term beginning Jan 22, 1997. Reelected 2000, current term expires Jan 2007. Born Bronx New York Feb 10, 1944. Jewish. Educated at Monmouth College B.S. 1965 and Suffolk University Law School J.D. 1968. Member Phi Alpha Delta. Admitted to practice Florida 1969, District of Columbia and New York. In legal practice Florida 1969-96 and Washington D.C. 1978-79.

Public Defender 1974-77 and Prosecutor 1977-78 City of North Miami Beach. Judge/Mediator Citizens Dispute Center 1978-81. Member The District of Columbia Bar, The Florida Bar and New York State Bar Association. Attended Florida Conference of County Court Judges Jan 1997, March 1997, Winter 1997, Summer 1997 and Winter 1998. Enjoys boating.

Office: 208 North Dade Justice Center, 15555 Biscayne Boulevard, Miami 33160.

Telephone: (305) 354-8772.

SCOLA, Jacqueline H. *(Judge, Florida Circuit Court Eleventh Judicial Circuit)*

Office: 603 Gerstein Justice Building, 1351 N.W. Twelfth Street, Miami 33125.

Telephone: (305) 548-5733.

SCOLA, Robert N., Jr. *(Judge, Florida Circuit Court Eleventh Judicial Circuit)* Appointed by Governor Lawton Chiles to term beginning Sept 1995. Elected 1996 and 2002. Current term expires Jan 2009. Served Criminal Division Oct 1995 to Jan 2001. Serves Family Division since Jan 2001. Educated at Brown University B.A. 1977 and Boston College M.A. J.D. cum laude 1980. Admitted to practice Florida 1980, Massachusetts 1981, Trial Bars of U.S. District Courts Northern 1981, Southern 1982 and Middle 1987 Districts of Florida and Eastern District of Michigan 1989 and U.S. Courts of Appeals Eleventh 1987 and Second 1990 Circuits. In legal practice Miami 1986-95.

Deputy Chief Assistant State Attorney and Major Crimes Prosecutor Dade County State Attorney's Office 1980-86. Co-author with H. Scott Fingerhut "To Seal or Not to Seal: When a Statute and Court Rule Conflict, Which Prevails?" LXIX No. 4 Florida B. Jour. April 1995 and "Tough Times in the Sunshine State: Florida Gets Tough on Crime but Defendants Aren't the Only

SCOLA, ROBERT N., JR.—*Continued*

Ones in Trouble" LXXIII No. 10 Florida B. Jour. Nov 1999. Adjunct Professor of Law University of Miami since 1994. Member Circuit Court Conflict Screening Committee 1992-95 and U.S. Attorney/Defense Attorney Liaison Committee 1994-95. Former Member Miami Chapter Florida Association of Criminal Defense Lawyers (Board of Directors 1990-95, President 1994-95). Member Florida Association for Women Lawyers, The Florida Bar (Member 1993-95 and Chairperson 1994 Grievance Committee 11E 1993-95, Member Criminal Rules of Procedure Committee since 1999) and Cuban American Bar Association. Instructor "Advanced Evidentiary Problems" Florida College for Advanced Judicial Studies 1998 and Florida Association of Criminal Defense Lawyers June 2000; "Avoiding Mistrials" Florida College for Advanced Judicial Studies 1998-99; "Post-Conviction Relief in Non-Capital Cases" Continuing Legal Education Seminar for Law Clerks of the District Courts of Appeal 1998, Conference of Circuit Court Judges 1998, Florida College for Advanced Judicial Studies 1999 and 2000 and Miami-Dade County State Attorney's Office 1999; "Tough Times in the Sunshine State: Florida's Enhanced Sentencing Provisions" Miami Chapter Florida Association of Criminal Defense Lawyers Sept 1999 and Criminal Law Section The Florida Bar Jan 2000; "Juror Misconduct" Florida Conference of County Court Judges Jan 2000 and Florida College for Advanced Judicial Studies May 2000; and "Jury Selection: *Melbourne* Issues" Florida College for Advanced Judicial Studies May 2000.

Office: 2025 Courthouse Center, 175 N.W. First Avenue, Miami 33128.

Telephone: (305) 349-5744.

Fax: (305) 349-6172

SCOTT, Robert C. *(Senior Judge, Florida Circuit Court Seventeenth Judicial Circuit)* Assumed Senior Judge status, serves by assignment.

Office: Broward County Courthouse, 201 S.E. Sixth Street, Fort Lauderdale 33301.

Telephone: (954) 831-7740.

SCRIVEN, Mary S. *(Magistrate Judge, United States District Court Middle District of Florida)* Appointed by U.S. District Court judges.

Office: 1034 U.S. Courthouse, 801 North Florida Avenue, Tampa 33602-3800.

Telephone: (813) 301-5540.

SEALS, James H. *(Judge, Florida Circuit Court Twentieth Judicial Circuit)* Former Judge, Lee County Court.

Office: Lee County Justice Center, 1700 Monroe Street, Fort Myers 33901.

Telephone: (239) 335-2441.

Fax: (239) 335-2586

SEAVER, William H. *(Senior Judge, Pasco County Court)* Elected 1964 to term beginning Jan 1965. Reelected 1968, 1972, 1976, 1980, 1984 and 1988. Assumed Senior Judge status July 1, 1992, serves by assignment. State Certified County Court Mediator, Family Court Mediator and Circuit Court Mediator. State Certified Arbitrator. General Master Sixth Judicial Circuit. Born Orlando Florida March 4, 1923. Presbyterian. Educated at University of Florida B.S.B.A. 1949 J.D. 1950. Member Delta Theta Phi. Admitted to practice Florida 1950. In legal practice Dade City 1951-72.

Acting Solicitor County Court of Record 1951-52. Prosecuting Attorney Pasco County 1963-64. Member The Florida Bar, Clearwater and Pasco County (Secretary 1954, Secretary-Treasurer 1955-56, Vice President 1958, President 1959) Bar Associations. Attended Conference of Juvenile Court Judges 1964-72, County Judges Clerks Conference 1964-72, Conference of County Judges 1964-98, Southeastern Conference of Juvenile Court Judges and Special Court Judges course, Juvenile Court Judges course and General Jurisdiction course The National Judicial College. USAF 1943-1946. Previously worked as Adjuster for Commercial Credit Corporation and Scientific Aide with U.S. Department of Agriculture. Democrat. Director Civil Defense 1951-53. Enjoys dancing, scuba diving, hunting, fishing, airboating, hypnotism and duplicate bridge.

Office: Judicial Building, 545 First Avenue North, St. Petersburg 33701.

Telephone: (727) 464-4470.

SEIDLIN, Larry S. *(Judge, Florida Circuit Court Seventeenth Judicial Circuit)* Appointed by Governor Bob Martinez to term beginning March 10, 1989. Elected to subsequent terms. Born New York New York May 24, 1950. Educated at Lehman College B.A. 1972 and University of Miami J.D. 1976. Admitted to practice Florida 1976. Began legal practice Fort Lauderdale 1976. Judge, Broward County Court Jan 1, 1979 to March 1989.

Assistant State Attorney Broward County 1976-78. Legal advisor to Sheriff Stack, Broward County Feb 1978 to Dec 1978. Author study guides "Policy Issues in Crime Control & Constitutional Law," "Marriage, The Family, and The Aged" and "Administration of Juvenile Justice" Nova University 1978-79. Instructor in Crime and Justice in North America; Policy Issues in Crime Control; Constitutional Law; Management Theory and Personnel Administration in Criminal Justice; and Advanced Administrative Functions, Managerial Effectiveness and Politics of Criminal Justice Nova University 1977-79. Member Broward County Bar Association. Enjoys jogging, tennis, racquetball and swimming.

Office: 822 Broward County Courthouse, 201 S.E. Sixth Street, Fort Lauderdale 33301.

Telephone: (954) 831-7815.

Fax: (954) 831-5572

SEIDMAN, Lee Jay *(Judge, Broward County Court)*

Office: South Regional Courthouse, 3550 Hollywood Boulevard, Hollywood 33021.

Telephone: (954) 831-7691.

Fax: (954) 831-0397

SEITZ, Patricia A. *(Judge, United States District Court Southern District of Florida)* Appointed for life by President Bill Clinton to term beginning Nov 16, 1998. Born Washington D.C. Sept 2, 1946. Educated at Kansas State University B.A. 1968 and Georgetown University Law Center J.D. 1973. Law Clerk to Hon. Charles R. Richey, U.S. District Court District of Columbia 1973-74. In legal practice 1974-96.

Director Office of Legal Counsel Executive Office of

SEITZ, PATRICIA A.—*Continued*

the President Office of National Drug Control Policy 1996-97. President The Florida Bar 1993-94.

Office: Federal Courthouse Square, Fifth Floor, 301 North Miami Avenue, Miami 33128.

Telephone: (305) 523-5530.

SELPH, Steven *(Judge, Polk County Court)*

Mailing address: P.O. Box 9000, Drawer J113, Bartow 33831-9000.

Telephone: (863) 534-4628.

SELTZER, Barry S. *(Magistrate Judge, United States District Court Southern District of Florida)* Appointed by U.S. District Court judges Nov 5, 1990 to term beginning March 18, 1991. Reappointed 1999, current term expires March 18, 2007. Born New York New York Nov 30, 1954. Jewish. Educated at Hamilton College B.A. magna cum laude 1976 and New York University M.B.A. 1980 J.D. 1980 LL.M. in Taxation 1984. Staff member 1977-78 and Note and Comment Editor 1978-79 New York University Review of Law and Social Change. Admitted to practice Florida 1980, U.S. District Court Middle District of Florida 1981, U.S. Courts of Appeals Fifth 1981 and Eleventh 1981 Circuits and U.S. Supreme Court 1988. In legal practice Tampa 1980-82. Judge, Broward County Court Feb 12, 1988 to March 17, 1991, appointed by Governor Bob Martinez.

Assistant U.S. Attorney Southern District of Florida 1984-88. Member Florida Conference of County Court Judges, American Judges Association, The Florida Bar, Broward County, Federal and American Bar Associations. Attended Florida Judicial College March 1988 and The National Judicial College 1989. Recipient Special Achievement Award from U.S. Justice Department 1986. President Justice Unit B'nai B'rith. Enjoys sports, triathlon (swimming, biking and running) and weightlifting.

Office: U.S. Courthouse, 299 East Broward Boulevard, Fort Lauderdale 33301.

Telephone: (954) 769-5450.

SEMENTO, Lawrence J. *(Judge, Florida Circuit Court Fifth Judicial Circuit)*

Mailing address: P.O. Box 7800, Tavares 32778-7800.

Office: Lake County Judicial Center, Tavares 32778.

Telephone: (352) 742-4212.

Fax: (352) 742-4229

SERAPHIN, Fred *(Judge, Dade County Court)*

Office: Dade County Courthouse, 73 West Flagler Street, Miami 33130.

Telephone: (305) 636-2262.

SESTAK, William G. *(Judge, Pasco County Court)*

Office: 111 West Pasco Government Center, 7530 Little Road, New Port Richey 34654.

Telephone: (727) 847-8184.

Fax: (727) 847-8046

SEXTON, Susan *(Judge, Florida Circuit Court Thirteenth Judicial Circuit)*

Office: 273A Hillsborough County Courthouse, 419 Pierce Street, Tampa 33602-4022.

Telephone: (813) 272-5211.

Fax: (813) 276-8015

SHACKELFORD, Jan *(Judge, Florida Circuit Court First Judicial Circuit)* Appointed by Governor Jeb Bush to term beginning 2000. Elected 2002, current term expires Jan 2009. Born Scott AFB Illinois July 1, 1964. Educated at Huntingdon College B.A. with honors 1985, Florida State University J.D. 1988 and University of West Florida M.A. 1994. Admitted to practice Florida 1988, U.S. District Court Northern District of Florida 1992, U.S. Court of Appeal Eleventh Circuit 1993 and U.S. Supreme Court 1994. In legal practice Jacksonville 1988-89 and Pensacola 1991-2000.

Assistant State Attorney 1989-91.

Office: M.C. Blanchard Judicial Building, 190 Governmental Center, Pensacola 32501.

Telephone: (850) 595-4453.

Fax: (850) 595-4455

SHAFER, Robert T., Jr. *(Senior Judge, Florida Circuit Court Twentieth Judicial Circuit)* Former Chief Judge. Assumed Senior Judge status, serves by assignment. Born Cincinnati Ohio Sept 11, 1929. Presbyterian. Educated at College of Wooster B.A. 1951 and University of Cincinnati College of Law J.D. 1956. Member Phi Delta Phi. Admitted to practice Florida 1956. In legal practice Fort Myers 1957-77.

Author Editorial Note and Case Note on Corporation Law University of Cincinnati Law Review 1955 and 1956. Executive Committee Florida Conference of Circuit Judges 1986-88. Member American Judicature Society, The Florida Bar (Board of Governors Junior Bar Section 1963-65), Lee County (President 1968) and American Bar Associations. Lieutenant USMC 1951-53. Recipient Bronze Star. Assistant Trust Officer First National Bank Fort Myers 1956-57. Republican. Member American Red Cross Lee County Chapter (Chairman 1962-63). Enjoys reading, jogging, bicycling, triathlons and traveling.

Office: Charlotte County Justice Center, 350 East Marion Avenue, Punta Gorda 33950.

Telephone: (239) 335-2299.

SHAHOOD, George A. *(Judge, Florida District Court of Appeal Fourth District)* Born Jacksonville Florida Feb 19, 1938. Episcopalian. Member St. John's Church (Vestryman). Educated at Emory University B.A. 1959 and Mercer University LL.B. 1968. Admitted to practice Florida 1968, U.S. District Court Southern District of Florida 1971 and U.S. Court of Appeals Fifth Circuit 1971. Began legal practice Dania 1968. Associate Municipal Judge 1969-75. Municipal Judge 1975-77. Judge, Broward County Court 1978-83. Former Judge, Florida Circuit Court Seventeenth Judicial Circuit.

Member Florida Conference of County Court Judges, The Florida Bar, South Broward, Broward County and American Bar Associations. E-4 U.S. Army 1960-62. Member Rotary Club of Dania, American Legion Post 304, Eureka Masonic Lodge 269 and Dania Chamber of Commerce. Enjoys traveling.

Mailing address: P.O. Box 3315, West Palm Beach 33402-3315.

Office: 1525 Palm Beach Lakes Boulevard, West Palm Beach 33401.

Telephone: (561) 242-7210.

Fax: (561) 242-2100

SHAMES, Mark I. *(Judge, Florida Circuit Court Sixth Judicial Circuit)*

Office: 545 First Avenue North, Room 200, St. Petersburg 33701.

Telephone: (727) 582-7734.

Fax: (727) 582-7409

SHAPIRO, Bernard S. *(Judge, Florida Circuit Court Eleventh Judicial Circuit)* Assumed office Jan 1991. Elected to subsequent terms. Born Detroit Michigan March 24, 1949. Educated at Eastern Michigan University B.A. 1970 and University of Miami J.D. 1973. Admitted to practice Florida 1973 and Michigan 1973. In legal practice Miami Florida Oct 1973 to Jan 1987. Judge, Dade County Court Jan 1987 to Jan 1991.

Member The Florida Bar, State Bar of Michigan and Dade County Bar Association. Enjoys coin collecting, boating and traveling.

Office: 175 N.W. First Avenue, Suite 2128, Miami 33128.

Telephone: (305) 349-5732.

SHAPIRO, Martin *(Judge, Dade County Court)*

Office: 15555 Biscayne Boulevard, Room 207, Miami 33125.

Telephone: (305) 354-8771.

SHAPIRO, Sidney B. *(Judge, Florida Circuit Court Eleventh Judicial Circuit)* Elected 1982 to term beginning Jan 4, 1983. Reelected 1988, 1994 and 2000. Current term expires Jan 2007. Born New York New York Nov 20, 1943. Educated at U.S. Merchant Marine Academy 1965 and University of Florida School of Law J.D. 1970. Research Assistant to Hon. Charles A. Carroll, Florida District Court of Appeal Third District 1970-71. Member Phi Alpha Delta. Admitted to practice Florida 1971, U.S. Courts of Appeals Fifth 1971 and Eleventh 1981 Circuits and U.S. Supreme Court 1974. Began legal practice Miami 1971.

Assistant Attorney City of Miami 1971-72. Attorney City of North Miami Beach 1978-82. Adjunct Professor of Paralegal Studies University of Miami 1979-87. Member The Florida Bar. Lieutenant j.g. USNR 1965-70. Marine Engineer 1965-67.

Office: 309 Dade County Courthouse, 73 West Flagler Street, Miami 33130.

Telephone: (305) 349-7135.

SHARP, George Kendall *(Senior Judge, United States District Court Middle District of Florida)* Appointed for life by President Ronald Reagan. Assumed Senior status Jan 1, 2000, serves by assignment. Born Chicago Illinois Dec 30, 1934. Protestant. Educated at Yale University B.A. 1957 and University of Virginia J.D. 1963. Admitted to practice Florida 1963. Began legal practice Vero Beach. Judge, Florida Circuit Court Nineteenth Judicial Circuit 1979-84. Captain USN 1957 (currently USNR).

Office: 635 U.S. Courthouse, 80 North Hughey Avenue, Orlando 32801.

Telephone: (407) 835-4260.

SHARP, Winifred J. *(Judge, Florida District Court of Appeal Fifth District)* Appointed by Governor Robert Graham Oct 1979. Retained by election 1980, 1986, 1992 and 1998. Current term expires Jan 2005. Former Chief Judge. Born New Castle Pennsylvania June 26, 1936. Religious affiliation: Disciples of Christ. Educated at Vassar B.A. 1958, University of Virginia 1958-59 and Stanford University LL.B. 1961. Associate Notes Editor and Staff Stanford Law Review 1960-61. Member Phi Beta Kappa and Order of the Coif. Admitted to practice California 1962 and Florida 1964. Began legal practice Washington D.C. 1961. In legal practice Orlando 1963-79.

Author "CLE-Real Property III, Landlord and Tenant Chapter" The Florida Bar 1976 and "Instruments of the Third Kind" The Florida B. Jour. June 1978. Member National Association of Women Judges, Florida Association of Women Judges, State Bar of California, The Florida Bar, Volusia County, Orange County and American Bar Associations. Worked on outline and lecture materials for courses on U.C.C. Article 9, 1977 and 1979. Member Central Christian Church of Orlando. Enjoys tennis, swimming, horses and art.

Office: 300 South Beach Street, Daytona Beach 32114.

Telephone: (386) 947-1518.

Fax: (386) 947-1563

SHAW, Leander J., Jr. *(Senior Justice, Florida Supreme Court)* Appointed by Governor Robert Graham Jan 1983. Retained by election 1984, 1990 and 1996. Chief Justice 1990-92. Assumed Senior Justice status, serves by assignment. Born Salem Virginia Sept 6, 1930. Educated at West Virginia State College B.A. 1952 and Howard University J.D. 1957. Awarded honorary LL.D. West Virginia State College 1986, Nova University 1991 and Washington and Lee University 1991 and honorary Ph.D. Florida International University 1990. Admitted to practice Florida 1960, U.S. District Court Southern District of Florida 1960, U.S. Court of Appeals Eleventh Circuit 1961 and U.S. Supreme Court 1982. In legal practice Jacksonville 1960-69 and 1972-74. Judge, Florida Industrial Relations Commission 1974-79, appointed by Governor Reubin Askew. Judge, Florida District Court of Appeal First District 1979-83, appointed by Governor Robert Graham.

Assistant Public Defender Duval County 1965-69. Assistant State Attorney Florida 1969-72. Assistant Professor of Law Florida A. & M. University 1957-60. Ex-Officio Advisor to Traffic Court Review Committee 1984-93. Designated Director The Florida Bar Foundation 1985-92. Advisor Racial and Ethnic Bias Study Commission 1989-91, Supreme Court Committee on Fairness since 1997, Florida Standard Jury Instructions—Criminal since 1998, Florida Rules of Criminal Procedure since 1998 and Florida Rules of Judicial Administration since 1999. Chairman Governor's Criminal Justice Task Force 1991. Board of Directors National Center for State Courts 1992-94 and American Judicature Society 1992-96. Member Judicial Fellows Program of The Supreme Court of the United States 1992-95. Member The Florida Bar (Judicial Nominating Procedures Committee 1983-86, Commission on Children 1990-91, Board of Directors 1990-92), Tallahassee, National and American (Chairman Board of Elections 1985) Bar Associations. Presenter Conference of Attorney Generals of the African Nations Abuja Nigeria Sept 1991. Recipient Florida Humanist of the Year Award 1991, Ben Franklin Award from Suncoast Tiger Bay Club 1992 and Gertrude E. Rush Award from National Bar Association 1995. Artillery Officer Korean War 1952-54. Board of Visitors Florida State University College of Law since 1994. Past Chairman Jacksonville Opportunities Industrialization Center Board. Former Member Police Advisory Committee and Human Relations Council. Member Florida Association of Voluntary Agencies for Caribbean Action.

Office: Supreme Court Building, 500 South Duval Street, Tallahassee 32399-1925.

SHELFER, James O. *(Judge, Leon County Court)*
Office: Leon County Courthouse, 301 South Monroe Street, Tallahassee 32301.
Telephone: (850) 577-4309.
Fax: (850) 922-0070

SHEPARD, Clifford B., Jr. *(Senior Judge, Florida Circuit Court Fourth Judicial Circuit)* Assumed office Jan 1, 1973. Elected to subsequent terms. Former Chief Judge. Assumed Senior Judge status, serves by assignment. Born Jacksonville Florida Aug 30, 1919. Protestant. Educated at University of Florida B.S.B.A. 1942 LL.B. 1948 replaced by J.D. 1967. Member Alpha Kappa Psi and Phi Alpha Delta (Justice 1947-48). Admitted to practice Florida 1948. Began legal practice Jacksonville 1948. Judge, Duval County Small Claims Court 1965-70. Judge, Duval County Juvenile Court 1970-73.

Former Director of Board Legal Aid Association of Duval County. Vice President 1967-68 and Secretary-Treasurer 1968-69 Small Claims Judges Association of Florida. Member Juvenile Court Rules Committee Florida Council of Juvenile Judges 1970-73, Federal-State Judicial Coordinating Council since 1981, Judicial Advisory Board State of Florida since 1981, Florida Conference of Circuit Court Judges (Chairman Elect 1983-84, Chairman 1984-85), The Florida Bar, Jacksonville and American Bar Associations. Graduate National College of Juvenile Justice 1971 and National College of State Trial Judges 1973. Captain U.S. Army Artillery 1942-46. Enjoys hunting, fishing and sports.
Office: Duval County Courthouse, 330 East Bay Street, Jacksonville 32202.
Telephone: (904) 630-1693.

SHERRILL, William C., Jr. *(Magistrate Judge, United States District Court Northern District of Florida)* Appointed by U.S. District Court judges.
Office: U.S. Courthouse, 111 North Adams Street, Tallahassee 32301-7717.
Telephone: (850) 521-3621.

SHEVIN, Robert L. *(Judge, Florida District Court of Appeal Third District)* Appointed by Governor Lawton Chiles to term beginning June 24, 1996. Retained by election 1998, current term expires Jan 3, 2005.. Born Miami Florida Jan 19, 1934. Educated at University of Florida B.A. 1955 and University of Miami J.D. magna cum laude 1957. Case Note Editor University of Miami Law Review. Recipient American Jurisprudence Awards in Constitutional Law, Civil Procedure, Criminal Law, Real Property Law and Bills and Notes. Member Phi Delta Phi, Pi Lambda Phi, Phi Kappa Phi, Omicron Delta Kappa and Florida Blue Key. Admitted to practice Florida 1957 and U.S. Court of Appeals District of Columbia Circuit 1990. In legal practice Miami Jan 1979 to June 21, 1996.

Attorney General Florida 1971-79. City Attorney Miami Beach 1979-80. Chairman Interim Committee on Crime and Law Enforcement 1965. Chairman Select Committee to Investigate Organized Crime and Law Enforcement 1967 and Member Interim Study Committee on Urban Affairs 1968 Florida Legislature. Member Florida Tax Reform Commission 1968, Florida Constitutional Revision Commission 1978 and Federal Judicial Nominating Commission of Florida 1995. Member Committee on Rule Making Process since 1996 and Chairman Jury Trials Innovation Committee 1999-2001 Judicial Management Council. Member National Association of Attorneys General, The Association of Trial Lawyers of America, American Judicature Society, The Florida Bar (Chairman and Member Judicial Administration, Selection and Tenure Committee 1995-96), Dade County, American and International Bar Associations. Recipient Judicial Community Service Award from Greater Miami Jewish Federation 1998, Judicial Achievement Award from Academy of Florida Trial Lawyers 2000, Award for Exemplary Public Service and Leadership from Dade County Trial Lawyers Association, Miami-Dade Chapter Florida Association for Women Lawyers and Dade County Defense Bar Association 2001, Allen Morris Award for Outstanding Freshman Legislator, Intergovernmental Award from U.S. Department of Housing and Urban Development, Furtherance of Justice Award from Florida Prosecuting Attorneys Association and Distinguished Service Award from Florida Sheriff's Association. Named Outstanding Young Man of Florida by Florida Jaycees. Member House of Representatives 1964-66 and Senate 1966-70 Florida. Chairman Housing Finance Authority of Dade County 1980-82 and Florida State Athletic Commission 1984-87. Board of Directors Florida Citizens Against Crime 1985-93 and Florida Crime Commission since 1993. Member Judicial Reform Committee Greater Miami Chamber of Commerce 1993, Executive Committee Miami Citizens Against Crime and Visiting Committee University of Miami Law School. Board of Trustees Beacon Council since 1993. Chair Partners for Safe Neighborhoods 1994. Member Advisory Committee 75th Anniversary League of Women Voters 1995, Leadership Circle United Way of Dade County, Masonic Lodge Jackson #1, Scottish Rite and Mahi Shrine.
Office: 2001 S.W. 117th Avenue, Miami 33175-1716.
Telephone: (305) 229-3200.
Fax: (305) 229-3206

SHINHOLSER, Olin W. *(Judge, Florida Circuit Court Tenth Judicial Circuit)* Former Judge, Highlands County Court, appointed by Governor Bob Martinez to term beginning Dec 22, 1989.
Office: 309 Highlands County Courthouse, 430 South Commerce Avenue, Sebring 33870.
Telephone: (863) 402-6614.
Fax: (863) 402-6575

SHOEMAKER, Wayne *(Judge, Orange County Court)*
Office: 435 Orange County Courthouse, 425 North Orange Avenue, Orlando 32801.
Telephone: (407) 836-0530.

SHORE, Brent D. *(Judge, Duval County Court)* Elected Sept 3, 1996 to term beginning Jan 7, 1997. Reelected Sept 5, 2000, current term expires Jan 1, 2007. Born Charlotte North Carolina Aug 16, 1947. Presbyterian. Educated at University of Florida B.S. 1969 J.D. 1971. Member Phi Delta Phi. Admitted to practice Florida 1972, District of Columbia 1972, U.S. District Court District of Columbia 1972 and U.S. Court of Appeals Fifth 1973 and Eleventh 1973 Circuits. In legal practice Jacksonville 1978-96.

Attorney Federal Communications Commission 1972-73. Assistant State Attorney 1973-78. Member The Florida Bar and Jacksonville Bar Association.
Office: 300 Duval County Courthouse, 330 East Bay Street, Jacksonville 32202.
Telephone: (904) 630-2566.
Fax: (904) 630-2979

SHUTTER, Steven G. *(Judge, Broward County Court)* Appointed by Governor Robert Graham to term beginning July 11, 1981. Elected 1982, 1986, 1990, 1994 and 1998. Current term expires Jan 2005. Born Brooklyn New York June 8, 1944. Jewish. Educated at Tufts University B.A. 1966 and New York University Law School J.D. 1969. Managing Editor Annual Survey of American Law 1968-69. Admitted to practice New York 1970, U.S. Court of Military Appeals 1971, Florida 1973 and U.S. Supreme Court 1975. Began legal practice Denver Colorado 1969. In legal practice Washington D.C. 1970-72 and Pembroke Pines Florida 1972-78. Chief General Master, Florida Circuit Court Seventeenth Judicial Circuit 1978-81.

Trial Attorney Denver Legal Services 1969-70. Chief Prosecutor City of Pembroke Pines 1972-78. Author "Criminal Procedure Update" Annual Survey of American Law Oceana Publishers 1968, "Dissolution in the 1980's" The Florida Bar May 1980, "Federal Child Kidnapping Prevention Act" 55 Florida B. Jour. 479, June 1981 and "Federal Child Support Legislation" The Florida Bar Nov 1983. Important Decisions: Lauderhill v. Jackson 4 Fla. Supp. 2d 116, 1983 and State v. DeVant (right to counsel at DUI videotapings) 5 Fla. Supp. 2d 1984. Adjunct Professor of Litigation and Trial Advocacy Nova Southeastern University 1987-2003. Member Florida Conference of County Court Judges (Vice President), American Judges Association and The Florida Bar (Executive Committee Family Law Section 1981-85). Lecturer Dissolution of Marriage The Florida Bar. Graduate The National Judicial College 1983 and American Academy of Judicial Education. 1984. Faculty member Florida Prosecutor/Public Defender Training Program 1984 and Sentencing Misdemeanors The National Judicial College. Named Florida Judge of the Year by Crime Watch of Florida 1983, Broward County Judge of the Year by Crime Stoppers 1983 and Adjunct Professor of the Year by Nova Southeastern University 2001. Recipient Knights of Pythias Humanitarian Award 1983. City of Tamarac proclaimed "Judge Steven Shutter Day" Dec 14, 1983. Coach varsity soccer team American Heritage High School 1987-89 and varsity soccer team 1990-93 and golf team 1990-2003 University School.

Office: 270 West Regional Courthouse, 100 North Pine Island Road, Plantation 33324.
Telephone: (954) 831-7571.

SIEG, Peter K. *(Judge, Florida Circuit Court Eighth Judicial Circuit)* Former Judge, Alachua County Court, elected to term beginning Jan 1991.
Office: 304 Alachua County Courthouse, 201 East University Avenue, Gainesville 32601.
Telephone: (352) 374-3651.
Fax: (352) 374-5238

SIEGEL, Andrew L. *(Judge, Florida Circuit Court Seventeenth Judicial Circuit)*
Office: 304 Broward County Courthouse, 201 S.E. Sixth Street, Fort Lauderdale 33301.

SIEGEL, Paul *(Judge, Florida Circuit Court Eleventh Judicial Circuit)*
Office: 412 Dade County Courthouse, 73 West Flagler Street, Miami 33130.
Telephone: (305) 349-7144.

SIERRA, Monica L. *(Judge, Florida Circuit Court Thirteenth Judicial Circuit)*
Office: 419 Pierce Street, Tampa 33602-4022.
Telephone: (813) 272-5777.

SIGLER, Victoria S. *(Judge, Florida Circuit Court Eleventh Judicial Circuit)* Former Judge, Dade County Court, elected to term beginning Jan 3, 1995.
Office: 1351 N.W. Twelfth Street, Room 713, Miami 33125.
Telephone: (305) 548-5618.

SILBERMAN, Morris *(Judge, Florida District Court of Appeal Second District)* Appointed by Governor Jeb Bush to term beginning Jan 2, 2001. Retained by election 2002, current term expires Jan 2009. Born Philadelphia Pennsylvania. Educated at Tulane University B.A. 1979 and University of Florida J.D. 1982. Law Clerk to Hon. Herboth S. Ryder, Florida District Court of Appeal Second District 1982-84. Admitted to practice Florida 1982. In legal practice Sarasota 1984-86 and Clearwater 1986-2000.
Mailing address: P.O. Box 327, Lakeland 33802-0327.
Office: 1005 East Memorial Boulevard, Lakeland 33801.
Telephone: (863) 499-2290.

SILVER, Roger A. *(Judge, Dade County Court)*
Office: 73 West Flagler Street, Miami 33130.
Telephone: (305) 375-4801.

SILVERMAN, David E. *(Judge, Brevard County Court)*
Office: 160 Melbourne Courthouse, 50 South Nieman Avenue, Melbourne 32901-1261.
Telephone: (321) 952-4703.
Fax: (321) 952-4681

SILVERMAN, Scott J. *(Judge, Florida Circuit Court Eleventh Judicial Circuit)* Elected 1999. Born Silver Spring Maryland. Jewish. Educated at University of Miami B.B.A. magna cum laude 1978 and University of Tulsa College of Law J.D. 1981. Recipient Flammang Academic Scholarship. Member Phi Kappa Phi, Beta Gamma Sigma, Omicron Delta Epsilon, Alpha Lambda Delta and Phi Delta Phi. Law Clerk to Hon. Fredricka G. Smith, Florida Circuit Court Eleventh Judicial Circuit 1983. Admitted to practice Oklahoma 1981, U.S. District Courts Eastern 1981, Northern 1981 and Western 1981 Districts of Oklahoma and Southern District of Florida 1983, U.S. Court of Appeals Tenth Circuit 1981, Florida 1983 and U.S. Tax Court 1983. In legal practice Coconut Grove 1983-85 and Miami 1985-91. Judge, Dade County Court Jan 1991 to 1999.

Assistant Attorney General Oklahoma 1981-82. Author "Think 'Mandatory Penalties' Before You Drink" *The Miami Herald* Dec 23, 1991, "Juror Discrimination: Addressing *Neil* and *Slappy* Challenges" The Florida Bar Criminal Law Section Newsletter June 1992 and "Recovering Attorney Fees from Publicly Represented Criminal Defendants" Florida B. Jour. May 1996. Co-author with R. J. Potash "Impairment of Earning Capacity as an Element of Damages" Florida B. Jour. Nov 1990; with M. C. Lando "Domestic Violence: A View from the Bench" *The Miami Herald* Oct 26, 1991; and with J. T. Colby "Expanding the Role of Jurors in Florida Courts" Florida B. Jour. Oct 1991. Editorial Board Florida B. Jour. and Florida Bar News 1992-95. Member since 1994 and Chairman 1998 and 2002 Judicial Ethics

SILVERMAN, SCOTT J.—*Continued*

Advisory Committee, Member Technology Commission since 1996 Florida Supreme Court. Member since 1997 and Chairman 1999-2000 Committee on the Rules of Judicial Administration. Member Florida Conference of County Court Judges (Chairman Technology Committee 1996-98, Member Criminal Rules Committee, Finance Committee, Resource Committee, Traffic Court Rules and Review Committee, Education Committee), American Judges Association, The Florida Bar and Oklahoma Bar Association. Recipient Harvey Ford Leadership Award from Florida Conference of County Court Judges 1998 and Herbert Harley Award from American Judicature Society 2000.

Office: 712 Gerstein Justice Building, 1351 N.W. 12th Street, Miami 33125.

Telephone: (305) 548-5613.

Fax: (305) 548-5612

Website address: http://www.techjudge.com

SILVERNAIL, J. Preston *(Judge, Florida Circuit Court Eighteenth Judicial Circuit)* Former Chief Judge. Born Jasper Alabama Aug 24, 1947. Methodist. Educated at University of Florida B.A. 1972 M.B.A. with honors 1976 and St. Mary's University J.D. with honors 1977. Member Phi Alpha Delta, Omicron Delta Kappa and Florida Blue Key. Admitted to practice Florida 1977 and U.S. District Court Middle District of Florida 1980. In legal practice Melbourne 1977-92. Former Judge, Brevard County Court, appointed by Governor Lawton Chiles to term beginning Nov 18, 1992.

Member American Inns of Court, Florida Conference of County Court Judges, American Judicature Society, The Florida Bar and Brevard County Bar Association. Sergeant E-5 U.S. Army 1967-69. Board of Directors Brevard County Parks and Recreation District, Melbourne Art Festival and Kiwanis. Enjoys playing golf, snow skiing and reading.

Office: Moore Justice Center, Second Floor, 2825 Judge Fran Jamieson Way, Viera 32940-8006.

Telephone: (321) 617-7262.

Fax: (321) 617-7264

SILVERTOOTH, Lynn N. *(Senior Judge, Florida Circuit Court Twelfth Judicial Circuit)* Assumed Senior Judge status, serves by assignment.

Mailing address: P.O. Box 48927, Sarasota 34230.

Office: 2002 Ringling Boulevard, Sarasota 34237.

Telephone: (941) 861-7800.

SIMMS, Robert J. *(Judge, Florida Circuit Court Thirteenth Judicial Circuit)* Elected to term beginning Jan 1991. Reelected 1996 and 2002. Current term expires Jan 2009.

Office: 121 Annex, 800 East Kennedy Boulevard, Tampa 33602-4146.

Telephone: (813) 272-6879.

Fax: (813) 276-2329

SIMONS, Stuart M. *(Judge, Florida Circuit Court Eleventh Judicial Circuit)*

Office: 405 Dade County Courthouse, 73 West Flagler Street, Miami 33130.

Telephone: (305) 349-4121.

SIMONTON, Andrea M. *(Magistrate Judge, United States District Court Southern District of Florida)* Appointed by U.S. District Court judges to term beginning April 1, 1999. Term expires 2007. Educated at Florida International University B.S.W. 1973 and University of Miami J.D. cum laude 1978. Member and Research Editor University of Miami Law Review. Law Clerk to Hon. James Lawrence King, U.S. District Court Southern District of Florida 1978-79. Admitted to practice Florida 1978.

Assistant U.S. Attorney Southern District of Florida Dec 1983 to Oct 1993 and Sept 1996 to April 1999. Deputy General Counsel Federal Bureau of Investigation Oct 1993 to Sept 1996.

Office: 131 U.S. Courthouse, 300 N.E. First Avenue, Miami 33132.

Telephone: (305) 523-5930.

SIMPSON, Raymond L. *(Senior Judge, Duval County Court)* Assumed Senior Judge status, serves by assignment.

Office: Duval County Courthouse, 330 East Bay Street, Jacksonville 32202.

Telephone: (904) 630-1693.

SINGBUSH, William *(Judge, Florida Circuit Court Fifth Judicial Circuit)* Elected to term beginning Jan 1991. Reelected 1996 and 2002. Current term expires Jan 2009.

Office: Marion County Judicial Center, 110 N.W. First Avenue, Ocala 34475.

Telephone: (352) 401-7815.

Fax: (352) 401-7819

SINGLETARY, G. Richard *(Judge, Florida Circuit Court Fifth Judicial Circuit)* Assumed office Oct 6, 1989. Elected to subsequent terms. Former Judge, Lake County Court.

Mailing address: P.O. Box 7800, Tavares 32778-7800.

Office: Lake County Judicial Center, Tavares 32778.

Telephone: (352) 747-4209.

Fax: (352) 742-4229

SIRMONS, Don T. *(Judge, Florida Circuit Court Fourteenth Judicial Circuit)* Former Chief Judge. Former Judge, Bay County Court.

Mailing address: P.O. Box 831, Panama City 32402.

Office: 300 East Fourth Street, Panama City 32401.

Telephone: (850) 747-5322.

Fax: (850) 747-5159

SJOSTROM, Jonathan *(Judge, Florida Circuit Court Second Judicial Circuit)*

Office: 365-I Leon County Courthouse, 301 South Monroe Street, Tallahassee 32301.

Telephone: (850) 577-4321.

Fax: (850) 922-0327

SKIDMORE, Thomas D. *(Judge, Sumter County Court)* Elected Nov 8, 1988 to term beginning Jan 3, 1989. Reelected 1992, 1996 and 2000. Current term expires Jan 2007. Born Newark New Jersey Dec 25, 1950. Roman Catholic. Educated at Clemson University B.A. 1972 and Vermont Law School J.D. with honors 1976. Admitted to practice Florida 1977, U.S. District Court Middle District of Florida 1978, U.S. Courts of Appeals Fifth 1980 and Eleventh 1983 Circuits and U.S. Supreme Court 1980. In legal practice Bushnell 1976-88.

Instructor Lake Sumter Community College 1977-84. President Tri County Bar Association 1985. Member Florida Conference of County Court Judges (Vice President 1990-93), American Judges Association, The Florida Bar (Grievance Committee 1987-88) and American Bar Association. Recipient Friend of Education Award

SKIDMORE, THOMAS D.—*Continued*
from Sumter County 1990 and Distinguished Leadership Award from Florida Conference of County Court Judges 1991. Enjoys sports.
Office: Sumter County Courthouse, 225 East McCollum Avenue, Bushnell 33513.
Telephone: (352) 793-0250.
Fax: (352) 793-0252

SKIEVASKI, Kim A. *(Judge, Florida Circuit Court First Judicial Circuit)* Elected to term beginning Jan 1991. Reelected 1996 and 2002. Current term expires Jan 2009. Born Eglin AFB Florida Dec 15, 1952. Methodist. Educated at Florida State University B.A. magna cum laude 1977 J.D. with honors 1981. Admitted to practice Florida 1982. USN 1972-76.
Office: Judicial Building, Fifth Floor, 190 Governmental Center, Pensacola 32501.
Telephone: (850) 595-4456.
Fax: (850) 595-4458

SKINNER, John H. *(Judge, Florida Circuit Court Fourth Judicial Circuit)* Former Judge, Duval County Court.
Office: 224 Duval County Courthouse, 330 East Bay Street, Jacksonville 32202.
Telephone: (904) 630-2592.
Fax: (904) 630-2979

SKOLNIK, Peter *(Judge, Broward County Court)* Elected to term beginning Jan 1991. Reelected 1994 and 1998. Current term expires Jan 2005.
Office: 780 Broward County Courthouse, 201 S.E. Sixth Street, Fort Lauderdale 33301.
Telephone: (954) 831-7835.

SLAUGHTER, William R., II *(Judge, Suwannee County Court)* Appointed by Governor Lawton Chiles Feb 7, 1994.
Office: Suwanee County Courthouse, 200 South Ohio Avenue, Live Oak 32064.
Telephone: (386) 362-3431.
Fax: (386) 364-4116

SLOAN, James D. *(Judge, Hendry County Court)*
Mailing address: P.O. Box 1695, Labelle 33975.
Office: Hendry County courthouse, Labelle 33935.
Telephone: (863) 675-5227.
Fax: (863) 675-5248

SLOM, Samuel J. *(Judge, Dade County Court)*
Office: 513 Gerstein Justice Building, 1351 N.W. Twelfth Street, Miami 33125.
Telephone: (305) 548-5187.

SLOOP, John R. *(Judge, Seminole County Court)* Elected to term beginning Jan 1991. Reelected 1994 and 1998. Current term expires Jan 2005. Born Ohio 1948. Methodist. Educated at University of Maryland B.S. 1974 and Florida State University J.D. 1981. Admitted to practice Florida 1981 and U.S. District Courts Middle 1981 and Southern 1981 Districts of Florida. In legal practice central Florida area 1984-91.
Vice President Florida Conference of County Court Judges 1994-95. Instructor semi-annual conferences. Member Habitat for Humanity, Boy Scouts of America, Kiwanis and Optimists. Interests include eliminating substandard housing in Seminole County, legal research and instruction and water sports.
Office: Seminole County Courthouse, 301 North Park Avenue, Sanford 32771-1292.
Telephone: (407) 665-4106.
Fax: (407) 665-4261

SMILEY, Elijah *(Judge, Bay County Court)*
Mailing address: P.O. Box 2269, Panama City 32402.
Office: Bay County Courthouse, Panama City 32402.
Telephone: (850) 747-5205.
Fax: (850) 747-5629

SMITH, C. McFerrin, III *(Judge, Florida Circuit Court Seventh Judicial Circuit)* Former Chief Judge.
Office: Volusia County Courthouse, 101 North Alabama Avenue, DeLand 32724.
Telephone: (386) 736-5945.
Fax: (386) 943-7076

SMITH, Charles E. *(Senior Judge, Florida Circuit Court Nineteenth Judicial Circuit)* Assumed Senior Judge status, serves by assignment.
Office: 218 South Second Street, Fort Pierce 34950.
Telephone: (772) 462-1472.

SMITH, Frederick D. *(Judge, Florida Circuit Court Eighth Judicial Circuit)* Born Gainesville Florida Feb 1, 1943. Educated at University of Florida B.S.J.M. with honors 1970 J.D. 1973. Admitted to practice Florida 1973, U.S. District Courts Northern 1974 and Middle 1975 Districts of Florida and U.S. Courts of Appeals Fifth 1981 and Eleventh 1981 Circuits. In legal practice Jacksonville 1973-74 and Gainesville 1975-86. Former Judge, Alachua County Court, appointed by Governor Robert Graham to term beginning July 23, 1986.
Author "Loss of Consortium: The Wife's Cause of Action" University of Florida L. Rev. 1970. Adjunct Professor University of Florida Law School since 1987. President Elect Eighth Judicial Circuit Bar Association 1986 (resigned to accept judicial appointment). First Lieutenant U.S. Army 1964-68.
Office: 409 Alachua County Courthouse, 201 East University Avenue, Gainesville 32601.
Telephone: (352) 374-3652.
Fax: (352) 374-5238

SMITH, Fredricka G. *(Judge, Florida Circuit Court Eleventh Judicial Circuit)*
Office: 416 Dade County Courthouse, 73 West Flagler Street, Miami 33130.
Telephone: (305) 349-7157.

SMITH, Gilbert A. *(Senior Judge, Florida Circuit Court Twelfth Judicial Circuit)* Former Chief Judge. Assumed Senior Judge status, serves by assignment.
Mailing address: P.O. Box 48927, Sarasota 34230.
Office: 2002 Ringling Boulevard, Sarasota 34237.
Telephone: (941) 861-7800.

SMITH, John Roger *(Judge, Volusia County Court)*
Office: Volusia County Courthouse, 101 North Alabama Avenue, DeLand 32724.
Telephone: (386) 736-5948.

SMITH, Joseph E. *(Judge, Levy County Court)* Appointed by Governor Lawton Chiles to term beginning June 21, 1993. Elected 1994 and 1998. Current term expires Jan 2005. Methodist. Educated at Florida State University B.S. 1964 and University of Florida J.D.

SMITH, JOSEPH E.—*Continued*

1968. Admitted to practice Florida 1989. In legal practice Bronson 1969-93.

Assistant State Attorney 1975-93. Member Eighth Judicial Circuit Bar Association.

Mailing address: P.O. Box 327, Bronson 32621.
Telephone: (352) 486-5224.
Fax: (352) 486-5384

SMITH, L. Ralph, Jr. *(Judge, Florida Circuit Court Second Judicial Circuit)*

Office: 365-J Leon County Courthouse, 301 South Monroe Street, Tallahassee 32301.
Telephone: (850) 577-4312.
Fax: (850) 922-0327

SMITH, Larry G. *(Senior Judge, Florida District Court of Appeal)* Appointed by Governor Robert Graham March 30, 1979. Retained by election 1980, 1986 and 1992. Chief Judge 1987-89. Assumed Senior Judge status July 31, 1994, serves by assignment. Born Montgomery Alabama Aug 6, 1924. Educated at University of Alabama and University of Florida LL.B. 1949. Admitted to practice Florida 1949, U.S. District Courts Northern 1950 and Middle 1962 Districts of Florida and U.S. Supreme Court 1970. Began legal practice Panama City 1949. In legal practice Orlando 1960-64 and Panama City 1964-72. Judge, Florida Circuit Court Fourteenth Circuit Jan 1, 1973 to March 30, 1979.

Member Airport Authority of Panama City 1952-55. Assistant State Attorney 1953-57. Research Aide Florida Supreme Court 1958-60. Member 1968-72 and Vice Chairman 1972 Florida Board of Bar Examiners. Member Florida Court Educational Council 1985-91 and Florida Supreme Court Bench/Bar Commission 1990-91. Member American Judicature Society, St. Andrews Bay American Inn of Court, Florida Conference of District Court of Appeal Judges (President 1986-87), Florida Conference of Circuit Court Judges (Chairman Public Information and Media Relations Committee 1975-76), The Florida Bar (Media Relations Committee 1976-78 and Committee on Legal Education and Admissions to the Bar), Bay County, Orange County (Secretary Executive Council 1963-64), Fourteenth Judicial Circuit (Secretary 1953, Grievance Committee 1967-70) and American Bar Associations. Lieutenant j.g. USNR 1943-45. Member First United Methodist Church.

Office: 4115 West Seventeenth Street, Panama City 32401.
Telephone: (850) 763-7034.

SMITH, Maura T. *(Judge, Florida Circuit Court Ninth Judicial Circuit)*

Office: 1145 Orange County Courthouse, 425 North Orange Avenue, Orlando 32801.
Telephone: (407) 836-0540.
Fax: (407) 836-0451

SMITH, Radford W. *(Senior Judge, Pinellas County Court)* Assumed Senior Judge status, serves by assignment.

Office: Judicial Building, 545 First Avenue North, St. Petersburg 33701.
Telephone: (727) 464-4470.

SMITH, Rupert Jasen *(Senior Judge, Florida Circuit Court Nineteenth Judicial Circuit)* Appointed by Governor Robert Graham to term beginning Sept 25, 1981. Elected Nov 2, 1982 and Nov 1988. Assumed Senior Judge status, serves by assignment. Born Fort Pierce Florida Jan 10, 1924. Educated at University of Florida B.A. 1949 LL.B. 1950. Admitted to practice Florida 1950 and U.S. District Court Southern District of Florida 1951. In legal practice Fort Pierce 1950-81.

Representative Florida State Legislature 1956-62. Member The Florida Bar and St. Lucie County Bar Association. Attended conferences on Criminal Law University of Virginia Summer 1983, on Civil Law Harvard Law School Summer 1986 and on General Law Stanford University Summer 1987. USAS 1943-46 and Jan 1951 to Dec 1952. Enjoys playing golf and hunting.

Office: 218 South Second Street, Fort Pierce 34950.
Telephone: (772) 462-1472.

SMITH, Thomas B. *(Judge, Florida Circuit Court Ninth Judicial Circuit)*

Office: Orange County Courthouse, 425 North Orange Avenue, Orlando 32801.
Telephone: (407) 836-2119.
Fax: (407) 836-0450

SMITH, W. Bruce *(Judge, Florida Circuit Court Tenth Judicial Circuit)*

Mailing address: P.O. Box 9000, Drawer J-132, Bartow 33831-9000.
Telephone: (863) 534-4653.

SNOW, Lurana S. *(Magistrate Judge, United States District Court Southern District of Florida)* Appointed by U.S. District Court judges. Former Chief Magistrate Judge.

Office: U.S. Courthouse, 299 East Broward Boulevard, Fort Lauderdale 33301.
Telephone: (954) 769-5460.

SNYDER, Arthur I. *(Senior Judge, Florida Circuit Court Eleventh Judicial Circuit)* Assumed Senior Judge status, serves by assignment.

Office: 511 Dade County Courthouse, 73 West Flagler Street, Miami 33130.
Telephone: (305) 349-7001.

SNYDER, Howard T. *(Magistrate Judge, United States District Court Middle District of Florida)* Appointed by U.S. District Court judges.

Mailing address: P.O. Box 649, Jacksonville 32201-0649.
Telephone: (904) 549-1960.

SOLOMON, Harold *(Senior Judge, Florida Circuit Court Eleventh Judicial Circuit)* Assumed Senior Judge status, serves by assignment.

Office: 511 Dade County Courthouse, 73 West Flagler Street, Miami 33130.
Telephone: (305) 349-7001.

SOTO, Bertila *(Judge, Florida Circuit Court Eleventh Judicial Circuit)* Former Judge, Dade County Court.

Office: 413 Gerstein Justice Building, 1351 N.W. Twelfth Street, Miami 33125.
Telephone: (305) 548-5170.
Fax: (305) 548-5236

SOUD, A. C., Jr. *(Judge, Florida Circuit Court Fourth Judicial Circuit)*

Office: 224 Duval County Courthouse, 330 East Bay Street, Jacksonville 32202.
Telephone: (904) 630-2532.
Fax: (904) 630-2979

SOUTHWOOD, John D. *(Senior Judge, Florida Circuit Court Fourth Judicial Circuit)* Assumed Senior Judge status, serves by assignment. Born Paris Kentucky Jan 9, 1934. Methodist. Educated at University of Oklahoma B.B.A. 1956 and Florida State University J.D. with honors 1969. Admitted to practice Florida 1969, U.S. District Court Middle District of Florida 1969 and U.S. Supreme Court 1973. Former Judge, Duval County Court, elected to term beginning Jan 5, 1975.

With Office of the Public Defender at Jacksonville 1969. Member Conference of Florida County Court Judges (President 1979), Jacksonville and American (1970-73) Bar Associations. Democratic Committeeman 1966-68.

Office: Duval County Courthouse, 330 East Bay Street, Jacksonville 32202.

Telephone: (904) 630-1693.

SPAULDING, Karla R. *(Magistrate Judge, United States District Court Middle District of Florida)* Appointed by U.S. District Court judges.

Office: 596 U.S. Courthouse, 80 North Hughey Avenue, Orlando 32801.

Telephone: (407) 835-4320.

SPECHLER, Jay S. *(Judge, Broward County Court)* Elected 1988 to term beginning Jan 1989. Reelected 1992, 1996 and 2000. Current term expires Jan 2007. Born Jacksonville Florida Dec 4, 1952. Educated at University of Florida B.S. and Nova University J.D. Admitted to practice Florida 1979 and New York.

Office: 425 Broward County Courthouse, 201 S.E. Sixth Street, Fort Lauderdale 33301.

Telephone: (954) 831-7307.

Fax: (954) 831-5572

SPEISER, Mark A. *(Judge, Florida Circuit Court Seventeenth Judicial Circuit)* Elected 1982 to term beginning Jan 4, 1983. Reelected 1988, 1994 and 2000. Current term expires Jan 2007. Born Holyoke Massachusetts Oct 28, 1947. Jewish. Educated at American University B.S. with honors 1969, University of North Carolina J.D. 1972 and Georgetown University LL.M. in Taxation 1976. Member Tau Epsilon Phi. Admitted to practice Florida 1972 and District of Columbia 1974. In legal practice Washington D.C. 1972-74 and 1977-78, New York City 1974-76, Miami 1976-77 and Fort Lauderdale 1978-82 Florida.

Member The District of Columbia Bar, The Florida Bar and Broward County Bar Association. Chairman Broward County Juvenile Detention Center Advisory Board. Secretary Broward County Mental Health Advisory Board. Member Knights of Pythias. Enjoys sports and scuba diving.

Office: 905A Broward County Courthouse, 201 S.E. Sixth Street, Fort Lauderdale 33301.

Telephone: (954) 831-7805.

Fax: (954) 831-5784

SPENCER, W. Thomas *(Senior Judge, Florida Circuit Court Eleventh Judicial Circuit)* Assumed Senior Judge status, serves by assignment.

Office: 511 Dade County Courthouse, 73 West Flagler Street, Miami 33130.

Telephone: (305) 349-7001.

SPOTO, Keith P. *(Judge, Polk County Court)*

Mailing address: P.O. Box 9000, Drawer J-152, Bartow 33831-9000.

Office: Polk County Courthouse, Bartow 33830.

Telephone: (863) 534-5862.

Fax: (863) 534-5832

SPRINGSTEAD, Jack *(Judge, Florida Circuit Court Fifth Judicial Circuit)* Assumed office Oct 6, 1989. Elected to subsequent terms.

Office: Hernando County Courthouse, 20 North Main Street, Brooksville 34601.

Telephone: (352) 754-4281.

Fax: (352) 754-4265

SPRINKEL, George A., IV *(Judge, Florida Circuit Court Ninth Judicial Circuit)* Assumed office Jan 2, 1990. Elected to subsequent terms. Born Richmond Virginia Oct 5, 1941. Educated at University of Florida B.A. in Political Science 1964 J.D. 1968. Admitted to practice Florida 1969. Began legal practice Orlando. Judge, Orlando County Court Jan 1977 to Jan 1990.

Member The Florida Bar, Orange County and American Bar Associations. U.S. Army. Former member Central Florida Young Democrats (President 1969-70). Board of Directors Thee Door of Central Florida, Easter Seal Society of Central Florida, Central Florida University of Florida Alumni Association (National Vice President) and Virginia Heights Civic Association (Past President). Member First Congregational Church of Winter Park and Executive Committee Orlando Yacht Club. Enjoys sailing, softball, golf and tennis.

Office: 1715 Orange County Courthouse, 425 North Orange Avenue, Orlando 32801.

Telephone: (407) 836-2040.

STAFFORD, Leonard L. *(Senior Judge, Florida Circuit Court Seventeenth Judicial Circuit)* Elected to term beginning Jan 1991. Reelected 1996. Assumed Senior Judge status, serves by assignment. Born Valley Alabama Feb 4, 1935. Educated at University of Alabama, Jacksonville State University B.S. 1958 and University of Miami J.D. 1963. Judge, Fort Lauderdale Municipal Court 1973-77. Judge, Broward County Court May 1986 to Jan 1991. First Lieutenant U.S. Army 1958-60.

Office: Broward County Courthouse, 201 S.E. Sixth Street, Fort Lauderdale 33301.

Telephone: (954) 831-7740.

STAFFORD, William Henry, Jr. *(Senior Judge, United States District Court Northern District of Florida)* Appointed for life by President Gerald R. Ford to term beginning May 30, 1975. Former Chief Judge. Assumed Senior status, serves by assignment. Born Masury Ohio May 11, 1931. Episcopalian. Educated at Temple University B.S. 1953 LL.B. 1956 replaced by J.D. 1968. Admitted to practice Florida 1961, U.S. District Court Northern District of Florida 1962, U.S. Court of Appeals Fifth Circuit 1969 and U.S. Supreme Court 1970. Began legal practice Pensacola 1961.

Founding President Tallahassee American Inns of Court. Member The Florida Bar. Lieutenant j.g. USN 1957-60. Republican. Enjoys walking and traveling.

Office: U.S. Courthouse, 111 North Adams Street, Tallahassee 32301-7717.

Telephone: (850) 521-3611.

STANCIL, Hale R. *(Judge, Florida Circuit Court Fifth Judicial Circuit)* Assumed office Nov 18, 1993.

STANCIL, HALE R.—*Continued*

Born Ocala Florida Jan 3, 1946. Religious affiliation: Disciples of Christ. Educated at Central Florida Community College A.A. 1966, University of Florida B.S.B.A. 1968 and Stetson University College of Law J.D. 1973. Member Phi Delta Phi and Alpha Kappa Psi. Admitted to practice Florida 1973. In legal practice Ocala 1973-82. Judge, Marion County Court, Jan 4, 1983 to Nov 17, 1993.

With Public Defender's Office 1974-78. Lecturer on Self Defense Under Florida Law Women's Handgun Safety Course Central Florida Community College. Recipient Outstanding Citizenship Award 1985, Good Government Award 1986, Distinguished Service Award from Florida Council on Crime and Delinquency 1986 and Outstanding Service Award as Chairman of the Program Committee from Ocala Lions Club 1986. Corporal USMC 1969-71. Founding Director West Central Florida Driver Improvement, Inc. (President 1987-91). Member First Christian Church of Ocala (Chairman of the Board 1981-82 and Elder), Ocala Lions Club (President 1980-81), Morocco Temple, Ocala Shrine Club, Marion Dunn Lodge 19 (Vigilance Committee), Marion County Chamber of Commerce, Florida Council on Crime and Delinquency, Sons of the American Revolution, American Legion Post 27 (Commander 1981-82) and Disabled American Veterans Chapter 68 (Commander 1985).

Office: Sumter County Courthouse, 225 East McCollum Avenue, Bushnell 33513.
Telephone: (352) 793-0280.
Fax: (352) 568-6645

STARNES, Hugh E. *(Judge, Florida Circuit Court Twentieth Judicial Circuit)* Appointed by Governor Reubin O'Donovan Askew to term beginning June 1, 1978. Elected 1984, 1990, 1996 and 2002. Current term expires Jan 2009. Former Chief Judge. Born Fort Myers Florida Sept 25, 1940. Educated at University of Florida B.A. 1962 LL.B. 1964. Member Phi Delta Phi. Admitted to practice Florida 1965. Began legal practice Fort Myers 1965.

Member Lee County and American Bar Associations. Specialist Five U.S. Army 1965-71 and Florida National Guard. Chairman City of Fort Myers Community Relations Board. Enjoys ranching and sports.

Office: Lee County Justice Center, 1700 Monroe Street, Fort Myers 33901.
Telephone: (239) 335-2257.
Fax: (239) 477-2069

STEELE, John E. *(Judge, United States District Court Middle District of Florida)* Magistrate Judge 1991-2000. Appointed Judge for life by President Bill Clinton to term beginning July 28, 2000. Born Detroit Michigan 1949. Educated at University of Detroit B.A. 1971 J.D. 1973. In legal practice 1988-91.

Office: U.S. Courthouse, 2110 First Street, Fort Myers 33901.
Telephone: (239) 461-2140.

STEIN, Harry *(Senior Judge, Florida Circuit Court Eighteenth Judicial Circuit)* Appointed by Governor Lawton Chiles to term beginning Sept 1, 1992. Elected 1992. Assumed Senior Judge status, serves by assignment. Born Camden New Jersey Sept 25, 1929. Jewish. Educated at University of Miami LL.B. 1955. Admitted to practice Florida 1955. In legal practice Miami 1955-63 and Melbourne 1963-80. Judge, Brevard County Court 1981-92.

Assistant City Attorney Miami 1960-63. City Attorney Palm Bay 1967-68. Chief Assistant Solicitor Brevard County 1971-73. Assistant State Attorney 1973-77. Domestic Relations Commissioner Brevard County 1979-80. Member Brevard County Bar Association. Corporal USAF 1951-52. Enjoys swimming, diving, biking, reading, bridge, tennis and racquetball.

Office: Moore Justice Center, 2825 Judge Fran Jamieson Way, Viera 32940-8006.
Telephone: (321) 637-5555.

STEIN, Linda S. *(Judge, Dade County Court)*
Office: 209 North Dade Justice Center, 15555 Biscayne Boulevard, Miami 33160.
Telephone: (305) 354-8773.

STEINBECK, Margaret Ogilvie *(Judge, Florida Circuit Court Twentieth Judicial Circuit)*
Office: Charlotte County Justice Center, 350 East Marion Avenue, Punta Gorda 33950.
Telephone: (941) 637-2186.
Fax: (941) 637-2283

STEINBERG, Ralph *(Senior Judge, Florida Circuit Court Thirteenth Judicial Circuit)* Assumed Senior Judge status, serves by assignment. Born Trenton New Jersey Oct 21, 1930. Jewish. Educated at University of Tampa B.S. 1953 and Stetson University J.D. 1959. Admitted to practice Florida 1959. Began legal practice Tampa 1959. Judge, Hillsborough County Court 1978-83.

Assistant Public Defender Hillsborough County 1972-75. Member The Association of Trial Lawyers of America, Bay Area Trial Lawyers Association (Secretary 1968), Academy of Florida Trial Lawyers, Florida Conference of County Court Judges, Florida Conference of Circuit Court Judges (Chairman Civil Justice Section 1986-87, member Executive Committee 1986-87), Commercial Law League of America, The Florida Bar, Hillsborough County, Tampa and American Bar Associations. Instructor Florida Judicial College 1985 and 1986. Corporal Specialist Fourth Class U.S. Army 1953-55. Democrat. Official and Team Manager Senior and Pony League Baseball for ten years. Board of Directors Jewish Community Center of Tampa and Tampa Jewish Federation. President two years, Vice President five years and Board of Directors eight years Hillel School of Tampa. Member Beth Israel (Board of Directors, Past President, Vice President and Secretary). Enjoys music, musical instruments and athletics.

Office: Hillsborough County Courthouse, 419 Pierce Street, Tampa 33602-4022.
Telephone: (813) 272-5894.

STEINHARDT, Raphael *(Judge, Dade County Court)* Elected to term beginning Jan 1991. Reelected 1994 and 1998. Current term expires Jan 2005.

Office: 210 North Dade Justice Center, 15555 Biscayne Boulevard, Miami 33160.
Telephone: (305) 354-8761.

STEINMEYER, F. E., III *(Senior Judge, Florida Circuit Court Second Judicial Circuit)* Appointed by Governor Bob Martinez Feb 8, 1989. Elected to subse-

STEINMEYER, F. E., III—*Continued*

quent terms. Assumed Senior Judge status, serves by assignment.

Office: Leon County Courthouse, 301 South Monroe Street, Tallahassee 32301.
Telephone: (850) 577-4420.

STEPHENS, Debra Moses *(Judge, Palm Beach County Court)*
Office: 9.2203 Palm Beach County Courthouse, 205 North Dixie Highway, West Palm Beach 33401.
Telephone: (561) 355-2534.
Fax: (561) 355-3841

STEPHENSON, Gene R. *(Judge, Florida Circuit Court Eighteenth Judicial Circuit)*
Office: Juvenile Justice Center, 190 Bush Boulevard, Sanford 32773-6196.
Telephone: (407) 665-4269.

STERN, Kenneth D. *(Judge, Florida Circuit Court Fifteenth Judicial Circuit)* Born Atlantic City New Jersey Sept 29, 1941. Jewish. Educated at Ohio University A.B. 1963 and Cleveland State University J.D. 1967. Editor-in-Chief Cleveland-Marshall Law Review 1967. Law Clerk to Hon. Joseph Silbert, Ohio Court of Appeals 1967-69. Member Phi Alpha Delta. Admitted to practice Florida 1967. In legal practice Boca Raton 1981-99. Traffic Magistrate, Palm Beach County Court 1991-95. Former Judge, Palm Beach County Court, appointed by Governor Jeb Bush March 7, 1999 to term beginning May 3, 1999.

Assistant U.S. Attorney Southern District of Florida Feb 1978 to Aug 1981. Trial Attorney Antitrust Division U.S. Department of Justice. Author "Firemen's Recovery from Negligent Landowners" Cleveland-Marshall L. Rev. June 1967. Member Palm Beach County Trial Lawyers Association, Palm Beach County Association of Criminal Defense Lawyers, Academy of Florida Trial Lawyers, Florida Association of Criminal Defense Lawyers, Florida Academy of Certified Mediators Inc., National Association of Criminal Defense Lawyers, American Arbitration Association, Council for Marriage Preservation and Divorce Resolution (Founding Member) and South Palm Beach County Bar Association (Director 1983-93, President 1991-92). Attended Arbitration Training and Certification 1989 and Mediation Training and Certification 1994 American Arbitration Association. Recipient Judicial Service Award from South Palm Beach County Bar Association June 2000.

Office: Palm Beach County Courthouse, 205 North Dixie Highway, West Palm Beach 33401.
Telephone: (561) 355-6115.

STETSON, Brad *(Judge, Florida Circuit Court Fourth Judicial Circuit)* Elected to term beginning Jan 1991. Reelected 1996 and 2002. Current term expires Jan 2009. Serves Family Law Division since 2001. Born Providence Rhode Island July 13, 1949. Educated at San Diego State University B.A. 1973 and University of Florida J.D. 1979. Admitted to practice Florida 1979, U.S. District Court Southern District of Florida 1980 and U.S. Court of Appeals Fifth Circuit 1980.

Assistant State Attorney and Director Special Prosecution Felony Division Aug 1979 to July 1990. Member Inns of Court. Board Member North Florida Council of Boy Scouts, YWCA and All Saints Nursing Home. Member Catholic Lawyers Guild and Christian Legal Society. Enjoys playing with his kids, coaching soccer, swimming and playing tennis and guitar.

Office: Duval County Courthouse, 330 East Bay Street, Jacksonville 32202.
Telephone: (904) 630-2111.
Fax: (904) 630-2979

STETTIN, Herbert *(Senior Judge, Florida Circuit Court Eleventh Judicial Circuit)* Assumed Senior Judge status, serves by assignment.
Office: 511 Dade County Courthouse, 73 West Flagler Street, Miami 33130.
Telephone: (305) 349-7001.

STEVENSON, W. Matthew *(Judge, Florida District Court of Appeal Fourth District)* Appointed by Governor Lawton Chiles Nov 10, 1993. Retained by election. Educated at Florida State University B.A. 1975 J.D. 1978. Editorial Board Florida State University Law Review 1976-77. Law Clerk to Hon. Joseph Woodrow Hatchett, Florida Supreme Court and U.S. Court of Appeals Fifth Circuit 1979-80. Judge, Florida Circuit Court Fifteenth Judicial Circuit Jan 2, 1990 to 1994, appointed by Governor Bob Martinez.

Assistant Public Defender Fifteenth Judicial Circuit 1978-79. Mediator Mediation Inc. 1987-90. Member Palm Beach County Criminal Justice Task Force 1993-94. Member Emeritus Craig S. Barnard American Inns of Court. Member American Arbitration Association, National Council of Juvenile and Family Court Judges, The Florida Bar, Palm Beach County and National Bar Associations. Board Member Boys and Girls Club of Palm Beach County 1991-93. Board of Trustees Palm Beach Atlantic College since 1994. Advisory Board Pre-Law Magnet Program Palm Beach Lakes Community High School since 1998. Certified high school varsity football referee Florida High School Activities Association.

Mailing address: P.O. Box 3315, West Palm Beach 33402-3315.
Office: 1525 Palm Beach Lakes Boulevard, West Palm Beach 33401.
Telephone: (561) 242-2058.
Fax: (561) 242-2096

STODDARD, Ralph C. *(Judge, Florida Circuit Court Thirteenth Judicial Circuit)* Elected Sept 1996 to term beginning Jan 5, 1997. Reelected 2002, current term expires Jan 2009. Born Goshen New York July 24, 1948. Roman Catholic. Educated at University of South Florida B.A. 1969 and University of Florida J.D. 1975. Admitted to practice Florida 1976, U.S. District Court Middle District of Florida 1976, U.S. Court of Appeals Eleventh Circuit 1996 and U.S. Supreme Court. In legal practice Brandon 1976-96.

Member Family Law Inn of Court, Hillsborough Association of Women Lawyers, The Florida Bar, Brandon, Plant City and Hillsborough County Bar Associations. Staff Sergeant USAF 1969-73. Past President Kiwanis Club of Greater Brandon. Enjoys cycling, sailing, backpacking and music.

Office: 335 Hillsborough County Courthouse, 419 Pierce Street, Tampa 33602-4022.
Telephone: (813) 276-2059.
Fax: (813) 276-8015

STONE, Barry J. *(Judge, Florida District Court of Appeal Fourth District)* Assumed office 1986. Retained by election, current term expires Jan 2007. Chief Judge

STONE, BARRY J.—*Continued*

1997-99. Educated at University of Florida B.A. 1960 J.D. 1963. In legal practice 1963-79. Judge, Florida Circuit Court Seventeenth Judicial Circuit 1979-86.

President Florida Conference of District Court of Appeal Judges 1999. President Stephen R. Booher Inn of Court and North Broward Bar Association. Member Broward County Bar Association. Chairman Pompano Beach Planning Board. Member Broward County Mental Health Board.

Mailing address: P.O. Box 3315, West Palm Beach 33402-3315.

Office: 1525 Palm Beach Lakes Boulevard, West Palm Beach 33401.

Telephone: (561) 242-7222.

Fax: (561) 242-2100

STONE, William F. *(Judge, Florida Circuit Court First Judicial Circuit)*

Office: Okaloosa County Courthouse, 101 James Lee Boulevard, Crestview 32536.

Telephone: (850) 689-5735.

Fax: (850) 689-5749

STREITFELD, Jeffrey E. *(Judge, Florida Circuit Court Seventeenth Judicial Circuit)* Elected to term beginning Jan 1991. Reelected 1996 and 2002. Current term expires Jan 2009.

Office: 920 Broward County Courthouse, 201 S.E. Sixth Street, Fort Lauderdale 33301.

Telephone: (954) 831-7809.

Fax: (954) 831-5572

STRICKLAND, J. Tim *(Senior Judge, Florida Circuit Court Tenth Judicial Circuit)* Elected to term beginning 1976. Reelected to subsequent terms. Assumed Senior Judge status, serves by assignment. Born Tampa Florida Aug 17, 1939. Educated at Duke University A.B. in Economics 1962 and Emory University LL.B. 1966. Member Delta Theta Phi and Kappa Kappa Psi. In legal practice Lakeland 1967-73. Judge, St. Leo Municipal Court 1969-70. Judge, Lakeland Municipal Court 1971-72. Judge 1972-76 and Administrative Judge 1975-76, Polk County Court.

Assistant Solicitor Polk County 1968-69. Prosecutor Lakeland Municipal Court 1970-71 and Mulberry Municipal Court 1970-72. Mulberry City Attorney 1970-72. Member Academy of Florida Trial Lawyers, American Judicature Society, The Florida Bar (Committee on the Implementation of Article V), Polk County, Tenth Judicial Circuit and American Bar Associations. Attended Academy of Judicial Education 1972, Florida Institute for the Judiciary 1972, The National Judicial College 1973, 1976, 1978, and 1982 (Faculty Advisor 1984), County Judges College at Gainesville 1975 and County Judges Educational Conference at Tampa 1976. Nominated for Florida Municipal Court Judge's Award 1972 and American Bar Association's Annual Traffic Court Award 1972. Recipient Lakeland City Commission's Citation for Excellence in Judicial Administration as Lakeland Municipal Judge, Award for Judicial Services from Lakeland Police Benefit Association 1972 and Outstanding Young Man Award from Lakeland Jaycees 1972. Selected by Florida Supreme Court as member Bicentennial Committee of the Bar and Judiciary 1976. Established Polk County's first D.W.I. Rehabilitation Course. Introduced first Defensive Driving Course to Polk County Municipal Court 1972. Chairman Polk County March of Dimes 1969. Board member Lakeland YMCA 1970-72. Member Bartow Kiwanis Club, Elks Lodge 1291, Lakeland Jaycees 1967-71, Masonic Lodge 91 and First United Methodist Church of Lakeland.

Mailing address: P.O. Box 9000, Drawer J-133, Bartow 33831-9000.

Office: 255 North Broadway, Bartow 33830.

Telephone: (863) 534-4690.

STRICKLAND, Stan *(Judge, Florida Circuit Court Ninth Judicial Circuit)* Former Judge, Orange County Court.

Office: 1115 Orange County Courthouse, 425 North Orange Avenue, Orlando 32801.

Telephone: (407) 836-2121.

STRINGER, Thomas E., Sr. *(Judge, Florida District Court of Appeal Second District)* Term expires Jan 2007. Born Peekskill New York July 8, 1944. Episcopalian. Educated at New York University B.A. 1967 and Stetson University College of Law J.D. 1974. Admitted to practice Florida 1974, U.S. District Court Middle District of Florida 1974 and U.S. Court of Appeals Fifth Circuit 1977. In legal practice Tampa 1976-84. Judge, Hillsborough County Court 1984-88. Former Judge, Florida Circuit Court Thirteenth Judicial Circuit, appointed by Governor Bob Martinez to term beginning Jan 1988.

Life Member National Bar Association (Judicial Council). Member George Edgecomb Bar Association and Hillsborough County Bar Association. Captain USAF 1967-71.

Mailing address: 801 East Twiggs Street, Suite 600, Tampa 33602.

Telephone: (813) 272-3430.

Fax: (813) 229-6534

STROKER, R. James *(Judge, Florida Circuit Court Ninth Judicial Circuit)* Former Chief Judge. Former Judge, Orange County Court.

Office: 2030 Orange County Courthouse, 425 North Orange Avenue, Orlando 32801.

Telephone: (407) 836-2026.

STURGIS, Radford R. *(Judge, Lee County Court)* Appointed by Governor Robert Graham to term beginning Sept 8, 1981. Elected 1982, 1986, 1990, 1994 and 1998. Current term expires Jan 2005. Administrative Judge since 1984 and Administrative Juvenile Judge since Jan 1992. Former Chief Judge. Born Atlanta Georgia Aug 2, 1948. Presbyterian. Educated at St. Johns River Junior College A.A. 1968 and Florida State University B.A. 1970 J.D. 1973. Law Clerk to Hon. Everett Richardson, Florida Circuit Court Fourth Judicial Circuit 1971. Admitted to practice Florida 1973. Began legal practice Fort Myers 1973. In legal practice Cape Coral 1979-81.

Assistant State Attorney 1973-79. Author "Stop & Frisk" 1981 and "Drinking and Driving in Florida" 1986 Florida B. Jour. Important Decisions: State v. Rahn (D.U.I. is a misdemeanor) 1984; State v. Shell (incarceration of juveniles) 1985; and State v. Perrine (no sixth amendment right to counsel, D.U.I.) 1987. Instructor Florida Police Academy 1976-79. Member Florida Prosecuting Attorneys Association, National District Attorneys Association, The Florida Bar (Publication Chairman and Executive Counsel 1973 Criminal Law Section) and Lee County Bar Association (Secretary 1979 and President Elect 1981). Attended Florida Judicial College 1982

STURGIS, RADFORD R.—*Continued*
and The National Judicial College 1982-85. Captain USAR 1972-80. Previously worked in door-to-door sales, soda and paper delivery, restaurants and supermarkets. Political affiliation: Nonpartisan. Instructor Lee County School Board Adult Education Program 1977-84. Member Covenant Presbyterian Church (Elder and Deacon), Big Brothers, Mental Health Board and YMCA Junior Basketball Program. Enjoys golf, basketball, softball, volleyball, the stock market and reading nonfiction.

Office: Lee County Justice Center, 1700 Monroe Street, Fort Myers 33901.
Telephone: (239) 335-2278.
Fax: (239) 335-2587

SUAREZ, Richard J. *(Judge, Dade County Court)*
Office: Gerstein Justice Building, 1351 N.W. Twelfth Street, Miami 33125.
Telephone: (305) 548-5191.

SULLIVAN, Irene *(Judge, Florida Circuit Court Sixth Judicial Circuit)*
Office: Criminal Justice Center, 14250 49th Street North, Clearwater 33762.
Telephone: (727) 453-7103.
Fax: (727) 464-6744

SULLIVAN, Kirby *(Senior Judge, Glades County Court)* Elected to term beginning Jan 8, 1985. Reelected 1988 and 1992. Assumed Senior Judge status, serves by assignment. Born Brunswick County North Carolina Oct 2, 1927. Baptist. Educated at University of North Carolina A.B. 1948 J.D. 1950. Editor North Carolina Law Review 1948-50. Member Phi Beta Kappa. Admitted to practice North Carolina 1950, Florida 1970, U.S. District Court 1971 and U.S. Supreme Court 1971. Began legal practice Southport North Carolina 1950. In legal practice Winter Park and Orlando 1970 and Moore Haven 1979 Florida.

Solicitor Brunswick County North Carolina 1950-51. Author "Workmen's Compensation, Accidental Result, Sufficiency for Recovery" 27 North Carolina L. Rev. 599 June 1949 and "Restraint of Trade—Fair Trade Acts—Constitutionality" 28 North Carolina L. Rev. 336 April 1950. President Thirteenth Judicial District North Carolina Bar Association 1967-68. First Lieutenant U.S. Army JAGC 1951-53. USAR 1953-60. Democrat. North Carolina House of Representatives 1955-57. Chairman Brunswick County North Carolina Democratic Executive Committee 1958-60 and 1962-64. Member North Carolina State Democratic Executive Committee 1960-62 and 1964-66. Moderator Brunswick Baptist Association North Carolina 1964-66. Board of Trustees Cape Fear Technical Institute 1964-70 (Commencement Speaker 1967). Past District Governor Lions. Past State Vice President Jaycees. Life Member VFW and American Legion. Enjoys photography and travel.

Office: Charlotte County Justice Center, 350 East Marion Avenue, Punta Gorda 33950.
Telephone: (239) 335-2299.

SWANSON, Ronald *(Judge, Santa Rosa County Court)*
Office: Santa Rosa County Courthouse, 6865 S.W. Caroline Street, Milton 32570.
Telephone: (850) 623-0135.
Fax: (850) 983-1006

SWARTZ, Jeffrey D. *(Judge, Dade County Court)* Elected to term beginning Jan 3, 1995. Reelected 1998, current term expires Jan 2005.
Office: Miami Beach District Court, 1130 Washington Avenue, Miami Beach 33139.
Telephone: (305) 535-4240.
Fax: (305) 535-4235

SWIGERT, William Theron, Sr. *(Judge, Florida Circuit Court Fifth Judicial Circuit)* Appointed by Governor Reubin Askew to term beginning Sept 23, 1974. Elected 1980, 1986, 1992 and 1998. Current term expires Jan 2005. Chief Judge 1989 to June 30, 2001. Born Oak Park Illinois May 24, 1936. Educated at Florida State University B.S. 1958 and University of Florida College of Law J.D. with honors 1961, Symposium Editor University of Florida Law Review. Member Phi Alpha Delta. Admitted to practice Florida 1961, U.S. District Court, U.S. Court of Appeals Fifth Circuit, U.S. Supreme Court and U.S. Tax Court. In legal practice Ocala 1961-73. Judge, Marion County Court Aug 20, 1973 to Sept 22, 1974.

City Attorney Belleview 1963-70. City Prosecutor Ocala 1969-70. Author "Transfer of the Mortgagee's Interest in Florida" and "Dower in Florida" University of Florida L. Rev. Member Governor's Advisory Council to Department of Offender Rehabilitation 1977-79. President 1996-99 and Organizational and Charter Member D. R. Smith American Inn of Court. Board of Directors Public Policy Institute 1999. Member American Judicature Society, The Florida Bar, Marion County (Treasurer 1967, Vice President 1968 and President 1969) and American Bar Associations. Graduate National College of the State Judiciary 1974, American Academy of Judicial Education 1975, National College of Juvenile Justice 1977, Trial Judges Academy 1978, American Academy of Judicial Education 1984, Chief Judges Specialty Court 1992 and Statewide Pro-Bono Attorney Plan 1992. Attended "Economics for State Judges" University of Kansas 1998 and "Judicial Reasoning" American Academy of Judicial Education 2001. Listed in *Outstanding Young Men of America* 1965, 1969, 1970 and 1971, *Florida Lives* 1966 and *Who's Who in the South and Southwest* 1967-68 and 1969-70. Recipient Distinguished Service Award 1965 and Good Government Award 1973 from Ocala Jaycees, Resolution of Appreciation Award for Government Services from Ocala City Council 1973, Award for Outstanding Contribution to Criminal Justice System from Florida Council on Crime and Delinquency 1981 and Certificates of Appreciation from Drug Court and Teen Court Marion County Court Alternative Programs 1997, 1998, 1999 and 2000, Ocala Chess Club, Boy Scouts of America and Veterans of Foreign Wars. Captain USAR 1961-66. Mayor City of Ocala 1973-75. Chairman Multiple Sclerosis Drive 1970-73. Former Chairman Sunshine Christmas Festival. Former member Ocala Jaycees (Director, Vice President, President 1963-64). Director Boy Scouts of America and Ocala Civil Defense. Lifetime honorary member Florida Sheriffs Association. Member First United Methodist Church (Administrative Board, President Methodist Men's Club), Ocala-Marion County Chamber of Commerce, Committee of 100, Sigma Chi Alumni Club Florida State University (Director and President 1964-65, National Director 1971-72), Golden Hills Turf and Country Club, Metropolitan Dinner Club (Director), Eighth Street Elementary PTA (President 1965-66), Ocala Toastmasters Club, Kiwanis Club, Elks Club and University of Florida

SWIGERT, WILLIAM THERON, SR.—*Continued*

Alumni Association. Cub Scout leader. Enjoys handball, reading and traveling.

Mailing address: 110 N.W. First Avenue, Room 4017, Ocala 34475.

Office: Marion County Judicial Center, Ocala 34475.

Telephone: (352) 401-6763.

Fax: (352) 401-6789

TANNER, Sharon Howard *(Judge, Duval County Court)* Elected to term beginning Jan 8, 1985. Reelected 1988, 1992, 1996 and 2000. Current term expires Jan 2007. Born Jacksonville Florida June 11, 1952. Presbyterian. Educated at University of Florida B.S. 1974 J.D. 1978. Member Chi Omega. Admitted to practice Florida 1978. Began legal practice Jacksonville 1978.

Member The Florida Bar and Jacksonville Bar Association.

Office: Duval County Courthouse, 330 East Bay Street, Jacksonville 32202.

Telephone: (904) 630-2575.

Fax: (904) 630-2979

TARBUCK, Joseph Q. *(Senior Judge, Florida Circuit Court First Judicial Circuit)* Appointed by Governor Robert Graham July 30, 1982. Elected 1982, 1988 and 1994. Assumed Senior Judge status, serves by assignment. Educated at Florida State University B.S. 1957 and University of Florida LL.B. 1959. Admitted to practice Florida 1959. In legal practice Pensacola 1959-82.

Office: Judicial Building, 190 Governmental Center, Pensacola 32501.

Telephone: (850) 595-4400.

TAYLOR, Arthur Howard *(Senior Judge, Florida Circuit Court Eleventh Judicial Circuit)* Elected Nov 3, 1992 to term beginning Jan 5, 1993. Served Family Division. Assumed Senior Judge status, serves by assignment. Born Newton Massachusetts April 11, 1930. Presbyterian. Educated at Boston University A.A. 1950 J.D. 1954. Admitted to practice Florida 1959, U.S. Court of Appeals for the Armed Forces 1960, U.S. Supreme Court 1964 and U.S. Court of Appeals Eleventh Circuit 1981. In legal practice Miami 1975-92.

Member American Judges Association, The Florida Bar, Dade County (Chairman Legal Referral Committee) and American Bar Associations. Attended Florida Advanced Judicial College and numerous Florida Circuit Judges conferences. Lieutenant Colonel U.S. Army JAGC 1954-74 (Military Judge 1969-74). Member Miami Shores Code Enforcement 1982-87. Member Masons Village Lodge #315, Scottish Rite and Shriners.

Office: 511 Dade County Courthouse, 73 West Flagler Street, Miami 33130.

Telephone: (305) 349-7001.

TAYLOR, Carole Y. *(Judge, Florida District Court of Appeal Fourth District)* Assumed office 1998. Term expires Jan 2007. Educated at University of North Carolina B.A. 1971 J.D. 1974. Admitted to practice North Carolina 1974, Florida 1977, U.S. District Courts Northern and Southern Districts of Florida and Eastern and Middle Districts of North Carolina and U.S. Court of Appeals Eleventh Circuit. Judge, Broward County Court 1991-95. Judge, Florida Circuit Court Seventeenth Judicial Circuit March 13, 1995 to 1998.

Staff Attorney Legal Aid Society of Durham County 1974-76 and New Hanover Legal Services 1976-77. Associate University Attorney University of Florida 1977-79. Assistant Public Defender 1979-82. Assistant U.S. Attorney 1982-83. Vice President Florida Chapter National Bar Association 1980-81. Founding Member and Vice President T. J. Reddick Bar Association 1987. Member Florida Association of Women Lawyers, The Florida Bar, The North Carolina State Bar, Broward County, Palm Beach County and Federal Bar Associations. Board of Directors Boys and Girls Clubs of Broward County.

Mailing address: P.O. Box 3315, West Palm Beach 33402-3315.

Office: 1525 Palm Beach Lakes Boulevard, West Palm Beach 33401.

Telephone: (561) 242-2073.

Fax: (561) 242-2095

TAYLOR, L. Haldane *(Judge, Florida Circuit Court Fourth Judicial Circuit)* Assumed office June 10, 1991. Elected to subsequent terms. Former Judge, Duval County Court.

Office: Duval County Courthouse, 330 East Bay Street, Jacksonville 32202.

Telephone: (904) 630-2583.

Fax: (904) 630-2979

TAYLOR, Sandra F. *(Judge, Florida Circuit Court Sixteenth Judicial Circuit)* Former Chief Judge. Former Judge, Monroe County Court.

Office: 400 Monroe County Courthouse, 502 Whitehead Street, Key West 33040.

Telephone: (305) 292-3480.

Fax: (305) 292-3434

TENCH, Benjamin M. *(Senior Judge, Florida Circuit Court Eighth Judicial Circuit)* Elected to term beginning 1973. Former Chief Judge. Assumed Senior Judge status, serves by assignment. Born Gainesville Florida Oct 23, 1919. Educated at University of Florida B.A. 1941 and University of Virginia LL.B. 1947. Admitted to practice Virginia 1948 and Florida 1949. Gainesville Municipal Judge 1949-54. Judge, Alachua County Felony Court of Record 1971-73.

Assistant State Attorney Eighth Judicial Circuit of Florida 1959-62. Special Assistant Attorney General of Florida 1967-68. Assistant Public Defender Eighth Judicial Circuit of Florida 1968-69. Member The Florida Bar and Eighth Judicial Circuit Bar Association. Major USAS 1941-47. U.S. Foreign Service 1962-66. Democrat. Member First Presbyterian Church. Enjoys reading, tennis and golf.

Office: Alachua County Courthouse, 201 East University Avenue, Gainesville 32601.

Telephone: (352) 374-3648.

TEPPER, Lynn *(Judge, Florida Circuit Court Sixth Judicial Circuit)* Elected July 1988. Reelected 1994 and 2000. Current term expires Jan 2007. Born Amityville New York Aug 7, 1952. Jewish. Educated at Bard College B.A. 1974 and Stetson University College of Law J.D. 1977. Law Clerk to Chief Bankruptcy Judge Alexander Paskay, U.S. District Court Middle District of Florida. Admitted to practice Florida 1977, U.S. District Court Middle District of Florida 1977, U.S. Court of Appeals Eleventh Circuit 1977 and U.S. Supreme Court 1987. In legal practice Hudson and Port Richey 1980-84. Judge, Pasco County Court 1985-88.

Published in Family Law Quarterly Florida Bar Journal. Member The Florida Bar (Alternative Dispute Reso-

TEPPER, LYNN—*Continued*

lution Committee 1988, Steering Committee for CLE Manual on Arbitration in Florida 1988-90, Bench/Bar Commission 1990-91, Bench/Bar Implementation Commission 1992-95) and American Bar Association (Standing Committee on Law and Literacy since 1993). Florida Representative "Equal Justice" 1993, "Mental Health and Development Disabilities and Defendants" 1994 and "The Child Tribal Welfare Act" 1994 The National Judicial College. Faculty Member Criminal Law Florida Advanced Judicial Studies College 1993-97 and American Academy of Judicial Education 1997. Presenter Annual Meeting American Bar Association 1994. Inducted into Berner High School Hall of Fame 1987. Named Humanitarian of the Year by Florida Animal Control Association 1988, Woman of the Year by Calusa Business & Professional Women 1988-89, Public Citizen of the Year by Tampa Bay Unit National Association of Social Workers 1991 and Public Citizen of the Year by Florida Literacy Coalition 1994. Recipient Law Enforcement Commendation by Sons of the American Revolution 1990 and Broken Slingshot Award from San Antonio Boys' Village 1990. Board of Governors Bard College 1982-92. Member Multi-Agency Coordinating Council since 1987, Commission on Minimum Standards for Batterer's Intervention Program since 1994 and Florida Domestic Violence Implementation Task Force 1994-97. President Probationer's Educational Growth of Florida since 1992. Enjoys snow skiing, traveling and reading.

Office: 106C Dade City Courthouse, 38053 Live Oak Avenue, Dade City 33523.

Telephone: (352) 521-4370.

Fax: (352) 521-4107

TERRELL, Terry D. *(Judge, Florida Circuit Court First Judicial Circuit)* Appointed by Governor Lawton Chiles Feb 18, 1992 to term beginning March 20, 1992. Elected 1992 and 1998. Current term expires Jan 2005. Born Seattle Washington June 21, 1948. Catholic. Educated at University of West Florida B.A. with honors 1973 and Florida State University J.D. 1976. Admitted to practice Florida 1977, U.S. District Court Northern District of Florida 1979, U.S. Supreme Court 1980 and U.S. Court of Appeals Eleventh Circuit 1981. In legal practice Pensacola 1979.

Assistant Public Defender 1977-79 and Chief Assistant Public Defender 1979-92 First Judicial Circuit. Adjunct Professor of Tort and Juvenile Law University of West Florida 1980-85. Member Children's Court Improvement Committee 1998-2002 and Family Court Steering Committee. President Pensacola Inn of Court American Inns of Court 2000-02. Mentor Judge Coordinator First Circuit. Former Member Florida Public Defender Association. Honorary Member Pensacola Criminal Defense Attorneys Association (Charter Director). Member Escambia-Santa Rosa Bar Association. Lecturer Death Penalty Seminars Florida Public Defender Association 1980-91. Faculty Member Juvenile Law Florida College of Advanced Judicial Studies 1993-2000. Served to First Lieutenant U.S. Army 1966-69. President, Vice President, Treasurer and Member Community Drug and Alcohol Commission 1980-92. Member Juvenile Justice Board 1992-95 and Escambia County Juvenile Justice Council 1992-95. Enjoys skiing, traveling, flying and playing golf.

Office: M.C. Blanchard Judicial Building, 190 West Government Street, Pensacola 32501.

Telephone: (850) 595-4464.

Fax: (850) 595-0392

THARPE, Chet A. *(Judge, Florida Circuit Court Thirteenth Judicial Circuit)* Elected to term beginning Jan 1991. Reelected 1996 and 2002. Current term expires Jan 2009.

Office: 317 Tower, 801 East Twiggs Street, Tampa 33602-3554.

Telephone: (813) 272-6850.

THOMAS, Cheryl K. *(Judge, Hillsborough County Court)* Appointed by Governor Jeb Bush to term beginning Jan 2001. Elected 2002, current term expires Jan 2009. Born Tampa Florida Aug 11, 1958. Educated at Hillsborough Community College A.A. 1977 and University of Florida B.A. 1979 J.D. 1981. Admitted to practice Florida 1982 and U.S. District Court Middle District of Florida 1993. In legal practice Tampa July 1993 to June 1997.

Assistant State Attorney Feb 1983 to May 1984 Orange County and Osceola County and May 1984 to May 1986 Pinellas County and Pasco County. Senior Trial Attorney Florida Department of Transportation Oct 1989 to July 1992. Bar Counsel The Florida Bar July 1992 to June 1993. Litigation and Trial Attorney Office of the Attorney General June 1997 to Jan 3, 2001. Co-chair Membership Committee Hillsborough County Bar 1992. Member Hillsborough Association of Women Lawyers, George Edgecomb Bar, The Florida Bar (Grievance Committee 13 E 1998) and National Bar Association. Captain U.S. Army JAGC July 1986 to June 1992.

Office: 204 Hillsborough County Courthouse, 419 Pierce Street, Tampa 33602.

THOMAS, Patricia V. *(Judge, Florida Circuit Court Fifth Judicial Circuit)*

Office: 311 Citrus County Courthouse, 110 North Apopka Avenue, Inverness 34450.

Telephone: (352) 341-6701.

Fax: (352) 341-6796

THOMAS, Teretha L. *(Judge, Dade County Court)*

Office: 1-4 Coral Gables District Court, 3100 Ponce De Leon, Miami 33134.

Telephone: (305) 569-2506.

THOMPSON, Emerson R., Jr. *(Chief Judge, Florida District Court of Appeal Fifth District)* Assumed office March 15, 1993. Retained by election, current term expires Jan 2007. Chief Judge since 2000. Educated at University of Florida B.A. 1970 and Florida State University J.D. 1973. Judge, Orange County Court 1976-80. Judge 1980-93 and Chief Judge 1989-91, Florida Circuit Court Ninth Judicial Circuit.

Assistant State Attorney Ninth Judicial District 1973-76. Former Adjunct Professor Valencia Community College. Founder and Past President American Inns of Court #123. Former Member Executive Committee Florida Conference of Circuit Court Judges and Commission on Racial and Ethnic Bias Florida Supreme Court. Member American Judicature Society, Paul C. Perkins Bar Association, The Florida Bar, Orange County and

THOMPSON, EMERSON R., JR.—*Continued*

National (Florida Chapter) Bar Associations. Faculty Member The National Judicial College since 1987.

Office: 300 South Beach Street, Daytona Beach 32114.
Telephone: (386) 947-1576.
Fax: (386) 947-4138

THOMPSON, James R. *(Judge, Florida Circuit Court Twentieth Judicial Circuit)* Former Judge, Lee County Court.

Office: Lee County Justice Center, 1700 Monroe Street, Fort Myers 33901.
Telephone: (239) 335-2831.
Fax: (239) 335-2264

THORPE, Janet C. *(Judge, Florida Circuit Court Ninth Judicial Circuit)*

Office: 1720 Orange County Courthouse, 425 North Orange Avenue, Orlando 32801.
Telephone: (407) 836-1486.
Fax: (407) 835-5030

THREADGILL, Edward F. *(Senior Judge, Florida District Court of Appeal)* Former Chief Judge. Assumed Senior Judge status, serves by assignment. Former Judge, Polk County Court. Former Judge, Florida Circuit Court Tenth Judicial Circuit.

Office: 1005 East Memorial Boulevard, Lakeland 33801.
Telephone: (863) 499-2290.

TIMMERMAN, Wayne S. *(Judge, Florida Circuit Court Thirteenth Judicial Circuit)*

Office: 364 Hillsborough County Courthouse, 419 Pierce Street, Tampa 33602-4022.
Telephone: (813) 307-4751.

TINLIN, Charles J. *(Judge, St. Johns County Court)* Elected Nov 1990 to term beginning Jan 8, 1991. Reelected July 1994 and 1998. Current term expires Jan 2005. Born Fort Wayne Indiana Jan 12, 1955. Protestant. Educated at Flagler College B.A. 1979 and California Western School of Law J.D. 1985. Admitted to practice Florida 1985, U.S. District Court Middle District of Florida 1985 and U.S. Tax Court 1986. In legal practice St. Augustine 1985-87.

Assistant State Attorney St. Augustine 1987-90.

Office: St. Johns County Judicial Center, 4010 Lewis Speedway, St. Augustine 32095.
Telephone: (904) 823-2378.

TITUS, Becky A. *(Judge, Florida Circuit Court Twelfth Judicial Circuit)* Former Judge, Sarasota County Court.

Mailing address: P.O. Box 48927, Sarasota 34230.
Office: 2002 Ringling Boulevard, Sarasota 34237.
Telephone: (941) 861-7898.
Fax: (941) 861-7911

TOBIN, David L. *(Senior Judge, Florida Circuit Court Eleventh Judicial Circuit)* Appointed by Governor Bob Martinez to term beginning Sept 1987. Elected 1988 and 1994. Assumed Senior Judge status, serves by assignment. Born Miami Florida Jan 5, 1928. Educated at University of Miami B.S.E.S. 1949 J.D. 1961. Member Phi Alpha Delta. Admitted to practice Florida 1961, U.S. District Court 1961 and U.S. Supreme Court 1965. In legal practice Miami 1961-87.

Instructor in Trial Practice Dade Community College 1988-90. Board of Directors Coral Gables Bar Association 1964 and Dade County Bar Association 1974. USAFR 1950-55.

Office: 511 Dade County Courthouse, 73 West Flagler Street, Miami 33130.
Telephone: (305) 349-7001.

TOBIN, Victor *(Judge, Florida Circuit Court Seventeenth Judicial Circuit)*

Office: 5910 Broward County Courthouse, 201 S.E. Sixth Street, Fort Lauderdale 33301.
Telephone: (954) 831-6332.

TODD, Alan C. *(Judge, Orange County Court)* Appointed by Governor Bob Martinez to term beginning Jan 29, 1990. Elected to subsequent terms.

Office: 420 Orange County Courthouse, 425 North Orange Avenue, Orlando 32801.
Telephone: (407) 836-2266.

TOLTON, William Jeremiah, Jr. *(Judge, Florida Circuit Court First Judicial Circuit)* Appointed by Governor Reubin Askew to term beginning Aug 1, 1976. Elected 1976, 1982, 1988, 1994 and 2000. Current term expires Jan 2007. Born Pensacola Florida Dec 9, 1937. Methodist. Educated at Washington and Lee University B.A. 1960 LL.B. 1964. Admitted to practice Florida 1965. In legal practice Fort Walton Beach 1965-76.

Attorney Okaloosa County Commissioners 1968-72. City Attorney Valparaiso 1970-72. Part-time Instructor in Business Law Okaloosa-Walton Junior College 1965-66. Member The Florida Bar and Okaloosa-Walton Bar Association (honorary). Democrat. Florida State Representative 1972-76. Enjoys golf, tennis and reading.

Office: Okaloosa County Courthouse Annex, Box 15, 1250 North Eglin Parkway, Shalimar 32579-1234.
Telephone: (850) 651-7482.
Fax: (850) 651-7334

TOMBRINK, Richard, Jr. *(Judge, Florida Circuit Court Fifth Judicial Circuit)* Appointed by Governor Bob Martinez Dec 1, 1988 to term beginning Jan 20, 1989. Elected Nov 4, 1990, Nov 1996 and Nov 2002. Current term expires Jan 2009. Administrative Judge Hernando County since 1989. Organized and presided over initial Drug Court and Domestic Violence Court Hernando County. Born Brooksville Florida April 18, 1950. Roman Catholic. Educated at Florida State University B.S. cum laude 1972 and University of Florida J.D. 1977. Member Phi Delta Phi. Admitted to practice Florida 1977 and U.S. District Court Middle District of Florida 1978. In legal practice Brooksville 1977-88.

Author Chapter 23 "Interpleader" *Florida Civil Practice Before Trial* 5th ed. 1999 and Chapter 2 "Grounds for Dissolution and Effect of Fault" *Florida Dissolution of Marriage* I 6th ed. 2002 The Florida Bar CLE. Charter President Citrus-Hernando Inns of Court. Former Member Academy of Florida Trial Lawyers and The Association of Trial Lawyers of America. Member American Judges Association, American Judicature Society, The Florida Bar, Hernando County (President 1980), Tri-County (Secretary 1982) and American Bar Associations. Named Boss of the Year by Hernando County Legal Secretaries Association 1980 and by American Business Woman's Association 1987. Listed in *Marquis' Who's Who of Emerging Leaders of America* 1990 and *Who's Who in American Law* 1996-97. Participated as Associate Judge on the Florida District Court of Appeals Fifth District Nov 1996. E-4 U.S. Army 1973-75. For-

TOMBRINK, RICHARD, JR.—*Continued*

mer Member Board of Directors Pasco-Hernando Community College Foundation, Inc. Former Member Committee of 100, Downtown Development Association and Hernando County Historical Association. Member Chamber of Commerce, Florida Conservation Association, Red Mule Runners and Kiwanis. Enjoys all sports, gardening and reading.

Office: 20 North Main Street, Room 359, Brooksville 34601.

Telephone: (352) 754-4280.

TORPY, Vincent G., Jr. *(Judge, Florida District Court of Appeal Fifth District)* Former Judge, Florida Circuit Court Eighteenth Judicial Circuit.

Office: 300 South Beach Street, Daytona Beach 32114.

Telephone: (386) 947-1522.

Fax: (386) 947-1565

TOWNSEND, Richard R. *(Judge, Clay County Court)* Appointed by Governor Lawton Chiles Nov 18, 1993 to term beginning Jan 1994. Elected 1998, current term expires Jan 2005. Born Buffalo New York Nov 14, 1947. Educated at Centre College of Kentucky B.A. 1969 and Florida State University College of Law J.D. with honors 1972. Admitted to practice Florida 1972. In legal practice 1975-93. U.S. Army JAGC 1972-75.

Mailing address: P.O. Box 1018, Green Cove Springs 32043.

Office: Clay County Courthouse, Green Cove Springs 32043.

Telephone: (904) 278-4730.

Fax: (904) 278-4728

TRACHMAN, Lisa G. *(Judge, Broward County Court)* Elected to term beginning Jan 3, 1995. Reelected 1998, current term expires Jan 2005.

Office: 453 Broward County Courthouse, 201 S.E. Sixth Street, Fort Lauderdale 33301.

Telephone: (954) 831-6033.

Fax: (954) 831-5572

TRAWICK, Daryl E. *(Judge, Florida Circuit Court Eleventh Judicial Circuit)* Former Judge, Dade County Court.

Office: 711 Gerstein Justice Building, 1351 N.W. Twelfth Street, Miami 33125.

Telephone: (305) 548-5110.

Fax: (305) 548-5610

TRAYNOR, J. Michael *(Judge, Florida Circuit Court Seventh Judicial Circuit)*

Office: St. Johns County Judicial Center, 4010 Lewis Speedway, St. Augustine 32095.

Telephone: (904) 823-2386.

Fax: (904) 823-2393

TROWBRIDGE, C. Pfeiffer *(Senior Judge, Florida Circuit Court Nineteenth Judicial Circuit)* Elected to term beginning Dec 29, 1960. Reelected to subsequent terms. Former Chief Judge. Assumed Senior Judge status, serves by assignment. Born Ottawa Illinois Aug 24, 1928. Congregationalist. Educated at Denison University B.A. 1950 and University of Virginia J.D. 1953. Editor-in-Chief Virginia Law Review 1952-53. Member Phi Delta Phi, Scribes and Order of the Coif. Admitted to practice Virginia 1952 and Florida 1956. Began legal practice Stuart Florida 1956.

Author "Domicile Problems of Winter Residents" 11 Miami Law Quarterly 375, 1957, reprinted in 7 L. Rev. Digest 33, 1957; "Priorities Between Construction Mortgages and Mechanics' Liens" 35 Florida B. Jour. 178, 1961; "Male Inequities in Family Law" 37 Florida B. Jour. 1022, 1963; "Mimeograph Divorce Cases" 37 Florida B. Jour. 10, 1965; and "Computerization of Divorce Cases" 45 Florida B. Jour. 18, 1971. Contributor Chapter on Factors and Commission Merchants Vol. 10, 1959, Chapter on Master and Servant and Chapter on Mayhem Vol. 16, 1961, Chapter on Rape Vol. 20, 1963, Chapter on Sundays and Holidays Vol. 22, 1964, and Chapter on Usages and Customs Vol. 24, 1965 *Florida Law & Practice.* Member The Florida Bar, Martin County (President 1960) and Virginia Bar Associations. First Lieutenant U.S. Army JAGC 1953-56. Member Rotary Club, Civil Air Patrol, U.S. Coast Guard Auxiliary, Masons (Florida and Ohio), Mensa and Intertel.

Office: 218 South Second Street, Fort Pierce 34950.

Telephone: (772) 462-1472.

TUNIS, Dava J. *(Judge, Dade County Court)*

Office: 236 Courthouse Center, 175 N.W. First Avenue, Miami 33128.

Telephone: (305) 349-5702.

TURNER, Eugene C. *(Judge, Collier County Court)* Appointed by Governor Robert Graham to term beginning Jan 1983. Elected 1984, 1988, 1992, 1996 and 2000. Current term expires Jan 2007. Born Farmville Virginia July 20, 1944. Methodist. Educated at University of South Florida B.A. 1966 and University of Baltimore J.D. 1974. Admitted to practice Florida 1976. In legal practice Naples 1977-84.

Assistant State Attorney Twentieth Judicial Circuit 1974-77. Member The Association of Trial Lawyers of America, Collier County (Director 1979, Treasurer 1980) and American (Sections: Family Law, Criminal Justice, Real Property, Probate and Trust Law, Taxation) Bar Associations. Attended The National Judicial College 1985. Assistant County Planner Pinellas County 1967-68. Junior high school teacher Hillsborough County 1969. Board of Directors and President 1987 North Naples Rotary. Director North Naples United Methodist Church. Member Boy Scouts of America (Membership Committee). President Child Protection Team. Enjoys snow skiing, jogging and marathon running.

Office: Collier County Government Complex, Bldg. L, 3301 Tamiami Trail East, Naples 34112.

Telephone: (239) 774-8125.

Fax: (239) 774-9654

TURNER, George B. *(Judge, Brevard County Court)*

Office: Moore Justice Center, Third Floor, 2825 Judge Fran Jamieson Way, Viera 32940.

Telephone: (321) 617-7284.

Fax: (321) 617-7278

TURNER, Larry Gibbs *(Judge, Florida Circuit Court Eighth Judicial Circuit)*

Office: 415 Alachua County Courthouse, 201 East University Avenue, Gainesville 32601.

Telephone: (352) 337-6137.

Fax: (352) 374-5238

TURNER, Thomas W. *(Judge, Florida Circuit Court Ninth Judicial Circuit)*

Office: Orange County Courthouse, 425 North Orange Avenue, Orlando 32801.

TURNOFF, William C. *(Magistrate Judge, United States District Court Southern District of Florida)* Appointed by U.S. District Court judges to term beginning Feb 24, 1986. Reappointed 1994 and 2002. Current term expires 2010. Chief Magistrate Judge 1994-97. Born Philadelphia Pennsylvania Nov 19, 1948. Jewish. Educated at Franklin & Marshall College A.B. cum laude 1970 and Cornell University J.D. 1973. Associate Editor Cornell International Law Journal 1971-73. Member Phi Beta Kappa, Pi Gamma Mu and Phi Alpha Theta. Admitted to practice Pennsylvania 1973 and Florida 1977.

Assistant District Attorney Philadelphia 1973-80. Assistant U.S. Attorney Miami 1980-86 (Chief Major Crimes Section 1982-86). Member 1983-86 and Chairman 1985-86 Grievance Committee The Florida Bar. Recipient Special Achievement Awards from Department of Justice 1983 and 1986, Honor Award from U.S. Secret Service 1986, Judicial Distinction Award from Florida Association of Criminal Defense Lawyers 1992 and Judicial Community Service Award from Greater Miami Jewish Federation 1999. Board of Directors 1987-94, Vice President 1990-91 and President 1991-92 Bench-Bar Unit B'nai B'rith.

Office: U.S. Courthouse, 300 N.E. First Avenue, Miami 33132.
Telephone: (305) 523-5710.

TYGART, Frederick B. *(Judge, Florida Circuit Court Fourth Judicial Circuit)*
Office: Duval County Courthouse, 330 East Bay Street, Jacksonville 32202.
Telephone: (904) 630-2536.
Fax: (904) 630-2979

ULMER, Ray E., Jr. *(Judge, Florida Circuit Court Sixth Judicial Circuit)* Former Chief Judge.
Office: 200 Judicial Building, 545 First Avenue North, St. Petersburg 33701.
Telephone: (727) 582-7733.
Fax: (727) 582-7409

UNGARO-BENAGES, Ursula M. *(Judge, United States District Court Southern District of Florida)* Appointed for life by President George Bush to term beginning 1992. Born Miami Beach Florida Jan 29, 1951. Educated at University of Miami B.A. 1973 and University of Florida J.D. 1975. In legal practice Miami 1976-87. Judge, Florida Circuit Court Eleventh Judicial Circuit 1987-92.
Office: Federal Courthouse Square, 301 North Miami Avenue, Miami 33128-7788.
Telephone: (305) 523-5550.

VACCARO, Dorothy L. *(Judge, Pinellas County Court)*
Office: Pinellas County Courthouse, 14250 49th Street North, Clearwater 33762.
Telephone: (727) 453-7262.
Fax: (727) 464-6484

VAN NORTWICK, William A., Jr. *(Judge, Florida District Court of Appeal First District)* Appointed by Governor Lawton Chiles June 17, 1994. Retained by election. Born Morehead City North Carolina Aug 21, 1945. Educated at Duke University A.B 1967 and University of Florida J.D. with honors 1970. Executive Editor University of Florida Law Review 1968-70. In legal practice Jacksonville 1970-94.

Board of Directors 1982-87 and President 1985-87 Florida Legal Services. Fellow Florida Bar Foundation (Board of Directors 1985-94 and President 1993-94) and American Bar Foundation. Member American Judicature Society, The Florida Bar and American Bar Association. Board of Directors Jacksonville Track Club 1977-81 and Child Development Services of Northeast Florida, Inc. (Head Start) 1990-91. Board of Directors since 1990 and Treasurer 1994 Florida-Georgia Blood Alliance, Inc. (Blood Bank). Race Director River Run 15,000, 1980. Member Leadership Jacksonville, Jacksonville Art Museum and Rotary Club.

Office: 301 Martin Luther King Jr. Boulevard, Tallahassee 32399-1850.
Telephone: (850) 487-1000.
Fax: (850) 921-4768

VAUGHN, Dan L. *(Judge, Florida Circuit Court Nineteenth Judicial Circuit)* Former Judge, St. Lucie County Court, elected to term beginning Jan 1991.
Office: 216 Courthouse Addition, 218 South Second Street, Fort Pierce 34950.
Telephone: (772) 462-1462.
Fax: (772) 462-1456

VENZER, Ellen Sue *(Judge, Dade County Court)* Elected to term beginning Jan 3, 1995. Reelected 1998, current term expires Jan 2005.
Office: 1-6 Coral Gables District Court, 3100 Ponce de Leon, Coral Gables 33134.
Telephone: (305) 569-2502.

VERNON, Susan *(Judge, Monroe County Court)* Elected to term beginning Jan 1991. Reelected 1994 and 1998. Current term expires Jan 2005.
Office: Monroe County Courthouse Annex, Third Floor, 500 Whitehead Street, Key West 33040.
Telephone: (305) 292-3517.
Fax: (305) 292-3434

VILLANTI, Craig C. *(Judge, Florida Circuit Court Sixth Judicial Circuit)*
Office: 104 West Pasco Judicial Center, 7530 Little Road, New Port Richey 34654.
Telephone: (727) 847-8922.
Fax: (727) 847-8924

VINSON, Roger *(Chief Judge, United States District Court Northern District of Florida)* Appointed for life by President Ronald Reagan to term beginning Nov 4, 1983. Born Cadiz Kentucky Feb 19, 1940. Baptist. Educated at U.S. Naval Academy B.S. 1962 and Vanderbilt University J.D. 1971. Wilson Merit Scholar 1969-71. Staff member Vanderbilt Law Review 1969-71. Admitted to practice Florida 1971. Began legal practice Pensacola 1971. Lieutenant (aviator) USN 1962-68.
Office: 517 U.S. Courthouse, One North Palafox Street, Pensacola 32501-5625.
Telephone: (850) 435-8444.

VITALE, Linda *(Judge, Florida Circuit Court Seventeenth Judicial Circuit)*
Office: 998 Broward County Courthouse, 201 S.E. Sixth Street, Fort Lauderdale 33301.
Telephone: (954) 831-7779.
Fax: (954) 831-5572

VITUNAC, Ann E. *(Magistrate Judge, United States District Court Southern District of Florida)* Appointed by U.S. District Court judges.
Office: 423 Federal Building, 701 Clematis Street, West Palm Beach 33401.
Telephone: (561) 803-3440.

VOGEL, Christine K. *(Judge, Hillsborough County Court)*
Office: 9 County Office Building, Plant City 33566.
Telephone: (813) 757-3846.

VOLZ, Edward J., Jr. *(Judge, Lee County Court)* Elected July 1990 to term beginning Jan 1991. Reelected 1994 and 1998. Current term expires Jan 2005. Born Bronx New York May 8, 1946. Roman Catholic. Educated at Villanova University B.S. 1968 and Fordham University J.D. 1971. Admitted to practice New York 1971, Florida 1982 and U.S. District Courts Eastern and Southern Districts of New York and Middle District of Florida.
Assistant District Attorney Suffolk County New York 1972-74 and 1978-83. Assistant Town Attorney Islip New York 1976-78. Assistant State Attorney Twentieth Judicial Circuit Florida 1983-90. Assistant U.S. Attorney Middle District of Florida 1988-90. Adjunct Professor Florida Gulf Coast University since 1986 and Edison Community College. Circuit Representative Florida Conference of County Court Judges. Member The Florida Bar, Lee County and New York State Bar Associations. Counsel to Legislature Suffolk County New York 1974-76. Developed and presides over Lee County Adult Drug Court Program. Past President and Former Treasurer Fort Myers Lions Club. Former Chairman and Former Member Lee County Finance and Housing Authority. Former Member Board of Directors Swim Florida. Former Member Board of Directors and Coach Fort Myers Little League. Advisory Board Criminal Justice Program Florida Gulf Coast University. Member Advisory Committee Paralegal Program Edison Community College. Volunteer Judge Teen Court. Active in Drug Awareness Program Elks Lodge #1288. Nationally Certified Swimming Official U.S. Swimming.
Office: Lee County Justice Center, 1700 Monroe Street, Fort Myers 33901.
Telephone: (239) 335-2860.
Fax: (239) 335-2588

VONHOF, Gary L. *(Judge, Florida Circuit Court Fifteenth Judicial Circuit)* Assumed office Jan 2, 1990. Elected to subsequent terms. Current term expires Jan 2009. Born Rochester New York March 6, 1941. United Methodist. Educated at Calvin College B.A. 1969 and Syracuse University College of Law J.D. 1972. Admitted to practice Florida 1972. In legal practice West Palm Beach 1972-87. Judge, Palm Beach County Court 1987-89, appointed by Governor Robert Martinez. USAF 1959-63.
Office: South County Courthouse, 200 West Atlantic Avenue, Delray Beach 33444.
Telephone: (561) 274-1430.

WALKER, David Seth *(Senior Judge, Florida Circuit Court Sixth Judicial Circuit)* Elected 1972 to term beginning Jan 2, 1973. Reelected 1978, 1984, 1990 and 1996. Assumed Senior Judge status, serves by assignment. Born Atlanta Georgia Sept 12, 1940. Catholic. Educated at Wake Forest University B.A. 1962 and Stetson University LL.B. 1965. College Chapel Speaker. Admitted to practice Florida 1965. Began legal practice St. Petersburg 1965. Judge, Pinellas County Court Jan 1971 to 1972. Visiting Judge, Florida District Court of Appeal Second District 1973.
Assistant State Attorney 1968-70. Important Decisions: Reorganization of Guardianship Rules & Procedures 1972, Approval of Pinellas County Dual Taxation Plan 1975, Ruling upon Constitutionality of Pinellas Planning Council 1976 and Propriety of Zoning of Wetlands for Esthetic and Environmental Purposes 1978. Member Association of Florida Trial Lawyers, The Association of Trial Lawyers of America, Pinellas County Trial Lawyers Association, American Judicature Society, The Florida Bar, St. Petersburg and American Bar Associations. Gulfport City Councilman 1968-70. President Science Center of Pinellas County 1967-69. Director Child and Family Developmental Center 1968-76. Chairman Troop Committee Boy Scouts of America. Member Sertoma International, St. Petersburg Yacht Club and Aircraft Owners and Pilots Association. Enjoys home repair, canoeing, golf, reading and photography.
Office: Judicial Building, 545 First Avenue North, St. Petersburg 33701.
Telephone: (727) 464-4470.

WALKER, Jill C. *(Judge, Wakulla County Court)* Elected to term beginning Jan 1991. Reelected 1994 and 1998. Current term expires Jan 2005.
Office: Wakulla County Courthouse, 3056 Crawfordville Highway, Crawfordville 32327.
Telephone: (850) 926-0943.
Fax: (850) 926-5117

WALLACE, Waddell A., III *(Judge, Florida Circuit Court Fourth Judicial Circuit)*
Office: Duval County Courthouse, 330 East Bay Street, Jacksonville 32202.
Telephone: (904) 630-7154.
Fax: (904) 630-2979

WALLER, Margaret T. *(Judge, Florida Circuit Court Ninth Judicial Circuit)* Former Judge, Osceola County Court.
Office: Two Courthouse Square, Suite 6465, Kissimmee 34741.
Telephone: (407) 343-2499.
Fax: (407) 343-2401

WALSH, J. David *(Judge, Florida Circuit Court Seventh Judicial Circuit)* Appointed by Governor Jeb Bush Feb 26, 2001. Elected 2002, current term expires Jan 6, 2009. Educated at Wake Forest University 1977.
Office: 304 Courthouse Annex, 125 East Orange Avenue, Daytona Beach 32114.
Telephone: (386) 257-6091.
Fax: (386) 257-6077

WALSH, Thomas J., Jr. *(Judge, St. Lucie County Court)*
Office: 250 N.W. Country Club Drive, Port St. Lucie 34986.
Telephone: (772) 871-5339.
Fax: (772) 871-5340

WARD, Diane V. *(Judge, Florida Circuit Court Eleventh Judicial Circuit)*
Office: 208 Juvenile Justice Center, 3300 N.W. 27th Avenue Miami 33142.
Telephone: (305) 638-6234.

WARNER, Martha C. *(Judge, Florida District Court of Appeal Fourth District)* Assumed office 1989. Chief Judge July 1, 1999 to June 30, 2001. Educated at Colorado College B.A. magna cum laude 1971, University of Chicago Law School 1971-72, University of Florida College of Law J.D. with high honors 1974 and University of Virginia LL.M. in Judicial Process 1995. Editorial Board University of Florida Law Review. Member Phi Beta Kappa, Phi Kappa Phi and Order of the Coif. Admitted to practice Florida 1974, U.S. Court of Appeals Eleventh Circuit 1982 and U.S. Supreme Court 1985. In legal practice 1974-85. Judge, Florida Circuit Court Nineteenth Judicial Circuit 1986-88.

Member American Inns of Court, The Florida Bar and Martin County Bar Association. Chair Board of Directors Presbyterian Early Learning School 1981-87. Board of Directors Martin County Unit American Heart Association 1982-89 and Martin County Council for the Arts 1996-99. Chair High School Juried Art Shows 1997-99. Deacon First United Presbyterian Church 1987-91. Member Chancel Choir Palm Presbyterian Church.

Mailing address: P.O. Box 3315, West Palm Beach 33402-3315.

Office: 1525 Palm Beach Lakes Boulevard, West Palm Beach 33401.

Telephone: (561) 242-2023.

Fax: (561) 242-2016

WARREN, Stasia *(Judge, Volusia County Court)* Elected to term beginning Jan 1991. Reelected 1994 and 1998. Current term expires Jan 2005.

Office: Justice Center, 251 North Ridgewood Avenue, Daytona Beach 32114.

Telephone: (386) 239-7855.

Fax: (386) 239-7833

WATSON, John W., III *(Judge, Florida Circuit Court Seventh Judicial Circuit)* Appointed by Governor Robert Graham to term beginning Nov 3, 1986. Elected to subsequent terms. Current term expires Jan 2005. Born Los Angeles California June 16, 1944. Baptist. Educated at Orlando Junior College A.A. 1964, Florida Southern College B.A. 1967 and Florida State University J.D. 1970. Member Phi Delta Phi. Admitted to practice Florida 1970. In legal practice Ormond Beach and Daytona Beach Dec 1974 to Dec 1984.

Assistant State Attorney Seventh Judicial Circuit Aug 1973 to Nov 1986. Member The Florida Bar.

Office: Courthouse Annex, 125 East Orange Avenue, Daytona Beach 32114.

Telephone: (386) 257-6072.

Fax: (386) 248-8122

WATSON, Richard O. *(Senior Judge, Florida Circuit Court Seventh Judicial Circuit)* Appointed by Governor Reubin Askew to term beginning June 10, 1977. Elected 1978, 1984 and 1990. Former Chief Judge. Assumed Senior Judge status, serves by assignment. Born St. Augustine Florida Jan 22, 1933. Educated at University of Florida B.S.J. 1955 LL.B. with honors 1960. Member Phi Kappa Phi and Order of the Coif. Admitted to practice Florida 1960. In legal practice Fort Lauderdale 1960-63 and St. Augustine 1963-77.

Assistant Public Defender 1964-68 and Assistant State Attorney 1969-77 Florida Seventh Judicial Circuit. City Commissioner St. Augustine 1975-77. Member St. Johns County and American Bar Associations. Recipient Distinguished Citizens Award from Boy Scouts of America. Named Paul Harris Fellow by Rotary. Former Major Florida National Guard.

Office: 101 North Alabama Avenue, De Land 32724.

Telephone: (386) 257-6097.

WATTLES, Bob *(Judge, Florida Circuit Court Ninth Judicial Circuit)* Elected Nov 1994 to term beginning Jan 1, 1995. Reelected Nov 2000, current term expires Jan 2007. Born Portsmouth Virginia March 14, 1947. Educated at University of Florida B.S.J. 1967 J.D. 1972. Admitted to practice Florida 1973, New York and District of Columbia. In legal practice Orlando Florida 1978-94.

Member U.S. Supreme Court Bar Association, The District of Columbia Bar, Orange County, New York State and Federal Bar Associations. Enjoys fishing and judging. Personal Statement or Quote: "Get it right."

Mailing address: P.O. Box 3306, Orlando 32802.

Office: 1140 Orange County Courthouse, 425 North Orange Avenue, Orlando 32801.

Telephone: (407) 836-0545.

Fax: (407) 835-5148

WEATHERBY, Michael *(Judge, Florida Circuit Court Fourth Judicial Circuit)*

Office: 204 Duval County Courthouse, 330 East Bay Street, Jacksonville 32202.

Telephone: (904) 630-2524.

Fax: (904) 630-8300

WEBB, William R. *(Judge, Florida Circuit Court Sixth Judicial Circuit)* Elected to term beginning Jan 3, 1995. Reelected 2000, current term expires Jan 2007.

Office: 104 West Pasco Judicial Center, 7530 Little Road, New Port Richey 34654.

Telephone: (727) 847-8172.

WEBSTER, Peter *(Judge, Florida District Court of Appeal First District)* Appointed by Governor Lawton Chiles Nov 1991. Retained by election, current term expires Jan 2007. Born Framingham Massachusetts Feb 12, 1949. Educated at Georgetown University B.S.F.S. magna cum laude 1971 and Duke University School of Law J.D. with distinction 1974. Member Phi Beta Kappa, Phi Alpha Theta and Phi Eta Sigma. Law Clerk to Hon. Gerald Bard Tjoflat, U.S. District Court Middle District of Florida 1974-75. In legal practice Florida 1975-85. Judge, Florida Circuit Court Fourth Judicial Circuit 1986-91.

Master of the Bench Chester Bedell American Inn of Court 1988-92. Former Member Florida Academy of Trial Lawyers, The Association of Trial Lawyers of America, Federal and American (National Conference of State Trial Judges) Bar Associations. Member Tallahassee American Inn of Court, American Judicature Society, The Florida Bar, Jacksonville and Tallahassee Bar Associations. Board of Directors Jacksonville Area Legal Aid 1978-83, River Region Human Services, Inc. 1986-88 and Duke Alumni Club of Greater Jacksonville 1988-90. Advisory Board PACE Center for Girls, Inc. 1986-91. Committee Member Shawnee District North Florida Council Boy Scouts of America 1974-78. Officer and Executive Board Suwannee River Area Council Boy Scouts of America since 1992.

Office: 301 Martin Luther King Jr. Boulevard, Tallahassee 32399-1850.

Telephone: (850) 487-1000.

Fax: (850) 921-4768

WEINBERG, Richard G. *(Senior Judge, Florida Circuit Court Seventh Judicial Circuit)* Appointed by Governor Robert Graham to term beginning Sept 20, 1981. Elected 1982, 1988 and 1994. Assumed Senior Judge status, serves by assignment. Born New York New York March 18, 1932. Educated at University of Florida B.S.B.A. 1953 LL.B. 1959 replaced by J.D. Contributor University of Florida Law Review 1958. Member Scabbard & Blade. Admitted to practice Florida 1959. Began legal practice St. Augustine 1959. Judge, St. Augustine Municipal Court 1963-73.

Former Attorney St. Augustine Beach Airport Authority. Instructor in Legal Ethics University of Florida School of Law 1969-80. President Florida Municipal Judges Association 1965. Member The Florida Bar, St. Johns County and American 1959-81 Bar Associations. Instructor in Law Enforcement Certification for State of Florida 1980-84. First Lieutenant U.S. Army 1953-55. Brigadier General Florida National Guard Infantry 1984-89 (retired). Previously worked for Barnett Banks. Director YMCA. Advisor to USO. Member St. Augustine Jaycees (Secretary) and military officer clubs. Enjoys archery, running and tennis.

Office: 101 North Alabama Avenue, De Land 32724.
Telephone: (386) 257-6097.

WEINSTEIN, Peter M. *(Judge, Florida Circuit Court Seventeenth Judicial Circuit)*

Office: 4880 Broward County Courthouse, 201 S.E. Sixth Street, Fort Lauderdale 33301.
Telephone: (954) 831-5506.

WELCH, Thomas F. *(Judge, Bay County Court)* Elected to term beginning Jan 1991. Reelected 1994 and 1998. Current term expires Jan 2005.

Mailing address: P.O. Box 2269, Panama City 32402.
Office: Bay County Courthouse, Panama City 32401.
Telephone: (850) 747-5211.
Fax: (850) 747-5629

WELLS, Charles Talley *(Justice, Florida Supreme Court)* Appointed by Governor Lawton Chiles to term beginning June 16, 1994. Retained by election Nov 1996 and Nov 2002. Current term expires Jan 2009. Chief Justice 2000-02. Born Orlando Florida March 4, 1939. Methodist. Educated at University of Florida B.A. 1961 J.D. 1964. Member Phi Beta Sigma and Florida Blue Key. Admitted to practice Florida 1965, U.S. District Courts Middle 1965 and Southern 1976 Districts of Florida, U.S. Court of Appeals Fifth (now Eleventh) Circuit 1966, U.S. Supreme Court 1969 and U.S. Court of Federal Claims 1990. Board Certified as a Specialist in Civil Trial Law by The Florida Bar. In legal practice 1964-68, 1970-75 and 1976-94. Certified Mediator Florida Circuit Court (Civil) 1990 and U.S. District Court 1990.

Trial Attorney U.S. Department of Justice 1969. Fellow American Bar Foundation. Member The Florida Bar, Tallahassee, Orange County and American Bar Associations. Recipient Distinguished Alumnus Award from University of Florida. Inducted into University of Florida Hall of Fame. Recipient Award of Excellence from Orange County Legal Aid Society. USAR.

Office: Supreme Court Building, 500 South Duval Street, Tallahassee 32399-1925.
Telephone: (850) 921-1096.
Fax: (850) 922-2188

WELLS, Kelvin C. *(Judge, Okaloosa County Court)*

Office: Okaloosa County Courthouse, 1250 North Eglin Parkway, Shalimar 32579.
Telephone: (850) 651-7449.
Fax: (850) 651-7278

WELLS, Linda Ann *(Judge, Florida District Court of Appeal Third District)*

Office: 2001 S.W. 117th Street, Miami 33175-1716.
Telephone: (305) 229-3200.
Fax: (305) 229-3206

WENNET, Richard I. *(Judge, Florida Circuit Court Fifteenth Judicial Circuit)*

Office: Palm Beach County Courthouse, 205 North Dixie Highway, West Palm Beach 33401.
Telephone: (561) 355-2315.

WESSEL, John D. *(Judge, Florida Circuit Court Fifteenth Judicial Circuit)*

Office: 205 North Dixie Highway, Courtroom 11D, West Palm Beach 33401.
Telephone: (561) 355-6570.

WHATLEY, James W. *(Judge, Florida District Court of Appeal Second District)* Appointed by Governor Lawton Chiles Nov 30, 1994 to term beginning Jan 1995. Retained by election. Born Miami Florida May 12, 1947. Educated at University of Miami 1969 J.D. 1972. In legal practice Miami 1972-81 and Sarasota County 1982-88. Judge, Florida Circuit Court Twelfth Judicial Circuit Jan 1989 to Jan 1995, appointed by Governor Bob Martinez.

Mailing address: P.O. Box 327, Lakeland 33802-0327.
Office: 1005 East Memorial Boulevard, Lakeland 33801.
Telephone: (863) 499-2290.
Fax: (863) 413-2649

WHITE, Alice Blackwell *(Judge, Florida Circuit Court Ninth Judicial Circuit)* Appointed by Governor Lawton Chiles to term beginning April 15, 1992. Elected Sept 1992 and 1998. Current term expires Jan 2005. Educated at Furman University B.A. 1977 and University of South Carolina School of Law J.D. 1980. Managing Editor South Carolina Law Review. In legal practice Florida June 1980 to March 1991.

Member since 1991, Trustee 1993, President/Trustee Sept 1, 1994 to Aug 31, 1995 and President Sept 1, 1995 to Aug 31, 1996 American Inns of Court #123. Secretary 1993-94, Circuit Court Judicial Representative, Orange County Bar Association Representative and Trustee Legal Aid Society of the Orange County Bar Association. Member Central Florida Association for Women Lawyers (Treasurer 1982-83) and Orange County Bar Association (Chairperson Speaker's Bureau 1983-84, Member 1985-89, Co-Chair 1987, Chair 1987-89 and Chairperson Subcommittee for Judge's Reception Federal and State Trial Practice Committee, Member Judicial Relations Committee 1989-90, Trustee Educational Fund 1990-91, Secretary 1990-91, Co-Chair Professionalism Committee 1994-95). Author/Lecturer on "Denouement" 1983 and 1985 and on "Thickening the Plot" 1987 Basic Commercial Litigation Seminar and on "Trial Ethics" Evidence Code Seminar 1994 and 1995 Young Lawyers Division The Florida Bar. Speaker on "The Role of the Guardian Ad Litem in a Criminal Case" Guardian Ad Litem Training Seminar The Legal Aid Society of the Orange County Bar Association 1992-93. Panelist work-

WHITE, ALICE BLACKWELL—*Continued*

shop on "New Reporters v. Jurors" 22nd Annual Media-Law Conference The Florida Bar 1996. Faculty Member on "DUI for Experienced County and Circuit Judges" and "Sentencing" Advanced Judicial College 1996. Recipient award in recognition of exemplary performance and dedication to providing quality services and fair treatment to victims and witnesses of crime from Sex Crimes/Child Abuse Unit Office of the State Attorney Ninth Judicial Circuit in observance of Victim's Rights Week April 26, 1990 and Pro Bono Award of Excellence from Legal Aid Society of Orange County Bar Association, Inc. Aug 21, 1990. Member Associate Board Loch Haven Art Center 1981-82 and Florida Symphony Association 1982-83. Board of Trustees 1984-88 and First Vice President 1986-88 Orlando Community Concert Association. Chairperson Music Committee 1986-87, Member Board of Trustees 1989-91, Vice Chair Long Range Planning Committee 1990-91, Vice Moderator 1992-94, Moderator 1995-96 and Member Chancel Choir and Brass Ensemble First Congregational Church of Winter Park. Member 1987-90 and Chairperson 1988-90 Transportation Permit Board Orlando. Board of Directors Central Florida Crimeline Program, Inc. 1990-91.

Office: 2035 Orange County Courthouse, 425 North Orange Avenue, Orlando 32801.

Telephone: (407) 836-2084.

Fax: (407) 835-5018

WHITE, Patrick A. *(Magistrate Judge, United States District Court Southern District of Florida)* Appointed by U.S. District Court judges to term beginning April 2, 2003.

Office: U.S. Courthouse, 300 N.E. First Avenue, Miami 33132.

Telephone: (305) 523-5100.

WHITE, William P., Jr. *(Judge, Escambia County Court)*

Office: Judicial Building, 190 Governmental Center, Pensacola 32501.

Telephone: (850) 595-4433.

Fax: (850) 595-4435

WHITE-LABORA, Deborah *(Judge, Dade County Court)*

Office: 2122 Courthouse Center, 175 N.W. First Avenue, Miami 33128.

Telephone: (305) 349-5750.

Fax: (305) 349-6177

WHITEHEAD, Reginald K. *(Judge, Florida Circuit Court Ninth Judicial Circuit)* Former Judge, Orange County Court.

Office: Orange County Courthouse, 425 North Orange Avenue, Orlando 32801.

Telephone: (407) 836-2028.

Fax: (407) 835-5070

WHITTEMORE, James D. *(Judge, United States District Court Middle District of Florida)* Appointed for life by President Bill Clinton to term beginning May 27, 2000. Born Walterboro South Carolina Aug 19, 1952. Educated at University of Florida B.S.B.A. 1974 and Stetson University College of Law J.D. 1977. In legal practice Florida 1977 and 1981-90. Judge, Florida Circuit Court Thirteenth Judicial Circuit Feb 1, 1990 to May 26, 2000, appointed by Governor Bob Martinez.

Assistant Federal Public Defender 1978-81.

Office: U.S. Courthouse, 801 North Florida Avenue, Tampa 33602.

Telephone: (813) 301-5400.

WIGGINS, David C. *(Judge, Florida Circuit Court Fourth Judicial Circuit)* Appointed by Governor Bob Martinez to term beginning Jan 1, 1988. Elected to subsequent terms. Born Richmond Virginia Sept 24, 1946. Episcopalian. Educated at Florida State University B.S. 1968 and Cumberland School of Law of Samford University J.D. 1972. Admitted to practice Florida 1972, U.S. Court of Appeals 1980 and U.S. Supreme Court 1980. Began legal practice Jacksonville 1972. Judge, Duval County Court March 8, 1982 to Dec 31, 1987.

Former Assistant Attorney. Member Jacksonville and American Bar Associations.

Office: 208 Duval County Courthouse, 330 East Bay Street, Jacksonville 32202.

Telephone: (904) 630-2111.

Fax: (904) 630-2979

WILD, Joe A. *(Judge, Indian River County Court)*

Office: 263 Indian River County Courthouse, 2000 Sixteenth Avenue, Vero Beach 32960.

Telephone: (772) 770-5072.

Fax: (772) 770-5477

WILKES, William A. *(Judge, Florida Circuit Court Fourth Judicial Circuit)* Former Judge, Clay County Court.

Mailing address: P.O. Drawer 1845, Green Cove Springs 32043.

Office: Clay County Courthouse, Green Cove Springs 32043.

Telephone: (904) 269-6338.

Fax: (904) 278-4728

WILL, Joseph G. *(Judge, Florida Circuit Court Seventh Judicial Circuit)*

Office: Volusia County Justice Center, 251 North Ridgewood Avenue, Daytona Beach 32114.

Telephone: (386) 257-6033.

Fax: (386) 257-6077

WILLIAMS, Amy M. *(Judge, Pinellas County Court)*

Office: Criminal Justice Center, 14250 49th Street North, Clearwater 33762.

Telephone: (727) 464-6460

WILLIAMS, Charles E. *(Judge, Florida Circuit Court Twelfth Judicial Circuit)*

Mailing address: P.O. Box 1000, Bradenton 34206.

Office: 1115 Manatee Avenue West, Bradenton 34205.

Telephone: (941) 749-7139.

Fax: (407) 742-5957

WILLIAMS, Elijah H. *(Judge, Florida Circuit Court Seventeenth Judicial Circuit)*

Office: 446 Broward County Courthouse, 201 S.E. Sixth Street, Fort Lauderdale 33301.

Telephone: (954) 831-6974.

Fax: (954) 831-5572

WILLIAMS, Joseph M. *(Judge, Baker County Court)* Elected Nov 3, 1992 to term beginning Jan 5, 1993. Reelected 1996 and 2000. Current term expires

WILLIAMS, JOSEPH M.—*Continued*

Jan 2007. Born Jacksonville Florida Sept 28, 1964. Educated at University of Florida B.A. 1986 and Stetson University College of Law J.D. 1989. Admitted to practice Florida 1989, Georgia 1989, U.S. Court of Appeals Eleventh Circuit 1990 and U.S. District Courts Middle 1992 and Southern 1992 Districts of Florida. In legal practice Tavernier 1989-92 and Macclenny 1992-93.

Office: 100 Baker County Courthouse, 339 East Macclenny Street, Macclenny 32063.
Telephone: (904) 259-3575.
Fax: (904) 259-1451

WILLIAMS, Kenneth L. *(Judge, Florida Circuit Court First Judicial Circuit)* Elected Sept 4, 1990 to term beginning Jan 1991. Reelected 1996 and 2002. Current term expires Jan 2009. Born Jacksonville Florida Jan 28, 1951. Educated at Oakwood College B.A. 1972 and University of Florida J.D. 1979. Admitted to practice Florida 1980 and U.S. District Court Middle District of Florida 1984. Judge, Escambia County Court July 16, 1986 to Jan 1991, appointed by Governor Robert Graham.

Assistant State Attorney March 1979 to July 1986. Adjunct Professor of Evidence and Forensic Science Pensacola Junior College since 1986. Member Florida Conference of County Court Judges, Florida Conference of Circuit Court Judges, The Florida Bar, Escambia-Santa Rosa County and Gulf Coast Bar Associations. Attended Traffic Adjudication Seminar Florida Judicial College and Evidence and Writing Seminar The National Judicial College. Previously employed as salesman for Lever Brothers Co., Metropolitan Life Insurance Company, Burroughs Corporation and Blossom Home Builders. Democrat. Board of Directors YMCA and Community Drug & Alcohol Commission. Member NAACP, SCLC, Center of Excellence and Pensacola Bicentennial Commission. Enjoys diving, basketball, jogging, bird watching and golf.

Office: Judicial Building, 190 Governmental Center, Pensacola 32501.
Telephone: (850) 595-4465.
Fax: (850) 595-0360

WILLIAMS, O. Edgar, Jr. *(Senior Judge, Florida Circuit Court Seventeenth Judicial Circuit)* Assumed Senior Judge status, serves by assignment.

Office: Broward County Courthouse, 201 S.E. Sixth Street, Fort Lauderdale 33301.
Telephone: (954) 831-7740.

WILLIAMS, Robert E. *(Judge, Nassau County Court)*

Mailing address: P.O. Box 768, Fernandina Beach 32035.
Office: Nassau County Courthouse, Fernandina Beach 32034.
Telephone: (800) 958-3496.
Fax: (904) 321-5787

WILLIAMSON, Michael G. *(Judge, United States Bankruptcy Court Middle District of Florida)* Appointed by U.S. Court of Appeals Eleventh Circuit judges to term beginning March 1, 2000. Born 1951. Educated at Duke University B.S. 1973 and Georgetown University J.D. 1976.

Office: 1054 U.S. Courthouse, 801 North Florida Avenue, Tampa 33602-3899.
Telephone: (813) 301-5520.

WILSON, Thomas G. *(Magistrate Judge, United States District Court Middle District of Florida)* Appointed by U.S. District Court judges.

Office: U.S. Courthouse, 801 North Florida Avenue, Tampa 33602-3800.
Telephone: (813) 301-5588.

WILSON, Thomas S., Jr. *(Judge, Florida Circuit Court Eleventh Judicial Circuit)* Appointed by Governor Bob Martinez June 13, 1990. Elected to subsequent terms.

Office: 524 Dade County Courthouse, 73 West Flagler Street, Miami 33130.
Telephone: (305) 349-7161.

WINESETT, Sherra *(Judge, Florida Circuit Court Twentieth Judicial Circuit)*

Office: Charlotte County Justice Center, 350 East Marion Avenue, Punta Gorda 33950.
Telephone: (941) 637-2257.
Fax: (941) 637-2283

WINIKOFF, Jeffrey *(Judge, Florida Circuit Court Fifteenth Judicial Circuit)*

Office: Palm Beach County Courthouse, 205 North Dixie Highway, West Palm Beach 33401.

WITTEN, Fred N. *(Judge, Gulf County Court)*

Office: Gulf County Courthouse, 1000 Cecil Costin Sr. Boulevard, Port St. Joe 32456.
Telephone: (850) 227-1141.
Fax: (850) 227-1142

WOLF, James R. *(Judge, Florida District Court of Appeal First District)* Appointed by Governor Bob Martinez June 19, 1990. Retained by election. Born Newark New Jersey June 15, 1950. Educated at Rutgers University A.B. 1972 and University of Miami J.D. 1975. Recipient American Jurisprudence Award in Civil Procedure. In legal practice Palm Beach 1980-83.

Assistant State Attorney Fifteenth Judicial Circuit 1975-78. Assistant City Attorney West Palm Beach 1978-80. Member Florida Municipal Attorneys' Association, Conference of Appellate Court Judges and The Florida Bar. General Counsel Florida League of Cities 1983-90.

Office: 301 Martin Luther King Jr. Boulevard, Tallahassee 32399-1850.
Telephone: (850) 487-1000.
Fax: (850) 921-4768

WOLFE, Mark *(Judge, Hillsborough County Court)* Assumed office March 2000. Educated at University of Notre Dame B.B.A. 1978 and University of Miami School of Law J.D. 1981. Admitted to practice Florida 1981, U.S. Court of Appeals Eleventh Circuit 1981, U.S. District Courts Southern 1981 and Middle 1983 Districts of Florida, Trial Bar of U.S. District Court Southern District of Florida 1982, New York 1989 and U.S. Supreme Court 1990. Board Certified as a Specialist in Appellate Practice by The Florida Bar 1996. In legal practice Tampa June 1986 to Feb 2000. Traffic Court Magistrate, Hillsborough County Court Dec 1989 to Sept 1992.

WOLFE, MARK—*Continued*

With Office of the Public Defender May 1983 to June 1986. Member The Florida Bar (Judicial Nomination Procedures Committee since 1998) and Hillsborough County Bar Association (Co-chair Law Week 2001 and 2002). Member United Way Keel Club.

Office: 801 East Twiggs Street, Room 225, Tampa 33602.

Telephone: (813) 272-6852.

Fax: (813) 276-8015

WOODARD, W. Wayne *(Judge, Charlotte County Court)* Appointed by Governor Bob Martinez to term beginning Jan 2, 1990. Elected to subsequent terms.

Office: Charlotte County Justice Center, 350 East Marion Avenue, Punta Gorda 33950.

Telephone: (941) 637-2266.

Fax: (941) 637-2283

WOODSON, J. William *(Senior Judge, Florida Circuit Court Eighteenth Judicial Circuit)* Assumed Senior Judge status, serves by assignment.

Office: Moore Justice Center, 2825 Judge Fran Jamieson Way, Viera 32940-8006.

Telephone: (321) 637-5555.

WORTHEN, Freddie J. *(Judge, Volusia County Court)* Appointed by Governor Bob Martinez to term beginning March 7, 1989. Elected to subsequent terms.

Office: Courthouse Annex, 125 East Orange Avenue, Daytona Beach 32114.

Telephone: (386) 257-6070.

WRIGHT, Karla Foreman *(Judge, Polk County Court)*

Mailing address: P.O. Box 9000, Drawer J-147, Bartow 33831.

Telephone: (863) 534-5820.

Fax: (863) 534-5832

WRIGHT, William Leon *(Judge, Florida Circuit Court Fourteenth Judicial Circuit)*

Mailing address: P.O. Box 976, Marianna 32447.

Telephone: (850) 482-9078.

Fax: (850) 482-9123

WRIGHT, Zebedee W. *(Judge, Broward County Court)*

Office: 310 Broward County Courthouse, 201 S.E. Sixth Street, Fort Lauderdale 33301.

Telephone: (954) 831-7841.

Fax: (954) 831-5572

WROBLE, Arthur G. *(Judge, Florida Circuit Court Fifteenth Judicial Circuit)* Elected Sept 5, 2000 to term beginning Jan 1, 2001. Term expires Dec 31, 2007. Born Taylor Pennsylvania Jan 21, 1948. Roman Catholic. Educated at University of Florida B.S.B.A. 1970 M.B.A. 1971 J.D. 1973. Admitted to practice Florida 1973, U.S. District Courts Southern 1974, Middle 1982 and Northern 1986 Districts of Florida, U.S. Courts of Appeals Fifth 1974 and Eleventh 1981 Circuits, U.S. Supreme Court 1976 and U.S. Court of Appeals for the Armed Forces 1990. In legal practice Palm Beach 1973-82 and 1987-89, West Palm Beach 1982-87 and 1992-2001 and Lake Worth 1989-92.

Director Alternate Sentencing Program Palm Beach County Public Defenders' Office 1983-2000. Editor Mechanic's Lien Legal Forms & Worksheets 1981 and Legal Forms and Worksheets 1982 Young Lawyers Section The Florida Bar. Director 1979-81 and President 1984-85 Palm Beach County Bar Association. President 1980-81 and Director since 1981 Guild of Catholic Lawyers of Palm Beach County, Inc. Board of Governors Young Lawyers Section 1979-83, Member CLE Committee 1982-89 and Voluntary Bar Liaison Committee 1984-91 and Board of Governors 1985-89 The Florida Bar. Director Florida Council of Bar Association Presidents 1986-91 and The Florida Bar Foundation 1989-93. Member U.S. Magistrate Selection Panel Southern District of Florida 1987. Director 1995-2001 and President 1999-2000 West Palm Beach Chapter American Inn of Court LIV. Former Member South Palm Beach County Bar Association. Member Florida Association of Women Lawyers, Hispanic Bar Association (Palm Beach County) and J. Malcolm Cunningham Bar Association. Recipient Outstanding Catholic Lawyer Award from Guild of Catholic Lawyers 1993 and Outstanding Citizen Award from West Palm Beach Kiwanis 1994. Inducted in Bishop Moore High School Athletic Hall of Fame 1997. Listed in *Who's Who in America* 50th-54th ed. and *Who's Who in American Law* 2nd-11th ed. Lieutenant Colonel USAR JAGC (retired). Eagle Scout Boy Scouts of America 1962. Director since 1980 and President 1990-2000 West Palm Beach Kiwanis Club Foundation, Inc. Co-chairman Professional Development United Way 1984-85. Director Central Palm Beach County Chamber of Commerce 1989-96 and Palm Glades Council Girl Scouts of America since 1996. Graduate and Director Leadership Palm Beach County 1990-92.

Office: 205 North Dixie Highway, West Palm Beach 33401.

Telephone: (561) 355-1560.

YACUCCI, Philip J. *(Judge, St. Lucie County Court)*

Office: 218 South Second Street, Fort Pierce 34950.

Telephone: (772) 462-1957.

YANCEY, James Alan *(Judge, Polk County Court)*

Mailing address: P.O. Box 9000, Drawer J-102, Bartow 33831-9000.

Office: Polk County Courthouse, Bartow 33830.

Telephone: (863) 534-4576.

YAWN, Theron A., Jr. *(Senior Judge, Florida Circuit Court Eighth Judicial Circuit)* Elected 1972 to term beginning Jan 3, 1973. Reelected to subsequent terms. Chief Judge 1977. Assumed Senior Judge status, serves by assignment. Born Jackson County Florida Oct 7, 1926. Presbyterian. Educated at University of Florida A.A. 1948 LL.B. 1951. Admitted to practice Florida 1951. Began legal practice Starke 1951. Judge, Bradford County Court 1953-73.

Chairman Florida Conference of Circuit Court Judges 1982-83. Private USAAC 1945-47.

Office: Alachua County Courthouse, 201 East University Avenue, Gainesville 32601.

Telephone: (352) 374-3648.

YERMAN, Mark J. *(Judge, Citrus County Court)* Appointed by Governor Lawton Chiles Oct 28, 1993.

Office: Citrus County Courthouse, 110 North Apopka Avenue, Inverness 34450.

Telephone: (352) 341-6713.

Fax: (352) 341-6791

YOUNG, David H. *(Judge, Florida Circuit Court Eleventh Judicial Circuit)* Elected to term beginning Jan 1, 2001. Term expires Dec 31, 2006. Born Miami Flori-

YOUNG, DAVID H.—*Continued*

da April 24, 1959. Educated at Tulane University B.A. 1981 and University of Miami J.D. 1984. Admitted to practice Florida 1985. In legal practice Miami Jan 1, 1988 to Dec 31, 1991. Former Judge, Dade County Court.

Assistant State Attorney April 1, 1985 to Dec 31, 1987. Member Adopt-a-Pet. Enjoys collecting penguins. Personal Statement or Quote: "Get involved in your community. Always strive to improve the administration of justice."

Office: 420 Gerstein Justice Building, 1351 N.W. Twelfth Avenue, Miami 33125.

Telephone: (305) 548-5178.

YOUNG, George C. *(Senior Judge, United States District Court Middle District of Florida)* Appointed for life by President John F. Kennedy to term beginning 1961. Chief Judge 1973-81. Assumed Senior status, serves by assignment. Born Cincinnati Ohio Aug 4, 1916. Educated at University of Florida A.B. 1938 LL.B. 1940 and Harvard University 1947. Member Order of the Coif, Florida Blue Key, Phi Beta Kappa, Phi Kappa Phi and Phi Delta Phi. Admitted to practice Florida 1940. In legal practice Winter Haven 1940-41, Miami 1947 and Jacksonville 1953-61.

Assistant U.S. Attorney Jacksonville 1952. Member Committee on Administration of Federal Magistrates System Judicial Conference of the U.S., American Judicature Society, The American Law Institute, The Florida Bar (Governor 1960-61), Jacksonville (Past President) and American (Special Committee for Administration of Criminal Justice) Bar Associations. Lieutenant s.g. USNR 1942-46. Administrative and Legislative Assistant to Senator Smathers 1948-52. Board of Directors Jacksonville United Cerebral Palsy Association 1953-60. Member Rollins College Alumni Association (President 1968-69).

Office: 630 U.S. Courthouse, 80 North Hughey Avenue, Orlando 32801.

Telephone: (407) 835-4280.

ZABEL, Sarah *(Judge, Florida Circuit Court Eleventh Judicial Circuit)*

Office: 73 Flagler Street, Miami 33130.

Telephone: (305) 349-7353.

ZACK, Robert S. *(Judge, Broward County Court)* Elected Nov 1988 to term beginning Jan 2, 1989. Reelected Sept 1992, Sept 1996 and Sept 2000. Current term expires Dec 31, 2006. Born Detroit Michigan May 31, 1943. Educated at Boston University B.S.B.A. 1965 and Wayne State University J.D. 1968. Admitted to practice Michigan 1968 and Florida 1973. In legal practice Detroit Michigan 1968-73 and Fort Lauderdale Florida 1973-88.

Instructor in Commercial Litigation and Torts American Paralegal Institute Barry University 1990-91. Instructor Broward County Police Academy 1990-93 and National Institute for Paralegal Training 1991-92. Adjunct Professor of Paralegal Studies Rollins College 1992-95. Member Florida Conference of County Court Judges (Past President, Former Treasurer). Instructor in Sentencing Alternatives Florida Conference of County Court Judges and in Sentencing Alternatives Advanced Traffic Adjudication Seminar. Enjoys fishing, boating, exercising and golf.

Office: 333 Broward County Courthouse, 201 S.E. Sixth Street, Fort Lauderdale 33301.

Telephone: (954) 831-7293.

Fax: (954) 831-7255

ZEIDWIG, Howard M. *(Judge, Florida Circuit Court Seventeenth Judicial Circuit)*

Office: 4850 Broward County Courthouse, 201 S.E. Sixth Street, Fort Lauderdale 33301.

Telephone: (954) 831-7763.

Fax: (954) 831-8587

ZELLER, Sharon L. *(Judge, Broward County Court)*

Office: 214 South Regional Courthouse, 3550 Hollywood Boulevard, Hollywood 33021.

Telephone: (954) 831-0306.

ZLOCH, William J. *(Chief Judge, United States District Court Southern District of Florida)* Appointed for life by President Ronald Reagan to term beginning Nov 29, 1985. Chief Judge since July 2, 2000.

Chairman Financial Disclosure Committee Judicial Conference of the U.S. 1993. Member The Florida Bar. Recipient President's Award from Broward County Bar Association 1982-83 and President's Pro Bono Service Award for Seventeenth Judicial Circuit from The Florida Bar March 13, 1985. Lieutenant USN 1967-69.

Office: U.S. Courthouse, 299 East Broward Boulevard, Fort Lauderdale 33301.

Telephone: (954) 769-5480.

GEORGIA

Capital ATLANTA

UNITED STATES DISTRICT COURTS DISTRICTS OF GEORGIA

Within Georgia there are three United States District Courts. For descriptive information refer to the United States Courts section.

MIDDLE DISTRICT consists of seven divisions.

Albany Division includes Baker, Calhoun, Dougherty, Early, Miller, Mitchell, Turner and Worth counties. The court sits at Albany.

Americus Division includes Ben Hill, Crisp, Dooly, Lee, Macon, Schley, Sumter, Terrell, Webster and Wilcox counties. The court sits at Americus.

Athens Division includes Clarke, Elbert, Franklin, Greene, Hart, Madison, Morgan, Oconee, Oglethorpe and Walton counties. The court sits at Athens.

Columbus Division includes Chattahoochee, Clay, Harris, Marion, Muscogee, Quitman, Randolph, Stewart, Talbot and Taylor counties. The court sits at Columbus.

Macon Division includes Baldwin, Bibb, Bleckley, Butts, Crawford, Hancock, Houston, Jasper, Jones, Lamar, Monroe, Peach, Pulaski, Putnam, Twiggs, Upson, Washington and Wilkinson counties. The court sits at Macon.

Thomasville Division includes Brooks, Colquitt, Decatur, Grady, Seminole and Thomas counties. The court sits at Thomasville.

Valdosta Division includes Berrien, Clinch, Cook, Echols, Irwin, Lanier, Lowndes and Tift counties. The court sits at Valdosta.

Chief Judge
W. Louis Sands

Judges
Hugh Lawson
Clay D. Land
C. Ashley Royal

Senior Judges
Wilbur Dawson Owens, Jr.
Duross Fitzpatrick

Clerk
Gregory J. Leonard
P.O. Box 128
Macon, Georgia 31202-0128
(478) 752-3497

NORTHERN DISTRICT consists of four divisions.

Atlanta Division includes Cherokee, Clayton, Cobb, DeKalb, Douglas, Fulton, Gwinnett, Henry, Newton and Rockdale counties. The court sits at Atlanta.

Gainesville Division includes Banks, Barrow, Dawson, Fannin, Forsyth, Gilmer, Habersham, Hall, Jackson, Lumpkin, Pickens, Rabun, Stephens, Towns, Union and White counties. The court sits at Gainesville.

Newnan Division includes Carroll, Coweta, Fayette, Haralson, Heard, Meriwether, Pike, Spalding and Troup counties. The court sits at Newnan.

Rome Division includes Bartow, Catoosa, Chattooga, Dade, Floyd, Gordon, Murray, Paulding, Polk, Walker and Whitfield counties. The court sits at Rome.

Chief Judge
Orinda D. Evans

Judges

Harold L. Murphy	J. Owen Forrester
Jack T. Camp	Julie E. Carnes
Clarence Cooper	Willis B. Hunt, Jr.
Thomas W. Thrash, Jr.	Richard W. Story
Charles Pannell, Jr.	Beverly B. Martin

Senior Judges

William C. O'Kelley	Charles A. Moye, Jr.
G. Ernest Tidwell	Robert L. Vining, Jr.
Marvin H. Shoob	Horace T. Ward

Clerk
Luther D. Thomas
2211 U.S. Courthouse
75 Spring Street S.W.
Atlanta, Georgia 30303-3361
(404) 215-1600

SOUTHERN DISTRICT consists of six divisions.

Augusta Division includes Burke, Columbia, Glascock, Jefferson, Lincoln, McDuffie, Richmond, Taliaferro, Warren and Wilkes counties. The court sits at Augusta.

Brunswick Division includes Appling, Camden, Glynn, Jeff Davis, Long, McIntosh and Wayne counties. The court sits at Brunswick.

Dublin Division includes Dodge, Johnson, Laurens, Montgomery, Telfair, Treutlen and Wheeler counties. The court sits at Dublin.

Savannah Division includes Bryan, Chatham, Effingham and Liberty counties. The court sits at Savannah.

Statesboro Division includes Bulloch, Candler, Emanuel, Evans, Jenkins, Screven, Tattnall and Toombs counties. The court sits at Statesboro.

Waycross Division includes Atkinson, Bacon, Brantley, Charlton, Coffee, Pierce and Ware counties. The court sits at Waycross.

Chief Judge
Dudley H. Bowen, Jr.

Judges
Berry Avant Edenfield
William T. Moore, Jr.

UNITED STATES DISTRICT COURTS DISTRICTS OF GEORGIA—*Continued*

Senior Judge
Anthony A. Alaimo

Clerk
Scott Poff
P.O. Box 8286
Savannah, Georgia 31412-8286
(912) 650-4020

UNITED STATES MAGISTRATE JUDGES OF GEORGIA

MIDDLE DISTRICT
Claude W. Hicks, Jr.
Richard L. Hodge
G. Mallon Faircloth

NORTHERN DISTRICT

Joel M. Feldman	Gerrilyn G. Brill
E. Clayton Scofield, III	C. Christopher Hagy
Janet F. King	Linda T. Walker
Alan J. Baverman	Susan S. Cole
Walter E. Johnson	

SOUTHERN DISTRICT
G. R. Smith
James E. Graham
W. Leon Barfield

UNITED STATES BANKRUPTCY COURTS OF GEORGIA

MIDDLE DISTRICT

Chief Judge
Robert F. Hershner, Jr.

Judges
John T. Laney III
James D. Walker, Jr.

Bankruptcy Clerk
William E. Tanner
P.O. Box 1957
Macon, Georgia 31202-1957
(478) 752-3506

NORTHERN DISTRICT

Chief Judge
Stacey W. Cotton

Judges

W. Homer Drake, Jr.	Joyce Bihary
Margaret H. Murphy	Robert E. Brizendine
James E. Massey	Coleman Ray Mullins
Paul W. Bonapfel	

Bankruptcy Clerk
W. Yvonne Evans
1340 U.S. Courthouse
75 Spring Street S.W.
Atlanta, Georgia 30303-3367
(404) 215-1000

SOUTHERN DISTRICT

Chief Judge
John S. Dalis

Judge
Lamar W. Davis, Jr.

Bankruptcy Clerk
Michael F. McHugh
P.O. Box 8347
Savannah, Georgia 31412-8347
(912) 650-4100

SUPREME COURT OF GEORGIA

The Supreme Court is Georgia's court of last resort. The court consists of seven justices elected at nonpartisan elections for staggered six-year terms. Vacancies may be filled by the governor from a list of candidates provided by the Judicial Nominating Commission. Newly appointed justices serve for the remainder of the unexpired term. The chief justice and the presiding justice are elected by peer vote to two-year terms; a second, consecutive two-year term is permitted. Retirement is mandatory at age seventy-five or on the last day of the term in which the justice turns seventy, whichever is later; however, the governor may appoint retired justices to serve as senior judges.

The court has exclusive appellate jurisdiction in all cases involving the construction of a treaty or of the United States or Georgia constitutions; the constitutionality of a law, ordinance or constitutional provision; and contested elections. The court has general appellate jurisdiction in areas of land title, equity, divorce and alimony, the validity or construction of wills, capital felonies, extraordinary remedies, or cases certified to it by the Court of Appeals. The court may consider cases brought up from the Court of Appeals by certiorari or cases on which the Court of Appeals is equally divided, and may answer any question of law from any state or federal appellate court. The court has rule-making authority over the Superior, State, Juvenile, Probate and Magistrate Courts. The court regulates admission to the bar and may issue all writs necessary to the exercise of proper jurisdiction.

The court sits en banc at Atlanta but may hold sessions at other locations around the state. Terms of court begin in January, April and September; oral arguments are heard each month, except August and December.

Chief Justice
Norman S. Fletcher

Presiding Justice
Leah Sears

Justices
Robert Benham
Carol W. Hunstein
George H. Carley
Hugh P. Thompson
Preston Harris Hines

Senior Judges
Richard Bell
G. Conley Ingram

Clerk
Sherie M. Welch
244 Washington Street S.W., Suite 572
Atlanta, Georgia 30334
(404) 656-3470

SUPREME COURT OF GEORGIA—*Continued*

Administrative Office of the Courts

David L. Ratley
Director
244 Washington Street S.W., Suite 300
Atlanta, Georgia 30334
(404) 656-5171

COURT OF APPEALS OF GEORGIA

The Court of Appeals is Georgia's intermediate appellate court. The court consists of a chief judge and eleven judges elected at nonpartisan elections for staggered six-year terms. Vacancies are filled by the governor from a list of candidates provided by the Judicial Nominating Commission. Newly appointed judges serve for the remainder of the unexpired term. The chief judge, usually the judge most senior in service who has not previously served as chief judge, is elected by peer vote to a two-year term. The chief judge names judges to panels each year and appoints a presiding judge to head each panel. The chief judge and the presiding judges form the executive council to handle certain administrative matters. Retirement is mandatory at age seventy-five or on the last day of the term in which the judge turns seventy, whichever is later; however, the governor may appoint retired judges to serve as senior judges.

The court has appellate jurisdiction in all civil and criminal matters where exclusive jurisdiction is not reserved to the Supreme Court or conferred on other courts. Cases heard by the court include civil claims for damages, child custody cases, workers' compensation claims and criminal cases other than capital felonies. The court may also certify legal questions to the Supreme Court.

Panel decisions are final unless there is a dissent; the case is then decided by a combined panel of judges. The court may also have all judges decide the case. If, after a hearing by the full court, the judges are equally divided, the case is transferred for decision to the Supreme Court. Terms of court begin January, April and September. The court sits at Atlanta.

Chief Judge

J. D. Smith

Judges

Gary B. Andrews
G. Alan Blackburn
Frank M. Eldridge
M. Yvette Miller
Herbert E. Phipps
Alfred Harris Adams
Edward Hodgson Johnson
John H. Ruffin, Jr.
Anne Elizabeth Barnes
John J. Ellington
Charles B. Mikell, Jr.

Senior Judges

Dorothy Toth Beasley
Braswell D. Deen, Jr.
William L. McMurray, Jr.
Arnold Shulman
John W. Sognier

SUPERIOR COURTS OF GEORGIA

The Superior Courts are Georgia's courts of general trial jurisdiction. Judges are elected from their respective circuits in nonpartisan elections for four-year terms. Vacancies may be filled by the governor from a list of candidates provided by the Judicial Nominating Commission. A chief judge handles administrative tasks in each circuit, but method of selection and length of term vary from circuit to circuit. The forty-nine judicial circuits are divided into ten judicial districts for administrative purposes. An administrative judge is elected by peer vote in each district. Administrative judges may assign Superior Court judges, with their approval, to serve in other counties or circuits as needed. Retirement is mandatory at age seventy-five or at the end of the term in which the judge turns seventy; however, the governor may appoint retired judges to serve as senior judges in any court in the state.

The courts have exclusive original jurisdiction over trials in felony cases and in cases involving divorce, equity and questions of title to land. The courts also exercise jurisdiction over civil law actions and misdemeanors and over juveniles who commit violent felonies. The courts have appellate jurisdiction over inferior courts as provided by law and may issue writs necessary to the exercise of proper jurisdiction.

The courts sit at the county seats.

ALAPAHA JUDICIAL CIRCUIT includes Atkinson, Berrien, Clinch, Cook and Lanier counties. The court sits at Pearson, Nashville, Homerville, Adel and Lakeland.

Chief Judge

Brooks E. Blitch, III

Judge

Carson Dane Perkins

ALCOVY JUDICIAL CIRCUIT includes Newton and Walton counties. The court sits at Covington and Monroe.

Chief Judge

Marvin Williams Sorrells

Judges

John M. Ott
Samuel D. Ozburn
Horace J. Johnson, Jr.

APPALACHIAN JUDICIAL CIRCUIT includes Fannin, Gilmer and Pickens counties. The court sits at Blue Ridge, Ellijay and Jasper.

Chief Judge

Brenda S. Weaver

Judge

Roger E. Bradley

ATLANTA JUDICIAL CIRCUIT includes Fulton County. The court sits at Atlanta.

Chief Judge

Elizabeth E. Long

Judges

Philip F. Etheridge
Alice D. Bonner
Gail S. Tusan
Stephanie B. Manis
Wendy L. Shoob
Constance C. Russell
T. Jackson Bedford, Jr.
John J. Goger
Jerry W. Baxter
M. Gino Brogdon, Sr.
Thelma Wyatt Cummings Moore
Alford J. Dempsey, Jr.
Bensonetta Tipton Lane
Doris L. Downs
Cynthia D. Wright
Melvin K. Westmoreland
Rowland W. Barnes
Marvin Arrington, Jr.

SUPERIOR COURTS OF GEORGIA—*Continued*

ATLANTIC JUDICIAL CIRCUIT includes Bryan, Evans, Liberty, Long, McIntosh and Tattnall counties. The court sits at Pembroke, Claxton, Hinesville, Ludowici, Darien and Reidsville.

Chief Judge
David L. Cavender

Judges
Albert Rahn, III
Robert L. Russell, III
Charles Paul Rose, Jr.

AUGUSTA JUDICIAL CIRCUIT includes Burke, Columbia and Richmond counties. The court sits at Waynesboro, Appling and Augusta.

Chief Judge
William M. Fleming, Jr.

Judges
Albert Pickett
Carl C. Brown, Jr.
Neal W. Dickert
James G. Blanchard, Jr.
J. Carlisle Overstreet
Robert L. Allgood
Duncan Wheale

BELL-FORSYTH JUDICIAL CIRCUIT includes Forsyth County. The court sits at Cumming.

Chief Judge
Richard S. Gault

Judge
Jeffrey S. Bagley

BLUE RIDGE JUDICIAL CIRCUIT includes Cherokee County. The court sits at Canton.

Chief Judge
Frank C. Mills, III

Judge
N. Jackson Harris

BRUNSWICK JUDICIAL CIRCUIT includes Appling, Camden, Glynn, Jeff Davis and Wayne counties. The court sits at Baxley, Woodbine, Brunswick, Hazlehurst and Jesup.

Chief Judge
James R. Tuten, Jr.

Judges
Amanda F. Williams
E. M. Wilkes, III
Stephen G. Scarlett

CHATTAHOOCHEE JUDICIAL CIRCUIT includes Chattahoochee, Harris, Marion, Muscogee, Talbot and Taylor counties. The court sits at Cusseta, Hamilton, Buena Vista, Columbus, Talbotton and Butler.

Chief Judge
Kenneth B. Followill

Judges
John D. Allen
Douglas Pullen
Robert Glenn Johnston, III
Frank J. Jordan, Jr.
Roxann Gray Daniel

CHEROKEE JUDICIAL CIRCUIT includes Bartow and Gordon counties. The court sits at Cartersville and Calhoun.

Chief Judge
Shepherd Lee Howell

Judges
David K. Smith
G. Carey Nelson

CLAYTON JUDICIAL CIRCUIT includes Clayton County. The court sits at Jonesboro.

Chief Judge
Matthew O. Simmons

Judges
Deborah C. Benefield
Albert Collier

COBB JUDICIAL CIRCUIT includes Cobb County. The court sits at Marietta.

Chief Judge
Michael Stoddard

Judges
Dorothy A. Robinson
Mary Ellen Staley
S. Lark Ingram
Robert Flournoy, III
George H. Kreeger
James G. Bodiford
Kenneth O. Nix
Adele Grubbs

CONASAUGA JUDICIAL CIRCUIT includes Murray and Whitfield counties. The court sits at Chatsworth and Dalton.

Chief Judge
William T. Boyett

Judges
Jack Partain
Robert B. Adams
M. Cindy Morris

CORDELE JUDICIAL CIRCUIT includes Ben Hill, Crisp, Dooly and Wilcox counties. The court sits at Fitzgerald, Cordele, Vienna and Abbeville.

Chief Judge
Whitfield R. Forrester

Judge
John C. Pridgen

COWETA JUDICIAL CIRCUIT includes Carroll, Coweta, Heard, Meriwether and Troup counties. The court sits at Carrollton, Newnan, Franklin, Greenville and LaGrange.

Chief Judge
William F. Lee, Jr.

Judges
Allen B. Keeble
Quillian Baldwin, Jr.
Aubrey Duffey
John Simpson

DOUGHERTY JUDICIAL CIRCUIT includes Dougherty County. The court sits at Albany.

Chief Judge
Loring Albert Gray, Jr.

SUPERIOR COURTS OF GEORGIA—*Continued*

Judges
Willie E. Lockette
Stephen S. Goss

DOUGLAS JUDICIAL CIRCUIT includes Douglas County. The court sits at Douglasville.

Chief Judge
Robert J. James

Judges
David T. Emerson
Donald B. Howe

DUBLIN JUDICIAL CIRCUIT includes Johnson, Laurens, Treutlen and Twiggs counties. The court sits at Wrightsville, Dublin, Soperton and Jeffersonville.

Chief Judge
H. Gibbs Flanders, Jr.

Judge
Stan Smith

EASTERN JUDICIAL CIRCUIT includes Chatham County. The court sits at Savannah.

Chief Judge
Perry Brannen, Jr.

Judges
Michael L. Karpf
Penny Haas Freesemann
John E. Morse, Jr.
James F. Bass, Jr.
Louisa Abbott

ENOTAH JUDICIAL CIRCUIT includes Lumpkin, Towns, Union and White counties. The court sits at Dahlonega, Hiawassee, Blairsville and Cleveland.

Chief Judge
Hugh W. Stone

Judge
David Eugene Barrett

FLINT JUDICIAL CIRCUIT includes Henry County. The court sits at McDonough.

Chief Judge
William H. Craig

Judge
Arch W. McGarity

GRIFFIN JUDICIAL CIRCUIT includes Fayette, Pike, Spalding and Upson counties. The court sits at Fayetteville, Zebulon, Griffin and Thomaston.

Chief Judge
Paschal A. English, Jr.

Judges
Johnnie L. Caldwell, Jr.
Christopher C. Edwards
Tommy Richard Hankinson

GWINNETT JUDICIAL CIRCUIT includes Gwinnett County. The court sits at Lawrenceville.

Chief Judge
K. Dawson Jackson

Judges
Richard T. Winegarden
Michael C. Clark
Debra Kaplan Turner
R. Timothy Hamil
Fred A. Bishop, Jr.
Melodie Snell Conner
William M. Ray, II

HOUSTON JUDICIAL CIRCUIT includes Houston County. The court sits at Perry.

Chief Judge
George F. Nunn, Jr.

Judge
Edward D. Lukemire

LOOKOUT MOUNTAIN JUDICIAL CIRCUIT includes Catoosa, Chattooga, Dade and Walker counties. The court sits at Ringgold, Summerville, Trenton and LaFayette.

Chief Judge
Jon B. Wood

Judges
Kristina Cook Connelly
Wm. Ralph Hill, Jr.
Ralph Van Pelt, Jr.

MACON JUDICIAL CIRCUIT includes Bibb, Crawford and Peach counties. The court sits at Macon, Knoxville and Fort Valley.

Chief Judge
Tommy Day Wilcox

Judges
G. Bryant Culpepper
Martha C. Christian
S. Phillip Brown
Lamar W. Sizemore, Jr.

MIDDLE JUDICIAL CIRCUIT includes Candler, Emanuel, Jefferson, Toombs and Washington counties. The court sits at Metter, Swainsboro, Louisville, Lyons and Sandersville.

Chief Judge
Walter C. McMillan, Jr.

Judge
Kathy Palmer

MOUNTAIN JUDICIAL CIRCUIT includes Habersham, Rabun and Stephens counties. The court sits at Clarkesville, Clayton and Toccoa.

Chief Judge
E. H. "Bucky" Woods, III

Judge
James E. Cornwell, Jr.

NORTHEASTERN JUDICIAL CIRCUIT includes Dawson and Hall counties. The court sits at Dawsonville and Gainesville.

Chief Judge
C. Andrew Fuller

Judges
John E. Girardeau
Kathlene F. Gosselin
Bonnie Chessher Oliver

SUPERIOR COURTS OF GEORGIA—*Continued*

NORTHERN JUDICIAL CIRCUIT includes Elbert, Franklin, Hart, Madison and Oglethorpe counties. The court sits at Elberton, Carnesville, Hartwell, Danielsville and Lexington.

Chief Judge
John H. Bailey, Jr.

Judges
Lindsay A. Tise, Jr.
Thomas L. Hodges

OCMULGEE JUDICIAL CIRCUIT includes Baldwin, Greene, Hancock, Jasper, Jones, Morgan, Putnam and Wilkinson counties. The court sits at Milledgeville, Greensboro, Sparta, Monticello, Gray, Madison, Eatonton and Irwinton.

Chief Judge
William A. Prior, Jr.

Judges
John Lee Parrott
Hulane Evans George
James Levi Cline, Jr.
Hugh V. Wingfield, III

OCONEE JUDICIAL CIRCUIT includes Bleckley, Dodge, Montgomery, Pulaski, Telfair and Wheeler counties. The court sits at Cochran, Eastman, Mount Vernon, Hawkinsville, McRae and Alamo.

Chief Judge
Phillip R. West

Judge
H. Frederick Mullis, Jr.

OGEECHEE JUDICIAL CIRCUIT includes Bulloch, Effingham, Jenkins and Screven counties. The court sits at Statesboro, Springfield, Millen and Sylvania.

Chief Judge
William E. Woodrum, Jr.

Judges
John R. Turner
F. Gates Peed

PATAULA JUDICIAL CIRCUIT includes Clay, Early, Miller, Quitman, Randolph, Seminole and Terrell counties. The court sits at Fort Gaines, Blakely, Colquitt, Georgetown, Cuthbert, Donalsonville and Dawson.

Chief Judge
Joe C. Bishop

Judge
Ronnie Joe Lane

PAULDING JUDICIAL CIRCUIT includes Paulding County. The court sits at Dallas.

Chief Judge
William A. Foster, III

Judge
Tonny S. Beavers

PIEDMONT JUDICIAL CIRCUIT includes Banks, Barrow and Jackson counties. The court sits at Homer, Winder and Jefferson.

Chief Judge
Robert W. Adamson

Judges
T. David Motes
Joseph H. Booth

ROCKDALE JUDICIAL CIRCUIT includes Rockdale County. The court sits at Conyers.

Chief Judge
Sidney L. Nation

Judge
David B. Irwin

ROME JUDICIAL CIRCUIT includes Floyd County. The court sits at Rome.

Chief Judge
Robert G. Walther

Judges
Walter J. Matthews
F. Larry Salmon
Tami P. Colston

SOUTHERN JUDICIAL CIRCUIT includes Brooks, Colquitt, Echols, Lowndes and Thomas counties. The court sits at Quitman, Moultrie, Statenville, Valdosta and Thomasville.

Chief Judge
H. Arthur McLane

Judges
Harry Jay Altman, II
Frank D. Horkan
Richard M. Cowart

SOUTH GEORGIA JUDICIAL CIRCUIT includes Baker, Calhoun, Decatur, Grady and Mitchell counties. The court sits at Newton, Morgan, Bainbridge, Cairo and Camilla.

Chief Judge
A. Wallace Cato

Judge
J. Richard Porter, III

SOUTHWESTERN JUDICIAL CIRCUIT includes Lee, Macon, Schley, Stewart, Sumter and Webster counties. The court sits at Leesburg, Oglethorpe, Ellaville, Lumpkin, Americus and Preston.

Chief Judge
R. Rucker Smith

Judges
George M. Peagler, Jr.
John V. Harper

STONE MOUNTAIN JUDICIAL CIRCUIT includes DeKalb County. The court sits at Decatur.

Chief Judge
Michael E. Hancock

Judges

Robert P. Mallis	Hilton Fuller
Daniel M. Coursey, Jr.	Robert J. Castellani
Clarence F. Seeliger	Linda Warren Hunter
Gail C. Flake	Anne Workman
Cynthia J. Becker	

SUPERIOR COURTS OF GEORGIA—*Continued*

TALLAPOOSA JUDICIAL CIRCUIT includes Haralson and Polk counties. The court sits at Buchanan and Cedartown.

Chief Judge
Michael L. Murphy

Judge
Richard C. Sutton

TIFTON JUDICIAL CIRCUIT includes Irwin, Tift, Turner and Worth counties. The court sits at Ocilla, Tifton, Ashburn and Sylvester.

Chief Judge
Gary C. McCorvey

Judge
J. Harvey Davis

TOOMBS JUDICIAL CIRCUIT includes Glascock, Lincoln, McDuffie, Taliaferro, Warren and Wilkes counties. The court sits at Gibson, Lincolnton, Thomson, Crawfordville, Warrenton and Washington.

Chief Judge
E. Purnell Davis, II

Judge
Roger W. Dunaway, Jr.

TOWALIGA JUDICIAL CIRCUIT includes Butts, Lamar and Monroe counties. The court sits at Jackson, Barnesville and Forsyth.

Chief Judge
E. Byron Smith

Judge
Thomas H. Wilson

WAYCROSS JUDICIAL CIRCUIT includes Bacon, Brantley, Charlton, Coffee, Pierce and Ware counties. The court sits at Alma, Nahunta, Folkston, Douglas, Blackshear and Waycross.

Chief Judge
Clarence D. Blount

Judges
Stephen L. Jackson
Dwayne Hamilton Gillis

WESTERN JUDICIAL CIRCUIT includes Clarke and Oconee counties. The court sits at Athens and Watkinsville.

Chief Judge
Lawton E. Stephens

Judges
Steve C. Jones
David R. Sweat

SENIOR SUPERIOR COURT JUDGES

Stephen Edwin Boswell
George H. Bryant
James L. Bullard
Willard H. Chason
Frank S. Cheatham, Jr.
John D. Crosby
Joe C. Crumbley
George B. Culpepper, III
F. Marion Cummings
Dubignion Douglas
J. Emory Findley
Robert E. Flournoy, Jr.
John A. Frazier
Joel James Fryer
Arthur W. Fudger
Joseph J. Gaines
Jack N. Gunter
Marvin B. Hartley, Jr.
John R. Harvey
W. Colbert Hawkins
James W. Head
Ralph Hicks
Elmo Holt
George A. Horkan, Jr.
William H. Ison
Isaac Jenrette
A. Richard Kenyon
William R. Killian
Kenneth Kilpatrick
H. Lamar Knight
W. D. Knight
John H. Land
John S. Langford, Jr.
Don A. Langham
Roy M. Lilly
Joseph E. Loggins
H. W. Lott
Faye Sanders Martin
Rufe E. McCombs
L. A. McConnell, Jr.
T. Penn McWhorter
Bobby C. Milam
Ben J. Miller
C. Cloud Morgan
Tracy Moulton, Jr.
Bernard J. Mulherin, Sr.
William J. Neville
James B. O'Connor
George E. Oliver
James W. Oxendine
Clarence L. Peeler, Jr.
Robert Thomas Pope
Robert L. Royal
Robert Lee Scoggin
Oscar D. Smith, Jr.
William J. Smith
Homer W. Stark
Robert B. Struble
A. Blenn Taylor, Jr.
Coy H. Temples
William Malcolm Towson, Sr.
Joseph B. Tucker
Clarence Vaughn, Jr.
James H. Weeks
Andrew J. Whalen, Jr.
Elisha Mullins Whisnant
Jere F. White
Watson L. White
Dan Peace Winn
Charles A. Wofford

STATE COURTS OF GEORGIA

The State Courts are courts of limited jurisdiction established in some counties in Georgia. There are currently State Courts operating in 70 of the 159 counties. The courts were first established in 1970 from a combination of existing county-funded courts. Effective July 1, 1984, constitutional and statutory provisions granted State Courts uniform jurisdiction and provided for judges to be elected in nonpartisan elections. Judges serve full time in Bibb, Bulloch, Carroll, Chatham, Cherokee, Clarke, Clayton, Cobb, Coweta, DeKalb, Dougherty, Douglas, Effingham, Fayette, Forsyth, Fulton, Glynn, Gwinnett, Henry, Houston, Lowndes, Muscogee, Richmond, Rockdale, Spalding, Troup and Walker counties; all other State Court judges serve part time except in Hall County where they may serve either. Judges are elected by the voters in their respective counties for four-year terms. Vacancies and new judgeships may be filled by the governor from a list of candidates provided by the Judicial Nominating Commission. Retired judges may be appointed by the governor to serve as senior judges.

The courts have criminal jurisdiction over trials of nonfelony criminal cases and civil jurisdiction over all general civil actions, regardless of amount claimed, except when jurisdiction is vested in the Superior Court. The courts may issue and hear applications for search and arrest warrants, hold courts of inquiry and conduct preliminary felony hearings. The courts have appellate jurisdiction to review decisions of lower courts as provided by statute.

The courts sit at the county seats.

†Also serves Juvenile Court

STATE COURTS OF GEORGIA—*Continued*

County	Judge
Appling	Emmett P. Johnson, Jr.
Bacon	William J. Edgar
Baldwin	Alan W. Thrower
Bibb	William P. Adams
Brooks	William R. Folsom
Bryan	Jack E. Carney, Jr.
Bulloch	Gary L. Mikell
Burke	Jerry Daniel
Candler	Ogden Doremus
Carroll	Robert H. Sullivan
Chatham	H. Gregory Fowler
	Ronald E. Ginsberg
Chattooga	Carlton H. Vines
Cherokee	C. J. Gober, Jr.
	William Alan Jordan
Clarke	N. Kent Lawrence
Clayton	Harold G. Benefield
	Morris E. Braswell
	John C. Carbo, III
	Linda S. Cowen
Clinch	Berrien L. Sutton†
Cobb	Melodie Howard Clayton
	M. Russell Carlisle, Jr.
	David Darden
	Irma Glover
	Toby Batson Prodgers
	Kathryn Johnson Tanksley
	Bridgette Campbell
	Nancy M. Campbell
	Roland R. Castellanos
	Beverly M. Collins
Coffee	Earl M. McRae, Jr.
Colquitt	Richard T. Kent
Coweta	John Herbert Cranford
Decatur	George C. Floyd
DeKalb	Edward E. Carriere, Jr.
	J. Antonio DelCampo
	Janis Gordon
	John Panos
	Wayne M. Purdom
	Mathew Robins
	Alvin T. Wong
Dougherty	John F. Salter, Sr.
Douglas	W. O'Neal Dettmering, Jr.
Early	Thomas H. Baxley
Effingham	Ronald Thompson
Elbert	Richard D. Campbell
Emanuel	William H. McWhorter, Jr.
Evans	Ron Hallman
Fayette	W. Fletcher Sams
Forsyth	David L. Dickinson
	Philip C. Smith
Fulton	Albert L. Thompson
	Diane E. Bessen
	Brenda Hill Cole
	Myra H. Dixon
	Susan B. Forsling
	John R. Mather
	Henry M. Newkirk
	Patsy Y. Porter
	Penny Brown Reynolds
Glynn	Orion L. Douglass, Sr.
Grady	John W. Bass, Sr.
Gwinnett	Howard Cook
	David M. Fuller
	Joseph Iannazzone
	Robert W. Mock, Sr.
	Pamela D. South
Habersham	Linton Kim Crawford, Jr.
Hall	Charles S. Wynne
	Rob Chambers
Henry	Ben Studdard, III
	James T. Chafin, III
Houston	Bob Richardson
Jackson	Jerry C. Gray
Jeff Davis	Ken W. Smith†
Jefferson	John R. Murphy, III
Jenkins	R. H. Reeves, III
Liberty	Leon M. Braun, Jr.
Long	Richard D. Phillips
Lowndes	Kelly D. Turner
McIntosh	Dale Jenkins
Miller	Robert M. Thomas
Mitchell	Michael Bankston
Muscogee	Andy Prather
	Maureen C. Gottfried
Pierce	Franklin D. Rozier, Jr.
Putnam	Jesse Copelan, Jr.
Richmond	Gayle B. Hamrick
	Richard A. Slaby
	David D. Watkins
Rockdale	William F. Todd, Jr.
Screven	Lisa M. Gross
Spalding	Sidney R. Esary
Stephens	Alton M. Adams
Sumter	Michael A. Fenessy
Tattnall	B. Daniel Dubberly, III
Thomas	Elliott P. McCollum, Jr.
Tift	Larry B. Mims
Toombs	Malcolm F. Bryant, Jr.
Treutlen	Donald Gillis
Troup	Jeannette L. Little
Turner	John Holland
Walker	Charles D. Peppers, Sr.
Ware	Douglas L. Gibson
Washington	Robert W. Wommack, Jr.
Wayne	Raymond S. Gordon, Jr.
Worth	Clarence A. Miller

JUVENILE COURTS OF GEORGIA

The Juvenile Courts are courts of special jurisdiction in Georgia established in some circuits. In circuits without a separate Juvenile Court judge, Superior Court judges hear juvenile cases. Judges are appointed by the Superior Court of their respective circuits for four-year terms, except in Rome Judicial Circuit where judges are elected for four-year terms. Associate judges are appointed by the Superior Court of their respective circuits or by the appointed judge in circuits with Juvenile Courts and serve at the pleasure of the appointing court. Associate judges may assist Juvenile Court and Superior Court judges with juvenile cases.

In circuits which have established Juvenile Courts, the courts have exclusive original jurisdiction in cases of delinquent and unruly children under the age of seventeen and deprived children under the age of eighteen. The courts have concurrent jurisdiction with the Superior Court in cases involving capital felonies, custody and

JUVENILE COURTS OF GEORGIA—*Continued*

child support cases and in proceedings to terminate parental rights. The courts also have jurisdiction over minors enlisting in the military, consent to marriage for minors and cases involving the Interstate Compact on Juveniles. Appeals are to the Court of Appeals or the Supreme Court.

The courts sit at the county seats.

*Also serves as Chief Magistrate
†Also serves State Court
‡Associate Judge

ALAPAHA JUDICIAL CIRCUIT includes Atkinson, Berrien, Clinch, Cook and Lanier counties. The court sits at Pearson, Nashville, Homerville, Adel and Lakeland.

Judges
George A. Bessonette
Berrien L. Sutton†

ALCOVY JUDICIAL CIRCUIT includes Newton and Walton counties. The court sits at Covington and Monroe.

Judges
George J. Hearn, III
Billy J. Waters

APPALACHIAN JUDICIAL CIRCUIT includes Fannin, Gilmer and Pickens counties. The court sits at Blue Ridge, Ellijay and Jasper.

Judges
William L. Reilly
Lynne M. Massaro‡

ATLANTA JUDICIAL CIRCUIT includes Fulton County. The court sits at Atlanta.

Judges
Nina Hickson
Charles G. Hodges‡
David Getachew-Smith‡
Juliette Wiltshire Scales‡
Sanford J. Jones
George G. Blau, III‡
Sharon N. Hill‡

ATLANTIC JUDICIAL CIRCUIT includes Bryan, Evans, Liberty, Long, McIntosh and Tattnall counties. The court sits at Pembroke, Claxton, Hinesville, Ludowici, Darien and Reidsville.

Judges
Benjamin P. Brinson
Luz Cloy
Linnie Darden, III

AUGUSTA JUDICIAL CIRCUIT includes Burke, Columbia and Richmond counties. The court sits at Waynesboro, Appling and Augusta.

Judges
Herbert E. Kernaghan
Preston B. Lewis, Jr.
Douglas J. Flanagan

BELL-FORSYTH JUDICIAL CIRCUIT includes Forsyth County. The court sits at Cumming.

Judges
J. Russell Jackson
Pamela Boles

BLUE RIDGE JUDICIAL CIRCUIT includes Cherokee County. The court sits at Canton.

Judges
Ellen McElyea
John B. Sumner

BRUNSWICK JUDICIAL CIRCUIT includes Appling, Camden, Glynn, Jeff Davis and Wayne counties. The court sits at Baxley, Woodbine, Brunswick, Hazlehurst and Jesup.

Judges
Terry K. Floyd
Donald E. Manning
Ken W. Smith†
J. Alexander Johnson
O. T. "Terry" Nichols*
Sophia C. Butler‡

CHATTAHOOCHEE JUDICIAL CIRCUIT includes Chattahoochee, Harris, Marion, Muscogee, Talbot and Taylor counties. The court sits at Cusseta, Hamilton, Buena Vista, Columbus, Talbotton and Butler.

Judges
Aaron Cohn
E. Wayne Jernigan
Warner L. Kennon

CHEROKEE JUDICIAL CIRCUIT includes Bartow and Gordon counties. The court sits at Cartersville and Calhoun.

Judges
J. Lane Bearden
Velma Tilley

CLAYTON JUDICIAL CIRCUIT includes Clayton County. The court sits at Jonesboro.

Judges
Karlton Van Banke
Tracy Graham
Steve Teske‡

COBB JUDICIAL CIRCUIT includes Cobb County. The court sits at Marietta.

Judges
Juanita Stedman
Sallie Walker Paist
Stephen Schuster
Carrie T. Harris‡

CONASAUGA JUDICIAL CIRCUIT includes Murray and Whitfield counties. The court sits at Chatsworth and Dalton.

Judge
Connie Maples Blaylock

CORDELE JUDICIAL CIRCUIT includes Ben Hill, Crisp, Dooly and Wilcox counties. The court sits at Fitzgerald, Cordele, Vienna and Abbeville.

Judge
T. Christopher Hughes

COWETA JUDICIAL CIRCUIT includes Carroll, Coweta, Heard, Meriwether and Troup counties. The court sits at Carrollton, Newnan, Franklin, Greenville and LaGrange.

Judges
Daniel P. Camp
Michael Key

JUVENILE COURTS OF GEORGIA—*Continued*

Joseph P. MacNabb
David Jasper Turner, Jr.

DOUGHERTY JUDICIAL CIRCUIT includes Dougherty County. The court sits at Albany.

Judges
Herbie Solomon
Richard Brooker‡

DOUGLAS JUDICIAL CIRCUIT includes Douglas County. The court sits at Douglasville.

Judge
Peggy H. Walker

DUBLIN JUDICIAL CIRCUIT includes Johnson, Laurens, Treutlen and Twiggs counties. The court sits at Wrightsville, Dublin, Soperton and Jeffersonville.

Judges
William L. Tribble, Sr.
Elizabeth Rutrough‡

EASTERN JUDICIAL CIRCUIT includes Chatham County. The court sits at Savannah.

Judges
John W. Beam, Jr.
Juan C. Ayala‡

ENOTAH JUDICIAL CIRCUIT includes Lumpkin, Towns, Union and White counties. The court sits at Dahlonega, Hiawassee, Blairsville and Cleveland.

Judges
Charles B. Brown
Michelle Vaughan

FLINT JUDICIAL CIRCUIT includes Henry County. The court sits at McDonough.

Judges
A. J. Welch, Jr.
William P. Bartles

GRIFFIN JUDICIAL CIRCUIT includes Fayette, Pike, Spalding and Upson counties. The court sits at Fayetteville, Zebulon, Griffin and Thomaston.

Judges
A. Ronald Cook
Tarey Schell‡

GWINNETT JUDICIAL CIRCUIT includes Gwinnett County. The court sits at Lawrenceville.

Judges
Robert V. Rodatus
Stephen E. Franzen
Robert S. Jones‡

HOUSTON JUDICIAL CIRCUIT includes Houston County. The court sits at Perry.

Judge
Deborah A. Edwards

LOOKOUT MOUNTAIN JUDICIAL CIRCUIT includes Catoosa, Chattooga, Dade and Walker counties. The court sits at Ringgold, Summerville, Trenton and LaFayette.

Judges
J. Michael Giglio
F. Bryant Henry, Jr.
McCracken "Ken" Poston
William Jerry Westbrook

MACON JUDICIAL CIRCUIT includes Bibb, Crawford and Peach counties. The court sits at Macon, Knoxville and Fort Valley.

Judges
Thomas J. Matthews
Quintress J. Gilbert

MIDDLE JUDICIAL CIRCUIT includes Candler, Emanuel, Jefferson, Toombs and Washington counties. The court sits at Metter, Swainsboro, Louisville, Lyons and Sandersville.

Judges
Tom Rawlings
Sarah M. Peacock‡
Mauri DeWaun Gray‡

MOUNTAIN JUDICIAL CIRCUIT includes Habersham, Rabun and Stephens counties. Jurisdiction is handled by the superior court.

NORTHEASTERN JUDICIAL CIRCUIT includes Dawson and Hall counties. The court sits at Dawsonville and Gainesville.

Judges
Cliff L. Jolliff
Mary R. Carden‡

NORTHERN JUDICIAL CIRCUIT includes Elbert, Franklin, Hart, Madison and Oglethorpe counties. The court sits at Elberton, Carnesville, Hartwell, Danielsville and Lexington.

Judges
Susanne Burton
Margaret N. Dyal

OCMULGEE JUDICIAL CIRCUIT includes Baldwin, Greene, Hancock, Jasper, Jones, Morgan, Putnam and Wilkinson counties. The court sits at Milledgeville, Greensboro, Sparta, Monticello, Gray, Madison, Eatonton and Irwinton.

Judge
Philip Spivey

OCONEE JUDICIAL CIRCUIT includes Bleckley, Dodge, Montgomery, Pulaski, Telfair and Wheeler counties. The court sits at Cochran, Eastman, Mount Vernon, Hawkinsville, McRae and Alamo.

Judges
W. Dennis Mullis
Sarah Wall

OGEECHEE JUDICIAL CIRCUIT includes Bulloch, Effingham, Jenkins and Screven counties. Jurisdiction is handled by the superior court.

PATAULA JUDICIAL CIRCUIT includes Clay, Early, Miller, Quitman, Randolph, Seminole and Terrell counties. The court sits at Fort Gaines, Blakely, Colquitt, Georgetown, Cuthbert, Donalsonville and Dawson.

JUVENILE COURTS OF GEORGIA—*Continued*

Judges

Edward Ross Collier
Ronald H. Rentz

PAULDING JUDICIAL CIRCUIT includes Paulding County. The court sits at Dallas.

Judges

Sandra Miller
Lani Skipper‡

PIEDMONT JUDICIAL CIRCUIT includes Banks, Barrow and Jackson counties. The court sits at Homer, Winder and Jefferson.

Judge

Kevin J. Guidry

ROCKDALE JUDICIAL CIRCUIT includes Rockdale County. The court sits at Conyers.

Judge

William Schneider

ROME JUDICIAL CIRCUIT includes Floyd County. The court sits at Rome.

Judges

Timothy A. Pape
Terri Burkhalter‡

SOUTHERN JUDICIAL CIRCUIT includes Brooks, Colquitt, Echols, Lowndes and Thomas counties. The court sits at Quitman, Moultrie, Statenville, Valdosta and Thomasville.

Judges

Stephen H. Andrews
Allen D. Denton
O. Wayne Ellerbee
William M. McIntosh
Vann K. Parrott‡

SOUTH GEORGIA JUDICIAL CIRCUIT includes Baker, Calhoun, Decatur, Grady and Mitchell counties. The court sits at Newton, Morgan, Bainbridge, Cairo and Camilla.

Judges

Edwin J. Perry, III
Randall E. Chew*

SOUTHWESTERN JUDICIAL CIRCUIT includes Lee, Macon, Schley, Stewart, Sumter and Webster counties. The court sits at Leesburg, Oglethorpe, Ellaville, Lumpkin, Americus and Preston.

Judge

Lisa C. Jones

STONE MOUNTAIN JUDICIAL CIRCUIT includes DeKalb County. The court sits at Decatur.

Judges

Gregory A. Adams
Robin S. Nash
Linda Bratton Haynes‡
Desiree Sutton Peagler‡

TALLAPOOSA JUDICIAL CIRCUIT includes Haralson and Polk counties. The court sits at Buchanan and Cedartown.

Judges

Mark H. Murphy
Thomas M. Rego‡
G. Randall Williams‡

TIFTON JUDICIAL CIRCUIT includes Irwin, Tift, Turner and Worth counties. The court sits at Ocilla, Tifton, Ashburn and Sylvester.

Judges

Holli G. Martin
Fred W. Rigdon, Jr.‡

TOOMBS JUDICIAL CIRCUIT includes Glascock, Lincoln, McDuffie, Taliaferro, Warren and Wilkes counties. The court sits at Gibson, Lincolnton, Thomson, Crawfordville, Warrenton and Washington.

Judge

Harold A. Hinesley

TOWALIGA JUDICIAL CIRCUIT includes Butts, Lamar and Monroe counties. The court sits at Jackson, Barnesville and Forsyth.

Judge

Sharon J. Whitwell

WAYCROSS JUDICIAL CIRCUIT includes Bacon, Brantley, Charlton, Coffee, Pierce and Ware counties. The court sits at Alma, Nahunta, Folkston, Douglas, Blackshear and Waycross.

Judges

Marion C. Pritchard
John B. Adams

WESTERN JUDICIAL CIRCUIT includes Clarke and Oconee counties. The court sits at Athens and Watkinsville.

Judges

James E. McDonald, Jr.
Sara M. McArthur
Robin W. Shearer‡

PROBATE COURTS OF GEORGIA

The Probate Courts, formerly known as Courts of Ordinary, are courts of limited jurisdiction in Georgia. Most judges are elected in partisan elections by the voters in their respective counties for four-year terms; judges in twenty-five counties are elected in nonpartisan elections.

The courts have exclusive original jurisdiction over probate of wills, administration of estates, appointment of guardians and involuntary hospitalization of incapacitated adults and other dependent individuals. If provided by statute, jurisdiction extends to holding habeas corpus hearings, supervising local elections and presiding over criminal preliminary hearings. In counties without State Courts, the courts may also try state game and fish law violations as well as traffic cases. In certain cases, the courts may also issue search and arrest warrants. Jury trial is by right in civil cases in counties with populations over 96,000 where the judge has been admitted to practice law for at least seven years. Appeals are to the Court of Appeals or the Supreme Court.

PROBATE COURTS OF GEORGIA—*Continued*

The courts sit at each county seat.

*Also serves as Chief Magistrate

County	Judge
Appling	Diane Hallman
Atkinson	Jeffery Paulk McGowan
Bacon	Joe Boatright*
Baker	Angela Hendricks*
Baldwin	Todd A. Blackwell
Banks	Betty Thomas
Barrow	Tammy S. Brown
Bartow	Mitchell Scoggins
Ben Hill	Tommy Walton Ash
Berrien	Susan W. Griner
Bibb	William J. Self, II
Bleckley	Kenneth Powell
Brantley	Johnnie E. Crews
Brooks	Jo Ann K. Collins
Bryan	Sam Davis, Jr.
Bulloch	Lee H. DeLoach
Burke	Preston B. Lewis, III
Butts	Vicki W. Johnston
Calhoun	Annie Doris Holder*
Camden	Martin Gillette
Candler	Charles Elliot Beasley
Carroll	Betty B. Cason
Catoosa	Greg Grayson
Charlton	Robert F. Phillips
Chatham	Harris Lewis
Chattahoochee	Kenneth Van Horn
Chattooga	Jonathan Marlin Payne
Cherokee	Kipling L. McVay
Clarke	Susan P. Tate
Clay	Melessa Shivers
Clayton	Eugene E. Lawson
Clinch	Karleen S. O'Berry
Cobb	David Dodd
Coffee	Troy C. Paul
Colquitt	Aileen H. Dunn
Columbia	Pat Hardaway
Cook	Louise Cowart
Coweta	Mary T. Cranford
Crawford	Sara Paravis
Crisp	Belinda F. Griffin
Dade	Jan Ellison
Dawson	Jennifer Evans Burt
Decatur	Tripp Barwick
DeKalb	William Marion Guess, Jr.
Dodge	John Kelley
Dooly	Dwayne D. Forehand
Dougherty	Nancy Smith Stephenson
Douglas	James T. Baker
Early	Tonya Holley*
Echols	Carl L. Rodgers*
Effingham	Frances Y. Seckinger
Elbert	Susan Sexton
Emanuel	Don E. Wilkes
Evans	Darin McCoy
Fannin	Linda K. Davis
Fayette	Martha King Stephenson
Floyd	Steven Burkhalter
Forsyth	Joyce W. Hawkins
Franklin	Eddy Fowler
Fulton	Pinkie T. Toomer
Gilmer	Margaret E. Huff
Glascock	Denise Dallas
Glynn	vacancy
Gordon	Johnny R. Parker
Grady	Sadie W. Voyles
Greene	Laverne C. Ogletree*
Gwinnett	Walter J. Clarke, II
Habersham	Ann Frye Adams-Jarrell
Hall	Patti Palmour Cornett
Hancock	Edith J. Ingram
Haralson	Eddie Hulsey
Harris	Martha M. Hartley
Hart	Bob Smith
Heard	Joseph Bledsoe
Henry	Del Buttrill
Houston	Janice Davidson Spires
Irwin	Virginia S. Turner
Jackson	Margaret Deadwyler
Jasper	Kathy Tyler
Jeff Davis	Jeffrey C. Chavis
Jefferson	Quillian L. Bryant, Jr.
Jenkins	Wanda Burke
Johnson	Mary Jo Buxton
Jones	J. Mike Greene*
Lamar	Kathryn B. Martin
Lanier	Judy B. Mullis
Laurens	Helen Woodard Harper
Lee	John Dennis Wheaton
Liberty	Nancy K. Aspinwall
Lincoln	Lee D. Moss*
Long	Marie H. Middleton*
Lowndes	Ruby K. Sirmans
Lumpkin	Michael Chastain
Macon	Mack S. McCarty
Madison	Donald H. Royston
Marion	James R. "Bump" Welch*
McDuffie	Albert E. "Gene" Wells
McIntosh	Gordon S. Shuman
Meriwether	Stiles Allen Estes
Miller	Brenda G. McNease*
Mitchell	Susan Taylor
Monroe	Karen Pitman
Montgomery	Rubie Nell Sanders
Morgan	Michael F. Bracewell
Murray	Dale Adams
Muscogee	Julia W. Lumpkin
Newton	Henry A. Baker*
Oconee	David Anglin
Oglethorpe	Beverly W. Nation
Paulding	Deborah Andersen
Peach	Deborah W. Hunnicutt
Pickens	Denny Rodney Gibson
Pierce	Brenda Howard
Pike	Lynn Brandenburg
Polk	Joyce B. Jones
Pulaski	Jeffrey W. Jones
Putnam	Patrice Howard
Quitman	Robert T. Bennett*
Rabun	Larry E. Cannon
Randolph	Linda E. Jackson
Richmond	Isaac Jolles
Rockdale	Lillis J. Brown
Schley	Marie M. Giddens
Screven	Debbie Wells
Seminole	J. E. Earnest*

PROBATE COURTS OF GEORGIA—*Continued*

Spalding	DeWitt Simonton, Jr.
Stephens	Glenda Ernest
Stewart	Jimmy B. Brazier
Sumter	Judy Reeves
Talbot	Joe S. Johnson, Jr.*
Taliaferro	Martha R. Mayo*
Tattnall	Sharon J. McCall
Taylor	Ronnie A. Parker*
Telfair	Dianne M. Walker
Terrell	Nancy Fryer
Thomas	Vickie Burnette
Tift	Lillian S. Radford
Toombs	Jackie O. Driskell
Towns	Wayne Garrett*
Treutlen	Grace B. Proctor*
Troup	Donald W. Boyd
Turner	Penny E. Thomas
Twiggs	Bob Powell
Union	Charles Dwain Brackett
Upson	Gary Hamby
Walker	Foye L. Johnson
Walton	H. Greg Adams
Ware	Marcus Lee Sweat, Jr.
Warren	Lucy J. Bryant
Washington	Rachel T. Lord
Wayne	Christine Burch
Webster	Lorene Tindol*
Wheeler	Roy O. Braswell, Jr.*
White	Garrison Baker
Whitfield	Ray Broadrick
Wilcox	Betty J. Anderson
Wilkes	Jim Burton
Wilkinson	Vivian L. Cummings*
Worth	Virginia Andrews

MAGISTRATE COURTS OF GEORGIA

The Magistrate Courts are courts of limited jurisdiction located in each of the 159 counties in Georgia. The courts were established July 1, 1983, by constitutional and statutory provisions to replace Justice of the Peace Courts, Small Claims Courts, previously existing Magistrate Courts and the County Court of Echols County. Initially, chief magistrates were appointed by the Superior Court in each respective circuit. Currently, most chief magistrates are elected in partisan elections for four-year terms. One or more magistrates are appointed by the chief magistrate; terms run concurrently with that of the chief magistrate who appointed them. Judges of other limited jurisdiction courts may serve as chief magistrates or magistrates as provided by law. Retired magistrates may be appointed by the governor to serve as senior judges.

The courts have jurisdiction over applications for and the issuance of search and arrest warrants, county ordinance violations, dispossessory actions, distress warrants and misdemeanor violations of bad check laws as well as misdemeanor violations of shoplifting, possession of marijuana and criminal trespass. The courts have civil jurisdiction in cases in which the amount in controversy does not exceed $15,000 except when jurisdiction is vested exclusively with the Superior Court. The courts may hold misdemeanor and felony preliminary hearings, administer oaths, issue subpoenas and punish contempts by a fine of up to $200 and/or imprisonment of up to ten days. Appeals are de novo to the State Court or Superior Court.

The courts sit at the county seats.

†Also serves Juvenile Court
#Also serves Probate Court
*Also serves Civil Court
‡Also serves Municipal Court of Columbus

County	Chief Magistrate
Appling	Donald W. Sears
Atkinson	Hilda James
Bacon	Joe Boatright#
Baker	Angela Hendricks#
Baldwin	Shane Geeter
Banks	Henry D. Banks
Barrow	June Schuenemann
Bartow	Thomas E. Moseley
Ben Hill	Shirley R. Ely
Berrien	S. H. Barker
Bibb	William C. Randall*
Bleckley	Helen J. Hart
Brantley	M. Louise Cheshire
Brooks	Joyce Miskiel
Bryan	Dale Mitchum
Bulloch	June B. Braswell
Burke	Curtis St. Germaine
Butts	James F. Trimble
Calhoun	Annie Doris Holder#
Camden	Harvey L. Fry
Candler	Judd Drake
Carroll	Alton P. Johnson
Catoosa	Donald Ray Caldwell
Charlton	Reginald F. Todd
Chatham	John W. Andre, Jr.
Chattahoochee	Hendon H. Griffin
Chattooga	Tracy L. Maddux
Cherokee	Charles T. Robertson, II
Clarke	Patricia D. Barron
Clay	Judy M. Cooper
Clayton	Michael P. Baird
Clinch	Annie Ruth Steedley
Cobb	Frank R. Cox
Coffee	Betty S. Lanier
Colquitt	Mose M. Kinsey
Columbia	David L. Huguenin
Cook	Ellen Wood
Coweta	James C. Stripling
Crawford	Juanita Childres
Crisp	Guy Douglas Pfeiffer
Dade	Thomas Wayne Reed
Dawson	Paul Payne
Decatur	Ralph C. Smith, Jr.
DeKalb	Winston P. Bethel
Dodge	Charles E. Nelson
Dooly	William A. Willis
Dougherty	Baxter C. Howell
Douglas	Susan S. Camp
Early	Tonya Holley#
Echols	Carl L. Rodgers#
Effingham	Preston G. Exley
Elbert	Lanie J. Simmons
Emanuel	Charles G. Brewer
Evans	Alvin N. Lewis
Fannin	Ronald L. Newton
Fayette	Charles Floyd
Floyd	Jerry Wood

MAGISTRATE COURTS OF GEORGIA—*Continued*

Forsyth	Barbara Cole
Franklin	Wm. David Buffington
Fulton	Joann Bayneum
Gilmer	Roger Kincaid
Glascock	Misty May
Glynn	Timothy L. Barton
Gordon	Max Fuller
Grady	D. Larry Bearden
Greene	Laverne C. Ogletree#
Gwinnett	Warren P. Davis
Habersham	James N. Butterworth
Hall	Bernard E. Roberts, III
Hancock	Shirley R. Ingram
Haralson	Evan Lee Stapler
Harris	W. Ken Askew
Hart	Selma Cheely
Heard	Donna Jean Burnham
Henry	Judy Hayes
Houston	David M. Pierce
Irwin	Paula Daniels
Jackson	Billy Chandler
Jasper	Kenneth G. Jackson
Jeff Davis	Chris A. Davenport
Jefferson	Murry Bowman
Jenkins	Janice Wilson Cheney
Johnson	Joe W. Rowland
Jones	J. Mike Greene#
Lamar	Brenda Williamson
Lanier	Charles R. Shaw
Laurens	Thomas C. Bobbitt, III
Lee	James R. Thurman
Liberty	Melinda Anderson
Lincoln	Lee D. Moss#
Long	Marie H. Middleton#
Lowndes	George H. Hart, Jr.
Lumpkin	William Jeffrey Lowe
Macon	Linda S. Rodgers
Madison	Harry F. Rice
Marion	James R. "Bump" Welch#
McDuffie	Robert H. Cofer, II
McIntosh	Ralph E. Poppell
Meriwether	Jack A. Todd
Miller	Brenda G. McNease#
Mitchell	Randall E. Chew†
Monroe	Frank N. Wilder, IV
Montgomery	James L. McCall, Jr.
Morgan	Connie J. Holt
Murray	Steve Hampton
Muscogee	H. Haywood Turner, III‡
Newton	Henry A. Baker#
Oconee	S. Ben Parker
Oglethorpe	Gail Smith
Paulding	Martin E. Valbuena
Peach	Laurens C. Lee
Pickens	Larry Ray
Pierce	Glenda Dowling
Pike	Priscilla Killingsworth
Polk	Rick Crawford
Pulaski	Carlette W. Gibson
Putnam	Ellen I. Pierce
Quitman	Robert T. Bennett#
Rabun	Frank Sutton
Randolph	Linda F. Bantz
Richmond	William D. Jennings, III*
Rockdale	Clarence R. Horne, Jr.
Schley	Robert Larry Wall
Screven	Michael Grady Jenkins
Seminole	J. E. Earnest#
Spalding	Rita L. Cavanaugh
Stephens	Dale P. Smith
Stewart	George E. Hancock
Sumter	Shirley S. Duke
Talbot	Joe S. Johnson, Jr.#
Taliaferro	Martha R. Mayo#
Tattnall	Susie W. Rowland
Taylor	Ronnie A. Parker#
Telfair	Vickie B. Scarborough
Terrell	Linda Freeman
Thomas	Grace D. Garland
Tift	Doug Jones
Toombs	Ezra J. Aaron
Towns	Wayne Garrett#
Treutlen	Grace B. Proctor#
Troup	Vickie Sue McWaters
Turner	Craig E. Poole
Twiggs	Kenneth E. Fowler
Union	Johnnie M. Garmon
Upson	Danny C. Bentley
Walker	Jerry Day
Walton	Dan F. Pierce
Ware	Lawton G. Taylor, Sr.
Warren	S. D. Pearson
Washington	Clayton C. Sheppard
Wayne	O. T. "Terry" Nichols†
Webster	Lorene Tindol#
Wheeler	Roy O. Braswell, Jr.#
White	Joy Parks
Whitfield	Barrett W. Whittemore
Wilcox	Alec Glenn Dorsey
Wilkes	Rosa Lee Martin
Wilkinson	Vivian L. Cummings#
Worth	Jean A. Powers

CIVIL COURTS OF GEORGIA

The Civil Courts are courts of limited jurisdiction established in Bibb and Richmond counties. Judges are elected for four-year terms.

The Civil Courts exist in place of the original City Courts. Each has jurisdiction to issue warrants, handle misdemeanor and felony preliminaries and hold jury trials. In Bibb County, Civil Court judges may hear civil law cases in which the amount in controversy is less than $7,500; in Richmond County, the amount in controversy must be less than $25,000.

The courts sit at Macon and Augusta.

*Also serves as Chief Magistrate

County	Judge
Bibb	William C. Randall*
	William M. Shurling, III
Richmond	William D. Jennings, III*
	H. Scott Allen

MUNICIPAL COURT OF COLUMBUS

The Municipal Court of Columbus is a court of limited jurisdiction in Muscogee County. The judge is elected for a four-year term.

The court has countywide jurisdiction in civil and

MUNICIPAL COURT OF COLUMBUS—*Continued*

landlord-tenant cases when the amount in controversy does not exceed $7,500. The court also has countywide criminal jurisdiction over misdemeanor guilty pleas and preliminary hearings. The court may issue warrants and hold jury trials in civil cases.

The court sits at Columbus.

---

*Also serves as Chief Magistrate

Judge
H. Haywood Turner, III*

COUNTY RECORDER'S COURTS OF GEORGIA

The County Recorder's Courts of Chatham, DeKalb, Gwinnett and Muscogee counties are courts of limited jurisdiction in Georgia. The method of selecting judges and their length of terms vary among counties.

The courts have jurisdiction to issue criminal warrants, handle criminal case preliminaries and hear and determine cases involving violation of all county ordinances.

The courts sit at the county seats.

County	Judge
Chatham	Lawrence G. Dillon
	LeRoy Burke, III
	Charles C. Brooks
	William A. Dowell
Columbus-Muscogee	Michael P. Cielinski
	Mary A. Buckner
	Michael E. Joyner
DeKalb	R. Joy Walker
	Angela T. Butts
	J. Phillip Hancock
	Ralph E. Merck
	Stephen W. Nicholas
	Nelly F. Withers
Gwinnett	Robert S. Jones
	Michael Greene
	Patti Muise
Muscogee	See Columbus-Muscogee

CITY COURT OF ATLANTA

The City Court of Atlanta was created to assist in the enforcement of traffic laws in the City of Atlanta. The court consists of a chief judge and ten judges appointed by the mayor and subject to retention vote at the second general city election following the date of appointment. Retired judges may serve as senior judges.

The court has jurisdiction over all crimes and offenses under the law of the State relating to and regulating traffic except where the Superior Court has been given exclusive jurisdiction.

Chief Judge
Edward L. Baety

Judges

Andrew J. Hairston
Lenwood A. Jackson
Julie M. T. Walker
Crystal Gaines
Nina M. Radakovich
Calvin S. Graves
Gary E. Jackson
Lisa Young Smith

Senior Judges
Joe Browne
Carson B. Shafer

MUNICIPAL COURT OF ATLANTA

The Municipal Court of Atlanta is a court of limited jurisdiction in Georgia. The court consists of a chief judge and nine judges initially appointed by the mayor. Judges run in the next general election following their appointment for four-year terms.

The court handles preliminary hearings for criminal violations occurring within the city of Atlanta.

Chief Judge
Barbara A. Harris

Judges

Elaine L. Carlisle
Deborah S. Greene
Catherine E. Malicki
William F. Riley, Jr.
vacancy
Clinton E. Deveaux
Howard R. Johnson
Andrew A. Mickle
vacancy

MUNICIPAL COURTS OF GEORGIA

Georgia's local Municipal Courts are courts of limited jurisdiction located in most of the state's incorporated towns and cities. The Municipal Courts were originally established as courts of incorporated municipalities with varying names, such as City Courts, Mayor's Courts, Municipal Courts, Recorder's Courts or Police Courts. All except the City Court of Atlanta were classified as Municipal Courts by the 1983 state constitution. The majority of municipal judges are appointed to office for one-year terms; however, some are elected as provided by individual municipal charters.

The courts have jurisdiction to try local traffic offenses and cases involving violations of municipal ordinances and concurrent jurisdiction over shoplifting cases and cases involving one ounce or less of marijuana and may try violations of the criminal trespass laws. The courts may also issue criminal warrants, conduct preliminary hearings and provide fines and penalties for offenses of simple assault and simple battery.

There are approximately 415 Municipal Courts in operation throughout the state.

Georgia Counties and County Seats

Appling
Baxley

Atkinson
Pearson

Bacon
Alma

Baker
Newton

Baldwin
Milledgeville

Banks
Homer

Barrow
Winder

Bartow
Cartersville

Ben Hill
Fitzgerald

Berrien
Nashville

Bibb
Macon

Bleckley
Cochran

Brantley
Nahunta

Brooks
Quitman

Bryan
Pembroke

Bulloch
Statesboro

Burke
Waynesboro

Butts
Jackson

Calhoun
Morgan

Camden
Woodbine

Candler
Metter

Carroll
Carrollton

Catoosa
Ringgold

Charlton
Folkston

Chatham
Savannah

Chattahoochee
Cusseta

Chattooga
Summerville

Cherokee
Canton

Clarke
Athens

Clay
Fort Gaines

Clayton
Jonesboro

Clinch
Homerville

Cobb
Marietta

Coffee
Douglas

Colquitt
Moultrie

Columbia
Appling

Cook
Adel

Coweta
Newnan

Crawford
Knoxville

Crisp
Cordele

Dade
Trenton

Dawson
Dawsonville

Decatur
Bainbridge

DeKalb
Decatur

Dodge
Eastman

Dooly
Vienna

Dougherty
Albany

Douglas
Douglasville

Early
Blakely

Echols
Statenville

Effingham
Springfield

Elbert
Elberton

Emanuel
Swainsboro

Evans
Claxton

Fannin
Blue Ridge

Fayette
Fayetteville

Floyd
Rome

Forsyth
Cumming

Franklin
Carnesville

Fulton
Atlanta

Gilmer
Ellijay

Glascock
Gibson

Glynn
Brunswick

Gordon
Calhoun

Grady
Cairo

Greene
Greensboro

Gwinnett
Lawrenceville

Habersham
Clarkesville

Hall
Gainesville

Hancock
Sparta

Haralson
Buchanan

Harris
Hamilton

Hart
Hartwell

Heard
Franklin

Henry
McDonough

Houston
Perry

Irwin
Ocilla

Jackson
Jefferson

Jasper
Monticello

Jeff Davis
Hazlehurst

Jefferson
Louisville

Jenkins
Millen

Johnson
Wrightsville

Jones
Gray

Lamar
Barnesville

Lanier
Lakeland

Laurens
Dublin

Lee
Leesburg

Liberty
Hinesville

Lincoln
Lincolnton

Long
Ludowici

Lowndes
Valdosta

Lumpkin
Dahlonega

Macon
Oglethorpe

Madison
Danielsville

Marion
Buena Vista

McDuffie
Thomson

McIntosh
Darien

Meriwether
Greenville

Miller
Colquitt

Mitchell
Camilla

Monroe
Forsyth

Montgomery
Mount Vernon

Morgan
Madison

COUNTIES AND COUNTY SEATS—*Continued*

Murray
Chatsworth

Muscogee
Columbus

Newton
Covington

Oconee
Watkinsville

Oglethorpe
Lexington

Paulding
Dallas

Peach
Fort Valley

Pickens
Jasper

Pierce
Blackshear

Pike
Zebulon

Polk
Cedartown

Pulaski
Hawkinsville

Putnam
Eatonton

Quitman
Georgetown

Rabun
Clayton

Randolph
Cuthbert

Richmond
Augusta

Rockdale
Conyers

Schley
Ellaville

Screven
Sylvania

Seminole
Donalsonville

Spalding
Griffin

Stephens
Toccoa

Stewart
Lumpkin

Sumter
Americus

Talbot
Talbotton

Taliaferro
Crawfordville

Tattnall
Reidsville

Taylor
Butler

Telfair
McRae

Terrell
Dawson

Thomas
Thomasville

Tift
Tifton

Toombs
Lyons

Towns
Hiawassee

Treutlen
Soperton

Troup
LaGrange

Turner
Ashburn

Twiggs
Jeffersonville

Union
Blairsville

Upson
Thomaston

Walker
LaFayette

Walton
Monroe

Ware
Waycross

Warren
Warrenton

Washington
Sandersville

Wayne
Jesup

Webster
Preston

Wheeler
Alamo

White
Cleveland

Whitfield
Dalton

Wilcox
Abbeville

Wilkes
Washington

Wilkinson
Irwinton

Worth
Sylvester

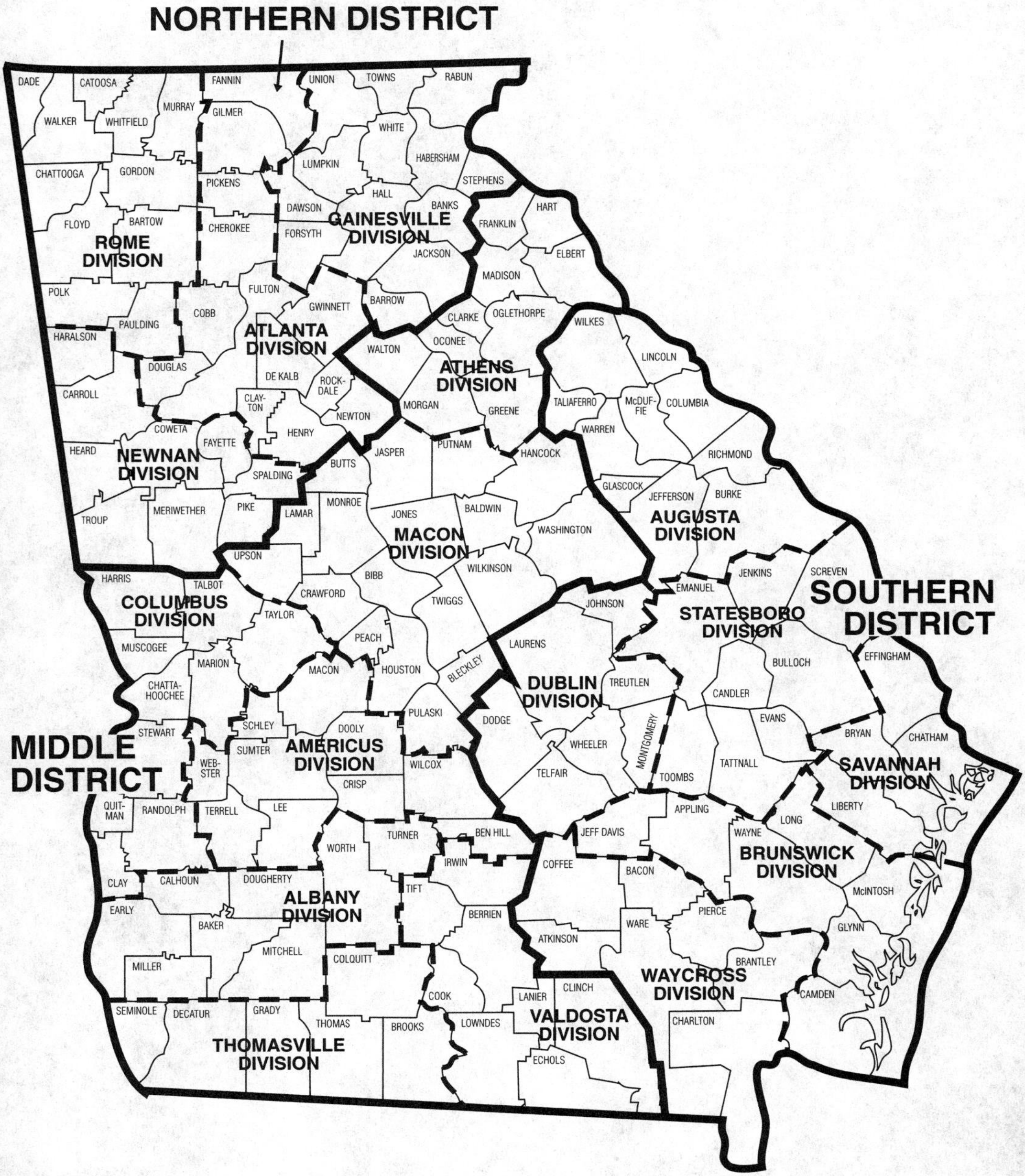
NORTHERN DISTRICT
MIDDLE DISTRICT
SOUTHERN DISTRICT
ROME DIVISION
GAINESVILLE DIVISION
ATLANTA DIVISION
ATHENS DIVISION
NEWNAN DIVISION
AUGUSTA DIVISION
MACON DIVISION
COLUMBUS DIVISION
STATESBORO DIVISION
DUBLIN DIVISION
AMERICUS DIVISION
SAVANNAH DIVISION
BRUNSWICK DIVISION
ALBANY DIVISION
WAYCROSS DIVISION
VALDOSTA DIVISION
THOMASVILLE DIVISION
DADE
CATOOSA
WALKER
WHITFIELD
MURRAY
FANNIN
GILMER
UNION
TOWNS
RABUN
WHITE
HABERSHAM
LUMPKIN
STEPHENS
CHATTOOGA
GORDON
PICKENS
DAWSON
HALL
BANKS
FLOYD
BARTOW
CHEROKEE
FORSYTH
FRANKLIN
HART
JACKSON
ELBERT
POLK
FULTON
MADISON
COBB
GWINNETT
BARROW
PAULDING
CLARKE
OGLETHORPE
WILKES
HARALSON
WALTON
OCONEE
LINCOLN
DOUGLAS
DE KALB
ROCK-DALE
CARROLL
CLAY-TON
MORGAN
GREENE
TALIAFERRO
McDUF-FIE
COLUMBIA
NEWTON
COWETA
HENRY
WARREN
FAYETTE
HEARD
JASPER
PUTNAM
HANCOCK
RICHMOND
BUTTS
SPALDING
GLASCOCK
JEFFERSON
BURKE
MONROE
LAMAR
PIKE
MERIWETHER
TROUP
JONES
BALDWIN
WASHINGTON
UPSON
JENKINS
SCREVEN
WILKINSON
HARRIS
TALBOT
BIBB
EMANUEL
CRAWFORD
JOHNSON
TWIGGS
TAYLOR
PEACH
LAURENS
MUSCOGEE
BULLOCH
EFFINGHAM
MARION
BLECKLEY
HOUSTON
MACON
CHATTA-HOOCHEE
TREUTLEN
CANDLER
PULASKI
EVANS
STEWART
SCHLEY
DOOLY
DODGE
MONTGOMERY
BRYAN
CHATHAM
WHEELER
SUMTER
WEB-STER
WILCOX
CRISP
TELFAIR
TOOMBS
TATTNALL
QUIT-MAN
RANDOLPH
TERRELL
LEE
LIBERTY
APPLING
LONG
BEN HILL
TURNER
JEFF DAVIS
WAYNE
WORTH
IRWIN
COFFEE
CLAY
CALHOUN
DOUGHERTY
BACON
McINTOSH
TIFT
EARLY
BAKER
BERRIEN
WARE
PIERCE
GLYNN
MITCHELL
ATKINSON
MILLER
COLQUITT
BRANTLEY
CLINCH
COOK
LANIER
CAMDEN
SEMINOLE
DECATUR
GRADY
THOMAS
BROOKS
LOWNDES
CHARLTON
ECHOLS

UNITED STATES DISTRICT COURTS DISTRICTS OF GEORGIA

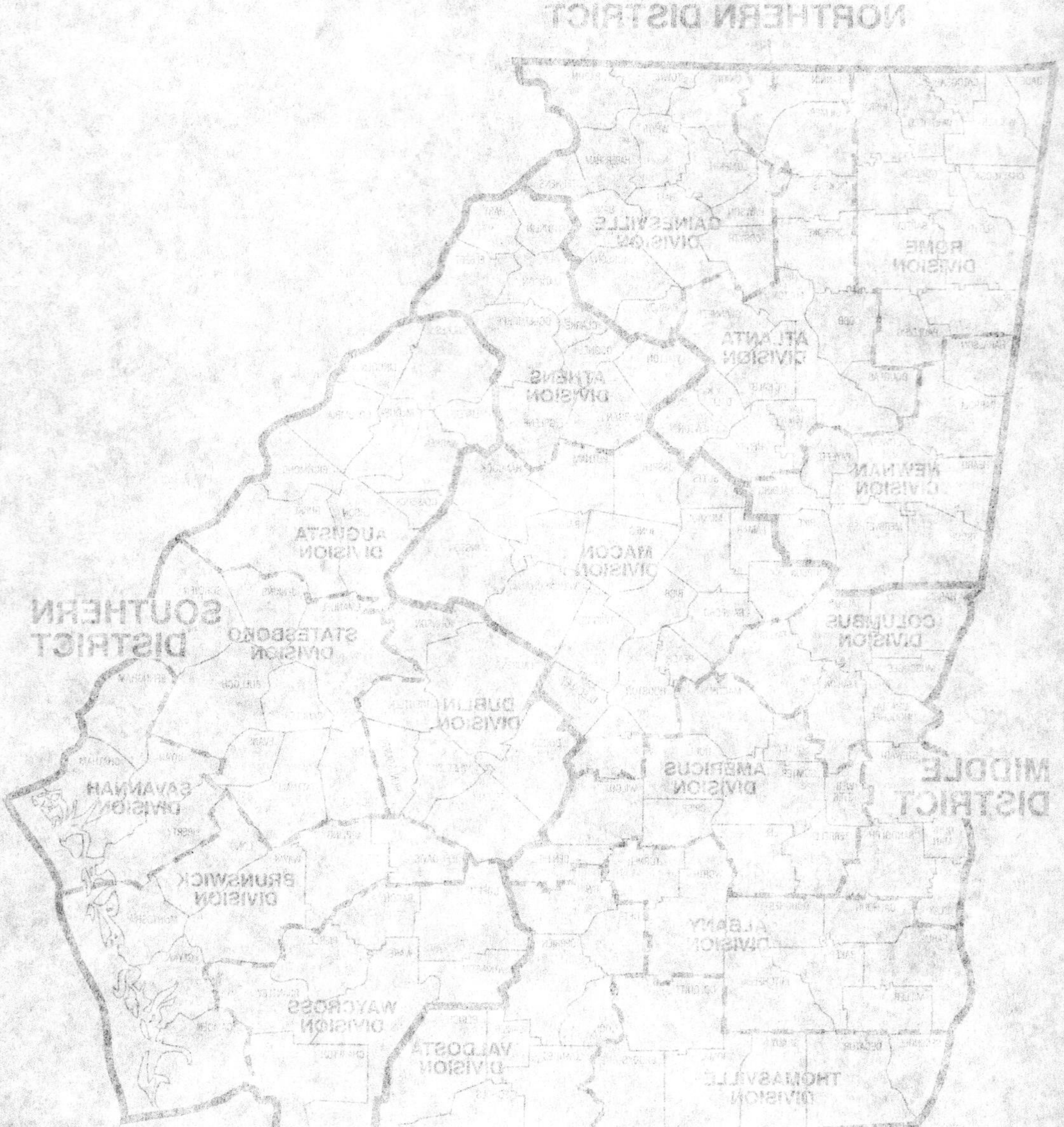
NORTHERN DISTRICT
MIDDLE DISTRICT
SOUTHERN DISTRICT
GAINESVILLE DIVISION
ROME DIVISION
ATLANTA DIVISION
ATHENS DIVISION
NEWNAN DIVISION
AUGUSTA DIVISION
MACON DIVISION
STATESBORO DIVISION
COLUMBUS DIVISION
DUBLIN DIVISION
AMERICUS DIVISION
SAVANNAH DIVISION
BRUNSWICK DIVISION
ALBANY DIVISION
WAYCROSS DIVISION
VALDOSTA DIVISION
THOMASVILLE DIVISION

UNITED STATES DISTRICT COURTS DISTRICTS OF GEORGIA

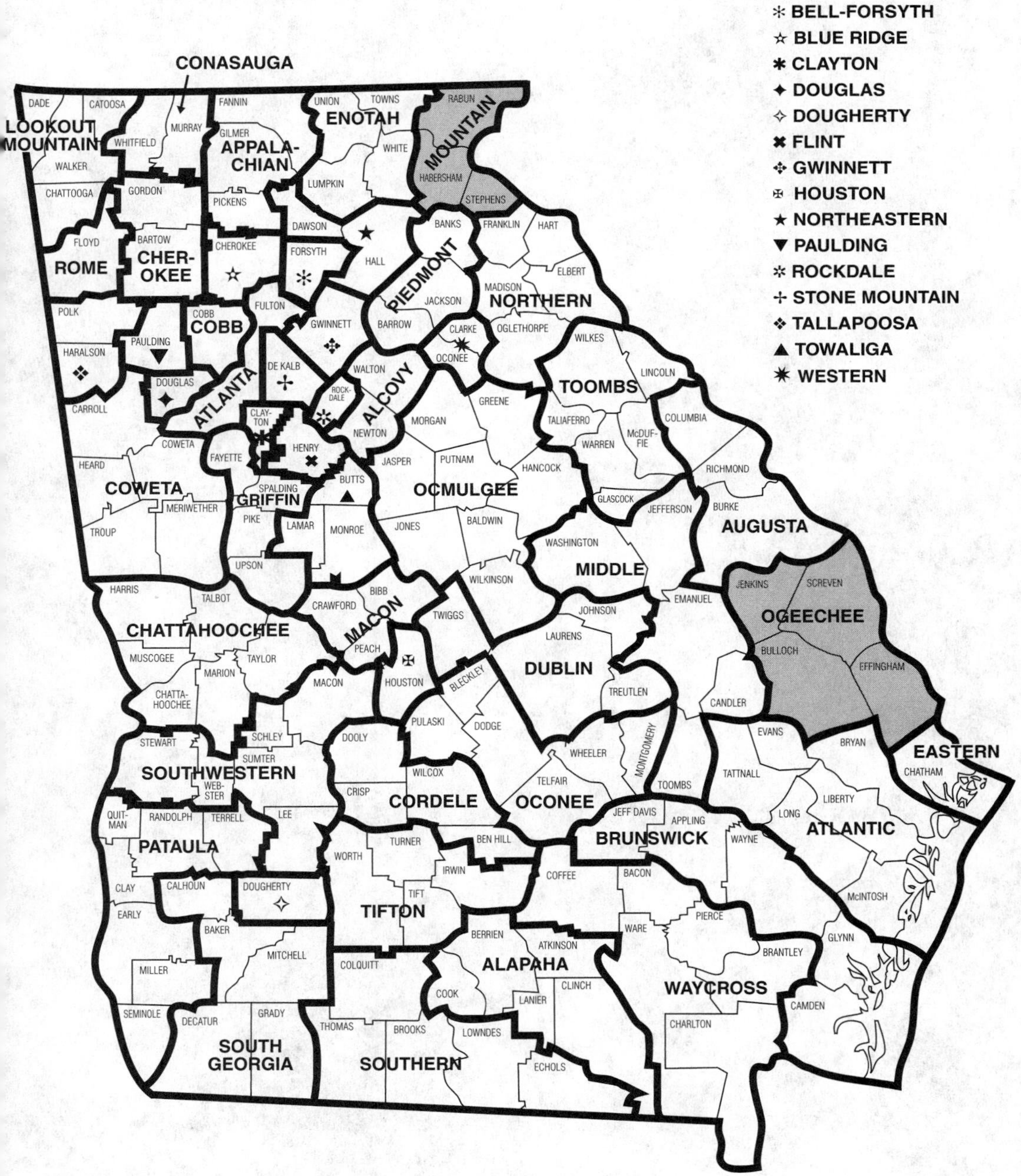

BELL-FORSYTH
BLUE RIDGE
CLAYTON
DOUGLAS
DOUGHERTY
FLINT
GWINNETT
HOUSTON
NORTHEASTERN
PAULDING
ROCKDALE
STONE MOUNTAIN
TALLAPOOSA
TOWALIGA
WESTERN
CONASAUGA
LOOKOUT MOUNTAIN
APPALACHIAN
ENOTAH
MOUNTAIN
ROME
CHEROKEE
COBB
PIEDMONT
NORTHERN
ATLANTA
ALCOVY
TOOMBS
COWETA
GRIFFIN
OCMULGEE
AUGUSTA
MIDDLE
CHATTAHOOCHEE
MACON
OGEECHEE
DUBLIN
SOUTHWESTERN
CORDELE
OCONEE
EASTERN
BRUNSWICK
ATLANTIC
PATAULA
TIFTON
ALAPAHA
WAYCROSS
SOUTH GEORGIA
SOUTHERN
DADE
CATOOSA
WALKER
WHITFIELD
MURRAY
FANNIN
GILMER
UNION
TOWNS
RABUN
WHITE
HABERSHAM
STEPHENS
LUMPKIN
CHATTOOGA
GORDON
PICKENS
DAWSON
BANKS
FRANKLIN
HART
FLOYD
BARTOW
CHEROKEE
FORSYTH
HALL
ELBERT
MADISON
JACKSON
POLK
COBB
FULTON
GWINNETT
BARROW
CLARKE
OGLETHORPE
WILKES
HARALSON
PAULDING
DE KALB
WALTON
OCONEE
LINCOLN
DOUGLAS
ROCKDALE
CARROLL
CLAYTON
NEWTON
GREENE
MORGAN
COLUMBIA
TALIAFERRO
COWETA
FAYETTE
HENRY
McDUFFIE
WARREN
HEARD
JASPER
PUTNAM
HANCOCK
RICHMOND
BUTTS
SPALDING
MERIWETHER
GLASCOCK
JEFFERSON
BURKE
PIKE
LAMAR
MONROE
JONES
BALDWIN
TROUP
WASHINGTON
UPSON
WILKINSON
HARRIS
TALBOT
BIBB
JENKINS
SCREVEN
CRAWFORD
TWIGGS
JOHNSON
EMANUEL
LAURENS
MUSCOGEE
TAYLOR
PEACH
BULLOCH
EFFINGHAM
MARION
HOUSTON
BLECKLEY
MACON
TREUTLEN
CANDLER
CHATTAHOOCHEE
SCHLEY
PULASKI
DODGE
STEWART
DOOLY
SUMTER
WHEELER
MONTGOMERY
EVANS
BRYAN
WEBSTER
WILCOX
TELFAIR
TATTNALL
CHATHAM
CRISP
TOOMBS
QUITMAN
RANDOLPH
TERRELL
LEE
JEFF DAVIS
APPLING
LIBERTY
LONG
TURNER
BEN HILL
WAYNE
WORTH
IRWIN
CLAY
CALHOUN
DOUGHERTY
COFFEE
BACON
TIFT
McINTOSH
EARLY
BAKER
WARE
PIERCE
BERRIEN
ATKINSON
GLYNN
MITCHELL
BRANTLEY
MILLER
COLQUITT
CLINCH
COOK
LANIER
CAMDEN
SEMINOLE
GRADY
DECATUR
THOMAS
BROOKS
LOWNDES
CHARLTON
ECHOLS
JUVENILE JURISDICTION HANDLED BY SUPERIOR COURT

JUDICIAL CIRCUITS OF GEORGIA SUPERIOR COURTS AND GEORGIA JUVENILE COURTS

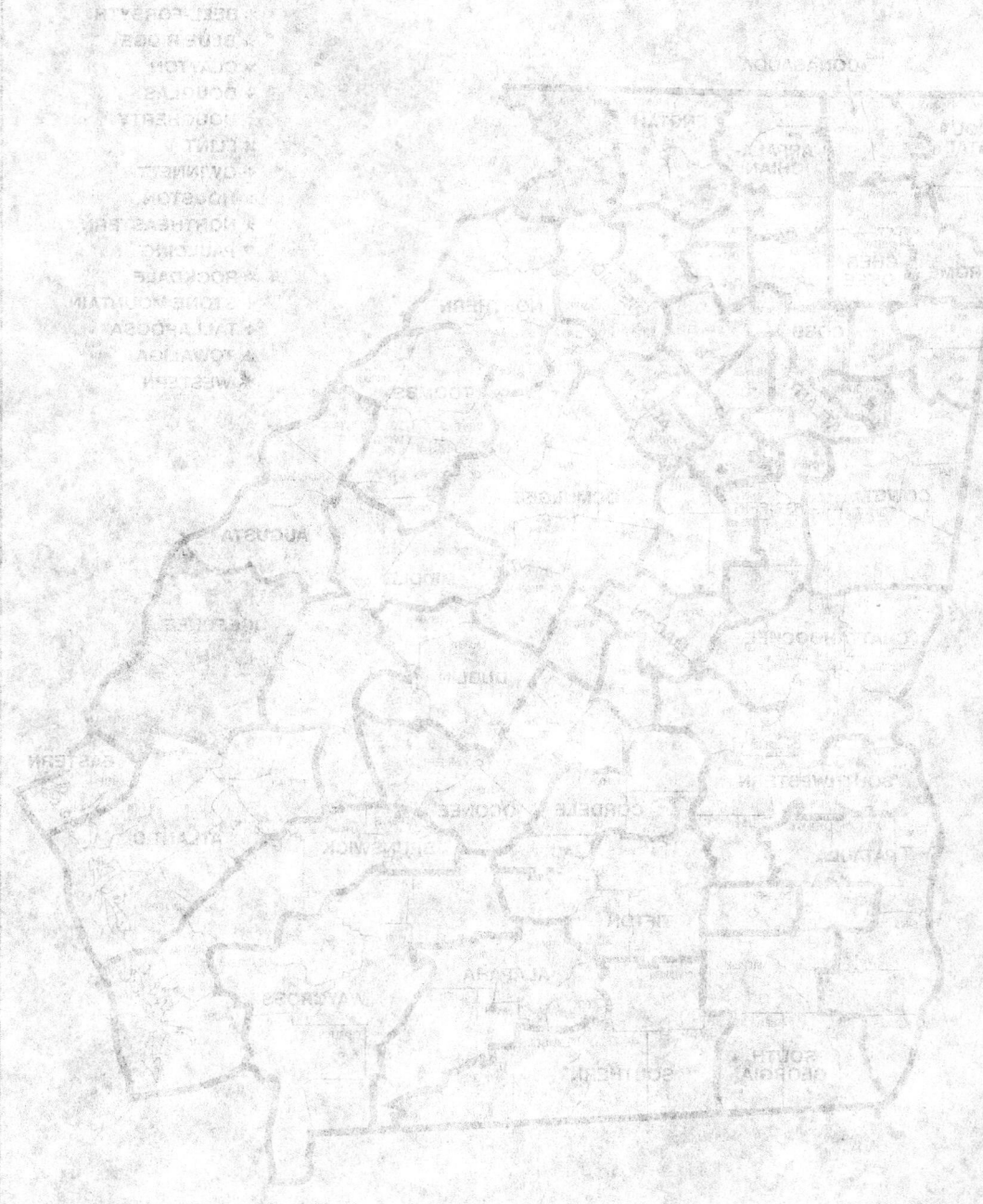

GEORGIA

AARON, Ezra J. *(Chief Magistrate, Magistrate Court of Toombs County)* Assumed office 1983. Elected to subsequent terms. Born Claxton Georgia May 8, 1930. Southern Baptist. Justice of the Peace nine years. Judge, Small Claims Court March 1, 1975 to July 1983. City Councilman 1962-66. Sergeant USAS 1948-52.

Office: 147 Jerry Avenue, Lyons 30436.
Telephone: (912) 526-8984.
Fax: (912) 526-8985

ABBOTT, Louisa *(Judge, Superior Court of Georgia Eastern Judicial Circuit)*

Office: 203 Chatham County Courthouse, 133 Montgomery Street, Savannah 31401.
Telephone: (912) 652-7162.
Fax: (912) 652-7164
E-mail address: labbott@chathamcounty.org

ADAMS, Alfred Harris *(Judge, Court of Appeals of Georgia)* Born Augusta Georgia March 14, 1948. Baptist. Educated at Mercer University B.A. 1970 J.D. 1971. Admitted to practice Georgia 1971, U.S. District Court Northern District of Georgia 1971, U.S. Court of Appeals Fifth Circuit 1974 and U.S. Supreme Court 1982. In legal practice Marietta since 1971. Judge, Municipal Court of Marietta 1982-83. Former Judge and Chief Judge, State Court of Cobb County, appointed by Governor Joe Frank Harris to term beginning Jan 4, 1985.

Assistant District Attorney Cobb Judicial Circuit 1971-73. County Administrator 1980-85. Author "Due Process in Hospital Staff Selection—Exclusion Controversies" GSHA Hospital Law Seminar 1977. Member State Bar of Georgia and Cobb County Bar Association (Bar Representative Board of Directors Cobb County Symposium, Inc. 1978-81, President Younger Lawyers Section 1979, Member Executive Committee 1980, Secretary-Treasurer Trial Lawyers Section 1982 and Chairman Legal Economics Committee 1982). Member Cobb-Kennestone Hospital Guild. Board of Directors Cobb County Symposium, Inc. and Cobb County Youth Museum, Inc.

Office: 334 State Judicial Building, Atlanta 30334.
Telephone: (404) 656-3455.

ADAMS, Alton M. *(Judge, State Court of Stephens County)* Appointed by Governor George D. Busbee to term beginning June 11, 1979. Elected 1984, 1988, 1992, 1996 and 2000. Current term expires Dec 31, 2004. Serves part time. Born Toccoa Georgia March 30, 1945. Baptist. Trustee First Baptist Church of Toccoa. Educated at Mercer University B.S. cum laude 1967 J.D. magna cum laude 1971. Georgia Survey Editor Mercer University Law Review 1970-71. Member Kappa Sigma and Phi Delta Phi. Admitted to practice Georgia 1971. Began legal practice Toccoa 1971.

Member Mountain Judicial Circuit (President 1974-75) and Stephens County (President 1983-84) Bar Associations. Past President Toccoa-Stephens County Chamber of Commerce and Currahee Arts Council, Inc. and Toccoa Elementary Parent Teacher Organization.

Mailing address: P.O. Box 488, Toccoa 30577-0488.
Telephone: (706) 886-3401.
Fax: (706) 282-1954
E-mail address: adamslawfirm@alltel.net

ADAMS, Dale *(Judge, Probate Court of Murray County)*

Office: 115 Fort Street, Chatsworth 30705.
Telephone: (706) 695-3812.
Fax: (706) 517-1340
E-mail address: mcprobate@alltel.net

ADAMS, Gregory A. *(Judge, Juvenile Court of Georgia Stone Mountain Judicial Circuit)* Appointed to term beginning June 24, 1994. Reappointed 1998 and 2002. Current term expires June 24, 2006. Currently serves as Chief Judge.

Office: 3631 Camp Circle, Decatur 30032.
Telephone: (404) 294-2727.
Fax: (404) 294-2981
E-mail address: GAADAMS@co.dekalb.ga.us

ADAMS, H. Greg *(Judge, Probate Court of Walton County)* Elected to term beginning Jan 1, 1981. Reelected 1984, 1988, 1992, 1996 and 2000. Current term expires Dec 31, 2004. Born Walton Georgia Dec 5, 1944. Methodist. Educated at Georgia State University B.S. 1976 and University of Georgia M.Ed. 1978. Chief Magistrate, Magistrate Court of Walton County 1981-92.

Research and Development Manager International Loss Control Institute Loganville Georgia. Democrat. Founder Georgia Association of Paraplegics. Enjoys movies and sports.

Mailing address: P.O. Box 629, Monroe 30655-0629.
Telephone: (770) 267-1345.
Fax: (770) 267-1417
E-mail address: gadams@co.walton.ga.us

ADAMS, John B. *(Judge, Juvenile Court of Georgia Waycross Judicial Circuit)* Appointed.

Mailing address: P.O. Box 607, Folkston 31537-0607.
Office: 203 West Main Street, Folkston 31537.
Telephone: (912) 496-2567.
Fax: (912) 496-4737
E-mail address: jbacga@planttel.net

ADAMS, Robert B. *(Judge, Superior Court of Georgia Conasauga Judicial Circuit)*

Mailing address: P.O. Box 596, Dalton 30722-0596.
Telephone: (706) 278-4251.
Fax: (706) 275-7573
E-mail address: badams@ocsonline.com

ADAMS, William P. *(Judge, State Court of Bibb County)* Elected Nov 1998 to term beginning Jan 1, 1999. Reelected Aug 2002, current term expires Jan 1, 2007. Born Macon Georgia Feb 7, 1952. Methodist. Educated at University of Georgia B.B.A. with honors 1974 and Mercer University J.D. with honors 1977. Staff member Mercer Law Review 1976-77. Admitted to practice Georgia 1977 and U.S. District Court Middle District of Georgia 1977. In legal practice Macon 1977-78 and 1986-98.

Assistant U.S. Attorney Middle District of Georgia 1978-86. Member State Bar of Georgia, Macon (Presi-

ADAMS, WILLIAM P.—*Continued*

dent 1996-97), Federal (President Middle Georgia Chapter 1992-93) and American Bar Associations. Named Kiwanian of the Year 1992. President Elect and Member Kiwanis Club. Involved in activities with church and Little League. Enjoys sports.
Mailing address: P.O. Box 5086, Macon 31213-7199.
Office: 500 Bibb County Courthouse, Macon 31201.
Telephone: (478) 621-6676.
Fax: (478) 621-6326
E-mail address: badams@co.bibb.ga.us

ADAMS-JARRELL, Ann Frye *(Judge, Probate Court of Habersham County)*
Mailing address: P.O. Box 625, Clarkesville 30523.
Telephone: (706) 754-2013.
Fax: (706) 754-5093

ADAMSON, Robert W. *(Chief Judge, Superior Court of Georgia Piedmont Judicial Circuit)* Magistrate Oct 12, 1992 to Dec 31, 1992. Elected Judge to term beginning Jan 1, 1993. Reelected to terms beginning Jan 1, 1997 and Jan 1, 2001. Current term expires Dec 31, 2004. Born Turin Georgia Sept 19, 1941. Religious affiliation: Disciples of Christ. Educated at University of Georgia B.S.A. 1964 J.D. 1971. Member Phi Alpha Delta (Vice Justice Georgia Chapter 1970), Omega Delta Kappa and Blue Key. Admitted to practice Georgia 1971, U.S. District Court District of Georgia 1975, U.S. Court of Appeals Fifth Circuit 1975 and U.S. Supreme Court 1978. In legal practice Winder 1971-92.
Member Winder-Barrow Industrial Building Authority 1992. Member State Bar of Georgia, Piedmont (Past President) and American Bar Associations. Captain U.S. Army March 1964 to Aug 1968 (Vietnam 1966-67). Member Barrow County Chamber of Commerce (President 1992), Grid Iron Society and Rotary Club of Winder (Past President). Enjoys farming, hunting, fishing and cooking.
Mailing address: P.O. Box 39, Homer 30547-0039.
Telephone: (706) 677-6282.
Fax: (706) 677-2329

ALAIMO, Anthony A. *(Senior Judge, United States District Court Southern District of Georgia)* Appointed for life by the President. Former Chief Judge. Assumed Senior status, serves by assignment. Educated at Ohio Northern University A.B. and Emory University J.D. Admitted to practice 1948.
Mailing address: P.O. Box 944, Brunswick 31521-0944.
Telephone: (912) 280-1340.

ALLEN, H. Scott *(Judge, Civil Court of Richmond County)* Also serves as Magistrate, Magistrate Court of Richmond County.
Office: 314 Municipal Building, Augusta 30911.
Telephone: (706) 821-2385.
Fax: (706) 821-2381

ALLEN, John D. *(Judge, Superior Court of Georgia Chattahoochee Judicial Circuit)* Appointed by Governor Zell Miller to term beginning Oct 27, 1993. Elected 1994, 1998 and 2002. Current term expires Dec 31, 2006. Former Judge, State Court of Muscogee County.
Mailing address: P.O. Box 1340, Columbus 31902-1340.
Telephone: (706) 653-4277.
Fax: (706) 653-4275

ALLGOOD, Robert L. *(Judge, Superior Court of Georgia Augusta Judicial Circuit)* Appointed by Governor Zell Miller to term beginning Sept 21, 1995. Elected 1996 and 2000. Current term expires Dec 31, 2004.
Office: 312 City-County Building, 530 Greene Street, Augusta 30911.
Telephone: (706) 821-2835.
Fax: (706) 721-1091

ALTMAN, Harry Jay, II *(Judge, Superior Court of Georgia Southern Judicial Circuit)* Appointed by Governor Zell Miller to term beginning Aug 8, 1994. Elected 1996 and 2000. Current term expires 2004. Born Thomasville Georgia March 3, 1951. Jewish. Educated at Washington and Lee University B.A. cum laude 1972 and University of Georgia J.D. magna cum laude 1975. Admitted to practice Georgia 1975 and Florida 1977. In legal practice Thomasville 1975-94.
Board of Governors 1982-94.
Mailing address: P.O. Box 1734, Thomasville 31799-1734.
Telephone: (229) 228-6276.
Fax: (229) 225-4128
E-mail address: thosct@rose.net

ANDERSEN, Deborah *(Judge, Probate Court of Paulding County)* Elected to term beginning Jan 1, 2001. Born Douglas County Georgia Sept 15, 1953. Baptist.
Attends Probate Judges Seminar annually. Republican. Enjoys working with youth groups in church and traveling.
Office: 25 Courthouse Square, First Floor, Dallas 30132.
Telephone: (770) 443-7541.
Fax: (770) 443-7631
E-mail address: deborah.andersen@paulding.gov

ANDERSON, Betty J. *(Judge, Probate Court of Wilcox County)*
Office: Wilcox County Courthouse, 103 North Broad Street, Abbeville 31001.
Telephone: (229) 467-2220.
Fax: (229) 467-2000

ANDERSON, Melinda *(Chief Magistrate, Magistrate Court of Liberty County)*
Mailing address: P.O. Box 912, Hinesville 31310-0912.
Telephone: (912) 368-2063.
Fax: (912) 876-2474
E-mail address: melinda.anderson@gsccca.org

ANDRE, John W., Jr. *(Chief Magistrate, Magistrate Court of Chatham County)* Elected to term beginning Jan 1, 1985. Reelected 1988, 1992, 1996 and 2000. Current term expires Dec 31, 2004. Born Savannah Georgia Jan 9, 1934. Lutheran. Educated at Armstrong State College B.B.A. 1969 and John Marshall Law School LL.B. 1973. Admitted to practice Georgia 1973. Began legal practice Savannah 1973.
Commissioner Chatham County 1977-80. Engineman Second Class USN 1952-56.
Office: 133 Montgomery Street, Room 300, Savannah 31401.
Telephone: (912) 652-7187.
Fax: (912) 652-7550

ANDREWS, Gary B. *(Judge, Court of Appeals of Georgia)* Former Chief Judge. Currently serves as Pre-

ANDREWS, GARY B.—*Continued*
siding Judge. Educated at University of Georgia B.B.A. J.D. Judge, Superior Court of Georgia Lookout Mountain Judicial Circuit 1980-85.

Appointed to Public Service Commission 1985-90. Attended The National Judicial College 1981.

Office: 334 State Judicial Building, Atlanta 30334.
Telephone: (404) 656-3456.
Fax: (404) 651-8139

ANDREWS, Stephen H. *(Judge, Juvenile Court of Georgia Southern Judicial Circuit)* Appointed.
Mailing address: P.O. Drawer 70, Thomasville 31799.
Telephone: (229) 226-5308.
Fax: (229) 228-9108
E-mail address: seery@bellsouth.net

ANDREWS, Virginia *(Judge, Probate Court of Worth County)*
Office: 201 North Main Street, Room 12, Sylvester 31791.
Telephone: (229) 776-8207.
Fax: (229) 776-1540

ANGLIN, David *(Judge, Probate Court of Oconee County)* Former Chief Magistrate, Magistrate Court of Oconee County.
Mailing address: P.O. Box 54, Watkinsville 30677-0054.
Telephone: (706) 769-3936.
Fax: (706) 769-3934
E-mail address: danglin@oconee.ga.us

ARRINGTON, Marvin S., Jr. *(Judge, Superior Court of Georgia Atlanta Judicial Circuit)*
Office: T5655 Justice Center Tower, 185 Central Avenue S.W., Atlanta 30303.
Telephone: (404) 730-6907.

ASH, Tommy Walton *(Judge, Probate Court of Ben Hill County)* Elected to term beginning Jan 1, 1997. Reelected 2000, current term expires Dec 31, 2004.
Office: Ben Hill County Courthouse, 111 South Sheridan Street, Fitzgerald 31750.
Telephone: (229) 426-5137.
Fax: (229) 426-5486
E-mail address: bhcoprob@ga.quik.com

ASKEW, W. Ken *(Chief Magistrate, Magistrate Court of Harris County)*
Mailing address: P.O. Box 347, Hamilton 31811-0347.
Telephone: (706) 628-4977.
Fax: (706) 628-5416

ASPINWALL, Nancy K. *(Judge, Probate Court of Liberty County)*
Mailing address: P.O. Box 28, Hinesville 31310-0028.
Telephone: (912) 876-3635.
Fax: (912) 876-3589

AYALA, Juan C. *(Associate Judge, Juvenile Court of Georgia Eastern Judicial Circuit)* Appointed.
Office: 197 Carl Griffin Drive, Savannah 31405.
Telephone: (912) 652-6700.
Fax: (912) 652-6741

BAETY, Edward L. *(Chief Judge, City Court of Atlanta)*
Office: 104 Trinity Avenue S.W., Atlanta 30303.
Telephone: (404) 658-6919.
Fax: (404) 658-7125

BAGLEY, Jeffrey S. *(Judge, Superior Court of Georgia Bell-Forsyth Judicial Circuit)* Appointed by Governor Roy Barnes to term beginning Aug 25, 2001. Born Forsyth County Georgia July 10, 1961. Baptist. Educated at Georgia Institute of Technology B.S.C.E. with honors 1983 and Emory University School of Law J.D. 1987. Admitted to practice Georgia 1987, U.S. District Court Northern District of Georgia 1987 and U.S. Court of Appeals Eleventh Circuit 1990. In legal practice Cumming 1987-96. Former Part-time Judge, Juvenile Court of Forsyth County, appointed by Governor Zell Miller to term beginning Jan 1, 1997. Judge, State Court of Forsyth County Jan 1, 1997 to 2001, appointed by Governor Zell Miller.

Member Lawyers Club of Atlanta, State Bar of Georgia, Atlanta, Forsyth County (President 1990-91) and American Bar Associations. Lecturer "Civil Litigation for Younger Lawyers" State Bar of Georgia. Member South Forsyth Rotary Club. Enjoys gardening and antique cars.

Office: 100 Courthouse Square, Suite 150, Cumming 30040.
Telephone: (770) 205-4660.
Fax: (770) 205-4661
E-mail address: jsbagley@co.forsyth.ga.us

BAILEY, John H., Jr. *(Chief Judge, Superior Court of Georgia Northern Judicial Circuit)* Appointed by Governor Zell Miller Nov 1995 to term beginning Jan 1, 1996. Elected Nov 1996 and Nov 2000. Current term expires Dec 31, 2004. Chief Judge since Aug 1, 1999. Born Elberton Georgia Oct 7, 1948. Roman Catholic. Educated at Georgia College B.S. 1970 and John Marshall Law School J.D. 1979. Admitted to practice Georgia 1979 and U.S. District Court Middle District of Georgia 1979. In legal practice Elberton 1979-96.

Assistant District Attorney 1985-90 and Chief Assistant District Attorney 1990-96 Northern Circuit of Georgia. Member Elberton and Northern Circuit Bar Associations. Faculty Advisor Career Prosecutor Course 1989. Attended Career Prosecutor Course National College of District Attorneys and General Jurisdiction Course The National Judicial College. Member Elberton Rotary Club. Enjoys travel, golf, hunting, fishing and antiques.

Mailing address: P.O. Box 645, Elberton 30635.
Office: Elbert County Courthouse, Elberton 30635.
Telephone: (706) 283-2046.
Fax: (706) 213-2079

BAIRD, Michael P. *(Chief Magistrate, Magistrate Court of Clayton County)* Elected to term beginning Jan 1, 1997. Reelected 2000, current term expires Dec 31, 2004.
Office: Justice Center, 9151 Tara Boulevard, Jonesboro 30236.
Telephone: (770) 477-3444.
Fax: (770) 473-5750

BAKER, Garrison *(Judge, Probate Court of White County)* Assumed office Sept 20, 1983. Elected 1984, 1988, 1992, 1996 and 2000. Current term expires Dec 31, 2004.
Office: 59 South Main Street, Suite H, Cleveland 30528.
Telephone: (706) 865-4141.
Fax: (706) 865-1324

BAKER, Henry A. *(Judge, Probate Court of Newton County and Chief Magistrate, Magistrate Court of New-*

BAKER, HENRY A.—*Continued*

ton County) Elected Probate Judge to term beginning Jan 1, 1977. Reelected 1980, 1984, 1988, 1992, 1996 and 2000. Current term expires Dec 31, 2004. Born Newton County Georgia Nov 9, 1944. Methodist. Educated at Georgia Southern College B.S.Ed. 1967 and Georgia State University M.Ed. 1975.

Member Georgia Probate Judges Association. Sergeant U.S. Army 1969-72. Teacher Newton County School System. Member Covington Kiwanis Club and American Legion Post 32.

Office: 1132 Usher Street N.W., Room 148, Covington 30014.
Telephone: (770) 784-2050.
Fax: (770) 784-2145

BAKER, James T. *(Judge, Probate Court of Douglas County)*
Office: 8700 Hospital Drive, Douglasville 30134.
Telephone: (770) 920-7249.
Fax: (770) 920-7381

BALDWIN, Quillian, Jr. *(Judge, Superior Court of Georgia Coweta Judicial Circuit)* Appointed by Governor Zell Miller to term beginning Sept 26, 1995. Elected 1996 and 2000. Current term expires Dec 31, 2004.
Mailing address: P.O. Box 1364, LaGrange 30241.
Telephone: (706) 883-1633.
Fax: (706) 883-1639

BANKE, Karlton Van *(Judge, Juvenile Court of Georgia Clayton Judicial Circuit)* Appointed. Currently serves as Presiding Judge.
Office: Clayton County Courthouse, Annex 3 Third Floor, Jonesboro 30236-3694.
Telephone: (770) 477-3270.
Fax: (770) 477-3255
E-mail address: KVBanke@bellsouth.net

BANKS, Henry D. *(Chief Magistrate, Magistrate Court of Banks County)*
Mailing address: P.O. Box 364, Homer 30547-0364.
Telephone: (706) 677-6270.
Fax: (706) 677-6215

BANKSTON, Michael *(Judge, State Court of Mitchell County)* Elected to term beginning Jan 1, 1997. Reelected 2000, current term expires Dec 31, 2004. Serves part time.
Mailing address: P.O. Box 385, Camilla 31730-0385.
Telephone: (229) 336-0461.
Fax: (229) 336-0463
E-mail address: mbanks@camillaga.net

BANTZ, Linda F. *(Chief Magistrate, Magistrate Court of Randolph County)*
Mailing address: P.O. Box 6, Cuthbert 31740-0006.
Telephone: (229) 732-6182.
Fax: (229) 732-5781
E-mail address: magjudge@alltel.net

BARFIELD, W. Leon *(Magistrate Judge, United States District Court Southern District of Georgia)* Appointed by U.S. District Court judges to term beginning Aug 31, 1993. Reappointed 2001, current term expires Aug 31, 2009. Born Moultrie Georgia Sept 8, 1947. Protestant. Educated at Abraham Baldwin College A.A. 1969 and University of Georgia B.S. 1973 J.D. 1976. Law Clerk to Hon. Elie L. Holton, Georgia Superior Court Waycross Circuit 1976-77. Member Phi Beta Kappa and Phi Kappa Phi. Admitted to practice Georgia 1976 and U.S. District Court Southern District of Georgia 1981.

Assistant District Attorney Augusta 1979-81. Assistant U.S. Attorney Savannah 1981-93. U.S. Army Oct 3, 1967 to May 23, 1969.
Mailing address: P.O. Box 1504, Augusta 30903-1504.
Telephone: (706) 849-4420.

BARKER, S. H. *(Chief Magistrate, Magistrate Court of Berrien County)*
Mailing address: P.O. Box 103, Nashville 31639-0103.
Telephone: (229) 686-7019.
Fax: (229) 686-6328

BARNES, Anne Elizabeth *(Judge, Court of Appeals of Georgia)* Elected Nov 3, 1998 to term beginning Jan 1, 1999. Term expires Dec 31, 2004. Born Atlanta Georgia Sept 25, 1955. Educated at Georgia State University B.A. magna cum laude 1979 and University of Georgia School of Law J.D. 1983. Member Phi Kappa Phi, Omicron Delta Kappa, Golden Key and Blue Key. Admitted to practice Georgia 1984. In legal practice Savannah and Atlanta 1984-96 and Decatur 1996-98.

Former Vice President Georgia Trial Lawyers Association. Fellow Lawyers Foundation of Georgia. Member Domestic Violence Committee Judicial Council of Georgia, Old War Horse Lawyers Club, Lamar Inns of Court, Lawyers Club of Atlanta, GABEO, Georgia Association of Black Women Attorneys, Georgia Association of Women Lawyers, Institute of Judicial Administration, National Association of Women Judges, American Judicature Society, State Bar of Georgia, Atlanta (Membership Committee), DeKalb, Gate City and American Bar Associations. Attended Appellate Judges Seminar New York University July 1999. Past President Morningside Wood Homeowners Association. Member Commerce Club and Georgia Public Policy Foundation, St. Martin in the Fields Episcopal Church and Atlanta Track Club. Completed Peachtree Road Race more than 10 times.
Office: 334 State Judicial Building, Atlanta 30334.
Telephone: (404) 656-3454.
Fax: (404) 463-8303

BARNES, Rowland W. *(Judge, Superior Court of Georgia Atlanta Judicial Circuit)* Appointed by Governor Zell Miller to term beginning Aug 5, 1998. Elected 2000, current term expires Dec 31, 2004. Born Cheyenne Wyoming April 25, 1940. Educated at Lebanon Valley College B.S. 1962 and Emory University J.D. 1972. Listed in *Who's Who Among American Colleges and Universities* 1961-62. Admitted to practice Georgia 1972 and U.S. Court of Appeals Eleventh Circuit. In legal practice Atlanta 1974-98. Former part-time Judge, Municipal Courts of Hapeville and Fairburn. Former Magistrate, Magistrate Court of Fulton County.

Attorney Department of Housing and Urban Development 1972-74. Member State Bar of Georgia, Atlanta and South Fulton Bar Associations. Air National Guard Aug 9, 1962 to Jan 28, 1968. USAF Jan 28, 1968 to June 30, 1969.
Office: 136 Pryor Street, Suite C-848, Atlanta 30303-3653.
Telephone: (404) 335-8667.
Fax: (404) 224-0551
E-mail address: rowland.barnes@fultoncourt.org

BARRETT, David Eugene *(Judge, Superior Court of Georgia Enotah Judicial Circuit)* Appointed by Gover-

BARRETT, DAVID EUGENE—*Continued*

nor Zell Miller to term beginning Aug 10, 1992. Elected to term beginning Jan 1, 1995. Reelected 1998 and 2002. Current term expires Dec 31, 2006. Born Hiawassee Georgia June 25, 1955. Baptist. Educated at University of Georgia B.A. summa cum laude 1977 J.D. cum laude 1980. Member Phi Beta Kappa and Phi Kappa Phi. Admitted to practice Georgia 1980 and U.S. District Courts Middle 1980 and Northern 1980 Districts of Georgia. In legal practice Athens 1980-84 and Hiawassee 1984-92. Former Judge, Hiawassee Recorder's Court.

Member State Bar of Georgia, Enotah, Mountain Judicial (Treasurer 1987-88, Vice President 1988-89, President 1989-90), Western Judicial (Secretary 1983-84) and American Bar Associations. Instructor in Domestic Relations Practice Family Law Institute 1994, Deprivation Practice in Juvenile Court Council of Juvenile Court Judges 1994 and Institute of Continuing Legal Education. Recipient Distinguished Service Award NE Georgia Board of Realtors 1988. Former Board Member Fledglings, Inc. (child advocacy agency). Board of Directors Towns County Hospital 1986-88. Member Towns County Chamber of Commerce and White County Chamber of Commerce. Enjoys gardening.

Office: 59 South Main Street, Suite K, Cleveland 30528-4501.
Telephone: (706) 865-6135.
Fax: (706) 865-2682
E-mail address: debarrett55@yahoo.com

BARRON, Patricia D. *(Chief Magistrate, Magistrate Court of Clarke County)*
Mailing address: P.O. Box 1868, Athens 30603.
Office: 325 East Washington Street, Athens 30601.
Telephone: (706) 613-3310.
Fax: (706) 613-3314

BARTLES, William P. *(Judge, Juvenile Court of Georgia Flint Judicial Circuit)* Appointed. Former part-time Judge, Juvenile Courts of Butts, Lamar and Monroe Counties.
Office: 43 Lawrenceville Street, McDonough 30253-3294.
Telephone: (770) 954-2086.
Fax: (770) 898-7597
E-mail address: bbartles@co.henry.ga.us

BARTON, Timothy L. *(Chief Magistrate, Magistrate Court of Glynn County)*
Office: 701 H Street, Brunswick 31520.
Telephone: (912) 554-7250.
Fax: (912) 267-5677

BARWICK, Tripp *(Judge, Probate Court of Decatur County)*
Mailing address: P.O. Box 234, Bainbridge 39818-0234.
Telephone: (229) 248-3016.
Fax: (229) 248-3858

BASS, James F., Jr. *(Judge, Superior Court of Georgia Eastern Judicial Circuit)* Appointed by Governor Zell Miller to term beginning May 18, 1995. Elected 1996 and 2000. Current term expires Dec 31, 2004.
Office: 421 Chatham County Courthouse, 133 Montgomery Street, Savannah 31401.
Telephone: (912) 652-7154.
Fax: (912) 652-7512

BASS, John W., Sr. *(Judge, State Court of Grady County)* Serves part time.
Mailing address: P.O. Box 88, Cairo 39828-0088.
Office: 311 North Broad Street, Cairo 39828.
Telephone: (229) 377-2424.

BAVERMAN, Alan J. *(Magistrate Judge, United States District Court Northern District of Georgia)* Appointed by U.S. District Court judges to term beginning Feb 1, 2001.
Office: 1702 U.S. Courthouse, 75 Spring Street S.W., Atlanta 30303-3309.
Telephone: (404) 215-1395.

BAXLEY, Thomas H. *(Judge, State Court of Early County)* Appointed by Governor Zell Miller to term beginning Nov 6, 1995. Elected 1996 and 2000. Current term expires Dec 31, 2004. Serves part time.
Mailing address: P.O. Box 670, Blakely 39823-0670.
Telephone: (229) 723-3426.
Fax: (229) 723-6464
E-mail address: tbaxley@alltel.net

BAXTER, Jerry W. *(Judge, Superior Court of Georgia Atlanta Judicial Circuit)* Born Atlanta Georgia Sept 17, 1949. Episcopalian. Educated at University of Georgia B.B.A. 1971 J.D. 1974. Admitted to practice Georgia 1974. Former Judge, State Court of Fulton County, appointed by Governor Joe Frank Harris to term beginning Sept 1985.

Assistant Solicitor General June 1974 to April 1976 and Assistant District Attorney April 1976 to Sept 1985 Litigation Section Fulton County. Member Atlanta Lawyers Club, District Attorneys Association of Georgia, National College of District Attorneys, Council of State Court Judges, American Judges Association, State Bar of Georgia, Atlanta, Gate City and American Bar Associations.

Office: T4855 Justice Center Tower, 185 Central Avenue S.W., Atlanta 30303.
Telephone: (404) 224-3740.
Fax: (404) 224-3748
E-mail address: jerry.baxter@fultoncourt.org

BAYNEUM, Joann *(Chief Magistrate, Magistrate Court of Fulton County)*
Office: C-669 Fulton County Courthouse, 136 Pryor Street S.W., Atlanta 30303-3435.
Telephone: (404) 730-4552.
Fax: (404) 893-2683

BEAM, John W., Jr. *(Judge, Juvenile Court of Georgia Eastern Judicial Circuit)* Appointed.
Office: 197 Carl Griffin Drive, Savannah 31405.
Telephone: (912) 652-6703.
Fax: (912) 652-6744
E-mail address: JWBeam@wpo.co.chatham.ga.us

BEARDEN, D. Larry *(Chief Magistrate, Magistrate Court of Grady County)* Elected Sept 3, 1992. Reelected to term beginning Jan 1, 1997 and 2001. Current term expires Jan 1, 2005. Born Cairo Georgia July 23, 1948. Baptist.

Member Second Judicial District Council of Magistrate Court Judges of Georgia (Vice President 1995, President 1996). Communications Technician USN 1969-73. Member Chamber of Commerce, Grady County Historical Society, Theatre Historical Society of America

BEARDEN, D. LARRY—*Continued*

and Will Rogers Motion Picture Pioneers. Interests include motion picture theatres (palaces and small town).
Office: 250 North Broad Street, Cairo 31728-0250.
Telephone: (229) 377-4132.
Fax: (229) 377-4127
E-mail address: lbearden@alltel.net *or* judgebearden-@yahoo.com

BEARDEN, J. Lane *(Judge, Juvenile Court of Georgia Cherokee Judicial Circuit)* Appointed.
Office: 100 Court Street, Calhoun 30701.
Telephone: (706) 625-6959.
Fax: (706) 602-2337
E-mail address: beardenlaw@aol.com

BEASLEY, Charles Elliot *(Judge, Probate Court of Candler County)* Assumed office Oct 20, 1980. Elected at special election to term beginning Jan 1, 1981. Reelected 1984, 1988, 1992, 1996 and 2000. Current term expires Dec 31, 2004. Born Candler County Georgia Jan 24, 1939. Religious affiliation: Free Will Baptist. Former Chief Magistrate, Magistrate Court of Candler County.
Pastor Friendship Free Will Baptist Church near Twin City. Member Kiwanis Club (President 1989). Enjoys fishing.
Office: Courthouse Square, Metter 30439.
Telephone: (912) 685-2357.
Fax: (912) 685-5130

BEASLEY, Dorothy Toth *(Senior Judge, Court of Appeals of Georgia)* Appointed by Governor Joe Frank Harris to term beginning Nov 5, 1984. Elected to term beginning Jan 1, 1987. Reelected 1992. Former Chief Judge and Presiding Judge. Assumed Senior status, serves when called. Born Garfield New Jersey Oct 5, 1937. Lutheran. Educated at St. Lawrence University B.A. with honors 1959, American University LL.B. 1964 and University of Virginia LL.M. in Judicial Process 1984. Daish Scholar American University. Casenote Editor American University Law Review. Law Clerk to Circuit Court Arlington County Virginia Feb 1964 to Feb 1966. Member Mortar Board St. Lawrence University. Admitted to practice District of Columbia 1964, Virginia 1965, Georgia 1969 and U.S. Supreme Court 1971. In legal practice Arlington Virginia 1966-67 and Atlanta Georgia 1968-69. Judge, State Court of Fulton County April 25, 1977 to Nov 5, 1984, appointed by Governor George Busbee.
Assistant Attorney General Georgia 1969-73. Assistant U.S. Attorney 1973-77 (Chief of General Crimes Section 1976-77). Adjunct Faculty Emory University Law School 1973-74. Chairman Study Group on American Bar Association Draft of Standards on the Legal Status of Prisoners. President Georgia Association of Women Lawyers 1975-76. Member American Judicature Society (Former member Board of Directors), The American Law Institute and State Bar of Georgia (Committees on Correctional Facilities and Services 1975-85, Designation of Areas of Practice 1979-82, Judicial Procedure and Administration and Delay and Costs Reduction). Grantee-participant National Endowment for Humanities Seminar for Lawyers 1976. Attended The National Judicial College 1977 and 1979, seminar for Appellate Judges New York University July 1986 and seminar on "Justice and Society" Aspen Institute Aug 1986. Participant Leadership Atlanta 1974-75 and Leadership Georgia 1982. Member Study Group on Education 1975-76 and Vice President 1977 Alumni Association. Advisory member Georgia Commission on Children and Youth. Church Council member and former member Board of Directors Lutheran Towers.
Mailing address: 450 High Point Road N.E., Atlanta 30342.
E-mail address: beasleydt@aol.com

BEAVERS, Tonny S. *(Judge, Superior Court of Georgia Paulding Judicial Circuit)* Appointed by Governor Roy Barnes to term beginning July 1, 2002. Former Associate Judge, Juvenile Court of Paulding County. Former Chief Magistrate, Magistrate Court of Paulding County.
Office: Paulding County Courthouse, 11 Courthouse Square, Dallas 30132.
Telephone: (678) 363-2900.
Fax: (678) 363-2902

BECKER, Cynthia J. *(Judge, Superior Court of Georgia Stone Mountain Judicial Circuit)*
Office: 556 North McDonough Street, Room 801, Decatur 30030.
Telephone: (404) 371-2691.
Fax: (404) 371-3044
E-mail address: cjbecker@co.dekalb.ga.us

BEDFORD, T. Jackson, Jr. *(Judge, Superior Court of Georgia Atlanta Judicial Circuit)* Elected to term beginning Jan 1, 1997. Reelected 2000, current term expires Dec 31, 2004.
Office: T4955 Justice Center Tower, 185 Central Avenue S.W., Atlanta 30303.
Telephone: (404) 730-4604.
Fax: (404) 730-6019
E-mail address: tjackson.bedford@fultoncounty.org

BELL, Richard *(Senior Judge, Supreme Court of Georgia)* Assumed office as Justice. Assumed Senior status, serves when called.
Mailing address: 794 Allgood Road, Stone Mountain 30083.

BENEFIELD, Deborah C. *(Judge, Superior Court of Georgia Clayton Judicial Circuit)*
Office: 4JC202 Banke Justice Center, 9151 Tara Boulevard, Jonesboro 30236.
Telephone: (770) 477-3436.
Fax: (770) 477-3465

BENEFIELD, Harold G. *(Judge, State Court of Clayton County)* Appointed by Governor Joe Frank Harris to term beginning March 18, 1983. Elected 1984, 1988, 1992, 1996 and 2000. Current term expires Dec 31, 2004. Currently serves as Chief Judge. Born Atlanta Georgia Feb 3, 1951. United Methodist. Member Jones Memorial First United Methodist Church. Educated at Georgia Institute of Technology B.S. 1973 and Mercer University J.D. 1976. Member Phi Delta Phi. Admitted to practice Georgia 1976. Began legal practice Forest Park 1976. In legal practice Morrow and Jonesboro 1980-83.
Assistant District Attorney Clayton Judicial Circuit 1977-80. Member American Judges Association, State Bar of Georgia, Atlanta and Clayton County Bar Associations. Enjoys racquetball, golf, tennis and family activities.
Office: Justice Center, 9151 Tara Boulevard, Jonesboro 30236.

BENEFIELD, HAROLD G.—*Continued*
Telephone: (770) 477-3375.
Fax: (770) 473-5991
E-mail address: JUDGEHB@bellsouth.net

BENHAM, Robert *(Justice, Supreme Court of Georgia)* Appointed by Governor Joe Frank Harris Dec 1989. Elected July 17, 1990, 1996 and 2002. Current term expires Dec 31, 2008. Former Presiding Justice and Chief Justice. First African-American to serve as Chief Justice in Georgia. Born Cartersville Georgia Sept 25, 1946. Baptist. Educated at Tuskegee University B.S. 1967, University of Georgia J.D. 1970 and University of Virginia LL.M. 1989. Member Phi Alpha Delta 1970. Admitted to practice Georgia 1970. Began legal practice Carterville 1971. Judge, Court of Appeals of Georgia April 3, 1984 to Dec 1989, appointed by Governor Joe Frank Harris. Captain U.S. Army. Enjoys woodworking.
Office: 527 State Judicial Building, Atlanta 30334.
Telephone: (404) 656-3476.
Fax: (404) 657-4329

BENNETT, Robert T. *(Judge, Probate Court of Quitman County and Chief Magistrate, Magistrate Court of Quitman County)* Appointed Probate Judge by Governor Zell Miller to term beginning May 1, 1991. Elected 1992, 1996 and 2000. Current term expires Dec 31, 2004. Born Eufaula Alabama June 20, 1940. Baptist.
Mailing address: P.O. Box 7, Georgetown 31754-0007.
Telephone: (229) 334-2224.
Fax: (229) 334-6826

BENTLEY, Danny C. *(Chief Magistrate, Magistrate Court of Upson County)* Appointed to term beginning Oct 22, 1993. Elected 1996 and 2000. Current term expires Dec 31, 2004.
Mailing address: P.O. Box 890, Thomaston 30286-0890.
Telephone: (706) 647-6891.
Fax: (706) 647-1248
E-mail address: bentfarm@yahoo.com

BESSEN, Diane E. *(Judge, State Court of Fulton County)*
Office: T3855 Justice Center Tower, 185 Central Avenue S.W., Atlanta 30303.
Telephone: (404) 730-7760.
Fax: (404) 224-0572

BESSONETTE, George A. *(Judge, Juvenile Court of Georgia Alapaha Judicial Circuit)* Former Associate Judge. Appointed Judge. Currently serves as Presiding Judge.
Mailing address: P.O. Box 148, Homerville 31634.
Telephone: (912) 487-1215.
Fax: (912) 487-1227
E-mail address: georgeb1954@yahoo.com

BETHEL, Winston P. *(Chief Magistrate, Magistrate Court of DeKalb County)* Former Chief Judge, Recorder's Court of DeKalb County.
Office: 807 DeKalb County Courthouse, Decatur 30030.
Telephone: (404) 371-4766.
Fax: (404) 371-2986
E-mail address: wpbethel@co.dekalb.ga.us

BIHARY, Joyce *(Judge, United States Bankruptcy Court Northern District of Georgia)*
Office: 1431 U.S. Courthouse, 75 Spring Street S.W., Atlanta 30303-3367.
Telephone: (404) 215-1030.

BISHOP, Fred A., Jr. *(Judge, Superior Court of Georgia Gwinnett Judicial Circuit)* Appointed by Governor Zell Miller to term beginning July 1991. Elected June 1996 and 2000. Current term expires Dec 31, 2004. Currently serves as Administrative Judge District Nine. Educated at Auburn University B.A.E. 1965 and John Marshall University Law School J.D. 1972. Admitted to practice Georgia 1972 and U.S. Court of Appeals Eleventh Circuit. In legal practice Lawrenceville 1974-87. Chief Magistrate, Magistrate Court of Gwinnett County 1983-87. Judge, State Court of Gwinnett County 1987-91.
Office: Gwinnett Justice Center, 75 Langley Drive, Lawrenceville 30045.
Telephone: (770) 822-8650.
Fax: (770) 822-8641
E-mail address: bishopfr@co.gwinnett.ga.us

BISHOP, Joe C. *(Chief Judge, Superior Court of Georgia Pataula Judicial Circuit)* Born Richland Georgia Jan 6, 1957. Baptist. Educated at Valdosta State College B.F.A. with honors 1979 and University of Georgia J.D. 1982. Admitted to practice Georgia 1982 and U.S. District Courts Middle 1982 and Northern 1989 Districts of Georgia. Judge, Recorder's Court of Terrell County 1985-90. Judge, Juvenile Court of Terrell County 1988-94.
County Attorney Terrell County 1985-91. Member Sherwood Baptist Church and Rotary.
Mailing address: P.O. Box 759, Dawson 39842-0759.
Telephone: (229) 995-4994.
Fax: (229) 995-2062
E-mail address: tcll@surfsouth.com

BLACKBURN, G. Alan *(Judge, Court of Appeals of Georgia)* Elected to term beginning 1992. Reelected 1998, current term expires 2004. Former Chief Judge. Currently serves as Presiding Judge. Born East Bend North Carolina May 6, 1939. Educated at John Marshall University Law School LL.B. 1968 and University of Virginia School of Law LL.M. in Judicial Process 2001. Admitted to practice Georgia 1972. In legal practice Decatur and Fulton County 1972-85 and Cobb County 1985-92.
Former Member Georgia Trial Lawyers Association and Georgia Association of Administrative Law Judges. Charter Member Georgia Association of Criminal Defense Lawyers. Member State Bar of Georgia, Cobb County and American Bar Associations. Former Chairman Advisory Board Cobb County Salvation Army. Former Chairman Board of Directors New Horizons Ministries. Board of Directors Georgia Chapter National Committee for the Prevention of Child Abuse.
Office: 334 State Judicial Building, Atlanta 30334.
Telephone: (404) 656-3451.
Fax: (404) 463-6211
E-mail address: lynchm@appeals.courts.state.ga.us

BLACKWELL, Todd A. *(Judge, Probate Court of Baldwin County)* Elected to term beginning Nov 4,

BLACKWELL, TODD A.—*Continued*

1998. Reelected 2000, current term expires Dec 31, 2004.

Office: 121 North Wilkinson Street, Suite 109, Milledgeville 31061.
Telephone: (478) 445-4807.
Fax: (478) 445-5178
E-mail address: baldwin.probate@yahoo.com

BLANCHARD, James G., Jr. *(Judge, Superior Court of Georgia Augusta Judicial Circuit)* Former Associate Judge and Judge, Juvenile Court of Georgia Augusta Judicial Circuit.

Superior Court office: City-County Building, 530 Greene Street, Augusta 30911.
Telephone: (706) 842-2837.
Fax: (706) 721-1091
E-mail address: blanchardj@gajudges.org

BLAU, George G., III *(Associate Judge, Juvenile Court of Georgia Atlanta Judicial Circuit)* Appointed to term beginning 1986. Reappointed 1996. Born Columbus Georgia April 10, 1936. Religious affiliation: Disciples of Christ. Educated at University of Georgia M.S. 1958, Vanderbilt University M.Div. 1961 and Woodrow Wilson College of Law J.D. 1977. Admitted to practice Georgia 1977, U.S. District Court Northern District of Georgia 1977 and U.S. Court of Appeals 1977. In legal practice Atlanta 1977-86.

Intake Attorney Fulton County Juvenile Court 1984-96. Member Council of Juvenile Court Judges of Georgia, National Council of Juvenile and Family Court Judges and Atlanta Bar Association. Enjoys ballroom dancing, big band music and artworks of Chagall.

Office: 395 Pryor Street S.W., Atlanta 30312-2713.
Telephone: (404) 224-4841.
E-mail address: gblau@mindspring.com

BLAYLOCK, Connie Maples *(Judge, Juvenile Court of Georgia Conasauga Judicial Circuit)* Former Associate Judge. Appointed Judge to term beginning July 1, 1996. Reappointed 2000, current term expires July 1, 2004.

Office: 301 West Crawford Street, Dalton 30720.
Telephone: (706) 278-6558.
Fax: (706) 272-7018
E-mail address: tblay@alltel.net

BLEDSOE, Joseph *(Judge, Probate Court of Heard County)*

Mailing address: P.O. Box 478, Franklin 30217-0478.
Telephone: (706) 675-3353.
Fax: (706) 675-0819
E-mail address: hcpcga@hotmail.com

BLITCH, Brooks E., III *(Chief Judge, Superior Court of Georgia Alapaha Judicial Circuit)*

Mailing address: P.O. Box 335, Homerville 31634-0335.
Telephone: (912) 487-2280.
Fax: (912) 487-3241

BLOUNT, Clarence D. *(Chief Judge, Superior Court of Georgia Waycross Judicial Circuit)* Term expires Dec 31, 2004.

Mailing address: P.O. Box 1258, Waycross 31502.
Office: Ware County Courthouse, Waycross 31502.
Telephone: (912) 287-4320.
Fax: (912) 287-4814

BOATRIGHT, Joe *(Judge, Probate Court of Bacon County and Chief Magistrate, Magistrate Court of Bacon County)*

Mailing address: P.O. Box 389, Alma 31510-0389.
Telephone: (912) 632-7661 (probate), 632-5961 (magistrate).
Fax: (912) 632-7662

BOBBITT, Thomas C., III *(Chief Magistrate, Magistrate Court of Laurens County)* Elected to term beginning Jan 1, 1997. Reelected 2000, current term expires Dec 31, 2004.

Mailing address: P.O. Box 1676, Dublin 31040-1676.
Office: 308 Roosevelt Street, Dublin 31040.
Telephone: (478) 272-5010.
Fax: (478) 275-0035
E-mail address: tbobbitt@nlamerica.com

BODIFORD, James G. *(Judge, Superior Court of Georgia Cobb Judicial Circuit)* Elected to term beginning Jan 1, 1995. Reelected Nov 1998 and 2002. Current term expires Dec 31, 2006. Chief Magistrate, Magistrate Court of Cobb County 1985-94.

Office: 30 Waddell Street, Marietta 30090-9642.
Telephone: (770) 528-1822.
Fax: (770) 528-8141

BOLES, Pamela *(Judge, Juvenile Court of Georgia Bell-Forsyth Judicial Circuit)* Appointed.

Office: 112 West Maple Street, Suite 5, Cumming 30040.
Telephone: (770) 781-3099.
Fax: (770) 781-3089

BONAPFEL, Paul W. *(Judge, United States Bankruptcy Court Northern District of Georgia)* Appointed by U.S. Court of Appeals Eleventh Circuit judges to term beginning April 10, 2002. Term expires April 2016.

Office: 1492 U.S. Courthouse, 75 Spring Street S.W., Atlanta 30303-3367.
Telephone: (404) 215-1018.

BONNER, Alice D. *(Judge, Superior Court of Georgia Atlanta Judicial Circuit)* Former Judge, State Court of Fulton County.

Office: T5955 Justice Center Tower, 185 Central Avenue S.W., Atlanta 30303.
Telephone: (404) 730-4166.
Fax: (404) 730-4705

BOOTH, Joseph H. *(Judge, Superior Court of Georgia Piedmont Judicial Circuit)*

Mailing address: P.O. Box 685, Winder 30680-0685.
Telephone: (770) 307-3032.
Fax: (770) 307-3033

BOSWELL, Stephen Edwin *(Senior Judge, Superior Court of Georgia)* Appointed by Governor George D. Busbee to term beginning Sept 13, 1982. Elected 1986 and 1990. Assumed Senior status, serves when called. Born Hogansville Georgia Feb 3, 1947. Methodist. Educated at University of Georgia A.B. 1969 J.D. 1974. Admitted to practice Georgia 1974, U.S. Court of Appeals 1975 and U.S. Supreme Court 1975. In legal practice Jonesboro 1974-82.

Vice Chairman Electronic Data Processing Committee 1988-90 and Georgia Court Automation Commission since 1990. Member State Bar of Georgia (Board of Governors 1977-82), Clayton County (President 1977-78)

BOSWELL, STEPHEN EDWIN—*Continued*

and American (Committee on Technology and the Future of the Courts Judicial Administrative Division) Bar Associations. Instructor Computer Classes ICLE since 1986 and Magistrate Training Council since 1986. First Lieutenant U.S. Army 1969-71. Democrat. President Arts Clayton, Inc. 1986-87. Chairman Board of Directors Dance Theatre of Georgia, Inc. 1990-91 and Trust Company Bank of Clayton County. Member Administrative Board Jonesboro Methodist Church. Member Kiwanis Club, Masons and Mundy's Mill Homeowner's Association. Enjoys running.

Office: Banke Justice Center, 9151 Tara Boulevard, Jonesboro 30236.
Telephone: (770) 477-3432.
Fax: (770) 473-5827

BOWEN, Dudley H., Jr. *(Chief Judge, United States District Court Southern District of Georgia)* Appointed for life by President Jimmy Carter to term beginning 1979. Chief Judge since 1997. Born Augusta Georgia June 25, 1941. Educated at University of Georgia A.B. 1964 LL.B. 1965. In legal practice Augusta 1965-66, 1968-72 and 1975-79. Judge, U.S. Bankruptcy Court Southern District of Georgia 1972-75.

Mailing address: P.O. Box 2106, Augusta 30903-2106.
Telephone: (706) 849-4440.

BOWMAN, Murry *(Chief Magistrate, Magistrate Court of Jefferson County)* Elected to term beginning Jan 1, 1989. Reelected 1992, 1996 and 2000. Current term expires Dec 31, 2004. Born Jefferson County Georgia Nov 11, 1953. Methodist. Educated at Georgia College A.A.

Attended Institute of Continuing Judicial Education University of Georgia. Recipient several certificates of appreciation for community service from local governments and several military awards. Georgia Air National Guard. Previously employed as police chief.

Mailing address: P.O. Box 749, Louisville 30434-0749.
Telephone: (478) 625-8834.
Fax: (478) 625-9736
E-mail address: Judgm1@aol.com

BOYD, Donald W. *(Judge, Probate Court of Troup County)*

Office: 900 Dallis Street, LaGrange 30240.
Telephone: (706) 883-1690.
Fax: (706) 812-7933

BOYETT, William T. *(Chief Judge, Superior Court of Georgia Conasauga Judicial Circuit)*

Mailing address: P.O. Box 2582, Dalton 30722-2582.
Telephone: (706) 278-3340.
Fax: (706) 275-7567
E-mail address: wboyett@ocsonline.com

BRACEWELL, Michael Frederick *(Judge, Probate Court of Morgan County)* Elected to term beginning Jan 1, 1993. Reelected 1996 and 2000. Current term expires Dec 31, 2004. Born Atlanta Georgia May 29, 1947. Methodist. Educated at University of Georgia B.B.A. 1970.

Member Georgia County Officers Association, Council of Probate Judges of Georgia and National College of Probate Judges. Energy Services Representative Georgia Power Co. 1970-80. Previously employed by Baldwin Realty Inc. 1981-92. Chairman Morgan County Democratic Executive Committee 1984-92. Member Madison-Morgan Cultural Center and Chamber of Commerce. Interested in historic preservation.

Mailing address: P.O. Box 857, Madison 30650-0857.
Telephone: (706) 343-6500.
Fax: (706) 343-6465
E-mail address: mbracewell@morganga.org

BRACKETT, Charles Dwain *(Judge, Probate Court of Union County)* Elected to term beginning Jan 1, 1997. Reelected 2000, current term expires Dec 31, 2004. Former Chief Magistrate, Magistrate Court of Union County, appointed to term beginning Jan 1, 1997.

Office: 114 Courthouse Street, Suite 8, Blairsville 30512.
Telephone: (706) 439-6006.
Fax: (706) 439-6009

BRADLEY, Roger E. *(Judge, Superior Court of Georgia Appalachian Judicial Circuit)*

Office: 9A South Side Square, Ellijay 30540.
Telephone: (706) 515-2027.
Fax: (706) 515-2028
E-mail address: bradleyr@gajudges.org

BRANDENBURG, Lynn *(Judge, Probate Court of Pike County)* Elected to term beginning Jan 1, 1997. Reelected 2000, current term expires Dec 31, 2004.

Mailing address: P.O. Box 324, Zebulon 30295-0324.
Telephone: (770) 567-8734.
Fax: (770) 567-2019

BRANNEN, Perry, Jr. *(Chief Judge, Superior Court of Georgia Eastern Judicial Circuit)* Appointed by Governor George D. Busbee to term beginning June 11, 1979. Elected 1980, 1984, 1988, 1996 and 2000. Current term expires Dec 31, 2004. Administrative Judge First District 1985-87. Born Savannah Georgia June 16, 1940. Episcopalian. Educated at Washington and Lee University A.B. cum laude 1962 and University of Georgia LL.B. 1965. Member Phi Delta Phi. Admitted to practice Georgia 1964, U.S. District Court Southern District of Georgia 1967 and U.S. Court of Appeals Fifth Circuit 1974. Began legal practice Savannah 1967.

Member Judicial Council of Georgia 1985-87, Council of Superior Court Judges (Executive Committee since 1985, Secretary-Treasurer 1988-89, President 1990-91), State Bar of Georgia (Executive Committee Younger Lawyers Section 1974-75) and Savannah Bar Association. Captain U.S. Army 1965-67. Recipient Army Commendation Medal 1967.

Office: 422 Chatham County Courthouse, 133 Montgomery Street, Savannah 31401.
Telephone: (912) 652-7158.
Fax: (912) 652-7522
E-mail address: pbrannenjr@aol.com

BRASWELL, June B. *(Chief Magistrate, Magistrate Court of Bulloch County)*

Mailing address: P.O. Box 1004, Statesboro 30459-1004.
Telephone: (912) 764-6458, 756-4520.
Fax: (912) 489-6731

BRASWELL, Morris E. *(Judge, State Court of Clayton County)* Elected to term beginning Jan 1, 1997. Reelected 2000, current term expires Dec 31, 2004.

Office: Justice Center, 9151 Tara Boulevard, Jonesboro 30236.

BRASWELL, MORRIS E.—*Continued*

Telephone: (770) 472-8000.
Fax: (770) 472-8004
E-mail address: judgsbras@hotmail.com

BRASWELL, Roy O., Jr. *(Judge, Probate Court of Wheeler County and Chief Magistrate, Magistrate Court of Wheeler County)*
Mailing address: P.O. Box 477, Alamo 30411-0477.
Telephone: (912) 568-7133.
Fax: (912) 568-1743

BRAUN, Leon M., Jr. *(Judge, State Court of Liberty County)* Elected July 1992 to term beginning Jan 1993. Reelected Nov 1996 and Nov 2000. Current term expires Jan 2005. Serves part time. Born Savannah Georgia Feb 19, 1955. Baptist. Educated at Armstrong State College and John Marshall Law School. Admitted to practice Georgia 1981 and U.S. District Courts Middle and Southern Districts of Georgia. In legal practice Hinesville since 1981. Judge, Municipal Court of Midway 1985-93. Judge, Municipal Court of Pembroke 1991-93.

City Attorney Gumbranch since 1981. President Council of State Court Judges of Georgia 2001-02. Member State Bar of Georgia. Attended CLE courses for state court judges. Advisory Board First Citizens Bank 1996-2002. Sunday School Director and Trustee Friendship Baptist Church. Enjoys golfing, fishing and hunting.
Office: 103 Memorial Drive, Hinesville 31313.
Telephone: (912) 876-7101.
Fax: (912) 876-8088
E-mail address: LBraun@coastalnow.net

BRAZIER, Jimmy B. *(Judge, Probate Court of Stewart County)* Elected to term beginning Jan 1, 1977. Reelected to subsequent terms. Current term expires Dec 31, 2004. Born Richland Georgia Sept 16, 1951. Baptist. Member First Baptist Church (deacon). Educated at Georgia Southwestern College B.S.E. 1974 and Atlanta Law School J.D. 1989. Admitted to practice Georgia 1989. Began legal practice Lumpkin. Democrat. Enjoys football, hunting, golf, softball, baseball and fishing.
Mailing address: P.O. Box 876, Lumpkin 31815-0876.
Telephone: (229) 838-4394.
Fax: (229) 838-9084
E-mail address: jimmybrazier@cs.com

BREWER, Charles G. *(Chief Magistrate, Magistrate Court of Emanuel County)*
Office: 107 North Main Street, Swainsboro 30401-3541.
Telephone: (478) 237-7278.
Fax: (478) 237-2593

BRILL, Gerrilyn G. *(Magistrate Judge, United States District Court Northern District of Georgia)* Appointed by U.S. District Court judges.
Office: 1690 U.S. Courthouse, 75 Spring Street S.W., Atlanta 30303-3361.
Telephone: (404) 215-1365.

BRINSON, Benjamin P. *(Judge, Juvenile Court of Georgia Atlantic Judicial Circuit)* Appointed. Currently serves as Chief Judge.
Mailing address: P.O. Box 667, Claxton 30417.
Telephone: (912) 739-2533.
Fax: (912) 739-2513
E-mail address: bpbrinson@aol.com

BRIZENDINE, Robert E. *(Judge, United States Bankruptcy Court Northern District of Georgia)* Appointed by U.S. Court of Appeals Eleventh Circuit judges.
Office: 1234 U.S. Courthouse, 75 Spring Street S.W., Atlanta 30303-3367.
Telephone: (404) 215-1014.

BROADRICK, Ray *(Judge, Probate Court of Whitfield County)*
Office: 301 West Crawford Street, Dalton 30720.
Telephone: (706) 275-7400.
Fax: (706) 275-7486
E-mail address: rbroadrick@whitfieldcounty.com

BROGDON, M. Gino, Sr. *(Judge, Superior Court of Georgia Atlanta Judicial Circuit)* Former Judge, State Court of Fulton County, appointed by Governor Zell Miller to term beginning March 8, 1996.
Office: T8905 Justice Center Tower, 185 Central Avenue S.W., Atlanta 30303.
Telephone: (404) 730-4335.
Fax: (404) 730-7160

BROOKER, Richard *(Associate Judge, Juvenile Court of Georgia Dougherty Judicial Circuit)* Appointed.
Mailing address: P.O. Box 1827, Albany 31702-1827.
Telephone: (229) 431-2162.
Fax: (229) 434-2665
E-mail address: doughertycojuvct@mindspring.com

BROOKS, Charles C. *(Judge, Recorder's Court of Chatham County)*
Office: 133 Montgomery Street, Room 104, Savannah 31401.
Telephone: (912) 652-7433.
Fax: (912) 652-7412

BROWN, Carl C., Jr. *(Judge, Superior Court of Georgia Augusta Judicial Circuit)* Appointed by Governor Zell Miller to term beginning Dec 5, 1994. Elected 1996 and 2000. Current term expires Dec 31, 2004.
Office: 320 City-County Building, 530 Greene Street, Augusta 30911-4406.
Telephone: (706) 821-2347.
Fax: (706) 721-4476

BROWN, Charles B. *(Judge, Juvenile Court of Georgia Enotah Judicial Circuit)* Appointed. Currently serves as Presiding Judge.
Mailing address: P.O. Box 24, Helen 30545-0024.
Telephone: (706) 878-2124.
Fax: (706) 878-1687
E-mail address: charlesbbrown@hotmail.com

BROWN, Lillis J. *(Judge, Probate Court of Rockdale County)* Elected Nov 1992 to term beginning Jan 1, 1993. Reelected Nov 1996 and Nov 2000. Current term expires Jan 2004. Born Atlanta Georgia March 19, 1952. Baptist. Educated at Mercer University. Magistrate, Magistrate Court of Rockdale County 1985-89.

Member Council of Probate Court Judges of Georgia, Probate Judges Training Council of Georgia and Magistrate Judges Training Council of Georgia. Attended American Judicial Academy for Non-Attorney Judges 1978 and National Judicial Leadership Institute 2001-02. Member Rockdale County Republican Party. Member Leadership Rockdale County 1999. Past President Rockdale Council of Child Abuse and Pilot Club of Conyers,

BROWN, LILLIS J.—*Continued*
Inc. Enjoys gardening and traveling. Personal Statement or Quote: "Be prepared, be forthcoming and be sincere."
Office: 107 Rockdale County Courthouse, 922 Court Street N.E., Conyers 30012.
Telephone: (770) 929-4057.
Fax: (770) 918-6463
E-mail address: lillis.brown@rockdalecounty.org

BROWN, S. Phillip *(Judge, Superior Court of Georgia Macon Judicial Circuit)* Appointed by Governor Zell Miller to term beginning Jan 1, 1996. Elected 1996 and 2000. Current term expires Dec 31, 2004.
Office: 310 Bibb County Courthouse, Macon 31201.
Telephone: (478) 621-6328.
Fax: (478) 621-6580

BROWN, Tammy S. *(Judge, Probate Court of Barrow County)*
Office: 30 North Broad Street, Winder 30680.
Telephone: (770) 307-3045.
Fax: (770) 867-8041

BROWNE, Joe *(Senior Judge, City Court of Atlanta)* Appointed by mayor. Assumed Senior status, serves when called.
Office: 104 Trinity Avenue S.W., Atlanta 30303.
Telephone: (404) 658-6919.
Fax: (404) 658-7125

BRYANT, George H. *(Senior Judge, Superior Court of Georgia)* Former Chief Judge Northern Judicial Circuit. Assumed Senior status, serves when called.
Mailing address: P.O. Box 821, Hartwell 30643.
Telephone: (706) 377-3898.

BRYANT, Lucy J. *(Judge, Probate Court of Warren County)*
Mailing address: P.O. Box 364, Warrenton 30828-0364.
Telephone: (706) 465-2227.
Fax: (706) 465-1300

BRYANT, Malcolm F., Jr. *(Judge, State Court of Toombs County)* Serves part time.
Mailing address: P.O. Box 28, Vidalia 30475-0028.
Office: 502 Jackson Street, Vidalia 30474.
Telephone: (912) 537-9021.
Fax: (912) 537-3807

BRYANT, Quillian L., Jr. *(Judge, Probate Court of Jefferson County)* Elected to term beginning Jan 1, 1960. Reelected to subsequent terms. Born Richmond Georgia Oct 22, 1929. Educated at University of Georgia LL.B.
Mailing address: P.O. Box 307, Louisville 30434-0307.
Telephone: (478) 625-3258.
Fax: (478) 625-0245

BUCKNER, Mary A. *(Judge, Recorder's Court of Columbus-Muscogee County)*
Mailing address: P.O. Box 709, Columbus 31902-0709.
Telephone: (706) 653-4256.

BUFFINGTON, William David *(Chief Magistrate, Magistrate Court of Franklin County)*
Mailing address: P.O. Box 467, Carnesville 30521-0467.
Telephone: (706) 384-7473.
Fax: (706) 384-4346

BULLARD, James L. *(Senior Judge, Superior Court of Georgia)* Assumed Senior status, serves when called.
Office: 30 Waddell Street, Marietta 30090-9642.
Telephone: (770) 528-1880.
Fax: (770) 528-8103

BURCH, Christine *(Judge, Probate Court of Wayne County)*
Office: 174 North Brunswick Street, Jesup 31546.
Telephone: (912) 427-5940.
Fax: (912) 427-5944

BURKE, LeRoy, III *(Judge, Recorder's Court of Chatham County)* Appointed to term beginning April 12, 1993. Elected 1994 and 1998. Born Suffolk Virginia. Roman Catholic. Educated at Hampton University B.A. 1971 and Woodrow Wilson College of Law J.D. 1979. Admitted to practice Georgia 1979 and U.S. District Courts Northern 1979 and Southern 1985 Districts of Georgia. In legal practice Atlanta 1979-84 and Savannah 1984-89.
Office: 133 Montgomery Street, Room 104, Savannah 31401.
Telephone: (912) 652-7429.
Fax: (912) 652-7412
E-mail address: lburke@ci.savannah.ga.us

BURKE, Wanda *(Judge, Probate Court of Jenkins County)*
Mailing address: P.O. Box 904, Millen 30442-0904.
Telephone: (478) 982-5581.
Fax: (478) 982-2829

BURKHALTER, Steven *(Judge, Probate Court of Floyd County)* Elected to term beginning Jan 1, 1997. Reelected 2000, current term expires Dec 31, 2004.
Office: 201 Floyd County Administrative Offices, Three Government Plaza, Rome 30161.
Telephone: (706) 291-5136.
Fax: (706) 291-5189
E-mail address: burkhals@floydcountyga.org

BURKHALTER, Terri *(Associate Judge, Juvenile Court of Georgia Rome Judicial Circuit)*
Office: Three Government Plaza, Suite 202, Rome 30161.
Telephone: (706) 291-5180.
Fax: (706) 291-5247
E-mail address: terriburkhalter@aol.com

BURNETTE, Vickie *(Judge, Probate Court of Thomas County)*
Mailing address: P.O. Box 1582, Thomasville 31799-1582.
Telephone: (229) 225-4116.
Fax: (229) 227-1698
E-mail address: probate@surfsouth.com

BURNHAM, Donna Jean *(Chief Magistrate, Magistrate Court of Heard County)*
Mailing address: P.O. Box 395, Franklin 30217-0395.
Telephone: (706) 675-3002.
Fax: (706) 675-0819
E-mail address: peapodpard2@hotmail.com

BURT, Jennifer Evans *(Judge, Probate Court of Dawson County)* Elected to term beginning Jan 1, 1997. Reelected 2000, current term expires Dec 31, 2004.
Office: 25 Tucker Avenue, Suite 102, Dawsonville 30534.
Telephone: (706) 344-3580.
Fax: (706) 265-6155

BURTON, Jim *(Judge, Probate Court of Wilkes County)*
Office: 23 East Court Street, Room 422, Washington 30673.
Telephone: (706) 678-2523.
Fax: (706) 678-4854
E-mail address: jim.burton@gscca.org

BURTON, Susanne *(Judge, Juvenile Court of Georgia Northern Judicial Circuit)* Appointed.
Mailing address: P.O. Box 166, Lexington 30648-0166.
Telephone: (706) 743-8910.
Fax: (706) 743-3130

BUTLER, Sophia C. *(Associate Judge, Juvenile Court of Georgia Brunswick Judicial Circuit)* Appointed.
Office: 132 West Parker Street, Baxley 31513-0658.
Telephone: (912) 366-9000.
Fax: (912) 367-5883
E-mail address: sbutler@jajlaw.com

BUTTERWORTH, James N. *(Chief Magistrate, Magistrate Court of Habersham County)*
Mailing address: P.O. Box 738, Cornelia 30531.
Telephone: (706) 778-2294.
Fax: (706) 776-3371

BUTTRILL, Del *(Judge, Probate Court of Henry County)* Elected at special election to term beginning Jan 29, 1982. Reelected 1984, 1988, 1992, 1996 and 2000. Current term expires Dec 31, 2004. Also serves Traffic Court of Henry County. Born DeKalb County Georgia Jan 27, 1941. Baptist. Ordained Minister Feb 11, 1970. Educated at Presbyterian College 1960 and Atlanta Law School 1984.
President Del Buttrill Construction Company six years. Member County Officers Association of Georgia, Georgia Probate Judges Association and National College of Probate Judges. Attended The National Judicial College 1984. Previously worked in hospital and lab equipment sales fourteen years. Enjoys woodworking, art and photography.
Office: 99 Sims Street, McDonough 30253.
Telephone: (770) 954-2303.
Fax: (770) 954-2308
E-mail address: dbuttrill@co.henry.ga.us

BUTTS, Angela T. *(Judge, Recorder's Court of DeKalb County)*
Office: 3630 Camp Circle, Decatur 30032-1394.
Telephone: (404) 294-2635.
Fax: (404) 294-2148

BUXTON, Mary Jo *(Judge, Probate Court of Johnson County)*
Mailing address: P.O. Box 264, Wrightsville 31096-0264.
Telephone: (478) 864-3316.
Fax: (478) 864-0528
E-mail address: maryjobuxton@gascсca.com

CALDWELL, Donald Ray *(Chief Magistrate, Magistrate Court of Catoosa County)* Elected to term beginning Jan 1, 1997. Reelected 2000, current term expires Dec 31, 2004.
Office: 7694 Nashville Street, Ringgold 30736.
Telephone: (706) 935-3114.
Fax: (706) 965-9036

CALDWELL, Johnnie L., Jr. *(Judge, Superior Court of Georgia Griffin Judicial Circuit)* Appointed by Governor Zell Miller to term beginning July 27, 1995. Elected 1996 and 2000. Current term expires Dec 31, 2004.
Mailing address: P.O. Box 916, Thomaston 30286-0916.
Telephone: (706) 646-2523.
Fax: (706) 646-2527

CAMP, Daniel P. *(Judge, Juvenile Court of Georgia Coweta Judicial Circuit)* Appointed.
Office: 203 Tanner Street, Carrollton 30117.
Telephone: (770) 832-2482.
Fax: (770) 830-7950
E-mail address: dan@wigginsandcamp.com

CAMP, Jack T. *(Judge, United States District Court Northern District of Georgia)* Appointed for life by President Ronald Reagan to term beginning May 27, 1988. Born Newnan Georgia Oct 30, 1943. Presbyterian. Educated at The Citadel B.A. 1965 and University of Virginia M.A. 1967 J.D. 1973. Recipient Ford Foundation Fellowship Graduate School of Arts and Sciences University of Virginia 1966-67. Admitted to practice Alabama 1973, Georgia 1975 and U.S. District Courts Northern 1973 and Southern 1973 Districts of Alabama and Middle 1975, Northern 1975 and Southern 1975 Districts of Georgia. In legal practice Birmingham Alabama 1973-75 and Newnan Georgia 1975-88.
Member Federal Judges Association, State Bar of Georgia (Board of Governors 1988-89), Newnan-Coweta, Coweta Circuit (Secretary 1977, President 1978) and American Bar Associations. Captain U.S. Army 1967-70 USAR 1970-86. Recipient Vietnam Campaign Medal, Vietnam Service Medal and National Defense Service Medal 1967-70 and Bronze Star Medal 1969. Member Newnan Presbyterian Church, Kiwanis Club of Newnan, Newnan Historical Society, Georgia Trust for Historic Preservation, University of Virginia Alumni Association and Alumni Association of The Citadel.
Mailing address: P.O. Box 939, Newnan 30264-0939.
Telephone: (678) 423-3020.

CAMP, Susan S. *(Chief Magistrate, Magistrate Court of Douglas County)*
Mailing address: P.O. Box 99, Douglasville 30133-0099.
Telephone: (770) 920-7215.
Fax: (770) 920-7547

CAMPBELL, Bridgette *(Judge, State Court of Cobb County)* Serves Division Two.
Office: 12 East Park Square, Marietta 30090.
Telephone: (770) 423-6800.
Fax: (770) 423-6804

CAMPBELL, Nancy M. *(Judge, State Court of Cobb County)* Elected to term beginning Jan 1, 1987. Reelected 1990, 1994, 1998 and 2002. Current term expires Dec 31, 2006. Serves Division Two. Born Texas. Educated at West Georgia College, Kennesaw State College

CAMPBELL, NANCY M.—*Continued*

and Woodrow Wilson College of Law J.D. 1978. Admitted to practice Georgia 1978.

Assistant Solicitor, Division Coordinator and Administrative Assistant Cobb County Solicitor's Office. Member Council of State Court Judges of Georgia and Cobb County Bar Association.

Office: 12 East Park Square, Marietta 30090.
Telephone: (770) 528-1751.
Fax: (770) 528-1753

CAMPBELL, Richard D. *(Judge, State Court of Elbert County)* Serves part time.

Mailing address: P.O. Box 1056, Elberton 30635.
Office: 313 Heard Street, Elberton 30635-2436.
Telephone: (706) 283-5000.
Fax: (706) 283-5002
E-mail address: pacllp@elberton.net

CANNON, Larry E. *(Judge, Probate Court of Rabun County)* Elected to term beginning Jan 1, 1985. Reelected 1988, 1992, 1996 and 2000. Current term expires Dec 31, 2004. Born Clayton Georgia Aug 19, 1944. Baptist Minister. Member Lions Club.

Office: 25 Courthouse Square, Suite 215, Clayton 30525.
Telephone: (706) 782-3614.
Fax: (706) 782-9278

CARBO, John C., III *(Judge, State Court of Clayton County)*

Office: Justice Center, 9151 Tara Boulevard, Jonesboro 30236.
Telephone: (770) 477-4500.
Fax: (770) 477-4595
E-mail address: jccarbo3@aol.com

CARDEN, Mary R. *(Associate Judge, Juvenile Court of Georgia Northeastern Judicial Circuit)* Appointed.

Mailing address: P.O. Box 311, Gainesville 30503-0311.
Telephone: (770) 531-6927.
Fax: (770) 531-6940

CARLEY, George H. *(Justice, Supreme Court of Georgia)* Appointed by Governor Zell Miller March 16, 1993. Elected 1994 and 2000. Term expires Dec 31, 2006. Born Jackson Mississippi Sept 24, 1938. Educated at University of Georgia A.B. 1960 LL.B. 1962. Member Alpha Tau Omega, Pi Sigma Alpha and Phi Delta Phi. Admitted to practice Georgia 1961. Began legal practice Atlanta 1961. In legal practice Decatur 1963-79. Judge April 5, 1979 to March 15, 1993, Chief Judge 1989-90 and Presiding Judge 1991-93, Court of Appeals of Georgia, appointed by Governor George D. Busbee.

Member Georgia Commission on Dispute Resolution, Old Warhorse Lawyers Club (Secretary 1995), Joseph Henry Lumpkin American Inn of Court (President 1993-95), Lawyers Club of Atlanta, Georgia Bar Foundation, State Bar of Georgia and American Bar Association. Chairman Georgia Law Related Education Consortium 1994-95. Member House of Representatives Georgia 1966. Member University of Georgia Law School Association Council 1986-91 (President 1989-90). Trustee Georgia Legal History Foundation, Inc. Board of Visitors University of Georgia School of Law. Involved with Georgia and National High School Mock Trial Competitions since 1988. Member Pythagoras Lodge 41 Masons, Atlanta Consistory Scottish Rite and Decatur Rotary Club. Communicant Holy Trinity Episcopal Church Decatur.

Office: 536 State Judicial Building, Atlanta 30334.
Telephone: (404) 656-3471.
Fax: (404) 657-7576

CARLISLE, Elaine L. *(Judge, Municipal Court of Atlanta)* Appointed by Mayor Andrew Young to term beginning 1990. Elected 2001, current term expires 2005. Born Gary Indiana Jan 30. Presbyterian. Educated at Howard University B.A. 1977 and John Marshall University Law School J.D. cum laude 1982. Admitted to practice Georgia 1983, U.S. Court of Appeals Eleventh Circuit and U.S. Supreme Court.

City Solicitor Atlanta 1982-89. Director District Five National Association of Women Judges. Representative District Two Municipal Court Judges Association. Member American Judges Association. Diamond Life Member Atlanta Alumnae Chapter Delta Sigma Theta Sorority, Inc.

Office: 170 Garnett Street S.W., Atlanta 30335.
Telephone: (404) 865-8103.
Fax: (404) 658-6805
E-mail address: ecarlisle@mindspring.com

CARLISLE, M. Russell, Jr. *(Judge, State Court of Cobb County)* Elected 1986 to term beginning Jan 1, 1987. Reelected 1990 and 1994. Appointed to Division One by Governor Zell Miller to term beginning Dec 21, 1995. Elected 1996 and 2000. Current term expires Dec 31, 2004. Born Columbus Georgia Jan 9, 1949. Methodist. Educated at University of Georgia A.B. 1971 and John Marshall Law School J.D. 1975. Member Sigma Delta Kappa. Admitted to practice Georgia 1975, U.S. District Court Northern District of Georgia 1977 and U.S. Court of Appeals Eleventh Circuit 1982. In legal practice Lilburn 1975-76 and Marietta 1976-86.

Assistant Solicitor Cobb County 1977-78. Author "Electronic Home Confinement" Georgia State B. Jour. 1988. Member State Bar of Georgia and Cobb County Bar Association. Instructor at numerous state level seminars and served three times as group discussion leader at The National Judicial College. Enjoys bicycling, reading, boating and classic cars.

Office: 12 East Park Square, Marietta 30090-9637.
Telephone: (770) 528-1761.
Fax: (770) 528-1770
E-mail address: rcarlisle@cobbcounty.org

CARNES, Julie E. *(Judge, United States District Court Northern District of Georgia)* Appointed for life by President George Bush to term beginning 1992. Born Atlanta Georgia Oct 31, 1950. Educated at University of Georgia B.A. 1972 J.D. 1975. Law Clerk to Hon. Lewis R. Morgan, U.S. Court of Appeals Fifth Circuit 1975-77.

Assistant U.S. Attorney 1978-90 and Appellate Chief Criminal Division 1987-89 Northern District of Georgia. Member U.S. Attorney General's Advisory Committee on Sentencing Guidelines 1988-90. Member since 1989, Special Counsel 1989 and U.S. Sentencing Commissioner 1990-92 U.S. Sentencing Commission.

Office: 2167 U.S. Courthouse, 75 Spring Street S.W., Atlanta 30303-3361.
Telephone: (404) 215-1510.

CARNEY, Jack E., Jr. *(Judge, State Court of Bryan County)* Serves part time.

Mailing address: P.O. Box 787, Pembroke 31321-0787.
Telephone: (912) 653-4500.
Fax: (912) 653-3391
E-mail address: jcarney@g-net.net

CARRIERE, Edward E., Jr. *(Judge, State Court of DeKalb County)* Appointed by Governor Zell Miller to term beginning Jan 5, 1998. Elected Nov 1998 and 2002. Current term expires Dec 31, 2006.

Office: 210 Callaway Building, 120 West Trinity Place, Decatur 30030.
Telephone: (404) 687-7130.
Fax: (404) 687-7156
E-mail address: carriere@co.dekalb.ga.us

CASON, Betty B. *(Judge, Probate Court of Carroll County)* Elected to term beginning Jan 1, 1997. Reelected 2000, current term expires Dec 31, 2004.

Office: 204 Carroll County Courthouse, Carrollton 30117.
Telephone: (770) 830-5840.
Fax: (770) 830-5995
E-mail address: ccprobat@bellsouth.net

CASTELLANI, Robert J. *(Judge, Superior Court of Georgia Stone Mountain Judicial Circuit)* Appointed by Governor Joe Frank Harris to term beginning Dec 1, 1984. Elected 1986, 1990, 1994, 1998 and 2002. Current term expires Dec 31, 2006. Former Chief Judge. Born Syracuse New York July 4, 1941. Presbyterian. Educated at Hobart College B.A. 1963 and Emory Law School J.D. 1966. Member Bryan Society. Admitted to practice Georgia 1965. In legal practice Atlanta 1965-82. Magistrate, U.S. District Court Northern District of Georgia 1982-84.

Assistant Attorney General Georgia 1967-73. First Assistant U.S. Attorney 1977-82. Adjunct Professor of Law Emory University School of Law. President Lamar American Inn of Court since 1992. Member Council of Superior Court Judges of Georgia (Chairman Rules Committee), American Judicature Society, DeKalb Lawyers Association, State Bar of Georgia, Atlanta, DeKalb and American Bar Associations. Attended various introductory and advanced courses The National Judicial College 1985, 1987, 1989 and 1992.

Office: 402 DeKalb County Courthouse, 556 North McDonough Street, Decatur 30030.
Telephone: (404) 371-2457.
Fax: (404) 687-3511

CASTELLANOS, Roland R. *(Judge, State Court of Cobb County)* Serves Division Two.

Office: 12 East Park Square, Marietta 30090.
Telephone: (770) 528-1700.
Fax: (770) 528-1788

CATO, A. Wallace *(Chief Judge, Superior Court of Georgia South Georgia Judicial Circuit)* Appointed by Governor George D. Busbee to term beginning May 17, 1978. Elected to subsequent terms. Current term expires Dec 31, 2004. Currently serves as Administrative Judge District Two.

Mailing address: P.O. Box 65, Bainbridge 39818-0065.
Telephone: (229) 246-1111.
Fax: (229) 246-5265
E-mail address: wcato@surfsouth.com

CAVANAUGH, Rita L. *(Chief Magistrate, Magistrate Court of Spalding County)* Former Magistrate. Elected Chief Magistrate to term beginning Jan 1, 1997. Reelected 2000, current term expires Dec 31, 2004.

Office: 132 East Solomon Street, Griffin 30223.
Telephone: (770) 467-4336.
Fax: (770) 467-0081
E-mail address: ritacavanaugh@hotmail.com

CAVENDER, David L. *(Chief Judge, Superior Court of Georgia Atlantic Judicial Circuit)* Elected to term beginning Jan 1, 1983. Reelected 1986, 1996 and 2000. Current term expires Dec 31, 2004. Chief Judge since June 1, 1999. Born Waycross Georgia Nov 23, 1947. Baptist. Educated at Georgia Southern College B.A. 1969 and University of Georgia J.D. cum laude 1975. Member Alpha Tau Omega. Admitted to practice Georgia 1975. Began legal practice Waycross 1975. In legal practice Hinesville 1979-82.

Member State Bar of Georgia and American Bar Association. Specialist Five U.S. Army 1969-72. Member Hinesville Lions Club. Enjoys fishing, tennis and jogging.

Mailing address: P.O. Box 713, Hinesville 31310-0713.
Telephone: (912) 368-2250.
Fax: (912) 368-6622

CHAFIN, James T., III *(Judge, State Court of Henry County)*

Mailing address: P.O. Box 2000, McDonough 30253.
Telephone: (770) 898-9550.
Fax: (770) 898-9601
E-mail address: JimChafin@worldnet.att.net

CHAMBERS, Rob *(Judge, State Court of Hall County)* Appointed by Governor Zell Miller to term beginning Dec 7, 1998.

Office: 200 Main Street, Suite 100, Gainesville 30501-3708.
Telephone: (770) 534-3770.
Fax: (770) 534-1441

CHANDLER, Billy *(Chief Magistrate, Magistrate Court of Jackson County)* Appointed to term beginning July 1, 1983. Elected to term beginning Jan 1, 1985. Reelected 1988, 1992, 1996 and 2000. Current term expires Jan 1, 2005. Also serves as Judge, Commerce Municipal Court, appointed to term beginning Jan 8, 1990. Born Banks County Georgia Dec 30, 1939. Baptist. Justice of the Peace 1970-83.

Councilman-at-large City of Commerce 1973-74 and 1977-78. Democrat. Deacon First Baptist Church, Commerce. 32° Scottish Rite Mason. Lifetime Colonel Georgia Jaycees Rebel Corps. Past President Commerce Jaycees. Board of Trustees First Baptist Church Commerce. Member Hudson Masonic Lodge 294 and Commerce Athletic Booster Club. Enjoys sports, fishing, golf and swimming.

Mailing address: P.O. Box 751, Commerce 30529-0015.
Telephone: (706) 335-6545.
Fax: (706) 335-5221

CHASON, Willard H. *(Senior Judge, Superior Court of Georgia)* Appointed by Governor George D. Busbee to term beginning Dec 29, 1982. Elected 1984, 1988

CHASON, WILLARD H.—*Continued*
and 1992. Assumed Senior status, serves when called. Born Grady County Georgia Aug 26, 1924. United Methodist. Educated at Mercer University Walter F. George School of Law J.D. cum laude 1950. Staff member Mercer Law Review 1949. Member Pi Kappa Phi and Delta Theta Phi. Admitted to practice Georgia 1950. In legal practice Cairo 1950-82.
State Court Solicitor Grady County 1960-66. Member State Bar of Georgia. USNR 1943-46. Member Rotary Club. Enjoys farming.
Mailing address: P.O. Box 774, Cairo 39828-0774.
Telephone: (229) 378-1060.

CHASTAIN, Michael *(Judge, Probate Court of Lumpkin County)*
Office: 99 Courthouse Hill, Suite C, Dahlonega 30533-0278.
Telephone: (706) 864-3847.
Fax: (706) 864-9271

CHAVIS, Jeffrey C. *(Judge, Probate Court of Jeff Davis County)*
Mailing address: P.O. Box 446, Hazelhurst 31539-0446.
Office: Jeff Davis County Courthouse, Hazelhurst 31539.
Telephone: (912) 375-6626.
Fax: (912) 375-0378

CHEATHAM, Frank Sellars, Jr. *(Senior Judge, Superior Court of Georgia)* Appointed by Governor Jimmy Carter to term beginning March 31, 1972. Elected to subsequent terms. Former Chief Judge Eastern Judicial Circuit. Assumed Senior status, serves when called. Born Savannah Georgia Jan 11, 1924. Methodist. Educated at Armstrong Junior College 1944 and University of Georgia A.B. 1946 LL.B. 1948. Member Blue Key Honor Society, Omicron Delta Kappa and Phi Delta Phi. Admitted to practice Georgia 1948 and U.S. Supreme Court 1968. Began legal practice Savannah 1948.
Author "The Making of a Court Administrator" Judicature Oct 1976. Member Judicial Council of Georgia, Judicial Planning Committee of Georgia (Chairman 1978), Council of Superior Court Judges of Georgia (Secretary-Treasurer 1978-79, President 1980), State Crime Commission, American Judicature Society, State Bar of Georgia (Disciplinary Board 1967-70), Savannah (President 1969) and American Bar Associations. Selected Outstanding Young Man of Georgia 1951. Democrat. Georgia House of Representatives 1953-60 (Chairman House Appropriations Committee 1957-60). President Kiwanis Club 1969. Board President YMCA 1963-67. Board of Directors First Bank of Savannah 1969-72 and since 1980. Board of Trustees Candler General Hospital 1971-76. Member Board of Curators Georgia Historical Society and Savannah Symphony Society Board 1979-82. Enjoys photography.
Office: 426 Chatham County Courthouse, 133 Montgomery Street, Savannah 31401-3241.
Telephone: (912) 652-7150.
Fax: (912) 652-7130

CHEELY, Selma *(Chief Magistrate, Magistrate Court of Hart County)*
Mailing address: P.O. Box 698, Hartwell 30643-0698.
Telephone: (706) 376-6817.
Fax: (706) 376-6821
E-mail address: sc30643@hotmail.com

CHENEY, Janice Wilson *(Chief Magistrate, Magistrate Court of Jenkins County)* Appointed to term beginning July 5, 1983. Reappointed to subsequent terms. Born Millen Georgia March 19, 1955. Baptist.
Mailing address: P.O. Box 892, Millen 30442-0892.
Telephone: (478) 982-5580.
Fax: (478) 982-4911

CHESHIRE, M. Louise *(Chief Magistrate, Magistrate Court of Brantley County)*
Mailing address: P.O. Box 998, Nahunta 31553-0998.
Telephone: (912) 462-6780.
Fax: (912) 462-5538

CHEW, Randall E. *(Judge, Juvenile Court of Georgia South Georgia Judicial Circuit and Chief Magistrate, Magistrate Court of Mitchell County)* Former Presiding Judge Juvenile Court.
Juvenile Court mailing address: P.O. Box 664, Pelham 31779-0664.
Telephone: (229) 294-4460.
Fax: (229) 294-4951
Magistrate Court office: 30 North Court Avenue, Camilla 31730.
Telephone: (229) 336-2077.
Fax: (229) 336-2039
E-mail address: rechew@surfsouth.com

CHILDRES, Juanita *(Chief Magistrate, Magistrate Court of Crawford County)*
Mailing address: P.O. Box 568, Roberta 31078-0568.
Telephone: (478) 836-4439.
Fax: (478) 836-4340

CHRISTIAN, Martha C. *(Judge, Superior Court of Georgia Macon Judicial Circuit)*
Office: 310 Bibb County Courthouse, Macon 31201.
Telephone: (478) 621-6620.
Fax: (478) 621-6583

CIELINSKI, Michael P. *(Judge, Recorder's Court of Columbus-Muscogee County)* Serves as Chief Judge.
Mailing address: P.O. Box 1882, Columbus 31901-1882.
Telephone: (706) 653-0354.
Fax: (706) 323-1722
E-mail address: jwaters44@mindspring.com

CLARK, Michael C. *(Judge, Superior Court of Georgia Gwinnett Judicial Circuit)* Elected to term beginning Jan 1, 1992. Reelected 1996 and 2000. Current term expires Dec 31, 2004. Born Macon Georgia July 20, 1952. Educated at University of Georgia B.S. 1976 J.D. 1980 and University of Nevada Reno M.J.S. 2003. Admitted to practice Georgia 1980.
Assistant District Attorney Gwinnett Judicial Circuit 1981-83. Enjoys scuba diving and writing.
Office: 75 Langley Drive, Lawrenceville 30045.
Telephone: (770) 822-8607.
Fax: (770) 822-8637
E-mail address: sagemich@mindspring.com

CLARKE, Walter J., II *(Judge, Probate Court of Gwinnett County)* Elected Nov 1992 to term beginning Jan 1, 1993. Reelected Nov 1996 and 2000. Current term expires Dec 31, 2004. Educated at University of Georgia B.B.A. 1970, Georgia College M.B.A. 1972 and

CLARKE, WALTER J., II—*Continued*
Woodrow Wilson College of Law J.D. 1981. Admitted to practice Georgia 1982.

Office: Gwinnett Justice Center, 75 Langley Drive, Lawrenceville 30045-6900.
Telephone: (770) 822-8250.
Fax: (770) 822-8267

CLAYTON, Melodie Howard *(Judge, State Court of Cobb County)* Elected Nov 1992 to term beginning Jan 1, 1993. Reelected 1996 and 2000. Current term expires Dec 31, 2004. Currently serves as Chief Judge. Serves Division One. Born San Antonio Texas Sept 4, 1953. Methodist. Educated at University of Georgia and Woodrow Wilson College of Law J.D. with honors 1980. Admitted to practice Georgia 1980, U.S. District Court Northern District of Georgia 1980, U.S. Court of Appeals Eleventh Circuit 1983 and U.S. Supreme Court 1984. In legal practice Austell 1980-85 and 1989-92.

Chief Assistant Solicitor State Court of Cobb County 1985-89. President Council of State Court Judges of Georgia 2002-03. Member State Bar of Georgia (Bench and Bar Committee, Team Coach Mock Trial Program Younger Lawyers Division), Atlanta (Judicial Section) and Cobb County Bar Associations.

Office: 12 East Park Square, Suite 3B, Marietta 30090-9637.
Telephone: (770) 528-1741.
Fax: (770) 528-1740

CLINE, James Levi, Jr. *(Judge, Superior Court of Georgia Ocmulgee Judicial Circuit)* Appointed by Governor Zell Miller to term beginning July 25, 1995. Elected 1996 and 2000. Current term expires Dec 31, 2004.

Mailing address: P.O. Box 3069, Eatonton 31024-3069.
Telephone: (706) 485-7530.
Fax: (706) 485-7549

CLOY, Luz *(Judge, Juvenile Court of Georgia Atlantic Judicial Circuit)* Appointed.

Mailing address: P.O. Box 622, Darien 31305.
Telephone: (912) 437-2818.
Fax: (912) 437-6635

COFER, Robert H., II *(Chief Magistrate, Magistrate Court of McDuffie County)*

Mailing address: P.O. Box 252, Thomson 30824-0252.
Office: 337 Main Street, Thomson 30824.
Telephone: (706) 597-2618.
Fax: (706) 595-2041

COHN, Aaron *(Judge, Juvenile Court of Georgia Chattahoochee Judicial Circuit)* Appointed to term beginning Jan 1, 1965. Reappointed to subsequent terms. Born Columbus Georgia March 3, 1916. Jewish. Educated at University of Georgia J.D. 1938. Member Blue Key. Admitted to practice Georgia 1938. Began legal practice Columbus 1938.

Chief Vote Registrar Muscogee County 1961-65. Author "Dual Challenge of Juvenile Justice" Georgia B. Jour. 1975. Guest Lecturer Georgia Police Academy in Atlanta since 1975, Columbus College since 1972, and Southeastern Police Institute University of Georgia since 1974. Lecturer Criminal Justice Division Columbia State University. Member State Bar of Georgia and Columbus Bar Association. Colonel U.S. Army 1940-46. Democrat.

Mailing address: P.O. Box 1340, Columbus 31902-1340.
Office: Consolidated Government Center, Columbus 31902.
Telephone: (706) 653-4289.
Fax: (706) 653-4388

COLE, Barbara *(Chief Magistrate, Magistrate Court of Forsyth County)*

Office: 121 Dahlonega Street, Cumming 30040.
Telephone: (770) 781-2211.
Fax: (770) 844-7581
E-mail address: bacole@co.forsyth.ga.us

COLE, Brenda Hill *(Judge, State Court of Fulton County)* Appointed by Governor Zell Miller to term beginning Aug 5, 1998. Elected 2000, current term expires Dec 31, 2004. Born Joaquin Texas Jan 25, 1943. United Methodist. Educated at Spelman College B.A. 1963, Clark Atlanta University M.S.L.S. 1967 and Emory University J.D. 1977. Admitted to practice Georgia 1977 and West Virginia 1983.

Assistant Attorney General Fiscal Affairs Division Georgia Sept 1977 to June 1982. Attorney West Virginia Department of Corrections Dec 1982 to May 1984. Assistant Attorney General Tax Division Feb 1985 to March 1986 and Deputy Attorney General Environment and Energy Division April 1986 to May 1988 West Virginia. Assistant Attorney General Environmental Division Sept 1988 to May 1995, Senior Assistant Attorney General and Division Director Business and Professional Regulations June 1995 to Dec 1995 and Deputy Attorney General Regulated Industries and Professions Dec 1995 to Aug 1998 Georgia. Board Member *Women Looking Ahead* News Magazine since 1995. Member Lawyers Club of Atlanta, Georgia Association of Black Women Attorneys, Georgia Association of Women Lawyers, The West Virginia State Bar, State Bar of Georgia, Atlanta, Gate City and American Bar Associations. Librarian Atlanta University Sept 1970 to 1974. Board of Trustees Gammon Theological Seminary since 1982 and Michael C. Carlos Museum Emory University 1990-2002. Founder 1989, Chair 1989-98 and Member since 1989 Clark Atlanta University Guild. Board Member Legal Committee General Council of Finance and Administration The United Methodist Church 1992-2001, Atlanta Community Food Bank 1994-99, Big Brothers Big Sisters of Atlanta, Inc. 1995-99 and Atlanta Women's Foundation since 1999. Member Executive Committee Law Alumni Association Emory University 1997-2001, Cascade United Methodist Church, Dogwood City Chapter Links, Inc. and Chautauqua Circle. Enjoys reading, sports and music.

Office: T3905 Justice Center Tower, 185 Central Avenue, Atlanta 30303-3643.
Telephone: (404) 730-4311.
Fax: (404) 730-8182
E-mail address: brenda.cole@cjisful.net

COLE, Susan S. *(Magistrate Judge, United States District Court Northern District of Georgia)* Appointed by U.S. District Court judges to term beginning March 7, 2002.

Office: 106 U.S. Courthouse, 121 Spring Street S.E., Gainsville 30501.
Telephone: (678) 450-2790.

COLLIER, Albert *(Judge, Superior Court of Georgia Clayton Judicial Circuit)* Elected to term beginning Jan 1, 1999. Reelected 2002, current term expires Dec 31, 2006.
Office: Banke Justice Center, 9151 Tara Boulevard, Jonesboro 30236.
Telephone: (770) 477-3440.
Fax: (770) 473-5992

COLLIER, Edward Ross *(Judge, Juvenile Court of Georgia Pataula Judicial Circuit)* Appointed. Serves part time. Educated at University of Georgia A.B. 1986 and Mercer University J.D. 1990. Admitted to practice Georgia 1990.
Mailing address: P.O. Box 577, Dawson 39842-0577.
Telephone: (229) 995-5657.
Fax: (229) 995-6667
E-mail address: ed@colliergamble.com

COLLINS, Beverly M. *(Judge, State Court of Cobb County)* Serves Division Two.
Office: 12 East Park Square, Marietta 30090.
Telephone: (770) 528-1771.
Fax: (770) 528-1774

COLLINS, Jo Ann K. *(Judge, Probate Court of Brooks County)*
Mailing address: P.O. Box 665, Quitman 31643-0665.
Telephone: (229) 263-5567.
Fax: (229) 263-7559

COLSTON, Tami P. *(Judge, Superior Court of Georgia Rome Judicial Circuit)*
Office: Three Government Plaza, Suite 324, Rome 30161.
Telephone: (706) 290-6077.
Fax: (706) 290-6081
E-mail address: tamicolston@aol.com

CONNELLY, Kristina Cook *(Judge, Superior Court of Georgia Lookout Mountain Judicial Circuit)*
Mailing address: P.O. Box 179, Summerville 30747-0179.
Telephone: (706) 857-0715.
Fax: (706) 857-0726

CONNER, Melodie Snell *(Judge, Superior Court of Georgia Gwinnett Judicial Circuit)* Appointed by Governor Zell Miller to term beginning July 1, 1998. Elected 2000, current term expires Dec 31, 2004. Judge, State Court of Gwinnett County Oct 28, 1993 to June 30, 1998, appointed by Governor Zell Miller.
Office: Gwinnett Justice Center, 75 Langley Drive, Lawrenceville 30045.
Telephone: (770) 822-8660.
Fax: (770) 822-8662
E-mail address: connerme@co.gwinnett.ga.us

COOK, A. Ronald *(Judge, Juvenile Court of Georgia Griffin Judicial Circuit)* Appointed to term beginning Sept 16, 1985. Reappointed 1988, 1992, 1996 and 2000. Current term expires July 1, 2004. Born Butts County Georgia Feb 25, 1929. Baptist. Educated at John Marshall Law School LL.B. 1968.
Mailing address: P.O. Box 360, Griffin 30224-0360.
Office: 433 East Solomon Street, Griffin 30224.
Telephone: (770) 228-3911.
Fax: (770) 228-9477
E-mail address: A.RonaldCook@juno.com

COOK, Howard *(Judge, State Court of Gwinnett County)* Serves as Chief Judge.
Office: Gwinnett Justice Center, 75 Langley Drive, Lawrenceville 30045.
Telephone: (770) 822-8508.
Fax: (770) 822-8535
E-mail address: cookho@co.gwinnett.ga.us

COOPER, Clarence *(Judge, United States District Court Northern District of Georgia)* Appointed for life by President Bill Clinton to term beginning 1994. Born Decatur Georgia May 5, 1942. Educated at Clark College B.A. 1964, Emory University School of Law J.D. 1967 and Harvard University M.P.A. 1978. Judge, Municipal Court of Atlanta 1975-80. Judge, Superior Court of Georgia Atlanta Judicial Circuit 1980-90. Judge, Court of Appeals of Georgia 1990-94.
Attorney Atlanta Legal Aid Society 1967. Assistant District Attorney Fulton County 1968 and 1970-75.
Office: 1721 U.S. Courthouse, 75 Spring Street S.W., Atlanta 30303-3361.
Telephone: (404) 215-1390.

COOPER, Judy M. *(Chief Magistrate, Magistrate Court of Clay County)*
Mailing address: P.O. Box 73, Fort Gaines 31751-0073.
Telephone: (229) 768-2841.
Fax: (229) 768-3443
E-mail address: judy.cooper@clay.gsccca.org

COPELAN, Jesse, Jr. *(Judge, State Court of Putnam County)* Elected to term beginning Jan 1, 1997. Reelected 2000, current term expires Dec 31, 2004. Serves part time.
Mailing address: P.O. Box 3099, Eatonton 31024-3099.
Telephone: (706) 485-9410.
Fax: (706) 485-9921
E-mail address: jcjr@hom.net

CORNETT, Patti Palmour *(Judge, Probate Court of Hall County)* Elected Nov 1992 to term beginning Jan 1, 1993. Reelected 1996 and 2000. Current term expires Dec 31, 2004. Born Gainesville Georgia Jan 26, 1935. Methodist/Episcopalian. Educated at University of Georgia, University of Arkansas, Brenau College and Woodrow Wilson College of Law J.D. Admitted to practice Georgia 1987 and U.S. District Court Northern District of Georgia. In legal practice Gainesville, Hall County, Dawson County and Forsyth County.
Member Gainesville-Northeast Bar Association. Attended numerous seminars. Former Member Rotary International. Member and Officer Benevolent and Protective Order of Elks (BPOE) Auxiliary and American Legion Auxiliary. Member Georgia Commission on Language Interpreters.
Office: 123 Hall County Courthouse, 225 Green Street, Gainesville 30501.
Telephone: (770) 536-7180.
Fax: (770) 531-4946
E-mail address: pcornett.probatecourt@hallcounty.org

CORNWELL, James E., Jr. *(Judge, Superior Court of Georgia Mountain Judicial Circuit)* Elected to term beginning Jan 1, 1999. Reelected 2002, current term expires Dec 31, 2006.
Mailing address: P.O. Box 758, Toccoa 30577.

CORNWELL, JAMES E., JR.—*Continued*

Telephone: (706) 886-7525.
Fax: (706) 886-1259
E-mail address: scjudge@alltel.net

COTTON, Stacey W. *(Chief Judge, United States Bankruptcy Court Northern District of Georgia)*
Office: 1415 U.S. Courthouse, 75 Spring Street S.W., Atlanta 30303-3367.
Telephone: (404) 215-1026.

COURSEY, Daniel M., Jr. *(Judge, Superior Court of Georgia Stone Mountain Judicial Circuit)* Elected to term beginning Jan 1, 1983. Reelected 1986, 1990, 1994, 1998 and 2002. Current term expires Dec 31, 2006. Former Chief Judge.
Office: 900 DeKalb County Courthouse, 556 North McDonough Street, Decatur 30030.
Telephone: (404) 371-4710.
Fax: (404) 371-2993
E-mail address: dcrobiso@co.dekalb.ga.us

COWART, Louise *(Judge, Probate Court of Cook County)* Former Chief Magistrate, Magistrate Court of Cook County.
Office: 212 North Hutchinson Avenue, Adel 31620.
Telephone: (229) 896-3941.
Fax: (229) 896-6083

COWART, Richard M. *(Judge, Superior Court of Georgia Southern Judicial Circuit)* Appointed by Governor Zell Miller to term beginning Sept 13, 1995. Elected 1996 and 2000. Current term expires Dec 31, 2004. Born Valdosta Georgia Oct 13, 1951. Methodist. Educated at Valdosta State College B.A. 1973 and Mercer University J.D. 1976. Member Omicron Delta Kappa, Kappa Alpha Order and Phi Delta Phi. Admitted to practice Georgia 1976. Began legal practice Valdosta 1976. Judge, Valdosta Recorder's Court 1978-83. Judge, State Court of Lowndes County Sept 1983 to Sept 12, 1995, appointed by Governor Joe Frank Harris.
Former Member Council of State Court Judges of Georgia (President 1992-93) and Judicial Council of Georgia. Member Council of Superior Court Judges of Georgia, American Judicature Society, State Bar of Georgia, Valdosta (President 1986-87) and American Bar Associations. Member Park Avenue United Methodist Church (Lay Leader). President Valdosta Rotary Club 1987-88.
Mailing address: P.O. Box 806, Valdosta 31603-0806.
Telephone: (229) 333-7620.
Fax: (229) 245-5308

COWEN, Linda S. *(Judge, State Court of Clayton County)* Appointed by Governor Zell Miller to term beginning Dec 20, 1995. Elected 1996 and 2000. Current term expires Dec 31, 2004. Former Chief Judge.
Office: 3JC302 Justice Center, 9151 Tara Boulevard, Jonesboro 30236.
Telephone: (770) 477-3392.
Fax: (770) 603-4149
E-mail address: lscowen@mindspring.com

COX, Frank R. *(Chief Magistrate, Magistrate Court of Cobb County)*
Office: 32 Waddell Street, Third Floor, Marietta 30090-9656.
Telephone: (770) 528-8931.
Fax: (770) 528-8947
E-mail address: fcox@cobbcounty.org

CRAIG, William H. *(Chief Judge, Superior Court of Georgia Flint Judicial Circuit)* Also Administrative Judge District Six.
Office: Henry County Courthouse, One Courthouse Square, Second Floor, McDonough 30253-3293.
Telephone: (770) 954-2107.
Fax: (770) 954-2083

CRANFORD, John Herbert *(Judge, State Court of Coweta County)* Appointed by Governor Zell Miller to term beginning May 27, 1998. Elected 2000, current term expires Dec 31, 2004.
Mailing address: P.O. Box 1925, Newnan 30264-1925.
Telephone: (770) 254-2645.
Fax: (770) 252-6408

CRANFORD, Mary T. *(Judge, Probate Court of Coweta County)*
Office: 22 East Broad Street, Newnan 30263-1973.
Telephone: (770) 254-2640.
Fax: (770) 254-2648
E-mail address: cowetaprobate@mindspring.com

CRAWFORD, Linton Kim, Jr. *(Judge, State Court of Habersham County)* Elected to term beginning Jan 1, 1997. Reelected 2000, current term expires Dec 31, 2004. Serves part time.
Mailing address: P.O. Box 220, Clarkesville 30523.
Telephone: (706) 754-0834.
Fax: (706) 754-0836
E-mail address: kimcrawford@alltel.net

CRAWFORD, Rick *(Chief Magistrate, Magistrate Court of Polk County)*
Mailing address: P.O. Box 225 Cedartown 30125.
Telephone: (770) 748-4090.
Fax: (770) 749-1445
E-mail address: rickcraw@bellsouth.net

CREWS, Johnnie E. *(Judge, Probate Court of Brantley County)* Former Magistrate, Magistrate Court of Brantley County.
Mailing address: P.O. Box 207, Nahunta 31553-0207.
Telephone: (912) 462-5192.
Fax: (912) 462-8360

CROSBY, John D. *(Senior Judge, Superior Court of Georgia)* Elected at special election to term beginning Nov 1, 1980. Reelected 1984, 1988, 1992 and 1996. Former Chief Judge Tifton Judicial Circuit. Assumed Senior status Dec 31, 2000, serves when called. Born Cook County Georgia Nov 30, 1939. Methodist. Member Tifton First United Methodist Church. Educated at University of Georgia B.B.A. 1961 LL.B. 1963. Contributor Georgia Law Review 1962. Member Alpha Gamma Rho. Admitted to practice Georgia 1963. In legal practice Tifton since 1964. Judge, State Court of Tift County 1971-79.
Member Tifton City Commission 1967-71. Member Georgia Council of Superior Court Judges, American Judicature Society, State Bar of Georgia and Tifton Bar Association. Member First United Methodist Church of Tifton and Tifton Rotary Club. Enjoys golf, hunting, fishing and boating.
Mailing address: P.O. Box 891, Tifton 31793-0891.
Telephone: (229) 386-7906.
Fax: (229) 386-7977

CRUMBLEY, Joe C. *(Senior Judge, Superior Court of Georgia)* Appointed by Governor George Busbee to term beginning May 24, 1977. Elected to subsequent terms. Former Chief Judge Clayton Judicial Circuit. Assumed Senior status Dec 31, 1992, serves when called.

Mailing address: 373 Parkwood Way, Jonesboro 30236.

CULPEPPER, G. Bryant *(Judge, Superior Court of Georgia Macon Judicial Circuit)* Currently serves as Administrative Judge District Three.

Office: 310 Bibb County Courthouse, Macon 31201.
Telephone: (478) 621-6575.
Fax: (478) 621-6582
E-mail address: bculpepper@co.bibb.ga.us

CULPEPPER, George B., III *(Senior Judge, Superior Court of Georgia)* Appointed to term beginning Aug 15, 1967. Assumed Senior status Jan 1, 1983, serves when called. Born Fort Valley Georgia Dec 26, 1920. Methodist. Educated at Mars Hill Junior College 1940 and Mercer University LL.B. 1943. Admitted to practice Georgia 1946. Began legal practice Fort Valley 1946.

Member State Bar of Georgia. USNR 1942-45.

Mailing address: 5300 Zebulon Road, Apartment 2228, Macon 31210.

CUMMINGS, F. Marion *(Senior Judge, Superior Court of Georgia)* Appointed by Governor Joe Frank Harris to term beginning Nov 22, 1988. Elected 1990, 1994 and 1998. Former Chief Judge Tallapoosa Judicial Circuit. Assumed Senior status, serves when called. Born Rome Georgia Nov 11, 1938. Methodist. Educated at Florida State University B.S. 1962 and Mercer University J.D. 1967. Staff member 1965 and Senior Editor 1966-67 Mercer Law Review. Chief Justice Honor Court. Member Phi Alpha Delta. Admitted to practice Georgia 1967, U.S. District Courts Middle 1967 and Northern 1983 Districts of Georgia and U.S. Court of Appeals Eleventh Circuit 1981. In legal practice Cedartown 1967-88.

Solicitor State Court of Polk County 1971-74. Former Member Rome-Polk County-Chatooga County Young Lawyers Association (President 1974), Georgia Trial Lawyers Association and The Association of Trial Lawyers of America. Member State Bar of Georgia, Tallapoosa Circuit (President 1977 and 1984) and American Bar Associations. Specialist Five (Parachutist Badge) U.S. Army 1958-60 USAR 1960-61. Previously worked as sales representative National Gypsum Co. 1962 and claims representative Liberty Mutual Insurance Co. 1964.

Office: 203 Polk County Courthouse, Cedartown 30125.
Telephone: (770) 749-2118.
Fax: (770) 749-2123
E-mail address: cummingsm@sidebar.com

CUMMINGS, Vivian L. *(Judge, Probate Court of Wilkinson County and Chief Magistrate, Magistrate Court of Wilkinson County)* Elected Probate Judge to term beginning Jan 1, 1997. Reelected 2000, current term expires Dec 31, 2004. Appointed Chief Magistrate to term beginning Jan 1, 1997. Elected 2000, current term expires Dec 31, 2004.

Mailing address: P.O. Box 201, Irwinton 31042-0201.
Telephone: (478) 946-2222.
Fax: (478) 946-3810

CUMMINGS MOORE, Thelma Wyatt *(Judge, Superior Court of Georgia Atlanta Judicial Circuit)* Appointed by Governor Joe Frank Harris to term beginning 1990. Elected 1992, 1996 and 2000. Current term expires Dec 2004. Chief Judge 1998-2000. Born Amarillo Texas July 6, 1945. Methodist. Educated at University of California B.A. in French 1965, Illinois Institute of Technology (Fellowship in Psychodynamics) and Emory University J.D. with distinction 1971. John Hay Whitney Fellow 1969-70 and National Urban League Fellow 1969-71. Recipient American Jurisprudence Awards in Commercial Law, Mortgages and Administrative Law and Appellate Advocacy Award 1970. Member Alpha Kappa Alpha, Phi Delta Phi and Order of the Coif. Admitted to practice Georgia 1971. Began legal practice Atlanta 1971. Senior Judge pro hac vice, Atlanta Municipal Court 1977-78. Judge, City Court of Atlanta 1980-85. Former Judge, State Court of Fulton County, elected to term beginning 1985.

Chairperson License Review Board City of Atlanta 1974-75. Author "The Incompetence of a Husband and Wife to Testify so as to Illegitimate a Child" Georgia State B. Jour. 1970. Important Decision: State v. McIntire 1978. Visiting Assistant Professor of Law Emory University 1974-75. Former Board Member National Center for State Courts. Member State Bar of Georgia, Gate City and National (Member and Former Chair Judicial Council) Bar Associations. Recipient Atlanta Business and Professional Women's Award 1970. Named Most Outstanding Young Woman in Atlanta 1970 and One of the Most Outstanding Young Women in America 1977. Listed in *Who's Who in American Law*. Former Cooperating Attorney NAACP Legal Defense and Educational Fund and Washington Research Project. Former Counsel Youth Citizenship Fund. Board of Trustees Emory University. Fellow National Urban League. Enjoys horticulture, dressmaking, painting and poetry writing.

Office: T4905 Justice Center Tower, 185 Central Avenue S.W., Atlanta 30303.
Telephone: (404) 730-4305.
Fax: (404) 730-0162

DALIS, John S. *(Chief Judge, United States Bankruptcy Court Southern District of Georgia)*

Mailing address: P.O. Box 1487, Augusta 30903-1487.
Telephone: (706) 724-4439.

DALLAS, Denise *(Judge, Probate Court of Glascock County)*

Mailing address: P.O. Box 277, Gibson 30810-0277.
Telephone: (706) 598-3241.
Fax: (706) 598-2471

DANIEL, Jerry *(Judge, State Court of Burke County)* Serves part time.

Office: 722 Shadrack Street, Waynesboro 30830.
Telephone: (706) 554-5522.
Fax: (706) 437-9200

DANIEL, Roxann Gray *(Judge, Superior Court of Georgia Chattahoochee Judicial Circuit)*

Mailing address: P.O. Box 1340, Columbus 31902-1340.
Telephone: (706) 653-4266.
Fax: (706) 653-4268

DANIELS, Paula *(Chief Magistrate, Magistrate Court of Irwin County)*
Office: 207 South Irwin Avenue, Suite 3, Ocilla 31774.
Telephone: (229) 468-7671.
Fax: (229) 468-9672
E-mail address: ptdmaget@surfsouth.com

DARDEN, David *(Judge, State Court of Cobb County)* Serves Division One.
Office: 12 East Park Square, Marietta 30090.
Telephone: (770) 427-9977.

DARDEN, Linnie, III *(Judge, Juvenile Court of Georgia Atlantic Judicial Circuit)* Appointed.
Mailing address: P.O. Box 105, Hinesville 31310.
Telephone: (912) 876-0111.
Fax: (912) 368-2979
E-mail address: ldarden@clds.net

DAVENPORT, Chris A. *(Chief Magistrate, Magistrate Court of Jeff Davis County)* Elected to term beginning Jan 1, 1997. Reelected 2000, current term expires Dec 31, 2004.
Mailing address: P.O. Box 568, Hazlehurst 31539-0568.
Telephone: (912) 375-6630.
Fax: (912) 375-6629
E-mail address: jdmagco@bellsouth.net

DAVIS, E. Purnell, II *(Chief Judge, Superior Court of Georgia Toombs Judicial Circuit)* Term expires Dec 31, 2004.
Mailing address: P.O. Box 66, Warrenton 30828-0066.
Telephone: (706) 465-3946.
Fax: (706) 465-1808

DAVIS, J. Harvey *(Judge, Superior Court of Georgia Tifton Judicial Circuit)*
Mailing address: P.O. Box 806, Tifton 31793-0806.
Telephone: (229) 386-7906.
Fax: (229) 386-7977

DAVIS, Lamar W., Jr. *(Judge, United States Bankruptcy Court Southern District of Georgia)* Former Chief Judge.
Mailing address: P.O. Box 8347, Savannah 31412-8347.
Telephone: (912) 650-4109.

DAVIS, Linda K. *(Judge, Probate Court of Fannin County)*
Office: 420 West Main Street, Suite 2, Blue Ridge 30513.
Telephone: (706) 632-3011.
Fax: (706) 632-7167

DAVIS, Sam, Jr. *(Judge, Probate Court of Bryan County)*
Mailing address: P.O. Box 418, Pembroke 31321-0418.
Telephone: (912) 653-3856.
Fax: (912) 653-3845
E-mail address: samdavis@bryan-county.org

DAVIS, Warren P. *(Chief Magistrate, Magistrate Court of Gwinnett County)* Magistrate 1984-87. Appointed Chief Magistrate Sept 1987. Elected 1988, 1992, 1996 and 2000. Current term expires Dec 31, 2004. Born Portland Maine Dec 23, 1950. Educated at New York University B.A. and Columbia Southern School of Law LL.B. Admitted to practice Georgia 1979 and U.S. Courts of Appeals Fifth 1979 and Eleventh 1986 Circuits. In legal practice Atlanta 1979-94.
Instructor Brenau College 1983-87. Member State Bar of Georgia and American Bar Association. Instructor Seminar on Domestic Violence 1992 and 1994. Recipient Public Safety Award 1992. Republican. Enjoys flying.
Office: Gwinnett Justice Center, 75 Langley Drive, Lawrenceville 30045-6900.
Telephone: (770) 822-8080.
Fax: (770) 822-8075
E-mail address: daviswa@co.gwinnett.ga.us

DAY, Jerry *(Chief Magistrate, Magistrate Court of Walker County)*
Office: 102 Napier Street, LaFayette 30728-2914.
Telephone: (706) 638-1217.
Fax: (706) 638-1218
E-mail address: magistrate@co.walker.ga.us

DEADWYLER, Margaret *(Judge, Probate Court of Jackson County)* Elected July 21, 1992 to term beginning Jan 1, 1993. Reelected July 9, 1996 and 2000. Current term expires Dec 31, 2004. Born Jackson County Georgia March 11, 1948. Baptist.
Office: Jackson County Courthouse, 85 Washington Street, Jefferson 30549.
Telephone: (706) 367-6366.
Fax: (706) 367-2468

DEEN, Braswell D., Jr. *(Senior Judge, Court of Appeals of Georgia)* Appointed by Governor Carl E. Sanders to term beginning June 24, 1965. Elected 1966, 1972, 1978 and 1984. Former Chief Judge and Former Presiding Judge. Assumed Senior status Dec 31, 1990, serves when called. Born McRae Georgia Aug 16, 1925. Methodist. Educated at University of Georgia B.A. 1948 LL.B. 1950. Member Pi Kappa Alpha (President) and Delta Theta Phi (Vice Dean). Admitted to practice Georgia 1950. Began legal practice Alma 1950.
Co-author *Georgia Appellate Judiciary* Harrison Publishing Co. 1987. Author *Deen's List: ABC's on ADR* and *Trial by Combat!* Former Professor in Constitutional Law and Appellate Advocacy at evening law schools. Former Adjunct Professor of Origins (creation and evolution) Oglethorpe University. Former Instructor in Chess Emory University. National lecturer "Crime Causes and Cures" and "Origins: Evolution vs. Non-Evolution Law and Science Perspective!" Member State Bar of Georgia and American Bar Association. Named one of five Outstanding Young Men in Georgia by Georgia Jaycees 1955. Recipient Knotz Bennett Cup for Outstanding Citizen of Year 1956, Citation of Merit for Outstanding Contribution to Older People in Georgia from Georgia Gerontology Society 1967 and Georgia Good Citizenship Award from National Sons of the American Revolution 1980. USMC. Recipient Purple Heart. Georgia House of Representatives 1951-52, 1953-54, 1955-56 and 1959-60 (Authored Georgia Women's Jury Bill, Chairman Vocational Education Subcommittee House Education Committee). Trustee Georgia Legal History Foundation. President Georgia Chess Association. Georgia Chess Review Representative, winning second place in 1964 Georgia State Chess Championship

DEEN, BRASWELL D., JR.—*Continued*
and second place in Jacksonville Florida Chess Open 1964. Active in various church and civic organizations.
Mailing address: 4715 Kittyhawk Place N.E., Atlanta 30342.

DelCAMPO, J. Antonio *(Judge, State Court of DeKalb County)*
Office: 804 DeKalb County Courthouse, 556 North McDonough Street, Decatur 30030.
Telephone: (404) 371-2350
Fax: (404) 371-2014
E-mail address: delcampo@co.dekalb.ga.us

DeLOACH, Lee H. *(Judge, Probate Court of Bulloch County)*
Mailing address: P.O. Box 1005, Statesboro 30459-1005.
Telephone: (912) 489-8749.
Fax: (912) 764-8740
E-mail address: probatecourt@bulloch.net

DEMPSEY, Alford J., Jr. *(Judge, Superior Court of Georgia Atlanta Judicial Circuit)* Appointed by Governor Zell Miller to term beginning May 31, 1995. Elected 1996 and 2000. Current term expires Dec 31, 2004.
Office: T5855 Justice Center Tower, 185 Central Avenue S.W., Atlanta 30303-3653.
Telephone: (404) 302-8527.
Fax: (404) 335-2862
E-mail address: alford.dempsey@fultoncourt.org

DENTON, Allen D. *(Judge, Juvenile Court of Georgia Southern Judicial Circuit)* Appointed.
Mailing address: P.O. Box 329, Quitman 31643-0329.
Telephone: (229) 263-7173.
Fax: (229) 263-8324

DETTMERING, W. O'Neal, Jr. *(Judge, State Court of Douglas County)*
Office: Douglas County Courthouse, Fourth Floor, 8700 Hospital Drive, Douglasville 30134.
Telephone: (770) 489-5235.
Fax: (770) 489-5242
E-mail address: ndettmering@co.douglas.ga.us

DEVEAUX, Clinton E. *(Judge, Municipal Court of Atlanta)* Appointed by mayor.
Office: 170 Garnett Street S.W., Atlanta 30303.
Telephone: (404) 865-8104.
Fax: (404) 658-6805
E-mail address: cedeveaux@ci.atlanta.ga.us

DICKERT, Neal W. *(Judge, Superior Court of Georgia Augusta Judicial Circuit)* Elected to term beginning Jan 1, 1997. Reelected 2000, current term expires Dec 31, 2004.
Office: 312 City-County Building, 530 Greene Street, Augusta 30911-4406.
Telephone: (706) 821-2837.
Fax: (706) 721-1091
E-mail address: nd7727@co.richmond.ga.us

DICKINSON, David L. *(Judge, State Court of Forsyth County)* Currently serves as Chief Judge.
Office: 100 West Courthouse Square, Suite 30, Cumming 30040.
Telephone: (770) 781-2130.
Fax: (770) 886-2821
E-mail address: dldickinson@forsythco.com

DILLON, Lawrence G. *(Judge, Recorder's Court of Chatham County)* Serves as Chief Judge.
Office: 133 Montgomery Street, Room 104, Savannah 31401.
Telephone: (912) 652-7431.
Fax: (912) 652-7412
E-mail address: Ldillon@ci.savannah.ga.us

DIXON, Myra H. *(Judge, State Court of Fulton County)*
Office: T3655 Justice Center Tower, 185 Central Avenue S.W., Atlanta 30303.
Telephone: (404) 730-4295.
Fax: (404) 224-0573

DODD, David *(Judge, Probate Court of Cobb County)*
Office: 32 Waddell Street, Marietta 30060.
Telephone: (770) 528-1990.
Fax: (770) 528-1996
E-mail address: probatecourt@cobbcounty.org

DOREMUS, Ogden *(Judge, State Court of Candler County)* Elected Aug 1984 to term beginning Jan 1, 1985. Reelected 1988, 1992, 1996 and 2000. Current term expires Jan 1, 2005. Serves part time. Born Atlanta Georgia April 23, 1921. Methodist. Educated at Emory University B.A. 1946 J.D. with honors 1949. Editor Emory Law Journal 1947-48. Member Phi Alpha Delta. Admitted to practice Georgia 1947, U.S. District Courts Northern 1948, Middle 1948 and Southern 1951 Districts of Georgia and U.S. Courts of Appeals Fifth 1948 and Eleventh 1981 Circuits. In legal practice Atlanta 1947-60, Savannah 1960-72 and Metter 1960-2002.
Former Couunty/City Attorney. Instructor Woodrow Wilson College of Law 1950-54 and Georgia Southern University 1976-80. President 1990-91 Council of State Court Judges of Georgia (Chairman Legislative Committee 1998 and Uniform Rules Committee 1998). Member Judicial Council of Georgia, State Bar of Georgia (Chairman Insurance Law Section 1962-70 and 1985-90, Member Court Futures Committee 1998), Middle District and American (Chairman Committee on Environmental Law Section of General Practice 1962-68) Bar Associations. Chairman Insurance Law Section Annual Institute for Insurance Law 1978-86 and Institute of Trial Advocacy Georgia 1980-86. Attended Bi-Annual Judicial Conferences Institute of Continuing Judicial Education 1985-96 and seminars on Insurance Law and Environmental Law State Bar of Georgia. Honoree and First Recipient Ogden Doremus Award from Council of State Court Judges 1998. First Lieutenant USAAC ETO 1942-46. Political affiliation: nonpartisan. Member Georgia Democratic Executive Committee 1962-66 and Chatham County Democratic Executive Committee. Member Single Trial Court Study Commission 1998. Member Atlanta City Council 1950-54, Willow Lake Golf Club, Savannah Chatham Club and Forrest City Gun Club. Enjoys tennis, photography and hiking.
Mailing address: P.O. Box 702, Metter 30439-0702.
Telephone: (912) 685-6464.
Fax: (912) 685-2160
E-mail address: doremus@pineland.net *or* odoremus-@excite.com

DORSEY, Alec Glenn *(Chief Magistrate, Magistrate Court of Wilcox County)* Appointed to term beginning July 1, 1983. Reappointed 1984, 1988, 1992, 1996 and 2000. Current term expires Dec 31, 2004. Born Macon

DORSEY, ALEC GLENN—*Continued*

Georgia Sept 29, 1943. Baptist. Member Abbeville First Baptist Church (Deacon since 1976). Educated at Emory-at-Oxford College A.D. 1963 and Georgia Southern College B.B.A. 1966. Member Alpha Phi Omega and Phi Kappa Alpha. Justice of the Peace, Wilcox County 1979-83.

Member Georgia Courts of Limited Jurisdiction, Inc. and Georgia Council of Magistrate Court Judges, Inc. (State Secretary since July 1983). Petty Officer Second Class USN 1966-68. Partner Dorsey Realty since 1959. President Dorsey State Bank since 1987 (Vice President 1967-87). President Dorsey Chevrolet, Inc. 1969-80 and Dorsey Oil Company, Inc. 1985-92. City Councilman Jan 1968 to Dec 1969 and Mayor Jan 1970 to Dec 1976 Abbeville. Member Abbeville Volunteer Fire Department Nov 1969 to 1985 and Ocmulgee Festival Committee 1983. Boy Scout Troop Advisor 1984. County Chairman and Area Board member Heart of Georgia Community Action Council for ten years. President Wilcox County Chamber of Commerce for 5 years. Member Abbeville Lions Club (President 2002). Enjoys fishing, hunting, working, coin collecting and treasure hunting.

Office: 103 North Broad Street North, Room 102, Abbeville 31001.
Telephone: (229) 467-2442.
Fax: (229) 467-2000

DOUGLAS, Dubignion *(Senior Judge, Superior Court of Georgia)* Appointed by Governor George D. Busbee to term beginning Jan 1, 1981. Elected 1982 and 1986. Assumed Senior status, serves when called. Born Irwin County Georgia May 24, 1924. Baptist. Educated at Berry College 1947-48 and Mercer University J.D. 1951. Admitted to practice Georgia 1951. Began legal practice Dublin 1951. Judge, Dublin City Court 1952-58. Judge, State Court of Laurens County July 11, 1977 to Jan 1, 1981.

Member State Bar of Georgia (Former member Board of Governors). Sergeant U.S. Army 1945-46. Democrat. Representative Georgia General Assembly 1966-70. Enjoys gardening and music.

Mailing address: 1408 Edgewood Drive, Dublin 31021.

DOUGLASS, Orion L., Sr. *(Judge, State Court of Glynn County)* Elected 1992 to term beginning Jan 1993. Reelected Nov 1996 and 2000. Current term expires Dec 31, 2004. Born Savannah Georgia Feb 22, 1947. Presbyterian. Educated at Holy Cross College A.B. 1968 and Washington University School of Law J.D. 1971. Admitted to practice Georgia 1973, Missouri 1973, U.S. District Courts Northern 1974 and Southern 1984 Districts of Georgia and U.S. Supreme Court 1984. In legal practice Atlanta 1974 and Brunswick 1974-92. Judge, Brunswick Municipal Court 1981-92.

Attended The National Judicial College Reno Nevada Sept 1993. Enjoys golf, music and family.

Office: 701 H Street, Suite 105, Brunswick 31521.
Telephone: (912) 554-7349.
Fax: (912) 267-5642
E-mail address: orionldouglass@glynncounty.org

DOWELL, William A. *(Judge, Recorder's Court of Chatham County)*

Mailing address: P.O. Box 10133, Savannah 31412.
Telephone: (912) 233-8017.
Fax: (912) 234-6430
E-mail address: tybeelaw@mindspring.com

DOWLING, Glenda *(Chief Magistrate, Magistrate Court of Pierce County)*

Office: 2 Courthouse, 3550 U.S. Highway 84 West, Blackshear 31516.
Telephone: (912) 449-2027.
Fax: (912) 449-2103
E-mail address: glendadowling@yahoo.com

DOWNS, Doris L. *(Judge, Superior Court of Georgia Atlanta Judicial Circuit)* Appointed by Governor Zell Miller to term beginning March 4, 1996. Elected 1996 and 2000. Current term expires Dec 31, 2004.

Office: T7955 Justice Center Tower, 185 Central Avenue S.W., Atlanta 30303-3643.
Telephone: (404) 730-4991.
Fax: (404) 335-2828

DRAKE, Judd *(Chief Magistrate, Magistrate Court of Candler County)*

Mailing address: P.O. Box 826, Metter 30439.
Office: Two S.E. Broad Street, Metter 30439.
Telephone: (912) 685-3039.
Fax: (912) 685-6806

DRAKE, W. Homer, Jr. *(Judge, United States Bankruptcy Court Northern District of Georgia)* Appointed by U.S. District Court judges to term beginning Sept 1, 1964. Reappointed 1971 and 1979. Reappointed by U.S. Court of Appeals Eleventh Circuit judges 1985 and May 20, 1999. Current term expires May 20, 2013. Born Colquitt Georgia Nov 21, 1932. Educated at Mercer University A.B. 1954 LL.B. 1956. Law Clerk to Hon. Lewis R. Morgan, U.S. District Court Northern District of Georgia 1961-64. Admitted to practice Georgia 1956. In legal practice Atlanta 1976-79.

Co-author *Chapter 13 Practice and Procedure* 1983 and *Chapter 11 Reorganizations* 2nd ed. 1998 West Group. Author *Bankruptcy Practice for the General Practitioner* West Group 3rd ed. 1995 and various other articles in bankruptcy law journals and periodicals. President National Conference of Bankruptcy Judges 1972-73. Member Committee on the Administration of the Bankruptcy System Judicial Conference of the U.S. 1989-95. Founder and Advisor Southeastern Bankruptcy Law Institute. Fellow American College of Bankruptcy. First Recipient David W. Pollard Achievement Award for Contributions to Bankruptcy Law and Practice from Atlanta Bar Association 1994. Walter Homer Drake Professor of Law Mercer University Walter F. George School of Law established by Southeastern Bankruptcy Law Institute 1996. First Lieutenant JAGC 1956-60. Board of Trustees Mercer University.

Mailing address: P.O. Box 1408, Newnan 30264-1408.
Office: 18 Greenville Street, Newnan 30263.
Telephone: (678) 423-3080.
Fax: (678) 423-3099

DRISKELL, Jackie O. *(Judge, Probate Court of Toombs County)*

Mailing address: P.O. Box 1370, Lyons 30436.
Office: Toombs County Courthouse, Lyons 30436.
Telephone: (912) 526-8696.
Fax: (912) 526-1008

DUBBERLY, B. Daniel, III *(Judge, State Court of Tattnall County)* Elected July 1994 to term beginning Jan 1, 1995. Reelected July 1998 and 2002. Current

DUBBERLY, B. DANIEL, III—*Continued*
term expires Jan 1, 2007. Serves part time. Born Claxton Georgia May 17, 1957. Baptist. Educated at Mercer University A.B. 1980 and Woodrow Wilson College of Law J.D. 1983. Admitted to practice Georgia 1984, U.S. District Court Southern District of Georgia 1984, U.S. Court of Appeals Eleventh Circuit 1993 and U.S. Supreme Court 1994. In legal practice Glennville.

Solicitor State Court of Tattnall County 1991-94. Member Atlantic Bar Association. Member Rotary Club and Lions Club.

Mailing address: P.O. Box 458, Glennville 30427-0458.
Telephone: (912) 654-3952.
Fax: (912) 654-3912
E-mail address: dubmcgov@cybersouth.com

DUFFEY, Aubrey *(Judge, Superior Court of Georgia Coweta Judicial Circuit)* Appointed by Governor Zell Miller to term beginning Sept 26, 1995. Elected 1996 and 2000. Current term expires Dec 31, 2004. Former Judge, State Court of Carroll County.

Mailing address: P.O. Box 338, Carrollton 30112-0338.
Telephone: (770) 830-5871.
Fax: (770) 830-5996

DUKE, Shirley S. *(Chief Magistrate, Magistrate Court of Sumter County)*

Mailing address: P.O. Box 563, Americus 31709-0563.
Telephone: (229) 928-4524.
Fax: (229) 928-4527
E-mail address: sduke@sumter-ga.com

DUNAWAY, Roger W., Jr. *(Judge, Superior Court of Georgia Toombs Judicial Circuit)* Elected to term beginning Jan 1, 1997. Reelected 2000, current term expires Dec 31, 2004.

Mailing address: P.O. Box 480, Thomson 30824.
Telephone: (706) 595-2126.
Fax: (706) 595-8930

DUNN, Aileen H. *(Judge, Probate Court of Colquitt County)* Elected at special election to term beginning Dec 7, 1982. Reelected 1984, 1988, 1992, 1996 and 2000. Current term expires Dec 31, 2004. Born Colquitt County Georgia May 21, 1944. Methodist.

Recipient Frances Duncan Award for outstanding achievement in election administration by a county superintendent of elections by Secretary of State Max Cleland 1992. Real Estate Appraiser 1962-70. Legal Secretary 1972-82. Enjoys reading and needlework.

Mailing address: P.O. Box 264, Moultrie 31776-0264.
Telephone: (229) 616-7415.
Fax: (229) 616-7403
E-mail address: ahg31776@yahoo.com

DYAL, Margaret N. *(Judge, Juvenile Court of Georgia Northern Judicial Circuit)* Former Associate Judge. Appointed Judge.

Mailing address: P.O. Box 57, Lavonia 30553-0057.
Telephone: (706) 356-4062.
Fax: (706) 356-8653
E-mail address: dyalatty@alltel.com

EARNEST, J. E. *(Judge, Probate Court of Seminole County and Chief Magistrate, Magistrate Court of Seminole County)*

Office: Seminole County Courthouse, Donalsonville 31745.
Telephone: (229) 524-5256.
Fax: (229) 524-8644

EDENFIELD, Berry Avant *(Judge, United States District Court Southern District of Georgia)* Appointed for life by President Jimmy Carter to term beginning Nov 9, 1978. Former Chief Judge. Born Bulloch County Georgia Aug 2, 1934. Protestant. Educated at University of Georgia B.B.A. 1956 LL.B. 1958. Admitted to practice Georgia 1958, U.S. District Court Southern District of Georgia 1963, U.S. Court of Appeals Fifth Circuit 1969 and U.S. Supreme Court 1971. In legal practice Statesboro 1958-78.

Former Member Georgia State Senate.

Mailing address: P.O. Box 9865, Savannah 31412-0065.
Telephone: (912) 650-4080.

EDGAR, William J. "Sam" *(Judge, State Court of Bacon County)* Serves part time.

Mailing address: P.O. Box 467, Alma 31510.
Telephone: (912) 632-7777.
Fax: (912) 632-6480
E-mail address: skedgar@almatel.net

EDWARDS, Christopher C. *(Judge, Superior Court of Georgia Griffin Judicial Circuit)* Elected to term beginning Jan 1, 1999. Reelected 2002, current term expires Dec 31, 2006. Born Sept 29, 1955. Educated at Vanderbilt University B.A. and Nova University Center for the Study of Law J.D. Admitted to practice Georgia 1981.

Member Council of Superior Court Judges of Georgia (Committees on Pattern Jury Charge, Benchbook and Uniform Rules).

Office: 140 Stonewall Avenue West, Suite 211, Fayetteville 30214.
Telephone: (770) 460-5730.
Fax: (770) 719-9752
E-mail address: judgeedwards@admin.co.fayette.ga.us

EDWARDS, Deborah A. *(Judge, Juvenile Court of Georgia Houston Judicial Circuit)* Appointed to term beginning July 1, 1996. Reappointed 2000, current term expires July 1, 2004.

Office: 202 Carl Vinson Parkway, Warner Robins 31088.
Telephone: (478) 542-2060.
Fax: (478) 922-4279
E-mail address: dedwards@houstoncountyga.org

ELDRIDGE, Frank M. *(Judge, Court of Appeals of Georgia)* Appointed by Governor Zell Miller to term beginning July 16, 1996. Elected 1998, current term expires Dec 31, 2004. Born Atlanta Georgia March 26, 1939. Educated at Vanderbilt University B.A. 1962 J.D. 1965 and New York University LL.M. in Taxation 1966. Admitted to practice Georgia 1965. Judge and Chief Judge, Superior Court of Georgia Atlanta Judicial Circuit April 15, 1979 to July 15, 1996.

Office: 334 State Judicial Building, Atlanta 30334.
Telephone: (404) 657-9405.
Fax: (404) 657-8893
E-mail address: eldridgf@appeals.courts.state.ga.us

ELLERBEE, O. Wayne *(Judge, Juvenile Court of Georgia Southern Judicial Circuit)* Appointed.
Mailing address: P.O. Box 25, Valdosta 31603-0025.
Telephone: (229) 242-2211.
E-mail address: wellerbee@datasys.net

ELLINGTON, John J. *(Judge, Court of Appeals of Georgia)* Appointed by Governor Roy Barnes to term beginning July 12, 1999. Elected 2000, current term expires Dec 31, 2006. Born Vidalia Georgia Oct 26, 1960. Educated at University of Georgia B.B.A. 1982 J.D. 1985. Admitted to practice Georgia 1985. Judge, State Court of Treutlen County 1991-99. Former Judge, Municipal Courts of Glenwood, Lyons, Mount Vernon, Reidsville, Soperton and Uvalda.
Member Atlanta Lawyer's Club. Past President Vidalia Rotary Club and Soperton Lions Club. Eagle Scout Alumni Chairman Troop #56 Boy Scouts of America.
Office: 334 State Judicial Building, Atlanta 30334.
Telephone: (404) 463-3026.
Fax: (404) 463-3027

ELLISON, Jan *(Judge, Probate Court of Dade County)*
Mailing address: P.O. Box 605, Trenton 30752-0605.
Telephone: (706) 657-4414.
Fax: (706) 657-4305

ELY, Shirley R. *(Chief Magistrate, Magistrate Court of Ben Hill County)* Appointed by Governor Zell Miller to term beginning Feb 4, 1994. Reappointed May 17, 1994. Elected 1996 and 2000. Current term expires Dec 31, 2004. Born Dooly County Georgia Feb 16, 1937. Baptist.
Member Council of Magistrate Court Judges of Georgia (Legislative Committee 1995-96). Board of Trustees Alternative Dispute Resolution Cordele Judicial Circuit. Member Georgia Commission on Family Violence. Attended Institute of Continuing Judicial Education of Georgia University of Georgia School of Law. Member Committee on Child Abuse Protocol Ben Hill County. Member Order of the Eastern Star of Georgia. Enjoys exercising and reading.
Mailing address: P.O. Box 1163, Fitzgerald 31750-1163.
Telephone: (229) 426-5133.
Fax: (229) 426-5123

EMERSON, David T. *(Judge, Superior Court of Georgia Douglas Judicial Circuit)*
Office: Douglas County Courthouse, 8700 Hospital Drive, Douglasville 30134.
Telephone: (770) 920-7227.
Fax: (770) 920-7377
E-mail address: demerson@co.douglas.ga.us

ENGLISH, Paschal A., Jr. *(Chief Judge, Superior Court of Georgia Griffin Judicial Circuit)* Term expires Dec 31, 2004.
Office: Government Annex, 145 Johnson Avenue, Fayetteville 30214.
Telephone: (770) 461-2150.
Fax: (770) 460-6175

ERNEST, Glenda *(Judge, Probate Court of Stephens County)*
Office: 205 North Alexander Street, Room 108, Toccoa 30577.
Telephone: (706) 886-2828.
Fax: (706) 886-2631

ESARY, Sidney R. *(Judge, State Court of Spalding County)* Elected to term beginning Jan 1, 2001. Term expires Dec 31, 2004. Born Montgomery Alabama March 1, 1947. Presbyterian. Educated at Davidson College B.A. 1969 and University of Georgia School of Law J.D. 1972. Admitted to practice Georgia 1972. In legal practice Griffin 1972-2000.
Mailing address: P.O. Box 843, Griffin 30224.
Office: 132 East Solomon Street, Griffin 30223.
Telephone: (770) 467-4474.
Fax: (770) 467-4475
E-mail address: judgesidesary@aol.com

ESTES, Stiles Allen *(Judge, Probate Court of Meriwether County)* Elected to term beginning Nov 4, 1998. Reelected July 2000, current term expires Dec 31, 2004. Born Greenville Georgia Oct 16, 1945. Methodist. Educated at Mercer University B.A. 1967.
Member Council of Probate Court Judges of Georgia.
Mailing address: P.O. Box 608, Greenville 30222-0608.
Office: 100 Court Square, Greenville 30222.
Telephone: (706) 672-4952.
Fax: (706) 672-9465

ETHERIDGE, Philip F. *(Judge, Superior Court of Georgia Atlanta Judicial Circuit)* Appointed by Governor George D. Busbee to term beginning Dec 9, 1981. Elected 1982, 1988, 1992, 1996 and 2000. Current term expires Dec 31, 2004. Former Chief Judge. Born Atlanta Georgia June 8, 1942. Christian. Educated at University of Notre Dame 1962 and University of Georgia B.A. 1965 J.D. 1966. Recipient Outstanding Graduate Award from University of Georgia 1966. Member Gridiron. Admitted to practice Georgia 1965. Began legal practice Athens 1965. In legal practice Atlanta 1966-78. Judge Jan 1, 1979 to Dec 8, 1981 and Chief Judge Sept 1, 1981 to Dec 8, 1981, State Court of Fulton County.
Adjunct Professor of Law Emory University School of Law 1984-98. President Council of Superior Court Judges of Georgia 1994-95. Member American Judicature Society, Lawyers Club of Atlanta, State Bar of Georgia, Atlanta and American Bar Associations. Faculty member Atlanta College of Trial Advocacy 1981 and 1983-88 and National Institute for Trial Advocacy, Boulder Colorado 1986-87 and 1989. Georgia Air National Guard 1966-72. Enjoys running and hiking.
Office: T8705 Justice Center Tower, 185 Central Avenue S.W., Atlanta 30303-3643.
Telephone: (404) 730-4182.
Fax: (404) 657-8439

EVANS, Orinda D. *(Chief Judge, United States District Court Northern District of Georgia)* Appointed for life by President Jimmy Carter to term beginning 1979. Chief Judge since Sept 1, 1999. Born Savannah Georgia April 23, 1943. Educated at Duke University A.B. 1965 and Emory University School of Law J.D. 1968. In legal practice Atlanta 1968-79.
Counsel Atlanta Crime Commission 1970-71.
Office: 1988 U.S. Courthouse, 75 Spring Street S.W., Atlanta 30303-3361.
Telephone: (404) 215-1490.

EXLEY, Preston G. *(Chief Magistrate, Magistrate Court of Effingham County)* Elected to term beginning

EXLEY, PRESTON G.—*Continued*

Jan 1, 1997. Reelected 2000, current term expires Dec 31, 2004.
Mailing address: P.O. Box 819, Springfield 31329-0819.
Telephone: (912) 754-2124.
Fax: (912) 754-4893

FAIRCLOTH, G. Mallon *(Magistrate Judge, United States District Court Middle District of Georgia)* Appointed by U.S. District Court judges to term beginning July 1, 1999. Term expires 2007.
Mailing address: P.O. Box 117, Columbus 31902-0117.
Telephone: (706) 649-7860.

FELDMAN, Joel M. *(Magistrate Judge, United States District Court Northern District of Georgia)* Appointed by U.S. District Court judges to term beginning Oct 23, 1974. Reappointed 1981, 1989 and 1997. Current term expires Oct 24, 2005. Born Atlanta Georgia Jan 2, 1941. Jewish. Educated at Emory University B.A. 1962 LL.B. 1964 J.D. 1971. Admitted to practice Georgia 1963.
Assistant Attorney General of Georgia 1966-68. Assistant District Attorney Fulton County 1968-72 and 1974. Member Naval Reserve Lawyers Association, Federal Magistrate Judges Association, State Bar of Georgia, Atlanta and Federal Bar Associations. Airman Third Class USAFR 1964. Captain (retired) USNR JAGC 1964-92 (Reserve Military Judge Navy-Marine Corps Trial Judiciary 1981-92). Assistant Legislative Counsel General Assembly of Georgia 1964-66. Legislative Assistant and Legal Counsel to Senator Sam Nunn 1973-74. Member Naval Reserve Association (President Atlanta Chapter 1982-83 and Southeast District 1983-84), Navy League of U.S. (President Atlanta Council 1985-86) and Naval Order of U.S. (President 1990-91).
Office: 1619 U.S. Courthouse, 75 Spring Street S.W., Atlanta 30303-3361.
Telephone: (404) 215-1375.

FENNESSY, Michael A. *(Judge, State Court of Sumter County)* Serves part time.
Mailing address: P.O. Box 507, Americus 31709-0507.
Telephone: (229) 924-6175.
Fax: (229) 924-8509

FINDLEY, J. Emory *(Senior Judge, Superior Court of Georgia)* Assumed Senior status Jan 1, 1995, serves when called.
Mailing address: P.O. Box 426, Claxton 30417-0426.
Office: Evans County Courthouse, Claxton 30417.
Telephone: (912) 739-0035.
E-mail address: efindley@frontiernet.net

FITZPATRICK, Duross *(Senior Judge, United States District Court Middle District of Georgia)* Appointed for life by President Ronald Reagan Nov 13, 1985 to term beginning Jan 1, 1986. Former Chief Judge. Assumed Senior status Feb 1, 2001, serves by assignment. Born Macon Georgia Oct 19, 1934. Episcopalian. Educated at University of the South and University of Georgia B.S.F. 1961 LL.B. 1966. Member Sigma Alpha Epsilon. Admitted to practice Georgia 1965 and U.S. District Courts Middle 1967 and Northern 1985 Districts of Georgia. In legal practice Cochran 1967-85.
Important Decisions: Smith v. Kemp (death penalty for retarded person) 664 F. Supp. 500 M.D. Ga. 1987; Thomas G. Waller, et al. v. Ozzy Osbourne, CBS, Inc., CBS Records, Inc., et al. 763 F. Supp. 1144 M.D. Ga. 1991; and CMAX/Cleveland, Inc., dba Computermax v. UCR, et al. 804 F. Supp. 337 M.D. Ga. 1992. Instructor in Trial Techniques Emory University 1983-88. Member Chief Justice's Commission on Professionalism Supreme Court of Georgia 1992-98. Board of Directors Federal Judges Association 1999-2001. Fellow Georgia Bar Foundation and American Bar Foundation. Master of the Bench William A. Bootle Chapter American Inns of Court. Member State Bar of Georgia (Board of Governors 1976, Executive Committee Board of Governors 1979, President Elect 1983-84, President 1984-85), Oconee (President 1970) and Macon Bar Associations. Attended course Advanced Trial Advocacy Skills National Institute for Trial Advocacy March 1983. Sergeant USMC 1954-57. Forester U.S. Forest Service and private business 1961-63. Republican. Member Georgia Forest Research Council 1976-82. Member Richland Restoration League, Inc. (President 1986-87). Manages own farm and timberland for timber production. Enjoys hunting, American history, travel and photography. Personal Statement or Quote: "The trial of lawsuits requires that all participants (the judge, jury and each lawyer) do their utmost to carry out their duties in a professional manner. If any of the above fails in that obligation, the likelihood of an unjust verdict is greatly increased."
Mailing address: P.O. Box 1014, Macon 31202-1014.
Telephone: (478) 752-3500.

FLAKE, Gail C. *(Judge, Superior Court of Georgia Stone Mountain Judicial Circuit)* Former Judge, State Court of DeKalb County.
Office: 504 DeKalb County Courthouse, 556 North McDonough Street, Decatur 30030.
Telephone: (404) 371-2909.
Fax: (404) 371-2788

FLANAGAN, Douglas J. *(Judge, Juvenile Court of Georgia Augusta Judicial Circuit)* Appointed to term beginning 2000. Term expires Oct 2004. Serves part time. Born Brooklyn New York Oct 30, 1946. Educated at Augusta State University B.B.A. J.D. LL.M. Admitted to practice Georgia 1977. In legal practice Augusta.
Past President Augusta Chapter Federal Bar Association. U.S. Army.
Office: 401 Walton Way, Augusta 30901.
Telephone: (706) 821-1201.
E-mail address: dougjflan@aol.com

FLANDERS, H. Gibbs, Jr. *(Chief Judge, Superior Court of Georgia Dublin Judicial Circuit)* Appointed by Governor Zell Miller to term beginning Sept 27, 1993. Elected 1996 and 2000. Current term expires Dec 31, 2004.
Mailing address: P.O. Box 2100, Dublin 31040-2100.
Telephone: (478) 272-0061.
Fax: (478) 275-9180

FLEMING, William M., Jr. *(Chief Judge, Superior Court of Georgia Augusta Judicial Circuit)* Appointed by Governor Lester Maddox May 8, 1968. Elected to subsequent terms. Born Winston-Salem North Carolina Oct 20, 1924. Catholic. Educated at University of Georgia LL.B. 1950. Admitted to practice Georgia 1950. Began legal practice Augusta 1950.
Member State Bar of Georgia and Augusta Bar Association. Sergeant USAAC 1943-45. Richmond County

FLEMING, WILLIAM M., JR.—*Continued*

Representative Georgia Legislature 1959-68. Democrat. Enjoys tennis, fishing and hunting.

Office: 305 City-County Building, 530 Greene Street, Augusta 30911.
Telephone: (706) 821-2357.
Fax: (706) 721-1089
E-mail address: wf1175@co.richmond.ga.us

FLETCHER, Norman S. *(Chief Justice, Supreme Court of Georgia)* Appointed by Governor Joe Frank Harris Dec 28, 1989. Elected Nov 1990, 1996 and 2002. Current term expires 2008. Former Presiding Justice. Born Fitzgerald Georgia July 10, 1934. Educated at University of Georgia B.A. 1956 LL.B. 1958 and University of Virginia LL.M. 1995. Member Omicron Delta Kappa, Phi Delta Theta, Phi Delta Phi and Blue Key. In legal practice Rome 1958-63 and LaFayette 1963-89.

City Attorney LaFayette 1965-89. Attorney Walker County 1973-88. Special Assistant Attorney General 1979-89. President Lookout Mountain Bar Association 1973-74. Fellow American Bar Foundation and Georgia Bar Foundation. Master Joseph Henry Lumpkin Inn of Court. Board of Visitors University of Georgia School of Law 1989-95 (Chairman 1994-95). Commissioner General Assembly Presbyterian Church USA 1984-85. Past President LaFayette Rotary Club. Former Board Member LaFayette Chamber of Commerce. Member and Ruling Elder Peachtree Presbyterian Church Atlanta.

Office: 507 State Judicial Building, Atlanta 30334.
Telephone: (404) 656-3477.
Fax: (404) 657-4211

FLOURNOY, Robert, III *(Judge, Superior Court of Georgia Cobb Judicial Circuit)*
Office: 30 Waddell Street, Marietta 30090.
Telephone: (678) 581-5400.
Fax: (678) 581-5407

FLOURNOY, Robert E., Jr. *(Senior Judge, Superior Court of Georgia)* Appointed by Governor Joe Frank Harris to term beginning July 14, 1987. Elected 1988, 1992 and 1996. Former Chief Judge Cobb Judicial Circuit. Assumed Senior status, serves when called. Born Atlanta Georgia Sept 30, 1930. Baptist. Educated at Emory University A.B. 1951 and University of Georgia J.D. 1952. Law Clerk to Hon. Ralph H. Pharr, Superior Court of Georgia Atlanta Judicial Circuit 1953. Member Phi Delta Phi, Pi Sigma Alpha, Omicron Delta Kappa and Kappa Alpha. Admitted to practice Georgia 1952. In legal practice Atlanta 1954-57 and Marietta 1957-87.

Assistant Attorney City of Smyrna 1957-63 and Cobb County 1957-64. Deputy Assistant Attorney General Georgia 1961-84. Attorney Lake Acworth Authority 1963-66. Mayor Marietta 1982-85. Member Lawyers Club of Atlanta, American Judicature Society, State Bar of Georgia (Board of Governors 1972-76), Cobb County (President 1966-67) and American Bar Associations. Attended General Jurisdiction Course The National Judicial College July 1988, American Academy of Judicial Education June 1990, annual Superior Court Judges Seminar and annual State Bar Convention. Captain USAF 1952-53. Member Georgia Legislature 1963-64. Chairman Executive Committee Cobb County Democratic Party 1965-69. President Cobb Landmarks and Historical Society 1986-87. Member Atlanta Regional Commission 1981-85 (Parliamentarian, Member Executive Committee), Downtown Marietta Development Authority and First Baptist Church of Marietta.

Office: 30 Waddell Street, Marietta 30090-9642.
Telephone: (770) 528-1880.
Fax: (770) 528-8103

FLOYD, Charles *(Chief Magistrate, Magistrate Court of Fayette County)*
Mailing address: P.O. Box 1076, Fayetteville 30214-1076.
Telephone: (770) 461-2116.
Fax: (770) 719-2357

FLOYD, George C. *(Judge, State Court of Decatur County)* Serves part time.
Mailing address: P.O. Box 1026, Bainbridge 39818.
Telephone: (229) 246-5694.
Fax: (229) 246-6732
E-mail address: gcfloyd@hotmail.com

FLOYD, Terry K. *(Judge, Juvenile Court of Georgia Brunswick Judicial Circuit)* Appointed.
Mailing address: P.O. Drawer 766, St. Marys 31558-0766.
Telephone: (912) 882-4348.
Fax: (912) 882-3758
E-mail address: tkfloyd@net-magic.net

FOLLOWILL, Kenneth B. *(Chief Judge, Superior Court of Georgia Chattahoochee Judicial Circuit)* Appointed by Governor George Busbee to term beginning May 17, 1978. Elected to subsequent terms. Born Hammond Indiana Nov 30, 1935. Episcopalian. Educated at University of the South B.A. 1956 and Emory University LL.B. 1960. Member Kappa Alpha Order, Phi Delta Phi and Pi Gamma Mu. Admitted to practice Georgia 1960. Began legal practice Columbus 1960. Judge, State Court of Muscogee County Feb 1970 to May 1978.

City Court Solicitor Columbus 1965-70. Instructor in Commercial Law American Institute of Banking 1964. Past Chairman Governor's Criminal Justice Coordinating Council. Member Columbus Younger Lawyers Section (Past President), State Trial Judges and Solicitors Association of Georgia (Past President), Judicial Council of Georgia (Past Secretary, Vice Chairman and Chairman), Chattahoochee Judicial Circuit Bar Association (Past President) and State Bar of Georgia. Sergeant USAR 1958-64. Member Columbus Metropolitan Boys Clubs Advisory Board and Columbus Country Club. Former Vice President and Board Vice Chairman First Federal Savings and Loan Association. Enjoys hunting, fishing and music.

Mailing address: P.O. Box 1340, Columbus 31902-1340.
Telephone: (706) 653-4270.
Fax: (706) 653-4269
E-mail address: followill@mindspring.com

FOLSOM, William R. *(Judge, State Court of Brooks County)* Elected to term beginning Jan 1, 1997. Reelected 2000, current term expires Dec 31, 2004. Serves part time.
Office: 111 East Adair Street, Valdosta 31601.
Telephone: (229) 244-0382.
Fax: (229) 244-0109
E-mail address: wfolsom@datasys.net

FOREHAND, Dwayne D. *(Judge, Probate Court of Dooly County)*
Mailing address: P.O. Box 304, Vienna 31092-0304.
Telephone: (229) 268-4217.
Fax: (229) 268-6142

FORRESTER, J. Owen *(Judge, United States District Court Northern District of Georgia)* Appointed for life by President Ronald Reagan to term beginning 1981. Born Columbus Georgia April 27, 1939. Educated at Georgia Institute of Technology B.S. 1961 and Emory University School of Law LL.B. 1966. In legal practice Atlanta 1967-69. Magistrate, U.S. District Court Northern District of Georgia 1976-81.
Assistant U.S. Attorney Northern District of Georgia 1969-76. Staff Attorney Callaway for Governor Committee 1966-67.
Office: 1921 U.S. Courthouse, 75 Spring Street S.W., Atlanta 30303-3361.
Telephone: (404) 215-1310.

FORRESTER, Whitfield R. *(Chief Judge, Superior Court of Georgia Cordele Judicial Circuit)* Appointed by Governor George D. Busbee to term beginning June 9, 1980. Elected 1982, 1986, 1996 and 2000. Current term expires Dec 31, 2004. Born Crisp County Georgia Jan 3, 1925. Baptist. Educated at North Georgia College 1942 and University of Georgia J.D. 1948. Member Phi Delta Phi. Admitted to practice Georgia 1948. In legal practice Cordele 1948-80.
Former City Attorney Cordele. Former Attorney Crisp County Power Commission. Member State Bar of Georgia, Cordele Judicial Circuit and American Bar Associations. Captain U.S. Army.
Mailing address: P.O. Box 701, Cordele 31010-0701.
Telephone: (229) 276-2620.
Fax: (229) 276-2652

FORSLING, Susan B. *(Judge, State Court of Fulton County)* Appointed by Governor Zell Miller to term beginning Oct 17, 1997. Elected Nov 1998 and 2002. Current term expires Dec 31, 2006.
Office: T2955 Justice Center Tower, 185 Central Avenue S.W., Atlanta 30303.
Telephone: (404) 730-4510.
Fax: (404) 224-0577
E-mail address: susanforsling@co.fulton.ga.us

FOSTER, William A., III *(Chief Judge, Superior Court of Georgia Paulding Judicial Circuit)* Formerly served Tallapoosa Judicial Circuit.
Office: 201 Paulding County Courthouse, 11 Courthouse Square, Dallas 30132.
Telephone: (770) 443-7551.
Fax: (770) 443-7554

FOWLER, Eddy *(Judge, Probate Court of Franklin County)* Elected to term beginning Jan 1, 1997. Reelected 2000, current term expires Dec 31, 2004.
Mailing address: P.O. Box 207, Carnesville 30521-0207.
Telephone: (706) 384-2403.
Fax: (706) 384-2636

FOWLER, H. Gregory *(Judge, State Court of Chatham County)* Appointed by Governor Zell Miller to term beginning May 18, 1995. Elected 1996 and 2000. Current term expires Dec 31, 2004. Currently serves as Chief Judge.
Office: 430 Chatham County Courthouse, 133 Montgomery Street, Savannah 31401-3239.
Telephone: (912) 652-7565.
Fax: (912) 652-7566

FOWLER, Kenneth E. *(Chief Magistrate, Magistrate Court of Twiggs County)*
Mailing address: P.O. Box 146, Jeffersonville 31044-0146.
Telephone: (478) 945-3428.
Fax: (478) 945-2083

FRANZEN, Stephen E. *(Judge, Juvenile Court of Georgia Gwinnett Judicial Circuit)* Appointed.
Office: Gwinnett Justice Center, 75 Langley Drive, Lawrenceville 30045.
Telephone: (770) 822-8349.
Fax: (770) 822-8062
E-mail address: franzest@co.gwinnett.ga.us

FRAZIER, John A. *(Senior Judge, Superior Court of Georgia)* Appointed by Governor Jimmy Carter to term beginning Dec 30, 1974. Elected to term beginning Jan 1, 1975. Reelected 1978, 1982 and 1986. Retired Aug 1, 1988. Assumed Senior status, serves when called. Born Floyd County Georgia Nov 29, 1918. Episcopalian. Educated at LaSalle Extension University LL.B. Admitted to practice Georgia 1950. In legal practice Savannah and Rome 1950-74. Judge, Juvenile Court of Floyd County 1964-74.
Member State Bar of Georgia, Rome and American Bar Associations. Corporal USAAC April 1943 to Feb 1946.
Office: 2499 North Broad Street N.E., Rome 30161-5319.
Telephone: (706) 234-3079.

FREEMAN, Linda *(Chief Magistrate, Magistrate Court of Terrell County)* Elected to term beginning Jan 1, 1997. Reelected 2000, current term expires Dec 31, 2004.
Mailing address: P.O. Box 793, Dawson 31742-0793.
Telephone: (229) 995-3757.
Fax: (229) 995-4496

FREESEMANN, Penny Haas *(Judge, Superior Court of Georgia Eastern Judicial Circuit)* Appointed by Governor Zell Miller to term beginning May 18, 1995. Elected 1996 and 2000. Current term expires Dec 31, 2004. Judge, State Court of Chatham County Oct 7, 1993 to May 17, 1995.
Office: 204 Chatham County Courthouse, 133 Montgomery Street, Savannah 31401.
Telephone: (912) 652-7252.
Fax: (912) 652-7254
E-mail address: phfreese@wpo.co.chatham.ga.us

FRY, Harvey L. *(Chief Magistrate, Magistrate Court of Camden County)* Appointed Magistrate 1995. Elected Chief Magistrate 2000. Term expires Dec 31, 2004. Also Judge Pro Tem, Woodbine Municipal Court. Born Ashland Kansas Feb 26, 1946. Methodist.
Officer USN (retired). Board of Directors Chamber of Commerce and Coastal Zone Management Advisory Council. Member Camden County Rotary, Woodbine Li-

FRY, HARVEY L.—*Continued*

ons and VFW. Interests include U.S. history, hunting, pistol matches and antique tractors.
Mailing address: P.O. Box 386, Woodbine 31569-0386.
Telephone: (912) 576-5658.
Fax: (912) 576-7955
E-mail address: magcourt@eagnet.com

FRYER, Joel James *(Senior Judge, Superior Court of Georgia)* Appointed by Governor Jimmy Carter to term beginning July 1, 1974. Elected to subsequent terms. Former Chief Judge Atlanta Judicial Circuit. Assumed Senior status, serves when called. Born Cleveland Ohio Dec 1, 1928. Educated at University of Georgia B.B.A. 1950 LL.B. 1951. Admitted to practice Georgia 1951. Began legal practice Atlanta 1951. Judge, Civil Court of Fulton County 1971-74.
Author "The Omnibus Hearing: Benefit or Burden for State Courts?" 28 Mercer L. Rev. 329, 1976. Member State Bar of Georgia, Atlanta and American Bar Associations. First Lieutenant U.S. Army 1951-53. Democrat.
Office: C-956 Fulton County Courthouse, 136 Pryor Street, Atlanta 30303.
Telephone: (404) 730-4264.
Fax: (404) 224-0940
E-mail address: FRYERJ@mindspring.com

FRYER, Nancy *(Judge, Probate Court of Terrell County)* Elected to term beginning Jan 1, 1997. Reelected 2000, current term expires Dec 31, 2004.
Mailing address: P.O. Box 67, Dawson 31742-0067.
Telephone: (229) 995-5515.
Fax: (229) 995-5574
E-mail address: probatefryer@hotmail.com

FUDGER, Arthur W. *(Senior Judge, Superior Court of Georgia)* Appointed by Governor George D. Busbee to term beginning Nov 1, 1977. Elected to subsequent terms. Former Chief Judge Tallapoosa Judicial Circuit. Assumed Senior status, serves when called. Born Jacksonville Florida Nov 1, 1933. United Methodist. Educated at Georgia Institute of Technology B.S. 1958 and Emory University J.D. 1967. Admitted to practice Georgia 1967. Began legal practice Dallas Georgia 1967. Judge, Dallas Recorder's Court 1969-77.
City Attorney Hiram 1967-73. Attorney Paulding County School Board 1971-75. County Attorney Paulding County 1972-76. Member State Bar of Georgia (Board of Governors 1977-79), Tallapoosa Judicial Circuit (President 1976) and American Bar Associations. Recipient District Award of Merit from Boy Scouts of America 1977. Airman USAF 1954-56. Democrat. Member Paulding County Chamber of Commerce (President 1970), Paulding County Civitian Club (President 1977) and Cobb, Douglas, Paulding TB Association (President 1971). District Commissioner Boy Scouts 1974-77. Scout Master Troop 773, 1975-77. Enjoys skiing, camping and boating.
Office: 203 Paulding County Courthouse, Dallas 30132.
Telephone: (770) 443-7551.
Fax: (770) 445-7657
E-mail address: a_fudger@hotmail.com

FULLER, C. Andrew *(Chief Judge, Superior Court of Georgia Northeastern Judicial Circuit)* Appointed by Governor Zell Miller to term beginning July 29, 1993. Elected 1994, 1998 and 2002. Current term expires Dec 31, 2006.
Mailing address: P.O. Box 3362, Gainesville 30503-3362.
Telephone: (770) 531-6861.
Fax: (770) 533-7678

FULLER, David M. *(Judge, State Court of Gwinnett County)*
Office: Gwinnett Justice Center, 75 Langley Drive, Lawrenceville 30045-6935.
Telephone: (770) 822-8503.
Fax: (770) 822-8536
E-mail address: fullerda@co.gwinnett.ga.us

FULLER, Hilton *(Judge, Superior Court of Georgia Stone Mountain Judicial Circuit)* Elected to term beginning Jan 1, 1981. Reelected 1984, 1988, 1992, 1996 and 2000. Current term expires Dec 31, 2004. Former Chief Judge. Born Atlanta Georgia Feb 16, 1941. Methodist. Educated at University of Florida and Emory University B.A. 1964 LL.B. 1964 replaced by J.D. Winner Moot Court competition Emory University School of Law. Chief Justice Honor Court. Staff member Journal of Public Law. Admitted to practice Georgia 1964 and U.S. Supreme Court. In legal practice Atlanta 1964-80.
Adjunct Professor of Law Georgia State University. Former member Sentence Review Panel. Member Uniform Rules Revision Committee for Superior Courts. Former Judicial Associate Editor *Courts, Health, Science and the Law* Georgetown University Medical and Law Centers. Chair Georgia Courts Automation Commission. Member Council of Superior Court Judges of Georgia (Secretary-Treasurer 1986-87, President 1986-87). Member Old War Horse Lawyers Club, American Judicature Society, State Bar of Georgia, Decatur-DeKalb, Atlanta and American (National Conference of State Trial Judges Judicial Administration Division) Bar Associations. Graduate The National Judicial College. Former faculty member National Institute of Trial Advocacy, Institute for Court Management and The National Judicial College. Former coach Decatur-DeKalb YMCA youth soccer league. Member Decatur First United Methodist Church and Advisory Board Justice Center of Atlanta, Inc. Active in civic, community and church affairs.
Office: 306 DeKalb County Courthouse, 556 North McDonough Street, Decatur 30030.
Telephone: (404) 371-2211.
Fax: (404) 371-3062
E-mail address: hmfuller@co.dekalb.ga.us

FULLER, Max *(Chief Magistrate, Magistrate Court of Gordon County)*
Mailing address: P.O. Box 1025, Calhoun 30703-1025.
Telephone: (706) 629-6818.
Fax: (706) 602-1751

GAINES, Crystal *(Judge, City Court of Atlanta)* Appointed by mayor.
Office: 104 Trinity Avenue, Atlanta 30303.
Telephone: (404) 658-6919.
Fax: (404) 658-7125
E-mail address: cagaines@ci.atlanta.ga.us

GAINES, Joseph J. *(Senior Judge, Superior Court of Georgia)* Former Chief Judge Western Judicial Circuit. Assumed Senior status, serves when called.
Mailing address: P.O. Box 8045, Athens 30603-8045.
Telephone: (706) 613-3161.
Fax: (706) 613-3169

GARLAND, Grace D. *(Chief Magistrate, Magistrate Court of Thomas County)*
Mailing address: P.O. Box 879, Thomasville 31799-0879.
Telephone: (229) 225-3334.
Fax: (229) 225-3342

GARMON, Johnnie M. *(Chief Magistrate, Magistrate Court of Union County)*
Office: 114 Courthouse Street, Suite 10, Blairsville 30512.
Telephone: (706) 439-6008.
Fax: (706) 439-6104

GARRETT, Wayne *(Judge, Probate Court of Towns County and Chief Magistrate, Magistrate Court of Towns County)* Appointed Chief Magistrate July 1983. Elected 1984, 1988, 1992, 1996 and 2000. Current term expires Dec 31, 2004. Born Hiawassee Georgia Nov 10, 1934.
Sergeant U.S. Army 1951-54. Member Masons and VFW. Enjoys water sports and outdoor activities.
Office: 48 River Street, Suite E, Hiawassee 30546.
Telephone: (706) 896-3467.
Fax: (706) 896-1772

GAULT, Richard S. *(Chief Judge, Superior Court of Georgia Bell-Forsyth Judicial Circuit)* Formerly served Blue Ridge Judicial Circuit. Former Judge, State Court of Cherokee-Forsyth Counties.
Office: 100 West Courthouse Square, Suite 160, Cumming 30040.
Telephone: (770) 781-2133.
Fax: (770) 888-8862
E-mail address: rsgault@co.forsyth.ga.us

GEETER, Shane *(Chief Magistrate, Magistrate Court of Baldwin County)*
Mailing address: P.O. Box 1565, Milledgeville 31061-1565.
Office: Baldwin County Courthouse, Milledgeville 30161.
Telephone: (478) 445-4446.
Fax: (478) 445-5918
E-mail address: smg1@accucomm.net

GEORGE, Hulane Evans *(Judge, Superior Court of Georgia Ocmulgee Judicial Circuit)* Appointed by Governor Zell Miller to term beginning May 25, 1994. Elected 1996 and 2000. Current term expires Dec 31, 2004.
Mailing address: P.O. Box 1050, Milledgeville 31059-1050.
Telephone: (478) 445-4270.
Fax: (478) 445-2622
E-mail address: hgeorge@accucomm.net

GETACHEW-SMITH, David *(Associate Judge, Juvenile Court of Georgia Atlanta Judicial Circuit)* Appointed.
Office: Justice Center, 395 Pryor Street S.W., Third Floor, Atlanta 30312.
Telephone: (404) 224-4851.
Fax: (404) 730-1121

GIBSON, Carlette W. *(Chief Magistrate, Magistrate Court of Pulaski County)*
Mailing address: P.O. Box 667, Hawkinsville 31036-0667.
Telephone: (478) 783-1357.
Fax: (478) 892-3308

GIBSON, Denny Rodney *(Judge, Probate Court of Pickens County)* Elected to term beginning Jan 1, 1977. Reelected 1984, 1988, 1992, 1996 and 2000. Current term expires Dec 31, 2004. Born Pickens County Georgia July 9, 1947. Baptist. Democrat. Member Gospel Quartet and Masons.
Office: 50 North Main Street, Suite C, Jasper 30143.
Telephone: (706) 253-8756.
Fax: (706) 253-8910
E-mail address: pickensprobatejudge@hotmail.com

GIBSON, Douglas L. *(Judge, State Court of Ware County)* Serves part time.
Mailing address: P.O. Box 1589, Waycross 31502-1589.
Telephone: (912) 283-3858.
Fax: (912) 283-3806
E-mail address: gibsonspivey@wayxcable.com

GIDDENS, Marie M. *(Judge, Probate Court of Schley County)* Elected at special election to term beginning Feb 27, 1990. Reelected 1992, 1996 and 2000. Current term expires Dec 31, 2004. Born Eastman Georgia Sept 8, 1928. Baptist.
Secretary Champion Home Builders Co. 1964-89. Member Ellaville Baptist Church. Worked with husband in their funeral home business 1961 to Dec 31, 1998.
Mailing address: P.O. Box 385, Ellaville 31806-0385.
Telephone: (229) 937-2905.
Fax: (229) 937-5588

GIGLIO, J. Michael *(Judge, Juvenile Court of Georgia Lookout Mountain Judicial Circuit)* Former Associate Judge. Appointed Judge.
Mailing address: P.O. Box 1600, Ringgold 30736-1600.
Telephone: (706) 935-4901.
Fax: (706) 935-4909
E-mail address: JMGIGLIO@msn.com

GILBERT, Quintress J. *(Judge, Juvenile Court of Georgia Macon Judicial Circuit)* Appointed to term beginning Feb 1, 1997. Reappointed 2000, current term expires Dec 31, 2004.
Office: 505 Bibb County Courthouse, Macon 31201.
Telephone: (478) 621-6359.
Fax: (478) 621-6448
E-mail address: qgilbert@co.bibb.ga.us

GILLETTE, Martin *(Judge, Probate Court of Camden County)*
Mailing address: P.O. Box 818, Woodbine 31569-0818.
Telephone: (912) 576-3785.
Fax: (912) 576-5484
E-mail address: girlfriday31569@yahoo.com

GILLIS, Donald *(Judge, State Court of Treutlen County)* Serves part time.
Mailing address: P.O. Box 2015, Dublin 31040-2015.

GILLIS, DONALD—*Continued*

Telephone: (912) 529-3881, (478) 272-3545.
Fax: (478) 272-8853
E-mail address: gillis@nlamerica.com

GILLIS, Dwayne Hamilton *(Judge, Superior Court of Georgia Waycross Judicial Circuit)* Appointed by Governor Roy Barnes to term beginning May 31,2001. Elected Aug 2001, current term expires Jan 1, 2007. Born Dec 15, 1960. Baptist. Educated at South Georgia College A.S. 1984, Valdosta State College B.S. 1987 and Mercer University School of Law J.D. 1990. Admitted to practice Georgia 1990. In legal practice Douglas since June 1, 1990. Judge, Municipal Court of Douglas April 1992 to May 31, 2001. Part-time Judge, Juvenile Courts of Bacon, Brantley, Charlton, Coffee, Pierce, and Ware Counties Oct 2000 to May 31, 2001.

Member State Bar of Georgia, Douglas (Vice President 1992-93, President 1993-94) and American Bar Associations. Patrol Officer Douglas Police Department 1983-84. Shift Commander St. Mary's Police Department 1984-87.

Office: Coffee County Courthouse, 101 South Peterson Avenue, Suite B-2, Douglas 31533.
Telephone: (912) 384-0587.
Fax: (912) 384-0701

GINSBERG, Ronald E. *(Judge, State Court of Chatham County)* Appointed by Governor Zell Miller to term beginning May 18, 1995. Elected 1996 and 2000. Current term expires Dec 31, 2004.

Office: 209 Chatham County Courthouse, 133 Montgomery Street, Savannah 31401.
Telephone: (912) 652-7556.
Fax: (912) 652-7557
E-mail address: reginsbe@chathamcounty.org

GIRARDEAU, John E. *(Judge, Superior Court of Georgia Northeastern Judicial Circuit)* Former Chief Judge.

Mailing address: P.O. Box 49, Gainesville 30503-0049.
Telephone: (770) 531-6996.
Fax: (770) 531-7105
E-mail address: judgegirardeau@mindspring.com

GLOVER, Irma *(Judge, State Court of Cobb County)* Appointed by Governor Zell Miller to term beginning Dec 21, 1995. Elected 1996 and 2000. Current term expires Dec 31, 2004. Serves Division One. Former Judge, Juvenile Court of Cobb County.

Office: 12 East Park Square, Marietta 30090.
Telephone: (770) 528-1711.
Fax: (770) 528-1733
E-mail address: iglover@cobbcounty.org

GOBER, C. J., Jr. *(Judge, State Court of Cherokee County)* Currently serves as Chief Judge. Former Judge, Juvenile Court of Cherokee County.

Office: 90 North Street, Suite 170, Canton 30114.
Telephone: (770) 720-6343.
Fax: (770) 479-2173
E-mail address: cjgober@co.cherokee.ga.us

GOGER, John J. *(Judge, Superior Court of Georgia Atlanta Judicial Circuit)* Appointed by Governor Zell Miller to term beginning Aug 5, 1998. Elected Nov 1999, current term expires Dec 31, 2004. Born New Jersey March 8, 1947. Educated at Xavier University B.S. cum laude 1969 and Boston College J.D. 1973. Editor Boston College Law Review 1972-73. Law Clerk to Hon. Newell Edenfield, U.S. District Court Northern District of Georgia 1973-74. Admitted to practice Georgia 1974. In legal practice Atlanta 1974-95. Judge, State Court of Fulton County June 1995 to Aug 1998, appointed by Governor Zell Miller.

Author "Standing: Suits Against Federal Regulatory and Administrative Agencies" 13, 289, 1971 and "The Billy Rose Case" 14, 183, 1972 Boston College Industry & Commerce L. Rev. Editor and Author *Daniel's Georgia Handbook of Criminal Evidence* and *Daniel's Georgia Criminal Trial Practice.* Board of Advisors Annual Survey of Bankruptcy Law 1979-84 and Lecturer Art and the Law Seminar 1984-89 and Trial Techniques Program 1985-93 Emory University School of Law. Adjunct Professor of Trial Advocacy Georgia State University Law School 1994-97. Member Atlanta Division Northern District of Georgia Panel of U.S. Bankruptcy Trustees 1979-95. Treasurer National Association of Bankruptcy Trustees 1983-84. Member Georgia Association of Criminal Defense Lawyers (Treasurer 1979-95), State Bar of Georgia, Atlanta (Chair Bar Poll and Election Committee 1983-84), Gate City (Board of Directors 1997) and American Bar Associations. Chairman Board of Directors Lullwater School 1975-79. Board of Directors Metro Atlanta Advisory Drug Council 1981-83, Atlanta Easter Seals 1987-89, Atlanta Volunteer Lawyers Foundation 1995-98 and Arthritis Foundation 1997-2000. Board of Directors 1983-90 and President 1987-88 Georgia Volunteer Lawyers for the Arts, Inc. Member Public Relations Committee Buckhead Christian Ministry 1995-96. Program Facilitator Leadership Atlanta 1997-2000.

Office: 185 Central Avenue, Suite T-4705, Atlanta 30303.
Telephone: (404) 335-8671.
Fax: (404) 224-0550
E-mail address: john.goger@fultoncourt.org

GORDON, Janis *(Judge, State Court of DeKalb County)*

Office: 604 DeKalb County Courthouse, 556 North McDonough Street, Decatur 30030.
Telephone: (404) 371-2354

GORDON, Raymond S., Jr. *(Judge, State Court of Wayne County)* Elected to term beginning Jan 1, 1979. Reelected 1982, 1986, 1990, 1994, 1998 and 2002. Current term expires Dec 31, 2006. Serves part time.

Mailing address: P.O. Box 787, Jesup 31598-0787.
Telephone: (912) 427-9582.
Fax: (912) 427-9531
E-mail address: g&h@jesup.net

GOSS, Stephen S. *(Judge, Superior Court of Georgia Dougherty Judicial Circuit)* Appointed by Governor Roy Barnes. Former part-time Judge, Juvenile Court of Dougherty County.

Mailing address: P.O. Box 1827, Albany 31702-1827.
Telephone: (229) 434-2683.
Fax: (229) 434-2174

GOSSELIN, Kathlene F. *(Judge, Superior Court of Georgia Northeastern Judicial Circuit)* Appointed by Governor Zell Miller to term beginning June 3, 1998. Elected Nov 2000, current term expires Dec 31, 2004. Born Chicago Illinois Jan 2, 1956. Episcopalian. Educated at Southern Illinois University B.A. with honors 1976 and University of Chicago J.D. 1980. Admitted to

GOSSELIN, KATHLENE F.—*Continued*

practice Georgia 1980. In legal practice Atlanta 1980-81 and Gainesville 1981-87. Judge and Chief Judge, State Court of Hall County Jan 1, 1987 to June 2, 1998.

Member State Bar of Georgia, Gainesville-Northeastern and American Bar Associations.

Mailing address: P.O. Box 1778, Gainesville 30503.
Telephone: (770) 531-6990.
Fax: (770) 533-7679

GOTTFRIED, Maureen C. *(Judge, State Court of Muscogee County)* Appointed by Governor Zell Miller to term beginning Nov 22, 1995. Elected July 1996 and 2001. Current term expires Dec 31, 2005. Born March 14, 1961. Educated at Trinity College B.A. 1983 and University of Georgia School of Law J.D. 1986. Recipient Presidential Scholarship. Member Order of Metis.

Chief Assistant Solicitor Aug 1986 to Jan 1993 and Solicitor Jan 1993 to Nov 1995 State Court of Muscogee County. Member Columbus Younger Lawyer's Club, State Bar of Georgia, Columbus and American Bar Associations. Instructor Seminar on Prosecution of DUI's 1992, 1993, 1994, 1995 and 1996 and Basic Litigation Course 1994, 1995 and 1996 Prosecuting Attorney's Council. Board Member Girls, Inc. and Child Advocacy Center. Member Network for Professionals and Executives, Fraternal Order of Police Auxiliary and Exchange Club of Columbus. Assistant soccer coach CYSA.

Mailing address: P.O. Box 1340, Columbus 31902-1340.
Telephone: (706) 653-4322.
Fax: (706) 653-4321
E-mail address: mgottfried@columbusga.org

GRAHAM, James E. *(Magistrate Judge, United States District Court Southern District of Georgia)* Appointed by U.S. District Court judges.

Mailing address: P.O. Box 250, Brunswick 31521-0250.
Telephone: (912) 280-1360.

GRAHAM, Tracy *(Judge, Juvenile Court of Georgia Clayton Judicial Circuit)* Former Associate Judge. Appointed Judge.

Office: 121 South McDonough Street, Jonesboro 30236-3694.
Telephone: (770) 477-3270.
Fax: (770) 477-3255
E-mail address: tracygraham@bellsouth.net

GRAVES, Calvin S. *(Judge, City Court of Atlanta)*
Office: 104 Trinity Avenue S.W., Atlanta 30303.
Telephone: (404) 658-6919.
Fax: (404) 658-7125

GRAY, Jerry C. *(Judge, State Court of Jackson County)* Serves part time.
Office: 66 Washington Street, Jefferson 30549.
Telephone: (706) 367-2122.
Fax: (706) 367-2468

GRAY, Loring Albert, Jr. *(Chief Judge, Superior Court of Georgia Dougherty Judicial Circuit)* Appointed by Governor Joe Frank Harris to term beginning Jan 21, 1986. Elected Aug 1986, 1996 and 2000. Current term expires Dec 31, 2004. Born Portsmouth Virginia June 8, 1947. Episcopalian. Educated at Albany Junior College A.A. cum laude 1971 and University of Georgia A.B. cum laude 1972 J.D. 1975. Member Phi Alpha Delta. Admitted to practice Georgia 1975 and U.S. Courts of Appeals Fifth 1976 and Eleventh 1981 Circuits. In legal practice Albany 1979-86.

Assistant District Attorney Dougherty Judicial Circuit 1976-79. City Court Prosecutor and Police Advisor 1979-86. Member State Bar of Georgia, Dougherty Judicial Circuit (President 1984-85) and American Bar Associations. Attended General Jurisdiction Course The National Judicial College July 1986. Instructor in Basic Computers Institute of Continuing Judicial Education. E-5 USN 1966-71. Recipient Navy Unit Citation, Good Conduct Medal, Armed Forces Expeditionary Medal, Vietnam Service Medal (with one star) and Vietnam Campaign Medal. Political affiliation: Independent. Assisted in campaigns of Congressman Charles Hatcher (D-Georgia) and Governor Joe Frank Harris (D-Georgia). Active in Albany Museum of Art, Albany Little Theatre and Albany Art Festival (Chairman 1982). Enjoys art, music, hunting, fishing, computers and cycling.

Mailing address: P.O. Box 1827, Albany 31702-1827.
Telephone: (229) 431-3242.
Fax: (229) 878-3153

GRAY, Mauri DeWaun *(Associate Judge, Juvenile Court of Georgia Middle Judicial Circuit)* Appointed.
Mailing address: P.O. Box 1015, Sandersville 31082.
Telephone: (478) 552-3227.
Fax: (478) 522-8807

GRAYSON, Greg *(Judge, Probate Court of Catoosa County)*
Office: Catoosa County Justice Building, 875 LaFayette Street, Ringgold 30736-1799.
Telephone: (706) 935-3511.
Fax: (706) 935-3519
E-mail address: grayson@catt.com

GREENE, Deborah S. *(Judge, Municipal Court of Atlanta)* Appointed by mayor.
Office: 170 Garnett Street S.W., Atlanta 30303.
Telephone: (404) 865-8100.
Fax: (404) 658-6859

GREENE, J. Mike *(Judge, Probate Court of Jones County and Chief Magistrate, Magistrate Court of Jones County)* Elected Probate Judge Nov 1981. Reelected to subsequent terms. Elected Chief Magistrate to term beginning Jan 1, 1985. Reelected 1988, 1992, 1996 and 2000. Current term expires Dec 31, 2004. Born Jones County Georgia March 14, 1956. Baptist. Educated at Middle Georgia College 1976 and Georgia College B.S.B.A. 1978.

Mailing address: P.O. Box 1359, Gray 31032-1359.
Telephone: (478) 986-6668.
Fax: (478) 986-1715

GREENE, Michael *(Judge, Recorder's Court of Gwinnett County)* Former Associate Judge, Juvenile Court of Gwinnett County.
Office: Gwinnett Justice Center, 75 Langley Drive, Lawrenceville 30245-6900.
Telephone: (770) 822-8383.
Fax: (770) 822-8394
E-mail address: greenmi@co.gwinnett.ga.us

GRIFFIN, Belinda F. *(Judge, Probate Court of Crisp County)* Court Clerk seven years. Elected Judge to term beginning Oct 30, 1985. Reelected 1988, 1992, 1996

GRIFFIN, BELINDA F.—*Continued*

and 2000. Current term expires Dec 31, 2004. Born Crisp County Georgia Aug 12, 1960. Southern Baptist.

President Southwest Georgia Probate Judges Association 1994-95 and 1997-98.

Mailing address: P.O. Box 26, Cordele 31010-0026.
Telephone: (229) 276-2621.
Fax: (229) 273-9184

GRIFFIN, Hendon H. *(Chief Magistrate, Magistrate Court of Chattahoochee County)*

Mailing address: P.O. Box 120, Cusseta 31805-0120.
Telephone: (706) 989-3643.
Fax: (706) 989-0396

GRINER, Susan W. *(Judge, Probate Court of Berrien County)* Elected to term beginning Jan 1, 2001. Term expires Jan 1, 2005. Born Lowndes Georgia Nov 16, 1946. Methodist.

Member Woman's Club. Participant church, school and community activities. Enjoys spending time with children and grandchildren, fishing, traveling, gardening and cooking.

Office: 2 Berrien County Courthouse, 101 East Marion Avenue, Nashville 31639.
Telephone: (229) 686-5213.
Fax: (229) 686-9495

GROSS, Lisa M. *(Judge, State Court of Screven County)* Elected to term beginning Jan 1, 1997. Reelected 2000, current term expires Dec 31, 2004. Serves part time.

Mailing address: P.O. Box 33, Newington 30446.
Office: 700 Oliver Highway, Newington 30446.
Telephone: (912) 857-3534.
Fax: (912) 857-4861
E-mail address: southernx@planters.net

GRUBBS, Adele *(Judge, Superior Court of Georgia Cobb Judicial Circuit)* Former Judge, Juvenile Court of Cobb County.

Office: 30 Waddell Street, Marietta 30090.
Telephone: (770) 528-1826.
Fax: (770) 528-1830
E-mail address: agrubbs@cobbcounty.org

GUESS, William Marion, Jr. *(Judge, Probate Court of DeKalb County)* Elected to term beginning Jan 1, 1973. Reelected to subsequent terms. Current term expires Dec 31, 2004. Born Atlanta Georgia Oct 19, 1942. Methodist. Educated at Emory University A.B. 1966 J.D. 1967. Admitted to practice Georgia 1969. Began legal practice Atlanta 1969.

Author *Guardianship: The Law in Georgia* Harrison & Co., *Probate and Administration: The Law in Georgia* Harrison & Co. and "Georgia Probate Notes" published in Probate Courts monthly newsletter. Member Judicial Council of Georgia, Atlanta Lawyers Club, State Bar of Georgia, Atlanta and Decatur-DeKalb Bar Associations. Board of Trustees Georgia Institute for Continuing Judicial Education. Enjoys swimming and skin diving.

Office: 103 DeKalb County Courthouse, 556 North McDonough Street, Decatur 30030.
Telephone: (404) 371-2718.
Fax: (404) 371-7055
E-mail address: wmguess@co.dekalb.ga.us

GUIDRY, Kevin J. *(Judge, Juvenile Court of Georgia Piedmont Judicial Circuit)* Appointed.

Mailing address: P.O. Box 628, Winder 30680-0628.
Telephone: (770) 307-0048.
Fax: (770) 307-4522
E-mail address: piedmontjc@hotmail.com

GUNTER, Jack N. *(Senior Judge, Superior Court of Georgia)* Elected to term beginning Jan 1, 1973. Reelected to subsequent terms. Former Chief Judge Mountain Judicial Circuit. Assumed Senior status, serves when called.

Mailing address: 1643 Camp Creek Road, Cornelia 30531.

HAGY, C. Christopher *(Magistrate Judge, United States District Court Northern District of Georgia)* Appointed by U.S. District Court judges.

Office: 1756 U.S. Courthouse, 75 Spring Street S.W., Atlanta 30303-3361.
Telephone: (404) 215-1440.

HAIRSTON, Andrew J. *(Judge, City Court of Atlanta)* Appointed by Mayor Andrew J. Young to term beginning April 4, 1982. Retained by election. Serves Traffic Division. Former Chief Judge. Born Clemmons North Carolina July 8, 1932. Minister Church of Christ. Educated at Paul Quinn College B.S. with honors 1955 B.A. with honors 1956, John Marshall Law School J.D. with honors 1969, Woodrow Wilson College of Law LL.M. 1971, Texas Christian University Th.M. 1978, Emory University D.MIN. 1999 and University of Nevada M.J.S. 1999. Admitted to practice Georgia 1971. In legal practice Atlanta 1971-76.

Assistant Solicitor General State Court of Fulton County 1976-78 and City Solicitor 1978-82 Atlanta. Instructor John Marshall Law School 1970-76. Member State Bar of Georgia, Gate City, National and American Bar Associations. Colonel USAS Chaplaincy since 1965. Member Operation Breadbasket and Concerned Black Clergy. Enjoys sports and exercise.

Office: 104 Trinity Avenue S.W., Atlanta 30303.
Telephone: (404) 658-6919.
Fax: (404) 658-7125
E-mail address: ahairston@ci.atlanta.ga.us

HALLMAN, Diane *(Judge, Probate Court of Appling County)* Elected to term beginning Jan 1, 1977. Reelected to subsequent terms. Current term expires Jan 1, 2005. Born Baxley Georgia Dec 22, 1943. Religious affiliation: Non-Denominational. Political affiliation: Non-Partisan. Enjoys reading and traveling.

Office: B Appling County Courthouse, 36 South Main Street, Baxley 31513.
Telephone: (912) 367-8114.
Fax: (912) 367-8166

HALLMAN, Ron *(Judge, State Court of Evans County)* Serves part time.

Mailing address: P.O. Box 980, Claxton 30417.
Office: 802 West Main Street, Claxton 30417.
Telephone: (912) 739-3868.

HAMBY, Gary *(Judge, Probate Court of Upson County)*

Mailing address: P.O. Box 906, Thomaston 30286-0012.
Telephone: (706) 647-7015.
Fax: (706) 646-3341
E-mail address: garyhamby@msn.com

HAMIL, R. Timothy *(Judge, Superior Court of Georgia Gwinnett Judicial Circuit)* Former Judge, State Court of Gwinnett County, elected Nov 1998 to term beginning Jan 1, 1999.

Office: Gwinnett Justice Center, 75 Langley Drive, Lawrenceville 30045.
Telephone: (770) 822-8548.
Fax: (770) 822-8536
E-mail address: hamiltim@co.gwinnett.ga.us

HAMPTON, Steve *(Chief Magistrate, Magistrate Court of Murray County)*

Office: 121 Fourth Avenue, Chatsworth 30705.
Telephone: (706) 695-3021.
Fax: (706) 695-7525

HAMRICK, Gayle B. *(Judge, State Court of Richmond County)* Currently serves as Chief Judge. Serves Division One.

Office: A-246 Law Enforcement Center, 401 Walton Way, Augusta 30901.
Telephone: (706) 821-1167.
Fax: (706) 821-1251
E-mail address: gh1196@co.richmond.ga.us

HANCOCK, George E. *(Chief Magistrate, Magistrate Court of Stewart County)* Elected to term beginning Jan 1, 1997. Reelected 2000, current term expires Dec 31, 2004.

Mailing address: P.O. Box 712, Lumpkin 31815-0712.
Telephone: (229) 838-0505.
Fax: (229) 838-0016

HANCOCK, J. Phillip *(Judge, Recorder's Court of DeKalb County)*

Office: 1549 Clairmont Road, Suite 106B, Decatur 30033.
Telephone: (404) 486-7400.
Fax: (404) 486-7403
E-mail address: phanc46268@aol.com

HANCOCK, Michael E. *(Chief Judge, Superior Court of Georgia Stone Mountain Judicial Circuit)* Appointed by Governor Zell Miller to term beginning May 3, 1991. Currently serves as Administrative Judge Fourth District. Born Gainesville Georgia Aug 19, 1949. Educated at Georgia State University B.S. 1973 and Emory University J.D. 1978. Law Clerk to Hon. Romae Powell, Juvenile Court of Fulton County 1976. Admitted to practice Georgia 1979. Began legal practice Atlanta 1979. Chief Judge, Recorder's Court of DeKalb County July 1, 1983 to May 1991.

Assistant Public Defender Fulton County 1979-81. Assistant Public Defender 1981-82 and Assistant Solicitor 1983 DeKalb County. Member DeKalb Lawyers Association (Founder and President Emeritus), State Bar of Georgia, Decatur-DeKalb and American Bar Associations. Recipient Black Male Achiever Award from Southern Bell/Bell-South Company 1991. Member Class of Leadership DeKalb 1992-93. Enjoys operating a computer bulletin board service.

Office: 403 DeKalb County Courthouse, 556 North McDonough Street, Decatur 30030-3356.
Telephone: (404) 371-2344.
Fax: (404) 371-2002
E-mail address: mehancoc@co.dekalb.ga.us

HANKINSON, Tommy Richard *(Judge, Superior Court of Georgia Griffin Judicial Circuit)*

Mailing address: P.O. Box 1527, Griffin 30224.
Office: 132 East Solomon Street, Griffin 30223.
Telephone: (770) 467-4329.
Fax: (770) 467-4333

HARDAWAY, Pat *(Judge, Probate Court of Columbia County)* Elected to term beginning Jan 1, 1981. Reelected to subsequent terms. Current term expires Dec 31, 2004. Born Gurnsey Wyoming Oct 24, 1935. Educated at University of Georgia.

Personal Statement or Quote: "It is one of the most beautiful compensations of this life that no one can sincerely try to help another without helping oneself" (Ralph Waldo Emerson).

Mailing address: P.O. Box 525, Appling 30802-0525.
Telephone: (706) 541-1254.
Fax: (706) 541-4001
E-mail address: phardaway@co.columbia.ga.us

HARPER, Helen Woodard *(Judge, Probate Court of Laurens County)* Chief Court Clerk Jan 13, 1968 to Dec 31, 1980. Elected Judge to term beginning Jan 1, 1981. Reelected 1984, 1988, 1992, 1996 and 2000. Current term expires Dec 31, 2004. Born Laurens County Georgia Nov 26, 1945. Baptist.

President County Officers Association 1997. Named Member of the Year by Area 27 MH/MR Advisory Council 1990, Pilot of the Year 1991 and Officer of the Year by County Officers Association of Georgia 1991. Democrat. Member Laurens County Democratic Executive Committee since 1981. Secretary Area 27 MH/MR Advisory Council. President 1991-92 and Board of Directors Pilot Club of Dublin. Vice President 1990-91 and Board Member Chamber of Commerce. Chairman St. Patrick's Arts and Craft Show 1997 and Miss St. Patrick's Scholarship Program Pageant 1997. Vice Chairman Dublin-Laurens County Chamber of Commerce 1997. Board Member Heart Fund. Charter Member Women of the Moose. Member Elks Auxiliary and Marie Baptist Church, Dublin. President Blarney Stone 1988-89. Vice Chairman Dublin-Laurens County St. Patrick Committee 1993. Enjoys quilting, reading and walking.

Mailing address: P.O. Box 2098, Dublin 31040-2098.
Telephone: (478) 272-2566.
Fax: (478) 277-2932

HARPER, John V. *(Judge, Superior Court of Georgia Southwestern Judicial Circuit)*

Mailing address: P.O. Box 784, Americus 31709-0784.
Telephone: (229) 924-2269.
Fax: (229) 924-1614
E-mail address: johnvharper@hotmail.com

HARRIS, Barbara A. *(Chief Judge, Municipal Court of Atlanta)* Appointed by Mayor Andrew Young to term beginning April 19, 1981. Retained by election 1985, 1989, 1993, 1997 and 2001. Current term expires Dec 31, 2005. Born Atlanta Georgia July 18, 1951. United Methodist. Educated at Harvard-Radcliffe College A.B. cum laude 1973 and University of Michigan J.D. 1976. Law Clerk to Hon. Charles Longstreet Weltner, Superior Court of Georgia Atlanta Judicial Circuit 1976. Member Phi Alpha Delta. Admitted to practice Georgia 1976 and U.S. District Court Northern District of Georgia 1976.

Assistant U.S. Attorney Northern District of Georgia 1977-82. Member Supreme Court Commission on Equal-

HARRIS, BARBARA A.—*Continued*

ity, Supreme Court Commission on Substance Abuse, Judicial Council of Georgia, National Conference of Bar Examiners, State Bar of Georgia, Gale City, National and American (Co-chair Committee on Minorities 1995-96 and Member Executive Committee National Conference of Special Court Judges Judicial Administration Division) Bar Associations. Member Leadership Atlanta, Drifters, Inc. and NAACP.
Office: 170 Garnett Street S.W., Atlanta 30303.
Telephone: (404) 865-8102.
Fax: (404) 658-6805
E-mail address: BAHarris@ci.atlanta.ga.us

HARRIS, Carrie T. *(Associate Judge, Juvenile Court of Georgia Cobb Judicial Circuit)* Appointed.
Office: 1738 County Services Parkway S.W., Suite 250, Marietta 30008.
Telephone: (770) 528-2228.
Fax: (770) 528-2576
E-mail address: carrieinga@hotmail.com

HARRIS, N. Jackson *(Judge, Superior Court of Georgia Blue Ridge Judicial Circuit)* Former Judge, Juvenile Court of Cherokee County, appointed to term beginning Jan 1, 1997.
Office: 90 North Street, Suite 260, Canton 30114.
Telephone: (770) 479-0454.
Fax: (770) 345-3276
E-mail address: jharris@brjc.net

HART, George H., Jr. *(Chief Magistrate, Magistrate Court of Lowndes County)*
Mailing address: P.O. Box 1349, Valdosta 31603-1349.
Telephone: (229) 333-5112.
Fax: (229) 333-7616

HART, Helen J. *(Chief Magistrate, Magistrate Court of Bleckley County)*
Office: Courthouse Annex, 306 S.E. Second Street, Cochran 31014.
Telephone: (478) 934-3202.
Fax: (478) 934-7826
E-mail address: lahhart@accucomm.net

HARTLEY, Martha M. *(Judge, Probate Court of Harris County)* Elected to term beginning Nov 5, 1998. Reelected 2000, current term expires Dec 31, 2004. Born LaGrange Georgia July 28, 1947. Baptist. Educated at Georgia College A.B. 1969, Emory University M.L.S. 1970 and University of Georgia J.D. cum laude 1980. Law Clerk to Chief Judge Anthony A. Alaimo, U.S. District Court Southern District of Georgia 1980-81. Admitted to practice Georgia 1980. Began legal practice Douglasville 1981.
Member State Bar of Georgia. Charter Member Harris County Rotary Club.
Mailing address: P.O. Box 569, Hamilton 31811.
Telephone: (706) 628-5038.
Fax: (706) 628-7322

HARTLEY, Marvin B., Jr. *(Senior Judge, Superior Court of Georgia)* Appointed by Governor George D. Busbee to term beginning May 24, 1977. Elected 1978, 1982, 1986 and 1996. Assumed Senior status, serves when called. Born Sandersville Georgia Jan 13, 1933. Educated at University of Georgia A.B.J. 1959 J.D. 1961. Admitted to practice Georgia 1961. Judge, State Court of Toombs County Jan 1, 1977 to May 23, 1977.
Member State Bar of Georgia (Former member Board of Governors) and Middle Judicial Circuit Bar Association. U.S. Army 1953-55. Past President Lyons Jaycees, Lyons Lions Club and Lyons-Toombs County Chamber of Commerce.
Mailing address: 273 North Victory Drive, Lyons 30436.

HARVEY, John R. *(Senior Judge, Superior Court of Georgia)* Elected to term beginning March 1974. Reelected to subsequent terms. Former Chief Judge Atlantic Judicial Circuit. Assumed Senior status, serves when called. Born Bulloch County Georgia July 5, 1935. Methodist. Educated at University of Georgia B.B.A. and J.D. Admitted to practice Georgia 1966. Began legal practice Pembroke 1966.
Solicitor State Court of Bryan County 1970-74 and Pembroke City Court 1967-74. Member Atlantic Bar Association 1966. Sergeant USAS 1957-59.
Mailing address: P.O. Box 1018, Pembroke 31321-1018.

HAWKINS, Joyce W. *(Judge, Probate Court of Forsyth County)* Elected to term beginning Aug 1976. Reelected to subsequent terms. Current term expires Dec 31, 2004. Born Forsyth County Georgia Sept 6, 1940. Methodist. Former Chief Magistrate, Magistrate Court of Forsyth County.
Office: 101 Forsyth County Courthouse Annex, 112 West Maple Street, Cumming 30040.
Telephone: (770) 781-2140.
Fax: (770) 886-2839

HAWKINS, William Colbert *(Senior Judge, Superior Court of Georgia)* Appointed by Governor Lester Garfield Maddox to term beginning Feb 4, 1969. Elected to subsequent terms. Assumed Senior status March 29, 1984, serves when called. Born Walton County Georgia June 20, 1914. Baptist. Educated at University of Georgia A.B. 1937 J.D. 1939. Member Sphinx, Omicron Delta Kappa and Blue Key. Admitted to practice Georgia 1939, U.S. Court of Appeals Fifth Circuit and U.S. Supreme Court. Began legal practice Sylvania 1939.
Member State Bar of Georgia and American Bar Association. Colonel USAR JAGC. Georgia General Assembly 1951-52 and 1955-58. Member Masons and Shriners.
Mailing address: P.O. Box 439, Sylvania 30467-0439.
Telephone: (912) 564-2091.

HAYES, Judy *(Chief Magistrate, Magistrate Court of Henry County)* Elected to term beginning Jan 1, 1983. Reelected 1986, 1990, 1994, 1998 and 2002. Current term expires Dec 31, 2006. Chief Magistrate since July 1, 1983. Born Red Bay Alabama Feb 20, 1941. Presbyterian. Judge, Henry County Small Claims Court Jan 3, 1983 to June 30, 1983.
Member Uniform Rules Committee, Training Committee, Legislative Committee, BenchBook Committee and Executive Committee and Past Vice President Council of Magistrate Court Judges of Georgia.
Office: 30 Atlanta Street, McDonough 30253-2108.
Telephone: (770) 954-2111.
Fax: (770) 954-2144
E-mail address: jhayes@co.henry.ga.us

HAYNES, Linda Bratton *(Associate Judge, Juvenile Court of Georgia Stone Mountain Judicial Circuit)* Appointed.
Office: 1947 East Gate Drive, Stone Mountain 30087.
Telephone: (404) 294-2916.
Fax: (404) 297-3907
E-mail address: lbhaynes@co.dekalb.ga.us

HEAD, James W. *(Senior Judge, Superior Court of Georgia)* Elected to term beginning Jan 1, 1985. Reelected 1988 and 1992. Assumed Senior status Feb 1, 1995, serves when called. Former Judge, State Court of Chatham County. Former Judge, Juvenile Court of Chatham County.
Office: 415 West Broughton Street, Suite 112, Savannah 31401.
Telephone: (912) 652-7167, 651-2040.
Fax: (912) 651-6378

HEARN, George J., III *(Judge, Juvenile Court of Georgia Alcovy Judicial Circuit)* Appointed.
Office: Law Enforcement Center, 1425-A South Madison Avenue, Monroe 30655.
Telephone: (770) 267-1346.
Fax: (770) 267-8313
E-mail address: ghearn@co.walton.ga.us

HENDRICKS, Angela *(Judge, Probate Court of Baker County and Chief Magistrate, Magistrate Court of Baker County)*
Mailing address: P.O. Box 548, Newton 39870-0548.
Telephone: (229) 734-3007 (probate), 734-3009 (magistrate).
Fax: (229) 734-8822.

HENRY, F. Bryant, Jr. *(Judge, Juvenile Court of Georgia Lookout Mountain Judicial Circuit)* Appointed to term beginning Sept 2, 1997. Reappointed Oct 1, 2000, current term expires Sept 30, 2004.
Mailing address: P.O. Box 601, LaFayette 30728-0601.
Telephone: (706) 638-3044.
Fax: (706) 639-1776
E-mail address: bhnh1971@aol.com

HERSHNER, Robert F., Jr. *(Chief Judge, United States Bankruptcy Court Middle District of Georgia)* Appointed by U.S. District Court judges to term beginning Dec 1, 1980. Reappointed by U.S. Court of Appeals Eleventh Circuit judges. Born Sumter South Carolina Jan 21, 1944. Methodist. Educated at Mercer University A.B. 1966 J.D. 1969. Associate Editor Mercer University Law Review 1968-69. Member Phi Delta Phi. Admitted to practice Georgia 1971. Began legal practice Macon 1972.
Consultant to Norton *Bankruptcy Law and Practice* Callaghan & Co. since 1984. Member 1990-99 and Chair 1994-99 Committee on Bankruptcy Judge Education The Federal Judicial Center. Governor, Vice President 1996-97 and President Oct 1997 to Oct 1998 National Conference of Bankruptcy Judges. Board Member Federal Judicial Center since March 14, 2001. Member State Bar of Georgia and Macon Bar Association. Captain U.S. Army 1970-75.
Mailing address: P.O. Box 86, Macon 31202-0086.
Telephone: (478) 752-3505.

HICKS, Claude W., Jr. *(Magistrate Judge, United States District Court Middle District of Georgia)* Appointed by U.S. District Court judges to term beginning Oct 1, 1983. Reappointed 1986, 1994 and 2002. Current term expires 2010. Served part time 1983-86. Born Jacksonville Florida Oct 18, 1945. Baptist. Educated at Furman University B.A. 1967 and Mercer University J.D. 1970. Member Sigma Alpha Epsilon and Phi Delta Phi. Admitted to practice Georgia 1970, U.S. District Court Middle District of Georgia 1970, U.S. Supreme Court 1978 and U.S. Court of Appeals Eleventh Circuit 1981. In legal practice Macon 1970-86.
Member State Bar of Georgia and Macon Bar Association. Captain U.S. Army JAGC 1974-75. Board of Deacons Highland Hills Baptist Church. Member Idle Hour Golf and Country Club.
Mailing address: P.O. Box 48, Macon 31202-0048.
Telephone: (478) 752-8125.

HICKS, Ralph *(Senior Judge, Superior Court of Georgia)* Assumed Senior status, serves when called.
Mailing address: 3435 Valley Road N.W., Atlanta 30305-1148.

HICKSON, Nina *(Judge, Juvenile Court of Georgia Atlanta Judicial Circuit)* Appointed to term beginning May 10, 1999. Currently serves as Chief Presiding Judge.
Assistant U.S. Attorney. Associate General Counsel Primerica Financial Services.
Office: 395 Pryor Street S.W., Suite J241, Atlanta 30312.
Telephone: (404) 224-4811.
Fax: (404) 335-2732
E-mail address: nrhickson4@hotmail.com

HILL, Sharon N. *(Associate Judge, Juvenile Court of Georgia Atlanta Judicial Circuit)* Appointed.
Office: Justice Center, 395 Pryor Street S.W., Third Floor, Atlanta 30312.
Telephone: (404) 224-4871.
Fax: (404) 730-1121
E-mail address: snhill@mindspring.com

HILL, Wm. Ralph, Jr. *(Judge, Superior Court of Georgia Lookout Mountain Judicial Circuit)* Appointed by Governor Zell Miller to term beginning Feb 1, 1995. Elected July 9, 1996, current term expires Dec 31, 2004. Born LaGrange Georgia April 12, 1943. Presbyterian. Educated at Furman University B.A. 1965 and University of Georgia LL.B. 1968. Member Phi Alpha Delta. Admitted to practice Georgia 1968, U.S. District Court Northern District of Georgia 1970, U.S. Courts of Appeals Fifth 1970 and Eleventh 1985 Circuits and U.S. Supreme Court 1976. In legal practice Newnan July 1970 to Oct 1970, Augusta Oct 1970 to April 1971 and LaFayette Sept 1973 to Feb 1995.
Assistant District Attorney Lookout Mountain Judicial Circuit May 1971 to Sept 1973. Lifetime Fellow Roscoe Pound American Trial Lawyers Foundation. Member Georgia Association of Criminal Defense Lawyers, Georgia Trial Lawyers Association, Christian Legal Society, National Association of Criminal Defense Lawyers, Inc., The Association of Trial Lawyers of America, State Bar of Georgia (Board of Governors 1984-92, Law Revision Committee) and Lookout Mountain Bar Association. Attended General Jurisdiction Course The National Judicial College July 1995 and "A Judge's Philosophy of Law and Judging" Cambridge Massachusetts July 1998 and "No Reversals—Correct Rulings: Evidence in Action" Bar Harbor Maine Aug 2000 American Academy of Judicial Education. Captain U.S. Army April

HILL, WM. RALPH, JR.—*Continued*

1968 to June 1970. Recipient Army Commendation Medal, Bronze Star Medal, Republic of Viet Nam Service Medal and National Defense Service Medal. Deacon First Baptist Church of LaFayette. Member Gideons International, American Legion, VFW, Masons and Scottish Rite. Enjoys reading, fishing and hiking.
Mailing address: P.O. Box 525, LaFayette 30728.
Telephone: (706) 638-6394.
Fax: (706) 638-0641

HINES, Preston Harris *(Justice, Supreme Court of Georgia)* Appointed by Governor Zell Miller to term beginning July 26, 1995. Elected to subsequent term. Born Atlanta Georgia Sept 6, 1943. Educated at Emory University A.B. in Political Science 1965 J.D. 1968. Member Phi Delta Phi and Sigma Alpha Epsilon. Research Assistant Atlanta Bar Association Police-Community Relations Committee 1967. Admitted to practice Georgia 1968 and U.S. District Court Northern District of Georgia 1973. Law Clerk to Senior Judge, Civil Court of Fulton County 1968-69. In legal practice Marietta 1969-74. Judge, State Court of Cobb County May 8, 1974 to Dec 31, 1982. Judge, Superior Court of Georgia Cobb Judicial Circuit Jan 1, 1983 to July 25, 1995.

Co-author *You and the Law* a booklet published by the Atlanta Bar Association Police-Community Relations Committee 1967. Former Chairman Plan Development Subcommittee. Former member Records Retention and Destruction Judicial Planning Committee, State Crime Commission and Georgia Judicial Council. Member State Bar of Georgia (Chairman Law Day Committee 1975, member Executive Committee of Younger Lawyers Section 1974-76), Cobb Judicial Circuit (Secretary 1972-73, Chairman Law Day Committee 1972) and American Bar Associations. Selected one of Five Outstanding Young Men of the Year by Georgia Jaycees 1975 and Boss of the Year by Cobb County Legal Secretaries Association 1975-76 and 1983-84. Chairman Attorney's Division Cobb County United Appeal 1972. Participant Leadership Georgia 1975 and Leadership Atlanta 1978-79. President Cobb County YMCA 1976. Co-treasurer Cobb Landmarks Society, Inc. 1976-77. Former member Board of Directors Cobb County Emergency Aid Association, Inc., Cobb-Marietta Girls Club, Inc., Georgia Chapter Leukemia Society of America, Cobb County Children's Center, Metro Atlanta Red Cross and First Presbyterian Day Kindergarten. Former Member Kiwanis Club of Marietta (Former Member Board of Directors, Chairman Key Club Committee, Former Chairman Spiritual Aims Committee and Past President). Board of Directors Kennesaw College Foundation, Inc. Member First Presbyterian Church of Marietta (Clerk of Session and Elder, Chairman Board of Deacons 1982) and Atlanta Sigma Alpha Epsilon Alumni Association.
Office: 533 State Judicial Building, Atlanta 30334.
Telephone: (404) 656-3473.
Fax: (404) 651-8566
E-mail address: bricej@supreme.courts.state.ga.us

HINESLEY, Harold A. *(Judge, Juvenile Court of Georgia Toombs Judicial Circuit)* Appointed.
Mailing address: P.O. Box 342, Warrenton 30828.
Office: 202 Court Square, Warrenton 30828.
Telephone: (706) 465-3238.
E-mail address: hhinesley@cpapronet.com

HODGE, Richard L. *(Magistrate Judge, United States District Court Middle District of Georgia)* Appointed by U.S. District Court judges.
Mailing address: P.O. Box 87, Albany 31702-0087.
Telephone: (229) 430-8577.

HODGES, Charles G. *(Associate Judge, Juvenile Court of Georgia Atlanta Judicial Circuit)* Appointed. Currently serves as Chief Associate Judge.
Office: Justice Center, 395 Pryor Street S.W., Fourth Floor, Atlanta 30312.
Telephone: (404) 224-4712.
Fax: (404) 730-1121

HODGES, Thomas L. *(Judge, Superior Court of Georgia Northern Judicial Circuit)* Appointed by Governor Roy Barnes to term beginning Oct 21, 1999. Elected 2000, current term expires Jan 1, 2005. Born Atlanta Georgia April 20, 1948. Methodist. Educated at Emory University B.A. 1969 and University of Georgia J.D. cum laude 1972. Staff member Georgia Law Review 1971-72. Admitted to practice Georgia 1972 and U.S. District Courts Middle and Southern Districts. In legal practice Augusta 1972-77 and Elberton 1978-99. Judge, Municipal Court of Comer 1991-99. Part-time Judge, State Court of Elbert County 1993-99. Former Court Administrator, Georgia Tenth Judicial District.

Solicitor State Court of Elbert County 1981-92. Special Assistant Attorney General DFCS 1989-92. Author "Estate Planning: The Use of Insurance to Fund Stock Purchase Agreements" 9 Georgia State B. Jour. 303, 1973. Member Elberton (President 1990-91) and Northern Circuit (President 1980-81) Bar Associations. District Chairman Broad River District Boy Scouts of America 1982-87. Former Member Elberton Optimist Club (President 1982-83). Former Little League baseball coach. Member Elbert County Chamber of Commerce (Former Director, Treasurer and Awards Chairman), Kiwanis Club of Elberton (President 1988-89 and 1998-99), First United Methodist Church (Former Lay Leader, Former Member Board of Stewards, Choir President, Liturgist) and United Methodist Men. Part-time Sunday school teacher.
Mailing address: P.O. Box 950, Hartwell 30643.
Telephone: (706) 376-7151.
Fax: (706) 856-2329

HOLDER, Annie Doris *(Judge, Probate Court of Calhoun County and Chief Magistrate, Magistrate Court of Calhoun County)*
Mailing address: P.O. Box 87, Morgan 31766-0087.
Telephone: (229) 849-2115.
Fax: (229) 849-2117
E-mail address: projudgeholder@alltel.net

HOLLAND, John *(Judge, State Court of Turner County)* Serves part time.
Mailing address: P.O. Box 824 Ashburn 31714-0824.
Office: 320 North Street, Ashburn 31714.
Telephone: (229) 567-2824.

HOLLEY, Tonya *(Judge, Probate Court of Early County and Chief Magistrate, Magistrate Court of Early County)*
Office: 8 Early County Courthouse, 30 Courthouse Square, Blakely 31723-1832.
Telephone: (229) 723-3454.
Fax: (229) 723-5246
E-mail address: tonyaholley@alltel.net

HOLT, Connie J. *(Chief Magistrate, Magistrate Court of Morgan County)*
Mailing address: P.O. Box 589, Madison 30650.
Telephone: (706) 342-3088.
Fax: (706) 343-6364
E-mail address: cholt@morganga.org

HOLT, Elmo *(Senior Judge, Superior Court of Georgia)* Assumed Senior status, serves when called.
Office: 214 North Fulton Annex, 7741 Roswell Road, Atlanta 30350.
Telephone: (770) 649-7368.

HORKAN, Frank D. *(Judge, Superior Court of Georgia Southern Judicial Circuit)* Former Judge, State Court of Colquitt County.
Mailing address: P.O. Box 2227, Moultrie 31776-2227.
Telephone: (229) 616-7445.
Fax: (229) 616-7447

HORKAN, George Arthur, Jr. *(Senior Judge, Superior Court of Georgia)* Assumed office Aug 16, 1972. Elected to subsequent terms. Former Chief Judge Southern Judicial Circuit. Assumed Senior status, serves when called. Born Moultrie Georgia March 9, 1926. Educated at Mercer University A.B. 1950 and University of Georgia J.D. 1952. Editor Georgia Bar Journal 1952. Admitted to practice Georgia 1952. In legal practice Moultrie 1952-69. Judge, Moultrie Municipal Court 1957-69.
District Attorney Southern Judicial Circuit Moultrie 1969-72. Author "Pre-Trial Motions in Criminal Cases in Georgia" 1975. Member Georgia Criminal Justice Council 1975-76, Judicial Qualifications Commission of Georgia and Georgia Council of Superior Court Judges. Adult Advisor Moultrie Youth Center.
Mailing address: P.O. Box 682, Moultrie 31776-0682.
Telephone: (229) 616-7445.
Fax: (229) 616-7447

HORNE, Clarence R., Jr. *(Chief Magistrate, Magistrate Court of Rockdale County)* Magistrate 1987-93. Elected Chief Magistrate to term beginning Jan 1, 1993. Reelected 1996 and 2000. Current term expires Dec 31, 2004. Born Atlanta Georgia Nov 21, 1943. Presbyterian. Educated at Emory University A.B. 1965 and Woodrow Wilson College of Law J.D. magna cum laude 1976. In legal practice Conyers 1978-2001.
Mailing address: P.O. Box 289, Conyers 30012-0289.
Telephone: (770) 929-4014.
Fax: (770) 785-2496

HOWARD, Brenda *(Judge, Probate Court of Pierce County)*
Mailing address: P.O. Box 406, Blackshear 31516-0406.
Telephone: (912) 449-2029.
Fax: (912) 449-2006

HOWARD, Patrice *(Judge, Probate Court of Putnam County)* Elected to term beginning Jan 1, 1997. Reelected 2000, current term expires Dec 31, 2004.
Office: 100 South Jefferson Avenue, Eatonton 31024.
Telephone: (706) 485-5476, 485-9761.
Fax: (706) 485-2515
E-mail address: putnamprobate@surfsouth.com

HOWE, Donald B. *(Judge, Superior Court of Georgia Douglas Judicial Circuit)* Appointed by Governor Zell Miller to term beginning July 8, 1998. Elected 2000, current term expires Dec 31, 2004. Born Bremen Georgia July 14, 1938. Roman Catholic. Educated at Emory University 1956-58 and University of Georgia A.B. 1960 LL.B. 1962. Chief Justice Honor Court 1961-62. Member Blue Key. Admitted to practice Georgia 1961, U.S. District Courts Northern 1962 and Middle 1978 Districts of Georgia, U.S. Courts of Appeals Fifth 1972 and Eleventh 1981 Circuits and U.S. Supreme Court 1973. In legal practice Tallapoosa 1966-90 and Douglasville 1990-98.
Assistant U.S. Attorney Tallapoosa Judicial Circuit 1966-71. Member Georgia Trial Lawyers Association, The Association of Trial Lawyers of America, American Judicature Society, State Bar of Georgia, Federal and American Bar Associations. Captain U.S. Army JAGC 1963-66. Enjoys golfing, gardening and fishing. Personal Statement or Quote: "Be prompt, professional and pleasant."
Office: 8700 Hospital Drive, Douglasville 30134.
Telephone: (770) 920-7417.

HOWELL, Baxter C. *(Chief Magistrate, Magistrate Court of Dougherty County)*
Mailing address: P.O. Box 1827, Albany 31702-1827.
Telephone: (229) 431-2149.
Fax: (229) 434-2692
E-mail address: bax51@aol.com

HOWELL, Shepherd Lee *(Chief Judge, Superior Court of Georgia Cherokee Judicial Circuit)* Appointed by Governor Joe Frank Harris to term beginning Jan 17, 1990. Elected 1990, 1994, 1998 and 2002. Current term expires Dec 31, 2006. Born Cartersville Georgia Jan 12, 1954. Methodist. Educated at West Georgia College B.S. cum laude 1977 and Cumberland School of Law of Samford University J.D. 1980. Admitted to practice Georgia 1980, U.S. District Court District of Georgia 1980 and U.S. Court of Appeals Fifth Circuit 1980. In legal practice Cartersville 1980-90.
Member State Bar of Georgia and Cartersville Bar Association (Treasurer 1989-90). Enjoys outdoor recreation.
Office: 135 West Cherokee Avenue, Suite 322, Cartersville 30120.
Telephone: (770) 387-5124.
Fax: (770) 606-2397

HUFF, Margaret E. *(Judge, Probate Court of Gilmer County)*
Office: Gilmer County Courthouse, One West Side Square, Ellijay 30540-1098.
Telephone: (706) 635-4763.
Fax: (706) 635-4761

HUGHES, T. Christopher *(Judge, Juvenile Court of Georgia Cordele Judicial Circuit)* Appointed to term beginning Oct 1, 1999. Reappointed 2000, current term expires Sept 30, 2004. Born Fitzgerald Georgia Nov 11, 1959. Baptist. Educated at University of Georgia A.B. 1981 J.D. 1984. Admitted to practice Georgia 1984. In legal practice Fitzgerald 1984-2000. Judge, Fitzgerald Municipal Court Sept 1, 1995 to Sept 30, 2000.
Mailing address: P.O. Box 5149, Fitzgerald 31750.
Office: 413 South Grant Street, Fitzgerald 31750.
Telephone: (229) 426-5638.
Fax: (229) 426-5639
E-mail address: judgechughes@mchsi.com

HUGUENIN, David L. *(Chief Magistrate, Magistrate Court of Columbia County)*
Mailing address: P.O. Box 777, Evans 30809-0777.
Telephone: (706) 868-3316.
Fax: (706) 868-3314

HULSEY, Eddie *(Judge, Probate Court of Haralson County)*
Mailing address: P.O. Box 620, Buchanan 30113-0620.
Telephone: (770) 646-2008.
Fax: (770) 646-3419

HUNNICUTT, Deborah W. *(Judge, Probate Court of Peach County)* Former Magistrate, Magistrate Court of Peach County.
Mailing address: P.O. Box 327, Fort Valley 31030-0327.
Telephone: (478) 825-2313.
Fax: (478) 825-2678

HUNSTEIN, Carol W. *(Justice, Supreme Court of Georgia)* Term expires 2006. Born Miami Florida Aug 16, 1944. Religious affiliation: Church of God. Educated at Miami-Dade Junior College A.A. 1970, Florida Atlantic University B.S. 1972 and Stetson University J.D. 1976. Recipient Clint Green Award in Trial Practice 1976. Member Sigma Delta Kappa. Admitted to practice Georgia 1976, U.S. District Court 1978, U.S. Court of Appeals 1978 and U.S. Supreme Court 1989. In legal practice Atlanta 1976-84. Judge, Superior Court of Georgia Stone Mountain Judicial Circuit 1984-92.
Chair Georgia Commission on Gender Bias in the Judicial System since 1989. President Elect Council of Superior Court Judges of Georgia since 1990. Member Atlanta Lawyers Club, DeKalb Lawyers Association, Georgia Association of Women Lawyers, National Association of Women Judges (Director 1988-90), State Bar of Georgia, Decatur-DeKalb and American (Judicial Administration Division) Bar Associations. Instructor numerous CLE seminars sponsored by State Bar of Georgia, Georgia Association of Criminal Defense Lawyers, Georgia Trial Lawyers Association and Decatur-DeKalb Bar Association. Attended or instructed various CLE and Continuing Judicial Education programs University of Georgia and Georgia State University. Judge National Institute for Trial Advocacy Emory University. Recipient Clint Green Award for Trial Advocacy 1976 and Women Who Have Made a Difference Award from DeKalb Women's Network 1986. Member Advisory Board Neighborhood Justice Center, Commercial Real Estate Women's Association, Advisory Board Atlanta Women's Network and Abigails. Enjoys gardening.
Office: 523 State Judicial Building, Atlanta 30334.
Telephone: (404) 656-3475.
Fax: (404) 657-9586

HUNT, Willis B., Jr. *(Judge, United States District Court Northern District of Georgia)* Appointed for life by President Bill Clinton to term beginning 1995. Born Malden Massachusetts Dec 10, 1932. Educated at Emory University LL.B. 1954 and University of Virginia School of Law LL.M. 1990. In legal practice Clearwater Florida 1959-60, Atlanta Georgia 1960-67 and Perry and Warner Robbins Georgia 1967-71. Judge, Superior Court of Georgia Houston Judicial Circuit 1971-86. Justice and Chief Justice, Supreme Court of Georgia 1986-95.
Office: 1788 U.S. Courthouse, 75 Spring Street S.W., Atlanta 30303-3361.
Telephone: (404) 215-1450.

HUNTER, Linda Warren *(Judge, Superior Court of Georgia Stone Mountain Judicial Circuit)* Former Judge, State Court of DeKalb County.
Office: 505 DeKalb County Courthouse, 556 North McDonough Street, Decatur 30030.
Telephone: (404) 371-2525.
Fax: (404) 371-4754

IANNAZZONE, Joseph *(Judge, State Court of Gwinnett County)*
Office: Gwinnett Justice Center, 75 Langley Drive, Lawrenceville 30045-6935.
Telephone: (770) 822-8550.
Fax: (770) 822-8645
E-mail address: iannazjo@co.gwinnett.ga.us

INGRAM, Edith J. *(Judge, Probate Court of Hancock County)* Elected to term beginning Jan 1, 1969. Reelected 1972, 1976, 1980, 1984, 1988, 1992, 1996 and 2000. Current term expires Jan 1, 2005. Born Hancock County Georgia Jan 16, 1942. Baptist. Educated at Fort Valley State College B.S. Member Delta Sigma Theta.
Office: 601 Courthouse Square, Sparta 31087-0481.
Telephone: (706) 444-5343.
Fax: (706) 444-8024

INGRAM, G. Conley *(Senior Judge, Supreme Court of Georgia)* Justice 1973-77. Assumed Senior status, serves when called. Currently serves Superior Court of Georgia. In legal practice Atlanta 1977-98. Former Judge, Juvenile Court of Cobb County. Former Judge, Superior Court of Georgia Cobb Judicial Circuit.
Office: 30 Waddell Street, Marietta 30090.
Telephone: (770) 528-1880.
Fax: (770) 528-8103

INGRAM, S. Lark *(Judge, Superior Court of Georgia Cobb Judicial Circuit)* Appointed by Governor Zell Miller to term beginning Nov 21, 1995. Elected 1996 and 2000. Current term expires Dec 31, 2004. Former Judge, State Court of Cobb County.
Office: 30 Waddell Street, Marietta 30090.
Telephone: (770) 528-1831.
Fax: (770) 528-1834

INGRAM, Shirley R. *(Chief Magistrate, Magistrate Court of Hancock County)* Elected to term beginning Jan 1, 1999. Reelected 2002, current term expires Dec 31, 2006.
Office: 603 Courthouse Square, Sparta 31087.
Telephone: (706) 444-6234.
Fax: (706) 444-6178

IRWIN, David B. *(Judge, Superior Court of Georgia Rockdale Judicial Circuit)* Elected to term beginning Jan 1, 1999. Reelected 2002, current term expires Dec 31, 2006.
Office: 922 Court Street N.E., Room 200A, Conyers 30012-4540.
Telephone: (770) 929-4082.
Fax: (770) 929-4084

ISON, William H. *(Senior Judge, Superior Court of Georgia)* Appointed by Governor George Busbee May

ISON, WILLIAM H.—*Continued*

24, 1977 to term beginning July 1, 1977. Elected 1978, 1982, 1986, 1990, 1994 and 1998. Former Chief Judge Clayton Judicial Circuit. Assumed Senior status, serves when called. Born Spalding County Georgia Jan 24, 1935. Protestant. Educated at John Marshall Law School LL.B. 1968. Admitted to practice Georgia 1968. Began legal practice Jonesboro 1968.

Assistant District Attorney 1969-72 and District Attorney 1973-77 Clayton Judicial Circuit. Member State Bar of Georgia (Chairman Criminal Law Section 1977-78), Clayton County (Treasurer 1974-75, Secretary 1975-76, President 1976-77) and American Bar Associations. E-5 USN 1954-59. Democrat. Member Masons, Scottish Rite, Shriners and Kiwanis. Enjoys hunting and fishing.

Office: Banke Justice Center, 9151 Tara Boulevard, Jonesboro 30236.
Telephone: (770) 477-3432.
Fax: (770) 473-5993

JACKSON, Gary E. *(Judge, City Court of Atlanta)* Appointed by Mayor Bill Campbell to term beginning Dec 11, 2000. Retained by election 2001, current term expires 2005. Born 1952. Educated at Wharton School University of Pennsylvania B.S. 1972 and University of Georgia School of Law J.D. cum laude 1975. Senior Editor University of Georgia Law Review. Admitted to practice Georgia 1975 and New York 1985. In legal practice Atlanta Georgia 1976-2000. Magistrate, Magistrate Court of Fulton County 1986-2000. Judge pro hac vice, Municipal Court of Atlanta 1995-2000.

Member State Bar of Georgia, Atlanta, Gate City and Stonewall Bar Associations. Member Golf Collectors Society.

Office: 104 Trinity Street S.W., Atlanta 30303.
Telephone: (404) 658-6919.

JACKSON, J. Russell *(Judge, Juvenile Court of Georgia Bell-Forsyth Judicial Circuit)* Former Associate Judge. Appointed Judge to term beginning July 12, 2001. Term expires July 12, 2005. Former Associate Judge, Juvenile Court of Cherokee County.

Office: 112 West Maple Street, Suite 5, Cumming 30040.
Telephone: (770) 781-3099.
Fax: (770) 781-3089
E-mail address: jrjackson@co.forsyth.ga.us

JACKSON, K. Dawson *(Chief Judge, Superior Court of Georgia Gwinnett Judicial Circuit)* Chief Judge since Jan 1, 1999.

Office: Gwinnett Justice Center, 75 Langley Drive, Lawrenceville 30045.
Telephone: (770) 822-8619.
Fax: (770) 822-8642
E-mail address: jacksonda@co.gwinnett.ga.us

JACKSON, Kenneth G. *(Chief Magistrate, Magistrate Court of Jasper County)*

Office: 126 West Greene Street, Suite 301, Monticello 31064.
Telephone: (706) 468-4909.
Fax: (706) 468-4928
E-mail address: jaspermagistrate@hotmail.com

JACKSON, Lenwood A. *(Judge, City Court of Atlanta)*

Office: 260 Central Avenue, Atlanta 30303.
Telephone: (404) 658-7048.
Fax: (404) 658-6508
E-mail address: lajackson@ci.atlanta.ga.us

JACKSON, Linda E. *(Judge, Probate Court of Randolph County)*

Mailing address: P.O. Box 424, Cuthbert 39840-0424.
Telephone: (229) 732-2671.
Fax: (229) 732-5781

JACKSON, Stephen L. *(Judge, Superior Court of Georgia Waycross Judicial Circuit)* Elected to term beginning Jan 1, 1997. Reelected 2000, current term expires Dec 31, 2004.

Office: Pierce County Courthouse, Blackshear 31516.
Telephone: (912) 449-2220.
Fax: (912) 449-2222

JAMES, Hilda *(Chief Magistrate, Magistrate Court of Atkinson County)*

Mailing address: P.O. Box 674, Pearson 31642-0674.
Telephone: (912) 422-7158.
Fax: (912) 422-7989
E-mail address: magjudge@planttel.net

JAMES, Robert J. *(Chief Judge, Superior Court of Georgia Douglas Judicial Circuit)* Former Administrative Judge Seventh District.

Mailing address: P.O. Box 794, Douglasville 30133.
Telephone: (770) 920-7265.
Fax: (770) 920-7376

JENKINS, Dale *(Judge, State Court of McIntosh County)* Appointed by Governor Zell Miller to term beginning Oct 11, 1993. Elected 1994, 1998 and 2002. Current term expires Dec 31, 2006. Serves part time.

Mailing address: P.O. Box 1168, Darien 31305-1168.
Telephone: (912) 437-3440.
Fax: (912) 437-2315
E-mail address: dalelaw@darientel.net

JENKINS, Michael Grady *(Chief Magistrate, Magistrate Court of Screven County)* Elected Aug 1992 to term beginning Jan 1, 1993. Reelected 1996 and 2000. Current term expires Dec 31, 2004. Born Millen Georgia March 25, 1961. Presbyterian. Educated at Georgia Southern College B.S. 1984.

Member Chief Magistrate Association. Attends required continuing education courses. Member Rotary Club. Enjoys hunting and fishing.

Mailing address: P.O. Box 64, Sylvania 30467.
Telephone: (912) 564-7375.
Fax: (912) 564-5618

JENNINGS, William D., III *(Judge, Civil Court of Richmond County and Chief Magistrate, Magistrate Court of Richmond County)* Appointed by Governor Joe Frank Harris 1987. Elected 1988, 1992, 1996 and 2000. Current term expires Dec 31, 2004. Serves as Chief Judge for Civil Court. Born Atlanta Georgia 1951. Episcopalian. Educated at University of Georgia A.B.J. 1973 and Cumberland School of Law of Samford University J.D. 1977. Admitted to practice Georgia 1978.

Office: 317 Municipal Building, Augusta 30911.
Telephone: (706) 821-2516.
Fax: (706) 821-2381

JENRETTE, Isaac *(Senior Judge, Superior Court of Georgia)* Former Chief Judge Atlanta Judicial Circuit. Assumed Senior status, serves when called.
Office: T8905 Justice Center Tower, 185 Central Avenue S.W., Atlanta 30303.
Telephone: (404) 730-4335.
Fax: (404) 335-2863

JERNIGAN, E. Wayne *(Judge, Juvenile Court of Georgia Chattahoochee Judicial Circuit)* Appointed.
Mailing address: P.O. Box 1340, Columbus 31902-1340.
Office: Consolidated Government Center, Columbus 31902.
Telephone: (706) 653-4289.
Fax: (706) 653-4288

JOHNSON, Alton P. *(Chief Magistrate, Magistrate Court of Carroll County)*
Mailing address: P.O. Box 338, Carrollton 30117-0338.
Telephone: (770) 830-5874.

JOHNSON, Edward Hodgson *(Judge, Court of Appeals of Georgia)* Appointed by Governor Zell Miller to term beginning Feb 28, 1992. Elected Nov 3, 1992 and 1998. Current term expires Dec 31, 2004. Former Chief Judge. Currently serves as Presiding Judge. Born Newnan Georgia Sept 9, 1948. Educated at Georgia State University A.B. in History 1971 M.A. 1989, Vanderbilt University School of Law J.D. 1973 and University of Virginia School of Law LL.M. 1995. Member Phi Alpha Theta and Kappa Sigma. Began legal practice Atlanta. Judge, State Court of Fulton County Dec 15, 1980 to Dec 31, 1988. Judge, Superior Court of Georgia Atlanta Judicial Circuit Jan 1, 1989 to Feb 27, 1992.
Author "Contempt of Court in Georgia" Georgia State B. Jour. 1986 and "Strangers in a Strange Land: The Soviet Legal System" The Atlanta Lawyer Atlanta Bar Association Spring 1987. Adjunct Professor of Law in Pre-trial Civil Litigation 1982-93 and Civil Damages 1985-93 Emory University School of Law. Member Georgia State Crime Commission 1977-78 (Chairman Task Force on Criminal Justice Information Systems), Georgia Educational Improvement Council 1978-80 and White House Conference on Regulatory Reform Washington D.C. Jan 1980. Member American Judicature Society, Atlanta Lawyers Club, State Bar of Georgia, Gate City, North Fulton, Atlanta (Bench and Bar Planning Committee) and American (Committees on Judicial Education and Court and Community Judicial Administration Division) Bar Associations. Participant General Jurisdiction Trial Judges Course The National Judicial College 1981. Instructor Tutorial Program to assist minority law students preparing for Bar exam Gate City Bar Association 1981-84, Atlanta Bar Association National Institute for Trial Advocacy Program for Trial Lawyers 1981-84, Misdemeanor Practice Seminar 1982 and Orientation Seminar for New Judges 1982-84 ICLE Athens. Faculty member National Institute for Trial Advocacy Program Boulder Colorado 1984. Recipient WSB 750 Award for drafting and sponsoring Georgia's Shoplifting Statute and sponsoring Georgia Consumers' Utility Council Law. Recipient Outstanding Service in the Field of Crime Prevention Award from Georgia State Crime Commission 1977-78, Outstanding Service for Georgia and Its Retail Industry Award from Georgia Retail Association, Friend of the Children Award for work in area of juvenile justice from United Way Council for Children 1978 and Award for Legislative Work in the Field of Public Education from Atlanta Association of Educators 1979. Named one of Outstanding Young Men in America 1979 and 1982. Legal Counsel to Georgia Senate Judiciary Committee 1975 and Georgia Lieutenant Governor 1976. Georgia State Senator 34th District (Civil Law Subcommittee, Judiciary Committee, Primary and Secondary Education Subcommittee, Education Committee, Rules Committee, Special Judiciary Committee, Appropriations Committee and Vice Chairman Fulton County Senate Delegation) 1977-80. Advisory Board Fulton County Adjustment Center since 1981. Chair Georgia Law-Related Education Consortium of Vinson Institute of Government University of Georgia 1995-98. Board of Directors Christian City, Inc. (Co-chairman Administrative Committee).
Office: 334 State Judicial Building, Atlanta 30334.
Telephone: (404) 656-3452.
Fax: (404) 657-4210

JOHNSON, Emmett P., Jr. *(Judge, State Court of Appling County)* Serves part time.
Mailing address: P.O. Box 304, Baxley 31515-0304.
Office: 442 North Boulevard, Baxley 31513.
Telephone: (912) 367-2476.

JOHNSON, Foye L. *(Judge, Probate Court of Walker County)*
Mailing address: P.O. Box 436, LaFayette 30728-0436.
Telephone: (706) 638-2852.
Fax: (706) 638-2869

JOHNSON, Horace J., Jr. *(Judge, Superior Court of Georgia Alcovy Judicial Circuit)*
Office: Courthouse Annex 6, 116 South Broad Street, Monroe 30655.
Telephone: (770) 267-1491.
Fax: (770) 267-1365

JOHNSON, Howard R. *(Judge, Municipal Court of Atlanta)* Appointed by mayor.
Office: 170 Garnett Street S.W., Atlanta 30303.
Telephone: (404) 865-8100.
Fax: (404) 658-6859

JOHNSON, J. Alexander *(Judge, Juvenile Court of Georgia Brunswick Judicial Circuit)* Appointed to term beginning Dec 1, 1993. Elected 1998 and 2002. Current term expires 2006.
Office: 132 West Parker Street, Baxley 31513-0658.
Telephone: (912) 366-9000.
Fax: (912) 367-5883
E-mail address: jajohnson@jajlaw.com

JOHNSON, Joe S., Jr. *(Judge, Probate Court of Talbot County and Chief Magistrate, Magistrate Court of Talbot County)*
Mailing address: P.O. Box 157, Talbotton 31827-0157.
Telephone: (706) 665-8866.
Fax: (706) 665-8240

JOHNSON, Walter E. *(Magistrate Judge, United States District Court Northern District of Georgia)* Appointed by U.S. District Court judges to term beginning March 18, 2002.
Office: 600 East First Street, Room 322, Rome 30161.
Telephone: (706) 378-4090.

JOHNSTON, Robert Glenn, III *(Judge, Superior Court of Georgia Chattahoochee Judicial Circuit)* Appointed by Governor Zell Miller to term beginning Oct 23, 1995. Elected 1996 and 2000. Current term expires Dec 31, 2004. Born Columbus Georgia Sept 3, 1948. Presbyterian. Educated at Presbyterian College B.A. 1970 and Emory University J.D. 1973. Admitted to practice Georgia 1973. Began legal practice Columbus 1973. Judge, State Court of Muscogee County Feb 1, 1983 to Oct 22, 1995.

Solicitor State Court of Muscogee County June 1977 to Feb 1983. Member State Judges and Solicitors Association and State Bar of Georgia. Captain USAR (infantry) 1967-74. Member Rotary Club. Enjoys golf.

Mailing address: P.O. Box 1340, Columbus 31902-1340.

Telephone: (706) 653-4281.

Fax: (706) 653-4279

JOHNSTON, Vicki W. *(Judge, Probate Court of Butts County)*

Office: 25 Third Street, Suite 7, Jackson 30233-1965.

Telephone: (770) 775-8204.

Fax: (770) 775-8004

JOLLES, Isaac *(Judge, Probate Court of Richmond County)* Elected to term beginning Nov 4, 1998. Reelected 2000, current term expires Dec 31, 2004.

Office: 530 Greene Street, Room 401, Augusta 30911.

Telephone: (706) 821-2431.

Fax: (706) 821-2442

JOLLIFF, Cliff L. *(Judge, Juvenile Court of Georgia Northeastern Judicial Circuit)* Appointed.

Mailing address: P.O. Box 311, Gainesville 30503-0311.

Telephone: (770) 531-6927.

Fax: (770) 531-6940

E-mail address: CJolliff@hallcounty.org

JONES, Doug *(Chief Magistrate, Magistrate Court of Tift County)*

Mailing address: P.O. Box 214, Tifton 31793-0214.

Telephone: (229) 386-7907.

Fax: (229) 386-7978

E-mail address: djones@tiftcounty.org

JONES, Jeffrey W. *(Judge, Probate Court of Pulaski County)* Elected to term beginning Jan 1, 1993. Reelected 1996 and 2000. Current term expires Dec 31, 2004. Born Americus Georgia Oct 1, 1964. Baptist. Educated at Georgia Southern University B.B.A. 1987.

Office: Pulaski County Courthouse, Hawkinsville 31036.

Telephone: (478) 783-2061.

Fax: (478) 783-9219

JONES, Joyce B. *(Judge, Probate Court of Polk County)* Appointed to term beginning July 1, 1991. Elected 1992, 1996 and 2000. Current term expires Dec 31, 2004.

Office: 102 Polk County Courthouse, Cedartown 30125.

Telephone: (770) 749-2128.

Fax: (770) 749-2150

JONES, Lisa C. *(Judge, Juvenile Courts of Georgia Southwestern Judicial Circuit)* Appointed.

Mailing address: P.O. Drawer 607, Americus 31709.

Telephone: (229) 928-4569.

Fax: (229) 928-4572

E-mail address: juvjudge@sowega.net

JONES, Robert S. *(Associate Judge, Juvenile Court of Georgia Gwinnett Judicial Circuit and Judge, Recorder's Court of Gwinnett County)* Appointed Associate Judge. Currently serves as Chief Judge Recorder's Court.

Office: Gwinnett Justice Center, 75 Langley Drive, Lawrenceville 30045-6900.

Telephone: (770) 822-8289.

Fax: (770) 822-8394

E-mail address: jonesrob@co.gwinnett.ga.us

JONES, Sanford J. *(Judge, Juvenile Court of Georgia Atlanta Judicial Circuit)* Appointed. Former Chief Presiding Judge.

Office: 395 Pryor Street S.W., Chambers 4606, Atlanta 30303.

Telephone: (404) 224-4821.

Fax: (404) 335-2936

E-mail address: judgesjones@aol.com

JONES, Steve C. *(Judge, Superior Court of Georgia Western Judicial Circuit)* Appointed by Governor Zell Miller to term beginning Dec 1, 1995. Elected 1996 and 2000. Current term expires Dec 31, 2004.

Mailing address: P.O. Box 1623, Athens 30603-1623.

Telephone: (706) 613-3780.

Fax: (706) 613-3782

E-mail address: affirm@mindspring.com

JORDAN, Frank J., Jr. *(Judge, Superior Court of Georgia Chattahoochee Judicial Circuit)*

Mailing address: P.O. Box 1340, Columbus 31902-1340.

Telephone: (706) 653-4667.

Fax: (706) 653-4316

JORDAN, William Alan *(Judge, State Court of Cherokee County)*

Office: 90 North Street, Suite 130, Canton 30114.

Telephone: (770) 345-3364.

Fax: (770) 345-3366

E-mail address: wajlawyer1@yahoo.com

JOYNER, Michael E. *(Judge, Recorder's Court of Columbus-Muscogee County)*

Mailing address: P.O. Box 681, Columbus 31902-0681.

Office: 924 Second Avenue, Columbus 31902.

Telephone: (706) 324-5253.

Fax: (706) 327-9786

KARPF, Michael L. *(Judge, Superior Court of Georgia Eastern Judicial Circuit)* Appointed by Governor Zell Miller to term beginning Aug 5, 1993. Elected 1994, 1998 and 2002. Current term expires Dec 31, 2006. Currently serves as Administrative Judge District One. Former Judge, Recorder's Court of Chatham County. Former Judge, State Court of Chatham County.

Office: 212 Chatham County Courthouse, 133 Montgomery Street, Savannah 31401.

Telephone: (912) 652-7460.

Fax: (912) 652-7242

E-mail address: mkarpf@wpo.co.chatham.ga.us

KEEBLE, Allen B. *(Judge, Superior Court of Georgia Coweta Judicial Circuit)* Term expires Dec 31, 2004. Former Judge, State Court of Troup County.
Office: 201 Colonial Building, 119 Ridley Avenue, LaGrange 30240.
Telephone: (706) 883-1730.
Fax: (706) 883-1639
E-mail address: judgekeeble@mindspring.com

KELLEY, John *(Judge, Probate Court of Dodge County)*
Mailing address: P.O. Box 514, Eastman 31023-0514.
Telephone: (478) 374-3775.
Fax: (478) 374-9197

KENNON, Warner L. *(Judge, Juvenile Court of Georgia Chattahoochee Judicial Circuit)* Former Associate Judge, appointed to term beginning 1994. Appointed Judge. Also Guardian, Muscogee County since 1989. Born Emory University Georgia Sept 18, 1953. Educated at Oglethorpe University B.B.A. 1976 and John Marshall Law School J.D. 1979. Admitted to practice Georgia 1979 and U.S. District Court Middle District of Georgia 1980. In legal practice Columbus. Guardian Ad Litem, Juvenile Court of Columbus 1989-94.
Member National Panel of Construction Arbitrators American Arbitration Association, National Council of Juvenile and Family Court Judges, State Bar of Georgia (Fiduciary Law Section), Columbus and Chattahoochee (President 1994-95) Bar Associations. President Mental Health Association of Columbus 1990-92. Board of Directors Boys Club of Columbus since 1997. Member Columbus Chamber of Commerce.
Mailing address: P.O. Box 1340, Columbus 31902-1340.
Office: Consolidated Government Center, Columbus 31902.
Telephone: (706) 653-4289.
Fax: (706) 653-4288
E-mail address: wkennon@columbusga.org

KENT, Richard T. *(Judge, State Court of Colquitt County)* Elected to term beginning Jan 1, 1997. Reelected 2000, current term expires Dec 31, 2004. Serves part time.
Mailing address: P.O. Box 1654, Moultrie 31776.
Telephone: (229) 985-1957.
E-mail address: rkent44@yahoo.com

KENYON, A. Richard *(Senior Judge, Superior Court of Georgia)* Appointed 1965. Elected to subsequent terms. Former Chief Judge. Assumed Senior status, serves when called. Born Gainesville Georgia. Educated at Davidson College A.B. 1940 and University of Georgia LL.B. summa cum laude 1946. Member Phi Beta Kappa. Admitted to practice Georgia 1942. Began legal practice Gainesville 1946.
Former Hall County Attorney. Participant 1967 and Faculty Advisor 1971 National College of State Trial Judges. Faculty Advisor Maryland Crime and Corrections Workshop for Judges 1969. Lecturer and Faculty Advisor Seminars for Trial Judges in Texas, Alabama, Arkansas, Kentucky and Georgia. Named Rotary Man of the Year. U.S. Army Infantry WWII. Recipient Silver Star and Bronze Star. Georgia Legislature 1947-48. Member Gainesville Board of Education (Past Chairman) and Georgia Association for Mental Health (Past President). Kiwanian.
Mailing address: 1084 Park Street, Gainesville 30501.

KERNAGHAN, Herbert E. *(Judge, Juvenile Court of Georgia Augusta Judicial Circuit)* Former Associate Judge. Appointed Judge. Currently serves as Chief Judge.
Office: 401 Walton Way, Room A113, Augusta 30901.
Telephone: (706) 821-1185.
E-mail address: ps2205@co.richmond.ga.us

KEY, Michael *(Judge, Juvenile Court of Georgia Coweta Judicial Circuit)* Appointed.
Mailing address: P.O. Box 2210, LaGrange 30241-2210.
Telephone: (706) 884-6601.
Fax: (706) 884-5909
E-mail address: michaelkey@charter.net

KILLIAN, William R. *(Senior Judge, Superior Court of Georgia)* Appointed by Governor George D. Busbee to term beginning Aug 1, 1977. Elected to subsequent terms. Assumed Senior status 1991, serves when called. Born Gadsden Alabama Nov 15, 1920. Presbyterian. Educated at University of Georgia J.D. 1943. Admitted to practice Georgia 1947. In legal practice Brunswick 1947-77. Judge, Brunswick Recorder's Court 1952-53. U.S. Commissioner, U.S. District Court Southern District of Georgia 1958.
Member Georgia Crime Commission 1975-76, State Bar of Georgia, Brunswick (President 1958) and Brunswick Judicial Circuit (Vice President 1976-77) Bar Associations. U.S. Army 1943-46. Attended University of Basel (Switzerland) and University of Nancy (France) in U.S. Army Information and Education Programs 1945-46. Georgia General Assembly 1955-64.
Mailing address: Glynn County Courthouse, Brunswick 31521.
Telephone: (912) 554-7369.
Fax: (912) 261-3849

KILLINGSWORTH, Priscilla *(Chief Magistrate, Magistrate Court of Pike County)*
Mailing address: P.O. Box 466, Zebulon 30295-0466.
Telephone: (770) 567-2004.
Fax: (770) 567-2023

KILPATRICK, Kenneth *(Senior Judge, Superior Court of Georgia)* Appointed by Governor Joe Frank Harris to term beginning Aug 27, 1985. Elected 1986, 1990 and 1994. Served Clayton Judicial Circuit. Assumed Senior status Jan 1, 1999, serves when called. Born Forest Park Georgia Nov 5, 1933. Protestant. Educated at Georgia State University B.B.A. 1954 and University of Georgia LL.B. 1956. Admitted to practice Georgia 1956. Served USN.
Mailing address: 6412 State Highway 60, Suches 30572.

KINCAID, Roger *(Chief Magistrate, Magistrate Court of Gilmer County)* Elected to term beginning Jan 1, 1997. Reelected 2000, current term expires Dec 31, 2004.
Mailing address: One Westside Square, Box 5, Ellijay 30540.
Office: #53 Sand Street, Ellijay 30540.
Telephone: (706) 635-2515.
Fax: (706) 635-7756

KING, Janet F. *(Magistrate Judge, United States District Court Northern District of Georgia)* Appointed

KING, JANET F.—*Continued*

by U.S. District Court judges to term beginning Oct 20, 1998. Term expires 2006.

Office: 1613 U.S. Courthouse, 75 Spring Street S.W., Atlanta 30303-3361.

Telephone: (404) 215-1385.

KINSEY, Mose M. *(Chief Magistrate, Magistrate Court of Colquitt County)* Appointed to term beginning Jan 1, 2001. Term expires Dec 31, 2004. Born Norman Park Georgia July 29, 1953. Southern Baptist. Educated at Fresno Pacific College B.A. with honors 1996 and Albany State University with honors 2002.

Member Council of Magistrate Judges of Georgia. Mentor to two students at local alternative school. Interests include raising cattle. Personal Statement or Quote: "The buck stops here!"

Mailing address: P.O. Box 70, Moultrie 31768.

Telephone: (229) 616-7450.

Fax: (229) 616-7494

KNIGHT, H. Lamar *(Senior Judge, Superior Court of Georgia)* Assumed Senior status, serves when called.

Office: 209 Carroll County Courthouse, Carrollton 30117.

Telephone: (770) 830-5852.

Fax: (770) 830-5996

KNIGHT, W. D. *(Senior Judge, Superior Court of Georgia)* Appointed by Governor George Busbee to term beginning May 24, 1977. Elected to subsequent terms. Former Chief Judge Alapaha Judicial Circuit. Assumed Senior status, serves when called. Born Ray City Georgia March 2, 1934. Member First Baptist Church of Nashville. Educated at Valdosta State College B.S. 1955 and University of Georgia School of Law J.D. 1958. Member Kappa Alpha. Admitted to practice Georgia 1958. Began legal practice Nashville 1958.

Member State Bar of Georgia, Alapaha (Past President) and American Bar Associations. Georgia National Guard. Democrat. City Council Ray City 1959. Georgia House of Representatives 1961-67. Former Secretary Berrien County Industrial Building Authority. Member New Lois Community Club (Past President), Berrien Civic Club (Past President), Circlestone Country Club (Past President) and Berrien County Heart Association (Past President). Former member Berrien County Jaycees. Former Pony League team coach, manager and coach girls softball team and Boy Scout Troop Scout Master.

Mailing address: P.O. Box 846, Nashville 31639-0846.

Telephone: (229) 686-7400.

Fax: (229) 686-7992

KREEGER, George H. *(Judge, Superior Court of Georgia Cobb Judicial Circuit)* Appointed by Governor Joe Frank Harris to term beginning July 1, 1984. Elected 1986, 1990, 1994, 1998 and 2002. Current term expires Dec 31, 2006. Currently serves as Administrative Judge District Seven. Born Atlanta Georgia July 6, 1941. Methodist. Educated at University of Georgia B.S.Ed. 1963 J.D. 1966. Member Sigma Pi and Phi Delta Phi. Admitted to practice Georgia 1966. Began legal practice Marietta 1966. Judge, State Court of Cobb County 1979-84.

Member State Bar of Georgia and Cobb Judicial Circuit Bar Association. Captain USAR 1966-72. Georgia House of Representatives 1969-76.

Office: 30 Waddell Street, Marietta 30090.

Telephone: (770) 528-1837.

Fax: (770) 528-1842

LAND, Clay D. *(Judge, United States District Court Middle District of Georgia)* Appointed for life by President George W. Bush to term beginning Dec 28, 2001. Born March 24, 1960. Educated at University of Georgia B.B.A. magna cum laude 1982 J.D. cum laude 1985. Editorial Board Georgia Law Review 1983-84. Member Order of the Coif. Admitted to practice Georgia 1985. In legal practice Columbus 1985-2001.

Member State Senate Georgia 1995-2000.

Mailing address: P.O. Box 2017, Columbus 31902.

Telephone: (706) 649-7812.

LAND, John H. *(Senior Judge, Superior Court of Georgia)* Elected to term beginning Jan 1, 1965. Reelected 1968, 1972, 1976, 1980 and 1984. Former Chief Judge. Assumed Senior status, serves when called. Born Columbus Georgia June 12, 1918. Baptist. Educated at University of Georgia LL.B. 1939. Admitted to practice Georgia 1939. Began legal practice Columbus 1939.

Solicitor General 1955-64. Member State Bar of Georgia. Major U.S. Army Coast Artillery Anti-aircraft 1941-45. Democrat. Georgia State Senator 1949-50. Member Columbus Exchange Club, Masons, Shriners, American Legion and Veterans of Foreign Wars. Enjoys hunting and fishing.

Mailing address: 6848 Copper Oaks Court, Columbus 31904.

LANE, Bensonetta Tipton *(Judge, Superior Court of Georgia Atlanta Judicial Circuit)* Appointed by Governor Zell Miller to term beginning May 31, 1995. Elected 1996 and 2000. Current term expires Dec 31, 2004. Former Judge, City Court of Atlanta.

Office: T1955 Justice Center Tower, 185 Central Avenue S.W., Atlanta 30303.

Telephone: (404) 302-8535.

Fax: (404) 335-2864

E-mail address: bensonetta.lane@fultoncourt.org

LANE, Ronnie Joe *(Judge, Superior Court of Georgia Pataula Judicial Circuit)* Former part-time Judge, Juvenile Court of Seminole County, appointed to term beginning June 16, 1994.

Mailing address: P.O. Box 636, Donalsonville 31745-0636.

Telephone: (229) 524-2149.

Fax: (229) 524-8817

E-mail address: rjlane@surfsouth.com

LANEY, John T., III *(Judge, United States Bankruptcy Court Middle District of Georgia)* Appointed by U.S. Court of Appeals Eleventh Circuit judges to term beginning Oct 1, 1986. Reappointed Oct 1, 2000, current term expires Sept 30, 2014. Born Columbus Georgia March 27, 1942. Presbyterian. Educated at Mercer University A.B. 1964 LL.B. magna cum laude 1966 replaced by J.D. Co-Editor-in-Chief Mercer Law Review 1965-66. Member Phi Alpha Delta. Admitted to practice Georgia 1965, U.S. Courts of Appeals Fifth 1966 and Eleventh 1981 Circuits and U.S. Court of Military Appeals 1967. In legal practice Columbus 1970-86.

Important Decision: In re Bullington (confirmation of family farmer Chapter 12 case holding Chapter 12 con-

LANEY, JOHN T., III—*Continued*

stitutional) 16 B.C.D. 1206, 80 B.R. 590, CCH Bankr. Dec 72, 138, 17 C.B.C.2d 1438 aff'd D.C. 89 B.R. 1010 Dec 18, 1987, aff'd 878 F.2d 354, 11th Circuit 1989; rehearing denied en banc 889 F.2d 276, 1989. Member National Conference of Bankruptcy Judges, American Judicature Society, Columbus Bar Association, Inc. (President 1985-86), State Bar of Georgia (Chairman General Practice and Trial Section 1983-84; Member 1982-85, Chairman 1984-85 and Vice Chairman Review Panel 1986-87 State Disciplinary Board) and American Bar Association. Captain JAGC U.S. Army 1966-70. Board of Directors Columbus Legal Aid Society, Inc. 1972-77 (President), Georgia Indigent Legal Services, Inc. 1973-77 and Metropolitan Boys Club of Columbus, Inc. 1973-86 (President 1979). Member Rotary Club of East Columbus. Enjoys amateur radio (K4BAI) and tennis.
Mailing address: P.O. Box 1540, Columbus 31902-1540.
Telephone: (706) 649-7840.

LANGFORD, John S., Jr. *(Senior Judge, Superior Court of Georgia)* Elected to term beginning Jan 1, 1973. Former Chief Judge Atlanta Judicial Circuit. Assumed Senior status Jan 1, 1989, serves when called. Born Atlanta Georgia July 4, 1931. Episcopalian. Educated at Auburn University B.S. 1953 and Emory University LL.B. 1958. Admitted to practice Georgia 1957. Began legal practice Atlanta 1957. Judge, Civil Court of Fulton County May 1, 1966 to Jan 1, 1968. Judge, Juvenile Court of Fulton County Jan 1, 1968 to Jan 1, 1973.
Member American Judicature Society, Lawyers Club of Atlanta, State Bar of Georgia, Atlanta and American Bar Associations. Instructor National College of the State Judiciary 1974 and American Academy of Judicial Education 1970-71, 1975-76, 1978-81 and 1984-88. First Lieutenant USAF 1954-55.
Office: C927 Fulton County Courthouse, 136 Pryor Street S.W., Atlanta 30303-3406.
Telephone: (404) 730-4530.

LANGHAM, Don A. *(Senior Judge, Superior Court of Georgia)* Appointed to term beginning 1985. Assumed Senior status Sept 1, 1997, serves when called. Former Judge, State Court of Fulton County.
Office: C-927 Fulton County Courthouse, 136 Pryor Street S.W., Atlanta 30303.
Telephone: (404) 730-4287.
Fax: (404) 657-8808

LANIER, Betty S. *(Chief Magistrate, Magistrate Court of Coffee County)* Elected to term beginning Jan 1, 1997. Reelected 2000, current term expires Dec 31, 2004.
Office: 101 South Peterson Avenue, Douglas 31533.
Telephone: (912) 384-1381.
Fax: (912) 384-0291

LAWRENCE, N. Kent *(Judge, State Court of Clarke County)* Currently serves as Chief Judge.
Office: 300 East Washington Street, Suite 425, Athens 30601.
Telephone: (706) 613-3200.
Fax: (706) 613-3204
E-mail address: kentlawrence@co.clarke.ga.us

LAWSON, Eugene E. *(Judge, Probate Court of Clayton County)*
Office: Clayton County Courthouse, Annex 3, 121 South McDonough Street, Jonesboro 30236.
Telephone: (770) 477-3299.
Fax: (770) 477-3306

LAWSON, Hugh *(Judge, United States District Court Middle District of Georgia)* Appointed for life by President Bill Clinton to term beginning Jan 19, 1996. Born Hawkinsville Georgia Sept 23, 1941. Methodist. Educated at Emory University A.B. 1963 LL.B. 1964. Member Chi Phi and Phi Delta Phi. Admitted to practice Georgia 1965. Began legal practice Hawkinsville 1965. Judge Aug 1, 1979 to Jan 18, 1996 and Former Chief Judge, Superior Court of Georgia Oconee Judicial Circuit.
Mailing address: P.O. Box 838, Macon 31202-0838.
Telephone: (478) 752-3591.

LEE, Laurens C. *(Chief Magistrate, Magistrate Court of Peach County)* Appointed to term beginning April 1995. Elected Nov 1996 and 2000. Current term expires Jan 1, 2005. Also Judge pro tem, Juvenile Courts of Peach and Crawford Counties since 1994. Born Fort Valley Georgia April 11, 1958. Baptist. Educated at Georgia College B.S. 1981 and Mercer University J.D. 1984. Admitted to practice Georgia 1984 and U.S. District Court Middle District of Georgia 1984. In legal practice Perry 1986-88 and Fort Valley since 1988.
Assistant District Attorney Ogeechee Judicial Circuit 1984-85. Public Defender Twiggs County since 1987. Instructor in Real Estate for Paralegals Georgia College 1994-96. Member State Bar of Georgia and Peach-Crawford Bar Association. Attended Annual Chief Magistrate Recertification Institute of Continuing Judicial Education of Georgia and numerous CLE courses. Republican. Interests include politics, sports, antique cars, reading and travel.
Office: 700 Spruce Street, Building A, Fort Valley 31030.
Telephone: (478) 825-2060.
Fax: (478) 825-1893

LEE, William F., Jr. *(Chief Judge, Superior Court of Georgia Coweta Judicial Circuit)* Elected Aug 1980 to term beginning Jan 1, 1981. Reelected 1984, 1988, 1992, 1996 and 2000. Current term expires Dec 31, 2004. Born Newnan Georgia Feb 13, 1943. Baptist. Educated at University of Georgia A.B. 1966 J.D. 1967. Law Clerk to Hon. Lewis R. Morgan, U.S. Court of Appeals Fifth Circuit 1968-69. Member Sigma Alpha Epsilon and Phi Delta Phi. Admitted to practice Georgia 1967, U.S. District Court Northern District of Georgia 1968, U.S. Court of Appeals Fifth Circuit 1968 and U.S. Supreme Court 1970. In legal practice Atlanta 1969-1972 and Newnan 1972-75.
District Attorney 1975-80. Member Council of Superior Court Judges of Georgia, State Bar of Georgia and American Bar Association. Lecturer on Evidence 1984 and Damages 1986 Georgia Trial Lawyers Association. Faculty Advisor The National Judicial College 1990. Member Newnan Rotary Club.
Mailing address: P.O. Box 8, Newnan 30264-0008.
Telephone: (770) 253-8175.
Fax: (770) 253-6274

LEWIS, Alvin N. *(Chief Magistrate, Magistrate Court of Evans County)* Appointed to term beginning

LEWIS, ALVIN N.—*Continued*

April 1, 1986. Reappointed 1988, 1992, 1996 and 2000. Current term expires Dec 31, 2004. Born Chicago Illinois March 14, 1953. Baptist. Educated at Georgia Southern College B.B.A. 1974.

Owner Snap Lewis Insurance Agency, Inc. Enjoys hunting and woodworking.

Office: 7 Courthouse Annex, Claxton 30417-1765.
Telephone: (912) 739-3745.
Fax: (912) 739-8856

LEWIS, Harris *(Judge, Probate Court of Chatham County)*

Mailing address: P.O. Box 8344, Savannah 31412.
Office: 133 Montgomery Street, Room 509, Savannah 31401.
Telephone: (912) 652-7264.
Fax: (912) 652-7262

LEWIS, Preston B., Jr. *(Judge, Juvenile Court of Georgia Augusta Judicial Circuit)* Former Associate Judge. Appointed Judge.

Mailing address: P.O. Box 88, Waynesboro 30830-0088.
Office: 211 East Sixth Street, Waynesboro 30830.
Telephone: (706) 554-3955.
Fax: (706) 554-0350

LEWIS, Preston B., III *(Judge, Probate Court of Burke County)* Elected to term beginning Jan 1, 1997. Reelected 2000, current term expires Dec 31, 2004.

Mailing address: P.O. Box 322, Waynesboro 30830-0322.
Telephone: (706) 554-3000.
Fax: (706) 554-6693

LILLY, Roy M. *(Senior Judge, Superior Court of Georgia)* Appointed by Governor George D. Busbee to term beginning April 15, 1979. Elected 1982, 1986 and 1990. Assumed Senior status 1994, serves when called. Born Brooks County Georgia May 10, 1919. Methodist. Educated at Norman Junior College 1938 and Mercer University LL.B. 1940. Member Phi Delta Theta. Admitted to practice Georgia 1941. Began legal practice Thomasville 1941. Part-time Judge, Juvenile Court of Thomas County 1978-79.

Judicial Fellow American College of Trial Lawyers. Member State Bar of Georgia. Lieutenant USN WWII. Mayor Thomasville 1962-71.

Mailing address: P.O. Box 71, Thomasville 31799-0071.

LITTLE, Jeannette L. *(Judge, State Court of Troup County)* Appointed by Governor Joe Frank Harris 1986. Elected 1988, 1992, 1996 and 2000. Current term expires Dec 31, 2004. Born Troup County Georgia Oct 20, 1954. Baptist. Educated at Furman University, LaGrange College B.A. cum laude 1976 and Mercer University J.D. magna cum laude 1979. Staff member Mercer Law Review 1978-79. Admitted to practice Georgia 1979. Began legal practice LaGrange 1979. Judge, Troup County Small Claims Court 1979-81. Chief Magistrate, Magistrate Court of Troup County 1982-86.

Office: 119 Ridley Avenue, Suite 201, LaGrange 30240.
Telephone: (706) 883-1727.
Fax: (706) 883-1639
E-mail address: judgelittle@mindspring.com

LOCKETTE, Willie E. *(Judge, Superior Court of Georgia Dougherty Judicial Circuit)* Elected to term beginning Jan 1, 1997. Reelected 2000, current term expires Dec 31, 2004. Former Chief Magistrate, Magistrate Court of Dougherty County.

Mailing address: P.O. Box 1827, Albany 31702-1827.
Telephone: (229) 431-2186.
Fax: (229) 431-2174

LOGGINS, Joseph E. *(Senior Judge, Superior Court of Georgia)* Assumed office Nov 1, 1978. Elected to subsequent terms. Former Chief Judge Lookout Mountain Judicial Circuit. Assumed Senior status, serves when called.

Mailing address: P.O. Box 464, Summerville 30747-0464.

LONG, Elizabeth E. *(Chief Judge, Superior Court of Georgia Atlanta Judicial Circuit)* Also Administrative Judge District Five.

Office: T8655 Justice Center Tower, 185 Central Avenue S.W., Atlanta 30303.
Telephone: (404) 730-4570.
Fax: (404) 730-4127

LORD, Rachel T. *(Judge, Probate Court of Washington County)* Elected to term beginning Jan 1, 1989. Reelected 1992, 1996 and 2000. Current term expires Dec 31, 2004. Born Washington County Georgia March 3, 1945. Nazarene. Hobbies include reading, cross-stitching and hiking.

Mailing address: P.O. Box 669, Sandersville 31082-0669.
Telephone: (478) 552-3304.
Fax: (478) 552-7424

LOTT, H. W. *(Senior Judge, Superior Court of Georgia)* Elected to term beginning Jan 1, 1961. Reelected to subsequent terms. Assumed Senior status Jan 1, 1981, serves when called. Born Lenox Georgia Dec 13, 1924. Catholic. Educated at Emory University and Mercer University. Admitted to practice Georgia 1951. Began legal practice Nashville 1951.

Member State Bar of Georgia and American Bar Association. U.S. Army 1943-46. Georgia State Representative 1957-61.

Mailing address: P.O. Box 348, Lenox 31637-0348.

LOWE, William Jeffrey *(Chief Magistrate, Magistrate Court of Lumpkin County)* Elected to term beginning Jan 1, 1997. Reelected 2000, current term expires Dec 31, 2004. Born Lumpkin County April 12, 1958. Baptist.

Personal Statement or Quote: "Giving both sides a fair shake."

Office: 99 Courthouse Hill, Suite F, Dahlonega 30533.
Telephone: (706) 864-7760.
Fax: (706) 867-8643

LUKEMIRE, Edward D. *(Judge, Superior Court of Georgia Houston Judicial Circuit)* Appointed by Governor Zell Miller to term beginning Sept 13, 1996. Elected 1996 and 2000. Current term expires Dec 31, 2004.

Office: Houston County Courthouse, 201 Perry Parkway, Perry 31069.
Telephone: (478) 218-4850.
Fax: (478) 218-4855

LUMPKIN, Julia W. *(Judge, Probate Court of Muscogee County)* Elected to term beginning Nov 4, 1998. Reelected 2000, current term expires Dec 31, 2004.
Mailing address: P.O. Box 1340, Columbus 31902-1340.
Telephone: (706) 653-4333.

MacNABB, Joseph P. *(Judge, Juvenile Court of Georgia Coweta Judicial Circuit)* Appointed.
Mailing address: P.O. Box 220, Newnan 30264-0220.
Telephone: (770) 253-3282.
Fax: (770) 251-7262
E-mail address: joseph@rjm-pc.com

MADDUX, Tracy L. *(Chief Magistrate, Magistrate Court of Chattooga County)* Appointed to term beginning April 10, 1997. Elected 2001, current term expires 2005.
Office: 10017 Commerce Street, Summerville 30747-1356.
Telephone: (706) 857-0711.
Fax: (706) 857-0675

MALICKI, Catherine E. *(Judge, Municipal Court of Atlanta)* Appointed by mayor.
Office: 170 Garnett Street S.W., Atlanta 30303.
Telephone: (404) 865-8100.
Fax: (404) 658-6859

MALLIS, Robert P. *(Judge, Superior Court of Georgia Stone Mountain Judicial Circuit)* Term expires Dec 31, 2004. Former Chief Judge.
Office: 905 DeKalb County Courthouse, 556 North McDonough Street, Decatur 30030.
Telephone: (404) 371-7010.
Fax: (404) 687-3546
E-mail address: RPMALLIS@co.dekalb.ga.us

MANIS, Stephanie B. *(Judge, Superior Court of Georgia Atlanta Judicial Circuit)* Appointed by Governor Zell Miller to term beginning May 31, 1995. Elected 1996 and 2000. Current term expires Dec 31, 2004.
Office: T5905 Justice Center Tower, 185 Central Avenue S.W., Atlanta 30303.
Telephone: (404) 302-8540.
Fax: (404) 302-8544
E-mail address: stephanie.manis@fultoncourt.org

MANNING, Donald E. *(Judge, Juvenile Court of Georgia Brunswick Judicial Circuit)* Appointed.
Office: Courthouse Annex, 1725 Reynolds Street, Brunswick 31520.
Telephone: (912) 554-7039.
Fax: (912) 267-5629
E-mail address: dmanning@glynncounty.org

MARTIN, Beverly B. *(Judge, United States District Court Northern District of Georgia)* Appointed for life by President Bill Clinton to term beginning Aug 4, 2000. Born Macon Georgia Aug 7, 1955. Educated at Stetson University B.A. 1976 and University of Georgia J.D. 1981. In legal practice Georgia 1981-94.

Assistant Attorney General State Law Department Georgia 1984-94. Assistant U.S. Attorney 1994-97 and U.S. Attorney 1997-2000 Middle District of Georgia.
Office: 2388 U.S. Courthouse, 75 Spring Street S.W., Atlanta 30303-3309.
Telephone: (404) 215-1540.

MARTIN, Faye Sanders *(Senior Judge, Superior Court of Georgia)* Appointed by Governor George D. Busbee to term beginning Nov 1, 1978. Elected 1980, 1984, 1988 and 1996. Former Chief Judge Ogeechee Judicial Circuit. Assumed Senior status, serves when called. First woman appointed Superior Court Judge by a Governor of Georgia. First woman Chief Judge Superior Court of Georgia. Born Bulloch County Georgia Feb 6, 1934. Baptist. Educated at Georgia Southern College 1952-54 and Woodrow Wilson College of Law 1955-56. Awarded honorary J.D. Woodrow Wilson College of Law 1981. Admitted to practice Georgia 1956, U.S. District Court Southern District of Georgia 1957 and U.S. Supreme Court 1978. First woman admitted to practice Bulloch County Georgia. In legal practice Statesboro 1956-78. Ex officio Justice of the Peace 1957-68.

Member Georgia Superior Courts Sentence Review Panel 1980 and 1985, Georgia Association of Women Lawyers (Vice President 1959-60), Georgia Council of Juvenile Court Judges, Georgia Council of Superior Court Judges, National Association of Women Judges, National Council of Juvenile and Family Court Judges, State Bar of Georgia, Bulloch County (Secretary-Treasurer 1956-72), Ogeechee Judicial and American Bar Associations. Attended The National Judicial College 1978 and The Institute for Court Management San Diego California 1980. Listed in *Who's Who of American Women, Who's Who in the South and Southwest, Dictionary of International Biography, Who's Who in Law, Who's Who in Georgia, Men and Women of Distinction* 1979 and *The World's Who's Who of Women* 1979. Recipient Diploma of Distinction and Distinguished Certificate of Merit from International Biographical Centre Manchester England. Named one of four Notable Bulloch County Women at Georgia's 250th Birthday Celebration 1983. Recipient Georgia Southern College Distinguished Alumni Award for outstanding service to college and community Oct 1984. Worked as legal secretary 1952-54. Member Statesboro Primitive Baptist Church, Georgia Southern College Alumni Association, Zeta Tau Alpha Alumni Association and Woodrow Wilson College of Law Alumni Association. Enjoys fishing and cooking.
Mailing address: P.O. Box 803, Statesboro 30459.
Telephone: (912) 764-1706.
Fax: (912) 764-7632

MARTIN, Holli G. *(Judge, Juvenile Court of Georgia Tifton Judicial Circuit)* Appointed.
Mailing address: P.O. Box 7090, Tifton 31793.
Telephone: (229) 386-7904.
Fax: (229) 386-7977
E-mail address: hmartin@tiftcounty.org

MARTIN, Kathryn B. *(Judge, Probate Court of Lamar County)*
Office: 326 Thomaston Street, Box 6, Barnesville 30204-1612.
Telephone: (770) 358-5155.
Fax: (770) 358-5348

MARTIN, Rosa Lee *(Chief Magistrate, Magistrate Court of Wilkes County)*
Office: 23 East Court Street, Room 427, Washington 30673.
Telephone: (706) 678-1881.
Fax: (706) 678-1865

MASSARO, Lynne M. *(Associate Judge, Juvenile Court of Georgia Appalachian Judicial Circuit)* Appointed.
Mailing address: P.O. Box 111, Blue Ridge 30513.
Telephone: (706) 632-7591.
Fax: (706) 632-5354

MASSEY, James E. *(Judge, United States Bankruptcy Court Northern District of Georgia)* Appointed by U.S. Court of Appeals Eleventh Circuit judges.
Office: 1215 U.S. Courthouse, 75 Spring Street S.W., Atlanta 30303-3367.
Telephone: (404) 215-1010.

MATHER, John R. *(Judge, State Court of Fulton County)* Appointed by Governor Zell Miller to term beginning March 8, 1996. Elected 1996 and 2000. Current term expires Dec 31, 2004.
Office: T2905 Justice Center Tower, 185 Central Avenue S.W., Atlanta 30303-3643.
Telephone: (404) 730-4110.
Fax: (404) 224-0576
E-mail address: john.mather@cjisful.net

MATTHEWS, Thomas J. *(Judge, Juvenile Court of Georgia Macon Judicial Circuit)* Appointed to term beginning Feb 1, 1997. Reappointed 2000, current term expires Dec 31, 2004. Former Presiding Judge. Currently serves as Chief Judge.
Office: 505 Bibb County Courthouse, Macon 31201.
Telephone: (478) 621-6356.
Fax: (478) 621-6482
E-mail address: tmatthews@co.bibb.ga.us

MATTHEWS, Walter J. *(Judge, Superior Court of Georgia Rome Judicial Circuit)*
Office: 320 Floyd County Courthouse, Three Government Plaza, Rome 30161.
Telephone: (706) 291-5126.
Fax: (706) 291-5297

MAY, Misty *(Chief Magistrate, Magistrate Court of Glascock County)*
Mailing address: P.O. Box 201, Gibson 30810-0201.
Telephone: (706) 598-2013.
Fax: (706) 598-3577
E-mail address: cmjmmay@netcape.net

MAYO, Martha R. *(Judge, Probate Court of Taliaferro County and Chief Magistrate, Magistrate Court of Taliaferro County)* Elected Judge to term beginning Jan 1, 1997. Reelected 2000, current term expires Dec 31, 2004. Appointed Chief Magistrate Jan 1, 1997. Elected 2000, current term expires Dec 31, 2004.
Mailing address: P.O. Box 264, Crawfordville 30631-0264.
Telephone: (706) 456-2253.
Fax: (706) 456-2904

McARTHUR, Sara M. *(Judge, Juvenile Court of Georgia Western Judicial Circuit)* Former Associate Judge. Appointed Judge.
Mailing address: P.O. Box 893, Athens 30603-0893.
Telephone: (706) 353-7736.
Fax: (706) 354-4713
E-mail address: saramcarthur@hotmail.com

McCALL, James L., Jr. *(Chief Magistrate, Magistrate Court of Montgomery County)* Appointed to term beginning Jan 1, 1997. Reappointed 2000, current term expires Dec 31, 2004. Born Jacksonville Florida June 9, 1956. Baptist.
Mailing address: P.O. Box 174, Mount Vernon 30445-0174.
Telephone: (912) 594-6414.
Fax: (912) 594-6414
E-mail address: mccalllarry@hotmail.com

McCALL, Sharon J. *(Judge, Probate Court of Tattnall County)*
Mailing address: P.O. Box 699, Reidsville 30453-0699.
Telephone: (912) 557-6719.
Fax: (912) 557-3976

McCARTY, Mack S. *(Judge, Probate Court of Macon County)* Elected to term beginning Jan 1, 1989. Reelected 1992, 1996 and 2000. Current term expires Dec 31, 2004. Born Meriwether County Georgia Sept 25, 1943. Lutheran. Educated at University of Georgia B.B.A. 1967.
Mailing address: P.O. Box 216, Oglethorpe 31068-0216.
Telephone: (478) 472-7685.
Fax: (478) 472-5643

McCOLLUM, Elliott P., Jr. *(Judge, State Court of Thomas County)* Serves part time.
Office: 118 Imperial Drive, Thomasville 31792.
Telephone: (229) 226-8856.
Fax: (229) 228-4478

McCOMBS, Rufe E. *(Senior Judge, Superior Court of Georgia)* Elected to term beginning Jan 1, 1983. Reelected 1986. Assumed Senior status, serves when called. Born Decatur Georgia Aug 14, 1919. Presbyterian. Educated at Duke University and University of Georgia B.S. 1940 J.D. 1942. Member Phi Beta Kappa. Admitted to practice Georgia 1941. Judge, Columbus Municipal Court Sept 1975 to June 1978. Judge, State Court of Muscogee County June 21, 1978 to Dec 31, 1982.
Important Decision: Terry McCants et al. v. Taylor County Board of Tax Commissioners et al. 1988. Member Columbus Lawyers Club, State Bar of Georgia and American Bar Association. Democrat. Board member Family Counseling.
Mailing address: P.O. Box 6453, Columbus 31917-6453.

McCONNELL, L. A., Jr. *(Senior Judge, Superior Court of Georgia)* Former Chief Judge Houston Judicial Circuit. Assumed Senior status, serves when called. Former Judge, State Court of Houston County.
Office: Houston County Courthouse, 800 Carroll Street, Perry 31069.
Telephone: (478) 988-1277.
Fax: (478) 987-5058

McCORVEY, Gary C. *(Chief Judge, Superior Court of Georgia Tifton Judicial Circuit)* Elected to term beginning Jan 1, 1997. Reelected 2000, current term expires Dec 31, 2004.
Mailing address: P.O. Box 7090, Tifton 31793-7090.
Telephone: (229) 386-7904.
Fax: (229) 386-7977
E-mail address: mccorveyg@gajudges.org

McCOY, Darin *(Judge, Probate Court of Evans County)*
Mailing address: P.O. Box 852, Claxton 30417-0852.
Office: 123 West Main Street, Claxton 30417.
Telephone: (912) 739-4080.
Fax: (912) 739-4077
E-mail address: judgemccoy@hotmail.com

McDONALD, James E., Jr. *(Judge, Juvenile Court of Georgia Western Judicial Circuit)* Appointed.
Office: 115 Clarke County Courthouse, 325 East Washington Street, Athens 30601.
Telephone: (706) 613-3300.
Fax: (706) 613-3306
E-mail address: robjm@attglobal.net

McELYEA, Ellen *(Judge, Juvenile Court of Georgia Blue Ridge Judicial Circuit)* Appointed.
Office: 90 North Street, Suite 240, Canton 30114.
Telephone: (770) 704-2373.
Fax: (770) 479-2870
E-mail address: judgemcelyea@juvenilecourt.com

McGARITY, Arch W. *(Judge, Superior Court of Georgia Flint Judicial Circuit)* Appointed by Governor Zell Miller to term beginning June 29, 1995. Elected 1996 and 2000. Current term expires Dec 31, 2004.
Office: Henry County Courthouse, One Courthouse Square, Third Floor, McDonough 30253-3293.
Telephone: (770) 954-2118.
Fax: (770) 954-2947
E-mail address: awm8439@yahoo.com

McGOWAN, Jeffery Paulk *(Judge, Probate Court of Atkinson County)* Elected to term beginning Jan 1, 1997. Reelected 2000, current term expires Dec 31, 2004.
Mailing address: P.O. Box 855, Pearson 31642-0855.
Telephone: (912) 422-3552.
Fax: (912) 422-7842

McINTOSH, William M. *(Judge, Juvenile Court of Georgia Southern Judicial Circuit)* Appointed.
Mailing address: P.O. Box 250, Moultrie 31776-0250.
Telephone: (229) 985-5881.
Fax: (229) 985-0659
E-mail address: wmcmc@alltel.net

McLANE, H. Arthur *(Chief Judge, Superior Court of Georgia Southern Judicial Circuit)* Appointed by Governor Joe Frank Harris to term beginning July 29, 1983. Elected 1984, 1988, 1996 and 2000. Current term expires Dec 31, 2004. Administrative Judge District Two 1998-2002. Born Valdosta Georgia April 2, 1939. Member Park Avenue United Methodist Church. Educated at Emory University B.A. 1961 and University of Georgia J.D. 1964. Member Omicron Delta Kappa, Phi Kappa Phi and Blue Key. Recipient Phi Delta Phi Prize from law school. Admitted to practice Georgia 1963 and U.S. Supreme Court 1972. Judge, State Court of Lowndes County Jan 1, 1974 to July 29, 1983.
County Attorney Lowndes County 1965-72. Instructor Valdosta State College 1976. President Council of Superior Court Judges of Georgia 1995-96. Member American Judicature Society, State Bar of Georgia, Valdosta (President 1974) and Southern Judicial Circuit (Vice President 1981) Bar Associations. Recipient Outstanding Young Men of America Award 1972. Listed in *Who's Who in the South and Southwest.* Board of Directors Valdosta Boys Club (President 1971-72), Georgia Sheriffs' Boys' Ranch (Chairman 1982-83) and Valdosta Rotary Club (President 1984-85). Member Valdosta Country Club (President 1972), Chamber of Commerce (President 1985) and Gridiron Secret Society. Enjoys tennis, golf, hunting and woodworking.
Mailing address: P.O. Box 1349, Valdosta 31603-1349.
Telephone: (229) 333-5130.
Fax: (229) 245-5223

McMILLAN, Walter C., Jr. *(Chief Judge, Superior Court of Georgia Middle Judicial Circuit)* Former Administrative Judge District Eight.
Mailing address: P.O. Box 1015, Sandersville 31082-1015.
Telephone: (478) 552-3227.
Fax: (478) 552-8807
E-mail address: mcmillanw@gajudges.org

McMURRAY, William L., Jr. *(Senior Judge, Court of Appeals of Georgia)* Former Presiding Judge. Assumed Senior status, serves when called.
Mailing address: 4540 Holliston Road, Atlanta 30360.

McNEASE, Brenda G. *(Judge, Probate Court of Miller County and Chief Magistrate, Magistrate Court of Miller County)*
Office: 155 South First Street, Room 110, Colquitt 39837-1284.
Telephone: (229) 758-4110.
Fax: (229) 758-8133
E-mail address: mcll@surfsouth.com

McRAE, Earl M., Jr. *(Judge, State Court of Coffee County)* Serves part time.
Mailing address: P.O. Box 1968, Douglas 31534.
Telephone: (912) 384-5610.
Fax: (912) 384-0291
E-mail address: judgemcrae@alltel.net

McVAY, Kipling Louise *(Judge, Probate Court of Cherokee County)* Elected to term beginning Jan 1, 1997. Reelected 2000, current term expires Jan 1, 2005. Admitted to practice Georgia 1976, U.S. District Court Northern District of Georgia 1976 and U.S. Supreme Court 1979. In legal practice Canton 1979-1997. State Administrative Law Judge 1983-97. Judge Pro Tem, Juvenile Court of Cherokee County 1989.
Office: 340 Cherokee County Justice Center, 90 North Street, Canton 30114.
Telephone: (770) 479-0541.
Fax: (770) 720-6318
E-mail address: klmrss@aol.com

McWATERS, Vickie Sue *(Chief Magistrate, Magistrate Court of Troup County)*
Office: 119 Ridley Avenue, Suite 101, LaGrange 30240.
Telephone: (706) 883-1695.
Fax: (706) 883-1632
E-mail address: vsmch2os@mindspring.com

McWHORTER, T. Penn *(Senior Judge, Superior Court of Georgia)* Appointed by Governor Joe Frank Harris to term beginning July 8, 1986. Elected 1988, 1992, 1996 and 2000. Former Chief Judge Piedmont Judicial Circuit. Former Administrative Judge Tenth Judicial District. Assumed Senior status, serves when called. Born Winder Georgia Jan 15, 1934. Methodist. Educated at Emory-at-Oxford Junior College 1951-53, Emory University B.A. 1955 and University of Georgia J.D. 1958.

MCWHORTER, T. PENN—*Continued*

Member Alpha Tau Omega and Phi Delta Phi. Admitted to practice Georgia 1958 and U.S. District Court Middle District of Georgia. In legal practice Atlanta 1958-60 and Winder 1960-86.

City Attorney Winder 1961-86 and Statham 1968-86. Member Continuing Legal Education Committee 1982-87, Disciplinary Review Panel 1986-89, The Association of Trial Lawyers of America, Council of Superior Court Judges of Georgia, Council of Juvenile Court Judges of Georgia, Judicial Council of Georgia, American Judicature Society, State Bar of Georgia (Board of Governors 1970-84), Piedmont (President 1962-63) and American Bar Associations. Attended General Jurisdiction Course The National Judicial College 1987, Juvenile Court seminars Judicial Continuing Legal Education and New Judges Orientation Seminar. E-4 Georgia National Guard 1958-64. Previously worked part time in newspaper delivery and lawn service, for U.S. Post Office and as short-order cook, waiter, Southern Bell lineman, grocery store employee, Benson Old Home Fruitcake salesman and retail clothing clerk. Formerly with Committee on Un-American Activities U.S. House of Representatives. Past President Jaycees, Kiwanis Club (Former Lieutenant Governor Seventh District), Chamber of Commerce, Athletic Booster Club, Yargo District Boy Scouts, ARC Committee and The Critic's Choice Theater. Chairman Administrative Board Methodist Church. Trustee Methodist Children's Home and United Methodist Church (Lay leader and certified lay speaker). Public address announcer for local high school. Enjoys golf, football, acting and speaking.

Mailing address: 10 Olevia Street, Winder 30680.

McWHORTER, William H., Jr. *(Judge, State Court of Emanuel County)* Serves part time.

Mailing address: P.O. Box 99, Swainsboro 30401-0099.
Office: 109 East Moring Street, Swainsboro 30401.
Telephone: (478) 237-7551.
Fax: (478) 237-7514

MERCK, Ralph E. *(Judge, Recorder's Court of DeKalb County)*

Office: 3630 Camp Circle, Decatur 30032-1394.
Telephone: (404) 294-2635.
Fax: (404) 294-2148

MICKLE, Andrew A. *(Judge, Municipal Court of Atlanta)* Appointed by Mayor Maynard Jackson Nov 1981 to term beginning Jan 11, 1982. Elected Nov 1985, 1989, 1993, 1997 and 2001. Current term expires Jan 1, 2006. Born New York New York April 19, 1950. Russian Orthodox. Educated at Harvard University A.B. cum laude 1972 and Emory University School of Law J.D. 1976. Admitted to practice Georgia 1976, U.S. District Court District of Georgia 1976 and District of Columbia 1994. In legal practice Atlanta 1976-78.

Assistant Public Defender and Deputy Public Defender 1978-80 and Public Defender 1980-81 Atlanta. Instructor Atlanta Law School 1980 and 1990-92 and Criminal Justice Department Georgia State University since 1983. Member State Bar of Georgia and Atlanta Bar Association. Attended The National Judicial College 1982, Legal Study Forum of Soviet Union 1985 and 1986 and numerous Institute for Court Management Seminars. Member Municipal Court Training Council 1992-97. Instructor Institute of Continuing Judicial Education of Georgia since 1992. Enjoys tennis, jogging, home improvement, gardening, reading and Braves games.

Office: 170 Garnett Street S.W., Atlanta 30303.
Telephone: (404) 865-8100.
Fax: (404) 658-6859
E-mail address: aamickle@ci.atlanta.ga.us

MIDDLETON, Marie H. *(Judge, Probate Court of Long County and Chief Magistrate, Magistrate Court of Long County)* Elected Judge July 9, 1996 to term beginning Jan 1, 1997. Reelected 2000, current term expires Dec 31, 2004. Born Wayne County Georgia Nov 30, 1954. Baptist. Enjoys reading, hunting and fishing.

Mailing address: P.O. Box 426, Ludowici 31316-0426.
Telephone: (912) 545-2315.
Fax: (912) 545-2150

MIKELL, Charles B., Jr. *(Judge, Court of Appeals of Georgia)* Educated at Princeton University A.B. 1963, University of North Carolina and University of Georgia J.D. with honors 1976. Senior Editor Georgia Law Review 1975-76. Member Order of the Coif. Admitted to practice Georgia 1976 and South Carolina 1977. Former Judge, State Court of Chatham County. Former Judge, Superior Court of Georgia Eastern Judicial Circuit.

Office: 334 State Judicial Building, Atlanta 30334.
Telephone: (404) 656-3459.
Fax: (404) 463-3027
E-mail address: cmikelljr@aol.com

MIKELL, Gary L. *(Judge, State Court of Bulloch County)*

Mailing address: P.O. Box 1688, Statesboro 30459.
Telephone: (912) 764-8605.
Fax: (912) 489-1730
E-mail address: bcjudge@frontiernet.net

MILAM, Bobby C. *(Senior Judge, Superior Court of Georgia)* Appointed by Governor Joe Frank Harris to term beginning July 1, 1983. Elected 1984, 1988, 1992 and 1996. Former Chief Judge Appalachian Judicial Circuit. Assumed Senior status, serves when called. Born Fairburn Georgia Dec 15, 1930. Baptist. Educated at University of Georgia B.A. 1957 and University of Georgia Lumpkin School of Law LL.B. with honors 1959. Articles Editor Georgia Law Review 1958. Law Clerk to Hon. Jessie M. Wood, Superior Court of Georgia two years. Member Phi Sigma Alpha and Phi Kappa Phi. Admitted to practice Georgia 1958, U.S. District Court Northern District of Georgia 1961 and U.S. Court of Appeals Fifth Circuit 1961. In legal practice Blue Ridge 1966-83.

Assistant U.S. Attorney Northern District of Georgia 1961-65. Member Blue Ridge Judicial Circuit Bar Association 1966-83. Member State Bar of Georgia, Appalachian Judicial Circuit and American Bar Associations. Staff Sergeant USMC 1950-54. Worked for National Biscuit Co. 1949-50 and Lockheed Aircraft Corp. 1954-55. Democrat. Enjoys hunting, swimming and walking.

Mailing address: P.O. Box 576, Blue Ridge 30513.
Telephone: (706) 632-2656.
Fax: (706) 258-3070

MILLER, Ben J. *(Senior Judge, Superior Court of Georgia)* Appointed by Governor George Busbee to term beginning July 1, 1977. Elected to subsequent

MILLER, BEN J.—*Continued*
terms. Former Chief Judge Griffin Judicial Circuit. Assumed Senior status, serves when called.
Mailing address: P.O. Box 1527, Griffin 30224-1527.
Telephone: (770) 467-4329.
Fax: (770) 467-4333

MILLER, Clarence A. *(Judge, State Court of Worth County)* Serves part time.
Mailing address: P.O. Box 190, Sylvester 31791-0190.
Telephone: (229) 776-3396.
Fax: (229) 776-9582

MILLER, M. Yvette *(Judge, Court of Appeals of Georgia)* Appointed by Governor Roy Barnes to term beginning July 12, 1999. Elected Nov 2000, current term expires Dec 31, 2006. First African-American woman to serve on Court of Appeals of Georgia. Born Macon Georgia June 21, 1955. Educated at Mercer University B.A. cum laude 1977 J.D. 1980 and Emory University School of Law LL.M. in Litigation 1988. Law Clerk to Hon. William H. Alexander, State Court of Fulton County. In legal practice Jesup. Part-time Magistrate, Magistrate Court of Fulton County 1985-89. Former Administrative Law Judge and Director Judge Appellate Division, Georgia State Board of Workers' Compensation. Former Judge, State Court of Fulton County, appointed by Governor Zell Miller to term beginning Nov 1, 1996.

Former Assistant District Attorney Fulton County. Former Senior Associate Counsel to MARTA. Former Vice President and Past President Elect Georgia Association of Black Women Attorneys. Former Board Member Georgia Association of Women Lawyers. Former Member Supreme Court Committee on Substance Abuse and the Courts. Chair Supreme Court Commission on Public Trust and Confidence. Fellow Lawyers Foundation of Georgia. Member Lamar Inn of Court, Lawyers Club of Atlanta, State Bar of Georgia, Atlanta, Gate City, National and American Bar Associations. Former Board Member Young Women's Christian Association of Greater Atlanta. Former Member Board of Trustees Leadership Georgia. Former Member Mercer University Law School Alumni Board of Directors. Board of Directors Kids' Chance, Inc. Board of Visitors Mercer University Law School. Member National Alliance for the Mentally Ill, Delta Sigma Theta Sorority, Inc. and Cascade United Methodist Church.
Office: 434 State Judicial Building, Atlanta 30334.
Telephone: (404) 463-3032.
Fax: (404) 656-4717
E-mail address: millery@appeals.courts.state.ga.us

MILLER, Sandra *(Judge, Juvenile Court of Georgia Paulding Judicial Circuit)* Appointed.
Office: 217A Main Street, Dallas 30132.
Telephone: (770) 445-9452.

MILLS, Frank C., III *(Chief Judge, Superior Court of Georgia Blue Ridge Judicial Circuit)* Appointed by Governor George D. Busbee to term beginning Feb 9, 1981. Elected 1984, 1988, 1992, 1996 and 2000. Current term expires Dec 31, 2004. Born DeKalb County Georgia July 7, 1948. Episcopalian. Educated at Emory University B.A. 1970 and University of Georgia School of Law J.D. 1973. Member Chi Phi. Admitted to practice Georgia 1973 and U.S. District Court Northern District of Georgia 1973. Began legal practice Canton 1973.

Chief Assistant District Attorney 1974-78 and District Attorney 1978-81 Blue Ridge Judicial Circuit. Author "Annual Survey of Georgia Law—Criminal Law" 43 No. 1 Mercer L. Rev. 175-242, 45 No. 1 Mercer L. Rev. 135-214 and 46 No. 1 Mercer L. Rev. Member Georgia District Attorneys Association 1974-81, Georgia Council of Superior Court Judges, Blue Ridge, Canton and American Bar Associations. Recipient Distinguished District Attorney Award from Georgia District Attorneys Association 1979, Silver Beaver Award from National Council of Boy Scouts of America 1995 and Chief Justice Robert Benham Award for Community Service from State Bar of Georgia and Community Service Task Force 1999. Named Outstanding Young Man of America for Cherokee County by Jaycees 1982. Member Leadership Georgia, Inc. 1982. Captain USAR 1973. Member Canton Lions Club, Cherokee County Chamber of Commerce, Cherokee County Humane Society (Director), University of Georgia Alumni Association (District Vice President and Board of Managers), University of Georgia Law School Council (District Representative) and Canton Golf Club. Interests include photography, camping, swimming, scouting, chess and the Georgia Bulldogs.
Office: 90 North Street, Suite 270, Canton 30114-2789.
Telephone: (770) 479-2302.
Fax: (770) 704-2333
E-mail address: fmills@brjc.net

MIMS, Larry B. *(Judge, State Court of Tift County)* Serves part time.
Mailing address: P.O. Box 1, Tifton 31793.
Office: 223 East Second Street, Suite B, Tifton 31794.
Telephone: (229) 382-7470.
Fax: (229) 382-7478
E-mail address: lmims@friendlycity.net

MISKIEL, Joyce *(Chief Magistrate, Magistrate Court of Brooks County)*
Mailing address: P.O. Box 387, Quitman 31643-0387.
Telephone: (229) 263-9989.
Fax: (229) 263-7847
E-mail address: jmiskiel@surfsouth.com

MITCHUM, Dale *(Chief Magistrate, Magistrate Court of Bryan County)* Appointed to term beginning March 1, 1997. Reappointed 2000, current term expires Dec 31, 2004.
Mailing address: P.O. Box 670, Pembroke 31321-0670.
Telephone: (912) 653-3861, 756-4520.
Fax: (912) 653-4603

MOCK, Robert W., Sr. *(Judge, State Court of Gwinnett County)* Former Judge, Recorder's Court of Gwinnett County.
Office: Gwinnett Justice Center, 75 Langley Drive, Lawrenceville 30045-6935.
Telephone: (770) 822-8515.
Fax: (770) 822-8513
E-mail address: mockro@co.gwinnett.ga.us

MOORE, William T., Jr. *(Judge, United States District Court Southern District of Georgia)* Appointed for life by President Bill Clinton to term beginning Oct 31, 1994. Born Bainbridge Georgia May 7, 1940. Episcopalian. Educated at Georgia Military College A.A. with

MOORE, WILLIAM T., JR.—*Continued*

distinction 1960, University of Georgia 1961 J.D. 1964 and University of Virginia School of Law LL.M. 2001. Member Kappa Alpha, Phi Delta Phi and Gridiron Secret Society. Admitted to practice Georgia 1964, U.S. District Court Southern District of Georgia 1964, U.S. Courts of Appeals Fifth 1979 and Eleventh 1979 Circuits and U.S. Supreme Court 1980. In legal practice Savannah 1964-94.

U.S. Attorney Southern District of Georgia 1977-81. Professor of Business Law Savannah State College late 1960s. Member U.S. Attorney General's Advisory Committee 1978-81. Fellow American Board of Criminal Lawyers. Member Committee on Criminal Law Judicial Conference of the U.S., Eleventh Circuit District Judges Association, Federal Judges Association, State Bar of Georgia and Federal Bar Association. Recipient Distinguished Alumni Award from Georgia Military College 1978, Special Appreciation Award from Georgia Bureau of Investigation 1980 and Bureau of Alcohol, Tobacco and Firearms U.S. Department of Treasury 1980, Extraordinary Service Award from Savannah Chapter Federal Bar Association 1980 and Distinguished Letterman's Award from Baseball Letterman's Club University of Georgia 2001. Enjoys jogging, golf, weight training, boating and reading.

Mailing address: P.O. Box 10245, Savannah 31412-0445.

Office: 308 U.S. Courthouse, 125 Bull Street, Savannah 31401.

Telephone: (912) 650-4173.

Fax: (912) 650-4177

MORGAN, C. Cloud *(Senior Judge, Superior Court of Georgia)* Assumed Senior status, serves when called.

Office: 310 Bibb County Courthouse, Macon 31201.

Telephone: (478) 749-6650.

Fax: (478) 749-6529

MORRIS, M. Cindy *(Judge, Superior Court of Georgia Conasauga Judicial Circuit)*

Mailing address: P.O. Box 732, Dalton 30722.

Telephone: (706) 278-0047.

Fax: (706) 275-9060

MORSE, John E., Jr. *(Judge, Superior Court of Georgia Eastern Judicial Circuit)* Appointed by Governor Zell Miller to term beginning May 18, 1995. Elected 1996 and 2000. Current term expires Dec 31, 2004. Former Judge and Chief Judge, State Court of Chatham County.

Office: 213 Chatham County Courthouse, 133 Montgomery Street, Savannah 31401.

Telephone: (912) 652-7236.

Fax: (912) 652-7361

E-mail address: JEMorse@wpo.co.chatham.ga.us

MOSELEY, Thomas E. *(Chief Magistrate, Magistrate Court of Bartow County)* Elected to term beginning Jan 1, 1997. Reelected 2000, current term expires Dec 31, 2004.

Office: 135 West Cherokee Avenue, Suite 225, Cartersville 30120.

Telephone: (770) 387-5070.

Fax: (770) 387-5073

MOSS, Lee D. *(Judge, Probate Court of Lincoln County and Chief Magistrate, Magistrate Court of Lincoln County)*

Mailing address: P.O. Box 205, Lincolnton 30817-0205.

Telephone: (706) 359-5528.

Fax: (706) 359-5520

MOTES, T. David *(Judge, Superior Court of Georgia Piedmont Judicial Circuit)* Appointed by Governor Zell Miller to term beginning Jan 1, 1996. Elected 1996 and 2000. Current term expires Dec 31, 2004. Born Winder Georgia Dec 6, 1954. Educated at University of Georgia A.B. 1977 J.D. 1980. Admitted to practice Georgia 1980. Judge, State Court of Jackson County Jan 1, 1989 to Dec 31, 1995.

Assistant District Attorney Piedmont Judicial Circuit 1981-88.

Mailing address: P.O. Box 670, Jefferson 30549-0670.

Telephone: (706) 367-6370.

Fax: (706) 367-2273

MOULTON, Tracy, Jr. *(Senior Judge, Superior Court of Georgia)* Appointed by Governor Zell Miller to term beginning July 28, 1995. Elected 1996. Assumed Senior status, serves when called. Former Judge, State Court of Early County.

Mailing address: P.O. Drawer 687, Blakely 31723.

Telephone: (229) 723-8454.

Fax: (229) 723-3134

MOYE, Charles A., Jr. *(Senior Judge, United States District Court Northern District of Georgia)* Appointed for life by President Richard M. Nixon to term beginning Oct 23, 1970. Former Chief Judge. Assumed Senior status Jan 1, 1988, serves by assignment. Born Atlanta Georgia July 13, 1918. Congregationalist. Educated at Emory University A.B. 1939 J.D. 1943. Admitted to practice Georgia 1943.

Member Lawyers Club of Atlanta, The American Law Institute, American Bar Foundation, State Bar of Georgia, Atlanta, Federal and American Bar Associations. Republican.

Office: 2342 U.S. Courthouse, 75 Spring Street S.W., Atlanta 30303-3361.

Telephone: (404) 215-1340.

MUISE, Patti *(Judge, Recorder's Court of Gwinnett County)*

Office: Gwinnett Justice Center, 75 Langley Drive, Lawrenceville 30245-6900.

Telephone: (770) 822-8169.

Fax: (770) 822-8173

E-mail address: muisepa@co.gwinnett.ga.us

MULHERIN, Bernard J., Sr. *(Senior Judge, Superior Court of Georgia)* Appointed by Governor George D. Busbee to term beginning March 7, 1980. Elected 1980, 1982, 1986, 1990 and 1994. Served Augusta Judicial Circuit. Assumed Senior status Jan 1, 1999, serves when called. Born Augusta Georgia Aug 21, 1932. Catholic. Educated at Spring Hill College B.S. 1954 and University of Georgia LL.B. cum laude 1958. Assistant Editor University of Georgia Law Review 1958. Member Phi Kappa Phi. Admitted to practice Georgia 1958. Began legal practice Augusta 1958.

Special Agent FBI 1959-60. Important Decision: Blackburn v. Blackburn. Member State Bar of Georgia, Augusta and American Bar Associations. First Lieuten-

MULHERIN, BERNARD J., SR.—*Continued*

ant U.S. Army 1954-56. City Council Augusta 1973-80. Member Boys Club (President 1985) and Knights of Columbus (State Deputy 1970-72). Enjoys golf.

Office: 902 City-County Building, 530 Greene Street, Augusta 30911.

Telephone: (706) 821-2574.

MULLINS, Coleman Ray *(Judge, United States Bankruptcy Court Northern District of Georgia)* Appointed by U.S. Court of Appeals Eleventh Circuit judges to term beginning Feb 29, 2000. Term expires 2014.

Office: 1270 U.S. Courthouse, 75 Spring Street S.W., Atlanta 30303-3308.

Telephone: (404) 215-1002.

MULLIS, H. Frederick, Jr. *(Judge, Superior Court of Georgia Oconee Judicial Circuit)* Appointed by Governor Zell Miller to term beginning March 29, 1996. Elected 1996 and 2000. Current term expires Dec 31, 2004.

Mailing address: P.O. Box 4248, Eastman 31023-4248.

Telephone: (478) 374-9800.

Fax: (478) 374-0009

E-mail address: judgefm@progressivetel.com

MULLIS, Judy B. *(Judge, Probate Court of Lanier County)* Elected to term beginning Sept 21, 1988. Reelected 1992, 1996 and 2000. Current term expires Jan 1, 2005. Born Lowndes County Georgia Nov 8, 1953. Southern Baptist.

Executive Board Council of Probate Court Judges of Georgia. Member Probate Judges Training Council. Past President Georgia Election Officials Association. Member Lakeland Lions Club and Lanier County Chamber of Commerce. Enjoys piano and choir music.

Office: 100 Main Street, Lakeland 31635.

Telephone: (229) 482-3668.

Fax: (229) 482-8333

E-mail address: lcpcjam@yahoo.com

MULLIS, W. Dennis *(Judge, Juvenile Court of Georgia Oconee Judicial Circuit)* Appointed.

Mailing address: P.O. Box 429, Cochran 31014.

Office: 202 Cherry Street, Cochran 31014.

Telephone: (478) 934-6352.

Fax: (478) 934-6352

E-mail address: dmullis1@communicomm.com

MURPHY, Harold L. *(Judge, United States District Court Northern District of Georgia)* Appointed for life by President Jimmy Carter to term beginning Aug 11, 1977. Born Haralson County Georgia March 31, 1927. Methodist. Educated at West Georgia College, University of Mississippi and University of Georgia Law School LL.B. 1949. Member Sigma Alpha Epsilon and Phi Delta Phi. Admitted to practice Georgia 1949, U.S. District Court Northern District of Georgia 1949 and U.S. Courts of Appeals Fifth 1956 and Eleventh 1981 Circuits. In legal practice Buchanan 1949-64 and Tallapoosa 1964-71. Judge, Superior Court of Georgia Tallapoosa Judicial Circuit 1971-77.

Fellow American Bar Foundation. Member Joseph Henry Lumpkin American Inn of Court (Past President), American Judicature Society, Eleventh Circuit District Judges Association, State Bar of Georgia, Tallapoosa Circuit and American Bar Associations. Frequent seminar lecturer. USN 1945-46. Representative General Assembly of Georgia 1951-61. Member First United Methodist Church.

Mailing address: P.O. Drawer 53, Rome 30162-0053.

Telephone: (706) 291-5626.

MURPHY, John R., III *(Judge, State Court of Jefferson County)* Elected to term beginning Jan 1, 1997. Reelected 2000, current term expires Dec 31, 2004. Serves part time.

Mailing address: P.O. Box 31, Louisville 30434-0031.

Telephone: (478) 625-7281.

Fax: (478) 625-8200

E-mail address: jmurphy_amhlaw@bellsouth.net

MURPHY, Margaret H. *(Judge, United States Bankruptcy Court Northern District of Georgia)*

Office: 1290 U.S. Courthouse, 75 Spring Street S.W., Atlanta 30303-3367.

Telephone: (404) 215-1006.

MURPHY, Mark H. *(Judge, Juvenile Court of Georgia Tallapoosa Judicial Circuit)* Appointed to term beginning July 1, 1997. Reappointed 2001, current term expires June 30, 2005. Christian. Educated at Georgia State University J.D. 1992. Student Writing Editor Georgia Law Review 1991-92. Admitted to practice Georgia 1992 and U.S. District Court Northern District of Georgia 1992. In legal practice Bremen 1992-97. Chief Magistrate, Magistrate Court of Haralson County Jan 1, 1989 to July 1, 2001.

Author "A Constitutional Analysis of Compulsory School Attendance Laws in the Southeast: Do They Unlawfully Interfere with Alternatives to Public Education?" Georgia State University L. Rev. 1992 and *Georgia Juvenile Practice and Procedure* Harrison Publishing Company 4th ed.

Mailing address: P.O. Box 969, Buchanan 30113-0969.

Office: Haralson County Courthouse, Buchanan 30113.

Telephone: (770) 646-2025.

Fax: (770) 646-1508

MURPHY, Michael L. *(Chief Judge, Superior Court of Georgia Tallapoosa Judicial Circuit)* Appointed to term beginning Dec 3, 1998. Elected 2000, current term expires Dec 31, 2004.

Mailing address: P.O. Box 186, Buchanan 30113-0186.

Telephone: (770) 646-2018.

Fax: (770) 646-2019

E-mail address: murph10@mindspring.com

NASH, Robin S. *(Judge, Juvenile Court of Georgia Stone Mountain Judicial Circuit)* Appointed.

Office: 3631 Camp Circle, Decatur 30032.

Telephone: (404) 294-2753.

Fax: (404) 294-2956

E-mail address: rsnash@co.dekalb.ga.us

NATION, Beverly W. *(Judge, Probate Court of Oglethorpe County)*

Mailing address: P.O. Box 70, Lexington 30648-0070.

Telephone: (706) 743-5350.

Fax: (706) 743-3514

NATION, Sidney L. *(Chief Judge, Superior Court of Georgia Rockdale Judicial Circuit)* Chief Judge since

NATION, SIDNEY L.—*Continued*

Jan 1, 1999. Former Judge, State Court of Rockdale County.

Mailing address: P.O. Box 289, Conyers 30012-0289.
Telephone: (770) 918-6300.
Fax: (770) 918-6460
E-mail address: FSHCMP@aol.com

NELSON, Charles E. *(Chief Magistrate, Magistrate Court of Dodge County)*
Office: 5018 Courthouse Circle, Suite 202, Eastman 31023.
Telephone: (478) 374-7243.
Fax: (478) 374-5716

NELSON, G. Carey *(Judge, Superior Court of Georgia Cherokee Judicial Circuit)*
Office: 135 West Cherokee Avenue, Suite 340, Cartersville 30120.
Telephone: (770) 387-5122.
Fax: (770) 606-2241
E-mail address: nelsonc@bartowga.org

NEVILLE, William J. *(Senior Judge, Superior Court of Georgia)* Appointed by Governor Joe Frank Harris to term beginning Jan 1, 1985. Elected to subsequent terms. Assumed Senior status, serves when called. Born Statesboro Georgia Feb 11, 1923. Missionary Baptist. Educated at Mercer University J.D. 1949. Chief Justice, Court of Honor and Court of Corrections 1948-49. Member Phi Alpha Delta and Sigma Alpha Epsilon. Admitted to practice Georgia 1948. Began legal practice Macon 1948. In legal practice Statesboro 1949. Judge, Recorder's Court of Bulloch County 1953-84.

County Attorney Bulloch County 1953-84. Instructor in Business Law Georgia Southern College 1962-65. President Circuit Bar Association 1976-81. Major U.S. Army 1940-68 (retired). Georgia House of Representatives 1951-52. Member Kiwanis. President Law Alumni 1958. Past President Jaycees. Enjoys flying, boating, fishing and architecture.

Mailing address: P.O. Box 683, Statesboro 30459.

NEWKIRK, Henry M. *(Judge, State Court of Fulton County)* Appointed by Governor Zell Miller to term beginning Aug 5, 1998. Elected Nov 2000, current term expires Dec 31, 2004. Born Cleveland Ohio 1953. Methodist. Educated at Florida State University B.S. 1976 and Woodrow Wilson College of Law J.D. 1982. Law Clerk to Hon. Thomas Jerome Dillon, Juvenile Court of Fulton County 1981-82. Admitted to practice Georgia 1983 and U.S. District Court Northern District of Georgia 1983.

Assistant Solicitor General DeKalb County 1984-86. Senior Assistant District Attorney Fulton County 1986-98. Member Lawyers Club of Atlanta, Georgia Association of Black Women Attorneys, Gate City, North Fulton, South Fulton, Stonewall and Atlanta Bar Associations. Instructor New Judge Training 2000 and 2001. Youth Coach. Enjoys skiing, motorcycling and running.

Office: 185 Central Avenue S.W., Suite 2655, Atlanta 30303.
Telephone: (404) 224-0493.
Fax: (404) 224-0578
E-mail address: henry.newkirk@co.fulton.ga.us

NEWTON, Ronald L. *(Chief Magistrate, Magistrate Court of Fannin County)* Elected to term beginning Jan 1, 1989. Reelected 1992, 1996 and 2000. Current term expires Dec 31, 2004. Also Judge, McCaysville Municipal Court, appointed to term beginning Jan 1991. Born McCaysville Georgia Nov 29, 1960. Baptist. Educated at Truett-McConnell College. Attends Institute of Continuing Judicial Education of Georgia University of Georgia School of Law annually.

Office: 420 West Main Street, Suite 7, Blue Ridge 30513.
Telephone: (706) 632-5558.
Fax: (706) 632-8236

NICHOLAS, Stephen W. *(Judge, Recorder's Court of DeKalb County)*
Office: 23 North Avondale Road, Avondale Estates 30002.
Telephone: (404) 296-7976.
Fax: (404) 296-9902

NICHOLS, O. T. "Terry" *(Judge, Juvenile Court of Georgia Brunswick Judicial Circuit and Chief Magistrate, Magistrate Court of Wayne County)* Appointed Judge to term beginning Nov 21, 1977. Reappointed to subsequent terms.

Mailing address: P.O. Box 27, Jesup 31598-0027.
Telephone: (912) 427-5960.
Fax: (912) 427-5944
E-mail address: terryn@accessatc.net

NIX, Kenneth O. *(Judge, Superior Court of Georgia Cobb Judicial Circuit)* Appointed by Governor Zell Miller to term beginning Dec 1, 1995. Elected 1996 and 2000. Current term expires Dec 31, 2004. Born Atlanta Georgia Oct 4, 1939. Member Bethany United Methodist Church. Educated at Presbyterian College 1957-59 and Emory University B.S. 1961 LL.B. 1964. Admitted to practice Georgia 1965. Began legal practice Atlanta 1965. In legal practice Smyrna 1970. Judge, Recorder's Court of Smyrna 1970-71. Judge Jan 1, 1983 to Nov 30, 1995 and Former Chief Judge, State Court of Cobb County.

Important Decision: Presiding Judge in largest verdict case ($11,032,000) in the State Court of Cobb County Jan 1985. Professor John Marshall Law School 1992-2000. Member State Bar of Georgia and Cobb County Bar Association. Attended General Jurisdiction course July 15 to Aug 10, 1984, Legal Writing course July 1985 and Medical and Scientific Evidence course Sept 1987 The National Judicial College. Faculty Advisor The National Judicial College 1991, 1996 and 2001. Named Outstanding Young Man of the Year by Smyrna Jaycees 1973. Recipient Distinguished Service Award from Cobb County Chamber of Commerce 1974, Presidential Citation as Outstanding Legislator from Georgia Association for Health, Physical Education and Recreation 1978, Friend of the Year Award from Cobb County Association of Educators 1980 and 1982, "Me Smyrna" Citizen of the Year Award from Smyrna Oakdale/Moose Lodge 1996 and Ogden Doremus Award for Lifetime Contribution to the judicial, legal and humanitarian communities 1997. Republican. Delegate to County, District and State Republican Conventions 1970-82. Member Georgia House of Representatives 1973-83 (Caucus Secretary 1977-83, Chairman Cobb County Legislative Delegation 1982-83). Trustee and Chairman State PTA Legislative and Citizenship 1981-82 Southern Tech Foundation. Trustee Life University since 1993. President and Director Smyrna Seniors Softball Association since 1999. Member Metropolitan Football League (Director 1979-81), Cobb County Midget Football Conference

NIX, KENNETH O.—*Continued*
(Past Commissioner), Cobb County Unit American Cancer Society, Smyrna Bicentennial Committee (Steering Committee and Legal Council) and Smyrna Rotary Club. Interests include coaching football, basketball and baseball, playing softball and officiating high school football and baseball.

Office: 30 Waddell Street, Marietta 30090-9642.
Telephone: (770) 528-1888.
Fax: (770) 528-8105

NUNN, George F., Jr. *(Chief Judge, Superior Court of Georgia Houston Judicial Circuit)* Term expires Dec 31, 2004.

Office: Houston County Courthouse, 800 Carroll Street, Perry 31069.
Telephone: (478) 987-2110.
Fax: (478) 987-8781

O'BERRY, Karleen S. *(Judge, Probate Court of Clinch County)*

Mailing address: P.O. Box 364, Homerville 31634-0364.
Telephone: (912) 487-5523.
Fax: (912) 487-3083

O'CONNOR, James B. *(Senior Judge, Superior Court of Georgia)* Elected to term beginning Jan 1, 1965. Reelected to subsequent terms. Assumed Senior status, serves when called. Born Dodge County Georgia Jan 17, 1929. Baptist. Educated at Duke University A.B. 1948 and Mercer University J.D. 1951. Admitted to practice Georgia 1950.

Past President Council of Superior Court Judges of Georgia. Member Judicial Council of Georgia (Vice Chairman), State Bar of Georgia, Oconee and American Bar Associations. First Lieutenant U.S. Army JAGC 1952-55. Democrat. Member Rotary Club. Enjoys quail hunting.

Mailing address: 977 Jay Bird Springs Road, Chauncey 31011.

OGLETREE, Laverne C. *(Judge, Probate Court of Greene County and Chief Magistrate, Magistrate Court of Greene County)*

Office: 113 Greene County Courthouse, 113 North Main Street, Greensboro 30642.
Telephone: (706) 453-3346.
Fax: (706) 453-7649
E-mail address: ogletreel@hotmail.com

O'KELLEY, William C. *(Senior Judge, United States District Court Northern District of Georgia)* Appointed for life by President Richard M. Nixon to term beginning Oct 23, 1970. Former Chief Judge. Assumed Senior status, serves by assignment. Member Alien Terrorist Removal Court since 1996. Born Atlanta Georgia Jan 2, 1930. Member Wieuca Road Baptist Church. Educated at Emory University A.B. 1951 LL.B. 1953. Member Omicron Delta Kappa and Sigma Chi. Admitted to practice Georgia 1952. Began legal practice Atlanta 1952. In legal practice Atlanta 1961-70.

Assistant U.S. Attorney Atlanta 1959-61. Important Decisions: F.A.I.R. v. Volpe 1973; Georgia v. U.S. 411 U.S. 526, 1973; Barclays Bank D.C.O. v. Mercantile National Bank 1974; Bryan v. Brock & Blevins Co. 1974; and Tyler v. Vickery 1975. Member Judicial Conference of the U.S. (Committee on Administration of Criminal Law 1979-82, Subcommittee on Jury Trials in Complex Criminal Cases 1981-82, Executive Committee 1983-84, Advisory Committee on Criminal Rules 1984-87), Federal Judicial Center (Committee on Orientation of Newly Appointed District Judges 1985-87, Board of Directors 1987-91), District Judges Association of the Fifth Circuit (Secretary-Treasurer 1976-77, Vice President 1977-78, President-elect 1978-79, President 1979-80), Lawyers Club of Atlanta, State Bar of Georgia and American Bar Association. Captain USAFR 1953-66. General Counsel Georgia Republican Party 1968-70. Member Peachtree-Atlanta Kiwanis Club and Atlanta Athletic Club. Enjoys farming and other outdoor activities.

Office: 1942 U.S. Courthouse, 75 Spring Street S.W., Atlanta 30303-3309.
Telephone: (404) 215-1530.
Fax: (404) 215-1538

OLIVER, Bonnie Chessher *(Judge, Superior Court of Georgia Northeastern Judicial Circuit)* Appointed by Governor Roy Barnes to term beginning Sept 27, 1999. Judge, State Court of Hall County June 11, 1998 to Sept 26, 1999, appointed by Governor Zell Miller.

Mailing address: P.O. Box 409, Gainesville 30503-0409.
Telephone: (770) 297-2333.
Fax: (770) 297-2337
E-mail address: judgeoliver@mindspring.com

OLIVER, George E. *(Senior Judge, Superior Court of Georgia)* Appointed by Governor Lester Maddox to term beginning June 17, 1970. Elected to subsequent terms. Assumed Senior status Jan 1, 1985, serves when called. Born Covington Georgia Sept 20, 1914. Methodist. Educated at Presbyterian College A.B. 1936 and University of Georgia J.D. 1939. Admitted to practice Georgia 1939. In legal practice Savannah. Former Judge, Recorder's Court 1955-63 and State Court 1963-70.

Member American Judicature Society, State Bar of Georgia, Savannah and American Bar Associations. Lieutenant USCG 1942-46. Grand Master Masons Georgia 1973. Potentate Alee Temple Shrine 1964. Member Legal Aid Society, Scottish Rite 33°, Sons of the American Revolution (Past President), Society of Colonial Wars and St. Andrews Society. Enjoys reading and beach walking.

Office: 415 Broughton Street, Suite 112, Savannah 31401.
Telephone: (912) 652-7166, 652-7486.
Fax: (912) 651-6378

OTT, John M. *(Judge, Superior Court of Georgia Alcovy Judicial Circuit)* Term expires Dec 31, 2004.

Office: 1132 Usher Street N.W., Room 220, Covington 30014.
Telephone: (770) 784-2080.
Fax: (770) 784-2130
E-mail address: jott@co.newton.ga.us

OVERSTREET, J. Carlisle *(Judge, Superior Court of Georgia Augusta Judicial Circuit)* Appointed by Governor Zell Miller to term beginning Nov 1, 1991. Elected to term beginning Jan 1, 1993. Reelected 1996 and 2000. Current term expires Dec 31, 2004. Born Augusta Georgia March 31, 1945. Presbyterian. Educated at Augusta College A.B. 1967 and Mercer University Law School J.D. 1970. Member Phi Delta Phi (President and Secretary). Admitted to practice Georgia 1971. In legal

OVERSTREET, J. CARLISLE—*Continued*

practice Augusta 1970-91. Judge, Municipal Court of Augusta 1988-91.

Member Council of Superior Court Judges of Georgia (Chairman Personnel Committee since 1996, Member Budget Committee since 2000, Secretary-Treasurer since 2000), State Bar of Georgia and Augusta Bar Association. Member Augusta Country Club and Rotary Club of Augusta. Enjoys golf.

Office: 320 City-County Building, 530 Greene Street, Augusta 30911.
Telephone: (706) 821-2444.
Fax: (706) 721-4476

OWENS, Wilbur Dawson, Jr. *(Senior Judge, United States District Court Middle District of Georgia)* Appointed for life by President Richard M. Nixon to term beginning March 1, 1972. Former Chief Judge. Assumed Senior status, serves by assignment. Born Albany Georgia Feb 1, 1930. Presbyterian. Educated at Emory University and University of Georgia J.D. 1952. Staff member Georgia Law Review 1950-52. Member Phi Delta Phi. Admitted to practice Georgia 1952 and U.S. Supreme Court 1967. In legal practice Albany 1954-55 and Macon 1965-72.

Assistant U.S. Attorney Macon 1962-65. Member State Bar of Georgia, Macon and American Bar Associations. Staff Judge Advocate USAF 1952-54. First Lieutenant promoted to Captain USAFR. Vice President and Trust Officer Bank of Albany 1955-59. Secretary Treasurer Southwestern Mortgage Corporation 1959-62. Member First Presbyterian Church, Idle Hour Golf and Country Club and Rotary Club.

Mailing address: P.O. Box 65, Macon 31202-0065.
Telephone: (478) 752-3491.

OXENDINE, James W. *(Senior Judge, Superior Court of Georgia)* Served Gwinnett Judicial Circuit. Assumed Senior status, serves when called.

Office: 75 Langley Drive, Lawrenceville 30045.
Telephone: (770) 822-8602.
Fax: (770) 822-8676

OZBURN, Samuel D. *(Judge, Superior Court of Georgia Alcovy Judicial Circuit)* Appointed by Governor Zell Miller to term beginning Jan 1, 1996. Elected 1996 and 2000. Current term expires Dec 31, 2004.

Office: 1132 Usher Street N.W., Room 214, Covington 30014.
Telephone: (770) 784-2180.
Fax: (770) 788-3770

PAIST, Sallie Walker *(Judge, Juvenile Court of Georgia Cobb Judicial Circuit)* Former Associate Judge. Appointed Judge.

Office: 1738 County Services Parkway S.W., Marietta 30008.
Telephone: (770) 528-2444.
Fax: (770) 528-2576
E-mail address: spaist@cobbcounty.org

PALMER, Kathy *(Judge, Superior Court of Georgia Middle Judicial Circuit)*

Mailing address: P.O. Box 330, Swainsboro 30401.
Telephone: (478) 237-3260.
Fax: (478) 237-0949
E-mail address: kspalmer@pineland.net

PANNELL, Charles A., Jr. *(Judge, United States District Court Northern District of Georgia)* Appointed for life by President Bill Clinton to term beginning Dec 1, 1999. Born DeKalb County Georgia Jan 24, 1946. Educated at University of Georgia B.A. 1967 J.D. 1970. In legal practice 1972-76. Judge, Superior Court of Georgia Conasauga Judicial Circuit 1979-99.

Assistant U.S. Attorney Northern District of Georgia 1971-72. Special Assistant Attorney General Law Department Georgia 1974-76. District Attorney Conasauga Judicial Circuit 1977-79.

Office: 2367 U.S. Courthouse, 75 Spring Street S.W., Atlanta 30303-3361.
Telephone: (404) 215-1580.

PANOS, John *(Judge, State Court of DeKalb County)*

Office: 604 DeKalb County Courthouse, 556 North McDonough Street, Decatur 30030.
Telephone: (404) 371-2354

PAPE, Timothy A. *(Judge, Juvenile Court of Georgia Rome Judicial Circuit)* Elected to term beginning Jan 1, 1983. Reelected 1986, 1990, 1994, 1998 and 2002. Current term expires Dec 31, 2006. Born Pittsfield Massachusetts Jan 3, 1948. Methodist. Educated at Mercer University B.A. cum laude 1970 and University of Georgia J.D. 1977. Admitted to practice Georgia 1977 and U.S. District Court Northern District of Georgia 1977. In legal practice Rome since 1977.

Assistant District Attorney 1977-79. Member Floyd County Child Abuse Protocol Committee, Rome/Floyd County Commission on Children and Youth (President 1992-93), Council of Juvenile Court Judges of Georgia (President 1991-92), Georgia Courts Automation Commission, National Council of Juvenile and Family Court Judges, State Bar of Georgia and Rome Bar Association (President 1986-87). Member Advisory Board Boy Scouts of America since 1985, Advisory Board Coosa Valley Mental Health and Mental Retardation, Board of Directors Floyd Training and Service Center for the Mentally Retarded (President 1985-86 and 1994-95) and Breakfast Optimist Club of Rome (President 1982-83 and 1990-91, Secretary Treasurer 1983-85). Participant Leadership Rome 1986. Member Exchange Club of Rome. Enjoys backpacking, canoeing, fishing, jogging and photography.

Office: 202 Floyd County Courthouse, Three Government Plaza, Rome 30161.
Telephone: (706) 291-5263.
Fax: (706) 291-5247
E-mail address: papet@floydcountyga.org

PARAVIS, Sara *(Judge, Probate Court of Crawford County)*

Mailing address: P.O. Box 1028, Roberta 31078-1028.
Telephone: (478) 836-3313.
Fax: (478) 836-4111

PARKER, Johnny R. *(Judge, Probate Court of Gordon County)*

Mailing address: P.O. Box 669, Calhoun 30703-0669.
Telephone: (706) 629-7314.
Fax: (706) 629-4698

PARKER, Ronnie A. *(Judge, Probate Court of Taylor County and Chief Magistrate, Magistrate Court of Taylor County)*

Mailing address: P.O. Box 536, Butler 31006-0536.

PARKER, RONNIE A.—*Continued*
Telephone: (478) 862-3357.
Fax: (478) 862-5334

PARKER, S. Ben *(Chief Magistrate, Magistrate Court of Oconee County)*
Mailing address: P.O. Box 1099, Watkinsville 30677.
Telephone: (706) 769-3940.
Fax: (706) 769-3948

PARKS, Joy *(Chief Magistrate, Magistrate Court of White County)*
Office: 59 South Main Street, Cleveland 30528.
Telephone: (706) 865-6636.
Fax: (706) 865-7738
E-mail address: jparks@whitecounty.net

PARROTT, John Lee *(Judge, Superior Court of Georgia Ocmulgee Judicial Circuit)* Appointed by Governor Joe Frank Harris to term beginning Dec 14, 1987. Elected 1988, 1992, 1996 and 2000. Current term expires Dec 31, 2004. Educated at The Citadel B.A. 1971 and University of Georgia School of Law J.D. 1974.
Mailing address: P.O. Box 111, Monticello 31064-0111.
Telephone: (706) 468-4906.
Fax: (706) 468-4929

PARROTT, Vann K. *(Associate Judge, Juvenile Court of Georgia Southern Judicial Circuit)* Appointed.
Mailing address: P.O. Box 329, Quitman 31643.
Telephone: (229) 263-8833.
Fax: (229) 263-8324

PARTAIN, Jack *(Judge, Superior Court of Georgia Conasauga Judicial Circuit)* Appointed by Governor Zell Miller to term beginning Dec 1, 1995. Elected 1996 and 2000. Current term expires Dec 31, 2004.
Mailing address: P.O. Box 2535, Dalton 30722-2535.
Telephone: (706) 278-6713.
Fax: (706) 278-6714
E-mail address: jpartain@ocsonline.com

PAUL, Troy C. *(Judge, Probate Court of Coffee County)* Elected to term beginning Jan 1, 1981. Reelected 1984, 1988, 1992, 1996 and 2000. Current term expires Jan 1, 2005. Born Coffee County Georgia March 9, 1944. Missionary Baptist.
E-6 Army National Guard 1965-76. Democrat. Member Carver Baptist Church, Douglas Chamber of Commerce, Mental Health Association and Farm Bureau.
Office: Coffee County Courthouse, 101 South Peterson Avenue, Douglas 31533.
Telephone: (912) 384-5213.
Fax: (912) 384-0291

PAYNE, Jonathan Marlin *(Judge, Probate Court of Chattooga County)* Elected to term beginning Feb 28, 1975. Reelected to subsequent terms. Born Memphis Tennessee Aug 22, 1948. Church of Christ. Educated at Snead State Junior College and Georgia State University. Former Chief Magistrate, Magistrate Court of Chattooga County.
Appointed to Probate Judges Scholarship Committee 1978. Corporal USMC 1967-72. Member Young Democrats of Georgia. Delegate State Democratic Charter Convention 1975. County Coordinator for Auburn University Athletics. Hobbies include fishing, hunting and guns.
Mailing address: P.O. Box 467, Summerville 30747-0467.
Telephone: (706) 857-0709.
Fax: (706) 857-0877
E-mail address: jonm1966p@yahoo.com

PAYNE, Paul *(Chief Magistrate, Magistrate Court of Dawson County)*
Mailing address: P.O. Box 254, Dawsonville 30534-0254.
Telephone: (706) 344-3730.
Fax: (706) 344-3537

PEACOCK, Sarah M. *(Associate Judge, Juvenile Court of Georgia Middle Judicial Circuit)* Appointed.
Mailing address: P.O. Box 869, Lyons 30436.
Telephone: (912) 526-3437.
Fax: (912) 526-9387

PEAGLER, Desiree Sutton *(Associate Judge, Juvenile Court of Georgia Stone Mountain Judicial Circuit)* Appointed to term beginning Sept 22, 1997.
Office: 3631 Camp Circle, Decatur 30032-1399.
Telephone: (404) 294-2946.
Fax: (404) 294-2143
E-mail address: dpeagler@usa.net

PEAGLER, George M., Jr. *(Judge, Superior Court of Georgia Southwestern Judicial Circuit)*
Mailing address: P.O. Box 784, Americus 31709-0784.
Telephone: (229) 924-5839.
Fax: (229) 924-3312
E-mail address: judgepeagler@yahoo.com

PEARSON, S. D. *(Chief Magistrate, Magistrate Court of Warren County)*
Mailing address: P.O. Box 203, Warrenton 30828-0203.
Telephone: (706) 465-3123.
Fax: (706) 465-1300

PEED, F. Gates *(Judge, Superior Court of Georgia Ogeechee Judicial Circuit)* Born Statesboro Georgia April 9, 1954. Presbyterian. Educated at University of Georgia B.S. 1976 M.A. 1977 and Mercer University J.D. cum laude 1982. Member Phi Alpha Delta. Admitted to practice Georgia 1982, U.S. District Courts Middle, Northern and Southern Districts and U.S. Court of Appeals Eleventh Circuit. In legal practice Statesboro since 1982. Former part-time Judge, State Court of Bulloch County, elected to term beginning Jan 1, 1997.
Bulloch County Solicitor 1994 to Dec 31, 1996. Member Georgia Defense Lawyers Association, Georgia Trial Lawyers Association, The Association of Trial Lawyers of America, State Bar of Georgia (Overview Committee), Bulloch County, Ogeechee Circuit and American Bar Associations. Member Georgia Society of Public Accountants. Statesboro Rotary Club, Downtown Statesboro Development Authority and Trinity Presbyterian Church. Enjoys hunting.
Mailing address: P.O. Box 967, Statesboro 30459.
Telephone: (912) 764-6095.
Fax: (912) 489-3148
E-mail address: fgpfox@frontiernet.net

PEELER, Clarence Lee, Jr. *(Senior Judge, Superior Court of Georgia)* Elected to term beginning July 1,

PEELER, CLARENCE LEE, JR.—*Continued*

1965. Reelected to subsequent terms. Assumed Senior status 1984, serves when called. Born Athens Georgia Oct 30, 1918. Protestant. Educated at The Citadel B.A. 1939, Emory University 1946 and Atlanta Law School LL.B. 1950. Admitted to practice Georgia 1946. Began legal practice Decatur 1946. In legal practice Decatur 1956-65.

Assistant Solicitor Stone Mountain Judicial Circuit 1948-56. Captain U.S. Army 1942-45. Democrat.

Mailing address: 615 Ridgecrest Road N.E., Atlanta 30307.

PEPPERS, Charles Donald, Sr. *(Judge, State Court of Walker County)* Appointed by Governor Joe Frank Harris to term beginning May 6, 1985. Elected 1986, 1990, 1994, 1998 and 2002. Current term expires Dec 31, 2006. Born LaFayette Georgia July 24, 1945. Baptist. Educated at University of Chattanooga B.S. 1968 and Atlanta Law School 1978. Admitted to practice Georgia 1978. In legal practice LaFayette since 1978. Attended various seminars for State Court judges.

Mailing address: P.O. Box 1316, LaFayette 30728-1316.
Telephone: (706) 638-1664.
Fax: (706) 639-1776

PERKINS, Carson Dane *(Judge, Superior Court of Georgia Alapaha Judicial Circuit)* Elected to term beginning Jan 1, 1997. Reelected 2000, current term expires Dec 31, 2004.

Mailing address: P.O. Box 606, Nashville 31639-0606.
Telephone: (229) 686-2180.
Fax: (229) 686-2597
E-mail address: dane@surfsouth.com

PERRY, Edwin J., III *(Judge, Juvenile Court of Georgia South Georgia Judicial Circuit)* Appointed to term beginning Oct 1, 1991. Reappointed to subsequent terms. Current term expires Jan 1, 2005. Currently serves as Presiding Judge. Born Bainbridge Georgia Jan 21, 1948. Christian. Educated at University of Georgia A.B. cum laude 1970 J.D. 1974. Member Phi Beta Kappa and Phi Kappa Phi. Admitted to practice Georgia 1974. In legal practice Bainbridge since 1974. Former Chief Magistrate, Magistrate Court of Decatur County.

Member State Bar of Georgia.

Mailing address: P.O. Box 542, Bainbridge 39818-0542.
Telephone: (229) 246-2271.
Fax: (229) 246-2216
E-mail address: splwyr@surfsouth.com

PFEIFFER, Guy Douglas *(Chief Magistrate, Magistrate Court of Crisp County)* Appointed to term beginning July 1, 1983. Elected 1984, 1988, 1992, 1996 and 2000. Current term expires Dec 31, 2004. Also serves as Judge, Municipal Court of Arabi since 2000. Born Belleville Illinois Jan 19, 1946. United Methodist. Member First Methodist Church of Cordele. Educated at St. Louis University 1964, University of Illinois B.S.M.E. 1968 and Emory University J.D. with distinction 1975. Law Clerk to Chief Justice Virgil Kirk, Navajo Nation Tribal Courts 1973-74. Member Triangle Fraternity. Admitted to practice Georgia 1975. Began legal practice Cordele 1975. Former Judge pro tem, Juvenile Courts of Ben Hill, Crisp, Dooly and Wilcox Counties.

Co-author Monograph "Misdemeanor Bad Check Jurisdiction in Magistrate Court" Council of Magistrate Court Judges 1987. Member Georgia Commission on Gender Bias 1989-91 and Georgia Commission on Dispute Resolution 1996-2002. Moderator Magistrate Court Task Force for Georgia Court Futures Project. Associate Member National Center for State Courts. Member American Judges Association, American Judicature Society, State Bar of Georgia, Cordele Judicial Circuit and American (Committee on Part-Time Judicial Officers National Conference of Special Court Judges Judicial Administration Division) Bar Associations. Instructor Magistrate Judges Recertification Course Georgia ICJE since 1984. Recipient Service Award from Council of Magistrate Court Judges of Georgia 1987 and 1991. Captain USAF 1968-72. Member Advisory Council to Georgia Public TV 1979-82, Cordele Rotary Club (President 1980), Cordele-Crisp County Chamber of Commerce (President 1985) and American Cancer Society (Crisp County President 1979). Interests include the performing arts, roses, golf, travel and community services.

Office: 210 South Seventh Street, Room 102, Cordele 31015.
Telephone: (229) 276-2618.
Fax: (229) 276-2675
E-mail address: pfeiffer@planttel.net

PHILLIPS, Richard D. *(Judge, State Court of Long County)* Serves part time.

Mailing address: P.O. Box 69, Ludowici 31316-0069.
Telephone: (912) 545-2191.
Fax: (912) 545-2505

PHILLIPS, Robert F. *(Judge, Probate Court of Charlton County)* Elected to term beginning Jan 1, 1997. Reelected 2000, current term expires Dec 31, 2004.

Office: Charlton County Courthouse, 100 South Third Street, Folkston 31537.
Telephone: (912) 496-2230.
Fax: (912) 496-1156

PHIPPS, Herbert E. *(Judge, Court of Appeals of Georgia)* Appointed by Governor Roy Barnes to term beginning July 12, 1999. Born Baker County Georgia Dec 20, 1941. Educated at Morehouse College B.A. 1964 and Case Western Reserve University School of Law J.D. 1971. Editor Case Western Reserve Law Review. Member Sigma Pi Phi. In legal practice 1983-95. Associate Judge, State Court of Dougherty County 1980-88. Judge, Juvenile Court of Dougherty County 1988-95. Judge, Superior Court of Georgia Dougherty Judicial Circuit June 30, 1995 to 1999, appointed by Governor Zell Miller.

Past President Dougherty Circuit Bar Association. Member C. B. King Bar Association, State Bar of Georgia (Former Member Board of Governors), Atlanta and American Bar Associations. Past President Albany Association for Retarded Citizens, Albany Sickle Cell Foundation, Faith Fund Foundation and The Criterion Club. Former Member Board of Directors Albany Technical Institute. Board of Directors Security Bank & Trust Company of Albany.

Office: 334 State Judicial Building, Atlanta 30334.
Telephone: (404) 656-3457.
Fax: (404) 651-8139

PICKETT, Albert *(Judge, Superior Court of Georgia Augusta Judicial Circuit)* Term expires Dec 31, 2004.
Office: 305 City-County Building, 530 Greene Street, Augusta 30911.
Telephone: (706) 821-2365.
Fax: (706) 721-1089

PIERCE, Dan F. *(Chief Magistrate, Magistrate Court of Walton County)*
Mailing address: P.O. Box 1188, Monroe 30655-1188.
Telephone: (770) 267-1385.
Fax: (770) 266-1512
E-mail address: dpierce@co.walton.ga.us

PIERCE, David M. *(Chief Magistrate, Magistrate Court of Houston County)* Appointed to term beginning Jan 1, 1997. Reappointed 2000, current term expires Dec 31, 2004.
Office: 89 Cohen Walker Drive, Warner Robins 31088-5817.
Telephone: (478) 987-4695.
Fax: (478) 987-5249
E-mail address: dpierce@houstoncountyga.org

PIERCE, Ellen I. *(Chief Magistrate, Magistrate Court of Putnam County)* Appointed to term beginning Jan 1, 1997. Elected 2000, current term expires Dec 31, 2006.
Office: 108 South Madison Avenue, Suite 101, Eatonton 31024.
Telephone: (706) 485-4306.
Fax: (706) 484-1814

PITMAN, Karen *(Judge, Probate Court of Monroe County)* Elected to term beginning Nov 4, 1998. Reelected 2000, current term expires Dec 31, 2004.
Mailing address: P.O. Box 187, Forsyth 31029.
Telephone: (478) 994-7036.
Fax: (478) 994-7054

POOLE, Craig E. *(Chief Magistrate, Magistrate Court of Turner County)* Elected to term beginning Jan 1, 1985. Reelected 1988, 1992, 1996 and 2000. Current term expires Dec 31, 2004. Born Turner County Georgia June 23, 1959. Methodist.
Radio Operator Turner County Sheriff's Department April 1, 1978 to Dec 31, 1984. Democrat. Enjoys hunting, fishing and family activities.
Office: 219 East College Avenue, Room 2, Ashburn 31714.
Telephone: (229) 567-3155.
E-mail address: cpoole@surfsouth.com

POPE, Robert Thomas *(Senior Judge, Superior Court of Georgia)* Appointed by Governor George D. Busbee to term beginning Oct 10, 1978. Elected Nov 13, 1978, Nov 1982, Nov 1986, 1990, 1994 and 1998. Former Chief Judge Cherokee Judicial Circuit. Assumed Senior status, serves when called. Administrative Judge, Seventh Judicial Administrative District 1992-94. Born Atlanta Georgia Dec 29, 1940. Member Calhoun First United Methodist Church. Educated at Georgia Institute of Technology B.S.I.M. 1963, Emory University J.D. with distinction 1966 and New York University LL.M. 1970. Recipient BNA Award 1966 and American Jurisprudence Award in Antitrust 1966. Member Bryan Society. Editorial Board Journal of Public Law 1966. Admitted to practice Georgia 1965, U.S. Supreme Court 1970, U.S. District Court Northern District of Georgia 1976 and U.S. Court of Appeals Fifth Circuit 1977. Began legal practice Atlanta 1966. In legal practice Calhoun since 1970.
Instructor U.S. Military Academy at West Point 1966-70. Member Judicial Council of Georgia 1992-94. Member Council of Superior Court Judges of Georgia (Vice Chairman Drafting Committee Uniform Superior Court Rules, Member Executive Committee), American Judicature Society, State Bar of Georgia, Cherokee Judicial Circuit and Calhoun Bar Associations. Instructor in Commercial Law American Banking Association 1971. Captain U.S. Army JAGC 1966-70. Enjoys bluegrass music, canoeing and backpacking.
Mailing address: 108 Buena Vista Drive, Calhoun 30701.

POPPELL, Ralph E. *(Chief Magistrate, Magistrate Court of McIntosh County)* Elected to term beginning Jan 1, 1985. Reelected 1988, 1992, 1996 and 2000. Current term expires Dec 31, 2004. Born Long County Georgia Oct 17, 1936. Protestant. Educated at University of Maryland in Police Administration.
Police Officer Washington D.C. 1960-70 (retired). Specialist Five USAF 1954-58. Democrat. Member Masons and International Police Association. Enjoys private piloting, boating and fishing.
Mailing address: P.O. Box 1661, Darien 31305.
Telephone: (912) 437-4888.
Fax: (912) 437-2768
E-mail address: magctt@darientel.net

PORTER, J. Richard, III *(Judge, Superior Court of Georgia South Georgia Judicial Circuit)* Elected to term beginning Jan 1, 1997. Reelected 2000, current term expires Dec 31, 2004.
Mailing address: P.O. Box 729, Cairo 39828-0729.
Telephone: (229) 377-7349.
Fax: (229) 378-1032
E-mail address: judgejrp@surfsouth.com

PORTER, Patsy Y. *(Judge, State Court of Fulton County)* Appointed by Governor Zell Miller to term beginning March 8, 1996. Elected 1996 and 2000. Current term expires Dec 31, 2004.
Office: T2855 Justice Center Tower, 185 Central Avenue S.W., Atlanta 30303.
Telephone: (404) 730-4345.
Fax: (404) 224-0575

POSTON, McCracken "Ken" *(Judge, Juvenile Court of Georgia Lookout Mountain Judicial Circuit)* Appointed. Serves part time.
Mailing address: P.O. Box 1600, Ringgold 30736.
Telephone: (706) 935-4901.
Fax: (706) 935-4909
E-mail address: mcposton@mindspring.com

POWELL, Bob *(Judge, Probate Court of Twiggs County)*
Mailing address: P.O. Box 307, Jeffersonville 31044-0307.
Telephone: (478) 945-3390.
Fax: (478) 945-6070

POWELL, Kenneth *(Judge, Probate Court of Bleckley County)* Elected to term beginning Jan 1, 1997. Reelected 2000, current term expires Dec 31, 2004.
Office: 306 S.E. Second Street, Cochran 31014.
Telephone: (478) 934-3204.
Fax: (478) 934-3205
E-mail address: bcpj@communicomm.com

POWERS, Jean A. *(Chief Magistrate, Magistrate Court of Worth County)*
Mailing address: P.O. Box 64, Sylvester 31791-0064.
Telephone: (229) 776-8210.

PRATHER, Andy *(Judge, State Court of Muscogee County)* Appointed by Governor Zell Miller to term beginning Jan 21, 1994. Elected to subsequent terms. Current term expires Dec 31, 2006. Currently serves as Chief Judge.
Mailing address: P.O. Box 1340, Columbus 31902-1340.
Telephone: (706) 653-4318.

PRIDGEN, John C. *(Judge, Superior Court of Georgia Cordele Judicial Circuit)* Appointed by Governor Roy Barnes to term beginning September 27, 1999. Reelected 2000, current term expires Dec 31, 2004. Born Macon Georgia June 10, 1950. Methodist. Educated at University of Georgia B.B.A. 1972 J.D. 1975. Admitted to practice Georgia 1975.
District Attorney Cordele Judicial Circuit Jan 1, 1987 to Sept 26, 1999.
Mailing address: P.O. Box 5025, Cordele 31010-5025.
Office: 210 Crisp County Courthouse, 210 South Seventh Street, Cordele 31015.
Telephone: (229) 276-2619.
Fax: (229) 276-2629
E-mail address: pridgenj@gajudges.org

PRIOR, William A., Jr. *(Chief Judge, Superior Court of Georgia Ocmulgee Judicial Circuit)* Term expires Dec 31, 2004.
Mailing address: P.O. Box 728, Madison 30650-0728.
Telephone: (706) 342-0672.
Fax: (706) 342-3730

PRITCHARD, Marion C. *(Judge, Juvenile Court of Georgia Waycross Judicial Circuit)* Appointed. Currently serves as Presiding Judge.
Mailing address: P.O. Box 556, Waycross 31502-0556.
Office: 801 Grove Avenue, Waycross 31501.
Telephone: (912) 287-4345.
Fax: (912) 287-4347

PROCTOR, Grace B. *(Judge, Probate Court of Treutlen County and Chief Magistrate, Magistrate Court of Treutlen County)*
Office: Treutlen County Courthouse Annex, 114 Second Street South, Soperton 30457-1438.
Telephone: (912) 529-3342.
Fax: (912) 529-6838

PRODGERS, Toby Batson *(Judge, State Court of Cobb County)* Appointed by Governor Zell Miller to term beginning Dec 21, 1995. Elected 1996 and 2000. Current term expires Dec 31, 2004. Serves Division One.
Office: 12 East Park Square, Marietta 30090.
Telephone: (770) 528-1731.
Fax: (770) 528-1736

PULLEN, Douglas *(Judge, Superior Court of Georgia Chattahoochee Judicial Circuit)* Appointed by Governor Zell Miller to term beginning Oct 23, 1995. Elected 1996 and 2000. Current term expires Dec 31, 2004.
Mailing address: P.O. Box 1340, Columbus 31902-1340.
Telephone: (706) 653-4273.
Fax: (706) 653-4569

PURDOM, Wayne M. *(Judge, State Court of DeKalb County)* Appointed by Governor Zell Miller to term beginning July 9, 1998. Elected 2000, current term expires Dec 31, 2004. Born Philadelphia Pennsylvania April 14, 1953. Methodist. Educated at Yale University B.A. cum laude 1974 and Emory University J.D. 1977 LL.M. 1980. Admitted to practice Georgia 1977. Began legal practice Decatur 1977. Part-time Associate Magistrate 1983-84 and Chief Magistrate Jan 1, 1985 to July 8, 1998, Magistrate Court of DeKalb County.
Member Georgia Trial Lawyers Association, State Bar of Georgia, Decatur-DeKalb and American Bar Associations. Democrat. Active in judicial campaigns 1980-84. Treasurer South Decatur Community Center, Inc. 1981-83.
Office: 605 DeKalb County Courthouse, 556 North McDonough Street, Decatur 30030.
Telephone: (404) 687-7180.
Fax: (404) 687-7185
E-mail address: wpurdom@randomc.com

RADAKOVICH, Nina M. *(Judge, City Court of Atlanta)*
Office: 104 Trinity Avenue S.W., Atlanta 30303.
Telephone: (404) 658-6919.
Fax: (404) 658-7961
E-mail address: nradakovich@ci.atlanta.ga.us

RADFORD, Lillian S. *(Judge, Probate Court of Tift County)*
Mailing address: P.O. Box 792, Tifton 31793-0792.
Telephone: (229) 386-7936.
Fax: (229) 386-7913

RAHN, Albert, III *(Judge, Superior Court of Georgia Atlantic Judicial Circuit)* Elected to term beginning Jan 1, 1995. Current term expires Dec 31, 2006. Former Judge, State Court of Tattnall County.
Mailing address: P.O. Box 280, Reidsville 30453-0280.
Telephone: (912) 557-6393.
Fax: (912) 557-4415

RANDALL, William C. *(Chief Magistrate, Magistrate Court of Bibb County and Judge, Civil Court of Bibb County)* Currently serves as Chief Judge Civil Court.
Office: 111 Bibb County Courthouse, 601 Mulberry Street, Macon 31201.
Telephone: (478) 621-6338.
Fax: (478) 621-6470
E-mail address: wrandall@co.bibb.ga.us

RAWLINGS, Tom *(Judge, Juvenile Court of Georgia Middle Judicial Circuit)* Appointed.
Mailing address: P.O. Box 5746, Sandersville 31082.
Telephone: (478) 553-0012.
Fax: (478) 552-8807
E-mail address: tcrawlings@hotmail.com

RAY, Larry *(Chief Magistrate, Magistrate Court of Pickens County)*
Office: 50 North Main Street, Jasper 30143.
Telephone: (706) 253-8747.
Fax: (706) 253-8750

RAY, William M., II *(Judge, Superior Court of Georgia Gwinnett Judicial Circuit)*
Office: Gwinnett Justice Center, 75 Langley Drive, Lawrenceville 30045.
Telephone: (770) 822-8613.
Fax: (770) 822-8637
E-mail address: raywi@co.gwinnett.ga.us

REED, Thomas Wayne *(Chief Magistrate, Magistrate Court of Dade County)* Elected to term beginning Jan 1, 1993. Reelected 1996 and 2000. Current term expires Dec 31, 2004. Born Fort Campbell Kentucky March 15, 1950. Southern Baptist.
Member Council of Magistrate Court Judges of Georgia and State Bar of Georgia. Attended Institute of Continuing Judicial Education of Georgia University of Georgia School of Law Feb 1993. U.S. Army 1970. Former Police Officer Los Angeles Police Department.
Mailing address: P.O. Box 1263, Trenton 30752-1263.
Telephone: (706) 657-4113.
Fax: (706) 657-8618

REEVES, Judy *(Judge, Probate Court of Sumter County)*
Mailing address: P.O. Box 246, Americus 31709-0246.
Telephone: (229) 928-4551.
Fax: (229) 928-4622
E-mail address: judyr@sumter-ga.com

REEVES, R. H., III *(Judge, State Court of Jenkins County)* Elected to term beginning Jan 1, 1999. Reelected 2002, current term expires Dec 31, 2006. Serves part time. Born Jenkins County Georgia Feb 21, 1942. United Methodist. Educated at Emory University B.A. 1964 J.D. 1967. Admitted to practice Georgia 1966.
Certified Lay Speaker United Methodist Church. Enjoys music.
Mailing address: P.O. Box 690, Millen 30442-0690.
Office: 724 East Winthrope Avenue, Millen 30442.
Telephone: (478) 982-5812.
Fax: (478) 982-5900
E-mail address: rhreevesiii@bellsouth.net

REGO, Thomas M. *(Associate Judge, Juvenile Court of Georgia Tallapoosa Judicial Circuit)* Appointed.
Mailing address: P.O. Box 276, Tallapoosa 30176.
Telephone: (770) 574-7686.
Fax: (770) 574-7052
E-mail address: tmrego@earthlink.com

REILLY, William L. *(Judge, Juvenile Court of Georgia Appalachian Judicial Circuit)* Former Associate Judge. Appointed Judge.
Mailing address: P.O. Box 2153, Blue Ridge 30513.
Telephone: (706) 632-2225.
Fax: (706) 632-0451
E-mail address: barrister@tds.net

RENTZ, Ronald H. *(Judge, Juvenile Court of Georgia Pataula Judicial Circuit)* Appointed to term beginning March 11, 1982. Reappointed March 11, 1990, 1994, 1998 and 2002. Current term expires March 2006. Born Greenville South Carolina Aug 2, 1946. Methodist. Educated at Gordon Military College 1964-65 and University of Georgia A.B. 1968 J.D. 1972. Recipient scholastic medal for top 10% of freshman class Gordon Military College 1965. Member Phi Delta Phi. Admitted to practice Georgia 1972 and U.S. District Courts Middle 1973 and Southern 1973 Districts of Georgia. Began legal practice Augusta 1972. In legal practice Colquitt 1976-93.
Solicitor State Court of Miller County 1976-80. Member Council of Juvenile Court Judges of Georgia (President 1994-95), State Bar of Georgia, Pataula (President 1978) and American Bar Associations. E-4 USAR 1968-72. Board of Directors Southwest Georgia Hospital since 1990. Member Lions Club (Past President, Board of Directors twelve years). Enjoys golf, tennis and football.
Mailing address: P.O. Box 217, Colquitt 31737-0217.
Telephone: (229) 758-5575.
Fax: (229) 758-3038
E-mail address: rhrentz@surfsouth.com

REYNOLDS, Penny Brown *(Judge, State Court of Fulton County)* Appointed by Governor Roy Barnes. Educated at Georgia State University B.S. cum laude J.D. Member Alpha Kappa Alpha. Admitted to practice Georgia.
Former Assistant Attorney General Georgia. Executive Council to Governor Roy Barnes. Co-editor *Women and the Law: A Guide to Women's Legal Rights in Georgia.* Board of Directors Gate City Bar Association. Barrister Lamar Inn of Court. Member Georgia Association of Women Lawyers, Georgia Association of Black Women Attorneys, National Association of Women Lawyers and American Bar Associations. Recipient "Woman of Wonder Award" 2000 from National Council of Negro Women, Inc. and Quaker Oats Co. Named Outstanding African American by Allstate Insurance Company, one of Georgia's 100 Most Powerful and Influential Women by *Women Looking Ahead News Magazine*, one of "Atlanta's Top 100 Black Women of Influence" by Atlanta Business League and National Community Leader of the Year by National Council of Negro Woman, Inc. and Quaker Oats Co. Former Member Georgia Commission on Women. Advisory Board Georgia Legislative Black Caucus, Georgia Coalition of Black Women, Inc. and Metropolitan Atlanta Chapter National Coalition of 100 Black Women. Board of Directors Atlanta Branch NAACP. Member Finance Committee and Chairperson Capitol Improvement Fund. Coordinator Midway Summer Institute, Midway Clothes Closet and After School Program. Member Atlanta Black/Jewish Coalition and International Women's Forum, Inc. Enjoys reading. Personal Statement or Quote: "To whom much is given, much is required."
Office: T3705 Justice Center Tower, 185 Central Avenue S.W., Atlanta 30303.
Telephone: (404) 730-4330.
Fax: (404) 224-0570

RICE, Harry F. *(Chief Magistrate, Magistrate Court of Madison County)*
Mailing address: P.O. Box 6, Danielsville 30633-0006.
Telephone: (706) 795-5679.
Fax: (706) 795-2222

RICHARDSON, Bob *(Judge, State Court of Houston County)* Appointed by Governor Joe Frank Harris to term beginning Sept 18, 1985. Elected 1986, 1990, 1994, 1998 and 2002. Current term expires Dec 31, 2006. Born Tifton Georgia June 17, 1940. Methodist.

RICHARDSON, BOB—*Continued*
Educated at Southern Methodist University B.A. 1962 and University of Georgia J.D. 1965. Admitted to practice Georgia 1971. In legal practice Perry and Warner Robins 1971-85. First Lieutenant U.S. Army Artillery 1965-68.
Office: 202 Carl Vinson Parkway, Warner Robins 31088.
Telephone: (478) 542-2013.
Fax: (478) 328-2161
E-mail address: brichardson@houstoncountyga.org

RIGDON, Fred W., Jr. *(Associate Judge, Juvenile Court of Georgia Tifton Judicial Circuit)* Appointed.
Mailing address: P.O. Box 1701, Tifton 31793.
Office: 424 Tift Avenue, Tifton 31794.
Telephone: (229) 382-7494.
Fax: (229) 386-5451
E-mail address: fwrigdon@friendlycity.net

RILEY, William F., Jr. *(Judge, Municipal Court of Atlanta)* Appointed by mayor.
Office: 170 Garnett Street S.W., Atlanta 30303.
Telephone: (404) 865-8100.
Fax: (404) 658-6859
E-mail address: wfriley@ci.atlanta.ga.us

ROBERTS, Bernard E., III *(Chief Magistrate, Magistrate Court of Hall County)*
Mailing address: P.O. Drawer 1435, Gainesville 30503-1435.
Telephone: (770) 531-6912.
Fax: (770) 531-6917

ROBERTSON, Charles T., II *(Chief Magistrate, Magistrate Court of Cherokee County)* Elected to term beginning Jan 1, 2001. Term expires Dec 31, 2004. Born Atlanta Georgia June 21, 1957. Methodist. Educated at Kennesaw State University B.S. with honors 1988 and John Marshall University J.D. with honors 1992. Admitted to practice Georgia 1993, U.S. District Court Northern District of Georgia 1993 and U.S. Tax Court 1993. In legal practice Woodstock 1995-2001.
Author *How to File for Divorce in Georgia* and *How to Start a Georgia Business* Sphinx Publishing. Member Cobb County and Cherokee County Bar Associations. General Counsel Cherokee Republican Party 1995-99.
Office: 90 North Street, Suite 150, Canton 30114.
Telephone: (770) 479-8516.
Fax: (770) 720-6323
E-mail address: CROBERTSON@CCCOURT.COM
Website address: www.cccourt.com

ROBINS, Mathew *(Judge, State Court of DeKalb County)*
Office: 304 DeKalb County Courthouse, 556 North McDonough Street, Decatur 30030.
Telephone: (404) 371-2300.
Fax: (404) 371-2731
E-mail address: MROB@randomc.com

ROBINSON, Dorothy A. *(Judge, Superior Court of Georgia Cobb Judicial Circuit)* Elected 1980. Reelected to subsequent terms. First woman to serve as a superior court judge in the circuit. Former Chief Judge and Administrative Judge District Seven. Born New York Oct 4, 1937. Roman Catholic. Educated at St. John's University B.B.A. 1961 and St. Louis University J.D. 1967. Admitted to practice Georgia 1967. Began legal practice Marietta 1967. Judge, Cobb County State Court Jan 1973 to 1980, appointed by Governor Jimmy Carter (first woman to serve as judge of a court of record in Georgia). Justice Pro Hac Vice, Supreme Court of Georgia 1985.
President Georgia Association of Women Lawyers 1973-74 and State Trial Judges and Solicitors Association of Georgia 1979-80. Chairman of the Board 1991 and Board of Trustees Institute of Continuing Judicial Education. State Court Representative 1980-81 and Superior Court Representative Judicial Council of Georgia. Member Executive Committee Georgia Council of Superior Court Judges. Member State Bar of Georgia and Cobb County Bar Association. Graduate The National Judicial College. Chairman Board of Trustees Cobb County Symposium, Inc. 1979-80. Member Marietta Rotary Club (Director Community Services 1991-92) and St. Joseph's Church. Enjoys running, tennis and biking.
Office: 30 Waddell Street, Marietta 30090.
Telephone: (770) 528-1843.
Fax: (770) 528-1881

RODATUS, Robert V. *(Judge, Juvenile Court of Georgia Gwinnett Judicial Circuit)* Appointed. Currently serves as Presiding Judge. Born Pittsburgh Pennsylvania Jan 30, 1952. Catholic. Educated at University of Pittsburgh 1970, Georgia Southwestern College B.A. cum laude 1973 and Mercer University J.D. 1976. Assistant Editor Mercer Law Review 1975-76. Law Clerk to Superior Court of Georgia Gwinnett Judicial Circuit. Member Delta Theta Phi. Admitted to practice Georgia 1976. Began legal practice Lawrenceville 1976. In legal practice Norcross 1981. Chief Judge, Recorder's Court of Gwinnett County 1985-92.
Senior Assistant District Attorney Trial Division Gwinnett Judicial Circuit 1983-84. Member National Association of District Attorneys, American Judicature Society, State Bar of Georgia and Gwinnett County Bar Association. Member Lions Club and Knights of Columbus. Enjoys marathons.
Office: Gwinnett Justice Center, 75 Langley Drive, Lawrenceville 30045.
Telephone: (770) 822-8282.
Fax: (770) 822-8062
E-mail address: rodatus@mindspring.com

RODGERS, Carl L. *(Judge, Probate Court of Echols County and Chief Magistrate, Magistrate Court of Echols County)*
Mailing address: P.O. Box 118, Statenville 31648-0118.
Telephone: (229) 559-7526.
Fax: (229) 559-8128
E-mail address: judgerodgers@planttel.net

RODGERS, Linda S. *(Chief Magistrate, Magistrate Court of Macon County)*
Mailing address: P.O. Box 605, Oglethorpe 31068-0605.
Telephone: (478) 472-8509.
Fax: (478) 472-5643

ROSE, Charles Paul, Jr. *(Judge, Superior Court of Georgia Atlantic Judicial Circuit)*
Mailing address: P.O. Box 1246, Hinesville 31310.
Telephone: (912) 877-4770.
Fax: (912) 877-2015

ROWLAND, Joe W. *(Chief Magistrate, Magistrate Court of Johnson County)* Born Johnson County Georgia Dec 25, 1928. Methodist. Educated at Mercer University A.B. 1951 LL.B. 1952. Admitted to practice Georgia 1952. Former Judge, State Court of Johnson County, elected to term beginning Jan 1, 1960.

County Attorney Johnson County 1970-92. Democrat.

Mailing address: P.O. Box 227, Wrightsville 31096-0227.

Telephone: (478) 864-3350.

Fax: (478) 864-1343

E-mail address: rowland@nlamerica.com

ROWLAND, Susie W. *(Chief Magistrate, Magistrate Court of Tattnall County)* Elected to term beginning Jan 1, 1989. Reelected 1992, 1996 and 2000. Current term expires Dec 31, 2004. Born Montgomery County Georgia May 8, 1940. Baptist.

Deputy Clerk 1972-87 and Chief Deputy 1976-87 Superior and State Court Clerk's office. Attended Seminar Institute of Continuing Judicial Education Savannah June 1992. Enjoys cooking, sewing, fishing and yard work.

Mailing address: P.O. Box 513, Reidsville 30453-0513.

Telephone: (912) 557-4372.

Fax: (912) 557-3136

ROYAL, C. Ashley *(Judge, United States District Court Middle District of Georgia)* Appointed for life by President George W. Bush to term beginning Dec 28, 2001.

Mailing address: P.O. Box 129, Macon 31202.

Telephone: (478) 752-3445.

ROYAL, Robert L. *(Senior Judge, Superior Court of Georgia)* Elected to term beginning Jan 1, 1973. Reelected 1976, 1980 and 1984. Assumed Senior status Jan 1, 1989, serves when called. Born Sycamore Georgia Jan 14, 1921. Baptist. Educated at University of Georgia A.B. 1942 J.D. 1944. Member Phi Beta Kappa. Admitted to practice Georgia 1943. Judge, State Court of Floyd County 1971-72.

Member State Bar of Georgia and Rome Bar Association. Democrat. Member Noon Optimist Club.

Mailing address: 10 Vineland Drive N.W., Rome 30165-1424.

ROYSTON, Donald H. *(Judge, Probate Court of Madison County)*

Mailing address: P.O. Box 207, Danielsville 30633-0207.

Telephone: (706) 795-3354.

Fax: (706) 795-5933

ROZIER, Franklin D., Jr. *(Judge, State Court of Pierce County)* Elected to term beginning Jan 1, 1999. Reelected 2002, current term expires Dec 31, 2006. Serves part time.

Mailing address: P.O. Box 186, Blackshear 31516-0186.

Telephone: (912) 449-4493.

Fax: (912) 449-4485

RUFFIN, John H., Jr. *(Judge, Court of Appeals of Georgia)* Appointed by Governor Zell Miller to term beginning Aug 24, 1994. Currently serves as Presiding Judge. Born Waynesboro Georgia. Educated at Morehouse College and Howard University School of Law. Admitted to practice Georgia 1961, U.S. District Courts Middle and Southern Districts of Georgia, U.S. Court of Appeals Eleventh Circuit and U.S. Supreme Court. Judge, Superior Court of Georgia Augusta Judicial Circuit 1986-94.

Member Georgia Association of Criminal Defense Lawyers, Georgia Conference of Black Lawyers, Inc., Council of Superior Court Judges of Georgia, Council of Juvenile Court Judges of Georgia, American Judicature Society, State Bar of Georgia, Atlanta, Augusta, National and American Bar Associations.

Office: 334 State Judicial Building, Atlanta 30334.

Telephone: (404) 656-3458.

Fax: (404) 651-8139

E-mail address: ruffinj@appeals.courts.state.ga.us

RUSSELL, Constance C. *(Judge, Superior Court of Georgia Atlanta Judicial Circuit)* Appointed by Governor Zell Miller to term beginning March 4, 1996. Elected 1996 and 2000. Current term expires Dec 31, 2004.

Office: T5705 Justice Center Tower, 185 Central Avenue S.W., Atlanta 30303.

Telephone: (404) 335-2803.

Fax: (404) 335-2814

RUSSELL, Robert L., III *(Judge, Superior Court of Georgia Atlantic Judicial Circuit)* Appointed by Governor Zell Miller to term beginning Aug 9, 1995. Elected 1996 and 2000. Current term expires Dec 31, 2004.

Mailing address: P.O. Box 581, Darien 31305-0581.

Telephone: (912) 437-3033.

Fax: (912) 437-3034

RUTROUGH, Elizabeth *(Associate Judge, Juvenile Court of Georgia Dublin Judicial Circuit)* Appointed.

Mailing address: P.O. Box 2069, Dublin 31040.

Telephone: (478) 272-4131.

Fax: (478) 272-1639

ST. GERMAINE, Curtis *(Chief Magistrate, Magistrate Court of Burke County)*

Mailing address: P.O. Box 401, Waynesboro 30830-0401.

Telephone: (706) 554-4281.

Fax: (706) 554-8772

E-mail address: cjudgecurt@aol.com

SALMON, F. Larry *(Judge, Superior Court of Georgia Rome Judicial Circuit)* Elected to term beginning Jan 1, 1989. Reelected 1992, 1996 and 2000. Current term expires Dec 31, 2004. Born Rome Georgia March 29, 1938. Baptist. Educated at University of Georgia B.B.A. 1962 J.D. 1963. Member Phi Delta Phi. Admitted to practice Georgia 1962, U.S. District Courts Middle 1962 and Northern 1963 Districts of Georgia, U.S. Courts of Appeals Fifth and Eleventh Circuits and U.S. Supreme Court. In legal practice Rome 1963-69 and 1985-89.

Assistant Solicitor General 1966-69 and District Attorney 1969-85 Rome Judicial Circuit. Visiting Instructor in Evidence Regional Police Academy Floyd College 1983-85. President District Attorneys Association of Georgia 1976. Chairman Prosecuting Attorney's Council of Georgia 1979 and 1982-83. Vice Chairman Georgia Courts Automation Commission 1992-95. Member State Bar of Georgia (Chairman Criminal Law Section 1973-74) and American Bar Association. Attended The National Judicial College. Member Judicial Planning Commission of Georgia 1979-82, Criminal Justice Coordinating Commit-

SALMON, F. LARRY—*Continued*

tee of Georgia 1982-83 and Georgia Crime Commission. Interests include basketball and computers.

Office: 312 Floyd County Courthouse, Three Government Plaza, Rome 30161.
Telephone: (706) 291-5121.
Fax: (706) 291-5278
E-mail address: salmon1@floydsuperiorcourt.org

SALTER, John F., Sr. *(Judge, State Court of Dougherty County)*
Mailing address: P.O. Box 1827, Albany 31702-1827.
Telephone: (229) 431-2152.
Fax: (229) 431-3282
E-mail address: salterjohnsalter@netscape.net

SAMS, W. Fletcher *(Judge, State Court of Fayette County)* Elected to term beginning Jan 1, 1997. Reelected 2000, current term expires Dec 31, 2004.
Mailing address: P.O. Box 1659, Fayetteville 30214.
Telephone: (770) 716-0836.
Fax: (770) 716-8948
E-mail address: fletcher@admin.co.fayette.ga.us

SANDERS, Rubie Nell *(Judge, Probate Court of Montgomery County)*
Mailing address: P.O. Box 444, Mt. Vernon 30445-0444.
Telephone: (912) 583-2681.
Fax: (912) 583-4343
E-mail address: rmoxsand@hotmail.com

SANDS, W. Louis *(Chief Judge, United States District Court Middle District of Georgia)* Appointed for life by President Bill Clinton to term beginning 1994. Chief Judge since Feb 2, 2001. Born Bradley Georgia April 12, 1949. Educated at Mercer University B.A. 1971 J.D. 1974. In legal practice Macon 1987-91. Judge, Superior Court of Georgia Macon Judicial Circuit 1991-93.

Assistant District Attorney Macon Judicial Circuit 1975-78. Assistant U.S. Attorney Middle District of Georgia 1978-87.
Mailing address: P.O. Box 1705, Albany 31702-1705.
Telephone: (229) 430-8553.

SCALES, Juliette Wiltshire *(Associate Judge, Juvenile Court of Georgia Atlanta Judicial Circuit)* Appointed.
Office: Justice Center, 395 Pryor Street, Third Floor, Atlanta 30312.
Telephone: (404) 224-4881.
Fax: (404) 730-1121

SCARBOROUGH, Vickie B. *(Chief Magistrate, Magistrate Court of Telfair County)* Elected to term beginning Jan 1, 1997. Reelected 2000, current term expires Dec 31, 2004.
Office: 128 East Oak Street, Suite 5, McRae 31055.
Telephone: (229) 868-6772.
Fax: (229) 868-7956
E-mail address: vscar_2000@yahoo.com

SCARLETT, Stephen G. *(Judge, Superior Court of Georgia Brunswick Judicial Circuit)*
Office: Glynn County Courthouse, 701 H Street, Box 203, Brunswick 31520.
Telephone: (912) 554-7356.
Fax: (912) 267-0895

SCHELL, Tarey *(Associate Judge, Juvenile Court of Georgia Griffin Judicial Circuit)* Appointed.
Office: 165 South Jeff Davis Drive, Fayetteville 30214.
Telephone: (770) 460-7125.
Fax: (770) 460-0170

SCHNEIDER, William *(Judge, Juvenile Court of Georgia Rockdale Judicial Circuit)* Former Associate Judge. Appointed Judge.
Mailing address: P.O. Box 452, Conyers 30012-0452.
Telephone: (770) 388-5077.
Fax: (770) 388-5035
E-mail address: william.schneider@rockdalecounty.org

SCHUENEMANN, June *(Chief Magistrate, Magistrate Court of Barrow County)*
Office: 30 North Broad Street, Room 321, Winder 30680.
Telephone: (770) 307-3050.
Fax: (770) 868-1440

SCHUSTER, Stephen *(Judge, Juvenile Court of Georgia Cobb Judicial Circuit)* Appointed.
Office: 1738 County Services Parkway S.W., Marietta 30008.
Telephone: (770) 528-2426.
Fax: (770) 528-2232
E-mail address: stephen.schuster@cobbcounty.org

SCOFIELD, E. Clayton, III *(Magistrate Judge, United States District Court Northern District of Georgia)* Appointed by U.S. District Court judges to term beginning May 1998. Term expires May 2006. Born Atlanta Georgia June 4, 1950. Educated at Duke University B.A. cum laude 1972 and University of Georgia J.D. cum laude 1975. Notes Editor Georgia Law Review 1973-75. Law Clerk to Hon. Anthony A. Alaimo, U.S. District Court Southern District of Georgia 1975-77. Admitted to practice Georgia 1975, U.S. District Courts Southern 1975 and Northern Districts of Georgia and U.S. Courts of Appeals Fifth and Eleventh Circuits. In legal practice Atlanta 1977-98.

Member Atlanta Lawyers Club, Atlanta (President 1996) and American Bar Associations.
Office: 1683 U.S. Courthouse, 75 Spring Street S.W., Atlanta 30303-3361.
Telephone: (404) 215-1380.

SCOGGIN, Robert Lee "Bob" *(Senior Judge, Superior Court of Georgia)* Elected Sept 1962 to term beginning Jan 1, 1963. Reelected to subsequent terms. Assumed Senior status Dec 30, 1974, serves when called. Appointed Judge Emeritus by Governor Jimmy Carter Dec 30, 1974. Born Rome Georgia Jan 13, 1923. Baptist. Educated at Berry College B.S. 1944. Awarded honorary LL.D. John Marshall Law School 1969. Admitted to practice Georgia 1947. Began legal practice Rome 1947.

Assistant Solicitor Rome Judicial Circuit 1951-52. Member State Bar of Georgia and Rome Judicial Circuit Bar Association. Attended National Judicial College University of Pennsylvania 1967. Lieutenant j.g. USN 1944-46. Democrat. Georgia House of Representatives 1949-62 (Speaker Pro Tem 1961-62). Member Civitan, Masons, American Legion, VFW, Amvets and Elks.
Mailing address: P.O. Box 578, Woodbine 31569.

SCOGGINS, Mitchell *(Judge, Probate Court of Bartow County)*
Office: 133 West Cherokee Avenue, Suite 243A, Cartersville 30120-3101.
Telephone: (770) 387-5075.
Fax: (770) 387-5074

SEARS, Donald W. *(Chief Magistrate, Magistrate Court of Appling County)* Elected to term beginning Jan 1, 1999. Reelected 2002, current term expires Dec 31, 2006.
Mailing address: P.O. Box 366, Baxley 31515-0366.
Telephone: (912) 367-8116.
Fax: (912) 367-8182

SEARS, Leah *(Presiding Justice, Supreme Court of Georgia)* Born Heidelberg Germany June 13, 1955. Presbyterian. Educated at Cornell University B.S. with honors 1976, Emory University School of Law J.D. 1980 and University of Nevada Reno 1987 and 1989. Member Alpha Kappa Alpha. Admitted to practice Georgia 1980, U.S. District Court Northern District of Georgia 1980 and U.S. Court of Appeals Eleventh Circuit 1981. In legal practice Atlanta 1980-85. Judge pro hac vice 1982-85 and Judge 1985-88, City Court of Atlanta. Former Judge, Superior Court of Georgia Atlanta Judicial Circuit, elected to term beginning Jan 1, 1989. First woman to serve on Superior Court of Georgia Atlanta Judicial Circuit 1989. First black woman and youngest judge to serve Superior Court of Georgia.

Author "Buckle Up" *Southline* Feb 1987; "Should Blacks Celebrate the Constitution" *Southline* Sept 1987; "The Importance of Our Courts of First Resort" *Court Review Magazine* Nov 1987, excerpted in *The Fulton County Daily Report* July 9, 1987 and *The National Law Journal* Oct 19, 1987; "Alienation from Courts a Barrier to Rural Justice" *The Atlanta Journal/ Constitution* Jan 1988; and "Settlement Week: A View from the Bench" *The Atlanta Lawyer* Feb 1991. Important Decisions: The Atlanta Journal and The Atlanta Constitution, a Division of Cox Enterprises, Inc., a Delaware Corporation, and Mark Sherman, individually and as one of the staff writers v. Carole Dortch, in her official capacity as Director of the Bureau of General Services for the City of Atlanta and the Bureau of General Services for the City of Atlanta Sept 1990 and Rebecka L. Mendenhall v. Steven P. Garvey Feb 1990. Board Member Georgia Association for Women Lawyers. Founding President and Committee Member Georgia Association of Black Women Attorneys. Member National Association of Women Judges (Board Member Women Judges' Fund for Justice, Member Committee on Judicial Selection and Resolutions and National Task Force on Gender Bias in the Court), American Judicature Society, State Bar of Georgia (Chair Alcohol and Drug Awareness Counselors and Executive Council Young Lawyers Section, Advisory Member Public Relations Committee, Member Committee to Advise Office of General Counsel and Commission on Children and the Courts), Atlanta, Gate City, National and American Bar Associations.

Leader "You Be the Judge Seminar" National Association of Women Judges Feb 1990. Attended Professional Ethics and Malpractice Seminar ICLE Dec 14, 1990. Recipient Award for Community Service from Atlanta Chapter NAACP 1988, Distinguished Leadership Award for Outstanding Service in the Judiciary 1988 and Certificate of Appreciation from Fulton County 1989. Honored in Salute to African-American Business and Professional Women by *Dollars and Sense Magazine* 1990 and as Black Woman of Achievement by Southern Bell 1990. Featured in 1990-91 Calendar of Black History Southern Bell 1990. Named Outstanding Young Woman of America by Jaycees. First black female attorney with a large Atlanta law firm. Previously worked as reporter for *Columbus Ledger* Columbus Georgia 1976-77. Founder Battered Women's Project of Columbus Georgia. Executive Committee Member Greater Atlanta Club National Association of Negro Business and Professional Women (Past President). Board Member AMC Cancer Research Center, Atlanta Chapter American Red Cross and Affordable Houses, Inc. Board Nominee Georgia Chapter The National Council of Christians and Jews. Advisory Board Member Outdoor Activity Nature Center. Recruiter Southeastern Region Cornell University Alumni Club. Former Member Leadership Atlanta. Member National Association of Alcoholism and Drug Abuse Counselors, American Business Women's Association, The Georgia Addiction Counselor's Association, Joint Center for Political Studies, The High Museum of Art Member's Guild, Women's Forum of Georgia, Inc. of International Women's Forum, Kiwanis Club of Central Atlanta and Ebenezer Baptist Church. Hobbies include writing.
Office: 501 State Judicial Building, Atlanta 30334.
Telephone: (404) 656-3474.
Fax: (404) 657-6997
E-mail address: searsl@supreme.courts.state.ga.us

SECKINGER, Frances Y. *(Judge, Probate Court of Effingham County)*
Mailing address: P.O. Box 387, Springfield 31329-0387.
Office: 901 Pine Street, Springfield 31329.
Telephone: (912) 754-2112.
Fax: (912) 754-7516
E-mail address: fseckinger@effinghamcounty.org

SEELIGER, Clarence F. *(Judge, Superior Court of Georgia Stone Mountain Judicial Circuit)* Elected to term beginning Jan 1, 1985. Reelected 1988, 1992, 1996 and 2000. Current term expires Dec 31, 2004. Born Seattle Washington Nov 23, 1940. Episcopalian. Educated at University of Washington B.A. 1963 and Emory University School of Law J.D. 1970. Member Acacia Fraternity and Phi Alpha Delta. Admitted to practice Georgia 1970. Began legal practice Atlanta 1970. In legal practice Decatur 1971-80. Judge, State Court of DeKalb County 1981-84.

Member State Bar of Georgia, Decatur-DeKalb, Atlanta and American Bar Associations. Recipient Human Relations Award for Government from DeKalb Community Relations Commissions 1983 and Order of Pythagoras Award for community service from Acacia Fraternity 1989. Captain USAF 1963-67. Member DeKalb County Elections Board 1975-79 (Chairman 1979). Member and Treasurer Board for Trinity Child Development Center (Decatur Head Start 1985-88). Interests include walking, basketball and reading history and politics.
Office: 303 DeKalb County Courthouse, 556 North McDonough Street, Decatur 30030.
Telephone: (404) 371-2336.
Fax: (404) 371-2066
E-mail address: cseelig@co.dekalb.ga.us

SELF, William J., II *(Judge, Probate Court of Bibb County)* Elected at special election to term beginning April 18, 1989. Reelected Nov 3, 1992, Nov 5, 1996

SELF, WILLIAM J., II—*Continued*

and 2000. Current term expires Dec 31, 2004. Born Macon Georgia Jan 17, 1949. Baptist. Educated at University of Georgia B.B.A. 1971 J.D. 1974. Admitted to practice Georgia 1974 and U.S. District Court Middle District of Georgia 1974. In legal practice Macon 1974-89.

Member Council of Probate Judges of Georgia, American Judges Association, State Bar of Georgia, Macon and American Bar Associations.

Mailing address: P.O. Box 6518, Macon 31208-6518.
Office: 207 Bibb County Courthouse, Macon 31201.
Telephone: (478) 621-6494.
Fax: (478) 621-6686
E-mail address: wself@co.bibb.ga.us

SEXTON, Susan *(Judge, Probate Court of Elbert County)*

Office: Elbert County Courthouse, Elberton 30635-1800.
Telephone: (706) 283-2016.
Fax: (706) 283-9668

SHAFER, Carson B. *(Senior Judge, City Court of Atlanta)* Appointed by mayor. Assumed Senior status, serves when called.

Office: 104 Trinity Avenue S.W., Atlanta 30303.
Telephone: (404) 658-6919.
Fax: (404) 658-7125

SHAW, Charles R. *(Chief Magistrate, Magistrate Court of Lanier County)*

Office: Lanier County Courthouse, 100 Main Street, Lakeland 31635.
Telephone: (229) 482-2207.
Fax: (229) 482-8333
E-mail address: laniermag@usa.net

SHEARER, Robin W. *(Associate Judge, Juvenile Court of Georgia Western Judicial Circuit)* Appointed.

Office: 115 Clarke County Courthouse, 325 East Washington Street, Athens 30601.
Telephone: (706) 613-3300.
Fax: (706) 613-3306
E-mail address: rwshearer1@aol.com

SHEPPARD, Clayton C. *(Chief Magistrate, Magistrate Court of Washington County)* Elected to term beginning Jan 1, 1997. Reelected 2000, current term expires Dec 31, 2004.

Mailing address: P.O. Box 1053, Sandersville 31082-1053.
Telephone: (478) 552-3591.
Fax: (478) 552-7424

SHIVERS, Melessa *(Judge, Probate Court of Clay County)*

Mailing address: P.O. Box 448, Fort Gaines 39851.
Office: 210 South Washington, Fort Gaines 39851.
Telephone: (229) 768-2445.
Fax: (229) 768-2710

SHOOB, Marvin H. *(Senior Judge, United States District Court Northern District of Georgia)* Appointed for life by President Jimmy Carter to term beginning 1979. Assumed Senior status Sept 30, 1991, serves by assignment. Born Walterboro South Carolina Feb 23, 1923. Educated at University of Georgia School of Law J.D. 1948. In legal practice Atlanta 1948-79.

Office: 1767 U.S. Courthouse, 75 Spring Street S.W., Atlanta 30303-3361.
Telephone: (404) 215-1470.

SHOOB, Wendy L. *(Judge, Superior Court of Georgia Atlanta Judicial Circuit)* Appointed by Governor Zell Miller to term beginning March 4, 1996. Elected 1996 and 2000. Current term expires Dec 31, 2004. Born Atlanta Georgia Feb 14, 1954. Educated at University of Virginia B.A. with distinction 1974 and Mercer University J.D. 1977. Admitted to practice Georgia 1978 and U.S. District Court Northern District of Georgia 1978. In legal practice Atlanta 1987-92. Judge, State Court of Fulton County 1992-96.

Trial Attorney U.S. Equal Employment Opportunity Commission Denver Colorado and Los Angeles California 1978-79. Assistant District Attorney Fulton County 1979-87. Member Georgia Association for Women Lawyers (Past President), Council of Superior Court Judges of Georgia, National Association of Women Judges, State Bar of Georgia (Investigative Panel 1991-92, Board of Governors 1992-96, Disciplinary Rules and Procedures Committee 1992-96) and Atlanta Bar Association (Judicial Selection and Tenure Committee 1990-92, Board of Directors 1990-95). Listed in *Who's Who Among Rising Young Americans* 1992. Board of Directors Metropolitan Atlanta YMCA. Member Leadership Atlanta 1994, Junior League of Atlanta and Lawyers Club of Atlanta.

Office: T7905 Justice Center Tower, 185 Central Avenue, Atlanta 30303-3643.
Telephone: (404) 335-2812.
Fax: (404) 335-2824

SHULMAN, Arnold *(Senior Judge, Court of Appeals of Georgia)* Appointed by Governor George D. Busbee to term beginning Jan 7, 1977. Elected to subsequent terms. Assumed Senior status, serves when called. Born Philadelphia Pennsylvania. Jewish. Educated at Emory University and University of Georgia School of Law J.D. Admitted to practice Georgia 1937. In legal practice Atlanta 1937-77.

Author five editions *Georgia Practice and Procedure.* Professor Atlanta Law School 1960-75. Adjunct Professor Georgia State University College of Law 1983-85. Member Lawyers Club of Atlanta, State Bar of Georgia, Atlanta and American Bar Associations. Served First Infantry to Captain Air Corps 1941-46. Law Member General Court Martial 1944.

Mailing address: 1527 September Chase, Decatur 30033.

SHUMAN, Gordon S. *(Judge, Probate Court of McIntosh County)* Elected to term beginning Jan 1, 1985. Reelected 1988, 1992, 1996 and 2000. Current term expires Dec 31, 2004. Born Bryan County Georgia Sept 17, 1935. Baptist. Judge, Small Claims Court of McIntosh County 1980-83. Chief Magistrate, Magistrate Court of McIntosh County 1983-84.

Interests include church activities, fishing and hunting.
Mailing address: P.O. Box 453, Darien 31305-0453.
Telephone: (912) 437-6636.
Fax: (912) 437-6635

SHURLING, William M., III *(Judge, Civil Court of Bibb County)*
Office: 101 Bibb County Courthouse, Macon 31201.
Telephone: (478) 621-6505.

SIMMONS, Lanie J. *(Chief Magistrate, Magistrate Court of Elbert County)* Appointed to term beginning July 20, 1996. Elected 2000, current term expires Dec 31, 2004.
Mailing address: P.O. Box 763, Elberton 30635-0763.
Telephone: (706) 283-2027.
Fax: (706) 283-2004

SIMMONS, Matthew O. *(Chief Judge, Superior Court of Georgia Clayton Judicial Circuit)*
Office: 9151 Tara Boulevard, Jonesboro 30236.
Telephone: (770) 477-3484.
Fax: (770) 477-3487
E-mail address: Mattsimmons.CSCJ@hotoffice.net

SIMONTON, DeWitt W., Jr. *(Judge, Probate Court of Spalding County)* Elected at special election to term beginning Dec 1985. Reelected 1988, 1992, 1996 and 2000. Current term expires Dec 31, 2004. Born Griffin Georgia Nov 22, 1932. Baptist. Educated at West Georgia College 1951 and Atlanta Business College 1952.
Staff Sergeant USAF 1953-57. Former Coroner of Spalding County. Member First Baptist Church.
Office: Spalding County Courthouse, 132 East Solomon Street, Griffin 30223.
Telephone: (770) 467-4340.
Fax: (770) 467-4243

SIMPSON, John *(Judge, Superior Court of Georgia Coweta Judicial Circuit)* Elected to term beginning Jan 1, 1997. Reelected 2000, current term expires Dec 31, 2004.
Mailing address: P.O. Box 338, Carrollton 30112.
Telephone: (770) 830-5855.
Fax: (770) 830-5857

SIRMANS, Ruby K. *(Judge, Probate Court of Lowndes County)*
Mailing address: P.O. Box 72, Valdosta 31603-0072.
Telephone: (229) 333-5103.
Fax: (229) 333-7646

SIZEMORE, Lamar W., Jr. *(Judge, Superior Court of Georgia Macon Judicial Circuit)*
Office: 310 Bibb County Courthouse, Macon 31201.
Telephone: (478) 621-6535.
Fax: (478) 621-6581
E-mail address: lsizemore@co.bibb.ga.us

SKIPPER, Lani *(Associate Judge, Juvenile Court of Georgia Paulding Judicial Circuit)* Appointed.
Office: 367 West Memorial Drive, Dallas 30132.
Telephone: (770) 445-4438.

SLABY, Richard A. *(Judge, State Court of Richmond County)* Appointed by Governor Zell Miller to term beginning July 23, 1997. Elected 1998 and 2002. Current term expires Dec 31, 2006. Serves Division One. Former Associate Judge, Juvenile Court of Richmond County.
Office: A-211 Law Enforcement Center, 401 Walton Way, Augusta 30901.
Telephone: (706) 821-2582.
Fax: (706) 821-1177
E-mail address: rs1319@co.richmond.ga.us

SMITH, Bob *(Judge, Probate Court of Hart County)*
Mailing address: P.O. Box 1159, Hartwell 30643-1159.
Telephone: (706) 376-2565.
Fax: (706) 376-9032
E-mail address: probatecourt@hartcom.net

SMITH, Dale P. *(Chief Magistrate, Magistrate Court of Stephens County)*
Office: 205 North Alexander Street, Room 107, Toccoa 30577.
Telephone: (706) 886-6205.
Fax: (706) 886-5569

SMITH, David K. *(Judge, Superior Court of Georgia Cherokee Judicial Circuit)* Appointed by Governor Roy Barnes Jan 3, 2001. Elected Aug 20, 2002, current term expires Dec 31, 2006. Born Rome Georgia Oct 15, 1960. Baptist. Educated at Emory University B.A. 1982 and University of Georgia 1985. Admitted to practice Georgia 1985. In legal practice Calhoun 1985-2001.
Member State Bar of Georgia and Gordon County Bar Association.
Mailing address: P.O. Box 1809, Calhoun 30703-1809.
Telephone: (706) 629-7763.

SMITH, E. Byron *(Chief Judge, Superior Court of Georgia Towaliga Judicial Circuit)* Term expires Jan 1, 2005. Former Judge, Superior Court of Georgia Flint Judicial Circuit.
Mailing address: P.O. Box 5, Barnesville 30204.
Office: Lamar County Courthouse, Barnesville 30204.
Telephone: (770) 358-5156.
Fax: (770) 358-5314

SMITH, G. R. *(Magistrate Judge, United States District Court Southern District of Georgia)* Appointed by U.S. District Court judges to term beginning 1988. Reappointed 1996, current term expires 2004.
Mailing address: P.O. Box 8286, Savannah 31412.
Telephone: (912) 650-4020.

SMITH, Gail *(Chief Magistrate, Magistrate Court of Oglethorpe County)*
Mailing address: P.O. Box 356, Lexington 30648-0356.
Telephone: (706) 743-8321.
Fax: (706) 743-3177

SMITH, J. D. *(Chief Judge, Court of Appeals of Georgia)* Former Presiding Judge. Former Judge and Chief Judge, Superior Court of Georgia Northeastern Judicial Circuit.
Office: 407 State Judicial Building, Atlanta 30334.
Telephone: (404) 656-3453.

SMITH, Ken W. *(Judge, State Court of Jeff Davis County and Judge, Juvenile Court of Georgia Brunswick Judicial Circuit)* Former Associate Judge. Appointed Judge Juvenile Court.
Mailing address: P.O. Drawer 1745, Hazlehurst 31539-1745.
Office: 53 South Tallahassee Street, Hazlehurst 31539.
Telephone: (912) 375-7797.
Fax: (912) 375-7736
E-mail address: kwslaw1@bellsouth.net

SMITH, Lisa Young *(Judge, City Court of Atlanta)* Appointed by mayor.
Office: 104 Trinity Avenue, Atlanta 30303.
Telephone: (404) 658-6919.
Fax: (404) 658-7125
E-mail address: lsmith@ci.atlanta.ga.us

SMITH, Oscar D., Jr. *(Senior Judge, Superior Court of Georgia)* Elected to term beginning Jan 1, 1970. Reelected to subsequent terms. Assumed Senior status, serves when called. Born Columbus Georgia July 21, 1920. Member First Presbyterian Church. Educated at Georgia Southwestern College 1938-40 and University of Virginia 1946-47. Admitted to practice Georgia 1947. Judge, Columbus City Court 1962-69.
Member Columbus Lawyers Club and State Bar of Georgia. Major USAS 1941-45. Member Reserve Officers Association.
Mailing address: 1243 Forest Avenue, Columbus 31906-2535.

SMITH, Philip C. *(Judge, State Court of Forsyth County)*
Office: 100 West Courthouse Square, Suite 200, Cumming 30040.
Telephone: (770) 781-2136.

SMITH, R. Rucker *(Chief Judge, Superior Court of Georgia Southwestern Judicial Circuit)* Elected 1992 to term beginning Jan 4, 1993. Reelected 1996 and 2000. Current term expires Jan 1, 2005. Born Americus Georgia Oct 15, 1953. Methodist. Educated at University of Florida B.A. 1976 and Emory University LL.B. 1979. Admitted to practice Georgia 1979, U.S. District Courts Northern 1979 and Middle 1982 Districts of Georgia, U.S. Courts of Appeals Fifth 1980 and Eleventh 1981 Circuits and U.S. Tax Court 1982. In legal practice Atlanta 1979-81.
Assistant 1981-83 and Chief Assistant 1983-92 District Attorney Southwestern Judicial Circuit. Board of Governors State Bar of Georgia. Member Council of Superior Court Judges of Georgia. Named Outstanding Young Man of Sumter County by Jaycees 1984. Member Rules Committee Georgia State Democratic Committee Atlanta since 1990. President Sumter Historical Society 1991 and Sumter County Council on Child Abuse 1992. Member Kiwanis. Enjoys tennis, golf and running.
Mailing address: P.O. Box 784, Americus 31709-0784.
Telephone: (229) 928-4554.
Fax: (229) 928-4552
E-mail address: smithr@gajudges.org

SMITH, Ralph C., Jr. *(Chief Magistrate, Magistrate Court of Decatur County)*
Office: 912 Spring Creek Road, Box 3, Bainbridge 31717-3556.
Telephone: (229) 248-3014.
Fax: (229) 248-3862

SMITH, Stan *(Judge, Superior Court of Georgia Dublin Judicial Circuit)* Elected July 2000 to term beginning Jan 1, 2001. Term expires Dec 31, 2004. Born Macon Georgia Jan 16, 1951. Baptist. Educated at Mercer University A.B. 1973 J.D. 1977 and Georgia College 1974. Admitted to practice Georgia 1977. In legal practice Dublin 1979-2000. Former Part-time Judge, Juvenile Court of Laurens County.
Mailing address: P.O. Box 2069, Dublin 31040-2069.
Telephone: (478) 272-4131.
Fax: (478) 272-1639

SMITH, William J. *(Senior Judge, Superior Court of Georgia)* Served Chattahoochee Judicial Circuit. Assumed Senior status, serves when called.
Mailing address: P.O. Box 1340, Columbus 31902-1340.
Telephone: (706) 653-4265.
Fax: (706) 653-4268
E-mail address: smithwill@mindspring.com

SOGNIER, John W. *(Senior Judge, Court of Appeals of Georgia)* Assumed Senior status, serves when called.
Mailing address: 5675 Lake Island Drive, Atlanta 30327.

SOLOMON, Herbie *(Judge, Juvenile Court of Georgia Dougherty Judicial Circuit)* Appointed.
Mailing address: P.O. Box 1827, Albany 31702-1827.
Telephone: (229) 431-2162.
Fax: (229) 434-2665
E-mail address: hsololaw@surfsouth.com

SORRELLS, Marvin Williams *(Chief Judge, Superior Court of Georgia Alcovy Judicial Circuit)* Appointed by Governor Joe Frank Harris to term beginning Sept 1, 1988. Elected 1988, 1996 and 2000. Current term expires Dec 31, 2004. Currently serves as Administrative Judge District Ten. Born Walton County Georgia Dec 7, 1936. Educated at University of Georgia B.B.A. 1959 LL.B. 1962. Admitted to practice Georgia 1961, U.S. District Court 1962 and U.S. Court of Appeals Fifth Circuit 1963. Began legal practice Monroe 1963. Judge, Juvenile Court of Walton County 1973-88.
Sheriff 1962 and Deputy Sheriff 1962 to Aug 13, 1963 Walton County. Probation Officer 1964-68 and Referee 1968-73 Juvenile Court. Member Council of Juvenile Court Judges of Georgia, State Bar of Georgia, Walton County (Past President) and Alcovy (President 1973-74, Chairman Grievance Committee 1975) Bar Associations. Member and Elder First Christian Church. Enjoys woodwork and the study of history.
Mailing address: P.O. Box 805, Monroe 30655-0805.
Telephone: (770) 267-1339.
Fax: (770) 267-1396

SOUTH, Pamela D. *(Judge, State Court of Gwinnett County)*
Office: Gwinnett Justice Center, 75 Langley Drive, Lawrenceville 30045-6935.
Telephone: (770) 822-8554.
Fax: (770) 822-8513
E-mail address: southpam@co.gwinnett.ga.us

SPIRES, Janice Davidson *(Judge, Probate Court of Houston County)* Elected to term beginning Jan 1, 1997. Reelected 2000, current term expires Dec 31, 2004.
Mailing address: P.O. Box 1801, Perry 31069-1801.
Telephone: (478) 987-2770.
Fax: (478) 988-4500
E-mail address: hcprobate2002@yahoo.com

SPIVEY, Philip *(Judge, Juvenile Court of Georgia Ocmulgee Judicial Circuit)* Appointed.
Mailing address: P.O. Box 1810, Milledgeville 31059.
Office: Baldwin County Courthouse, Milledgeville 31059.
Telephone: (478) 445-7060.
Fax: (478) 445-7059
E-mail address: juvenilect@alltel.net

STALEY, Mary Ellen *(Judge, Superior Court of Georgia Cobb Judicial Circuit)* Elected to term beginning Jan 1, 1993. Reelected 1996 and 2000. Current term expires Dec 31, 2004. Born Memphis Tennessee March 4, 1953. Educated at West Georgia University B.A. with honors 1975 and University of Georgia J.D. 1978. Admitted to practice Georgia 1978 and U.S. Supreme Court 1982. Magistrate, Magistrate Court of Cobb County 1982-83. Associate Judge 1983-84 and Judge 1984-92, State Court of Cobb County.
Assistant District Attorney Cobb Judicial Circuit 1978-82. Member Executive Committee Weltner Family Law Inns of Court. Member Council of Superior Court Judges of Georgia, American Judicature Society, State Bar of Georgia and Cobb County Bar Association. Named American Business Woman of the Year by American Business Women's Association 1987, one of Ten Outstanding Young Women of America 1987 and YWCA Woman of Achievement 1994. Former Chair Cobb Art Board. Past President Marietta Civitan Club. Member Marietta Kiwanis Club.
Office: 30 Waddell Street, Marietta 30090.
Telephone: (770) 528-1816.
Fax: (770) 528-1821

STAPLER, Evan Lee *(Chief Magistrate, Magistrate Court of Haralson County)*
Mailing address: P.O. Box 1040, Buchanan 30113.
Telephone: (770) 646-2015.
Fax: (770) 646-2017

STARK, Homer W. *(Senior Judge, Superior Court of Georgia)* Appointed by Governor George Busbee to term beginning July 1, 1977. Elected to subsequent terms. Assumed Senior status Jan 1, 1999, serves when called.
Office: 75 Langley Drive, Lawrenceville 30045.
Telephone: (770) 822-8616.
Fax: (770) 822-8642

STEDMAN, Juanita *(Judge, Juvenile Court of Georgia Cobb Judicial Circuit)* Appointed. Former Chief Judge. Currently serves as Presiding Judge.
Office: 1738 County Services Parkway S.W., Marietta 30008.
Telephone: (770) 528-2224.
Fax: (770) 528-2232
E-mail address: jdstedman@cobbcounty.org

STEEDLEY, Annie Ruth *(Chief Magistrate, Magistrate Court of Clinch County)*
Office: 100 Courthouse Square, Homerville 31634.
Telephone: (912) 487-2514.
Fax: (912) 487-3658
E-mail address: chief1@surfsouth.com

STEPHENS, Lawton E. *(Chief Judge, Superior Court of Georgia Western Judicial Circuit)* Appointed by Governor Zell Miller to term beginning May 1, 1991. Elected 1996 and 2000. Current term expires Dec 31, 2004. Born Athens Georgia Nov 14, 1954. Presbyterian. Educated at University of North Carolina B.A. 1977 and University of Georgia School of Law J.D. 1981. Member Phi Delta Phi and Gridiron. Admitted to practice Georgia 1981, U.S. District Courts Middle and Southern Districts of Georgia and U.S. Court of Appeals Eleventh Circuit. In legal practice Athens 1981-91.
Assistant Solicitor State Court of Clarke County 1986-87. Important Decisions: Doe v. Red & Black Publishing Co. (freedom of information) 437 SE 2d 474, 1993; Hospital Authority of Clarke County v. Martin (punitive damages) 438 SE 2d 103, 1993; and Martin v. State (search and seizure) 448 SE 2d 57, 1993. Chairman of Board Institute for Continuing Judicial Education. Member Council of Superior Court Judges of Georgia (Immediate Past President) and State Bar of Georgia. Attended General Jurisdiction Course The National Judicial College. Recipient Arch Award from University of Georgia Alumni Society. State Representative Georgia House of Representatives 1987-91. Enjoys water skiing and coaching baseball and basketball.
Mailing address: P.O. Box 8064, Athens 30603-8064.
Telephone: (706) 613-3175.
Fax: (706) 613-3179

STEPHENSON, Martha King *(Judge, Probate Court of Fayette County)* Elected to term beginning Jan 1, 1993. Reelected 1996 and 2000. Current term expires Dec 31, 2004. Born Atlanta Georgia Sept 22, 1930. Methodist. Educated at Mercer University 1952 and Woodrow Wilson College of Law J.D. cum laude 1980. Admitted to practice Georgia 1980, U.S. District Court District of Georgia 1981 and U.S. Court of Appeals Eleventh Circuit 1981. In legal practice Fayetteville 1980-93.
Member Fayette County Zoning Board of Appeals 1990-93. Member State Bar of Georgia and Fayette County Bar Association (Former Secretary-Treasurer). Participant in twenty-one hours of continuing judicial education 1992 and twelve hours of continuing legal education annually. Republican. Board Member Youth Protection Home. Board of Trustees First United Methodist Church. Member Fayette County Chamber of Commerce. Enjoys piano and organ music and oil painting.
Office: 145 Johnson Avenue, Fayetteville 30214-2079.
Telephone: (770) 461-9555.
Fax: (770) 460-8685

STEPHENSON, Nancy Smith *(Judge, Probate Court of Dougherty County)* Elected Nov 1992 to term beginning Jan 1, 1993. Reelected Nov 1996 and Nov 2000. Current term expires Dec 31, 2004. Born Tifton Georgia. Methodist. Educated at University of Georgia A.B. 1978 J.D. 1981. Admitted to practice Georgia 1981 and U.S. Court of Appeals Eleventh Circuit 1981. In legal practice Albany 1987-92.
Assistant District Attorney Dougherty County 1985-87. Member Southwest Georgia Probate Judges Association, Council of Probate Court Judges of Georgia and Dougherty Bar Association. Board of Directors Southwest Georgia Council on Aging and Albany Community Hospice. Board of Trustees Deerfield Windsor Academy.
Mailing address: P.O. Box 1827, Albany 31702.
Office: 225 Pine Avenue, Suite 124, Albany 31701.
Telephone: (229) 431-2102.
Fax: (229) 434-2694
E-mail address: NSSPROBATE@netscape.net

STODDARD, Michael *(Chief Judge, Superior Court of Georgia Cobb Judicial Circuit)* Former Judge, State Court of Cobb County.
Office: 30 Waddell Street, Marietta 30090.
Telephone: (770) 528-1849.
Fax: (770) 528-1854

STONE, Hugh W. *(Chief Judge, Superior Court of Georgia Enotah Judicial Circuit)*
Office: 114 Courthouse Street, Box 2, Blairsville 30512.
Telephone: (706) 439-6100.
Fax: (706) 439-6099

STORY, Richard W. *(Judge, United States District Court Northern District of Georgia)* Appointed for life by President Bill Clinton to term beginning Feb 10, 1998. Born Augusta Georgia May 3, 1953. United Methodist. Educated at LaGrange College B.A. 1975 and University of Georgia J.D. 1978. Admitted to practice Georgia 1978 and U.S. District Court Northern District of Georgia 1978. In legal practice Gainesville 1978-86. Part-time Judge, Juvenile Court of Hall County 1985-86. Chief Judge, Superior Court of Georgia Northeastern Judicial Circuit July 8, 1986 to Feb 9, 1998.
Member State Bar of Georgia and Gainesville-Northeastern Bar Association.
Office: 2121 U.S. Courthouse, 75 Spring Street S.W., Atlanta 30303-3361.
Telephone: (404) 215-1350.

STRIPLING, James C. *(Chief Magistrate, Magistrate Court of Coweta County)* Elected to term beginning Jan 1, 1997. Reelected 2000, current term expires Dec 31, 2004.
Office: 34 East Broad Street, Newnan 30263-1923.
Telephone: (770) 254-2610.
Fax: (770) 254-2614
E-mail address: jstripling@coweta.ga.us

STRUBLE, Robert B. *(Senior Judge, Superior Court of Georgia)* Former Chief Judge Mountain Judicial Circuit. Assumed Senior status Jan 1, 1999, serves when called.
Mailing address: 302 Willowdell Drive, Toccoa 30577.
E-mail address: pbstrub2@yahoo.com

STUDDARD, Ben, III *(Judge, State Court of Henry County)* Elected to term beginning Jan 1, 1999. Reelected 2002, current term expires Dec 31, 2006.
Office: 40 Atlanta Street, Suite 200, McDonough 30253.
Telephone: (770) 898-7612.
Fax: (770) 898-7616
E-mail address: bstuddard@co.henry.ga.us

SULLIVAN, Robert H. *(Judge, State Court of Carroll County)* Appointed by Governor Zell Miller to term beginning Dec 20, 1995. Elected 1996 and 2000. Current term expires Dec 31, 2004.
Mailing address: P.O. Box 338, Carrollton 30117-0338.
Telephone: (770) 830-5850.
Fax: (770) 830-5996

SUMNER, John B. *(Judge, Juvenile Court of Georgia Blue Ridge Judicial Circuit)* Appointed.
Office: 90 North Street, Suite 230, Canton 30114.
Telephone: (770) 479-2198.
Fax: (770) 479-2870
E-mail address: jsleagal@msn.com

SUTTON, Berrien L. *(Judge, State Court of Clinch County and Judge, Juvenile Court of Georgia Alapaha Judicial Circuit)* Elected to term beginning 1980. Reelected 1984, 1988, 1992, 1996 and 2000. Current term expires Dec 31, 2004. Serves part time. Appointed Juvenile Judge 2000. Born Douglas Georgia July 24, 1949. Baptist. Educated at South Georgia College A.S. 1968, Valdosta State College B.S. cum laude 1972 and University of Georgia J.D. 1975. E-4 U.S. Army 1970-72.
Mailing address: P.O. Box 496, Homerville 31634-0496.
Telephone: (912) 487-5273.
Fax: (912) 487-2112
E-mail address: BSutton749@aol.com

SUTTON, Frank *(Chief Magistrate, Magistrate Court of Rabun County)* Elected to term beginning Jan 1, 2003. Born Lenox Georgia Feb 2, 1934. Independent study of law 1959-61. Admitted to practice Georgia 1961, U.S. District Courts Middle and Northern Districts of Georgia, U.S. Courts of Appeals Fifth and Eleventh Circuits and U.S. Supreme Court. In legal practice Clayton since 1961. Former Judge, Municipal Court of Mountain City. Former Judge, Municipal Court of Clayton.
City Attorney Clayton and Mountain City for 15 years. County Attorney Tift and Rabun counties. Member State Bar of Georgia. Personal Statement or Quote: "Keep it short."
Mailing address: P.O. Box 977, Clayton 30525.
Office: 39 Screamer Drive, Clayton 30525.
Telephone: (706) 782-3595.
Fax: (706) 782-6899

SUTTON, Richard C. *(Judge, Superior Court of Georgia Tallapoosa Judicial Circuit)*
Office: 105 Polk County Courthouse, Cedartown 30125.
Telephone: (770) 749-6790.
Fax: (770) 749-6793

SWEAT, David R. *(Judge, Superior Court of Georgia Western Judicial Circuit)*
Mailing address: P.O. Box 1706, Athens 30603.
Telephone: (706) 613-3186.
Fax: (706) 613-3187

SWEAT, Marcus Lee, Jr. *(Judge, Probate Court of Ware County)* Elected to term beginning Jan 1, 1985. Reelected 1988, 1992, 1996 and 2000. Current term expires Dec 31, 2004. Born Waycross Georgia Aug 30, 1923. Methodist. Educated at Emory University.
Previously worked in packing house sales Sunnyland Foods Thomasville thirty-six years.
Office: 123 Ware County Courthouse, 800 Church Street, Waycross 31501.
Telephone: (912) 287-4315, 287-4316.
Fax: (912) 287-4317

TANKSLEY, Kathryn Johnson *(Judge, State Court of Cobb County)* Serves Division One.
Office: 166 Anderson Street S.E., Suite 225, Marietta 30060.
Telephone: (770) 424-1500.

TATE, Susan P. *(Judge, Probate Court of Clarke County)* Elected Nov 1996 to term beginning Jan 1, 1997. Reelected Nov 2000, current term expires Dec 31, 2004. Born Monroe Georgia July 10, 1950. Christian. Educated at University of Georgia B.A. with honors 1972 J.D. with honors 1975. Admitted to practice Georgia 1975, U.S. District Court Northern District of Georgia 1981, U.S. Courts of Appeals Fifth 1981 and Eleventh 1982 Circuits and U.S. Supreme Court 1987. In legal practice Athens 1982-97.

Assistant Regional Counsel 1975-80 and Deputy Regional Counsel 1980-82 U.S. Department of Energy. Vice President Council of Probate Court Judges of Georgia. Member National College of Probate Court Judges, State Bar of Georgia and Western Circuit Bar Association (Former Secretary and President).

Office: Clarke County Courthouse, 325 East Washington Street, Athens 30601.
Telephone: (706) 613-3320.
Fax: (706) 613-3323

TAYLOR, A. Blenn, Jr. *(Senior Judge, Superior Court of Georgia)* Former Chief Judge Brunswick Judicial Circuit. Assumed Senior status, serves when called. Former Administrative Judge District One.

Mailing address: 4311 Eighth Street, East Beach, St. Simons Island 31522.
E-mail address: judgebt@yahoo.com

TAYLOR, Lawton G., Sr. *(Chief Magistrate, Magistrate Court of Ware County)* Magistrate 1990-95. Elected Chief Magistrate to term beginning Jan 1, 1997. Reelected 2000, current term expires Dec 31, 2004. Born Jacksonville Florida Aug 25, 1934. Baptist. Educated at Florida State University.

Member Masons, Scottish Rite, York Rite, Shriners, Elks, Lion's Club and Exchange Club. Enjoys fishing and hunting.

Mailing address: P.O. Box 17, Waycross 31502-0017.
Office: 201 State Street, Room 102, Waycross 31501.
Telephone: (912) 287-4373.
Fax: (912) 287-4377
E-mail address: lgtaylorsr@wayxcable.com

TAYLOR, Susan *(Judge, Probate Court of Mitchell County)*

Mailing address: P.O. Box 229, Camilla 31730-0229.
Telephone: (229) 336-2015.
Fax: (229) 336-2004

TEMPLES, Coy H. *(Senior Judge, Superior Court of Georgia)* Appointed May 7, 1974. Elected to term beginning Jan 1975. Reelected to subsequent terms. Former Chief Judge Conasauga Judicial Circuit. Assumed Senior status, serves when called. Born Register Georgia Oct 11, 1936. Presbyterian. Educated at The Citadel A.B. 1958 and Emory University J.D. 1966. Admitted to practice Georgia 1966. In legal practice Dalton 1967-74. Judge, Juvenile Court of Whitfield County 1971-74.

Member State Bar of Georgia. Captain U.S. Army 1958-64. Member First Presbyterian Church of Dalton. Enjoys hiking and backpacking.

Mailing address: 701 Ridgewood Lane, Dalton 30720.

TESKE, Steve *(Associate Judge, Juvenile Court of Georgia Clayton Judicial Circuit)* Appointed.

Office: Courthouse Annex 3, Jonesboro 30236.
Telephone: (770) 477-3260.
Fax: (770) 477-3255
E-mail address: steske@bellsouth.net

THOMAS, Betty *(Judge, Probate Court of Banks County)* Elected Nov 7, 2000 to term beginning Jan 1, 2001. Term expires Dec 31, 2004. Born Banks County Georgia. Baptist. Educated at Piedmont College B.S. with honors 1979. Political affiliation: nonpartisan.

Mailing address: P.O. Box 7, Homer 30547.
Office: Banks County Courthouse, 144 Yonah Road, Homer 30547.
Telephone: (706) 677-6250.
Fax: (706) 677-2337

THOMAS, Penny E. *(Judge, Probate Court of Turner County)*

Mailing address: P.O. Box 2506, Ashburn 31714-2506.
Telephone: (229) 567-2151.
Fax: (229) 567-0358

THOMAS, Robert M. *(Judge, State Court of Miller County)* Serves part time.

Office: 21 Jeterville Road, Colquitt 31737.
Telephone: (229) 758-5666.
Fax: (229) 758-9006

THOMPSON, Albert L. *(Judge, State Court of Fulton County)* Elected to term beginning Jan 1, 1985. Reelected 1988, 1992, 1996 and 2000. Current term expires Dec 31, 2004. Currently serves as Chief Judge. Born Atlanta Georgia Nov 12, 1946. Roman Catholic. Educated at Morehouse College B.A. 1969 and Boston College J.D. 1972. Admitted to practice Georgia 1974. In legal practice 1978. Magistrate, Magistrate Court of Fulton County 1980-84.

House Counsel H. J. Russell Company 1972. Member State Bar of Georgia, Atlanta, Gate City and National Bar Associations. Worked for Small Business Administration 1977. Enjoys woodworking and tennis.

Office: T3955 Justice Center Tower, 185 Central Avenue S.W., Atlanta 30303.
Telephone: (404) 730-4497.
Fax: (404) 224-0574

THOMPSON, Hugh P. *(Justice, Supreme Court of Georgia)* Appointed by Governor Zell Miller to term beginning March 1, 1994. Elected to subsequent terms. Current term expires Dec 31, 2006. Born Montezuma Georgia July 7, 1943. Episcopalian. Educated at Emory University and Mercer University Walter F. George School of Law J.D. 1969. Member Alpha Tau Omega and Phi Delta Phi. Admitted to practice Georgia 1970. Began legal practice Milledgeville 1970. Judge, Recorder's Court of Milledgeville 1971-79. Judge, Baldwin County Court 1973-79. Former Judge and Chief Judge, Superior Court of Georgia Ocmulgee Judicial Circuit June 6, 1979 to Feb 28, 1994, appointed by Governor George D. Busbee.

Instructor in Business Law Georgia College 1971-72. Member Judicial Council of Georgia 1982, State Bar of Georgia, Baldwin County and Ocmulgee Judicial Circuit Bar Associations. Recipient Distinguished Service Award from Baldwin County Jaycees 1972. Named Outstanding Young Man of Baldwin County 1972. Former member Rotary Club and Milledgeville Jaycees. Interests include hunting, rose gardening, golf and fishing.

Office: 514 State Judicial Building, Atlanta 30334.

THOMPSON, HUGH P.—*Continued*
Telephone: (404) 656-3472.
Fax: (404) 651-8642
E-mail address: kilpatrs@supreme.courts.state.ga.us

THOMPSON, Ronald *(Judge, State Court of Effingham County)*
Mailing address: P.O. Box 697, Rincon 31326-0697.
Office: 6162 Highway 21 South, Rincon 31326.
Telephone: (912) 826-5344.

THRASH, Thomas W., Jr. *(Judge, United States District Court Northern District of Georgia)* Appointed for life by President Bill Clinton to term beginning 1997. Born Birmingham Alabama May 8, 1951. Educated at University of Virginia B.A. 1973 and Harvard Law School J.D. 1976. In legal practice Atlanta 1976-77 and 1981-97.
Assistant District Attorney Fulton County 1977-80.
Office: 2188 U.S. Courthouse, 75 Spring Street S.W., Atlanta 30303-3361.
Telephone: (404) 215-1550.

THROWER, Alan W. *(Judge, State Court of Baldwin County)* Elected to term beginning Jan 1, 1999. Reelected 2002, current term expires Dec 31, 2006. Serves part time.
Office: 202 Baldwin County Courthouse, Milledgeville 31061.
Telephone: (478) 452-5442.
Fax: (478) 451-5257

THURMAN, James R. *(Chief Magistrate, Magistrate Court of Lee County)* Elected to term beginning Jan 1, 1997. Reelected 2000, current term expires Dec 31, 2004.
Mailing address: P.O. Box 522, Leesburg 31763-0522.
Telephone: (229) 759-6016.
Fax: (229) 759-3303
E-mail address: jrthurman@lee.ga.us

TIDWELL, G. Ernest *(Senior Judge, United States District Court Northern District of Georgia)* Appointed for life by President Jimmy Carter to term beginning 1979. Chief Judge 1996-99. Assumed Senior status Oct 8, 1999, serves by assignment. Born Atlanta Georgia Aug 1, 1931. Educated at Emory University School of Law LL.B. 1954. In legal practice Atlanta 1954-66. Judge, Civil Court of Fulton 1968-71. Judge, Superior Court of Georgia Atlanta Judicial Circuit 1971-79.
Executive Assistant Attorney General State of Georgia 1966-68. Associate General Counsel State Bar of Georgia 1965-66. Legal Aide to House Floor Leader General Assembly Georgia 1964-66.
Office: 1967 U.S. Courthouse, 75 Spring Street S.W., Atlanta 30303-3361.
Telephone: (404) 215-1460.

TILLEY, Velma *(Judge, Juvenile Court of Georgia Cherokee Judicial Circuit)* Appointed.
Office: 135 West Cherokee Avenue, Suite 333, Cartersville 30120-3181.
Telephone: (770) 387-5039.
Fax: (770) 387-5044
E-mail address: vctilley1@yahoo.com

TINDOL, Lorene *(Judge, Probate Court of Webster County and Chief Magistrate, Magistrate Court of Webster County)* Elected Judge to term beginning Jan 1, 1999. Reelected 2002, current term expires Dec 31, 2006.
Mailing address: P.O. Box 135, Preston 31824-0135.
Telephone: (229) 828-3615.
Fax: (229) 828-3616

TISE, Lindsay A., Jr. *(Judge, Superior Court of Georgia Northern Judicial Circuit)* Elected to term beginning Jan 1, 1997. Reelected 2000, current term expires Dec 31, 2004.
Mailing address: P.O. Box 709, Carnesville 30521.
Telephone: (706) 384-4377.
Fax: (706) 384-4384

TODD, Jack A. *(Chief Magistrate, Magistrate Court of Meriwether County)*
Mailing address: P.O. Box 702, Greenville 30222-0702.
Office: 124 North Court Square, Greenville 30222.
Telephone: (706) 672-1247.
Fax: (706) 672-1172

TODD, Reginald F. *(Chief Magistrate, Magistrate Court of Charlton County)* Elected to term beginning Jan 1, 1997. Reelected 2000, current term expires Dec 31, 2004.
Office: 100 County Street, Folkston 31537.
Telephone: (912) 496-2617.
Fax: (912) 496-2560

TODD, William F., Jr. *(Judge, State Court of Rockdale County)* Elected July 21, 1992 to term beginning Jan 1, 1993. Reelected 1996 and 2000. Current term expires Dec 31, 2004. Born San Diego California April 29, 1954. Methodist. Educated at University of Georgia B.A. with honors 1976 J.D. 1979. Admitted to practice Georgia 1979 and U.S. District Courts Southern 1979 and Middle 1982 Districts of Georgia. In legal practice Thomasville 1981-82.
Assistant District Attorney Statesboro 1979-81 and Conyers 1983-92. Member Atlanta Lawyers Club, State Bar of Georgia and Rockdale County Bar Association. Faculty Instructor Basic Litigation Course Prosecuting Council of Georgia Aug 1989-94. Named Chairman of the Year 1985 and Officer of the Year 1988 by Rockdale County Jaycees. Recipient Sid Herring Memorial Award from Rockdale County Jaycees 1992. Member Council for Battered Women, Church Pre-school and Administrative Boards, Rockdale Prevention Alliance and Rotary Club. Enjoys running, camping, reading and chess.
Office: 310 Rockdale County Courthouse, 922 Court Street N.E., Conyers 30012.
Telephone: (770) 929-4020.
Fax: (770) 918-6695
E-mail address: william.todd@rockdalecounty.org

TOOMER, Pinkie T. *(Judge, Probate Court of Fulton County)* Appointed to term beginning March 1, 2002. Term expires Dec 31, 2004. Born Charleston West Virginia Dec 17, 1950. Educated at Boston University B.A. 1972 M.A. 1974 and Emory University J.D. 1976. Law Clerk to Hon. Floyd Ernest Propst, III, Probate Court of Fulton County 1977-78. Admitted to practice Georgia 1977 and U.S. District Court Northern District of Georgia 1977. Part-time Magistrate, Magistrate Court of Fulton County 1991-2002.
Member Georgia Association of Black Women Attorneys, Council of Probate Court Judges of Georgia, Na-

TOOMER, PINKIE T.—*Continued*

tional College of Probate Judges and Gate City Bar Association.

Office: 185 Central Avenue S.W., Room T2705, Atlanta 30303.
Telephone: (404) 730-4690.
Fax: (404) 730-7698
E-mail address: pinkie.toomer@mail.co.fulton.ga.us

TOWSON, William Malcolm, Sr. *(Senior Judge, Superior Court of Georgia)* Appointed by Governor George Busbee to term beginning June 29, 1977. Elected 1978, 1980, 1984, 1988, 1992 and 1996. Former Chief Judge Dublin Judicial Circuit. Assumed Senior status, serves when called. Administrative Judge, Eighth Judicial Administrative District Jan 1994 to June 30, 1998. Born Laurens County Georgia May 31, 1923. Methodist. Educated at University of Georgia LL.B. cum laude 1949. Student Editor Georgia Bar Journal and Chief Justice Law School Honor Court. Admitted to practice Georgia 1949. Began legal practice Dublin 1949. Judge, State Court of Laurens County Jan 1, 1969 to June 28, 1977.

Former Dublin City Attorney, Laurens County Attorney, East Dublin City Attorney and Laurens County School Board Attorney. Member State Disciplinary Board, State Bar of Georgia, Dublin Judicial Circuit and American Bar Associations. Staff Sergeant USAS 1945-46. Georgia State Senate General Assembly 1961-62. Laurens County Representative General Assembly 1963-64. Enjoys fishing, hunting, boating and gardening.

Mailing address: 225 Evergreen Road, Dublin 31021.
E-mail address: WilliamTowson.CSCJ@hotoffice.net

TRIBBLE, William L., Sr. *(Judge, Juvenile Court of Georgia Dublin Judicial Circuit)* Appointed.

Office: Laurens County Courthouse, Dublin 31021.
Telephone: (478) 272-8623.
E-mail address: county1@bellsouth.net

TRIMBLE, James F. *(Chief Magistrate, Magistrate Court of Butts County)*

Mailing address: P.O. Box 457, Jackson 30233.
Telephone: (770) 775-8220.
Fax: (770) 775-1945
E-mail address: bc_mag@bellsouth.net

TUCKER, Joseph B. *(Senior Judge, Superior Court of Georgia)* Appointed to term beginning Aug 1, 1983. Elected to subsequent terms. Former Chief Judge Lookout Mountain Judicial Circuit. Assumed Senior status Sept 1, 1996, serves when called. Born Ringgold Georgia Jan 28, 1933. Baptist. Educated at Mercer University A.B. 1954 and Walter F. George Law School Mercer University LL.B. 1956. Admitted to practice Georgia 1956, U.S. District Courts Middle 1956 and Northern 1964 Districts of Georgia and U.S. Court of Appeals Fifth Circuit 1964. Began legal practice Macon 1956. Part-time Judge, Juvenile Court of Catoosa County 1975-83.

City Attorney Ringgold 1958-78. County Attorney 1962-73. Member Lookout Mountain Bar Association (President 1972) and State Bar of Georgia. Named one of Outstanding Young Men of Georgia 1965. Democrat (Executive Committee 1959-63). Georgia House of Representatives 1963-66. Enjoys fishing and hunting.

Mailing address: 346 Old County Road, Ringgold 30736.

TURNER, David Jasper, Jr. *(Judge, Juvenile Court of Georgia Coweta Judicial Circuit)* Appointed to term beginning Nov 1, 1976. Reappointed 1982, 1988, 1992, 1996 and 2000. Current term expires 2004. Also Judge, Manchester and Shiloh Municipal Courts. Born Atlanta Georgia April 9, 1942. Methodist. Educated at Mercer University J.D. 1967. Editorial Board Mercer Law Review 1965-67. Member Sigma Nu, Phi Delta Phi and Blue Key. Admitted to practice Georgia 1967. In legal practice Atlanta 1967-70 and Manchester since 1970. Judge, Greenville Municipal Court 1975-77. Former Judge, Warm Springs Municipal Court and Woodbury Municipal Court.

Member Georgia Trial Lawyers Association, The Association of Trial Lawyers of America and State Bar of Georgia. Specialist 4 Army National Guard 1967-73. Member Greenville United Methodist Church.

Mailing address: P.O. Drawer 450, Manchester 31816-0450.
Office: 133 West Main Street, Manchester 31816.
Telephone: (706) 846-8427.
Fax: (706) 846-5241

TURNER, Debra Kaplan *(Judge, Superior Court of Georgia Gwinnett Judicial Circuit)* Elected to term beginning Jan 1, 1999. Reelected 2002, current term expires Dec 31, 2006.

Office: Gwinnett Justice Center, 75 Langley Drive, Lawrenceville 30045.
Telephone: (770) 822-8623.
Fax: (770) 822-8645
E-mail address: willisw@co.gwinnett.ga.us

TURNER, H. Haywood, III *(Chief Magistrate, Magistrate Court of Muscogee County and Judge, Municipal Court of Columbus)*

Mailing address: P.O. Box 1340, Columbus 31902-1340.
Telephone: (706) 653-4390.
Fax: (706) 653-4559

TURNER, John R. *(Judge, Superior Court of Georgia Ogeechee Judicial Circuit)* Elected to term beginning Jan 1, 1997. Reelected 2000, current term expires Dec 31, 2004. Former Chief Judge. Former Judge, State Court of Bulloch County.

Mailing address: P.O. Box 1453, Statesboro 30459-1453.
Telephone: (912) 764-9607.
Fax: (912) 764-3835

TURNER, Kelly D. *(Judge, State Court of Lowndes County)* Appointed by Governor Zell Miller to term beginning Dec 20, 1995. Elected 1996 and 2000. Current term expires Dec 31, 2004. Former part-time Judge, Juvenile Court of Lowndes County.

Mailing address: P.O. Box 1661, Valdosta 31603-1661.
Telephone: (229) 671-2600.
Fax: (229) 671-3441
E-mail address: kturner@lowndescounty.com

TURNER, Virginia S. *(Judge, Probate Court of Irwin County)*

Office: 202 South Irwin Avenue, Ocilla 31774.
Telephone: (229) 468-5138
Fax: (229) 468-5702

TUSAN, Gail S. *(Judge, Superior Court of Georgia Atlanta Judicial Circuit)* Appointed by Governor Zell

TUSAN, GAIL S.—*Continued*

Miller to term beginning May 31, 1995. Elected 1996 and 2000. Current term expires Dec 31, 2004. Former Judge, State Court of Fulton County.
Office: T8955 Justice Center Tower, 185 Central Avenue S.W., Atlanta 30303.
Telephone: (404) 302-8520.
Fax: (404) 302-8524
E-mail address: gail.tusan@co.fulton.ga.us

TUTEN, James R., Jr. *(Chief Judge, Superior Court of Georgia Brunswick Judicial Circuit)* Term expires Dec 31, 2004.
Mailing address: P.O. Box 1473, Brunswick 31521-1473.
Telephone: (912) 554-7372.
Fax: (912) 264-8145

TYLER, Kathy *(Judge, Probate Court of Jasper County)*
Office: 126 West Greene Street, Room 201, Monticello 31064.
Telephone: (706) 468-4903.
Fax: (706) 468-4926
E-mail address: jprobate@hom.net

VALBUENA, Martin E. *(Chief Magistrate, Magistrate Court of Paulding County)*
Mailing address: P.O. Box 1125, Dallas 30132.
Telephone: (770) 443-2204.
Fax: (770) 443-6613

VAN HORN, Kenneth *(Judge, Probate Court of Chattahoochee County)*
Mailing address: P.O. Box 119, Cusseta 31805-0119.
Telephone: (706) 989-3603.
Fax: (706) 989-2005
E-mail address: judgevanhorn@aol.com

VAN PELT, Ralph, Jr. *(Judge, Superior Court of Georgia Lookout Mountain Judicial Circuit)* Appointed by Governor Zell Miller to term beginning Sept 20, 1996. Elected 1998 and 2002. Current term expires Dec 31, 2006.
Office: 206 Catoosa County Courthouse, 875 LaFayette Street, Ringgold 30736.
Telephone: (706) 965-4047.
Fax: (706) 965-6246

VAUGHAN, Michelle *(Judge, Juvenile Court of Georgia Enotah Judicial Circuit)* Appointed to term beginning May 1, 1998. Reappointed 2003, current term expires 2007. Born Marietta Georgia Feb 28, 1967. Educated at University of Georgia B.A. 1988 J.D. 1991. Admitted to practice Georgia 1991. In legal practice Cobb County 1991-95 and Union County 1995-2000.
Mailing address: P.O. Box 1657, Blairsville 30514-1657.
Telephone: (706) 745-7052.
Fax: (706) 745-0062
E-mail address: mvaughan@alltel.net

VAUGHN, Clarence R., Jr. *(Senior Judge, Superior Court of Georgia)* Former Chief Judge Rockdale Judicial Circuit. Assumed Senior status, serves when called.
Office: 922 Court Street N.E., Suite 250C, Conyers 30012.
Telephone: (770) 929-4023.
Fax: (770) 918-6460

VINES, Carlton H. *(Judge, State Court of Chattooga County)* Serves part time.
Mailing address: P.O. Box 498, Summerville 30747-0498.
Telephone: (706) 857-0704.
Fax: (706) 857-0726
E-mail address: chattoogastatecourt@hotmail.com

VINING, Robert L., Jr. *(Senior Judge, United States District Court Northern District of Georgia)* Appointed for life by President Jimmy Carter to term beginning 1979. Chief Judge 1995-96. Assumed Senior status March 31, 1996, serves by assignment. Born Chatsworth Georgia March 30, 1931. Educated at University of Georgia B.A. 1959 J.D. 1959. In legal practice Dalton 1958-69. Judge, Superior Court of Georgia Conasauga Judicial Circuit 1969-79.
Solicitor General Conasauga Judicial Circuit 1963-68.
Mailing address: P.O. Box 6226, Rome 30162-6226.
Telephone: (706) 378-4070.

VOYLES, Sadie W. *(Judge, Probate Court of Grady County)* Elected to term beginning Jan 1, 2001. Term expires Dec 31, 2004. Born Cairo Georgia April 16, 1942.
Director and Member Kiwanis Club of Cairo. Member Pilot Club of Cairo.
Office: 250 North Broad Street, Box 1, Cairo 39828.
Telephone: (229) 377-4621.
Fax: (229) 377-4127

WALKER, Dianne M. *(Judge, Probate Court of Telfair County)*
Office: 128 East Oak Street, Suite 1, McRae 31055-1604.
Telephone: (229) 868-6038.
Fax: (229) 868-7620
E-mail address: judgedw@msn.com

WALKER, James D., Jr. *(Judge, United States Bankruptcy Court Middle District of Georgia)* Appointed by U.S. Court of Appeals Eleventh Circuit judges. Former Judge, U.S. Bankruptcy Court Southern District of Georgia.
Mailing address: P.O. Box 64, Macon 31202-0064.
Telephone: (478) 752-8293.

WALKER, Julie M. T. *(Judge, City Court of Atlanta)*
Office: 260 Central Avenue, Atlanta 30303.
Telephone: (404) 658-6926.
Fax: (404) 658-7053
E-mail address: jmtwalker@ci.atlanta.ga.us

WALKER, Linda T. *(Magistrate Judge, United States District Court Northern District of Georgia)* Appointed by U.S. District Court judges to term beginning Jan 2, 2000. Term expires 2008.
Office: 1629 U.S Courthouse, 75 Spring Street S.W., Atlanta 30303-3309.
Telephone: (404) 215-1370.

WALKER, Peggy H. *(Judge, Juvenile Court of Georgia Douglas Judicial Circuit)* Former Associate Judge. Appointed Judge.
Office: 8700 Hospital Drive, Douglasville 30134.
Telephone: (770) 920-7245.
Fax: (770) 920-7380
E-mail address: Pwalker@co.douglas.ga.us

WALKER, R. Joy *(Judge, Recorder's Court of DeKalb County)* Currently serves as Chief Judge.
Office: 3630 Camp Circle, Decatur 30032.
Telephone: (404) 294-2635.
Fax: (404) 294-2148

WALL, Robert Larry *(Chief Magistrate, Magistrate Court of Schley County)*
Mailing address: P.O. Box 372, Ellaville 31806-0372.
Telephone: (229) 937-5581.
Fax: (229) 937-5188

WALL, Sarah *(Judge, Juvenile Court of Georgia Oconee Judicial Circuit)* Appointed.
Office: 5124 Norman Street, Eastman 31023.
Telephone: (478) 374-4346.
Fax: (478) 374-0168
E-mail address: hwlaw@accucomm.net

WALTHER, Robert G. *(Chief Judge, Superior Court of Georgia Rome Judicial Circuit)*
Office: Three Government Plaza, Suite 310, Rome 30161.
Telephone: (706) 291-5124.
Fax: (706) 290-6080

WARD, Horace T. *(Senior Judge, United States District Court Northern District of Georgia)* Appointed for life by President Jimmy Carter to term beginning Dec 29, 1979. Assumed Senior status, serves by assignment. Born LaGrange Georgia July 29, 1927. Member Friendship Baptist Church at Atlanta. Educated at Morehouse College A.B. with high honors 1949, Atlanta University M.A. 1950 and Northwestern University J.D. 1959. Member Phi Alpha Delta, Alpha Phi Alpha and Sigma Pi Phi. Admitted to practice Georgia 1960. In legal practice Atlanta 1960-74. Judge, State Court of Fulton County July 1, 1974 to Jan 24, 1977. Judge, Superior Court of Georgia Atlanta Judicial Circuit Jan 25, 1977 to Dec 28, 1979.

Claims Authorizer U.S. Social Security Administration 1959-60. Deputy City Attorney Atlanta 1969-70. Assistant Fulton County Attorney 1971-74. Instructor in Political Science University of Arkansas at Pine Bluff (formerly Arkansas A.M. & N. College) 1950-51. Instructor Alabama State College 1951-53 and 1955-56. Lecturer in Business Law and School Law Atlanta University 1965-70. Member Governor's Commission of Court Reorganization and Structure, Atlanta Lawyers Club, State Bar of Georgia (Criminal Law Committee, Law Revision Committee, Disciplinary Tribunal for Atlanta Judicial Circuit and Bench and Bar Committee), Gate City (President 1972-74, Past Vice President and Treasurer), Atlanta (Judicial Administration Committee, Police Community Relations Committee, Consumer Affairs Committee and Judicial Selection and Tenure Committee), National (Chairman Judicial Council 1978-79) and American Bar Associations. Listed in "City Shapers: Saluting 200 Who Shaped Atlanta" Atlanta Magazine May 1976. U.S. Army 1953-55 (one year in Korea). Georgia State Senate 1964-74 (Senate Judiciary Committee for seven years, Senate Rules Committee, County and Urban Affairs Committee, Senate Committees on Business Trade and Commerce and Penal Correctional Affairs and MARTA Overview Committee). Member State Democratic Executive Committee 1966-74. Alternate Delegate Democratic Convention 1968. Member Fulton County Executive Committee 1967-72 and Charter Commission of City of Atlanta 1971-72. Former member Georgia Advisory Committee U.S. Civil Rights Commission, Metropolitan Atlanta Commission on Crime and Delinquency (Board of Trustees), Fledgling Foundation, Inc. (Board of Trustees), Judicial Selection Commission of City of Atlanta and Lawyers Committee for Civil Rights Under Law. Former member Board of Directors Atlanta Legal Aid Society, Atlanta Urban League and Federal Defender Program Northern District of Georgia. Past Assisting Lawyer NAACP Legal Defense & Education Fund, Inc. Member NAACP and YMCA.
Office: 2388 U.S. Courthouse, 75 Spring Street S.W., Atlanta 30303-3361.
Telephone: (404) 215-1330.

WATERS, Billy J. *(Judge, Juvenile Court of Georgia Alcovy Judicial Circuit)* Appointed to term beginning Sept 2, 1997. Reappointed 2002, current term expires 2006.
Office: 1132 Usher Street, Room 119, Covington 30014.
Telephone: (770) 784-2060.
Fax: (770) 784-2065
E-mail address: bwaters@co.newton.ga.us

WATKINS, David D. *(Judge, State Court of Richmond County)* Appointed by Governor Zell Miller to term beginning July 23, 1997. Elected 1998 and 2002. Current term expires Dec 31, 2006. Serves Division Two.
Office: A-211 Law Enforcement Center, 401 Walton Way, Augusta 30901.
Telephone: (706) 821-2825.
Fax: (706) 821-1177
E-mail address: dw8057@co.richmond.ga.us

WEAVER, Brenda S. *(Chief Judge, Superior Court of Georgia Appalachian Judicial Circuit)* Appointed by Governor Zell Miller to term beginning April 2, 1996. Elected 1996 and 2000. Current term expires Dec 31, 2004.
Mailing address: P.O. Box 545, Jasper 30143-0545.
Telephone: (706) 253-8729.
Fax: (706) 253-8734

WEEKS, James H. *(Senior Judge, Superior Court of Georgia)* Appointed by Governor George D. Busbee to term beginning Nov 15, 1982. Elected 1984, 1988 and 1996. Assumed Senior status, serves when called. Born Ensley Alabama Aug 23, 1924. Methodist. Educated at Auburn University B.S. 1948 and Emory University LL.B. 1961 replaced by J.D. 1970. Admitted to practice Georgia 1960 and Alabama 1961. In legal practice Decatur Georgia 1961-82.
Important Decision: State v. Turnipseed 186 Ga. App. 278, 1988. Member Alabama State Bar, State Bar of Georgia, Decatur-DeKalb and Atlanta Bar Associations. Sergeant USAAC 1942-46. Enjoys golf, reading and grandchildren.
Office: 909 DeKalb County Courthouse, 556 North McDonough Street, Decatur 30030.
Telephone: (404) 371-4700.
Fax: (404) 371-2817
E-mail address: jhweeks@co.dekalb.ga.us

WELCH, A. J., Jr. *(Judge, Juvenile Court of Georgia Flint Judicial Circuit)* Appointed to term beginning 1975. Reappointed to subsequent terms. Currently serves as Chief Judge. Serves part time. Born McDonough Georgia. Educated at University of Georgia B.A. with honors 1966 and Mercer University School of Law J.D. with honors 1969. Staff member Mercer Law Review. In legal practice Atlanta since 1970. Former part-time Judge, Juvenile Courts of Butts, Lamar and Monroe Counties.

President Council of Juvenile Court Judges of Georgia 1999. Board of Governors State Bar of Georgia. Member Judicial Council of Georgia. Chairman Henry County Chamber of Commerce. Elder and Chairman Finance Committee McDonough Presbyterian Church.

Mailing address: P.O. Box 10, McDonough 30253.
Telephone: (770) 957-3937.
E-mail address: bwelch@swblawfirm.com

WELCH, James R. "Bump" *(Judge, Probate Court of Marion County and Chief Magistrate, Magistrate Court of Marion County)* Assumed office as Probate Judge 1969. Elected to subsequent terms. Current term expires Dec 31, 2004. Born Columbus Georgia Dec 12, 1939. Methodist. Educated at Georgia Southwestern College.

E-4 USAF 1961-65. Democrat. Active in church associations. Enjoys golf, hunting and fishing.

Mailing address: P.O. Box 207, Buena Vista 31803-0207.
Telephone: (229) 649-5542.
Fax: (229) 649-2059
E-mail address: bumpw@sowega.net

WELLS, Albert E. "Gene" *(Judge, Probate Court of McDuffie County)*

Mailing address: P.O. Box 2028, Thomson 30824-2028.
Telephone: (706) 595-2124.
Fax: (706) 597-2644

WELLS, Debbie *(Judge, Probate Court of Screven County)*

Office: 216 Mims Road, Suite 107, Sylvania 30467.
Telephone: (912) 564-2783.
Fax: (912) 564-9139
E-mail address: screvenprobate@yahoo.com

WEST, Phillip R. *(Chief Judge, Superior Court of Georgia Oconee Judicial Circuit)* Currently serves as Administrative Judge District Eight.

Mailing address: P.O. Box 1058, Eastman 31023-1058.
Telephone: (478) 374-7731.
Fax: (478) 374-0344

WESTBROOK, William Jerry *(Judge, Juvenile Court of Georgia Lookout Mountain Judicial Circuit)* Appointed to term beginning Feb 1983. Reappointed Feb 1989, Jan 1993, 1996 and 2000. Current term expires Dec 31, 2004. Serves part time. Born Trion Georgia June 22, 1938. Educated at Furman University and Woodrow Wilson College of Law J.D. 1961. Admitted to practice Georgia 1961. In legal practice Summerville since 1964. Judge, State Court of Chattooga County 1966-72. Juvenile Referee 1973-83.

Board of Governors State Bar of Georgia 1968-72 and 1986-94. Fellow Georgia Bar Foundation. U.S. Army 1961-63.

Mailing address: P.O. Box 427, Summerville 30747-0427.
Telephone: (706) 857-1622.
Fax: (706) 857-2480
E-mail address: jerry@watersprite.com

WESTMORELAND, Melvin K. *(Judge, Superior Court of Georgia Atlanta Judicial Circuit)* Appointed by Governor Zell Miller to term beginning Sept 24, 1997. Elected 1998 and 2002. Current term expires Dec 31, 2006. Former Judge, State Court of Fulton County.

Office: T4655 Justice Center Tower, 185 Central Avenue S.W., Atlanta 30303.
Telephone: (404) 335-2570.
Fax: (404) 335-2865
E-mail address: melvin.westmoreland@co.fulton.ga.us

WHALEN, Andrew J., Jr. *(Senior Judge, Superior Court of Georgia)* Former Chief Judge Griffin Judicial Circuit. Assumed Senior status October 8, 1998, serves when called.

Mailing address: P.O. Box 627, Griffin 30224-0627.

WHEALE, Duncan *(Judge, Superior Court of Georgia Augusta Judicial Circuit)* Elected to term beginning Jan 1, 1999. Reelected 2002, current term expires Dec 31, 2006.

Office: 311 City-County Building, 530 Greene Street, Augusta 30911.
Telephone: (706) 261-1910.
Fax: (706) 821-1976

WHEATON, John Dennis *(Judge, Probate Court of Lee County)* Elected to term beginning Jan 1, 1985. Reelected 1988, 1992, 1996 and 2000. Current term expires Dec 31, 2004. Born Elmira New York April 20, 1943. Baptist.

Previously self-employed. Member First Baptist Church of Leesburg (Chairman Personnel Committee). Licensed commercial pilot with instrument rating. Enjoys flying and part-time farming.

Mailing address: P.O. Box 592, Leesburg 31763-0592.
Telephone: (229) 759-6006.
Fax: (229) 759-3345

WHISNANT, Elisha Mullins *(Senior Judge, Superior Court of Georgia)* Appointed by Governor George Busbee to term beginning Jan 1, 1978. Elected to subsequent terms. Former Chief Judge Chattahoochee Judicial Circuit. Assumed Senior status Sept 1, 1995, serves when called. Born Waverly Hall Georgia Feb 28, 1928. Baptist. Educated at Walter F. George Law School Mercer University LL.B. 1950. Admitted to practice Georgia 1950. Began legal practice Hamilton 1950. In legal practice Columbus since 1958.

District Attorney Chattahoochee Judicial Circuit June 1, 1970 to Dec 31, 1977. Member District Attorneys Association of Georgia, Council of Superior Court Judges of Georgia, Columbus Lawyers Club and State Bar of Georgia. Member Georgia Criminal Law Study 1962-68. Sergeant U.S. Army 1950-52. Democrat. Georgia State Senate 1961-62. Enjoys quail hunting.

Mailing address: 216 Tenth Street, Columbus 31901.

WHITE, Jere F. *(Senior Judge, Superior Court of Georgia)* Elected to term beginning Jan 1, 1977. Reelected 1980, 1984 and 1988. Former Chief Judge Cherokee Judicial Circuit. Assumed Senior status, serves when called. Born Cartersville Georgia Sept 14, 1923. Presbyterian. Educated at Auburn University 1941-42 and Atlanta Law School LL.B. 1948. Admitted to practice Georgia 1949. In legal practice Cartersville 1952-76.

Solicitor General Cherokee Judicial Circuit 1963-68.

WHITE, JERE F.—*Continued*

Member State Bar of Georgia and Cherokee and Cartersville Bar Association (President). Named Bartow County Young Man of the Year 1957. Lieutenant j.g. USN 1943-45. Democrat. Member First Presbyterian Church of Cartersville (Elder). Enjoys golf, gardening and yard work.

Mailing address: 55 Arrowhead Drive, Cartersville 30120.

WHITE, Watson L. *(Senior Judge, Superior Court of Georgia)* Elected to term beginning Jan 1, 1979. Reelected 1982, 1986 and 1990. Former Chief Judge Cobb Judicial Circuit. Assumed Senior status Jan 1, 1995, serves when called. Former Judge, State Court of Cobb County.

Office: 30 Waddell Street, Marietta 30090-9642.
Telephone: (770) 528-1880.
Fax: (770) 528-8103

WHITTEMORE, Barrett W. *(Chief Magistrate, Magistrate Court of Whitfield County)*

Mailing address: P.O. Box 386, Dalton 30722-0386.
Office: 210 North Thornton Avenue, Dalton 30720.
Telephone: (706) 278-5052.
Fax: (706) 278-8810
E-mail address: Barrett@whittemore.com

WHITWELL, Sharon J. *(Judge, Juvenile Court of Georgia Towaliga Judicial Circuit)* Appointed. Currently serves as Chief Judge.

Office: 15 Butts County Courthouse, 25 Third Street, Jackson 30233.
Telephone: (770) 775-8026.

WILCOX, Tommy Day *(Chief Judge, Superior Court of Georgia Macon Judicial Circuit)* Appointed by Governor George D. Busbee to term beginning Oct 1981. Elected to subsequent terms. Current term expires Dec 31, 2004. Former Administrative Judge District Three. Born Dec 27, 1942. Methodist. Member Vineville Methodist Church. Educated at Mercer University A.B. 1965 J.D. 1973. Admitted to practice Georgia.

Member State Bar of Georgia (Board of Governors, State Disciplinary Board). Lieutenant USN 1966-69. Member Macon Exchange Club.

Office: 310 Bibb County Courthouse, Macon 31201.
Telephone: (478) 621-6545.
Fax: (478) 621-6618

WILDER, Frank N., IV *(Chief Magistrate, Magistrate Court of Monroe County)* Elected to term beginning Jan 1, 1985. Reelected 1988, 1992, 1996 and 2000. Current term expires Dec 31, 2004. Born Monroe County Georgia July 20, 1959. Methodist.

Appointee Governor's Commission to study family violence and make recommendations to the governor and general assembly. Instructor in issues of spouse abuse Magistrate Court Training Council. Certified Instructor Georgia Public Safety Training Center, specializing in spouse abuse and search and seizure law. Previously worked in law enforcement and musical entertainment. Co-owner Left Banque Restaurant. Interested in issues concerning domestic violence. Enjoys music, fishing, gardens, history and physical fitness.

Mailing address: P.O. Box 974, Forsyth 31029-0974.
Telephone: (478) 994-7018.
Fax: (478) 994-7284
E-mail address: magistrate@redi.net

WILKES, Don E. *(Judge, Probate Court of Emanuel County)*

Mailing address: P.O. Box 70, Swainsboro 30401.
Telephone: (478) 237-7091.
Fax: (478) 237-2633

WILKES, E. M., III *(Judge, Superior Court of Georgia Brunswick Judicial Circuit)* Appointed by Governor Zell Miller to term beginning Sept 28, 1993. Elected to subsequent terms. Current term expires Dec 31, 2004. Born Jeff Davis County Georgia March 27, 1946. Methodist. Educated at Georgia Institute of Technology B.S. in General Management 1972 and Mercer University J.D. 1975. Admitted to practice Georgia 1975. Began legal practice Hazlehurst 1975. Judge, Hazlehurst Municipal Court 1977-83. Judge, Juvenile Court of Jeff Davis County Sept 1, 1979 to Sept 27, 1993. Judge, State Court of Jeff Davis County June 19, 1984 to Sept 27, 1993, appointed by Governor Joe Frank Harris.

Attorney City of Hazlehurst Jan 1, 1984 to June 30, 1987. Member Georgia Trial Lawyers Association, The Association of Trial Lawyers of America, State Bar of Georgia, Hazlehurst-Baxley and American Bar Associations. First Lieutenant U.S. Army 1967-70. Member Hazlehurst Rotary Club.

Mailing address: P.O. Drawer 1540, Hazlehurst 31539-1540.
Office: Jeff Davis County Courthouse, 100 Jeff Davis Street, Hazlehurst 31539.
Telephone: (912) 375-6632.
Fax: (912) 375-6634
E-mail address: wilkesem@altamaha.net

WILLIAMS, Amanda F. *(Judge, Superior Court of Georgia Brunswick Judicial Circuit)*

Office: Glynn County Courthouse, 701 H Street, Box 202, Brunswick 31520.
Telephone: (912) 554-7364.
Fax: (912) 264-8281

WILLIAMS, G. Randall *(Associate Judge, Juvenile Court of Georgia Tallapoosa Judicial Circuit)* Appointed Aug 15, 1999. Also serves as Judge pro tem, Probate Court of Paulding County since 2002. Born Gainesville Georgia Oct 16, 1946. Religious affiliation: Non-Denominational. Educated at State University of New York A.A. 1973, LaSalle Extension University LL.B. 1969 and Woodrow Wilson College of Law J.D. 1976. Admitted to practice Georgia 1978, U.S. District Court Northern District of Georgia 1978, U.S. Tax Court 1978, U.S. Court of Appeals Eleventh Circuit 1980 and U.S. Supreme Court 1998. In legal practice Dallas Georgia since 1992.

Tax Law Specialist Internal Revenue Service Feb 1976 to Sept 1980. Attorney ADP Pension Services, Inc. Oct 1981 to Dec 1982. Member State Bar of Georgia and Paulding County Bar Association. Member Christian Legal Society. Interests include photography and computers. Personal Statement or Quote: "There but for the grace of God go I" (Winston Churchill).

Mailing address: P.O. Box 471, Dallas 30132.
Office: Haralson County Courthouse, Highway 120, Buchanan 30113.
Telephone: (770) 443-1532.
Fax: (770) 943-3232
E-mail address: grw2@bellsouth.net

WILLIAMSON, Brenda *(Chief Magistrate, Magistrate Court of Lamar County)* Elected to term beginning Jan 1, 1997. Reelected 2000, current term expires Dec 31, 2004.
Office: Waller Detention Center, 121 Roberta Drive, Barnesville 30204.
Telephone: (770) 358-5154.
Fax: (770) 358-5214

WILLIS, William A. *(Chief Magistrate, Magistrate Court of Dooly County)*
Mailing address: P.O. Box 336, Vienna 31092-0336.
Telephone: (229) 268-4324.
Fax: (229) 268-3585

WILSON, Thomas H. *(Judge, Superior Court of Georgia Towaliga Judicial Circuit)*
Mailing address: P.O. Box 950, Forsyth 31029.
Office: One Courthouse Square, Second Floor, Forsyth 31029.
Telephone: (478) 994-7658.
Fax: (478) 994-7660

WINEGARDEN, Richard Thomas *(Judge, Superior Court of Georgia Gwinnett Judicial Circuit)* Appointed by Governor Joe Frank Harris to term beginning July 9, 1987. Elected 1988, 1992, 1996 and 2000. Current term expires Dec 31, 2004. Former Administrative Judge District Nine. Born Wyandotte Michigan July 8, 1949. Christian. Educated at University of Michigan B.B.A. 1971 and Wayne State University J.D. 1974. Member Chi Psi. Admitted to practice Georgia 1974. Began legal practice Lawrenceville 1974. Judge pro tem, Norcross City Court 1982-83. Judge, State Court of Gwinnett County 1983-87.
Assistant District Attorney Gwinnett County 1974-76.
Office: Gwinnett Justice Center, 75 Langley Drive, Lawrenceville 30045.
Telephone: (770) 822-8605.
Fax: (770) 822-8641
E-mail address: flo@co.gwinnett.ga.us

WINGFIELD, Hugh V., III *(Judge, Superior Court of Georgia Ocmulgee Judicial Circuit)* Appointed by Governor Zell Miller to term beginning July 7, 1998. Elected 2000, current term expires Dec 31, 2004.
Mailing address: P.O. Drawer 1539, Gray 31032.
Telephone: (478) 986-6501.
Fax: (478) 986-3549

WINN, Dan Peace *(Senior Judge, Superior Court of Georgia)* Appointed by Governor Carl Sanders. Elected 1966, 1970, 1974, 1978, 1982 and 1986. Former Chief Judge Tallapoosa Judicial Circuit. Assumed Senior status, serves when called. Born Douglasville Georgia Sept 19, 1921. Methodist. Educated at Young Harris College 1939-41 and Emory University LL.B. 1948. Admitted to practice Georgia 1948, U.S. District Court District of Georgia 1949 and U.S. Supreme Court 1959. Began legal practice Cedartown 1948.
Assistant Attorney General Georgia 1948. Solicitor Polk County City Court 1951-59. Solicitor General Tallapoosa Judicial Circuit 1959-67. Member Council of Superior Court Judges of Georgia (President 1970-71), American Judges Association, State Bar of Georgia, Tallapoosa and American Bar Associations. President District Attorneys Association. First Lieutenant USMCR 1942-45 and Major USMCR. Recipient Distinguished Flying Cross Air Medal. Member Optimist Club, Masons, VFW (Life member) and American Legion. Enjoys golf and tennis.
Mailing address: 735 North Marshall Street, Cedartown 30125.

WITHERS, Nelly F. *(Judge, Recorder's Court of DeKalb County)*
Office: 3630 Camp Circle, Decatur 30032-1394.
Telephone: (404) 294-2635.
Fax: (404) 294-2148
E-mail address: nfwithers@co.dekalb.ga.us

WOFFORD, Charles A. *(Senior Judge, Superior Court of Georgia)* Appointed by Governor Lester Garfield Maddox July 1, 1967. Elected to subsequent terms. Assumed Senior status Jan 1, 1981, serves when called. Born Atlanta Georgia Nov 29, 1914. Presbyterian (Elder since 1955, former Chairman Board of Deacons, former Treasurer and Sunday School Superintendent). Educated at Atlanta Law School LL.B. 1943 LL.M. 1945 and Webster University LL.D. 1946. Life member Sigma Delta Kappa. Admitted to practice Georgia 1943, U.S. District Court District of Georgia and U.S. Court of Appeals Fifth Circuit. Began legal practice Atlanta 1943. Judge, Atlanta Municipal Court 1954-58. Judge, Criminal Court of Fulton County 1959-67.
Member American Judicature Society, Fulton Lawyers Association, Atlanta Lawyers Club, Atlanta and American Bar Associations. Past President Overland Guaranty and Insurance Agency, Inc. Charter President Atlanta Law School Alumni Association. Past Grand President Sigma Delta Kappa. Past Vice Chairman Scottish Rite Hospital for Crippled Children. President Scottish Rite Foundation of Georgia. Life member Masons, Shriners, M.O.V.P.E.R., Order of the Eastern Star, Knights of Pythias, Loyal Order of Moose, Eagles and Sons of Confederate Veterans.
Mailing address: 636 Virginia Avenue N.E., Atlanta 30306.

WOMMACK, Robert W., Jr. *(Judge, State Court of Washington County)* Serves part time.
Mailing address: P.O. Box 348, Sandersville 31082.
Office: 114 Myrtle Way, Sandersville 31802.
Telephone: (478) 552-2150.
Fax: (478) 552-2148

WONG, Alvin T. *(Judge, State Court of DeKalb County)* Elected to term beginning Jan 1, 1999. Reelected 2002, current term expires Dec 31, 2006.
Office: 608 DeKalb County Courthouse, 556 North McDonough Street, Decatur 30030.
Telephone: (404) 371-2591.
Fax: (404) 687-3820
E-mail address: atwong@co.dekalb.ga.us

WOOD, Ellen *(Chief Magistrate, Magistrate Court of Cook County)*
Office: 1000 County Farm Road, Adel 31620.
Telephone: (229) 896-3151.
Fax: (229) 896-5186

WOOD, Jerry *(Chief Magistrate, Magistrate Court of Floyd County)* Elected to term beginning Jan 1, 1997. Reelected 2000, current term expires Dec 31, 2004.
Office: 3 Government Plaza, Suite 227, Rome 30161.
Telephone: (706) 291-5250.
Fax: (706) 291-5269
E-mail address: woodj@floydcountyga.org

WOOD, Jon B. *(Chief Judge, Superior Court of Georgia Lookout Mountain Judicial Circuit)*
Mailing address: P.O. Box 1185, LaFayette 30728-1185.
Telephone: (706) 638-1650.
Fax: (706) 638-1654
E-mail address: Jonbwood@aol.com

WOODRUM, William E., Jr. *(Chief Judge, Superior Court of Georgia Ogeechee Judicial Circuit)*
Mailing address: P.O. Box 805, Millen 30442-0805.
Telephone: (478) 982-0109.
Fax: (912) 764-4947

WOODS, E. H. "Bucky", III *(Chief Judge, Superior Court of Georgia Mountain Judicial Circuit)* Chief Judge since Jan 1, 1999.
Mailing address: P.O. Box 485, Clarkesville 30523-0485.
Telephone: (706) 754-6274.
Fax: (706) 754-4722

WORKMAN, Anne *(Judge, Superior Court of Georgia Stone Mountain Judicial Circuit)* Appointed by Governor Zell Miller to term beginning July 9, 1998. Elected 2000, current term expires Dec 31, 2004. Born Woodruff South Carolina Oct 13, 1947. Baptist. Educated at Duke University A.B. 1969 and Emory University J.D. 1972. Associate Editor Journal of Public Law 1970-71. Member Phi Delta Phi. Admitted to practice Georgia 1972 and South Carolina 1973. In legal practice Decatur July 1979 to Feb 1983. Judge pro tem, Juvenile Court of DeKalb County Oct 1981 to Jan 1983. Associate Judge, Recorder's Court of DeKalb County July 1982 to March 1983. Judge March 1983 to Dec 1984 and Chief Magistrate Sept 1984 to Dec 1984, Magistrate Court of DeKalb County. Judge, State Court of DeKalb County Jan 1, 1985 to July 8, 1998.

Solicitor Juvenile Court of DeKalb County Nov 1973 to July 1979. Consultant Attorney Division of Children and Youth Georgia Department of Human Resources 1979-83. Adjunct Professor Emory University Law School 1974-88. Member Executive Committee Council of Magistrate Judges of Georgia 1983-84, Georgia Commission on Gender Bias in the Judicial System 1989-91 and Commission on Family Violence 1992-96. Member Lawyers Club of Atlanta, National Council of Juvenile and Family Court Judges, Council of State Court Judges of Georgia (President 1988-89), State Bar of South Carolina, State Bar of Georgia (Board of Governors since March 1993), Atlanta (Chair Judicial Section 1993-94), Decatur-DeKalb and American Bar Associations. Named One of "Ten Women Who Have Made a Difference in DeKalb" by DeKalb Network for Women and DeKalb YWCA Nov 1985. Recipient Community Service Award from Emory Legal Association of Women Students Emory School of Law Nov 1986 and Golden Apple Award for an Elected Official for contributions in the cause of mentally ill and mentally retarded citizens June 1994. Member Leadership Atlanta 1990. Member Junior League of DeKalb County and Druid Hills Civic Association. Member Task Force on Domestic Violence and Task Force on Child Sexual Abuse of DeKalb County. Enjoys traveling and gourmet cooking.

Office: 310 Callaway Building, 120 West Trinity Place, Decatur 30030.
Telephone: (404) 371-2338.

WRIGHT, Cynthia D. *(Judge, Superior Court of Georgia Atlanta Judicial Circuit)* Appointed by Governor Zell Miller to term beginning Nov 1, 1996. Elected July 1998 and July 2002. Current term expires Dec 31, 2006. Born June 8, 1954. Educated at Wesleyan College A.B. 1974 and University of Georgia School of Law J.D. 1977. Admitted to practice Georgia 1977. In legal practice Atlanta. Judge, State Court of Fulton County Jan 5, 1995 to Oct 31, 1996, appointed by Governor Zell Miller.

Instructor Emory University School of Law 1995. Attended The National Judicial College July 1996 and various Superior Court Judges seminars. Assistant Executive Counsel to Governor George D. Busbee. Executive Counsel to Governor Zell Miller 1991-94. Enjoys golf, baseball, reading, skiing, hiking and traveling.

Office: T8855 Justice Center Tower, 185 Central Avenue S.W., Atlanta 30303.
Telephone: (404) 730-4185.
Fax: (404) 335-2883
E-mail address: cynthia.wright@fultoncourt.org

WYNNE, Charles S. *(Judge, State Court of Hall County)* Currently serves as Chief Judge. Former Chief Magistrate, Magistrate Court of Hall County, elected to term beginning Jan 1, 1997.
Mailing address: P.O. Box 737, Gainesville 30503-0737.
Telephone: (770) 531-7007.
Fax: (770) 531-3975
E-mail address: cwynne@mindspring.com

HAWAII

Capital HONOLULU

UNITED STATES DISTRICT COURT DISTRICT OF HAWAII

The court sits at Honolulu. For descriptive information refer to the United States Courts section.

Chief Judge
David Alan Ezra

Judges
Helen W. Gillmor
Susan Oki Mollway

Senior Judges
Samuel Pailthorpe King
Alan C. Kay

Clerk
Walter A.Y.H. Chinn
C-338 Federal Building
300 Ala Moana Boulevard
Honolulu, Hawaii 96850-0338
(808) 541-1300

UNITED STATES MAGISTRATE JUDGES OF HAWAII

Barry M. Kurren
David E. Faucher
Leslie E. Kobayashi
Kevin S. C. Chang
Carolyn M. Shattuck

UNITED STATES BANKRUPTCY COURT OF HAWAII

Judge
Robert J. Faris

Recalled Judge
Lloyd King

Bankruptcy Clerk
Mark Van Allsburg
250L First Hawaiian Tower
1132 Bishop Street
Honolulu, Hawaii 96813-2830
(808) 522-8100

HAWAII SUPREME COURT

The Supreme Court is Hawaii's court of last resort. The court consists of a chief justice and four associate justices. Justices are appointed for initial ten-year terms by the governor with the consent of the Senate from a list compiled by the Judicial Selection Commission. The Judicial Selection Commission determines whether a justice shall be retained in office. Justices must retire at age 70.

The court has appellate jurisdiction over all questions of law or fact brought before it from any other agency or court. The court has original jurisdiction in extraordinary writs and may issue other writs necessary to the exercise of proper jurisdiction. The court has exclusive jurisdiction in the examination, licensing and disciplining of attorneys and in determining judicial fitness. The court also has superintending control over all inferior courts.

The court sits at Honolulu.

Chief Justice
Ronald T. Y. Moon

Associate Justices
Steven H. Levinson
Paula A. Nakayama
Simeon R. Acoba, Jr.
James E. Duffy, Jr.

Clerk
Darrell N. Phillips
Ali'iolani Hale
417 South King Street
Honolulu, Hawaii 96813-2902
(808) 539-4919

Administrative Director of the Courts
Rick Keller
Ali'iolani Hale
417 South King Street
Honolulu, Hawaii 96813-2902
(808) 539-4900

HAWAII INTERMEDIATE COURT OF APPEALS

The Intermediate Court of Appeals was created by the Hawaiian Legislature in 1979. The court consists of a chief judge and three associate judges. Judges are appointed for initial ten-year terms by the governor with the consent of the Senate from a list compiled by the Judicial Selection Commission. The Judicial Selection Commission determines whether a judge shall be retained in office. Judges must retire at age 70. The chief judge is chosen through a merit selection plan for a ten-year term.

The court has concurrent jurisdiction with the Supreme Court with the exception of the examination, licensing and disciplining of attorneys, as well as questions reserved by a federal appellate court, which fall under the Supreme Court's exclusive jurisdiction. Cases may be transferred between the Supreme Court and Intermediate Court of Appeals at the discretion of the chief justice. The court may issue writs necessary to the exercise of proper jurisdiction.

The court sits at Honolulu.

Chief Judge
James S. Burns

HAWAII INTERMEDIATE COURT OF APPEALS—*Continued*

Associate Judges
Corinne K. A. Watanabe
John Lim
Daniel R. Foley

HAWAII CIRCUIT COURTS

The Circuit Courts are Hawaii's courts of general jurisdiction. Judges are appointed for initial ten-year terms by the governor with the consent of the Senate from a list compiled by the Judicial Selection Commission. The Judicial Selection Commission determines whether a judge shall be retained in office. Judges must retire at age 70. A chief judge as well as two deputy chief judges may be assigned to each circuit by the chief justice. The Family Court is a division of the Circuit Courts. In the First Circuit, three circuit judges are assigned specifically to the Family Court by the chief justice; one of these serves as a Senior Family Court Judge. In other circuits, the chief judges also serve as Senior Family Court Judges.

The courts have exclusive jurisdiction in probate, guardianship and criminal felony cases, as well as in civil cases when the amount in controversy exceeds $20,000. The courts have concurrent jurisdiction with the District Courts in civil nonjury cases when the amount in controversy is between $10,000 and $20,000. The courts may also hear cases involving mechanics' liens and misdemeanor violations transferred from the District Court for jury trial. The Family Court Division has jurisdiction over youths, and youths over eighteen in situations defined by statute, and over adults involved in family law cases. All jury trials are held in the Circuit Courts.

There are four circuits consisting of the First, Second, Third and Fifth; the Fourth Circuit consolidated with the Third in 1943. The courts sit at times and places prescribed by state law.

---

*Also serves as Senior Family Court Judge

FIRST JUDICIAL CIRCUIT includes Honolulu County. The court sits at Honolulu.

Chief Judge
Colleen K. Hirai

Deputy Chief Judges
Karen Blondin (Civil)
Dan T. Kochi (Criminal)

Judges

Karen Ahn	Derrick H. M. Chan
Gary W. B. Chang	Virginia Lea Crandall
Dexter D. Del Rosario	Reynaldo D. Graulty
Eden Elizabeth Hifo	Victoria S. Marks
Sabrina McKenna	Marie N. Milks
Rhonda A. Nishimura	Richard K. Perkins
Richard Pollack	Karl K. Sakamoto
Sandra A. Simms	Michael Anthony Town
Wilfred K. Watanabe	Michael D. Wilson

Senior Family Court Judge
Frances Q. F. Wong

Family Court Judges
Steven S. Alm
Marcia J. Waldorf

SECOND JUDICIAL CIRCUIT includes Maui County and the Kalaupapa settlement in Kalawao, Molokai. The court sits at Lanai, Molokai and Wailuku.

Chief Judge
Shackley F. Raffetto*

Judges
Joel E. August
Joseph E. Cardoza

THIRD JUDICIAL CIRCUIT includes Hawaii County. The court sits at Hilo, Honokaa, Kamuela, Ka'u, Kohala and Kona.

Chief Judge
Ronald Ibarra*

Judges
Greg Nakamura*
vacancy

FIFTH JUDICIAL CIRCUIT includes Kauai County. The court sits at Lihue.

Chief Judge
George M. Masuoka*

Judge
Clifford L. Nakea

HAWAII DISTRICT COURTS

The District Courts are courts of limited jurisdiction in Hawaii. Judges are appointed for initial six-year terms by the chief justice with consent of the Senate from a list compiled by the Judicial Selection Commission. The Judicial Selection Commission determines whether a judge shall be retained in office. A deputy chief judge may be assigned to each circuit by the chief justice. Per diem judges are also appointed by the chief justice to serve on an as-needed basis. District judges may be assigned specifically to the Family Court division of the Circuit Court by the chief justice.

The courts have exclusive civil jurisdiction in cases involving less than $10,000 and concurrent jurisdiction with the Circuit Courts in cases when the amount in controversy is between $10,000 and $20,000. The courts exercise exclusive criminal jurisdiction in traffic and ordinance violations, conduct preliminary felony hearings and hear criminal misdemeanors punishable by a fine and/or imprisonment not exceeding one year when a jury trial is not demanded.

Boundaries of the District Courts are identical to those of the Circuit Courts.

---

*Also serves as Family Court Judge

FIRST JUDICIAL CIRCUIT includes Honolulu County. The court sits at Ewa, Koolauloa, Koolaupoko, Wahiawa, Waialua and Waianae.

Deputy Chief Judge
Colette Y. Garibaldi

HAWAII DISTRICT COURTS—*Continued*

Judges

Bert I. Ayabe
Leslie A. Hayashi
Faye M. Koyanagi
David Lo
Russel S. Nagata
Clarence A. Pacarro
Fa'auuga To'oto'o
Hilary Benson Gangnes
Gerald H. Kibe
Lono J. Lee
Christopher McKenzie
Rhonda Nishimura
Barbara Richardson

Family Court Judges

Michael F. Broderick
Darryl Y. C. Choy
Linda K.C. Luke
Karen M. Radius
Bode Amilale Uale
R. Mark Browning
Kenneth E. Enright
Paul T. Murakami
Allene R. Suemori

SECOND JUDICIAL CIRCUIT includes Maui County and the Kalaupapa settlement in Kalawao, Molokai. The court sits at Hana, Lahaina, Lanai (Island), Makawao and Molokai (Island).

Deputy Chief Judge

Douglas H. Ige

Judges

Reinette W. Cooper
Rhonda I. L. Loo

Family Court Judges

Eric G. Romanchak
Geronimo Valdriz, Jr.

THIRD JUDICIAL CIRCUIT includes Hawaii County. The court sits at Hamakua, Hilo, Ka'u, Kona, North Hilo, North Kohala, Puna and South Kohala.

Deputy Chief Judge

vacancy

Judges

Joseph P. Florendo, Jr.
Matthew S. K. Pyun
vacancy

Family Court Judges

Aley K. Auna, Jr.
Ben H. Gaddis
Terence T. Yoshioka

FIFTH JUDICIAL CIRCUIT includes Kauai County. The court sits at Hanalei, Kawaihau, Koloa, Lihue and Waimea.

Deputy Chief Judge

Calvin K. Murashige*

Judge

Trudy K. Senda

HAWAII LAND COURT

The Land Court is a court of statewide special jurisdiction in Hawaii administering the Torrens Title System of land registration. Its two judges are assigned by the chief justice from among the First Circuit Court judges.

The court has jurisdiction over applications for original registration of land, petitions for subdivisions, designations and deletions of easements, accretions and erosions of Land Court lands, clarifications and updating of status for Land Court property. All appeals are taken directly to the Supreme Court.

The court sits at Honolulu.

HAWAII TAX APPEAL COURT

The Tax Appeal Court is a court of statewide special jurisdiction in Hawaii. Its judge is assigned by the chief justice from among the First Circuit Court judges.

The court has original appellate jurisdiction over all disputes between tax assessor and taxpayer including excise, liquor, income, property and insurance tax matters. All appeals are taken directly to the Supreme Court.

The court sits at Honolulu and convenes in the other circuits at least once per year to hear disputes concerning real property taxes.

Hawaii Counties and County Seats

Hawaii

Hilo

Honolulu

Honolulu

Kauai

Lihue

Maui

Wailuku

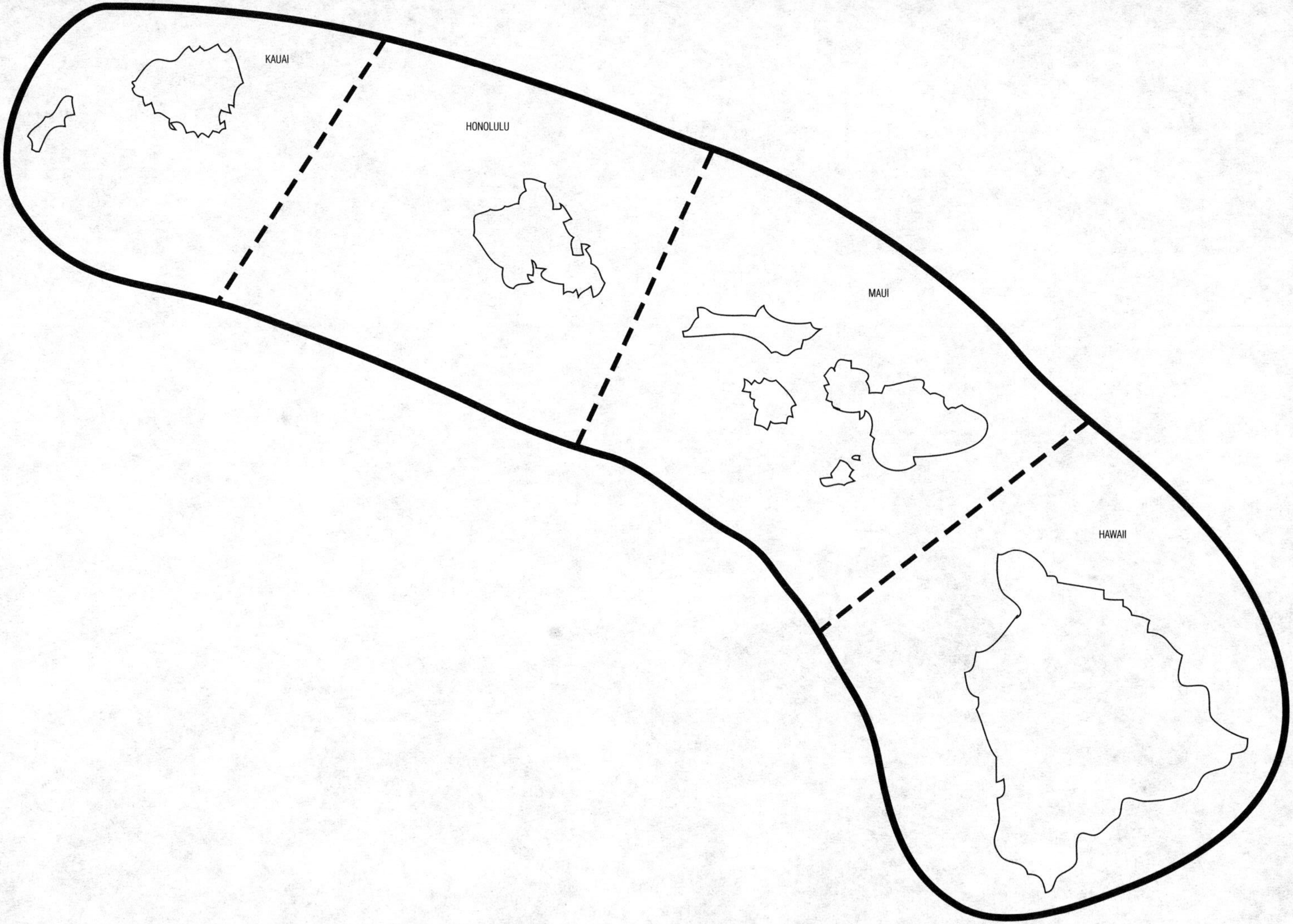
KAUAI
HONOLULU
MAUI
HAWAII

UNITED STATES DISTRICT COURT DISTRICT OF HAWAII

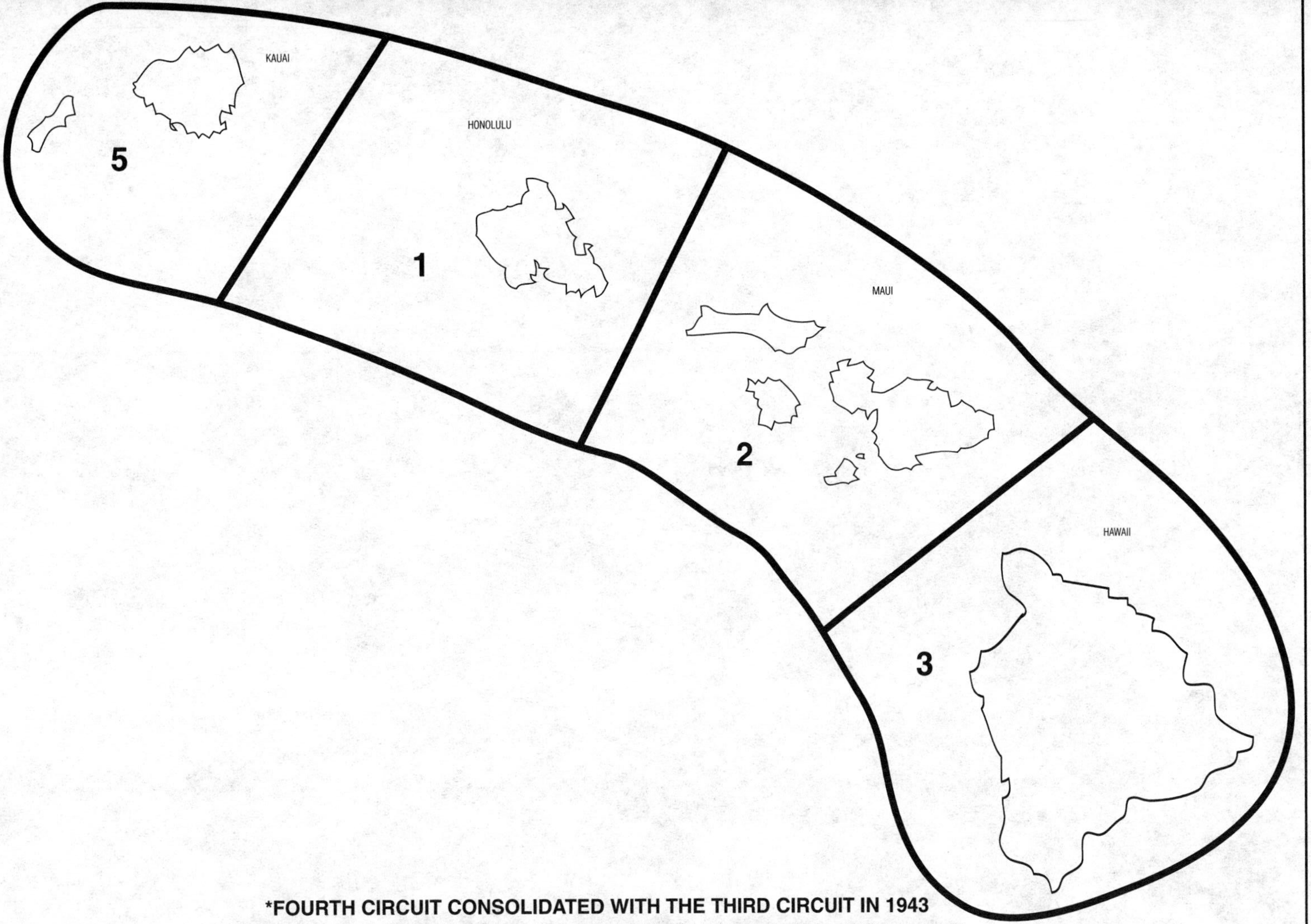
KAUAI
HONOLULU
MAUI
HAWAII
5
1
2
3

*FOURTH CIRCUIT CONSOLIDATED WITH THE THIRD CIRCUIT IN 1943

JUDICIAL CIRCUITS OF HAWAII CIRCUIT COURTS AND HAWAII DISTRICT COURTS*

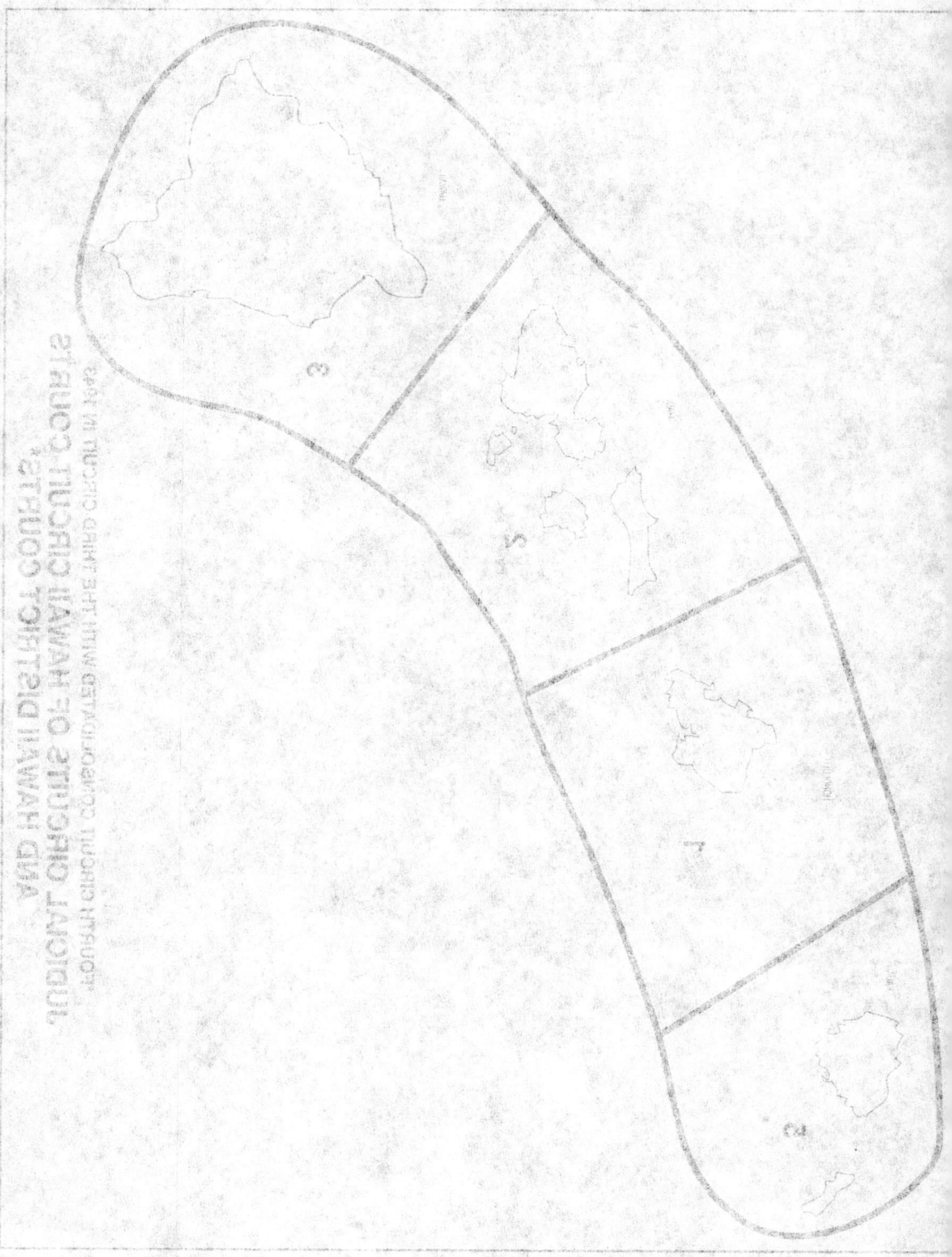

HAWAII

ACOBA, Simeon R., Jr. *(Associate Justice, Hawaii Supreme Court)* Appointed by Governor Benjamin J. Cayetano to term beginning May 19, 2000. Term expires May 18, 2010. Born Honolulu Hawaii March 11, 1944. Methodist. Educated at University of Hawaii B.A. with honors 1966 and Northwestern University J.D. 1969. Law Clerk to Chief Justice William S. Richardson, Hawaii Supreme Court 1969-70. Admitted to practice Hawaii 1969. Began legal practice Honolulu 1969. In legal practice 1973-80. Per Diem Judge, Hawaii District Court First Circuit 1979-80. Judge, Hawaii Circuit Court First Circuit June 16, 1980 to May 25, 1994. Associate Justice, Hawaii Intermediate Court of Appeals May 26, 1994 to May 18, 2000.

Housing Officer and Special Assistant to the President University of Hawaii 1970-71. Hawaii Deputy Attorney General 1971-73. Staff Attorney House of Representatives 1975. Special Attorney Division of Occupational Safety and Health Department of Labor 1975-77, Campaign Spending Commission 1976 and Public Utilities Division 1976-77 State of Hawaii. Instructor Legal Methods Seminars 1977-78 and Trial Practice Seminars 1976-77 University of Hawaii School of Law and Criminal Law 1992-2002 Hawaii Pacific University. Director Legal Aid Society of Hawaii 1975-76. Hawaii Supreme Court Bar Examiner 1975-79. Subcommittee Chairman Supreme Court Committee on Pattern Civil Jury Instructions 1990-91. Chairman ad hoc Committee on Jury Master List 1992. Member Hearing Committee Office of Disciplinary Counsel 1978-79, Medical Claims Conciliation Board 1978-79, Committee to Consider the Adoption of ABA Model Rules of Professional Conduct 1989-91 and Committee on Judicial Evaluation and Dues Hawaii State Trial Judges Association 1991. Member The Association of Trial Lawyers of America, Hawaii State (Director Young Lawyers Section 1973, Judicial Administration Committee 1992-94) and American Bar Associations. Recipient Liberty Bell Award from Hawaii State Bar Association 1964. Member Governor's Conference on the Year Two Thousand 1970, Citizens Committee on the Administration of Justice 1972, State Drug Abuse Commission 1975-76 and State of Hawaii Filipino Celebration Executive Committee 1991. Director Hawaii Mental Health Association 1975-77, Nuuanu YMCA 1975-78 and Kalanianaole Athletic Club Board 1977-87.

Office: Ali'iolani Hale, 417 South King Street, Honolulu 96813-2902.

Telephone: (808) 539-4725.

AHN, Karen *(Judge, Hawaii Circuit Court First Judicial Circuit)* Appointed by Governor Benjamin J. Cayetano to term beginning May 10, 2000. Term expires May 9, 2010. Judge, Hawaii District Court First Circuit June 3, 1994 to May 9, 2000, appointed by Chief Justice Ronald T. Y. Moon.

Office: Ka'ahumanu Hale, 777 Punchbowl Street, Honolulu 96813-5093.

Telephone: (808) 539-4066.

ALM, Steven S. *(Family Court Judge, Hawaii Circuit Court First Judicial Circuit)* Appointed by Governor Benjamin J. Cayetano to term beginning May 14, 2001. Term expires May 13, 2011.

Office: Kauikeaouli Hale, Eleventh Floor, 1111 Alakea Street, Honolulu 96813-2807.

Telephone: (808) 538-5882.

AUGUST, Joel E. *(Judge, Hawaii Circuit Court Second Judicial Circuit)* Appointed by Governor Benjamin J. Cayetano to term beginning June 10, 2002. Term expires June 9, 2012.

Office: Hoapili Hale, Suite 106, 2145 Main Street, Wailuku 96793-1679.

Telephone: (808) 244-2955.

AUNA, Aley K., Jr. *(Family Court Judge, Hawaii District Court Third Judicial Circuit)* Appointed by Chief Justice to term beginning April 4, 2000. Term expires April 3, 2006.

Mailing address: P.O. Box 1007, Hilo 96721-1007.

Office: 345 Kekuanaoa Street, Room 40, Hilo 96720-4388.

Telephone: (808) 329-7377.

AYABE, Bert I. *(Judge, Hawaii District Court First Judicial Circuit)* Appointed by Chief Justice Ronald T. Y. Moon to term beginning June 6, 2003. Term expires June 5, 2009.

Office: Kauikeaouli Hale, Eleventh Floor, 1111 Alakea Street, Honolulu 96813-2897.

BLONDIN, Karen *(Deputy Chief Judge, Hawaii Circuit Court First Judicial Circuit)* Appointed by Governor John D. Waihee, III to term beginning May 11, 1992. Retained by the Judicial Selection Commission to term beginning May 11, 2002, current term expires May 10, 2012. Currently serves Civil Division.

Office: Ka'ahumanu Hale, 777 Punchbowl Street, Honolulu 96813-5093.

Telephone: (808) 539-4116.

BRODERICK, Michael F. *(Family Court Judge, Hawaii District Court First Judicial Circuit)* Appointed by Chief Justice Ronald T. Y. Moon to term beginning June 6, 2003. Term expires June 5, 2009.

Mailing address: P.O. Box 3498, Honolulu 96811-3498.

Office: Ka'ahumanu Hale, 777 Punchbowl Street, Honolulu 96813-5093.

BROWNING, R. Mark *(Family Court Judge, Hawaii District Court First Judicial Circuit)* Former Per Diem Family Court Judge. Appointed Family Court Judge by Chief Justice Ronald T. Y. Moon to term beginning June 6, 1997. Retained by the Judicial Selection Commission June 6, 2003, current term expires June 5, 2009.

Mailing address: P.O. Box 3498, Honolulu 96811-3498.

Office: Ka'ahumanu Hale, 777 Punchbowl Street, Honolulu 96813-5093.

Telephone: (808) 539-4441.

BURNS, James S. *(Chief Judge, Hawaii Intermediate Court of Appeals)* Appointed by Governor George R. Ariyoshi to term beginning 1980. Retained by the Judi-

BURNS, JAMES S.—*Continued*

cial Selection Commission 1992 and May 2002. Current term expires May 13, 2012. Chief Judge since May 14, 1982. Born Honolulu Hawaii April 19, 1937. Educated at Benedictine College B.S. 1959 and Villanova University J.D. 1962. Admitted to practice Hawaii 1962. Judge, Hawaii Circuit Court First Circuit (Family and Civil Court Divisions) 1977-80.

Office: Kapuaiwa Building, Second Floor, 426 Queen Street, Honolulu 96813.

Telephone: (808) 539-4750.

CARDOZA, Joseph E. *(Judge, Hawaii Circuit Court Second Judicial Circuit)* Appointed by Governor Benjamin J. Cayetano to term beginning June 24, 1999. Term expires June 23, 2009.

Office: Hoapili Hale, Suite 106, 2145 Main Street, Wailuku 96793-1679.

Telephone: (808) 244-2860.

CHAN, Derrick H. M. *(Judge, Hawaii Circuit Court First Judicial Circuit)* Appointed by Governor Benjamin J. Cayetano to term beginning Aug 25, 2000. Term expires Aug 24, 2010.

Office: 111 Alakea Street, Courtroom 5B, Honolulu 96813-2807.

Telephone: (808) 538-5193.

CHANG, Gary W. B. *(Judge, Hawaii Circuit Court First Judicial Circuit)* Appointed by Governor Benjamin J. Cayetano to term beginning June 1, 1999. Term expires May 31, 2009.

Office: Ka'ahumanu Hale, 777 Punchbowl Street, Honolulu 96813-5093.

Telephone: (808) 539-4084.

CHANG, Kevin S. C. *(Magistrate Judge, United States District Court District of Hawaii)* Appointed by U.S. District Court judges to term beginning Dec 19, 2000. Term expires Dec 18, 2008. Former Presiding Administrative Judge, Hawaii Circuit Court First Circuit April 30, 1993 to Dec 19, 2000, appointed by Governor John D. Waihee, III.

Office: C-209 Federal Building, 300 Ala Moana Boulevard, Honolulu 96850-0209.

Telephone: (808) 541-1308.

CHOY, Darryl Y. C. *(Family Court Judge, Hawaii District Court First Judicial Circuit)* Appointed by Chief Justice William S. Richardson to term beginning Jan 4, 1982. Retained by the Judicial Selection Commission Jan 4, 1988, 1994 and Jan 4, 2000. Current term expires Jan 3, 2006. Born Honolulu Hawaii Aug 23, 1946. Congregationalist. Educated at Marquette University B.S.B.A. 1968 and University of Santa Clara J.D. cum laude 1972. Honorary Member University of Santa Clara Law Review. Law Clerk to Hon. Norito Kawakami, Hawaii Circuit Court First Circuit 1972-73. Member Phi Alpha Delta. Admitted to practice Hawaii 1972 and U.S. District Court 1972. Began legal practice Honolulu 1972. Hearings Officer, Hawaii Public Employment Relations Board 1973-75 and Department of Regulatory Agencies 1975-81.

Member Hawaii State Board of Bar Examiners 1979-95. Member Hawaii State (Attorney/Client Coordinating Committee 1977-78) and American Bar Associations. Chairperson task force to develop and establish statewide Juvenile Justice Information System since 1985 and implementation team to computerize First Circuit Family Court since 1988. Enjoys music and hunting.

Mailing address: P.O. Box 3498, Honolulu 96811-3498.

Office: Ka'ahumanu Hale, 777 Punchbowl Street, Honolulu 96813-5093.

Telephone: (808) 539-4435.

COOPER, Reinette W. *(Judge, Hawaii District Court Second Judicial Circuit)* Appointed by Chief Justice Ronald T. Y. Moon to term beginning May 7, 2001. Term expires May 6, 2007.

Office: 2145 Main Street, Suite 137, Wailuku 96793-1679.

Telephone: (808) 244-2730.

CRANDALL, Virginia Lea *(Judge, Hawaii Circuit Court First Judicial Circuit)* Appointed by Governor John D. Waihee, III to term beginning April 1, 1991. Retained by the Judicial Selection Commission 2001, current term expires March 31, 2011. Former Presiding Administrative Judge Civil Division.

Office: Ka'ahumanu Hale, 777 Punchbowl Street, Honolulu 96813-5093.

Telephone: (808) 539-4054.

DEL ROSARIO, Dexter D. *(Judge, Hawaii Circuit Court First Judicial Circuit)* Appointed by Governor John D. Waihee, III to term beginning April 15, 1994. Term expires April 14, 2004. Former Judge, Hawaii District Court First Circuit.

Office: Ka'ahumanu Hale, 777 Punchbowl Street, Honolulu 96813-5093.

Telephone: (808) 539-4078.

DUFFY, James E., Jr. *(Associate Justice, Hawaii Supreme Court)* Appointed by Governor Linda Lingle to term beginning June 27, 2003. Term expires June 26, 2013.

Office: Ali'iolani Hale, 417 South King Street, Honolulu 96813-2902.

Telephone: (808) 539-4747.

ENRIGHT, Kenneth E. *(Family Court Judge, Hawaii District Court First Judicial Circuit)* Appointed by Chief Justice Ronald T. Y. Moon to term beginning Feb 28, 1997. Retained by the Judicial Selection Commission Feb 28, 2003, current term expires Feb 27, 2009.

Mailing address: P.O. Box 3498, Honolulu 96811-3498.

Office: Ka'ahumanu Hale, 777 Punchbowl Street, Honolulu 96813-5093.

Telephone: (808) 539-4433.

EZRA, David Alan *(Chief Judge, United States District Court District of Hawaii)* Appointed for life by President Ronald Reagan to term beginning 1988. Chief Judge since Nov 30, 1999. Born Columbus Ohio June 27, 1947. Educated at St. Mary's University B.B.A. 1969 J.D. 1972. In legal practice Honolulu 1972-88.

Office: C-400 Federal Building, 300 Ala Moana Boulevard, Honolulu 96850-0400.

Telephone: (808) 541-1907.

FARIS, Robert J. *(Judge, United States Bankruptcy Court District of Hawaii)* Appointed by U.S. Court of

FARIS, ROBERT J.—*Continued*

Appeals Ninth Circuit judges to term beginning Feb 14, 2002. Term expires Feb 2016.
Office: 250L First Hawaiian Tower, 1132 Bishop Street, Honolulu 96813-2830.
Telephone: (808) 522-8111.
E-mail address: Robert_Faris@hib.uscourts.gov

FAUCHER, David E. *(Magistrate Judge, United States District Court District of Hawaii)* Appointed by U.S. District Court judges. Serves part time.
Mailing address: P.O. Box 832, APO AP 96558.
Telephone: (808) 421-0011.

FLORENDO, Joseph P., Jr. *(Judge, Hawaii District Court Third Judicial Circuit)* Appointed by Chief Justice to term beginning Nov 3, 1986. Retained by the Judicial Selection Commission 1992 and Nov 3, 1998. Current term expires Nov 2, 2004.
Mailing address: P.O. Box 4879, Hilo 96720-4879.
Office: 205 State Building, 75 Aupuni Street, Hilo 96720-4253.
Telephone: (808) 322-8710.

FOLEY, Daniel R. *(Associate Judge, Hawaii Intermediate Court of Appeals)* Appointed by Governor Benjamin J. Cayetano to term beginning Oct 02, 2000. Term expires Oct 1, 2010.
Office: Kapuaiwa Building, Second Floor, 426 Queen Street, Honolulu 96813.
Telephone: (808) 539-4698.

GADDIS, Ben H. *(Family Court Judge, Hawaii District Court Third Judicial Circuit)* Appointed by Chief Justice Herman T. F. Lum to term beginning May 17, 1989. Retained by the Judicial Selection Commission May 17, 1995 and May 2001. Current term expires May 16, 2007.
Mailing address: P.O. Box 1007, Hilo 96721-1007.
Office: 345 Kekuanaoa Street, Room 40, Hilo 96720-4388.
Telephone: (808) 934-5700.

GANGNES, Hilary Benson *(Judge, Hawaii District Court First Judicial Circuit)* Appointed by Chief Justice Ronald T. Y. Moon to term beginning May 22, 2002. Term expires May 21, 2008.
Office: Kauikeaouli Hale, Eleventh Floor, 1111 Alakea Street, Honolulu 96813-2897.
Telephone: (808) 538-5227.

GARIBALDI, Colette Y. *(Deputy Chief Judge, Hawaii District Court First Judicial Circuit)* Appointed by Chief Justice Ronald T. Y. Moon to term beginning Feb 28, 1997. Retained by the Judicial Selection Commission Feb 28, 2003, current term expires Feb 27, 2009.
Office: Kauikeaouli Hale, 11th Floor, 1111 Alakea Street, Honolulu 96813-2897.
Telephone: (808) 538-5000.

GILLMOR, Helen W. *(Judge, United States District Court District of Hawaii)* Appointed for life by President Bill Clinton to term beginning 1994. Educated at Queens College of the City University of New York B.A. 1965 and Boston University School of Law LL.B. 1968. In legal practice Boston Massachusetts 1968-69, El Paso Texas 1969, Camden Maine 1970 and Honolulu Hawaii 1971-72, 1974-77 and 1985-94. Per Diem Family Court Judge 1977-83 and Per Diem Judge 1983-85, Hawaii District Court First Circuit. Law Clerk to Chief Justice William S. Richardson, Hawaii Supreme Court 1972. Deputy Public Defender Honolulu 1972-74.
Office: C-435 Federal Building, 300 Ala Moana Boulevard, Honolulu 96850-0435.
Telephone: (808) 541-3502.

GRAULTY, Reynaldo D. *(Judge, Hawaii Circuit Court First Judicial Circuit)* Appointed by Governor Benjamin J. Cayetano to term beginning March 5, 1999. Term expires March 4, 2009.
Office: Ka'ahumanu Hale, 777 Punchbowl Street, Honolulu 96813-5093.
Telephone: (808) 539-4109.

HAYASHI, Leslie A. *(Judge, Hawaii District Court First Judicial Circuit)* Per Diem Judge Aug 11, 1989 to Nov 1990. Appointed Judge by Chief Justice Herman T. F. Lum to term beginning Nov 5, 1990. Retained by the Judicial Selection Commission Nov 5, 1996 and Nov 5, 2002. Current term expires Nov 4, 2008. Born Tokyo Japan Aug 3, 1954. Protestant. Educated at Stanford University B.A. with distinction 1976 and Georgetown University Law Center J.D. 1979. Admitted to practice Illinois 1980, Hawaii 1981, U.S. District Courts Northern District of Illinois 1980 and District of Hawaii 1981 and U.S. Courts of Appeals Seventh 1980 and Ninth 1982 Circuits. In legal practice Honolulu Hawaii 1980-88.
Court Annexed Arbitrator 1985-90. In-house Counsel ACRO, Inc. Aug 1988 to Oct 1990. Author "Canadian Pacific Cases: Kinoshita & Nakashima: What Really Happened to the Employer?" XXII No. 1 Hawaii B. Jour. 1989 and *Model Associates' Orientation Program* Young Lawyers Division 1991. Author "Guardianship," "Landlord-Tenant," "Resolving Fee Disputes," "Five Tips to Remember if You are Sued," "Hawaii's Courts" and "Title VII of the Civil Rights Act of 1964" and Co-editor *Our Rights, Our Lives: A Guide to Women's Legal Rights in Hawaii* Jan 1990, Jan 1991 and Jan 1997. Editor *Alternatives to Incarceration* 1990 and *The Law & You: A Directory of Law-Related Education Programs* 1991 Young Lawyers Division. Co-author "Blanco: Why a Reasonable Person with a Gun Cannot Cause an Accident" Hawaii B. Jour. Nov. 1993. Arbitrator American Arbitration Association since 1990. Bencher American Inns of Court since 1992. Co-chair Judicial ad hoc Committee to Study Gender Bias 1986-89. Member Judicial Committee on ADR and Criminal Law 1993-95. Board Member Attorneys and Judges Assistance Program Board Jan 2, 1994 to Jan 1, 1997. Member Hawaii Supreme Court Committee on Equality and Access to the Courts (Member since 1990, Vice Chair 1993, Co-chair since 1993), Judicial Permanent Committee on Rules of Penal Procedure and Circuit Court Criminal Rules 1991-97, Hawaii Women's Legal Fund (Director 1986-88 and 1992-94, Secretary 1991), Hawaii Women Lawyers (Secretary 1984, Vice President 1985, President 1986), Hawaii State Trial Judges Association (Executive Committee 1993-97), Hawaii State (Director 1987-88, Vice-President/President Elect 1989, President 1990 Young Lawyers Division, Chair Standing Committee on the Delivery of Legal Services to the Public 1988-89, Board of Directors 1988-90, Executive Committee 1990, Liaison for Hawaii State Trial Judges Association 1991-95, Member since 1991, Co-chair 1993 and 1996 and Chair 1994 Standing Committee on Law-Related Education), Illinois State and American Bar Associations.

HAYASHI, LESLIE A.—*Continued*

Attorney Delegate to first Hawaii State Judicial Conference 1985-87. Board of Directors Hawaii Institute for Continuing Legal Education 1989. Guest Speaker People's Law School since 1990. Member Judiciary's Law-Related Education Conference 1992. Judiciary Representative to National Conference of Special Court Judges American Bar Association Aug 1992. Faculty Member since 1995 and Instructor on Advanced Administrative Law 1995-97, 1999-2000 and 2002 The National Judicial College. Named Outstanding Attorney of the Year by Hawaii Women Lawyers 1989 and Woman of the Year 1992. Recipient Justice Award Young Lawyers Division Hawaii State Bar Association 1995. Listed in *Foremost Women of the 20th Century, Outstanding Young Women of America, Prominent People in Hawaii, Who's Who in American Law, Who's Who in American Women, Who's Who of Emerging Leaders* and *Who's Who Among Rising Young Americans.* Co-founder and Director Hawaii Women's Consortium 1985. Executive Director Hawaii Lawyers Care June 1988 to Aug 1989. Anchor Legal Line KGMB Live at Five News Program Sept 1988 to Oct 1990. Executive Board Judiciary History Center 1990-93 and Board Member Friends of the Judiciary History Center since 1995. Founding Member 1994 and President since 1995 Hawaii Friends of Civic and Law-Related Education. Author *Fables from the Garden, Fables from the Sea* and *Fables from the Deep* (children's books). Enjoys watercolors, ballet and writing.

Office: Kauikeaouli Hale, 11th Floor, 1111 Alakea Street, Honolulu 96813-2897.

Telephone: (808) 538-5003.

HIFO, Eden Elizabeth *(Judge, Hawaii Circuit Court First Judicial Circuit)* Appointed by Governor John D. Waihee, III to term beginning April 30, 1993. Retained by the Judicial Selection Commission April 30, 2003, current term expires April 2013.

Office: Ka'ahumanu Hale, 777 Punchbowl Street, Honolulu 96813-5093.

Telephone: (808) 539-4025.

HIRAI, Colleen K. *(Chief Judge, Hawaii Circuit Court First Judicial Circuit)* Appointed by Governor John D. Waihee, III to term beginning May 6, 1994. Term expires May 5, 2004.

Office: Ka'ahumanu Hale, 777 Punchbowl Street, Honolulu 96813-5093.

Telephone: (808) 539-4640.

IBARRA, Ronald *(Chief Judge, Hawaii Circuit Court Third Judicial Circuit)* Appointed by Governor John D. Waihee, III to term beginning May 10, 1989. Retained by the Judicial Selection Commission May 10, 1999, current term expires May 9, 2009. Former Senior Family Court Judge. Born Kona Hawaii. Educated at University of Hawaii B.B.A. 1970, Santa Clara University School of Law J.D. with honors 1976 and Georgetown University Law Center LL.M. Admitted to practice Hawaii 1976, U.S. District Court District of Hawaii 1976 and U.S. Court of Appeals District of Columbia Circuit 1977. In legal practice Kailua-Kona 1981.

Deputy Prosecutor 1977-81, Corporation Counsel 1985-87 and Managing Director 1987-88 County of Hawaii. Chairperson Probate Rules Committee. Member Judicial Education Committee, Rules of Civil Procedure Committee, Criminal Pattern Jury Instructions Committee and Civil Pattern Jury Instructions Committee. Member Hawaii State Trial Judges Association and Hawaii State Bar Association. Recipient Fred Schutte Award for meritorious service to bar and profession from Hawaii State Bar Association 2002. First Lieutenant U.S. Army 1970-72. Lieutenant Colonel USAR 1994.

Mailing address: P.O. Box 1970, Kealakekua 96750-1970.

Office: 240 Keakealani Building, 79-7579A Haukapila Street, Kealakekua 96750.

Telephone: (808) 322-8755.

IGE, Douglas H. *(Deputy Chief Judge, Hawaii District Court Second Judicial Circuit)* Appointed by Chief Justice Ronald T. Y. Moon to term beginning June 28, 1996. Retained by the Judicial Selection Commission June 28, 2002, current term expires June 27, 2008. Formerly served as Family Court Judge.

Office: 2145 Main Street, Suite 137, Wailuku 96793-1679.

Telephone: (808) 244-2714.

KAY, Alan C. *(Senior Judge, United States District Court District of Hawaii)* Appointed for life by President Ronald Reagan July 3, 1986 to term beginning Jan 2, 1987. Former Chief Judge. Assumed Senior status Jan 2, 2000, serves by assignment. Born Honolulu Hawaii July 5, 1932. Christian. Educated at Princeton University B.A. 1957 and University of California Boalt Hall School of Law LL.B. 1960. Member Phi Delta Phi. Admitted to practice Hawaii 1960, U.S. District Court District of Hawaii 1960 and U.S. Court of Appeals Ninth Circuit 1962. In legal practice Honolulu 1960-86.

Counselor Aloha Inn American Inn of Court since 1987. Member Ninth Circuit Pacific Islands Committee since 1994, Ninth Circuit Judicial Council, Federal Judges Association, Hawaii State (Executive Committee 1972-73, Board of Directors Real Estate Section 1983-86) and American Bar Associations. Corporal USMC 1953-55. Republican. Director Legal Aid Society 1968-71, Bank of Hawaii 1971-86, Fellowship of Christian Athletes 1978-83, Good News Mission (prison ministry) 1980-86 and Economic Development Corporation of Honolulu 1985-86. Steering Committee Fuller Theological Seminary Hawaii 1985-86. Board of Regents International College and Graduate School since 1994. Enjoys sports and reading.

Office: C-415 Federal Building, 300 Ala Moana Boulevard, Honolulu 96850-0415.

Telephone: (808) 541-1904.

KIBE, Gerald H. *(Judge, Hawaii District Court First Judicial Circuit)* Appointed by Chief Justice Ronald T. Y. Moon Oct 24, 1994 to term beginning Jan 6, 1995. Retained by the Judicial Selection Commission Jan 6, 2001, current term expires Jan 5, 2007. Born Wailuku Maui Hawaii Oct 28, 1952. Educated at Drake University B.A. 1974 and Northwestern University J.D. 1977. Law Clerk to Associate Justice Thomas S. Ogata, Hawaii Supreme Court 1977-79. Admitted to practice Hawaii 1977, U.S. District Court District of Hawaii 1979 and U.S. Court of Appeals Ninth Circuit 1983. In legal practice Honolulu 1981-83.

Assistant Disciplinary Counsel 1979-81 and Chief Disciplinary Counsel 1983-94 Hawaii Supreme Court.

KIBE, GERALD H.—*Continued*

Member Hawaii State and American Bar Associations. Board Member Palama Settlement.

Office: Kauikeaouli Hale, 11th Floor, 1111 Alakea Street, Honolulu 96813-2897.

Telephone: (808) 538-5004.

KING, Lloyd *(Recalled Judge, United States Bankruptcy Court District of Hawaii)* Appointed Judge by U.S. Court of Appeals Ninth Circuit judges. Appointed Recalled Judge by the Judicial Council of the Ninth Circuit.

Office: 250L First Hawaiian Tower, 1132 Bishop Street, Honolulu 96813-2830.

Telephone: (808) 522-8111.

KING, Samuel Pailthorpe *(Senior Judge, United States District Court District of Hawaii)* Appointed to serve during good behavior by President Richard M. Nixon to term beginning July 1972. Assumed Senior status, serves by assignment. Born Hankow China April 13, 1916. Episcopalian. Educated at Yale University B.S. 1937 LL.B. 1940. Member Order of the Coif. Admitted to practice Hawaii 1940 and District of Columbia 1940. In legal practice Honolulu 1940-61 and 1970-72. Part-time District Magistrate, City and County of Honolulu 1956-61. Judge, Hawaii Circuit Court 1961-70.

Co-editor and co-translator *The Theory and Practice of Go* by O. Korschelt, Tuttle 1965. Faculty member National College of the State Judiciary and National Institute for Trial Advocacy 1968-70, 1972-73, 1976 and 1984. Captain USNR active duty 1942-46 (retired). Republican.

Office: C-461 Federal Building, 300 Ala Moana Boulevard, Honolulu 96850-0461.

Telephone: (808) 541-1900.

KOBAYASHI, Leslie E. *(Magistrate Judge, United States District Court District of Hawaii)* Appointed by U.S. District Court judges to term beginning Aug 2, 1999. Term expires Aug 1, 2007.

Office: C-353 Federal Building, 300 Ala Moana Boulevard, Honolulu 96850-0353.

Telephone: (808) 541-1331.

KOCHI, Dan T. *(Deputy Chief Judge, Hawaii Circuit Court First Judicial Circuit)* Appointed by Governor John D. Waihee, III to term beginning April 15, 1994. Term expires April 14, 2004. Former Senior Family Court Judge. Currently serves Criminal Division.

Office: Ka'ahumanu Hale, 777 Punchbowl Street, Honolulu 96813-5093.

Telephone: (808) 539-4580.

KOYANAGI, Faye M. *(Judge, Hawaii District Court First Judicial Circuit)* Appointed by Chief Justice Ronald T. Y. Moon to term beginning June 10, 2003. Term expires June 9, 2009.

Office: Kauikeaouli Hale, Eleventh Floor, 1111 Alakea Street, Honolulu 96813-2897.

KURREN, Barry M. *(Magistrate Judge, United States District Court District of Hawaii)* Appointed by U.S. District Court judges to term beginning March 2, 1992. Reappointed to term beginning March 2, 2000, current term expires March 1, 2008. Born Pittsburgh Pennsylvania March 24, 1951. Jewish. Educated at University of Hawaii B.A. with highest honors 1973 J.D. 1977. Law Clerk to Hon. Martin Pence, U.S. District Court District of Hawaii 1977-78. Admitted to practice Hawaii 1977, U.S. District Court District of Hawaii 1977 and U.S. Court of Appeals Ninth Circuit 1977. In legal practice Honolulu 1978-91. Judge, Hawaii District Court First Circuit 1991-92.

Adjunct Professor of Law University of Hawaii since 1994. Bencher American Inn of Court IV. Member Federal Magistrate Judges Association, Hawaii State and American Bar Associations. Lecturer or Panelist at numerous seminars on various subjects including Pretrial and Trial Practice and Federal Rules of Civil Procedure and Evidence. Enjoys jogging, playing tennis and traveling.

Office: C-229 Federal Building, 300 Ala Moana Boulevard, Honolulu 96850-0229.

Telephone: (808) 541-1306.

LEE, Lono J. *(Judge, Hawaii District Court First Judicial Circuit)* Appointed by Chief Justice Ronald T. Y. Moon to term beginning June 10, 2003. Term expires June 9, 2009.

Office: Kauikeaouli Hale, Eleventh Floor, 1111 Alakea Street, Honolulu 96813-2897.

LEVINSON, Steven H. *(Associate Justice, Hawaii Supreme Court)* Appointed by Governor John D. Waihee, III to term beginning April 7, 1992. Retained by the Judicial Selection Commission April 2002, current terms expires April 7, 2012. Born Cincinnati Ohio June 8, 1946. Jewish. Educated at Stanford University B.A. with distinction 1968 and University of Michigan Law School J.D. 1971. Staff member University of Michigan Journal of Law Reform 1970-71. Law Clerk to Hon. Bernard H. Levinson, Hawaii Supreme Court 1971-72. Admitted to practice Hawaii 1972, U.S. District Court District of Hawaii 1972 and U.S. Court of Appeals Ninth Circuit 1972. In legal practice Honolulu 1972-89. Judge, Hawaii Circuit Court First Circuit Feb 1989 to April 1992.

Author "The Language of Involuntary Mental Hospitalization: A Study in Sound and Fury" University of Michigan Journal of Law Reform 1970. Important Decisions 1992-97: Birmingham v. Fodor's Travel Publications, Inc. 73 Haw. 359, 833 P.2d 70, 1992; Cho Mark v. K & K International 73 Haw. 509, 836 P.2d 1057, 1992; State v. Quino 74 Haw. 161, 176, 840 P.2d 358, 365, 1992, cert denied U.S. 113 S. Ct. 1849, 123 L.Ed. 2d 472, 1993; Briones v. State 74 Haw. 442, 469, 848 P.2d 966, 979, 1993; State v. Kelekolio 74 Haw. 479, 849 P.2d 58, 1993; Baehr v. Lewin 74 Haw. 530, 852 P.2d 44, recon. granted in part 74 Haw. 645, 875 P.2d 225, 1993; AIG Hawaii Ins. Co. v. Estate of Caraang 74 Haw. 620, 851 P.2d 321, 1993; State v. Bonnell 75 Haw. 124, 856 P.2d 1265, 1993; Richardson v. City and County of Honolulu 76 Haw. 46, 868 P.2d 1193, recon. denied 76 Haw. 247, 871 P.2d 795, 1994; In re Doe, Born January 5, 1976 76 Haw. 85, 869 P.2d 1304, 1994; State v. Furutani 76 Haw. 172, 873 P.2d 51, 1994; State v. Hoey 77 Haw. 17, 881 P.2d 504, 1994; Dawes v. First Ins. Co. of Hawaii Ltd. 77 Haw. 117, 883 P.2d 38, recon. denied 77 Haw. P.2d 1994; State v. Gaylord 78 Haw. 127, 890 P.2d 1166, 1995; State v. Pone 78 Haw. 262, 892 P.2d 455, 1995; Dines v. Pacific Ins. Co. 78 Haw. 325, 893 P.2d 176, recon. denied 78 Haw. 474, 896 P.2d 930, 1995; Housing Fin. & Dev. Corp. v. Castle 79 Haw. 64, 898 P.2d 576, 1995; State v. Kinnane 79 Haw. 46, 897 P.2d 973, 1995; State v. Holborn 80 Haw. 27, 904 P.2d 912, recon. denied 80

LEVINSON, STEVEN H.—*Continued*
Haw. 187, 907 P.2d 773, 1995; State v. Wallace 80 Haw. 382, 910 P.2d 695, 1996; State v. Merino 81 Haw. 198, 915 P.2d 672, 1996; Mathewson v. Aloha Airlines, Inc. 82 Haw. 57, 919 P.2d 969, 1996; Brown v. KFC Nat'l Mgt. Co. 82 Haw. 226, 921 P.2d 146, recon. denied 82 Haw. 360, 922 P.2d 973, 1996; State v. Lee 83 Haw. 267, 925 P.2d 1091, 1996; State v. Trainor 83 Haw. 250, 925 P.2d 818, 1996; Gray v. Administrative Dir. of the Court 84 Haw. 138, 931 P.2d 580, 1997; State v. Soto 84 Haw. 229, 933 P.2d 66, 1997; State v. Cornelio 84 Haw. 476, 935 P.2d 1021, 1997; State v. Quitog 85 Haw. 129, 938 P.2d 559, 1997; Tabieros v. Clark Equip. Co. 85 Haw. 336, 944 P.2d 1279, 1997; State v. Hoang 86 Haw. 48, 947 P.2d 360, 1997; and Estate of John Doe v. Paul Revere Ins. Group 86 Haw. 262, 948 P.2d 1103, 1997.

Important Decisions 1998-99: State v. Mallan 86 Haw. 440, 454, 950 P.2d 178, 192, 1998; Chun v. Board of Trustees of the Employees' Retirement System of the State of Hawaii 87 Haw. 152, 952 P.2d 1215, 1998; Korean Buddhist Dae Won Sa Temple of Hawaii v. Sullivan 87 Haw. 217, 953 P.2d 1315, 1998; Ozaki v. AOAO of Discovery Bay 87 Haw. 265, 954 P.2d 644, 1998 cert; State v. Tabigne 88 Haw. 296, 966 P.2d 608, 1998; State v. Christian 88 Haw. 407, 967 P.2d 239, 1998; Roxas v. Marcos 89, Haw. 91, 969 P.2d 1209, 1998 recon. denied 89 Haw. P.2d 1999; Leong v. Sears Roebuck & Co. 89 Haw. 204, 970 P.2d 972, 1998; State v. Medeiros 89 Haw. 361, 973 P.2d 736, 1999; Jenkins v. Liberty Newspapers Limited Partnership 89 Haw. 254, 971 P.2d 1089, 1999; State v. Stocker 90 Haw. 85, 976 P.2d 399, 1999; Potter v. Hawaii Newspaper Agency 89 Haw. 411, 974 P.2d 51, 1999; Ruf v. Honolulu Police Dept. 89 Haw. 315, 972 P.2d 1081 recon. denied Haw. P.2d 1999; State v. Dudoit 90 Haw. 262, 978 P.2d 700 recon. denied Haw. P.2d 1999; Taylor v. Government Employees Ins. Co. 90 Haw. 302, 978 P.2d 740, 1999; State v. Cabrera 90 Haw. 359, 978 P.2d 797, 1999; Pelosi v. Wailea Ranch Estates 91 Haw. 478, 985 P.2d 1045 recon. denied Haw. P.2d 1999 cert; State v. Kotis 91 Haw. 319, 984 P.2d 78, recon. denied Haw. P.2d 1999; State v. Ortiz 91 Haw. 181, 981 P.2d 1127, 1999; Leslie v. Estate of Tavares 91 Haw. 394, 984 P.2d 1220, 1999; Roes v. FHP, Inc. 91 Haw. 470, 985 P.2d 661, 1999; State v. Sua 92 Haw. 61, 987 P.2d 959, 1999 cert; State v. Viernes 92 Haw. 130, 988 P.2d 195, 1999; Dairy Road Partners v. Island Ins. Co. 92 Haw. 398, 992 P.2d 93, 2000; Chun v. Board of Trustees of ERS 92 Haw. 432, 992 P.2d 127, 2000; State v. Jenkins 93 Haw. 87, 997 P.2d 13, 2000; State v. Valentine 93 Haw. 199, 998 P.2d 479, 2000; Flor v. Holguin 94 Haw. 70, 9 P.3d 382, 2000; Crichfield v. Grand Wailea Co. 93 Haw. 477, 6 P.3d 349, 2000; State v. Ah Loo 94 Haw. 207, 10 P.3d 728, 2000 cert; Hawaii Community Federal Credit Union v. Keka 94 Haw. 213, 11 P.3d 1, 2000; and Casumpang v. ILWU, Local 142 No. 22726, 2000.

Former Chairperson Advisory Committee to Conduct a Comprehensive Review of The Hawaii Penal Code Hawaii State Judicial Council. Former Court Liaison Justice Committee to Consider Adoption of the ABA Model Rules of Professional Conduct. Former Member Committee on AIDS Policy and Standing Committee on Pattern Criminal Jury Instructions Hawaii State Judiciary. Former Member Working Group Center for Alternative Dispute Resolution and Chief Justice's Standing Committee on Delay Reduction in the Circuit Courts. Former Member The Association of Trial Lawyers of America. Member Hawaii State (Director Young Lawyers Division 1975-76, Director 1982-84) and American (Judicial Administration Division) Bar Associations. Attended General Jurisdiction I and II courses Sept 1989, Sept 1991 and Oct 1991, Assembly Member since 1990 and State Judicial Leader since 1991 The National Judicial College. Attended all Hawaii State Judicial conferences and education projects since 1989. Attended basic and advanced Appellate Judges seminars June 1994 and June 1995 New York University Institute of Judicial Administration. Member Temple Emanu-el.

Office: Ali'iolani Hale, 417 South King Street, Honolulu 96813-2902.

Telephone: (808) 539-4735.

LIM, John *(Associate Judge, Hawaii Intermediate Court of Appeals)* Appointed by Governor Benjamin J. Cayetano to term beginning June 1, 1999. Term expires May 31, 2009. Former Family Court Judge, Hawaii District Court First Circuit, appointed by Chief Justice. Former Judge, Hawaii Circuit Court First Circuit, appointed by Governor Benjamin J. Cayetano.

Office: Kapuaiwa Building, Second Floor, 426 Queen Street, Honolulu 96813.

Telephone: (808) 539-4751.

LO, David *(Judge, Hawaii District Court First Judicial Circuit)* Appointed by Chief Justice Ronald T. Y. Moon to term beginning Aug 23, 2000. Term expires Aug 22, 2006.

Office: Kauikeaouli Hale, 11th Floor, 1111 Alakea Street, Honolulu 96813-2897.

Telephone: (808) 538-5010.

LOO, Rhonda I. L. *(Judge, Hawaii District Court Second Judicial Circuit)* Appointed by Chief Justice Ronald T. Y. Moon to term beginning May 1, 1997. Retained by the Judicial Selection Commission May 1, 2003, current term expires April 30, 2009.

Office: Hoapili Hale, 2145 Main Street, Suite 137, Wailuku 96793-1679.

Telephone: (808) 244-2723.

LUKE, Linda K.C. *(Family Court Judge, Hawaii District Court First Judicial Circuit)* Former Per Diem Family Court Judge. Appointed Judge by Chief Justice Herman T. F. Lum to term beginning Dec 29, 1986. Retained by the Judicial Selection Commission 1992 and Dec 29, 1998. Current term expires Dec 28, 2004.

Mailing address: P.O. Box 3498, Honolulu 96811-3498.

Office: Ka'ahumanu Hale, 777 Punchbowl Street, Honolulu 96813-5093.

Telephone: (808) 539-4432.

MARKS, Victoria S. *(Judge, Hawaii Circuit Court First Judicial Circuit)* Appointed by Governor John D. Waihee, III to term beginning May 26, 1994. Term expires May 25, 2004. Former Presiding Administrative Judge Criminal Division. Former Family Court Judge, Hawaii District Court First Circuit, appointed by Chief Justice Herman T. F. Lum.

Office: Ka'ahumanu Hale, 777 Punchbowl Street, Honolulu 96813-5093.

Telephone: (808) 539-4012.

MASUOKA, George M. *(Chief Judge, Hawaii Circuit Court Fifth Judicial Circuit)* Appointed by Governor John D. Waihee, III to term beginning July 8, 1988. Retained by the Judicial Selection Commission July 8, 1998, current term expires July 7, 2008. Also serves as Senior Family Court Judge.
Office: 3059 Umi Street, Room 101, Lihue 96766-1809.
Telephone: (808) 246-3322.

McKENNA, Sabrina *(Judge, Hawaii Circuit Court First Judicial Circuit)* Appointed by Governor Benjamin J. Cayetano to term beginning June 30, 1995. Term expires June 29, 2005. Former Family Court Judge. Former Judge, Hawaii District Court First Circuit, appointed by Chief Justice.
Office: Ka'ahumanu Hale, 777 Punchbowl Street, Honolulu 96813-5093.
Telephone: (808) 539-4220.

McKENZIE, Christopher P. *(Judge, Hawaii District Court First Judicial Circuit)* Per Diem Family Court Judge July 1995 to 2002. Appointed by Chief Justice Ronald T. Y. Moon to term beginning May 22, 2002. Term expires May 21, 2008.
Office: Kauikeaouli Hale, Eleventh Floor, 1111 Alakea Street, Honolulu 96813-2897.
Telephone: (808) 538-5011.

MILKS, Marie N. *(Judge, Hawaii Circuit Court First Judicial Circuit)* Appointed by Governor George R. Ariyoshi to term beginning March 16, 1984. Retained by the Judicial Selection Commission 1994, current term expires March 15, 2004. Former Presiding Administrative Judge Criminal Division.
Office: Ka'ahumanu Hale, 777 Punchbowl Street, Honolulu 96813-5093.
Telephone: (808) 539-4100.

MOLLWAY, Susan Oki *(Judge, United States District Court District of Hawaii)* Appointed for life by President Bill Clinton to term beginning Aug 4, 1998. Born Honolulu Hawaii Nov 6, 1950. Educated at University of Hawaii B.A. with distinction 1971 M.A. 1973 and Harvard Law School J.D. cum laude 1981. Editor-in-Chief Harvard Civil Rights-Civil Liberties Law Review 1980-81. Member Phi Beta Kappa, Phi Kappa Phi and Alpha Lambda Delta. Admitted to practice Hawaii 1981, U.S. District Court District of Hawaii 1981, U.S. Court of Appeals Ninth Circuit 1981 and U.S. Supreme Court 1993. In legal practice Honolulu 1981-98.
Contributing Author *Called From Within—Early Women Lawyers of Hawaii* University of Hawaii Press 1992. Adjunct Professor of Law University of Hawaii School of Law 1987-88. Former Secretary and Director Hawaii Women's Legal Foundation. Former Director Hawaii Women Lawyer's Association and Hawaii Justice Foundation. Former Arbitrator Court-Annexed Arbitration Program. Member District Judges Association, Federal Judges Association, American Judicature Society, The American Law Institute and National Asian Pacific American Bar Association. Recipient Outstanding Woman Lawyer of the Year Award from Hawaii Women Lawyers Association 1987 and Trailblazer Award from National Asian Pacific American Bar Association 1998. Instructor Department of English University of Hawaii 1973-75. Lecturer on English language Takushoku University 1975-76. Editor of English-language books about Asia Charles E. Tuttle Co. in Tokyo 1976-78. Former Member Board of Directors Hawaii Chapter American Civil Liberties Union.
Office: 300 Ala Moana Boulevard, Room C-409, Honolulu 96850-0409.
Telephone: (808) 541-1720.
Fax: (808) 541-1724

MOON, Ronald T. Y. *(Chief Justice, Hawaii Supreme Court)* Appointed by Governor John D. Waihee, III to term beginning March 1990. Retained by the Judicial Selection Commission March 31, 1993 and March 2003. Current term expires March 2013. Chief Justice since March 31, 1993. Born Honolulu Hawaii September 4, 1940. Congregationalist. Educated at Coe College B.A. 1962 and University of Iowa LL.B. 1965. Law Clerk to Chief Judge Martin Pence, U.S. District Court District of Hawaii 1965-66. Admitted to practice Hawaii 1966, U.S. District Court District of Hawaii 1966 and U.S. Court of Appeals Ninth Circuit 1972. In legal practice Honolulu 1966-82. Judge, Hawaii Circuit Court First Circuit 1982-90.
Adjunct Professor of Pretrial Litigation University of Hawaii 1986-88. Bencher American Inns of Court IV. Member American Board of Trial Advocates (President Hawaii Chapter 1986-95, National Secretary 1989-90), The Association of Trial Lawyers of America, American Judicature Society, Hawaii State and American Bar Associations. Participated as lecturer, panelist, moderator or guest speaker at numerous events including seminars on various subjects including Circuit Court rules, settlement and trial procedures and techniques, alternative dispute resolution and legal ethics. Enjoys gardening and orchid growing.
Office: Ali'iolani Hale, 417 South King Street, Honolulu 96813-2902.
Telephone: (808) 539-4700.

MURAKAMI, Paul T. *(Family Court Judge, Hawaii District Court First Judicial Circuit)* Appointed by Chief Justice Ronald T. Y. Moon to term beginning June 7, 2002. Term expires June 6, 2008.
Mailing address: P.O. Box 3498, Honolulu 96811-3498.
Office: Ka'ahumanu Hale, 777 Punchbowl Street, Honolulu 96813-5093.
Telephone: (808) 539-4434.

MURASHIGE, Calvin K. *(Deputy Chief Judge, Hawaii District Court Fifth Judicial Circuit)* Appointed by Chief Justice Ronald T. Y. Moon to term beginning June 25, 1999. Term expires June 24, 2005. Also serves as Family Court Judge. Born Lihue Hawaii Oct 26, 1945. Protestant. Educated at Hamilton College A.B. 1967 and George Washington University National Law Center J.D. 1973. Admitted to practice Hawaii 1974. In legal practice Lihue 1980-99.
Deputy Prosecuting Attorney Kauai County 1974-80. Lieutenant USNR 1969-78. Major Hawaii Air National Guard 1978-89.
Office: 3059 Umi Street, Room 111, Lihue 96766-1809.
Telephone: (808) 246-3391.

NAGATA, Russel S. *(Judge, Hawaii District Court First Judicial Circuit)* Appointed by Chief Justice Herman T. F. Lum to term beginning Oct 5, 1992. Retained

NAGATA, RUSSEL S.—*Continued*
by the Judicial Selection Commission Oct 5, 1998, current term expires Oct 4, 2004.
Office: Kauikeaouli Hale, 11th Floor, 1111 Alakea Street, Honolulu 96813-2897.
Telephone: (808) 538-5007.

NAKAMURA, Greg *(Judge, Hawaii Circuit Court Third Judicial Circuit)* Appointed by Governor John D. Waihee, III to term beginning April 18, 1994. Term expires April 17, 2004. Also serves as Senior Family Court Judge. Former Judge, Hawaii District Court Third Circuit, appointed by Chief Justice Herman T. F. Lum.
Mailing address: P.O. Box 1007, Hilo 96721-1007.
Office: 75 Aupuni Street, Room 205, Hilo 96720-4253.
Telephone: (808) 961-7464.

NAKAYAMA, Paula A. *(Associate Justice, Hawaii Supreme Court)* Appointed by Governor John D. Waihee, III to term beginning April 22, 1993. Retained by the Judicial Selection Commission April 2003, current term expires April 2013. Educated at University of California at Davis and University of California Hastings College of the Law J.D. Admitted to practice Hawaii 1979. Former Judge, Hawaii Circuit Court First Circuit.
Former Deputy Prosecuting Attorney City and County of Honolulu.
Office: Ali'iolani Hale, 417 South King Street, Honolulu 96813-2902.
Telephone: (808) 539-4720.

NAKEA, Clifford L. *(Judge, Hawaii Circuit Court Fifth Judicial Circuit)* Appointed by Governor Benjamin J. Cayetano to term beginning Sept 22, 2000. Term expires Sept 21, 2010. Born Honolulu Hawaii Nov 6, 1943. Catholic. Educated at St. Mary's College B.A. 1965 and University of San Francisco J.D. 1971. Member McAuliffe Society. Admitted to practice Hawaii 1971, U.S. District Court District of Hawaii 1971 and U.S. Court of Appeals Ninth Circuit 1971. Began legal practice Honolulu 1971. In legal practice Lihue 1974-80. Judge and Administrative Judge, Hawaii District Court Fifth Circuit June 27, 1980 to Sept 21, 2000.
Deputy Prosecutor Honolulu 1971-73 and Kauai 1973-74. Member Kauai County and Hawaii State Bar Associations. Director Kauai Museum and YMCA. Finance Chairman St. Catharine's Church. Interests include athletics, home improvements and travel.
Office: 3016 Umi Street, Room 212, Lihue 96766.
Telephone: (808) 632-2600.

NISHIMURA, Rhonda *(Judge, Hawaii Circuit Court First Judicial Circuit)* Appointed by Governor Linda Lingle to term beginning June 20, 2003. Term expires June 19, 2013. Judge, Hawaii District Court First Judicial Circuit June 6, 1997 to June 4, 2003.
Office: Ka'ahumanu Hale, 777 Punchbowl Street, Honolulu 96813-5093.
Telephone: (808) 539-4767.

PACARRO, Clarence A. *(Judge, Hawaii District Court First Judicial Circuit)* Appointed by Chief Justice Ronald T. Y. Moon to term beginning June 7, 2002. Term expires June 6, 2008.
Office: Kauikeaouli Hale, Eleventh Floor, 1111 Alakea Street, Honolulu 96813-2897.
Telephone: (808) 538-5005.

PERKINS, Richard K. *(Judge, Hawaii Circuit Court First Judicial Circuit)* Appointed by Governor John D. Waihee, III to term beginning May 6, 1994. Term expires May 5, 2004. Former Family Court Judge and Presiding Administrative Judge. Currently serves Criminal Division.
Office: Ka'ahumanu Hale, 777 Punchbowl Street, Honolulu 96813-5093.
Telephone: (808) 539-4044.

POLLACK, Richard *(Judge, Hawaii Circuit Court First Judicial Circuit)* Appointed by Governor Benjamin J. Cayetano to term beginning May 10, 2000. Term expires May 9, 2010.
Office: Ka'ahumanu Hale, 777 Punchbowl Street, Honolulu 96813-5093.
Telephone: (808) 539-4686.

PYUN, Matthew S. K. *(Judge, Hawaii District Court Third Judicial Circuit)* Appointed by Chief Justice Ronald T. Y. Moon to term beginning May 14, 2003. Term expires May 13, 2009.
Mailing address: P.O. Box 4879, Hilo 96720-4879.
Office: 205 State Building, 75 Aupuni Street, Hilo 96720-4253.

RADIUS, Karen M. *(Family Court Judge, Hawaii District Court First Judicial Circuit)* Appointed by Chief Justice Ronald T. Y. Moon to term beginning Dec 9, 1994. Retained by the Judicial Selection Commission Dec 9, 2000, current term expires Dec 8, 2006.
Mailing address: P.O. Box 3498, Honolulu 96811-3498.
Office: Ka'ahumanu Hale, 777 Punchbowl Street, Honolulu 96813-5093.
Telephone: (808) 539-4373.

RAFFETTO, Shackley F. *(Chief Judge, Hawaii Circuit Court Second Judicial Circuit)* Appointed by Governor John D. Waihee, III to term beginning June 9, 1994. Term expires June 8, 2004. Also serves as Senior Family Court Judge.
Office: Hoapili Hale, Suite 106, 2145 Main Street, Wailuku 96793-1679.
Telephone: (808) 244-2980.

RICHARDSON, Barbara *(Judge, Hawaii District Court First Judicial Circuit)* Appointed by Chief Justice Ronald T. Y. Moon to term beginning May 5, 2000. Term expires May 4, 2006.
Office: Kauikeaouli Hale, 11th Floor, 1111 Alakea Street, Honolulu 96813-2897.
Telephone: (808) 538-5017.

ROMANCHAK, Eric G. *(Family Court Judge, Hawaii District Court Second Judicial Circuit)* Per Diem Judge 1978-82. Appointed Judge by Chief Justice William S. Richardson to term beginning Oct 29, 1982. Retained by the Judicial Selection Commission 1988, 1994 and Oct 29, 2000. Current term expires Oct 28, 2006. Former Administrative Judge. Born Biloxi Mississippi Aug 15, 1944. Catholic. Educated at University of Michigan A.B. 1966 and Willamette University College of Law J.D. 1970. Law Clerk to Chief Justice William S. Richardson, Hawaii Supreme Court 1970-71. Member Phi Delta Theta. Admitted to practice Hawaii 1970. Be-

ROMANCHAK, ERIC G.—*Continued*

gan legal practice Wailuku 1971. In legal practice Kahului 1976.

Member Hawaii State and American Bar Associations.

Office: 2145 Main Street, Wailuku 96793-1679.

Telephone: (808) 244-2700.

SAKAMOTO, Karl K. *(Judge, Hawaii Circuit Court First Judicial Circuit)* Appointed by Governor Benjamin J. Cayetano to term beginning June 1, 2000. Term expires May 31, 2010. Educated at University of Hawaii B.A. with distinction 1978 J.D. 1982. Member Phi Beta Kappa and Phi Kappa Phi. In legal practice Hawaii March 1989 to Oct 1991.

Senior/Deputy Public Defender Oct 1982 to March 1989. Senior/Enforcement Attorney Oct 1991 to April 1997 and Deputy Executive Director since April 1997 Hawaii Civil Rights Commission.

Office: 1111 Alakea Street, Courtroom 5B, Honolulu 96813-2921.

Telephone: (808) 539-4150.

SENDA, Trudy K. *(Judge, Hawaii District Court Fifth Judicial Circuit)* Appointed by Chief Justice Ronald T. Y. Moon to term beginning May 4, 2001. Term expires May 3, 2007.

Office: 3059 Umi Street, Room 111, Lihue 96766-1809.

Telephone: (808) 246-3366.

SHATTUCK, Carolyn M. *(Magistrate Judge, United States District Court District of Hawaii)* Appointed by U.S. District Court judges to term beginning March 1, 2001. Term expires February 2005. Serves part time.

Mailing address: P.O. Box 1274, APO AP 96555.

Telephone: (805) 355-3276.

SIMMS, Sandra A. *(Judge, Hawaii Circuit Court First Judicial Circuit)* Appointed by Governor John D. Waihee, III to term beginning May 26, 1994. Term expires May 25, 2004. Former Judge, Hawaii District Court First Circuit.

Office: 1111 Alakea Street, Courtroom 5C, Honolulu 96813-2807.

Telephone: (808) 538-5236.

SUEMORI, Allene R. *(Family Court Judge, Hawaii District Court First Judicial Circuit)* Appointed by Chief Justice to term beginning March 31, 1993. Retained by the Judicial Selection Commission March 31, 1999, current term expires March 30, 2005.

Mailing address: P.O. Box 3498, Honolulu 96811-3498.

Office: Ka'ahumanu Hale, 777 Punchbowl Street, Honolulu 96813-5093.

Telephone: (808) 539-4439.

TO'OTO'O, Fa'auuga *(Judge, Hawaii District Court First Judicial Circuit)* Appointed by Chief Justice Ronald T. Y. Moon to term beginning Dec 9, 1994. Retained by the Judicial Selection Commission Dec 9, 2000, current term expires Dec 8, 2006.

Office: Kauikeaouli Hale, 11th Floor, 1111 Alakea Street, Honolulu 96813-2897.

Telephone: (808) 538-5021.

TOWN, Michael Anthony *(Judge, Hawaii Circuit Court First Judicial Circuit)* Appointed by Governor John D. Waihee, III to term beginning April 30, 1993. Retained by the Judicial Selection Commission April 30, 2003, current term expires April 2013. Former Senior Family Court Judge. Born San Diego California Oct 24, 1940. Episcopalian. Educated at Stanford University B.A. 1962, University of California Hastings College of the Law J.D. with honors 1968 and Yale University LL.M. in Constitutional Law 1969. Comment Editor Hastings Law Journal. Law Clerk to Hon. Bernard H. Levinson, Hawaii Supreme Court 1969-70. Member Order of the Coif. Admitted to practice California 1968, Hawaii 1970 and U.S. District Court District of Hawaii 1970. Family Court Judge, Hawaii District Court First Circuit Dec 21, 1979 to 1993, appointed by Governor William S. Richardson.

Athletic Director La Universidad del Cauca Popayan Columbia and New Site Evaluator Peace Corps 1962-64. Supervising Attorney 1970-78 and Deputy Director 1979 Legal Aid Society of Hawaii. Author "The Decision to Disobey: A View of Symbolic Civil Disobedience" 8 Hawaii B. Jour. 5, 1970 reviewed in 56 ABA Jour. 1010 Oct 1970 and "Public Access to Beaches in Hawaii: A Social Necessity" 10 Hawaii B. Jour. 3, 1973. Adjunct Professor of Law University of Hawaii William S. Richardson School of Law since 1982. Member National Council of Juvenile and Family Court Judges (Children in Placement Committee since 1981), State Bar of California, Hawaii State and American (Judicial Administration Division) Bar Associations. Grantee and Fellow National Endowment for the Humanities "Law and Justice" American University Aug 1975 and "Theories of Adjudication" Yale Law School 1981. Member Social Concerns Commission Diocese of Hawaii Episcopal Church since 1980 and Hawaii Committee on the Humanities since 1980.

Office: Ka'ahumanu Hale, 777 Punchbowl Street, Honolulu 96813-5093.

Telephone: (808) 539-4074.

UALE, Bode Amilale *(Family Court Judge, Hawaii District Court First Judicial Circuit)* Per Diem Family Court Judge Aug 1991 to Oct 1992. Appointed Family Court Judge by Chief Justice to term beginning Oct 27, 1992. Retained by the Judicial Selection Commission Oct 27, 1998, current term expires Oct 26, 2004. Lead Judge Juvenile Division 1993-96 and June 1999 to Aug 2000. Currently serves Domestic Division. Church of Jesus Christ of Latter-Day Saints. Educated at Brigham Young University B.A. cum laude 1979 and University of Hawaii School of Law J.D. 1984. Admitted to practice Hawaii 1984. In legal practice Honolulu April 1989 to Oct 1992.

Deputy Public Defender Hawaii Oct 1984 to April 1989. Member Hawaii State Trial Judges Association and National Council of Juvenile and Family Court Judges. Lead Judge for Hawaii Diversion Project Model Courts and Victims Act Model Courts National Council of Juvenile and Family Court Judges. Recipient Distinguished Service to Children and Families Award from Child and Parents Advocates Section Hawaii State Bar Association 1994 and Honored Alumnus Award for Division of Social Sciences from Alumni Association Brigham Young University at Laie Feb 1999. Advisory Board Member "Ho'o Imi Ola" Minority Admissions Program John A. Burns School of Medicine University of Hawaii and Asian/Pacific Islander Youth Violence Prevention Center. Volunteer Speaker "No Hope in Dope" Drug Prevention Program Honolulu Police Department. Venturing Crew Advisor Boy Scouts of America. Enjoys singing and playing guitar and ukulele. Per-

UALE, BODE AMILALE—*Continued*

sonal Statement or Quote: "Preparation is the key to competent client representation."

Mailing address: P.O. Box 3498, Honolulu 96811-3498.

Office: Ka'ahumanu Hale, 777 Punchbowl Street, Honolulu 96813-5093.

Telephone: (808) 539-4438.

VALDRIZ, Geronimo, Jr. *(Family Court Judge, Hawaii District Court Second Judicial Circuit)* Appointed by Chief Justice Ronald T. Y. Moon to term beginning May 26, 2000. Term expires May 25, 2006.

Office: 2145 Main Street, Wailuku 96793-1679.

Telephone: (808) 244-2700.

WALDORF, Marcia J. *(Family Court Judge, Hawaii Circuit Court First Judicial Circuit)* Appointed by Governor Benjamin J. Cayetano to term beginning June 18, 2002. Term expires June 17, 2012. Judge and Administrative Judge, Hawaii District Court First Judicial Circuit Jan 3, 1985 to June 17, 2002.

Office: 1111 Alakea Street, Courtroom 8B, Honolulu 96813-2921.

Telephone: (808) 538-5874.

WATANABE, Corinne K. A. *(Associate Judge, Hawaii Intermediate Court of Appeals)* Appointed by Governor John D. Waihee, III to term beginning May 11, 1992. Retained by the Judicial Selection Commission May 2002, current term expires May 10, 2012.

Office: Kapuaiwa Building, Second Floor, 426 Queen Street, Honolulu 96813.

Telephone: (808) 539-4752.

WATANABE, Wilfred K. *(Judge, Hawaii Circuit Court First Judicial Circuit)* Appointed by Governor George R. Ariyoshi to term beginning April 30, 1985. Retained by the Judicial Selection Commission April 30, 1995, current term expires April 29, 2005. Former Judge, Hawaii District Court First Circuit.

Office: Ka'ahumanu Hale, 777 Punchbowl Street, Honolulu 96813-5093.

Telephone: (808) 539-4060.

WILSON, Michael D. *(Judge, Hawaii Circuit Court First Judicial Circuit)* Appointed by Governor Benjamin J. Cayetano to term beginning May 10, 2000. Term expires May 9, 2010. Former Family Court Judge.

Office: Ka'ahumanu Hale, 777 Punchbowl Street, Honolulu 96813-5093.

Telephone: (808) 539-4006.

WONG, Frances Q. F. *(Senior Family Court Judge, Hawaii Circuit Court First Judicial Circuit)* Appointed Judge by Governor John D. Waihee, III to term beginning May 11, 1992. Retained by the Judicial Selection Commission to term beginning May 11, 2002, current term expires May 10, 2012. Born Hong Kong Nov 24, 1951. United Church of Christ. Educated at University of Hawaii B.Ed. 1973 and University of Southern California J.D. 1977. Admitted to practice Hawaii 1977. Began legal practice Honolulu 1977. Per Diem Judge Dec 1983 to Feb 1986 and Family Court Judge Feb 1986 to May 1992, Hawaii District Court First Circuit.

Member Hawaii Women Lawyers, American Judicature Society and Hawaii State Bar Association.

Office: Ka'ahumanu Hale, 777 Punchbowl Street, Honolulu 96813-5093.

Telephone: (808) 539-4440.

YOSHIOKA, Terence T. *(Family Court Judge, Hawaii District Court Third Judicial Circuit)* Appointed by Chief Justice Ronald T. Y. Moon to term beginning April 28, 2000. Term expires April 27, 2006.

Mailing address: P.O. Box 1007, Hilo 96721-1007.

Office: 345 Kekuanaoa Street, Room 40, Hilo 96720-4388.

Telephone: (808) 934-5700.

IDAHO

Capital BOISE

UNITED STATES DISTRICT COURT DISTRICT OF IDAHO

Within Idaho, exclusive of Yellowstone National Park (which is under the jurisdiction of the United States District Court District of Wyoming), there is one United States District Court. The court sits at Boise, Coeur d'Alene, Moscow and Pocatello. For descriptive information refer to the United States Courts section.

Chief Judge
B. Lynn Winmill

Judge
Edward J. Lodge

Clerk
Cameron S. Burke
U.S. Courthouse, MSC 039
550 West Fort Street
Boise, Idaho 83724
(208) 334-1361

UNITED STATES MAGISTRATE JUDGES OF IDAHO

Mikel H. Williams
Larry M. Boyle

UNITED STATES BANKRUPTCY COURT OF IDAHO

Chief Judge
Jim D. Pappas

Judge
Terry L. Myers

Bankruptcy Clerk
Cameron S. Burke
U.S. Courthouse, MSC 039
550 West Fort Street
Boise, Idaho 83724
(208) 334-1074

IDAHO SUPREME COURT

The Supreme Court is Idaho's court of last resort. The court consists of a chief justice and four justices elected at large in nonpartisan elections for staggered six-year terms. Vacancies are filled by the governor from a list of candidates provided by the Judicial Council. Newly appointed justices run for election to six-year terms at the primary election immediately preceding completion of the unexpired term. The chief justice is elected by peer vote to a four-year term.

The court has final appellate jurisdiction over decisions of the Court of Appeals, interim orders and final judgments of the District Court, orders of the Industrial Accident Commission and the Public Utilities Commission and criminal cases imposing sentences of capital punishment. The court has original jurisdiction to hear claims against the state and disciplinary actions against attorneys and to issue extraordinary writs and all other writs necessary to the exercise of proper jurisdiction. The court exercises general supervisory and administrative control over the lower courts.

The court sits en banc at Boise, Coeur d'Alene, Lewiston, Pocatello and Twin Falls.

Chief Justice
Linda Copple Trout

Justices
Gerald F. Schroeder
Wayne L. Kidwell
Daniel T. Eismann
Roger S. Burdick

Retired Justice
Jesse R. Walters, Jr.

Clerk
Frederick C. Lyon
Supreme Court Building
451 West State Street
Boise, Idaho 83720-0101
(208) 334-2210

Administrative Director of the Courts
Patricia Tobias
Supreme Court Building
451 West State Street
Boise, Idaho 83720-0101
(208) 334-2246

IDAHO COURT OF APPEALS

The Court of Appeals, which began operation on Jan 4, 1982, is Idaho's court of intermediate appellate jurisdiction. The court consists of a chief judge and two judges elected in nonpartisan elections for staggered six-year terms. Vacancies are filled by the governor from a list of candidates provided by the Judicial Council. Newly appointed judges run for election to six-year terms at the primary election immediately preceding completion of the unexpired term. A chief judge is appointed by the chief justice to serve a two-year term and may be reappointed. Active or retired district judges, retired Supreme Court justices and retired Court of Appeals judges may be assigned to the court as needed.

The court has appellate jurisdiction over cases assigned by the Supreme Court. The Court of Appeals may not hear cases involving claims against the state, extraordinary writs, appeals from imposition of capital punishment or appeals from the Industrial Accident Commission or Public Utilities Commission. The Supreme Court may review any decision of the court, but

IDAHO COURT OF APPEALS—*Continued*

in most cases the decisions of the Court of Appeals are final.

The court sits en banc at Boise and may sit elsewhere as needed.

Chief Judge
Karen L. Lansing

Judges
Darrel R. Perry
Sergio A. Gutierrez

IDAHO DISTRICT COURT

The District Court is Idaho's trial court of general jurisdiction. Judges are elected in nonpartisan elections in each of the seven judicial districts for four-year terms. Vacancies are filled by the governor from a list of candidates provided by the Judicial Council. Newly appointed judges run for election to four-year terms at the primary election immediately preceding the completion of the unexpired term. An administrative judge is elected by peer vote to serve an unspecified term in each district. A Magistrate Division is established in each district with judges of the Magistrate Division initially appointed by a District Magistrates Commission for two-year terms; subsequent four-year terms are by retention vote in county elections. There is at least one resident Magistrate Division judge for each county.

The court exercises original jurisdiction over civil and criminal cases including personal injury and other torts, contracts, domestic relations, felonies, post-conviction review and habeas corpus. The court exercises appellate jurisdiction over cases from the Magistrate Division, Small Claims Department and state agencies and boards. The Magistrate Division has jurisdiction of civil actions involving not more than $10,000, preliminary hearings on felony matters and full jurisdiction of misdemeanor cases. The division also handles probate and juvenile matters and domestic relations cases and may issue arrest and search warrants. A Small Claims Department is established in the Magistrate Division with jurisdiction in civil actions up to $4,000. In the Fifth Judicial District there is a division called Snake River Basin Adjudication which was created to handle water disputes.

The court sits at the county seats.

FIRST JUDICIAL DISTRICT includes Benewah, Bonner, Boundary, Kootenai and Shoshone counties. The court sits at St. Maries, Sandpoint, Bonners Ferry, Coeur d'Alene and Wallace.

Administrative Judge
Charles W. Hosack

Judges
Fred M. Gibler
John Patrick Luster
John T. Mitchell
Steven Verby

Resident County	Judge of Magistrate Division
Benewah	Patrick R. McFadden
Bonner	Barbara A. Buchanan
	Debra A. Heise
	Don L. Swanstrom
Boundary	Justin W. Julian
Kootenai	Robert B. Burton
	Eugene A. Marano
	Benjamin R. Simpson
	Barry E. Watson
	Scott L. Wayman
Shoshone	Daniel J. McGee

SECOND JUDICIAL DISTRICT includes Clearwater, Idaho, Latah, Lewis and Nez Perce counties. The court sits at Orofino, Grangeville, Moscow, Nezperce and Lewiston.

Administrative Judge
John R. Stegner

Judges
Carl B. Kerrick
Jeff M. Brudie
John Bradbury

Resident County	Judge of Magistrate Division
Clearwater	Orin Lee Squire
Idaho	Michael J. Griffin
Latah	William C. Hamlett
Lewis	Stephen L. Calhoun
Nez Perce	Jay P. Gaskill
	Gregory K. Kalbfleisch
	Kent J. Merica

THIRD JUDICIAL DISTRICT includes Adams, Canyon, Gem, Owyhee, Payette and Washington counties. The court sits at Council, Caldwell, Emmett, Murphy, Payette and Weiser.

Administrative Judge
James C. Morfitt

Judges
Gregory M. Culet
Stephen W. Drescher
Renae Hoff
Juneal Kerrick

Resident County	Judge of Magistrate Division
Adams	James C. Peart
Canyon	Gary D. DeMeyer
	Bradly S. Ford
	Todd Joyner
	Frank Kotyk
	James A. "J.R." Schiller
	Robert M. Taisey, Jr.
Gem	Gordon W. Petrie
Owyhee	Thomas J. Ryan
Payette	William B. Dillon, III
	A. Lynne Krogh
Washington	Gregory F. Frates

FOURTH JUDICIAL DISTRICT includes Ada, Boise, Elmore and Valley counties. The court sits at Boise, Idaho City, Mountain Home and Cascade.

Administrative Judge
Darla S. Williamson

Judges

Deborah A. Bail	Cheri C. Copsey
Joel D. Horton	Michael R. McLaughlin
Thomas F. Neville	Kathryn A. Sticklen
Michael Wetherell	Ronald J. Wilper

IDAHO DISTRICT COURT—*Continued*

Resident County	Judge of Magistrate Division
Ada	Christopher M. Bieter
	Russell A. Comstock
	David E. Day
	R. Michael Dennard
	John F. Dutcher
	Timothy L. Hansen
	Charles L. Hay
	Terry R. McDaniel
	Carolyn M. Minder
	Thomas R. Morden
	Michael Oths
	Richard Allan Schmidt
	L. Kevin Swain
	John C. Vehlow
	Thomas P. Watkins
Boise	Patricia G. Young
Elmore	David C. Epis
	John R. Sellman
Valley	Henry R. Boomer

FIFTH JUDICIAL DISTRICT includes Blaine, Camas, Cassia, Gooding, Jerome, Lincoln, Minidoka and Twin Falls counties. The court sits at Hailey, Fairfield, Burley, Gooding, Jerome, Shoshone, Rupert and Twin Falls.

Administrative Judge
vacancy

Judges

Monte B. Carlson
John C. Hohnhorst
John M. Melanson
Nathan W. Higer
James J. May
R. Barry Wood

Resident County	Judge of Magistrate Division
Blaine	Robert J. Elgee
Camas	John F. Varin
Cassia	Michael R. Crabtree
	Roy C. Holloway
Gooding	Kevin P. Cassidy
Jerome	Thomas H. Borresen
Lincoln	Mark A. Ingram
Minidoka	Larry R. Duff
Twin Falls	Charles P. Brumbach
	Howard D. Smyser
	Randy J. Stoker

SIXTH JUDICIAL DISTRICT includes Bannock, Bear Lake, Caribou, Franklin, Oneida and Power counties. The court sits at Pocatello, Paris, Soda Springs, Preston, Malad City and American Falls.

Administrative Judge
Don L. Harding

Judges

Peter D. McDermott
N. Randy Smith
William H. Woodland

Resident County	Judge of Magistrate Division
Bannock	Gaylen L. Box
	R. Ted Israel
	Dan C. McDougall
	Bryan K. Murray
	Boyd Barnard White, II
Bear Lake	Orene Lynn Brower
Caribou	Ronald M. Hart
Franklin	Eric Hunn
Oneida	David L. Evans
Power	Mark Beebe

SEVENTH JUDICIAL DISTRICT includes Bingham, Bonneville, Butte, Clark, Custer, Fremont, Jefferson, Lemhi, Madison and Teton counties. The court sits at Blackfoot, Idaho Falls, Arco, Dubois, Challis, St. Anthony, Rigby, Salmon, Rexburg and Driggs.

Administrative Judge
James C. Herndon

Judges

Gregory S. Anderson
Brent J. Moss
Richard T. St. Clair
Jon J. Shindurling

Resident County	Judge of Magistrate Division
Bingham	R. James Archibald
	Ryan W. Boyer
Bonneville	Earl Blower
	Linda J. Cook
	L. Mark Riddoch
Butte	Ralph Savage
Clark	William Hollerich
Custer	Charles L. Roos
Fremont	Keith M. Walker
Jefferson	Michael B. Kennedy
Lemhi	Jerry R. Meyers
Madison	Mark S. Rammell
Teton	Colin W. Luke

Idaho Counties and County Seats

Ada
Boise

Adams
Council

Bannock
Pocatello

Bear Lake
Paris

Benewah
St. Maries

Bingham
Blackfoot

Blaine
Hailey

Boise
Idaho City

Bonner
Sandpoint

Bonneville
Idaho Falls

Boundary
Bonners Ferry

Butte
Arco

Camas
Fairfield

Canyon
Caldwell

Caribou
Soda Springs

Cassia
Burley

COUNTIES AND COUNTY SEATS—*Continued*

Clark
Dubois

Clearwater
Orofino

Custer
Challis

Elmore
Mountain Home

Franklin
Preston

Fremont
St. Anthony

Gem
Emmett

Gooding
Gooding

Idaho
Grangeville

Jefferson
Rigby

Jerome
Jerome

Kootenai
Coeur d'Alene

Latah
Moscow

Lemhi
Salmon

Lewis
Nezperce

Lincoln
Shoshone

Madison
Rexburg

Minidoka
Rupert

Nez Perce
Lewiston

Oneida
Malad City

Owyhee
Murphy

Payette
Payette

Power
American Falls

Shoshone
Wallace

Teton
Driggs

Twin Falls
Twin Falls

Valley
Cascade

Washington
Weiser

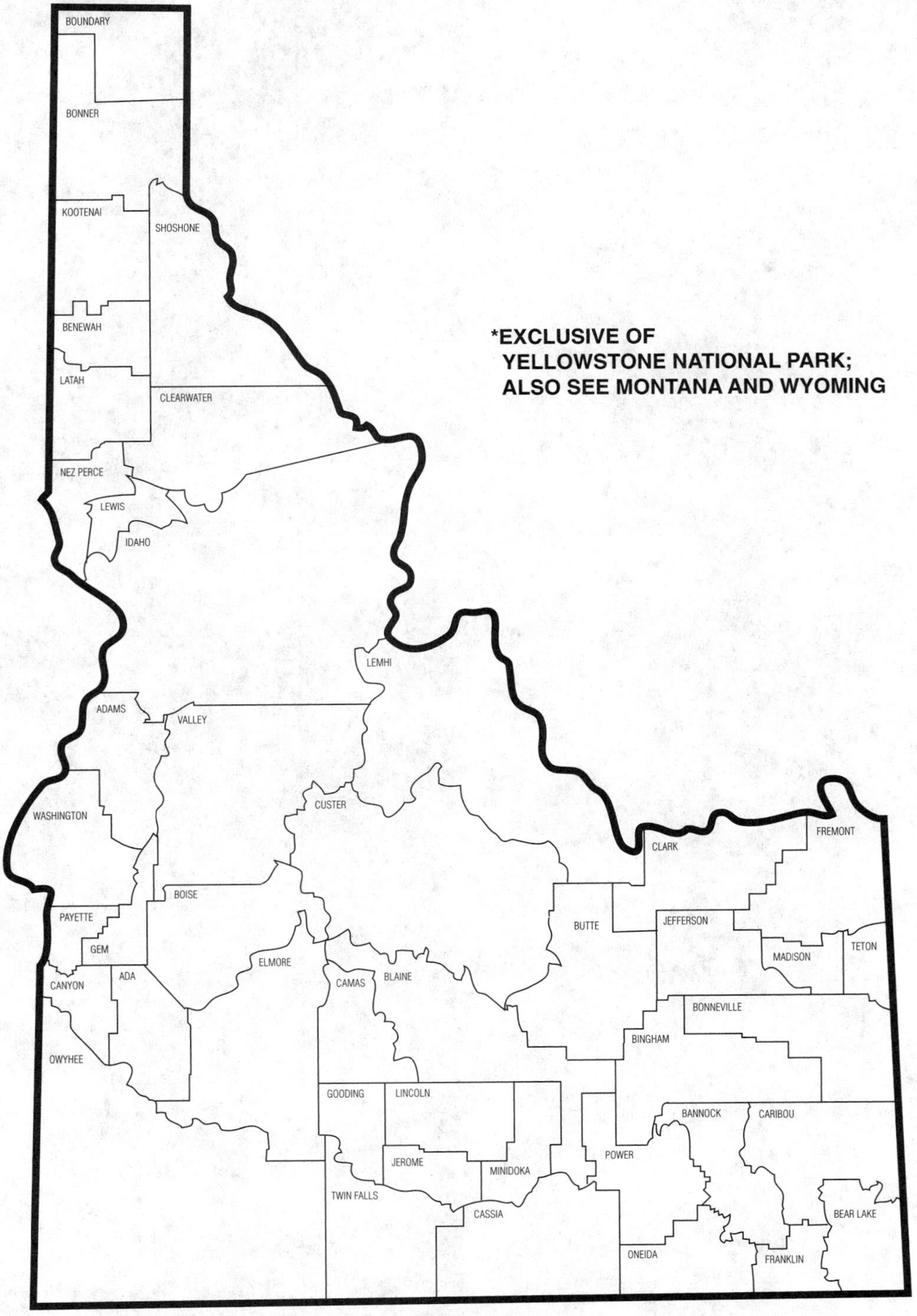
BOUNDARY
BONNER
KOOTENAI
SHOSHONE
BENEWAH
LATAH
CLEARWATER
NEZ PERCE
LEWIS
IDAHO
LEMHI
ADAMS
VALLEY
CUSTER
WASHINGTON
CLARK
FREMONT
BOISE
PAYETTE
BUTTE
JEFFERSON
TETON
MADISON
GEM
ELMORE
CANYON
ADA
CAMAS
BLAINE
BONNEVILLE
BINGHAM
OWYHEE
GOODING
LINCOLN
BANNOCK
CARIBOU
POWER
JEROME
MINIDOKA
TWIN FALLS
CASSIA
BEAR LAKE
ONEIDA
FRANKLIN

*EXCLUSIVE OF
YELLOWSTONE NATIONAL PARK;
ALSO SEE MONTANA AND WYOMING

UNITED STATES DISTRICT COURT DISTRICT OF IDAHO*

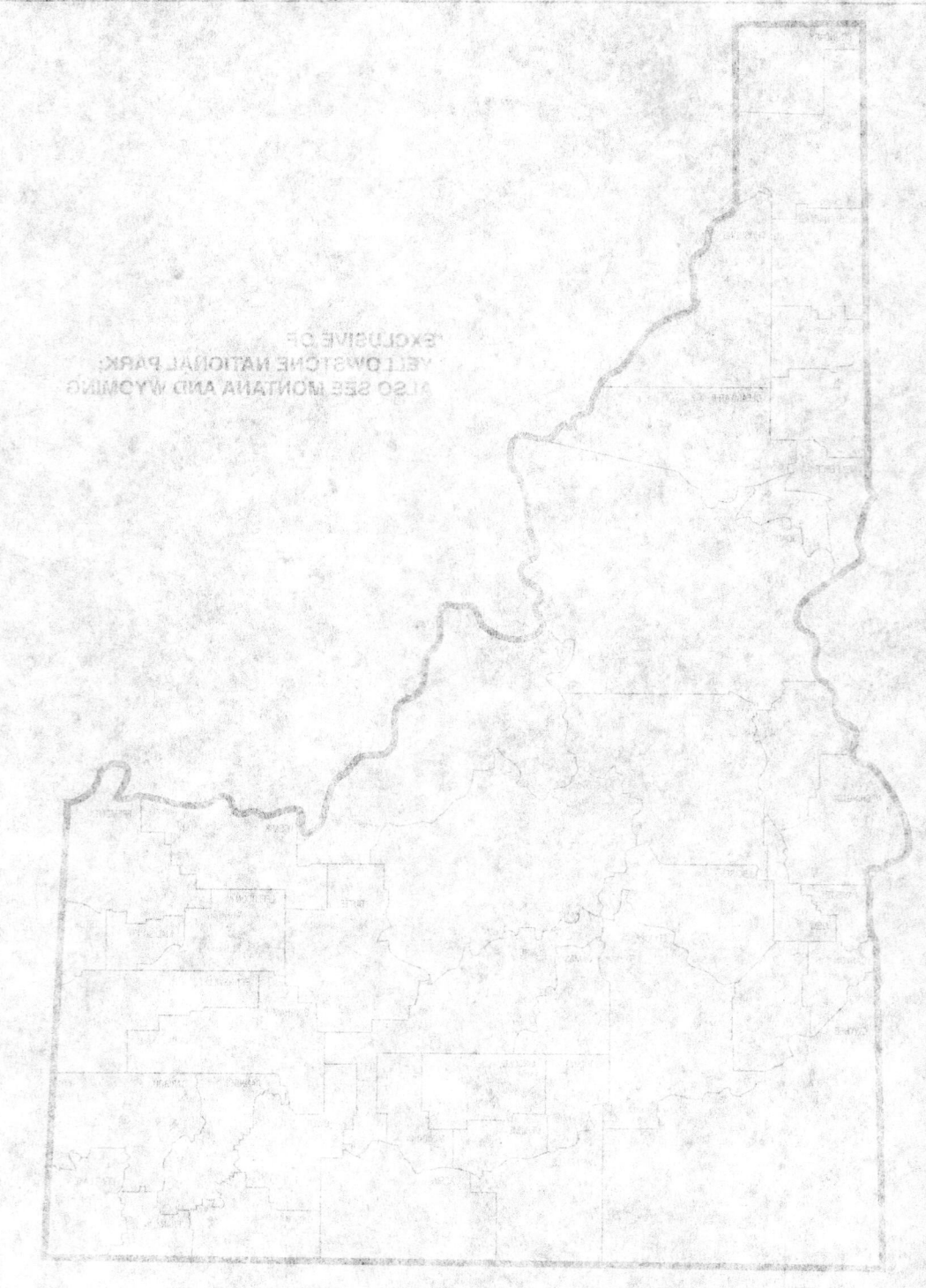

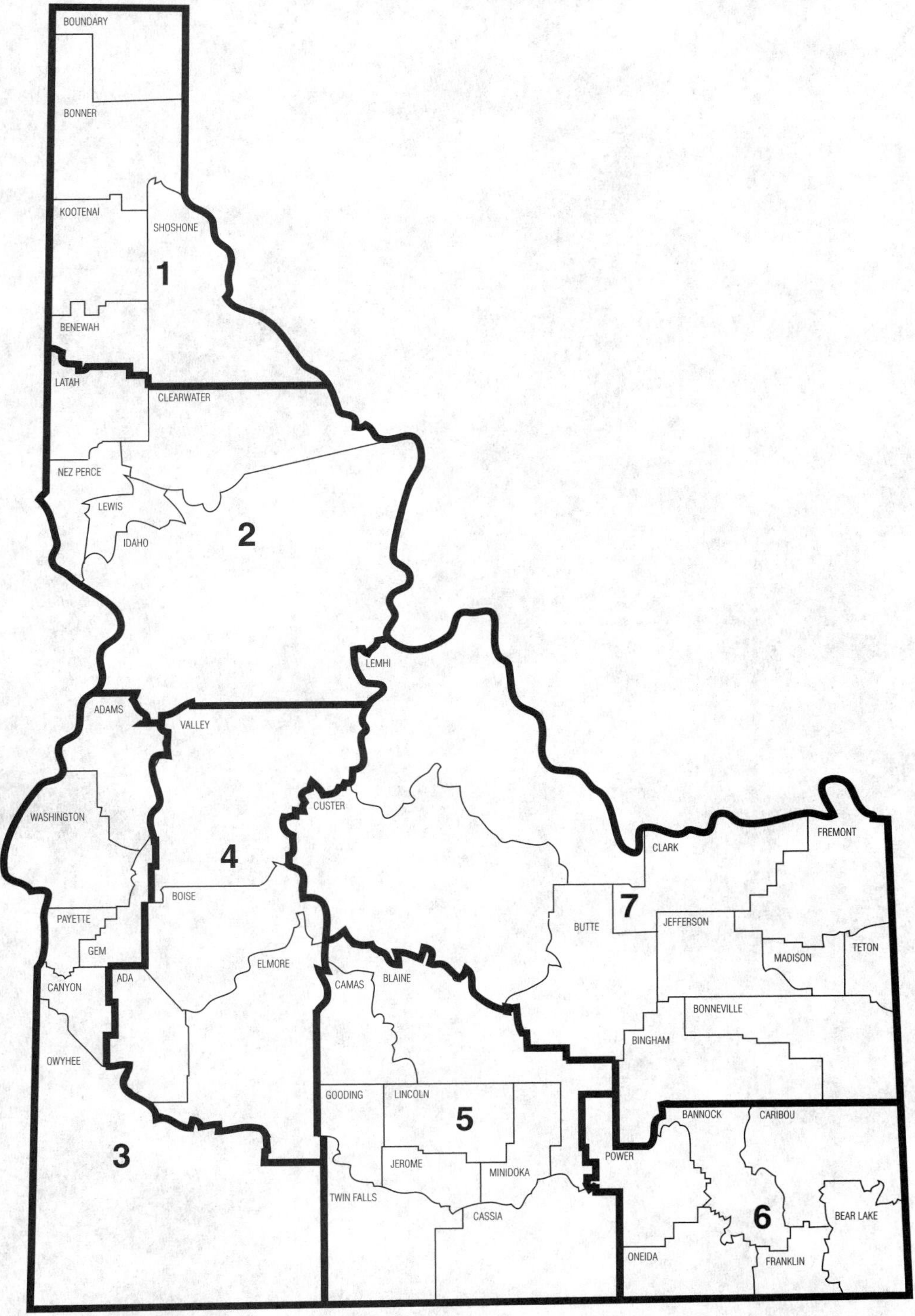
BOUNDARY
BONNER
KOOTENAI
SHOSHONE
1
BENEWAH
LATAH
CLEARWATER
NEZ PERCE
LEWIS
IDAHO
2
LEMHI
ADAMS
VALLEY
CUSTER
WASHINGTON
4
BOISE
CLARK
FREMONT
7
BUTTE
JEFFERSON
MADISON
TETON
PAYETTE
GEM
ELMORE
CANYON
ADA
CAMAS
BLAINE
BONNEVILLE
BINGHAM
OWYHEE
GOODING
LINCOLN
5
BANNOCK
CARIBOU
3
JEROME
MINIDOKA
POWER
TWIN FALLS
CASSIA
6
BEAR LAKE
ONEIDA
FRANKLIN

JUDICIAL DISTRICTS OF IDAHO DISTRICT COURT

IDAHO

ANDERSON, Gregory S. *(Judge, Idaho District Court Seventh Judicial District)*
Office: 605 North Capital Avenue, Idaho Falls 83402.
Telephone: (208) 529-1350.
Fax: (208) 529-1300

ARCHIBALD, R. James *(Judge, Idaho District Court Seventh Judicial District Magistrate Division)* Appointed to term beginning Jan 2003. Serves Bingham County.
Office: 501 North Maple, #402, Blackfoot 83221-1700.
Telephone: (208) 785-8040.
Fax: (208) 785-8057

BAIL, Deborah A. *(Judge, Idaho District Court Fourth Judicial District)*
Office: Ada County Courthouse, 200 West Front Street, Boise 83702-7300.
Telephone: (208) 287-7561.
Fax: (208) 287-7529

BEEBE, Mark *(Judge, Idaho District Court Sixth Judicial District Magistrate Division)* Appointed to term beginning Sept 15, 1985. Retained by election Nov 1988, Nov 1992, Nov 1996 and Nov 2000. Current term expires Jan 2005. Serves Power County. Born Moscow Idaho Jan 8, 1948. Educated at Boise State University B.A. and University of Idaho J.D. Admitted to practice Idaho 1974. In legal practice American Falls 1974-85.
Prosecuting Attorney 1978-85. Member Portneuf Inns of Court. National Guard E-4. Enjoys golf, basketball, fly fishing, skiing, waterfowl hunting and weightlifting.
Office: 543 Bannock, American Falls 83211.
Telephone: (208) 226-7619.
Fax: (208) 226-7612

BIETER, Christopher M. *(Judge, Idaho District Court Fourth Judicial District Magistrate Division)* Serves Ada County.
Office: 200 West Front Street, Boise 83702-7300.
Telephone: (208) 287-7621.
Fax: (208) 287-7499

BLOWER, Earl *(Judge, Idaho District Court Seventh Judicial District Magistrate Division)* Serves Bonneville County.
Office: 605 North Capital Avenue, Idaho Falls 83402.
Telephone: (208) 529-1350.
Fax: (208) 529-1300

BOOMER, Henry R. *(Judge, Idaho District Court Fourth Judicial District Magistrate Division)* Appointed Feb 2001. Serves Valley County.
Mailing address: P.O. Box 1350, Cascade 83611.
Office: Valley County Courthouse, Cascade 83611.
Telephone: (208) 382-7178.
Fax: (208) 382-7184

BORRESEN, Thomas H. *(Judge, Idaho District Court Fifth Judicial District Magistrate Division)* Serves Jerome County.
Office: 310 Jerome County Courthouse, 300 North Lincoln, Jerome 83338.
Telephone: (208) 324-8811.
Fax: (208) 324-2719

BOX, Gaylen L. *(Judge, Idaho District Court Sixth Judicial District Magistrate Division)* Serves Bannock County.
Mailing address: P.O. Box 4847, Pocatello 83205.
Telephone: (208) 236-7255.
Fax: (208) 236-7012

BOYER, Ryan W. *(Judge, Idaho District Court Seventh Judicial District Magistrate Division)* Appointed to term beginning Feb 1, 1999. Retained by election 2000, current term expires 2004. Serves Bingham County. Educated at Brigham Young University B.A. and University of Idaho M.S. J.D. In legal practice Idaho Falls 1987-99.
Former City Attorney Arco City.
Office: 501 North Maple, #402, Blackfoot 83221-1700.
Telephone: (208) 785-8040.
Fax: (208) 785-8057

BOYLE, Larry M. *(Magistrate Judge, United States District Court District of Idaho)* Appointed by U.S. District Court judges to term beginning April 1, 1992. Currently serves as Chief Magistrate Judge. Born Seattle Washington June 23, 1943. In legal practice Idaho Falls 1973-86. Former Judge, Idaho District Court Seventh Judicial District. Former Justice, Idaho Supreme Court.
Office: 630 U.S. Courthouse, MSC 040, 550 West Fort Street, Boise 83724.
Telephone: (208) 334-9010.

BRADBURY, John *(Judge, Idaho District Court Second Judicial District)* Elected 2002 to term beginning Jan 2003. Term expires Jan 2007.
Office: Idaho County Courthouse, Grangeville 83530.
Telephone: (208) 983-2776.
Fax: (208) 983-2376

BROWER, Orene Lynn *(Judge, Idaho District Court Sixth Judicial District Magistrate Division)* Appointed to term beginning April 1, 1989. Retained by election Nov 1990, Nov 1994, Nov 1998 and Nov 2002. Current term expires Jan 2007. Serves Bear Lake County. Born Pocatello Idaho July 13, 1955. Church of Jesus Christ of Latter-day Saints. Educated at State University of New York B.S. 1980 and University of Idaho J.D. 1982. Admitted to practice Idaho 1983 and U.S. District Court District of Idaho 1983. In legal practice Montpelier 1983-89.
Prosecuting Attorney Bear Lake County 1985-89.
Mailing address: P.O. Box 190, Paris 83261.
Telephone: (208) 945-2208.
Fax: (208) 945-2780

BRUDIE, Jeff M. *(Judge, Idaho District Court Second Judicial District)* Appointed by Governor Dirk Kempthorne June 2001.

Mailing address: P.O. Box 896, Lewiston 83501.
Office: Nez Perce County Courthouse, Lewiston 83501.
Telephone: (208) 799-3057.
Fax: (208) 799-3058

BRUMBACH, Charles P. *(Judge, Idaho District Court Fifth Judicial District Magistrate Division)* Serves Twin Falls County.

Mailing address: P.O. Box 126, Twin Falls 83303-0126.
Office: 427 Shoshone Street North, Twin Falls 83301.
Telephone: (208) 736-4032.
Fax: (208) 736-4155

BUCHANAN, Barbara A. *(Judge, Idaho District Court First Judicial District Magistrate Division)* Serves Bonner County.

Office: 215 South First Avenue, Sandpoint 83864.
Telephone: (208) 265-1446.
Fax: (208) 265-1468

BURDICK, Roger S. *(Justice, Idaho Supreme Court)* Appointed by Governor Dirk Kempthorne June 26, 2003. Judge, Idaho District Court Fifth Judicial District Magistrate Division Sept 1981 to Sept 1993. Former Administrative Judge, Idaho District Court Fifth Judicial District, appointed by Governor Cecil D. Andrus Sept 1993.

Mailing address: P.O. Box 83720, Boise 83720-0101.
Office: 451 West State Street, Boise 83720.
Telephone: (208) 334-2210.

BURTON, Robert B. *(Judge, Idaho District Court First Judicial District Magistrate Division)* Serves Kootenai County.

Mailing address: P.O. Box 9000, Coeur d'Alene 83816-9000.
Telephone: (208) 446-1104.

CALHOUN, Stephen L. *(Judge, Idaho District Court Second Judicial District Magistrate Division)* Serves Lewis County.

Mailing address: P.O. Box 39, Nezperce 83543.
Office: Lewis County Courthouse, Nezperce 83543.
Telephone: (208) 937-2251.
Fax: (208) 937-9233

CARLSON, Monte B. *(Judge, Idaho District Court Fifth Judicial District)*

Office: Cassia County Courthouse, 1459 Overland Avenue, Burley 83318.
Telephone: (208) 878-7152.
Fax: (208) 878-1010

CASSIDY, Kevin P. *(Judge, Idaho District Court Fifth Judicial District Magistrate Division)* Serves Gooding County.

Mailing address: P.O. Box 477, Gooding 83330.
Office: 624 Main Street, Gooding 83330.
Telephone: (208) 934-4261.
Fax: (208) 934-4408

COMSTOCK, Russell A. *(Judge, Idaho District Court Fourth Judicial District Magistrate Division)* Serves Ada County.

Office: 200 West Front Street, Boise 83702-7300.
Telephone: (208) 287-7471.
Fax: (208) 287-7499

COOK, Linda J. *(Judge, Idaho District Court Seventh Judicial District Magistrate Division)* Assumed office Jan 1, 1976. Retained by election 1978, 1982, 1986, 1990, 1994, 1998 and 2002. Current term expires Jan 2007. Serves Bonneville County. Born Idaho Falls Idaho Feb 13, 1944. Church of Jesus Christ of Latter-Day Saints. Educated at Brigham Young University B.S. 1965 M.S. 1968 and University of Idaho J.D. 1973. Admitted to practice Idaho 1973. Began legal practice Idaho Falls 1973.

Author "Legal Status of Homemakers" I.W.Y. Commission Government Printing Office 1977. Enjoys carpentry, woodworking and photography.

Office: 605 North Capital Avenue, Idaho Falls 83402.
Telephone: (208) 529-1350.
Fax: (208) 529-1300

COPSEY, Cheri C. *(Judge, Idaho District Court Fourth Judicial District)*

Office: Ada County Courthouse, 200 West Front Street, Boise 83702-7300.
Telephone: (208) 287-7534.
Fax: (208) 287-7529

CRABTREE, Michael R. *(Judge, Idaho District Court Fifth Judicial District Magistrate Division)* Serves Cassia County.

Office: Cassia County Courthouse, 1459 Overland Avenue, Burley 83318.
Telephone: (208) 878-0180.
Fax: (208) 878-1003

CULET, Gregory M. *(Judge, Idaho District Court Third Judicial District)* Judge of Magistrate Division June 1, 1980 to 2001. Appointed District Judge by Governor Dirk Kempthorne Oct 2001. Born San Antonio Texas Dec 18, 1951. Educated at University of Idaho B.A. in Political Science 1974 J.D. 1978. Admitted to practice Idaho 1978. Began legal practice Caldwell 1978.

Former Chief Deputy Criminal Prosecutor. Instructor in Business Law Treasure Valley Community College Oregon 1986-89. Chair Supreme Court Committee on Juvenile Rules. Member Idaho State Bar. Enjoys camping, fishing, hiking, skiing and outdoor activities.

Office: 1115 Albany Street, Caldwell 83605.
Telephone: (208) 454-7370.
Fax: (208) 454-7442

DAY, David E. *(Judge, Idaho District Court Fourth Judicial District Magistrate Division)* Appointed to term beginning July 1, 1995. Retained by election Jan 1999 and 2002. Current term expires Jan 2007. Serves Ada County. Born Council Idaho Sept 15, 1953. Educated at University of Idaho B.S. 1973 J.D. cum laude 1983. Staff member Idaho Law Review 1982-83. Admitted to practice Idaho 1984, Oregon 1986, U.S. District Courts District of Idaho 1984 and District of Oregon 1989 and U.S. Court of Appeals Ninth Circuit 1986. In legal practice Boise Idaho Jan 1984 to June 1995.

Advisory Board *The Advocate* 1996-99. Member Exam Committee Idaho State Bar since 2000. Chair Subcommittee to draft uniform family law forms Idaho Supreme Court. Social Work/Psychology Specialist U.S. Army 1974-77. Restaurant Manager Pizza Hut of Idaho, Inc. June 1978 to May 1979. Department Manager Sears

DAY, DAVID E.—*Continued*
May 1979 to Aug 1981. Interests include law, personal computers, camping, hiking and reading.
Office: 200 West Front Street, Boise 83702-7300.
Telephone: (208) 287-7473.
Fax: (208) 287-7499

DeMEYER, Gary D. *(Judge, Idaho District Court Third Judicial District Magistrate Division)* Serves Canyon County.
Office: 1115 Albany Street, Caldwell 83605.
Telephone: (208) 454-7376.
Fax: (208) 454-7525

DENNARD, R. Michael *(Judge, Idaho District Court Fourth Judicial District Magistrate Division)* Serves Ada County.
Office: 200 West Front Street, Boise 83702-7300.
Telephone: (208) 287-7475.
Fax: (208) 287-7499

DILLON, William B., III *(Judge, Idaho District Court Third Judicial District Magistrate Division)* Appointed to term beginning March 31, 1986. Retained by election. Current term expires Jan 2005. Serves Payette County. Born Omaha Nebraska Aug 19, 1950. Educated at Creighton University 1968-69 and University of Nebraska B.A. 1972 LL.M. 1977. Moot Court. Admitted to practice Idaho 1978.
Deputy Prosecuting Attorney Caldwell 1978-82. Deputy Attorney General Boise 1982-86. Attended Idaho Judicial Conference July 1986, Idaho New Judge Seminar Sept 1986, Magistrate Institute Nov 1986 and The National Judicial College March 1987. Second Lieutenant U.S. Army 1973-75. Member Kiwanis, Flyfishers of Idaho and Gem State Flyfishers. Enjoys fly fishing, hunting, backpacking, photography and skeet shooting.
Office: 1130 Third Avenue North, Payette 83661.
Telephone: (208) 642-6019.
Fax: (208) 642-6011

DRESCHER, Stephen W. *(Judge, Idaho District Court Third Judicial District)* Former Administrative Judge.
Mailing address: P.O. Box 670, Weiser 83672.
Telephone: (208) 414-1700.
Fax: (208) 414-3925

DUFF, Larry R. *(Judge, Idaho District Court Fifth Judicial District Magistrate Division)* Serves Minidoka County.
Mailing address: P.O. Box 368, Rupert 83350.
Office: Eighth and G Streets, Rupert 83350.
Telephone: (208) 436-7186.
Fax: (208) 436-5857

DUTCHER, John F. *(Judge, Idaho District Court Fourth Judicial District Magistrate Division)* Appointed to term beginning Jan 25, 1982. Retained by election 1984, 1988, 1992, 1996 and 2000. Current term expires Jan 1, 2005. Serves Ada County. Born Philadelphia Pennsylvania Sept 6, 1944. Educated at California State University at Northridge B.A. 1971 and Southwestern University J.D. 1974. Admitted to practice Idaho 1975. Began legal practice Caldwell 1975. In legal practice Boise 1977-82.
Deputy Prosecuting Attorney Canyon County 1975-77 and Ada County 1977-82. Deputy City Attorney Caldwell 1976-77. Guest Lecturer Boise State University since 1977 and Idaho Post Academy (Law Enforcement). Lecturer on Juvenile Law, Crime and Society and Victim's Rights. Drafted and graded questions for state bar exam. Advisory Board Guardian Ad Litem (CASA) Program 1984-85. Supreme Court Juvenile Rules Committee 1984-85 and Evidence Rules Committee since 1986. Member National Council of Juvenile and Family Court Judges and Editorial Advisory Board "The Advocate" Idaho State Bar since 1985. Member Ada County Sexual Abuse Task Force since 1986. Core member and host site judge for Office of Juvenile Justice and Delinquency Prevention's National Initiative on Private Sector Probation. Member Governor's Commission on Children and Youth since 1985. Instructor annual judicial conferences and "New Judges Orientation" training. E-4 U.S. Army 1962-65. Member National Ski Patrol since 1979. Enjoys skiing, hunting and fishing.
Office: 200 West Front Street, Boise 83702-7300.
Telephone: (208) 287-7477.
Fax: (208) 287-7499

EISMANN, Daniel T. *(Justice, Idaho Supreme Court)* Elected May 23, 2000 to term beginning Jan 2, 2001. Term expires Jan 2007. Born Eugene Oregon. Educated at University of Idaho College of Law J.D. cum laude 1976. Staff member Idaho Law Review. Law Clerk to Hon. Charles R. Donaldson, Idaho Supreme Court 1976. Moot Court. Judge, Idaho District Court Third Judicial District Magistrate Division, appointed 1986. Judge 1995 to Jan 1, 2001 and Former Administrative Judge, Idaho District Court Fourth Judicial District.
Member Boise Chapter Inns of Court, Ada County Domestic Violence Task Force and Idaho State Bar. Established and presided over Ada County Drug Court. U.S. Army. Recipient two Purple Hearts and three medals for heroism. Co-founder Children's Voices, Inc. Volunteer Canyon Area United Way.
Mailing address: P.O. Box 83720, Boise 83720-0101.
Office: 451 West State Street, Boise 83702.
Telephone: (208) 334-2149.

ELGEE, Robert J. *(Judge, Idaho District Court Fifth Judicial District Magistrate Division)* Serves Blaine County.
Office: 106 Blaine County Courthouse, 201 Second Avenue South, Hailey 83333.
Telephone: (208) 788-5524.
Fax: (208) 788-5527

EPIS, David C. *(Judge, Idaho District Court Fourth Judicial District Magistrate Division)* Serves Elmore County.
Office: 150 South Fourth East, Mountain Home 83647.
Telephone: (208) 587-2125.
Fax: (208) 587-2134

EVANS, David L. *(Judge, Idaho District Court Sixth Judicial District Magistrate Division)* Serves Oneida County.
Office: 10 Court Street, Malad 83252.
Telephone: (208) 766-4285.
Fax: (208) 766-2990

FORD, Bradly S. *(Judge, Idaho District Court Third Judicial District Magistrate Division)* Serves Canyon County.
Office: 1115 Albany Street, Caldwell 83605.

FORD, BRADLY S.—*Continued*
Telephone: (208) 454-7365.
Fax: (208) 454-7525

FRATES, Gregory F. *(Judge, Idaho District Court Third Judicial District Magistrate Division)* Appointed Dec 2001. Serves Washington County.
Office: 485 East Third Street, Payette 83672.
Telephone: (208) 414-2232.
Fax: (208) 414-2335

GASKILL, Jay P. *(Judge, Idaho District Court Second Judicial District Magistrate Division)* Appointed Dec 2001. Serves Nez Perce County.
Mailing address: P.O. Box 896, Lewiston 83501.
Office Nez Perce County Courthouse, Lewiston 83501.
Telephone: (208) 799-3050.
Fax: (208) 799-3058

GIBLER, Fred M. *(Judge, Idaho District Court First Judicial District)* Appointed by Governor Dirk Kempthorne June 2001. Born Grangeville Idaho 1950. Educated at University of Idaho B.S. 1972 J.D. 1976. Admitted to practice Idaho 1976, U.S. Courts of Appeals Ninth 1983 and District of Columbia 1993 Circuits and U.S. Court of Federal Claims 1993.
Member Idaho State Bar, First Judicial District and American Bar Associations.
Mailing address: P.O. Box 527, Wallace 83873-0527.
Office: Shoshone County Courthouse, 700 Bank Street, Wallace 83873-2355.
Telephone: (208) 752-1266.
Fax: (208) 753-3581

GRIFFIN, Michael J. *(Judge, Idaho District Court Second Judicial District Magistrate Division)* Serves Idaho County.
Office: Idaho County Courthouse, 320 West Main, Grangeville 83530.
Telephone: (208) 983-2776.
Fax: (208) 983-2376

GUTIERREZ, Sergio A. *(Judge, Idaho Court of Appeals)* Appointed by Governor Dirk Kempthorne Jan 2002. Elected May 2002. Born Chihuahua México May 6, 1954. Religious affiliation: Nazarene. Educated at Boise State University B.A. cum laude 1980 and University of California Hastings College of the Law J.D. Student Intern to Hon. Cruz Reynoso, California Supreme Court 1983. Admitted to practice Idaho 1983, U.S. District Court District of Idaho 1983 and U.S. Court of Appeals Ninth Circuit 1991. In legal practice Caldwell 1983-93. Judge, Idaho District Court Third Judicial District Dec 1, 1993 to Jan 2002, appointed by Governor Cecil D. Andrus.
Director Farmworker Law Unit Idaho Legal Aid Services, Inc. 1985-90. Special Deputy Attorney General Idaho 1991-92. Member Idaho District Judges Association and Idaho State Bar. Attended general jurisdiction courses The National Judicial College 1995 and Appellate Judges Seminar New York University School of Law 2002. Enjoys triathlons, running, tennis and biking.
Mailing address: P.O. Box 83720, Boise 83720-0101.
Office: 537 West Bannock, Boise 83720.
Telephone: (208) 334-5166.

HAMLETT, William C. *(Judge, Idaho District Court Second Judicial District Magistrate Division)* Serves Latah County.
Mailing address: P.O. Box 8068, Moscow 83843.
Office: Latah County Courthouse, Moscow 83843.
Telephone: (208) 883-2255.
Fax: (208) 883-2259

HANSEN, Timothy L. *(Judge, Idaho District Court Fourth Judicial District Magistrate Division)* Serves Ada County.
Office: 200 West Front Street, Boise 83702-7300.
Telephone: (208) 287-7483.
Fax: (208) 287-7499

HARDING, Don L. *(Administrative Judge, Idaho District Court Sixth Judicial District)* Elected May 1994 to term beginning Jan 1, 1995. Reelected 1998 and 2002. Current term expires 2007. Born St. Anthony Idaho Sept 13, 1937. Church of Jesus Christ of Latter-Day Saints. Educated at George Washington University B.B.A. in Accounting 1964 J.D. 1970. Admitted to practice Idaho 1972, U.S. District Court District of Idaho 1972 and U.S. Tax Court 1974. In legal practice Malad 1972-77 and Soda Springs 1983-94. Judge, Idaho District Court Sixth Judicial District Magistrate Division 1977-83.
Prosecuting Attorney Oneida County 1973-77. Deputy Prosecuting Attorney Caribou County 1983-88. Corporate Counsel for numerous small corporations 1983-94. Member American Association of Attorney-Certified Public Accountants and Idaho State Bar. Member Rotary Club of Soda Springs.
Office: 159 South Main Street, Soda Springs 83276.
Telephone: (208) 547-2146.
Fax: (208) 547-4759

HART, Ronald M. *(Judge, Idaho District Court Sixth Judicial District Magistrate Division)* Serves Caribou County.
Mailing address: P.O. Box 775, Soda Springs 83276.
Telephone: (208) 547-2146.
Fax: (208) 547-4759

HAY, Charles L. *(Judge, Idaho District Court Fourth Judicial District Magistrate Division)* Serves Ada County.
Office: 6300 West Denton, Boise 83704.
Telephone: (208) 364-3066.
Fax: (208) 364-3010

HEISE, Debra A. *(Judge, Idaho District Court First Judicial District Magistrate Division)* Serves Bonner County.
Office: 215 South First Avenue, Sandpoint 83864.
Telephone: (208) 265-1446.
Fax: (208) 265-1468

HERNDON, James C. *(Administrative Judge, Idaho District Court Seventh Judicial District)*
Office: 501 North Maple, #310, Blackfoot 83221-1700.
Telephone: (208) 785-8040.
Fax: (208) 785-8057

HIGER, Nathan W. *(Judge, Idaho District Court Fifth Judicial District)* Judge of Magistrate Division Dec 1977 to 1999. Appointed District Judge by Governor Dirk Kempthorne to term beginning March 30, 1999.

HIGER, NATHAN W.—*Continued*

Former Judge, Snake River Basin Adjudication. Educated at University of Washington School of Law J.D.

Mailing address: P.O. Box 126, Twin Falls 83303-0126.

Office: 427 Shoshone Street North, Twin Falls 83301-6153.

Telephone: (208) 736-4172.

Fax: (208) 736-4155

HOFF, Renae *(Judge, Idaho District Court Third Judicial District)* Former Judge of Magistrate Division, appointed to term beginning Sept 1, 1990. Elected District Judge 2002 to term beginning Jan 2003. Term expires Jan 2007. Born Caldwell Idaho Feb 23, 1951. Educated at College of Idaho B.A. cum laude 1979 and Southwestern University School of Law J.D. 1981. Admitted to practice Idaho 1981, U.S. District Court District of Idaho 1981 and U.S. Court of Appeals Ninth Circuit 1986. In legal practice Caldwell 1981-90.

City Prosecutor Homedale 1987-90. City Attorney Marsing 1987-90. Board Member Idaho Volunteer Policy Council (Chair 1992-95) and Idaho Legal Aid Services 1986-90. Member Domestic Assault & Battery Advisory Board 1995-96 and Chair Civil Protection Order Committee 1996-2000 Idaho Supreme Court. Court Member Idaho Team to Implement the Violence Against Women Act 1996-2001. Ad Hoc Committee on the Nampa Courts 1998-99. President Idaho Association of Magistrate Judges 1998-2001. Member Canyon County Lawyers (President 1990), Idaho Women Lawyers, National Association of Women Judges, Idaho State Bar and Third District Bar Association (Secretary 1990). Moderator People's Law School 1989 and Access to Justice Conference on Domestic Relations 1992. Instructor in Testifying in Court Police Officer's Training Academy 1991. Recipient Equal Access to Justice Award for pro bono work from Idaho State Bar 1988 and 1993 and Outstanding Service Award from Idaho State Bar 1996. Chair Idaho Volunteer Lawyers 1994-97. Member Canyon County Campus Committee Boise State University 2000-01.

Office: 1115 Albany Street, Caldwell 83605.

Telephone: (208) 454-7371.

Fax: (208) 454-7442

HOHNHORST, John C. *(Judge, Idaho District Court Fifth Judicial District)* Appointed by Governor Dirk Kempthorne Aug 1, 2001. Elected 2002, current term expires Jan 2007. Born Jerome Idaho Dec 25, 1952. Educated at University of Idaho B.S. 1975 J.D. cum laude 1978. Staff member Idaho Law Review 1977-78. Admitted to practice Idaho 1978, U.S. District Court District of Idaho 1978, U.S. Court of Appeals Ninth Circuit 1980, U.S. Supreme Court 1987 and U.S. Court of Federal Claims. In legal practice Twin Falls 1978-2001.

Member American College of Trial Lawyers (Judiciary Committee), American Academy of Appellate Lawyers and Idaho State Bar (Commissioner 1990-93, President 1993). Precinct Committeeman Republican Central Committee Twin Falls County 1999-2001. Board of Directors Twin Falls Chamber of Commerce 1989. Member Dean's Advisory Council University of Idaho College of Law 1996-2003. Member Planning/Zoning Commission Twin Falls.

Mailing address: P.O. Box 126, Twin Falls 83303-0126.

Office: 427 Shoshone Street North, Twin Falls 83301-6153.

Telephone: (208) 736-4047.

Fax: (208) 736-4002

HOLLERICH, William *(Judge, Idaho District Court Seventh Judicial District Magistrate Division)* Appointed to term beginning Feb 1, 1999. Retained by election. Serves Clark County. Born Illinois. Educated at University of Idaho College of Law J.D.

Criminal Defense Attorney and Prosecutor 1979-94 and Military Judge 1994-99 USMC JAGC.

Mailing address: P.O. Box 205, Dubois 83423.

Office: Clark County Courthouse, Dubois 83423.

Telephone: (208) 374-5402, 529-1350.

Fax: (208) 374-5609

HOLLOWAY, Roy C. *(Judge, Idaho District Court Fifth Judicial District Magistrate Division)* Serves Cassia County.

Office: Cassia County Courthouse, 1459 Overland Avenue, Burley 83318.

Telephone: (208) 878-0180.

Fax: (208) 878-1003

HORTON, Joel D. *(Judge, Idaho District Court Fourth Judicial District)* Judge of Magistrate Division 1988-96. Appointed District Judge by Governor Philip E. Batt to term beginning July 1, 1996. Elected 1998 and 2002. Current term expires Jan 2007. Born Nampa Idaho Oct 30, 1959. Educated at University of Washington B.A. 1982 and University of Idaho J.D. cum laude 1985. Admitted to practice Idaho 1985 and U.S. District Court District of Idaho 1985. In legal practice Lewiston 1985-86 and Twin Falls 1986-88.

Office: Ada County Courthouse, 200 West Front Street, Boise 83702-7300.

Telephone: (208) 287-7544.

Fax: (208) 287-7529

HOSACK, Charles W. *(Administrative Judge, Idaho District Court First Judicial District)*

Mailing address: P.O. Box 9000, Coeur d'Alene 83816-9000.

Telephone: (208) 446-1106.

HUNN, Eric *(Judge, Idaho District Court Sixth Judicial District Magistrate Division)* Appointed to term beginning June 2002. Serves Franklin County.

Office: 39 West Oneida, Preston 83263.

Telephone: (208) 852-0877.

Fax: (208) 852-2926

INGRAM, Mark A. *(Judge, Idaho District Court Fifth Judicial District Magistrate Division)* Appointed April 2001. Serves Lincoln County.

Mailing address: P.O. Drawer A, Shoshone 83352.

Office: 111 West B Street, Shoshone 83352.

Telephone: (208) 886-2173.

Fax: (208) 886-2458

ISRAEL, R. Ted *(Judge, Idaho District Court Sixth Judicial District Magistrate Division)* Serves Bannock County.

Mailing address: P.O. Box 4847, Pocatello 83205.

ISRAEL, R. TED—*Continued*

Telephone: (208) 236-7322.
Fax: (208) 236-7012

JOYNER, Todd *(Judge, Idaho District Court Third Judicial District Magistrate Division)* Appointed to term beginning Jan 2003. Serves Canyon County.

Office: 120 Ninth Avenue South, Nampa 83651.
Telephone: (208) 467-2171.
Fax: (208) 466-0423

JULIAN, Justin W. *(Judge, Idaho District Court First Judicial District Magistrate Division)* Appointed Jan 2001. Serves Boundary County.

Mailing address: P.O. Box 419, Bonners Ferry 83805.
Telephone: (208) 267-5504.
Fax: (208) 267-6624

KALBFLEISCH, Gregory K. *(Judge, Idaho District Court Second Judicial District Magistrate Division)* Serves Nez Perce County.

Mailing address: P.O. Box 896, Lewiston 83501.
Office: Nez Perce County Courthouse, Lewiston 83501.
Telephone: (208) 799-3050.
Fax: (208) 799-3058

KENNEDY, Michael B. *(Judge, Idaho District Court Seventh Judicial District Magistrate Division)* Serves Jefferson County.

Mailing address: P.O. Box 71, Rigby 83442.
Telephone: (208) 745-7736.
Fax: (208) 745-6636

KERRICK, Carl B. *(Judge, Idaho District Court Second Judicial District)* Magistrate Judge 1993 to Jan 31, 1999. Appointed Judge by Governor Dirk Kempthorne to term beginning Feb 1, 1999. Educated at University of Idaho J.D. In legal practice McCall 1987-93.

Former Prosecuting Attorney Valley County.

Mailing address: P.O. Box 896, Lewiston 83501.
Office: Nez Perce County Courthouse, Lewiston 83501.
Telephone: (208) 799-3141.
Fax: (208) 799-3058

KERRICK, Juneal *(Judge, Idaho District Court Third Judicial District)* Judge of Magistrate Division Jan 1987 to April 2002. Appointed District Judge by Governor Dirk Kempthorne April 2002.

Office: 1115 Albany Street, Caldwell 83605.
Telephone: (208) 454-7370.
Fax: (208) 454-7442

KIDWELL, Wayne L. *(Justice, Idaho Supreme Court)* Elected Nov 1998 to term beginning Jan 4, 1999. Term expires Jan 2005. Educated at University of Idaho B.A. J.D. Admitted to practice Idaho 1964.

Former Prosecuting Attorney Ada County. Former Associate Deputy U.S. Attorney General. Former Attorney General Idaho. Former State Senator and State Senate Majority Leader.

Mailing address: P.O. Box 83720, Boise 83720-0101.
Office: 451 West State Street, Boise 83702-6057.
Telephone: (208) 334-3186.

KOTYK, Frank *(Judge, Idaho District Court Third Judicial District Magistrate Division)* Appointed to term beginning July 1, 2002. Serves Canyon County.

Office: 1115 Albany Street, Caldwell 83605.
Telephone: (208) 454-7376.
Fax: (208) 454-7525

KROGH, A. Lynne *(Judge, Idaho District Court Third Judicial District Magistrate Division)* Appointed to term beginning Dec 2, 1996. Retained by election Nov 3, 1998 and 2002. Current term expires 2007. Serves Payette County. Born Warrensburg Missouri July 2, 1958. Educated at Colorado State University B.A. with honors 1981 and University of Colorado J.D. 1984. Admitted to practice Colorado 1984 and Idaho 1985.

Deputy Attorney General Idaho Department of Water Resources 1985-96. Author "The 1986 Idaho Water Rights Adjudication Statute" 23, 1986-87 and "Injury and Enlargement in Idaho Water Right Transfers" 27, 249, 1990-91 Idaho L. Rev.; "Water Rights Adjudication Handbook" *Idaho Water Law Handbook* Idaho Department of Water Resources 1987; and "Water Right Adjudications in the Western States: Procedures, Constitutionality, Problems & Solutions" 15 Land and Water L. Rev. 1, 1995. Member Idaho State Bar (Legislative Information Committee 1989-96, Bar Exam Grading Committee since 1992). Attended Rocky Mountain Regional Program National Institute for Trial Advocacy Denver Colorado Aug 1992 and General Jurisdiction Program The National Judicial College Reno Nevada Aug 1996. Instructor Western States Water Rights Adjudication Conference 1992-96. Chairperson Idaho Department of Water Resources Blood Drive 1986-91. Member Red Cross.

Office: 1130 Third Avenue North, Payette 83661.
Telephone: (208) 642-6019.
Fax: (208) 642-6011

LANSING, Karen L. *(Chief Judge, Idaho Court of Appeals)* Appointed by Governor Cecil D. Andrus to term beginning June 8, 1993. Elected 1998, current term expires 2005. Born Kendrick Idaho June 23, 1950. Educated at University of Idaho B.A. with honors 1972 and University of Washington J.D. with honors 1978. Member Order of the Coif. Admitted to practice Idaho 1978, U.S. District Court District of Idaho 1978 and U.S. Court of Appeals Ninth Circuit 1982. In legal practice Boise 1979-93.

Assistant City Attorney Boise 1978-79. Chair Evidence Rules Advisory Committee and Member Appellate Rules Advisory Committee and Public Record Act Advisory Committee Idaho Supreme Court. Member American Inns of Court Boise Chapter, Idaho State Bar (Former Member Law Day Committee, Member Workers' Compensation Section) and American Bar Association. Speaker "Implied Covenant of Good Faith" Continuing Legal Education Idaho State Bar 1992. Attended Appellate Seminar Boston Massachusetts Sept 1993 and Sun Valley Idaho July 1994 American Bar Association, Appellate Seminar New York University June 1994 and Five-State Judicial Conference July 1994. Recipient Pro Bono Award from Idaho State Bar 1993. Personnel Analyst Idaho Personnel Commission 1972 and 1973. Planner Idaho State Planning Agency 1973-75. Former Member Policy Council Idaho Volunteer Lawyers Program and Boise City Civil Service Commission. Board of Directors Boise YWCA (Vice President 1989). Chair Small Business Education Committee Boise Area Chamber of

LANSING, KAREN L.—*Continued*

Commerce. Member Literacy Lab of Boise (volunteer teacher, Member Board of Directors, Past President). Enjoys gardening and reading.
Mailing address: P.O. Box 83720, Boise 83720-0101.
Office: 537 West Bannock, Boise 83702.
Telephone: (208) 334-5168.

LODGE, Edward J. *(Judge, United States District Court District of Idaho)* Appointed for life by President George Bush to term beginning Nov 27, 1989. Chief Judge 1992-99. Born Caldwell Idaho Dec 3, 1933. Educated at College of Idaho B.A. 1957 and University of Idaho LL.B. 1961. In legal practice Idaho 1960-63. Judge, Canyon County Probate Court 1963-65. Judge 1965-88 and Former Administrative Judge, Idaho District Court Third Judicial District. Judge, U.S. Bankruptcy Court District of Idaho 1988-89.
Office: U.S. Courthouse, MSC 040, 550 West Fort Street, Boise 83724.
Telephone: (208) 334-9270.

LUKE, Colin W. *(Judge, Idaho District Court Seventh Judicial District Magistrate Division)* Serves Teton County.
Office: 89 North Main Street, Suite 5, Driggs 83422-5141.
Telephone: (208) 354-2239, 529-1350.
Fax: (208) 354-8496

LUSTER, John Patrick *(Judge, Idaho District Court First Judicial District)* Judge of Magistrate Division July 1, 1986 to July 31, 2000. Appointed District Judge by Governor Dirk Kempthorne to term beginning Aug 1, 2000. Born Fort Walton Beach Florida March 14, 1952. Christian. Educated at California State College at San Bernardino B.A. 1973 and Gonzaga University J.D. 1976. Admitted to practice Idaho 1977, Utah 1977 and U.S. District Court District of Idaho 1977. In legal practice Coeur d'Alene Idaho 1980 to July 1986.
Deputy Prosecuting Attorney Blaine County March 1980 to August 1980. Public Defender Kootenai County March 1979 to Jan 1980. Instructor in Business Law North Idaho College 1980-81. Attended General Jurisdiction Course The National Judicial College March 1986 and Magistrate Training Institute Idaho Supreme Court Nov 1987 and Nov 1988. E-5 USMCR 1970-72. Democrat. Candidate Kootenai County Prosecuting Attorney 1980. Enjoys skiing, fly fishing, backpacking and triathlon.
Mailing address: P.O. Box 9000, Coeur d'Alene 83816-9000.
Office: 324 West Garden Avenue, Coeur d'Alene 83814-2100.
Telephone: (208) 769-4423.
Fax: (208) 769-4496

MARANO, Eugene A. *(Judge, Idaho District Court First Judicial District Magistrate Division)* Serves Kootenai County.
Mailing address: P.O. Box 9000, Coeur d'Alene 83816-9000.
Telephone: (208) 446-1102.

MAY, James J. *(Judge, Idaho District Court Fifth Judicial District)* Born American Falls Idaho Dec 16, 1925. Educated at University of Idaho B.A. 1949 J.D. 1951. Member Phi Alpha Delta. Admitted to practice Washington 1952, Idaho 1953 and U.S. Supreme Court 1960. In legal practice Twin Falls Idaho 1952-86.
Public Defender Twin Falls County 1970. Prosecuting Attorney Twin Falls County 1961-66. President Idaho Prosecuting Attorney Association 1966. Member Idaho Judicial Council 1989-95, Idaho Law Foundation (Board of Directors 1982-92, President 1992), National District Attorneys Association, California Trial Lawyers Association, National Criminal Defense Lawyers Association, The Association of Trial Lawyers of America (Board of Governors 1981-84), Idaho Trial Lawyers Association (President 1971-74, Board of Governors 1971-84), Western Trial Lawyers Association (Board of Governors 1972-86, President 1984), Idaho State Bar (Commissioner 1978-80, President 1980), Fifth Judicial District (President 1965-66), Washington State and American (Membership Chairman Section of Insurance, Negligence and Compensation Law 1971-72) Bar Associations. Lecturer on Economics of Law Practice University of Idaho School of Law. Presenter on Criminal Law San Diego and Civil Law Las Vegas annual meeting and semi-annual meeting American Trial Lawyers Association and on criminal defense side of seminar Judge Advocate General Officers Camp Pendleton California. Participant Civil and Criminal Seminars University of Idaho School of Law, CLE on Trial Practice Colorado Trial Lawyers and Western Trial Lawyers Association annual meeting Hawaii, CLE on Civil and Criminal Trial Practice Idaho Trial Lawyers Association and CLE on Evidence, Real Estate, Criminal Law and Orientation for New Lawyers Idaho Law Foundation. Recipient Outstanding Service Award from Idaho State Bar 1992 and Hon. George Granata Jr. Award for Professionalism as a Trial Judge 1999. USN 1944-47. Member Twin Falls Chamber of Commerce (Board of Directors 1983-86 and President 1986).
Office: 201 Second Avenue South, Suite 110, Hailey 83333.
Telephone: (208) 788-5526.
Fax: (208) 788-5512

McDANIEL, Terry R. *(Judge, Idaho District Court Fourth Judicial District Magistrate Division)* Serves Ada County.
Office: 200 West Front Street, Boise 83702-7300.
Telephone: (208) 287-7485.
Fax: (208) 287-7499

McDERMOTT, Peter D. *(Judge, Idaho District Court Sixth Judicial District)* Appointed by Governor John Evans to term beginning April 2, 1981. Reelected 1982, 1986, 1990, 1994, 1998 and 2002. Current term expires Jan 2007. Former Administrative Judge. Born Pocatello Idaho Sept 23, 1939. Catholic. Educated at Idaho State University B.A. 1964 and University of Idaho College of Law J.D. with honors 1968. Admitted to practice Idaho 1968 and U.S. District Court District of Idaho 1968. In legal practice Pocatello 1968-81.
Member Idaho Trial Lawyers Association, Idaho District Judges Association (President 1983-84) and Idaho State Bar. Instructor in Federal Rules of Evidence The National Judicial College 1991 and 1992. Enjoys gardening, fishing, hunting, baseball and all outdoor sports.
Mailing address: P.O. Box 4131, Pocatello 83205.
Telephone: (208) 236-7242.
Fax: (208) 236-7012

McDOUGALL, Dan C. *(Judge, Idaho District Court Sixth Judicial District Magistrate Division)* Serves Bannock County.
Mailing address: P.O. Box 4847, Pocatello 83205.
Telephone: (208) 236-7252.
Fax: (208) 236-7012

McFADDEN, Patrick R. *(Judge, Idaho District Court First Judicial District Magistrate Division)* Appointed to term beginning Feb 17, 1995. Retained by election 1998, current term expires 2004. Serves Benewah County. Born St. Maries Idaho Oct 10, 1956. Educated at University of Idaho B.S. 1979 J.D. 1984. Admitted to practice Idaho 1984. In legal practice St. Maries 1984-95.
Office: 701 College Avenue, St. Maries 83861.
Telephone: (208) 245-3241.
Fax: (208) 245-3046

McGEE, Daniel J. *(Judge, Idaho District Court First Judicial District Magistrate Division)* Serves Shoshone County.
Office: 700 Bank Street, Wallace 83873.
Telephone: (208) 752-1266.
Fax: (208) 752-4271

McLAUGHLIN, Michael Robert *(Judge, Idaho District Court Fourth Judicial District)* Judge of Magistrate Division 1991-97. Appointed District Judge by Governor Philip E. Batt Dec 27, 1997. Elected May 1998 and 2002. Current term expires Jan 2007. Former Administrative Judge. Born Boise Idaho July 11, 1950. Catholic. Educated at University of Idaho B.A. 1973 J.D. 1976. Member Phi Alpha Delta. Admitted to practice Idaho 1977. In legal practice Mountain Home 1977-80 and 1984-91.
Prosecuting Attorney Elmore County 1981-83.
Office: Ada County Courthouse, 200 West Front Street, Boise 83702-7300.
Telephone: (208) 287-7551.
Fax: (208) 287-7529

MELANSON, John M. *(Judge, Idaho District Court Fifth Judicial District)* Judge of Magistrate Division Jan 3, 1995 to Dec 31, 2000. Appointed District Judge by Governor Dirk Kempthorne Dec 2000. Born Norwalk Connecticut. Educated at Idaho State University B.B.A. 1978 and University of Idaho J.D. 1981. Admitted to practice Idaho 1981, U.S. District Court District of Idaho 1981 and U.S. Court of Appeals Ninth Circuit 1988. In legal practice Buhl 1981-95.
City Prosecutor Buhl 1985-95. Member Idaho State Bar and Fifth District Bar Association. Recipient Pro Bono Award from Idaho State Bar 1994. Staff Sergeant U.S. Army 1968-70.
Mailing address: P.O. Box 474, Rupert 83350.
Telephone: (208) 436-9041.
Fax: (208) 436-5272

MERICA, Kent J. *(Judge, Idaho District Court Second Judicial District Magistrate Division)* Appointed to term beginning 1999. Serves Nez Perce County. Educated at University of Idaho College of Law J.D. In legal practice Lewiston 1982-99.
Former Public Defender Lewiston.
Mailing address: P.O. Box 896, Lewiston 83501.
Office: Nez Perce County Courthouse, Lewiston 83501.
Telephone: (208) 799-3050.
Fax: (208) 799-3058

MEYERS, Jerry R. *(Judge, Idaho District Court Seventh Judicial District Magistrate Division)* Serves Lemhi County.
Office: 206 Courthouse Drive, Salmon 83467.
Telephone: (208) 756-3115.
Fax: (208) 756-4673

MINDER, Carolyn M. *(Judge, Idaho District Court Fourth Judicial District Magistrate Division)* Serves Ada County.
Office: 200 West Front Street, Boise 83702-7300.
Telephone: (208) 287-7623.
Fax: (208) 287-7499

MITCHELL, John T. *(Judge, Idaho District Court First Judicial District)* Appointed by Governor Dirk Kempthorne Oct 2001.
Mailing address: P.O. Box 9000, Coeur d'Alene, 83816-9000.
Office: 324 West Garden Avenue, Coeur d'Alene, 83814-2100.
Telephone: (208) 446-1103.

MORDEN, Thomas R. *(Judge, Idaho District Court Fourth Judicial District Magistrate Division)* Appointed to term beginning Aug 31, 1981. Retained by election. Serves Ada County. Born Detroit Michigan Sept 11, 1946. Educated at Boise State University B.A. 1972 and Idaho State University J.D. 1978. Admitted to practice Idaho 1978. Began legal practice Hailey 1978.
Support Enforcement Officer Idaho Attorney General's Office 1972-74. Prosecutor 1979 and Public Defender 1979-81. Member Idaho Trial Lawyers Association 1979-81, National Council of Juvenile and Family Court Judges and Idaho State Bar. Specialist Four U.S. Army 1964-68. Worked as croupier 1969 and log scaler 1974-75. Democrat. Board of Directors Guardian Ad Litem Program since 1981. Enjoys hunting, fishing, camping, reading and horses.
Office: 200 West Front Street, Boise 83702-7300.
Telephone: (208) 287-7625.
Fax: (208) 287-7499

MORFITT, James C. *(Administrative Judge, Idaho District Court Third Judicial District)* Former Judge of Magistrate Division.
Office: 1115 Albany Street, Caldwell 83605.
Telephone: (208) 454-7371.
Fax: (208) 454-7442

MOSS, Brent J. *(Judge, Idaho District Court Seventh Judicial District)* Former Judge of Magistrate Division. Appointed District Judge by Governor Cecil D. Andrus to term beginning 1993. Elected to subsequent terms.
Mailing address: P.O. Box 389, Rexburg 83440.
Telephone: (208) 356-6880.
Fax: (208) 356-6880

MURRAY, Bryan K. *(Judge, Idaho District Court Sixth Judicial District Magistrate Division)* Appointed to term beginning Nov 1, 1993. Retained by election Nov 1996 and Nov 2000. Current term expires Jan 2005. Serves Bannock County. Born Bakersfield California March 12, 1956. Church of Jesus Christ of Latter-Day Saints. Educated at Idaho State University B.A. 1980 and University of Idaho J.D. 1982. Admitted to practice Idaho 1983, U.S. District Court District of Idaho 1983

MURRAY, BRYAN K.—*Continued*
and U.S. Court of Appeals Ninth Circuit 1986. In legal practice Pocatello.
Mailing address: P.O. Box 4847, Pocatello 83205.
Telephone: (208) 234-1087.
Fax: (208) 234-1094

MYERS, Terry L. *(Judge, United States Bankruptcy Court District of Idaho)* Appointed by U.S. Court of Appeals Ninth Circuit Judges to term beginning Aug 1, 1998. Term expires 2012. Educated at Idaho State University B.A. with high honors 1976 and University of Idaho J.D. summa cum laude 1980. Law Clerk to Idaho Supreme Court 1980-81 and to U.S. Bankruptcy Court District of Idaho 1981-84. Admitted to practice Idaho 1980. In legal practice Boise 1984-98.
Member National Conference of Bankruptcy Judges, American Bankruptcy Institute and Idaho State Bar.
Office: U.S. Courthouse, MSC 040, 550 West Fort Street, Boise 83724.
Telephone: (208) 334-9341.

NEVILLE, Thomas F. *(Judge, Idaho District Court Fourth Judicial District)* Former Judge of Magistrate Division.
Office: Ada County Courthouse, 200 West Front Street, Boise 83702-7300.
Telephone: (208) 287-7521.
Fax: (208) 287-7529

OTHS, Michael *(Judge, Idaho District Court Fourth Judicial District Magistrate Division)* Appointed to term beginning Feb 2003. Serves Ada County.
Office: 200 West Front Street, Boise 83702-7300.
Telephone: (208) 287-7481.
Fax: (208) 287-7499

PAPPAS, Jim D. *(Chief Judge, United States Bankruptcy Court District of Idaho)* Appointed by U.S. Court of Appeals Ninth Circuit judges.
Office: U.S. Courthouse, MSC 042, 550 West Fort Street, Boise 83724.
Telephone: (208) 334-9571.

PEART, James C. *(Judge, Idaho District Court Third Judicial District Magistrate Division)* Serves Adams County.
Mailing address: P.O. Box 48, Council 83612.
Telephone: (208) 253-4233.
Fax: (208) 253-4880

PERRY, Darrel R. *(Judge, Idaho Court of Appeals)* Former Chief Judge. Born Fairfield California Sept 18, 1954. Christian. Educated at University of Idaho B.S. 1976 J.D. 1979. Member Phi Gamma Delta. Admitted to practice Idaho 1979 and U.S. District Court District of Idaho 1979. Began legal practice Lewiston 1979. Former Judge, Idaho District Court Second Judicial District Magistrate Division, appointed to term beginning Jan 1, 1982.
Formerly with Public Defender's Office. Member Idaho State Bar and Clearwater Bar Association.
Mailing address: P.O. Box 83720, Boise 83720-0101.
Office: 537 West Bannock, Boise 83702-5758.
Telephone: (208) 334-5170.

PETRIE, Gordon W. *(Judge, Idaho District Court Third Judicial District Magistrate Division)* Serves Gem County.
Office: 415 East Main Street, Room 300, Emmett 83617.
Telephone: (208) 365-4221.
Fax: (208) 365-6172

RAMMELL, Mark S. *(Judge, Idaho District Court Seventh Judicial District Magistrate Division)* Appointed to term beginning June 1992. Retained by election Nov 1994, 1998 and 2002. Current term expires Jan 2007. Serves Madison County. Born Driggs Idaho Dec 18, 1958. Mormon. Educated at Brigham Young University B.A. 1983 and Willamette University J.D. 1986. Admitted to practice Idaho 1986, Utah 1991 and U.S. District Court District of Utah 1991. In legal practice Rexburg Idaho 1986-92.
District Attorney 1991-92. Instructor Ricks College 1992. Member Idaho Trial Lawyers Association and The Association of Trial Lawyers of America. Attended Advanced Evidence and Legal Writing The National Judicial College. Enjoys fishing and spending time with family.
Mailing address: P.O. Box 389, Rexburg 83440.
Telephone: (208) 356-9383.
Fax: (208) 356-5425

RIDDOCH, L. Mark *(Judge, Idaho District Court Seventh Judicial District Magistrate Division)* Appointed to term beginning Nov 1, 1983. Retained by election 1986, 1990, 1994, 1998 and Nov 5, 2002. Current term expires Jan 2007. Serves Bonneville County. Also serves Child Protection and Parent Drug Court since Oct 1, 2002. Born Seattle Washington Oct 28, 1947. Educated at Brigham Young University B.A. 1971 M.A. 1972 and University of Puget Sound J.D. 1975. Law Clerk to Hon. J. Ray Durstsch, District Judge Fourth Judicial District 1976. Admitted to practice Idaho 1976, U.S. Claims Court 1977, U.S. Court of Appeals Ninth Circuit 1978 and U.S. Supreme Court 1981.
Assistant Attorney General 1976-78 and Deputy Attorney General 1978-83 Idaho. House Counsel Department of Lands State Land Board 1978-83.
Office: 605 North Capital Avenue, Idaho Falls 83402.
Telephone: (208) 529-1350.

ROOS, Charles L. *(Judge, Idaho District Court Seventh Judicial District Magistrate Division)* Serves Custer County.
Office: P.O. Box 385, Challis 83226.
Telephone: (208) 879-2359, 588-2277.
Fax: (208) 879-5246

RYAN, Thomas J. *(Judge, Idaho District Court Third Judicial District Magistrate Division)* Serves Owyhee County.
Mailing address: P.O. Box 128, Murphy 83650.
Telephone: (208) 495-2806.
Fax: (208) 495-1226

ST. CLAIR, Richard T. *(Judge, Idaho District Court Seventh Judicial District)* Appointed by Governor Philip E. Batt March 27, 1996 to term beginning May 7, 1996. Reelected May 12, 1998 and May 7, 2002. Current term expires Dec 31, 2006. Born Idaho Falls Idaho June 1, 1947. Educated at University of Idaho B.S. 1969 J.D. 1972 and George Washington University National Law Center LL.M. 1975. Notes Editor Idaho Law Review

ST. CLAIR, RICHARD T.—*Continued*

1970-72. Admitted to practice Idaho 1972, U.S. District Court District of Idaho 1972, U.S. Court of Appeals for the Armed Forces 1972 and U.S. Court of Federal Claims 1975. In legal practice Idaho Falls 1975-96.

Member American Judges Association. Captain U.S. Army Legal Services Agency JAGC 1972-75.

Office: 605 North Capital Avenue, Idaho Falls 83402.
Telephone: (208) 529-1350.
Fax: (208) 529-1300

SAVAGE, Ralph *(Judge, Idaho District Court Seventh Judicial District Magistrate Division)* Appointed to term beginning Jan 2003. Serves Butte County.

Mailing address: P.O. Box 171, Arco 83213.
Telephone: (208) 527-8259, 529-1350.
Fax: (208) 527-3445

SCHILLER, James A. "J.R." *(Judge, Idaho District Court Third Judicial District Magistrate Division)* Serves Canyon County.

Office: 1115 Albany Street, Caldwell 83605.
Telephone: (208) 454-6612.
Fax: (208) 454-7525

SCHMIDT, Richard Allan *(Judge, Idaho District Court Fourth Judicial District Magistrate Division)* Appointed to term beginning Jan 1975. Retained by election. Current term expires Jan 2007. Serves Ada County. Born San Mateo California June 9, 1945. Educated at San Jose State College B.A. in Political Science 1967 and San Francisco Law School LL.B. 1973. Member Lambda Chi Alpha. Admitted to practice California 1978 and Idaho 1980.

Member Idaho State Bar and State Bar of California. Attended National College of the State Judiciary 1975, 1976 and 1977. Previously worked for Wells Fargo Bank Trust Department and Matthew Bender Publishing Company San Francisco. Member Boy Scouts of America. Amateur radio operator. Enjoys camping and hunting.

Office: 200 West Front Street, Boise 83702-7300.
Telephone: (208) 287-7627.
Fax: (208) 287-7499

SCHROEDER, Gerald F. *(Justice, Idaho Supreme Court)* Appointed by Governor Philip E. Batt Jan 20, 1995. Elected to subsequent terms. Born Boise Idaho Sept 13, 1939. Educated at College of Idaho B.A. magna cum laude 1961 and Harvard University J.D. 1964. Admitted to practice Idaho 1965. Began legal practice Boise 1965. Judge, Ada County Probate Court 1969-71. Judge of Magistrate Division 1971 to Dec 8, 1975 and Former Administrative Judge, Idaho District Court Fourth Judicial District, appointed Administrative Judge to term beginning Dec 9, 1975.

Author *Idaho Probate Procedure* Idaho State Bar 1971, "Developments in the Enforcement of Parental and State Standards in Juvenile Proceedings" Idaho L. Rev. 1974 and "The Altered Role of the Court and the UPC" UPC Notes Nov 1974. Contributor *The Uniform Probate Code Study Materials* The American Law Institute 1973-74. Contributing Author *Justice for the Times* Idaho Law Foundation 1990. Adjunct Faculty Boise State University 1986-95. Member District Judges Association, American Judicature Society and Idaho State Bar. Former member Governor's Council on Crime and Delinquency. Instructor Boise Bar Review since 1973 and legal education classes in approximately 13 states. Named one of Outstanding Young Men of America 1969, Portrait of a Distinguished Citizen and Idaho Statesman 1974. Listed in *Who's Who in American Law* 1977. Toll Fellow National Council of State Governments 1989. Board of Directors Boise Racquet and Swim Club and Boise Philharmonic. Former member Idaho Mental Health Association. Former Board member Boise Opera Association.

Mailing address: P.O. Box 83720, Boise 83720-0101.
Office: 451 West State Street, Boise 83702-6057.
Telephone: (208) 334-3324.

SELLMAN, John R. *(Judge, Idaho District Court Fourth Judicial District Magistrate Division)* Appointed July 1, 1976. Retained by election. Serves Elmore County. Born Boise Idaho Feb 3, 1943. Catholic. Educated at Idaho State University B.A. 1967 and University of Idaho J.D. 1968. Member Phi Alpha Delta. Admitted to practice Idaho 1968. Began legal practice Murphy 1969. In legal practice Mountain Home 1970.

Owyhee County Prosecuting Attorney 1969-70. Elmore County Public Defender Nov 1972 to June 1976. Author article in "Family Advocate" American Bar Association 1979. Member Idaho Magistrates Association, Idaho State Bar, Elmore County and American Bar Associations. Private U.S. Army 1968-69. Enjoys hunting, fishing, carpentry, stained glass and golf.

Office: 150 South Fourth East, Mountain Home 83647.
Telephone: (208) 587-2124.
Fax: (208) 587-2134

SHINDURLING, Jon J. *(Judge, Idaho District Court Seventh Judicial District)*

Office: 605 North Capital Avenue, Idaho Falls 83402.
Telephone: (208) 529-1350.
Fax: (208) 529-1300

SIMPSON, Benjamin R. *(Judge, Idaho District Court First Judicial District Magistrate Division)* Serves Kootenai County.

Mailing address: P.O. Box 9000, Coeur d'Alene 83816-9000.
Telephone: (208) 446-1110.

SMITH, N. Randy *(Judge, Idaho District Court Sixth Judicial District)*

Mailing address: P.O. Box 4165, Pocatello 83205.
Telephone: (208) 236-7244.
Fax: (208) 236-7012

SMYSER, Howard D. *(Judge, Idaho District Court Fifth Judicial District Magistrate Division)* Appointed Jan 2001. Serves Twin Falls County.

Mailing address: P.O. Box 126, Twin Falls 83303-0126.
Office: 427 Shoshone Street North, Twin Falls 83303.
Telephone: (208) 736-4119.
Fax: (208) 736-4155

SQUIRE, Orin Lee *(Judge, Idaho District Court Second Judicial District Magistrate Division)* Appointed to term beginning 1999. Retained by election Jan 8, 2001. Current term expires Jan 2005. Serves Clearwater County. Educated at University of Idaho College of Law J.D.

Former City Attorney Orofino, Weippe and Pierce.

SQUIRE, ORIN LEE—*Continued*

Former Deputy Prosecutor Clearwater County. USN twenty-two years.
Mailing address: P.O. Box 586, Orofino 83544.
Office: Clearwater County Courthouse, Orofino 83544.
Telephone: (208) 476-5596.
Fax: (208) 476-5159

STEGNER, John R. *(Administrative Judge, Idaho District Court Second Judicial District)* Assumed office as Judge. Elected to subsequent terms.
Mailing address: P.O. Box 8068, Moscow 83843.
Office: Latah County Courthouse, Moscow 83843.
Telephone: (208) 883-2255.
Fax: (208) 883-2259

STICKLEN, Kathryn A. *(Judge, Idaho District Court Fourth Judicial District)* Elected to term beginning Jan 4, 1999. Elected to subsequent term. Educated at University of Utah College of Law J.D. Admitted to practice Idaho 1976 and Utah 1976. In legal practice Boise.
Former Counsel Idaho State Insurance Fund. Member Idaho State Bar Professional Conduct Board Hearing/Review Committee and Idaho Supreme Court Appellate Rules Committee. Honored as one of the first 100 women admitted to Utah State Bar Jan 1999.
Office: Ada County Courthouse, 200 West Front Street, Boise 83702-7300.
Telephone: (208) 287-7531.
Fax: (208) 287-7529

STOKER, Randy J. *(Judge, Idaho District Court Fifth Judicial District Magistrate Division)* Appointed to term beginning Jan 2003. Serves Twin Falls County.
Mailing address: P.O. Box 126, Twin Falls 83303-0126.
Office: 427 Shoshone Street North, Twin Falls 83303-0126.
Telephone: (208) 736-4118.
Fax: (208) 736-4002

SWAIN, L. Kevin *(Judge, Idaho District Court Fourth Judicial District Magistrate Division)* Appointed Feb 2001. Serves Ada County.
Office: 200 West Front Street, Boise 83702-7300.
Telephone: (208) 287-7633.
Fax: (208) 287-7499

SWANSTROM, Don L. *(Judge, Idaho District Court First Judicial District Magistrate Division)* Serves Bonner County. Also serves as Trial Court Administrator.
Office: 215 South First Avenue, Sandpoint 83864.
Telephone: (208) 265-1444, 769-4440.
Fax: (208) 265-1499, 664-0639

TAISEY, Robert M., Jr. *(Judge, Idaho District Court Third Judicial District Magistrate Division)* Serves Canyon County.
Office: 1115 Albany Street, Caldwell 83605.
Telephone: (208) 454-7365.
Fax: (208) 454-7525

TROUT, Linda Copple *(Chief Justice, Idaho Supreme Court)* Appointed by Governor Cecil D. Andrus to term beginning Oct 1992. Elected 1996. Re-elected May 2002. Born Tokyo Japan Sept 1, 1951. Educated at University of Idaho B.A. 1973 J.D. 1977. Admitted to practice Idaho 1977. Began legal practice Lewiston 1977. Judge of Magistrate Division 1982-88 and District Judge 1991-92, Idaho District Court Second Judicial District.
Instructor University of Idaho College of Law 1983 and 1988. Member Idaho State Bar and Clearwater Bar Association (President 1980-81).
Mailing address: P.O. Box 83720, Boise 83720-0101.
Office: 451 West State Street, Boise 83702-6057.
Telephone: (208) 334-2207.

VARIN, John F. *(Judge, Idaho District Court Fifth Judicial District Magistrate Division)* Serves Camas County.
Mailing address: P.O. Box 430, Fairfield 83327.
Office: Camas County Courthouse, Fairfield 83327.
Telephone: (208) 764-2238.
Fax: (208) 764-2349

VEHLOW, John C. *(Judge, Idaho District Court Fourth Judicial District Magistrate Division)* Appointed to term beginning Aug 1, 1987. Retained by election Nov 1990, Nov 8, 1994, 1998 and 2002. Current term expires Jan 2007. Serves Ada County. Born New York New York June 18, 1946. Religious affiliation: Church of the Nazarene. Educated at University of Texas B.A. 1969, Texas A&M University M.A. 1972 and St. Mary's University School of Law J.D. 1974. Admitted to practice Idaho 1975, U.S. District Court District of Idaho 1975 and U.S. Supreme Court 1978. In legal practice Kuna 1980-81.
Deputy Attorney General Idaho Department of Fish and Game 1976-80. Member Idaho State Bar. USMCR 1967-73. Enjoys bass fishing.
Office: 6300 West Denton Street, Boise 83704.
Telephone: (208) 364-3049.
Fax: (208) 364-3010

VERBY, Steven *(Judge, Idaho District Court First Judicial District)* Elected 2002 to term beginning Jan 2003. Term expires Jan 2007.
Office: Bonner County Courthouse, 215 South First Avenue, Sandpoint 83864.
Telephone: (208) 265-1445.
Fax: (208) 263-0896

WALKER, Keith M. *(Judge, Idaho District Court Seventh Judicial District Magistrate Division)* Serves Fremont County.
Office: 151 West First North, Room 15, St. Anthony 83445.
Telephone: (208) 624-7401.
Fax: (208) 624-4607

WALTERS, Jesse R., Jr. *(Retired Justice, Idaho Supreme Court)* Appointed by Governor Philip E. Batt Sept 2, 1997. Elected 1998. Retired July 31, 2003. Born Rexburg Idaho Dec 26, 1938. Church of Jesus Christ of Latter-Day Saints. Educated at Ricks College, University of Washington 1962, University of Idaho B.A. 1961 LL.B. J.D. 1963 and University of Virginia LL.M. 1990. Law Clerk to Chief Justice E. T. Knudson, Idaho Supreme Court 1963-64. Admitted to practice Idaho 1963, U.S. District Court District of Idaho 1964 and U.S. Court of Appeals Ninth Circuit 1970. Began legal practice Boise 1963. Judge, Idaho District Court Fourth Judicial District Aug 17, 1977 to Jan 3, 1982. Judge and Chief Judge, Idaho Court of Appeals Jan 4, 1982 to 1997, appointed by Governor John V. Evans.
Executive Committee Member 1985-86, Secretary 1991-92, Treasurer 1992-93 and President 1994-95

WALTERS, JESSE R., JR.—*Continued*

Council of Chief Judges of Courts of Appeal. Board of Directors American Judicature Society. Member Idaho Trial Lawyers Association, The Association of Trial Lawyers of America, Idaho State Bar and Boise Bar Association. Republican. Precinct Committeeman 1976. Past President Boise Jaycees and Boise Vista Lions. Past National Director U.S. Jaycees. Member Elks Lodge 310 and Eagle Lodge 115. Enjoys skiing, hunting, fishing and golf.

Mailing address: P.O. Box 83720, Boise 83720-0101.
Office: 451 West State Street, Boise 83702.
Telephone: (208) 334-3464.

WATKINS, Thomas P. *(Judge, Idaho District Court Fourth Judicial District Magistrate Division)* Appointed to term beginning Jan 4, 1999. Retained by election. Current term expires Jan 2005. Serves Ada County. Born Boise Idaho. Educated at University of New Mexico and University of Idaho College of Law.

Deputy Attorney/Prosecutor (Chief Criminal Division three years) City of Boise six years. With Criminal Division three years and Chief Deputy Complex Crimes Unit 1994-96 Office of Idaho Attorney General. Chief Counsel Idaho Department of Law Enforcement 1996-98.

Office: 200 West Front Street, Boise 83702-7300.
Telephone: (208) 287-7631.
Fax: (208) 287-7659

WATSON, Barry E. *(Judge, Idaho District Court First Judicial District Magistrate Division)* Serves Kootenai County.

Mailing address: P.O. Box 9000, Coeur d'Alene 83816-9000.
Telephone: (208) 446-1109.

WAYMAN, Scott L. *(Judge, Idaho District Court First Judicial District Magistrate Division)* Appointed Jan 2001. Serves Kootenai County.

Mailing address: P.O. Box 9000, Coeur d'Alene 83816-9000.
Telephone: (208) 446-1108.

WETHERELL, Michael *(Judge, Idaho District Court Fourth Judicial District)* Elected 2002 to term beginning Jan 2003. Term expires Jan 2007.

Office: Ada County Courthouse, 200 West Front Street, Boise 83702-7300.
Telephone: (208) 287-7541, 382-4150, 392-4452.
Fax: (208) 287-7529

WHITE, Boyd Barnard, II *(Judge, Idaho District Court Sixth Judicial District Magistrate Division)* Appointed Jan 8, 1983 to term beginning April 1, 1983. Retained by election 1984, 1988, 1992, 1996 and 2000. Current term expires Jan 2005. Serves Bannock County. Born Brigham City Utah Sept 24, 1943. Church of Jesus Christ of Latter-Day Saints. Educated at Brigham Young University B.S. 1968 J.D. cum laude 1977. Admitted to practice Idaho 1977. Began legal practice Pocatello 1977.

Member Idaho Supreme Court Misdemeanor Rules Committee. Captain U.S. Army 1968-74. Recipient Bronze Star. Enjoys fishing, hunting and computer programming.

Mailing address: P.O. Box 4847, Pocatello 83205.
Telephone: (208) 236-7236.
Fax: (208) 236-7012

WILLIAMS, Mikel H. *(Magistrate Judge, United States District Court District of Idaho)* Appointed by U.S. District Court judges.

Office: U.S. Courthouse, MSC 040, 550 West Fort Street, Boise 83724.
Telephone: (208) 334-9330.

WILLIAMSON, Darla S. *(Administrative Judge, Idaho District Court Fourth Judicial District)* Appointed Judge of Magistrate Division Aug 1, 1979. Appointed District Judge by Governor Dirk Kempthorne Jan 1, 2001. Administrative Judge since Oct 2, 2001. Born Monterey Park California Feb 28, 1944. Protestant. Educated at Willamette University B.A. 1968 and University of Idaho J.D. 1972. Member Psi Chi. Admitted to practice Idaho 1972 and U.S. District Court District of Idaho 1972. In legal practice McCall 1972-79.

Prosecuting Attorney Valley County 1976-78. Former Member Rural Courts Committee, Idaho Rules of Evidence Committee, Idaho Rules of Civil Procedure Committee, Fairness and Equality Committee, Idaho Child Support Guidelines Committee and Technology Committee. Past President Idaho Magistrate Judges' Association. First Lieutenant (flight nurse) USAFR 1965-74. Member McCall Task Force 1973-74 and Advisory Board Ida-Ore Regional Planning Commission 1974-76. Enjoys softball, skiing and fishing.

Office: Ada County Courthouse, 200 West Front Street, Boise 83702-7300.
Telephone: (208) 287-7564, 587-2123.
Fax: (208) 287-7529

WILPER, Ronald J. *(Judge, Idaho District Court Fourth Judicial District)* Appointed by Governor Philip E. Batt to term beginning Jan 1, 1999. Born Idaho. Educated at Boise State University and University of Idaho College of Law.

Former Chief Criminal Deputy Canyon County Prosecutor's Office.

Office: Ada County Courthouse, 200 West Front Street, Boise 83702-7300.
Telephone: (208) 287-7554.
Fax: (208) 287-7529

WINMILL, B. Lynn *(Chief Judge, United States District Court District of Idaho)* Appointed for life by President William Jefferson Clinton to term beginning Aug 1995. Chief Judge since June 1, 1999. Born Blackfoot Idaho March 18, 1952. Educated at Idaho State University B.A. 1974 and Harvard Law School J.D. 1977. In legal practice Denver Colorado 1977-79 and Pocatello Idaho 1979-87. Judge and Administrative Judge, Idaho District Court Sixth Judicial District 1987-95.

Office: U.S. Courthouse, MSC 040, 550 West Fort Street, Boise 83724.
Telephone: (208) 334-9145.

WOOD, R. Barry *(Judge, Idaho District Court Fifth Judicial District)* Former Judge of Magistrate Division. Former Administrative Judge. Former Presiding Judge, Snake River Basin Adjudication.

Mailing address: P.O. Box 27, Gooding 83330.
Office: 624 Main Street, Gooding 83330.
Telephone: (208) 934-4861.
Fax: (208) 934-4408

WOODLAND, William H. *(Judge, Idaho District Court Sixth Judicial District)* Former Judge of Magistrate Division. Appointed District Judge May 25, 1978

WOODLAND, WILLIAM H.—*Continued*

to term beginning July 1, 1978. Elected to subsequent terms. Former Administrative Judge. Born Pocatello Idaho Feb 16, 1941. Church of Jesus Christ of Latter-Day Saints. Educated at Ricks College 1960, Idaho State University B.A. 1966 and University of Utah J.D. 1971. Admitted to practice Utah 1971 and Idaho 1973. Began legal practice Salt Lake City Utah 1971. In legal practice Pocatello Idaho 1975-78.

Founding Member and Past President Portneuf Inns of Court. Member Idaho State Bar, Utah State Bar and American Bar Association. Attended The National Judicial College 1978. Member Idaho State Civic Symphony Board. Enjoys horseback riding, mountaineering and woodworking.

Mailing address: P.O. Box 4126, Pocatello 83205.

Telephone: (208) 236-7250.

Fax: (208) 236-7012

YOUNG, Patricia G. *(Judge, Idaho District Court Fourth Judicial District Magistrate Division)* Serves Boise County.

Mailing address: P.O. Box 126, Idaho City 83631.

Telephone: (208) 392-4452, 287-7487.

Fax: (208) 392-6712

ILLINOIS

Capital SPRINGFIELD

UNITED STATES DISTRICT COURTS DISTRICTS OF ILLINOIS

Within Illinois there are three United States District Courts. For descriptive information refer to the United States Courts section.

CENTRAL DISTRICT consists of Adams, Brown, Bureau, Cass, Champaign, Christian, Coles, DeWitt, Douglas, Edgar, Ford, Fulton, Greene, Hancock, Henderson, Henry, Iroquois, Kankakee, Knox, Livingston, Logan, Macon, Macoupin, Marshall, Mason, McDonough, McLean, Menard, Mercer, Montgomery, Morgan, Moultrie, Peoria, Piatt, Pike, Putnam, Rock Island, Sangamon, Schuyler, Scott, Shelby, Stark, Tazewell, Vermilion, Warren and Woodford counties. The court sits at Champaign/Urbana, Danville, Peoria, Quincy, Rock Island and Springfield.

Chief Judge
Joe Billy McDade

Judges
Michael M. Mihm
Michael P. McCuskey
Jeanne E. Scott

Senior Judges
Harold Albert Baker
Richard Henry Mills

Clerk
John M. Waters
151 Federal Building
600 East Monroe Street
Springfield, Illinois 62701
(217) 492-4020

NORTHERN DISTRICT consists of two divisions.

Eastern Division includes Cook, DuPage, Grundy, Kane, Kendall, Lake, La Salle and Will counties. The court sits at Chicago and Wheaton.

Western Division includes Boone, Carroll, DeKalb, Jo Daviess, Lee, McHenry, Ogle, Stephenson, Whiteside and Winnebago counties. The court sits at Freeport and Rockford.

Chief Judge
Charles P. Kocoras

Judges
Charles R. Norgle, Sr.
James B. Zagel
Wayne R. Andersen
Ruben Castillo
David H. Coar
Robert W. Gettleman
Rebecca R. Pallmeyer
Matthew F. Kennelly
James F. Holderman, Jr.
Suzanne B. Conlon
Philip G. Reinhard
Blanche M. Manning
Elaine E. Bucklo
Joan B. Gottschall
William J. Hibbler
Ronald A. Guzman
Joan Humphrey Lefkow
Amy J. St. Eve
John W. Darrah

Senior Judges
John F. Grady
James B. Moran
William T. Hart
Paul E. Plunkett
Brian Barnett Duff
George M. Marovich
Marvin E. Aspen
Milton I. Shadur
John A. Nordberg
Harry D. Leinenweber
James H. Alesia
George W. Lindberg

Clerk
Michael W. Dobbins
U.S. Courthouse
219 South Dearborn Street
Chicago, Illinois 60604
(312) 435-5670

SOUTHERN DISTRICT includes Alexander, Bond, Calhoun, Clark, Clay, Clinton, Crawford, Cumberland, Edwards, Effingham, Fayette, Franklin, Gallatin, Hamilton, Hardin, Jackson, Jasper, Jefferson, Jersey, Johnson, Lawrence, Madison, Marion, Massac, Monroe, Perry, Pope, Pulaski, Randolph, Richland, St. Clair, Saline, Union, Wabash, Washington, Wayne, White and Williamson counties. The court sits at Alton, Benton, Cairo and East St. Louis.

Chief Judge
G. Patrick Murphy

Judges
J. Phil Gilbert
David R. Herndon
Michael J. Reagan

Senior Judges
James L. Foreman
William D. Stiehl

Clerk
Norbert G. Jaworski
P.O. Box 249
East St. Louis, Illinois 62202-0249
(618) 482-9371

UNITED STATES MAGISTRATE JUDGES OF ILLINOIS

CENTRAL DISTRICT
David G. Bernthal
Byron Cudmore
John A. Gorman

NORTHERN DISTRICT
Edward A. Bobrick
Martin C. Ashman
Morton Denlow
Nan R. Nolan
Geraldine Soat Brown
P. Michael Mahoney
Arlander Keys
Ian H. Levin
Sidney I. Schenkier
Michael T. Mason

UNITED STATES DISTRICT COURTS DISTRICTS OF ILLINOIS—*Continued*

SOUTHERN DISTRICT

Gerald B. Cohn
Philip M. Frazier
Clifford J. Proud

Recalled Magistrate Judge

Charles H. Evans (Central District)

UNITED STATES BANKRUPTCY COURTS OF ILLINOIS

CENTRAL DISTRICT

Chief Judge

Gerald D. Fines

Judges

Larry Lee Lessen
Thomas L. Perkins

Recalled Judge

William V. Altenberger

Bankruptcy Clerk

Hardin W. Hawes
226 Federal Building
600 East Monroe Street
Springfield, Illinois 62701-1626
(217) 492-4551

NORTHERN DISTRICT

Chief Judge

Eugene R. Wedoff

Judges

Jack B. Schmetterer
John H. Squires
Carol A. Doyle
Pamela S. Hollis
Jacqueline P. Cox
Susan Pierson Sonderby
Manuel Barbosa
Bruce W. Black
A. Benjamin Goldgar

Recalled Judges

John D. Schwartz
Robert E. Ginsberg

Bankruptcy Clerk

Kenneth Gardner
U.S. Courthouse
219 South Dearborn Street
Chicago, Illinois 60604
(312) 435-6036

SOUTHERN DISTRICT

Judge

Kenneth J. Meyers

Bankruptcy Clerk

Wayne Bannert
P.O. Box 309
East St. Louis, Illinois 62202-0309
(618) 482-9400

SUPREME COURT OF ILLINOIS

The Supreme Court is Illinois' court of last resort. The state is divided into five judicial districts for electoral purposes only. The court consists of a chief justice and six justices initially elected at partisan elections in each judicial district for ten-year terms. Thereafter, justices may run on a retention vote for additional terms without party affiliation. Three of the justices are elected from the First Judicial District and one from each of the four other districts. A chief justice is elected by peer vote for a three-year term. Retirement is mandatory at age seventy-five; however, retired justices may be assigned by the court to serve on a recall basis.

The court has discretionary original jurisdiction in cases relating to revenue, mandamus, prohibition or habeas corpus and has exclusive jurisdiction over matters of redistricting of the General Assembly and the ability of the governor to hold office. The court hears direct appeals from the Circuit Courts in cases involving capital punishment and hears appeals from the Appellate Court in cases involving constitutional issues. The court has general administrative control over all courts in the state.

Four justices constitute a quorum, and the concurrence of four is necessary for a decision. The court sits en banc at Springfield and Chicago and recesses during February, April, July, August, October and December.

FIRST JUDICIAL DISTRICT includes Cook County.

SECOND JUDICIAL DISTRICT includes Boone, Carroll, DeKalb, DuPage, Jo Daviess, Kane, Kendall, Lake, Lee, McHenry, Ogle, Stephenson and Winnebago counties.

THIRD JUDICIAL DISTRICT includes Bureau, Fulton, Grundy, Hancock, Henderson, Henry, Iroquois, Kankakee, Knox, La Salle, Marshall, McDonough, Mercer, Peoria, Putnam, Rock Island, Stark, Tazewell, Warren, Whiteside and Will counties.

FOURTH JUDICIAL DISTRICT includes Adams, Brown, Calhoun, Cass, Champaign, Clark, Coles, Cumberland, DeWitt, Douglas, Edgar, Ford, Greene, Jersey, Livingston, Logan, Macon, Macoupin, Mason, McLean, Menard, Morgan, Moultrie, Piatt, Pike, Sangamon, Schuyler, Scott, Vermilion and Woodford counties.

FIFTH JUDICIAL DISTRICT includes Alexander, Bond, Christian, Clay, Clinton, Crawford, Edwards, Effingham, Fayette, Franklin, Gallatin, Hamilton, Hardin, Jackson, Jasper, Jefferson, Johnson, Lawrence, Madison, Marion, Massac, Monroe, Montgomery, Perry, Pope, Pulaski, Randolph, Richland, St. Clair, Saline, Shelby, Union, Wabash, Washington, Wayne, White and Williamson counties.

Chief Justice

Mary Ann G. McMorrow

Justices

Charles E. Freeman
Robert R. Thomas
Rita B. Garman
Thomas R. Fitzgerald
Thomas L. Kilbride
Philip J. Rarick

Clerk

Juleann Hornyak
Supreme Court Building
200 East Capitol Avenue
Springfield, Illinois 62701
(217) 782-2035

SUPREME COURT OF ILLINOIS—*Continued*

Director
Cynthia Y. Cobbs
222 North LaSalle Street, 13th Floor
Chicago, Illinois 60601
(312) 793-3250

ILLINOIS APPELLATE COURT

The Appellate Court is Illinois' court of intermediate appellate jurisdiction. The state is divided into five judicial districts, and the Supreme Court prescribes the number of appellate divisions within each judicial district. At least three judges are assigned to each division by the Supreme Court. Judges are initially elected at partisan elections in each judicial district for ten-year terms. Subsequent ten-year terms are by retention vote. In the absence of a law, vacancies may be filled by Supreme Court appointment. A presiding judge is elected in each division by peer vote to a one-year term. Retirement is mandatory at age seventy-five; however, retired judges may be assigned by the Supreme Court to serve on a recall basis.

The court hears appeals of all final decisions of the Circuit Courts except those cases heard directly by the Supreme Court. The court may exercise any original jurisdiction it finds necessary and reviews administrative actions as provided by law. All decisions of the court are final unless the Supreme Court grants leave to appeal.

The court sits in one or more divisions in each judicial district as specified below. With the approval of the chief justice, a division may sit at any location in the state. The districts are defined in the Illinois Supreme Court section. The presiding judge of a division designates the judges to sit in panels of three each. The concurrence of two judges is necessary for a decision.

---

*Circuit Court judge sitting by assignment

FIRST JUDICIAL DISTRICT sits at Chicago.

DIVISION ONE

Judges
Jill Kathleen McNulty
Joseph Gordon
Denise Margaret O'Malley
James G. Fitzgerald Smith

DIVISION TWO

Judges
Anne M. Burke
Robert Cahill
Margaret Stanton McBride

DIVISION THREE

Judges
Leslie E. South
Shelvin Louise Marie Hall
Thomas E. Hoffman
Rodolfo Garcia*
Warren D. Wolfson*

DIVISION FOUR

Judges
Allen Hartman
Mary Jane Theis
Alan J. Greiman*
Themis N. Karnezis*

DIVISION FIVE

Judges
Calvin C. Campbell
Patrick J. Quinn
Neil F. Hartigan
Ellis E. Reid*

DIVISION SIX

Judges
John Patrick Tully
Sheila M. O'Brien
Michael J. Gallagher
Margaret O'Mara Frossard*

SECOND JUDICIAL DISTRICT sits at Elgin.

Judges
John J. Bowman
Thomas E. Callum
R. Peter Grometer*
Susan F. Hutchinson
Robert D. McLaren
Robert E. Byrne*
Barbara Gilleran Johnson
Frederick J. Kapala*
Jack O'Malley

THIRD JUDICIAL DISTRICT sits at Ottawa.

Judges
Tobias "Toby" Barry
Tom M. Lytton
Daniel L. Schmidt
William E. Holdridge
Mary W. McDade
Kent F. Slater

FOURTH JUDICIAL DISTRICT sits at Springfield.

Judges
Thomas R. Appleton*
James A. Knecht
Sue E. Myerscough
John W. Turner
Robert W. Cook
John T. McCullough
Robert J. Steigmann

FIFTH JUDICIAL DISTRICT sits at Mount Vernon.

Judges
Melissa A. Chapman
Richard P. Goldenhersh
Clyde L. Kuehn
Thomas M. Welch
James K. Donovan*
Terrence J. Hopkins
Gordon E. Maag

ILLINOIS CIRCUIT COURTS

The Circuit Courts are Illinois' courts of general jurisdiction. The state is divided into twenty-two judicial circuits. Three circuits, Cook County, the Twelfth Circuit and the Eighteenth Circuit, consist of a single county. The other nineteen judicial circuits are composed of two or more contiguous counties as provided by law. Each judicial circuit has one unified Circuit Court. Circuit judges are initially elected at partisan elections in each circuit for six-year terms. Subsequent six-year terms are by retention vote. In the absence of a law, vacancies may be filled by Supreme Court appointment. The circuit judges appoint associate judges in their respective circuits on a merit basis for four-year terms. Associate judges' duties are prescribed by Supreme Court rules.

ILLINOIS CIRCUIT COURTS—*Continued*

The Supreme Court has the authority to temporarily assign circuit judges to any court and associate judges to any Circuit Court. A chief judge is elected in each circuit by peer vote to serve at the pleasure of the judges of that circuit. Retirement is mandatory at age seventy-five; however, with their consent retired judges may be recalled by the Supreme Court. Retired associate judges may be assigned only as associate judges.

The courts have original jurisdiction of all justiciable matters except those in which the Supreme Court has exclusive jurisdiction. The courts may review administrative actions as provided by law.

The courts sit at the county seats and elsewhere as needed.

---

*Assigned to Appellate Court

FIRST JUDICIAL CIRCUIT includes Alexander, Jackson, Johnson, Massac, Pope, Pulaski, Saline, Union and Williamson counties. The court sits at Cairo, Murphysboro, Vienna, Metropolis, Golconda, Mound City, Harrisburg, Jonesboro and Marion.

Chief Judge

Michael J. Henshaw

Circuit Judges

Mark Monroe Boie
Mark H. Clarke
Ronald R. Eckiss
Terry J. Foster
Donald Lowery
Paul S. Murphy
Phillip G. Palmer, Sr.
William G. Schwartz
Stephen L. Spomer
Bruce D. Stewart
William J. Thurston
David W. Watt, Jr.
James R. Williamson

Associate Judges

Rodney A. Clutts
Kimberly L. Dahlen
Thomas H. Jones
E. Dan Kimmel
Brocton D. Lockwood
John A. Speroni
William H. Wilson

SECOND JUDICIAL CIRCUIT includes Crawford, Edwards, Franklin, Gallatin, Hamilton, Hardin, Jefferson, Lawrence, Richland, Wabash, Wayne and White counties. The court sits at Robinson, Albion, Benton, Shawneetown, McLeansboro, Elizabethtown, Mount Vernon, Lawrenceville, Olney, Mount Carmel, Fairfield and Carmi.

Chief Judge

James M. Wexstten

Circuit Judges

Larry O. Baker
David M. Correll
Larry D. Dunn
Don Al Foster
David K. Frankland
Terry H. Gamber
Bennie Joe Harrison
Robert M. Hopkins
Loren P. Lewis
Stephen G. Sawyer
Thomas H. Sutton
George W. Timberlake
E. Kyle Vantrease
Barry Leon Vaughan

Associate Judges

Kathleen M. Alling
Leo T. Desmond
Kimbara Graham Harrell
James V. Hill
Robert W. Lewis

THIRD JUDICIAL CIRCUIT includes Bond and Madison counties. The court sits at Greenville and Edwardsville.

Chief Judge

Edward C. Ferguson

Circuit Judges

Nicholas G. Byron
Ann Callis
Phillip J. Kardis
John Knight
A. Andreas Matoesian
George J. Moran
Charles Romani, Jr.
Daniel J. Stack

Associate Judges

Thomas W. Chapman
Barbara L. Crowder
Ellar Duff
James Hackett
Clarence Harrison, II
Lola P. Maddox
Lewis E. Mallott
Ralph J. Mendelsohn
Nelson F. Metz
Richard L. Tognarelli

FOURTH JUDICIAL CIRCUIT includes Christian, Clay, Clinton, Effingham, Fayette, Jasper, Marion, Montgomery and Shelby counties. The court sits at Taylorville, Louisville, Carlyle, Effingham, Vandalia, Newton, Salem, Hillsboro and Shelbyville.

Chief Judge

S. Gene Schwarm

Circuit Judges

John P. Coady
Patrick L. Duke
Patrick J. Hitpas
Michael P. Kiley
Kelly D. Long
Kathleen P. Moran
David L. Sauer
Steven P. Seymour
Ronald D. Spears
Sherri L. E. Tungate
Michael R. Weber

Associate Judges

William J. Becker
James J. Eder
James R. Harvey
Mark M. Joy
John W. McGuire
Dennis Middendorff
David W. Slater

FIFTH JUDICIAL CIRCUIT includes Clark, Coles, Cumberland, Edgar and Vermilion counties. The court sits at Marshall, Charleston, Toledo, Paris and Danville.

Chief Judge

James R. Glenn

Circuit Judges

Claudia J. Anderson
H. Dean Andrews
Dale A. Cini
Michael D. Clary
Craig H. DeArmond
Millard Scott Everhart
Thomas J. Fahey
Gary W. Jacobs
Tracy W. Resch
Mitchell K. Shick
Ashton C. Waller, Jr.

Associate Judges

James K. Borbely
David W. Lewis
Teresa K. Righter
Joseph P. Skowronski, Jr.
Gordon R. Stipp

SIXTH JUDICIAL CIRCUIT includes Champaign, DeWitt, Douglas, Macon, Moultrie and Piatt counties. The court sits at Urbana, Clinton, Tuscola, Decatur, Sullivan and Monticello.

Chief Judge

John P. Shonkwiler

ILLINOIS CIRCUIT COURTS—*Continued*

Circuit Judges

Arnold F. Blockman
Harry E. Clem
Thomas J. Difanis
Dan L. Flannell
John K. Greanias
Michael Q. Jones
Frank W. Lincoln
Katherine M. McCarthy
Theodore E. Paine
Stephen H. Peters
J. G. Townsend
Albert G. Webber

Associate Judges

Holly F. Clemons
James Coryell
Scott B. Diamond
Ann A. Einhorn
Jeffrey B. Ford
Chris E. Freese
John R. Kennedy
Heidi N. Ladd
Thomas E. Little
Timothy J. Steadman
Lisa Holder White

SEVENTH JUDICIAL CIRCUIT includes Greene, Jersey, Macoupin, Morgan, Sangamon and Scott counties. The court sits at Carrollton, Jerseyville, Carlinville, Jacksonville, Springfield and Winchester.

Chief Judge

Thomas P. Carmody

Circuit Judges

Thomas R. Appleton*
Lois A. Bell
Donald M. Cadagin
James W. Day
Robert J. Eggers
Leslie J. Graves
Patrick W. Kelley
Joseph P. Koval
Richard T. Mitchell
Thomas G. Russell
Leo J. Zappa, Jr.

Recalled Circuit Judge

Dennis L. Schwartz

Associate Judges

Diane L. Brunton
Charles J. Gramlich
Robert T. Hall
Roger W. Holmes
Theodis P. Lewis
John A. Mehlick
Steven H. Nardulli
Tim P. Olson
George H. Ray
Stuart H. Shiffman

EIGHTH JUDICIAL CIRCUIT includes Adams, Brown, Calhoun, Cass, Mason, Menard, Pike and Schuyler counties. The court sits at Quincy, Mount Sterling, Hardin, Virginia, Havana, Petersburg, Pittsfield and Rushville.

Chief Judge

Thomas L. Brownfield

Circuit Judges

Dennis K. Cashman
Richard D. Greenlief
Bob Hardwick, Jr.
Alesia A. McMillen
M. Carol Pope
Michael R. Roseberry
Mark A. Schuering
David K. Slocum
Scott Walden
Robert L. Welch

Associate Judges

Mark A. Drummond
Diane M. Lagoski
Thomas J. Ortbal
Chet W. Vahle
John C. Wooleyhan

NINTH JUDICIAL CIRCUIT includes Fulton, Hancock, Henderson, Knox, McDonough and Warren counties. The court sits at Lewistown, Carthage, Oquawka, Galesburg, Macomb and Monmouth.

Chief Judge

William D. Henderson

Circuit Judges

Harry C. Bulkeley
David R. Hultgren
Stephen C. Mathers
James B. Stewart
David F. Stoverink
Eugene Taylor
Ronald C. Tenold
David L. Vancil, Jr.

Associate Judges

Steven R. Bordner
John R. Clerkin
Richard H. Gambrell
Larry W. Heiser
Gregory K. McClintock
Patricia A. Walton

TENTH JUDICIAL CIRCUIT includes Marshall, Peoria, Putnam, Stark and Tazewell counties. The court sits at Lacon, Peoria, Hennepin, Toulon and Pekin.

Chief Judge

John A. Barra

Circuit Judges

J. Peter Ault
Stuart P. Borden
Michael E. Brandt
Kevin R. Galley
Richard E. Grawey
Stephen A. Kouri
James E. Shadid
Scott A. Shore
Joe R. Vespa

Associate Judges

Erik I. Blanc
Glenn H. Collier
David J. Dubicki
Chris L. Fredericksen
Timothy M. Lucas
Jerelyn D. Maher
Richard D. McCoy
Brian Mark Nemenoff
Albert L. Purham, Jr.
Rebecca R. Steenrod

ELEVENTH JUDICIAL CIRCUIT includes Ford, Livingston, Logan, McLean and Woodford counties. The court sits at Paxton, Pontiac, Lincoln, Bloomington and Eureka.

Chief Judge

John P. Freese

Circuit Judges

Donald D. Bernardi
David L. Coogan
Ronald C. Dozier
Harold J. Frobish
John B. Huschen
Steve Pacey
G. Michael Prall
Charles G. Reynard
Elizabeth A. Robb
James E. Souk

Associate Judges

Donald A. Behle
William D. DeCardy
Scott D. Drazewski
Charles M. Feeney, III
Kevin P. Fitzgerald
Charles H. Frank
Robert L. Freitag
Paul G. Lawrence
Randolph R. Spires

TWELFTH JUDICIAL CIRCUIT includes Will County. The court sits at Joliet.

Chief Judge

Stephen D. White

Circuit Judges

Carla J. Alessio Goode
Amy M. Bertani-Tomczak
Herman S. Haase
Gerald R. Kinney
Rodney B. Lechwar
Susan T. O'Leary
Daniel J. Rozak
Richard C. Schoenstedt
Richard J. Siegel

Associate Judges

Barbara Jean Badger
Robert J. Baron
Cathy Block
Thomas A. Dunn

ILLINOIS CIRCUIT COURTS—*Continued*

James E. Garrison
Lawrence C. Gray
Ludwig J. Kuhar, Jr.
William G. McMenamin
Marzell Richardson, Jr.
Edwin B. Grabiec
Kathleen G. Kallan
Robert C. Lorz
Gilbert L. Niznik

THIRTEENTH JUDICIAL CIRCUIT includes Bureau, Grundy and La Salle counties. The court sits at Princeton, Morris and Ottawa.

Chief Judge
Robert L. Carter

Circuit Judges
Marc Bernabei
James A. Lanuti
Cynthia M. Raccuglia
Eugene P. Daugherity
Robert C. Marsaglia
H. Chris Ryan, Jr.

Associate Judges
William P. Balestri
William R. Banich
James L. Brusatte
A. Scott Madson
Lance R. Peterson

FOURTEENTH JUDICIAL CIRCUIT includes Henry, Mercer, Rock Island and Whiteside counties. The court sits at Cambridge, Aledo, Rock Island and Morrison.

Chief Judge
Jeffrey W. O'Connor

Circuit Judges
Joseph F. Beatty
James G. Conway, Jr.
Ted Hamer
Timothy J. Slavin
James T. Teros
Mark A. VandeWiele
Walter D. Braud
Danny A. Dunagan
Lori R. Lefstein
Charles H. Stengel
Larry S. Vandersnick

Associate Judges
John L. Bell
Alan G. Blackwood
John L. Hauptman
Dana R. McReynolds
Carol M. Pentuic
Thomas C. Berglund
Michael P. Brinn
John R. McClean, Jr.
James J. Mesich
Vicki Wright

FIFTEENTH JUDICIAL CIRCUIT includes Carroll, Jo Daviess, Lee, Ogle and Stephenson counties. The court sits at Mount Carroll, Galena, Dixon, Oregon and Freeport.

Chief Judge
Stephen C. Pemberton

Circuit Judges
Barry R. Anderson
Val Gunnarsson
William A. Kelly
Michael Mallon
David T. Fritts
Charles R. Hartman
Tomas M. Magdich

Associate Judges
Charles T. Beckman
John F. Joyce
John E. Payne
Theresa L. Ursin
David L. Jeffrey
Kathleen O. Kauffmann
Victor Sprengelmeyer

SIXTEENTH JUDICIAL CIRCUIT includes DeKalb, Kane and Kendall counties. The court sits at Sycamore, Geneva and Yorkville.

Chief Judge
Philip L. DiMarzio

Circuit Judges
Judith M. Brawka
Michael J. Colwell
Douglas R. Engel
Joseph M. Grady
Donald C. Hudson
Gene Louis Nottolini
Robert B. Spence
James M. Wilson
F. Keith Brown
James T. Doyle
Donald J. Fabian
R. Peter Grometer*
Kurt Klein
Timothy Q. Sheldon
Grant Steven Wegner

Associate Judges
Allen M. Anderson
James Donnelly
James R. Edwards
James C. Hallock
Richard J. Larson
Mary Karen Simpson
Stephen Sullivan
Leonard J. Wojtecki
Franklin D. Brewe
Wiley W. Edmondson
Patricia P. Golden
Robert L. Janes
Thomas E. Mueller
Robbin J. Stuckert
William H. Weir

SEVENTEENTH JUDICIAL CIRCUIT includes Boone and Winnebago counties. The court sits at Belvidere and Rockford.

Chief Judge
Gerald F. Grubb

Circuit Judges
Rosemary Collins
Janet R. Holmgren
Joseph G. McGraw
Richard W. Vidal
Timothy R. Gill
Frederick J. Kapala*
R. L. Pirrello
Kathryn E. Zenoff

Associate Judges
Robert G. Coplan
John Todd Kennedy
Steven M. Nash
J. Edward Prochaska
R. Craig Sahlstrom
John R. Truitt
Ronald J. White
Patrick L. Heaslip
Angus S. More, Jr.
Steven L. Nordquist
Gary Pumilia
Brian Dean Shore
Steven G. Vecchio

EIGHTEENTH JUDICIAL CIRCUIT includes DuPage County. The court sits at Wheaton.

Chief Judge
Robert K. Kilander

Circuit Judges
Robert J. Anderson
George J. Bakalis
Robert E. Byrne*
Edward R. Duncan, Jr.
Rodney W. Equi
Kenneth Moy
Hollis L. Webster
C. Stanley Austin
Michael J. Burke
Kathryn E. Creswell
John T. Elsner
Ann B. Jorgensen
Perry R. Thompson
Bonnie M. Wheaton

Recalled Circuit Judge
Stephen J. Culliton

Associate Judges
Kenneth A. Abraham
John W. Demling
Thomas C. Dudgeon
Blanche Hill Fawell
Dorothy F. French
James W. Jerz
James J. Konetski
Richard A. Lucas
Joseph S. Bongiorno
Peter J. Dockery
Mark W. Dwyer
William I. Ferguson
Nicholas J. Galasso
Bruce R. Kelsey
Patrick J. Leston
Brian R. McKillip

ILLINOIS CIRCUIT COURTS—*Continued*

Jane H. Mitton
Kenneth L. Popejoy
Elizabeth Walter Sexton
Kenneth W. Torluemke
Cary B. Pierce
Thomas J. Riggs
Terence M. Sheen
George J. Sotos
Eugene A. Wojcik

Recalled Associate Judge

Paul Noland

NINETEENTH JUDICIAL CIRCUIT includes Lake and McHenry counties. The court sits at Waukegan and Woodstock.

Chief Judge

Margaret J. Mullen

Circuit Judges

Ward S. Arnold
Michael T. Caldwell
David M. Hall
Raymond J. McKoski
Victoria A. Rossetti
Christopher C. Starck
Henry C. Tonigan, III
Stephen E. Walter
James K. Booras
John R. Goshgarian
Maureen P. McIntyre
Sharon Prather
Mary S. Schostok
Michael J. Sullivan
Jane D. Waller

Associate Judges

Thomas F. Baker
Terrence J. Brady
Valerie Boettle Ceckowski
Helen R. Franks
Donald H. Geiger
Mitchell L. Hoffman
Patrick N. Lawler
Victoria L. Martin
Jorge L. Ortiz
Theodore S. Potkonjak
Emilio B. Santi
Joseph R. Waldeck
Diane E. Winter
John D. Bolger
George Bridges
Joseph P. Condon
Wallace B. Dunn
Michael John Fritz
Gordon E. Graham
Brian P. Hughes
Sarah P. Lessman
Gary Neddenriep
John T. Phillips
John G. Radosevich
Thomas R. Smoker
Charles P. Weech
Gerald M. Zopp, Jr.

TWENTIETH JUDICIAL CIRCUIT includes Monroe, Perry, Randolph, St. Clair and Washington counties. The court sits at Waterloo, Pinckneyville, Chester, Belleville and Nashville.

Chief Judge

Jan V. Fiss

Circuit Judges

James W. Campanella
James K. Donovan*
Annette A. Eckert
Robert J. Hillebrand
Robert P. LeChien
Milton S. Wharton
Lloyd A. Cueto
Dennis B. Doyle
Jerry D. Flynn
Lloyd A. Karmeier
Michael J. O'Malley

Associate Judges

Richard Aguirre
Laninya Cason
John Goodwin
Vincent J. Lopinot
Alexis Otis-Lewis
Stephen R. Rice
Patrick M. Young
Walter C. Brandon, Jr.
Ellen A. Dauber
Dennis Hatch
Scott Mansfield
James M. Radcliffe
William A. Schuwerk

TWENTY-FIRST JUDICIAL CIRCUIT includes Iroquois and Kankakee counties. The court sits at Watseka and Kankakee.

Chief Judge

Kendall O. Wenzelman

Circuit Judges

Kathy Bradshaw Elliott
J. Gregory Householter
Gordon Lee Lustfeldt
Clark Erwin Erickson
Michael J. Kick
Susan Sumner Tungate

Recalled Circuit Judge

Charles E. Glennon

Associate Judges

Michael D. Kramer
William O. Schmidt
David A. Youck

CIRCUIT COURT OF COOK COUNTY includes Cook County. The court sits at Chicago.

Chief Judge

Timothy C. Evans

Circuit Judges

Martin S. Agran
Patricia Banks
Carole K. Bellows
Richard B. Berland
Robert W. Bertucci
Janice L. Bierman
Margaret Ann Brennan
Cynthia Brim
Rodney Hughes Brooks
Mary M. Brosnahan
Charles P. Burns
Anthony L. Burrell
Diane Gordon Cannon
Thomas R. Chiola
Mary Ellen Coghlan
Melvin J. Cole
Claudia Conlon
Maureen E. Connors
Wilbur E. Crooks
Daniel P. Darcy
David Delgado
Barbara J. Disko
Christopher Donnelly
John T. Doody, Jr.
Loretta C. Douglas
Loretta Eadie-Daniels
Lynn M. Egan
James R. Epstein
Thomas Fecarotta, Jr.
Peter A. Felice
Denise K. Filan
Thomas E. Flanagan
John J. Fleming
Peter Flynn
Lester D. Foreman
Rodolfo Garcia*
Vincent M. Gaughan
Francis W. Glowacki
Francis X. Golniewicz, Jr.
Alan J. Greiman*
Patrick S. Grossi
Catherine M. Haberkorn
Sophia H. Hall
Marsha D. Hayes
Shelli Williams Hayes
Nancy J. Arnold
Ronald F. Bartkowicz
Gerald C. Bender
Andrew Berman
Paul P. Biebel, Jr.
Richard J. Billik, Jr.
Eileen M. Brewer
Philip L. Bronstein
Janet Adams Brosnahan
James R. Brown
Edward R. Burr
Bernetta D. Bush
Thomas F. Carmody, Jr.
Evelyn B. Clay
Matthew E. Coghlan
Sharon Johnson Coleman
Clayton J. Crane
Lisa R. Curcio
Thomas M. Davy
Donald M. Devlin
Francis J. Dolan
David Donnersberger
Deborah M. Dooling
Jennifer Duncan-Brice
James D. Egan
Richard J. Elrod
Candace Jean Fabri
Roger G. Fein
Raymond A. Figueroa
Kathy M. Flanagan
James P. Flannery, Jr.
Susan G. Fleming
Nicholas R. Ford
Raymond Funderburk
Sheldon Gardner
James J. Gavin
Allen S. Goldberg
Robert E. Gordon
Llwellyn Greene-Thapedi
Susan Ruscitti Grussel
William J. Haddad
La Quietta J. Hardy-Campbell
Michael T. Healy

ILLINOIS CIRCUIT COURTS—*Continued*

Curtis Heaston
Michael J. Hogan
Leo E. Holt
Garritt E. Howard
Arnette R. Hubbard
Anthony A. Iosco
Aaron Jaffe
Dorothy F. Jones
Daniel E. Jordan
James J. Jorzak
Themis N. Karnezis*
Michael R. Keehan
Carol A. Kelly
Kathleen G. Kennedy
Dorothy K. Kinnaird
Robert J. Kowalski
Bertina E. Lampkin
Diane Joan Larsen
Marjorie C. Laws
David G. Lichtenstein
Thomas J. Lipscomb
Robert Lopez Cepero
Noreen V. Love
Stuart F. Lubin
Daniel J. Lynch
John K. Madden
William O. Maki
LeRoy K. Martin, Jr.
Mary Anne Mason
Carol Pearce McCarthy
Barbara A. McDonald
Patrick E. McGann
Dennis M. McGuire
Paddy H. McNamara
Barbara M. Meyer
Judy I. Mitchell-Davis
John J. Moran, Jr.
John Emmett Morrissey
Lisa Ruble Murphy
Joyce Marie Murphy Gorman
P. Scott Neville, Jr.
Julia M. Nowicki
Stuart A. Nudelman
Edward P. O'Brien
William T. O'Brien
James P. O'Malley
Margaret O'Mara Frossard*
Stuart E. Palmer
Kathleen M. Pantle
William Michael Phelan
Edward N. Pietrucha
Lee Preston
Thomas P. Quinn
Ralph Reyna
Barbara Riley
James G. Riley
Thomas D. Roti
James T. Ryan
Leida Gonzalez Santiago
Colleen F. Sheehan
Nancy Drew Sheehan
Richard A. Siebel
James F. Henry
Thomas L. Hogan
Vanessa A. Hopkins
Nathaniel Howse, Jr.
Cheyrl D. Ingram
Moshe Jacobius
Raymond L. Jagielski
Rickey Jones
Edward R. Jordan
Paul A. Karkula
Joseph Kazmierski, Jr.
Daniel J. Kelley
James W. Kennedy
Kerry M. Kennedy
John P. Kirby
William G. Lacy
Joanne L. Lanigan
Jeffrey Lawrence
Casandra Lewis
Marcella C. Lipinski
Daniel M. Locallo
Gay-Lloyd Lott
Michele F. Lowrance
Marvin P. Luckman
Daniel Joseph Lynch
William D. Maddux
Marcia Maras
Patricia Martin Bishop
Veronica B. Mathein
James P. McCarthy
Susan J. McDunn
Sheila McGinnis
Kathleen M. McGury
Colleen McSweeney-Moore
Anthony S. Montelione
Dennis J. Morrissey
Mary A. Mulhern
Michael J. Murphy
Elliott Muse, Jr.
Marya Nega
Lewis Nixon
Thomas E. Nowinski
Donald J. O'Brien, Jr.
Joan M. O'Brien
Lawrence O'Gara
William P. O'Malley
William D. O'Neal
Sandra R. Otaka
Thomas P. Panichi
Sebastian T. Patti
Donna Phelps Felton
Edmund Ponce de Leon
Robert J. Quinn
Ellis E. Reid*
James L. Rhodes
Daniel A. Riley
Ronald C. Riley
Maureen Durkin Roy
Nancy S. Salyers
Drella Savage
Stephen A. Schiller
Kevin M. Sheehan
Lon W. Shultz
Henry R. Simmons, Jr.
Henry M. Singer
Irwin J. Solganick
John O. Steele
Victoria A. Stewart
Jane Louise Stuart
Laura M. Sullivan
Fred G. Suria, Jr.
Shelley Sutker-Dermer
Lawrence Terrell, Sr.
Karen T. Tobin
Michael P. Toomin
Sandra Tristano
John D. Turner, Jr.
Joseph J. Urso
Raul Vega
Richard F. Walsh
Edward Washington, II
Daniel S. Weber
Camille E. Willis
Warren D. Wolfson*
Anthony L. Young
Susan F. Zwick
Maura Slattery Boyle
Cheryl A. Starks
David P. Sterba
Paul Stralka
Daniel J. Sullivan
Sharon M. Sullivan
Donald J. Suriano
Bill Taylor
Mary Maxwell Thomas
Amanda S. Toney
Charles M. Travis
Edna M. Turkington
Valarie E. Turner
James Michael Varga
Kenneth J. Wadas
John A. Ward
Cyril J. Watson
Alexander P. White
Gregory J. Wojkowski
E. Kenneth Wright, Jr.
Frank G. Zelezinski

Recalled Circuit Judges

Henry A. Budzinski
Allen A. Freeman
Leonard L. Levin
Benjamin E. Novoselsky
Darryl B. Simko
Lori M. Wolfson
Robert E. Cusack
Thomas V. Gainer, Jr.
Allan W. Masters
James S. Quinlan, Jr.
Charles R. Winkler

Associate Judges

Sam L. Amirante
William J. Aukstik
Mark J. Ballard
Consuelo E. Bedoya
J. Martin Berry
Adam D. Bourgeois, Jr.
William Stewart Boyd
Michael Brown
Dennis J. Burke
Frank B. Castiglione
Timothy J. Chambers
Gloria G. Coco
Thomas J. Condon
Noreen M. Daly
Frank DeBoni
Grace G. Dickler
James P. Etchingham
Howard Lewis Fink
Lawrence P. Fox
Edwin A. Gausselin
Susan Fox Gillis
J. B. Grogan
R. Morgan Hamilton
Earl B. Hoffenberg
Ann Houser
John J. Hynes
Arthur L. Janura, Jr.
Jordan Kaplan
Nancy J. Katz
Lynne Kawamoto
Randye A. Kogan
John G. Laurie
James B. Linn
Patrick F. Lustig
Thaddeus S. Machnik
John J. Mannion
Edward A. Antonietti
Reginald H. Baker
Robert P. Bastone
Helaine L. Berger
Samuel J. Betar, III
Preston L. Bowie, Jr.
Stephen Y. Brodhay
Gary L. Brownfield
Joseph N. Casciato
Donna L. Cervini
Joseph M. Claps
Susan M. Coleman
Abishi C. Cunningham
Ronald S. Davis
Dennis A. Dernbach
James G. Donegan
Fé Fernandez
Lawrence E. Flood
Sheldon C. Garber
Daniel T. Gillespie
Gregory R. Ginex
Gilbert J. Grossi
Miriam E. Harrison
Patricia B. Holmes
Colleen A. Hyland
Marianne Jackson
Sandi G. Johnson-Speh
Pamela G. Karahalios
Richard A. Kavitt
Carol A. Kipperman
Lambros J. Kutrubis
Neil J. Linehan
Mark J. Lopez
Joseph M. Macellaio
Jeffrey A. Malak
Charles M. May

ILLINOIS CIRCUIT COURTS—*Continued*

Brendan J. McCooey
William F. McGlynn
Clifford L. Meacham
George M. Morrissey
James V. Murphy II
Raymond Myles
Rita M. Novak
Gregory M. O'Brien
Jerome M. Orbach
Donald Panarese, Jr.
Alfred J. Paul
William G. Pileggi
Michael J. Pope
Dennis J. Porter
Wayne D. Rhine
Elizabeth Loredo Rivera
Stanley J. Sacks
James M. Schreier
Terrence V. Sharkey
Michele M. Simmons
Terence B. Smith
Eddie A. Stephens
Michael W. Stuttley
John D. Tourtelot
Rena M. Van Tine
Daniel G. Welter
Martin E. McDonough
Brigid Mary McGrath
Daniel R. Miranda
J. Patrick Morse
Michael J. Murray
Paul J. Nealis
James M. Obbish
Thomas J. O'Hara
Marcia B. Orr
Luciano Panici
Arthur C. Perivolidis
Nicholas T. Pomaro
Charles E. Porcellino
Jesse Gregory Reyes
Hyman Riebman
Mary K. Rochford
James J. Ryan
Marcus R. Salone
John J. Scotillo
Karen G. Shields
Robert M. Smierciak
James F. Stack
Richard A. Stevens
Thomas R. Sumner
Thomas M. Tucker
John A. Wasilewski
LaBrenda E. White
Walter Williams
William S. Wood
Willie B. Wright
Gerald T. Winiecki
Leon Wool
Michael C. Zissman

Recalled Associate Judge

David A. Erickson

ILLINOIS COURT OF CLAIMS

The Court of Claims is a quasi-judicial court in Illinois that is part of the legislative branch. The court consists of a chief justice and six judges appointed by the governor with the advice and consent of the Senate for six-year terms.

The court has exclusive jurisdiction of all claims against the state founded in law, in contract or upon administrative or executive regulations, except claims concerning the Workers' Compensation Act or the Workers' Occupational Diseases Act. The court also has exclusive jurisdiction over claims of unjustly served time in state prisons and claims in tort where damages do not exceed $100,000, except in motor vehicle cases.

The court sits at Chicago and Springfield.

Chief Justice

Andrew Raucci

Judges

David A. Epstein
Frederick J. Hess
Randy Patchett
Robert G. Frederick
Norma Jann
Zack Stamp

Illinois Counties and County Seats

Adams
Quincy

Alexander
Cairo

Bond
Greenville

Boone
Belvidere

Brown
Mount Sterling

Bureau
Princeton

Calhoun
Hardin

Carroll
Mount Carroll

Cass
Virginia

Champaign
Urbana

Christian
Taylorville

Clark
Marshall

Clay
Louisville

Clinton
Carlyle

Coles
Charleston

Cook
Chicago

Crawford
Robinson

Cumberland
Toledo

DeKalb
Sycamore

DeWitt
Clinton

Douglas
Tuscola

DuPage
Wheaton

Edgar
Paris

Edwards
Albion

Effingham
Effingham

Fayette
Vandalia

Ford
Paxton

Franklin
Benton

Fulton
Lewistown

Gallatin
Shawneetown

Greene
Carrollton

Grundy
Morris

Hamilton
McLeansboro

Hancock
Carthage

Hardin
Elizabethtown

Henderson
Oquawka

Henry
Cambridge

Iroquois
Watseka

Jackson
Murphysboro

Jasper
Newton

Jefferson
Mount Vernon

Jersey
Jerseyville

Jo Daviess
Galena

Johnson
Vienna

Kane
Geneva

Kankakee
Kankakee

Kendall
Yorkville

Knox
Galesburg

Lake
Waukegan

La Salle
Ottawa

Lawrence
Lawrenceville

Lee
Dixon

COUNTIES AND COUNTY SEATS—*Continued*

Livingston
Pontiac

Logan
Lincoln

Macon
Decatur

Macoupin
Carlinville

Madison
Edwardsville

Marion
Salem

Marshall
Lacon

Mason
Havana

Massac
Metropolis

McDonough
Macomb

McHenry
Woodstock

McLean
Bloomington

Menard
Petersburg

Mercer
Aledo

Monroe
Waterloo

Montgomery
Hillsboro

Morgan
Jacksonville

Moultrie
Sullivan

Ogle
Oregon

Peoria
Peoria

Perry
Pinckneyville

Piatt
Monticello

Pike
Pittsfield

Pope
Golconda

Pulaski
Mound City

Putnam
Hennepin

Randolph
Chester

Richland
Olney

Rock Island
Rock Island

St. Clair
Belleville

Saline
Harrisburg

Sangamon
Springfield

Schuyler
Rushville

Scott
Winchester

Shelby
Shelbyville

Stark
Toulon

Stephenson
Freeport

Tazewell
Pekin

Union
Jonesboro

Vermilion
Danville

Wabash
Mount Carmel

Warren
Monmouth

Washington
Nashville

Wayne
Fairfield

White
Carmi

Whiteside
Morrison

Will
Joliet

Williamson
Marion

Winnebago
Rockford

Woodford
Eureka

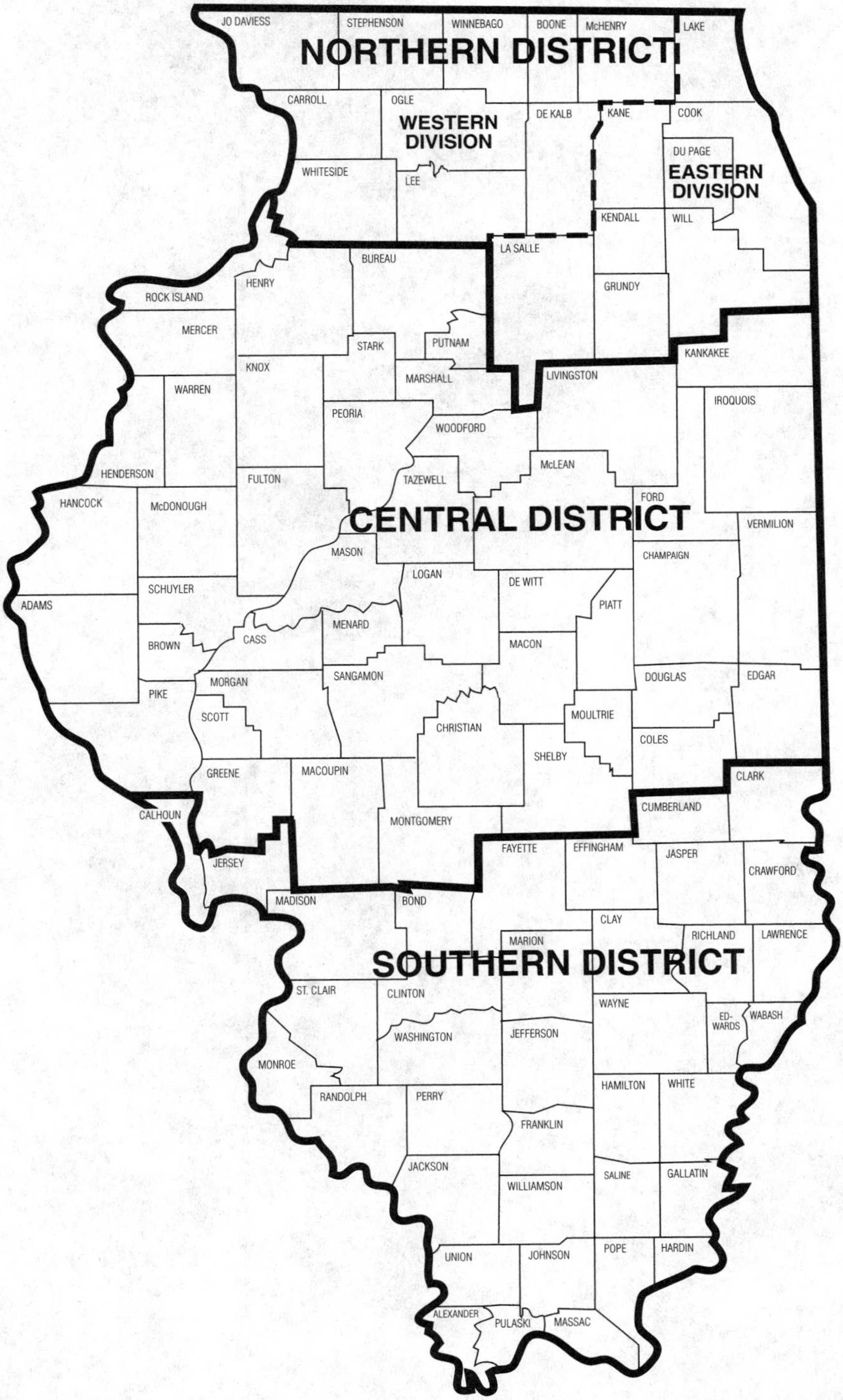
NORTHERN DISTRICT
WESTERN DIVISION
EASTERN DIVISION
CENTRAL DISTRICT
SOUTHERN DISTRICT
JO DAVIESS
STEPHENSON
WINNEBAGO
BOONE
McHENRY
LAKE
CARROLL
OGLE
DE KALB
KANE
COOK
DU PAGE
WHITESIDE
LEE
KENDALL
WILL
LA SALLE
GRUNDY
BUREAU
ROCK ISLAND
HENRY
MERCER
STARK
PUTNAM
KANKAKEE
KNOX
MARSHALL
LIVINGSTON
WARREN
IROQUOIS
PEORIA
WOODFORD
McLEAN
HENDERSON
FULTON
TAZEWELL
FORD
HANCOCK
McDONOUGH
VERMILION
MASON
CHAMPAIGN
LOGAN
DE WITT
SCHUYLER
ADAMS
PIATT
MENARD
CASS
BROWN
MACON
MORGAN
SANGAMON
DOUGLAS
EDGAR
PIKE
SCOTT
MOULTRIE
CHRISTIAN
COLES
SHELBY
GREENE
MACOUPIN
CLARK
CALHOUN
MONTGOMERY
CUMBERLAND
FAYETTE
EFFINGHAM
JASPER
JERSEY
CRAWFORD
MADISON
BOND
CLAY
MARION
RICHLAND
LAWRENCE
ST. CLAIR
CLINTON
WAYNE
ED-
WARDS
WABASH
WASHINGTON
JEFFERSON
MONROE
HAMILTON
WHITE
RANDOLPH
PERRY
FRANKLIN
JACKSON
SALINE
GALLATIN
WILLIAMSON
UNION
JOHNSON
POPE
HARDIN
ALEXANDER
PULASKI
MASSAC

UNITED STATES DISTRICT COURTS DISTRICTS OF ILLINOIS

JO DAVIESS
STEPHENSON
WINNEBAGO
BOONE
McHENRY
LAKE
CARROLL
OGLE
DE KALB
KANE
COOK
2
DU PAGE
WHITESIDE
LEE
1
KENDALL
WILL
LA SALLE
BUREAU
HENRY
GRUNDY
ROCK ISLAND
3
MERCER
STARK
PUTNAM
KNOX
KANKAKEE
MARSHALL
LIVINGSTON
WARREN
IROQUOIS
PEORIA
WOODFORD
McLEAN
HENDERSON
FULTON
TAZEWELL
HANCOCK
McDONOUGH
FORD
VERMILION
MASON
CHAMPAIGN
LOGAN
SCHUYLER
DE WITT
ADAMS
PIATT
MENARD
4
CASS
BROWN
MACON
SANGAMON
MORGAN
DOUGLAS
EDGAR
PIKE
SCOTT
MOULTRIE
CHRISTIAN
COLES
SHELBY
GREENE
MACOUPIN
CLARK
CALHOUN
CUMBERLAND
MONTGOMERY
FAYETTE
EFFINGHAM
JASPER
JERSEY
CRAWFORD
MADISON
BOND
CLAY
MARION
RICHLAND
LAWRENCE
CLINTON
ST. CLAIR
WAYNE
ED-WARDS
WABASH
WASHINGTON
JEFFERSON
MONROE
5
RANDOLPH
PERRY
HAMILTON
WHITE
FRANKLIN
JACKSON
SALINE
GALLATIN
WILLIAMSON
UNION
JOHNSON
POPE
HARDIN
ALEXANDER
PULASKI
MASSAC

JUDICIAL DISTRICTS OF ILLINOIS APPELLATE COURT

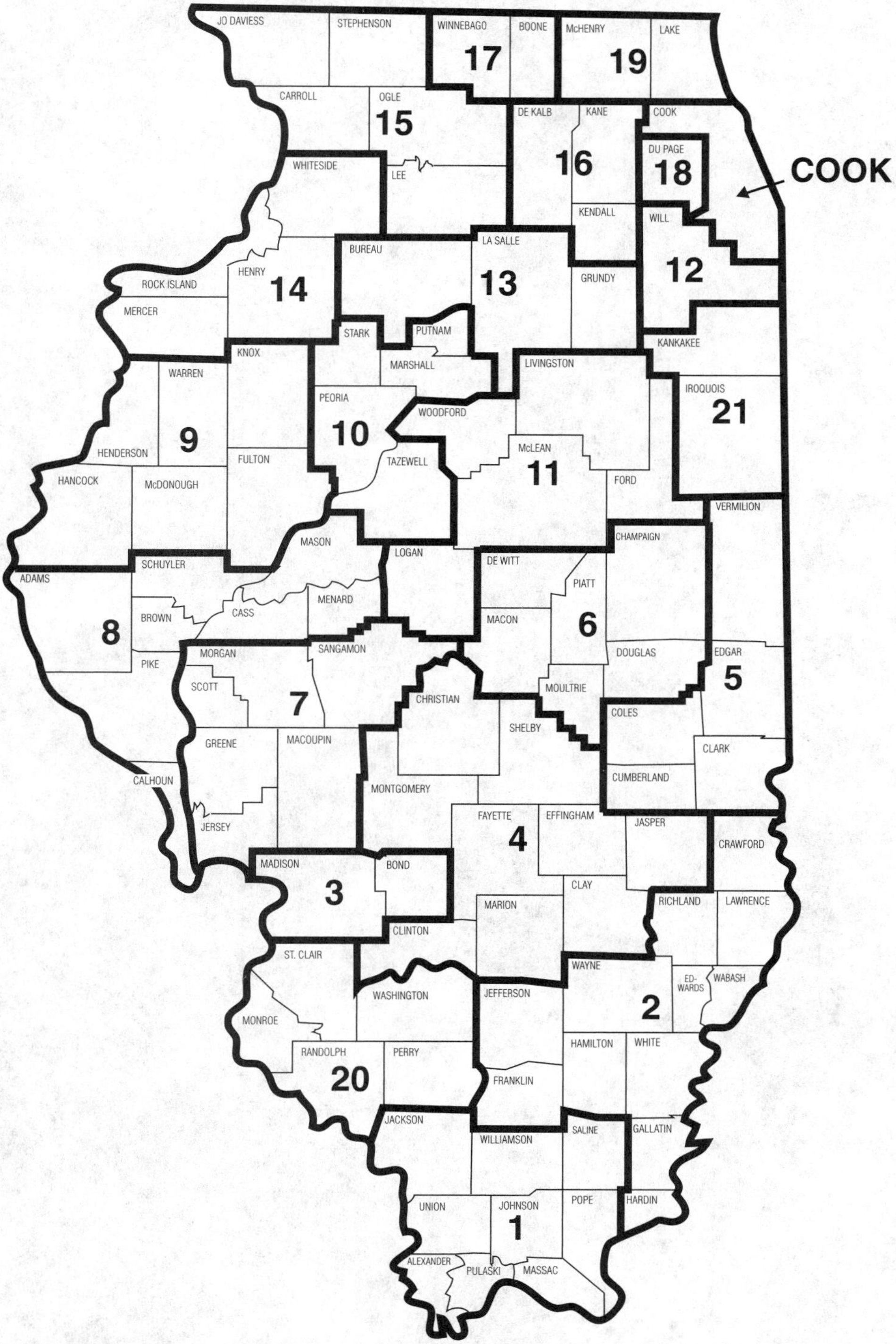
JO DAVIESS
STEPHENSON
WINNEBAGO
BOONE
17
McHENRY
LAKE
19
CARROLL
OGLE
15
DE KALB
KANE
COOK
16
DU PAGE
18
COOK
WHITESIDE
LEE
KENDALL
WILL
12
BUREAU
LA SALLE
GRUNDY
HENRY
14
13
ROCK ISLAND
MERCER
STARK
PUTNAM
KANKAKEE
KNOX
MARSHALL
LIVINGSTON
WARREN
PEORIA
IROQUOIS
21
WOODFORD
10
9
HENDERSON
TAZEWELL
McLEAN
11
FULTON
HANCOCK
McDONOUGH
FORD
VERMILION
MASON
CHAMPAIGN
LOGAN
DE WITT
SCHUYLER
ADAMS
PIATT
MENARD
CASS
BROWN
MACON
6
8
SANGAMON
MORGAN
DOUGLAS
EDGAR
PIKE
5
SCOTT
7
MOULTRIE
CHRISTIAN
COLES
SHELBY
GREENE
MACOUPIN
CLARK
CALHOUN
CUMBERLAND
MONTGOMERY
FAYETTE
EFFINGHAM
JASPER
JERSEY
4
CRAWFORD
MADISON
BOND
CLAY
3
RICHLAND
LAWRENCE
MARION
CLINTON
ST. CLAIR
WAYNE
ED-
WARDS
WABASH
WASHINGTON
JEFFERSON
2
MONROE
HAMILTON
WHITE
RANDOLPH
PERRY
20
FRANKLIN
JACKSON
SALINE
GALLATIN
WILLIAMSON
UNION
JOHNSON
POPE
HARDIN
1
ALEXANDER
PULASKI
MASSAC

JUDICIAL CIRCUITS OF ILLINOIS CIRCUIT COURTS

ILLINOIS

ABRAHAM, Kenneth A. *(Associate Judge, Illinois Circuit Court Eighteenth Judicial Circuit)*

Office: 505 North County Farm Road, Wheaton 60187.

Telephone: (630) 682-6497.

AGRAN, Martin S. *(Circuit Judge, Illinois Circuit Court of Cook County)*

Office: 2808 R. J. Daley Center, Chicago 60602.

Telephone: (312) 603-3894.

AGUIRRE, Richard *(Associate Judge, Illinois Circuit Court Twentieth Judicial Circuit)*

Office: County Building, 10 Public Square, Belleville 62220.

Telephone: (618) 277-7325.

ALESIA, James H. *(Senior Judge, United States District Court Northern District of Illinois)* Appointed for life by President Ronald Reagan to term beginning June 24, 1987. Assumed Senior status Feb 1, 1998, serves by assignment. Educated at Loyola University of Chicago B.S. 1956 and Chicago-Kent College of Law LL.B. 1960 replaced by J.D. Member Phi Alpha Delta. Admitted to practice Illinois 1960, U.S. District Courts Northern District of Illinois 1960, District of Minnesota 1970, District of South Dakota 1971, Northern District of Texas 1979, District of Hawaii 1980 and Eastern District of Wisconsin 1980, U.S. Courts of Appeals Seventh 1961, Eighth 1970 and Ninth 1980 Circuits, Minnesota 1970, U.S. Supreme Court 1971 and Trial Bar of U.S. District Court Northern District of Illinois 1982. U.S. Administrative Law Judge, Department of Halth and Human Services Social Security Administration 1973-80 and U.S. Occupational Safety and Health Review Commission 1980-82.

Assistant General Attorney, General Attorney and Assistant General Counsel Chicago & North Western Transportation Company 1963-70. Assistant U.S. Attorney Northern District of Illinois 1971-73. Assembly Representative Illinois State Bar Association 1978-84. Charter Life Fellow Illinois Bar Foundation. Member Justinian Society of Lawyers, Celtic Legal Society, Federal and American Bar Associations.

Office: U.S. Courthouse, 219 South Dearborn Street, Chicago 60604.

Telephone: (312) 435-7614.

ALESSIO GOODE, Carla J. *(Circuit Judge, Illinois Circuit Court Twelfth Judicial Circuit)* Former Associate Judge.

Office: Will County Courthouse, 14 West Jefferson Street, Joliet 60432.

Telephone: (815) 727-8540.

ALLING, Kathleen M. *(Associate Judge, Illinois Circuit Court Second Judicial Circuit)*

Mailing address: P.O. Box 1266, Mount Vernon 62864.

Office: Jefferson County Courthouse, Mount Vernon 62864.

Telephone: (618) 244-8005.

ALTENBERGER, William V. *(Recalled Judge, United States Bankruptcy Court Central District of Illinois)* Appointed Judge by U.S. Court of Appeals Seventh Circuit judges to term beginning Dec 23, 1985. Reappointed Dec 1999. Former Chief Judge. Appointed Recalled Judge by the Judicial Council of the Seventh Circuit. Born East St. Louis Illinois July 10, 1935. Educated at University of Illinois B.S. 1957 LL.B. 1963. Admitted to practice Illinois 1963. In legal practice Peoria 1963-85. First Lieutenant USAF 1957-60.

Office: Federal Building, 100 N.E. Monroe Street, Peoria 61602.

Telephone: (309) 671-7290.

AMIRANTE, Sam L. *(Associate Judge, Illinois Circuit Court of Cook County)* Appointed to term beginning Dec 8, 1988. Reappointed to subsequent terms. Born Chicago Illinois. Roman Catholic. Educated at Loyola University of Chicago B.S. 1970 J.D. 1974. Member Phi Alpha Delta, Justinian Society and Columbian Society. Admitted to practice Illinois 1974, U.S. District Court Northern District of Illinois 1975, U.S. Supreme Court 1983 and Trial Bar of U.S. District Court Northern District of Illinois. In legal practice Park Ridge 1978-88.

Assistant Public Defender Cook County 1974-78. Trial Defense Attorney for serial killer John Wayne Gacy 1978-80. Municipal Prosecutor Village of Norridge 1978-88. Author "Missing Child Act of 1984" ISEARCH LAW 1984 and "*People v. Barnes,* George Orwell's *1984* Revisited: Unbridled and Impermissible Use of Computer Power in the Modern Age" 28 No. 4 Loyola University of Chicago L. Jour. Summer 1997. Adjunct Professor Harper College. Member Illinois Judges Association. Attended The National Judicial College. Recipient Award of Excellence from Save a Life Foundation 1999 and Four Chaplains Award for selfless service to humanity without regard to race, religion or creed from USMC 2000. Sergeant USMCR 1970-76. Candidate for State Senator 1984. Enjoys coaching baseball and football.

Office: 2121 Euclid, Room 205-A, Rolling Meadows 60008.

Telephone: (847) 818-2286.

ANDERSEN, Wayne R. *(Judge, United States District Court Northern District of Illinois)* Appointed for life by President George Bush to term beginning Nov 1991. Born Chicago Illinois July 30, 1945. United Church of Christ. Educated at Harvard University B.A. with honors 1967 and University of Illinois J.D. 1970. Admitted to practice Illinois 1970 and U.S. District Court Northern District of Illinois 1972. In legal practice Chicago 1972-81. Circuit Judge, Circuit Court of Cook County 1984-91.

Illinois Deputy Secretary of State 1981-84. Member Chicago Bar Association.

Office: U.S. Courthouse, 219 South Dearborn Street, Chicago 60604.

Telephone: (312) 435-7619.

ILLINOIS

ANDERSON, Allen M. *(Associate Judge, Illinois Circuit Court Sixteenth Judicial Circuit)* Appointed.

Office: 400A Kane County Judicial Center, 37W777 Route 38, St. Charles 60175.

Telephone: (630) 232-3440.

ANDERSON, Barry R. *(Circuit Judge, Illinois Circuit Court Fifteenth Judicial Circuit)* Former Associate Judge.

Office: Stephenson County Courthouse, 15 North Galena Street, Freeport 61032.

Telephone: (815) 235-8288.

ANDERSON, Claudia J. *(Circuit Judge, Illinois Circuit Court Fifth Judicial Circuit)*

Office: Seven North Vermilion Street, Danville 61832.

Telephone: (217) 431-2559.

ANDERSON, Robert J. *(Circuit Judge, Illinois Circuit Court Eighteenth Judicial Circuit)* Former Associate Judge.

Office: DuPage County Courthouse, 505 North County Farm Road, Wheaton 60187.

Telephone: (630) 682-6548.

ANDREWS, H. Dean *(Circuit Judge, Illinois Circuit Court Fifth Judicial Circuit)* Former Associate Judge. Assumed office as Circuit Judge.

Office: Edgar County Courthouse, 115 West Court Street, Paris 61944.

Telephone: (217) 466-5125.

ANTONIETTI, Edward A. *(Associate Judge, Illinois Circuit Court of Cook County)*

Office: 727 West 111th Street, Chicago 60628.

Telephone: (773) 660-2439.

APPLETON, Thomas R. *(Circuit Judge, Illinois Circuit Court Seventh Judicial Circuit)* Elected to term beginning Dec 7, 1992. Retained by election 1998, current term expires 2004. Currently on assignment by Supreme Court of Illinois as Judge, Illinois Appellate Court Fourth Judicial District. Born Chicago Illinois. Lutheran. Educated at Augustana College at Rock Island B.A. 1971, University of Illinois M.A. 1972 and Illinois Institute of Technology, Chicago-Kent College of Law J.D. 1976. Articles Editor Chicago-Kent Law Review 1974-76. Law Clerk to Hon. James C. Craven, Illinois Appellate Court District Four 1976-77. Admitted to practice Illinois 1976, U.S. Supreme Court 1979, U.S. District Court Southern District of Illinois and U.S. Court of Appeals Seventh Circuit. In legal practice Springfield 1980-92.

Member Illinois Judges Association, Sangamon County and Illinois State Bar Associations. Member Springfield Municipal Opera, Springfield Area Soccer Association and Goodwill Industries.

Office: 214 South Sixth Street, Suite 200, Springfield 62701.

Telephone: (217) 558-0365.

ARNOLD, Nancy J. *(Circuit Judge, Illinois Circuit Court of Cook County)*

Office: 2502 R. J. Daley Center, Chicago 60602.

Telephone: (312) 603-6008.

ARNOLD, Ward S. *(Circuit Judge, Illinois Circuit Court Nineteenth Judicial Circuit)* Associate Judge Feb 16, 1984 to June 30, 1995. Assumed office as Circuit Judge 1995. Born Belvidere Illinois Nov 22, 1945. Lutheran. Educated at University of Illinois B.S. 1968 and John Marshall Law School J.D. 1973. Member Phi Alpha Delta. Admitted to practice Illinois 1973, U.S. District Court Northern District of Illinois 1973, U.S. Supreme Court 1978 and U.S. Trial Bar 1983. Began legal practice Woodstock 1973. In legal practice Marengo 1975-84.

Assistant Public Defender McHenry County 1973-75. Member Illinois Judges Association, McHenry County (Board of Governors 1976-82), Illinois State (Assembly 1980-86) and American Bar Associations. Specialist Five U.S. Army 1968-70.

Office: McHenry County Courthouse, 2200 Seminary Avenue, Woodstock 60098.

Telephone: (815) 334-4355.

ASHMAN, Martin C. *(Magistrate Judge, United States District Court Northern District of Illinois)* Appointed by U.S. District Court judges Jan 1995. Reappointed Jan 2003, current term expires Jan 30, 2011. Born Chicago Illinois May 5, 1931. Jewish. Educated at DePaul University J.D. 1953. Contributing writer DePaul Law Review 1952. Admitted to practice Illinois 1953. In legal practice Chicago 1953-87. Circuit Judge, Illinois Circuit Court of Cook County July 27, 1987 to Dec 1994.

Commissioner Illinois Court of Claims 1974-87. Corporation Counsel Village of Morton Grove 1977-87. Author "Handgun Control by Local Government" Northern Kentucky L. Rev. 1982. Member National Institute of Municipal Law Officers 1977-87. Former Member The Association of Trial Lawyers of American and Illinois Trial Lawyers Association. Member Decalogue Society of Lawyers (Board of Managers 1988), Illinois Judges Association, Chicago, Illinois State and American Bar Associations. Lecturer Municipal Ordinance Drafting course National Institute of Municipal Law Officers 1982 and Loyola University. Petty Officer Third Class USNR 1952-58. Trustee Village of Morton Grove 1971-74. Involved in various charities. Enjoys writing, reading and travel. Personal Statement or Quote: "Be prepared."

Office: U.S. Courthouse, 219 South Dearborn Street, Chicago 60604.

Telephone: (312) 435-5624.

ASPEN, Marvin E. *(Senior Judge, United States District Court Northern District of Illinois)* Appointed for life by President Jimmy Carter July 24, 1979. Chief Judge July 1, 1995 to June 30, 2002. Assumed Senior status July 1, 2002, serves by assignment. Born Chicago Illinois July 11, 1934. Educated at Loyola University B.S. and Northwestern University J.D. 1958. Admitted to practice Illinois 1958, U.S. District Court Northern District of Illinois 1959, U.S. Court of Appeals Seventh Circuit 1960 and U.S. Supreme Court 1962. Began legal practice Chicago 1958. Circuit Judge, Illinois Circuit Court of Cook County Sept 16, 1971 to July 23, 1979.

Assistant State's Attorney Cook County 1960-63. Assistant Corporation Counsel City of Chicago 1964-70. Former Member Board of Editors *Chicago Bar Record* and Editorial Board *Criminal Justice* Section of Criminal Justice American Bar Association. Board Member American Bar Association Journal. Author "Criminal Law for the Layman" 1971, "Criminal Evidence for Police" 1972 and "The Search for Renewed Civility in Litigation" 28 Valparaiso University L. Rev. 513, 1994. Edward Avery Harriman Adjunct Professor of Law Northwestern University School of Law. Former Member and Draftsman Committee to Revise the Illinois Criminal Code of 1961,

ASPEN, MARVIN E.—*Continued*

Former Chairman Associate Rules Committee and Committee on Ordinance Violation Problems, Former Vice Chairman Committee on Pattern Jury Instructions in Criminal Cases Illinois Supreme Court. Former Member Committee on the Administration of the Bankruptcy System and Trial Bar Implementation Committee Judicial Conference of the U.S. and Federal Bar Examination Committee National Conference of Bar Examiners. Former Commissioner Illinois Law Enforcement Commission and Governor's Advisory Commission on Criminal Justice. Board of Trustees American Inns of Court Foundation. Board Member American Bar Foundation. Chair Committee on Civility Seventh Federal Judicial Circuit 1991-92. Member Standing Committee on Federal Judicial Improvements, Federal Judicial Center (Past Chair Director Search Committee, Board Member), Chicago (Former Member Board of Managers, Chairman Criminal Law Committee, Member Special Commission on Criminal Justice, Committee on Committees, Continuing Legal Education Committee, Development of Law Committee and Civil Disorder Committee), Illinois State (Former Chairman Public Relations Committee, Corrections Committee, Fair Trial/Free Press Committee and Criminal Law Committee) and American (Former Member Board of Governors, Former Chairperson Executive Committee National Conference of Federal Trial Judges Judicial Administration Division, Former Chairperson Committee on Rules of Criminal Procedure, Former Member Adjunct Committee on Fair Trial-Free Press in Criminal Law Issues and Council Member Section of Criminal Justice, Former Chairperson Liaison with the Judiciary, Former Member Committee on Jury Comprehension Study, Co-chair Institute for Trial Practice Task Force, Council Member Section of Litigation, Member Section of Criminal Justice, Member House of Delegates, President ABA Museum) Bar Associations.

Faculty Member National Institute for Trial Advocacy, The National Judicial College and Federal Judicial Center. Lecturer on judicial management, trial bar rules, continuing legal education and complex litigation at judicial conferences and trial advocacy programs in the U.S. and abroad. Chairman Advisory Committee for Short Courses (Post Law School Educational Program) Northwestern University School of Law. Planner and Participant legal seminars at Harvard University, Emory University, University of Florida, Oxford University, England, University of Bologna, Italy, University of Nuremberg, Germany, University of Cairo, Egypt, University of Zimbabwe, Royal University of Malta, University of the Philippines and University of Madrid, Spain. Special Faculty NITA Advanced Trial Advocacy Program (introduces British trial techniques to experienced American litigators) and American Bar Association program (acquaints Scottish lawyers with modern litigation and technology). Recipient Herbert Harley Award (in recognition of services in promoting the effective administration of justice) from American Judicature Society 1999, Award for Significant Practical Achievement for Excellence and Innovation for Alternative Dispute Resolutions and Dispute Management from Center for Public Resources, Award of Merit from Northwestern University Alumni Association and National Center for Freedom of Information Studies Award. Named Person of the Year by *Chicago Lawyer* 1995. Former Chairman Advisory Board Institute of Criminal Justice John Marshall Law School. Former Member Cook County Board of Corrections and Board of the John Howard Association. Former Member Visiting Committee and Past President Alumni Association Northwestern University School of Law. Former Member Project on Plea Bargaining in the United States Georgetown University Law Center. Former Member Visiting Committee University of Chicago Law School. Member Visiting Committee Northern Illinois University College of Law.

Office: U.S. Courthouse, 219 South Dearborn Street, Chicago 60604.

Telephone: (312) 435-5696.

AUKSTIK, William J. *(Associate Judge, Illinois Circuit Court of Cook County)*

Office: 10220 South 76th Avenue, Room 210A, Bridgeview 60455.

Telephone: (708) 974-6541.

AULT, J. Peter *(Circuit Judge, Illinois Circuit Court Tenth Judicial Circuit)* Former Associate Judge. Assumed office as Circuit Judge.

Office: Tazewell County Courthouse, 342 Court Street, Pekin 61554-4281.

Telephone: (309) 477-2201.

AUSTIN, C. Stanley *(Circuit Judge, Illinois Circuit Court Eighteenth Judicial Circuit)* Former Associate Judge.

Office: DuPage County Courthouse, 505 North County Farm Road, Wheaton 60187.

Telephone: (630) 682-6480.

BADGER, Barbara Jean *(Associate Judge, Illinois Circuit Court Twelfth Judicial Circuit)*

Office: 14 West Jefferson, Joliet 60432.

Telephone: (815) 727-8540.

BAKALIS, George J. *(Circuit Judge, Illinois Circuit Court Eighteenth Judicial Circuit)* Appointed Associate Judge Sept 5, 1990. Reappointed July 1991. Elected Circuit Judge to term beginning Dec 2, 1996. Retained by election 2002, current term expires Dec 2008. Born Berwyn Illinois Dec 10, 1941. Greek Orthodox. Educated at Lake Forest College B.S. with honors 1963, Northwestern University M.A.T. 1964 and DePaul University J.D. 1969. Admitted to practice Illinois 1969 and U.S. District Court Northern District of Illinois 1973. In legal practice Bensenville 1973-75 and Bloomingdale 1975-90.

Author various articles DuPage County B. Jour. Member Illinois Judges Association and DuPage County Bar Association. Attended General Jurisdiction Reno Nevada and Issues in Domestic Relations Orlando Florida The National Judicial College and Criminal Law State of Illinois. Instructor in Domestic Relations DuPage County Bar Association. Previously employed as high school and college instructor 1963-68. Enjoys baseball, books and automobiles.

Office: DuPage County Courthouse, 505 North County Farm Road, Wheaton 60187.

Telephone: (630) 682-7300.

BAKER, Harold Albert *(Senior Judge, United States District Court Central District of Illinois)* Appointed for life by President Jimmy Carter to Eastern District of Illinois to term beginning September 23, 1978. Reassigned to Central District of Illinois March 31, 1979. Chief Judge 1984-91. Assumed Senior status Oct 4, 1994, serves by assignment. Born Mount Kisco New York Oct 4, 1929. Educated at Columbia University and Universi-

BAKER, HAROLD ALBERT—*Continued*
ty of Illinois at Urbana-Champaign A.B. 1951 J.D. 1956. In legal practice Champaign 1956-78.
Senior Counsel President's Commission on CIA Activities in the U.S. 1975.
Office: 338 U.S. Courthouse, 201 South Vine Street, Urbana 61801.
Telephone: (217) 373-5835.

BAKER, Larry O. *(Circuit Judge, Illinois Circuit Court Second Judicial Circuit)* Term expires 2004.
Mailing address: P.O. Box 223, Elizabethtown 62931.
Telephone: (618) 287-8891.

BAKER, Reginald H. *(Associate Judge, Illinois Circuit Court of Cook County)*
Office: 16501 South Kedzie Parkway, Markham 60426.
Telephone: (708) 210-4170.

BAKER, Thomas F. *(Associate Judge, Illinois Circuit Court Nineteenth Judicial Circuit)*
Office: 2200 North Seminary Avenue, Woodstock 60098.
Telephone: (815) 334-4385.

BALESTRI, William P. *(Associate Judge, Illinois Circuit Court Thirteenth Judicial Circuit)*
Office: 707 Etna Road, Ottawa 61350.
Telephone: (815) 434-8276.

BALLARD, Mark J. *(Associate Judge, Illinois Circuit Court of Cook County)*
Office: 1340 South Michigan, Room 501, Chicago 60605.
Telephone: (312) 341-2861.

BANICH, William R. *(Associate Judge, Illinois Circuit Court Thirteenth Judicial Circuit)*
Office: LaSalle County Courthouse, 119 West Madison, Ottawa 61350.
Telephone: (815) 434-4457.

BANKS, Patricia *(Circuit Judge, Illinois Circuit Court of Cook County)*
Office: 2505 R. J. Daley Center, Chicago 60602.
Telephone: (312) 603-4347.

BARBOSA, Manuel *(Judge, United States Bankruptcy Court Northern District of Illinois)* Appointed by U.S. Court of Appeals Seventh Circuit judges March 23, 1998. Term expires 2012. Educated at Illinois Benedictine College B.A. 1969 and John Marshall Law School J.D. 1977.
Member Kane County, Winnebago County, Illinois State and American Bar Associations. Chairman Illinois Human Rights Commission 1980-98.
Office: Federal Building, 211 South Court Street, Rockford 61101.
Telephone: (815) 987-4366.

BARON, Robert J. *(Associate Judge, Illinois Circuit Court Twelfth Judicial Circuit)*
Office: 14 West Jefferson Street, Joliet 60432.
Telephone: (815) 727-8540.

BARRA, John A. *(Chief Judge, Illinois Circuit Court Tenth Judicial Circuit)* Term expires Dec 2006.
Office: 215 Peoria County Courthouse, 324 Main Street, Peoria 61602.
Telephone: (309) 672-6047.

BARRY, Tobias "Toby" *(Judge, Illinois Appellate Court Third Judicial District)* Appointed Nov 4, 2002. Born Chicago Illinois April 12, 1924. Roman Catholic. Educated at Marquette University Ph.B. 1949 and University of Notre Dame J.D. 1952. Admitted to practice Illinois 1952. Began legal practice La Salle and Ladd 1952. Judge, Illinois Appellate Court Third Judicial District Dec 2, 1974 to Dec 1, 1994.
Instructor in Business Law La Salle Peru Oglesby Junior College 1958-59. Past President Illinois Judges Association. Member American Judicature Society, Bureau County, La Salle County, Illinois State and American Bar Associations. Surgical Corpsman Third Class USN PTO 1942-45. Democrat. State Representative 1960-74. Bureau County Democratic Chairman 1962-74.
Office: 226 Fox River Center, 110 East Main, Ottawa 61350.
Telephone: (815) 433-5321.

BARTKOWICZ, Ronald F. *(Circuit Judge, Illinois Circuit Court of Cook County)* Former Associate Judge.
Office: 2101 R. J. Daley Center, Chicago 60602.
Telephone: (312) 603-5910.

BASTONE, Robert P. *(Associate Judge, Illinois Circuit Court of Cook County)*
Office: 400 R. J. Daley Center, Chicago 60602.
Telephone: (312) 603-2600.

BEATTY, Joseph F. *(Circuit Judge, Illinois Circuit Court Fourteenth Judicial Circuit)* Term expires 2008.
Office: Rock Island County Courthouse, 210 Fifteenth Street, Rock Island 61201.
Telephone: (309) 786-4451.

BECKER, William J. *(Associate Judge, Illinois Circuit Court Fourth Judicial Circuit)*
Office: Three Briarcreek, Breese 62230.
Telephone: (217) 532-9501.

BECKMAN, Charles T. *(Associate Judge, Illinois Circuit Court Fifteenth Judicial Circuit)* Appointed Sept 16, 1999. Term expires 2003. Born Decatur Illinois Oct 26, 1949. Presbyterian. Educated at Eastern Illinois University B.S. 1971 and John Marshall Law School J.D. with distinction 1975. Admitted to practice Illinois 1975. In legal practice Dixon 1978-99.
Office: 309 South Galena Avenue, Dixon 61021.
Telephone: (815) 284-5254.
Fax: (815) 284-5205
E-mail address: cbeckman@leecourt.com

BEDOYA, Consuelo E. *(Associate Judge, Illinois Circuit Court of Cook County)*
Office: 5600 Old Orchard Road, Room 231, Skokie 60077.
Telephone: (847) 470-7200.

BEHLE, Donald A. *(Associate Judge, Illinois Circuit Court Eleventh Judicial Circuit)* Appointed.
Office: Logan County Courthouse, Lincoln 62656.
Telephone: (217) 732-7652.

BELL, John L. *(Associate Judge, Illinois Circuit Court Fourteenth Judicial Circuit)* Appointed to term beginning Aug 1, 1995. Reappointed June 1999, current term expires 2003. Born Davenport Iowa Feb 16, 1953. Lutheran. Educated at University of Southern Mississippi B.S. 1974 and Thomas M. Cooley Law School J.D. 1982. Admitted to practice Illinois 1983 and U.S. District Court Central District of Illinois 1983.

BELL, JOHN L.—*Continued*

Assistant Public Defender Rock Island County 1984-95. Member Illinois Judges Association (Board of Directors).

Office: 408 Rock Island County Courthouse, 210 Fifteenth Street, Rock Island 61201.
Telephone: (309) 786-4451.

BELL, Lois A. *(Circuit Judge, Illinois Circuit Court Seventh Judicial Circuit)*
Office: Scott County Courthouse, 35 East Market Street, Winchester 62694.
Telephone: (217) 742-3173.

BELLOWS, Carole K. *(Circuit Judge, Illinois Circuit Court of Cook County)* Appointed to term beginning Oct 1986. Retained by election, current term expires Dec 2006. Born Chicago Illinois May 24, 1935. Educated at University of Illinois B.A. 1957 and Northwestern University School of Law J.D. 1960.
Office: 1602 R. J. Daley Center, Chicago 60602.
Telephone: (312) 603-4823.

BENDER, Gerald C. *(Circuit Judge, Illinois Circuit Court of Cook County)*
Office: 2801 R. J. Daley Center, Chicago 60602.
Telephone: (312) 603-3893.

BERGER, Helaine L. *(Associate Judge, Illinois Circuit Court of Cook County)*
Office: 1502 R. J. Daley Center, Chicago 60602.
Telephone: (312) 603-6039.

BERGLUND, Thomas C. *(Associate Judge, Illinois Circuit Court Fourteenth Judicial Circuit)*
Office: Mercer County Courthouse, Aledo 61231.
Telephone: (309) 582-7122.

BERLAND, Richard B. *(Circuit Judge, Illinois Circuit Court of Cook County)* Term expires 2004.
Office: 2310 R. J. Daley Center, Chicago 60602.
Telephone: (312) 603-6054.

BERMAN, Andrew *(Circuit Judge, Illinois Circuit Court of Cook County)*
Office: 1100 South Hamilton, Chicago 60612.
Telephone: (312) 433-4757.

BERNABEI, Marc *(Circuit Judge, Illinois Circuit Court Thirteenth Judicial Circuit)*
Office: 700 South Main Street, Princeton 61356.
Telephone: (815) 879-3091.

BERNARDI, Donald D. *(Circuit Judge, Illinois Circuit Court Eleventh Judicial Circuit)* Associate Judge Nov 1991 to 1996. Elected Circuit Judge Nov 1996. Retained by election 2002, current term expires Dec 2008. Born Spring Valley Illinois May 8, 1951. Educated at Knox College 1973 and Western New England College School of Law J.D. 1978. Admitted to practice Illinois 1978, U.S. District Court Central District of Illinois 1980 and U.S. Supreme Court 1985.

State's Attorney Livingston County 1982-91. Instructor Police Training Institute University of Illinois 1989-90. Guest Lecturer Department of Criminal Justice Sciences Illinois State University. Member McLean County and Illinois State Bar Associations. Attended The National Judicial College 1992 and 1997. Member Treatment Advisory Board of the Baby Fold and Bloomington Kiwanis Club. Interests include antique automobiles and fishing.

Office: McLean County Law and Justice Center, 104 West Front Street, Bloomington 61701.
Telephone: (309) 888-5257.

BERNTHAL, David G. *(Magistrate Judge, United States District Court Central District of Illinois)* Appointed by U.S. District Court judges. Born Danville Illinois April 18, 1950. Educated at University of Illinois A.B. cum laude 1972 J.D. 1976. Admitted to practice Illinois 1976 and U.S. District Court Central District of Illinois 1976. In legal practice Danville 1976-86. Associate Judge, Illinois Circuit Court Fifth Judicial Circuit, appointed to term beginning Jan 1, 1987.

Seventh Circuit Representative Board of Editors Federal Courts Law Review. Member Federal Magistrate Judges Association and Champaign County Bar Association. Member Rotary International and Champaign Country Club.

Office: 114 U.S. Courthouse, 201 South Vine Street, Urbana 61802.
Telephone: (217) 373-5839.

BERRY, J. Martin *(Associate Judge, Illinois Circuit Court of Cook County)* Appointed. Educated at Illinois Institute of Technology, Chicago-Kent College of Law J.D. 1974.
Office: 10220 South 76th Avenue, Bridgeview 60455.
Telephone: (708) 974-6535.

BERTANI-TOMCZAK, Amy M. *(Circuit Judge, Illinois Circuit Court Twelfth Judicial Circuit)* Appointed to term beginning Dec 5, 1994. Elected Nov 5, 1996. Retained by election 2002, current term expires Dec 2008. Born Joliet Illinois April 1, 1957. Roman Catholic. Educated at St. Mary's University of San Antonio B.A. in Political Science 1979 and Thomas M. Cooley Law School J.D. cum laude 1985. Editor-in-Chief Thomas M. Cooley Law Review 1983-85. Admitted to practice Michigan 1985 and Illinois 1986.

Assistant State's Attorney Will County Jan 1986 to Dec 1992. Assistant Attorney General State of Illinois Feb 1993 to Dec 1994. Member Criminal Law and Probation Administration Illinois Judicial Conference since Jan 1995. Attended conference on the death penalty and New Judges Seminar. Member Exchange Club of Joliet and Joliet Region Chamber of Commerce. Enjoys reading, water skiing, computers, aerobics and jogging.

Office: 464 Will County Courthouse, 14 West Jefferson Street, Joliet 60432.
Telephone: (815) 727-8909.

BERTUCCI, Robert W. *(Circuit Judge, Illinois Circuit Court of Cook County)* Elected to term beginning Dec 7, 1992. Retained by election 1998, current term expires Dec 2004. Born Chicago Illinois Nov 25, 1956. Educated at Triton Community College A.A. 1976, Lake Forest College B.A. 1979 and Illinois Institute of Technology, Chicago-Kent College of Law J.D. with high honors 1983. Admitted to practice Illinois 1983. In legal practice Chicago 1992.

Assistant State's Attorney Cook County 1983-92. Member Justinian Law Society (Executive Committee), Illinois Judges Association (Board of Directors 1994-2000) and Chicago Bar Association. Attended Constitutional Criminal Procedure course July 1993 and Handling Capital Cases course Jan 1996 The National Judicial College. Recipient Bar and Gavel Award for out-

BERTUCCI, ROBERT W.—*Continued*

standing service to the college, community and the law profession from Student Bar Association Chicago-Kent College of Law 1983 and David Award for great expectations for achievement in law from Italian Sons and Daughters of America 1993. Past President Advisory Council Chicago Park District. Past Chairman Elmwood Park Planning Commission. Interests include family, tennis and travel.
Office: 1713 R. J. Daley Center, Chicago 60602.
Telephone: (312) 603-4579.

BETAR, Samuel J., III *(Associate Judge, Illinois Circuit Court of Cook County)*
Office: 1401 R. J. Daley Center, Chicago 60602.
Telephone: (312) 603-4371.

BIEBEL, Paul P., Jr. *(Circuit Judge, Illinois Circuit Court of Cook County)*
Office: 2600 South California, Room 101, Chicago 60608.
Telephone: (773) 869-3160.

BIERMAN, Janice L. *(Circuit Judge, Illinois Circuit Court of Cook County)* Former Associate Judge.
Office: 2121 Euclid, Room 203-A, Rolling Meadows 60008.
Telephone: (847) 818-2279.

BILLIK, Richard J., Jr. *(Circuit Judge, Illinois Circuit Court of Cook County)*
Office: 2201 R. J. Daley Center, Chicago 60602.
Telephone: (312) 603-6064.

BLACK, Bruce W. *(Judge, United States Bankruptcy Court Northern District of Illinois)* Appointed by U.S. Court of Appeals Seventh Circuit judges to term beginning Aug 13, 2001. Born Peoria Illinois May 16, 1944. Educated at Bradley University B.A. magna cum laude 1966 and University of Illinois J.D. 1971. Article Editor Illinois Law Forum 1969-71. Law Clerk to Hon. Robert D. Morgan, U.S. District Court Central District of Illinois 1971-72. Admitted to practice Illinois 1971. Judge and Chief Judge, Illinois Circuit Court Tenth Judicial Circuit Dec 15, 1985 to 2001.
State Attorney Tazewell County 1976-85.
Office: 662 U.S. Courthouse, 219 South Dearborn Street, Chicago 60604.
Telephone: (312) 435-6867.

BLACKWOOD, Alan G. *(Associate Judge, Illinois Circuit Court Fourteenth Judicial Circuit)*
Office: Rock Island County Courthouse, 210 Fifteenth Street, Rock Island 61201.
Telephone: (309) 786-4451.

BLANC, Erik I. *(Associate Judge, Illinois Circuit Court Tenth Judicial Circuit)*
Office: 210 Peoria County Courthouse, 324 Main Street, Peoria 61602.
Telephone: (309) 672-6047.

BLOCK, Cathy *(Associate Judge, Illinois Circuit Court Twelfth Judicial Circuit)*
Office: Will County Courthouse, 14 West Jefferson, Joliet 60432.
Telephone: (815) 727-8540.

BLOCKMAN, Arnold F. *(Circuit Judge, Illinois Circuit Court Sixth Judicial Circuit)*
Office: Champaign County Courthouse, Courtroom D, 101 East Main, Urbana 61801.
Telephone: (217) 384-3702.

BOBRICK, Edward A. *(Magistrate Judge, United States District Court Northern District of Illinois)* Appointed by U.S. District Court judges.
Office: U.S. Courthouse, 219 South Dearborn Street, Chicago 60604.
Telephone: (312) 435-5361.

BOIE, Mark Monroe *(Circuit Judge, Illinois Circuit Court First Judicial Circuit)* Elected to term beginning Dec 1, 2000. Term expires Dec 1, 2006. Born St. Louis Missouri June 20, 1967. Educated at University of Mississippi at Oxford B.A. 1989 and John Marshall Law School J.D. 1997. Admitted to practice Illinois 1997 and U.S. District Court Southern District of Illinois 1997. In legal practice Anna 1997-2000.
Office: Union County Courthouse, 309 West Market Street, Jonesboro 62952.
Telephone: (618) 833-8114.

BOLGER, John D. *(Associate Judge, Illinois Circuit Court Nineteenth Judicial Circuit)*
Office: 2200 Seminary Avenue, Woodstock 60098.
Telephone: (815) 334-4385.

BONGIORNO, Joseph S. *(Associate Judge, Illinois Circuit Court Eighteenth Judicial Circuit)*
Office: DuPage County Courthouse, 505 North County Farm Road, Wheaton 60187-3907.
Telephone: (630) 682-7300.

BOORAS, James K. *(Circuit Judge, Illinois Circuit Court Nineteenth Judicial Circuit)* Former Associate Judge. Assumed office as Circuit Judge.
Office: Lake County Courthouse, 18 North County Street, Waukegan 60085.
Telephone: (847) 377-3859.

BORBELY, James K. *(Associate Judge, Illinois Circuit Court Fifth Judicial Circuit)*
Office: Vermilion County Courthouse, Seven North Vermilion, Danville 61832.
Telephone: (217) 431-2559.

BORDEN, Stuart P. *(Circuit Judge, Illinois Circuit Court Tenth Judicial Circuit)* Former Associate Judge.
Office: 215 Peoria County Courthouse, 324 Main Street. Peoria 61602.
Telephone: (309) 672-6047.

BORDNER, Steven R. *(Associate Judge, Illinois Circuit Court Ninth Judicial Circuit)*
Office: Fulton County Courthouse, 100 North Main Street, Lewistown 61542.
Telephone: (309) 547-3041.

BOURGEOIS, Adam D., Jr. *(Associate Judge, Illinois Circuit Court of Cook County)*
Office: 1303 R. J. Daley Center, Chicago 60602.
Telephone: (312) 603-5660.

BOWIE, Preston L., Jr. *(Associate Judge, Illinois Circuit Court of Cook County)*
Office: 2600 South California, Room 203, Chicago 60608.
Telephone: (773) 869-7413.

BOWMAN, John J. *(Judge, Illinois Appellate Court Second Judicial District)* Elected to term beginning Dec 1990. Retained by election 2000, current term expires Dec 2010. Born Oak Park Illinois Jan 13, 1930. Educated at University of Illinois B.S. 1952 and John Marshall Law School J.D. 1959. Admitted to practice Illinois 1959. Circuit Judge, Illinois Circuit Court Eighteenth Judicial Circuit 1976-90.

Deputy Public Defender 1965-73 and State's Attorney 1973-76 DuPage County. President DuPage County Bar Association 1971-72. USAS 1952-54.

Office: 17 West 682 Butterfield Road #302, Oakbrook Terrace 60181.

Telephone: (630) 620-1466.

BOYD, William Stewart *(Associate Judge, Illinois Circuit Court of Cook County)*

Office: 1605 R. J. Daley Center, Chicago 60602.

Telephone: (312) 603-4836.

BRADY, Terrence J. *(Associate Judge, Illinois Circuit Court Nineteenth Judicial Circuit)* Appointed April 27, 1977. Reappointed to subsequent terms. Born Chicago Illinois Dec 24, 1940. Educated at College of St. Thomas B.A. cum laude 1963 and University of Illinois J.D. 1968. Notes Editor Illinois Law Forum 1967-68. Admitted to practice Illinois 1969, U.S. District Court Northern District of Illinois 1970 and U.S. Court of Appeals Seventh Circuit 1971. In legal practice Crystal Lake 1969-70 and Waukegan 1970-77. Hearing Officer, Illinois Pollution Control Board 1972-77.

Author "The Informer's Privilege in Criminal Cases" Illinois Law Forum Fall 1967, "Major Traffic Charges Such as DWI: The Double Standard Forged Under Distinctions Between State and Ordinance Cases" Illinois B. Jour. Jan 1982, Pension Chapter *Illinois Judges Manual* Illinois Judges Association 1983, 1986 and 1992, "The Illinois Domestic Violence Act: A Selective Critique" Loyola University at Chicago B. Jour., Booklet "Illinois Judicial Benefits" Illinois Judges Association Dec 1989 and 1992 and "Settle It" 1998, "The Six Steps of a Jury Trial" 1999, "Civil Discovery—Rule 213—Keys to Compliance" 1999 and "Lake County's Domestic Violence Court" *The Docket* Lake County Bar Association. Editorial Board *The Docket* Lake County Bar Association 1994-95 and 2001-02. Lecturer and Author "SCR 213—2000 Update" Civil Seminar May 2000, *The Docket* Sept 2000 and "213 Issues" and "Expert Witness Issues" 2001-02 Lake County Bar Association; "Expert Testimony—A Guide" Nineteenth Circuit Judicial Education Seminar Oct 2000 and *The Docket* Jan 2001. Former Member Illinois Probation and Court Services Association, The Association of Trial Lawyers of America, American Arbitration Association, Illinois Trial Lawyers Association and American Bar Association. Member Task Force on Domestic Violence Illinois Attorney General's Office 1990 and Statewide Advisory Committee Domestic Violence Protocol for Illinois Judges The Administrative Office of the Illinois Court 1995. Contributing Member Long Range Planning Committee 1999-2000 and Member and Senior Associate Judge Executive Committee Nineteenth Judicial Circuit. Member Illinois Judges Association (Pension Committee since 1984, Board of Governors since 1987, Member Committee of Committees 1986-87, Chairman Insurance Committee since 1989), Board of Directors), Lake County (Chairman Medical Legal Committee 1974, Board of Governors 1974, Vice Chairman Younger Members Executive Committee 1972-73, Secretary and Vice Chairman Grievance Committee 1971-73 and 1975-78, Chairman Traffic Committee 1983-84, Member Probate Committee 1983-85, Court Rules Committee 1984-85, Family Law Committee 1987-91 and Civil Law Committee since 1992) and Illinois State (Task Force on drafting legislative revisions of Illinois Domestic Violence Act 1988-92, Member 1994-95, Secretary 1997, Vice Chair 1998, Chair 1999 and Ex-officio Judicial Advisory Polls Committee, Member Bench and Bar Section Committee) Bar Associations.

Attended Annual Illinois Judge Seminars since 1977; "General Jurisdiction" 1979, "Alcohol—Drug Substance Abuse" 1983, "Sentencing Misdemeanants" 1985 and "Management of High Volume Courts" 1988 The National Judicial College; "Evidence" Oakbrook 1982, "Criminal Law" Rockford 1986, "Divorce—Family Law" Rockford 1986, "Jury Trials" 1995, "Literature and Law" 1995 and "Court Management in Civil and Criminal Jury Trials" 1999 Illinois Judicial Conference; "Basic Probate" 1984 and "Business Evaluation—Divorce" 1985 ICLE Chicago; Domestic Violation Conference Illinois Coalition Against Domestic Violence Springfield 1985 and 1986; Child Support Collection Task Force Conference Illinois Department of Public Aid Lincolnshire 1986; "Judges and the Media" Conference University of Illinois Champaign-Urbana, co-sponsored by Illinois Judges Association May 1988; "Conference on Professionalism" Illinois State Bar Association 1992; "Civil Law—Selected Tort Topics" seminar Administrative Office of Illinois Supreme Court May 1994; and "Civil Mediation" The National Judicial College 1999. Panelist "Access to Civil Justice" Conference Illinois State Bar Association 1992. Member Joint Judicial Education Committee for Illinois Judicial Conference 1992. Lecturer Annual Illinois Associate Judge Seminars (Chairman Traffic Committee 1985 and Domestic Relations—Domestic Violence 1987 and Member Evidence Committee 1986 and Coordinating Committee since 1989). Lecturer on "New Legislation-Court Costs in Illinois" Statewide Illinois Traffic Conference, Peoria June 1982, "Traffic Law Update-1983" Lake County Bar Association Seminar Oct 1983, "State Pension for Illinois Judges" New Judges Meetings, Chicago Jan and Aug 1984, "Property—Support Issues" Seminar Family Law Committee Lake County Bar Association, Waukegan June 1988, "Illinois Judicial Benefits" Illinois Judges Association Conference since Dec 1989, New Judges Meeting since Dec 1990, "Pretrials and Negotiations" Statewide Seminar Illinois Judicial Conference 1996 and "Jury Trials: The Judicial Perspective" The National Judicial College Reno Nov 1997. Liaison/Lecturer "Ethics" Associate Judges Seminar, Chicago March 1990. Speaker/Lecturer "Family Law—Stress" 1991 and "Civil Law Issues" 1992 Seminar Lake County Bar Association. Keynote Speaker "Child Support Enforcement" Illinois Association of Child Support Enforcers 1991 and Swearing in Installation of Associate Judges 19th Judicial Circuit June 1995. Discussion Leader "Advanced Evidence" seminar 1994 and Visiting Judicial Faculty 1997 The National Judicial College. Author and Lecturer "Pretrials and Negotiations" Statewide Judicial Seminar Illinois Judicial Conference 1997; "Settlement Skills" Seminar 1997, "Domestic Violence Court" 1997, "Mechanics of Jury Trials" Seminar 1998 and "Illinois Supreme Court Rule 213 Discovery Issues" Seminar 1999 Lake County Bar Association; and "Closing Arguments—Civil Jury

BRADY, TERRENCE J.—*Continued*

Trials" Educational Conference Nineteenth Judicial Circuit 1999. Alternate Faculty Member "Chancery, and Miscellaneous Remedies" 2000 and "Settlement Techniques" Illinois Judicial Conference 2002. Invited Member "Law and Economics" seminar University of Kansas 2000 and "Judicial Faculty Development" The National Judicial College 2000 and Illinois Judicial Conference 2000. Judge National High School Mock Trial Championship Competition Illinois State Bar Association 1994. E-4 U.S. Army 1963-64 and 1968-69. Member Delegation of American Judges Mexican Government's Judicial Visitation Program, Mexico City Mexico 2001. Member Libertyville Tennis Club. Enjoys tennis, golf, running, downhill skiing, reading and writing.

Office: Lake County Courthouse, 18 North County Street, Waukegan 60085.
Telephone: (847) 377-3600.

BRANDON, Walter C., Jr. *(Associate Judge, Illinois Circuit Court Twentieth Judicial Circuit)*
Office: 10 Public Square, Belleville 62220.
Telephone: (618) 277-7325.

BRANDT, Michael E. *(Circuit Judge, Illinois Circuit Court Tenth Judicial Circuit)* Appointed Associate Judge Aug 3, 1993. Reappointed July 1, 1995. Elected Circuit Judge Dec 1998. Born Chicago Illinois March 5, 1950. Educated at University of Illinois at Chicago B.A. 1972 and John Marshall University Law School J.D. 1976. Admitted to practice Illinois 1976, U.S. District Courts Northern 1976 and Central 1980 Districts of Illinois and U.S. Court of Appeals Seventh Circuit 1982. In legal practice Peoria 1982-93.

Assistant State's Attorney Peoria County 1977-82. Part-time Instructor Illinois Central College since 1997. Member Illinois Judges Association, Peoria County, Tazewell County, Illinois State and American Bar Associations.

Office: Peoria County Courthouse, 324 Main Street, Peoria 61602.
Telephone: (309) 672-6047.
E-mail address: JDGBRANDT@AOL.COM

BRAUD, Walter D. *(Circuit Judge, Illinois Circuit Court Fourteenth Judicial Circuit)*
Office: 210 Fifteenth Street, Rock Island 61201.
Telephone: (309) 786-4451.

BRAWKA, Judith M. *(Circuit Judge, Illinois Circuit Court Sixteenth Judicial Circuit)* Associate Judge Jan 11, 1991 to Dec 1, 2002. Elected Circuit Judge to term beginning Dec 2, 2002. Term expires Nov 30, 2008. Born Nov 24, 1954. Educated at DePaul University B.A. summa cum laude 1975 and Northwestern University School of Law J.D. cum laude 1978. Member Order of the Coif. Admitted to practice Illinois 1978.

Assistant Public Defender 1978-86 and Public Defender 1986-90 Kane County. Member Illinois Judges Association, Kane County, Illinois State and American Bar Associations.

Office: Kane County Judicial Center, 37W777 Route 38, St. Charles 60175-7536.
Telephone: (630) 232-3440.

BRENNAN, Margaret Ann *(Circuit Judge, Illinois Circuit Court of Cook County)*
Office: 1303 R. J. Daley Center, Chicago 60602.
Telephone: (312) 603-7959.

BREWE, Franklin D. *(Associate Judge, Illinois Circuit Court Sixteenth Judicial Circuit)*
Office: Kane County Judicial Center, 37W777 Route 38, St. Charles 60175.
Telephone: (630) 406-7110.

BREWER, Eileen M. *(Circuit Judge, Illinois Circuit Court of Cook County)*
Office: 1303 R. J. Daley Center, Chicago 60602.
Telephone: (312) 603-7959.

BRIDGES, George *(Associate Judge, Illinois Circuit Court Nineteenth Judicial Circuit)*
Office: Lake County Courthouse, 18 North County Street, Waukegan 60085.
Telephone: (847) 377-3712.

BRIM, Cynthia *(Circuit Judge, Illinois Circuit Court of Cook County)*
Office: 10220 South 76th Avenue, Bridgeview 60455.
Telephone: (708) 974-6542.

BRINN, Michael P. *(Associate Judge, Illinois Circuit Court Fourteenth Judicial Circuit)* Appointed to term beginning Jan 12, 1981. Reappointed to subsequent terms. Born Rock Island Illinois May 20, 1948. Catholic. Educated at St. Ambrose College B.A. magna cum laude 1973 and University of Illinois J.D. 1976. Admitted to practice Illinois 1976. Began legal practice Rock Island 1976.

Member Illinois Judges Association and Rock Island County Bar Association. Petty Officer Second Class USN 1966-70.

Office: Rock Island County Courthouse, 210 Fifteenth Street, Rock Island 61201.
Telephone: (309) 786-4451.

BRODHAY, Stephen Y. *(Associate Judge, Illinois Circuit Court of Cook County)*
Office: 1100 South Hamilton Avenue, Chicago 60612.
Telephone: (312) 433-4756.

BRONSTEIN, Philip L. *(Circuit Judge, Illinois Circuit Court of Cook County)*
Office: 2202 R. J. Daley Center, Chicago 60602.
Telephone: (312) 603-4643.

BROOKS, Rodney Hughes *(Circuit Judge, Illinois Circuit Court of Cook County)*
Office: 1100 South Hamilton, Room G-36S, Chicago 60612.
Telephone: (312) 433-4757.

BROSNAHAN, Janet Adams *(Circuit Judge, Illinois Circuit Court of Cook County)*
Office: 1303 R. J. Daley Center, Chicago 60602.
Telephone: (312) 603-7959.

BROSNAHAN, Mary M. *(Circuit Judge, Illinois Circuit Court of Cook County)*
Office: 2600 South California Avenue, Chicago 60608.
Telephone: (773) 869-3160.

BROWN, F. Keith *(Circuit Judge, Illinois Circuit Court Sixteenth Judicial Circuit)* Former Associate Judge.
Office: 400 Kane County Judicial Center, 37W777 Route 38, St. Charles 60175-7536.
Telephone: (630) 232-5820.

BROWN, Geraldine Soat *(Magistrate Judge, United States District Court Northern District of Illinois)* Appointed by U.S. District Court judges to term beginning June 19, 2000.
Office: U.S. Courthouse, 219 South Dearborn Street, Chicago 60604.
Telephone: (312) 435-5612.

BROWN, James R. *(Circuit Judge, Illinois Circuit Court of Cook County)*
Office: 1303 R. J. Daley Center, Chicago 60602.
Telephone: (312) 603-7959.

BROWN, Michael *(Associate Judge, Illinois Circuit Court of Cook County)* Appointed to term beginning Nov 1999. Term expires 2003. Born Chicago Illinois March 12, 1955. Religious affiliation: United Church of Christ. Educated at Chicago State University B.S. 1977 and Illinois Institute of Technology, Chicago-Kent College of Law J.D. with honors 1987. Member Kappa Alpha Psi, Bar and Gavel Society and Moot Court Society. Admitted to practice Illinois 1987, U.S. District Court Northern District of Illinois 1987 and Trial Bar of U.S. District Court Northern District of Illinois 1992.
Assistant State's Attorney 1987-99 and Deputy Chief Narcotics 1997-99 Cook County State's Attorney Office. Member Committee on Law And Probation Administration Illinois Judicial Conference 2001. Member Illinois Judges Association, Illinois Judicial Council and Cook County Bar Association. Member J. M. Harlan High School Alumni Association, Chicago State University Alumni Association and Trinity United Church of Christ.
Office: 1100 South Hamilton, Chicago 60612.
Telephone: (312) 433-4757.
E-mail address: mibrown@cookcounty.gov

BROWNFIELD, Gary L. *(Associate Judge, Illinois Circuit Court of Cook County)*
Office: 10220 South 76th Avenue, Bridgeview 60455.
Telephone: (708) 974-6535.

BROWNFIELD, Thomas L. *(Chief Judge, Illinois Circuit Court Eighth Judicial Circuit)* Elected to term beginning Dec 1, 1986. Retained by election 1992 and 1998. Current term expires Nov 2004. Chief Judge since Dec 1, 2001. Born Springfield Illinois Feb 9, 1949. Protestant. Educated at Western Illinois University B.S. with honors 1971 and University of Denver College of Law J.D. 1976. Admitted to practice Colorado 1976 and Illinois 1977. In legal practice Havana 1977-86 and Mason City 1982-86 Illinois.
State's Attorney Mason County Feb 1, 1978 to Nov 30, 1984. Instructor Spoon River College since 1987. Member Article V Rules Committee 1989-93 and Judicial Facilitator Judicial Performance Evaluation Program since 1993 Supreme Court of Illinois. Member Illinois Judges Association (Speaker's Bureau since 1995), National Conference Of State Trial Judges (Former Member Committees on Criminal Justice, Jury Management and International Relations), American Judges Association, Mason County (President 1983), Illinois State and American Bar Associations. Enjoys woodcarving, tennis, scuba diving, fishing and hunting.
Office: Mason County Courthouse, 125 North Plum Street, Havana 62644.
Telephone: (309) 543-3628.

BRUNTON, Diane L. *(Associate Judge, Illinois Circuit Court Seventh Judicial Circuit)*
Office: Macoupin County Courthouse, 201 East Main Street, Carlinville 62626.
Telephone: (217) 854-3181.

BRUSATTE, James L. *(Associate Judge, Illinois Circuit Court Thirteenth Judicial Circuit)*
Office: LaSalle County Courthouse, 119 West Madison Street, Ottawa 61350.
Telephone: (815) 434-4457.

BUCKLO, Elaine E. *(Judge, United States District Court Northern District of Illinois)* Magistrate Judge Dec 19, 1985 to 1994. Appointed Judge for life by President Bill Clinton Oct 17, 1994. Born Boston Massachusetts Oct 1, 1944. Educated at St. Louis University A.B. cum laude 1966 and Northwestern University J.D. magna cum laude 1972. Articles Editor Northwestern University Law Review 1971-72. Law Clerk to Hon. Robert Sprecher, U.S. Court of Appeals Seventh Circuit 1972-73. Admitted to practice California 1973, U.S. District Courts Northern District of California 1973 and Northern District of Illinois 1974, Illinois 1974 and U.S. Court of Appeals Seventh Circuit. In legal practice Chicago Illinois 1974-85.
Author "Scienter and Rule 10b-5" Northwestern University L. Rev. 1972 and "The Supreme Court Attempts to Define Scienter" Stanford L. Rev. 1977. Associate Editor *Litigation* American Bar Association 1979-86. Visiting Professor University of California at Davis 1978-80. Vice President 1976-77 and President 1977-78 Chicago Council of Lawyers. Board of Directors 1992-93, Secretary 1993-94 and Treasurer 1994 Federal Magistrate Judges Association. Member Civil Justice Reform Act Committee Northern District of Illinois 1992-94 and Advisory Committee to Magistrate Judges Division Administrative Office of the U.S. Courts 1993-94. Member Committee on Law and Literacy Section of Special Committees and Commissions American Bar Association 1995-98 and Committee on Administration of Magistrate Judge System Judicial Conference since 1998. Member Chicago (Secretary Development in the Law Committee 1982-83, Vice Chairman 1988-89, Chairman 1989-90) and Federal (Treasurer 1988-89, Secretary 1989-90, Vice President 1990-92 and President 1992-93 Chicago Chapter) Bar Associations. Member Visiting Committee Northern Illinois University College of Law since 1994 and Visiting Committee Northwestern University School of Law 1996-99.
Office: 1988 U.S. Courthouse, 219 South Dearborn Street, Chicago 60604.
Telephone: (312) 435-7610.

BUDZINSKI, Henry A. *(Recalled Circuit Judge, Illinois Circuit Court of Cook County)* Retired, serves by recall.
Office: 1803 R. J. Daley Center, Chicago 60602.
Telephone: (312) 603-7545.

BULKELEY, Harry Clifford *(Circuit Judge, Illinois Circuit Court Ninth Judicial Circuit)* Appointed Associate Judge Nov 15, 1982. Reappointed to subsequent terms. Elected Circuit Judge to term beginning Dec 5, 1994. Reelected Nov 7, 2000, current term expires Dec 2006. Born Galesburg Illinois Sept 1, 1949. Presbyterian. Educated at University of Texas-Austin B.B.A. 1971 and Illinois Institute of Technology, Chicago-Kent College of Law J.D. with honors 1974. Editor Chicago-Kent

BULKELEY, HARRY CLIFFORD—*Continued*

Law Review 1973-74. Member Theta Xi and Phi Alpha Delta. Admitted to practice Illinois 1974. Began legal practice Princeton 1974. In legal practice Galesburg 1974-82.

Author "Does a Landlord Have a Duty to Mitigate Damages When a Tenant Abandons During the Lease?" Illinois B. Jour. 1980. Instructor Carl Sandburg Junior College 1978-81. Member Knox County (President 1982-83), Illinois State 1974-83 and American since 1974 Bar Associations. Republican. Public Guardian and Administrator Knox County 1978-82.

Office: Knox County Courthouse, 200 South Cherry Street, Galesburg 61401.

Telephone: (309) 343-3121.

BURKE, Anne M. *(Judge, Illinois Appellate Court First Judicial District Division Two)* Appointed to term beginning Aug 1995. Elected 1996, current term expires 2006. Formerly served Division Three. Born Chicago Illinois Feb 3, 1944. Educated at DePaul University B.A. 1976 and Illinois Institute of Technology, Chicago-Kent College of Law J.D. 1983. Admitted to practice U.S. District Court Northern District of Illinois 1983, U.S. Court of Appeals Seventh Circuit 1985 and Trial Bar of U.S. District Court Northern District of Illinois 1987. Judge, Illinois Court of Claims 1987-94, appointed by Governor James R. Thompson.

Special Counsel for Child Welfare Services to Governor Jim Edgar.

Office: 160 North LaSalle Street, Room N1509, Chicago 60601.

Telephone: (312) 793-4841.

BURKE, Dennis J. *(Associate Judge, Illinois Circuit Court of Cook County)*

Office: 1100 South Hamilton, Chicago 60612.

Telephone: (312) 433-4756.

BURKE, Michael J. *(Circuit Judge, Illinois Circuit Court Eighteenth Judicial Circuit)* Appointed Associate Judge. Assumed office as Circuit Judge.

Office: DuPage County Courthouse, 505 North County Farm Road, Wheaton 60187.

Telephone: (630) 682-7792.

BURNS, Charles P. *(Circuit Judge, Illinois Circuit Court of Cook County)*

Office: 1500 Maybrook Drive, Room 127, Maywood 60153.

Telephone: (708) 865-6060.

BURR, Edward R. *(Circuit Judge, Illinois Circuit Court of Cook County)* Associate Judge Aug 6, 1984 to Dec 4, 1988. Elected Circuit Judge to term beginning Dec 5, 1988. Retained by election 1994 and 2000. Current term expires Dec 2, 2006. Born Chicago Illinois July 14, 1931. Educated at University of Illinois B.A. 1953 and Northwestern University J.D. 1958. Member Phi Alpha Delta. Admitted to practice Illinois 1958, U.S. District Court Northern District of Illinois 1958, U.S. Court of Appeals Seventh Circuit 1958, U.S. Supreme Court 1964, Trial Bar of U.S. District Court Northern District of Illinois 1983 and U.S. Court of Appeals for the Armed Forces. Began legal practice Chicago. Former Hearing Officer, Board of Appeals Cook County.

Former Assistant Corporation Counsel Chicago. Former Special Counsel to City Council Committee on Police, Fire, Civil Service, Schools and Municipal Institutions. Author "Litigation Involving Pro Se Parties" and "Litigation in Cook County: The View from the Bench, Closing Arguments" IICLE, "The Law of Contempt in Illinois" Loyola University of Chicago L. Jour. 19 No. 3 Spring 1988 distributed as reference book to all Illinois judges by Illinois Supreme Court and "Illinois Premises Liability: A Primer with Cases" Chicago Bar Association April 2000. Lecturer Illinois Institute of Technology, Chicago-Kent College of Law 1986, University of Miami, Ohio 1986 and University of Chicago Law School 1986-87. Adjunct Professor of Law John Marshall Law School since 1987 and Illinois Institute of Technology, Chicago-Kent College of Law 1991-92. Panel Member Federal Defender Program U.S. District Court Northern District of Illinois. Fellow Illinois Bar Foundation. Member Decalogue Society of Lawyers, Illinois Academy of Criminology, American Board of Trial Advocates (National Board of Directors 2000), Illinois Judges Association (Board of Directors since 2000), Women's Bar Association of Illinois, American Judicature Society (National Board of Directors 1998-2000), Chicago and Illinois State Bar Associations. Faculty Member Illinois Judicial Conference (Vice Chairman Committee on Contracts 1986 and Chairman Committee on Contempt 1987), Professional Development Program for New Associate Judges Circuit Court of Cook County 1985-90 and American Academy of Judicial Education since 1988. Participant "Life as a Judicial Officer in the 21st Century" Illinois Judicial Conference Regional Seminar May 6-7, 1999, "Scientific Evidence and Expert Testimony" The National Judicial College July 23-28, 2000 and Environmental Law Seminar for Judges USEPA Oct 26, 2000. Moderator/Faculty Member "Preparing and Litigating Premises Liability Cases" Chicago Bar Association April 6, 2000. Colonel USAF 1953-84 (retired). Private pilot.

Office: 2504 R. J. Daley Center, Chicago 60602.

Telephone: (312) 603-6014.

BURRELL, Anthony L. *(Circuit Judge, Illinois Circuit Court of Cook County)*

Office: 1303 R. J. Daley Center, Chicago 60602.

Telephone: (312) 603-7959.

BUSH, Bernetta D. *(Circuit Judge, Illinois Circuit Court of Cook County)* Elected to term beginning Dec 7, 1992. Retained by election Nov 1998, current term expires Dec 2004. Serves Chancery Division since March 7, 2000. Born Chicago Illinois. Baptist. Educated at Northeastern Illinois University B.A. 1970 M.A. with honors 1973 and DePaul University College of Law J.D. 1977. Admitted to practice Illinois 1977, U.S. District Court Northern District of Illinois 1978 and U.S. Court of Appeals Seventh Circuit 1978. In legal practice Chicago 1977-92.

Legal Advisor Judicare Project of the Legal Service Corporation in Chicago 1977-78 and Illinois State Board of Education 1979-92. Contributor *County Division Handbook for Conducting Jury Trials* 1998. Instructor in Criminal Justice and Business Law Center for Inner City Studies Northeastern Illinois University. Member Constitutional Rights Foundation 1982, Law Bridges Program Chicago Bar Foundation 1997 and Judicial Mentoring Program Circuit Court of Cook County 1997-98. Member Illinois Judicial Council (Board of Directors), Women Judges Association, Illinois Judges Association (Board of Directors), Chicago, Cook County and National Bar Associations. Panelist Landlord-Tenant seminar

BUSH, BERNETTA D.—*Continued*

Chicago Bar Association April 1994, "Women Leaders in 2010" Morraine Valley Community College April 1996, "Appellate Techniques" John Marshall College of Law 1996 and 1997, Urban League-Community Forum Feb 1998 and "Using Financial and Economic Experts in Litigation and the Effects of *Daubert*" Judicial Council and Board of Governors Mid-Winter Meeting National Bar Association, San Juan Puerto Rico Jan 17-21, 2001. Lecturer "Mental Health and Adoption Laws" Loyola College of Law March 1996. Discussion Leader "Dispute Resolutions" The National Judicial College March 1997. Recipient Certificate of Appreciation from Constitutional Rights Foundation 1981, YLS Certificate Award from Chicago Bar Association 1986, Outstanding Service Award from Cultural Linguistic Approach Follow Through Project 1997 and Meritorious Service Award from Illinois Judicial Council 1998. Named Outstanding Alumni by Northeastern Illinois University 1997. Curriculum Coordinator Head Start and Teacher Adult Education Chicago Board of Education. Program Consultant Cultural Linguistic Curriculum Northeastern Illinois University 1972-76. Evaluator North Central Accreditation Association 1978-91. Member Education Commission of the States 1981 and Illinois Commission on Children 1981-84. Board of Trustees City Colleges of Chicago 1988-90. Board of Directors Woodlawn Community Development Corporation since 1993. Member Advisory Board Grateful House 1997-98. Member Chicago Chapter NAACP, National Black Business and Professional Women, Operation PUSH, Cosmopolitan Community Church and Gap Community Organization.

Office: 2008 Daley Center, 50 West Washington, Chicago 60602.

Telephone: (312) 603-5926.

Fax: (312) 603-6787

BYRNE, Robert E. *(Circuit Judge, Illinois Circuit Court Eighteenth Judicial Circuit)* Appointed Associate Judge to term beginning Sept 1, 1986. Reappointed 1987. Elected Circuit Judge 1992. Retained by election 1998, current term expires Dec 2004. Currently on assignment by Supreme Court of Illinois as Judge, Illinois Appellate Court Second Judicial District since Feb 2001. Born Oak Park Illinois July 10, 1941. Educated at Loyola University at Chicago B.S. 1964 J.D. 1967. Admitted to practice Illinois 1968 and U.S. District Court Northern District of Illinois 1968. In legal practice Chicago and Wheaton 1968-86.

Author "Illinois Court Annexed Mandatory Arbitration" Chicago Bar Record 1990 and "Alternative Dispute Resolution" DuPage Bar Briefs 1990. Member International Association of Trial Judges, DuPage County, Illinois State and American Bar Associations. Instructor on Alternative Dispute Resolution DuPage County Bar Association 1986, 1987 and 1989; Illinois Judges Association Conference 1989-90; Conferences on Arbitration Chicago Bar Association 1989-90; and Arbitration Institute of Court Management 1991. Attended courses on General Jurisdiction, Juvenile Law, Alternative Dispute Resolution and Computers.

Office: 500 Roosevelt Road, Suite 300, Glen Ellyn 60137.

Telephone: (630) 790-7820.

BYRON, Nicholas G. *(Circuit Judge, Illinois Circuit Court Third Judicial Circuit)* Appointed Associate Judge Feb 2, 1981. Reappointed 1984. Appointed Circuit Judge to term beginning Jan 17, 1989. Elected 1990. Retained by election 1996 and 2002. Current term expires Dec 2008. Former Chief Judge. Born Lansing Michigan Oct 28, 1929. Greek Orthodox. Educated at Johns Hopkins University A.B. 1953 and Washington University J.D. 1958. Admitted to practice Missouri 1958 and Illinois 1964. Began legal practice Clayton Missouri 1958. In legal practice Belleville 1964 and Edwardsville 1969 Illinois.

State's Attorney Madison County Illinois 1972-80. Board of Directors and Vice President National District Attorneys Association. President Illinois States Attorneys Association. First Lieutenant U.S. Army Infantry 1953-55. Democrat.

Office: Madison County Courthouse, 155 North Main Street, Edwardsville 62025.

Telephone: (618) 692-6200.

CADAGIN, Donald M. *(Circuit Judge, Illinois Circuit Court Seventh Judicial Circuit)*

Office: 722 Sangamon County Complex, 200 South Ninth Street, Springfield 62701.

Telephone: (217) 753-6391.

CAHILL, Robert *(Judge, Illinois Appellate Court First Judicial District Division Two)* Elected Nov 1992. Born Oak Park Illinois April 7, 1936. Roman Catholic. Educated at Loyola University A.B. 1959 and Loyola Law School 1966. Member Phi Alpha Delta. Admitted to practice Illinois 1966. Began legal practice Springfield 1966. In legal practice Chicago. Former Associate Judge, Illinois Circuit Court of Cook County, appointed to term beginning July 1, 1983.

School Board Evanston Illinois 1973-76. Former Legislative Draftsman and Assistant State's Attorney. Author "University and Urban Community Involvement" University of Illinois 1970. Member Chicago Bar Association. E-4 U.S. Army 1959-61.

Office: 160 North LaSalle Street, Room S1605, Chicago 60601.

Telephone: (312) 793-5416.

CALDWELL, Michael T. *(Circuit Judge, Illinois Circuit Court Nineteenth Judicial Circuit)* Former Associate Judge. Elected Circuit Judge Nov 2002.

Office: 2200 North Seminary, Woodstock 60098.

Telephone: (815) 334-4352.

CALLIS, Ann *(Circuit Judge, Illinois Circuit Court Third Judicial Circuit)* Former Associate Judge.

Office: 310 Madison County Courthouse, 155 North Main, Edwardsville 62025.

Telephone: (618) 692-7040.

CALLUM, Thomas E. *(Judge, Illinois Appellate Court Second Judicial District)* Appointed Feb 2001. Born Evergreen Park Illinois May 18, 1944. Educated at St. Joseph's College B.A. with honors 1966 and Illinois Institute of Technology, Chicago-Kent College of Law J.D. with distinction 1973. In legal practice Wheaton 1980-86. Associate Judge 1986-94, Circuit Judge 1994 to Feb 2001 and Chief Judge Feb 1999 to Feb 2001, Illinois Circuit Court Eighteenth Judicial Circuit.

Assistant State's Attorney Cook County 1973-78.

CALLUM, THOMAS E.—*Continued*

Deputy Chief Criminal Division DuPage County State's Attorney Office 1978-80.

Office: Unit A3, 100 West Roosevelt Road, Suite 101, Wheaton 60187.

Telephone: (630) 668-6009.

CAMPANELLA, James W. *(Circuit Judge, Illinois Circuit Court Twentieth Judicial Circuit)*

Office: Perry County Courthouse, One Public Square, Pinckneyville 62274-1172.

Telephone: (618) 357-6079.

CAMPBELL, Calvin C. *(Judge, Illinois Appellate Court First Judicial District Division Five)* Elected to term beginning Dec 4, 1978. Retained by election 1988 and 1998. Current term expires 2008. Former Presiding Judge Division Six. Born Roanoke Virginia Aug 20, 1924. Methodist. Educated at Howard University A.B. 1948 and University of Chicago J.D. 1951. Admitted to practice Illinois 1951. Began legal practice Chicago 1951. Circuit Judge, Illinois Circuit Court of Cook County 1977-78.

Illinois Assistant Attorney General 1957-77. Member Cook County and Illinois State Bar Associations. Recipient Outstanding Public Service Award from Attorney General's office 1976. U.S. Army 1943-45.

Office: 160 North LaSalle Street, Room S1508, Chicago 60601.

Telephone: (312) 793-5442.

CANNON, Diane Gordon *(Circuit Judge, Illinois Circuit Court of Cook County)*

Office: 2600 South California Avenue, Chicago 60608.

Telephone: (773) 869-3049.

CARMODY, Thomas F., Jr. *(Circuit Judge, Illinois Circuit Court of Cook County)*

Office: 10220 South 76th Avenue, Bridgeview 60455.

Telephone: (708) 974-6535.

CARMODY, Thomas P. *(Chief Judge, Illinois Circuit Court Seventh Judicial Circuit)* Elected to term beginning Dec 3, 1990. Retained by election Nov 1996 and Nov 2002. Current term expires 2008. Chief Judge since Jan 1, 2003. Born Chicago Illinois June 21, 1932. Roman Catholic. Educated at Blackburn College B.A. 1954 and University of Notre Dame J.D. 1957. Admitted to practice Illinois 1957. In legal practice Carlinville 1957-90.

State's Attorney Macoupin County 1964-72. Member Macoupin County and Illinois State Bar Associations. Participant Committee on Sanctions in Civil Cases and Instructor 1992 Annual Conference of Circuit Judges. Democrat. Member Elks (Past Exalted Ruler) and Knights of Columbus. Enjoys reading and spectator sports.

Office: Macoupin County Courthouse, 201 East Main Street, Carlinville 62626.

Telephone: (217) 854-3211.

CARTER, Robert L. *(Chief Judge, Illinois Circuit Court Thirteenth Judicial Circuit)* Appointed Associate Judge July 1979. Elected Circuit Judge Nov 1988. Retained by election 1994 and 2000. Current term expires Dec 2006. Chief Judge since 1993. Born Springfield Illinois Feb 25, 1946. Educated at University of Illinois A.B. 1968 J.D. 1974 and Sangamon State University M.A. 1974. Law Clerk to Hon. Howard C. Ryan, Illinois Supreme Court 1974-75. Admitted to practice Illinois 1974 and U.S. District Court Northern District of Illinois 1974. In legal practice Ottawa 1975-79.

Co-author Chapter in *Illinois Contract Law* Illinois Continuing Legal Education 1986-90. Instructor in Business Law Illinois Valley Community College 1976-92. Member ad hoc Committee to Study the Organization and Function of the Illinois Judicial Conference 1990-91. Member Special Committee on Capital Cases Supreme Court of Illinois since 2001. Chair Conference of Chief Judges since Dec 2002. Member Judicial Ethics Advisory Committee on Family Violence Issues. Member Illinois Judicial Conference (Executive Committee since 2001), Illinois Judges Association (President 1995, Board of Directors), La Salle County and Illinois State Bar Associations. Frequent lecturer on jury trials, evidence, contempt and domestic relations at judicial education programs since 1980. Member 1981-86 and Chairman 1985-86 Associate Judge Seminar Coordinating Committee and Conference. Member 1983-91 and Chairman 1989-91 Illinois Subcommittee on Judicial Education. Member Study Committee on Complex Litigation Illinois Judicial Conference since 1986. Member Judicial Mentor Training Committee 1998, Chairman Judicial Mentor Committee since 2003. Member Planning Committee Illinois Judicial Academy 2003. Faculty Mentor Illinois Advanced Judicial Academy 2001. Former Faculty Member Negotiation and Mediation National Institute of Trial Advocacy. E-5 U.S. Army 1969-70. Vietnam Veteran. Member American Legion (Former Post Commander) and VFW.

Office: 204 La Salle County Courthouse, 119 West Madison Street, Ottawa 61350.

Telephone: (815) 434-0770.

CASCIATO, Joseph N. *(Associate Judge, Illinois Circuit Court of Cook County)* Appointed to term beginning June 1982. Elected at special election to term beginning June 12, 1984. Born Chicago Illinois Dec 2, 1949. Roman Catholic. Educated at Loyola University B.A. 1971 and DePaul University J.D. 1974. Dean's List 1974. Law Clerk to Illinois Circuit Court of Cook County 1972-73. Member Lex Legio and Justinian Law Society. Admitted to practice Illinois 1974, U.S. District Court District of Illinois 1974 and U.S. Supreme Court 1981. Began legal practice Chicago 1974.

Assistant Corporation Counsel City of Chicago 1974-80. Adjunct Professor DePaul University since 1985. Member Illinois Judges Association and Chicago Bar Association. Recipient Bancroft-Whitney Award for Commercial Law Excellence. Enjoys golf, music and opera.

Office: 2208 R. J. Daley Center, Chicago 60602.

Telephone: (312) 603-6068.

CASHMAN, Dennis K. *(Circuit Judge, Illinois Circuit Court Eighth Judicial Circuit)* Associate Judge 1979-82. Appointed Circuit Judge to term beginning Dec 1, 1982. Elected Nov 1984. Retained by election 1990, Nov 1996 and 2002. Current term expires Dec 2008. Presiding Judge Adams County since 1988. Born Quincy Illinois May 19, 1945. Presbyterian. Educated at University of Illinois B.S. 1967 and Chicago-Kent College of Law J.D. 1970. Admitted to practice Illinois 1970. In legal practice Macomb 1970-71 and Quincy 1971-79.

Former Chief Assistant State's Attorney McDonough County. Vice Chairman 1985 and Chairman 1986 Evi-

CASHMAN, DENNIS K.—*Continued*

dence Committee Illinois Judicial Conference. Member Illinois Judges Association (Co-chair Judicial Discipline Committee 1999-2002, Member President's Task Force 2002), American Judicature Society, American Judges Association, Adams County (President 1988-90) and Illinois State Bar Associations. Attended courses on Criminal Evidence 1986, Civil Litigation 1990, Dispute Resolution Skills 1996 and Civil Mediation 2001 The National Judicial College and Law and Science and the Highly Effective Judge Illinois Judicial Academy June 2001. Recipient Liberty Bell Award from Adams County Bar Association 1994 and Sexual Assault Prevention and Intervention Services Justice Award 1996. Member 1976-79 and President 1978-79 Quincy Board of Education. Enjoys golfing, reading and traveling.

Office: Adams County Courthouse, 521 Vermont Street, Quincy 62301.

Telephone: (217) 277-2065.

CASON, Laninya *(Associate Judge, Illinois Circuit Court Twentieth Judicial Circuit)*

Office: 10 Public Square, Belleville 62220.

Telephone: (618) 277-6832.

CASTIGLIONE, Frank B. *(Associate Judge, Illinois Circuit Court of Cook County)*

Office: 16501 South Kedzie Parkway, Markham 60426.

Telephone: (708) 210-4170.

CASTILLO, Ruben *(Judge, United States District Court Northern District of Illinois)* Appointed for life by President Bill Clinton to term beginning May 13, 1994. Educated at Loyola University of Chicago B.A. 1976 and Northwestern University J.D. 1979. Admitted to practice Illinois 1979, U.S. District Court Northern District of Illinois 1979 and U.S. Court of Appeals Seventh Circuit 1984.

Assistant U.S. Attorney Special Prosecution Division Northern District of Illinois 1984-88. Director and Regional Counsel Chicago Office Mexican-American Legal Defense and Educational Fund 1988-91. Vice President Chicago Council of Lawyers 1991-93. Board Member Federal Judges Association since 1997. Member American Bar Association. Board of Overseers Chicago-Kent College of Law since 1992. Board Member Chicago Humanities Festival since 1997.

Office: U.S. Courthouse, 219 South Dearborn Street, Chicago 60604.

Telephone: (312) 435-5878.

CECKOWSKI, Valerie Boettle *(Associate Judge, Illinois Circuit Court Nineteenth Judicial Circuit)*

Office: 18 North County Street, Waukegan 60085.

Telephone: (847) 377-7979.

CERVINI, Donna L. *(Associate Judge, Illinois Circuit Court of Cook County)*

Office: 400 R. J. Daley Center, Chicago 60602.

Telephone: (312) 603-2600.

CHAMBERS, Timothy J. *(Associate Judge, Illinois Circuit Court of Cook County)*

Office: 5600 Old Orchard Road, Skokie 60077.

Telephone: (847) 470-7223.

CHAPMAN, Melissa A. *(Judge, Illinois Appellate Court Fifth Judicial District)*

Office: #2 Ginger Creek Village, Glen Carbon 62034.

Telephone: (618) 656-0644.

CHAPMAN, Thomas William *(Associate Judge, Illinois Circuit Court Third Judicial Circuit)*

Office: Madison County Courthouse, 155 North Main Street, Edwardsville 62025.

Telephone: (618) 692-6200.

CHIOLA, Thomas R. *(Circuit Judge, Illinois Circuit Court of Cook County)*

Office: 1505 R. J. Daley Center, Chicago 60602.

Telephone: (312) 603-4848.

CINI, Dale A. *(Circuit Judge, Illinois Circuit Court Fifth Judicial Circuit)* Former Associate Judge.

Office: Coles County Courthouse, Second Floor, 651 Jackson, Charleston 61920.

Telephone: (217) 348-0541.

CLAPS, Joseph M. *(Associate Judge, Illinois Circuit Court of Cook County)*

Office: 1100 South Hamilton, Chicago 60612.

Telephone: (312) 433-5011.

CLARKE, Mark H. *(Circuit Judge, Illinois Circuit Court First Judicial Circuit)* Former Associate Judge.

Office: 2000 Washington Avenue, Cairo 62914.

Telephone: (618) 734-0509.

CLARY, Michael D. *(Circuit Judge, Illinois Circuit Court Fifth Judicial Circuit)*

Office: Seven North Vermilion Street, Danville 61832.

Telephone: (217) 431-2559.

CLAY, Evelyn B. *(Circuit Judge, Illinois Circuit Court of Cook County)*

Office: 2600 South California, Room 101, Chicago 60608.

Telephone: (773) 869-7443.

CLEM, Harry E. *(Circuit Judge, Illinois Circuit Court Sixth Judicial Circuit)* Former Associate Judge.

Office: Champaign County Courthouse, 101 East Main Street, Urbana 61801.

Telephone: (217) 384-3868.

CLEMONS, Holly F. *(Associate Judge, Illinois Circuit Court Sixth Judicial Circuit)* Appointed.

Office: Champaign County Courthouse, 101 East Main Street, Urbana 61801.

Telephone: (217) 384-1218.

CLERKIN, John R. *(Associate Judge, Illinois Circuit Court Ninth Judicial Circuit)* Appointed to term beginning Feb 1989. Reappointed 1991, 1995 and 1999. Current term expires 2003. Born Chicago Illinois July 27, 1951. Roman Catholic. Educated at Northwestern University B.A. 1973 and John Marshall Law School J.D. 1976. Admitted to practice Illinois 1977 and U.S. District Court Central District of Illinois 1979.

State's Attorney McDonough County 1979-89. Member McDonough County and Illinois State Bar Associations.

Office: McDonough County Courthouse, Macomb 61455.

Telephone: (309) 837-4891.

CLUTTS, Rodney A. *(Associate Judge, Illinois Circuit Court First Judicial Circuit)*
Office: Union County Courthouse, Jonesboro 62952.
Telephone: (618) 833-8114.

COADY, John P. *(Circuit Judge, Illinois Circuit Court Fourth Judicial Circuit)* Former Associate Judge.
Office: Christian County Courthouse, Taylorville 62568.
Telephone: (217) 824-4810.

COAR, David H. *(Judge, United States District Court Northern District of Illinois)* Bankruptcy Judge Oct 14, 1986 to Oct 31, 1994. Appointed Judge for life by President Bill Clinton Nov 1, 1994. Born Birmingham Alabama Aug 11, 1943. Educated at Syracuse University B.A. 1964, Loyola University J.D. 1969 and Harvard Law School LL.M. 1970. Admitted to practice Illinois 1969 and Alabama 1971. In legal practice Mobile Alabama 1971 and Birmingham Alabama 1972-74.
Legal Defense and Education Fund NAACP 1970-71. U.S. Trustee Northern District of Illinois 1979-82. Associate Professor DePaul University Law School 1974-79 and 1982-86. Fellow American College of Bankruptcy. Member Legal Club of Chicago, National Bankruptcy Conference, Cook County, Chicago, National and Federal Bar Associations. Sergeant E-5 USMCR 1965-71.
Office: U.S. Courthouse, 219 South Dearborn Street, Chicago 60604.
Telephone: (312) 435-5648.

COCO, Gloria G. *(Associate Judge, Illinois Circuit Court of Cook County)*
Office: 1135 Ashland Avenue, River Forest 60305.
Telephone: (312) 341-2745.

COGHLAN, Mary Ellen *(Circuit Judge, Illinois Circuit Court of Cook County)*
Office: 9100 West Hillcrest Lane, Palos Park 60464.
Telephone: (773) 869-7446.

COGHLAN, Matthew E. *(Circuit Judge, Illinois Circuit Court of Cook County)* Elected to term beginning Dec 4, 2000. Term expires Dec 2006. Born Evergreen Park Illinois April 4, 1962. Catholic. Educated at University of Illinois B.A. 1984 J.D. 1987. Admitted to practice Illinois 1987 and U.S. District Court Northern District of Illinois.
Assistant State's Attorney Cook County Sept 1987 to Dec 2000. Special Assistant U.S. Attorney Northern District of Illinois 1992. Member Illinois Judges Association, Illinois State and American Bar Associations. Democrat. Firefighter Chicago March 1997 to Oct 2000.
Office: 1340 South Michigan Avenue, Suite 701, Chicago 60605.
E-mail address: mcoghlan38@aol.com

COHN, Gerald B. *(Magistrate Judge, United States District Court Southern District of Illinois)* Appointed by U.S. District Court judges to term beginning May 1, 1981. Reappointed 1989 and 1997. Current term expires April 30, 2005. Born Springfield Illinois Dec 28, 1939. Jewish. Educated at Illinois College B.A. 1961 and University of Chicago J.D. 1964. Member Sigma Pi. Admitted to practice Illinois 1965, U.S. District Court District of Illinois 1965 and U.S. Supreme Court 1975. Began legal practice Chicago 1965. In legal practice East Alton 1968 and Bethalto 1970.
Member The Association of Trial Lawyers of America, American Judicature Society, Alton-Wood River (President 1973), Madison County (President 1975), Illinois State (Chairman Judicial Advisory Poll and member Assembly) and American Bar Associations. Sergeant U.S. Army 1965-67. Republican. Member Rotary Club (President 1976) and Chamber of Commerce (President 1977). Enjoys photography, equestrian sports, sailing and racquetball.
Mailing address: P.O. Box 2587, East St. Louis 62202-2587.
Telephone: (618) 482-9376.

COLE, Melvin J. *(Circuit Judge, Illinois Circuit Court of Cook County)*
Office: 3008 R. J. Daley Center, Chicago 60602.
Telephone: (312) 603-7503.

COLEMAN, Sharon Johnson *(Circuit Judge, Illinois Circuit Court of Cook County)*
Office: 2001 R. J. Daley Center, Chicago 60602.
Telephone: (312) 603-5915.

COLEMAN, Susan M. *(Associate Judge, Illinois Circuit Court of Cook County)*
Office: 1500 Maybrook Drive, Maywood 60153.
Telephone: (708) 865-6060.

COLLIER, Glenn H. *(Associate Judge, Illinois Circuit Court Tenth Judicial Circuit)*
Office: Peoria County Courthouse, 324 Main Street, Peoria 61602.
Telephone: (309) 672-6927.

COLLINS, Rosemary *(Circuit Judge, Illinois Circuit Court Seventeenth Judicial Circuit)* Former Associate Judge.
Office: Winnebago County Courthouse, 400 West State Street, Rockford 61101.
Telephone: (815) 987-2503.

COLWELL, Michael J. *(Circuit Judge, Illinois Circuit Court Sixteenth Judicial Circuit)* Former Associate Judge. Assumed office as Circuit Judge. Term expires Dec 2008. Former Chief Judge. Born Aurora Illinois July 8, 1947. Roman Catholic. Educated at Loras College B.A. 1969 and DePaul University J.D. 1972. Admitted to practice Illinois 1972 and U.S. District Court Northern District of Illinois 1972. In legal practice Aurora 1972-84. Served Illinois Appellate Court by special assignment.
Office: Kane County Courthouse, 100 South Third Street, Geneva 60134.
Telephone: (630) 232-3440.

CONDON, Joseph P. *(Associate Judge, Illinois Circuit Court Nineteenth Judicial Circuit)*
Office: McHenry County Courthouse, 2200 North Seminary Avenue, Woodstock 60098.
Telephone: (815) 338-2040.

CONDON, Thomas J. *(Associate Judge, Illinois Circuit Court of Cook County)*
Office: 16501 South Kedzie Parkway, Markham 60426.
Telephone: (708) 210-4170.

CONLON, Claudia *(Circuit Judge, Illinois Circuit Court of Cook County)*
Office: 5600 Old Orchard Road, Stokie 60077.
Telephone: (847) 470-5946.

CONLON, Suzanne B. *(Judge, United States District Court Northern District of Illinois)* Appointed for life by

CONLON, SUZANNE B.—*Continued*

President Ronald Reagan to term beginning 1988. Born Portland Oregon Jan 17, 1939. Educated at Mundelein College B.A. 1963, Loyola University of Chicago J.D. 1968 and University of London Diploma in Foreign and Comparative Law 1971. Law Clerk to Hon. Edwin Robson, U.S. District Court Northern District of Illinois 1968-71. In legal practice Chicago 1972-75.

Assistant U.S. Attorney Northern District of Illinois 1976-77 and 1982-86 and Central District of California 1977-82. Assistant General Counsel 1986 and Executive Director 1986-87 U.S. Sentencing Commission. Special Counsel to Associate U.S. Attorney General Stephen S. Trott 1988.

Office: U.S. Courthouse, 219 South Dearborn Street, Chicago 60604.
Telephone: (312) 435-5595.

CONNORS, Maureen E. *(Circuit Judge, Illinois Circuit Court of Cook County)* Former Associate Judge.
Office: 1814 R. J. Daley Center, Chicago 60602.
Telephone: (312) 603-6469.

CONWAY, James G., Jr. *(Circuit Judge, Illinois Circuit Court Fourteenth Judicial Circuit)*
Office: 100 S.E. Third Avenue, Third Floor, Aledo 61231.
Telephone: (309) 582-7711.

COOGAN, David L. *(Circuit Judge, Illinois Circuit Court Eleventh Judicial Circuit)* Former Associate Judge.
Office: Logan County Courthouse, Lincoln 62656.
Telephone: (217) 732-7013.

COOK, Robert W. *(Judge, Illinois Appellate Court Fourth Judicial District)* Elected 1994. Term expires 2004. Born Springfield Illinois Nov 6, 1943. Catholic. Educated at Quincy College 1961-63 and University of Illinois A.B. 1965 J.D. 1967. Editor University of Illinois Law Forum 1966-67. Admitted to practice Illinois 1968 and U.S. Supreme Court 1973. Began legal practice Quincy 1970. Circuit Judge, Illinois Circuit Court Eighth Judicial Circuit March 1, 1983 to 1994. Served Illinois Appellate Court by special assignment 1991-94.

Author "Jurisdiction in Dissolution of Marriage Cases" Jan 1989 and "Allowing Child Victims' Hearsay under Section 115-10: A Critical Analysis" Nov 2001 Illinois B. Jour. Chairman Regional Seminar on Children in the Law Illinois Judicial Conference 1990-91. Member Illinois State Bar Association (Committee on Civil Practice and Procedure 1980-83). Lecturer New Judge's Seminar 1990-94, Civil Evidence 1994-95 and Recent Statutes Dealing with Hearsay 1999-2000. Captain USMC 1967-70.

Office: 608 Vermont Street, Second Floor, Quincy 62301.
Telephone: (217) 221-2500.

COPLAN, Robert G. *(Associate Judge, Illinois Circuit Court Seventeenth Judicial Circuit)*
Office: 400 West State Street, Rockford 61101.
Telephone: (815) 987-5464.

CORRELL, David M. *(Circuit Judge, Illinois Circuit Court Second Judicial Circuit)* Term expires 2004.
Office: Crawford County Courthouse, Robinson 62454.
Telephone: (618) 544-7471.

CORYELL, James *(Associate Judge, Illinois Circuit Court Sixth Judicial Circuit)*
Office: Macon County Courts Facility, 253 East Wood Street, Decatur 62523.
Telephone: (217) 424-1442.

COX, Jacqueline P. *(United States Bankruptcy Court Northern District of Illinois)* Appointed by U.S. Court of Appeals Seventh Circuit judges to term beginning Feb 3, 2003. Term expires Feb 2017. Former Associate Judge and Circuit Judge, Illinois Circuit Court of Cook County.
Office: 656 U.S. Courthouse, 219 South Dearborn Street, Chicago 60604.
Telephone: (312) 435-5679.

CRANE, Clayton J. *(Circuit Judge, Illinois Circuit Court of Cook County)*
Office: 2600 South California Avenue, Chicago 60608.
Telephone: (773) 869-7432.

CRESWELL, Kathryn E. *(Circuit Judge, Illinois Circuit Court Eighteenth Judicial Circuit)* Former Associate Judge.
Office: DuPage County Courthouse, 505 North County Farm Road, Wheaton 60187.
Telephone: (630) 682-6477.

CROOKS, Wilbur E. *(Circuit Judge, Illinois Circuit Court of Cook County)* Elected to term beginning Dec 1996. Retained by election 2002, current term expires 2008. Serves Criminal Division. Born Chicago Illinois Dec 9, 1940. Protestant. Educated at DePaul University J.D. 1976. Admitted to practice Illinois 1978.

Assistant State's Attorney Cook County 1978-96. Member Illinois Judges Association, Chicago, Cook County and National Bar Associations. Role Model "We Care" Program. Member Male Chorus Calvary MB Church. Enjoys fishing, hunting and basketball.

Office: 2600 South California Avenue, Chicago 60608.
Telephone: (773) 869-3160.

CROWDER, Barbara L. *(Associate Judge, Illinois Circuit Court Third Judicial Circuit)* Appointed to term beginning Jan 8, 1999. Reappointed May 1999, current term expires 2003. Born Mattoon Illinois Feb 3, 1956. Educated at University of Illinois B.A. 1978 J.D. 1981. Member Phi Alpha Delta. Admitted to practice Illinois 1981 and U.S. District Court Southern District of Illinois 1981. In legal practice Peru 1981-82 and Edwardsville 1985-99 Illinois.

Assistant State's Attorney Madison County 1982-85. Co-author Chapter "Parentage" *Family Law Handbook* Illinois State Bar Association 1996. Author numerous articles "Family Law Newsletter" Illinois State Bar Association 1990-99 and Chapter "Maintenance" *Illinois Family Law* IICLE 1998. Instructor in Business Law Belleville Area College 1985. Board of Directors Illinois Judges Association since 2000. Member Metro-East Women Lawyers (President 1986), Madison County and Illinois State (Chair Family Law Section Council 1997-98) Bar Associations. Instructor People's Law School sponsored by Madison County Bar Association and Illinois State Bar Association 1990, 1995 and 1998, Family Law Updates Illinois State Bar Association 1995-2000 and "Drafting Marital Separation Agreements" IICLE 1999 and 2000. Named Outstanding Working Woman of Illi-

CROWDER, BARBARA L.—*Continued*

nois by Illinois Federation of Business and Professional Women 1989. Recipient Distinguished Service Award from Family Law Section Illinois State Bar Association 1995-96. Democratic Committeewoman 1984-98. Member Edwardsville Business and Professional Women (President 1987-88 and 1995-96). Enjoys children, travel and reading.

Office: Madison County Courthouse, 155 North Main Street, Edwardsville 62025.

Telephone: (618) 692-6200.

E-mail address: BarbCrowdr@aol.com

CUDMORE, Byron *(Magistrate Judge, United States District Court Central District of Illinois)* Appointed Sept 1, 1997. Educated at University of Illinois B.S. with honors 1974 and Southern Illinois University J.D. 1977. Admitted to practice Illinois 1977.

Office: 600 East Monroe Street, Room 124, Springfield 62701.

Telephone: (217) 492-4396.

Fax: (217) 492-4596

CUETO, Lloyd A. *(Circuit Judge, Illinois Circuit Court Twentieth Judicial Circuit)*

Office: 10 Public Square, Belleville 62220.

Telephone: (618) 277-6600.

CULLITON, Stephen J. *(Recalled Circuit Judge, Illinois Circuit Court Eighteenth Judicial Circuit)* Former Associate Judge. Assumed office as Circuit Judge. Retired, serves by recall.

Office: DuPage County Courthouse, 505 North County Farm Road, Wheaton 60187.

Telephone: (630) 682-7537.

CUNNINGHAM, Abishi C. *(Associate Judge, Illinois Circuit Court of Cook County)*

Office: 1105 R. J. Daley Center, Chicago 60602.

Telephone: (312) 603-4535.

CURCIO, Lisa R. *(Circuit Judge, Illinois Circuit Court of Cook County)*

Office: 1303 R. J. Daley Center, Chicago 60602.

Telephone: (312) 603-7959.

CUSACK, Robert E. *(Recalled Circuit Judge, Illinois Circuit Court of Cook County)* Appointed to term beginning June 15, 1973. Elected. Retained by election to subsequent terms. Retired, serves by recall. Born Chicago Illinois May 9, 1917. Catholic. Educated at University of Chicago B.A. 1938 and University of Michigan J.D. 1941. Admitted to practice Illinois 1942. Began legal practice Chicago 1942.

Member Chicago, Illinois State and American Bar Associations. U.S. Army 1942-45. Democrat. Enjoys golf and tennis.

Office: 1801 R. J. Daley Center, Chicago 60602.

Telephone: (312) 603-4684.

DAHLEN, Kimberly L. *(Associate Judge, Illinois Circuit Court First Judicial Circuit)*

Office: Jackson County Courthouse, Murphysboro 62966.

Telephone: (618) 687-7330.

DALY, Noreen M. *(Associate Judge, Illinois Circuit Court of Cook County)*

Office: 1100 South Hamilton, Chicago 60612.

Telephone: (312) 433-4756.

DARCY, Daniel P. *(Circuit Judge, Illinois Circuit Court of Cook County)*

Office: 2600 South California Avenue, Chicago 60608.

Telephone: (773) 869-3160.

DARRAH, John W. *(Judge, United States District Court Northern District of Illinois)* Appointed for life by President Bill Clinton to term beginning Sept 1, 2000. Born Chicago Illinois Dec 11, 1938. Educated at Loyola University School of Law J.D. Admitted to practice Illinois 1969 and Trial Bar of U.S. District Court Northern District of Illinois 1983. Circuit Judge 1986-2000 and Presiding Judge Chancery Division June 1992 to May 1994, Illinois Circuit Court Eighteenth Judicial Circuit.

Former Special General Counsel Board of Election Commission, Former Deputy Public Defender Felony Division, Former Assistant State's Attorney and Former Supervisor Criminal Division DuPage County. Former Special Assistant Attorney General. Former Attorney Advisor Federal Trade Commission. Adjunct Professor of Law since 1976 and Faculty Advisor National Moot Court Competition since 1988 Northern Illinois University College of Law. Adjunct Professor of Law John Marshall Law School 2002. Past President DuPage American Inns of Court and DuPage County Bar Association. Former Assembly Member Illinois State Bar Association. Member Federal Judges Association, American Judicature Society and Federal Circuit Bar Associations. Faculty Member National Institute for Trial Advocacy. Panelist Jury Trials and Evidence Illinois Judicial Conference. Adjunct Faculty Member and Panelist Workshop for Law School American Bar Association. Named Professor of the Year by Northern Illinois University 1992 and 1995. Recipient Board of Directors Award from DuPage County Bar Association 1995. Former Republican Precinct Committeeman Bloomingdale Township Republican Organization DuPage County. Public Administrator and Public Guardian DuPage County. Past President DuPage County Legal Aid Society. Former Member Board of Directors DuPage County Youth Services Coalition. Former Member Citizens Advisory Council School District 89 and School District 200.

Office: 219 South Dearborn Street, Chambers 1288, Chicago 60604.

Telephone: (312) 435-5619.

DAUBER, Ellen A. *(Associate Judge, Illinois Circuit Court Twentieth Judicial Circuit)*

Office: County Building, 10 Public Square, Belleville 62220.

Telephone: (618) 277-7325.

DAUGHERITY, Eugene P. *(Circuit Judge, Illinois Circuit Court Thirteenth Judicial Circuit)*

Office: 119 West Madison Street, Ottawa 61350.

Telephone: (815) 434-0400.

DAVIS, Ronald S. *(Associate Judge, Illinois Circuit Court of Cook County)*

Office: 1307 R. J. Daley Center, Chicago 60602.

Telephone: (312) 603-3480.

DAVY, Thomas M. *(Circuit Judge, Illinois Circuit Court of Cook County)* Elected Nov 3, 1992 to term beginning Dec 7, 1992. Retained by election 1998, current term expires Dec 2004. Born Chicago Illinois Oct 13, 1946. Catholic. Educated at Loyola University B.A. 1968 and DePaul University College of Law J.D. 1971.

DAVY, THOMAS M.—*Continued*

Admitted to practice Illinois 1971, U.S. District Court Northern District of Illinois 1971, Trial Bar of U.S. District Court Northern District of Illinois 1987 and U.S. Court of Appeals Seventh Circuit 1987. Court Coordinator, Illinois Circuit Court of Cook County 1971-74.

Assistant State's Attorney Cook County 1974-92. Author "Prosecutor Immunity: The Impact of *Burns v. Reed*" *The Prosecutor* 1992 and "Absolute Immunity Defense in Civil Rights Actions" Law Enforcement Legal Defense Manual 1992. Member Catholic Lawyers Guild and Illinois Judges Association. Attended Illinois Judicial Conference, American Academy of Judicial Education and The National Judicial College seminars. Honored by Hickory Hills Police Department 1986, Fifth District Police Chiefs Association 1987 and Fifth District State's Attorneys Office 1987. Auxiliary policeman Western Springs 1991-92. Former Lector and Parish Council Member St. John of the Cross Church. Enjoys running.

Office: 10220 South 76th Avenue, Room 101B, Bridgeview 60455.

Telephone: (708) 974-6537.

DAY, James W. *(Circuit Judge, Illinois Circuit Court Seventh Judicial Circuit)* Elected to term beginning 1990. Retained by election 1996 and 2002. Current term expires 2008.

Office: Greene County Courthouse, 519 North Main, Carrollton 62016.

Telephone: (217) 942-6731.

DeARMOND, Craig H. *(Circuit Judge, Illinois Circuit Court Fifth Judicial Circuit)*

Office: Vermilion County Courthouse, Seven North Vermilion, Danville 61832.

Telephone: (217) 431-2558.

DeBONI, Frank *(Associate Judge, Illinois Circuit Court of Cook County)*

Office: 2452 West Belmont, Chicago 60618.

Telephone: (773) 404-3304.

DeCARDY, William D. *(Associate Judge, Illinois Circuit Court Eleventh Judicial Circuit)* Appointed to term beginning Feb 15, 1973. Reappointed to subsequent terms. Born Chicago Illinois May 27, 1942. Educated at University of Illinois B.S. 1964 J.D. 1966. Law Clerk to Idaho Supreme Court 1967. Admitted to practice Illinois 1966 and Idaho 1967. Began legal practice Champaign Illinois 1967.

Counsel to Illinois State Senate President pro tem 1969.

Office: Law and Justice Center, 104 West Front Street, Bloomington 61701.

Telephone: (309) 888-5245.

DELGADO, David *(Circuit Judge, Illinois Circuit Court of Cook County)*

Office: 2810 R. J. Daley Center, Chicago 60602.

Telephone: (312) 603-3914.

DEMLING, John W. *(Associate Judge, Illinois Circuit Court Eighteenth Judicial Circuit)* Appointed.

Office: DuPage County Courthouse, 505 North County Farm Road, Wheaton 60187.

Telephone: (630) 682-7292.

DENLOW, Morton *(Magistrate Judge, United States District Court Northern District of Illinois)* Appointed by U.S. District Court judges to term beginning March 1, 1996. Term expires March 2004. Educated at Washington University A.B. cum laude 1969 and Northwestern University School of Law J.D. cum laude 1972. Member Order of the Coif. Admitted to practice Illinois 1972, U.S. District Court Northern District of Illinois 1973, U.S. Court of Appeals Seventh Circuit 1973 and U.S. Supreme Court 1989. In legal practice 1971-96.

Director of Professional Services Chicago Regional Office Jams/Endispute 1995-96. Author "My Rookie Year on the Bench" Chicago Bar Association Record 62 Sept 1997, "Steps to an Effective Settlement Conference: Before You Come to the Table" ABA Pretrial Practice & Discovery Newsletter 3 Fall 1997, "Steps to an Effective Settlement Conference: At the Table" 3 Winter 1998 ABA Practice & Discovery Newsletter, "Mediation of Commercial Disputes: A Useful Tool for Trial Lawyers and Their Clients" Chicago Bar Record 30 Sept 1995 and Dispute Resolution Journal American Arbitration Association 79 Oct-Dec 1995, "Summary Judgment: Boon or Burden" *The Judges' Journal* American Bar Association 26 Summer 1998, "Trial on the Papers: An Alternative to Cross Motions for Summary Judgment" 46 *The Federal Lawyer* 30 Aug 1999 and "Justice Should Emphasize People, Not Paper" 83 *Judicature: The Journal of the American Judicature Society* 50 Sept-Oct 1999. Senior Lecturer on Law Loyola University School of Law 1983-95. Adjunct Professor of Trial Advocacy Northwestern University School of Law 1990-91. Member Executive Committee Center for Analysis of Alternative Dispute Resolution Systems, Alternative Dispute Resolution Committee U.S. District Court Northern District of Illinois, Chicago (Board of Managers), Decalogue, Illinois State, Federal and American Bar Associations. Faculty Member National Institute for Trial Advocacy since 1988. Lecturer Northwestern University Corporation Counsel Institute, National Employment Lawyers Association, American Intellectual Property Law Association, Chicago Bar Association, Illinois State Bar Association, Federal Bar Association and American Bar Association. Member Advisory Committee Dispute Resolution Research Center J. L. Kellogg Graduate School of Management.

Office: U.S. Courthouse, 219 South Dearborn Street, Chicago 60604.

Telephone: (312) 435-5856.

DERNBACH, Dennis A. *(Associate Judge, Illinois Circuit Court of Cook County)*

Office: 2600 South California Avenue, Room 301, Chicago 60608.

Telephone: (773) 869-7455.

DESMOND, Leo T. *(Associate Judge, Illinois Circuit Court Second Judicial Circuit)* Appointed to term beginning Aug 15, 1981. Reappointed to subsequent terms. Born Chicago Illinois June 13, 1950. Roman Catholic. Educated at Millikin University B.S. with honors 1973 and DePaul University J.D. 1977. Law Clerk to Hon. John M. Karns and Hon. George Kasserman, Illinois Appellate Court Fifth Judicial District 1977-79. Admitted to practice Illinois 1977. Began legal practice Benton 1978.

Assistant State's Attorney Franklin County 1980-81. Member Illinois Judges Association and Illinois State Bar Association.

Office: Franklin County Courthouse, Benton 62812.

Telephone: (618) 438-6003.

DEVLIN, Donald M. *(Circuit Judge, Illinois Circuit Court of Cook County)* Elected to term beginning Dec 2, 1996. Retained by election 2002, current term expires Dec 2008. Born Monmouth Illinois Jan 4, 1946. Educated at Beloit College B.A. cum laude 1968 and University of Missouri J.D. 1973. Member Phi Alpha Delta. Admitted to practice Illinois 1974 and U.S. District Court Northern District of Illinois 1975. In legal practice Chicago 1992-96.

Assistant State's Attorney Cook County 1974-92. Member Illinois Judges Association, Chicago and Illinois State Bar Associations. USN 1968-70. Republican. Chairman Winnetka Planning Commission 1995-96.

Office: 2307 R. J. Daley Center, Chicago 60602.
Telephone: (312) 603-6482.

DIAMOND, Scott B. *(Associate Judge, Illinois Circuit Court Sixth Judicial Circuit)* Appointed to term beginning Dec 1, 1980. Reappointed 1983, 1987, 1991, 1995 and 1999. Current term expires 2003. Born Chicago Illinois Nov 27, 1946. Jewish. Educated at University of Illinois B.S. 1968 and Illinois Institute of Technology, Chicago-Kent College of Law J.D. with honors 1971. Admitted to practice Illinois 1971. Began legal practice Decatur 1971.

Former Assistant State's Attorney and Public Defender. Instructor in Business Law Richland Community College since 1980. Member Illinois Judicial Association.

Office: 225 Macon County Courts Facility, 253 East Wood, Decatur 62523.
Telephone: (217) 424-1484.

DICKLER, Grace G. *(Associate Judge, Illinois Circuit Court of Cook County)*

Office: 5600 Old Orchard Road, Room 240, Skokie 60077.
Telephone: (847) 470-7200.

DIFANIS, Thomas J. *(Circuit Judge, Illinois Circuit Court Sixth Judicial Circuit)*

Office: Champaign County Courthouse, 101 East Main Street, Urbana 61801.
Telephone: (217) 384-3866.

DiMARZIO, Philip L. *(Chief Judge, Illinois Circuit Court Sixteenth Judicial Circuit)* Elected to term beginning Dec 3, 1988. Retained by election Nov 1994 and 2000. Current term expires Dec 2006. Born DeKalb Illinois Feb 22, 1949. Educated at Northern Illinois University B.A. 1970 and University of Illinois J.D. 1973 LL.M. 1981. Member Justinian Society. Admitted to practice Illinois 1973 and U.S. District Court Northern District of Illinois 1973. In legal practice Sycamore 1975-81.

Assistant State's Attorney Cook County 1973-75. State's Attorney DeKalb County 1984-88. Instructor in Business Law 1979-84 and Executive M.B.A. Law Course and White Collar Crime 1981-84 Northern Illinois University. Master American Inn of Court. Member DeKalb County and Kane County Bar Associations.

Office: Kane County Judicial Center, 37W777 Route 38, St. Charles 60175-7536.
Telephone: (630) 406-7156.

DISKO, Barbara J. *(Circuit Judge, Illinois Circuit Court of Cook County)* Former Associate Judge. Assumed office as Circuit Judge. Term expires Dec 2006.

Office: 1606 R. J. Daley Center, Chicago 60602.
Telephone: (312) 603-4829.

DOCKERY, Peter J. *(Associate Judge, Illinois Circuit Court Eighteenth Judicial Circuit)*

Office: 505 North County Farm Road, Wheaton 60187.
Telephone: (630) 682-6408.

DOLAN, Francis J. *(Circuit Judge, Illinois Circuit Court of Cook County)*

Office: 1503 R. J. Daley Center, Chicago 60602.
Telephone: (312) 603-4852.

DONEGAN, James G. *(Associate Judge, Illinois Circuit Court of Cook County)*

Office: 1506 R. J. Daley Center, Chicago 60602.
Telephone: (312) 603-5545.

DONNELLY, Christopher J. *(Circuit Judge, Illinois Circuit Court of Cook County)*

Office: 16501 South Kedzie Parkway, Markham 60426.
Telephone: (708) 210-4170.

DONNELLY, James *(Associate Judge, Illinois Circuit Court Sixteenth Judicial Circuit)*

Office: DeKalb County Courthouse, 133 West State Street, Sycamore 60178.
Telephone: (815) 895-7175.

DONNERSBERGER, David R. *(Circuit Judge, Illinois Circuit Court of Cook County)* Former Associate Judge.

Office: 2206 R. J. Daley Center, Chicago 60602.
Telephone: (312) 603-6348.

DONOVAN, James K. *(Circuit Judge, Illinois Circuit Court Twentieth Judicial Circuit)* Assumed office 2001. On assignment by Supreme Court of Illinois as Judge, Illinois Appellate Court Fifth Judicial District since Sept 2002. Born East St. Louis Illinois Aug 12, 1952. Educated at Southern Illinois University at Carbondale B.S. and St. Louis University School of Law J.D. In legal practice 1981-82 and 1994-2001. Associate Judge 1983-87 and Circuit Judge 1987-94, Illinois Circuit Court Twentieth Judicial Circuit.

Office: 333 Salem Place, Suite 130, Fairview Heights 62208.
Telephone: (618) 632-1050.

DOODY, John T., Jr. *(Circuit Judge, Illinois Circuit Court of Cook County)*

Office: 1303 R. J. Daley Center, Chicago 60602.
Telephone: (312) 603-7959.

DOOLING, Deborah M. *(Circuit Judge, Illinois Circuit Court of Cook County)*

Office: 2304 R. J. Daley Center, Chicago 60602.
Telephone: (312) 603-6010.

DOUGLAS, Loretta C. *(Circuit Judge, Illinois Circuit Court of Cook County)* Associate Judge 1984-90. Assumed office as Circuit Judge. Term expires Dec 2008. Born Chicago Illinois Feb 5, 1943. Catholic. Educated at Loyola University of Chicago B.S. 1965 J.D. 1968 and George Washington University National Law Center LL.M. 1977. In legal practice Chicago 1968-84.

President Women's Bar Association of Illinois 1981-82. Board of Governors Illinois State Bar Association. Enjoys skiing and golfing.

Office: 10220 South 76th Avenue, Bridgeview 60455.
Telephone: (708) 974-6540.

DOUGLAS, LORETTA C.—*Continued*

Fax: (708) 974-6021
E-mail address: HerHonor@msn.com

DOYLE, Carol A. *(Judge, United States Bankruptcy Court Northern District of Illinois)* Appointed by U.S. Court of Appeals Seventh Circuit judges to term beginning July 26, 1999. Term expires July 2013. Educated at University of Iowa B.B.A. with distinction 1978 and Loyola University School of Law J.D. with distinction 1982. Law Clerk to Hon. John A. Nordberg, U.S. District Court Northern District of Illinois 1982-85. In legal practice Chicago 1985-99.

Office: U.S. Courthouse, 219 South Dearborn Street, Chicago 60604.
Telephone: (312) 435-6010.

DOYLE, Dennis B. *(Circuit Judge, Illinois Circuit Court Twentieth Judicial Circuit)*

Office: Monroe County Courthouse, 100 South Main, Waterloo 62298.
Telephone: (618) 939-8681.

DOYLE, James T. *(Circuit Judge, Illinois Circuit Court Sixteenth Judicial Circuit)* Former Associate Judge.

Office: 400A Kane County Judicial Center, 37W777 Route 38, St. Charles 60175-7536.
Telephone: (630) 232-3440.

DOZIER, Ronald C. *(Circuit Judge, Illinois Circuit Court Eleventh Judicial Circuit)* Circuit Judge 1987-88. Associate Judge 1989-90. Appointed Circuit Judge to term beginning March 29, 1991. Elected Nov 1992 and Nov 1998. Current term expires Dec 2004. Born Mill Shoals Illinois Oct 20, 1946. Roman Catholic. Educated at University of Illinois B.A. 1968 J.D. 1973. Admitted to practice Illinois 1973.

Assistant State's Attorney 1973-76 and State's Attorney 1976-87 McLean County. President Illinois State's Attorneys Association 1984. Member Illinois Juvenile Justice Commission 1990-2000. Member McLean County and Illinois State Bar Associations. E-5 U.S. Army Corps of Engineers 1969-90. Vietnam Veteran. Republican. Member Illinois Dangerous Drugs Commission 1982-86 and Illinois DUI Task Force 1983-84. Member Walk to Emmaus and Cursillo and Christian Legal Society. Member Southern Cherokee tribe (Native American Indian).

Office: 523 Law and Justice Center, 104 West Front Street, Bloomington 61701.
Telephone: (309) 888-5215.

DRAZEWSKI, Scott D. *(Associate Judge, Illinois Circuit Court Eleventh Judicial Circuit)* Former Circuit Judge.

Office: McLean County Law and Justice Center, 104 West Front Street, Bloomington 61701.
Telephone: (309) 888-5001.

DRUMMOND, Mark A. *(Associate Judge, Illinois Circuit Court Eighth Judicial Circuit)*

Office: Adams County Courthouse, 521 Vermont Street, Quincy 62301.
Telephone: (217) 277-2058.

DUBICKI, David J. *(Associate Judge, Illinois Circuit Court Tenth Judicial Circuit)*

Office: 215 Peoria County Courthouse, 324 Main Street, Peoria 61602-1363.
Telephone: (309) 672-6036.

DUDGEON, Thomas C. *(Associate Judge, Illinois Circuit Court Eighteenth Judicial Circuit)*

Office: DuPage County Courthouse, 505 North County Farm Road, Wheaton 60187.
Telephone: (630) 682-7300.

DUFF, Brian Barnett *(Senior Judge, United States District Court Northern District of Illinois)* Appointed for life by President Ronald Reagan to term beginning Oct 25, 1985. Assumed Senior status, serves by assignment. Born Dallas Texas Sept 15, 1930. Roman Catholic. Educated at University of Notre Dame A.B. in English 1953 and DePaul University College of Law J.D. 1962. Admitted to practice Illinois 1962, Massachusetts 1962, U.S. District Court Northern District of Illinois 1962 and U.S. Supreme Court 1968. In legal practice Chicago 1969-76. Circuit Judge, Illinois Circuit Court of Cook County 1976-85.

Lecturer Loyola University School of Law 1978-79. Adjunct Professor John Marshall Law School since 1985. Member Illinois Appellate Lawyers Association, Chicago and American Bar Associations. Lieutenant j.g. USN 1953-56. Enjoys travel, history, the arts, sports and teaching children of all ages.

Office: U.S. Courthouse, 219 South Dearborn Street, Chicago 60604.
Telephone: (312) 435-5541.

DUFF, Ellar *(Associate Judge, Illinois Circuit Court Third Judicial Circuit)* Appointed to term beginning Oct 5, 1987. Reappointed 1991, 1995 and 1999. Current term expires 2003. Born Catron Missouri April 13, 1949. Christian. Educated at University of Missouri-Columbia B.S.Ed. 1976 J.D. 1981. Admitted to practice Illinois 1982, Missouri 1982 and U.S. District Courts Western District of Missouri 1982 and Southern District of Illinois 1983.

Office: 221 Madison County Courthouse, 155 North Main Street, Edwardsville 62025.
Telephone: (618) 692-7040.

DUKE, Patrick L. *(Circuit Judge, Illinois Circuit Court Fourth Judicial Circuit)*

Mailing address: P.O. Box 100, Louisville 62858.
Telephone: (618) 665-3838.

DUNAGAN, Danny A. *(Circuit Judge, Illinois Circuit Court Fourteenth Judicial Circuit)* Appointed Associate Judge to term beginning July 1, 1987. Assumed office as Circuit Judge. Term expires 2008. Born Danville Illinois May 20, 1946. Educated at Southern Illinois University B.A. 1968 and University of Illinois J.D. 1975. Admitted to practice Illinois 1975 and U.S. District Court Northern District of Illinois 1975. In legal practice Morrison 1978-87.

Member Whiteside County (Secretary 1976-77), Illinois State and American Bar Associations. E-5 U.S. Army 1968-71. Previously employed as teacher 1968.

Office: Whiteside County Courthouse, 200 East Knox, Morrison 61270.
Telephone: (815) 772-5170.

DUNCAN, Edward R., Jr. *(Circuit Judge, Illinois Circuit Court Eighteenth Judicial Circuit)* Appointed As-

DUNCAN, EDWARD R., JR.—*Continued*

sociate Judge Aug 17, 1987. Reappointed July 1, 1991. Appointed Circuit Judge to term beginning Dec 5, 1994. Elected 1996. Retained by election 2002, current term expires Dec 2008. Born Joliet Illinois Oct 23, 1945. Presbyterian. Educated at Cornell University B.A. 1967 and University of Illinois J.D. 1972. Admitted to practice Illinois 1972 and U.S. District Court Northern District of Illinois 1972. In legal practice Chicago 1972-75 and Wheaton 1975-87.

Co-author with Roger K. O'Reilly chapters "Investigation" and 'Pre-Trial Discovery" in *Proving Fault in Automobile Accident Cases* Illinois Institute for Continuing Legal Education 1978. Instructor College of DuPage since 1988. Member Illinois Judges Association, DuPage County and Illinois State Bar Associations. Attended courses on General Jurisdiction 1988 and Court Management 1989 The National Judicial College. Captain USAR 1967-73. Recipient Army Commendation Medal 1968 and Bronze Star and first oak leaf cluster 1969. Republican. Member VFW. Enjoys children and reading.

Office: DuPage County Courthouse, 505 North County Farm Road, Wheaton 60187.

Telephone: (630) 682-7164.

DUNCAN-BRICE, Jennifer *(Circuit Judge, Illinois Circuit Court of Cook County)*

Office: 2207 R. J. Daley Center, Chicago 60602.

Telephone: (312) 603-6058.

DUNN, Larry D. *(Circuit Judge, Illinois Circuit Court Second Judicial Circuit)*

Office: Richland County Courthouse, Olney 62450.

Telephone: (618) 392-3421.

DUNN, Thomas A. *(Associate Judge, Illinois Circuit Court Twelfth Judicial Circuit)*

Office: Will County Courthouse, 14 West Jefferson, Joliet 60432.

Telephone: (815) 727-8530.

DUNN, Wallace B. *(Associate Judge, Illinois Circuit Court Nineteenth Judicial Circuit)* Appointed to term beginning May 1, 1986. Reappointed 1991, 1995 and 1999. Current term expires July 2003. Born Chicago Illinois Nov 28, 1940. Educated at University of Illinois B.S. 1963 and DePaul College of Law J.D. 1965. Member Nu Beta Epsilon. Admitted to practice Illinois 1965 and U.S. District Courts Southern 1965 and Northern 1967 Districts of Illinois. In legal practice Chicago 1965-74 and Highwood 1974-86.

Corporation Counsel City of Highwood 1969-86. Member Lake County Zoning Board of Appeals 1980-86. Author "Summary of Illinois Mental Health Code" Northwest Suburban Bar Association Journal 1964. Contributor Lake County Bar Association Journal 1996. Member Jefferson Inn American Inns of Court, Illinois Judges Association, McHenry County, Lake County (Chairman Municipal Law Committee 1978) and Illinois State (Assembly since 1992, Council Member Civil Practice and Procedures Section since 2000) Bar Associations. Presented Program on Conduct of a Civil Jury Trial Associate Judge Seminar Committee Illinois Judicial Conference 1992. Recipient Certificate of Appreciation from Governor's Advisory Council.

Office: Lake County Courthouse, 18 North County Street, Waukegan 60085.

Telephone: (847) 377-3600.

DWYER, Mark W. *(Associate Judge, Illinois Circuit Court Eighteenth Judicial Circuit)*

Office: 505 North County Farm Road, Room 2015, Wheaton 60187.

Telephone: (630) 682-7300.

EADIE-DANIELS, Loretta *(Circuit Judge, Illinois Circuit Court of Cook County)*

Office: 16501 South Kedzie Parkway, Markham 60426.

Telephone: (708) 210-4170.

ECKERT, Annette A. *(Circuit Judge, Illinois Circuit Court Twentieth Judicial Circuit)* Former Associate Judge.

Office: County Building, 10 Public Square, Belleville 62220.

Telephone: (618) 277-6600.

ECKISS, Ronald R. *(Circuit Judge, Illinois Circuit Court First Judicial Circuit)*

Office: Williamson County Courthouse, 200 Jefferson Street, Marion 62959.

Telephone: (618) 997-1301.

EDER, James J. *(Associate Judge, Illinois Circuit Court Fourth Judicial Circuit)*

Office: 1001 South First Street, Effingham 62401.

Telephone: (217) 342-4831.

EDMONDSON, Wiley W. *(Associate Judge, Illinois Circuit Court Sixteenth Judicial Circuit)*

Office: 400A Kane County Judicial Center, 37W777 Route 38, St. Charles 60175-7536.

Telephone: (630) 232-3440.

EDWARDS, James R. *(Associate Judge, Illinois Circuit Court Sixteenth Judicial Circuit)*

Office: 37W777 Route 38, St. Charles 60175.

Telephone: (630) 232-3440.

EGAN, James D. *(Circuit Judge, Illinois Circuit Court of Cook County)* Former Associate Judge.

Office: 2600 South California, Chicago 60608.

Telephone: (773) 869-3208.

EGAN, Lynn M. *(Circuit Judge, Illinois Circuit Court of Cook County)*

Office: 2401 R. J. Daley Center, Chicago 60602.

Telephone: (312) 603-4811.

EGGERS, Robert J. *(Circuit Judge, Illinois Circuit Court Seventh Judicial Circuit)* Former Associate Judge.

Office: 732 Sangamon County Complex, 200 South Ninth Street, Springfield 62701.

Telephone: (217) 753-6735.

EINHORN, Ann A. *(Associate Judge, Illinois Circuit Court Sixth Judicial Circuit)*

Office: Champaign County Courthouse, 101 East Main Street, Urbana 61801.

Telephone: (217) 384-1284.

ELLIOTT, Kathy Bradshaw *(Circuit Judge, Illinois Circuit Court Twenty-first Judicial Circuit)* Former Associate Judge, appointed to term beginning Jan 1997. Assumed office as Circuit Judge. Born Beecher Illinois July 11, 1951. Protestant. Educated at Southern Illinois University B.S. 1972, University of Hawaii M.S.W.

ELLIOTT, KATHY BRADSHAW—*Continued*

1976 and Chicago-Kent College of Law J.D. 1984. Admitted to practice Illinois 1984.
First Assistant State's Attorney Kankakee 1988-97.
Office: Kankakee County Courthouse, 450 East Court Street, Kankakee 60901.
Telephone: (815) 936-4695.

ELROD, Richard J. *(Circuit Judge, Illinois Circuit Court of Cook County)*
Office: 2501 R. J. Daley Center, Chicago 60602.
Telephone: (312) 603-7991.

ELSNER, John T. *(Circuit Judge, Illinois Circuit Court Eighteenth Judicial Circuit)* Appointed.
Office: DuPage County Courthouse, 505 North County Farm Road, Wheaton 60187.
Telephone: (630) 682-7300.

ENGEL, Douglas R. *(Circuit Judge, Illinois Circuit Court Sixteenth Judicial Circuit)* Former Associate Judge. Assumed office as Circuit Judge. Term expires 2008.
Office: DeKalb County Courthouse, 133 West State Street, Sycamore 60178.
Telephone: (815) 895-7160.

EPSTEIN, David A. *(Judge, Illinois Court of Claims)* Appointed by Governor Jim Edgar.
Office: 30 North LaSalle Street, Suite 2900, Chicago 60602.
Telephone: (312) 553-1479.

EPSTEIN, James R. *(Circuit Judge, Illinois Circuit Court of Cook County)*
Office: 5600 Old Orchard Road, Skokie 60077.
Telephone: (847) 470-7220.

EQUI, Rodney W. *(Circuit Judge, Illinois Circuit Court Eighteenth Judicial Circuit)* Former Associate Judge.
Office: DuPage County Courthouse, 505 North County Farm Road, Wheaton 60187.
Telephone: (630) 682-6862.

ERICKSON, Clark Erwin *(Circuit Judge, Illinois Circuit Court Twenty-first Judicial Circuit)* Appointed to term beginning Sept 1, 1995. Elected Nov 5, 1996. Retained by election 2002, current term expires Dec 2008. Born Ironwood Michigan March 23, 1948. Baptist. Educated at University of Illinois B.S. 1971 M.B.A. 1976 J.D. 1976. Admitted to practice Illinois 1976 and U.S. District Court Central District of Illinois 1979.
State's Attorney Kankakee County 1992-95. Member Illinois Judges Association and Illinois State Bar Association. Enjoys fiction-writing.
Office: Kankakee County Courthouse, 450 East Court Street, Kankakee 60901.
Telephone: (815) 937-2915.

ERICKSON, David A. *(Recalled Associate Judge, Illinois Circuit Court of Cook County)* Appointed Associate Judge. Retired, serves by recall.
Office: 1100 South Hamilton Avenue, Chicago 60612.
Telephone: (312) 433-4756.

ETCHINGHAM, James P. *(Associate Judge, Illinois Circuit Court of Cook County)*
Office: 1500 Maybrook Drive, Room 287, Maywood 60153.
Telephone: (708) 865-6060.

EVANS, Charles H. *(Recalled Magistrate Judge, United States District Court Central District of Illinois)* Appointed Magistrate Judge by U.S. District Court judges. Appointed Recalled Magistrate Judge by the Judicial Council of the Seventh Circuit.
Office: 110 Federal Building, 600 East Monroe Street, Springfield 62701.
Telephone: (217) 492-4810.

EVANS, Timothy C. *(Chief Judge, Illinois Circuit Court of Cook County)*
Office: 2600 R. J. Daley Center, Chicago 60602.
Telephone: (312) 603-6000.

EVERHART, Millard Scott *(Circuit Judge, Illinois Circuit Court Fifth Judicial Circuit)*
Office: 651 Jackson Avenue, Second Floor, Charleston 61920.
Telephone: (217) 849-3871.

FABIAN, Donald J. *(Circuit Judge, Illinois Circuit Court Sixteenth Judicial Circuit)* Former Associate Judge.
Office: Kane County Judicial Center, 37W777 Route 38, St. Charles 60175.
Telephone: (630) 232-3441.

FABRI, Candace Jean *(Circuit Judge, Illinois Circuit Court of Cook County)*
Office: 1100 South Hamilton Avenue, Chicago 60612.
Telephone: (312) 433-7811.

FAHEY, Thomas J. *(Circuit Judge, Illinois Circuit Court Fifth Judicial Circuit)* Term expires Dec 2006.
Office: Vermilion County Courthouse, Seven North Vermilion, Danville 61832.
Telephone: (217) 431-2559.

FAWELL, Blanche Hill *(Associate Judge, Illinois Circuit Court Eighteenth Judicial Circuit)* Appointed.
Office: DuPage County Courthouse, 505 North County Farm Road, Wheaton 60187.
Telephone: (630) 682-7300.

FECAROTTA, Thomas P., Jr. *(Circuit Judge, Illinois Circuit Court of Cook County)*
Office: 2121 Euclid, Room 204A, Rolling Meadows 60008.
Telephone: (847) 818-2279.

FEENEY, Charles M., III *(Associate Judge, Illinois Circuit Court Eleventh Judicial Circuit)* Appointed to term beginning Dec 1, 2000. Born Bloomington Illinois Sept 22, 1963. Methodist. Educated at University of Illinois B.A. 1985 and Washington University J.D. 1988. Admitted to practice Illinois 1988. In legal practice El Paso Illinois Nov 15, 1991 to Nov 4, 1998.
State's Attorney Woodford County Nov 4, 1998 to Dec 1, 2000. Instructor in Business Law Eureka College. Member Woodford County and Illinois State Bar Associations. USMC JAGC.
Office: Woodford County Courthouse, 117 East County Street, Eureka 61530.
Telephone: (309) 467-7330.
E-mail address: charlesf@mclean.gov

FEIN, Roger G. *(Circuit Judge, Illinois Circuit Court of Cook County)*
Office: 1303 R. J. Daley Center, Chicago 60602.
Telephone: (312) 603-7959.

FELICE, Peter A. *(Circuit Judge, Illinois Circuit Court of Cook County)*
Office: 1303 R. J. Daley Center, Chicago 60602.
Telephone: (312) 603-7959.

FERGUSON, Edward C. *(Chief Judge, Illinois Circuit Court Third Judicial Circuit)* Former Associate Judge. Assumed office as Circuit Judge. Term expires 2008. Former Chief Judge.
Office: Madison County Courthouse, 155 North Main Street, Edwardsville 62025.
Telephone: (618) 692-6200.

FERGUSON, William I. *(Associate Judge, Illinois Circuit Court Eighteenth Judicial Circuit)* Appointed.
Office: 505 North County Farm Road, Wheaton 60187.
Telephone: (630) 682-6502.

FERNANDEZ, Fé *(Associate Judge, Illinois Circuit Court of Cook County)* Appointed to term beginning Dec 1997. Term expires 2003. Serves Domestic Relations Division. Born Havana Cuba. Educated at Loyola University of Chicago B.A. cum laude 1975 and DePaul University J.D. 1978. Admitted to practice Illinois 1978, U.S. District Court Northern District of Illinois 1978 and U.S. Court of Appeals Seventh Circuit 1978. In legal practice Evanston 1981-97.
With Office of the State Appellate Defender 1978-81. Instructor Roosevelt University 1990-91 and Loyola University of Chicago since 1994. Member Hispanic Lawyers of Illinois, Illinois Judges Association, American Judicature Society and Chicago Bar Association.
Office: 32 West Randolph, Room 1402R, Chicago 60601.
Telephone: (312) 609-3790.

FIGUEROA, Raymond A. *(Circuit Judge, Illinois Circuit Court of Cook County)*
Office: 3002 R. J. Daley Center, Chicago 60602.
Telephone: (312) 603-6667.

FILAN, Denise K. *(Circuit Judge, Illinois Circuit Court of Cook County)*
Office: 1340 South Michigan Avenue, Room 602, Chicago 60605.
Telephone: (312) 341-2889.

FINES, Gerald D. *(Chief Judge, United States Bankruptcy Court Central District of Illinois)* Appointed by U.S. Court of Appeals Seventh Circuit judges to term beginning Aug 18, 1987. Reappointed Aug 18, 2001, current term expires Aug 18, 2015. Chief Judge since June 1, 2000. Born Taylorville Illinois Jan 26, 1940. Educated at Eastern Illinois University B.S. 1965 M.S. 1967 and University of Kentucky J.D. 1970. Admitted to practice Kentucky 1970, District of Columbia 1972 and Illinois 1976. In legal practice Springfield Illinois 1987.
Deputy Director and Acting Director of U.S. Attorneys U.S. Department of Justice 1970-76. U.S. Attorney Central District of Illinois 1977-86. Instructor in Commercial Law Eastern Illinois University 1966-67. Member The District of Columbia Bar, U.S. Court of Federal Claims, U.S. Supreme Court and Illinois State Bar Associations. Corporal U.S. Army 1958-60.
Office: 127 Federal Building, 201 North Vermilion Street, Danville 61832.
Telephone: (217) 431-4817.

FINK, Howard Lewis *(Associate Judge, Illinois Circuit Court of Cook County)* Appointed to term beginning 1982. Reappointed 1988, 1991, 1995 and 1999. Current term expires 2003. Born Chicago Illinois. Educated at University of Wisconsin B.S. with honors 1957 and Harvard University LL.B. 1960. Member Voluntary Defenders. Admitted to practice Illinois 1960 and New Mexico 1973. In legal practice Chicago Illinois since 1960.
Attorney-Advisor Federal Trade Commission 1960-61. Attorney Antitrust Division and Civil Rights Division U.S. Department of Justice 1961-66. Regional General Counsel Executive Office of the President O.E.O. 1966. Assistant U.S. Attorney 1966-67 and Special Assistant Attorney General 1969-71 Illinois. Member Illinois Judges Association, State Bar of New Mexico, Chicago, Northwest Suburban and West Suburban Bar Associations. Attended Sentencing Misdemeanors course 1984 and Advanced Evidence course 1988 The National Judicial College. Recipient Man of Year Award from Wilmette Junior Chamber of Commerce 1975. Village Trustee Wilmette.
Office: 2121 Euclid, Room 103-A, Rolling Meadows 60008.
Telephone: (847) 818-2534.

FISS, Jan V. *(Chief Judge, Illinois Circuit Court Twentieth Judicial Circuit)* Former Associate Judge.
Office: County Building, 10 Public Square, Belleville 62220.
Telephone: (618) 277-6600.

FITZGERALD, Kevin P. *(Associate Judge, Illinois Circuit Court Eleventh Judicial Circuit)*
Office: McLean County Law and Justice Center, 104 West Front Street, Bloomington 61701.
Telephone: (309) 888-5290.

FITZGERALD, Thomas R. *(Justice, Supreme Court of Illinois)* Born Chicago Illinois July 10, 1941. Roman Catholic. Educated at Loyola University 1959-63 and John Marshall Law School LL.B with honors 1968 replaced by J.D. 1970. Honorary LL.D. John Marshall Law School June 1999. Associate Editor The John Marshall Journal of Practice and Procedure Fall 1968. Member Phi Alpha Delta. Admitted to practice Illinois 1968 and U.S. District Court Northern District of Illinois 1968. Former Circuit Judge, Illinois Circuit Court of Cook County, elected to term beginning Dec 6, 1976.
Assistant State's Attorney Cook County 1968-76. Part-time Instructor Legal Writing 1968-70 and Practice Court Judge 1969-73 John Marshall Law School. Part-time Instructor 1977-82, Adjunct Professor since 1982 and Assistant Coordinator Trial Advocacy Program since 1986 Illinois Institute of Technology, Chicago-Kent College of Law. Coach National Champion Trial Advocacy Team Chicago-Kent Law School 1988. Board of Directors Lawyer's Assistance Program since 1986. Chairman Cook County Principals Committee. Member Illinois Truth in Sentencing Commission since 1996. Member Supreme Court Planning and Oversight Committee for Judicial Performance Evaluation, Illinois Judicial Ethics Committee, Governor's Task Force on Crime and Corrections, Cook County Coordinating Council, Judicial Advisory Council, Illinois Supreme Court Special Commission on the Administration of Justice, Illinois Judicial Conference (Member Study Committee on Jury Utilization 1979, Committee on Criminal Law 1986, Regional Committee on Criminal Law 1990 and Supreme Court Committee on Jury Instructions in Criminal Cases since

FITZGERALD, THOMAS R.—*Continued*
1994; Chairman Committee on Sentencing 1981, Committee on Instructions New Judges Seminar 1982-88, Study Committee on the Right to Trial by Jury 1983, Committee on Evidence 1984, Committee on Criminal Law 1987 and Committee on Criminal Law and Probation Administration since 1993), Chicago Inn of Court, Illinois Judges Association (Board of Directors 1981-84 and 1990-95, Treasurer 1985, Secretary 1986, Second Vice President 1988, First Vice President 1989 and President 1990), Chicago (Juvenile Law Committee 1969, Criminal Law Committee 1975-83, Constitutional Law Committee 1976-86, Judiciary Committee since 1987, Traffic Law Committee 1988-89, Board of Managers 1989-91, Chairman 1991-93 and Member since 1991 Long Range Planning Committee) and Illinois State Bar Associations. Faculty Member Conference Einstein Institute for Science, Health and the Courts Aug 1998. Recipient Distinguished Service Award from The John Marshall Law School Alumni Association 1987 and Man of the Year Award from Celtic Lawyers March 1999. USNR 1963-68. Past President Queen of the Universe School Board 1973-74.

Office: 160 North LaSalle, Room N2013, Chicago 60601.
Telephone: (312) 793-5460.

FLANAGAN, Kathy M. *(Circuit Judge, Illinois Circuit Court of Cook County)* Elected to term beginning Dec 8, 1988. Retained by election Dec 1994 and 2000. Current term expires Dec 2006. Born Chicago Illinois Nov 25, 1952. Roman Catholic. Educated at St. Xavier College B.A. 1974 and John Marshall Law School J.D. 1979. Admitted to practice Illinois 1979 and U.S. Court of Appeals Seventh Circuit 1979. In legal practice Chicago 1979-80 and Oak Lawn 1980-88.

Attended numerous seminars for Chicago Bar Association, Illinois State Bar Association, Illinois Institute for Continuing Legal Education, National Business Institute, American Society of Certified Public Accountants, Northwest Suburban Bar, Southwest Bar Association and South Suburban Bar. Faculty Member Illinois Judicial Conference. Democrat.

Office: 2210 R. J. Daley Center, Chicago 60602.
Telephone: (312) 603-6066.

FLANAGAN, Thomas E. *(Circuit Judge, Illinois Circuit Court of Cook County)*
Office: 1610 R. J. Daley Center, Chicago 60602.
Telephone: (312) 603-4834.

FLANNELL, Dan L. *(Circuit Judge, Illinois Circuit Court Sixth Judicial Circuit)* Term expires Dec 2006.
Office: Moultrie County Courthouse, 10 South Main Street, Sullivan 61951.
Telephone: (217) 728-4521.

FLANNERY, James P., Jr. *(Circuit Judge, Illinois Circuit Court of Cook County)* Appointed June 1988. Elected 1990. Retained by election 1996 and 2002. Current term expires Dec 2008. Born Chicago Illinois Feb 27, 1950. Educated at Illinois Institute of Technology B.S. 1973 and John Marshall Law School J.D. 1976. Admitted to practice Illinois 1976.
Office: 2603 R. J. Daley Center, Chicago 60602.
Telephone: (312) 603-6414.
E-mail address: jpflann@cookcountygov.com

FLEMING, John J. *(Circuit Judge, Illinois Circuit Court of Cook County)*
Office: 2600 South California, Chicago 60608.
Telephone: (773) 869-3373.

FLEMING, Susan G. *(Circuit Judge, Illinois Circuit Court of Cook County)*
Office: 1604 R. J. Daley Center, Chicago 60602.
Telephone: (312) 603-4824.

FLOOD, Lawrence E. *(Associate Judge, Illinois Circuit Court of Cook County)*
Office: 400 R. J. Daley Center, Chicago 60602.
Telephone: (312) 603-2600.

FLYNN, Jerry D. *(Circuit Judge, Illinois Circuit Court Twentieth Judicial Circuit)* Appointed Associate Judge to term beginning Oct 7, 1975. Appointed Circuit Judge to term beginning Sept 1, 1988. Elected 1992. Retained by election 1998, current term expires 2004. Born Moline Illinois May 20, 1948. Roman Catholic. Educated at Lewis College 1966-67, Illinois College B.A. 1970 and St. Louis University J.D. 1974. Member Sigma Pi. Admitted to practice Illinois 1974. Began legal practice Red Bud 1974.

Member Illinois Associate Judge Coordinating Committee 1984-88, Committee on Enforcement of Judgments 1985, Committee on Contempt 1987, Committee on Pro Se Litigation 1988 and Subcommittee on Prison Litigation since 1996. Member Illinois Judges Association (Board of Directors since 1985), East St. Louis, Randolph County, St. Clair County and Illinois State Bar Associations. Graduate The National Judicial College 1986 and 1988. Named Illinois College Young Alumnus of 1982 and Illinois College Alumnus of the Year 1988. USAR 1970-75. Member Advisory Board Boy Scouts since 1986. Member Knights of Columbus, Lions Club and American Legion.

Office: Randolph County Courthouse, Chester 62233.
Telephone: (618) 826-2712.

FLYNN, Peter *(Circuit Judge, Illinois Circuit Court of Cook County)* Appointed to term beginning May 17, 1999. Elected Nov 4, 2000, current term expires Dec 4, 2006. Born Bronxville New York July 23, 1942. Roman Catholic. Educated at Harvard College B.A. magna cum laude 1963 and Yale Law School LL.B. 1966. Admitted to practice Illinois 1969. In legal practice Chicago 1969-99.

Assistant Lecturer on Law University of Ife, Nigeria Jan 1967 to Jan 1969. Member Chicago Lincoln Inn of Court, American Law Institute, Illinois State and American Bar Associations. Volunteer U.S. Peace Corps Nigeria 1967-69. Member 1979-85 and Chairman 1983-85 Plan Commission and Trustee 1985-89 Village of Olympia Fields. Judge/Adviser Moot Court. Enjoys history, classical piano, classical guitar, sailing, poetry and theater.

Office: 2408 R. J. Daley Center, Chicago 60602.
Telephone: (312) 603-4158.

FORD, Jeffrey B. *(Associate Judge, Illinois Circuit Court Sixth Judicial Circuit)* Appointed to term beginning July 1, 1985. Reappointed 1987, 1991, 1995 and 1999. Current term expires July 2003. Born Chicago Illinois June 26, 1951. Jewish. Educated at University of Illinois-Urbana B.S. 1973 J.D. 1976. Member Phi Beta Kappa and Phi Kappa Phi. Admitted to practice Illinois

FORD, JEFFREY B.—*Continued*

1976, Florida 1977 and U.S. District Court Central District of Illinois 1979.

Adjunct Instructor University of Illinois Police Training Institute since 1980. Member The Florida Bar and American Bar Association. Instructor in Traffic Law Update Judicial Conference March 1987. Presenter Illinois Department of Alcohol and Substance Abuse Conference 1988, 1989 and 1990 and DUI Judicial Education Conferences June 1990-98.

Office: Champaign County Courthouse, 101 East Main Street, Urbana 61801.

Telephone: (217) 384-1292.

FORD, Nicholas R. *(Circuit Judge, Illinois Circuit Court of Cook County)*

Office: 2600 South California, Room 101, Chicago 60608.

Telephone: (773) 869-3160.

FOREMAN, James L. *(Senior Judge, United States District Court Southern District of Illinois)* Appointed for life by President Richard M. Nixon to term beginning March 7, 1972. Chief Judge 1979-92. Assumed Senior status June 1, 1992, serves by assignment. Born Metropolis Illinois May 12, 1927. Protestant. Educated at University of Illinois B.S. 1950 J.D. 1952. Admitted to practice Illinois 1952. Began legal practice Metropolis 1952. In legal practice 1952-72.

Illinois Assistant Attorney General 1953-60. State's Attorney Massac County 1960-64. Member Judicial Conference Committee on Judicial Resources. Named Alumni of the Month by University of Illinois College of Law 1973. USN 1945-46. Past President Metropolis Chamber of Commerce and Metropolis Board of Education. Member First Christian Church.

Office: U.S. Courthouse, 301 West Main Street, Benton 62812-1362.

Telephone: (618) 439-7740.

FOREMAN, Lester D. *(Circuit Judge, Illinois Circuit Court of Cook County)* Former Associate Judge. Assumed office as Circuit Judge. Term expires 2004.

Office: 2308 R. J. Daley Center, Chicago 60602.

Telephone: (312) 603-6052.

FOSTER, Don Al *(Circuit Judge, Illinois Circuit Court Second Judicial Circuit)* Term expires 2008.

Office: Gallatin County Courthouse, Shawneetown 62984.

Telephone: (618) 269-3094.

FOSTER, Terry J. *(Circuit Judge, Illinois Circuit Court First Judicial Circuit)* Appointed Associate Judge to term beginning Dec 6, 1982. Elected Circuit Judge Dec 5, 1988. Retained by election Nov 8, 1994 and 2000. Current term expires Dec 2006. Born Eldorado Illinois Oct 2, 1948. Baptist. Educated at Southern Illinois University B.A. 1969 and University of Illinois J.D. 1972. Member Phi Alpha Delta. Admitted to practice Illinois 1972 and U.S. District Court Southern District of Illinois 1973. In legal practice Metropolis 1972-82.

Member Illinois Judges Association and Illinois State Bar Association.

Office: Massac County Courthouse, Metropolis 62960.

Telephone: (618) 524-7038.

FOX, Lawrence P. *(Associate Judge, Illinois Circuit Court of Cook County)* Appointed to term beginning Oct 24, 1986. Reappointed 1987, 1991, 1995 and 1999. Current term expires 2003. Born Chicago Illinois Aug 31, 1949. Catholic. Educated at John Carroll University A.B. cum laude 1971 and Loyola University of Chicago J.D. 1975. Admitted to practice Illinois 1975 and U.S. District Court Northern District of Illinois 1975. In legal practice Oak Park 1983-86.

Assistant Public Defender Cook County 1975-83. Instructor in Trial Advocacy DePaul University College of Law since 1984.

Office: 2600 South California, Room 301, Chicago 60608.

Telephone: (773) 869-7437.

FRANK, Charles H. *(Associate Judge, Illinois Circuit Court Eleventh Judicial Circuit)* Appointed to term beginning May 1, 1982. Reappointed to subsequent terms. Born Berwyn Illinois May 20, 1948. Lutheran. Educated at Illinois State University B.S.B.A. and John Marshall Law School J.D. with high honors. Admitted to practice Illinois 1977. Began legal practice Pontiac 1977.

Assistant State's Attorney 1978-82. Member Livingston County and Illinois State Bar Associations. E-5 USAR 1970-76. Republican. Board member Cancer Society and Sheltered Rehabilitation Workshop.

Office: Livingston County Courthouse, Pontiac 61764.

Telephone: (815) 844-5166.

FRANKLAND, David K. *(Circuit Judge, Illinois Circuit Court Second Judicial Circuit)*

Mailing address: P.O. Box 149, Albion 62806.

Telephone: (618) 445-3414.

FRANKS, Helen R. *(Associate Judge, Illinois Circuit Court Nineteenth Judicial Circuit)*

Office: Lake County Courthouse, 18 North County Street, Waukegan 60085.

Telephone: (847) 377-3747.

FRAZIER, Philip M. *(Magistrate Judge, United States District Court Southern District of Illinois)* Appointed by U.S. District Court judges to term beginning May 1987. Reappointed 1995 and May 2003. Current term May 2011.

Office: U.S. Courthouse, 301 West Main Street, Benton 62812-1362.

Telephone: (618) 439-7750.

FREDERICK, Robert G. *(Judge, Illinois Court of Claims)* Appointed by Governor Jim Edgar to term beginning July 1992. Reappointed 1998, current term expires July 2004. Born Evanston Illinois Feb 11, 1948. Protestant. Educated at Northern Illinois University B.S. 1969 and University of Illinois J.D. with honors 1972. Member Phi Delta Phi and Order of the Coif. Admitted to practice Illinois 1972, U.S. District Court Central District of Illinois 1974, U.S. Court of Appeals Seventh Circuit 1975 and U.S. Supreme Court 1978. In legal practice Evanston 1972 and Urbana 1972-2002.

Assistant State's Attorney Champaign County 1972-75. Public Defender Champaign County 1975-79. Instructor in Business Law at Parkland Junior College 1978-81. Instructor University of Illinois Police Training Institute 1985-92. Member Illinois State and American Bar Associations. Republican. Enjoys fishing, golf and travel.

Office: 129 West Main, Urbana 61801.

Telephone: (217) 367-9025.

FREDERICKSEN, Chris L. *(Associate Judge, Illinois Circuit Court Tenth Judicial Circuit)*
Office: Peoria County Courthouse, 324 Main Street, Peoria 61602-1363.
Telephone: (309) 672-6944.

FREEMAN, Allen A. *(Recalled Circuit Judge, Illinois Circuit Court of Cook County)* Retired, serves by recall.
Office: 2110 R. J. Daley Center, Chicago 60602.
Telephone: (312) 603-3386.

FREEMAN, Charles E. *(Justice, Supreme Court of Illinois)* Elected to term beginning Dec 3, 1990. Retained by election Dec 2000, current term expires Dec 2010. Former Chief Justice. First African-American to serve on Supreme Court of Illinois. Born Richmond Virginia Dec 12, 1933. Presbyterian. Educated at Virginia Union University B.A. 1954 and John Marshall Law School J.D. 1962. Awarded honorary LL.D. John Marshall Law School. Admitted to practice Illinois 1962. In legal practice Chicago 1962-1976. Circuit Judge, Illinois Circuit Court of Cook County 1976-86. Justice, Illinois Appellate Court First Judicial District 1986-90.
Assistant Illinois Attorney General 1964. Assistant State's Attorney 1964. Assistant Attorney Board of Election Commissioners 1964-65. Arbitrator Illinois Industrial Commission Jan 1965 to Sept 1973. Commissioner Illinois Commerce Commission Sept 1973 to Dec 1976. Member Illinois Judicial Council, Illinois Judges Association, American Judges Association, American Judicature Society, Chicago, Cook County, DuPage County and Illinois State Bar Associations. Recipient Kenneth E. Wilson Award, Certificate of Merit, Ida Platt Award, Presidential Award and Judicial Award from Cook County Bar Association; Kenneth Wilson Memorial Award and Meritorious Service Award from Illinois Judicial Council; Guardians Award of Appreciation; Certificate of Merit from John Marshall Law School Alumni Association; Certificate of Achievement from International Christian Fellowship Missions; Earl B. Dickerson Award from Chicago Bar Association; Certificate of Recognition from Task Force on Opportunities for Minorities in the Judicial Administration and The Commission on Opportunities for Minorities in the Profession American Bar Association; and Cornelius Francis Stradford Award from State's Attorney of Cook County. Specialist Three U.S. Army as Courts and Boards Reporter in Korea 1956-58. Property and Insurance Consultant Cook County Department of Public Aid 1959-64. Member Conference to Fulfill These Rights (Board of Directors), Englewood Businessmen and Civic League (Past Vice President) and Garfield Park Community Growth Center, Inc. (Board of Directors). Hobbies include photography and collecting cameo glass and soapstone.
Office: 160 North LaSalle Street, Room N2014, Chicago 60601.
Telephone: (312) 793-5480.

FREESE, Chris E. *(Associate Judge, Illinois Circuit Court Sixth Judicial Circuit)*
Office: 10 Moultrie County Courthouse, 10 South Main Street, Sullivan 61951.
Telephone: (217) 728-7123.

FREESE, John P. *(Chief Judge, Illinois Circuit Court Eleventh Judicial Circuit)* Appointed Associate Judge to term beginning Aug 16, 1982. Elected Circuit Judge 1992. Retained by election 1998, current term expires 2004. Chief Judge since 2000. Born Bloomington Illinois Sept 17, 1947. United Methodist. Educated at Illinois State University B.S. magna cum laude 1969 and University of Michigan J.D. 1972. Admitted to practice Michigan 1972, Illinois 1976 and U.S. District Court Central District of Illinois 1979. In legal practice Bloomington Illinois 1976-82.
Member American Judicature Society, McLean County, Illinois State and American Bar Associations. Faculty member at several judicial seminars Administrative Office of Illinois Courts. Lieutenant USN JAGC 1973-76. McLean County Board of Supervisors 1979-82. Board of Directors Salvation Army and McLean County Compact. Board of Trustees Illinois Symphony Orchestra. Member First United Methodist Church, Normal Illinois. Enjoys walking, bicycle riding and reading.
Office: Law and Justice Center, 104 West Front Street, Bloomington 61701.
Telephone: (309) 888-5222.

FREITAG, Robert L. *(Associate Judge, Illinois Circuit Court Eleventh Judicial Circuit)*
Office: McLean County Law and Justice Center, 104 West Front Street, Bloomington 61701.
Telephone: (309) 888-5220.

FRENCH, Dorothy F. *(Associate Judge, Illinois Circuit Court Eighteenth Judicial Circuit)*
Office: 505 North County Farm Road, Wheaton 60187.
Telephone: (630) 682-7300.

FRITTS, David T. *(Circuit Judge, Illinois Circuit Court Fifteenth Judicial Circuit)*
Mailing address: P.O. Box 304, Dixon 61021.
Office: Lee County Courts Building, Dixon 61021.
Telephone: (815) 284-5257.

FRITZ, Michael John *(Associate Judge, Illinois Circuit Court Nineteenth Judicial Circuit)* Appointed to term beginning Oct 14, 1986. Reappointed 1987, 1991, 1995 and 1999. Current term expires 2003. Born Milwaukee Wisconsin Feb 12, 1950. Episcopalian. Educated at Carroll College B.S. 1972 and John Marshall Law School J.D. 1976. Admitted to practice Wisconsin 1976, U.S. District Court Eastern District of Wisconsin 1976 and Illinois 1983. In legal practice Milwaukee Wisconsin 1976-77 and West Bend Wisconsin 1980-83.
Assistant District Attorney Waukesha Wisconsin 1977-80. City Attorney West Bend Wisconsin 1980-83. First Deputy State's Attorney Lake County Illinois 1983-86. Member Illinois Judges Association and State Bar of Wisconsin. Attends numerous legal and judicial conferences, seminars and CLE.
Office: Lake County Courthouse, 18 North County Street, Waukegan 60085.
Telephone: (847) 377-3600.

FROBISH, Harold J. *(Circuit Judge, Illinois Circuit Court Eleventh Judicial Circuit)* Former Associate Judge.
Office: Livingston County Courthouse, Pontiac 61764.
Telephone: (815) 844-5171.

FUNDERBURK, Raymond *(Circuit Judge, Illinois Circuit Court of Cook County)*
Office: 1504 R. J. Daley Center, Chicago 60602.
Telephone: (312) 603-4812.

GAINER, Thomas V., Jr. *(Recalled Circuit Judge, Illinois Circuit Court of Cook County)* Retired, serves by recall.
Office: 400 R. J. Daley Center, Chicago 60602.
Telephone: (312) 603-2600.

GALASSO, Nicholas J. *(Associate Judge, Illinois Circuit Court Eighteenth Judicial Circuit)*
Office: DuPage County Judicial Center, 505 North County Farm Road, Wheaton 60187.
Telephone: (630) 682-7186.

GALLAGHER, Michael J. *(Judge, Illinois Appellate Court First Judicial District Division Six)* Born Evergreen Park Illinois Feb 7, 1953. Educated at University of Illinois at Chicago B.A. with honors 1975 and Chicago-Kent College of Law J.D. with honors 1978. Editor Chicago-Kent Law Review. Law Clerk to Hon. William G. Clark, Supreme Court of Illinois 1979-81. In legal practice 1981-88. Former Circuit Judge, Illinois Circuit Court of Cook County, appointed to term beginning 1988. Served Illinois Appellate Court First Judicial District Division One by special assignment.
Staff Attorney U.S. Securities and Exchange Commission 1978-79. Member Illinois Judges Association, Women's Bar Association of Illinois and Chicago Bar Association.
Office: 160 North LaSalle Street, Room N1709, Chicago 60601.
Telephone: (312) 793-5406.

GALLEY, Kevin R. *(Circuit Judge, Illinois Circuit Court Tenth Judicial Circuit)* Associate Judge March 1, 2001 to Dec 2, 2002. Elected Circuit Judge Nov 5, 2002. Born Ottawa Illinois June 22, 1954. Roman Catholic. Educated at University of Illinois at Urbana-Champaign B.A. 1976 and St. Louis University J.D. 1980. Admitted to practice Illinois 1980.
Public Defender Marshall County 1980-2001. Member Marshall County and Illinois State Bar Associations. Member Marshall County Summer Baseball League.
Office: 324 Main Street, Peoria 61602.
Telephone: (309) 672-6037.

GAMBER, Terry H. *(Circuit Judge, Illinois Circuit Court Second Judicial Circuit)* Former Chief Judge.
Mailing address: P.O. Box 1266, Mount Vernon 62864.
Telephone: (618) 244-8005.

GAMBRELL, Richard H. *(Associate Judge, Illinois Circuit Court Ninth Judicial Circuit)*
Office: Hancock County Courthouse, Carthage 62321.
Telephone: (309) 837-4891.

GARBER, Sheldon C. *(Associate Judge, Illinois Circuit Court of Cook County)* Appointed June 17, 1985. Reappointed July 1, 1987, July 1, 1991, July 1, 1995 and July 1999. Current term expires 2003. Born Chicago Illinois July 19, 1938. Jewish. Educated at John Marshall Law School J.D. 1964. Member Nu Beta Epsilon. Admitted to practice Illinois 1964. In legal practice Chicago 1964-85.
Office: 1404 R. J. Daley Center, Chicago 60602.
Telephone: (312) 603-4864.

GARCIA, Rodolfo *(Circuit Judge, Illinois Circuit Court of Cook County)* Assumed office Dec 1996. Served Criminal Division April 1997 to March 2003. On assignment by Supreme Court of Illinois as Judge, Illinois Appellate Court First Judicial District Division Three since March 2003. Educated at University of Illinois at Champaign-Urbana B.S. in Economics and University of Chicago J.D. Began legal practice 1983.
Office: 160 North LaSalle Street, Chicago 60601.

GARDNER, Sheldon *(Circuit Judge, Illinois Circuit Court of Cook County)* Appointed Associate Judge June 15, 1988. Reappointed June 27, 1991. Elected Circuit Judge Nov 1992. Retained by election 1998. Current term expires Dec 2004. Born Chicago Illinois May 27, 1928. Educated at University of Chicago A.B. with honors 1946 and Illinois Institute of Technology, Chicago-Kent College of Law J.D. 1953. Admitted to practice Illinois 1954, U.S. District Court Northern District of Illinois 1955, U.S. Courts of Appeals Fifth 1985 and Seventh 1985 Circuits and U.S. Supreme Court 1986. In legal practice 1954-73 and 1976-88.
Deputy State's Attorney and Chief Civil Division Office of State's Attorney Cook County 1973-76. Village Attorney Justice 1981-83. Author "Increasing the Effectiveness of the Criminal Prosecutor Through Creative Use of the Civil Courts" 10 No. 4 *The Prosecutor* National District Attorneys Association 1974-76; Civil Remedies Chapter "Economic Crime Project" *Manual of Investigation and Prosecution of Economic Crimes;* "Candidate's Guide to Filing for Political Office in Illinois" and "The Role of the Prosecutor in Vote Fraud" Chicago Community Trust—Project Leap Publication; and "Liabilities and Immunities of Prosecutors and Other Local Officials Under the Federal Civil Rights Acts" *The Prosecutor's Deskbook* 2nd ed. National District Attorneys Association. Co-author with Celeste E. Kralovec "Federal Protections of Individual Rights in Local Elections" 13 John Marshall L. Rev. 701, 1980 and Chapter 5 "The Illinois Civil War Over Transportation Facility Sovereign Immunity" *Transportation Negligence 1984* Illinois Institute for Continuing Legal Education 5-1, 1984. Co-author Chapter 1 and General Editor "Getting on the Ballot" *Election Law Practice Handbook 1985* Illinois Institute for Continuing Legal Education 1985. Instructor John Marshall Law School Graduate Division 1974-75, Illinois Institute of Technology, Chicago-Kent College of Law 1977-78 and Loyola University School of Law. Adjunct Instructor in Human Services Administration Spertus College of Judaica. Former Member, Chairman Corporate Civil Committee 1974-75, National Board Member 1974-76, Board of Directors 1977-81 and General Counsel 1980 National District Attorneys Association. Former Member Illinois State's Attorney Association and Federal Bar Association. Arbitrator American Arbitration Association. Member Decalogue Society of Lawyers (Board of Directors 1976 and 1990-91), Illinois Judges Association, Chicago (Former Member and Chair Election Law Committee 1985-87, Former Member Matrimonial Law Committee, Committee on Candidates and Local Government Law Committee), Illinois State (Former Member Family Law Committee and Administrative Law Committee) and American Bar Associations. Participant "The Prosecutor's Use of Civil Remedies" March 1974, "The Use of Civil Remedies to Combat Consumer Fraud" March 1975, "The Prosecutor and The Press" Annual Meeting Aug 1975, "Choosing Between Civil, Criminal and Administrative Remedies for Consumer Fraud Units" Economic Crimes Unit Winter 1975 and "Prosecutorial Immunity" March 1976 National District Attorneys Association; "Relating Between County Boards and State's Attorneys in Illinois" Annual Meet-

GARDNER, SHELDON—*Continued*

ing Illinois State's Attorneys Association 1975; "County Government—Illinois Special District" IICLE Chicago, Springfield and Rockford 1977; "The Liability Crisis in County Government" National Association of Counties, National Association of County Civil Attorneys and National District Attorneys Association San Diego Feb 1980, Chicago Oct 1979 and Atlanta June 1979; "Transportation Facility Negligence" American Bar Association Tampa Feb 1985; "Representing the Business of Politics" May 1986 and "Creative Use of Civil Remedies" Young Lawyers Division Chicago Bar Association; "Making Effective Use of Pretrials in Settling Domestic Relations Cases" Law Education Series Illinois State Bar Association Dec 1990; and "Administrative and Judicial Review of Candidates Petition Challenges" Project Leap Seminar. Moderator "Illinois Real Estate Taxation" Illinois Institute for Continuing Legal Education Chicago May 1979. Planning Chairman and Participant "Legal Aspects of a Political Campaign: Candidates, Parties, Contributions" Committee on Continuing Professional Education American Bar Association Arlington April 1980 and "Transportation Negligence" Illinois Institute for Continuing Legal Education July 1984. Panelist "For the Plaintiff: Settlement Procedures and Techniques in the Public Facility" Liability Conference Illinois Institute for Continuing Legal Education Oct 1985. Recipient Award for Services as Co-chairman Israel Bond Dinner March 1974. Parliamentarian Cook County Republican Convention April 1988. Former State Chairman Independent Voters of Illinois. Former Member Executive Committee Republican Party of Evanston, Illinois. Chair Convention Committee and Member Executive Committee National Unity Party. Political Analyst Dave Baum Today WMAQ-TV. Former Executive Vice President South East Community Organization. Founding Chairman/Board Member Project LEAP (Legal Elections in All Precincts). Chairman Property Value Maintenance Committee. Board Member Chicago Jewish Historical Society. Instructor Elderhostel Program Jewish Community Centers of Chicago since 1993. Member Evanston Zoning Board of Appeals 1977-85, Beth Emet Synagogue (Reform), Chicago Loop Synagogue (Traditional) and American Jewish Historical Society.

Office: 2306 R. J. Daley Center, Chicago 60602.
Telephone: (312) 603-6048.

GARMAN, Rita B. *(Justice, Supreme Court of Illinois)* Assumed office Feb 2001. Elected Nov 5, 2002, current term expires 2012. Born Aurora Illinois Nov 19, 1943. Methodist. Educated at University of Illinois B.S. with highest honors 1965 and University of Iowa J.D. with distinction 1968. Member Mortar Board, Beta Gamma Sigma and Phi Kappa Phi. Admitted to practice Illinois 1968 and Iowa 1968. Associate Judge Jan 7, 1974 to 1986 and Circuit Judge 1986 to July 16, 1995, Illinois Circuit Court Fifth Judicial Circuit. Judge, Illinois Appellate Court Fourth Judicial District, appointed to term beginning July 17, 1995.

Assistant State's Attorney Vermilion County 1969-73. Member Vermilion County, Iowa State and Illinois State Bar Associations. Republican.

Office: 3607 North Vermilion, Suite 1, Danville 61832-1478.
Telephone: (217) 431-8928.

GARRISON, James E. *(Associate Judge, Illinois Circuit Court Twelfth Judicial Circuit)*
Office: 14 West Jefferson Street, Joliet 60432.
Telephone: (815) 727-8540.

GAUGHAN, Vincent M. *(Circuit Judge, Illinois Circuit Court of Cook County)*
Office: 2600 South California, Chicago 60608.
Telephone: (773) 869-3190.

GAUSSELIN, Edwin A., Jr. *(Associate Judge, Illinois Circuit Court of Cook County)*
Office: 16501 South Kedzie Parkway, Markham 60426.
Telephone: (708) 210-4170.

GAVIN, James J. *(Circuit Judge, Illinois Circuit Court of Cook County)*
Office: 16501 South Kedzie Parkway, Markham 60426.
Telephone: (708) 210-4170.

GEIGER, Donald H. *(Associate Judge, Illinois Circuit Court Nineteenth Judicial Circuit)*
Office: Lake County Courthouse, 18 North County Street, Waukegan 60085.
Telephone: (847) 377-3757.

GETTLEMAN, Robert W. *(Judge, United States District Court Northern District of Illinois)* Appointed for life by President Bill Clinton to term beginning Oct 21, 1994. Born May 5, 1943. Educated at University of Florida 1963, Boston University B.S.B.A. cum laude 1965 and Northwestern University School of Law J.D. cum laude 1968. Law Clerk to Hon. Latham Castle and Hon. Luther M. Swygert, U.S. Court of Appeals Seventh Circuit 1968-70. In legal practice 1970-94.

Member Chicago Council of Lawyers, Chicago and American Bar Associations.

Office: U.S. Courthouse, 219 South Dearborn Street, Chicago 60604.
Telephone: (312) 435-5543.

GILBERT, J. Phil *(Judge, United States District Court Southern District of Illinois)* Appointed for life by President George Bush to term beginning Oct 1, 1992. Former Chief Judge. Born Carbondale Illinois March 11, 1949. Methodist. Educated at University of Illinois B.S. 1971 and Loyola University School of Law J.D. 1974. Member Phi Alpha Delta. Admitted to practice Illinois 1974. In legal practice Carbondale 1974-88. Circuit Judge, Illinois Circuit Court First Judicial Circuit 1988-92.

Member and Chairman Illinois State Board of Elections 1978-87. Member Jackson County and Illinois State Bar Associations.

Office: U.S. Courthouse, 301 West Main Street, Benton 62812-1362.
Telephone: (618) 435-3779.

GILL, Timothy R. *(Circuit Judge, Illinois Circuit Court Seventeenth Judicial Circuit)* Former Associate Judge.
Office: Winnebago County Courthouse, 400 West State Street, Rockford 61101.
Telephone: (815) 987-3062.

GILLERAN JOHNSON, Barbara *(Judge, Illinois Appellate Court Second Judicial District)* Former Asso-

GILLERAN JOHNSON, BARBARA—*Continued*

ciate Judge and Circuit Judge, Illinois Circuit Court Nineteenth Judicial Circuit.
Office: 236 Robert Parker Coffin Road, Long Grove 60047.
Telephone: (847) 821-1763.

GILLESPIE, Daniel T. *(Associate Judge, Illinois Circuit Court of Cook County)*
Office: 1106 R. J. Daley Center, Chicago 60602.
Telephone: (312) 603-4548.

GILLIS, Susan Fox *(Associate Judge, Illinois Circuit Court of Cook County)* Elected to term beginning Nov 1, 1999. Term expires 2003. Born Cleveland Ohio June 13, 1943. Educated at DePaul University B.A. 1982 and Illinois Institute of Technology, Chicago-Kent College of Law J.D. 1988. Admitted to practice Illinois 1988 and U.S. District Court Northern District of Illinois 1988. In legal practice Chicago May 1988 to Oct 1999.
President 1994-95 and Member Foundation Board Women's Bar Association of Illinois. President National Association of Women Lawyers 1998-99. Board of Directors Chicago Bar Association 1995-97. Member Illinois Judges Association, Illinois State and American Bar Associations. Recipient Young Alumni Award from Illinois Institute of Technology, Chicago-Kent College of Law 1996, Golden Gavel Award from CARPLS 2000 and Special Service Award from Grateful House 2000. Board of Directors Grateful House 1994-2000 and CARPLS 1996-98. Enjoys quilting and travel.
Office: 1708 R. J. Daley Center, Chicago 60602.
Telephone: (312) 603-4098.
E-mail address: SFOXGILLIS@AOL.COM

GINEX, Gregory R. *(Associate Judge, Illinois Circuit Court of Cook County)*
Office: 1500 Maybrook Drive, Maywood 60153.
Telephone: (708) 865-6060.

GINSBERG, Robert E. *(Recalled Judge, United States Bankruptcy Court Northern District of Illinois)* Appointed Judge by U.S. Court of Appeals Seventh Circuit judges to term beginning June 6, 1985. Reappointed Dec 1999. Appointed Recalled Judge by the Judicial Council of the Seventh Circuit 2002. Born Cambridge Massachusetts Jan 4, 1945. Educated at Brown University B.A. 1966, American University J.D. 1969 and Harvard Law School LL.M. 1974. Staff member American University Law Review. Member Phi Delta Phi. Admitted to practice District of Columbia 1969, U.S. District Courts District of Columbia 1970 and Northern District of Illinois 1975 and U.S. Court of Appeals Seventh Circuit 1980. In legal practice Chicago 1977-85.
Trial Attorney Branch of Reorganization Division of Corporate Regulation U.S. Securities and Exchange Commission 1969-73. Inquiry Panel/Hearing Board Member Illinois Attorney Registration and Disciplinary Commission 1977-85. Vice Chair National Bankruptcy Review Commission. Author "Bankruptcy Law, Seventh Circuit Survey" 53 Chicago-Kent L. Rev. 190, 1977; "Introduction to the Symposium: The Bankruptcy Reform Act of 1978—A Primer" 28 DePaul L. Rev. 923, 1979; "The Bankruptcy Reform Act of 1978, Creditors' Rights Handbook" 1980 IICLE; "The Bankruptcy Improvements Act—The Creditors Strike Back" 3, 1982 and "The Bankruptcy Improvements Act—An Update" 235, 1983 Northern Illinois L. Rev.; and *Treatise on Bankruptcy Law* Prentice Hall 1985, 2nd ed. 1989 (Supp. 1990). Co-author "Overview of the Bankruptcy Reform Act, Bankruptcy Practice Handbook" IICLE 1981 and with Hon. Robert D. Martin *Bankruptcy: Text, Statute Rules, Forms* 4th ed. Aspen Law and Business 1996. Important Decisions: In re Tek-Aids Industries (pre-petition security interest in general intangibles and proceeds does not cover proceeds of a preference action) 145 B.R. 253, 1985; Matter of Reda (no jury trials in preference actions) 60 B.R. 178, 1986; and In re Alvi (debt incurred on charge cards is dischargeable since use of card is not representative of anything) 191 B.R. 724, 1996. Professor of Law DePaul University College of Law 1974-85. Visiting Professor of Law University of Illinois Spring 1984. Fellow American College of Bankruptcy. Chair Bankruptcy Education Committee. Member Federal Judicial Center (Board Member 1987-91), National Bankruptcy Conference, National Conference of Bankruptcy Judges, American Bankruptcy Institute, Bankruptcy Planning Group, Southwestern Legal Foundation and Chicago Bar Association (Bankruptcy and Reorganization Committee 1984-85). Faculty Member Bankruptcy Judges' Educational Seminars Federal Judicial Center 1984-85. Lecturer or Conference Chair numerous CLE conferences and seminars. Enjoys skiing, golf, ice hockey and history.
Office: U.S. Courthouse, 219 South Dearborn Street, Chicago 60604.
Telephone: (312) 435-5530.

GLENN, James R. *(Chief Judge, Illinois Circuit Court Fifth Judicial Circuit)* Elected 1998. Born Mattoon Illinois Dec 23, 1959. Presbyterian. Educated at University of Illinois A.B. 1982 and Southern Illinois University J.D. 1985. Admitted to practice Illinois 1985. In legal practice Mattoon 1985-98.
Member Coles-Cumberland, Edgar County and Illinois State Bar Associations. Republican. Enjoys coaching youth sports.
Office: Coles County Courthouse, Second Floor, 651 Jackson Avenue, Charleston 61920.
Telephone: (217) 348-9407.
Fax: (217) 348-7395
E-mail address: JGlenn@co.coles.il.us

GLENNON, Charles Edward *(Recalled Circuit Judge, Illinois Circuit Court Twenty-first Judicial Circuit)* Appointed to Eleventh Judicial Circuit to term beginning Jan 1, 1976. Elected Nov 1976. Retained by election. Former Chief Judge. Retired, serves by recall. Born Monticello Illinois April 5, 1942. Episcopalian. Educated at University of Illinois B.A. 1964 J.D. 1966. Admitted to practice Illinois 1966 and U.S. Supreme Court 1974. In legal practice Pontiac 1968-73 and Dwight 1973-75.
Dwight Village Attorney 1973-75. Author and Lecturer on Domestic Relations and Custody Disputes. Fellow The Illinois Bar Foundation. Member Illinois Council of Juvenile and Family Court Judges, Illinois Judges Association, Livingston County and Illinois State Bar Associations. E-5 U.S. Army 1966-68. Republican. Former Member Dwight Community Chest. Chairman Advisory Board Pontiac Salvation Army 1976. Member Regional Planning Commission, Livingston County Commission

GLENNON, CHARLES EDWARD—*Continued*

on Children and Youth, Dwight Chamber of Commerce (Board of Directors 1974-75), Lions, Rotary and Elks.

Office: Kankakee County Courthouse, 450 East Court Street, Kankakee 60901.

Telephone: (815) 937-2915.

GLOWACKI, Francis W. *(Circuit Judge, Illinois Circuit Court of Cook County)* Former Associate Judge. Assumed office as Circuit Judge 1979.

Office: 2121 Euclid, Room 210-A, Rolling Meadows 60008.

Telephone: (847) 818-2535.

GOLDBERG, Allen S. *(Circuit Judge, Illinois Circuit Court of Cook County)*

Office: 2303 R. J. Daley Center, Chicago 60602.

Telephone: (312) 603-6078.

GOLDEN, Patricia P. *(Associate Judge, Illinois Circuit Court Sixteenth Judicial Circuit)*

Office: DeKalb County Courthouse, 133 West State Street, Sycamore 60178.

Telephone: (815) 895-7160.

GOLDENHERSH, Richard P. *(Judge, Illinois Appellate Court Fifth Judicial District)* Assumed office 1988. Term expires Dec 2008. Born East St. Louis Illinois July 16, 1944. Educated at Washington University A.B. 1966 J.D. 1969. Associate Judge 1975-82 and Circuit Judge 1982-88, Illinois Circuit Court Twentieth Judicial Circuit.

Past President Illinois Judges Association. Member St. Clair County and Illinois State Bar Associations.

Office: 56 South 65th Street, Suite 6, Belleville 62223.

Telephone: (618) 397-9733.

GOLDGAR, A. Benjamin *(Judge, United States Bankruptcy Court Northern District of Illinois)* Appointed by U.S. Court of Appeals Seventh Circuit judges to term beginning Feb 3, 2003. Term expires Feb 2, 2017. Born Appleton Wisconsin Jan 15, 1957. Educated at Brown University A.B. magna cum laude 1979 and Northwestern University School of Law J.D. 1982. Editorial Board Journal of Criminal Law and Criminology. Member Phi Beta Kappa. Admitted to practice Illinois 1982, U.S. District Courts Northern 1982 and Central 1991 Districts of Illinois and Eastern District of Wisconsin 1989, U.S. Courts of Appeals Seventh 1985, Eighth 2001, District of Columbia 2001 and Eleventh 2002 Circuits, Trial Bar of U.S. District Court Northern District of Illinois 1988 and U.S. Supreme Court 1991. In legal practice Chicago Illinois 1982-95.

Assistant Attorney General 1995-2003 and Supervising Attorney 1997-2003 Civil Appeals Division Office of the Illinois Attorney General.

Office: 219 South Dearborn, Room 668, Chicago 60604.

Telephone: (312) 435-5642.

GOLNIEWICZ, Francis X., Jr. *(Circuit Judge, Illinois Circuit Court of Cook County)*

Office: 1500 Maybrook Drive, Maywood 60153.

Telephone: (708) 865-6060.

GOODWIN, John *(Associate Judge, Illinois Circuit Court Twentieth Judicial Circuit)* Appointed to term beginning March 6, 1989. Reappointed 1991, 1995 and 1999. Current term expires 2003. Born East St. Louis Illinois June 22, 1948. Catholic. Educated at Southern Illinois University A.B. 1970 and St. Louis University J.D. 1973. Associate Editor St. Louis University Law Journal 1971-72. Law Clerk to Hon. Edward C. Eberspacher, Illinois Appellate Court District Five 1972-73. Admitted to practice Illinois 1974 and U.S. District Court Southern District of Illinois 1974. In legal practice East St. Louis and Belleville 1978-89.

Assistant State's Attorney 1973-78. City Prosecutor East St. Louis 1980-84. Author "Judicially Refining the Missouri Long-Arm Statute: A Tort as The Minimum Contact" 16 No. 2 St. Louis University L. Jour. Winter 1971. Associate Professor of Business Law McKendree College 1989-98. Member East St. Louis, St. Clair County and Illinois State Bar Associations. Recipient Public Service Award from St. Clair County 1978, Boy Scouts National Award for Distinguished Service to Youth 1988 and Public Service Award from U.S. Department of Justice 1991. Executive Board Boy Scouts of America. Member Rotary (Past President). Enjoys snow boarding and motorcycling.

Office: County Building, 10 Public Square, Belleville 62220.

Telephone: (618) 277-7325.

GORDON, Joseph *(Judge, Illinois Appellate Court First Judicial District Division One)* Appointed 1989. Elected 1990. Retained by election 2000, current term expires Dec 2010. Formerly served Division Two. Born Chicago Illinois Dec 4, 1932. Educated at Roosevelt University B.A. 1954 and Northwestern University School of Law J.D. 1960. Law Clerk to Hon. Julius J. Hoffman, U.S. District Court Northern District of Illinois 1960-61. Circuit Judge, Illinois Circuit Court of Cook County 1976-83 and 1988-89.

Office: 160 North LaSalle Street, Room S1908, Chicago 60601.

Telephone: (312) 793-4503.

GORDON, Robert E. *(Circuit Judge, Illinois Circuit Court of Cook County)*

Office: 1403 R. J. Daley Center, Chicago 60602.

Telephone: (312) 603-4157.

GORMAN, John A. *(Magistrate Judge, United States District Court Central District of Illinois)* Appointed by U.S. District Court judges to term beginning Feb 18, 2000. Term expires Feb 2008. Former Circuit Judge and Chief Judge, Illinois Circuit Court Tenth Judicial Circuit.

Office: 211 U.S. Courthouse, 100 N.E. Monroe Street, Peoria 61602.

Telephone: (309) 671-7140.

Fax: (309) 671-7141

GOSHGARIAN, John Robert *(Circuit Judge, Illinois Circuit Court Nineteenth Judicial Circuit)* Appointed Associate Judge to term beginning Aug 1983. Elected Circuit Judge to term beginning Dec 1, 1986. Retained by election 1992 and 1998. Current term expires Dec 2004. Former Chief Judge. Born Waukegan Illinois April 27, 1946. Catholic. Educated at Northwestern University B.A. 1968 and University of Illinois J.D. 1971. Admitted to practice Illinois 1972, U.S. District Court District of Illinois, U.S. Supreme Court and U.S. Court of Appeals. Began legal practice Waukegan 1972. In legal practice Round Lake 1974-83.

Former Public Administrator, Public Guardian, Assistant State's Attorney and Assistant Attorney General Lake County. Member Lake County and Illinois State

GOSHGARIAN, JOHN ROBERT—*Continued*

Bar Associations. Republican. Former Trustee Village of Round Lake. President Beach Park Lions.

Office: Lake County Courthouse, 18 North County Street, Waukegan 60085-4359.

Telephone: (847) 377-3702.

GOTTSCHALL, Joan B. *(Judge, United States District Court Northern District of Illinois)* Magistrate Judge 1984-96. Appointed Judge for life by President Bill Clinton to term beginning 1996. Educated at Smith College B.A. cum laude 1969 and Stanford Law School J.D. 1973. In legal practice 1973-76 and 1978-82.

Staff Attorney Federal Defender Program 1976-78. Attorney Office of Legal Counsel University of Chicago 1983-84. Member Rules Committee and Chair Anti-Discrimination Task Force U.S. District Court Northern District of Illinois. Member American Law Institute, Women's Bar Association of Illinois, Chicago and American Bar Associations. Board of Directors Constitutional Rights Foundation of Chicago and Illinois Humanities Council. Board of Directors Martin Marty Center and Member and Former Chair Visiting Committee University of Chicago Divinity School. Founder The Second Tuesday Group.

Office: U.S. Courthouse, 219 South Dearborn Street, Chicago 60604.

Telephone: (312) 435-5640.

GRABIEC, Edwin B. *(Associate Judge, Illinois Circuit Court Twelfth Judicial Circuit)*

Office: Will County Courthouse, 14 West Jefferson Street, Joliet 60432.

Telephone: (815) 727-8556.

GRADY, John F. *(Senior Judge, United States District Court Northern District of Illinois)* Appointed for life by President Gerald R. Ford to term beginning Jan 5, 1976. Former Chief Judge. Assumed Senior status, serves by assignment. Born Chicago Illinois May 23, 1929. Educated at Northwestern University B.S. 1952 J.D. 1954. Associate Editor Northwestern University Law Review. Member Phi Beta Kappa. Admitted to practice Illinois 1955. Began legal practice Chicago 1955. In legal practice Waukegan 1963-76. Assistant U.S. Attorney Northern District of Illinois 1956-61.

Office: U.S. Courthouse, 219 South Dearborn Street, Chicago 60604.

Telephone: (312) 435-5848.

GRADY, Joseph M. *(Circuit Judge, Illinois Circuit Court Sixteenth Judicial Circuit)*

Office: 400B Kane County Judicial Center, 37W777 Route 38, St. Charles 60175.

Telephone: (630) 232-5820.

GRAHAM, Gordon E. *(Associate Judge, Illinois Circuit Court Nineteenth Judicial Circuit)*

Office: 2200 North Seminary, Woodstock 60098.

Telephone: (815) 338-2040.

GRAHAM HARRELL, Kimbara *(Associate Judge, Illinois Circuit Court Second Judicial Circuit)*

Mailing address: P.O. Box 1266, Mount Vernon 62864.

Telephone: (618) 244-8007.

GRAMLICH, Charles J. *(Associate Judge, Illinois Circuit Court Seventh Judicial Circuit)* Appointed.

Office: 532 Sangamon County Complex, 200 South Ninth Street, Springfield 62701.

Telephone: (217) 753-6738.

GRAVES, Leslie J. *(Circuit Judge, Illinois Circuit Court Seventh Judicial Circuit)*

Office: Sangamon County Complex, 200 South Ninth Street, Springfield 62701.

Telephone: (217) 753-6823.

GRAWEY, Richard E. *(Circuit Judge, Illinois Circuit Court Tenth Judicial Circuit)* Term expires 2008.

Office: Tazewell County Courthouse, 342 Court Street, Pekin 61554-4281.

Telephone: (309) 477-2201.

GRAY, Lawrence C. *(Associate Judge, Illinois Circuit Court Twelfth Judicial Circuit)*

Office: Will County Courthouse, 14 West Jefferson Street, Joliet 60432.

Telephone: (815) 727-8540.

GREANIAS, John K. *(Circuit Judge, Illinois Circuit Court Sixth Judicial Circuit)* Term expires Dec 2006.

Office: 3A Macon County Courts Facility, 253 East Wood, Decatur 62523.

Telephone (217) 424-1467.

GREENE-THAPEDI, Llwellyn *(Circuit Judge, Illinois Circuit Court of Cook County)* Elected to term beginning Dec 1992. Retained by election 1998, current term expires Dec 2004. Born Guthrie Oklahoma Aug 19. Christian. Educated at Langston University B.A. cum laude 1953, University of Saskatchewan M.A. 1972 and Loyola University of Chicago J.D. 1976. Admitted to practice Illinois 1976 and U.S. District Court Northern District of Illinois 1976. In legal practice Chicago 1976-92.

Instructor in Business Law Chicago State University. President Cook County Bar Association. Board Member Women's Bar Association of Illinois, Chicago and National Bar Associations. Member Illinois Judicial Council, Illinois Judges Association, Women Judges Association, International Association of Women Judges and Illinois State Bar Association. Enjoys writing poetry, singing and creating collages.

Office: 16501 South Kedzie Parkway, Markham 60426.

Telephone: (708) 210-4170.

GREENLIEF, Richard D. *(Circuit Judge, Illinois Circuit Court Eighth Judicial Circuit)*

Mailing address: P.O. Box 486, Hardin 62047.

Office: Calhoun County Courthouse, Hardin 62047.

Telephone: (618) 576-2432.

GREIMAN, Alan J. *(Circuit Judge, Illinois Circuit Court of Cook County)* Appointed July 10, 1987. Currently on assignment by Supreme Court of Illinois as Judge, Illinois Appellate Court First Judicial District Division Four. Formerly served Division Five. Born Chicago Illinois Dec 29, 1931. Jewish. Educated at University of Illinois B.S. 1953 LL.B. 1955. Admitted to practice Illinois 1955. In legal practice Chicago 1955-87.

Chairman Executive Committee Illinois Appellate Court. Member Women's, Chicago and Illinois State Bar

GREIMAN, ALAN J.—*Continued*

Associations. Former member Illinois House of Representatives (Assistant Majority Leader).

Office: 160 North LaSalle Street, Room N1711, Chicago 60601.

Telephone: (312) 793-4483.

GROGAN, J. B. *(Associate Judge, Illinois Circuit Court of Cook County)*

Office: 1310 R. J. Daley Center, Chicago 60602.

Telephone: (312) 603-4411.

GROMETER, R. Peter *(Circuit Judge, Illinois Circuit Court Sixteenth Judicial Circuit)* Associate Judge 1985-92. Elected Circuit Judge 1992. Retained by election Nov 2000, current term expires 2006. Former Chief Judge. Currently on assignment by Supreme Court of Illinois as Judge, Illinois Appellate Court Second Judicial District. Born Aurora Illinois. Educated at Michigan State University B.S. 1968 and University of Illinois J.D. 1973. Admitted to practice Illinois 1973. In legal practice Aurora 1973-85.

Office: 75 South Randall Road, Suite 200, North Aurora 60542.

Telephone: (630) 844-8989.

GROSSI, Gilbert J. *(Associate Judge, Illinois Circuit Court of Cook County)*

Office: 1500 Maybrook Drive, Chicago 60153.

Telephone: (708) 865-6060.

GROSSI, Patrick S. *(Circuit Judge, Illinois Circuit Court of Cook County)* Former Associate Judge. Assumed office as Circuit Judge. Term expires 2004.

Office: 10220 South 76th Avenue, Bridgeview 60455.

Telephone: (708) 974-6898.

GRUBB, Gerald F. *(Chief Judge, Illinois Circuit Court Seventeenth Judicial Circuit)* Appointed Associate Judge to term beginning Feb 13, 1987. Reappointed July 1, 1987 and July 1, 1991. Assumed office as Circuit Judge. Born Belvidere Illinois Sept 9, 1947. Educated at Northern Illinois University B.S. 1969 and John Marshall Law School J.D. 1975. Admitted to practice Illinois 1975 and U.S. District Court Northern District of Illinois 1986. In legal practice Belvidere 1975-87.

Assistant City Attorney 1975-76. Assistant State's Attorney 1976-80 and State's Attorney 1980-87. Former Member Illinois State's Attorneys Association and National District Attorneys Association. Member Illinois Judges Association and Illinois State Bar Association. Assistant Judge "DUI and Courts" The National Judicial College Sept 1987.

Office: 601 North Main Street, Belvidere 61008.

Telephone: (815) 544-0371.

GRUSSEL, Susan Ruscitti *(Circuit Judge, Illinois Circuit Court of Cook County)*

Office: 5600 Old Orchard Road, Skokie 60077.

Telephone: (847) 470-7200.

GUNNARSSON, Val *(Circuit Judge, Illinois Circuit Court Fifteenth Judicial Circuit)*

Mailing address: P.O. Box 211, Mount Carroll 61053.

Office: 301 Main Street, Mount Carroll 61053.

Telephone: (815) 244-0276.

GUZMAN, Ronald A. *(Judge, United State District Court Northern District of Illinois)* Magistrate Judge 1990-99. Appointed Judge for life by President Bill Clinton to term beginning Nov 16, 1999. Born Rio Piedras Puerto Rico Nov 18, 1948. Educated at Lehigh University B.A. 1970 and New York University School of Law J.D. 1973. In legal practice 1973-74 and Chicago 1980-90.

Assistant State's Attorney Cook County 1975-80. Staff Attorney Association House of Chicago 1980-84.

Office: U.S. Courthouse, 219 South Dearborn Street, Chicago 60604.

Telephone: (312) 435-5363.

HAASE, Herman S. *(Circuit Judge, Illinois Circuit Court Twelfth Judicial Circuit)* Appointed Associate Judge to term beginning Feb 15, 1977. Elected Circuit Judge Dec 1978. Retained by election 1984, 1990, 1996 and 2002. Current term expires 2008. Former Chief Judge. Born Chicago Illinois March 22, 1942. Lutheran. Educated at Blackburn College B.A. 1963 and Northwestern University J.D. 1966. Member Phi Alpha Delta. Admitted to practice Illinois 1970. In legal practice Joliet 1974-77. Served on assignment by Illinois Supreme Court as Judge, Illinois Appellate Court Third Judicial District 1991-92.

Assistant State's Attorney 1970-74. Adjunct Professor in Business Law Lewis University Romeoville 1980-84. Member Will County Bar Association. Attended Automation of Courts 1987 and Mediation Course 2002 The National Judicial College and Law and Organizational Economics Seminar University of Kansas 2001. Lieutenant USNR 1966-69. Republican. Republican Precinct Committeeman Wheatland Township 1976. Board of Directors Marianjoy Rehabilitation Hospital and Camelot Homeowners Association. Member Joliet Rotary Club. Enjoys computers, reading and classical music.

Office: River Valley Justice Center, 3210 West McDonough Street, Joliet 60431.

Telephone: (815) 730-7167.

HABERKORN, Catherine M. *(Circuit Judge, Illinois Circuit Court of Cook County)*

Office: 5600 Old Orchard Road, Room 119, Skokie 60077.

Telephone: (847) 470-7219.

HACKETT, James *(Associate Judge, Illinois Circuit Court Third Judicial Circuit)*

Office: Madison County Courthouse, 155 North Main Street, Edwardsville 62025.

Telephone: (618) 692-7040.

HADDAD, William J. *(Circuit Judge, Illinois Circuit Court of Cook County)* Appointed to term beginning Jan 24, 2003. Term expires Dec 6, 2004.

Office: 400 R. J. Daley Center, Chicago 60602.

Telephone: (312) 603-2600.

HALL, David M. *(Circuit Judge, Illinois Circuit Court Nineteenth Judicial Circuit)* Former Associate Judge.

Office: Lake County Courthouse, 18 North County Street, Waukegan 60085.

Telephone: (847) 377-3789.

HALL, Robert T. *(Associate Judge, Illinois Circuit Court Seventh Judicial Circuit)*

Office: 614 Sangamon County Building, 200 South Ninth, Springfield 62701.

Telephone: (217) 753-6825.

HALL, Shelvin Louise Marie *(Judge, Illinois Appellate Court First Judicial District Division Three)* Elected Nov 7, 2000. Term expires 2010. Born Cuero Texas June 15, 1948. Baptist. Educated at Hampton Institute B.A. 1970 and Boston University J.D. 1974. Admitted to practice Texas 1975, U.S. District Court Southern District of Texas 1976, Illinois 1982 and U.S. Supreme Court 1982. In legal practice Houston Texas 1974-80. Former Circuit Judge, Illinois Circuit Court of Cook County, appointed to term beginning Jan 11, 1991. Served Illinois Appellate Court by special assignment.

General Counsel Illinois Department of Human Rights. Instructor in Legal Advocacy John Marshall Law School 1989-90. Member Education Committee Illinois Judicial Conference. Member Black Women Lawyers Association of Chicago, Illinois Judicial Council (Board Member since 1992, Secretary 1994-95, Chairperson 1996-97, Member Executive Committee), Illinois Judges Association, National Association of Women Judges, Women's Bar Association of Illinois, Chicago, Cook County (Board Member 1983-94, Vice President 1990), Illinois State, National (Board Member 1977-94, Vice President 1985, Chair Elect 1997-98 and Chairperson 1998-99 Judicial Council) and American Bar Associations. Instructor Family Law Seminar National Bar Association Aug 1994, in Ethics Dec 1994 and in Civil Jury Trial Practice 1997 New Judges Seminar and Domestic Relations Seminar June 1995 Illinois Judicial Conference. Recipient Sampson Award from Illinois Judicial Council, Judicial Award from Cook County Bar Association, Pinnacle Award from *Being Single Magazine*, Speakers Award from National Association of Real Estate Brokers, Young Lawyers Division Award and Women's Division Award from National Bar Association and Luke Moore Award from PUSH/EXCEL, Inc. Speaker Martin Luther King Day Loyola Law School Jan 1995. Democrat. Legislative Director to U.S. Congressman Mickey Leland 1980-82. Board Member Lutheran Family Mission 1995-97. Former Board Member Legal Assistance Foundation of Chicago. Former Chair Christian Care Department and Department of Christian Education. Member Friendship Baptist Church (Youth Director 1995-97). Interests include theatre, opera and public speaking at numerous churches and civic and legal organizations.

Office: 160 North LaSalle, Room S1910, Chicago 60601.
Telephone: (312) 793-5438.
Fax: (312) 793-2596

HALL, Sophia H. *(Circuit Judge, Illinois Circuit Court of Cook County)* Elected to term beginning Dec 2, 1980. Retained by election 1986, 1992 and 1998. Current term expires 2004. Born Chicago Illinois. Educated at University of Wisconsin-Madison B.S. 1964 and Northwestern University Law School J.D. 1967. Member Phi Kappa Phi. Admitted to practice Illinois 1967, U.S. District Court Northern District of Illinois 1967, U.S. Court of Appeals Seventh Circuit 1970 and U.S. Supreme Court 1971. In legal practice Chicago 1967-80.

Office: 2301 R. J. Daley Center, Chicago 60602.
Telephone: (312) 603-3733.

HALLOCK, James C. *(Associate Judge, Illinois Circuit Court Sixteenth Judicial Circuit)*
Office: 400 Kane County Judicial Center, 37W777 Route 38, St. Charles 60175-7536.
Telephone: (630) 232-5820.

HAMER, Ted *(Circuit Judge, Illinois Circuit Court Fourteenth Judicial Circuit)*
Office: Henry County Courthouse, Cambridge 61238.
Telephone: (309) 937-3523.

HAMILTON, R. Morgan *(Associate Judge, Illinois Circuit Court of Cook County)*
Office: 1508 R. J. Daley Center, Chicago 60602.
Telephone: (312) 603-4808.

HARDWICK, Bob, Jr. *(Circuit Judge, Illinois Circuit Court Eighth Judicial Circuit)*
Mailing address: P.O. Box 137, Virginia 62691.
Office: 100 East Springfield Street, Virginia 62691.
Telephone: (217) 452-3841.

HARDY-CAMPBELL, La Quietta J. *(Circuit Judge, Illinois Circuit Court of Cook County)*
Office: 3006 R. J. Daley Center, Chicago 60602.
Telephone: (312) 603-6417.

HARRISON, Bennie Joe *(Circuit Judge, Illinois Circuit Court Second Judicial Circuit)*
Office: Wayne County Courthouse, Fairfield 62837.
Telephone: (618) 842-4926.

HARRISON, Clarence W., II *(Associate Judge, Illinois Circuit Court Third Judicial Circuit)*
Office: Madison County Courthouse, 155 North Main Street, Edwardsville 62025.
Telephone: (618) 692-7040.

HARRISON, Miriam E. *(Associate Judge, Illinois Circuit Court of Cook County)*
Office: 1812 R. J. Daley Center, Chicago 60602.
Telephone: (312) 603-6492.

HART, William T. *(Senior Judge, United States District Court Northern District of Illinois)* Appointed for life by President Ronald Reagan to term beginning 1982. Assumed Senior status June 1, 1996, serves by assignment. Born Joliet Illinois Feb 4, 1929. Educated at Loyola University of Chicago School of Law J.D. 1951. In legal practice Chicago 1956-82.

Assistant U.S. Attorney Northern District of Illinois 1954-56. Special Assistant State Attorney General 1957-58. Special Assistant State's Attorney Cook County 1960.

Office: U.S. Courthouse, 219 South Dearborn Street, Chicago 60604.
Telephone: (312) 435-5776.

HARTIGAN, Neil F. *(Judge, Illinois Appellate Court First Judicial District Division Five)*
Office: 160 North LaSalle Street, Room S1911, Chicago 60601.
Telephone: (312) 793-4484.

HARTMAN, Allen *(Judge, Illinois Appellate Court First Judicial District Division Four)* Elected to term beginning 1978. Retained by election 1988 and 1998. Current term expires 2008. Former Chairman Executive Committee. Currently serves as Presiding Judge. Born Chicago Illinois July 1, 1927. Educated at Northwestern University J.D. 1959. Associate Editor Northwestern University Law Review. Law Clerk to Hon. Ulysses S. Schwartz and Hon. John T. Dempsey, Illinois Appellate Court. Justice Phi Alpha Delta Fuller Chapter. Admitted to practice Illinois 1959. Circuit Judge, Illinois Circuit Court of Cook County 1973-78.

Assistant Corporation Counsel 1961-62, General

HARTMAN, ALLEN—*Continued*
Counsel to Corporation Counsel 1965-70, and First Assistant Corporation Counsel 1971 and 1973 City of Chicago. Executive Director Chicago Home Rule Commission 1972. Editor and Contributor "Chicago Home Rule Commission Report." Contributor *Practical Lawyers Manual of Trial and Appellate Practice* and *Callaghan's Federal Lawyer's Manual.* Author "Legal Ethics" Chicago Bar Record, "Judicial Decision Making" and "Legal Writing: A Judge's Perspective" Illinois B. Jour., "Survey of the Illinois Law of Procedure" and "The Why's and Whynot's of Jury Trial Judicial Comments on Evidence" Loyola L. Jour. Co-author *Illinois Lawyer's Manual* Lawyers Cooperative Publishing Co. Adjunct Professor of Illinois Civil Litigation, Analysis of Code of Civil Procedure, Supreme Court Rules and Case Law Loyola University School of Law. Former Chairman Subcommittee on Judicial Education Executive Committee Illinois Supreme Court. Member Illinois Supreme Court Rules Committee. Lecturer on Motions, Appellate Practice and Contemporary Legal Problems CLE and Young Lawyers Sections Chicago Bar Association. Chairman and Lecturer Committees on Evidence, Motion Practice, Civil Law Development, Negligence and Strict Liability, Judicial Discretion and Judicial Notice and Subcommittee on Judicial Education Illinois Judicial Conference Regional Seminars. Contributor Institute of Government and Public Affairs Symposium on Home Rule in Illinois and Northwestern University Law Review Symposium on Uniform Commercial Code in Illinois.
Office: 160 North LaSalle Street, Room N1909, Chicago 60601.
Telephone: (312) 793-5412.

HARTMAN, Charles R. *(Circuit Judge, Illinois Circuit Court Fifteenth Judicial Circuit)*
Office: Stephenson County Courthouse, 15 North Galena, Freeport 61032.
Telephone: (815) 235-8285.

HARVEY, James R. *(Associate Judge, Illinois Circuit Court Fourth Judicial Circuit)*
Office: 15051 East 1200th Avenue, Effingham 62401.
Telephone: (217) 342-4065.

HATCH, Dennis *(Associate Judge, Illinois Circuit Court Twentieth Judicial Circuit)*
Office: 10 Public Square, Belleville 62220.
Telephone: (618) 277-7325.

HAUPTMAN, John L. *(Associate Judge, Illinois Circuit Court Fourteenth Judicial Circuit)*
Office: Whiteside County Courthouse, Morrison 61270.
Telephone: (815) 772-5245.

HAYES, Marsha D. *(Circuit Judge, Illinois Circuit Court of Cook County)*
Office: 1710 R. J. Daley Center, Chicago 60602.
Telephone: (312) 603-4096.

HAYES, Shelli Williams *(Circuit Judge, Illinois Circuit Court of Cook County)*
Office: 1410 R. J. Daley Center, Chicago 60602.
Telephone: (312) 603-4871.

HEALY, Michael T. *(Circuit Judge, Illinois Circuit Court of Cook County)* Appointed to term beginning Sept 1, 1999. Elected Dec 4, 2000, current term expires Dec 2006. Born Chicago Illinois 1946. Educated at University of Illinois at Chicago B.A. 1968 and DePaul University College of Law J.D. 1972. Admitted to practice Illinois 1972. In legal practice Chicago 1972-2000.
Office: 5555 West Grand Avenue, Chicago 60639.
Telephone: (773) 804-6154.

HEASLIP, Patrick L. *(Associate Judge, Illinois Circuit Court Seventeenth Judicial Circuit)*
Office: 400 West State Street, Rockford 61101.
Telephone: (815) 987-3062.

HEASTON, Curtis *(Circuit Judge, Illinois Circuit Court of Cook County)* Former Associate Judge. Assumed office as Circuit Judge. Term expires Dec 2006.
Office: 1100 South Hamilton, Room 8004, Chicago 60612.
Telephone: (312) 433-4757.

HEISER, Larry W. *(Associate Judge, Illinois Circuit Court Ninth Judicial Circuit)*
Office: McDonough County Courthouse, Macomb 61455.
Telephone: (309) 837-4891.

HENDERSON, William D. *(Chief Judge, Illinois Circuit Court Ninth Judicial Circuit)* Former Associate Judge. Assumed office as Circuit Judge. Term expires 2004.
Office: 130 South Lafayette, Suite 30, Macomb 61455.
Telephone: (309) 837-9278.

HENRY, James F. *(Circuit Judge, Illinois Circuit Court of Cook County)* Former Associate Judge.
Office: 2104 R. J. Daley Center, Chicago 60602.
Telephone: (312) 603-3384.

HENSHAW, Michael J. *(Chief Judge, Illinois Circuit Court First Judicial Circuit)* Elected to term beginning Dec 4, 1978. Retained by election 1984, 1990, 1996 and 2002. Current term expires 2008. Born Harrisburg Illinois Nov 21, 1944. Baptist. Educated at Southeastern Illinois College A.A. 1965, Southern Illinois University B.A. 1967 and Illinois Institute of Technology, Chicago-Kent College of Law J.D. 1971. Admitted to practice Illinois 1971. Began legal practice Harrisburg 1971.
State's Attorney Saline County 1972-76. Member Saline County and Illinois State Bar Associations. Democrat.
Office: Saline County Courthouse, Harrisburg 62946.
Telephone: (618) 253-8741.

HERNDON, David R. *(Judge, United States District Court Southern District of Illinois)* Appointed for life by President Bill Clinton April 23, 1998 to term beginning Nov 16, 1998. Born Sedalia Missouri Aug 23, 1953. Methodist. Educated at Southern Illinois University B.A. 1974 J.D. 1977. Member Phi Alpha Delta. Admitted to practice Illinois 1977, Missouri 1979, U.S. District Courts Eastern 1979 and Western 1979 Districts of Missouri and Southern 1979 and Central 1981 Districts of Illinois, U.S. Court of Appeals Seventh Circuit 1987 and U.S. Supreme Court 1989. In legal practice East Alton Illinois 1977-79, St. Louis Missouri 1979-80 and Wood River Illinois 1980-91. Associate Judge, Illinois Circuit Court Third Judicial Circuit 1991-98.
Office: 750 Missouri Avenue, East St. Louis 62201.
Telephone: (618) 482-9077.

HERNDON, DAVID R.—*Continued*

Fax: (618) 482-9195
E-mail address: judge_herndon@ilsd.uscourts.gov

HESS, Frederick J. *(Judge, Illinois Court of Claims)* Appointed by Governor Jim Edgar.
Office: 325 South High, Belleville 62220.
Telephone: (618) 234-8636.

HIBBLER, William J. *(Judge, United States District Court Northern District of Illinois)* Appointed for life by President Bill Clinton to term beginning July 2, 1999. Born Kennedy Alabama Aug 7, 1946. Educated at University of Illinois at Chicago B.S. 1969 and DePaul University J.D. 1973. In legal practice Chicago 1977-81. Associate Judge, Illinois Circuit Court of Cook County 1986-99.
Assistant State's Attorney Cook County 1973-77 and 1981-86.
Office: 1746 U.S. Courthouse, 219 South Dearborn Street, Chicago 60604.
Telephone: (312) 435-5613.

HILL, James V. *(Associate Judge, Illinois Circuit Court Second Judicial Circuit)*
Mailing address: P.O. Box 89, Robinson 62454.
Office: Crawford County Courthouse, Robinson 62454.
Telephone: (618) 544-7471.

HILLEBRAND, Robert J. *(Circuit Judge, Illinois Circuit Court Twentieth Judicial Circuit)* Appointed Associate Judge to term beginning May 12, 1989. Reappointed June 1991, June 1995 and 1999. Assumed office as Circuit Judge. Born Rockford Illinois Nov 1, 1940. Roman Catholic. Educated at University of Illinois A.B. 1962 LL.B. 1965. Law Clerk to Hon. Joseph Goldenhersh, Illinois Supreme Court 1971-73. Admitted to practice Illinois 1965, U.S. District Courts Southern 1965 and Central Districts of Illinois 1966 and U.S. Court of Appeals Seventh Circuit 1966. In legal practice East St. Louis 1965-81 and Belleville 1981-89.
Assistant Public Defender St. Clair County 1973-75. Assistant Corporation Counsel City of East St. Louis 1975-77. Member Illinois Judges Association, American Judges Association and American Bar Association (National Conference of State Trial Judges Judicial Administration Division). Member Subcommittee on Judicial Education Executive Committee Judicial Conference since 1991 and Committee on Judicial Performance Education since 1991 Illinois Supreme Court. Instructor Civil Jury Trial Associate Judge Seminar 1991.
Office: 1158 Windermere Run, O'Fallon 62269.
Telephone: (618) 277-7325.

HITPAS, Patrick J. *(Circuit Judge, Illinois Circuit Court Fourth Judicial Circuit)* Appointed to term beginning Aug 14, 1992. Elected Nov 1992. Retained by election Nov 1998, current term expires Nov 30, 2004. Born St. Louis Missouri Nov 4, 1947. Catholic. Educated at St. Joseph's College B.S. cum laude 1969 and St. Louis University J.D. 1972. Admitted to practice Illinois 1972 and Missouri 1972. In legal practice Belleville Illinois 1974-76 and Carlyle Illinois 1980-92.
State's Attorney Clinton County Illinois 1976-80. Member Illinois Judges Association and Illinois State Bar Association. Speaker at seminars Illinois State Bar Association. Enjoys golfing, traveling and reading.
Mailing address: P.O. Box 150, Carlyle 62231.
Telephone: (618) 594-0165.

HOFFENBERG, Earl B. *(Associate Judge, Illinois Circuit Court of Cook County)*
Office: 1340 South Michigan Avenue, Room 202, Chicago 60605.
Telephone: (312) 341-2710.

HOFFMAN, Mitchell L. *(Associate Judge, Illinois Circuit Court Nineteenth Judicial Circuit)*
Office: Lake County Courthouse, 18 North County Street, Waukegan 60085.
Telephone: (847) 377-3502.

HOFFMAN, Thomas E. *(Judge, Illinois Appellate Court First Judicial District Division Three)* Elected 1994. Former Presiding Judge. Formerly served Division Four. Born Chicago Illinois Dec 23, 1947. Educated at Loyola University of Chicago B.B.A. 1969 and John Marshall Law School J.D. 1971. Associate Judge 1984-88 and Circuit Judge 1988-94, Illinois Circuit Court of Cook County. Served Illinois Appellate Court First Judicial District by special assignment 1993-94.
Trustee and Vice Chairman Judges' Retirement Board and Member Executive Committee Illinois Judicial Conference. Member Chicago Inn of Court, Justinian Law Society and Chicago Bar Association. President John Marshall Law School Alumni Association 1996.
Office: 160 North LaSalle Street, Room N1610, Chicago 60601.
Telephone: (312) 793-5432.

HOGAN, Michael J. *(Circuit Judge, Illinois Circuit Court of Cook County)* Term expires Dec 2006.
Office: 2601 R. J. Daley Center, Chicago 60602.
Telephone: (312) 603-5415.

HOGAN, Thomas L. *(Circuit Judge, Illinois Circuit Court of Cook County)*
Office: 2101A R. J. Daley Center, Chicago 60602.
Telephone: (312) 603-5905.

HOLDERMAN, James F., Jr. *(Judge, United States District Court Northern District of Illinois)* Appointed for life by President Ronald Reagan to term beginning May 1, 1985. Born May 30, 1946. Educated at University of Illinois B.S. 1968 J.D. 1971. Law Clerk to U.S. District Court District of Illinois 1971-72. In legal practice Chicago 1978-85.
Assistant U.S. Attorney 1972-78. Member American Bar Association.
Office: U.S. Courthouse, 219 South Dearborn Street, Chicago 60604.
Telephone: (312) 435-5632.

HOLDRIDGE, William E. *(Judge, Illinois Appellate Court Third Judicial District)* Elected to term beginning Dec 1994. Term expires Dec 2004. Former Presiding Judge. Born Peoria Illinois March 30, 1948. Catholic. Educated at Illinois State University B.S.Ed. with honors 1970 M.S. with honors 1971, University of Illinois Ph.D. with honors 1974 and Southern Illinois University J.D. with honors 1984. Law Clerk to Hon. James D. Heiple, Illinois Appellate Court Third Judicial District 1985-90. Admitted to practice Illinois 1984, Missouri 1984 and U.S. District Courts Central 1985 and Northern 1985 Districts of Illinois. In legal practice Peoria Il-

HOLDRIDGE, WILLIAM E.—*Continued*

linois 1984-90. Circuit Judge, Illinois Circuit Court Ninth Judicial Circuit 1990-94.

Corporate Counsel Central Illinois Agencies and Mass Mutual 1984-90. City Attorney Farmington 1988-90. Director Administrative Office of Illinois Courts 1997. Member Illinois Judges Association, Peoria, Fulton County and Illinois State Bar Associations. Attended numerous courses The National Judicial College and seminars Illinois State Bar Association. Republican. Member Rotary International, Ancient Order of Hibernians, Knights of Columbus and Farmington and Canton Chambers of Commerce. Interests include agriculture, antique and collectible automobiles and farm tractors.

Office: 207 Main Street, Suite 600, Peoria 61602.

Telephone: (309) 671-3190.

HOLLIS, Pamela S. *(Judge, United States Bankruptcy Court Northern District of Illinois)* Appointed by U.S. Court of Appeals Seventh Circuit judges to term beginning Jan 27, 2003. Term expires Jan 2017.

Office: 648 U.S. Courthouse, 219 South Dearborn Street, Chicago 60604.

Telephone: (312) 435-5534.

HOLMES, Patricia B. *(Associate Judge, Illinois Circuit Court of Cook County)*

Office: 1100 South Hamilton Avenue, Chicago 60612.

Telephone: (312) 433-4756.

HOLMES, Roger W. *(Associate Judge, Illinois Circuit Court Seventh Judicial Circuit)* Appointed to term beginning Feb 15, 1988. Reappointed 1991, 1995 and 1999. Current term expires 2003. Born Chicago Illinois May 5, 1951. Methodist. Educated at University of Illinois B.S. with high honors 1973 J.D. 1976. Member Delta Sigma Pi. Admitted to practice Illinois 1976 and U.S. District Court Central District of Illinois 1976. In legal practice Springfield 1976-88.

Member Sangamon County Bar Association (Vice President 1988, President 1989). Vice Chairman Sheriff's Deputy Merit Commission Sangamon County 1987-88. Officer Springfield Municipal Opera. Enjoys model railroading, music and cooking.

Office: 718 County Complex, 200 South Ninth Street, Springfield 62701.

Telephone: (217) 753-6737.

HOLMGREN, Janet R. *(Circuit Judge, Illinois Circuit Court Seventeenth Judicial Circuit)* Former Associate Judge.

Office: Winnebago County Courthouse, Second Floor, 400 West State, Rockford 61101.

Telephone: (815) 987-3062.

HOLT, Leo E. *(Circuit Judge, Illinois Circuit Court of Cook County)* Elected to term beginning Dec 1, 1986. Retained by election 1992 and 1998. Current term expires 2004. Born Chicago Illinois July 2, 1927. Educated at Roosevelt University and John Marshall Law School LL.B. 1959. Admitted to practice Illinois 1959, U.S. District Courts Northern District of Illinois 1959 and Eastern District of Wisconsin 1975, U.S. Court of Appeals Seventh Circuit 1964 and U.S. Supreme Court 1968. In legal practice Chicago 1959-73 and Harvey 1973-86.

Member Illinois Judicial Council and Cook County Bar Association. Attended The National Judicial College. Corporal USAF 1947-49. Enjoys hunting.

Office: 2600 South California Avenue, Chicago 60608.

Telephone: (773) 869-7452.

HOPKINS, Robert M. *(Circuit Judge, Illinois Circuit Court Second Judicial Circuit)* Elected to term beginning Dec 1992. Retained by election 1998, current term expires Dec 2004. Currently serves as Resident Judge Lawrence County. Born Peoria Illinois Oct 2, 1951. Roman Catholic. Educated at Illinois State University B.A. with honors 1973 and University of Illinois J.D. 1983. Member Delta Theta Phi. Admitted to practice Illinois 1983, U.S. District Courts Southern 1984 and Central 1986 Districts of Illinois. In legal practice Lawrenceville 1983-92.

Member Illinois Judges Association and Illinois State Bar Association. Attended New Judge's Seminar 1992, Conduct of a Felony Jury Trial 1994, Juvenile Law Mini-Seminar and Criminal Law Evidence Seminar. Member Red Hills Settler's Association, Lawrenceville Kiwanis Club and Lawrence County Industrial Development Council. Interests include canoeing, hiking, choir and genealogy.

Office: Lawrence County Courthouse, Lawrenceville 62439.

Telephone: (618) 943-4421.

HOPKINS, Terrence J. *(Judge, Illinois Appellate Court Fifth Judicial District)* Elected Nov 1994. Term expires Dec 2004. Presiding Judge Dec 1995 to Dec 1996. Born West Frankfort Illinois March 6, 1948. Roman Catholic. Educated at Southern Illinois University B.A. 1970 and St. Louis University J.D. 1974. Admitted to practice Illinois 1974 and U.S. District Court Southern District of Illinois 1974. Began legal practice West Frankfort 1974. Former Circuit Judge and Chief Judge, Illinois Circuit Court Second Judicial Circuit, appointed to term beginning June 1, 1983.

State's Attorney Franklin County Dec 1976 to June 1983. Member The Association of Trial Lawyers of America, Illinois Judges Association, Franklin County and Jefferson County Bar Associations. Democrat. Past Exalted Ruler West Frankfort Elks. Retired coach sixth grade basketball program.

Office: 2929 Broadway, Suite 7, Mt. Vernon 62864.

Telephone: (618) 244-8304.

HOPKINS, Vanessa A. *(Circuit Judge, Illinois Circuit Court of Cook County)* Elected to term beginning 1996. Retained by election 2002, current term expires Dec 2008. Currently serves Civil Jury Division. Educated at Chicago State University B.S. 1986, Roosevelt University M.B.A. 1988 and Northern Illinois University College of Law J.D. 1993. In legal practice Chicago 1994-96.

Faculty Member Northeastern University, Kishwaukee College, DeVry Institute of Technology and Roosevelt University. Board of Directors and Co-chairperson Membership Committee Illinois Judges Association. Board of Directors Illinois Judicial Council. Named Outstanding Young Alumna for College of Law by Northern Illinois University Alumni Association 1999. Recipient Outstanding Women Student Leadership Award and Outstanding Contribution to Law School Community Award from Northern Illinois University and Bridge Builders Award from Rainbow PUSH Organization. Board of Directors Committee to Improve Education in South Shore.

HOPKINS, VANESSA A.—*Continued*

Board of Visitors Northern Illinois University College of Law. Parent Network Advisory Board Nancy B. Jefferson Alternative School. Chairperson Existing Programs Committee Juvenile Mentoring and Early Intervention Coalition Rainbow PUSH Organization.
Office: 1510 R. J. Daley Center, Chicago 60602.
Telephone: (312) 603-4805.

HOUSEHOLTER, J. Gregory *(Circuit Judge, Illinois Circuit Court Twenty-first Judicial Circuit)* Associate Judge 1992-96. Elected Circuit Judge to term beginning Dec 2, 1996. Retained by election 2002, current term expires Dec 2008. Born Oakland California July 8, 1945. Roman Catholic. Educated at University of Notre Dame B.A. in Economics 1967 and Valparaiso University School of Law J.D. 1973. Admitted to practice Illinois 1973 and U.S. District Court Central District of Illinois 1973. In legal practice Kankakee 1973-92.
Special Assistant Attorney General Illinois 1975-78 and 1981-83. Assistant Public Defender Kankakee County 1989-92. Co-author "An Overview of Industrial Vocational Rehabilitation Statutes and Approaches" 74 Illinois B. Jour. 342 March 1986. Member Kankakee County and Illinois State (Assembly Member 1982-88 and 1993-96) Bar Associations. E-4 U.S. Army 1968-70.
Office: Kankakee County Courthouse, 450 East Court Street, Kankakee 60901.
Telephone: (815) 937-2920.

HOUSER, Ann *(Associate Judge, Illinois Circuit Court of Cook County)* Appointed to term beginning Oct 24, 1986. Reappointed to subsequent terms. Born Owensville Indiana March 24, 1943. Educated at Roosevelt University B.S.B.A. 1969 and DePaul College of Law J.D. 1971. Admitted to practice Illinois 1972.
Office: 1107 R. J. Daley Center, Chicago 60602.
Telephone: (312) 603-4536.

HOWARD, Garritt E. *(Circuit Judge, Illinois Circuit Court of Cook County)*
Office: 5600 Old Orchard Road, Room 130, Skokie 60077.
Telephone: (847) 470-7200.

HOWSE, Nathaniel R., Jr. *(Circuit Judge, Illinois Circuit Court of Cook County)*
Office: 1711 R. J. Daley Center, Chicago 60602.
Telephone: (312) 603-6547.

HUBBARD, Arnette R. *(Circuit Judge, Illinois Circuit Court of Cook County)* Serves Law Division.
Office: 2809 R. J. Daley Center, Chicago 60602.
Telephone: (312) 603-4283.

HUDSON, Donald C. *(Circuit Judge, Illinois Circuit Court Sixteenth Judicial Circuit)* Former Associate Judge.
Office: 400 Kane County Judicial Center, 37W777 Route 38, St. Charles 60175-7536.
Telephone: (630) 406-7158.

HUGHES, Brian P. *(Associate Judge, Illinois Circuit Court Nineteenth Judicial Circuit)*
Office: 18 North County Street, Waukegan 60085.
Telephone: (847) 377-7980.

HULTGREN, David R. *(Circuit Judge, Illinois Circuit Court Ninth Judicial Circuit)* Elected to term beginning Dec 7, 1992. Retained by election 1998, current term expires Dec 2004. Born Geneseo Illinois April 30, 1951. Educated at Augustana College B.A. cum laude 1973 and University of North Carolina J.D. 1978. Law Clerk to Hon. Albert Scott, Illinois Appellate Court Third Judicial District 1978-86. Member Phi Delta Phi. Admitted to practice Illinois 1978, U.S. Tax Court 1982, U.S. District Court Central District of Illinois and U.S. Court of Appeals Seventh Circuit. In legal practice Monmouth 1978-92.
Republican. Member Illinois House of Representatives 1987-92.
Office: Knox County Courthouse, Galesburg 61401.
Telephone: (309) 345-3874.

HUSCHEN, John B. *(Circuit Judge, Illinois Circuit Court Eleventh Judicial Circuit)*
Office: 117 East Court Street, Eureka 61530.
Telephone: (309) 467-2131.

HUTCHINSON, Susan Fayette *(Judge, Illinois Appellate Court Second Judicial District)* Elected to term beginning Dec 5, 1994. Term expires Dec 2004. Born Monmouth Illinois April 1, 1950. Educated at Quincy University B.A. 1971 and DePaul University College of Law J.D. 1977. Admitted to practice Illinois 1977, U.S. District Court Northern District of Illinois 1978 and U.S. Supreme Court 1989. Associate Judge 1981-92 and Circuit Judge 1992-94, Illinois Circuit Court Nineteenth Judicial Circuit.
Assistant State's Attorney McHenry County 1977-81. Member Jefferson Inn and DeKalb Inn American Inns of Court, National Association of Women Judges (Former District Director), Illinois State (Special Committee on Women and the Law) and American Bar Associations.
Mailing address: P.O. Box 880, Woodstock 60098.
Office: 1700 South Eastwood Drive, Woodstock 60098.
Telephone: (815) 338-5875.

HYLAND, Colleen A. *(Associate Judge, Illinois Circuit Court of Cook County)*
Office: 400 R. J. Daley Center, Chicago 60602.
Telephone: (312) 603-2600.

HYNES, John J. *(Associate Judge, Illinois Circuit Court of Cook County)*
Office: 1303 R. J. Daley Center, Chicago 60602.
Telephone: (312) 603-7959.

INGRAM, Cheyrl D. *(Circuit Judge, Illinois Circuit Court of Cook County)*
Office: 1500 Maybrook Drive, Maywood 60153.
Telephone: (708) 865-6060.

IOSCO, Anthony A. *(Circuit Judge, Illinois Circuit Court of Cook County)*
Office: 1340 South Michigan Avenue, Room 702, Chicago 60605.
Telephone: (312) 341-2892.

JACKSON, Marianne *(Associate Judge, Illinois Circuit Court of Cook County)*
Office: 1100 South Hamilton, Chicago 60612.
Telephone: (312) 433-6961.

JACOBIUS, Moshe *(Circuit Judge, Illinois Circuit Court of Cook County)*
Office: 1901 R. J. Daley Center, Chicago 60602.
Telephone: (312) 603-6556.

JACOBS, Gary W. *(Circuit Judge, Illinois Circuit Court Fifth Judicial Circuit)* Former Associate Judge. Elected Circuit Judge to term beginning Dec 7, 1992. Retained by election 1998, current term expires Dec 2004.
Office: Coles County Courthouse, Second Floor, 651 Jackson, Charleston 61920.
Telephone: (217) 348-0541.

JAFFE, Aaron *(Circuit Judge, Illinois Circuit Court of Cook County)* Term expires 2004.
Office: 2405 R. J. Daley Center, Chicago 60602.
Telephone: (312) 603-3343.

JAGIELSKI, Raymond L. *(Circuit Judge, Illinois Circuit Court of Cook County)*
Office: 1702 R. J. Daley Center, Chicago 60602.
Telephone: (312) 603-6040.

JANES, Robert L. *(Associate Judge, Illinois Circuit Court Sixteenth Judicial Circuit)*
Office: 37W777 Route 38, Suite 400A, St. Charles 60175.
Telephone: (630) 406-7113.

JANN, Norma *(Judge, Illinois Court of Claims)* Appointed by governor.
Office: 233 East Wacker Drive, Suite 1811, Chicago 60601.
Telephone: (312) 504-9003.

JANURA, Arthur L., Jr. *(Associate Judge, Illinois Circuit Court of Cook County)*
Office: 2121 Euclid, Room 207-A, Rolling Meadows 60008.
Telephone: (847) 818-2535.

JEFFREY, David L. *(Associate Judge, Illinois Circuit Court Fifteenth Judicial Circuit)*
Office: Stephenson County Courthouse, 15 North Galena Avenue, Freeport 61032.
Telephone: (815) 235-8286.

JERZ, James W. *(Associate Judge, Illinois Circuit Court Eighteenth Judicial Circuit)*
Office: DuPage County Courthouse, 505 North County Farm Road, Wheaton 60187.
Telephone: (630) 682-7354.

JOHNSON-SPEH, Sandi G. *(Associate Judge, Illinois Circuit Court of Cook County)*
Office: 10220 South 76th Avenue, Room 103A, Bridgeview 60455.
Telephone: (708) 974-6300.

JONES, Dorothy F. *(Circuit Judge, Illinois Circuit Court of Cook County)*
Office: 1308 R. J. Daley Center, Chicago 60602.
Telephone: (312) 603-3484.

JONES, Michael Q. *(Circuit Judge, Illinois Circuit Court Sixth Judicial Circuit)* Former Associate Judge. Assumed office as Circuit Judge.
Office: Champaign County Courthouse, 101 East Main Street, Urbana 61801.
Telephone: (217) 384-3895.

JONES, Rickey *(Circuit Judge, Illinois Circuit Court of Cook County)*
Office: 2600 South California Avenue, Chicago 60608.
Telephone: (773) 869-3323.

JONES, Thomas H. *(Associate Judge, Illinois Circuit Court First Judicial Circuit)*
Mailing address: P.O. Box 388, Murphysboro 62966.
Telephone: (618) 687-7330.

JORDAN, Daniel E. *(Circuit Judge, Illinois Circuit Court of Cook County)*
Office: 5600 Old Orchard Road, Room 123, Skokie 60077.
Telephone: (847) 470-7200.

JORDAN, Edward R. *(Circuit Judge, Illinois Circuit Court of Cook County)* Appointed Aug 1, 1994. Elected to term beginning Dec 1, 1994. Retained by election 2000, current term expires 2006. Serves Domestic Relations Division. Born Chicago Illinois Aug 13, 1936. Educated at Roosevelt University B.A. 1970 and John Marshall Law School J.D. 1972. Admitted to practice Illinois 1973, U.S. District Court Northern District of Illinois 1973, U.S. Court of Appeals Seventh Circuit 1982 and Trial Bar of U.S. District Court Northern District of Illinois 1985. In legal practice Chicago April 19, 1973 to April 30, 1983 and Wheeling May 1, 1983 to July 31, 1994.

Author "DNA Results are Admissible in Illinois" 35 No. 1 Aug 1991, "Paternity Settlement Does *Not* Bar Future Action for Support" 35 No. 8 May 1992 and "Family Law Applications of Supreme Court Rule 220" 37 No. 1 Sept 1993 Family Law Newsletter Illinois State Bar Association. Member Committee to Study Caseflow Management in the Law Division 1979, Bar Association Liaison Committee 1979-81, Chair Qualified Arbitrator Mandatory Arbitration Program 1991-94, Cochair Committee to Study Attorney Fee Legislation 1998 and Chair Subcommittee on Judicial Manpower Illinois Circuit Court of Cook County. Former Member Small Firm Committee Chicago Bar Association. Member Decalogue Society of Lawyers (Board of Managers 1973-76, Executive Secretary 1976-77, Second Vice President 1977-78, First Vice President 1978-79, President 1979-80), Illinois Judges Association, National Council of Juvenile and Family Court Judges, Women's Bar Association of Illinois, Northwest Suburban, Illinois State (Council Member Family Law Section 1989-93 and since 2001, Chairman Parentage Subcommittee 1991-93) and American Bar Associations.

Guest Lecturer "Divorce Taxation and Family Planning" Jan 1997 and "The Accountant's Role in Divorce Litigation" Sept 1998 DePaul University Graduate School of Taxation. Participant "The Child as Witness, Legal and Psychological Perspectives" Symposium The Behavioral Science and Legal Forum, Inc. Oct 29, 1998, "Divorce Law: Not the Black Sheep Anymore" Roundtable Discussion 12 No. 140 Illinois Legal Times Dec 1998, "Advanced Seminar on Leading Edge Financial Issues" Panel Illinois Chapter American Academy of Matrimonial Lawyers Feb 12, 1999, "Divorce University IV" Panel The Lilac Tree May 1, 1999, "Marital or Non-Marital, You Make the Call" Panel Jan 17, 2000, "Financial Fundamentals of Divorce" Panel June 2000 and "Child Custody Trial: What You Need to Know" Panel Young Lawyers Section May 14, 2001 Chicago Bar Association, "What Makes an Expert—Now That We Have 'Daubert'?" Jan 15, 2001 and "Using Contempt as an Enforcement Tool" National Child Support Enforcement Association Aug 13, 2001. Organizer and Presenter "Nuts and Bolts for the Domestic Relations Division, A Guide for Bench and Bar" Judges of the

JORDAN, EDWARD R.—*Continued*

Domestic Relations Division Illinois Circuit Court of Cook County Oct 28, 1999. Master Teacher "Preparation and Presentation of a Domestic Relations Trial" IICLE Nov 2, 2001, Jan 25, 2002, Oct 8, 2002 and Oct 10, 2002. Moderator First Annual Family Law Conference IICLE April 11, 2002. Guest Speaker "Developments in the Domestic Relations Division" Circuit Court Committee Chicago Bar Association Sept 12, 2002. Panelist "Discovery: Strategies and Methods for Getting What You Want" Young Lawyers Section Chicago Bar Association Sept 25, 2002. Recipient Certificate of Appreciation for Participation in Chicago Bar Association program of Continuing Legal Education 1982 and Hebrew University Law School Perpetual Fellowship Award from Decalogue Society of Lawyers July 22, 2001. U.S. Army 1958-61. Recipient Good Conduct Medal Aug 1961.

Office: 3010 R. J. Daley Center, Chicago 60602.
Telephone: (312) 603-4894.

JORGENSEN, Ann B. *(Circuit Judge, Illinois Circuit Court Eighteenth Judicial Circuit)* Former Associate Judge.

Office: DuPage County Courthouse, 505 North County Farm Road, Wheaton 60187.
Telephone: (630) 682-7325.

JORZAK, James J. *(Circuit Judge, Illinois Circuit Court of Cook County)*

Office: 1108 R. J. Daley Center, Chicago 60602.
Telephone: (312) 603-4542.

JOY, Mark M. *(Associate Judge, Illinois Circuit Court Fourth Judicial Circuit)* Appointed to term beginning July 1982. Reappointed 1987, 1991, 1995 and 1999. Current term expires 2003. Born Chicago Illinois Dec 15, 1948. Educated at Eastern Illinois University B.A. with honors 1970 M.A. with honors 1975 and Loyola University J.D. 1976. Staff member Loyola Law Journal 1975-76. Admitted to practice Illinois 1976. Began legal practice Hillsboro.

Office: Montgomery County Courthouse, 120 North Main Street, Hillsboro 62049.
Telephone: (217) 532-9501.

JOYCE, John F. *(Associate Judge, Illinois Circuit Court Fifteenth Judicial Circuit)*

Mailing address: P.O. Box 211, Mount Carroll 61053.
Office: 301 North Main, Mount Carroll 61053.
Telephone: (815) 244-0274.

KALLAN, Kathleen G. *(Associate Judge, Illinois Circuit Court Twelfth Judicial Circuit)*

Office: Will County Courthouse, 14 West Jefferson, Joliet 60432.
Telephone: (815) 727-8553.

KAPALA, Frederick J. *(Circuit Judge, Illinois Circuit Court Seventeenth Judicial Circuit)* Associate Judge 1982 to Dec 5, 1994. Elected Circuit Judge to term beginning Dec 5, 1994. Retained by election 2000, current term expires Dec 2006. Currently on assignment by Supreme Court of Illinois as Judge, Illinois Appellate Court Second Judicial District since Dec 1, 2001. Born Rockford Illinois. Educated at Marquette University magna cum laude and University of Illinois College of Law. Moot Court Board. Member Phi Beta Kappa and Pi Gamma Mu. Admitted to practice Illinois, Florida, Wisconsin, U.S. District Court Northern District of Illinois, U.S. Court of Appeals Seventh Circuit, U.S. Court of Federal Claims, U.S. Tax Court and U.S. Supreme Court. In legal practice Rockford Illinois 1977-82. Presiding Judge, Juvenile Court 1989-91.

Assistant State's Attorney Winnebago County 1975-77. Special Assistant Attorney General Consumer Protection Division Northern Illinois 1981-82. Instructor "Medical-Legal Implications for Emergency Medical Care" University of Illinois College of Medicine. Member Court Facilities Pilot Program Department of Children and Family Services, The Association of Trial Lawyers of America, Illinois Council of Juvenile and Family Court Judges, Illinois Judges Association, National Council of Juvenile and Family Court Judges, American Judges Association, American Judicature Society, The Florida Bar, State Bar of Wisconsin, Boone County, Winnebago County, Illinois State and American Bar Associations. Attended Illinois Judicial Conference seminars, National College of Juvenile and Family Law and The National Judicial College. Instructor "Judges and Police: Working for Families Through Community Resources" and "At Risk Youth: Children in Custody" Northwest Illinois Children's Conference, "CASA Within the System" Illinois Court Appointed Special Advocate Workshop and advocate training CASA programs Winnebago County and Boone County. Recipient Outstanding Young Men of America Award. Captain U.S. Army and USAR 1970-80. Board of Directors Barbara Olson Center of Hope and Evergreen Recover Center. Criminal Justice Advisory Board Rockford College. Member Mayor's Youth Policy. Advisory Council, Family Violence Coordinating Council Seventeenth Judicial Circuit, Illinois Family Violence Coordinating Council, Criminal Justice Fact-finding Committee of Winnebago County, Metro Rockford Juvenile Crime and Delinquency Task Force, Court Appointed Special Advocate Program of Winnebago County, Children's Advocacy Project, Multi Agency Board, Youth Services Network and Rotary Club of Rockford.

Office: Winnebago County Courthouse, 400 West State Street, Rockford 61101.
Telephone: (815) 987-2503.

KAPLAN, Jordan *(Associate Judge, Illinois Circuit Court of Cook County)*

Office: 3007 R. J. Daley Center, Chicago 60602.
Telephone: (312) 603-5018.

KARAHALIOS, Pamela G. *(Associate Judge, Illinois Circuit Court of Cook County)* Appointed to term beginning June 19, 1988. Reappointed July 1, 1991, July 1, 1995 and 1999. Current term expires 2003. Born Chicago Illinois Sept 29, 1952. Greek Orthodox. Educated at Lewis University B.A. 1976 J.D. 1978. Admitted to practice Illinois 1978.

With State's Attorney's Office Cook County 1978-88. Member Illinois Judges Association, Women Judges Association, Women's Bar Association of Illinois, Hellenic, Chicago, Northwest Suburban and Illinois State Bar Associations.

Office: 2121 Euclid, Room 209-A, Rolling Meadows 60008.
Telephone: (847) 818-2535.

KARDIS, Phillip J. *(Circuit Judge, Illinois Circuit Court Third Judicial Circuit)* Term expires 2008.
Office: 2000 Edison, Granite City 62040.
Telephone: (618) 692-6200.

KARKULA, Paul A. *(Circuit Judge, Illinois Circuit Court of Cook County)*
Office: 400 R. J. Daley Center, Chicago 60602.
Telephone: (312) 603-2600.

KARMEIER, Lloyd A. *(Circuit Judge, Illinois Circuit Court Twentieth Judicial Circuit)* Elected to term beginning Dec 1, 1986. Retained by election 1992 and 1998. Current term expires Dec 2004. Born Okawville Illinois Jan 12, 1940. Lutheran. Educated at University of Illinois B.S. 1962 LL.B. 1964 replaced by J.D. 1968. Law Clerk to Hon. Byron O. House, Illinois Supreme Court 1964-68. Member Phi Delta Phi and Beta Sigma Psi. Admitted to practice Illinois 1964 and U.S. District Court District of Illinois 1973. In legal practice Nashville 1964-86.
Assistant State's Attorney 1964-68 and State's Attorney 1968-72 Washington County. Law Clerk to Hon. James L. Foreman, U.S. District Court Eastern District of Illinois 1972-73. Member Washington County (Secretary), Illinois State and American Bar Associations. Chairman Washington County Chapter American Red Cross. President and Treasurer Nashville Jaycees.
Office: Washington County Courthouse, Nashville 62263.
Telephone: (618) 327-3612.

KARNEZIS, Themis N. *(Circuit Judge, Illinois Circuit Court of Cook County)* Former Associate Judge. Currently on assignment by Supreme Court of Illinois as Judge, Illinois Appellate Court First Judicial District Division Four. Born Chicago Illinois Sept 18, 1942. Catholic. Educated at University of Detroit B.S. 1965 and John Marshall Law School J.D. 1970. Admitted to practice Illinois 1970 and U.S. District Court District of Illinois 1970. Began legal practice Chicago 1970.
Assistant State's Attorney 1970-74. Prosecutor Village of Hazelcrest 1974-82 and City of Country Club Hills 1974-82. Member Illinois Judges Association, Hellenic (Director), Chicago, Southwest Suburban (Director) and Illinois State (Assembly) Bar Associations. Director Beverly Improvement Association.
Office: 160 North LaSalle Street, Room N1511, Chicago 60601.
Telephone: (312) 793-5413.

KATZ, Nancy J. *(Associate Judge, Illinois Circuit Court of Cook County)* Appointed.
Office: 1902 R. J. Daley Center, Chicago 60602.
Telephone: (312) 603-5921.

KAUFFMANN, Kathleen O. *(Associate Judge, Illinois Circuit Court Fifteenth Judicial Circuit)*
Office: Ogle County Courthouse, Fourth and Washington, Oregon 61061.
Telephone: (815) 732-3201.

KAVITT, Richard A. *(Associate Judge, Illinois Circuit Court of Cook County)*
Office: 2121 Euclid, Room 208-A, Rolling Meadows 60008.
Telephone: (847) 818-2535.

KAWAMOTO, Lynne *(Associate Judge, Illinois Circuit Court of Cook County)*
Office: 1806 R. J. Daley Center, Chicago 60602.
Telephone: (312) 603-6440.

KAZMIERSKI, Joseph G., Jr. *(Circuit Judge, Illinois Circuit Court of Cook County)*
Office: 2600 South California Avenue, Room 207, Chicago 60608.
Telephone: (773) 869-7425.

KEEHAN, Michael R. *(Circuit Judge, Illinois Circuit Court of Cook County)*
Office: 155 West 51st Street, Chicago 60609.
Telephone: (773) 373-8877.

KELLEY, Daniel J. *(Circuit Judge, Illinois Circuit Court of Cook County)*
Office: 1500 Maybrook Drive, Room 148, Maywood 60153.
Telephone: (708) 865-6401.

KELLEY, Patrick W. *(Circuit Judge, Illinois Circuit Court Seventh Judicial Circuit)*
Office: 716 Sangamon County Complex, 200 South Ninth Street, Springfield 62701.
Telephone: (217) 753-6813.

KELLY, Carol A. *(Circuit Judge, Illinois Circuit Court of Cook County)*
Office: 1100 South Hamilton, Room G24-N, Chicago 60612.
Telephone: (312) 433-4757.

KELLY, William A. *(Circuit Judge, Illinois Circuit Court Fifteenth Judicial Circuit)* Term expires 2008. Former Chief Judge.
Office: Jo Daviess County Courthouse, 330 North Bench Street, Galena 61036.
Telephone: (815) 777-0037.

KELSEY, Bruce R. *(Associate Judge, Illinois Circuit Court Eighteenth Judicial Circuit)*
Office: DuPage County Courthouse, 505 North County Farm Road, Wheaton 60187.
Telephone: (630) 682-7300.

KENNEDY, James W. *(Circuit Judge, Illinois Circuit Court of Cook County)*
Office: 1804 R. J. Daley Center, Chicago 60602.
Telephone: (312) 603-6498.

KENNEDY, John R. *(Associate Judge, Illinois Circuit Court Sixth Judicial Circuit)*
Office: Champaign County Courthouse, 101 East Main, Urbana 61801.
Telephone: (217) 384-3702.

KENNEDY, John Todd *(Associate Judge, Illinois Circuit Court Seventeenth Judicial Circuit)*
Office: 601 North Main Street, Belvidere 61008-2600.
Telephone: (815) 544-0371.

KENNEDY, Kathleen G. *(Circuit Judge, Illinois Circuit Court of Cook County)*
Office: 32 West Randolph, Room 1403, Chicago 60602.
Telephone: (312) 609-3790.

KENNEDY, Kerry M. *(Circuit Judge, Illinois Circuit Court of Cook County)*
Office 1303 R. J. Daley Center, Chicago 60602.
Telephone: (312) 603-7959.

KENNELLY, Matthew F. *(Judge, United States District Court Northern District of Illinois)* Appointed for life by President Bill Clinton to term beginning June 22, 1999. Born Oct 6, 1956. Educated at University of Notre Dame B.A. summa cum laude 1978 and Harvard Law School J.D. magna cum laude 1981. Law Clerk to Hon. Prentice H. Marshall, U.S. District Court Northern District of Illinois 1982-84. In legal practice Chicago 1981-82 and 1984-99.

Office: 1778 U.S. Courthouse, 219 South Dearborn Street, Chicago 60604.

Telephone: (312) 435-5618.

KEYS, Arlander *(Magistrate Judge, United States District Court Northern District of Illinois)* Appointed by U.S. District Court judges to term beginning Feb 1995. Reappointed Feb 2003, current term expires Feb 20, 2011. Presiding Magistrate Judge since Oct 1998. Educated at DePaul University B.A. 1972 J.D. 1975. Admitted to practice Illinois 1975. Administrative Law Judge June 1986 to April 1988 and Chief Administrative Law Judge April 1988 to Jan 1995 Office of Hearings and Appeals Social Security Administration U.S. Department of Health and Human Services.

Trial Attorney National Labor Relations Board 1975-80. Regional Attorney Federal Labor Relations Authority June 1980 to June 1986. Adjunct Professor of Administrative Law John Marshall Law School since 1999. Member Advisory Committee Study of Rules of Practice and Internal Operating Procedures of District and Bankruptcy Courts. Member Illinois Judicial Council, Chicago (Committee on Minority Federal Jury Service), Cook County, Seventh Circuit (Liaison for the U.S. District Court), Federal (Former Member Board of Directors, Treasurer 1999-2000, Secretary 2000-01 and Second Vice President 2001-02 Chicago Chapter) and American Bar Associations. USMC 1963-67. Second Vice President Just the Beginning Foundation 2001-02.

Office: 2240 U.S. Courthouse, 219 South Dearborn Street, Chicago 60604.

Telephone: (312) 435-5630.

KICK, Michael J. *(Circuit Judge, Illinois Circuit Court Twenty-first Judicial Circuit)*

Office: Kankakee County Courthouse, 450 East Court Street, Kankakee 60901.

Telephone: (815) 937-2926.

KILANDER, Robert K. *(Chief Judge, Illinois Circuit Court Eighteenth Judicial Circuit)*

Office: 505 North County Farm Road, Wheaton 60187.

Telephone: (630) 682-7303.

KILBRIDE, Thomas L. *(Justice, Supreme Court of Illinois)* Elected 2000. Born LaSalle Illinois. Educated at St. Mary's College B.A. magna cum laude 1978 and Antioch School of Law J.D. 1981. Admitted to practice U.S. District Court Central District of Illinois and U.S. Court of Appeals Seventh Circuit. In legal practice Rock Island for 20 years.

Former Board Member, Former Vice President and Past President Illinois Township Attorneys Association. Former Volunteer Lawyer and Charter Member Illinois Pro Bono Center. Member Rock Island County and Illinois State Bar Associations. Former Member Rock Island Human Relations Commission. Volunteer Legal Advisor Community Caring Conference and Quad City Harvest, Inc. Charter Chairman Quad Cities Interfaith Sponsoring Committee.

Office: 1819 Fourth Avenue, Rock Island 61201.

Telephone: (309) 794-3608.

KILEY, Michael P. *(Circuit Judge, Illinois Circuit Court Fourth Judicial Circuit)* Elected to term beginning Dec 7, 1992. Retained by election 1998, current term expires 2004. Born Chicago Illinois June 1, 1951. Roman Catholic. Educated at University of Illinois B.A 1973 and John Marshall University Law School J.D. 1977. Admitted to practice Illinois 1977 and U.S. District Court Central District of Illinois. In legal practice Shelbyville 1977-92.

Assistant State's Attorney 1977-80 and State's Attorney 1984-92 Shelby County. Instructor in Business Law Sparks Business College 1984-92. Member Shelby County (Past President) and Illinois State Bar Associations. Named in Outstanding Young Men of America. Recipient Outstanding Prosecution Awards from Growing Strong Sexual Assault Center, Illinois Department of Conservation and Illinois Association of Arson Investigation. Democrat. Member Rotary, Moose, Chamber of Commerce and Knights of Columbus. Enjoys sports and family activities.

Office: Shelby County Courthouse, Shelbyville 62565.

Telephone: (217) 774-3622.

KIMMEL, E. Dan *(Associate Judge, Illinois Circuit Court First Judicial Circuit)* Appointed Dec 17, 1990. Reappointed July 1, 1991, July 1, 1995 and July 1, 1999. Current term expires 2003. Born Du Quoin Illinois May 5, 1937. Methodist. Educated at University of Illinois B.S. 1959 J.D. 1965. Admitted to practice Illinois 1967 and U.S. District Court Southern District of Illinois 1975. In legal practice Carbondale 1967-90.

Member Jackson County and Illinois State Bar Associations. Captain USAF 1959-65.

Office: Jackson County Courthouse, Murphysboro 62966.

Telephone: (618) 687-7332.

E-mail address: edankimmel@yahoo.com

KINNAIRD, Dorothy Kirie *(Circuit Judge, Illinois Circuit Court of Cook County)* Appointed Jan 11, 1991. Elected 1992. Retained by election. Serves Chancery Division. Presiding Judge since Jan 2002. Educated at Lawrence University B.A. 1971 and DePaul University College of Law J.D. 1974. In legal practice Illinois 1978-1991.

Assistant State's Attorney Cook County 1975-78. Village Attorney Franklin Park 1978-91. Instructor in Law, Legal Writing and Research Illinois Institute of Technology, Chicago-Kent College of Law 1978-80. Board of Directors 1978-99 and President 1989-91 Center for Conflict Resolution. Secretary Chicago Bar Association 1985-87. Board of Directors Chicago Bar Foundation since 1999. Member Committee on Complex Litigation since 2000. Member since 2000 and Vice Chair since 2001 Judicial Mentor Committee Illinois Judicial Conference. Former Member Illinois Trial Lawyers Association and Women's Bar Association of Illinois. Member Hellenic, Illinois State and American Bar Associations. Presenter "Termination of Parental Rights/Adoptions" Juvenile Law Seminar Nov 1994 and "Preliminary Injunctions" Chancery and Miscellaneous Remedies Seminar March 1996 Illinois Judicial Conference and "Temporary Restraining Orders and Preliminary Injunction Practice" Chancery and Special Remedies Jan 17, 1996, "Prelimi-

KINNAIRD, DOROTHY KIRIE—*Continued*
nary Injunctions and Temporary Restraining Orders" Motion Practice in the Law and Chancery Divisions Jan 20, 2000 and "Litigation Strategies for Practice in the Chancery Division" Civil Practice—Perspectives from the Bench Jan 31, 2001 Chicago Bar Association CLE. Chair Mentoring Committee New Judge Mentoring Program Cook County since 1999. Faculty Member "Judicial Conduct, Courtroom Management and Ethical Issues in Handling Judicial Life" New Judge Seminar Dec 2001, "Managing High Profile Cases" Education Conference Feb 2002 and March 2002 and Bankruptcy Law for State Court Judges June 2002 Illinois Judicial Conference. Member Winnetka Congregational Church since 1976. Board of Directors Trinity High School 1993-99.

Office: 2403 R. J. Daley Center, Chicago 60602.
Telephone: (312) 603-4181.

KINNEY, Gerald R. *(Circuit Judge, Illinois Circuit Court Twelfth Judicial Circuit)* Appointed Dec 1994. Elected Nov 1996. Retained by election 2002, current term expires Dec 2008. Born Joliet Illinois April 3, 1950. Catholic. Educated at Southern Illinois University B.A. with honors 1972 and Loyola University School of Law J.D. 1975. Admitted to practice Illinois 1975, U.S. District Court Northern District of Illinois, Trial Bar of U.S. District Court Northern District of Illinois and U.S. Supreme Court. In legal practice Joliet 1975-94.

Important decision: imposed death penalty on child killer Timothy Buss 1996. Member Illinois Trial Lawyers Association, Will County (President 1987-88), Illinois State and American Bar Associations. Republican. Enjoys fishing, children, sports and travel.

Office: 462 Will County Courthouse, 14 West Jefferson Street, Joliet 60432.
Telephone: (815) 727-8537.

KIPPERMAN, Carol A. *(Associate Judge, Illinois Circuit Court of Cook County)*
Office: 1500 Maybrook Drive, Room 289, Maywood 60153.
Telephone: (708) 865-6060.

KIRBY, John P. *(Circuit Judge, Illinois Circuit Court of Cook County)*
Office: 2600 South California, Chicago 60608.
Telephone: (773) 869-3373.

KLEIN, Kurt *(Circuit Judge, Illinois Circuit Court Sixteenth Judicial Circuit)* Appointed Associate Judge. Assumed office as Circuit Judge.
Office: 133 West State Street, Sycamore 60178.
Telephone: (815) 895-7160.

KNECHT, James A. *(Judge, Illinois Appellate Court Fourth Judicial District)* Elected 1986. Retained by election 1996, current term expires Dec 2006. Former Presiding Judge. Born Lincoln Illinois 1944. Educated at Illinois State University and University of Illinois College of Law J.D. with honors 1973. Editor University of Illinois Law Review. Law Clerk to Hon. Robert C. Underwood, Supreme Court of Illinois 1973-74. Member Order of the Coif. Associate Judge 1975-78 and Circuit Judge 1978-86, Illinois Circuit Court Eleventh Judicial Circuit.

Co-founder and Past Charter President Robert C. Underwood Inn of Court. Fellow Illinois Bar Foundation. Member Appellate Lawyers Association, Illinois Judges Association, American Judicature Society, McLean County and Illinois State Bar Associations. Board of Directors Illinois State University Foundation Board and Institute for Collaborative Solutions.

Office: 318 West Washington Street, Bloomington 61701.
Telephone: (309) 829-3715.

KNIGHT, John *(Circuit Judge, Illinois Circuit Court Third Judicial Circuit)* Elected to term beginning 2000. Born St. Louis Missouri 1952. Educated at Greenville College B.S.B.A. 1977 and Washington University J.D. 1981.

State's Attorney Bond County Jan 1983 to Dec 2000. U.S. Army 1972-74.

Office: Bond County Courthouse, 200 West College Avenue, Greenville 62246.
Telephone: (618) 664-0730.
Fax: (618) 664-4676
E-mail address: judgeknight@gvc.net

KOCORAS, Charles P. *(Chief Judge, United States District Court Northern District of Illinois)* Appointed for life by President Jimmy Carter to term beginning Nov 1980. Chief Judge since July 1, 2002. Educated at Wilson Junior College Chicago 1956-58 and DePaul University B.S. in Accounting 1961 J.D. 1969. Valedictorian DePaul University 1969. Member Beta Alpha Psi. Admitted to practice Illinois 1969.

Former Trial Attorney, former Deputy Chief Criminal and Special Prosecutions Divisions, First Assistant U.S. Attorney July 1975 to July 1977 and Assistant U.S. Attorney July 1977 to Oct 1977 U.S. Department of Justice Chicago. Chairman Illinois Commerce Commission Nov 1977 to Jan 1979. Instructor in Trial Practice for senior students John Marshall Law School since 1975. Member Federal Criminal Jury Instruction Committee Seventh Federal Circuit. Member Chicago Bar Association (Committee on Evaluation of Candidates Investigation Division). Seminar Lecturer IICLE and Chicago Bar Association. Recipient Chicago Tribune Award for Outstanding Guardsman 1965, Department of Justice Special Commendation Award for Outstanding Service 1974 and Department of Justice Director's Award for Superior Performance as Assistant United States Attorney 1976. Illinois National Guard 1961-67 (active duty May 1961 to Nov 1961). Revenue Agent, Instructor, District Conferee and Estate Tax Examiner U.S. Internal Revenue Service Chicago 1962-69.

Office: U.S. Courthouse, 219 South Dearborn Street, Chicago 60604.
Telephone: (312) 435-5600.

KOGAN, Randye A. *(Associate Judge, Illinois Circuit Court of Cook County)*
Office: 2209 R. J. Daley Center, Chicago 60602.
Telephone: (312) 603-6056.

KONETSKI, James J. *(Associate Judge, Illinois Circuit Court Eighteenth Judicial Circuit)*
Office: 505 North County Farm Road, Wheaton 60187.
Telephone: (630) 682-7300.

KOURI, Stephen A. *(Circuit Judge, Illinois Circuit Court Tenth Judicial Circuit)*
Office: 215 Peoria County Courthouse, 324 Main Street, Peoria 61602-1363.
Telephone: (309) 672-6047.

KOVAL, Joseph P. *(Circuit Judge, Illinois Circuit Court Seventh Judicial Circuit)* Appointed to term beginning July 1, 1976. Elected 1976. Retained by election Nov 1982, 1988, 1994 and 2000. Current term expires Dec 2006. Former Chief Judge. Born Mount Olive Illinois March 16, 1929. Roman Catholic. Educated at Blackburn College A.A. 1950 and University of Illinois B.A. 1952 LL.B. 1954. Admitted to practice Illinois 1955. Began legal practice Carlinville Jan 1958. Hearing Officer, Illinois Department of Aeronautics 1961-69.

Employed by Illinois Legislative Reference Bureau 1956-57. State's Attorney Macoupin County 1972-76. Member Illinois Judges Association, American Judicature Society and Macoupin County Bar Association. Corporal U.S. Army 1954-56. Democrat. Member Knights of Columbus.

Office: Macoupin County Courthouse, 201 East Main Street, Carlinville 62626.

Telephone: (217) 854-3211.

KOWALSKI, Robert J. *(Circuit Judge, Illinois Circuit Court of Cook County)* Former Associate Judge.

Office: 2121 Euclid, Room 102-A, Rolling Meadows 60008.

Telephone: (847) 818-2534.

KRAMER, Michael D. *(Associate Judge, Illinois Circuit Court Twenty-first Judicial Circuit)*

Office: Kankakee County Courthouse, 450 East Court Street, Kankakee 60901.

Telephone: (815) 937-2915.

KUEHN, Clyde L. *(Judge, Illinois Appellate Court Fifth Judicial District)* Former Circuit Judge, Illinois Circuit Court Twentieth Judicial Circuit. Served Illinois Appellate Court Fifth Judicial District by special assignment.

Office: 23 Public Square, Suite 450, Belleville 62220.

Telephone: (618) 236-8610.

KUHAR, Ludwig J., Jr. *(Associate Judge, Illinois Circuit Court Twelfth Judicial Circuit)*

Office: Will County Courthouse, 14 West Jefferson, Joliet 60432.

Telephone: (815) 727-8540.

KUTRUBIS, Lambros J. *(Associate Judge, Illinois Circuit Court of Cook County)*

Office: 1303 R. J. Daley Center, Chicago 60602.

Telephone: (312) 603-4639.

LACY, William G. *(Circuit Judge, Illinois Circuit Court of Cook County)*

Office: 2600 South California, Chicago 60608.

Telephone: (773) 869-3160.

LADD, Heidi N. *(Associate Judge, Illinois Circuit Court Sixth Judicial Circuit)* Appointed to term beginning Aug 23, 1999. Educated at University of Illinois B.A. with high distinction 1978 J.D. 1982. Admitted to practice Illinois 1982 and U.S. District Court Central District of Illinois 1984.

Assistant State's Attorney Lead Prosecutor Champaign County 1982-99. Instructor in Trial Advocacy University of Illinois College of Law since 1994. Member East Central Illinois Women's Attorney Association, Illinois Judges Association, Champaign County and Illinois State Bar Associations. Instructor in Trial Advocacy Illinois Appellate Prosecutor since 1994. Instructor in Trial Advocacy and DNA Evidence National District Attorneys Association 1999. Presenter on Trial Advocacy and DNA Evidence Attorneys Associations in Illinois, Minnesota and Iowa 1994-99.

Office: Champaign County Courthouse, 101 East Main Street, Urbana 61801.

Telephone: (217) 384-3715.

LAGOSKI, Diane M. *(Associate Judge, Illinois Circuit Court Eighth Judicial Circuit)*

Office: Brown County Courthouse, Mount Sterling 62353.

Telephone: (217) 773-3200.

LAMPKIN, Bertina E. *(Circuit Judge, Illinois Circuit Court of Cook County)* Appointed Associate Judge to term beginning July 2, 1987. Elected Circuit Judge 1992. Retained by election 1998, current term expires 2004. Born Chicago Illinois Dec 20, 1948. Methodist. Educated at Roosevelt University B.A. 1975 and DePaul University College of Law J.D. 1974. Recipient Lex Legio Scholarship 1973. Admitted to practice Illinois 1974, U.S. District Court District of Illinois 1975 and U.S. Court of Appeals Seventh Circuit 1975.

Assistant State's Attorney Cook County 1974-85. Senior Attorney Corporation Counsel's Office Chicago 1985-87. Author "Supervision From the Prosecutor's Point of View" Illinois State Bar Association Newsletter 1976. Member Illinois Judges Association, Illinois Judicial Council, Chicago (Vice Chair Judicial Evaluation Committee), Cook County (Treasurer and Second Vice President) and Illinois State Bar Associations. Associate Judge New Judge Seminar IICLE Nov 1987 and Problems in Criminal Evidence The National Judicial College Nov 1988. Instructor in Criminal Law New Judge Seminar since 1988 and Domestic Violence 1997 and 1998 IICLE. Recipient Outstanding Service Award from Cook County Bar Association 1978. Previously employed as cashier and bookkeeper by A&P Stores. Member Christian Methodist Episcopal Church (Missionary, Steward, choir member, youth counselor, former youth tutor and Sunday School teacher). Enjoys roller skating, singing and comedies.

Office: 2600 South California, Room 506, Chicago 60608.

Telephone: (773) 869-3196.

LANIGAN, Joanne L. *(Circuit Judge, Illinois Circuit Court of Cook County)*

Office: 2571 R. J. Daley Center, Chicago 60602.

Telephone: (312) 603-4467.

LANUTI, James A. *(Circuit Judge, Illinois Circuit Court Thirteenth Judicial Circuit)* Former Associate Judge.

Office: Criminal Justice Center, 707 Etna Road, Ottawa 61350.

Telephone: (815) 434-8285.

LARSEN, Diane Joan *(Circuit Judge, Illinois Circuit Court of Cook County)*

Office: 2203 R. J. Daley Center, Chicago 60602.

Telephone: (312) 603-6062.

LARSON, Richard J. *(Associate Judge, Illinois Circuit Court Sixteenth Judicial Circuit)*

Office: Kane County Courthouse, 100 South Third Street, Geneva 60134.

Telephone: (630) 232-3441.

LAURIE, John G. *(Associate Judge, Illinois Circuit Court of Cook County)* Appointed to term beginning May 7, 1981. Reappointed to subsequent terms. Born Oak Park Illinois Aug 1, 1945. Catholic. Educated at St. Mary's College B.A. 1967 and DePaul University J.D. 1970. Member Alpha Kappa Psi. Admitted to practice Illinois 1970 and Wisconsin 1970. Began legal practice Chicago 1970.
Member Chicago and Northwest Bar Associations.
Office: 1501 R. J. Daley Center, Chicago 60602.
Telephone: (312) 603-4827.

LAWLER, Patrick N. *(Associate Judge, Illinois Circuit Court Nineteenth Judicial Circuit)*
Office: Lake County Courthouse, 18 North County Street, Waukegan 60085.
Telephone: (847) 377-3743.

LAWRENCE, Jeffrey *(Circuit Judge, Illinois Circuit Court of Cook County)*
Office: 3003 R. J. Daley Center, Chicago 60602.
Telephone: (312) 603-5278.

LAWRENCE, Paul G. *(Associate Judge, Illinois Circuit Court Eleventh Judicial Circuit)*
Office: McLean County Law and Justice Center, 104 West Front Street, Bloomington 61701.
Telephone: (309) 888-5243.

LAWS, Marjorie C. *(Circuit Judge, Illinois Circuit Court of Cook County)*
Office: 2600 South California Avenue, Chicago 60608.
Telephone: (773) 869-3049.

LeCHIEN, Robert P. *(Circuit Judge, Illinois Circuit Court Twentieth Judicial Circuit)* Former Associate Judge.
Office: County Building, 10 Public Square, Belleville 62220.
Telephone: (618) 277-7325.

LECHWAR, Rodney B. *(Circuit Judge, Illinois Circuit Court Twelfth Judicial Circuit)* Former Associate Judge. Assumed office as Circuit Judge. Term expires 2004. Former Chief Judge.
Office: 439 Will County Courthouse, 14 West Jefferson, Joliet 60432.
Telephone: (815) 727-8540.

LEFKOW, Joan Humphrey *(Judge, United States District Court Northern District of Illinois)* Appointed for life by President Bill Clinton to term beginning Sept 1, 2000. Born Kansas Jan 9, 1944. Episcopalian. Educated at Wheaton College A.B. 1965 and Northwestern University J.D. 1971. Editorial Board Northwestern University Law Review. Law Clerk to Hon. Thomas E. Fairchild, U.S. Court of Appeals Seventh Circuit. Admitted to practice Illinois 1971, U.S. District Court Northern District of Illinois 1972 and U.S. Courts of Appeals Seventh 1972 and Fifth 1980 Circuits. Began legal practice Chicago 1972. Administrative Law Judge 1975-77 and Chief Administrative Law Judge 1977-79, Illinois Fair Employment Practices Commission. Former Magistrate, U.S. District Court Northern District of Illinois, appointed by U.S. District Court judges to term beginning Nov 9, 1982. Former Judge, U.S. Bankruptcy Court Northern District of Illinois, appointed by U.S. Court of Appeals Seventh Circuit judges.
Attorney Legal Assistance Foundation of Chicago 1972-75. Executive Director Cook County Legal Assistance Foundation 1981-82. Author Casenotes "An Expansion of the Stevedoring Contractors Remedies Against the Shipowner in Admiralty" 65 Northwestern University L. Rev. 506 and "Workmen's Compensation and Protective Legislation for Women" 65 Northwestern University L. Rev. 1024. Instructor University of Miami Law School 1980-81. Democrat.
Office: 1956 U.S. Courthouse, 219 South Dearborn Street, Chicago 60604.
Telephone: (312) 435-5832.

LEFSTEIN, Lori R. *(Circuit Judge, Illinois Circuit Court Fourteenth Judicial Circuit)*
Office: 210 Fifteenth Street, Room 408, Rock Island 61201.
Telephone: (309) 558-3286.

LEINENWEBER, Harry Daniel *(Senior Judge, United States District Court Northern District of Illinois)* Appointed for life by President Ronald Reagan to term beginning Jan 17, 1986. Assumed Senior status, serves by assignment. Born Joliet Illinois June 3, 1937. Roman Catholic. Educated at University of Notre Dame A.B. in History cum laude 1958 and University of Chicago Law School J.D. 1962. Admitted to practice Illinois 1962, U.S. District Court Northern District of Illinois 1967 and Trial Bar of U.S. District Court Northern District of Illinois 1983. In legal practice Joliet 1962-86.
City Attorney Joliet 1963-67. Special Prosecutor Will County 1968-70. Instructor University of Illinois-Chicago Fall since 1988. Member Illinois Judicial Advisory Council 1973-84. Board of Directors Law Club of Chicago 1996-98. Former Member Illinois Trial Lawyers Association, Will County Legal Assistance (Board member 1982-86), Will County (Board member 1984-86) and Illinois State Bar Associations. Commissioner since 1976, Member Executive Committee 1992-94 and Life Member since 1996 National Conference of Commissioners on Uniform State Laws. Attended Seventh Circuit Judicial Conference annually since May 1986 and Federal Judges Association Conference Oct 1986. Instructor Legislative Process Seminar University of Illinois since 1988. Member National Advisory Committee University of Illinois Institute of Government and Public Affairs since 1998. Republican. Precinct Committeeman 1966-86. Member Illinois General Assembly House of Representatives 42nd District 1973-83 (Chairman Judiciary I Committee 1981-83). Delegate Republican National Convention 1980. Special Counsel Village of Park Forest 1967-74, Village of Bolingbrook 1975-77 and Will County Forest Preserve 1977. Former Member American Interprofessional Institute and American Cancer Society. Board Member Good Shepherd Manor since 1981.
Office: U.S. Courthouse, 219 South Dearborn Street, Chicago 60604.
Telephone: (312) 435-7612.

LESSEN, Larry Lee *(Judge, United States Bankruptcy Court Central District of Illinois)* Appointed by U.S. District Court judges to term beginning 1973. Reappointed by U.S. Court of Appeals Seventh Circuit judges. Former Chief Judge. Born Lincoln Illinois Dec 25, 1939. Educated at University of Illinois B.A.S. 1960 LL.B. 1962. Law Clerk to Hon. Casper Platt, U.S. District Court District of Illinois 1962-64. Admitted to practice Illinois 1962 and U.S. District Court Eastern District of Illinois 1964. In legal practice at Danville 1967-85.

LESSEN, LARRY LEE—*Continued*
Magistrate, U.S. District Court Central District of Illinois 1973-84.

Assistant State's Attorney Vermilion County 1964-67. Assistant Attorney General Illinois 1968-70. Danville City Attorney 1971-73. Member Lincoln-Douglas Inn of Court, National Conference of Bankruptcy Judges (Board of Governors), Sangamon County, Vermilion County, Federal and American (Judicial Administration Division) Bar Associations. Past President Danville Family Service Bureau.

Office: 226 Federal Building, 600 East Monroe Street, Springfield 62701-1626.

Telephone: (217) 492-4566.

LESSMAN, Sarah P. *(Associate Judge, Illinois Circuit Court Nineteenth Judicial Circuit)*

Office: Lake County Courthouse, 18 North County Street, Waukegan 60085.

Telephone: (847) 377-3401.

LESTON, Patrick J. *(Associate Judge, Illinois Circuit Court Eighteenth Judicial Circuit)* Appointed to term beginning Oct 1995. Reappointed to subsequent term. Born Maywood Illinois May 2, 1948. Educated at University of Illinois B.S. 1970 and Northwestern University School of Law J.D. cum laude 1973. Admitted to practice Illinois 1973, U.S. District Court Northern District of Illinois and U.S. Court of Appeals Seventh Circuit. In legal practice 1973-95.

Editor Young Lawyers Division Newsletter Illinois State Bar Association 1983. Author "Report on Professionalism" Illinois State Bar Association 1988, "Proof Requirement for Leaving the Scene" 7 Illinois State Bar Association Traffic Laws Newsletter 3 Jan 1998 and "Going South (Travel in Antarctica)" 10, 3 Oct 1997 and "Judicial Tips: Domestic Relations" 21 Oct 2000 DuPage Bar Brief. Member DuPage Inns of Court, Justinian Law Society, Illinois Judges Association (Board of Directors since 1998, Co-chair Benefits and Pension since 1998), Chicago, DuPage County (Chair 1976, Vice Chair 1984-86 and President 1987 Young Lawyers Division, Chair Lawyers Referral 1985, Chair Judiciary Committee 1988, General Counsel 1990-91), Illinois State (Member since 1981 and Agenda Chair 1985-86 Assembly, Secretary 1983, Vice Chair 1984 and Chair 1985 Young Lawyers Division, Member Special Committee on Professionalism 1985, Board of Governors 1990-98) and American (Committee on Economics of Law Office Management 1981, Illinois Delegate Young Lawyers Division Assembly 1982-85) Bar Associations. Instructor "Construction Litigation After Moorman" 1985, "Basic Guide to Incorporation" 1987, "Section 1031 (Starker) Tax Deferred Exchanges" 1990, Trial Advocacy Course 1995-2000 and "Rule to Show Cause/ Contempt" Family Law seminar May 2000 DuPage County Bar Association and "Efficient Residential Real Estate Closings" ATLF 1989. Ethics Moderator Eighteenth Judicial Circuit Institute Day Jan 2000. Enjoys travel, golf, scuba, volleyball and skiing.

Office: 505 North County Farm Road, Wheaton 60187.

Telephone: (630) 682-7300.

LEVIN, Ian H. *(Magistrate Judge, United States District Court Northern District of Illinois)* Appointed by U.S. District Court judges 1997. Educated at University of Illinois 1957-59 and DePaul University B.S. 1961 J.D. cum laude 1966. Law Secretary to Hon. Daniel P. Ward, Supreme Court of Illinois Nov 1966 to Oct 1969. In legal practice Sept 1973 to Sept 1989. Former Circuit Judge, Illinois Circuit Court of Cook County, appointed to term beginning Sept 1989.

Chief Appeals Division Public Defender Cook County Oct 1969 to Sept 1973. Special Counsel to Chicago Board of Election Commissioners. Co-author "Continuing Legal Education for Judges" Women's Bar Association of Illinois News 1990 and IICLE Election Law Chapter "State Court Litigation and Its Impact on Federal Litigation" 1991. CPA 1961. Founding Member Appellate Lawyers Association 1968. Member Chicago (Judiciary Committee 1991), Illinois State and American Bar Associations. Lecturer "Impact of New Illinois Drug Laws" Institute of Criminal Justice 1972 and Law in American Society Project 1972. Revenue Agent Internal Revenue Service Feb 1962 to Nov 1966. Judge Regional Moot Court Competition 1974 and Mock Trial Advocacy Competition 1990 and 1991. Board Member DePaul University College of Law Alumni Association since 1992. Member Civil Rights Committee Anti-Defamation League since 1990.

Office: U.S. Courthouse, 219 South Dearborn Street, Chicago 60604.

Telephone: (312) 435-6060.

LEVIN, Leonard L. *(Recalled Circuit Judge, Illinois Circuit Court of Cook County)* Retired, serves by recall.

Office: 2106 R. J. Daley Center, Chicago 60602.

Telephone: (312) 603-3388.

LEWIS, Casandra *(Circuit Judge, Illinois Circuit Court of Cook County)*

Office: 1303 R. J. Daley Center, Chicago 60602.

Telephone: (312) 603-7959.

LEWIS, David W. *(Associate Judge, Illinois Circuit Court Fifth Judicial Circuit)*

Office: Edgar County Courthouse, 115 West Court Street, Paris 61944.

Telephone: (217) 466-7472.

LEWIS, Loren "Larry" P. *(Circuit Judge, Illinois Circuit Court Second Judicial Circuit)* Appointed to term beginning Jan 18, 1978. Elected Nov 1978. Retained by election 1984, 1990, 1996 and 2002. Current term expires 2008. Born Berwyn Illinois March 2, 1942. Baptist. Educated at University of Illinois B.A. with honors 1964 J.D. 1967. Member Tau Kappa Epsilon. Admitted to practice Illinois 1967 and U.S. District Court Southern District of Illinois 1967. In legal practice Benton 1967-78.

State's Attorney Franklin County 1972-76. Member Illinois Judges Association, Franklin County (President 1973) and Illinois State Bar Associations. Captain 1967-69 and Special Deputy to the Chief Counsel Missile Command 1968 U.S. Army. Member American Legion, Benton Elks Lodge 1234, Rotary Club, Boneyard Bocce Ball Club and bridge clubs. Enjoys bridge, gardening and fishing.

Office: Franklin County Courthouse, Benton 62812.

Telephone: (618) 438-6003.

LEWIS, Robert W. *(Associate Judge, Illinois Circuit Court Second Judicial Circuit)* Appointed Jan 2001. Term expires 2003. Born Christopher Illinois Sept 17, 1949. Educated at University of Illinois B.A. 1971 and Florida State University J.D. cum laude 1974. Admitted

LEWIS, ROBERT W.—*Continued*

to practice Illinois 1974, U.S. District Court Southern District of Illinois 1974 and U.S. Court of Appeals Seventh Circuit 1976. In legal practice Benton 1974-2001.

Member Franklin County (Past President) and Illinois State Bar Associations. Affiliated with Boys Scouts of America for 35 years. Past President Benton Rotary Club and Benton Lion's Club. Held numerous positions with First United Methodist Church Benton Illinois.

Office: Franklin County Courthouse, Benton 62812.

Telephone: (618) 438-6003.

LEWIS, Theodis P. *(Associate Judge, Illinois Circuit Court Seventh Judicial Circuit)*

Office: County Complex, 200 South Ninth Street, Springfield 62701.

Telephone: (217) 546-2701.

LICHTENSTEIN, David G. *(Circuit Judge, Illinois Circuit Court of Cook County)* Appointed to term beginning Jan 30, 1987. Elected Nov 1988. Retained by election Nov 1994 and 2000. Current term expires Dec 2006. Born Chicago Illinois July 13, 1945. Educated at Washington University A.B. 1968 J.D. 1974 and New York University M.A. 1971. Admitted to practice Illinois 1974, Missouri 1975, New York 1980, U.S. District Court Southern District of Illinois, Trial Bar of U.S. District Court Northern District of Illinois, U.S. Courts of Appeals Fourth, Fifth, Seventh, Eighth, Eleventh and District of Columbia Circuits and U.S. Supreme Court. In legal practice Springfield 1975-78 and Chicago 1978-87 Illinois.

Assistant Attorney General Illinois 1975-79. Legal Counsel to Attorney General Illinois 1983-87.

Office: 2204 R. J. Daley Center, Chicago 60602.

Telephone: (312) 603-4646.

LINCOLN, Frank W. *(Circuit Judge, Illinois Circuit Court Sixth Judicial Circuit)* Elected to term beginning Dec 1, 1984. Retained by election 1990, 1996 and 2002. Current term expires Dec 1, 2008. Born Tuscola Illinois Nov 17, 1938. United Methodist. Educated at DePauw University A.B. 1961 and University of Illinois J.D. 1964. Admitted to practice Illinois 1964, U.S. District Court Southern District of Illinois 1964 and U.S. Tax Court 1981. In legal practice Tuscola 1964-84.

Assistant State's Attorney 1964-68 and State's Attorney 1968-72 Douglas County. Member Douglas County (Past President, Secretary-Treasurer and Vice President) and Illinois State (Former Assembly Member) Bar Associations. Tuscola City Alderman 1980-84.

Mailing address: P.O. Box 284, Tuscola 61953.

Office: Douglas County Courthouse, Tuscola 61953.

Telephone: (217) 253-4121.

LINDBERG, George W. *(Senior Judge, United States District Court Northern District of Illinois)* Appointed for life by President George Bush. Assumed Senior status June 21, 2001, serves by assignment. Born Crystal Lake Illinois June 21, 1932. Episcopalian. Educated at Northwestern University B.S. 1954 J.D. 1957. Admitted to practice Illinois 1958, U.S. District Court Northern District of Illinois 1958 and U.S. Supreme Court 1978. In legal practice Crystal Lake 1968-73. Former Presiding Justice, Illinois Appellate Court Second Judicial District.

Deputy Illinois Attorney General 1977-78. Former lecturer Northwestern University. Republican. State Representative Illinois General Assembly 1967-73. Illinois State Comptroller 1973-77.

Office: U.S. Courthouse, 219 South Dearborn Street, Chicago 60604.

Telephone: (312) 435-5355.

LINEHAN, Neil J. *(Associate Judge, Illinois Circuit Court of Cook County)*

Office: 2600 South California Avenue, Chicago 60608.

Telephone: (773) 869-3160.

LINN, James B. *(Associate Judge, Illinois Circuit Court of Cook County)*

Office: 2600 South California, Chicago 60608.

Telephone: (773) 869-7428.

LIPINSKI, Marcella Carmen *(Circuit Judge, Illinois Circuit Court of Cook County)* Elected Nov 7, 2000. Term expires 2006. Born Chicago Illinois June 20, 1942. Catholic. Educated at Chicago State University B.A. cum laude 1976 and John Marshall Law School J.D. 1980. Admitted to practice Illinois 1980.

Assistant Public Defender Cook County 1986-2000. Member Advocates Society, Illinois Judges Association and South Suburban Bar Association. Democrat. Church Lector. Enjoys family life, crafts and piano.

Office: 16501 South Kedzie Parkway, Markham 60426.

Telephone: (708) 210-4170.

LIPSCOMB, Thomas J. *(Circuit Judge, Illinois Circuit Court of Cook County)*

Office: 1303 R. J. Daley Center, Chicago 60602.

Telephone: (312) 603-7959.

LITTLE, Thomas E. *(Associate Judge, Illinois Circuit Court Sixth Judicial Circuit)*

Office: Macon County Courts Facility, 253 East Wood Street, Decatur 62523.

Telephone: (217) 424-1437.

LOCALLO, Daniel M. *(Circuit Judge, Illinois Circuit Court of Cook County)* Associate Judge June 13, 1986 to Nov 1992. Elected Circuit Judge Nov 3, 1992. Retained by election 1998, current term expires Dec 2004. Served Criminal Felony Division 1992-99. Serves Law Division since March 15, 1999. Born Chicago Illinois Oct 28, 1952. Roman Catholic. Educated at University of Illinois B.S. in Finance 1974 and John Marshall Law School J.D. 1977. Admitted to practice Illinois 1977 and U.S. District Court Northern District of Illinois 1978.

Assistant State's Attorney Cook County 1978-83. Assistant Corporation Counsel Torts Division Chicago Sept 1985 to June 1986. Co-editor Newsletter Criminal Law Section Illinois State Bar Association 1988-91. Author "Use of Blood in Reckless Homicide and DUI Cases" 1989 and "The Right to Fitness Hearings for Defendants on Psychotropic Drugs" 1997 Illinois B. Jour, Article 36 Forfeiture Related Decisions 1965-99, Summary of Death Penalty Decision 1978-2002 and Traffic Related Decisions 1986-2001. Co-author *Manual for Complex Civil Litigation and Manual for Complex Criminal Litigation.* Adjunct Professor John Marshall Law School 2001-02. Member Associate Judge Coordinating Council 1988-91. Member Executive Committee 1992-2001 and Complex Litigation Committee 1995-2001 Illinois Judicial Conference. Member Supreme Court Committee to Study and Reform the Illinois Death Penalty since April

LOCALLO, DANIEL M.—*Continued*

6, 1999. Member Justinian Law Society, Illinois Judicial Council, Illinois Judges Association and Illinois State Bar Association (Council Chair Criminal Law Section June 1997 to June 1998). Instructor Associate Judge Conference 1988-91. Democrat. Member St. Eugene Grammar School Board. Enjoys golf, family activities, gardening, cooking and coaching cross-country, basketball, volleyball and baseball. Personal Statement or Quote: "What is popular is not always right; what is right is not always popular."
Office: 1912 R. J. Daley Center, Chicago 60602.
Telephone: (312) 603-5940.

LOCKWOOD, Brocton D. *(Associate Judge, Illinois Circuit Court First Judicial Circuit)*
Office: Saline County Courthouse, Harrisburg 62946.
Telephone: (618) 253-8741.

LONG, Kelly D. *(Circuit Judge, Illinois Circuit Court Fourth Judicial Circuit)*
Office: Montgomery County Courthouse, 120 North Main Street, Hillsboro 62049.
Telephone: (217) 532-9601.

LOPEZ, Mark J. *(Associate Judge, Illinois Circuit Court of Cook County)* Appointed.
Office: 1603A R. J. Daley Center, Chicago 60602.
Telephone: (312) 603-4841.

LOPEZ CEPERO, Robert *(Circuit Judge, Illinois Circuit Court of Cook County)*
Office: 2309 R. J. Daley Center, Chicago 60602.
Telephone: (312) 603-4804.

LOPINOT, Vincent J. *(Associate Judge, Illinois Circuit Court Twentieth Judicial Circuit)*
Office: St. Clair County Building, 10 Public Square, Belleville 62220.
Telephone: (618) 277-6600.

LORZ, Robert C. *(Associate Judge, Illinois Circuit Court Twelfth Judicial Circuit)*
Office: Will County Courthouse, 14 West Jefferson Street, Joliet 60432.
Telephone: (815) 727-8544.

LOTT, Gay-Lloyd *(Circuit Judge, Illinois Circuit Court of Cook County)*
Office: 2302 R. J. Daley Center, Chicago 60602.
Telephone: (312) 603-6041.

LOVE, Noreen V. *(Circuit Judge, Illinois Circuit Court of Cook County)*
Office: 1303 R. J. Daley Center, Chicago 60602.
Telephone: (312) 603-7959.

LOWERY, Donald *(Circuit Judge, Illinois Circuit Court First Judicial Circuit)* Term expires 2004.
Office: Pope County Courthouse, Golconda 62938.
Telephone: (618) 683-3941.

LOWRANCE, Michele F. *(Circuit Judge, Illinois Circuit Court of Cook County)*
Office: 2002 R. J. Daley Center, Chicago 60602.
Telephone: (312) 603-5913.

LUBIN, Stuart F. *(Circuit Judge, Illinois Circuit Court of Cook County)*
Office: 1100 South Hamilton, Room G30-S, Chicago 60612.
Telephone: (312) 433-4757.

LUCAS, Richard A. *(Associate Judge, Illinois Circuit Court Eighteenth Judicial Circuit)*
Office: DuPage County Courthouse, 505 North County Farm Road, Wheaton 60187.
Telephone: (630) 682-6481.

LUCAS, Timothy M. *(Associate Judge, Illinois Circuit Court Tenth Judicial Circuit)*
Office: 215 Peoria County Courthouse, 324 Main Street, Peoria 61602.
Telephone: (309) 672-6047.

LUCKMAN, Marvin P. *(Circuit Judge, Illinois Circuit Court of Cook County)*
Office: 3150 West Flournoy Street, Chicago 60612.
Telephone: (773) 265-8936.

LUSTFELDT, Gordon Lee *(Circuit Judge, Illinois Circuit Court Twenty-first Judicial Circuit)*
Office: Iroquois County Courthouse, 550 South Tenth Street, Watseka 60970.
Telephone: (815) 432-6965.

LUSTIG, Patrick F. *(Associate Judge, Illinois Circuit Court of Cook County)*
Office: 1303 R. J. Daley Center, Chicago 60602.
Telephone: (312) 603-7959.

LYNCH, Daniel J. *(Circuit Judge, Illinois Circuit Court of Cook County)* Elected Nov 1984 to term beginning Dec 1, 1984. Retained by election 1990, 1996 and 2002. Current term expires Dec 2008. Born Evergreen Park Illinois May 23, 1943. Roman Catholic. Educated at Xavier University B.S., Ohio University M.A. and DePaul University College of Law J.D. Admitted to practice Illinois 1970 and U.S. District Court Northern District of Illinois.

Corporation Counsel City of Chicago 1970-76. Assistant Attorney Chicago Board of Education 1976-79. Chief Attorney Cook County Assessors Office 1979-81. Author "Computer Generated Evidence: The Impact of Computer Technology on Traditional Rules of Evidence" 20 No. 4 Loyola University of Chicago L. Jour. 1989. Instructor St. Xavier College and in Business Law Moraine Valley Community College 1970-90. Member Chicago Bar Association. Attended Computer and Evidence courses The National Judicial College and many courses on evidence and criminal and civil procedure at the local level. Former Member Oak Lawn Chapter Barbershop Chorus. Board of Directors Men of Tomitine. Board Member Beverly Improvement Association. Enjoys travel, mechanics, boating and history.
Office: 10220 South 76th Avenue, Bridgeview 60455.
Telephone: (708) 974-6534.

LYNCH, Daniel Joseph *(Circuit Judge, Illinois Circuit Court of Cook County)*
Office: 1103 R. J. Daley Center, Chicago 60602.
Telephone: (312) 603-4531.

LYTTON, Tom M. *(Judge, Illinois Appellate Court Third Judicial District)* Elected to term beginning Dec 7, 1992. Retained by election 2002, current term expires Dec 5, 2012. Born Raleigh North Carolina Oct 6, 1943. Jewish. Educated at Northwestern University B.A. with honors 1965 J.D. 1968 and International School of Law, The Hague Netherlands 1967. Admitted to practice Illinois 1968, U.S. District Court Central District of Illinois 1968, California 1976, Arizona 1986 and U.S. Court of

LYTTON, TOM M.—*Continued*

Appeals Seventh Circuit. In legal practice East Moline Illinois 1973-92.

Author "Crossing State Lines to Practice Law" American University L. Rev. 1970. Important Decisions: Estate of Charles v. Siegfried 623 N.E.2d 1021, 1993; Berard v. Eagle Air et al. 629 N.E.2d 221, 1994; Bazydlo v. Volant 636 N.E.2d 1107, 1994; Knox County v. Mid State Coal 640 N.E.2d 4, 1994; and Meyer v. McKeown 641 N.E.2d 1212, 1994. Member Illinois Judges Association, State Bar of Arizona, State Bar of California and Illinois State Bar Association. Attended Appellate Judges Seminar New York University 1993. Board Member Black Hawk College 1978-82. Enjoys reading and running.

Office: 1515 Fifth Avenue, Suite 305, Moline 61265.
Telephone: (309) 757-9458.
Fax: (309) 757-9460
E-mail address: tlytton@court.state.il.us

MAAG, Gordon E. *(Judge, Illinois Appellate Court Fifth Judicial District)* Appointed 1992. Elected 1994, current term expires 2004. Born East St. Louis Illinois Feb 21, 1951. Educated at St. Louis University B.A. 1973, University of Mississippi J.D. 1979 and University of Virginia School of Law LL.M. 2001. In legal practice 1979-89. Associate Judge, Illinois Circuit Court Third Judicial Circuit 1989-92.

Member Illinois Trial Lawyers Association, Illinois State and American Bar Associations.

Office: 1410 Niedringhaus Avenue, Granite City 62040.
Telephone: (618) 451-7638.

MACELLAIO, Joseph M. *(Associate Judge, Illinois Circuit Court of Cook County)*

Office: 16501 South Kedzie Parkway, Markham 60426.
Telephone: (708) 210-4170.

MACHNIK, Thaddeus S. *(Associate Judge, Illinois Circuit Court of Cook County)* Appointed.

Office: 3001 R. J. Daley Center, Chicago 60602.
Telephone: (312) 603-7957.

MADDEN, John K. *(Circuit Judge, Illinois Circuit Court of Cook County)* Appointed Associate Judge 1984. Elected Circuit Judge 1992. Retained by election 1998, current term expires 2004. Born Chicago Illinois Jan 27, 1943. Catholic. Educated at Marquette University B.A. 1965 J.D. 1968. Admitted to practice Wisconsin 1968, Illinois 1971 and Colorado 1971.

Office: 2108 R. J. Daley Center, Chicago 60602.
Telephone: (312) 603-6024.

MADDOX, Lola P. *(Associate Judge, Illinois Circuit Court Third Judicial Circuit)* Appointed to term beginning July 1, 1979. Reappointed to subsequent terms. Current term expires 2003. Born Alton Illinois May 21, 1949. United Church of Christ. Educated at Illinois State University B.S. 1971 and Duke University J.D. 1975. Admitted to practice Illinois 1975, U.S. District Court Southern District of Illinois 1975 and U.S. Supreme Court 1979. In legal practice Alton 1975-79.

Member Alton WoodRiver, Madison County and Illinois State Bar Associations. Attended "Alcohol and the Courts" The National Judicial College 1989 and annual and periodic seminars Administrative Office of the Illinois Courts.

Office: Madison County Courthouse, 155 North Main Street, Edwardsville 62025.
Telephone (618) 692-7040.

MADDUX, William D. *(Circuit Judge, Illinois Circuit Court of Cook County)*

Office: 2005 R. J. Daley Center, Chicago 60602.
Telephone: (312) 603-6343.

MADSON, A. Scott *(Associate Judge, Illinois Circuit Court Thirteenth Judicial Circuit)*

Office: 700 South Main Street, Princeton 61354.
Telephone: (815) 875-4534.

MAGDICH, Tomas M. *(Circuit Judge, Illinois Circuit Court Fifteenth Judicial Circuit)* Term expires 2004.

Mailing address: P.O. Box 348, Dixon 61021.
Office: Lee County Courthouse, Dixon 61021.
Telephone (815) 284-5253.

MAHER, Jerelyn D. *(Associate Judge, Illinois Circuit Court Tenth Judicial Circuit)* Former Circuit Judge.

Office: Tazewell County Courthouse, 342 Court Street, Pekin 61554-4281.
Telephone: (309) 477-2201.

MAHONEY, P. Michael *(Magistrate Judge, United States District Court Northern District of Illinois)* Appointed by U.S. District Court judges.

Office: Federal Building, 211 South Court Street, Rockford 61101.
Telephone: (815) 987-4360.

MAKI, William O. *(Circuit Judge, Illinois Circuit Court of Cook County)*

Office: 2006 R. J. Daley Center, Chicago 60602.
Telephone: (312) 603-5923.

MALAK, Jeffrey A. *(Associate Judge, Illinois Circuit Court of Cook County)*

Office: 1810 R. J. Daley Center, Chicago 60602.
Telephone: (312) 603-6499.

MALLON, Michael *(Circuit Judge, Illinois Circuit Court Fifteenth Judicial Circuit)* Former Associate Judge.

Office: Ogle County Courthouse, Box 297, Oregon 61061.
Telephone: (815) 732-1163.

MALLOTT, Lewis E. *(Associate Judge, Illinois Circuit Court Third Judicial Circuit)*

Office: Madison County Courthouse, 155 North Main Street, Edwardsville 62025.
Telephone: (618) 692-6200.

MANNING, Blanche M. *(Judge, United States District Court Northern District of Illinois)* Appointed for life by President Bill Clinton to term beginning Aug 1994. Born Chicago Illinois Dec 12, 1934. Catholic. Educated at Chicago Teacher's College B.Ed. 1961, Roosevelt University M.A. 1972, John Marshall Law School J.D. 1967 and University of Virginia School of Law LL.M. 1992. Member Zeta Chapter Kappa Beta Pi. Admitted to practice Illinois 1967, U.S. District Court Northern District of Illinois 1967, U.S. Supreme Court 1971 and U.S. Court of Appeals Seventh Circuit 1978. Associate Judge 1979-86 and Circuit Judge 1986-87, Illinois Circuit Court of Cook County. Justice, Illinois Ap-

MANNING, BLANCHE M.—*Continued*

pellate Court First Judicial District March 1987 to Aug 1994.

Assistant State's Attorney Cook County 1968-73. Supervisory Trial Attorney U.S. Equal Employment Opportunity Commission 1973-77. General Attorney United Airlines 1977-78. Assistant U.S. Attorney Northern District of Illinois 1978-79. Instructor in Law in an Urban Society Malcolm X College 1969-70 and in Appellate Advocacy NCBL College of Law 1978-79. Adjunct Faculty DePaul College of Law since 1992. Former Member Education Subcommittee Appellate Judges Conference American Bar Association 1991-94. Fellow American Bar Foundation. Member Illinois Judicial Council (Treasurer 1982-85, Chairman 1988-89), National Judicial Council, Women's Bar Association of Illinois, Cook County (Second Vice President 1973, Board of Directors 1973 and 1987-89) and National Bar Associations. Vice Chair and Panelist "Finality of Judgments and Appealibility of Orders" Circuit and Appellate Judges Seminar Illinois Judicial Conference Sept 1988. Member Teaching Team Trial Advocacy Workshop Harvard Law School 1991-96 and University of Chicago 1993-95. Listed in *Who's Who Among Black Americans* and *International Who's Who Among Professional Women in the World.* Recipient Judicial Award 1979 and 1987 and Kenneth E. Wilson Judge of the Year Award 1986 from Cook County Bar Association; Black Judiciary Award from We Can Foundation, Inc. 1980; Community Recognition Award from National Association of Negro Business and Professional Women's Clubs, Inc. 1981; Edith S. Sampson Memorial Award from Illinois Judicial Council 1985; Certificate of Appreciation from Young Lawyers Section Chicago Bar Association 1985; Award of Excellence in Judicial Administration from Women's Bar Association of Illinois 1986; Distinguished Alumna Award from Chicago State University 1986; Resolution in Recognition of Outstanding Efforts from Coordinating Committee Illinois Judicial Conference 1985-87; "We Care" Role Model Award from Chicago Police Department and Chicago Public Schools We Care Program 1987 and 1988; Black Rose Award from League of Black Women 1987; Thurgood Marshall Award from Illinois Institute of Technology, Chicago-Kent College of Law BALSA Chapter 1988; Professional Achievement Award from Roosevelt University Alumni Association 1988; and Distinguished Alumnus Award from John Marshall Law School 1988. Elementary school teacher Chicago Board of Education 1961-67. Board of Trustees Sherwood Conservatory of Music. Board of Directors Alumni Association Chicago State University and Advisory Council Lawyers' Assistants Program Roosevelt University. Participant in "We Care" Role Model Program. Member Chicago Bar Association symphony orchestra. Plays saxophone and clarinet. Enjoys golf and tennis.

Office: U.S. Courthouse, 219 South Dearborn Street, Chicago 60604.

Telephone: (312) 435-7608.

MANNION, John J. *(Associate Judge, Illinois Circuit Court of Cook County)* Appointed to term beginning Jan 4, 1984. Reappointed 1987, 1991, 1995 and 1999. Current term expires 2003. Born Chicago Illinois Nov 24, 1936. Roman Catholic. Educated at Loyola University B.S. 1968 and Illinois Institute of Technology, Chicago-Kent College of Law J.D. 1974. Admitted to practice Illinois 1974.

State's Attorney Cook County 1974-84. Instructor in Criminal Law Morning Valley Community College 1984-86. Member Chicago Bar Association. Airman Second Class USAF 1957-60. With Chicago Police Department 1961-74 (Homicide detective 1965-71, Sergeant 1971-74).

Office: 10220 South 76th Avenue, Room 107, Bridgeview 60455.

Telephone: (708) 974-6310.

MANSFIELD, Scott *(Associate Judge, Illinois Circuit Court Twentieth Judicial Circuit)*

Office: County Building, 10 Public Square, Belleville 62220.

Telephone: (618) 277-6600.

MARAS, Marcia *(Circuit Judge, Illinois Circuit Court of Cook County)*

Office: 1711 R. J. Daley Center, Chicago 60602.

Telephone: (312) 603-4324.

MAROVICH, George M. *(Senior Judge, United States District Court Northern District of Illinois)* Appointed for life by President Ronald Reagan to term beginning 1988. Assumed Senior status Jan 2, 2000, serves by assignment. Born East Hazel Crest Illinois Jan 2, 1931. Eastern Orthodox. Educated at University of Illinois B.S. 1952 J.D. 1954. Admitted to practice Illinois 1955. Began legal practice Richton Park 1955. In legal practice South Holland 1959-76. Circuit Judge, Illinois Circuit Court of Cook County 1976-88.

Member Chicago, South Suburban (President 1960) and Illinois State Bar Associations. Republican. Chairman Thornton Community College Board 1970-76 and South Holland Police and Fire Commission 1966-76. Member South Holland Lions Club and Lansing Sportsmen's Club. Enjoys golf, reading, tennis and racquetball.

Office: U.S. Courthouse, 219 South Dearborn Street, Chicago 60604.

Telephone: (312) 435-5590.

MARSAGLIA, Robert C. *(Circuit Judge, Illinois Circuit Court Thirteenth Judicial Circuit)* Appointed Associate Judge. Assumed office as Circuit Judge.

Office: Grundy County Courthouse, Morris 60450.

Telephone: (815) 941-3254.

MARTIN, LeRoy K., Jr. *(Circuit Judge, Illinois Circuit Court of Cook County)*

Office: 1303 R. J. Daley Center, Chicago 60602.

Telephone: (312) 603-7959.

MARTIN, Victoria L. *(Associate Judge, Illinois Circuit Court Nineteenth Judicial Circuit)*

Office: Lake County Courthouse, 18 North County Street, Waukegan 60085.

Telephone: (847) 377-3798.

MARTIN BISHOP, Patricia *(Circuit Judge, Illinois Circuit Court of Cook County)* Elected to term beginning Dec 1996. Retained by election 2002, current term expires Dec 2008. Served Child Protection Division Dec 1996 to July 1998 and Law Division July 1998 to Jan 2000. Presiding Judge Child Protection Division since Jan 2000. Born Chicago Illinois April 27, 1959. Educated at University of Nairobi, Kenya 1979, Middlebury College B.S. with honors 1981 and Northern Illinois University College of Law J.D. 1985.

MARTIN BISHOP, PATRICIA—*Continued*

Assistant Public Defender Sixth District Feb 1986 to Sept 1988 and Early Entry Unit Sept 1988 to Oct 1989, Attorney Trial Supervisor Early Entry Unit Oct 1989 to Oct 1992 and Sixth District Oct 1992 to Jan 1994 and Deputy Chief Fifth District Jan 1994 to Dec 1996 Cook County. Member Committee on Racial, Ethnic and Sexual Orientation Awareness in the Circuit Court of Cook County. Member Illinois Judicial Council, Illinois Judges Association, American Judges Association, Chicago, Cook County, Illinois State and U.S. Supreme Court Bar Associations. Board Member Pro Bono Advocates, Dr. Charles E. Gavin Memorial Foundation and Campaign for a Drug Free Westside. Board of Visitors Northern Illinois University. Member Families and Children Leadership Subcabinet and New Faith Baptist Church.

Office: 1100 South Hamilton Avenue, Chicago 60612.

Telephone: (312) 433-4756.

MASON, Mary Anne *(Circuit Judge, Illinois Circuit Court of Cook County)*

Office: 1100 South Hamilton, Room G030, Chicago 60612.

Telephone: (312) 433-4757.

MASON, Michael T. *(Magistrate Judge, United States District Court Northern District of Illinois)* Appointed by U.S. District Court judges to term beginning Sept 29, 2001.

Office: U.S. Courthouse, 219 South Dearborn Street, Chicago 60604.

Telephone: (312) 435-5610.

MASTERS, Allan W. *(Recalled Circuit Judge, Illinois Circuit Court of Cook County)* Retired, serves by recall.

Office: 32 West Randolph, Room 1404R, Chicago 60602.

Telephone: (312) 603-3790.

MATHEIN, Veronica B. *(Circuit Judge, Illinois Circuit Court of Cook County)*

Office: 3009 R. J. Daley Center, Chicago 60602.

Telephone: (312) 603-4279.

MATHERS, Stephen C. *(Circuit Judge, Illinois Circuit Court Ninth Judicial Circuit)* Associate Judge 1978-80. Elected Circuit Judge Nov 4, 1980. Retained by election 1986, 1992 and 1998. Current term expires 2004. Born Galesburg Illinois Nov 1, 1946. Educated at Northwestern University B.A. 1968 and University of Illinois J.D. 1974. Admitted to practice Illinois 1974 and U.S. Supreme Court 1979. In legal practice Geneva 1974-75 and Galesburg 1975-78.

Assistant State's Attorney Kane County 1974-75. Instructor in Criminal Law Carl Sandburg Community College 1975-88. Guest Lecturer University of Illinois College of Law 1979-83 and 1987-93. Member Illinois Board of Admissions to the Bar 1994-97. Member Illinois Judges Association (Board of Directors 1993-2001, President 2000-01), Illinois State (Family Law Section Council 1984-88, Assembly 1988-92) and American Bar Associations. Faculty member Family Law Illinois Judicial Conference 1986, Illinois Institute for Continuing Legal Education 1988 and 1989 and LawEd Series Illinois State Bar Association 1989 and 1992. Faculty Lecturer Update Programs Family Law Section Illinois State Bar Association 1986, 1987 and 1988. Special Agent U.S. Army Military Intelligence 1968-71. Recipient Outstanding Community Achievement of Vietnam Era Veterans Award 1979. Trustee Galesburg Cottage Hospital 1980-96 and Galesburg Ambulance Service 1981-96 (President 1984-85 and 1986-87).

Office: Knox County Courthouse, 200 South Cherry Street, Galesburg 61401.

Telephone: (309) 345-3847.

MATOESIAN, A. Andreas *(Circuit Judge, Illinois Circuit Court Third Judicial Circuit)* Assumed office as Associate Judge 1979. Assumed office as Circuit Judge. Term expires 2004. Former Chief Judge.

Office: 405 Madison County Courthouse, 155 North Main, Edwardsville 62025.

Telephone: (618) 692-6200.

MAY, Charles M. *(Associate Judge, Illinois Circuit Court of Cook County)*

Office: 1100 South Hamilton Avenue, Room G18A, Chicago 60612.

Telephone: (312) 433-4757.

McBRIDE, Margaret Stanton *(Judge, Illinois Appellate Court First Judicial District Division Two)* Formerly served Division Three. Born Evanston Illinois Dec 28, 1951. Catholic. Educated at Newton College B.A. 1973 and DePaul University College of Law J.D. 1976. Admitted to practice Illinois 1976 and U.S. District Court Northern District of Illinois 1977. In legal practice Chicago 1976-77. Former Circuit Judge, Illinois Circuit Court of Cook County, appointed to term beginning July 2, 1987.

Assistant State's Attorney Cook County 1977-87. Faculty member National Institute for Trial Advocacy. Member Illinois Judges Association, National Association of Women Judges, Women's Bar Association of Illinois, Chicago and Illinois State Bar Associations. Attended Associate Judges Conference sponsored by Illinois Judges Conference 1988, 1989 and 1990.

Office: 160 North LaSalle, Room N1905, Chicago 60601.

Telephone: (312) 793-5462.

McCARTHY, Carol Pearce *(Circuit Judge, Illinois Circuit Court of Cook County)*

Office: 2811 R. J. Daley Center, Chicago 60602.

Telephone: (312) 603-3915.

McCARTHY, James P. *(Circuit Judge, Illinois Circuit Court of Cook County)*

Office: 1501 R. J. Daley Center, Chicago 60602.

Telephone: (312) 603-4854.

McCARTHY, Katherine M. *(Circuit Judge, Illinois Circuit Court Sixth Judicial Circuit)* Former Associate Judge. Assumed office as Circuit Judge.

Office: Macon County Courts Facility, 253 East Wood Street, Decatur 62526.

Telephone: (217) 424-1442.

McCLEAN, John R., Jr. *(Associate Judge, Illinois Circuit Court Fourteenth Judicial Circuit)* Appointed.

Office: Rock Island County Courthouse, 210 Fifteenth Street, Rock Island 61201.

Telephone: (309) 786-4451.

McCLINTOCK, Gregory K. *(Associate Judge, Illinois Circuit Court Ninth Judicial Circuit)*

Office: Warren County Courthouse, Monmouth 61462.

Telephone: (309) 734-3423.

McCOOEY, Brendan J. *(Associate Judge, Illinois Circuit Court of Cook County)*
Office: 2121 Euclid Avenue, Room 104-A, Rolling Meadows 60008.
Telephone: (847) 818-2529.

McCOY, Richard D. *(Associate Judge, Illinois Circuit Court Tenth Judicial Circuit)*
Office: Tazewell County Courthouse, 342 Court Street, Pekin 61554.
Telephone: (309) 477-2201.

McCULLOUGH, John T. *(Judge, Illinois Appellate Court Fourth Judicial District)* Elected to term beginning Dec 3, 1984. Retained by election Dec 5, 1994, current term expires Dec 2004. Presiding Judge Industrial Commission Division since 1991. Presiding Judge since Dec 2001. Born Streator Illinois June 15, 1931. Educated at Lincoln College 1949-51 and University of Illinois B.S. 1953 LL.B. 1955. Admitted to practice Illinois 1955. Began legal practice Lincoln and Mount Pulaski 1955. County Judge 1962-64. Associate Judge Jan 1964 to July 1971, Circuit Judge July 1971 to Dec 1984 and Chief Judge 1974-84, Illinois Circuit Court Eleventh Judicial Circuit.
Chairman State Conference of Chief Judges Illinois 1982-83 and 1984-85 and Illinois Appellate Court 2002. Named Courier Man of the Month Nov 1961. Recipient Distinguished Service Award from Lincoln Jaycees 1962. Listed in *Outstanding Young Men of America.* USAS 1955-57. Republican. Past Exalted Ruler, Trustee and Secretary Crippled Children's Trust Elks 914. Chairman All America City Commission 1963-64, Legislative Committee Lincoln Chamber of Commerce, Budget and Admissions Committee United Fund 1962-65 and Prairie Trails District Boy Scouts 1962-64. Member Mount Pulaski Chamber of Commerce. Board of Trustees St. Clara's Inc. and Lincoln College. President Lincoln Junior Achievement 1968-69.
Office: 111½ North Sangamon Street, Lincoln 62656.
Telephone: (217) 732-3193.

McCUSKEY, Michael P. *(Judge, Unites States District Court Central District of Illinois)* Appointed for life by President Bill Clinton to term beginning May 4, 1998. Born Peoria Illinois June 30, 1948. Educated at Illinois State University B.S. 1970 and St. Louis University J.D. 1975. Admitted to practice Illinois 1975 and U.S. District Court Central District of Illinois 1987. In legal practice Lacon 1975-88. Circuit Judge, Illinois Circuit Court Tenth Judicial Circuit 1988-90. Judge, Illinois Appellate Court Third Judicial District 1990-98.
Public Defender Marshall County 1976-88. Member Abraham Lincoln Inn American Inns of Court, Illinois Judges Association, Champaign County, Peoria County and Illinois State Bar Associations. Recipient Award of Excellence and Meritorious Service from Illinois Public Defenders Association 1991. Member Rotary Club of Urbana.
Office: U.S. Courthouse, 201 South Vine Street, Urbana 61802.
Telephone: (217) 373-5837.
Fax: (217) 373-5855

McDADE, Joe Billy *(Chief Judge, United States District Court Central District of Illinois)* Appointed for life by President George Bush to term beginning 1991. Chief Judge since Nov 19, 1998. Born Bellville Texas Dec 2, 1937. Educated at Bradley University B.S. 1959 M.S. 1960 and University of Michigan J.D. 1963. In legal practice Peoria 1968-82. Associate Judge 1982-88 and Circuit Judge 1988-91, Illinois Circuit Court Tenth Judicial District.
Staff Attorney Antitrust Division U.S. Department of Justice 1963-65. Executive Director Greater Peoria Legal Aid Society 1965-68.
Office: 122 Federal Building, 100 N.E. Monroe Street, Peoria 61602.
Telephone: (309) 671-7821.

McDADE, Mary W. *(Judge, Illinois Appellate Court Third Judicial District)* Born Columbia South Carolina Aug 1939. Educated at University of Michigan B.A. 1961 and University of Illinois J.D. 1984. Law Clerk to Hon. Michael M. Mihm, U.S. District Court Central District of Illinois 1984-86. Admitted to practice Illinois, U.S. District Courts Central and Northern Districts of Illinois, U.S. Court of Appeals Seventh Circuit and U.S. Supreme Court.
Member Peoria County, Illinois State and American Bar Associations. Chairman Board of Trustees Eureka College 1980-82.
Office: 401 S.W. Water Street, Suite 409, Peoria 61602.
Telephone: (309) 671-3003.

McDONALD, Barbara A. *(Circuit Judge, Illinois Circuit Court of Cook County)*
Office: 2103A R. J. Daley Center, Chicago 60602.
Telephone: (312) 603-5900.

McDONOUGH, Martin E. *(Associate Judge, Illinois Circuit Court of Cook County)*
Office: 16501 South Kedzie Parkway, Markham 60426.
Telephone: (708) 210-4170.

McDUNN, Susan J. *(Circuit Judge, Illinois Circuit Court of Cook County)*
Office: 1303 R. J. Daley Center, Chicago 60602.
Telephone: (312) 603-4645.

McGANN, Patrick E. *(Circuit Judge, Illinois Circuit Court of Cook County)* Former Associate Judge.
Office: 2508 R. J. Daley Center, Chicago 60602.
Telephone: (312) 603-4890.

McGINNIS, Sheila *(Circuit Judge, Illinois Circuit Court of Cook County)*
Office: 1303 R. J. Daley Center, Chicago 60602.
Telephone: (312) 603-7959.

McGLYNN, William F. *(Associate Judge, Illinois Circuit Court of Cook County)* Appointed to term beginning Nov 1, 1999. Term expires Nov 2003. Born Chicago Illinois Sept 14, 1948. Catholic. Educated at Northeastern Illinois University B.A. 1976 and John Marshall Law School J.D. with honors 1981. Member Phi Alpha Delta. Admitted to practice Illinois 1981, U.S. District Court Northern District of Illinois 1981 and Trial Bar of U.S. District Court Northern District of Illinois 1985. In legal practice Oak Brook and Palos Heights 1988-99.
Assistant State's Attorney Cook County 1981-86. Assistant Attorney General Illinois 1987-88. Member Illinois Judges Association and Chicago Bar Association.
Office: 16501 South Kedzie Parkway, Markham 60426.
Telephone: (708) 210-4170.

McGRATH, Brigid Mary *(Associate Judge, Illinois Circuit Court of Cook County)*
Office: 1908 R. J. Daley Center, Chicago 60602.
Telephone: (312) 603-5938.

McGRAW, Joseph G. *(Circuit Judge, Illinois Circuit Court Seventeenth Judicial Circuit)*
Office: Winnebago County Courthouse, 400 West State Street, Rockford 61101.
Telephone: (815) 987-2522.

McGUIRE, Dennis M. *(Circuit Judge, Illinois Circuit Court of Cook County)*
Office: 1303 R. J. Daley Center, Chicago 60602.
Telephone: (312) 603-7959.

McGUIRE, John W. *(Associate Judge, Illinois Circuit Court Fourth Judicial Circuit)*
Office: Marion County Courthouse, Salem 62881.
Telephone: (618) 548-3864.

McGURY, Kathleen M. *(Circuit Judge, Illinois Circuit Court of Cook County)*
Office: 1500 Maybrook Drive, Room 123, Maywood 60153.
Telephone: (708) 865-6060.

McINTYRE, Maureen P. *(Circuit Judge, Illinois Circuit Court Nineteenth Judicial Circuit)* Former Associate Judge. Assumed office as Circuit Judge.
Office: 2200 North Seminary Avenue, Woodstock 60098.
Telephone: (815) 334-4385.

McKILLIP, Brian R. *(Associate Judge, Illinois Circuit Court Eighteenth Judicial Circuit)*
Office: 505 North County Farm Road, Wheaton 60187.
Telephone: (630) 469-1824.

McKOSKI, Raymond J. *(Circuit Judge, Illinois Circuit Court Nineteenth Judicial Circuit)* Former Associate Judge. Former Chief Judge.
Office: Lake County Courthouse, 18 North County Street, Waukegan 60085.
Telephone: (847) 377-3854.

McLAREN, Robert D. *(Judge, Illinois Appellate Court Second Judicial District)* Elected to term beginning Dec 5, 1988. Retained by election 1998, current term expires Dec 2008. Former Presiding Judge. Born Oak Park Illinois Oct 1, 1944. Protestant. Educated at Monmouth College B.A. 1966 and Drake University Law School J.D. 1969. Member Phi Alpha Delta. Admitted to practice Illinois 1969, Iowa 1969 and U.S. District Court Northern District of Illinois 1972. In legal practice Elmhurst 1977-81. Associate Judge 1981-84 and Circuit Judge 1984-88, Illinois Circuit Court Eighteenth Judicial Circuit.

Assistant State's Attorney Chief of Civil Division DuPage County 1970-77. Former member Illinois State Bar Association (General Assembly). Member Illinois Judges Association. Lecturer on Real Estate Taxation Illinois State Bar Association 1975. Recipient Award of Merit from DuPage County Juvenile Officers Association. Enjoys tennis, golf and stereo music.
Office: 115 West Wesley, Suite 1, Wheaton 60187.
Telephone: (630) 682-3090.

McMENAMIN, William G. *(Associate Judge, Illinois Circuit Court Twelfth Judicial Circuit)*
Office: Will County Courthouse, 14 West Jefferson Street, Joliet 60432.
Telephone: (815) 727-8552.

McMILLEN, Alesia A. *(Circuit Judge, Illinois Circuit Court Eighth Judicial Circuit)*
Mailing address: P.O. Box 80, Rushville 62681.
Office: Schuyler County Courthouse, Rushville 62681.
Telephone: (217) 322-3211.

McMORROW, Mary Ann G. *(Chief Justice, Supreme Court of Illinois)* Elected Nov 1992. Retained by election 2002, current term expires Dec 2012. Born Chicago Illinois. Educated at Rosary College 1948-50 and Loyola University J.D. 1953. Awarded honorary LL.D. John Marshall Law School, LL.D. honoris causa Quincy University, Doctorate of Humanities honoris causa Lewis University and D.H.L. honoris causa Rosary College. Member Phi Alpha Delta. Admitted to practice Illinois 1953, U.S. District Court Northern District of Illinois 1970 and U.S. Supreme Court 1976. Circuit Judge, Illinois Circuit Court of Cook County 1976-85. Served Illinois Appellate Court by special assignment 1985. Former Judge, Illinois Appellate Court First Judicial District 1986-92 (Chairperson Executive Committee 1991).

Assistant State's Attorney Cook County 1955 (first woman to prosecute major criminal cases in Criminal Court Cook County). Member Wigmore Inns of Court (Master Bencher), The Advocates' Society, Illinois Judges Association (Board of Directors), National Association of Women Judges, American Judicature Society, Women's Bar Association of Illinois (President 1975-76), Chicago, Northwest Suburban and Illinois State Bar Associations. Recipient Medal of Excellence from Alumni Association Loyola University School of Law 1991, Tribute to Chicago Women Award from Midwest Women's Center 1993, Lawyer of the Year Award from Catholic Lawyers Guild 1993, Rerum Novarum Government Award from St. Joseph Seminary 1994 and Fellows Award for Distinguished Service to Law and Society from Illinois State Bar Association and Illinois Bar Foundation 1996. Named one of Chicago's 100 Most Influential Women by Crain's *Chicago Business* 1996. Invested a Dame of Sovereign Military Order of Malta. Board of Directors Loyola Law School Alumni Association.
Office: 160 North LaSalle Street, Room S2005, Chicago 60601.
Telephone: (312) 793-5470.

McNAMARA, Paddy H. *(Circuit Judge, Illinois Circuit Court of Cook County)* Elected to term beginning Dec 2, 1986. Retained by election 1992 and 1998. Current term expires 2004. Born Pasadena California Feb 6, 1943. Educated at University of California at Berkeley B.A. and DePaul University College of Law J.D. 1973. Admitted to practice Illinois 1973, U.S. District Court Northern District of Illinois 1973, U.S. Court of Appeals Seventh Circuit 1979 and U.S. Supreme Court 1983. In legal practice Chicago 1973-86.

Author "A Follow-up on *Hishon*" Illinois B. Jour. May 1986 and "Voir Dire in Civil Cases" Administrative Office of the Illinois Courts Sept 1995 republished by Chicago Bar Association. Member Supreme Court Committee on Illinois Civil Practice Jury Instructions since 1995. Member Chicago Council of Lawyers, Women's Bar Association of Illinois and Illinois Judges As-

MCNAMARA, PADDY H.—*Continued*

sociation. Seminar Participant IICLE 1986-88. Instructor National Institute for Trial Advocacy Northwestern University Law School 1988, 1989, 1990, 1994 and 1996. Board of Directors John Howard Association since 1984. Member Governor's Task Force on Mentally Ill Offenders 1987.
Office: 2404 R. J. Daley Center, Chicago 60602.
Telephone: (312) 603-6017.

McNULTY, Jill Kathleen *(Judge, Illinois Appellate Court First Judicial District Division One)* Elected to term beginning Dec 6, 1990. Retained by election 2000, current term expires Dec 2010. Formerly served Division Two. Born Peoria Illinois June 1, 1935. Catholic. Educated at Vassar College, Northwestern University B.A. 1957 J.D. 1960 and University of Washington. Board of Editors Northwestern University Law Review 1959-60. Admitted to practice Illinois 1960 and U.S. District Court Northern District of Illinois 1961. In legal practice Chicago 1960-79. Associate Judge 1979-82 and Circuit Judge 1982-90, Circuit Court of Cook County.
Author "The Right to Be Left Alone" American Criminal L. Rev. 1972, "The Juvenile's Right to Treatment" Santa Clara L. Rev. 1976 and "First Amendment v. Sixth Amendment: A Constitutional Battle in the Juvenile Courts" New Mexico L. Rev. 1980. Assistant Professor 1972-74, Associate Professor 1974-77 and Professor 1977-81 Illinois Institute of Technology, Chicago-Kent College of Law. Member Illinois Judicial Council (former Chair), Women's Bar Association of Illinois, Chicago, Cook County and Illinois State Bar Associations.
Office: 160 North LaSalle Street, Suite S1608, Chicago 60601.
Telephone: (312) 793-5407.

McREYNOLDS, Dana R. *(Associate Judge, Illinois Circuit Court Fourteenth Judicial Circuit)* Appointed to term beginning Dec 1990. Reappointed 1991, 1995 and 1999. Term expires Dec 2003. Born Bloomington Illinois July 29, 1950. Educated at University of Illinois B.S. 1972 and John Marshall Law School J.D. 1976. Admitted to practice Illinois 1976 and U.S. District Court Central District of Illinois 1976. In legal practice Kewanee 1976-90.
Public Defender Henry County 1978-90. Member Illinois Judges Association.
Mailing address: P.O. Box 451, Kewanee 61443.
Telephone: (309) 852-4738.

McSWEENEY-MOORE, Colleen *(Circuit Judge, Illinois Circuit Court of Cook County)* Appointed July 1, 1994. Elected Dec 1, 1994. Retained by election 2000, current term expires Dec 2006. Currently serves Criminal Division. Born Chicago Illinois July 17, 1955. Roman Catholic. Educated at University of Illinois B.A. 1978 and John Marshall University Law School J.D. 1982. Admitted to practice Illinois 1982 and U.S. Court of Appeals Seventh Circuit 1982.
Assistant State's Attorney Cook County 1983-94. Adjunct Professor of Trial Advocacy Illinois Institute of Technology, Chicago-Kent College of Law since 1995. Member Illinois Judges Association, Women's Bar Association of Illinois and Chicago Bar Association. Instructor in Trial Advocacy Illinois State Appellate Prosecutors 1996. Enjoys teaching and camping.
Office: 2600 South California Avenue, Room 706, Chicago 60608.
Telephone: (773) 869-3173.

MEACHAM, Clifford L. *(Associate Judge, Illinois Circuit Court of Cook County)*
Office: 2806 R. J. Daley Center, Chicago 60602.
Telephone: (312) 603-3904.

MEHLICK, John A. *(Associate Judge, Illinois Circuit Court Seventh Judicial Circuit)*
Office: County Complex, 200 South Ninth Street, Springfield 62701.
Telephone: (217) 753-6735.

MENDELSOHN, Ralph J. *(Associate Judge, Illinois Circuit Court Third Judicial Circuit)*
Office: Madison County Courthouse, 155 North Main Street, Edwardsville 62025.
Telephone: (618) 692-7040.

MESICH, James J. *(Associate Judge, Illinois Circuit Court Fourteenth Judicial Circuit)*
Office: Rock Island County Courthouse, 210 Fifteenth Street, Rock Island 61201.
Telephone: (309) 788-7331.

METZ, Nelson F. *(Associate Judge, Illinois Circuit Court Third Judicial Circuit)* Appointed to term beginning March 29, 2000. Born Alton Illinois July 30, 1946. Educated at Southern Illinois University B.A. with honors 1972 M.A. 1975 J.D. cum laude 1982. Admitted to practice Illinois 1982, U.S. District Court Southern District of Illinois 1982 and U.S. Court of Appeals Seventh Circuit 1984. In legal practice Alton 1982-2000.
Assistant State's Attorney Madison County 1984-2000. Member Illinois Judges Association, Alton-Wood River, Madison County and Illinois State Bar Associations. Member American Legion and Knights of Columbus.
Office: Madison County Courthouse, 155 North Main Street, Edwardsville 62025.
Telephone: (618) 692-6200.
E-mail address: nfmetz@co.madison.il.us

MEYER, Barbara M. *(Circuit Judge, Illinois Circuit Court of Cook County)*
Office: 1303 R. J. Daley Center, Chicago 60602.
Telephone: (312) 603-7959.

MEYERS, Kenneth J. *(Judge, United States Bankruptcy Court Southern District of Illinois)* Former Magistrate, U.S. District Court Southern District of Illinois, appointed by U.S. District Court judges 1975.
Mailing address: P.O. Box 309, East St. Louis 62202-0309.
Telephone: (618) 482-9307.

MIDDENDORFF, Dennis *(Associate Judge, Illinois Circuit Court Fourth Judicial Circuit)*
Office: Clinton County Courthouse, Carlyle 62231.
Telephone: (217) 532-9501.

MIHM, Michael M. *(Judge, United States District Court Central District of Illinois)* Appointed for life by President Ronald Reagan to term beginning Aug 1982. Chief Judge Nov 1991 to Nov 18, 1998. Born Amboy Illinois May 18, 1943. Roman Catholic. Educated at Loras College B.A. cum laude 1964 and St. Louis University J.D. 1967. Member Delta Theta Phi. Admitted to

MIHM, MICHAEL M.—*Continued*

practice Missouri 1967, Illinois 1967 and U.S. District Court Central District of Illinois 1968. In legal practice Peoria Illinois Dec 1980 to Aug 1982.

Assistant Prosecuting Attorney St. Louis County Missouri 1967-68. Assistant State's Attorney 1968-69 and State's Attorney 1972-80 Peoria County. Police Legal Advisor and Assistant Corporation Counsel City of Peoria 1969-72. Co-author *Illinois Pattern Jury Instructions, Criminal* 2nd ed. West Publishing Co. 1981, with Chief Judge Juan R. Torruella "Foreword: To Promote and Strengthen Judicial Independence and the Rule of Law in the Hemisphere" Conference of Supreme Courts of the Americas 40 St. Louis L. Jour. 969-983 Summer 1996 and with Judge Nancy Gertner "Teaching Judges How to Sentence" 11 No. 2 *Federal Sentencing Reporter* 96 Sept/Oct 1998. Author "Highlights from a Decade of Guideline Sentencing" 10 No. 1 *Federal Sentencing Reporter* 6 July/Aug 1997, "Pot, What Should the Penalties Be for Marijuana? 'Some Criminal Sanctions Must Remain'" 3 No. 7 Illinois Issues 5 and "Organized Effort Needed to Combat Fraud" 6 No. 5 ICPI Report 2. Adjunct Professor "Accelerated Trial Advocacy" John Marshall Law School since 1991. Member Illinois Supreme Court Special Committee on Criminal Jury Trial Instructions 1976-82 and Illinois Criminal Justice Information Council 1977-82. Representative of District Judges of the Seventh Circuit regarding formulation of U.S. Sentencing Guidelines 1987-88. Member Committee on the Judicial Branch 1987-93, Chairman Subcommittee on Long Range Planning 1992, Member since 1998 and Chairman Jan 13, 1994 to Oct 1995 Committee on International Judicial Relations and Member Executive Committee Oct 1995 to Oct 1997 Judicial Conference of the U.S. Founding Member Abraham Lincoln (President 1988-89), Clarence Darrow and August J. Scheineman American Inns of Court 1988-89. Member Committee on Education Programs 1991-94 and Federal-State Committee 1991-96 Seventh Circuit. Former National Vice President National Association of Policy Attorneys. Former Member Board of Directors National District Attorneys Association and Illinois State Bar Association Committee to Review Bail Laws in the State of Illinois. Member Peoria County Bar Association (Former Member Board of Directors). Faculty Case Management Seminar for Judges with 3-5 years on federal bench Federal Judicial Center 1991-93. Speaker "The Sentencing Guidelines" Seventh Circuit conferences and workshops 1991-95. Co-maker with Hon. Terry J. Hatter, Jr. "Criminal Pretrial Proceedings" Judge Orientation Video Federal Judicial Center 1992. Lecturer on American Legal System for judges and other court officials from the Russian Federation and other countries in Central and Eastern Europe and Central Asia and China Administrative Office of the U.S., Federal Judicial Center, U.S. Information Agency and State Department since 1993. Lecturer and Consultant "Program for Senior Judges from the Russian Federation on Issues of Court Governance and Management" Federal Judicial Center and Administrative Office of the U.S. Courts March 1997. Named Man of the Year by Penny Press 1976 and Outstanding Young Man of America by National Jaycees 1978. Recipient Charles C. Schlink "Good Government Award" from Peoria Jaycees 1977 and Award of Appreciation (for valuable contributions to the building of the Russian judicial system and judicial reform in Russia) from Council of Judges of the Russian Federation Oct 1999. Former Vice Chairman Illinois Dangerous Drugs Advisory Council. Former Member Board of Directors Phoenix Products, Peoria Salvation Army, State of Illinois T.A.S.C. (Treatment Alternatives to Street Crime) and W.D. Boyce Council Boys Scouts of America. Former Member Advisory Board Peoria Big Brothers-Big Sisters and Parents Board and Long Range Planning Committee Notre Dame High School. Former Member Board of Directors Proctor Health Care Foundation.

Office: 204 Federal Building, 100 N.E. Monroe Street, Peoria 61602.

Telephone: (309) 671-7113.

MILLS, Richard Henry *(Senior Judge, United States District Court Central District of Illinois)* Appointed for life by President Ronald Reagan 1985. Assumed Senior status, serves by assignment. Born Beardstown Illinois July 19, 1929. Educated at Illinois College B.A. 1951, Mercer University J.D. 1957 and University of Virginia LL.M. 1982. Board of Editors Mercer Law Review. President Phi Alpha Literary Society and Pi Kappa Delta. Member Phi Alpha Delta. Admitted to practice Illinois 1957, U.S. Court of Appeals Seventh Circuit 1959, U.S. Court of Military Appeals 1963 and U.S. Supreme Court 1963. In legal practice Virginia 1957-66. Circuit Judge, Illinois Circuit Court Eighth Judicial Circuit 1966-76. Served Illinois Appellate Court by special assignment 1969-74. Justice, Illinois Appellate Court Fourth Judicial District 1976 to Aug 27, 1985.

Legal Advisor Illinois Youth Commission 1958-60. State's Attorney Cass County 1960-64. Author Casenote "Corporations—Non-cumulative Preferred Stock" 8 Mercer L. Rev. 214, 1956; "Labor Law: Right to Work vs Union Shop" 45 ABA Jour. 711, 1959; "Illinois Youth Commission—Five Years Old" 48 Illinois B. Jour. 8, 1959; "Juvenile Delinquency—Also a Federal Problem" 49 ABA Jour. 44, 1963; "The Practicing Prosecutor—Beset With Conflicts" 54 Illinois B. Jour. 606, 1966; "The Prosecutor: Charging and 'Bargaining'" 511 University of Illinois Law Forum 3, 1966; "Promptness—A Legal Virtue" 2 The Institute Report (Illinois Institute for Continuing Legal Education) 22, 1973; "Jury Duty—Right and Responsibility" 12 The Judges' Journal 2, 1973; "The Continuing Legal Education of the Judges in Illinois" The Chicago Law Bulletin April 26, 1973; "Today's Laws—Tomorrow's Leaders" 63 Illinois B. Jour. 506 May 1975; "Continuing Judicial Education in Illinois" 14 The Judges' Journal 3, 1975; "Investing the New Judge" 65 Illinois B. Jour. 384, 1977; "The Illinois Appellate Court: A Chronicle and Breviary of Intermediate Review" Southern Illinois University L. Jour. 373, 1981; "On The Record" 64 Chicago Bar Record 96, 1982; "Caseload Explosion: The Appellate Response" 16 John Marshall L. Rev. 1, 1982; "Commentaries: To the New Lawyer" 12 Southern Illinois University L. Jour. 285, 1987; "Military Rules of Evidence: Adoption or Abrogation of the Common Law?" 22 Akron L. Rev. 329, 1989; and "Federal Practice" 49 Mercer L. Rev. 1045, 1998. Adjunct Professor Southern Illinois University School of Medicine since 1985. Founding President Lincoln-Douglas American Inn of Court #150 1991-93. Member Illinois Law Enforcement Commission 1977-83, Illinois Judges Association, Appellate Judges' Conference, Illinois Supreme Court Rules Committee 1963-85, Cass County (President 1962-64 and 1975-76), Sangamon County, Chicago, Illinois State (Chairman Criminal Law Section 1967-68 and Judicial Administration Sec-

MILLS, RICHARD HENRY—*Continued*

tion 1972-73) and American (Chair National Conference of Federal Trial Judges Judicial Administration Division 1999-2000) Bar Associations. Chairman Criminal Law Seminars for Judges Committee Illinois Judicial Conference 1971-78 and Illinois Courts Law Day 1973 and 1975. Presides in Trial Advocacy Program and Moot Court University of Illinois College of Law and Southern Illinois University School of Law. Attended The National Judicial College 1968 and 1972, faculty member 1975 and 1978.

Recipient George Washington Honor Medal from Freedoms Foundation at Valley Forge 1969, 1973, 1975 and 1983 and American Bar Association Award for Best Law Day Speech in the U.S. 1974. Served with Third Infantry Division Korean War. Colonel USAR (retired). Major General Illinois Militia. Recipient Bronze Star, Meritorious Service Medal with oak leaf cluster, Joint Service Commendation Medal, Good Conduct Medal, American Defense Medal, Korean Service Medal with battle star, United Nations Korean Service Medal, Armed Forces Reserve Medal, Army Reserve Components Achievement Medal, U.S. Presidential Unit Citation and Korean Presidential Unit Citation. Distinguished Eagle Scout, Silver Beaver and Silver Antelope Boy Scouts of America, Kiwanis Club (President 1963), Masonic Lodge (Master 1962), Springfield Consistory 33°, Ansar Shrine, Army and Navy Club, VFW, Reserve Officers Association and American Legion. Board of Trustees Passavant Hospital 1964-70 and Illinois College. Board of Visitors Mercer University School of Law 1977-84. President Boy Scout Council 1978-80.

Office: 117 U.S. Courthouse, 600 East Monroe Street, Springfield 62701.

Telephone: (217) 492-4340.

MIRANDA, Daniel R. *(Associate Judge, Illinois Circuit Court of Cook County)*

Office: 2803 R. J. Daley Center, Chicago 60602.

Telephone: (312) 603-3908.

MITCHELL, Richard T. *(Circuit Judge, Illinois Circuit Court Seventh Judicial Circuit)* Former Judge, Illinois Court of Claims, assumed office 1993.

Office: Morgan County Courthouse, 300 West State Street, Jacksonville 62650.

Telephone: (217) 245-8520.

MITCHELL-DAVIS, Judy I. *(Circuit Judge, Illinois Circuit Court of Cook County)* Elected Nov 6, 1990. Retained by election 1996 and 2002. Current term expires 2008. Supervising Judge Drug Treatment Court since Dec 1990. Educated at University of Chicago B.A. 1973 and DePaul University College of Law J.D. 1977. Pullman Scholar. In legal practice Chicago May 1978 to June 1979 and Oct 1981 to Jan 1990.

Assistant State's Attorney Cook County June 1979 to Sept 1981. Assistant Public Defender Appeals Division Cook County Jan 1990 to Nov 1990. Professor of Business Law Daniel Hale Williams University Oct 1977 to May 1978. Member Illinois Judges Association, Illinois Judicial Council, National Association of Drug Court Professionals, Women's, Black Women's, Chicago, Cook County, Illinois State and National Bar Associations. Attended Trial Practice Institute National College for Criminal Defense Summer 1983, General Jurisdiction Courses I and II The National Judicial College Fall 1991, Course on Mediation for Lawyers and Non-Lawyers Center for Conflict Resolution Summer 1995, Course on Mediation for Lawyers Mediation Institute of America, Inc. Spring 1996 and training for Drug Court Judges National Association of Drug Court Professionals Fall 1998. Inducted into Chicago Women's Hall of Fame 1991. Recipient Meritorious and Community Service Awards from Illinois Judicial Council and Cook County Bar Association, Community Role Model Award from Second Baptist Church and Chicago Coalition for Law Related Education in the Chicago Public Schools Award.

Office: 1500 Maybrook Drive, Maywood 60153.

Telephone: (708) 865-6060.

MITTON, Jane H. *(Associate Judge, Illinois Circuit Court Eighteenth Judicial Circuit)*

Office: DuPage County Courthouse, 505 North County Farm Road, Wheaton 60187.

Telephone: (630) 682-7519.

MONTELIONE, Anthony S. *(Circuit Judge, Illinois Circuit Court of Cook County)* Elected 1984. Retained by election 1990, 1996 and 2002. Current term expires 2008.

Office: 10220 South 76th Avenue, Room 205-L, Bridgeview 60455.

Telephone: (708) 974-6288.

MORAN, George J. *(Circuit Judge, Illinois Circuit Court Third Judicial Circuit)* Former Associate Judge. Assumed office as Circuit Judge. Term expires Dec 2006.

Office: Madison County Courthouse, 155 North Main Street, Edwardsville 62025.

Telephone: (618) 692-4459.

MORAN, James B. *(Senior Judge, United States District Court Northern District of Illinois)* Appointed for life by President Jimmy Carter to term beginning July 24, 1979. Assumed Senior status, serves by assignment. Born Evanston Illinois June 20, 1930. Episcopalian. Educated at University of Michigan B.A. in Economics with honors 1952 and Harvard University LL.B. magna cum laude 1957. Law Clerk to Hon. J. Edward Lumbard, U.S. Court of Appeals Second Circuit 1957-58. Member Phi Beta Kappa. Admitted to practice Illinois 1958. In legal practice Chicago 1958-79.

Member Chicago Council of Lawyers, Lawyers Club of Chicago, Chicago and Seventh Circuit Bar Associations. Sergeant U.S. Army 1952-54. Director Evanston Defender Program since 1975 and Woodlawn Community Development Corporation since 1978. Member General Assembly Illinois 1965-66. Director Gateway Foundation since 1968 (Past President, Vice President and Secretary) and Evanston City Council 1971-75. Enjoys sailing.

Office: U.S. Courthouse, 219 South Dearborn Street, Chicago 60604.

Telephone: (312) 435-5772.

MORAN, John J., Jr. *(Circuit Judge, Illinois Circuit Court of Cook County)*

Office: 2600 South California Avenue, Chicago 60608.

Telephone: (773) 869-3186.

MORAN, Kathleen P. *(Circuit Judge, Illinois Circuit Court Fourth Judicial Circuit)* Elected to term beginning Dec 1, 1994. Retained by election 2000, current term expires Dec 2006. Born St. Louis Missouri Aug 12,

MORAN, KATHLEEN P.—*Continued*

1950. Educated at Southern Illinois University B.A. with honors 1973 and University of Kansas J.D. 1976. Staff member University of Kansas Law Review. Law Clerk to Hon. Joseph Goldenhersh, Illinois Supreme Court 1976-78. Admitted to practice Illinois 1976. In legal practice Trenton 1978-94.

Office: Clinton County Courthouse, Carlyle 62231.
Telephone: (618) 594-2464.

MORE, Angus S., Jr. *(Associate Judge, Illinois Circuit Court Seventeenth Judicial Circuit)* Appointed to term beginning Jan 11, 1995. Reappointed July 1, 1995 and July 1999. Current term expires July 2003. Born Kankakee Illinois June 26, 1939. Presbyterian. Educated at University of Illinois A.B. 1961 and Washington College of Law of American University J.D. 1967. Member Delta Theta Phi. Admitted to practice Illinois 1967, U.S. District Court Northern District of Illinois 1968 and U.S. Court of Appeals Seventh Circuit 1970. In legal practice Rockford 1967-95.

Part-time Assistant Attorney General Consumer Fraud 1969-71 and Workers' Compensation 1974-83 Illinois. Member Illinois Judges Association and Winnebago County Bar Association. Captain U.S. Army Infantry 1961-67. Republican. Precinct Committeeman 1967-94. Member Rock Run Long Rifles, Inc., Northern Illinois Rifle and Pistol Club, Rockford Skeet Club, Rotary International and University Club of Rockford. Enjoys target shooting and hunting.

Office: Winnebago County Courthouse, 400 West State Street, Rockford 61101.
Telephone: (815) 987-3062.

MORRISSEY, Dennis J. *(Circuit Judge, Illinois Circuit Court of Cook County)*

Office: 400 R. J. Daley Center, Chicago 60602.
Telephone: (312) 603-2624.

MORRISSEY, George M. *(Associate Judge, Illinois Circuit Court of Cook County)*

Office: 16501 South Kedzie Parkway, Markham 60426.
Telephone: (708) 210-4170.

MORRISSEY, John Emmett *(Circuit Judge, Illinois Circuit Court of Cook County)* Elected Associate Judge at special election to term beginning July 1, 1983. Assumed office as Circuit Judge. Term expires Dec 2006. Born Chicago Illinois Dec 11, 1942. Roman Catholic. Educated at Bellarmine College B.S. 1966 and St. Louis University J.D. 1974. Admitted to practice Illinois 1974 and U.S. District Court District of Illinois 1974. Began legal practice Chicago 1974.

Former Member Illinois State Bar Association. Board of Directors Celtic Lawyers Society. Member Illinois Judges Association, Chicago and American Bar Associations. Captain U.S. Army 1966-69. Member Irish Fellowship Club. Enjoys golf, reading, raising his children, exercising and biking. Personal Statement or Quote: "Freedom of the press is an awesome privilege. Use it wisely and fairly."

Office: 2406 R. J. Daley Center, Chicago 60602.
Telephone: (312) 603-6020.
E-mail address: JMcGINL10@aol.com

MORSE, J. Patrick *(Associate Judge, Illinois Circuit Court of Cook County)*

Office: 5600 Old Orchard Road, Skokie 60077.
Telephone: (847) 470-7200.

MOY, Kenneth *(Circuit Judge, Illinois Circuit Court Eighteenth Judicial Circuit)* Elected to term beginning Nov 5, 1996. Retained by election 2002, current term expires Dec 2008. Born Chicago Illinois March 24, 1933. Lutheran. Educated at Elmhurst College B.S. 1955 and John Marshall Law School J.D. 1961. Law Clerk to Hon. William L. Guild, Illinois Appellate Court District Two. Admitted to practice Illinois 1961, U.S. District Court Northern District of Illinois and U.S. Court of Appeals Seventh Circuit. In legal practice Elmhurst 1961-86 and Clarendon Hills 1986-96.

Assistant State's Attorney DuPage County 1962-65. Township Attorney York 1964-69. Attorney Roselle School District 1965-66. Republican. Board Member DuPage County 1984-96. Board Member Mutual Citizen Board Blue Cross Blue Shield of Illinois. Member Kiwanis and Committee 100.

Office: 505 North County Farm Road, Wheaton 60187.
Telephone: (630) 682-7305.

MUELLER, Thomas E. *(Associate Judge, Illinois Circuit Court Sixteenth Judicial Circuit)*

Office: 37W777 Route 38, Room 400-A, St. Charles 60175.
Telephone: (630) 406-7148.

MULHERN, Mary A. *(Circuit Judge, Illinois Circuit Court of Cook County)*

Office: 2609 R. J. Daley Center, Chicago 60602.
Telephone: (312) 603-7834.

MULLEN, Margaret J. *(Chief Judge, Illinois Circuit Court Nineteenth Judicial Circuit)* Former Associate Judge.

Office: Lake County Courthouse, 18 North County Street, Waukegan 60085.
Telephone: (847) 377-3600.

MURPHY, G. Patrick *(Chief Judge, United States District Court Southern District of Illinois)* Appointed for life by President Bill Clinton to term beginning 1998. Chief Judge since Oct 3, 2000. Born Carbondale Illinois Dec 1, 1948. Educated at Southern Illinois University B.S. 1974 J.D. 1978. In legal practice Marion 1978-98.

Office: U.S. Courthouse, 750 Missouri Avenue, East St. Louis 62201-2954.
Telephone: (618) 482-9173.

MURPHY, James Vincent, II *(Associate Judge, Illinois Circuit Court of Cook County)* Appointed to term beginning June 17, 1985. Appointed to subsequent terms. Current term expires 2003. Born Evanston Illinois Jan 24, 1946. Roman Catholic. Educated at St. Mary's College B.A. with honors 1966 and DePaul University M.A. with honors 1972 J.D. 1974. Admitted to practice Illinois 1974, U.S. District Court Northern District of Illinois 1974 and U.S. Supreme Court 1980. In legal practice Chicago.

Corporation Counsel City of Chicago 1978-85. Author Chapter and Bibliography *International Criminal Law and Terrorism* 1974. Member Celtic Lawyer Society, West Suburban, Chicago, Illinois State and American Bar Associations. Recipient Constance Morris House

MURPHY, JAMES VINCENT, II—*Continued*

Award for service to victims of domestic violence 1989-2002, North River Committee President's Award, Uptown-Ravenswood Award and Northwest Neighborhood Award. U.S. Army Military Police 1967-73. Director Sauganash Community Association. Former President local Little League. Active in church. Enjoys reading good fiction, writing and playing sports such as golf, squash and tennis.

Office: 1500 Maybrook Drive, Room 119, Maywood 60153.

Telephone: (708) 865-6060.

MURPHY, Lisa Ruble *(Circuit Judge, Illinois Circuit Court of Cook County)*

Office: 2807 R. J. Daley Center, Chicago 60602.

Telephone: (312) 603-3898.

MURPHY, Michael J. *(Circuit Judge, Illinois Circuit Court of Cook County)* Appointed Associate Judge to term beginning 1985. Assumed office as Circuit Judge. Currently serves as Presiding Judge Cook County Division. Educated at Loyola University of Chicago B.S. in Economics 1964 and John Marshall Law School J.D. with honors 1971. Graduated first in law school class. Recipient American Jurisprudence Award in Constitutional Law, West Publishing Company prize for scholarly achievement in third year and post graduate scholarship to Lawyer's Institute. Elected to Order of John Marshall.

Assistant Attorney General Illinois 1971-76. Special Assistant U.S. Attorney 1974-76. Executive Director and Staff Attorney South East Chicago Commission 1976-85. Member 1980-84 and Vice Chair 1984 Inquiry Board and Member Hearing Board 1985 Attorney Registration and Disciplinary Commission. Part-time Instructor in Legal Research and Writing John Marshall Law School 1975-78. Faculty Member New Investigators Illinois Department of Revenue 1985. Board Member and Trained Intervenor Lawyers Assistance Program since 1983. Member Bench-Bar Relations Committee and Subcommittee on Criteria for Judicial Selection Chicago Bar Association 1989. Member Coordinating Committee and Liaison to Criminal Law Topical Committee 1988-89 and Vice Chairman 1989-90 Associate Judges Seminar. Instructor and Trial Judge Chicago Coalition for Law Related Education since 1984. Faculty Member Associate Judge Professional Development Orientation Program since 1986. Mock Trial Judge University of Chicago Law School since 1986, Loyola University Law School 1986, Young Lawyers Section Chicago Bar Association 1986 and John Marshall Law School 1989. Lecturer on "Defending Clients Charged with DUI" 1987-88 and "Litigation in Cook County: A View from the Bench" 1987 Illinois Institute for Continuing Legal Education; "Judicial Ethics" Associate Judges Seminar 1988; and "Alcohol and Drugs" The National Judicial College since 1988. Faculty Member Judicial Ethics Forum American Judicature Society Denver, Chicago and Washington D.C. 1988-89. Attended Seminars on "Domestic Violence Act" Illinois Coalition Against Domestic Violence 1985; "Constitutional Issues in Criminal Cases" 1986, "Wards of the Court" 1987, "Ethical Issues in Law and Society" 1987, "Evidence" 1987, "Management of a Civil Jury Trial" 1987, "Motion Practice in Civil Cases" 1989 and "Jury Management, Civil and Criminal" 1989 Illinois Judicial Conference; "Assessments and Appraisals" Assessment and Appraisal Institute University of Chicago 1987; "Judicial Writing" The National Judicial College 1988; and "Election Law" Illinois Institute of Continuing Education 1988. Previously employed as Savings and Loan Examiner Illinois 1964-65 and Criminal Investigator U.S. Department of the Treasury 1965-71. Board Member Mercy Hospital and Medical Center since 1976.

Office: 1701 R. J. Daley Center, Chicago 60602.

Telephone: (312) 603-6194.

MURPHY, Paul S. *(Circuit Judge, Illinois Circuit Court First Judicial Circuit)* Appointed to term beginning Jan 17, 1989. Elected Nov 6, 1990. Retained by election 1996 and 2002. Current term expires Dec 2008. Born Hartford Connecticut Jan 15, 1947. Catholic. Educated at Georgetown University A.B. 1969 and Boston College J.D. 1972. Admitted to practice Massachusetts 1972, U.S. Court of Military Appeals 1973, Illinois 1976 and U.S. District Court District of Illinois 1976. In legal practice Herrin Illinois 1976-89. U.S. Army Jan 1973 to Jan 1976.

Office: Williamson County Courthouse, Marion 62959.

Telephone: (618) 997-1301.

MURPHY GORMAN, Joyce Marie *(Circuit Judge, Illinois Circuit Court of Cook County)*

Office: 400 R. J. Daley Center, Chicago 60602.

Telephone: (312) 603-2600.

MURRAY, Michael J. *(Associate Judge, Illinois Circuit Court of Cook County)* Appointed July 3, 1987. Reappointed to subsequent terms. Born Sept 6, 1934. Educated at Villanova University B.S. 1957 and DePaul University College of Law J.D. 1962. In legal practice 1982-87. Former Hearing Officer, State Board of Elections.

Chief Attorney Board of Education Chicago 1973-81. Former Special Counsel City Colleges of Chicago. Lecturer on Criminal Justice St. Xavier College. Guest Lecturer on School Law Loyola University and Roosevelt University. Member Associate Judge Task Force 1993-97, Presiding Judges' Committee on Uniform Orders in Traffic Cases (Operation Babel) and Legislative Liaison Committee, Disciplinary Committee and Task Force on Judicial Immunity Illinois Judges Association. Chairman 1992 Associate Judge Seminar Committee on Conduct of a Civil Jury Trial II. Attended "Commercial Litigation" seminar May 1992, "Case Management of a Civil Jury Trial" seminar Oct 1992, "Developing a Systematic Approach to the Multiple DUI Offender" May 19-21, 1994 and "Education Conference 2002." Recipient Constance Morris House Recognition Award for working with survivors of domestic violence 1994. Legislative representative for the Board of Education to Illinois General Assembly 1962-70. Participant Judge 12th Annual John Marshall National Moot Court Competition and John Marshall Law School Trial Advocacy Program.

Office: 10220 South 76th Avenue, Room 201B, Bridgeview 60455.

Telephone: (708) 974-6532.

MUSE, Elliott, Jr. *(Circuit Judge, Illinois Circuit Court of Cook County)*

Office: 16501 South Kedzie Parkway, Markham 60426.

Telephone: (708) 210-4170.

MYERSCOUGH, Sue E. *(Judge, Illinois Appellate Court Fourth Judicial District)* Elected to term beginning Dec 7, 1998. Term expires Dec 2008. Born Springfield Illinois 1951. Catholic. Educated at Southern Illinois University B.A. with honors 1973 J.D. 1980 and University of Chicago M.A. 1974. Recipient Southern Illinois University Scholarship. President's Scholar. Articles Editor Southern Illinois University Law Journal 1979-80. Law Clerk to Hon. Harold Albert Baker, U.S. District Court Central District of Illinois 1980-81. Moot Court Finalist. Admitted to practice Illinois 1980 and U.S. Court of Appeals Seventh Circuit 1999. In legal practice Springfield 1981-87. Associate Judge 1987-90, Circuit Judge 1990-98, Presiding Judge 1995-98 and Chief Judge 1997-98, Illinois Circuit Court Seventh Judicial Circuit.

Author "Service Contracts—A Subject for State or Federal Regulation: Do Consumers Need Protection from the Service Contract Industry?" 4 Southern Illinois University L. Jour. 1979. Member Lincoln-Douglas Inn of Court, Appellate Trial Lawyers Association, The Association of Trial Lawyers of America, Illinois Judges Association, Sangamon County, Central Illinois Women's, Illinois State and American Bar Associations. Recipient Illinois Probation Recognition Award 1998, Women in Excellence Award from YWCA 2001, Hillary Rodham Clinton Leadership Award from Illinois Democratic Women 2002, Athena Award from Greater Springfield Chamber of Commerce 2002, Order of Barristers Award, Cross-Cultural Teaching Exchange Award, Distinguished Service Award from Sangamon County Probation and Sangamon County Board and Right Track Truancy Recognition Award. Named Honorary Member Illinois Women's Bar 2000. Democrat. Member Juvenile Justice Initiative, Women in Management State Youth Council, Youth Enrichment Services Committee and Eagles Club Lincoln Land Community College. Enjoys gourmet cooking, golf and walking.

Office: 500 South Sixth Street, Springfield 62701-1810.

Telephone: (217) 557-5490.

Fax: (217) 557-5487

MYLES, Raymond *(Associate Judge, Illinois Circuit Court of Cook County)* Appointed.

Office: 1303 R. J. Daley Center, Chicago 60602.

Telephone: (312) 603-7959.

NARDULLI, Steven H. *(Associate Judge, Illinois Circuit Court Seventh Judicial Circuit)*

Office: 200 South Ninth Street, Springfield 62701.

Telephone: (217) 753-6731.

NASH, Steven M. *(Associate Judge, Illinois Circuit Court Seventeenth Judicial Circuit)* Appointed 1990. Reappointed 1995 and 1999. Current term expires 2003. Born Rockford Illinois 1952. Educated at Rockford College B.A. 1974 and University of Illinois J.D. 1980. Admitted to practice Illinois.

Assistant State's Attorney 1980-90.

Office: Winnebago County Courthouse, 400 West State Street, Rockford 61101.

Telephone: (815) 987-3062.

NEALIS, Paul J. *(Associate Judge, Illinois Circuit Court of Cook County)*

Office: 16501 South Kedzie Parkway, Room 106, Markham 60426.

Telephone: (708) 210-4168.

NEDDENRIEP, Gary *(Associate Judge, Illinois Circuit Court Nineteenth Judicial Circuit)*

Office: Lake County Courthouse, 18 North County Street, Waukegan 60085.

Telephone: (847) 377-3794.

NEGA, Marya *(Circuit Judge, Illinois Circuit Court of Cook County)*

Office: 1603 R. J. Daley Center, Chicago 60602.

Telephone: (312) 603-4839.

NEMENOFF, Brian Mark *(Associate Judge, Illinois Circuit Court Tenth Judicial Circuit)* Appointed June 1986 to term beginning Aug 1, 1986. Reappointed 1987, 1991, 1995 and 1999. Current term expires 2003. Born Chicago Illinois Dec 3, 1947. Educated at Miami University B.A. 1970 and University of Illinois J.D. 1974. Law Clerk to Hon. Jay Alloy, Illinois Appellate Court Third Judicial District 1974-75. Member Omicron Delta Kappa. Admitted to practice Illinois 1974, U.S. District Court Central District of Illinois and U.S. Court of Appeals Seventh Circuit.

Assistant Corporate Counsel, Deputy Corporate Counsel and City Attorney Peoria 1976-86. General Counsel Peoria Civic Center 1976-86. Instructor in Business Law Illinois Central College 1976-77. Attended seminars sponsored by Illinois State Bar Association and Administrative Office of Illinois Courts. USAR 1970-76.

Office: Tazewell County Courthouse, 342 Court Street, Pekin 61554-4281.

Telephone: (309) 477-2201.

NEVILLE, P. Scott, Jr. *(Circuit Judge, Illinois Circuit Court of Cook County)*

Office: 1101 R. J. Daley Center, Chicago 60602.

Telephone: (312) 603-4415.

NIXON, Lewis *(Circuit Judge, Illinois Circuit Court of Cook County)*

Office: 400 R. J. Daley Center, Chicago 60602.

Telephone: (312) 603-2600.

NIZNIK, Gilbert L. *(Associate Judge, Illinois Circuit Court Twelfth Judicial Circuit)*

Office: Will County Courthouse, 14 West Jefferson, Joliet 60432.

Telephone: (815) 436-3835.

NOLAN, Nan R. *(Magistrate Judge, United States District Court Northern District of Illinois)* Appointed by U.S. District Court judges.

Office: 1870 U.S. Courthouse, 219 South Dearborn Street, Chicago 60604.

Telephone: (312) 435-5604.

NOLAND, Paul *(Recalled Associate Judge, Illinois Circuit Court Eighteenth Judicial Circuit)* Appointed. Retired, serves by recall.

Office: DuPage County Courthouse, 505 North County Farm Road, Wheaton 60187.

Telephone: (630) 682-7300.

NORDBERG, John A. *(Senior Judge, United States District Court Northern District of Illinois)* Appointed for life by President Ronald Reagan to term beginning May 6, 1982. Assumed Senior status June 18, 1994, serves by assignment. Born Evanston Illinois June 18, 1926. Educated at Carleton College 1943-44 and 1946-47 and University of Michigan J.D. 1950. Assistant Editor Michigan Law Review. Member Order of the Coif. Admitted to practice Illinois 1950. Began legal practice

NORDBERG, JOHN A.—*Continued*

Chicago 1950. Justice of the Peace and Magistrate 1957-65 and Circuit Judge 1976-82, Illinois Circuit Court of Cook County.

Editor-in-Chief Chicago B. Jour. Arbitrator American Arbitration Association. Member American Judicature Society, Law Club of Chicago, Legal Club of Chicago, Chicago, Illinois State and American Bar Associations. ETM/3 USN 1944-46. Member Glenview Community Church. Permanent Guest of Union League Club of Chicago. Enjoys golf and tennis.

Office: U.S. Courthouse, 219 South Dearborn Street, Chicago 60604.

Telephone: (312) 435-5781.

NORDQUIST, Steven L. *(Associate Judge, Illinois Circuit Court Seventeenth Judicial Circuit)* Appointed Dec 2, 1996. Reappointed July 1, 1999, current term expires 2003. Born Rockford Illinois April 20, 1951. Catholic. Educated at University of Illinois B.S. 1973 and Hamline University School of Law J.D. 1976. Member Phi Alpha Delta. Admitted to practice Illinois 1977, U.S. District Court District of Illinois 1977, Wisconsin 1984 and U.S. Supreme Court 1984. In legal practice Rockford Illinois April 1977 to Dec 1996.

Member Illinois Judges Association, Winn County, Illinois State and American Bar Associations. Republican. Member Ducks Unlimited, Pheasants Forever, Barbara Olson School of Hope and YMCA Rockford. Enjoys racquetball and scuba diving.

Office: 400 West State Street, Rockford 61101.

Telephone: (815) 987-3062.

Fax: (815) 987-3011

NORGLE, Charles Ronald, Sr. *(Judge, United States District Court Northern District of Illinois)* Appointed for life by President Ronald Reagan to term beginning Nov 1, 1984. Born March 3, 1937. Educated at Northwestern University B.B.A. 1964 and John Marshall Law School J.D. 1969. Admitted to practice Illinois 1969. Associate Judge 1973-77 and 1978-81 and Circuit Judge 1977-78 and 1981-84, Illinois Circuit Court Eighteenth Judicial Circuit.

Assistant State's Attorney 1969-71 and Deputy Public Defender 1971-73 DuPage County. Author "Significant Pretrial Restraint on Liberty" Illinois B. Jour. 1977. Instructor College of DuPage. Lecturer Police Training Institute University of Illinois. Adjunct Faculty Member Trial Advocacy John Marshall Law School and Northwestern University School of Law. Appointed by Chief Justice Rehnquist to Federal Defender Services Committee. Member Seventh Circuit Council Committee, Executive Committee District Court, Illinois Judges Association, American Judges Association, National Lawyers Club, DuPage County, Illinois State, Federal Circuit, Federal and American Bar Associations. Attended The National Judicial College 1975, 1978 and 1981. Recipient Distinguished Service Award from John Marshall Law School 1986. U.S. Army 1955-57.

Office: U.S. Courthouse, 219 South Dearborn Street, Chicago 60604.

Telephone: (312) 435-5634.

NOTTOLINI, Gene Louis *(Circuit Judge, Illinois Circuit Court Sixteenth Judicial Circuit)* Appointed Associate Judge to term beginning Dec 2, 1984. Assumed office as Circuit Judge. Term expires 2008. Former Chief Judge. Born Elgin Illinois July 9, 1944. Catholic. Educated at St. Louis University J.D. 1968. Admitted to practice Illinois 1968 and Missouri 1968. In legal practice Elgin Illinois 1968-84.

Office: 100 South Third Street, Geneva 60134.

Telephone: (630) 232-3441.

NOVAK, Rita M. *(Associate Judge, Illinois Circuit Court of Cook County)* Appointed to term beginning Nov 2, 1999. Term expires 2003. Serves Child Protection Division. Born Detroit Michigan Dec 8, 1949. Educated at Albion College B.A. cum laude 1972, DePaul University J.D. 1978 and Columbia University LL.M. 1981. Note and Comment Editor DePaul Law Review 1977-78. Law Clerk to Hon. John Powers Crowley, U.S. District Court Northern District of Illinois 1978-80. Admitted to practice Illinois 1978, U.S. District Court Northern District of Illinois 1978, U.S. Court of Appeals Seventh Circuit 1985 and U.S. Supreme Court 1987. Circuit Judge, Illinois Circuit Court of Cook County Nov 21, 1997 to Dec 2, 1998.

Assistant Attorney General Chief Civil Appeals Illinois 1991-97. Co-author with Douglas Somerlot "Delay on Appeal: A Process for Identifying Causes and Cures" 1988. Co-editor *The Gavel* Illinois Judges Association 2000-01. Assistant Professor of Civil Procedure, Remedies, Constitutional Law and Administrative Law Indiana University 1981-84. Member Chicago Council of Lawyers, Women's Bar Association of Illinois, Illinois Judges Association, Chicago and Illinois State Bar Associations.

Office: 1100 South Hamilton Avenue, Room C015, Chicago 60612.

Telephone: (312) 433-4756.

NOVOSELSKY, Benjamin E. *(Recalled Circuit Judge, Illinois Circuit Court of Cook County)* Retired, serves by recall.

Office: 1807 R. J. Daley Center, Chicago 60602.

Telephone: (312) 603-6472.

NOWICKI, Julia M. *(Circuit Judge, Illinois Circuit Court of Cook County)* Appointed Associate Judge to term beginning Jan 9, 1984. Reappointed 1987. Assumed office as Circuit Judge. Born Milwaukee Wisconsin May 11, 1948. Protestant. Educated at University of Wisconsin B.A. with honors 1971 and Loyola University J.D. 1975. Admitted to practice Illinois 1975, U.S. District Court Northern District of Illinois 1975, U.S. Court of Appeals Seventh Circuit 1980 and Trial Bar of U.S. District Court Northern District of Illinois 1982. Began legal practice Chicago 1975.

Lecturer on Criminal Law Cook County Department of Corrections 1981-83. Instructor in Trial Practice Loyola University School of Law 1981-84 and Federal Trial Bar Advocacy Course The Association of Trial Lawyers of America and Chicago Bar Association 1983-84. Member Illinois Governor's Advisory Council on Criminal Justice Legislation since 1975. Member Advocates Society, Illinois Trial Lawyers Association, Women's Bar Association of Illinois (Chair Trial Lawyers Section since 1982), Chicago and American Bar Associations. Enjoys scuba diving, soccer, tennis, cello and ballet.

Office: 2510 R. J. Daley Center, Chicago 60602.

Telephone: (312) 603-6032.

NOWINSKI, Thomas E. *(Circuit Judge, Illinois Circuit Court of Cook County)* Former Associate Judge.
Office: 10220 South 76th Avenue, Room 105A, Bridgeview 60455.
Telephone: (708) 974-6534.

NUDELMAN, Stuart A. *(Circuit Judge, Illinois Circuit Court of Cook County)* Former Associate Judge. Assumed office as Circuit Judge. Term expires Dec 2006.
Office: 2010 R. J. Daley Center, Chicago 60602.
Telephone: (312) 603-5932.

OBBISH, James M. *(Associate Judge, Illinois Circuit Court of Cook County)* Appointed. Educated at University of Illinois at Champaign-Urbana B.A. 1968 and DePaul University J.D. 1973. In legal practice Chicago May 1980 to Dec 1997.
Assistant State's Attorney Cook County May 1974 to May 1980.
Office: 1100 South Hamilton, Room C25, Chicago 60612.
Telephone: (312) 433-4756.
Fax: (312) 433-7899
E-mail address: jmobbis@cookcountygov.com

O'BRIEN, Donald J., Jr. *(Circuit Judge, Illinois Circuit Court of Cook County)*
Office: 1906 R. J. Daley Center, Chicago 60602.
Telephone: (312) 603-5935.

O'BRIEN, Edward P. *(Circuit Judge, Illinois Circuit Court of Cook County)*
Office: 1706 R. J. Daley Center, Chicago 60602.
Telephone: (312) 603-7892.

O'BRIEN, Gregory M. *(Associate Judge, Illinois Circuit Court of Cook County)*
Office: 1100 South Hamilton Avenue, Chicago 60612.
Telephone: (312) 433-4756.

O'BRIEN, Joan M. *(Circuit Judge, Illinois Circuit Court of Cook County)*
Office: 1100 South Hamilton Avenue, Room G034, Chicago 60612.
Telephone: (312) 433-4756.

O'BRIEN, Sheila M. *(Judge, Illinois Appellate Court First Judicial District Division Six)* Elected 1994. Formerly served Division One. Born Nov 8, 1955. Educated at University of Notre Dame B.A. 1977 J.D. 1980. Former Associate Judge, Illinois Circuit Court Twentieth Judicial Circuit, appointed to term beginning 1985.
Former Assistant Public Defender.
Office: 160 North LaSalle Street, Room N1906, Chicago 60601.
Telephone: (312) 793-5431.

O'BRIEN, William T. *(Circuit Judge, Illinois Circuit Court of Cook County)*
Office: 1303 R. J. Daley Center, Chicago 60602.
Telephone: (312) 603-7959.

O'CONNOR, Jeffrey W. *(Chief Judge, Illinois Circuit Court Fourteenth Judicial Circuit)* Term expires Dec 2006.
Office: 408 Rock Island County Courthouse, 210 Fifteenth Street, Rock Island 61201.
Telephone: (309) 786-4451.

O'GARA, Lawrence *(Circuit Judge, Illinois Circuit Court of Cook County)*
Office: 1303 R. J. Daley Center, Chicago 60602.
Telephone: (312) 603-7959.

O'HARA, Thomas J. *(Associate Judge, Illinois Circuit Court of Cook County)*
Office: 16501 South Kedzie Parkway, Markham 60426.
Telephone: (708) 210-4170.

O'LEARY, Susan T. *(Circuit Judge, Illinois Circuit Court Twelfth Judicial Circuit)*
Office: Will County Courthouse, 14 West Jefferson, Joliet 60432.
Telephone: (815) 727-8540.

OLSON, Tim P. *(Associate Judge, Illinois Circuit Court Seventh Judicial Circuit)*
Office: Morgan County Courthouse, Jacksonville 62650.
Telephone: (217) 243-5419.

O'MALLEY, Denise Margaret *(Judge, Illinois Appellate Court First Judicial District Division One)* Born Chicago Illinois March 15, 1940. Catholic. Educated at Mundelein College B.A. 1961, University of Chicago M.A. 1971 and John Marshall Law School J.D. 1981. Admitted to practice Illinois 1981. In legal practice Chicago 1981-92. Former Circuit Judge, Illinois Circuit Court of Cook County, elected to term beginning Dec 2, 1992.
Member Women's Bar Association of Illinois and Chicago Bar Association. Attended Evidence, Family Law and Advanced Evidence courses The National Judicial College. Democrat. Member Irish Fellowship Club, Parade Committee, Human Society and National Foundation for Women.
Office: 160 North LaSalle Street, Room S1510, Chicago 60601.
Telephone: (312) 793-5453.

O'MALLEY, Jack *(Judge, Illinois Appellate Court Second Judicial District)* Elected Nov 2000. Born Chicago Illinois 1951. Educated at Loyola University of Chicago B.S. magna cum laude, Cornell University Law School and University of Chicago Law School.
Office: 10329 Main Street, Richmond 60071.
Telephone: (815) 678-0089.

O'MALLEY, James P. *(Circuit Judge, Illinois Circuit Court of Cook County)*
Office: 10220 South 76th Avenue, Room 104-A, Bridgeview 60455.
Telephone: (708) 974-6534.

O'MALLEY, Michael J. *(Circuit Judge, Illinois Circuit Court Twentieth Judicial Circuit)* Term expires 2008.
Office: County Building, 10 Public Square, Belleville 62220.
Telephone: (618) 277-7325.

O'MALLEY, William P. *(Circuit Judge, Illinois Circuit Court of Cook County)*
Office: 2452 West Belmont, Chicago 60618.
Telephone: (773) 404-3315.

O'MARA FROSSARD, Margaret *(Circuit Judge, Illinois Circuit Court of Cook County)* Appointed Associate Judge Dec 8, 1988. Elected Circuit Judge Nov 15,

O'MARA FROSSARD, MARGARET—*Continued*

1994. Retained by election Nov 2000, current term expires Nov 2006. Currently on assignment by Supreme Court of Illinois as Judge, Illinois Appellate Court First Judicial District Division Six. Formerly served Illinois Appellate Court First Judicial District Division One. Born Chicago Illinois Nov 23, 1951. Educated at Northwestern University B.A. with honors 1973 and Illinois Institute of Technology, Chicago-Kent College of Law J.D. 1976. Contributing author Chicago-Kent Law Review 1975-76. Admitted to practice Illinois 1976, U.S. District Court Northern District of Illinois 1984 and Trial Bar of U.S. District Court Northern District of Illinois 1984.

Assistant State's Attorney Cook County 1976-88 (Deputy Supervisor Rape Prosecution Task Force 1980, Felony Trial Supervisor 1984-87, Chief Felony Trial Division 1987-88). Contributing writer "Sexual Assault: A Hospital/Community Protocol for Forensic and Medical Examination" 1985-86. Author "The Detainer Process: The Hidden Due Process Violation in Parole Revocation" 52 Chicago-Kent L. Rev. 716, "The Gary Dotson Case: A Practical Approach to Recantation Problems in a Major Media Case" National College of District Attorneys 1987, Chapter 8 "Pre-Trial Motions" *Federal Criminal Practice* IICLE 1987 and 1992, "Examining the Recanting Witness" *Litigation Magazine* American Bar Association 1988, "Case Note: *People v. Storms*" 15 No. 3 *The Gavel* 1992, "Foundation for Opinion Evidence and Chain of Custody" Judicial D.U.I. Training 1993, "Supreme Court Offers Guidance in Interpreting Code of Judicial Conduct" 16 No. 2 *The Gavel* 1993 and "Spoliation Evidence in Illinois: The Law After *Boyd v. Traveler's Insurance*" 28 Loyola University of Chicago L. Jour. 685, 1997. Important Decisions: Jackson v. Michael Reese Hospital (spoliation of evidence) 96-2395, Generes v. Stephen (plaintiff's post trial motion for judgment notwithstanding the verdict or in the alternative for a new trial) 84 M2 1045, People v. Finucane (state's motion to admit log book and card containing breathalyzer results into evidence in a driving under the influence of alcohol bench trial) Y2-563-353, Pappageorge/Haymes Ltd., an Illinois Corporation v. Sam Maniatis (jury trial contract case) 91 M2 0149, People v. Santoya and People v. Moses (motions to quash arrest and suppress evidence in driving under the influence of alcohol), O'Donnell v. S and Z Cab Company, an Illinois Corporation and Wade Sims (plaintiff's post-trial motion to set aside the verdict or to enter judgment notwithstanding the verdict) 89 M2 1487, Keys v. Crawford (personal injury trial) 90 M2 100196, Testa v. People (post conviction petition) P.C. 80-C-002825, Tamraz v. Sadeghloo (personal injury) 89 M2 1746, People v. Scott Welty, People v. Davis (circumstantial murder jury trial) and Glencoe v. Klotz (First Amendment, freedom of speech) 91 MC2006752.

Former Adjunct Professor Chicago-Kent College of Law and DePaul University College of Law. Adjunct Professor Northwestern University School of Law. Lecturer University of Chicago Law School and Cook County State's Attorney's Office. Member Judicial DUI Training Committee, House Judiciary II Subcommittee on Uniform Criminal Sentencing and National Advisory Committee on the Evidence Collection Project for Victims of Sexual Assault. Member Illinois Trial Lawyers Association, The Association of Trial Lawyers of America, National District Attorney's Association, National Institute of Trial Advocacy, NITA Advocates Association, Illinois Judges Association, National Women Judges Association, Women's Bar Association of Illinois, Chicago (Special Committee on Administration of Criminal Justice in Cook County, Judicial Evaluation Committee, In-Court Lawyer Referral Program, Vice Chair Criminal Law Committee), Illinois State, Seventh Circuit and American (Trial Practice Subcommittee, Sections: Judicial Administration Division, Tort and Insurance Practice, Litigation, Criminal Justice) Bar Associations. Faculty Member National Institute of Trial Advocacy, National College of District Attorneys, Federal Trial Bar Course Chicago Bar Association and Illinois Institute of Technology, Chicago-Kent Trial Advocacy Team. Panelist Civil Motion Practice NSBA, Anatomy of a Civil Case American Bar Association, Search and Seizure Associate Judge Seminar, Cook County Judges DUI Conference and Illinois Institute of Continuing Legal Education. Recipient McManus Award for recognition of a graduate who significantly reflects the school's philosophy and ideals 1992, Community Service Award from Illinois State Bar Association 1997 and Professional Service Award from NSBA 1997. Lecturer Chicago Osteopathic Hospital, City of Chicago Department of Human Services, Constitutional Rights Foundation/Chicago Project, Illinois Federation of Business and Professional Women, National Coalition Against Sexual Assault and Rush-Presbyterian St. Luke's College of Nursing. Panelist Continental Cablevision, MacNeil-Lehrer News Hour PBX-TV, 20/20 ABC-TV and WBBM-TV's Newsmakers. Member National Organization for Victim Assistance and Daniel Murphy Scholarship Foundation. Moderator Chicago Youth Center Lower North Cabrini Green Club. Enjoys running.

Office: 160 North LaSalle, Chicago 60601.
Telephone: (312) 793-4488.

O'NEAL, William D. *(Circuit Judge, Illinois Circuit Court of Cook County)*
Office: 16501 South Kedzie Parkway, Markham 60426.
Telephone: (708) 210-4170.

ORBACH, Jerome M. *(Associate Judge, Illinois Circuit Court of Cook County)*
Office: 5600 Old Orchard Road, Room 132, Skokie 60077.
Telephone: (847) 470-7200.

ORR, Marcia B. *(Associate Judge, Illinois Circuit Court of Cook County)*
Office: 5600 Old Orchard Road, Room 132, Skokie 60077.
Telephone: (847) 470-7200.

ORTBAL, Thomas J. *(Associate Judge, Illinois Circuit Court Eighth Judicial Circuit)*
Office: Adams County Courthouse, 521 Vermont Street, Quincy 62301.
Telephone: (217) 277-2036.

ORTIZ, Jorge L. *(Associate Judge, Illinois Circuit Court Nineteenth Judicial Circuit)*
Office: 18 North County Street, Waukegan 60085.
Telephone: (847) 377-3600.

OTAKA, Sandra R. *(Circuit Judge, Illinois Circuit Court of Cook County)*
Office: 1100 South Hamilton Avenue, Room G025, Chicago 60612.
Telephone: (312) 433-4756.

OTIS-LEWIS, Alexis *(Associate Judge, Illinois Circuit Court Twentieth Judicial Circuit)*
Office: County Building, 10 Public Square, Belleville 62220.
Telephone: (618) 277-7325.

PACEY, Steve *(Circuit Judge, Illinois Circuit Court Eleventh Judicial Circuit)* Appointed Aug 19, 1996. Elected Nov 3, 1998, current term expires Dec 2004. Born Urbana Illinois Nov 10, 1948. United Methodist. Educated at University of Illinois B.A. 1970 J.D. 1974. Admitted to practice Illinois 1974 and U.S. District Court Central District of Illinois 1975. In legal practice Paxton 1974-96. Commissioner, Illinois Court of Claims 1994-96.
President Ford County Bar Association 1991-97. Advisory Board Illinois Bar Foundation 1996-2001. Member Illinois Judges Association (Committee on Judicial Selection and Retention), Illinois Judicial Conference and Illinois State Bar Association (Chair Judicial Advisory Polls Committee 1993-94, Assembly Member 1994-2001, Secretary Judicial Evaluations Committee 1995-96, Board of Directors ISBA Mutual Insurance Company 1995-96, Member Special Committee on the Future of the Courts 2001-02, Chair Committee on Attorney Registration and Disciplinary Commission 2002-03). Speaker Continuing Legal Education Program Illinois State Bar Association 1996 and 1999. Recipient Honorable Mention Pro Bono Awards 1991 and Presidential Commendation 2000 from Illinois State Bar Association. Counselor and Instructor American Legion Boys State 1970-77. Board of Directors 1977-82 and Treasurer Community Resource & Counseling Center. President 1989 and Board of Directors 1985-94 Paxton Chamber of Commerce. Member Ford County Board 1990-96, Selective Service System Local Board 1990-2000 and Paxton Service Club (Secretary-Treasurer 1975-95). President 1993-94 and Board of Directors 1992-95 Paxton Day Care Center. Board of Directors 1994-96 and Treasurer PRIDE in Paxton. Host weekly legal issues program WPXN Radio 1991-97 and 1998-2001. Past Volunteer Legal Advisor Community Thrift Shop, Paxton Foundation, Paxton Day Care Center and Anabel Huling Early Learning Center in Rantoul. United Fund Volunteer. Park District Coach. Licensed Foster Parent. Red Cross Blood Donor.
Mailing address: P.O. Box 1, Paxton 60957.
Office: Ford County Courthouse, 200 West State Street, Paxton 60957.
Telephone: (217) 379-2814.
Fax: (217) 379-4400
E-mail address: circuit@paxton.net

PAINE, Theodore E. *(Circuit Judge, Illinois Circuit Court Sixth Judicial Circuit)* Former Associate Judge.
Office: 6B Macon County Courts Facility, 253 East Wood, Decatur 62523.
Telephone: (217) 424-1438.

PALLMEYER, Rebecca R. *(Judge, United States District Court Northern District of Illinois)* Magistrate Judge Oct 1, 1991 to 1998. Appointed Judge for life by President Bill Clinton Oct 26, 1998. Born Tokyo Japan Sept 13, 1954. Lutheran. Educated at Valparaiso University B.A. 1976 and University of Chicago J.D. 1979. Christ College Scholar. Recipient Joseph Henry Beale Award 1977. Law Clerk to Hon. Rosalie E. Wahl, Minnesota Supreme Court 1979-80. Member Alpha Lambda Delta, Phi Alpha Theta and Mortar Board. Admitted to practice Illinois 1980. In legal practice Chicago 1980-85. Administrative Law Judge, Illinois Human Rights Commission 1985-91.
Important Decisions: Zumbro, Inc. v. Merck & Co., Inc. 819 F. Supp. 1387 N.D. Ill. 1993; Mid America Title Co. v. Kirk 867 F. Supp.673 N.D. Ill. 1994 aff'd 59 F.3d 719, 7th Cir. cert. denied 516 U.S. 990, 1995; Pickett v. Prince 52 F. Supp.2d 893 N.D. Ill. 1999 aff'd 207 F.3d 402, 7th Cir. 2000; Milano v. United States 92 F. Supp.2d 269 N.D. Ill. 2000; DuPuy v. McDonald 141 F. Supp.2d 1090, 7th Cir. 2001; Vang v. Ashcroft 149 F. Supp.2d 1027 N.D. Ill. 2001; In re Mexico Money Transfer Litigation 164 F. Supp.2d 1002 N.D. Ill. 2000 aff'd 267 F.3d 743, 7th Cir. 2001; Fabri v. Pritikin-Fabri 221 F. Supp.2d 859, 7th Cir, 2001; and Nanda v. The Board of Trustees of the University of Illinois 2002 WL 1553330 N.D. Ill. aff'd 303 F.2d 817, 7th Cir. 2002. Instructor in Employment Discrimination Loyola Law School Spring 1989 and Spring 1991. Member Federal Magistrate Judges Association (Board of Directors 1994-97), National Association of Women Judges, Chicago (Secretary 1989-90 and Chair 1992-93 Development of the Law Committee, Co-chair Labor and Employment Committee 1989-91) and Federal (Board of Managers Chicago Chapter since 1995) Bar Associations. Speaks frequently on issues relating to employment law and civil practice. Member Judicial Resources Committee U.S. Judicial Conference 1994-2000. Recipient David C. Hilliard Award for outstanding committee service from Chicago Bar Association 1991, Alumni Achievement Award from Valparaiso University 2002 and Professional Achievement Award from Chicago-Kent College of Law 2002. Named Executive Magistrate Judge May 1996. Enjoys choral music, sewing and running.
Office: 2178 U.S. Courthouse, 219 South Dearborn Street, Chicago 60604.
Telephone: (312) 435-5636.

PALMER, Phillip G., Sr. *(Circuit Judge, Illinois Circuit Court First Judicial Circuit)* Former Associate Judge.
Office: Williamson County Courthouse, 200 Jefferson Street, Marion 62959.
Telephone: (618) 997-1301.

PALMER, Stuart E. *(Circuit Judge, Illinois Circuit Court of Cook County)*
Office: 2600 South California Avenue, Room 702, Chicago 60608.
Telephone: (773) 869-3167.

PANARESE, Donald D., Jr. *(Associate Judge, Illinois Circuit Court of Cook County)*
Office: 400 R. J. Daley Center, Chicago 60602.
Telephone: (312) 603-2600.

PANICHI, Thomas P. *(Circuit Judge, Illinois Circuit Court of Cook County)*
Office: 16501 South Kedzie Parkway, Markham 60426.
Telephone: (708) 210-4170.

PANICI, Luciano *(Associate Judge, Illinois Circuit Court of Cook County)*
Office: 400 R. J. Daley Center, Chicago 60602.
Telephone: (312) 603-2600.

PANTLE, Kathleen M. *(Circuit Judge, Illinois Circuit Court of Cook County)*
Office: 1100 South Hamilton Avenue, Chicago 60612.
Telephone: (312) 433-4757.

PATCHETT, Randy *(Judge, Illinois Court of Claims)* Appointed by Governor Jim Edgar.
Mailing address: P.O. Box 1176, Marion 62959.
Telephone: (618) 997-1984.

PATTI, Sebastian Thomas *(Circuit Judge, Illinois Circuit Court of Cook County)* Assumed office 1995. Born Feb 10, 1953. Educated at Duke University B.A. cum laude 1975 and University of Kansas School of Law J.D. 1978. Law Clerk to Hon. Herbert W. Walton, Kansas District Court District Ten 1977. Admitted to practice Illinois, Kansas, U.S. Courts of Appeals Sixth, Seventh, Eighth and Tenth Circuits and U.S. District Courts Central and Northern Districts of Illinois and District of Kansas.

Staff Attorney Environmental Law Institute 1979. Associate Regional Counsel U.S. Environmental Protection Agency 1979-95. Special Assistant U.S. Attorney Eastern District of Michigan 1994-95. Co-author with George C. Coggins "Resurrection and Expansion of the Migratory Bird Treaty Act" 50 University of Colorado L. Rev. 165 and "Emerging Law of Wildlife II: A Narrative Bibliography of Federal Wildlife Law" 4 Harvard Environmental L. Rev. 164. Commissioner Committee on Character and Fitness Supreme Court of Illinois since 1993. Recipient Bronze Medal for Toxics Litigation 1984 and 1988, Bronze Medal for Clean Water Act Litigation 1992 and Distinguished Service Award 1993 from U.S. Government. Vice-President S. Patti Construction Company 1974-78. Board of Directors Steppenwolf Theater Company since 1989. Board of Directors and pro bono Volunteer AIDS Legal Council of Chicago 1994-95. Pro bono Volunteer Cabrini Green Legal Aid Clinic 1994-95.
Office: 1111 R. J. Daley Center, Chicago 60602.
Telephone: (312) 603-4532.

PAUL, Alfred J. *(Associate Judge, Illinois Circuit Court of Cook County)*
Office: 1704 R. J. Daley Center, Chicago 60602.
Telephone: (312) 603-4821.

PAYNE, John E. *(Associate Judge, Illinois Circuit Court Fifteenth Judicial Circuit)* Appointed to term beginning Jan 2, 1985. Reappointed July 1, 1987, July 1, 1991, July 1, 1995 and 1999. Current term expires July 2003. Born Amboy Illinois Dec 4, 1948. Catholic. Educated at Loyola University B.A. with honors 1971 and Northwestern University J.D. 1974. Admitted to practice Illinois 1974.

State's Attorney Lee County 1976-80. Member Illinois Juvenile Judges Association, National Juvenile Judges Association and Lee County Bar Association.
Mailing address: P.O. Box 348, Dixon 61021.
Office: Lee County Courts Building, Dixon 61021.
Telephone: (815) 284-5264.

PEMBERTON, Stephen C. *(Chief Judge, Illinois Circuit Court Fifteenth Judicial Circuit)*
Mailing address: P.O. Box 455, Oregon 61061.
Office: Ogle County Courthouse, Oregon 61061.
Telephone: (815) 732-1161.

PENTUIC, Carol M. *(Associate Judge, Illinois Circuit Court Fourteenth Judicial Circuit)*
Office: Rock Island County Courthouse, 210 Fifteenth Street, Rock Island 61201.
Telephone: (309) 786-4451.

PERIVOLIDIS, Arthur C. *(Associate Judge, Illinois Circuit Court of Cook County)* Appointed to term beginning May 16, 1977. Reappointed to subsequent terms. Assigned to Probate Division since Sept 1978. Born Oak Park Illinois Nov 1, 1941. Educated at Lake Forest College B.A. 1964 and Northwestern University J.D. 1967. Member Phi Beta Kappa and Phi Eta Sigma. Admitted to practice Illinois 1967, U.S. District Court Northern District of Illinois 1967, U.S. Court of Appeals Seventh Circuit 1968 and U.S. Supreme Court 1974. In legal practice Chicago 1967-77.

Member Illinois Judges Association, Hellenic (Director and Officer since 1974), Northwest Suburban, Chicago (Chairman Judiciary and Bench-Bar Committee 1975-76, Young Lawyers Section Executive Committee 1975-77 and Director 1976-78) and Illinois State (Assembly 1980-86) Bar Associations. Recipient The David C. Hilliard Award for outstanding committee service that has benefited both the public and legal profession 1976, Certificates of Appreciation for improving Bench-Bar relations 1977 and 1978, Certificates of Appreciation from Chicago Bar Association Young Lawyers Section for service as Director 1976-78 and Certificates of Appreciation from Chicago Bar Association for service as Speaker since 1978. Member United Hellenic Voters of Illinois (Board of Legal Advisors 1976-77), Hellenic Professional Society of Illinois (Treasurer 1968-69, President 1969-70, Board member 1970-71), Order of AHEPA (Garfield Chapter 203), Masons, Scottish Rite, Shriners, Lawyers Shrine Club (President 1987), St. Nectarios Greek Orthodox Church (Board member 1975-76, Parish Board Secretary 1976, volunteer legal counsel, Chairman Land Acquisition Committee) and Sts. Peter and Paul Greek Orthodox Church.
Office: 1809 R. J. Daley Center, Chicago 60602.
Telephone: (312) 603-4463.

PERKINS, Thomas L. *(Judge, United States Bankruptcy Court Central District of Illinois)* Appointed by U.S. Court of Appeals Seventh Circuit judges to term beginning July 20, 2000. Term expires July 2014.
Office: 116 Federal Building, 100 N.E. Monroe Street, Peoria 61602.
Telephone: (309) 671-7075.

PETERS, Stephen H. *(Circuit Judge, Illinois Circuit Court Sixth Judicial Circuit)* Term expires Dec 2006.
Office: DeWitt County Courthouse, 201 West Washington, Clinton 61727.
Telephone: (217) 935-2584.

PETERSON, Lance R. *(Associate Judge, Illinois Circuit Court Thirteenth Judicial Circuit)*
Office: 111 East Washington, Morris 60450.
Telephone: (815) 941-3252.

PHELAN, William Michael *(Circuit Judge, Illinois Circuit Court of Cook County)*
Office: 10220 South 76th Avenue, Room 110, Bridgeview 60455.
Telephone: (708) 974-6542.

PHELPS FELTON, Donna *(Circuit Judge, Illinois Circuit Court of Cook County)*
Office: 2121 Euclid, Room 109, Rolling Meadows 60008.
Telephone: (847) 818-2094.

PHILLIPS, John T. *(Associate Judge, Illinois Circuit Court Nineteenth Judicial Circuit)*
Office: Lake County Courthouse, 18 North County Street, Waukegan 60085.
Telephone: (847) 377-4363.

PIERCE, Cary B. *(Associate Judge, Illinois Circuit Court Eighteenth Judicial Circuit)* Appointed July 19, 1991.
Office: 505 North County Farm Road, Wheaton 60187.
Telephone: (630) 682-6804.

PIETRUCHA, Edward N. *(Circuit Judge, Illinois Circuit Court of Cook County)*
Office: 1100 South Hamilton, Room G32S, Chicago 60612.
Telephone: (312) 433-4757.

PILEGGI, William G. *(Associate Judge, Illinois Circuit Court of Cook County)* Appointed.
Office: 1109 R. J. Daley Center, Chicago 60602.
Telephone: (312) 603-4533.

PIRRELLO, R. L. *(Circuit Judge, Illinois Circuit Court Seventeenth Judicial Circuit)* Term expires 2008.
Office: Winnebago County Courthouse, 400 West State Street, Rockford 61101.
Telephone: (815) 987-2520.

PLUNKETT, Paul E. *(Senior Judge, United States District Court Northern District of Illinois)* Appointed for life by President Ronald Reagan to term beginning Jan 17, 1983. Assumed Senior status, serves by assignment. Born Boston Massachusetts July 9, 1935. Educated at Harvard University B.S. 1957 LL.B. 1960. Admitted to practice Illinois 1960, U.S. District Court Northern District of Illinois 1961 and U.S. Court of Appeals Seventh Circuit 1963. In legal practice Chicago 1960-63 and 1966-83.
Assistant U.S. Attorney Northern District of Illinois 1963-66. Adjunct Professor of Trial Practice and Evidence John Marshall Law School 1976-80 and since 1984. Director Trial Practice Loyola Law School 1977-78. Member Legal Club of Chicago, American Inns of Court, Chicago (Civil Practice Committee since 1973) and Federal Bar Associations.
Office: U.S. Courthouse, 219 South Dearborn Street, Chicago 60604.
Telephone: (312) 435-5775.

POMARO, Nicholas T. *(Associate Judge, Illinois Circuit Court of Cook County)*
Office: 2121 Euclid, Room 106-A, Rolling Meadows 60008.
Telephone: (847) 818-2718.

PONCE DE LEON, Edmund *(Circuit Judge, Illinois Circuit Court of Cook County)*
Office: 1500 Maybrook Drive, Maywood 60153.
Telephone: (708) 865-6060.

POPE, M. Carol *(Circuit Judge, Illinois Circuit Court Eighth Judicial Circuit)*
Mailing address: P.O. Box 496, Petersburg 62675.
Telephone: (217) 632-2107.

POPE, Michael J. *(Associate Judge, Illinois Circuit Court of Cook County)*
Office: 2121 Euclid, Room 202-A, Rolling Meadows 60008.
Telephone: (847) 818-2279.

POPEJOY, Kenneth L. *(Associate Judge, Illinois Circuit Court Eighteenth Judicial Circuit)*
Office: 505 North County Farm Road, Wheaton 60187.
Telephone: (630) 682-7674.

PORCELLINO, Charles E. *(Associate Judge, Illinois Circuit Court of Cook County)*
Office: 2121 Euclid, Room 107-A, Rolling Meadows 60008.
Telephone: (847) 818-2094.

PORTER, Dennis J. *(Associate Judge, Illinois Circuit Court of Cook County)*
Office: 2600 South California Avenue, Room 604, Chicago 60608.
Telephone: (773) 869-3183.

POTKONJAK, Theodore S. *(Associate Judge, Illinois Circuit Court Nineteenth Judicial Circuit)*
Office: Lake County Courthouse, 18 North County Street, Waukegan 60085.
Telephone: (847) 377-3503.

PRALL, G. Michael *(Circuit Judge, Illinois Circuit Court Eleventh Judicial Circuit)* Former Associate Judge.
Office: McLean County Law and Justice Center, 104 West Front Street, Bloomington 61701.
Telephone: (309) 888-5284.

PRATHER, Sharon *(Circuit Judge, Illinois Circuit Court Nineteenth Judicial Circuit)* Former Associate Judge.
Office: McHenry County Courthouse, 2200 North Seminary, Woodstock 60098.
Telephone: (815) 338-2040.

PRESTON, Lee *(Circuit Judge, Illinois Circuit Court of Cook County)* Elected to term beginning Dec 5, 1994. Retained by election 2000, current term expires Dec 2006. Born Chicago Illinois Feb 6, 1944. Jewish. Educated at University of Illinois B.S. 1966, DePaul University College of Law J.D. 1972 and Spertus Institute of Jewish Studies 1976. Research Staff member DePaul Law Review 1971-72. Member Phi Alpha Delta. Admitted to practice Illinois 1972, U.S. District Court Northern District of Illinois 1972, U.S. Tax Court 1972 and Florida 1973.
Lecturer on Law and the Legislative Process Loyola University of Chicago 1987-92. Adjunct Professor of Law (Illinois Civil Procedure) Chicago-Kent College of Law since 1996. Member Decalogue Society of Lawyers, Jewish Judges Association of Illinois, Illinois Judges Association and Chicago Bar Association. U.S. Ar-

PRESTON, LEE—*Continued*

my 1968-70. Member Illinois House of Representatives (Chair Committee on Children and Family Law, Consumer Protection Committee and Civil Procedure Subcommittee Judiciary Committee) 1979-93.
Office: 2004 R. J. Daley Center, Chicago 60602.
Telephone: (312) 603-5918.
Fax: (312) 603-5199

PROCHASKA, J. Edward *(Associate Judge, Illinois Circuit Court Seventeenth Judicial Circuit)*
Office: Winnebago County Courthouse, 400 West State Street, Rockford 61101.
Telephone: (815) 544-3140.

PROUD, Clifford J. *(Magistrate Judge, United States District Court Southern District of Illinois)* Appointed by U.S. District Court judges.
Office: U.S. Courthouse, 750 Missouri Avenue, East St. Louis 62201-2954.
Telephone: (618) 482-9007.

PUMILIA, Gary *(Associate Judge, Illinois Circuit Court Seventeenth Judicial Circuit)*
Office: Winnebago County Courthouse, 400 West State Street, Rockford 61101.
Telephone: (815) 961-3239.

PURHAM, Albert L., Jr. *(Associate Judge, Illinois Circuit Court Tenth Judicial Circuit)*
Office: Peoria County Courthouse, 324 Main Street, Peoria 61602.
Telephone: (309) 672-6989.

QUINLAN, James S., Jr. *(Recalled Circuit Judge, Illinois Circuit Court of Cook County)* Former Associate Judge. Assumed office as Circuit Judge. Retired, serves by recall.
Office: 1904 R. J. Daley Center, Chicago 60602.
Telephone: (312) 603-5930.

QUINN, Patrick J. *(Judge, Illinois Appellate Court First Judicial District Division Five)* Elected 1996. Formerly served Division Six. Born Chicago Illinois Oct 1, 1953. Educated at University of Illinois at Chicago B.A. 1975 and John Marshall Law School J.D. 1980.
Assistant State's Attorney 1981-96, Supervisor Sixth Municipal District 1989-91 and Former Director Public Integrity Unit and Organized Crime Unit State's Attorney's Office Cook County.
Office: 160 North LaSalle Street, Room S1610, Chicago 60601.
Telephone: (312) 793-1391.

QUINN, Robert J. *(Circuit Judge, Illinois Circuit Court of Cook County)*
Office: 2804 R. J. Daley Center, Chicago 60602.
Telephone: (312) 603-3904.

QUINN, Thomas P. *(Circuit Judge, Illinois Circuit Court of Cook County)* Term expires 2004.
Office: 2410 R. J. Daley Center, Chicago 60602.
Telephone: (312) 603-6025.

RACCUGLIA, Cynthia M. *(Circuit Judge, Illinois Circuit Court Thirteenth Judicial Circuit)* Former Associate Judge.
Office: LaSalle County Courthouse, 119 West Madison, Ottawa 61350.
Telephone: (815) 434-6616.

RADCLIFFE, James M., III *(Associate Judge, Illinois Circuit Court Twentieth Judicial Circuit)*
Office: County Building, 10 Public Square, Belleville 62220.
Telephone: (618) 277-7325.

RADOSEVICH, John G. *(Associate Judge, Illinois Circuit Court Nineteenth Judicial Circuit)*
Office: Lake County Courthouse, 18 North County Street, Waukegan 60085.
Telephone: (847) 377-3786.

RARICK, Philip J. *(Justice, Supreme Court of Illinois)* Appointed by Supreme Court of Illinois Sept 5, 2002. Born Collinsville Illinois 1940. Catholic. Educated at Southern Illinois University B.S. 1962 and St. Louis University J.D. 1965. Admitted to practice Illinois 1965. Began legal practice Belleville 1965. In legal practice Collinsville 1966-75. Former Circuit Judge and Chief Judge, Illinois Circuit Court Third Judicial Circuit. Judge, Illinois Appellate Court Fifth Judicial District Dec 1988 to Sept 2002.
Assistant State's Attorney 1965-75. Township Attorney 1967-75 and City Attorney 1969-75 Collinsville. Jarvis Township Attorney 1972-75. Member Executive Committee and Study Committee on Complex Litigation Illinois Judicial Conference 1987-2001. Member Tri-City, Madison County and Illinois State Bar Associations.
Mailing address: P.O. Box 2050, Fairview Heights 62208.
Office: 333 Salem Place, Suite 170, Fairview Heights 62208.
Telephone: (618) 624-3242.
Fax: (618) 624-3254

RAUCCI, Andrew *(Chief Justice, Illinois Court of Claims)* Appointed by Governor George H. Ryan.
Mailing address: 3000 North Sheridan, Apartment 18D, Chicago 60657.

RAY, George H. *(Associate Judge, Illinois Circuit Court Seventh Judicial Circuit)*
Office: Sangamon County Complex, 200 South Ninth Street, Springfield 62701.
Telephone: (217) 753-6735.

REAGAN, Michael J. *(Judge, United States District Court Southern District of Illinois)* Appointed for life by President Bill Clinton to term beginning Oct 23, 2000. Born Albuquerque New Mexico March 27, 1954. Educated at Bradley University B.S. 1976 and St. Louis University J.D. 1980. In legal practice 1979-2000.
Assistant Public Defender St. Clair County 1996-2000.
Office: U.S. Courthouse, 750 Missouri Avenue, East St. Louis 62201.
Telephone: (618) 482-9225.

REID, Ellis E. *(Circuit Judge, Illinois Circuit Court of Cook County)* Appointed to term beginning Feb 25, 1985. Reappointed Dec 1, 1986. Elected Nov 8, 1988. Retained by election Nov 8, 1994 and Nov 7, 2000. Current term expires Dec 2006. Currently on assignment by Supreme Court of Illinois as Judge, Illinois Appellate Court First Judicial District Division Five since Nov 14, 2000. Born Chicago Illinois May 19, 1934. African Methodist Episcopal. Educated at University of Illinois B.A. 1956 and University of Chicago Law School J.D. 1959. Member Phi Delta Phi. Admitted to practice Illinois 1959, U.S. District Court Northern District of Illi-

REID, ELLIS E.—*Continued*

nois 1960, U.S. Court of Appeals Seventh Circuit 1960 and U.S. Supreme Court 1969. In legal practice Chicago 1959-85.

Hearing Examiner Illinois Fair Employment Practices Commission 1968-76. Special Assistant State's Attorney Cook County 1970-72. Member Illinois Supreme Court Rules Committee 1991-2001. Member Illinois Judicial Council (Chairman 1990-91), Illinois Judges Association (Board of Directors 1990-2001), Cook County (President 1970-72), Illinois State (Member of Assembly 1990-95) and National Bar Associations. Participant 1985-90, Faculty Member 1986-90 and Member Executive Committee 2002 Illinois Judicial Conference. Participant "Conducting the Civil Trial Course" 1987 and Faculty Member "Court Management for Judges and Court Administrators" 1994-95 The National Judicial College. Recipient Civil Rights Award from Cook County Bar Association 1970, Outstanding Alumnus Award from University of Chicago Law School B.A.L.S.A. Chapter 1977, First Congressional District of Illinois Award 1980, Leadership Award from Cook County Bar Association 1984, Civic Award from A.M.E. Ministerial Alliance 1985, Grand Polemarch's Certificate of Appreciation for Service as General Counsel of Kappa Alpha Psi 1985, Judicial Award from Cook County Bar Association 1985, Award of Honor for Outstanding Church, Civic and Community Services Rendered to Fallen Humanity from AMEC Ministerial Alliance of Chicago 1986, DMC-AMEC Distinguished Humanitarian Award for Outstanding Community Service 1986, Achievement Award for Contribution to Law from Chicago Alumni Chapter Kappa Alpha Psi 1988, Meritorious Service Award from Illinois Judicial Council 1988, Monarch Award for the category of Law Alpha Kappa Alpha's Salute to Black Men 1988, Kenneth E. Wilson Memorial Award 1991 and 1996, Lifetime Achievement Award from The Cultural Citizens Foundation for the Performing Arts 1999-2000, Push for Excellence Award 2000 and Stradford Award 2000. Captain USAR 1956-69. Member Chicago Alumni Chapter Kappa Alpha Psi, Bethel A.M.E. Church of Chicago (Trustee Board), Chicago Unicorns and Druids. Enjoys travel and writing.

Office: 160 North LaSalle Street, Room N1509, Chicago 60601.

Telephone: (312) 793-4403.

REINHARD, Philip G. *(Judge, United States District Court Northern District of Illinois)* Appointed for life by President George Bush Feb 12, 1992. Born La Salle Illinois Jan 12, 1941. Educated at University of Illinois B.A. 1962 J.D. 1964. Admitted to practice Illinois 1964. Circuit Judge, Illinois Circuit Court Seventeenth Judicial Circuit 1976-80. Justice and Presiding Justice, Illinois Appellate Court Second Judicial District 1980-91.

State's Attorney Winnebago County 1968-76. Commissioner Illinois Law Enforcement Commission 1977-83. President Illinois State's Attorneys Association 1973. Member Winnebago County Bar Association. Lecturer American Academy for Judicial Education since 1972.

Office: Federal Building, 211 South Court Street, Rockford 61101.

Telephone: (815) 987-4480.

RESCH, Tracy W. *(Circuit Judge, Illinois Circuit Court Fifth Judicial Circuit)* Elected to term beginning Dec 1990. Retained by election Nov 1996 and 2002. Current term expires Dec 2008. Born Paris Illinois Aug 10, 1949. Methodist. Educated at College of Wooster B.A. 1970 and University of Illinois J.D. 1973. Staff member and Legislative Review Editor University of Illinois Law Forum 1971-73. Law Clerk to U.S. District Court Southern District of Illinois 1973-74. Admitted to practice Illinois 1973 and U.S. District Court Southern District of Illinois 1973. In legal practice Effingham and Casey 1981-90.

Assistant Illinois Attorney General Criminal Justice Division 1974-76. State's Attorney Clark County 1976-81. Member Clark County and Illinois State Bar Associations.

Office: Clark County Courthouse, Marshall 62441.

Telephone: (217) 826-8713.

REYES, Jesse Gregory *(Associate Judge, Illinois Circuit Court of Cook County)* Elected to term beginning Dec 7, 1997. Serves First Municipal District and County Section Chancery Division. Born Chicago Illinois Oct 25, 1952. Catholic. Educated at University of Illinois B.A. 1979 and John Marshall Law School J.D. 1982. Member Gavel Society. Admitted to practice Illinois, U.S. District Court Northern District of Illinois and U.S. Supreme Court.

Senior Corporation Counsel Torts Division City of Chicago 1985-96. Attorney Chicago Public Schools 1996-97. Author *Premises Liability Law for Governmental Bodies* IICLE 1994 and 1999. Important Decision: People v. Xadrian McCraven (evidence based domestic violence trial) No. 1-99-2890, 2000. Member Hispanic Lawyers Association of Illinois, Catholic Lawyers Association of Illinois (Board Member), Illinois Judges Association (Third Vice President) Chicago (Former Secretary), Illinois State (Former Assembly Member), Puerto Rican and Hispanic National (Former Chair Judicial Convention) Bar Associations. Speaker "Judicial Ethics" 2000, "Persistent Drunk Driver: Sentencing Strategies" Seminar Series 2001-02 and "Managing Youthful and High Risk Offenders in DUI Cases" Seminar Series 2002-03 Illinois Judicial Conference; "Judicial Perspective" Domestic Violence Conference, Laredo Texas; and "Circuit Court Rules" Judicial Seminar Circuit Court of Cook County. Recipient Distinguished Service Award from John Marshall Law School 1990, Community Service Award from Latin American Police Association 1999, Achievement Award from Combined Law Enforcement Hispanic Heritage Committee 2000 and Person of the Year Award from Latin American Police Association 2002. Board Member Queen of Peace High School. Member John Marshall Law School Alumni Association (Past President, Board Member), Leukemia Society Teams in Training, American GI Forum and Leadership Greater Chicago Fellows. Enjoys running, bicycling and reading fiction and historical novels.

Office: 400 R. J. Daley Center, Chicago 60602.

Telephone: (312) 603-2600.

REYNA, Ralph *(Circuit Judge, Illinois Circuit Court of Cook County)* Former Associate Judge.

Office: 2600 South California Avenue, Room 504, Chicago 60608.

Telephone: (773) 869-3201.

REYNARD, Charles G. *(Circuit Judge, Illinois Circuit Court Eleventh Judicial Circuit)*
Office: McLean County Law and Justice Center, 104 West Front Street, Bloomington 61701.
Telephone: (309) 888-5215.

RHINE, Wayne D. *(Associate Judge, Illinois Circuit Court of Cook County)* Appointed to term beginning Jan 5, 1983. Reappointed July 1, 1983, July 1, 1987, July 1, 1991, July 1, 1995 and 1999. Current term expires 2003. Currently serves as Supervising Judge non-jury tort and contract cases. Born Chicago Illinois Dec 28, 1941. Jewish. Educated at University of Illinois at Chicago and DePaul University LL.B. 1965. Staff member DePaul Law Review 1963. Member Nu Beta Epsilon. Admitted to practice Illinois 1965 and U.S. District Courts Northern 1965 and Southern 1965 Districts of Illinois. In legal practice Chicago 1965-83.
Prosecutor Village of Calumet Park 1975-77. Author "Champerty & Maintenance" DePaul L. Rev. 1963. Important Decisions: Brentwood Nursing Center v. Visey (upheld the use of an additure) Sept 26, 1988 and People v. Delgado (first hearing under anti-stalking law upholding its constitutionality) July 26, 1992. Former Member Decalogue Society, The Advocates' Society, Illinois Judges Association and Northwest Suburban Bar Association. Lecturer Illinois Judicial Seminar. Attended The National Judicial College and other numerous conferences and seminars. Former Member and Officer 40th Ward Democratic Organization. Member Glenview Board of Zoning Appeal 1981-83 and Glenview Historical Society. Enjoys collecting stamps. Avid follower of Chicago Cubs.
Office: 1104 R. J. Daley Center, Chicago 60602.
Telephone: (312) 603-4546.

RHODES, James L. *(Circuit Judge, Illinois Circuit Court of Cook County)*
Office: 16501 South Kedzie Parkway, Markham 60426.
Telephone: (708) 210-4170.

RICE, Stephen R. *(Associate Judge, Illinois Circuit Court Twentieth Judicial Circuit)*
Office: County Building, 10 Public Square, Belleville 62220.
Telephone: (618) 277-7325.

RICHARDSON, Marzell L., Jr. *(Associate Judge, Illinois Circuit Court Twelfth Judicial Circuit)*
Office: Will County Courthouse, 14 West Jefferson Street, Joliet 60432.
Telephone: (815) 727-8540.

RIEBMAN, Hyman *(Associate Judge, Illinois Circuit Court of Cook County)*
Office: 400 R. J. Daley Center, Chicago 60602.
Telephone: (312) 603-2600.

RIGGS, Thomas J. *(Associate Judge, Illinois Circuit Court Eighteenth Judicial Circuit)*
Office: 2015 DuPage County Courthouse, 505 North County Farm Road, Wheaton 60187.
Telephone: (630) 682-7300.

RIGHTER, Teresa K. *(Associate Judge, Illinois Circuit Court Fifth Judicial Circuit)*
Office: Coles County Courthouse, Second Floor, 651 Jackson, Charleston 61920.
Telephone: (217) 348-0541.

RILEY, Barbara *(Circuit Judge, Illinois Circuit Court of Cook County)*
Office: 1901 R. J. Daley Center, Chicago 60602.
Telephone: (312) 603-3008.

RILEY, Daniel A. *(Circuit Judge, Illinois Circuit Court of Cook County)*
Office: 10220 South 76th Avenue, Bridgeview 60455.
Telephone: (708) 974-6288.

RILEY, James G. *(Circuit Judge, Illinois Circuit Court of Cook County)*
Office: 1808A R. J. Daley Center, Chicago 60602.
Telephone: (312) 603-4493.

RILEY, Ronald C. *(Circuit Judge, Illinois Circuit Court of Cook County)* Term expires Dec 2006.
Office: 16501 South Kedzie Parkway, Markham 60426.
Telephone: (708) 210-4170.

RIVERA, Elizabeth Loredo *(Associate Judge, Illinois Circuit Court of Cook County)*
Office: 1903 R. J. Daley Center, Chicago 60602.
Telephone: (312) 603-3009.

ROBB, Elizabeth A. *(Circuit Judge, Illinois Circuit Court Eleventh Judicial Circuit)* Former Associate Judge. Assumed office as Circuit Judge.
Office: McLean County Law and Justice Center, 104 West Front Street, Bloomington 61701.
Telephone: (309) 888-5254.

ROCHFORD, Mary K. *(Associate Judge, Illinois Circuit Court of Cook County)*
Office: 5600 Old Orchard Road, Skokie 60077.
Telephone: (847) 470-7200.

ROMANI, Charles, Jr. *(Circuit Judge, Illinois Circuit Court Third Judicial Circuit)* Appointed Associate Judge to term beginning Jan 1983. Assumed office as Circuit Judge. Term expires Dec 2006. Former Chief Judge. Born Litchfield Illinois July 23, 1947. Catholic. Educated at Western Illinois University B.A. 1969 and St. Louis University J.D. 1974. Member Theta Chi. Admitted to practice Illinois 1974. In legal practice Greenville 1976-83.
Assistant State's Attorney Madison County 1974-76. State's Attorney Bond County 1976-83. Former member National District Attorneys Association and American Bar Association. Member Illinois Judges Association and Illinois State Bar Association. Sergeant U.S. Army 1969-71.
Office: Madison County Courthouse, 155 North Main Street, Edwardsville 62025.
Telephone: (618) 692-6200.

ROSEBERRY, Michael R. *(Circuit Judge, Illinois Circuit Court Eighth Judicial Circuit)* Elected to term beginning Dec 1, 1990. Retained by election 1996 and 2002. Current term expires 2008. Born Rushville Illinois June 12, 1954. Methodist. Educated at Western Illinois University B.S. with honors 1976 and Washington University School of Law J.D. 1979. Admitted to practice Illinois 1979. In legal practice Pittsfield 1979-90.
State's Attorney Pike County 1980-84. Member Pike County and Illinois State Bar Associations. Republican. Enjoys golf and hunting.
Office: Pike County Courthouse, Pittsfield 62363.
Telephone: (217) 285-2025.

ROSSETTI, Victoria A. *(Circuit Judge, Illinois Circuit Court Nineteenth Judicial Circuit)* Former Associate Judge.
Office: Lake County Courthouse, 18 North County Street, Waukegan 60085.
Telephone: (847) 377-3708.

ROTI, Thomas D. *(Circuit Judge, Illinois Circuit Court of Cook County)* Elected to term beginning Dec 4, 2000. Term expires Dec 3, 2006. Born Evanston Illinois. Roman Catholic. Educated at Loyola University of Chicago B.S. 1967 J.D. cum laude 1970. Managing Editor Loyola University Law Journal 1969-70. Law Clerk to Hon. Frank J. McGarr, U.S. District Court Northern District of Illinois 1971-72. Admitted to practice Illinois 1970, U.S. District Court Northern District of Illinois 1971 and U.S. Court of Appeals Seventh Circuit 1972. In legal practice 1972-75.
Assistant General Counsel 1975-77 and Vice President and General Counsel 1977-95 Dominick's Finer Foods, Inc. Author "1969 Recent Decisions" Illinois B. Jour. 679-684, 1969. Member Justinian Law Society, Illinois Judges Association, Chicago, Illinois State and American Bar Associations. Presenter and Panel Member Food Safety 1986 and Handling Mass Torts and Saving the Business 1990 Food Marketing Institute. Round Table Participant *Corporate Legal Times* 1992. Attended New Judge Seminar 2000, Persistent Drunk Drivers Seminar 2001 and 2002 and Judicial Conference 2002. Major USAR 1967-83. Enjoys family, reading and American History.
Office: 409 R. J. Daley Center, Chicago 60602.
Telephone: (312) 603-2621.
E-mail address: tdroti@attbi.com

ROY, Maureen Durkin *(Circuit Judge, Illinois Circuit Court of Cook County)*
Office: 2105 R. J. Daley Center, Chicago 60602.
Telephone: (312) 603-4550.

ROZAK, Daniel J. *(Circuit Judge, Illinois Circuit Court Twelfth Judicial Circuit)* Appointed Associate Judge Feb 1995 to term beginning March 31, 1995. Reappointed July 1995 and 1999. Assumed office as Circuit Judge. Born Chicago Illinois Oct 24, 1951. Educated at Illinois State University B.S. 1973 and Loyola University School of Law J.D. 1976. Admitted to practice Illinois 1976, U.S. District Court Northern District of Illinois 1977, U.S. Court of Appeals Seventh Circuit 1978 and U.S. Supreme Court 1979. In legal practice Joliet and Braidwood 1980-95.
Assistant State's Attorney Will County 1976-80. Instructor in Business Law Joliet Junior College 1980-84. Member Illinois Judges Association, Will County and Illinois State Bar Associations. Member Will County Board 1980-82 and Will County Planning and Zoning Committee 1983-95. Member Braidwood Lions Club and Wilmington Moose Lodge. Interested in American Civil War.
Office: 444 Will County Courthouse, 14 West Jefferson Street, Joliet 60432.
Telephone: (815) 727-8540.

RUSSELL, Thomas G. *(Circuit Judge, Illinois Circuit Court Seventh Judicial Circuit)* Associate Judge 1983-90. Elected Circuit Judge to term beginning Dec 3, 1990. Retained by election 1996 and 2002. Current term expires 2008. Former Chief Judge. Born Fresno California Oct 26, 1948. Christian Scientist. Educated at Stanford University B.A. 1970 and University of the Pacific J.D. 1977. International Law Moot Court Honors Board. Law Intern to Chief Judge James Browning, U.S. Court of Appeals Ninth Circuit Winter 1977. Admitted to practice Illinois 1978, California 1978, District of Columbia 1981 and U.S. Supreme Court 1991. In legal practice Jerseyville Illinois Nov 1978 to Feb 1983.
Assistant State's Attorney Jersey County 1980-83. Author "Recent Developments in German and EEC Antimerger Law: A Comparative Study from an American Perspective" Comparative Law Yearbook Vol. 2 1978 Sijthoff and Noordhoff The Netherlands 1979. Co-chair Steering Committee Illinois Family Violence Coordinating Council since 2001. Former Member Coordinating Committee Associate Judges Seminar. Member Illinois Council of Juvenile and Family Court Judges (Former member Executive Committee), National Council of Juvenile and Family Court Judges, Illinois Judges Association and State Bar of California (inactive). Earned Graduate Diploma in Comparative Law from Center for International Legal Studies 1978. Board Member Great Rivers Land Trust since 2001 and District 100 Foundation since 2001. Member Jerseyville Rotary Club (President 1982-83).
Office: Jersey County Courthouse, 201 West Pearl Street, Jerseyville 62052.
Telephone: (618) 498-5571.

RYAN, H. Chris, Jr. *(Circuit Judge, Illinois Circuit Court Thirteenth Judicial Circuit)* Associate Judge 1989-92. Elected Circuit Judge to term beginning Dec 1992. Retained by election 1998, current term expires Dec 2004.
Office: Criminal Justice Center, 707 Etna Road, Ottawa 61350.
Telephone: (815) 434-8285.

RYAN, James J. *(Associate Judge, Illinois Circuit Court of Cook County)* Appointed to term beginning 1991. Reappointed 1995 and 1999. Current term expires 2003. Born Chicago Illinois March 1, 1951. Educated at Milton College B.A. 1973 and DePaul University College of Law J.D. 1976. Admitted to practice Illinois 1977.
Assistant Corporation Counsel Law Department City of Chicago 1977. Senior Attorney 1991. Member Chicago Bar Association.
Office: 10220 South 76th Avenue, Bridgeview 60455.
Telephone: (708) 974-6325.
Fax: (708) 974-6021

RYAN, James T. *(Circuit Judge, Illinois Circuit Court of Cook County)* Elected to term beginning 1996. Retained by election 2002, current term expires Dec 2008. Born Yonkers New York July 23, 1934. Roman Catholic. Educated at Lafayette College B.S. 1956, University of Wisconsin LL.B. 1959 and Marquette University M.B.A. Admitted to practice Wisconsin 1959, Illinois 1961 and U.S. Supreme Court 1963. In legal practice Illinois 1959-96.
Special State Attorney 1983-86. Member The Association of Trial Lawyers of America, State Bar of Wisconsin, Northwest Suburban, Chicago and Illinois State Bar Associations. Mayor Arlington Heights 1975-89. President Municipal League 1988.
Office: 2121 Euclid Avenue, Rolling Meadows 60008.
Telephone: (847) 818-2279.

SACKS, Stanley J. *(Associate Judge, Illinois Circuit Court of Cook County)*
Office: 2600 South California Street, Room 303, Chicago 60608.
Telephone: (773) 869-7449.

SAHLSTROM, R. Craig *(Associate Judge, Illinois Circuit Court Seventeenth Judicial Circuit)*
Office: 400 West State Street, Second Floor, Rockford 61101.
Telephone: (815) 987-3062.

ST. EVE, Amy J. *(Judge, United States District Court Northern District of Illinois)* Appointed for life by President George W. Bush to term beginning Aug 30, 2002.
Office: U.S. Courthouse, 219 South Dearborn Street, Chicago 60604.
Telephone: (312) 435-5686.

SALONE, Marcus R. *(Associate Judge, Illinois Circuit Court of Cook County)*
Office: 2600 South California Street, Room 308, Chicago 60608.
Telephone: (773) 869-7434.

SALYERS, Nancy S. *(Circuit Judge, Illinois Circuit Court of Cook County)*
Office: 5600 Old Orchard Road, Skokie 60077.
Telephone: (847) 470-7200.

SANTI, Emilio B. *(Associate Judge, Illinois Circuit Court Nineteenth Judicial Circuit)* Appointed to term beginning Jan 4, 1981. Reappointed to subsequent terms. Born Pescia Italy Nov 10, 1947. Roman Catholic. Educated at Marquette University B.A. 1969 and Ohio Northern University J.D. 1974. Member Alpha Phi Omega and Sigma Phi Epsilon. Admitted to practice Illinois 1974. Began legal practice Waukegan 1974.
Former Assistant State's Attorney. Member Illinois Trial Lawyers Association, Northwest Suburban, Lake County, Illinois State and American Bar Associations. E-5 U.S. Army 1969-71.
Office: Lake County Courthouse, 18 North County Street, Waukegan 60085.
Telephone: (847) 377-3718.

SANTIAGO, Leida Gonzalez *(Circuit Judge, Illinois Circuit Court of Cook County)*
Office: 1608 R. J. Daley Center, Chicago 60602.
Telephone: (312) 603-4832.

SAUER, David L. *(Circuit Judge, Illinois Circuit Court Fourth Judicial Circuit)* Former Associate Judge. Appointed Circuit Judge June 1986. Elected Nov 1988. Retained by election 1994 and 2000. Current term expires Dec 2006. Born Belleville Illinois July 4, 1952. Protestant. Educated at University of Illinois B.A. 1974 and Rutgers University-Camden J.D. 1977. Admitted to practice Illinois 1977.
Office: 55 Sherwood Drive, Centralia 62801.
Telephone: (618) 548-3864.

SAVAGE, Drella *(Circuit Judge, Illinois Circuit Court of Cook County)*
Office: 32 West Randolph, Room 1401R, Chicago 60602.
Telephone: (312) 609-3790.

SAWYER, Stephen G. *(Circuit Judge, Illinois Circuit Court Second Judicial Circuit)* Former Associate Judge. Elected Circuit Judge.
Office: Wabash County Courthouse, Mount Carmel 62863.
Telephone: (618) 262-8371.

SCHENKIER, Sidney I. *(Magistrate Judge, United States District Court Northern District of Illinois)* Appointed by U.S. District Court judges to term beginning Oct 30, 1998. Term expires 2006. Educated at Northwestern University B.S. with distinction 1976 J.D. magna cum laude 1979. Member Order of the Coif. Law Clerk to Hon. Marvin E. Aspen, U.S. District Court Northern District of Illinois Sept 1979 to Aug 1980. Admitted to practice Illinois 1979, U.S. District Court Northern District of Illinois 1979, U.S. Courts of Appeals Seventh 1981, Fifth 1982 and Ninth 1990 Circuits, Trial Bar of U.S. District Court Northern District of Illinois 1986 and U.S. Supreme Court 1990. In legal practice Chicago July 14, 1981 to Oct 29, 1998.
Author "Magistrate Judge Practice" *Federal Civil Practice* Illinois Institute for Continuing Legal Education 2000. Adjunct Professor Clinical Trial Advocacy Program Northwestern University School of Law since Sept 1986. Member Civil Justice Reform Act Advisory Group June 1995 to Oct 1997, Advisory Committee on Rules and Practice Feb 1996 to Oct 1998 and Rules Committee since 1999 U.S. District Court Northern District of Illinois. Member American Bar Association. Instructor Regional Program 1990, Program for Teaching NITA Instructors 1991, Expert Witness Program 1992, National Program 1993 and Midwest Deposition Program Spring 2001 National Institute for Trial Advocacy.
Office: 219 South Dearborn, Suite 1756, Chicago 60604.
Telephone: (312) 435-5609.
Fax: (312) 554-8677
E-mail address: sidney_schenkier@ilnd.uscourts.gov

SCHILLER, Stephen A. *(Circuit Judge, Illinois Circuit Court of Cook County)* Assumed office 1981. Term expires 2004. Born Chicago Illinois April 15, 1937. Educated at Roosevelt University B.S.C. in Finance and Economics 1958 and University of Chicago Law School J.D. 1961. National Defender Fellow University of Chicago 1965. In legal practice Chicago 1962-74 and 1980.
Assistant to Cook County Special Prosecutor 1960-61. Executive Director Chicago Crime Commission 1974-80. Author "More Light on a Low Visibility Function: The Need to Recognize and Structure Selective and Discriminatory Enforcement of Laws" Police L. Quar. published in three parts July 1972, October 1972 and January 1973, "The ABA Standards for Criminal Justice" 2 No. 2 Young Lawyer's Jour. 1, 1973, *ABA Standards for the Administration of Criminal Justice: Illinois' Compliance* Chicago Bar Association 1974, "Criminal Justice in America: A Critical Understanding" 3 No. 4 Journal of Criminal Justice Winter 1975, "Selective and Discriminatory Enforcement of Laws" Chapter 9 *Community Relations and the Administration of Justice* 1975, "Doing Justice—The Choice of Punishments" 67 No. 3 Journal of Criminal Law and Criminology Sept 1976, "Use of Force by Law Enforcement Officers" Police L. Quar. July 1978, "Illinois' New Sentencing Laws—The Effect on Sentencing in Cook County: Some Early Returns" 60 Chicago Bar Record 130 Nov-Dec 1978, "Justice Delayed: An Environmental Problem" 61 Chicago Bar Re-

SCHILLER, STEPHEN A.—*Continued*

cord 140 Nov-Dec 1979, "Illinois Sentencing Procedure" Chapter 2 *The Law of Sentencing* IICLE 1983 and "Changing Court, Changing System" Chapter 4 *Justice in Chicago* Loyola-Mellon Lecture Series 1984. Co-author with Peter Marikas "Criminal Courts and Local Legal Culture" 36 DePaul L. Rev. 327, 1987; and with Hon. Thomas Durkin *Grimes Criminal Law Outline* 1999 revised annually and with Penny J. White *Impact Decisions: Supreme Court of the United States* 2000-2001 Term and 2001-2002 Term The National Judicial College. Former Member Board of Editors Criminal Justice Review Georgia State University, Illinois State Bar Journal and Chicago Bar Record.

Associate Professor Department of Criminal Justice 1968-78, Director Administration of Criminal Justice Curriculum 1970-72 and Adjunct Professor Department of Criminal Justice since 1979 University of Illinois at Chicago. Adjunct Professor in Evidence Loyola University of Chicago School of Law since 1989. Former member Standing Committee on Police and Civil Disturbances Illinois Law Enforcement Commission 1972-74 and Illinois Governor's Committee on Competency to Stand Trial. Past Consultant to Cook County Sheriff Richard J. Elrod on the development of a Youth Services Division. Member State Task Force on Criminal Justice Information Systems 1975-78. Consultant on Education and Training Illinois Law Enforcement Commission and the Illinois State Board of Higher Education 1970-72. Advisory Board Evaluation Institute Westinghouse National Issues Center. Judge Miner Moot Court Competition Northwestern University Law School 1979-84 and Regional Trial Advocacy Competition conducted by American Bar Association and Illinois State Bar Association 1983-84. Current Decisions contributor to "Law Practice Alert" Newsletter of Professional Advancement Concepts Springfield Illinois 1984. Fellow Institute for Social and Policy Studies Yale University 1972. Member American Association of University Professors (Former member Executive Committee University of Illinois Chapter), Academy of Criminal Justice Sciences (Former Program Chairman 1972 National Meeting), Illinois Judges Association (Chairman program segment on problems in instructing juries in murder/voluntary manslaughter cases 1984), Illinois State's Attorneys Association (Legal Training Committee), Chicago (Former Chairman Association External Liaison Committee, Committee on Criminal Justice Standards, Subcommittee on Mental Health Legal-Medical Relations Committee and Committee on Prison Reform Young Lawyers Section; former Co-chairman Staff Services Project to study police board proceedings; former member Law Related Education Committee, Legal Education Committee, Candidate's Committee and Executive Committee Young Lawyers Section; Reporter Special Review Committee on Police Community Relations 1972; and Member Criminal Law Committee), Illinois State (Former Chairman Criminal Justice Section Council, former Editor Criminal Justice Section Newsletter, former Secretary Ad Hoc Committee on Amendment of the Bail Article of Illinois Constitution, former member Committee on Correctional Facilities and Committee on Constitutional Rights, member and Former Chairman Publications Committee) and American (Former Chairman Illinois/ABA Project on Standards for the Administration of Criminal Justice, Midwest Region Committee on Penal Reform Section of Young Lawyers and former member Committee to Improve Civil and Criminal Case Handling; member Rules of Criminal Procedure and Evidence Subcommittee Criminal Justice Committee and Committee on Crisis in the Jails National Conference of State Trial Judges) Bar Associations.

Co-chairman National Institute of Mental Health Conference on Community Mental Health Services Zion Illinois 1960. Reporter HEW/NCCJ/IACP-sponsored Regional Conferences on Delinquency Prevention and Juvenile Justice Atlanta, Boston, Chicago, Denver, Philadelphia and San Francisco 1971-72. Program Chairman Academy of Criminal Justice Sciences Annual Meeting Boston Massachusetts 1972. Faculty Illinois Judicial Conference on Criminal Law Seminars 1973, Program on Police Officer's Civil Rights Liability Institute for Criminal Justice Illinois Institute of Technology, Chicago-Kent College of Law 1977, Program on Self Defense and Justifiable Use of Force Institute for Criminal Justice Illinois Institute of Technology, Chicago-Kent College of Law 1979, Program on Arrest, Search and Seizure IICLE 1979, Seminar on the Law of Search and Seizure 1980 and Seminar on the Law of Homicide 1982 Institute of Criminal Justice John Marshall Law School, Program on the Law of Sentencing IICLE 1983, General Jurisdiction Program since 1983 and Program on the Law of Search and Seizure 1984 The National Judicial College and Program on Recent Decision of the U.S. Supreme Court sponsored by National Judicial College American Bar Association Annual Meeting 1984. Judge/Instructor Trial Advocacy Programs conducted by Illinois Institute of Technology, Chicago-Kent College of Law, Northwestern University and Loyola University Law Schools through IICLE 1979-84. Chairman Program on the Future of the Exclusionary Rule Illinois State Bar Association Annual Meeting 1981.

Presented papers on "A Social Science Approach to Teaching Law to Policemen" Illinois Conference on Community College Education 1968, "Moral Considerations in the Operation of a Police Investigative Unit" Major Cities Command Officers Training Conference for Commanders of Detective Units Zion Illinois 1968, "Riots and Rights: The Administration of Justice in Mass Civil Disturbances" Midwest Political Science Association Annual Meeting 1969, "In Re Gault and Contemporary Juvenile Justice" IACP Workshops for commanding officers of major city police departments University of Virginia, University of Georgia, Asilomar California and Warrenton Virginia 1970, "Public Confidence and the Criminal Justice System" Illinois Federation of Women's Clubs 1977, "Law and the Consumer Society" Chicago Board of Education Economics Forum 1977, "Organized Crime in the 1980s" National Conference on Organized Crime University of Southern California 1979 and "Criminal Justice: System or Non-System" (keynote address) Loyola University Symposium on Critical Issues in Criminal Justice 1980. Lecturer "Law in a New Land" series published by Law in American Society Project (project of Chicago Bar Association and Chicago Board of Education) as teaching materials in public schools 1966, Public Information Workshop Illinois Department of Law Enforcement 1980, "Current Issues in the Supreme Court of the United States in the 1980s" Symposium Saint Xavier College 1981 and "Professional Responsibility in the Practice of Criminal Law" Loyola University Law School 1981, 1983 and 1984. Panelist "Attorneys: Ethical Considerations in the Courtroom"

SCHILLER, STEPHEN A.—*Continued*

Citizens Look at Their Courts, Cook County Court Watching Program 1983 and "Fair Trial—Free Press" University of Illinois Champaign 1984. Participant studies on "Procedures for the Hospitalization and Discharge of the Mentally Ill" American Bar Foundation 1960-62 and "The Importance of Interrogation as an Investigative Tool" 1963-64. Participant Colloquium on "The Criminal Investigator: A Typology" Yale University 1972 and Conference on Prison Overcrowding in Illinois University of Illinois Champaign 1984. Listed in *Who's Who in American Law*. Past Chairman Chicago Alliance for Shaping a Safer City. Advisory Board Cook County Victim Witness Assistance Project, Inc. and Cook County Court Watching Project. Field Research Associate American Bar Foundation 1961-62. Community Advisory Board Junior League of Chicago. Board of Directors Constitutional Rights Foundation Chicago Project and John Howard Association. Medical Services Coordinator Chicago Operation Headstart 1968.

Office: 2402 R. J. Daley Center, Chicago 60602.

Telephone: (312) 603-5432.

SCHMETTERER, Jack B. *(Judge, United States Bankruptcy Court Northern District of Illinois)* Appointed by U.S. Court of Appeals Seventh Circuit judges to term beginning May 9, 1985. Reappointed Nov 6, 1999, current term expires 2013. Born Chicago Illinois April 11, 1931. Jewish. Educated at Yale University B.A. with honors 1952 LL.B. 1955 replaced by J.D. Member Phi Delta Phi. Admitted to practice Illinois 1955, U.S. District Courts Northern District of Illinois 1956 and District of Ohio 1973, U.S. Court of Appeals Seventh Circuit 1965, U.S. Tax Court 1981 and U.S. Claims Court 1982. In legal practice Chicago.

Assistant U.S. Attorney 1963-70 (Chief Civil Division 1966-68) and First Assistant U.S. Attorney 1968-70. First Assistant State's Attorney Cook County 1971-73. Author "Enforcement of Court Decrees" A.B.A. Jour. Aug 1958, "Role of United States Liens in Illinois Mortgage Foreclosures" Illinois State B. Jour. Feb 1966, "Suing Uncle Sam in Tort: Problems and Procedures for the Illinois Lawyer" Illinois State B. Jour. Aug 1967 and "Crisis in Cook County Criminal Justice System" VIII 2 Justinian L. Jour. July 1972. Co-author and Co-chairman "Program for Action" Chicago Bar Association Commission on Criminal Justice in Cook County June 1975. Former Visiting Professor of Evidence, Criminal Law and Procedure Criminal Justice Department University of Illinois. Instructor in Political Science Yale University 1954-55 and University of Georgia 1957-58. Member Decalogue Society, Law Club of Chicago, Legal Club of Chicago, Mackey-Wigmore Inn of Court, National Conference of Bankruptcy Judges, Federal (Former President Chicago chapter) and American Bar Associations. Recipient Citation from Leadership Council for Metropolitan Open Communities June 10, 1970. E-5 U.S. Army 1956-58. Northbrook Trustee North Shore Mass Transit District 1981-84. Board of Trustees Northbrook Village 1984-85. Former Board Member Cook County Court Watchers, Inc., Chicago Crime Commission and Better Government Association. Former Chair Northbrook Caucus and John Howard Association. Board Member and Vice President Just the Beginning Foundation. Enjoys cooking, government and gardening.

Office: U.S. Courthouse, 219 South Dearborn Street, Chicago 60604.

Telephone: (312) 435-5654.

SCHMIDT, Daniel L. *(Judge, Illinois Appellate Court Third Judicial District)*

Office: 401 S.W. Water Street, Suite 309, Peoria 61602.

Telephone: (309) 671-7659.

SCHMIDT, William O. *(Associate Judge, Illinois Circuit Court Twenty-first Judicial Circuit)*

Office: 450 East Court Street, Kankakee 60901.

Telephone: (815) 937-2993.

SCHOENSTEDT, Richard C. *(Circuit Judge, Illinois Circuit Court Twelfth Judicial Circuit)* Former Associate Judge.

Office: 14 West Jefferson Street, Joliet 60432.

Telephone: (815) 727-8540.

SCHOSTOK, Mary S. *(Circuit Judge, Illinois Circuit Court Nineteenth Judicial Circuit)* Former Associate Judge. Assumed office as Circuit Judge.

Office: Lake County Courthouse, 18 North County Street, Waukegan 60085.

Telephone: (847) 377-3846.

SCHREIER, James M. *(Associate Judge, Illinois Circuit Court of Cook County)* Appointed to term beginning May 15, 1977. Reappointed to subsequent terms. Born Chicago Illinois Sept 15, 1940. Roman Catholic. Educated at Georgetown University A.B. in Government 1962 and DePaul University J.D. 1965. Admitted to practice Illinois 1965 and U.S. District Court Northern District of Illinois 1965. Began legal practice Chicago 1965.

Assistant State's Attorney Criminal Division Cook County 1965-77. Author "Motions to Suppress and Quash" Illinois CLE 1979. Member Chicago Bar Association.

Office: 2600 South California Avenue, Chicago 60608.

Telephone: (773) 869-3170.

SCHUERING, Mark A. *(Circuit Judge, Illinois Circuit Court Eighth Judicial Circuit)* Associate Judge Sept 15, 1986 to Dec 3, 1990. Elected Circuit Judge to term beginning Dec 3, 1990. Retained by election to terms beginning Dec 2, 1996 and Dec 2, 2002. Current term expires 2008. Born Quincy Illinois Sept 7, 1953. Educated at Quincy University B.A. 1975 and St. Louis University J.D. cum laude 1978. Recipient Ralph Huck Scholarship for "Excellent Contributions to the Academic Community" from Quincy University 1975. Member Alpha Sigma Nu. Admitted to practice Illinois 1978, Missouri 1982 (inactive) and U.S. District Court Central District of Illinois 1981. In legal practice Quincy Illinois 1978-86.

Part-time Public Defender Adams County 1980-84. Author *Illinois Sentencing Manual* Illinois State Bar Association 1999. Adjunct Professor "The American Judicial Process" and "Violence and Victimization" since 1989 and Volunteer Coach Mock Trial Team Quincy University. Member Illinois Judges Association (Board of Directors, Member Illinois Judicial Ethics Committee), American Judges Association, American Judicature Society, Adams County (Co-chair People's Law School

SCHUERING, MARK A.—*Continued*

Committee, Chair Technology Committee) and Illinois State (Member and Former Chair Committee on Corrections and Sentencing) Bar Associations. Attended "Alcohol, Drugs and the Courts" Nov 1987, "Effective Sentencing and Probation Management" Oct 1993, "Dispute Resolution Skills" Oct 1996 and "Conducting the Trial" Nov 1998 and Discussion Leader "Traffic Court Proceedings" Nov 1988 The National Judicial College. Faculty Member Regional Seminars on Sentencing since 1997, Illinois New Judges' Seminar and Illinois DUI Judicial Training Programs. Presenter and Moderator People's Law School 1991, 1993 and 1998. Inducted into Quincy University Sports Hall of Fame (Tennis) 1985. Member Adams County Family Violence Council. Active with substance abuse prevention and literacy efforts.

Office: Adams County Courthouse, 521 Vermont Street, Quincy 62301.

Telephone: (217) 277-2050.

Fax: (217) 277-2072

E-mail address: mschuering@co.adams.il.us

SCHUWERK, William A., Jr. *(Associate Judge, Illinois Circuit Court Twentieth Judicial Circuit)* Appointed to term beginning Jan 6, 1989. Reappointed July 1, 1991, July 1, 1995 and 1999. Current term expires 2003. Born St. Louis Missouri Jan 28, 1948. Educated at University of Illinois A.B. 1970 and St. Louis University Law School J.D. 1973. Admitted to practice Illinois 1973 and U.S. District Court Southern District of Illinois 1975. In legal practice Chester 1973-76 and 1984-89.

State's Attorney Randolph County 1976-84. Member Illinois Judges Association and Illinois State Bar Association.

Office: Randolph County Courthouse, Chester 62233.

Telephone: (618) 826-5000.

SCHWARM, S. Gene *(Chief Judge, Illinois Circuit Court Fourth Judicial Circuit)*

Office: Fayette County Courthouse, 221 South Seventh Street, Vandalia 62471.

Telephone: (618) 283-5010.

SCHWARTZ, Dennis L. *(Recalled Circuit Judge, Illinois Circuit Court Seventh Judicial Circuit)* Appointed Associate Judge to term beginning April 1, 1973. Assumed office as Circuit Judge. Retired, serves by recall. Born St. Louis Missouri April 30, 1940. Presbyterian. Educated at University of Illinois, Milliken University B.S. 1962 and Washington University J.D. 1965. Admitted to practice Illinois 1966. Began legal practice Carlinville 1966.

Member Macoupin County Bar Association. Illinois National Guard 1965-71. Democrat. Enjoys golf and bowling.

Office: 200 South Ninth Street, Room 516, Springfield 62701.

Telephone: (217) 753-6733.

SCHWARTZ, John D. *(Recalled Judge, United States Bankruptcy Court Northern District of Illinois)* Appointed by U.S. Court of Appeals Seventh Circuit judges to term beginning Nov 2, 1984. Former Chief Judge. Appointed Recalled Judge by the Judicial Council of the Seventh Circuit. Born Chicago Illinois May 24, 1925. Educated at University of Chicago B.Phil. 1947 J.D. 1950. Assistant Business Manager University of Chicago Law Review. Admitted to practice Illinois 1951 and U.S. District Court Northern District of Illinois 1951. In legal practice Chicago 1951-84. Master-in-Chancery, Illinois Circuit Court of Cook County 1963.

Assistant U.S. Attorney Northern District of Illinois 1952-54. Author "Property of the Estate" IICLE 1985. Member Law Club of Chicago, Legal Club of Chicago (Secretary 1978-80, President 1988-89), Great Plains Bankruptcy Conference (Board of Directors), National Conference of Bankruptcy Judges, Decalogue Society of Lawyers, Chicago, Federal and American Bar Associations. Lecturer Seminar for Bankruptcy Practitioners IICLE 1986 and 1987. Flight Officer USAAC 1943-45. Board of Directors Foundation for Hearing and Speech Rehabilitation. Enjoys biking, skiing and travel.

Office: U.S. Courthouse, 219 South Dearborn Street, Chicago 60604.

Telephone: (312) 435-5652.

SCHWARTZ, William G. *(Circuit Judge, Illinois Circuit Court First Judicial Circuit)* Associate Judge 1986-90. Appointed Circuit Judge Oct 1, 1990. Elected 1992. Retained by election 1998, current term expires 2004. Born Oak Park Illinois Nov 14, 1949. Catholic. Educated at Southern Illinois University B.A. 1973 J.D. 1976. Admitted to practice Illinois 1976 and U.S. District Courts Eastern 1976 and Central 1983 Districts of Illinois. In legal practice Carbondale 1976-86.

State's Attorney Jackson County 1979-80. Author "Pre-hearing Dispositions" Juvenile Law IICLE 1976-89. Important Decisions: People v. Hamilton (constitutionality of Judicial Driving Permit in Illinois and hearing procedures) Illinois Supreme Court 1987. Instructor Southern Illinois University at Carbondale 1982-86. Member Jackson County and Illinois State (Chair Juvenile Law Committee) Bar Associations. Attended "Liability Crisis in County Government" National Association of Civil County Attorneys 1979, Trial Advocacy Seminar State's Attorneys Appellate Service Commission 1980 and "Processing DUI Cases in High Volume Courts" The National Judicial College 1987. Specialist Fifth Class U.S. Army 1968-71. Democratic Precinct Committeeman 1971-76. Member Murphysboro School Board 1984-86.

Mailing address: P.O. Box 388, Murphysboro 62966.

Telephone: (618) 687-7334.

SCOTILLO, John J. *(Associate Judge, Illinois Circuit Court of Cook County)*

Office: 2121 Euclid, Rolling Meadows 60008.

Telephone: (847) 818-2535.

SCOTT, Jeanne E. *(Judge, United States District Court Central District of Illinois)* Appointed for life by President Bill Clinton to term beginning Nov 30, 1998. Born Springfield Illinois Aug 17, 1948. Educated at Bradley University B.A. magna cum laude 1970 and Northwestern University School of Law J.D. 1973. Admitted to practice Illinois 1973 and U.S. District Court Central District of Illinois 1975. In legal practice Springfield 1978-79. Associate Judge March 26, 1979 to Dec 1988, Circuit Judge Dec 5, 1988 to Nov 1998, Presiding Judge Sangamon County 1990 to Dec 1994 and Chief Judge Dec 1992 to Dec 1994, Illinois Circuit Court Seventh Judicial Circuit.

Assistant State's Attorney Sangamon County 1973-78. Author "Women on the Illinois State Court Bench" Illi-

SCOTT, JEANNE E.—*Continued*

nois B. Jour. May 1986 and "Judge's Forum" J.D.C. Quarterly Fourth Quarter 1995.

Office: 319 Federal Building, 600 East Monroe Street, Springfield 62701.
Telephone: (217) 492-4000.

SEXTON, Elizabeth Walter *(Associate Judge, Illinois Circuit Court Eighteenth Judicial Circuit)* Appointed July 1996 to term beginning Aug 9, 1996. Reappointed June 1999, current term expires June 2004. Born Akron Ohio Dec 21, 1954. Episcopalian. Educated at Wittenberg University B.A. 1977 and Illinois Institute of Technology, Chicago-Kent College of Law J.D. with high honors 1984. Admitted to practice Illinois 1984 and U.S. District Court Northern District of Illinois. In legal practice Wheaton 1984-96.

Member DuPage Association of Women Lawyers, Illinois Judges Association, DuPage County (Board of Directors, Chair Children's Advocacy Committee) and Illinois State (Council Member Activities and Bar Membership Section) Bar Associations.

Office: 505 North County Farm Road, Wheaton 60187.
Telephone: (630) 682-7300.

SEYMOUR, Steven P. *(Circuit Judge, Illinois Circuit Court Fourth Judicial Circuit)* Term expires 2008.

Mailing address: P.O. Box 832, Effingham 62401-0832.
Telephone: (217) 342-4065.

SHADID, James E. *(Circuit Judge, Illinois Circuit Court Tenth Judicial Circuit)*

Office: 215 Peoria County Courthouse, 324 Main Street, Peoria 61602-1363.
Telephone: (309) 672-6047.

SHADUR, Milton I. *(Senior Judge, United States District Court Northern District of Illinois)* Appointed for life by President Jimmy Carter to term beginning June 24, 1980. Assumed Senior status June 25, 1992, serves by assignment. Born St. Paul Minnesota June 25, 1924. Educated at University of Chicago B.S. 1943 J.D. 1949. In legal practice 1949-80.

Member Judicial Conference Advisory Committee on Rules of Evidence since 1993.

Office: 2388 U.S. Courthouse, 219 South Dearborn Street, Chicago 60604.
Telephone: (312) 435-5766.

SHARKEY, Terrence V. *(Associate Judge, Illinois Circuit Court of Cook County)*

Office: 1100 South Hamilton Avenue, Room G026, Chicago 60612.
Telephone: (312) 433-4757.

SHEEHAN, Colleen F. *(Circuit Judge, Illinois Circuit Court of Cook County)*

Office: 1340 South Michigan Avenue, Chicago 60605.
Telephone: (312) 341-2871.

SHEEHAN, Kevin M. *(Circuit Judge, Illinois Circuit Court of Cook County)*

Office: 2600 South California, Chicago 60608.
Telephone: (773) 869-3373.

SHEEHAN, Nancy Drew *(Circuit Judge, Illinois Circuit Court of Cook County)*

Office: 1115 R. J. Daley Center, Chicago 60602.
Telephone: (312) 603-3523.

SHEEN, Terence M. *(Associate Judge, Illinois Circuit Court Eighteenth Judicial Circuit)*

Office: 505 North County Farm Road, Wheaton 60187.
Telephone: (630) 682-7300.

SHELDON, Timothy Q. *(Circuit Judge, Illinois Circuit Court Sixteenth Judicial Circuit)* Appointed Associate Judge to term beginning Dec 1, 1986. Reappointed 1987 and 1991. Assumed office as Circuit Judge. Born Chicago Illinois Dec 8, 1946. Episcopalian. Educated at Indiana University 1965-67, Wisconsin State University B.B.A. 1969 and John Marshall Law School J.D. 1975. Moot Court. Admitted to practice Illinois 1975 and U.S. District Court Northern District of Illinois 1975. In legal practice Elgin 1975-86.

Author "Character Testimony in Criminal Trials" Kane County Bar Briefs 1986. Member Illinois Trial Lawyers Association, Chicago, Kane County, Illinois State and American Bar Associations.

Office: Kane County Courthouse, 100 South Third Street, Geneva 60134.
Telephone: (630) 232-3441.

SHICK, Mitchell K. *(Circuit Judge, Illinois Circuit Court Fifth Judicial Circuit)*

Office: Coles County Courthouse, Second Floor, 651 Jackson Avenue, Charleston 61920.
Telephone: (217) 348-0538.

SHIELDS, Karen G. *(Associate Judge, Illinois Circuit Court of Cook County)* Appointed to term beginning Dec 2, 1997. Born Tampa Florida Sept 24, 1952. Educated at University of Illinois at Chicago B.A. in Political Science 1977 and DePaul University College of Law J.D. 1980. Admitted to practice Illinois 1980 and California 1990. In legal practice Chicago 1980-82, 1991-95 and Dec 1996 to Nov 1997. Associate Judge, Illinois Circuit Court of Cook County March 1995 to Dec 1996.

Assistant Public Defender Cook County 1982-91. Instructor in Trial Advocacy 2000-03. Member Chicago Council of Lawyers, Women's, Chicago and Illinois State Bar Associations. Enjoys travel and hiking.

Office: 2805 R. J. Daley Center, Chicago 60602.
Telephone: (312) 603-3897.

SHIFFMAN, Stuart H. *(Associate Judge, Illinois Circuit Court Seventh Judicial Circuit)* Appointed to term beginning July 1, 1983. Reappointed July 1, 1987, July 1, 1991, July 1, 1995 and 1999. Current term expires 2003. Born Chicago Illinois March 4, 1948. Jewish. Educated at Northwestern University B.A. 1970 and DePaul University J.D. 1974. Admitted to practice Illinois 1974. Began legal practice Springfield 1974.

Former Assistant State's Attorney Sangamon County and Assistant Attorney General Illinois. Author "More Pieces of the Puzzle" 75, 278, 1992, "Tale of Two Harlans" 76, 319, 1993, "Holmes, the Legal Scholar" 78, 54, 1994, "A Champion of Civil Liberties" 79, 94, 1995, "The Man and the Judge" 81, 214, 1998, "A Remarkable Man" 82, 293, 1999; "An Enduring Legacy" 84, 44, 2000; and "A Disturbing Portrait" 85, 45, 2001 *Judicature*; Review "David J. Brewer: The Life of a Supreme Court Justice" 39 *American Journal of Legal His-*

SHIFFMAN, STUART H.—*Continued*
tory 274, 1995; and "Judicial Biographies: A Sampling" 39 No. 3, 38, 2000, "The Constitution and the New Deal" 40 No. 2, 45, 2001 and "Law Without Values" 40 No. 3, 45, 2001 *Judges Journal.* Member Scribes Book Award Committee 1992-2002. Adjunct Professor University of Illinois at Springfield. Chairman Standing Committee on Gavel Awards American Bar Association 1989-90.
Office: 524 Sangamon County Complex, 200 South Ninth, Springfield 62701.
Telephone: (217) 753-6736.

SHONKWILER, John P. *(Chief Judge, Illinois Circuit Court Sixth Judicial Circuit)* Magistrate 1965-71. Associate Judge 1971-72. Appointed Circuit Judge 1972. Elected Nov 1974. Retained by election 1980, 1986, 1992 and 1998. Current term expires 2004. Chief Judge since Jan 1, 1994. Born Decatur Illinois April 5, 1933. Presbyterian. Educated at University of Illinois B.A. 1955 and Northwestern University J.D. 1962. Admitted to practice Illinois 1962. Began legal practice Monticello 1962.
Instructor State Coordinating Committee 1970-77. Member Governor's DUI Task Force 1984. President Associate Judges of Illinois 1970-71. Director since 1978 and President 1983 Illinois Judges Association. Captain USNR Intelligence since 1955. Republican.
Office: 306 Piatt County Courthouse, Monticello 61856.
Telephone: (217) 762-5861.

SHORE, Brian Dean *(Associate Judge, Illinois Circuit Court Seventeenth Judicial Circuit)*
Office: Winnebago County Courthouse, 400 West State Street, Rockford 61101.
Telephone: (815) 987-3062.

SHORE, Scott A. *(Circuit Judge, Illinois Circuit Court Tenth Judicial Circuit)* Elected to term beginning Dec 3, 1990. Retained by election 1996 and 2002. Current term expires 2008. Born Rockford Illinois Dec 23, 1952. Educated at University of Illinois B.A. 1974 and Southern Illinois University J.D. 1977. Admitted to practice Illinois 1977. In legal practice Hennepin 1977-90.
Member Illinois Judges Association and Illinois State Bar Association.
Office: 215 Peoria County Courthouse, 324 Main Street, Peoria 61602-1363.
Telephone: (309) 672-6047.

SHULTZ, Lon W. *(Circuit Judge, Illinois Circuit Court of Cook County)*
Office: 2600 South California, Room 306, Chicago 60608.
Telephone: (773) 869-7440.

SIEBEL, Richard A. *(Circuit Judge, Illinois Circuit Court of Cook County)* Elected to term beginning Dec 1998. Term expires Dec 2004. Born Chicago Illinois Feb 8, 1939. Educated at Brown University A.B. 1961 and Northwestern University School of Law J.D. 1964. Admitted to practice Illinois 1964, U.S. District Court Northern District of Illinois 1964 and U.S. Court of Appeals Seventh Circuit 1980. In legal practice Chicago 1968-98.
Member Illinois Judges Association, Chicago and Illinois State Bar Associations. USN JAG 1964-67.
Office: 2305 R. J. Daley Center, Chicago 60602.
Telephone: (312) 603-6034.

SIEGEL, Richard J. *(Circuit Judge, Illinois Circuit Court Twelfth Judicial Circuit)*
Office: Will County Courthouse, 14 West Jefferson, Joliet 60432.
Telephone: (815) 727-8540.

SIMKO, Darryl B. *(Recalled Circuit Judge, Illinois Circuit Court of Cook County)* Assumed office 2001. Retired, serves by recall. Educated at University of Notre Dame B.B.A. cum laude 1982 and Loyola University of Chicago School of Law J.D. 1985. Law Student Editor Chicago Bar Record. Law Clerk to Hon. Anthony John Scotillo, Illinois Circuit Court of Cook County 1985-87. Admitted to practice Illinois, U.S. District Courts Central and Northern Districts of Illinois and U.S. Courts of Appeals Sixth and Seventh Circuits.
Law Clerk to Hon. John M. O'Connor, Jr. and Hon. Francis Stanley Lorenz, Illinois Appellate Court First Judicial District 1988-92. Law Clerk to Hon. Charles E. Freeman, Illinois Supreme Court 1992-96. Senior Assistant Attorney General Office of the Attorney General Illinois 1996-2001. Co-author "Restrictive Covenants Not to Compete" *Chancery and Special Remedies Volume* IICLE supplement 1989 and "Principles of Appellate Review: A Lack of Consensus in Illinois Reviewing Courts" 3 No. 2 Appellate L. Rev. 1990. Author "Of Public Pensions, State Constitutional Contract Protection, and Fiscal Constraint" 69 No. 3 Temple L. Rev. 1996 and "Updating the Standard of Review for Petitions to Vacate Final Judgments" 86 No. 1 Illinois B. Jour. 1998. Adjunct Professor of Legal Writing since 1988 and Lecturer on Business Law 1991-99 Loyola University of Chicago. Member Judicial Performance Evaluation Committee 1999-2002 and Character and Fitness Committee 2000-01 Supreme Court of Illinois. Attended Chancery Practice Seminar IICLE 1987 and Fundamentals of Appellate Practice Seminar Bench/Bar Relations Committee Chicago Bar Association 1994.
Office: 400 R. J. Daley Center, Chicago 60602.
Telephone: (312) 603-2600.

SIMMONS, Henry R., Jr. *(Circuit Judge, Illinois Circuit Court of Cook County)*
Office: 2600 South California Avenue, Chicago 60608.
Telephone: (773) 869-3166.

SIMMONS, Michele M. *(Associate Judge, Illinois Circuit Court of Cook County)*
Office: 1100 South Hamilton Avenue, Chicago 60612.
Telephone: (312) 433-4756.

SIMPSON, Mary Karen *(Associate Judge, Illinois Circuit Court Sixteenth Judicial Circuit)* Appointed.
Office: 37W777 Route 38, Room 400A, St. Charles 60175.
Telephone: (630) 232-3442.

SINGER, Henry M. *(Circuit Judge, Illinois Circuit Court of Cook County)*
Office: 1303 R. J. Daley Center, Chicago 60602.
Telephone: (312) 603-7959.

SKOWRONSKI, Joseph P., Jr. *(Associate Judge, Illinois Circuit Court Fifth Judicial Circuit)* Appointed to

SKOWRONSKI, JOSEPH P., JR.—*Continued*

term beginning July 6, 1984. Reappointed July 1, 1987, July 1, 1991, July 1, 1995 and 1999. Current term expires 2003. Born Moline Illinois June 27, 1944. Roman Catholic. Educated at University of Illinois B.A. with honors 1966 J.D. 1969. Law Clerk to Hon. Henry S. Wise, U.S. District Court Eastern District of Illinois 1970-71. Admitted to practice Illinois 1969, U.S. District Court Eastern District of Illinois 1969 and U.S. Court of Appeals Seventh Circuit 1972. In legal practice Danville 1971-84.

VISTA Attorney Legal Aid Society Danville 1969-70. Part-time Assistant Public Defender Felony Division Vermilion County 1972-74. Special Defender for Juveniles and Mental Health Cases 1972-82 and for Juveniles 1982-84. Member Illinois Judges Association, Vermilion County, Illinois State and American Bar Associations. Participated in United Fund campaigns 1971-83. Member Danville District 118 School Board 1976-78, Vermilion County Council on Alcohol and Drug Abuse (now known as Pioneer Center) Board 1978-84, Center for Children's Services Board 1978-84, Danville Traffic Commission 1978-84 and various school district committees 1978-84. Active parent and speaker in local schools. Interested in genealogy.

Office: Vermilion County Courthouse, 7 North Vermilion, Danville 61832.

Telephone: (217) 431-2565.

SLATER, David W. *(Associate Judge, Illinois Circuit Court Fourth Judicial Circuit)* Appointed to term beginning Jan 1, 1985. Reappointed 1987, 1991, 1995 and 1999. Current term expires 2003. Born Pana Illinois April 10, 1951. Methodist. Educated at University of Illinois B.S. 1973 and John Marshall Law School J.D. with high honors 1976. Admitted to practice Illinois 1976.

Member Christian County, Illinois State and American Bar Associations. Member First United Methodist Church.

Office: Christian County Courthouse, Taylorville 62568.

Telephone: (217) 824-4810.

SLATER, Kent F. *(Judge, Illinois Appellate Court Third Judicial District)* Elected to term beginning Dec 3, 1990. Retained by election 2000, current term expires Dec 2010. Former Presiding Judge. Born Hampton Iowa Nov 25, 1945. Educated at University of Illinois B.S. 1968 and John Marshall Law School J.D. with honors 1975. Staff member John Marshall Law Review 1973-75. Admitted to practice Illinois 1975. In legal practice Macomb 1975-88. Circuit Judge, Illinois Circuit Court Ninth Judicial Circuit 1988-90.

Member McDonough County and Illinois State Bar Associations. First Lieutenant U.S. Army 1969-71. Member House of Representatives Illinois 1984-88.

Office: 219 North Randolph Street, Macomb 61455.

Telephone: (309) 833-1704.

SLATTERY BOYLE, Maura *(Circuit Judge, Illinois Circuit Court of Cook County)*

Office: 400 R. J. Daley Center, Chicago 60602.

Telephone: (312) 603-2600.

SLAVIN, Timothy J. *(Circuit Judge, Illinois Circuit Court Fourteenth Judicial Circuit)* Appointed Associate Judge to term beginning April 1, 1981. Reappointed 1983, 1987 and 1991. Elected Circuit Judge to term beginning Dec 7, 1992. Retained by election 1998, current term expires Dec 2004. Born Morrison Illinois April 18, 1951. Roman Catholic. Educated at University of Notre Dame B.A. cum laude 1973 and Boston College J.D. 1976. Admitted to practice Illinois 1976 and U.S. District Court Northern District of Illinois 1976. Began legal practice Morrison 1976.

Assistant State's Attorney 1976-79 and State's Attorney 1979-81 Whiteside County. Instructor in Family Law Blackhawk Community College. Former Member Governor's Commission for the Circuit Clerks, Illinois Judges Association (President 1999, Co-chair Judicial Discipline Committee), Whiteside County and Illinois State Bar Associations. Member 1988 and Vice Chair 1989 Judicial Ethics Committee Illinois Judicial Conference. Past President Morrison Jaycees. Former Chairman United Way Campaign. Past President Board of Directors Morrison Country Club. President and Board of Directors Self Help Enterprises (workshop for the disabled).

Office: Whiteside County Courthouse, Morrison 61270.

Telephone: (815) 772-5179.

SLOCUM, David K. *(Circuit Judge, Illinois Circuit Court Eighth Judicial Circuit)* Appointed March 1, 1975. Elected Nov 1, 1976. Retained by election 1982, 1988, 1994 and 2000. Current term expires Dec 2006. Former Chief Judge. Born Quincy Illinois Aug 6, 1941. Roman Catholic. Educated at Quincy College B.A. 1963 and University of Illinois J.D. 1971. Admitted to practice Illinois 1971. Began legal practice Quincy 1971.

Member Illinois Judges Association, Adams County, Brown County, Illinois State and American Bar Associations. Attended General Summer session The National Judicial College, Reno Nevada. Captain USAF 1963-68. Director Schuyler-Brown Historical Society and Saukee Area Council Boy Scouts. Member Optimist Club of Mount Sterling. Enjoys antiques and target shooting.

Mailing address: P.O. Box 142, Mount Sterling 62353.

Office: Brown County Courthouse, Mount Sterling 62353.

Telephone: (217) 773-2311.

SMIERCIAK, Robert M. *(Associate Judge, Illinois Circuit Court of Cook County)*

Office: 10220 South 76th Avenue, Bridgeview 60455.

Telephone: (708) 974-6899.

SMITH, James G. Fitzgerald *(Judge, Illinois Appellate Court First Judicial District Division One)* Born Chicago Illinois. Catholic. Educated at Marquette University A.B. 1966 B.S. 1966 and John Marshall Law School J.D. 1975. Admitted to practice Illinois 1975, U.S. District Court Northern District of Illinois 1975 and U.S. Court of Appeals for the Armed Forces 1995. Former Associate Judge and Circuit Judge, Illinois Circuit Court of Cook County, appointed to term beginning Aug 1989.

City Attorney Des Plaines 1979-89. Member Chicago, Northwest Suburban and Illinois State Bar Associations. Colonel USAR since 1968. President Glenbrook Fire District 1987-89.

Office: 160 North LaSalle Street, Room S1710, Chicago 60601.

Telephone: (312) 793-5404.

SMITH, Terence B. *(Associate Judge, Illinois Circuit Court of Cook County)*
Office: 400 R. J. Daley Center, Chicago 60602.
Telephone: (312) 603-2600.

SMOKER, Thomas R. *(Associate Judge, Illinois Circuit Court Nineteenth Judicial Circuit)*
Office: 18 North County Street, Waukegan 60085.
Telephone: (847) 377-3752.

SOLGANICK, Irwin J. *(Circuit Judge, Illinois Circuit Court of Cook County)* Term expires 2004.
Office: 2605 R. J. Daley Center, Chicago 60602.
Telephone: (312) 603-6551.

SONDERBY, Susan Pierson *(Judge, United States Bankruptcy Court Northern District of Illinois)* Appointed by U.S. Court of Appeals Seventh Circuit judges to term beginning Oct 1, 1986. Reappointed Dec 14, 1999, current term expires Oct 2014. Chief Judge July 20, 1998 to July 20, 2002. First Female Bankruptcy Judge. Born Chicago Illinois May 15, 1947. Presbyterian. Educated at Joliet Junior College 1967, University of Illinois B.A. 1969 and John Marshall Law School J.D. 1973. Dean's List Joliet Junior College 1967. James Scholar 1969. Certified under Illinois Supreme Court Rule 711 to practice as senior law student managing Illinois Attorney General's Consumer Fraud Branch Office. Member Alpha Delta Phi and Alpha Phi. Admitted to practice Illinois 1973, U.S. District Courts Northern 1973, Central 1978 and Southern 1978 Districts and U.S. Court of Appeals Seventh Circuit 1984. In legal practice Joliet 1972-78.

Assistant Attorney General Consumer Protection Division Litigation Section Office of the Attorney General June 1977 to April 1978. Assistant Attorney General and Chief Consumer Protection Division Office of the Illinois Attorney General May 1978 to Feb 1983. U.S. Trustee Northern District of Illinois March 1, 1983 to Sept 30, 1986. Author Chapter "The United States Trustee—Officers and Administrators" 1983 and Chapter "The United States Trustee and Case Administration" 1985 and supplement 1987 *Illinois Institute of Continuing Legal Education Bankruptcy Practice* IICLE; "Bankruptcy Court Reorganization Under the Bankruptcy Amendments and Federal Judgeship Act of 1984" 73 No. 1 The Credit World 10, 1984; "Bankruptcy Courts: Jurisdiction, Referral, Venue, Removal, Remand, Abstention and Appeals" 466, 7, 1988 and "United States Trustee System" 446, 757, 1988 *Current Developments in Bankruptcy and Reorganization 1988* PLI/Comm; "Trustees, Interim Trustees, United States Trustee: Powers and Duties" *Current Developments in Bankruptcy and Reorganization 1989* 490 PLI/Comm 7, 1989; "Discharge and Dischargeability" *Dealing with the Reorganizing Debtor 1990: Transactions, Negotiations and Litigation* 546 PLI/Comm 155, 1990; "Amendments to the Bankruptcy Rules and to the Official Forms" *Current Developments in Bankruptcy and Reorganization 1991* 572 PLI/Comm 69, 1991; and "Understanding Business Bankruptcy: How to Handle Everyday Problems" 576 PLI/Comm 75, 1991. Co-author with Lisa Ramsden "The Plan Process" *Representing the Trade Creditor and Landlord in Chapter 11 Cases* 632 PLI/Comm 621, 1992, with Dennise L. McCann "Amendments to the Bankruptcy Rules and to the Official Forms" *Current Developments in Bankruptcy and Reorganization 1992* 617 PLI/Comm 87, 1992 and with Kathleen M. McGuire "A Gray Area in Law? Recent Developments Relating to Conflicts of Interest and the Retention of Attorneys in Bankruptcy Cases" Commercial Law Journal Fall 2000.

Important Decisions: In re Convent Guardian Corporation (disposition of motion for abstention or remand) 87 B 2166, 1987; Federal Deposit Insurance Corporation v. Donald F. and Wanda L. Boebel (denying motion for summary judgment on complaint to determine dischargeability) 79 B.R. 381 Bankr. 1987; Wieboldt Stores, Inc. (approving settlement of the District Court leveraged buy-out action with Household Financial Corporation) 86 B 14850, 1987; Harris Trust & Savings Bank v. Wayne J. Klein Corporation (motion for summary judgment and validity of security interest) 83 B.R. 968 Bankr. 1988; Leroy G. Inskeep v. Simone et al. (order compelling discovery) 84 A 1246, 1988; Wieboldt Stores, Inc. (approving settlement of the District Court leveraged buy-out action with General Electric Capital Corporation) 86 B 14850, 1988; In re George and Kornelia Balhmalmi (the retroactive employment of professionals is not favored) 84 Bankr. 123, 1988; Richard Fogel v. Daniel Litza, MMS Terminals, Inc. and Affiliated Insurance Consultants, Inc. (opinion and order denying summary judgment on complaint to recover preferential payments) 87 A 1110, 1989; In re Michael G. Coan (opinion and order granting motion for turnover of funds) 86 B 7678, 1989; In re Convent Guardian Corp. (seminal case discussing fee applications and the payment of fees and reimbursement of expenses) 103 Bankr. 937, 1989; In re Tandem Enterprises, Ltd. (removal actions and "related to" jurisdiction) 124 Bankr. 283, 1991; In re Adventist Living Centers, Inc. (standards for compensation of accounts as professionals) 137 Bankr. 692, 1991; In re Adventist Living Centers, Inc. (fee application format and breakdown of compensable services, including conferencing) 127 Bankr. 701, 1991; In re Madison Management Group, Inc. (appointment of limited trustee and employment of professional manager) 137 Bankr. 275, 1992; In re Global Precious Commodities, Inc. and Global Commodities 143 B.R. 204 March 11, 1992; In re Ace Pecan Company, Inc. (personal jurisdiction over foreign defendants) 143 B.R. 696, 1992; In re Salem Mills, Inc. (third-party action related to underlying bankruptcy case by virtue of indemnity claims) 1992; In re Johnson (untimely or tardily filed claims not allowed in Chapter 13 context) 156 B.R. 557, 1993; In re FBN Food Services, Inc. (trustee may avoid transfers made by debtor to pay valid debts of corporate affiliate) 175 B.R. 671, 1994; In re Ransom (without first obtaining determination that tax debts were nondischargeable, IRS could not show cause to dismiss based on its contention that, because plan confirmation could not discharge individual debtor from nondischargeable debts, debtor could not bind IRS to his plan) 191 B.R. 720, 1995; In re Madison Management Group, Inc. (although Chapter 7 trustee who brought adversary proceeding against debtor's former parent corporations was entitled to disclosure of documents prepared for parent corporations while parent-subsidiary relationship was in place, attorney-client privilege remained as to third parties) 212 B.R. 894, 1997; In re Moran (disallowing reimbursement of litigation expenses where special counsel's contingent fee agreement did not provide for payment of expenses) 231 B.R. 290, 1998; In re Lake States Commodities, Inc. (determination of payout from estate to investor-creditors who had brought independent lawsuit against futures commodity merchant through which debtors con-

SONDERBY, SUSAN PIERSON—*Continued*
ducted business) 230 B.R. 602, 1999; In re Lake States Commodities, Inc. (denying summary judgment because genuine issues of material fact existed regarding alleged Ponzi scheme investor's "good faith" defense and whether investor gave reasonably equivalent value for subject transfers) 253 B.R. 866, 2000; In re Pincombe (holding that creditor refusing to withdraw discrimination charge in connection with administrative proceeding did not violate automatic stay) 256 B.R. 774, 2000; In re DeMert & Dougherty, Inc. (determining proceedings fell within court's "related to" jurisdiction) 271 B.R. 821, 2001; In re Dec (failure to include purported purchase option on bankruptcy schedules constituted affirmative action of concealment and supported equitable tolling of statute of limitations) 272 B.R. 218, 2001; In re Midway Indus. Contractors, Inc. (failure to disclose adverse interest and lack of disinterestedness warranted reduction in attorneys compensation) 272 B.R. 651, 2001; In re Anicom, Inc. (failure to establish excusable neglect warranted denial of retroactive employment of crisis manager) 273 B.R. 756, 2002; and In re Kmart Corp. (adopting breakpoint approach to determine whether percentage rent owing commercial landlord arose post petition for purposes of section 365(d)(3) of Code) 286 B.R. 345, 2002.

Lecturer "The United States Trustee and the Bankruptcy Code" Northern Illinois University College of Law Sept 12, 1983 and Sept 17, 1984 and Illinois Institute of Technology, Chicago-Kent College of Law March 29, 1984; "Developments Regarding the Bankruptcy Code" John Marshall Law School May 24, 1984; and "The Office of the United States Trustee" Illinois Institute of Technology, Chicago-Kent College of Law April 11, 1985. Adjunct Faculty DePaul University College of Law Jan 1986. Member Race and Gender Bias Task Force, Mediation Task Force and Biological Threat Special Task Force, former member Building Security Committee and former Chairperson Personnel Review Board U.S. District Court Northern District of Illinois. Former Member U.S. Trustee Advisory Committee, Civil Justice Reform Act Advisory Committee, Budget and Finance Council Administrative Office of the U.S. Courts, Commercial Law League of America (Executive Council Bankruptcy and Insolvency Section, Bankruptcy Committee, Vice Chairman Education Committee U.S. Trustee Review Committee, Coordination with National Conference of Bankruptcy Judges Committee), Chicago (Local Bankruptcy Rules Subcommittee Bankruptcy and Reorganization Committee), Sangamon County, Will County and American Bar Associations. Advisory Group Administrative Office U.S. Bankruptcy Judges. Fellow American College of Bankruptcy (Circuit Admissions Committee). Honorary Member Lawyers Club of Chicago and Chicago Chapter Federal Bar Association (Board Member). Member Planning Committee Judicial Conference of the Seventh Circuit, Judicial Local Bankruptcy Rules Committee, Nordic Law Club, Abraham Lincoln Marovitz Inn of Court (Former Master and Past President), The Association of Trial Lawyers of America, National Conference of Bankruptcy Judges (Legislative Outreach Committee, Liaison with Bankruptcy Review Commission Committee, National Bankruptcy Review Commission, Commercial Law League Liaison Committee, Chairperson Bankruptcy Judges Liaison Committee with U.S. Trustee's Office), American Bankruptcy Institute and Seventh Circuit Bar Association (Judicial Conference Planning Committee 2000, Former Treasurer). Law Faculty Federal Judicial Training Center, Practising Law Institute, U.S. Department of Justice, National Bankruptcy Institute and Illinois Continuing Education. Cited in over eighty biographical publications including *50th Edition of Who's Who in America, Who's Who in American Law, International Who's Who of Intellectuals, The World's Who's Who of Women, Who's Who in American Politics* and *2000 Notable Americans* and featured in "Illinois Issues" Jan 1981, *The Chicago Daily Law Bulletin* March 1, 1995 and *The Chicago Tribune* Jan 28, 1996. Named Joliet Business and Professional Women's Young Career Woman 1974 and one of six accomplished alumni John Marshall Law School during 90th Anniversary Year.

Keynote Speaker Joliet West High School National Honor Society Awards Banquet 1978, Business and Professional Women's District Conference 1982 and Commencement Speaker Joliet Junior College 1982. Recipient Leadership Award from International Organization of Women Executives 1980, Special Achievement Award Aug 1984 and Executive Office of U.S. Trustees Director's Award 1986 from Department of Justice, Distinguished Alumni Achievement Award from Joliet Junior College 1987, Distinguished Alumna Award from John Marshall Law School 1988 and Award for Distinguished Service to the Bench from American Bankruptcy Institute 1990. Honored by U.S. District Court, Women's Bar Association of Illinois and Chicago Bar Association Alliance of Women for being the First Female Bankruptcy Judge March 2000. Nominated "Outstanding Woman of 21st Century" by American Biographical Institute, Inc. Republican. Named Young Republican of the Year 1973 and Young Republican of Will County. Former Illinois State Republican Chairwoman 17th Congressional District. Board of Directors Land of Lincoln Girl Scout Council 1980-83 and John Marshall Law School Alumni Association. Board of Advisors and Executive Committee International Organization of Women Executives 1981. Chairman Clubs and Organizations Sangamon County United Way Capital Campaign 1982. Secretary State Fraudulent ID Committee 1982-83. Member Westminster Presbyterian Church 1978-83, Zonta Club of Springfield Area 1978-83 (President 1982), Aid to Retarded Citizens Capital Campaign 1981, Consumer Advisory Council to Federal Reserve Board 1981-84 (Chairman 1983), Henson Robinson Zoo Capital Campaign 1982, Family Service Center Capital Campaign 1982, Department of Insurance Task Force on Improper Claims Practices 1982, Secret Warranties Subcommittee Consumer Protection Committee National Association of Attorneys General 1982-83, Individual Guarantors Committee Goodman Theatre 1983-85 and Chicago Council on Foreign Relations 1984. Member Fourth Presbyterian Church since 1983, The Art Institute of Chicago since 1983, John Marshall Law School Alumni Association (Board of Directors since 1983, Second Vice President 1985, First Vice President 1986, Co-chairman 90th Anniversary Gala Celebration, ABA Review Accreditation Committee, Chairman Luncheon Lecture Series 1985-86, Chairman Distinguished Service Awards Committee 1986, Executive Committee Long-range Planning Committee since 1987), Zonta Club of the Chicago Waterfront since 1984 (Charter member), Union League Club of Chicago (Judicial Privileges) and Chicago Architec-

SONDERBY, SUSAN PIERSON—*Continued*

ture Foundation. Pilot. Enjoys travel, handwork and entertaining.

Office: U.S. Courthouse, 219 South Dearborn Street, Chicago 60604.

Telephone: (312) 435-5646.

SOTOS, George J. *(Associate Judge, Illinois Circuit Court Eighteenth Judicial Circuit)*

Office: 505 North County Farm Road, Wheaton 60187.

Telephone: (630) 682-7300.

SOUK, James E. *(Circuit Judge, Illinois Circuit Court Eleventh Judicial Circuit)* Associate Judge 1997-2002. Elected Circuit Judge Nov 2002. Term expires 2008. Born Beckley West Virginia July 5, 1945. Christian. Educated at West Virginia University A.B. with high honors 1966 and University of Illinois J.D. with honors 1974. Staff member University of Illinois Law Review 1972-73. Law Clerk to Hon. Robert C. Underwood, Illinois Supreme Court 1974-75. Member Phi Beta Kappa and Order of the Coif. Admitted to practice Illinois 1974 and U.S. District Courts Central 1976 and Northern 1976 Districts of Illinois. In legal practice Chicago 1975-76 and Urbana 1979-91.

Assistant State's Attorney Champaign County 1976-79. Chief Felony Prosecutor McLean County State's Attorney's Office 1991-97. Member Robert C. Underwood Inns of Court, Illinois Judges Association and McLean County Bar Association. Captain USAF 1967-71.

Office: 104 West Front Street, Room 4-A, Bloomington 61701.

Telephone: (309) 888-5252.

SOUTH, Leslie E. *(Judge, Illinois Appellate Court First Judicial District Division Three)* Elected Nov 1996. Educated at Loyola University of Chicago B.A. with honors 1976 and Northwestern University School of Law J.D. 1978. Associate Judge 1988-92 and Circuit Judge 1992-96, Illinois Circuit Court of Cook County.

Assistant Prosecutor Cook County 1978-82. Staff Attorney Chicago Transit Authority 1984-88. Former Chairperson Illinois Judicial Council. Member Illinois Judges Association, Women's Bar Association of Illinois, South Suburban and Cook County Bar Associations.

Office: 160 North LaSalle Street, Room N1607, Chicago 60601.

Telephone: (312) 793-5450.

SPEARS, Ronald D. *(Circuit Judge, Illinois Circuit Court Fourth Judicial Circuit)* Appointed to term beginning Aug 1, 1993. Elected Nov 1994. Retained by election 2000, current term expires 2006. Born July 30, 1951. Educated at Southern Illinois University J.D. summa cum laude 1977. Editor-in-Chief Southern Illinois University Law Journal. Law Clerk to Hon. J. Waldo Ackerman, U.S. District Court Central District of Illinois 1977-79. Admitted to practice Illinois, U.S. District Court Central District of Illinois, U.S. Court of Appeals Seventh Circuit and U.S. Supreme Court. In legal practice Taylorville 1979-93.

City Attorney Taylorville 1985-89 and 1993. Fellow Illinois State Bar Foundation and American Bar Foundation. Member Lincoln-Douglas Inn American Inns of Court, Illinois Judges Association (Board of Directors), Christian County (Past President), Illinois State (Chair Military Affairs Committee) and American Bar Associations. Colonel Illinois Army National Guard. Member Bethel Baptist Church (Moderator, Sunday School Teacher), Taylorville Optimist Club (Past President, District Lieutenant Governor), United Way of Taylorville and Vicinity (Board of Directors), Christian County YMCA (Board of Directors) and Southern Illinois University School of Law Alumni Association (Past President). Interests include public speaking, reading, bicycling and jogging.

Office: Christian County Courthouse, Taylorville 62568.

Telephone: (217) 824-4810.

SPENCE, Robert B. *(Circuit Judge, Illinois Circuit Court Sixteenth Judicial Circuit)*

Office: 400A Kane County Judicial Center, 37W777 Route 38, St. Charles 60175.

Telephone: (630) 232-3442.

SPERONI, John A. *(Associate Judge, Illinois Circuit Court First Judicial Circuit)*

Office: Williamson County Courthouse, 200 West Jefferson, Marion 62959.

Telephone: (618) 997-1301.

SPIRES, Randolph R. *(Associate Judge, Illinois Circuit Court Eleventh Judicial Circuit)*

Office: 112 West Madison Street, Pontiac 61764.

Telephone: (815) 844-5172.

SPOMER, Stephen L. *(Circuit Judge, Illinois Circuit Court First Judicial Circuit)* Elected to term beginning Aug 1978. Retained by election 1984, 1990, 1996 and 2002. Current term expires 2008. Former Chief Judge. Born Urbana Illinois April 14, 1949. Lutheran. Educated at Tulane University B.A. 1971 J.D. 1974. Member Pi Kappa Alpha. Admitted to practice Illinois 1974. Began legal practice Cairo 1974. In legal practice Metropolis 1976.

Public Defender 1975-76. State's Attorney Massac County 1976-78. Instructor in Business, Constitutional Law and Criminal Law Shawnee College 1976-77 and Ethics and Criminal Law Southern Illinois University 1989 and 1990. Member Illinois Judges Association and Illinois State Bar Association. President Cairo Rotary Club 1985-86. Enjoys tennis.

Office: Alexander County Courthouse, Cairo 62914.

Telephone: (618) 734-0509.

SPRENGELMEYER, Victor V. *(Associate Judge, Illinois Circuit Court Fifteenth Judicial Circuit)* Appointed to term beginning Oct 11, 1991. Reappointed 1995 and 1999. Current term expires 2003. Born Dubuque Iowa Dec 25, 1942. Roman Catholic. Educated at Loras College and University of Iowa LL.B. 1966. Author Iowa Law Review 1965-66. Admitted to practice Iowa 1966, Illinois 1967, Wisconsin 1980, U.S. District Courts Northern District of Illinois and Northern and Southern Districts of Iowa and U.S. Courts of Appeals Seventh and Eighth Circuits. In legal practice Dubuque Iowa 1966-91 and East Dubuque Illinois 1967-91.

Public Defender 1970-73 and State's Attorney 1973-76 Jo Daviess County.

Office: Jo Daviess County Courthouse, 330 North Bench Street, Galena 61036.

Telephone: (815) 777-0037.

SQUIRES, John H. *(Judge, United States Bankruptcy Court Northern District of Illinois)* Trustee 1984-87. Ap-

SQUIRES, JOHN H.—*Continued*

pointed Judge by U.S. Court of Appeals Seventh Circuit judges to term beginning Jan 1, 1988. Reappointed 2001, current term expires Dec 31, 2015. Born Urbana Illinois Oct 21, 1946. Roman Catholic. Educated at University of Illinois A.B. with honors 1968 J.D. 1971. Notes and Comments Editor University of Illinois Law Forum 1969-71. Admitted to practice Illinois 1971, U.S. District Court Southern District of Illinois 1972 and U.S. Tax Court 1978. In legal practice Springfield 1971-88.

Author Comment "Admissibility of Personal Checking Records" 1970 University of Illinois Law Form 288, 1970, "The Evolution of Bankruptcy in the Northern District of Illinois" 10 DePaul Business L. Jour. 29, 1997, "Fifteen Common Practice Errors and How to Avoid Them" 10 No. 9 *DCBA Brief* The Journal of the DuPage County Bar Association June 1998 and "A Brief Survey of Lien Stripping and Modification in Chapter 13 Plans" 12 No. *DCBA Brief* The Journal of the DuPage County Bar Association Feb 2000. Member American Bankruptcy Institute, The Lawyers Club, National Conference of Bankruptcy Judges and Federal Bar Association. Lecturer American Bankruptcy Institute, IICLE, Chicago Bar Association, DuPage County Bar Association, Sangamon County Bar Association, Winnebago County Bar Association, Commercial Law League of America and Illinois Credit Union League. USAF 1969. Member American Business Club and Union League Chicago Club.

Office: 676 U.S. Courthouse, 219 South Dearborn Street, Chicago 60604.
Telephone: (312) 435-7580.

STACK, Daniel J. *(Circuit Judge, Illinois Circuit Court Third Judicial Circuit)* Associate Judge 1986 to Jan 2003. Appointed Circuit Judge Jan 6, 2003. Term expires Dec 6, 2004. Born Granite City Illinois Nov 12, 1950. Roman Catholic. Educated at Benedictine College B.A. 1972 and St. Louis University J.D. 1976. Admitted to practice Illinois 1977 and U.S. District Court Eastern District of Illinois 1977. In legal practice Collinsville 1977-78 and Highland 1978-86.

Special Assistant Attorney General Consumer Fraud Division 1978-81 and Land Acquisition Division 1981-86. Member Illinois Trial Lawyers Association, American Trial Lawyers Association, Illinois Judges Association and Illinois State Bar Association. Chairman Evidence Section Illinois Judicial Conference 1991. Named Distinguished and Outstanding Lieutenant Governor and Distinguished Club President Optimist International. Specialist 5 USAR 1972-81. Vice Chairman College Young Democrats 1970-71. Chair Fundraising National Collegiate Committee Senator Henry M. Jackson for President and Republican Nominee for House of Representatives Twenty-first Congressional District 1978. Member Knights of Columbus, Masons Lodge #583 and American Legion. Life Member Optimist International. Enjoys fishing, boating, golf, snow and water skiing, ice skating and hunting.

Office: Madison County Courthouse, 155 North Main Street, Edwardsville 62025.
Telephone: (618) 692-7040.
Fax: (618) 692-7475
E-mail address: djstack@co.mad.il.us

STACK, James F. *(Associate Judge, Illinois Circuit Court of Cook County)*
Office: 10220 South 76th Avenue, Bridgeview 60455.
Telephone: (708) 974-6899.

STAMP, Zack *(Judge, Illinois Court of Claims)* Appointed by governor.
Office: 601 West Monroe Street, Springfield 62704.
Telephone: (217) 525-0700.

STARCK, Christopher C. *(Circuit Judge, Illinois Circuit Court Nineteenth Judicial Circuit)* Former Associate Judge.
Office: Lake County Courthouse, 18 North County Street, Waukegan 60085.
Telephone: (847) 377-3850.

STARKS, Cheryl A. *(Circuit Judge, Illinois Circuit Court of Cook County)*
Office: 2103 R. J. Daley Center, Chicago 60602.
Telephone: (312) 603-4183.

STEADMAN, Timothy J. *(Associate Judge, Illinois Circuit Court Sixth Judicial Circuit)*
Office: Macon County Courts Facility, 253 East Wood Street, Decatur 62523.
Telephone: (217) 424-1303.

STEELE, John O. *(Circuit Judge, Illinois Circuit Court of Cook County)* Former Associate Judge. Assumed office as Circuit Judge.
Office: 3004 R. J. Daley Center, Chicago 60602.
Telephone: (312) 603-4605.

STEENROD, Rebecca R. *(Associate Judge, Illinois Circuit Court Tenth Judicial Circuit)*
Office: Tazewell County Courthouse, 342 Court Street, Pekin 61554-4281.
Telephone: (309) 477-2201.

STEIGMANN, Robert James *(Judge, Illinois Appellate Court Fourth Judicial District)* Elected Nov 1994. Term expires Dec 2004. Former Presiding Judge. Born Chicago Illinois Dec 27, 1944. Jewish. Educated at University of Illinois B.S. 1965 J.D. 1968. Admitted to practice Illinois 1968. Began legal practice Springfield 1968. Circuit Judge, Illinois Circuit Court Sixth Judicial Circuit Dec 6, 1976 to Dec 1994. Served Illinois Appellate Court Fourth Judicial District by special assignment July 1989 to Dec 1994.

With State's Attorney's Office Sangamon County 1969-71 and Champaign County 1971-76. Author "Illinois Juvenile Court Practice" Illinois ICLE March 1970, "The Preliminary Hearing in Illinois" Aug 1978, "Prior Inconsistent Statements as Substantive Evidence in Illinois" Aug 1984, "First and Second Degree Murder in Illinois" May 1987 Illinois State B. Jour. and three volume treatise *Illinois Evidence Manual* 3rd ed. West Group 1995. Co-author *Illinois Evidentiary Foundations* April 1992. Editor Criminal Justice Section Newsletter of Illinois State Bar Association 1975-80. Important Decision: Costello v. Capital Cities Communications (dissenting opinion involving constitutional issue with regard to libel law) 153 Ill. App. 3d 956, 977, 1987. Adjunct Faculty University of Illinois College of Law. Board member Illinois Judges Association 1978-84 and 1989-91. Former Chairman Committee on Pattern Jury Instructions in Criminal Cases Illinois Supreme Court. Member American Judicature Society, Champaign County, Illinois State and American Bar Associations. Faculty

STEIGMANN, ROBERT JAMES—*Continued*

Member and Presenter to new judges on courts of review New York University School of Law Institute of Judicial Administration and National College of District Attorneys. Republican. Enjoys reading, sports and bridge.

Mailing address: P.O. Box 815, Urbana 61803-0815.
Office: 100 West Main, Urbana 61801.
Telephone: (217) 278-3131.

STENGEL, Charles H. *(Circuit Judge, Illinois Circuit Court Fourteenth Judicial Circuit)*
Office: Rock Island County Courthouse, 210 15th Street, Rock Island 61201.
Telephone: (309) 786-4451.

STEPHENS, Eddie A. *(Associate Judge, Illinois Circuit Court of Cook County)*
Office: 5600 Old Orchard Road, Skokie 60077.
Telephone: (847) 470-7200.

STERBA, David P. *(Circuit Judge, Illinois Circuit Court of Cook County)*
Office: 10220 South 76th Avenue, Room 201A, Bridgeview 60455.
Telephone: (708) 974-6321.

STEVENS, Richard A. *(Associate Judge, Illinois Circuit Court of Cook County)*
Office: 1100 South Hamilton Avenue, Chicago 60612.
Telephone: (312) 433-4756.

STEWART, Bruce D. *(Circuit Judge, Illinois Circuit Court First Judicial Circuit)*
Office: Saline County Courthouse, 10 East Poplar, Harrisburg 62946.
Telephone: (618) 253-8741.

STEWART, James B. *(Circuit Judge, Illinois Circuit Court Ninth Judicial Circuit)* Former Associate Judge.
Office: Knox County Courthouse, 200 South Cherry Street, Galesburg 61401.
Telephone: (309) 345-3847.

STEWART, Victoria A. *(Circuit Judge, Illinois Circuit Court of Cook County)*
Office: 727 East 111th Street, Chicago 60628.
Telephone: (773) 660-0346.

STIEHL, William D. *(Senior Judge, United States District Court Southern District of Illinois)* Appointed for life by President Ronald Reagan to term beginning Aug 1, 1986. Former Chief Judge. Assumed Senior status, serves by assignment. Born Belleville Illinois Dec 3, 1925. Methodist. Educated at University of North Carolina and St. Louis University LL.B. 1949. Member Sigma Alpha Epsilon. Admitted to practice Missouri 1949, Illinois 1950, U.S. District Court Southern District of Illinois and U.S. Court of Appeals Seventh Circuit. In legal practice Belleville Illinois 1950-86.

Assistant State's Attorney St. Clair County 1956-60. Special Assistant Attorney General Illinois 1970-73. Important Decisions: United States, National Rural Utilities Cooperatives Finance Corp. and Soyland Power Coop., Inc. v. Southwestern Electric Corp., Inc. (nuclear power plant; rural electric cooperative all requirements contract) 663 F. Supp. 897 S.D. Ill. 1987; Matta-Ballesteros v. Henman (writ of habeas corpus to return inmate to Honduras) 697 F. Supp. 1040 S.D. Ill. 1988; and Wilson v. Lane (writ of habeas corpus by others on behalf of death row inmate regarding competency of inmate to waive federal challenges to his sentence) 697 F. Supp. 1489 S.D. Ill. 1988, 697 F. Supp. 1500 S.D. Ill. 1988. President Belleville Bar Association 1957. Member The Association of Trial Lawyers of America, The Bar Association of Metropolitan St. Louis, St. Clair County, Illinois State and American Bar Associations. Commander USNR 1943-73 (retired). Vice President Illinois Young Republican Organization 1955-57. President St. Clair County Young Republican Organization 1954-55. Chairman St. Clair County Republican Central Committee 1960-66 and Republican Voters Registration Illinois 1964. Member Executive Committee Illinois Republican County Chairmen's Association 1960-66. Republican Precinct Committeeman 1960-72. Board of Governors Illinois Republican Citizens League 1961-65 and United Republican Fund of Illinois 1967-80. Treasurer 1966-74 and Vice Chairman 1978-82 Illinois Republican State Central Committee. State Central Committeeman 21st Congressional District of Illinois 1966-82. Presidential Elector for Illinois 1968. Southern Regional Coordinator Illinois Committee to Re-Elect the President 1971-72. Delegate Republican National Nominating Convention 1976. Member 1949-50 and 1954-56 and President 1956-57 Board of Education Belleville Township High School and Junior College. Member Illinois Constitution Study Commission 1966-69, Governor's Advisory Council 1969-73 and Community Advisory Council Small Business Administration 1970-72. Honorary Life Member Local 53 International Association of Fire Fighters AFL-CIO.

Mailing address: P.O. Box 249, East St. Louis 62202-0249.
Telephone: (618) 482-9231.

STIPP, Gordon R. *(Associate Judge, Illinois Circuit Court Fifth Judicial Circuit)*
Office: Vermilion County Courthouse, 7 North Vermilion, Danville 61832.
Telephone: (217) 431-2562.

STOVERINK, David F. *(Circuit Judge, Illinois Circuit Court Ninth Judicial Circuit)* Former Associate Judge.
Mailing address: P.O. Box 2, Carthage 62321.
Office: Hancock County Courthouse, Carthage 62321.
Telephone: (217) 357-2515.

STRALKA, Paul *(Circuit Judge, Illinois Circuit Court of Cook County)*
Office: 1100 South Hamilton Avenue, Chicago 60612.
Telephone: (312) 433-4757.

STUART, Jane Louise *(Circuit Judge, Illinois Circuit Court of Cook County)*
Office: 1406 R. J. Daley Center, Chicago 60602.
Telephone: (312) 603-4867.

STUCKERT, Robbin J. *(Associate Judge, Illinois Circuit Court Sixteenth Judicial Circuit)*
Office: 400A Kane County Judicial Center, 37W777 Route 38, St. Charles 60175.
Telephone: (630) 232-3442.

STUTTLEY, Michael W. *(Associate Judge, Illinois Circuit Court of Cook County)*
Office: 16501 South Kedzie Parkway, Room 099, Markham 60426.
Telephone: (708) 210-4170.

SULLIVAN, Daniel J. *(Circuit Judge, Illinois Circuit Court of Cook County)*
Office: 2121 Euclid, Room 105A, Rolling Meadows 60008.
Telephone: (847) 818-2534.

SULLIVAN, Laura M. *(Circuit Judge, Illinois Circuit Court of Cook County)*
Office: 1303 R. J. Daley Center, Chicago 60602.
Telephone: (312) 603-7959.

SULLIVAN, Michael J. *(Circuit Judge, Illinois Circuit Court Nineteenth Judicial Circuit)* Former Associate Judge. Term expires 2008.
Office: McHenry County Courthouse, 2200 North Seminary Avenue, Woodstock 60098.
Telephone: (815) 338-2040.

SULLIVAN, Sharon M. *(Circuit Judge, Illinois Circuit Court of Cook County)*
Office: 5600 Old Orchard Road, Skokie 60077.
Telephone: (847) 470-7209.

SULLIVAN, Stephen *(Associate Judge, Illinois Circuit Court Sixteenth Judicial Circuit)*
Office: 400 Kane County Judicial Center, 37W777 Route 38, St. Charles 60175.
Telephone: (630) 232-3442.

SUMNER, Thomas R. *(Associate Judge, Illinois Circuit Court of Cook County)*
Office: 2600 South California, Room 206, Chicago 60608.
Telephone: (773) 869-7416.

SURIA, Fred G., Jr. *(Circuit Judge, Illinois Circuit Court of Cook County)* Term expires Dec 2006.
Office: 2600 South California Avenue, Room 602, Chicago 60608.
Telephone: (773) 869-3181.

SURIANO, Donald J. *(Circuit Judge, Illinois Circuit Court of Cook County)*
Office: 1306 R. J. Daley Center, Chicago 60602.
Telephone: (312) 603-4197.

SUTKER-DERMER, Shelley *(Circuit Judge, Illinois Circuit Court of Cook County)*
Office: 5600 Old Orchard Road, Skokie 60077.
Telephone: (847) 470-7207.

SUTTON, Thomas H. *(Circuit Judge, Illinois Circuit Court Second Judicial Circuit)* Term expires Dec 2006. Former Chief Judge.
Office: 301 Jennifer Avenue, Carmi 62821.
Telephone: (618) 382-4758.

TAYLOR, Bill *(Circuit Judge, Illinois Circuit Court of Cook County)*
Office: 2005 R. J. Daley Center, Chicago 60602.
Telephone: (312) 603-5902.

TAYLOR, Eugene *(Circuit Judge, Illinois Circuit Court Ninth Judicial Circuit)* Appointed to term beginning Aug 9, 1999. Elected Nov 7, 2000, current term expires Nov 2005. Born Canton Illinois July 16, 1931. Christian. Educated at University of Illinois B.A. 1953 J.D. 1958. Admitted to practice Illinois 1958, U.S. Court of Appeals Seventh Circuit 1980 and U.S. Tax Court 1980. In legal practice Canton 1958-99. USAF 1954-56.
Office: Fulton County Courthouse, Lewiston 61542.
Telephone: (309) 547-3041.
E-mail address: cetaylor58@aol.com

TENOLD, Ronald C. *(Circuit Judge, Illinois Circuit Court Ninth Judicial Circuit)* Appointed Associate Judge to term beginning Dec 21, 1987. Reappointed 1991 and 1995. Elected Circuit Judge to term beginning Dec 2, 1996. Retained by election 2002, current term expires Dec 2008. Born Mason City Iowa March 12, 1946. Presbyterian. Educated at University of Iowa B.A. 1968 J.D. 1971. Admitted to practice Illinois 1971, Iowa 1971 and U.S. District Courts Southern District of Iowa 1973 and Southern District of Illinois 1977. In legal practice Monmouth Illinois 1971-87.
City Attorney Monmouth 1982-87. Former Member Illinois Trial Lawyers Association, Iowa State and American Bar Associations. Member Illinois Judges Association, Warren County and Illinois State Bar Associations. Republican. Member Monmouth Rotary Club. Enjoys golf, fishing and woodcarving. Personal Statement or Quote: "The Journey has always been about laughing together, loving each other, seeking adventure, believing in our dreams and making a difference . . . but sometimes we forget."
Office: Warren County Courthouse, 100 West Broadway, Monmouth 61462.
Telephone: (309) 734-7201.
E-mail address: rctenold@maplecity.com

TEROS, James T. *(Circuit Judge, Illinois Circuit Court Fourteenth Judicial Circuit)* Term expires Dec 2006.
Office: Rock Island County Courthouse, 210 Fifteenth Street, Rock Island 61201.
Telephone: (309) 786-4451.

TERRELL, Lawrence, Sr. *(Circuit Judge, Illinois Circuit Court of Cook County)* Elected to term beginning Dec 1, 1994. Retained by election 2000, current term expires Dec 2006. Educated at Illinois Wesleyan University B.A. 1972 and Vanderbilt University J.D. 1975. Member Omega Psi Phi. Admitted to practice Illinois 1976. In legal practice Chicago 1976-78.
Assistant State's Attorney Cook County 1978-85. Assistant Corporation Counsel Chicago 1987-94. Instructor in Political Science Chicago State University 1978-93. Member Illinois State Bar Association. Program Moderator "Traffic Law Hot Topics" Illinois State Bar Association CLE 1997. Attended Sentencing Misdemeanants Course The National Judicial College 1998. Recipient Commitment to Domestic Violence Victims Award from Constance Morris House 1995, Dedication to Westside Youth Award from Habilitative Services, Inc. 1995 and Civic Award from NAACP 1997.
Office: 1500 Maybrook Drive, Room 128, Maywood 60153.
Telephone: (708) 865-6062.

THEIS, Mary Jane *(Judge, Illinois Appellate Court First Judicial District Division Four)* Elected 1994. Formerly served Division Five. Born Chicago Illinois Feb 27, 1949. Educated at Loyola University of Chicago B.A. 1971 and University of San Francisco School of Law J.D. 1973. Associate Judge 1983-88 and Circuit Judge 1988-93, Illinois Circuit Court of Cook County.
Assistant Public Defender 1974-83. Member Illinois

THEIS, MARY JANE—*Continued*
Judges Association, Women's Bar Association of Illinois, Chicago and Illinois State Bar Associations.
Office: 160 North LaSalle Street, Room S1705, Chicago 60601.
Telephone: (312) 793-5422.

THOMAS, Mary Maxwell *(Circuit Judge, Illinois Circuit Court of Cook County)* Appointed to term beginning Aug 21, 1987. Elected 1988. Retained by election 1994 and 2000. Current term expires Dec 2006. Born Waukegan Illinois 1943. Educated at New Mexico State University B.A. 1966, University of Chicago Law School J.D. 1973 and University of Nevada at Reno Master of Judicial Studies 1996. Member Phi Kappa Phi, Pi Gamma Mu and Alpha Kappa Alpha. Admitted to practice Illinois 1973, U.S. District Court Northern District of Illinois 1973, U.S. Court of Appeals Seventh Circuit 1977 and U.S. Supreme Court 1980. In legal practice Chicago and Evanston 1973.
Assistant City Attorney Evanston 1974-77. Assistant U.S. Attorney Northern District of Illinois 1977-87. Author "The African American Male: Communication Gap Converts Justice into 'Just Us' System" 13 Harvard Blackletter L. Jour. Spring 1997. Member Illinois Judicial Council (Chairperson 1991-92), National Association of Women Judges, Cook County and National Bar Associations. Instructor "General Jurisdiction" 1994, "Advanced Evidence" 1995, "Great Issues in Law as Reflected in Literature" Summer 1995 and 1996 and "Judicial Writing" July 1997 The National Judicial College. Recipient Presidential Award from Cook County Bar Association 1987, Distinguished Service Award 1988, 1992 and 1996 and Edith Sampson Award 1989 from Illinois Judicial Council, National Black Prosecutors' Distinguished Service Award 1991 and Kentucky Colonel Award 1994. Named Woman of Distinction by *Ebony Man* Magazine 1992. Life Member NAACP. Member Second Baptist Church (Former Legal Counsel, Member Planning and Development Committee and Women's Month Committee), Alpha Kappa Alpha and Role Model Program. Enjoys running, swimming, reading, singing, writing and mentoring youth.
Office: 5600 Old Orchard Road, Room 219, Skokie 60077.
Telephone: (847) 470-5961.

THOMAS, Robert R. *(Justice, Supreme Court of Illinois)* Elected to term beginning Dec 4, 2000. Born Rochester New York Aug 7, 1952. Educated at University of Notre Dame B.A. 1974 and Loyola University School of Law J.D. 1981. Circuit Judge 1988-94 and Acting Chief Judge 1989-94, Illinois Circuit Court Eighteenth Judicial Circuit. Judge, Illinois Appellate Court Second Judicial District 1994-2000.
Member DuPage County Bar Association.
Office: 1776 South Naperville Road, Bldg. A Suite 207, Wheaton 60187.
Telephone: (630) 871-0025.

THOMPSON, Perry R. *(Circuit Judge, Illinois Circuit Court Eighteenth Judicial Circuit)* Former Associate Judge.
Office: 505 North County Farm Road, Wheaton 60187.
Telephone: (630) 682-7361.

THURSTON, William J. *(Circuit Judge, Illinois Circuit Court First Judicial Circuit)*
Office: Pulaski County Courthouse, 500 Illinois Avenue, Mound City 62936.
Telephone: (618) 748-9814.

TIMBERLAKE, George W. *(Circuit Judge, Illinois Circuit Court Second Judicial Circuit)* Associate Judge Feb 1, 1985 to Nov 2000. Elected Circuit Judge to term beginning Dec 2000. Term expires Dec 2006. Born Mount Carmel Illinois Nov 17, 1948. Educated at University of Illinois B.A. 1970 M.B.A. 1977 J.D. 1977. Law Clerk to Hon. Kenneth J. Meyers, U.S. District Court Southern District of Illinois 1978. Admitted to practice Illinois 1977. In legal practice Mount Carmel and Albion 1979-85.
Assistant Attorney General 1982-84. Author "Attorney Sanctions in Illinois under Illinois Supreme Court Rule 137" Loyola University of Chicago L. Rev. 1989 and Chapter "Diversion and Pre-Court Disposition" *Juvenile Law Handbook* Illinois Institute for Continuing Legal Education 2001. Member Illinois Judges Association, Jefferson County and Illinois State Bar Associations. Instructor in "Equitable Remedies," "AIDS and Civil Law" and "Sanctions" Illinois Judicial Conference. Democrat. Former Precinct Committeeman. President Big Brothers/Big Sisters and other children organizations.
Mailing address: P.O. Box 1266, Mt. Vernon 62864.
Telephone: (618) 244-8006.

TOBIN, Karen T. *(Circuit Judge, Illinois Circuit Court of Cook County)* Former Associate Judge.
Office: 2121 Euclid, Room 108-A, Rolling Meadows 60008.
Telephone: (847) 818-2718.

TOGNARELLI, Richard L. *(Associate Judge, Illinois Circuit Court Third Judicial Circuit)*
Office: Madison County Courthouse, 155 North Main Street, Edwardsville 62025.
Telephone: (618) 692-6200.

TONEY, Amanda S. *(Circuit Judge, Illinois Circuit Court of Cook County)*
Office: 1304 R. J. Daley Center, Chicago 60602.
Telephone: (312) 603-5007.

TONIGAN, Henry C., III *(Circuit Judge, Illinois Circuit Court Nineteenth Judicial Circuit)* Appointed Associate Judge to term beginning Aug 21, 1983. Reappointed July 1, 1987. Elected Circuit Judge 1992. Retained by election 1998, current term expires Dec 2004. Presiding Judge Felony Division 1992-94 and 1996-97, Divorce Division 1995-96 and Civil Division 1997-98 and since 2000. Former Chief Judge. Educated at Cornell College B.A. and Southern Methodist University J.D. Admitted to practice Illinois 1976 and U.S. District Court Northern District of Illinois 1976. In legal practice Waukegan 1976-83.
Office: Lake County Courthouse, 18 North County Street, Waukegan 60085.
Telephone: (847) 360-6356.

TOOMIN, Michael P. *(Circuit Judge, Illinois Circuit Court of Cook County)*
Office: 2600 South California Avenue, Chicago 60608.
Telephone: (773) 869-3042.

TORLUEMKE, Kenneth W. *(Associate Judge, Illinois Circuit Court Eighteenth Judicial Circuit)*
Office: DuPage County Courthouse, 505 North County Farm Road, Wheaton 60187.
Telephone: (630) 682-7300.

TOURTELOT, John D. *(Associate Judge, Illinois Circuit Court of Cook County)*
Office: 1100 South Hamilton, Room G026N, Chicago 60612.
Telephone: (312) 433-4757.

TOWNSEND, J. G. *(Circuit Judge, Illinois Circuit Court Sixth Judicial Circuit)* Associate Judge 1979-90. Elected Circuit Judge Nov 6, 1990. Retained by election 1996 and 2002. Current term expires 2008. Appointed Presiding Judge Champaign County Dec 2, 1996. Born Charleston West Virginia April 1, 1948. Lutheran. Educated at College of Emporia B.A. with honors 1972 and University of Illinois College of Law J.D. 1975. Member Phi Alpha Delta. Admitted to practice Illinois 1975. In legal practice Champaign 1975-79.
Fellow Illinois Bar Foundation and American Bar Foundation. Member Illinois Judges Association, Champaign County, Illinois State (Assembly Member, Bench and Bar Section Council 1986-90) and American (Committee on Ethics and Professional Responsibility National Conference of State Trial Judges Judicial Administration Division) Bar Associations. Faculty member Criminal Law Seminar Illinois Associate Judges Conference 1990. Named Boss of the Year Champaign County Legal Secretaries Association 1989. U.S. Army 1966-70 and USAR since 1970. Co-President Parent Teacher Fellowship St. John Lutheran School 1989-90. Member Community Advisory Board Junior League of Champaign-Urbana. Life Member Reserve Officers Association. Member National Eagle Scout Association. Vigil Honor Member Order of the Arrow and Executive Board Member Prairelands Council Boy Scouts of America. Member Special Forces Association, American Legion, VFW, AMVETS, University of Illinois Alumni Association.
Office: Champaign County Courthouse, 101 East Main Street, Urbana 61801.
Telephone: (217) 384-3704.

TRAVIS, Charles M. *(Circuit Judge, Illinois Circuit Court of Cook County)*
Office: 1303 R. J. Daley Center, Chicago 60602.
Telephone: (312) 603-7959.

TRISTANO, Sandra *(Circuit Judge, Illinois Circuit Court of Cook County)*
Office: 1303 R. J. Daley Center, Chicago 60602.
Telephone: (312) 603-7959.

TRUITT, John R. *(Associate Judge, Illinois Circuit Court Seventeenth Judicial Circuit)*
Office: Winnebago County Courthouse, 400 West State Street, Rockford 61101.
Telephone: (815) 987-3130.

TUCKER, Thomas M. *(Associate Judge, Illinois Circuit Court of Cook County)*
Office: 1500 Maybrook Drive, Room 281, Maywood 60153.
Telephone: (708) 865-6060.

TULLY, John Patrick *(Judge, Illinois Appellate Court First Judicial District Division Six)* Elected to term beginning Dec 3, 1990. Retained by election 2000, current term expires Dec 2010. Former Presiding Judge. Formerly served Division One. Born Chicago Illinois. Catholic. Educated at Chicago Teachers College B.E. 1957 and DePaul University College of Law J.D. 1970. Admitted to practice Illinois 1970 and U.S. District Courts Northern and Southern Districts of Illinois. In legal practice Chicago 1970-84. Circuit Judge, Illinois Circuit Court of Cook County 1984-90.
Author *Divorce Without Tears* Home Business Press 1982. Member Illinois State Bar Association. Attended Illinois judicial conferences 1985-90. Democrat. Enjoys reading, playing golf, running, writing and traveling.
Office: 160 North LaSalle Street, Room S1708, Chicago 60601.
Telephone: (312) 793-5403.

TUNGATE, Sherri L. E. *(Circuit Judge, Illinois Circuit Court Fourth Judicial Circuit)* Former Associate Judge. Assumed office as Circuit Judge.
Mailing address: RR 2, Box 233, Flora 62839.
Telephone: (217) 532-9501.

TUNGATE, Susan Sumner *(Circuit Judge, Illinois Circuit Court Twenty-first Judicial Circuit)* Associate Judge 1998-2002. Elected Circuit Judge 2002. Term expires Dec 2008. Born Danville Illinois July 25, 1947. Educated at Illinois Wesleyan University B.S. 1970 B.A. 1970 and Loyola University of New Orleans J.D. 1976. Admitted to practice Illinois 1976, Louisiana 1976 and U.S. Supreme Court 1985. In legal practice 1976-98.
Assistant Public Defender Iroquois County Illinois. Member Chicago, Illinois State and Louisiana State Bar Associations.
Office: 450 East Court Street, Kankakee 60901.
Telephone: (815) 936-4680.

TURKINGTON, Edna M. *(Circuit Judge, Illinois Circuit Court of Cook County)* Elected Nov 1992 to term beginning Dec 7, 1992. Retained by election 1998, current term expires Dec 2004. Educated at Roosevelt University B.A. 1965, DePaul University M.Ed. 1969 J.D. 1973. Recipient Reginald Heber Smith Fellowship 1973-74 and Ten Outstanding Young People's Award 1974. Member Pi Mu Epsilon. Admitted to practice Illinois 1974, U.S. District Court Northern District of Illinois 1975 and Trial Bar of U.S. District Court Northern District of Illinois 1975. In legal practice 1974-76 and 1989-90.
Assistant State's Attorney 1976-87 and April 1990 to Dec 1992 Cook County. General Counsel Committee on Committees, Rules and Ethics City Council of the City of Chicago 1987-88. Author "An Overview of the Illinois Statutory Summary Suspension Law with Respect to the Illinois Supreme Court Decision in *People v. Schaeffer*" 22 No. 3 *General Practice* Jan 1994 and 3 No. 3 *Traffic Laws and Courts* May 1994, "Recent Restrictions on the Use of Materials Obtained by Grand Jury Subpoena" 23 No. 1 *General Practice* July 1994, "Right to a Jury Trial in Civil Forfeiture Proceedings" 23 No. 5 *General Practice* March 1995, "*Housh v. Bowers:* Restrictions on the Impeachment by Prior Conviction in a Civil Action" 26 No. 6 *Bench and Bar* Dec 1995 and "Recent Restrictions upon a Local Public Entity's Liability for Willful and Wanton Conduct—The Local Government and Governmental Employees Tort Immunity Act Revisited" 25 No. 2 *General Practice* Jan 1997 Illinois State Bar Association. Member Illinois Judges Association, Illinois Judicial Council (Nominating

TURKINGTON, EDNA M.—*Continued*

Committee, Speaker's Bureau and Community Outreach Committee, Black History Committee, Law Day Committee), Women's Bar Association of Illinois, Cook County (Law Day Committee, Attorney Registration and Disciplinary Committee, Judicial Evaluation Committee, Mentor Young Lawyers Mentoring Program) and Illinois State (Council Member Bench and Bar Section and General Practice Section) Bar Associations. Recipient Meritorious Recognition Award from Cook County Bar Association 1993, prestigious award for compassion and fairness to African-American Community from South Suburban Ministers Fellowship 1994, Distinguished Service Award from Youth As Resources 1994, 1995 and 1996 and Friend of 4-H Award 1996. Honored for Outstanding Judicial Contributions by South Suburban Bar Association 1994. Administrative Assistant to Mayor Chicago 1988-89. Board Member Youth As Resources. Advisor Early Childhood Research and Intervention Program University of Illinois at Chicago. Trained intervener to assist drug dependent judges and lawyers Lawyer's Assistance Program. Graduation and Law Day Speaker Chicago Public Schools. Member Mentoring program for youth St. Mark Church.

Office: 1402 R. J. Daley Center, Chicago 60602.
Telephone: (312) 603-4863.

TURNER, John D., Jr. *(Circuit Judge, Illinois Circuit Court of Cook County)*

Office: 16501 South Kedzie Parkway, Markham 60426.
Telephone: (708) 210-4170.

TURNER, John W. *(Judge, Illinois Appellate Court Fourth Judicial District)* Appointed June 2001. Born Lincoln Illinois March 23, 1956. Educated at University of Illinois B.A. 1978 and DePaul University J.D. 1981. Member Phi Beta Kappa. In legal practice Lincoln 1984-2001.

Office: 119½ North Sangamon Street, Lincoln 62656.
Telephone: (217) 732-4043.

TURNER, Valarie E. *(Circuit Judge, Illinois Circuit Court of Cook County)*

Office: 1303 R. J. Daley Center, Chicago 60602.
Telephone: (312) 603-7959.

URSIN, Theresa L. *(Associate Judge, Illinois Circuit Court Fifteenth Judicial Circuit)* Appointed to term beginning Aug 26, 1999. Term expires 2003. Born Covington Kentucky Aug 30, 1956. Lutheran. Educated at University of Wisconsin B.A. with distinction 1978 and Northern Illinois University J.D. 1982. Law Clerk to Magistrate Judge Patrick M. Mahoney, U.S. District Court Northern District of Illinois 1984-88. Admitted to practice Illinois 1982. In legal practice Naperville 1982-84 and Freeport 1985-87.

Assistant State's Attorney Stephenson County 1987-99. Member Illinois Judges Association, National Council of Juvenile and Family Court Judges and Stephenson County Bar Association.

Office: Stephenson County Courthouse, 15 North Galena, Freeport 61032.
Telephone: (815) 235-8287.

URSO, Joseph J. *(Circuit Judge, Illinois Circuit Court of Cook County)* Associate Judge Nov 15, 1977 to June 30, 1994. Appointed Circuit Judge July 1, 1994. Elected to term beginning Dec 5, 1994. Retained by election Dec 2000, current term expires Dec 2006. Currently serves as Presiding Judge Third Municipal District. Born Dec 19, 1942. Educated at Northern Illinois University B.S. in Finance with honors 1966 and DePaul University J.D. 1969. Admitted to practice Illinois 1969 and U.S. District Court Northern District of Illinois 1969.

Assistant State's Attorney Cook County 1969-77. Supervisor Felony Review Unit 1973-77 and First Municipal District 1977. Author Chapter 1 "Screening Cases" *Prosecution of the Criminal Case* Illinois ICLE 1975. Lecturer at Chicago Police and Cook County Sheriff's Training Academies and Cook County State's Attorneys Training Seminars. Member National District Attorneys Association, Justinian Society of Lawyers, Chicago, Illinois State and American Bar Associations.

Office: 2121 Euclid, Rolling Meadows 60008.
Telephone: (847) 818-2286.

VAHLE, Chet W. *(Associate Judge, Illinois Circuit Court Eighth Judicial Circuit)* Appointed to term beginning July 1, 1987. Reappointed July 1, 1991, July 1, 1995 and 1999. Current term expires 2003. Born Quincy Illinois July 1, 1950. Lutheran. Educated at Quincy University B.A. 1972 and Valparaiso University J.D. 1976. Member Delta Theta Phi. Admitted to practice Illinois 1977, Florida 1978 and U.S. District Court Central District of Illinois 1979.

Public Defender 1977-80 and Assistant State's Attorney 1983-87 Adams County. Author "Dispositions in Neglect and Abuse Cases" Juvenile Law Handbook IICLE 1997 and 2001. Member Study Committee on Juvenile Justice Illinois Judicial Conference 1993-2002. Member since 1999 and Vice Chair since 2000 State Court Improvement Project. Member Special Committee on Child Custody Issues Supreme Court of Illinois since 2002. Member National Council of Juvenile and Family Court Judges (Chair 1996-98 and Co-chair 2002-03 Juvenile Law Committee, Member Board of Trustees 1997-2003, Vice Chair Family Violence Committee 1998-99, Co-chair Federal Legislation Committee 2002-03), Illinois Judges Association (Board of Directors 1995-2001, President's Task Force 2001-03, Co-chair Associate Judges Committee 2002-03) and Adams County Bar Association (Board of Directors 1993-2001). Presenter "Family Law Update" Illinois State Bar Association Dec 1992. Faculty Member "Issues in Hearing Child Sex Abuse Cases" March 1995 and "Juvenile Law" March 1996 and March 2001 Illinois Judicial Conference and "Compliance with Federal Foster Care Requirements" State Court Improvement Project 2002. Recipient Hope and Dignity Award from Quincy Area Network Against Domestic Abuse 1994, Champions in Adoption Award from Governor George H. Ryan 1999 and Humanitarian Award from Family Service Agency of Adams County 2000. Organizer Adams County Family Violence Council 1995. Enjoys hunting, fishing and traveling.

Office: Adams County Courthouse, 521 Vermont Street, Quincy 62301.
Telephone: (217) 277-2025.

VANCIL, David L., Jr. *(Circuit Judge, Illinois Circuit Court Ninth Judicial Circuit)*

Office: Warren County Courthouse, Monmouth 61462.
Telephone: (309) 837-9278.

VANDERSNICK, Larry S. *(Circuit Judge, Illinois Circuit Court Fourteenth Judicial Circuit)*
Mailing address: P.O. Box 9, Cambridge 61238.
Office: Henry County Courthouse, Cambridge 61238.
Telephone: (309) 786-4451.

VandeWIELE, Mark A. *(Circuit Judge, Illinois Circuit Court Fourteenth Judicial Circuit)*
Office: Rock Island County Courthouse, 210 Fifteenth Street, Rock Island 61201.
Telephone: (309) 558-3285.

VAN TINE, Rena M. *(Associate Judge, Illinois Circuit Court of Cook County)*
Office: 1100 South Hamilton Avenue, Chicago 60612.
Telephone: (312) 433-4756.

VANTREASE, E. Kyle *(Circuit Judge, Illinois Circuit Court Second Judicial Circuit)*
Office: Franklin County Courthouse, Benton 62812.
Telephone: (618) 438-6003.

VARGA, James Michael *(Circuit Judge, Illinois Circuit Court of Cook County)*
Office: 2606 R. J. Daley Center, Chicago 60602.
Telephone: (312) 603-4206.

VAUGHAN, Barry Leon *(Circuit Judge, Illinois Circuit Court Second Judicial Circuit)*
Office: Hamilton County Courthouse, McLeansboro 62859.
Telephone: (618) 643-2611.

VECCHIO, Steven G. *(Associate Judge, Illinois Circuit Court Seventeenth Judicial Circuit)*
Office: Winnebago County Courthouse, 400 West State Street, Rockford 61101.
Telephone: (815) 987-3062.

VEGA, Raul *(Circuit Judge, Illinois Circuit Court of Cook County)*
Office: 1303 R. J. Daley Center, Chicago 60602.
Telephone: (312) 603-7959.

VESPA, Joe R. *(Circuit Judge, Illinois Circuit Court Tenth Judicial Circuit)*
Office: 215 Peoria County Courthouse, 324 West Main Street, Peoria 61602-1363.
Telephone: (309) 672-6099.

VIDAL, Richard W. *(Circuit Judge, Illinois Circuit Court Seventeenth Judicial Circuit)* Former Associate Judge.
Office: Winnebago County Courthouse, 400 West State Street, Rockford 61101.
Telephone: (815) 987-3062.

WADAS, Kenneth J. *(Circuit Judge, Illinois Circuit Court of Cook County)* Elected to term beginning Dec 1, 1996. Retained by election 2002, current term expires Dec 2008. Born Chicago Illinois Nov 2, 1945. Roman Catholic. Educated at Loyola University of Chicago B.S. 1968 and John Marshall Law School J.D. 1975. Admitted to practice Illinois 1975, U.S. District Courts Central and Northern Districts of Illinois, U.S. Tax Court and U.S. Courts of Appeals Seventh, Eighth, Ninth, Tenth and Eleventh Circuits. In legal practice Chicago 1986-96.
Assistant State's Attorney Cook County 1976-86. Member Illinois Judges Association and Chicago Bar Association. Captain USMC 1968-71. Democrat. Enjoys gardening, cooking, golfing and reading.
Office: 2600 South California Avenue, Chicago 60608.
Telephone: (773) 869-7410.

WALDECK, Joseph R. *(Associate Judge, Illinois Circuit Court Nineteenth Judicial Circuit)*
Office: 18 North County Street, Waukegan 60085.
Telephone: (847) 377-4353.

WALDEN, Scott *(Circuit Judge, Illinois Circuit Court Eighth Judicial Circuit)* Appointed to term beginning June 26, 1995. Elected Nov 6, 1996. Retained by election Nov 5,2002, current term expires Dec 1, 2008. Born Elgin Illinois Aug 21, 1953. Educated at The Principia College B.A. 1975 and Valparaiso University J.D. 1978. Admitted to practice Illinois 1978 and U.S. District Court Central District of Illinois 1979. In legal practice Quincy 1978-88.
State's Attorney Adams County 1988-95. Instructor in Criminal Law Illinois Judicial Conference Seminars. Member Breakfast Kiwanis Club (Past President).
Office: Adams County Courthouse, 521 Vermont Street, Quincy 62301.
Telephone: (217) 277-2060.

WALLER, Ashton C., Jr. *(Circuit Judge, Illinois Circuit Court Fifth Judicial Circuit)* Former Associate Judge. Term expires 2008. Former Chief Judge.
Office: Coles County Courthouse, Second Floor, 651 Jackson, Charleston 61920.
Telephone: (217) 348-0545.

WALLER, Jane D. *(Circuit Judge, Illinois Circuit Court Nineteenth Judicial Circuit)* Associate Judge 1981-96. Elected Circuit Judge to term beginning Dec 2, 1996. Retained by election 2002, current term expires Nov 30, 2008. Chief Judge Dec 1, 2000 to Nov 30, 2002. Born Rapid City South Dakota Jan 27, 1946. Educated at Trinity College B.A. with honors 1968, Northwestern University M.A.T. 1969 and University of Illinois J.D. with honors 1973. Admitted to practice Illinois 1973 and U.S. District Court Northern District of Illinois 1973. In legal practice Waukegan 1973-81.
Member Illinois Judges Association, National Association of Women Judges, Lake County (President 1996-97) and Illinois State Bar Associations. Instructor in Civil and Criminal Evidence Illinois Judicial Conference 1996-97. Recipient Samuel S. Berger Award from Chicago Chapter Academy of Matrimonial Attorneys 1994. Republican.
Office: Lake County Courthouse, 18 North County Street, Waukegan 60085.
Telephone: (847) 377-3600.

WALSH, Richard F. *(Circuit Judge, Illinois Circuit Court of Cook County)*
Office: 1100 South Hamilton, Room G-28S, Chicago 60612.
Telephone: (312) 433-4757.

WALTER, Stephen E. *(Circuit Judge, Illinois Circuit Court Nineteenth Judicial Circuit)* Former Associate Judge. Term expires 2008. Former Chief Judge.
Office: Lake County Courthouse, 18 North County Street, Waukegan 60085.
Telephone: (847) 377-3777.

WALTON, Patricia A. *(Associate Judge, Illinois Circuit Court Ninth Judicial Circuit)*
Office: Knox County Courthouse, Galesburg 61401.
Telephone: (309) 345-3847.

WARD, John A. *(Circuit Judge, Illinois Circuit Court of Cook County)* Former Associate Judge.
Office: 2005 R. J. Daley Center, Chicago 60602.
Telephone: (312) 603-5907.

WASHINGTON, Edward, II *(Circuit Judge, Illinois Circuit Court of Cook County)*
Office: 1303 R. J. Daley Center, Chicago 60602.
Telephone: (312) 603-7959.

WASILEWSKI, John A. *(Associate Judge, Illinois Circuit Court of Cook County)*
Office: 10220 South 76th Avenue, Bridgeview 60455.
Telephone: (708) 974-6542.

WATSON, Cyril J. *(Circuit Judge, Illinois Circuit Court of Cook County)* Former Associate Judge.
Office: 2802 R. J. Daley Center, Chicago 60602.
Telephone: (312) 603-3900.

WATT, David W., Jr. *(Circuit Judge, Illinois Circuit Court First Judicial Circuit)* Appointed Associate Judge to term beginning June 7, 1982. Elected Circuit Judge to term beginning Dec 5, 1988. Retained by election 1994 and 2000. Current term expires Dec 2006. Presiding Judge since Sept 1990. Born Springfield Illinois April 19, 1943. Protestant. Educated at University of Wisconsin B.S. 1965 and University of Illinois J.D. 1968. Admitted to practice Illinois 1968 and U.S. Supreme Court 1977. In legal practice Murphysboro 1970-82.

Investigator Attorney General State of Illinois 1965-68. Assistant State's Attorney Jackson County 1968-70. Commissioner Illinois Appellate Defender Commission 1990-96. Author "Implied Consent: A Nuts and Bolts Approach." Life Patron Fellow Illinois Bar Foundation. Member Criminal Justice Council 1981-86 (Vice Chairman 1982), Illinois Judges Association (Director 1983-86), The Association of Trial Lawyers of America, American Judicature Society, Jackson County (Secretary 1968-69 and President 1978-80) and Illinois State (Assembly Delegate 1980-85, Board of Governors 1985-90) Bar Associations. Lecturer Criminal Justice Council and Drunk Driving Legislation update programs. Recipient Land of Lincoln Legal Assistance Foundation Award May 8, 1981 and Illinois Public Defender's Association Award June 15, 1984.
Mailing address: P.O. Box 388, Murphysboro 62966.
Telephone: (618) 687-7330.

WEBBER, Albert G. *(Circuit Judge, Illinois Circuit Court Sixth Judicial Circuit)*
Office: 253 East Wood Street, Decatur 62523.
Telephone: (217) 424-1464.

WEBER, Daniel S. *(Circuit Judge, Illinois Circuit Court of Cook County)* Term expires 2004.
Office: 1500 Maybrook Drive, Room 295, Maywood 60153.
Telephone: (708) 865-6060.

WEBER, Michael R. *(Circuit Judge, Illinois Circuit Court Fourth Judicial Circuit)* Associate Judge 1983-84. Elected Circuit Judge 1984. Retained by election 1990, 1996 and 2002. Current term expires 2008. Former Chief Judge. Born Olney Illinois June 17, 1947. Catholic. Educated at University of Illinois B.S. 1969 and St. Louis University J.D. cum laude 1973. Member Phi Delta Phi. Admitted to practice Illinois 1973. In legal practice Effingham 1973 and Newton 1980.

Member Supreme Court Committee on Post-Conviction Relief in Capital Cases, Child Support Advisory Committee of the Conference of Chief Judges, Illinois Judges Association and Illinois State Bar Association.
Mailing address: P.O. Box 366, Newton 62448.
Telephone: (618) 783-2524.

WEBSTER, Hollis L. *(Circuit Judge, Illinois Circuit Court Eighteenth Judicial Circuit)* Appointed Associate Judge July 1, 1991. Reappointed June 30, 1995. Appointed Circuit Judge Aug 15, 1995. Elected Nov 5, 1996. Retained by election 2002, current term expires Dec 2008. Born June 15, 1955. Educated at University of Illinois at Champaign-Urbana B.S. 1977 and Loyola University of Chicago J.D. 1982. Law Clerk to Hon. John A. Nordberg, U.S. District Court Northern District of Illinois 1982-83. Admitted to practice Illinois 1982. In legal practice Lisle 1983-91.

Author "Petrillo: Protection or Penalty? A View from the Defense" 12 No. 2 DuPage County Bar Association Bar News Nov 1987 and 32 No. 3 Young Lawyers Illinois State Bar Association Jan 1988; "Private Interviews with Plaintiff's Doctors" 30 No. 2 For the Defense Feb 1988; *Guide for the Defendant Doctor* Hinshaw and Culbertson Nov 1988; "Domestic Violence: A Summary for Civil Lawyers" 7 No. 3 DuPage County Bar Association Brief Nov 1994 and 4 No. 3 *IDC Quarterly* 3rd quarter 1994; "Enforcement in Domestic Violence Cases" 26 Loyola University at Chicago L. Jour. 1995; Foreword *The Complete Idiot's Guide to Protecting Yourself from Everyday Legal Hassles* by Brent Terry, MacMillan 1995; "Day in the Life Films: Probative and Prejudicial Plaintiff's Pictures" 2 No. 9 May-June 1991, "Equitable Thoughts" 3 No. 1 Sept 1991, "Can We Talk?" 3 No. 3 March 1991, "Petitions to Revoke: A Delicate Due Process Balance" 5 No. 8 April 1993, "Quality Assurance in the Judiciary: Education and Peer Review" 5 No. 9 May-June 1993, "Law vs. Morality: The Dilemma of Justice" 8 No. 3 Nov 1995, "The Dead-Man's Act: A Continuing Controversy" 9 No. 6 Feb 1997, "Judicial Practice Tips/Adjudication of Health Care Provider Liens" 9 No. 9 May 1997 and "Judicial Practice Tips/Trial Evidence" 10 No. 1 Aug 1997, 10 No. 3 Oct 1997 and 10 No. 10 July 1998 DuPage County Bar Association Brief; "Trial Practice Tips on Evidence" DuPage County Association of Women Lawyers Fifth Annual Trial Advocacy Seminar March 8, 1997; "Adjudication of Health Care Provider Liens" DuPage County Bar Association Appellate/Civil Law and Practice Seminar April 2, 1997; and "Professional Responsibility/The Supreme Court Judicial Mentoring Program" 11 No. 5 DuPage County Bar Association Brief Jan 1999. Co-author with Kathleen T. Zellner "Appellate Procedural Traps for the Unwary" 12 No. 10 DuPage County Bar Association Bar News June 1988; with Thomas A. Brabec "Tort Reform and Insurance Investigation Checklists" American States Insurance Seminar Sept 12, 1988; with Robert G. Black "Mandatory Court Annexed Arbitration in DuPage County" CNA Insurance Seminar May 25, 1989; with Daniel E. May "Hedonics: The Measure of Pleasure" 1 No. 2 DuPage County Bar Association Brief Nov 1989; with Stuart Nudelman *Mentor Manual* Administrative Office of Illinois Courts Aug 1998; and with Joseph M. Mannon "Judicial Prac-

WEBSTER, HOLLIS L.—*Continued*

tice Tips/Something About Sanctions" 12 No. 2 DuPage Bar Association Brief Oct 1999. Editor DuPage County Bar Association Monthly Journal 1991-93. Publication Board Member 1989-93 and Vice-Chair Civil Practice Committee 1990-91 DuPage County Bar Association. Member Education Committee Supreme Court since Feb 1, 2000. Faculty Judicial Training on D.U.I. Illinois Department of Alcohol and Substance Abuse 1991-94. Faculty Judicial Ethics 1992 and 1996, Domestic Violence 1995, Judicial Mentor Training 1998, Civil Pre-Trial Motion Practice 1999, Seminar 2000 and Civil Evidence Seminar 2000 and 2001 Illinois Judicial Conference. Graduate 1993 and Faculty Domestic Violence Course The National Judicial College. Faculty National Institute of Trial Advocacy DuPage County 1995 and 1998. Panel Speaker on Discovery Practices including Supreme Court Rule 213 DuPage County Bar Association Seminar 1999. Attended Bench-Bar Symposium DuPage County Bar Association 1999. Member DuPage County Advisory Board on Domestic Violence 1992-96.

Office: 505 North County Farm Road, Wheaton 60187.

Telephone: (630) 682-7789.

WEDOFF, Eugene R. *(Chief Judge, United States Bankruptcy Court Northern District of Illinois)* Appointed by U.S. Court of Appeals Seventh Circuit judges Sept 16, 1987. Reappointed 2001, current term expires 2015. Chief Judge since July 21, 2002. Educated at University of Chicago B.A. cum laude 1972 J.D. 1975.

Director American Bankruptcy Institute. Member National Conference of Bankruptcy Judges and American Bar Association.

Office: U.S. Courthouse, 219 South Dearborn Street, Chicago 60604.

Telephone: (312) 435-5644.

WEECH, Charles P. *(Associate Judge, Illinois Circuit Court Nineteenth Judicial Circuit)*

Office: 2200 North Seminary Avenue, Woodstock 60098.

Telephone: (815) 338-2040.

WEGNER, Grant Steven *(Circuit Judge, Illinois Circuit Court Sixteenth Judicial Circuit)* Former Associate Judge. Assumed office as Circuit Judge. Term expires 2008. Former Chief Judge.

Office: 37W777 Route 38, Box 400-A, St. Charles 60175.

Telephone: (630) 232-3440.

WEIR, William H. *(Associate Judge, Illinois Circuit Court Sixteenth Judicial Circuit)*

Office: 37W777 Route 38, St. Charles 60175.

Telephone: (630) 232-3221.

WELCH, Robert L. *(Circuit Judge, Illinois Circuit Court Eighth Judicial Circuit)* Elected 1978. Retained by election 1984, 1990, 1996 and 2002. Current term expires 2008. Former Chief Judge.

Office: Cass County Courthouse, Virginia 62691.

Telephone: (217) 277-2058.

WELCH, Thomas M. *(Judge, Illinois Appellate Court Fifth Judicial District)* Elected to term beginning Dec 1, 1980. Retained by election 1990 and 2000. Current term expires Dec 2010. Born St. Louis Missouri Feb 28, 1939. Religious affiliation: Evangelical. Educated at University of Illinois B.S. 1962 and University of Missouri J.D. 1965. Member Delta Chi and Phi Delta Phi. Admitted to practice Illinois 1965 and Missouri 1965. Began legal practice Collinsville Illinois 1965. Magistrate, Illinois Circuit Court 1965-71.

Assistant State's Attorney Madison County 1971-72. City Attorney Collinsville 1975-80. Member Tri-City, Madison County and Illinois State Bar Associations. Republican. Commercial instrument pilot. Enjoys restoring antique race cars and flying.

Mailing address: P.O. Box 625, Collinsville 62234.

Office: Crestmont, #2, Collinsville 62234.

Telephone: (618) 344-1299.

WELTER, Daniel G. *(Associate Judge, Illinois Circuit Court of Cook County)* Appointed to term beginning Oct 24, 1986. Reappointed 1991, 1995 and 1999. Current term expires 2003. Born Chicago Illinois March 11, 1949. Roman Catholic. Educated at Loyola University of Chicago A.B. 1971 and Illinois Institute of Technology, Chicago-Kent College of Law J.D. 1976. Admitted to practice Illinois 1976 and U.S. District Court Northern District of Illinois 1976. In legal practice Chicago 1976-77.

With Office of the Corporation Counsel 1977-81 and Chief Assistant Corporation Counsel 1981-86 City of Chicago. Member Catholic Lawyers Guild, Lawyers Assistance Program and Chicago Bar Association. Instructor The National Judicial College since 1989. Teaching Faculty Judicial DUI Training Illinois Department of Alcoholism and Substance Abuse (DASA). Sergeant Illinois National Air Guard 1972-78. Branch Manager Talman Federal Savings and Loan 1972-76. Ordained Deacon Roman Catholic Archdiocese of Chicago 1991. Board of Advisors Catholic Charities of Chicago since 1998. Vice Chairman Diaconate Council since 1998.

Office: 10220 South 76th Avenue, Room 202, Bridgeview 60455.

Telephone: (708) 974-6535.

WENZELMAN, Kendall O. *(Chief Judge, Illinois Circuit Court Twenty-first Judicial Circuit)*

Office: Kankakee County Courthouse, 450 East Court Street, Kankakee 60901.

Telephone: (815) 937-3650.

WEXSTTEN, James M. *(Chief Judge, Illinois Circuit Court Second Judicial Circuit)* Term expires Dec 2006.

Mailing address: P.O. Box 1197, Mount Vernon 62864.

Office: 105 South Sixth Street, Mount Vernon 62864.

Telephone: (618) 244-8036.

WHARTON, Milton S. *(Circuit Judge, Illinois Circuit Court Twentieth Judicial Circuit)* Appointed Associate Judge to term beginning Dec 6, 1976. Reappointed to subsequent terms. Assumed office as Circuit Judge. Term expires Dec 2006. Born St. Louis Missouri Sept 20, 1946. Roman Catholic. Educated at Southern Illinois University B.S. 1969 and DePaul University J.D. 1974. Admitted to practice Illinois 1975.

With St. Clair County Public Defender's Office at Belleville 1975. Member St. Clair County, Metro East (Vice President 1976) and Illinois State Bar Associations. Member Lions Club International.

Office: County Building, 10 Public Square, Belleville 62220.

Telephone: (618) 277-6600.

WHEATON, Bonnie M. *(Circuit Judge, Illinois Circuit Court Eighteenth Judicial Circuit)* Former Associate Judge.
Office: DuPage County Courthouse, 505 North County Farm Road, Wheaton 60187.
Telephone: (630) 682-7300.

WHITE, Alexander P. *(Circuit Judge, Illinois Circuit Court of Cook County)* Elected to term beginning Dec 1, 1986. Retained by election 1992 and 1998. Current term expires 2004. Currently serves as Supervising Judge Tax and Miscellaneous Law Section. Born Chicago Illinois March 30, 1932. Protestant. Educated at Northern Illinois University B.S. 1959, Chicago-Kent College of Law J.D. with honors 1964, John Marshall Law School LL.M. 1976 and DePaul University M.S. with honors 1977. Editor Chicago-Kent Law Review 1962-64. Law Clerk to Hon. John L. Lyons, Illinois Appellate Court 1964-67. Member Phi Delta Phi. Admitted to practice Illinois 1964, U.S. Court of Appeals Seventh Circuit 1968, U.S. Supreme Court 1968 and U.S. Court of Military Appeals 1968. In legal practice Chicago 1964-86.
Instructor Chicago-Kent College of Law 1970-75 and Northern Illinois University 1980-84. Member Chicago, Illinois State, Seventh Circuit and Federal (President Chicago Chapter 1980) Bar Associations. Colonel USMC 1954-86. Legal Assistant to President Cook County Board of Commissioners 1967-69 and to Governor of Illinois 1969. Executive Assistant to U.S. Senator 1969-70. Chairman Illinois Industrial Commission 1970-73.
Office: 2503 R. J. Daley Center, Chicago 60602.
Telephone: (312) 603-5533.

WHITE, LaBrenda E. *(Associate Judge, Illinois Circuit Court of Cook County)*
Office: 10220 South 76th Avenue, Room 209, Bridgeview 60455.
Telephone: (708) 974-6759.

WHITE, Lisa Holder *(Associate Judge, Illinois Circuit Court Sixth Judicial Circuit)*
Office: Macon County Courthouse, 253 East Wood Street, Decatur 62523.
Telephone: (217) 424-0857.

WHITE, Ronald J. *(Associate Judge, Illinois Circuit Court Seventeenth Judicial Circuit)*
Office: 400 West State Street, Rockford 61101.
Telephone: (815) 961-3247.

WHITE, Stephen D. *(Chief Judge, Illinois Circuit Court Twelfth Judicial Circuit)* Former Associate Judge.
Office: 439 Will County Courthouse, 14 West Jefferson Street, Joliet 60432.
Telephone: (815) 727-8453.

WILLIAMS, Walter *(Associate Judge, Illinois Circuit Court of Cook County)*
Office: 3150 West Flournoy, Chicago 60612.
Telephone: (773) 265-8936.

WILLIAMSON, James R. *(Circuit Judge, Illinois Circuit Court First Judicial Circuit)* Elected to term beginning Dec 4, 1978. Retained by election 1984, 1990, 1996 and 2002. Current term expires 2008. Born Carbondale Illinois Aug 31, 1945. Methodist. Educated at DePauw University B.A. 1967 and University of Arkansas at Fayetteville J.D. with high honors 1975. Associate Editor Arkansas Law Review 1974. Admitted to practice Illinois 1975, U.S. District Court Eastern District of Illinois 1978 and U.S. Supreme Court 1978. Began legal practice Vienna 1975.
State's Attorney Johnson County Dec 1976 to Dec 1978. Author "Search of the Person Incident to a Lawful Arrest" 28 Comment, Arkansas L. Rev. 1974. Member Illinois Bar Foundation, Illinois Judges Association and Illinois State Bar Association. Republican. Enjoys reading, outdoor activities, exercise (physical fitness) and collecting political and sports memorabilia and American collectibles.
Office: Johnson County Courthouse, Vienna 62995.
Telephone: (618) 658-8160.

WILLIS, Camille E. *(Circuit Judge, Illinois Circuit Court of Cook County)*
Office: 16501 South Kedzie Parkway, Markham 60426.
Telephone: (708) 210-4170.

WILSON, James M. *(Circuit Judge, Illinois Circuit Court Sixteenth Judicial Circuit)* Former Associate Judge. Term expires Dec 2006.
Mailing address: P.O. Box M, Yorkville 60560.
Office: Kendall County Courthouse, Yorkville 60560.
Telephone: (630) 553-4208.

WILSON, William H. *(Associate Judge, Illinois Circuit Court First Judicial Circuit)*
Office: Williamson County Courthouse, 200 Jefferson Street, Marion 62959.
Telephone: (618) 997-3335.

WINIECKI, Gerald T. *(Associate Judge, Illinois Circuit Court of Cook County)*
Office: 155 West 51st Street, Chicago 60609.
Telephone: (773) 373-8878.

WINKLER, Charles R. *(Recalled Circuit Judge, Illinois Circuit Court of Cook County)* Retired, serves by recall.
Office: 3005 R. J. Daley Center, Chicago 60602.
Telephone: (312) 603-4726.

WINTER, Diane E. *(Associate Judge, Illinois Circuit Court Nineteenth Judicial Circuit)*
Office: Lake County Circuit Court Branch B, 430 Lakehurst Road, Waukegan 60085.
Telephone: (847) 377-4368.

WOJCIK, Eugene A. *(Associate Judge, Illinois Circuit Court Eighteenth Judicial Circuit)*
Office: 505 North County Farm Road, Wheaton 60187.
Telephone: (630) 682-7300.

WOJKOWSKI, Gregory J. *(Circuit Judge, Illinois Circuit Court of Cook County)*
Office: 1409 R. J. Daley Center, Chicago 60602.
Telephone: (312) 603-4859.

WOJTECKI, Leonard J. *(Associate Judge, Illinois Circuit Court Sixteenth Judicial Circuit)*
Mailing address: P.O. Box M, Yorkville 60560.
Office: Kendall County Courthouse, Yorkville 60560.
Telephone: (630) 232-3440.

WOLFSON, Lori M. *(Recalled Circuit Judge, Illinois Circuit Court of Cook County)* Retired, serves by recall.
Office: 400 R. J. Daley Center, Chicago 60602.
Telephone: (312) 603-2600.

WOLFSON, Warren D. *(Circuit Judge, Illinois Circuit Court of Cook County)* Appointed to term beginning 1975. Elected 1976. Retained by election 1982, 1988, 1994 and 2000. Current term expires Dec 2006. On assignment by Supreme Court of Illinois as Judge, Illinois Appellate Court First Judicial District Division Three since Dec 1994. Born Chicago Illinois Feb 14, 1933. Educated at University of Illinois at Chicago B.S. 1955 and University of Illinois at Urbana-Champaign LL.B. 1957. Admitted to practice Illinois 1957, U.S. District Court Northern District of Illinois 1963, U.S. Court of Appeals Seventh Circuit 1965 and U.S. Supreme Court 1970.

Office: 160 North LaSalle, Room S1505, Chicago 60601.
Telephone: (312) 793-5408.

WOOD, William S. *(Associate Judge, Illinois Circuit Court of Cook County)* Appointed to term beginning June 1983. Reappointed July 1995 and 1999. Current term expires 2003. Born Chicago Illinois Dec 3, 1926. Educated at University of Iowa B.A. 1947 LL.B. 1950. Admitted to practice Iowa 1950 and Illinois 1956. In legal practice Chicago 1959-83.

Assistant State's Attorney Cook County 1956-59. Member Illinois Judicial Council, Illinois Judges Association and Cook County Bar Association. Private First Class U.S. Army Sept 1951 to Sept 1953. Enjoys golf, swimming and wrestling.

Office: 2600 South California, Room 101, Chicago 60608.
Telephone: (773) 869-3160.

WOOL, Leon *(Associate Judge, Illinois Circuit Court of Cook County)* Elected to term beginning Nov 1, 1999. Term expires 2003. Born Chicago Illinois Dec 10, 1937. Jewish. Educated at Drake University 1960 and DePaul University J.D. 1963. Admitted to practice Illinois 1963. In legal practice Chicago 1963-99.

First Deputy Attorney Chicago Transit 1987-97. Member Decalogue Society, Chicago, Illinois State and American Bar Associations.

Office: 1112 R. J. Daley Center, Chicago 60602.
Telephone: (312) 603-4539.

WOOLEYHAN, John C. *(Associate Judge, Illinois Circuit Court Eighth Judicial Circuit)* Appointed to term beginning Feb 25, 1983. Reappointed 1987, 1991, 1995 and 1999. Current term expires 2003. Born Quincy Illinois Feb 27, 1949. Protestant. Educated at College of William & Mary A.B. 1971 and Washington University J.D. 1974. Staff member Washington University Law Quarterly 1972-73. Member Phi Delta Phi. Admitted to practice Illinois 1975 and U.S. District Court Central District of Illinois 1975. Began legal practice Quincy 1975.

Public Defender 1976-80 and First Assistant State's Attorney 1980-83 Adams County. Member Illinois Judges Association, Adams County and Illinois State Bar Associations. Member Boy Scouts and YMCA.

Office: Adams County Courthouse, 521 Vermont Street, Quincy 62301.
Telephone: (217) 277-2025.

WRIGHT, E. Kenneth, Jr. *(Circuit Judge, Illinois Circuit Court of Cook County)*
Office: 1808 R. J. Daley Center, Chicago 60602.
Telephone: (312) 603-6466.

WRIGHT, Vicki *(Associate Judge, Illinois Circuit Court Fourteenth Judicial Circuit)*
Office: Whiteside County Courthouse, Morrison 61270.
Telephone: (309) 786-4451.

WRIGHT, Willie B. *(Associate Judge, Illinois Circuit Court of Cook County)*
Office: 5229 South Kimbark, Chicago 60615.
Telephone: (773) 804-6140.

YOUCK, David A. *(Associate Judge, Illinois Circuit Court Twenty-first Judicial Circuit)* Appointed.
Office: Iroquois County Courthouse, 550 South Tenth Street, Watseka 60970.
Telephone: (815) 432-6965.
Fax: (815) 432-3485
E-mail address: dayouck@prairienet.org

YOUNG, Anthony L. *(Circuit Judge, Illinois Circuit Court of Cook County)*
Office: 1601 R. J. Daley Center, Chicago 60602.
Telephone: (312) 603-4845.

YOUNG, Patrick M. *(Associate Judge, Illinois Circuit Court Twentieth Judicial Circuit)*
Office: 10 Public Square, Belleville 62220.
Telephone: (618) 277-7325.

ZAGEL, James B. *(Judge, United States District Court Northern District of Illinois)* Appointed for life by President Ronald Reagan to term beginning June 17, 1987. Born Chicago Illinois March 4, 1941. Educated at University of Chicago B.A. 1962 M.A. 1962 and Harvard University Law School J.D. 1963.

Member Committee of Codes of Conduct Judicial Conference 1987-94. Member Chicago and American Bar Associations.

Office: U.S. Courthouse, 219 South Dearborn Street, Chicago 60604.
Telephone: (312) 435-5713.

ZAPPA, Leo J., Jr. *(Circuit Judge, Illinois Circuit Court Seventh Judicial Circuit)* Former Chief Judge.
Office: 724 Sangamon County Complex, 200 South Ninth Street, Springfield 62701.
Telephone: (217) 753-6653.

ZELEZINSKI, Frank G. *(Circuit Judge, Illinois Circuit Court of Cook County)*
Office: 16501 South Kedzie Parkway, Markham 60426.
Telephone: (708) 210-4170.

ZENOFF, Kathryn E. *(Circuit Judge, Illinois Circuit Court Seventeenth Judicial Circuit)* Former Associate Judge.
Office: Winnebago County Courthouse, 400 West State Street, Rockford 61101.
Telephone: (815) 987-2503.

ZISSMAN, Michael C. *(Associate Judge, Illinois Circuit Court of Cook County)* Appointed to term beginning June 13, 1986. Reappointed June 30, 1987, June 30, 1991, June 30, 1995 and 1999. Current term expires 2003. Born Chicago Illinois. Educated at North Park College B.A. 1963 and DePaul University J.D. 1966. Admitted to practice Illinois 1967. In legal practice Chicago 1969-86.

Assistant State's Attorney Cook County 1967-69. Member Decalogue Society of Lawyers (Board Member

ZISSMAN, MICHAEL C.—*Continued*

since 1987), Illinois Judges Association (Board Member since 1988), Chicago, Illinois State and Asian-American Bar Associations. Frequent Lecturer Chicago Bar Association. Lecturer 1988 and Attendee since 1989 Illinois Judicial Conference. Legal Advisor Lake County Sheriff 1973-74. Board President North Park College Alumni Association. Enjoys stamp collecting and traveling.

Office: 1408 R. J. Daley Center, Chicago 60602.
Telephone: (312) 603-4869.

ZOPP, Gerald M., Jr. *(Associate Judge, Illinois Circuit Court Nineteenth Judicial Circuit)*

Office: 2200 North Seminary, Woodstock 60098.
Telephone: (815) 334-4385.

ZWICK, Susan F. *(Circuit Judge, Illinois Circuit Court of Cook County)*

Office: 2812 R. J. Daley Center, Chicago 60602.
Telephone: (312) 603-7551.

INDIANA

Capital INDIANAPOLIS

UNITED STATES DISTRICT COURTS DISTRICTS OF INDIANA

Within Indiana there are two United States District Courts. For descriptive information refer to the United States Courts section.

NORTHERN DISTRICT consists of three divisions.

Fort Wayne Division includes Adams, Allen, Blackford, DeKalb, Grant, Huntington, Jay, LaGrange, Noble, Steuben, Wells and Whitley counties. The court sits at Fort Wayne.

Hammond Division includes Benton, Carroll, Jasper, Lake, Newton, Porter, Tippecanoe, Warren and White counties. The court sits at Hammond and Lafayette.

South Bend Division includes Cass, Elkhart, Fulton, Kosciusko, La Porte, Marshall, Miami, Pulaski, St. Joseph, Starke and Wabash counties. The court sits at South Bend.

Chief Judge
Robert L. Miller, Jr.

Judges
Allen Sharp
James T. Moody
Rudy Lozano
Phillip Peter Simon

Senior Judge
William C. Lee

Clerk
Stephen R. Ludwig
315 Federal Building
& U.S. Courthouse
204 South Main Street
South Bend, Indiana 46601-2194
(574) 246-8000

SOUTHERN DISTRICT consists of four divisions.

Evansville Division includes Daviess, Dubois, Gibson, Martin, Perry, Pike, Posey, Spencer, Vanderburgh and Warrick counties. The court sits at Evansville.

Indianapolis Division includes Bartholomew, Boone, Brown, Clinton, Decatur, Delaware, Fayette, Fountain, Franklin, Hamilton, Hancock, Hendricks, Henry, Howard, Johnson, Madison, Marion, Monroe, Montgomery, Morgan, Randolph, Rush, Shelby, Tipton, Union and Wayne counties. The court sits at Indianapolis and Richmond.

New Albany Division includes Clark, Crawford, Dearborn, Floyd, Harrison, Jackson, Jefferson, Jennings, Lawrence, Ohio, Orange, Ripley, Scott, Switzerland and Washington counties. The court sits at New Albany.

Terre Haute Division includes Clay, Greene, Knox, Owen, Parke, Putnam, Sullivan, Vermillion and Vigo counties. The court sits at Terre Haute.

Chief Judge
Larry J. McKinney

Judges
Sarah Evans Barker
John D. Tinder
David F. Hamilton
Richard L. Young

Senior Judge
S. Hugh Dillin

Clerk
Laura A. Briggs
105 U.S. Courthouse
46 East Ohio Street
Indianapolis, Indiana 46204
(317) 229-3700

UNITED STATES MAGISTRATE JUDGES OF INDIANA

NORTHERN DISTRICT
Andrew P. Rodovich
Roger B. Cosbey
Theresa L. Springmann
Christopher A. Nuechterlein

SOUTHERN DISTRICT
Jordan D. Lewis
V. Sue Shields
Michael G. Naville
William T. Lawrence
William G. Hussmann, Jr.
Tim A. Baker

Recalled Magistrate Judges
John Paul Godich (Southern)
Kennard P. Foster (Southern)

UNITED STATES BANKRUPTCY COURTS OF INDIANA

NORTHERN DISTRICT

Chief Judge
Harry C. Dees, Jr.

Judge
Robert E. Grant

Recalled Judge
Kent Lindquist

UNITED STATES DISTRICT COURTS DISTRICTS OF INDIANA—*Continued*

Bankruptcy Clerk
James Bonini
P.O. Box 7003
South Bend, Indiana 46634-7003
(574) 968-2100

SOUTHERN DISTRICT

Chief Judge
Frank J. Otte

Judges
Basil H. Lorch, III
Anthony John Metz, III
James K. Coachys

Bankruptcy Clerk
John A. O'Neal
P.O. Box 44978
Indianapolis, Indiana 46244-0978
(317) 229-3800

INDIANA SUPREME COURT

The Supreme Court is Indiana's court of last resort. The court consists of a chief justice and four associate justices appointed for initial two-year terms by the governor from a list supplied by the Judicial Nominating Commission. Subsequent ten-year terms are by retention election. The chief justice is selected by the Judicial Nominating Commission from among the justices for a five-year term and is subject to reappointment.

The court has appellate jurisdiction in all criminal cases and under such terms and conditions as specified by rules. Appeals from a judgment imposing a sentence of death, life imprisonment or imprisonment for a term greater than fifty years for a single offense or those declaring a state or federal statute unconstitutional are taken directly to the Supreme Court. The court has original jurisdiction concerning admission to the bar, discipline of lawyers and judges, supervision of lower courts and the issuance of writs necessary to the exercise of proper jurisdiction. Upon petition, cases involving substantial questions of law, great public importance or emergencies may also be heard by the court.

Three judges constitute a quorum. The court sits at Indianapolis.

Chief Justice
Randall T. Shepard

Associate Justices
Brent E. Dickson
Frank Sullivan, Jr.
Robert D. Rucker
Theodore R. Boehm

Clerk
Brian Bishop
217 State House
200 West Washington Street
Indianapolis, Indiana 46204
(317) 232-1930

Supreme Court Administrator
Doug Cressler
315 State House
Indianapolis, Indiana 46204
(317) 232-2540

Executive Director
Lilia Judson
Division of State Court Administration
115 West Washington Street, Suite 1080
Indianapolis, Indiana 46204
(317) 232-2542

INDIANA COURT OF APPEALS

The Court of Appeals is Indiana's court of intermediate appellate jurisdiction and is divided into three geographic districts and two statewide at-large districts. Three judges serve each district and primarily review cases brought from their respective districts. Judges are appointed for initial two-year terms by the governor from a list supplied by the Judicial Nominating Commission. Subsequent ten-year terms are by retention election. The chief judge is elected by peer vote for a three-year term. In addition, a presiding judge is chosen in each district by a vote of the judges of that district.

The court has appellate jurisdiction over all cases except those where the Supreme Court has exclusive jurisdiction. The court may also review final decisions of various administrative agencies.

The court sits at Indianapolis.

Chief Judge
Sanford Michael Brook

FIRST DISTRICT includes Bartholomew, Boone, Brown, Clark, Clay, Crawford, Daviess, Dearborn, Decatur, Dubois, Fayette, Floyd, Fountain, Franklin, Gibson, Greene, Hancock, Harrison, Hendricks, Henry, Jackson, Jefferson, Jennings, Johnson, Knox, Lawrence, Martin, Monroe, Montgomery, Morgan, Ohio, Orange, Owen, Parke, Perry, Pike, Posey, Putnam, Randolph, Ripley, Rush, Scott, Shelby, Spencer, Sullivan, Switzerland, Union, Vanderburgh, Vermillion, Vigo, Warrick, Washington and Wayne counties.

Presiding Judge
Edward W. Najam, Jr.

Judges
L. Mark Bailey
John Gatch Baker

SECOND DISTRICT includes Adams, Blackford, Carroll, Cass, Clinton, Delaware, Grant, Hamilton, Howard, Huntington, Jay, Madison, Marion, Miami, Tippecanoe, Tipton, Wabash, Wells and White counties.

Presiding Judge
Ezra H. Friedlander

Judges
James S. Kirsch
Patrick D. Sullivan

THIRD DISTRICT includes Allen, Benton, DeKalb, Elkhart, Fulton, Jasper, Kosciusko, LaGrange, Lake, La Porte, Marshall, Newton, Noble, Porter, Pulaski, St. Joseph, Starke, Steuben, Warren and Whitley counties.

INDIANA COURT OF APPEALS—*Continued*

Presiding Judge
Sanford Michael Brook

Judges
Michael P. Barnes
Paul D. Mathias

FOURTH DISTRICT includes all counties of the state.

Presiding Judge
Carr L. Darden

Judges
Melissa S. Mattingly-May
Patricia A. Riley

FIFTH DISTRICT includes all counties of the state.

Presiding Judge
Margret G. Robb

Judges
John T. Sharpnack
Nancy Harris Vaidik

INDIANA TAX COURT

The Tax Court, established on July 1, 1986, is a court of limited appellate jurisdiction in Indiana. The judge is appointed by the governor for an initial two-year term from a list supplied by the Judicial Nominating Commission. Subsequent ten-year terms are by retention election.

The court has exclusive jurisdiction in original tax appeals, which are defined as cases that arise under state tax laws and which are initial appeals of a final determination made by the Department of Revenue or the State Board of Tax Commissioners. The court also maintains a small claims docket to process claims for refunds from the Department of Revenue that do not exceed $5,000 for any one year and appeals of final determination of assessed value made by the State Board of Tax Commissioners that do not exceed $15,000 for any one year. Appeals are to the Supreme Court.

The court sits at Indianapolis. However, a taxpayer may select to have all evidentiary hearings held in one of seven specifically designated counties.

Judge
Thomas G. Fisher

INDIANA CIRCUIT COURT

The Circuit Court is a court of general jurisdiction in Indiana. The state is divided into ninety circuits. Two of the judicial circuits consist of two counties; the remaining eighty-eight circuits consist of one county each. Judges are elected in partisan elections for six-year terms, except in Vanderburgh County where the judge is elected in a nonpartisan election. Vacancies are filled by the governor from a list supplied by the Judicial Nominating Commission.

The court has original jurisdiction in all civil and criminal matters except where exclusive jurisdiction is conferred upon one of the lower courts. In the absence of lower courts in any county, the Circuit Court assumes the jurisdiction normally reserved for that lower court. The court also has appellate jurisdiction over City and Town Courts. In twenty-two counties, a separate small claims docket has been established by law to hear civil claims of $3,000 or less and possessory actions between landlord and tenant when the amount in controversy does not exceed $3,000. In the remaining counties, small claims dockets have been established either in the Superior or County Courts.

The court sits at each county seat.

County	Judge
Adams	Frederick A. Schurger
Allen	Thomas J. Felts
Bartholomew	Stephen R. Heimann
Benton	Rex W. Kepner
Blackford	Bruce C. Bade
Boone	Steve David
Brown	Judith A. Stewart
Carroll	Joseph W. Carey
Cass	Julian L. Ridlen
Clark	Daniel Francis Donahue
Clay	Ernest E. Yelton
Clinton	Linley E. Pearson
Crawford	Kenneth Lynn Lopp
Daviess	Robert L. Arthur
Dearborn-Ohio	James D. Humphrey
Decatur	John A. Westhafer
DeKalb	Paul R. Cherry
Delaware	Robert L. Barnet, Jr.
	Richard A. Dailey
	John M. Feick
	Wayne J. Lennington
	Marianne L. Vorhees
Dubois	William E. Weikert
Elkhart	Terry C. Shewmaker
Fayette	Daniel Lee Pflum
Floyd	J. Terrence Cody
Fountain	Susan Orr Henderson
Franklin	J. Steven Cox
Fulton	Douglas B. Morton
Gibson	Walter H. Palmer
Grant	Thomas R. Hunt
Greene	David K. Johnson
Hamilton	Judith S. Proffitt
Hancock	Richard D. Culver
Harrison	Harris Lloyd Whitis
Hendricks	Jeffrey V. Boles
Henry	Mary G. Willis
Howard	Lynn Murray
Huntington	Mark A. McIntosh
Jackson	William E. Vance
Jasper	E. Duane Daugherty
Jay	Brian D. Hutchison
Jefferson-Switzerland	Ted R. Todd
Jennings	Jonathan W. Webster
Johnson	K. Mark Loyd
Knox	Sherry L. Biddinger Gregg
Kosciusko	Rex L. Reed
LaGrange	James "Scott" Vanderbeck
Lake	Lorenzo Arredondo
La Porte	Robert W. Gilmore, Jr.
Lawrence	Richard D. McIntyre, Sr.
Madison	Fredrick R. Spencer
Marion	Ted Sosin

INDIANA CIRCUIT COURT—*Continued*

Marshall	Michael D. Cook
Martin	R. Joseph Howell
Miami	Rosemary Higgins Burke
Monroe	Douglas R. Bridges
	E. Michael Hoff
	Marc R. Kellams
	Elizabeth N. Mann
	Viola J. Taliaferro
	Kenneth G. Todd
	David L. Welch
Montgomery	Thomas K. Milligan
Morgan	Mathew G. Hanson
Newton	Jeryl F. Leach
Noble	G. David Laur
Ohio	See Dearborn-Ohio
Orange	Larry R. Blanton
Owen	Frank Mattioda Nardi
Parke	Ronda R. Brown
Perry	James A. McEntarfer
Pike	Lee F. Baker
Porter	Mary R. Harper
Posey	James M. Redwine
Pulaski	Michael A. Shurn
Putnam	Diana LaViolette
Randolph	Jan L. Chalfant
Ripley	Carl H. Taul
Rush	Barbara Arnold Harcourt
St. Joseph	Terry A. Crone
Scott	James D. Kleopfer, Jr.
Shelby	Charles D. O'Connor, Jr.
Spencer	Wayne A. Roell
Starke	David P. Matsey
Steuben	Allen N. Wheat
Sullivan	Paul J. Pierson
Switzerland	See Jefferson-Switzerland
Tippecanoe	Donald L. Daniel
Tipton	Thomas R. Lett
Union	James R. Williams
Vanderburgh	Carl A. Heldt
Vermillion	Bruce V. Stengel
Vigo	David R. Bolk
Wabash	Daniel J. Vanderpool
Warren	Robert M. Hall
Warrick	David O. Kelley
Washington	Robert L. Bennett
Wayne	Douglas H. VanMiddlesworth
Wells	David L. Hanselman, Sr.
White	Robert W. Thacker
Whitley	James R. Heuer

INDIANA SUPERIOR COURTS

The Superior Courts are courts of general jurisdiction which exist in seventy-four counties in Indiana. With the exception of four counties, judges are elected by the voters in partisan elections for six-year terms. Vacancies are filled by the governor from a list supplied by the Judicial Nominating Commission. Judges in Lake and St. Joseph counties are appointed by the governor upon recommendation of a local nominating commission to serve an initial six-year term and thereafter run on a retention ballot. In Vanderburgh County, judges are elected in nonpartisan elections. Judges in Allen County are elected in a general election on a separate ballot without party designation, and vacancies are filled by the governor from a list of candidates nominated by the Allen County Judicial Nominating Commission. As of January 1996, the Marion Municipal Court consolidated with the Marion Superior Court.

The courts are individually created and regulated; therefore, jurisdiction varies from county to county. Generally, the Superior Courts have concurrent civil, criminal and appellate jurisdiction with the Circuit Court and have varying degrees of jurisdiction in probate and juvenile matters. In counties where there are no County Courts, small claims and minor offenses divisions are established in the Superior Courts.

The courts sit at the county seats.

County	Judge
Adams	James A. Heimann
Allen	David J. Avery
	Nancy Eshcoff Boyer
	Frances C. Gull
	Daniel G. Heath
	Stanley A. Levine
	Charles F. Pratt
	Kenneth R. Scheibenberger
	Stephen M. Sims
	John F. Surbeck, Jr.
Bartholomew	Roderick D. McGillivray
	Chris D. Monroe
Blackford	John W. Forcum
Boone	James R. Detamore
	Matthew C. Kincaid
Carroll	Jeffrey R. Smith
Cass	Richard A. Maughmer
	Thomas C. Perrone
Clark	Cecile A. Blau
	Steven Michael Fleece
	Jerry F. Jacobi
Clay	J. Blaine Akers
Clinton	Kathy R. Smith
Daviess	Dean A. Sobecki
Dearborn	G. Michael Witte
Decatur	W. Michael Wilke
DeKalb	Kevin P. Wallace
Dubois	Howard B. Lytton, Jr.
Elkhart	George W. Biddlecome
	David Bonfiglio
	L. Benjamin Pfaff
	Stephen E. Platt
	James W. Rieckhoff
	Olga H. Stickel
Fayette	Ronald T. Urdal
Floyd	Richard G. Striegel
Fulton	Wayne E. Steele
Gibson	Earl G. Penrod
Grant	Natalie R. Conn
	Randall Lee Johnson
	Jeffrey D. Todd
Greene	J. David Holt
Hamilton	Jerry M. Barr
	J. Richard Campbell
	William J. Hughes

INDIANA SUPERIOR COURTS—*Continued*

Hamilton—Cont.	Steven R. Nation
	Wayne A. Sturtevant
Hancock	Dan E. Marshall
	Terry K. Snow
Harrison	Roger D. Davis
Hendricks	David H. Coleman
	Robert W. Freese
	Karen M. Love
Henry	Michael D. Peyton
	Robert Witham
Howard	Stephen M. Jessup
	Dennis H. Parry
	Douglas A. Tate
Huntington	Jeffrey R. Heffelfinger
Jackson	Frank W. Guthrie
Jasper	J. Philip McGraw
Jay	Joel D. Roberts
Jefferson	Fred H. Hoying
Jennings	James Funke, Jr.
Johnson	Kevin Barton
	Cynthia S. Emkes
	Kim VanValer Shilts
Knox	W. Timothy Crowley
	Jim R. Osborne
Kosciusko	Duane G. Huffer
	James C. Jarrette
	Joe V. Sutton
LaGrange	George E. Brown
Lake	
County Division	Julie N. Cantrell
	Sheila Marie Moss
	Nicholas J. Schiralli
	Jesse M. Villalpando
Civil Division	James Danikolas
	William E. Davis
	Jeffery J. Dywan
	John R. Pera
	Robert A. Pete
	Diane Kavadias Schneider
	Gerald N. Svetanoff
Criminal Division	Joan Kouros
	Richard W. Maroc
	Clarence D. Murray
	Thomas P. Stefaniak, Jr.
Juvenile Division	Mary Beth Bonaventura
La Porte	Paul J. Baldoni
	William J. Boklund
	Walter P. Chapala
	Steven E. King
Lawrence	Michael A. Robbins
	William G. Sleva
Madison	Jack L. Brinkman
	Dennis D. Carroll
	Thomas Newman, Jr.
Marion	
Civil Division	Cynthia J. Ayers
	Thomas J. Carroll
	David J. Dreyer
	Steven H. Frank
	John F. Hanley
	Kenneth H. Johnson
	Patrick L. McCarty
	Gary L. Miller
	Robyn L. Moberly
Marion—Cont.	S. K. Reid
	Gerald S. Zore
Criminal Division	Robert R. Altice, Jr.
	Cale J. Bradford
	Linda E. Brown
	Sheila A. Carlisle
	Barbara A. Collins
	Jane Conley
	Patricia J. Gifford
	Evan D. Goodman
	John W. Hammel
	Grant Hawkins
	Reuben B. Hill
	Jane Magnus-Stinson
	William J. Nelson
	Rebekah Pierson-Treacy
	Tanya Walton Pratt
	Clark Rogers
	David A. Shaheed
	Mark D. Stoner
	William E. Young
Environmental and Community Division	Michael D. Keele
Juvenile Division	James W. Payne
Probate/Mental Health Division	Charles J. Deiter
Marshall	Robert O. Bowen
	Dean A. Colvin
Miami	Daniel C. Banina
Montgomery	David A. Ault
Morgan	Christopher L. Burnham
	Jane Spencer Craney
	G. Thomas Gray
Newton	Daniel J. Molter
Noble	Michael J. Kramer
	Stephen S. Spindler
Ohio-Switzerland	John D. Mitchell
Orange	R. Michael Cloud
Porter	William E. Alexa
	Roger V. Bradford
	David L. Chidester
	Julia M. Jent
	Jeffrey L. Thode
Posey	S. Brent Almon
Pulaski	Patrick B. Blankenship
Putnam	Robert J. Lowe
Randolph	Peter D. Haviza
Ripley	James B. Morris
Rush	David E. Northam
St. Joseph	William H. Albright
	Roland W. Chamblee, Jr.
	J. Jerome Frese
	Jenny Pitts Manier
	John M. Marnocha
	William T. Means
	Michael P. Scopelitis
	William C. Whitman
Scott	Nicholas L. South
Shelby	Russell J. Sanders
	Jack A. Tandy
Steuben	William C. Fee
Sullivan	Thomas E. Johnson
Switzerland	See Ohio-Switzerland
Tippecanoe	Thomas H. Busch
	Gregory J. Donat
	Donald C. Johnson
	Lesley A. Meade

INDIANA SUPERIOR COURTS—*Continued*

Tippecanoe—Cont.	Michael A. Morrissey
	Loretta H. Rush
Vanderburgh	Scott R. Bowers
	J. Douglas Knight
	Mary Margaret Lloyd
	Brett J. Niemeier
	Robert J. Pigman
	Robert J. Tornatta
	Wayne S. Trockman
Vigo	Phillip I. Adler
	Barbara L. Brugnaux
	Michael H. Eldred
	R. Jerome Kearns
Wabash	Michael L. Sposeep
Warrick	Robert R. Aylsworth
	Keith A. Meier
Washington	Frank Newkirk, Jr.
Wayne	Darrin M. Dolehanty
	Gregory A. Horn
	P. Thomas Snow
Wells	Everett E. Goshorn
White	Robert B. Mrzlack
Whitley	Michael D. Rush

INDIANA COUNTY COURTS

The County Courts are courts of limited jurisdiction in Indiana which were created by the General Assembly in 1975 to replace Justice of the Peace Courts. County Courts exist in three of the ninety-two counties. Judges are elected from their respective counties for six-year terms. Vacancies are filled by the governor from a list supplied by the Judicial Nominating Commission.

The courts have original and concurrent jurisdiction in all civil actions founded in contract or tort when the amount in question does not exceed $10,000, certain landlord-tenant actions, violations of local ordinances and class D felonies and misdemeanors and infractions. The courts have original exclusive jurisdiction in cases involving possession of property valued at less than $10,000. The courts also have a small claims docket, similar to that of the Circuit Court, where civil cases of up to $3,000 and landlord-tenant possessory actions when the rent due is $3,000 or less may be filed. The courts may conduct preliminary hearings in felony cases. Appeals from the County Courts are to the Court of Appeals.

The courts sit at the county seats unless otherwise indicated.

County	Judge
Floyd	Robert T. Hublar
Madison	Thomas L. Clem
	David W. Hopper
Montgomery	Peggy Quint Lohorn

ST. JOSEPH PROBATE COURT

The St. Joseph Probate Court is the only specialized probate court in Indiana. The judge is elected by the voters of the county for a six-year term. Vacancies are filled by the governor from a list supplied by the Judicial Nominating Commission.

The court has original jurisdiction in all matters pertaining to the probate of wills; appointment of guardians, assignees, executors, administrators and trustees; adoptions; and settlements of incompetents' estates. The court also has exclusive juvenile jurisdiction.

The court sits at South Bend.

Judge
Peter J. Nemeth

MARION COUNTY SMALL CLAIMS COURT

The Small Claims Court of Marion County is a court of limited jurisdiction consisting of nine divisions based on township lines. One judge is elected from each township by its respective township voters to a four-year term. Vacancies are filled by the governor from a list supplied by the Judicial Nominating Commission.

The court has countywide trial jurisdiction concurrent with the Circuit and Superior Courts in all civil actions founded in contract or tort in which the claim does not exceed $6,000, in actions for possession of property in which the claim does not exceed $6,000 and in landlord-tenant cases when the amount in question is less than $6,000. The court may also hear petitions for temporary protective orders. Appeals are de novo to the Marion Superior Court.

The court sits at Indianapolis.

Township Division	Judge
Center	Paula E. Lopossa
Decatur	Jeffrey A. Berg
Franklin	John Kitley
Lawrence	Terry N. Hursh
Perry	J. Myron Barnard
Pike	A. Douglas Stephens
Warren	Lori Kyle Endris
Washington	Lynda F. Huppert
Wayne	Robert Lutz

INDIANA CITY AND TOWN COURTS

Indiana's City and Town Courts are courts of limited jurisdiction which were scheduled to cease operation on December 31, 1979. Since that time several legislative amendments have extended their term. Beginning in 1982 and every fourth year thereafter, second and third class cities or towns may pass ordinances establishing or abolishing city or town courts. A City or Town Court which was in existence on January 1, 1981 may continue in operation until abolished by ordinance. Judges are elected for four-year terms by the voters of their city or town. Vacancies are filled by the governor from a list supplied by the Judicial Nominating Commission.

Jurisdiction of City Courts varies depending upon the size of the city. Generally, all City Courts have jurisdiction over city ordinance violations, misdemeanors and infractions and over civil cases when the amount in question does not exceed $500. In Lake County civil jurisdiction extends to cases in which the amount in controversy does not exceed $3,000. Lake County City Courts have criminal jurisdiction over violation of all state statutes but may impose fines only up to $1,000 or sentences of not more than one year. A City Court in a third class city which is not a county seat has civil jurisdiction of cases involving up to $3,000. Appeals are tried de novo in the Circuit or Superior Court of the county. Carmel City Court is a court of record, and appeals are taken to the Court of Appeals.

Town courts have exclusive jurisdiction over all viola-

INDIANA CITY AND TOWN COURTS—*Continued*

tions of town ordinances, misdemeanors and infractions. Appeals from judgments of a Town Court are also taken to the Circuit or Superior Court of the county.

City or Town	Judge
Alexandria	James L. King
Anderson	Donald R. Phillippe
Attica	Mark W. Mason
Aurora	Avis Rivera
Avon	Maureen T. Owen
Batesville	Joseph P. Radvansky
Bicknell	Jon McKinnon
Bluffton	Lyle J. Cotton
Brownsburg	Charles E. Hostetter
Bunker Hill	David G. Betzner
Burlington	John C. Adams
Butler	Richard L. Obendorf
Carmel	Gail Z. Bardach
Charlestown	George Waters
Clarksville	Joseph P. Weber
Clinton	Carl F. Cloyd
Crown Point	Herman L. Barber, Jr.
Delphi	Kimberly A. Cripe
DeMotte	Gregory Osborn
Dunkirk	Tommy D. Phillips, II
East Chicago	vacancy
Edgewood	Alan R. Miller
Elkhart	Charles H. Grodnik
Elwood	Veronica Mia Roby
Frankfort	George G. Ponton
Franklin	Robert D. Schafstall
Fremont	Marjorie L. Mertz
Gary	Deidre L. Monroe
Gas City	vacancy
Goshen	Cecelia J. McGregor
Greenwood	Lewis J. Gregory
Hagerstown	Rebecca L. Justice
Hammond	Jeffrey A. Harkin
Hobart	William J. Longer
Jamestown	Mary Ann Caldwell
Jeffersonville	Vicki L. Carmichael
Knightstown	Lewis Hayden Butler
Knox	Charles Hasnerl
Lake Station	Kristina C. Kantar
Lawrenceburg	Thomas G. Bauer
Lebanon	Patricia Crow
Lowell	Thomas W. Vanes
Marion	James F. Kocher
Martinsville	Mark Peden
Merrillville	George Paras
Monon	Judith E. Wood
Montpelier	Joe E. Kyle
Mooresville	Susan J. Leib
Muncie	Linda Ralu Smith Wolf
Nappanee	David W. Widmoyer
New Castle	John R. Lansinger
New Haven	Geoff Robison
Noblesville	Gregory L. Caldwell
North Manchester	Cheryl Anne Gohman
Peru	Jeffry Price
Plainfield	James D. Spencer
Portland	Michele Pensinger
Roanoke	Bobby G. Turpin
Rockport	Joseph C. Alvey
Schererville	Debbie A. Riga
Sharpsville	Evelyn R. Holman
Terre Haute	Michael J. Lewis
Thorntown	Donald G. Vaughn
Tipton	Lewis D. Harper
Union City	vacancy
Versailles	Cheryl A. Richmond
Wabash	Ruthanna Christle
Walkerton	Roger L. Huizenga
West Lafayette	Lori Stein Sabol
Whitestown	Wayne Cornwell
Whiting	William W. Ciesar, Jr.
Winchester	Evard E. Thompson
Yorktown	Timothy Gant
Zionsville	Christine J. Atkinson

Indiana Counties and County Seats

Adams
Decatur

Allen
Fort Wayne

Bartholomew
Columbus

Benton
Fowler

Blackford
Hartford City

Boone
Lebanon

Brown
Nashville

Carroll
Delphi

Cass
Logansport

Clark
Jeffersonville

Clay
Brazil

Clinton
Frankfort

Crawford
English

Daviess
Washington

Dearborn
Lawrenceburg

Decatur
Greensburg

DeKalb
Auburn

Delaware
Muncie

Dubois
Jasper

Elkhart
Goshen

Fayette
Connersville

Floyd
New Albany

Fountain
Covington

Franklin
Brookville

Fulton
Rochester

Gibson
Princeton

Grant
Marion

Greene
Bloomfield

Hamilton
Noblesville

Hancock
Greenfield

Harrison
Corydon

Hendricks
Danville

Henry
New Castle

Howard
Kokomo

Huntington
Huntington

Jackson
Brownstown

COUNTIES AND COUNTY SEATS—*Continued*

Jasper
Rensselaer

Jay
Portland

Jefferson
Madison

Jennings
Vernon

Johnson
Franklin

Knox
Vincennes

Kosciusko
Warsaw

LaGrange
LaGrange

Lake
Crown Point

La Porte
La Porte

Lawrence
Bedford

Madison
Anderson

Marion
Indianapolis

Marshall
Plymouth

Martin
Shoals

Miami
Peru

Monroe
Bloomington

Montgomery
Crawfordsville

Morgan
Martinsville

Newton
Kentland

Noble
Albion

Ohio
Rising Sun

Orange
Paoli

Owen
Spencer

Parke
Rockville

Perry
Cannelton

Pike
Petersburg

Porter
Valparaiso

Posey
Mount Vernon

Pulaski
Winamac

Putnam
Greencastle

Randolph
Winchester

Ripley
Versailles

Rush
Rushville

St. Joseph
South Bend

Scott
Scottsburg

Shelby
Shelbyville

Spencer
Rockport

Starke
Knox

Steuben
Angola

Sullivan
Sullivan

Switzerland
Vevay

Tippecanoe
Lafayette

Tipton
Tipton

Union
Liberty

Vanderburgh
Evansville

Vermillion
Newport

Vigo
Terre Haute

Wabash
Wabash

Warren
Williamsport

Warrick
Boonville

Washington
Salem

Wayne
Richmond

Wells
Bluffton

White
Monticello

Whitley
Columbia City

LA PORTE
ST. JOSEPH
ELKHART
LAGRANGE
STEUBEN
LAKE
PORTER
SOUTH BEND DIVISION
NOBLE
DE KALB
MARSHALL
STARKE
KOSCIUSKO
NORTHERN DISTRICT
WHITLEY
ALLEN
JASPER
NEWTON
PULASKI
FULTON
FORT WAYNE DIVISION
WABASH
MIAMI
HUNTINGTON
WELLS
ADAMS
WHITE
CASS
BENTON
CARROLL
HAMMOND DIVISION
GRANT
TIPPECANOE
HOWARD
BLACKFORD
JAY
WARREN
CLINTON
TIPTON
MADISON
DELAWARE
RANDOLPH
FOUNTAIN
MONTGOMERY
BOONE
HAMILTON
VERMILLION
HENRY
WAYNE
PARKE
HENDRICKS
MARION
HANCOCK
INDIANAPOLIS DIVISION
PUTNAM
RUSH
FAYETTE
UNION
SHELBY
VIGO
CLAY
JOHNSON
MORGAN
FRANKLIN
SOUTHERN DISTRICT
OWEN
DECATUR
TERRE HAUTE DIVISION
MONROE
BROWN
BARTHOLOMEW
RIPLEY
DEARBORN
SULLIVAN
GREENE
JENNINGS
JACKSON
LAWRENCE
OHIO
KNOX
DAVIESS
MARTIN
JEFFERSON
SWITZERLAND
WASHINGTON
SCOTT
ORANGE
NEW ALBANY DIVISION
CLARK
PIKE
GIBSON
DUBOIS
CRAWFORD
HARRISON
FLOYD
EVANSVILLE DIVISION
PERRY
POSEY
VANDER-BURGH
WARRICK
SPENCER
UNITED STATES DISTRICT COURTS DISTRICTS OF INDIANA

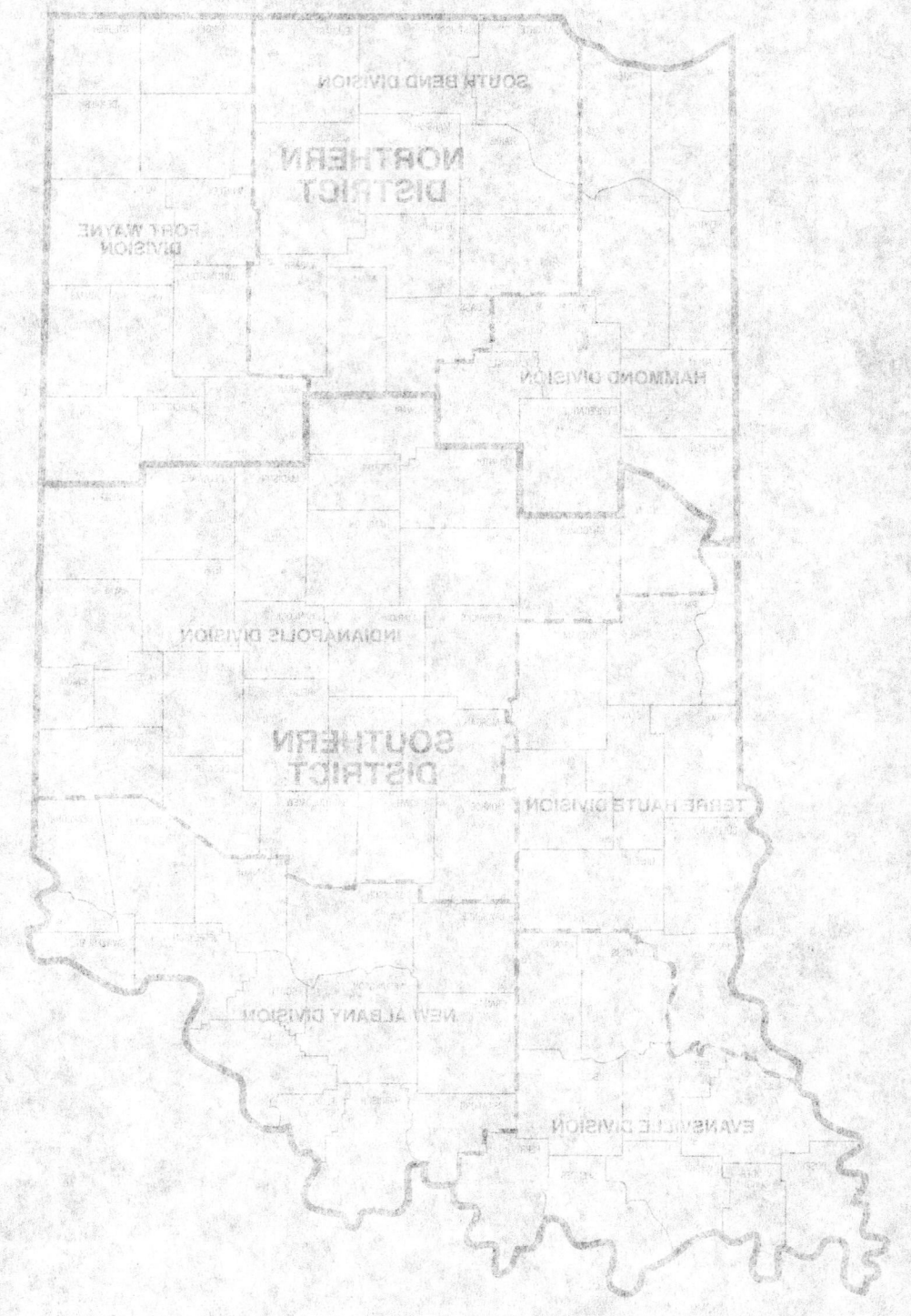

LA PORTE
ST. JOSEPH
ELKHART
LAGRANGE
STEUBEN
LAKE
PORTER
3
NOBLE
DE KALB
MARSHALL
STARKE
KOSCIUSKO
JASPER
WHITLEY
ALLEN
NEWTON
PULASKI
FULTON
WABASH
HUNTINGTON
MIAMI
WELLS
ADAMS
WHITE
CASS
BENTON
CARROLL
GRANT
TIPPECANOE
HOWARD
BLACKFORD
JAY
2
WARREN
CLINTON
TIPTON
MADISON
DELAWARE
FOUNTAIN
RANDOLPH
HAMILTON
MONTGOMERY
BOONE
VERMILLION
HENRY
WAYNE
PARKE
HENDRICKS
MARION
HANCOCK
PUTNAM
RUSH
FAYETTE
UNION
SHELBY
JOHNSON
VIGO
CLAY
MORGAN
FRANKLIN
OWEN
DECATUR
MONROE
BROWN
BARTHOLOMEW
RIPLEY
DEARBORN
SULLIVAN
GREENE
1
JENNINGS
JACKSON
LAWRENCE
OHIO
JEFFERSON
SWITZERLAND
KNOX
DAVIESS
MARTIN
WASHINGTON
SCOTT
ORANGE
CLARK
PIKE
GIBSON
DUBOIS
HARRISON
CRAWFORD
FLOYD
PERRY
POSEY
VANDER-
BURGH
WARRICK
SPENCER

DISTRICTS OF INDIANA COURT OF APPEALS

INDIANA

ADAMS, John C. *(Judge, Burlington Town Court)* Appointed by Governor Robert D. Orr to term beginning Dec 1, 1984. Elected Nov 1987, 1991, 1995 and 1999. Current term expires Dec 31, 2003.

Mailing address: P.O. Box 96, Burlington 46915.

Office: 101 West Seventh Street, Burlington 46915.

Telephone: (765) 566-3672.

ADLER, Phillip I. *(Judge, Vigo Superior Court)* Elected to term beginning Jan 1, 1997. Reelected 2002, current term expires Dec 31, 2008. Educated at Indiana University-Bloomington B.S. 1968 J.D. 1971.

Prosecutor Vigo County 1987-96. Democrat.

Office: 33 South Third Street, Terre Haute 47807-3434.

Telephone: (812) 462-3238.

E-mail address: bufsab2@aol.com

AKERS, J. Blaine *(Judge, Clay Superior Court)* Elected to term beginning Jan 1, 2001. Term expires Dec 31, 2006. Educated at Indiana State University B.S. 1977 and Indiana University-Indianapolis J.D. 1984.

City Attorney Brazil 1985-87. Deputy Prosecutor Clay County and Vigo County 1985-90. Chief Deputy Prosecuting Attorney Putnam County 1999. Member Public Relations Committee Judicial Conference of Indiana, Indiana Judges Association, Clay County and Indiana State Bar Associations. Democrat.

Office: 609 East National Avenue, Brazil 47834-2659.

Telephone: (812) 442-1442.

E-mail address: csc@claynet.com

ALBRIGHT, William H. *(Judge, St. Joseph Superior Court)* Appointed by Governor Robert D. Orr to term beginning Jan 6, 1984. Retained by election. Current term expires Dec 31, 2004. Former Chief Judge. Born Sharon Pennsylvania July 17, 1941. Episcopalian. Educated at Carnegie Institute of Technology B.S.M.E. 1963 and University of Notre Dame J.D. 1967. Moot Court. Member Tau Beta Pi and Pi Tau Sigma. Admitted to practice Indiana 1967. Began legal practice South Bend 1967.

Common Council Attorney 1975 and Prosecutor 1978 St. Joseph County. Member St. Joseph County and Indiana State Bar Associations. Republican.

Office: 101 South Main Street, South Bend 46601-1807.

Telephone: (574) 235-9542.

ALEXA, William E. *(Judge, Porter Superior Court)* Office: 16 East Lincolnway, Valparaiso 46383-5555.

Telephone: (219) 465-3411.

ALMON, S. Brent *(Judge, Posey Superior Court)* Mailing address: P.O. Box 604, Mount Vernon 47620-0604.

Office: Coliseum, 126 East Third Street, Mount Vernon 47620.

Telephone: (812) 838-1325.

ALTICE, Robert R., Jr. *(Judge, Marion Superior Court)* Elected to term beginning Jan 1, 2001. Term expires Dec 31, 2006. Serves Criminal Division. Educated at Miami University, Ohio B.A. 1983, Central Missouri State University M.S. 1984 and University of Missouri-Kansas City J.D. 1987.

Deputy Prosecuting Attorney and Chief Felony Division Marion County 1994-2000.

Office: 200 East Washington Street, Room W-241, Indianapolis 46204.

Telephone: (317) 327-4996.

Fax: (317) 327-4984

E-mail address: baltice@indygov.org

ALVEY, Joseph C. *(Judge, Rockport City Court)* Elected to term beginning Jan 1, 1992. Reelected 1995 and 1999. Current term expires Dec 31, 2003.

Mailing address: P.O. Box 151, Rockport 47635.

Office: 426 Main, Rockport 47635.

Telephone: (812) 649-2242.

ARREDONDO, Lorenzo *(Judge, Lake Circuit Court)* Elected to term beginning Jan 1, 1981. Reelected 1986, 1992 and 1998. Current term expires Dec 31, 2004. Educated at Indiana University A.B. 1965 M.S. in Secondary Education 1967 and University of San Francisco J.D. 1972. Admitted to practice Indiana 1974. Began legal practice East Chicago 1974. Judge, Lake County Court Jan 1, 1977 to Dec 31, 1980.

With the Offices of Lake County Prosecutor 1972-74 and Lake County Assistant Attorney 1974-76. Author "El Chicano y the Constitution, The Legacy of *Hernandez v. Texas,* Grand Jury Discrimination" 6 University of San Francisco L. Rev. 129, Oct 1971, "To Make a Good Decision . . . Law and Experience Alone Are Not Enough" 27 No. 4 The Judges Journal 23 Fall 1988 and "Combating Stereotypes: Sexism and Racism in Courts" 27 No. 4 Court Review 14 Fall 1989. Fellow Indiana Bar Foundation. Co-founder Calumet American Inns of Court. Member Indiana Judges Association (Board of Directors Judicial Conference 1983-85 and 1990-94, Board of Managers 1987-89), American Judicature Society (Board of Managers since 1996, Editorial Committee 1997-98, Executive Committee 1999-2003), Indiana State (Chair Committee on Opportunities for Minorities in the Profession 1995 and 2001, Member Board of Governors 1997-99), Hispanic National (President 1983) and American (Executive Committee National Conference of State Trial Court Judges 1981-84 and 1996-99, Special Committee Youth Education for Citizenship 1983-89, Committee on International Judiciaries 1987, Chair Task Force on Opportunities for Minorities in the Judiciary 1995) Bar Associations. Graduate Indiana Graduate Program for Judges 1997. Faculty Indiana Judicial College and The National Judicial College. Recipient Sherman Minton Judicial Excellence Award 1995 and Rabb Emison Achievement Award 1997.

Office: 2293 North Main Street, Crown Point 46307-1854.

Telephone: (219) 755-3488.

Fax: (219) 755-3484

E-mail address: lalaw@mail.icongrp.com

ARTHUR, Robert L. *(Judge, Daviess Circuit Court)* Appointed by Governor Robert D. Orr to term beginning Oct 15, 1982. Elected 1984, 1990, 1996 and 2002. Cur-

ARTHUR, ROBERT L.—*Continued*

rent term expires Dec 31, 2008. Born Sioux Falls South Dakota Jan 5, 1943. Methodist. Educated at Vincennes University 1963, Indiana State University B.S. 1966 and Indiana University at Indianapolis J.D. 1975. Law Clerk to Hon. Joe Lowdermilk, Indiana Court of Appeals 1973-75. Admitted to practice Indiana 1975. Began legal practice Washington Indiana 1975. Referee, Pike Circuit Court 1980-82.

Member Daviess County and Indiana State Bar Associations. Republican. Member Rotary and Elks Club. Enjoys golf, racquetball, bridge and music.

Mailing address: P.O. Box 268, Washington 47501.

Office: 200 East Walnut Street, Washington 47501-2759.

Telephone: (812) 254-8670.

E-mail address: circuit.court@daviess.org

ATKINSON, Christine J. *(Judge, Zionsville Town Court)* Elected to term beginning Feb 1, 2000. Term expires Dec 31, 2003. Educated at University of California at Davis B.S. 1971, California State University B.S. 1976 and Indiana University J.D. 1993.

Office: 110 South Fourth Street, Zionsville 46077.

Telephone: (317) 873-2469.

E-mail address: atkinson@qserve.net

AULT, David A. *(Judge, Montgomery Superior Court)* Elected to term beginning Jan 1, 1991. Reelected 1996 and 2002. Current term expires Dec 31, 2008. Born Rochester Indiana Jan 27, 1948. Episcopalian. Educated at Wabash College A.B. 1970 and Indiana University School of Law J.D. 1973. Law Clerk to Allen Superior Court 1973-74. Admitted to practice Indiana 1973 and U.S. District Courts Northern 1973 and Southern 1973 Districts of Indiana. In legal practice Crawfordsville 1974-91.

Member Judicial Conference of Indiana (Board of Directors 1994-96, Civil Instructions Committee), Indiana Judges Association (Board of Managers, Chairman Pro Bono Committee District 4), Montgomery County (Past President) and Indiana State Bar Associations.

Office: 100 East Main Street, Crawfordsville 47933-1715.

Telephone: (765) 364-6447.

Fax: (765) 364-6465

E-mail address: dault@wico.net

AVERY, David J. *(Judge, Allen Superior Court)* Appointed by Governor Frank O'Bannon to term beginning Aug 8, 2000. Term expires Dec 31, 2004. Educated at Illinois State University B.S. 1973 and Valparaiso University J.D. 1976.

Member Alternative Dispute Resolution Committee since 2000. Member Benjamin Harrison Inn of Court, Allen County and Indiana State Bar Associations.

Office: 715 South Calhoun, Room 316, Fort Wayne 46802-1805.

Telephone: (260) 449-7463.

E-mail address: djayavery@fwi.com

AYERS, Cynthia J. *(Judge, Marion Superior Court)* Elected to term beginning Jan 1, 1991, Reelected 1996 and 2002. Current term expires Dec 31, 2008. Serves Civil Division. Born Indianapolis Indiana Oct 19, 1947. Protestant. Educated at Indiana University B.A. 1974 M.A. 1978 J.D. 1982. Admitted to practice Indiana 1983 and U.S. District Court Southern District of Indiana 1983. In legal practice Indianapolis 1983-88. Magistrate, Marion Circuit Court 1988-90.

Deputy Prosecutor 1983-85. Trial Attorney Indiana Consumer Counselor 1985-88. Instructor in Business Law and Family Law Indiana Vocational Technical College 1985-86. Member Character and Fitness Committee since 1992 and Domestic Relations Committee since 1995 Indiana Supreme Court, Indianapolis (Board of Managers 1990-92), Marion County (Board of Managers 1990) and Indiana State Bar Associations. Attended Family Law Seminar Colorado Springs 1987, Legal Writing Seminar Harvard University 1991, Judicial Problem Solving 1996 and Evidence Seminar 1997 American Academy of Judicial Education and Court Management Seminar The National Judicial College Reno Nevada 1993. Attended 1990-97 and Faculty Member Sept 1992 Indiana Judicial Conference. Girls Incorporated Forum Series Honoree 1992. Recipient Citizen of the Year Award from National Association of Social Workers 1992 and Service Appreciation Award from International Girl Aid League 1992. Adult Probation Officer Marion County Probation 1972-75. Senior Parole Officer Indiana Department of Corrections 1975-83. Election Commissioner 1988 and 1989. Supporter Indianapolis Symphony Orchestra, Indianapolis Art Museum and Public Television. Enjoys reading and tennis.

Office: 200 East Washington Street, Room W442, Indianapolis 46204.

Telephone: (317) 327-5082.

E-mail address: cayers@indygov.org

AYLSWORTH, Robert R. *(Judge, Warrick Superior Court)* Appointed by Governor B. Evan Bayh July 1, 1993. Elected to term beginning Jan 1, 1995. Reelected Jan 1, 2001, current term expires Dec 31, 2006. Educated at University of Southern Indiana B.S. 1975 and Indiana University-Indianapolis J.D. magna cum laude 1979.

Deputy Prosecuting Attorney 1980-93 and Attorney Area Plan Commission 1988-93 Warrick County. Member Juvenile Justice Improvement Committee Judicial Conference of Indiana, Evansville, Warrick County, Indiana State and American Bar Associations. Democrat. Life Member Indiana University Alumni Association. Member University of Southern Indiana Alumni Association.

Office: 380 Warrick County Judicial Center, One County Square, Boonville 47601.

Telephone: (812) 897-6213.

Fax: (812) 897-6214

BADE, Bruce C. *(Judge, Blackford Circuit Court)* Appointed by Governor Otis Ray Bowen to term beginning July 1, 1975. Elected 1976, 1982, 1988, 1994 and 2000. Current term expires Dec 31, 2006. Educated at Butler University B.S. 1964 and Indiana University J.D. 1968.

Member Indiana Judges Association, Indiana Council of Juvenile and Family Court Judges and Blackford County Bar Association. Graduate Indiana Judicial College 1981. U.S. Army.

Office: 110 West Washington Street, Hartford City 47348-2251.

Telephone: (765) 348-2901.

BAILEY, L. Mark *(Judge, Indiana Court of Appeals First District)* Appointed by Governor Frank O'Bannon Jan 1998. Retained by election Nov 2000, current term expires Dec 31, 2010. Former Presiding Judge. Born

BAILEY, L. MARK—*Continued*

Greensburg Indiana Jan 21, 1957. Educated at University of Indianapolis B.A. 1978, Indiana University J.D. 1982 and Indiana Wesleyan University M.B.A. 1999. Admitted to practice Indiana 1982 and U.S. District Courts Northern 1982 and Southern 1982 Districts of Indiana. In legal practice Indianapolis 1982-90 and Greensburg 1988-90. Administrative Law Judge, Department of Health and Human Services Indiana 1988-90. Former Judge, Decatur County Court. Former Judge, Decatur Superior Court, elected to term beginning Jan 1, 1991.

Former Instructor in General Law, Legal Research and Business Law University of Indianapolis and Ivy Tech. Lecturer Purdue University School of Technology. Member Indiana Judges Association (Board of Managers 1996-2000), Indiana and American Bar Associations. Chair Indiana Pro Bono Commission 1999-2002. Chairman Local Coordinating Council Governor's Task Force for a Drug Free Indiana 1991-94.

Office: 200 West Washington Street, Room 425, Indianapolis 46204-2784.
Telephone: (317) 232-6897.
Fax: (812) 233-0392
E-mail address: lbailey@courts.state.in.us

BAKER, John Gatch *(Judge, Indiana Court of Appeals First District)* Appointed by Governor B. Evan Bayh June 2, 1989. Retained by election. Current term expires Dec 31, 2012. Former Presiding Judge. Born Indianapolis Indiana Oct 4, 1946. Methodist. Educated at Indiana University A.B. 1968 J.D. 1971 and University of Virginia LL.M. 1995. Admitted to practice Indiana 1971. Began legal practice Bloomington 1971. Judge, Monroe County Court Jan 1, 1976 to June 30, 1977. Judge, Monroe Superior Court July 1, 1977 to June 1, 1989. Former Presiding Judge, Indiana Court of Appeals First District, appointed to term June 2, 1989.

Member Indiana Judges Association (Board of Managers since 1979, Secretary-Treasurer 1983-84, Vice President 1985-86, President 1987-89), Judicial Conference of Indiana (Board of Directors 1978-88), American Judicature Society, Monroe County (Treasurer 1972-77), Indiana State and American Bar Associations. Captain USAR 1971-76. Democrat. Enjoys history, sailing, cross country skiing, golf and basketball.

Office: 200 West Washington Street, Room 419, Indianapolis 46204-2784.
Telephone: (317) 232-6895.
Fax: (317) 233-3093
E-mail address: jbaker@courts.state.in.us

BAKER, Lee F. *(Judge, Pike Circuit Court)* Elected to term beginning Jan 1, 2001. Term expires Dec 31, 2006. Educated at Indiana University-Bloomington B.S. 1992 J.D. 1995. USN 1983-88 and 1990-91.

Office: Courthouse, 801 Main Street, Petersburg 47567-0407.
Telephone: (812) 354-6026.
E-mail address: pikejudge@aol.com

BAKER, Tim A. *(Magistrate Judge, United States District Court Southern District of Indiana)* Appointed to term beginning Oct 1, 2001. Term expires 2009. Educated at Indiana University B.A. 1984 and Valparaiso University School of Law J.D. 1989. Law Clerk to Chief Judge Larry J. McKinney, U.S. District Court Southern District of Indiana 1989-91. In legal practice Indianapolis 1991-1995. Assistant U.S. Attorney Southern District of Indiana 1995-2001. Member Local Rules Advisory Committee Southern District of Indiana since 2000. Distinguished Fellow Indianapolis Bar Foundation 2002. Member Indianapolis Bar Association (Chair Labor and Employment Law Section 2000, Co-chair Law Student Division 2002-03, Board of Managers since 2003).

Office: 234 U.S. Courthouse, 46 East Ohio Street, Indianapolis 46204.
Telephone: (317) 229-3660.

BALDONI, Paul J. *(Judge, La Porte Superior Court)* Appointed by Governor Robert D. Orr to term beginning June 1, 1986. Elected to subsequent terms. Current term expires Dec 31, 2008. Born South Bend Indiana Sept 4, 1944. Catholic. Educated at Indiana University B.S. 1966 J.D. 1970. Member Phi Kappa Theta. Admitted to practice Indiana 1970. In legal practice La Porte 1973-76. Judge, La Porte County Court 1976-86.

State Public Defender's Office Indianapolis 1970-73. Member Indiana Judges Association, La Porte City (Past President) and La Porte County Bar Associations.

Office: 809 State Street, La Porte 46350.
Telephone: (219) 326-6808.
Fax: (219) 326-0556
E-mail address: lapsup03@netnitco.net

BANINA, Daniel C. *(Judge, Miami Superior Court)* Elected to term beginning Jan 1, 1997. Reelected 2002, current term expires Dec 31, 2008. Educated at St. Joseph's College B.S. 1979 and Valparaiso University J.D. 1982.

Chief Deputy Prosecutor Franklin County 1984-86 and Miami County 1987-96. President Miami County Bar Association since 1997. Member American Judges Association. Graduate The National Judicial College Reno Nevada 1997. Republican.

Office: 25 North Broadway, Peru 46970-2247.
Telephone: (765) 472-3901.
E-mail address: dcbanina@netusal.net

BARBER, Herman L., Jr. *(Judge, Crown Point City Court)* Elected to term beginning Jan 1, 1976. Reelected to subsequent terms. Current term expires Dec 31, 2003. Born Sharon Pennsylvania Feb 16, 1941. Presbyterian. Educated at DePauw University B.A. 1963 and Valparaiso University J.D. 1966. Admitted to practice Indiana 1966. Began legal practice Crown Point 1966.

Mailing address: P.O. Box 594, Crown Point 46307.
Office: Courthouse Square, Crown Point 46307.
Telephone: (219) 662-3243.

BARDACH, Gail Z. *(Judge, Carmel City Court)* Appointed by Governor Evan Bayh Feb 21, 1993. Elected 1995 and 1999. Current term expires Dec 31, 2003. Educated at Indiana University A.B. 1972 J.D. 1975.

Deputy Prosecuting Attorney Marion County 1975-77. Assistant U.S. Attorney Southern District of Indiana 1977-83.

Office: One Civic Square, Carmel 46032-1751.
Telephone: (317) 571-2440.
Fax: (317) 846-0835
E-mail address: gbardach@ci.carmel.in.us

BARKER, Sarah Evans *(Judge, United States District Court Southern District of Indiana)* Appointed for life by President Ronald Reagan to term beginning March 14, 1984. Chief Judge 1994-2000. Born Mishawaka Indiana June 10, 1943. Educated at Indiana Uni-

BARKER, SARAH EVANS—*Continued*
versity B.S. 1965 and Washington College of Law of American University J.D. 1969.

Assistant U.S. Attorney 1972-76, First Assistant U.S. Attorney 1976-77 and U.S. Attorney 1981-84 Southern District of Indiana. Legislative Assistant to U.S. Representative Gilbert Gude 1969 and U.S. Senator Charles H. Percy 1969-71. Special Counsel to U.S. Senate Government Operations Committee and Subcommittee on Investigations, Washington D.C. 1971-72. Director of Research/Director of Scheduling and Advance Senator Charles H. Percy Reelection Campaign 1972.

Office: 210 U.S. Courthouse, 46 East Ohio Street, Indianapolis 46204.

Telephone: (317) 229-3600.

BARNARD, J. Myron *(Judge, Marion County Small Claims Court Perry Township Division)* Appointed by Governor Edgar D. Whitcomb to term beginning Nov 1972. Elected 1974, 1978, 1982, 1986, 1990, 1994, 1998 and 2002. Current term expires 2006. Born Indianapolis Indiana June 8, 1935. United Church of Christ. Educated at Indiana Central College and American Institute of Banking.

Previously employed by Merchants Bank Indianapolis six years. Republican. Member Southport Jaycees (Past President), Scottish Rite Masonic Lodge and Mural Shine Ancient Landmark 319. Enjoys fishing and woodworking.

Office: 4925 South Shelby Street, Suite 100, Indianapolis 46227-4281.

Telephone: (317) 786-9242.

BARNES, Michael P. *(Judge, Indiana Court of Appeals Third District)* Appointed by Governor Frank O'Bannon to term beginning May 22, 2000. Retained by election 2002, current term expires Dec 31, 2012. Born Dec 2, 1947. Educated at St. Ambrose College B.A. 1970 and University of Notre Dame Law School J.D. 1973. In legal practice St. Joseph County 1973-78 and 1999-2000.

Deputy Prosecuting Attorney 1973-78 and Prosecuting Attorney 1979-98 St. Joseph County. Former Member National Board of Trial Advocacy. Chairman of the Board Indiana Prosecuting Attorneys Council 1982-83 and 1992-93 and American Prosecutor's Research Institute 1997-98. President St. Joseph County Bar Association 1992-93 and National District Attorneys Association 1995-96. Chairman Board of Regents National College of District Attorneys 1997-98. Member National Advisory Council on Violence Against Women 1997.

Office: 200 West Washington Street, Room 409, Indianapolis 46204-2784.

Telephone: (317) 232-6881.

E-mail address: mbarnes@courts.state.in.us

BARNET, Robert L., Jr. *(Judge, Delaware Circuit Court)* Elected to term beginning Jan 1, 1979. Reelected 1984, 1990, 1996 and 2002. Current term expires Dec 31, 2008. Educated at Ball State University B.S. 1968 and Indiana University J.D. 1971.

Chief Deputy Prosecutor 1972-74 and Public Defender 1977-78 Delaware County. Member Delaware County Bar Association (Secretary-Treasurer 1978).

Office: 100 West Washington Street, Muncie 47305-2869.

Telephone: (765) 747-7782.

Fax: (765) 747-7748

E-mail address: rbarnet@co.delaware.in.us

BARR, Jerry M. *(Judge, Hamilton Superior Court)* Appointed by Governor Otis Ray Bowen to term beginning July 1, 1979. Elected 1980, 1986, 1992 and 1998. Current term expires Dec 31, 2004. Educated at Yale University A.B. 1964 and University of Chicago J.D. 1967. Judge, Noblesville City Court 1972-74.

Deputy Prosecutor Hamilton County 1968. Member Probate Committee 1988-96 and Board of Directors 1994-98 Judicial Conference of Indiana. Member Indiana Judges Association (Board of Managers 1998-2001), Indiana Council of Juvenile and Family Court Judges, Hamilton County (President 1978-79), Indiana State and American Bar Associations. Graduate Indiana Judicial College 1985. Republican.

Office: One Hamilton Square, Suite 384, Noblesville 46060-2614.

Telephone: (317) 776-9647.

E-mail address: jmb@co.hamilton.in.us

BARTON, Kevin *(Judge, Johnson Superior Court)* Appointed by Governor Frank O'Bannon to term beginning Oct 2, 2000. Term expires Dec 31, 2006. Educated at Vanderbilt University B.A. magna cum laude 1977 and Indiana University-Indianapolis J.D. cum laude 1980. Note and Development Editor Indiana Law Review 1979-80. Member Phi Beta Kappa.

Deputy Prosecuting Attorney Johnson County 1982-89. President Johnson County Bar Association 2000. Republican.

Office: Five East Jefferson Street, Franklin 46131-2339.

Telephone: (317) 736-3710.

E-mail address: kbarton@co.johnson.in.us

BAUER, Thomas G. *(Judge, Lawrenceburg City Court)* Elected to term beginning Jan 1, 1996. Reelected to subsequent term. Current term expires Dec 31, 2003.

Private First Class U.S. Army 1961-63. Formerly employed by Dearborn Sheriff's Department.

Office: 349 Walnut Street, Lawrenceburg 47025-1909.

Telephone: (812) 537-2772.

E-mail address: lcc@seidata.com

BENNETT, Robert L. *(Judge, Washington Circuit Court)* Appointed by Governor Otis Ray Bowen to term beginning Aug 14, 1980. Elected to subsequent terms. Current term expires Dec 31, 2004. Educated at Indiana University-Bloomington B.S. 1966 J.D. 1973.

Chief Deputy Prosecutor Washington County 1974-80. Member Indiana Judges Association (Board of Managers 1986-89), Washington County, Indiana State and American Bar Associations. Graduate Indiana Judicial College 1989. USAF 1966-70. Democrat.

Office: Courthouse, 99 Public Square, Salem 47167-2098.

Telephone: (812) 883-5302.

E-mail address: circuit@blueriver.net

BERG, Jeffrey A. *(Judge, Marion County Small Claims Court Decatur Township Division)*

Office: 3750 South Foltz Street, Indianapolis 46241.

Telephone: (317) 241-2854.

BETZNER, David G. *(Judge, Bunker Hill Town Court)* Elected to term beginning Jan 1, 1980. Reelected 1983, 1987, 1991, 1995 and 1999. Current term expires

BETZNER, DAVID G.—*Continued*

Dec 31, 2003. Born Tipton Indiana Feb 14, 1954. Methodist.

Fire Chief Pipe Creek Fire Department Bunker Hill. Democrat. Treasurer Bunker Hill Jaycees. Trustee Bunker Hill United Methodist Church. Enjoys fishing and baseball.

Office: 144 West Broadway, Bunker Hill 46914.
Telephone: (765) 689-7494.

BIDDLECOME, George W. *(Judge, Elkhart Superior Court)* Elected to term beginning Jan 1, 1997. Reelected 2002, current term expires Dec 31, 2008. Educated at Wittenberg University B.A. cum laude 1970 and Duke University J.D. 1973.

Deputy Prosecuting Attorney 1974 and 1977-96 and Public Defender 1975 Elkhart County. Republican.

Office: 101 North Main Street, Goshen 46526-3232.
Telephone: (574) 535-6440.
E-mail address: hunt@bnin.net

BLANKENSHIP, Patrick B. *(Judge, Pulaski Superior Court)* Elected to term beginning Jan 1, 2001. Term expires Dec 31, 2006. Educated at Indiana University-Bloomington B.S. 1983 and Valparaiso University J.D. 1989.

Office: 300 Courthouse, 112 East Main Street, Winamac 46996-1208.
Telephone: (574) 946-3371.
E-mail address: pcsupct@pwrtc.com

BLANTON, Larry R. *(Judge, Orange Circuit Court)* Appointed by Governor Frank O'Bannon to term beginning July 21, 1997. Elected to subsequent term. Current term expires Dec 31, 2004. Educated at Campbellsville University B.S. 1969, Western Kentucky University M.P.A. 1984 and University of Louisville J.D. 1989.

Member Orange County, Louisville, Indiana State, Kentucky and American Bar Associations. Specialist 6 USAR 1966-72. Democrat.

Office: Courthouse, "O" Court Street, Paoli 47454-1321.
Telephone: (812) 723-2411.

BLAU, Cecile A. *(Judge, Clark Superior Court)* Elected to term beginning Jan 1, 1997. Reelected 2002, current term expires Dec 31, 2008. Educated at Northern Illinois University B.S. 1966, Indiana University M.S. 1969 and University of Louisville J.D. 1975.

Chair Criminal Benchbook Committee Judicial Conference of Indiana and District 14 Pro Bono Committee. Certified Fellow American Academy of Matrimonial Lawyers. Member Sherman Minton Inns of Court, Indiana Judges Association, Clark County and Indiana State Bar Associations. Democrat.

Office: 501 East Court Avenue, Jeffersonville 47130-4029.
Telephone: (812) 285-6333.
Fax: (812) 285-6380
E-mail address: cblau@protegra.net

BOEHM, Theodore R. *(Associate Justice, Indiana Supreme Court)* Appointed by Governor B. Evan Bayh to term beginning Aug 7, 1996. Retained by election, current term expires Dec 31, 2008. Educated at Brown University A.B. 1960 and Harvard University J.D. 1963.

Office: 200 West Washington Street, Room 324, Indianapolis 46204-2732.
Telephone: (317) 232-2547.
E-mail address: tboehm@courts.state.in.us

BOKLUND, William J. *(Judge, La Porte Superior Court)* Appointed by Governor B. Evan Bayh Dec 13, 1993. Elected Nov 5, 1996. Reelected 2002, current term expires Dec 31, 2008. Educated at Purdue University B.A. with honors 1973 and Valparaiso University School of Law J.D. 1977. Admitted to practice Indiana 1977, U.S. District Courts Southern 1977 and Northern 1979 Districts of Indiana and U.S. Supreme Court 1987. In legal practice La Porte 1978-93.

Director IV-D Child Support Division and Administrative Coordinator Welfare Fraud Division La Porte County. Adjunct Professor of Business Law Purdue University, North Central Campus. Democrat. Named Judge of the Year by Indiana Correctional Association 1977. Recipient Outstanding Part Time Teaching Award from Purdue University, North Central Campus 1998-99 and Excellence in Public Information and Education Award from Indiana Judges Association. Director National Child Support Enforcement Association 1989-92. President Indiana Child Support Alliance 1992-93.

Mailing address: P.O. Box 1091, Michigan City 46361.
Office: 300 West Michigan Street, Suite 116, Michigan City 46360.
Telephone: (219) 872-3101.
E-mail address: wboklund@bigfoot.com

BOLES, Jeffrey V. *(Judge, Hendricks Circuit Court)* Elected to term beginning Jan 1, 1979. Reelected 1984, 1990, 1996 and 2002. Current term expires Dec 31, 2008. Born Indianapolis Indiana Oct 22, 1941. Christian. Educated at Butler University A.B. 1965 and Indiana University School of Law J.D. 1974. Admitted to practice Indiana 1974, U.S. District Courts Southern 1974 and Northern 1977 Districts of Indiana, U.S. Court of Appeals Seventh Circuit 1975, U.S. Tax Court 1976 and U.S. Supreme Court 1978. In legal practice Danville 1972-79.

Instructor in School Law and Business Law Butler University since 1975 and adjunct faculty member Practical Trial Practice Indiana School of Law-Indianapolis and Banking Law University of Indianapolis. Fellow Indiana Bar Foundation. President Indianapolis Law Club 1986-87. Member Indiana Trial Lawyers Association, Indiana State Judges Association, Juvenile Judges Association, Hendricks County, Indianapolis and Indiana State (Committee on Judicial Improvement) Bar Associations. Graduate Indiana Judicial College 1986 and Economics Institute for State Judges University of Kansas 1998. Teacher Pittsboro High School 1967-72. Republican. President Hendricks County Historical Society 1988-89. Interested in school law and Indy racing league.

Mailing address: P.O. Box 349, Danville 46122-0349.
Telephone: (317) 745-9271.
Fax: (317) 745-9256
E-mail address: jvb4@iquest.net

BOLK, David R. *(Judge, Vigo Circuit Court)* Educated at Indiana University-Bloomington B.A. 1985 J.D. 1988. Former Judge, Terre Haute City Court, appointed by Governor B. Evan Bayh to term beginning Jan 5, 1991.

BOLK, DAVID R.—*Continued*

Member Terre Haute City and Indiana State Bar Associations. Democrat.

Office: 33 South Third, Terre Haute 47807-3434.
Telephone: (812) 462-3241.
E-mail address: bratnat3@gte.net

BONAVENTURA, Mary Beth *(Judge, Lake Superior Court)* Magistrate 1982-93. Appointed Judge by Governor B. Evan Bayh April 1, 1993. Retained by election 1998 and 2002. Current term expires Dec 31, 2008. Serves Juvenile Division. Educated at Marian College B.A. 1977 and Northern Illinois University J.D. 1981.

Deputy Prosecutor Lake County 1981-82. Board of Directors since 1993 and Vice President Indiana Council of Juvenile and Family Court Judges. Board of Trustees National Council of Juvenile and Family Court Judges (Chairman Delinquency Committee, Member Dependency, Abuse and Neglect Committee). Board of Managers Indiana Judges Association. Member Juvenile Justice Improvement Committee Judicial Conference of Indiana and Lake County Bar Association. Recipient recognition award for dedicated work from Lake County Bar Association 1982, recognition award for outstanding service to children from Hoosier Boys Town 1991, Morton B. Krantz Award for efforts and dedication toward community mental health 1994 and recognition award for Outstanding Judicial Leadership from National Gang Crime Research Center 1998. Honored for outstanding service to the Criminal Justice field by Calumet College of St. Joseph Criminal Justice Club 1996. Board of Directors American Red Cross, Lake County Mental Health Association and Southlake Mental Health Association. Advisory Board Community Corrections Lake County. Board Member Boys and Girls Club of America since 1993.

Office: 3000 West 93rd Avenue, Crown Point 46307.
E-mail address: judbon@netnitco.net

BONFIGLIO, David *(Judge, Elkhart Superior Court)* Elected to term beginning Jan 1, 2001. Term expires Dec 31, 2006. Educated at University of Notre Dame B.A. 1977 and Valparaiso University J.D. 1982. Magistrate, Elkhart Circuit Court 1985-2000.

Member Indiana Council of Juvenile and Family Court Judges, National Council of Juvenile and Family Court Judges, National Association of Drug Court Professionals, Indiana State and American Bar Associations. Republican.

Office: 315 South Second Street, Elkhart 46516.
Telephone: (574) 523-2374.
Fax: (574) 523-2392
E-mail address: dbonfi5665@aol.com

BOWEN, Robert O. *(Judge, Marshall Superior Court)* Elected to term beginning Jan 1, 1995. Reelected 2000, current term expires Dec 31, 2006. Born Bremen Indiana July 31, 1952. Lutheran. Educated at Indiana University B.S. 1974 and Valparaiso University J.D. 1977. Law Clerk to Indiana Supreme Court 1977-78. In legal practice Columbus 1978 and Bremen 1986-94. Judge, Marshall County Court 1981-86. Small Claims Referee, Whitley Superior Court 1987-93.

Indiana Legislative Services Agency 1978-80. Board of Managers Indiana Judges Association 1982-86. Member Marshall County and Indiana State Bar Associations. Republican.

Office: 211 West Madison Street, Suite 301, Plymouth 46563-1707.
Telephone: (574) 935-8740.
Fax: (574) 935-9967
E-mail address: robb@co.marshall.in.us

BOWERS, Scott R. *(Judge, Vanderburgh Superior Court)* Elected to term beginning Jan 1, 1985. Reelected 1990, 1996 and 2002. Current term expires Dec 31, 2008. Former Chief Judge. Educated at Indiana University A.B. 1972 and University of Houston J.D. 1975.

Deputy Prosecutor Evansville 1976-80 and 1984. Member Indiana Judges Association (Board of Managers 1991-94).

Office: 116 Courts Building, 825 Sycamore Street, Evansville 47708-1833.
Telephone: (812) 426-5400.
E-mail address: sbowers@vanderburghgov.org

BOYER, Nancy Eshcoff *(Judge, Allen Superior Court)* Referee 1990-91. Appointed Judge by Governor B. Evan Bayh Aug 2, 1991. Elected to subsequent term. Current term expires Dec 31, 2004. Educated at DePauw University B.A. cum laude 1973 and Indiana University-Indianapolis J.D. cum laude 1976.

Board of Directors Judicial Conference of Indiana 1996-98. Member Character and Fitness Committee Indiana Supreme Court and Allen County Bar Association. Member Indiana Commission for Continuing Legal Education 1991-96. Board of Directors Allen County Courthouse Preservation Trust.

Office: 715 South Calhoun Street, Room 318, Fort Wayne 46802-1805.
Telephone: (260) 449-7251.
E-mail address: nboyer@fwi.com

BRADFORD, Cale J. *(Judge, Marion Superior Court)* Elected to term beginning Jan 1, 1997. Reelected 2002, current term expires Dec 31, 2008. Serves Criminal Division. Educated at Indiana University B.S. 1982 J.D. 1986.

Assistant U.S. Attorney Southern District of Indiana June 1990 to Jan 1995. Chief Trial Deputy Marion County Prosecutor's Office 1995-96. Republican. Board of Directors Craine House.

Office: 200 East Washington Street, Room W-242, Indianapolis 46204-3307.
Telephone: (317) 327-4533.
E-mail address: cbradfor@indygov.org

BRADFORD, Roger V. *(Judge, Porter Superior Court)* Appointed by Governor Robert Orr to term beginning June 23, 1981. Elected 1984, 1990, 1996 and 2002. Current term expires Dec 31, 2008. Born Gary Indiana March 14, 1945. Lutheran. Educated at Indiana State University B.A. 1967 and Valparaiso University J.D. 1973. Admitted to practice Indiana 1973 and U.S. District Courts Southern 1973 and Northern 1973 Districts of Indiana. Began legal practice Portage 1973. Judge, Porter County Court 1979-81.

Adjunct Professor Valparaiso University School of Law. Member Porter County American Inns of Court, Indiana Judges Association, Porter County and Indiana State Bar Associations. Republican.

Office: 16 Lincolnway, #338, Valparaiso 46383-5555.
Telephone: (219) 465-3410.

BRADFORD, ROGER V.—*Continued*

Fax: (219) 465-3648
E-mail address: rbrad@porterco.org

BRIDGES, Douglas R. *(Judge, Monroe Circuit Court)* Assumed office Jan 1, 1991. Elected to subsequent term. Current term expires Dec 31, 2006. Born Indianapolis Indiana Feb 12, 1935. Episcopalian. Educated at Purdue University B.S.M.E. 1957 and Indiana University-Bloomington J.D. 1966. Member Phi Alpha Delta. Admitted to practice Indiana 1966 and U.S. District Court Southern District of Indiana 1966. In legal practice Bloomington Sept 1966 to Dec 1971 and Jan 1979 to Sept 1985. Judge, Monroe Superior Court 1972-78, appointed by Governor Edgar D. Whitcomb. Judge, Monroe Superior Court 1985-90, appointed by Governor Robert D. Orr.

Majority Attorney Indiana House of Representatives Jan 1971 to May 1971. Important Decision: Zoss v. Royal Chevrolet 197 (revocation of acceptance under UCC). Instructor in Law 1972-74 and Forensics 1975-76 Indiana University. Member Monroe County (President 1986), Indiana State and American Bar Associations. Graduate The National Judicial College 1973 and Indiana Judicial College Indiana Judicial Conference 1985. Lieutenant USN 1957-59 and USNR 1959-66. Previously employed as inspection engineer Phillips Petroleum Company Bartlesville Oklahoma. Republican. Member Indiana University Varsity Club (President), Boys Club Board (President), Rotary (President) and United Way. Enjoys bicycling, racquetball, gardening, spectator sports and travel.

Office: Courts Building, 301 North College Avenue, Bloomington 47401-3865.
Telephone: (812) 349-2644.
E-mail address: judgerandy@co.monroe.in.us

BRINKMAN, Jack L. *(Judge, Madison Superior Court)* Elected to term beginning Jan 1, 1979. Reelected 1984, 1990, 1996 and 2002. Current term expires Dec 31, 2008. Born Seymour Indiana June 23, 1950. Protestant. Educated at Indiana University at Indianapolis B.S. with honors 1972 J.D. with honors 1975. Admitted to practice Indiana 1975. Began legal practice Anderson 1975.

Member Indiana Council of Juvenile and Family Court Judges, National Council of Juvenile and Family Court Judges, Madison County and Indiana State Bar Associations. Democrat.

Office: 16 East Ninth Street, Anderson 46016-1574.
Telephone: (765) 641-9627.

BROOK, Sanford Michael *(Chief Judge, Indiana Court of Appeals and Presiding Judge, Indiana Court of Appeals Third District)* Appointed by Governor Frank O'Bannon Sept 16, 1998. Retained by election 2000, current term expires 2010. Chief Judge since 2002. Born South Bend Indiana June 23, 1949. Jewish. Educated at Indiana University at Bloomington B.A. with honors 1971 J.D. 1974. Admitted to practice Indiana 1974. In legal practice South Bend 1974-84. Former Judge, St. Joseph Superior Court, appointed by Governor Robert D. Orr to term beginning Jan 1, 1987.

Part-time Deputy City Attorney 1976-78, part-time Deputy Prosecuting Attorney 1979-83 and Deputy Prosecuting Attorney 1984-86 South Bend. Adjunct Associate Professor of Law University of Notre Dame Law School since 1987. Member St. Joseph County, Indiana State and American Bar Associations. Faculty member National Institute of Trial Advocacy since 1986. Democrat.

Office: 200 West Washington Street, Room 416, Indianapolis 46204-2784.
Telephone: (317) 232-6882.
E-mail address: sbrook@courts.state.in.us

BROWN, George E. *(Judge, LaGrange Superior Court)* Appointed by Governor Robert D. Orr to term beginning Jan 1, 1988. Elected 1990, 1996 and 2002. Current term expires Dec 31, 2008. Educated at Ball State University B.S. 1969 and DePaul University J.D. 1974. Admitted to practice Indiana 1974. Chief Deputy Prosecutor LaGrange County 1975-77. Judge, LaGrange County Court April 24, 1984 to Dec 31, 1987.

Office: 105 North Detroit Street, LaGrange 46761-1896.
Telephone: (260) 463-7396.
E-mail address: gebrown@ligtel.com

BROWN, Linda E. *(Judge, Marion Superior Court)* Commissioner 2000. Elected Judge to term beginning Jan 1, 2001. Term expires Dec 31, 2006. Serves Criminal Division. Educated at Indiana State University B.S. 1977 and Indiana University-Indianapolis J.D. 1991.

Public Defender Marion County 1996.

Office: 200 East Washington Street, Room E-608, Indianapolis 46204.
Telephone: (317) 327-3850.
E-mail address: lebrown@indygov.org

BROWN, Ronda R. *(Judge, Parke Circuit Court)* Elected to term beginning Jan 1, 1993. Reelected 1998, current term expires Dec 31, 2004. Born Clinton Indiana Oct 20, 1963. Methodist. Educated at Indiana State University B.S. 1986 and Valparaiso University School of Law J.D. 1989. Admitted to practice Indiana 1989 and U.S. District Courts Northern 1989 and Southern 1989 Districts of Indiana. In legal practice Rockville 1989-93.

Attorney Parke County 1989-93 and Town of Rockville 1989-93. Deputy Prosecuting Attorney Parke County 1991-93. Member Indiana Judges Association, Indiana Council of Juvenile and Family Court Judges, National Council of Juvenile and Family Court Judges and American Bar Association (Judicial Administration Division). Member National Federation of Republican Women. Enjoys horseback training and riding.

Office: 201 Courthouse, 116 West High Street, Rockville 47872-1782.
Telephone: (765) 569-5671.
E-mail address: pccourt@bloomingdaletel.com

BRUGNAUX, Barbara L. *(Judge, Vigo Superior Court)* Term expires Dec 31, 2008. Educated at St. Mary-of-the-Woods College B.A. 1970, The Ohio State University M.A. 1974 and Indiana University-Bloomington J.D. 1974. Judge pro tem Feb 1994 to June 1996 and Former Judge, Vigo County Court, appointed to term beginning June 12, 1996.

Deputy Prosecuting Attorney Vigo County 1987-94. Member Indiana Judges Association, National Association of Women Judges, Terre Haute and Indiana State Bar Associations. Democrat.

Office: 33 South Third Street, Terre Haute 47807.
Telephone: (812) 462-3266.
E-mail address: brugnauxb@aol.com

BURKE, Rosemary Higgins *(Judge, Miami Circuit Court)*
Office: 25 North Broadway, Peru 46970-2247.
Telephone: (765) 472-3901.

BURNHAM, Christopher L. *(Judge, Morgan Superior Court)* Magistrate 1986-93. Elected Judge July 1, 1993. Reelected 1998, current term expires Dec 31, 2004. Educated at Carroll College B.A. 1974 and Indiana University-Bloomington J.D. 1982. Magistrate, Morgan Circuit Court 1986-93.
Chief Deputy Prosecutor Morgan County 1983-85. Public Defender Hendricks Superior Court 1985-86. Adjunct Faculty Member Business Law Marian College 1985-86. Board of Directors 1994-2000 and Chair Juvenile Benchbook Committee 1995-99 Judicial Conference of Indiana. Board of Directors Indiana Council of Juvenile and Family Court Judges. Graduate Indiana Judicial College 1997. Captain USMC 1974-79. Lieutenant Colonel Indiana Air National Guard since 1980. Republican.
Office: 10 East Washington Street, Martinsville 46151-1482.
Telephone: (765) 349-5051.
E-mail address: cburnham@scican.net

BUSCH, Thomas H. *(Judge, Tippecanoe Superior Court)*
Office: 301 Main Street, Lafayette 47901-1354.
Telephone: (765) 423-9293.

BUTLER, Lewis Hayden *(Judge, Knightstown Town Court)* Appointed by Governor Frank O'Bannon to term beginning July 24, 1998. Elected 1999, current term expires Dec 31, 2003.
Office: 203 East Main Street, Knightstown 46148-1277.
Telephone: (765) 345-2803.

CALDWELL, Gregory L. *(Judge, Noblesville City Court)* Elected Nov 5, 1991 to term beginning Jan 1, 1992. Reelected 1995 and 1999. Current term expires Dec 31, 2003. Born Elwood Indiana March 11, 1942. Protestant. Educated at Indiana University A.B. 1964 J.D. 1968. Member Phi Delta Phi. Admitted to practice Indiana 1968, U.S. District Court Southern District of Indiana 1968, U.S. Court of Appeals Seventh Circuit 1968 and U.S. Supreme Court 1979. In legal practice Tipton 1968-72 and Noblesville since 1972.
Deputy Prosecutor Tipton County 1968-70 and Hamilton County 1972-77. Member Hamilton County Bar Association. Attended seminar on Advanced Evidence The National Judicial College July 1992.
Office: 135 South Ninth Street, Noblesville 46060-2608.
Telephone: (317) 776-6344.

CALDWELL, Mary Ann *(Judge, Jamestown Town Court)* Elected to term beginning Jan 1, 2000. Term expires Dec 31, 2003.
Office: 21 East Main Street, Jamestown 46147.
Telephone: (765) 676-6331.

CAMPBELL, J. Richard *(Judge, Hamilton Superior Court)* Elected to term beginning Jan 1, 1997. Reelected 2002, current term expires Dec 31, 2008. Educated at University of Evansville B.S. 1975 and Indiana University-Indianapolis J.D. 1983.
Deputy Prosecutor Hamilton County 1984-88. Member Hamilton County Bar Association. Assistant Director of Publications Indiana Judicial Center 1983-84. Member Fishers Planning Commission 1989-91. Republican.
Office: One Hamilton County Square, Suite 292, Noblesville 46060-2614.
Telephone: (317) 776-9612.
E-mail address: jrc@co.hamilton.in.us

CANTRELL, Julie N. *(Judge, Lake Superior Court)* Elected to term beginning Jan 1, 1997. Retained by election 2002, current term expires Dec 31, 2008. Serves County Division. Educated at Purdue University B.S. 1990 and University of Tulsa J.D. 1993.
Deputy Prosecuting Attorney Lake County 1993-96. Member Calumet Inns of Court. Instructor Northwest Indiana Law Enforcement Training Academy.
Office: 2293 North Main Street, Crown Point 46307-1854.
Telephone: (219) 755-3601.
E-mail address: ballenti@mail.icongrp.com

CAREY, Joseph W. *(Judge, Carroll Circuit Court)* Elected to term beginning Jan 1, 1991. Reelected 1996 and 2002. Current term expires Dec 31, 2008. Born Logansport Indiana May 25, 1926. Protestant. Educated at Indiana University B.S. 1950 LL.B. 1953. Member Phi Delta Phi. Admitted to practice Indiana 1953 and U.S. District Courts Northern 1953 and Southern 1953 Districts of Indiana. In legal practice Lafayette 1953-81. Magistrate, U.S. District Court Northern District of Indiana 1955-81.
Member Indiana Judges Association, Carroll County and Indiana State Bar Associations. Attended The National Judicial College 1990 and 1994. USNR 1944-1946. Republican.
Mailing address: P.O. Box 28, Delphi 46923-0028.
Telephone: (765) 564-3711.
E-mail address: jcarey@dcwi.com

CARLISLE, Sheila A. *(Judge, Marion Superior Court)* Elected to term beginning Jan 1, 2001. Term expires Dec 31, 2006. Serves Criminal Division. Educated at Indiana University-Bloomington B.S. 1985 J.D. 1987.
Deputy Prosecutor 1988-90 and Chief Trial Deputy Prosecutor 1995-2000 Marion County. Chief Deputy Prosecutor Johnson County 1991-94. Republican.
Office: 200 East Washington Street, Room T-401, Indianapolis 46204.
Telephone: (317) 327-8673.
E-mail address: scarlisl@indygov.org

CARMICHAEL, Vicki L. *(Judge, Jeffersonville City Court)* Elected to term beginning Jan 1, 2000. Term expires Dec 31, 2003. Educated at Indiana University Southeast B.A. 1984 and University of Louisville J.D. 1987.
Staff Attorney Kentucky Supreme Court 1987-88. Chief Public Defender 1989-94. Assistant Public Defender since 1994. Recipient Pro Bono Public Service Award from Clark-Floyd County 1997. Member Clark County, Kentucky and American Bar Associations. Democrat.
Office: 501 East Court Avenue, Room 263, Jeffersonville 47130-4029.
Telephone: (812) 285-6431.
E-mail address: vickilaw1@aol.com

CARROLL, Dennis D. *(Judge, Madison Superior Court)* Elected to term beginning Jan 1, 1981. Reelected 1986, 1992 and 1998. Current term expires Dec 31, 2004. Born Mount Vernon Illinois May 1, 1947. Mem-

CARROLL, DENNIS D.—*Continued*

ber North Anderson Church of God. Educated at Anderson University B.A. 1969 and Indiana University J.D. 1974. Admitted to practice Indiana 1974.
Office: 16 East Ninth Street, Anderson 46016-1574.
Telephone: (765) 641-9622.
Fax: (765) 640-4217

CARROLL, Thomas J. *(Judge, Marion Superior Court)* Assumed office Jan 1, 1996. Elected 2000, current term expires Dec 31, 2006. Serves Civil Division. Educated at Indiana University B.S. 1964 J.D. 1967. Bailiff Marion Municipal Court 1965-66. Judge, Marion Municipal Court Jan 1, 1988 to Dec 31, 1995, appointed by Governor Robert D. Orr.
U.S. Trustee U.S. Bankruptcy Court Southern District of Indiana 1978-87. Board of Managers Indiana Judges Association 1991-94. Member American Judges Association and Indianapolis Bar Association. Democrat.
Office: 200 East Washington Street, Room W542, Indianapolis 46204-3307.
Telephone: (317) 327-3870.
E-mail address: tcarroll@indygov.org

CHALFANT, Jan L. *(Judge, Randolph Circuit Court)* Elected to term beginning Jan 1, 1993. Reelected 1998, current term expires Dec 31, 2004. Educated at DePauw University B.A. 1964 and Indiana University-Bloomington J.D. 1968.
Prosecuting Attorney Randolph County 1975-87. Republican.
Office: Courthouse, 100 South Main Street, Winchester 47394-1888.
Telephone: (765) 584-7070.
E-mail address: judge99@connectiva.net

CHAMBLEE, Roland W., Jr. *(Judge, St. Joseph Superior Court)* Appointed by Governor B. Evan Bayh to term beginning July 1, 1990. Retained by election Nov 1992 and Nov 1998. Current term expires Dec 31, 2004. Born Nashville Tennessee Dec 23, 1951. Catholic. Educated at University of Notre Dame B.A. 1973 J.D. 1977. Admitted to practice Indiana 1977. In legal practice South Bend 1978-89. Magistrate, St. Joseph Circuit Court 1989-90.
Office: 101 South Main Street, Room 20, South Bend 46601-1807.
Telephone: (574) 235-9051.
E-mail address: rwcjr1251@aol.com

CHAPALA, Walter P. *(Judge, La Porte Superior Court)* Elected to term beginning Jan 1, 1991. Reelected 1996 and 2002. Current term expires Dec 31, 2008. Educated at Indiana University B.S. 1964 and Valparaiso University J.D. 1970.
Prosecuting Attorney La Porte County 1979-90. Democrat.
Office: 200 Courthouse, 300 Washington Street, Michigan City 46360.
Telephone: (219) 872-2505.

CHERRY, Paul R. *(Judge, DeKalb Circuit Court)* Elected to term beginning Jan 1, 1989. Reelected 1994 and 2000. Current term expires Dec 31, 2006. Born Charlotte Michigan Feb 24, 1951. Religious affiliation: United Brethren. Educated at Huntington College B.A. with honors 1973 and Ohio Northern University J.D. 1977. Admitted to practice Indiana 1978, Ohio 1978, U.S. District Courts Northern 1978 and Southern 1978 Districts of Indiana, U.S. Court of Appeals Seventh Circuit 1978 and U.S. Supreme Court 1981. In legal practice Auburn Indiana area 1978-88.
Deputy Prosecuting Attorney 1980-82 and Prosecuting Attorney 1983-88 DeKalb County. Instructor in Business Law and American Constitutional Development Huntington College since 1980. Member Indiana Prosecuting Attorneys Association 1983-88. Member Judicial Conference of Indiana, Indiana Judges Association, Christian Legal Society, DeKalb County and Indiana State Bar Associations. Named Sagamore of the Wabash by Governor of Indiana 1981, Honorary Secretary of State 1986 and Honorary Attorney General 1987. Republican. Member DeKalb Oratorio Chorus, and Board of Trustees Huntington College (Chairman). Enjoys reading and all sports.
Office: 100 South Main Street, Auburn 46706-2361.
Telephone: (260) 925-2764.

CHIDESTER, David L. *(Judge, Porter Superior Court)*
Office: 16 East Lincolnway, #228, Valparaiso 46383-5643.
Telephone: (219) 465-3412.

CHRISTLE, Ruthanna *(Judge, Wabash City Court)*
Office: 23 West Market Street, Wabash 46992-3128.
Telephone: (260) 563-4946.

CIESAR, William W., Jr. *(Judge, Whiting City Court)* Elected to term beginning Jan 1, 1996. Reelected 1999, current term expires Dec 31, 2003. Educated at Purdue University B.S. 1982 M.S. 1982, Valparaiso University J.D. 1988 and Chicago-Kent College of Law LL.M. 1997.
Member Chicago, Lake County, Indiana State and American Bar Associations.
Mailing address: P.O. Box 230, Whiting 46394.
Office: 1443-119th Street, Whiting 46394-1742.
Telephone: (219) 659-4688.
E-mail address: wccourt@whitingcitycourt.com

CLEM, Thomas L. *(Judge, Madison County Court)* Elected to term beginning Jan 1, 1991. Reelected 1996 and 2002. Current term expires Dec 31, 2008. Born Marion Indiana Sept 17, 1952. Educated at Ball State University B.A. with honors 1977 and Indiana University J.D. 1980. Admitted to practice Indiana 1981 and U.S. District Court Southern District of Indiana 1981.
Deputy Prosecutor Madison County 1985-90. Council Attorney Madison County 1988-90. Instructor in Criminal Law and Procedure Anderson University 1988. Member Indiana Judges Association, Madison County, Indiana State and American Bar Associations.
Office: 16 East Ninth Street, Anderson 46016-1576.
Telephone: (765) 641-9497.

CLOUD, R. Michael *(Judge, Orange Superior Court)* Elected to term beginning Jan 1, 1997. Reelected 2002, current term expires Dec 31, 2008. Educated at Indiana University A.B. 1980 J.D. 1985. Former Judge, Orange County Court, elected to term beginning Jan 1, 1997.
Chief Deputy Prosecutor Orange County 1985-97. Republican.
Office: County Complex Building, 205 East Main Street, Box 216, Paoli 47454.
Telephone: (812) 723-2403.
E-mail address: superiorcourt@co.orange.in.us

CLOYD, Carl F. *(Judge, Clinton City Court)* Elected to term beginning Jan 1, 1984. Reelected Nov 7, 1987, Nov 3, 1991, 1995 and Nov 2, 1999. Current term expires Dec 31, 2003. Born Clinton Indiana Sept 29, 1918. Religious affiliation: Disciples of Christ.

Sergeant USAS Infantry 1943-46. Employed by U.S. Postal Service 1938-80 (Postmaster Clinton 1961-80). Democrat. Elder First Christian Church. President Clinton Little League 1955. District Representative Little League Congress 1959-60. President Wabash Valley semi-pro league 1962. Worshipful Master 1963 and Secretary since 1970 Jerusalem Lodge 99 F&AM. 33° Scottish Rite Valley of Terre Haute. Presiding officer all York Rite bodies of Masonry KYCH 1970. State President National Association of Postmasters U.S. 1977. Vice President Indiana Postmasters Retired since 1987. Enjoys golf and gardening.

Office: 259 Vine Street, Clinton 47842-2199.
Telephone: (765) 832-9444.

COACHYS, James K. *(Judge, United States Bankruptcy Court Southern District of Indiana)* Appointed to term beginning Oct 1, 2000. Term expires 2014. Born Newark New Jersey Aug 5, 1946. Catholic. Educated at Butler University B.S. 1969 and Indiana University J.D. with honors 1974. Admitted to practice Indiana 1974 and U.S. District Court Southern District of Indiana 1974. In legal practice Franklin 1974-86. Juvenile Referee, Johnson Circuit Court 1987-88. Judge, Johnson Superior Court Jan 1, 1989 to Sept 30, 2000.

Author *Indiana Evidence Workshop Handbook* Professional Education Systems, Inc. 1989. Member Indiana Trial Lawyers Association, The Association of Trial Lawyers of America, Johnson County, Indiana State and American Bar Associations. Instructor Indiana Evidence Workshop Professional Education Systems, Inc. Oct 12, 1989. Staff Sergeant USAR 1969-76. Financial Analyst Ford Motor Co. 1969-72.

Office: 322 U.S. Courthouse, 46 East Ohio Street, Indianapolis 46204.
Telephone: (317) 229-3870.

CODY, J. Terrence *(Judge, Floyd Circuit Court)* Elected Nov 3, 1998 to term beginning Jan 1, 1999. Term expires Dec 31, 2004. Born New Albany Indiana Nov 7, 1949. Roman Catholic. Educated at Xavier University A.B. 1971 and Indiana University J.D. 1974. Admitted to practice Indiana 1974 and U.S. District Court Southern District of Indiana 1974. In legal practice New Albany 1974-99.

Member American Judicature Society, National Council of Family and Juvenile Court Judges, Indiana State and American Bar Associations. Democrat.

Office: 311 Hauss Square, Room 417, New Albany 47150-5856.
Telephone: (812) 948-5455.
Fax: (812) 948-4735
E-mail address: circuit@floydcounty.in.gov

COLEMAN, David H. *(Judge, Hendricks Superior Court)* Elected to term beginning Jan 1, 1991. Reelected 1996 and 2002. Current term expires Dec 31, 2008. Born Lafayette Indiana March 23, 1948. Protestant. Educated at Indiana State University B.S. 1970 and Indiana University School of Law J.D. 1974. Admitted to practice Indiana 1974 and U.S. District Court Southern District of Indiana 1974. In legal practice Danville 1974-90.

Prosecuting Attorney Hendricks County 1979-90. Board of Directors Indiana Judicial Conference. Member Indiana Judges Association, Hendricks County (President 1978-79) and Indiana State Bar Associations. Attended The National Judicial College Jan 1991, March 1991, Jan 1992, Jan 1993, Aug 1993 and Jan 1995. Teacher Brownsburg High School 1970-72. Member Danville Rotary Club.

Office: One Courthouse Square, #107, Danville 46122.
Telephone: (317) 745-9244.
Fax: (317) 745-9375
E-mail address: dcthejudge@aol.com

COLLINS, Barbara A. *(Judge, Marion Superior Court)* Elected to term beginning Jan 1, 2001. Term expires Dec 31, 2006. Serves Criminal Division. Educated at University of Illinois at Chicago B.S.N. 1977 and Indiana University M.S.N. 1981 J.D. 1984.

Office: 200 East Washington Street, Room E-643, Indianapolis 46204.
Telephone: (317) 327-3202.
E-mail address: bcollins@indygov.org

COLVIN, Dean A. *(Judge, Marshall Superior Court)* Appointed by Governor Robert D. Orr to term beginning April 7, 1986. Elected Nov 6, 1990, 1996 and 2002. Current term expires Dec 31, 2008. Served Marshall County Court April 7, 1986 to June 1, 1988. Born Marshall County Indiana April 15, 1952. Educated at Indiana University B.S. 1978 and Valparaiso University School of Law J.D. 1983. Admitted to practice Indiana 1983.

Deputy Attorney General Indiana 1983-84.

Office: 211 West Madison Street, Plymouth 46563.
Telephone: (574) 935-8763.
Fax: (574) 935-5041

CONLEY, Jane *(Judge, Marion Superior Court)* Serves Criminal Division.

Office: 9049 East Tenth Street, Indianapolis 46219.
Telephone: (317) 327-7995.

CONN, Natalie R. *(Judge, Grant Superior Court)* Elected to term beginning Jan 1, 1997. Reelected 2002, current term expires Dec 31, 2008. Born Marion Indiana Nov 22, 1967. Presbyterian. Educated at Indiana University-Bloomington B.S. 1990 and Pepperdine University J.D. 1993. Admitted to practice Indiana 1993 and U.S. District Courts Northern 1993 and Southern 1993 Districts of Indiana.

Deputy Prosecutor Grant County 1993-96. Republican. Member Indiana Judges Association, National Women Judges Association, Grant County and Indiana State Bar Associations. Named Indiana Outstanding Young Attorney of the Year 2001.

Office: 101 East Fourth Street, Room 306, Marion 46952-4010.
Telephone: (765) 668-8123.
Fax: (765) 651-2470
E-mail address: nconnlaw@hotmail.com

COOK, Michael D. *(Judge, Marshall Circuit Court)* Elected to term beginning Jan 1, 1981. Reelected 1986, 1992 and 1998. Current term expires Dec 31, 2004. Born Plymouth Indiana April 16, 1951. Protestant. Educated at Indiana University B.S. 1973 and Valparaiso University School of Law J.D. 1978. Admitted to practice Indiana 1978 and U.S. District Courts Northern and Southern Districts of Indiana. In legal practice Plymouth 1978. Judge, Marshall County Court 1978-80.

Member Indiana Judges Association (Secretary-Treas-

COOK, MICHAEL D.—*Continued*

urer 1990-93, Vice President 1993-95, President 1995-97), Indiana Council of Juvenile and Family Court Judges, National Council of Juvenile and Family Court Judges, American Judges Association, Marshall County, Indiana State and American Bar Associations. Graduate American Academy of Judicial Skills 1984 and Indiana Judicial College 1984. Republican.

Office: 501 North Center Street, Suite 301, Plymouth 46563-1707.

Telephone: (574) 935-8780.

Fax: (574) 936-4703

E-mail address: mcook@co.marshall.in.us

CORNWELL, Wayne *(Judge, Whitestown Town Court)* Appointed to term beginning Aug 1998. Elected 1999, current term expires Dec 31, 2003.

Mailing address: P.O. Box 155, Whitestown 46075-0155.

Office: 7 South Main Street, Whitestown 46075-9382.

Telephone: (765) 769-6557.

COSBEY, Roger B. *(Magistrate Judge, United States District Court Northern District of Indiana)* Appointed by U.S. District Court judges to term beginning Jan 3, 1990. Reappointed Jan 1998, current term expires Jan 2, 2006. Born Elkhart Indiana Jan 13, 1950, United Methodist. Educated at Western Michigan University B.A. 1972 and University of Toledo J.D. 1975. Admitted to practice Indiana 1975 and U.S. District Court Southern District of Indiana 1975. In legal practice Ligonier 1975-81. Judge, Noble Superior Court 1982-90.

Attorney City of Ligonier 1977-79, Ligonier Planning Commission 1977-79 and West Noble School Corporation 1977-81. Co-author with Hon. William C. Lee "Accelerated Dispute Resolution (ADR) in the United States District Court, Northern District of Indiana" *Alternative Dispute Resolution* Indiana CLE Forum 1991 and "The Administration of Civil Litigation in the Fort Wayne Division of the Northern District of Indiana" *Federal Court for the State Court Practitioner* Indiana CLE Forum 1994. Author "The Experience in the Northern District of Indiana with Mandatory Disclosures and the Impact of the Discovery Amendments" *Federal Civil Practice* Indiana CLE Forum 1994, "Overview of the Local Rules and the Applicability and Interpretation of Amended Rule 26(a)" *Current Issues in Criminal and Civil Law* Federal Bar Association 1994, "An Early Judicial Perspective on the Americans with Disabilities Act" *ADA: New Developments in the Law* Indiana CLE Forum 1994 and "Motion Practice Pointers" *Res Gestae* Sept 2000. Chairperson Local Rules Advisory Committee U.S. District Court Northern District of Indiana since 1999. Member Gender and Race Study Task Force U.S. Court of Appeals Seventh Circuit. Fellow Allen County Bar Foundation. Member Federal Magistrate Judges Association, American Judicature Society, Benjamin Harrison American Inns of Court (Counselor 1993-94, President-Elect 1994-95, President 1995-96), Allen County and Indiana State Bar Associations. Board of Directors Indiana Judicial Conference 1985-89. Graduate Indiana Judicial College 1987 and Automation Program for Judges at Introductory, Intermediate and Advanced Levels Federal Judicial Center. Panel Member "Third Party Liability After Tort Reform" 1996 and "Practical Tips for Success in Federal Civil Practice, Northern District of Indiana" 1997 Indiana CLE Forum. Presenter "Federal Court Practice for the Northern District" 1998, "The Trial of a Sexual Harassment Case" 1999 and "Advanced Employment Law" 2000 Indiana CLE Forum. Major USAR JAGC 1972-92. Member Fort Wayne Downtown Rotary Club, Fort Wayne Quest Club and Aldersgate United Methodist Church.

Office: 1130 Federal Building, 1300 South Harrison Street, Fort Wayne 46802.

Telephone: (260) 422-2406.

COTTON, Lyle J. *(Judge, Bluffton City Court)* Elected to term beginning Jan 1, 1988. Reelected Nov 1991, 1995 and 1999. Current term expires Dec 31, 2003. Born Fort Wayne Indiana April 3, 1928. United Methodist. Judge, Bluffton City Court 1963-71.

Member Indiana City Court Judges Association. Recipient Silver Beaver Award from Boy Scouts of America. Private USMC 1946-47. Representative New York Life Insurance Company since 1954. Republican. Member Boy Scouts of America, Order of the Eastern Star and 33° of Ancient and Accepted Scottish Rite. Past Grand Patron of Indiana Grand Chapter Masonic Lodge. Enjoys reading and bicycling.

Office: 204 East Market Street, Bluffton 46714-2197.

Telephone: (260) 824-3392.

E-mail address: ljgrcotton@parlorcity.com

COX, J. Steven *(Judge, Franklin Circuit Court)* Elected to term beginning Jan 1, 1995. Reelected 2000, current term expires Dec 31, 2006. Educated at Indiana University-Bloomington B.A. 1987 and Valparaiso University J.D. 1990.

Assistant Public Defender Franklin County 1990-92. Deputy Prosecutor Fayette County 1992-93. Republican.

Office: 459 Main Street, Brookville 47012-1405.

Telephone: (765) 647-4186.

E-mail address: fcounty@gte.net

CRANEY, Jane Spencer *(Judge, Morgan Superior Court)* Elected to term beginning 1996. Reelected 2002, current term expires Dec 31, 2008. Born Chicago Illinois April 17, 1954. Lutheran. Educated at Hanover College B.A. 1976 and Indiana University-Indianapolis 1979. Law Clerk to Hon. Stanley Miller, Indiana Court of Appeals 1979-80. Member Phi Alpha Delta. Admitted to practice Indiana 1979 and U.S. District Court Southern District of Indiana 1979. Judge, Morgan County Court Jan 1, 1991 to 1995.

Prosecuting Attorney Morgan County 1983-91. Board Member Indiana Judicial Conference and Indiana Judges Association 1997-2000. Member Task Force on Race and Gender Issues Indiana Supreme Court, Morgan County, Indiana State and American Bar Associations. Speaker Indiana Prosecuting Attorneys Council, Indiana State Police, Indiana Judicial Center, Association of Government Attorneys in Capitol Litigation and Indiana Continuing Legal Education Council. Honoree Girls Club, Inc. 1991. Republican. Member Governor's Task Force on Mental Health 1988-89 and Governor's Task Force on Prescription Drugs 1989-90. Board of Directors South Central Community Mental Health Association. President Rotary. Enjoys traveling and studying languages.

Mailing address: P.O. Box 1556, Martinsville 46151-1556.

Telephone: (765) 342-1040.

Fax: (765) 349-5504

E-mail address: judgejane@hotmail.com

CRIPE, Kimberly A. *(Judge, Delphi City Court)* Appointed by Governor Frank O'Bannon to term beginning Aug 23, 1999. Term expires Dec 31, 2003.
Office: 201 South Union Street, Delphi 46923-1531.
Telephone: (765) 564-2097.
E-mail address: kandk@carlnet.org

CRONE, Terry A. *(Judge, St. Joseph Circuit Court)* Master Commissioner 1986-89. Assumed office as Judge Feb 11, 1989. Elected to subsequent terms. Current term expires Dec 31, 2008. Educated at DePauw University B.A. 1974 and University of Notre Dame J.D. 1977.
County Attorney St. Joseph County 1980-86. Board of Managers Indiana Judges Association 1993. Democrat.
Office: 101 South Main Street, South Bend 46601-1807.
Telephone: (574) 235-9551.

CROW, Patricia *(Judge, Lebanon City Court)*
Office: 201 East Main Street, Lebanon 46052.
Telephone: (765) 482-8846.

CROWLEY, W. Timothy *(Judge, Knox Superior Court)* Elected to term beginning Jan 1, 1997. Reelected 2002, current term expires Dec 31, 2008. Educated at Indiana State University B.S 1973 M.S. 1977 and Indiana University J.D. 1985.
Certified Civil and Family Law Mediator 1993-96. High school teacher and coach Vincennes Lincoln High School 1973-82. Member Vincennes Park Board 1987-94 and Vincennes Community School Board 1995-96.
Office: Courthouse, 111 North Seventh Street, Vincennes 47591.
Telephone: (812) 885-2517.
Fax: (812) 895-4890
E-mail address: judgetc@wvc.net

CULVER, Richard D. *(Judge, Hancock Circuit Court)* Term expires Dec 31, 2006. Educated at Franklin College B.A. 1980 and Indiana University-Indianapolis J.D. 1983. Judge, Hancock County Court Oct 3, 1988 to 1992. Judge, Hancock Superior Court 1992-2000.
Deputy Prosecutor Hancock County 1988. Board of Directors Judicial Conference of Indiana 1997-99. Republican.
Office: Nine East Main Street, Room 302, Greenfield 46140-2320.
Telephone: (317) 462-1107.
E-mail address: culverr@webtv.net

DAILEY, Richard A. *(Judge, Delaware Circuit Court)* Elected to term beginning Jan 1, 1983. Reelected 1988, 1994 and 2000. Current term expires Dec 31, 2006. Educated at Ball State University A.B. 1964 M.A. 1980 and Indiana University J.D. 1967. Judge, Delaware County Court 1977-82.
Deputy Prosecutor Twenty-eighth Judicial Circuit 1968 and Forty-sixth Judicial Circuit 1970-72. Public Defender Forty-sixth Judicial Circuit 1973-74. Associate Professor of Political Science Ball State University 1975-77. Member Indiana Judges Association.
Office: Delaware County Justice Center, 100 West Washington Street, Muncie 47305.
Telephone: (765) 747-7784.
E-mail address: rdailey@co.delaware.in.us

DANIEL, Donald L. *(Judge, Tippecanoe Circuit Court)* Elected to term beginning Jan 1, 2003. Term expires Dec 31, 2008. Educated at Purdue University B.S. 1969 and Indiana University-Purdue University at Indianapolis J.D. 1974.
Office: Courthouse, 301 Main Street, Lafayette 47901.
Telephone: (765) 423-9343.
Fax: (765) 423-9116
E-mail address: DDaniel@county.tippecanoe.in.us

DANIKOLAS, James *(Judge, Lake Superior Court)* Appointed by Governor Otis Ray Bowen to term beginning Jan 1, 1977. Retained by election. Current term expires Dec 31, 2004. Serves Civil Division. Currently serves as Chief Judge. Born East Chicago Indiana Jan 24, 1936. Greek Orthodox. Educated at University of Michigan 1954-56, DePauw University 1956-57 and Valparaiso University J.D. 1960. Admitted to practice Indiana 1960. In legal practice East Chicago 1960-70.
Member American Judicature Society, Indiana State and American Bar Associations. Graduate The National Judicial College and Indiana Judicial College.
Office: 15 West Fourth Avenue, Gary 46402-1284.
Telephone: (219) 881-6157.
E-mail address: danikjx@lakecountyin.org

DARDEN, Carr L. *(Presiding Judge, Indiana Court of Appeals Fourth District)* Appointed by Governor B. Evan Bayh Oct 18, 1994 to term beginning Nov 28, 1994. Retained by election 1998, current term expires Dec 31, 2008. Born Springfield Tennessee July 21, 1937. Church of Christ. Educated at Indiana University B.S. 1966 J.D. 1970. Admitted to practice Indiana 1970 and U.S. District Courts Southern 1970 and Northern 1984 Districts of Indiana. In legal practice Indianapolis 1973-75 and 1982-89. Presiding Judge, Marion Municipal Court 1989-90. Presiding Judge, Marion Superior Court 1991-94.
State Deputy Public Defender and Chief Deputy Public Defender 1970-81. Public Defender Marion County 1982-88. Member Judicial Conference of Indiana, Indiana Judges Association, Indianapolis (Board of Managers), Marion County (Board of Managers), Indiana State, National (Judicial Council) and American Bar Associations. USAF 1955-59. Democrat.
Office: 115 West Washington Street, Suite 1270, Indianapolis 46204-3419.
E-mail address: cdarden@courts.state.in.us

DAUGHERTY, E. Duane *(Judge, Jasper Circuit Court)* Appointed by Governor Robert D. Orr to term beginning Feb 25, 1982. Elected 1982, 1988, 1994 and 2000. Current term expires Dec 31, 2006. Born Bedford Indiana July 31, 1935. Educated at Earlham College B.A. 1962 and Indiana University J.D. 1968. Member Phi Alpha Delta. Admitted to practice Indiana 1968. Began legal practice Covington 1968. In legal practice DeMotte 1972-82.
Deputy Prosecuting Attorney Jasper County Oct 1972 to Feb 1982. Member Jasper County (President 1983-84), Indiana State and American Bar Associations. U.S. Army 1956-59. USAR and Indiana National Guard 1959-68.
Office: Courthouse, 115 West Washington Street, Rensselaer 47978-2890.
Telephone: (219) 866-7766.
Fax: (219) 866-4943
E-mail address: jccircuit@liljasper.com

DAVID, Steve *(Judge, Boone Circuit Court)* Elected to term beginning Jan 1, 1995. Reelected 2000, current term expires Dec 31, 2006. Educated at Murray State

DAVID, STEVE—*Continued*
University 1979 and Indiana University-Indianapolis J.D. 1982.

Board of Directors Indiana Juvenile Justice Task Force. Member Juvenile Justice Improvement Committee Judicial Conference of Indiana, Indiana Judges Association, Indiana Council of Juvenile and Family Court Judges, National Council of Juvenile and Family Court Judges, Boone County and Indiana State Bar Associations. Lieutenant Colonel U.S. Army JAGC 1982-2001. Republican.

Office: 310 Courthouse Square, Lebanon 46052-2159.
Telephone: (765) 482-0530.
E-mail address: circuit@in-motion.net

DAVIS, Roger D. *(Judge, Harrison Superior Court)* Elected Nov 1996 to term beginning Jan 1, 1997. Reelected 2002, current term expires Dec 31, 2008. Democrat.

Office: 1445 Gardner Lane N.W., #3018, Corydon 47112-2070.
Telephone: (812) 738-8141.

DAVIS, William E. *(Judge, Lake Superior Court)* Appointed by Governor B. Evan Bayh Nov 21, 1994. Retained by election 1998, current term expires Dec 31, 2004. Serves Civil Division. Educated at Purdue University B.A. 1970 and Indiana University-Bloomington J.D. 1976. Civil Referee, East Chicago City Court Feb 1990 to Nov 1994.

Deputy Prosecutor Title IV-D 1977-78 and Public Defender Felony Division Nov 1985 to Feb 1990 Lake County. Member Civil Instructions Committee Judicial Conference of Indiana, James C. Kimbrough Law Association, East Chicago, Lake County, Indiana State, National and American Bar Associations. First Lieutenant U.S. Army Nov 1971 to July 1974. Board of Directors YMCA Hobart.

Office: Courthouse, 3711 Main Street, East Chicago 46312-2299.
Telephone: (219) 398-7386.

DEES, Harry C., Jr. *(Chief Judge, United States Bankruptcy Court Northern District of Indiana)* Appointed by U.S. Court of Appeals Seventh Circuit to term beginning Oct 1, 1986. Reappointed Oct 1, 2000, current term expires 2014. Chief Judge since Jan 9, 2003. Born California March 20, 1945. Educated at DePauw University B.A. 1967 and Indiana University-Bloomington J.D. 1974. Admitted to practice Indiana 1974, U.S. District Courts Southern 1974 and Northern 1986 Districts of Indiana and U.S. Court of Appeals Seventh Circuit 1986. In legal practice Terre Haute 1974-86. Referee, Vigo County Juvenile Court 1979-83.

Public Defender 1977-78, Welfare Attorney 1978 and Deputy Prosecutor 1983 Vigo County. Instructor Indiana State University 1984-86 and Notre Dame Law School 1988-2002. Member National Conference of Bankruptcy Judges, Terre Haute, St. Joseph County and Indiana State Bar Associations. Lieutenant Colonel JAG USAF 1967-71 and Air National Guard 1976-92. Member Rotary Club, Scottish Rite, Goodwill Industries and United Way. Enjoys history, reading, cars, traveling and swimming.

Mailing address: P.O. Box 7003, South Bend 46634-7003.
Telephone: (574) 968-2280.

DEITER, Charles J. *(Judge, Marion Superior Court)* Commissioner Civil Division 1976-77 and Probate Division 1978-91. Appointed Judge by Governor B. Evan Bayh Dec 2, 1991. Elected 1996 and 2002. Current term expires Dec 31, 2008. Serves Probate/Mental Health Division. Educated at Marian College B.A. 1959 and Indiana University-Bloomington LL.B. 1965.

Deputy Attorney General 1965-69. Staff Attorney Legal Services Organization 1969-76 and Legal Aid Society 1973-76. Indiana National Guard 1959-64. Democrat.

Office: 200 East Washington Street, Room T1721, Indianapolis 46204.
Telephone: (317) 327-5063.
E-mail address: cdeiter@indygov.org

DETAMORE, James R. *(Judge, Boone Superior Court)* Elected to term beginning Jan 1, 1991. Reelected 1996 and 2002. Current term expires Dec 31, 2008. Born Columbus Ohio Aug 10, 1938. Religious affiliation: Disciples of Christ. Educated at The Ohio State University and Indiana University B.S. with highest distinction 1978 J.D. cum laude 1983. Admitted to practice Indiana 1983, U.S. District Courts Northern 1983 and Southern 1983 Districts of Indiana and U.S. Supreme Court 1987. In legal practice Zionsville 1983-90.

Member Criminal Benchbook Committee Indiana Judges Association, Court Alcohol and Drug Program Advisory Committee Indiana Judicial Center, Boone County and Indiana State Bar Associations. Attended courses on Drugs and Alcohol in Courts April 1992, Domestic Violence Jan 1993, Constitutional Criminal Procedure July 1993, Special Problems in Criminal Evidence Jan 1994 and Drug Courts Nov 1996 The National Judicial College, Children of Divorce Ohio University April 1994 and Domestic Relations American Academy of Judicial Education Oct 1994. Graduate First Indiana Graduate Judges Program 1997 and Indiana Judicial College 1997. Rural mail carrier 1975-85. Owner of independent insurance agency 1975-90. Republican. Member Kiwanis Club.

Office: One Courthouse Square, Lebanon 46052-2159.
Telephone: (765) 482-6502.
Fax: (765) 483-4414
E-mail address: jdetamore@co.boone.in.us

DICKSON, Brent E. *(Associate Justice, Indiana Supreme Court)* Appointed by Governor Robert D. Orr to term beginning Jan 6, 1986. Retained by election Nov 8, 1988 and Nov 1998. Current term expires Dec 31, 2008. Born Gary Indiana July 18, 1941. Presbyterian. Educated at Purdue University B.A. 1964 and Indiana University School of Law J.D. 1968. Awarded honorary Doctor of Letters Purdue University 1996. Admitted to practice Indiana 1968, U.S. District Courts Northern 1968 and Southern 1968 Districts of Indiana, U.S. Court of Appeals Seventh Circuit 1972 and U.S. Supreme Court 1975. In legal practice Lafayette 1968-85.

Author "Renewing Lawyer Civility" 28 Valparaiso University L. Rev. 531, 1994 and "Lawyers and Judges as Framers of Indiana's 1851 Constitution" 30 Indiana L. Rev. 1997. Adjunct Professor Indiana University School of Law. Certified Civil Trial Advocate National Board of Trial Advocacy 1980. Former Member The Association of Trial Lawyers of America and Indiana Trial Lawyers Association (Board of Directors 1974-85). Member American Law Institute, Indiana Judges Association, Institute of Judicial Administration, American Judicature Society, Indianapolis, Indiana State, Seventh

DICKSON, BRENT E.—*Continued*
Circuit and American Bar Associations. Trained in Civil Mediation 1994.
Office: 200 West Washington Street, Room 306, Indianapolis 46204-2732.
Telephone: (317) 232-2549.
Fax: (317) 233-8706
E-mail address: bdickson@courts.state.in.us

DILLIN, S. Hugh *(Senior Judge, United States District Court Southern District of Indiana)* Appointed for life by President John F. Kennedy to term beginning Oct 7, 1961. Chief Judge 1982-84. Assumed Senior status. Born Petersburg Indiana June 9, 1914. Presbyterian. Educated at Indiana University A.B. 1936 LL.B. 1938. Awarded honorary LL.D. Indiana University 1992. Admitted to practice Indiana 1938. Began legal practice Petersburg 1938.
Indiana House of Representatives 1937-42 and 1951-52 (Minority Floor Leader 1951-52). Indiana Senate 1959-61 (Majority Floor Leader and President pro tem 1961). Important Decision: Indianapolis School Desegregation Case 1971. Member Judicial Panel on Multidistrict Litigation 1983-92, Judicial Conference of the U.S. 1979-82 (Executive Committee 1980-82, Court Administration Committee 1982-87, Chairman Subcommittee on Federal-State Relations 1982-87), Indianapolis, Indiana State and American Bar Associations. President Seventh Circuit Trial Judges Association 1977-79. Named Most Valuable Member of General Assembly 1951, 1959 and 1961. Captain U.S. Army 1943-46. Democrat.
Office: 255 U.S. Courthouse, 46 East Ohio Street, Indianapolis 46204.
Telephone: (317) 229-3610.

DOLEHANTY, Darrin M. *(Judge, Wayne Superior Court)*
Office: 301 East Main Street, Second Floor, Richmond 47374-4200.
Telephone: (765) 973-9269.

DONAHUE, Daniel Francis *(Judge, Clark Circuit Court)* Elected to term beginning Jan 1, 1987. Reelected 1992 and 1998. Current term expires Dec 31, 2004. Born Pittsburgh Pennsylvania Sept 1, 1940. Roman Catholic. Educated at John Carroll University A.B. 1962 and University of Louisville School of Law J.D. 1969. Admitted to practice Indiana 1969. In legal practice Jeffersonville 1970 and 1983-86.
Prosecuting Attorney Clark County 1971-82. Board of Directors 1973-82 and Chairman 1975-76 Indiana Prosecuting Attorneys Council. Board of Directors 1991-2001 and Chairman Domestic Relations Committee since 1995 Indiana Judicial Conference. Member Committee on Character and Fitness Indiana Supreme Court since 1990, State Public Defender Commission since 1996, Sherman Minton American Inn of Court, American Judicature Society, Clark County and Indiana State Bar Associations. Graduate Indiana Judicial College 1994. Participant Indiana Graduate Program for Judges 1996-97. First Lieutenant U.S. Army 1964-66. Chairman Clark County Democratic Central Committee 1970-74.
Office: 501 East Court Avenue, Jeffersonville 47130-4029.
Telephone: (812) 285-6308.
E-mail address: ddonahue@protegra.net

DONAT, Gregory J. *(Judge, Tippecanoe Superior Court)* Term expires Dec 31, 2008. Born Peru Indiana Sept 14, 1947. Roman Catholic. Educated at Ball State University B.S. 1970 and Indiana University J.D. 1972. Admitted to practice Indiana 1973, U.S District Courts Northern 1973 and Southern 1973 Districts of Indiana, U.S. Court of Appeals Seventh Circuit 1978 and U.S. Supreme Court 1980. Began legal practice Lafayette 1973. Judge, Lafayette City Court 1978-80. Former Judge, Tippecanoe County Court, elected to term beginning Jan 1, 1985.
Former Commissioner Indiana Emergency Medical Services Commission. Director Indiana Judicial Conference. Member Indiana State Bar Association (Director Young Lawyers Section). Discussion Group Leader The National Judicial College. Republican. President Tippecanoe County Lincoln Club. Director Community and Family Resource Center and Tippecanoe County Convention and Visitors Bureau. Enjoys snow skiing, water skiing, running and camping.
Office: 301 Main Street, Lafayette 47901.
Telephone: (765) 423-9266.
E-mail address: greggdonat@aol.com

DREYER, David J. *(Judge, Marion Superior Court)* Elected to term beginning Jan 1, 1997. Reelected 2002, current term expires Dec 31, 2008. Serves Civil Division. Educated at University of Notre Dame B.A. 1977 J.D. 1980. Recipient Reginald Heber Smith Community Lawyer Fellowship 1980-82.
Chief Counsel Marion County Prosecutor's Office 1991-94. Special Counsel Indiana 1995-96. Chair Community Relations Committee Judicial Conference of Indiana and District 8 Pro Bono Committee. Attended Indiana Graduate Program for Judges 1999. Democrat. Member Legal Services Organization 1980-86.
Office: 200 East Washington Street, Room T-1441, Indianapolis 46204.
Telephone: (317) 327-4160.
E-mail address: ddreyer@indygov.org

DYWAN, Jeffery J. *(Judge, Lake Superior Court)* Appointed by Governor B. Evan Bayh May 31, 1991. Retained by election. Current term expires Dec 31, 2006. Serves Civil Division. Educated at Purdue University B.S. 1971 and Valparaiso University J.D. 1974. In legal practice Griffith 1974-81 and Schererville 1981-91.
Deputy Prosecutor 1978-80 and Public Defender 1981-83 Lake County. Instructor Calumet College 1974-76 and Indiana Vocational and Technical College 1978. Member Alternative Dispute Resolution Committee 1993-99 and Civil Jury Instructions Committee Judicial Conference of Indiana. Member Subcommittee Mass Tort Litigation Committee Conference of Chief Justices. Member Indiana Judges Association, American Judicature Society, Lake County (Practice and Procedure Committee) and Indiana State Bar Associations. Attendee The National Judicial College Reno Nevada since 1998.
Office: 2293 North Main Street, Crown Point 46307.
Telephone: (219) 648-6150.
Fax: (219) 648-6155
E-mail address: jdywan@hotmail.com

ELDRED, Michael H. *(Judge, Vigo Superior Court)* Elected to term beginning Jan 1, 1981. Reelected to subsequent terms. Current term expires Dec 31, 2004. Born Terre Haute Indiana May 30, 1948. Educated at University of Notre Dame B.A. 1970 J.D. 1975. Staff member Notre Dame Law Review 1973. Law Clerk to Hon.

ELDRED, MICHAEL H.—*Continued*

Robert K. Rodibaugh, U.S. District Court Northern District of Indiana. Admitted to practice Indiana 1975. Began legal practice Washington D.C. 1975. In legal practice Terre Haute 1977.

Deputy Prosecuting Attorney Forty-third Judicial Circuit 1978-80. Visiting Lecturer Indiana State University since 1981. Republican. Member Leadership Terre Haute, Rotary Club, Family Services Association and Big Brothers/Big Sisters. Enjoys running.

Office: 33 South Third, Terre Haute 47807-3434.

Telephone: (812) 462-3295.

E-mail address: smeld4@aol.com

EMKES, Cynthia S. *(Judge, Johnson Superior Court)* Term expires Dec 31, 2008. Educated at Indiana University-Bloomington B.A. 1979 and Indiana University-Indianapolis J.D. cum laude 1985. Magistrate, Johnson Circuit Court 1987.

Board of Directors 1993-95 and Member Criminal Instructions Committee Judicial Conference of Indiana. Member Indiana Judges Association, Indiana Council of Juvenile and Family Court Judges, National Council of Juvenile and Family Court Judges, Johnson County (Secretary-Treasurer 1987), Indiana State and American Bar Associations. Graduate Indiana Judicial College 1996. Republican.

Office: Five East Jefferson Street, Franklin 46131-2339.

Telephone: (317) 736-3782.

E-mail address: cemkes@co.johnson.in.us

ENDRIS, Lori Kyle *(Judge, Marion County Small Claims Court Warren Township Division)* Appointed by Governor Frank O'Bannon to term beginning Jan 1, 2001. Elected Nov 5, 2002, current term expires Dec 31, 2006. Educated at Ball State University B.S. cum laude 1984 and Indiana University School of Law at Indianapolis J.D. 1987. Law Clerk to Indiana Court of Appeals 1988-92. Admitted to practice Indiana 1988. Environmental Law Judge, Office of Environmental Adjudication 1995-98.

Member Indianapolis and Indiana State Bar Associations.

Office: 501 North Post Road, Indianapolis 46219.

Telephone: (317) 897-2061.

Fax: (317) 895-4354.

FEE, William C. *(Judge, Steuben Superior Court)* Elected to term beginning Jan 1, 1987. Reelected to subsequent terms. Current term expires Dec 31, 2008. Educated at Purdue University B.A. 1977 and Case Western Reserve University J.D. 1980. Judge, Steuben County Court, Jan 1, 1985 to 1986.

Attorney Legal Services Program of Northern Indiana, Inc. 1980-84. Member Association of Family and Conciliation Courts, Indiana Judges Association, American Judicature Society and Indiana State Bar Association.

Office: 55 South Public Square, Angola 46703-0327.

Telephone: (260) 665-7712.

E-mail address: ssuperior.wcf@verizon.net

FEICK, John M. *(Judge, Delaware Circuit Court)*

Office: Delaware County Justice Center, 100 West Washington, Muncie 47305.

Telephone: (765) 747-7770.

FELTS, Thomas J. *(Judge, Allen Circuit Court)*

Office: 715 South Calhoun, Room 300, Fort Wayne 46802-1805.

Telephone: (260) 449-7602.

FISHER, Thomas G. *(Judge, Indiana Tax Court)* Appointed by Governor Robert D. Orr to term beginning July 1, 1986. Retained by election. Current term expires Dec 31, 2008. Educated at Earlham College A.B. 1962 and Indiana University LL.B. 1965.

Prosecuting Attorney Jasper County 1967-86.

Office: 115 West Washington Street, Suite 1160, Indianapolis 46204-2241.

Telephone: (317) 232-4694.

Fax: (317) 232-0644

E-mail address: tfisher@courts.state.in.us

FLEECE, Steven Michael *(Judge, Clark Superior Court)* Assumed office 1995. Term expires Dec 31, 2008. Born Louisville Kentucky April 13, 1950. Christian. Educated at St. Meinrad Seminary 1968-69, Indiana University A.B. in Journalism 1972 and University of Louisville J.D. 1982. Member Brandeis Society (top ten percent of class) University of Louisville 1982. Recipient American Law Book Company Award for Most Significant Contribution to Legal Scholarship 1982 and Greenebaum Award for Excellence in Legal Writing 1982. Editor-in-Chief Journal of Family Law 1981-82. Member Phi Kappa Phi, Omicron Delta Kappa and Phi Alpha Delta. Admitted to practice Indiana 1982 and U.S. District Courts Northern 1982 and Southern 1982 Districts of Indiana. Began legal practice Jeffersonville 1982. Judge, Clark County Court Jan 1, 1985 to 1995.

Quality Control Reviewer Indiana State Department of Public Welfare 1974-76. Caseworker Supervisor Clark County Department of Public Welfare 1976-79. Deputy Prosecutor Clark County 1983-84. Author "A Review of the Child Support Enforcement Program" Jour. of Family Law 1982. Member Indiana Judges Association, Clark County, Indiana State and American (Judicial Administration Division) Bar Associations. Democrat. Member Charleston Lions Club, Sons of the American Revolution, National Wildlife Federation and Sierra Club. Enjoys history, environmental issues, bicycling, hiking and canoeing.

Office: City-County Building, 501 East Court Avenue, Jeffersonville 47130.

Telephone: (812) 285-6316.

E-mail address: smfleece@hotmail.com

FORCUM, John W. *(Judge, Blackford Superior Court)* Term expires Dec 31, 2004. Born Anderson Indiana March 9, 1949. Presbyterian. Educated at Purdue University B.S. 1972 and Indiana University J.D. 1978. Admitted to practice Indiana 1978. Former Judge, Blackford County Court, elected to term beginning Jan 1, 1987.

City Attorney Hartford City 1984-85. Lieutenant Governor Kiwanis 1988-89. Enjoys woodworking, cars and fishing.

Office: 110 West Washington Street, Hartford City 47348-2251.

Telephone: (765) 348-1840.

FOSTER, Kennard P. *(Recalled Magistrate Judge, United States District Court Southern District of Indiana)* Appointed Magistrate Judge by U.S. District Court judges to term beginning May 16, 1986. Reappointed Nov 1994. Appointed Recalled Magistrate Judge by the

FOSTER, KENNARD P.—*Continued*
Judicial Council of the Seventh Circuit Nov 11, 2002. Born Urbana Illinois Aug 15, 1944. Catholic. Educated at Ball State University B.S. 1966 and Indiana University J.D. 1970. Staff Member Indiana Legal Forum 1970. Admitted to practice Indiana 1970 and U.S. Court of Appeals Seventh Circuit 1976. In legal practice Franklin 1971-76.

Assistant U.S. Attorney Southern District of Indiana 1976-86. Member Federal Bar Association (Chapter President).

Office: 269 U.S. Courthouse, 46 East Ohio Street, Indianapolis 46204.

Telephone: (317) 229-3620.

FRANK, Steven H. *(Judge, Marion Superior Court)* Assumed office Jan 1, 1996. Elected 2000, current term expires Dec 31, 2006. Serves Civil Division. Born Indianapolis Indiana March 23, 1944. Educated at Indiana University B.A. 1968 J.D. 1971. Law Clerk to Indiana Supreme Court 1970-72. Admitted to practice Indiana 1971. Began legal practice Indianapolis 1971. Judge, Marion Municipal Court Dec 5, 1977 to Dec 31, 1995, appointed by Governor Otis Ray Bowen.

Deputy Prosecutor Nineteenth Judicial Circuit Court 1972-74. Member Character and Fitness Committee Indiana Supreme Court, Indianapolis, Indiana State and American Bar Associations.

Office: 200 East Washington Street, Room W-407, Indianapolis 46204.

Telephone: (317) 327-4200.

E-mail address: sfrank@indygov.org

FREESE, Robert W. *(Judge, Hendricks Superior Court)* Elected to term beginning Jan 1, 2001. Term expires Dec 31, 2006. Educated at Marian College B.A. 1981 and Indiana University-Indianapolis J.D. 1984. Judge, Brownsburg Town Court 1992-95.

Chief Deputy Prosecutor Hendricks County 1995-2000. Member Hendricks County Bar Association. Republican.

Office: One Courthouse Square, Suite 106, Danville 46122-0365.

Telephone: (317) 745-9305.

FRESE, J. Jerome *(Judge, St. Joseph Superior Court)* Appointed by Governor Robert D. Orr Sept 1, 1985. Retained by election. Current term expires Dec 31, 2006. Educated at Loyola College B.A. 1953, Trinity College, Dublin Ireland M.Litt. 1962, University of Iowa Ph.D. 1973 and University of Notre Dame J.D. 1975.

Assistant U.S. Attorney Chicago Illinois 1976-81 and South Bend Indiana 1981-85. Member Indiana Judges Association. Faculty Member National Institute for Trial Advocacy Chicago Illinois 1981-82 and Indianapolis Indiana 1985.

Office: 101 South Main Street, South Bend 46601-1807.

Telephone: (574) 235-9563.

FRIEDLANDER, Ezra H. *(Presiding Judge, Indiana Court of Appeals Second District)* Appointed by Governor B. Evan Bayh to term beginning Dec 28, 1992. Retained by election 1996, current term expires Dec 31, 2006. Educated at Indiana University A.B. 1962 LL.B. 1965.

Deputy Prosecuting Attorney Lake County 1965-68. Deputy Prosecutor Marion County 1974-76. Fellow Indianapolis Bar Foundation and Indiana State Bar Foundation. Member Civil Instructions Committee Judicial Conference of Indiana, American Judicature Society, Indianapolis, Indiana State, Seventh Circuit and American Bar Associations.

Office: 200 West Washington Street, Room 411, Indianapolis 46204-2784.

Telephone: (317) 232-6892.

E-mail address: efriedla@courts.state.in.us

FUNKE, James, Jr. *(Judge, Jennings Superior Court)* Elected Nov 1996 to term beginning Jan 1, 1997. Reelected 2002, current term expires Dec 31, 2008. Born Cincinnati Ohio Feb 9, 1959. Baptist. Educated at Tri-State University B.A. 1981 and Indiana University-Indianapolis J.D. 1991. Admitted to practice Indiana 1991. Clerk, Jennings Circuit Court 1987-97.

Republican. Member Rotary Club. Enjoys baseball, hockey and jogging.

Mailing address: P.O. Box 490, Vernon 47282-0490.

Office: 25 Pike Street, Vernon 47282.

Telephone: (812) 346-9700.

E-mail address: jcsupcourt@seidata.com

GANT, Timothy *(Judge, Yorktown Town Court)* Appointed to term beginning Dec 1, 1996. Elected 1999, current term expires Dec 31, 2003.

Mailing address: P.O. Box 157, Yorktown 47396.

Office: 9730 West Smith Street, Box 14, Yorktown 47396-1198.

Telephone: (765) 759-4006.

Fax: (765) 759-4011

E-mail address: yorktowntowncourt@comcast.net

GIFFORD, Patricia J. *(Judge, Marion Superior Court)* Elected to term beginning Jan 1, 1979. Reelected 1984, 1990, 1996 2002. Current term expires Dec 31, 2008. Serves Criminal Division. Born Indianapolis Indiana April 13, 1938. Protestant. Educated at College of William & Mary A.B. 1960 and Indiana University J.D. 1968. Admitted to practice Indiana 1968 and U.S. District Court Southern District of Indiana 1968. Began legal practice Indianapolis 1968. Referee, Marion City Juvenile Court 1975-79.

Deputy Attorney General 1969-70 and Assistant State Attorney General 1970-72 Indiana. Deputy Prosecutor Marion County 1972-75. Member Indiana Judges Association, National Association of Women Judges, Indianapolis and Indiana State Bar Associations. Republican. Former Vice Committeewoman and Secretary Lawyers for a Sound Judiciary. Secretary State House Young Republicans. Board of Directors Indianapolis Legal Aid Society and Disciples of Christ Board of Church Extension (Vice Chairman 1979, Chairman 1980 and 1987). Member Daughters of the American Revolution. Enjoys painting and gardening.

Office: 200 East Washington Street, #W-203, Indianapolis 46204-3395.

Telephone: (317) 327-4525.

E-mail address: pgifford@indygov.org

GILMORE, Robert W., Jr. *(Judge, La Porte Circuit Court)* Elected to term beginning Jan 1, 1995. Reelected 2000, current term expires Dec 31, 2006. Educated at Dartmouth College B.A. 1967 and Indiana University-Bloomington J.D. 1971. Judge, City Court of Michigan City 1972-75.

First Deputy Prosecuting Attorney La Porte County

GILMORE, ROBERT W., JR.—*Continued*

1979-80. Second Lieutenant Indiana National Guard 1968-74. Member Human Rights Committee Michigan City 1972-78. Member Indiana Gaming Commission 1994.

Office: Courthouse, 813 Lincolnway, La Porte 46350-3429.

Telephone: (219) 326-6808.

E-mail address: gilbob@csinet.net

GODICH, John Paul *(Recalled Magistrate Judge, United States District Court Southern District of Indiana)* Appointed Magistrate Judge by U.S. District Court judges to term beginning Oct 1, 1973. Reappointed 1981, 1989 and 1997. Appointed Recalled Magistrate Judge by the Judicial Council of the Seventh Circuit Oct 1, 2001. Former Chief Magistrate Judge. Born Indianapolis Indiana Nov 30, 1944. Catholic. Educated at Princeton University A.B. cum laude 1966 and Yale University LL.B. 1969. Staff member Yale Law Journal 1967-69. Law Clerk to Hon. S. Hugh Dillin, U.S. District Court Southern District of Indiana 1969-71. Admitted to practice U.S. District Court Southern District of Indiana 1969, U.S. Court of Appeals Seventh Circuit 1970, Indiana 1971 and U.S. Tax Court 1972. In legal practice Indianapolis 1971-73.

Member Committee on the Administration of the Magistrate Judges System Judicial Conference of the U.S. 1987-94. President National Council of U.S. Magistrates 1988-89. Member American Judicature Society, Indianapolis, Indiana State, Seventh Circuit, Federal (President Indianapolis Chapter 1975-76) and American Bar Associations.

Office: 355 U.S. Courthouse, 46 East Ohio Street, Indianapolis 46204.

Telephone: (317) 229-3630.

GOHMAN, Cheryl Anne *(Judge, North Manchester Town Court)* Appointed by Governor Frank O'Bannon to term beginning Jan 1, 1999. Elected 1999, current term expires Dec 31, 2003.

First Deputy Clerk-Treasurer Town of North Manchester. Republican.

Office: 709 West Main Street, North Manchester 46962-1899.

Telephone: (260) 982-2031.

GOODMAN, Evan D. *(Judge, Marion Superior Court)* Assumed office Jan 1, 1996. Elected 2000, current term expires Dec 31, 2006. Serves Criminal Division. Educated at Indiana State University A.B. and University of Tulsa J.D. Court Administrator 1975-76 and Hearing Administrator 1977-81, Marion Probate Court. Judge and Presiding Judge, Marion Municipal Court Jan 1, 1982 to Dec 31, 1995, appointed by Governor Robert D. Orr.

Deputy Prosecutor Marion County 1970-73. Public Defender Marion Probate Court 1976-77. Member Governor's Commission for the Study of Mental Health Laws.

Office: 200 East Washington Street, Room W343, Indianapolis 46204.

Telephone: (317) 327-3229.

E-mail address: egoodman@indygov.org

GOSHORN, Everett E. *(Judge, Wells Superior Court)* Appointed by Governor Robert D. Orr July 1, 1986. Elected to subsequent terms. Current term expires Dec 31, 2008. Born Huntington Indiana Jan 15, 1945. Methodist. Educated at Purdue University B.S. 1967 and Indiana University J.D. 1970. Admitted to practice Indiana 1970. In legal practice Bluffton 1970-74. Judge, Wells County Court Jan 1, 1981 to June 30, 1986.

Prosecutor Wells County 1974-80. Member Indiana Judges Association, Indiana Prosecuting Attorneys Association (President Elect 1980), Wells County (President 1974), Indiana State and American Bar Associations. Graduate Indiana Judicial College. Lecturer on Small Claims Procedures in Indiana to newly elected judges. Former member Bluffton Rotary Club. Enjoys music, gardening and photography.

Office: 102 Market Street West, Bluffton 46714-2050.

Telephone: (260) 824-3287.

E-mail address: 90d01j@wellscounty.org

GRANT, Robert E. *(Judge, United States Bankruptcy Court Northern District of Indiana)* Appointed by U.S. Court of Appeals Seventh Circuit judges 1987.

Office: 2128 Federal Building, 1300 South Harrison Street, Fort Wayne 46802.

Telephone: (260) 426-2455.

GRAY, G. Thomas *(Judge, Morgan Superior Court)* Appointed by Governor Robert D. Orr to term beginning Jan 1, 1983. Elected 1984, 1990, 1996 and 2002. Current term expires Dec 31, 2008. Educated at DePauw University B.A. 1970 and Indiana University at Indianapolis J.D. 1973.

Deputy Prosecutor 1973-74 and Prosecuting Attorney 1976-82 Morgan County. Member Indiana Judges Association, Morgan County and Indiana State Bar Associations.

Mailing address: P.O. Box 1556, Martinsville 46151-1556.

Telephone: (765) 342-1030.

Fax: (765) 342-1098

GREGG, Sherry L. Biddinger *(Judge, Knox Circuit Court)* Elected Nov 1998 to term beginning Jan 1, 1999. Term expires Dec 31, 2004. Born Daviess County Indiana May 1, 1960. Educated at Vincennes University A.S. with highest honors 1980, University of Evansville B.S. magna cum laude 1982 and Indiana University School of Law J.D. 1985. Member Phi Delta Phi (President 1983-84). Admitted to practice Indiana 1986, U.S. District Courts Northern 1986 and Southern 1986 Districts of Indiana and U.S. Court of Appeals Seventh Circuit 1986. In legal practice Indianapolis 1986-89, Jasonville 1989-93 and Terre Haute 1993-99.

General Counsel Indiana State University 1993-99. Author "Designing a Campus Law Enforcement Internship Program" 23 No. 3 Campus Law Enforcement Journal May-June 1993; and "The Legal Ramifications of Student Internships" 10 No. 1 The Justice Professional 1997. Assistant Professor Department of Political Science 1989-91 and Department of Criminology 1991-93 Indiana State University. Lecturer Ph.D. Program in Education Administration 1999. Member Indiana Judges Association, American Judges Association, Knox County, Indiana State, Seventh Circuit and American Bar Associations. Named Outstanding Faculty Member Indiana State University 1992. Recipient Outstanding Alumni Faculty Citation from Vincennes University 1997 and Pacemaker Paddle Award from Vincennes University Student Government 1997. Democrat. Board Member Knox County Association of Retarded Citizens and Miss Northwest Territory Scholarship Organization, Inc. Advi-

GREGG, SHERRY L. BIDDINGER—*Continued*

sory Board Wabash Valley Regional Community Corrections. Member Knox County League of Women Voters, Indiana Partners in Politics and Sandborn Christian Church.

Office: Knox County Courthouse, 111 North Seventh Street, Vincennes 47591-2022.

Telephone: (812) 885-2527.

Fax: (812) 886-9414

E-mail address: kcircuit@wvc.net

GREGORY, Lewis J. *(Judge, Greenwood City Court)* Elected Nov 1995 to term beginning Jan 1, 1996. Reelected 1999, current term expires Dec 31, 2003. Born Muncie Indiana May 27, 1952. Presbyterian. Educated at Ball State University B.S. magna cum laude 1974 and Indiana University J.D. 1987. Admitted to practice Indiana 1988. In legal practice Indiana 1988-95.

Office: 186 Surina Way, Suite B, Greenwood 46143-1637.

Telephone: (317) 882-5129.

E-mail address: gregory@cityofgreenwood.com

GRODNIK, Charles H. *(Judge, Elkhart City Court)* Elected to term beginning Jan 1, 1992. Reelected 1995 and 1999. Current term expires Dec 31, 2003. Born Minneapolis Minnesota Sept 7, 1944. Educated at University of Minnesota B.A. 1966 J.D. 1969. Admitted to practice Indiana 1970. In legal practice Elkhart since 1971.

Certified Mediator. Member The Association of Trial Lawyers of America, Elkhart City (President 1992), Elkhart County and Indiana State (Family Law Section) Bar Associations. Member Elkhart County Election Board 1984-86.

Office: 229 South Second Street, Elkhart 46516-3192.

Telephone: (574) 522-5272.

E-mail address: chgrodnik@thornegrodnik.com

GULL, Frances C. *(Judge, Allen Superior Court)* Magistrate 1988-89. Elected to term beginning Jan 1, 1997. Reelected 2002, current term expires Dec 31, 2008. Educated at St. Joseph's College B.S. 1980 and Valparaiso University J.D. 1983.

Probate Commissioner/Misdemeanor Referee 1983-87, Deputy Prosecuting Attorney 1987-88 and Chief Deputy Prosecuting Attorney 1990-96 Allen County. Chair Mayor's Commission on Domestic Violence, Rape and Sexual Harassment. Member Daybreak Advisory Council.

Office: 715 South Calhoun Street, Room 314, Fort Wayne 46802-1805.

Telephone: (260) 449-7464.

E-mail address: fcgull@co.allen.in.us

GUTHRIE, Frank W. *(Judge, Jackson Superior Court)* Appointed by Governor Robert D. Orr to term beginning Jan 1, 1988. Elected 1990, 1996 and 2002. Current term expires Dec 31, 2008. Born Indianapolis Indiana Nov 24, 1947. Episcopalian. Educated at Wabash College B.A. 1970 and Indiana University at Bloomington J.D. 1973. Admitted to practice Indiana 1973. Began legal practice Seymour 1973. Judge, Jackson County Court Jan 1, 1976 to Dec 31, 1987.

Member Indiana Judges Association, Jackson County and Indiana State Bar Associations. Democrat.

Mailing address: P.O. Box 788, Seymour 47274-0788.

Office: 1420 Corporate Way, Seymour 47274.

Telephone: (812) 522-9677.

E-mail address: jcsupct@hsonline.net

HALL, Robert M. *(Judge, Warren Circuit Court)* Appointed by Governor Otis Ray Bowen to term beginning Jan 21, 1974. Elected Nov 1974, 1980, 1986, 1992 and 1998. Current term expires Dec 31, 2004. Born Danville Illinois Jan 14, 1944. Protestant. Educated at Indiana University at Bloomington A.B. 1966 J.D. 1969. Admitted to practice Indiana 1969. In legal practice Covington 1969-74.

Member Committee on Character and Fitness Indiana Supreme Court. Member Indiana Council of Juvenile and Family Court Judges, Indiana Judicial Conference, Indiana Judges Association, National Council of Juvenile and Family Court Judges, American Judicature Society, Fountain County (President 1972-73), Warren County, Indiana State and American Bar Associations. Graduate National College of the State Judiciary 1977 and Indiana Judicial College 1979. Republican. Member Covington Jaycees (President 1971-72) and Covington Lions Club (President 1973-74). Enjoys bowling.

Office: 5 Courthouse, 125 North Monroe, Williamsport 47993-1162.

Telephone: (765) 762-3604.

Fax: (765) 764-1692

E-mail address: rhall_wccourt@hotmail.com

HAMILTON, David F. *(Judge, United States District Court Southern District of Indiana)* Appointed for life by President Bill Clinton to term beginning Oct 28, 1994. Born Bloomington Indiana May 5, 1957. United Methodist. Educated at Haverford College B.A. magna cum laude 1979, University of Tuebingen, Germany and Yale Law School J.D. 1983. Fulbright Scholar. Law Clerk to Hon. Richard D. Cudahy, U.S. Court of Appeals Seventh Circuit 1983-84. Member Phi Beta Kappa. Admitted to practice Indiana 1984, U.S. District Court Southern District of Indiana 1984, U.S. Court of Appeals Seventh Circuit 1985 and U.S. Supreme Court 1992. In legal practice Indianapolis 1984-89 and 1991-94.

Counsel to Governor State of Indiana 1989-91.

Office: 330 U.S. Courthouse, 46 East Ohio Street, Indianapolis 46204.

Telephone: (317) 229-3640.

HAMMEL, John W. *(Judge, Marion Superior Court)* Serves Criminal Division.

Office: 200 East Washington Street, T1221, Indianapolis 46204.

Telephone: (317) 327-2490.

HANLEY, John F. *(Judge, Marion Superior Court)* Elected to term beginning Jan 1, 2001. Term expires Dec 31, 2006. Serves Civil Division. Educated at University of Notre Dame B.A. 1977 and Indiana University J.D. 1982. Judge, Marion Superior Court 1990-96.

Board of Managers Indiana Judges Association 1992-96. Democrat.

Office: 200 East Washington Street, #T-1421, Indianapolis 46204.

Telephone: (317) 327-3260.

Fax: (317) 327-3844

E-mail address: jhanley@indygov.org

HANSELMAN, David L., Sr. *(Judge, Wells Circuit Court)* Appointed by Governor Robert D. Orr to term

HANSELMAN, DAVID L., SR.—*Continued*

beginning Feb 6, 1981. Elected to subsequent terms. Current term expires Dec 31, 2006. Educated at DePauw University B.A. 1968 and Indiana University J.D. 1974. In legal practice Wells County 1974-81.

Past President Wells County Bar Association. Member Indiana Judges Association, Indiana Council of Juvenile and Family Court Judges, Indiana State and American Bar Associations. Captain USAF 1968-72.

Office: Courthouse, 102 Market Street West, Bluffton 46714-2050.

Telephone: (260) 824-6485.

E-mail address: 90c01j@wellscounty.org

HANSON, Mathew G. *(Judge, Morgan Circuit Court)* Elected to term beginning Jan 1, 2001. Term expires Dec 31, 2006. Educated at Wabash College A.B. 1991 and University of Toledo J.D. 1994.

Deputy Prosecuting Attorney Morgan County 1997-2000.

Mailing address: P.O. Box 1556, Martinsville 46151-1556.

Telephone: (765) 342-1020.

E-mail address: hanson@sciscan.net

HARCOURT, Barbara Arnold *(Judge, Rush Circuit Court)* Elected Nov 1988 to term beginning Jan 1, 1989. Reelected Nov 8, 1994 and 2000. Current term expires Dec 31, 2006. Born Rushville Indiana Dec 19, 1950. Episcopalian. Educated at Earlham College B.A. 1973, Indiana University School of Law J.D. magna cum laude 1987 and University of Nevada Reno Master's in Judicial Studies 1997. Business Editor Indiana Law Review 1986-87. Admitted to practice Indiana 1987.

Instructor in Probate Law The National Judicial College. Director Rush Welfare Department 1979-84.

Office: 100 East Second Street, Third Floor, Rushville 46173-1887.

Telephone: (765) 932-2078.

E-mail address: charcour@comsys.net

HARKIN, Jeffrey A. *(Judge, Hammond City Court)* Appointed by Governor Frank O'Bannon to term beginning April 12, 2001. Term expires Dec 31, 2003. Educated at University of Notre Dame B.A. 1973 and John Marshall Law School J.D. 1995. Democrat.

Office: 5925 Calumet Avenue, Hammond 46320-2575.

Telephone: (219) 853-6389.

HARPER, Lewis D. *(Judge, Tipton City Court)* Appointed by Governor Frank O'Bannon to term beginning May 6, 1997. Elected 1999, current term expires Dec 31, 2003.

Mailing address: P.O. Box 381, Tipton 46072-0381.

Office: 225 East Jefferson, Tipton 46072.

Telephone: (765) 675-7878.

HARPER, Mary R. *(Judge, Porter Circuit Court)* Elected to term beginning Jan 1, 1997. Reelected 2002, current term expires Dec 31, 2008. Educated at Colorado State University B.A. 1972 and Valparaiso University J.D. 1975. Judge, Porter County Court 1985 to May 31, 1986. Judge, Porter Superior Court 1986-96.

Deputy Prosecutor 1975-81 and Chief Deputy Prosecutor 1978-79 Porter County. Former Member Indiana Judicial Ethics Committee. Member Committee on Character and Fitness Indiana Supreme Court since 1986. Board of Managers Indiana Judges Association 1992-2000. Member Juvenile Justice Improvement Committee since 1997 and Probation Committee since 1998 Indiana Judicial Conference. Member Porter County Bar Association (President 1985-86).

Office: Courthouse, 16 Lincolnway, Valparaiso 46383-5555.

Telephone: (219) 465-3425.

E-mail address: d05@porterco.org

HASNERL, Charles *(Judge, Knox City Court)* Elected to term beginning Jan 1, 1996. Reelected 1999, current term expires Dec 31, 2003. Educated at Valparaiso University B.A. 1993. Republican.

Office: 101 West Washington Street, Knox 46534-1100.

Telephone: (574) 772-3766.

E-mail address: kcc@nitline.com

HAVIZA, Peter D. *(Judge, Randolph Superior Court)* Appointed by Governor Frank O'Bannon to term beginning Jan 1, 1999. Elected 2002, current term expires Dec 31, 2008. Educated at Indiana University-Bloomington B.A. 1969 and Indiana University-Indianapolis J.D. 1976. Member Phi Alpha Delta.

Town Attorney Parker City. Public Defender Randolph County 1978-98. Attorney Union School Corporation 1979-98, Randolph Central School Corporation 1981-98, WUR and Randolph County SWMD 1994-98. Member Randolph County and Indiana State Bar Associations. Petty Officer Second Class USN 1969-73. Democrat.

Office: 100 South Main Street, Winchester 47394-1892.

Telephone: (765) 584-7070.

E-mail address: judge205@connectiva.net

HAWKINS, Grant *(Judge, Marion Superior Court)* Elected to term beginning Jan 1, 2001. Term expires Dec 31, 2006. Serves Criminal Division.

Office: 200 East Washington Street, Room W-305, Indianapolis 46204-3337.

Telephone: (317) 327-4811.

E-mail address: ghawkins@indygov.org

HEATH, Daniel G. *(Judge, Allen Superior Court)* Elected to term beginning Jan 1, 1997. Reelected 2002, current term expires Dec 31, 2008. Educated at Indiana University-Bloomington B.A. 1975 and Indiana University-Indianapolis J.D. 1984.

Former Lecturer on Government and Pre-Law St. Francis College. Barrister Benjamin Harrison Inn of Court. Member Allen County Council 1993-96.

Office: 715 South Calhoun Street, Room 319, Fort Wayne 46802-1805.

Telephone: (260) 449-7633.

E-mail address: dheath@fwi.com

HEFFELFINGER, Jeffrey R. *(Judge, Huntington Superior Court)* Elected to term beginning July 1, 1988. Reelected 1990, 1996 and 2002. Current term expires Dec 31, 2008. Born Huntington Indiana Oct 31, 1954. Protestant. Educated at Huntington College B.A. summa cum laude 1977 and Indiana University J.D. 1980. Law Clerk to Hon. Linda Chezem, Lawrence County Court 1979-80. Admitted to practice Indiana 1980. Began legal practice Huntington 1980. Judge, Huntington County Court Jan 1, 1985 to July 1, 1988.

Instructor in Business Law Huntington College 1988. Former member Indiana State and American Bar Associ-

HEFFELFINGER, JEFFREY R.—*Continued*

ations. Member Indiana Judges Association and Huntington County Bar Association.

Office: 201 North Jefferson Street, Room 302, Huntington 46750-2867.

Telephone: (260) 358-4852.

E-mail address: jrheffelfinger@huntington.in.us

HEIMANN, James A. *(Judge, Adams Superior Court)* Elected Nov 1990 to term beginning Jan 1, 1991. Reelected Nov 1996 and 2002. Current term expires Dec 31, 2008. Born Decatur Indiana April 2, 1942. Catholic. Educated at St. Joseph's College B.S. cum laude 1964 and Indiana University School of Law J.D. 1967. Admitted to practice Indiana 1967. In legal practice Decatur 1972-90.

City Attorney Decatur 1972-76. Member Adams County and Indiana State Bar Associations. First Lieutenant U.S. Army 1967-70.

Mailing address: P.O. Box 569, Decatur 46733-0569.

Office: 122 South Third Street, Decatur 46733.

Telephone: (260) 724-5347.

E-mail address: superiorcourt@decaturnet.com

HEIMANN, Stephen R. *(Judge, Bartholomew Circuit Court)* Appointed by Governor B. Evan Bayh Oct 1, 1991. Elected to subsequent terms. Current term expires Dec 31, 2004. Educated at Wabash College B.A. 1977 and Indiana University-Indianapolis J.D. 1980.

Board of Directors Indiana Council of Juvenile and Family Court Judges since 1993. Board of Law Examiners since 1998. Democrat.

Office: 234 Washington Street, Columbus 47201-6750.

Telephone: (812) 379-1605.

E-mail address: sheimann@bartholomewco.com

HELDT, Carl A. *(Judge, Vanderburgh Circuit Court)* Appointed by Governor Frank O'Bannon to term beginning April 17, 1998. Elected 2000, current term expires Dec 31, 2006. Educated at Valparaiso University B.A. 1966 and Indiana University-Bloomington J.D. 1969.

Assistant City Attorney 1971. Deputy Prosecuting Attorney Evansville 1973-77. Assistant County Attorney 1993-96. Board of Directors Judicial Conference of Indiana since 2000. Member Evansville (President 1991-92). and Indiana State (House of Delegates 1991-99) Bar Associations.

Office: 210 Courts Building, 825 Sycamore Street, Evansville 47708-1885.

Telephone: (812) 435-5192.

E-mail address: caheldt@evansville.net

HENDERSON, Susan Orr *(Judge, Fountain Circuit Court)* Elected to term beginning Jan 1, 1999. Term expires Dec 31, 2004. Educated at Indiana University B.S. 1980 and University of Dayton School of Law J.D. 1984. Admitted to practice Indiana, U.S. District Courts Northern and Southern Districts of Indiana and Central District of Illinois and U.S. Supreme Court.

Deputy Prosecuting Attorney Fountain County 1984-90. Fellow Indiana Bar Foundation. Member Juvenile Benchbook Committee Judicial Conference of Indiana and Indiana State Bar Association (Delegate). Republican.

Mailing address: P.O. Box 97, Covington 47932-0097.

Office: 301 Fourth Street, Covington 47932-1237.

Telephone: (765) 793-3422.

E-mail address: ftncirct@k-inc.com

HEUER, James R. *(Judge, Whitley Circuit Court)* Appointed by Governor B. Evan Bayh April 1, 1992. Elected 1998, current term expires Dec 31, 2004. Educated at Purdue University B.S. 1971 and Indiana University J.D. 1974.

Chief Deputy Prosecutor Whitley County 1985-92. Member Juvenile Justice Improvement Committees Judicial Conference of Indiana. Republican.

Office: Courthouse, Third Floor, 101 West Van Buren Street, Columbia City 46725-2109.

Telephone: (260) 248-3115.

E-mail address: jheuer@whitleynet.org

HILL, Reuben B. *(Judge, Marion Superior Court)* Appointed by Governor Frank O'Bannon to term beginning Aug 12, 1999. Elected to subsequent term. Current term expires Dec 31, 2006. Serves Criminal Division. Republican.

Office: 200 East Washington Street, Room W-342, Indianapolis 46204.

Telephone: (317) 327-3237.

E-mail address: rehill@indygov.org

HOFF, E. Michael *(Judge, Monroe Circuit Court)* Elected to term beginning Jan 1, 1993. Reelected 1998, current term expires Dec 31, 2004. Educated at Indiana University-Bloomington B.A. 1972 J.D. 1975.

Deputy Prosecutor Monroe County 1978-79. Member Indiana Judges Association and Monroe County Bar Association. Democrat.

Office: Justice Building, 301 North College Avenue, Bloomington 47404-3865.

Telephone: (812) 349-2620.

E-mail address: mhoff@co.monroe.in.us

HOLMAN, Evelyn R. *(Judge, Sharpsville Town Court)* Elected Nov 1979 to term beginning Jan 1, 1980. Reelected Nov 1983, Nov 1987, Nov 1991, Nov 1995 and 1999. Current term expires Dec 31, 2003. Born Batesville Indiana June 21, 1943. Methodist. Educated at Ball State University B.S. 1965 M.A. 1968.

English teacher Tri-Central Junior High School and part-time school bus driver. Member Indiana City and Town Court Judges Association. Honorary member Fraternal Order of Police. Republican. Member Sharpsville Park Board, National Federation of Republican Women, Tipton County Republican Women, American Federation of Teachers and Homemakers' Forté Home Extension Club. Enjoys singing. Involved in community activities.

Mailing address: P.O. Box 14, Sharpsville 46068-0014.

Telephone: (765) 963-2911.

HOLT, J. David *(Judge, Greene Superior Court)* Appointed by Governor Robert D. Orr 1988 to term beginning Jan 1, 1989. Elected 1990, 1996 and 2002. Current term expires Dec 31, 2008. Born Bloomfield Indiana 1942. Presbyterian. Educated at Indiana University A.B. 1964 J.D. 1967. Admitted to practice Indiana 1967 and U.S. District Court Southern District of Indiana 1967. In legal practice Spencer 1971-72 and Bloomfield 1972-88.

Deputy Prosecuting Attorney Owen County 1971-72. Prosecuting Attorney Greene County 1975-82. Member Greene County and Indiana State Bar Associations. Lieutenant USN JAGC 1968-71. Republican.

Mailing address: P.O. Box 445, Bloomfield 47424-0445.

Telephone: (812) 384-3492.

HOLT, J. DAVID—*Continued*

Fax: (812) 384-8458
E-mail address: greenesuperior1@ncci.net

HOPPER, David W. *(Judge, Madison County Court)* Elected to term beginning Jan 1, 1997. Reelected 2002, current term expires Dec 31, 2008. Educated at Purdue University B.A. 1971, Ball State University M.A. 1974 and Indiana University J.D. 1978. Judge, Madison County Court 1981-90. Master Commissioner/Juvenile Referee, Hamilton County 1991-96.

Attorney Madison County Council 1995. Member Indiana Judges Association, Madison County, Indiana State and American Bar Associations. Graduate Indiana Judicial College 1986. Republican.

Office: 16 East Ninth Street, Anderson 46016-1576.
Telephone: (765) 641-9490.
E-mail address: dhopper@madisoncty.com

HORN, Gregory A. *(Judge, Wayne Superior Court)* Former Judge pro tem. Elected Judge Nov 5, 1996 to term beginning Jan 1, 1997. Reelected 2002, current term expires Dec 31, 2008. Born Muncie Indiana Feb 6, 1954. United Methodist. Educated at Indiana University-Bloomington A.B. 1976 and Indiana University-Indianapolis J.D. 1980. Member Phi Delta Phi. Admitted to practice Indiana 1980, U.S. District Court Southern District of Indiana 1980 and U.S. Supreme Court 1985. In legal practice Richmond 1980-97.

Corporate Counsel Northeastern Wayne schools 1988-96. Faculty 1987-90 and Instructor in Business Law and Criminal Justice since 1997 Indiana University-East. Member Wayne County, Indiana State (Civil Instructions Committee) and American Bar Associations. Speaker on Ethical Considerations in Family Practice 1992, Post Dissolution Modification Actions 1995 and Child Custody and Support in Indiana 1996 Indiana CLE Forum. Past President Alumni Association College of Arts and Sciences Indiana University. Republican. Director Leadership Wayne County, Absacold Youth Foundation and Boys Club.

Office: 301 East Main Street, Richmond 47374-4200.
Telephone: (765) 973-9260.
E-mail address: gregh@co.wayne.in.us

HOSTETTER, Charles E. *(Judge, Brownsburg Town Court)* Appointed to term beginning Jan 1, 1995. Elected 1999, current term expires Dec 31, 2003.

Office: 80 East Vermont, Brownsburg 46112.
Telephone: (317) 852-1192.

HOWELL, R. Joseph *(Judge, Martin Circuit Court)* Elected to term beginning Jan 1, 1993. Reelected 1998, current term expires Dec 31, 2004. Born Jasper Indiana Aug 18, 1963. Roman Catholic. Educated at Indiana University B.A. 1984 J.D. magna cum laude 1988. Editor-in-Chief Indiana Law Journal 1987-88. Law Clerk to Hon. Michael S. Kanne, U.S. Court of Appeals Seventh Circuit 1988-89. Member Delta Theta Phi and Order of the Coif. Admitted to practice Indiana 1988, U.S. District Courts Northern 1988 and Southern 1988 Districts of Indiana and U.S. Court of Appeals Seventh Circuit 1989. In legal practice Indianapolis 1989-92 and Loogootee 1992.

Member Indiana Judges Association, Indiana State and American Bar Associations. Democrat. Member Loogootee Jaycees, Loogootee Knights of Columbus, Loogootee Lions Club, Loogootee Optimist Club and Loogootee Moose Lodge.

Mailing address: P.O. Box 370, Shoals 47581-0370.
Office: Courthouse, Shoals 47581.
Telephone: (812) 247-3652.
Fax: (812) 247-3901
E-mail address: judgerjhowell@rtccom.net

HOYING, Fred H. *(Judge, Jefferson Superior Court)* Assumed office 1992. Elected 1996 and 2002. Current term expires Dec 31, 2008. Born Celina Ohio May 6, 1946. Catholic. Educated at St. Joseph's College at Rensselaer B.A. 1969 and University of Louisville J.D. with honors 1972. Admitted to practice Indiana 1972. Began legal practice Madison 1972. Judge, Jefferson County Court Jan 1, 1976 to 1992.

Instructor Ivy Tech 1978-87. Member Indiana Judges Association (Board of Managers 1980), Judicial Conference of Indiana (Board of Directors 1982-84), Indiana Judges Association and Jefferson County Bar Association. Democrat.

Office: 300 East Main Street, Madison 47250-3537.
Telephone: (812) 265-8914.
E-mail address: fhsup@jeffersoncoin.org

HUBLAR, Robert T. *(Judge, Floyd County Court)* Appointed by Governor Otis Ray Bowen to term beginning Jan 1, 1976. Elected to subsequent terms. Current term expires Dec 31, 2008. Born New Albany Indiana Aug 14, 1945. Catholic. Educated at Bellarmine Ursuline College B.S. 1967 and University of Louisville J.D. 1972. Admitted to practice Indiana 1974. Began legal practice 1974.

Member Floyd County and Indiana State Bar Associations. Democrat.

Office: 311 West First Street, Room 425, New Albany 47150-5856.
Telephone: (812) 948-5473.

HUFFER, Duane G. *(Judge, Kosciusko Superior Court)* Elected to term beginning Jan 1, 1997. Reelected 2002, current term expires Dec 31, 2008. Educated at Indiana University A.B. 1970 and Stetson University J.D. 1974. Republican.

Office: Justice Building, 121 North Lake Street, Warsaw 46580-2787.
Telephone: (574) 267-4444.
E-mail address: dhuffer@kcgov.com

HUGHES, William J. *(Judge, Hamilton Superior Court)* Appointed by Governor Robert D. Orr July 1, 1988. Elected to subsequent terms. Current term expires Dec 31, 2008. Educated at University of Evansville B.S. 1977 and Indiana University-Indianapolis J.D. 1980.

Board of Directors Indiana Judicial Center. Member Jury Committee Judicial Conference of Indiana, Indiana Judges Association (Board of Managers 1991-94), American Judicature Society, Hamilton County, Indiana State and American Bar Associations. Republican.

Office: 215 One Hamilton County Square, Suite 215, Noblesville 46060-2614.
Telephone: (317) 776-9709.
Fax: (317) 776-8587
E-mail address: wjh@co.hamilton.in.us

HUIZENGA, Roger L. *(Judge, Walkerton Town Court)* Elected to term beginning Jan 1, 1996. Reelected 1999, current term expires Dec 31, 2003.

Mailing address: P.O. Box 103, Walkerton 46574-0103.

Telephone: (574) 586-2340.

HUMPHREY, James D. *(Judge, Dearborn-Ohio Circuit Court)* Elected to term beginning Jan 1, 1999. Term expires Dec 31, 2004. Educated at Indiana University B.A. 1980 J.D. 1983.

Deputy Prosecuting Attorney 1984-86 and County Attorney 1995-98 Dearborn County. Prosecuting Attorney Dearborn County and Ohio County 1987-94. Republican.

Office: 215 West High Street, Lawrenceburg 47025-1999.

Telephone: (812) 537-8865.

Office: Courthouse, Main Street, Rising Sun 47040.

Telephone: (812) 438-2610.

E-mail address: jdh47025@yahoo.com

HUNT, Thomas R. *(Judge, Grant Circuit Court)* Appointed by Governor Otis Ray Bowen to term beginning Sept 22, 1980. Elected 1982, 1988, 1994 and 2000. Current term expires Dec 31, 2006. Educated at Indiana University B.S. 1970 J.D. 1973. Law Clerk to Indiana Court of Appeals 1971-73.

Member Indiana Judges Association (Board of Managers since 1999). Graduate Indiana Judicial College 1991. Republican.

Office: 101 East Fourth Street, Marion 46952-4010.

Telephone: (765) 664-5527.

E-mail address: abeone1803@hotmail.com

HUPPERT, Lynda F. *(Judge, Marion County Small Claims Court Washington Township Division)*

Office: 2184 East 54th Street, Indianapolis 46220.

Telephone: (317) 251-2148.

HURSH, Terry N. *(Judge, Marion County Small Claims Court Lawrence Township Division)* Elected to term beginning Jan 1, 1999. Reelected 2002, current term expires Dec 31, 2006. Born Fort Wayne Indiana March 19, 1956. Lutheran. Educated at Indiana University B.A. 1978, Ohio Northern University J.D. cum laude 1981 and Concordia University Theological Seminary M.Div. 1992. Admitted to practice Indiana 1981. In legal practice Fort Wayne 1981-92.

Attorney Board of Aviation Commission Fort Wayne 1981-82. City Attorney New Haven 1983-88. Member National Conference of Juvenile and Family Court Judges, American Judicature Society, Indianapolis, Allen County, Indiana State and American Bar Associations. President Lawrence Chamber of Commerce. Board Member Mexican Alliance of Indiana. Executive Director Lutheran Child and Family Services. Interests include family, children issues, juvenile justice and amateur radio (W9CQG). Personal Statement or Quote: "Know thyself" (Plato).

Office: 4455 McCoy Street, Lawrence 46226.

Telephone: (317) 377-7025.

Fax: (317) 545-1665

E-mail address: LawCT27@aol.com

HUSSMANN, William G., Jr. *(Magistrate Judge, United States District Court Southern District of Indiana)* Appointed by U.S. District Court judges to term beginning April 1, 1988. Reappointed 1996, current term expires April 1, 2004. Born Evansville Indiana Nov 29, 1950. Educated at Valparaiso University B.A. 1972 J.D. 1975. Admitted to practice Indiana 1976 and North Carolina 1976. In legal practice Wilmington North Carolina 1976-81.

Deputy Attorney General Indiana 1981-83. Staff Attorney Indiana Supreme Court Disciplinary Committee 1983-86 and Associated Insurance Co. 1986-88.

Office: 328 Federal Building, 101 N.W. Martin Luther King Blvd., Evansville 47708.

Telephone: (812) 434-6430.

HUTCHISON, Brian D. *(Judge, Jay Circuit Court)* Elected to term beginning Jan 1, 2001. Term expires Dec 31, 2006. Educated at Ball State University B.S. 1986 and Indiana University-Indianapolis J.D. 1995. Republican.

Office: 120 North Court Street, Portland 47371-2116.

Telephone: (260) 726-4044.

E-mail address: hutchisb@jayco.net

JACOBI, Jerry F. *(Judge, Clark Superior Court)* Elected to term beginning Jan 1, 1995. Reelected 2000, current term expires Dec 31, 2006. Educated at Indiana University B.A. 1976 and University of Dayton J.D. 1979.

Prosecuting Attorney Clark County 1983-89. Board of Directors Indiana Prosecuting Attorneys Council 1984-89. Member Clark County Bar Association. Democrat. Director Indiana Utility Consumer Counselor 1989-91.

Office: 501 East Court Avenue, Jeffersonville 47130-4029.

Telephone: (812) 285-6294.

E-mail address: jjacobi@protgra.net

JARRETTE, James C. *(Judge, Kosciusko Superior Court)* Term expires Dec 31, 2008. Educated at Butler University B.A. 1970 and Indiana University J.D. 1973. Former Judge, Kosciusko County Court, appointed by Governor Otis Ray Bowen to term beginning Sept 4, 1979.

Member Indiana Judges Association, Kosciusko County and Federal Bar Associations.

Office: 121 North Lake Street, Second Floor, Warsaw 46580-2785.

Telephone: (574) 372-2376.

E-mail address: jjarrette@kconline.com

JENT, Julia M. *(Judge, Porter Superior Court)* Appointed to term beginning Jan 8, 1997. Elected 1998, current term expires Dec 31, 2004. Educated at Indiana University B.S. 1979 and Valparaiso University J.D. 1982. U.S. Army 1965-66. Democrat.

Office: 3560 Willowcreek Road, Portage 46368-5995.

Telephone: (219) 759-2501.

E-mail address: jjent@porterco.org

JESSUP, Stephen M. *(Judge, Howard Superior Court)* Elected to term beginning Jan 1, 1995. Reelected 2000, current term expires Dec 31, 2006. Educated at Hanover College A.B. 1966 and Indiana University-Indianapolis J.D. 1969. Referee Howard Circuit Court 1978-94.

Former Member National Organization on Legal Problems in Education. Staff Indiana Judicial Study Commission. Member Ethics Committee Judicial Conference of

JESSUP, STEPHEN M.—*Continued*

Indiana. Republican. Former Member National School Board Association (School Attorney Division).

Office: 104 North Buckeye Street, Room 304, Kokomo 46901-9004.

Telephone: (765) 456-2201.

JOHNSON, David K. *(Judge, Greene Circuit Court)* Appointed by Governor Otis Ray Bowen to term beginning Sept 3, 1976. Elected 1978, 1984, 1990, 1996 and 2002. Current term expires Dec 31, 2008. Born Linton Indiana Feb 11, 1947. Methodist. Educated at Indiana University B.S. 1969 J.D. 1973. Admitted to practice Indiana 1973. Began legal practice Bloomfield 1973.

Deputy Prosecuting Attorney Greene County 1975-76. Member Indiana Judges Association, Greene County and Indiana State Bar Associations. Republican. Enjoys sports.

Mailing address: P.O. Box 231, Bloomfield 47424-0231.

Telephone: (812) 384-4325.

Fax: (812) 384-8458

E-mail address: greenecircuitcourt@ncci.net

JOHNSON, Donald C. *(Judge, Tippecanoe Superior Court)* Elected to term beginning Jan 1, 1991. Reelected 1996 and 2002. Current term expires Dec 31, 2008. Born Lafayette Indiana April 17, 1944. Educated at Indiana State University B.S. 1966 and Indiana University J.D. 1969. Member Pi Delta Phi. Admitted to practice Indiana 1969 and U.S. District Court Northern District of Indiana 1969. In legal practice Lafayette 1973-90.

Deputy Prosecuting Attorney 1970. Instructor in Law and Ethics Purdue University 1988-90. Member Indiana State and American (Judicial Administration Division) Bar Associations. Graduate 1990 and Faculty 1997 The National Judicial College. Special Agent FBI 1969-72.

Office: 301 Main Street, Lafayette 47901-1354.

Telephone: (765) 423-9107.

Fax: (765) 423-9133

E-mail address: djohnson@county.tippecanoe.in.us

JOHNSON, Kenneth H. *(Judge, Marion Superior Court)* Elected to term beginning Jan 1, 1979. Reelected 1984, 1990, 1996 and 2002. Current term expires Dec 31, 2008. Serves Civil Division. Currently serves as Presiding Judge. Born Knoxville Tennessee May 13, 1944. Member Colonial Hills Baptist Church. Educated at Xavier University 1965, Hanover College A.B. in Psychology 1966, Miami University Ph.D. candidate in Clinical Psychology 1967-68 and Indiana University School of Law at Indianapolis J.D. 1972. Staff member Indiana Law Review. Law Clerk and Bailiff to Hon. Addison M. Dowling, Marion Superior Court Jan 1, 1970 to April 1, 1973 (assisted in the writing of the Uni-Gov law, the consolidation of City and County government in Marion County Indiana). Recipient honors for Independent Study project and paper "An Electrodermographic Study of Tension in the Study of Interrupted and Uninterrupted Tasks." Member Beta Theta Pi. Admitted to practice Indiana 1972 and U.S. District Court Southern District of Indiana 1972. In legal practice Indianapolis 1973-78.

Former Counsel before the Public Service Commission of Indiana and the Internal Revenue Service. Former Assistant Corporation Counsel City of Indianapolis. Author "Practical Divorce Advocacy: Obtaining Custody for the Husband" ICLEF 1982. Important Decisions: LaVelle, et al. v. The Board of School Commissioners of the City of Indianapolis, et al. Marion Superior Court Civil Division Cause Number S280-0880 (1980); Indiana Department of State Revenue v. General Foods Corporation 427 N.E. 2d 665 (1981); F. Perry Ray v. The State Election Board 422 N.E. 2d 718 (1981), rehearing denied 425 N.E. 2d 240 (1981); State Board of Tax Commissioners v. The Rudrananda Ashram, Inc. Marion Superior Court Civil Division Cause Number S279-0471 (1982); Julia M. Carson and Knute F. Dobkins v. City of Indianapolis, Mayor William Hudnut, The City-County Council and the Capital Improvement Board of Managers of Marion County 430 N.E. 2d 788 (1982); Marion County Department of Public Welfare v. Methodist Hospital of Indiana, Inc. 436 N.E. 2d 123 (1982); Jean Johnson v. Lillie May Padilla M.D. 433 N.E. 2d 393 (1982); Capital Consolidated, Inc. v. Jane Ann Sargent and Samson Paper Company, Inc. Marion Superior Court Civil Division Cause Number S282-0079 (1983); In Re: The Marriage of Charles A. Melangton v. Marilyn K. Melangton Marion Superior Court Civil Division Cause Number S281-0855 (1983); and Jocelyn E. Tandy v. Harold Hawkins, et al. Marion Superior Court Civil Division Cause Number S283-0610 (1983).

Appointed by Chief Justice Givan to Civil Pattern Jury Instruction Committee for three year term in conjunction with the Indiana Judicial Center. Member National Conference of State Trial Court Judges, Christian Legal Society, Indiana Judges Association, Indianapolis and American (Judicial Administration Division) Bar Associations. Faculty member Indiana Judicial Center in orientation of new Indiana State Trial Court Judges, specializing in area of Domestic Relations Law 1980-83 and Indiana Continuing Legal Education Forum "Practical Divorce Advocacy" seminar Dec 1982. Guest Speaker on "Pre-Trial Conference and Stipulations Can Save You Time and Money" Aug 14, 1980, "Civil Trial Walk-Thru: The Voir Dire" and "Six Member Juries in Civil Cases" June 15, 1983 Indianapolis Bar Association. Presented paper "Changing Families: The View from the Bench" 19th Annual Conference Association of Family Conciliation Courts May 15, 1981. Guest Lecturer on Civil Trial Procedure Indiana University School of Law April 23, 1982. Participant "Ask a Judge Seminar" Indianapolis Bar Association Oct 1982. Named Best Reasonable Judge: Above Reproach in "The Best of Indianapolis" *Indianapolis* magazine May 1983. Republican. Marion County Republican Precinct Committeeman 1977-78. Board of Directors Christian Justice Center of Indianapolis, Inc. Advisory Board Paralegal Program for Indiana Central University and Salvation Army. Elder Faith Missionary Church. Member Indiana University Alumni Association, Boy Scouts of America (Speakers Bureau), Devon Civic League, Northeast Neighborhood Association (NENA) and The Friends of the Law School Art Gallery.

Office: 200 East Washington Street, Room W-443, Indianapolis 46204.

Telephone: (317) 327-4105.

E-mail address: hizoner@aol.com

JOHNSON, Randall Lee *(Judge, Grant Superior Court)* Elected to term beginning Jan 1, 2001. Term expires Dec 31, 2006. Born Marion Indiana March 31, 1949. Presbyterian. Educated at Ball State University B.S. 1971 and University of Louisville J.D. 1975. Admitted to practice Indiana 1975. In legal practice Marion 1975-92.

JOHNSON, RANDALL LEE—*Continued*

Deputy Prosecuting Attorney Grant County 1975-92. Corporate Counsel City of Marion 1992-2000. Member Grant County (President 1999) and Indiana State Bar Associations. Republican. Member Marion Rotary Club and National Rifle Association. Enjoys hunting, boating, fishing, camping and spending time with grandchildren.

Office: 101 East Fourth Street, Marion 46952.
Telephone: (765) 662-1719.
Fax: (765) 668-6541
E-mail address: rjohnson@grantcounty.net

JOHNSON, Thomas E. *(Judge, Sullivan Superior Court)* Assumed office 1988. Elected to subsequent terms. Current term expires Dec 31, 2008. Educated at Indiana University B.S. 1970 J.D. 1973. Judge, Sullivan-Greene County Court Jan 1, 1981 to 1988.

Prosecuting Attorney Sullivan County 1975-78. Member Indiana Judges Association, Sullivan County (President 1982-93) and Indiana State Bar Associations. Graduate Indiana Judicial College 1986. Democrat.

Office: 100 Courthouse Square, Room 301, Sullivan 47882-1592.
Telephone: (812) 268-6939.
E-mail address: judgetom@bigfoot.com

JUSTICE, Rebecca L. *(Judge, Hagerstown Town Court)* Appointed by Governor Frank O'Bannon to term beginning Jan 1, 1998. Elected 1999, current term expires Dec 31, 2003. Educated at Indiana University B.A. 1987 and J.D. 1991.

Office: 49 East College Street, Hagerstown 47346-1299.
Telephone: (765) 489-6172.
E-mail address: hager@info.com

KANTAR, Kristina C. *(Judge, Lake Station City Court)*

Office: 3701 Fairview Avenue, Lake Station 46405-2371.
Telephone: (219) 962-2145.

KEARNS, R. Jerome *(Judge, Vigo Superior Court)* Term expires Dec 31, 2004. Educated at Indiana State University B.S. 1961 and University of Louisville LL.B. 1966. Former Judge, Vigo County Court, elected to term beginning Jan 1, 1997.

U.S. Army 1958-60. Democrat. Representative Indiana General Assembly 1970-74 and 1986-94.

Office: 215 Wabash, Terre Haute 47807-3434.
Telephone: (812) 462-3263.
Fax: (812) 232-5183

KEELE, Michael D. *(Judge, Marion Superior Court)* Elected to term beginning Jan 1, 2001. Term expires Dec 31, 2006. Serves Environmental Division. Educated at Wabash College A.B. 1978 and Indiana University-Indianapolis J.D. 1982. Judge, Marion County Small Claims Court Pike Township Division 1989-2000.

Member Indianapolis Bar Association. Republican. Chief Counsel Department of Metropolitan Development 1984-89.

Office: 1525 Shelby Street, Indianapolis 46203.
Telephone: (317) 327-1028.
E-mail address: mkeele@indygov.org

KELLAMS, Marc R. *(Judge, Monroe Circuit Court)* Assumed office Jan 1, 1991. Elected to subsequent terms. Current term expires Dec 31, 2006. Educated at Indiana University A.B. 1975 J.D. 1978. Probate Commissioner 1979 and Juvenile Referee 1979-80, Monroe Circuit Court. Judge, Monroe Superior Court 1981-90.

Attorney Indiana University 1979-80. Adjunct Assistant Professor of Law Indiana University School of Law since 1983. Member Indiana Judges Association, Monroe County and Indiana State Bar Associations. Graduate Indiana Judicial College. USN 1968-72.

Office: Justice Building, 301 North College Avenue, Bloomington 47401-3865.
Telephone: (812) 349-2625.
E-mail address: judgekellams@co.monroe.in.us

KELLEY, David O. *(Judge, Warrick Circuit Court)*

Office: One County Square, Suite 360, Boonville 47601.
Telephone: (812) 897-6130.

KEPNER, Rex W. *(Judge, Benton Circuit Court)* Elected to term beginning Jan 1, 1997. Reelected 2002, current term expires Dec 31, 2008. Educated at Ball State University B.S. 1987 and Indiana University-Indianapolis J.D. 1990.

Chief Deputy Prosecutor Benton County 1991-96. Republican.

Office: 700 East Fifth Street, Fowler 47944-1528.
Telephone: (765) 884-0370.
E-mail address: kepner@localline.com

KINCAID, Matthew C. *(Judge, Boone Superior Court)*

Office: 307 Courthouse Square, Lebanon 46052-2159.
Telephone: (765) 482-0450.

KING, James L. *(Judge, Alexandria City Court)* Appointed by Governor Frank O'Bannon to term beginning March 12, 1999. Elected to subsequent term. Current term expires Dec 31, 2003.

Office: 125 North Wayne Street, Alexandria 46001-2051.
Telephone: (765) 724-2541.

KING, Steven E. *(Judge, La Porte Superior Court)* Elected to term beginning Jan 1, 1991. Reelected 1996 and 2002. Current term expires Dec 31, 2008. Born Valparaiso Indiana March 22, 1950. Educated at Ball State University B.S. with honors 1972 and Valparaiso University School of Law J.D. 1978. Associate Editor Valparaiso University Law Review. Law Clerk to Hon. Robert Staton, Indiana Court of Appeals Third District 1978-80 and Hon. Donald Hunter, Indiana Supreme Court 1981-83. Admitted to practice Indiana 1978.

Probate Commissioner La Porte Circuit Court 1983-90. Author "Interspousal Electronic Surveillance and Title III" 12 Valparaiso University L. Rev. 537, 1978, "Survey of Developments in Domestic Relations" 17 Indiana L. Rev. 173, 1984 and 18 Indiana L. Rev. 211, 1985. Member Indiana Judges Association, National Council of Juvenile and Family Court Judges and La Porte County Bar Association. Recipient Liberty Bell Award from Indiana State Bar Association 1990. Peace Corps Volunteer West Africa 1972-74. Teacher LaCrosse High School 1974-75. Member American Red Cross and Friends of the Library. Enjoys gardening and sports.

Office: 300 Washington Street, #202, Michigan City 46360.
Telephone: (219) 879-4453.
Fax: (219) 873-7002

KIRSCH, James S. *(Judge, Indiana Court of Appeals Second District)* Appointed by Governor B. Evan Bayh to term beginning March 5, 1994. Retained by election 1996, current term expires Dec 31, 2006. Former Presiding Judge. Born Indianapolis Indiana Dec 9, 1946. Roman Catholic. Educated at Butler University B.A. cum laude 1968 and Indiana University J.D. cum laude 1974. Staff member Indiana Law Review 1971-72. Member Phi Kappa Theta. Admitted to practice Indiana 1974, U.S. District Court Southern District of Indiana 1974 and U.S. Supreme Court 1979. In legal practice Indianapolis 1974-88. Judge pro tem Aug 1988 to June 1989 and Judge June 1989 to March 4, 1994, Marion County Superior Court.

Adjunct Faculty Member Butler University 1985-86. Visiting Professor of Law and Management Purdue University since 1991. Judge National Products Liability Moot Court Competition 1992. Distinguished Fellow 1984, Board of Directors since 1986 and President 1988-89 Indianapolis Bar Foundation. Member National Conference of Bar Presidents since 1986, Caucus of Metropolitan Bar Leaders since 1986, Judicial Ethics Committee since 1991 and Judicial Education Committee since 1993 Judicial Conference of Indiana and Council on State-Federal Judicial Relationships since 1992. Fellow American College of Trial Lawyers. Member Commercial Law League of America, Indiana Judges Association, Indianapolis (Board of Managers 1983-88, President 1987), Indiana State (House of Delegates since 1979, Task Force on Mandatory Continuing Legal Education 1985-86) and American (National Conference of State Trial Judges Judicial Administration Division) Bar Associations. Attended "Collection and Enforcement of a Judgment" 1980, "The Conflicting Public Image of Lawyers" 1987 and "The Future of Our Courts" 1993 Young Lawyers Division and "Mediation Expectations" Advanced Mediation Training Seminar 1992; Moderator and Panelist "Real Estate Foreclosures" 1982 and "Recent Developments in Indiana Law" 1984; and Moderator "Joint Custody in Indiana" 1982 and "Petitions to Transfer" 1985 Indianapolis Bar Association. Attended seminars on "The Legal System in Indiana—An Overview" Stanley K. Lacy Executive Leadership Series 1990 and "Indiana Matrimonial Law" 1990, "Post Judgment Collection" 1993, "Demonstrative Evidence" 1994 and "Stay of Execution Pending Appeal" Indiana Appellate Practice Seminar 1994 Indiana Continuing Legal Education Forum. Panelist and Moderator "Indiana Evidence Workshop" Professional Education Systems 1992. Attended seminars on "Judicial Ethics: Real Life Problems" Indiana Judicial College 1993, "Zoning and the Courts" Marion County Alliance of Neighborhood Associations 1993, "Judicial Ethics" Indiana Judicial Conference 1993, "Indiana's New Rules of Evidence" Indiana Evidence Workshop Professional Education Systems 1993 and "Marion County Court Update—The Crisis No Longer Looms, It is Here" Indiana Bar Association 1994. Participant National Conference on State-Federal Judicial Relationships 1992. Listed in *Who's Who in American Law* since 1984, *Who's Who in the Midwest* since 1988 and *Who's Who in America* since 1990. Named Sagamore of the Wabash 1987. Teacher Indianapolis Archdiocesan School System 1969-71. Democrat. Board of Directors Indianapolis Legal Aid Society 1979-86, Indianapolis Urban League since 1984, Community Service Council of Indiana since 1989 (Task Force on Services to the Elderly 1988, Treasurer 1991-92, Vice President 1992-94, President since 1995), United Way of Central Indiana (Vice Chair Allocations Subcommittee 1983 and Policy Planning since 1990, Chair Strategic Planning Committee and Evaluation Committee 1986-90, Member Key Club Leadership Council 1988) and Community Centers of Indianapolis (Chair Program Committee since 1990). Member Government Affairs Council 1983-85 and Participant Stanley K. Lacy Executive Leadership Training Series 1985-86 Indianapolis Chamber of Commerce. Member Task Force of Long-Range Plan Implementation Strategies United Way of Greater Indianapolis 1985. Board of Visitors Indiana University School of Law 1987-88. Board of Advisors Rose Hulman Institute since 1990. Enjoys reading, running and spectator sports.

Office: 200 West Washington Street, Room 433, Indianapolis 46204-2784.
Telephone: (317) 232-6909.
E-mail address: jkirsch@courts.state.in.us

KITLEY, John *(Judge, Marion County Small Claims Court Franklin Township Division)*
Office: 4531 Independence Square, Indianapolis 46203.
Telephone: (317) 784-1751.

KLEOPFER, James D., Jr. *(Judge, Scott Circuit Court)* Elected to term beginning Jan 1, 1981. Reelected 1986, 1992 and 1998. Current term expires Dec 31, 2004. Born Scottsburg Indiana Oct 16, 1942. Presbyterian. Educated at Indiana University B.S. 1964 and University of Louisville J.D. 1968. Member Phi Kappa Phi. Admitted to practice Indiana 1968 and U.S. District Court Southern District of Indiana 1968. Began legal practice Henryville 1968.

Attorney Scott County 1969-80 and Attorney Scott County Department of Public Welfare 1969-80. Member Indiana Judges Association, Indiana Juvenile Judges Association, Scott County and Indiana State Bar Associations. Democrat. Chairman Scott County Democratic Central Committee 1972-80.

Office: Courthouse, One East McClain Avenue, Scottsburg 47170-1848.
Telephone: (812) 752-8430.

KNIGHT, J. Douglas *(Judge, Vanderburgh Superior Court)* Elected Nov 1986 to term beginning Jan 1, 1987. Reelected Nov 1992 and 1998. Current term expires Dec 31, 2004. Born Evansville Indiana Nov 11, 1944. Educated at Indiana University B.A. 1966 and Cumberland School of Law of Samford University J.D. 1969. Admitted to practice Indiana 1969. In legal practice Evansville 1969-87.

Member American Inn of Court, Evansville, Indiana State and American Bar Associations. U.S. Army.

Office: 218 Courts Building, 825 Sycamore Street, Evansville 47708-1833.
Telephone: (812) 435-5112.
E-mail address: jdknight@vanderburghgov.org

KOCHER, James F. *(Judge, Marion City Court)* Appointed by Governor Robert D. Orr July 1987. Elected to subsequent terms. Current term expires Dec 31, 2003. Educated at Indiana University-Bloomington B.A. 1976 and Indiana University-Indianapolis J.D. 1979.

KOCHER, JAMES F.—*Continued*

Deputy Prosecutor Grant County 1980-81. Assistant City Attorney Marion 1981-84.

Office: 301 South Branson Street, Marion 46952-4052.

Telephone: (765) 668-4425.

KOUROS, Joan *(Judge, Lake Superior Court)* Appointed to term beginning Jan 12, 1997. Retained by election 2000. Current term expires Dec 31, 2006. Serves Criminal Division.

Office: Government Center, 2293 North Main Street, Crown Point 46307-1854.

Telephone: (219) 755-3500.

E-mail address: kourojx@lakecountyin.org

KRAMER, Michael J. *(Judge, Noble Superior Court)* Assumed office July 1999. Term expires Dec 31, 2008. Born Madison Indiana Feb 10, 1955. Roman Catholic. Educated at Ball State University B.S. 1977 and University of Dayton School of Law J.D. summa cum laude 1983. Associate Editor University of Dayton Law Review 1981-83. Member Phi Alpha Delta. Admitted to practice Indiana 1983 and U.S. District Courts Northern 1983 and Southern 1983 Districts of Indiana. In legal practice Terre Haute 1983-85 and Ligonier 1985-90. Judge, Noble County Court Jan 1, 1991 to July 1999.

Author "Patentability of a Process that Includes a Programmed Digital Computer" University of Dayton L. Rev. 1981. Member The American Law Institute, Indiana Judges Association, American Judges Association, Noble County (President 1989-91) and Indiana State Bar Associations. Democrat. President Courthouse Square Preservation Society 1990-93, Noble County Literacy Council 1991-93, Ligonier Rotary Club 1992-93 and Drug Free Noble County since 1995. Board of Directors Noble House since 1994. Enjoys history, photography and hiking.

Office: 101 North Orange Street, Albion 46701.

Telephone: (260) 636-2129.

E-mail address: mikekr@ligtel.com

KYLE, Joe E. *(Judge, Montpelier City Court)* Elected to term beginning Jan 1, 1996. Reelected 1999, current term expires Dec 31, 2003. Educated at Ball State University B.A. 1961, University of Wisconsin-Madison M.A. 1962, Indiana University-Bloomington M.A. 1967, Southern Methodist University J.D. 1970 and University of London, England B.C.J. 1973. Admitted to practice Indiana, Texas, U.S. District Court District of Indiana and U.S. Supreme Court.

Director Historic Woodlawn Trust and Blackford County Community Foundation, Inc. CEO Community Foundation of Montpelier, Inc. Democrat.

Office: 300 West Huntington Street, Montpelier 47359.

Telephone: (765) 728-5642.

E-mail address: judgejoe@parlorcity.com

LANSINGER, John R. *(Judge, New Castle City Court)* Elected to term beginning Jan 1, 1984. Reelected to subsequent terms. Current term expires Dec 31, 2003.

Office: 1217 Indiana Avenue, New Castle 47362.

Telephone: (765) 529-5720.

LAUR, G. David *(Judge, Noble Circuit Court)* Elected to term beginning Jan 1, 1999. Term expires Dec 31, 2004. Educated at The Ohio State University B.A. 1969 J.D. 1972.

Prosecutor Noble County 1974-98. Captain USAFR 1972-78. Democrat. President Prosecuting Attorney Association 1981. Board of Directors IPAC 1977-98 (Chair Pension and State Agency Committees), Indiana Law Enforcement Academy 1979-85 and Community Foundation Noble County since 1990.

Office: 101 North Orange Street, Albion 46701-1095.

Telephone: (260) 636-2128.

E-mail address: circourt@ligtel.com

LaVIOLETTE, Diana *(Judge, Putnam Circuit Court)* Elected to term beginning Jan 1, 1993. Reelected 1998, current term expires Dec 31, 2004. Educated at Texas Christian University B.A. 1967, Duquesne University M.A. 1973 and Indiana University-Indianapolis J.D. 1980.

Deputy Prosecutor 1981-86 and Chief Deputy Prosecutor 1987-92 Putnam County. Adjunct Professor of Political Science DePauw University. President Putnam County Bar Association 1992-94. Member Domestic Relations Committee Judicial Conference of Indiana. Republican.

Office: One Courthouse Square, Greencastle 46135-1503.

Telephone: (765) 653-5315.

Fax: (765) 653-0234

E-mail address: judge@ccrtc.com

LAWRENCE, William T. *(Magistrate Judge, United States District Court Southern District of Indiana)* Appointed by U.S. District Court judges to term beginning Nov 11, 2002.. Educated at Indiana University B.S. 1970 J.D. 1973. Master Commissioner 1983-96 and Judge Jan 1, 1997 to Nov 2002, Marion Circuit Court.

Fellow Indianapolis Bar Foundation. Board of Directors Judicial Conference of Indiana since 1997. Member Indiana Judges Association, Indianapolis, Indiana State and American Bar Associations. Republican.

Office: 243 U.S. Courthouse, 46 East Ohio Street, Indianapolis 46204.

Telephone: (317) 229-3610.

LEACH, Jeryl F. *(Judge, Newton Circuit Court)* Elected to term beginning Jan 1, 2001. Term expires Dec 31, 2006.

Mailing address: P.O. Box 101, Kentland 47951-0101.

Office: 201 North Third Street, Kentland 47951.

Telephone: (219) 474-5131.

E-mail address: jfllaw@ffni.com

LEE, William C. *(Senior Judge, United States District Court Northern District of Indiana)* Appointed for life by President Ronald Reagan 1981. Former Chief Judge. Assumed Senior status, serves by assignment. Born Fort Wayne Indiana Feb 2, 1938. Member Trinity English Lutheran Church (Church Council). Educated at Yale University A.B. 1959 and University of Chicago Law School J.D. 1962. Griffin Scholar and Weymouth Kirkland Scholar. Admitted to practice Indiana and U.S. District Court Northern District of Indiana. In legal practice Fort Wayne 1964-70 and 1973-81.

Deputy Prosecuting Attorney Allen County 1963-69 (Chief Deputy 1966-69). U.S. District Attorney Northern District of Indiana 1970-73. Contributing Author *Business and Commercial Litigation in the Federal Courts* West Publishing Company 1998. Author *Federal Jury Practice and Instructions* I West Publishing Company 1999. President Benjamin Harrison Inn of Court and American Inns of Court. Fellow American College of

LEE, WILLIAM C.—*Continued*

Trial Lawyers. Member Criminal Jury Instruction Committee and Judicial Council Member Bankruptcy Judge Screening Committee Seventh Circuit. Member Rules Revision Committee and Civil Justice Reform Act Advisory Committee Northern District of Indiana and Judicial Resources Committee Judicial Conference of the U.S. Co-chairman Fort Wayne Fine Arts Operating Fund Drive 1978. Board of Directors, Secretary, Vice President and President Fort Wayne Philharmonic Orchestra. Board of Directors Fort Wayne Fine Arts Foundation, Fort Wayne Civic Theatre, Neighbors, Inc., Fort Wayne Rotary Club, Embassy Theatre Foundation, Arts United of Greater Fort Wayne, Fort Wayne Ballet, Indiana Humanities Council and Lutheran School of Theology at Chicago. Board of Directors and Vice President Hospice of Fort Wayne, Inc. Board of Directors and President Legal Aid of Fort Wayne, Inc., North Side High School Alumni Association and Fort Wayne-Allen County Historical Society. Council Member and Vice President Trinity English Lutheran Church. Board of Trustees Fort Wayne Museum of Art. Board of Trustees, President and Chairman Scholarship Committee Fort Wayne Community Schools.

Office: 2145 Federal Building, 1300 South Harrison Street, Fort Wayne 46802.

Telephone: (260) 422-2841.

LEIB, Susan J. *(Judge, Mooresville Town Court)* Appointed by Governor Frank O'Bannon to term beginning July 30, 2001. Term expires Dec 31, 2003. Born Elkhart Indiana. Educated at Valparaiso University B.A. with distinction 1986 and Indiana University J.D. 1989. Admitted to practice Indiana and U.S. District Courts Northern and Southern Districts of Indiana. In legal practice Mooresville 1995-2001.

Corporate Counsel AFSCME 1995-2001. Member Morgan County, Indiana State and American Bar Associations. Republican.

Office: 26 South Indiana Street, Mooresville 46158.

Telephone: (317) 831-1330.

LENNINGTON, Wayne J. *(Judge, Delaware Circuit Court)* Appointed by Governor Frank O'Bannon to term beginning Sept 1, 1998. Elected 2002, current term expires Dec 31, 2008. Educated at Indiana University B.S. J.D. 1956. Bankruptcy Trustee 1978-98, Master Commissioner 1990-95 and Probate Commissioner 1995-98 Delaware County.

Office: Delaware County Justice Center, 100 West Washington Street, Muncie 47305.

Telephone: (765) 747-7772.

E-mail address: wlennington@co.delaware.in.us

LETT, Thomas R. *(Judge, Tipton Circuit Court)*

Office: Courthouse, 101 East Jefferson Street, Tipton 46072-1909.

Telephone: (765) 675-2791.

LEVINE, Stanley A. *(Judge, Allen Superior Court)* Appointed by Governor Frank O'Bannon to term beginning Jan 1, 1999. Elected 2002, current term expires Dec 31, 2008. Educated at Indiana University B.A. 1960 LL.B. 1963.

Legal Advisor Common Council of City of Fort Wayne 1984-95. Board of Directors Indiana Judges Association. Member Allen County (President 1977-78) and Indiana State Bar Associations. Captain Indiana Air National Guard 1963-71. Staff Judge Advocate 1967-71. President Legal Aid of Fort Wayne, Inc. 1975-76.

Office: 715 South Calhoun Street, Room 325, Fort Wayne 46802-1805.

Telephone: (260) 449-7258.

E-mail address: salevi@fwi.com

LEWIS, Jordan D. *(Magistrate Judge, United States District Court Southern District of Indiana)* Appointed by U.S. District Court judges to term beginning 1979. Serves part time. Educated at Indiana University School of Law J.D. 1959. U.S. Army 1952-55.

Mailing address: P.O. Box 1506, Terre Haute 47808-1506.

Telephone: (812) 232-2382.

LEWIS, Michael J. *(Judge, Terre Haute City Court)*

Office: City Hall, 17 Harding Avenue, Terre Haute 47808.

Telephone: (812) 232-0697.

LINDQUIST, Kent *(Recalled Judge, United States Bankruptcy Court Northern District of Indiana)* Former Chief Judge. Appointed Recalled Judge by the Judicial Council of the Seventh Circuit Jan 10, 2003.

Office: 5400 Federal Plaza, Suite 3600, Hammond 46230.

Telephone: (219) 852-3550.

LLOYD, Mary Margaret *(Judge, Vanderburgh Superior Court)* Elected to term beginning Jan 1, 2001. Term expires Dec 31, 2006. Born Evansville Indiana Feb 3, 1964. Roman Catholic. Educated at University of Evansville B.S. magna cum laude 1986 and Indiana University-Indianapolis School of Law J.D. 1991. Admitted to practice Indiana 1991.

Deputy Prosecuting Attorney Vanderburgh County 1992-2000. Member Indiana Judges Association and Evansville Bar Association.

Office: 825 Sycamore Street, Room 218, Evansville 47708-1833.

Telephone: (812) 435-5966.

E-mail address: mlloyd@vanderburghgov.org

LOHORN, Peggy Quint *(Judge, Montgomery County Court)* Elected to term beginning Jan 1, 2003. Term expires Dec 31, 2008. Born Hammond Indiana Oct 27, 1955. Christian. Educated at Purdue University B.A. 1977 and University of Indiana at Indianapolis J.D. 1982. Admitted to practice Indiana 1982 and U.S. District Courts Northern 1982 and Southern 1982 Districts of Indiana. In legal practice Crawfordsville 1982-85.

Deputy Prosecutor 1983-85 and Chief Deputy Prosecutor 1985-2002 Montgomery County. Past President Montgomery County Bar Association. Republican. Active in community service organizations and church. Enjoys Purdue sports.

Office: 100 East Main, Room 302, Crawfordsville 47933.

Telephone: (765) 364-6455.

E-mail address: plohorn@yahoo.com

LONGER, William J. *(Judge, Hobart City Court)* Elected to term beginning Jan 1, 1992. Reelected 1995 and 1999. Current term expires Dec 31, 2003. Born Vinton Iowa Oct 20, 1951. Methodist. Educated at Valparaiso University B.A. 1974 J.D. 1977. Member Delta Theta Phi. Admitted to practice Indiana 1977 and U.S. District Court Northern District of Indiana 1978. In legal practice Griffith 1977-79 and Hobart since 1979.

LONGER, WILLIAM J.—*Continued*

Deputy Prosecuting Attorney Lake County 1982-91. Assistant City Attorney Hobart 1986-87. Instructor in Business Law Calumet College 1978-79. Member Hobart, Lake County, Indiana State and American Bar Associations.

Office: 414 Main Street, Hobart 46342-4444.

Telephone: (219) 942-8218.

Fax: (219) 942-2697

E-mail address: court@hobart.city.in.us

LOPOSSA, Paula E. *(Judge, Marion County Small Claims Court Center Township Division)* Educated at Millikin University B.A. 1966 and Indiana University M.A.T. 1968 J.D. 1973. Hearing Judge, Alcoholic Beverage Commission 1989-90. Former Judge, Marion Superior Court, elected to term beginning Jan 1, 1991.

Deputy Prosecutor Marion County 1975-77. Assistant U.S. Attorney 1977-89. Member Criminal Instructions Committee Judicial Conference of Indiana. Democrat.

Office: G-5 City-County Building, 200 East Washington Street, Indianapolis 46204.

Telephone: (317) 327-5057.

LOPP, Kenneth Lynn *(Judge, Crawford Circuit Court)* Elected to term beginning Jan 1, 1993. Reelected 1998, current term expires Dec 31, 2004. Born Corydon Indiana. Roman Catholic. Educated at Indiana University B.A. 1978 and University of Louisville J.D. 1984. Admitted to practice Indiana 1984 and U.S. District Courts Northern 1984 and Southern 1984 Districts of Indiana. In legal practice Corydon 1984-92 and English 1985-92.

Public Defender Harrison County 1986. Prosecuting Attorney Crawford County 1987-92. Member Harrison/Crawford (President 1991) and Indiana State Bar Associations. Democrat. Lions Club.

Mailing address: P.O. Box 216, English 47118-0216.

Office: Courthouse, South Court Street, English 47118.

Telephone: (812) 338-3113.

E-mail address: klopp@aol.com

LORCH, Basil H., III *(Judge, United States Bankruptcy Court Southern District of Indiana)* Appointed by U.S. Court of Appeals Seventh Circuit judges.

Office: 207 Federal Building, 121 West Spring Street, New Albany 47150.

Telephone: (812) 948-5230.

LOVE, Karen M. *(Judge, Hendricks Superior Court)* Elected to term beginning Jan 1, 1995. Reelected 2000, current term expires Dec 31, 2006. Educated at Butler University B.S. 1978 and Indiana University-Indianapolis J.D. 1986.

Member Hendricks County and Indiana State Bar Associations.

Office: One Courthouse Square, Suite 108, Danville 46122-0243.

Telephone: (317) 745-9393.

LOWE, Robert J. *(Judge, Putnam Superior Court)* Elected to term beginning Jan 1, 1997. Reelected 2002, current term expires Dec 31, 2008. Educated at Marion College B.A. 1968 and Indiana University-Indianapolis J.D. 1974.

Prosecuting Attorney Putnam County 1987-96. U.S. Army 1969-70. Republican.

Office: One Courthouse Square, Greencastle 46135-1503.

Telephone: (765) 653-2658.

E-mail address: putsupct@indy.tds.net

LOYD, K. Mark *(Judge, Johnson Circuit Court)* Magistrate 1991-94. Appointed Judge by Governor B. Evan Bayh Nov 16, 1994. Elected 2000, current term expires Dec 31, 2006. Educated at Franklin College B.A. 1971, Ball State University M.S. 1981 and University of Dayton J.D. 1984.

Chief Deputy Prosecutor Johnson County 1988-90. Faculty Member Business Law IUPU at Columbus since 1981. Member Johnson County Bar Association. Republican.

Office: Five East Jefferson Street, Franklin 46131-2339.

Telephone: (317) 736-3705.

E-mail address: markloyd@co.johnson.in.us

LOZANO, Rudy *(Judge, United States District Court Northern District of Indiana)* Appointed for life by President Ronald Reagan to term beginning Feb 26, 1988. Born East Chicago Indiana July 10, 1942. Educated at Indiana University B.S. 1963 LL.B. 1966. In legal practice Merrillville 1966-88. USAR 1966-73.

Office: 5400 Federal Plaza, Suite 4300, Hammond 46320.

Telephone: (219) 852-3600.

LUTZ, Robert *(Judge, Marion County Small Claims Court Wayne Township Division)*

Office: 5401 West Washington Street, Indianapolis 46241.

Telephone: (317) 241-9573.

LYTTON, Howard B., Jr. *(Judge, Dubois Superior Court)* Elected to term beginning Jan 1, 1999. Term expires Dec 31, 2004. Educated at Oakland City University B.S. 1960 and Indiana University J.D. 1966.

Member Dubois County and Indiana State Bar Associations. U.S. Army. Secretary Indiana State Police Board 1989-93. Democrat.

Office: One Courthouse Square, Jasper 47546-3088.

Telephone: (812) 481-1692.

E-mail address: hvoelkell@juno.com

MAGNUS-STINSON, Jane *(Judge, Marion Superior Court)* Appointed by Governor B. Evan Bayh March 6, 1995. Elected Nov 5, 1996 and 2002. Current term expires Dec 31, 2008. Serves Criminal Division. Educated at Butler University B.S. 1979 and Indiana University J.D. 1983.

Counsel June 1991 to Feb 1995 and Deputy Chief of Staff Jan 1993 to Feb 1995 to Governor B. Evan Bayh. Adjunct Professor Indiana University since 1988. Member Code Revision Commission 1991-95. Member Indianapolis and Indiana State Bar Associations. Faculty Member National Institute for Trial Advocacy Indianapolis since 1990. Board of Visitors Indiana University School of Law.

Office: 200 East Washington Street, Room W-306, Indianapolis 46204-3337.

Telephone: (317) 327-5466.

E-mail address: jstinson@indygov.org

MANIER, Jenny Pitts *(Judge, St. Joseph Superior Court)* Appointed by Governor Frank O'Bannon to term

MANIER, JENNY PITTS—*Continued*

beginning Aug 17, 1998. Retained by election 2000. Current term expires Dec 31, 2006. Educated at University of Notre Dame B.A. 1982 J.D. 1985.

Staff Attorney Legal Services Program of Northern Indiana 1985-88. Chief Assistant City Attorney South Bend 1988-97. General Counsel Indiana Department of Commerce 1997-98. Member St. Joseph County and Indiana State Bar Associations.

Office: 101 South Main Street, South Bend 46601-1807.

Telephone: (574) 235-9550.

MANN, Elizabeth N. *(Judge, Monroe Circuit Court)* Assumed office Jan 1, 1991. Elected to subsequent terms. Current term expires Dec 31, 2004. Educated at Indiana University A.B. 1973 J.D. 1976. Judge, Monroe Superior Court July 20, 1989 to 1990.

County Attorney Monroe County 1981-84. Board of Directors Judicial Conference of Indiana 1993-94. Member Indiana Judges Association (Board of Managers 1991), American Judicature Society, Monroe County, Indiana State and American Bar Associations. Graduate Indiana Judicial College 1997. Attended Indiana Graduate Program for Judges 1997. Democrat.

Office: Courts Building, 301 North College Avenue, Bloomington 47401-3865.

Telephone: (812) 349-2635.

E-mail address: elizmann@co.monroe.in.us

MARNOCHA, John M. *(Judge, St. Joseph Superior Court)* Appointed by Governor Frank O'Bannon to term beginning Jan 1, 1999. Retained by election 2002, current term expires Dec 31, 2008. Currently serves as Chief Judge. Born South Bend Indiana Nov 18, 1954. Educated at Indiana University B.A. 1978 and Valparaiso University School of Law J.D. 1982. Admitted to practice Indiana 1982, U.S. District Court Northern District of Indiana 1982 and U.S. Court of Appeals Seventh Circuit. In legal practice South Bend 1982-90.

Deputy City Attorney South Bend 1982-85. Deputy Prosecuting Attorney 1986-94 and Chief Deputy Prosecuting Attorney 1994-99 St. Joseph County. Adjunct Assistant Professor of Law University of Notre Dame Law School.

Office: 101 South Main Street, South Bend 46601-1807.

Telephone: (574) 235-9769.

Fax: (574) 235-5097

E-mail address: jmmarnocha@netscape.net *and* jmarnoch@co.st-joseph.in.us

MAROC, Richard W. *(Judge, Lake Superior Court)* Appointed by Governor Otis Ray Bowen to term beginning Jan 1, 1979. Retained by election. Current term expires Dec 31, 2006. Serves Criminal Division. Born Hammond Indiana Oct 1, 1942. Catholic. Educated at St. Joseph's College B.A. 1964 and Indiana University J.D. 1968. Admitted to practice Indiana 1968. Began legal practice East Chicago 1968. In legal practice Hammond 1972. Commissioner, Lake Criminal Court 1972.

Deputy Prosecuting Attorney Lake County 1973-75. Former member East Chicago City, Hammond City, Indiana State and American Bar Associations. Sergeant E-6 U.S. Army. Member Indiana Save the Dunes Association. Amateur hockey player 1967-76. High school club hockey coach 1977-78. Enjoys canoeing, hiking and outdoor activities.

Office: Government Center, 2293 North Main Street, Crown Point 46307-1854.

Telephone: (219) 755-3500.

E-mail address: marocrw@lakecountyin.org

MARSHALL, Dan E. *(Judge, Hancock Superior Court)*

Office: Nine East Main Street, Room 106, Greenfield 46140-2320.

Telephone: (317) 462-1115.

MASON, Mark W. *(Judge, Attica City Court)* Elected to term beginning Jan 1, 1988. Reelected to subsequent terms. Current term expires Dec 31, 2003. Educated at Purdue University B.S. 1966 M.S.

Teacher Attica Consolidated Schools.

Office: 305 East Main Street, Attica 47918-1323.

Telephone: (765) 762-2467.

E-mail address: mmason@attica.k12.in.us

MATHIAS, Paul D. *(Judge, Indiana Court of Appeals Third District)* Appointed by Governor Frank O'Bannon to term beginning April 1, 2000. Retained by election 2002, current term expires Dec 31, 2012. Educated at Harvard University B.A. cum laude 1976 and Indiana University-Bloomington J.D. 1979. Referee 1985-89 and Former Judge, Allen Superior Court, appointed by Governor B. Evan Bayh July 24, 1989.

Board of Managers 1991-2001, Secretary-Treasurer July 1993 to July 1995, Vice President July 1995 to July 1997 and President 1997-99 Indiana Judges Association. Vice Chairman Judicial Technology and Automation Committee. Member Records Management Committee and Character and Fitness Committee Indiana Supreme Court and Indiana Federal-State Council.

Office: 421 State House, 200 West Washington Street, Indianapolis 46204-2784.

Telephone: (317) 232-6880.

Fax: (317) 233-3100

E-mail address: pmathias@courts.state.in.us

MATSEY, David P. *(Judge, Starke Circuit Court)* Magistrate 1978-92. Appointed Judge by Governor B. Evan Bayh July 1, 1992. Elected to term beginning Jan 1, 1993. Reelected 1998, current term expires Dec 31, 2004. Educated at Wabash College A.B. 1966 and Valparaiso University J.D. 1969.

Chairman Probation Committee Judicial Conference of Indiana. Board of Directors Indiana Judicial Conference. Member Indiana Judges Association, Indiana Council of Juvenile and Family Court Judges, Starke County, Indiana State and American Bar Associations. Graduate Indiana Judicial College 1995. Democrat.

Office: Courthouse, 53 East Washington Street, Knox 46534-1196.

Telephone: (574) 772-9146.

E-mail address: starkecircuit@skyenet.net

MATTINGLY-MAY, Melissa S. *(Judge, Indiana Court of Appeals Fourth District)* Appointed by Governor Frank O'Bannon April 9, 1998. Retained by election 2000, current term expires Dec 31, 2010. Former Presiding Judge. Educated at Indiana University-South Bend B.S. 1980 and Indiana University-Indianapolis J.D. 1984. In legal practice Evansville 1984-98.

Board Member Indiana Continuing Legal Education Forum and Indiana Bar Foundation. Fellow Indianapolis

MATTINGLY-MAY, MELISSA S.—*Continued*

Bar Association and Indiana Bar Foundation. Member Evansville, Indianapolis, Indiana State (Board of Governors 1992-94, Counsel to President 2000-01) and American Bar Associations.

Office: 115 West Washington Street, Suite 1270, Indianapolis 46204-3419.

Telephone: (317) 232-6907.

E-mail address: mmatting@courts.state.in.us

MAUGHMER, Richard A. *(Judge, Cass Superior Court)* Elected to term beginning Jan 1, 2001. Term expires Dec 31, 2006. Educated at University of Nebraska B.S. 1975 J.D. 1979.

Prosecuting Attorney Cass County 1986-2000. Member Cass County and Indiana State Bar Associations. Lieutenant Colonel USAF 1972-2001.

Office: Courthouse, 200 Court Parke, Logansport 46947.

Telephone: (574) 753-7736.

E-mail address: supcourt2@casscountygov.org

McCARTY, Patrick L. *(Judge, Marion Superior Court)* Elected to term beginning Jan 1, 1991. Reelected 1996 and 2002. Current term expires Dec 31, 2008. Serves Civil Division. Educated at Ball State University B.S. 1971 and Indiana University-Indianapolis J.D. 1974. Commissioner Probate Division Marion Superior Court 1977-78.

Deputy Prosecutor Marion County 1975-76. Democrat.

Office: 200 East Washington Street, Room W-406, Indianapolis 46204.

Telephone: (317) 327-4222.

E-mail address: pmccarty@indygov.org

McENTARFER, James A. *(Judge, Perry Circuit Court)* Elected to term beginning Jan 1, 2001. Term expires Dec 31, 2006. Educated at University of Evansville B.S. 1978 and Indiana University-Indianapolis J.D. 1981.

Deputy Prosecuting Attorney Marion County 1984-86 and Tell City 1986-95. Member Perry County and Indiana State Bar Associations. Democrat.

Office: Courthouse Square, 2219 Payne Street, Tell City 47586.

Telephone: (812) 547-7048.

E-mail address: pcc@psci.net

McGILLIVRAY, Roderick D. *(Judge, Bartholomew Superior Court)*

Office: 234 Washington Street, Columbus 47201-6750.

Telephone: (812) 379-1610.

McGRAW, J. Philip *(Judge, Jasper Superior Court)* Appointed by Governor Otis Ray Bowen to term beginning July 1, 1981. Elected 1984, 1990, 1996 and 2002. Current term expires Dec 31, 2008. Born Lafayette Indiana Jan 5, 1944. Roman Catholic. Educated at St. Joseph's College B.S. 1969 and Valparaiso University School of Law J.D. 1973. Admitted to practice Indiana 1973 and U.S. District Court Southern District of Indiana 1973. Judge, Jasper-White County Court 1976-78. Judge, Jasper County Court 1978-81.

Deputy Prosecutor Thirtieth Judicial Circuit 1973-76. Important Decision: Brant v. Lumen (contract action and civil rights) 515 N.E.2d 868 Ind. App. 3, 1987. Adjunct Professor of Business Law St. Joseph's College 1982-91. Member American Judicature Society, Indiana Judicial Association (Legislative Committee 1976-78, County Court Committee 1979-84), Jasper County (Law Day Chairman 1975 and 1981), Indiana State and American Bar Associations. Attended The National Judicial College. Graduate and Instructor Indiana Judicial College. Instructor Institute for State Trial Judges. Teaching Fellows St. Joseph's College since 1994. Named Outstanding Trial Judge of the State of Indiana by Indiana Trial Lawyers Association 1986. Republican. Chairman Jasper County Mental Health 1979. Director Jasper Superior Court Alcohol and Drug Abuse Program since 1981. Adult Leader 4-H Club 1965. Member Community Committee for Community Development since 1986 and Chairman Committee for Rensselaer Alumni 1987 St. Joseph's College. Member Rensselaer Jaycees (Internal Vice President 1975), Indiana Jaycees, Boy Scouts of America (Member since 1972 and President 1988-91 Executive Board Sagamore Council, Vice President Programming 1985-88, Properties Chairman 1985-88), Ohio Archaeological Society, Northwest Indiana Archaeological Society (Executive Vice President 1980-81, Chairman Bi-Annual Cultural Show), Rensselaer Rotary 1983-88, Sons of the American Legion, National Rifle Association, Pheasants Forever and Ducks Unlimited. Enjoys hunting, fishing and golf.

Office: 115 West Washington Street, Rensselaer 47978-2890.

Telephone: (219) 866-4971.

E-mail address: phil@liljasper.com

McGREGOR, Cecelia J. *(Judge, Goshen City Court)* Appointed by Governor Robert D. Orr to term beginning June 8, 1984. Elected 1987, 1991, 1995 and 1999. Current term expires Dec 31, 2003. Born Carroll Iowa Aug 6, 1952. Roman Catholic. Educated at Mount Mercy College B.A. summa cum laude 1974 and University of Notre Dame J.D. 1977. Admitted to practice Indiana 1978. Began legal practice Goshen 1978.

Author "Antenuptial Agreements—Then and Now" *Res Gestae* Indiana State Bar Association and Chapter "Legal Ethics in Probate Practice" *Indiana Probate Practice* Matthew Bender Co. Guardian Ad Litem Elkhart County 1978-83. Public Defender Elkhart Circuit Court 1978-84. Member Indiana Supreme Court Subcommittees on Accelerated Dispute Resolution and Judicial Ethics. Member Indiana Judges Association and Goshen City Bar Association. Recipient Outstanding Young Women of America Award 1978, Outstanding Alumni Award Oct 1982, Child Advocate Award 1983 and Benefactor Award from Association for Disabled of Elkhart County 1988. Republican. Board of Directors New Day Parent-Child Society 1982-83. Member Committee for Prevention of Sexual Abuse 1980-83 and Child Community Protection Team 1980-84 (Chairperson 1984). Secretary 1983-87 Center for Community Justice (formerly Elkhart County PACT). Enjoys writing, cooking, reading, gardening and photography.

Office: 111 East Jefferson Street, Suite 2, Goshen 46528-3717.

Telephone: (574) 533-9365.

McINTOSH, Mark A. *(Judge, Huntington Circuit Court)* Appointed by Governor Robert D. Orr to term beginning July 30, 1987. Elected 1988, 1994 and 2000. Current term expires Dec 31, 2006. Born Glasgow Kentucky Aug 31, 1933. Methodist. Educated at Michigan State University B.S. 1956 and Indiana University, Bloomington J.D. 1964. Member Sigma Chi. Admitted to practice Indiana 1964. In legal practice Huntington 1964-87. Judge, Huntington City Court 1966-70.

MCINTOSH, MARK A.—*Continued*

Member Huntington County, Indiana State and American Bar Associations. Previously employed as secondary school teacher. Republican. Member Rotary, Elks, United Way and local charities. Interested in Civil War history. Enjoys alpine and Nordic skiing and camping.

Office: 201 North Jefferson Street, Room 301, Huntington 46750-2800.

Telephone: (260) 358-4814.

E-mail address: mark.mcintosh@huntington.in.us

McINTYRE, Richard D., Sr. *(Judge, Lawrence Circuit Court)* Appointed by Governor Robert D. Orr Nov 21, 1988. Elected to subsequent terms. Current term expires Dec 31, 2008. Educated at University of Colorado B.A. 1978 and Indiana University-Bloomington J.D. 1981.

Board of Managers Indiana Judges Association 1991-99. Board of Directors Judicial Conference of Indiana 1993-99. Graduate Indiana Judicial College 1998. Republican. Representative Indiana General Assembly 1980-84.

Office: Courthouse, 916 Fifteenth Street, Bedford 47421.

Telephone: (812) 275-2421.

E-mail address: rdm@kiva.net

McKINNEY, Larry J. *(Chief Judge, United States District Court Southern District of Indiana)* Appointed for life by President Ronald Reagan to term beginning July 1987. Chief Judge since Jan 1, 2001. Educated at MacMurry College B.A. 1966 and Indiana University J.D. 1969. Former Judge, Johnson Circuit Court, elected to term beginning Jan 1, 1979.

Member Federal Judges Association.

Office: 204 U.S. Courthouse, 46 East Ohio Street, Indianapolis 46204.

Telephone: (317) 229-3650.

McKINNON, Jon *(Judge, Bicknell City Court)* Elected to term beginning Jan 1, 1992. Reelected 1995 and 1999. Current term expires Dec 31, 2003. Educated at Vincennes University.

Attended Indiana Law Enforcement Academy 1985. U.S. Army 1964-67. Democrat.

Mailing address: P.O. Box 127, Bicknell 47512-0127.

Office: 119 East Second Street, Bicknell 47512-2201.

Telephone: (812) 735-2255.

Fax: (812) 735-3171

E-mail address: jonmckinnon1@juno.com

MEADE, Lesley A. *(Judge, Tippecanoe Superior Court)*

Office: 301 Main Street, Lafayette 47901.

Telephone: (765) 423-9280.

MEANS, William T. *(Judge, St. Joseph Superior Court)* Appointed by Governor Robert D. Orr March 31, 1986. Retained by election. Current term expires Dec 31, 2006. Educated at University of Southern California A.B. 1950 and University of Michigan J.D. 1953. Judge, Mishawaka City Court 1964-71.

Assistant City Attorney Mishawaka 1972-79. Attorney Mishawaka Parks Board 1984-86. Member Indiana Judges Association, St. Joseph County, Indiana State and American Bar Associations.

Office: 101 South Main Street, South Bend 46601-1807.

Telephone: (574) 235-9769.

MEIER, Keith A. *(Judge, Warrick Superior Court)* Elected to term beginning Jan 1, 2001. Term expires Dec 31, 2006. Educated at Indiana State University at Evansville B.S. 1972 and Indiana University-Indianapolis J.D. 1975.

Police Legal Advisor Vanderburgh County 1976-80. Public Defender Warrick County 1980-90. Chief Deputy Prosecuting Attorney Second Judicial Circuit 1995-2001. Assistant Professor and Adjunct Faculty Member University of Evansville 1977-2001. Graduate FBI Academy 1977. Republican.

Office: One County Square, Suite 300, Boonville 47601-0666.

Telephone: (812) 897-6140.

E-mail address: kameagle@aol.com

MERTZ, Marjorie L. *(Judge, Fremont Town Court)* Appointed by Governor Otis Ray Bowen to term beginning Dec 1, 1975. Elected to subsequent terms. Current term expires Dec 31, 2003. Educated at The Ohio State University 1942-45. Justice of the Peace 1964-75.

Secretary-Treasurer 1982-84 and Secretary 1984-96 Indiana City and Town Court Judges Association. Republican.

Mailing address: P.O. Box 438, Fremont 46737-0438.

Office: 205 North Tolford Street, Fremont 46737.

Telephone: (260) 495-9849.

METZ, Anthony John, III *(Judge, United States Bankruptcy Court Southern District of Indiana)* Appointed by U.S. Court of Appeals Seventh Circuit judges to term beginning Nov 14, 1997. Term expires Nov 13, 2011. Lutheran. Educated at Indiana University B.S. 1969 J.D. 1972. Member Phi Alpha Delta. Admitted to practice Indiana 1972 and U.S. District Court Southern District of Indiana 1972. In legal practice Indianapolis 1972-85. Commissioner, Marion Circuit Court 1979-84. Judge, Marion Superior Court Jan 1, 1985 to Nov 13, 1997.

Deputy Attorney General 1972-76. Important Decision: Gallagher v. Indiana State Election Board (held voters' residency requirements constitutional) 598 N.E.2nd 510, 1992. Fellow Indiana Bar Foundation 1997. Member National Conference of Bankruptcy Judges, Indianapolis (Executive Committee Litigation Section 1986-98, Board of Managers 1989-91, Vice President 1993 and 1994), Indiana State (Delegate 1992-96) Bar Associations. Participant in numerous seminars for Indiana CLE Forum and Indianapolis Bar Association. Named Distinguished Fellow 1988 and Recipient President's Award 1988 from Indianapolis Bar Association. Member Indianapolis Lawyers Club, Indianapolis Museum of Art and Indianapolis Zoological Society.

Office: 317 U.S. Courthouse, 46 East Ohio Street, Indianapolis 46204.

Telephone: (317) 229-3880.

MILLER, Alan R. *(Judge, Edgewood Town Court)* Appointed by Governor B. Evan Bayh to term beginning April 1, 1995. Elected 1999, current term expires Dec 31, 2003. Educated at Wabash College A.B. 1983 and Valparaiso University J.D. 1986. Member Phi Delta Phi.

Member Madison County, Indiana State and American Bar Associations. Chair Board of Directors American Red Cross of Madison County 1996.

Office: 3405 Nichol Avenue, Anderson 46011-3060.

Telephone: (765) 649-5533.

MILLER, Gary L. *(Judge, Marion Superior Court)* Elected to term beginning Jan 1, 1991. Reelected 1996 and 2002. Current term expires Dec 31, 2008. Serves Civil Division. Educated at Indiana University-Bloomington A.B. 1977 and Indiana University-Indianapolis J.D. 1980.

Deputy Prosecutor Marion County 1979-83. Board of Directors Judicial Conference of Indiana 1996-98. Member Indianapolis and Indiana State Bar Associations. Republican.

Office: 200 East Washington Street, Room W-507, Indianapolis 46204-3307.
Telephone: (317) 327-3939.
E-mail address: gmiller@indygov.org

MILLER, Robert L., Jr. *(Chief Judge, United States District Court Northern District of Indiana)* Appointed for life by President Ronald Reagan to term beginning 1985. Chief Judge since Feb 3, 2003. Educated at Northwestern University B.S. 1972 and Indiana University J.D. 1975. Law Clerk to U.S. District Court 1975. Former Judge, St. Joseph County Superior Court, appointed to term beginning Jan 1, 1976.

Author *Indiana Practice: Indiana Evidence* vols. 12 and 13, 1984 and vols. 12, 13, 13A and 13B, 1995 West Publishing Co. Member The American Law Institute, Judicial Conference of the U.S., St. Joseph County, Indiana State and American Bar Associations.

Office: 325 Federal Building, 204 South Main Street, South Bend 46601.
Telephone: (574) 246-8080.

MILLIGAN, Thomas K. *(Judge, Montgomery Circuit Court)* Elected to term beginning Jan 1, 1975. Reelected 1980, 1986, 1992 and 1998. Current term expires Dec 31, 2004. Educated at Wabash College B.A. 1963 and Indiana University J.D. 1966.

Member Indiana Judges Association (Board of Managers 1990-97, Secretary-Treasurer 1997-99, Vice President 1999-2001, President 2001-03), Indiana Council of Juvenile and Family Court Judges (Board of Directors 1979-85, Secretary 1980-84), Montgomery County and Indiana State Bar Associations. Graduate Indiana Judicial College 1981.

Office: 100 East Main Street, Crawfordsville 47933-1715.
Telephone: (765) 364-6450.
Fax: (765) 364-7251
E-mail address: tkm@wico.net

MITCHELL, John D. *(Judge, Ohio-Switzerland Superior Court)* Elected to term beginning Jan 1, 1985. Reelected Nov 1990, 1996 and 2002. Current term expires Dec 31, 2008. Born Decatur County Indiana March 15, 1937. Episcopalian. Educated at Wabash College A.B. 1959 and Indiana University J.D. 1969. Admitted to practice Indiana 1969 and U.S. District Court Southern District of Indiana 1969. In legal practice Rising Sun 1969-84.

Member Indiana Judges Association, Dearborn-Ohio County, Indiana State and American Bar Associations. Attended seminars Indiana Judicial Conference. Airman Second Class USAFR 1960-65. Previously employed at Indiana Bureau of Motor Vehicles 1961-64 and Indiana Revenue Department 1968-69. Democrat. President Decatur County Young Democrats and Ohio County Young Democrats. Former member Rising Sun Rotary Club. Enjoys travel.

Mailing address: P.O. Box 185, Rising Sun 47040-0185.
Office: Main Street, Rising Sun 47040.
Telephone: (812) 438-3410.
Office: Courthouse, 212 West Main Street, Vevay 47043.
Telephone: (812) 427-3410.

MOBERLY, Robyn L. *(Judge, Marion Superior Court)* Commissioner Civil Division 1996. Elected to term beginning Jan 1, 1997. Reelected 2002, current term expires Dec 31, 2008. Serves Civil Division. Educated at Indiana University B.A. 1975 J.D. cum laude 1978.

Member Community Relations Committee 1997-2000, Board of Directors 1998-2000 and Criminal Benchbook Committee since 2000 Judicial Conference of Indiana. Member Indiana Judges Association, Indianapolis and Indiana State Bar Associations. Republican.

Office: 200 East Washington Street, T-1760, Indianapolis 46204.
Telephone: (317) 327-5087.
E-mail address: rmoberly@indygov.org

MOLTER, Daniel J. *(Judge, Newton Superior Court)* Appointed by Governor Robert D. Orr to term beginning Sept 15, 1986. Elected Nov 8, 1988, 1994 and 2000. Current term expires Dec 31, 2006. Born Indiana Nov 3, 1951. Catholic. Educated at Indiana State University B.S. 1973 and Northern Illinois University J.D. 1978. Admitted to practice Indiana 1978. In legal practice Kentland 1978-86. Interested in antique cars.

Mailing address: P.O. Box 143, Kentland 47951-0143.
Office: 201 North Third Street, Kentland 47951.
Telephone: (219) 474-5569.
E-mail address: kaderdan@ffni.com

MONROE, Chris D. *(Judge, Bartholomew Superior Court)* Elected to term beginning Jan 1, 1989. Reelected to subsequent terms. Current term expires Dec 31, 2006. Educated at Indiana University-Bloomington B.A. 1977 and Tulane University J.D. 1980.

Public Defender Bartholomew County 1983-87. Member Alternative Dispute Resolution Committee Judicial Conference of Indiana, Indiana State and American Bar Associations. Republican.

Mailing address: P.O. Box 924, Columbus 47201-0924.
Office: 234 Washington Street, Columbus 47202.
Telephone: (812) 379-1623.
E-mail address: cmonroe@iquest.net

MONROE, Deidre L. *(Judge, Gary City Court)* Appointed by Governor Frank O'Bannon to term beginning April 6, 2000. Term expires Dec 31, 2003. Educated at Indiana State University B.A. 1982 and Valparaiso University J.D. 1992.

Office: 1301 Broadway, Gary 46407-1538.
Telephone: (219) 881-1271.

MOODY, James T. *(Judge, United States District Court Northern District of Indiana)* Magistrate 1979-82. Appointed Judge for life by President Ronald Reagan to term beginning 1982. Born LaCenter Kentucky June 16, 1938. Protestant. Educated at Indiana University B.A. 1960 LL.B. 1963. Admitted to practice Indiana 1963.

MOODY, JAMES T.—*Continued*

Began legal practice Hobart 1963. Judge, Lake Superior Court 1973-79.

City Attorney East Gary 1964-73 and Hobart 1964-73. Republican. Enjoys most spectator sports, fishing and reading.

Office: 5400 Federal Plaza, Suite 4100, Hammond 46320.

Telephone: (219) 852-3460.

MORRIS, James B. *(Judge, Ripley Superior Court)* Elected to term beginning Jan 1, 1997. Reelected 2002, current term expires Dec 31, 2008. Educated at Indiana University-Bloomington B.S. 1970 and Indiana University-Indianapolis J.D. 1986.

Chief Deputy Prosecutor 1990-92 and Public Defender 1993-95 Ripley County. Chief Deputy Prosecutor Franklin County 1996. Republican.

Mailing address: P.O. Box 801, Versailles 47042.

Office: 115 North Main Street, Versailles 47042.

E-mail address: judgejimmorris@hotmail.com

MORRISSEY, Michael A. *(Judge, Tippecanoe Superior Court)* Elected to term beginning Jan 1, 2001. Term expires Dec 31, 2006. Educated at Purdue University B.S. 1976 and Indiana University J.D. 1984. Judge, West Lafayette City Court 1986-2000, appointed by Governor Robert D. Orr. Republican.

Office: 301 Main Street, Lafayette 47901.

Telephone: (765) 423-9750.

E-mail address: mmorrissey@county.tippecanoe.in.us

MORTON, Douglas B. *(Judge, Fulton Circuit Court)* Elected to term beginning Jan 1, 1979. Reelected 1984, 1990, 1996 and 2002. Current term expires Dec 31, 2008. Born Logansport Indiana July 6, 1946. Church of Christ (Elder). Educated at Wabash College B.A. 1968 and Duke University Law School J.D. 1971. Law Clerk to Hon. James E. Noland, U.S. District Court Southern District of Indiana 1971-72. Admitted to practice Indiana 1971, U.S. District Courts Northern 1971 and Southern 1971 Districts of Indiana, U.S. Tax Court 1971 and U.S. Court of Appeals Seventh Circuit 1972. Began legal practice Rochester 1972.

Board of Directors Indiana Judicial Conference 1989-92. Member Indiana Council of Juvenile and Family Court Judges, Indiana Judges Association (Board of Managers 1982-87), Fulton County and Indiana State Bar Associations. Speaker on "The Rights of Children in Dissolution of Marriage" Court Appointed Special Advocates Conference April and June 1990. Chairman Civil Benchbook Committee Indiana Judicial Center. Republican. Delegate Indiana Governor Library Conference 1990. Former Chairman Board of Trustees Fulton County Leadership Academy. Past President Rotary Club. Enjoys playing bridge and golf.

Office: 815 Main Street, Rochester 46975-1593.

Telephone: (574) 223-4339.

E-mail address: morton@rtcol.com

MOSS, Sheila Marie *(Judge, Lake Superior Court)* Appointed by Governor B. Evan Bayh to term beginning Feb 1, 1993. Retained by election 1996 and 2002. Current term expires Dec 31, 2008. Serves County Division. Born Gary Indiana Jan 18, 1956. Roman Catholic. Educated at Valparaiso University B.A. 1978 J.D. 1981. Admitted to practice Indiana 1981 and U.S. District Courts Northern 1982 and Southern 1982 Districts of Indiana. In legal practice Gary 1981-93.

Chief Deputy Prosecutor 1982-89 and Director Child Support Division 1989-93 Lake County. Member Indiana Judicial Council, American Judges Association and National Bar Association. Member National Urban League and NAACP. Enjoys gardening and playing chess.

Office: Government Center, 2293 North Main Street, Crown Point 46307-1854.

Telephone: (219) 738-3580.

E-mail address: sheila@mail.icongrp.com

MRZLACK, Robert B. *(Judge, White Superior Court)* Elected to term beginning Jan 1, 1997. Reelected 2002, current term expires Dec 31, 2008. Educated at Indiana University A.B. 1979 and Indiana University-Indianapolis J.D. 1982.

Prosecuting Attorney 1987-94 and Deputy Prosecuting Attorney 1995-96 White County. Republican.

Mailing address: P.O. Box 1005, Monticello 47960-1005.

Office: Courthouse, 110 North Main Street, Monticello 47960.

Telephone: (574) 583-9520.

E-mail address: mrzlack@monti.net

MURRAY, Clarence D. *(Judge, Lake Superior Court)* Magistrate County Division 1993-99. Appointed Judge by Governor Frank O'Bannon to term beginning 1999. Retained by election 2000, current term expires Dec 31, 2006. Serves Criminal Division. Educated at Tennessee State University B.S. 1970 and Valparaiso University J.D. 1986.

Deputy Prosecuting Attorney Lake County 1990-93.

Office: Government Center, 2293 North Main Street, Crown Point 46307-1854.

Telephone: (219) 755-3500.

E-mail address: murracd@lakecountyin.org

MURRAY, Lynn *(Judge, Howard Circuit Court)* Appointed by Governor B. Evan Bayh March 31, 1995. Elected Nov 5, 1996 and 2002. Current term expires Dec 31, 2008. Born Paterson New Jersey March 2, 1956. Methodist. Educated at Purdue University B.A. 1978 and Rutgers University J.D. 1981. Member Phi Alpha Delta. Admitted to practice Indiana 1981. In legal practice Lafayette 1981-82 and Kokomo 1983-95.

Supervising Attorney UAW Legal Services Plan 1983-95. Instructor in General Law I and II, Torts and Family Law Indiana University-Kokomo 1990-95. Member Indiana Judges Association, American Judges Association, Indiana Council of Juvenile and Family Court Judges and National Council of Juvenile and Family Court Judges. Attended The National Judicial College 1997, 1998, 1999 and 2000, Indiana Graduate Program for Judges 1998-99 and 2000, Indiana Judicial College 2002 and American Academy for Judicial Education 2002. Named Professional/Business Woman of the Year by Kokomo Academy of Women 1996. Democrat. Chairman Herrel State Senate Campaign 1994. Board of Directors Child Abuse Prevention Council and Community Corrections. Enjoys sailing and computers.

Office: 310 Howard County Courthouse, 117 North Main Street, Kokomo 46901-9004.

Telephone: (765) 456-2202.

Fax: (765) 456-2016

E-mail address: judgelhm@aol.com

NAJAM, Edward W., Jr. *(Presiding Judge, Indiana Court of Appeals First District)* Appointed by Governor Evan Bayh Dec 30, 1992. Retained by election 1996, current term expires Dec 31, 2006. Educated at Indiana University-Bloomington B.A. 1969 and Harvard University J.D. 1972. Member Phi Beta Kappa. In legal practice 1974-92.

Fellow Indianapolis and Indiana Bar Foundations. Member Committee on Rules of Practice and Procedure and Judicial Technology and Automation Committee Supreme Court. Member Indiana Judges Association, American Judicature Society, Indianapolis, Monroe County, Indiana State (Former Chair Appellate Practice Section) and American (Appellate Judges Conference Judicial Administration Division) Bar Associations. Administrative Assistant to Mayor of Bloomington 1972-74.

Office: 200 West Washington Street, Room 423, Indianapolis 46204-2784.

Telephone: (317) 232-6884.

E-mail address: enajam@courts.state.in.us

NARDI, Frank Mattioda *(Judge, Owen Circuit Court)* Elected to term beginning Jan 1, 1983. Reelected 1988, 1994 and 2000. Current term expires Dec 31, 2006. Born Clinton Indiana Aug 18, 1953. Presbyterian. Educated at Indiana University at Bloomington B.A. with honors 1975 J.D. 1979. Admitted to practice Indiana 1979. In legal practice Spencer 1979-82.

Deputy Prosecuting Attorney 1979-82 and Title IV-D Attorney 1979-82 Owen County. Member Indiana Judges Association, Indiana Council of Juvenile and Family Court Judges, National Council of Juvenile and Family Court Judges, Owen County and Tri-County Bar Associations. Board of Directors Judicial Conference of Indiana. Graduate Indiana Judicial College 1988. Democrat. Member Exchange Club, 4-H (Volunteer) and Spencer Presbyterian Church. Director Owen County Fair Board. Enjoys farming, gardening and reading.

Mailing address: P.O. Box 86, Spencer 47460-0086.

Office: Courthouse, 60 South Main Street, Spencer 47460.

Telephone: (812) 829-5030.

E-mail address: owencircourt@ccrtc.com

NATION, Steven R. *(Judge, Hamilton Superior Court)* Elected to term beginning Jan 1, 1995. Reelected 2000, current term expires Dec 31, 2006. Educated at Indiana University B.A. 1972 J.D. 1975.

Prosecuting Attorney Hamilton County June 1979 to Dec 1994. Assistant Professor University of Indianapolis. Chair Records Management Committee. Chair Judicial Ethics Committee and Member Trial Rule 77 Subcommittee Judicial Conference of Indiana. Member Hamilton County and Indiana State Bar Associations. Republican.

Office: One Hamilton County Square, Room 345, Noblesville 46060-2232.

Telephone: (317) 776-9655.

E-mail address: srn@co.hamilton.in.us

NAVILLE, Michael G. *(Magistrate Judge, United States District Court Southern District of Indiana)* Appointed by U.S. District Court judges to term beginning 1995. Reappointed 1999 and 2003. Current term expires April 2007. Serves part time. Educated at Indiana University 1973 and University of Louisville School of Law J.D. 1976. Began legal practice 1976.

President St. Elizabeth's Southern Indiana Maternity Home 1989-96.

Mailing address: P.O. Box 1343, New Albany 47151-1343.

Telephone: (812) 949-1000.

NELSON, William J. *(Judge, Marion Superior Court)* Elected to term beginning Jan 1, 2001. Term expires Dec 31, 2006. Serves Criminal Division. Educated at Indiana University-Bloomington B.S. 1981 and Indiana University-Indianapolis J.D. 1984. Judge, Marion County Small Claims Court Warren Township Division 1994-2000.

Prosecuting Attorney Marion County 1983-85. Fellow Indianapolis Bar Foundation. Member Indianapolis and Indiana State Bar Associations. Republican.

Office: 200 East Washington Street, Room E-607, Indianapolis 46204.

Telephone: (317) 327-4777.

E-mail address: wnelson@indygov.org

NEMETH, Peter J. *(Judge, St. Joseph Probate Court)* Appointed by Governor B. Evan Bayh March 15, 1993. Elected to subsequent terms. Current term expires Dec 31, 2006. Educated at University of Arizona B.A. 1963 and Columbia University LL.B. 1966.

Deputy Prosecutor South Bend 1967-72. Member Probate Committee Judicial Conference of Indiana. Member City Council South Bend 1972-76. Mayor South Bend 1976-80.

Office: Juvenile Justice Center, 1000 South Michigan Street, South Bend 46601-3426.

Telephone: (574) 235-5437.

E-mail address: judgenemeth@jjconline.org

NEWKIRK, Frank, Jr. *(Judge, Washington Superior Court)* Elected to term beginning Jan 1, 1993. Reelected 1998, current term expires Dec 31, 2004. Born Salem Indiana Feb 5, 1957. United Methodist. Educated at Indiana University B.A. 1978 J.D. 1981. Admitted to practice Indiana 1981. In legal practice Salem 1981-92.

Deputy Prosecuting Attorney 1981-82. State Representative Indiana House of Representatives 1984-92. Member Washington County Bar Association. Recipient Rotary International Overseas Study Scholarship 1978.

Office: County Detention Center, 801 Jackson Street, Salem 47167-1218.

Telephone: (812) 883-4949.

E-mail address: superior@blueriver.net

NEWMAN, Thomas, Jr. *(Judge, Madison Superior Court)* Elected to term beginning Jan 1, 1977. Reelected 1982, 1988, 1994 and 2000. Current term expires Dec 31, 2006. Chief Judge since 1979. Born Anderson Indiana May 21, 1941. Christian Scientist. Educated at American University B.A. 1965 M.A. 1970 and Indiana University J.D. cum laude 1972. Admitted to practice Indiana 1972. Began legal practice Anderson 1972. Judge, Madison County Court 1976.

Police Legal Advisor Madison County 1972-74. Member Indiana Judges Association (Director), Madison County, Indiana State and American Bar Associations. Democrat. Director Madison County Bicentennial Commission 1976. Former member City of Anderson Historic Preservation Commission (Past President). Member Women's Alternative, Inc. (Board of Directors), Indiana University Alumni Club (Board of Directors, Past President), Center for Mental Health (Past President Board of

NEWMAN, THOMAS, JR.—*Continued*

Directors), Boy Scouts of America (Membership Chairman Sakima District) and Exchange Club.

Office: 16 East Ninth Street, Anderson 46016-1572.

Telephone: (765) 641-9632.

E-mail address: tnewman@madisoncty.com

NIEMEIER, Brett J. *(Judge, Vanderburgh Superior Court)* Elected to term beginning Jan 1, 2001. Term expires Dec 31, 2006. Educated at Indiana State University at Evansville B.S. 1981 and Indiana University-Indianapolis J.D. 1985.

Office: 126 Courts Building, 825 Sycamore Street, Evansville 47708-1833.

Telephone: (812) 435-5125.

E-mail address: bniemeier@vanderburghgov.org

NORTHAM, David E. *(Judge, Rush Superior Court)* Term expires Dec 31, 2008. Educated at Hanover College B.A. 1971 and Indiana University-Indianapolis J.D. 1976. Judge, Rush County Court, elected to term beginning Jan 1, 1997.

Board of Managers Indiana Judges Association 1997-2000. Republican.

Office: 101 East Second Street, Rushville 46173.

Telephone: (765) 932-4646.

E-mail address: rushsupjudge@mynetisun.com

NUECHTERLEIN, Christopher A. *(Magistrate Judge, United States District Court Northern District of Indiana)* Appointed by U.S. District Court judges to term beginning Jan 10, 2000. Term expires Jan 10, 2008. Born 1951. Educated at Valparaiso University B.A. 1973 J.D. 1976. Law Clerk to Hon. Allen Sharp, U.S. District Court Northern District of Indiana 1976-78. In legal practice Goshen 1978-81.

Trial Attorney Land and Natural Resources Division 1983-85 and Criminal Division Fraud Section 1985-89 U.S. Department of Justice. Assistant Director Attorney General's Advocacy Institute 1987-88. Assistant U.S. Attorney 1989-98, Chief Special Prosecutions Unit 1993, Chief Criminal Division 1993-94 and Executive Assistant U.S. Attorney 1994-98 Eastern District of California. Assistant Commissioner and Chief Counsel Health Plan Enforcement Division California Department of Corporations 1998-2000. Member Robert A. Grant Inn of Court, Federal Magistrate Judges Association, St. Joseph County and Indiana State Bar Associations.

Office: 201 Federal Building, 204 South Main Street, South Bend 46601.

Telephone: (574) 246-8100.

OBENDORF, Richard L. *(Judge, Butler City Court)* Mailing address: P.O. Box 13, Butler 46721-0013.

Office: 120 West Main Street, Butler 46721.

Telephone: (219) 868-2441.

O'CONNOR, Charles D., Jr. *(Judge, Shelby Circuit Court)* Appointed by Governor Robert D. Orr to term beginning March 5, 1982. Elected Nov 1982, Nov 1988, 1994 and 2000. Current term expires Dec 31, 2006. Educated at University of Notre Dame A.B. 1968 and Indiana University at Indianapolis J.D. 1972. Judge, Shelby County Court 1976-77.

Office: 407 South Harrison Street, Shelbyville 46176-2170.

Telephone: (317) 392-6360.

Fax: (317) 392-6496

E-mail address: charles.oconnor@co.shelby.in.us

OSBORN, Gregory *(Judge, DeMotte Town Court)* Appointed by Governor Frank O'Bannon to term beginning Aug 8, 2000. Term expires Dec 31, 2003.

Mailing address: P.O. Box 678, DeMotte 46310.

Telephone: (219) 987-3831.

E-mail address: medshoppe11637@yahoo.com

OSBORNE, Jim R. *(Judge, Knox Superior Court)* Elected to term beginning Jan 1, 1988. Reelected to subsequent terms. Current term expires Dec 31, 2008. Born Vincennes Indiana June 30, 1945. Member Old Cathedral Parish. Educated at Vincennes University A.S. gold cord 1965 and Indiana State University B.S. with honors 1967 J.D. 1974. Admitted to practice Indiana 1974. In legal practice Vincennes 1975-76. Judge, Knox County Court Jan 1, 1976 to Dec 31, 1987.

Deputy Prosecutor Knox County 1975-76. Board of Advisors Indiana Judicial Center 1976-90. Member Knox County, Indiana State and American Bar Associations. Graduate Indiana Judicial College Sept 1983. Democrat. Past President Vincennes University Alumni Association. Executive Director Knox County Alcohol and Drug Referral Program since 1980. Board Member Vincennes University Foundation since 1985. Board of Directors and Vice President Old Northwest Corporation. Board of Advisors Salvation Army (Past President). Chairman of Board Indiana Military Museum. Member Kiwanis (Past President Vincennes Chapter). Enjoys collecting military and historical artifacts, presidential signatures and WWII vehicles.

Office: 620 Busseron Street, Vincennes 47591-2032.

Telephone: (812) 882-4962.

Fax: (812) 886-4244

OTTE, Frank J. *(Chief Judge, United States Bankruptcy Court Southern District of Indiana)* Appointed by U.S. Court of Appeals Seventh Circuit judges to term beginning Oct 1, 1986. Reappointed Oct 1, 2000, current term expires Sept 30, 2014. Born Indianapolis Indiana Feb 16, 1938. Educated at Indiana University B.S. 1960 J.D. 1966. Admitted to practice Indiana 1966 and U.S. District Court Southern District of Indiana 1966. In legal practice Indianapolis 1966-86.

Member Indianapolis and Indiana State Bar Associations. First Lieutenant U.S. Army 1960-63.

Office: 309 U.S. Courthouse, 46 East Ohio Street, Indianapolis 46204.

Telephone: (317) 229-3890.

OWEN, Maureen T. *(Judge, Avon Town Court)* Elected to term beginning Jan 1, 2000. Term expires Dec 31, 2003. Educated at Indiana University B.A. 1978 and University of Dayton J.D. 1985.

Deputy Attorney General 1987-1996. Republican.

Office: 6570 East U.S. Highway 36, Avon 46123-9178.

Telephone: (317) 272-5478.

PALMER, Walter H. *(Judge, Gibson Circuit Court)* Elected to term beginning Jan 1, 1977. Reelected 1982, 1988, 1994 and 2000. Current term expires Dec 31, 2006. Educated at University of Mississippi B.S. 1966 and University of Louisville J.D. 1972.

Board of Directors Judicial Conference of Indiana since 1996. Member Indiana Judges Association, Indiana Trial Lawyers Association, American Judicature Society, Gibson County, Indiana State and American Bar Associations. Graduate Indiana Judicial College 1984. Attended

PALMER, WALTER H.—*Continued*
Indiana Graduate Program for Judges 1997. Democrat. Lieutenant U.S. Public Health Service 1966-68.
Mailing address: P.O. Box 168, Princeton 47670-0168.
Office: 101 North Main Street, Princeton 47670-1562.
Telephone: (812) 385-4885.
E-mail address: wpalm@sigecom.net

PARAS, George *(Judge, Merrillville Town Court)* Elected to term beginning Jan 1, 1996. Reelected 1999, current term expires Dec 31, 2003. Educated at Valparaiso University B.A. 1973, Birmingham School of Law and Valparaiso University J.D. 1980. Judge/Referee Gary City Court 1983-95.
Member American Judges Association and Lake County Bar Association. Democrat.
Office: 7820 Broadway, Merrillville 46410.
Telephone: (219) 756-6185.

PARRY, Dennis H. *(Judge, Howard Superior Court)* Appointed by Governor Otis Ray Bowen to term beginning April 26, 1980. Elected 1980, 1986, 1992 and 1998. Current term expires Dec 31, 2004. Born Gary Indiana Aug 4, 1941. Presbyterian. Educated at Ball State University B.S. 1965 and Valparaiso University J.D. 1969. Admitted to practice Indiana 1969 and U.S. District Court Southern District of Indiana 1969. Began legal practice Kokomo 1969.
Public Defender 1969-74, Prosecuting Attorney 1975-78 and Chief Deputy Prosecuting Attorney 1979 Howard County. Member Indiana State Judges Association, Howard County (Secretary-Treasurer 1969-70) and Indiana State Bar Associations. Sergeant U.S. Army 1959-63. Member 1st Brigade 3rd Infantry (The Old Guard) Fort Myers Virginia 1962-63. Previously worked as a teacher.
Office: 104 Buckeye, Suite 300, Kokomo 46901.
Telephone: (765) 456-2200.
E-mail address: judgedhp@yahoo.com

PAYNE, James W. *(Judge, Marion Superior Court)* Elected to term beginning Jan 1, 1985. Reelected 1990, 1996 and 2002. Current term expires Dec 31, 2008. Serves Juvenile Division. Born St. Louis Missouri Oct 3, 1946. Protestant. Educated at DePauw University B.A. 1968 and Indiana University J.D. 1972. Member Sigma Chi and Phi Delta Phi. Admitted to practice Indiana 1972 and U.S. District Court Southern District of Indiana 1972. In legal practice Indianapolis 1972-84.
Prosecutor City of Indianapolis 1980-84. Member National Council of Family and Juvenile Court Judges (Trustee), Indianapolis, Indiana State and American Bar Associations. Republican. Scoutmaster Troop 510. Active in Pike Youth Baseball League, Pike Youth Basketball League and First Baptist Youth Athletic Program.
Office: 2451 North Keystone Avenue, Indianapolis 46218.
Telephone: (317) 921-4841.
E-mail address: jpayne@indygov.org

PEARSON, Linley E. *(Judge, Clinton Circuit Court)* Elected to term beginning Jan 1, 1995. Reelected 2000, current term expires Dec 31, 2006. Educated at The Citadel B.A. 1966, Butler University M.B.A. 1970 and Indiana University J.D. 1970. Law Clerk to Indiana Supreme Court 1969-70.
Prosecuting Attorney Clinton County 1971-80. Attorney General Indiana 1981-92. Member Clinton County Bar Association. Republican. Member Society Attorney General Emeritus.
Office: 355 Courthouse Square, Frankfort 46041-1964.
Telephone: (765) 659-6345.
E-mail address: lpearson@mintel.net

PEDEN, Mark *(Judge, Martinsville City Court)* Elected to term beginning Jan 1, 1980. Reelected to subsequent terms. Current term expires Dec 31, 2003. Educated at Indiana University A.B. 1964 J.D. 1967.
Deputy Attorney General 1969-72. USAR 1968. Republican.
Mailing address: P.O. Box 1415, Martinsville 46151-1415.
Office: 59 South Jefferson Street, Martinsville 46151.
Telephone: (765) 342-1259.

PENROD, Earl G. *(Judge, Gibson Superior Court)* Appointed to term beginning Jan 1, 1985. Elected 1986, 1992 and 1998. Current term expires Dec 31, 2004. Educated at University of Louisville A.B. 1977 J.D. 1980. Judge, Gibson County Court 1983-84.
Member Indiana Judges Association, American Judges Association, Gibson County and Indiana State Bar Associations.
Office: 101 North Main Street, Princeton 47670-1562.
Telephone: (812) 386-6237.
E-mail address: egpenrod@gibsoncounty.net

PENSINGER, Michele *(Judge, Portland City Court)* Elected to term beginning Jan 1, 2000. Term expires Dec 31, 2003.
Office: 321 North Meridian Street, Portland 47371-1905.
Telephone: (260) 726-9395.
E-mail address: raymiller@jayco.net

PERA, John R. *(Judge, Lake Superior Court)* Appointed by Governor Frank O'Bannon to term beginning Sept 16, 2000. Term expires Dec 31, 2004. Serves Civil Division. Educated at Indiana University A.B. 1972 and Valparaiso University J.D. 1975.
President Lake County Bar Association 1997. Member Civil Instructions Committee. Democrat. Board President Legal Services of Northwest Indiana 1986-89.
Office: 2293 North Main Street, Crown Point 46307.
Telephone: (219) 755-3199.
E-mail address: jrpera@lakecountyin.org

PERRONE, Thomas C. *(Judge, Cass Superior Court)* Elected Nov 3, 1998 to term beginning Jan 1, 1999. Term expires Dec 31, 2004. Born Logansport Indiana Dec 3, 1948. Educated at Purdue University B.S.I.M. 1970 and University of Baltimore J.D. with honors 1976. Member Heuisler Honor Society. Admitted to practice Indiana 1977 and Illinois 1983. In legal practice Chicago Illinois 1982-88 and Logansport Indiana 1992-98.
Deputy City Attorney Logansport 1992-98. Member Indiana Judges Association, Cass County and Indiana State Bar Associations. Lieutenant j.g. USN 1970-72. Director of Administration Mississippi Governor's Office 1988-92.
Office: 200 Court Park, Room 401, Logansport 46947-3194.
Telephone: (574) 753-7735.
Fax: (574) 753-7845
E-mail address: supcourt1@casscountygov.org

PETE, Robert A. *(Judge, Lake Superior Court)* Former Magistrate. Appointed Judge by Governor Frank O'Bannon. Serves Civil Division. Educated at University of Notre Dame B.A. 1974 and Indiana University-Bloomington J.D. 1977.

Office: Courthouse, 232 Russell Street, Hammond 46320-1829.

Telephone: (219) 931-3440.

PEYTON, Michael D. *(Judge, Henry Superior Court)* Elected to term beginning Jan 1, 1997. Reelected 2002, current term expires Dec 31, 2008. Educated at DePauw University A.B. 1965 and Indiana University-Bloomington J.D. 1968.

Public Defender 1973-76 and Probate Commissioner 1981-86 Henry County. USAF 1968-72. Democrat.

Office: 320 Justice Center, 1215 Race Street, New Castle 47362.

Telephone: (765) 529-6408.

PFAFF, L. Benjamin *(Judge, Elkhart Superior Court)* Elected to term beginning Jan 1, 1997. Reelected 2002, current term expires Dec 31, 2008. Educated at Hillsdale College B.L.S. 1980 and Thomas M. Cooley Law School J.D. 1983.

Deputy Prosecuting Attorney Elkhart County Oct 1983 to Dec 1996. Member Community Relations Committee 1998-2000 and Criminal Instructions Committee since 2000 Judicial Conference of Indiana. Member Indiana Judges Association, Elkhart City, Elkhart County, Indiana State and American Bar Associations. Republican. Chair Advisory Board Elkhart City Community Corrections since 1999.

Office: 315 South Second Street, Elkhart 46516-3138.

Telephone: (574) 523-2231.

E-mail address: judgepfaff@aol.com

PFLUM, Daniel Lee *(Judge, Fayette Circuit Court)* Appointed by Governor Robert D. Orr to term beginning Jan 4, 1985. Elected 1986, 1992 and 1998. Current term expires Dec 31, 2004. Born Connersville Indiana Aug 6, 1947. Catholic. Educated at Indiana University B.A. 1970 J.D. 1975. Admitted to practice Indiana 1975 and U.S. District Court Southern District of Indiana 1975. Began legal practice Indianapolis 1975. In legal practice 1975-84.

Chief Probation Officer Fayette County 1979-84. Deputy Attorney General Indiana 1975-78. Member Fayette County (Secretary 1976-78) and Indiana State Bar Associations. Republican. Former Coach for YMCA and Boys Club Youth Soccer. Board of Directors Dunn Mental Health Center. Member Kiwanis, United Way, Big Brothers/Big Sisters and church parish council and committees. Enjoys photography, travel, skiing and tennis.

Office: 401 Central Avenue, Connersville 47331-1981.

Telephone: (765) 825-1331.

E-mail address: circuit@courthouse.co.fayette.in.us

PHILLIPPE, Donald R. *(Judge, Anderson City Court)* Elected to term beginning Jan 1, 1972. Reelected to subsequent terms. Current term expires Dec 31, 2003. Born Cutler Indiana April 9, 1933. Episcopalian. Educated at Ball State University B.S. 1959 and Indiana University J.D. 1963. Admitted to practice Indiana 1964, U.S. District Court 1964, U.S. Supreme Court 1969 and U.S. Court of Appeals 1972. Began legal practice Anderson 1964.

Accountant 1954-64. Deputy Prosecutor Anderson 1964-71. Member The Association of Trial Lawyers of America, Madison County and Indiana State Bar Associations. TM3 USN 1954-56. Democrat. Member Noon Optimists, Masons, Shriners, Scottish Rite, York Rite, American Legion and 40 and 8.

Mailing address: P.O. Box 2100, Anderson 46011-2100.

Office: 120 East Eighth Street, Anderson 46016-1505.

Telephone: (765) 648-6090.

E-mail address: dphillippe@cityofanderson.com

PHILLIPS, Tommy D., II *(Judge, Dunkirk City Court)* Appointed by Governor Frank O'Bannon to term beginning Oct 3, 2000. Term expires Dec 31, 2003. Educated at Indiana Wesleyan University B.S. cum laude 1978 and Ball State University M.A. 1983.

Office: 131 South Main Street, Dunkirk 47336-1288.

Telephone: (765) 768-6565.

E-mail address: cityofdunkirk@aol.com

PIERSON, Paul J. *(Judge, Sullivan Circuit Court)* Judge pro tem Sept 26, 1990 to Dec 31, 1990. Elected Judge to term beginning Jan 1, 1991. Reelected 1996 and 2002. Current term expires Dec 31, 2008. Educated at Indiana State University B.S. 1976, Butler University 1977-78 and California Western School of Law J.D. 1982.

Board of Directors Judicial Conference of Indiana 1994-96. Member Indiana Judges Association, Indiana Council of Juvenile and Family Court Judges, Indiana Correctional Association, American Judicature Society, Sullivan County and Indiana State Bar Associations. Graduate Indiana Judicial College 1996. USAR 1968-74. Democrat.

Office: 306 Courthouse, 100 Courthouse Square, Sullivan 47882-1592.

Telephone: (812) 268-4411.

E-mail address: judgepj@custom.net

PIERSON-TREACY, Rebekah *(Judge, Marion Superior Court)* Master Commissioner 1995-2000. Elected Judge to term beginning Jan 1, 2001. Term expires Dec 31, 2006. Serves Criminal Division. Educated at Purdue University B.A. 1984 and Indiana University-Bloomington J.D. 1988.

Former Deputy Prosecuting Attorney Marion County. Commissioner Protection and Advocacy Commission. Member Indianapolis, Marion County and Indiana State Bar Associations. Democrat.

Office: 200 East Washington Street, Room W-442, Indianapolis 46204.

Telephone: (317) 327-8881.

Fax: (317) 327-8886

E-mail address: rptreacy@indygov.org

PIGMAN, Robert J. *(Judge, Vanderburgh Superior Court)* Elected to term beginning Jan 1, 1999. Term expires Dec 31, 2004. Educated at University of Southern Indiana B.S. 1974 and Indiana University J.D. 1977.

Prosecuting Attorney Vanderburgh County 1983-90.

Office: 118 Courts Building, 825 Sycamore Street, Evansville 47708-1833.

Telephone: (812) 435-5410.

E-mail address: rpigman@vanderburghgov.org

PLATT, Stephen E. *(Judge, Elkhart Superior Court)* Appointed by Governor Robert D. Orr to term beginning Feb 16, 1982. Elected 1982, 1988, 1994 and 2000. Current term expires Dec 31, 2006. Currently serves as

PLATT, STEPHEN E.—*Continued*
Chief Judge. Born Logansport Indiana May 24, 1945. Roman Catholic. Educated at Valparaiso University B.A. 1967 J.D. 1970. Admitted to practice Indiana 1970. In legal practice Elkhart 1970-78. Judge, Elkhart County Court 1979-82.

Staff Attorney Elkhart County Legal Aid 1971-74. Deputy Prosecutor Elkhart County 1975-78. Important Decision: Doe v. Smith (abortion) 1988. Member Indiana Judges Association, Indiana Council of Juvenile and Family Court Judges, Elkhart City, Elkhart County, Indiana State and American Bar Associations.

Office: 315 South Second Street, Elkhart 46516-3138.
Telephone: (574) 523-2340.
Fax: (574) 523-2345
E-mail address: splatt@elkhartcounty.com

PONTON, George G. *(Judge, Frankfort City Court)* Elected to term beginning Jan 1, 1984. Reelected 1987, 1991, 1995 and 1999. Current term expires Dec 31, 2003. Educated at University of Notre Dame B.S.C. 1954 and Indiana University-Indianapolis J.D. 1971.

Town Attorney Monon 1976-2000. Member The Indiana Association of Trial Lawyers, Clinton County and Indiana State Bar Associations. Captain USAF 1954-56. Democrat.

Office: 301 East Clinton Street, Frankfort 46041.
Telephone: (765) 654-4469.

PRATT, Charles F. *(Judge, Allen Superior Court)* Referee 1983-85. Magistrate 1985-98. Elected Judge to term beginning Jan 1, 1999. Term expires Dec 31, 2004. Educated at Indiana-Purdue University at Fort Wayne B.A. 1976 and Indiana University-Indianapolis J.D. 1979.

Instructor Indiana-Purdue University at Fort Wayne. Member Allen County Bar Association.

Office: 715 South Calhoun Street, Room 208, Fort Wayne 46802-1805.
Telephone: (260) 449-7303.
E-mail address: cpratt@co.allen.in.us

PRATT, Tanya Walton *(Judge, Marion Superior Court)* Master Commissioner Criminal Division Sept 1993 to Dec 1996. Elected Nov 5, 1996 to term beginning Jan 1, 1997. Reelected 2002, current term expires Dec 31, 2008. Presiding Judge Criminal Division since Jan 1, 1997. Educated at Spelman College B.A. cum laude 1981 and Howard University J.D. 1984. In legal practice Indianapolis.

Public Defender Marion County. Fellow Indianapolis Bar Association (Member Steering Committee for 2000 Convention Women Lawyers Division). Member Indianapolis American Inn of Court, Indiana Judges Association (District 11 Representative), National Association of Women Judges, The Association of Trial Lawyers of America, American Judges Association, Indianapolis (Board of Managers), Marion County (Board of Directors), Indiana State, National and American Bar Associations. Attended The National Judicial College, Indiana Judicial Center Legislation Seminar, Bench and Bar Conference, Indiana Judicial Conference, National Association of Women Judges seminars, Judicial College Seminar and National Bar Association Conference. Democrat. Member NAACP, Delta Sigma Theta, Inc. and St. Joan of Arc Catholic Church.

Office: 200 East Washington Street, Room W-202, Indianapolis 46204-3336.
Telephone: (317) 327-3528.
E-mail address: tpratt@indygov.org

PRICE, Jeffry *(Judge, Peru City Court)* Elected to term beginning Jan 1, 2000. Term expires Dec 31, 2003.
Office: 35 South Broadway, Peru 46970-2231.
Telephone: (765) 472-3339.
E-mail address: jgprice@comteck.com

PROFFITT, Judith S. *(Judge, Hamilton Circuit Court)* Appointed by Governor Robert D. Orr to term beginning July 6, 1983. Elected 1984, 1990, 1996 and 2002. Current term expires Dec 31, 2008. Educated at Butler University B.S. 1967 and Indiana University at Indianapolis J.D. 1971.

Research Analyst Indiana Criminal Law Study Commission 1971-74 and Indiana Juvenile Code Study Commission 1974-75. Lecturer Indiana University at Indianapolis 1975-76. Section Director Indiana Lawyers Commission 1975-76. Member Indiana Judges Association, Hamilton County, Indiana State (Secretary 1979 and Chairman Family Law Section) and American Bar Associations.

Office: One Hamilton Square, Room 337, Noblesville 46060-2662.
Telephone: (317) 776-9646.
E-mail address: jsp@co.hamilton.in.us

RADVANSKY, Joseph P. *(Judge, Batesville City Court)* Appointed by Governor Robert D. Orr Sept 1, 1987. Elected to subsequent terms. Current term expires Dec 31, 2003. Educated at Purdue University 1952-66.

Indiana State policeman 1956-77 (retired). USN 1948-52.

Office: Memorial Building, 132 South Main Street, Batesville 47006.
Telephone: (812) 933-6102.

REDWINE, James M. *(Judge, Posey Circuit Court)* Elected to term beginning Jan 1, 1983. Reelected 1988, 1994 and 2000. Current term expires Dec 31, 2006. Educated at Indiana University B.A. 1968 J.D. 1970. Candidate Masters of Judicial Studies University of Nevada. Judge, Posey County Court 1981-82.

Deputy Prosecutor Vanderburgh County 1972-75. Chief Deputy Prosecutor 1976-78 and County Attorney 1979-80 Posey County. Lecturer Indiana State University at Evansville 1976. Member Indiana Judges Association, Posey County and Indiana State Bar Associations. Attended The National Judicial College 1986. Graduate Indiana Judicial College 1986. Member Owen Dunn Post 5 American Legion, Mount Vernon Elks, Boxers Den of Evansville, Mount Vernon Chamber of Commerce and First Christian Church. USAF.

Mailing address: P.O. Box 745, Mount Vernon 47620-0745.
Office: 112 East Main, Room 310, Mount Vernon 47620.
Telephone: (812) 838-0745.
E-mail address: pcc@comsource.net

REED, Rex L. *(Judge, Kosciusko Circuit Court)* Elected to term beginning Jan 1, 1995. Reelected 2000, current term expires Dec 31, 2006. Educated at Purdue

REED, REX L.—*Continued*
University B.S.C.E. 1964 and Indiana University-Bloomington J.D. 1969.

Member Kosciusko County, Indiana State and American Bar Associations. Captain U.S. Army 1964-69. Republican.

Office: 121 North Lake Street, Second Floor, Warsaw 46580-2785.
Telephone: (574) 372-2402.
Fax: (574) 372-2406
E-mail address: rreed@kcgov.com

REID, S. K. *(Judge, Marion Superior Court)* Elected to term beginning Jan 1, 2001. Term expires Dec 31, 2006. Serves Civil Division.

Office: 200 East Washington Street, Room T-1442, Indianapolis 46204.
Telephone: (317) 327-4166.
E-mail address: sreid@indygov.org

RICHMOND, Cheryl A. *(Judge, Versailles Town Court)* Appointed by Governor Frank O'Bannon to term beginning May 6, 1998. Elected to subsequent term. Current term expires Dec 31, 2003. Democrat.

Mailing address: P.O. Box 134, Versailles 47042-0134.
Telephone: (812) 689-6111.

RIDLEN, Julian L. *(Judge, Cass Circuit Court)* Elected to term beginning Jan 1, 1995. Reelected 2000, current term expires Dec 31, 2006. Educated at Anderson University B.A. 1963 and George Washington University J.D. 1967. Judge, Logansport City Court April 1969 to June 1978.

Treasurer State of Indiana Feb 10, 1979 to Feb 9, 1987. Member Indiana Council of Juvenile and Family Court Judges, American Judicature Society and Indiana State Bar Association. Republican.

Office: 200 Court Park, Room 412, Logansport 46947-3194.
Telephone: (574) 753-7730.
E-mail address: cccourt@cgc.com

RIECKHOFF, James W. *(Judge, Elkhart Superior Court)* Term expires Dec 31, 2008. Educated at Amherst College A.B. 1962 and Northwestern University J.D. 1965. Judge, Elkhart County Court Feb 22, 1982 to 1995, appointed by Governor Robert D. Orr.

Board of Directors Judicial Conference of Indiana 1984-96. Member Elkhart City, Elkhart County and Indiana State Bar Associations. U.S. Army 1966-71, JAGC 1967-71, Military Judge 1969-71. Chairman Elkhart County Community Corrections Advisory Board 1992-99.

Office: 315 South Second Street, Elkhart 46516-3138.
Telephone: (574) 523-2245.
Fax: (574) 523-2323

RIGA, Debbie A. *(Judge, Schererville Town Court)* Elected Nov 1999 to term beginning Jan 1, 2000. Term expires Dec 31, 2003. Born Indiana Dec 7, 1956. Catholic. Educated at Indiana University B.S.C.J. and Valparaiso University School of Law J.D. Admitted to practice Indiana 1993.

Office: 25 East Joliet Street, Schererville 46375.
Telephone: (219) 865-5579.

RILEY, Patricia A. *(Judge, Indiana Court of Appeals Fourth District)* Appointed by Governor B. Evan Bayh Jan 3, 1994. Retained by election 1996, current term expires Dec 31, 2006. Former Presiding Judge. Educated at Indiana University-Bloomington B.A. 1971 and Indiana University-Indianapolis J.D. 1974. Judge, Jasper Superior Court 1990-93.

Deputy Prosecutor Marion County 1975-77. Public Defender Marion County 1978-80 and Jasper County 1987-89. Member Legal Services Organization 1978. Board of Managers Indiana Judges Association 1991-93. Board of Directors National Association of Women Judges. Member Jasper County, Marion County, Indiana State (Board of Governors 1995-97, Women in the Law Committee, Improvements in the Judicial System Committee, Joint Committee on Bench and Bar on Gender Issues in the Profession) and American Bar Associations. Attended Indiana Graduate Program for Judges 1997.

Office: 1270 National City Center, 115 West Washington Street, Indianapolis 46204-3419.
Telephone: (317) 232-6902.
E-mail address: priley@courts.state.in.us

RIVERA, Avis *(Judge, Aurora City Court)* Appointed by Governor Frank O'Bannon to term beginning Aug 1, 1997. Elected to subsequent term. Current term expires Dec 31, 2003.

Mailing address: P.O. Box 158, Aurora 47001-0158.
Office: 218 Third Street, Aurora 47001.
Telephone: (812) 926-1985.

ROBB, Margret G. *(Presiding Judge, Indiana Court of Appeals Fifth District)* Appointed by Governor Frank O'Bannon to term beginning July 1998. Term expires Dec 31, 2004. Educated at Purdue University B.S. 1970 M.S. 1972 and Indiana University School of Law J.D. 1978. In legal practice 1978-98.

Deputy Public Defender 1982-92. Registered Mediator Civil and Family Law. Trustee Chapter 7 and 11 U.S. Bankruptcy Panel 1986-98. Founding Chair and President Governor's Commission on the Status of Women 1973. Secretary Tippecanoe County Bar Association 1980. Member Governance Committee IOLTA 1995-97 and State Board of Law Examiners 1998-99. Fellow Indiana Bar Foundation (Fellows Secretary since 1999) and American Bar Foundation. Vice Chair Committee for Improvement in the Judiciary since 1999. Chair Supreme Court Committee on Creation of Family Courts. Member Indiana Child Support Advisory Committee, Federal Advisory Committee on Local Rules of Court, Federal Advisory Committee for the Expediting of Federal Legislation, Indiana Judges Association, National Association of Women Judges (Board of Directors since 1999), American Judicature Society, Indianapolis and Indiana State (Secretary 1994-95, Chair Editorial Board 1995-96 and Bankruptcy-Creditor's Rights Section 1998-99, Co-chair Written Publications Committee 1996-97, Member Board of Governors 1997-99) Bar Associations. Awardee "Celebrating 100 Years of Women in the Legal Profession" by Indiana State Bar Association. Member since 1990 (Treasurer 1994-95, Vice President 1995-96, President 1996-97) Alumni Board of Directors and Member Centennial Committee Indiana University School of Law.

Office: 1270 National City Center, 115 West Washington Street, Indianapolis 46204-3419.
Telephone: (317) 233-3688.
E-mail address: mrobb@courts.state.in.us

ROBBINS, Michael A. *(Judge, Lawrence Superior Court)*

ROBBINS, MICHAEL A.—*Continued*

Office: Courthouse Annex, 1410 I Street, Bedford 47421-3852.
Telephone: (812) 275-3124.

ROBERTS, Joel D. *(Judge, Jay Superior Court)* Appointed by Governor Robert D. Orr Jan 1, 1989. Elected to subsequent terms. Current term expires Dec 31, 2008. Educated at Rose Polytechnic Institute B.S.C.E. 1968 and Indiana University-Indianapolis J.D. 1974.

Deputy Prosecutor Jay County 1976-88. Member Indiana Judges Association and Indiana State Bar Association. Republican.

Office: 120 North Court Street, Portland 47371-2116.
Telephone: (260) 726-9761.
E-mail address: jaysupct@co.jay.in.us

ROBISON, Geoff *(Judge, New Haven City Court)* Appointed by Governor Frank O'Bannon to term beginning Jan 1, 2000. Elected to subsequent term. Current term expires Dec 31 2006.

Office: 815 Lincoln Highway East, New Haven 46774.
Telephone: (260) 748-7878.
E-mail address: chief7025@aol.com

ROBY, Veronica Mia *(Judge, Elwood City Court)* Appointed by Governor Frank O'Bannon to term beginning Jan 14, 1998. Elected 1999, current term expires Dec 31, 2003. Educated at Ball State University B.S. 1993 M.A. 1994 and Temple University School of Law J.D. 1997.

Member Madison County Bar Association. Board of Directors Cottageview Children's Center, Inc.

Office: 1601 Main Street, Elwood 46036-2024.
Telephone: (765) 552-2655.
E-mail address: vmroby@hotmail.com

RODOVICH, Andrew P. *(Magistrate Judge, United States District Court Northern District of Indiana)* Appointed by U.S. District Court judges to term beginning May 3, 1982. Reappointed May 1990 and May 1998. Current term expires May 2006. Born Hammond Indiana Feb 24, 1948. Educated at Valparaiso University B.A. with senior honors and distinction 1970 J.D. with distinction 1973. Member Delta Theta Phi. Admitted to practice Indiana 1973, U.S. District Court Northern District of Indiana 1974 and U.S. Court of Appeals Seventh Circuit 1977. Referee, Hammond City Court 1978.

Chief Deputy Prosecutor Lake County 1979-82. Adjunct Professor Valparaiso Law School since 1985. Member Council of U.S. Magistrates, Lake County and Indiana State Bar Associations.

Office: 5400 Federal Plaza, Suite 3700, Hammond 46320.
Telephone: (219) 852-6600.
Fax: (219) 852-6611

ROELL, Wayne A. *(Judge, Spencer Circuit Court)* Appointed by Governor Otis Ray Bowen to term beginning Dec 5, 1978. Elected 1978, 1984, 1990, 1996 and 2002. Current term expires Dec 31, 2008. Born Huntingburg Indiana Sept 26, 1949. United Methodist. Educated at University of Evansville B.A. magna cum laude 1971 and Vanderbilt University School of Law J.D. 1975. Admitted to practice Indiana 1975 and U.S. District Court Southern District of Indiana 1975. In legal practice Boonville 1975-77 and Dale 1977-78.

Instructor in Criminal Justice Vincennes University Jasper Center 1987. Member Spencer County and Indiana State Bar Associations. Graduate Indiana Judicial College. Member Rockport Area Chamber of Commerce, Dale Chamber of Commerce and Spencer County Historical Society.

Mailing address: P.O. Box 152, Rockport 47635-0152.
Office: 200 Main Street, Rockport 47635.
Telephone: (812) 649-6025.
E-mail address: warnklr@psci.net

ROGERS, Clark *(Judge, Marion Superior Court)* Elected to term beginning Jan 1, 2001. Term expires Dec 31, 2006. Serves Criminal Division. Educated at DePauw University B.A. 1985 and University of Dayton J.D. 1989. Magistrate, Marion County 1991-2000.

Public Defender Marion County 1989-90. Member Indianapolis and Indiana State Bar Associations. Republican.

Office: 200 East Washington Street, Room G-024, Indianapolis 46204.
Telephone: (317) 327-4437.
E-mail address: chrogers@indygov.org

RUCKER, Robert D. *(Associate Justice, Indiana Supreme Court)* Appointed by Governor Frank O'Bannon. Term expires Dec 31, 2004. Educated at Indiana University Northwest A.B. 1974, Valparaiso University J.D. 1976 and University of Virginia LL.M. 1998. Former Judge and Presiding Judge, Indiana Court of Appeals Fifth District, appointed by Governor B. Evan Bayh Jan 1, 1991.

Deputy Prosecuting Attorney Lake County 1979-86. City Attorney Gary 1987-89. Member American Judicature Society, Marion County, Indiana State and National Bar Associations. U.S. Army 1966-68.

Office: 200 West Washington Street, Room 324, Indianapolis 46204-2732.
Telephone: (317) 232-2544.
E-mail address: rrucker@courts.state.in.us

RUSH, Loretta H. *(Judge, Tippecanoe Superior Court)* Elected to term beginning Jan 1, 1999. Term expires Dec 31, 2004. Educated at Purdue University B.A. 1980 and Indiana University J.D. 1983.

Member Juvenile Benchbook Committee Judicial Conference of Indiana since 1999 and Judicial Technology and Automation Committee Indiana Supreme Court. Member Indiana Council of Juvenile and Family Court Judges (Board of Directors since 2000), Indiana Judges Association, Tippecanoe County and Indiana State Bar Associations.

Office: 301 Main Street, Lafayette 47901-1354.
Telephone: (765) 423-9295.
E-mail address: lrush@county.tippecanoe.in.us

RUSH, Michael D. *(Judge, Whitley Superior Court)* Appointed by Governor B. Evan Bayh Dec 2, 1991. Elected to subsequent terms. Current term expires Dec 31, 2004. Educated at Hanover College B.A. 1967 and Valparaiso University J.D. 1973.

County Attorney Whitley County 1989-91. Associate Faculty of Public Policy courses in Family Law, American Culture and Criminal Law. Indiana University-Purdue University at Fort Wayne. Member Judicial Education Committee Judicial Conference of Indiana 1992-2000. Member Indiana Judges Association, Whitley

RUSH, MICHAEL D.—*Continued*

County (President 1981-84) and Indiana State Bar Associations. U.S. Army 1968-70. Democrat.

Office: 101 West Van Buren Street, Third Floor, Columbia City 46725-2109.

Telephone: (260) 248-3119.

E-mail address: mrush@whitleynet.org

SABOL, Lori Stein *(Judge, West Lafayette City Court)* Appointed by Governor Frank O'Bannon to term beginning Jan 18, 2001. Term expires Dec. 31, 2003. Educated at Indiana University B.A. 1975 J.D. 1982. In legal practice Lafayette since Oct 1982.

Member Tippecanoe County Bar and Indiana State Bar Association. Trained Mediator. Involved with the GAL/CASA Program (Former Foster Parent).

Office: 609 West Navajo Street, West Lafayette 47906-1995.

Telephone: (765) 775-5155.

SANDERS, Russell J. *(Judge, Shelby Superior Court)* Elected to term beginning Jan 1, 1997. Reelected 2002, current term expires Dec 31, 2008. Educated at Indiana University B.A. 1971 and Indiana University-Indianapolis J.D. 1975. USAR 1968-74. Republican.

Office: 407 South Harrison Street, Shelbyville 46176-2170.

Telephone: (317) 392-6340.

E-mail address: russ.sanders@co.shelby.in.us

SCHAFSTALL, Robert D. *(Judge, Franklin City Court)* Elected to term beginning Jan 1, 1972. Reelected 1975, 1979, 1983, 1987, 1991, 1995 and 1999. Current term expires Dec 31, 2003. Educated at Franklin College B.A. 1966 and Indiana University J.D. 1971.

Mailing address: P.O. Box 385, Franklin 46131-2496.

Office: 359 South Main Street, Franklin 46131.

Telephone: (317) 736-3620.

E-mail address: schafstall@iquest.net

SCHEIBENBERGER, Kenneth R. *(Judge, Allen Superior Court)* Appointed by Governor Evan Bayh to term beginning Jan 4, 1992. Elected 1998, current term expires Dec 31, 2004. Serves Criminal Division. Educated at Indiana University B.A. 1972 J.D. 1976.

Member Criminal Instructions Committee 1996-2001 and Jury Committee 2002 and Board of Directors 1998-99 Judicial Conference of Indiana. Board of Directors Indiana Association of Drug Court Professionals. Member National Association of Drug Court Professionals and Allen County Bar Association.

Office: 715 South Calhoun Street, Room 305, Fort Wayne 46802-1805.

Telephone: (260) 449-7563.

Fax: (260) 449-7495

E-mail address: kscheib@mail.fwi.com

SCHIRALLI, Nicholas J. *(Judge, Lake Superior Court)* Appointed by governor Jan 1, 1976. Retained by elections. Current term expires Dec 31, 2008. Serves County Division. Born Gary Indiana June 28, 1948. Catholic. Educated at University of Notre Dame B.A. 1970, University of Denver 1971 and Indiana University J.D. 1973. Admitted to practice Indiana 1974. Began legal practice Merrillville 1974. Justice of the Peace, Calumet Township 1973-75. Judge, Lake County Court Jan 1, 1977 to 1988.

Member Indiana Judges Association, Lake County and Indiana State Bar Associations. Democrat.

Office: Government Center, 2293 North Main Street, Crown Point 46307-1854.

Telephone: (219) 881-6171.

SCHNEIDER, Diane Kavadias *(Judge, Lake Superior Court)* Court Executive/Referee Juvenile Division 1986-93. Magistrate 1993-2000. Appointed Judge by Governor Frank O'Bannon to term beginning July 26, 2000. Term expires Dec 31, 2004. Serves Civil Division. Born Hammond Indiana Sept 22, 1948. Educated at Purdue University B.A. 1971 and Valparaiso University School of Law J.D. 1982. Law Clerk to Lake Superior Court 1983. Member Phi Alpha Delta. Admitted to practice Indiana 1982 and U.S. District Courts Northern 1982 and Southern 1982 Districts of Indiana. In legal practice East Chicago 1984-86.

Member National Council of Juvenile and Family Court Judges 1989-93 and Indiana Supreme Court Commission on Race and Gender Fairness 2001-03. Fellow Indiana Bar Foundation. Member Women Lawyers Association, Indiana Judges Association (Board of Directors since 2001), Indiana Judicial Conference (Board of Directors since 2002), National Association of Women Judges (Board of Directors since 2001), American Judicature Society, East Chicago, Lake County (Board of Managers 1990-91; Secretary 1992-94; Social and Program Co-chair 1994; Chair of Delegates since 1996; Member Bench Bar Planning Committee 1997; Former Member Women and Minorities Section, Legislation Committee and Committee on Library and Judicial Facilities; Family Law Section) and Indiana State (House of Delegates since 1988; Member State Legislation Committee 1991-98, Committee on Improvements in the Judicial System since 1991, Long Range Planning Committee 1993-95 and 2001 and Nominating Committee 1999 and 2001; Chair Credentials and Admissions Committee 1993; Member since 1993 and Chair 1999-2001 Committee on Women in the Law; Board of Governors 1995-97; Member Planning Committee 1997 and General Chair 1999 Spring Meeting; Council Member 2001 and Secretary/Treasurer 2001-02 PLEADS Section; General Practice Section) Bar Associations.

Presenter Bench-Bar Conference Indiana State Bar Association 1996. Member Magistrates Committee since 1996, Presenter New Magistrates Orientation Program 1999 and Chair 2000-02 Indiana Judicial Conference. Member Program Committee and Panelist Indiana Women in the Law Conference 2000. Board of Directors 1991-92, Vice President 1992-93 and President 1993-95 Alumni Association Valparaiso University School of Law. Attorney Volunteer Coach "We the People" Constitution Study Program for Grade 5 Elliott School 1998-2000. Participant Project Peace Training 1999. Judge, Indiana District One "We the People" Regional Competition for middle school and high school students 1999 and 2000. Attorney Team Member Project Peace Program Wilbur Wright Middle School 2000. Speaker on Legal Careers in Government Service and Participant Alumni Contact Program Career Services Department Valparaiso University School of Law. Member Theta Phi Collegiate Sorority Northern Indiana-Illinois Alumni Association.

Office: 232 Russell Street, Hammond 46320.

Telephone: (219) 933-2890.

Fax: (219) 933-0123

E-mail address: dks922@aol.com

SCHURGER, Frederick A. *(Judge, Adams Circuit Court)* Appointed by Governor Frank O'Bannon to term beginning Aug 2, 1999. Elected 2000, current term expires Dec 31, 2006. Educated at Wabash College B.A. 1968 and Indiana University J.D. 1972.
Mailing address: P.O. Box 610, Decatur 46733-0610.
Telephone: (260) 724-5307.
Fax: (260) 724-5308
E-mail address: fschurger@co.adams.in.us

SCOPELITIS, Michael P. *(Judge, St. Joseph Superior Court)* Appointed by Governor Frank O'Bannon to term beginning Oct 1, 2000. Retained by election 2002, current term expires Dec 31, 2008. Educated at Niagara University B.A. 1968 and Notre Dame Law School J.D. 1971.
Office: 219 Lincolnway West, Mishawaka 46544-1989.
Telephone: (574) 235-6219.

SHAHEED, David A. *(Judge, Marion Superior Court)* Serves Criminal Division.
Office: 200 East Washington Street, Room T441, Indianapolis 46204.
Telephone: (317) 327-5353.

SHARP, Allen *(Judge, United States District Court Northern District of Indiana)* Appointed for life by President Richard M. Nixon to term beginning Nov 1, 1973. Former Chief Judge. Born Washington D.C. Feb 11, 1932. Christian. Educated at Indiana State University 1950-53, George Washington University B.A. 1954, Indiana University J.D. 1957 and Butler University M.A. in History 1986. Admitted to practice Indiana 1957. In legal practice Williamsport eleven years. Judge, Indiana Court of Appeals 1969-73.
Author "Social Security Disability Cases Pose New Challenge to the Trial Bar" Trial Magazine 1968, "Social Security Disability Cases" ABA Jour. 1969 and "Social Security Disability Cases: A Challenge to the Trial Bar" *Res Gestae* 1969. Member West Central Bar of Indiana, Warren County, Indiana State, Seventh Circuit and American Bar Associations. Lieutenant Colonel USAFR since 1957. Republican.
Office: 124 Federal Building, 204 South Main Street, South Bend 46601.
Telephone: (574) 246-8170.

SHARPNACK, John T. *(Judge, Indiana Court of Appeals Fifth District)* Appointed by Governor B. Evan Bayh to term beginning Jan 1, 1991. Retained by election. Current term expires Dec 31, 2004. Former Presiding Judge. Chief Judge 1992-2001. Educated at University of Cincinnati A.B. 1955 LL.B. 1960.
Attorney Antitrust Division U.S. Department of Justice 1960-63. Board of Directors 1992-2001 Judicial Conference of Indiana. Board of Managers Indiana Judges Association 1992-2001. Fellow American College of Trial Lawyers. U.S. Army 1955-57.
Office: 115 West Washington Street, Room 1270, Indianapolis 46204-3419.
Telephone: (317) 233-3672.

SHEPARD, Randall T. *(Chief Justice, Indiana Supreme Court)* Appointed by Governor Robert D. Orr to term beginning Sept 6, 1985. Retained by election Nov 1988 and Nov 1998. Current term expires Dec 31, 2008. Born Lafayette Indiana Dec 24, 1946. Methodist. Educated at Princeton University A.B. cum laude 1969, Yale University Law School J.D. 1972 and University of Virginia LL.M. 1995. Member Phi Delta Phi. Admitted to practice Indiana 1972 and U.S. District Court Southern District of Indiana 1972. Began legal practice Washington D.C. 1972. In legal practice Evansville 1979-80. Judge, Vanderburgh Superior Court Jan 1, 1981 to Sept 5, 1985.
Special Assistant to the Under Secretary of Transportation Washington D.C. 1972-74. Executive Assistant to the Mayor of Evansville 1974-79. Author "Changing the Constitutional Jurisdiction of the Indiana Supreme Court" 63 Indiana L. Jour. 669, 1988, "Second Wind for the Indiana Bill of Rights" 22 Indiana L. Rev. 700, 1989, "Land Use Regulation in the Rehnquist Court: The Fifth Amendment and Judicial Intervention" 38 Catholic University L. Rev. 847, 1989 and "Campaign Speech: Restraint and Liberty in Judicial Ethics" 9 Georgetown Journal of Legal Ethics 1059, 1996. Important Decisions: White v. State (post-conviction relief standards for guilty pleas) 497 NE 2d 893, 1986; State Election Board v. Bayh (residency requirement for governor) 521 NE 2d 1313, 1988; and Matter of Sue Ann Lawrence (termination of life-sustaining medical treatment) 579 NE 2d 32, 1991. Member Indiana Judges Association (Director 1983 and since 1987), American Judicature Society, Evansville (Director 1983-84), Indianapolis, Indiana State and American (Council Member 1991-2001 and Chair 1999-2000 Section of Legal Education and Admissions to the Bar, Member since 1992 and Chair 1996-97 Executive Committee Appellate Judges Conference) Bar Associations. Recipient Friend of the Media Award from Society of Professional Journalists—Sigma Delta Chi 1979, Distinguished Service Award from Evansville Jaycees 1982, Herbert Harley Award from American Judicature Society 1992 and Silver Beaver Award from Boy Scouts of America 2002. Republican. Citizens Advisory Committee on Transportation Quality U.S. Department of Transportation 1975-77. Vice Chairman Vanderburgh County Republican Central Committee 1977-80. Chairman State Student Assistance Commission of Indiana 1981-85, Indiana Commission on the Bicentennial of the U.S. Constitution 1986-92 and Historic Landmarks Foundation of Indiana since 1989. Member National Trust for Historic Preservation (Chairman Board of Advisors and Trustee 1983-85 and 1987-96), Family and Children's Service (President 1983-84) and Conrad Baker Foundation (President 1978-84). Enjoys travel.
Office: 200 West Washington Street, Room 304, Indianapolis 46204-2732.
Telephone: (317) 232-2550.
E-mail address: rshepard@courts.state.in.us

SHEWMAKER, Terry C. *(Judge, Elkhart Circuit Court)* Elected to term beginning Jan 1, 1999. Term expires Dec 31, 2004. Educated at Indiana State University B.S. cum laude 1969, DePaul University College of Law and University of Notre Dame Law School J.D. 1975.
Deputy Prosecuting Attorney 1975-93 and Chief Deputy Prosecuting Attorney 1994-98 Elkhart County. Republican.
Office: 101 North Main Street, Goshen 46526-3232.
Telephone: (574) 523-2245.
E-mail address: tshewmaker@aol.com

SHIELDS, V. Sue *(Magistrate Judge, United States District Court Southern District of Indiana)* Appointed by U.S. District Court judges 1994. Reappointed Jan

SHIELDS, V. SUE—*Continued*

2002, current term expires Jan 2010. Born Wilmore Kentucky Jan 1, 1939. Methodist. Educated at Ball State University A.B. 1959 and Indiana University LL.B. with honors 1961. Staff member Law Journal. Member Order of the Coif. Admitted to practice Indiana 1961. Judge, Hamilton Superior Court 1965-78. Judge, Indiana Court of Appeals Second District 1978-94.

With the Office of the Internal Revenue Service Regional Counsel 1961 and Office of the Indiana Attorney General 1962-64. Active member various state and local bar associations.

Office: 256 U.S. Courthouse, 46 East Ohio Street, Indianapolis 46204.
Telephone: (317) 229-3670.

SHILTS, Kim VanValer *(Judge, Johnson Superior Court)* Elected to term beginning Jan 1, 1997. Reelected 2002, current term expires Dec 31, 2008. Born Franklin Indiana June 6, 1962. Educated at Indiana University B.A. 1984 J.D. 1991 and University of Minnesota 1985-88. Admitted to practice Indiana 1991. Magistrate, Johnson Circuit Court 1994-96. Republican.

Office: Five East Jefferson Street, Franklin 46131-2339.
Telephone: (317) 738-4425.
Fax: (317) 738-4458
E-mail address: kimvanvalershilts@co.johnson.in.us

SHURN, Michael A. *(Judge, Pulaski Circuit Court)* Temporary Judge 1984-94. Elected Judge to term beginning Jan 1, 1995. Reelected 2000, current term expires Dec 31, 2006. Educated at Indiana Central College B.A. 1971 and Indiana University-Indianapolis J.D. 1976. Articles Editor Indiana Law Review 1975-76. Law Clerk to Indiana Court of Appeals Second District 1976-77.

Faculty Indiana Department of Education. Member Probation Committee Judicial Conference of Indiana, Indiana Judges Association, Indiana Council of Juvenile and Family Court Judges, National Council of Juvenile and Family Court Judges, American Judges Association, American Judicature Society, Pulaski County, Indiana State and American Bar Associations. Faculty Indiana Judicial Center CLE and Probation Officer Training Indiana State Bar Association CLE. U.S. Army JAGC 1971-73. Democrat. Member Pulaski County Community Foundation, Pulaski County Historical Society, Inc. (Past President), Pulaski County Chamber of Commerce, Inc. (Past President), Kiwanis Club of Winamac, Indiana, Inc. (Past President), Pulaski County Drug Free Council, Academic Boosters Club, Athletic Boosters Club and Music Boosters Club Eastern Pulaski Community School Corporation, Winamac Community High School Parent Advisory Committee, Pulaski County Community Systemwide Response Program, Pulaski County Early Intervention Planning Council, Cassl Pulaski Community Corrections Program, Pulaski County CASA/GAL Program and Pulaski County Alternative Education Program for Suspended and Expelled Students. Elder Pulaski Presbyterian Church. Lay Pastor Presbytery of Wabash Valley Presbyterian Church. Assistant Scoutmaster Boy Scout Troop 229. Club Leader Pulaski County 4-H Club.

Office: 310 Courthouse, 112 East Main Street, Winamac 46996-1208.
Telephone: (574) 946-3851.
E-mail address: 66c01@pwrtc.com

SIMON, Phillip Peter *(Judge, United States District Court Northern District of Indiana)* Appointed for life by President George W. Bush to term beginning March 31, 2003.

Office: 1128 Federal Building, 1300 South Harrison Street, Fort Wayne 46802.
Telephone: (260) 423-3050.

SIMS, Stephen M. *(Judge, Allen Superior Court)* Elected to term beginning Jan 1, 1997. Reelected 2002, current term expires Dec 31, 2008. Educated at Indiana University-Bloomington B.A. 1969 and Indiana University-Indianapolis J.D. 1973. Magistrate/Hearing Officer, Allen Circuit Court 1995-96.

Prosecuting Attorney Thirty-eighth Judicial Circuit 1983-94. Chair Juvenile Justice Improvement Committee Judicial Conference of Indiana since 1999. U.S. Army National Guard 1967-75. Chair Community Corrections Board Allen County since 1990.

Office: 715 South Calhoun Street, Room 208, Fort Wayne 46802-1805.
Telephone: (260) 449-7284.
E-mail address: stephen.sims@co.allen.in.us

SLEVA, William G. *(Judge, Lawrence Superior Court)* Appointed by Governor B. Evan Bayh to term beginning Jan 1, 1996. Elected 2002, current term expires Dec 31, 2008. Born Chicago Illinois March 22, 1952. Roman Catholic. Educated at University of Illinois B.S. 1974 and Indiana University J.D. Law Clerk to Hon. Robert L. Bayt, U.S. Bankruptcy Court Southern District of Indiana 1981-83. Admitted to practice Indiana 1981 and U.S. District Court Southern District of Indiana. In legal practice Bedford 1983-89. Judge, Lawrence County Court Jan 1, 1989 to 1995.

Councilman Lawrence County Council 1987-89.

Office: Courthouse Annex, 1420 I Street, Bedford 47421.
Telephone: (812) 275-4161.
E-mail address: wgskiva.net

SMITH, Jeffrey R. *(Judge, Carroll Superior Court)* Appointed by Governor Robert D. Orr to term beginning July 1, 1988. Elected 1990, 1996 and 2002. Current term expires Dec 31, 2008. Born Logansport Indiana June 26, 1947. Christian. Educated at Wabash College A.B. 1969 and Indiana University J.D. 1972. Admitted to practice Indiana 1972. In legal practice Delphi 1972-87. Prosecuting Attorney Carroll County 1979-87.

Office: 101 West Main Street, Delphi 46923-1566.
Telephone: (765) 564-2136.
E-mail address: smithjhl@remconline.net

SMITH, Kathy R. *(Judge, Clinton Superior Court)* Appointed by Governor B. Evan Bayh July 1, 1990. Elected to subsequent terms. Current term expires Dec 31, 2008. Educated at Ball State University B.S. 1974 and Indiana University-Indianapolis J.D. 1980. Judge, Clinton County Court Jan 1, 1983 to June 30, 1990.

Chief Deputy Prosecutor Clinton County 1981-83. Member Clinton County Bar Association (Vice President 1982).

Office: 320 Courthouse Square, Frankfort 46041-1963.
Telephone: (765) 659-6341.
E-mail address: ksmith7@mintel.net

SNOW, P. Thomas *(Judge, Wayne Superior Court)* Elected to term beginning Jan 1, 1989. Reelected to subsequent terms. Current term expires Dec 31, 2006. Edu-

SNOW, P. THOMAS—*Continued*

cated at Ball State University B.S. 1969 and Indiana University-Indianapolis J.D. 1972.

Adjunct Faculty Member Indiana University East. Board of Directors 1991-95 and Member Judicial Administration Committee since 1992 Judicial Conference of Indiana. Member Indiana Judges Association and Indiana State Bar Association. Graduate Indiana Judicial College 1995. Republican.

Office: 301 East Main Street, Richmond 47374-4200.
Telephone: (765) 973-9259.
E-mail address: toms@co.wayne.in.us

SNOW, Terry K. *(Judge, Hancock Superior Court)*
Office: Nine East Main Street, Room 303, Greenfield 46140-2320.
Telephone: (317) 462-1148.

SOBECKI, Dean A. *(Judge, Daviess Superior Court)*
Office: 200 East Walnut Street, Washington 47501-2759.
Telephone: (812) 254-8671.

SOSIN, Ted *(Judge, Marion Circuit Court)*
Office: 200 East Washington Street, Room W506, Indianapolis 46204.
Telephone: (317) 327-4010.

SOUTH, Nicholas L. *(Judge, Scott Superior Court)* Appointed by Governor B. Evan Bayh to term beginning March 20, 1991. Elected to subsequent terms. Current term expires Dec 31, 2004. Educated at Indiana University Southeast A.B. 1977 and Indiana University-Indianapolis J.D. 1980.

Public Defender Scott Circuit Court 1981. Counsel Scott County School District No. 2 1981-91. Deputy Prosecuting Attorney Scott County 1987-91. Member Indiana Judges Association, Scott County and Indiana State Bar Associations. U.S. Army 1966-69. Democrat.

Office: One East McClain Avenue, Scottsburg 47170-1848.
Telephone: (812) 752-8464.
E-mail address: nlsouth89@hotmail.com

SPENCER, Fredrick R. *(Judge, Madison Circuit Court)* Elected to term beginning Jan 1, 1983. Reelected 1988, 1994 and 2000. Current term expires Dec 31, 2006. Born Anderson Indiana Feb 7, 1938. Episcopalian. Educated at Ball State University B.S. 1964 and Indiana University at Indianapolis J.D. 1971. Admitted to practice Indiana 1971, U.S. District Court Southern District of Indiana 1971 and U.S. Tax Court 1971. Began legal practice Anderson 1971.

Deputy Attorney General Indiana 1971. Deputy City Attorney Anderson 1972-79. Adjunct Faculty Anderson University Spring 1986. Member Madison County and American Bar Associations. Faculty Indiana Trial Lawyers Seminar Dec 1988. Specialist Four U.S. Army Communications Intelligence 1956-59.

Office: Madison County Government Center, Box 29, 16 East Ninth Street, Anderson 46016-1575.
Telephone: (765) 641-9436.

SPENCER, James D. *(Judge, Plainfield Town Court)* Appointed Aug 1, 1989. Elected to subsequent terms. Current term expires Dec 31, 2003. Educated at University of Illinois B.S. 1968 M.S. 1970 and Southern Illinois University School of Law J.D. 1977. Law Clerk to Illinois Appellate Court Fourth Judicial District 1977-79.

Assistant General Counsel Amax Coal Company 1979-93. Treasurer City and Town Court Judges Association since 1991. Member Indianapolis, Hendricks County and Indiana State Bar Associations. U.S. Army 1971-74. Republican.

Mailing address: P.O. Box 634, Plainfield 46168-0634.
Office: 1075 West Main Street, Plainfield 46168.
Telephone: (317) 838-3710.
Fax: (317) 838-3474

SPINDLER, Stephen S. *(Judge, Noble Superior Court)* Appointed by Governor B. Evan Bayh to term beginning Jan 3, 1990. Elected to subsequent terms. Current term expires Dec 31, 2006. Educated at New York University A.B. cum laude 1966 J.D. 1973. Member Phi Beta Kappa.

Chief Deputy Prosecuting Attorney Noble County 1975-90. Member Indiana Supreme Court Advisory Commission GAL/CASA and Indiana Commission on Mental Health. Member Indiana Supreme Court Rules Committee since 1995, Indiana Judges Association, Indiana Council of Juvenile and Family Court Judges, National Council of Juvenile and Family Court Judges, Association of Family and Conciliation Courts, American Judicature Society, Noble County, Indiana State and American Bar Associations. Graduate Indiana Judicial College 1995. Attended Indiana Graduate Program for Judges 1997. Democrat. Board of Directors Northeast Indiana CASA, Inc.

Office: 101 North Orange Street, Albion 46701-1095.
Telephone: (260) 636-3205.
E-mail address: supctl@ligtel.com

SPOSEEP, Michael L. *(Judge, Wabash Superior Court)* Elected 1996. Reelected 2002, current term expires Dec 31, 2008. Born Fort Wayne Indiana Dec 17, 1944. Jewish. Educated at Indiana University A.B. 1966 J.D. 1969. Member Sigma Alpha Mu. Admitted to practice Indiana 1969. Judge, Wabash City Court 1976-80. Judge, Wabash County Court Jan 1, 1981 to 1995.

Attorney National Labor Relations Board 1969. Member Indiana Judges Association, Wabash County and Indiana State Bar Associations. Graduate Indiana Judicial College 1987. Republican. Enjoys golf, boating, fishing and skiing.

Office: One West Hill Street, Wabash 46992-3151.
Telephone: (260) 563-0661.
E-mail address: msposeep@hotmail.com

SPRINGMANN, Theresa L. *(Magistrate Judge, United States District Court Northern District of Indiana)* Appointed by U.S. District Court judges to term beginning March 23, 1995. Reappointed March 2003, current term expires March 23, 2011. Educated at Indiana University B.A. summa cum laude 1977 and University of Notre Dame J.D. 1980. Judicial Clerk to Hon. James T. Moody, Lake Superior Court 1980-83. In legal practice Merrilllville 1984-95.

Member Calumet Chapter American Inns of Court, Federal Magistrate Judges Association, Lake County and Indiana State Bar Associations.

Office: 5400 Federal Plaza, Suite 3500, Hammond 46320.
Telephone: (219) 852-6700.

STEELE, Wayne E. *(Judge, Fulton Superior Court)* Elected to term beginning Jan 1, 2001. Term expires Dec 31, 2006. Educated at Indiana University-

STEELE, WAYNE E.—*Continued*

Bloomington B.S. 1974, Indiana University-Purdue University Indianapolis M.S. 1977 and Gonzaga University School of Law J.D. 1981.

Prosecuting Attorney Montgomery County 1983-90. Town Attorney Akron and Kewanna 1993-2000. Attorney 1993-2000, Public Defender 1997-98 and Chief Deputy Prosecuting Attorney 1998-2000 Fulton County. Past President Fulton County Bar Association. USN 1972-75.

Office: 815 Main Street, Rochester 46975-1593.
Telephone: (574) 223-3506.
E-mail address: molly@rtcol.com

STEFANIAK, Thomas P., Jr. *(Judge, Lake Superior Court)* Appointed by Governor Frank O'Bannon to term beginning Jan 22, 2001. Retained by election 2002, current term expires Dec 31, 2008. Serves Criminal Division. Educated at St. Joseph's College B.S. 1987 and Valparaiso University J.D. 1990. Former Judge, Hammond City Court, elected to term beginning Jan 1, 1996.

Deputy Prosecutor Lake County 1990-95. Member Lake County Bar Association (Board of Managers 1993-95). Democrat.

Office: Government Center, 2293 North Main Street, Crown Point 46307-1854.
Telephone: (219) 755-3500.
E-mail address: stefatp@lakecountyin.org

STENGEL, Bruce V. *(Judge, Vermillion Circuit Court)* Elected to term beginning Jan 1, 1995. Reelected 2000, current term expires Dec 31, 2006. Educated at Indiana University B.S. 1973 J.D. 1976.

Prosecuting Attorney 1979-92. Attorney North Vermillion Community School Corporation 1980-94 and Vermillion County Council 1993-94. City Attorney Clinton 1982-84. Member Juvenile Benchbook Committee Judicial Conference of Indiana since 1998. Member Indiana Judges Association, American Judges Association, Indiana State and American Bar Associations. Democrat.

Mailing address: P.O. Box 70, Newport 47966-0070.
Office: Courthouse, 255 South Main Street, Newport 47966.
Telephone: (765) 492-3044.
E-mail address: judgebvs@ccsdana.net

STEPHENS, A. Douglas *(Judge, Marion County Small Claims Court Pike Township Division)* Elected to term beginning Jan 1, 2003. Term expires Dec 31, 2006. Born Shelbyville Indiana March 1, 1959. Church of Jesus Christ of Latter-Day Saints. Educated at Indiana University B.A. 1981, Whittier College School of Law and Indiana University School of Law J.D. 1987. Admitted to practice Indiana 1988 and U.S. District Court Northern District of Indiana 1989. In legal practice Indianapolis since 1988.

Assistant Corporation Counsel City of Indianapolis 1988-91. Member Indianapolis Bar Association. Democrat.

Office: 5665 Lafayette Road, Suite B, Indianapolis 46234.
Telephone: (317) 293-1842.
Fax: (317) 290-8319
E-mail address: indylaws@aol.com

STEWART, Judith A. *(Judge, Brown Circuit Court)* Referee 1988-90. Elected to term beginning Jan 1, 2001. Term expires Dec 31, 2006. Educated at Butler University B.A. 1979 and Indiana University-Indianapolis J.D. 1982. Judge, Brown Circuit Court 1991-93.

U.S. Attorney Southern District of Indiana 1993-2000. Member American Judicature Society, Brown County, Indiana State, Seventh Circuit and American Bar Associations.

Mailing address: P.O. Box 85, Nashville 47448-0085.
Office: 20 East Main, Nashville 47448.
Telephone: (812) 988-7557.
E-mail address: jstewart@kiva.net

STICKEL, Olga H. *(Judge, Elkhart Superior Court)* Term expires Dec 31, 2008. Born Germany Dec 28, 1947. Eastern Orthodox. Educated at Indiana University A.B. 1970 M.L.S. 1972 J.D. 1976. Member Alpha Lambda Delta. Admitted to practice Indiana 1976. Began legal practice Goshen 1977. Judge, Goshen City Court 1978-84. Judge, Elkhart County Court 1984-95.

Member Goshen City Bar Association (Former Vice President, Past President).

Office: 101 North Main Street, Goshen 46526-3232.
Telephone: (574) 535-6463.
Fax: (574) 535-6401

STONER, Mark D. *(Judge, Marion Superior Court)* Elected to term beginning Jan 1, 2001. Term expires Dec 31, 2006. Serves Criminal Division. Educated at University of Virginia B.A. 1977 and Indiana University-Indianapolis J.D. 1981.

Senior Deputy Prosecutor Marion County 1979-2000.
Office: 200 East Washington Street, Room E-648, Indianapolis 46204.
Telephone: (317) 327-3211.
E-mail address: mstoner@indygov.org

STRIEGEL, Richard G. *(Judge, Floyd Superior Court)* Elected to term beginning Jan 1, 1979. Reelected 1984, 1990, 1996 and 2002. Current term expires Dec 31, 2008. Educated at Purdue University B.S. in Chemical Engineering 1966 and University of Louisville J.D. 1973.

Public Defender Floyd Circuit Court 1974-78. Member Indiana Judges Association (Board of Managers 1980-82) and Floyd County Bar Association. Board of Directors Indiana Judicial Center 1986-90.

Office: 311 West First Street, Room 200, New Albany 47150-5856.
Telephone: (812) 948-5450.

STURTEVANT, Wayne A. *(Judge, Hamilton Superior Court)* Elected to term beginning Jan 1, 1997. Reelected 2002, current term expires Dec 31, 2008. Educated at Butler University B.A. 1973 and Indiana University-Indianapolis J.D. 1977.

Deputy Prosecutor 1980-85 and Chief Deputy Prosecutor 1985-96 Hamilton County. Republican.

Office: One Hamilton County Square, #297, Noblesville 46060-2232.
Telephone: (317) 776-8263.
E-mail address: was@co.hamilton.in.us

SULLIVAN, Frank, Jr. *(Associate Justice, Indiana Supreme Court)* Appointed by Governor Evan Bayh Nov 1, 1993. Retained by election Nov 1996, current term expires Dec 31, 2006. Born South Bend Indiana March 21, 1950. Educated at Dartmouth College A.B. 1972, Indiana University-Bloomington J.D. 1982 and University of Virginia LL.M. 2001. In legal practice Indianapolis 1982-89.

SULLIVAN, FRANK, JR.—*Continued*

Member Juvenile Justice Improvement Committee Judicial Conference of Indiana, Indiana Judges Association, Indiana Council of Juvenile and Family Court Judges, National Council of Juvenile and Family Court Judges, American Judicature Society, Indianapolis, Marion County, Indiana State and American Bar Associations. State Budget Director Indiana 1989-93. Staff U.S. Representatives J. Edward Roush 1973 and John Brademas 1974-79.

Office: 200 West Washington Street, Room 321, Indianapolis 46204-2732.

Telephone: (317) 232-2548.

Fax: (317) 233-8691

E-mail address: fsullivan@courts.state.in.us

SULLIVAN, Patrick D. *(Judge, Indiana Court of Appeals Second District)* Elected to term beginning Jan 1, 1969. Retained by election 1972, 1982, 1992 and 2002. Current term expires Dec 31, 2012. Presiding Judge 1971, 1974, 1977, 1978, 1998 and 2001. Born Huntington Indiana Aug 9, 1932. Educated at Washington and Lee University B.A. in History 1956 law degree cum laude 1958. Member Omicron Delta Kappa, Sigma Chi, Pi Alpha Nu, Pi Sigma Alpha and Phi Delta Phi. President Law School Board of Governors. Board of Editors Law Review. Recipient Harrison B. Tweed Trophy National Moot Court Best Brief Award representing Washington and Lee University School of Law Dec 1957. Admitted to practice Indiana, U.S. District Courts Northern and Southern Districts of Indiana, U.S. Court of Appeals Seventh Circuit and U.S. Supreme Court. In legal practice Indianapolis 1961-65. Senior Commissioner, Marion Probate Court 1963-64. Judge, Marion Municipal Court 1965-69.

Deputy Attorney General Indiana 1958-61. Lecturer on American Diplomatic History Indiana University 1973 and "Law and Public Policy" Indiana University and Purdue University 1989, 1990 and 1991. Adjunct Professor of Law 1974-78 and Visiting Professor "Indiana Judicial Process" Indiana University at Indianapolis. Lecturer Indiana Bar Review Course. Lecturer "Law and the Layman" in adult education courses. Member Lawyers Club of Indianapolis, Advisory Committee of Indiana Supreme Court on Revision of Rules of Procedure and Practice, Appellate Judges Conference of ABA, Indianapolis Lawyers Commission, U.S. Government Evaluation Project-Juvenile Law Centers San Francisco 1973, Indianapolis, Indiana State and American Bar Associations. Faculty member Appellate Judges Seminars. Recipient First Annual Man of the Year Award by Knights of St. Peter Claver Indianapolis 1972. U.S. Navy 1952-54. Member Indiana Flood Control Advisory Committee and Community Services Council Legislative Committee. Co-founder and Director Martin Inn Inc. (halfway house). Director Indianapolis Indians Professional Baseball Club.

Office: 200 West Washington Street, Room 420, Indianapolis 46204-2784.

Telephone: (317) 232-6889.

SURBECK, John F., Jr. *(Judge, Allen Superior Court)* Appointed by Governor Robert D. Orr to term beginning Feb 5, 1988. Elected 1990, 1996 and 2002. Current term expires Dec 31, 2008. Born Evansville Indiana March 31, 1946. Catholic. Educated at Indiana University B.S. 1968 J.D. 1971. Law Clerk to Hon. Alfred W. Moellering, Allen Superior Court Sept 1971 to Sept 1972. Admitted to practice Indiana 1971 and U.S. District Courts Northern 1971 and Southern 1971 Districts of Indiana. In legal practice Fort Wayne 1972-88.

Deputy Public Defender and Public Defender Allen County 1972-88. Board of Directors Indiana Public Defender Council 1980-88 (Chairman 1986-88). Instructor in Evidence and Administrative Law Indiana University/Purdue University Spring and Fall 1990. Member Indiana Judges Association, Allen County, Indiana State and American Bar Associations. Board of Directors Three Rivers Festival and Boy Scouts of America. Member Steering Committees for Drug Free Indiana and Allen County Drug and Alcohol Consortium. Enjoys bicycling.

Office: 715 South Calhoun Street, Room 302, Fort Wayne 46802-1805.

Telephone: (260) 449-7583.

E-mail address: jsurbeck@fwi.com

SUTTON, Joe V. *(Judge, Kosciusko Superior Court)* Elected to term beginning Jan 1, 1997. Reelected 2002, current term expires Dec 31, 2008. Educated at Ball State University B.S. 1977 M.A. 1980 and Indiana University-Indianapolis J.D. 1988.

Deputy Prosecutor Kosciusko County 1990-96. Republican.

Office: Justice Building, 121 North Lake Street, Warsaw 46580.

Telephone: (574) 372-2394.

E-mail address: jsutton@kcgov.com

SVETANOFF, Gerald N. *(Judge, Lake Superior Court)* Appointed by Governor Robert D. Orr to term beginning July 1, 1981. Retained by election 1984, 1990, 1996 and 2002. Current term expires Dec 31, 2008. Serves Civil Division. Born Gary Indiana Dec 10, 1935. Educated at Indiana University B.S. 1958 LL.B. 1960 and Northwestern University graduate work in law 1972. Law Clerk to Indiana Supreme Court 1961-62. Admitted to practice Indiana 1960 and Illinois 1960. Began legal practice Gary Indiana 1960. In legal practice Indianapolis 1965-73 and Gary 1973-81 Indiana.

Author "Compensation for Victims of Violent Crime—Existing Sources vs. A State Plan" *Res Gestae* 1973. Member Indiana Judges Association and Indiana State Bar Association. Recipient Gary Community Mental Health Center Award 1984.

Office: 15 West Fourth Avenue, Gary 46402-1238.

Telephone: (219) 881-6146.

Fax: (219) 881-6168

TALIAFERRO, Viola J. *(Judge, Monroe Circuit Court)* Magistrate 1989-95. Appointed Judge by Governor B. Evan Bayh to term beginning July 1, 1995. Elected 1998, current term expires Dec 31, 2004. Educated at Virginia State College B.S. 1947, Johns Hopkins University M.L.A. 1969 and Indiana University-Bloomington J.D. 1977.

Board of Managers Indiana Judges Association since 1998. Member American Law Institute. Previously employed as Social Worker Maryland Department of Welfare Baltimore and Teacher and Department Head Baltimore City Public Schools Maryland. Democrat.

Office: Courts Building, 301 North College Avenue, Bloomington 47401-3865.

Telephone: (812) 349-2629.

E-mail address: taliafey@co.monroe.in.us

TANDY, Jack A. *(Judge, Shelby Superior Court)* Assumed office Jan 1, 1989. Elected 1990, 1996 and 2002. Current term expires Dec 31, 2008. Born Indianapolis Indiana Feb 21, 1957. Educated at Wabash College B.A. magna cum laude 1979 and Indiana University at Indianapolis J.D. 1982. Member Phi Beta Kappa and Tau Kappa Epsilon. Admitted to practice Indiana 1982. Began legal practice Indianapolis 1982. In legal practice Shelbyville 1983. Judge, Shelby County Court, Jan 1, 1985 to Dec 31, 1988.

Member Shelby County and Indiana State Bar Associations. Republican.

Office: 407 South Harrison Street, Basement #1, Shelbyville 46176-2170.

Telephone: (317) 392-6350.

E-mail address: jack.tandy@co.shelby.in.us

TATE, Douglas A. *(Judge, Howard Superior Court)*

Office: 117 North Main Street, Kokomo 46901-9004.

Telephone: (765) 456-2220.

TAUL, Carl H. *(Judge, Ripley Circuit Court)* Elected to term beginning Jan 1, 1991. Reelected 1996 and 2002. Current term expires Dec 31, 2008. Educated at Ball State University B.S. 1972 and Indiana University-Indianapolis J.D. 1976.

Prosecuting Attorney Ripley County 1983-86. U.S. Army 1966-68. Democrat.

Mailing address: P.O. Box 445, Versailles 47042-0445.

Telephone: (812) 689-6226.

Fax: (812) 689-6104

E-mail address: ripleyckt@hotmail.com

THACKER, Robert W. *(Judge, White Circuit Court)* Appointed by Governor Robert D. Orr to term beginning Nov 30, 1987. Elected 1988, 1994 and 2000. Current term expires Dec 31, 2006. Born Lafayette Indiana April 12, 1948. Educated at Northwestern University B.A. 1970 and Indiana University J.D. 1973. Admitted to practice Indiana 1973 and Wyoming 1974. In legal practice Monticello Indiana 1974-87. Enjoys reading, golf and all spectator and participating sports.

Mailing address: P.O. Box 230, Monticello 47960-0230.

Office: Courthouse, Monticello 47960.

Telephone: (574) 583-5032.

E-mail address: thacker@monti.net

THODE, Jeffrey L. *(Judge, Porter Superior Court)* Elected to term beginning Jan 1, 1995. Reelected 2000, current term expires Dec 31, 2006. Educated at Valparaiso University B.S. 1982 J.D. 1985. Probate Commissioner Porter County 1992-94.

Deputy Prosecuting Attorney Porter County 1990-92. Member American Inns of Court, Indiana Council of Juvenile and Family Court Judges and Porter County Bar Association. Republican.

Office: 3560 Willowcreek Road, Portage 46368.

Telephone: (219) 759-2501.

E-mail address: jthode@porterco.org

THOMPSON, Evard E. *(Judge, Winchester City Court)* Elected Nov 7, 1995 to term beginning Jan 1, 1996. Reelected Nov 2, 1999, current term expires Dec 31, 2003. Born Carlos Indiana July 22, 1926. Protestant.

Petty Officer Third Class USN Nov 1944 to May 1946. Treasurer Randolph County Jan 1987 to Dec 31, 1994. Member and Elder. (Member Choir and Quartet) Church of Christ. Enjoys golfing, fishing, boating and gardening.

Mailing address: P.O. Box 408, Winchester 47394-0408.

Office: 113 East Washington Street, Winchester 47394.

Telephone: (765) 584-9331.

TINDER, John D. *(Judge, United States District Court Southern District of Indiana)* Appointed for life by President Ronald Reagan to term beginning Aug 10, 1987. Born Indianapolis Indiana Feb 17, 1950. Educated at Indiana University B.S. 1972 J.D. 1975. Law Clerk to Office of U.S. Attorney 1974. In legal practice Indianapolis 1977-84.

Assistant U.S. Attorney 1974-77 and U.S. Attorney 1984-87 Southern District of Indiana. Public Defender Criminal Court 1977-78 and Chief Trial Deputy Prosecutor's Office 1979-82 Marion County.

Office: 304 U.S. Courthouse, 46 East Ohio Street, Indianapolis 46204.

Telephone: (317) 229-3680.

TODD, Jeffrey D. *(Judge, Grant Superior Court)*

Office: 101 East Fourth Street, Marion 46952-4010.

Telephone: (765) 664-9532.

TODD, Kenneth G. *(Judge, Monroe Circuit Court)* Assumed office Jan 1, 1991. Elected 1996 and 2002. Current term expires Dec 31, 2008. Born Batesville Indiana Sept 13, 1945. Protestant. Educated at Indiana University B.A. 1967 J.D. 1970. Admitted to practice Indiana 1970. Began legal practice Bloomington 1970. Probate Commissioner, Monroe Circuit Court 1976-78. Judge, Monroe Superior Court Jan 1, 1979 to Dec 31, 1990.

Member Indiana Judges Association, Monroe County and Indiana State Bar Associations. Captain USAF 1970-74 (Military Judge 1971-72 and Prosecutor Second Judicial District 1972-74). Republican.

Office: Courts Building, 301 North College Avenue, Bloomington 47401-3865.

Telephone: (812) 349-2630.

E-mail address: kgtodd@co.monroe.in.us

TODD, Ted R. *(Judge, Jefferson-Switzerland Circuit Court)* Elected to term beginning Jan 1, 1989. Reelected 1994 and 2000. Current term expires Dec 31, 2006. Born Goshen Indiana Nov 22, 1939. Episcopalian. Educated at Wabash College A.B. 1961 and Duke University School of Law LL.B. 1964. Admitted to practice Indiana 1964 and U.S. District Court Southern District of Indiana 1964. In legal practice Madison 1964-88.

Member 1989-98 and President 1995-96 Indiana State Board of Law Examiners. Democrat.

Office: 300 East Main Street, Madison 47250-3537.

Telephone: (812) 265-8930.

Fax: (812) 265-8946

Office: Courthouse, Vevay 47043.

Telephone: (812) 427-3410.

E-mail address: ttcir@jeffersoncoin.org

TORNATTA, Robert J. *(Judge, Vanderburgh Superior Court)* Magistrate 1995-97. Appointed Judge by Governor Frank O'Bannon to term beginning Dec 11, 1997. Elected 2000, current term expires Dec 31, 2006. Educated at Indiana University-Bloomington B.A. 1982 J.D. 1985. Law Clerk to Chief Judge Gene E. Brooks, U.S.

TORNATTA, ROBERT J.—*Continued*

District Court Southern District of Indiana 1986-88. Court Administrator, Vanderburgh Superior Court 1991.
Office: 225 Courts Building, 825 Sycamore Street, Evansville 47708-1849.
Telephone: (812) 426-5202.
E-mail address: rtornatta@vanderburghgov.org

TROCKMAN, Wayne S. *(Judge, Vanderburgh Superior Court)* Appointed by Governor Frank O'Bannon to term beginning Feb 9, 1999. Elected 2000, current term expires Dec 31, 2006. Educated at University of Southern Indiana B.S. 1981 and Indiana University J.D. 1985.
Assistant City Attorney Evansville 1991-98.
Office: 120 Civic Center Complex, 825 Sycamore Street, Evansville 47708-1833.
Telephone: (812) 435-5405.
E-mail address: wtrock@evansville.net

TURPIN, Bobby G. *(Judge, Roanoke Town Court)* Appointed to term beginning July 18, 1996. Elected 1999, current term expires Dec 31, 2003. Educated at Harbor College 1964-66.
Member City and Town Court Legislative Committee, National Judges Association and Indiana State Bar Association. Graduate National Judicial College 2000. USNR 1961-64. Member Town Council 1984-92.
Mailing address: P.O. Box 159, Roanoke 46783-1591.
Office: 141 West Third Street, Roanoke 46783.
Telephone: (260) 672-3273.

URDAL, Ronald T. *(Judge, Fayette Superior Court)*
Office: 401 Central Avenue, Connersville 47331-1981.
Telephone: (765) 825-1775.

VAIDIK, Nancy Harris *(Judge, Indiana Court of Appeals Fifth District)* Appointed by Governor Frank O'Bannon to term beginning Feb 2000. Retained by election 2002, current term expires Dec 31, 2012. Born Lafayette Indiana June 24, 1955. Educated at Valparaiso University B.A. with honors 1977 J.D. 1980. Admitted to practice Indiana 1980, U.S. District Court Northern District of Indiana and U.S. Supreme Court 1989. In legal practice Merrillville 1986-93. Former Judge, Porter Superior Court, elected to term beginning Jan 1, 1993.
Deputy Prosecutor 1980-83 and Chief Deputy Prosecutor 1983-86 Porter County. Adjunct Professor of Trial Advocacy Valparaiso University since 1986. Member Indiana Judges Association, Porter County and Indiana State Bar Associations. Instructor in Indiana Trial Skills 1994 and 1995 and Alternative Sentences 1994 Indiana Continuing Legal Education Forum.
Office: 200 West Washington Street, Room 409, Indianapolis 46204-3419.
Telephone: (317) 234-0883.
Fax: (317) 233-0392
E-mail address: nvaidik@courts.state.in.us

VANCE, William E. *(Judge, Jackson Circuit Court)* Appointed by Governor Frank O'Bannon to term beginning Jan 1, 1999. Elected 2000, current term expires Dec 31, 2006. Educated at Ball State University B.S. 1965 M.A. 1968 and Indiana University-Indianapolis J.D. 1974. Democrat.
Mailing address: P.O. Box 315, Brownstown 47220-0315.
Telephone: (812) 358-6133.
Fax: (812) 358-4689
E-mail address: bvancirc@seidata.com

VANDERBECK, James "Scott" *(Judge, LaGrange Circuit Court)* Elected Nov 1996 to term beginning Jan 1, 1997. Reelected 2002, current term expires Dec 31, 2008. Born Niles Michigan April 1953. Educated at Michigan State University B.S. 1977 and Valparaiso University J.D. 1984. Admitted to practice Indiana 1984 and U.S. Supreme Court 1988. In legal practice LaGrange 1984-96.
Attorney LaGrange County Department of Public Welfare, Sunny Brook RV and Howe Military School. Member Indiana Judges Association (Probate Committee) and Indiana State Bar Association.
Mailing address: P.O. Box 31, LaGrange 46761-0031.
Office: 105 North Detroit Street, LaGrange 46761.
Telephone: (260) 499-6358.
Fax: (260) 463-7848
E-mail address: lacirct@ligtel.com

VANDERPOOL, Daniel J. *(Judge, Wabash Circuit Court)* Elected to term beginning Jan 1, 1987. Reelected 1992 and 1998. Current term expires Dec 31, 2004. Born Wabash Indiana Sept 27, 1956. Educated at Huntington College B.A. magna cum laude 1977 and Indiana University School of Law J.D. magna cum laude 1980. Member Phi Alpha Delta and Order of the Coif. Admitted to practice Indiana 1980. Judge, Wabash City Court 1985-87.
Member Indiana Judges Association, American Judges Association, National Council of Juvenile and Family Court Judges and Indiana State Bar Association. Board of Directors Indiana Judicial Conference.
Office: One West Hill Street, Wabash 46992-3151.
Telephone: (260) 563-0661.
E-mail address: judgev@ctlnet.com

VANES, Thomas W. *(Judge, Lowell Town Court)* Elected to term beginning Jan 1, 2000. Term expires Dec 31, 2003. Born Hammond Indiana Sept 28, 1950. Educated at University of Notre Dame B.A. cum laude 1972 and Indiana University School of Law J.D. 1975. Admitted to practice Indiana 1975. In legal practice Merrillville Sept 1989 to 1999.
Deputy Prosecuting Attorney March 1976 to Sept 1989 and Assistant Public Defender (Felony) Sept 1989 to 1999 Lake County. Enjoys gardening.
Mailing address: P.O. Box 15, Lowell 46356.
Office: 501 East Main Street, Lowell 46356.
Telephone: (219) 696-7794.
E-mail address: lowelltwnct@xvi.net

VanMIDDLESWORTH, Douglas H. *(Judge, Wayne Circuit Court)* Elected to term beginning Jan 1, 1985. Reelected 1990, 1996 and 2002. Current term expires Dec 31, 2008. Born Clifton New Jersey May 10, 1942. Educated at Indiana University B.A. 1968 and Indiana University-Indianapolis J.D. 1975. Admitted to practice Indiana 1976. Began legal practice Richmond 1976.
Former Deputy Attorney General Indiana and Chief Trial Deputy Wayne County Prosecutor's Office. Member Wayne County and Indiana State Bar Associations. USN Photo Intelligence. Republican.
Office: Administration Building, 301 East Main Street, Richmond 47374-4200.
Telephone: (765) 973-9266.
E-mail address: dougv@co.wayne.in.us

VAUGHN, Donald G. *(Judge, Thorntown Town Court)* Appointed by Governor B. Evan Bayh April 10,

VAUGHN, DONALD G.—*Continued*

1991. Elected 1995 and 1999. Current term expires Dec 31, 2003. Judge, Thorntown Town Court 1975-88.

Vice President City and Town Court Judges Association 1994-2002. Republican. Member Sugar Creek Volunteer Fire Department 1989-99.

Office: 101 West Main Street, Thorntown 46071-1127.

Telephone: (765) 436-2200.

VILLALPANDO, Jesse M. *(Judge, Lake Superior Court)* Appointed by Governor Frank O'Bannon to term beginning July 1, 2000. Term expires Dec 31, 2006. Serves County Division. Born East Chicago Indiana July 4, 1959. Educated at Indiana University B.A. 1981 J.D. 1984 and Purdue University M.B.A. 2000. Admitted to practice Indiana 1985. In legal practice East Chicago 1985-2000.

City Attorney East Chicago 1995-2000. Member Indiana Judges Association, National Council of Juvenile and Family Court Judges, East Chicago, Lake County and Indiana State Bar Associations. State Representative Indiana General Assembly Dec 19, 1983 to June 30, 2000. Volunteer Cub Scouts and Girl Scouts. Member St. Mary Catholic Church. Magician. Personal Statement or Quote: "It is good advice for all to aspire to The Boy Scout Oath of 'Be Prepared.'"

Office: Courthouse, 232 Russell Street, Hammond 46320.

Telephone: (219) 933-2841.

E-mail address: villajm@lakecountyin.org

VORHEES, Marianne L. *(Judge, Delaware Circuit Court)*

Office: Delaware County Justice Center, 100 West Washington, Muncie 47305-2867.

Telephone: (765) 747-7780.

WALLACE, Kevin P. *(Judge, DeKalb Superior Court)* Appointed by Governor B. Evan Bayh March 9, 1989. Elected to subsequent terms. Current term expires Dec 31, 2008. Educated at University of Notre Dame B.A. 1975 and University of Toledo J.D. 1979.

City Attorney Garrett 1986-89. Deputy Public Defender DeKalb County 1986-89. Board of Directors Judicial Conference of Indiana since 1993. Democrat.

Office: 100 South Main Street, Auburn 46706-2361.

Telephone: (260) 925-4723.

E-mail address: dksupct@locl.net

WATERS, George *(Judge, Charlestown City Court)* Elected to term beginning Jan 1, 1988. Reelected 1991, 1995 and Nov 1999. Current term expires Dec 31, 2003. Educated at Indiana University. Former Justice of the Peace, Washington Township.

USN 1943-45. Secretary and Treasurer Local 79 International Guard Union. Democrat.

Office: 304 Main Cross Street, Charlestown 47111-1230.

Telephone: (812) 256-3422.

WEBER, Joseph P. *(Judge, Clarksville Town Court)* Appointed by Governor Robert D. Orr to term beginning Jan 20, 1986. Elected 1987, 1991, 1995 and 1999. Current term expires Dec 31, 2003. Born New Albany Indiana Feb 11, 1952. Catholic. Educated at Indiana University Southeast.

Previously worked as landscape architect. Democrat. Post Precinct Committeeman.

Office: 2000 Broadway, Clarksville 47129-3298.

Telephone: (812) 283-1505.

WEBSTER, Jonathan W. *(Judge, Jennings Circuit Court)* Elected to term beginning Jan 1, 1997. Reelected 2002, current term expires Dec 31, 2008. Educated at University of Louisville B.A. 1979 J.D. 1982. Referee Ripley Circuit Court 1988-96.

Deputy Prosecutor Jennings County 1986-88. Member Civil Benchbook Committee Judicial Conference of Indiana since 1997. Board of Managers Indiana Judges Association 1998-2001. Republican. Board of Directors Jennings Villa, Inc.

Mailing address: P.O. Box 386, Vernon 47282-0386.

Telephone: (812) 352-3082.

Fax: (812) 352-3085

E-mail address: circuit@hsonline.net

WEIKERT, William E. *(Judge, Dubois Circuit Court)* Elected to term beginning Jan 1, 1997. Reelected 2002, current term expires Dec 31, 2008. Educated at Indiana University-Bloomington B.A. 1967 J.D. 1970.

Chief Deputy Prosecuting Attorney 1975-78 and Prosecuting Attorney 1979-96 Fifty-seventh Circuit. USAR 1970-97. Democrat.

Office: One Courthouse Square, Room 206, Jasper 47546-3088.

Telephone: (812) 481-7020.

E-mail address: clerk@duboiscounty.org

WELCH, David L. *(Judge, Monroe Circuit Court)* Elected to term beginning Jan 1, 1991. Reelected 1996 and 2002. Current term expires Dec 31, 2008. Presiding Judge 1998-99. Born Indianapolis Indiana March 12, 1951. Christian. Educated at Indiana University A.B. 1973 and George Mason University School of Law J.D. 1981. Admitted to practice Indiana 1983 and U.S. District Courts Northern 1983 and Southern 1983 Districts of Indiana. In legal practice Bloomington 1983-91.

Deputy Attorney Monroe County 1983-85. Town Attorney Nashville 1984-90. Instructor "Law and Society" and "Administrative Law" Indiana University School of Public and Environmental Affairs 1983-88 and "Business Law" Indiana Vocational Technical College 1985. Presiding Judge Monroe County Board of Judges 1998-99. Chair Community Relations Committee Indiana Judicial Conference 1998 and Media/Judiciary Study Committee 1998. Member Indiana Public Trust Working Group National Public Trust and Confidence in the Judiciary Initiative 1999. Member Christian Legal Society, Indiana Judges Association (Judicial Independence Committee), American Judicature Society, Monroe County, Indiana State and American Bar Associations. Graduate Indiana Judicial College 1996 and Indiana Graduate Program for Judges 1999. Matriculated in Master's Degree of Judicial Studies The National Judicial College. First Lieutenant USAR 1973-81 (retired). Second Lieutenant Indiana National Guard. Confidential Assistant to Administrator Veterans Administration. Legislative Assistant U.S. Senate Veterans Committee. Democrat. Former Commissioner Dr. Martin Luther King Commission. Former President Habitat for Humanity of Monroe County, Inc. Former Chair Monroe County Community Corrections Advisory Board and Board of Directors Leadership Bloomington/Monroe County Alumni, Inc. Board of Directors Monroe County NAACP. Former Board Member Monroe County American Red Cross. Chair Justice Fel-

WELCH, DAVID L.—*Continued*

lowship Indiana Advisory Board. Member Prison Fellowship Indiana State Council, Bloomington Rotary Club and American Legion Post 18.

Office: Courts Building, 301 North College Avenue, Bloomington 47401-3865.

Telephone: (812) 349-2640.

E-mail address: judgedlwelch@co.monroe.in.us

WESTHAFER, John A. *(Judge, Decatur Circuit Court)* Elected to term beginning Jan 1, 1977. Reelected 1982, 1988, 1994 and 2000. Current term expires Dec 31, 2006. Born Greensburg Indiana Aug 16, 1940. Presbyterian. Educated at Purdue University A.B. 1962 and George Washington University J.D. 1965. Admitted to practice Indiana 1966. Began legal practice Lafayette 1966. Republican.

Office: 150 Courthouse Square, Suite 6, Greensburg 47240-2089.

Telephone: (812) 663-8455.

E-mail address: circuitcourt@decaturcounty.in.gov

WHEAT, Allen N. *(Judge, Steuben Circuit Court)* Elected to term beginning Jan 1, 1995. Reelected 2000, current term expires Dec 31, 2006. Educated at Indiana University B.S. 1971 J.D. 1976.

Deputy Prosecuting Attorney Steuben County 1984-85. Member Indiana Judges Association, Indiana Council of Juvenile and Family Court Judges, American Judges Association, Steuben County, Indiana State and American Bar Associations. Attended Indiana Graduate Program for Judges 1999. U.S. Army 1971-73. Republican. Board of Directors Steuben County Education Opportunity Center and Northeast Indiana CASA, Inc.

Office: 55 South Public Square, Angola 46703-0327.

Telephone: (260) 668-1000.

Fax: (260) 665-1913

E-mail address: scircuit.anw@verizon.net

WHITIS, Harris Lloyd *(Judge, Harrison Circuit Court)* Elected Nov 7, 1998 to term beginning Jan 1, 1999. Term expires Dec 31, 2004. Born Indianapolis Indiana May 26, 1946. Educated at Indiana University A.B. 1968 and University of Kentucky College of Law J.D. 1971. Admitted to practice Indiana 1971. In legal practice Corydon 1971-98.

Prosecuting Attorney Third Judicial Circuit 1975-82. Director Harrison County Community Foundation.

Mailing address: P.O. Box 428, Corydon 47112-0428.

Telephone: (812) 738-2191.

Fax: (812) 738-7502

E-mail address: hlwhitis@aye.net

WHITMAN, William C. *(Judge, St. Joseph Superior Court)* Appointed by Governor Otis Ray Bowen to term beginning Jan 1, 1981. Retained by election 1984, 1990, 1996 and 2002. Current term expires Dec 31, 2008. Born South Bend Indiana Sept 9, 1940. Episcopalian. Educated at Duke University B.A. 1962 and Indiana University School of Law LL.B. 1965. Admitted to practice Indiana 1966. Began legal practice South Bend 1966.

Public Defender 1969-71 and Deputy Prosecuting Attorney 1971-79 St. Joseph County. Member St. Joseph County and Indiana State Bar Associations. E-6 USAR 1965-71.

Office: 100 South Main Street, South Bend 46601-1807.

Telephone: (574) 235-9591.

WIDMOYER, David W. *(Judge, Nappanee City Court)* Elected to term beginning Jan 1, 1980. Reelected 1983, 1987, 1991, 1995 and 1999. Current term expires Dec 31, 2003. Educated at DePauw University A.B. 1953. Republican.

Mailing address: P.O. Box 29, Nappanee 46550-0029.

Office: 300 West Lincoln Avenue, Nappanee 46550.

Telephone: (574) 773-2112.

WILKE, W. Michael *(Judge, Decatur Superior Court)* Appointed by Governor Frank O'Bannon to term beginning April 13, 1998. Elected 2002, current term expires Dec 31, 2008. Educated at Butler University B.A. 1965 and Indiana University-Indianapolis J.D. 1969.

City Attorney Greensburg 1976-79. Deputy Prosecuting Attorney Decatur County 1986-98. Member Indiana Judges Association, Decatur County and Indiana State Bar Associations. Democrat.

Office: 150 Courthouse Square, Suite 9, Greensburg 47240-2074.

Telephone: (812) 663-8523.

E-mail address: superiorcourt@decaturcounty.in.gov

WILLIAMS, James R. *(Judge, Union Circuit Court)* Elected to term beginning Jan 1, 1999. Term expires Dec 31, 2004. Educated at Wabash College A.B. summa cum laude 1988 and Indiana University J.D. 1991.

Member Delaware County, Union County, Indiana State (Improvements in Judiciary Subcommittee) and American Bar Associations. Republican.

Office: 26 West Union Street, Liberty 47353-1350.

Telephone: (765) 458-5934.

E-mail address: uccourt@earthlink.net

WILLIS, Mary G. *(Judge, Henry Circuit Court)* Probate Commissioner 1997-2002. Elected Judge to term beginning Jan 1, 2003. Born Portsmouth Virginia Nov 18, 1966. Methodist. Educated at Ball State University B.S. cum laude 1988 and Indiana University at Indianapolis J.D. 1991. Member Phi Alpha Delta. Admitted to practice Indiana 1991, U.S. District Courts Northern 1991 and Southern 1991 Districts of Indiana and U.S. Supreme Court 1995. In legal practice Greenfield 1991-96.

Member Pro Bono Council District 6 Indiana Judges Association.

Office: 1215 Race Street, Suite 340, New Castle 47362.

Telephone: (765) 529-1516.

Fax: (765) 599-2498

E-mail address: mwillis@henryco.net

WITHAM, Robert *(Judge, Henry Superior Court)*

Office: 220 Justice Center, 1215 Race Street, New Castle 47362.

Telephone: (765) 521-2554.

WITTE, G. Michael *(Judge, Dearborn Superior Court)* Born Batesville Indiana Jan 14, 1957. Roman Catholic. Educated at Indiana University B.A. 1979 J.D. 1982. Member Tau Kappa Epsilon and Phi Delta Phi. Admitted to practice Indiana 1982, U.S. District Court Southern District of Indiana 1982 and U.S. Court of Ap-

WITTE, G. MICHAEL—*Continued*

peals Seventh Circuit 1983. In legal practice Aurora 1982-84. Former Judge, Dearborn County Court, elected to term beginning Jan 1, 1985.

Deputy Prosecutor Dearborn County 1983-84. Author "Pre-Adjudication Intervention in Alcohol-Related Cases" *The Judges Journal* Summer 1998. Judicial Fellow National Highway Traffic Safety Administration 1995-98. Member Indiana Judges Association, American Judges Association, Dearborn-Ohio Counties, Indiana State and American Bar Associations. Faculty National Judicial College since 1999. Faculty for legal programs sponsored by American Bar Association, National Highway Traffic Safety Administration, National Center for State Courts, National Criminal Justice Association, Indiana Judicial Center and Indiana CLE Forum. Named Outstanding Young Hoosier Indiana Jaycees 1989. Recipient District Award of Merit Boy Scouts of America 1988 and TKE Triangle Award Tau Kappa Epsilon 1989. Republican. Member Habitat for Humanity, Dearborn Jaycees, Sons of the American Legion, Knights of Columbus, Indiana University Alumni Association, Boy Scouts of America, YMCA and Dearborn County Chamber of Commerce. Enjoys bicycling, basketball, travel, snow skiing, carpentry and hiking.

Office: 215 West High Street, Lawrenceburg 47025.

Telephone: (812) 537-8874.

E-mail address: gmwitte@hotmail.com

WOLF, Linda Ralu Smith *(Judge, Muncie City Court)* Elected to term beginning Jan 1, 1988. Reelected Nov 1991, 1995 and 1999. Current term expires Dec 31, 2003. Born La Porte Indiana Jan 22, 1954. United Methodist. Educated at Hanover College B.A. cum laude 1976 and Indiana University School of Law J.D. 1979. Admitted to practice Indiana 1979 and U.S. District Court Southern District of Indiana 1979. In legal practice Winamac 1979-80 and Muncie since 1980.

Assistant Professor of Criminal Justice and Criminology 1990-91 and 1992-93. Instructor in Political Science (legal research and writing) 1991-92. Member Indiana Association of City and Town Court Judges and Muncie Bar Association (President 1987). Democrat. Board of Directors Family Services of Delaware County and Riley-Jones Club.

Office: Muncie City Hall, 300 North High Street, Muncie 47305-1644.

Telephone: (765) 747-4703.

WOOD, Judith E. *(Judge, Monon Town Court)* Appointed by Governor Frank O'Bannon to term beginning Jan 1, 1998. Elected 1999, current term expires Dec 31, 2003. Educated at Minot State University B.A. 1987 and Butler University M.B.A. 1993.

Mailing address: P.O. Box 657, Monon 47959.

Telephone: (219) 253-6441.

YELTON, Ernest E. *(Judge, Clay Circuit Court)* Appointed by Governor Otis Ray Bowen to term beginning Oct 1, 1979. Elected 1980, 1986, 1992 and 1998. Current term expires Dec 31, 2004. Born Indianapolis Indiana May 23, 1948. Presbyterian. Educated at Indiana University A.B. 1970 J.D. with honors 1974. Admitted to practice Indiana 1974. In legal practice Brazil Indiana 1974-79. Judge, Clay County Court 1979.

Member Indiana Judges Association (Board of Managers since 1983, Secretary-Treasurer since 1987), Indiana Juvenile and Family Court Judges Association, National Council of Juvenile and Family Court Judges, Clay County and Indiana State Bar Associations.

Office: 609 East National Avenue, Brazil 47834-2659.

Telephone: (812) 442-1442.

E-mail address: ccc@claynet.com

YOUNG, Richard L. *(Judge, United States District Court Southern District of Indiana)* Appointed for life by President Bill Clinton to term beginning March 25, 1998. Born Davenport Iowa Jan 3, 1953. Catholic. Educated at Drake University B.A. 1975 and George Mason University School of Law J.D. 1980. Admitted to practice Indiana 1980, Virginia 1980 and U.S. District Court Southern District of Indiana 1980. In legal practice Evansville Indiana 1980-90. Judge, Vanderburgh Circuit Court Jan 4, 1990 to 1998, appointed by Governor Evan Bayh.

Corporate Counsel City of Evansville 1985-88. President Evansville Bar Association 1994-95.

Office: 310 U.S. Courthouse Building, 101 N.W. Martin Luther King Blvd., Evansville 47708.

Telephone: (812) 465-6431.

E-mail address: rly@insd.uscourts.gov

YOUNG, William E. *(Judge, Marion Superior Court)* Elected to term beginning Jan 1, 2001. Term expires Dec 31, 2006. Serves Criminal Division. Educated at Indiana University B.S. 1984 J.D 1987.

Administrator Marion County Public Defender Agency 1994. Republican.

Office: 200 East Washington Street, Room G-96, Indianapolis 46204.

Telephone: (317) 327-3533.

E-mail address: wyoung@indygov.org

ZORE, Gerald S. *(Judge, Marion Superior Court)* Appointed by Governor Otis Ray Bowen to term beginning Dec 23, 1974. Elected 1978, 1984, 1990, 1996 and 2002. Current term expires Dec 31, 2008. Serves Civil Division. Born Indianapolis Indiana Oct 14, 1941. Catholic. Educated at Marian College A.B. 1963 and Indiana University J.D. 1968. Member St. Thomas More Society. Admitted to practice Indiana 1968, U.S. District Court Southern District of Indiana 1968 and District of Columbia 1971. In legal practice Washington D.C. 1968-71 and Indianapolis Indiana 1971-74. Appeals Referee, Indiana Personnel Division 1968.

Deputy Attorney General Indiana 1968-69. Trial Attorney and Legal Advisor to Commissioner Federal Trade Commission 1969-71. Deputy Prosecutor Marion County 1972-74. Member Judicial Conference of Indiana, Indiana Judges Association, American Judicature Society, Indianapolis, Marion County, Indiana State and American Bar Associations. Board of Trustees Marian College. Board of Directors Cathedral High School, Flanner House of Indianapolis, Inc., Indiana University School of Law Indianapolis Alumni Association and Noble of Indiana. Advisory Board Big Sisters of Greater Indianapolis, Inc.

Office: 200 East Washington Street, Room W-541, Indianapolis 46204.

Telephone: (317) 327-3901.

E-mail address: gzore@indygov.org

IOWA

Capital DES MOINES

UNITED STATES DISTRICT COURTS DISTRICTS OF IOWA

Within Iowa there are two United States District Courts. For descriptive information refer to the United States Courts section.

NORTHERN DISTRICT consists of four divisions.

Cedar Rapids Division includes Benton, Cedar, Grundy, Hardin, Iowa, Jones, Linn and Tama counties. The court sits at Cedar Rapids.

Central Division includes Butler, Calhoun, Carroll, Cerro Gordo, Emmet, Franklin, Hamilton, Hancock, Humboldt, Kossuth, Palo Alto, Pocahontas, Webster, Winnebago, Worth and Wright counties. The court sits at Fort Dodge and Mason City.

Eastern Division includes Allamakee, Black Hawk, Bremer, Buchanan, Chickasaw, Clayton, Delaware, Dubuque, Fayette, Floyd, Howard, Jackson, Mitchell and Winneshiek counties. The court sits at Dubuque and Waterloo.

Western Division includes Buena Vista, Cherokee, Clay, Crawford, Dickinson, Ida, Lyon, Monona, O'Brien, Osceola, Plymouth, Sac, Sioux and Woodbury counties. The court sits at Sioux City.

Chief Judge
Mark W. Bennett

Judge
Linda R. Reade

Senior Judges
Edward J. McManus
Donald E. O'Brien

Clerk
James D. Hodges, Jr.
P.O. Box 74710
Cedar Rapids, Iowa 52407-4710
(319) 286-2300

SOUTHERN DISTRICT consists of six divisions.

Central Division includes Boone, Dallas, Greene, Guthrie, Jasper, Madison, Marion, Marshall, Polk, Poweshiek, Story and Warren counties. The court sits at Des Moines.

Davenport Division includes Clinton, Johnson, Muscatine, Scott and Washington counties. The court sits at Davenport.

Eastern Division includes Des Moines, Henry, Lee, Louisa and Van Buren counties. The court sits at Keokuk.

Ottumwa Division includes Appanoose, Davis, Jefferson, Keokuk, Mahaska, Monroe and Wapello counties. The court sits at Ottumwa.

Southern Division includes Adair, Adams, Clarke, Decatur, Lucas, Ringgold, Taylor, Union and Wayne counties. The court sits at Creston.

Western Division includes Audubon, Cass, Fremont, Harrison, Mills, Montgomery, Page, Pottawattamie and Shelby counties. The court sits at Council Bluffs.

Chief Judge
Ronald E. Longstaff

Judges
Robert W. Pratt
James E. Gritzner

Senior Judges
Harold D. Vietor
Charles R. Wolle

Clerk
James R. Rosenbaum
P.O. Box 9344
Des Moines, Iowa 50306-9344
(515) 284-6248

UNITED STATES MAGISTRATE JUDGES OF IOWA

NORTHERN DISTRICT
John A. Jarvey
Paul A. Zoss

SOUTHERN DISTRICT
Celeste F. Bremer
Ross A. Walters
Thomas J. Shields

Recalled Magistrate Judge
Richard William Peterson (Southern)

UNITED STATES BANKRUPTCY COURTS OF IOWA

NORTHERN DISTRICT

Chief Judge
Paul J. Kilburg

Judge
William L. Edmonds

Bankruptcy Clerk
Sean F. McAvoy
P.O. Box 74890
Cedar Rapids, Iowa 52407-4890
(319) 286-2200

SOUTHERN DISTRICT

Judge
Lee M. Jackwig

UNITED STATES DISTRICT COURTS DISTRICTS OF IOWA—*Continued*

Recalled Judge
Russell J. Hill

Bankruptcy Clerk
Mary M. Weibel
P.O. Box 9264
Des Moines, Iowa 50306-9264
(515) 284-6230

IOWA SUPREME COURT

The Supreme Court is Iowa's court of last resort. The court consists of a chief justice and six justices. Justices are appointed by the governor from a list of nominees selected by a judicial nominating commission. Justices stand for retention for eight-year terms at the first general election following one year in office. The chief justice is elected by peer vote and serves for the duration of the eight-year term. Retirement is mandatory at age seventy-two; however, retired justices may serve as senior judges by assignment of the court for up to thirteen weeks per year until age seventy-eight.

The court has general appellate jurisdiction in civil and criminal cases including questions concerning the constitutionality of a legislative or executive act. The Supreme Court hears or transfers to the Court of Appeals all cases appealed from the District Court except those concerning real estate interests when the amount involves less than $3,000 (or small claims actions when the amount in controversy is $4,000 or less) unless the trial judge certifies that the cause is one in which appeals should be allowed. The court hears appeals from final judgments and interlocutory orders and also exercises discretionary review over any matters transferred to the Court of Appeals for decision. The court has original jurisdiction in such cases as reapportionment, bar discipline and the issuance of temporary injunctions and may grant writs of certiorari in cases where a District Court is alleged to have exceeded its jurisdiction or otherwise acted illegally. The court exercises administrative and supervisory control over the trial courts.

The court sits en banc at Des Moines and holds session all year.

Chief Justice
Louis A. Lavorato

Justices

Mark S. Cady	James H. Carter
Jerry L. Larson	Linda K. Neuman
Michael J. Streit	Marsha K. Ternus

Clerk
R. K. Richardson
Iowa Judicial Branch Building
1111 East Court Avenue
Des Moines, Iowa 50319
(515) 281-5911

Court Administrator
William J. O'Brien
Office of the Court Administrator
Iowa Judicial Branch Building
1111 East Court Avenue
Des Moines, Iowa 50319
(515) 281-5241

IOWA COURT OF APPEALS

The Court of Appeals is a court of intermediate appellate jurisdiction in Iowa. The court consists of a chief judge and eight judges appointed by the governor from a list of nominees selected by a judicial nominating commission. Judges stand for retention for six-year terms at the first general election following one year in office. The chief judge is elected by peer vote for a two-year term. Retirement is mandatory at age seventy-two; however, retired judges may serve as senior judges by assignment of the Supreme Court for up to thirteen weeks per year until age seventy-eight.

The court has appellate jurisdiction over all civil and criminal actions, post-conviction remedy proceedings, small claims actions, writs, orders and other proceedings. The court hears only those cases which are transferred to it by the Supreme Court. The court's decisions are final unless the Supreme Court grants a further review. The court may issue writs relevant to its jurisdiction.

The court usually sits in panels of three. The court sits at Des Moines.

Chief Judge
Rosemary Shaw Sackett

Judges

Larry J. Eisenhauer	Daryl L. Hecht
Terry Lee Huitink	Robert E. Mahan
John C. Miller	Anuradha Vaitheswaran
Gayle Nelson Vogel	Van D. Zimmer

IOWA DISTRICT COURT

The District Court is Iowa's court of general trial jurisdiction. The court is financially and structurally unified and consists of eight judicial districts, with five districts subdivided for electoral purposes. The court is served by district judges, district associate judges, alternate district associate judges, referees, senior judges and judicial magistrates. District judges are appointed by the governor from a list of nominees submitted by a district nominating commission. After one year, appointees must stand for retention in judicial elections for six-year terms. On June 30, 1973, Municipal Court judges became district associate judges. Prior to 1981, full-time magistrates were appointed by nominating commissions in each district to replace district associate judges who were not retained in office. Effective January 1, 1981, full-time magistrates were renamed district associate judges. District associate judges are nominated by a county judicial appointing commission and appointed by a majority vote of the district judges of each district. After one year, appointees stand for retention in general elections in each district for four-year terms. In counties having only one district associate judge, a nominating commission may appoint an alternate district associate judge to a four-year term to serve in the temporary absence of the district associate judge. Associate juvenile judges and associate probate judges may be appointed by the chief judge at the recommendation of a nominating committee of judges of the district. Associate juvenile judges and associate probate judges serve at the pleasure of the judges. Part-time magistrates, now known as judicial magistrates, are appointed by a county magistrate appointing commission for four-year terms. In districts requiring three or more judicial magistrates, a district associate judge may be appointed by the chief

IOWA DISTRICT COURT—*Continued*

judge of the district with the approval of a majority of the judges within that district. Each district has a chief judge appointed by the chief justice, with the approval of the Supreme Court, for a two-year term. Retirement is mandatory at age seventy-two; however, retired district judges and district associate judges may serve as senior judges by assignment of the Supreme Court for up to thirteen weeks per year until age seventy-eight.

The court has general and original jurisdiction over civil and criminal cases including probate and juvenile matters. Judicial magistrates have jurisdiction over criminal offenses in which the punishment does not exceed a fine of $500 and/or thirty days imprisonment, search warrants, small claims and replevin involving civil actions in which the amount in controversy is $4,000 or less and actions for forcible entry or for detainer of real estate where no question of title is involved, preliminary hearings when acting as committing magistrates in felonies and indictable misdemeanors, and miscellaneous actions as provided by law. District associate judges have the same jurisdiction as judicial magistrates and in addition have jurisdiction over civil actions for money judgments in which the amount in controversy does not exceed $10,000, indictable misdemeanors, felonies involving drunk driving, and juvenile cases when designated as a judge of the juvenile court by the chief judge of the judicial district. In some districts, juvenile cases may be handled by associate juvenile judges. Probate cases may be handled by associate probate judges in some districts. District judges possess the full jurisdiction over all matters of the court.

The court sits at each county seat and as specified. Except for office facilities at the local level, the Iowa Judicial Department is funded entirely by the state.

FIRST JUDICIAL DISTRICT includes Allamakee, Black Hawk, Buchanan, Chickasaw, Clayton, Delaware, Dubuque, Fayette, Grundy, Howard and Winneshiek counties. The court sits at Waukon, Waterloo, Independence, New Hampton, Elkader, Manchester, Dubuque, West Union, Grundy Center, Cresco and Decorah.

Chief Judge

Alan L. Pearson

District Judges

James C. Bauch — John J. Bauercamper
James L. Beeghly — Thomas N. Bower
Karl D. Briner — Stephen C. Clarke
Robert J. Curnan — Lawrence H. Fautsch
Jon C. Fister — Todd A. Geer
Margaret L. Lingreen — George L. Stigler
Bruce B. Zager

District Associate Judges

Nathan A. Callahan — James D. Coil
Richard R. Gleason — Jeffrey L. Harris
J. G. Johnson — Joseph M. Moothart
Randal J. Nigg

Associate Juvenile Judges

Alan D. Allbee
Daniel L. Block
Jane M. Mylrea

SECOND JUDICIAL DISTRICT includes Boone, Bremer, Butler, Calhoun, Carroll, Cerro Gordo, Floyd, Franklin, Greene, Hamilton, Hancock, Hardin, Humboldt, Marshall, Mitchell, Pocahontas, Sac, Story, Webster, Winnebago, Worth and Wright counties. The court sits at Boone, Waverly, Allison, Rockwell City, Carroll, Mason City, Charles City, Hampton, Jefferson, Webster City, Garner, Eldora, Dakota City, Marshalltown, Osage, Pocahontas, Sac City, Nevada, Fort Dodge, Forest City, Northwood and Clarion.

Chief Judge

Ronald H. Schechtman

District Judges

Carl D. Baker — Stephen P. Carroll
David R. Danilson — James M. Drew
Timothy J. Finn — Allan L. Goode
John S. Mackey — Bryan H. McKinley
Gary L. McMinimee — Michael J. Moon
William C. Ostlund — William J. Pattinson
Paul W. Riffel — Dale E. Ruigh
Jon S. Scoles — Joel E. Swanson
Kurt L. Wilke

District Associate Judges

Fredrick Edward Breen — Carlynn D. Grupp
Thomas R. Hronek — Peter B. Newell
Steven J. Oeth — Kim M. Riley
Steven P. VanMarel

Associate Juvenile Judges

Victor G. Lathrop
Gerald W. Magee
James A. McGlynn

THIRD JUDICIAL DISTRICT includes Buena Vista, Cherokee, Clay, Crawford, Dickinson, Emmet, Ida, Kossuth, Lyon, Monona, O'Brien, Osceola, Palo Alto, Plymouth, Sioux and Woodbury counties. The court sits at Storm Lake, Cherokee, Spencer, Denison, Spirit Lake, Estherville, Ida Grove, Algona, Rock Rapids, Onawa, Primghar, Sibley, Emmetsburg, LeMars, Orange City and Sioux City.

Chief Judge

Michael S. Walsh

District Judges

John D. Ackerman — Patrick M. Carr
Don E. Courtney — John P. Duffy
Duane E. Hoffmeyer — Edward A. Jacobson
David A. Lester — Jeffrey A. Neary
Frank B. Nelson — James D. Scott
Mary Jane Sokolovske — Gary E. Wenell

District Associate Judges

Donald J. Bormann — Robert J. Dull
Todd A. Hensley — Timothy T. Jarman
David C. Larson — Patrick C. McCormick
Donavon D. Schaefer

Associate Juvenile Judges

Brian L. Michaelson
Mary L. Timko

FOURTH JUDICIAL DISTRICT includes Audubon, Cass, Fremont, Harrison, Mills, Montgomery, Page, Pottawattamie and Shelby counties. The court sits at Audubon, Atlantic, Sidney, Logan, Glenwood, Red Oak, Clarinda, Avoca, Council Bluffs and Harlan.

Chief Judge

Charles L. Smith, III

IOWA DISTRICT COURT—*Continued*

District Judges

Gordon C. Abel
James S. Heckerman
Timothy O'Grady
Keith E. Burgett
J. C. Irvin
James M. Richardson

District Associate Judges

Gary K. Anderson
Mark J. Eveloff
Kathleen A. Kilnoski

FIFTH JUDICIAL DISTRICT includes Adair, Adams, Clarke, Dallas, Decatur, Guthrie, Jasper, Lucas, Madison, Marion, Polk, Ringgold, Taylor, Union, Warren and Wayne counties. The court sits at Greenfield, Corning, Osceola, Adel, Leon, Guthrie Center, Newton, Chariton, Winterset, Knoxville, Des Moines, Mount Ayr, Bedford, Creston, Indianola and Corydon.

Chief Judge

Arthur E. Gamble

District Judges

George W. Bergeson
Robert J. Blink
Darrell J. Goodhue
Gregory A. Hulse
Paul R. Huscher
William H. Joy
Gary G. Kimes
Martha L. Mertz-La Follette
Donna L. Paulsen
Glenn E. Pille
Karen A. Romano
Douglas F. Staskal
Robert D. Wilson
Richard G. Blane, II
David L. Christensen
Dale B. Hagen
Michael Huppert
Robert A. Hutchison
Peter A. Keller
John D. Lloyd
Joel D. Novak
Eliza J. Ovrom
Sherman Phipps
Artis I. Reis
Scott D. Rosenberg
Dennis J. Stovall

District Associate Judges

James D. Birkenholz
Richard B. Clogg
Carol S. Egly
Odell G. McGhee
Thomas W. Mott
Joe E. Smith
Gregory D. Brandt
Carol L. Coppola
Louise M. Jacobs
Cynthia M. Moisan
William A. Price
Terry L. Wilson

Associate Juvenile Judges

Constance Cohen
Karla J. Fultz

Associate Probate Judge

Ruth B. Klotz

SIXTH JUDICIAL DISTRICT includes Benton, Iowa, Johnson, Jones, Linn and Tama counties. The court sits at Vinton, Marengo, Iowa City, Anamosa, Cedar Rapids and Toledo.

Chief Judge

David M. Remley

District Judges

Larry J. Conmey
David S. Good
Kristin L. Hibbs
Thomas L. Koehler
L. Vern Robinson
William L. Thomas
Denver D. Dillard
Patrick R. Grady
Thomas M. Horan
Amanda P. Potterfield
Douglas S. Russell

District Associate Judges

Nancy A. Baumgartner
Sylvia A. Lewis
Robert E. Sosalla
Stephen C. Gerard, II
Michael J. Newmeister
Jane Frances Spande

Associate Juvenile Judge

Susan F. Flaherty

SEVENTH JUDICIAL DISTRICT includes Cedar, Clinton, Jackson, Muscatine and Scott counties. The court sits at Tipton, Clinton, Maquoketa, Muscatine and Davenport.

Chief Judge

John A. Nahra

District Judges

Bobbi M. Alpers
J. Hobart Darbyshire
Patrick J. Madden
Charles H. Pelton
David H. Sivright, Jr.
Nancy S. Tabor
Mark D. Cleve
James E. Kelley
Gary D. McKenrick
David E. Schoenthaler
Mark J. Smith

District Associate Judges

Mary E. Howes
Douglas C. McDonald
John G. Mullen
Arlen J. Van Zee
James A. Weaver

EIGHTH JUDICIAL DISTRICT includes Appanoose, Davis, Des Moines, Henry, Jefferson, Keokuk, Lee, Louisa, Mahaska, Monroe, Poweshiek, Van Buren, Wapello and Washington counties. The court sits at Centerville, Bloomfield, Burlington, Mount Pleasant, Fairfield, Sigourney, Fort Madison, Keokuk, Wapello, Oskaloosa, Albia, Montezuma, Keosauqua, Ottumwa and Washington.

Chief Judge

James Q. Blomgren

District Judges

Mary Ann Brown
William L. Dowell
Robert David Fahey, Jr.
E. Richard Meadows, Jr.
Michael R. Mullins
Richard J. Vogel
Daniel P. Wilson
Cynthia Howard Danielson
John G. Linn
Dan F. Morrison
Annette J. Scieszinski

District Associate Judges

Kirk A. Daily
Lucy J. Gamon
Mark E. Kruse
Michael R. Stewart
Michael G. Dieterich
Joel J. Kamp
Gary R. Noneman

Associate Juvenile Judge

William S. Owens

Iowa Counties and County Seats

Adair
Greenfield

Adams
Corning

Allamakee
Waukon

Appanoose
Centerville

Audubon
Audubon

Benton
Vinton

Black Hawk
Waterloo

Boone
Boone

Bremer
Waverly

Buchanan
Independence

Buena Vista
Storm Lake

Butler
Allison

Calhoun
Rockwell City

Carroll
Carroll

Cass
Atlantic

Cedar
Tipton

Cerro Gordo
Mason City

Cherokee
Cherokee

Chickasaw
New Hampton

Clarke
Osceola

Clay
Spencer

Clayton
Elkader

Clinton
Clinton

Crawford
Denison

Dallas
Adel

Davis
Bloomfield

Decatur
Leon

Delaware
Manchester

Des Moines
Burlington

Dickinson
Spirit Lake

Dubuque
Dubuque

Emmet
Estherville

Fayette
West Union

Floyd
Charles City

Franklin
Hampton

Fremont
Sidney

Greene
Jefferson

Grundy
Grundy Center

Guthrie
Guthrie Center

Hamilton
Webster City

Hancock
Garner

Hardin
Eldora

Harrison
Logan

Henry
Mount Pleasant

Howard
Cresco

Humboldt
Dakota City

Ida
Ida Grove

Iowa
Marengo

Jackson
Maquoketa

Jasper
Newton

Jefferson
Fairfield

Johnson
Iowa City

Jones
Anamosa

Keokuk
Sigourney

Kossuth
Algona

Lee
Fort Madison

Linn
Cedar Rapids

Louisa
Wapello

Lucas
Chariton

Lyon
Rock Rapids

Madison
Winterset

Mahaska
Oskaloosa

Marion
Knoxville

Marshall
Marshalltown

Mills
Glenwood

Mitchell
Osage

Monona
Onawa

Monroe
Albia

Montgomery
Red Oak

Muscatine
Muscatine

O'Brien
Primghar

Osceola
Sibley

Page
Clarinda

Palo Alto
Emmetsburg

Plymouth
LeMars

Pocahontas
Pocahontas

Polk
Des Moines

Pottawattamie
Council Bluffs

Poweshiek
Montezuma

Ringgold
Mount Ayr

Sac
Sac City

Scott
Davenport

Shelby
Harlan

Sioux
Orange City

Story
Nevada

Tama
Toledo

Taylor
Bedford

Union
Creston

Van Buren
Keosauqua

Wapello
Ottumwa

Warren
Indianola

Washington
Washington

Wayne
Corydon

Webster
Fort Dodge

Winnebago
Forest City

Winneshiek
Decorah

Woodbury
Sioux City

Worth
Northwood

Wright
Clarion

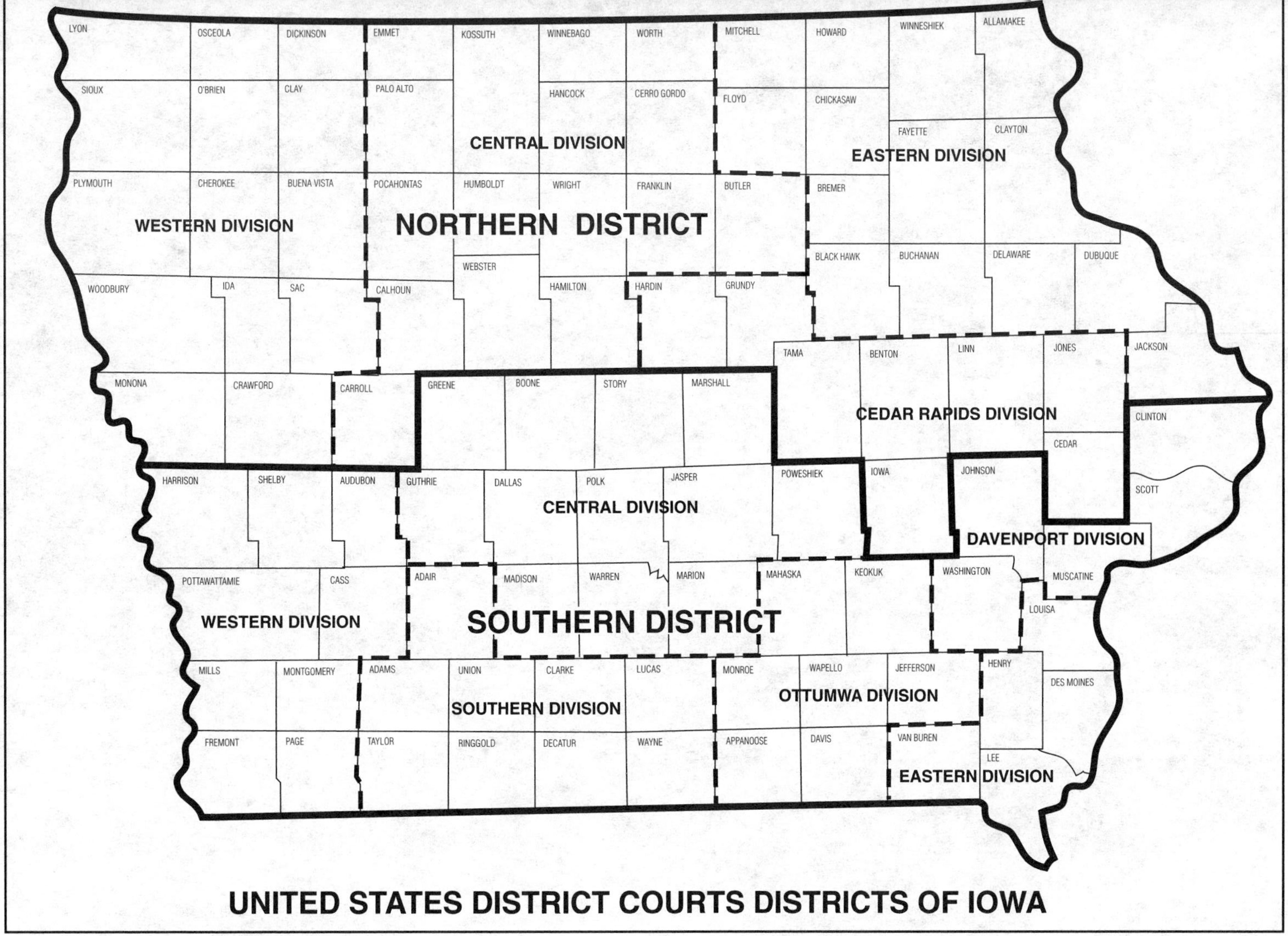
NORTHERN DISTRICT
WESTERN DIVISION
CENTRAL DIVISION
EASTERN DIVISION
CEDAR RAPIDS DIVISION
SOUTHERN DISTRICT
CENTRAL DIVISION
DAVENPORT DIVISION
WESTERN DIVISION
SOUTHERN DIVISION
OTTUMWA DIVISION
EASTERN DIVISION
LYON
OSCEOLA
DICKINSON
EMMET
KOSSUTH
WINNEBAGO
WORTH
MITCHELL
HOWARD
WINNESHIEK
ALLAMAKEE
SIOUX
O'BRIEN
CLAY
PALO ALTO
HANCOCK
CERRO GORDO
FLOYD
CHICKASAW
FAYETTE
CLAYTON
PLYMOUTH
CHEROKEE
BUENA VISTA
POCAHONTAS
HUMBOLDT
WRIGHT
FRANKLIN
BUTLER
BREMER
BLACK HAWK
BUCHANAN
DELAWARE
DUBUQUE
WEBSTER
WOODBURY
IDA
SAC
CALHOUN
HAMILTON
HARDIN
GRUNDY
TAMA
BENTON
LINN
JONES
JACKSON
MONONA
CRAWFORD
CARROLL
GREENE
BOONE
STORY
MARSHALL
CLINTON
CEDAR
HARRISON
SHELBY
AUDUBON
GUTHRIE
DALLAS
POLK
JASPER
POWESHIEK
IOWA
JOHNSON
SCOTT
POTTAWATTAMIE
CASS
ADAIR
MADISON
WARREN
MARION
MAHASKA
KEOKUK
WASHINGTON
MUSCATINE
LOUISA
MILLS
MONTGOMERY
ADAMS
UNION
CLARKE
LUCAS
MONROE
WAPELLO
JEFFERSON
HENRY
DES MOINES
FREMONT
PAGE
TAYLOR
RINGGOLD
DECATUR
WAYNE
APPANOOSE
DAVIS
VAN BUREN
LEE
UNITED STATES DISTRICT COURTS DISTRICTS OF IOWA

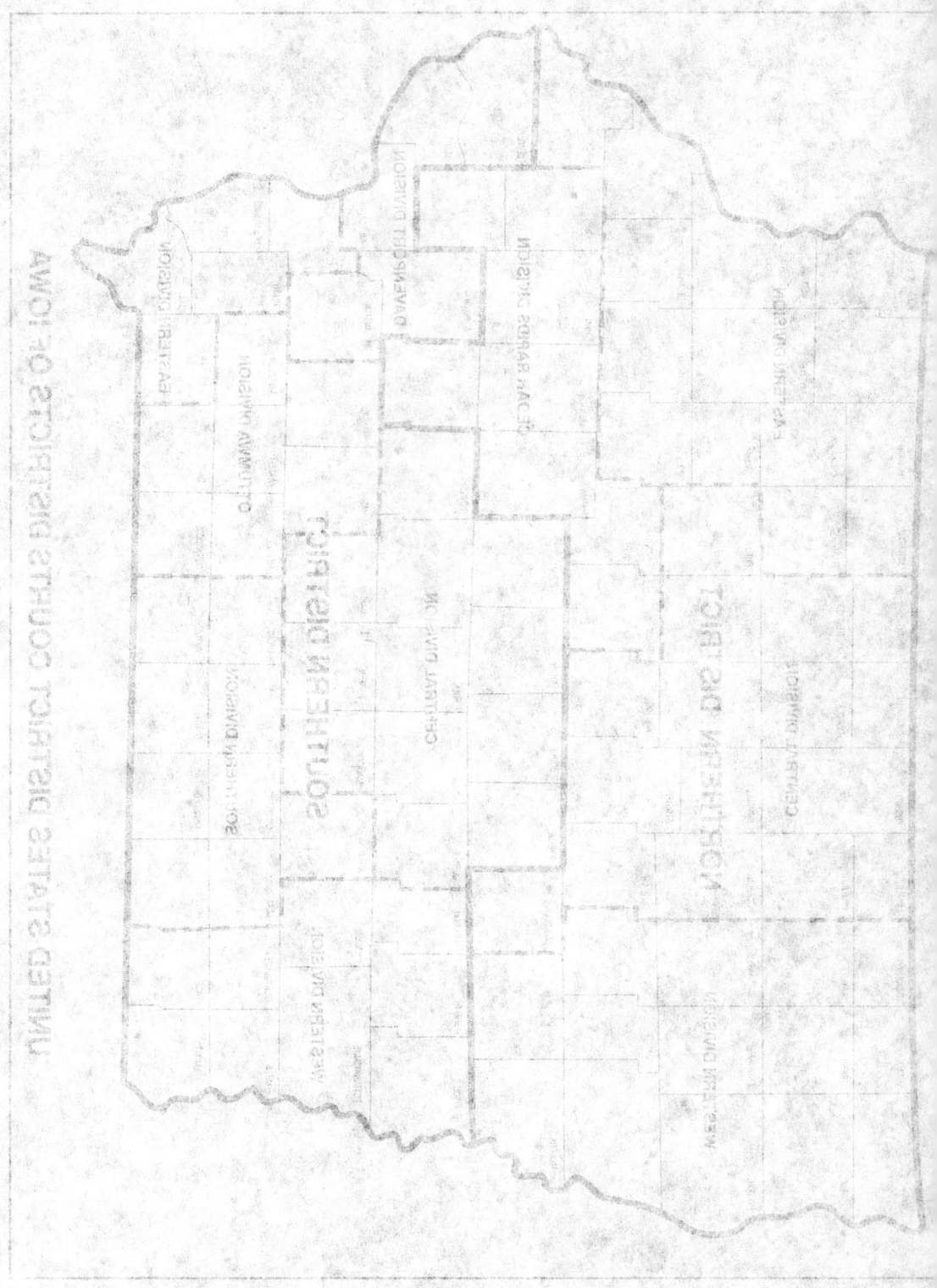

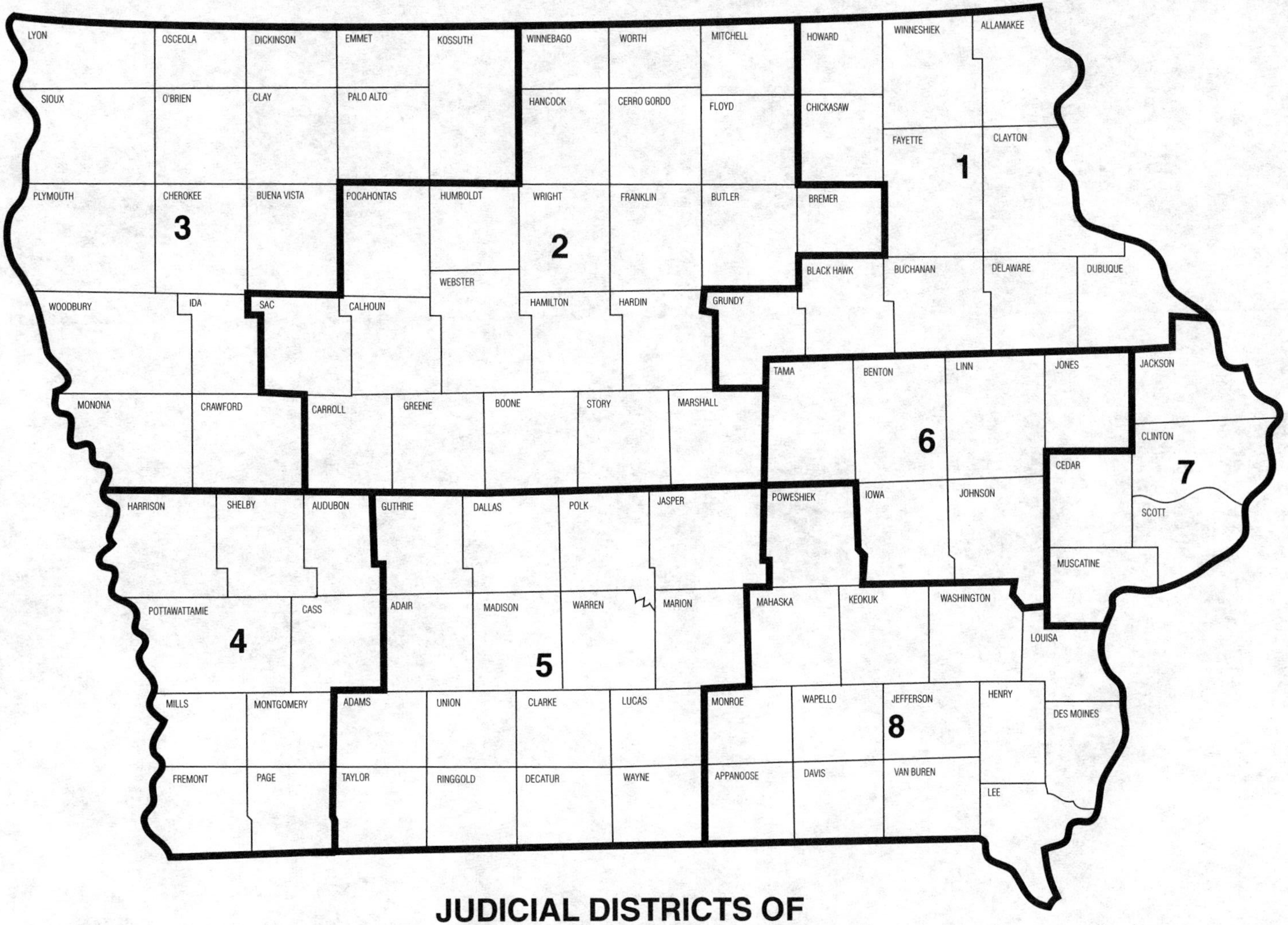
LYON
OSCEOLA
DICKINSON
EMMET
KOSSUTH
WINNEBAGO
WORTH
MITCHELL
HOWARD
WINNESHIEK
ALLAMAKEE
SIOUX
O'BRIEN
CLAY
PALO ALTO
HANCOCK
CERRO GORDO
FLOYD
CHICKASAW
FAYETTE
CLAYTON
1
PLYMOUTH
CHEROKEE
BUENA VISTA
POCAHONTAS
HUMBOLDT
WRIGHT
FRANKLIN
BUTLER
BREMER
3
2
WEBSTER
BLACK HAWK
BUCHANAN
DELAWARE
DUBUQUE
WOODBURY
IDA
SAC
CALHOUN
HAMILTON
HARDIN
GRUNDY
TAMA
BENTON
LINN
JONES
JACKSON
MONONA
CRAWFORD
CARROLL
GREENE
BOONE
STORY
MARSHALL
6
CLINTON
CEDAR
7
HARRISON
SHELBY
AUDUBON
GUTHRIE
DALLAS
POLK
JASPER
POWESHIEK
IOWA
JOHNSON
SCOTT
MUSCATINE
POTTAWATTAMIE
CASS
ADAIR
MADISON
WARREN
MARION
MAHASKA
KEOKUK
WASHINGTON
4
LOUISA
5
MILLS
MONTGOMERY
ADAMS
UNION
CLARKE
LUCAS
MONROE
WAPELLO
JEFFERSON
HENRY
DES MOINES
8
FREMONT
PAGE
TAYLOR
RINGGOLD
DECATUR
WAYNE
APPANOOSE
DAVIS
VAN BUREN
LEE

JUDICIAL DISTRICTS OF IOWA DISTRICT COURT

IOWA

ABEL, Gordon C. *(District Judge, Iowa District Court Fourth Judicial District)* Former District Associate Judge. Appointed District Judge by Governor Terry E. Branstad.

Mailing address: P.O. Box 476, Council Bluffs 51502.
Office: 227 South Sixth Street, Council Bluffs 51501.
Telephone: (712) 328-5793.

ACKERMAN, John D. *(District Judge, Iowa District Court Third Judicial District)* Appointed by Governor Terry E. Branstad.

Office: Woodbury County Courthouse, 620 Douglas Street, Sioux City 51101.
Telephone: (712) 279-6608.

ALLBEE, Alan D. *(Associate Juvenile Judge, Iowa District Court First Judicial District)* Appointed by the Chief Judge and serves at the pleasure of the judges.

Mailing address: P.O. Box 458, West Union 52175.
Office: Fayette County Courthouse, 114 North Vine Street, West Union 52175.
Telephone: (563) 422-3355.

ALPERS, Bobbi M. *(District Judge, Iowa District Court Seventh Judicial District)* Appointed by Governor Terry E. Branstad to term beginning June 22, 1992. Retained by election Nov 2000, current term expires Dec 31, 2006. Educated at University of Dubuque B.A. with honors 1973 and University of Iowa M.A. 1975 J.D. 1983. Admitted to practice Iowa 1983.

Member Iowa Judges Association, National Council of Juvenile and Family Court Judges, National Association of Women Judges, American Judicature Society, Scott County Bar and Iowa State Bar Association.

Office: Scott County Courthouse, 416 West Fourth Street, Davenport 52801.
Telephone: (563) 326-8606.

ANDERSON, Gary K. *(District Associate Judge, Iowa District Court Fourth Judicial District)* Appointed.

Mailing address: P.O. Box 476, Council Bluffs 51502.
Office: 227 South Sixth Street, Council Bluffs 51501.
Telephone: (712) 328-4700.

BAKER, Carl D. *(District Judge, Iowa District Court Second Judicial District)* Appointed by governor.

Office: Marshall County Courthouse, 17 East Main Street, Marshalltown 50158.
Telephone: (641) 754-6336.

BAUCH, James C. *(District Judge, Iowa District Court First Judicial District)* Appointed by Governor Terry E. Branstad to term beginning April 1, 1985. Retained by election Nov 1988, 1992 and 1998. Current term expires Dec 31, 2004. Born Marshalltown Iowa March 26, 1945. Methodist. Educated at University of Iowa B.A. 1967 J.D. 1969. Member Delta Upsilon and Phi Delta Phi. Admitted to practice Iowa 1969.

Assistant County Attorney 1978-82 and County Attorney 1983-85 Black Hawk County. Member Black Hawk County and Iowa State Bar Associations. First Lieutenant USMC 1969-72.

Office: Black Hawk County Courthouse, 316 East Fifth Street, Waterloo 50703.
Telephone: (319) 833-3285.

BAUERCAMPER, John J. *(District Judge, Iowa District Court First Judicial District)* Appointed by governor.

Mailing address: P.O. Box 248, Waukon 52172-0248.
Office: Allamakee County Courthouse, 110 Allamakee Street, Waukon 52172.
Telephone: (563) 568-3318.

BAUMGARTNER, Nancy A. *(District Associate Judge, Iowa District Court Sixth Judicial District)* Appointed.

Mailing address: P.O. Box 1468, Cedar Rapids 52406.
Office: Linn County Courthouse, Third Avenue Bridge, Cedar Rapids 52406.
Telephone: (319) 398-3920.

BEEGHLY, James L. *(District Judge, Iowa District Court First Judicial District)* Appointed by Governor Terry E. Branstad Dec 15, 1983, nominated by special election to term beginning Jan 1, 1984. Retained by election 1986, 1992 and 1998. Current term expires Dec 31, 2004. Born Conrad Iowa Nov 19, 1941. Lutheran (ELCA). Educated at Iowa State University B.S. 1967, Stout State College M.S. 1969 and University of Iowa J.D. 1974. Admitted to practice Iowa 1974. Began legal practice West Union 1974. Juvenile Court Referee 1979-80.

County Attorney Fayette County 1978-79. Board of Directors First Judicial District Department of Correctional Services and Chairman Board of Directors Area I Child Support Recovery Unit. Member Association of Trial Lawyers of Iowa, Iowa Judges Association (Secretary/Treasurer 1992-93, President Elect 1993-94, President 1994-95), The Association of Trial Lawyers of America, Black Hawk County 1981-83, Fayette County 1974-80 (Secretary-Treasurer 1975-76, Vice President 1976-77, President 1977-78), Iowa State and American Bar Associations. Petty Officer Second Class USN 1959-62. Previously worked sales and service 1963-65 and as production manager 1967-68 Spreads-All, Inc. Secondary school teacher Waukon Iowa 1969-72. Member Rotary International 1974-80 and Lions Club 1981-83. Enjoys bow hunting, fishing, canoeing and woodworking.

Mailing address: P.O. Box 458, West Union 52175.
Office: Fayette County Courthouse, 114 North Vine Street, West Union 52175.
Telephone: (563) 422-3591.

BENNETT, Mark W. *(Chief Judge, United States District Court Northern District of Iowa)* Magistrate Judge Southern District of Iowa 1991-94. Appointed Judge for life by President Bill Clinton to term beginning Aug 26, 1994. Chief Judge since Dec 30, 1999. Born Milwaukee Wisconsin June 4, 1950. Educated at Gustavus Adolphus College B.A. 1972 and Drake University Law School J.D. 1975. In legal practice Des Moines 1975-91.

BENNETT, MARK W.—*Continued*

General Counsel Iowa Civil Liberties Union 1975-89. Special Prosecutor Committee of Professional Ethics and Conduct Iowa State Bar 1987. Lecturer on Law and Trial Advocacy University of Iowa College of Law 1984-85. Instructor Drake University Trial Advocacy Institute 1987-89. Supervising Attorney Legal Ethics Clinic Drake University Law School 1981-83.

Office: 311 U.S. Courthouse, 320 Sixth Street, Sioux City 51101.

Telephone: (712) 233-3909.

BERGESON, George W. *(District Judge, Iowa District Court Fifth Judicial District)* Appointed by governor.

Office: 212 Polk County Courthouse, 500 Mulberry Street, Des Moines 50309.

Telephone: (515) 286-3846.

BIRKENHOLZ, James D. *(District Associate Judge, Iowa District Court Fifth Judicial District)* Appointed.

Office: 212 Polk County Courthouse, 500 Mulberry Street, Des Moines 50309.

Telephone: (515) 286-3863.

BLANE, Richard G., II *(District Judge, Iowa District Court Fifth Judicial District)* Appointed by Governor Terry E. Branstad Jan 1, 1995 to term beginning Feb 1, 1995. Retained by election Nov 1996 and 2002. Current term expires Dec 31, 2008. Born Chicago Illinois June 6, 1949. Educated at Drake University B.A. 1970 J.D. 1973. Admitted to practice Iowa 1973, U.S. District Courts Southern 1973 and Northern 1975 Districts of Iowa and U.S. Court of Appeals Eighth Circuit 1975. In legal practice Des Moines 1979-95.

Assistant Attorney Polk County 1973-78. First Assistant U.S. Attorney Southern District of Iowa 1978-79. Instructor Drake University Law School since 1995. Member Blackstone Inn of Court (President 1998-2000), Polk County (Board of Directors 1992-95) and Iowa State Bar Associations. Attended National Institute for Trial Advocacy 1976 and The National Judicial College 1995. Enjoys golfing, running, sailing and skiing.

Office: 406 Polk County Courthouse, 500 Mulberry Street, Des Moines 50309.

Telephone: (515) 286-3848.

E-mail address: Richard.Blane@jb.state.ia.us

BLINK, Robert J. *(District Judge, Iowa District Court Fifth Judicial District)* Appointed by Governor Terry E. Branstad.

Office: 212 Polk County Courthouse, 500 Mulberry Street, Des Moines 50309.

Telephone: (515) 286-3852.

BLOCK, Daniel L. *(Associate Juvenile Judge, Iowa District Court First Judicial District)* Appointed by the Chief Judge and serves at the pleasure of the judges.

Office: Black Hawk County Courthouse, 316 East Fifth Street, Waterloo 50703.

Telephone: (319) 833-3297.

BLOMGREN, James Q. *(Chief Judge, Iowa District Court Eighth Judicial District)* Appointed by Governor Terry E. Branstad 1998. Chief Judge since 2001. Born Des Moines Iowa. Educated at University of Iowa B.A. 1969 and University of Virginia J.D. 1972. In legal practice 1973-98.

Mailing address: P.O. Box 1168, Oskaloosa 52577.

Office: Mahaska County Courthouse, Oskaloosa 52577.

Telephone: (641) 673-4139.

BORMANN, Donald J. *(District Associate Judge, Iowa District Court Third Judicial District)* Appointed to term beginning July 2000. Retained by election, current term expires Dec 31, 2006. Born Emmetsburg Iowa Feb 25, 1942. Educated at University of South Dakota B.A. 1964 J.D. 1966. Editor-in-Chief South Dakota Law Review 1965-66. Law Clerk to Hon. Axel J. Beck, U.S. District Court District of South Dakota 1966-67. Admitted to practice Iowa 1966 and South Dakota 1966. In legal practice Emmetsburg Iowa May 1968 to July 1, 2000.

Attorney Rosebud Indian Reservation 1967-68. Member Palo Alto County (President 1975-2000), Iowa State and American Bar Associations. Member Horizon's of Palo Alto County. Enjoys spectator sports and reading.

Mailing address: P.O. Box 387, Emmetsburg 50536.

Telephone: (712) 852-4712.

Fax: (712) 852-2247

BOWER, Thomas N. *(District Judge, Iowa District Court First Judicial District)* Former District Associate Judge. Appointed District Judge by Governor Terry E. Branstad.

Office: Black Hawk County Courthouse, 316 East Fifth Street, Waterloo 50703.

Telephone: (319) 833-3295.

BRANDT, Gregory D. *(District Associate Judge, Iowa District Court Fifth Judicial District)* Appointed.

Office: 212 Polk County Courthouse, 500 Mulberry Street, Des Moines 50309.

Telephone: (515) 286-2187.

BREEN, Fredrick Edward *(District Associate Judge, Iowa District Court Second Judicial District)* Appointed to term beginning May 2, 1988. Retained by election Nov 1990, 1994, 1998 and 2002. Current term expires Dec 31, 2006. Born Fort Dodge Iowa Nov 26, 1938. Educated at Swarthmore College B.A. 1960 and University of Chicago Law School J.D. 1964. Law Clerk to Hon. Henry Burman, Illinois Appellate Court 1964-65. Admitted to practice Illinois 1964, Iowa 1972 and U.S. District Court Northern District of Iowa 1978. In legal practice Chicago Illinois 1965-72 and Fort Dodge Iowa 1972-88. Hospitalization Referee, Iowa District Court 1976-80.

First Assistant Attorney Webster County Iowa 1980-84. Member Iowa State Bar Association. Attended General Jurisdiction Course The National Judicial College 1989. Research Assistant American Judicature Society 1963-64. Enjoys vocal music and reading.

Office: Webster County Courthouse, 701 Central Avenue, Fort Dodge 50501.

Telephone: (515) 573-1438.

BREMER, Celeste F. *(Magistrate Judge, United States District Court Southern District of Iowa)* Appointed by U.S. District Court judges to term beginning Jan 1985. Reappointed 1988, 1990 and 1998. Current term expires Jan 2006. Chief Magistrate Judge 1991-98. Born San Francisco California 1953. Educated at St. Ambrose College B.A. magna cum laude 1974 and Uni-

BREMER, CELESTE F.—*Continued*
versity of Iowa College of Law J.D. 1977. Admitted to practice Iowa 1977, U.S. District Courts Northern 1978 and Southern 1978 Districts of Iowa, U.S. Court of Appeals Eighth Circuit 1978, California 1988 and U.S. Supreme Court 1989. In legal practice Davenport 1977-82.

Assistant County Attorney Scott County 1977-79. Assistant Attorney General Iowa 1979. Legal Department Deere & Co. 1982-85 and Economy Forms Corporation 1986-90. Co-author with W. Scott Simmer "One Day in Court: Suggestions for Implementing Summary Jury Trials in Iowa" Drake L. Rev. Spring 1987 and "'Fair and Effective' Prisoner Grievance Systems: Some Practical Suggestions" 14 St. Louis University Public L. Rev. 41, 1994. Author "You Have Been Arrested: Your Rights in English and Spanish" video for use in U.S. District Courts 1998. Faculty member Drake University College of Law 1985-90. Member Polk County Women Attorneys, Iowa Organization of Women Attorneys, National Association of Women Judges, Polk County (Chair pro bono Volunteer Lawyer Committee 1985-90), Iowa State and American Bar Associations. Recipient Mason Ladd Legal Writing Award (third place) from Iowa State Bar Association Young Lawyers Section 1986 and Volunteer Attorney Service Award from Legal Services Corporation of Iowa 1986.

Office: 429 U.S. Courthouse, 123 East Walnut Street, Des Moines 50309-2036.

Telephone: (515) 284-6200.

Fax: (515) 284-7392

BRINER, Karl D. *(District Judge, Iowa District Court First Judicial District)* Appointed by governor.

Office: Black Hawk County Courthouse, 316 East Fifth Street, Waterloo 50703.

Telephone: (319) 833-3289.

BROWN, Mary Ann *(District Judge, Iowa District Court Eighth Judicial District)* Appointed by Governor Tom Vilsack.

Mailing address: P.O. Box 158, Burlington 52601.

Office: Des Moines County Courthouse, 513 North Main Street, Burlington 52601.

Telephone: (319) 753-8202.

BURGETT, Keith E. *(District Judge, Iowa District Court Fourth Judicial District)* Appointed by governor.

Mailing address: P.O. Box 476, Council Bluffs 51502.

Office: 227 South Sixth Street, Council Bluffs 51501.

Telephone: (712) 328-5755.

CADY, Mark S. *(Justice, Iowa Supreme Court)* Appointed by Governor Terry E. Branstad to term beginning 1998. Retained by election. Born Rapid City South Dakota July 12, 1953. Presbyterian. Educated at Drake University B.S. 1975 J.D. 1978. Law Clerk to Iowa District Court Second Judicial District 1978-79. Admitted to practice Iowa 1978. Began legal practice Fort Dodge 1979. District Associate Judge Jan 3, 1983 to May 5, 1986 and District Judge May 6, 1986 to Feb 17, 1994, Iowa District Court Second Judicial District. Judge Feb 18, 1994 to 1997 and Chief Judge 1997-1998 Iowa Court of Appeals, appointed by Governor Terry E. Branstad.

Assistant Webster County Attorney 1979-80. Author "Curbing Litigation Abuse and Misuse: A Judicial Approach" 36 Drake L. Rev. 483, 1987 and "Advocating Personal Values in Advocacy" 52 Iowa Lawyers 9 May 1992. Adjunct Instructor in Business Law Buena Vista College since 1980.

Office: Judicial Branch Building, 1111 East Court Avenue, Des Moines 50319.

Telephone: (515) 576-6843.

CALLAHAN, Nathan A. *(District Associate Judge, Iowa District Court First Judicial District)* Appointed.

Office: Black Hawk County Courthouse, 316 East Fifth Street, Waterloo 50703.

Telephone: (319) 833-3302.

CARR, Patrick M. *(District Judge, Iowa District Court Third Judicial District)* Appointed by Governor Terry E. Branstad.

Office: 4 Clay County Courthouse, 215 West Fourth Street, Spencer 51301.

Telephone: (712) 262-1038.

CARROLL, Stephen P. *(District Judge, Iowa District Court Second Judicial District)* Appointed by governor.

Mailing address: P.O. Box 28, Hampton 50441.

Office: Franklin County Courthouse, 12 First Avenue N.W., Hampton 50441.

Telephone: (641) 456-5621.

CARTER, James H. *(Justice, Iowa Supreme Court)* Appointed by Governor Robert D. Ray Aug 4, 1982. Retained by election. Born Waverly Iowa Jan 18, 1935. Religious affiliation: Disciples of Christ. Educated at University of Iowa B.A. 1956 J.D. 1960. Member Order of the Coif. Board of Editors Iowa Law Review. Admitted to practice Iowa 1960. Judge, Iowa District Court 1973-76. Judge, Iowa Court of Appeals 1976-82, appointed by Governor Robert D. Ray.

Member Linn County, Iowa State and American Bar Associations.

Office: Judicial Branch Building, 1111 East Court Avenue, Des Moines 50319.

Telephone: (319) 398-3920.

CHRISTENSEN, David L. *(District Judge, Iowa District Court Fifth Judicial District)* Appointed by governor.

Mailing address: P.O. Box 306, Bedford 50833.

Office: Taylor County Courthouse, 403 Jefferson Street, Bedford 50833.

Telephone: (515) 286-3859.

CLARKE, Stephen C. *(District Judge, Iowa District Court First Judicial District)* Former Associate Juvenile Judge. Appointed District Judge by Governor Terry E. Branstad.

Office: Black Hawk County Courthouse, 316 East Fifth Street, Waterloo 50703.

Telephone: (319) 833-3291.

CLEVE, Mark D. *(District Judge, Iowa District Court Seventh Judicial District)* Appointed by governor. Retained by election 2000, current term expires Dec 31, 2006. Born Davenport Iowa June 8, 1955. Educated at University of Iowa B.A. 1977 J.D. with distinction 1981. Member Phi Beta Kappa. Admitted to practice Iowa 1981, U.S. District Courts Northern 1986 and Southern 1986 Districts of Iowa, U.S. Court of Appeals Eighth Circuit 1988 and U.S. Supreme Court 1989. In legal practice Davenport 1984-98.

CLEVE, MARK D.—*Continued*

Member Dillon Inn of Court, Iowa Judges Association, Scott County and Iowa State Bar Associations.

Office: Scott County Courthouse, 416 West Fourth Street, Davenport 52801.

Telephone: (563) 326-8783.

CLOGG, Richard B. *(District Associate Judge, Iowa District Court Fifth Judicial District)* Appointed.

Mailing address: P.O. Box 379, Indianola 50125.

Office: Warren County Courthouse, 115 North Howard Street, Indianola 50125.

Telephone: (515) 961-1036.

COHEN, Constance *(Associate Juvenile Judge, Iowa District Court Fifth Judicial District)* Appointed June 30, 1994 and serves at the pleasure of the judges. Born St. Louis Missouri May 26, 1950. Jewish. Educated at Drake University B.S.Ed. 1972 M.S.E. 1977 J.D. 1987. Listed in *Who's Who in American Law Schools.* Law Clerk to Hon. Glenn E. Pille, Iowa District Court Fifth Judicial District 1986. Admitted to practice Iowa 1987 and U.S. District Court Southern District of Iowa. In legal practice Redfield 1987-93.

Assistant County Attorney Dallas County 1987-93. Special Assistant Attorney General Iowa Department of Justice 1993-94. Adjunct Professor of Juvenile Law Drake University Law School since 1997. Chair Juvenile Court Officers Training Committee Iowa Supreme Court. Member Polk County Women Attorneys, Iowa Organization of Women Attorneys (President 1990), Blackstone Inn of Court, National Council of Juvenile and Family Court Judges (Board of Trustees since 1996, Lead Judge Model Court since March 2000, Chair Permanency Planning Committee), Women Judges Association, Iowa Judges Association (Chair Juvenile Court Committee), Dallas County (President 1989), Polk County and Iowa State Bar Associations. Presenter Foster and Adoptive Parents Training 1997-2002 and Very Important Partners Training 1998-2002 CASA, "Issues in Juvenile Justice" Iowa Court Improvement Project, "Evidentiary Issues in Juvenile Court" Iowa State Bar Association, "Basic Legal Issues" and "Testifying in Juvenile Court" Child Protection Training Academy (CPTA) and "Improving Educational Outcomes for Youth in Foster Care" and "What Does AGFA Want?" National Council of Juvenile and Family Court Judges. Recipient awards from Iowa County Attorneys Association 1994, CASA 1997 and Porter Avenue Center for Education 1999; and annual awards from Very Important Partners 1998-2002. Member The Mentoring Project. Volunteer various work with temple. Enjoys reading, hiking, biking and motorcycling.

Office: 212 Polk County Courthouse, 500 Mulberry Street, Des Moines 50309.

Telephone: (515) 286-3037.

COIL, James D. *(District Associate Judge, Iowa District Court First Judicial District)* Appointed to term beginning Aug 1, 1986. Retained by election Nov 1988, 1992, 1996 and 2000. Current term expires Dec 31, 2004. Born Des Moines Iowa July 18, 1951. Protestant. Educated at Simpson College B.A. 1973 and Creighton University J.D. 1977. Admitted to practice Iowa 1977. In legal practice Grundy Center 1983-84 and Waterloo 1984-86.

Special Prosecutor Judicial District 1-B 1977-79. Assistant County Attorney 1979-83 and First Assistant County Attorney 1983 Black Hawk County. Assistant County Attorney Grundy County 1983-84. Instructor in intermediate police science courses Hawkeye Institute of Technology 1984-85. Member Iowa Judges Association (Board of Directors 1989-93), Black Hawk County and Iowa State Bar Associations. Technical Sergeant Iowa Air National Guard 1970-78.

Office: Black Hawk County Courthouse, 316 East Fifth Street, Waterloo 50703.

Telephone: (319) 833-3304.

Fax: (319) 833-3270

CONMEY, Larry J. *(District Judge, Iowa District Court Sixth Judicial District)* Former Part-time Judicial Magistrate. Appointed District Judge by governor.

Mailing address: P.O. Box 19, Anamosa 52205.

Office: Jones County Courthouse, Main Street, Anamosa 52205.

Telephone: (319) 462-2275.

COPPOLA, Carol L. *(District Associate Judge, Iowa District Court Fifth Judicial District)* Appointed.

Office: 212 Polk County Courthouse, 500 Mulberry Street, Des Moines 50309.

Telephone: (515) 286-3904.

COURTNEY, Don E. *(District Judge, Iowa District Court Third Judicial District)* Appointed by governor Tom Vilsack.

Office: Kossuth County Courthouse, 114 West State Street, Algona 50511.

Telephone: (515) 295-5540.

CURNAN, Robert J. *(District Judge, Iowa District Court First Judicial District)* Appointed by Governor Robert D. Ray to term beginning Oct 1980. Retained by election. Born Davenport Iowa Dec 5, 1938. Educated at Coe College B.A. with honors 1961 and University of Minnesota LL.B. with honors 1964. Staff member University of Minnesota Law Review. Admitted to practice Minnesota 1964 and Iowa 1965. Began legal practice Annandale Minnesota 1964. In legal practice Dubuque Iowa 1965. Dubuque County Attorney 1971-80.

Office: Dubuque County Courthouse, 720 Central Avenue, Dubuque 52001.

Telephone: (563) 589-4447.

DAILY, Kirk A. *(District Associate Judge, Iowa District Court Eighth Judicial District)* Appointed.

Office: Wapello County Courthouse, 101 West Fourth Street, Ottumwa, 52501.

Telephone: (641) 683-1951.

DANIELSON, Cynthia Howard *(District Judge, Iowa District Court Eighth Judicial District)* Appointed by governor.

Mailing address: P.O. Box 176, Mt. Pleasant 52641.

Office: Henry County Courthouse, 100 East Washington, Mt. Pleasant 52641.

Telephone: (319) 385-2538.

DANILSON, David R. *(District Judge, Iowa District Court Second Judicial District)* Former Judicial Magistrate. Former District Associate Judge, appointed to term beginning July 1, 1987. Appointed District Judge by Governor Terry E. Branstad. Born Perry Iowa March 10, 1954. Educated at Iowa State University B.S. 1976 and Creighton University School of Law J.D. 1979. Admitted to practice Nebraska 1979 and Iowa 1980. Began le-

DANILSON, DAVID R.—*Continued*
gal practice Boone Iowa 1980. Judicial Hospitalization Referee 1980.

Director Iowa Judges Association 1998-2002. Member District 2B (Director 1986), Boone County (President 1982) and Iowa State Bar Associations. Faculty member Iowa Magistrate Conference 1985-89. Director Boone County Fair Board 1983-89. Member Boone Chamber of Commerce (Co-chairman Agriculture Committee 1984, Chairman Legislative Committee 1986). President Boone Estate and Financial Planners 1984. Director Boone County Prevention and Community Services 1985. Trustee National Court Reporters Foundation since 2001. Enjoys golf, college football and bicycling.

Office: Boone County Courthouse, 201 State Street, Boone 50036.

Telephone: (515) 433-0567.

DARBYSHIRE, J. Hobart *(District Judge, Iowa District Court Seventh Judicial District)* Appointed by Governor Terry E. Branstad to term beginning 1995. Retained by election 1996 and 2002. Current term expires Dec 31, 2008. Educated at Morningside College B.A. 1964 and University of Iowa J.D. 1967. Law Clerk to Justice Clay LeGrand, Iowa Supreme Court 1967-68. Admitted to practice Iowa 1967 and U.S. District Court Southern District of Iowa 1972. In legal practice Davenport 1968-79 and 1985-95. Part-time Magistrate Judge, U.S. District Court Southern District of Iowa 1972-79. District Judge, Iowa District Court Seventh Judicial District 1979-85, appointed by Governor Robert D. Ray.

Office: Scott County Courthouse, 416 West Fourth Street, Davenport 52801.

Telephone: (563) 326-8789.

E-mail address: hdarbysh@jb.state.ia.us

DIETERICH, Michael G. *(District Associate Judge, Iowa District Court Eighth Judicial District)* Appointed.

Mailing address: P.O. Box 158, Burlington 52601.

Office: Des Moines County Courthouse, 513 North Main Street, Burlington 52601.

Telephone: (319) 753-8240.

DILLARD, Denver D. *(District Judge, Iowa District Court Sixth Judicial District)* Appointed by Governor Tom Vilsack.

Mailing address: P.O. Box 1468, Cedar Rapids 52406.

Office: Linn County Courthouse, Third Avenue Bridge, Cedar Rapids 52406.

Telephone: (319) 398-3920.

DOWELL, William L. *(District Judge, Iowa District Court Eighth Judicial District)* Appointed by governor.

Mailing address: P.O. Box 158, Burlington 52601.

Office: Des Moines County Courthouse, 513 North Main Street, Burlington 52601.

Telephone: (319) 753-8229.

DREW, James M. *(District Judge, Iowa District Court Second Judicial District)* Appointed by governor.

Office: Cerro Gordo County Courthouse, 220 North Washington, Mason City 50401.

Telephone: (641) 456-5626.

DUFFY, John P. *(District Judge, Iowa District Court Third Judicial District)* Appointed by governor.

Mailing address: P.O. Box 1186, Storm Lake 50588.

Office: Buena Vista County Courthouse, 215 East Fifth Street, Storm Lake 50588.

Telephone: (712) 749-2546.

DULL, Robert J. *(District Associate Judge, Iowa District Court Third Judicial District)* Appointed.

Office: Plymouth County Courthouse, 215 Fourth Avenue S.E., Le Mars 51031.

Telephone: (712) 546-8195.

EDMONDS, William L. *(Judge, United States Bankruptcy Court Northern District of Iowa)* Appointed by U.S. Court of Appeals Eighth Circuit judges Aug 1987. Reappointed 2001, current term expires 2015. Former Chief Judge. Born New York New York March 1, 1944. Educated at University of Missouri at Columbia B.A. 1966 M.A. 1969 and University of Iowa J.D. with honors 1978. Member Order of the Coif. Admitted to practice Iowa 1978, U.S. District Courts Northern 1978 and Southern 1978 Districts of Iowa and U.S. Court of Appeals Eighth Circuit 1978. In legal practice Sioux City 1978-87.

Member Woodbury County and Iowa State Bar Associations.

Office: U.S. Courthouse, 320 Sixth Street, Sioux City 51101.

Telephone: (712) 233-3949.

EGLY, Carol S. *(District Associate Judge, Iowa District Court Fifth Judicial District)* Judicial Magistrate July 1, 1980 to March 1986. Appointed District Associate Judge to term beginning March 1986. Retained by election Nov 1990, 1994, 1998 and 2002. Current term expires Dec 31, 2006. Born 1949. Educated at St. Olaf College B.A. 1971 and Drake University J.D. 1974. Admitted to practice Iowa 1974 and Minnesota 1977. Began legal practice Des Moines Iowa 1979.

Assistant Attorney General State of Iowa 1974-78.

Office: 212 Polk County Courthouse, 500 Mulberry Street, Des Moines 50309.

Telephone: (515) 286-3909.

EISENHAUER, Larry J. *(Judge, Iowa Court of Appeals)* Appointed by Governor Tom Vilsack 2001. Born Emporia Kansas. Educated at Emporia State University B.A. 1968 and Drake University Law School J.D. 1974. In legal practice 1985-93. Associate Juvenile Judge and District Judge, Iowa District Court Fifth Judicial District 1994-2001, appointed by Governor Terry E. Branstad.

Office: Judicial Branch Building, 1111 East Court Avenue, Des Moines 50319.

Telephone: (515) 281-5221.

EVELOFF, Mark J. *(District Associate Judge, Iowa District Court Fourth Judicial District)* Appointed.

Mailing address: P.O. Box 476, Council Bluffs 51502.

Office: 227 South Sixth Street, Council Bluffs 51501.

Telephone: (712) 328-5864.

FAHEY, Robert David, Jr. *(District Judge, Iowa District Court Eighth Judicial District)* District Associate Judge 1981-84. Appointed District Judge by Governor Terry E. Branstad to term beginning Nov 1984. Retained by election Nov 1986, Nov 1992 and 1998. Current term expires Dec 31, 2004. Born Mount Pleasant Iowa Nov 13, 1949. Episcopalian. Educated at University of Notre Dame A.B. with honors 1972 J.D. 1975. Admitted to practice Iowa 1975, U.S. District Courts Northern 1975 and Southern 1975 Districts of Iowa and U.S. Supreme Court 1975. In legal practice Fort Madison 1978-

FAHEY, ROBERT DAVID, JR.—*Continued*

81. Hearing Officer, Iowa Occupational Safety and Health Review Board 1975-77 and Iowa Department of Revenue 1977-78.

Assistant County Attorney Lee County 1978-81. Faculty Advisor General Jurisdiction The National Judicial College Summer 1988. Board of Directors YMCA (Fort Madison). District Chairman Boy Scouts of America. Vestry of St. Luke's Church.

Mailing address: P.O. Box 1443, Fort Madison 52627.
Office: North Lee County Courthouse, 701 Avenue F, Fort Madison 52627.
Telephone: (800) 582-2304.

FAUTSCH, Lawrence H. *(District Judge, Iowa District Court First Judicial District)* Former District Associate Judge. Appointed District Judge by governor.
Office: Dubuque County Courthouse, 720 Central Avenue, Dubuque 52001.
Telephone: (563) 589-4584.

FINN, Timothy J. *(District Judge, Iowa District Court Second Judicial District)* Appointed by Governor Terry E. Branstad Dec 1987. Retained by election 1990, 1996 and 2002. Current term expires Dec 31, 2008. Born Jefferson Iowa Nov 3, 1948. Educated at University of Iowa B.A. 1971 and Drake University Law School J.D. 1974. Law Clerk to Justice K. David Harris, Iowa Supreme Court 1974-75. Admitted to practice Iowa 1974 and U.S. District Courts Northern and Southern Districts of Iowa. In legal practice Ames 1975-87.
Mailing address: P.O. Box 408, Nevada 50201.
Office: Story County Courthouse, 900 Sixth Street, Nevada 50201.
Telephone: (515) 382-7434.

FISTER, Jon C. *(District Judge, Iowa District Court First Judicial District)* Appointed by governor.
Office: Black Hawk County Courthouse, 316 East Fifth Street, Waterloo 50703.
Telephone: (319) 833-3287.

FLAHERTY, Susan F. *(Associate Juvenile Judge, Iowa District Court Sixth Judicial District)* Appointed by the Chief Judge and serves at the pleasure of the judges.
Mailing address: P.O. Box 1468, Cedar Rapids 52406.
Office: Linn County Courthouse, Third Avenue Bridge, Cedar Rapids 52406.
Telephone: (319) 398-3984.

FULTZ, Karla J. *(Associate Juvenile Judge, Iowa District Court Fifth Judicial District)* Appointed by the Chief Judge and serves at the pleasure of the judges.
Office: 212 Polk County Courthouse, 500 Mulberry Street, Des Moines 50309.
Telephone: (515) 286-3756.

GAMBLE, Arthur E. *(Chief Judge, Iowa District Court Fifth Judicial District)* Appointed by Governor Terry E. Branstad to term beginning July 15, 1983. Retained by election 1984, 1990, 1996 and 2002. Current term expires Dec 31, 2008. Born Des Moines Iowa Dec 21, 1952. Catholic. Educated at University of Iowa B.A. 1975 J.D. with honors 1978. Moot Court Board. Member Phi Delta Phi. Admitted to practice Iowa 1978. Began legal practice Des Moines 1978.

President C. Edwin Moore American Inn of Court 1996-98. Chair Iowa Supreme Court Task Force on Court Security 1999. Member Iowa Confidential Records Council 1984-86, Iowa Judges Association (President 1997-98), Polk County, Iowa State (Uniform Court Instructions Committee 1986-92) and American Bar Associations. Attended The National Judicial College 1984.
Office: 212 Polk County Courthouse, 500 Mulberry Street, Des Moines 50309.
Telephone: (515) 286-3853.

GAMON, Lucy J. *(District Associate Judge, Iowa District Court Eighth Judicial District)* Appointed.
Office: Keokuk County Courthouse, 101 South Main Street, Sigourney 52591.
Telephone: (641) 622-2210.

GEER, Todd A. *(District Judge, Iowa District Court First Judicial District)* Appointed by Governor Terry E. Branstad.
Mailing address: P.O. Box 345, Grundy Center 50638.
Office: Grundy County Courthouse, 706 G Avenue, Grundy Center 50638.
Telephone: (319) 824-5244.

GERARD, Stephen C., II *(District Associate Judge, Iowa District Court Sixth Judicial District)* Appointed.
Mailing address: P.O. Box 2510, Iowa City 52240.
Office: Johnson County Courthouse, 417 South Clinton Street, Iowa City 52240.
Telephone: (319) 338-9236.

GLEASON, Richard R. *(District Associate Judge, Iowa District Court First Judicial District)* Appointed.
Office: Dubuque County Courthouse, 720 Central Avenue, Dubuque 52001.
Telephone: (563) 589-4451.

GOOD, David S. *(District Judge, Iowa District Court Sixth Judicial District)* Appointed by governor.
Mailing address: P.O. Box 1468, Cedar Rapids 52406.
Office: Linn County Courthouse, Third Avenue Bridge, Cedar Rapids 52406.
Telephone: (319) 398-3920.

GOODE, Allan L. *(District Judge, Iowa District Court Second Judicial District)* District Associate Judge 1986-88. Appointed District Judge by Governor Terry E. Branstad to term beginning March 3, 1988. Retained by election 1990, 1996 and 2002. Current term expires Dec 31, 2008. Born Bloomfield Iowa June 25, 1941. Presbyterian. Educated at University of Iowa B.A. 1963 J.D. 1966. Member Phi Delta Phi. Admitted to practice Iowa 1966. In legal practice Fort Dodge 1966-86.

Member Iowa Judges Association and Iowa State Bar Association. Completes fifteen hours of CLE annually. Republican.

Office: Webster County Courthouse, 701 Central Avenue, Fort Dodge 50501.
Telephone: (515) 573-1438.

GOODHUE, Darrell J. *(District Judge, Iowa District Court Fifth Judicial District)* Appointed by Governor Terry E. Branstad to term beginning Jan 10, 1986. Retained by election Nov 8, 1988, Nov 8, 1994 and 2000. Current term expires Dec 31, 2006. Born Carlisle Iowa April 3, 1940. Religious affiliation: Society of Friends (Quaker). Educated at Simpson College B.A. summa cum laude 1962 and Drake University J.D. 1964. Assistant Editor Drake Law Review 1963-64. Member Order of the Coif. Admitted to practice Iowa 1964. In legal practice Indianola 1964-86.

City Attorney Indianola 1965-67 and 1969-86. County

GOODHUE, DARRELL J.—*Continued*

Attorney Warren County 1967-68. Part-time Instructor Criminal Justice Program Simpson College 1972-80. Member Iowa State and American Bar Associations. Attended The National Judicial College 1986. Lieutenant USNR 1966-70. Member Board of Trustees since 1986 and Chairman Academic Affairs Committee since 1990 Simpson College. Enjoys fishing.

Mailing address: P.O. Box 379, Indianola 50125.

Office: Warren County Courthouse, 115 North Howard Street, Indianola 50125.

Telephone: (515) 286-3859.

GRADY, Patrick R. *(District Judge, Iowa District Court Sixth Judicial District)* Associate Juvenile Judge 1989-95. Appointed District Judge by Governor Terry E. Branstad to term beginning July 28, 1995. Retained by election Nov 5, 1996 and 2002. Current term expires Dec 31, 2008. Born Davenport Iowa Jan 21, 1954. Roman Catholic. Educated at Creighton University B.A. cum laude 1975 and University of Iowa J.D. 1979. Admitted to practice Iowa 1979, U.S. District Courts Northern 1979 and Southern 1979 Districts of Iowa, U.S. Court of Appeals Eighth Circuit 1980 and U.S. Supreme Court 1980. In legal practice Davenport 1979-80.

Public Defender 1980-89.

Mailing address: P.O. Box 5488, Cedar Rapids 52406.

Telephone: (319) 398-3984.

GRITZNER, James E. *(Judge, United States District Court Southern District of Iowa)* Appointed for life by President George W. Bush to term beginning March 1, 2002. Born Charles City Iowa 1947. Educated at Dakota Wesleyan University B.A. 1969, University of Northern Iowa M.A. 1974 and Drake University Law School J.D. 1979. In legal practice 1979-2002.

Office: U.S. Courthouse, 123 East Walnut Street, Des Moines 50309.

Telephone: (515) 284-6248.

GRUPP, Carlynn D. *(District Associate Judge, Iowa District Court Second Judicial District)* Appointed.

Office: Cerro Gordo County Courthouse, 220 North Washington Street, Mason City 50401.

Telephone: (641) 421-3047.

HAGEN, Dale B. *(District Judge, Iowa District Court Fifth Judicial District)* Appointed by governor.

Mailing address: P.O. Box 379, Indianola 50125.

Office: Warren County Courthouse, 115 North Howard Street, Indianola 50125.

Telephone: (515) 286-3859.

HARRIS, Jeffrey L. *(District Associate Judge, Iowa District Court First Judicial District)* Appointed.

Mailing address: P.O. Box 345, Grundy Center 50638.

Office: Grundy County Courthouse, 706 G Avenue, Grundy Center 50638.

Telephone: (319) 824-5229.

HECHT, Daryl L. *(Judge, Iowa Court of Appeals)* Appointed by Governor Tom Vilsack 1999. Educated at Morningside College B.A 1974 and University of South Dakota J.D. 1977. In legal practice Sioux City 1977-99.

Member Woodbury County Judicial Magistrate Nominating Commission and Woodbury County Compensation Commission. Board of Directors Boys and Girls Home and Family Services. Member Morningside College Alumni Association.

Office: Judicial Branch Building, 1111 East Court Avenue, Des Moines 50319.

Telephone: (515) 281-6711.

HECKERMAN, James S. *(District Judge, Iowa District Court Fourth Judicial District)* Former District Associate Judge. Appointed District Judge by Governor Terry E. Branstad.

Mailing address: P.O. Box 476, Council Bluffs 51502.

Office: 227 South Sixth Street, Council Bluffs 51501.

Telephone: (712) 328-5756.

HENSLEY, Todd A. *(District Associate Judge, Iowa District Court Third Judicial District)* Appointed.

Office: Woodbury Law Enforcement Center, 407 Seventh Street, Sioux City 51101.

Telephone: (712) 279-6027.

HIBBS, Kristin L. *(District Judge, Iowa District Court Sixth Judicial District)* Appointed by Governor Terry E. Branstad Oct 28, 1987. Retained by election.

Mailing address: P.O. Box 2510, Iowa City 52244-2510.

Office: Johnson County Courthouse, 417 South Clinton Street, Iowa City 52240.

Telephone: (319) 356-6070.

HILL, Russell J. *(Recalled Judge, United States Bankruptcy Court Southern District of Iowa)* Appointed Recalled Judge by the Judicial Council of the Eighth Circuit. Former Chief Judge. Born Williams Iowa Sept 11, 1931. Educated at St. Olaf College B.A. 1952 and University of Iowa J.D. 1959. Admitted to practice Iowa 1959 and California 1962. Began legal practice San Diego California 1962. In legal practice Webster City Iowa 1966-72. Police Judge, Webster City 1969-72. Former District Judge, Iowa District Court Second Judicial District, appointed by Governor Robert D. Ray to term beginning May 25, 1972.

Lieutenant USNR 1952-56.

Office: 447 U.S. Courthouse Annex, 110 East Court Avenue, Des Moines 50309-2049.

Telephone: (515) 284-6400.

HOFFMEYER, Duane E. *(District Judge, Iowa District Court Third Judicial District)* Appointed by governor.

Office: Woodbury County Courthouse, 620 Douglas Street, Sioux City 51101.

Telephone: (712) 279-6608.

HORAN, Thomas M. *(District Judge, Iowa District Court Sixth Judicial District)* Appointed by governor.

Mailing address: P.O. Box 1468, Cedar Rapids 52406.

Office: Linn County Courthouse, Third Avenue Bridge, Cedar Rapids 52406.

Telephone: (319) 398-3920.

HOWES, Mary E. *(District Associate Judge, Iowa District Court Seventh Judicial District)* Appointed.

Office: Scott County Courthouse, 416 West Fourth Street, Davenport 52801.

Telephone: (563) 326-8780.

HRONEK, Thomas R. *(District Associate Judge, Iowa District Court Second Judicial District)* Appointed to term beginning July 18, 1982. Retained by election. Born Vinton Iowa May 18, 1947. Educated at Loras College B.A. with honors 1969 and Northwestern Uni-

HRONEK, THOMAS R.—*Continued*

versity J.D. with honors 1972. Admitted to practice Iowa 1972, U.S. District Court District of Iowa 1973 and U.S. Court of Appeals Eighth Circuit 1973.
Mailing address: P.O. Box 408, Nevada 50201.
Office: Story County Courthouse, 900 Sixth Street, Nevada 50201.
Telephone: (515) 382-6581.

HUITINK, Terry Lee *(Judge, Iowa Court of Appeals)* Appointed by Governor Terry E. Branstad. Born Orange City Iowa Dec 2, 1951. Religious affiliation: Reformed Church in America. Educated at University of Iowa B.A. 1974 and Drake University J.D. 1976. Associate Editor Drake Law Review 1975-76. Law Clerk to Hon. Leo E. Oxberger, Iowa Court of Appeals 1977. Admitted to practice Iowa 1977 and U.S. District Court Northern District of Iowa 1978. In legal practice Ireton 1977-88. Juvenile Court Referee 1981-88. Former District Judge, Iowa District Court Third Judicial District, appointed by Governor Terry E. Branstad to term beginning April 1, 1988.
Member Iowa Judges Association and Iowa State Bar Association.
Office: Judicial Branch Building, 1111 East Court Avenue, Des Moines 50319.
Telephone: (515) 281-5222.

HULSE, Gregory A. *(District Judge, Iowa District Court Fifth Judicial District)* Appointed by Governor Terry E. Branstad.
Office: Dallas County Courthouse, 801 Court Street, Adel 50003.
Telephone: (515) 993-5816.

HUPPERT, Michael *(District Judge, Iowa District Court Fifth Judicial District)* Appointed by governor.
Office: 212 Polk County Courthouse, 500 Mulberry Street, Des Moines 50309.
Telephone: (515) 286-3125.

HUSCHER, Paul R. *(District Judge, Iowa District Court Fifth Judicial District)* Appointed by Governor Terry E. Branstad.
Office: Dallas County Courthouse, 801 Court Street, Adel 50003.
Telephone: (515) 993-6885.

HUTCHISON, Robert A. *(District Judge, Iowa District Court Fifth Judicial District)* Appointed by governor.
Office: 212 Polk County Courthouse, 500 Mulberry Street, Des Moines 50309.
Telephone: (515) 286-3861.

IRVIN, J. C. *(District Judge, Iowa District Court Fourth Judicial District)* Appointed by governor.
Mailing address: P.O. Box 263, Clarinda 51632.
Office: Page County Courthouse, 112 East Main Street, Clarinda 51632.
Telephone: (712) 328-5795.

JACKWIG, Lee M. *(Judge, United States Bankruptcy Court Southern District of Iowa)* Appointed by U.S. Court of Appeals Eighth Circuit judges. Former Chief Judge.
Office: 443 U.S. Courthouse Annex, 110 East Court Avenue, Des Moines 50309-2050.
Telephone: (515) 284-6229.

JACOBS, Louise M. *(District Associate Judge, Iowa District Court Fifth Judicial District)* Appointed.
Office: 212 Polk County Courthouse, 500 Mulberry Street, Des Moines 50309.
Telephone: (515) 286-3450.

JACOBSON, Edward A. *(District Judge, Iowa District Court Third Judicial District)* Appointed by Governor Tom Vilsack.
Office: Ida County Courthouse, 401 Moorehead Street, Ida Grove 51445.
Telephone: (712) 364-2620.

JARMAN, Timothy T. *(District Associate Judge, Iowa District Court Third Judicial District)* Appointed to term beginning Aug 1, 1997. Retained by election. Educated at Loras College B.A. magna cum laude 1977 and University of Iowa J.D. 1980.
Member Woodbury County and Iowa State Bar Associations.
Office: 407 Seventh Street, Sioux City 51101.
Telephone: (712) 279-6025.
Fax: (712) 279-9564

JARVEY, John A. *(Magistrate Judge, United States District Court Northern District of Iowa)* Appointed by U.S. District Court judges.
Office: 211 U.S. Courthouse, 101 First Street S.E., Cedar Rapids 52401.
Telephone: (319) 286-2340.

JOHNSON, J. G. *(District Associate Judge, Iowa District Court First Judicial District)* Appointed.
Mailing address: P.O. Box 458, West Union 52175.
Office: Fayette County Courthouse, 114 North Vine Street, West Union 52175.
Telephone: (563) 422-5694.

JOY, William H. *(District Judge, Iowa District Court Fifth Judicial District)* Appointed by Governor Terry E. Branstad to term beginning Aug 9, 1989. Retained by election 1990, 1996 and 2002. Current term expires Dec 31, 2008. Born Perry Iowa Jan 4, 1943. Methodist. Educated at University of Iowa B.A. 1967 J.D. 1968. Admitted to practice Iowa 1968. In legal practice Perry 1968-89.
Mailing address: P.O. Box 605, Perry 50220.
Telephone: (515) 286-3859.
E-mail address: wmjoy@aol.com

KAMP, Joel J. *(District Associate Judge, Iowa District Court Eighth Judicial District)* Full-time Judicial Magistrate April 15, 1977 to Dec 31, 1980. Assumed office as District Associate Judge Jan 1, 1981. Retained by election. Born Fort Madison Iowa May 1, 1944. Christian Scientist. Educated at University of Iowa B.A. 1966 and University of Mississippi J.D. 1970. Admitted to practice Mississippi 1970 and Iowa 1971. Began legal practice Keokuk Iowa 1971. Part-time Judicial Magistrate, Iowa District Court Eighth Judicial District July to Sept 1973.
Instructor in Criminal Law Burlington Junior College 1975-76. Member Iowa State Bar Association. Republican.
Mailing address: P.O. Box 1443, Fort Madison 52627.
Office: North Lee County Courthouse, 701 Avenue F, Fort Madison 52627.
Telephone: (319) 372-3351.

KELLER, Peter A. *(District Judge, Iowa District Court Fifth Judicial District)* Appointed by Governor Terry E. Branstad March 27, 1986. Retained by election 1988, 1994 and 2000. Current term expires Dec 31, 2006. Born Dallas Center Iowa Jan 18, 1938. Lutheran. Educated at Iowa State University 1957-59, University of Utah 1959-60 and Drake University J.D. 1963. Admitted to practice Iowa 1963, Florida 1965, U.S. Court of Military Appeals 1968, U.S. Supreme Court 1968 and U.S. District Court Southern District of Iowa 1972. Began legal practice Orlando Florida 1966. In legal practice Dallas Center Iowa 1970-86.

Former member The Florida Bar. Member Iowa State Bar Association. Colonel USAF JAG 1963-70 and USAFR 1971-94. Precinct Chairperson Republican Party of Iowa 1972-86. Member Rotary Club, church board and Commercial Club. Enjoys fishing, camping and golf.

Office: Dallas County Courthouse, 801 Court Street, Adel 50003.

Telephone: (515) 286-3859.

KELLEY, James E. *(District Judge, Iowa District Court Seventh Judicial District)* Appointed by Governor Robert D. Ray to term beginning Sept 1, 1981. Retained by election 1982, 1988, 1994 and 2000. Current term expires Dec 31, 2006. Born Des Moines Iowa April 22, 1941. Roman Catholic. Educated at University of Notre Dame B.A. 1963, University of Iowa J.D. 1966 and University of Nevada Masters of Judicial Studies 1993. Articles Editor Iowa Law Review 1965-66. Member Order of the Coif. Admitted to practice Iowa 1966. Began legal practice Davenport 1966.

Author "Juror Stress: A Trial Judge's Perspective" 43 Drake L. Rev. 97, 1994. Member 1973-81 and Chairman 1975-81 City of Davenport Housing Advisory and Appeals Board. Chair Subcommittee on Records Management and Retention Iowa Judicial Council since 1987. Member Iowa Judges Association (President 1996-97), Scott County, Iowa State (Chair Jury Instructions Committee 2000-01) and American Bar Associations. Lecturer on Time Management for Judges Dec 1983, Performance Evaluations of Court Reporters Dec 1985, Probate Procedures Dec 1986, Media and the Courts Dec 1994 and Iowa Sexual Predator Civil Commitment Law June 2001 Iowa Judges Association Continuing Legal Education. Member Handel Oratorio Society 1967-84. Vice President United Way of Quad Cities 1978-79. Enjoys running, music and photography.

Office: Scott County Courthouse, 416 West Fourth Street, Davenport 52801.

Telephone: (563) 326-8608.

KILBURG, Paul J. *(Chief Judge, United States Bankruptcy Court Northern District of Iowa)* Appointed by U.S. Court of Appeals Eighth Circuit judges. Chief Judge since Aug 18, 1999. Former District Judge, Iowa District Court Sixth Judicial District.

Mailing address: P.O. Box 74890, Cedar Rapids 52407-4890.

Telephone: (319) 286-2230.

KILNOSKI, Kathleen A. *(District Associate Judge, Iowa District Court Fourth Judicial District)* Appointed.

Mailing address: P.O. Box 476, Council Bluffs 51502.

Office: 227 South Sixth Street, Council Bluffs 51501.

Telephone: (712) 328-5863.

KIMES, Gary G. *(District Judge, Iowa District Court Fifth Judicial District)* Appointed by Governor Terry E. Branstad.

Office: Clarke County Courthouse, 100 South Main, Osceola 50213.

Telephone: (641) 342-3111.

KLOTZ, Ruth B. *(Associate Probate Judge, Iowa District Court Fifth Judicial District)* Appointed by the Chief Judge and serves at the pleasure of the judges.

Office: 212 Polk County Courthouse, 500 Mulberry Street, Des Moines 50309.

Telephone: (515) 286-3790.

KOEHLER, Thomas L. *(District Judge, Iowa District Court Sixth Judicial District)* Full-time Judicial Magistrate 1979-80. District Associate Judge 1981-82. Appointed District Judge by Governor Robert D. Ray to term beginning Jan 15, 1982. Retained by elections. Born Henry Illinois July 15, 1937. Roman Catholic. Educated at University of Iowa LL.B. 1962. Admitted to practice 1962. Began legal practice Cedar Rapids 1962.

Assistant County Attorney Linn County 1965-69. Member Iowa Judges Association and Linn County Bar Association.

Mailing address: P.O. Box 1468, Cedar Rapids 52406.

Office: Linn County Courthouse, Third Avenue Bridge, Cedar Rapids 52406.

Telephone: (319) 398-3920.

KRUSE, Mark E. *(District Associate Judge, Iowa District Court Eighth Judicial District)* Appointed.

Mailing address: P.O. Box 158, Burlington 52601.

Office: Des Moines County Courthouse, 513 North Main Street, Burlington 52601.

Telephone: (319) 752-8245.

LARSON, David C. *(District Associate Judge, Iowa District Court Third Judicial District)* Former Alternate District Associate Judge. Appointed District Associate Judge.

Mailing address: P.O. Drawer ON, Spirit Lake 51360.

Office: Dickinson County Courthouse, Hill and Eighteenth Street, Spirit Lake 51360.

Telephone: (712) 336-1586.

LARSON, Jerry L. *(Justice, Iowa Supreme Court)* Appointed by Governor Robert D. Ray to term beginning Aug 25, 1978. Retained by election, current term expires Dec 31, 2004. Born Harlan Iowa May 17, 1936. Baptist. Educated at University of Iowa B.A. 1958 J.D. 1960. Staff member Iowa Law Review. Admitted to practice Iowa 1960. Judge, Iowa District Court Fourth Judicial District 1975-78.

Shelby County Attorney 1965-68.

Office: Judicial Branch Building, 1111 East Court Avenue, Des Moines 50319.

Telephone: (712) 755-2366.

LATHROP, Victor G. *(Associate Juvenile Judge, Iowa District Court Second Judicial District)* Former Associate Probate Judge. Appointed Associate Juvenile Judge by the Chief Judge 2000 and serves at the pleasure of the judges. Born Rockford Illinois April 27, 1950. Educated at Illinois State University B.S. 1972 and Drake University Law School J.D. 1975. Admitted to practice Iowa 1976. In legal practice Ames 1977-85.

Former Member Story County Bar Association. Member Iowa Judges Association, National Council of Juvenile and Family Court Judges and Iowa State Bar Asso-

LATHROP, VICTOR G.—*Continued*
ciation. Executive Director Story County Legal Aide Society 1976-77.
Mailing address: P.O. Box 408, Nevada 50201.
Office: Story County Courthouse, 900 Sixth Street, Nevada 50201.
Telephone: (515) 382-7434.

LAVORATO, Louis A. *(Chief Justice, Iowa Supreme Court)* Appointed by Governor Terry E. Branstad to term beginning Feb 12, 1986. Retained by election. Born Des Moines Iowa Sept 29, 1934. Educated at Drake University B.S.B.A. 1959 J.D. 1962. In legal practice Des Moines 1962-79. Judge 1979-86 and Chief Judge 1983-86, Iowa District Court Fifth Judicial District.
Member Iowa Judges Association (Former Chair Uniform Court Instruction Committee, former Co-chair Legislative Committee, President Elect). Speaker at several Continuing Legal Education forums for lawyers, judges and magistrates. U.S. Army 1953-55.
Office: Judicial Branch Building, 1111 East Court Avenue, Des Moines 50319.
Telephone: (515) 281-3952.

LESTER, David A. *(District Judge, Iowa District Court Third Judicial District)* Appointed by governor.
Office: Emmet County Courthouse, 609 First Avenue North, Estherville 51334.
Telephone: (712) 362-4567.

LEWIS, Sylvia A. *(District Associate Judge, Iowa District Court Sixth Judicial District)* Appointed.
Mailing address: P.O. Box 2510, Iowa City 52240.
Office: Johnson County Courthouse, 417 South Clinton Street, Iowa City 52240.
Telephone: (319) 398-3984.

LINGREEN, Margaret L. *(District Judge, Iowa District Court First Judicial District)* Appointed by governor.
Mailing address: P.O. Box 376, Decorah 52101.
Office: Winneshiek County Courthouse, 1111 Bine Street, Decorah 52101.
Telephone: (563) 382-3770.

LINN, John G. *(District Judge, Iowa District Court Eighth Judicial District)* Appointed by governor.
Mailing address: P.O. Box 158, Burlington 52601.
Office: Des Moines County Courthouse, 513 North Main Street, Burlington 52601.
Telephone: (319) 385-2538.

LLOYD, John D. *(District Judge, Iowa District Court Fifth Judicial District)* Appointed by Governor Tom Vilsack.
Office: Clarke County Courthouse, 100 South Main, Osceola 50213.
Telephone: (641) 342-6096.

LONGSTAFF, Ronald E. *(Chief Judge, United States District Court Southern District of Iowa)* Appointed Magistrate Judge by U.S. District Court judges to term beginning March 1, 1976. Reappointed 1984. Appointed Judge for life by the President. Born Pittsburg Kansas Feb 14, 1941. Lutheran. Educated at Kansas State College B.S. 1962 and University of Iowa J.D. 1965. Member Omicron Delta Kappa. Law Clerk to Judge Roy L. Stephenson 1965. Admitted to practice Iowa 1965.
Author Comment 49 Iowa L. Rev. 161, 1963; Comment 49 Iowa L. Rev. 560, 1964; and Note 49 Iowa L. Rev. 1224, 1964. Instructor Drake University Law School 1973-74. Member Iowa State Bar Association. Republican.
Office: 115 U.S. Courthouse, 123 East Walnut Street, Des Moines 50309-2036.
Telephone: (515) 284-6235.

MACKEY, John S. *(District Judge, Iowa District Court Second Judicial District)* Part-time Judicial Magistrate 1988-90. Appointed District Judge by Governor Terry E. Branstad Feb 20, 1990 to term beginning May 1, 1990. Retained by election Nov 3, 1992 and 1998. Current term expires Dec 31, 2004. Born Mechanicsville Iowa Aug 9, 1957. Lutheran. Educated at University of Iowa B.A. 1978 and University of Oklahoma J.D. 1982. Admitted to practice Iowa 1983, U.S. District Courts Northern 1983 and Southern 1984 Districts of Iowa and U.S. Court of Appeals Eighth Circuit 1987. In legal practice Mason City 1983-90.
Member Iowa Judges Association, American Judicature Society, Cerro Gordo County, District 2A and Iowa State Bar Associations. Enjoys fishing and reading.
Mailing address: P.O. Box 70, Garner 50438.
Office: Hancock County Courthouse, 855 State Street, Garner 50438.
Telephone: (641) 923-3521.

MADDEN, Patrick J. *(District Judge, Iowa District Court Seventh Judicial District)* Appointed by governor.
Mailing address: P.O. Box 8010, Muscatine 52761.
Office: Juvenile Court Services, 401 Walnut, Muscatine 52761.
Telephone: (563) 263-6634.

MAGEE, Gerald W. *(Associate Juvenile Judge, Iowa District Court Second Judicial District)* Appointed by the Chief Judge Jan 1992. Born Dunkerton Iowa July 20, 1943. Protestant. Educated at University of Iowa B.A. 1965 J.D. 1967. Admitted to practice Iowa 1967. In legal practice Jefferson 1967-92.
City Attorney (part time) City of Jefferson 1975-92. Member Iowa Judges Association and Iowa State Bar Association.
Office: Floyd County Courthouse, 101 South Main Street, Charles City 50616.
Telephone: (641) 228-7779.

MAHAN, Robert E. *(Judge, Iowa Court of Appeals)* Appointed by governor. Born Carroll Iowa Oct 23, 1946. Catholic. Educated at Iowa State University B.S. 1969 and University of Iowa J.D. 1973. Admitted to practice Iowa 1973. In legal practice Waterloo 1973-78. Judicial Magistrate July 20, 1978 to Dec 31, 1980. District Associate Judge Jan 1, 1981 to Jan 4, 1987 and Former District Judge, Iowa District Court First Judicial District.
Assistant County Attorney Black Hawk County 1976-78. Instructor in Juvenile and Family Law University of Northern Iowa since 1977. Member National Association of Juvenile Court Judges, Black Hawk County, Iowa State and American Bar Associations.
Office: Judicial Branch Building, 1111 East Court Avenue, Des Moines 50319.
Telephone: (515) 281-6711.

McCORMICK, Patrick C. *(District Associate Judge, Iowa District Court Third Judicial District)* Appointed.
Office: Woodbury Law Enforcement Center, 407 Seventh Street, Sioux City 51101.
Telephone: (712) 279-6026.

McDONALD, Douglas C. *(District Associate Judge, Iowa District Court Seventh Judicial District)* Appointed.
Office: Scott County Courthouse, 416 West Fourth Street, Davenport 52801.
Telephone: (563) 326-8780.

McGHEE, Odell G. *(District Associate Judge, Iowa District Court Fifth Judicial District)* Appointed.
Office: 212 Polk County Courthouse, 500 Mulberry Street, Des Moines 50309.
Telephone: (515) 286-3854.

McGLYNN, James A. *(Associate Juvenile Judge, Iowa District Court Second Judicial District)* Appointed by the Chief Judge and serves at the pleasure of the judges.
Mailing address: P.O. Box 845, Webster City 50595.
Office: Hamilton County Courthouse, Webster City 50595.
Telephone: (515) 832-9607.

McKENRICK, Gary D. *(District Judge, Iowa District Court Seventh Judicial District)* Former District Associate Judge. Appointed District Judge by governor.
Office: Scott County Courthouse, 416 West Fourth Street, Davenport 52801.
Telephone: (563) 326-8736.

McKINLEY, Bryan H. *(District Judge, Iowa District Court Second Judicial District)* Appointed by governor.
Office: Mitchell County Courthouse, 508 State Street, Osage 50461.
Telephone: (641) 732-3726.

McMANUS, Edward J. *(Senior Judge, United States District Court Northern District of Iowa)* Appointed for life by President John F. Kennedy to term beginning 1962. Former Chief Judge. Assumed Senior status, serves by assignment. Born Keokuk Iowa Feb 9, 1920. Catholic. Educated at St. Ambrose College (now St. Ambrose College and Marycrest College) 1936-38 and University of Iowa B.A. 1940 J.D. 1942. Admitted to practice Iowa 1942. Began legal practice Keokuk 1942.
Keokuk City Attorney 1946-55. State Senator 1955-59. Lieutenant Governor of Iowa 1959-61. Lieutenant (aviator) USNR 1942-46. Democrat.
Office: 329 U.S. Courthouse, 101 First Street S.E., Cedar Rapids 52401.
Telephone: (319) 286-2350.

McMINIMEE, Gary L. *(District Judge, Iowa District Court Second Judicial District)* Appointed by governor.
Mailing address: P.O. Box 867, Carroll 51401.
Office: Carroll County Courthouse, Sixth and Main Streets, Carroll 51401.
Telephone: (712) 792-9241.

MEADOWS, E. Richard, Jr. *(District Judge, Iowa District Court Eighth Judicial District)* Former District Associate Judge July 1, 1989 to 1998. Appointed District Judge by governor. Retained by election Nov 2000, current term expires 2006. Born Williamsburg Virginia March 29, 1947. Lutheran. Educated at James Madison University B.S. 1974 M.Ed. 1976 and Drake University J.D. 1985. Admitted to practice Iowa 1986. In legal practice Ottumwa 1986-89.
Member Iowa Judges Association, Wapello County and Iowa State Bar Associations. Petty Officer Second Class (E-5) USCG 1968-72. School Psychologist Area Education Agency 15 1976-79. Computer Programmer John Deere Ottumwa Works 1979-82. Council member First Lutheran Church. Enjoys racquetball and golf.
Office: Wapello County Courthouse, 101 West Fourth Street, Ottumwa 52501.
Telephone: (641) 683-1983.

MERTZ-LA FOLLETTE, Martha L. *(District Judge, Iowa District Court Fifth Judicial District)* Appointed by Governor Tom Vilsack.
Mailing address: P.O. Box 497, Knoxville 50138.
Office: Marion County Courthouse, Knoxville 50138.
Telephone: (641) 828-2210.

MICHAELSON, Brian L. *(Associate Juvenile Judge, Iowa District Court Third Judicial District)*
Office: Trosper-Hoyt Building, 822 Douglas Street, Sioux City 51101.
Telephone: (712) 279-6467.

MILLER, John C. *(Judge, Iowa Court of Appeals)* Appointed by Governor Tom Vilsack to term beginning Sept 1999. Retained by election 2000, current term expires Dec 31, 2006. Educated at University of Iowa B.A. 1969 J.D. with distinction 1975. Judge and Chief Judge, Iowa District Court Eighth Judicial District March 1981 to Sept 1999.
Office: Judicial Branch Building, 1111 East Court Avenue, Des Moines 50319.
Telephone: (515) 281-7651.

MOISAN, Cynthia M. *(District Associate Judge, Iowa District Court Fifth Judicial District)* Appointed.
Office: 212 Polk County Courthouse, 500 Mulberry Street, Des Moines 50309.
Telephone: (515) 286-2070.

MOON, Michael J. *(District Judge, Iowa District Court Second Judicial District)* Appointed by governor.
Office: Marshall County Courthouse, 17 East Main Street, Marshalltown 50158.
Telephone: (641) 754-1615.

MOOTHART, Joseph M. *(District Associate Judge, Iowa District Court First Judicial District)* Appointed.
Office: Black Hawk County Courthouse, 316 East Fifth Street, Waterloo 50703.
Telephone: (319) 833-3308.

MORRISON, Dan F. *(District Judge, Iowa District Court Eighth Judicial District)* Appointed by Governor Robert D. Ray to term beginning Jan 24, 1983. Retained by election 1984, 1990, 1996 and 2002. Current term expires Dec 31, 2008. Born Sigourney Iowa Nov 16, 1947. Methodist. Educated at University of Northern Iowa B.A. 1970 and Drake University J.D. 1975. Member Pi Gamma Mu and Phi Kappa Phi. Admitted to practice Iowa 1976 and U.S. District Courts Northern 1976 and Southern 1976 Districts of Iowa. In legal practice Sigourney 1976-83. Part-time Judicial Magistrate, Iowa District Court Eighth Judicial District 1976-80.
Sigourney City Attorney 1977-82. Member Keokuk County, Iowa State and American Bar Associations. Po-

MORRISON, DAN F.—*Continued*

litical affiliation: Independent. Member Jaycees and Boy Scouts of America. Enjoys sports.

Office: Keokuk County Courthouse, 101 South Main Street, Sigourney 52591.

Telephone: (641) 622-2210.

MOTT, Thomas W. *(District Associate Judge, Iowa District Court Fifth Judicial District)* Judicial Magistrate Dec 8, 1975 to Nov 30, 1980. Appointed District Associate Judge to term beginning Dec 1, 1980. Retained by election 1982, 1986, 1990, 1994, 1998 and 2002. Current term expires Dec 31, 2006. Born Knoxville Iowa Sept 18, 1945. Educated at University of Iowa B.A. 1972 J.D. with honors 1975. Admitted to practice Iowa 1975. Began legal practice Newton 1975.

Office: 104 Jasper County Courthouse, 101 First Street North, Newton 50208.

Telephone: (641) 792-6307.

MULLEN, John G. *(District Associate Judge, Iowa District Court Seventh Judicial District)* Appointed by Governor Terry E. Branstad to term beginning Nov 26, 1986. Retained by election Dec 1990, 1994, 1998 and 2002. Current term expires Dec 31, 2006. Born Tucson Arizona Oct 17, 1949. Protestant. Educated at University of Illinois B.S. 1971 and Drake University J.D. 1974. Admitted to practice Iowa 1975. In legal practice Davenport 1978-86.

Assistant Attorney General Iowa Jan 1975 to Dec 1977. Member National Council of Juvenile and Family Court Judges, Scott County and Iowa State Bar Associations.

Office: Scott County Courthouse, 416 West Fourth Street, Davenport 52801.

Telephone: (563) 326-8780.

MULLINS, Michael R. *(District Judge, Iowa District Court Eighth Judicial District)* Appointed by governor Tom Vilsack. Educated at Southwest Baptist University B.A. 1974, University of Iowa M.S.W. 1976 and Drake University Law School J.D. with honors 1982. Editor-in-Chief Drake Law Review 1981-82. Member Order of the Coif. Admitted to practice Iowa 1982. In legal practice Washington Iowa 1982-2001.

Mailing address: P.O. Box 391, Washington 52353.

Office: Washington County Courthouse, Washington 52353.

Telephone: (319) 653-7764.

MYLREA, Jane M. *(Associate Juvenile Judge, Iowa District Court First Judicial District)* Appointed by the Chief Judge and serves at the pleasure of the judges.

Office: Dubuque County Courthouse, 720 Central Avenue, Dubuque 52001.

Telephone: (563) 589-4463.

NAHRA, John A. *(Chief Judge, Iowa District Court Seventh Judicial District)* District Associate Judge 1985-86. Appointed District Judge by Governor Terry E. Branstad to term beginning Oct 8, 1986. Retained by election 1988, 1994 and 2000. Current term expires Dec 31, 2006. Born Davenport Iowa July 3, 1953. Educated at DePaul University B.A. 1975 and Creighton University J.D. 1978. Admitted to practice Iowa 1978. In legal practice Davenport 1978-85.

Lead Judge Iowa Permanency Planning Task Force 1987-88 and Seventh Judicial District Reasonable Efforts Model Court Project 1989-92. Iowa Judicial Department Member Out-of-State Placement of Iowa's Children Committee and Problem-Child Target Committee 1988-89. Member Supreme Court Family Court Study Committee 1989-90, Secure Unit Advisory Committee Mental Health Institute, Independence Iowa 1989-90 and Legislative Committee on Implementation of Family Courts 1990. Member Iowa Judges Association (Chair Juvenile Laws Committee 1986-88 and Court Administration and Technology Committee 1988-93, Board of Directors 1988-92, Co-chairman Legislative Committee 1993-2001, Secretary/Treasurer 2000-01, Vice President 2001-02, President since 2002), National Council of Juvenile and Family Court Judges (Court-Appointed Special Advocate Committee 1989-90, Community Relations Committee 1989-91 and 1994-95, Permanency Planning Advisory Committee 1989-91 and 1994-97), American Judicature Society, Scott County, Iowa State and American (National Conference of State Trial Judges Judicial Administration Division since 1986) Bar Associations.

Office: Scott County Courthouse, 416 West Fourth Street, Davenport 52801.

Telephone: (563) 326-8606.

NEARY, Jeffrey A. *(District Judge, Iowa District Court Third Judicial District)* Appointed by Governor Tom Vilsack.

Office: Woodbury County Courthouse, 620 Douglas Street, Sioux City 51101.

Telephone: (712) 279-6034.

NELSON, Frank B. *(District Judge, Iowa District Court Third Judicial District)* Appointed by Governor Terry E. Branstad to term beginning March 7, 1988. Retained by election. Born Ringsted Iowa July 16, 1932. Congregational. Educated at Iowa State University B.S. 1954 and University of Iowa J.D. 1959. Admitted to practice Iowa 1959 and U.S. District Courts Northern 1960 and Southern 1960 Districts of Iowa. In legal practice Spencer 1959-88.

Member Iowa Judges Association, Iowa State (Board of Governors 1978-79) and American Bar Associations. First Lieutenant U.S. Army 1954-56.

Office: 4 Clay County Courthouse, 215 West Fourth Street, Spencer 51301.

Telephone: (712) 262-1214.

NEUMAN, Linda K. *(Justice, Iowa Supreme Court)* Appointed by Governor Terry E. Branstad to term beginning 1986. Retained by election. Born Chicago Illinois June 18, 1948. Educated at University of Colorado B.A. Regent Scholar 1970 J.D. 1973 and University of Virginia LL.M. 1998. In legal practice Davenport 1974-79. Magistrate Scott County 1980-82. District Judge, Iowa District Court Seventh Judicial District 1982-86.

Adjunct Faculty University of Iowa Graduate School of Social Work 1981. Fellow American Bar Foundation. Member Commission on Continuing Legal Education 1974-81, Council on Judicial Selection 1986-88 and Chairperson Commission on Planning for the 21st Century Iowa Supreme Court. Advisor National Center for State Courts Study of Appellate Court Case Processing, Colloquy for State Appellate Court Judges University of Virginia Center for Biomedical Ethics and University of New Mexico Institute of Public Law Project on Bioethics Education for the State Judiciary. Member Iowa Organization of Women Attorneys, Dillon American Inn of Court, U.S. Association of Constitutional Law, Iowa Judges Association (Education Committee, Legislative Committee), National Association of Women Judges (Di-

NEUMAN, LINDA K.—*Continued*

rector representing Iowa, Missouri and Wisconsin 1984-86), American Judicature Society, Scott County (Chair Magistrate Appointing Commission 1985, Grievance Committee and Public Relations Committee, Member Executive Committee), Iowa State and American (Member Committee on Standards of Judicial Administration and Chairperson National Conference of Appellate Judges Judicial Administration Division) Bar Associations. Annual Linda K. Neuman Award for the Professions established by Quad Cities Women's Encouragement Board 1987. Recipient Exceptional Achievement Award from Mississippi Valley Girl Scout Council 1988 and Award for Distinguished Achievement from University of Colorado 1989. Vice President and Trust Officer Bettendorf Bank & Trust Company and Des Moines National Bank 1979-80. Former Director Marriage and Family Counseling Service of Scott and Rock Island Counties (President 1978-79), Quad Cities United Way (Executive Committee 1978-81), Vera French Community Mental Health Center, Scott County Board of Social Welfare, Scott County Library Foundation, Bettendorf Chamber of Commerce and The Maternal Health Center. Trustee St. Ambrose University. Member Alumni Advisory Board University of Colorado School of Law 1986-88. Member St. Peters Episcopal Church. Enjoys music, bicycling, skiing and sailing.

Office: Judicial Branch Building, 1111 East Court Avenue, Des Moines 50319.

Telephone: (563) 326-8668.

NEWELL, Peter B. *(District Associate Judge, Iowa District Court Second Judicial District)* Appointed.

Mailing address: P.O. Box 328, Waverly 50677.

Office: Bremer County Courthouse, 415 East Bremer Avenue, Waverly 50677.

Telephone: (319) 352-0520.

NEWMEISTER, Michael J. *(District Associate Judge, Iowa District Court Sixth Judicial District)* Appointed.

Mailing address: P.O. Box 1468, Cedar Rapids 52406.

Office: Linn County Courthouse, Third Avenue Bridge, Cedar Rapids 52406.

Telephone: (319) 398-3920.

NIGG, Randal J. *(District Associate Judge, Iowa District Court First Judicial District)* Appointed.

Office: Dubuque County Courthouse, 720 Central Avenue, Dubuque 52001.

Telephone: (563) 583-4465.

NONEMAN, Gary R. *(District Associate Judge, Iowa District Court Eighth Judicial District)* Appointed to term beginning July 1, 1987. Retained by election 1988, 1992, 1996 and 2000. Current term expires Dec 31, 2004. Born Fort Collins Colorado Oct 8, 1955. Methodist. Educated at Iowa State University B.A. with honors 1977 and University of Iowa J.D. with honors 1980. Member Order of the Coif. Admitted to practice Iowa 1980, U.S. District Courts Southern 1980 and Northern 1981 Districts of Iowa, U.S. Court of Appeals Eighth Circuit 1983, U.S. Court of Military Appeals 1983 and U.S. Supreme Court 1983. In legal practice Albia 1980-82 and Keokuk 1982-87.

Assistant Public Defender Lee County 1982-87. Member Iowa Judges Association (Member since 1992 and Chairman since 1996 Judicial Ethics Committee, Member Legislative Committee since 1992), Iowa State (Criminal Law Committee 1985-90) and American Bar Associations. Attended Criminal Defense Conference State Bar of Georgia 1983, Criminal Defense Seminar Northwestern University 1986 and Special Courts Program The National Judicial College 1988. Attended and instructed numerous Iowa Public Defender Association and Iowa Judges Association seminars. Recipient "Gold Seal" Judicial Award from Iowa Coalition Against Domestic Violence 1988 and 1989, Distinguished Presidents Award from Kiwanis Club 1990-91 and Crime Victims Service Certificate from U.S. Department of Justice 1990. Member Kiwanis Club. Former Member Keokuk Park Board and Keokuk Historical Preservation Board.

Mailing address: P.O. Box 725, Keokuk 52632.

Office: South Lee County Courthouse, 25 North Seventh Street, Keokuk 52632.

Telephone: (319) 524-2921.

NOVAK, Joel D. *(District Judge, Iowa District Court Fifth Judicial District)* Appointed by governor.

Office: 212 Polk County Courthouse, 500 Mulberry Street, Des Moines 50309.

Telephone: (515) 286-3849.

O'BRIEN, Donald E. *(Senior Judge, United States District Court Northern District of Iowa)* Appointed for life by President Jimmy Carter to term beginning 1978. Former Chief Judge. Assumed Senior status Dec 30, 1992, serves by assignment. Born Marcus Iowa Sept 30, 1923. Catholic. Educated at Trinity College and Creighton University LL.B. 1948. Member Gamma Eta Gamma. Admitted to practice Iowa 1948 and U.S. Supreme Court 1962. In legal practice Sioux City 1948-60 and 1967-77. Municipal Judge 1959-60.

County Attorney Woodbury County 1955-59. U.S. Attorney Northern District of Iowa 1961-67. Member Budget Committee 1985-95 and Eighth Circuit Representative 1990-97 Judicial Conference of the U.S. Member Woodbury County and Iowa State Bar Associations. First Lieutenant USAF 1942-45. Counsel U.S. House of Representatives Subcommittee 1977-78.

Mailing address: P.O. Box 267, Sioux City 51102-0267.

Telephone: (712) 233-3916.

OETH, Steven J. *(District Associate Judge, Iowa District Court Second Judicial District)* Appointed.

Office: Boone County Courthouse, 201 State Street, Boone 50036.

Telephone: (515) 433-0569.

O'GRADY, Timothy *(District Judge, Iowa District Court Fourth Judicial District)* Appointed by Governor Terry E. Branstad.

Mailing address: P.O. Box 476, Council Bluffs 51502.

Office: 227 South Sixth Street, Council Bluffs 51501.

Telephone: (712) 328-5794.

OSTLUND, William C. *(District Judge, Iowa District Court Second Judicial District)* Appointed by governor.

Office: Greene County Courthouse, 114 North Chestnut, Jefferson 50129.

Telephone: (515) 576-0581.

OVROM, Eliza J. *(District Judge, Iowa District Court Fifth Judicial District)* Appointed by governor.

Office: 212 Polk County Courthouse, 500 Mulberry Street, Des Moines 50309.

Telephone: (515) 286-3889.

OWENS, William S. *(Associate Juvenile Judge, Iowa District Court Eighth Judicial District)* Appointed by the Chief Judge and serves at the pleasure of the judges.
Office: Wapello County Courthouse, 101 West Fourth Street, Ottumwa 52501.
Telephone: (641) 683-1791.

PATTINSON, William J. *(District Judge, Iowa District Court Second Judicial District)* Appointed by governor.
Mailing address: P.O. Box 408, Nevada 50201.
Office: Story County Courthouse, 900 Sixth Street, Nevada 50201.
Telephone: (515) 382-6581.

PAULSEN, Donna L. *(District Judge, Iowa District Court Fifth Judicial District)* Appointed by governor.
Office: 212 Polk County Courthouse, 500 Mulberry Street, Des Moines 50309.
Telephone: (515) 286-2058.

PEARSON, Alan L. *(Chief Judge, Iowa District Court First Judicial District)* Full-time Judicial Magistrate Oct 1976 to Dec 1981. District Associate Judge Jan 1, 1981 to Oct 29, 1985. Appointed District Judge by Governor Terry E. Branstad to term beginning Oct 30, 1985. Retained by election. Born Ames Iowa April 13, 1946. Lutheran. Educated at Iowa State University B.S. 1968 and University of Iowa J.D. with distinction 1971. Board of Editors Iowa Law Review. Member Order of the Coif. Admitted to practice Iowa 1971. Began legal practice Dubuque 1972.
Staff Attorney Dubuque Area Legal Services 1972-73. Assistant County Attorney Dubuque County 1973-76. Former Co-chair Supreme Court Advisory Committee on the Administration of Juvenile Court Offices. Member Iowa Criminal and Juvenile Justice Planning Commission, Iowa Judges Association (Former Chair Juvenile Laws Committee, former member Workshop Committee and Associate Judges Committee) and American Bar Association. Former Faculty Advisor School of Instruction for Magistrates, Juvenile Court Conference and Iowa Judges Conference. Participant 1977 and Faculty Advisor 1981 The National Judicial College. Attended numerous training programs for juvenile court officers, social workers and child care agencies.
Office: Dubuque County Courthouse, 720 Central Avenue, Dubuque 52001.
Telephone: (563) 589-4464.

PELTON, Charles H. *(District Judge, Iowa District Court Seventh Judicial District)* Appointed by governor.
Mailing address: P.O. Box 2957, Clinton 52732.
Office: Clinton County Courthouse, 612 North Second Street, Clinton 52732.
Telephone: (563) 243-6210.

PETERSON, Richard William *(Recalled Magistrate Judge, United States District Court Southern District of Iowa)* U.S. Commissioner 1958-70. Appointed Magistrate by U.S. District Court judges to term beginning Dec 1970. Retired. Appointed Recalled Magistrate Judge by the Judicial Council of the Eighth Circuit. Born Council Bluffs Iowa Sept 29, 1925. Lutheran. Educated at University of Iowa B.A. 1949 J.D. with distinction 1951. Member Delta Sigma Rho and Omicron Delta Kappa. Admitted to practice Iowa 1951, U.S. District Court Southern District of Iowa 1951 and U.S. Supreme Court 1991. In legal practice Council Bluffs 1951-75. Trust Officer First National Bank Council Bluffs 1975-77. Author "The Federal Magistrates Act" Iowa L. Rev. Oct 1970, "To Further the Administration of Justice" June 1972 and "Justice South of the Border" Feb 1976 American Judicature Society and "The Court Moves West" Southside Press of the Midlands 1988. Fellow American Bar Foundation. Member Pottawattamie County, Southwest Iowa, Iowa State, Federal, American and Inter-American Bar Associations. Corporal U.S. Army 1943-45 and First Lieutenant USAF 1950-55. Republican. President Historical Society of the U.S. Courts in the Eight Circuit since 1989. Member 1958-64 and President 1962-63 Board of Education Council Bluffs Community School District. Mason. Enjoys reading.
Office: 25 Main Place, Council Bluffs 51503.
Telephone: (712) 325-9000.

PHIPPS, Sherman *(District Judge, Iowa District Court Fifth Judicial District)* Appointed by Governor Tom Vilsack.
Office: Decatur County Courthouse, 207 North Main Street, Leon 50144.
Telephone: (515) 286-3198.

PILLE, Glenn E. *(District Judge, Iowa District Court Fifth Judicial District)* Appointed by governor.
Office: 212 Polk County Courthouse, 500 Mulberry Street, Des Moines 50309.
Telephone: (515) 286-3856.

POTTERFIELD, Amanda P. *(District Judge, Iowa District Court Sixth Judicial District)* Appointed by governor.
Mailing address: P.O. Box 2510, Iowa City 52244-2510.
Office: Johnson County Courthouse, 417 South Clinton Street, Iowa City 52240.
Telephone: (319) 356-6060.

PRATT, Robert W. *(Judge, United States District Court Southern District of Iowa)* Appointed for life by President Bill Clinton Jan 7, 1997 to term beginning July 1, 1997. Born Emmetsburg Iowa. Roman Catholic. Educated at Loras College B.A. and Creighton University J.D. Staff Editor Creighton Law Review. Admitted to practice Nebraska 1972 and Iowa 1973. In legal practice Des Moines Iowa 1975-97.
Important Decisions: Hindman v. Transkrit Corp. 145 F.3d 986 8th Cir. 1998, Wilcutts v. Apfel 143 F.3d 1143 8th Cir. 1998, Planned Parenthood of Greater Iowa, Inc. v. Miller 30 F. Supp. 2d 1157 S.D. Iowa 1998 and Beard v. Flying J, Inc. 116 F. Supp. 2d 1077 S.D. Iowa 2000.
Office: 429 U.S. Courthouse, 123 East Walnut Street, Des Moines 50309.
Telephone: (515) 284-6254.
E-mail address: Robert_Pratt@IASD.USCourts.gov

PRICE, William A. *(District Associate Judge, Iowa District Court Fifth Judicial District)* Appointed.
Office: 212 Polk County Courthouse, 500 Mulberry Street, Des Moines 50309.
Telephone: (515) 286-3903.

READE, Linda R. *(Judge, United States District Court Northern District of Iowa)* Appointed for life by President George W. Bush to term beginning Nov 26,

READE, LINDA R.—*Continued*

2002. Former District Judge, Iowa District Court Fifth Judicial District.

Office: 101 First Street S.E., Suite 304, Cedar Rapids 52401.

Telephone: (319) 286-2330.

REIS, Artis I. *(District Judge, Iowa District Court Fifth Judicial District)* Former District Associate Judge. Appointed District Judge by governor.

Office: 212 Polk County Courthouse, 500 Mulberry Street, Des Moines 50309.

Telephone: (515) 286-3899.

REMLEY, David M. *(Chief Judge, Iowa District Court Sixth Judicial District)* Appointed by governor.

Mailing address: P.O. Box 19, Anamosa 52205.

Office: Jones County Courthouse, Main Street, Anamosa 52205.

Telephone: (319) 462-2275.

RICHARDSON, James M. *(District Judge, Iowa District Court Fourth Judicial District)* Appointed by governor.

Office: 6 Audubon County Courthouse, 318 Leroy Street, Audubon 50025.

Telephone: (712) 563-2766.

RIFFEL, Paul W. *(District Judge, Iowa District Court Second Judicial District)* Appointed by Governor Terry E. Branstad to term beginning March 19, 1984. Retained by election 1986, 1992 and 1998. Current term expires Dec 31, 2004. Born Burlington Iowa Aug 11, 1946. Roman Catholic. Educated at Drake University B.A. 1968 J.D. 1973. Member Phi Alpha Delta. Admitted to practice Iowa 1973. In legal practice Waverly 1973-84.

City Attorney Waverly 1973-76. County Attorney Bremer County 1976-84. Member Iowa Judges Association (Board of Directors 1988-94), Iowa County Attorneys Association (Legislative Committee 1978-79, Department of Criminal Investigation Advisory Committee 1981-82, Board of Directors 1982-83), American Judicature Society, Bremer County (President 1973-76), District 2A and Iowa State Bar Associations. Enjoys golf, biking and racquetball.

Mailing address: P.O. Box 328, Waverly 50677.

Office: Bremer County Courthouse, 415 East Bremer Avenue, Waverly 50677.

Telephone: (319) 352-5040.

RILEY, Kim M. *(District Associate Judge, Iowa District Court Second Judicial District)* Appointed to term beginning Oct 6, 2000. Retained by election. Born South Dakota Jan 24, 1963. Educated at Sioux Falls College B.A. 1985 and University of South Dakota J.D. 1988. Staff member South Dakota Law Review 1987. Law Clerk to South Dakota Circuit Court Sixth Judicial Circuit 1988-89. Admitted to practice Iowa 1990.

Chief Local Public Defender Marshalltown Iowa 1991-2000. Assistant County Attorney Carroll County. Member Iowa Judges Association and National Association of Women Judges. Member Advisory Board Salvation Army. Interests include traveling, reading and Yorkshire terriers.

Office: Marshall County Courthouse, 17 East Main Street, Marshalltown 50158.

Telephone: (641) 754-1612.

E-mail address: Kim.Riley@jb.state.ia.us

ROBINSON, L. Vern *(District Judge, Iowa District Court Sixth Judicial District)* Appointed by Governor Terry E. Branstad.

Mailing address: P.O. Box 2510, Iowa City 52244-2510.

Office: Johnson County Courthouse, 417 South Clinton Street, Iowa City 52240.

Telephone: (319) 356-6070.

ROMANO, Karen A. *(District Judge, Iowa District Court Fifth Judicial District)* District Associate Judge April 1996 to Dec 2001. Appointed District Judge by Governor Tom Vilsack Dec 19, 2001. Term expires Dec 31, 2004. Educated at Creighton University B.A. cum laude 1983 and University of Iowa College of Law J.D. with distinction 1986. Admitted to practice Iowa 1987 and U.S. District Courts Northern 1987 and Southern 1987 Districts of Iowa.

Assistant County Attorney Polk County Sept 1987 to April 1996.

Office: Polk County Courthouse, 500 Mulberry Street, Des Moines 50309.

Telephone: (515) 286-3906.

Fax: (515) 286-3858

E-mail address: Karen.Romano@jb.state.ia.us

ROSENBERG, Scott D. *(District Judge, Iowa District Court Fifth Judicial District)* Former District Associate Judge. Appointed District Judge by Governor Terry E. Branstad.

Office: 212 Polk County Courthouse, 500 Mulberry Street, Des Moines 50309.

Telephone: (515) 286-3900.

RUIGH, Dale E. *(District Judge, Iowa District Court Second Judicial District)* Appointed by Governor Robert D. Ray to term beginning Oct 1, 1981. Retained by election 1982, 1988, 1994 and 2000. Current term expires Dec 31, 2006. Born Mason City Iowa March 28, 1949. Methodist. Educated at Iowa State University B.S. with honors 1971 and University of Iowa J.D. with high distinction 1974. Member Order of the Coif. Admitted to practice Iowa 1974. Began legal practice Ames 1974. Judicial Magistrate, Iowa District Court Second Judicial District 1975-77.

Member Blackstone Inn of Court, Iowa Judges Association and Iowa State Bar Association.

Office: Story County Courthouse, Nevada 50201.

Telephone: (515) 382-7434.

RUSSELL, Douglas S. *(District Judge, Iowa District Court Sixth Judicial District)* Appointed by governor.

Mailing address: P.O. Box 2510, Iowa City 52244-2510.

Office: Johnson County Courthouse, 417 South Clinton Street, Iowa City 52240.

Telephone: (319) 356-6070.

SACKETT, Rosemary Shaw *(Chief Judge, Iowa Court of Appeals)* Appointed by Governor Terry E. Branstad to term beginning Aug 1983. Retained by election 1984, 1990, 1996 and 2002. Current term expires Dec 31, 2008. Born Fort Dodge Iowa Jan 17, 1940. Catholic. Educated at Buena Vista University B.A. with honors 1960, Drake University J.D. 1963 and University of Virginia LL.M. 1990. Member Kappa Beta Pi. Admitted to practice Iowa 1963 and U.S. District Court Northern District of Iowa 1963. In legal practice Pocahontas 1963-64 and Spencer 1964-83.

SACKETT, ROSEMARY SHAW—*Continued*

Author "Terminating Parental Rights of the Handicapped" XXV Family Law Quarterly 1991. Member American Bar Association (Program Chair 1997, President 1999-2000). Republican Presidential Committee Person 1966-71. Member Okoboji Yacht Club, writers groups and church. Enjoys writing poetry and children's stories.

Office: Judicial Branch Building, 1111 East Court Avenue, Des Moines 50319.

Telephone: (515) 281-7651.

SCHAEFER, Donavon D. *(District Associate Judge, Iowa District Court Third Judicial District)* Appointed.

Office: Cherokee County Courthouse, 520 West Main Street, Cherokee 51012.

Telephone: (712) 279-6748.

SCHECHTMAN, Ronald H. *(Chief Judge, Iowa District Court Second Judicial District)* Appointed by Governor Terry E. Branstad June 29, 1987 to term beginning Aug 14, 1987. Retained by election 1988, 1994 and 2000. Current term expires Dec 31, 2006. Born Greeley Iowa Feb 17, 1933. Roman Catholic. Educated at University of Iowa B.Sc. 1954 J.D. 1958. Note and Comment Writer Iowa Law Review 1956-58. Member Phi Delta Phi. Admitted to practice Iowa 1958. In legal practice Carroll 1958-87.

Member Iowa Judges Association, Carroll County and Iowa State Bar Associations. Participant General Jurisdiction The National Judicial College Summer 1988. Mayor City of Carroll 1976-80. Vice Chairperson Iowa Department of Economic Development 1980-87 and Iowa Jobs Commission 1982-86. Enjoys fishing, writing, reading, history and mushrooming.

Mailing address: P.O. Box 867, Carroll 51401.

Office: Carroll County Courthouse, Sixth and Main Streets, Carroll 51401.

Telephone: (712) 792-4350.

SCHOENTHALER, David E. *(District Judge, Iowa District Court Seventh Judicial District)* Appointed by Governor Terry E. Branstad to term beginning Nov 1, 1992. Retained by election Nov 1994 and 2000. Current term expires Dec 31, 2006. Born Maquoketa Iowa Nov 29, 1940. Educated at University of Iowa B.A. 1962 J.D. with honors 1964. Board of Editors Iowa Law Review 1963-64. Admitted to practice Iowa 1964. In legal practice Maquoketa 1964-92.

Office: Scott County Courthouse, 416 West Fourth Street, Davenport 52801.

Telephone: (563) 326-8709.

Fax: (563) 326-8218

SCIESZINSKI, Annette J. *(District Judge, Iowa District Court Eighth Judicial District)* Appointed by Governor Terry E. Branstad.

Office: Monroe County Courthouse, 10 Benton Avenue East, Albia 52531.

Telephone: (641) 932-7160.

SCOLES, Jon S. *(District Judge, Iowa District Court Second Judicial District)* Appointed by governor. Retained by election. Born Charles City Iowa 1951. Educated at University of Northern Iowa B.A. 1973 and University of Iowa J.D. 1979. Admitted to practice Iowa 1979.

Member Iowa Defense Counsel Association, Cerro Gordo County, Iowa State and American Bar Associations.

Office: Cerro Gordo County Courthouse, 220 North Washington, Mason City 50401.

Telephone: (641) 421-3099.

SCOTT, James D. *(District Judge, Iowa District Court Third Judicial District)* Appointed by governor.

Mailing address: P.O. Box 47, Orange City 51041.

Office: Sioux County Courthouse, Orange City 51041.

Telephone: (712) 737-2246.

SHIELDS, Thomas J. *(Magistrate Judge, United States District Court Southern District of Iowa)* Former part-time Magistrate Judge. Appointed full-time Magistrate Judge by U.S. District Court judges June 9, 2000. Current term expires June 9, 2008. Educated at College of William & Mary B.A. 1969 and Indiana University J.D. 1972. Law Clerk to Hon. William C. Stuart, U.S. District Court Southern District of Iowa 1972-74. Admitted to practice Indiana 1972, Iowa 1973, U.S. Tax Court 1973, U.S. Courts of Appeals Eighth 1980 and Seventh 1992 Circuits and U.S. Supreme Court 1995.

Fellow American College of Trial Lawyers. Member Iowa Academy of Trial Lawyers, American Board of Trial Advocates, Indiana State and Iowa State Bar Associations.

Office: 215 Federal Building, 131 East Fourth Street, Davenport 52801-1516.

Telephone: (563) 322-6692.

Fax: (563) 324-7145

SIVRIGHT, David H., Jr. *(District Judge, Iowa District Court Seventh Judicial District)* Appointed by Governor Terry E. Branstad to term beginning March 15, 1992. Retained by election 1994 and 2000. Current term expires Dec 31, 2006. Born Gary Indiana Nov 22, 1943. Protestant. Educated at Kansas University B.A. 1966 J.D. 1969. Admitted to practice Iowa 1969, U.S. District Courts Southern 1969 and Northern 1974 Districts of Iowa and U.S. Court of Appeals Eighth Circuit 1977. In legal practice Clinton 1969-92.

Instructor Clinton Citizen's Police Academy since 1995. Member Iowa Judges Association (Board of Directors since 1999), Iowa State and American (Judicial Division) Bar Associations. Attended The National Judicial College.

Mailing address: P.O. Box 2957, Clinton 52732.

Office: Clinton County Courthouse, 612 North Second Street, Clinton 52732.

Telephone: (563) 243-6210.

E-mail address: dsivrigh@jb.state.ia.us

SMITH, Charles L., III *(Chief Judge, Iowa District Court Fourth Judicial District)* Appointed by Governor Terry E. Branstad to term beginning Jan 2, 1990. Retained by election Nov 4, 1992 and 1998. Current term expires Dec 31, 2004. Born Omaha Nebraska Dec 20, 1945. Educated at Creighton University J.D. 1970. Member Phi Alpha Delta. Admitted to practice Nebraska 1970, Iowa 1971 and U.S. District Courts District of Nebraska 1970 and Southern District of Iowa 1971. In legal practice Missouri Valley Iowa 1970-89.

County Attorney Harrison County 1973-74. Member Iowa Judges Association and Iowa State Bar Association.

Mailing address: P.O. Box 476, Council Bluffs 51502.

Office: 227 South Sixth Street, Council Bluffs 51501.

Telephone: (712) 328-5759.

SMITH, Joe E. *(District Associate Judge, Iowa District Court Fifth Judicial District)* Appointed to term beginning Sept 17, 1999. Retained by election Nov 7, 2000, current term expires Dec 31, 2004. Born Butte Montana Dec 4, 1943. Episcopalian. Educated at University of Colorado B.S. 1967, University of Texas, El Paso M.A., University of Missouri-Columbia Ph.D. 1977 and Drake University J.D. 1989. Admitted to practice Iowa 1989.

Attorney II, Iowa Employment Appeal Board Office 1989-95. Public Defender Des Moines Adult Office 1995-99. Member Polk County and Iowa State (Legal Aid Committee since 1995) Bar Associations. Instructor Small Claims CLE Polk County Bar Association Nov 1999. Recipient Pro Bono Award from Iowa State Bar Association July 1998. Named Outstanding Volunteer by Polk County Bar Association 1998. Board Member Legal Aid Society of Polk County 1996-99. Interested in historic preservation, Russian history and classical music.

Office: 500 Mulberry Street, Des Moines 50309.
Telephone: (515) 286-3907.
Fax: (515) 286-3858
E-mail address: joe.smith@j.b.state.ia.us

SMITH, Mark J. *(District Judge, Iowa District Court Seventh Judicial District)* Appointed by Governor Terry E. Branstad.

Office: Scott County Courthouse, 416 West Fourth Street, Davenport 52801.
Telephone: (563) 326-8605.

SOKOLOVSKE, Mary Jane *(District Judge, Iowa District Court Third Judicial District)* Former District Associate Judge. Appointed District Judge by governor.

Office: Woodbury County Courthouse, 620 Douglas Street, Sioux City 51101.
Telephone: (712) 279-6608.

SOSALLA, Robert E. *(District Associate Judge, Iowa District Court Sixth Judicial District)* Appointed to term beginning March 15, 1982. Retained by election. Born Carrington North Dakota Sept 25, 1947. Catholic. Educated at Wayne State College B.A. with honors 1969 and University of Iowa J.D. 1972. Admitted to practice Iowa 1972. Began legal practice Cedar Rapids 1972.

Member Linn County and Iowa State Bar Associations.

Mailing address: P.O. Box 1468, Cedar Rapids 52406.
Office: Linn County Courthouse, Third Avenue Bridge, Cedar Rapids 52406.
Telephone: (319) 398-3920.

SPANDE, Jane Frances *(District Associate Judge, Iowa District Court Sixth Judicial District)* Appointed to term beginning Aug 1985. Retained by election Nov 1986, Nov 1990, Nov 1994, 1998 and 2002. Current term expires Dec 31, 2006. Born Minnesota Aug 21, 1950. Educated at Mankato State University B.S. magna cum laude 1972 and University of Iowa J.D. with honors 1977. Admitted to practice Iowa 1977. In legal practice Cedar Rapids 1979-85.

Assistant County Attorney Linn County Aug 1977 to Oct 1979 (full time) and Oct 1979 to Aug 1985 (part time). Member Iowa Judges Association. High School Social Studies Teacher and Librarian 1972-75. Enjoys reading, gardening, needlepoint and cooking.

Mailing address: P.O. Box 1468, Cedar Rapids 52406.
Office: Linn County Courthouse, Third Avenue Bridge, Cedar Rapids 52406.
Telephone: (319) 398-3920.

STASKAL, Douglas F. *(District Judge, Iowa District Court Fifth Judicial District)* Former District Associate Judge. Appointed District Judge by Governor Tom Vilsack.

Office: 212 Polk County Courthouse, 500 Mulberry Street, Des Moines 50309.
Telephone: (515) 286-3646.

STEWART, Michael R. *(District Associate Judge, Iowa District Court Eighth Judicial District)* Appointed.

Office: Poweshiek County Courthouse, 302 East Main Street, Montezuma 50171.
Telephone: (641) 623-5463.

STIGLER, George L. *(District Judge, Iowa District Court First Judicial District)* Former District Associate Judge, appointed to term beginning March 27, 1978. Appointed District Judge by Governor Terry E. Branstad to term beginning Feb 1, 1985. Retained by election Nov 1986, 1992 and 1998. Current term expires Dec 31, 2004. Born Durant Mississippi July 8, 1950. Methodist. Educated at University of Northern Iowa B.A. 1972 and University of Iowa J.D. 1975. Admitted to practice Iowa 1975, U.S. District Courts Northern 1980 and Southern 1980 Districts of Iowa and U.S. Court of Appeals Eighth Circuit 1980. Began legal practice Waterloo 1975.

Former Assistant County Attorney. Instructor Hawkeye Institute of Technology 1977-78. Member Black Hawk County, Iowa State and American Bar Associations.

Office: Black Hawk County Courthouse, 316 East Fifth Street, Waterloo 50703.
Telephone: (319) 291-2489.

STOVALL, Dennis J. *(District Judge, Iowa District Court Fifth Judicial District)* Appointed by Governor Terry E. Branstad.

Office: 212 Polk County Courthouse, 500 Mulberry Street, Des Moines 50309.
Telephone: (515) 286-3905.

STREIT, Michael J. *(Justice, Iowa Supreme Court)* Appointed by Governor Tom Vilsack. Born Sheldon Iowa. Educated at University of Iowa B.A. 1972 and University of San Diego School of Law J.D. 1975. In legal practice Chariton 1975-83. District Judge, Iowa District Court Fifth Judicial District 1983-96. Former Judge, Iowa Court of Appeals, appointed by Governor Terry E. Branstad to term beginning 1996.

Assistant County Attorney and Attorney Lucas County. Member Supreme Court Education Advisory Committee, Judges Association Education Committee, Iowa Judicial Institute, Supreme Court Judicial Technology Committee, Bencher and Blackstone Inn of Court.

Office: Judicial Branch Building, 1111 East Court Avenue, Des Moines 50319.
Telephone: (515) 281-5174.

SWANSON, Joel E. *(District Judge, Iowa District Court Second Judicial District)* Appointed by governor.
Mailing address: P.O. Box 867, Carroll 51401.
Office: Carroll County Courthouse, Sixth and Main Streets, Carroll 51401.
Telephone: (712) 464-3175.

TABOR, Nancy S. *(District Judge, Iowa District Court Seventh Judicial District)* Associate Juvenile Judge 1994-99. Appointed District Judge by Governor Tom Vilsack to term beginning Sept 3, 1999. Retained by election Nov 2000, current term expires Dec 31, 2006. Born Morristown New Jersey Aug 5, 1958. United Methodist. Educated at William Paterson College of New Jersey B.S. 1982 and University of Wyoming College of Law J.D. 1986. Member Phi Alpha Delta. Admitted to practice Wyoming 1986, U.S. District Court District of Wyoming 1986, U.S. Court of Appeals Tenth Circuit 1987, Iowa 1990 and U.S. Supreme Court 1991. In legal practice Douglas Wyoming 1987-89 and Maquoketa Iowa 1992-99.
Assistant County Attorney Clinton County Iowa 1989-92. Member Iowa Judges Association, National Association of Women Judges, Wyoming State Bar and Iowa State Bar Association (Iowa Select Committee on Juvenile Justice Task Force 1995-99). Presenter on concurrent jurisdiction between juvenile and district court Iowa Juvenile Court Conference Sept 2000. Member General Federation of Woman's Club. Enjoys reading and puppet ministry.
Office: Jackson County Courthouse, 201 West Platt Street, Maquoketa 52060.
Telephone: (563) 652-4946.
E-mail address: Nancy.Tabor@jb.state.ia.us

TERNUS, Marsha K. *(Justice, Iowa Supreme Court)* Appointed by Governor Terry E. Branstad 1993. Retained by election 1994 and 2002. Current term expires Dec 31, 2010. Born Vinton Iowa. Educated at University of Iowa B.A. with honors and high distinction 1972 and Drake University Law School J.D. with honors 1977. Member Phi Beta Kappa and Order of the Coif. Editor-in-Chief Drake University Law Review. In legal practice Des Moines.
Member Iowa Supreme Court Commission on Planning for the 21st Century, MultiState Performance Test Policy Committee National Conference of Bar Examiners, Iowa Jury Instructions Committee, Polk County (Past President) and Iowa State (Board of Governors) Bar Associations. Board of Directors Polk County Legal Aid Society. President Board of Counselors Drake University Law School.
Office: Judicial Branch Building, 1111 East Court Avenue, Des Moines 50319.
Telephone: (515) 281-3953.

THOMAS, William L. *(District Judge, Iowa District Court Sixth Judicial District)* Appointed by governor.
Mailing address: P.O. Box 1468, Cedar Rapids 52406.
Office: Linn County Courthouse, Third Avenue Bridge, Cedar Rapids 52406.
Telephone: (319) 398-3920.

TIMKO, Mary L. *(Associate Juvenile Judge, Iowa District Court Third Judicial District)* Appointed by the Chief Judge and serves at the pleasure of the judges.
Mailing address: P.O. Box 1186, Storm Lake 50588.
Office: Buena Vista County Courthouse, 215 East Fifth Street, Storm Lake 50588.
Telephone: (712) 749-2568.

VAITHESWARAN, Anuradha *(Judge, Iowa Court of Appeals)* Appointed by governor 1999. Born Hyderabad, India. Educated at Grinnell College 1980 and University of Iowa M.A. 1984 J.D. 1984. Law Clerk to Hon. Charles R. Wolle, Iowa Supreme Court.
Attorney Legal Services Corporation of Iowa and Iowa Attorney General's Office. Member C. Edwin Moore Inns of Court, Polk County and Iowa State Bar Associations. Member Polk County Women's Association.
Office: Judicial Branch Building, 1111 East Court Avenue, Des Moines 50319.
Telephone: (515) 281-5221.

VANMAREL, Steven P. *(District Associate Judge, Iowa District Court Second Judicial District)* Appointed.
Mailing address: P.O. Box 408, Nevada 50201.
Office: Story County Courthouse, 900 Sixth Street, Nevada 50201.
Telephone: (515) 382-6581.

VAN ZEE, Arlen J. *(District Associate Judge, Iowa District Court Seventh Judicial District)* Full-time Judicial Magistrate Jan 1, 1975 to Dec 31, 1980. Assumed office as District Associate Judge Jan 1, 1981. Retained by election. Born Oskaloosa Iowa June 1, 1945. Religious affiliation: Christian Reformed. Educated at Central College magna cum laude in Political Science 1970 and University of Iowa J.D. with honors 1973. Admitted to practice Iowa 1973. Began legal practice Clinton 1973.
Member Iowa Judges Association and Clinton County Bar Association.
Mailing address: P.O. Box 2957, Clinton 52733-2957.
Office: Clinton County Courthouse, 612 North Second Street, Clinton 52732.
Telephone: (563) 243-6210.

VIETOR, Harold D. *(Senior Judge, United States District Court Southern District of Iowa)* Appointed for life by President Jimmy Carter to term beginning May 21, 1979. Former Chief Judge. Assumed Senior status, serves by assignment. Born Parkersburg Iowa Dec 29, 1931. Educated at University of Iowa B.A. 1955 J.D. 1958. Law Clerk to Hon. Martin VanOosterhout, U.S. Court of Appeals 1958-59. Member Order of the Coif. Judge, Iowa District Court Sixth Judicial District 1965-79.
Member Federal Judges Association and Iowa State Bar Association.
Office: U.S. Courthouse, 123 East Walnut Street, Des Moines 50309-2038.
Telephone: (515) 284-6237.

VOGEL, Gayle Nelson *(Judge, Iowa Court of Appeals)* Appointed by Governor Terry E. Branstad to term beginning 1996. Retained by election. Born Rockford Illinois. Educated at Rockford College B.A. cum laude 1971 and Drake University Law School J.D. 1983. Member Order of the Coif. In legal practice Knoxville.
Member Iowa Judges Association (Ethics Committee, Grievance Commission 1988-96), C. Edwin Moore Inn of Court, Marion County, District 5A, Iowa State and

VOGEL, GAYLE NELSON—*Continued*
American Bar Associations. Named Business Woman of the Year by Chamber of Commerce 1994.
Office: Judicial Branch Building, 1111 East Court Avenue, Des Moines 50319.
Telephone: (515) 281-5221.

VOGEL, Richard J. *(District Judge, Iowa District Court Eighth Judicial District)* Appointed by Governor Robert D. Ray June 1978. Retained by election 1992 and 1998. Current term expires Dec 31, 2004. Born Grinnell Iowa Sept 30, 1940. Catholic. Educated at St. Ambrose College (now St. Ambrose College and Marycrest College) B.A. 1962 and University of Iowa LL.B. 1965. Admitted to practice Iowa 1965 and U.S. District Court Southern District of Iowa 1966. Began legal practice Grinnell 1965.
Office: Poweshiek County Courthouse, 302 East Main, Montezuma 50171.
Telephone: (641) 623-5463.

WALSH, Michael S. *(Chief Judge, Iowa District Court Third Judicial District)* Appointed District Judge by governor.
Office: Woodbury County Courthouse, 620 Douglas Street, Sioux City 51101.
Telephone: (712) 279-6608.

WALTERS, Ross A. *(Magistrate Judge, United States District Court Southern District of Iowa)* Appointed by U.S. District Court judges. Born Cleveland Ohio Dec 29, 1949. Educated at Pennsylvania State University B.A. with honors 1971 and University of Iowa J.D. with honors 1977. Project Editor Iowa Law Review. Law Clerk to Hon. William C. Hanson, U.S. District Courts Northern and Southern Districts of Iowa 1977-79. Admitted to practice Iowa 1977, U.S. District Courts Northern and Southern Districts of Iowa and U.S. Court of Appeals Eighth Circuit. In legal practice Des Moines 1979-90. Former District Judge, Iowa District Court Fifth Judicial District, appointed by Governor Terry E. Branstad to term beginning March 9, 1990.
Member Iowa Judges Association and Iowa State Bar Association. Lieutenant USNR 1971-74.
Office: 407 U.S. Courthouse, 123 East Walnut Street, Des Moines 50309.
Telephone: (515) 284-6217.

WEAVER, James A. *(District Associate Judge, Iowa District Court Seventh Judicial District)* Appointed to term beginning May 1, 1981. Retained by election. Born Sterling Illinois June 21, 1953. Protestant. Educated at Augustana College B.A. 1976 and University of Iowa J.D. 1978. Admitted to practice Iowa 1979. In legal practice Muscatine 1980-81.
Director Muscatine Legal Services 1979-80. Assistant Muscatine County Attorney 1980-81. Member Iowa Judges Association and Iowa State Bar Association.
Office: 401 East Third Street, Muscatine 52761-4134.
Telephone: (563) 263-4424.
Fax: (563) 262-4168
E-mail address: james.a.weaver@jb.state.ia.us

WENELL, Gary E. *(District Judge, Iowa District Court Third Judicial District)* Appointed by governor.
Office: Woodbury County Courthouse, 620 Douglas Street, Sioux City 51101.
Telephone: (712) 279-6608.

WILKE, Kurt L. *(District Judge, Iowa District Court Second Judicial District)* Appointed by governor.
Office: Webster County Courthouse, 701 Central Avenue, Fort Dodge 50501.
Telephone: (515) 573-2191.

WILSON, Daniel P. *(District Judge, Iowa District Court Eighth Judicial District)* Appointed by Governor Terry E. Branstad.
Mailing address: P.O. Box 400, Centerville 52544.
Office: Appanoose County Courthouse, Centerville 52544.
Telephone: (641) 856-6101.

WILSON, Robert D. *(District Judge, Iowa District Court Fifth Judicial District)* Appointed by Governor Terry E. Branstad.
Office: 212 Polk County Courthouse, 500 Mulberry Street, Des Moines 50309.
Telephone: (515) 286-3391.

WILSON, Terry L. *(District Associate Judge, Iowa District Court Fifth Judicial District)* Appointed.
Mailing address: P.O. Box 497, Knoxville 50138.
Office: Marion County Courthouse, Knoxville 50138.
Telephone: (641) 828-2207.

WOLLE, Charles R. *(Senior Judge, United States District Court Southern District of Iowa)* Appointed for life by President Ronald Reagan to term beginning 1987. Former Chief Judge. Assumed Senior status Oct 16, 2001, serves by assignment. Born Sioux City Iowa Oct 16, 1935. Methodist. Educated at Harvard College A.B. 1959 and Iowa College of Law J.D. with honors 1961. Notes Editor Iowa Law Review 1960-61. Member Phi Delta Phi. Admitted to practice Iowa 1961 and U.S. District Courts Northern 1961 and Southern 1961 Districts of Iowa. Began legal practice Sioux City 1961. Judge, Iowa District Court Third Judicial District 1981-83. Justice, Iowa Supreme Court 1983-87.
Fellow American College of Trial Lawyers 1979. Member Iowa State and American Bar Associations. Instructor The National Judicial College since 1983. Sergeant E-5 USAR 1961-67. Board of Directors Sioux City Symphony and Sioux City Chamber of Commerce. Enjoys running, tennis, literature, music and travel.
Mailing address: P.O. Box 545, Genoa, Nevada 89411-0545.
Office: 103 U.S. Courthouse, 123 East Walnut Street, Des Moines 50309-2039.
Telephone: (515) 284-6289.

ZAGER, Bruce B. *(District Judge, Iowa District Court First Judicial District)* Appointed by Governor Tom Vilsack.
Office: Black Hawk County Courthouse, 316 East Fifth Street, Waterloo 50703.
Telephone: (319) 833-3312.

ZIMMER, Van D. *(Judge, Iowa Court of Appeals)* Appointed by governor to term beginning Jan 4, 1999. Educated at University of Iowa B.A. 1969 J.D. 1972. District Judge, Iowa District Court Sixth Judicial District 1985-99.
Assistant County Attorney Linn County. Prosecutor Iowa Attorney General's Office. Assistant U.S. Attorney Northern District of Iowa. Chair Courts and Community Committee Iowa Judges Association. Faculty Iowa An-

ZIMMER, VAN D.—*Continued*

nual New Judge Orientation Program since 1992. U.S. Army 1972-73.

Office: Judicial Branch Building, 1111 East Court Avenue, Des Moines 50319.

Telephone: (515) 281-5223.

ZOSS, Paul A. *(Magistrate Judge, United States District Court Northern District of Iowa)* Appointed by U.S. District Court judges.

Office: 216 U.S. Courthouse, 320 Sixth Street, Sioux City 51101.

Telephone: (712) 233-3869.

KANSAS

Capital TOPEKA

UNITED STATES DISTRICT COURT DISTRICT OF KANSAS

The court sits at Dodge City, Fort Scott, Hutchinson, Kansas City, Lawrence, Leavenworth, Salina, Topeka and Wichita. For descriptive information refer to the United States Courts section.

Chief Judge
John W. Lungstrum

Judges
Monti L. Belot
Kathryn H. Vratil
John Thomas Marten
Carlos Murguia
Julie A. Robinson

Senior Judges
Wesley E. Brown
Richard Dean Rogers
Sam A. Crow
G. Thomas Van Bebber

Clerk
Ralph L. DeLoach
259 U.S. Courthouse
500 State Avenue
Kansas City, Kansas 66101-2430
(913) 551-5734

UNITED STATES MAGISTRATE JUDGES OF KANSAS

Karen M. Humphreys
Donald W. Bostwick
David J. Waxse
James P. O'Hara
K. Gary Sebelius

Recalled Magistrate Judges
John Thomas Reid
Gerald L. Rushfelt

UNITED STATES BANKRUPTCY COURT OF KANSAS

Chief Judge
Robert E. Nugent

Judges
James A. Pusateri
John T. Flannagan
Janice Miller Karlin

Bankruptcy Clerk
Fred W. Jamison
167 U.S. Courthouse
401 North Market Street
Witchita, Kansas 67202
(316) 269-6486

KANSAS SUPREME COURT

The Supreme Court is Kansas' court of last resort. The court consists of a chief justice and six justices appointed by the governor from nominations submitted by a Supreme Court nominating commission. Newly appointed justices serve initial one-year terms and then stand for retention for six-year terms. The most senior justice in continuous terms of service serves as chief justice. Retirement is mandatory at age seventy; however, justices who turn seventy while in office may finish their current term. Retired justices may serve by assignment of the court.

The court has original jurisdiction in proceedings in quo warranto, mandamus and habeas corpus and such jurisdiction as provided by law. Direct appeal to the court, rather than to the Court of Appeals, is required in cases involving Class A felonies or when a statute is declared unconstitutional. Decisions of the Court of Appeals may be reviewed at the discretion of the court. The court exercises exclusive jurisdiction over admission to the bar and the discipline of attorneys and judges and also exercises general administrative authority over all lower courts.

The court sits en banc at Topeka and usually recesses in August.

Chief Justice
Kay McFarland

Justices

Donald L. Allegrucci	Robert E. Davis
Lawton R. Nuss	Marla J. Luckert
Robert Gernon	vacancy

Clerk
Carol G. Green
374 Kansas Judicial Center
301 Southwest Tenth Avenue
Topeka, Kansas 66612
(785) 296-3229

Judicial Administrator
Howard Schwartz
Kansas Judicial Center
301 Southwest Tenth Avenue
Topeka, Kansas 66612-1507
(785) 296-4873

KANSAS COURT OF APPEALS

The Court of Appeals is the intermediate appellate court of Kansas. The court consists of a chief judge and ten judges appointed by the governor from nominations submitted by a Supreme Court nominating commission. Judges serve initial one-year terms and then stand for retention for four-year terms. The chief judge is designated by and serves at the pleasure of the Supreme Court. Retirement is mandatory at age seventy; however,

KANSAS COURT OF APPEALS—*Continued*

judges who turn seventy while in office may finish their current term. Retired judges may serve by assignment of the Supreme Court.

The court has statewide jurisdiction over appeals in civil and criminal matters arising in the District Court, except where the Supreme Court has exclusive jurisdiction. The court may review administrative actions as provided by law and may issue writs necessary to the exercise of proper jurisdiction. Appeals to the Supreme Court are a matter of right when a constitutional issue arises for the first time as a result of a Court of Appeals decision.

The court may sit in panels of three judges at the discretion of the chief judge. The court sits at Topeka or anywhere in the state as required.

Chief Judge
Gary W. Rulon

Judges

Jerry G. Elliott	Robert J. Lewis, Jr.
George Joseph Pierron, Jr.	Henry W. Green, Jr.
David S. Knudson	Christel E. Marquardt
Lee A. Johnson	Carol A. Beier
Richard Greene	Tom Malone

KANSAS DISTRICT COURT

The District Court is Kansas' court of general jurisdiction. The court is served by judges and magistrate judges. In seventeen of the thirty-one judicial districts, judges and magistrate judges are initially appointed by the governor from names submitted by district nominating commissions for one-year terms and then stand for retention for four-year terms. In the thirteenth, fourteenth, fifteenth, sixteenth, seventeenth, eighteenth, nineteenth, twentieth, twenty-second, twenty-third, twenty-fourth, twenty-sixth, twenty-seventh and twenty-ninth judicial districts, judges are elected in partisan elections for four-year terms. The term "administrative judge" was changed to "chief judge" effective July 1, 1999. Chief judges are appointed by the Supreme Court and serve two-year terms. Retirement is mandatory at age seventy; however, judges who turn seventy while in office may finish their current term. Retired judges may serve by assignment of the Supreme Court.

The court has original jurisdiction in civil, criminal, juvenile and probate matters. District judges possess the full original jurisdiction of the court and have appellate jurisdiction over cases arising in Municipal Courts and from cases heard by magistrate judges. They may also review administrative actions as provided by law. Magistrate judges have criminal jurisdiction over misdemeanors and may conduct preliminary felony examinations. Their civil jurisdiction is concurrent with that of district judges, with the following exceptions: they do not have jurisdiction over civil matters in any action, other than an action seeking judgement for an unsecured debt not sounding in tort and arising out of a contract for the provision of goods, services, or money, in which the amount of controversy, exclusive of interest and costs, exceeds $10,000; over actions against the state or any officers of the state; over certain actions regarding real estate; over actions for divorce, separate maintenance or custody of minor children; over writs of habeas corpus, mandamus and quo warranto; and over receiverships, declaratory judgments, injunctions or class actions.

The court generally sits at the county seats within each judicial district, though other locations may be designated by the chief judge of each district with approval of the Supreme Court.

FIRST JUDICIAL DISTRICT includes Atchison and Leavenworth counties. The court sits at Atchison and Leavenworth.

Chief Judge
David J. King

Judges
Gunnar A. Sundby
Martin J. Asher
Frederick N. Stewart
Philip C. Lacey
Robert J. Bednar

SECOND JUDICIAL DISTRICT includes Jackson, Jefferson, Pottawatomie and Wabaunsee counties. The court sits at Holton, Oskaloosa, Westmoreland and Alma.

Chief Judge
Tracy D. Klinginsmith

Judge
Gary L. Nafziger

Magistrate Judges
Dennis Lee Reiling
Steven M. Roth
Blaine A. Carter

THIRD JUDICIAL DISTRICT includes Shawnee County. The court sits at Topeka.

Chief Judge
Richard D. Anderson

Judges

Jan W. Leuenberger	Jean M. Schmidt
Eric S. Rosen	James M. Macnish, Jr.
Terry L. Bullock	Franklin R. Theis
Frank Yeoman, Jr.	Charles Andrews, Jr.
Daniel L. Mitchell	Matthew J. Dowd
David E. Bruns	Thomas R. Conklin
Nancy E. Parrish	

FOURTH JUDICIAL DISTRICT includes Anderson, Coffey, Franklin and Osage counties. The court sits at Garnett, Burlington, Ottawa and Lyndon.

Chief Judge
James J. Smith

Judges
Phillip M. Fromme
Thomas H. Sachse

Magistrate Judges
Jon Stephen Jones
Edwin R. Smith

FIFTH JUDICIAL DISTRICT includes Chase and Lyon counties. The court sits at Cottonwood Falls and Emporia.

Chief Judge
Merlin G. Wheeler

KANSAS DISTRICT COURT—*Continued*

Judges
John O. Sanderson
W. Lee Fowler

Magistrate Judge
John Riggs Conklin

SIXTH JUDICIAL DISTRICT includes Bourbon, Linn and Miami counties. The court sits at Fort Scott, Mound City and Paola.

Chief Judge
Stephen D. Hill

Judges
Richard M. Smith
Gerald W. Hart

Magistrate Judge
Rebecca Stephan

SEVENTH JUDICIAL DISTRICT includes Douglas County. The court sits at Lawrence.

Chief Judge
Robert W. Fairchild

Judges
Jack A. Murphy
Jean F. Shepherd
Michael J. Malone
Paula B. Martin

EIGHTH JUDICIAL DISTRICT includes Dickinson, Geary, Marion and Morris counties. The court sits at Abilene, Junction City, Marion and Council Grove.

Chief Judge
Michael F. Powers

Judges
Benjamin J. Sexton
Larry E. Bengtson
Steven L. Hornbaker
David R. Platt

Magistrate Judges
John E. Barker
Thomas H. Ball

NINTH JUDICIAL DISTRICT includes Harvey and McPherson counties. The court sits at Newton and McPherson.

Chief Judge
Richard B. Walker

Judges
Marty Joe Dickinson
Carl B. Anderson, Jr.

TENTH JUDICIAL DISTRICT includes Johnson County. The court sits at Olathe.

Chief Judge
Patrick D. McAnany

Judges
Peter V. Ruddick
Thomas M. Sutherland
Stephen R. Tatum
Janice D. Russell
Allen R. Slater
James F. Vano
Gerald T. Elliott
James Franklin Davis
Steve Leben
Larry McClain
Thomas H. Bornholdt
Brenda Cameron
John Anderson, III
John P. Bennett
Thomas E. Foster
Lawrence E. Sheppard
William O. Isenhour, Jr.

Magistrate Judges
Michael H. Farley
Linda S. Trigg
James E. Phelan

ELEVENTH JUDICIAL DISTRICT includes Cherokee, Crawford and Labette counties. The court sits at Columbus, Girard, Pittsburg, Oswego and Parsons.

Chief Judge
John C. Gariglietti

Judges
A. J. Wachter
David F. Brewster
Robert J. Fleming
Donald R. Noland
Daniel L. Brewster

Magistrate Judge
Bill W. Lyerla

TWELFTH JUDICIAL DISTRICT includes Cloud, Jewell, Lincoln, Mitchell, Republic and Washington counties. The court sits at Concordia, Mankato, Lincoln, Beloit, Belleville and Washington.

Chief Judge
Thomas M. Tuggle

Magistrate Judges
Kathryn Carter
Brian Grace
John Eyer
John L. Bingham
Bonnie J. Wilson
Terry N. Taylor

THIRTEENTH JUDICIAL DISTRICT includes Butler, Elk and Greenwood counties. The court sits at El Dorado, Howard and Eureka.

Chief Judge
John E. Sanders

Judges
Charles M. Hart
Dale L. Pohl
Mike Ward

Magistrate Judges
Martina M. Hubbell
Rebecca Lindamood

FOURTEENTH JUDICIAL DISTRICT includes Chautauqua and Montgomery counties. The court sits at Sedan, Independence and Coffeyville.

Chief Judge
Judd Dent

Judges
Roger Gossard
Russell D. Canaday

Magistrate Judge
David A. Casement

FIFTEENTH JUDICIAL DISTRICT includes Cheyenne, Logan, Rawlins, Sheridan, Sherman, Thomas and Wallace counties. The court sits at St. Francis, Oakley, Atwood, Hoxie, Goodland, Colby and Sharon Springs.

KANSAS DISTRICT COURT—*Continued*

Chief Judge
Jack L. Burr

Judge
Glenn D. Schiffner

Magistrate Judges
Tamara L. Zimbelman
John Cahoj
Richard J. Ress
Richard L. Kvasnicka
Steve Unruh
Pat Carroll

SIXTEENTH JUDICIAL DISTRICT includes Clark, Comanche, Ford, Gray, Kiowa and Meade counties. The court sits at Ashland, Coldwater, Dodge City, Cimarron, Greensburg and Meade.

Chief Judge
Daniel L. Love

Judges
E. Leigh Hood
Van Z. Hampton

Magistrate Judges
Michael A. Freelove
Loren L. Cronin
Joey E. Duncan
Ann L. Dixson
Keith Whitney

SEVENTEENTH JUDICIAL DISTRICT includes Decatur, Graham, Norton, Osborne, Phillips and Smith counties. The court sits at Oberlin, Hill City, Norton, Osborne, Phillipsburg and Smith Center.

Chief Judge
William B. Elliott

Magistrate Judges
Barbara Stites
Deb Anderson
Bonnie M. Leidig
John E. Bremer
Jacqueline E. Thornton
Keith Hooper

EIGHTEENTH JUDICIAL DISTRICT includes Sedgwick County. The court sits at Wichita.

Chief Judge
Richard T. Ballinger

Judges
Karl W. Friedel
Daniel T. Brooks
Gregory L. Waller
Ben Burgess
Paul W. Clark
James Fleetwood
Rebecca L. Pilshaw
Terry L. Pullman
Mark Vining
Douglas R. Roth
William Sioux Woolley
Warren Wilbert
vacancy
James L. Burgess
David W. Kennedy
Harold E. Flaigle
Timothy G. Lahey
Michael Corrigan
Eric Yost
David Kaufman
Tony Powell
Clark V. Owens II
Joseph Bribiesca
Timothy H. Henderson
Karen L. Langston

NINETEENTH JUDICIAL DISTRICT includes Cowley County. The court sits at Winfield and Arkansas City.

Chief Judge
J. Michael Smith

Judges
Robert L. Bishop
James T. Pringle, Jr.

TWENTIETH JUDICIAL DISTRICT includes Barton, Ellsworth, Rice, Russell and Stafford counties. The court sits at Great Bend, Ellsworth, Lyons, Russell and St. John.

Chief Judge
Barry A. Bennington

Judges
Hannelore Kitts
J. Michael Keeley

Magistrate Judges
Dale L. Urbanek
Don L. Alvord
Marty K. Clark
Timarie Ann Walters

TWENTY-FIRST JUDICIAL DISTRICT includes Clay and Riley counties. The court sits at Clay Center and Manhattan.

Chief Judge
Paul E. Miller

Judges
Meryl D. Wilson
David L. Stutzman

Magistrate Judge
Paul Wright

TWENTY-SECOND JUDICIAL DISTRICT includes Brown, Doniphan, Marshall and Nemaha counties. The court sits at Hiawatha, Troy, Marysville and Seneca.

Chief Judge
James A. Patton

Judge
John L. Weingart

Magistrate Judges
Roy M. Roper
Gerri Wybo-Vopata
James B. O'Connor

TWENTY-THIRD JUDICIAL DISTRICT includes Ellis, Gove, Rooks and Trego counties. The court sits at Hays, Gove, Stockton and WaKeeney.

Chief Judge
Edward Bouker

Judge
Thomas L. Toepfer

Magistrate Judges
Lois Werner
Douglas Bigge
Richard Flax

TWENTY-FOURTH JUDICIAL DISTRICT includes Edwards, Hodgeman, Lane, Ness, Pawnee and Rush counties. The court sits at Kinsley, Jetmore, Dighton, Ness City, Larned and La Crosse.

Chief Judge
Bruce T. Gatterman

KANSAS DISTRICT COURT—*Continued*

Magistrate Judges

Danny Smith
Shelley Selfridge
David Buster
Philip T. Kyle
James R. Kepple
Leonard A. Mastroni

TWENTY-FIFTH JUDICIAL DISTRICT includes Finney, Greeley, Hamilton, Kearny, Scott and Wichita counties. The court sits at Garden City, Tribune, Syracuse, Lakin, Scott City and Leoti.

Chief Judge
Philip C. Vieux

Judges
Robert J. Frederick
Michael L. Quint
Thomas F. Richardson

Magistrate Judges

C. Ann Wilson
Kevin G. Campbell
Janna K. DeLissa
Rebecca Crotty
Donna L. J. Blake
Jim Collins
Peter J. Ramirez

TWENTY-SIXTH JUDICIAL DISTRICT includes Grant, Haskell, Morton, Seward, Stanton and Stevens counties. The court sits at Ulysses, Sublette, Elkhart, Liberal, Johnson and Hugoton.

Chief Judge
T. Keith Wilson

Judges
Tom R. Smith
Kim R. Schroeder

Magistrate Judges
Margaret L. Alford
Tom B. Webb
Roseanna K. Volden
Mary P. Plummer
Verna Kay McQueen

TWENTY-SEVENTH JUDICIAL DISTRICT includes Reno County. The court sits at Hutchinson.

Chief Judge
Steven R. Becker

Judges
Richard Rome
Timothy J. Chambers
Patricia Macke Dick

TWENTY-EIGHTH JUDICIAL DISTRICT includes Ottawa and Saline counties. The court sits at Minneapolis and Salina.

Chief Judge
Daniel L. Hebert

Judges
Jerome P. Hellmer
George R. Robertson
Danny D. Boyer

Magistrate Judge
Adrian A. Lapka

TWENTY-NINTH JUDICIAL DISTRICT includes Wyandotte County. The court sits at Kansas City.

Chief Judge
Philip L. Sieve

Judges

John J. Bukaty, Jr.
John McNally
J. Dexter Burdette
Robert L. Serra
David P. Mikesic
David W. Boal
Daniel Duncan
Muriel Harris
Thomas L. Boeding
George A. Groneman
Cordell D. Meeks, Jr.
R. Wayne Lampson
Jan A. Way
Michael Grosko
Ernest Johnson

THIRTIETH JUDICIAL DISTRICT includes Barber, Harper, Kingman, Pratt and Sumner counties. The court sits at Medicine Lodge, Anthony, Kingman, Pratt and Wellington.

Chief Judge
Larry T. Solomon

Judges
Robert J. Schmisseur
Thomas H. Graber
R. Scott McQuin

Magistrate Judges
Scott L. McGuire
Richard Befort
James Mathis

THIRTY-FIRST JUDICIAL DISTRICT includes Allen, Neosho, Wilson and Woodson counties. The court sits at Iola, Erie, Chanute, Fredonia and Yates Center.

Chief Judge
C. Fred Lorentz, II

Judges
Daniel D. Creitz
Timothy E. Brazil

Magistrate Judges
Thomas M. Saxton, Jr.
Leo Gensweider

KANSAS MUNICIPAL COURTS

Kansas Municipal Courts are courts of limited jurisdiction. Judges are appointed by the municipality, except in Reno and Sedgwick counties where district judges make the appointments. Cities have the constitutional power to establish municipal courts.

The courts have original jurisdiction over violations of city ordinances. Appeals are heard de novo in the District Court.

Kansas Counties and County Seats

Allen
Iola

Anderson
Garnett

Atchison
Atchison

Barber
Medicine Lodge

Barton
Great Bend

Bourbon
Fort Scott

Brown
Hiawatha

Butler
El Dorado

Chase
Cottonwood Falls

Chautauqua
Sedan

Cherokee
Columbus

Cheyenne
St. Francis

Clark
Ashland

Clay
Clay Center

Cloud
Concordia

Coffey
Burlington

Comanche
Coldwater

Cowley
Winfield

Crawford
Girard

Decatur
Oberlin

Dickinson
Abilene

Doniphan
Troy

Douglas
Lawrence

Edwards
Kinsley

Elk
Howard

Ellis
Hays

Ellsworth
Ellsworth

Finney
Garden City

Ford
Dodge City

Franklin
Ottawa

Geary
Junction City

Gove
Gove

Graham
Hill City

Grant
Ulysses

Gray
Cimarron

Greeley
Tribune

Greenwood
Eureka

Hamilton
Syracuse

Harper
Anthony

Harvey
Newton

Haskell
Sublette

Hodgeman
Jetmore

Jackson
Holton

Jefferson
Oskaloosa

Jewell
Mankato

Johnson
Olathe

Kearny
Lakin

Kingman
Kingman

Kiowa
Greensburg

Labette
Oswego

Lane
Dighton

Leavenworth
Leavenworth

Lincoln
Lincoln

Linn
Mound City

Logan
Oakley

Lyon
Emporia

Marion
Marion

Marshall
Marysville

McPherson
McPherson

Meade
Meade

Miami
Paola

Mitchell
Beloit

Montgomery
Independence

Morris
Council Grove

Morton
Elkhart

Nemaha
Seneca

Neosho
Erie

Ness
Ness City

Norton
Norton

Osage
Lyndon

Osborne
Osborne

Ottawa
Minneapolis

Pawnee
Larned

Phillips
Phillipsburg

Pottawatomie
Westmoreland

Pratt
Pratt

Rawlins
Atwood

Reno
Hutchinson

COUNTIES AND COUNTY SEATS—*Continued*

Republic
Belleville

Rice
Lyons

Riley
Manhattan

Rooks
Stockton

Rush
La Crosse

Russell
Russell

Saline
Salina

Scott
Scott City

Sedgwick
Wichita

Seward
Liberal

Shawnee
Topeka

Sheridan
Hoxie

Sherman
Goodland

Smith
Smith Center

Stafford
St. John

Stanton
Johnson

Stevens
Hugoton

Sumner
Wellington

Thomas
Colby

Trego
WaKeeney

Wabaunsee
Alma

Wallace
Sharon Springs

Washington
Washington

Wichita
Leoti

Wilson
Fredonia

Woodson
Yates Center

Wyandotte
Kansas City

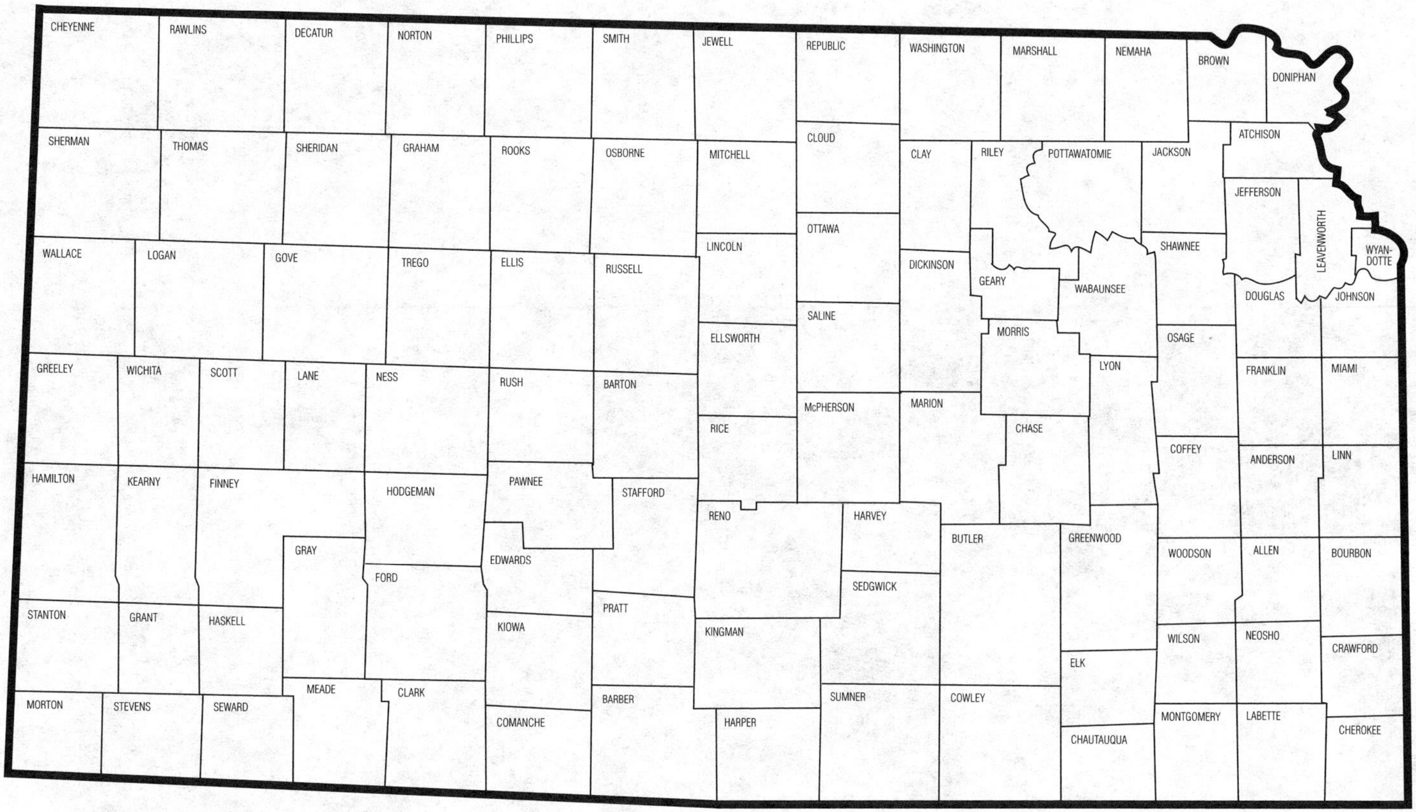
CHEYENNE
RAWLINS
DECATUR
NORTON
PHILLIPS
SMITH
JEWELL
REPUBLIC
WASHINGTON
MARSHALL
NEMAHA
BROWN
DONIPHAN
SHERMAN
THOMAS
SHERIDAN
GRAHAM
ROOKS
OSBORNE
MITCHELL
CLOUD
CLAY
RILEY
POTTAWATOMIE
JACKSON
ATCHISON
JEFFERSON
LEAVENWORTH
WYAN-
DOTTE
WALLACE
LOGAN
GOVE
TREGO
ELLIS
RUSSELL
LINCOLN
OTTAWA
DICKINSON
GEARY
WABAUNSEE
SHAWNEE
DOUGLAS
JOHNSON
SALINE
ELLSWORTH
MORRIS
OSAGE
GREELEY
WICHITA
SCOTT
LANE
NESS
RUSH
BARTON
McPHERSON
MARION
LYON
FRANKLIN
MIAMI
RICE
CHASE
COFFEY
ANDERSON
LINN
HAMILTON
KEARNY
FINNEY
HODGEMAN
PAWNEE
STAFFORD
RENO
HARVEY
BUTLER
GREENWOOD
WOODSON
ALLEN
BOURBON
GRAY
FORD
EDWARDS
SEDGWICK
STANTON
GRANT
HASKELL
KIOWA
PRATT
KINGMAN
WILSON
NEOSHO
CRAWFORD
ELK
MORTON
STEVENS
SEWARD
MEADE
CLARK
COMANCHE
BARBER
HARPER
SUMNER
COWLEY
MONTGOMERY
LABETTE
CHEROKEE
CHAUTAUQUA

UNITED STATES DISTRICT COURT DISTRICT OF KANSAS

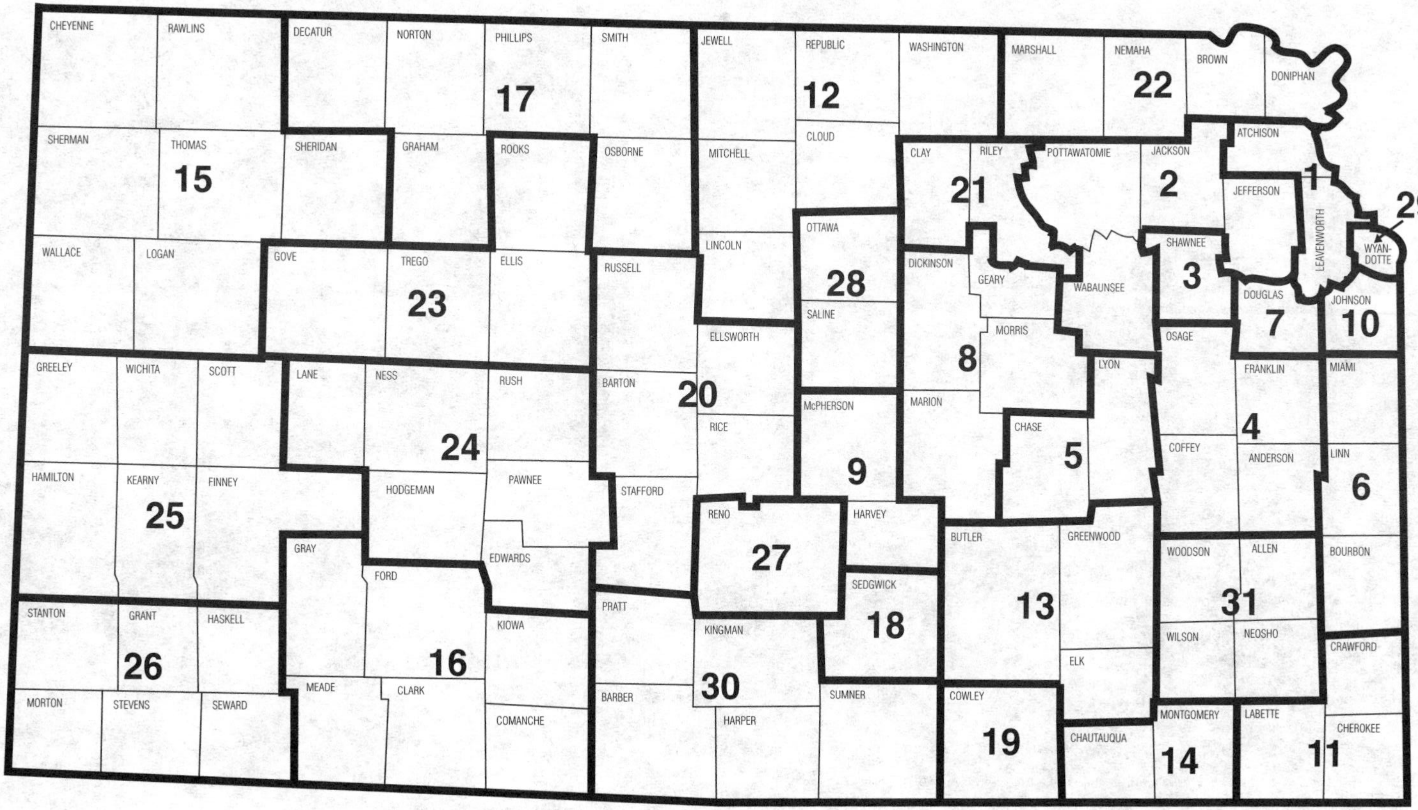
CHEYENNE
RAWLINS
DECATUR
NORTON
PHILLIPS
SMITH
JEWELL
REPUBLIC
WASHINGTON
MARSHALL
NEMAHA
BROWN
DONIPHAN
SHERMAN
THOMAS
SHERIDAN
GRAHAM
ROOKS
OSBORNE
MITCHELL
CLOUD
CLAY
RILEY
POTTAWATOMIE
JACKSON
ATCHISON
JEFFERSON
LEAVENWORTH
WYAN-DOTTE
WALLACE
LOGAN
GOVE
TREGO
ELLIS
RUSSELL
LINCOLN
OTTAWA
DICKINSON
GEARY
WABAUNSEE
SHAWNEE
DOUGLAS
JOHNSON
SALINE
ELLSWORTH
MORRIS
OSAGE
GREELEY
WICHITA
SCOTT
LANE
NESS
RUSH
BARTON
RICE
McPHERSON
MARION
LYON
FRANKLIN
MIAMI
CHASE
COFFEY
ANDERSON
LINN
HAMILTON
KEARNY
FINNEY
HODGEMAN
PAWNEE
STAFFORD
RENO
HARVEY
BUTLER
GREENWOOD
WOODSON
ALLEN
BOURBON
GRAY
FORD
EDWARDS
SEDGWICK
KIOWA
PRATT
KINGMAN
WILSON
NEOSHO
CRAWFORD
STANTON
GRANT
HASKELL
ELK
MORTON
STEVENS
SEWARD
MEADE
CLARK
COMANCHE
BARBER
HARPER
SUMNER
COWLEY
CHAUTAUQUA
MONTGOMERY
LABETTE
CHEROKEE
1
2
3
4
5
6
7
8
9
10
11
12
13
14
15
16
17
18
19
20
21
22
23
24
25
26
27
28
29
30
31

JUDICIAL DISTRICTS OF KANSAS DISTRICT COURT

KANSAS

ALFORD, Margaret L. *(Magistrate Judge, Kansas District Court Twenty-sixth Judicial District)*
Office: Grant County Courthouse, 108 South Glenn, Ulysses 67880.
Telephone: (620) 356-2146.
Fax: (620) 424-1192
E-mail address: windhven@pld.com

ALLEGRUCCI, Donald L. *(Justice, Kansas Supreme Court)* Appointed by Governor John Carlin to term beginning Jan 12, 1987. Retained by election. Born Pittsburg Kansas Sept 19, 1936. Educated at Pittsburg State University A.B. 1959 and Washburn University of Topeka J.D. 1963. Member Phi Alpha Delta. Admitted to practice Kansas 1963 and U.S. District Court District of Kansas 1963. Began legal practice El Dorado 1963. In legal practice Pittsburg 1968. Administrative Judge, Kansas District Court Eleventh Judicial District Feb 10, 1982 to Jan 11, 1987.

Assistant County Attorney 1963-67. State Senator 1976-80. Kansas Public Relations Board 1981-82. Instructor Pittsburg State University 1969-72. Member Crawford County and Kansas Bar Associations. Sergeant USAF 1959-60. Executive Director Mid-Kansas CAP Inc. Member Democratic State Committee 1974-80. Democratic candidate fifth Congressional district 1978. Former Board of Directors YMCA. Past President Heart Association. Former member Coty Humane Commission. Enjoys tennis, hunting, basketball, camping and gardening.
Office: 315 Kansas Judicial Center, 301 S.W. Tenth Avenue, Topeka 66612-1507.
Telephone: (785) 296-3807.

ALVORD, Don L. *(Magistrate Judge, Kansas District Court Twentieth Judicial District)* Elected to term beginning Jan 13, 1981. Reelected 1984, 1988, 1992, 1996 and 2000. Current term expires Jan 2005. Also serves as Municipal Court Judge Hoisington since 1984 and Chase since 1986. Born Kansas Dec 26, 1950. Educated at Washburn University of Topeka B.A. 1972 J.D. 1975. Member Tau Kappa Epsilon and Phi Alpha Delta. Admitted to practice Kansas 1975 and U.S. District Court District of Kansas 1975. In legal practice Lyons and Sterling 1975-81.

Referee Employment Security Division Kansas Department of Human Resources 1978-80. Member Kansas District Magistrate Judges Association, Rice County (Secretary 1976, Vice President 1977, President 1978), Southwest Kansas and Kansas Bar Associations. Democrat. Member Park Commission City of Sterling (Former Chairman) and Rice County Historical Society. Enjoys guitar, camping, hiking, climbing and mountain bike riding.
Office: Rice County Courthouse, Third Floor, 101 West Commercial Street, Lyons 67554-2797.
Telephone: (620) 257-2384.
Fax: (620) 257-3826

ANDERSON, Carl B., Jr. *(Judge, Kansas District Court Ninth Judicial District)* Former Administrative Judge.
Mailing address: P.O. Box 1106, McPherson 67460.
Office: McPherson County Courthouse, McPherson 67460.
Telephone: (620) 241-4474.
Fax: (620) 241-1372
E-mail address: judgea@kscourt.net

ANDERSON, Deb *(Magistrate Judge, Kansas District Court Seventeenth Judicial District)*
Mailing address: P.O. Box 70, Norton 67654.
Office: Norton County Courthouse, Norton 67654.
Telephone: (785) 877-5735.
Fax: (785) 877-5722

ANDERSON, John, III *(Judge, Kansas District Court Tenth Judicial District)*
Office: Johnson County Courthouse, 100 North Kansas Avenue, Olathe 66061-3273.
Telephone: (913) 715-3900.
Fax: (913) 715-3317
E-mail address: John.Anderson@jocoks.com

ANDERSON, Richard D. *(Chief Judge, Kansas District Court Third Judicial District)*
Office: 304 Shawnee County Courthouse, 200 S.E. Seventh Street, Topeka 66603-3922.
Telephone: (785) 233-8200.
Fax: (785) 291-4917
E-mail address: randerson@shawneecourt.org

ANDREWS, Charles, Jr. *(Judge, Kansas District Court Third Judicial District)*
Office: 400 Shawnee County Courthouse, 200 S.E. Seventh Street, Topeka 66603-3922.
Telephone: (785) 233-8200.
Fax: (785) 291-4917
E-mail address: candrews@shawneecourt.org

ASHER, Martin J. *(Judge, Kansas District Court First Judicial District)*
Mailing address: P.O. Box 408, Atchison 66002.
Office: Atchison County Courthouse, Atchison 66002.
Telephone: (913) 367-7400.
Fax: (913) 367-1171
E-mail address: atdo2@ponyexpress.net

BALL, Thomas H. *(Magistrate Judge, Kansas District Court Eighth Judicial District)*
Office: Morris County Courthouse, 501 West Main, Council Grove 66846.
Telephone: (620) 767-6838.
Fax: (620) 767-6488
E-mail address: mrmj2@cablerocket.com

BALLINGER, Richard T. *(Chief Judge, Kansas District Court Eighteenth Judicial District)*
Office: 6-3 Sedgwick County Courthouse, 525 North Main Street, Wichita 67203-3773.
Telephone: (316) 383-7941.
Fax: (316) 383-7560
E-mail address: rballing@dc18.org

BARKER, John E. *(Magistrate Judge, Kansas District Court Eighth Judicial District)*
Mailing address: P.O. Box 127, Abilene 67410.
Office: Dickinson County Courthouse, Abilene 67410.
Telephone: (785) 263-3041.
Fax: (785) 263-4407
E-mail address: mj1@oz-online.net

BECKER, Steven R. *(Chief Judge, Kansas District Court Twenty-seventh Judicial District)* Appointed by Governor John Carlin to term beginning April 1981. Elected Nov 1986. Reelected to subsequent terms. Current term expires Jan 2007. Born Hutchinson Kansas Aug 31, 1947. Educated at Washburn University of Topeka B.B.A. 1972 J.D. 1975. Admitted to practice Kansas 1975. Began legal practice Hutchinson 1975.
Member American Judges Association and Reno County Bar Association. Attended The National Judicial College 1982.
Office: Reno County Courthouse, 206 West First Street, Hutchinson 67501.
Telephone: (620) 694-2953.
Fax: (620) 694-2958
E-mail address: steveb@dist27.reno.ks.us

BEDNAR, Robert J. *(Judge, Kansas District Court First Judicial District)*
Office: 4074 Leavenworth Justice Center, 601 South Third Street, Leavenworth 66048-2868.
Telephone: (913) 684-0715.
Fax: (913) 684-0492
E-mail address: rbednar@lvcoks.com

BEFORT, Richard *(Magistrate Judge, Kansas District Court Thirtieth Judicial District)*
Mailing address: P.O. Box 467, Anthony 67003.
Office: Harper County Courthouse, 201 North Jennings Avenue, Anthony 67003.
Telephone: (620) 842-3721.
Fax: (620) 842-6025

BEIER, Carol A. *(Judge, Kansas Court of Appeals)* Appointed by Governor Bill Graves Dec 1999 to term beginning Feb 22, 2000. Retained by election Nov 2002, current term expires Jan 2008. Born Kansas City Kansas Sept 27, 1958. Episcopalian. Educated at University of Kansas B.S. with honors 1981 J.D. with honors 1985. Rice Scholar. Recipient American Jurisprudence Awards in Torts and Administrative Law. Articles Editor University of Kansas Law Review 1984-85. Law Clerk to Hon. James K. Logan, U.S. Court of Appeals Tenth Circuit 1985-86. Member Kappa Tau Alpha, Phi Kappa Phi and Order of the Coif. Admitted to practice Kansas 1985, U.S. District Court District of Kansas 1985, U.S. Court of Appeals Tenth Circuit 1986 and District of Columbia 1988. In legal practice Washington D.C. 1987-88 and Wichita Kansas 1993-2000.
Staff Attorney National Women's Law Center 1986-87. Author Note Evidence "The Psychotherapist-Patient Privilege—The Sixth Circuit Does the Decent Thing: In re *Zuniga*" 33 University of Kansas L. Rev. 385, 1985 and Essay "Civic Duty and Civic Risk: The Supreme Court Throws the Balance Out of Whack" 34 Washburn L. Jour. 495 May 1995. Co-author with Greenberger "Affirmative Action, The Women's Economic Justice Agenda—Ideas for the States" 45 The National Center for Policy Alternatives 1987, "Understanding Sexual Harassment, Sexual Harassment—How to Develop and Implement Effective Policies" National Association of Manufacturers 1987 and "Federal Funding of Discrimination—The Impact of *Grove City College v. Bell*" National Women's Law Center 1987; with Campbell and Kolker "The Tax Reform Act of 1986: The Return for Women" National Women's Law Center 1988; and with Banoun "Warehousing and Parking" 21 Review of Securities and Communications Regulation 39 Standard & Poor's 1988. Lecturer Emporia State University 1985 and Wichita State University 1994-95. Visiting Assistant Professor University of Kansas School of Law 1989-90. Member Kansas Board of Law Examiners since 1995. Member Kansas Bar Foundation, American Judicature Society, Wichita Women Attorneys Association (Vice President/President Elect 1992-93, President 1993-94), Women Attorney Association of Topeka, Kansas Women Attorneys Association (Co-founder 1994, Secretary 1994-96, Co-chair Lindsborg Conference 2002 Program Committee), National Association of Women Judges (District Representative District 10 Kansas since 2002), The District of Columbia Bar, Wichita (Chair Pro Bono Committee 1991-93 and Professional Diversity Committee 1995-96, Member Bar-O-Meter Committee 1991, Professional Diversity Committee 1991-2000, Law Day Committee since 1991), Kansas (Committee on Professionalism, Equality and Quality of Life 1992-94, Media Law Committee 1995-96) and American (Committee on White Collar Crime 1987-90) Bar Associations.
Presenter Recent Kansas Appellate Cases 31st Judicial District Wilson County Bar Association 2000, "Telling Your Story at Trial" Kansas Women Attorneys Association 2000, "Views From the Bench" Oct 2000 and Recent Developments in Kansas Criminal Law 2001 Kansas Trial Lawyers Association, Recent Decisions and Hot Issues Kansas Supreme Court Judicial Conference 2001, Appellate Practice and Brief Writing 2001 and Appellate Practice 2001 Topeka Bar Association, Recent Kansas Appellate Cases 2001 and Appellate Seminar 2002 Wyandotte County Bar Association, Recent Developments in Kansas Criminal Law 2001 and Recent Cases and Hot Topics Criminal Law Institute 2002 Kansas Bar Association, Law Review Symposium on Women and the Law University of Kansas School of Law 2001, "Intersection with State Law" 2002 and Appellate Practice Seminar 2002 Wichita Bar Association, "Recent Kansas Cases and Hot Topics" Criminal Law Institute Kansas Bar Association 2002 and Kansas Association of Legal Assistants 2002 and "Recent Kansas Decisions and Hot Issues" Department of Administration of Kansas 2002. Recipient Pro Bono Certificate from Kansas Bar Association June 1998 and "40 under 40" Award from Wichita Business Journal 1998. Graduate Leadership Wichita 1994. Member Community Council Advisory Board Wichita State University Center for Women's Studies 1995-2000. Volunteer and Tutor Hyde Elementary School since 1995. Leader Girl Scout Brownies 1996-98. Chair Nominating Committee Kansas Appleseed 1998-99. Volunteer Site Council Whitsun Elementary School 2001-02. Member since 2001 and Vice President since 2002 Board of Governors Kansas University Law Society. Enjoys running and reading current fiction.
Office: Kansas Judicial Center, 301 S.W. Tenth Avenue, Topeka 66612-1507.
Telephone: (785) 296-5412.
Fax: (785) 296-7079
E-mail address: beierc@kscourts.org

BELOT, Monti L. *(Judge, United States District Court District of Kansas)* Appointed for life by Presi-

BELOT, MONTI L.—*Continued*

dent George Bush to term beginning Nov 25, 1991. Born Kansas City Missouri March 4, 1943. Educated at University of Kansas B.A. 1965 J.D. 1968. In legal practice Kansas City 1976-83 and Coffeyville 1983-91.

Assistant U.S. Attorney 1973-76 and Special Assistant to U.S. Attorney 1976-78 Topeka.

Office: 111 U.S. Courthouse, 401 North Market Street, Wichita 67202.
Telephone: (316) 269-6519.

BENGTSON, Larry E. *(Judge, Kansas District Court Eighth Judicial District)*
Mailing address: P.O. Box 1147, Junction City 66441.
Office: Geary County Courthouse, Junction City 66441.
Telephone: (785) 762-5221.
Fax: (785) 762-4420
E-mail address: dj2@oz-online.net

BENNETT, John P. *(Judge, Kansas District Court Tenth Judicial District)*
Office: Johnson County Courthouse, 100 North Kansas Avenue, Olathe 66061-3273.
Telephone: (913) 715-3920.
Fax: (913) 715-3317
E-mail address: John.Bennett@jocoks.com

BENNINGTON, Barry A. *(Chief Judge, Kansas District Court Twentieth Judicial District)* Appointed by Governor John Carlin to term beginning Nov 24, 1980. Elected Nov 1982, Nov 1986, Nov 1990, Nov 1994, Nov 1998 and 2002. Current term expires Jan 2007. Born St. Louis Missouri Jan 27, 1941. Methodist. Educated at Kansas University B.S. 1963 J.D. 1967. Member Phi Alpha Delta. Admitted to practice Kansas 1967 and U.S. District Court District of Kansas 1967. In legal practice St. John 1967-80.

County Attorney 1970-74. Author "Search and Seizure of Students' Property" 7 No. 7 *School Law Newsletter* 1973. Executive Board Kansas District Judges Association. Member Kansas Bar Association (Board of Governors). Attended General Jurisdiction course 1981 and "Law, Ethics and Justice" 1989 The National Judicial College and state and local CLE seminars. USMCR.

Mailing address: P.O. Box 608, St. John 67576-0608.
Office: Stafford County Courthouse, 209-215 North Broadway, St. John 67576.
Telephone: (620) 549-3370.
Fax: (620) 549-3298
E-mail address: chambers@stjohnks.net

BIGGE, Douglas *(Magistrate Judge, Kansas District Court Twenty-third Judicial District)*
Office: Rooks County Courthouse, 115 North Walnut, Stockton 67669.
Telephone: (785) 425-6718.
Fax: (785) 425-6568
E-mail address: debigge@hotmail.com

BINGHAM, John L. *(Magistrate Judge, Kansas District Court Twelfth Judicial District)* Appointed by Governor Bill Graves.
Office: Jewell County Courthouse, 307 North Commercial, Mankato 66956.
Telephone: (785) 378-4030.
Fax: (785) 378-4035
E-mail address: jwlcodc@ruraltel.net

BISHOP, Robert L. *(Judge, Kansas District Court Nineteenth Judicial District)* Elected to term beginning Jan 10, 1977. Reelected to subsequent terms. Former Administrative Judge. Born Anthony Kansas Dec 6, 1932. Educated at Southwestern College B.A. cum laude 1956 and University of Kansas LL.B. 1959. Admitted to practice Kansas 1959. In legal practice Winfield 1959-77.

Member Kansas District Judges Association (President 1982), Cowley County (President 1972), Kansas and American Bar Associations. U.S. Army 1953-55. Republican.

Mailing address: P.O. Box 472, Winfield 67156.
Office: Cowley County Courthouse, Winfield 67156.
Telephone: (620) 221-5470.
Fax: (620) 221-1097
E-mail address: rlbishop@cowleycourt.com

BLAKE, Donna L. J. *(Magistrate Judge, Kansas District Court Twenty-fifth Judicial District)*
Mailing address: P.O. Box 745, Syracuse 67878-0745.
Office: Hamilton County Courthouse, Syracuse 67878.
Telephone: (620) 384-5129.
Fax: (620) 384-7806
E-mail address: dollyq@pld.com

BOAL, David W. *(Judge, Kansas District Court Twenty-ninth Judicial District)*
Office: Wyandotte County Court Svcs. Bldg., 711 Armstrong, Kansas City 66101.
Telephone: (913) 573-4193.
Fax: (913) 573-4195
E-mail address: Dboal@wycokck.org

BOEDING, Thomas L. *(Judge, Kansas District Court Twenty-ninth Judicial District)*
Office: Wyandotte County Courthouse, 710 North Seventh Street, Kansas City 66101.
Telephone: (913) 573-4104.
Fax: (913) 573-8105
E-mail address: Tboeding@wycokck.org

BORNHOLDT, Thomas H. *(Judge, Kansas District Court Tenth Judicial District)*
Office: Johnson County Courthouse, 100 North Kansas Avenue, Olathe 66061-3273.
Telephone: (913) 715-3850.
Fax: (913) 715-3317
E-mail address: Thomas.Bornholdt@jocoks.com

BOSTWICK, Donald W. *(Magistrate Judge, United States District Court District of Kansas)* Appointed by U.S. District Court judges to term beginning July 22, 1999. Term expires 2007.
Office: 403 U.S. Courthouse, 401 North Market Street, Wichita 67202.
Telephone: (316) 269-6114.

BOUKER, Edward *(Chief Judge, Kansas District Court Twenty-third Judicial District)*
Mailing address: P.O. Box 8, Hays 67601.
Office: Ellis County Courthouse, 1204 Fort Street, Hays 67601.
Telephone: (785) 628-9418.
Fax: (785) 628-8415
E-mail address: edbouker@hotmail.com

BOYER, Danny D. *(Judge, Kansas District Court Twenty-eighth Judicial District)*
Mailing address: P.O. Box 1760, Salina 67402-1760.
Office: Saline County Courthouse, 300 West Ash, Salina 67401.
Telephone: (785) 309-5840.
Fax: (785) 309-5845
E-mail address: dan.boyer@saline.org

BRAZIL, Timothy E. *(Judge, Kansas District Court Thirty-first Judicial District)*
Office: Neosho County Courthouse, 102 South Lincoln, Chanute 66720.
Telephone: (620) 431-5730.
Fax: (620) 431-5710
E-mail address: tbrazil@chanuteks.com

BREMER, John E. *(Magistrate Judge, Kansas District Court Seventeenth Judicial District)*
Office: Decatur County Courthouse, 120 East Hall, Box 89, Oberlin 67749.
Telephone: (785) 475-8108.
Fax: (785) 475-8170
E-mail address: dcmj@theclassic.net

BREWSTER, Daniel L. *(Judge, Kansas District Court Eleventh Judicial District)* Elected to term beginning Jan 10, 1977. Retained by election. Current term expires Jan 2005. Born Joplin Missouri May 15, 1947. Protestant. Educated at Kansas State College-Pittsburg B.A. 1969 and Washburn University of Topeka J.D. 1972. Admitted to practice Kansas 1972. Judge, Labette County Probate, Juvenile and County Court April 15, 1976 to Jan 9, 1977.
Labette County Attorney 1973-76. Member Kansas Bar Association. Attended The National Judicial College 1977.
Office: Labette County Courthouse, 201 South Central, Parsons 67357.
Telephone: (620) 421-4120.
Fax: (620) 421-3633

BREWSTER, David F. *(Judge, Kansas District Court Eleventh Judicial District)* Appointed by Governor John Carlin to term beginning Feb 8, 1982. Retained by election 1984, 1988, 1992, 1996 and 2000. Current term expires Jan 2005. Former Administrative Judge. Born Joplin Missouri May 25, 1944. Presbyterian. Educated at Oklahoma University B.A. 1965 and Washburn University J.D. 1968. Admitted to practice Kansas 1968 and U.S. District Court District of Kansas 1968. In legal practice Baxter Springs 1968-82.
County Attorney Cherokee County 1971-74. Member Kansas District Judges Association and Kansas Bar Association. USAR 1968-74.
Mailing address: P.O. Box 189, Columbus 66725-0189.
Office: Cherokee County Courthouse, Columbus 66725.
Telephone: (620) 429-3518.
Fax: (620) 429-1130
E-mail address: bookster@11thjd.org

BRIBIESCA, Joseph *(Judge, Kansas District Court Eighteenth Judicial District)*
Office: 8-2 Sedgwick County Courthouse, 525 North Main Street, Wichita 67203-3373.
Telephone: (316) 383-7601.
Fax: (316) 383-7560
E-mail address: jbribies@dc18.org

BROOKS, Daniel T. *(Judge, Kansas District Court Eighteenth Judicial District)*
Office: Juvenile Department Court Building, 1015 South Minnesota Street, Wichita 67211-2730.
Telephone: (316) 383-7487.
Fax: (316) 383-8000
E-mail address: dtbrooks@dc18.org

BROWN, Wesley Ernest *(Senior Judge, United States District Court District of Kansas)* Bankruptcy Referee April 1, 1958 to April 11, 1962. Appointed Judge for life by President John F. Kennedy to term beginning April 12, 1962. Assumed Senior status, serves by assignment. Born Hutchinson Kansas June 22, 1907. Protestant. Educated at University of Kansas 1925-29 and University of Missouri LL.B. 1933. Member Delta Theta Phi and Order of the Bench and Robe. Admitted to practice Kansas 1933, Missouri 1933, U.S. District Court 1938 and U.S. Supreme Court 1944. Began legal practice Hutchinson Kansas 1933. Former Judge, Temporary Emergency Court of Appeals of the U.S., appointed by U.S. Supreme Court Chief Justice Warren Earl Burger.
County Attorney Reno County 1935-39. Author "A Primer on Wage Earner Plans Under Chapter XIII, With Specimen Forms" Business Lawyer Vol. XVII No. 3, April 1962. Member Topeka, Wichita, Reno County, Kansas (Executive Council 1950-65, President 1964-65), Federal and American Bar Associations. Lieutenant USNR (Line Officer) 1944-46. Enjoys working, golfing and bridge.
Office: 414 U.S. Courthouse, 401 North Market Street, Wichita 67202.
Telephone: (316) 269-6497.

BRUNS, David E. *(Judge, Kansas District Court Third Judicial District)* Appointed by Governor Bill Graves 1999. Born Kansas City Kansas 1959. Educated at University of Kansas B.S. with distinction 1981 and Washburn University of Topeka J.D. with honors 1984. Notes Editor Washburn Law Journal 1983-84. Admitted to practice Kansas 1984 and U.S. District Court District of Kansas 1984.
Author "Administrative Law: Deletion of Confidential Material from Official Public Records" 22 Washburn L. Jour. 364, 1983 and Kansas Chapter 50 State Products Liability Guide West Publishing Co. 1994. Adjunct Professor of Pretrial Advocacy Washburn University School of Law since 1996. Member Sam A. Crow Inns of Court, American Judicature Society, Topeka, Kansas and American Bar Associations.
Office: 308 Shawnee County Courthouse, 200 S.E. Seventh Street, Topeka 66603-3922.
Telephone: (785) 233-8200.
Fax: (785) 291-4917
E-mail address: dbruns@shawneecourt.org

BUKATY, John J., Jr. *(Judge, Kansas District Court Twenty-ninth Judicial District)* Appointed by Governor John Carlin to term beginning Aug 22, 1986. Elected 1986, 1988, 1992, 1996 and 2000. Current term expires Jan 2005. Born Kansas City Missouri Nov 5, 1944. Roman Catholic. Educated at Regis College B.S. 1966 and University of Kansas J.D. 1969. Member Phi Alpha Delta. Admitted to practice Kansas 1969, U.S. District Court District of Kansas 1972 and U.S. Court of Ap-

BUKATY, JOHN J., JR.—*Continued*

peals Tenth Circuit 1980. In legal practice Kansas City 1972-86.

Assistant District Attorney Wyandotte County 1972-75. Municipal Court Prosecutor Kansas City 1975-83. Member Kansas City, Wyandotte County (Secretary 1978, President 1992), Kansas and American Bar Associations. First Lieutenant U.S. Army 1969-71. Board member Family and Children's Service, Inc. Member District Committee Boy Scouts of America. Enjoys racquetball, skiing, reading and golf.

Office: Wyandotte County Courthouse, Third Floor, 710 North Seventh Street, Kansas City 66101.
Telephone: (913) 573-2917.
Fax: (913) 573-4354
E-mail address: Jbukaty@wycokck.org

BULLOCK, Terry L. *(Judge, Kansas District Court Third Judicial District)* Appointed by Governor Robert F. Bennett 1976. Retained by election. Former Administrative Judge. Born Herington Kansas Sept 29, 1939. Episcopalian. Educated at Kansas State University A.B. cum laude 1961 and University of Kansas J.D. with distinction 1964. Sections Editor Kansas Law Review. Burdick Scholar and Judge Willard M. Benton Scholar. Member Phi Eta Sigma, Phi Kappa Phi, Blue Key, Interfraternity Council (Vice President), Chancery Pre-law Society (President), Phi Delta Phi and Order of the Coif. In legal practice Topeka 1964-76. Served Kansas Court of Appeals by special appointment.

Important Opinions: 6 Kan. App. 2d 24, 42, 157, 244, 833, 844, 963; 7 Kan. App. 2d 246, 259, 441, 445, 463, 467; 9 Kan. App. 2d 96, 108, 133, 151; 10 Kan. App. 2d 34, 39; No. 57,975 and No. 57,176 Oct 24, 1985; No. 57,605 Oct 31, 1985; and 223 Kan. 947-959. Adjunct Professor of Ethics and Professional Responsibility Washburn University of Topeka School of Law. Distinguished Visiting Professor University of Kansas School of Law. Former member Kansas Supreme Court Advisory Committee on Procedures for the Discipline of Attorneys and District Nominating Commission Third Judicial District. President Legal Services for Prisoners, Inc. (pro bono publico project providing legal assistance to indigent prison inmates and intern training for law students). Life Fellow The American Bar Foundation. Member Civil Code Advisory Committee Kansas Judicial Council, American Judicature Society, Topeka (Former Member Ethics and Grievance Committee and Executive Committee, Former Chairman Continuing Legal Education Committee and Washburn Law Institute Committee), Kansas (Former Board Member and Past President Young Lawyers Section, Former Member Executive Council, Member and Former General Chairman Ethics and Grievance Committee, Member Special Commission Studying the Reorganization of Governing Structure of the Bar, Chairman Legal Advertising Committee, Legal Specialization Committee and Commission on the Future of the Legal Profession) and American Bar Associations. Lecturer on Agency, Partnership and Master Servant Law Washburn and University of Kansas Bar Review Institutes and on Consumer Protection, Legal Ethics, Civil and Criminal Trial Procedures, Appellate Practice, Medical Malpractice and Commercial Transactions for law schools, bar association CLE and trial practice institutes. Recipient President's Outstanding Service Award from Kansas Bar Association 1977-78, 1979 and 1981, Lifetime Professionalism Award 1996 and Alumni Medallion from Delta Upsilon International Fraternity. Past President Community Resources Council of Topeka and Topeka Knife and Fork Club. Former Vestryman St. David's Parish. Former Delegate Legislative Convention Diocese of Kansas. Board of Governors and Past President University of Kansas School of Law. Board of Directors Delta Upsilon (International President, former member Board of Trustees Educational Foundation), Dr. Karl Menninger Distinguished Lectureship Series and The Villages (national organization providing homes for homeless youngsters). Lecturer Associated Clubs (national Knife and Fork Club Association). Member Grace Cathedral (Former Vestryman), Topeka Festival Singers, Masons, Blue Lodge and Scottish Rite bodies. Enjoys music.

Office: 410 Shawnee County Courthouse, 200 S.E. Seventh Street, Topeka 66603-3922.
Telephone: (785) 233-8200.
Fax: (785) 291-4917
E-mail address: tbullock@shawneecourt.org

BURDETTE, J. Dexter *(Judge, Kansas District Court Twenty-ninth Judicial District)*

Office: Wyandotte County Court Services Bldg., First Floor, 812 North Seventh Street, Kansas City 66101.
Telephone: (913) 573-2967.
Fax: (913) 573-8105
E-mail address: Dburdette@wycokck.org

BURGESS, Ben *(Judge, Kansas District Court Eighteenth Judicial District)*

Office: Sedgwick County Courthouse, Fourth Floor, 525 North Main Street, Wichita 67203-3773.
Telephone: (316) 383-7442.
Fax: (316) 383-7560
E-mail address: bburgess@dc18.org

BURGESS, James L. *(Judge, Kansas District Court Eighteenth Judicial District)*

Office: Juvenile Department Court Building, 1015 South Minnesota Street, Wichita 67211.
Telephone: (316) 383-7487.
Fax: (316) 383-8000
E-mail address: jburgess@dc18.org

BURR, Jack L. *(Chief Judge, Kansas District Court Fifteenth Judicial District)* Assumed office 1979. Elected to subsequent terms. Born Toronto Kansas 1942. Educated at Wichita State University B.A. 1967 and Washburn University of Topeka J.D. 1970. Admitted to practice Kansas 1970.

Member Kansas and American Bar Associations.

Office: 201 Sherman County Courthouse, 813 Broadway, Goodland 67735.
Telephone: (785) 899-4850.
Fax: (785) 899-4858
E-mail address: jburr@goodland.ixks.com

BUSTER, David *(Magistrate Judge, Kansas District Court Twenty-fourth Judicial District)*

Mailing address: P.O. Box 270, Larned 67550-0270.
Office: Pawnee County Courthouse, Larned 67550.
Telephone: (620) 285-6937.
Fax: (620) 285-3665
E-mail address: dbuster@pawnee.kscoxmail.com

CAHOJ, John *(Magistrate Judge, Kansas District Court Fifteenth Judicial District)*

Mailing address: P.O. Box 753, Hoxie 67740.

CAHOJ, JOHN—*Continued*
Office: Sheridan County Courthouse, Hoxie 67740.
Telephone: (785) 675-3221.
Fax: (785) 675-2256
E-mail address: sdcojudge@ruraltel.net

CAMERON, Brenda *(Judge, Kansas District Court Tenth Judicial District)*
Office: Johnson County Courthouse, 100 North Kansas Avenue, Olathe 66061-3273.
Telephone: (913) 715-3870.
Fax: (913) 715-3317
E-mail address: Brenda.Cameron@jocoks.com

CAMPBELL, Kevin G. *(Magistrate Judge, Kansas District Court Twenty-fifth Judicial District)*
Mailing address: P.O. Box 64, Lakin 67860.
Office: Kearny County Courthouse, Lakin 67860.
Telephone: (620) 355-6451.
Fax: (620) 355-7462

CANADAY, Russell D. *(Judge, Kansas District Court Fourteenth Judicial District)* Elected to term beginning Jan 9, 1989. Reelected Nov 3, 1992, Nov 5, 1996 and 2000. Current term expires Jan 2005. Born Topeka Kansas Nov 9, 1953. Nazarene. Educated at Washburn University of Topeka B.A. 1975 J.D. 1978. Admitted to practice Kansas 1978 and Colorado 1985.
Office: 201 Montgomery County Courthouse, 300 East Main, Independence 67301.
Telephone: (620) 330-1080.
Fax: (620) 331-6120

CARROLL, Pat *(Magistrate Judge, Kansas District Court Fifteenth Judicial District)*
Mailing address: P.O. Box 257, Atwood 67730.
Office: Rawlins County Courthouse, Atwood 67730.
Telephone: (785) 626-3271.
Fax: (785) 626-3350

CARTER, Blaine A. *(Magistrate Judge, Kansas District Court Second Judicial District)*
Office: Wabaunsee County Courthouse, 215 Kansas, Alma 66401.
Telephone: (785) 765-2406.
Fax: (785) 765-2487

CARTER, Kathryn *(Magistrate Judge, Kansas District Court Twelfth Judicial District)* Appointed to term beginning July 1, 1987. Retained by election. Born Cuyahoga Falls Ohio April 21, 1952. Educated at University of Kansas B.A. 1973 J.D. 1986. Admitted to practice Kansas 1986 and U.S. District Court District of Kansas 1986.
Member American Bar Association. Recipient Pacesetter Award from Cloud County Community Resources Council 1990.
Office: Cloud County Courthouse, 811 Washington, Concordia 66901.
Telephone: (785) 243-8130.
Fax: (785) 243-8188
E-mail address: kc@dustdevil.com

CASEMENT, David A. *(Magistrate Judge, Kansas District Court Fourteenth Judicial District)*
Mailing address: P.O. Box 306, Sedan 67361-0306.
Office: Chautauqua County Courthouse, 215 North Chautauqua, Sedan 67361.
Telephone: (620) 725-5874.
Fax: (620) 725-3027

CHAMBERS, Timothy J. *(Judge, Kansas District Court Twenty-seventh Judicial District)*
Office: Reno County Courthouse, 206 West First Street, Hutchinson 67501.
Telephone: (620) 694-2963.
Fax: (620) 694-2958
E-mail address: timothyc@dist27.reno.ks.us

CLARK, Marty K. *(Magistrate Judge, Kansas District Court Twentieth Judicial District)*
Mailing address: P.O. Box 876, Russell 67665-0876.
Office: Russell County Courthouse, Fourth and Main, Russell 67665.
Telephone: (785) 483-5641.
Fax: (785) 483-2448
E-mail address: racejudge@yahoo.com

CLARK, Paul W. *(Judge, Kansas District Court Eighteenth Judicial District)*
Office: 7-1 Sedgwick County Courthouse, 525 North Main Street, Wichita 67203-3773.
Telephone: (316) 383-7122.
Fax: (316) 383-7560
E-mail address: pclark@dc18.org

COLLINS, Jim *(Magistrate Judge, Kansas District Court Twenty-fifth Judicial District)* Appointed by Governor Bill Graves.
Office: Scott County Courthouse, 303 Court Street, Scott City 67871.
Telephone: (620) 872-7208.
Fax: (620) 872-3683
E-mail address: jcollins@wbsnet.org

CONKLIN, John Riggs *(Magistrate Judge, Kansas District Court Fifth Judicial District)*
Mailing address: P.O. Box 529, Cottonwood Falls 66845.
Office: Chase County Courthouse, Cottonwood Falls 66845.
Telephone: (620) 273-6319.
Fax: (620) 273-6890
E-mail address: conklin05@hotmail.com

CONKLIN, Thomas R. *(Judge, Kansas District Court Third Judicial District)*
Office: 307 Shawnee County Courthouse, 200 S.E. Seventh Street, Topeka 66603-3922.
Telephone: (785) 233-8200.
Fax: (785) 291-4917

CORRIGAN, Michael *(Judge, Kansas District Court Eighteenth Judicial District)* Elected at public election to term beginning Jan 10, 1977. Reelected 1980, 1984, 1988, 1992 and 1996 and 2000. Current term expires Jan 2005. Former Administrative Judge. Born Wichita Kansas Sept 1, 1936. Catholic. Educated at Wichita State University B.A. and University of Kansas J.D. Admitted to practice Kansas 1961. Began legal practice Wichita 1961. Juvenile Court Judge 1971-77.
Author "The Juvenile Court and Community Involvement" Osgoode Hall L. Jour. Aug 1972. Member Kansas Special Court Judges Association (President 1976), Kansas District Court Judges Association (President 1986), Wichita, Kansas and American Bar Associations. Republican. Board of Directors Junior Achievement of

CORRIGAN, MICHAEL—*Continued*

Wichita, Big Brothers and Big Sisters of Wichita and Wichita Guidance Center. Enjoys tennis and reading.
Office: 9-3 Sedgwick County Courthouse, 525 North Main Street, Wichita 67203-3773.
Telephone: (316) 383-7474.
Fax: (316) 383-7560
E-mail address: mcorriga@distcrt18.state.ks.us

CREITZ, Daniel D. *(Judge, Kansas District Court Thirty-first Judicial District)*
Mailing address: P.O. Box 630, Iola 66749.
Office: Allen County Courthouse, Iola 66749.
Telephone: (620) 365-1426.
Fax: (620) 365-1429
E-mail address: dancreitz@acdc.kscoxmail.com

CRONIN, Loren L. *(Magistrate Judge, Kansas District Court Sixteenth Judicial District)*
Mailing address: P.O. Box 722, Coldwater 67029.
Office: Comanche County Courthouse, Coldwater 67029.
Telephone: (620) 582-2966.
Fax: (620) 582-2603

CROTTY, Rebecca *(Magistrate Judge, Kansas District Court Twenty-fifth Judicial District)* Appointed by Governor Bill Graves.
Mailing address: P.O. Box 798, Garden City 67846-0798.
Office: Finney County Courthouse, Garden City 67846.
Telephone: (620) 271-6112.
Fax: (620) 271-6141
E-mail address: judge06@finneycounty.org

CROW, Sam A. *(Senior Judge, United States District Court District of Kansas)* Part-time Magistrate June 1, 1973 to Sept 15, 1975. Full-time Magistrate Sept 15, 1975 to Dec 10, 1981. Appointed Judge for life by President Ronald Reagan to term beginning Dec 10, 1981. Assumed Senior Status Nov 15, 1996, serves by assignment. Born Topeka Kansas May 5, 1926. Episcopalian. Educated at University of Kansas B.A. 1949 and Washburn University School of Law J.D. 1952. Member Washburn Law Review Board. Admitted to practice Kansas 1952, U.S. District Court District of Kansas 1952, U.S. Military Court of Appeals 1953, U.S. Supreme Court 1962 and U.S. Court of Appeals 1963. In legal practice Topeka 1952-75.

Lecturer Washburn University School of Law. Member Advisory Committee on Criminal Rules 1990-96, Subcommittee on Evidentiary Rules 1991-96 and Liaison to Subcommittee on Criminal Case Management Court Administration and Case Management Committee 1994-96 and to the Tenth Circuit 1996 Judicial Conference of the U.S. Member Attorney Disciplinary Committee U.S. District Court District of Kansas since 1999. Founder The Honorable Sam A. Crow American Inn of Court (President 1992-95). Former Member Wichita Lawyers Club and Judicial Council for the Tenth Circuit. Fellow Kansas Bar Foundation and Academy International Law and Science. Member Topeka Lawyers Club (Secretary 1964-65, President 1965-66), Kansas Trial Lawyers Association (Secretary 1959-60, President 1960-61, Board of Directors), American Judicature Society, International Academy of Law and Science, Topeka (Chairman Judicial Reform Committee, Bench and Bar Committee and Criminal Law Committee), Wichita, Kansas (Chairman Military Law Section 1965, 1967, 1970, 1972, 1974 and 1975, Trustee 1970-76) and American Bar Associations. Guest Lecturer on the U.S. Magistrate Courts University of Virginia at Charlottesville May 1979. Faculty National Institute for Trial Advocacy 1984 and 1985, U.S. Attorney General's Trial Advocacy Institute for Department of Justice, Washington D.C. 1985, 1986 and 1990, "Nuts & Bolts" Orientation for New Lawyers Wichita Bar Association 1988, 1989 and 1990. Recipient Distinguished Service Award from Washburn University School of Law June 9, 2000 and Distinguished Service Award from Topeka Bar Association 2000. Inducted in Topeka High School Hall of Fame Oct 22, 2000. Listed in *Who's Who in America.* Colonel USAR JAGC 1953-86 (retired). Cub Master 1957-60 and Board of Review 1960-70 Boy Scouts of America. Chairman 1959 and Board of Directors 1960-65 Kansas March of Dimes. Vestry Grace Episcopal Church 1960-65. Board of Directors Riverside Hospital 1986-92. Board of Governors Washburn University School of Law Alumni 1993-99. Member Shawnee County Historical Society, Shawnee Country Club, American Legion, Rotary Club and Shriners. Enjoys golf, snow skiing, horses and travel.
Office: 430 Federal Building, 444 S.E. Quincy Street, Topeka 66683.
Telephone: (785) 295-2626.

DAVIS, James Franklin *(Judge, Kansas District Court Tenth Judicial District)*
Office: Johnson County Courthouse, 100 North Kansas Avenue, Olathe 66061-3273.
Telephone: (913) 715-3800.
Fax: (913) 715-3317
E-mail address: James.Davis@jocoks.com

DAVIS, Robert E. *(Justice, Kansas Supreme Court)* Appointed by Governor Joan Finney 1993. Retained by election. Born Topeka Kansas Aug 28, 1939. Catholic. Educated at Creighton University B.A. 1961 and Georgetown University Law Center J.D. 1964. Staff member Georgetown Law Journal. Admitted to practice Kansas, U.S. District Court District of Kansas, U.S. Court of Appeals Tenth Circuit, U.S. Court of Military Review, U.S. Court of Appeals for the Armed Forces, U.S. Tax Court and U.S. Supreme Court. Magistrate Judge Leavenworth County 1969-76. Judge, Kansas District Court First Judicial District 1984-86, appointed by Governor John Carlin. Judge, Kansas Court of Appeals 1986-93, appointed by Governor John Carlin.

Board Attorney Kansas State Board of Pharmacy 1972-84. General Counsel and Director Leavenworth National Bank and Trust Company 1972-84. County Attorney Leavenworth County 1980-84. Author Note "Hartigan's Wake: Analysis of the Validity of Alabama Divorces in Sister States" 52 Georgetown L. Jour. 572, 1964. Instructor in Management and Business Law U.S. Penitentiary and U.S. Disciplinary Barracks Fort Leavenworth inmates Kansas City Kansas Community College 1985. Adjunct Professor of Business Law Master of Arts program Webster University 1985. Adjunct Professor of Law since 1990 and Instructor in Criminal Law 1992 University of Kansas School of Law. Guest Lecturer on "The Art of Advocacy" Washburn University School of Law 1991 and on "Child in Need of Care" University of Kansas School of Social Welfare 1993. Director and President Community Corrections Board Leavenworth County 1980-84. Member Permanency Planning Com-

DAVIS, ROBERT E.—*Continued*

mittee since 1985, Liaison for Kansas Lawyer Specialization 1993, Liaison for Alternate Dispute Resolution 1993 and Chair Rules Committee 1993 Kansas Supreme Court. Member Task Force on Female Offenders Kansas Department of Corrections 1990. Member Governor's Adoption Reform Task Force 1994. Former Member Kansas Trial Lawyers Association, The Association of Trial Lawyers of America, Kansas District Judges Association, National Council of Juvenile and Family Court Judges and Leavenworth County Bar Association (President 1977). Member American Inns of Court, American Judges Association, Kansas and American Bar Associations.

Attended New Judge Orientation Program University of Kansas 1985, General Jurisdiction Course for Trial Judges 1985 and Juvenile and Family Law Course 1990 The National Judicial College, Instruction for Lawyers and Judges Harvard Law School 1985, National Institute on Child Sexual Abuse Victims Seminar National Council of Juvenile and Family Court Judges 1985, Appellate Judicial Writing Program Stanford Law School 1988, Constitutional Law Conference Bureau of National Affairs Washington D.C. 1990 and National Round Table on Lawyer Specialty Certification Standing Committee on Specialization American Bar Association Washington D.C. 1993. Participant "Women, Families and Reproduction: Judicial Decision Making" Washington D.C. 1991 and National Symposium on "Court-Connected Dispute Resolution" National Center for State Courts Orlando Florida 1993. Guest Lecturer on Appellate Advocacy University of Kansas Appellate Advocacy Instructors 1991, Leavenworth County Bar Association in conjunction with Fort Leavenworth JAGC Law Day 1993 and Atchison County Bar Law Day 1993. Guest Instructor-Lecturer "Appellate Brief Writing and Oral Argument" CLE Seminar for Government Attorneys Topeka 1994. Team Leader "Leadership Institute in Judicial Education" Women Judges' Fund Appalachian State University 1994. Recipient Distinguished Service Award from Leavenworth Jaycees 1972. Captain U.S. Army JAGC 1964-67. Democrat. Member 1968-84, Director 1968-70 and Treasurer 1969 Leavenworth Chamber of Commerce. President Leavenworth County Handicapped Association 1968-71 and Leavenworth Council on Alcohol 1981-83. Member Leavenworth Kiwanis Club 1968-75, Leavenworth Jaycees 1969-73, Eagles Lodge 1969-84, Association of the United States Army 1970-80 and Governor's Advisory Commission on Alcoholism 1971-76. Director Leavenworth Historical Society 1970-75. Member 1974-84 and Chair 1980-84 Board of Trustees Saint John Hospital Leavenworth Kansas. Council Member Saint Mary College 1975-84.

Office: 313 Kansas Judicial Center, 301 S.W. Tenth Avenue, Topeka 66612-1507.
Telephone: (785) 296-5128.

DeLISSA, Janna K. *(Magistrate Judge, Kansas District Court Twenty-fifth Judicial District)* Appointed by Governor Bill Graves to term beginning Dec 8, 1997. Retained by election Nov 2000, current term expires Jan 2005. Born Syracuse Kansas 1959. Protestant. Educated at Oklahoma Baptist University B.A. magna cum laude 1981 and University of Kansas M.B.A. 1985 J.D. 1985. Admitted to practice Kansas 1985. In legal practice Leoti 1987-97.

County Attorney Wichita County 1987-97. Member Kansas District Magistrate Judges Association (Board of Directors) and Kansas Bar Association.

Mailing address: P.O. Box 968, Leoti 67861-0968.
Office: Wichita County Courthouse, Leoti 67861.
Telephone: (620) 375-4454.
Fax: (620) 375-2999
E-mail address: janna@pld.com

DENT, Judd *(Chief Judge, Kansas District Court Fourteenth Judicial District)*

Office: 201 Montgomery County Courthouse, 300 East Main Street, Independence 67301.
Telephone: (620) 330-1080.
Fax: (620) 331-6120
E-mail address: jurist@kancom.net

DICK, Patricia Macke *(Judge, Kansas District Court Twenty-seventh Judicial District)*

Office: Reno County Courthouse, 206 West First Street, Hutchinson 67501.
Telephone: (620) 694-2970.
Fax: (620) 694-2958
E-mail address: pattym@dist27.reno.ks.us

DICKINSON, Marty Joe *(Judge, Kansas District Court Ninth Judicial District)*

Mailing address: P.O. Box 665, Newton 67114-0665.
Office: Harvey County Courthouse, Newton 67114.
Telephone: (316) 284-6898.
Fax: (316) 283-4601
E-mail address: judgej@kscourt.net

DIXSON, Ann L. *(Magistrate Judge, Kansas District Court Sixteenth Judicial District)*

Office: Kiowa County Courthouse, 211 East Florida, Greensburg 67054.
Telephone: (620) 723-3317.
Fax: (620) 723-2970
E-mail address: kcll@midway.net

DOWD, Matthew J. *(Judge, Kansas District Court Third Judicial District)* Elected to term beginning Jan 10, 1977. Retained by election. Born Oklahoma City Oklahoma July 5, 1939. Catholic. Educated at Rockhurst College B.A. 1960, Marquette University 1961-62, University of Kansas LL.B. 1963 and Wichita State University M.A. in Criminal Justice 1984. Member Alpha Sigma Nu. Admitted to practice Kansas 1963, U.S. District Court District of Kansas, U.S. Court of Appeals Tenth Circuit, U.S. Court of Military Appeals and U.S. Supreme Court. In legal practice Hutchinson 1963-71 and Topeka 1971-75.

Kansas Assistant Attorney General 1971-72. Shawnee County Counselor 1973-76. Author "Kansas Property Taxpayer Remedies" 11 Washburn L. Jour. 65, 1971. Adjunct Professor of Criminal Justice Washburn University. Member Topeka, Shawnee County and Kansas Bar Associations. Attended The National Judicial College 1977. Lieutenant Colonel USAR JAG (retired).

Office: 322 Shawnee County Courthouse, 200 S.E. Seventh Street, Topeka 66603-3922.
Telephone: (785) 233-8200.
Fax: (785) 291-4917

DUNCAN, Daniel *(Judge, Kansas District Court Twenty-ninth Judicial District)*

Office: Wyandotte County Courthouse, Third Floor, 710 North Seventh Street, Kansas City 66101.
Telephone: (913) 573-2911.

DUNCAN, DANIEL—*Continued*

Fax: (913) 573-4354
E-mail address: ADuncan@wycokck.org

DUNCAN, Joey E. *(Magistrate Judge, Kansas District Court Sixteenth Judicial District)* Elected to term beginning Jan 8, 2001. Term expires Jan 2005. Born Great Bend Kansas March 3, 1957. Christian.

Member Kansas District Magistrate Judges Association and National Judges Association. Republican. Umpire for youth and adult softball and baseball. Interests include Bible studies and gold. Personal Statement or Quote: "A hundred years from now it will not matter with what rank you retired, how much money you made, or how many cases you worked, but the world may be different because you were important in the life of a child."

Mailing address: P.O. Box 487, Cimarron 67835.
Office: Gray County Courthouse, Cimarron 67835.
Telephone: (620) 855-3425.
Fax: (620) 855-7037

ELLIOTT, Gerald T. *(Judge, Kansas District Court Tenth Judicial District)*

Office: Johnson County Courthouse, 100 North Kansas Avenue, Olathe 66061-3273.
Telephone: (913) 715-3780.
Fax: (913) 715-3317
E-mail address: Gerald.Elliott@jocoks.com

ELLIOTT, Jerry G. *(Judge, Kansas Court of Appeals)* Appointed by Governor Mike Hayden to term beginning 1987. Retained by election. Born Fort Scott Kansas Nov 25, 1936. Educated at Hutchinson Community College, University of Kansas A.B. 1958 and Kansas University LL.B. with distinction 1964. Recipient C. C. Stewart Award. Editor-in-Chief Kansas Law Review. Law Clerk to Hon. Wesley Ernest Brown, U.S. District Court District of Kansas. Member Pi Sigma Alpha and Order of the Coif. In legal practice Wichita.

Former Member Kansas Continuing Legal Education Commission. Fellow Kansas Bar Foundation. Member Wichita Bar Association (Past President). Past President Wichita Council of Camp Fire, Kansas Chapter Leukemia Society of America, Wichita Legal Aid Society and Accent on Kids (Ronald McDonald Houses). Former Board member Music Theatre of Wichita.

Office: 324 Kansas Judicial Center, 301 S.W. Tenth Avenue, Topeka 66612-1507.
Telephone: (785) 296-5405.

ELLIOTT, William B. *(Chief Judge, Kansas District Court Seventeenth Judicial District)*

Office: Graham County Courthouse, 410 North Pomeroy, Hill City 67642.
Telephone: (785) 421-2495.
Fax: (785) 421-5463
E-mail address: belliott@ruraltel.net

EYER, John *(Magistrate Judge, Kansas District Court Twelfth Judicial District)* Born Everest Kansas June 5, 1952. Educated at Washburn University of Topeka B.B.A. 1974 J.D. 1977.

County Attorney Washington 1979-92.

Mailing address: P.O. Box 8, Belleville 66935-0008.
Office: Republic County Courthouse, 1800 M Street, Belleville 66935.
Telephone: (785) 527-5691, 527-5675.
Fax: (785) 527-5029
E-mail address: rcmj@nckcn.com

FAIRCHILD, Robert W. *(Chief Judge, Kansas District Court Seventh Judicial District)* Appointed by Governor Bill Graves Jan 31, 1996 to term beginning March 8, 1996. Retained by election. Chief Judge since 2001. Born Kansas City Missouri March 19, 1948. Educated at Texas Tech University B.A. with honors 1990 and University of Kansas J.D. 1973. Managing Editor Kansas Law Review 1971-73. Member Order of the Coif. Admitted to practice Kansas 1973 and U.S. District Court District of Kansas 1973. In legal practice Lawrence 1973-96.

County Counselor Douglas County 1986-96. Author "Resolving Community Disputes Through Mediation" *Kansas Government Journal* League of Kansas Municipalities 1996 and Chapter on Divorce Mediation *Practitioner's Guide to Kansas Family Law* Kansas Bar Association 1997. Adjunct Professor of Alternative Dispute Resolution University of Kansas School of Law 1993-98. Attended The National Judicial College Sept 1997. Captain USAFR 1972-80.

Office: Judicial Center, 111 East Eleventh Street, Lawrence 66044-2966.
Telephone: (785) 832-5265.
Fax: (785) 838-2455
E-mail address: rfairchild@douglas-county.com

FARLEY, Michael H. *(Magistrate Judge, Kansas District Court Tenth Judicial District)* Appointed by Governor Bill Graves.

Office: Johnson County Courthouse, 100 North Kansas Avenue, Olathe 66061-3273.
Telephone: (913) 715-3572.
Fax: (913) 715-3317
E-mail address: michael.farley@jocoks.com

FLAIGLE, Harold E. *(Judge, Kansas District Court Eighteenth Judicial District)*

Office: Juvenile Department Court Building, 1015 South Minnesota Street, Wichita 67211-2730.
Telephone: (316) 383-7487.
Fax: (316) 383-8000
E-mail address: hflaigle@dc18.org

FLANNAGAN, John T. *(Judge, United States Bankruptcy Court District of Kansas)* Appointed by U.S. Court of Appeals Tenth Circuit judges.

Office: 125 U.S. Courthouse, 500 State Avenue, Kansas City 66101-2416.
Telephone: (913) 551-6726.

FLAX, Richard *(Magistrate Judge, Kansas District Court Twenty-third Judicial District)*

Office: Trego County Courthouse, 216 North Main, Wakeeney 67672.
Telephone: (785) 743-2148.
Fax: (785) 743-2726
E-mail address: rflax@ruraltel.net

FLEETWOOD, James *(Judge, Kansas District Court Eighteenth Judicial District)*

Office: 10-3 Sedgwick County Courthouse, 525 North Main Street, Wichita 67203-3773.
Telephone: (316) 383-7623.
Fax: (316) 383-7560
E-mail address: jfleetwo@dc18.org

FLEMING, Robert J. *(Judge, Kansas District Court Eleventh Judicial District)*
Office: Labette County Courthouse, 201 South Central, Parsons 67357.
Telephone: (620) 421-1410.
Fax: (620) 421-3633
E-mail address: judgefleming@sbcglobal.net

FOSTER, Thomas E. *(Judge, Kansas District Court Tenth Judicial District)* Appointed by Governor Bill Graves.
Office: Johnson County Courthouse, 100 North Kansas Avenue, Olathe 66061-3273.
Telephone: (913) 715-3860.
Fax: (913) 715-3317
E-mail address: thomas.foster@jocoks.com

FOWLER, W. Lee *(Judge, Kansas District Court Fifth Judicial District)*
Office: Lyon County Courthouse, 430 Commercial, Emporia 66801.
Telephone: (620) 341-3293.
Fax: (620) 341-3497
E-mail address: lee_fowler@hotmail.com

FREDERICK, Robert J. *(Judge, Kansas District Court Twenty-fifth Judicial District)*
Mailing address: P.O. Box 798, Garden City 67846-0798.
Office: Finney County Courthouse, Garden City 67846.
Telephone: (620) 271-6103.
Fax: (620) 271-6141
E-mail address: judge02@finneycounty.org

FREELOVE, Michael A. *(Magistrate Judge, Kansas District Court Sixteenth Judicial District)* Elected to term beginning Jan 14, 1981. Reelected 1984, 1988, 1992, 1996 and 2000. Current term expires Jan 2005. Born Albuquerque New Mexico Oct 13, 1946. Protestant. Educated at Colorado State University A.A. 1969.
Deputy Sheriff Clark County 1975-80. Emergency Medical Technician and County Ambulance Director 1976-80. Staff Sergeant USAF 1966-70. Republican. Member Planning Commission City of Ashland, Masons, Kiwanis Club and Jaycees. Leader Cub Scouts and 4-H. Instructor in hunting safety. Interests include raising Quarter Horses.
Mailing address: P.O. Box 790, Ashland 67831-0790.
Office: Clark County Courthouse, Ashland 67831.
Telephone: (620) 635-2717.
Fax: (620) 635-2155
E-mail address: juez@ucom.net

FRIEDEL, Karl W. *(Judge, Kansas District Court Eighteenth Judicial District)* Appointed by Governor Mike Hayden Aug 20, 1987 to term beginning Oct 1, 1987. Elected Nov 1988, 1992, 1996 and 2000. Current term expires Jan 2005. Born Fort Scott Kansas Oct 24, 1936. Episcopalian. Educated at Wichita State University B.A. 1959 and Washburn University School of Law J.D. 1964. Admitted to practice Kansas 1964, U.S. District Court District of Kansas 1964, U.S. Court of Appeals Tenth Circuit 1965 and U.S. Supreme Court 1971. In legal practice Wichita 1964-87.
Member Kansas District Judges Association, Wichita and Kansas Bar Associations. Member St. John's Episcopal Church.
Office: 10-1 Sedgwick County Courthouse, 525 North Main Street, Wichita 67203-3773.
Telephone: (316) 383-7191.
Fax: (316) 383-7560
E-mail address: kfriedel@dc18.org

FROMME, Phillip M. *(Judge, Kansas District Court Fourth Judicial District)* Former Magistrate Judge Coffey County. Appointed Judge by Governor Bill Graves.
Mailing address: P.O. Box 330, Burlington 66839-0330.
Office: Coffey County Courthouse, Burlington 66839.
Telephone: (620) 364-8628.
Fax: (620) 364-8535
E-mail address: frommecoffeyco@hotmail.com

GARIGLIETTI, John C. *(Chief Judge, Kansas District Court Eleventh Judicial District)* Elected to term beginning Jan 10, 1977. Retained by election 1980, 1984, 1988, 1992, 1996 and 2000. Current term expires Jan 2005. Born Pittsburg Kansas Sept 30, 1943. Protestant. Educated at Kansas State College-Pittsburg B.S.S.W. 1966 and Washburn University of Topeka J.D. 1969. Member Law Student Exchange Study Program in Yugoslavia, England, Germany and France. Member Phi Alpha Delta. Admitted to practice Kansas 1969 and U.S. District Court District of Kansas 1969. Began legal practice Pittsburg 1969. Judge, Pittsburg City Court (Crawford County) Jan 15, 1976 to Jan 9, 1977.
Board of Directors John's Sport Center, Inc. Instructor of Business Government and Society Pittsburg State University 1990-92. Member The Association of Trial Lawyers of America, Kansas District Judges Association (Executive Committee), Crawford County (President 1976), Southeast Kansas and Kansas Bar Associations. Sponsor and Law Advisor Boy Scouts of America Explorer Post. Member Toyota Land Cruiser Association. Enjoys cars, guns, golf, fishing, antiques and sports card collecting.
Mailing address: P.O. Box 1348, Pittsburg 66762.
Office: Crawford County Courthouse, 602 North Locust, Pittsburg 66762.
Telephone: (620) 231-3570.
Fax: (620) 231-0316
E-mail address: johng@11thjd.org

GATTERMAN, Bruce T. *(Chief Judge, Kansas District Court Twenty-fourth Judicial District)* Elected 2002 to term beginning Jan 13, 2003. Term expires Jan 2007. Born Kinsley Kansas Aug 25, 1953. Methodist. Educated at Kansas State University B.S. cum laude 1975 and Washburn University J.D. 1978. Admitted to practice Kansas 1978 and U.S. District Court District of Kansas 1978. In legal practice Larned 1978-2002. Judge, Larned Municipal Court 1980-2002.
Attorney Board of Education 1980-2002. City Attorney Lewis 1989-2002. Member Kansas District Judges Association, Southwest Kansas, Kansas and American Bar Associations. Republican. Board of Directors Fort Larned Historical Society. Board Member Jordan Library. Enjoys golfing and traveling.
Mailing address: P.O. Box K, Larned 67550.
Office: 715 Broadway, Larned 67550.
Telephone: (620) 285-2247.
Fax: (620) 285-3665
E-mail address: 24thcj@pawnee.kscoxmail.com

GENSWEIDER, Leo *(Magistrate Judge, Kansas District Court Thirty-first Judicial District)*
Mailing address: P.O. Box 228, Yates Center 66783.
Office: Woodson County Courthouse, Yates Center 66783.
Telephone: (620) 625-8610, 625-8611.
Fax: (620) 625-8674

GERNON, Robert *(Justice, Kansas Supreme Court)* Appointed by Governor Bill Graves to term beginning Jan 13, 2003. Born Sabetha Kansas July 29, 1943. Educated at University of Kansas B.S. in Business Administration 1966, Washburn University School of Law J.D. 1969 and University of Virginia School of Law LL.M. in Judicial Process 2001. In legal practice 1970-79. Judge 1979-80 and Administrative Judge 1981-87 Kansas District Court Twenty-second Judicial District. Judge 1988-2003, Kansas Court of Appeals, appointed by Governor Mike Hayden to term beginning 1988.

Former Assistant Attorney and Former Probation and Presentence Investigator Shawnee County. Former County Attorney and County Counselor 1971-75 Brown County. Member Kansas District Judges Association, Kansas and American Bar Associations. Former Faculty Advisor The National Judicial College.
Office: 314 Kansas Judicial Center, 301 S.W. Tenth Avenue, Topeka 66612-1507.
Telephone: (785) 296-5364.

GOSSARD, Roger *(Judge, Kansas District Court Fourteenth Judicial District)*
Office: Montgomery County Courthouse, 102 West Seventh, Suite A, Coffeyville 67337.
Telephone: (620) 251-6052.
Fax: (620) 251-2734

GRABER, Thomas H. *(Judge, Kansas District Court Thirtieth Judicial District)* Elected to term beginning Jan 10, 1977. Retained by election 1980, 1984, 1988, 1992, 1996 and 2000. Current term expires Jan 2005. Born Wichita Kansas April 19, 1942. United Methodist. Educated at Wichita State University B.A. and Washburn University of Topeka J.D. Member Lambda Chi Alpha and Phi Alpha Delta. Admitted to practice Kansas 1967. Began legal practice Wichita 1967. In legal practice Mulvane 1974. Judge, Mulvane Municipal Court 1970-76. Judge, Belle Plaine Municipal Court 1973-76.

Member Sumner County Alcohol and Drug Advisory Committee since 1982. President Board of Directors Sumner County Mental Health Center 1984. Member Sumner County Bar Association (President 1977).
Mailing address: P.O. Box 399, Wellington 67152.
Office: Sumner County Courthouse, Wellington 67152.
Telephone: (620) 326-5936.
Fax: (620) 326-5365

GRACE, Brian *(Magistrate Judge, Kansas District Court Twelfth Judicial District)*
Office: Lincoln County Courthouse, 216 East Lincoln Avenue, Lincoln 67445.
Telephone: (785) 524-4754.

GREEN, Henry W., Jr. *(Judge, Kansas Court of Appeals)* Appointed by Governor Joan Finney to term beginning 1993. Retained by election. Born Leavenworth Kansas Jan 15, 1949. Educated at Kansas State University B.S. 1972 and University of Kansas School of Law J.D. 1975. In legal practice 1975-93. U.S. Panel of Bankruptcy Trustees District of Kansas 1979-93.

Past President Leavenworth County Bar Association. Member Kansas Board of Discipline of Attorneys, Topeka, Kansas and American Bar Associations. Pro Bono Counsel Buffalo Soldier Monument Committee.
Office: 267 Kansas Judicial Center, 301 S.W. Tenth Avenue, Topeka 66612-1507.
Telephone: (785) 296-5409.

GREENE, Richard *(Judge, Kansas Court of Appeals)* Appointed by Governor Kathleen Sebelius to term beginning June 18, 2003.
Office: Kansas Judicial Center, 310 S.W. Tenth Avenue, Topeka 66612-1507.
Telephone: (785) 296-3229.

GRONEMAN, George A. *(Judge, Kansas District Court Twenty-ninth Judicial District)* Appointed by Governor Joan Finney March 1993. Elected 1994, 1998 and 2002. Current term expires Jan 2007. Born Kansas City Missouri June 13, 1944. Lutheran. Educated at University of Kansas B.A. 1966 and University of Missouri-Kansas City J.D. 1969. Editorial Board University of Missouri-Kansas City Law Review 1967-69. Admitted to practice Kansas 1969, U.S. District Court District of Kansas 1969 and U.S. Court of Appeals Tenth Circuit 1972. In legal practice Kansas City June 1969 to March 1993. Justice of the Peace, Kansas City Jan 1967 to Jan 1970. Judge, Kansas City Municipal Court Sept 1976 to March 1993.

Member Kansas Municipal Judges Association (President 1984-85), Kansas District Judges Association, Wyandotte County, Kansas and American Bar Associations. Attended The National Judicial College 1993. First Lieutenant USMC 1970-74. Democrat. Past President University of Kansas Young Democrats and Wyandotte County Young Democrats.
Office: Wyandotte County Courthouse, 710 North Seventh Street, Kansas City 66101.
Telephone: (913) 573-2929.
Fax: (913) 573-4354
E-mail address: GGroneman@wycokck.org

GROSKO, Michael *(Judge, Kansas District Court Twenty-ninth Judicial District)* Elected Nov 1996 to term beginning Jan 1997. Reelected 2000, current term expires Jan 2005. Born Kansas City Kansas Oct 26, 1952. Catholic. Educated at Kansas University B.A. 1974 and Washburn University J.D. 1977. Admitted to practice Kansas 1977.

Assistant District Attorney Wyandotte County 1977-96. Member National Association of County and District Attorneys, Wyandotte County, Kansas and American Bar Associations. Attended General Jurisdiction course The National Judicial College 1997 and Economics Institute for State Judges Kansas University 1998. Democrat. Member State of Kansas Child Safety and Permanency Review Panel, State of Kansas SRS Continuous Quality Improvement Panel and Wyandotte County Juvenile Corrections Advisory Board.
Office: Wyandotte County Court Svcs. Bldg., 711 Armstrong, Kansas City 66101.
Telephone: (913) 573-4192.
Fax: (913) 573-4195
E-mail address: Mgrosko@wycokck.org

HAMPTON, Van Z. *(Judge, Kansas District Court Sixteenth Judicial District)* Appointed by Governor Bill Graves to term beginning Aug 1, 1995. Elected Nov 5, 1996 and 2000. Current term expires Jan 1, 2005. Born

HAMPTON, VAN Z.—*Continued*

Dodge City Kansas April 10, 1955. Protestant. Educated at Fort Hays State University B.S. in Agriculture 1977, Oral Roberts University J.D. 1987 and University of Arkansas at Fayetteville LL.M. 1990. Admitted to practice Kansas 1987, U.S. District Court District of Kansas 1987 and Colorado 1990. In legal practice Dodge City Kansas 1988-95.

Instructor in Agricultural Law University of Arkansas at Fayetteville 1987-88.

Mailing address: P.O. Box 197, Dodge City 67801.
Office: Ford County Courthouse, Dodge City 67801.
Telephone: (620) 227-4561.
Fax: (620) 227-6799
E-mail address: vhampton@16thdistrict.net

HARRIS, Muriel *(Judge, Kansas District Court Twenty-ninth Judicial District)*

Office: Wyandotte County Courthouse, First Floor, 710 North Seventh Street, Kansas City 66101.
Telephone: (913) 573-2914.
Fax: (913) 281-4354
E-mail address: Myharris@wycokck.org

HART, Charles M. *(Judge, Kansas District Court Thirteenth Judicial District)*

Office: 201 Butler County Courthouse, 121 South Gordy, El Dorado 67042.
Telephone: (316) 322-4356.
Fax: (316) 322-4365
E-mail address: judgehart@yahoo.com

HART, Gerald W. *(Judge, Kansas District Court Sixth Judicial District)*

Mailing address: P.O. Box 868, Fort Scott 66701.
Office: Bourbon County Courthouse, Fort Scott 66701.
Telephone: (620) 223-1380.
Fax: (620) 223-5303

HEBERT, Daniel L. *(Chief Judge, Kansas District Court Twenty-eighth Judicial District)* Appointed by Governor John Carlin to term beginning May 1, 1984. Retained by election 1986, 1990, 1994, 1998 and 2002. Current term expires Jan 2007. Born Salina Kansas Oct 17, 1944. Educated at St. Benedict's College B.A. magna cum laude 1966 and University of Notre Dame Law School J.D. 1969. Staff member and Editor Notre Dame Lawyer 1968-69. Member Gray's Inn. Admitted to practice Illinois 1969 and Kansas 1973. In legal practice Chicago Illinois 1969-73 and Salina Kansas 1973-84.

City Prosecutor Salina 1978-81. Member Kansas District Judges Association, Salina-Ottawa County (President 1981), Kansas and American Bar Associations. Attended course on General Jurisdiction The National Judicial College Fall 1984.

Mailing address: P.O. Box 1760, Salina 67402-1760.
Office: Saline County Courthouse, 300 West Ash, Salina 67401.
Telephone: (785) 309-5837.
Fax: (785) 309-5845
E-mail address: dan.hebert@saline.org

HELLMER, Jerome P. *(Judge, Kansas District Court Twenty-eighth Judicial District)*

Mailing address: P.O. Box 1760, Salina 67402-1760.
Office: Saline County Courthouse, 300 West Ash, Salina 67401.
Telephone: (785) 309-5839.
Fax: (785) 309-5845
E-mail address: jerome.hellmer@saline.org

HENDERSON, Timothy H. *(Judge, Kansas District Court Eighteenth Judicial District)*

Office: Juvenile Department Court Building, 1015 South Minnesota Street, Wichita 67211-2730.
Telephone: (316) 383-7487.
Fax: (316) 383-8000
E-mail address: thenders@dc18.org

HILL, Stephen D. *(Chief Judge, Kansas District Court Sixth Judicial District)* Appointed by Governor John Carlin to term beginning Jan 12, 1981. Retained by election. Current term expires Jan 2007. Born Fort Scott Kansas Dec 18, 1950. Christian. Educated at University of Kansas B.A. 1972 and Washburn University of Topeka School of Law J.D. 1973. Member Phi Alpha Delta and Order of Barristers. Admitted to practice Kansas 1975, U.S. District Court District of Kansas 1975 and U.S. Supreme Court 1980. Began legal practice Mound City 1975.

Member Kansas Trial Lawyers Association, American Judges Association, Miami County, Kansas and American Bar Associations. Democrat. Member Masonic Lodge and Lions Club. Hobbies include golf, fishing and gardening.

Mailing address: P.O. Box 187, Paola 66071.
Office: Miami County Courthouse, Paola 66071.
Telephone: (913) 294-3644.
Fax: (913) 294-2535
E-mail address: jhill@classicnet.net

HOOD, E. Leigh *(Judge, Kansas District Court Sixteenth Judicial District)*

Mailing address: P.O. Box 197, Dodge City 67801.
Office: Ford County Courthouse, Dodge City 67801.
Telephone: (620) 227-4604.
Fax: (620) 227-6799
E-mail address: lhood@16thdistrict.net

HOOPER, Keith *(Magistrate Judge, Kansas District Court Seventeenth Judicial District)*

Mailing address: P.O. Box 273, Smith Center 66967-0273.
Office: Smith County Courthouse, Smith Center 66967.
Telephone: (785) 282-5140.
Fax: (785) 282-5145
E-mail address: khooper@ruraltel.net

HORNBAKER, Steven L. *(Judge, Kansas District Court Eighth Judicial District)* Appointed by Governor Bill Graves.

Mailing address: P.O. Box 1147, Junction City 66441.
Office: Geary County Courthouse, Junction City 66441.
Telephone: (785) 762-5221.
Fax: (785) 762-4420
E-mail address: dj4@oz-online.net

HUBBELL, Martina M. *(Magistrate Judge, Kansas District Court Thirteenth Judicial District)*

Mailing address: P.O. Box 306, Howard 67349.
Office: Elk County Courthouse, Howard 67349.
Telephone: (620) 374-3532.
Fax: (620) 374-3531
E-mail address: judge@terraworld.net

HUMPHREYS, Karen M. *(Magistrate Judge, United States District Court District of Kansas)* Appointed by U.S. District Court judges. Former Judge, Kansas District Court Eighteenth Judicial District.
Office: 322 U.S. Courthouse, 401 North Market Street, Wichita 67202.
Telephone: (316) 269-6164.

ISENHOUR, William O., Jr. *(Judge, Kansas District Court Tenth Judicial District)* Appointed by Governor Joan Finney July 1994 to term beginning Sept 1, 1994. Retained by election 1996 and 2000. Current term expires Jan 2005. Born Kansas City Kansas May 11, 1942. Episcopalian. Educated at University of Missouri at Kansas City B.A. 1964 J.D. 1968. Law Clerk to Hon. Arthur J. Stanley, Jr., U.S. District Court District of Kansas 1968-69. Member Phi Delta Phi and Omicron Delta Kappa. Admitted to practice Kansas 1968, U.S. District Court District of Kansas 1968, U.S. Court of Appeals Tenth Circuit and U.S. Supreme Court 1982. In legal practice Mission 1968-94. Judge, Merriam Municipal Court 1969-71.
Member Kansas Trial Lawyers Association, Kansas City Metropolitan, Johnson County and Kansas Bar Associations.
Office: Johnson County Courthouse, 100 North Kansas Avenue, Olathe 66061-3273.
Telephone: (913) 715-3910.
Fax: (913) 715-3317
E-mail address: William.Isenhour@jocoks.com

JOHNSON, Ernest *(Judge, Kansas District Court Twenty-ninth Judicial District)*
Office: Wyandotte County Courthouse, Justice Complex, 710 North Seventh Street, Kansas City 66101.
Telephone: (913) 573-2987.
Fax: (913) 573-8170
E-mail address: Ejohnson@wycokck.org

JOHNSON, Lee A. *(Judge, Kansas Court of Appeals)* Appointed by Governor Bill Graves. Born Caldwell Kansas June 28, 1947. Educated at University of Kansas B.S.B.A. 1969 and Washburn University School of Law J.D. summa cum laude 1980.
City Attorney Caldwell 1987-97. Member Sumner County (President 1992) and Kansas Bar Associations. Mayor City of Caldwell 1975-76. Member Sumner Mental Health Board.
Office: 325 Kansas Judicial Center, 301 S.W. Tenth Avenue, Topeka 66612-1507.
Telephone: (785) 296-5407.

JONES, Jon Stephen *(Magistrate Judge, Kansas District Court Fourth Judicial District)*
Office: Osage County Courthouse, 717 Topeka Avenue, Lyndon 66451.
Telephone: (785) 828-4514.
Fax: (785) 828-4704

KARLIN, Janice Miller *(Judge, United States Bankruptcy Court District of Kansas)* Appointed by U.S. Court of Appeals Tenth Circuit judges to term beginning Oct 17, 2002. Term expires Oct 16, 2016.
Office: 225 U.S. Courthouse, 444 S.E. Quincy Street, Topeka 66683-3502.
Telephone: (785) 295-2646.

KAUFMAN, David *(Judge, Kansas District Court Eighteenth Judicial District)*
Office: 11-1 Sedgwick County Courthouse, 525 North Main Street, Wichita 67203-3773.
Telephone: (316) 383-7302.
Fax: (316) 383-7560
E-mail address: dkaufman@dc18.org

KEELEY, J. Michael *(Judge, Kansas District Court Twentieth Judicial District)* Elected Nov 1992 to term beginning Jan 13, 1993. Reelected 1996 and 2000. Current term expires Jan 2005. Born Minneola Kansas Oct 5, 1957. Catholic. Educated at Washburn University B.S. 1979 J.D. 1982. Admitted to practice Kansas 1982 and U.S. District Court District of Kansas 1982. In legal practice Great Bend 1982-92.
Member Kansas and American Bar Associations. Attended The National Judicial College 1992. Member school board. Leader Boy Scouts. Enjoys hunting, fishing and coaching and playing sports.
Office: 306 Barton County Courthouse, 1400 Main, Great Bend 67530-4098.
Telephone: (620) 793-1863.
Fax: (620) 793-1860
E-mail address: judgekeeley@hotmail.com

KENNEDY, David W. *(Judge, Kansas District Court Eighteenth Judicial District)* Appointed by Governor Robert F. Bennett to term beginning April 28, 1978. Elected 1978, 1982, 1986, 1990, 1994, 1998 and 2002. Current term expires Jan 2007. Born Lyons Kansas Nov 5, 1941. Episcopalian. Educated at University of Kansas B.S. 1965 LL.B. 1968. Member Phi Alpha Delta. Admitted to practice Kansas 1968. In legal practice Wichita 1968-78.
Member Kansas District Judges Association (Past President) and Kansas Bar Association. Member Wichita Downtown Lions (Former member Board of Directors, former Third Vice President, former First Vice President, former Secretary, Past President).
Office: 10-2 Sedgwick County Courthouse, 525 North Main Street, Wichita 67203-3773.
Telephone: (316) 383-7641.
Fax: (316) 383-7560
E-mail address: dkennedy@dc18.org

KEPPLE, James R. *(Magistrate Judge, Kansas District Court Twenty-fourth Judicial District)*
Mailing address: P.O. Box 445, Ness City 67560.
Office: Ness County Courthouse, Ness City 67560.
Telephone: (785) 798-3200.
Fax: (785) 798-3348
E-mail address: nsdmj@gbta.net

KING, David J. *(Chief Judge, Kansas District Court First Judicial District)*
Office: 4099 Leavenworth Justice Center, 601 South Third Street, Leavenworth 66048-2868.
Telephone: (913) 684-0718.
Fax: (913) 684-0492
E-mail address: dking@lvcoks.com

KITTS, Hannelore *(Judge, Kansas District Court Twentieth Judicial District)*
Office: 306 Barton County Courthouse, 1400 Main, Great Bend 67530-4098.
Telephone: (620) 793-1863.
Fax: (620) 793-1860
E-mail address: hkcourthouse@msn.com

KLINGINSMITH, Tracy D. *(Chief Judge, Kansas District Court Second Judicial District)*
Office: Jackson County Courthouse, 400 New York, Holton 66436.
Telephone: (785) 364-2191.
Fax: (785) 364-3804

KNUDSON, David S. *(Judge, Kansas Court of Appeals)* Appointed by Governor Bill Graves to term beginning 1995. Retained by election. Born Goodland Kansas Aug 22, 1941. Educated at University of Kansas B.S. in Business Administration 1963 and Washburn University School of Law J.D. 1966. Judge 1981-83 and Administrative Judge 1983-95, Kansas District Court Twenty-eighth Judicial District.

Former Assistant City Attorney Wichita. Former Saline County Attorney. Member Kansas Continuing Legal Education Commission, Kansas Judicial Council, American Judicature Society, Colorado, Kansas and American Bar Associations. Member Rotary International. Enjoys running, cycling, triathlons and marathons.

Office: 278 Kansas Judicial Center, 301 S.W. Tenth Avenue, Topeka 66612-1507.
Telephone: (785) 296-5410.

KVASNICKA, Richard L. *(Magistrate Judge, Kansas District Court Fifteenth Judicial District)*
Office: Logan County Courthouse, 710 West Second Street, Oakley 67748.
Telephone: (785) 672-4284.
Fax: (785) 672-3517
E-mail address: lgdc@ruraltel.net

KYLE, Philip T. *(Magistrate Judge, Kansas District Court Twenty-fourth Judicial District)* Elected to term beginning Jan 1985. Reelected 1988, 1992, 1996 and 2000. Current term expires Jan 2005. Born Wichita Kansas Jan 7, 1941. Educated at Wichita State University B.A. 1965, Emporia State University M.S. 1971, University of Kansas M.P.A. with honors 1977, Washburn University of Topeka J.D. with honors 1977 and University of Missouri LL.M. 1984. Admitted to practice Kansas 1978.

Member Bar Association of the Twenty-fourth Judicial District of Kansas, Hodgeman County, Kansas and American Bar Associations. Attended The National Judicial College 1986.

Mailing address: P.O. Box 187, Jetmore 67854-0187.
Office: Hodgeman County Courthouse, Jetmore 67854.
Telephone: (620) 357-8434.
Fax: (620) 357-6216
E-mail address: hgdistct@pld.com

LACEY, Philip C. *(Judge, Kansas District Court First Judicial District)* Appointed by Governor Joan Finney Nov 21, 1991 to term beginning Jan 6, 1992. Retained by election Nov 8, 1994, 1998 and 2002. Current term expires Jan 2007. Born Hoisington Kansas Nov 8, 1940. Catholic. Educated at Fort Hays State University B.S. 1963 and University of Kansas J.D. 1970. Admitted to practice Kansas 1971. In legal practice Atchison 1971-90.

Member Kansas and American Bar Associations. Captain USMC April 1964 to Nov 1968.

Mailing address: P.O. Box 408, Atchison 66002.
Office: Atchison County Courthouse, Atchison 66002.
Telephone: (913) 367-7400.
Fax: (913) 367-1171

LAHEY, Timothy G. *(Judge, Kansas District Court Eighteenth Judicial District)*
Office: 8-1 Sedgwick County Courthouse, 525 North Main Street, Wichita 67203-3773.
Telephone: (316) 383-7261.
Fax: (316) 383-7560
E-mail address: tlahey@dc18.org

LAMPSON, R. Wayne *(Judge, Kansas District Court Twenty-ninth Judicial District)*
Office: Wyandotte County Courthouse, First Floor, 710 North Seventh Street, Kansas City 66101.
Telephone: (913) 573-2806.
Fax: (913) 281-4354
E-mail address: wlampson@wycokck.org

LANGSTON, Karen L. *(Judge, Kansas District Court Eighteenth Judicial District)*
Office: 7-2 Sedgwick County Courthouse, 525 North Main Street, Wichita 67203-3373.
Telephone: (316) 660-4700.
Fax: (316) 383-7560
E-mail address: klangsto@dc18.org

LAPKA, Adrian A. *(Magistrate Judge, Kansas District Court Twenty-eighth Judicial District)* Elected to term beginning Jan 10, 1977. Retained by election 1980, 1984, 1988, 1992, 1996 and 2000. Current term expires Jan 2005. Born Great Bend Kansas April 30, 1949. Educated at Pampa Vocational and Technical Institute (Accounting) 1972 and Police Academy.

Police Officer 1972-77. Recipient Merit Award for Outstanding Performance of Duty and Fish and Game Merit Award for Outstanding Activity in Hunter's Safety Program. E-4 U.S. Army Paratroopers 1966-69. Republican. Enjoys bass fishing.

Office: Ottawa County Courthouse, 307 North Concord, Minneapolis 67467.
Telephone: (785) 392-2917.
Fax: (785) 392-3626
E-mail address: alapka@nckcn.com

LEBEN, Steve *(Judge, Kansas District Court Tenth Judicial District)* Appointed by Governor Joan Finney to term beginning Sept 17, 1993. Retained by election Nov 1994, 1998 and 2002. Current term expires Jan 2007. Born Eureka Kansas June 23, 1956. Educated at University of Kansas B.S. 1978 J.D. 1982. Staff member and Associate Editor Kansas Law Review 1980-82. Member Order of the Coif, Phi Kappa Phi and Mortar Board. Admitted to practice Missouri 1982, Kansas 1983, U.S. District Courts Western District of Missouri 1982 and District of Kansas 1983, U.S. Court of Appeals Tenth Circuit 1985 and U.S. Supreme Court 1987. In legal practice Kansas City Missouri 1982-84 and Overland Park Kansas 1984-93.

Author "Rule 11 Sanctions: The Special Problem of Local Counsel" Journal of the Kansas Bar Association 17 June 1989, "Survey of Kansas Law: Administrative Law" 37 Kansas L. Rev. 679, 1989, "Challenging and Defending Agency Actions in Kansas" Journal of the Kansas Bar Association 22 June-July 1995, Chapter "Civil Procedure and Evidence for the Family Lawyer" *Practitioner's Guide to Kansas Family Law* Kansas Bar Association 1997, "May Fault Be Considered in Deciding Financial Issues in Divorce Cases? Yes, When a Fault-Based Divorce is Granted" Journal of the Kansas Bar Association 29 June/July 1998, "Evidence for the Family Lawyer: Intrafamily Wiretapping, the Fifth

LEBEN, STEVE—*Continued*

Amendment and Other Selected Topics" Journal of the Kansas Bar Association 24 March 1999 and "Public Trust and Confidence in the Courts: A National Conference and Beyond" *Court Review* 4 Fall 1999. Co-author with Mark D. Hinderks "Restoring the Common in the Law: A Proposal for the Elimination of Rules Prohibiting the Citation of Unpublished Opinions in Kansas and the Tenth Circuit" 31 Washburn L. Jour. 155, 1992, "Long-Arm Jurisdiction in Kansas" Journal of the Kansas Bar Association 26 May 1993, "On the Admissibility of Expert Testimony in Kansas" Journal of the Kansas Bar Association 24 Nov 1997 and with Megan Moriarty "A Kansas Approach to Custodial Parent Move-Away Cases" 37 Washburn L. Jour. 497, 1998. Board of Editors Journal of the Kansas Bar Association since 1993. Editor two volumes *Practitioner's Guide to Kansas Family Law* Kansas Bar Association 1997 and *Court Review* American Judges Association since 1998. Important Decision: McCarthy v. City of Leawood (approving use of home rule powers to enact impact fees in area of new development) aff'd 257 Kan. 566, 894 P.2d 836, 1995. Member American Judges Association (Board of Governors since 1999), Kansas (President Administrative Law Section 1992-93, Board of Governors 1993-2000) and American (Committee on State Administrative Law Section of Administrative Law and Regulatory Practice since 1994) Bar Associations. Frequent CLE presenter in Kansas on administrative law, family law, evidence and civil procedure topics. Recipient Outstanding Young Lawyer in Kansas Award from Kansas Bar Association 1993 and Distinguished Service Award from National Center for State Courts 2003.

Office: Johnson County Courthouse, 100 North Kansas Avenue, Olathe 66061-3273.
Telephone: (913) 715-3820.
Fax: (913) 715-4000
E-mail address: steve.leben@jocoks.com

LEIDIG, Bonnie M. *(Magistrate Judge, Kansas District Court Seventeenth Judicial District)* Elected Nov 1992 to term beginning Jan 11, 1993. Reelected 1996 and 2000. Current term expires Jan 2005. Born Dodge City Kansas July 31, 1944. Religious affiliation: Wesleyan. Educated at Fort Hays State University B.S. 1967. Interests include agriculture.

Mailing address: P.O. Box 564, Phillipsburg 67661-0564.
Office: Phillips County Courthouse, Phillipsburg 67661.
Telephone: (785) 543-6830.
Fax: (785) 543-6832

LEUENBERGER, Jan W. *(Judge, Kansas District Court Third Judicial District)*

Office: 300 Shawnee County Courthouse, 200 S.E. Seventh Street, Topeka 66603-3922.
Telephone: (785) 233-8200.
Fax: (785) 291-4917
E-mail address: stindall@shawneecourt.org

LEWIS, Robert J., Jr. *(Judge, Kansas Court of Appeals)* Appointed by Governor Mike Hayden to term beginning Jan 24, 1989. Retained by election Nov 1990, Nov 1994, Nov 1998 and 2002. Current term expires Jan 2007. Born Atwood Kansas July 28, 1939. Catholic. Educated at University of Kansas B.A. 1961 J.D. 1963 and University of Virginia LL.M. in Judicial Process 1998. Staff member Kansas Law Review. Member Phi Delta Phi and Order of the Coif. Admitted to practice Kansas 1963. In legal practice Atwood 1964-89.

County Attorney Rawlins County 1968-72. Author Comment Cigarette/Cancer case Kansas L. Rev. 1962 and "The Kansas Sentencing Guidelines Act" 38 Washburn L. Jour. Spring 1999. President Topeka Inns of Court. Member Kansas Board of Law Examiners, Kansas and American Bar Associations. Recipient Award for Courageous Advocacy from American College of Trial Lawyers March 1991. Member Kansas Sentencing Commission, Friends of the Topeka Zoo, Downtown Topeka Rotary Club, Jayhawker Club and Williams Fund. Enjoys walking, astronomy and reading.

Office: 263 Kansas Judicial Center, 301 S.W. Tenth Avenue, Topeka 66612-1507.
Telephone: (785) 296-5411.

LINDAMOOD, Rebecca *(Magistrate Judge, Kansas District Court Thirteenth Judicial District)*

Office: Greenwood County Courthouse, 311 North Main, Eureka 67045.
Telephone: (620) 583-8155.
Fax: (620) 583-8154
E-mail address: BeckyL@Fox-net.net

LORENTZ, C. Fred, II *(Chief Judge, Kansas District Court Thirty-first Judicial District)* Appointed by Governor John Carlin to term beginning Nov 20, 1979. Retained by election 1982, 1986, 1990, 1994, 1998 and 2002. Current term expires Jan 2007. Born Kansas City Kansas Sept 3, 1944. Methodist. Educated at Baker University 1962-63, Kansas State College B.S. 1966 and Washburn University J.D. 1969. Member Delta Tau Delta and Phi Alpha Delta. Admitted to practice Kansas 1969 and U.S. District Court District of Kansas 1969. Began legal practice Fredonia 1969.

Attorney Wilson County 1970-74. Kansas House of Representatives 1974-78. Member Governor's Committee on Criminal Administration 1976-79. Member Kansas Judicial Council, Kansas Judges Association (Past President), American Judges Association and Kansas Bar Association. Specialist Five Army National Guard 1969-75. Member Wilson County Fair Association (Past President) and Fredonia Arts Council. Enjoys reading, sports and yard work.

Mailing address: P.O. Box 246, Fredonia 66736.
Office: Wilson County Courthouse, Fredonia 66736.
Telephone: (620) 378-4361.
Fax: (620) 378-4531

LOVE, Daniel L. *(Chief Judge, Kansas District Court Sixteenth Judicial District)*

Mailing address: P.O. Box 197, Dodge City 67801.
Office: Ford County Courthouse, Dodge City 67801.
Telephone: (620) 227-4620.
Fax: (620) 227-4644
E-mail address: dlove@16thdistrict.net

LUCKERT, Marla J. *(Justice, Kansas Supreme Court)* Appointed by Governor Bill Graves to term beginning Jan 13, 2003. Born Goodland Kansas July 20, 1955. Educated at Washburn University of Topeka B.A. 1977 J.D. 1980. Technical editor Washburn Law Journal. Admitted to practice Kansas 1980. Began legal practice Topeka 1980. Judge and Chief Judge, Kansas

LUCKERT, MARLA J.—*Continued*

District Court Third Judicial District, appointed by Governor Joan Finney 1992.

Office: 388 Kansas Judicial Center, 301 S.W. Tenth Avenue, Topeka 66612-1507.

Telephone: (785) 296-4900.

LUNGSTRUM, John W. *(Chief Judge, United States District Court District of Kansas)* Appointed for life by President George Bush to term beginning Nov 5, 1991. Chief Judge since Jan 1, 2001. Born Topeka Kansas Nov 2, 1945. Educated at Yale University B.A. magna cum laude 1967 and University of Kansas School of Law J.D. 1970. Editor-in-Chief University of Kansas Law Review 1969-70. Member Phi Beta Kappa, Phi Delta Phi and Order of the Coif. Admitted to practice Kansas 1970, California 1970, U.S. District Courts District of Kansas and Central District of California and U.S. Court of Appeals Tenth Circuit. In legal practice Los Angeles California 1970-71 and Lawrence Kansas Dec 1972 to Nov 1991.

Lecturer on Law 1973-82, 1986, 1989-91 and 1993-95 and Visiting Professor from the Judiciary of Contracts, Evidence, Trial Advocacy and Civil Procedure since 1996 University of Kansas School of Law. Chair District of Kansas Bench/Bar and Rules Committee 1995-2000. Former Chair Committee on Court Administration and Case Management Judicial Conference of the U.S. Former Member Tenth Circuit Judicial Council. Fellow American Inns of Court, Kansas Bar Foundation and American Bar Foundation. Member Douglas County (President 1982), Johnson County, Wyandotte County, Kansas (Vice Chair Subcommittee on Litigation Legislative Committee, Continuing Legal Education Committee and Bench/Bar Committee) and American Bar Associations. Faculty Trial Tactics and Techniques Institute Kansas Bar Association College of Advocacy. Lecturer Douglas County, Johnson County, Kansas City Metropolitan and Kansas Bar Associations and Kansas Judicial Conference. Lieutenant U.S. Army 1971-72. Recipient Army Commendation Medal. Board of Trustees, Stewardship Chairman and Member Senior Pastor Search Committee Plymouth Congregational Church. Enjoys basketball, family activities, hiking and skiing.

Office: 517 U.S. Courthouse, 500 State Avenue, Kansas City 66101-2436.

Telephone: (913) 551-6740.

LYERLA, Bill W. *(Magistrate Judge, Kansas District Court Eleventh Judicial District)* Appointed to term beginning Jan 1, 1991. Retained by election Nov 1992, 1996 and 2000. Current term expires Jan 2005. Born Joplin Missouri Oct 29, 1951. Christian. Educated at Missouri South State College A.S. 1973.

Member National Association of Family and Juvenile Court Judges, Kansas District Magistrate Judges Association (Second Vice President 1994-95 and President 1996-98), National Judges Association and American Judges Association. Attended General Jurisdiction April 1991, Sentencing Misdemeanants May 1994 and Traffic Court Proceedings The National Judicial College. Chief of Police Galena Kansas Police Department 1983-85. Sergeant Cherokee County Sheriff's Department 1985-89. Democrat. Enjoys woodworking, dancing and children.

Mailing address: P.O. Box 189, Columbus 66725.

Office: Cherokee County Courthouse, Columbus 66725.

Telephone: (620) 429-3877.

Fax: (620) 429-1130

E-mail address: blyerla@11thjd.org

MACNISH, James Martin, Jr. *(Judge, Kansas District Court Third Judicial District)* Appointed by Governor Robert Bennett to term beginning Nov 1, 1977. Retained by election Nov 1978, Nov 1982, Nov 1986, Nov 1990, Nov 1994, Nov 1998 and Nov 2002. Current term expires Jan 2007. Assigned Judge Kansas Court of Appeals since 1986. Assigned Judge Kansas Supreme Court Oct 1990, Nov 1991, June 1993 and Dec 2000. Born Richmond Heights Missouri Sept 3, 1935. Protestant. Educated at Washington University A.B. 1957 J.D. 1964. Member Sigma Chi and Phi Delta Phi. Admitted to practice Missouri 1964, U.S. District Court Eastern District of Missouri 1964, Kansas 1967, U.S. District Court District of Kansas 1967, U.S. Court of Appeals Tenth Circuit 1969 and U.S. Supreme Court 1971. Began legal practice St. Louis Missouri 1964. In legal practice Topeka Kansas 1967-77. Judge, Topeka Municipal Court 1973-77.

Member Kansas Sentencing Commission 1989-99. Member Kansas District Judges Association, American Judicature Society, Bar Association of Metropolitan St. Louis, The Missouri Bar, Topeka, Kansas and American Bar Associations. Recipient Honorary Life Member Award Washburn School of Law Association 1985. Captain USMC 1958-61. Member 1971-85 and Chairman 1974-75 Board of Regents Washburn University of Topeka.

Office: 401 Shawnee County Courthouse, 200 S.E. Seventh Street, Topeka 66603-3922.

Telephone: (785) 233-8200.

Fax: (785) 291-4917

E-mail address: jmacnish@shawneecourt.org

MALONE, Michael J. *(Judge, Kansas District Court Seventh Judicial District)* Appointed by Governor John Carlin to term beginning July 15, 1982. Retained by election. Current term expires Jan 2005. Former Chief Judge. Born Raymond Kansas Jan 16, 1948. Catholic. Educated at Kansas State University B.A. 1970 and University of Kansas J.D. 1973. Member Delta Upsilon and Blue Key. Admitted to practice Kansas 1973. Began legal practice Lawrence 1973.

Douglas County District Attorney 1977-82. Author "Prosecutor Inquisition: Tool or Abuse of Investigation" Law Enforcement Review 1981. Adjunct Professor University of Kansas Law School since 1983. Member Standing Subcommittee on Criminal Law Kansas Judicial Council, Kansas District Judges Association and Douglas County Bar Association. Faculty member National Institute of Trial Advocacy 1982-90 and National College on Judicial Conduct and Ethics. Participant The National Judicial College 1983. First Lieutenant U.S. Army 1973-74.

Office: Judicial Center, 111 East 11th, Lawrence 66044-2966.

Telephone: (785) 832-5124.

Fax: (785) 838-5456

E-mail address: mmalone@douglas-county.com

MALONE, Tom *(Judge, Kansas Court of Appeals)* Appointed by Governor Kathleen Sebelius March 2003. Educated at Kansas Newman College and Washburn University School of Law J.D. with honors 1979. In legal practice Wichita. Former Judge, Kansas District Court Eighteenth Judicial District Jan 1991 to 2003.

Office: 277 Kansas Judicial Center, 301 S.W. Tenth Avenue, Topeka 66612-1507.

Telephone: (785) 296-5364.

MARQUARDT, Christel E. *(Judge, Kansas Court of Appeals)* Appointed by Governor Bill Graves to term beginning 1995. Retained by election 1996 and 2000. Current term expires Jan 2005. Born Chicago Illinois Aug 26, 1935. Educated at Missouri Western State College B.S. 1970 and Washburn University School of Law J.D. 1974. Managing Editor Washburn Law Journal 1974. In legal practice 1974-95.

Hearing Examiner Topeka Human Relations Commission 1975-77. Member Kansas (President 1987-88) and American (Board of Governors since 1999) Bar Associations.

Office: 264 Kansas Judicial Center, 301 S.W. Tenth Avenue, Topeka 66612-1507.

Telephone: (785) 296-6146.

E-mail address: MARQUARDT@KSCOURTS.ORG

MARTEN, John Thomas *(Judge, United States District Court District of Kansas)* Appointed for life by President Bill Clinton to term beginning Jan 4, 1996. Born Topeka Kansas Nov 24, 1951. Educated at Washburn University B.A. 1973 J.D. 1976. Law Clerk to Hon. Tom Clark, U.S. Supreme Court 1976-77. In legal practice Omaha Nebraska 1977-80, Minneapolis Minnesota 1980-81 and McPherson Kansas 1981-96.

Office: 232 U.S. Courthouse, 401 North Market Street, Wichita 67202.

Telephone: (316) 269-6578.

MARTIN, Paula B. *(Judge, Kansas District Court Seventh Judicial District)*

Office: Judicial Center, 111 East Eleventh, Lawrence 66044-2966.

Telephone: (785) 832-5323.

Fax: (785) 838-2454

E-mail address: pmartin@douglas-county.com

MASTRONI, Leonard A. *(Magistrate Judge, Kansas District Court Twenty-fourth Judicial District)*

Mailing address: P.O. Box 387, La Crosse 67548.

Office: Rush County Courthouse, La Crosse 67548.

Telephone: (785) 222-2718.

Fax: (785) 222-2748

E-mail address: jmastron@gbta.net

MATHIS, James *(Magistrate Judge, Kansas District Court Thirtieth Judicial District)*

Mailing address: P.O. Box 495, Kingman 67068.

Office: Kingman County Courthouse, 130 North Spruce Street, Kingman 67068.

Telephone: (620) 532-5151.

Fax: (620) 532-2952

McANANY, Patrick D. *(Chief Judge, Kansas District Court Tenth Judicial District)* Appointed by Governor Bill Graves June 16, 1995. Retained by election. Chief Judge since Jan 2000. Born Sweetwater Texas Nov 18, 1943. Educated at Rockhurst College B.A. 1965 and University of Missouri at Kansas City School of Law J.D. 1968 LL.M. 1971. In legal practice Kansas City 1968-71 and Kansas City and Johnson County 1973-95.

Antitrust Counsel 1971-73. Former Adjunct Instructor in Business Law Rockhurst College. Adjunct Faculty in Trial Advocacy University of Kansas School of Law. Member Kansas Supreme Court Nominating Commission 1993-95. Former Director Association of Family and Conciliation Courts. President Earl E. O'Connor Inn of Court. Director and Treasurer Johnson County Bar Foundation. Member Judicial Advisory Board Law and Organizational Economics Center, Kansas District Judges Association (Executive Committee), American Judicature Society, American Judges Association, Johnson County and Kansas Bar Associations. Speaker CLE programs. Past President and Chairman Lenexa Chamber of Commerce and Kansas Opera Theatre, Inc. Former Director Children's Art Foundation. Member Lyric Opera Guild and Overland Park Civic Orchestra (violin section).

Office: Johnson County Courthouse, 100 North Kansas Avenue, Olathe 66061-3273.

Telephone: (913) 715-3880.

Fax: (913) 715-3886

E-mail address: patrick.mcanany@jocoks.com

McCLAIN, Larry *(Judge, Kansas District Court Tenth Judicial District)* Former Administrative Judge.

Office: Johnson County Courthouse, 100 North Kansas Avenue, Olathe 66061-3273.

Telephone: (913) 715-3840.

Fax: (913) 715-3847

E-mail address: Larry.McClain@jocoks.com

McFARLAND, Kay *(Chief Justice, Kansas Supreme Court)* Appointed by Governor Robert F. Bennett to term beginning 1977. Retained by election. Chief Justice since 1995. Born Coffeyville Kansas July 20, 1935. Protestant. Educated at Washburn University of Topeka B.A. magna cum laude 1957 J.D. 1964. Admitted to practice Kansas 1964. Began legal practice Topeka 1964. Judge, Shawnee County Probate and Juvenile Court Jan 1971 to Jan 1973. Judge, Kansas District Court Third Judicial District 1973-77.

Member Women Attorneys Association of Topeka, Topeka and Kansas Bar Associations. Republican.

Office: 307 Kansas Judicial Center, 301 S.W. Tenth Avenue, Topeka 66612-1507.

Telephone: (785) 296-5322.

McGUIRE, Scott L. *(Magistrate Judge, Kansas District Court Thirtieth Judicial District)*

Office: Barber County Courthouse, 118 East Washington, Medicine Lodge 67104.

Telephone: (620) 886-5639.

Fax: (620) 886-5854

E-mail address: smcguire@cyberlodg.com

McNALLY, John *(Judge, Kansas District Court Twenty-ninth Judicial District)*

Office: Wyandotte County Courthouse, Third Floor, 710 North Seventh Street, Kansas City 66101.

Telephone: (913) 573-2920.

Fax: (913) 281-4354

E-mail address: Jmcnally@wycokck.org

McQUEEN, Verna Kay *(Magistrate Judge, Kansas District Court Twenty-sixth Judicial District)* Elected to term beginning Jan 10, 1977. Reelected 1980, 1984, 1988, 1992, 1996 and 2000. Current term expires Jan 2005. Born Hugoton Kansas Aug 25, 1936. Christian.

MCQUEEN, VERNA KAY—*Continued*

Member Southwest Kansas Judges Association, Kansas District Magistrate Judges Association and National Judges Association.

Office: Stevens County Courthouse, 200 East Sixth Street, Hugoton 67951.

Telephone: (620) 544-2695.

Fax: (620) 544-2528

McQUIN, R. Scott *(Judge, Kansas District Court Thirtieth Judicial District)* Former Magistrate Judge.

Mailing address: P.O. Box 399, Wellington 67152.

Office: Sumner County Courthouse, Wellington 67152.

Telephone: (620) 326-5936.

Fax: (620) 326-5365

MEEKS, Cordell D., Jr. *(Judge, Kansas District Court Twenty-ninth Judicial District)* Appointed by Governor John Carlin Oct 9, 1980 to term beginning Jan 1, 1981. Elected 1982, 1986, 1990, 1994, 1998 and 2002. Current term expires Jan 1, 2007. Born Kansas City Kansas Dec 17, 1942. Religious affiliation: African Methodist Episcopal. Educated at University of Kansas B.A. 1964 J.D. 1967 and University of Pennsylvania Law School 1968. Recipient Reginald Heber Smith Fellowship. Member Omicron Delta Kappa, Phi Alpha Delta, Alpha Phi Alpha and Sigma Pi Phi. Admitted to practice Kansas 1967, U.S. District Court District of Kansas 1968, U.S. Court of Appeals Tenth Circuit 1969, U.S. Court of Military Appeals 1971, U.S. Supreme Court 1971 and U.S. Army Court of Military Review 1990. In legal practice Kansas City 1967-81. Judge, Kansas City Municipal Court 1976-81.

Special Assistant Attorney General Kansas Workmen's Compensation Fund 1976-78. Instructor in How to Buy and Sell Real Estate 1967-68 and World History 1970 Kansas City Community College (Kansas). Instructor National Institute of Trial Advocacy since 1986. Member Kansas Municipal Judges Association (President 1980-81), American Judges Association, American Judicature Society, Wyandotte County, Kansas and American (Member Committee on Ethics and Professional Responsibility National Conference of State Trial Judges Judicial Administration Division since 1986) Bar Associations. Member Attorney General's Commission on Crime Prevention 1986-91. Attended Traffic Court Seminar National College of the State Judiciary May 1976, seminar on "Practicalities of Judging: Jurisprudence and the Humanities" Harvard Law School June 1978, General Jurisdiction Course The National Judicial College Oct 1981, Military Judge Course The Judge Advocate General's School June 1990 and Graduate U.S. Army War College 1997. Recipient Outstanding Service Award from United Way 1983, Black Man of Distinction Award from Friends of Yates 1983, Distinguished Service Award from American Lung Association of Kansas 1986, Distinguished Service Award from NAACP 1986, Boss of the Year Award from Wyandotte County Legal Secretaries Association 1986, Blacks in Government Award for Contributions in the Field of Law 1988, President's Award from Greater Kansas City Chapter of SCLC 1990, Kansas City Spirit Award 1994, Distinguished Service Award 1995 and Distinguished Alumnus Award 2001 from University of Kansas, Distinguished Service Award from Park College 1995, Silver Beaver Award from Heart of America Council Boy Scouts of America 1996, Fred Ellsworth Medallion from University of Kansas Alumni Association 2002 and Leadership Award from Metropolitan Family Violence Coalition 2002. Named one of the 100 Most Influential African Americans in Kansas City by *Kansas City Globe* 1992-98, Outstanding Public Citizen of the Year-Kansas by Missouri-Kansas Chapter National Association of Social Workers 1994 and Most Influential African American in the State of Kansas 1998. Inducted into Mid America Education Hall of Fame 2001.

Colonel JAGC Kansas Army National Guard 1984-2001 (retired). Staff Judge Advocate 35th Infantry Division ARNG. JAG 1989-90. State JAG Kansas National Guard 1989-90. Senior Military Judge 1990-2001. Democrat. President 1984-85 and Former Member Board of Governors University of Kansas Law School. Member Kansas Commission on the Bicentennial of the U.S. Constitution 1987-91 and Kansas Commission on Veteran's Affairs since 1997. President Kansas Chapter 1988-89 and Chairman National Board 2001-02 American Lung Association. President Visiting Nurse Association of Greater Kansas City 1989-91. Board of Directors American Red Cross of Greater Kansas City 1989-95. Board of Trustees First A.M.E. Church since 1989. Chairman Board of Directors United Way of Wyandotte County 1990-91 and Wyandotte Health Foundation 1998-2002. National Board of Trustees 1990-94 and Co-Chair Greater Kansas City Region 1993-97 National Conference of Christians and Jews. President Midwest Bioethics Center 1995-97. Vice President for Operations, Heart of America Council Boy Scouts of America 1996-99. Chair National Board of Directors University of Kansas Alumni Association 1997-98. Past President Wyandotte County Legal Aid Society, Wyandotte County Junior Achievement, Wyandotte County Law Library and Substance Abuse Center of Eastern Kansas. Member Wyandotte County Red Cross (President 1973-75), Wyandotte County Mental Health Association (President 1981-83), Economic Opportunity Foundation (President 1981-84) and National Mental Health Association (Board of Directors 1980-83). Enjoys jazz piano, table tennis and swimming.

Office: Wyandotte County Courthouse, 710 North Seventh Street, Kansas City 66101.

Telephone: (913) 573-2926.

Fax: (913) 281-4354

MIKESIC, David P. *(Judge, Kansas District Court Twenty-ninth Judicial District)* Elected Nov 1976 to term beginning Jan 10, 1977. Reelected 1980, 1984, 1988, 1992, Nov 1996 and 2000. Current term expires Jan 2005. Born Wyandotte County Kansas May 6, 1944. Catholic. Educated at Kansas State College B.A. 1966, University of Kansas B.S.E. 1967 and University of Arkansas J.D. 1971. Admitted to practice Kansas 1971. Began legal practice Kansas City 1971.

With Wyandotte County District Attorney's Office 1971-77. Member Kansas House of Representatives 1973-77. Member Kansas Judicial Council (Advisory Committee on Mental Code Revision since 1991), National and State District Attorneys Associations 1973-77, Kansas District Court Judges Association (Executive Committee since 1991, President) and American Bar Association. Democrat. Board of Directors Metropolitan Organization to Counter Sexual Assault. Member Slavic-American Civic Club of Kansas City and Wyandotte

MIKESIC, DAVID P.—*Continued*

County Young Democrat Club. Enjoys fishing and travel.

Office: Wyandotte County Courthouse, First Floor, 710 North Seventh Street, Kansas City 66101.
Telephone: (913) 573-2834.
Fax: (913) 573-4136

MILLER, Paul E. *(Chief Judge, Kansas District Court Twenty-first Judicial District)* Appointed by Governor John Carlin to term beginning Nov 30, 1982. Retained by election. Born Oklahoma Feb 7, 1947. Educated at Kansas State University B.A. 1969 and University of Kansas J.D. 1972. Member Delta Upsilon. Admitted to practice Kansas 1972 and U.S. District Court District of Kansas 1972. Began legal practice Manhattan 1972. Judge, Manhattan Municipal Court 1977-82.

Riley County Attorney 1975-76. Instructor in Business Law Kansas State University since 1973. Member Kansas District Judges Association, Riley County, Central Kansas, Kansas and American Bar Associations.

Mailing address: P.O. Box 158, Manhattan 66505-0158.
Office: Riley County Courthouse, Manhattan 66502.
Telephone: (785) 537-6371.
Fax: (785) 565-6849
E-mail address: pem247@aol.com

MITCHELL, Daniel L. *(Judge, Kansas District Court Third Judicial District)*

Office: B-8 Shawnee County Courthouse, 200 S.E. Seventh Street, Topeka 66603-3922.
Telephone: (785) 233-8200.
Fax: (785) 291-4917
E-mail address: dmitchel@shawneecourt.org

MURGUIA, Carlos *(Judge, United States District Court District of Kansas)* Appointed for life by President Bill Clinton to term beginning Sept 22, 1999. Born Kansas City Kansas Sept 21, 1957. Educated at University of Kansas B.S. 1979 J.D. 1982. In legal practice Kansas City 1982-87. Judge, Kansas District Court Twenty-ninth Judicial District 1990-99.

Coordinator Immigration Amnesty Program El Centro, Inc. 1985-90.

Office: 537 U.S. Courthouse, 500 State Avenue, Kansas City 66101.
Telephone: (913) 551-5817.
Fax: (913) 551-5831

MURPHY, Jack A. *(Judge, Kansas District Court Seventh Judicial District)*

Office: Judicial Center, 111 East 11th, Lawrence 66044-2966.
Telephone: (785) 832-5248.
Fax: (785) 838-2454
E-mail address: jmurphy@douglas-county.com

NAFZIGER, Gary L. *(Judge, Kansas District Court Second Judicial District)*

Mailing address: P.O. Box 327, Oskaloosa 66066.
Office: Jefferson County Courthouse, Oskaloosa 66066.
Telephone: (785) 863-2461.
Fax: (785) 863-2369

NOLAND, Donald R. *(Judge, Kansas District Court Eleventh Judicial District)*

Mailing address: P.O. Box 69, Girard 66743.
Office: Crawford County Courthouse, Girard 66743.
Telephone: (620) 724-6213.
Fax: (620) 724-4987

NUGENT, Robert E. *(Chief Judge, United States Bankruptcy Court District of Kansas)* Appointed by U.S. Court of Appeals Tenth Circuit judges to term beginning June 14, 2000. Term expires June 14, 2014. Chief Judge Bankruptcy Court since Oct 28, 2002. Also Judge, Bankruptcy Appellate Panel Tenth Circuit. Selected by the Judicial Council of the Tenth Circuit to term beginning March 5, 2002. Born May 2, 1955. Educated at University of Kansas B.A. 1977 J.D. 1980.

Office: 104 U.S. Courthouse, 401 North Market Street, Wichita 67202.
Telephone: (316) 269-6404.

NUSS, Lawton R. *(Justice, Kansas Supreme Court)* Appointed by Governor Bill Graves Aug 2002. Born Salina Kansas Dec 30, 1952. Educated at University of Kansas B.A. 1975 J.D. 1982. In legal practice Salina 1982-2002.

Office: 389 Kansas Judicial Center, 301 S.W. Tenth Avenue, Topeka 66612-1507.
Telephone: (785) 296-4898.

O'CONNOR, James B. *(Magistrate Judge, Kansas District Court Twenty-second Judicial District)*

Mailing address: P.O. Box 213, Seneca 66538-0213.
Office: Nemaha County Courthouse, 607 Nemaha, Seneca 66538.
Telephone: (785) 336-2146.
Fax: (785) 336-6450

O'HARA, James P. *(Magistrate Judge, United States District Court District of Kansas)* Appointed by U.S. District Court judges to term beginning April 17, 2000. Term expires 2008. Born Detroit Michigan May 14, 1955. Episcopalian. Educated at University of Nebraska B.A. 1977 and Creighton University J.D. cum laude 1980. Staff member Creighton Law Review 1978-80. Law Clerk to Hon. C. Arlen Beam and Hon. Robert V. Denney, U.S. District Court District of Nebraska 1980-82. Admitted to practice Nebraska 1980 (inactive), Missouri 1982 (inactive), Kansas 1983, U.S. District Court District of Kansas 1983, U.S. Court of Appeals Tenth Circuit 1983 and U.S. Supreme Court 1984. In legal practice Overland Park Kansas and Kansas City Missouri 1982-2000.

Member Kansas City Metropolitan Bar Association, Johnson County and Kansas (Board of Editors since 1984) Bar Associations. Personal Statement or Quote: "Please strive to adhere to the four C's of effective advocacy, i.e. be complete, concise, civil, and thus credible."

Office: 208 U.S. Courthouse, 500 State Avenue, Kansas City 66101.
Telephone: (913) 551-6710.
Fax: (913) 551-6532
E-mail address: judge_ohara@ksd.uscourts.gov

OWENS, Clark V., II *(Judge, Kansas District Court Eighteenth Judicial District)*

Office: 6-1 Sedgwick County Courthouse, 525 North Main Street, Wichita 67203-3773.

OWENS, CLARK V., II—*Continued*

Telephone: (316) 383-7661.
Fax: (316) 383-7560
E-mail address: cowens@dc18.org

PARRISH, Nancy E. *(Judge, Kansas District Court Third Judicial District)*
Office: 303 Shawnee County Courthouse, 200 S.E. Seventh Street, Topeka 66603-3922.
Telephone: (785) 233-8200.
Fax: (785) 291-4917
E-mail address: nparrish@shawneecourt.org

PATTON, James A. *(Chief Judge, Kansas District Court Twenty-second Judicial District)* Elected Nov 1994 to term beginning Jan 9, 1995. Reelected 1998 and 2002. Current term expires Jan 2007. Born Sabetha Kansas Nov 20, 1949. Educated at Kansas State University B.A. 1971 and Washburn University School of Law J.D. 1975. Member Phi Delta Phi. Admitted to practice Kansas 1975 and U.S. District Court District of Kansas 1975. Colonel Kansas Army National Guard JAGC 1971-2001.
Mailing address: P.O. Box 417, Hiawatha 66434.
Office: Brown County Courthouse, Hiawatha 66434.
Telephone: (785) 742-3522.
Fax: (785) 742-3506
E-mail address: jpatton@rainbowtel.net

PHELAN, James E. *(Magistrate Judge, Kansas District Court Tenth Judicial District)*
Office: Johnson County Courthouse, 100 North Kansas Avenue, Olathe 66061-3273.
Telephone: (913) 715-3577.
Fax: (913) 715-3317
E-mail address: James.Phelan@jocoks.com

PIERRON, George Joseph, Jr. *(Judge, Kansas Court of Appeals)* Appointed by Governor Mike Hayden to term beginning Dec 11, 1990. Retained by election 1992, 1996 and 2000. Current term expires Jan 2005. Born Kansas City Kansas May 16, 1947. Catholic. Educated at Rockhurst College A.B. 1968 and University of Kansas J.D. 1971. Member Alpha Sigma Nu, Phi Alpha Delta and Pi Kappa Alpha. Admitted to practice Kansas 1971, U.S. District Court District of Kansas 1971 and U.S. Supreme Court 1978. In legal practice Olathe and Spring Hill 1971-73. Judge, Spring Hill Municipal Court 1972. Judge, Kansas District Court Tenth Judicial District 1982-90.
Assistant County Attorney and District Attorney 1971-82. Author "Child Abuse and Neglect—The Legal Challenge" Kansas B. Jour. 1977, "Analysis of K.S.A. 60-460 (dd)" Kansas B. Jour. 1983 and "Analysis of Child Hearsay" ABA National Legal Resource Center for Child Advocacy and Protection 1985. Co-author "Bringing the Appellate Courts to the People" 35 No. 2 Judges' Journal 10 Spring 1996. Member Kansas District Judges Association, American Judicature Society, Johnson County (Secretary 1976), Kansas and American (Co-chair Mediation and Arbitration Committee Section of Family Law) Bar Associations. Attended The National Judicial College 1983. Named Jaycees Outstanding Young Man of Olathe 1976. Recipient National Leadership Award from National Committee for the Prevention of Child Abuse 1986. Republican. County Chairman Young Republicans. Precinct Committeeman. Board of Directors Mid America Health Systems Agency 1978-81. Member and Chairman Kansas Children and Youth Advisory Committee. Chairman Olathe Community Blood Association. President Olathe Community Theatre Association. Member Rotary International (Past President), Kansas Committee for the Prevention of Child Abuse (Past President), Johnson County Mental Health Association (Board of Directors 1973-79) and Johnson County Mental Health Center Citizen Advisory Group.
Office: 277 Kansas Judicial Center, 301 S.W. Tenth Avenue, Topeka 66612-1507.
Telephone: (785) 296-5408.

PILSHAW, Rebecca L. *(Judge, Kansas District Court Eighteenth Judicial District)* Appointed by Governor Joan Finney to term beginning Dec 14, 1993. Elected 1994, 1996 and 2000. Current term expires Dec 31, 2004. Born Madisonville Kentucky June 30, 1952. United Methodist. Educated at Avila College B.A. with honors 1980 and University of Kansas J.D. 1984. Admitted to practice Kansas 1984. In legal practice Wichita 1987-93.
Assistant City Attorney Wichita 1984. Assistant District Attorney Sedgwick County 1984-87. Instructor in Business Law and Procurement Law Newman University since 1995. Member Sedgwick County and Kansas Bar Associations.
Office: 9-1 Sedgwick County Courthouse, 525 North Main Street, Wichita 67203-3773.
Telephone: (316) 383-7533.
Fax: (316) 383-7085
E-mail address: rpilshaw@dc18.org

PLATT, David R. *(Judge, Kansas District Court Eighth Judicial District)*
Mailing address: P.O. Box 1147, Junction City 66441.
Office: Geary County Courthouse, Junction City 66441.
Telephone: (785) 762-5221.
Fax: (785) 762-4420
E-mail address: dj5@oz-online.net

PLUMMER, Mary P. *(Magistrate Judge, Kansas District Court Twenty-sixth Judicial District)*
Mailing address: P.O. Box 913, Johnson 67855-0913.
Office: Stanton County Courthouse, 201 North Main, Johnson 67855.
Telephone: (620) 492-2220.
Fax: (620) 492-6410

POHL, Dale L. *(Judge, Kansas District Court Thirteenth Judicial District)*
Office: 201 Butler County Courthouse, 121 South Gordy, El Dorado 67042.
Telephone: (316) 322-4351.
Fax: (316) 322-4365
E-mail address: dalepohl@hotmail.com

POWELL, Tony *(Judge, Kansas District Court Eighteenth Judicial District)*
Office: Sedgwick County Courthouse, Fourth Floor, 525 North Main Street, Wichita 67203-3773.
Telephone: (316) 660-3246.
Fax: (316) 383-7560
E-mail address: tpowell@dc18.org

POWERS, Michael F. *(Chief Judge, Kansas District Court Eighth Judicial District)* Appointed by Governor Joan Finney to term beginning May 29, 1991. Retained by election 1996 and 2000. Current term expires Jan 2005. Chief Judge since Jan 1994. Born Iola Kansas

POWERS, MICHAEL F.—*Continued*

Nov 9, 1954. Methodist. Educated at Emporia State University B.S.E. with honors 1977 and University of Kansas J.D. 1980. Admitted to practice Kansas 1980. In legal practice Council Grove 1983-91.

Morris County Attorney 1980-91. Member Public Defender Advisory Committee Kansas Judicial Council 1987-89, Attorney General's Victims' Rights Task Force 1988-89 and Judicial Education Committee Office of Judicial Administration 1994-95. Former Member National District Attorneys Association, Kansas County and District Attorneys Association and Morris County Bar Association. Convener for Community Planning Team for Juvenile Justice Eighth Judicial District since 1997, Member Task Force on Permanency Planning Kansas Supreme Court (Acting Chairman 1997-98), American Judges Association, American Judicature Society, Kansas District Judges Association and Kansas Bar Association. Panel Member and Discussion Leader Legal System/Death Penalty Workshop with high school classes Marion High School 1993 and 1994. Presenter Law Related Education Workshop Marion County Special Education Cooperative 1994, 1995 and 1996. Recipient Service to Scouting Award from Council Grove Cub Scout Pack 65 1987-88, Certificate of Appreciation in recognition of outstanding community service from Mayor of Council Grove 1988, Sponsoring Agency Award for distinguished service from Kansas Department of Social and Rehabilitation Services 1996 and Distinguished Service Award from Kansas Association of Court Services Officers 1997. County Chairman 1981-90 and Delegate to State Committee 1986-90 Democratic Party. Board of Directors Wah-Shun-Gah Days Committee 1984 and 1985. Board of Directors 1987-94, Executive Board 1989-94 and President 1992-93 Emporia State University Alumni Association. Committee Chairman 1990, Board of Directors and Past President Council Grove Chamber of Commerce. Commission Member 1992-93, Assistant Coach and Head Coach Youth Baseball Team and Assistant Coach Youth Softball Team Marion Summer Baseball/Softball Commission. Organizational Member 1996 and Board of Directors 1997 and 1998 Chingawassa Days Committee. Assistant Coach and Head Coach Youth Baseball Team Council Grove Recreation Commission Summer Baseball Program. Former Member Morris County Resource, Conservation and Development Board and Morris County Child Protection Team. Merit Badge Counselor Marion Boy Scouts. Eagle Scout. Former Member Eagles Scout Review Committee and District Advancement Committee Council Grove Boy Scouts. Member Marion Kiwanis Club, Council Grove Kiwanis Club (Distinguished Club President 1984) and Building Improvement Team/Site Council Florence Middle School.

Mailing address: P.O. Box 298, Marion 66861-0298.
Office: Marion County Courthouse, Marion 66861.
Telephone: (620) 382-2104.
Fax: (620) 382-2259
E-mail address: mndj3@southwind.net

PRINGLE, James T., Jr. *(Judge, Kansas District Court Nineteenth Judicial District)*

Mailing address: P.O. Box 1152, Arkansas City 67005.
Telephone: (620) 441-4520.
Fax: (620) 442-7213
E-mail address: jpringle@cowleycourt.com

PULLMAN, Terry L. *(Judge, Kansas District Court Eighteenth Judicial District)*

Office: 5-5 Sedgwick County Courthouse, 525 North Main Street, Wichita 67203-3773.
Telephone: (316) 383-7381.
Fax: (316) 383-7560
E-mail address: tpullman@dc18.org

PUSATERI, James A. *(Judge, United States Bankruptcy Court District of Kansas)* Appointed by U.S. District Court judges Dec 27, 1976. Reappointed Dec 15, 1986. Former Chief Judge Bankruptcy Court. Also Judge, Bankruptcy Appellate Panel Tenth Circuit. Selected by the Judicial Council of the Tenth Circuit. Born Kansas City Missouri May 20, 1938. Roman Catholic. Educated at University of Kansas B.A. 1960 J.D. 1963. Member Sigma Alpha Epsilon. Admitted to practice Kansas 1963, U.S. District Court District of Kansas 1963 and U.S. Court of Appeals Tenth Circuit 1965. In legal practice Olathe 1963-65, Prairie Village 1965-69 and Kansas City 1969-76.

City Councilman Prairie Village 1967-69. Assistant U.S. Attorney Kansas City Kansas 1969-76. Author "Section 1111(b) of the Bankruptcy Code: How Much Does the Debtor Have to Pay and When Should the Creditor Elect" American Bankruptcy L. Jour. Spring 1984. Member National Conference of Bankruptcy Judges, American Bankruptcy Institute, Topeka and Kansas Bar Associations.

Office: 215 U.S. Courthouse, 444 S.E. Quincy Street, Topeka 66683-3502.
Telephone: (785) 295-2786.

QUINT, Michael L. *(Judge, Kansas District Court Twenty-fifth Judicial District)*

Mailing address: P.O. Box 798, Garden City 67846-0798.
Office: Finney County Courthouse, Garden City 67846.
Telephone: (620) 271-6105.
Fax: (620) 271-6141
E-mail address: judge03@finneycounty.org

RAMIREZ, Peter J. *(Magistrate Judge, Kansas District Court Twenty-fifth Judicial District)* Appointed by Governor Bill Graves.

Mailing address: P.O. Box 798, Garden City 67846-0798.
Office: Finney County Courthouse, Garden City 67846.
Telephone: (620) 271-6111.
Fax: (620) 271-6141
E-mail address: judge05@finneycounty.org

REID, John Thomas *(Recalled Magistrate Judge, United States District Court District of Kansas)* Appointed Magistrate Judge by U.S. District Court judges to term beginning Oct 31, 1984. Reappointed Dec 1, 1987 and Dec 1995. Retired June 30, 1999. Appointed Recalled Magistrate Judge by the Judicial Council of the Tenth Circuit. Born Newton Kansas July 4, 1929. Catholic. Educated at Wichita State University B.A. 1955 and Washburn University of Topeka J.D. 1958. Member Phi Alpha Delta. Admitted to practice Kansas 1958. Began legal practice Newton 1958. Former Municipal Judge, Newton and North Newton. Probate Judge, Harvey County 1961-67. Associate Judge, Kansas District Court Ninth Judicial District 1980-84.

Former Mayor City of Newton. Former Attorney Harvey County. Former Sedgwick City Attorney. Former Sedgwick School Board Attorney. Former Counselor Harvey County. Member Harvey County and Kansas Bar Associations. Corporal U.S. Army 1951-53. Enjoys reading and sports.

Office: 132 U.S. Courthouse, 401 North Market Street, Wichita 67202.

Telephone: (316) 269-6411.

REILING, Dennis Lee *(Magistrate Judge, Kansas District Court Second Judicial District)* Elected to term beginning Jan 10, 1975. Retained by election. Administrative/Chief Tribal Judge, The Prairie Band Potawatowi Nation since Jan 8, 1999. Born Leavenworth Kansas Oct 21, 1946. Presbyterian. Educated at Kansas State College-Emporia B.S.B. 1970.

Founder Kappa Epsilon Chapter Tau Kappa Epsilon Washburn University. President Oskaloosa Rotary Club.

Mailing address: P.O. Box 327, Oskaloosa 66066.

Office: Jefferson County Courthouse, Oskaloosa 66066.

Telephone: (785) 863-2471.

Fax: (785) 863-2369

E-mail address: dennisreiling@hotmail.com

RESS, Richard J. *(Magistrate Judge, Kansas District Court Fifteenth Judicial District)* Appointed by Governor John Carlin to term beginning Dec 15, 1983. Elected 1984, 1988, 1992, 1996 and 2000. Current term expires Jan 2005. Also serves as Judge, Colby Municipal Court since 1983, Brewster Municipal Court since 1992 and Rexford Municipal Court since 1997. Born Wells Minnesota Oct 9, 1952. Roman Catholic. Educated at Colby Community Junior College A.A. 1972, Kansas State University B.A. 1974 and Washburn University of Topeka J.D. 1979. Admitted to practice Kansas 1982. Began legal practice Colby 1982.

Deputy County Attorney Thomas County 1982-83. Instructor Criminal Justice Department Colby Community Junior College 1987-95. Member Kansas Municipal Judges Association (Board of Directors 1985-95, President 1993-94), Kansas Trial Attorneys Association, National Judges Association, Thomas County (Treasurer 1983-89), Northwest Kansas, Kansas and American Bar Associations. Instructor Kansas Municipal Judges Conference June 1986, 1993 and 1994. President Colby Swim Club. Board of Directors Kansas Sudden Infant Death Syndrome Foundation, Pioneer Memorial Library of Colby and Sacred Heart Catholic Grade School. Member Rotary. Enjoys hunting, military history, cartography and golfing.

Mailing address: P.O. Box 881, Colby 67701.

Office: Thomas County Courthouse, Colby 67701.

Telephone: (785) 462-4545.

Fax: (785) 462-2291

E-mail address: rress@thomascounty.com

RICHARDSON, Thomas F. *(Judge, Kansas District Court Twenty-fifth Judicial District)*

Mailing address: P.O. Box 798, Garden City 67846-0798.

Office: Finney County Courthouse, Garden City 67846.

Telephone: (620) 271-6107.

Fax: (620) 271-6141

E-mail address: judge04@finneycounty.org

ROBERTSON, George R. *(Judge, Kansas District Court Twenty-eighth Judicial District)*

Mailing address: P.O. Box 1760, Salina 67402-1760.

Office: Saline County Courthouse, 300 West Ash, Salina 67401.

Telephone: (785) 309-5838.

Fax: (785) 309-5845

E-mail address: george.robertson@saline.org

ROBINSON, Julie A. *(Judge, United States District Court District of Kansas)* Appointed for life by President George W. Bush to term beginning Dec 14, 2001. Educated at University of Kansas School of Law.

Office: 405 U.S. Courthouse, 444 Southeast Quincy Street, Topeka 66683.

Telephone: (785) 295-7637.

ROGERS, Richard Dean *(Senior Judge, United States District Court District of Kansas)* Appointed for life by President Gerald R. Ford to term beginning Aug 11, 1975. Assumed Senior status, serves by assignment. Born Oberlin Kansas Dec 29, 1921. Presbyterian. Educated at Kansas State University B.S. 1943 and University of Kansas J.D. 1947. Admitted to practice Kansas 1947. In legal practice Manhattan 1947-75.

Manhattan City Commissioner 1951-53 and 1959-63. Riley County Attorney 1954-58. State Representative 1963-67. State Senator 1968-75. President Kansas Senate 1975. Manhattan Mayor 1952 and 1963. Instructor in Business Law Kansas State University 1948-52. Member Kansas and American Bar Associations. Captain USAF 1943-45. Republican. Republican State Chairman 1962-64. Enjoys golf, tennis, hunting and fishing.

Office: 410 Federal Building, 444 S.E. Quincy Street, Topeka 66683.

Telephone: (785) 295-2735.

ROME, Richard *(Judge, Kansas District Court Twenty-seventh Judicial District)*

Office: Reno County Courthouse, 206 West First Street, Hutchinson 67501.

Telephone: (620) 694-2963.

Fax: (620) 694-2958

E-mail address: dickr@dist27.reno.ks.us

ROPER, Roy M. *(Magistrate Judge, Kansas District Court Twenty-second Judicial District)*

Mailing address: P.O. Box 295, Troy 66087.

Office: Doniphan County Courthouse, Troy 66087.

Telephone: (785) 985-3583.

Fax: (785) 985-2402

ROSEN, Eric S. *(Judge, Kansas District Court Third Judicial District)* Appointed by Governor Joan Finney March 1993. Retained by election. Served Kansas Court of Appeals by special assignment. Born Topeka Kansas May 25, 1953. Jewish. Educated at University of Kansas B.S. with honors 1975 M.S. with honors 1976 and Washburn University J.D. 1984. Admitted to practice Kansas 1985, U.S. District Court District of Kansas 1985 and U.S. Court of Appeals Tenth Circuit 1985. In legal practice Topeka 1989-93.

Assistant District Attorney Shawnee County 1985-88. Associate General Counsel and Kansas Securities Commissioner 1988-90. Adjunct Professor of Law Washburn University 1989-94. Member Koch Crime Commission, Topeka American Inns of Court, American Judges Association, American Judicature Society, Topeka, Kansas and American Bar Associations. Lecturer Menninger

ROSEN, ERIC S.—*Continued*

School of Law and Psychiatry, Career Prosecutor Course National College of District Attorneys June 1989, The National Judicial College Sept 1993 and Economic Institute for Judges Kansas University April 1997. Named Kansan of Distinction for Law 1999. Recipient Victims' Service Award for Outstanding Judge from Attorney General 2000 and Humanitarian Award from Martin Luther King—Living the Dream Foundation Jan 2002. President Topeka High School Site Council. Youth Basketball and Baseball Coach. Member Jerome Horton Foundation, Topeka High Booster Club and YMCA. Enjoys music, reading and traveling.

Office: 405 Shawnee County Courthouse, 200 S.E. Seventh Street, Topeka 66603-3922.

Telephone: (785) 233-8200.

Fax: (785) 291-4917

E-mail address: erosen@shawneecourt.org

ROTH, Douglas R. *(Judge, Kansas District Court Eighteenth Judicial District)*

Office: 5-3 Sedgwick County Courthouse, 525 North Main Street, Wichita 67203.

Telephone: (316) 383-7146.

Fax: (316) 383-7560

E-mail address: droth@dc18.org

ROTH, Steven M. *(Magistrate Judge, Kansas District Court Second Judicial District)* Appointed by Governor Joan Finney to term beginning Oct 15, 1993. Retained by election. Educated at Fort Hays State University B.A. 1986 and Washburn University School of Law J.D. 1989. Admitted to practice Kansas, U.S. District Court District of Kansas and U.S. Court of Appeals Tenth Circuit. In legal practice Topeka Jan 1989 to Oct 1993.

Professor of American History and Western Civilizations Highland Community College. Previously worked as resident manager of apartment complex and as farmer/rancher of a 1300 acre farm. Board of Directors Enterprise Academy. Member Audit Committee Shawnee Mission Medical Center. Member Interagency Council for Youth. Volunteer Topeka Rescue Mission and various state and local election campaigns. Interested in law, history, philosophy, politics, theology, human relations, literature, art and agriculture.

Mailing address: P.O. Box 129, Westmoreland 66549.

Office: Pottawatomie County Courthouse, Westmoreland 66549.

Telephone: (785) 457-3392.

Fax: (785) 457-2107

E-mail address: ptcourts@kansas.net

RUDDICK, Peter V. *(Judge, Kansas District Court Tenth Judicial District)*

Office: Johnson County Courthouse, 100 North Kansas Avenue, Olathe 66061-3273.

Telephone: (913) 715-3750.

Fax: (913) 715-3317

E-mail address: Peter.Ruddick@jocoks.com

RULON, Gary W. *(Chief Judge, Kansas Court of Appeals)* Appointed by Governor Mike Hayden to term beginning 1988. Retained by election. Born Manhattan Kansas May 18, 1941. Educated at Washburn University of Topeka B.A. 1969 J.D. 1971. Admitted to Kansas 1971. In legal practice Emporia 1972-79 and 1980-81. Administrative Judge, Kansas District Court Fifth Judicial District 1981-88. Staff Attorney Central Staff U.S. Court of Appeals Tenth Circuit Jan 1980 to Aug 1980. Member Kansas and American Bar Associations.

Office: 268 Kansas Judicial Center, 301 S.W. Tenth Avenue, Topeka 66612-1507.

Telephone: (785) 296-6184.

RUSHFELT, Gerald L. *(Recalled Magistrate Judge, United States District Court District of Kansas)* Appointed Magistrate Judge by U.S. District Court judges to term beginning Sept 9, 1985. Reappointed Sept 9, 1993. Appointed Recalled Magistrate Judge by the Judicial Council of the Tenth Circuit. Born Kansas City Kansas Aug 4, 1929. Reorganized Church of Jesus Christ of Latter-day Saints. Educated at Graceland College A.A. 1949 and University of Kansas B.A. 1953 LL.B. 1958. Member Phi Alpha Delta. Admitted to practice Kansas 1958, U.S. District Court District of Kansas 1958 and U.S. Court of Appeals Tenth Circuit 1968. In legal practice Kansas City 1958-73, Overland Park 1973-85 and Prairie Village 1973-85. Judge pro tem, Leawood Municipal Court 1978-85.

Instructor Trial Advocacy Critique University of Kansas 1980-92. Fellow American College of Trial Lawyers, International Society of Barristers and American Board of Trial Advocates. Member Earl E. O'Connor Inn of Court, Johnson County (President 1986-87), Kansas and American Bar Associations. Participant CLE seminars. Corporal U.S. Army 1953-55. Previously worked for Union Pacific Railroad Co. 1947-50, Toedman Cabs 1951-53, Rock Island Railroad Co. 1955-56 and K. C. Terminal Railway Co. 1956-58. Member Roeland Park City Council 1964-69. Board of Directors Wyandotte County Family and Children's Service 1968-75. Member Johnson County Human Relations Commission 1969-76. Board of Trustees Park College Parkville Missouri 1987-97. Board of Governors University of Kansas School of Law 1990-93.

Office: 219 U.S. Courthouse, 500 State Avenue, Kansas City 66101-2428.

Telephone: (913) 551-6716.

RUSSELL, Janice D. *(Judge, Kansas District Court Tenth Judicial District)* Appointed by Governor John Carlin to term beginning Sept 1, 1985. Retained by election Nov 1986, Nov 1990, Nov 1994, 1998 and 2002. Current term expires Jan 2007. Born Fort Scott Kansas Feb 4, 1950. Educated at University of Kansas B.A. 1971 M.A. 1973 J.D. 1977. Member Phi Beta Kappa. Law Clerk to Hon. Joe H. Swinehart, Kansas Court of Appeals 1977-79. Admitted to practice Kansas 1977. In legal practice Johnson County 1981-85.

Assistant District Attorney Johnson County 1979-81. Member American Judicature Society, Johnson County (Secretary 1981) and Kansas Bar Associations. Democrat. Charter member Johnson County Business Women's Association (Vice President 1979-80). Board of Directors since 1980 and President Johnson County Substance Abuse Services, Inc.

Office: Johnson County Courthouse, 100 North Kansas Avenue, Olathe 66061-3273.

Telephone: (913) 715-3810.

Fax: (913) 715-3317

E-mail address: Janice.Russell@jocoks.com

SACHSE, Thomas H. *(Judge, Kansas District Court Fourth Judicial District)*
Mailing address: P.O. Box 637, Ottawa 66067-0637.
Office: Franklin County Courthouse, New Court Building, Ottawa 66067.
Telephone: (785) 242-6000, 242-6052.
Fax: (785) 242-5970
E-mail address: tsachse@franklincoks.org

SANDERS, John E. *(Chief Judge, Kansas District Court Thirteenth Judicial District)*
Mailing address: P.O. Box 425, Eureka 67045.
Office: Greenwood County Courthouse, Eureka 67045.
Telephone: (620) 583-8150.
Fax: (620) 583-8152
E-mail address: DeeJudge@fox-net.net

SANDERSON, John O. *(Judge, Kansas District Court Fifth Judicial District)* Appointed by Governor Mike Hayden to term beginning April 8, 1988. Retained by election Nov 1990, Nov 1994, 1998 and 2002. Current term expires Jan 2007. Born Osceola Iowa Aug 2, 1938. Protestant. Educated at Iowa State University B.S. 1960 and University of Kansas J.D. 1973. Admitted to practice Kansas 1973, U.S. District Court District of Kansas 1973 and U.S. Court of Appeals Tenth Circuit 1976. In legal practice Emporia 1973-88.
Member Lyon-Chase Counties, Kansas and American Bar Associations. U.S. Army 1960-70. Colonel USAR 1970-90.
Office: Lyon County Courthouse, 430 Commercial, Emporia 66801.
Telephone: (620) 341-3292.
Fax: (620) 342-8005
E-mail address: johnsanderson@hotmail.com

SAXTON, Thomas M., Jr. *(Magistrate Judge, Kansas District Court Thirty-first Judicial District)* Appointed to term beginning Jan 29, 1989. Retained by election Nov 6, 1990, Nov 8, 1994, 1998 and 2002. Current term expires Jan 2007. Also serves as Judge, Iola Municipal Court since 1991. Born Iola Kansas June 16, 1951. Catholic. Educated at Pittsburgh State University B.S. 1977.
Member Kansas District Magistrate Judges Association (Vice President, Chairman Legislative Committee and Technology Committee), Kansas Municipal Judges Association, National Judges Association, National Council of Juvenile and Family Court Judges, Allen County and Thirty-first District Bar Associations. Judicial Certification District Magistrate Judge 1989.
Mailing address: P.O. Box 630, Iola 66749.
Office: Allen County Courthouse, Iola 66749.
Telephone: (620) 365-1425.
Fax: (620) 365-1429
E-mail address: tomsaxton@acdc.kscoxmail.com

SCHIFFNER, Glenn D. *(Judge, Kansas District Court Fifteenth Judicial District)*
Mailing address: P.O. Box 805, Colby 67701.
Office: Thomas County Courthouse, Colby 67701.
Telephone: (785) 462-4540.
Fax: (785) 462-2291
E-mail address: judge@colby.ixks.com

SCHMISSEUR, Robert J. *(Judge, Kansas District Court Thirtieth Judicial District)* Appointed by Governor John Carlin to term beginning July 31, 1986. Retained by election 1988, 1992, 1996 and 2000. Current term expires Jan 2005. Born Belleville Illinois Jan 22, 1952. Catholic. Educated at University of Illinois B.S. with honors 1974 and University of Kansas J.D. 1977. Admitted to practice Kansas 1977. In legal practice Pratt 1977-86.
Member Pratt County and Southwest Kansas (Chairman Continuing Legal Education Committee) Bar Associations. Enjoys hunting, fishing and gardening.
Mailing address: P.O. Box 984, Pratt 67124.
Office: Pratt County Courthouse, Pratt 67124.
Telephone: (620) 672-4102.
Fax: (620) 672-2902
E-mail address: rjs@prattcounty.org

SCHMIDT, Jean M. *(Judge, Kansas District Court Third Judicial District)*
Office: 411 Shawnee County Courthouse, 200 S.E. Seventh Street, Topeka 66603-3922.
Telephone: (785) 233-8200.
Fax: (785) 291-4130

SCHROEDER, Kim R. *(Judge, Kansas District Court Twenty-sixth Judicial District)*
Office: Stevens County Courthouse, 200 East Sixth, Hugoton 67951.
Telephone: (620) 428-6500.
Fax: (620) 544-2528
E-mail address: jschroed@pld.com

SEBELIUS, K. Gary *(Magistrate Judge, United States District Court District of Kansas)* Appointed by U.S. District Court judges to term beginning Feb 21, 2003.
Office: 420 U.S. Courthouse, 444 S.E. Quincy Street, Topeka 66683.
Telephone: (785) 295-2734.

SELFRIDGE, Shelley *(Magistrate Judge, Kansas District Court Twenty-fourth Judicial District)*
Mailing address: P.O. Box 188, Dighton 67839.
Office: Lane County Courthouse, Dighton 67839.
Telephone: (620) 397-2807.
Fax: (620) 397-5526
E-mail address: lanedmj@st-tel.net

SERRA, Robert L. *(Judge, Kansas District Court Twenty-ninth Judicial District)*
Office: Wyandotte County Courthouse, Basement, 710 North Seventh Street, Kansas City 66101.
Telephone: (913) 573-2961.
Fax: (913) 573-4135
E-mail address: Rserra@wycokck.org

SEXTON, Benjamin J. *(Judge, Kansas District Court Eighth Judicial District)*
Mailing address: P.O. Box 127, Abilene 67410.
Office: Dickinson County Courthouse, Abilene 67410.
Telephone: (785) 263-3010.
Fax: (785) 263-4407
E-mail address: dj1@oz-online.com

SHEPHERD, Jean F. *(Judge, Kansas District Court Seventh Judicial District)*
Office: Judicial Center, 111 East 11th, Lawrence 66044-2966.
Telephone: (785) 832-5230.
Fax: (785) 838-2455
E-mail address: jshepherd@douglas-county.com

SHEPPARD, Lawrence E. *(Judge, Kansas District Court Tenth Judicial District)*
Office: Johnson County Courthouse, 100 North Kansas Avenue, Olathe 66061-3273.
Telephone: (913) 715-3890.
Fax: (913) 715-3317
E-mail address: Lawrence.Sheppard@jocoks.com

SIEVE, Philip L. *(Chief Judge, Kansas District Court Twenty-ninth Judicial District)* Appointed by Governor John Carlin to term beginning Dec 1980. Elected to subsequent terms. Current term expires Jan 2007. Born Kansas City Kansas Nov 8, 1941. Catholic. Educated at Kansas University B.A. 1964 and Washburn University School of Law J.D. 1967. Member Phi Alpha Delta. Admitted to practice Kansas 1967. In legal practice Kansas City Kansas 1967-72.
Member Wyandotte County, Kansas and American Bar Associations. Attends American Bar Association conventions annually. Enjoys sailing and playing golf.
Office: Wyandotte County Courthouse, Third Floor, 710 North Seventh Street, Kansas City 66101.
Telephone: (913) 573-2923.
Fax: (913) 573-8171
E-mail address: Psieve@wycokck.org

SLATER, Allen R. *(Judge, Kansas District Court Tenth Judicial District)*
Office: Johnson County Courthouse, 100 North Kansas Avenue, Olathe 66061-3273.
Telephone: (913) 715-3830.
Fax: (913) 715-3317
E-mail address: Allen.Slater@jocoks.com

SMITH, Danny *(Magistrate Judge, Kansas District Court Twenty-fourth Judicial District)*
Mailing address: P.O. Box 232, Kinsley 67547.
Office: Edwards County Courthouse, Kinsley 67547.
Telephone: (620) 659-2672.
Fax: (620) 659-2998
E-mail address: eddistmj@midway.net

SMITH, Edwin R. *(Magistrate Judge, Kansas District Court Fourth Judicial District)*
Mailing address: P.O. Box 637, Ottawa 66067-0637.
Office: Franklin County Courthouse, New Court Building, Ottawa 66067.
Telephone: (785) 242-6000.
Fax: (785) 242-5970
E-mail address: esmith@franklincoks.org

SMITH, J. Michael *(Chief Judge, Kansas District Court Nineteenth Judicial District)*
Mailing address: P.O. Box 472, Winfield 67156.
Office: Cowley County Courthouse, Winfield 67156.
Telephone: (620) 221-5471.
Fax: (620) 221-1097
E-mail address: jmsmith@cowleycourt.com

SMITH, James J. *(Chief Judge, Kansas District Court Fourth Judicial District)* Appointed by Governor John Carlin to term beginning July 31, 1979. Retained by election 1980, 1984, 1988, 1992, 1996 and 2000. Current term expires Jan 2005. Born St. Paul Kansas July 8, 1942. Catholic. Educated at Rockhurst College B.A. 1963, Georgetown University and Washburn University of Topeka J.D. 1966. Admitted to practice Kansas 1966. In legal practice Humboldt 1968-79.
Member Fourth Judicial District and Kansas Bar Associations. Specialist Five U.S. Army 1966-68.
Mailing address: P.O. Box 305, Garnett 66032.
Office: Anderson County Courthouse, Garnett 66032.
Telephone: (785) 448-6886.
Fax: (785) 448-3230
E-mail address: jamesjs@aceks.com

SMITH, Richard M. *(Judge, Kansas District Court Sixth Judicial District)*
Office: Linn County Courthouse, 315 Main Street, Mound City 66056.
Telephone: (913) 795-2622.
Fax: (913) 795-2004

SMITH, Tom R. *(Judge, Kansas District Court Twenty-sixth Judicial District)*
Office: Stevens County Courthouse, 200 East Sixth, Hugoton 67951.
Telephone: (620) 544-2484.
Fax: (620) 544-2528
E-mail address: 26judge1@pld.com

SOLOMON, Larry T. *(Chief Judge, Kansas District Court Thirtieth Judicial District)* Appointed by Governor Mike Hayden to term beginning June 18, 1989. Retained by election Nov 1990, Nov 1994, Nov 1998 and Nov 2002. Current term expires Jan 2007. Chief Judge since 1991. Born Wichita Kansas July 29, 1950. Protestant. Educated at Wichita State University B.A. 1972 and Washburn University School of Law J.D. 1976. Recipient Irvine E. Ungerman Award for Outstanding Legal Clinician 1976. Member Phi Delta Phi (Magister 1976). Admitted to practice Kansas 1976 and U.S. District Court District of Kansas 1976. In legal practice Kingman 1976-89. Judge, Kansas Municipal Court Cunningham 1979-81.
County Attorney Kingman County 1981-85. City Attorney Kingman 1987-89. Chairman Kansas Commission on Alternate Dispute Resolution 1994-2000. Chairman Non-Judicial Salary Initiative Kansas Supreme Court 2002. Member Kansas District Judges Association (Treasurer 1999-2000 and President since 2003 Executive Committee), Kingman County (Treasurer 1976-77, President 1978-83) and Kansas Bar Associations. Attended The National Judicial College. Enjoys jazz, wildflowers, native grass and natural habitat gardening.
Mailing address: P.O. Box 495, Kingman 67068-0495.
Office: Kingman County Courthouse, Kingman 67068.
Telephone: (620) 532-5151.
Fax: (620) 532-2952
E-mail address: lts@kmdistrictcourt.kscoxmail.com

STEPHAN, Rebecca *(Magistrate Judge, Kansas District Court Sixth Judicial District)*
Mailing address: P.O. Box 868, Fort Scott 66701.
Office: Bourbon County Courthouse, Fort Scott 66701.
Telephone: (620) 223-1830.
Fax: (620) 223-5303

STEWART, Frederick N. *(Judge, Kansas District Court First Judicial District)*
Office: 4076 Leavenworth Justice Center, 601 South Third Street, Leavenworth 66048-2868.
Telephone: (913) 684-0720.
Fax: (913) 684-0492

STITES, Barbara *(Magistrate Judge, Kansas District Court Seventeenth Judicial District)*
Office: Graham County Courthouse, 410 North Pomeroy Avenue, Hill City 67642.
Telephone: (785) 421-2224, 421-3458.
Fax: (785) 421-5463
E-mail address: ghmc@ruraltel.net

STUTZMAN, David L. *(Judge, Kansas District Court Twenty-first Judicial District)*
Mailing address: P.O. Box 158, Manhattan 66505-0158.
Office: Riley County Courthouse, Manhattan 66502.
Telephone: (785) 537-6373.
Fax: (785) 565-6849
E-mail address: stutzman@interkan.net

SUNDBY, Gunnar A. *(Judge, Kansas District Court First Judicial District)*
Office: 4094 Leavenworth Justice Center, 601 South Third Street, Leavenworth 66048-2868.
Telephone: (913) 684-0407.
Fax: (913) 684-0492

SUTHERLAND, Thomas M. *(Judge, Kansas District Court Tenth Judicial District)*
Office: Johnson County Courthouse, 100 North Kansas Avenue, Olathe 66061-3273.
Telephone: (913) 715-3770.
Fax: (913) 715-3317
E-mail address: thomas.sutherland@jocoks.com

TATUM, Stephen R. *(Judge, Kansas District Court Tenth Judicial District)*
Office: Johnson County Courthouse, 100 North Kansas Avenue, Olathe 66061-3273.
Telephone: (913) 715-3790.
Fax: (913) 715-3317
E-mail address: Stephen.Tatum@jocoks.com

TAYLOR, Terry N. *(Magistrate Judge, Kansas District Court Twelfth Judicial District)* Appointed to term beginning May 1, 1989. Retained by election Nov 1990, Nov 1994, 1998 and 2002. Current term expires Jan 2007. Also serves as Municipal Court Judge Washington since 1990 and Hanover since 1991. Born Cuero Texas May 7, 1940. Methodist.
Under Sheriff 1978-82 and Sheriff 1982-89 Washington County. Member Kansas Municipal Judges Association, Kansas District Magistrate Judges Association, National Judges Association and American Judges Association. Attended The National Judicial College May 20, 1990. Senior Master Sergeant USAF 1957-78. Member American Legion, Veterans of Foreign Wars, Masonic Lodge, Rotary and Lions Club. Enjoys farming and sports, especially high school and college sports as a fan and booster club supporter.
Office: Washington County Courthouse, 214 C Street, Washington 66968.
Telephone: (785) 325-2953.
Fax: (785) 325-2557
E-mail address: wcdc@washingtonks.net

THEIS, Franklin R. *(Judge, Kansas District Court Third Judicial District)* Elected to term beginning Jan 1977. Retained by non-partisan retention election 1980, 1984, 1988, 1992, 1996 and 2000. Current term expires Jan 2005. Born Arkansas City Kansas Jan 30, 1942. Educated at Kansas University B.A. 1964 J.D. 1967. Member Delta Upsilon. Admitted to practice Kansas 1967, U.S. District Court District of Kansas 1967 and U.S. Court of Appeals Tenth Circuit 1969. In legal practice Arkansas City 1967-68 and Topeka and Lawrence 1968-76.
Assistant U.S. Attorney Topeka 1968-69. Governor's Pardon and Extradition Attorney 1969-71. Chief Attorney and Assistant Attorney General Kansas Department of Administration 1971-75. Member Kansas Adult Authority 1975. Member Kansas District Judges Association, Topeka and Kansas Bar Associations. Nominated to court vacancy by Kansas Supreme Court Nominating Commission Oct 1992. Democrat.
Office: 324 Shawnee County Courthouse, 200 S.E. Seventh Street, Topeka 66603-3922.
Telephone: (785) 233-8200.
Fax: (785) 291-4917
E-mail address: ftheis@shawneecourt.org

THORNTON, Jacqueline Ehret *(Magistrate Judge, Kansas District Court Seventeenth Judicial District)* Elected Nov 10, 1992 to term beginning Jan 11, 1993. Reelected Nov 12, 1996 and Nov 7, 2000. Current term expires Jan 8, 2005. Born Denver Colorado April 23, 1950. Lutheran. Educated at University of Kansas B.A. 1973. Judge, Osborne Municipal Court 1987-93.
Member Northwest Kansas District Magistrate Judges Association (Secretary 1995-97), Kansas District Magistrate Judges Association (Board of Directors 1995-97), National Judges Association and National Council of Juvenile and Family Court Judges. Member VFW Auxiliary.
Mailing address: P.O. Box 160, Osborne 67473.
Office: Osborne County Courthouse, 423 West Main Street, Osborne 67473.
Telephone: (785) 346-2442.
Fax: (785) 346-5992

TOEPFER, Thomas L. *(Judge, Kansas District Court Twenty-third Judicial District)*
Mailing address: P.O. Box 8, Hays 67601.
Office: Ellis County Courthouse, 1204 Fort Street, Hays 67601.
Telephone: (785) 628-9422.
Fax: (785) 628-8415
E-mail address: ttoepfer@eaglecom.net

TRIGG, Linda S. *(Magistrate Judge, Kansas District Court Tenth Judicial District)* Appointed by Governor Bill Graves.
Office: Johnson County Courthouse, 100 North Kansas Avenue, Olathe 66061-3273.
Telephone: (913) 715-3322.
Fax: (913) 715-3317
E-mail address: linda.trigg@jocoks.com

TUGGLE, Thomas M. *(Chief Judge, Kansas District Court Twelfth Judicial District)*
Mailing address: P.O. Box 423, Concordia 66901.
Office: Cloud County Courthouse, Concordia 66901.
Telephone: (785) 243-8125.
Fax: (785) 243-8188, 243-8128
E-mail address: tmt@dustdevil.com

UNRUH, Steve *(Magistrate Judge, Kansas District Court Fifteenth Judicial District)*
Mailing address: P.O. Box 8, Sharon Springs 67758.
Office: Wallace County Courthouse, Sharon Springs 67758.

UNRUH, STEVE—*Continued*
Telephone: (785) 852-4989.
Fax: (785) 852-4271
E-mail address: wacodmj@pld.com

URBANEK, Dale L. *(Magistrate Judge, Kansas District Court Twentieth Judicial District)*
Office: Ellsworth County Courthouse, 210 North Kansas Avenue, Ellsworth 67439-3118.
Telephone: (785) 472-3832.
Fax: (785) 472-5712

VAN BEBBER, G. Thomas *(Senior Judge, United States District Court District of Kansas)* Magistrate Judge 1982-89. Appointed Judge for life by President George Bush to term beginning Dec 8, 1989. Assumed Senior status Dec 31, 2000, serves by assignment. Born St. Joseph Missouri Oct 21, 1931. Educated at University of Kansas B.A. 1953 LL.B. 1955. Editorial Board Kansas Law Review. Member Order of the Coif and Phi Delta Phi. Admitted to practice Kansas 1955, U.S. District Court District of Kansas 1955 and U.S. Court of Appeals Tenth Circuit 1961. In legal practice Troy 1955-59 and 1961-82.
Assistant U.S. Attorney Kansas 1959-61. County Attorney Doniphan County 1963-69. Chairman Kansas Corporation Commission Kansas 1975-79. Member American Judicature Society, Johnson County, Wyandotte County, Kansas and American Bar Associations. Member House of Representatives Kansas Jan 1973 to May 1975. Chairman Doniphan County Republican Central Committee 1964-73.
Office: 529 U.S. Courthouse, 500 State Avenue, Kansas City 66101-2437.
Telephone: (913) 551-6721.

VANO, James F. *(Judge, Kansas District Court Tenth Judicial District)* Former Magistrate Judge, appointed by Governor Bill Graves.
Office: Johnson County Courthouse, 100 North Kansas Avenue, Olathe 66061-3273.
Telephone: (913) 715-3760.
Fax: (913) 715-3317
E-mail address: james.vano@jocoks.com

VIEUX, Philip C. *(Chief Judge, Kansas District Court Twenty-fifth Judicial District)* Appointed by Governor John Carlin 1982. Retained by election 1988, 1992, 1996 and 2000. Current term expires Jan 2005.
Mailing address: P.O. Box 798, Garden City 67846-0798.
Office: Finney County Courthouse, Garden City 67846.
Telephone: (620) 271-6100.
Fax: (620) 271-6141
E-mail address: judge01@finneycounty.org

VINING, Mark *(Judge, Kansas District Court Eighteenth Judicial District)*
Office: Sedgwick County Courthouse, Fourth Floor, 525 North Main Street, Wichita 67203-3773.
Telephone: (316) 383-7201.
Fax: (316) 383-7560
E-mail address: mvining@dc18.org

VOLDEN, Roseanna K. *(Magistrate Judge, Kansas District Court Twenty-sixth Judicial District)*
Mailing address: P.O. Box 825, Elkhart 67950.
Office: Morton County Courthouse, Elkhart 67950.
Telephone: (620) 697-4839.
Fax: (620) 697-4289
E-mail address: rvolden@elkhart.com

VRATIL, Kathryn H. *(Judge, United States District Court District of Kansas)* Appointed for life by President George Bush Oct 9, 1992. Born April 21, 1949. Educated at University of Kansas B.A. 1971 J.D. 1975 and Exeter University, England 1971-72. Watkins Scholar. Staff member 1973-74 and Note and Comment Editor 1974-75 Kansas Law Review. Law Clerk to Hon. Earl E. O'Connor, U.S. District Court District of Kansas 1975-78. Member Phi Kappa Phi, Mortar Board and Order of the Coif. Admitted to practice Kansas 1975, Missouri 1978, U.S. District Courts District of Kansas 1975 and Western 1978 and Eastern 1985 Districts of Missouri and U.S. Courts of Appeals Eighth 1978, Tenth 1980 and Eleventh 1983 Circuits. In legal practice 1978-92. Judge, Prairie Village Municipal Court 1990-92.
Author Casenote "*Calloway v. City of Overland Park* 211 Kan. 646, 508 P.2d 902 (1972)" 22 Kansas L. Rev 151, 1973; "The Misrepresentation Defense in Causal Relation States: A Primer" XXVI No. 4 Tort & Insurance L. Jour. 832 American Bar Association Summer 1991 and "Notes From the Bench" 42 Kansas L. Rev. 1, 1993. Board of Editors The Journal of the Kansas Bar Association 1992-95. Former Member Kansas Municipal Judges Association and The Missouri Bar (Federal Practice and Procedure Committee, Business Law Committee and Commercial Law Committee, Vice Chair Legal Assistants Committee 1990-91). Board of Directors Kansas Legal Services, Inc. 1991-92. Fellow Johnson County Bar Foundation, Kansas Bar Foundation (Fellows Committee since 1993) and American Bar Foundation. Master The Kansas Inn of Court since 1993. Member Association of Women Lawyers of Kansas City, Lawyers' Association of Kansas City, National Association of Women Judges, Federal Judges Association, American Judicature Society, The Kansas City Metropolitan (Federal Courts Committee since 1992, Commercial Bankruptcy Committee since 1992), Johnson County (Judicial Evaluation Committee 1991-92, Bench Bar Conference Committee since 1991), Wyandotte County, Kansas (Editorial Delegate Litigation Section 1991-92, Member Legal Aid and Referral Committee since 1991, Committee on Professionalism, Equality and Quality since 1993) and American (Federal Practice Committee on Revisions to Federal Rules of Civil Procedure 1983, Committees on Commercial Banking and Financial Transactions Litigation, Corporate Counsel Litigation, Business Torts Litigation, Creditors' Rights Litigation and Employment and Labor Relations Law Section of Litigation since 1983, Committees on Commercial Torts, Corporate Counsel and Life Insurance Law Section of Tort and Insurance Practice 1991-93, Section of Business Law, Judicial Administration Division) Bar Associations. Attended Advanced Course National Institute for Trial Advocacy July 1989, Sentencing Misdemeanants The National Judicial College April 21-26, 1991, Video Orientation for Newly Appointed District Judges Dec 1992, National Workshop for District Judges I March 1993, Program on Science and Law Arizona State University March-April 1993, Orientation Seminar for Newly Appointed District Judges June 1993 and Sentencing Institute Aug 1993.
Listed in *International Who's Who of Women* 1980, *Who's Who in American Law* 1993, *The World Who's Who of Women* 1994, *Who's Who of American Women*

VRATIL, KATHRYN H.—*Continued*

1994, *Who's Who in the Midwest* 1994 and 1995 and *Who's Who in America* 1994 and 1995. Named one of Outstanding Young Women of America 1981. Program Chairman 1977-78, Recording Secretary 1978-79, Board of Directors 1978-80, First Vice President 1979-80 and Historian 1980-81 Friends of the Johnson County Library. Co-chair Young Marrieds Program 1978-80, Mariners Board 1980-81 and Video Task Force 1988, Sunday School Teacher 1979-80, Shepherd-Deacon 1979-81, Member Stewardship Committee 1980 Adult Ministry Committee 1981-84 and Search Committee for Director of Ministries and Administration 1991-92, Chairman Sanctuary Task Force 1986-88, and Board of Trustees 1990-93 Village Presbyterian Church. Board of Governors University of Kansas Law Society 1978-91. Board of Directors Friends of Montessori, Inc. 1984-85. Member Development Committee since 1985, Alumni Board Kansas City Chapter 1990-92, National Board of Directors since 1991, Board of Governors Adams Alumni Center since 1992, Learned Club since 1992, Chancellors Club since 1993 and Williams Educational Fund since 1993 University of Kansas Alumni Association. Member The Central Exchange 1990-92 (Administrative Council 1991-92, Chair Annual Meeting Committee 1991-92), Political Training Institute Overland Park Chamber of Commerce 1991, Strategic Planning Committee City of Prairie Village 1991-92 and Kansas City Tomorrow 1991-92. National Advisory Board Center for Environmental Education and Training University of Kansas since 1993. Chairman Rhodes Scholar Selection Committee Kansas since 1994. Member Homestead Country Club (Membership Chairman 1983-84, Vice President 1984-85, President 1985-86), Junior League of Kansas City, Kansas (Board of Directors 1982-84 and 1985-86), Native Sons and Daughters of Kansas, Kansas City Tomorrow Alumni Association, Kansas State Historical Society, The Supreme Court Historical Society, Overland Park Rotary and University Club.

Office: 511 U.S. Courthouse, 500 State Avenue, Kansas City 66101-2435.
Telephone: (913) 551-6550.

WACHTER, A. J. *(Judge, Kansas District Court Eleventh Judicial District)*
Mailing address: P.O. Box 1348, Pittsburg 66762.
Office: Crawford County Courthouse, 602 North Locust, Pittsburg 66762.
Telephone: (620) 231-3570.
Fax: (620) 231-0316

WALKER, Richard B. *(Chief Judge, Kansas District Court Ninth Judicial District)* Appointed by Governor John Carlin to term beginning Dec 17, 1984. Retained by election 1986, 1990, 1994, 1998 and 2002. Current term expires 2007. Born Newton Kansas July 20, 1948. United Methodist. Educated at Bethel College B.A. with high distinction 1970 and University of Kansas J.D. 1973. Member Phi Delta Phi. Admitted to practice Kansas 1973, U.S. District Court District of Kansas 1973, U.S. Supreme Court 1977 and U.S. Court of Appeals Tenth Circuit 1982. Began legal practice Newton 1973.

State Representative 72nd District of Kansas 1972-77. Chief Legislative Assistant to U.S. Senator James B. Pearson 1977-78. Member Kansas Adult Authority Parole Board 1979-82 and Kansas Coordinating Council on Criminal Justice. City Attorney Newton and Halstead 1982-84. Member since 1989 and Chairman 1997-2000 Kansas Sentencing Commission. Member Harvey County, Kansas and American Bar Associations. Republican. Past President Kauffman Museum Association. Board of Directors Kansas State Historical Society.

Mailing address: P.O. Box 665, Newton 67114-0665.
Office: Harvey County Courthouse, Newton 67114.
Telephone: (316) 284-6888.
Fax: (316) 283-4601
E-mail address: judgew@kscourt.net

WALLER, Gregory L. *(Judge, Kansas District Court Eighteenth Judicial District)* Appointed by Governor Joan Finney to term beginning April 30, 1993. Elected Nov 1994, 1998 and 2002. Current term expires Jan 2007. Born Hutchinson Kansas Oct 17, 1948. Catholic. Educated at Washburn University B.A. with honors 1970 J.D. 1972. Member Phi Alpha Delta. Admitted to practice Kansas 1973, U.S. District Court District of Kansas 1973 and U.S. Court of Appeals Tenth Circuit 1973. In legal practice Wichita 1973-75.

Assistant District Attorney Sedgwick County 1975-93. Member National Center for State Courts, Kansas District Judges Association, Wichita and Kansas Bar Associations. Attended Kansas Judicial Conference and The National Judicial College. Democrat.

Office: 6-2 Sedgwick County Courthouse, 525 North Main Street, Wichita 67203-3773.
Telephone: (316) 383-7031.
Fax: (316) 383-7560
E-mail address: gwaller@dc18.org

WALTERS, Timarie Ann *(Magistrate Judge, Kansas District Court Twentieth Judicial District)*
Mailing address: P.O. Box 365, St. John 67576-0365.
Office: Stafford County Courthouse, St. John 67576.
Telephone: (620) 549-3295.
Fax: (620) 549-3298
E-mail address: magistrate@stjohnks.net

WARD, Mike *(Judge, Kansas District Court Thirteenth Judicial District)* Elected Nov 1998 to term beginning Jan 11, 1999. Reelected Nov 2002, current term expires Jan 12, 2007. Born El Dorado Kansas July 9, 1955. Catholic. Educated at University of Missouri B.S. cum laude 1977 and University of Kansas J.D. 1980. Admitted to practice Kansas 1980. In legal practice El Dorado 1983-99.

County Attorney Butler County 1987-99. Co-author with Professor George Coggins *The Law of Wildlife Management on the Federal Public Lands* University of Kansas School of Law 1980. Member Kansas Bar Association. Named Outstanding Prosecutor of the Year in Kansas 1995. Enjoys golfing, coaching and youth activities.

Office: 201 Butler County Judicial Building, 121 South Gordy, El Dorado 67042.
Telephone: (316) 322-4360.
Fax: (316) 322-4365
E-mail address: judgeward@hotmail.com

WAXSE, David J. *(Magistrate Judge, United States District Court District of Kansas)* Appointed by U.S. District Court judges to term beginning October 4, 1999. Term expires 2007. Educated at University of Kansas B.A. and Columbia University J.D.

ADR Judicial Officer District of Kansas. Co-author *Kansas Employment Law Handbook* 1991 supplements 1992 and 1995; and Chapter on Civil Rights *Kansas An-*

WAXSE, DAVID J.—*Continued*

nual Survey Kansas Bar Association 1990-99. Lecturer on Law University of Kansas School of Law. Former Chair and Member Kansas Commission on Judicial Qualifications 1992-99. Former Member Kansas Justice Commission, Civil Justice Reform Act Advisory Committee and Mediation Panel U.S. District Court District of Kansas and National Board Lawyer's Committee for Civil Rights Under Law. Board Member American Judicature Society. Fellow Kansas Bar Foundation and American Bar Foundation. Member Federal Magistrate Judge's Association, Kansas City Metropolitan (Civil Rights Law Committee), Johnson County, Wyandotte County, Kansas (Past President, Delegate American Bar Association House of Delegates) and American (Judicial Division) Bar Associations. Former National Board Member ACLU.

Office: 219 U.S. Courthouse, 500 State Avenue, Kansas City 66101-2428.
Telephone: (913) 551-5405.

WAY, Jan A. *(Judge, Kansas District Court Twenty-ninth Judicial District)*
Office: Wyandotte County Courthouse, 710 North Seventh Street, Kansas City 66101.
Telephone: (913) 573-2810.
Fax: (913) 573-4135
E-mail address: Jway@wycokck.org

WEBB, Tom B. *(Magistrate Judge, Kansas District Court Twenty-sixth Judicial District)*
Mailing address: P.O. Box 517, Sublette 67877.
Office: Haskell County Courthouse, Sublette 67877.
Telephone: (620) 675-8231.
Fax: (620) 675-8599
E-mail address: judwebb@pld.com

WEINGART, John L. *(Judge, Kansas District Court Twenty-second Judicial District)*
Mailing address: P.O. Box 417, Hiawatha 66434.
Office: Brown County Courthouse, Hiawatha 66434.
Telephone: (785) 742-2236.
Fax: (785) 742-3506

WERNER, Lois *(Magistrate Judge, Kansas District Court Twenty-third Judicial District)*
Mailing address: P.O. Box 97, Gove 67736.
Office: Gove County Courthouse, Gove 67736.
Telephone: (785) 938-2235.
Fax: (785) 938-2312

WHEELER, Merlin G. *(Chief Judge, Kansas District Court Fifth Judicial District)* Appointed by Governor Mike Hayden to term beginning April 6, 1990. Retained by election Nov 1992, Nov 1996 and 2000. Current term expires Jan 2005. Born Dodge City Kansas Sept 10, 1952. Educated at Emporia State University B.A. with honors 1974 and Washburn University J.D. cum laude 1977. Member Phi Alpha Delta. Admitted to practice Kansas 1977 and U.S. District Court District of Kansas 1977. In legal practice Emporia 1977-90.

Member Lyon/Chase County (President 1985) and Kansas (President Corporation, Banking and Business Law Committee 1988) Bar Associations.

Office: Lyon County Courthouse, 430 Commercial, Emporia 66801.
Telephone: (620) 341-3296.
Fax: (620) 342-8005
E-mail address: merlinwheeler@hotmail.com

WHITNEY, Keith *(Magistrate Judge, Kansas District Court Sixteenth Judicial District)*
Mailing address: P.O. Box 623, Meade 67864.
Office: Meade County Courthouse, Meade 67864.
Telephone: (620) 873-8760.
Fax: (620) 873-8759
E-mail address: Whitneyk@alltel.net

WILBERT, Warren *(Judge, Kansas District Court Eighteenth Judicial District)*
Office: 10-4 Sedgwick County Courthouse, 525 North Main Street, Wichita 67203-3773.
Telephone: (316) 383-8293.
Fax: (316) 383-7560
E-mail address: wwilbert@dc18.org

WILSON, Bonnie J. *(Magistrate Judge, Kansas District Court Twelfth Judicial District)*
Office: Mitchell County Courthouse, 115 South Hersey, Beloit 67420.
Telephone: (785) 738-2151.
Fax: (785) 738-4101
E-mail address: mcdcjudge@nckcn.com

WILSON, C. Ann *(Magistrate Judge, Kansas District Court Twenty-fifth Judicial District)* Elected to term beginning Jan 13, 1975. Retained by election 1976, 1980, 1984, 1988, 1992, 1996 and 2000. Current term expires Jan 2005. Also serves Tribune Municipal Court, Leoti Municipal Court and Horace Municipal Court. Born Okmulgee Oklahoma April 5, 1942. Roman Catholic. Educated at Western Wyoming Junior College 1960-61 and Colby Community College A.A. 1978.

Member Kansas District Magistrate Judges Association, Kansas Municipal Judges Association and National Judges Association. Earned Certificate of Qualification Kansas Supreme Court July 11, 1977 and Certificate of Completion General Session The National Judicial College Nov 18, 1983. Recipient Achievement Award from Kansas District Magistrate Judges Association Oct 11, 1988 and Samuel I. Mason Award for Outstanding District Magistrate Judge of Kansas Oct 20, 1997. Member Juvenile Corrections Advisory Board.

Mailing address: P.O. Box 516, Tribune 67879.
Office: Greeley County Courthouse, Tribune 67879.
Telephone: (620) 376-4258.
Fax: (620) 376-2351
E-mail address: glcodmj@sunflowertelco.com

WILSON, Meryl D. *(Judge, Kansas District Court Twenty-first Judicial District)*
Mailing address: P.O. Box 158, Manhattan 66505-0158.
Office: Riley County Courthouse, Manhattan 66502.
Telephone: (785) 537-6372.
Fax: (785) 537-6382
E-mail address: mwilson@co.riley.ks.us

WILSON, T. Keith *(Chief Judge, Kansas District Court Twenty-sixth Judicial District)*
Office: 103 Seward County Courthouse, 415 North Washington, Liberal 67901.
Telephone: (620) 626-3262.
Fax: (620) 626-3302
E-mail address: tkwilson@swko.net

WOOLLEY, William Sioux *(Judge, Kansas District Court Eighteenth Judicial District)*
Office: 5-4 Sedgwick County Courthouse, 525 North Main Street, Wichita 67203-3773.
Telephone: (316) 383-7107.
Fax: (316) 383-7560
E-mail address: wwoolley@dc18.org

WRIGHT, Paul *(Magistrate Judge, Kansas District Court Twenty-first Judicial District)*
Mailing address: P.O. Box 203, Clay Center 67432.
Office: Clay County Courthouse, Clay Center 67432.
Telephone: (785) 632-2636.
Fax: (785) 632-2651
E-mail address: ccdisjud@kansas.net

WYBO-VOPATA, Gerri *(Magistrate Judge, Kansas District Court Twenty-second Judicial District)*
Mailing address: P.O. Box 86, Marysville 66508-0086.
Office: Marshall County Courthouse, 1201 Broadway, Marysville 66508.
Telephone: (785) 562-5301, 562-3281.
Fax: (785) 562-2458
E-mail address: judgewybovopata@netscape.net

YEOMAN, Frank, Jr. *(Judge, Kansas District Court Third Judicial District)*
Office: 310 Shawnee County Courthouse, 200 S.E. Seventh Street, Topeka 66603-3922.
Telephone: (785) 233-8200.
Fax: (785) 291-4917

YOST, Eric *(Judge, Kansas District Court Eighteenth Judicial District)*
Office: 6-4 Sedgwick County Courthouse, 525 North Main Street, Wichita 67203-3773.
Telephone: (316) 383-7809.
Fax: (316) 383-7560
E-mail address: eyost@dc18.org

ZIMBELMAN, Tamara L. *(Magistrate Judge, Kansas District Court Fifteenth Judicial District)*
Mailing address: P.O. Box 646, St. Francis 67756.
Office: Cheyenne County Courthouse, St. Francis 67756.
Telephone: (785) 332-8860.
Fax: (785) 332-8851
E-mail address: judgez55@hotmail.com

KENTUCKY

Capital FRANKFORT

UNITED STATES DISTRICT COURTS DISTRICTS OF KENTUCKY

Within Kentucky, there are two United States District Courts. For descriptive information refer to the United States Courts section.

EASTERN DISTRICT includes Anderson, Bath, Bell, Boone, Bourbon, Boyd, Boyle, Bracken, Breathitt, Campbell, Carroll, Carter, Clark, Clay, Elliott, Estill, Fayette, Fleming, Floyd, Franklin, Gallatin, Garrard, Grant, Greenup, Harlan, Harrison, Henry, Jackson, Jessamine, Johnson, Kenton, Knott, Knox, Laurel, Lawrence, Lee, Leslie, Letcher, Lewis, Lincoln, Madison, Magoffin, Martin, Mason, McCreary, Menifee, Mercer, Montgomery, Morgan, Nicholas, Owen, Owsley, Pendleton, Perry, Pike, Powell, Pulaski, Robertson, Rockcastle, Rowan, Scott, Shelby, Trimble, Wayne, Whitley, Wolfe and Woodford counties. The court sits at Ashland, Catlettsburg, Covington, Frankfort, Jackson, Lexington, London, Pikeville and Richmond.

Chief Judge
Karl S. Forester

Judges
Joseph Martin Hood
Jennifer B. Coffman
Karen K. Caldwell
Danny C. Reeves
David L. Bunning

Senior Judges
William O. Bertelsman
G. Wix Unthank
Henry Rupert Wilhoit, Jr.

Clerk
Leslie G. Whitmer
P.O. Drawer 3074
Lexington, Kentucky 40588-3074
(859) 233-2503

WESTERN DISTRICT includes Adair, Allen, Ballard, Barren, Breckenridge, Bullitt, Butler, Caldwell, Calloway, Carlisle, Casey, Christian, Clinton, Crittenden, Cumberland, Daviess, Edmonson, Fulton, Graves, Grayson, Green, Hancock, Hardin, Hart, Henderson, Hickman, Hopkins, Jefferson, Larue, Livingston, Logan, Lyon, Marion, Marshall, McCracken, McLean, Meade, Metcalfe, Monroe, Muhlenberg, Nelson, Ohio, Oldham, Russell, Simpson, Spencer, Taylor, Todd, Trigg, Union, Warren, Washington and Webster counties. The court sits at Bowling Green, Louisville, Owensboro and Paducah.

Chief Judge
John G. Heyburn II

Judges
Charles R. Simpson, III
Jennifer B. Coffman
Thomas B. Russell
Joseph H. McKinley, Jr.

Senior Judge
Edward H. Johnstone

Clerk
Jeffrey A. Apperson
106 U.S. Courthouse
601 West Broadway
Louisville, Kentucky 40202
(502) 625-3520

UNITED STATES MAGISTRATE JUDGES OF KENTUCKY

EASTERN DISTRICT
J. B. Johnson, Jr.
Peggy E. Patterson
J. Gregory Wehrman
James B. Todd

WESTERN DISTRICT
W. David King
C. Cleveland Gambill
James D. Moyer
E. Robert Goebel

UNITED STATES BANKRUPTCY COURTS OF KENTUCKY

EASTERN DISTRICT

Chief Judge
William S. Howard

Judge
Joseph M. Scott, Jr.

Recalled Judge
Joe Lee

Bankruptcy Clerk
Jerry D. Truitt
P.O. Box 1111
Lexington, Kentucky 40588-1111
(859) 233-2608

WESTERN DISTRICT

Chief Judge
David T. Stosberg

Judges
Joan Lloyd Cooper
Thomas H. Fulton

UNITED STATES DISTRICT COURTS DISTRICTS OF KENTUCKY—*Continued*

Bankruptcy Clerk
Diane S. Robl
546 U.S. Courthouse
601 West Broadway
Louisville, Kentucky 40202-2264
(502) 627-5700

KENTUCKY SUPREME COURT

The Supreme Court is Kentucky's court of last resort. The state is divided into seven Supreme Court districts for electoral purposes. One justice is elected on a nonpartisan basis from each district for an eight-year term. Vacancies may be filled by the governor. The chief justice is elected by peer vote for a four-year term. Retired justices may serve as special judges.

The court exercises appellate jurisdiction over civil and criminal matters, with direct review over sentences of death, life imprisonment or imprisonment of more than twenty years. The court may be petitioned directly to hear appeals when a public issue is in question and may issue all writs necessary to the exercise of proper jurisdiction.

The court sits at Frankfort.

DISTRICT ONE includes Allen, Ballard, Butler, Caldwell, Calloway, Carlisle, Christian, Crittenden, Fulton, Graves, Hickman, Hopkins, Livingston, Logan, Lyon, Marshall, McCracken, McLean, Muhlenberg, Simpson, Todd, Trigg and Webster counties.

DISTRICT TWO includes Barren, Breckinridge, Bullitt, Daviess, Edmonson, Grayson, Hancock, Hardin, Hart, Henderson, Meade, Ohio, Union and Warren counties.

DISTRICT THREE includes Adair, Anderson, Bell, Casey, Clay, Clinton, Cumberland, Green, Jackson, Knox, Larue, Laurel, Leslie, Lincoln, Marion, McCreary, Metcalfe, Monroe, Nelson, Owsley, Pulaski, Rockcastle, Russell, Spencer, Taylor, Washington, Wayne and Whitley counties.

DISTRICT FOUR includes Jefferson County.

DISTRICT FIVE includes Bourbon, Boyle, Clark, Estill, Fayette, Franklin, Garrard, Jessamine, Lee, Madison, Mercer, Powell, Scott and Woodford counties.

DISTRICT SIX includes Bath, Boone, Bracken, Campbell, Carroll, Fleming, Gallatin, Grant, Harrison, Henry, Kenton, Lewis, Mason, Nicholas, Oldham, Owen, Pendleton, Robertson, Shelby and Trimble counties.

DISTRICT SEVEN includes Boyd, Breathitt, Carter, Elliott, Floyd, Greenup, Harlan, Johnson, Knott, Lawrence, Letcher, Magoffin, Martin, Menifee, Montgomery, Morgan, Perry, Pike, Rowan and Wolfe counties.

Chief Justice
Joseph E. Lambert

Justices

William Cooper	John William Graves
Martin E. Johnstone	James E. Keller
Janet L. Stumbo	Donald C. Wintersheimer

Clerk
Susan Stokley Clary
235 State Capitol Building
700 Capitol Avenue
Frankfort, Kentucky 40601-3415
(502) 564-5444

Administrative Director
Cicely Jaracz Lambert
Administrative Office of the Courts
100 Millcreek Park
Frankfort, Kentucky 40601-9230
(502) 573-2350

KENTUCKY COURT OF APPEALS

The Court of Appeals is Kentucky's court of intermediate appellate jurisdiction. Two judges are elected for eight-year terms on a nonpartisan basis from each of the seven Supreme Court electoral districts. Vacancies may be filled by the governor. The chief judge is elected by peer vote for a four-year term. Retired judges may serve as special judges.

The court has appellate jurisdiction from final and interlocutory judgments, convictions and orders or decrees of the Circuit Court unless such actions involve a judgment dissolving marriage or were rendered on an appeal from District Court. The court may also review cases concerning decisions of administrative agencies and issue all writs necessary to the exercise of proper jurisdiction.

The court sits in panels of not less than three judges at various locations in the state.

Chief Judge
Thomas D. Emberton

Judges

Matthew J. Baker	David Barber
David C. Buckingham	Sara Walter Combs
R. W. Dyche, III	Daniel T. Guidugli
Joseph R. Huddleston	Rick A. Johnson
William L. Knopf	William McAnulty, Jr.
Lewis G. Paisley	Wilfrid Schroder
Julia K. Tackett	

KENTUCKY CIRCUIT COURT

The Circuit Court is Kentucky's court of general jurisdiction. Judges are elected from their respective circuits for eight-year terms. Vacancies may be filled by the governor. In circuits where there is more than one judge, a chief judge may be elected by peer vote for a two-year term. The Family Court, which is a division of the Circuit Courts, began as a pilot project in 1991 and was permanently established by the voters in 2002. At present about one-third of the counties have family courts; these courts should be established in all counties within ten years. Judges are assigned specifically to the Family Court by the chief justice. Retired judges may serve as special judges.

The court has original jurisdiction of all law and equity matters not exclusively delegated to some other court. The court has jurisdiction in all cases of real estate title questions, contested probate matters, equity and in cases when the amount in controversy exceeds $4,000. Circuit Court also has appellate jurisdiction of judgments and final orders of District Courts. The Family Court division

KENTUCKY CIRCUIT COURT—*Continued*

has jurisdiction over family-related matters including dissolution of marriage, child custody, support and visitation, paternity and status offenses. The court is authorized to review actions and decisions of most administrative agencies, special districts and boards, such proceedings being original actions, not appeals.

There are fifty-seven judicial circuits, with court held in each county and as designated by the Supreme Court.

*Serves Family Court

FIRST JUDICIAL CIRCUIT includes Ballard, Carlisle, Fulton and Hickman counties. The court sits at Wickliffe, Bardwell, Hickman and Clinton.

Judge
William L. Shadoan

SECOND JUDICIAL CIRCUIT includes McCracken County. The court sits at Paducah.

Judges
Craig Z. Clymer
Robert Jeffrey Hines
Cynthia Sanderson*

THIRD JUDICIAL CIRCUIT includes Christian County. The court sits at Hopkinsville.

Judges
John L. Atkins
Judy A. Hall*
Edwin Morton White

FOURTH JUDICIAL CIRCUIT includes Hopkins County. The court sits at Madisonville.

Judge
Charles W. Boteler, Jr.

FIFTH JUDICIAL CIRCUIT includes Crittenden, Union and Webster counties. The court sits at Marion, Morganfield and Dixon.

Judges
Tommy W. Chandler
William Mitchell*

SIXTH JUDICIAL CIRCUIT includes Daviess County. The court sits at Owensboro.

Judges
Thomas O. Castlen
Henry McHenry Griffin, III

SEVENTH JUDICIAL CIRCUIT includes Logan and Todd counties. The court sits at Russellville and Elkton.

Judge
Tyler L. Gill

EIGHTH JUDICIAL CIRCUIT includes Warren County. The court sits at Bowling Green.

Judges
Margaret R. Huddleston*
Thomas Richards Lewis
John D. Minton, Jr.

NINTH JUDICIAL CIRCUIT includes Hardin County. The court sits at Elizabethtown.

Judges
Thomas Steven Bland
Janet P. Coleman
Kelly Mark Easton

TENTH JUDICIAL CIRCUIT includes Hart, Larue and Nelson counties. The court sits at Munfordville, Hodgenville and Bardstown.

Judge
Larry D. Raikes

ELEVENTH JUDICIAL CIRCUIT includes Green, Marion, Taylor and Washington counties. The court sits at Greensburg, Lebanon, Campbellsville and Springfield.

Judges
Allan Ray Bertram
Doughlas M. George

TWELFTH JUDICIAL CIRCUIT includes Henry, Oldham and Trimble counties. The court sits at New Castle, La Grange and Bedford.

Judges
Karen Conrad*
Paul Weil Rosenblum*

THIRTEENTH JUDICIAL CIRCUIT includes Garrard and Jessamine counties. The court sits at Lancaster and Nicholasville.

Judge
Hunter Daugherty

FOURTEENTH JUDICIAL CIRCUIT includes Bourbon, Scott and Woodford counties. The court sits at Paris, Georgetown and Versailles.

Judges
Paul F. Isaacs
Robert B. Overstreet

FIFTEENTH JUDICIAL CIRCUIT includes Carroll, Grant and Owen counties. The court sits at Carrollton, Williamstown and Owenton.

Judge
Stephen L. Bates

SIXTEENTH JUDICIAL CIRCUIT includes Kenton County. The court sits at Covington and Independence.

Judges
Gregory Bartlett
Steven R. Jaeger
Douglas M. Stephens
Patricia M. Summe

SEVENTEENTH JUDICIAL CIRCUIT includes Campbell County. The court sits at Newport and Alexandria.

Judges
Michael Foellger*
Leonard L. Kopowski
William J. Wehr

KENTUCKY CIRCUIT COURT—*Continued*

EIGHTEENTH JUDICIAL CIRCUIT includes Harrison, Nicholas, Pendleton and Robertson counties. The court sits at Cynthiana, Carlisle, Falmouth and Mount Olivet.

Judges
Robert W. McGinnis
David Melcher*

NINETEENTH JUDICIAL CIRCUIT includes Bracken, Fleming and Mason counties. The court sits at Brooksville, Flemingsburg and Maysville.

Judge
John Worthy McNeill

TWENTIETH JUDICIAL CIRCUIT includes Greenup and Lewis counties. The court sits at Greenup and Vanceburg.

Judge
Lewis Dunn Nicholls

TWENTY-FIRST JUDICIAL CIRCUIT includes Bath, Menifee, Montgomery and Rowan counties. The court sits at Owingsville, Frenchburg, Mount Sterling and Morehead.

Judges
William Mains
Beth Lewis Maze

TWENTY-SECOND JUDICIAL CIRCUIT includes Fayette County. The court sits at Lexington.

Judges
John R. Adams
Thomas L. Clark
Mary C. Noble
Gary D. Payne*
Jo Ann Wise*
Kimberly N. Bunnell*
Sheila R. Isaac
Rebecca M. Overstreet
Laurance VanMeter

TWENTY-THIRD JUDICIAL CIRCUIT includes Estill, Lee and Owsley counties. The court sits at Irvine, Beattyville and Booneville.

Judge
William W. Trude, Jr.

TWENTY-FOURTH JUDICIAL CIRCUIT includes Johnson, Lawrence and Martin counties. The court sits at Paintsville, Louisa and Inez.

Judges
Stephen N. Frazier*
Daniel R. Sparks

TWENTY-FIFTH JUDICIAL CIRCUIT includes Clark and Madison counties. The court sits at Winchester and Richmond.

Judges
Julia Hylton Adams
William T. Jennings
Jean Chenault Logue*
Jeffrey M. Walson*

TWENTY-SIXTH JUDICIAL CIRCUIT includes Harlan County. The court sits at Harlan.

Judge
Ron Johnson

TWENTY-SEVENTH JUDICIAL CIRCUIT includes Knox and Laurel counties. The court sits at Barbourville and London.

Judges
Lewis B. Hopper
Roderick Messer

TWENTY-EIGHTH JUDICIAL CIRCUIT includes Lincoln, Pulaski and Rockcastle counties. The court sits at Stanford, Somerset and Mount Vernon.

Judges
William T. Cain
Debra Lambert*
Daniel J. Venters

TWENTY-NINTH JUDICIAL CIRCUIT includes Adair and Casey counties. The court sits at Columbia and Liberty.

Judge
James G. Weddle

THIRTIETH JUDICIAL CIRCUIT includes Jefferson County. The court sits at Louisville.

Judges
Lisabeth Hughes Abramson
Denise G. Clayton
Patty Walker Fitzgerald*
Stephen M. George*
Juda Maria Hellmann*
Tom McDonald
Stephen K. Mershon
Kathleen Voor Montano*
Joseph W. O'Reilly*
Ann O'Malley Shake
Barry Willett
Jerry Bowles*
Joan L. Byer*
Ken Conliffe
Eleanore Garber*
Kevin L. Garvey*
Hugh Smith Haynie*
Thomas John Knopf
Judith McDonald-Burkman
Geoffrey P. Morris
Stephen P. Ryan
James M. Shake
Thomas B. Wine

THIRTY-FIRST JUDICIAL CIRCUIT includes Floyd County. The court sits at Prestonsburg.

Judges
Danny P. Caudill
John David Caudill
Julie Paxton*

THIRTY-SECOND JUDICIAL CIRCUIT includes Boyd County. The court sits at Ashland.

Judges
C. David Hagerman
Marc I. Rosen

THIRTY-THIRD JUDICIAL CIRCUIT includes Perry County. The court sits at Hazard.

Judge
Douglas C. Combs

THIRTY-FOURTH JUDICIAL CIRCUIT includes McCreary and Whitley counties. The court sits at Whitley City, Williamsburg and Corbin.

Judges
Paul Braden
Jerry D. Winchester

KENTUCKY CIRCUIT COURT—*Continued*

THIRTY-FIFTH JUDICIAL CIRCUIT includes Pike County. The court sits at Pikeville.

Judges
Eddy Coleman
Charles E. Lowe
Larry E. Thompson*

THIRTY-SIXTH JUDICIAL CIRCUIT includes Knott and Magoffin counties. The court sits at Hindman and Salyersville.

Judge
J. Robert Morgan

THIRTY-SEVENTH JUDICIAL CIRCUIT includes Carter, Elliott and Morgan counties. The court sits at Grayson, Sandy Hook and West Liberty.

Judges
Kristi Hogg Gossett*
Samuel C. Long

THIRTY-EIGHTH JUDICIAL CIRCUIT includes Butler, Edmonson, Hancock and Ohio counties. The court sits at Morgantown, Brownsville, Hawesville and Hartford.

Judge
Ronnie C. Dortch

THIRTY-NINTH JUDICIAL CIRCUIT includes Breathitt, Powell and Wolfe counties. The court sits at Jackson, Stanton and Campton.

Judge
Wm. Larry Miller

FORTIETH JUDICIAL CIRCUIT includes Clinton, Cumberland and Monroe counties. The court sits at Albany, Burkesville and Tompkinsville.

Judge
Eddie Lovelace

FORTY-FIRST JUDICIAL CIRCUIT includes Clay, Jackson and Leslie counties. The court sits at Manchester, McKee and Hyden.

Judges
Eugene Clark*
R. Cletus Maricle

FORTY-SECOND JUDICIAL CIRCUIT includes Calloway and Marshall counties. The court sits at Murray and Benton.

Judge
Dennis R. Foust

FORTY-THIRD JUDICIAL CIRCUIT includes Barren and Metcalfe counties. The court sits at Glasgow and Edmonton.

Judges
William Mitchell Nance*
Phillip Patton

FORTY-FOURTH JUDICIAL CIRCUIT includes Bell County. The court sits at Pineville and Middlesboro.

Judge
James L. Bowling

FORTY-FIFTH JUDICIAL CIRCUIT includes McLean and Muhlenberg counties. The court sits at Calhoun and Greenville.

Judge
David H. Jernigan

FORTY-SIXTH JUDICIAL CIRCUIT includes Breckinridge, Grayson and Meade counties. The court sits at Hardinsburg, Leitchfield and Brandenburg.

Judges
Robert Allen Miller
Sam H. Monarch

FORTY-SEVENTH JUDICIAL CIRCUIT includes Letcher County. The court sits at Whitesburg.

Judge
Samuel T. Wright

FORTY-EIGHTH JUDICIAL CIRCUIT includes Franklin County. The court sits at Frankfort.

Judges
Roger Crittenden
William Louis Graham
O. Reed Rhorer*

FORTY-NINTH JUDICIAL CIRCUIT includes Allen and Simpson counties. The court sits at Scottsville and Franklin.

Judge
William R. Harris

FIFTIETH JUDICIAL CIRCUIT includes Boyle and Mercer counties. The court sits at Danville and Harrodsburg.

Judges
Darren W. Peckler
Bruce Petrie*

FIFTY-FIRST JUDICIAL CIRCUIT includes Henderson County. The court sits at Henderson.

Judges
Sheila Nunley Farris*
Stephen Hayden

FIFTY-SECOND JUDICIAL CIRCUIT includes Graves County. The court sits at Mayfield.

Judge
John T. Daughaday

FIFTY-THIRD JUDICIAL CIRCUIT includes Anderson, Shelby and Spencer counties. The court sits at Lawrenceburg, Shelbyville and Taylorsville.

Judge
William F. Stewart

FIFTY-FOURTH JUDICIAL CIRCUIT includes Boone and Gallatin counties. The court sits at Burlington and Warsaw.

Judges
Joseph F. Bamberger
Linda Rae Bramlage*

FIFTY-FIFTH JUDICIAL CIRCUIT includes Bullitt County. The court sits at Shepherdsville.

Judge
Thomas L. Waller

KENTUCKY CIRCUIT COURT—*Continued*

FIFTY-SIXTH JUDICIAL CIRCUIT includes Caldwell, Livingston, Lyon and Trigg counties. The court sits at Princeton, Smithland, Eddyville and Cadiz.

Judge
Bill Cunningham

FIFTY-SEVENTH JUDICIAL CIRCUIT includes Russell and Wayne counties. The court sits at Jamestown and Monticello.

Judge
Robert Wilson

KENTUCKY DISTRICT COURT

The District Court is a court of limited jurisdiction in Kentucky, combining the Quarterly, County, Justice and Police Courts which were abolished January 1, 1978. Judges are elected from their respective districts in nonpartisan elections for four-year terms. Vacancies may be filled by the governor. In districts where there is more than one judge, a chief judge may be selected by peer vote for a two-year term. Retired judges may serve as special judges.

The court has exclusive original jurisdiction of all misdemeanors except when the charge is joined with an indictment for a felony and of civil cases in which the amount does not exceed $4,000, ordinance violations, uncontested probate matters and cases relating to juveniles or minors. The court also has concurrent jurisdiction with the Circuit Court to conduct preliminary hearings in felony cases and may, upon motion and for good cause shown, reduce the charge to a misdemeanor. Each District Court has a Small Claims Division which handles cases involving $1,500 or less.

There are sixty judicial districts, with court held at each county seat and other cities as assigned by the Supreme Court.

FIRST JUDICIAL DISTRICT includes Fulton and Hickman counties. The court sits at Hickman and Clinton.

Judge
Hunter Whitesell

SECOND JUDICIAL DISTRICT includes McCracken County. The court sits at Paducah.

Judges
Bard Kevin Brian
Donna L. Dixon

THIRD JUDICIAL DISTRICT includes Christian County. The court sits at Hopkinsville.

Judges
James G. Adams, Jr.
Arnold Lynch

FOURTH JUDICIAL DISTRICT includes Hopkins County. The court sits at Madisonville.

Judges
Logan Calvert
Robert F. Soder

FIFTH JUDICIAL DISTRICT includes Crittenden, Union and Webster counties. The court sits at Marion, Morganfield and Dixon.

Judge
C. René Williams

SIXTH JUDICIAL DISTRICT includes Daviess County. The court sits at Owensboro.

Judges
Joseph Castlen
Lisa A. Jones
David C. Payne

SEVENTH JUDICIAL DISTRICT includes Logan and Todd counties. The court sits at Russellville and Elkton.

Judge
Sue Carol Browning

EIGHTH JUDICIAL DISTRICT includes Warren County. The court sits at Bowling Green.

Judges
JoAnn Spinks Coleman
Brent J. Potter
Sam C. Potter, Jr.

NINTH JUDICIAL DISTRICT includes Hardin County. The court sits at Elizabethtown.

Judges
Kimberly W. Shumate
John David Simcoe

TENTH JUDICIAL DISTRICT includes Hart and Larue counties. The court sits at Munfordville and Hodgenville.

Judge
Clyde Derek Reed

ELEVENTH JUDICIAL DISTRICT includes Green, Marion, Taylor and Washington counties. The court sits at Greensburg, Lebanon, Campbellsville and Springfield.

Judges
James L. Avritt
Connie Phillips

TWELFTH JUDICIAL DISTRICT includes Henry, Oldham and Trimble counties. The court sits at New Castle, La Grange and Bedford.

Judges
Jerry D. Crosby, II
Diana E. Wheeler

THIRTEENTH JUDICIAL DISTRICT includes Garrard, Jessamine and Lincoln counties. The court sits at Lancaster, Nicholasville and Stanford.

Judges
Janet Carroll Booth
William Oliver

FOURTEENTH JUDICIAL DISTRICT includes Bourbon, Scott and Woodford counties. The court sits at Paris, Georgetown and Versailles.

Judges
Vanessa Dickson
Mary Jane Phelps

FIFTEENTH JUDICIAL DISTRICT includes Carroll, Grant and Owen counties. The court sits at Carrollton, Williamstown and Owenton.

KENTUCKY DISTRICT COURT—*Continued*

Judges
Thomas Funk
James Purcell

SIXTEENTH JUDICIAL DISTRICT includes Kenton County. The court sits at Covington.

Judges
Douglas Grothaus
Ann Ruttle
Martin J. Sheehan
Frank Trusty

SEVENTEENTH JUDICIAL DISTRICT includes Campbell County. The court sits at Newport and Alexandria.

Judges
Gregory Popovich
Karen Thomas

EIGHTEENTH JUDICIAL DISTRICT includes Harrison, Nicholas, Pendleton and Robertson counties. The court sits at Cynthiana, Carlisle, Falmouth and Mount Olivet.

Judge
William Probus

NINETEENTH JUDICIAL DISTRICT includes Bracken, Fleming and Mason counties. The court sits at Brooksville, Flemingsburg and Maysville.

Judge
W. Todd Walton, II

TWENTIETH JUDICIAL DISTRICT includes Greenup and Lewis counties. The court sits at Greenup and Vanceburg.

Judge
Robert B. Conley

TWENTY-FIRST JUDICIAL DISTRICT includes Bath, Menifee, Montgomery and Rowan counties. The court sits at Owingsville, Frenchburg, Mount Sterling and Morehead.

Judges
John R. Cox
William Lane

TWENTY-SECOND JUDICIAL DISTRICT includes Fayette County. The court sits at Lexington.

Judges
Pamela Goodwine
David Hayse
Kevin M. Horne
Maria Ransdell
Megan Thornton

TWENTY-THIRD JUDICIAL DISTRICT includes Estill, Lee and Owsley counties. The court sits at Irvine, Beattyville and Booneville.

Judge
Ralph E. McClanahan, II

TWENTY-FOURTH JUDICIAL DISTRICT includes Johnson, Lawrence and Martin counties. The court sits at Paintsville, Louisa and Inez.

Judges
John Kevin Holbrook
Susan Johnson

TWENTY-FIFTH JUDICIAL DISTRICT includes Clark and Madison counties. The court sits at Winchester and Richmond.

Judges
Brandy Oliver Brown
William G. Clouse, Jr.

TWENTY-SIXTH JUDICIAL DISTRICT includes Harlan County. The court sits at Harlan.

Judge
Phillip Hamm

TWENTY-SEVENTH JUDICIAL DISTRICT includes Knox and Laurel counties. The court sits at Barbourville and London.

Judges
Michael Caperton
John Knox Mills

TWENTY-EIGHTH JUDICIAL DISTRICT includes Pulaski and Rockcastle counties. The court sits at Somerset and Mount Vernon.

Judges
Michael L. Henry
Walter Flippin Maguire

TWENTY-NINTH JUDICIAL DISTRICT includes Adair and Casey counties. The court sits at Columbia and Liberty.

Judge
Roger Elliot

THIRTIETH JUDICIAL DISTRICT includes Jefferson County. The court sits at Louisville.

Judges

Donald Armstrong, Jr.	Judith Bartholomew
Angela McCormick Bisig	Sheila Anne Collins
Kevin Delahanty	Sean Delahanty
Deborah Deweese	Jacquelyn Poole Eckert
Matthew K. Eckert	Paula Fitzgerald
Janice Martin	Martin McDonald
Claude R. Prather	William P. Ryan, Jr.
Michele Stengel	Joan Antoinette "Toni" Stringer
Virginia Whittinghill	

THIRTY-FIRST JUDICIAL DISTRICT includes Floyd County. The court sits at Prestonsburg.

Judges
James R. Allen
Eric D. Hall

THIRTY-SECOND JUDICIAL DISTRICT includes Boyd County. The court sits at Catlettsburg.

Judges
George W. Davis
Gerald Brock Reams

THIRTY-THIRD JUDICIAL DISTRICT includes Perry County. The court sits at Hazard.

Judge
Leigh Anne Stephens

KENTUCKY DISTRICT COURT—*Continued*

THIRTY-FOURTH JUDICIAL DISTRICT includes McCreary and Whitley counties. The court sits at Whitley City, Corbin and Williamsburg.

Judges
Dan Ballou
David Burton

THIRTY-FIFTH JUDICIAL DISTRICT includes Pike County. The court sits at Pikeville.

Judges
Kelsey Evans Friend
Darrel H. Mullins

THIRTY-SIXTH JUDICIAL DISTRICT includes Knott and Magoffin counties. The court sits at Hindman and Salyersville.

Judge
Kimberly Childers

THIRTY-SEVENTH JUDICIAL DISTRICT includes Carter, Elliott and Morgan counties. The court sits at Grayson, Sandy Hook and West Liberty.

Judge
Kimberly I. Gevedon

THIRTY-EIGHTH JUDICIAL DISTRICT includes Butler, Edmonson, Hancock and Ohio counties. The court sits at Morgantown, Brownsville, Hawesville and Hartford.

Judges
Renona Carol Browning
John M. McCarty

THIRTY-NINTH JUDICIAL DISTRICT includes Breathitt, Powell and Wolfe counties. The court sits at Jackson, Stanton and Campton.

Judge
Kenny Profitt

FORTIETH JUDICIAL DISTRICT includes Clinton, Russell and Wayne counties. The court sits at Albany, Jamestown and Monticello.

Judges
D. Jeffrey Choate
James Lawson
Philip R. Morgan

FORTY-FIRST JUDICIAL DISTRICT includes Clay, Jackson and Leslie counties. The court sits at Manchester, McKee and Hyden.

Judges
Oscar G. House
Renee Helene Muncy

FORTY-SECOND JUDICIAL DISTRICT includes Calloway County. The court sits at Murray.

Judge
Jeanné Carroll

FORTY-THIRD JUDICIAL DISTRICT includes Barren and Metcalfe counties. The court sits at Glasgow and Edmonton.

Judge
Barlow Ropp

FORTY-FOURTH JUDICIAL DISTRICT includes Bell County. The court sits at Pineville.

Judge
Robert Vincent Costanzo

FORTY-FIFTH JUDICIAL DISTRICT includes McLean and Muhlenberg counties. The court sits at Calhoun and Greenville.

Judge
Brian Wiggins

FORTY-SIXTH JUDICIAL DISTRICT includes Breckinridge, Grayson and Meade counties. The court sits at Hardinsburg, Leitchfield and Brandenburg.

Judges
Shan Embry
Tom Lively

FORTY-SEVENTH JUDICIAL DISTRICT includes Letcher County. The court sits at Whitesburg.

Judge
James T. Wood

FORTY-EIGHTH JUDICIAL DISTRICT includes Franklin County. The court sits at Frankfort.

Judges
William G. Hart
Thomas Dawson Wingate

FORTY-NINTH JUDICIAL DISTRICT includes Allen and Simpson counties. The court sits at Scottsville and Franklin.

Judge
Frank Wakefield

FIFTIETH JUDICIAL DISTRICT includes Boyle and Mercer counties. The court sits at Danville and Harrodsburg.

Judge
Jeff Dotson

FIFTY-FIRST JUDICIAL DISTRICT includes Henderson County. The court sits at Henderson.

Judges
Kenton J. Watson
Robert Wiederstein

FIFTY-SECOND JUDICIAL DISTRICT includes Graves County. The court sits at Mayfield.

Judge
Deborah Crooks

FIFTY-THIRD JUDICIAL DISTRICT includes Anderson, Shelby and Spencer counties. The court sits at Lawrenceburg, Shelbyville and Taylorsville.

Judges
Linda S. Armstrong
Michael Harrod

FIFTY-FOURTH JUDICIAL DISTRICT includes Boone and Gallatin counties. The court sits at Burlington and Warsaw.

Judges
Michael Collins
Charles T. Moore

KENTUCKY DISTRICT COURT—*Continued*

FIFTY-FIFTH JUDICIAL DISTRICT includes Bullitt County. The court sits at Shepherdsville.

Judges
A. Bailey Taylor
Rebecca Ward

FIFTY-SIXTH JUDICIAL DISTRICT includes Caldwell, Livingston, Lyon and Trigg counties. The court sits at Princeton, Smithland, Eddyville and Cadiz.

Judges
Jill Clark
William McCaslin

FIFTY-SEVENTH JUDICIAL DISTRICT includes Nelson County. The court sits at Bardstown.

Judge
Bob Heaton

FIFTY-EIGHTH JUDICIAL DISTRICT includes Marshall County. The court sits at Benton.

Judge
Jack Telle

FIFTY-NINTH JUDICIAL DISTRICT includes Ballard and Carlisle counties. The court sits at Wickliffe and Bardwell.

Judge
Louis Keith Myers

SIXTIETH JUDICIAL DISTRICT includes Cumberland and Monroe counties. The court sits at Burkesville and Tompkinsville.

Judge
Steve D. Hurt

Kentucky Counties and County Seats

Adair
Columbia

Allen
Scottsville

Anderson
Lawrenceburg

Ballard
Wickliffe

Barren
Glasgow

Bath
Owingsville

Bell
Pineville

Boone
Burlington

Bourbon
Paris

Boyd
Catlettsburg

Boyle
Danville

Bracken
Brooksville

Breathitt
Jackson

Breckinridge
Hardinsburg

Bullitt
Shepherdsville

Butler
Morgantown

Caldwell
Princeton

Calloway
Murray

Campbell
Newport

Carlisle
Bardwell

Carroll
Carrollton

Carter
Grayson

Casey
Liberty

Christian
Hopkinsville

Clark
Winchester

Clay
Manchester

Clinton
Albany

Crittenden
Marion

Cumberland
Burkesville

Daviess
Owensboro

Edmonson
Brownsville

Elliott
Sandy Hook

Estill
Irvine

Fayette
Lexington

Fleming
Flemingsburg

Floyd
Prestonsburg

Franklin
Frankfort

Fulton
Hickman

Gallatin
Warsaw

Garrard
Lancaster

Grant
Williamstown

Graves
Mayfield

Grayson
Leitchfield

Green
Greensburg

Greenup
Greenup

Hancock
Hawesville

Hardin
Elizabethtown

Harlan
Harlan

Harrison
Cynthiana

Hart
Munfordville

Henderson
Henderson

Henry
New Castle

Hickman
Clinton

Hopkins
Madisonville

Jackson
McKee

Jefferson
Louisville

Jessamine
Nicholasville

Johnson
Paintsville

Kenton
Covington

Knott
Hindman

Knox
Barbourville

Larue
Hodgenville

Laurel
London

Lawrence
Louisa

Lee
Beattyville

Leslie
Hyden

Letcher
Whitesburg

Lewis
Vanceburg

COUNTIES AND COUNTY SEATS—*Continued*

Lincoln
Stanford

Livingston
Smithland

Logan
Russellville

Lyon
Eddyville

Madison
Richmond

Magoffin
Salyersville

Marion
Lebanon

Marshall
Benton

Martin
Inez

Mason
Maysville

McCracken
Paducah

McCreary
Whitley City

McLean
Calhoun

Meade
Brandenburg

Menifee
Frenchburg

Mercer
Harrodsburg

Metcalfe
Edmonton

Monroe
Tompkinsville

Montgomery
Mount Sterling

Morgan
West Liberty

Muhlenberg
Greenville

Nelson
Bardstown

Nicholas
Carlisle

Ohio
Hartford

Oldham
La Grange

Owen
Owenton

Owsley
Booneville

Pendleton
Falmouth

Perry
Hazard

Pike
Pikeville

Powell
Stanton

Pulaski
Somerset

Robertson
Mount Olivet

Rockcastle
Mount Vernon

Rowan
Morehead

Russell
Jamestown

Scott
Georgetown

Shelby
Shelbyville

Simpson
Franklin

Spencer
Taylorsville

Taylor
Campbellsville

Todd
Elkton

Trigg
Cadiz

Trimble
Bedford

Union
Morganfield

Warren
Bowling Green

Washington
Springfield

Wayne
Monticello

Webster
Dixon

Whitley
Williamsburg

Wolfe
Campton

Woodford
Versailles

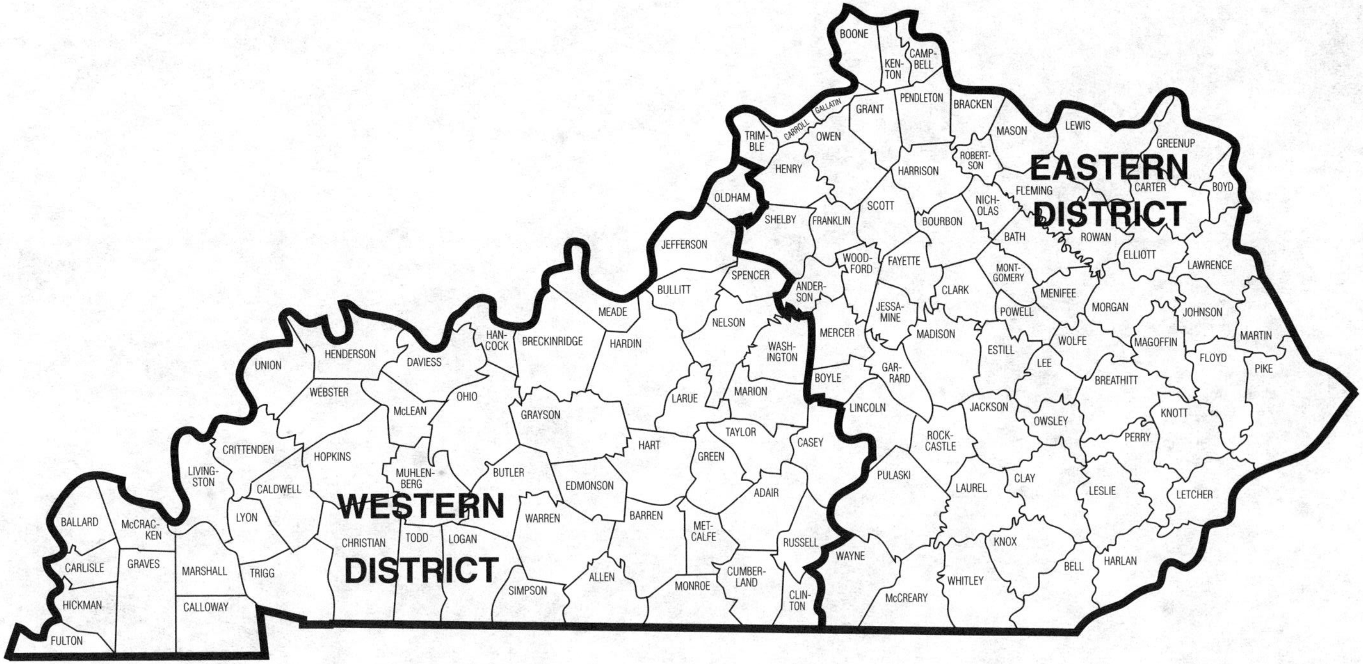
EASTERN DISTRICT
WESTERN DISTRICT
BOONE
KEN-TON
CAMP-BELL
GALLATIN
CARROLL
TRIM-BLE
GRANT
PENDLETON
BRACKEN
MASON
LEWIS
GREENUP
BOYD
CARTER
OWEN
HENRY
OLDHAM
SHELBY
FRANKLIN
SCOTT
HARRISON
ROBERT-SON
NICH-OLAS
FLEMING
BOURBON
BATH
ROWAN
ELLIOTT
LAWRENCE
JEFFERSON
WOOD-FORD
FAYETTE
MONT-GOMERY
SPENCER
ANDER-SON
CLARK
MENIFEE
MORGAN
JOHNSON
BULLITT
NELSON
JESSA-MINE
POWELL
MARTIN
MEADE
MERCER
MADISON
WOLFE
MAGOFFIN
FLOYD
PIKE
HAN-COCK
BRECKINRIDGE
HARDIN
WASH-INGTON
ESTILL
LEE
BREATHITT
UNION
HENDERSON
DAVIESS
BOYLE
GAR-RARD
MARION
WEBSTER
OHIO
LARUE
LINCOLN
JACKSON
OWSLEY
KNOTT
McLEAN
GRAYSON
TAYLOR
PERRY
CRITTENDEN
HOPKINS
HART
CASEY
ROCK-CASTLE
LIVING-STON
MUHLEN-BERG
BUTLER
GREEN
PULASKI
CLAY
CALDWELL
EDMONSON
ADAIR
LAUREL
LESLIE
LETCHER
BALLARD
McCRAC-KEN
LYON
CHRISTIAN
TODD
LOGAN
WARREN
BARREN
MET-CALFE
KNOX
RUSSELL
CARLISLE
GRAVES
MARSHALL
TRIGG
WAYNE
BELL
HARLAN
HICKMAN
SIMPSON
ALLEN
MONROE
CUMBER-LAND
WHITLEY
McCREARY
CALLOWAY
CLIN-TON
FULTON

UNITED STATES DISTRICT COURTS DISTRICTS OF KENTUCKY

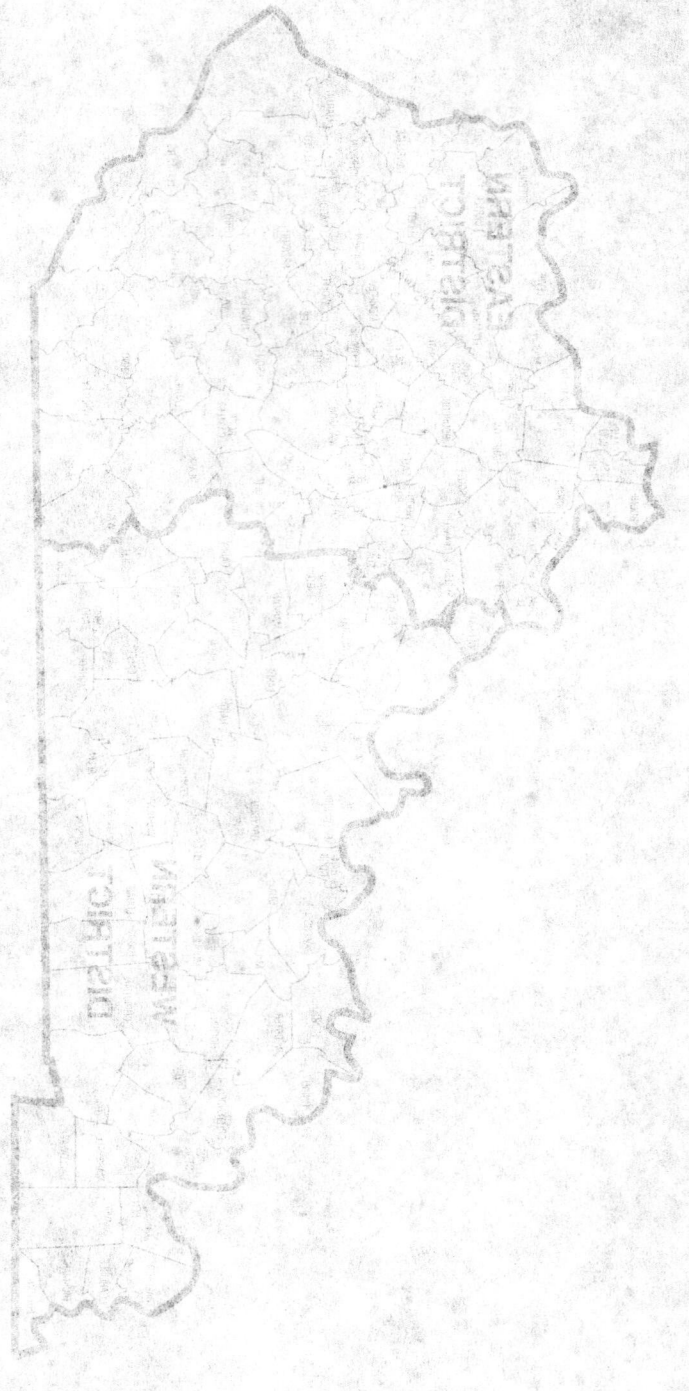

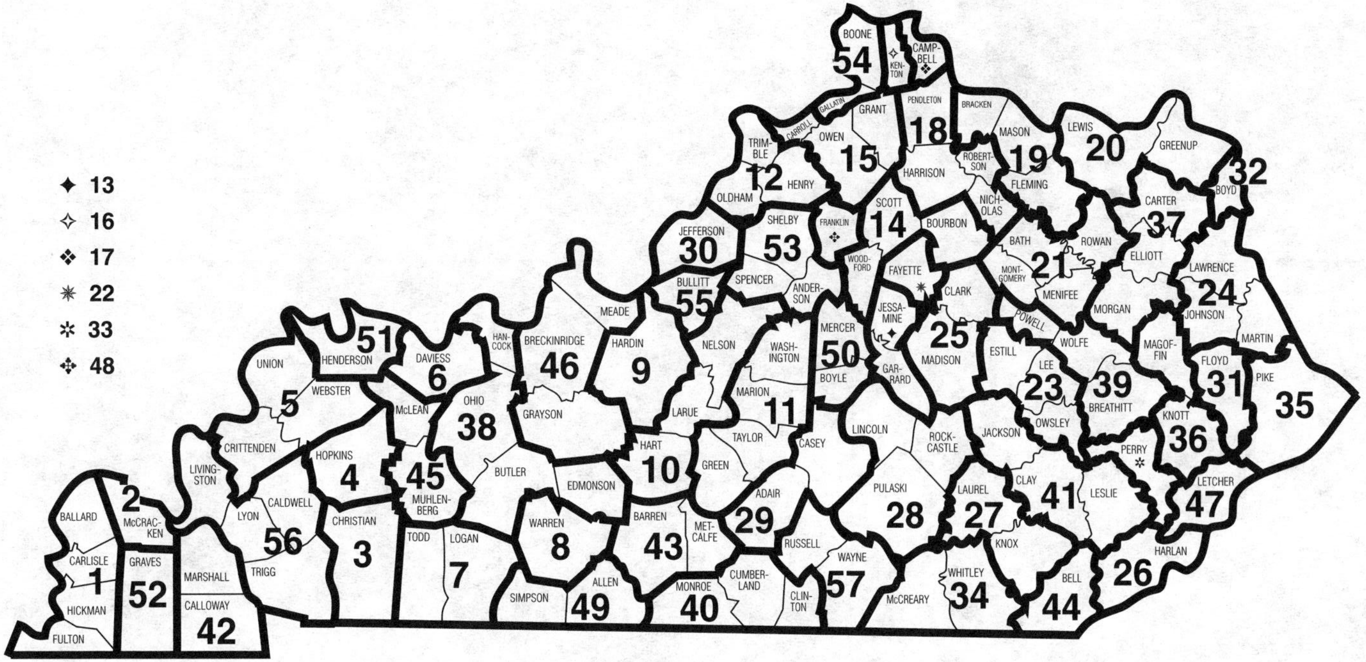
✦ 13
✧ 16
❖ 17
✷ 22
✲ 33
✣ 48
BOONE
54
KEN-TON
CAMP-BELL
GRANT
PENDLETON
18
BRACKEN
MASON
19
LEWIS
20
GREENUP
32
BOYD
GALLATIN
CARROLL
TRIM-BLE
OWEN
15
12
HENRY
OLDHAM
HARRISON
ROBERT-SON
FLEMING
CARTER
37
SCOTT
14
NICH-OLAS
JEFFERSON
30
SHELBY
53
FRANKLIN
BOURBON
BATH
21
ROWAN
ELLIOTT
LAWRENCE
24
WOOD-FORD
FAYETTE
MONT-GOMERY
MENIFEE
BULLITT
55
SPENCER
ANDER-SON
CLARK
MORGAN
JOHNSON
MARTIN
JESSA-MINE
POWELL
25
MERCER
50
WOLFE
MAGOF-FIN
FLOYD
31
PIKE
35
MEADE
HARDIN
9
NELSON
WASH-INGTON
BOYLE
GAR-RARD
MADISON
ESTILL
LEE
23
39
BREATHITT
HAN-COCK
BRECKINRIDGE
46
51
HENDERSON
DAVIESS
6
UNION
5
WEBSTER
McLEAN
OHIO
38
GRAYSON
LARUE
MARION
11
OWSLEY
KNOTT
36
JACKSON
CRITTENDEN
HOPKINS
4
45
MUHLEN-BERG
BUTLER
EDMONSON
HART
10
TAYLOR
CASEY
LINCOLN
ROCK-CASTLE
PERRY
LIVING-STON
GREEN
ADAIR
29
PULASKI
28
LAUREL
27
CLAY
41
LESLIE
LETCHER
47
2
McCRAC-KEN
BALLARD
LYON
CALDWELL
56
CHRISTIAN
3
WARREN
8
BARREN
43
MET-CALFE
RUSSELL
KNOX
HARLAN
CARLISLE
1
GRAVES
52
MARSHALL
TRIGG
TODD
LOGAN
7
SIMPSON
ALLEN
49
MONROE
40
CUMBER-LAND
CLIN-TON
WAYNE
57
McCREARY
WHITLEY
34
BELL
44
26
HICKMAN
FULTON
CALLOWAY
42

JUDICIAL CIRCUITS OF KENTUCKY CIRCUIT COURT

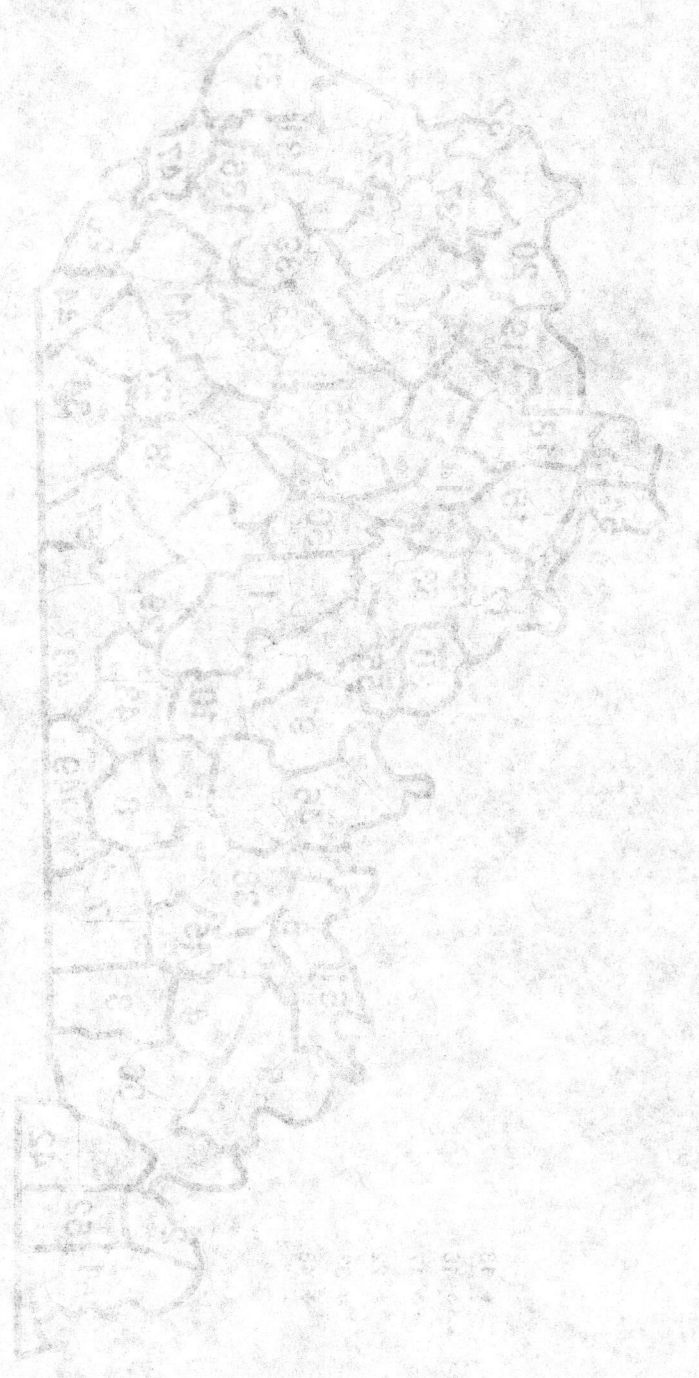

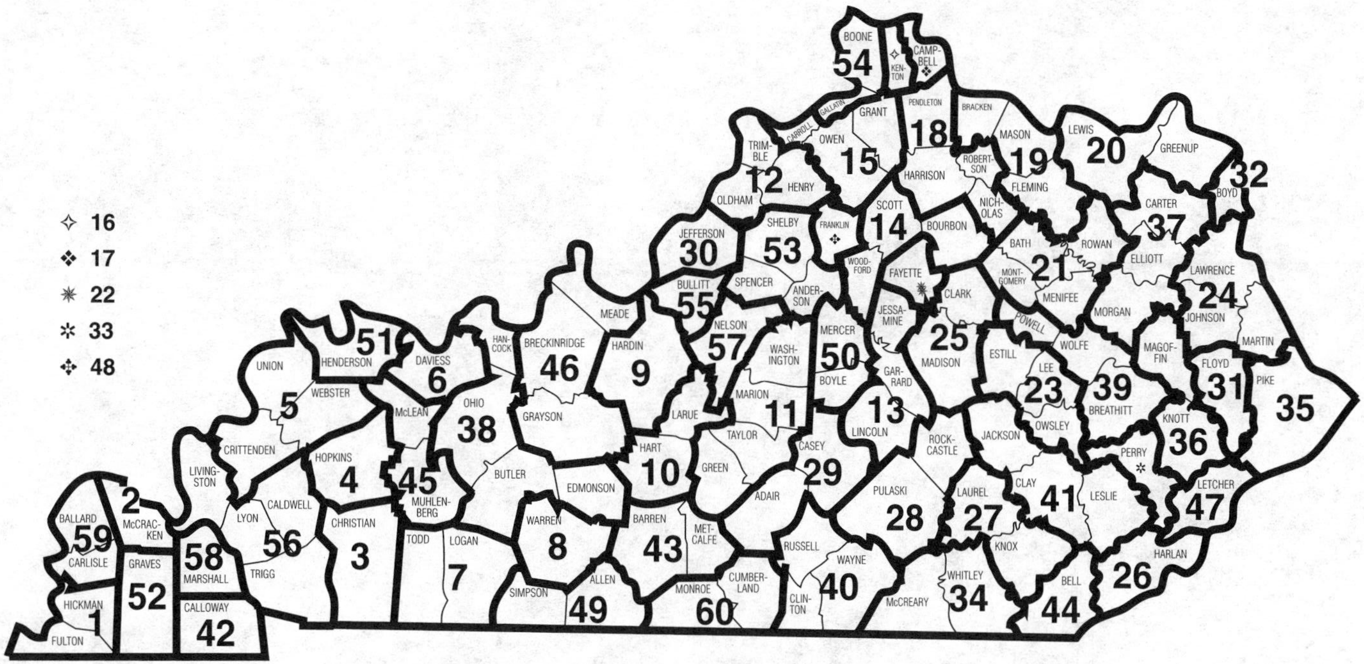

✧ 16
❖ 17
✷ 22
✲ 33
✣ 48
BOONE 54
KEN-TON
CAMP-BELL
GALLATIN
CARROLL
GRANT
PENDLETON
18
BRACKEN
MASON
19
LEWIS
20
GREENUP
32
BOYD
TRIM-BLE
12
HENRY
OWEN
15
HARRISON
ROBERT-SON
FLEMING
OLDHAM
JEFFERSON
30
SHELBY
53
FRANKLIN
SCOTT
14
BOURBON
NICH-OLAS
CARTER
37
BATH
ROWAN
21
ELLIOTT
MONT-GOMERY
MENIFEE
LAWRENCE
24
JOHNSON
MARTIN
WOOD-FORD
FAYETTE
CLARK
BULLITT
55
SPENCER
ANDER-SON
NELSON
57
WASH-INGTON
MERCER
50
BOYLE
JESSA-MINE
25
MADISON
POWELL
WOLFE
MORGAN
MAGOF-FIN
FLOYD
31
PIKE
35
UNION
HENDERSON
51
DAVIESS
6
HAN-COCK
BRECKINRIDGE
46
MEADE
HARDIN
9
WEBSTER
5
McLEAN
OHIO
38
GRAYSON
LARUE
MARION
11
GAR-RARD
13
LINCOLN
ESTILL
LEE
23
39
BREATHITT
KNOTT
36
CRITTENDEN
HOPKINS
4
45
MUHLEN-BERG
BUTLER
HART
10
TAYLOR
GREEN
CASEY
29
ROCK-CASTLE
JACKSON
OWSLEY
PERRY
LIVING-STON
EDMONSON
ADAIR
PULASKI
28
LAUREL
27
CLAY
41
LESLIE
LETCHER
47
BALLARD
59
CARLISLE
2
McCRAC-KEN
LYON
CALDWELL
56
CHRISTIAN
3
TODD
LOGAN
7
WARREN
8
BARREN
43
MET-CALFE
RUSSELL
WAYNE
40
KNOX
HARLAN
26
GRAVES
52
58
MARSHALL
TRIGG
SIMPSON
ALLEN
49
MONROE
60
CUMBER-LAND
CLIN-TON
McCREARY
WHITLEY
34
BELL
44
HICKMAN
1
FULTON
CALLOWAY
42

JUDICIAL DISTRICTS OF KENTUCKY DISTRICT COURT

' Forster-Long, Inc. *THE AMERICAN BENCH: Judges of the Nation*

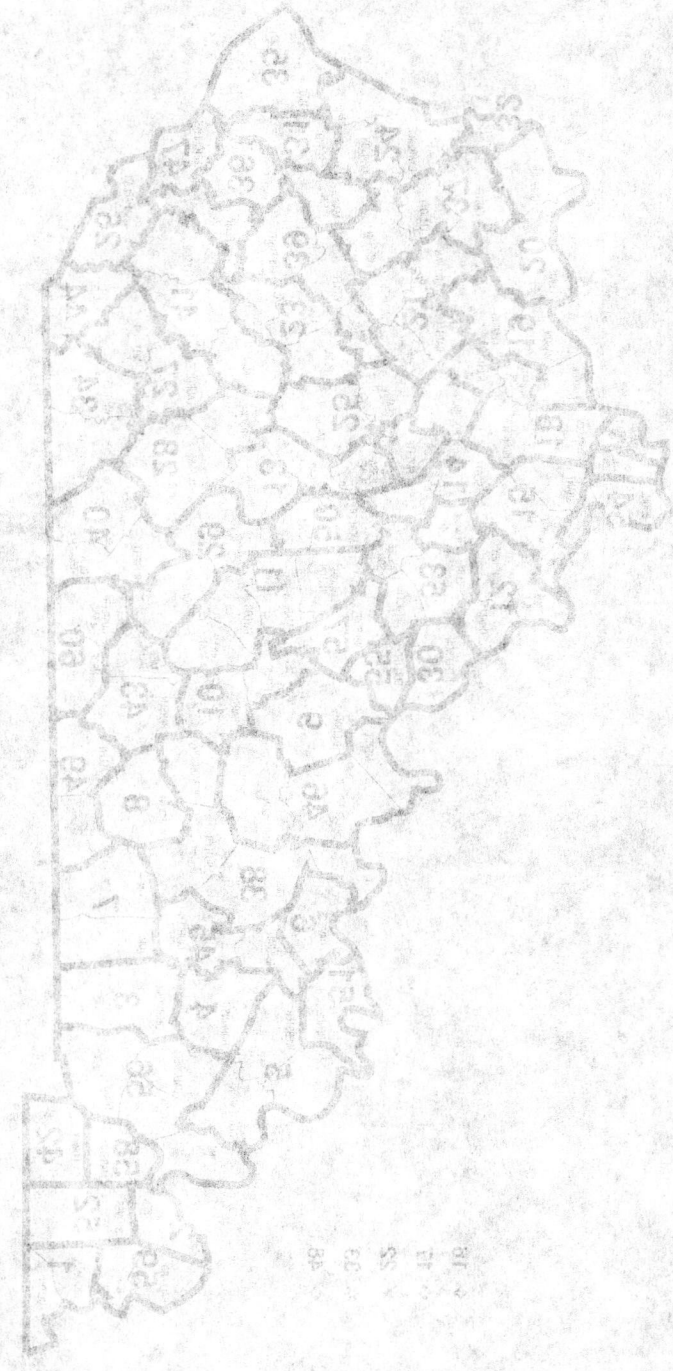

KENTUCKY

ABRAMSON, Lisabeth Hughes *(Judge, Kentucky Circuit Court Thirtieth Judicial Circuit)* Term expires Jan 2007. Former Judge, Kentucky Court of Appeals.

Office: Judicial Center, 700 West Jefferson Street, Louisville 40202.

Telephone: (502) 595-4919.

ADAMS, James G., Jr. *(Judge, Kentucky District Court Third Judicial District)* Elected Nov 1993 to term beginning Jan 4, 1994. Reelected Nov 1998 and 2002. Current term expires Jan 2007. Born Hopkinsville Kentucky Nov 4, 1954. Educated at University of Kentucky B.A. 1976 and Chase Law School of Northern Kentucky University J.D. 1979. Admitted to practice Kentucky 1979 and U.S District Court Western District of Kentucky 1980. In legal practice Hopkinsville 1979-93.

Chief Assistant Attorney Christian County 1982-93. Member Kentucky District Judges Association (Executive Board since 1996, Education Committee since 2001), Christian County (President 1982-83) and Kentucky Bar Associations. Attended The National Judicial College. Faculty Member Kentucky District Judges College. Recipient Boss of the Year Award from Hopkinsville Legal Secretaries Association 1983. Named Christian County Outstanding Young Man 1983. Democrat. Member Rotary Club and First United Methodist Church. Enjoys hunting, boating and playing golf. Active in church choir.

Office: Christian County Justice Center, 100 Justice Way, Hopkinsville 42240.

Telephone: (270) 889-6544.

Fax: (270) 889-6003

E-mail address: JamesAdams@mail.aoc.state.ky.us

ADAMS, John R. *(Judge, Kentucky Circuit Court Twenty-second Judicial Circuit)* Term expires Jan 2007. Former Judge, Kentucky District Court Twenty-second Judicial District.

Office: 572 Fayette County Courthouse, 120 North Limestone, Lexington 40507.

Telephone: (859) 246-2216.

ADAMS, Julia Hylton *(Judge, Kentucky Circuit Court Twenty-fifth Judicial Circuit)* Appointed by Governor Brereton C. Jones to term beginning Oct 1, 1993. Elected at special election to term beginning Jan 1, 1995. Reelected 1999, current term expires Jan 2007. Born Lexington Kentucky Aug 7, 1953. United Methodist. Administrative Board First United Methodist Church. Educated at Transylvania University B.A. with honors 1974 and University of Kentucky College of Law J.D. 1977. Member Chi Omega and Phi Delta Phi. Admitted to practice Kentucky 1978. Began legal practice Winchester 1978. Former Judge, Kentucky District Court Twenty-fifth Judicial District, appointed by Governor Martha Layne Collins to term beginning Jan 10, 1984.

Co-chair Attorney General's Task Force for Domestic Violence. Member Kentucky Crime Commission, Kentucky Supreme Court Task Force, Christian Legal Society, District Judges Association of Kentucky, Inc. (President), Kentucky Association of Circuit Judges (President, Member Education Committee, Judicial Instructor), American Judges Association and Kentucky Bar Association. Named Young Careerist by Business and Professional Women 1981, Outstanding Judge by Kentucky Bar Association 2001 and Outstanding Trial Judge by Kentucky Academy of Trial Attorneys 2002. Chairman United Way of Clark County, Big Brothers/Big Sisters of Winchester and State Commission on Student Discipline. Board member University of Kentucky Clark County Alumni Association.

Mailing address: P.O. Box 313, Winchester 40392.

Telephone: (859) 737-7263.

Fax: (859) 737-7100

ALLEN, James R. *(Judge, Kentucky District Court Thirty-first Judicial District)* Term expires Jan 2007.

Mailing address: P.O. Box 587, Prestonsburg 41653-0587.

Telephone: (606) 886-6195.

ARMSTRONG, Donald E., Jr. *(Judge, Kentucky District Court Thirtieth Judicial District)* Elected Nov 1998 to term beginning Jan 3, 1999. Reelected Nov 2002, current term expires Jan 2007. Chief Regional District Judge since Jan 2003. Born Louisville Kentucky Sept 4, 1950. Presbyterian. Educated at Vanderbilt University B.A. 1972 and University of Louisville J.D. 1975. Admitted to practice Kentucky 1975, U.S. District Courts Western 1975 and Eastern 1998 Districts of Kentucky, U.S. Court of Appeals Sixth Circuit 1978 and U.S. Supreme Court 1980. In legal practice Louisville 1975-98.

Assistant County Attorney Jefferson County 1989-97. Member Louisville, Kentucky and American Bar Associations.

Office: Hall of Justice, 600 West Jefferson Street, Louisville 40202.

Telephone: (502) 595-4632.

Fax: (502) 595-3270

E-mail address: DonaldA@mail.aoc.state.ky.us

ARMSTRONG, Linda S. *(Judge, Kentucky District Court Fifty-third Judicial District)* Term expires Jan 2007.

Mailing address: P.O. Box 669, Shelbyville 40066-0669.

Telephone: (502) 633-4130.

ATKINS, John L. *(Judge, Kentucky Circuit Court Third Judicial Circuit)* Term expires Jan 2007.

Office: Christian County Justice Center, 100 Justice Way, Hopkinsville 42240.

Telephone: (270) 889-6537.

AVRITT, James L. *(Judge, Kentucky District Court Eleventh Judicial District)* Term expires Jan 2007. Formerly served Thirty-seventh Judicial District.

Mailing address: P.O. Box 627, Lebanon 40033-0627.

Telephone: (270) 699-9951.

BAKER, Matthew J. *(Judge, Kentucky Court of Appeals)* Current term expires Jan 2007.

Office: A-102 The Corporate Centre, 401 Frederica Street, Owensboro 42301-3012.

Telephone: (270) 687-7235.

KENTUCKY

BALLOU, Dan *(Judge, Kentucky District Court Thirty-fourth Judicial District)* Elected Nov 2002. Term expires Jan 2007.

Mailing address: P.O. Box 329, Williamsburg 40769.
Telephone: (606) 549-5669.

BAMBERGER, Joseph F. *(Judge, Kentucky Circuit Court Fifty-fourth Judicial Circuit)* Term expires Jan 2007. Born Covington Kentucky Aug 14, 1942. Catholic. Educated at Xavier University A.B. 1965 and University of Kentucky J.D. 1969. Admitted to practice Kentucky 1970. In legal practice Warsaw 1970 and Florence 1976. Former Judge, Kentucky District Court Fifty-fourth Judicial District.

Former City Attorney Warsaw, Prosecutor City of Walton and Assistant Commonwealth Attorney. E-5 USAR 1966-72.

Mailing address: P.O. Box 480, Burlington 41005.
Telephone: (859) 586-6565.

BARBER, David *(Judge, Kentucky Court of Appeals)* Elected to term beginning Jan 3, 2000. Term expires Jan 2007. Born Martin Kentucky 1953. Educated at Transylvania University B.A. and University of Louisville School of Law J.D. Administrative Law Judge, Kentucky Department of Workers' Claims 1991-95.

City Attorney Martin 1981-85. Attorney Board of Education 1981-85 and County Attorney 1985 Floyd County. Member Judicial Nominating Commission Kentucky Department of Worker's Claims 1995-99. General Counsel to House of Representatives Kentucky 1990.

Office: 2980 KY Route 321, Prestonburg 41653-9105.
Telephone: (606) 886-0795.

BARTHOLOMEW, Judith *(Judge, Kentucky District Court Thirtieth Judicial District)* Term expires Jan 2007.

Office: Hall of Justice, 600 West Jefferson Street, Louisville 40202.
Telephone: (502) 595-4162.

BARTLETT, Gregory *(Judge, Kentucky Circuit Court Sixteenth Judicial Circuit)* Term expires Jan 2007.

Office: 701 Kenton County Justice Center, 230 Madison Avenue, Covington 41011.
Telephone: (859) 292-6530.

BATES, Stephen L. *(Judge, Kentucky Circuit Court Fifteenth Judicial Circuit)* Master Commissioner 1983-85. Term expires Jan 2007. Born Covington Kentucky July 24, 1950. Baptist. Educated at University of Kentucky B.B.A. 1972 and University of Louisville J.D. 1977. Admitted to practice Kentucky 1978. In legal practice Williamstown 1978-86. Former Judge, Kentucky District Court Fifteenth Judicial District, elected to term beginning Jan 4, 1986.

E-4 U.S. Army 1973-75. Member, Sunday School Teacher and Director and Deacon Dry Ridge Baptist Church. Enjoys golfing, basketball, boxing and reading.

Office: Grant County Courthouse, 101 North Main Street, Williamstown 41097.
Telephone: (859) 824-7516.

BERTELSMAN, William O. *(Senior Judge, United States District Court Eastern District of Kentucky)* Appointed for life by President Jimmy Carter to term beginning Nov 28, 1979. Assumed Senior status Feb 1, 2001, serves by assignment. Former Chief Judge. Born Kentucky Jan 31, 1936. Catholic. Educated at Xavier University B.A. summa cum laude 1958 and University of Cincinnati College of Law J.D. 1961 (graduated first in class). Associate Editor Cincinnati Law Review. Member Order of the Coif. Admitted to practice Kentucky 1961 and Ohio 1962. In legal practice Newport 1962-79.

City Attorney and Prosecutor City of Highland Heights 1962-69. Co-author with Philipps *Kentucky Rules of Procedure Annotated* West Publishing Co. 1984 and supplements (2 volumes). Author quarterly articles on various subjects *Kentucky Bench and Bar* Kentucky Bar Association. Adjunct Professor of Law Federal Jurisdiction Chase Law School of Northern Kentucky University since 1989. Instructor in Corporations 1965, Civil Procedure 1966-67 and Equity 1968-72 University of Cincinnati College of Law. Member Standing Committee on Practice and Procedure 1989-95. Liaison Member Advisory Committee on Civil Rules 1989-95. Member Plaintiffs' Lead Counsel Committee for Beverly Hills Fire Litigation. Captain U.S. Army Artillery 1963-64. Board member and officer Campbell County Chamber of Commerce (later merged into Northern Kentucky Chamber of Commerce) 1967-69. Board member Northern Kentucky Chamber of Commerce 1969-78 (President 1974).

Mailing address: P.O. Box 1012, Covington 41012-1012.
Telephone: (859) 392-7900.

BERTRAM, Allan Ray *(Judge, Kentucky Circuit Court Eleventh Judicial Circuit)* Term expires Jan 2007.

Office: 1 Courthouse, 203 North Court Street, Campbellsville 42718.
Telephone: (270) 465-6603.

BISIG, Angela McCormick *(Judge, Kentucky District Court Thirtieth Judicial District)* Elected Nov 2002. Term expires Jan 2007.

Office: Hall of Justice, 600 West Jefferson Street, Louisville 40202.
Telephone: (502) 595-3013.

BLAND, Thomas Steven *(Judge, Kentucky Circuit Court Ninth Judicial Circuit)* Term expires Jan 2007. Former Judge, Kentucky District Court Ninth Judicial District.

Office: Hardin County Justice Center, 120 East Dixie Avenue, Elizabethtown 42701-1469.
Telephone: (270) 766-5003.

BOOTH, Janet Carroll *(Judge, Kentucky District Court Thirteenth Judicial District)*

Office: Jessamine County Court Complex, 107 North Main Street, Nicholasville 40356-1200.
Telephone: (859) 885-5615.

BOTELER, Charles W., Jr. *(Judge, Kentucky Circuit Court Fourth Judicial Circuit)* Assumed office 1991. Term expires Jan 2007. Currently serves as Vice Chief Regional Circuit Judge. Judge, Kentucky District Court Fourth Judicial District 1980-91.

Office: 36 Courthouse, 30 Main, Madisonville 42431.
Telephone: (270) 824-7422.

BOWLES, Jerry *(Judge, Kentucky Circuit Court Thirtieth Judicial Circuit)* Term expires Jan 2007. Serves Family Court.

Office: 220 Judicial Center, 700 West Jefferson Street, Louisville 40202-4730.
Telephone: (502) 595-4502.

BOWLING, James L. *(Judge, Kentucky Circuit Court Forty-fourth Judicial Circuit)* Term expires Jan 2007. Former Judge, Kentucky District Court Forty-fourth Judicial District.
Mailing address: P.O. Box 751, Pineville 40977.
Telephone: (606) 337-5949.

BRADEN, Paul *(Judge, Kentucky Circuit Court Thirty-fourth Judicial Circuit)* Term expires Jan 2007.
Office: Circuit Judges Office, 1019 Cumberland Falls Highway, Corbin 40701.
Telephone: (606) 528-3013.

BRAMLAGE, Linda Rae *(Judge, Kentucky Circuit Court Fifty-fourth Judicial Circuit)* Term expires Jan 2007. Serves Family Court.
Mailing address: P.O. Box 991, Burlington 41005-0991.
Office: Old Courthouse, Burlington 41005.
Telephone: (859) 334-3520.

BRIAN, Bard Kevin *(Judge, Kentucky District Court Second Judicial District)*
Office: McCracken County Courthouse, 301 South Sixth Street, Paducah 42003.
Telephone: (270) 575-7261.

BROWN, Brandy Oliver *(Judge, Kentucky District Court Twenty-fifth Judicial District)*
Mailing address: P.O. Box 277, Richmond 40475-0277.
Telephone: (859) 624-4719.

BROWNING, Renona Carol *(Judge, Kentucky District Court Thirty-eighth Judicial District)* Term expires Jan 2007.
Office: Community Center, 130 East Washington Street, Hartford 42347.
Telephone: (270) 298-3223.

BROWNING, Sue Carol *(Judge, Kentucky District Court Seventh Judicial District)* Term expires Jan 2007.
Mailing address: P.O. Box 488, Russellville 42276.
Telephone: (270) 726-8080.
Fax: (270) 726-8080

BUCKINGHAM, David C. *(Judge, Kentucky Court of Appeals)* Term expires Jan 2007. Born Murray Kentucky Oct 29, 1951. Educated at Murray State University B.A. cum laude 1974 and University of Louisville J.D. 1977. Admitted to practice Kentucky 1977. Began legal practice Murray 1977. Judge, Kentucky District Court Forty-second Judicial District 1981-86. Judge, Kentucky Circuit Court Forty-second Judicial Circuit 1987 to 1996.
Assistant County Attorney 1978-81. Member Calloway County and Kentucky Bar Associations. Democrat.
Office: 312 South Eighth Street, Murray 42071.
Telephone: (270) 753-4324.
Fax: (270) 759-4394

BUNNELL, Kimberly N. *(Judge, Kentucky Circuit Court Twenty-second Judicial Circuit)* Assumed office Jan 6, 2003. Term expires Jan 2007. Serves Family Court. Former Judge, Kentucky District Court Twenty-second Judicial District.
Office: 120 North Limestone Street, Lexington 40507.
Telephone: (859) 246-2247.
Fax: (859) 246-2139
E-mail address: KimBunnell@mail.aoc.state.ky.us

BUNNING, David L. *(Judge, United States District Court Eastern District of Kentucky)* Appointed for life by President George W. Bush to term beginning Feb 21, 2002. Born Fort Thomas Kentucky 1966. Educated at University of Kentucky B.A. 1988 J.D. 1991.
Assistant U.S. Attorney Eastern District of Kentucky 1991-2002.
Office: 35 West Fifth Street, Room 410, Covington 41011.
Telephone: (859) 392-7907.

BURTON, David *(Judge, Kentucky District Court Thirty-fourth Judicial District)* Term expires Jan 2007.
Office: 805 South Main Street, Corbin 40701-1822.
Telephone: (606) 528-4430.

BYER, Joan L. *(Judge, Kentucky Circuit Court Thirtieth Judicial Circuit)* Term expires Jan 2007. Serves Family Court.
Office: 220 Judicial Center, 700 West Jefferson Street, Louisville 40202-4730.
Telephone: (502) 595-4656.

CAIN, William T. *(Judge, Kentucky Circuit Court Twenty-eighth Judicial Circuit)* Appointed by Governor Brereton C. Jones to term beginning Aug 1992. Elected Nov 1992 and 1999. Current term expires Jan 2007. Born Lexington Kentucky July 23, 1942. Episcopalian. Educated at University of Kentucky B.A. 1965 J.D. with distinction 1968. Staff member Kentucky Law Journal 1966-68. Member Delta Theta Phi and Order of the Coif. Admitted to practice Kentucky 1968. In legal practice Somerset 1968-84. Judge, Kentucky District Court Twenty-eighth Judicial District 1984-92.
Associate Instructor in U.S. and State Government Business Law Somerset Community College 1990-92. Member Pulaski County, Kentucky (House of Delegates 1978-84) and American Bar Associations. Member 1976-84 and Chairman 1978-81 Somerset Independent Board of Education.
Mailing address: P.O. Box 1324, Somerset 42502.
Office: Pulaski County Courthouse, Main Street, Somerset 42501.
Telephone: (606) 677-4098.
Fax: (606) 677-4182

CALDWELL, Karen K. *(Judge, United States District Court Eastern District of Kentucky)* Appointed for life by President George W. Bush to term beginning Nov 13, 2001. Born Stanford Kentucky 1956. Educated at Transylvania University B.A. 1977 and University of Kentucky College of Law J.D. 1980. In legal practice Kentucky 1993-2001.
Assistant U.S. Attorney 1987-90 and U.S. Attorney 1991-93 Eastern District of Kentucky.
Office: 310 South Main Street, Suite 434, London 40741.
Telephone: (606) 877-7950.

CALVERT, Logan *(Judge, Kentucky District Court Fourth Judicial District)* Elected Nov 2002. Term expires Jan 2007.
Office: Hopkins County Courthouse, 30 South Main Street, Madisonville 42431.
Telephone: (270) 824-7513.

CAPERTON, Michael *(Judge, Kentucky District Court Twenty-seventh Judicial District)* Term expires Jan 2007.
Mailing address: P.O. Box 2424, London 40743-2424.
Office: Judicial Annex 1, 107 South Broad Street, London 40741.
Telephone: (606) 864-7241.

CARROLL, Jeanné *(Judge, Kentucky District Court Forty-second Judicial District)* Elected Nov 2002. Term expires Jan 2007.
Office: 312 North Fourth Street, Murray 42071.
Telephone: (270) 753-0059.

CASTLEN, Joseph *(Judge, Kentucky District Court Sixth Judicial District)*
Office: Daviess County Judicial Center, 100 East Second Street, Owensboro 42303.
Telephone: (270) 687-7217.

CASTLEN, Thomas O. *(Judge, Kentucky Circuit Court Sixth Judicial Circuit)* Appointed by Governor Brereton C. Jones to term beginning Aug 14, 1995. Elected Nov 1995 and 1999. Current term expires Jan 2007. Born Owensboro Kentucky July 30, 1951. Catholic. Educated at Brescia College B.A. 1976 and Chase Law School of Northern Kentucky University J.D. 1979. Admitted to practice Kentucky 1980. In legal practice Owensboro 1980-85.
Commonwealth's Attorney Sixth Judicial Circuit Daviess County 1985-95. Member Daviess County and Kentucky Bar Associations. U.S. Army July 1969 to April 1972.
Office: 416 Judicial Complex, 100 East Second Street, Owensboro 42303.
Telephone: (270) 687-7228.
Fax: (270) 687-7999
E-mail address: TOMCASTLEN@mail.aoc.state.ky.us

CAUDILL, Danny P. *(Judge, Kentucky Circuit Court Thirty-first Judicial Circuit)* Term expires Jan 2007. Former Judge, Kentucky District Court Thirty-first Judicial District.
Office: Floyd County Justice Center, 127 South Lake Drive, Prestonsburg 41653.
Telephone: (606) 886-2424.

CAUDILL, John David *(Judge, Kentucky Circuit Court Thirty-first Judicial Circuit)* Term expires Jan 2007. Former Vice Chief Regional Circuit Judge.
Office: Floyd County Justice Center, 127 South Lake Drive, Prestonsburg 41653.
Telephone: (606) 886-0956.

CHANDLER, Tommy W. *(Judge, Kentucky Circuit Court Fifth Judicial Circuit)* Elected Nov 1991 to term beginning Jan 1, 1992. Reelected 1999, current term expires Jan 2007. Born Dixon Kentucky Jan 31, 1937. Baptist. Educated at Murray State University and University of Kentucky LL.B. Co-editor Kentucky Law Journal. Member Phi Alpha Delta and Order of the Coif. Admitted to practice Kentucky 1965. In legal practice Providence 1965-91.
Former City Attorney Providence City, Attorney Webster County and Commonwealth's Attorney Fifth Judicial District. Member Kentucky Bar Association.
Mailing address: P.O. Box 159, Providence 42450.
Office: 114 East Main Street, Providence 42450.
Telephone: (270) 667-9318.

CHILDERS, Kimberly *(Judge, Kentucky District Court Thirty-sixth Judicial District)* Elected Nov 2002. Term expires Jan 2007.
Mailing address: P.O. Box 728, Hindman 41822-0728.
Telephone: (606) 785-3078.

CHOATE, D. Jeffrey *(Judge, Kentucky District Court Fortieth Judicial District)* Term expires Jan 2007.
Office: Clinton County Courthouse, Box 213, 104 Washington Street, Albany 42602-0213.
Telephone: (606) 387-7008.

CLARK, Eugene *(Judge, Kentucky Circuit Court Forty-first Judicial Circuit)* Term expires Jan 2007. Serves Family Court.
Office: 114 Lawyer Street, Manchester 40962.
Telephone: (606) 599-0948.

CLARK, Jill *(Judge, Kentucky District Court Fifty-sixth Judicial District)* Term expires Jan 2007.
Mailing address: P.O. Box 674, Cadiz 42211.
Telephone: (270) 522-7979.

CLARK, Thomas L. *(Judge, Kentucky Circuit Court Twenty-second Judicial Circuit)* Term expires Jan 2007. Former Judge, Kentucky District Court Twenty-second Judicial District.
Office: 511 Fayette County Courthouse, 120 North Limestone, Lexington 40507.
Telephone: (859) 246-2533.

CLAYTON, Denise G. *(Judge, Kentucky Circuit Court Thirtieth Judicial Circuit)* Term expires Jan 2007. Born Louisville Kentucky April 28, 1952. Protestant. Educated at Defiance College B.A. cum laude and University of Louisville J.D. Admitted to practice Kentucky 1976, U.S. District Court Western District of Kentucky 1980 and U.S. Court of Appeals Sixth Circuit 1987. In legal practice Louisville 1978-85. Former Judge, Kentucky District Court Thirtieth Judicial District, appointed by Governor Paul E. Patton to term beginning Dec 3, 1996.
Estate Tax Attorney Internal Revenue Service 1976-78. Director Student Legal Services University of Louisville 1978-87. Staff Attorney 1987-91 and Associate Director 1991-96 Legal Aid Society. Instructor Paralegal Program University of Louisville since 1985. President Kentucky Chapter National Bar Association 1993-95. Former Member Board of Directors Louisville Bar Association and Women Lawyers Association. Member Kentucky Bar Association. Recipient Distinguished Alumna Award from University of Louisville. Member Governor's Criminal Justice Response Team. Former Board Member YWCA. Enjoys reading and walking.
Office: Judicial Center, 700 West Jefferson Street, Louisville 40202.
Telephone: (502) 595-4604.
Fax: (502) 595-0057

CLOUSE, William G., Jr. *(Judge, Kentucky District Court Twenty-fifth Judicial District)* Elected Nov 1993 to term beginning Jan 1994. Reelected Nov 1998 and 2002. Current term expires Jan 2007. Born Richmond Kentucky Jan 21, 1952. Catholic. Educated at Eastern Kentucky University B.S. 1974 and Chase Law School of Northern Kentucky University J.D. 1978. Admitted to practice Kentucky 1978, U.S. District Court Eastern District of Kentucky 1979, U.S. Court of Appeals Sixth Circuit 1979 and U.S. Supreme Court 1986. In legal practice Richmond 1978 and 1985-94.

CLOUSE, WILLIAM G., JR.—*Continued*

County Attorney Madison County 1979-85. Adjunct Faculty of Business Law Eastern Kentucky University 1978-79. Member Madison County and Kentucky Bar Associations. Recipient Consumer Advocate Award. Named Distinguished Alumni of Eastern Kentucky University. Former Kentucky State Senator Twenty-second District. Board member Leadership of Madison County. Coach Model Laboratory Mock Trial. One of the founders of Meals on Wheels.

Mailing address: P.O. Box 277, Richmond 40475-0277.

Office: Hall of Justice, Richmond 40475.

Telephone: (859) 624-4719, 624-4716.

CLYMER, Craig Z. *(Judge, Kentucky Circuit Court Second Judicial Circuit)* Elected Nov 1999 to term beginning Jan 2000. Term expires Jan 2007. Born Paducah Kentucky Jan 5, 1954. Baptist. Educated at Eastern Kentucky University B.S. 1977, Murray State University 1985 and Chase Law School of Northern Kentucky University J.D. with honors 1988. Law Clerk to Magistrate Judge, U.S. District Court Western District of Kentucky 1988-91. Admitted to practice Kentucky 1988 and U.S. District Courts Eastern 1989 and Western 1989 Districts of Kentucky. Judge, Kentucky District Court Second Judicial District 1994-99.

Member McCracken County and Kentucky Bar Associations. Enjoys horse riding and training, hunting, fishing and farming.

Office: McCracken County Courthouse, 301 South Sixth Street, Paducah 42003.

Telephone: (270) 575-7400.

Fax: (270) 575-7137

E-mail address: CraigC@mail.aoc.state.ky.us

COFFMAN, Jennifer B. *(Judge, United States District Court Eastern District of Kentucky and Judge, United States District Court Western District of Kentucky)* Appointed for life by President Bill Clinton to term beginning Oct 22, 1993. Born Union City Tennessee Jan 8, 1948. Presbyterian. Educated at University of Kentucky B.A. 1969 M.S. 1971 J.D. 1978. Staff member University of Kentucky Law Review 1977-78. Admitted to practice Kentucky 1978, U.S. District Courts Eastern 1979 and Western 1985 Districts of Kentucky and U.S. Court of Appeals Sixth Circuit 1981. In legal practice Lexington 1978-93.

Author "Kentucky Rape Shield Act—One Step Too Far" 66 No. 2 Kentucky L. Jour. 1977-78, "Restoration of Property: Illusory Barrier to Interspousal" 67 No. 1 Kentucky L. Jour. 1978-79 and "Wrongful Discharge" Fayette County Bar News July-Aug 1989. Co-author Chapter "Harassment of Employees" Kentucky Employment Law 1992. Instructor in Legal Writing 1979-81. Member Sixth Circuit Pattern Jury Instructions Committee, Judicial Resources Committee, CJRA Advisory Committee, Fayette County and Kentucky Bar Associations. Convention Chair Kentucky Bar Association 1992. Inducted into University of Kentucky College of Law Hall of Fame. Recipient Kentucky Bar Center Award from Kentucky Bar Association. Board of Directors YWCA of Lexington 1986-92. Member Second Presbyterian Church of Lexington 1993-96 and Dean Search Committee University of Kentucky.

Mailing address: P.O. Box 2228, Lexington 40588.

Telephone: (859) 233-2453.

COLEMAN, Eddy *(Judge, Kentucky Circuit Court Thirty-fifth Judicial Circuit)* Term expires Jan 2007.

Office: 435 Justice Building, 172 Division Street, Pikeville 41501.

Telephone: (606) 433-7554.

COLEMAN, Janet P. *(Judge, Kentucky Circuit Court Ninth Judicial Circuit)* Term expires Jan 2007. Former Judge, Kentucky District Court Ninth Judicial District.

Office: Hardin County Justice Center, 120 East Dixie Avenue, Elizabethtown 42701-4169.

Telephone: (270) 766-5039.

COLEMAN, JoAnn Spinks *(Judge, Kentucky District Court Eighth Judicial District)* Appointed by Governor Wallace G. Wilkinson to term beginning Aug 12, 1991. Elected to subsequent terms. Current term expires Jan 2007. Born Smiths Grove Kentucky. Baptist. Educated at Western Kentucky University B.A. and University of Louisville J.D. Member Phi Alpha Delta. Admitted to practice Kentucky 1979.

Assistant Commonwealth's Attorney 1980-91. Member Bowling Green Bar Association. Member Bowling Green Noon Lions Club, Chamber of Commerce and District Executive Council Boy Scouts of America. Trustee Living Hope Baptist Church. Enjoys sports, crafts, working with Cub Scouts and camping.

Office: 201 Warren County Justice Center, 1001 Center Street, Bowling Green 42101-2191.

Telephone: (270) 746-7405.

COLLINS, Michael *(Judge, Kentucky District Court Fifty-fourth Judicial District)* Term expires Jan 2007.

Mailing address: P.O. Box 886, Burlington 41005-0886.

Office: Washington Square, Burlington 41005.

Telephone: (859) 334-2230.

COLLINS, Sheila Anne *(Judge, Kentucky District Court Thirtieth Judicial District)* Term expires Jan 2007.

Office: Hall of Justice, 600 West Jefferson, Louisville 40202.

Telephone: (502) 595-4995.

COMBS, Douglas C. *(Judge, Kentucky Circuit Court Thirty-third Judicial Circuit)* Term expires Jan 2007. Former Judge, Kentucky District Court Thirty-third Judicial District.

Office: 481 Main Street, Hazard 41701.

Telephone: (606) 435-6004.

COMBS, Sara Walter *(Judge, Kentucky Court of Appeals)* Appointed by Governor Brereton C. Jones to term beginning Jan 31, 1994. Elected Nov 8, 1994 and 1999. Current term expires Jan 2007. Born Louisville Kentucky Aug 24, 1948. Catholic. Educated at University of Louisville B.A. (Valedictorian) 1970 M.A. 1971 J.D. with second class honors 1979. Honorary Member Phi Beta Kappa (Distinguished Service 1996). Admitted to practice Kentucky 1980 and U.S. District Courts Eastern 1985 and Western 1985 Districts of Kentucky. In legal practice Lexington, Louisville and Stanton. Associate Justice, Kentucky Supreme Court 1993.

City Attorney Stanton 1992-93. Instructor Night Division University of Louisville School of Law 1987-89 and French I and II Lees College 1993-94. Member Women Lawyers of Jefferson County, Kentucky Academy of Trial Attorneys, National Association of Women Judges, Louisville and Kentucky Bar Associations. Attended The National Judicial College Summer 1994.

COMBS, SARA WALTER—*Continued*
Named Distinguished Alumnus by University of Louisville Law School 1994 and Arts and Sciences Alumni Fellow by University of Louisville 1996. Vice President and General Counsel Naegele Outdoor Advertising Company 1982-89. Member Justice Committee Kentucky Appalachian Task Force, Kentucky Appalachian Commission, Kentucky Department for Libraries and Archives, Kentucky Historical Society, Kentucky Independent College Foundation, Kentucky Women's Leadership Network and State Advisory Council on Libraries. Interests include education, gardening and cooking.
Mailing address: P.O. Box 709, Stanton 40380-0709.
Office: 323 East College Avenue, Stanton 40380.
Telephone: (606) 663-0651.

CONLEY, Robert B. *(Judge, Kentucky District Court Twentieth Judicial District)* Term expires Jan 2007.
Office: Courthouse Annex, 101 Harrison Street, Greenup 41144.
Telephone: (606) 473-6339.

CONLIFFE, Ken *(Judge, Kentucky Circuit Court Thirtieth Judicial Circuit)* Term expires Jan 2007.
Office: Judicial Center, 700 West Jefferson Street, Louisville 40202.
Telephone: (502) 595-3012.

CONRAD, Karen *(Judge, Kentucky Circuit Court Twelfth Judicial Circuit)* Term expires Jan 2007. Serves Family Court.
Office: Oldham County Courthouse, 100 West Main Street, La Grange 40031.
Telephone: (502) 222-1692.
Fax: (502) 222-5684

COOPER, Joan Lloyd *(Judge, United States Bankruptcy Court Western District of Kentucky)* Appointed by U.S. Court of Appeals Sixth Circuit judges to term beginning Dec 22, 1999. Term expires 2013.
Office: 541 U.S. Courthouse, 601 West Broadway, Louisville 40202-2264.
Telephone: (502) 627-5525.
Fax: (502) 627-5573

COOPER, William *(Justice, Kentucky Supreme Court)* Assumed office 1996. Elected 1999, current term expires Jan 2007. Educated at University of Kentucky B.A. 1963 J.D. with high distinction 1970. Editor-in-Chief Kentucky Law Journal 1969-70. Member Sigma Phi Epsilon, Omicron Delta Kappa and Order of the Coif. In legal practice 1970-79. Judge, Kentucky Circuit Court Ninth Judicial Circuit Feb 1979 to Nov 1996.

Member since 1995 and Chair since 2000 Kentucky Evidence Rules Review Commission. Chair Supreme Court Criminal Rules Committee since 1997. Former Member Kentucky Association of Circuit Judges. Charter Life Fellow Kentucky Bar Foundation. Member Kentucky Bar Association. Member since 1963 and Fellow 1985 Alumni Association and Board of Directors 1982-88 and President 1986-87 Law Alumni Association University of Kentucky. Advocate 1971-79 and Member Third-Degree Council 1455 since 1971 Knights of Columbus. Member since 1971 and Judge Advocate Post 113 1971-79 and Department of Kentucky 1978-79 American Legion. Member Elizabethtown Rotary Club since 1974 and St. James Catholic Church.
Office: Hardin County Justice Center, 120 East Dixie Avenue, Elizabethtown 42701-1469.
Telephone: (270) 766-5179.

COSTANZO, Robert Vincent *(Judge, Kentucky District Court Forty-fourth Judicial District)*
Mailing address: P.O. Box 306, Pineville 40977.
Office: Bell County Courthouse, Pineville 40977.
Telephone: (606) 337-1149.

COX, John R. *(Judge, Kentucky District Court Twenty-first Judicial District)* Term expires Jan 2007. Currently serves as Vice Chief Regional District Judge.
Mailing address: P.O. Box 9, Morehead 40351.
Telephone: (606) 784-6888.

CRITTENDEN, Roger *(Judge, Kentucky Circuit Court Forty-eighth Judicial Circuit)* Term expires Jan 2007. Former Judge, Kentucky District Court Forty-eighth Judicial District.
Office: Courthouse, 214 St. Clair Street, Frankfort 40601.
Telephone: (502) 564-8383.
Fax: (502) 564-0096

CROOKS, Deborah *(Judge, Kentucky District Court Fifty-second Judicial District)* Elected Nov 2002. Term expires Jan 2007.
Office: Graves County Courthouse, 100 East Broadway, Mayfield 42066.
Telephone: (270) 247-0580.

CROSBY, Jerry D., II *(Judge, Kentucky District Court Twelfth Judicial District)* Currently serves as Chief Regional District Judge.
Office: 100 West Main Street, La Grange 40031.
Telephone: (502) 222-7447.

CUNNINGHAM, Bill *(Judge, Kentucky Circuit Court Fifty-sixth Judicial Circuit)* Term expires Jan 2007.
Mailing address: P.O. Box 790, Eddyville 42038-0790.
Telephone: (270) 388-5182.

DAUGHADAY, John T. *(Judge, Kentucky Circuit Court Fifty-second Judicial Circuit)* Elected to term beginning Jan 1984. Reelected 1991 and 1999. Current term expires Jan 2007. Born Graves County Kentucky Dec 31, 1944. Member First Christian Church. Educated at University of Kentucky B.A. 1968 J.D. 1970. Member Delta Theta Phi. Admitted to practice Kentucky 1970. Began legal practice Lexington 1970. Judge, Kentucky District Court Fifty-second Judicial District 1978-83.

City Attorney Lexington 1970-71. Alcoholic Beverage Administrator Lexington Jan to Aug 1977. Past Chairman Mayfield Planning and Zoning Board and Board of Adjustments. Instructor in Law American Institute of Banking Fall 1975. Former member Fayette County and Graves County Bar Associations. Member District Judges Education Committee 1978-79, Kentucky Association of Circuit Judges (President), Kentucky (Former member Children's Rights Committee) and American Bar Associations. Attended Trial Judges Academy American Academy of Judicial Education 1979, "Prison Crowding" National Academy of Corrections 1986 and "Restitution Programs in Judicial and Family Courts" National College of Juvenile Justice. Named Outstanding

DAUGHADAY, JOHN T.—*Continued*

Young Man of America 1972 and 1978 and Outstanding Young Man of Year by Mayfield-Graves County Jaycees 1978. President Mayfield-Graves County Cancer Society 1973-75 and South Highland Golf and Country Club 1976-77. Chairman Professional Committee United Fund 1974. Board of Directors J. U. Kevil Foundation 1972-76 and Kentucky Cancer Society 1975. Former Chairman American Cancer Crusade Graves County. Enjoys goose and duck hunting, golf and classical music.

Office: Courthouse, 100 East Broadway, Mayfield 42066.

Telephone: (270) 247-8726.

DAUGHERTY, Hunter *(Judge, Kentucky Circuit Court Thirteenth Judicial Circuit)* Term expires Jan 2007. Former Judge, Kentucky District Court Thirteenth Judicial District.

Office: 101 North Main Street, Nicholasville 40356.

Telephone: (859) 885-6722.

DAVIS, George W. *(Judge, Kentucky District Court Thirty-second Judicial District)* Term expires Jan 2007. Former Chief Regional District Judge.

Mailing address: P.O. Box 315, Catlettsburg 41129.

Office: 2800 Louisa Street, Catlettsburg 41129.

Telephone: (606) 739-5444.

DELAHANTY, Kevin *(Judge, Kentucky District Court Thirtieth Judicial District)* Term expires Jan 2007. Former Chief Regional District Judge.

Office: Hall of Justice, 600 West Jefferson Street, Louisville 40202.

Telephone: (502) 595-4957.

DELAHANTY, Sean *(Judge, Kentucky District Court Thirtieth Judicial District)* Term expires Jan 2007.

Office: Hall of Justice, 600 West Jefferson Street, Louisville 40202.

Telephone: (502) 595-4991.

DEWEESE, Deborah *(Judge, Kentucky District Court Thirtieth Judicial District)* Term expires Jan 2007.

Office: Hall of Justice, 600 West Jefferson Street, Louisville 40202.

Telephone: (502) 595-4696.

DICKSON, Vanessa *(Judge, Kentucky District Court Fourteenth Judicial District)* Elected Nov 2002. Term expires Jan 2007.

Office: 310 Main Street, Paris 40362.

Telephone: (859) 987-5562.

DIXON, Donna L. *(Judge, Kentucky District Court Second Judicial District)* Term expires Jan 2007. Currently serves as Vice Chief Regional District Judge.

Office: Courthouse, 301 South Sixth Street, Paducah 42003.

Telephone: (270) 575-7261.

DORTCH, Ronnie C. *(Judge, Kentucky Circuit Court Thirty-eighth Judicial Circuit)* Appointed by Governor Brereton C. Jones to term beginning March 25, 1992. Elected Nov 1992 and 1999. Current term expires Jan 2007. Born Hartford Kentucky Feb 1, 1945. Christian. Educated at Murray State University B.S. 1967, Western Kentucky University M.A. 1970 and Mississippi College School of Law J.D. 1978. Member Delta Theta Phi. Admitted to practice Mississippi 1978, Kentucky 1985 and U.S. District Courts Southern District of Mississippi 1978 and Western District of Kentucky 1985. In legal practice Jackson Mississippi 1978-85 and Hartford Kentucky 1985-86.

City Attorney Hartford and Commonwealth's Attorney Thirty-eighth Judicial Circuit 1986-92. Enjoys playing golf and reading.

Mailing address: P.O. Box 169, Hartford 42347.

Office: Washington Street, Hartford 42347.

Telephone: (270) 298-7250.

DOTSON, Jeff *(Judge, Kentucky District Court Fiftieth Judicial District)* Elected Nov 2002. Term expires Jan 2007.

Office: 224 South Main Street, Harrodsburg 40330-2306.

Telephone: (859) 734-6343.

DYCHE, R. W., III *(Judge, Kentucky Court of Appeals)* Appointed by Governor Martha L. Collins to term beginning June 17, 1986. Elected to subsequent terms. Current term expires Jan 2007. Born London Kentucky April 12, 1951. Religious affiliation: Disciples of Christ. Educated at Centre College of Kentucky A.B. 1972 and University of Kentucky College of Law J.D. 1975. Admitted to practice Kentucky 1975 and U.S. District Court Eastern District of Kentucky 1975. In legal practice London 1975-78. Judge, Kentucky District Court Twenty-seventh Judicial District 1978-86.

Mailing address: P.O. Box 5190, London 40745-5190.

Office: National City Bank Building, Fourth Floor, 400 South Main Street, London 40741.

Telephone: (606) 864-7661.

EASTON, Kelly Mark *(Judge, Kentucky Circuit Court Ninth Judicial Circuit)* Appointed by Governor Paul E. Patton to term beginning 2000. Elected Nov 2000, current term expires Jan 2007. Born Louisville Kentucky Oct 18, 1963. Educated at University of Kentucky B.A. with high distinction 1985, Oxford University, England International Graduate Summer School 1985 and University of Kentucky College of Law J.D. 1988. Staff member Journal of Mineral Law and Policy 1986-87. Member Delta Theta Phi, Phi Beta Kappa and Order of the Coif. Admitted to practice Kentucky 1988, U.S. District Courts Eastern and Western Districts of Kentucky, U.S. Court of Appeals Sixth Circuit and U.S. Court of Federal Claims. In legal practice Louisville 1988-90 and Elizabethtown 1990-2000.

Assistant Commonwealth Attorney Hardin County 1990-92. Member Hardin County (Past President, Chairman Scholarship Committee) and Kentucky Bar Associations. Board of Directors Horse Cave Theatre. Member Valley View Baptist Church. Interested in genealogy, theater, reading history, tennis and basketball.

Office: Hardin County Justice Center, 120 East Dixie, Elizabethtown 42701.

Telephone: (270) 766-5259.

Fax: (270) 765-5253

ECKERT, Jacquelyn Poole *(Judge, Kentucky District Court Thirtieth Judicial District)* Term expires Jan 2007.

Office: Hall of Justice, 600 West Jefferson Street, Louisville 40202.

Telephone: (502) 595-4983.

ECKERT, Matthew K. *(Judge, Kentucky District Court Thirtieth Judicial District)* Term expires Jan 2007.
Office: Hall of Justice, 600 West Jefferson Street, Louisville 40202.
Telephone: (502) 595-4992.

ELLIOT, Roger *(Judge, Kentucky District Court Twenty-ninth Judicial District)* Term expires Jan 2007. Former Chief Regional District Judge.
Mailing address: P.O. Box 790, Liberty 42539.
Office: Courthouse, Main Street, Liberty 42539.
Telephone: (606) 787-6761.

EMBERTON, Thomas D. *(Chief Judge, Kentucky Court of Appeals)* Term expires Jan 2007.
Mailing address: P.O. Box 450, Edmonton 42129-0450.
Office: 101 Stockton Street, Edmonton 42129.
Telephone: (270) 432-5800.

EMBRY, Shan *(Judge, Kentucky District Court Forty-sixth Judicial District)* Elected Nov 2002. Term expires Jan 2007.
Mailing address: P.O. Box 275, Leitchfield 42754.
Telephone: (270) 259-5890.

FARRIS, Sheila Nunley *(Judge, Kentucky Circuit Court Fifty-first Judicial Circuit)* Term expires Jan 2007. Serves Family Court.
Office: Five North Main Street, Henderson 42420.
Telephone: (270) 869-0460.

FITZGERALD, Patty Walker *(Judge, Kentucky Circuit Court Thirtieth Judicial Circuit)* Term expires Jan 2007. Serves Family Court.
Office: 220 Judicial Center, 700 West Jefferson, Louisville 40202-4730.
Telephone: (502) 595-4047.

FITZGERALD, Paula *(Judge, Kentucky District Court Thirtieth Judicial District)* Term expires Jan 2007.
Office: Hall of Justice, 600 West Jefferson Street, Louisville 40202.
Telephone: (502) 595-4994.

FOELLGER, Michael *(Judge, Kentucky Circuit Court Seventeenth Judicial Circuit)* Assumed office Jan 6, 2003. Term expires Jan 2007. Serves Family Court. Former Judge and Former Chief Regional District Judge, Kentucky District Court Seventeenth Judicial District.
Office: 600 Columbia Street, Newport 41071.
Telephone: (859) 292-6322.

FORESTER, Karl S. *(Chief Judge, United States District Court Eastern District of Kentucky)* Appointed for life by President Ronald Reagan to term beginning 1988. Chief Judge since Jan 1, 2001. Born Harlan Kentucky May 2, 1940. Educated at University of Kentucky B.A. 1962 J.D. 1966. In legal practice Harlan 1966-88.
Mailing address: P.O. Box 2165, Lexington 40588-2165.
Telephone: (859) 233-2625.

FOUST, Dennis R. *(Judge, Kentucky Circuit Court Forty-second Judicial Circuit)* Term expires Jan 2007. Former Judge, Kentucky District Court Fifty-eighth Judicial District.
Office: 80 Judicial Drive, Unit 101, Benton 42025.
Telephone: (270) 527-1480.

FRAZIER, Stephen N. *(Judge, Kentucky Circuit Court Twenty-fourth Judicial Circuit)* Elected to term beginning Jan 2, 1984. Reelected 1991 and 1999. Current term expires Jan 2007. Chief Regional Judge Mountain Administrative Region since June 1, 1986. Serves Family Court. Born Dayton Ohio Nov 27, 1943. Protestant. Educated at Pikeville College B.S. 1965 and University of Louisville School of Law J.D. 1969. Admitted to practice Kentucky 1969. In legal practice Paintsville 1969-70 and 1974-84 and Louisville 1970-74. Judge, Kentucky District Court Twenty-fourth Judicial District 1978.
Former City Attorney Paintsville Kentucky. Assistant Commonwealth Attorney Jefferson County 1973-74. Assistant County Attorney Johnson County 1975-76. Assistant Professor of History, Political Science and Business Law and Associate Professor of Political Science, Real Estate Law and Business Law Prestonburg Community College since 1991. Member Kentucky Retirement and Judicial Removal Committee. Member Kentucky and American Bar Associations. Recipient Chief Justice's Special Service Award presented by Kentucky Supreme Court Chief Justice and Kentucky Bar Association. Former Board Member and Chairman Paul B. Hall Regional Medical Center. Board Member The Southern College of Osteopathic Medicine.
Mailing address: P.O. Box 907, Paintsville 41240.
Office: Courthouse, Paintsville 41240.
Telephone: (606) 789-6701.

FRIEND, Kelsey Evans *(Judge, Kentucky District Court Thirty-fifth Judicial District)*
Office: 326 Hall of Justice, 172 Division Street, Pikeville 41501.
Telephone: (606) 433-7561.

FULTON, Thomas H. *(Judge, United States Bankruptcy Court Western District of Kentucky)* Appointed by U.S. Court of Appeals Sixth Circuit judges to term beginning Dec 6, 2002. Term expires Dec 5, 2016.
Office: 528 U.S. Courthouse, 601 West Broadway, Louisville 40202-2264.
Telephone: (502) 627-5550.

FUNK, Thomas *(Judge, Kentucky District Court Fifteenth Judicial District)* Term expires Jan 2007.
Office: Grant County Court House, Main Street, Williamstown 41097.
Telephone: (859) 824-7516.

GAMBILL, C. Cleveland *(Magistrate Judge, United States District Court Western District of Kentucky)* Appointed by U.S. District Court judges.
Office: 200 U.S. Courthouse, 601 West Broadway, Louisville 40202.
Telephone: (502) 625-3830.

GARBER, Eleanore *(Judge, Kentucky Circuit Court Thirtieth Judicial Circuit)* Assumed office Jan 6, 2003. Term expires Jan 2007. Serves Family Court. Former Judge, Kentucky District Court Thirtieth Judicial District.
Office: 220 Judicial Center, 700 West Jefferson Street, Louisville 40202-4730.
Telephone: (502) 595-4988.

GARVEY, Kevin L. *(Judge, Kentucky Circuit Court Thirtieth Judicial Circuit)* Assumed office Jan 6, 2003. Term expires Jan 2007. Serves Family Court. Educated at University of Louisville B.A. 1975 J.D. 1979. Admitted to practice Kentucky 1979, U.S. District Court Western District of Kentucky 1979 and U.S. Supreme Court.

GARVEY, KEVIN L.—*Continued*

Judge 1981 to 2003, Chief Judge 1996 and 1997 and Chief Judge Family Court Jan 2002 to Jan 5, 2003, Kentucky District Court Thirtieth Judicial District.

Board of Directors Louisville Bar Association. Recipient Youth Ministry Volunteer Award for involvement with high school youth from Archdiocese of Louisville. Member State Technology Committee. Enjoys coaching youth teams in volleyball, basketball and baseball.

Office: Jefferson County Judicial Center, 700 West Jefferson Street, Louisville 40202.

Telephone: (502) 595-4043.

Fax: (502) 595-3482

GEORGE, Doughlas M. *(Judge, Kentucky Circuit Court Eleventh Judicial Circuit)* Assumed office Jan 1998. Elected Nov 1999, current term expires Jan 1, 2007. Born Lebanon Kentucky Oct 5, 1953. Roman Catholic. Educated at University of Kentucky B.S. in Accounting 1975 and University of Louisville School of Law J.D. cum laude 1977. Recipient Torts and Criminal Procedure Book Awards. Member Beta Alpha Psi and Sigma Alpha Epsilon. Admitted to practice Kentucky 1978. In legal practice Louisville May 1978 to Feb 1979 and Springfield 1979-84. Master Commissioner, Washington Circuit Court Feb 1980 to April 1981. Trial Commissioner, Washington District Court April 1981 to Jan 1984. Judge, Kentucky District Court Eleventh Judicial District Jan 1984 to Jan 1998.

Member Kentucky Association of Circuit Judges and Kentucky Bar Association.

Mailing address: P.O. Box 328, Springfield 40069.

Telephone: (859) 336-3903.

GEORGE, Stephen M. *(Judge, Kentucky Circuit Court Thirtieth Judicial Circuit)* Assumed office Jan 6, 2003. Term expires Jan 2007. Serves Family Court. Former Judge, Kentucky District Court Thirtieth Judicial District.

Office: 220 Judicial Center, 700 West Jefferson Street, Louisville 40202.

Telephone: (502) 595-4998.

GEVEDON, Kimberly I. *(Judge, Kentucky District Court Thirty-seventh Judicial District)*

Mailing address: P.O. Box 216, West Liberty 41472.

Office: Morgan County Courthouse, West Liberty 41472.

Telephone: (606) 743-3866.

GILL, Tyler L. *(Judge, Kentucky Circuit Court Seventh Judicial Circuit)* Appointed by Governor Brereton C. Jones to term beginning August 17, 1995. Elected Nov 1999, current term expires Jan 2007. Born Hopkinsville Kentucky Nov 26, 1958. Christian. Educated at Western Kentucky University B.A. 1980 and University of Kentucky J.D. 1984. Law Clerk to Hon. Edward H. Johnstone, U.S. District Court Western District of Kentucky Summer 1983. Member Phi Delta Phi. Admitted to practice Kentucky 1984 and U.S. District Courts Western 1987 and Eastern 1988 Districts of Kentucky. In legal practice Elkton 1984-93. Judge, Kentucky District Court Seventh Judicial District 1993-95.

Instructor in Business Law Hopkinsville Community College 1991. Member Kentucky and American Bar Associations. Attended Special Jurisdiction 1995 and General Jurisdiction 1997 The National Judicial College. Holds commercial pilot's license with instrument rating.

Mailing address: P.O. Box 667, Russellville 42276.

Office: 200 West Fourth Street, Russellville 42276.

Telephone: (270) 726-2242.

E-mail address: Tyler_L_Gill@yahoo.com

GOEBEL, E. Robert *(Magistrate Judge, United States District Court Western District of Kentucky)* Appointed by U.S. District Court judges.

Office: Federal Building, 423 Frederica Street, Owensboro 42301.

Telephone: (270) 689-4450.

GOODWINE, Pamela *(Judge, Kentucky District Court Twenty-second Judicial District)* Currently serves as Chief Regional District Judge.

Office: 150 North Limestone, Room 531, Lexington 40507-1151.

Telephone: (859) 246-2247.

GOSSETT, Kristi Hogg *(Judge, Kentucky Circuit Court Thirty-seventh Judicial Circuit)* Assumed office Jan 6, 2003. Term expires Jan 2007. Serves Family Court.

Office: Carter County Courthouse, Second Floor, 300 West Main Street, Grayson 41143.

Telephone: (606) 475-1801.

GRAHAM, William Louis *(Judge, Kentucky Circuit Court Forty-eighth Judicial Circuit)* Term expires Jan 2007. Currently serves as Chief Regional Circuit Judge. Born March 3, 1946. Protestant. Educated at Davidson College B.A. 1968 and University of Kentucky J.D. 1971. Admitted to practice Kentucky 1971. Began legal practice Frankfort 1971. Judge, Franklin County Juvenile Court 1972-74. Judge, Kentucky District Court Forty-eighth Judicial District 1978-83.

Member Kentucky Bar Association. Captain U.S. Army Signal Corps 1973-78. Democrat. Former member Franklin County Democratic Executive Committee. Field representative for U.S. Senator Walter Huddleston 1975-77.

Office: Courthouse, 214 St. Clair Street, Frankfort 40601.

Telephone: (502) 564-8382.

GRAVES, John William "Bill" *(Justice, Kentucky Supreme Court)* Term expires Jan 2007. Born Paducah Kentucky Oct 17, 1935. Roman Catholic. Educated at University of Notre Dame B.S.Ch. 1957, University of Louisville School of Medicine 1957-58 and University of Kentucky J.D. 1963. Law Clerk to Chief Justice James B. Milliken, Kentucky Supreme Court 1963-64. Admitted to practice Kentucky 1963 and Illinois 1969. Began legal practice Paducah Kentucky 1965. Justice of the Peace, McCracken County 1966-70. Trial Commissioner, Paducah Police Court 1970 and McCracken County Quarterly Court 1971. Judge, Kentucky District Court Second Judicial District 1984-88. Former Judge, Kentucky Circuit Court Second Judicial Circuit.

Control Chemist Metropolis Illinois 1959-60. Paducah Police Court Prosecutor 1966. Instructor in Business Law Paducah Community College 1968-70 and Military Justice Murray State University. Former Director Kentucky Association of Trial Attorneys Western Kentucky Legal Services. Member McCracken County (Former Secretary-Treasurer), Kentucky and American Bar Associations. Colonel USAR JAGC 1959-94 (retired). Previ-

GRAVES, JOHN WILLIAM "BILL"—*Continued*

ously worked as paper boy, stock boy and truck driver. Past President Reserve Officers Association and Woodmen of the World. Former Exalted Ruler Elks. Former President Travelers Protective Association. Director Paducah Chapter Full Gospel Businessmen's Fellowship International. Consumer member Kentucky State Board of Podiatry 1980-90. Counsel and former Director Mental Retardation Board Paducah Cooperative Ministry. Active in scouting and youth sports. Enjoys golf, camping and fishing.

Mailing address: P.O. Box 993, Paducah 42002-0993.
Office: 222 Kentucky Avenue, Paducah 42003.
Telephone: (270) 575-7039.

GRIFFIN, Henry McHenry, III *(Judge, Kentucky Circuit Court Sixth Judicial Circuit)* Term expires Jan 2007. Born Owensboro Kentucky May 19, 1953. Methodist. Educated at Western Kentucky University B.A. 1975 and University of Kentucky College of Law J.D. Admitted to practice Kentucky 1980. Former Judge, Kentucky District Court Sixth Judicial District, elected to term beginning Jan 6, 1986.

Assistant County Attorney Daviess County 1981-86. Member American Judicature Society and Kentucky Bar Association. Recipient CLE Award. Former Chair Advisory Board Salvation Army. Advisory Board Big Brothers/Big Sisters 1983-90. Chair Mary Kendall Methodist Home Board. Board of Directors Volunteer Center. Enjoys golf, basketball and outdoor activities.

Office: Judicial Center, 100 East Second Street, Owensboro 42303.
Telephone: (270) 687-7226.

GROTHAUS, Douglas *(Judge, Kentucky District Court Sixteenth Judicial District)* Term expires Jan 2007.

Office: Kenton County Justice Center, Fourth Floor, 230 Madison, Covington 41011.
Telephone: (859) 292-6576.

GUIDUGLI, Daniel T. *(Judge, Kentucky Court of Appeals)* Appointed by Governor Paul E. Patton to term beginning 1996. Elected 1999, current term expires Jan 2007. Born Campbell County Kentucky 1952. Educated at Northern Kentucky University B.A. and Chase Law School of Northern Kentucky University J.D. Former Judge, Kentucky District Court Seventeenth Judicial District.

Former Assistant County Attorney. Member Northern Kentucky Bar Association. Recipient Outstanding Young Man of America Award 1984. Member Northern Kentucky University Alumni Association.

Office: One Moock Road, Suite 4, Newport 41071.
Telephone: (859) 291-9966.
Fax: (859) 291-0657

HAGERMAN, C. David *(Judge, Kentucky Circuit Court Thirty-second Judicial Circuit)* Appointed by Governor Brereton C. Jones to term beginning 1993. Elected 1999, current term expires Jan 2007.

Mailing address: P.O. Box 417, Catlettsburg 41129.
Office: 2800 Louisa Street, Catlettsburg 41129.
Telephone: (606) 739-6122.

HALL, Eric D. *(Judge, Kentucky District Court Thirty-first Judicial District)* Term expires Jan 2007.

Mailing address: P.O. Box 335, Allen 41601.
Telephone: (606) 886-6670.

HALL, Judy A. *(Judge, Kentucky Circuit Court Third Judicial Circuit)* Term expires Jan 2007. Serves Family Court.

Office: Christian County Justice Center, Second Floor, 100 Justice Way, Hopkinsville 42240.
Telephone: (270) 889-6038.

HAMM, Phillip *(Judge, Kentucky District Court Twenty-sixth Judicial District)* Term expires Jan 2007.

Mailing address: P.O. Box 838, Harlan 40831.
Office: Harlan County Courthouse, Central Street, Harlan 40831.
Telephone: (606) 573-7209.

HARRIS, William R. *(Judge, Kentucky Circuit Court Forty-ninth Judicial Circuit)* Term expires Jan 2007. Currently serves as Vice Chief Regional Circuit Judge.

Mailing address: P.O. Box 262, Franklin 42135-0262.
Office: Courthouse, Public Square, Franklin 42134.
Telephone: (270) 586-8058.

HARROD, Michael *(Judge, Kentucky District Court Fifty-third Judicial District)* Term expires Jan 2007. Currently serves as Vice Chief Regional District Judge.

Office: 311 Main Street, Shelbyville 40065.
Telephone: (502) 633-6313.

HART, William G. *(Judge, Kentucky District Court Forty-eighth Judicial District)* Term expires Jan 2007. Former Chief Judge.

Office: Franklin County Courthouse, 214 St. Clair Street, Frankfort 40601.
Telephone: (502) 564-7073.

HAYDEN, Stephen *(Judge, Kentucky Circuit Court Fifty-first Judicial Circuit)* Term expires Jan 2007. Former Judge, Kentucky District Court Fifty-first Judicial District.

Mailing address: P.O. Box 675, Henderson 42420.
Office: First and Main Streets, Henderson 42420.
Telephone: (270) 827-1295.

HAYNIE, Hugh Smith *(Judge, Kentucky Circuit Court Thirtieth Judicial Circuit)* Assumed office Jan 6, 2003. Term expires Jan 2007. Serves Family Court. Born Greensboro North Carolina Sept 29, 1958. Educated at College of William & Mary B.A. 1982 and University of Louisville School of Law J.D. 1991. Staff member Journal of Family Law. Admitted to practice Kentucky 1991. Judge, Kentucky District Court Thirtieth Judicial District Dec 1, 2000 to Jan 5, 2003, appointed by Governor Paul E. Patton.

Assistant Commonwealth Attorney Nov 1991 to Nov 2000. Prosecutor Louisville 1991-2000. Member National Council of Juvenile and Family Court Judges, Louisville and Kentucky Bar Associations.

Office: 402 Judicial Center, 700 West Jefferson Street, Louisville 40202.
Telephone: (502) 595-4996.
Fax: (502) 595-4484
E-mail address: hughhaynie@mail.aoc.state.ky.us

HAYSE, David *(Judge, Kentucky District Court Twenty-second Judicial District)* Term expires Jan 2007.

Office: 150 North Limestone, Room 531, Lexington 40507-1151.
Telephone: (859) 246-2247.

HEATON, Bob *(Judge, Kentucky District Court Fifty-seventh Judicial District)* Term expires Jan 2007.
Mailing address: P.O. Box 331, Bardstown 40004.
Office: Nelson County Courthouse, Bardstown 40004.
Telephone: (502) 348-2012.

HELLMANN, Juda Maria *(Judge, Kentucky Circuit Court Thirtieth Judicial Circuit)* Term expires Jan 2007. Serves Family Court.
Office: 220 Judicial Center, 700 West Jefferson Street, Louisville 40202-4730.
Telephone: (502) 595-4969.

HENRY, Michael L. *(Judge, Kentucky District Court Twenty-eighth Judicial District)* Term expires Jan 2007.
Office: Pulaski County Courthouse, Main Street, Somerset 42501.
Telephone: (606) 677-4112.

HEYBURN, John G., II *(Chief Judge, United States District Court Western District of Kentucky)* Appointed for life by President George Bush to term beginning Aug 28, 1992. Chief Judge since Dec 1, 2001. Born Boston Massachusetts Nov 12, 1948. Episcopalian. Educated at Harvard College A.B. 1970 and University of Kentucky J.D. 1976. National Moot Court Team. Member Barristers. Admitted to practice Kentucky 1976 and U.S. District Court Western District of Kentucky. In legal practice Louisville 1976-92.
Chair Louisville-Jefferson County Crime Commission 1985-88. Member Louisville, Kentucky and American Bar Associations. Chair Budget Committee Judicial Conference of the U.S.
Office: 239 U.S. Courthouse, 601 West Broadway, Louisville 40202.
Telephone: (502) 625-3620.

HINES, Robert Jeffrey *(Judge, Kentucky Circuit Court Second Judicial Circuit)* Term expires Jan 2007. Born Ohio Sept 26, 1955. Episcopalian. Educated at Paducah Community College A.A., Murray State University B.S. 1976 and University of Louisville School of Law J.D. 1979. Member Phi Alpha Delta. Admitted to practice Kentucky 1980 and U.S. District Court Western District of Kentucky 1980. In legal practice Paducah 1980-89. Former Judge, Kentucky District Court Second Judicial District, elected to term beginning Jan 3, 1990.
Assistant Commonwealth Attorney 1980-81. Assistant County Attorney 1981-89. Member Kentucky Bar Association.
Office: McCracken County Courthouse, 301 South Sixth Street, Paducah 42003.
Telephone: (270) 575-7292.

HOLBROOK, John Kevin *(Judge, Kentucky District Court Twenty-fourth Judicial District)*
Mailing address: P.O. Box 1247, Paintsville 41240.
Office: Paintsville Courthouse, Paintsville 41240.
Telephone: (606) 789-8636.

HOOD, Joseph Martin *(Judge, United States District Court Eastern District of Kentucky)* Former Magistrate. Appointed Judge for life by President George Bush. Born Ashland Kentucky Oct 14, 1942. Catholic. Educated at University of Kentucky B.S. 1965 J.D. 1972. Member Phi Delta Phi. Admitted to practice Kentucky 1973. Began legal practice Catlettsburg 1973.
Member Boyd County and Kentucky Bar Associations. Captain U.S. Army 1966-70. Member Knights of Columbus. Enjoys sports.
Mailing address: P.O. Box 2227, Lexington 40588-2227.
Telephone: (859) 233-2415.

HOPPER, Lewis B. *(Judge, Kentucky Circuit Court Twenty-seventh Judicial Circuit)* Term expires Jan 2007. Currently serves as Chief Regional Circuit Judge. Former Judge, Kentucky District Court Twenty-seventh Judicial District.
Mailing address: P.O. Box 749, Barbourville 40906.
Telephone: (606) 546-3470.

HORNE, Kevin M. *(Judge, Kentucky District Court Twenty-second Judicial District)* Term expires Jan 2007. Former Chief Regional District Judge.
Office: 150 North Limestone, Room 531, Lexington 40507-1151.
Telephone: (859) 246-2247.

HOUSE, Oscar G. *(Judge, Kentucky District Court Forty-first Judicial District)* Term expires Jan 2007.
Office: 79 Highway 80, Suite 2, Manchester 40962.
Telephone: (606) 598-6170.

HOWARD, William S. *(Chief Judge, United States Bankruptcy Court Eastern District of Kentucky)* Appointed by U.S. Court of Appeals Sixth Circuit judges.
Mailing address: P.O. Box 576, Lexington 40588-0576.
Telephone: (859) 233-2465.

HUDDLESTON, Joseph Russell *(Judge, Kentucky Court of Appeals)* Appointed by Governor Wallace G. Wilkinson to term beginning March 15, 1991. Elected Nov 1991 and 1999. Current term expires Jan 2007. Born Glasgow Kentucky Feb 5, 1937. Episcopalian. Educated at Princeton University A.B. 1959 and University of Virginia J.D. 1962 LL.M. 1997. Member Phi Alpha Delta. Admitted to practice Kentucky 1962, U.S. District Courts Western 1962 and Eastern 1968 Districts of Kentucky, U.S. Court of Appeals Sixth Circuit 1963, U.S. Supreme Court 1970 and U.S. Tax Court 1980. In legal practice Bowling Green 1962-87. Judge 1987-91 and Chief Judge 1990-91, Kentucky Circuit Court Eighth Judicial Circuit.
Author of numerous articles for *The Advocate* Kentucky Academy of Trial Attorneys and other bar periodicals. Instructor in Government Western Kentucky University 1962-63, Trial Advocacy University of Kentucky 1985 and Jurisprudence People's Law School. Member Kentucky Committee for Criminal Law Revision (drafted new penal code) 1969-71. Member Western Kentucky University Legal Advisory Council 1980-82. Member Supreme Court Advisory Committee on Civil Rules 1983-89. Member Gender Fairness in the Courts Committee since 1990. Member Committees on Law-Related Education 1991 and Child Support Guidelines 1991. Fellow American Bar Foundation. Member Southern Kentucky Estate Planning Council (Vice President 1982, President 1983), Kentucky Civil Rules Committee, Kentucky Crime Commission (Courts Committee 1972-76, Chairman Corrections Committee 1976-77, Member Executive Committee 1976-77), Kentucky Penal Code Commission, Kentucky Academy of Trial Attorneys (Board of Governors 1969-70 and 1975-86, Secretary 1976, Vice President 1977 and President 1978), The Association of Trial Lawyers of America (State Delegate

HUDDLESTON, JOSEPH RUSSELL—*Continued*

1981-82), Bowling Green (President 1972), Kentucky (House of Delegates 1971-80) and American Bar Associations. Attended The National Judicial College 1989; American Academy of Judicial Education Harvard Law School 1990; Graduate Program for Appellate Judges University of Virginia School of Law 1993-94; and Law and Organizational Economics University of Kansas 1997. Lecturer Kentucky Crime Commission. Speaker on several occasions for Kentucky Bar Association and Kentucky Academy of Trial Attorneys annual conventions. Seminar Speaker for The Association of Trial Lawyers of America. Recipient Henry V. Pennington Outstanding State Trial Judge Award from Kentucky Academy of Trial Attorneys 1990. Listed in *Who's Who in America*, *Who's Who in American Law* and *Best Lawyers in America* 1983 and 1987. Democrat. Former Member Bowling Green-Warren County Chamber of Commerce (Chairman Transportation Committee 1984 and Governmental Affairs Committee 1986, Director 1987-90) and Bowling Green-Warren County Jaycees (Co-chairman Southern Kentucky Fair 1963). Moderator and Organizer People's Law School 1986. Director Bowling Green Girls Club. Member Rotary Club. Enjoys sailing, camping, fishing and reading.

Office: 101 Thoroughbred Square, 1945 Scottsville Road, Bowling Green 42104.

Telephone: (270) 746-7867.

Fax: (270) 746-7870

HUDDLESTON, Margaret R. *(Judge, Kentucky Circuit Court Eighth Judicial Circuit)* Term expires Jan 2007. Serves Family Court.

Office: 304 Warren County Justice Center, 1001 Center Street, Bowling Green 42102-2192.

Telephone: (270) 746-7144.

HURT, Steve D. *(Judge, Kentucky District Court Sixtieth Judicial District)* Currently serves as Vice Chief Regional District Judge. Former Judge, Kentucky District Court Twenty-ninth Judicial District.

Mailing address: P.O. Box 750, Burkesville 42717.

Telephone: (270) 864-5600.

ISAAC, Sheila R. *(Judge, Kentucky Circuit Court Twenty-second Judicial Circuit)* Term expires Jan 2007. Former Judge, Kentucky District Court Twenty-second Judicial District.

Office: Fayette County Courthouse, 215 West Main Street, Lexington 40507.

Telephone: (859) 246-2531.

ISAACS, Paul F. *(Judge, Kentucky Circuit Court Fourteenth Judicial Circuit)* Term expires Jan 2007.

Office: Justice Center, 119 North Hamilton Street, Georgetown 40324.

Telephone: (502) 863-4781.

JAEGER, Steven R. *(Judge, Kentucky Circuit Court Sixteenth Judicial Circuit)* Term expires Jan 2007. Former Judge, Kentucky District Court Sixteenth Judicial District.

Office: 600 Kenton County Justice Center, 230 Madison Avenue, Covington 41011.

Telephone: (859) 292-6538.

JENNINGS, William T. *(Judge, Kentucky Circuit Court Twenty-fifth Judicial Circuit)* Term expires Jan 2007. Currently serves as Vice Chief Regional Circuit Judge. Former Judge, Kentucky District Court Twenty-fifth Judicial District.

Office: Courthouse, 101 West Main Street, Richmond 40475.

Telephone: (859) 624-4750.

JERNIGAN, David H. *(Judge, Kentucky Circuit Court Forty-fifth Judicial Circuit)* Term expires Jan 2007.

Mailing address: P.O. Box 567, Greenville 42345.

Office: Courthouse, Main Street, Greenville 42345.

Telephone: (270) 338-5930.

JOHNSON, J. B., Jr. *(Magistrate Judge, United States District Court Eastern District of Kentucky)* Part-time Magistrate Judge 1987-96. Appointed full-time Magistrate Judge by U.S. District Court judges to term beginning April 24, 1996. Term expires April 24, 2004. Born Williamsburg Kentucky Aug 31, 1936. Religious affiliation: Disciples of Christ. Educated at University of Kentucky B.S. 1958 J.D. 1961. Member Phi Delta Phi. Admitted to practice Kentucky 1961 and U.S. District Court Eastern District of Kentucky 1965. In legal practice Williamsburg 1964-73 and 1984-96. Judge, Kentucky Circuit Court Thirty-fourth Judicial Circuit 1973-84.

City Attorney Williamsburg 1965-73. Important Decision: Noble v. Sartori (medical malpractice liability for refusal to treat emergency room patient) S.Ct. Ky. 799 S.W.2d 8, 1990. Member Kentucky Association of Trial Attorneys, The Association of Trial Lawyers of America, Kentucky and American Bar Associations. Captain JAG USAF 1961-64. Enjoys hunting.

Office: 310 South Main Street, Room 351, London 40741.

Telephone: (606) 877-7940.

JOHNSON, Rick A. *(Judge, Kentucky Court of Appeals)* Elected Nov 1991 to term beginning Jan 1992. Reelected 1999, current term expires Jan 2007. Born Symsonia Kentucky May 1, 1955. Methodist. Educated at Western Kentucky University B.S. with honors 1976 and George Washington University J.D. 1979. Admitted to practice Kentucky 1979. In legal practice Mayfield 1979-91 and Paducah.

Member American Judges Association, Graves County, McCracken County, Kentucky and American Bar Associations. Named Outstanding Young Leader Mayfield-Graves County Jaycees 1988. Recipient Lovey Raburn Award from Western Kentucky Regional Mental Health-Mental Retardation Board, Inc. 1994. Democrat. Member Graves County Democratic Executive Committee 1983-87. Past President Mayfield-Graves County Chamber of Commerce and Paducah Lions Club. Former Chair Western Kentucky Regional Mental Health-Mental Retardation Board, Inc. Board Member Mayfield-Graves County Local Development Board.

Office: 2380 State Route 45 North, Mayfield 42066.

Telephone: (270) 247-1052.

JOHNSON, Ron *(Judge, Kentucky Circuit Court Twenty-sixth Judicial Circuit)* Elected Nov 1991 to term beginning Jan 3, 1992. Reelected Nov 1999, current term expires Jan 2, 2007. Born Benham Kentucky Sept 20, 1946. Methodist. Educated at University of Kentucky A.B. 1968 J.D. with honors 1973. Staff member Kentucky Law Journal 1971-73. Admitted to practice Kentucky 1973 and U.S. District Court Eastern District of

JOHNSON, RON—*Continued*

Kentucky 1974. In legal practice Pikeville 1973-80 and Harlan 1980-92.

Assistant Commonwealth's Attorney Thirty-fifth Judicial Circuit 1974-80. Commonwealth's Attorney Twenty-sixth Judicial Circuit 1980-92. Instructor in Business Law Southeast Community College University of Kentucky 1982-83. Former Member Kentucky Commonwealth Attorneys Association. Member Kentucky Judges Association, Harlan County, Pike County (Past President) and Kentucky Bar Associations. Attended Judicial College for Kentucky Circuit Judges and Special Judicial Writing Seminar sponsored by Kentucky Administrative Office of the Courts. Recipient The Carroll M. Redford Award as Kentucky's Outstanding Prosecutor 1988. Named Kentucky's Outstanding Judge by Kentucky Bar Association 1998. Captain U.S. Army Infantry (active duty) 1968-70 and USAR 1970-75. Recipient Silver Star Medal for gallantry in combat. Political affiliation: Independent. Past President Harlan Boys Choir Support Group. Former Board Member Tri-City Little League. Lay Speaker Benham United Methodist Church. Member VFW Post 5171 and Rotary International. Enjoys shooting, gardening, golfing and reading. Interested in history.

Mailing address: P.O. Drawer L, Harlan 40831.

Office: 210 East Central Street, Suite 302, Harlan 40831.

Telephone: (606) 573-3242.

Fax: (606) 573-1280

E-mail address: RonJohnson@mail.state.ky.us

JOHNSON, Susan *(Judge, Kentucky District Court Twenty-fourth Judicial District)* Term expires Jan 2007. Currently serves as Chief Regional District Judge.

Mailing address: P.O. Box 1247, Paintsville 41240.

Telephone: (606) 789-8636.

JOHNSTONE, Edward H. *(Senior Judge, United States District Court Western District of Kentucky)* Appointed for life by President Jimmy Carter Oct 1977. Chief Judge 1985-90. Assumed Senior status Oct 22, 1993, serves by assignment. Born Sao Paulo Brazil April 26, 1922. Educated at University of Kentucky College of Law J.D. 1949. In legal practice Princeton 1949-76. City Judge, Kentucky Police Court Princeton 1954-69. Judge, Kentucky Circuit Court Fifty-sixth Judicial Circuit 1976-77.

City Attorney Princeton 1952-54, Kuttawa 1954-76 and Fredonia 1954-76.

Office: 219 Federal Building, 501 Broadway Street, Paducah 42001.

Telephone: (270) 415-6450.

JOHNSTONE, Martin E. *(Justice, Kentucky Supreme Court)* Elected Nov 1996. Reelected Nov 1998, current term expires Jan 2007. Born Louisville Kentucky April 29, 1949. Christian. Educated at Western Kentucky University B.A. with honors 1971 and University of Louisville J.D. 1975. Member Alpha Tau Omega. Admitted to practice Kentucky 1975. Began legal practice Louisville 1975. Magisterial Judge 1976-78. Judge and Chief Judge, Kentucky District Court Thirtieth Judicial District 1978-1983. Judge and Chief Judge, Kentucky Circuit Court Thirtieth Judicial Circuit Jan 1984 to 1993. Judge and Chief Judge pro tem, Kentucky Court of Appeals 1993-96.

Instructor Institute for Paralegal Studies 1982-84. Member Kentucky Circuit Judges Association, American Judges Association, Louisville and Kentucky Bar Associations. Named Judge of the Year by Louisville Bar Association 1980 and 1999 and Trial Judge of the Year by Kentucky Academy of Trial Attorneys 1991. Recipient Distinguished Alumni Award from University of Louisville School of Law 1997. Enjoys canoeing, camping, fishing and skiing.

Office: 1000 Judicial Center, 700 West Jefferson Street, Louisville 40202-2761.

Telephone: (502) 595-3199.

JONES, Lisa A. *(Judge, Kentucky District Court Sixth Judicial District)* Elected Nov 2002. Term expires Jan 2007.

Office: 100 East Second Street, Owensboro 42303.

KELLER, James E. *(Justice, Kentucky Supreme Court)* Appointed by Governor Paul E. Patton to term beginning May 1999. Born Harlan Kentucky Aug 13, 1942. Methodist. Educated at Eastern Kentucky University and University of Kentucky J.D. 1965. Admitted to practice Kentucky 1966. Began legal practice Lexington 1966. Master Commissioner 1969-76 and Judge Nov 1976 to May 1999, Kentucky Circuit Court Twenty-second Judicial Circuit, appointed by Governor Julian Carroll.

Member Fayette County and Kentucky Bar Associations.

Office: 155 East Main Street, Suite 200, Lexington 40507-1332.

Telephone: (859) 246-2220.

KING, W. David *(Magistrate Judge, United States District Court Western District of Kentucky)* Appointed by U.S. District Court judges to term beginning Sept 1979. Reappointed 1987 and 1995. Current term expires 2003. Born Paducah Kentucky Jan 29, 1945. Methodist. Educated at Murray State University B.S. 1967 and University of Kentucky J.D. 1972. Admitted to practice Kentucky 1972 and U.S. District Court Western District of Kentucky 1973. Began legal practice Paducah 1972.

Member McCracken County, Kentucky and American Bar Associations. Sergeant U.S. Army 1968-70 (Tactical Operations Sergeant with First Field Force Vietnam IFFV 1970). Recipient Bronze Star 1970 and Staff Service Honor Medal (Republic of Vietnam 1970). Democrat.

Office: 330 U.S. Courthouse, 501 Broadway Street, Paducah 42001.

Telephone: (270) 415-6470.

KNOPF, Thomas John *(Judge, Kentucky Circuit Court Thirtieth Judicial Circuit)* Elected 1991 to term beginning Jan 1992. Reelected 1999, current term expires Jan 2007. Born Louisville Kentucky Sept 10, 1948. Catholic. Educated at Xavier University B.S. 1970 and University of Louisville J.D. 1973. Admitted to practice Kentucky 1973. Former Chief Judge, Kentucky District Court Thirtieth Judicial District.

Member Louisville and Kentucky Bar Associations. Faculty Member The National Judicial College.

Office: 810 Judicial Center, 700 West Jefferson Street, Louisville 40202-4724.

Telephone: (502) 595-4311.

KNOPF, William L. *(Judge, Kentucky Court of Appeals)* Elected Nov 1995 and Nov 1999. Current term expires Jan 2007. Born Louisville Kentucky Nov 22, 1954. Catholic. Educated at Loyola University of New

KNOPF, WILLIAM L.—*Continued*

Orleans B.B.A. 1976 and University of Louisville Louis D. Brandeis School of Law J.D. 1978. Admitted to practice Kentucky 1979, U.S. District Court Western District of Kentucky 1979 and U.S. Court of Appeals Sixth Circuit 1980. In legal practice Louisville 1981-84. Judge, Kentucky District Court Thirtieth Judicial District 1984-89. Judge, Kentucky Circuit Court Thirtieth Judicial Circuit 1989-95.

Assistant Commonwealth's Attorney Louisville 1979-81. Board of Directors Kentucky Bar Foundation. Member Kentucky Criminal Justice Council, Louisville and Kentucky Bar Associations.

Office: Jefferson County Judicial Center, 700 West Jefferson Street, Suite 1020, Louisville 40202-4724.

Telephone: (502) 595-3440.

Fax: (502) 595-3442

E-mail address: williamknopf@mail.aoc.state.ky.us

KOPOWSKI, Leonard L. *(Judge, Kentucky Circuit Court Seventeenth Judicial Circuit)* Elected 1983 to term beginning Jan 1, 1984. Reelected 1991 and 1999. Current term expires Jan 2, 2007. Former Chief Judge. Born Cleveland Ohio July 18, 1947. Catholic. Educated at Xavier University B.S. 1969 and Case Western Reserve University J.D. 1972. Admitted to practice Ohio 1972, Kentucky 1973, U.S. District Courts Southern District of Ohio 1973 and Eastern District of Kentucky 1973 and U.S. Court of Appeals Sixth Circuit 1976. Began legal practice Cincinnati Ohio 1972. In legal practice Newport Kentucky 1973. Judge, Kentucky District Court Seventeenth Judicial District 1978-83.

Attorney City of Highland Heights 1974-78. Instructor Chase Law School of Northern Kentucky University 1980-84. Member Cincinnati and Kentucky Bar Associations. Member Jaycees, Boy Scouts of America, Knights of Columbus, Elks, Senior Citizen Board and YMCA Board. Enjoys outdoor sports, hunting and fishing.

Office: 330 York Street, Newport 41071.

Telephone: (859) 292-6303.

LAMBERT, Debra *(Judge, Kentucky Circuit Court Twenty-eighth Judicial Circuit)* Term expires Jan 2007. Serves Family Court.

Office: 203 East Mount Vernon Street, Suite B, Somerset 42501-1412.

Telephone: (606) 677-4186.

LAMBERT, Joseph E. *(Chief Justice, Kentucky Supreme Court)* Elected Nov 1986 to term beginning Jan 5, 1987. Reelected Nov 8, 1994 and Nov 5, 2002. Current term expires Jan 2011. Chief Justice since Oct 2, 1998. Born Berea Kentucky May 23, 1948. Baptist. Educated at Georgetown College B.S. 1970 and University of Louisville School of Law J.D. 1974. Honorary LL.D. Georgetown College 1999, Eastern Kentucky University 1999 and Chase Law School of Northern Kentucky University 2002. Law Clerk to Hon. Rhodes Bratcher, U.S. District Court Western District of Kentucky 1974-75. Admitted to practice Kentucky 1974, U.S. District Courts Western 1975 and Eastern 1976 Districts of Kentucky and U.S. Supreme Court 1978. In legal practice Mount Vernon 1975-87.

Board of Directors National Association of Drug Court Professionals since 2001 and National Conference of Chief Justices since 2001. Attended Appellate Judges' Seminar Series American Bar Association and Institute of Judicial Administration New York University School of Law 1987 and 1992. Named Outstanding Judge of Kentucky 2000. Recipient Kentucky Public Advocate Award 2001 and Distinguished Alumni Award from University of Louisville School of Law. Republican. Staff member for U.S. Senator John Sherman Cooper 1970-71. Board of Regents Eastern Kentucky University 1988-92.

Office: 230 State Capitol Building, Frankfort 40601.

Telephone: (502) 564-4162.

Fax: (502) 564-1933

LANE, William *(Judge, Kentucky District Court Twenty-first Judicial District)* Elected Nov 2002. Term expires Jan 2007.

Office: Montgomery County Courthouse, One Court Street, Mount Sterling 40353.

Telephone: (606) 498-6622.

LAWSON, James *(Judge, Kentucky District Court Fortieth Judicial District)* Elected Nov 2002. Term expires Jan 2007.

Office: 215 East Cumberland Street, Albany 42602.

LEE, Joe *(Recalled Judge, United States Bankruptcy Court Eastern District of Kentucky)* Appointed Judge by U.S. Court of Appeals Sixth Circuit judges. Former Chief Judge. Appointed Recalled Judge by the Judicial Council of the Sixth Circuit.

Mailing address: P.O. Box 1111, Lexington 40588-1111.

Telephone: (859) 233-2814.

LEWIS, Thomas Richards *(Judge, Kentucky Circuit Court Eighth Judicial Circuit)* Appointed by Governor Wallace G. Wilkinson to term beginning 1991. Elected 1991 to term beginning Jan 1992. Reelected 1999, current term expires Jan 2007. Born Lexington Kentucky April 15, 1946. Methodist. Educated at Western Kentucky University A.B. 1969 and Samford University J.D. 1975. Law Clerk to Kentucky Supreme Court and Kentucky Court of Appeals 1975-76. Member Phi Alpha Delta and Pi Kappa Alpha. Admitted to practice Kentucky 1975. Began legal practice Frankfort 1975. In legal practice Bowling Green 1977. Judge, Kentucky District Court Eighth Judicial District 1984-91.

Assistant State Public Defender Frankfort Aug 1976 to Dec 1977. Assistant Commonwealth Attorney Eighth Judicial District Bowling Green Dec 1977 to Jan 1984. Instructor in Business Law Western Kentucky University 1986-89. Member Warren County, Kentucky and American Bar Associations. Named Outstanding Young Lawyer for Kentucky 1977. E-5 U.S. Army 1969-71. Democrat. Member Warren County Drug Task Force 1986-87 and Governor's Task Force Against Drugs 1986-88. Board of Directors Jaycees, Comprehensive Care, Boys Club, Spouse Abuse Center and Boys Youth Home.

Office: 404 Warren County Justice Center, 1001 Center Street, Bowling Green 42101-2193.

Telephone: (270) 746-7412.

Fax: (270) 746-7141

E-mail address: ThomasLewis@mail.aoc.state.ky.us

LIVELY, Tom *(Judge, Kentucky District Court Forty-sixth Judicial District)* Term expires Jan 2007.

Office: Grayson County Judicial Complex, 125 East White Oak Street, Leitchfield 42754.

Telephone: (270) 259-6785.

LOGUE, Jean Chenault *(Judge, Kentucky Circuit Court Twenty-fifth Judicial Circuit)* Assumed office

LOGUE, JEAN CHENAULT—*Continued*

1999. Term expires Jan 2007. Serves Family Court. Born May 29, 1962. Educated at Eastern Kentucky University B.B.A. 1984 and University of Kentucky College of Law J.D. 1988. Staff member Kentucky Law Journal 1986-88. Member Kappa Alpha Theta, Sigma Tau Pi, Omicron Delta Pi and Order of Omega. Admitted to practice Kentucky, U.S. District Court Eastern District of Kentucky and U.S. Supreme Court. In legal practice Lexington 1988-90 and Richmond 1990-99.

Assistant County Attorney Madison County 1990-93. Assistant Commonwealth's Attorney Twenty-fifth Judicial Circuit 1993-97. City Attorney Richmond 1997-99. Board of Directors Kentucky Bar Foundation 1998-99. Member Circuit Judges' Education Committee since 2001 and Status Offender Work Group Juvenile Justice Committee Kentucky Criminal Justice Council since 2001. Member Madison County (Secretary and Treasurer 1992-93, Vice President 1993-94, President 1994-95) and Kentucky (Board Member Young Lawyers Section 1991-92, Secretary Government Law Section since 1998) Bar Associations. Named Woman of the Year by Richmond Business and Professional Women's Club 1999. Recipient Outstanding Service Award from Kentucky Citizen Foster Care Review Board 2001. Board of Directors Richmond Chamber of Commerce 1990-95, Patti A. Clay Foundation, Inc. 1999-2001 and C.A.S.A. of Clark and Madison Counties, Inc. since 1999. Advisory Board Member Salvation Army Richmond 1992-95. Advisory Board Member Preschool since 1999 and Member First Presbyterian Church. Former Member Junior League of Lexington and Richmond Rotary Club. Member Society of Boonesboro, Alumni Association Eastern Kentucky University and Patti A. Clay Hospital Auxiliary.

Mailing address: P.O. Box 1415, Richmond 40476-1415.
Telephone: (859) 625-0601.

LONG, Samuel C. *(Judge, Kentucky Circuit Court Thirty-seventh Judicial Circuit)* Appointed by Governor Martha L. Collins to term beginning July 1987. Elected Nov 1987, 1991 and 1999. Current term expires Jan 2007. Born West Liberty Kentucky July 4, 1944. Christian. Educated at University of Kentucky B.A. 1966 J.D. 1969. Admitted to practice Kentucky 1969. In legal practice West Liberty 1971. Judge, Kentucky District Court Thirty-seventh Judicial District 1978-87.

Morgan County Attorney 1974-77. Member Kentucky and American Bar Associations. U.S. Army 1969-71. Member Lions Club (District Governor), Masons and Shriners.

Mailing address: P.O. Box 456, West Liberty 41472.
Telephone: (606) 743-4075.
Fax: (606) 743-2633

LOVELACE, Eddie *(Judge, Kentucky Circuit Court Fortieth Judicial Circuit)* Term expires Jan 2007.
Office: 104 Cumberland Street, Albany 42602.
Telephone: (606) 387-5986.

LOWE, Charles E. *(Judge, Kentucky Circuit Court Thirty-fifth Judicial Circuit)* Term expires Jan 2007.
Office: Hall of Justice Building, 172 Division Street, Pikeville 41501.
Telephone: (606) 433-7551.

LYNCH, Arnold *(Judge, Kentucky District Court Third Judicial District)* Elected Nov 2002. Term expires Jan 2007.
Office: 216 West Seventh Street, Hopkinsville 42240.
Telephone: (270) 889-6544.

MAGUIRE, Walter Flippin *(Judge, Kentucky District Court Twenty-eighth Judicial District)* Elected to term beginning Jan 1978. Reelected 1985, 1989, 1993, 1998 and 2002. Current term expires Jan 2007. One of Kentucky's original 113 District Court judges. Born Lexington Kentucky May 17, 1943. Methodist. Educated at Wake Forest College 1961 and University of Kentucky B.A. 1965 J.D. 1968. Member Academic and Leadership Societies, Omicron Delta Kappa and Phi Delta Phi. Admitted to practice Kentucky 1968. In legal practice Lexington 1970-72 and Somerset 1974-78.

Staff Attorney Departments of Commerce and Personnel Commonwealth of Kentucky 1968-69. Special Assistant in Criminal Justice Council of State Governments 1973-74. Assistant Attorney General Commonwealth of Kentucky 1982. Volunteer Faculty member Intensive Course in Trial Advocacy University of Kentucky College of Law 1983-90. Member State Judicial Council 1978-82, Kentucky District Court Judges Executive Committee elected Sept 1996, Pulaski County and Kentucky Bar Associations. Attended The National Judicial College 1978, "Humanities and the Law" 1979 and "Judicial Fact Finding and Decision Making" 1989 Harvard Law School and numerous state and regional judicial conferences. Fellow National Endowment for the Humanities University of Virginia College of Law 1979. Recipient Public Service Award from Pulaski County Outdoorsmen 1981. Associate Dean of Students 1969-73, Chairman Personnel Grievance Committee 1982-86 and former Associate Director Tobacco and Health Research Institute University of Kentucky. One of Kentucky's first Congressional Interns under Representative Tim Lee Carter 1965. Staff member for U.S. Senator John Sherman Cooper Summer 1967. Republican candidate for State Representative 1975. Chairman Pulaski County Republican Campaign committee 1975. Member Dean of Arts and Sciences Advisory Board University of Kentucky. Member and Co-founder Pulaski Heritage (preservation) and Kiwanis. Enjoys reading, hiking and sports activities.

Office: Courthouse, Main Street, Somerset 42501.
Telephone: (606) 677-4112.
Fax: (606) 677-4140

MAINS, William *(Judge, Kentucky Circuit Court Twenty-first Judicial Circuit)* Term expires Jan 2007.
Mailing address: P.O. Box 855, Morehead 40351.
Office: 627 East Main Street, Morehead 40351.
Telephone: (606) 784-5190.

MARICLE, R. Cletus *(Judge, Kentucky Circuit Court Forty-first Judicial Circuit)* Term expires Jan 2007.
Office: 79 Highway 80, Suite 1, Manchester 40962.
Telephone: (606) 598-5251.

MARTIN, Janice *(Judge, Kentucky District Court Thirtieth Judicial District)* Term expires Jan 2007.
Office: Hall of Justice, 600 West Jefferson, Louisville 40202.
Telephone: (502) 595-4999.

MAZE, Beth Lewis *(Judge, Kentucky Circuit Court Twenty-first Judicial Circuit)* Appointed by Governor Paul E. Patton to term beginning July 21, 2000. Elected Nov 3, 2000, current term expires Jan 2007. Born Lexington Kentucky Feb 28, 1963. Baptist. Educated at University of Kentucky B.S. with honors 1985 J.D. 1988. Admitted to practice Kentucky 1988 and U.S. District Court Eastern District of Kentucky 1988. In legal practice Mt. Sterling 1993-2000.

Assistant Attorney General Oct 17, 1988 to Sept 1, 1989. Assistant Commonwealth Attorney June 1, 1993 to July 20, 2000. Member Kentucky Academy of Trial Attorneys, The Association of Trial Lawyers of America and Kentucky Bar Association.

Mailing address: P.O. Box 1267, Mt. Sterling 40353.
Telephone: (859) 498-0488.
E-mail address: bethmaze@mail.aoc.state.ky.us

McANULTY, William E., Jr. *(Judge, Kentucky Court of Appeals)* Elected Nov 1998. Term expires Jan 2007. Born Indianapolis Indiana 1947. Educated at Indiana University and University of Louisville M.A.T. and J.D. Judge 1984-90 and 1993-98 and Chief Judge 1998, Kentucky Circuit Court Thirtieth Judicial Circuit.

Member Louisville and Kentucky Bar Associations. Named Henry V. Pennington Outstanding Judge of the Year by Kentucky Trial Attorneys Association 1997. Recipient Thomas C. Simons Distinguished Leadership Award from Leadership Louisville Foundation 1997.

Office: 1010 Judicial Center, 700 West Jefferson Street, Louisville 40202-2799.
Telephone: (502) 595-3430.

McCARTY, John M. *(Judge, Kentucky District Court Thirty-eighth Judicial District)*

Mailing address: P.O. Box 189, Hawesville 42348.
Office: 170 Main Cross Street, Hawesville 42348.
Telephone: (270) 298-3223.

McCASLIN, William *(Judge, Kentucky District Court Fifty-sixth Judicial District)* Term expires Jan 2007.

Office: Courthouse, 100 West Court Street, Princeton 42445.
Telephone: (270) 365-6656.

McCLANAHAN, Ralph E., II *(Judge, Kentucky District Court Twenty-third Judicial District)* Term expires Jan 2007. Currently serves as Chief Regional District Judge.

Office: 130 Main Street, Second Floor, Irvine 40336-1049.
Telephone: (606) 723-2000.

McDONALD, Martin *(Judge, Kentucky District Court Thirtieth Judicial District)* Term expires Jan 2007.

Office: Hall of Justice, 600 West Jefferson, Louisville 40202.
Telephone: (502) 595-4990.

McDONALD, Tom *(Judge, Kentucky Circuit Court Thirtieth Judicial Circuit)* Term expires Jan 2007. Born Louisville Kentucky Feb 10, 1955. Roman Catholic. Educated at University of Louisville B.A. cum laude 1977 J.D. 1980. Member Phi Alpha Delta. Admitted to practice Kentucky 1980, U.S. District Court Western District of Kentucky 1981 and U.S. Supreme Court 1984. In legal practice Louisville 1980-83. Former Judge, Kentucky District Court Thirtieth Judicial District, elected to term beginning Dec 14, 1983.

Assistant County Prosecutor 1980-83. Author "Alleviating the Trauma of the Abused Child in Our Courts" Louisville Lawyer Magazine 1986, "Confidentiality and the Press: A Two Edged Sword" Communications Manual for CASA Program 1987 and "Who Speaks for the Child" Children Today Magazine. Lecturer on Litigation and Business Organizations and Transactions University of Louisville since 1985. Member Jefferson County Juvenile Justice Commission, Court Appointed Special Advocate Project of Kentucky (Chairman Board of Directors), National Court Appointed Special Advocate Association (President 1988-90) National Council of Juvenile and Family Court Judges, Louisville, Kentucky and American Bar Associations. Attended National College of Juvenile Justice 1985. Faculty member National College of Juvenile and Family Law since 1986.

Presentations and seminars conducted: "How to Testify and Win in Court" Jefferson County Department for Human Services, Louisville Kentucky Feb 1986; "Agency Court Relations" Rockefeller College of Public Affairs and Policy and New York State Department of Social Services, Albany New York March 20, 1986; "Challenges of Rural vs Urban Judicial Programs" National Court Appointed Special Advocate Association and National Council of Juvenile and Family Court Judges, Indianapolis Indiana May 5, 1986; "Kids on the Street: A View from the Bench on Status Offenders" Ohio Association of Juvenile and Family Court Judges, Columbus Ohio June 18, 1986; "A View from the Bench: The Judicial Role in Community Coordination" The Kentucky Juvenile Justice Commission, Louisville Kentucky June 24, 1986; "A View from the Bench: The Court Appointed Special Advocate" Office of Juvenile Justice Delinquency Prevention U.S. Department of Justice, Boston Massachusetts July 15, 1986; "The Future of Child Protective Services" National Association of Public Child Welfare Administrators, Washington D.C. Sept 16, 1986; "A View from the Bench: The Court Appointed Special Advocate" National Court Appointed Special Advocate Association, Chicago Illinois Sept 20, 1986; "A View from the Bench: The Court Appointed Special Advocate" National College of Juvenile and Family Law, Reno Nevada Oct 15, 1986; "A View from the Bench: The Court Appointed Special Advocate" National Council of Juvenile and Family Court Judges, Reno Nevada June 17, 1987; "Permanency Planning for Children—A View from the Bench: Federal Adoption Assistance and Child Welfare Act of 1980" Blue Ridge Institute and National Council of Juvenile and Family Court Judges, Black Mountain North Carolina Aug 4, 1987 and South Carolina Department of Social Services, Columbia South Carolina Aug 21, 1987; "A View from the Bench: Court Appointed Special Advocates" National Council of Juvenile and Family Court Judges, Reno Nevada Oct 29, 1987; "Volunteers in the Courts" National Council of Juvenile and Family Court Judges and the National District Attorneys Association, Reno Nevada March 13, 1989; and "Ensuring High Quality Representation for Children: What Role Can Judges Play?" April 7, 1990 and "The Correlation Between Domestic Violence, Child Abuse and Juvenile Delinquency" April 8, 1990 Harvard Law School. Testified before U.S. Senate Committee on the Judiciary on "Innovative Responses to Child Abuse and Judicial Procedures" May 16, 1989. Recipient Continuing Judicial Education Recognition Award. Listed in *Who's Who in American Law.* Board of Directors Jefferson County Child Abuse Authority, Jefferson County Spouse Abuse Center, Project Find and KIPDA Council

MCDONALD, TOM—*Continued*
on Aging. Member Kentucky Task Force on Permanency Planning, Kentucky Task Force on Dispositional Alternatives for Foster Children and National Eagle Scouts Association. Enjoys sailing and tennis.

Office: Jefferson County Judicial Center, 700 West Jefferson Street, Louisville 40202.

Telephone: (502) 595-4327.

McDONALD-BURKMAN, Judith *(Judge, Kentucky Circuit Court Thirtieth Judicial Circuit)* Appointed by Governor Paul E. Patton to term beginning Aug 26, 1998. Elected Nov 2, 1998 and Nov 4, 1999. Current term expires Jan 2007. Born Louisville Kentucky Dec 14, 1958. Catholic. Educated at University of Louisville B.S. with honors 1981 M.A.T. 1983 J.D. with honors 1987. Recipient Brandeis Scholar Award 1987. Admitted to practice Kentucky 1987 and U.S. District Court Western District of Kentucky 1987. In legal practice Louisville 1987 to Aug 1998.

Instructor 1981-93 and 1992 and Adjunct Assistant Professor 1992-95 University of Louisville. Co-chair Jefferson County Family Court Advisory Committee 1996-98. Member Jefferson County Courts Facility Advisory Council 1996-99. Former Member Kentucky Bar Association for Women, Kentucky Academy of Trial Attorneys and Women Lawyers Association of Jefferson County. Member Kentucky Association of Circuit Judges, American Judges Association, Louisville (Continuing Legal Education Program Committee 1992-94, Committee on Continuing Legal Education since 2000), Kentucky (Joint Study for Judicial Concerns since 1997) and American (Judicial Division) Bar Associations. Attended The National Judicial College Reno Nevada April 1999, Kentucky Circuit Judges College Sept 1999, Jan 2000, Oct 2001 and Sept 2002 and Kentucky Bar Association Nov 1999. Lecturer CLE Programs Kentucky Academy of Trial Attorneys, Louisville Bar Association and Kentucky Bar Association. Recipient Richard Revell Family Law Practitioner of the Year Award from Louisville Bar Association 1996. Teacher of Health Sciences Assumption High School 1982-83. Board of Trustees Ursuline Campus Schools, Inc. 1992-98. Mentor Family Law Team Louisville Pro Bono Consortium 1996-98. Former Member Cystic Fibrosis Annual Walk-A-Thon Committee. Member Our Lady of Lourdes Athletic Committee since 1999 and St. Joseph Child Development Center Parent Advisory Committee since 1999.

Office: Jefferson County Judicial Center, 700 West Jefferson, Louisville 40202.

Telephone: (502) 595-4356.

Fax: (502) 595-3496

E-mail address: judymb@mail.aoc.state.ky.us

McGINNIS, Robert W. *(Judge, Kentucky Circuit Court Eighteenth Judicial Circuit)* Appointed by Governor Wallace G. Wilkinson to term beginning Oct 30, 1989. Elected Nov 1989, Nov 1991 and 1999. Current term expires Jan 2007. Currently serves as Vice Chief Regional Circuit Judge. Born Danville Kentucky June 15, 1953. Christian. Educated at Eastern Kentucky University B.B.A. 1975 and Chase Law School of Northern Kentucky University J.D. 1978. Admitted to practice Kentucky 1978. In legal practice Butler 1978-84. Judge, Kentucky District Court Eighteenth Judicial District 1984-89.

Member Kentucky Circuit Judges Association and Kentucky Bar Association. E-5 Kentucky National Guard 1972-78. Democrat. Member Butler Lions Club. Enjoys athletics, reading and history.

Office: 115 Justice Center, 115 Court Street, Cynthiana 41031.

Telephone: (859) 234-3431.

McKINLEY, Joseph H., Jr. *(Judge, United States District Court Western District of Kentucky)* Appointed for life by President Bill Clinton to term beginning 1995. Born Owensboro Kentucky June 9, 1954. Educated at University of Kentucky B.S. 1976 and University of Louisville School of Law J.D. 1979. In legal practice Owensboro 1979-91. Judge, Kentucky Circuit Court Sixth Judicial Circuit 1992-95.

Commissioner Kentucky Oil and Gas Commission 1982-90. Assistant County Attorney Daviess County 1985-87. Hearing Officer Natural Resources and Environmental Protection Cabinet 1990-91.

Office: 206 Federal Building, 423 Frederica Street, Owensboro 42301.

Telephone: (270) 689-4430.

McNEILL, John Worthy *(Judge, Kentucky Circuit Court Nineteenth Judicial Circuit)* Term expires Jan 2007.

Office: 100 West Third Street, Maysville 41056.

Telephone: (606) 564-9736.

MELCHER, David *(Judge, Kentucky Circuit Court Eighteenth Judicial Circuit)* Assumed office Jan 6, 2003. Term expires Jan 2007. Serves Family Court. Former Judge, Kentucky District Court Eighteenth Judicial District.

Office: 2 Harrison County Justice Center, 115 Court Street, Cynthiana 41031.

Telephone: (859) 234-1918.

MERSHON, Stephen K. *(Judge, Kentucky Circuit Court Thirtieth Judicial Circuit)* Term expires Jan 2007. Former Judge, Kentucky District Court Thirtieth Judicial District.

Office: 802 Judicial Center, 700 West Jefferson, Louisville 40202.

Telephone: (502) 595-4103.

Fax: (502) 595-0057

MESSER, Roderick *(Judge, Kentucky Circuit Court Twenty-seventh Judicial Circuit)* Elected to term beginning Jan 1992. Reelected 1999, current term expires Jan 2007. Born Barbourville Kentucky May 3, 1952. Protestant. Educated at University of Kentucky B.A. 1973 J.D. 1976. Judge, Kentucky District Court Twenty-seventh Judicial District 1984-92.

Mailing address: P.O. Box 5189, London 40745-5189.

Office: Courthouse, London 40741.

Telephone: (606) 878-8111.

MILLER, Robert Allen *(Judge, Kentucky Circuit Court Forty-sixth Judicial Circuit)* Appointed by Governor Paul Patton to term beginning Jan 15, 1999. Elected Nov 1999, current term expires Jan 2007. Educated at Centre College of Kentucky B.A. and University of Kentucky J.D. Admitted to practice Kentucky 1979. In legal practice Brandenburg 1979-99.

Attorney Meade County 1986-99. Member Kentucky Bar Association. Attended Advanced Course in Evidence

MILLER, ROBERT ALLEN—*Continued*
The National Judicial College. Member Brandenburg Rotary Club.
Mailing address: P.O. Box 245, Brandenburg 40108.
Telephone: (270) 422-7800.
E-mail address: RobertMiller@mail.aoc.state.ky.us

MILLER, Wm. Larry *(Judge, Kentucky Circuit Court Thirty-ninth Judicial Circuit)* Term expires Jan 2007.
Mailing address: P.O. Box 430, Campton 41301.
Office: Courthouse, Campton 41301.
Telephone: (606) 668-7590.

MILLS, John Knox *(Judge, Kentucky District Court Twenty-seventh Judicial District)* Term expires Jan 2007. Currently serves as Chief Regional District Judge.
Mailing address: P.O. Box 314, Barbourville 40906.
Telephone: (606) 864-7241.

MINTON, John D., Jr. *(Judge, Kentucky Circuit Court Eighth Judicial Circuit)* Term expires Jan 2007. Former Chief Regional Circuit Judge.
Office: 401 Warren County Justice Center, 1001 Center Street, Bowling Green 42101-2193.
Telephone: (270) 746-7408.

MITCHELL, William *(Judge, Kentucky Circuit Court Fifth Judicial Circuit)* Assumed office Jan 6, 2003. Term expires Jan 2007. Serves Family Court. Former Judge, Kentucky District Court Fifth Judicial District.
Office: 60 U.S. Highway 41-A South, Dixon 42409.
Telephone: (270) 639-5094.

MONARCH, Sam H. *(Judge, Kentucky Circuit Court Forty-sixth Judicial Circuit)* Term expires Jan 2007. Born March 9, 1945. Educated at Murray State University B.S. 1968 M.S. 1969 and University of Louisville J.D. 1976. Admitted to practice Kentucky 1977 and U.S. Supreme Court. In legal practice Hardinsburg 1980-92.
Commonwealth Attorney 1987 to Dec 1991.
Mailing address: P.O. Box 147, Hardinsburg 40143.
Telephone: (270) 756-6278.
Fax: (270) 756-1280

MONTANO, Kathleen Voor *(Judge, Kentucky Circuit Court Thirtieth Judicial Circuit)* Assumed office Jan 6, 2003. Term expires Jan 2007. Serves Family Court. Judge, Kentucky District Court Thirtieth Judicial District July 1998 to Jan 5, 2003.
Office: 600A Judicial Center, 700 West Jefferson, Louisville Kentucky 40202.
Telephone: (502) 595-4699.
Fax: (502) 595-3324

MOORE, Charles T. *(Judge, Kentucky District Court Fifty-fourth Judicial District)* Appointed by Governor Wallace G. Wilkinson to term beginning Jan 1990. Elected to subsequent terms. Current term expires Jan 2007. Born Covington Kentucky July 28, 1952. Educated at Northern Kentucky University B.S. in Accounting 1975, Xavier University M.A. 1977 and Chase Law School of Northern Kentucky University J.D. 1980. Admitted to practice Kentucky 1980.
Domestic Relations Commissioner 1988-90. Member American Judges Association and Northern Kentucky and Kentucky Bar Associations. Lecturer on Domestic Violence Kentucky Bar Association 1992. Attended General Jurisdiction Advanced Studies Course The National Judicial College. Member Boone County Ethics Commission and Boone County Businessmen's Association.
Mailing address: P.O. Box 886, Burlington 41005.
Office: Washington Square, Burlington 41005.
Telephone: (859) 334-2230.

MORGAN, J. Robert *(Judge, Kentucky Circuit Court Thirty-sixth Judicial Circuit)* Term expires Jan 2007. Former Judge, Kentucky District Court Thirty-sixth Judicial District.
Mailing address: P.O. Box 867, Hindman 41822.
Office: Main Street, Hindman 41822.
Telephone: (606) 785-3842, 785-9273.

MORGAN, Philip R. *(Judge, Kentucky District Court Fortieth Judicial District)*
Mailing address: P.O. Box 55, Monticello 42633.
Telephone: (606) 348-7799.

MORRIS, Geoffrey P. *(Judge, Kentucky Circuit Court Thirtieth Judicial Circuit)* Elected to term beginning Jan 6, 1992. Reelected 1999, current term expires Jan 2007. Former Chief Regional Circuit Judge. Educated at University of Louisville B.A. 1965 J.D. 1970. Member Phi Alpha Delta. Admitted to practice Kentucky 1971, U.S. District Court Western District of Kentucky and U.S. Court of Appeals Sixth Circuit. In legal practice Louisville 1971-73 and 1982-91.
Chief Trial Attorney Public Defender's Office 1973-76. Senior Prosecutory Attorney Commonwealth's Attorney Office 1976-82. Member Louisville Bar Association (President Academy of Justice 1975-76, Chairman Criminal Practice 1978-79, Vice President and President 1979-81). Instructor in Closing Arguments Kentucky Judicial College 1982. Recipient Pro Bono Service Award from Louisville Bar Association 1990. Private First Class USMCR 1963-65. Peace Corps Volunteer 1965-67. Member Leadership Louisville 1980-81.
Office: Judicial Center, 700 West Jefferson Street, Louisville 40202.
Telephone: (502) 595-4400.

MOYER, James D. *(Magistrate Judge, United States District Court Western District of Kentucky)* Appointed by U.S. District Court judges.
Office: 208 U.S. Courthouse, 601 West Broadway, Louisville 40202.
Telephone: (502) 625-3930.

MULLINS, Darrel H. *(Judge, Kentucky District Court Thirty-fifth Judicial District)* Appointed by Governor Paul E. Patton to term beginning Sept 6, 1996. Elected Nov 5, 1996, Nov 1998 and 2002. Current term expires Jan 2007. Born Pikeville Kentucky Sept 20, 1950. Methodist. Educated at Pikeville College B.S. 1978, Eastern Kentucky University M.A. 1979 and Chase Law School of Northern Kentucky University J.D. 1989. Admitted to practice Kentucky 1989. In legal practice Pikeville 1989-90.
Assistant Commonwealth's Attorney Thirty-fifth Judicial District 1990-96. Member Kentucky Bar Association.
Office: 311 Hall of Justice, 172 Division Street, Pikeville 41501.
Telephone: (606) 433-7562.

MUNCY, Renee Helene *(Judge, Kentucky District Court Forty-first Judicial District)* Elected Nov 1989 to term beginning Jan 1 1990. Reelected 1993, 1998 and 2002. Current term expires Jan 2007. Born Hazard Ken-

MUNCY, RENEE HELENE—*Continued*

tucky Oct 5, 1959. Southern Baptist. Educated at University of Kentucky B.A. 1981 and Northern Kentucky University J.D. 1985. Member Order of the Curia. Admitted to practice Kentucky 1985 and U.S. District Court Eastern District of Kentucky 1986. In legal practice Hyden 1985-86 and Hazard 1986-89.

Member Kentucky District Judges Association, Inc. and Kentucky Bar Association. Enjoys horseback riding.

Mailing address: P.O. Box 1840, Hyden 41749.
Office: 2230 Main Street, Room 101, Hyden 41749.
Telephone: (606) 672-3350.

MYERS, Louis Keith *(Judge, Kentucky District Court Fifty-ninth Judicial District)* Term expires Jan 2007.

Mailing address: P.O. Box 485, Wickliffe 42087.
Telephone: (270) 335-5138.

NANCE, William Mitchell *(Judge, Kentucky Circuit Court Forty-third Judicial Circuit)* Assumed office Jan 6, 2003. Term expires Jan 2007. Serves Family Court. Born Glasgow Kentucky Feb 24, 1951. Southern Baptist. Educated at Harvard University A.B. cum laude 1973 and University of Louisville School of Law J.D. 1977. Admitted to practice Kentucky 1977 and U.S. District Court Western District of Kentucky 1978. In legal practice Glasgow 1977-2000. Judge, Kentucky District Court Forty-third Judicial District 2000 to Jan 5, 2003.

Member American Judges Association, American Judicature Society, Barren County, Kentucky and American Bar Associations. Member Sons of the American Revolution and Masons.

Office: 202 Courthouse Square, Glasgow 42141.
Telephone: (270) 651-9923.
Fax: (270) 651-5524

NICHOLLS, Lewis Dunn *(Judge, Kentucky Circuit Court Twentieth Judicial Circuit)* Term expires Jan 2007. Born Lexington Kentucky May 20, 1950. Methodist. Educated at Morehead University B.S. 1972 M.S. 1974 and Chase Law School of Northern Kentucky University J.D. 1980. Admitted to practice Kentucky 1981. Began legal practice Greenup 1981. Former Judge, Kentucky District Court Twentieth Judicial District, appointed by Governor Martha Layne Collins to term beginning Feb 13, 1984.

Member Kentucky Bar Association. Captain U.S. Army 1974-77. Enjoys reading and swimming.

Office: Courthouse Annex, 101 Harrison Street, Greenup 41144.
Telephone: (606) 473-7165.

NOBLE, Mary C. *(Judge, Kentucky Circuit Court Twenty-second Judicial Circuit)* Term expires Jan 2007. Former Chief Regional Circuit Judge.

Office: 566 Fayette County Courthouse, 120 North Limestone, Lexington 40507.
Telephone: (859) 246-2212.

OLIVER, William *(Judge, Kentucky District Court Thirteenth Judicial District)* Term expires Jan 2007.

Office: 305 County Court Complex, Third Floor, 107 North Main Street, Nicholasville 40356.
Telephone: (859) 885-5615.
Fax: (859) 885-1715

O'REILLY, Joseph W. *(Judge, Kentucky Circuit Court Thirtieth Judicial Circuit)* Assumed office Jan 6, 2003. Term expires Jan 2007. Serves Family Court. Born Oak Park Illinois Nov 30, 1949. Roman Catholic. Educated at University of Notre Dame A.B. 1971 J.D. 1974. Admitted to practice Kentucky 1974, U.S. District Courts Western 1975 and Eastern 1989 Districts of Kentucky, U.S. Court of Appeals Sixth Circuit 1982, U.S. Supreme Court 1987 and North Carolina 1995. Judge, Kentucky District Court Thirtieth Judicial District Nov 2000 to Jan 5, 2003, appointed by Governor Paul E. Patton.

Associate General Counsel Blue Cross and Blue Shield of Kentucky Sept 1989 to May 1995. General Counsel Kentucky Public Protection and Regulation Cabinet Sept 1997 to Nov 2000. Former Assistant County Attorney Jefferson County.

Office: Judicial Center, 700 West Jefferson Street, Louisville 40202-4730.
Telephone: (502) 595-4993.
Fax: (502) 595-3495

OVERSTREET, Rebecca M. *(Judge, Kentucky Circuit Court Twenty-second Judicial Circuit)* Elected to term beginning Nov 28, 1988. Reelected 1991 and 1999. Current term expires Jan 2007. Born Lexington Kentucky Feb 7, 1952. Educated at Eastern Kentucky University A.A. 1973 B.S. with distinction 1974 and University of Kentucky College of Law J.D. 1977. Staff member Kentucky Law Journal. Member Phi Delta Phi. Admitted to practice Kentucky 1977 and Florida 1978. Judge, Kentucky District Court Twenty-second Judicial District 1982-88.

Assistant Commonwealth Attorney Lexington 1977-82. Author "The Juror Becomes Expert" 65 Kentucky L. Jour. 1976-77 and "Criminal Law Survey" Kentucky L. Jour. 1980. Co-author "Before and After the Quinlan Case" 65 Kentucky L. Jour. 823, 1976-77. Adjunct Professor University of Kentucky College of Law 1979 and Eastern Kentucky University 1980. Member The Florida Bar, Fayette County (Treasurer 1979) and Kentucky Bar Associations. Named to Hall of Distinguished Alumni Eastern Kentucky University. Board of Directors McDowell Cancer Network, Inc. 1982-88 and Diabetes Center of Excellence 1983-88 (Advisory Board). Member Institutional Review Board Humana Hospital 1984-88 and Spouse Abuse Committee YWCA 1987-90. Former Member Drug Free Advisory Board Fayette County Schools. Member Southland Christian Church.

Office: 503 Fayette County Courthouse, 120 North Limestone, Lexington 40507.
Telephone: (859) 246-2218.
Fax: (859) 246-2139

OVERSTREET, Robert B. *(Judge, Kentucky Circuit Court Fourteenth Judicial Circuit)* Term expires Jan 2007. Born Danville Kentucky July 15, 1947. Presbyterian. Educated at University of Kentucky B.S. in Accounting 1969 J.D. 1973. Admitted to practice Kentucky 1973. Began legal practice Versailles 1973. Former Judge, Kentucky District Court Fourteenth Judicial District, appointed by Governor Martha Layne Collins to term beginning Jan 11, 1984.

Member Woodford County, Kentucky and American Bar Associations.

Office: 103 South Main, Room 304, Versailles 40383.
Telephone: (859) 873-3109.

PAISLEY, Lewis G. *(Judge, Kentucky Court of Appeals)* Term expires Jan 2007. Former Judge, Kentucky District Court Twenty-second Judicial District. Former

PAISLEY, LEWIS G.—*Continued*
Judge, Kentucky Circuit Court Twenty-second Judicial Circuit.

Office: 177 North Upper, Suite 101, Lexington 40507-1100.

Telephone: (859) 246-2053.

PATTERSON, Peggy E. *(Magistrate Judge, United States District Court Eastern District of Kentucky)* Appointed by U.S. District Court judges to term beginning Aug 24, 1990. Reappointed Aug 24, 1998, current term expires Aug 23, 2006. Educated at Centre College of Kentucky B.A. 1972, Oxford University, England 1972-73 and University of Kentucky College of Law J.D. 1976. Law Clerk to Hon. Howard David Hermansdorfer, U.S. District Court Eastern District of Kentucky 1976-78. In legal practice 1978-90.

Member American Judicature Society, Boyd County, Kentucky, Federal (Kentucky Chapter) and American Bar Associations. Board of Trustees Centre College of Kentucky since 1999.

Office: 210 Federal Building, 1405 Greenup Avenue, Ashland 41101.

Telephone: (606) 329-2952.

PATTON, Phillip *(Judge, Kentucky Circuit Court Forty-third Judicial Circuit)* Term expires Jan 2007.

Office: 300 Courthouse Square, Glasgow 42141.

Telephone: (270) 651-2744.

PAXTON, Julie *(Judge, Kentucky Circuit Court Thirty-first Judicial Circuit)* Appointed by Governor Paul E. Patton June 16, 1999 to term beginning July 19, 1999. Elected Nov 2, 1999, current term expires Jan 2007. Serves Family Court. Born Lexington Kentucky Feb 27, 1958. Methodist. Educated at University of Kentucky B.A. 1980 and Chase Law School of Northern Kentucky University J.D. 1986. Law Clerk to Hon. John D. Miller, Kentucky Court of Appeals 1986-87. Admitted to practice Kentucky 1986. In legal practice Prestonburg since 1987.

Assistant Attorney Floyd County 1987-89. Member Floyd County and Kentucky Bar Associations. Sunday School Teacher First United Methodist Church since 1988. Board of Directors Jenny Wiley Theatre since 1988. Member since 1992 and President Chapter G 1998-2000 PEO.

Office: Floyd County Justice Center, 127 South Lake Drive, Prestonsburg 41653.

Telephone: (606) 886-9901.

Fax: (606) 886-9995

PAYNE, David C. *(Judge, Kentucky District Court Sixth Judicial District)* Appointed by Governor Paul E. Patton to term beginning June 22, 1998. Elected Nov 1998 and Nov 2002. Current term expires Jan 2007. Born Owensboro Kentucky Feb 1, 1955. Catholic. Educated at Western Kentucky University B.S. 1977 and University of Louisville J.D. 1980. Admitted to practice Kentucky 1980, Texas 1982 and U.S. Supreme Court 1991. In legal practice Austin Texas 1990-95 and Owensboro Kentucky 1995-98.

Assistant Attorney General Texas 1983-90. Member Kentucky District Judges Association, Inc., State Bar of Texas, Daviess County and Kentucky Bar Associations. Political affiliation: Non-partisan.

Office: Daviess County Judicial Center, 100 East Second Street, Owensboro 42303.

Telephone: (270) 687-7214.

Fax: (270) 687-7210

PAYNE, Gary D. *(Judge, Kentucky Circuit Court Twenty-second Judicial Circuit)* Term expires Jan 2007. Currently serves as Chief Regional Judge. Serves Family Court. Born Paducah Kentucky. Catholic. Educated at Pepperdine University B.A. 1976 and University of Kentucky J.D. 1978. Admitted to practice Kentucky 1979 and U.S. District Courts Eastern and Western Districts of Kentucky. In legal practice Lexington 1981-86. Former Judge, Kentucky District Court Twenty-second Judicial District, appointed by Governor Wallace G. Wilkinson to term beginning Nov 1988.

Instructor in Business Law College of Business and Economics University of Kentucky since 1981. Member Fayette and Kentucky Bar Associations. E-6 USMC 1970-76. Colonel Kentucky National Guard JAG.

Office: 553 Fayette County Courthouse, 120 North Limestone, Lexington 40507.

Telephone: (859) 246-2214.

Fax: (859) 246-2139

PECKLER, Darren W. *(Judge, Kentucky Circuit Court Fiftieth Judicial Circuit)* Term expires Jan 2007. Educated at Southern Illinois University B.A. 1969 and University of Kentucky J.D. 1972. Admitted to practice Kentucky 1972. Began legal practice Danville 1972. Judge, Danville Police Court 1975-77. Former Judge and Former Chief Regional District Judge, Kentucky District Court Fiftieth Judicial District, elected to term beginning Jan 2, 1978.

Office: Boyle County Courthouse, Second Floor, 321 West Main, Danville 40422.

Telephone: (859) 239-7009.

PETRIE, Bruce *(Judge, Kentucky Circuit Court Fiftieth Judicial Circuit)* Assumed office Jan 6, 2003. Term expires Jan 2007. Serves Family Court. Former Judge, Kentucky District Court Fiftieth Judicial District.

Office: Boyle County Courthouse, Third Floor, 321 Main Street, Danville 40422.

Telephone: (859) 239-7291.

PHELPS, Mary Jane *(Judge, Kentucky District Court Fourteenth Judicial District)* Term expires Jan 2007. Currently serves as Vice Chief Regional District Judge.

Office: Courthouse Annex, 103 Main Street, Versailles 40383.

Telephone: (859) 879-9871.

PHILLIPS, Connie *(Judge, Kentucky District Court Eleventh Judicial District)* Term expires Jan 2007.

Mailing address: P.O. Box 4189, Campbellsville 42719.

Telephone: (270) 465-8424.

POPOVICH, Gregory *(Judge, Kentucky District Court Seventeenth Judicial District)* Term expires Jan 2007.

Office: 600 Columbia Street, Newport 41071.

Telephone: (859) 292-6322.

POTTER, Brent J. *(Judge, Kentucky District Court Eighth Judicial District)* Appointed by Governor Paul E.

POTTER, BRENT J.—*Continued*

Patton to term beginning 2000. Currently serves as Vice Chief Regional District Judge.
Office: 202 Warren County Justice Center, 1001 Center Street, Bowling Green 42101-2191.
Telephone: (270) 746-7060.

POTTER, Sam C., Jr. *(Judge, Kentucky District Court Eighth Judicial District)* Elected Nov 5, 1996 and Nov 2002. Current term expires Jan 2007. Born Bowling Green Kentucky Feb 23, 1959. Educated at University of Kentucky B.S. 1981 and Salmon P. Chase College of Law J.D. 1984. Admitted to practice Kentucky 1984. In legal practice Bowling Green 1984-96.
Attended Special Court Jurisdiction Advances program March 9-21, 1997.
Mailing address: P.O. Box 1504, Bowling Green 42102-1504.
Office: 203 Warren County Justice Center, 1001 Center Street, Bowling Green 42101-2191.
Telephone: (270) 746-7028.
Fax: (270) 746-7116

PRATHER, Claude R. *(Judge, Kentucky District Court Thirtieth Judicial District)* Elected Nov 2002. Term expires Jan 2007.
Office: Hall of Justice, 600 West Jefferson, Louisville 40202.
Telephone: (502) 595-4610.

PROBUS, William *(Judge, Kentucky District Court Eighteenth Judicial District)* Term expires Jan 2007.
Office: 2 Harrison County Justice Center, 115 Court Street, Cynthiana 41031.
Telephone: (859) 234-1918.

PROFITT, Kenny *(Judge, Kentucky District Court Thirty-ninth Judicial District)* Term expires Jan 2007.
Mailing address: P.O. Box 1000, Stanton 40380.
Office: Court Street, Stanton 40380.
Telephone: (606) 663-4123.

PURCELL, James *(Judge, Kentucky District Court Fifteenth Judicial District)* Elected Nov 2002. Term expires Jan 2007.
Office: 101 North Main Street, Williamstown 41097.
Telephone: (859) 824-0189.

RAIKES, Larry D. *(Judge, Kentucky Circuit Court Tenth Judicial Circuit)* Appointed by Governor John Y. Brown, Jr. to term beginning March 26, 1983. Elected 1983, 1991 and 1999. Current term expires Jan 2007. Born Marion County Kentucky Aug 1, 1939. Baptist. Educated at University of Kentucky B.A. 1960 LL.B. 1962. Member Sigma Nu. Admitted to practice Kentucky 1962. Began legal practice Hodgenville 1962.
Attorney Larue County 1970-78. Member Kentucky Association of Circuit Judges, Kentucky and American Bar Associations. Democrat. Enjoys sports, reading and painting.
Office: 200 Court Square, Bardstown 40004.
Telephone: (502) 348-7313.
Fax: (502) 348-2702

RANSDELL, Maria *(Judge, Kentucky District Court Twenty-second Judicial District)* Term expires Jan 2007.
Office: 150 North Limestone, Room 531, Lexington 40507-1151.
Telephone: (859) 246-2247.

REAMS, Gerald Brock *(Judge, Kentucky District Court Thirty-second Judicial District)*
Office: Courthouse Annex, 2800 Louisa Street, Catlettsburg 41129.
Telephone: (606) 739-5525.

REED, Clyde Derek *(Judge, Kentucky District Court Tenth Judicial District)*
Office: Larue County Courthouse, 209 West High Street, Hodgenville 42748.
Telephone: (270) 358-9501.

REEVES, Danny C. *(Judge, United States District Court Eastern District of Kentucky)* Appointed for life by President George W. Bush to term beginning Dec 31, 2001. Born Corbin Kentucky 1957. Educated at Eastern Kentucky University B.A. 1978 and Chase Law School of Northern Kentucky University J.D. 1981. Law Clerk to Hon. Eugene E. Siler, Jr., U.S. District Courts Eastern and Western Districts of Kentucky 1981-83. In legal practice 1983-2001.
Office: 300 South Main Street, Suite 444, London 40741.
Telephone: (606) 877-7960.

RHORER, O. Reed *(Judge, Kentucky Circuit Court Forty-eighth Judicial Circuit)* Term expires Jan 2007. Serves Family Court. Born Frankfort Kentucky. Southern Baptist. Educated at Vanderbilt University B.A. 1975 and University of Kentucky College of Law J.D. 1978. Admitted to practice Kentucky 1978 and U.S. Court of Appeals Sixth Circuit. In legal practice Lexington 1978-86. Former Judge, Kentucky District Court Forty-eighth Judicial District, appointed by Governor Wallace G. Wilkinson to term beginning Jan 28, 1991.
Staff Attorney Federal Land Bank Louisville 1986-88. Assistant to Revenue Secretary Commonwealth of Kentucky 1988-91. Member Kentucky Bar Association.
Office: 321 West Main Street, Frankfort 40601-1803.
Telephone: (502) 564-2278.

ROPP, Barlow *(Judge, Kentucky District Court Forty-third Judicial District)* Term expires Jan 2007. Currently serves as Vice Chief Regional District Judge.
Mailing address: P.O. Box 1359, Glasgow 42142-1359.
Telephone: (270) 651-9839.

ROSEN, Marc I. *(Judge, Kentucky Circuit Court Thirty-second Judicial Circuit)* Term expires Jan 2007. Former Judge, Kentucky District Court Thirty-second Judicial District.
Mailing address: P.O. Box 417, Catlettsburg 41129.
Office: 2800 Louisa Street, Catlettsburg 41129.
Telephone: (606) 739-5844.

ROSENBLUM, Paul Weil *(Judge, Kentucky Circuit Court Twelfth Judicial Circuit)* Term expires Jan 2007. Serves Family Court. Born Louisville Kentucky Dec 20, 1949. Jewish. Educated at Boston University B.A. in Psychology 1972 and University of Louisville J.D. 1975. Member Beta Theta Pi. Admitted to practice Kentucky 1975. In legal practice La Grange 1975-85. Former Judge, Kentucky District Court Twelfth Judicial District, appointed by Governor Martha Layne Collins to term beginning Jan 18, 1985.
Assistant Attorney Oldham County 1978-85. Member Oldham County (Past President), Kentucky and American Bar Associations. Democrat. Board of Directors Legal Aid and Head Start. Member Kentucky Humane So-

ROSENBLUM, PAUL WEIL—*Continued*

ciety, Big Brothers-Big Sisters Task Force for Oldham County, Oldham County Juvenile Justice Task Force, Henry County Spouse Abuse Task Force, Oldham County Spouse Abuse Task Force and Oldham County Chamber of Commerce. Enjoys reading, photography, travel and gourmet cooking.

Office: Oldham County Courthouse, 100 West Main Street, La Grange 40031-1116.

Telephone: (502) 222-1692.

RUSSELL, Thomas B. *(Judge, United States District Court Western District of Kentucky)* Appointed for life by President Bill Clinton. Born Louisville Kentucky 1945. Educated at Western Kentucky University B.A. 1967 and University of Kentucky J.D. 1970. Managing Editor Kentucky Law Journal 1969-70. Member Phi Delta Phi and Order of the Coif. Admitted to practice Kentucky 1970.

Director Kentucky Bar Foundation. Fellow American Bar Foundation and American College of Trial Lawyers. Member McCracken County (President 1989-90), Kentucky (Chair Insurance and Negligence Section 1982-83, Insurance Committee 1985-86 and Alternative Dispute Resolution Committee 1988-89, Member Board of Governors 1984-93, President 1991-92) and American (Chair Automobile Law Committee 1983-84 and Public Relations Committee 1987-89 Section of Tort and Insurance Practice) Bar Associations.

Office: 307 Federal Building, 501 Broadway Street, Paducah 42001.

Telephone: (270) 415-6430.

RUTTLE, Ann *(Judge, Kentucky District Court Sixteenth Judicial District)* Term expires Jan 2007.

Office: Kenton County Justice Center, Fourth Floor, 230 Madison, Covington 41011.

Telephone: (859) 292-6576.

RYAN, Stephen P. *(Judge, Kentucky Circuit Court Thirtieth Judicial Circuit)* Term expires Jan 2007. Born Louisville Kentucky June 3, 1952. Catholic. Educated at University of Louisville B.S. J.D. Admitted to practice Kentucky 1981 and U.S. District Courts Eastern and Western Districts of Kentucky. Magistrate, Jefferson County 1985-87. Former Judge, Kentucky District Court Thirtieth Judicial District, elected to term beginning Nov 13, 1987.

Member Kentucky Academy of Trial Attorneys, The Association of Trial Lawyers of America, Louisville and Kentucky Bar Associations. U.S. Army 1972-74. Democrat. Enjoys barefoot water skiing and golf.

Office: Judicial Center, 700 West Jefferson Street, Louisville 40202.

Telephone: (502) 595-4799.

RYAN, William P., Jr. *(Judge, Kentucky District Court Thirtieth Judicial District)* Appointed by Governor Wallace G. Wilkinson to term beginning April 20, 1990. Elected Nov 1990, 1993, 1998 and 2002. Current term expires Jan 2007. Currently serves as Chief Regional District Judge. Born Louisville Kentucky. Roman Catholic. Educated at University of Louisville 1981 J.D. 1986. Admitted to practice Kentucky 1986, U.S. District Court District of Kentucky 1987 and U.S. Supreme Court 1992. In legal practice Louisville 1986-90.

Member American Judicature Society.

Office: Hall of Justice, 600 West Jefferson Street, Louisville 40202.

Telephone: (502) 595-4997.

SANDERSON, Cynthia E. *(Judge, Kentucky Circuit Court Second Judicial Circuit)* Assumed office Jan 6, 2003. Term expires Jan 2007. Serves Family Court. Born Mayfield Kentucky Jan 19, 1957. Catholic. Educated at University of Kentucky B.A. 1977 and Chase Law School of Northern Kentucky University J.D. 1981. Admitted to practice Kentucky 1981, U.S. District Court Western District of Kentucky 1983 and U.S. Court of Appeals Sixth Circuit 1987. Former Judge, Kentucky District Court Second Judicial District, appointed by Governor Paul E. Patton.

Fellow American Academy of Matrimonial Lawyers.

Office: 301 South Sixth Street, Paducah 42003.

Telephone: (270) 575-7133, 575-7134.

SCHRODER, Wilfrid *(Judge, Kentucky Court of Appeals)* Assumed office 1991. Elected 1999, current term expires Jan 2007. Born Fort Mitchell Kentucky April 19, 1946. Educated at University of Kentucky B.A. 1968 J.D. 1970 and University of Missouri LL.M. 1971. Admitted to practice Kentucky 1970, Missouri 1972, U.S. Supreme Court 1973, U.S. District Courts Eastern and Western Districts of Kentucky and U.S. Court of Appeals Sixth Circuit. In legal practice Covington Kentucky 1975-83. Hearing Officer Kentucky Personnel Board 1981-83. Judge 1983 to July 9, 1991 and Juvenile Judge August 1986 to July 1987 Kentucky District Court Sixteenth Judicial District.

Civil Defense Attorney Legal Aid and Defenders' Society of Kansas City 1970-71. Corporate Attorney St. Paul Insurance Company, Kansas City 1971-72. Deposition and Hearing Attorney Workers' Compensation Special Fund 1975-80. Criminal Defense Attorney Public Defender Society of Northern Kentucky 1975-81. Attorney Northern Kentucky Area Planning Commission 1978-80. City Attorney Newport 1982 and 1983. Author "Preservation of Historic Areas in Kentucky" 62 Kentucky L. Jour. 940, 1974 and "Attorney Fees in Probate" Northern Kentucky Bar Association Newsletter Nov 1989. Assistant Professor Chase Law School of Northern Kentucky University Fall 1972 to Summer 1975. Faculty Supervisor Municipal Revision Task Force funded by Spindletop Research Foundation Summer 1975. Board of Directors Northern Kentucky Legal Aid Society 1974 and 1975. Trustee Public Defender Society of Northern Kentucky 1981 and 1982. Member Municipal Attorneys League 1982, Kenton County (Professional Conduct Committee 1983) and Kentucky Bar Associations. Board of Directors Hope Cottage (for dependent children) 1986-94. Member Lexington-Fayette County Planning Commission 1970 (Zoning Technician and Secretary to Board of Adjustment), American Society of Planning Officials 1971, ad hoc Committee on Landlord-Tenant Relations of Covington City Commissioners 1974 and 1975, Covington FOPA since 1983, Task Force to Study Redevelopment of Urban Areas (LRC) 1983 and Covington Committee on Street Kids 1986-87.

Office: 2734 Chancellor Drive, Suite 109, Crestview Hill 41017-3443.

Telephone: (859) 292-6574.

SCOTT, Joseph M., Jr. *(Judge, United States Bankruptcy Court Eastern District of Kentucky)* Appointed by U.S. Court of Appeals Sixth Circuit judges. Former Chief Judge.
Mailing address: P.O. Box 1111, Lexington 40588-1111.
Telephone: (859) 233-2814.

SHADOAN, William L. *(Judge, Kentucky Circuit Court First Judicial Circuit)* Elected to term beginning Jan 1984. Reelected 1991 and 1999. Current term expires Jan 2007. Currently serves as Chief Regional Circuit Judge. Born Galesburg Illinois July 12, 1931. Methodist. Member Wickliffe United Methodist Church (Trustee and Official Board). Educated at Centre College of Kentucky, University of Kentucky A.B. 1955 and University of Louisville J.D. 1961. Admitted to practice Kentucky 1961 and U.S. District Court District of Kentucky 1962. Special Judge, Kentucky Supreme Court 1985.
Member Governor Julian M. Carroll's Special Advisory Committee on County Government, Attorney General Steven's Committee on the Prosecution System in Kentucky and Kentucky Legislative Flood Control Commission. Vice Chairman Certificate of Need and Licensure Board. Chairman Kentucky County Officials Compensation Board. Member Kentucky Prosecutors Advisory Council, Kentucky County Attorneys Association (President 1975-76), The Association of Trial Lawyers of America, First Judicial District (President 1968-69), Kentucky and American Bar Associations. Listed in *Who's Who in the South and Southwest* and *Kentucky Lives.* Captain U.S. Army 1955-61. Vice Chairman Mississippi River Parkway Commission. Pilot District 4 Great River Road Commission. Chairman Purchase Area Crime Council. Board of Directors and Executive Committee Purchase Area Development District. Co-chairman County Bicentennial Committees 1974 and 1976. Past President Wickliffe P.T.A., Wickliffe Chamber of Commerce and Ballard County Country Club. Board of Directors Mental Health and Retardation. Commissioner Wickliffe Baseball and Football Little Leagues. Member Kentucky Historical Society Executive Committee, Health Planning Council, Health Service Agency West, Social Service Advisory Committee, 32° Masons Lodge #625, Shriner Rizpah Temple, Elks, American Legion Post 3, Wickliffe Lions Club (Past President) and Order of Eastern Star 516.
Office: Ballard County Courthouse, Box 578, Court Street, Wickliffe 42087.
Telephone: (270) 335-5189.

SHAKE, Ann O'Malley *(Judge, Kentucky Circuit Court Thirtieth Judicial Circuit)* Term expires Jan 2007. Former Judge, Kentucky District Court Thirtieth Judicial District.
Office: Judicial Center, 700 West Jefferson Street, Louisville 40202.
Telephone: (502) 595-3011.

SHAKE, James M. *(Judge, Kentucky Circuit Court Thirtieth Judicial Circuit)* Appointed by Governor Brereton C. Jones to term beginning 1993. Elected 1999, current term expires Jan 2007. Currently serves as Chief Regional Circuit Judge.
Office: Judicial Center, 700 West Jefferson, Louisville 40202.
Telephone: (502) 595-4062.

SHEEHAN, Martin J. *(Judge, Kentucky District Court Sixteenth Judicial District)* Elected to term beginning Jan 1, 1994. Reelected Nov 1998 and 2002. Current term expires Jan 2007. Born Cincinnati Ohio Oct 26, 1957. Catholic. Educated at Northern Kentucky University B.A. 1980 and Chase Law School of Northern Kentucky University J.D. 1983. Admitted to practice Kentucky 1983, Ohio 1984 and U.S. District Court Eastern District of Kentucky 1984. In legal practice Ludlow Kentucky 1985-94.
Adjunct Professor of Juvenile Law Chase Law School of Northern Kentucky University since 1996. Member Northern Kentucky Bar Association. Member House of Representatives Kentucky 1989-94.
Office: 230 Madison Avenue, Suite 500, Covington 41011.
Telephone: (859) 292-6561.

SHUMATE, Kimberly W. *(Judge, Kentucky District Court Ninth Judicial District)* Term expires Jan 2007.
Office: Hardin County Justice Center, 120 East Dixie Avenue, Elizabethtown 42701-1469.
Telephone: (270) 766-5005.

SIMCOE, John David *(Judge, Kentucky District Court Ninth Judicial District)*
Office: Hardin County Justice Center, 120 East Dixie Avenue, Elizabethtown 42701-1469.
Telephone: (270) 766-5004.

SIMPSON, Charles R., III *(Judge, United States District Court Western District of Kentucky)* Appointed for life by President Ronald Reagan Aug 4, 1986. Former Chief Judge. Born Cleveland Ohio July 8, 1945. Roman Catholic. Educated at University of Louisville B.A. 1967 J.D. 1970. Admitted to practice Kentucky 1970 and U.S. District Court Western District of Kentucky 1971. In legal practice Louisville 1971-86.
Board of Directors Louisville Bar Foundation. Master Louis D. Brandeis Inns of Court. Member Federal Judges Association, Louisville (Board of Directors 1981 and 1992-93), Kentucky, Federal Circuit and Federal Bar Associations. Board of Directors University of Louisville Law Alumni Association.
Office: 247 U.S. Courthouse, 601 West Broadway, Louisville 40202.
Telephone: (502) 625-3600.

SODER, Robert F. *(Judge, Kentucky District Court Fourth Judicial District)* Appointed by Governor Wallace G. Wilkinson to term beginning July 1991. Elected Nov 1991, Nov 1993, Nov 1998 and 2002. Current term expires Jan 2007. Born Lexington Kentucky 1954. Methodist. Educated at University of Kentucky B.A. 1976 and University of Louisville J.D. 1979. Member Delta Theta Phi. Admitted to practice Kentucky 1979 and U.S. District Court Western District of Kentucky 1981. In legal practice Madisonville 1979-91.
Attended Advanced Course "Special Court Jurisdiction" The National Judicial College Nov 1992.
Office: Hopkins County Courthouse, 30 South Main Street, Madisonville 42431.
Telephone: (270) 824-7512.

SPARKS, Daniel R. *(Judge, Kentucky Circuit Court Twenty-fourth Judicial Circuit)* Term expires Jan 2007.

SPARKS, DANIEL R.—*Continued*

Former Judge, Kentucky District Court Twenty-fourth Judicial District.

Mailing address: P.O. Box 1209, Paintsville 41240.
Office: 219 Courthouse, Paintsville 41240.
Telephone: (606) 789-6861.

STENGEL, Michele *(Judge, Kentucky District Court Thirtieth Judicial District)*

Office: Hall of Justice, 600 West Jefferson Street, Louisville 40202.
Telephone: (502) 595-4989.

STEPHENS, Douglas M. *(Judge, Kentucky Circuit Court Sixteenth Judicial Circuit)* Appointed by Governor John Y. Brown to term beginning March 7, 1983. Elected Nov 1983, 1991 and 1999. Current term expires Jan 2007. Former Chief Regional Circuit Judge. Born Covington Kentucky Feb 24, 1942. Educated at Villa Madonna College (now Thomas More College) 1964 and Catholic University of America LL.B. 1967. Admitted to practice Kentucky 1967. In legal practice Covington 1967-77. Judge, Kentucky District Court Sixteenth Judicial District 1978-83.

Part-time Faculty member Thomas More College 1979-85. Member Kentucky Circuit Judges Association, Northern Kentucky and Kentucky Bar Associations.

Office: 700 Kenton County Judicial Center, 230 Madison Avenue, Covington 41011.
Telephone: (859) 292-6533.

STEPHENS, Leigh Anne *(Judge, Kentucky District Court Thirty-third Judicial District)* Elected Nov 2002. Term expires Jan 2007.

Office: 481 Main Street, Hazard 41702.
Telephone: (606) 435-6007.

STEWART, William F. *(Judge, Kentucky Circuit Court Fifty-third Judicial Circuit)* Elected to term beginning Jan 1992. Reelected 1999, current term expires Jan 2007. Born Mobile Alabama Feb 18, 1945. Protestant. Educated at University of Kentucky B.S. 1968 and University of Louisville J.D. 1975. Admitted to practice Kentucky 1976. In legal practice Shelbyville 1976-86. Judge, Kentucky District Court Fifty-third Judicial District 1986-92.

Member Kentucky Association of Trial Attorneys and Kentucky Bar Association. Lieutenant j.g. USN Vietnam 1966-71.

Mailing address: P.O. Box 1327, Shelbyville 40066-3327.
Office: 535½ Main Street, Shelbyville 40065.
Telephone: (502) 633-3412.

STOSBERG, David T. *(Chief Judge, United States Bankruptcy Court Western District of Kentucky)* Appointed by U.S. Court of Appeals Sixth Circuit judges. Also Judge, Bankruptcy Appellate Panel Sixth Circuit. Selected by the Judicial Council of the Sixth Circuit.

Office: 533 U.S. Courthouse, 601 West Broadway, Louisville 40202-2264.
Telephone: (502) 627-5575.

STRINGER, Joan Antoinette "Toni" *(Judge, Kentucky District Court Thirtieth Judicial District)*

Office: 600 West Jefferson, Louisville 40202.
Telephone: (502) 595-4960.

STUMBO, Janet L. *(Justice, Kentucky Supreme Court)* Elected Nov 1993 to term beginning Jan 1994. Reelected 1996, current term expires Jan 2005. Born Prestonburg Kentucky. Educated at Morehead State University and University of Kentucky College of Law. Staff Attorney to Hon. Harris S. Howard, Kentucky Court of Appeals. In legal practice 1982 and 1989. Judge, Kentucky Court of Appeals Jan 1990 to Jan 1994 (first woman from seventh judicial district elected to court of appeals and first to be elected without being appointed).

Former Assistant County Attorney Floyd County. Co-author chapter "Appeals of Workers' Compensation in Kentucky" 2nd ed. 1996. Chair Civil Rules Committee. Court Representative Board of Directors Kentucky Bar Foundation. Board of Trustees Kentucky Bar Center. Board of Directors 1983-89 and Board Chair 1984-89 Appalachian Research and Defense Fund of Kentucky, Inc. Elected to Alumni Association Hall of Fame Morehead State University 1990. Recipient Hall of Justice Award from Kentucky Women Advocates 1991 and 1995, Bull's Eye Award from Women in State Government Network 1995 and Women Lawyers of Achievement Award from Kentucky Bar Association for Women 1996.

Office: 311 North Arnold Avenue, Suite 502, Prestonburg 41653-1279.
Telephone: (606) 886-9288.

SUMME, Patricia M. *(Judge, Kentucky Circuit Court Sixteenth Judicial Circuit)* Elected Nov 8, 1994 to term beginning Dec 9, 1994. Reelected 1999, current term expires Jan 2007. Chief Judge Kenton Circuit Court 1998-99. Catholic. Educated at Xavier University B.A. 1975 and Salmon P. Chase College of Law Northern Kentucky University J.D. 1979. Admitted to practice Kentucky 1979 and Ohio 1980. In legal practice Fort Wright Kentucky 1979-94.

Law Clerk to Attorney Joseph L. Summe 1978-79. City Attorney Fort Wright 1982 to Nov 1994 and Ludlow 1990 to Nov 1994. Member Chief Justice's Task Force on Security 2000-01. Member Northern Kentucky (Chair Legislative Committee 1985-86 and Family Law Committee 1988-90, Secretary 1986-87, Member Women Lawyers Section, Real Estate Committee, Municipal Attorney Committee, Local Rules Committee) and Kentucky (House of Delegates since 1987, Joint Study Commission on Judicial Concerns since 1997, Hearing Officer) Bar Associations. Recipient Reverend Martin Luther King Vision and Unity Award from Northern Kentucky NAACP 2002. Member Board of Overseers 1987-88, President Elect 1988, Chair of Personnel Committee 1988-95 and Board of Trustees 1988-2000 Redwood School and Rehabilitation Center. Board Member Xavier Alumni 1987-89, Notre Dame Academy School Board and Kenton Foster Care Review Board. Member Salmon P. Chase College of Law Alumni Club (Treasurer 1982 and President 1983-85). Member St. Agnes Parish Council 1982-86, Youth Group Leader 1983-86, Bi-Centennial Committee Chamber of Commerce 1992, Committee of Codification Kentucky Department for Libraries and Archives. Former volunteer Women's Crisis Center.

Office: 601 Kenton County Justice Center, 230 Madison Avenue, Covington 41011.
Telephone: (859) 292-6531.
Fax: (859) 292-6384

TACKETT, Julia K. *(Judge, Kentucky Court of Appeals)* Elected Nov 1999. Term expires Jan 2007. Long-

TACKETT, JULIA K.—*Continued*
est-serving woman judge in Kentucky. Educated at University of Kentucky B.A. J.D. Law Clerk to Chief Justice, Kentucky Supreme Court. Judge, Kentucky District Court Twenty-second Judicial District 1978-99.

Assistant Commonwealth's Attorney Fayette County. Federal Public Defender Eastern District of Kentucky. Member Kentucky Bar Association (House of Delegates, Past President Young Lawyers Section). Board of Trustees University of Kentucky. Past President University of Kentucky National Alumni Association. Member University of Kentucky Lafferty Society and College of Law Visiting Committee. Board of Advisors Lexington Public Library.

Office: 140 Tate Building, 125 Lisle Industrial Avenue, Lexington 40511-2062.

Telephone: (859) 246-2734.

TAYLOR, A. Bailey *(Judge, Kentucky District Court Fifty-fifth Judicial District)* Term expires Jan 2007.

Mailing address: P.O. Box 586, Shepherdsville 40165.

Office: 149 North Walnut Street, Shepherdsville 40165.

Telephone: (502) 543-2243.

TELLE, Jack *(Judge, Kentucky District Court Fifty-eighth Judicial District)* Elected Nov 2002. Term expires Jan 2007.

Office: Marshall County Courthouse, 1101 Main Street, Benton 42025.

THOMAS, Karen *(Judge, Kentucky District Court Seventeenth Judicial District)* Term expires Jan 2007. Currently serves as Chief Regional District Judge.

Office: 600 Columbia Street, Newport 41071.

Telephone: (859) 292-6322.

THOMPSON, Larry E. *(Judge, Kentucky Circuit Court Thirty-fifth Judicial Circuit)* Elected Nov 1999 to term beginning Jan 1, 2000. Term expires Jan 2007. Serves Family Court. Born Iaegar West Virginia Dec 11, 1955. Church of Christ. Educated at Eastern Kentucky University B.S. 1983 and Chase Law School of Northern Kentucky University J.D. 1986. Admitted to practice West Virginia 1987 and Kentucky 1988. In legal practice Williamson West Virginia 1987-95. Judge, Kentucky District Court Thirty-fifth Judicial District 1995-2000.

Member Kentucky and West Virginia Bar Associations.

Office: BB&T Bank Building, Fourth Floor, 164 Main Street, Pikeville 41501-1184.

Telephone: (606) 433-7061.

E-mail address: LarryThompson@mail.aoc.state.ky.us

THORNTON, Megan *(Judge, Kentucky District Court Twenty-second Judicial District)* Term expires Jan 2007.

Office: 150 North Limestone, Room 531, Lexington 40507-1151.

Telephone: (859) 246-2247.

TODD, James B. *(Magistrate Judge, United States District Court Eastern District of Kentucky)* Appointed by U.S. District Court judges to term beginning March 31, 1994. Reappointed 2002, current term expires March 2010. Educated at University of Kentucky B.S. 1963 J.D. 1966. In legal practice 1975-94.

Member Kentucky Bar Association.

Mailing address: P.O. Box 2058, Lexington 40588-2058.

Telephone: (859) 233-2697.

TRUDE, William W., Jr. *(Judge, Kentucky Circuit Court Twenty-third Judicial Circuit)* Elected Nov 1991 to term beginning Jan 6, 1992. Reelected 1999, current term expires Jan 2007. Born Du Bois Pennsylvania Jan 1, 1953. Methodist. Educated at Eastern Kentucky University B.B.A. with honors 1980 and University of Kentucky J.D. 1983. Member Phi Alpha Delta and Phi Kappa Phi. Admitted to practice Kentucky 1983 and U.S. District Courts Eastern 1984 and Western 1986 Districts of Kentucky.

Member Kentucky Association of Circuit Judges, Madison County and Kentucky Bar Associations. E-4 USMC 1970-74. Enjoys golfing, hunting, boating and fishing.

Office: 204 Courthouse, 130 Main Street, Irvine 40336.

Telephone: (606) 723-3320.

Fax: (606) 723-8231

TRUSTY, Frank *(Judge, Kentucky District Court Sixteenth Judicial District)* Term expires Jan 2007.

Office: 230 Madison Avenue, Suite 500, Covington 41011.

Telephone: (859) 292-6561.

UNTHANK, G. Wix *(Senior Judge, United States District Court Eastern District of Kentucky)* Appointed for life by President Jimmy Carter to term beginning June 1980. Assumed Senior status June 14, 1988, serves by assignment. Born Tway Kentucky June 14, 1923. Presbyterian. Educated at University of Miami 1950. Admitted to practice Florida 1950 and Kentucky 1950. In legal practice Harlan 1957-66. Judge, Kentucky District Court Twenty-sixth Judicial District 1950-57.

Assistant U.S. Attorney Lexington 1966-69. Commonwealth Attorney Harlan County 1970-80. Member American Judicature Society, The Florida Bar, Kentucky and American Bar Associations. Recipient Decorated Purple Heart, Bronze Star and combat infantry badge.

Mailing address: P.O. Box 5112, London 40745-5112.

Telephone: (606) 878-2731.

VanMETER, Laurance *(Judge, Kentucky Circuit Court Twenty-second Judicial Circuit)* Term expires Jan 2007. Former Judge, Kentucky District Court Twenty-second Judicial District.

Office: 534 Fayette County Courthouse, 120 North Limestone, Lexington 40507.

Telephone: (859) 246-2703.

VENTERS, Daniel J. *(Judge, Kentucky Circuit Court Twenty-eighth Judicial Circuit)* Elected Nov 6, 1983 to term beginning Jan 1984. Reelected 1991 and 1999. Current term expires Jan 2007. Serves as Chief Judge. Born Charleston West Virginia April 13, 1950. Educated at The Ohio State University B.S. 1972 and University of Kentucky J.D. 1975. Admitted to practice Kentucky 1975 and U.S. District Court Eastern District of Kentucky 1977. In legal practice Somerset 1975-79. Judge, Kentucky District Court Twenty-eighth Judicial District 1979-84, appointed by Governor Julian Carroll.

Assistant Commonwealth's Attorney 1975-79. Instruc-

VENTERS, DANIEL J.—*Continued*
tor in American Government Somerset Community College 1992-93. Member Kentucky Commonwealth's Attorneys Association 1975-79, Kentucky Association of Circuit Judges, National District Attorneys Association 1975-79, Circuit Judges Association of Kentucky, Inc., Pulaski County, Kentucky and American (National Conference of State Trial Judges Judicial Administration Division) Bar Associations. Recipient Outstanding Trial Judge Award from Kentucky Academy of Trial Attorneys 1986.
Mailing address: P.O. Box 1324, Somerset 42502.
Office: Main Street, Somerset 42501.
Telephone: (606) 677-4091.

WAKEFIELD, Frank *(Judge, Kentucky District Court Forty-ninth Judicial District)* Term expires Jan 2007. Currently serves as Vice Chief Regional District Judge.
Mailing address: P.O. Box 413, Franklin 42135.
Office: Courthouse, Main Street, Franklin 42134.
Telephone: (270) 586-8717.

WALLER, Thomas L. *(Judge, Kentucky Circuit Court Fifty-fifth Judicial Circuit)* Term expires Jan 2007.
Mailing address: P.O. Box 97, Shepherdsville 40165.
Telephone: (502) 543-4776.

WALSON, Jeffrey M. *(Judge, Kentucky Circuit Court Twenty-fifth Judicial Circuit)* Assumed office Jan 6, 2003. Term expires Jan 2007. Serves Family Court. Born Clark County Kentucky 1962. Protestant. Educated at Georgetown College B.S. 1984 and University of Kentucky College of Law J.D. 1987. Admitted to practice Kentucky 1987, U.S. District Court Eastern District of Kentucky 1988 and U.S. Supreme Court 1994. In legal practice Winchester 1987-93. Judge, Kentucky District Court Twenty-fifth Judicial District Oct 14, 1993 to Jan 5, 2003, appointed by Governor Brereton C. Jones.
Assistant Commonwealth's Attorney 1988-93. Instructor in Real Estate Law Eastern Kentucky University. President Kentucky District Judges Association, Inc. since 2000. Member Clark County, Madison County and Kentucky Bar Associations. Presenter/Lecturer Kentucky District Judges' College, Kentucky District Judges' Orientation and Kentucky Court Improvement Project.
Mailing address: P.O. Box 877, Winchester 40391.
Office: Clark Judicial Center, Winchester 40391.
Telephone: (859) 737-7491.

WALTON, W. Todd, II *(Judge, Kentucky District Court Nineteenth Judicial District)* Term expires Jan 2007.
Office: 100 Court Square, Second Floor, Room 205, Flemingsburg 41041.
Telephone: (606) 845-1037.
E-mail address: Todd_Walton@mail.aoc.state.ky.us

WARD, Rebecca *(Judge, Kentucky District Court Fifty-fifth Judicial District)* Term expires Jan 2007.
Mailing address: P.O. Box 586, Shepherdsville 40165.
Telephone: (502) 543-2243.

WATSON, Kenton J. *(Judge, Kentucky District Court Fifty-first Judicial District)* Term expires Jan 2007.
Mailing address: P.O. Box 675, Henderson 42419.
Office: Henderson County Courthouse, Henderson 42420.
Telephone: (270) 826-4755.

WEDDLE, James G. *(Judge, Kentucky Circuit Court Twenty-ninth Judicial Circuit)* Elected Nov 2, 1999 to term beginning Jan 3, 2000. Term expires Jan 2007. Born Casey County Kentucky March 21, 1941. Baptist. Educated at University of Kentucky J.D. 1966. Admitted to practice Kentucky 1966, U.S. District Courts Western 1969 and Eastern 1988 Districts of Kentucky and U.S. Supreme Court 1971. In legal practice Liberty 1966-1999.
Attorney Casey County 1970-85. Member Kentucky Association of Circuit Judges and Kentucky Bar Association. Enjoys a good book.
Mailing address: P.O. Box 307, Liberty 42539.
Telephone: (606) 787-6991.
E-mail address: jamesweddle@mail.aoc.state.ky.us

WEHR, William J. *(Judge, Kentucky Circuit Court Seventeenth Judicial Circuit)* Appointed by Governor Wallace G. Wilkinson to term beginning Oct 1988. Elected to subsequent terms. Current term expires Jan 2, 2007. Currently serves as Chief Regional Circuit Judge. Born July 13, 1950. Educated at University of Kentucky B.A. 1972 and Chase Law School of Northern Kentucky University J.D. 1976. Admitted to practice Kentucky 1976, U.S. District Courts Eastern 1976 and Western 1976 Districts of Kentucky, U.S. Court of Appeals Sixth Circuit 1980 and U.S. Supreme Court 1980. In legal practice Newport 1976-88.
Assistant County Attorney 1978-88. Guest Lecturer on Administrative Practice 1981, 1983 and 1988 and Criminal Law 1987 Chase Law School of Northern Kentucky University. President Campbell County Bar Association 1984. Member Cincinnati Bar Association/Northern Kentucky Bar Association Task Force 1990. Member Kentucky Association of Circuit Judges, The Association of Trial Lawyers of America, National Association of District Attorneys, Cincinnati, Northern Kentucky (Treasurer 1985, President 1987, Chairman Long Range Planning Commission 1988), Kentucky and American Bar Associations. Attended American Academy of Judicial Training Washington D.C. 1989 and The National Judicial College Reno Nevada 1990. Recipient Continuing Education Award from Kentucky Bar Association 1990. Listed in *Who's Who in American Law* 4th and 5th editions. USCGR 1968-74. Previously employed as ward service manager St. Elizabeth Hospital 1972-76. Board Member 1980-87 and President 1984-86 Senior Citizens of Northern Kentucky, Inc. Member and Chairman Campbell County Mental Health/Mental Retardation Allocation Committee since 1986. Member Fort Thomas Optimist Club (School coordinator "Just Say No" program St. Catherine's School since 1987), St. Catherine of Siena Parish, Fraternal Order of Police, Newport Elks, Loyal Boosters, Campbell County Jaycees and alumni clubs of University of Kentucky, Northern Kentucky University and Chase Law School. Sponsors various youth athletic teams in soccer, baseball and basketball.
Office: Courthouse, 330 York Street, Newport 41071.
Telephone: (859) 292-6301.

WEHRMAN, J. Gregory *(Magistrate Judge, United States District Court Eastern District of Kentucky)* Part-time Magistrate Judge Nov 1975 to Jan 1992. Appointed full-time Magistrate Judge by U.S. District Court judges to term beginning Jan 1992. Reappointed Jan 2000, cur-

WEHRMAN, J. GREGORY—*Continued*

rent term expires Jan 2008. Born Covington Kentucky Jan 3, 1944. Roman Catholic. Educated at University of Florida 1962-64, University of Cincinnati B.A. 1966 and University of Kentucky J.D. 1969. Admitted to practice Kentucky 1969 and Florida 1969. Began legal practice Covington Kentucky 1969.

Member Northern Kentucky and Federal Bar Association.

Mailing address: P.O. Box 1229, Covington 41012-1229.

Telephone: (859) 392-7909.

WHEELER, Diana E. *(Judge, Kentucky District Court Twelfth Judicial District)* Master Commissioner and Family Court Commissioner 2000-02. Elected Nov 2002 to term beginning Jan 6, 2003. Term expires Jan 2007. Born Bedford Kentucky Aug 9, 1962. Catholic. Educated at University of Kentucky B.S. cum laude 1984 J.D. 1987. Admitted to practice Kentucky 1987. In legal practice La Grange 1988-2002.

Staff Attorney to Hon. Dennis A. Fritz, Kentucky Circuit Court Twelfth Judicial Circuit 1987-88. Former Member American Bar Association. Member Oldham County and Kentucky Bar Associations. Board Member Host House, YMCA and Rose Haven. Member La Grange Rotary and Oldham Business and Professional Women. Enjoys reading and swimming.

Office: 100 West Main Street, La Grange 40031.

Telephone: (502) 222-7447.

Fax: (502) 222-3047

E-mail address: dianawheeler@mail.aoc.state.ky.us

WHITE, Edwin Morton *(Judge, Kentucky Circuit Court Third Judicial Circuit)* Elected 1983 to term beginning Jan 3, 1984. Reelected 1991 and 1999. Current term expires Jan 2007. Born Birmingham Alabama March 27, 1948. Episcopalian. Educated at University of the South B.S. 1970 and University of Kentucky College of Law J.D. 1973. Law Clerk to Hon. B. T. Moynahan, Jr., U.S. District Court Eastern District of Kentucky. Admitted to practice Kentucky 1973. Began legal practice Lexington 1973. In legal practice Hopkinsville since 1974. Judge, Kentucky District Court 1981-83.

Instructor in Real Estate Law University of Kentucky at Hopkinsville Community College 1976-80. Member Christian County and Kentucky Bar Associations. First Lieutenant USAF 1974. Vice Chairman Penny Royal Mental Health Association 1976-78. Board of Trustees University of the South 1982-85. President Kentucky Golf Association 1984-85. Member Vestry Grace Episcopal Church 1987 and Rotary Club. Enjoys golf and skiing.

Office: Christian County Justice Center, 100 Justice Way, Hopkinsville 42240.

Telephone: (270) 889-6536.

WHITESELL, Hunter *(Judge, Kentucky District Court First Judicial District)* Term expires Jan 2007.

Mailing address: P.O. Box 198, Hickman 42050.

Office: Courthouse, Hickman 42050.

Telephone: (270) 236-2839.

WHITTINGHILL, Virginia *(Judge, Kentucky District Court Thirtieth Judicial District)* Elected to term beginning Nov 27, 1989. Reelected 1993, 1998 and 2002. Current term expires Jan 2007. Educated at University of Louisville B.A. in Psychology 1975 J.D. 1978. Managing Editor Journal of Law and Education 1976-78. Admitted to practice Kentucky 1978.

Trial Commissioner Kentucky Circuit Court Thirtieth Judicial Circuit 1984-89. Member National Association of Women Judges, Louisville and Kentucky Bar Associations.

Office: Hall of Justice, 600 West Jefferson Street, Louisville 40202.

Telephone: (502) 595-4611.

WIEDERSTEIN, Robert *(Judge, Kentucky District Court Fifty-first Judicial District)* Term expires Jan 2007.

Mailing address: P.O. Box 675, Henderson 42419.

Office: Courthouse, Henderson 42420.

Telephone: (270) 826-4755.

WIGGINS, Brian *(Judge, Kentucky District Court Forty-fifth Judicial District)* Elected Nov 2002. Term expires Jan 2007.

Mailing address: P.O. Box 274, Greenville 42345.

Office: 109 East Main Cross, Greenville 42345.

Telephone: (270) 338-0995.

WILHOIT, Henry Rupert, Jr. *(Senior Judge, United States District Court Eastern District of Kentucky)* Appointed for life by President Ronald Reagan to term beginning October 23, 1981. Chief Judge Sept 20, 1998 to Dec 30, 2000. Assumed Senior status Dec 31, 2000, serves by assignment. Born Grayson Kentucky Feb 11, 1935. Religious affiliation: Christian Church. Educated at University of Kentucky LL.B. 1960. Admitted to practice Kentucky 1960, U.S. District Court Eastern District of Kentucky 1961 and U.S. Court of Appeals Sixth Circuit 1972. Began legal practice Grayson 1960.

Attorney City of Grayson 1962-66. Attorney Carter County 1966-70. Fellow American College of Trial Lawyers. Member Kentucky Bar Association (President 1981). Recipient Distinguished Service Award from University of Kentucky Alumni Association 1980. National President University of Kentucky Alumni Association 1977. Trustee University of Kentucky 1988-94.

Office: Federal Building, 1405 Greenup Avenue, Ashland 41105.

Telephone: (606) 329-2592.

WILLETT, Barry *(Judge, Kentucky Circuit Court Thirtieth Judicial Circuit)* Elected to term beginning Jan 1, 2000. Term expires Jan 2007. Born Louisville Kentucky 1957. Educated at University of Kentucky B.A. 1980 and University of Louisville School of Law J.D. 1983. Admitted to practice Kentucky 1985. In legal practice Louisville 1985-2000.

Office: 601 Judicial Center, 700 West Jefferson Street, Louisville 40402-4730.

Telephone: (502) 595-4054.

Fax: (502) 595-3482

E-mail address: BarryWillett@mail.aoc.state.ky.us

WILLIAMS, C. René *(Judge, Kentucky District Court Fifth Judicial District)* Term expires Jan 2007. Currently serves as Chief Regional District Judge.

Mailing address: P.O. Box 126, Dixon 42409.

Office: Webster County Courthouse, Dixon 42409.

Telephone: (270) 639-5506.

WILSON, Robert *(Judge, Kentucky Circuit Court Fifty-seventh Judicial Circuit)* Term expires Jan 2007.

WILSON, ROBERT—*Continued*

Former Judge, Kentucky District Court Fortieth Judicial District.
Mailing address: P.O. Box 10, Jamestown 42629.
Office: Courthouse, Jamestown 42629.
Telephone: (270) 343-2131.

WINCHESTER, Jerry D. *(Judge, Kentucky Circuit Court Thirty-fourth Judicial Circuit)* Term expires Jan 2007. Currently serves as Vice Chief Regional Circuit Judge.
Office: 1019 Cumberland Falls Highway, Corbin 40701.
Telephone: (606) 528-3013.

WINE, Thomas B. *(Judge, Kentucky Circuit Court Thirtieth Judicial Circuit)* Elected Nov 1991 to term beginning Jan 6, 1992. Reelected 1999, current term expires Jan 2, 2007. Former Chief Regional Circuit Judge. Born Louisville Kentucky May 21, 1955. Christian. Educated at University of Louisville B.A. 1977 J.D. 1980. Admitted to practice Kentucky 1980 and U.S. District Courts Eastern 1981 and Western 1981 Districts of Kentucky. In legal practice Louisville 1991-92.
Member Louisville, Kentucky and American Bar Associations. Nominated Judge of the Year by Louisville Bar Association 1997. Enjoys camping and gardening. Interested in genealogy.
Office: Judicial Center, 700 West Jefferson Street, Louisville 40202.
Telephone: (502) 595-4294.
Fax: (502) 595-3496

WINGATE, Thomas Dawson *(Judge, Kentucky District Court Forty-eighth Judicial District)*
Office: Franklin County Courthouse, 214 St. Clair Street, Frankfort 40601.
Telephone: (502) 564-7073.
Fax: (502) 564-3711

WINTERSHEIMER, Donald C. *(Justice, Kentucky Supreme Court)* Elected 1982 to term beginning Jan 1, 1983. Reelected 1990 and 1998. Current term expires Jan 2007. Born Covington Kentucky April 21, 1932. Catholic. Educated at Thomas More College A.B. 1953, Xavier University M.A. 1957 and University of Cincinnati J.D. 1959. Honorary Doctor of Laws Northern Kentucky University 1999. Member Phi Delta Phi and Tau Kappa Alpha. Admitted to practice Kentucky 1959 and Ohio 1959. In legal practice Covington Kentucky and Cincinnati Ohio 1959-76. Judge, Kentucky Court of Appeals 1976-83.
Covington City Solicitor 1962-76. Instructor Thomas More College 1969-76. Adjunct Professor of Law Chase Law School of Northern Kentucky University since 1983. Past President Kentucky Municipal Attorneys Association. Chairman Kentucky Continuing Judicial Education Commission and Kentucky Criminal Rules Committee since 1988. Member Institute of Judicial Administration, American Judicature Society, Cincinnati, Kenton County, Kentucky (Member IOLTA Committee), Ohio State and American Bar Associations. Recipient Community Service Award 1970 and named Outstanding Teacher 1973 Thomas More College. Recipient Certificate of Appreciation from City of Covington Bicentennial Committee 1976 and Kentucky Bar Association CLE Recognition Award 1981-82, 1987-88, 1989-90, 1991-92 and 1993-94. Corporal U.S. Army 1953-55. Past President Thomas More Alumni Association. Democrat. Enjoys softball and tennis.
Mailing address: P.O. Box 387, Covington 41012.
Telephone: (859) 292-6300.
Fax: (859) 292-6377

WISE, Jo Ann *(Judge, Kentucky Circuit Court Twenty-second Judicial Circuit)* Appointed by Governor Paul E. Patton to term beginning Jan 13, 2003. Term expires Jan 2007. Serves Family Court.
Office: 120 North Limestone, Lexington 40507-1151.
Telephone: (859) 246-2214.

WOOD, James T. *(Judge, Kentucky District Court Forty-seventh Judicial District)* Term expires Jan 2007.
Office: 156 Main Street, Suite 101C, Whitesburg 41858.
Telephone: (606) 633-4222.

WRIGHT, Samuel T. *(Judge, Kentucky Circuit Court Forty-seventh Judicial Circuit)* Appointed by Governor Brereton C. Jones to term beginning 1993. Elected 1999, current term expires Jan 2007. Former Judge, Kentucky District Court Forty-seventh Judicial District.
Office: Courthouse, 101 West Main Street, Whitesburg 41858.
Telephone: (606) 633-2259.

LOUISIANA

Capital BATON ROUGE

UNITED STATES DISTRICT COURTS DISTRICTS OF LOUISIANA

Within Louisiana there are three United States District Courts. For descriptive information refer to the United States Courts section.

EASTERN DISTRICT includes Assumption, Jefferson, Lafourche, Orleans, Plaquemines, St. Bernard, St. Charles, St. James, St. John the Baptist, St. Tammany, Tangipahoa, Terrebonne and Washington parishes. The court sits at New Orleans and Houma.

Chief Judge
Helen G. Berrigan

Judges

Martin L. C. Feldman
Stanwood Duval, Jr.
Eldon E. Fallon
Ivan L. R. Lemelle
Carl J. Barbier
Jay C. Zainey
Sarah S. Vance
G. Thomas Porteous, Jr.
Mary Ann Vial Lemmon
Kurt D. Engelhardt
Lance M. Africk

Senior Judges

Frederick Jacob Reagan Heebe
Adrian G. Duplantier
A. J. McNamara
Marcel Livaudais, Jr.
Charles Schwartz, Jr.
Morey L. Sear
Peter H. Beer
Henry A. Mentz, Jr.

Clerk
Loretta G. Whyte
C151 U.S. Courthouse
500 Camp Street
New Orleans, Louisiana 70130-3367
(504) 589-7600

MIDDLE DISTRICT includes Ascension, East Baton Rouge, East Feliciana, Iberville, Livingston, Pointe Coupee, St. Helena, West Baton Rouge and West Feliciana parishes. The court sits at Baton Rouge.

Chief Judge
Frank J. Polozola

Judges
Ralph E. Tyson
James J. Brady

Senior Judge
John V. Parker

Clerk
Lawrence Talamo
Federal Building
777 Florida Street
Baton Rouge, Louisiana 70801-1712
(225) 389-3500

WESTERN DISTRICT includes Acadia, Allen, Avoyelles, Beauregard, Bienville, Bossier, Caddo, Calcasieu, Caldwell, Cameron, Catahoula, Claiborne, Concordia, DeSoto, East Carroll, Evangeline, Franklin, Grant, Iberia, Jackson, Jefferson Davis, Lafayette, La Salle, Lincoln, Madison, Morehouse, Natchitoches, Ouachita, Rapides, Red River, Richland, Sabine, St. Landry, St. Martin, St. Mary, Tensas, Union, Vermilion, Vernon, Webster, West Carroll and Winn parishes. The court sits at Alexandria, Lafayette, Lake Charles, Monroe, Opelousas and Shreveport.

Chief Judge
Richard T. Haik

Judges
Rebecca F. Doherty
Tucker L. Melancon
Robert G. James

Senior Judges
Tom Stagg
F. A. Little, Jr.
Donald E. Walter
James T. Trimble, Jr.

Clerk
Robert H. Shemwell
1167 U.S. Courthouse
300 Fannin Street
Shreveport, Louisiana 71101-3083
(318) 676-4273

UNITED STATES MAGISTRATE JUDGES OF LOUISIANA

EASTERN DISTRICT

Alma L. Chasez
Joseph C. Wilkinson, Jr.
Karen Wells Roby
Louis Moore, Jr.
Sally A. Shushan
Daniel E. Knowles, III

MIDDLE DISTRICT

Stephen C. Riedlinger
Christine A. Noland
Docia L. Dalby

WESTERN DISTRICT

Mildred E. Methvin
Roy S. Payne
Karen L. Hayes
Robert H. Shemwell
Alonzo P. "Lon" Wilson
James D. Kirk

UNITED STATES BANKRUPTCY COURTS OF LOUISIANA

EASTERN DISTRICT

Chief Judge
Thomas M. Brahney, III

Judge
Jerry A. Brown

UNITED STATES DISTRICT COURTS DISTRICTS OF LOUISIANA—*Continued*

Bankruptcy Clerk
Warren A. Cuntz, Jr.
601 Federal Building
501 Magazine Street
New Orleans, Louisiana 70130
(504) 589-7878

MIDDLE DISTRICT

Judge
Douglas D. Dodd

Bankruptcy Clerk
J. Lynn Burkett
119 U.S. Courthouse
707 Florida Street
Baton Rouge, Louisiana 70801
(225) 389-0211

WESTERN DISTRICT

Chief Judge
Gerald H. Schiff

Judges
Stephen V. Callaway
Henley A. Hunter

Bankruptcy Clerk
J. Barry Dunford
2201 U.S. Courthouse
300 Fannin Street
Shreveport, Louisiana 71101-3089
(318) 676-4267

SUPREME COURT OF LOUISIANA

The Supreme Court is Louisiana's court of last resort. The state is divided into seven Supreme Court districts for electoral purposes. The court consists of a chief justice and six associate justices elected for ten-year terms. Vacancies are filled within one year by special election called by the governor. In the interim, the vacancy is filled by Supreme Court appointment. The justice most senior in service is designated the chief justice and serves in that capacity as long as he serves the court. Retirement is generally mandatory at age seventy; however, retired justices may serve in any court in the state by assignment of the Supreme Court.

The court has appellate jurisdiction over cases in which an ordinance or law has been declared unconstitutional, capital cases in which the death penalty has been imposed and over all issues involved in a civil action properly before it. The court has exclusive original jurisdiction over disciplinary proceedings against attorneys, petitions for discipline of judges and fact questions affecting its own appellate jurisdiction. The court has discretionary review of decisions of the Courts of Appeal. The court has supervisory and administrative control over the lower courts and may issue writs necessary to the exercise of proper jurisdiction.

The court sits en banc at New Orleans.

DISTRICT ONE includes portions of Jefferson Parish; portions of Orleans Parish; and St. Helena, St. Tammany, Tangipahoa and Washington parishes.

DISTRICT TWO includes Allen, Beauregard, Bossier, Caddo, DeSoto, Evangeline, Natchitoches, Red River, Sabine, Vernon and Webster parishes.

DISTRICT THREE includes Acadia, Avoyelles, Calcasieu, Cameron, Jefferson Davis, Lafayette, St. Landry and Vermilion parishes.

DISTRICT FOUR includes Bienville, Caldwell, Catahoula, Claiborne, Concordia, East Carroll, Franklin, Grant, Jackson, La Salle, Lincoln, Madison, Morehouse, Ouachita, Rapides, Richland, Tensas, Union and West Carroll and Winn parishes.

DISTRICT FIVE includes Ascension, East Baton Rouge, East Feliciana, Iberville, Livingston, Pointe Coupee, West Baton Rouge and West Feliciana parishes.

DISTRICT SIX includes portions of Jefferson Parish and Assumption, Iberia, Lafourche, Plaquemines, St. Bernard, St. Charles, St. James, St. John the Baptist, St. Martin, St. Mary and Terrebonne parishes.

DISTRICT SEVEN includes portions of Jefferson Parish and portions of Orleans Parish.

Chief Justice
Pascal F. Calogero, Jr.

Justices

Jeffrey P. Victory	Jeannette Theriot Knoll
Chet D. Traylor	Catherine D. Kimball
Bernette Joshua Johnson	John L. Weimer

Clerk
John Tarlton Olivier
Supreme Court Building
301 Loyola Avenue
New Orleans, Louisiana 70112-1814
(504) 568-5707

Judicial Administrator
Hugh M. Collins
1555 Poydras Street, Suite 1540
New Orleans, Louisiana 70112-3701
(504) 568-5747

LOUISIANA COURTS OF APPEAL

The Courts of Appeal are Louisiana's courts of intermediate appellate jurisdiction. The state is divided into five circuits with a court in each circuit. Each circuit is subdivided into districts. The judges are elected to ten-year terms in elections held in their respective districts or at large within their circuits. The judge on each court most senior in service is designated the chief judge and serves in this capacity as long as he serves the court. Retirement is generally mandatory at age seventy; however, retired judges may serve any court in the state by assignment of the Supreme Court.

The courts have appellate jurisdiction over all civil cases, over all matters from the Family and Juvenile Courts and over all criminal cases triable by a jury except when appealable directly to the Supreme Court or to the District Courts. The courts' jurisdiction is limited to questions of law and fact in civil cases and law only in criminal cases. The courts may issue writs necessary to the exercise of proper jurisdiction.

LOUISIANA COURTS OF APPEAL—*Continued*

Each court usually sits in panels of three judges, but may sit in larger panels or en banc as needed. The courts sit at each circuit.

FIRST CIRCUIT includes Ascension, Assumption, East Baton Rouge, East Feliciana, Iberville, Lafourche, Livingston, Pointe Coupee, St. Helena, St. Mary, St. Tammany, Tangipahoa, Terrebonne, Washington, West Baton Rouge and West Feliciana parishes. The court sits at Baton Rouge.

Chief Judge

Burrell J. Carter

Judges

Frank Foil
Randolph H. Parro
James E. Kuhn
John T. Pettigrew
Edward J. "Jimmy" Gaidry
Vanessa Guidry-Whipple
Brady M. Fitzsimmons
John Michael Guidry
Robert D. Downing
J. Michael McDonald
Page McClendon

SECOND CIRCUIT includes Bienville, Bossier, Caddo, Caldwell, Claiborne, DeSoto, East Carroll, Franklin, Jackson, Lincoln, Madison, Morehouse, Ouachita, Red River, Richland, Tensas, Union, Webster, West Carroll and Winn parishes. The court sits at Shreveport.

Chief Judge

Henry N. Brown, Jr.

Judges

Felicia Toney Williams
Gay C. Gaskins
Charles B. Peatross
D. Milton Moore, III
James E. Stewart, Sr.
J. Jay Caraway
R. Harmon Drew, Jr.

THIRD CIRCUIT includes Acadia, Allen, Avoyelles, Beauregard, Calcasieu, Cameron, Catahoula, Concordia, Evangeline, Grant, Iberia, Jefferson Davis, Lafayette, La Salle, Natchitoches, Rapides, Sabine, St. Landry, St. Martin, Vermilion and Vernon parishes. The court sits at Lake Charles.

Chief Judge

Ned E. Doucet, Jr.

Judges

Ulysses G. Thibodeaux
John D. Saunders
Sylvia R. Cooks
Jimmie C. Peters
Michael G. Sullivan
Elizabeth A. Pickett
Billie Colombaro Woodard
Oswald A. Decuir
Marc T. Amy
Glenn B. Gremillion
Billy H. Ezell

FOURTH CIRCUIT includes Orleans, Plaquemines and St. Bernard parishes. The court sits at New Orleans.

Chief Judge

William H. Byrnes, III

Judges

Joan Bernard Armstrong
Patricia Rivet Murray
Dennis R. Bagneris, Sr.
Terri Fleming Love
David S. Gorbaty
Edwin A. Lombard
Charles Robert Jones
James F. McKay, III
Michael E. Kirby
Max N. Tobias, Jr.
Leon A. Cannizzaro, Jr.

FIFTH CIRCUIT includes Jefferson, St. Charles, St. James and St. John the Baptist parishes. The court sits at Gretna.

Chief Judge

Edward A. Dufresne, Jr.

Judges

Sol Gothard
Thomas F. Daley
Marion F. Edwards
Walter J. Rothschild
James L. Cannella
Susan M. Chehardy
Clarence E. McManus

LOUISIANA DISTRICT COURTS

The District Courts are Louisiana's courts of general trial jurisdiction. The state is divided into forty-one judicial districts with a District Court established in each district, except in Orleans Parish, which has both a Criminal District Court and a Civil District Court. The Criminal District Court has twelve judges and one magistrate judge; the Civil District Court has fourteen judges. Judges (including the magistrate judge) are elected by the voters in their respective districts for six-year terms. Chief judges for the individual districts are elected by peer vote for a term designated by the court. Retirement is generally mandatory at age seventy; however, retired judges may continue to serve by assignment of the Supreme Court.

The courts have original jurisdiction in all civil and criminal matters except in Orleans Parish and the First, Nineteenth and Twenty-fourth Judicial Districts, where the Family and Juvenile Courts have exclusive jurisdiction over certain types of cases. In Orleans Parish, violations of municipal ordinances are tried by the Municipal and Traffic Courts. In civil cases, the courts have concurrent jurisdiction with the City Courts when the amount in controversy is between $10,000 and $25,000; with the Parish Courts, generally up to $20,000; and with the Justice of the Peace Courts when the amount in controversy does not exceed $3,000. The courts exercise concurrent jurisdiction with the City Courts over misdemeanors and over juvenile matters in parishes without a separate Juvenile Court. Appeals from the City, Municipal, Traffic and Mayor's Courts are generally heard in the District Courts; cases tried under a state statute are appealed directly to the Courts of Appeal. The District Courts also exercise appellate jurisdiction over Justice of the Peace Courts in parishes where no Parish Court exists. In addition, the Orleans Parish Criminal District Court has supervisory control over the Municipal Court and Traffic Court of New Orleans.

The courts sit at each parish seat.

ORLEANS PARISH CIVIL DISTRICT includes Orleans Parish. The court sits at New Orleans.

Judges

Carolyn Gill-Jefferson
Roland L. Belsome
Madeleine Landrieu
Robin M. Giarrusso
Piper D. Griffin
Herbert A. Cade
C. Hunter King
Rosemary Ledet
Lloyd J. Medley
Yada T. Magee
Michael G. Bagneris
Nadine M. Ramsey
Kern Reese
Ethel Simms Julien

ORLEANS PARISH CRIMINAL DISTRICT includes Orleans Parish. The court sits at New Orleans.

LOUISIANA DISTRICT COURTS—*Continued*

Judges

Charles L. Elloie
Benedict J. Willard
Calvin Johnson
Julian A. Parker
Raymond C. Bigelow
Arthur L. Hunter, Jr.
Patrick G. Quinlan
Frank A. Marullo, Jr.
Dennis J. Waldron
Camille Buras
Darryl Derbigny
Terry Q. Alarcon

Magistrate Judge

Gerard J. Hansen

FIRST JUDICIAL DISTRICT includes Caddo Parish. The court sits at Shreveport.

Judges

Robert P. Waddell
Scott J. Crichton
B. Woodrow Nesbitt, Jr.
Charles R. Scott
Roy L. Brun
Ramona Emanuel
Leon L. Emanuel, III
John D. Mosely, Jr.
Jeanette G. Garrett
Michael R. Walker

SECOND JUDICIAL DISTRICT includes Bienville, Claiborne and Jackson parishes. The court sits at Arcadia, Homer and Jonesboro.

Judges

Jenifer Ward Clason
Jimmy C. Teat
Glenn Fallin

THIRD JUDICIAL DISTRICT includes Lincoln and Union parishes. The court sits at Ruston and Farmerville.

Judges

Cynthia T. Woodard
R. Wayne Smith
Jay B. McCallum

FOURTH JUDICIAL DISTRICT includes Morehouse and Ouachita parishes. The court sits at Bastrop and Monroe.

Judges

Jimmy N. Dimos
Wilson Rambo
Marcus R. Clark
Carl Van Sharp
Alvin R. Sharp
Sharon Ingram Marchman
John Larry Lolley
C. Wendell Manning
Benjamin Jones

FIFTH JUDICIAL DISTRICT includes Franklin, Richland and West Carroll parishes. The court sits at Winnsboro, Rayville and Oak Grove.

Judges

Glen W. Strong
Glynn D. Roberts
Edwin Rudolph McIntyre, Jr.

SIXTH JUDICIAL DISTRICT includes East Carroll, Madison and Tensas parishes. The court sits at Lake Providence, Tallulah and St. Joseph.

Judges

Michael E. Lancaster
John D. Crigler

SEVENTH JUDICIAL DISTRICT includes Catahoula and Concordia parishes. The court sits at Harrisonburg and Vidalia.

Judges

Kathy J. Johnson
Leo Boothe

EIGHTH JUDICIAL DISTRICT includes Winn Parish. The court sits at Winnfield.

Judge

Jim W. Wiley

NINTH JUDICIAL DISTRICT includes Rapides Parish. The court sits at Alexandria.

Judges

Donald T. Johnson
F. Rae Swent
B. Dexter Ryland
Harry F. Randow
Thomas M. Yeager
W. Ross Foote
George C. Metoyer, Jr.

TENTH JUDICIAL DISTRICT includes Natchitoches Parish. The court sits at Natchitoches.

Judges

Eric R. Harrington
Monty L. Doggett

ELEVENTH JUDICIAL DISTRICT includes DeSoto and Sabine parishes. The court sits at Mansfield and Many.

Judges

Robert E. Burgess
Charles B. Adams
Stephen B. Beasley

TWELFTH JUDICIAL DISTRICT includes Avoyelles Parish. The court sits at Marksville.

Judges

Mark Anthony Jeansonne
William J. Bennett

THIRTEENTH JUDICIAL DISTRICT includes Evangeline Parish. The court sits at Ville Platte.

Judges

J. Larry Vidrine
Thomas F. Fuselier

FOURTEENTH JUDICIAL DISTRICT includes Calcasieu Parish. The court sits at Lake Charles.

Judges

D. Kent Savoie
Guy E. Bradberry
Patricia H. Minaldi
G. Michael Canaday
Lilynn A. Cutrer
David Painter
Robert L. Wyatt
Wilford Dan Carter
Alcide J. Gray

FIFTEENTH JUDICIAL DISTRICT includes Acadia, Lafayette and Vermilion parishes. The court sits at Crowley, Lafayette and Abbeville.

Judges

John D. Trahan
J. Byron Hébert
Herman C. Clause
Durwood W. Conque
Thomas R. Duplantier
Patrick L. Michot
Phyllis Montgomery Keaty
Jules D. Edwards, III
Edward D. Rubin
Glennon P. Everett
David Blanchet
Kristian Earles
Marilyn C. Castle

LOUISIANA DISTRICT COURTS—*Continued*

SIXTEENTH JUDICIAL DISTRICT includes Iberia, St. Martin and St. Mary parishes. The court sits at New Iberia, St. Martinville and Franklin.

Judges

Gerard B. Wattigny
Paul J. deMahy
John E. Conery
William D. Hunter
Keith R. J. Comeaux
Edward M. Leonard, Jr.
Charles L. Porter
Lori A. Landry

SEVENTEENTH JUDICIAL DISTRICT includes Lafourche Parish. The court sits at Thibodaux.

Judges

John E. LeBlanc
Jerome J. Barbera, III
Walter I. Lanier
A. Bruce Simpson
F. Hugh LaRose

EIGHTEENTH JUDICIAL DISTRICT includes Iberville, Pointe Coupee and West Baton Rouge parishes. The court sits at Plaquemine, New Roads and Port Allen.

Judges

James J. Best
J. Robin Free
Alvin Batiste, Jr.
Jack T. Marionneaux

NINETEENTH JUDICIAL DISTRICT includes East Baton Rouge Parish. The court sits at Baton Rouge.

Judges

Todd Hernandez
Donald R. Johnson
Louis R. Daniel
Janice G. Clark
William A. Morvant
Timothy E. Kelley
Richard D. Anderson
Anthony Marabella, Jr.
R. Michael Caldwell
Curtis A. Calloway
Bonnie F. Jackson
Michael R. Erwin
Kay Bates
Jewel E. Welch, Jr.
Wilson Fields

TWENTIETH JUDICIAL DISTRICT includes East Feliciana and West Feliciana parishes. The court sits at Clinton and St. Francisville.

Judges

George H. Ware, Jr.
William G. Carmichael

TWENTY-FIRST JUDICIAL DISTRICT includes Livingston, St. Helena and Tangipahoa parishes. The court sits at Livingston, Greensburg and Amite.

Judges

Wayne Ray Chutz
Bruce Charles Bennett
Robert Morrison, III
M. Douglas Hughes
Brenda Bedsole Ricks
Jefferson Hughes, III
Ernest G. Drake, Jr.
Zorraine M. Waguespack

TWENTY-SECOND JUDICIAL DISTRICT includes St. Tammany and Washington parishes. The court sits at Covington and Franklinton.

Judges

Raymond S. Childress
Elaine W. Di Miceli
Patricia T. Hedges
Peter J. Garcia
William J. Burris
Martin E. Coady
Larry J. Green
Donald M. Fendlason
Reginald Badeaux, III
William J. Knight

TWENTY-THIRD JUDICIAL DISTRICT includes Ascension, Assumption and St. James parishes. The court sits at Donaldsonville, Napoleonville and Convent.

Judges

Ralph Tureau
Thomas Kliebert, Jr.
Guy Holdridge
Pegram J. Mire, Jr.
Alvin Turner, Jr.

TWENTY-FOURTH JUDICIAL DISTRICT includes Jefferson Parish. The court sits at Gretna.

Judges

Joan S. Benge
Fredericka H. Wicker
Alan J. Green
Robert M. Murphy
Greg Gerard Guidry
Patrick J. McCabe
Robert A. Pitre
Kernan A. Hand
Jo Ellen Grant
Stephen J. Windhorst
Martha E. Sassone
Charles V. Cusimano, II
Henry G. Sullivan, Jr.
Hans J. Liljeberg
Ross P. LaDart
Melvin C. Zeno

TWENTY-FIFTH JUDICIAL DISTRICT includes Plaquemines Parish. The court sits at Pointe-a-la-Hache.

Judges

Anthony D. Ragusa, Jr.
William A. Roe

TWENTY-SIXTH JUDICIAL DISTRICT includes Bossier and Webster parishes. The court sits at Benton and Minden.

Judges

Dewey E. Burchett, Jr.
Ford E. Stinson, Jr.
Cecil Paxton Campbell, II
John M. Robinson
Bruce M. Bolin

TWENTY-SEVENTH JUDICIAL DISTRICT includes St. Landry Parish. The court sits at Opelousas.

Judges

James T. Genovese
Aaron Frank McGee, III
Alonzo Harris
Donald W. Hebert

TWENTY-EIGHTH JUDICIAL DISTRICT includes La Salle Parish. The court sits at Jena.

Judge

J. P. Mauffray, Jr.

TWENTY-NINTH JUDICIAL DISTRICT includes St. Charles Parish. The court sits at Hahnville.

Judges

Emile R. St. Pierre
Kirk R. Granier
Robert A. Chaisson

THIRTIETH JUDICIAL DISTRICT includes Vernon Parish. The court sits at Leesville.

Judges

Vernon B. Clark
John C. Ford
Lester P. Kees

LOUISIANA DISTRICT COURTS—*Continued*

THIRTY-FIRST JUDICIAL DISTRICT includes Jefferson Davis Parish. The court sits at Jennings.

Judge
Wendell Reive Miller

THIRTY-SECOND JUDICIAL DISTRICT includes Terrebonne Parish. The court sits at Houma.

Judges
George J. Larke, Jr.
John R. Walker
Timothy Claude Ellender
David W. Arceneaux
Randy Bethancourt

THIRTY-THIRD JUDICIAL DISTRICT includes Allen Parish. The court sits at Oberlin.

Judges
Joel G. Davis
Patricia C. Cole

THIRTY-FOURTH JUDICIAL DISTRICT includes St. Bernard Parish. The court sits at Chalmette.

Judges
Robert A. Buckley
Manuel A. Fernandez
Wayne George Cresap
Kirk A. Vaughn
Jacques A. Sanborn

THIRTY-FIFTH JUDICIAL DISTRICT includes Grant Parish. The court sits at Colfax.

Judge
Allen A. Krake

THIRTY-SIXTH JUDICIAL DISTRICT includes Beauregard Parish. The court sits at DeRidder.

Judges
Stuart S. Kay, Jr.
Herman I. Stewart

THIRTY-SEVENTH JUDICIAL DISTRICT includes Caldwell Parish. The court sits at Columbia.

Judge
Don C. Burns

THIRTY-EIGHTH JUDICIAL DISTRICT includes Cameron Parish. The court sits at Cameron.

Judge
H. Ward Fontenot

THIRTY-NINTH JUDICIAL DISTRICT includes Red River Parish. The court sits at Coushatta.

Judge
Lewis O. Sams

FORTIETH JUDICIAL DISTRICT includes St. John the Baptist Parish. The court sits at Edgard.

Judges
Madeline Jasmine
Mary Hotard Becnel
J. Sterling Snowdy

LOUISIANA FAMILY AND JUVENILE COURTS

Family and Juvenile Courts are courts of special jurisdiction in Louisiana. There are four Juvenile Courts, located in Caddo, East Baton Rouge, Jefferson and Orleans parishes. East Baton Rouge Parish also has the only Family Court. Judges are elected for six-year terms by voters of their respective parishes, except in Orleans Parish where Juvenile Court judges are elected to eight-year terms. Retirement is generally mandatory at age seventy; however, retired judges may serve by assignment of the Supreme Court.

The Juvenile Courts have exclusive original jurisdiction over delinquency cases involving persons under the age of twenty-one who commit delinquent acts before attaining the age of seventeen, except in those instances where juveniles who have reached the age of fifteen are charged with first degree murder, second degree murder, aggravated rape or aggravated kidnapping; in these cases, jurisdiction is transferred to the appropriate court exercising criminal jurisdiction over the charged offenses. Some Juvenile Courts also have exclusive original jurisdiction to try an adult for contributing to the delinquency of children, criminal neglect of family, improper supervision, and any other misdemeanor enacted for the protection of the physical, moral or mental well-being of children. The Juvenile Courts have original jurisdiction in all adoption proceedings involving unemancipated children under the age of seventeen. The Family Court in East Baton Rouge Parish has exclusive jurisdiction over divorce actions; annulment of marriage; establishment and disavowal of the paternity of children; spousal and child support; and custody and visitation of children. In parishes not having Juvenile Courts, the District Courts and City Courts exercise concurrent jurisdiction over the above matters.

CADDO PARISH JUVENILE COURT sits at Shreveport.

Judges
David N. Matlock
Paul Young
Vernon Claville

EAST BATON ROUGE PARISH FAMILY COURT sits at Baton Rouge.

Judges
Jennifer Luse
Luke A. LaVergne
Toni M. Higginbotham
Annette M. Lassalle

EAST BATON ROUGE PARISH JUVENILE COURT sits at Baton Rouge.

Judges
Kathleen Stewart Richey
Pamela Taylor Johnson

JEFFERSON PARISH JUVENILE COURT sits at Harvey.

Judges
Ann Murry Keller
Andrea Price Janzen
Nancy Amato Konrad

ORLEANS PARISH JUVENILE COURT sits at New Orleans.

LOUISIANA FAMILY AND JUVENILE COURTS—*Continued*

Judges

Ernestine S. Gray
Yvonne Hughes
Anita Hamann Ganucheau
C. Hearn Taylor
Lawrence L. Lagarde
Mark Doherty

LOUISIANA CITY, MUNICIPAL AND TRAFFIC COURTS

The City Courts are Louisiana's principal courts of limited jurisdiction and may be established in cities with populations exceeding 5,000. Judges are generally elected for six-year terms by the voters of their respective wards; however, some terms may be for shorter or longer periods, depending on the municipality. In courts having more than one judge, the judge having served the longest is designated the senior judge of the court. In Orleans Parish, the court is divided into First and Second City Courts, which exercise civil jurisdiction; a Municipal Court, which handles misdemeanor cases except traffic cases; and a Traffic Court. Retirement is generally mandatory at age seventy; however, retired judges may serve by assignment of the Supreme Court.

Outside Orleans Parish, City Courts have criminal jurisdiction in cases not punishable at hard labor, including violations of parish and city ordinances, state DWI cases, peace bonds and preliminary examinations in non-capital cases. The courts exercise concurrent jurisdiction with the District Courts in juvenile matters except where there is a separate Juvenile Court. The courts have civil jurisdiction, concurrent with the District Courts, in cases when the amount in dispute does not exceed amounts ranging from $10,000 to $25,000 (depending on the court), except for those matters in which Parish Courts have no jurisdiction, and except in matters involving tutorship, curatorship, emancipation and partition proceedings. The City Courts may also establish small claims divisions for claims of up to $3,000. Within Orleans Parish, the Municipal Court has exclusive original jurisdiction over municipal ordinances excluding traffic. The Traffic Court has exclusive original jurisdiction over violations of municipal traffic ordinances.

City	Judge
Abbeville	Edward B. Broussard
Alexandria	Richard E. Starling, Jr.
Baker	Mark D. Plaisance
Bastrop	Merwin M. Brandon, Jr.
Baton Rouge	Laura Prosser Davis
	Trudy White
	Alex W. Wall
	Yvette M. Alexander
	Suzan S. Ponder
Bogalusa	Robert J. Black
Bossier City	Thomas A. Wilson, Jr.
Breaux Bridge	Randy P. Angelle
Bunkie	James H. Mixon
Crowley	Barrett Harrington
Denham Springs	Charles W. Borde, Jr.
Eunice	Lynette Young Feucht
Franklin	Terry G. Breaux
Hammond	Grace Bennett Gasaway
Houma	Jude Thaddeus Fanguy
Jeanerette	Cameron B. Simmons
Jennings	C. Steve Gunnell
Kaplan	Frank LeMoine
Lafayette	Frances Moran Bouillion
	Douglas James Saloom
Lake Charles	Thomas P. Quirk
	John S. Hood
Leesville	Elvin C. Fontenot, Jr.
Marksville	Angelo J. Piazza, III
Minden	John C. Campbell
Monroe	Tammy D. Lee
	B. Scott Leehy
	Daryl Blue
Morgan City	Kim P. Stansbury
Natchitoches	Fred S. Gahagan
New Iberia	Robert L. Segura
New Orleans	
First City Court	Charles A. Imbornone
	Angélique A. Reed
	Sonja M. Spears
Second City Court	Mary K K Norman
Municipal Court	John A. Shea
	Bruce J. McConduit
	Sean P. Early
	Paul N. Sens
Traffic Court	Dennis Jude Dannel
	Robert E. Jones
	Paul A. Bonin
	Ronald J. Sholes
Oakdale	Perrell Fuselier
Opelousas	Kenneth Boagni, Jr.
Pineville	Phillip J. Terrell
Plaquemine	William C. Dupont
Port Allen	William T. Kleinpeter
Rayne	James M. Cunningham
Ruston	Danny Tatum
Shreveport	R. Lee Irvin
	Charles W. Kelly
	LaLeshia Walker Alford
	Randy E. Collins
Slidell	Gary J. Dragon
Springhill	John B. Slattery
Sulphur	Charles Schrumpf
Thibodaux	David M. Richard
Vidalia	George C. Murray, Jr.
Ville Platte	Donald J. Launey
West Monroe	Jim Norris
Winnfield	Jacque D. Derr
Winnsboro	Ann McIntyre
Zachary	Lonny A. Myles

LOUISIANA PARISH COURTS

Three Parish Courts are established in Louisiana: two in Jefferson Parish and one in Ascension Parish. Jefferson Parish is divided into First Parish Court and Second Parish Court. Judges are elected for six-year terms by the voters of their respective wards. In courts having more than one judge, the judge having served the longest is designated the senior judge of the court. Retirement is generally mandatory at age seventy; however, retired judges may serve by assignment of the Supreme Court.

Parish Court jurisdiction is similar to that of the City Courts. The courts have concurrent jurisdiction with the District Courts over criminal offenses which are punishable by fines of $1,000 or less, imprisonment not exceeding six months, or both. The courts have concurrent civil jurisdiction with the District Courts in cases when the amount in controversy is up to $20,000.

LOUISIANA PARISH COURTS—*Continued*

Parish	Judge
Ascension	Marilyn M. Lambert
Jefferson	
First Parish Court	Rebecca M. Olivier
	George W. Giacobbe
Second Parish Court	Roy M. Cascio
	Stephen Grefer

LOUISIANA LOWER COURTS

JUSTICE OF THE PEACE COURTS are established in cities not having City Courts. Justices are elected for six-year terms. The courts have original civil jurisdiction concurrent with the District Courts in cases up to $3,000, excluding suits involving title to real estate, the right to public office, divorce proceedings, suits against public bodies and executory proceedings. Concurrent jurisdiction extends to suits for possession or ownership of movable property not exceeding $2,000; suits by landowners or lessors for eviction of occupants or tenants of leased commercial properties and farmlands where the amount of monthly rent does not exceed $2,000, regardless of the amount of rent due or the amount of rent owing for the unexpired term of the lease; and suits by landowners or lessors for the eviction of occupants or tenants of leased residential premises, regardless of the amount of rent due or the amount of rent owing for the unexpired term of the lease. Justices may exercise criminal jurisdiction as committing magistrates and for the issuance of peace bonds.

MAYOR'S COURTS are municipal courts that have jurisdiction over violations of municipal ordinances. Mayors and appointed magistrates are granted the power of imposing imprisonment as well as the power of committing magistrate.

Louisiana Parishes and Parish Seats

Acadia
Crowley

Allen
Oberlin

Ascension
Donaldsonville

Assumption
Napoleonville

Avoyelles
Marksville

Beauregard
DeRidder

Bienville
Arcadia

Bossier
Benton

Caddo
Shreveport

Calcasieu
Lake Charles

Caldwell
Columbia

Cameron
Cameron

Catahoula
Harrisonburg

Claiborne
Homer

Concordia
Vidalia

DeSoto
Mansfield

East Baton Rouge
Baton Rouge

East Carroll
Lake Providence

East Feliciana
Clinton

Evangeline
Ville Platte

Franklin
Winnsboro

Grant
Colfax

Iberia
New Iberia

Iberville
Plaquemine

Jackson
Jonesboro

Jefferson
Gretna

Jefferson Davis
Jennings

Lafayette
Lafayette

Lafourche
Thibodaux

La Salle
Jena

Lincoln
Ruston

Livingston
Livingston

Madison
Tallulah

Morehouse
Bastrop

Natchitoches
Natchitoches

Orleans
New Orleans

Ouachita
Monroe

Plaquemines
Pointe-a-la-Hache

Pointe Coupee
New Roads

Rapides
Alexandria

Red River
Coushatta

Richland
Rayville

Sabine
Many

St. Bernard
Chalmette

St. Charles
Hahnville

St. Helena
Greensburg

St. James
Convent

St. John the Baptist
Edgard

St. Landry
Opelousas

St. Martin
St. Martinville

St. Mary
Franklin

PARISHES AND PARISH SEATS—*Continued*

St. Tammany
Covington

Tangipahoa
Amite

Tensas
St. Joseph

Terrebonne
Houma

Union
Farmerville

Vermilion
Abbeville

Vernon
Leesville

Washington
Franklinton

Webster
Minden

West Baton Rouge
Port Allen

West Carroll
Oak Grove

West Feliciana
St. Francisville

Winn
Winnfield

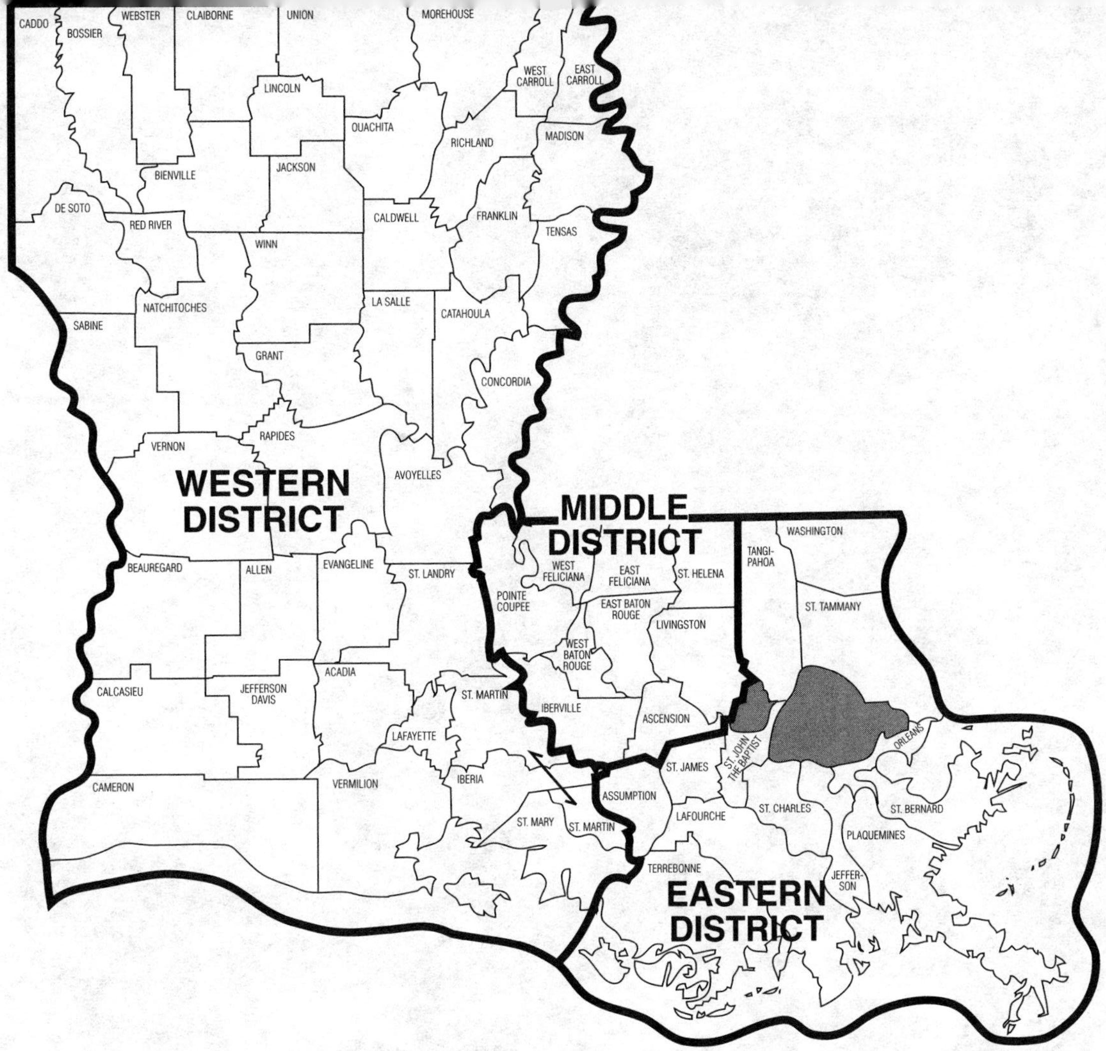
CADDO
BOSSIER
WEBSTER
CLAIBORNE
UNION
MOREHOUSE
WEST CARROLL
EAST CARROLL
LINCOLN
OUACHITA
RICHLAND
MADISON
BIENVILLE
JACKSON
DE SOTO
RED RIVER
CALDWELL
FRANKLIN
TENSAS
WINN
LA SALLE
CATAHOULA
NATCHITOCHES
SABINE
GRANT
CONCORDIA
RAPIDES
VERNON
AVOYELLES
WESTERN DISTRICT
MIDDLE DISTRICT
WASHINGTON
TANGI-PAHOA
WEST FELICIANA
EAST FELICIANA
ST. HELENA
BEAUREGARD
ALLEN
EVANGELINE
ST. LANDRY
POINTE COUPEE
EAST BATON ROUGE
ST. TAMMANY
LIVINGSTON
WEST BATON ROUGE
ACADIA
JEFFERSON DAVIS
CALCASIEU
ST. MARTIN
IBERVILLE
ASCENSION
LAFAYETTE
ORLEANS
ST. JOHN THE BAPTIST
ST. JAMES
IBERIA
CAMERON
VERMILION
ASSUMPTION
ST. CHARLES
ST. BERNARD
LAFOURCHE
ST. MARY
ST. MARTIN
PLAQUEMINES
TERREBONNE
JEFFER-SON
EASTERN DISTRICT

UNITED STATES DISTRICT COURTS DISTRICTS OF LOUISIANA

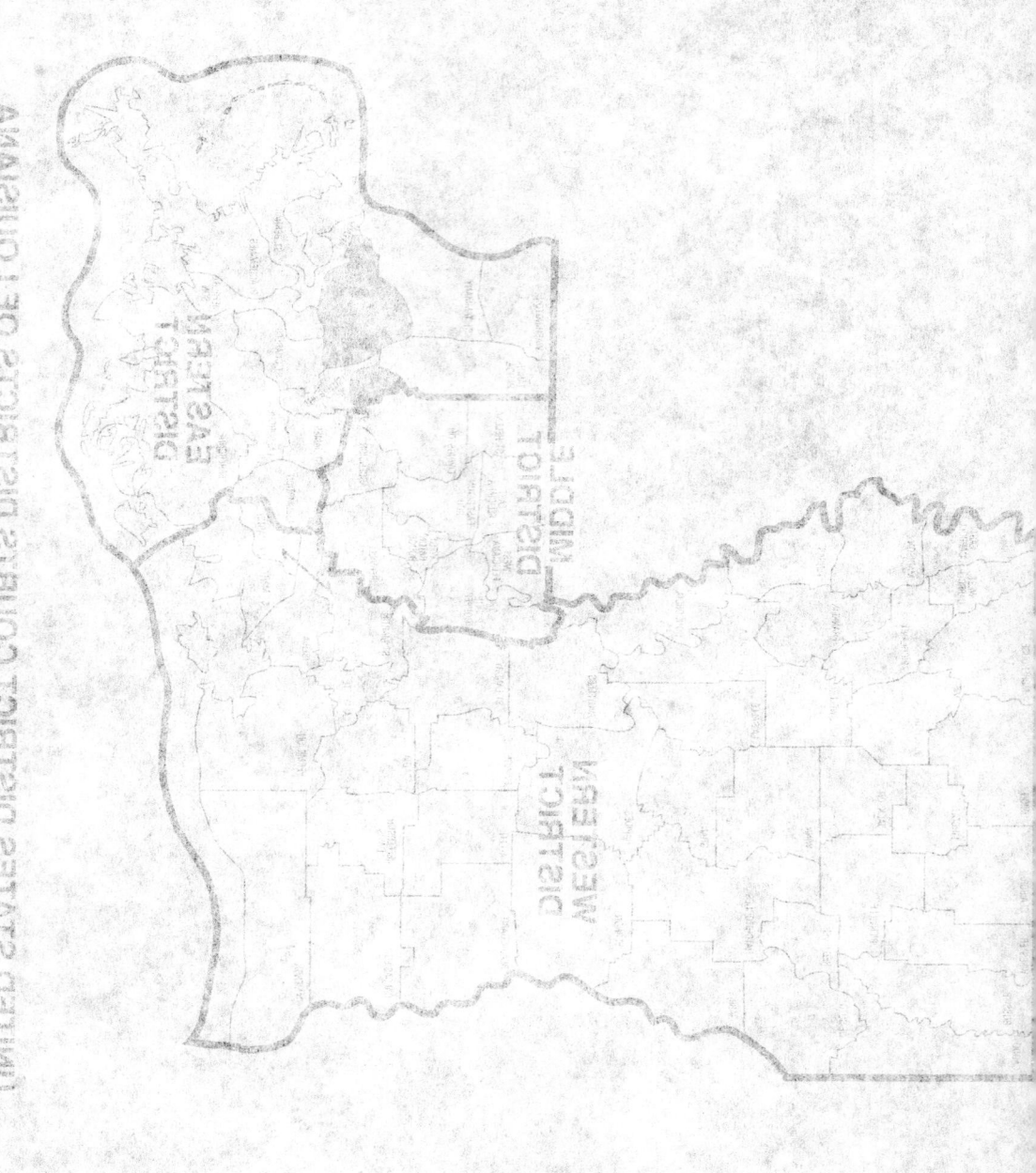

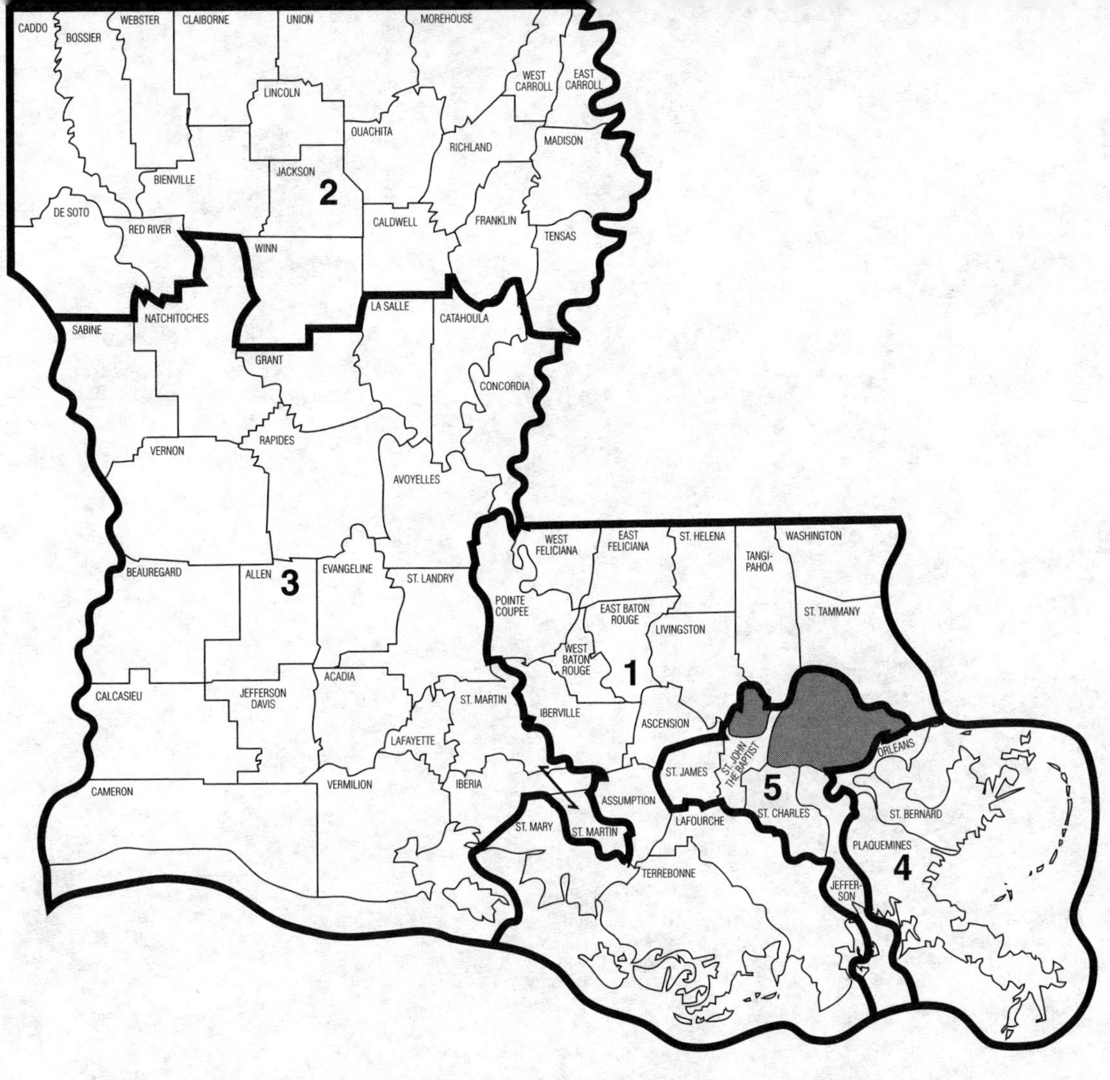
CADDO
BOSSIER
WEBSTER
CLAIBORNE
UNION
MOREHOUSE
WEST CARROLL
EAST CARROLL
LINCOLN
OUACHITA
RICHLAND
MADISON
JACKSON
2
BIENVILLE
DE SOTO
RED RIVER
CALDWELL
FRANKLIN
TENSAS
WINN
LA SALLE
CATAHOULA
NATCHITOCHES
SABINE
GRANT
CONCORDIA
RAPIDES
VERNON
AVOYELLES
WEST FELICIANA
EAST FELICIANA
ST. HELENA
TANGI-PAHOA
WASHINGTON
BEAUREGARD
ALLEN
3
EVANGELINE
ST. LANDRY
POINTE COUPEE
EAST BATON ROUGE
LIVINGSTON
ST. TAMMANY
WEST BATON ROUGE
1
CALCASIEU
JEFFERSON DAVIS
ACADIA
ST. MARTIN
IBERVILLE
ASCENSION
LAFAYETTE
ST. JOHN THE BAPTIST
ORLEANS
ST. JAMES
5
CAMERON
VERMILION
IBERIA
ASSUMPTION
ST. CHARLES
ST. BERNARD
LAFOURCHE
ST. MARY
ST. MARTIN
PLAQUEMINES
4
TERREBONNE
JEFFER-SON

CIRCUITS OF LOUISIANA COURTS OF APPEAL

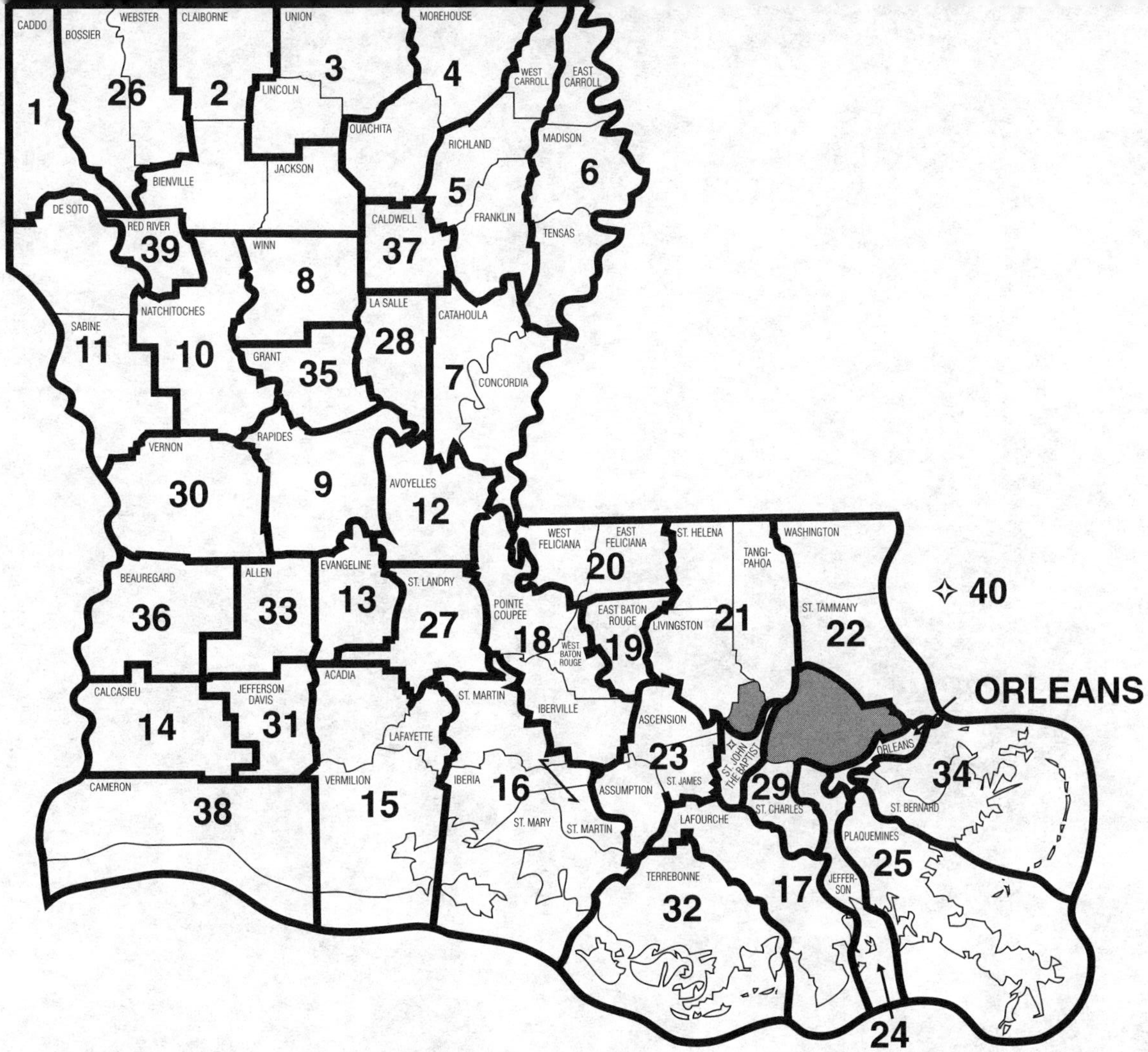
CADDO
BOSSIER
WEBSTER
CLAIBORNE
UNION
MOREHOUSE
WEST CARROLL
EAST CARROLL
LINCOLN
OUACHITA
RICHLAND
MADISON
BIENVILLE
JACKSON
FRANKLIN
TENSAS
DE SOTO
RED RIVER
CALDWELL
WINN
NATCHITOCHES
LA SALLE
CATAHOULA
SABINE
GRANT
CONCORDIA
RAPIDES
VERNON
AVOYELLES
WEST FELICIANA
EAST FELICIANA
ST. HELENA
TANGI-PAHOA
WASHINGTON
BEAUREGARD
ALLEN
EVANGELINE
ST. LANDRY
POINTE COUPEE
EAST BATON ROUGE
LIVINGSTON
ST. TAMMANY
WEST BATON ROUGE
ACADIA
CALCASIEU
JEFFERSON DAVIS
ST. MARTIN
IBERVILLE
ASCENSION
ORLEANS
LAFAYETTE
ST. JOHN THE BAPTIST
ST. JAMES
ST. CHARLES
ST. BERNARD
CAMERON
VERMILION
IBERIA
ASSUMPTION
ST. MARY
LAFOURCHE
PLAQUEMINES
TERREBONNE
JEFFER-SON
1
2
3
4
5
6
7
8
9
10
11
12
13
14
15
16
17
18
19
20
21
22
23
24
25
26
27
28
29
30
31
32
33
34
35
36
37
38
39
40

JUDICIAL DISTRICTS OF LOUISIANA DISTRICT COURTS

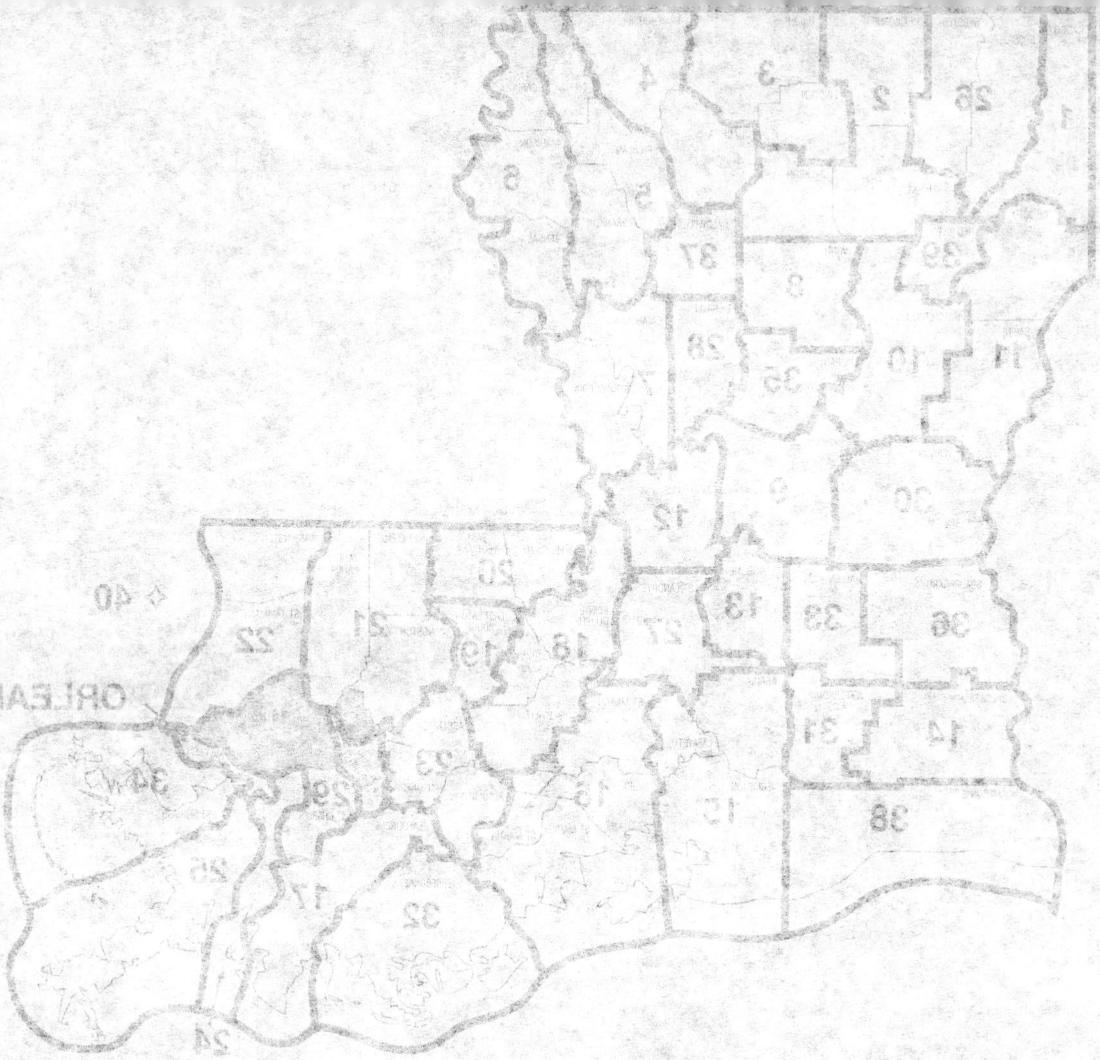
ORLEANS
40
1
2
3
4
5
6
7
8
9
10
11
12
13
14
15
16
17
18
19
20
21
22
23
24
25
26
27
28
29
30
31
32
33
34
35
36
37
38
39

JUDICIAL DISTRICTS OF LOUISIANA DISTRICT COURTS

LOUISIANA

ADAMS, Charles B. *(Judge, Louisiana District Court Eleventh Judicial District)* Currently serves as Chief Judge.
Mailing address: P.O. Box 1350, Mansfield 71052.
Telephone: (318) 872-2291.

AFRICK, Lance M. *(Judge, United States District Court Eastern District of Louisiana)* Former Magistrate Judge. Appointed Judge for life by President George W. Bush.
Office: B335 Federal Building, 501 Magazine Street, New Orleans 70130.
Telephone: (504) 589-7605.

ALARCON, Terry Q. *(Judge, Louisiana District Court Orleans Parish Criminal District)* Former Judge, New Orleans Traffic Court.
Office: 2700 Tulane Avenue, New Orleans 70119.
Telephone: (504) 826-5105.

ALEXANDER, Yvette Mansfield *(Judge, Baton Rouge City Court)*
Office: 233 St. Louis Street, Baton Rouge 70821-3438.
Telephone: (225) 389-5006.

ALFORD, LaLeshia Walker *(Judge, Shreveport City Court)* Elected to term beginning Sept 1997. Reelected 2002, current term expires Dec 31, 2008. First African-American elected to Shreveport City Court. Born Shreveport Louisiana March 18, 1961. Educated at North Texas State University, Texas Woman's University B.S. magna cum laude 1983 and Tulane University School of Law J.D. 1988. Editor-in-Chief National Black Law Journal. Admitted to practice Louisiana 1989. In legal practice New Orleans and Shreveport 1988-96.

Assistant District Attorney 1992-97. Staff Attorney Office of Family Support State of Louisiana. Executive Director National Judicial Council National Bar Association 2001. Former Pupil Harry K. Booth American Inns of Court. Member Shreveport Black Lawyer's Association, National Association of Women Judges, Shreveport and Louisiana Bar Associations. Participant Criminal Law Delegation to China People to People Ambassador Program Rutgers University Sept 8, 2000 to Sept 21, 2000. Recipient Brotherhood Award from National Council of Christians and Jews 1979, Community Services Award from National Council of Negro Women 1984, Legal Services Award from Caddo Community Action Agency 1996 and President's Award from NAACP 2001. Named Outstanding Law Student of America 1987-88. Previously worked as a music therapist Pinecrest State School and Caddo Parish School. Past President Shreveport Youth Symphony. President One Church—One Offender Reentry Program. Board Member Renzi Center. Assistant Superintendent, Teacher Sunday School and Church musician First Church of God in Christ. Member Property Standard Board, League of Women Voters, and Quota Club. Writer, motivational speaker, musician and composer.
Office: 1244 Texas Avenue, Shreveport 71101.
Telephone: (318) 673-5890.

AMY, Marc T. *(Judge, Louisiana Court of Appeal Third Circuit)*
Office: 122 North State Street, Abbeville 70510-5417.
Telephone: (337) 898-1222.

ANDERSON, Richard D. *(Judge, Louisiana District Court Nineteenth Judicial District)*
Office: 222 St. Louis Street, Suite 679, Baton Rouge 70802.
Telephone: (225) 389-4731.

ANGELLE, Randy P. *(Judge, Breaux Bridge City Court)* Elected to term beginning Jan 1, 1991. Reelected 1996 and 2002. Current term expires Dec 31, 2008. Born Lafayette Louisiana Aug 15, 1952. Catholic. Educated at University of Southwestern Louisiana B.A. 1975 and Loyola University J.D. 1977. Member Phi Kappa Phi, Phi Delta Phi and St. Thomas More Society. Admitted to practice Louisiana 1977, U.S. District Courts Western 1978 and Middle 1982 Districts of Louisiana and U.S. Court of Appeals Fifth Circuit 1982. In legal practice Lafayette since 1977.

Member Louisiana Trial Lawyers Association, Lafayette Parish, Louisiana State and American Bar Associations. Louisiana National Guard 1971-77. Member St. Bernard Elementary School Board, Kiwanis Club and Chamber of Commerce. Enjoys fishing, hunting, golf, coaching youth baseball and all sports.
Office: 101 Berard Street, Breaux Bridge 70517.
Telephone: (337) 332-4117.

ARCENEAUX, David W. *(Judge, Louisiana District Court Thirty-second Judicial District)*
Mailing address: P.O. Box 3780, Houma 70361.
Telephone: (985) 873-6570.

ARMSTRONG, Joan Bernard *(Judge, Louisiana Court of Appeal Fourth Circuit)* Assumed office Aug 1984. Born New Orleans Louisiana. Educated at Xavier University B.A. and Loyola University J.D. Judge, Orleans Parish Juvenile Court 1974-84.
Office: 1515 Poydras Street, New Orleans 70112.
Telephone: (504) 592-0913.

BADEAUX, Reginald T., III *(Judge, Louisiana District Court Twenty-second Judicial District)* Elected to term beginning Jan 1, 1998. Reelected 2001, current term expires Dec 31, 2007. Born New Orleans Louisiana April 11, 1955. Catholic. Educated at Southeastern Louisiana University B.A. 1980 and Loyola University School of Law J.D. 1984. Admitted to practice Louisiana 1984. In legal practice May 1, 1984 to Jan 1, 1998.

Assistant District Attorney Twenty-second Judicial District Sept 20, 1990 to Sept 20, 1997. Member Inns of Court, Louisiana Association of Drug Court Professionals and Louisiana State Bar Association. Republican. Board Member Habitat for Humanity, United Theatre Artists and Youth Service Bureau. Enjoys family, reading, theater and film. Personal Statement or Quote: "Quality of justice is elusive."
Office: 501 East Boston Street, Covington 70433.
Telephone: (985) 875-2150.
E-mail address: Judgertb@fastband.com

BAGNERIS, Dennis Raymond, Sr. *(Judge, Louisiana Court of Appeal Fourth Circuit)* Elected to term beginning Jan 1, 1999. Term expires Dec 31, 2008. Born New Orleans Louisiana June 10, 1948. Educated at Xavier University B.A. 1970 M.A. 1977 and Tulane University of Louisiana School of Law J.D. 1981. Admitted to practice Louisiana 1982.

Guest Lecturer Sophia University Tokyo Japan 1991, International Government Club Tokyo Japan 1991 and Government Council Gifu Japan 1991. Recipient Appreciation Award from Concerned Citizens for Better Government 1985, Certificate of Merit from City of New Orleans 1992, Outstanding Legislator Award from Victims and Citizens Against Crime 1992, Appreciation Award from Louisiana Association of the Deaf 1993, Appreciation Award from Reality House 1994 and Legislator of the Year Award from ARC of Louisiana 1994. Named Senator of the Year by LFT 1990 and Outstanding Alumnus by Tulane University 1995. Case worker Louisiana Department of Public Welfare 1970-72. Probation officer New Orleans Alcohol Safety Action Project 1972-74. Senator 1983-98 and President pro tempore 1992-99 Senate Louisiana. President Louisiana Legislative Black Caucus 1989-90.

Office: 1515 Poydras Street, Seventh Floor, New Orleans 70112.

Telephone: (504) 592-0901.

BAGNERIS, Michael G. *(Judge, Louisiana District Court Orleans Parish Civil District)* Former Chief Judge.

Office: 421 Loyola Avenue, Room 304, New Orleans 70112.

Telephone: (504) 592-9337.

BARBERA, Jerome J., III *(Judge, Louisiana District Court Seventeenth Judicial District)* Currently serves as Chief Judge.

Mailing address: P.O. Box 29, Thibodaux 70302-0029.

Telephone: (985) 446-0517.

BARBIER, Carl J. *(Judge, United States District Court Eastern District of Louisiana)* Appointed for life by President Bill Clinton to term beginning October 12, 1998. Born New Orleans Louisiana Aug 21, 1944. Catholic. Educated at Southeastern Louisiana University B.A. with honors 1966 and Loyola University School of Law J.D. with honors 1970. Associate Editor Loyola Law Review 1968-70. Law Clerk to Hon. William Redmann, Louisiana Court of Appeal Fourth Circuit 1969-70 and Hon. Fred Cassibry, U.S. District Court Eastern District of Louisiana 1970-71. Member Alpha Sigma Nu. Admitted to practice Louisiana 1970, U.S. District Court Eastern District of Louisiana 1970 and U.S. Court of Appeals Fifth Circuit 1971. In legal practice New Orleans 1971-98.

Member Jefferson, New Orleans, Louisiana State, Federal and American Bar Associations. Enjoys jogging, reading and traveling.

Office: C322 U.S. Courthouse, 500 Camp Street, New Orleans 70130.

Telephone: (504) 589-7525.

E-mail address: Barbier@laed.uscourts.gov

BATES, Kay *(Judge, Louisiana District Court Nineteenth Judicial District)* Currently serves as Chief Judge.

Office: 222 St. Louis Street, Baton Rouge 70801.

Telephone: (225) 389-4787.

BATISTE, Alvin, Jr. *(Judge, Louisiana District Court Eighteenth Judicial District)* Currently serves as Chief Judge.

Mailing address: P.O. Box 241, Plaquemine 70765-0241.

Telephone: (225) 687-5230.

BEASLEY, Stephen B. *(Judge, Louisiana District Court Eleventh Judicial District)*

Mailing address: P.O. Box 9, Many 71449.

Telephone: (318) 256-9789.

BECNEL, Mary Hotard *(Judge, Louisiana District Court Fortieth Judicial District)* Currently serves as Chief Judge.

Mailing address: P.O. Box 357, Edgard 70049.

Telephone: (985) 497-5508.

BEER, Peter H. *(Senior Judge, United States District Court Eastern District of Louisiana)* Appointed for life by President Jimmy Carter Nov 27, 1979. Assumed Senior status, serves by assignment. Born New Orleans Louisiana April 12, 1928. Jewish. Educated at Tulane University of Louisiana B.B.A. 1949 LL.B. with honors 1951 and University of Virginia School of Law LL.M. 1986. Member Omicron Delta Kappa and Phi Delta Phi. Presiding Judge Tulane Moot Court. Admitted to practice Louisiana 1952, U.S. Court of Military Appeals 1954 and U.S. Supreme Court 1954. Began legal practice New Orleans 1952. Judge, Louisiana Court of Appeal Fourth Circuit Oct 1974 to Dec 1979.

Author "Keeping Up with the Jones Act" Tulane L. Rev. 1987. Part-time faculty member University of Virginia School of Law and Tulane University School of Law. Vice Chairman Committee to Study Louisiana Appellate Caseloads and Procedures. Member National Judicial Council of State and Federal Courts since Jan 13, 1994. Member Judicial Conference of the U.S. (State-Federal Committee), New Orleans, Louisiana State and American Bar Associations. Nominated to serve on U.S. Sentencing Commission by Chief Justice of the U.S. Supreme Court and Judicial Conference of the U.S. Sept 23, 1997. Served to Sergeant U.S. Army Infantry 1945-47 and Captain USAF 1952-54. Recipient Soldiers Medal, Bronze Star and Air Force Commendation Medal. Political affiliation: Independent. Member New Orleans City Council 1970-74 (Vice President 1972-74, Acting President 1974). Vice President New Orleans Home for Jewish Aged and Bureau of Governmental Research. Board member Touro Infirmary and New Orleans Public Library. Member Southern Yacht Club. Enjoys sailing, golf and fishing.

Office: C121 U.S. Courthouse, 500 Camp Street, New Orleans 70130-3384.

Telephone: (504) 589-7510.

BELSOME, Roland L. *(Judge, Louisiana District Court Orleans Parish Civil District)*

Office: 421 Loyola Avenue, New Orleans 70112.

Telephone: (504) 592-9209.

BENGE, Joan S. *(Judge, Louisiana District Court Twenty-fourth Judicial District)*

Office: 200 Derbigny Street, Gretna 70053.

Telephone: (504) 364-3850.

BENNETT, Bruce Charles *(Judge, Louisiana District Court Twenty-first Judicial District)* Elected to term beginning April 4, 1988. Reelected 1990, 1996 and 2002. Current term expires Dec 31, 2008. Born Amite Louisi-

BENNETT, BRUCE CHARLES—*Continued*
ana Sept 21, 1952. Christian. Educated at Louisiana State University B.S. 1972 J.D. 1975. Recipient Dean Henry George McMahon Scholarship senior year. Admitted to practice Louisiana 1975, U.S. Court of Military Appeals 1976, U.S. Supreme Court 1976 and U.S. District Courts Eastern 1979 and Middle 1979 Districts of Louisiana. In legal practice Hammond 1979-88. Magistrate, Independence Town Court 1985-88.
Town Attorney Independence 1984-88. Instructor in Criminal Law Los Angeles Community College Overseas Branch 1977-78, University of Maryland Overseas Branch 1978-79 and Southeastern Louisiana University 1989-2002. Member Bar of the Supreme Court of the United States, Louisiana Trial Lawyers Association, American Trial Lawyers Association, Louisiana District Judges Association and Twenty-first Judicial District Bar Association. Attended General Jurisdiction course Sept 1988 and Complex Litigation course The National Judicial College. Captain USAF JAGC 1975-79. Democrat. Member Tangipahoa Parish Democratic Executive Committee 1983-87. Member Hammond Exchange Club (Former President) and Hammond Housing Authority (Former Chairman). Enjoys tennis, golf and amateur little theatre.
Mailing address: P.O. Box 788, Amite 70422.
Telephone: (985) 748-9445.

BENNETT, William J. *(Judge, Louisiana District Court Twelfth Judicial District)* Currently serves as Chief Judge.
Mailing address: P.O. Box 84, Marksville 71351.
Telephone: (318) 253-9418.

BERRIGAN, Helen G. *(Chief Judge, United States District Court Eastern District of Louisiana)* Appointed for life by President Bill Clinton to term beginning 1994. Chief Judge since Nov 28, 2001. Born New Rochelle New York April 15, 1948. Educated at University of Wisconsin B.A. 1969, American University M.A. 1971 and Louisiana State University Law Center J.D. 1977. In legal practice New Orleans 1978-94.
Staff Attorney Governor's Pardon, Parole and Rehabilitation Commission 1977-78.
Office: C556 U.S. Courthouse, 500 Camp Street, New Orleans 70130-3353.
Telephone: (504) 589-7515.

BEST, James J. *(Judge, Louisiana District Court Eighteenth Judicial District)*
Mailing address: P.O. Box 536, New Roads 70760.
Telephone: (225) 638-5532.

BETHANCOURT, Randy *(Judge, Louisiana District Court Thirty-second Judicial District)*
Office: 7856 Main Street, Suite 236, Houma 70360.
Telephone: (985) 873-6580.

BIGELOW, Raymond C. *(Judge, Louisiana District Court Orleans Parish Criminal District)* Elected Oct 1993 to term beginning Dec 1, 1993. Reelected Sept 1996, current term expires Dec 31, 2003. Born Houma Louisiana May 27, 1947. Catholic. Educated at University of New Orleans 1979 and Tulane University School of Law J.D. 1982. Admitted to practice Louisiana 1982. In legal practice Lake Charles 1982-83.
Assistant District Attorney New Orleans 1983-93.
Office: 2700 Tulane Avenue, New Orleans 70119.
Telephone: (504) 827-3480.

BLACK, Robert J. *(Judge, Bogalusa City Court)*
Mailing address: P.O. Box 518, Bogalusa 70429-0518.
Telephone: (985) 732-6204.

BLANCHET, David *(Judge, Louisiana District Court Fifteenth Judicial District)*
Mailing address: P.O. Box 3407, Lafayette 70502.
Telephone: (337) 269-5729.

BLUE, Daryl *(Judge, Monroe City Court)*
Mailing address: P.O. Box 777, Monroe 71210.
Telephone: (318) 329-2580.

BOAGNI, Kenneth, Jr. *(Judge, Opelousas City Court)* Elected to term beginning Jan 1, 1973. Reelected 1978, 1984, 1990, 1996 and 2002. Current term expires Dec 31, 2008. Serves part time. Born Opelousas Louisiana Aug 24, 1936. Roman Catholic. Member Queen of Angels Catholic Church (Board of Directors). Educated at University of Southwestern Louisiana B.A. 1961 and Tulane University LL.B. 1961. Admitted to practice Louisiana 1961. Began legal practice Opelousas 1961.
Member Committee to Write Louisiana Juvenile Code 1980, State Committee to Write Louisiana Small Claims Legislation 1981, Louisiana Trial Lawyers Association, Louisiana City Judges Association (Secretary-Treasurer 1978, Vice President 1979 and President 1980), Louisiana Juvenile Judges Association (Secretary-Treasurer 1975, Vice President 1976 and President 1977) and St. Landry Parish Bar Association (Secretary 1964, Treasurer 1965 and Vice President 1966). Named Sertoma Man of the Year by Opelousas Sertoma Club 1973, Kiwanian of the Year by Opelousas Kiwanis Club 1974, Boss of the Year by St. Landry Secretaries Association 1978 and Citizen of the Year by City of Opelousas 1984. U.S. Army 1957-63. Democrat. Elected to St. Landry Parish Democratic Executive Committee (served 22 years). President Louisiana State Team Four Bridge Championships twelve years. Board of Directors Opelousas Kiwanis Club, Opelousas Chamber of Commerce and Sacred Heart Academy Grand Coteau. Chairman St. Landry Heart Fund Tennis Tournament eleven years. Life Master American Contract Bridge League. Interests include antiques, bridge, tennis, gardening and attending football and basketball events.
Mailing address: P.O. Box 1999, Opelousas 70571-1999.
Telephone: (337) 948-2570.

BOLIN, Bruce M. *(Judge, Louisiana District Court Twenty-sixth Judicial District)* Currently serves as Chief Judge.
Mailing address: P.O. Box 310, Benton 71006.
Telephone: (318) 965-2217.

BONIN, Paul A. *(Judge, New Orleans Traffic Court)*
Office: 727 South Broad Street, New Orleans 70119.
Telephone: (504) 827-5064.

BOOTHE, Leo *(Judge, Louisiana District Court Seventh Judicial District)* Elected to term beginning Jan 1, 1991. Reelected 1996 and 2002. Current term expires Dec 31, 2008. Currently serves as Chief Judge. Born Harrisonburg Louisiana Dec 8, 1941. Protestant. Educated at Louisiana State University B.A. 1965 J.D. 1970. Staff member Louisiana Law Review 1967-69. Law Clerk to Hon. J. Cleveland Fruge, U.S. Court of Appeals Third Circuit 1969-70. Admitted to practice Louisiana 1970, U.S. District Court Western District of Louisiana 1971 and U.S. Court of Appeals Fifth Circuit

BOOTHE, LEO—*Continued*

1978. In legal practice Columbia 1970-71 and Jonesville 1971-90.

Member Seventh Judicial District and Louisiana State Bar Associations. Enjoys fishing, hunting and raising cattle.

Mailing address: P.O. Drawer 600, Harrisonburg 71340.

Telephone: (318) 744-5414.

BORDE, Charles W., Jr. *(Judge, Denham Springs City Court)* Elected to term beginning Jan 1, 1991. Reelected 1996 and 2002. Current term expires Dec 31, 2008. Born Hattiesburg Mississippi Oct 10, 1947. Methodist. Educated at Louisiana State University B.A. 1969 and Loyola School of Law J.D. 1972. Admitted to practice Louisiana 1972 and U.S. District Court Middle District of Louisiana 1972. In legal practice Denham Springs since 1972.

Member Louisiana City Court Judges Association, Louisiana Council of Juvenile and Family Court Judges, Livingston Parish (Past President), Twenty-first Judicial District, Louisiana State and American Bar Associations.

Office: 400 Mayor Herbert Hoover Avenue, Denham Springs 70726-3613.

Telephone: (225) 665-5505.

BOUILLION, Frances Moran *(Judge, Lafayette City Court)* Assumed office May 1994. Currently serves as Senior Judge. Born March 20, 1945. Educated at St. Mary College B.S. 1967 and Louisiana State University Law Center J.D. 1987. Law Clerk to Hon. John M. Duhe, Jr., U.S. District Court Western District of Louisiana 1987-88. Admitted to practice Louisiana 1987, U.S. District Courts Middle 1988, Western 1988 and Eastern 1989 Districts of Louisiana and U.S. Court of Appeals Fifth Circuit 1989. In legal practice Lafayette 1988-94.

Adjunct Professor Louisiana State University Law Center since 1996. Member Merit Selection Panel for Magistrate Judges U.S. District Court Western District of Louisiana. Certified Mediator American Arbitration Association. Member Executive Committee since 1995, Team Leader 1995 and 1996 and Program Chair 1996 and 1997 Acadiana Inn of Court. Member Acadiana Association of Women Attorneys (Chair Community Outreach Committee 1991-92), Lafayette Volunteer Lawyers Association, Louisiana City Judges Association (Treasurer 1996-97), Louisiana Council of Juvenile and Family Court Judges, Louisiana State Judges Association, American Judges Association, Lafayette Parish, Louisiana State (Assistant Bar Examiner since 1994) and American (Sections: Litigation, Business Law, Criminal Justice) Bar Associations. Participant "Psychological Advocacy, Attorneys and Use of Blind Test Data" Louisiana Psychological Association Annual Meeting, New Orleans Louisiana Nov 1991; "Women and the Law" Acadiana Association of Women Attorneys and the Lafayette Center for Displaced Homemakers, Lafayette Louisiana Aug 1992; "What to Expect in Court" Seminar on Shoplifting Louisiana State Department of Justice, Lafayette Louisiana Sept 1995; and "Improving the Working Relationships Between Schools and Court" Lafayette Parish School Board, Lafayette Louisiana Sept 25, 1996. Guest Lecturer "Social Security—Nuts and Bolts" University of Southwest Louisiana Feb 1996. Inducted into Louisiana State University Law Center Hall of Fame 1988. Claims Representative 1967-72, Operations Analyst 1972-74 and Operations Supervisor 1974-84 Social Security Administration. Member Leadership Lafayette 1992-93. Board of Directors Goodwill Industries of Acadiana March 1992 to Dec 1996 (Chair Environmental Concerns Committee, Member Rehabilitation Committee).

Mailing address: P.O. Drawer 3344, Lafayette 70502-3344.

Telephone: (337) 291-8777.

BRADBERRY, Guy E. *(Judge, Louisiana District Court Fourteenth Judicial District)*

Mailing address: P.O. Box 3210, Lake Charles 70602.

Telephone: (337) 437-3363.

BRADY, James J. *(Judge, United States District Court Middle District of Louisiana)* Appointed for life by President Bill Clinton to term beginning May 29, 2000. Educated at Southeastern Louisiana University B.A. 1966 and Louisiana State University J.D. 1969. In legal practice Alexandria, Baton Rouge and New Orleans for 23 years and Washington D.C. Jan 1, 1993 to 1996.

Former Adjunct Instructor in Political Science Louisiana State University. Former Member Louisiana State Board of Tax Appeals. Member 1971-97 and Chairman 1985-96 Democratic State Central Committee of Louisiana. Delegate Democratic Mid-term Convention 1974 and Democratic National Convention 1980, 1984, 1988, 1992 and 1996. Member 1985-96 and Vice Chair 1990-96 Democratic National Committee. President Association of State Democratic Chairs 1990-96. Presidential Elector 1992.

Office: 369 Federal Building, 777 Florida Street, Baton Rouge 70801-1712.

Telephone: (225) 389-4030.

Fax: (225) 389-4031

BRAHNEY, Thomas M., III *(Chief Judge, United States Bankruptcy Court Eastern District of Louisiana)*

Office: 601 Federal Building, 501 Magazine Street, New Orleans 70130.

Telephone: (504) 589-7800.

BRANDON, Merwin M., Jr. *(Judge, Bastrop City Court)* Elected 1984 to term beginning Jan 1, 1985. Reelected 1990, 1996 and 2002. Current term expires Dec 31, 2008.

Mailing address: P.O. Box 391, Bastrop 71221-0391.

Telephone: (318) 283-0257.

BREAUX, Terry G. *(Judge, Franklin City Court)*

Office: 317 Willow Street, Franklin 70538.

Telephone: (337) 828-3858.

BROUSSARD, Edward B. *(Judge, Abbeville City Court)*

Mailing address: P.O. Box 251, Abbeville 70511-0251.

Telephone: (337) 893-1513.

BROWN, Henry N., Jr. *(Chief Judge, Louisiana Court of Appeal Second Circuit)*

Mailing address: P.O. Box 1528, Shreveport 71165-1528.

Telephone: (318) 227-3765.

BROWN, Jerry A. *(Judge, United States Bankruptcy Court Eastern District of Louisiana)* Appointed by U.S. Court of Appeals Fifth Circuit judges to term beginning Aug 27, 1992. Term expires Aug 26, 2006. Born Detroit

BROWN, JERRY A.—*Continued* Michigan Jan 31, 1932. Baptist. Educated at Murray State University B.A. with honors 1954 and Tulane University J.D. with honors 1959. Assistant Editor Tulane Law Review 1958-59. Law Clerk to Hon. John Minor Wisdom, U.S. Court of Appeals Fifth Circuit 1959-60. Member Phi Delta Phi. Admitted to practice Louisiana 1959, Kentucky 1959, U.S. District Courts Eastern 1960 and Western 1966 Districts of Louisiana and Western District of Kentucky 1980 and U.S. Court of Appeals Fifth Circuit 1960.

Important Decisions: In re Tahkenitch Tree Farm Partnership 156 B.R. 525, Bankr. E.D. La. 1993; In re Inter Urban Broadcasting of Cincinnati, Inc. 180 B.R. 153, 75 A.F.T.R.2d 95-887 Bankr. L. Rep. 76,411 Bankr. E.D. La. 1995; In re Miller 196 B.R. 334 Bankr. E.D. La. 1996; In re Totina 198 B.R. 673, 29 Bankr. Ct. Dec. 515 Bankr. L. Rep. 77,108 Bankr. E.D. La.; In re Treasure Bay Corp. 205 B.R. 490, 30 Bankr. Ct. Dec 483 Bankr. S.D. Miss. 1997; In re Treasure Bay Corp. 212 B.R. 520 Bankr. S.D. Miss. 1997; In re Johnson 89 F.3d 240, 5th Cir. 1996 (adopting opinion of Bankruptcy Court); In re Guiding Light Corp. 217 B.R. 493 Bankr. E.D. La. 1998; In re Pallet Reefer Co. 233 B.R. 687 Bankr. E.D. La. 1999; In re AMGAM Assoc. 239 B.R. 737 Bankr. S.D. Miss. 1999; In re O'Neil Theatres, Inc. 257 B.R. 806 Bankr. E.D. La. 2000; In re Schwegmann Giant Supermarkets Partnership 264 B.R. 823 Bankr. E.D. La. 2001; and In re Babcock & Wilcox Co. 274 B.R. 230 Bankr. E.D. La. 2002. Member Inns of Court, Bar Association of the Fifth Federal Circuit, New Orleans, Louisiana, Kentucky and American Bar Associations. Enjoys basketball, jogging, skiing and Dixieland jazz. Interested in antique cars.

Office: 501 Magazine Street, Suite 741A, New Orleans 70130.
Telephone: (504) 589-7886.

BRUN, Roy L. *(Judge, Louisiana District Court First Judicial District)*
Office: 501 Texas Street, Room 404, Shreveport 71101.
Telephone: (318) 677-5340.

BUCKLEY, Robert A. *(Judge, Louisiana District Court Thirty-fourth Judicial District)*
Office: 1101 West St. Bernard Highway, Chalmette 70043.
Telephone: (504) 278-4414.

BURAS, Camille *(Judge, Louisiana District Court Orleans Parish Criminal District)*
Office: 2700 Tulane Avenue, New Orleans 70119.
Telephone: (504) 827-3430.

BURCHETT, Dewey E., Jr. *(Judge, Louisiana District Court Twenty-sixth Judicial District)* Elected to term beginning Oct 13, 1988. Reelected 1990, 1996 and 2002. Current term expires Dec 31, 2008. Born Shreveport Louisiana Nov 18, 1939. Presbyterian. Educated at Louisiana State University B.A. 1962 J.D. 1970. Member Phi Alpha Delta. Admitted to practice Louisiana 1970, U.S. District Court Western District of Louisiana 1970 and U.S. Court of Appeals Fifth Circuit 1970. In legal practice Bossier City 1970-88.

City Attorney Bossier City 1976-77. Attorney Bossier Levee District 1979-88. Member Louisiana State and American Bar Associations. Attended Louisiana Judicial College 1989 and 1990. Captain USAF 1962-67. Democrat. Executive Committee 1971-79 and Chairman Bossier Parish Democratic Party. Lieutenant Colonel Louisiana Civil Air Patrol. Member Bossier Chamber of Commerce. Enjoys golfing and flying airplanes.

Mailing address: P.O. Box 310, Benton 71006.
Telephone: (318) 965-2217.

BURGESS, Robert E. *(Judge, Louisiana District Court Eleventh Judicial District)*
Mailing address: P.O. Box 1299, Mansfield 71052.
Telephone: (318) 872-1366.

BURNS, Don C. *(Judge, Louisiana District Court Thirty-seventh Judicial District)*
Office: 201 Main Street, Columbia 71418.
Telephone: (318) 649-6404.

BURRIS, William J. *(Judge, Louisiana District Court Twenty-second Judicial District)*
Mailing address: P.O. Box 608, Franklinton 70438.
Telephone: (985) 839-7840.

BYRNES, William H., III *(Chief Judge, Louisiana Court of Appeal Fourth Circuit)* Elected to term beginning Jan 1, 1982. Reelected 1992 and 2002. Current term expires Dec 31, 2012. Born New Orleans Louisiana Feb 23, 1943. Catholic. Educated at Louisiana State University B.S. 1965 and Loyola University of the South J.D. 1968. Member Phi Delta Theta. Admitted to practice Louisiana 1968. Began legal practice New Orleans 1968. Louisiana State Representative 1975-81.

Office: 1515 Poydras Street, Seventh Floor, New Orleans 70112.
Telephone: (504) 592-0941.

CADE, Herbert A. *(Judge, Louisiana District Court Orleans Parish Civil District)*
Office: 421 Loyola Avenue, New Orleans 70112.
Telephone: (504) 592-9232.

CALDWELL, R. Michael *(Judge, Louisiana District Court Nineteenth Judicial District)* Elected Sept 1996 to term beginning Jan 1, 1997. Reelected Aug 2002, current term expires Dec 31, 2008. Born Baton Rouge Louisiana Sept 28, 1949. Episcopalian. Educated at Tulane University B.A. 1971 and Louisiana State University J.D. 1974. Law Clerk to Hon. Lewis S. Doherty, III, Louisiana District Court Nineteenth Judicial District 1974-75. Admitted to practice Louisiana 1974, U.S. District Courts Middle 1975, Western 1978 and Eastern 1979 Districts of Louisiana and U.S. Court of Appeals Fifth Circuit 1982. In legal practice Baton Rouge 1975-96.

Editor *Workers' Compensation Update Report* Committee on Workers' Compensation and Liability American Bar Association 1990 and Update Report "Workers' Compensation in 1991" Louisiana State Bar Association. Co-editor Update Report "Workers' Compensation in 1990" Louisiana State Bar Association. Former Member Wex S. Malone American Inn of Court, The Defense Research Institute, Inc. (Workers' Compensation Committee), Federation of Insurance and Corporate Counsel (Workers' Compensation Committee, Publications and Membership Committee) and American Bar Association (Committee on Workers' Compensation and Employers' Liability Law Section of Tort and Insurance Practice). Member Baton Rouge (Workers' Compensation Committee) and Louisiana State (ad hoc Committee on Proposed Modifications in Professional Disciplinary Procedures,

CALDWELL, R. MICHAEL—*Continued*

Bench/Bar Liaison Committee) Bar Associations. Mediator Personal Injury Litigation Claims for Arbitration Forums, Inc., Dallas Texas and Alternative Dispute Resolution Corporation, Baton Rouge Louisiana. Speaker "Managing the Workers' Compensation Case" Crawford & Company and Neuromedical Center of Baton Rouge May 1989, "The Statutory Employer Defense" Federation of Insurance and Corporate Counsel Annual Meeting Aug 1990 and "Workers' Compensation" Summer School for Lawyers Louisiana State Bar Association 1991. Faculty Member "Workers' Compensation in Louisiana" Sept 1989, Jan 1990 and July 1995, "Louisiana Labor and Employment Law" Jan 1990 and "Advanced Workers' Compensation in Louisiana" May 1990 and May 1991 National Business Institute seminars. Guest Lecturer on Workers' Compensation Louisiana State University Law Center Nov 1990 and March 1993 and Southern University Law Center March 1991 and 1995. Seminar Chairperson "Exploring Current Issues in Louisiana Workers' Compensation" Louisiana State Bar Association Dec 1995. Advisory Board Health South Corporation. Chancellor 1988-90, Vestry Member 1991-94, Member Parish Commission on Ministry, Lector, Lay Eucharistic Minister and Liturgical Master of Ceremonies St. Luke's Episcopal Church.

Office: 864 Governmental Building, 222 St. Louis Street, Baton Rouge 70801.

Telephone: (225) 389-4734.

CALLAWAY, Stephen V. *(Judge, United States Bankruptcy Court Western District of Louisiana)* Former Chief Judge.

Office: 4400 U.S. Courthouse, 300 Fannin Street, Shreveport 71101-3088.

Telephone: (318) 676-4269.

CALLOWAY, Curtis A. *(Judge, Louisiana District Court Nineteenth Judicial District)* Elected to term beginning 1992. Reelected 1996 and 2002. Current term expires Dec 2008. Born Birmingham Alabama Dec 10, 1939. Baptist. Educated at Miles College B.A. 1962 and Southern University J.D. 1965. Member Kappa Alpha Psi. Admitted to practice Louisiana 1969. In legal practice Baton Rouge 1969-88. Judge, Baton Rouge City Court 1989-92.

Member American Judges Association, Baton Rouge (Member 1974-79 and Vice President 1979-81 Lawyer Referral Committee), Louisiana State, National and American Bar Associations. Attended City and Juvenile Conference 1979-92, Evidence Seminar 1989-92, Spring Judges Conference 1989-92 and Fall Judges Conference 1989-92 Louisiana Judicial College. USMC 1965-68. Member Baton Rouge Black Alcoholism Council, Baton Rouge Marine Institute and Metropolitan Area Law League. Enjoys golfing, coaching soccer and working in the church.

Office: 222 St. Louis Street, Suite 831, Baton Rouge 70802.

Telephone: (225) 389-4737.

CALOGERO, Pascal F., Jr. *(Chief Justice, Supreme Court of Louisiana)* Elected Associate Justice 1972 to term beginning Jan 10, 1973. Reelected 1974, 1988 and 1998. Current term expires Dec 31, 2008. Chief Justice since April 9, 1990. Born New Orleans Louisiana Nov 9, 1931. Educated at Loyola University School of Law J.D. with honors 1954 and University of Virginia LL.M. 1992. Awarded honorary D.H.L. Loyola University School of Law. President Student Editorial Board Loyola Law Review. Member Blue Key, Phi Alpha Delta and Alpha Sigma Nu. President St. Thomas More Law Club. Admitted to practice Louisiana 1954. In legal practice 1958-72.

Attorney to Louisiana Wildlife and Fisheries Commission 1960-62 and Louisiana Stadium and Exposition District 1970-73. Instructor in Business Law Louisiana State University at New Orleans (now University of New Orleans). Lecturer Loyola University School of Law. Former Representative to Louisiana Supreme Court Committee on Judicial Ethics and to National Center for State Courts. Former Chairman Supreme Court Budgetary Control Board. Member Fourth Circuit Judges Association, Louisiana Trial Lawyers Association, American Judicature Society, New Orleans, New Orleans Criminal Courts, Louisiana State and American Bar Associations. Attended Appellate Judges' course New York University 1973. Recipient honorary title Cavaliere Ufficiale from President of Italian Republic 1974 and Americanism Award (Civis Illustris Medal) from Unico Grand Order of Dr. Filippo Mazzei. Captain U.S. Army JAGC 1954-57. Democrat. Elected member Louisiana Democratic State Central Committee. Louisiana Delegate Democratic National Convention 1968. Democratic Nominee for Presidential Electoral College 1968. Member Greater New Orleans Italian Cultural Society.

Office: 301 Loyola Avenue, New Orleans 70112.

Telephone: (504) 568-5727.

CAMPBELL, Cecil Paxton, II *(Judge, Louisiana District Court Twenty-sixth Judicial District)* Elected to term beginning Jan 1, 1979. Reelected to subsequent terms. Born Shreveport Louisiana Jan 6, 1948. Member First United Methodist Church of Bossier City (Administrative Board). Educated at Northwestern State University and Louisiana State University J.D. 1973. Admitted to practice Louisiana 1973 and U.S. District Court Western District of Louisiana 1973. Began legal practice Bossier City 1973.

Assistant City Attorney Bossier City 1973-74. Assistant District Attorney Twenty-sixth Judicial District 1975-76. Chief Assistant Twenty-sixth Judicial District Indigent Defender Board 1976-78. Member Louisiana Juvenile Judges Association, Louisiana District Judges Association, Bossier Parish, Louisiana State and American Bar Associations. Democrat. Director Youth Services Camp. Sustaining member Paul Harris and Boy Scouts of America. Member Bossier Jaycees, Southern Amateur Athletic Union (Official), Bossier Rotary Club (President), Bossier YMCA (Board of Directors), Bossier Disaster Relief (Chairman) and Indian Y-Guides (Chairman). Enjoys hunting, fishing, softball, boxing and gun collecting.

Mailing address: P.O. Box 310, Benton 71006.

Telephone: (318) 965-2217.

CAMPBELL, John C. *(Judge, Minden City Court)*

Mailing address: P.O. Box 968, Minden 71058-0968.

Telephone: (318) 377-4308.

CANADAY, G. Michael *(Judge, Louisiana District Court Fourteenth Judicial District)*

Mailing address: P.O. Box 3210, Lake Charles 70602.

Telephone: (337) 437-3530.

CANNELLA, James L. *(Judge, Louisiana Court of Appeal Fifth Circuit)* Elected to term beginning Oct 30,

CANNELLA, JAMES L.—*Continued*

1991. Reelected 1994, current term expires Dec 31, 2004. Born New Orleans Louisiana Aug 14, 1943. Christian. Educated at University of New Orleans B.A. 1966 and Loyola University School of Law J.D. 1967. Member Delta Theta Phi. Admitted to practice Louisiana 1967. In legal practice New Orleans 1967-81. Judge, Louisiana District Court Twenty-fourth Judicial District 1982-91.

Member American Judges Association, American Judicature Society, Jefferson Parish, Louisiana State and American Bar Associations. E-5 USAR 1961-67. Republican.

Mailing address: P.O. Box 489, Gretna 70054.

Telephone: (504) 376-1440.

CANNIZZARO, Leon A., Jr. *(Judge, Louisiana Court of Appeal Fourth Circuit)* Born New Orleans Louisiana Feb 3, 1953. Roman Catholic. Educated at University of New Orleans B.A. 1975 and Loyola University School of Law J.D. 1978. Admitted to practice Louisiana 1978. In legal practice New Orleans 1983-86. Assistant District Attorney Orleans Parish Dec 1978 to Oct 1983. Judge, Louisiana District Court Orleans Parish Criminal District Feb 10, 1986 to Dec 31, 2002.

Office: 1515 Poydras Street, Seventh Floor, New Orleans 70112.

Telephone: (504) 592-0933.

CARAWAY, J. Jay *(Judge, Louisiana Court of Appeal Second Circuit)* Elected 1996. Served as Justice ad hoc, Supreme Court of Louisiana Spring 2001. Born June 24, 1953. Educated at Louisiana Tech University B.S. 1975 M.B.A. 1976 and Louisiana State University Law Center J.D. with honors 1980. Inducted into Louisiana State University Law Center Hall of Fame. Member Order of the Coif. In legal practice Shreveport for 15 years.

President Second Circuit Judges Association 1997-2001. Board Member Louisiana Judicial College since 1998. Louisiana Representative National Symposium on the Future of Judicial Branch Education 1999. Member Mandatory Continuing Education Committee Louisiana State Bar Association 2000-02. Member Harry V. Booth American Inn of Court since 1998. Former Member Advisory Council Louisiana State University Mineral Law Institute. Member Asbury United Methodist Church Bossier City, Bossier City Lions Club and Planning Committee Benton Chapter Ducks Unlimited.

Office: 430 Fannin Street, Shreveport 71101.

Telephone: (318) 227-3724.

CARMICHAEL, William G. *(Judge, Louisiana District Court Twentieth Judicial District)*

Mailing address: P.O. Box 2758, St. Francisville 70775.

Telephone: (225) 635-4363.

CARTER, Burrell J. *(Chief Judge, Louisiana Court of Appeal First Circuit)* Elected at special election 1981 to term beginning Jan 1, 1982. Reelected 1990 and 2002. Current term expires Dec 31, 2012. Served as Justice ad hoc, Supreme Court of Louisiana 1982 and 1995. Served as Judge ad hoc, Louisiana Court of Appeal Fourth Circuit 1989. Born Baton Rouge Louisiana June 17, 1935. Methodist. Educated at Louisiana State University LL.B. 1958 replaced by J.D. Recipient Honors Award and Criminal Law Award Louisiana State University Law Center. Associate Editor Louisiana State University Law Review 1957-58. Law Clerk to Chief Judge Robert S. Ellis, Louisiana Court of Appeal First Circuit March 1961 to Sept 1961 and Aug 1962 to Jan 1963. Member Order of the Coif, Phi Kappa Phi and Phi Delta Phi. Admitted to practice Louisiana 1958, U.S. District Court Eastern District of Louisiana 1959, U.S. Supreme Court 1962, U.S. Court of Military Appeals 1962 and U.S. Court of Appeals Fifth Circuit 1973. In legal practice Greensburg 1958-74. Judge, Louisiana District Court Twenty-first Judicial District 1974-81.

Mayor Greensburg 1962-64. Board of Alderman Greensburg. Author "Garnishment in Louisiana" 18 Louisiana L. Rev. 446, 1958 and "Price v. Coppus Engineering Association" 515 So.2d 589 La. App. 1st Cir. 1987 writ denied 516 So.2d 133 La. 1987 Lead Case in American Law Reports. Member Louisiana Council of Juvenile Court Judges, National Council of Juvenile Court Judges, National College of Probate Judges, American Judges Association, American Judicature Society, Baton Rouge, Twenty-first Judicial District (Vice President 1968-69, President 1970-72), Louisiana State, Federal and American (Appellate Judges Conference Judicial Administration Division since 1982) Bar Associations. Attended Judge Advocate General's Corps Civil Law Course University of Virginia 1962, Louisiana Judicial College Seminars since 1976, Appellate Judges Conference Seminars American Bar Association since 1982 and Judicial Writing Course 1989 and Computers in the Courts 1991 The National Judicial College. Instructor Recent Developments in Law Louisiana Judicial College 1987 and Effective Appellate Advocacy Twenty-first Judicial District Bar Association 1988. Inducted into Paul M. Herbert Law Center Hall of Fame Louisiana State University 1987. Captain USAR JAGC 1962-68 (active 1961-62). Democrat. Member Greensburg Methodist Church, American Red Cross, Boy Scouts of America and American Legion (Post Commander, Judge Advocate Sixth District 1989-93, Department Judge Advocate 1992-93). Enjoys fishing.

Mailing address: P.O. Box 309, Greensburg 70441.

Telephone: (225) 222-4171.

CARTER, Wilford Dan *(Judge, Louisiana District Court Fourteenth Judicial District)* Elected to term beginning Oct 12, 1992. Reelected 1996 and 2002. Current term expires Dec 31, 2008. Born Lake Charles Louisiana Dec 8. Baptist. Educated at McNeese State University B.S. 1972 and Southern University J.D. 1975. Member Kappa Alpha Psi. Admitted to practice Louisiana 1974 and U.S. District Courts Eastern 1978, Middle 1978 and Western 1978 Districts of Louisiana. In legal practice Lake Charles 1974-92.

Former City Councilman Lake Charles. Former State Representative Louisiana. Member Louisiana State, National and American Bar Associations. U.S. Army Security Agency. Democrat. Member Cornerstone 229, John G. Lewis Consistory, Alkade Temple 153, American Legion 551, VFW 7321 and McNeese State University Alumni Association. Enjoys reading and writing.

Mailing address: P.O. Box 3210, Lake Charles 70602.

Telephone: (337) 437-3530.

CASCIO, Roy M. *(Judge, Second Parish Court Jefferson Parish)* Currently serves as Senior Judge.

Office: 200 Derbigny Street, Second Floor, Gretna 70053.

Telephone: (504) 364-2800.

CASTLE, Marilyn C. *(Judge, Louisiana District Court Fifteenth Judicial District)* Elected Nov 5, 1998 to term beginning Jan 1, 1999. Reelected Aug 23, 2002, current term expires Dec 31, 2008. Born Opelousas Louisiana Jan 2, 1953. Methodist. Educated at Louisiana State University B.A. 1973 and Louisiana State University Law Center J.D. 1976. Admitted to practice Louisiana 1976, U.S. District Courts Eastern, Middle and Western Districts of Louisiana and U.S. Court of Appeals Fifth Circuit. In legal practice Lafayette 1979-98.

Assistant District Attorney Nineteenth Judicial District 1976-79. Member Louisiana District Judges Association, Lafayette Parish (Board of Directors 1987-90, President 1990) and Louisiana State (Board of Governors 1995-97, Member House of Delegates 1998) Bar Associations.

Mailing address: P.O. Box 27, Lafayette 70502.
Office: 800 South Buchanan Street, Lafayette 70501.
Telephone: (337) 261-5130.
Fax: (337) 261-5134

CHAISSON, Robert A. *(Judge, Louisiana District Court Twenty-ninth Judicial District)* Currently serves as Chief Judge.

Mailing address: P.O. Box 424, Hahnville 70057-0424.
Telephone: (985) 783-2923.

CHASEZ, Alma L. *(Magistrate Judge, United States District Court Eastern District of Louisiana)* Appointed by U.S. District Court judges.

Office: B347 Federal Building, 501 Magazine Street, New Orleans 70130.
Telephone: (504) 589-7610.

CHEHARDY, Susan M. *(Judge, Louisiana Court of Appeal Fifth Circuit)* Former Judge, Louisiana District Court Twenty-fourth Judicial District.

Mailing address: P.O. Box 489, Gretna 70054.
Telephone: (504) 376-1446.

CHILDRESS, Raymond S. *(Judge, Louisiana District Court Twenty-second Judicial District)*
Mailing address: P.O. Drawer 608, Franklinton 70438.
Telephone: (985) 839-7845.

CHUTZ, Wayne Ray *(Judge, Louisiana District Court Twenty-first Judicial District)*
Mailing address: P.O. Box 788, Amite 70422.
Telephone: (985) 748-9445.

CLARK, Janice G. *(Judge, Louisiana District Court Nineteenth Judicial District)*
Office: 222 St. Louis Street, Suite 816, Baton Rouge 70802.
Telephone: (225) 389-5012.

CLARK, Marcus R. *(Judge, Louisiana District Court Fourth Judicial District)*
Office: 300 St. John Street, Room 400, Monroe 71201.
Telephone: (318) 361-2296.

CLARK, Vernon B. *(Judge, Louisiana District Court Thirtieth Judicial District)* Elected Sept 21, 1996 to term beginning Jan 1, 1997. Reelected 2002, current term expires Dec 31, 2008. Born Eunice Louisiana Nov 28, 1951. Baptist. Educated at Northwestern State University B.S. with honors 1973 and Loyola University J.D. 1976. Admitted to practice Louisiana 1976, U.S. District Courts Eastern 1976 and Western 1976 Districts of Louisiana and U.S. Court of Appeals Fifth Circuit 1976. In legal practice Leesville 1976-96.

Assistant District Attorney Thirtieth Judicial District 1985-89. Member Louisiana Judges Association, American Judges Association, Thirtieth Judicial District Court and Louisiana State Bar Associations. Board of Directors Red River Delta Law Enforcement Planning Council, Chamber of Commerce and Lion's Club. Enjoys golfing, gardening and hunting.

Mailing address: P.O. Drawer 1700, Leesville 71496-1700.
Telephone: (337) 239-2147.

CLASON, Jenifer Ward *(Judge, Louisiana District Court Second Judicial District)* Elected to term beginning Jan 1991. Reelected 1996 and 2002. Current term expires Dec 31, 2008. Currently serves as Chief Judge. First woman elected Judge of Louisiana District Court Second Judicial District. Born Washington D.C. April 11, 1946. Educated at Mary Washington College of University of Virginia B.A. 1968 and University of Georgia School of Law J.D. cum laude 1976. Staff member Georgia Journal of International and Comparative Law. Recipient Ratner Scholarship. Admitted to practice Georgia 1976, Louisiana 1977 and U.S. District Court Western District of Louisiana 1979. In legal practice Shreveport Louisiana and Homer Louisiana 1980-90.

Attorney Claiborne Council on Aging. Member Task Force on Women in the Courts Louisiana Supreme Court. State Hearing Officer Federal Handicapped Children's Act (P.L. 94-142) and State Exceptional Children's Act. Public Defender and President Second Judicial District Indigent Defender Board. Instructor in Business Law Louisiana Tech University 1977-79. Member Federal-State Judicial Council, American Judicature Society, State Bar of Georgia, Claiborne Parish (Former Secretary, Past President), Louisiana State (Nominating Committee, House of Delegates) and American Bar Associations. Presented seminars to law enforcement departments in Claiborne, Bienville and Webster Parishes. Panelist Speaker Louisiana Defense Lawyers Association and Shreveport Inn of Court. Speaker Summer School for Lawyers and Public Defenders Louisiana State Bar Association. Recipient Outstanding Woman of Achievement Award from Louisiana Tech Women's Faculty Coalition 1992. Biology teacher Robert Smalls High School 1969-70. Speaker and Organizer Louisiana Bicentennial Commission. Vice President and President Homer Public School PTA. Vestry member St. John's Episcopal Church. Member Homer Chamber of Commerce (President), Claiborne Industrial Development Foundation, Homer Industrial Development Foundation, Lake Claiborne Promotional Association, Homer Lions Club and American Heart Association.

Office: Claiborne Parish Courthouse, Homer 71040.
Telephone: (318) 927-3550.

CLAUSE, Herman C. *(Judge, Louisiana District Court Fifteenth Judicial District)*
Mailing address: P.O. Box 3998, Lafayette 70502.
Telephone: (337) 269-5702.

CLAVILLE, Vernon *(Judge, Caddo Parish Juvenile Court)*
Office: 1835 Spring Street, Shreveport 71101.
Telephone: (318) 226-6751.

COADY, Martin E. *(Judge, Louisiana District Court Twenty-second Judicial District)*
Office: 428 East Boston Street, Room 207, Covington 70433.
Telephone: (985) 898-2567.

COLE, Patricia C. *(Judge, Louisiana District Court Thirty-third Judicial District)*
Mailing address: P.O. Drawer A, Oberlin 70655.
Telephone: (337) 639-2256.

COLLINS, Randy E. *(Judge, Shreveport City Court)*
Office: 1244 Texas Avenue, Shreveport 71101.
Telephone: (318) 673-5879.

COMEAUX, Keith R. J. *(Judge, Louisiana District Court Sixteenth Judicial District)*
Office: 300 Iberia Street, Suite 210, New Iberia 70560-4585.
Telephone: (337) 369-4410.

CONERY, John E. *(Judge, Louisiana District Court Sixteenth Judicial District)*
Mailing address: P.O. Box 596, Franklin 70538.
Telephone: (337) 828-4100.

CONQUE, Durwood W. *(Judge, Louisiana District Court Fifteenth Judicial District)* Elected to term beginning Dec 17, 1987. Reelected 1990, 1996 and 2002. Current term expires Dec 31, 2008. Born Lafayette Louisiana July 21, 1946. Roman Catholic. Educated at University of St. Thomas B.A. cum laude 1967 and Louisiana State University J.D. 1972. Admitted to practice Louisiana 1973, U.S. Supreme Court 1976, U.S. District Courts Districts of Louisiana and U.S. Courts of Appeals Fifth and Sixth Circuits. In legal practice Abbeville 1973-87.
City Attorney Abbeville 1981-87. Specialist Fifth Class U.S. Army 1970-72. Democrat. Member Abbeville Kiwanis Club. Enjoys music and wood carving.
Office: 100 North State Street, Suite 210, Abbeville 70510.
Telephone: (337) 898-4315.

COOKS, Sylvia R. *(Judge, Louisiana Court of Appeal Third Circuit)*
Mailing address: P.O. Box 16577, Lake Charles 70616.
Telephone: (337) 235-2196.

CRESAP, Wayne George *(Judge, Louisiana District Court Thirty-fourth Judicial District)* Born April 22, 1947. Educated at Louisiana State University B.S. 1969, Loyola University at New Orleans M.B.A. 1973 and Tulane University School of Law J.D. 1973. Moot Court Team Southern Regional Interschool Competition 1971 and International Law Moot Court Competition 1972. Member Phi Alpha Delta. Admitted to practice Louisiana 1974, U.S. District Court Eastern District of Louisiana 1974, U.S. Court of Appeals Fifth Circuit 1974 and U.S. Supreme Court 1977. In legal practice 1974-99. Judge ad hoc, New Orleans First City Court 1982-92.
Assistant City Attorney III New Orleans 1974-78. Legal Advisor Sheriff's Office St. Bernard Parish 1988-99. Curator ad hoc for Abused and Neglected Children Orleans Parish Juvenile Court 1982-92. Officer Fourth and Fifth Circuit Judges Association since 2000. Past President St. Bernard Parish Bar Association. Former Member Louisiana Trial Lawyers Association, Louisiana State and American Bar Associations. U.S. Army 1969. Served to Major Louisiana Army National Guard. Notary Public 1974. State Representative at Large Louisiana State National Guard Association 1980-83. Charter Member, Chairman Board of Directors and President St. Bernard Chapter Alliance for Good Government 1990-92. St. Bernard Representative Regional Planning Commission 1992-97. Charter Member "Speak Up for St. Bernard" Speaker's Bureau 1996. Board of Directors St. Bernard Youth Foundation. Certified Counsel Capital Program Louisiana Indigent Defense Assistance Board. Life Member Special Forces Association since 1987 and St. Bernard Chapter #550 Vietnam Veterans of America.
Office: 1101 West St. Bernard Highway, Chalmette 70043.
Telephone: (504) 278-4425.

CRICHTON, Scott J. *(Judge, Louisiana District Court First Judicial District)*
Office: 501 Texas Street, Suite 300D, Shreveport 71101.
Telephone: (318) 226-6818.

CRIGLER, John D. *(Judge, Louisiana District Court Sixth Judicial District)* Elected to term beginning March 5, 1993. Reelected 1996 and 2002. Current term expires Dec 31, 2008. Currently serves as Chief Judge. Born Newellton Louisiana March 31, 1952. Baptist. Educated at Louisiana State University J.D. 1977. Admitted to practice Louisiana 1977, U.S. District Court Western District of Louisiana and U.S. Court of Appeals Fifth Circuit. In legal practice St. Joseph 1977.
Assistant District Attorney Sixth Judicial District 1978-93. Member Louisiana Council of Juvenile and Family Court Judges, National Council of Juvenile and Family Court Judges, American Judicature Society, Sixth Judicial District, Louisiana State and American Bar Associations.
Mailing address: P.O. Box 708, St. Joseph 71366.
Telephone: (318) 766-3233.

CUNNINGHAM, James M. *(Judge, Rayne City Court)*
Mailing address: P.O. Box 31, Rayne 70578.
Telephone: (337) 334-9677.

CUSIMANO, Charles V., II *(Judge, Louisiana District Court Twenty-fourth Judicial District)*
Office: 200 Derbigny Street, Gretna 70053.
Telephone: (504) 364-3929.

CUTRER, Lilynn A. *(Judge, Louisiana District Court Fourteenth Judicial District)*
Mailing address: P.O. Box 3210, Lake Charles 70602.
Telephone: (337) 437-3363.

DALBY, Docia L. *(Magistrate Judge, United States District Court Middle District of Louisiana)* Appointed by U.S. District Court judges.
Office: 265 Federal Building, 777 Florida Street, Baton Rouge 70801-1712.
Telephone: (225) 389-3602.

DALEY, Thomas F. *(Judge, Louisiana Court of Appeal Fifth Circuit)* Elected Jan 1996 to term beginning March 1, 1996. Born Neptune New Jersey Oct 17, 1953. Catholic. Educated at Rutgers University B.A. 1975 and Loyola University School of Law J.D. 1978. Admitted to practice Louisiana 1978, U.S. District Court District of Columbia, U.S. Courts of Appeals Fifth and Eighth Circuits and U.S. Supreme Court. In legal practice La-

DALEY, THOMAS F.—*Continued*

Place 1978-84. Judge Jan 1991 to Feb 1996 and Chief Judge 1991-94, Louisiana District Court Fortieth Judicial District. Ad hoc Judge, Louisiana Court of Appeal Fifth Circuit Aug 1993, Oct 1993 and Aug 1994.

Assistant District Attorney and Parish Attorney St. John the Baptist Parish 1984-89. Part-time Professor of Criminal Justice Delgado Community College 1981-82. Adjunct Professor Louisiana State University Law Center 1998-2003. Assistant Bar Examiner for Louisiana Bar 1993-2002. Member Louisiana and American Bar Associations. Lecturer Louisiana Judicial College 1993-2003 and Louisiana State Bar Association CLE 1994-2003. Board Member Belle Terre II Civic Association (Past President). Board of Directors 4-H Foundation. Chairman St. John Shade Tree Committee. Member St. John Clean Green Committee and Adopt A Road Program. Monsignor Bergeron Council Knights of Columbus. Catechism Instructor and Parishioner St. Joan of Arc Catholic Church.

Mailing address: P.O. Box 489, Gretna 70054.
Telephone: (504) 376-1426.

DANIEL, Louis R. *(Judge, Louisiana District Court Nineteenth Judicial District)*

Office: 222 St. Louis Street, Suite 634, Baton Rouge 70802.
Telephone: (225) 389-4711.

DANNEL, Dennis Jude *(Judge, New Orleans Traffic Court)* Elected to term beginning Jan 1, 1989. Reelected 1996, current term expires Dec 31, 2004. Currently serves as Senior Judge. Born New Orleans Louisiana April 25, 1943. Catholic. Educated at Louisiana State University J.D. Admitted to practice Louisiana 1975 and U.S. District Court Eastern District of Louisiana. Began legal practice New Orleans.

Attorney Justice Department U.S. Attorney's Office 1976-79 and Public Defender's Office 1979-82. Member New Orleans, Louisiana State and American Bar Associations. E-4 USN Fleet Marine Force 1961-65. Previously employed at U.S. Post Office and Chevron Oil Company. Democrat. Enjoys tennis, reading and foreign languages.

Office: 727 South Broad Street, New Orleans 70119.
Telephone: (504) 827-5000.

DAVIS, Joel G. *(Judge, Louisiana District Court Thirty-third Judicial District)* Elected Sept 1996. Reelected 2002, current term expires Dec 31, 2008. Currently serves as Chief Judge. Born Alexandria Louisiana March 23, 1961. Roman Catholic. Educated at University of Louisiana at Lafayette B.S. 1984 and Tulane University School of Law J.D. 1990. Law Clerk to Hon. Earl Ernest Veron 1990, Hon. John M. Shaw 1991 and Hon. Richard T. Haik 1992, U.S. District Court Western District of Louisiana. Admitted to practice Louisiana 1990 and U.S. District Courts Eastern 1990, Middle 1990 and Western 1990 Districts of Louisiana. In legal practice Oakdale.

Mailing address: P.O. Box 496, Oberlin 70655.
Telephone: (337) 639-2266.
Fax: (337) 639-4310
E-mail address: judgedavis@centurytel.net

DAVIS, Laura Prosser *(Judge, Baton Rouge City Court)*

Office: 233 St. Louis Street, Baton Rouge 70802.
Telephone: (225) 389-3021.

DECUIR, Oswald A. *(Judge, Louisiana Court of Appeal Third Circuit)*

Mailing address: P.O. Box 10505, New Iberia 70562-0505.
Telephone: (337) 369-3540.

deMAHY, Paul J. *(Judge, Louisiana District Court Sixteenth Judicial District)* Elected Nov 4, 1986 to term beginning Dec 1, 1986. Reelected 1990, 1996 and 2002. Current term expires Dec 31, 2008. Born St. Martinville Louisiana Aug 11, 1949. Roman Catholic. Educated at University of Louisiana at Lafayette B.A. 1973 and Louisiana State University Law Center J.D. 1973. Member Phi Alpha Delta. Admitted to practice Louisiana 1973, U.S. District Courts Western 1975 and Eastern 1982 Districts of Louisiana, U.S. Court of Appeals Fifth Circuit 1982 and U.S. Supreme Court 1982. In legal practice St. Martinville 1973-86 and Lafayette 1983-86.

City Attorney St. Martinville 1974-86. Chief Defender Indigent Defender Board Sixteenth Judicial District 1986. Member Louisiana Trial Lawyers Association (Board of Governors 1982-85), Louisiana Association of Criminal Defense Lawyers (Honorary member), Louisiana District Judges Association, Louisiana Council of Juvenile and Family Court Judges, American Judges Association, National Council of Juvenile and Family Court Judges, Louisiana State and American Bar Associations. Recipient St. Martinville Outstanding Young Man Award 1978 and Professional of the Year Award from St. Martin Association for Retarded Citizens 1984. Republican. Member Knights of Columbus, Kiwanis and J.C.I. Senate. Enjoys triathlons.

Mailing address: P.O. Box 7, St. Martinville 70582.
Telephone: (337) 394-2216.

DERBIGNY, Darryl *(Judge, Louisiana District Court Orleans Parish Criminal District)*

Office: 2700 Tulane Avenue, New Orleans 70119.
Telephone: (504) 827-3458.

DERR, Jacque D. *(Judge, Winnfield City Court)*

Mailing address: P.O. Box 908, Winnfield 71483.
Telephone: (318) 628-4844.

Di MICELI, Elaine W. *(Judge, Louisiana District Court Twenty-second Judicial District)* Elected Nov 5, 1996 to term beginning Jan 1, 1997. Reelected 2002, current term expires Dec 31, 2008. Born New Orleans Louisiana March 8, 1943. Roman Catholic. Educated at Loyola University B.B.A. with honors 1967 M.B.A. 1972 J.D. 1977. Staff member Loyola Law Review. Admitted to practice Louisiana 1977 and Texas 1995. In legal practice Slidell Louisiana 1977-96 and New Orleans Louisiana 1990-95.

Assistant District Attorney St. Tammany Parish 1978. City Attorney Slidell 1983-90. Instructor in Business Law Delgado College. Member Slidell (Past President), St. Tammany Parish (Former Treasurer), Louisiana State (Former Chair Public Law Section) and American Bar Associations. Graduate The National Judicial College 1997. Republican. Member Business and Professional

DI MICELI, ELAINE W.—*Continued*

Women and Chamber of Commerce. Enjoys fishing and gourmet cooking.
Office: 301 North New Hampshire Street, Covington 70433.
Telephone: (985) 898-2562.

DIMOS, Jimmy N. *(Judge, Louisiana District Court Fourth Judicial District)*
Office: 300 St. John Street, Monroe 71201.
Telephone: (318) 361-2285.

DODD, Douglas D. *(Judge, United States Bankruptcy Court Middle District of Louisiana)* Appointed by U.S. Court of Appeals Fifth Circuit judges to term beginning May 2, 2002. Term expires May 2016.
Office: 236 U.S. Courthouse, 707 Florida Street, Baton Rouge 70801.
Telephone: (225) 389-0371.

DOGGETT, Monty L. *(Judge, Louisiana District Court Tenth Judicial District)* Currently serves as Chief Judge.
Mailing address: P.O. Box 775, Natchitoches 71458-0775.
Telephone: (318) 357-2209.

DOHERTY, Mark *(Judge, Orleans Parish Juvenile Court)*
Office: 421 Loyola Avenue, New Orleans 70112.
Telephone: (504) 565-7381.

DOHERTY, Rebecca F. *(Judge, United States District Court Western District of Louisiana)* Appointed for life by President George Bush to term beginning 1991. Born Fort Worth Texas June 3, 1952. Educated at Northwestern State University B.A. 1973 M.A. 1975 and Louisiana State University Law Center J.D. 1981. In legal practice Lafayette 1981-91.
Office: 4900 U.S. Courthouse, 800 Lafayette Street, Lafayette 70501.
Telephone: (337) 593-5050.

DOUCET, Ned E., Jr. *(Chief Judge, Louisiana Court of Appeal Third Circuit)* Elected to term beginning Jan 1, 1979. Reelected 1984 and 1994. Current term expires Dec 31, 2004. Born Kaplan Louisiana June 1, 1943. Catholic. Educated at Northwestern University B.S. 1965 and Loyola University J.D. 1970. Admitted to practice Louisiana 1970. Began legal practice Crowley 1970. In legal practice Kaplan 1972-78.
City Attorney Kaplan 1974-76. Louisiana State Senate April 1976 to Dec 31, 1978. Member Vermilion Parish, Louisiana State and American Bar Associations. Louisiana National Guard. Democrat. Member Kaplan Rotary Club (Charter President), Louisiana Municipal Association, Louisiana Intracoastal Seaway Association (Board of Directors), Kaplan Industrial Committee (Coordinator), American Legion, Knights of Columbus, Abbeville Chamber of Commerce and Kaplan Jaycees. Enjoys golf and dancing.
Office: 556 Jefferson Street, Suite 201, Lafayette 70501.
Telephone: (337) 262-1202.

DOWNING, Robert D. *(Judge, Louisiana Court of Appeal First Circuit)* Born Baton Rouge Louisiana Aug 2, 1949. Former Judge, Louisiana District Court Nineteenth Judicial District, elected to term beginning Jan 1, 1985.
Mailing address: P.O. Box 4408, Baton Rouge 70821.
Telephone: (225) 342-0703.

DRAGON, Gary J. *(Judge, Slidell City Court)*
Office: 501 Bouscaren Street, Slidell 70458.
Telephone: (985) 643-1274.

DRAKE, Ernest G., Jr. *(Judge, Louisiana District Court Twenty-first Judicial District)*
Mailing address: P.O. Box 788, Amite 70422.
Telephone: (985) 748-9445.

DREW, R. Harmon, Jr. *(Judge, Louisiana Court of Appeal Second Circuit)* Elected July 1998 to term beginning Jan 1, 1999. Term expires Dec 31, 2008. Born Shreveport Louisiana Nov 11, 1946. Episcopalian. Educated at Louisiana State University B.S. 1968 J.D. 1971. Member Phi Delta Phi. Admitted to practice Louisiana 1972. Judge, Minden City Court 1984-88. Judge, Louisiana District Court Twenty-sixth Judicial District 1988-98.
Assistant District Attorney Twenty-sixth Judicial District 1974-84. Co-author "True Blue Drew Book: Louisiana Criminal Laws." Instructor Bossier Parish Community College, Northwestern State University and Louisiana State University at Shreveport. Bandleader Harmon Drew Super Group.
Office: 430 Fannin Street, Shreveport 71101.
Telephone: (318) 227-3720.
Fax: (318) 227-3775
E-mail address: rhdrew@lasccoa.state.la.us

DUFRESNE, Edward A., Jr. *(Chief Judge, Louisiana Court of Appeal Fifth Circuit)* Elected to term beginning May 1, 1982. Reelected 1992 and 2002. Current term expires Dec 31, 2012. Born New Orleans Louisiana Oct 26, 1938. Catholic. Educated at Loyola University B.B.A. 1960 J.D. 1963. Member Delta Theta Phi and Blue Key. Admitted to practice Louisiana 1963. Began legal practice Hahnville 1963. Judge, Louisiana District Court Twenty-ninth Judicial District 1979-82.
Clerk of Court St. Charles Parish 1963-78. Member American Judicature Society, Twenty-ninth Judicial District, Louisiana State and American Bar Associations. Previously worked in real estate. Democrat. Member Knights of Columbus and Lions Club. Enjoys outdoor activities, hunting, horseback riding, playing cards and reading.
Mailing address: P.O. Box 489, Gretna 70054.
Telephone: (504) 376-1435.

DUPLANTIER, Adrian G. *(Senior Judge, United States District Court Eastern District of Louisiana)* Appointed for life by President Jimmy Carter. Assumed Senior status, serves by assignment. Born New Orleans Louisiana March 5, 1929. Catholic. Educated at Loyola University J.D. cum laude 1949 and University of Virginia Law School LL.M. in Judicial Process 1988. Editorial Board 1947-48 and Editor-in-Chief 1948-49 Loyola Law Review. Recipient Loyola University Law School Faculty Award 1949. Law Clerk to Louisiana Civil District Court Orleans Parish 1949-50. Member Alpha Sigma Nu. Honorary member Order of the Coif Louisiana State University. Admitted to practice Louisiana 1950, U.S. Supreme Court 1954 and U.S. Court of Military Appeals 1955. Began legal practice New Orleans 1950. Civil Court Judge, Louisiana District Court

DUPLANTIER, ADRIAN G.—*Continued*

Orleans District 1974-78, appointed by Governor Edwin W. Edwards.

First Assistant District Attorney New Orleans 1954-56. Co-author *Louisiana Formulary, Criminal Procedure* Bobbs-Merrill 1970. Lecturer English Department Loyola University 1948-50. Professor (part-time) in Civil and Criminal Procedures and Contracts since 1952 and Lecturer in Dental Jurisprudence 1960-67 Loyola University Law School. Visiting Professor of Louisiana Civil Procedure Tulane University Law School 1976. District Judge Representative for Fifth Circuit Judicial Conference of the United States 1982-85. Member Judicial Conference of the U.S. (Committee on the Bicentennial of the Constitution 1986-91, Chairman Subcommittee Conference on Bill of Rights Bicentennial 1991, Member 1992-96 and Chairman since 1996 Advisory Committee on Bankruptcy Rules). Member New Orleans, Louisiana State (recipient Award for Professional Services 1960) and American Bar Associations. Named Junior Chamber of Commerce Outstanding Young Man in Greater New Orleans 1960. Recipient New Orleans Association for Retarded Children Meritorious Service Award 1966 and State of Louisiana Certificate of Merit from governor for outstanding service 1970. USNR. Democrat. Louisiana State Senator 1960-74. Delegate Democratic National Convention 1964. Past President Loyola University Law School Alumni Association, Associated Catholic Charities of New Orleans and Social Welfare Planning Council of Greater New Orleans. Advisory Board St. Mary's Dominican College, Ursuline Academy, Jesuit High School, Mt. Carmel Academy, Convent of Good Shepherd and New Orleans Area Boy Scouts. Chairman Boys Hope New Orleans since 1980.

Office: C205 U.S. Courthouse, 500 Camp Street, New Orleans 70130-3363.

Telephone: (504) 589-7535.

DUPLANTIER, Thomas R. *(Judge, Louisiana District Court Fifteenth Judicial District)*

Mailing address: P.O. Box 3612, Lafayette 70502-3612.

Telephone: (337) 269-5722.

DUPONT, William C. *(Judge, Plaquemine City Court)*

Mailing address: P.O. Box 1017, Plaquemine 70765.

Telephone: (225) 687-7236.

DUVAL, Stanwood R., Jr. *(Judge, United States District Court Eastern District of Louisiana)* Appointed for life by President Bill Clinton to term beginning Oct 31, 1994. Educated at Louisiana State University B.A. 1964 J.D. 1966. In legal practice Houma 1966-94.

Assistant City Attorney 1970-72. Parish Attorney Terrebonne Parish Consolidated Government 1988-92. Delegate and Member Committee on Executive Branch Louisiana Constitutional Convention 1973. Member Indigent Defender Board 1976-82 and Advisory Committee on Appellate Rules Judicial Conference of the U.S. 1997-2000. Council Member Louisiana State Law Institute 1996-2000. President Tulane Inns of Court 2001. Former Member Committee to Write Rules of Procedure.

Office: C368 U.S. Courthouse, 500 Camp Street, New Orleans 70130.

Telephone: (504) 589-7540.

EARLES, Kristian *(Judge, Louisiana District Court Fifteenth Judicial District)*

Mailing address: P.O. Box 1980, Crowley 70527-1980.

EARLY, Sean P. *(Judge, New Orleans Municipal Court)*

Office: 727 South Broad Street, Room 105, New Orleans 70119.

Telephone: (504) 827-5081.

EDWARDS, Jules D., III *(Judge, Louisiana District Court Fifteenth Judicial District)* Elected Nov 3, 1992 to term beginning Jan 1, 1993. Elected to subsequent term. Currently serves as Chief Judge. Born New Orleans Louisiana Nov 13, 1957. Catholic. Educated at Loyola University B.A. J.D. and Louisiana State University M.P.A. Admitted to practice Louisiana 1984 and U.S. District Courts Eastern and Western Districts of Louisiana. In legal practice New Orleans 1985-87 and Lafayette 1987-92.

Member American Judges Association, Louisiana State, National and American Bar Associations. Attended Civil Mediation Course The National Judicial College 1996 and Law and Organizational Economics Center Institute for State Judges Sept 28, 1996 to Oct 4, 1996 and Dec 14, 1996 to Dec 20, 1996. Recipient Louisiana Longevity Medal. Major Louisiana Army National Guard. Recipient The Army Commendation Medal with Second Oak Leaf Cluster, Achievement Medal and National Defense Service Medal. Member Louisiana ESGR and American Legion Post 504. Enjoys reading, films and physical fitness.

Office: 800 South Buchanan Street, Fourth Floor, Lafayette 70501.

Telephone: (337) 269-5708.

EDWARDS, Marion F. *(Judge, Louisiana Court of Appeal Fifth Circuit)* Former Judge, Louisiana District Court Twenty-fourth Judicial District.

Mailing address: P.O. Box 489, Gretna 70054.

Telephone: (504) 376-1415.

ELLENDER, Timothy Claude *(Judge, Louisiana District Court Thirty-second Judicial District)* Assumed office Sept 15, 1982. Elected to term beginning Jan 1, 1985. Reelected 1990, 1996 and 2002. Current term expires Dec 31, 2008. Born Houma Louisiana Oct 28, 1944. Catholic. Educated at Louisiana State University B.A. 1966 and Loyola University J.D. 1970. Admitted to practice Louisiana 1970. Began legal practice Houma 1970.

Member Louisiana Trial Lawyers Association, The Association of Trial Lawyers of America and Louisiana State Bar Association. Enjoys shrimping and gardening.

Office: 7856 Main Street, Houma 70360.

Telephone: (985) 873-6560.

ELLOIE, Charles L. *(Judge, Louisiana District Court Orleans Parish Criminal District)*

Office: 2700 Tulane Avenue, New Orleans 70119.

Telephone: (504) 827-3490.

EMANUEL, Leon L., III *(Judge, Louisiana District Court First Judicial District)*

Office: 501 Texas Street, Room 300A, Shreveport 71101.

Telephone: (318) 226-6812.

EMANUEL, Ramona *(Judge, Louisiana District Court First Judicial District)*

Office: 501 Texas Street, Room 300A, Shreveport 71101.

Telephone: (318) 226-6822.

ENGELHARDT, Kurt D. *(Judge, United States District Court Eastern District of Louisiana)* Appointed for life by President George W. Bush to term beginning Dec 14, 2001.

Office: C367 U.S. Courthouse, 500 Camp Street, New Orleans 70130.

Telephone: (504) 589-7645.

ERWIN, Michael R. *(Judge, Louisiana District Court Nineteenth Judicial District)* Elected to term beginning Jan 1, 1991. Reelected 1996 and 2002. Current term expires Dec 31, 2008. Born Franklinton Louisiana Jan 17, 1950. Catholic. Educated at Southeastern Louisiana University B.A. in Political Science 1972, Louisiana State University B.A. in Criminal Justice 1976 and Southern University Law Center J.D. 1979. Admitted to practice Louisiana 1979. In legal practice Baton Rouge 1979-82.

Chief of Trials and First Assistant District Attorney 1988-90. Member Louisiana District Attorneys Association (Board of Directors 1987-90, Representative Committee to write Louisiana Evidence Code 1988-89), Baton Rouge and Louisiana State Bar Associations. Instructor in Louisiana Evidence Code Louisiana District Attorneys Association Aug 1989 and Baton Rouge Bench/Bar Conference. Recipient Distinguished Alumni Award Southern University 1992. Democrat. Coach American Legion Youth Baseball twelve years. Enjoys golf and spectator sports.

Office: 222 St. Louis Street, Room 658, Baton Rouge 70802.

Telephone: (225) 389-4765.

EVERETT, Glennon P. *(Judge, Louisiana District Court Fifteenth Judicial District)*

Mailing address: P.O. Drawer 503, Crowley 70527-0503.

Telephone: (337) 788-8814.

EZELL, Billy H. *(Judge, Louisiana Court of Appeal Third Circuit)* Former Judge, Louisiana District Court Fourteenth Judicial District.

Mailing address: P.O. Box 16577, Lake Charles 70602.

Telephone: (337) 433-9403.

FALLIN, Glenn *(Judge, Louisiana District Court Second Judicial District)*

Office: 100 Courthouse Drive, Room 208, Arcadia 71001.

Telephone: (318) 263-7412.

FALLON, Eldon E. *(Judge, United States District Court Eastern District of Louisiana)* Appointed for life by President Bill Clinton May 10, 1995 to term beginning June 26, 1995. Born New Orleans Louisiana Feb 16, 1939. Catholic. Educated at Tulane University B.A. with honors 1960 J.D. with honors 1962 and Yale Law School LL.M. 1963. Admitted to practice Louisiana 1962, U.S. District Courts Eastern 1962, Middle 1962 and Western 1980 Districts of Louisiana, U.S. Court of Appeals Fifth Circuit 1962 and U.S. Supreme Court 1989. In legal practice New Orleans 1962-95.

Editor-in-Chief Louisiana Bar Journal 1981-82. Author *Trial Handbook for Louisiana Lawyers* 1981 and 2nd ed. 1992 Lawyers Co-operative Publishing Company and *Offshore Oil Field Litigation—Cases and Materials* Tulane University School of Law. Adjunct Professor of Law Tulane Law School 1975-96. Fellow Louisiana Bar Foundation (Secretary-Treasurer 1992, Vice President 1993-95, President 1995-96) and American College of Trial Lawyers (State Chair 1991-92 and 1992-93). Life Member American Bar Foundation. Member American Board of Trial Advocates, The Association of Trial Lawyers of America (State Committee 1968-70 and 1976-77, Secretary-Treasurer 1981-82, Vice Chair 1983-84 and Chair 1984-85 Admiralty Section), The Maritime Law Association of the U.S., Society of American Law Teachers, Louisiana Trial Lawyers Association (Board of Governors 1969-70 and 1980-81), New Orleans, Louisiana State (Council Member Section on Insurance, Negligence, Admiralty and Compensation Law 1972-73, Member Committee on Prepaid Legal Services 1975, Chair Committee on Continuing Legal Education 1979-81, Secretary-Treasurer 1981-82, Chair Medical/Legal Interprofessional Committee 1983-84, President Elect 1984-85, President 1985-86) and American (Committee on Jury Trials 1970-71) Bar Associations. Lecturer Appellate Practice Seminar Jan 1990, "Ethics of Getting and Keeping and Losing Clients" June 1992 and "Professionalism for the Trial Lawyer" 1997 Louisiana State Bar Association; "Elements of Damage in Maritime Personal Injury and Death Claims—An Update" Louisiana Trial Lawyers Association April 1990; "Negotiations and Settlement" Litigation Institute Tulane University School of Law Nov 1991; "Practical Procedures for Handling a Multi-Party Suit Through a Plaintiff's Committee—The Big Case" Tulane CLE Program Nov 1993; "Destination: Federal Court" Federal Practice New Orleans 1996; "Maritime Law—View from the Bench" The Association of Trial Lawyers of America Convention San Diego 1997; and "Proving Damages under Maritime Law" Tulane Admiralty Law Institute 1997. Panelist "Judicial Ethics and Conduct Discussion" Louisiana Judicial College March 1990. Lecturer Dec 1990 and Moderator/ Commentator Dec 1993 Last Chance Seminar Louisiana Trial Lawyers Association. Keynote Speaker MidWinter Convention American Trial Lawyers Association Feb 1995. Recipient President's Awards 1980 and 1988 and Lifetime Achievement Award for efforts in Pro Bono service 1987 Louisiana State Bar Association, Louisiana Médaille De La Ville De Paris 1983, National Pro Bono Publico Award from American Bar Association 1987 and Outstanding Lawyer in Louisiana from Louisiana Bar Foundation 1989. Listed in *Best Lawyers in America* and *Who's Who in American Law*. Sergeant E-5 Army National Guard 1957-65. Chair Board Louisiana Supreme Court Historical Society since 1992.

Office: C456 U.S. Courthouse, 500 Camp Street, New Orleans 70130.

Telephone: (504) 589-7545.

FANGUY, Jude Thaddeus *(Judge, Houma City Court)* Elected Sept 16, 1978 to term beginning Jan 1, 1979. Reelected 1984, 1990, 1996 and 2002. Current term expires Dec 31, 2008. Born Houma Louisiana Aug 20, 1942. Roman Catholic. Educated at St. Joseph Seminary 1960-61, Nicholls State University 1961-64 and Louisiana State University J.D. 1967. Listed in *Who's Who in American Colleges and Universities* 1964. Admitted to practice Louisiana 1967.

Member Louisiana Trial Lawyers Association, The Association of Trial Lawyers of America, Terrebonne

FANGUY, JUDE THADDEUS—*Continued*

Parish, Louisiana State and American Bar Associations. Named Outstanding Young Man of America 1970. President Houma-Terrebonne Jaycees 1971-72 and Louisiana Junior Miss Pageant, Inc. 1973-74. Chairman Terrebonne Parish Flood Appeals Board 1976-78.

Office: 7887 Main Street, Houma 70360.

Telephone: (985) 868-4232.

FELDMAN, Martin L. C. *(Judge, United States District Court Eastern District of Louisiana)* Appointed for life by President Ronald Reagan Oct 12, 1983. Born St. Louis Missouri Jan 28, 1934. Jewish. Member Temple Sinai (Former Trustee). Educated at Tulane University B.A. 1955 J.D. with honors 1957. Assistant Editor Tulane University Law Review 1955-57. Law Clerk to Hon. John Minor Wisdom, U.S. Court of Appeals Fifth Circuit 1957-59. Member Order of the Coif. Winner Nathan Burkan Memorial Copyright Law Competition 1957. Admitted to practice Louisiana 1957 and Missouri 1957. Began legal practice New Orleans Louisiana 1959.

Vice President Wembley Industries, Inc. Chairman Board of Directors Cox Cable New Orleans, Inc. Special Counsel to Governor David C. Treen 1981-83. Author "A Puzzle Under the Federal Impleader Rule," "Employee Management Committees and the Labor Management Relations Act of 1947," "The Relationship Between Copyright and Unfair Competition Principles," "Some Tax Problems Under the Proposed Revision of the Louisiana Trust Estates Law" (Address to Louisiana State Bar Convention Annual Meeting 1963), " 'Trafficking' in Net Operating Loss Corporations—Revisited," "Planning for Employers' Payments to Widows," "The Shareholders' Agreement," "Revenue Ruling 71-497: IRS Renovates an Old Obstacle Course," "A Constitutional Amendment to Require Fiscal Balance—Economic Panacea or Pandora's Box?" and "State Takeover Statutes—A Constitutional Confrontation." Member The American Law Institute, The Missouri Bar, New Orleans, Louisiana State and American (Section of Business Law) Bar Associations. Lecturer on Taxation Arkansas-Louisiana-Texas Tax Institute, Louisiana State Bar Convention and Tulane University Tax Institute. Lecturer on Corporate Law Louisiana State Bar Association CLE seminars and Louisiana State Bar Convention. Recipient Distinguished Service Award Louisiana Tech University 1981 and National Tree of Life Award Jewish National Fund 1983. Captain U.S. Army JAGC 1957-63. Republican. Nixon-Lodge District Campaign Manager 1960. Co-chairman of Finance Treen for Congress 1962. Parish Election Day Chairman Lyons for Governor 1963 and Goldwater-Miller 1964. Louisiana Republican State Central Committee 1964-74. General Counsel and Chairman State Law Committee Republican Party of Louisiana 1965-72. Chairman Sponsors Committee New Orleans Dinner for Richard Nixon 1966. State Board Director Louisiana Republican Action Council 1966-72. Chairman Advisory Committee New Orleans Dinner for Senator Charles Percy 1967. Delegate Republican National Convention 1968 and 1972. Chairman Special Events Nixon-Agnew Committee of New Orleans 1968. Parliamentarian Louisiana Republican State Central Committee 1968-72. Arrangements Chairman Southern Regional Republican Conference 1969. Co-chairman Testimonial Dinner for Vice President Agnew 1970. Advisor to Secretary of Health, Education & Welfare Region VI 1972-73. Advisory Council on National Security and International Affairs Republican National Committee 1978-80. Member and former Vice Chairman Orleans Parish Republican Executive Committee. Former Finance Chairman Greater Metropolitan New Orleans Area (First and Second Congressional Districts). Former Deputy Vice Chairman Young Republican Federation of Louisiana.

Director New Orleans Regional Advisory Board Anti-Defamation League (Former Chairman). National Secretary and member National Executive Committee National Commission of the Anti-Defamation League. Board of Trustees WYES-TV (Chairman 1977-79). Board of Managers Touro Infirmary (President since 1982). Board of Directors Public Broadcasting Service. Director Advisory Board Friends of the University of New Orleans Library. Member Charter Revision Advisory Committee City of New Orleans, Mayor's Revenue Revision Task Force 1979-80 and Dean's Council Tulane School of Law. Former member Board of Directors New Orleans Jewish Family and Children's Service (Past President), New Orleans Speech and Hearing Center (Past Vice President), Loyola University Institute of Politics (Past President), New Orleans Inter-Racial Council of Business Opportunity, City of New Orleans Audubon Park Commission, New Orleans Development Services and Ballet Hysell. Former Trustee New Orleans Jewish Welfare Federation (Chairman Community Relations Committee 1970-72). Former member Finance Committee New Orleans Museum of Art and Orleans Parish Election Reforms Council Board of Election Supervisors (Chairman Subcommittee on Election Commissioners). Former Corporation Counsel Community Endowment Foundation New Orleans Jewish Welfare Federation. Interests include tennis, reading mysteries and historical novels and collecting scrimshaw.

Office: C555 U.S. Courthouse, 500 Camp Street, New Orleans 70130-3318.

Telephone: (504) 589-7550.

FENDLASON, Donald M. *(Judge, Louisiana District Court Twenty-second Judicial District)* Elected Oct 1995 to term beginning Jan 1, 1996. Reelected Oct 1996 and 2002. Current term expires Dec 31, 2008. Born Oct 2, 1937. Baptist. Educated at Southeastern Louisiana University B.A. 1959 and Loyola University School of Law J.D. 1964. Admitted to practice Louisiana 1964. In legal practice Bogalusa 1964-96. Judge, Bogalusa City Court 1987-95.

City Attorney Bogalusa 1970-78. Former Assistant District Attorney. President Louisiana City Judges Association 1992-93 and Louisiana Council of Juvenile and Family Court Judges since 2001. Member American Judges Association and Louisiana State Bar Association. Named Judge of the Year by Louisiana CASA 2000. Recipient Humanitarian Award from Arthritis Foundation. Associate Member Republican Professional Women's Club. Member Habitat for Humanity, Youth Services Bureau, Arthritis Foundation and Camp Fire. Enjoys hunting, fishing and cycling.

Office: 428 East Boston Street, Room 201, Covington 70433.

Telephone: (985) 898-2772.

FERNANDEZ, Manuel A. *(Judge, Louisiana District Court Thirty-fourth Judicial District)*

Office: 1101 West St. Bernard Highway, Chalmette 70043.

Telephone: (504) 278-4420.

FEUCHT, Lynette Young *(Judge, Eunice City Court)*
Mailing address: P.O. Box 591, Eunice 70535.
Telephone: (337) 457-6535.

FIELDS, Wilson *(Judge, Louisiana District Court Nineteenth Judicial District)*
Office: 222 St. Louis Street, Suite 780, Baton Rouge 70802.
Telephone: (225) 389-8741.

FITZSIMMONS, Brady M. *(Judge, Louisiana Court of Appeal First Circuit)* Elected 1994 to term beginning Jan 1, 1995. Term expires Dec 31, 2004. Born New Orleans Louisiana July 17, 1941. Catholic. Educated at Spring Hill College B.A., Louisiana State University M.A. and Loyola University of the South J.D. Admitted to practice Louisiana 1975. Began legal practice Covington. Judge, Louisiana District Court Twenty-second Judicial District Oct 1988 to Dec 31, 1994.

Former Public Defender Louisiana. Former Assistant District Attorney (Chief Criminal Division) Louisiana District Court Twenty-second Judicial District. Former Faculty Member English Department Southeastern Louisiana University and Loyola University of the South. Adjunct Faculty Member Loyola University Law School. Fellow St. Thomas More Inn of Court. Member National Council of Juvenile and Family Court Judges (Former member Pediatric and Adolescent Medicine Committee), Louisiana Bar Foundation, American Judges Association, Louisiana State (Former Member Section on Composition and Administration of the Judiciary) and American (Committee on Sole Practitioners and Small Firms Judicial Administration Division 1989-90) Bar Associations. Faculty Member Legal Skills Program and Guest Panelist Annual Louisiana Association of Defense Counsel Seminar. Faculty Member Gulf Coast Regional National Institute for Trial Advocacy. Moderator "Composition and Administration of the Judiciary" Louisiana State Bar Association Annual Meeting. Speaker "Depositions from A to Z" Louisiana State Bar Association Seminar. Judge Mentor Program 1996. Presided over "The Masters in Trial" American Board of Trial Advocates. Faculty Advisor The National Judicial College Feb 1992. Instructor New Orleans Police Academy. Guest Lecturer Louisiana State Police Academy. Authored poetry appearing in *Southern Review* and *America* magazines.
Office: 832 East Boston Street, Unit 16, Covington 70433.
Telephone: (985) 893-3676.

FOIL, Frank *(Judge, Louisiana Court of Appeal First Circuit)* Former Judge, Louisiana District Court Nineteenth Judicial District.
Mailing address: P.O. Box 4408, Baton Rouge 70821.
Telephone: (225) 342-0901.

FONTENOT, Elvin C., Jr. *(Judge, Leesville City Court)*
Mailing address: P.O. Box 1486, Leesville 71496.
Telephone: (337) 238-1531.

FONTENOT, H. Ward *(Judge, Louisiana District Court Thirty-eighth Judicial District)* Currently serves as Chief Judge.
Mailing address: P.O. Box 578, Cameron 70631.
Telephone: (337) 775-5649.

FOOTE, W. Ross *(Judge, Louisiana District Court Ninth Judicial District)* Elected to term beginning Jan 1, 1991. Reelected 1996 and 2002. Current term expires Dec 31, 2008. Born Alexandria Louisiana Oct 1, 1952. Methodist. Educated at Duke University B.A. 1974 and Louisiana State University J.D. Member Omicron Delta Kappa. Admitted to practice Louisiana 1978 and U.S. District Courts Eastern 1978 and Western 1978 Districts of Louisiana. In legal practice Alexandria 1978-91.

Adjunct Professor in Succession Procedure Louisiana College 1986-87. Chair Louisiana Judicial Mentoring Project since 1995, Louisiana Judicial Retreat Project since 1998 and Judicial European Development Initiative for Louisiana District Judges. Member Advisory Committee on Technology National Center for State Courts 1995-98, Committee for New Judgeships Louisiana Judicial Council 1997-98, Long-Range Planning Committee Louisiana Supreme Court, Louisiana District Judges Association (Executive Committee, Supreme Court Computer Information Systems Committee, State Criminal Bench Book Revisions Committee), Alexandria, Louisiana State and American Bar Associations. Attended annual courses Louisiana Judicial College 1991-2000, General Jurisdiction and Writing courses The National Judicial College 1992 and Seminar on Basic Issues of Science Federal Judicial Center 1997. Instructor in Jury Trial Bench/Bar Conference 1992. Trial Judge Speaker Falling Leaves Seminar 1993. Speaker Louisiana Judicial College 1994-97. Faculty Member The National Judicial College Reno Nevada 1999-2000. Recipient President's Award from Louisiana State Bar Association 1997. Democrat. Past President YMCA. Scout Executive Board. Board Member March of Dimes and Louisiana Boys & Girls Club. Captain United Way. Enjoys tennis, sailing, cycling, travel and wines.
Mailing address: P.O. Box 1431, Alexandria 71309-1431.
Telephone: (318) 443-6893.

FORD, John C. *(Judge, Louisiana District Court Thirtieth Judicial District)* Elected October 1996 to term beginning Dec 1996. Reelected to subsequent term. Currently serves as Chief Judge. Born Leesville Louisiana June 24, 1939. Catholic. Educated at Northwestern State University B.S. 1966 and Loyola University School of Law J.D. 1973. Admitted to practice Louisiana 1973, U.S. District Courts Eastern 1974, Middle 1974 and Western 1974 Districts of Louisiana and U.S. Court of Appeals Fifth Circuit 1974. In legal practice Leesville 1973-96.

Member Louisiana Trial Lawyers Association, Vernon and Louisiana State Bar Associations. Specialist Four U.S. Army 1962-65. Police Juror District 8 Vernon Parish 1991-96. Enjoys hunting and fishing.
Mailing address: P.O. Drawer 1700, Leesville 71496-1700.
Telephone: (337) 239-3584.
E-mail address: judge@worldnetla.net

FREE, J. Robin *(Judge, Louisiana District Court Eighteenth Judicial District)*
Mailing address: P.O. Box 724, Port Allen 70767.
Telephone: (225) 336-2419.

FUSELIER, Perrell *(Judge, Oakdale City Court)*
Mailing address: P.O. Box 565, Oakdale 71463.
Telephone: (318) 335-1121.

FUSELIER, Thomas F. *(Judge, Louisiana District Court Thirteenth Judicial District)*
Mailing address: P.O. Box 1057, Ville Platte 70586.
Telephone: (337) 363-5608.

GAHAGAN, Fred S. *(Judge, Natchitoches City Court)*
Mailing address: P.O. Box 70, Natchitoches 71458-0070.
Telephone: (318) 352-6666.

GAIDRY, Edward J. "Jimmy" *(Judge, Louisiana Court of Appeal First Circuit)* Assumed office Sept 6, 2002. Born Houma Louisiana May 20, 1942. Admitted to practice Louisiana 1967, U.S. District Court Eastern District of Louisiana 1968 and U.S. Supreme Court 1971. Began legal practice Terrebonne Parish 1967. Former Judge ad hoc, Houma City Court. Judge, Louisiana District Court Thirty-second Judicial District Jan 1, 1985 to 2002.

Assistant City Attorney and City Attorney Houma 1970-71. Assistant District Attorney 1972-73. Former Special Prosecutor for District Attorney's Office. Former Attorney for Houma-Terrebonne Airport Commission. Member Subcommittee on Judicial Selection Louisiana District Judges Association. Member American Judges Association, The Association of Trial Lawyers of America, Louisiana Trial Lawyers Association, Terrebonne Parish, Louisiana State and American Bar Associations. Former member Board of Directors Gulf Coast Conservation Association. Board member Houma-Terrebonne Chamber of Commerce, Knights of Columbus, Terrebonne Sportsmen's League, Houma Lions Club, Terreanian Carnival Club, Louisiana State University Alumni Association and Vandebilt Alumni Association.
Mailing address: P.O. Box 1916, Houma 70361.
Telephone: (985) 853-1300.

GANUCHEAU, Anita Hamann *(Judge, Orleans Parish Juvenile Court)* Elected Dec 8, 1979 to term beginning Jan 1, 1980. Reelected 1988 and 1996. Current term expires Dec 31, 2004. Born Birmingham Alabama Nov 24, 1943. Catholic. Educated at Loyola University B.S.M.T. magna cum laude 1965 and Tulane University J.D. 1971. Staff member Tulane Law Review 1969-71. Member Order of the Coif. Admitted to practice Louisiana 1971, U.S. District Court Eastern District of Louisiana 1972 and U.S. Court of Appeals Fifth Circuit 1972. Began legal practice New Orleans 1971.

Author articles in 44 Tulane L. Rev. 363, 1970, 45 Tulane L. Rev. 211, 1970 and 4 Southern University L. Rev. 16, 1977. Instructor Tulane University Paralegal Studies 1981-83. Member Louisiana Association of Juvenile and Family Court Judges, National Council of Juvenile and Family Court Judges, Louisiana Fourth and Fifth Circuit Judges Association, Louisiana Association for Women Attorneys, Louisiana State and American Bar Associations.
Office: 421 Loyola Avenue, New Orleans 70112.
Telephone: (504) 565-7383.

GARCIA, Peter J. *(Judge, Louisiana District Court Twenty-second Judicial District)*
Office: 329 North New Hampshire Street, Covington 70433.
Telephone: (985) 898-2565.

GARRETT, Jeanette G. *(Judge, Louisiana District Court First Judicial District)*
Office: 501 Texas Street, Suite 300 D, Shreveport 71101.
Telephone: (318) 226-6811.

GASAWAY, Grace Bennett *(Judge, Hammond City Court)* Elected Nov 1996 to term beginning Jan 1, 1997. Reelected 2002, current term expires Dec 31, 2008. Born Hammond Louisiana June 16, 1961. Episcopalian. Educated at Louisiana State University B.A. 1982 J.D. 1985. Admitted to practice Louisiana 1986 and U.S. District Courts Eastern and Middle Districts of Louisiana. In legal practice Hammond since 1986.

Charter Board Member Southeastern Louisiana Delinquency Prevention Council. Board of Trustees Louisiana Council of Juvenile and Family Court Judges. Judge Advocate Region Two State Judge Advocate Network. Member Florida Parishes American Inns of Court, Florida Parishes Judges Association, Louisiana City Judges Association, National Council of Juvenile and Family Court Judges, Twenty-first Judicial District (Past President, Former Vice President, Former Secretary/Treasurer), Louisiana State and American Bar Associations. Graduate The National Judicial College 1998. Recipient Annie Award for Outstanding Woman of the Year in Government from Southeastern Louisiana University and Hammond Chamber of Commerce 1999. Democrat. Past President Options, Inc. Former Member Board of Directors Tangipahoa Association for Retarded Citizens. Past President and Board of Directors Richard Murphy Hospice Foundation. Board of Directors Hammond Chamber of Commerce (Committee Service-Membership, Education). Advisory Council Graduate Counseling Southeastern Louisiana University. Delegate Summit on Youth Louisiana's Promise. Trainer/Educator Court Appointed Special Advocates and on Law Enforcement and Criminal Justice Leadership Tangipahoa. Lieutenant Krewe of Omega. Team Captain Relay for Life American Cancer Society. Vestry Member Grace Memorial Episcopal Church since 1998.
Office: 303 East Thomas Street, Hammond 70401.
Telephone: (985) 542-3465.
E-mail address: gasaway_gb@hammond.org

GASKINS, Gay C. *(Judge, Louisiana Court of Appeal Second Circuit)* Elected 1995. Born April 22, 1953. Educated at Centenary College B.A. 1975 and Louisiana State University Law Center J.D. 1982. In legal practice Shreveport 1986-90. Former Judge, Shreveport City Court, elected to term beginning 1990.

Assistant District Attorney Caddo Parish 1982-90. President Second Circuit Judges Association since 2003. Louisiana Court of Appeal Liaison to Shreveport Bar Association. Member Harry V. Booth Inn of Court, Shreveport, Louisiana State and American Bar Associations.
Office: 430 Fannin Street, Shreveport 71101.
Telephone: (318) 227-3770.

GENOVESE, James T. *(Judge, Louisiana District Court Twenty-seventh Judicial District)*
Mailing address: P.O. Box 777, Opelousas 70571-0777.
Telephone: (337) 948-0588.

GIACOBBE, George W. *(Judge, First Parish Court Jefferson Parish)* Elected Dec 1, 1988. Reelected to terms beginning Jan 1, 1990, Jan 1, 1996 and Jan 1,

GIACOBBE, GEORGE W.—*Continued*

2002. Current term expires Dec 31, 2007. Currently serves as Senior Judge. Born New Orleans Louisiana Jan 9, 1945. Catholic. Educated at Louisiana State University B.S. 1967 and Loyola University School of Law J.D. 1973. Admitted to practice Louisiana 1973 and U.S. District Court Eastern District of Louisiana 1973. In legal practice Kenner Oct 1973 to Nov 1988. Magistrate, Kenner City Court Feb 7, 1987 to Nov 30, 1988.

Assistant City Attorney Feb 1978 to April 1980 and City Attorney April 1980 to Feb 1987 Kenner. Member Louisiana City Judges Association, Fourth and Fifth Circuit Judges Association (Past President, Treasurer), American Judicial Society, Jefferson, Louisiana State and American Bar Associations. Enjoys fishing, reading and golfing.

Office: 924 David Drive, Metairie 70003.
Telephone: (504) 736-8977.
Fax: (504) 736-8995
E-mail address: george@jeffparishcourts.com

GIARRUSSO, Robin M. *(Judge, Louisiana District Court Orleans Parish Civil District)*
Office: 421 Loyola Avenue, Room 411, New Orleans 70112.
Telephone: (504) 592-9333.

GILL-JEFFERSON, Carolyn W. *(Judge, Louisiana District Court Orleans Parish Civil District)* Currently serves as Chief Judge.
Office: 421 Loyola Avenue, Room 314, New Orleans 70112.
Telephone: (504) 592-9200.

GORBATY, David S. *(Judge, Louisiana Court of Appeal Fourth Circuit)* Former Judge, Louisiana District Court Thirty-fourth Judicial District.
Office: 1515 Poydras Street, Seventh Floor, New Orleans 70112.
Telephone: (504) 556-9990.

GOTHARD, Sol *(Judge, Louisiana Court of Appeal Fifth Circuit)* Elected 1986. Reelected to subsequent term. Born Bronx New York Nov 1, 1930. Jewish. Educated at City College of the City University of New York B.A. in Sociology, Western Reserve University (now Case Western Reserve University) M.S. in Social Work, Tulane University of Louisiana and Loyola University at New Orleans LL.B. J.D. Admitted to practice Louisiana 1962. In legal practice Metairie 1962-72. Judge and Chief Judge, Jefferson Parish Juvenile Court Oct 6, 1972 to 1986.

Former Probation Officer, Probation Supervisor and Assistant Director of Probation New Orleans Juvenile Court. Professor Loyola University, Tulane University Graduate School of Social Work and Southern University of New Orleans Graduate School of Social Work. Past President Louisiana Council of Juvenile Court Judges. Member Jefferson Parish, Louisiana State and American Bar Associations. Attended National College of Juvenile Justice. Named Citizen of the Year by Louisiana State Chapter National Association of Social Workers 1983 and Alumnus of the Year by Mandel School of Applied Social Sciences Case Western Reserve University 1989. Recipient Alfred E. Clay Award for significant contributions to children from Children's Bureau of Greater New Orleans 1983. Private First Class U.S. Army 1953-55. Democrat. Member National Association of Social Workers and Academy of Certified Social Workers. Board of Directors American Professional Society on the Abuse of Children (APSAC).
Mailing address: P.O. Box 489, Gretna 70054.
Telephone: (504) 376-1420.

GRANIER, Kirk R. *(Judge, Louisiana District Court Twenty-ninth Judicial District)*
Mailing address: P.O. Box 424, Hahnville 70057-0424.
Telephone: (985) 783-2923.

GRANT, Jo Ellen *(Judge, Louisiana District Court Twenty-fourth Judicial District)* Elected Dec 1990 to term beginning Jan 1991. Reelected 1996 and 2002. Current term expires Dec 31, 2008. Chief Judge 1998-99. Born Coshocton Ohio Dec 24, 1942. Methodist. Educated at The Ohio State University B.S. 1964 and Tulane University School of Law J.D. 1976. Admitted to practice Louisiana 1976 and U.S. District Court Eastern District of Louisiana 1977. In legal practice Gretna 1976-90.

Assistant District Attorney 1977-90. Instructor Trial Advocacy Program Tulane University School of Law 1992-97 and Louisiana State University 1992-99. Member Fourth and Fifth Circuit Judges Association, Fifth Circuit Judges Association, Louisiana District Judges Association (Board Member 1996-99), Jefferson, Louisiana State (Professionalism and Quality of Life Committee since 1996) and American Bar Associations. Lecturer on Professionalism. Recipient Outstanding Judicial Award from Victims and Citizens Against Crime 1998. Republican. Enjoys golfing, reading, knitting and cooking.
Office: Gretna Courthouse Annex Building, Gretna 70053.
Telephone: (504) 364-3910.
Fax: (504) 365-3392
E-mail address: joelleng@24jdc.co.jefferson.la.us

GRAY, Alcide J. *(Judge, Louisiana District Court Fourteenth Judicial District)*
Mailing address: P.O. Box 3210, Lake Charles 70602.
Telephone: (337) 437-3530.

GRAY, Ernestine S. *(Judge, Orleans Parish Juvenile Court)* Elected Nov 6, 1984. Reelected 1986, 1994 and 2002. Current term expires Dec 31, 2010. Currently serves as Chief Judge. Born Denmark South Carolina 1946. Educated at Spelman College B.A. 1970 and Louisiana State University School of Law J.D. 1976. Member Delta Sigma Theta. Admitted to practice Louisiana 1976.

Trial Attorney Baton Rouge Legal Aid Society, Attorney General's Office Louisiana and U.S. Equal Employment Opportunity Commission. Chair Task Force on Welfare Reform 1991. Consulting Editor Journal of Emotional Behavior since 1992. Board Member Louisiana Bar Foundation 1991-97, Legal Aid Bureau since 1985 and Court Appointed Special Advocates since 1990. Chair Task Force on Welfare Reform 1991 and Advisory Committee on Court Improvement Program Supreme Court of Louisiana since 1995. Co-Chair Mayor's Task Force on Children, Youth and Families 1994. Member Louisiana Children's Code Committee, New Orleans Association of Black Women Attorneys, Louisiana Commission on Law Enforcement, Louisiana Council of Juvenile and Family Court Judges (Secretary-Treasurer 1989-90, Vice President 1990-91, President 1991-92), Louis A. Martinet Society (Treasurer 1998-99,

GRAY, ERNESTINE S.—*Continued*

Secretary, Vice President, President), National Association of Women Judges, Association for Women Attorneys, American Judges Association, Louisiana State, National and American (Committee on Bias 1991, Co-chair 1991 and Chair 1992 Committee on Permanency Planning, Secretary 1997-98, Treasurer 1998-99 and Vice President since 1999 National Council of Juvenile and Family Court Judges) Bar Associations. Presenter "Managing Diversity and the Colors of Juvenile Justice" Chicago Illinois Nov 18, 1991 Chicago Illinois, "Maintaining Families—Continuing to Make Reasonable Efforts Work" Covington Georgia Dec 12, 1991, "NCJFCJ Protocol for Making Reasonable Efforts to Preserve Families in Drug Related Dependency Cases" New York Regional Substance Abuse Training Westchester New York Feb 28-29, 1992 and Syracuse New York Feb 10-11, 1992, "NCJFCJ Protocol in Drug Related Dependency Cases" Annual Conference National Court Appointed Special Advocates Association Nashville Tennessee May 16-19, 1992, "Reasonable Efforts" National Conference of State Legislatures Scottsdale Arizona Jan 2-4, 1994 and "The National Summit on Children Exposed to Violence" Safe from the Start Washington D.C. June 22-24, 1999. Instructor Gulf Coast Regional Program National Institute for Trial Advocacy. Named One of 100 Women in the Forefront 1986, Volunteer of the Year by Metropolitan YMCA 1991, YMCA Role Model 1993 and Woman of Distinction by Patricia Richelle Day Care Center 1995. Recipient Outstanding Achievement in Law Award from Omega Psi Phi 1986, Flaschner Award from American Bar Association 1995, TOP Award from Family Service of Greater New Orleans 1997 and Ernest N. Morial Judicial Pacesetter Award from Louis A. Martinet Legal Society 1999.

Chair Dropout Prevention Task Force Orleans Parish School Board 1985-86. Board Member United Way of Greater New Orleans 1987-93, One Church One Child since 1985, YMCA since 1987 (Chair 1998-99), New Orleans Job Corps Community Relations Board since 1988 (Chair 1990-94), New Orleans Marine Institute 1990-99 (Chair 1995-97), Milne Boys' Home FOCUS (intensive home-based family preservation program) since 1990, Louisiana Special Olympics 1991-94, Institute of Mental Hygiene 1991-99, Volunteers of America since 1992 (Chair 1997-99), National Council of Negro Women of Greater New Orleans since 1993, Travelers Aid Society 1995-97, Boys and Girls Club 1995-97, YWCA since 1996 (Secretary since 1998) and New Orleans Youth at Risk 1997. Member Steering Committee Task Force on Early Childhood Education New Orleans Public School 1990. Member New Orleans Chapter Links, Inc. (President 1994-96) and New Orleans Chapter National Alumnae Association of Spelman College (President 1995-97). Enjoys running, reading and traveling.

Office: 421 Loyola Avenue, New Orleans 70112.
Telephone: (504) 565-7326.

GREEN, Alan J. *(Judge, Louisiana District Court Twenty-fourth Judicial District)*

Office: 200 Derbigny Street, Room 302, Gretna 70053.
Telephone: (504) 364-3866.

GREEN, Larry J. *(Judge, Louisiana District Court Twenty-second Judicial District)* Currently serves as Chief Judge.

Office: 428 East Boston Street, Room 203, Covington 70433.
Telephone: (985) 898-2710.

GREFER, Stephen *(Judge, Second Parish Court Jefferson Parish)*

Office: 200 Derbigny Street, Gretna 70053.
Telephone: (504) 364-2800.

GREMILLION, Glenn B. *(Judge, Louisiana Court of Appeal Third Circuit)* Elected 1995 and 1996. Current term expires Dec 31, 2006. Born Natchez Mississippi June 29, 1946. Catholic. Educated at Louisiana Tech University B.S. 1968 and Loyola University of New Orleans Law School J.D. 1976. Staff member Loyola Law Review 1975-76. Member Tau Kappa Epsilon. Admitted to practice Louisiana 1976. Began legal practice Ferriday 1976. Former Judge and Chief Judge, Louisiana District Court Seventh Judicial District Dec 1, 1983 to 1995.

Assistant District Attorney 1976-81. Prosecutor City of Vidalia 1979-82. Member Seventh Judicial District (President 1981-83) and Louisiana State Bar Associations. Captain USAF 1969-73. Lieutenant Colonel Louisiana National Guard since 1989. Democrat. Member Louisiana Democratic Central Committee 1980-84. Member Rotary Club of Ferriday, Ferriday Jaycees and Ferriday Chamber of Commerce. Enjoys golf and tennis.

Office: 1400 Highway 65, Ferriday 71334.
Telephone: (318) 757-2322.

GRIFFIN, Piper D. *(Judge, Louisiana District Court Orleans Parish Civil District)*

Office: 421 Loyola Avenue, New Orleans 70112.
Telephone: (504) 592-9226.

GUIDRY, Greg Gerard *(Judge, Louisiana District Court Twenty-fourth Judicial District)* Elected to term beginning Oct 2000. Reelected 2002, current term expires Dec 2008. Born New Orleans Louisiana July 2, 1960. Catholic. Educated at Louisiana State University B.A. magna cum laude 1982 J.D. 1985. Member Order of the Coif. In legal practice New Orleans 1985-89.

Assistant Attorney General Louisiana 1989-90. Assistant U.S. Attorney Eastern District of Louisiana 1990-2000. Member The Federalist Society. Recipient Special Award for Excellence of Performance in the Administration of Criminal Justice from Chief Postal Inspectors. Republican. Board of Advisors New Orleans Catholic Charities, Rotary Club and American Quarter Horse Association. Enjoys raising and showing American Quarter Horses.

Office: Courthouse Annex Building, Gretna 70053.
Telephone: (504) 364-3884.
E-mail address: GregG@24JDC.co.jefferson.la.us

GUIDRY, John Michael *(Judge, Louisiana Court of Appeal First Circuit)* Elected to term beginning 1997. Educated at Louisiana State University B.A. 1983 and Southern University Law Center J.D. cum laude 1987. In legal practice Baton Rouge 1987-97.

Assistant Parish Attorney Baton Rouge 1988-91. Instructor Law Center since 1988 and Political Science Department since 1993 Southern University. Member Louis A. Martinet Legal Society, American Judges Association, Baton Rouge, Louisiana State, National and American Bar Associations. Legislative Assistant 1980-

GUIDRY, JOHN MICHAEL—*Continued*

88, Assistant Clerk 1984-88 and State Representative 1992-93 Louisiana House of Representatives. State Senator Louisiana Senate 1993-97. Deacon Fairview Baptist Church.

Mailing address: P.O. Box 4408, Baton Rouge 70821-4408.

Telephone: (225) 342-1065.

E-mail address: jguidry@la-fcca.org

GUIDRY-WHIPPLE, Vanessa *(Judge, Louisiana Court of Appeal First Circuit)*

Office: 7910 Main Street, Suite 410, Houma 70360.

Telephone: (985) 876-4034.

GUNNELL, C. Steve *(Judge, Jennings City Court)*

Mailing address: P.O. Box 609, Jennings 70546.

Telephone: (337) 821-5514.

HAIK, Richard T. *(Chief Judge, United States District Court Western District of Louisiana)* Appointed for life by the President. Chief Judge since May 31, 2002. Born New Iberia Louisiana March 1, 1950. Catholic. Educated at University of Southwestern Louisiana B.S. 1972 and Loyola Law School J.D. 1975. Member Delta Theta Phi. Admitted to practice Louisiana 1975 and U.S. District Courts Eastern 1980 and Western 1980 Districts of Louisiana. In legal practice New Iberia 1975-84. Former Chief Judge and Judge, Louisiana District Court Sixteenth Judicial District, elected to term beginning Oct 5, 1984.

Former member Board of Governors Louisiana Trial Lawyers Association. Member Association of Juvenile Judges, Louisiana District Judges Association (Treasurer, Executive Committee, Judicial Budget Committee), Louisiana State and American Bar Associations. Attended Spring and Fall Judges Conference and Juvenile Seminar Houston Texas. Captain Louisiana National Guard 1972-79. Mechanized Company Commander OCS 156th Infantry 1977-79. USAR 1980-84. Previously employed with Vacco Wireline, Loffland Brothers and Wilson Downhole. Republican. Coach Little League and Flag Football. Former member Cajun Kiwanis Club. Member American Legion, Iberia Retarded Citizens Association and St. Edward's School Board. Enjoys fishing, riding horses and racquetball.

Office: 4200 U.S. Courthouse, 800 Lafayette Street, Lafayette 70501.

Telephone: (337) 593-5100.

HAND, Kernan A. *(Judge, Louisiana District Court Twenty-fourth Judicial District)*

Office: 200 Derbigny Street, Room 201, Gretna 70053.

Telephone: (504) 364-3903.

HANSEN, Gerard J. *(Magistrate Judge, Louisiana District Court Orleans Parish Criminal District)* Elected to term beginning Nov 20, 1978. Reelected to subsequent terms.

Office: 2700 Tulane Avenue, New Orleans 70119.

Telephone: (504) 827-3440.

HARRINGTON, Barrett *(Judge, Crowley City Court)* Elected to term beginning Jan 1, 1983. Reelected 1990, 1996 and 2002. Current term expires Dec 31, 2008. Born Alexandria Louisiana Feb 15, 1936. Catholic. Educated at Louisiana State University B.S. 1958 and Tulane University J.D. 1962. Admitted to practice Louisiana 1962 and U.S. District Courts Eastern 1969 and Western 1969 Districts of Louisiana. In legal practice Crowley.

Assistant District Attorney Fifteenth Judicial District 1970-72. Founding Director Indigent Defender Board Fifteenth Judicial District. Member Police and Civil Service Boards Crowley. Board of Governors Louisiana Trial Lawyers Association (three terms). Member Louisiana State and Federal Bar Associations. Instructor in Criminal Law State Fire Marshal's Office Baton Rouge. Captain U.S. Army Airborne. Member Acadiana Chapter 82nd Airborne Division Association and Central Gulf Coast Special Forces Association. Chairman International Rice Festival. Eyesight Committee Chairman Crowley Lions Club thirty years. Member American Legion Post 15. Enjoys scuba diving and equestrian activities including fox hunting and endurance riding.

Mailing address: P.O. Box 225, Crowley 70526.

Telephone: (337) 788-4118.

HARRINGTON, Eric R. *(Judge, Louisiana District Court Tenth Judicial District)*

Mailing address: P.O. Box 775, Natchitoches 71458-0775.

Telephone: (318) 357-2210.

HARRIS, Alonzo *(Judge, Louisiana District Court Twenty-seventh Judicial District)* Elected May 1993. Reelected Sept 1996 and 2002. Current term expires Dec 31, 2008. Currently serves as Chief Judge. Born Opelousas Louisiana June 20, 1961. Baptist. Educated at Southern University B.S. 1983 J.D. 1986. Member Delta Theta Phi. Admitted to practice Louisiana 1987. Began legal practice Opelousas.

Member Louisiana Judicial College, Third Circuit Judges Association, National Council of Juvenile and Family Court Judges and Louisiana State Bar Association. Attended Annual Judges Spring Conference Louisiana State Bar Association April 1999 and Summer School for Judges San Destin Florida June 1999. Member Opelousas Rotary Club. Interests include basketball, golf, fishing and showing cattle with children.

Mailing address: P.O. Drawer 478, Opelousas 70571.

Telephone: (337) 948-0584.

HAYES, Karen L. *(Magistrate Judge, United States District Court Western District of Louisiana)* Appointed by U.S. District Court judges to term beginning June 1997. Reappointed 2001, current term expires 2005. Serves part time. Educated at Louisiana State University B.A. 1976, Northeast Louisiana University M.A. 1981 and Mississippi College School of Law J.D. with special distinction 1990. Law Clerk to Hon. Donald E. Walter, U.S. District Court Western District of Louisiana 1990-91. Admitted to practice Louisiana 1990 and U.S. Court of Appeals Fifth Circuit 1991. In legal practice Monroe since 1991.

Mailing address: P.O. Box 3087, Monroe 71210-3087.

Telephone: (318) 387-2441.

HEBERT, Donald W. *(Judge, Louisiana District Court Twenty-seventh Judicial District)* Elected to term beginning Nov 1999. Reelected 2002, current term expires Dec 31, 2008. Born Opelousas Louisiana Aug 4, 1948. Educated at University of Louisiana at Lafayette B.S. 1974 and Louisiana State University J.D. 1977. Admitted to practice Louisiana 1978 and U.S. District Courts Eastern 1978, Middle 1978 and Western 1978

HEBERT, DONALD W.—*Continued*
Districts of Louisiana. In legal practice Opelousas 1978-99.

Member Louisiana Council of Juvenile and Family Court Judges, Louisiana District Judges Association, National Council of Juvenile and Family Court Judges, St. Landry Parish and Louisiana State Bar Associations. USN 1968-72. Democrat. Member Louisiana Democratic State Central Committee 1988-92. Member St. Landry Chamber of Commerce and Rotary International. Enjoys playing tennis, fishing and reading.

Mailing address: P.O. Box 868, Opelousas 70571.
Telephone: (337) 948-0580.
E-mail address: Donald.W.Hebert@hotmail.com

HÉBERT, J. Byron *(Judge, Louisiana District Court Fifteenth Judicial District)* Elected at special election to term beginning Oct 3, 1980. Reelected 1984, 1990, 1996 and 2002. Current term expires Dec 31, 2008. Born Abbeville Louisiana July 28, 1943. Roman Catholic. Educated at Louisiana State University B.A. 1966 J.D. 1970. Law Clerk to Hon. Richard J. Putnam, U.S. District Court Western District of Louisiana 1970-75. Member Sigma Alpha Epsilon, Phi Alpha Delta and Phi Eta Sigma. Admitted to practice Louisiana 1970. Began legal practice Abbeville 1970. Magistrate, U.S. District Court Western District of Louisiana July 1, 1975 to July 10, 1980.

Member National Council of Juvenile and Family Court Judges, Vermilion Parish and Louisiana State Bar Associations. Democrat. Advisory Board Mount Carmel Elementary School 1981-84. Board of Trustees Academy of the Sacred Heart 1991-99. Active in Abbey Players Community Theatre since 1977. Chevalier Confrérie de L'Omelette Géante d'Abbeville Louisiana. Volunteer Tour Guide Abbeville. Interests include piano, bridge, travel and photography.

Office: 220 Courthouse Building, 100 North State Street, Abbeville 70510.
Telephone: (337) 898-4315.

HEDGES, Patricia T. *(Judge, Louisiana District Court Twenty-second Judicial District)*
Office: 510 East Boston Street, Room 201, Covington 70433.
Telephone: (985) 898-2564.

HEEBE, Frederick Jacob Reagan *(Senior Judge, United States District Court Eastern District of Louisiana)* Appointed for life by President Lyndon B. Johnson to term beginning May 2, 1966. Former Chief Judge. Assumed Senior status, serves by assignment. Born Gretna Louisiana Aug 25, 1922. Methodist. Educated at Tulane University of Louisiana B.A. 1943 LL.B. 1949. Member Phi Beta Kappa and Moot Court. Admitted to practice Louisiana 1949. Began legal practice Gretna 1949. Judge, Louisiana District Court Twenty-fourth Judicial District 1961-66.

Vice Chairman Jefferson Parish Council 1958-60. Member American Judicature Society, New Orleans, Louisiana State, Federal and American Bar Associations. Captain U.S. Army Infantry 1944-46. Democrat. Chairman Jefferson Parish Board of Public Welfare 1953-55. Charter member Community Welfare Council Jefferson Parish 1957. Member Board of Directors Social Welfare Planning Council, New Orleans Regional Mental Center and Clinic and West Bank Association for Retarded. Active in Westside District Boy Scouts. Enjoys golf.

Office: U.S. Courthouse, 500 Camp Street, New Orleans 70130.
Telephone: (504) 589-7721.

HERNANDEZ, Todd *(Judge, Louisiana District Court Nineteenth Judicial District)*
Office: 222 St. Louis Street, Suite 619, Baton Rouge 70802.
Telephone: (225) 389-4706.

HIGGINBOTHAM, Toni M. *(Judge, East Baton Rouge Parish Family Court)*
Office: 222 St. Louis Street, Room 958, Baton Rouge 70802.
Telephone: (225) 389-4673.

HOLDRIDGE, Guy *(Judge, Louisiana District Court Twenty-third Judicial District)* Elected Nov 1990 to term beginning Jan 1, 1991. Reelected 1996 and 2002. Current term expires Dec 31, 2008. Born Gonzales Louisiana June 30, 1953. Catholic. Educated at Louisiana State University B.A. 1974 J.D. 1978. Member Phi Kappa Phi, Delta Theta Phi and Order of the Coif. Admitted to practice Louisiana 1978. In legal practice 1978-91. Judge ad hoc, Ascension Parish Court 1983-91.

City Attorney Gonzales 1982-91. Family Law Editor *Trial Brief.* Author *"Aldinger v. Howard:* A Possible Problem for Pendent Parties" 37 Louisiana L. Rev. 1977 and "Louisiana's Useful Class Action: *Williams v. State*" 38 Louisiana L. Rev. Member Twenty-third Judicial District Indigent Defender Board, Twenty-third Judicial District and Louisiana State (House of Delegates) Bar Associations. Inducted into Louisiana Law Center Hall of Fame. Member Rotary Club, Mayor's Prayer Breakfast Committee, Knights of Columbus and St. Theresa Ushers Association.

Office: 828-202 South Irma Boulevard, Gonzales 70737.
Telephone: (225) 621-8500.

HOOD, John S. *(Judge, Lake Charles City Court)* Elected Oct 1984 to term beginning Jan 1, 1985. Reelected 1990, 1996 and 2002. Current term expires Dec 31, 2008. Born Lake Charles Louisiana April 6, 1949. Presbyterian. Educated at Louisiana State University B.A. 1971 J.D. 1975. Law Clerk to Louisiana District Court Fourteenth Judicial District 1975-76. Admitted to practice Louisiana 1975. In legal practice Lake Charles 1976-84.

Mailing address: P.O. Box 1664, Lake Charles 70602.
Telephone: (337) 491-1305.

HUGHES, Jefferson D., III *(Judge, Louisiana District Court Twenty-first Judicial District)*
Mailing address: P.O. Box 907, Walker 70785.
Telephone: (225) 686-7461.

HUGHES, M. Douglas *(Judge, Louisiana District Court Twenty-first Judicial District)*
Mailing address: P.O. Box 788, Amite 70422.
Telephone: (985) 748-9445.

HUGHES, Yvonne *(Judge, Orleans Parish Juvenile Court)*
Office: 421 Loyola Avenue, New Orleans 70112.
Telephone: (504) 565-7370.

HUNTER, Arthur L., Jr. *(Judge, Louisiana District Court Orleans Parish Criminal District)*
Office: 2700 Tulane Avenue, New Orleans 70119.
Telephone: (504) 826-5503.

HUNTER, Henley A. *(Judge, United States Bankruptcy Court Western District of Louisiana)* Appointed by U.S. Court of Appeals Fifth Circuit judges to term beginning July 31, 1987. Reappointed July 31, 2001, current term expires July 30, 2015. Former Chief Judge. Born Shreveport Louisiana May 27, 1944. Educated at University of Arkansas B.A. 1966 and Louisiana State University School of Law J.D. 1969. Law Clerk to Louisiana Court of Appeal Second Circuit 1969-70. Member Phi Alpha Delta. Admitted to practice Louisiana 1969. In legal practice Shreveport 1970-87.

Member American Judicature Society, National Conference of Bankruptcy Judges, Alexandria, Louisiana State and American Bar Associations. Instructor "Debtor-or-Creditor Relations" Legal Assistants Program Conferences and Institutes Department 1979-87. Speaker "Recent Developments in Legislation and Jurisprudence" Sept 1988, Sept 21-22, 1989, Sept 12-13, 1991, Sept 17-18, 1992 and Sept 22-23, 1994 and Recent Development Seminar Baton Rouge Nov 15, 1995, Nov 5-6, 1998, Oct 21-22, 1999, Oct 26-27, 2000, Nov 8-9, 2001 and Oct 24-25, 2002; and "Recent Developments in Legislation and Jurisprudence" Seminar Monroe Oct 31, 1996, Oct 8-9, 1998 and Oct 5-6, 2000. Panelist "Bankruptcy Litigation and Practice" Professional Education Systems Nov 1988, U.S. Trustees Seminar Shreveport Jan 29-30, 1998 and Aug 12, 2001, Pro Bono Project CLE Seminar Marksville Dec 3, 1999; and Southwest Louisiana Bankruptcy Bar Association Sept 25, 2000 and Oct 22, 2002.
Office: 300 Jackson Street, Suite 201, Alexandria 71301-8357.
Telephone: (318) 443-8083.

HUNTER, William D. *(Judge, Louisiana District Court Sixteenth Judicial District)* Former Chief Judge.
Mailing address: P.O. Box 1029, Franklin 70538.
Telephone: (337) 828-4100.

IMBORNONE, Charles A. *(Judge, New Orleans First City Court)* Currently serves as Senior Judge.
Office: 421 Loyola Avenue, Room 202, New Orleans 70112.
Telephone: (504) 592-9240.

IRVIN, R. Lee *(Judge, Shreveport City Court)* Elected Oct 1990 to term beginning Jan 1, 1991. Reelected 1996 and 2002. Current term expires Dec 31, 2008. Born Shreveport Louisiana Sept 6, 1955. Catholic. Educated at Northeast Louisiana University and Louisiana State University J.D. Admitted to practice Louisiana 1980 and U.S. District Courts Middle 1980 and Western 1980 Districts of Louisiana.
Office: 1244 Texas Avenue, Shreveport 71101.
Telephone: (318) 673-5870.

JACKSON, Bonnie F. *(Judge, Louisiana District Court Nineteenth Judicial District)*
Office: 222 St. Louis Street, Suite 682, Baton Rouge 70802.
Telephone: (225) 389-4755.

JAMES, Robert G. *(Judge, United States District Court Western District of Louisiana)* Appointed for life by President Bill Clinton to term beginning Oct 31, 1998. Born Ruston Louisiana June 19, 1946. Educated at Louisiana Tech University B.A. 1968 and Louisiana State University Law Center J.D. 1971. In legal practice Ruston 1971-98. Judge, Ruston City Court 1985-98.
Mailing address: P.O. Drawer 3107, Monroe 71210-3107.
Telephone: (318) 322-6230.

JANZEN, Andrea Price *(Judge, Jefferson Parish Juvenile Court)*
Mailing address: P.O. Box 1900, Harvey 70059.
Telephone: (504) 367-3500.

JASMINE, Madeline *(Judge, Louisiana District Court Fortieth Judicial District)* Elected to term beginning Jan 2, 1991. Reelected 1996 and 2002. Current term expires Dec 31, 2008. Senior Judge since 1996. Born New Orleans Louisiana March 8, 1953. Baptist. Educated at Dillard University B.A. magna cum laude 1975 and Loyola University School of Law J.D. 1978. Admitted to practice Louisiana 1978, U.S. District Court Eastern District of Louisiana 1978 and U.S. Court of Appeals Fifth Circuit 1978. In legal practice Edgard 1978-90.

Assistant District Attorney 1979-90. Founding Member New Orleans Association of Black Women Attorneys. Member Louisiana Task Force on Racial and Ethnic Fairness in the Courts, Metropolitan District Law Enforcement Planning and Action Commission (President 1998-99), Louis A. Martinet Legal Society, Fourth and Fifth Circuit Court Judges Association, Louisiana District Judges Association, National Association of Women Judges, National Council of Juvenile and Family Court Judges, Fortieth Judicial District, Louisiana State, National and American Bar Associations. Attended Recent Developments in Law Seminar Sept 1991, New Judges Seminar Dec 13, 1991, Spring Judges Conference annually April 1991 to April 1998 and since 2000 and Summer School for Judges annually since June 1991 Louisiana State University. Recipient Ernest N. Morial Judicial Pacesetter Award from Louis A. Martinet Legal Society 1992. Former Substitute Teacher St. John the Baptist Parish School. Former Coordinator St. Jude Children's Research Hospital Bike-A-Thon. Coach High School Moot Court Competition five years. Member Scholarship Committee Woman's Auxiliary Second District Missionary Association, Louisiana, Inc. Interests include working with young people. Actively involved in community and church activities.
Mailing address: P.O. Box 277, Edgard 70049.
Telephone: (985) 497-3315.

JEANSONNE, Mark Anthony *(Judge, Louisiana District Court Twelfth Judicial District)*
Office: 312 North Main Street, Marksville 71351.
Telephone: (318) 253-9418.

JOHNSON, Bernette Joshua *(Justice, Supreme Court of Louisiana)* Appointed to term beginning Oct 31, 1994. Educated at Spelman College B.A. 1964 and Louisiana State University J.D. 1969. Judge 1984-94 and Chief Judge 1994, Louisiana District Court Orleans Parish Civil District.

Law Intern Civil Rights Division U.S. Department of Justice. Legal Services Attorney New Orleans Legal Assistance Corporation. Organizer CLE Program and Chair CLE Committee Louis A. Martinet Legal Society. Named as one of Outstanding Women on the Bench by New Orleans Association of Black Women Attorneys and Woman of the Year by LaBelle West Chapter

JOHNSON, BERNETTE JOSHUA—*Continued*
American Business Women Association 1994. First recipient of Ernest N. Morial Award from New Orleans Legal Assistance Corporation Recipient Daniel Byrd Award and A. P. Tureaud Citizenship Award from Louisiana State Conference NAACP. Community organizer Legal Defense and Education Fund NAACP. Former Member Executive Committee National Alumnae Association Spelman College. Former Chair New Orleans Chapter Southern Christian Leadership Conference SCLC/Women. Board Member New Orleans YWCA and New Orleans Legal Assistance Corporation. Chair Board of Directors Greater St. Stephen Full Gospel Baptist Church Learning Center.

Office: 301 Loyola Avenue, New Orleans 70112.
Telephone: (504) 568-8062.

JOHNSON, Calvin *(Judge, Louisiana District Court Orleans Parish Criminal District)*
Office: 2700 Tulane Avenue, New Orleans 70119.
Telephone: (504) 827-3482.

JOHNSON, Donald R. *(Judge, Louisiana District Court Nineteenth Judicial District)* Former Judge, Baton Rouge City Court.
Office: 222 St. Louis Street, Suite 623, Baton Rouge 70802.
Telephone: (225) 389-4717.

JOHNSON, Donald T. *(Judge, Louisiana District Court Ninth Judicial District)*
Mailing address: P.O. Drawer 1431, Alexandria 71309.
Telephone: (318) 443-6893.

JOHNSON, Kathy J. *(Judge, Louisiana District Court Seventh Judicial District)*
Mailing address: P.O. Drawer 600, Harrisonburg 71340.
Telephone: (318) 744-5414.

JOHNSON, Pamela Taylor *(Judge, East Baton Rouge Parish Juvenile Court)*
Office: 8333 Veterans Memorial Boulevard, Baton Rouge 70807.
Telephone: (225) 354-1208.

JONES, Benjamin *(Judge, Louisiana District Court Fourth Judicial District)* Elected Aug 20, 1992 to term beginning Sept 25, 1992. Reelected 1996 and 2002. Current term expires Dec 31, 2008. Born Lake Providence Louisiana Sept 26, 1943. Baptist. Educated at Southern University B.A. with honors 1966 and Boston College Law School J.D. 1969. Admitted to practice Massachusetts 1969, Louisiana 1979, U.S. Court of Appeals Fifth Circuit 1981 and U.S. Supreme Court 1989. In legal practice Monroe 1979-92.

Legal Services Attorney Dec 1971 to Oct 1973. Assistant U.S. Attorney District of Massachusetts 1973-75. Special Assistant Attorney General 1990-92. Chairman Board of Appeal (Chief Administrative Law Judge) Boston Massachusetts 1977-79. Important Decisions (while temporarily serving on Louisiana Court of Appeal): State v. Lamb (forfeiture) No. 26,257 La. Ct. App. Oct 26, 1994 and Davidson v. Shreveport Airport Authority (civil service) No. 26,172 La. Ct. App. Oct 26, 1994. Former President Fourth Judicial District Bar Association and Louisiana District Judges Association. Member Louisiana Judiciary Commission, Fred Fudickar American Inn of Court and Louis A. Martinet Legal Society. Attended General Jurisdiction Course The National Judicial College Fall 1993. Instructor 1996 Fall Judges Conference and Dec 1996 New Judges Conference The Louisiana Judicial College. Recipient plaque for service as President Fourth Judicial District Bar Association. Served to Captain U.S. Army Intelligence March 1970 to Nov 1971. Deputy Legal Counsel to Governor Michael S. Dukakis Massachusetts 1975-77. General Counsel School Board Monroe City 1985-92. Chairman Board of Trustees Zion Traveler Baptist Church. Board of Directors United Way. Enjoys music, reading, playing chess, watching most sports, reading to children and teaching them board, card, memory and logic games.

Office: 300 St. John Street, Monroe 71201.
Telephone: (318) 361-2257.

JONES, Charles Robert *(Judge, Louisiana Court of Appeal Fourth Circuit)* Elected to term beginning Jan 1, 1992. Reelected 2001, current term expires Dec 31, 2011. Born New Orleans Louisiana Sept 10, 1944. Catholic. Educated at Xavier University of Louisiana B.S. 1971 and Loyola University School of Law J.D. 1975. Admitted to practice Louisiana 1975. In legal practice 1978-83 and 1985-91.

Assistant District Attorney Orleans Parish 1975-78. Member Orleans Indigent Defender Program 1978-79. State Representative Louisiana 1984-91. Important Decisions: Harris v. Pizza Hut et al. 455 So. 2d 1364 (established the law in Louisiana as to the duty owed to an invitee by a commercial restaurant to provide a safe place) and State of Louisiana v. Robert Bonds (defendant, a black New Orleans Police Officer, was charged with the murder of a white uptown motorist, the jury returned a not guilty verdict). Member Louis A. Martinet Legal Society, Fourth and Fifth Circuit Judges Association, Louisiana Association of Circuit Court Judges, Louisiana State (Judicial Council), National (Judicial Council) and American (Appellate Judges Conference) Bar Associations. Faculty Member National Institute of Trial Advocacy. Listed in *Who's Who Among African Americans*. Recipient Distinguished Service Award from City of New Orleans 1975; Golden Apple Award 1984, 1985, 1987, 1988 and 1990; Certificate of Merit from City of New Orleans 1985 and 1990; and Outstanding Achievement Award from Louisiana Legislative Black Caucus 1991. Named Legislator of the Year 1985 and 1987. U.S. Army 1962-65. Counselor Orleans Parish Prison Rehabilitation Program 1974-75. Former Member Board of Directors St. Luke's Community Center. Former Member Louisiana Legislative Black Caucus, National Black Caucus of State Legislators and National Council of State Legislators. Board of Directors Treme Cultural and Enrichment Program.

Office: 1515 Poydras Street, Seventh Floor, New Orleans 70112.
Telephone: (504) 592-0917.

JONES, Robert E. *(Judge, New Orleans Traffic Court)*
Office: 727 South Broad Street, New Orleans 70119.
Telephone: (504) 827-5002.

JULIEN, Ethel Simms *(Judge, Louisiana District Court Orleans Parish Civil District)*
Office: 421 Loyola Avenue, Room 312, New Orleans 70112.
Telephone: (504) 592-9254.

KAY, Stuart S., Jr. *(Judge, Louisiana District Court Thirty-sixth Judicial District)* Currently serves as Chief Judge. Former Judge, DeRidder City Court.
Mailing address: P.O. Box 1148, DeRidder 70634-1148.
Telephone: (337) 463-7993.

KEATY, Phyllis Montgomery *(Judge, Louisiana District Court Fifteenth Judicial District)*
Mailing address: P.O. Box 53288, Lafayette 70505-3288.
Telephone: (337) 261-5125.

KEES, Lester P. *(Judge, Louisiana District Court Thirtieth Judicial District)*
Mailing address: P.O. Drawer 1700, Leesville 71496-1700.
Telephone: (337) 239-3584.

KELLER, Ann Murry *(Judge, Jefferson Parish Juvenile Court)*
Mailing address: P.O. Box 1900, Harvey 70059.
Telephone: (504) 367-3500.

KELLEY, Timothy E. *(Judge, Louisiana District Court Nineteenth Judicial District)*
Office: 222 St. Louis Street, Suite 857, Baton Rouge 70802.
Telephone: (225) 389-4728.

KELLY, Charles W. *(Judge, Shreveport City Court)* Currently serves as Senior Judge.
Office: 1244 Texas Avenue, Shreveport 71101.
Telephone: (318) 673-5885.

KIMBALL, Catherine D. "Kitty" *(Justice, Supreme Court of Louisiana)* Elected Nov 1992. Reelected 1998, current term expires Dec 31, 2008. Born Alexandria Louisiana Feb 7, 1945. Educated at Louisiana State University J.D. 1970. Law Clerk to U.S. District Court Western District of Louisiana 1970. In legal practice 1975-82. Judge and Chief Judge, Louisiana District Court Eighteenth Judicial District Dec 1982 to 1992.

Special Counsel Louisiana Attorney General's Office 1971-73. General Counsel Louisiana Commission on Law Enforcement and Administration of Criminal Justice 1973-81. Assistant District Attorney Eighteenth Judicial District 1978-82. Chairperson Technology Committee and Case Management Information System Task Force and Former Member Committee on the Judicial Electoral Process Supreme Court of Louisiana. Chair Judicial Budgetary Control Board. Former Member Louisiana District Judges Association (First Vice President, Executive Committee), Louisiana Juvenile Judges Association, Louisiana Task Force on Women in the Courts, Governor's Commission on Child Support, Economic Justice for All Task Force, Automated Fingerprint Identification Selection Committee, National Conference of State Trial Judges, American Judicature Society, The Association of Trial Lawyers of America and Eighteenth Judicial District Bar Association. Member National Integration Resource Center Task Force U.S. Department of Justice, Justice Funding Commission, Louisiana Coordinating Council on Domestic Violence, Wex Malone American Inn of Court, State-Federal Judicial Council and Louisiana State Bar Association. Named One of the Top 25 Women of Achievement by Baton Rouge Business Report 1997. Recipient Outstanding Judicial Award from Victims and Citizens Against Crime, Inc. Inducted into Louisiana State University Law Center Hall of Fame. National Alumni Board and Past President Alumni Association Louisiana State University Law Center. Member Leadership Louisiana 1999.
Office: 301 Loyola Avenue, New Orleans 70112.
Telephone: (504) 568-7757.

KING, C. Hunter *(Judge, Louisiana District Court Orleans Parish Civil District)*
Office: 421 Loyola Avenue, Room 406, New Orleans 70112.
Telephone: (504) 592-9250.

KIRBY, Michael E. *(Judge, Louisiana Court of Appeal Fourth Circuit)* Born Port Sulphur Louisiana April 6, 1948. Catholic. Educated at Louisiana State University B.A. 1970 J.D. 1973. Moot Court Board. Member Phi Alpha Theta and Mu Sigma Rho. Admitted to practice Louisiana 1974. Began legal practice Port Sulphur 1974. Former Judge, Louisiana District Court Twenty-fifth Judicial District, elected to term beginning Jan 1, 1985.

Former Counselor Louisiana State Firemen's Association. Member Plaquemines (Past President 1981-82), Louisiana State and American Bar Associations. Member Plaquemines Parish Council 1974-84 (President 1982-83), Plaquemines Parish Fair and Orange Festival, Jaycees, Knights of Columbus, Port Sulphur Volunteer Fire Department, Retarded Citizens Association and Council on Aging. Enjoys bicycle riding, golf, music and walking.
Office: 1515 Poydras Street, Seventh Floor, New Orleans 70112.
Telephone: (504) 568-2600.

KIRK, James D. *(Magistrate Judge, United States District Court Western District of Louisiana)* Appointed by U.S. District Court judges Dec 15, 1997. Term expires Dec 14, 2005.
Office: 331 Federal Building, 515 Murray Street, Alexandria 71301.
Telephone: (318) 473-7510.

KLEINPETER, William T. *(Judge, Port Allen City Court)*
Mailing address: P.O. Box 93, Port Allen 70767.
Telephone: (225) 346-4702.
E-mail address: pacitycourt@EATEL.com

KLIEBERT, Thomas, Jr. *(Judge, Louisiana District Court Twenty-third Judicial District)*
Mailing address: P.O. Box 105, Convent 70723.
Telephone: (225) 869-5517.

KNIGHT, William J. "Rusty" *(Judge, Louisiana District Court Twenty-second Judicial District)*
Office: 428 East Boston Street, Room 205, Covington 70433.
Telephone: (985) 898-2730.

KNOLL, Jeannette Theriot *(Justice, Supreme Court of Louisiana)* Elected to term beginning Jan 1, 1997. Born Baton Rouge Louisiana Jan 23, 1944. Catholic. Educated at Loyola University B.S. 1966 J.D. 1969 and University of Virginia School of Law LL.M. 1996. Member Tri Phi. Admitted to practice Louisiana 1969. Began legal practice in Marksville 1969. Judge, Louisiana Court of Appeal Third Circuit Jan 1, 1982 to 1996.

First Assistant District Attorney Twelfth Judicial District Court 1972-82. Member American Judicature Society, National Association of Women Judges, Avoyelles Parish (Secretary-Treasurer 1969-70, Vice President

KNOLL, JEANNETTE THERIOT—*Continued*
1970-71 and President 1971-72), Louisiana State and American Bar Associations.
Office: 301 Loyola Avenue, New Orleans 70112.
Telephone: (504) 568-5720.

KNOWLES, Daniel E., III *(Magistrate Judge, United States District Court Eastern District of Louisiana)* Appointed by U.S. District Court judges to term beginning Jan 6, 2003.
Office: C114 U.S. Courthouse, 500 Camp Street, New Orleans 70130.
Telephone: (504) 589-7575.

KONRAD, Nancy Amato *(Judge, Jefferson Parish Juvenile Court)* Elected to term beginning Aug 1980. Reelected 1984, 1990, 1996 and 2002. Current term expires 2008. Born New Orleans Louisiana May 11, 1941. Catholic. Educated at Loyola University of the South B.S. 1962 J.D. 1965. Member Phi Alpha Delta. Admitted to practice Louisiana 1965. Began legal practice Gretna 1965.

Advisory Board Juvenile Corrections Program and Juvenile Justice Commission.Member Juvenile Justice Work Group You Who Coalition. Member Louisiana Council of Juvenile and Family Court Judges (President 1989, Treasurer), Louisiana Law Institute (Children's Code Revision Committee), American Judges Association, National Council of Juvenile and Family Court Judges, National Association of Women Judges, Jefferson Parish and Louisiana State Bar Associations. Recipient Adjutor Hominum Award from Loyola University 1993, Judge Richard Ware Award from Louisiana Children's Trust Fund 1999, Families in Need of Services Award from Louisiana Families in Need of Services Association (FINS) 1999 and Champion for Children Award from Prevent Child Abuse Louisiana 1999. Named Public Elected Official of the Year by Louisiana Chapter National Association of Social Workers 2000. Former Co-lead Judge Louisiana Task Force for Foster Care Reform. Chair Louisiana Children's Code Project. Member Louisiana Children's Cabinet, Louisiana Association of Elected Women and Italian American Society Jefferson Auxiliary.
Mailing address: P.O. Box 1900, Harvey 70059.
Telephone: (504) 367-3500.

KRAKE, Allen A. *(Judge, Louisiana District Court Thirty-fifth Judicial District)* Currently serves as Chief Judge.
Office: 200 Main Street, Suite 202, Colfax 71417.
Telephone: (318) 627-3244.

KUHN, James E. *(Judge, Louisiana Court of Appeal First Circuit)* Elected to term beginning Jan 1, 1995. Born Hammond Louisiana Oct 31, 1946. Roman Catholic. Educated at Southeastern Louisiana University B.S. 1968 and Loyola University School of Law J.D. 1972. Member Phi Delta Phi. Admitted to practice Louisiana 1973, U.S. Supreme Court 1978 and Colorado 1995. In legal practice Hammond 1973-74 and Denham Springs 1974-91. Judge, Louisiana District Court Twenty-first Judicial District Jan 1, 1991 to Dec 31, 1994.

Former Assistant District Attorney Twenty-first Judicial District. Instructor in Government and Criminal Justice Southeastern Louisiana University since 1991. Member Colorado and Louisiana State Bar Associations. Louisiana National Guard 1968-74.
Office: 103 North Sixth Street, Ponchatoula 70454.
Telephone: (985) 386-6082.
Fax: (985) 370-7271

LaDART, Ross P. *(Judge, Louisiana District Court Twenty-fourth Judicial District)* Elected to term beginning May 10, 1999. Reelected 2002, current term expires Dec 31, 2008. Born New Orleans Louisiana June 25, 1942. Catholic. Educated at University of Southern Mississippi B.S. 1964 and South Texas College of Law J.D. 1968. Admitted to practice Louisiana 1969, U.S. District Court Eastern District of Louisiana 1970, U.S. Court of Appeals Fifth Circuit 1973 and U.S. Supreme Court 1974. Began legal practice Gretna.

Assistant Parish Attorney Jefferson Parish 1971-78. Hearing Examiner and Special Assistant Personnel Appeals Board and Department of Personnel 1978-98. Instructor Loyola University 1975-76. Adjunct Professor Delgado Community College 1998. Member Louisiana Council of Juvenile and Family Court Judges, Fourth and Fifth Circuit Judges Association, Jefferson Parish, Louisiana State and American Bar Associations. Attended General Jurisdiction Course The National Judicial College June 1999. Recipient Monte M. Lemann Award from Louisiana Civil Service League. Member Our Lady of Visitation Parish Church.
Office: 200 Derbigny Street, Gretna 70053.
Telephone: (504) 364-3959.
E-mail address: RossL@24jdc.co.jefferson.la.us

LAGARDE, Lawrence L. *(Judge, Orleans Parish Juvenile Court)* Elected Sept 1986 to term beginning Jan 1, 1987. Reelected Oct 1994 and 2002. Current term expires Dec 31, 2010. Born New Orleans Louisiana. Catholic. Educated at Loyola University B.B.A. 1964 J.D. 1964. Admitted to practice Louisiana 1964 and U.S. District Court Eastern District of Louisiana 1964. In legal practice New Orleans 1964-86.

Public Defender Orleans Parish Juvenile Court 1970-72. Member Blue Ridge Association of Juvenile Court Judges (Past President), Louisiana Council of Juvenile and Family Court Judges (Past President), National Council of Juvenile and Family Court Judges, New Orleans and Louisiana State Bar Associations.
Office: 421 Loyola Avenue, New Orleans 70112.
Telephone: (504) 565-7327.

LAMBERT, Marilyn M. *(Judge, Ascension Parish Court)*
Office: 828 South Irma Boulevard, Room 209, Gonzales 70737.
Telephone: (225) 621-8504.
E-mail address: mlambert@ascensioncourthouse.org

LANCASTER, Michael E. *(Judge, Louisiana District Court Sixth Judicial District)* Elected Oct 23, 1999 to term beginning Dec 1, 1999. Reelected Oct 2002, current term expires Dec 31, 2008. Born Baton Rouge Louisiana April 13, 1948. Catholic. Educated at Louisiana State University B.A. 1972 J.D. 1972. Member Phi Delta Theta. Admitted to practice Louisiana 1973 and U.S. District Courts Western 1973 and Middle Districts of Louisiana. In legal practice Tallulah, Lancaster and Baxter 1973-99.

Assistant District Attorney Sixth Judicial District

LANCASTER, MICHAEL E.—*Continued*
1991-99. Member Sixth Judicial District (Past President), Louisiana State and American Bar Associations.
Mailing address: P.O. Box 1271, Tallulah 71284-1271.
Office: Madison Parish Courthouse, 100 North Cedar Street, Tallulah 71282.
Telephone: (318) 574-2712.
Fax: (318) 574-0534

LANDRIEU, Madeleine *(Judge, Louisiana District Court Orleans Parish Civil District)* Assumed office July 3, 2001.
Office: 421 Loyola Avenue, New Orleans 70112.
Telephone: (504) 592-9214.

LANDRY, Lori A. *(Judge, Louisiana District Court Sixteenth Judicial District)*
Mailing address: P.O. Box 626, St. Martinville 70582.
Telephone: (337) 394-2253.

LANIER, Walter I. *(Judge, Louisiana District Court Seventeenth Judicial District)*
Mailing address: P.O. Box 511, Thibodaux 70302.
Telephone: (985) 446-1381.

LARKE, George J., Jr. *(Judge, Louisiana District Court Thirty-second Judicial District)*
Office: 7856 Main Street, Suite 200, Houma 70360.
Telephone: (985) 873-6540.

LAROSE, F. Hugh *(Judge, Louisiana District Court Seventeenth Judicial District)*
Office: 201 Green Street, Second Floor, Thibodaux 70302.
Telephone: (985) 446-1381.

LASSALLE, Annette M. *(Judge, East Baton Rouge Parish Family Court)*
Office: 222 St. Louis Street, Room 978, Baton Rouge 70802.
Telephone: (225) 389-4678.

LAUNEY, Donald J. *(Judge, Ville Platte City Court)*
Mailing address: P.O. Box 147, Ville Platte 70586.
Telephone: (337) 363-1500.

LaVERGNE, Luke A. *(Judge, East Baton Rouge Parish Family Court)* Elected Oct 3, 1992 to term beginning Jan 1, 1993. Reelected Sept 9, 1996 and 2002. Current term expires Dec 31, 2008. Born Lawtell Louisiana May 7, 1938. Catholic. Educated at University of Nebraska B.G.S. cum laude 1969, Southern Illinois University M.S. 1974 and Louisiana State University J.D. 1982. Member Phi Delta Phi and Phi Beta Sigma. Admitted to practice Louisiana 1982, U.S. District Courts Middle 1982, Eastern 1983 and Western 1983 Districts of Louisiana and U.S. Supreme Court 1991.
Assistant District Attorney 1982-84. Assistant Parish Attorney 1990-92. Member Louisiana State, National (Judicial Council) and American Bar Associations. Captain USAF 1956-79 (retired). Democrat. Parish Democratic Committee 1990-92. Board of Directors YMCA and OLOL College. Former member Boy Scouts of America. Enjoys woodworking, golfing, watching old movies and traveling.
Office: 222 St. Louis Street, Room 948, Baton Rouge 70802.
Telephone: (225) 389-7657.

LeBLANC, John E. *(Judge, Louisiana District Court Seventeenth Judicial District)* Elected Nov 3, 1998 to term beginning Dec 10, 1998. Born Thibodaux Louisiana May 20, 1959. Catholic. Educated at Louisiana State University B.S. 1981 J.D. 1985. Admitted to practice Louisiana 1986. In legal practice Thibodaux 1986-98.
Assistant Indigent Defender Seventeenth Judicial District 1991-98. Member Louisiana District Judges Association, Lafourche Parish (Former Secretary/Treasurer, Former Vice President, Past President) and Louisiana State Bar Associations. Enjoys golf.
Mailing address: P.O. Box 231, Thibodaux 70302-0231.
Telephone: (985) 447-3780.

LEDET, Rosemary *(Judge, Louisiana District Court Orleans Parish Civil District)*
Office: 421 Loyola Avenue, Room 302, New Orleans 70112.
Telephone: (504) 592-9204.

LEE, Tammy D. *(Judge, Monroe City Court)*
Mailing address: P.O. Box 777, Monroe 71210.
Telephone: (318) 329-2580.

LEEHY, B. Scott *(Judge, Monroe City Court)* Elected Sept 21, 1996 to term beginning Jan 1, 1997. Reelected Aug 23, 2002, current term expires Dec 31, 2008. Born Monroe Louisiana Aug 11, 1962. Roman Catholic. Educated at Northeast Louisiana University B.A. 1986 and Mississippi College School of Law J.D. 1989. Member Phi Alpha Delta. Admitted to practice Louisiana 1990 and U.S. District Court Western District of Louisiana 1990. In legal practice Monroe 1990-97.
Assistant District Attorney Fourth Judicial District 1990-97. Member Louisiana City Judges Association, Louisiana Council of Juvenile and Family Court Judges, Fourth Judicial District and Louisiana State Bar Associations. Republican. Member Rotary Club, Optimist Club and Chamber of Commerce. Enjoys hunting, traveling, skiing and water sports.
Mailing address: P.O. Box 777, Monroe 71210.
Telephone: (318) 329-2580.
Fax: (318) 329-2622

LEMELLE, Ivan L. R. *(Judge, United States District Court Eastern District of Louisiana)* Magistrate Judge Oct 3, 1984 to 1998. Appointed Judge for life by President Bill Clinton April 13, 1998. Born Opelousas Louisiana June 29, 1950. Catholic. Educated at Xavier University of Louisiana B.S. cum laude 1971 and Loyola University School of Law J.D. 1974. Herbert Lehman Scholar. Ford Foundation and Earl Warren Legal Fund Scholar. NAACP Scholar. Dr. Martin Luther King, Jr. Scholar. Recipient Youth Motivation Task Force Commendations from National Alliance of Business. Member Blue Key 1972. Law Clerk to Hon. Robert F. Collins 1972-74. Member Alpha Phi Alpha and Alpha Kappa Mu. Admitted to practice Louisiana 1974, U.S. District Court Eastern District of Louisiana 1975, U.S. Court of Appeals Fifth Circuit 1983 and U.S. Supreme Court 1984. Began legal practice New Orleans 1974. Judge ad hoc, New Orleans Municipal Court 1981. Judge ad hoc, New Orleans First City Court 1982-83.
Assistant District Attorney Parish of Orleans 1974-77. Assistant City Attorney New Orleans 1977-78. Assistant Attorney General Louisiana Department of Justice 1980-84. Lecturer on Business Law Xavier University of Louisiana 1974-75 and Evidence Loyola University Criminal Justice Program 1977-78. Guest Lecturer Tulane and Loyola Universities Law Clinical programs. Member

LEMELLE, IVAN L. R.—*Continued*

Martinet Society, Louisiana, National, and Federal Bar Associations. Participant Hastings College of Advocacy Summer Trial Advocacy Program 1977. President Sigma Lambda Alumni Chapter of Alpha Phi Alpha Fraternity Inc. Ex-officio Board member Industrial Development Board City of New Orleans. Ex-officio Advisory Board New Orleans Jazz and Heritage Foundation. Former legal advisor on EEO and AAP to Metro Regional Planning Commission. Enjoys fishing, swimming, baseball, volleyball, football, chess and backgammon.

Office: C525 U.S. Courthouse, 500 Camp Street, New Orleans 70130.

Telephone: (504) 589-7555.

LEMMON, Mary Ann Vial *(Judge, United States District Court Eastern District of Louisiana)* Appointed for life by President Bill Clinton to term beginning July 26, 1996. Born Hahnville Louisiana Nov 22, 1941. Catholic. Educated at Loyola Law School J.D. with honors 1964. Editor-in-Chief Loyola Law Review 1964. Admitted to practice Louisiana 1964. Judge, Louisiana District Court Twenty-ninth Judicial District May 1, 1982 to July 25, 1996.

Member Bench-Bar Liaison Committee Louisiana Judicial College, Bench Book Advisory Committee, Louisiana District Judges Association (Executive Committee), Louisiana Bar Foundation and American Bar Association (Program Chair National Conference of State Trial Judges and National Conference of Federal Trial Judges). Member Visiting Committee Loyola University School of Law.

Office: C406 U.S. Courthouse, 500 Camp Street, New Orleans 70130.

Telephone: (504) 589-7565.

LeMOINE, Frank *(Judge, Kaplan City Court)*

Office: 511 North Cushing Avenue, Kaplan 70548.

Telephone: (337) 643-6611.

LEONARD, Edward M., Jr. *(Judge, Louisiana District Court Sixteenth Judicial District)*

Mailing address: P.O. Box 252, Franklin 70538.

Telephone: (337) 828-4100.

LILJEBERG, Hans J. *(Judge, Louisiana District Court Twenty-fourth Judicial District)*

Office: Courthouse Annex, Gretna 70053.

Telephone: (504) 364-3941.

LITTLE, F. A., Jr. *(Senior Judge, United States District Court Western District of Louisiana)* Appointed for life by President Ronald Reagan to term beginning Oct 1984. Chief Judge 1996 to May 30, 2002. Assumed Senior status May 30, 2002, serves by assignment. Born Minneapolis Minnesota Oct 26, 1936. Educated at Tulane University B.A. 1958 J.D. 1961. Admitted to practice Louisiana 1961. In legal practice New Orleans 1961-65 and Alexandria 1965-84.

Mailing address: P.O. Box 1031, Alexandria 71309-1031.

Telephone: (318) 473-7375.

LIVAUDAIS, Marcel, Jr. *(Senior Judge, United States District Court Eastern District of Louisiana)* Former Magistrate, appointed to term beginning Sept 1, 1977. Appointed Judge for life by President Ronald Reagan. Assumed Senior status, serves by assignment. Born New Orleans Louisiana March 3, 1925. Educated at Tulane University of Louisiana B.A. 1945 J.D. 1949. Admitted to practice Louisiana 1949. Began legal practice New Orleans 1949.

Member New Orleans (President 1975-76), Louisiana State and Federal Bar Associations. Lieutenant j.g. USN WWII and Korean Conflict.

Office: C405 U.S. Courthouse, 500 Camp Street, New Orleans 70130-3317.

Telephone: (504) 589-7560.

LOLLEY, John Larry *(Judge, Louisiana District Court Fourth Judicial District)* Born Monroe Louisiana Oct 30, 1945. Baptist. Educated at Northeast Louisiana University B.A. 1968 and Loyola University at New Orleans J.D. 1971. Admitted to practice Louisiana 1972 and U.S. District Court Western District of Louisiana 1973. Began legal practice Monroe 1972. Former Judge, Monroe City Court.

Member Louisiana City Judges Association, Louisiana State and American Bar Associations. First Lieutenant U.S. Army Air Defense Artillery 1966-68 and USAR since 1970. Democrat. Member Monroe Rotary Club.

Office: 300 St. John Street, Suite 400, Monroe 71201.

Telephone: (318) 361-2260.

LOMBARD, Edwin A. *(Judge, Louisiana Court of Appeal Fourth Circuit)*

Office: 1515 Poydras Street, Seventh Floor, New Orleans 70112.

Telephone: (504) 592-0909.

LOVE, Terri Fleming *(Judge, Louisiana Court of Appeal Fourth Circuit)* Former Judge, Louisiana District Court Orleans Parish Civil District.

Office: 1515 Poydras Street, Seventh Floor, New Orleans 70112.

Telephone: (504) 592-0921.

LUSE, Jennifer *(Judge, East Baton Rouge Parish Family Court)* Currently serves as Chief Judge.

Office: 222 St. Louis Street, Room 983, Baton Rouge 70802.

Telephone: (225) 389-4676.

MAGEE, Yada T. *(Judge, Louisiana District Court Orleans Parish Civil District)* Former Chief Judge.

Office: 421 Loyola Avenue, Room 302, New Orleans 70112.

Telephone: (504) 592-9216.

MANNING, C. Wendell *(Judge, Louisiana District Court Fourth Judicial District)*

Office: 300 St. John Street, Suite 400, Monroe 71201.

Telephone: (318) 361-2270.

MARABELLA, Anthony J., Jr. *(Judge, Louisiana District Court Nineteenth Judicial District)*

Office: 222 St. Louis Street, Baton Rouge 70801.

Telephone: (225) 389-4722.

MARCHMAN, Sharon Ingram *(Judge, Louisiana District Court Fourth Judicial District)*

Office: 300 St. John Street, Suite 400, Monroe 71201.

Telephone: (318) 361-2291.

MARIONNEAUX, Jack T. *(Judge, Louisiana District Court Eighteenth Judicial District)* Former Chief Judge.

Mailing address: P.O. Box 758, Plaquemine 70764.

Telephone: (225) 687-5220.

MARULLO, Frank A., Jr. *(Judge, Louisiana District Court Orleans Parish Criminal District)* Appointed by Governor Edwin Edwards to term beginning Sept 1974. Elected to subsequent terms. Current term expires Dec 31, 2008. Born New Orleans Louisiana Dec 31, 1939. Catholic. Educated at University of Southern Mississippi B.S. and Loyola University J.D. Charter member Phi Alpha Delta. Admitted to practice Louisiana.

Former Project Chief Criminal Court Renaissance Project. Former Member Committee on Time Standards for Courts of Appeal and Fourth and Fifth Circuit District Judges Association. Member Committee on the Governor's Prison Overcrowding Task Force, Louisiana Sentencing Commission, Louisiana District Judges Association (Past President, Chairman Legislative Committee), American Justinian Society of Jurists (Past President), American Judges Association, Louisiana State and American (Former Vice President National Committee on Rights of Victims) Bar Associations. Recipient Special Recognition Award from Executive Office of the President for his creation and involvement in the Drug Courts of Criminal District Court, Cavaliere from President of the Republic of Italy, Medal of St. Louis, King of France and Medal of the Order of Lawyers for the Court of Paris. Member Louisiana House of Representatives 1971-74 (Chairman Joint Legislative Committee on Correction, Member House Ways and Means Committee, Health and Welfare Committee, Labor and Industry Committee, Judiciary Committee, Transition Team to 1974 Constitutional Convention). Former Member Mayor's Council on Criminal Justice and Mayor's Council for Drug War. Past President New Orleans Athletic Club. Chairman of the Board Cabrini High School. Member Knights of Columbus, Carrollton Businessman's Association and Italian American Marching Club. Enjoys collecting clocks, automatic musical instruments and coins.

Office: 2700 Tulane Avenue, New Orleans 70119.
Telephone: (504) 827-3450.

MATLOCK, David N. *(Judge, Caddo Parish Juvenile Court)* Currently serves as Chief Judge.

Office: 1835 Spring Street, Shreveport 71101.
Telephone: (318) 226-6755.

MAUFFRAY, J. P., Jr. *(Judge, Louisiana District Court Twenty-eighth Judicial District)* Elected to term beginning Dec 8, 1994. Reelected July 12, 1996 and 2002. Current term expires Dec 31, 2008. Currently serves as Chief Judge. Born New Orleans Louisiana Nov 18, 1943. Catholic. Educated at Tulane University B.S. 1965 and Louisiana State University J.D. 1973. Law Clerk to Hon. Paul B. Landry, Jr., Louisiana Court of Appeal First Circuit 1974-75. Admitted to practice Louisiana 1974, U.S. District Courts Middle 1976 and Western 1976 Districts of Louisiana, U.S. Supreme Court 1977 and U.S. Court of Appeals Fifth Circuit 1981. In legal practice Baton Rouge 1974-75 and Jena 1976-94.

Special Assistant District Attorney Twenty-eighth Judicial District 1975-76. Member Louisiana State Bar Association.

Mailing address: P.O. Box 1890, Jena 71342-1890.
Telephone: (318) 992-2002.

McCABE, Patrick J. *(Judge, Louisiana District Court Twenty-fourth Judicial District)*

Office: 200 Derbigny Street, Gretna 70053.
Telephone: (504) 364-3890.

McCALLUM, Jay B. *(Judge, Louisiana District Court Third Judicial District)*

Office: 100 East Bayou Street, Suite 202, Farmerville 71241.
Telephone: (318) 368-9734.

McCLENDON, Page *(Judge, Louisiana Court of Appeal First Circuit)*

Mailing address: P.O. Box 339, Ponchatoula 70454.
Telephone: (985) 624-3310.

McCONDUIT, Bruce J. *(Judge, New Orleans Municipal Court)*

Office: 727 South Broad Street, New Orleans 70119.
Telephone: (504) 827-5085.

McDONALD, J. Michael *(Judge, Louisiana Court of Appeal First Circuit)* Elected to term beginning Jan 1, 2003. Term expires Dec 31, 2012. Born Baton Rouge Louisiana March 11, 1946. Educated at Louisiana State University. Judge, Louisiana District Court Nineteenth Judicial District Dec 6, 1986 to Dec 31, 2002.

Assistant District Attorney 1977-82. Interests include coaching high school soccer.

Office: 1600 North Third Street, Baton Rouge 70802.
Telephone: (225) 342-1021.

McGEE, Aaron Frank, III *(Judge, Louisiana District Court Twenty-seventh Judicial District)* Elected July 1994 to term beginning Jan 1, 1995. Reelected July 1996 and Sept 2002. Current term expires Dec 31, 2008. Born Eunice Louisiana Dec 20, 1939. Catholic. Educated at Spring Hill College B.S. 1960 and Tulane University School of Law LL.B. 1963. Member Phi Alpha Delta. Admitted to practice Louisiana 1961.

Louisiana National Guard. Member Eunice Lions Club. Enjoys hunting and fishing.

Mailing address: P.O. Box 1116, Opelousas 70571.
Telephone: (337) 948-0586.

McINTYRE, Ann *(Judge, Winnsboro City Court)*

Office: 1308 Cornell Street, Winnsboro 71295.
Telephone: (318) 435-4508.

McINTYRE, Edwin Rudolph, Jr. *(Judge, Louisiana District Court Fifth Judicial District)* Elected Sept 14, 1996 to term beginning Jan 1, 1997. Reelected 2002, current term expires Dec 31, 2008. Former Chief Judge. Born Winnsboro Louisiana Jan 10, 1952. United Methodist. Educated at Louisiana State University B.S. 1973 J.D. 1977. Admitted to practice Louisiana 1977 and U.S. District Court Western District of Louisiana 1982. In legal practice Winnsboro 1977-96. Judge, Winnsboro City Court 1993-96.

Assistant District Attorney Fifth Judicial District 1979-92. Co-author *Louisiana Law Enforcement Handbook* 6th ed. Dec 1990. Judicial Fellow Louisiana Bar Foundation. Member Louisiana Juvenile Judges Association, Louisiana District Judges Association, Louisiana District Attorneys Association, Fifth Judicial District and Louisiana State Bar Associations. President Franklin Parish Catfish Festival 1988, Franklin Parish Chamber of Commerce 1991, Winnsboro Rotary Club 1994, Winnsboro Lions Club 1995, Winnsboro Gideon Camp 1999 and Franklin Parish Tourist Commission. SME Chairman

MCINTYRE, EDWIN RUDOLPH, JR.—*Continued*

Boy Scouts of America. Chairman First United Methodist Church Council. Enjoys tennis, gardening and traveling.

Mailing address: P.O. Box 106, Winnsboro 71295.
Telephone: (318) 435-7111.

McKAY, James F., III *(Judge, Louisiana Court of Appeal Fourth Circuit)* Elected March 7, 1989. Reelected Aug 23, 2002, current term expires Dec 31, 2012. Born New Orleans Louisiana Feb 22, 1947. Catholic. Educated at University of Louisiana at Lafayette B.A. 1969 and Loyola University J.D. 1974. Member Delta Theta Phi and St. Thomas More Law Club. Admitted to practice Louisiana 1974. Began legal practice New Orleans 1974. Former Judge, Louisiana District Court Orleans Parish Criminal District, elected at special election to term beginning Dec 14, 1982.

Member Louisiana District Judges Association, Louisiana Trial Lawyers Association, Louisiana State and American Bar Associations. Democrat. Louisiana Democratic State Central Committee 1980-82. President Firemen's Charitable and Benevolent Association. Board of Directors DeLaSalle Alumni Association. Member Knights of Columbus, Ancient Order of Hibernians and Renaissance Committee. Enjoys tennis and golf.

Office: 1515 Poydras Street, Seventh Floor, New Orleans 70112.
Telephone: (504) 592-0929.

McMANUS, Clarence E. *(Judge, Louisiana Court of Appeal Fifth Circuit)* Born New Orleans Louisiana June 3, 1934. Protestant. Educated at Tulane University B.B.A. 1958 J.D. 1961. Moot Court. Member Delta Sigma Phi and Phi Delta Phi. Admitted to practice Louisiana 1961. Began legal practice Metairie. Former Judge, Louisiana District Court Twenty-fourth Judicial District, elected at special election June 17, 1982.

Assistant District Attorney Jefferson Parish 1970-82. Member Jefferson Parish, Louisiana State, Federal and American Bar Associations. Republican. Member Elks and Lions Club.

Mailing address: P.O. Box 489, Gretna 70054.
Telephone: (504) 376-1430.

McNAMARA, A. J. *(Senior Judge, United States District Court Eastern District of Louisiana)* Appointed for life by President Ronald Reagan to term beginning 1982. Chief Judge Feb 27, 1999 to June 9, 2001. Assumed Senior status June 9, 2001, serves by assignment. Born New Orleans Louisiana June 9, 1936. Educated at Louisiana State University B.S. 1959 and Loyola University School of Law at New Orleans J.D. 1968. Law Clerk to Hon. Herbert W. Christenberry, U.S. District Court Eastern District of Louisiana 1966-68. In legal practice New Orleans 1968-82.

Louisiana State Representative 1976-80.

Office: C367 U.S. Courthouse, 500 Camp Street, New Orleans 70130-3342.
Telephone: (504) 589-7570.

MEDLEY, Lloyd J. *(Judge, Louisiana District Court Orleans Parish Civil District)*

Office: 421 Loyola Avenue, New Orleans 70112.
Telephone: (504) 592-9222.

MELANCON, Tucker L. *(Judge, United States District Court Western District of Louisiana)* Appointed for life by President Bill Clinton to term beginning 1994. Born Bryan Texas Feb 3, 1946. Educated at Louisiana State University B.S. 1968 and Tulane University School of Law J.D. 1973. In legal practice Marksville 1973-93.

Office: 4700 U.S. Courthouse, 800 Lafayette Street, Lafayette 70501.
Telephone: (337) 593-5065.

MENTZ, Henry A., Jr. *(Senior Judge, United States District Court Eastern District of Louisiana)* Appointed for life by President Ronald Reagan to term beginning June 30, 1982. Assumed Senior status July 1992, serves by assignment. Born New Orleans Louisiana Nov 10, 1920. Episcopalian. Educated at Tulane University B.A. 1941 and Louisiana State University LL.B. 1943. Board of Editors Louisiana Law Review 1942-43. Chief Justice Louisiana State University Honor Court 1942. Admitted to practice Louisiana 1943, U.S. District Court Eastern District of Louisiana 1944 and U.S. Court of Appeals 1960. In legal practice New Orleans 1943 and Hammond 1946-82.

Assistant Executive Counsel to Governor 1948. City Attorney Hammond 1954-61. Member Twenty-first Judicial District (President 1974-76) and Louisiana State (Chairman Standing Committee on Indigent Defenders 1980-81) Bar Associations. Important Decisions: U.S. Environmental Protection Agency v. New Orleans Public Service, Inc. (explicates state law covering moveables and immoveables) by designation 826 F.2d 361, 5th Cir. 1987; In re Shell Oil Refinery (trial plan) 136 F.R.D. 588 E.D. La. 1991; and In re Shell Oil Refinery (court approval of class settlement and attorney fees) 155 F.R.D. 552 E.D. La. 1993. Recipient AMVETS Distinguished Service Award 1950, Louisiana Civil Service League Award (Honorary Chairman) and Delta Tau Delta Distinguished Service Chapter. Staff Sergeant U.S. Army Infantry 1943-46. Recipient Northern France and Central Germany Battle Stars. Republican. Board of Trustees WYES Educational TV. Board of Advisors Southeastern Louisiana University. Executive Committee Council for a Better Louisiana. President Louisiana Civil Service League 1978-81. Member Louisiana Board of Election Supervisors 1980-82 and Christian Pavilion Committee World's Fair. Vestryman Christ Church Cathedral since 1985. Member Boston Club, Essex Club, Sons of the American Revolution, Masons, St. George Society (President) and Society for Music and Performing Arts (Chairman).

Office: C114 U.S. Courthouse, 500 Camp Street, New Orleans 70130.
Telephone: (504) 589-7575.

METHVIN, Mildred E. *(Magistrate Judge, United States District Court Western District of Louisiana)* Appointed by U.S. District Court judges June 10, 1983. Reappointed 1991 and 1999. Current term expires June 10, 2007. Born Alexandria Louisiana Oct 24, 1952. Catholic. Educated at H. Sophie Newcomb Memorial College B.A. 1974, Tulane University School of Law and Georgetown University Law Center J.D. 1976. Member Phi Beta Kappa. Admitted to practice District of Columbia 1977 and Louisiana 1977. Began legal practice Alexandria Louisiana 1977. In legal practice Shreveport Louisiana 1979 and Charleston West Virginia 1981.

Previously worked for U.S. Attorney's Office and Department of Interior. Founder American Inn of Court of Acadiana. Member National Association of Women Judges, Federal Magistrate Judges Association, The District

METHVIN, MILDRED E.—*Continued*

of Columbia Bar and Louisiana State Bar Association. Enjoys bicycling, painting and gardening.

Office: 3500 U.S. Courthouse, 800 Lafayette Street, Lafayette 70501.

Telephone: (337) 593-5140.

METOYER, George C., Jr. *(Judge, Louisiana District Court Ninth Judicial District)* Elected Oct 8, 1992 to term beginning Dec 1, 1992. Reelected 1996 and 2002. Current term expires Dec 2008. Born Alexandria Louisiana June 3, 1958. Catholic. Educated at University of Southwestern Louisiana B.A. 1980 and Southern University Law Center J.D. 1983. Admitted to practice Louisiana 1984 and U.S. District Court Middle District of Louisiana 1984. In legal practice Alexandria 1984-92.

Assistant District Attorney Louisiana District Court Ninth Judicial District 1983-92. Member Louisiana District Judges Association, American Judges Association, The Association of Trial Lawyers of America, Alexandria, Louisiana State, Federal and American Bar Associations. Instructor Conference on Domestic Violence and Family Matters 1993. Board of Advisors St. James Catholic Church. Advisory Board Renaissance Juvenile Home. Member Louisiana Child Support Enforcement Association and Cattlemen Association. Enjoys raising cattle and horses, golfing and swimming.

Office: 701 Murray Street, Alexandria 71301.

Telephone: (318) 443-6893.

MICHOT, Patrick L. "Rick" *(Judge, Louisiana District Court Fifteenth Judicial District)* Elected Nov 6, 1990 to term beginning Jan 1, 1991. Reelected 1996 and 2002. Current term expires Dec 31, 2008. Born Nov 15, 1948. Educated at University of Southwestern Louisiana B.S.B.A. 1970 and Gonzaga University J.D. 1982. Admitted to practice Louisiana 1983, U.S. District Court Western District of Louisiana 1983 and U.S. Courts of Appeals Third 1983 and Fifth 1985 Circuits. In legal practice Lafayette 1983-90. Lieutenant j.g. USN 1968-74.

Mailing address: P.O. Box 3075, Lafayette 70502.

Telephone: (337) 269-5724.

MILLER, Wendell Reive *(Judge, Louisiana District Court Thirty-first Judicial District)* Elected Oct 1996 to term beginning Jan 1, 1997. Reelected 2002, current term expires Dec 31, 2008. Currently serves as Chief Judge. Born Crowley Louisiana Dec 2, 1953. Religious affiliation: Church of Christ. Educated at McNeese State University B.S. 1974 and Louisiana State University Law Center J.D. 1978. Admitted to practice Louisiana 1979 and U.S. District Courts Eastern, Middle and Western Districts of Louisiana. In legal practice Jennings 1979-96. Judge, Jennings City Court 1993-96.

District Attorney Thirty-first Judicial District 1985-90. Member Louisiana Council of Juvenile and Family Court Judges, American Judges Association, Jefferson Davis Parish, Southwest Louisiana and Louisiana State Bar Associations. Representative Louisiana Republican State Central Committee 1992-93. Board Member Zigler Museum. Interested in books.

Office: 300 State Street, Suite 202, Jennings 70546.

Telephone: (337) 824-3506.

MINALDI, Patricia H. *(Judge, Louisiana District Court Fourteenth Judicial District)* Assumed office 1997. First woman to hold this office. Educated at Wesleyan University B.A. cum laude 1980, Boston University School of Law 1982 and Tulane University School of Law J.D. 1983. Admitted to practice Louisiana 1983.

With Orleans Parish District Attorney's Office 1983-85. Felony Assistant District Attorney Calcasieu Parish 1985-96. Treasurer 1998-99, Secretary 1999-2000, Second Vice President 2000-01, First Vice President 2001-02 and President since 2002 Executive Committee Louisiana District Judges Association. Chairman Governor's Post-Conviction DNA Testing Advisory Commission 2000-01. Former Member Louisiana District Attorneys Association and National District Attorneys Association. Barrister Alfred J. Tate Inn of Court. Member Southwest Louisiana and Louisiana State (Former Chairman Crime Victims' Services Committee, Former Member Mandatory CLE Committee) Bar Associations. Presenter "Arson Investigation and Legal Aspects" Louisiana State University Sept 1992; "Judicial Responses to Domestic Violence" 1998 Family Violence Symposium April 23-24, 1998; "The Most Effective Trial Tactics: A View from the Bench" 1999 Jazz Festival Seminar Louisiana State Bar Association April 30, 1999; "Capital Murder—Insights into Voir Dire and Related Issues" Annual Conference Judges' Association of the Third Circuit Court of Appeal Nov 11-13, 1999; and "Criminal Law and Procedure Colloquium" April 13-14, 2000 and "Problems in Louisiana Civil Procedure and Evidence" Feb 23, 2001 Louisiana Judicial College. Recipient Trial Advocacy Award from The Association of Government Attorneys in Capital Litigation 1993-94 and "Court of Honor" Award from Crimefighters of Southwest Louisiana 1998. Former Member Board of Directors YMCA, Crime Stoppers and Family and Youth Counseling Agency. Former Den Leader Boy Scouts of America. Former Member Republican Women's Club. Chairman Community Advisory Board, Forensic Interview Protocol Committee, Interagency Protocol Committee and Medical Protocol Committee Child Advocacy Center. Sustaining Member and Former Member Board of Directors Junior League of Lake Charles. Member Louisiana Republican Elected Women and Advisory Committee McNeese State University College of Nursing.

Mailing address: P.O. Box 3210, Lake Charles 70602.

Telephone: (337) 437-3530.

MIRE, Pegram J., Jr. *(Judge, Louisiana District Court Twenty-third Judicial District)* Former Judge, Ascension Parish Court.

Office: 114 Nicholls Street, Donaldsonville 70346.

Telephone: (225) 473-8714.

MIXON, James H. *(Judge, Bunkie City Court)* Elected to term beginning Jan 1, 1979. Reelected 1984, 1990, 1996 and 2002. Current term expires Dec 31, 2008. Born Alexandria Louisiana Nov 1, 1944. Member Calvary Episcopal Church (Senior Warden). Educated at Louisiana State University B.S. 1967 J.D. 1973. Admitted to practice Louisiana 1973. In legal practice Marksville 1973-74 and Bunkie 1974-91.

Member Louisiana City Judges Association, Louisiana Juvenile Judges Association, American Judges Association, Avoyelles Parish, Louisiana State and American Bar Associations. Democrat. Member Bunkie Chamber of Commerce, Avoyelles Country Club (Vice President), Bunkie Rotary Club and Bunkie Quarterback Club. Enjoys golf, fishing and hunting.

Mailing address: P.O. Box 74, Bunkie 71322.

Telephone: (318) 346-7250.

MOORE, D. Milton, III *(Judge, Louisiana Court of Appeal Second Circuit)* Elected Oct 2002 to term beginning Jan 1, 2003. Term expires Dec 31, 2012. Born Monroe Louisiana Dec 24, 1951. Catholic. Educated at Louisiana State University B.A. 1973 J.D. 1976. Admitted to practice Louisiana 1976, U.S. District Courts Eastern and Western Districts of Louisiana and U.S. Court of Appeals Fifth Circuit. In legal practice Monroe 1976-88. Judge 1989-2002 and Chief Judge 1997-98, Louisiana District Court Fourth Judicial District.

Fellow Louisiana Bar Foundation. Member Judiciary Commission of Louisiana (Chair since 2001), Louisiana District Judges Association, Fred Fudickar Jr. American Inn of Court, American Judicature Society, American Judges Association, Louisiana Bar Foundation, Fourth Judicial District, Louisiana State and American Bar Associations. Democrat. Member 1980-88 and Chairman 1986-88 Monroe City Council. Member Monroe Rotary Club. Enjoys golfing, running and reading.

Office: 130 DeSiard Street, Suite 309, Monroe 71201.
Telephone: (318) 325-6244.
Fax: (318) 325-6473
E-mail address: mmoore@lasccoa.state.la.us

MOORE, Louis, Jr. *(Magistrate Judge, United States District Court Eastern District of Louisiana)* Appointed by U.S. District Court judges.

Office: B419 Federal Building, 501 Magazine Street, New Orleans 70130.
Telephone: (504) 589-7625.

MORRISON, Robert H., III *(Judge, Louisiana District Court Twenty-first Judicial District)* Currently serves as Chief Judge.

Mailing address: P.O. Box 788, Amite 70422.
Telephone: (985) 748-9445.

MORVANT, William A. *(Judge, Louisiana District Court Nineteenth Judicial District)* Elected to term beginning Jan 1, 1997. Reelected 2002, current term expires Dec 31, 2008. Born Thibodaux Louisiana Nov 3, 1956. Catholic. Educated at Spring Hill College B.S. 1979 and Louisiana State University Law Center J.D. 1985. Law Clerk to Hon. Felix H. Savoie, Jr., Louisiana Court of Appeals First Circuit 1985-86. Admitted to practice Louisiana 1985, U.S. Supreme Court 1985 and U.S. Court of Appeals Fifth Circuit 1986. In legal practice Baton Rouge 1986-97.

Member Baton Rouge, Louisiana State and American Bar Associations. Attended The National Judicial College. Board Member Baton Rouge CYO, Paula Manship YMCA and Family Service of Greater Baton Rouge. Member Advisory Board I-CARE and RCIA St. Aloysius Catholic Church. Enjoys golf, tennis and fishing.

Office: 222 St. Louis Street, Room 880, Baton Rouge 70802.
Telephone: (225) 389-4714.

MOSELY, John D., Jr. *(Judge, Louisiana District Court First Judicial District)*

Office: 501 Texas Street, Suite 620, Shreveport 71101.
Telephone: (318) 226-6966.

MURPHY, Robert M. *(Judge, Louisiana District Court Twenty-fourth Judicial District)*

Office: Annex Building, 200 Derbigny Street, Gretna 70053.
Telephone: (504) 364-3876.

MURRAY, George C., Jr. *(Judge, Vidalia City Court)* Elected to term beginning Dec 13, 1978. Reelected 1980, 1986, 1992 and 1998. Current term expires Dec 31, 2004. Born Ferriday Louisiana July 27, 1942. Roman Catholic. Educated at Northeast Louisiana University B.A. 1965 and Louisiana State University J.D. 1971. Admitted to practice Louisiana 1971. Began legal practice Vidalia 1971.

Member Seventh Judicial District (Secretary-Treasurer, President 1976-78) and Louisiana State Bar Associations. Captain U.S. Army Quartermaster Corps 1966-68.

Mailing address: P.O. Box 1030, Vidalia 71373.
Telephone: (318) 336-6255.
Fax: (318) 336-5801
E-mail address: gmurray@telepak.net

MURRAY, Patricia Rivet *(Judge, Louisiana Court of Appeal Fourth Circuit)* Assumed office 1994. Born New Orleans Louisiana Oct 14, 1944. Educated at Tulane University B.A. 1982 J.D. 1984. In legal practice 1984-94.

Office: 1515 Poydras Street, Seventh Floor, New Orleans 70112.
Telephone: (504) 592-0945.

MYLES, Lonny A. *(Judge, Zachary City Court)*

Mailing address: P.O. Box 310, Zachary 70791.
Telephone: (225) 654-0044.

NESBITT, B. Woodrow, Jr. *(Judge, Louisiana District Court First Judicial District)*

Office: 501 Texas Street, Room 300B, Shreveport 71101.
Telephone: (318) 226-6819.

NOLAND, Christine A. *(Magistrate Judge, United States District Court Middle District of Louisiana)* Appointed by U.S. District Court judges.

Office: 375 Federal Building, 777 Florida Street, Baton Rouge 70801-1712.
Telephone: (225) 389-3592.

NORMAN, Mary K K *(Judge, New Orleans Second City Court)* Clerk 1990-94. Elected Judge March 1994 to term beginning May 1994. Reelected Nov 1994 and 2000. Current term expires Dec 31, 2006. Born Monroe Louisiana June 11, 1945. Catholic. Educated at Louisiana Tech University B.A. 1967 and Tulane University J.D. 1970. Law Clerk to Hon. James C. Gulotta, Louisiana Court of Appeal Fourth Circuit 1971-72. Admitted to practice Louisiana 1970. In legal practice New Orleans 1979-94.

Assistant City Attorney Orleans Parish 1976-78. Member Louisiana City Judges Association, Fourth and Fifth Circuit Judges Association, Louisiana Trial Lawyers Association, National Association of Women Judges, New Orleans (Breast Cancer Committee), Louisiana State and American Bar Associations. Member Lieutenant Governor's Committee on Juvenile Justice. President Board of Directors Our Lady of Holy Cross College Library. Board Member Louisiana State University Medical School (Committee on Alcohol and Substance Abuse). Active in many charitable organizations. Enjoys traveling and dancing.

Office: 225 Morgan Street, New Orleans 70114.
Telephone: (504) 368-4099.
E-mail address: kknorman@acadiacom.net

NORRIS, Jim *(Judge, West Monroe City Court)*
Office: 2303 North Seventh Street, West Monroe 71291.
Telephone: (318) 396-2767.

OLIVIER, Rebecca M. *(Judge, First Parish Court Jefferson Parish)*
Office: 924 David Drive, Metairie 70003.
Telephone: (504) 736-8913.

PAINTER, David *(Judge, Louisiana District Court Fourteenth Judicial District)* Elected to term beginning Jan 1, 1997. Reelected 2002, current term expires Dec 31, 2008. Currently serves as Chief Judge. Born Watchez Mississippi June 2, 1937. Episcopalian. Educated at Tulane University B.B.A. 1959 LL.B. 1962. Admitted to practice Louisiana 1962 and U.S. Supreme Court 1983. In legal practice Lake Charles 1962-96.
Member Louisiana Trial Lawyers Association (President 1987), The Association of Trial Lawyers of America (Board of Governors 1988-90) and Louisiana State Bar Association (Board of Governors 1994-96). Democrat. Member City Council Lake Charles 1984-96.
Mailing address: P.O. Box 3210, Lake Charles 70602.
Telephone: (337) 437-3530.
E-mail address: PainterDavid@msn.com

PARKER, John V. *(Senior Judge, United States District Court Middle District of Louisiana)* Appointed for life by President Jimmy Carter to term beginning 1979. Chief Judge 1979-98. Assumed Senior status Oct 31, 1998, serves by assignment. Born Baton Rouge Louisiana Oct 14, 1928. Educated at Louisiana State University B.A. 1949 J.D. 1952. In legal practice Baton Rouge 1954-79.
Assistant Parish Attorney East Baton Rouge Parish 1956-66. U.S. Army 1952-54. USAR 1954-64.
Office: 355 Federal Building, 777 Florida Street, Baton Rouge 70801-1712.
Telephone: (225) 389-3568.

PARKER, Julian A. *(Judge, Louisiana District Court Orleans Parish Criminal District)*
Office: 2700 Tulane Avenue, New Orleans 70119.
Telephone: (504) 827-3462.

PARRO, Randolph H. *(Judge, Louisiana Court of Appeal First Circuit)* Elected to term beginning 1993. Former Judge, Louisiana District Court Seventeenth Judicial District.
Mailing address: P.O. Box 5177, Thibodaux 70302.
Telephone: (985) 447-2185.

PAYNE, Roy S. *(Magistrate Judge, United States District Court Western District of Louisiana)* Appointed by U.S. District Court judges to term beginning Nov 1, 1987. Reappointed Nov 1, 1995, current term expires Oct 31, 2003. Born New Orleans Louisiana Aug 30, 1952. Methodist. Educated at University of Virginia B.A. with distinction 1974, Louisiana State University J.D. 1977 and Harvard Law School LL.M. 1980. Associate Editor Louisiana Law Review 1975-77. Law Clerk to Hon. Tom Stagg, U.S. District Court Western District of Louisiana 1977-79. Member Phi Kappa Phi and Order of the Coif. Admitted to practice Louisiana 1977, U.S. District Court Western District of Louisiana 1980, U.S. Court of Appeals Fifth Circuit 1981 and U.S. Supreme Court 1983. In legal practice Shreveport 1980-87.
Author Note "Due Process for Drivers" 36 Louisiana L. Rev. 852, 1976 and Comment "The Co-conspirator's Exception to the Hearsay Rule: The Limits of Its Logic" 37 Louisiana L. Rev. 1101, 1977. Instructor in Appellate Advocacy New England School of Law 1979-80 and Criminal Evidence Louisiana State University 1990-93. Member Harry V. Booth American Inn of Court (Secretary-Treasurer 1990-96, President 1996-98), Louisiana Association of Defense Counsel (Board of Directors 1986-87), Judicial Council of the Fifth Circuit (Magistrate's Committee 1990-98) and Louisiana State Bar Association (Legal Aid Committee 1986-87). Faculty member numerous CLE seminars Louisiana Association of Defense Counsel and Louisiana State Bar Association. Recipient Judicial Appreciation Award Shreveport Bar Association Pro Bono Project 1989. Republican. Chairman Northwest Louisiana Legal Services, Inc. 1984-85.
Office: 4300 U.S. Courthouse, 300 Fannin Street, Shreveport 71101-3087.
Telephone: (318) 676-3265.

PEATROSS, Charles B. *(Judge, Louisiana Court of Appeal Second Circuit)* Elected July 1996. Born May 27, 1940. Educated at Tulane University B.B.A. 1963 J.D. 1964. Admitted to practice Louisiana and Colorado.
City Attorney Shreveport 1983-86. Louisiana State Chairman National Institute of Municipal Law Officers 1984-86. Member Harry V. Booth Inn of Court, Shreveport Bar and Louisiana Bar Association. Representative to Louisiana House of Delegates 1974-94. Member 1978-82 and Chairman 1982 Shreveport City Council. Chairman Board of Directors Shreveport-Bossier Metropolitan YMCA 1980-82.
Mailing address: P.O. Box 1528, Shreveport 71165-1528.
Telephone: (318) 227-3750.

PETERS, Jimmie C. *(Judge, Louisiana Court of Appeal Third Circuit)* Elected to term beginning 1994. Reelected to term beginning 1996, current term expires 2006. Born Alexandria Louisiana Jan 8, 1943. Baptist. Educated at Louisiana State University B.S.C.E. 1968 J.D. 1970. Member Phi Alpha Delta. Admitted to practice Louisiana 1970, U.S. District Courts Middle 1971, Western 1971 and Eastern 1977 Districts of Louisiana, U.S. Court of Appeals Fifth Circuit 1975 and U.S. Supreme Court 1975. In legal practice Jena 1970-85. Judge, Louisiana District Court Twenty-eighth Judicial District, Jan 1, 1985 to 1994.
City Attorney Jena, Olla, Tullos and Urania 1974-84. Assistant District Attorney Louisiana District Court Twenty-eighth Judicial District 1985-88. Adjunct Faculty Member in Law Louisiana College since 1986. Instructor Alexandria Police Academy since 1998 and Rapides Parish Sheriff's Training Academy since 2000. Former Member Louisiana Trial Lawyers Association, Louisiana Municipal Attorneys Association (Secretary 1976-77, Vice President 1977-78, President 1978-79), Louisiana District Judges Association, Louisiana Council of Juvenile and Family Court Judges and National Council of Juvenile and Family Court Judges. Member Red River Delta Law Enforcement Planning Council (Board of Directors since 1985, Project Priority Committee since 1992, Treasurer since 1996), LaSalle Parish Drug Task Force, Crossroads—American Inns of Court of Alexandria-Pineville (Executive Committee 1995-2001, Secretary 1997-98, Vice President 1998-99, President 1999-2000), Twenty-eighth Judicial District (Vice President 1976-77, President 1977-78), Louisiana State (House of Delegates 1972-79, Long Range Planning Committee

PETERS, JIMMIE C.—*Continued*

1996, Judicial Council Committee on Court Costs 1996-97, Central Louisiana Steering Committee of Citizens Summit on Justice Reform Committee since 1996) and American Bar Associations. Speaker and Panelist on legal topics at numerous bench and bar seminars and civic and social organizations. Named Outstanding Young Man of Jena 1972-73. Member 1970-85, President 1972 and Coach for 15 years Jena Dixie Youth Baseball Program. Member Jena Kiwanis Club 1970-99, First Baptist Church since 1970 and Alexandria Lions Club 1995-96. Member 1970-75 and President 1972-73 Jena Jaycees. Member 1988-92, Vice Chairman 1989-90 and Chairman 1990-91 Child and Adolescent Service System Program Statewide Committee. Board of Directors LaSalle Association for the Developmentally Delayed 1990-96. Executive Board Member Louisiana Federation of Families for Children's Mental Health 1993-95. Enjoys snow skiing, golfing and fishing.

Mailing address: P.O. Box 1380, Jena 71342.
Office: 3150 North First Street, Suite C, Jena 71342.
Telephone: (318) 992-6125.
Fax: (318) 992-6147

PETTIGREW, John T. *(Judge, Louisiana Court of Appeal First Circuit)* Elected to term beginning Jan 1999. Term expires Dec 31, 2008. Born Houma Louisiana Oct 24, 1947. Roman Catholic. Educated at Louisiana State University B.A. 1969 J.D. 1972. Member Phi Delta Phi and Sigma Chi. Admitted to practice Louisiana 1973, U.S. District Courts Eastern 1974 and Western 1982 Districts of Louisiana and U.S. Court of Appeals Fifth Circuit 1982. In legal practice Houma 1973-90. Judge ad hoc Houma City Court 1975-89. Judge, Louisiana District Court Thirty-second Judicial District Jan 1, 1991 to Dec 31, 1998.

Adjunct Professor of Government Nicholls State University 1992-2000. Member Louisiana Council of Juvenile and Family Court Judges, Louisiana District Judges Association, American Judicature Society, American Judges Association, Terrebonne, Louisiana State and American Bar Associations. Attended annual CLE seminars sponsored by Louisiana Judiciary. Captain U.S. Army 1979. Democrat. Member and Vice Chairman Terrebonne Democratic Executive Committee 1975-90. Appointed Member Terrebonne Notarial Commission 1973-82 and General Hospital District Governing Board Hospital District 1, 1979-81. Assistant Coach Bantam Football. Member Houma Carnival Club. Enjoys fishing, hunting, bowling and golfing.

Mailing address: P.O. Box 7035, Houma 70361.
Telephone: (985) 872-3522.

PIAZZA, Angelo J., III *(Judge, Marksville City Court)*

Mailing address: P.O. Box 429, Marksville 71351.
Telephone: (318) 253-6423.

PICKETT, Elizabeth A. *(Judge, Louisiana Court of Appeal Third Circuit)* Former Judge, Louisiana District Court Eleventh Judicial District.

Mailing address: P.O. Box 70, Many 71449.
Telephone: (318) 256-4180.

PITRE, Robert A. *(Judge, Louisiana District Court Twenty-fourth Judicial District)*

Office: 200 Derbigny Street, Gretna 70053.
Telephone: (504) 364-3895.

PLAISANCE, Mark D. *(Judge, Baker City Court)*

Mailing address: P.O. Box 1, Baker 70704-0001.
Telephone: (225) 778-1866.

POLOZOLA, Frank J. *(Chief Judge, United States District Court Middle District of Louisiana)* Magistrate 1973-80. Appointed Judge for life by President Jimmy Carter May 29, 1980. Chief Judge since Sept 1, 1998. Catholic. Educated at Louisiana State University 1959-62 J.D. 1965. Law Clerk to Hon. E. Gordon West, U.S. District Court Middle District of Louisiana 1965-66. Admitted to practice Louisiana 1965. Began legal practice Baton Rouge 1966.

Instructor Louisiana State University Law Center 1975-95 and Southern University Law School 1980 and 1983-86. Member National Council of U.S. Magistrates 1973-80 (President 1979-80), Fifth Circuit District Judges Association (Past President), Federal Judges Association, Federal (President Baton Rouge 1969), Baton Rouge and Louisiana State Bar Associations. Enjoys fishing, hunting and cooking.

Office: 313 Federal Bldg. & U.S. Courthouse, 777 Florida Street, Baton Rouge 70801-1712.
Telephone: (225) 389-3576.

PONDER, Suzan S. *(Judge, Baton Rouge City Court)*

Mailing address: P.O. Box 3438, Baton Rouge 70821.
Telephone: (225) 389-3095.

PORTEOUS, G. Thomas, Jr. *(Judge, United States District Court Eastern District of Louisiana)* Appointed for life by President Bill Clinton. Born New Orleans Louisiana Dec 15, 1946. Catholic. Educated at Louisiana State University B.A. in Economics 1968 J.D. 1971. Member Phi Alpha Delta. Admitted to practice Louisiana 1971, U.S. Court of Appeals Fifth Circuit, U.S. District Court Eastern District of Louisiana and U.S. Supreme Court. Began legal practice 1971. Judge pro tem Aug 1984 to Dec 1984 and Former Judge, Louisiana District Court Twenty-fourth Judicial District, elected to term beginning Jan 1, 1985.

Special Counsel Louisiana Department of Justice 1971-73. Assistant District Attorney Chief Felony Complaint Division 1973-74 and Felony Supervisor since 1976 Jefferson Parish District Attorney's Office. Attorney City of Harahan since 1982. Instructor in Criminal Law, Criminal Procedure and Constitutional Law St. Mary's Dominican College and Criminal Law and Criminal Procedures Jefferson Parish Sheriff Office training academy. Member Louisiana District Attorneys Association (Past President Assistant's Section), Jefferson Parish, Louisiana State and American Bar Associations. Participant Career Prosecutor Course National College of District Attorneys Aug 1973 and Problems in Louisiana Evidence Seminar March 1976 and Criminal Law Seminar Sept 1976 Louisiana State University School of Law. Attended Louisiana District Attorneys Association Annual Conference 1975-77. Former President St. Clement of Rome Men's Club. Football and baseball coach and basketball referee Johnny Bright Playground.

Office: C206 U.S. Courthouse, 500 Camp Street, New Orleans 70130-3325.
Telephone: (504) 589-7585.

PORTER, Charles L. *(Judge, Louisiana District Court Sixteenth Judicial District)*

Office: 300 Iberia Street, Suite 210, New Iberia 70560.
Telephone: (337) 369-4410.

QUINLAN, Patrick G. *(Judge, Louisiana District Court Orleans Parish Criminal District)*
Office: 2700 Tulane Avenue, New Orleans 70119.
Telephone: (504) 827-3476.

QUIRK, Thomas P. *(Judge, Lake Charles City Court)* Elected to term beginning Jan 1, 1979. Reelected 1984, 1990, 1996 and 2002. Current term expires Dec 31, 2008. Currently serves as Senior Judge. Born Nov 18, 1944. Educated at Louisiana State University B.S. 1966 J.D. 1969. Law Clerk to Hon. Edwin Hunter, U.S. District Court Western District of Louisiana 1970. Admitted to practice Louisiana, U.S. District Courts Central and Western Districts of Louisiana, U.S. Court of Appeals Fifth Circuit and U.S. Tax Court.

Former Auditor Louisiana Internal Revenue Service. Former Teacher Spencer Business College. Member Louisiana City Court Judges Association, Louisiana Council of Juvenile Court Judges, Southwest Louisiana Trial Lawyers Association, Louisiana Trial Lawyers Association, The Association of Trial Lawyers of America, Southwest Louisiana, Louisiana State and American Bar Associations. Recipient VFW Humanitarian Award 1981, American Legion Memorial Award 1981-82, Kiwanis Club Outstanding Citizen Award 1981-82, Calcasieu Area Safety Council Community Service Award 1982, Insurance Women of Lake Charles Community Service Award 1982, National Law Journal Award 1982 and Louisiana Highway Safety Commission Award of Merit 1983. Enjoys fishing and cooking.
Mailing address: P.O. Box 1664, Lake Charles 70602.
Telephone: (337) 491-1305.

RAGUSA, Anthony D., Jr. *(Judge, Louisiana District Court Twenty-fifth Judicial District)*
Office: 301 Main Street, Belle Chasse 70037.
Telephone: (504) 297-5221.

RAMBO, Wilson *(Judge, Louisiana District Court Fourth Judicial District)*
Office: 300 St. John Street, Fourth Floor, Monroe 71201.
Telephone: (318) 361-2250.

RAMSEY, Nadine M. *(Judge, Louisiana District Court Orleans Parish Civil District)*
Office: 421 Loyola Avenue, New Orleans 70112.
Telephone: (504) 592-9230.

RANDOW, Harry F. *(Judge, Louisiana District Court Ninth Judicial District)*
Mailing address: P.O. Drawer 1431, Alexandria 71309-1431.
Telephone: (318) 443-6893.

REED, Angélique A. *(Judge, New Orleans First City Court)* Elected Oct 3, 1998 to term beginning Jan 1, 1999. Term expires Dec 31, 2005. Born Washington D.C. May 23, 1960. Catholic. Educated at Xavier University B.S. 1982 and Loyola University School of Law J.D. 1982. Law Clerk to Hon. Miriam G. Waltzer, Louisiana District Court Orleans District 1984-86. Member Alpha Kappa Alpha. Admitted to practice Louisiana 1985 and U.S. District Court Eastern District of Louisiana 1986. In legal practice New Orleans 1985-98.

Assistant City Attorney New Orleans 1986-98. Former Board Member New Orleans Pro Bono Project. Board of Governors Louisiana Trial Lawyers Association. Member Task Force on Alternative Dispute Resolution Supreme Court of Louisiana, Louis A. Martinet Legal Society (Past President), Association of Women Attorneys and National Bar Association (Board of Governors). Instructor "Eviction Process: Tenant's Rights" and "Jamaking Me Learn" CLE. Recipient Gillis Long Public Service Award from Loyola University School of Law. Democrat. Former Board Member YWCA, Coalition of 100 Black Women and Junior Associated Catholic Charities. Past President Independent Women's Organization. Associate Member Committee of 21. Board of Directors Dryades YMCA. Advisory Board Carver School-Based Health Clinic and Day Care. Training Graduate Metropolitan Area Committee Leadership and United Way Volunteer Leadership. Member Louisiana League of Good Government, Broadmoor Improvement Association, Persons Plus Program Velocity Foundation, NAACP, League of Women Voters, New Orleans Volunteers in Court, St. Matthias Catholic Church (Parish Council) and New Orleans Chapter Links, Inc.
Office: 421 Loyola Avenue, New Orleans 70112.
Telephone: (504) 592-9243.

REESE, Kern *(Judge, Louisiana District Court Orleans Parish Civil District)*
Office: 421 Loyola Avenue, Room 303, New Orleans 70112.
Telephone: (504) 592-9236.

RICHARD, David M. *(Judge, Thibodaux City Court)* Elected at special election to term beginning Nov 9, 1976. Reelected to subsequent terms. Born Thibodaux Louisiana April 11, 1945. Catholic. Educated at Nicholls State University B.S. with honors 1967 and Louisiana State University J.D. 1970. President Nicholls State University Honor Board. Admitted to practice Louisiana 1970. Began legal practice Thibodaux 1970.

City Attorney Thibodaux 1974-76. Member Lafourche Parish Bar Association (Secretary-Treasurer 1976-77, Vice President since 1977). Recipient Thibodaux's Outstanding Young Man Award 1976. Democrat. Enjoys golf, tennis, fishing, dancing and dining.
Mailing address: P.O. Box 568, Thibodaux 70302.
Telephone: (985) 446-7238.

RICHEY, Kathleen Stewart *(Judge, East Baton Rouge Parish Juvenile Court)* Elected to term beginning Jan 1991. Reelected 1996 and 2002. Current term expires Dec 31, 2008. Born Baton Rouge Louisiana Jan 6, 1954. Presbyterian. Educated at Louisiana Tech University B.A. magna cum laude 1975 and Louisiana State University J.D. 1978. Candidate Louisiana Law Review 1976-78. Law Clerk to Hon. Daniel W. LeBlanc, Louisiana District Court Nineteenth Judicial District 1978-79. Admitted to practice Louisiana 1978. In legal practice Baton Rouge 1979-90.

Assistant Public Defender 1979-90. Instructor Juvenile Law Enforcement Officer's Continuing Education 1980-82. Adjunct Professor Political Science Department Louisiana State University 1995. Member Baton Rouge Criminal Defense Bar, Louisiana Association of Criminal Defense Lawyers, Baton Rouge and Louisiana State Bar Associations. Instructor in Family Law Bench Bar Conference and Juvenile Law Louisiana Association of Criminal Defense Lawyers. Attended "Juvenile Justice" National Legal Aid and Defender Association. Trainer Louisiana Judicial College since 1993. Board of Directors Baton Rouge Area Alcohol and Drug Center, Inc. Member Human and Legal Rights Committee Special Children's Village. Task Force Chairman, Troop Leader and Board of Directors Big Buddy Program Audubon

RICHEY, KATHLEEN STEWART—*Continued*

Girl Scout Council. Member Epilepsy Association of Baton Rouge. Enjoys camping, reading, music and needlework.

Office: 8333 Veterans Memorial Boulevard, Baton Rouge 70807.

Telephone: (225) 354-1230.

RICKS, Brenda Bedsole *(Judge, Louisiana District Court Twenty-first Judicial District)* Elected to term beginning Nov 15, 1996. Reelected 2002, current term expires Dec 31, 2008. Born Baton Rouge Louisiana Sept 18, 1951. Church of Christ. Educated at Southeastern Louisiana University B.A. with honors 1973 and Southern University J.D. 1984. Admitted to practice Louisiana 1984. In legal practice Amite 1984-96.

Assistant District Attorney Twenty-first Judicial District 1987-95. Contract Attorney Louisiana Department of CYFS. Member Florida Parishes Inns of Court, National Association of Women Judges, American Judicature Society, Twenty-first Judicial, Louisiana State and American Bar Associations. Attended General Jurisdiction, Handling Capital Cases, Forensic, Medical and Scientific Evidence The National Judicial College. Republican. Member Amite and Hammond Republican Women's Clubs, Amite and Hammond Chambers of Commerce, Amite City Museum and Denham Springs Arts Council.

Mailing address: P.O. Box 788, Amite 70422.

Telephone: (985) 748-9445.

RIEDLINGER, Stephen C. *(Magistrate Judge, United States District Court Middle District of Louisiana)* Appointed by U.S. District Court judges May 1986. Reappointed May 1994 and May 2002. Current term expires May 2010. Educated at Louisiana State University B.A. 1971 J.D. 1977. Admitted to practice Louisiana 1977. In legal practice Baton Rouge 1977-86.

Office: 260 Federal Building, 777 Florida Street, Baton Rouge 70801-1712.

Telephone: (225) 389-3584.

ROBERTS, Glynn D. *(Judge, Louisiana District Court Fifth Judicial District)* Elected to term beginning Nov 8, 1983. Reelected 1984, 1990, 1996 and 2002. Current term expires Dec 31, 2008. Born Delhi Louisiana May 14, 1945. Baptist. Educated at Louisiana Tech University B.S. 1967 and Louisiana State University J.D. 1970. Member Phi Alpha Delta and Delta Sigma Pi. Admitted to practice Louisiana 1970 and U.S. District Court Western District of Louisiana. In legal practice Lake Charles 1970-73 and Rayville 1973-83.

Assistant District Attorney Louisiana District Court Fifth Judicial District 1979-83. Member Louisiana District Judges Association, Fred Fudickar Jr. American Inn of Court, Fifth District, Louisiana State and American Bar Associations. Democrat.

Mailing address: P.O. Drawer 90, Rayville 71269.

Office: Richland Parish Courthouse, Third Floor, Rayville 71269.

Telephone: (318) 728-4111.

Fax: (318) 728-7003

ROBINSON, John M. *(Judge, Louisiana District Court Twenty-sixth Judicial District)* Born Springhill Louisiana April 15, 1949. Methodist. Educated at Louisiana State University B.S. 1971 J.D. 1974. Law Clerk to Hon. James L. Dennis, Louisiana Court of Appeal Second Circuit 1974-75. Member Phi Kappa Phi and Phi Delta Phi. Admitted to practice Louisiana 1974 and U.S. District Court Western District of Louisiana 1975. In legal practice Mansfield 1975-76 and Springhill since 1976. Former Judge, Springhill City Court, elected to term beginning Dec 1, 1986.

Member Louisiana Council of Juvenile and Family Court Judges (President 1990-91) and Webster Parish Bar Association (President 1988). E-6 Louisiana Army National Guard 1969-76. Democrat. Board of Directors Springhill-Cullen Chamber of Commerce. Member Springhill Lions (Past President) and Springhill Shriners (Past President). Coach Dixie Youth Baseball. Enjoys working out, jogging, golf and hunting.

Mailing address: P.O. Box 310, Benton 71006.

Telephone: (318) 965-2217.

ROBY, Karen Wells *(Magistrate Judge, United States District Court Eastern District of Louisiana)* Appointed by U.S. District Court judges to term beginning Feb 22, 1999. Term expires Feb 22, 2007.

Office: B437 Federal Building, 501 Magazine Street, New Orleans 70130.

Telephone: (504) 589-7615.

ROE, William A. *(Judge, Louisiana District Court Twenty-fifth Judicial District)* Currently serves as Chief Judge.

Office: 301 Main Street, Belle Chasse 70037.

Telephone: (504) 297-5210.

ROTHSCHILD, Walter J. *(Judge, Louisiana Court of Appeal Fifth Circuit)* Judge pro tem Nov 15, 2000 to Jan 5, 2001. Elected to term beginning Jan 6, 2001. Reelected 2002, current term expires Dec 31, 2012. Born Dec 28, 1936. Catholic. Educated at Louisiana State University at New Orleans B.A. 1965 and Loyola University School of Law J.D. 1973. Member St. Thomas Moore Inn of Court. Admitted to practice Louisiana 1973, U.S. District Court Eastern District of Louisiana 1976, U.S. Court of Appeals Fifth Circuit 1976 and U.S. Supreme Court 1977. In legal practice New Orleans 1979-84. Judge, Louisiana District Court Twenty-fourth Judicial District 1995-2001.

Assistant U.S. Attorney Eastern District of Louisiana 1989-91. Assistant District Attorney Jefferson Parish 1991-95. Instructor Our Lady of Holy Cross College Fall 1999. Member Jefferson Parish and Louisiana State Bar Associations. Corporal USMC 1957-60. Republican. Enjoys exercising.

Mailing address: P.O. Box 489, Gretna 70054.

Office: 101 Derbigny Street, Suite 207, Gretna 70053.

Telephone: (504) 376-1410.

Fax: (504) 376-1401

E-mail address: wrothschild@fifthcircuit.org

RUBIN, Edward D. *(Judge, Louisiana District Court Fifteenth Judicial District)*

Office: 800 South Buchanan Street, Fourth Floor, Lafayette 70501.

Telephone: (337) 232-8211.

RYLAND, B. Dexter *(Judge, Louisiana District Court Ninth Judicial District)* Currently serves as Chief Judge.

Mailing address: P.O. Box 1431, Alexandria 71309.

Telephone: (318) 443-6893.

ST. PIERRE, Emile R. *(Judge, Louisiana District Court Twenty-ninth Judicial District)*
Mailing address: P.O. Box 424, Hahnville 70057-0424.
Telephone: (985) 783-3209.

SALOOM, Douglas James *(Judge, Lafayette City Court)* Elected to term beginning Nov 1995. Reelected 1996 and 2002. Current term expires Dec 31, 2008. Born Lafayette Louisiana June 27, 1960. Catholic. Educated at University of Louisiana at Lafayette B.S. cum laude 1982 and Tulane University J.D. 1985. Admitted to practice Louisiana 1985 and U.S. District Court Western District of Louisiana. In legal practice Lafayette Oct 1985 to Nov 1995.
Public Defender 1988-95. Member Louisiana City Judges Association (President 2001-02), American Judges Association, Lafayette Parish, Louisiana State and American Bar Associations. Named Eagle Scout 1975. Chairman Lafayette Chapter National Eagle Scout Association.
Mailing address: P.O. Drawer 3344, Lafayette 70502-3344.
Telephone: (337) 291-8761.
Fax: (337) 291-8759

SAMS, Lewis O. *(Judge, Louisiana District Court Thirty-ninth Judicial District)* Currently serves as Chief Judge.
Mailing address: P.O. Box 401, Coushatta 71019.
Telephone: (318) 932-6206.

SANBORN, Jacques A. *(Judge, Louisiana District Court Thirty-fourth Judicial District)*
Office: 1101 West St. Bernard Highway, Chalmette 70043.
Telephone: (504) 278-4417.

SASSONE, Martha E. *(Judge, Louisiana District Court Twenty-fourth Judicial District)* Elected to term beginning Jan 1, 1991. Reelected 1996 and 2002. Current term expires Dec 31, 2008. Former Chief Judge. Educated at University of New Orleans B.A. 1975 and Loyola University School of Law J.D. 1979. Admitted to practice Louisiana 1980, U.S. Supreme Court 1989 and U.S. District Court.
Office: 200 Derbigny Street, Gretna 70053.
Telephone: (504) 364-3922.

SAUNDERS, John D. *(Judge, Louisiana Court of Appeal Third Circuit)* Assumed office 1992. Born June 4, 1943. Educated at Louisiana State University B.A. J.D. In legal practice 1984-90.
Member Louisiana Commission on Criminal Justice and Sentencing Commission. Member Evangeline Parish and Louisiana State Bar Associations. Recipient President's Special Recognition Award from Louisiana Association of Educators 1989. Democrat. State Senator Louisiana 1975-92 (Chair Judiciary C Committee, Member Insurance and Revenue and Fiscal Affairs Committees). Past Vice President Jaycees and Mamou Youth, Inc. Former Secretary Louisiana State University Alumni Association.
Mailing address: P.O. Box 566, Ville Platte 70586.
Telephone: (337) 363-5629.

SAVOIE, D. Kent *(Judge, Louisiana District Court Fourteenth Judicial District)*
Mailing address: P.O. Box 3210, Lake Charles 70602-3210.
Telephone: (337) 437-3530.

SCHIFF, Gerald H. *(Chief Judge, United States Bankruptcy Court Western District of Louisiana)* Appointed by U.S. Court of Appeals Fifth Circuit judges to term beginning Aug 28, 1992. Current term expires Aug 27, 2006. Chief Judge since June 1, 2000. Born Opelousas Louisiana Sept 27, 1941. Jewish. Educated at Louisiana State University B.S. 1963 J.D. 1967. Member Phi Alpha Delta, Omicron Delta Kappa and Order of the Coif. Admitted to practice Louisiana 1967, U.S. District Courts Western 1978 and Middle 1990 Districts of Louisiana and U.S. Court of Appeals Fifth Circuit 1981. In legal practice Opelousas 1969-92.
Member Bankruptcy Bar Association of Southwest Louisiana (Vice President, Board of Directors 1988-89) and St. Landry Bar Association (President 1979). Speaker seminars sponsored by Louisiana Bar Association, Louisiana State University and Gillis W. Long Poverty Law Center of Loyola Law School. Captain U.S. Army 1967-69. Enjoys golf.
Office: Federal Building, 231 South Union Street, Opelousas 70570.
Telephone: (337) 942-8243.

SCHRUMPF, Charles *(Judge, Sulphur City Court)*
Office: 802 South Huntington Street, Sulphur 70663.
Telephone: (337) 527-7006.

SCHWARTZ, Charles, Jr. *(Senior Judge, United States District Court Eastern District of Louisiana)* Appointed for life by President Gerald R. Ford to term beginning June 21, 1976. Assumed Senior status, serves by assignment. Born New Orleans Louisiana Aug 22, 1922. Educated at Tulane University of Louisiana B.A. 1943 LL.B. 1947 replaced by J.D. Board of Editors Tulane Law Review. Member Phi Beta Kappa. Admitted to practice Louisiana 1947. Began legal practice New Orleans 1947.
Adjunct Professor of Law Tulane University. Member Judicial Conference of the U.S. (Committee on the Implementation of the Jury System 1981-87), Fifth Circuit District Judges Association (President 1983-84), New Orleans, Louisiana State and American Bar Associations. Major USAR 1942-76 (retired). Republican. Elected to Orleans Parish Republican Executive Committee 1960, 1963, 1967 and 1971 (Secretary 1960 and Chairman 1964-75) and to Republican State Central Committee 1961, 1963, 1967, 1971 and 1975. Active in United Way, Community Chest and Cancer Association. Past President Lakewood Country Club.
Office: C317 U.S. Courthouse, 500 Camp Street, New Orleans 70130.
Telephone: (504) 589-7590.

SCOTT, Charles R. *(Judge, Louisiana District Court First Judicial District)* Elected to term beginning Jan 1, 1985. Reelected 1990, 1996 and 2002. Current term expires Dec 31, 2008. Currently serves as Chief Judge. Born Natchitoches Louisiana July 3, 1947. Methodist. Educated at Northwestern State University of Louisiana 1965-68 and Louisiana State University J.D. 1971. Member Phi Alpha Delta. Admitted to practice Louisiana 1971 and U.S. District Court District of Louisiana.

SCOTT, CHARLES R.—*Continued*

Began legal practice Shreveport 1971. Judge, Shreveport City Court 1980-82.

Assistant City Attorney Shreveport 1973-82. Instructor Shreveport Police Academy 1980-84. Member Governor's Commission on Child Support 1984-85, Louisiana Trial Lawyers Association, The Association of Trial Lawyers of America, Shreveport, Louisiana State and American Bar Associations.

Office: 501 Texas Street, Room 300H, Shreveport 71101-5401.

Telephone: (318) 226-6836.

SEAR, Morey L. *(Senior Judge, United States District Court Eastern District of Louisiana)* Appointed for life by President Gerald R. Ford to term beginning May 1976. Former Chief Judge. Assumed Senior status Oct 31, 2000, serves by assignment. Born New Orleans Louisiana Feb 26, 1929. Jewish. Educated at Tulane University of Louisiana LL.B. 1950. Member Zeta Beta Tau, Order of the Coif and Order of Barristers. Admitted to practice Louisiana 1950. In legal practice New Orleans 1955-71. Former Judge, Temporary Emergency Court of Appeals of the U.S.

Assistant District Attorney 1953-55. Special Counsel New Orleans Aviation Board 1956-60. Adjunct Professor Tulane University of Louisiana School of Law since 1976. Director Extern Program in Federal Court Tulane University and Loyola Law School. Member Judicial Conference of the U.S. (Former member Committee on Implementation of the Federal Magistrates System, Former Chairman Advisory Committee on Bankruptcy Rules, Member ad hoc Committee on Bankruptcy Legislation and Executive Committee, Chairman Committee on the Administration of the Bankruptcy System), New Orleans, Louisiana State and American Bar Associations. Captain USMC 1951-53. Republican. Past President Congregation Temple Sinai. Board of Governors Tulane Medical Center. President Board of Trustees Tulane Medical Center Hospital and Clinic. Enjoys fishing, boating and bicycling.

Office: C256 U.S. Courthouse, 500 Camp Street, New Orleans 70130.

Telephone: (504) 589-7500.

SEGURA, Robert L. *(Judge, New Iberia City Court)*

Office: 457 East Main Street, Room 206, New Iberia 70560.

Telephone: (337) 369-2334.

SENS, Paul N. *(Judge, New Orleans Municipal Court)*

Office: 727 South Broad Street, New Orleans 70119.

Telephone: (504) 827-5086.

SHARP, Alvin R. *(Judge, Louisiana District Court Fourth Judicial District)* Elected to term beginning Jan 1, 1997. Reelected 2002, current term expires Dec 31, 2008. Born West Monroe Louisiana April 3, 1964. Baptist. Educated at Southern University B.A. cum laude 1986 J.D. cum laude 1989 and Emory University LL.M. 1990. Merit Scholar. Editor-in-Chief Southern University Law Review 1988-89. Member Delta Theta Phi. Admitted to practice Louisiana 1990. In legal practice Monroe 1990-97. City Prosecutor 1992-96. Prince Hall Mason. Enjoys collecting coins and stamps.

Office: 300 St. John Street, Monroe 71201.

Telephone: (318) 361-2298.

E-mail address: asharp@4jdc.com

SHEA, John A. *(Judge, New Orleans Municipal Court)* Elected to term beginning Jan 1, 1979. Reelected 1986, 1994 and 2002. Current term expires Dec 31, 2010. Currently serves as Senior Judge. Born New Orleans Louisiana May 9, 1934. Catholic. Educated at Loyola University LL.B. 1958. Admitted to practice Louisiana 1958. Began legal practice New Orleans 1959.

Member Fourth and Fifth Circuit Judges Association, New Orleans Trial Judges Association, Louisiana City Court Judges Association, Louisiana District Court Judges Association, Louisiana Trial Lawyers Association, American Justinian Society, American Judicature Society, American Judges Association, The Association of Trial Lawyers of America, Louisiana State and American Bar Associations. Captain USAR JAGC 1958-66. Democrat. Member Louisiana State Democratic Central Committee 1970-79. Hobbies include golf, cooking and woodwork.

Office: 727 South Broad Street, New Orleans 70119.

Telephone: (504) 827-5081.

SHEMWELL, Robert H. *(Magistrate Judge, United States District Court Western District of Louisiana)* Appointed by U.S. District Court judges to term beginning Aug 3, 1984. Reappointed 1992 and 2000. Current term expires 2008. Also serves as Clerk of Court since 1975. Born Shreveport Louisiana Oct 25, 1941. Episcopalian. Educated at Louisiana State University LL.B. 1967 J.D. 1968. Member Phi Delta Phi. Admitted to practice Louisiana 1967. Began legal practice Baton Rouge 1967.

Assistant U.S. Attorney U.S. District Court Western District of Louisiana 1970-75. Member Shreveport and Louisiana Bar Associations. Republican.

Office: 1167 U.S. Courthouse, 300 Fannin Street, Shreveport 71101-3083.

Telephone: (318) 676-4273.

SHOLES, Ronald J. *(Judge, New Orleans Traffic Court)* Former Judge, Louisiana District Court Orleans Parish Civil District.

Office: 727 South Broad Street, New Orleans 70119.

Telephone: (504) 827-5099.

SHUSHAN, Sally A. *(Magistrate Judge, United States District Court Eastern District of Louisiana)* Appointed by U.S. District Court judges to term beginning Feb 1, 1999. Term expires Feb 1, 2007.

Office: B345 Federal Building, 501 Magazine Street, New Orleans 70130.

Telephone: (504) 589-7620.

SIMMONS, Cameron B. *(Judge, Jeanerette City Court)*

Mailing address: P.O. Box 268, Jeanerette 70544.

Telephone: (337) 276-5603.

SIMPSON, A. Bruce *(Judge, Louisiana District Court Seventeenth Judicial District)*

Mailing address: P.O. Box 1122, Thibodaux 70302.

Telephone: (985) 448-1291.

SLATTERY, John B. *(Judge, Springhill City Court)*

Mailing address: P.O. Box 86, Springhill 71075.

Telephone: (318) 539-4213.

SMITH, R. Wayne *(Judge, Louisiana District Court Third Judicial District)*
Mailing address: P.O. Box 388, Ruston 71273-0388.
Telephone: (318) 251-5121.

SNOWDY, J. Sterling *(Judge, Louisiana District Court Fortieth Judicial District)* Elected Nov 5, 1996 to term beginning Jan 1, 1997. Reelected Oct 5, 2002, current term expires Dec 31, 2008. Born New Orleans Louisiana April 24, 1959. Roman Catholic. Educated at University of New Orleans B.S. 1981 and Loyola University School of Law J.D. 1984. Admitted to practice Louisiana 1986 and U.S. District Courts Eastern 1986, Middle 1986 and Western 1986 Districts of Louisiana. In legal practice Reserve 1986-89 and LaPlace 1989-96.

Member Louisiana State, Federal and American Bar Associations. Enjoys music, theater and gardening.

Office: St. John the Baptist Courthouse, Edgard 70049.

Telephone: (985) 497-5580.

SPEARS, Sonja M. *(Judge, New Orleans First City Court)* Elected Nov 3, 1998 to term beginning Jan 1, 1999. Term expires Dec 31, 2004. Born Brookline Massachusetts May 31, 1964. Baptist. Educated at Tufts University B.A. 1986 and Tulane University J.D. 1991. Moot Court Board 1989-91. Admitted to practice Louisiana 1991 and U.S. District Court Eastern District of Louisiana 1992. In legal practice New Orleans 1991-98.

Adjunct Professor of Trial Advocacy Tulane University School of Law since 1999. Member Louis A. Martinet Legal Society, New Orleans, National and American Bar Associations.

Office: 421 Loyola Avenue, Room 200, New Orleans 70112.

Telephone: (504) 592-9247.

E-mail address: spears@orleanscdc.com

STAGG, Tom *(Senior Judge, United States District Court Western District of Louisiana)* Appointed for life by the President to term beginning 1974. Former Chief Judge. Assumed Senior status March 1, 1991, serves by assignment. Born Shreveport Louisiana Jan 19, 1923. Educated at Louisiana State University B.A. 1943 J.D. 1949. Admitted to practice Louisiana 1949. In legal practice Shreveport 1949-74.

Member Shreveport, Louisiana State and American Bar Associations. Captain U.S. Army Infantry ETO 1943-46. Recipient Bronze Star and Purple Heart with oak leaf cluster. Republican. Delegate Republican National Conventions 1956, 1960, 1964, 1968 and 1972. Member Republican National Committee for Louisiana 1964-72 (Executive Committee 1964-68). Vice President King Hardware Company 1955-74. President Abe Meyer Corporation 1960-74 and Stagg Investments Inc. 1964-74. Managing partner Pierremont Mall Shopping Center 1963-74. Chairman Governor's Tidelands Advisory Council 1969-70. Delegate Louisiana Constitutional Convention (Chairman Rules Committee and Committee on Executive Department). Member Shreveport Airport Authority 1967-73 (Chairman 1970-73), Governor's Advisory Committee on Offshore Revenues 1972-74, Shreveport Junior Chamber of Commerce (President 1955-56), Louisiana Junior Chamber of Commerce (Vice President 1956-57) and Photographic Society of America.

Office: 4100 U.S. Courthouse, 300 Fannin Street, Shreveport 71101-3091.

Telephone: (318) 676-3260.

STANSBURY, Kim P. *(Judge, City Court of Morgan City)*
Mailing address: P.O. Box 1577, Morgan City 70381.
Telephone: (985) 384-2718.

STARLING, Richard E., Jr. *(Judge, Alexandria City Court)*
Mailing address: P.O. Box 30, Alexandria 71309.
Telephone: (318) 449-5151.

STEWART, Herman I. *(Judge, Louisiana District Court Thirty-sixth Judicial District)*
Mailing address: P.O. Box 1148, DeRidder 70634.
Telephone: (337) 463-7993.

STEWART, James E., Sr. *(Judge, Louisiana Court of Appeal Second Circuit)* Elected to term beginning Sept 1, 1994. Term expires Aug 2004. Born Shreveport Louisiana Aug 11, 1955. Educated at University of New Orleans B.A. in Political Science 1977 and Loyola University School of Law J.D. 1980. Life Member Omega Psi Phi (Past President). Admitted to practice Louisiana 1980, U.S. District Court Western District of Louisiana and U.S. Court of Appeals Fifth Circuit. Judge, Louisiana District Court First Judicial District Jan 1991 to Aug 1994.

Assistant City Attorney Shreveport Oct 1980 to Jan 1982. Assistant District Attorney Feb 1982 to 1983, Misdemeanor Assistant 1983-84, Felony Assistant 1984-85, Section Chief 1985-87, Division Chief 1987 to Sept 1989 and First Assistant District Attorney Oct 1989 to Dec 1990 Caddo Parish. Member Louisiana Sentencing Guidelines Commission, Louisiana Court of Appeals Association, Harry V. Booth Inn of Court, Shreveport, Louisiana State (Assistant Bar Examiner), National (Judicial Council) and American Bar Associations. Attended Annual Summer School for Judges Louisiana Judicial College. Instructor in Criminal Litigation Division of Continuing Education and Public Service Louisiana State University. Eagle Scout 1970. Named one of Outstanding Young Men of America 1980 and 1983. Recipient Legal Profession Award 1989 and Legal Services Award 1990 from Caddo Community Action Agency; Man of the Year Award 1991 and 1992 from Rho Omega Chapter Omega Psi Phi; and Paul Lynch Award 1993. Inducted into C. E. Byrd High School Hall of Fame 1991. Member United Methodist Travel Seminar to Africa 1974. Founder Project About Face (program to expose inner-city youth to the risks of a life of crime). Past President Laurel Street ECE School PTA. Chairman Pastor-Parish Relations Committee and Wills and Legacy Committee St. James United Methodist Church. Board of Directors C. E. Byrd High School Alumni Association. Founder and Coach West Shreveport Little League. T-Ball Coach Shreveport Little League.

Mailing address: P.O. Box 1528, Shreveport 71165.

Telephone: (318) 227-3740.

STINSON, Ford E., Jr. *(Judge, Louisiana District Court Twenty-sixth Judicial District)*
Mailing address: P.O. Box 310, Benton 71006.
Telephone: (318) 965-2217.

STRONG, Glen W. *(Judge, Louisiana District Court Fifth Judicial District)* Elected to term beginning Oct 5, 1984. Reelected 1990, 1996 and 2002. Current term expires Dec 31, 2008. Born Oak Grove Louisiana Nov 5, 1948. Baptist. Educated at Northeast Louisiana University and Louisiana State University J.D. 1975. Admitted

STRONG, GLEN W.—*Continued*

to practice Louisiana 1975 and U.S. District Court Western District of Louisiana 1976. In legal practice Monroe 1975-76 and Oak Grove 1976-84.

Past member Louisiana Trial Lawyers Association. Member Fifth District (President 1979) and Louisiana State Bar Associations. Democrat. Delegate to Louisiana Democratic Convention 1980-84. Member since 1976, President 1983 and District Governor 1987 Oak Grove Lions Club. Enjoys camping, hunting, fishing, raising Limousin cattle and paint horses.

Mailing address: P.O. Drawer 1208, Oak Grove 71263.

Telephone: (318) 428-4284.

SULLIVAN, Henry G., Jr. *(Judge, Louisiana District Court Twenty-fourth Judicial District)*

Office: 200 Derbigny Street, Gretna 70053.

Telephone: (504) 364-3935.

SULLIVAN, Michael G. *(Judge, Louisiana Court of Appeal Third Circuit)* Born Effingham Illinois Dec 2, 1941. Catholic. Educated at Spring Hill College B.S. 1964 and Loyola University School of Law J.D. 1973. Member Phi Delta Phi. Admitted to practice Louisiana 1973. Began legal practice Lafayette 1973. Former Judge, Lafayette City Court, elected to term beginning Jan 1, 1984.

Member National Council of Juvenile and Family Court Judges, American Judges Association, Lafayette Parish, Louisiana State and American Bar Associations. Sergeant U.S. Army 1966-69. Member Rotary International and Boy Scouts of America (Executive Director Evangeline Area Council). Enjoys tennis.

Mailing address: P.O. Box 2548, Lafayette 70502.

Telephone: (337) 269-9686.

SWENT, F. Rae *(Judge, Louisiana District Court Ninth Judicial District)*

Office: 701 Murray Street, Alexandria 71301.

Telephone: (318) 443-6893.

TATUM, Danny *(Judge, Ruston City Court)*

Mailing address: P.O. Box 1821, Ruston 71273-1821.

Telephone: (318) 251-8614.

TAYLOR, C. Hearn *(Judge, Orleans Parish Juvenile Court)*

Office: 421 Loyola Avenue, New Orleans 70112.

Telephone: (504) 565-7315.

TEAT, Jimmy C. *(Judge, Louisiana District Court Second Judicial District)*

Mailing address: P.O. Box 100, Jonesboro 71251.

Telephone: (318) 259-3442.

TERRELL, Phillip J. *(Judge, Pineville City Court)*

Mailing address: P.O. Box 3671, Pineville 71361.

Telephone: (318) 449-5656.

THIBODEAUX, Ulysses Gene *(Judge, Louisiana Court of Appeal Third Circuit)*

Mailing address: P.O. Box 16577, Lake Charles 70616.

Telephone: (337) 433-9403.

TOBIAS, Max N., Jr. *(Judge, Louisiana Court of Appeal Fourth Circuit)* Born New Orleans Louisiana Sept 9, 1947. Jewish. Educated at Tulane University of Louisiana B.A. 1971 J.D. 1971. Law Clerk to Hon. John A. Dixon, Jr., Supreme Court of Louisiana 1971-72. Member Delta Theta Phi. Admitted to practice Louisiana 1971, U.S. District Court Eastern District of Louisiana 1972, U.S. Courts of Appeals Fifth 1972 and Federal 1972 Circuits, U.S. Tax Court 1972, U.S. Claims Court 1972, U.S. Court of International Trade 1972 and U.S. Supreme Court 1974. In legal practice New Orleans 1972-86. Former Judge, Louisiana District Court Orleans Parish Civil District, elected to term beginning Feb 28, 1986.

Member American Judicature Society, New Orleans and American Bar Associations. Attended The National Judicial College. Democrat. Delegate Constitutional Convention of Louisiana 1973-74. Enjoys jogging, fishing and hiking.

Office: 1515 Poydras Street, Seventh Floor, New Orleans 70112.

Telephone: (504) 592-0937.

TRAHAN, John D. *(Judge, Louisiana District Court Fifteenth Judicial District)* Elected Sept 21, 1996 to term beginning Jan 1, 1997. Reelected 2002, current term expires Dec 31, 2008. Born Crowley Louisiana Nov 15, 1957. Catholic. Educated at University of Southwestern Louisiana B.S. 1979 and Louisiana State University J.D. 1982. Law Clerk to Hon. Edmond L. Guidry, Jr., Louisiana Court of Appeal Third Circuit 1982-84. Admitted to practice Louisiana 1982. In legal practice Crowley 1984-96.

Member John M. Duhe, Jr. American Inn of Court, Judges Association of the Third Circuit Court of Appeal, American Judicature Society, American Judges Association, Acadia Parish and Louisiana State Bar Associations. Member Alumni Association University of Southwestern Louisiana and Louisiana State University and Knights of Columbus. Enjoys golf, tennis, jogging and reading.

Mailing address: P.O. Box 1366, Crowley 70527-1366.

Telephone: (337) 788-8817.

TRAYLOR, Chet D. *(Justice, Supreme Court of Louisiana)* Elected to term beginning Jan 1, 1997. Term expires Dec 31, 2006. Born Columbia Louisiana. Methodist. Educated at Northeast Louisiana University B.A. 1969 and Loyola University School of Law J.D. 1974. Judge, Louisiana District Court Fifth Judicial District 1985 to Dec 31, 1996.

Assistant District Attorney Franklin Parish 1975-76. Former Legal Advisor Louisiana State Police. Former Investigator Organized Crime and Racketeering Unit Louisiana Department of Justice. Served to Sergeant E-5 U.S. Army Military Police. Founding Board Member Winnsboro Economic Development Foundation. Former Board Member Winnsboro Lion's Club and Franklin Parish Mental Health Association. Former First President Winnsboro Ducks Unlimited. Founder John Adams Chapter Greenwings. Life Member National Rifle Association. Member Rocky Mountain Conservation Fund.

Office: 301 Loyola Avenue, Second Floor, New Orleans 70112.

Telephone: (504) 568-5744.

TRIMBLE, James T., Jr. *(Senior Judge, United States District Court Western District of Louisiana)* Magistrate Judge 1986-91. Appointed Judge for life by President George Bush to term beginning Sept 12, 1991. Assumed Senior status Sept 13, 2002, serves by assignment. Born Bunkie Louisiana Sept 13, 1932. Southern Baptist. Educated at University of Southwest Louisiana

TRIMBLE, JAMES T., JR.—*Continued*
and Louisiana State University B.A. 1955 LL.B. 1956 replaced by J.D. Admitted to practice Louisiana 1956. In legal practice Alexandria 1959-86.
Member Louisiana Bar Foundation, Federal Judges Association, Southwest Louisiana and Louisiana State Bar Associations. USAF JAG 1956-59.
Office: 237 U.S. Courthouse, 611 Broad Street, Lake Charles 70601.
Telephone: (337) 437-3884.

TUREAU, Ralph *(Judge, Louisiana District Court Twenty-third Judicial District)* Elected Nov 1996 to term beginning Jan 1, 1997. Reelected 2002, current term expires Dec 31, 2008. Currently serves as Chief Judge. Born Gonzales Louisiana Dec 15, 1945. Catholic. Educated at Louisiana State University B.A. 1967 J.D. 1971. Admitted to practice Louisiana 1971 and U.S. District Courts Eastern, Middle and Western Districts of Louisiana. In legal practice Gonzales 1971-97.
Assistant District Attorney 1979-97. Parish Attorney Ascension County 1991-97. Member Rotary Club. Enjoys scuba diving, hunting and fishing.
Mailing address: P.O. Box 1919, Gonzales 70707-1919.
Telephone: (225) 621-8500.

TURNER, Alvin, Jr. *(Judge, Louisiana District Court Twenty-third Judicial District)* Former Chief Judge.
Office: 828-202 South Irma Boulevard, Gonzales 70737.
Telephone: (225) 621-8500.

TYSON, Ralph E. *(Judge, United States District Court Middle District of Louisiana)* Appointed for life by President Bill Clinton to term beginning Aug 10, 1998. Born Baton Rouge Louisiana Aug 13, 1948. Educated at Louisiana State University B.A. 1970 J.D. 1973. In legal practice Louisiana 1973-88. Judge, Baton Rouge City Court 1988-93. Judge, Louisiana District Court Nineteenth District Judicial District 1993-98.
Office: 301 Federal Building, 777 Florida Street, Baton Rouge 70801-1712.
Telephone: (225) 389-3634.

VANCE, Sarah S. *(Judge, United States District Court Eastern District of Louisiana)* Appointed for life by President Bill Clinton to term beginning 1994. Born Donaldsonville Louisiana Jan 16, 1950. Educated at Louisiana State University B.A. 1971 and Tulane University School of Law J.D. 1978. In legal practice New Orleans 1978-94.
Office: C255 U.S. Courthouse, 500 Camp Street, New Orleans 70130.
Telephone: (504) 589-7595.

VAN SHARP, Carl *(Judge, Louisiana District Court Fourth Judicial District)* Elected Sept 1, 1992 to term beginning Jan 1, 1993. Reelected 1996 and 2002. Current term expires Dec 31, 2008. Born Monroe Louisiana June 25, 1958. Baptist. Educated at Northeast Louisiana University B.A. with honors 1979 and Louisiana State University J.D. 1982. Admitted to practice Louisiana 1982. In legal practice Monroe 1982-84.
City Attorney Monroe 1984-92. Member National and American Bar Associations.
Office: 300 St. John Street, Monroe 71201.
Telephone: (318) 361-2250.

VAUGHN, Kirk A. *(Judge, Louisiana District Court Thirty-fourth Judicial District)* Former Chief Judge.
Office: 1101 West St. Bernard Highway, Chalmette 70043.
Telephone: (504) 278-4433.

VICTORY, Jeffrey P. *(Justice, Supreme Court of Louisiana)* Elected to term beginning Jan 1, 1995. Term expires Dec 31, 2004. Born Shreveport Louisiana Jan 29, 1946. Baptist. Educated at Centenary College B.A. 1967 and Tulane University 1971. Staff member Tulane Law Review 1968-71. In legal practice Shreveport 1971-81. Judge, Louisiana District Court First Judicial District Jan 1, 1982 to Dec 31, 1990. Judge, Louisiana Court of Appeal Second Circuit Jan 1, 1991 to Dec 31, 1994.
Member Shreveport, Louisiana State and American Bar Associations. Louisiana National Guard 1969-75. Enjoys tennis, motorcycles and classic cars.
Office: 301 Loyola Avenue, New Orleans 70112.
Telephone: (504) 568-5733.

VIDRINE, J. Larry *(Judge, Louisiana District Court Thirteenth Judicial District)*
Mailing address: P.O. Box 371, Ville Platte 70586.
Telephone: (337) 363-5516.

WADDELL, Robert P. "Bobby" *(Judge, Louisiana District Court First Judicial District)* Elected Oct 6, 1990 to term beginning Nov 15, 1990. Reelected 1996 and 2002. Current term expires Dec 31, 2008. Born Shreveport Louisiana May 19, 1948. United Methodist. Educated at Louisiana Tech University B.S. 1971 and Louisiana State University J.D. 1974. Admitted to practice Louisiana 1974. In legal practice Shreveport 1974-90.
Assistant District Attorney Caddo Parish 1976-79. State Representative Louisiana 1979-90.
Office: 501 Texas Street, Room 300C, Shreveport 71101.
Telephone: (318) 226-6816.

WAGUESPACK, Zorraine M. *(Judge, Louisiana District Court Twenty-first Judicial District)*
Mailing address: P.O. Box 788, Amite 70422.
Telephone: (985) 748-9445.

WALDRON, Dennis J. *(Judge, Louisiana District Court Orleans Parish Criminal District)* Elected at special election to term beginning Feb 10, 1982. Reelected 1984, 1990, 1996 and 2002. Current term expires Dec 31, 2008. Currently serves as Chief Judge. Born New Orleans Louisiana March 9, 1947. Roman Catholic. Educated at University of New Orleans B.A. 1969 and Loyola University J.D. with honors 1973. Casenote and Comment Writer Loyola Law Review 1970-73. Admitted to practice Louisiana 1973. Began legal practice New Orleans 1973.
Assistant District Attorney 1974-81. First Assistant District Attorney Orleans Parish 1980-81. Lecturer on Criminal Law City College of Loyola University since 1975. Adjunct Professor of Criminal Law Loyola University School of Law. Member Louisiana Judges Association, Louisiana State and American Bar Associations. Enjoys jogging and reading.
Office: 2700 Tulane Avenue, New Orleans 70119.
Telephone: (504) 827-3473.

WALKER, John R. *(Judge, Louisiana District Court Thirty-second Judicial District)*
Mailing address: P.O. Box 3564, Houma 70361-3564.
Telephone: (985) 873-6550.

WALKER, Michael R. *(Judge, Louisiana District Court First Judicial District)*
Office: 501 Texas Street, Suite C, Shreveport 71101.
Telephone: (318) 226-6823.

WALL, Alex W. *(Judge, Baton Rouge City Court)*
Mailing address: P.O. Box 3438, Baton Rouge 70821.
Telephone: (225) 389-3346.

WALTER, Donald E. *(Senior Judge, United States District Court Western District of Louisiana)* Appointed for life by President Ronald Reagan to term beginning 1985. Assumed Senior status Nov 30, 2001, serves by assignment. Born Jennings Louisiana March 15, 1936. Educated at Louisiana State University B.A. 1961 J.D. 1964. In legal practice Lake Charles 1964-69 and Shreveport 1978-85.
U.S. Attorney Western District of Louisiana 1969-77.
Office: 4200 U.S. Courthouse, 300 Fannin Street, Shreveport 71101-3059.
Telephone: (318) 676-3175.

WARE, George H., Jr. *(Judge, Louisiana District Court Twentieth Judicial District)*
Mailing address: P.O. Box 529, Clinton 70722.
Telephone: (225) 683-0613.

WATTIGNY, Gerard B. *(Judge, Louisiana District Court Sixteenth Judicial District)* Elected Oct 21, 1995 to term beginning Dec 5, 1995. Reelected Sept 26, 1996 and 2001. Current term expires Dec 31, 2007. Currently serves as Chief Judge. Born New Iberia Louisiana April 10, 1942. Episcopalian. Educated at University of Louisiana at Lafayette and Louisiana State University J.D. 1967. Member Blue Key. Admitted to practice Louisiana 1967. In legal practice New Iberia 1967-95.
Member Louisiana State and American Bar Associations. Democrat.
Office: 300 Iberia Street, Suite 210, New Iberia 70560.
Telephone: (337) 369-4410.

WEIMER, John L. *(Justice, Supreme Court of Louisiana)* Elected to term beginning Dec 13, 2001. Term expires Dec 2011. Educated at Nicholls State University B.S. with honors 1976 and Louisiana State University J.D. 1980. In legal practice 1988-95. Judge Pro Tem 1993 and Judge 1995-98, Louisiana District Court Seventeenth Judicial District. Judge, Louisiana Court of Appeal First Circuit June 1, 1998 to Dec 12, 2001.
Adjunct Professor of Business Law 1983-88 and 1996-98 and Faculty Member 1988-95 Nicholls State University. Regional Co-chairman Citizens' Summit on Justice Reform 1997. Delegate House of Delegates Louisiana State Bar Association. Listed in *Who's Who Among American Teachers* 1994 and 1995. Recipient Presidential Award for Teaching Excellence 1995, Outstanding Judicial Award from Victims and Citizens Against Crime 1996 and Outstanding Jurist Award from Crimefighters 1998. Director Free Enterprise Program Nicholls State University 1995.
Office: 301 Loyola Avenue, New Orleans 70112.
Telephone: (504) 568-5723.

WELCH, Jewel E., Jr. *(Judge, Louisiana District Court Nineteenth Judicial District)* Elected Oct 1994 to term beginning Jan 1, 1995. Reelected 1996 and 2002. Current term expires Dec 31, 2008. Former Chief Judge. Born Baton Rouge Louisiana. Baptist. Educated at University of Maryland B.S. magna cum laude 1977 and Louisiana State University Law Center J.D. 1980. Member Phi Kappa Phi. Admitted to practice Louisiana 1980 and U.S. District Courts Eastern 1980 and Middle 1980 Districts of Louisiana. In legal practice Zachary and Baton Rouge 1980-94.
Office: 222 St. Louis Street, Suite 757, Baton Rouge 70802.
Telephone: (225) 389-8820.

WHITE, Trudy *(Judge, Baton Rouge City Court)*
Office: 233 St. Louis Street, Baton Rouge 70802.
Telephone: (225) 389-3025.

WICKER, Fredericka H. *(Judge, Louisiana District Court Twenty-fourth Judicial District)*
Office: 200 Derbigny Street, Room 206, Gretna 70053.
Telephone: (504) 364-3859.

WILEY, Jim W. *(Judge, Louisiana District Court Eighth Judicial District)* Currently serves as Chief Judge.
Mailing address: P.O. Box 71, Winnfield 71483.
Telephone: (318) 628-4596.

WILKINSON, Joseph C., Jr. *(Magistrate Judge, United States District Court Eastern District of Louisiana)* Appointed by U.S. District Court judges.
Office: B409 Federal Building, 501 Magazine Street, New Orleans 70130.
Telephone: (504) 589-7630.

WILLARD, Benedict J. *(Judge, Louisiana District Court Orleans Parish Criminal District)*
Office: 2700 Tulane Avenue, New Orleans 70119.
Telephone: (504) 827-3434.

WILLIAMS, Felicia Toney *(Judge, Louisiana Court of Appeal Second Circuit)* Elected to term beginning Nov 6, 1992. Reelected Oct 2002, current term expires 2012. Born Newellton Louisiana Nov 26, 1956. Baptist. Educated at Southern University 1977 J.D. 1980. Editor-in-Chief Southern University Law Review 1979-80. Law Clerk to Louisiana Supreme Court 1981-82. Member Delta Theta Phi and Alpha Kappa Alpha. Admitted to practice Louisiana 1981 and U.S. District Court Western District of Louisiana 1982. In legal practice Tallulah 1982-90. Former Judge, Louisiana District Court Sixth Judicial District.
Assistant District Attorney 1982-90. Member Association of Women Judges, National Association of Female Attorneys, American Judicature Society, Louisiana State and American Bar Associations. Girl Scout Leader. Member Eastern Star. Enjoys softball. Interests include youth development and the elderly.
Mailing address: P.O. Box 1528, Shreveport 71165-1528.
Telephone: (318) 227-3744.

WILSON, Alonzo P. "Lon" *(Magistrate Judge, United States District Court Western District of Louisiana)* Appointed by U.S. District Court judges to term beginning Dec 17, 1991. Born Baton Rouge Louisiana March 7, 1953. Educated at Louisiana State University Law

WILSON, ALONZO P. "LON"—*Continued*

Center 1974. Admitted to practice Louisiana 1974. In legal practice Alexandria 1974-91.
Office: 209 U.S. Courthouse, 611 Broad Street, Lake Charles 70601.
Telephone: (337) 437-3874.

WILSON, Thomas A., Jr. *(Judge, City Court of Bossier City)*
Office: 620 Benton Road, Bossier City 71111.
Telephone: (318) 741-8595.

WINDHORST, Stephen J. *(Judge, Louisiana District Court Twenty-fourth Judicial District)*
Office: 200 Derbigny Street, Room 104, Gretna 70053.
Telephone: (504) 364-3916.

WOODARD, Billie Colombaro *(Judge, Louisiana Court of Appeal Third Circuit)* Elected to term beginning 1992. Educated at College of William & Mary B.A. in Psychology 1967, Loyola University School of Law J.D. 1981 and University of Virginia School of Law LL.M. 1998.

Author *You and the Law* 1993. Lead Author *Louisiana Civil Trial Procedure* Practice Series West Group since 1997. Former Instructor in Law McNeese State University. Founder and President Judge Albert Tate, Jr. Inn of Court 1994-98. Member National Annual Committee 1995 and Judicial Relations Committee 1998 American Inns of Court. Board of Governors Louisiana Judicial College since 1995. Member Appellate Court Performance Standards Commission 1996. Member National Association of Women Judges, American Judges Association, Southwest Louisiana, Louisiana State, Federal and American Bar Associations. Lecturer and Trainer Professionalism and Quality of Life Committee Louisiana State Bar Association 1998. Presenter of seminars on numerous areas of the law to local organizations. Selected as Pacesetter by John C. Stennis Center for Women in Public Service 1999 and 2000. Creator and Host "You and the Law" KPLC-TV Lake Charles 1981-94. Member Media Advisory Committee Campaign for the Children 1998. Formerly with International Corporate Division Citibank New York New York. Former Administrator of Obstetrics and Gynecology Medical College of Virginia and Department of Psychology University of Houston. Former Coordinator of Medical Education Texas Heart Institute, Texas Children's Hospital and St. Luke's Episcopal Hospital Houston Texas. Creator "Youth and the Law" (a program designed to give youth hands on experience with all levels of the court system, especially juvenile court). Co-host "Building Bridges" (a half hour television program). Creator, producer and host "Youth and the Law" (a one hour television special). Former President Artists Civic Theatre and Studio. Former Member Business and Professional Women's Association.
Office: 1000 Main Street, Lake Charles 70615.
Telephone: (337) 433-9403.

WOODARD, Cynthia T. *(Judge, Louisiana District Court Third Judicial District)* Former Chief Judge.
Mailing address: P.O. Box 388, Ruston 71273.
Telephone: (318) 251-5121.

WYATT, Robert L. *(Judge, Louisiana District Court Fourteenth Judicial District)*
Mailing address: P.O. Box 3210, Lake Charles 70602.
Telephone: (337) 437-3530.

YEAGER, Thomas M. *(Judge, Louisiana District Court Ninth Judicial District)*
Mailing address: P.O. Drawer 1431, Alexandria 71309-1431.
Telephone: (318) 443-6893.

YOUNG, Paul *(Judge, Caddo Parish Juvenile Court)*
Office: 1835 Spring Street, Shreveport 71101.
Telephone: (318) 226-6755.

ZAINEY, Jay C. *(Judge, United States District Court Eastern District of Louisiana)* Appointed for life by President George W. Bush to term beginning Feb 19, 2002. Educated at University of New Orleans B.S. 1973 and Louisiana State University Law Center J.D. 1975. Admitted to practice Texas 1998, Louisiana, U.S. District Courts Eastern, Middle and Western Districts of Louisiana, U.S. Court of Appeals Fifth Circuit and U.S. Supreme Court. In legal practice Louisiana April 1976 to 2002. Judge ad hoc, First Parish Court Jefferson Parish. Judge ad hoc, Jefferson Parish Juvenile Court. Traffic Hearing Officer, Jefferson Parish East Bank.

Former ex officio member Louisiana Judicial College, Louisiana Law Institute and The American Law Institute. Fellow Louisiana Bar Foundation. Member Committee on Judicial Ethics Supreme Court of Louisiana, St. Thomas More Inn of Court, St. Thomas More Catholic Lawyers Association, The Federalist Society, Southern Conference of Bar Association Presidents, National Conference of Bar Association Presidents (Executive Council), National Lawyers Association, Jefferson (President 1990-91), Louisiana State (President 1995-96, Chairman Victims of Crime Compensation Committee and Section of Negligence, Workman's Compensation and Insurance Law) and American (House of Delegates) Bar Associations. Faculty Member Louisiana Association of Defense Counsel Trial Academy. Recipient Director's Award from Legal Services Project, Award for "Outstanding Service" from Executive Council National Conference of Bar Association Presidents, Recognition Award from Community Action Committee Louisiana State Bar Association and Law Day Award from Jefferson Bar Association Auxiliary. USAFR Jan 1971 to April 1976. Board of Directors Jefferson Performing Arts Society. President "Extra Mile" Jefferson Parish Human Services Association), Parent's Club Jesuit High School and Parish Council St. Catherine of Siena Church. Board of Visitors Ave Maria School of Law. Member Old Metairie Road Business Association, Jefferson Chamber of Commerce and President's Committee on Mental Retardation Task Force.
Office: C-508 U.S. Courthouse, 500 Camp Street, New Orleans 70130-3367.
Telephone: (504) 589-7590.

ZENO, Melvin C. *(Judge, Louisiana District Court Twenty-fourth Judicial District)* Currently serves as Chief Judge.
Office: 200 Derbigny Street, Gretna 70053.
Telephone: (504) 364-3975.

MAINE

Capital AUGUSTA

UNITED STATES DISTRICT COURT DISTRICT OF MAINE

The court sits at Bangor and Portland. For descriptive information refer to the United States Courts section.

Chief Judge
George Z. Singal

Judge
D. Brock Hornby

Senior Judge
Gene Carter

Clerk
William S. Brownell
Federal Courthouse
156 Federal Street
Portland, Maine 04101
(207) 780-3357

UNITED STATES MAGISTRATE JUDGES OF MAINE

William S. Brownell
David M. Cohen
Margaret J. Kravchuk

UNITED STATES BANKRUPTCY COURT OF MAINE

Chief Judge
James B. Haines, Jr.

Judge
Louis H. Kornreich

Bankruptcy Clerk
Celia E. Strickler
537 Congress Street
Second Floor
Portland, Maine 04101-3318
(207) 780-3482

MAINE SUPREME JUDICIAL COURT

The Supreme Judicial Court is Maine's court of last resort. The court consists of a chief justice and six associate justices appointed by the governor with consent of the legislature for seven-year terms. Upon retirement, justices may be appointed to active retired status by the governor with consent of the legislature for seven-year terms in either the Supreme Judicial Court or the Superior Court.

The court hears appeals of civil and criminal cases from the Superior Court and District Court, appeals from final judgments, orders and decrees of the Probate Court, appeals of decisions of the Public Utilities Commission and the Workers' Compensation Commission's Appellate Division, interlocutory criminal appeals and appeals of decisions from a single justice of the court. Single justices have civil jurisdiction in nonjury cases except divorce or annulment of marriage and upon assignment may sit in the Superior or District Court to hear cases. In addition, single justices handle admission to the bar and bar disciplinary proceedings. The court makes decisions regarding legislative apportionment and renders advisory opinions concerning important questions of law when requested by the governor, Senate or House of Representatives. The court has supervisory control over the lower courts and may issue writs necessary to the exercise of proper jurisdiction. Three justices are appointed by the chief justice to serve as the Appellate Division for the review of criminal sentences of one year or more.

The court sits at Portland ten times a year.

Chief Justice
Leigh I. Saufley

Associate Justices

Donald G. Alexander	Susan W. Calkins
Robert W. Clifford	Howard H. Dana, Jr.
Jon D. Levy	Paul L. Rudman

Active Retired Justices
James P. Archibald
Samuel W. Collins, Jr.

Clerk
James C. Chute
P.O. Box 368
Cumberland County Courthouse
142 Federal Street
Portland, Maine 04112-0368
(207) 822-4146

State Court Administrator
James T. Glessner
P.O. Box 4820
62 Elm Street
Portland, Maine 04112
(207) 822-0710

MAINE SUPERIOR COURT

The Superior Court has jurisdiction over criminal and non-family civil matters and is the jury court for Maine. Justices are appointed by the governor with consent of the legislature for seven-year terms. The chief justice serves as administrative head of the court. Upon retirement, justices may be appointed to active retired status by the governor with consent of the legislature for seven-year terms.

The court has original jurisdiction exclusively or concurrently with other courts over all matters that are not within the exclusive jurisdiction of the District Court. The Superior Court is the only court where civil and criminal jury trials are held.

MAINE SUPERIOR COURT—*Continued*

The court sits at each county seat.

Chief Justice
Nancy Mills

Justices

John R. Atwood
Roland A. Cole
Thomas E. Delahanty, II
Ellen A. Gorman
Thomas E. Humphrey
Joseph M. Jabar
Andrew Mead
Thomas D. Warren
G. Arthur Brennan
Robert E. Crowley
Paul A. Fritzsche
Jeffrey L. Hjelm
E. Allen Hunter
Donald H. Marden
Kirk Studstrup

Active Retired Justices
Carl O. Bradford
Stephen L. Perkins

MAINE DISTRICT COURT

The District Court is a court of limited jurisdiction in Maine. Judges are appointed by the governor with consent of the legislature for seven-year terms. The chief justice of the Supreme Judicial Court designates a chief judge and deputy chief judge. The chief justice may also assign district judges to sit on the Superior Court. Upon retirement, judges may be appointed to active retired status by the governor with consent of the legislature for seven-year terms. On March 15, 2001, the Maine Administrative Court was absorbed by the Maine District Court's jurisdiction and is no longer a separate entity.

The court has original jurisdiction in nonfelony criminal cases and civil violations and may accept guilty pleas and conduct probable cause hearings in felony cases. The court has exclusive jurisdiction in divorce, termination of parental rights and protection from abuse cases. It has concurrent jurisdiction with the Superior Court in all nonjury civil matters. The court also has certain specified equitable jurisdiction including, but not limited to, cases involving unfair trade practices and local land use violations. The court has exclusive jurisdiction over juvenile matters and small claims cases that do not exceed $4,500. The court may also hear mental health, forcible entry and detainer, quiet title and foreclosure cases.

The court sits at each county seat and may also sit at other cities as designated by the legislature.

Chief Judge
Vendean V. Vafiades

Deputy Chief Judge
Robert E. Mullen

Judges

William R. Anderson
John B. Beliveau
Douglas A. Clapp
Ronald A. Daigle
E. Paul Eggert
Christine Foster
Peter J. Goranites
Jessie B. Gunther
Andre G. Janelle
Rick E. Lawrence
John D. McElwee
John C. Nivison
John V. Romei
Bernard C. Staples
Michael N. Westcott
Patricia G. Worth
Roland Beaudoin
Jane S. Bradley
Paul A. Cote, Jr.
Wayne R. Douglas
Joseph H. Field
Rae Ann French
David B. Griffiths
Andrew M. Horton
John David Kennedy
James E. MacMichael
Ann M. Murray
Keith A. Powers
Ronald D. Russell
Kevin L. Stitham
Joyce A. Wheeler

Active Retired Judges
Bernard M. Devine
Courtland D. Perry, II

MAINE PROBATE COURTS

The Probate Courts are courts of limited jurisdiction in Maine. Each county has a probate court with judges elected by the voters of their respective counties for four-year terms.

The courts have jurisdiction over probate matters including administration of estates, wills, adoption, guardianship and name changes, subject to appeal to the Superior Court. In inheritance tax abatement cases and in other cases when parties agree, direct appeal may be made to the Supreme Judicial Court. The courts also have concurrent jurisdiction with the Supreme Judicial Court on matters of equity relating to the administration of estates, wills and trusts.

The courts sit at the county seats.

Maine Counties and County Seats

Androscoggin
Auburn

Aroostook
Houlton

Cumberland
Portland

Franklin
Farmington

Hancock
Ellsworth

Kennebec
Augusta

Knox
Rockland

Lincoln
Wiscasset

Oxford
South Paris

Penobscot
Bangor

Piscataquis
Dover-Foxcroft

Sagadahoc
Bath

Somerset
Skowhegan

Waldo
Belfast

Washington
Machias

York
Alfred

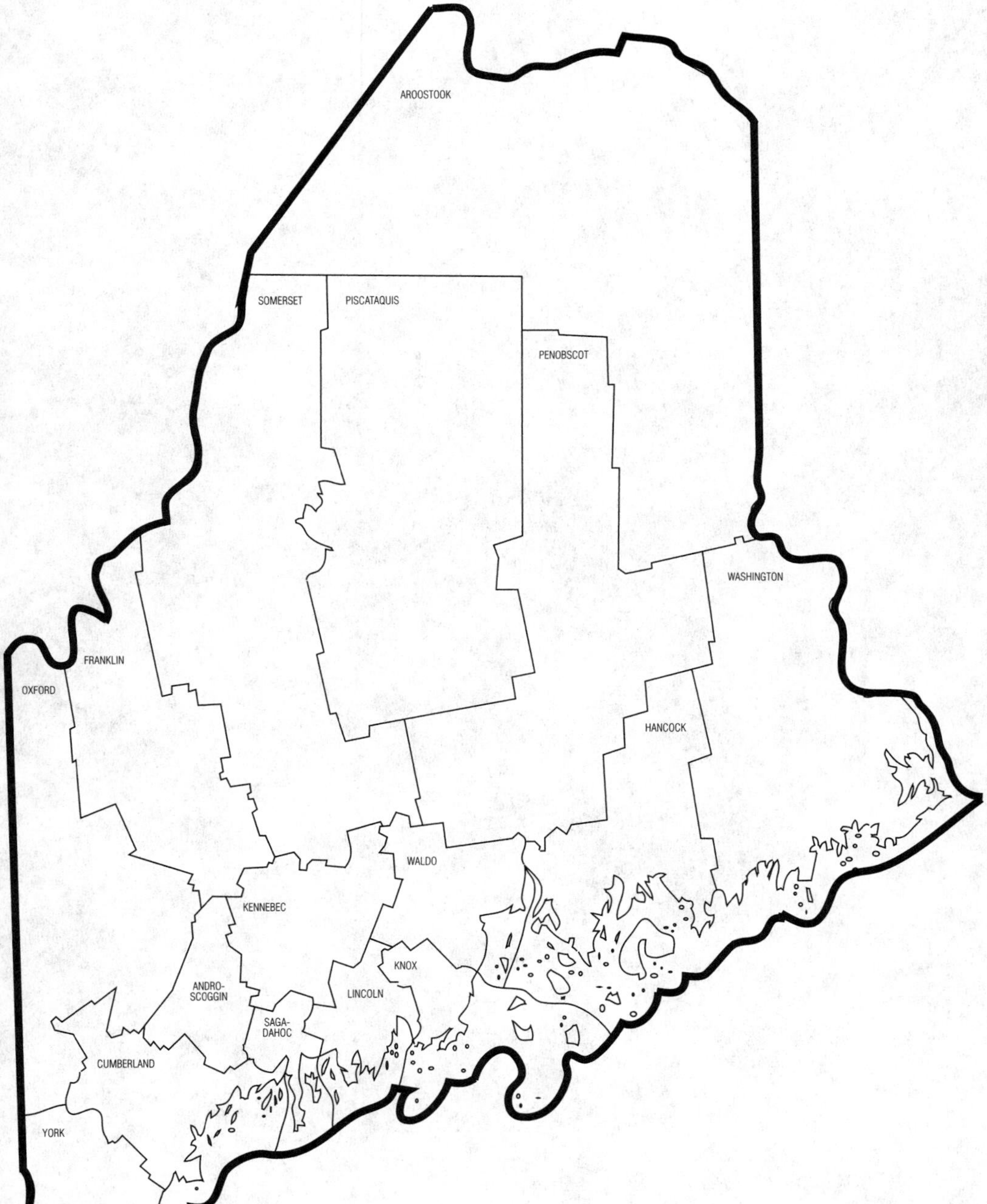
AROOSTOOK
SOMERSET
PISCATAQUIS
PENOBSCOT
WASHINGTON
FRANKLIN
OXFORD
HANCOCK
WALDO
KENNEBEC
KNOX
ANDRO-
SCOGGIN
LINCOLN
SAGA-
DAHOC
CUMBERLAND
YORK

UNITED STATES DISTRICT COURT DISTRICT OF MAINE

MAINE

ALEXANDER, Donald G. *(Associate Justice, Maine Supreme Judicial Court)* Appointed by Governor Angus S. King, Jr. to term beginning Sept 1998. Term expires Sept 2005. Educated at Bowdoin College A.B. with honors 1964 and University of Chicago Law School J.D. 1967. Admitted to practice District of Columbia 1968 (inactive), U.S. Supreme Court 1971 and Maine 1973. In legal practice Washington D.C. Judge, Maine District Court Dec 1978 to Feb 1980, appointed by Governor James B. Longley. Justice, Maine Superior Court Feb 1980 to Aug 1998, appointed by Governor Joseph E. Brennan.

Former Deputy and Assistant Attorney General Maine. Author *Maine Jury Instruction Manual* LEXIS Law Publishing 1985, 1990, 1996 and 4th ed. 2001; "Sentencing: Try Your Hand at It" 1, 336, 1986, "Sentencing: It's Part of the Criminal Process Too" 1, 300, 1986, "Some Thoughts on Improving Discovery and the Practice of Law" 4, 128, 1989, "Motion Day: Old Traditions, New Rules: A Guide to Survival" 5, 166, 1990, "Summary Judgment: An Old Remedy for New Times" 9, 128, 1994, "Let's Kick Abe Lincoln Out of the Courtroom: New Approaches to Conducting Trials" 10, 148, 1995, "Tips for Success in Summary Judgment Practice" 16, 172, 2001, "Ten Tips for Effective Objection Practice" 16, 214, 2001 and "Preparing for More Effective Closing Argument" 17, 194, 2002 Maine B. Jour.; and *Maine Rules of Civil Procedure with Advisory Committee Notes from 1981, Annotations and Commentary* 2003 and *Maine Appellate Practice* 2003. Instructor Trial Advocacy Workshop Harvard Law School since 1980. Court Liaison Advisory Committee on Maine Rules of Civil Procedure 1981-93 and since 1998. Member Committee on Judicial Responsibility and Disability 1990-96 and Criminal Law Advisory Committee 1993-98. Chair 1993-98 and Court Liaison since 1998 State Court Library Committee. Member Maine State Bar Association (CLE Committee since 1993). Instructor CLE programs Maine State Bar Association since 1981. Former Assistant Counsel Committee on Public Works U.S. Senate. Former Legislative Counsel National League of Cities and U.S. Conference of Mayors. Board of Directors Cleaves Law Library since 1998.

Mailing address: P.O. Box 368, Portland 04112-0368.
Office: Cumberland County Courthouse, 142 Federal Street, Portland 04101.
Telephone: (207) 822-4100.

ANDERSON, William R. *(Judge, Maine District Court)* Appointed by governor.
Office: 62 Union Street, Rockland 04841-2836.
Telephone: (207) 596-2240.

ARCHIBALD, James P. *(Active Retired Justice, Maine Supreme Judicial Court)* Appointed Associate Justice by Governor Kenneth Curtis to term beginning 1971. Appointed Active Retired Justice by Governor Joseph E. Brennan Jan 2, 1980. Reappointed Jan 2, 1987, May 9, 1994 and by Governor Angus S. King, Jr. 2001. Born Houlton Maine May 17, 1912. Unitarian. Educated at Bowdoin College B.A. 1934 and Boston University J.D. 1937. Received honorary LL.D. Ricker College 1971. Admitted to practice Maine 1937. In legal practice Houlton 1937-56. Justice, Maine Superior Court 1956-71.

Houlton Town Council 1940-44. Aroostook County Attorney 1942-44 and 1946-50. Corporation Counsel Houlton 1947-56. Special Assistant Attorney General Maine 1951-52. Member American Judicature Society, The American Law Institute, Aroostook County, Maine State and American Bar Associations. Recipient Silver Shingle Award from Boston University School of Law 1971 and Centennial Award 1972. Board of Directors Madigan Memorial Hospital. President 1971-77 and Board of Directors since 1971 Houlton Regional Hospital. Member Houlton School Committee 1947-57 and Masons.

Mailing address: P.O. Box 787, Houlton 04730-0787.
Office: Aroostook County Courthouse, Houlton 04730.
Telephone: (207) 532-6563.

ATWOOD, John R. *(Justice, Maine Superior Court)* Appointed by Governor John R. McKernan, Jr. to term beginning May 17, 1994. Reappointed by Governor Angus S. King, Jr. 2001, current term expires 2008. Born Brooklyn New York July 14, 1946. Episcopalian. Educated at University of Pennsylvania A.B. 1968 and Cornell University Law School J.D. 1971. Admitted to practice Maine 1971, U.S. District Court District of Maine and U.S. Supreme Court.

District Attorney District Six 1979-87. Commissioner Department of Public Safety 1987-97. E-4 U.S. Army Reserves. Chairman Republican Committee Knox County 1978-82.

Office: Kennebec County Courthouse, 95 State Street, Augusta 04330-5680.
Telephone: (207) 624-5830.

BEAUDOIN, Roland *(Judge, Maine District Court)* Assumed office March 15, 2001. Former Chief Judge, Maine Administrative Court.
Mailing address: P.O. Box 412, Portland 04112.
Telephone: (207) 822-4269.

BELIVEAU, John B. *(Judge, Maine District Court)* Appointed by Governor Joseph E. Brennan Oct 1984. Reappointed by Governor John R. McKernan, Jr. Feb 1988 and by Governor Angus S. King, Jr. 1995 and 2002. Current term expires 2009. Born Lewiston Maine Feb 17, 1937. Christian. Educated at University of Notre Dame B.A. Dean's List 1959, New York University M.B.A. 1961 and Georgetown University J.D. 1964. Member Phi Delta Phi. Admitted to practice Maine 1964, District of Columbia 1965 and U.S. District Court District of Maine 1964. In legal practice Lewiston and Auburn 1964-84. Former Judge-at-Large, Maine District Court.

Mayor Lewiston 1969-70. County Attorney Androscoggin County 1971-72. Judicial Liaison for Maine Court Appointed Special Advocates Program. Attended semiannual Judicial Committee Conference Maine State Bar Association 1984-91, Maine Judicial Conference 1984-91, American Academy of Judicial Education Fall 1989 and Substance Abuse and Alternative Society Pro-

BELIVEAU, JOHN B.—*Continued*

gram National Conference of State Courts Fall 1991. Enjoys jazz piano, handball, baseball, weight lifting, golfing and studying native North American history, Indian culture and lifestyle.

Mailing address: P.O. Box 1345, Lewiston 04243-1345.

Telephone: (207) 783-5403.

BRADFORD, Carl O. *(Active Retired Justice, Maine Superior Court)* Appointed by Governor Joseph E. Brennan to term beginning Oct 23, 1981. Reappointed 1989 and 1996. Current term expires 2005. Born Dallas Texas Nov 16, 1932. Roman Catholic. Educated at University of Detroit 1956-59 and University of Maine J.D. with honors 1962. Associate Editor University of Maine Law Review 1961-62. Admitted to practice Maine 1963, U.S. District Court District of Maine 1963, U.S. Court of Appeals First Circuit 1963 and U.S. Supreme Court 1978. In legal practice Freeport 1964-81.

Assistant Attorney General Augusta 1963. Commissioner Uniform State Laws 1972-76. Board of Directors National Center for State Courts 1996-99. Board of Trustees The National Judicial College since 2001. Member Maine Trial Lawyers Association (Board of Governors 1970-81, Secretary 1980-81), Maine State (Board of Governors 1970-81, Vice President 1974-76, President 1977) and American (House of Delegates 1978-81 and 1990-95, Delegate since 1984, Member 1985-95 and Chair 1991 Committee on Judicial Immunity, Member Nominating Committee 1986 and 1991, Vice Chair 1993-94, Chair Elect 1994-95 and Chair 1995-96 National Conference of State Trial Court Judges Judicial Administration Division; Board of Governors 1990-93; Search Committee for New ABA Executive Director 1990, Program Committee 1990-93 and Liaison to Section of Criminal Justice, National Conference of Special Court Judges and Government and Public Sector Lawyers Division 1990-93) Bar Associations. USNR 1951-57. AL3 USN 1953-55 (active duty). Democrat. Town Committee State Convention Delegate. Freeport Library Trustee 1964-72. Director 1968-1974 and Commodore 1972 Harraseeket Yacht Club. Coach Peewee Football 1976, Little League Baseball 1979-82 and Senior League Baseball 1983-85. Yarmouth Parent Teacher Council 1980-81. Corporator of Freeport Scholarship Foundation. Founder and Leader Port City Jazz, a jazz band playing jazz standards of the 20s, 30s and 40s. Plays lead trumpet, cornet and flugelhorn. Enjoys skiing, jogging, oil painting, silk screening, music and reading.

Mailing address: P.O. Box 287, Portland 04112-0287.

Office: Cumberland County Courthouse, 142 Federal Street, Portland 04101.

Telephone: (207) 822-4174.

Fax: (207) 822-4136

BRADLEY, Jane S. *(Judge, Maine District Court)* Appointed by governor.

Mailing address: P.O. Box 412, Portland 04112.

Telephone: (207) 822-4269.

BRENNAN, G. Arthur *(Justice, Maine Superior Court)* Appointed by governor. Former Judge-at-Large, Maine District Court.

Mailing address: P.O. Box 160, Alfred 04002-0160.

Office: York County Courthouse, Court Street, Alfred 04002.

Telephone: (207) 490-4943.

BROWNELL, William S. *(Magistrate Judge, United States District Court District of Maine)* Appointed by U.S. District Court judges to term beginning Jan 8, 1979. Subsequently reappointed. Serves part time. Also serves as Clerk of Court. Born Plainfield New Jersey May 8, 1946. Educated at University of Maine B.A. 1968 J.D. 1971.

Office: Federal Courthouse, 156 Federal Street, Portland 04101.

Telephone: (207) 780-3357.

CALKINS, Susan W. *(Associate Justice, Maine Supreme Judicial Court)* Appointed by Governor Angus S. King, Jr. to term beginning 1998. Educated at University of Colorado, University of Maine School of Law J.D. and University of Virginia LL.M. Former Judge, Maine District Court District Thirteen. Former Chief Judge, Maine District Court. Former Justice, Maine Superior Court.

Mailing address: P.O. Box 368, Portland 04112-0368.

Office: Cumberland County Courthouse, 142 Federal Street, Portland 04101.

Telephone: (207) 822-4135.

CARTER, Gene *(Senior Judge, United States District Court District of Maine)* Appointed for life by President Ronald Reagan to term beginning July 5, 1983. Former Chief Judge. Assumed Senior status Jan 2, 2003, serves by assignment. Born Milbridge Maine Nov 1, 1935. Educated at University of Maine B.A. 1958 and New York University School of Law LL.B. 1961. Honorary LL.D. University of Maine 1985. Recipient Elihu Root-Samuel J. Tilden Scholarship. Law Clerk to Hon. J. Spencer Bell, U.S. Court of Appeals Fourth Circuit. Member Phi Beta Kappa and Phi Kappa Phi. Admitted to practice Maine 1962. In legal practice Bangor 1965-80. Associate Justice, Supreme Judicial Court of Maine 1980-83.

Chairman Housing Authority City of Bangor 1973-78. Member 1966-75 and Chairman 1976-80 Supreme Judicial Court's Advisory Committee on the Maine Rules of Civil Procedure. Fellow American College of Trial Lawyers and International Society of Barristers. Former member The Defense Research Institute, Inc., American Judicature Society and American Bar Association. Member The American Law Institute, Maine Trial Lawyers Association, Penobscot County (Past President) and Maine State (Former Chairman Litigation Section) Bar Associations. Captain USAR JAGC.

Office: Federal Courthouse, 156 Federal Street, Portland 04101.

Telephone: (207) 780-3662.

CLAPP, Douglas A. *(Judge, Maine District Court)* Appointed to District Four by Governor Joseph E. Brennan to term beginning May 6, 1986. Appointed to District Twelve by Governor John R. McKernan, Jr. 1991. Reappointed by Governor Angus S. King, Jr. 1998, current term expires 2005. Born Walpole Massachusetts Sept 18, 1945. Educated at Ohio Wesleyan University B.A. in History 1967 and American University J.D. 1970. Admitted to practice Maryland 1971, Maine 1972, U.S. District Court District of Maine, U.S. Court of Appeals First Circuit and U.S. Supreme Court. In legal practice Pittsfield Maine 1972-82.

Commissioner Maine Workers' Compensation Com-

CLAPP, DOUGLAS A.—*Continued*
mission 1982-86. Member Maine Trial Lawyers Association, Maine State and American Bar Associations.
Mailing address: P.O. Box 525, Skowhegan 04976-0525.
Office: 47 Court Street, Skowhegan 04976.
Telephone: (207) 474-9518.

CLIFFORD, Robert W. *(Associate Justice, Maine Supreme Judicial Court)* Appointed by Governor Joseph E. Brennan to term beginning Aug 1, 1986. Reappointed 1993 and 2000. Current term expires 2007. Born Lewiston Maine May 2, 1937. Roman Catholic. Educated at Bowdoin College A.B. with honors in Political Science 1959, Boston College Law School J.D. 1962 and University of Virginia School of Law LL.M. 1998. Member Sigma Nu. Admitted to practice Maine 1962 and U.S. District Court 1965. In legal practice Lewiston 1962 and 1964-79. Justice June 8, 1979 to July 31, 1986 and Chief Justice Jan 1, 1984 to July 31, 1986, Maine Superior Court.
Member Lewiston City Council 1968-70 (President 1969). Mayor Lewiston 1971-72. Member Maine Senate 1973-76. Chairman Lewiston Charter Commission 1978-79. Member Androscoggin County and Maine State Bar Associations. Captain U.S. Army 1962-64. Member Auburn-Lewiston Kiwanis Club 1965-79 (President 1971-72).
Mailing address: P.O. Box 3488, Auburn 04212-3488.
Office: Androscoggin County Courthouse, Two Turner Street, Auburn 04210.
Telephone: (207) 783-5425.
Fax: (207) 783-5441

COHEN, David M. *(Magistrate Judge, United States District Court District of Maine)* Appointed by U.S. District Court judges to term beginning Oct 11, 1988. Reappointed Oct 11, 1996, current term expires Oct 10, 2004. Born Manchester New Hampshire Nov 8, 1942. Jewish. Educated at Bowdoin College A.B. with honors 1964 and Boston College Law School LL.B. with honors 1967. Member Order of the Coif. Admitted to practice Maine 1967, Massachusetts 1967 and U.S. District Court District of Maine 1967. In legal practice Portland Maine 1968-88.
Member Cumberland County and Maine State Bar Associations.
Office: Federal Courthouse, 156 Federal Street, Portland 04101.
Telephone: (207) 780-3360.

COLE, Roland A. *(Justice, Maine Superior Court)* Appointed by governor. Chief Justice 1995-97. Educated at University of Maine. Former Judge, Maine District Court District Ten, appointed by Governor Joseph E. Brennan to term beginning May 29, 1981.
Assistant County Attorney Washington County 1969-70. County Attorney 1973-74 and Public Administrator 1978-81 York County.
Mailing address: P.O. Box 287, Portland 04112-0287.
Office: Cumberland County Courthouse, 142 Federal Street, Portland 04101.
Telephone: (207) 822-4174.

COLLINS, Samuel W., Jr. *(Active Retired Justice, Maine Supreme Judicial Court)* Appointed Associate Justice by Governor John R. McKernan, Jr. to term beginning Sept 16, 1988. Appointed Active Retired Justice by governor. Born Caribou Maine Sept 17, 1923. Universalist. Educated at University of Maine B.A. 1944 and Harvard Law School LL.B. 1947. Member Phi Beta Kappa and Phi Kappa Phi. Admitted to practice Maine 1947, Massachusetts 1947, U.S. District Court District of Maine 1948 and U.S. Tax Court 1949. In legal practice Rockland Maine 1947-88.
State Senator Maine 1975-84. Member State Court Library Committee since 1988 and Judicial Legislative Committee since 1988. Clerk Intelligence Division U.S. War Department 1944.
Office: Knox County Courthouse, 62 Union Street, Rockland 04841.
Telephone: (207) 594-2254.

COTE, Paul A., Jr. *(Judge, Maine District Court)* Appointed by governor.
Mailing address: P.O. Box 1345, Lewiston 04243-1345.
Telephone: (207) 783-5403.

CROWLEY, Robert E. *(Justice, Maine Superior Court)* Appointed by governor. Born Boston Massachusetts June 1, 1946. Catholic. Educated at Georgetown University A.B. 1968 J.D. 1971. Admitted to practice Maine 1971 and Massachusetts 1972. Began legal practice Boston Massachusetts 1972. In legal practice Kennebunk Maine 1974. Former Judge, York County Probate Court, elected to term beginning Jan 1, 1983. Former Judge-at-Large, Maine District Court.
Former Instructor in Real Estate Law University of Southern Maine. President Maine Probate Judges Assembly 1986-87. Member York County and Maine State Bar Associations. Captain U.S. Army 1971-72.
Mailing address: P.O. Box 287, Portland 04112-0287.
Office: Cumberland County Courthouse, 142 Federal Street, Portland 04101.
Telephone: (207) 822-4151.

DAIGLE, Ronald A. *(Judge, Maine District Court)* Appointed by governor.
Office: 144 Sweden Street, Caribou 04736.
Telephone: (207) 493-3144.

DANA, Howard H., Jr. *(Associate Justice, Maine Supreme Judicial Court)* Appointed by Governor John R. McKernan, Jr. to term beginning 1993. Reappointed by Governor Angus S. King, Jr. 2000, current term expires 2007. Educated at Bowdoin College 1962, Cornell University J.D. 1966 LL.M. in Public Administration 1966 and University of Virginia LL.M. in Judicial Process 1998.
Mailing address: P.O. Box 368, Portland 04112-0368.
Office: Cumberland County Courthouse, 142 Federal Street, Portland 04101.
Telephone: (207) 822-4175.

DELAHANTY, Thomas E., II *(Justice, Maine Superior Court)* Appointed by Governor Joseph E. Brennan to term beginning Nov 4, 1983. Reappointed April 23, 1991 and 1998. Current term expires April 2005. Chief Justice June 1990 to June 1995. Born Lewiston Maine June 6, 1945. Roman Catholic. Educated at St. Michael's College B.A. 1967 and University of Maine J.D. 1970. Honorary LL.D. St. Michael's College 1997. Admitted to practice Maine 1970, U.S. District Court District of Maine 1970, U.S. Supreme Court 1979 and U.S. Court of Appeals First Circuit 1980. In legal practice Lewiston 1970-74 and 1981-83, Auburn 1975-80 and

DELAHANTY, THOMAS E., II—*Continued*
Portland 1980-81. Bail Commissioner 1981-83. Complaint Justice 1982-83.

Assistant County Attorney 1971-72 and County Attorney 1973-74 Androscoggin County. District Attorney Androscoggin, Franklin and Oxford Counties 1975-80. U.S. Attorney District of Maine 1980-81. Member National District Attorneys Association (Board of Directors 1973-79, Vice President 1979-80), Androscoggin County (Vice President 1982, President 1983) and Maine State (Board of Governors 1981-83) Bar Associations.

Mailing address: P.O. Box 3660, Auburn 04212-3660.
Office: Androscoggin County Courthouse, Two Turner Street, Auburn 04210.
Telephone: (207) 783-5440.

DEVINE, Bernard M. *(Active Retired Judge, Maine District Court)* Appointed by governor. Former Chief Judge.

Office: 205 Newbury Street, Portland 04101.
Telephone: (207) 822-4171.

DOUGLAS, Wayne R. *(Judge, Maine District Court)* Appointed by governor.

Office: 447 Main Street, Springvale 04083.
Telephone: (207) 459-1400.

EGGERT, E. Paul *(Judge, Maine District Court)* Appointed by Governor Angus S. King, Jr.

Mailing address: P.O. Box 412, Portland 04112.
Telephone: (207) 822-4269.

FIELD, Joseph H. *(Judge, Maine District Court)* Appointed by Governor John R. McKernan, Jr. July 1990 to term beginning Nov 1, 1990. Reappointed by Governor Angus S. King, Jr. 1997, current term expires 2004. Born Weston Massachusetts Dec 28, 1946. Unitarian. Educated at Harvard University A.B. with honors 1969 and University of Maine School of Law J.D. 1976. Admitted to practice Maine 1976, Massachusetts 1976, U.S. District Courts District of Maine 1976 and District of Massachusetts 1987, U.S. Court of Appeals First Circuit 1983 and U.S. Supreme Court 1985. In legal practice Brunswick Maine 1980-90.

Assistant District Attorney Prosecutorial District Six 1976-80. Member Maine Trial Lawyers Association and Maine State Bar Association. Commander USCGR 1969-92 (retired). Enjoys music and sailing.

Office: 147 New Meadow Road, West Bath 04530-9704.
Telephone: (207) 442-0200.

FOSTER, Christine *(Judge, Maine District Court)* Appointed by governor. Former Deputy Chief Judge.

Office: 25 Adams Street, Biddeford 04005.
Telephone: (207) 283-1147.

FRENCH, Rae Ann *(Judge, Maine District Court)* Appointed by Governor John R. McKernan, Jr. to term beginning 1991. Reappointed by Governor Angus S. King, Jr. to term beginning April 5, 2000, current term expires April 2007.

Office: 145 State Street, Augusta 04330-7495.
Telephone: (207) 287-8075.

FRITZSCHE, Paul A. *(Justice, Maine Superior Court)* Appointed by Governor Joseph E. Brennan to term beginning July 31, 1986. Reappointed by Governor John R. McKernan, Jr. 1993 and Governor Angus S. King, Jr. 2000. Current term expires Sept 1, 2007. Born Worcester Massachusetts July 20, 1950. Educated at Worcester Polytechnic Institute B.S. with honors 1972 and University of Maine School of Law J.D. with honors 1975. Admitted to practice Maine 1975, Massachusetts 1975, U.S. District Court District of Maine 1975 and U.S. Supreme Court 1979.

Attorney Pine Tree Legal Assistance 1975-81. Public Advocate Maine 1981-86.

Mailing address: P.O. Box 160, Alfred 04002-0160.
Office: York County Courthouse, Court Street 04002.
Telephone: (207) 324-5122.
Fax: (207) 490-2461

GORANITES, Peter J. *(Judge, Maine District Court)* Appointed by Governor John R. McKernan, Jr. March 4, 1988. Reappointed Nov 30, 1988, Nov 1995 and Nov 2002. Current term expires Nov 2009. Born Lewiston Maine Feb 3, 1948. Greek Orthodox. Educated at University of Maine B.A. 1970 J.D. 1973. Admitted to practice Maine 1973, U.S. District Court District of Maine 1973 and U.S. Supreme Court 1979. In legal practice Portland 1976-88.

Assistant Attorney General 1973-76. Instructor University of Maine 1974 and 1976. Member Cumberland and Maine State Bar Associations.

Mailing address: P.O. Box 412, Portland 04112.
Telephone: (207) 822-4269.

GORMAN, Ellen A. *(Justice, Maine Superior Court)* Appointed by Governor Angus S. King, Jr. Former Judge, Maine District Court.

Mailing address: P.O. Box 3660, Auburn 04212-3660.
Office: Androscoggin County Courthouse, Two Turner Street, Auburn 04210.
Telephone: (207) 783-5440.

GRIFFITHS, David B. *(Judge, Maine District Court)* Appointed by Governor John R. McKernan, Jr. to term beginning Sept 23, 1988. Reappointed 1995 and 2002. Current term expires Sept 2009. Born Presque Isle Maine Nov 14, 1936. Congregationalist. Educated at University of Maine, Orono B.A. 1958 and Boston University School of Law J.D. 1961. Admitted to practice Maine 1961 and U.S. District Court District of Maine 1962. In legal practice Presque Isle 1961-88.

Instructor University of Maine, Presque Isle 1967-74. Member Aroostook County (President 1987-88) and Maine State Bar Associations. Member 1985-88 and Chairman 1988 City Council Presque Isle. Member Presque Isle Industrial Council 1986-88. Past President Aroostook Mental Health Services, Inc. Director School Administrative District One 1967-69 and Maine State School Board Association 1968-69. Scoutmaster Troup 168 Boy Scouts of America 1975-85. Trustee Aroostook Medical Center since 1988. Senior Deacon and Trustee Presque Isle Congregational Church. Member Kiwanis Club and Presque Isle Country Club. Enjoys playing golf, biking, skiing, running, sailing, camping and photography.

Mailing address: P.O. Box 794, Presque Isle 04769.
Telephone: (207) 764-2055.

GUNTHER, Jessie B. *(Judge, Maine District Court)* Appointed by Governor James B. Longley Jan 21, 1976. Reappointed by Governor John R. McKernan, Jr. Sept 27, 1990 and Governor Angus S. King, Jr. 1997. Current term expires 2004. Born Philipsburg Montana Aug 4, 1947. Episcopalian. Educated at Wells College A.B. with honors 1969 and Dickinson School of Law J.D.

GUNTHER, JESSIE B.—*Continued*

with honors 1972. Staff member Dickinson Law Review 1971-72. Admitted to practice Maine 1972 and U.S. District Court District of Maine 1972. In legal practice Augusta 1972-76. Justice, Maine Superior Court 1980-86.

Instructor University College 1986-87 and Department of Public Administration 1989-90 University of Maine. Member Piscataquis County and Maine State Bar Associations.

Office: 73 Hammond Street, Bangor 04401.
Telephone: (207) 941-3040.

HAINES, James B., Jr. *(Chief Judge, United States Bankruptcy Court District of Maine)* Appointed by U.S. Court of Appeals First Circuit judges. Also Judge, Bankruptcy Appellate Panel First Circuit. Selected by the Judicial Council of the First Circuit.

Office: 537 Congress Street, Portland 04101.
Telephone: (207) 780-3653.

HJELM, Jeffrey L. *(Justice, Maine Superior Court)* Appointed by Governor Angus S. King, Jr. Former Judge, Maine District Court.

Office: Penobscot County Courthouse, 97 Hammond Street, Bangor 04401-4913.
Telephone: (207) 561-2310.

HORNBY, D. Brock *(Judge, United States District Court District of Maine)* Magistrate 1982-88. Appointed Judge for life by President George Bush to term beginning May 1990. Chief Judge 1996 to Jan 2, 2003. Born April 21, 1944. Educated at University of Western Ontario B.A. Honours 1965 and Harvard University J.D. cum laude 1969. Harvard Fellowship. Recipient Gold Medal for Academic Excellence. Supreme Court Note and Development Editor Harvard Law Review. Law Clerk to Hon. John Minor Wisdom, U.S. Court of Appeals Fifth Circuit 1969-70. Admitted to practice Maine, Virginia and U.S. Supreme Court. In legal practice Portland Maine 1974-82. Associate Justice, Supreme Judicial Court of Maine 1988-90.

Author "Innovations Break Asbestos Logjam" 3 *Maine Trial Practice* 33, 1987, "A Note of Sadness and a Note of Joy" 12 No. 2 Alternatives to the High Cost of Litigation 19, 1994, "Federal Court-Annexed ADR: After the Hoopla" 7 *FJC Directions* 26, 1994, "Appellate Judges: Think Before You Publish" 22 No. 2 *Litigation* 3, 1996, "Recent Judicial Conference Recommendations for Achieving Cost and Delay Reduction in the Federal Courts" 37 No. 2 *Judge's Journal* American Bar Association 12, 1998, "Embracing Change: Aligning People and Technology" 2 No. 8 FCCA Journal 5 Winter 1999 and "How Jurors See Us" 14 No. 3 Maine B. Jour. 174 July 1999. Assistant Professor 1970-73 and Associate Professor 1973-74 University of Virginia School of Law. Member Maine Law-Related Education Advisory Board 1994-98. Chair Committee on District Judge Education Federal Judicial Center 1995-98. Fellow Maine Bar Foundation (Board of Directors 1990-93) and American Bar Foundation. Advisor Project to Produce *Restatement (Third) of Restitution.* Member Subcommittee on Court ADR Program Design and Judicial Project Advisory Council CPR Institute for Dispute Resolution, The American Law Institute (Council Member), Judicial Conference of the U.S. (Subcommittee on Judicial Improvements 1985-88, Member 1990-2000 and Chair 1997-2000 Committee on Court Administration and Case Management, First Circuit District Judge Representative since 2000), Cumberland County, Maine State and American Bar Associations. Lecturer on civil and jury trial proceedings, case management and hearing techniques Federal Judicial Center since 1987 and Administrative Law Judges Social Security Administration 1991 and 1993. Board of Visitors University of Maine School of Law.

Office: Federal Courthouse, 156 Federal Street, Portland 04101.
Telephone: (207) 780-3280.

HORTON, Andrew M. *(Judge, Maine District Court)* Appointed by Governor Angus S. King, Jr.

Mailing address: P.O. Box 412, Portland 04112.
Telephone: (207) 822-4269.

HUMPHREY, Thomas E. *(Justice, Maine Superior Court)* Appointed by Governor Angus S. King, Jr. Former Judge and Deputy Chief Judge, Maine District Court.

Mailing address: P.O. Box 287, Portland 04112-0287.
Office: Cumberland County Courthouse, 142 Federal Street, Portland 04101.
Telephone: (207) 822-4151.

HUNTER, E. Allen *(Justice, Maine Superior Court)* Appointed by Governor Angus S. King, Jr.

Office: Aroostook County Courthouse, 144 Sweden Street, Caribou 04736-2399.
Telephone: (207) 947-8606.

JABAR, Joseph M. *(Justice, Maine Superior Court)* Appointed by Governor Angus S. King, Jr.

Mailing address: P.O. Box 725, Skowhegan 04976-0725.
Office: Somerset County Courthouse, Court Street, Skowhegan 04976.
Telephone: (207) 622-7475.

JANELLE, Andre G. *(Judge, Maine District Court)* Appointed by governor. Former Deputy Chief Judge.

Office: 25 Adams Street, Biddeford 04005.
Telephone: (207) 283-1147.

KENNEDY, John David *(Judge, Maine District Court)* Appointed by governor.

Mailing address: P.O. Box 95, Springvale 04083-0095.
Telephone: (207) 459-1400.

KORNREICH, Louis H. *(Judge, United States Bankruptcy Court District of Maine)* Appointed by U.S. Court of Appeals First Circuit judges to term beginning April 3, 2001. Term expires April 2015.

Mailing address: P.O. Box 1109, Bangor 04402-1109.
Office: Federal Building, Bangor 04401.
Telephone: (207) 945-0550.

KRAVCHUK, Margaret J. *(Magistrate Judge, United States District Court District of Maine)* Appointed by U.S. District Court judges to term beginning Jan 21, 2000. Term expires Jan 21, 2008. Born Pittsburgh Pennsylvania July 14, 1948. Educated at Bethany College B.A. summa cum laude 1970, Brown University M.A.T. 1971 and University of Maine J.D. 1976. Admitted to practice Maine 1976 and U.S. District Court District of Maine 1976. Judge, Maine District Court District Three Feb 8, 1985 to March 26, 1990, appointed by Governor Joseph Brennan. Justice and Chief Justice, Maine Supe-

KRAVCHUK, MARGARET J.—*Continued*
rior Court, March 27, 1990 to Jan 20, 2000, appointed by Governor John R. McKernan, Jr.
Mailing address: P.O. Box 2578, Bangor 04402-2578.
Telephone: (207) 945-0315.

LAWRENCE, Rick E. *(Judge, Maine District Court)* Appointed by Governor Angus S. King, Jr.
Mailing address: P.O. Box 412, Portland 04112.
Telephone: (207) 822-4269.

LEVY, Jon D. *(Associate Justice, Maine Supreme Judicial Court)* Appointed by Governor Angus S. King, Jr. to term beginning 2002. Former Judge, Deputy Chief Judge and Chief Judge, Maine District Court.
Mailing address: P.O. Box 368, Portland 04112-0368.
Office: Cumberland County Courthouse, 142 Federal Street, Portland 04101.
Telephone: (207) 822-4227.

MacMICHAEL, James E. *(Judge, Maine District Court)* Appointed by governor.
Mailing address: P.O. Box 525, Skowhegan 04976.
Telephone: (207) 474-9518.

MARDEN, Donald H. *(Justice, Maine Superior Court)* Appointed by governor. Born Waterville Maine 1936. Educated at University of Maine, Cornell University B.S. 1958 and Boston University J.D. 1964. Awarded honorary LL.D. Unity College 1979. Admitted to practice Maine 1964. In legal practice 1964-94.
Assistant County Attorney 1971-72 and County Attorney 1973-74 Kennebec County. Member Grievance Commission 1979-87 and Member 1984-91 Board of Overseers of Bar (State Judge Advocate 1984-86, Deputy Adjutant General 1986-94). Member Waterville, Kennebec County and Maine State Bar Associations. U.S. Army 1959-61, USAR 1961-64 and National Guard 1964-94. Board of Aldermen 1966-67 and Mayor 1968-69 Waterville.
Office: Kennebec County Courthouse, 95 State Street, Augusta 04330-5680.
Telephone: (207) 622-7475.
E-mail address: dhmarden@gwi.net

McELWEE, John D. *(Judge, Maine District Court)* Appointed by Governor Angus S. King, Jr.
Office: Municipal Building, Congress Street, Rumford 04276.
Telephone: (207) 364-7171.

MEAD, Andrew *(Justice, Maine Superior Court)* Appointed by Governor John R. McKernan, Jr. Reappointed 1999, current term expires June 1, 2006. Former Chief Justice. Born Glen Ridge New Jersey July 9, 1951. Congregationalist. Educated at University of Maine B.A. 1973 and New York Law School J.D. 1976. Admitted to practice Maine 1976. In legal practice Bangor 1976-90. Judge, Penobscot Tribal Court 1978-90.
President Maine State Bar Association since 1990.
Office: Penobscot County Courthouse, 97 Hammond Street, Bangor 04401-4913.
Telephone: (207) 561-2310.

MILLS, Nancy *(Chief Justice, Maine Superior Court)* Appointed by Governor John R. McKernan, Jr. to term beginning 1993. Reappointed by Governor Angus S. King, Jr. 2000, current term expires 2007. Former Judge-at-Large, Maine District Court.
Mailing address: P.O. Box 287, Portland 04112-0287.
Office: Cumberland County Courthouse, 142 Federal Street, Portland 04101.
Telephone: (207) 822-4174.

MULLEN, Robert E. *(Deputy Chief Judge, Maine District Court)* Appointed by governor.
Office: 129 Main Street, Farmington 04938.
Telephone: (207) 778-8200.

MURRAY, Ann M. *(Judge, Maine District Court)* Appointed by Governor Angus S. King, Jr.
Office: 73 Hammond Street, Bangor 04401.
Telephone: (207) 941-3040.

NIVISON, John C. *(Judge, Maine District Court)* Appointed by Governor Angus S. King, Jr.
Mailing address: P.O. Box 397, Waterville 04903-0397.
Office: 18 Colby Street, Waterville 04901.
Telephone: (207) 873-2103.

PERKINS, Stephen L. *(Active Retired Justice, Maine Superior Court)* Appointed by governor.
Mailing address: P.O. Box 287, Portland 04112-0287.
Office: Cumberland County Courthouse, 142 Federal Street, Portland 04101.
Telephone: (207) 822-4174.

PERRY, Courtland D., II *(Active Retired Judge, Maine District Court)* Appointed by Governor James B. Longley to term beginning Oct 13, 1976. Reappointed 1984, 1991 and 1998. Current term expires April 2005. Born Portland Maine July 28, 1936. Lutheran. Educated at University of Maine, University of Virginia LL.B. 1961 and George Washington University LL.M. 1968. Admitted to practice Maine 1961, U.S. District Court District of Maine 1962, U.S. Supreme Court 1968 and U.S. Court of Appeals First Circuit 1971.
Assistant Attorney General 1961-76. Author "Critique on Maine's Modified Durham Rule" Journal of Maine Medical Association 1966. Instructor Maine Criminal Justice Academy 1973-75. Member Augusta and Maine Jaycees 1962-70. Enjoys fishing.
Office: 145 State Street, Augusta 04330.
Telephone: (207) 287-8075.

POWERS, Keith A. *(Judge, Maine District Court)* Appointed by Governor Angus S. King, Jr.
Mailing address: P.O. Box 412, Portland 04112.
Telephone: (207) 822-4269.

ROMEI, John V. *(Judge, Maine District Court)* Appointed by governor.
Mailing address: P.O. Box 297, Machias 04654-0294.
Office: 47 Court Street, Machias 04654.
Telephone: (207) 255-3044.

RUDMAN, Paul L. *(Associate Justice, Maine Supreme Judicial Court)* Appointed by Governor John R. McKernan, Jr. to term beginning June 5, 1992. Reappointed 1999, current term expires June 4, 2006. Born Bangor Maine March 26, 1935. Jewish. Educated at Yale College A.B. 1957 and George Washington University National Law Center J.D. with honors 1960. Staff member George Washington University Law Review 1958-60. Member Phi Delta Phi. Admitted to practice Maine 1960 and District of Columbia 1960. In legal

RUDMAN, PAUL L.—*Continued*

practice Bangor Maine 1960-92. Captain Maine Air National Guard 1960-66.

Office: Penobscot County Courthouse, 97 Hammond Street, Bangor 04401-4913.

Telephone: (207) 561-2325.

RUSSELL, Ronald D. *(Judge, Maine District Court)* Appointed by governor.

Office: 73 Hammond Street, Bangor 04401.

Telephone: (207) 941-3040.

SAUFLEY, Leigh I. *(Chief Justice, Maine Supreme Judicial Court)* Appointed by Governor Angus S. King, Jr. Oct 1997. Chief Justice since Dec 6, 2001. First female chief justice to serve Maine Supreme Judicial Court. Educated at University of Maine at Orono 1976 and University of Maine School of Law J.D. 1980. Member Phi Beta Kappa. Judge-at-Large, Maine District Court 1990-93, appointed by Governor John R. McKernan, Jr. Justice, Maine Superior Court 1993-97, appointed by Governor John R. McKernan, Jr.

Mailing address: P.O. Box 368, Portland 04112-0368.

Office: Cumberland County Courthouse, 142 Federal Street, Portland 04101.

Telephone: (207) 822-4286.

SINGAL, George Z. *(Chief Judge, United States District Court District of Maine)* Appointed for life by President Bill Clinton to term beginning July 2000. Chief Judge since Jan 3, 2003. Born Florence Italy Oct 27, 1945. Educated at University of Maine B.A. 1967 and Harvard Law School J.D. 1970. In legal practice Maine 1970-2000. Complaint Justice, Bangor 1974.

Assistant County Attorney 1971-73.

Office: Federal Courthouse, 156 Federal Street, Portland 04101.

Telephone: (207) 780-3119.

STAPLES, Bernard C. *(Judge, Maine District Court)* Appointed by governor. Reappointed by Governor Angus S. King, Jr. to term beginning Feb 1996 and 2003. Current term expires Feb 2010. Born Rockland Maine Nov 4, 1932. Educated at Bates College A.B. 1955 and Boston University LL.B. 1961. Junior Editor Boston University Law Review 1959-61. Admitted to practice Maine 1961. In legal practice Bar Harbor 1963-89. Former Judge, Maine Probate Court.

County Attorney 1965-68. Member Maine Trial Judges Association, Hancock County, Maine State and American Bar Associations. Member Rotary Club.

Office: 50 State Street, Ellsworth 04605.

Telephone: (207) 667-7142.

STITHAM, Kevin L. *(Judge, Maine District Court)* Appointed by Governor Angus S. King, Jr.

Office: 59 East Main Street, Dover-Foxcroft 04426-1395.

Telephone: (207) 564-2240.

STUDSTRUP, Kirk *(Justice, Maine Superior Court)* Appointed by Governor Angus S. King, Jr. Oct 1997. Term expires 2004. Born Beloit Wisconsin July 11, 1944. Educated at Duke University B.A. 1967 and George Washington University J.D. 1974. Admitted to practice Maine 1974, U.S. District Court District of Maine 1975, U.S. Court of Appeals First Circuit 1977 and U.S. Supreme Court 1978. Judge and Chief Judge, Maine District Court 1984-97, appointed by Governor Joseph E. Brennan.

Member Maine State Bar Association. Lieutenant USNR July 1967 to April 1970.

Office: 95 State Street, Augusta 04330-5680.

Telephone: (207) 622-7475.

VAFIADES, Vendean V. *(Chief Judge, Maine District Court)* Appointed by Governor Angus S. King, Jr. Former Deputy Chief Judge.

Office: 145 State Street, Augusta 04330.

Telephone: (207) 287-8075.

WARREN, Thomas D. *(Justice, Maine Superior Court)* Appointed by Governor Angus S. King, Jr.

Mailing address: P.O. Box 287, Portland 04112-0287.

Office: Cumberland County Courthouse, 142 Federal Street, Portland 04101.

Telephone: (207) 822-4151.

WESTCOTT, Michael N. *(Judge, Maine District Court)* Appointed by governor. Former Chief Judge.

Mailing address: P.O. Box 249, Wiscasset 04578-0249.

Office: High Street, Wiscasset 04578.

Telephone: (207) 882-6363.

WHEELER, Joyce A. *(Judge, Maine District Court)* Appointed by Governor Angus S. King, Jr. Former Associate Judge, Maine Administrative Court.

Mailing address: P.O. Box 770, York 03909-0770.

Telephone: (207) 363-1230.

WORTH, Patricia G. *(Judge, Maine District Court)* Appointed by Governor Angus S. King, Jr.

Mailing address: P.O. Box 382, Belfast 04915.

Office: 103 Church Street, Belfast 04915.

Telephone: (207) 338-3107.

MARYLAND

Capital ANNAPOLIS

UNITED STATES DISTRICT COURT DISTRICT OF MARYLAND

United States District Court District of Maryland consists of two divisions. For descriptive information refer to the United States Courts section.

Northern Division includes Allegany, Anne Arundel, Baltimore, Caroline, Carroll, Cecil, Dorchester, Frederick, Garrett, Harford, Howard, Kent, Queen Anne's, Somerset, Talbot, Washington, Wicomico and Worcester counties and the city of Baltimore. The court sits at Baltimore, Cumberland and Denton.

Southern Division includes Calvert, Charles, Montgomery, Prince George's and St. Mary's counties. The court shall be held at a suitable site in Montgomery or Prince George's counties not more than five miles from the boundary of Montgomery and Prince George's counties.

Chief Judge

Benson Everett Legg

Judges

J. Frederick Motz
Peter J. Messitte
Catherine C. Blake
William D. Quarles
Deborah K. Chasanow
Alexander Williams, Jr.
Andre Maurice Davis
Richard D. Bennett

Senior Judges

Edward Skottowe Northrop
Frederic N. Smalkin
William M. Nickerson
Alexander Harvey, II
Walter E. Black, Jr.
Marvin J. Garbis

Clerk

Felicia C. Cannon
U.S. Courthouse
101 West Lombard Street
Baltimore, Maryland 21201-2690
(410) 962-2600

UNITED STATES MAGISTRATE JUDGES OF MARYLAND

Victor H. Laws, III
William Connelly
Paul W. Grimm
James K. Bredar
Beth P. Gesner
Jillyn K. Schulze
Susan K. Gauvey
Charles B. Day
Thomas M. DiGirolamo

UNITED STATES BANKRUPTCY COURT OF MARYLAND

Chief Judge

James F. Schneider

Judges

Paul Mannes
E. Stephen Derby
Duncan W. Keir

Bankruptcy Clerk

Mark Sammons
8308 U.S. Courthouse
101 West Lombard Street
Baltimore, Maryland 21201-2696
(410) 962-2688

COURT OF APPEALS OF MARYLAND

The Court of Appeals is Maryland's court of last resort. The court consists of a chief judge and six associate judges, one representing each of the seven appellate circuits. Judges are initially appointed by the governor and confirmed by the Senate and run for retention for ten-year terms at the next general election occurring at least one year after the appointment. Subsequent retention elections are held every ten years. Judges elected before 1977 served fifteen-year terms. From among the judges, the governor designates a chief judge as the constitutional administrative head of the courts system. Retirement is mandatory at age seventy; however, the court may recall retired judges for temporary service.

The court has exclusive appellate jurisdiction in criminal cases when judgment of death has been pronounced; when a question certified under the Uniform Certified Questions of Law Act is involved; or when a question on legislative redistricting or removal from certain offices is involved. The court exercises discretionary review of cases pending in or decided by the Court of Special Appeals and certain cases decided by a Circuit Court on appeal from the District Court or Motor Vehicle Administration when circumstances make review desirable and in the public interest. The court has rule-making and supervisory control over the lower courts and regulates admission to the bar and the conduct of its members and members of the bench.

The court sits en banc at Annapolis with five judges constituting a quorum.

FIRST APPELLATE CIRCUIT includes Caroline, Cecil, Dorchester, Kent, Queen Anne's, Somerset, Talbot, Wicomico and Worcester counties.

SECOND APPELLATE CIRCUIT includes Baltimore and Harford counties.

THIRD APPELLATE CIRCUIT includes Allegany, Carroll, Frederick, Garrett, Howard and Washington counties.

FOURTH APPELLATE CIRCUIT includes Prince George's County.

FIFTH APPELLATE CIRCUIT includes Anne Arundel, Calvert, Charles and St. Mary's counties.

COURT OF APPEALS OF MARYLAND—*Continued*

SIXTH APPELLATE CIRCUIT includes Baltimore City.

SEVENTH APPELLATE CIRCUIT includes Montgomery County.

Chief Judge
Robert M. Bell

Associate Judges

John C. Eldridge	Irma S. Raker
Alan M. Wilner	Dale R. Cathell
Glenn T. Harrell, Jr.	Lynne A. Battaglia

Clerk
Alexander L. Cummings
Courts of Appeal Building
361 Rowe Boulevard
Annapolis, Maryland 21401
(410) 260-1500
TTY (410) 260-1554

State Court Administrator
Frank Broccolina
Administrative Office of the Courts
Maryland Judicial Center
580 Taylor Avenue
Annapolis, Maryland 21401
(410) 260-1290

COURT OF SPECIAL APPEALS OF MARYLAND

The Court of Special Appeals is the intermediate appellate court in Maryland. The court is divided into the same appellate circuits as the Court of Appeals and consists of a chief judge and twelve associate judges, one elected to represent each of the seven appellate circuits and six elected to serve at large. Judges are initially appointed by the governor and confirmed by the Senate and run for retention for ten-year terms at the next general election occurring at least one year after the appointment. Subsequent retention elections are held every ten years. The chief judge is designated by the governor. Retirement is mandatory at age seventy; however, retired judges may be recalled for temporary service by the Court of Appeals.

The court has exclusive initial appellate jurisdiction over any reviewable judgment, decree, order or other action of a Circuit Court or an Orphans' Court except as provided by law. The court may also consider applications for leave to appeal in such areas as post conviction, habeas corpus matters involving denial of or excessive bail, inmate grievances, probation violations and victims' rights and from sentences entered upon guilty pleas.

The court may sit in panels of three judges, but a majority of the judges may order that any case be heard en banc. The court sits at Annapolis.

Chief Judge
Joseph F. Murphy, Jr.

Associate Judges

Arrie W. Davis	Ellen L. Hollander
James P. Salmon	James R. Eyler
Andrew L. Sonner	Deborah S. Eyler
James A. Kenney, III	Sally Denison Adkins
Peter B. Krauser	Mary Ellen Barbera
J. Frederick Sharer	Clayton Greene, Jr.

CIRCUIT COURTS OF MARYLAND

The Circuit Courts are courts of general unlimited trial jurisdiction in Maryland. There are twenty-four circuit courts grouped into eight judicial circuits: the first seven circuits each contain two or more counties; and on January 1, 1983, the former Supreme Bench of Baltimore City was consolidated into the Eighth Judicial Circuit. Judges are initially appointed by the governor and run for election to fifteen-year terms at the first general election occurring at least one year after appointment. The judges may be opposed by one or more qualified attorneys. If a judge's fifteen-year term expires the year before the next general election (held every other year), the governor appoints the judge to an interim appointment. At the next general election, the judge will again run for a fifteen-year term. Eight circuit administrative judges are appointed by the chief judge of the Court of Appeals to perform administrative duties in each of their respective circuits. They are assisted by county administrative judges. Retirement is mandatory at age seventy; however, retired judges may be recalled for temporary service by the Court of Appeals.

The Circuit Courts are the highest common law and equity courts of record exercising original jurisdiction within Maryland. The courts have full common law and equity powers and jurisdiction in all civil and criminal cases within their boundaries, and all the additional powers and jurisdiction conferred by the Constitution and by law, except where exclusive jurisdiction is conferred upon another court. The courts exercise appellate jurisdiction over the District Court, Orphans' Courts and certain administrative agencies. The courts have exclusive juvenile jurisdiction except in Montgomery County where the District Court exercises juvenile jurisdiction. The Circuit Courts of Montgomery and Harford counties also exercise Orphans' Court jurisdiction.

The courts sit at the county seats.

†County Administrative Judge

FIRST JUDICIAL CIRCUIT includes Dorchester, Somerset, Wicomico and Worcester counties. The courts sit at Cambridge, Princess Anne, Salisbury and Snow Hill.

Circuit Administrative Judge
Daniel M. Long† (Somerset)

County	Associate Judge
Dorchester	Donald F. Johnson†
Wicomico	D. William Simpson†
	Donald C. Davis
	Kathleen L. Beckstead
Worcester	Theodore R. Eschenburg†
	Thomas C. Groton, III

SECOND JUDICIAL CIRCUIT includes Caroline, Cecil, Kent, Queen Anne's and Talbot counties. The courts sit at Denton, Elkton, Chestertown, Centreville and Easton.

Circuit Administrative Judge
William S. Horne† (Talbot)

CIRCUIT COURTS OF MARYLAND—*Continued*

County	Associate Judge
Caroline	Karen A. Murphy Jensen†
Cecil	Dexter M. Thompson, Jr.†
	O. Robert Lidums
	Richard Eli Jackson
Kent	J. Frederick Price†
Queen Anne's	John W. Sause, Jr.†

THIRD JUDICIAL CIRCUIT includes Baltimore and Harford counties. The courts sit at Towson and Bel Air.

Circuit Administrative Judge
John Grason Turnbull, II† (Baltimore)

County	Associate Judge
Baltimore	John F. Fader, II
	Dana Mark Levitz
	Christian M. Kahl
	Thomas J. Bollinger, Sr.
	J. Norris Byrnes
	John O. Hennegan
	Lawrence R. Daniels
	Robert E. Cadigan
	Kathleen Gallogly Cox
	Robert N. Dugan
	Susan Souder
	Ruth A. Jakubowski
	Michael J. Finifter
	Vicki Ballou-Watts
	Patrick Cavanaugh
Harford	William O. Carr†
	Maurice W. Baldwin, Jr.
	Stephen M. Waldron
	Thomas E. Marshall
	Emory A. Plitt, Jr.

FOURTH JUDICIAL CIRCUIT includes Allegany, Garrett and Washington counties. The courts sit at Cumberland, Oakland and Hagerstown.

Circuit Administrative Judge
Frederick C. Wright, III† (Washington)

County	Associate Judge
Allegany	Gary George Leasure†
	W. Timothy Finan
Garrett	James L. Sherbin†
Washington	John H. McDowell
	W. Kennedy Boone, III
	Donald E. Beachley

FIFTH JUDICIAL CIRCUIT includes Anne Arundel, Carroll and Howard counties. The courts sit at Annapolis, Westminster and Ellicott City.

Circuit Administrative Judge
Diane O. Leasure† (Howard)

County	Associate Judge
Anne Arundel	Pamela L. North
	Ronald A. Silkworth
	Michael E. Loney
	Joseph P. Manck†
	Philip T. Caroom
	Nancy L. Davis-Loomis
	Paul A. Hackner
	David S. Bruce
Anne Arundel—Cont.	Michele Dane Jaklitsch
	Rodney C. Warren
Carroll	Luke K. Burns, Jr.
	Raymond E. Beck, Sr.†
	Michael M. Galloway
Howard	Raymond J. Kane, Jr.
	James B. Dudley
	Dennis M. Sweeney
	Lenore R. Gelfman

SIXTH JUDICIAL CIRCUIT includes Frederick and Montgomery counties. The courts sit at Frederick and Rockville.

Circuit Administrative Judge
Paul H. Weinstein† (Montgomery)

County	Associate Judge
Frederick	G. Edward Dwyer, Jr.†
	Mary Ann Stepler
	John H. Tisdale
	Julie R. Stevenson
Montgomery	DeLawrence Beard
	Paul A. McGuckian
	James L. Ryan
	Ann S. Harrington
	S. Michael Pincus
	D. Warren Donohue
	Michael D. Mason
	Durke G. Thompson
	Louise G. Scrivener
	Nelson W. Rupp, Jr.
	Patrick L. Woodward
	Eric M. Johnson
	Ann Newman Sundt
	William J. Rowan, III
	John W. Debelius, III
	Dennis M. McHugh
	Katherine D. Savage
	Marielsa A. Bernard
	Joseph Aloysius Dugan, Jr.

SEVENTH JUDICIAL CIRCUIT includes Calvert, Charles, Prince George's and St. Mary's counties. The courts sit at Prince Frederick, La Plata, Upper Marlboro and Leonardtown.

Circuit Administrative Judge
William D. Missouri† (Prince George's)

County	Associate Judge
Calvert	Warren J. Krug†
	Marjorie L. Clagett
Charles	Robert C. Nalley†
	Steven G. Chappelle
	Christopher C. Henderson
	Amy Janel Bragunier
Prince George's	Robert J. Woods
	Graydon S. McKee, III
	Steven I. Platt
	Larnzell Martin, Jr.
	Richard H. Sothoron, Jr.
	C. Philip Nichols, Jr.
	William B. Spellbring, Jr.
	Thomas P. Smith
	E. Allen Shepherd
	Sherrie L. Krauser
	Michele D. Hotten

CIRCUIT COURTS OF MARYLAND—*Continued*

Prince George's—Cont.	Sheila R. Tillerson Adams
	James J. Lombardi
	Toni E. Clarke
	Maureen M. Lamasney
	Herman C. Dawson
	Michael P. Whalen
	Ronald D. Schiff
	Julia Beth Weatherly
	Dwight David Jackson
	Melanie M. Shaw Geter
	Sean D. Wallace
St. Mary's	Marvin S. Kaminetz†
	C. Clarke Raley
	Karen H. Abrams

EIGHTH JUDICIAL CIRCUIT includes Baltimore City.

Circuit Administrative Judge
Ellen M. Heller†

Associate Judges

Joseph H. H. Kaplan	Thomas E. Noel
Clifton J. Gordy, Jr.	John N. Prevas
John C. Themelis	Paul A. Smith
Joseph P. McCurdy, Jr.	Martin P. Welch
Carol E. Smith	Albert J. Matricciani, Jr.
David W. Young	Thomas Waxter, Jr.
Bonita J. Dancy	Allen L. Schwait
Evelyn Omega Cannon	Marcella A. Holland
Alfred Nance	Stuart R. Berger
M. Brooke Murdock	Audrey J. S. Carrion
Wanda Keyes Heard	John M. Glynn
Kaye A. Allison	Lynn Kellene Stewart
John Philip Miller	Edward R. K. Hargadon
Shirley Marie Watts	
Althea M. Handy	

MARYLAND DISTRICT COURT

The District Court is a court of statewide limited jurisdiction in Maryland and is divided into twelve districts. Judges are appointed by the governor with the consent of the Senate for ten-year terms. The chief judge of the Court of Appeals designates one district court judge as chief judge of the court. An administrative judge for each district is appointed by the chief judge of the court. Retired judges may be recalled for temporary service by the Court of Appeals.

The court has exclusive civil jurisdiction when the amount in controversy is $2,500 or less and in cases involving landlord and tenant, forcible entry and detainer, replevin actions, peace orders and other cases as provided by law. The court has concurrent civil jurisdiction with the Circuit Court in actions when the amount in controversy is more than $2,500 but does not exceed $25,000 with limited exceptions. The court has exclusive criminal jurisdiction in cases when the penalty is less than three years imprisonment and/or a $2,500 fine and concurrent criminal jurisdiction with the Circuit Court in other misdemeanors and certain felony cases. The court may also hold felony preliminary hearings. The court holds no jury trials; a defendant who is entitled to and chooses a jury trial must proceed to the Circuit Court. Commissioners issue arrest warrants and set bail or collateral. The District Court exercises juvenile jurisdiction in Montgomery County only.

The court sits at the county seats and as specified.

Chief Judge
James N. Vaughan

DISTRICT ONE includes Baltimore City.

Administrative Judge
Keith E. Mathews

Associate Judges

Charlotte M. Cooksey	H. Gary Bass
Askew W. Gatewood, Jr.	Theodore B. Oshrine
Kathleen M. Sweeney	Barbara Baer Waxman
Jamey H. Weitzman	C. Yvonne Holt-Stone
Gale E. Rasin	Norman E. Johnson, Jr.
Nancy B. Shuger	Jack I. Lesser
Ben C. Clyburn	Charles A. Chiapparelli
Timothy J. Doory	George Lipman
John R. Hargrove, Jr.	Timothy D. Murphy
Emanuel Brown	Miriam Brown Hutchins
Nathan Braverman	Catherine J. O'Malley
Ronald Alan Karasic	Jeannie Jinkyung Hong
Halee F. Weinstein	

DISTRICT TWO includes Dorchester, Somerset, Wicomico and Worcester counties. The court sits at Cambridge, Princess Anne, Salisbury and Snow Hill.

Administrative Judge
John L. Norton, III

Associate Judges
R. Scott Davis
Richard R. Bloxom
Lloyd O. Whitehead
R. Patrick Hayman

DISTRICT THREE includes Caroline, Cecil, Kent, Queen Anne's and Talbot counties. The court sits at Denton, Elkton, Chestertown, Centreville and Easton.

Administrative Judge
James C. McKinney

Associate Judges
John T. Clark, III
William H. Adkins, III
Floyd L. Parks
Stephen J. Baker
Douglas H. Everngam

DISTRICT FOUR includes Calvert, Charles and St. Mary's counties. The court sits at Prince Frederick, La Plata and Leonardtown.

Administrative Judge
Stephen L. Clagett

Associate Judges
Gary S. Gasparovic
Richard A. Cooper
John F. Slade, III

DISTRICT FIVE includes Prince George's County. The court sits at Upper Marlboro.

Administrative Judge
Thurman H. Rhodes, Sr.

MARYLAND DISTRICT COURT—*Continued*

Associate Judges

Patrice E. Lewis
Thomas J. Love
Joel D. Worshtil
Hassan Ali El-Amin
Mark Thomas O'Brien
Leo Edward Green, Jr.
Josef B. Brown
Beverly J. Woodard
Robert Wilson Heffron
Jean Szekeres Baron
Richard Angelo Palumbo
Albert Willis Northrop

DISTRICT SIX includes Montgomery County. The court sits at Rockville.

Administrative Judge

Cornelius J. Vaughey

Associate Judges

Louis D. Harrington
Barry A. Hamilton
Mary E. McCormick
Michael John Algeo
Eugene Wolfe
Thomas L. Craven
Patricia L. Mitchell
Stephen P. Johnson
Gary Gilbert Everngam
Brian G. Kim

DISTRICT SEVEN includes Anne Arundel County. The court sits at Annapolis and Glen Burnie.

Administrative Judge

James W. Dryden

Associate Judges

Martha F. Rasin
Essom V. Ricks, Jr.
Megan B. Johnson
John Peter McKenna
Vincent A. Mulieri
Robert C. Wilcox
Jeffrey Michael Wachs

DISTRICT EIGHT includes Baltimore County. The court sits at Towson.

Administrative Judge

Alexandra N. Williams

Associate Judges

A. Gordon Boone, Jr.
Barbara R. Jung
Darryl G. Fletcher
Norman R. Stone, III
Nancy Maggitti Cohen
Jan Marshall Alexander
I. Marshall Seidler
G. Darrell Russell, Jr.
Robert J. Steinberg
Robert E. Cahill, Jr.
Dorothy Jean Wilson
Bruce Sewell Lamdin

DISTRICT NINE includes Harford County. The court sits at Bel Air.

Administrative Judge

Victor K. Butanis

Associate Judges

John L. Dunnigan
Mimi Cooper
Angela M. Eaves

DISTRICT TEN includes Carroll and Howard counties. The court sits at Westminster and Ellicott City.

Administrative Judge

JoAnn M. Ellinghaus-Jones

Associate Judges

Louis A. Becker, III
Neil E. Axel
Pamila J. Brown
Marc G. Rasinsky
Alice P. Clark
Sue-Ellen Hantman

DISTRICT ELEVEN includes Frederick and Washington counties. The court sits at Frederick and Hagerstown.

Administrative Judge

W. Milnor Roberts

Associate Judges

Frederick J. Bower
R. Noel Spence
Ralph H. France, II
Janice Rodnick Ambrose

DISTRICT TWELVE includes Allegany and Garrett counties. The court sits at Cumberland and Oakland.

Administrative Judge

Paul J. Stakem

Associate Judges

Ralph M. Burnett
Edward A. Malloy, Jr.

MARYLAND ORPHANS' COURTS

The Orphans' Courts are courts of special jurisdiction in Maryland and are established in Baltimore City and in each county except Montgomery and Harford counties, where the Circuit Court exercises Orphans' Court jurisdiction. Judges are elected from their respective counties for four-year terms. The chief judge in each county is designated by the governor and serves until the end of his term.

The courts have exclusive jurisdiction over matters involving probate, guardianships, orphans and the administration of estates and other matters as provided by law. Appeals may be taken to the Court of Special Appeals and, except in Montgomery and Harford counties, appeals may also be taken to the Circuit Court as trial de novo.

The courts sit at the county seats.

MARYLAND TAX COURT

The Tax Court is an Executive Branch agency of special statewide jurisdiction in Maryland and is not a Constitutional court of record. Judges are appointed by the governor for six-year terms. One of the judges is designated by the governor to be chief judge.

The Tax Court has jurisdiction over appeals in all tax cases and has the full power to hear, try and determine or remand any matter before it. The Tax Court is empowered to assess, classify, modify, change or alter any valuation, assessment, classification, tax or final order. Appeal is to the Circuit Court.

Maryland Counties and County Seats

Allegany
Cumberland

Anne Arundel
Annapolis

Baltimore
Towson

Baltimore City
(Independent City)

Calvert
Prince Frederick

Caroline
Denton

Carroll
Westminster

Cecil
Elkton

Charles
La Plata

Dorchester
Cambridge

Frederick
Frederick

Garrett
Oakland

Harford
Bel Air

Howard
Ellicott City

Kent
Chestertown

Montgomery
Rockville

Prince George's
Upper Marlboro

Queen Anne's
Centreville

St. Mary's
Leonardtown

Somerset
Princess Anne

Talbot
Easton

Washington
Hagerstown

Wicomico
Salisbury

Worcester
Snow Hill

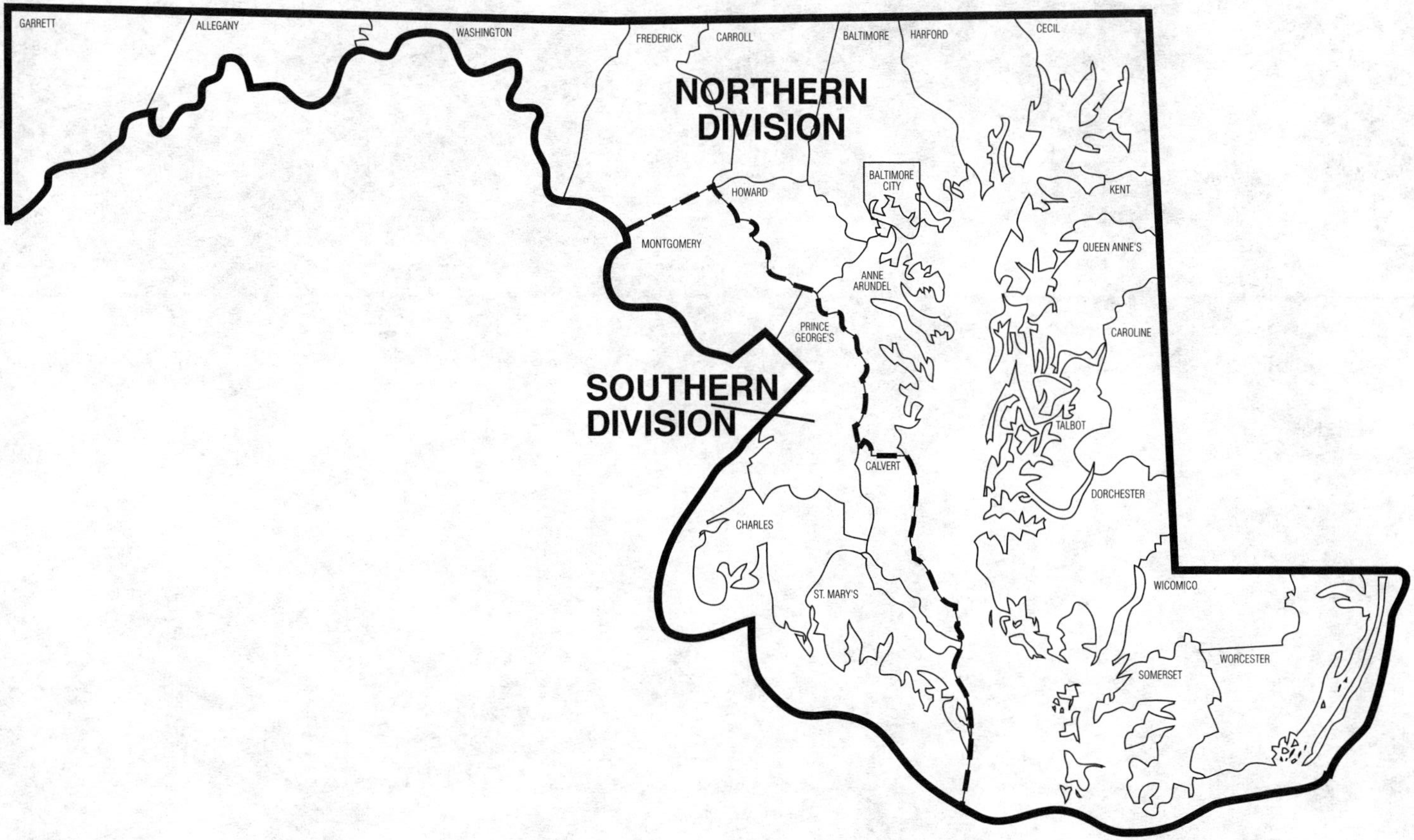
GARRETT
ALLEGANY
WASHINGTON
FREDERICK
CARROLL
BALTIMORE
HARFORD
CECIL
NORTHERN DIVISION
BALTIMORE CITY
HOWARD
KENT
MONTGOMERY
QUEEN ANNE'S
ANNE ARUNDEL
PRINCE GEORGE'S
CAROLINE
SOUTHERN DIVISION
TALBOT
CALVERT
DORCHESTER
CHARLES
WICOMICO
ST. MARY'S
WORCESTER
SOMERSET

DIVISIONS OF
UNITED STATES DISTRICT COURT DISTRICT OF MARYLAND

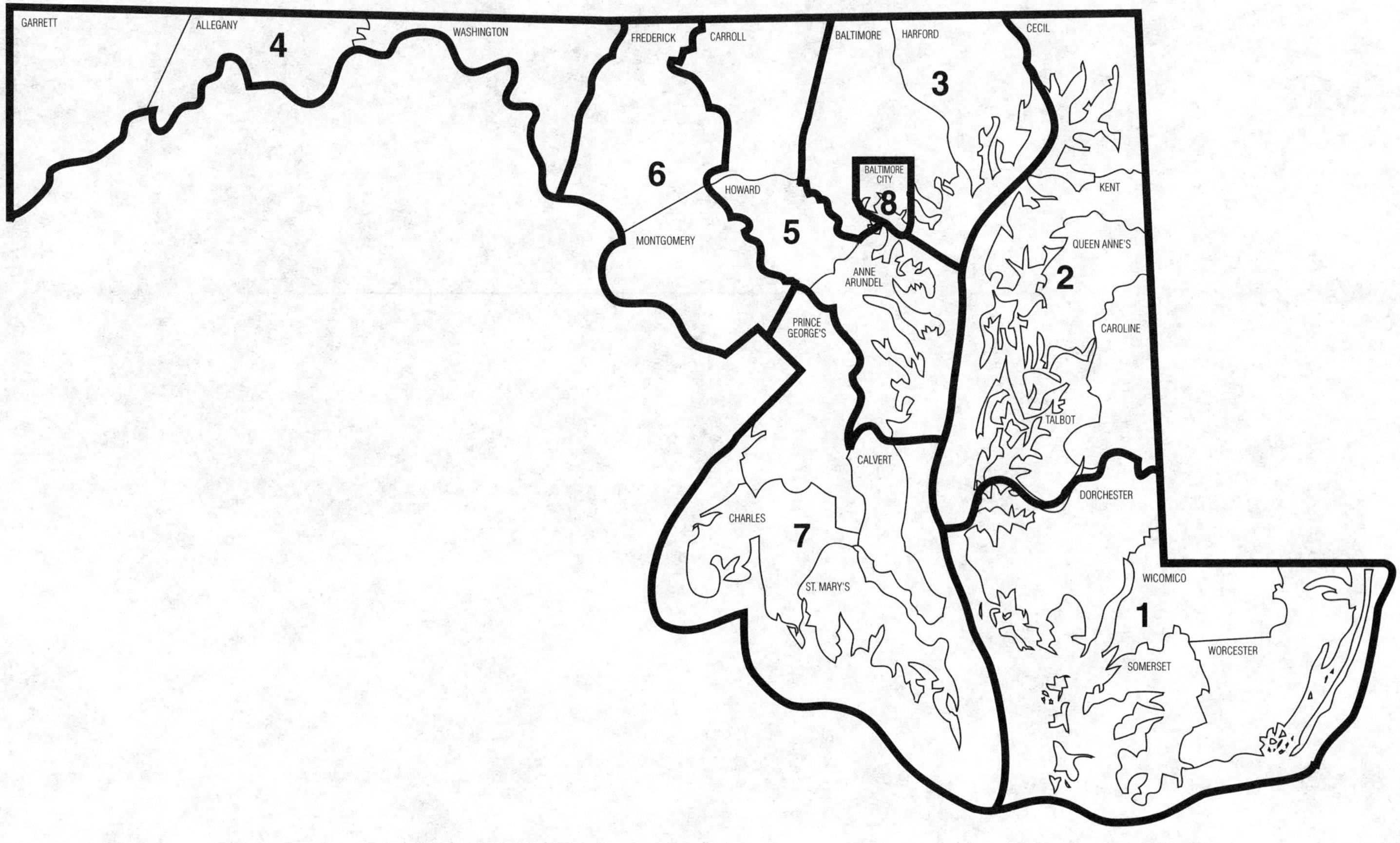
GARRETT
ALLEGANY
4
WASHINGTON
FREDERICK
CARROLL
BALTIMORE
HARFORD
CECIL
3
6
HOWARD
BALTIMORE CITY
8
KENT
5
MONTGOMERY
QUEEN ANNE'S
2
ANNE ARUNDEL
PRINCE GEORGE'S
CAROLINE
TALBOT
CALVERT
DORCHESTER
CHARLES
7
ST. MARY'S
WICOMICO
1
WORCESTER
SOMERSET

JUDICIAL CIRCUITS OF CIRCUIT COURTS OF MARYLAND

JUDICIAL CIRCUITS OF CIRCUIT COURTS OF MARYLAND

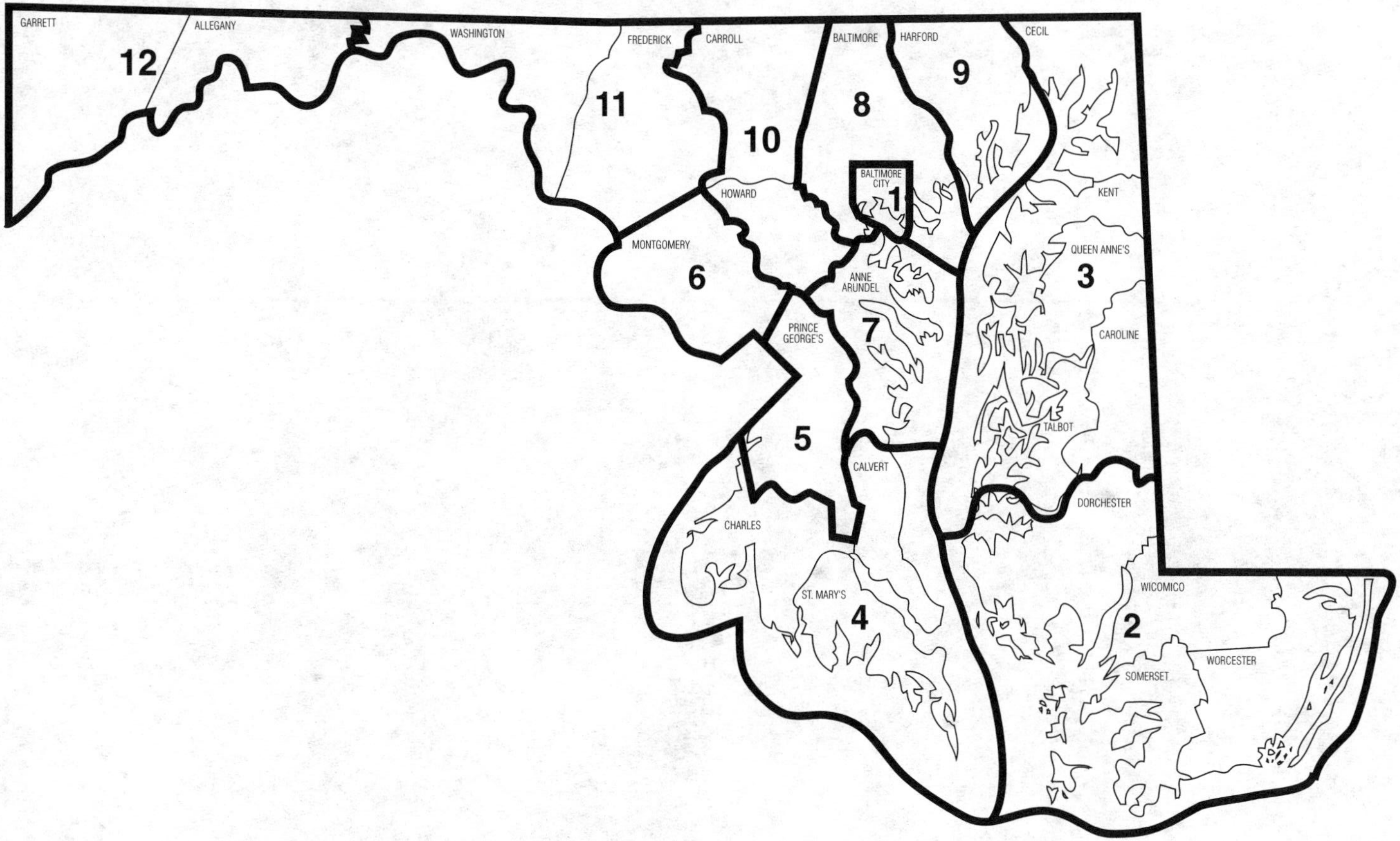
GARRETT
ALLEGANY
12
WASHINGTON
FREDERICK
CARROLL
11
10
BALTIMORE
HARFORD
8
9
CECIL
BALTIMORE CITY
1
HOWARD
MONTGOMERY
6
KENT
QUEEN ANNE'S
3
ANNE ARUNDEL
7
PRINCE GEORGE'S
CAROLINE
TALBOT
5
CALVERT
DORCHESTER
CHARLES
ST. MARY'S
4
WICOMICO
2
SOMERSET
WORCESTER

DISTRICTS OF MARYLAND DISTRICT COURT

MARYLAND

ABRAMS, Karen H. *(Associate Judge, Circuit Court for St. Mary's County, Seventh Judicial Circuit)*

Office: 41605 Courthouse Drive, Leonardtown 20650.

Telephone: (301) 475-4585.

ADKINS, Sally Denison *(Associate Judge, Court of Special Appeals of Maryland)* Appointed by Governor Parris N. Glendening to term beginning June 1998. Retained by election. Born Salisbury Maryland Jan 21, 1950. Educated at Lawrence University B.A. 1972 and University of Maryland School of Law with honors J.D. 1975. Law Clerk to Hon. Marvin H. Smith, Maryland Court of Appeals 1975-76. Admitted to practice Maryland 1976. In legal practice 1976-95. Associate Judge, Circuit Court for Wicomico County, First Judicial Circuit 1996-98.

Member Trial Court Judicial Nominating Commission First Judicial Circuit 1983-90, Ethics Commission Wicomico County 1986-96 and Attorney General's Advisory Council on Family Legal Needs of Low-Income Persons 1991-93. Fellow Maryland Bar Foundation. Member Women's Bar Association (President Eastern Shore Chapter 1990-92), Maryland State Bar Association, Inc., Wicomico County (President 1991-92) and American Bar Associations. Board of Directors Legal Aid Bureau 1980-84, Coastal Hospice, Inc. 1980-88, Mid-Delmarva Family Young Men's Christian Association (YMCA), Inc. 1981-91 and Organize, Unite, and Revitalize (OUR) Community, Inc. 1995-98. Member Greater Salisbury Committee, Inc. 1990-97.

Mailing address: P.O. Box 1029, Salisbury 21803-1029.

Telephone: (410) 334-6367.

ADKINS, William H., III *(Associate Judge, Maryland District Court District Three)* Appointed by Governor Harry Roe Hughes to term beginning Jan 9, 1984. Reappointed by Governor William D. Schaefer Jan 1994, current term expires Jan 2004. Born North Adams Massachusetts Nov 10, 1947. Episcopalian. Member Trinity Cathedral. Educated at Hartwick College B.A. 1970 and Catholic University of America School of Law J.D. 1973. Law Clerk to Hon. Philip M. Fairbanks, Maryland Circuit Court Sixth Judicial Circuit 1973-74. Member Phi Alpha Delta. Admitted to practice Maryland 1973 and District of Columbia 1974. In legal practice Rockville 1974-78, Snow Hill 1978-82 and Easton 1982-84.

Town Attorney Snow Hill 1979-81 and Preston 1982-84 Maryland. Assistant Defender Office of the Public Defender Maryland 1981. Author "Lawyer Specialization" Maryland B. Jour. 1979. Instructor in Paralegal program Warwick Technical Community College 1980-81. Member National Association of Criminal Defense Lawyers, The District of Columbia Bar, Maryland State Bar Association, Inc., Talbot County and American Bar Associations. Democrat. Board of Trustees Historic Easton, Inc. and Easton Academy of the Arts. Board of Directors Coral Arts Society. Member Tred Avon Yacht Club and Eastern Shore Sailing Association. Enjoys sailing, reading, classical music and gourmet cooking.

Office: 108 West Dover Street, Easton 21601.

Telephone: (410) 819-5850.

ALEXANDER, Jan Marshall *(Associate Judge, Maryland District Court District Eight)* Appointed by governor.

Office: 120 East Chesapeake Avenue, Towson 21286-5307.

Telephone: (410) 512-2050.

ALGEO, Michael John *(Associate Judge, Maryland District Court District Six)* Appointed by Governor Parris N. Glendening to term beginning 1999. Term expires 2009. Educated at West Chester University B.S. magna cum laude 1977 and Washington College of Law of American University J.D. 1984. Staff member International Law Journal 1981-82. Judicial Clerk to Hon. William M. Cave, Maryland Circuit Court Sixth Judicial Circuit 1985-86. In legal practice Rockville Maryland and Washington D.C. 1988-90.

Senior Assistant State's Attorney Montgomery County 1986-88 and 1990-99. Co-author Chapter 5 "Court Treatment of Personnel" Retrospective Report Select Committee on Gender Equality 2001. Guest Lecturer on Criminal Law University of Maryland since 1988. Instructor in Essay Bar Review Course "Maryland Civil Procedure" 1991-92 and in Legal Research, Legal Writing, Criminal Law, Civil Litigation, Contract Law, Corporate Law and Domestic Relations Montgomery College. Adjunct Professor of Criminal Trial Practice and Trial Techniques in Civil Litigation Washington College of Law of American University since 2000. Former Member National District Attorneys Association. Member Judicial Education Committee and Select Committee on Gender Equality Maryland District Court and Bar Association of Montgomery County (Executive Committee 1992-94, Judicial Selection Committee 1992-98, Panel Member Attorney Grievance Commission 1995-99, Chairman Nominations and Elections Committee 1996-97, Member Administration of Justice Committee 1997). Faculty Member "Motions in Circuit Court" Spring 1995 and "Handling Bond Reviews in District Court" CLE Fall 2000 Bar Association of Montgomery County and Trial Advocacy Course National District Attorneys Advocacy Center Columbia South Carolina July 1998. Recipient Most Creative Teacher Award Summer 1998 and Paralegal Faculty Service Award 1999 from Montgomery College. Named Distinguished Alumnus by Washington College of Law of American University 1999. Air Transportation Coordinator USAF 1970-76. Recipient Vietnam Service Medal and Vietnam Campaign Medal. Campaign Treasurer People for Potter 1990-92. Founding Chairperson Montgomery County Democratic Lawyers Club. Member Montgomery County Democratic Party. Cub Scout Assistant Pack 928, 1994-95. Panel Judge Siegal Moot Court Competition Catholic University School of Law Fall 1997. Charter Member Vietnam Veterans of America. Vice President Quail Ridge Homeowners Association. Eucharistic Minister St. Mary's Church. Volunteer and Participant "An Evening of Re-

ALGEO, MICHAEL JOHN—*Continued*

membrance for the Victims of September 11, 2001" Rockville Arts. Member American Legion Post 171. Enjoys reading, recreational sports, American history and composing music.

Office: 27 Court House Square, Rockville 20850-2325.

Telephone: (301) 279-1536.

E-mail address: Michael.Algeo@courts.state.md.us

ALLISON, Kaye A. *(Associate Judge, Circuit Court for Baltimore City, Eighth Judicial Circuit)*

Office: Courthouse, 100 North Calvert Street, Baltimore 21202.

Telephone: (410) 396-5074.

AMBROSE, Janice Rodnick *(Associate Judge, Maryland District Court District Eleven)* Appointed by Governor Parris N. Glendening.

Office: 100 West Patrick Street, Frederick 21701.

Telephone: (301) 694-2005.

AXEL, Neil E. *(Associate Judge, Maryland District Court District Ten)* Appointed by governor.

Office: 3451 Courthouse Drive, Ellicott City 21043-4377.

Telephone: (410) 480-7706.

BAKER, Stephen J. *(Associate Judge, Maryland District Court District Three)* Appointed by Governor Parris N. Glendening.

Office: 170 East Main Street, Elkton 21921-5943.

Telephone: (410) 996-0703.

BALDWIN, Maurice W., Jr. *(Associate Judge, Circuit Court for Harford County, Third Judicial Circuit)*

Office: 20 West Courtland Street, Bel Air 21014.

Telephone: (410) 638-3264.

BALLOU-WATTS, Vicki *(Associate Judge, Circuit Court for Baltimore County, Third Judicial Circuit)* Former Associate Judge, Maryland District Court District Eight, appointed by Governor Parris N. Glendening.

Office: County Courts Building, 401 Bosley Avenue, Towson 21204.

Telephone: (410) 887-2690.

BARBERA, Mary Ellen *(Associate Judge, Court of Special Appeals of Maryland)* Appointed by Governor Parris N. Glendening to term beginning Jan 4, 2002. Educated at Towson State University B.S. cum laude 1975 and University of Maryland School of Law J.D. 1984. Law Clerk to Hon. Robert L. Karwacki, Maryland Court of Special Appeals 1984. Admitted to practice Maryland 1984.

Assistant Attorney General 1985-89 and Deputy Chief Criminal Appeals Division 1989-98 Office of Attorney General. Deputy Legal Counsel 1998-99 and Legal Counsel 1999-2001 Office of Governor. Member Serjeants' Inn Law Club, Wranglers Law Club, Women's Bar Association and Maryland State Bar Association, Inc.

Office: Courts of Appeal Building, 361 Rowe Boulevard, Annapolis 21401.

Telephone: (410) 260-1482.

BARON, Jean Szekeres *(Associate Judge, Maryland District Court District Five)* Appointed by Governor Parris N. Glendening.

Office: 14735 Main Street, Suite 173B, Upper Marlboro 20772.

Telephone: (301) 952-4021.

BASS, H. Gary *(Associate Judge, Maryland District Court District One)* Appointed by governor.

Office: 5800 Wabash Avenue, Baltimore 21215-3330.

Telephone: (410) 878-8922.

BATTAGLIA, Lynne A. *(Associate Judge, Court of Appeals of Maryland)* Appointed by Governor Parris N. Glendening to term beginning Jan 26, 2001. Born Buffalo New York April 14, 1946. Educated at American University B.A. 1967 M.A. 1968, Georgetown University 1968 and University of Maryland School of Law J.D. 1974. Articles Editor Maryland Law Review. Member Order of the Coif. Admitted to practice Maryland 1974. In legal practice 1974-78.

Assistant U.S. Attorney 1978-81 and U.S. Attorney Aug 20, 1993 to Jan 26, 2001 District of Maryland. Senior Trial Attorney Office of Special Litigation U.S. Department of Justice 1984-88. Chief Criminal Investigations Division Office of Attorney General 1988-91. Chief of Staff to U.S. Senator Barbara A. Mikulski.

Office: Courts of Appeal Building, 361 Rowe Boulevard, Annapolis 21401.

Telephone: (410) 260-1565.

BEACHLEY, Donald E. *(Associate Judge, Circuit Court for Washington County, Fourth Judicial Circuit)* Former Part-time Magistrate Judge, U.S. District Court District of Maryland.

Office: 95 West Washington Street, Hagerstown 21740.

Telephone: (240) 313-2555.

BEARD, DeLawrence *(Associate Judge, Circuit Court for Montgomery County, Sixth Judicial Circuit)* Appointed by Governor Harry Roe Hughes to term beginning April 19, 1984. Elected Nov 1986 and 2001. Current term expires Nov 2016. Chief Judge since 1996. Born Okalona Arkansas Dec 26, 1937. Educated at University of Missouri B.A. in Political Science 1964, University of Baltimore School of Law J.D. 1970 and Georgetown University Law Center LL.M. 1977. Member Phi Beta Gamma and Alpha Phi Alpha (IUL Chapter). Admitted to practice Maryland 1974, U.S. District Court District of Maryland, U.S. Courts of Appeals Fourth and District of Columbia Circuits, U.S. Court of Claims, U.S. Court of Military Appeals, U.S. Supreme Court and U.S. Court of Customs and Patent Appeals. Began legal practice Rockville 1974. Judge, Maryland District Court District Six 1982-84.

Assistant State's Attorney 1974-79 and District Public Defender 1979-82 Montgomery County. Former Assistant Professorial Lecturer George Washington University College of General Studies and Graduate School of Forensic Science Washington D.C. Guest Lecturer Street Law Program Montgomery County Detention Center Rockville since 1979. Montgomery County Criminal Justice Commission 1979-82. Member Maryland State Bar Association, Inc. 1974-78, J. Franklyn Bourne Law Club 1978-82, National Association of Criminal Defense Lawyers 1979-82, Montgomery County since 1974, National since 1975 and American 1974-78 Bar Associations. Named Outstanding Citizen of the Year by Omega Psi

BEARD, DELAWRENCE—*Continued*

Phi Mu Nu Chapter 1982. Recipient Community Service Award from Montgomery County NAACP 1984. Former Senior Marketing Representative IBM Corporation Washington D.C. Board of Directors Suburban Maryland Fair Housing Bethesda 1973-75 and Children's Hospital Medical Center Washington D.C. 1973-81. Vice Chairman 1977, Chairman 1978 and Board of Directors 1981-84 Covenants Committee Country Place Citizens Association. Life member Montgomery County NAACP.

Office: Judicial Center, 50 Maryland Avenue, Rockville 20850.

Telephone: (240) 777-9296.

BECK, Raymond E., Sr. *(Associate Judge, Circuit Court for Carroll County, Fifth Judicial Circuit)* Also serves as County Administrative Judge Carroll County.

Office: 55 North Court Street, Westminster 21157.

Telephone: (410) 386-2616.

BECKER, Louis A., III *(Associate Judge, Maryland District Court District Ten)* Appointed by governor.

Office: 3451 Courthouse Drive, Ellicott City 21043-4377.

Telephone: (410) 461-0220.

BECKSTEAD, Kathleen Leonard *(Associate Judge, Circuit Court for Wicomico County, First Judicial Circuit)* Appointed by Governor Parris N. Glendening.

Mailing address: P.O. Box 198, Salisbury 21803-0198.

Office: 105 Courthouse, 101 North Division Street, Salisbury 21801.

Telephone: (410) 548-4822.

BELL, Robert M. *(Chief Judge, Court of Appeals of Maryland)* Assumed office 1991. Chief Judge since 1996. Born Rocky Mount North Carolina July 6, 1943. Educated at Morgan State College A.B. with honors 1966 and Harvard University J.D. 1969. Admitted to practice Maryland 1969. Began legal practice Baltimore. Judge, Maryland District Court District One Jan 1975 to Dec 1979, appointed by Governor Marvin Mandel. Judge, Circuit Court for Baltimore City 1980-84. Associate Judge, Court of Special Appeals of Maryland 1984-91.

Member The Bar Association of Baltimore City, Maryland State Bar Association, Inc., Monumental City, National and American Bar Associations.

Office: 634 Courthouse East, 111 North Calvert Street, Baltimore 21202.

Telephone: (410) 333-6396.

BENNETT, Richard D. *(Judge, United States District Court District of Maryland)* Appointed for life by President George W. Bush.

Office: U.S. Courthouse, 101 West Lombard Street, Baltimore 21201.

Telephone: (401) 962-3190.

Office: U.S. Courthouse, 6500 Cherrywood Lane, Greenbelt 20770.

Telephone: (301) 344-0054.

BERGER, Stuart R. *(Associate Judge, Circuit Court for Baltimore City, Eighth Judicial Circuit)* Appointed by Governor Parris N. Glendening to term beginning Dec 21, 1998. Elected 2000, current term expires 2015. Born Baltimore Maryland April 30, 1959. Jewish. Educated at Bucknell University B.A. with honors 1981 and University of Baltimore J.D. 1985. Staff member University of Baltimore Law Review 1982-84. Admitted to practice Maryland 1985, U.S. District Court District of Maryland 1985, U.S. Court of Appeals Fourth Circuit 1988 and U.S. Supreme Court 1996. In legal practice Baltimore 1985-98.

Author "Refusal to Allow Defendant to Introduce Testimony of Alibi Witness Was Neither an Abuse of Discretion Nor a Violation of Due Process When the Defendant Failed to Comply with Procedural Notice of Alibi Rule" 13 No. 2 University of Baltimore L. Rev. Member Maryland Bar Foundation, Bar Association of Baltimore City, Maryland State Bar Association, Inc., Federal and American Bar Associations. Democrat. Interests include reading, baseball and golf.

Office: 111 North Calvert Street, Room 436M, Baltimore 21202.

Telephone: (410) 396-5008.

Fax: (410) 545-7331

BERNARD, Marielsa A. *(Associate Judge, Circuit Court for Montgomery County, Sixth Judicial Circuit)* Former Associate Judge, Maryland District Court District Six, appointed by Governor Parris N. Glendening.

Office: 50 Maryland Avenue, Rockville 20850.

Telephone: (240) 777-9366.

BLACK, Walter E., Jr. *(Senior Judge, United States District Court District of Maryland)* Appointed for life by President Ronald Reagan to term beginning May 17, 1982. Chief Judge March 9, 1991 to Oct 21, 1994. Assumed Senior status Oct 21, 1994, serves by assignment. Born Baltimore Maryland July 7, 1926. Baptist. Educated at Harvard University A.B. magna cum laude 1946 LL.B. 1949. Admitted to practice Maryland 1949. In legal practice Baltimore 1949-53 and 1957-82.

Assistant U.S. Attorney 1953-55 and U.S. Attorney 1956-57 Maryland. Member The Bar Association of Baltimore City, Maryland State Bar Association, Inc. and American Bar Association. Republican. Alternate 1960 and Delegate 1964 Republican National Convention. Chairman Republican City Committee, Baltimore City 1962-66. Director Hospital for Consumptives of Maryland, Union Memorial Hospital and Baltimore Urban League.

Office: 7A U.S. Courthouse, 101 West Lombard Street, Baltimore 21201-2600.

Telephone: (410) 962-0107.

BLAKE, Catherine C. *(Judge, United States District Court District of Maryland)* Magistrate Judge 1987-95. Appointed Judge for life by President Bill Clinton to term beginning 1995. Educated at Radcliffe College B.A. magna cum laude 1972 and Harvard Law School J.D. cum laude 1975. In legal practice Boston 1975-77.

Assistant U.S. Attorney District of Maryland 1977-83. First Assistant U.S. Attorney 1983-85 and 1986-87. U.S. Attorney 1985-86.

Office: 7310 U.S. Courthouse, 101 West Lombard Street, Baltimore 21201-2600.

Telephone: (410) 962-3220.

BLOXOM, Richard R. *(Associate Judge, Maryland District Court District Two)* Appointed by Governor William D. Schaefer March 23, 1990. Reappointed by Governor Parris N. Glendening 2000, current term expires 2010. Born Chincoteague Virginia Sept 22, 1947. Baptist. Educated at University of Maryland B.S. 1969 and University of Virginia J.D. 1976. Admitted to practice Virginia 1976, U.S. Supreme Court 1978, Maryland

BLOXOM, RICHARD R.—*Continued*

1980 and U.S. Court of Appeals Fourth Circuit 1982. In legal practice Pocomoke City Maryland 1980-90. Captain USNR 1989-95.
Office: 301 Commerce Street, Snow Hill 21863.
Telephone: (410) 219-7830.

BOLLINGER, Thomas J., Sr. *(Associate Judge, Circuit Court for Baltimore County, Third Judicial Circuit)*
Office: County Courts Building, 401 Bosley Avenue, Towson 21204.
Telephone: (410) 887-2693.

BOONE, A. Gordon, Jr. *(Associate Judge, Maryland District Court District Eight)* Appointed by Governor Harry Roe Hughes to term beginning April 22, 1982. Reappointed by Governor William D. Schaefer 1992 and by Governor Parris N. Glendening 2002. Current term expires 2012. Born Baltimore Maryland Aug 21, 1933. Roman Catholic. Educated at Georgetown University 1952-53, University of Maryland 1957-60 and University of Baltimore LL.B. 1963. Court Bailiff to Circuit Court Judge 1960-63. Admitted to practice Maryland 1963. Began legal practice Towson 1963.
County Prosecutor 1963-68. County Public Defender 1968-73. City Prosecutor 1974-82. Instructor on Law Baltimore Police Department 1980-81. Member The Bar Association of Baltimore City and Maryland State Bar Association, Inc. Sergeant USAF 1953-57. Democrat. Elected to Democratic State Central Committee for twelve years. Member Elks. Enjoys boating.
Office: 120 East Chesapeake Avenue, Towson 21286-5307.
Telephone: (410) 512-2059.

BOONE, W. Kennedy, III *(Associate Judge, Circuit Court for Washington County, Fourth Judicial Circuit)*
Office: 95 West Washington Street, Hagerstown 21740.
Telephone: (240) 313-2560.

BOWER, Frederick J. *(Associate Judge, Maryland District Court District Eleven)* Appointed by governor. Former Administrative Judge.
Office: 100 West Patrick Street, Frederick 21701.
Telephone: (301) 694-2005.

BRAGUNIER, Amy Janel *(Associate Judge, Circuit Court for Charles County, Seventh Judicial Circuit)*
Mailing address: P.O. Box 970, La Plata 20646.
Office: 200 Charles Street, La Plata 20646.
Telephone: (301) 870-2459.

BRAVERMAN, Nathan *(Associate Judge, Maryland District Court District One)* Appointed by Governor Parris N. Glendening.
Office: 5800 Wabash Avenue, Baltimore 21215-3330.
Telephone: (410) 878-8206.

BREDAR, James K. *(Magistrate Judge, United States District Court District of Maryland)* Appointed by U.S. District Court judges to term beginning Jan 26, 1998. Term expires Jan 2006. Born Omaha Nebraska Feb 6, 1957. Educated at Harvard University B.A. cum laude 1979, Yale University 1981-82 and Georgetown University Law Center J.D. cum laude 1982. Editor American Criminal Law Review. Law Clerk to Richard P. Matsch, U.S. District Court District of Colorado 1983-84. Admitted to practice Colorado 1983, U.S. Supreme Court 1993 and Maryland 1995.
Project Director Vera Institute of Justice London England 1991-92. Federal Public Defender District of Maryland 1992-98. Author "Justice Informed: The Pre-Sentence Report Pilot Trials in the Crown Court" Her Majesty's Home Office Great Britain 1992 and "Moving Up the Day of Reckoning: Strategies for Attacking the Cracked Trials Problem" Criminal L. Rev. 1992. Member Bar Association of Baltimore City, Maryland State Bar Association, Inc. and Federal Bar Association (Board of Governors Maryland Chapter).
Office: 8C U.S. Courthouse, 101 West Lombard Street, Baltimore 21201.
Telephone: (410) 962-0950.
Fax: (410) 962-9031

BROWN, Emanuel *(Associate Judge, Maryland District Court District One)* Appointed by Governor Parris N. Glendening.
Office: 5800 Wabash Avenue, Baltimore 21215-3330.
Telephone: (410) 878-8107.

BROWN, Josef B. *(Associate Judge, Maryland District Court District Five)* Appointed by governor.
Office: 4990 Rhode Island Avenue, Hyattsville 20781.
Telephone: (301) 699-2777.

BROWN, Pamila J. *(Associate Judge, Maryland District Court District Ten)* Appointed by governor.
Office: 3451 Courthouse Drive, Ellicott City 21043-4377.
Telephone: (410) 461-0220.

BRUCE, David S. *(Associate Judge, Circuit Court for Anne Arundel County, Fifth Judicial Circuit)* Former Associate Judge, Maryland District Court District Seven, appointed by Governor Parris N. Glendening.
Office: Court House, Church Circle, Annapolis 21401.
Telephone: (410) 222-1264.

BURNETT, Ralph M. *(Associate Judge, Maryland District Court District Twelve)* Appointed by governor.
Office: 205 South Third Street, Oakland 21550-1526.
Telephone: (301) 334-8023.

BURNS, Luke K., Jr. *(Associate Judge, Circuit Court for Carroll County, Fifth Judicial Circuit)* Appointed by Governor Harry Roe Hughes to term beginning Sept 28, 1979. Elected to subsequent terms. Born Baltimore Maryland Jan 27, 1934. Educated at Fordham University A.B. 1957 and University of Baltimore LL.B. 1964. Member Sigma Delta Kappa. Admitted to practice Maryland 1964. Judge, Maryland District Court District Ten 1978-79, appointed by Governor Blair Lee III.
Member American Judges Association, Maryland State Bar Association, Inc. and Carroll County Bar Association.
Office: 55 North Court Street, Westminster 21157.
Telephone: (410) 386-2092.

BUTANIS, Victor K. *(Administrative Judge, Maryland District Court District Nine)* Appointed by governor.
Office: Two South Bond Street, Bel Air 21014-3737.
Telephone: (410) 836-4510.

BYRNES, J. Norris *(Associate Judge, Circuit Court for Baltimore County, Third Judicial Circuit)*
Office: County Courts Building, 401 Bosley Avenue, Towson 21204.
Telephone: (410) 887-2668.

CADIGAN, Robert E. *(Associate Judge, Circuit Court for Baltimore County, Third Judicial Circuit)*
Office: County Courts Building, 401 Bosley Avenue, Towson 21204.
Telephone: (410) 887-2674.

CAHILL, Robert Edward, Jr. *(Associate Judge, Maryland District Court District Eight)* Appointed by Governor Parris N. Glendening.
Office: 120 East Chesapeake Avenue, Towson 21286-5307.
Telephone: (410) 512-2050.

CANNON, Evelyn Omega *(Associate Judge, Circuit Court for Baltimore City, Eighth Judicial Circuit)* Appointed by Governor Parris N. Glendening Oct 31, 1996 to term beginning Dec 6, 1996. Elected Nov 1998, current term expires Nov 2013. Born New Orleans Louisiana Feb 23, 1950. Buddhist. Educated at University of New Orleans B.A. in History 1971 and Duke University School of Law J.D. 1974 LL.M. 1976. Admitted to practice North Carolina 1974, U.S. District Courts Middle 1974 and Eastern 1975 Districts of North Carolina and District of Maryland 1980, U.S. Court of Appeals Fourth Circuit 1975, District of Columbia 1976, Maryland 1980 and U.S. Supreme Court 1986.
Staff Attorney Public Defender Service District of Columbia 1976-77. Assistant Attorney General 1983-86, Principal Counsel Trial Litigation 1986-91 and Chief of Litigation 1991-96 Maryland Attorney General's Office. Assistant Professor University of Maryland School of Law 1977-83. Member Alliance of Black Women Attorneys, Women's Law Center, St. Thomas More Society, Maryland Bar Foundation, Bar Association of Baltimore City, Maryland State Bar Association, Inc. and Monumental Bar Association. Faculty National Institute of Trial Advocacy since 1976. Named one of Maryland's Top 100 Women 1997 and 2001 and Man for All Seasons by St. Thomas More 2000. Recipient Living History Award from National Association of Negro Business and Professional Women's Clubs, Inc. 1998. Honored by Coalition of 100 Black Women and Women Who Broke Glass Ceiling. Member Baltimore Shambhala Center and St. Vincent de Paul Catholic Church. Enjoys reading and travel. Personal Statement or Quote: "I will spend this life taking my armor off" (Pema Chodron).
Office: Courthouse East, 111 North Calvert Street, Baltimore 21202.
Telephone: (410) 545-6235.
E-mail address: Evelyn.Omega.Cannon-@courts.state.md.us

CAROOM, Philip T. *(Associate Judge, Circuit Court for Anne Arundel County, Fifth Judicial Circuit)*
Office: Court House, Church Circle, Annapolis 21401.
Telephone: (410) 222-1382.

CARR, William O. *(Associate Judge, Circuit Court for Harford County, Third Judicial Circuit)* Also serves as County Administrative Judge Harford County.
Office: 20 West Courtland Street, Bel Air 21014.
Telephone: (410) 638-3262.

CARRION, Audrey J. S. *(Associate Judge, Circuit Court for Baltimore City, Eighth Judicial Circuit)* Appointed by Governor Parris N. Glendening. Former Associate Judge, Maryland District Court District One.
Office: Courthouse, 100 North Calvert Street, Baltimore 21202.
Telephone: (410) 396-5130.

CATHELL, Dale R. *(Associate Judge, Court of Appeals of Maryland)* Appointed by Governor Parris N. Glendening. Born Berlin Maryland July 31, 1937. Episcopalian. Educated at University of Maryland and Eastern College (now University of Baltimore) LL.B. 1967. Admitted to practice Maryland 1967. In legal practice Ocean City 1967-80. Judge, Maryland District Court 1980-81. Associate Judge, Circuit Court for Worcester County, First Judicial Circuit March 1980 to Sept 1989, appointed by Governor Harry Roe Hughes. Former Associate Judge, Court of Special Appeals of Maryland, appointed by Governor William D. Schaefer Sept 1989.
Counsel Town of Ocean City 1970-78. Important Decisions: Baysinger v. Schmid Products Company (products liability) Jan 31, 1985 and Pasternak v. Go (riparian rights case) Feb 6, 1985. Instructor Worwic Community College 1976-78. Member Maryland State Bar Association, Inc. and Worcester County Bar Association. Recipient Award for Outstanding Contribution to Development and Progress of Ocean City 1973, Award for Outstanding and Dedicated Service to Worcester County Shoreline Community 1977 and Award for Outstanding Service to Legal Intern Program 1983 and 1984. Corporal USAF 1955-59. Enjoys tennis, reading, skiing, fishing and soccer.
Mailing address: P.O. Box 4306, Salisbury 21803-4306.
Telephone: (410) 543-6014.

CAVANAUGH, Patrick *(Associate Judge, Circuit Court for Baltimore County, Third Judicial Circuit)*
Office: County Courts Building, 401 Bosley Avenue, Towson 21204.
Telephone: (410) 887-6507.

CHAPPELLE, Steven G. *(Associate Judge, Circuit Court for Charles County, Seventh Judicial Circuit)*
Mailing address: P.O. Box 970, La Plata 20646.
Office: 200 Charles Street, La Plata 20646.
Telephone: (301) 932-3430.

CHASANOW, Deborah K. *(Judge, United States District Court District of Maryland)* Magistrate Judge 1987-93. Appointed Judge for life by President Bill Clinton to term beginning 1993. Born Washington D.C. April 23, 1948. Educated at Douglass College, Rutgers University B.A. 1970 and Stanford University Law School J.D. 1974. Law Clerk to Hon. David L. Cahoon, Maryland Circuit Court Circuit Six 1974-75. Member Phi Beta Kappa. Admitted to practice Maryland 1974 and District of Columbia 1975.
Chief Criminal Appeals Division Office of Attorney General 1979-87. Member Marlborough American Inn of Court (Past President), Wrangler's Law Club, National Association of Women Judges, Women's Bar Association, Maryland State Bar Association, Inc. and Prince George's County Bar Association. Governor's Advisory Board on Rape and Sexual Offenses 1982-84. Governor's Task Force to Review the Defense of Insanity 1982-84.
Office: 465A U.S. Courthouse, 6500 Cherrywood Lane, Greenbelt 20770-1293.
Telephone: (301) 344-0634.

CHIAPPARELLI, Charles A. *(Associate Judge, Maryland District Court District One)* Appointed by governor.
Office: 5800 Wabash Avenue, Baltimore 21215-3330.
Telephone: (410) 878-8107.

CLAGETT, Marjorie L. *(Associate Judge, Circuit Court for Calvert County, Seventh Judicial Circuit)* Appointed by governor.
Office: Calvert County Courthouse, 175 Main Street, Prince Frederick 20678.
Telephone: (410) 535-1600.

CLAGETT, Stephen L. *(Administrative Judge, Maryland District Court District Four)* Appointed by governor.
Office: Multi-Service Center, 200 Duke Street, Prince Frederick 20678-4136.
Telephone: (410) 535-2091.

CLARK, Alice P. *(Associate Judge, Maryland District Court District Ten)* Appointed by Governor Parris N. Glendening.
Office: 3451 Courthouse Drive, Ellicott City 21043-4377.
Telephone: (410) 461-0220.

CLARK, John T., III *(Associate Judge, Maryland District Court District Three)* Appointed by governor to term beginning 1979. Reappointed to subsequent terms.
Office: 120 Broadway, Centreville 21617-1092.
Telephone: (410) 758-5200.

CLARKE, Toni E. *(Associate Judge, Circuit Court for Prince George's County, Seventh Judicial Circuit)*
Office: Court House, 14735 Main Street, Upper Marlboro 20772.
Telephone: (301) 952-4988.

CLYBURN, Ben C. *(Associate Judge, Maryland District Court District One)* Appointed by governor.
Office: 5800 Wabash Avenue, Baltimore 21215-3330.
Telephone: (410) 878-8107.

COHEN, Nancy Maggitti *(Associate Judge, Maryland District Court District Eight)* Appointed by Governor Parris N. Glendening.
Office: 120 East Chesapeake Avenue, Towson 21286-5307.
Telephone: (410) 512-2050.

CONNELLY, William *(Magistrate Judge, United States District Court District of Maryland)* Appointed by U.S. District Court judges to term beginning March 31, 1995. Reappointed March 31, 2003, current term expires March 30, 2011. Born Washington D.C. Feb 11, 1952. Roman Catholic. Educated at University of Maryland B.A. 1973 J.D. 1976 and Georgetown University LL.M. 1979. Law Clerk to Circuit Court for Prince George's County 1976-77. Admitted to practice Maryland 1976 and District of Columbia 1979. In legal practice Camp Springs 1981-95. USAF 1977-81. USAFR since 1981.
Office: 355A U.S. Courthouse, 6500 Cherrywood Lane, Greenbelt 20770-5296.
Telephone: (301) 344-0627.
Fax: (301) 344-8434

COOKSEY, Charlotte Manning *(Associate Judge, Maryland District Court District One)* Appointed by Governor Harry Roe Hughes to term beginning July 20, 1983. Reappointed by Governor William D. Schaefer July 1993, current term expires July 20, 2003. Born Baltimore Maryland Oct 30, 1947. Protestant. Educated at Louisiana State University 1965, Newcomb College of Tulane University of Louisiana B.A. 1968, Loyola University J.D. 1971 and University of Cambridge, England. Staff member and Managing Editor Loyola Law Review 1969-71. Recipient American Jurisprudence Award for Excellence in Obligations 1970. Member Kappa Kappa Gamma. Admitted to practice Louisiana 1971, District of Columbia 1973 and Maryland 1976. Began legal practice New Orleans Louisiana 1971. Master-in-Chancery Division of Juvenile Causes Supreme Bench of Baltimore City 1979-83.
With Legal Aid Bureau, Inc. Baltimore Maryland 1972-74 and 1975-79 and U.S. Department of Justice Washington D.C. 1974-75. Author "Discovery by Defendants of the Results of the Prosecution's Unlawful Electronic Surveillance" Loyola L. Rev. 1969 and "The Battered Child Syndrome—Louisiana's Response to the Cry" Loyola L. Rev. 1971. Member Judicial Ethics Committee, National Association of Women Judges, Women's Law Center, The Bar Association of Baltimore City, Maryland State Bar Association, Inc., The District of Columbia Bar, Women's and Louisiana State Bar Associations. Attended Institute of Juvenile Justice 1980, National College of Juvenile and Family Court Judges 1980 and The National Judicial College 1985. Institution Counselor New Orleans Mental Health Center 1969-71. Member Governor's Commission on Mental Health.
Office: 10 Cherry Hill Road, Baltimore 21225-1159.
Telephone: (410) 355-4288.

COOPER, Mimi *(Associate Judge, Maryland District Court District Nine)* Appointed by Governor Parris N. Glendening.
Office: Two South Bond Street, Bel Air 21014-3737.
Telephone: (410) 836-4510.

COOPER, Richard A. *(Associate Judge, Maryland District Court District Four)* Appointed by Governor Parris N. Glendening.
Mailing address: P.O. Box 3070, La Plata 20646-3070.
Office: 200 Charles Street, La Plata 20646.
Telephone: (301) 932-3279.

COX, Kathleen Gallogly *(Associate Judge, Circuit Court for Baltimore County, Third Judicial Circuit)* Appointed by Governor Parris N. Glendening Jan 1999. Elected Nov 2000, current term expires Nov 2015. Born Washington D.C. Feb 18, 1955. Catholic. Educated at University of Notre Dame B.A. 1976 J.D. 1979. Associate Editor Notre Dame Law Review 1977-79. Law Clerk to Hon. James R. Miller, Jr., U.S. District Court District of Maryland 1979-81. Admitted to practice Maryland 1979, District of Columbia 1980, U.S. District Courts District of Maryland 1980 and District of Columbia, U.S. Court of Appeals Fourth Circuit and U.S. Supreme Court. In legal practice Towson Maryland 1989-99.
Assistant Federal Public Defender District of Maryland 1982-85. Member Bar Association of Baltimore City, Maryland State Bar Association, Inc. and American Bar Association.
Office: County Courts Building, 401 Bosley Avenue, Towson 21204.
Telephone: (410) 887-6510.
Fax: (410) 296-1324
E-mail address: KCox@CO.BA.MD.US

CRAVEN, Thomas L. *(Associate Judge, Maryland District Court District Six)* Appointed by governor.
Office: 27 Courthouse Square, Rockville 20850-2325.
Telephone: (301) 279-1551.

DANCY, Bonita J. *(Associate Judge, Circuit Court for Baltimore City, Eighth Judicial Circuit)*
Office: Courthouse East, 111 North Calvert Street, Baltimore 21202.
Telephone: (410) 396-5102.

DANIELS, Lawrence R. *(Associate Judge, Circuit Court for Baltimore County, Third Judicial Circuit)* Appointed by Governor William D. Schaefer Dec 21, 1993. Elected to subsequent term. Born New Haven Connecticut Aug 27, 1947. Roman Catholic. Educated at Johns Hopkins University B.A. 1969 and University of Connecticut School of Law J.D. 1972. Associate Editor Connecticut Law Review 1971-72. Admitted to practice Connecticut 1972, Hawaii 1974 and Maryland 1977. In legal practice Honolulu Hawaii 1978-79 and Towson Maryland 1979-89. Associate Judge, Maryland District Court District Eight Feb 2, 1989 to Dec 20, 1993, appointed by Governor William D. Schaefer.
Adjunct Professor University of Baltimore School of Law 1996-2001. President Justinian Law Society. Member Maryland State Bar Association Inc. (Board of Governors 1999-2000) and Baltimore County Bar Association (President 1997-98). Named Man of the Year by Justinian Law Society 1993. Recipient Law Day Award from Maryland Sons of Italy 1996. USAR (retired). Served in Operation Desert Storm. Director Associated Italian American Charities of Maryland and OSIA.
Office: County Courts Building, 401 Bosley Avenue, Towson 21204.
Telephone: (410) 887-4307.

DAVIS, Andre Maurice *(Judge, United States District Court District of Maryland)* Appointed for life by President Bill Clinton to term beginning Aug 1995. Born Baltimore Maryland Feb 11, 1949. Educated at University of Pennsylvania B.A. 1971 and University of Maryland J.D. cum laude 1978. Recipient Roger Howell Award 1978. Law Clerk to Hon. Frank A. Kaufman, U.S. District Court District of Maryland 1978-79 and Hon. Francis D. Murnaghan, Jr. U.S. Court of Appeals Fourth Circuit 1979-80. Member Phi Alpha Delta. Admitted to practice Maryland 1979 and U.S. Court of Appeals Fourth Circuit 1980. In legal practice Baltimore 1983-87. Associate Judge, Maryland District Court District One Aug 1987 to Dec 1990. Associate Judge, Circuit Court for Baltimore City, Eighth Judicial Circuit Dec 19, 1990 to Aug 1995, appointed by Governor William D. Schaefer.
Appellate Attorney Civil Rights Division U.S. Department of Justice 1980-81. Assistant U.S. Attorney District of Maryland 1981-83. Assistant Professor of Law 1984-87 and Adjunct Faculty Member since 1987 University of Maryland School of Law. President Legal Aid Bureau, Inc. 1985-87. Vice President and President Executive Committee Maryland Judicial Conference 1992-94. President Digges Inn American Inns of Court 1997-98. Former Member Board of Directors Judicial Institute of Maryland. Member American Inns of Court, The Bar Association of Baltimore City, Maryland State Bar Association, Inc. (Council Member Section on Correctional Reform since 1990), Monumental City and American (Member Executive Committee since 1999 and Vice Chair National Conference of Federal Trial Judges Judicial Division) Bar Associations. Faculty Member on General Jurisdiction, Products Liability and Professional Liability The National Judicial College since 1994. Director Baltimore Urban League 1975-78. Trustee Goucher College 1985-91. Board of Directors 1989-96 and since 2001 and Past President Big Brothers-Big Sisters of Central Maryland, Inc. President and Board Member Alumni Association 1993-2001, Co-chair Advisory Board "Community Law in Action" and Member Board of Visitors University of Maryland School of Law. Co-chair International Committee and Board Member Einstein Institute for Science, Health and the Courts. Board Member Open Society Institute-Baltimore. Enjoys photography.
Office: 5B U.S. Courthouse, 101 West Lombard Street, Baltimore 21201-2615.
Telephone: (410) 962-0801.
Fax: (410) 962-0820
E-mail address: judge_andre_davis@mdd.uscourts.gov

DAVIS, Arrie W. *(Associate Judge, Court of Special Appeals of Maryland)* Appointed by Governor William D. Schaefer to term beginning Dec 27, 1990. Retained by election. Current term expires Nov 2012. Born Baltimore Maryland July 21, 1940. Episcopalian. Educated at Morgan State University A.B. 1963 and University of New York M.A. 1966. Law Clerk to Hon. Joseph Carter, Supreme Bench of Baltimore City 1968. Member Alpha Phi Omega. Admitted to practice Maryland 1969, U.S. Supreme Court, U.S. District Court District of Maryland and U.S. Court of Appeals Fourth Circuit. Began legal practice Baltimore 1969. Judge, Maryland District Court 1981-83. Associate Judge, Circuit Court for Baltimore City, Eighth Judicial Circuit June 3, 1984 to Dec 26, 1990, appointed by Governor Harry Roe Hughes.
Assistant State's Attorney 1969-71. Assistant Attorney General Aug 1971 to March 1981. Instructor Morgan State University 1971-81 and Villa Julie College, Inc. 1972-80. English teacher in public schools 1963-69.
Office: 630 Courthouse East, 111 North Calvert Street, Baltimore 21202.
Telephone: (410) 333-3200.

DAVIS, Donald C. *(Associate Judge, Circuit Court for Wicomico County, First Judicial Circuit)*
Mailing address: P.O. Box 198, Salisbury 21803-0198.
Office: 105 Courthouse, 101 North Division Street, Salisbury 21801.
Telephone: (410) 548-4822.

DAVIS, R. Scott *(Associate Judge, Maryland District Court District Two)* Appointed by governor.
Office: 201 Baptist Street, Salisbury 21801.
Telephone: (410) 543-6600.

DAVIS-LOOMIS, Nancy L. *(Associate Judge, Circuit Court for Anne Arundel County, Fifth Judicial Circuit)* Former Associate Judge, Maryland District Court District Seven.
Office: Court House, Church Circle, Annapolis 21401.
Telephone: (410) 222-1205.

DAWSON, Herman C. *(Associate Judge, Circuit Court for Prince George's County, Seventh Judicial Circuit)*
Office: Court House, 14735 Main Street, Upper Marlboro 20772.
Telephone: (301) 952-3676.

DAY, Charles B. *(Magistrate Judge, United States District Court District of Maryland)* Appointed by U.S. District Court judges to term beginning Feb 18, 1997. Term expires Feb 17, 2005. Born Dothan Alabama April 12, 1957. Educated at University of Maryland B.S. in Criminal Justice 1978 J.D. 1984 and American University M.S. in Judicial Administration 1980. Admitted to practice Maryland 1985 and District of Columbia 1989. In legal practice 1989-97.

Office: 235A U.S. Courthouse, 6500 Cherrywood Lane, Greenbelt 20770-5295.

Telephone: (301) 344-0393.

DEBELIUS, John William, III *(Associate Judge, Circuit Court for Montgomery County, Sixth Judicial Circuit)* Appointed by Governor Parris N. Glendening June 2001. Elected Nov 2002, current term expires 2017. Born Newark New Jersey Nov 11, 1953. Educated at California State University at Northridge B.S. 1975 and University of Baltimore School of Law J.D. 1978. Comments Editor University of Baltimore Law Review 1977-78. Law Clerk to Hon. Philip M. Fairbanks, Maryland Circuit Court Sixth Judicial Circuit 1978-79. Admitted to practice Maryland 1978, District of Columbia, U.S. District Court District of Maryland, U.S. Court of Appeals Fourth Circuit and U.S. Supreme Court. In legal practice Gaithersburg Maryland 1979-2001.

Author "The Maryland Boulevard Rule, A Time for Change" 6 University of Baltimore L. Rev. 223, 1977. Board of Governors Maryland State Bar Association, Inc. 1994-96 and 1998-2000. President Montgomery County Bar Association 1997-98, Montgomery County Bar Foundation 1998-99 and Montgomery County Chapter American Inns of Court since 2003. Member House of Delegates American Bar Association 1998-2000. Member Gaithersburg Homeless Advisory Board. Volunteer Lord's Table Soup Kitchen. Enjoys sailing.

Office: Maryland Judicial Center, 50 Maryland Avenue, Rockville 20850.

Telephone: (240) 777-9212.

Fax: (240) 777-9216

DERBY, E. Stephen *(Judge, United States Bankruptcy Court District of Maryland)* Appointed by U.S. Court of Appeals Fourth Circuit judges to term beginning Dec 9, 1987. Reappointed Dec 9, 2001, current term expires Dec 2015. Born Boston Massachusetts 1938. Educated at Wesleyan University A.B. with distinction 1960 and Harvard Law School LL.B. cum laude 1965. Law Clerk to Hon. Harrison L. Winter, U.S. District Court District of Maryland and U.S. Court of Appeals Fourth Circuit 1965-66. Admitted to practice Maryland 1965, U.S. District Court District of Maryland 1966, U.S. Court of Appeals Fourth Circuit 1968 and U.S. Supreme Court 1973. In legal practice Baltimore 1966-71 and 1973-87.

Assistant Attorney General Maryland 1971-73. Adjunct Faculty University of Maryland School of Law 1986 and since 1989. Fellow American College of Bankruptcy. Member American Bankruptcy Institute, Bankruptcy Bar Association of Maryland, Maryland State Bar Association, Inc. and Anne Arundel County Bar Association.

Office: 9442 U.S. Courthouse, 101 West Lombard Street, Baltimore 21201-2696.

Telephone: (410) 962-7801.

DiGIROLAMO, Thomas M. *(Magistrate Judge, United States District Court District of Maryland)* Appointed by U.S. District Court judges Sept 18, 1998. Reappointed 2002, current term expires Sept 17, 2006. Serves part time. Born Plainfield New Jersey Nov 28, 1956. Educated at Rutgers College 1978 and Dickinson School of Law J.D. 1981. Judicial Clerk to Maryland Circuit Court Circuit Four. Admitted to practice U.S. District Court District of Maryland 1988 and U.S. Court of Appeals Fourth Circuit 1990. Member Omicron Delta Epsilon and Chi Psi.

Assistant State Attorney Washington County 1983-88. Member Federal Magistrates Judges Association, Maryland State Bar Association, Inc. and Washington County Bar Association. Chairman Washington County Animal Control Authority. Member Rotary Club of Hagerstown.

Mailing address: P.O. Box 4227, Hagerstown 21741-4227.

Telephone: (301) 739-8610.

DONOHUE, D. Warren *(Associate Judge, Circuit Court for Montgomery County, Sixth Judicial Circuit)* Appointed by governor.

Office: 50 Maryland Avenue, Rockville 20850.

Telephone: (240) 777-9226.

DOORY, Timothy J. *(Associate Judge, Maryland District Court District One)* Appointed by governor.

Office: 5800 Wabash Avenue, Baltimore 21215-3330.

Telephone: (410) 878-8926.

DRYDEN, James W. *(Administrative Judge, Maryland District Court District Seven)* Appointed by Governor William D. Schaefer.

Office: 251 Rowe Boulevard, Annapolis 21401.

Telephone: (410) 260-1360.

DUDLEY, James B. *(Associate Judge, Circuit Court for Howard County, Fifth Judicial Circuit)* Former Associate Judge, Maryland District Court District Ten.

Office: Court House, Ellicott City 21043.

Telephone: (410) 313-2145.

DUGAN, Joseph Aloysius, Jr. *(Associate Judge, Circuit Court for Montgomery County, Sixth Judicial Circuit)*

Office: 50 Maryland Avenue, Rockville 20850.

Telephone: (240) 777-9268.

DUGAN, Robert N. *(Associate Judge, Circuit Court for Baltimore County, Third Judicial Circuit)* Former Associate Judge, Maryland District Court District Eight.

Office: County Courts Building, 401 Bosley Avenue, Towson 21204.

Telephone: (410) 887-6531.

DUNNIGAN, John L. *(Associate Judge, Maryland District Court District Nine)* Appointed by governor.

Office: Two South Bond Street, Bel Air 21014-3737.

Telephone: (410) 836-4510.

DWYER, G. Edward, Jr. *(Associate Judge, Circuit Court for Frederick County, Sixth Judicial Circuit)* Also serves as County Administrative Judge Frederick County.

Office: 100 West Patrick Street, Frederick 21701.

Telephone: (301) 696-2973.

EAVES, Angela M. *(Associate Judge, Maryland District Court District Nine)* Appointed by Governor Parris N. Glendening.

Office: Two South Bond Street, Bel Air 21014-3737.

Telephone: (410) 836-4510.

EL-AMIN, Hassan Ali *(Associate Judge, Maryland District Court District Five)* Appointed by Governor Parris N. Glendening.
Office: 14735 Main Street, Suite 173B, Upper Marlboro 20772.
Telephone: (301) 952-4011.

ELDRIDGE, John C. *(Associate Judge, Court of Appeals of Maryland)* Appointed by Governor Marvin Mandel to term beginning Jan 1974. Retained by election 1976, 1991 and 2001. Current term expires Nov 2011. Born Baltimore Maryland Nov 13, 1933. Methodist. Educated at Harvard University A.B. cum laude 1955 and University of Maryland LL.B. cum laude 1959. Law Clerk to Hon. Simon E. Sobeloff, U.S. Court of Appeals Fourth Circuit 1959-61. Member Order of the Coif. Admitted to practice Maryland 1960 and District of Columbia 1960. In legal practice Annapolis 1969-73.
With U.S. Department of Justice 1961-69 (Assistant Chief Civil Appellate Section 1967-69). Chief Legislative Officer Office of the Governor of Maryland 1969-73. Important Decisions: Volkswagen of America, Inc. v. Young 272 Md. 201, 1974; Bowie Inn, Inc. v. City of Bowie 274 Md. 230, 1975; Phipps v. General Motors Corporation 278 Md. 337, 1976; Governor of Maryland v. Exxon Corp. 279 Md. 410 aff'd 437 U.S. 117, 98 S. Ct. 2207, 57 L. Ed. 2d 91, 1978; Kelley v. R. G. Industries 304 Md. 124, 497 A. 2d 1143, 1985.; State v. Burning Tree Club, Inc. 315 Md. 254, 554 A.2d 366, 1989; and Board of Trustees v. City of Baltimore 317 Md. 72, 562 A.2d 720, 1989. Member Maryland State Bar Association, Inc. and Anne Arundel County Bar Association.
Office: Courts of Appeal Building, 361 Rowe Boulevard, Annapolis 21401.
Telephone: (410) 260-1515.

ELLINGHAUS-JONES, JoAnn M. *(Administrative Judge, Maryland District Court District Ten)* Appointed by Governor William D. Schaefer.
Office: 101 North Court Street, Westminster 21157.
Telephone: (410) 386-2365.

ESCHENBURG, Theodore R. *(Associate Judge, Circuit Court for Worcester County, First Judicial Circuit)* Also serves as County Administrative Judge Worcester County.
Mailing address: P.O. Box 40, Snow Hill 21863.
Office: 104 Court House, One West Market Street, Snow Hill 21863.
Telephone: (410) 632-0700.

EVERNGAM, Douglas Howard *(Associate Judge, Maryland District Court District Three)* Appointed by Governor Parris N. Glendening.
Office: Multi-Service Center, 207 South Third Street, Denton 21629-1229.
Telephone: (410) 479-5800.

EVERNGAM, Gary Gilbert *(Associate Judge, Maryland District Court District Six)* Appointed by Governor Parris N. Glendening.
Office: 27 Court House Square, Rockville 20850-2325.
Telephone: (301) 279-1538.

EYLER, Deborah S. *(Associate Judge, Court of Special Appeals of Maryland)* Appointed by Governor Parris N. Glendening to term beginning 1997. Born New York New York Aug 11, 1952. Educated at New York University B.A. 1975 and University of Maryland School of Law J.D. with honors 1981. National Moot Court Team. Member Order of the Coif. Admitted to practice Maryland 1982. In legal practice Maryland 1982-97.
Chair Trial Courts Nominating Commission Baltimore County 1995-97. Chair Maryland Judicial Commission on Pro Bono since 1998. Member Maryland Bar Foundation, Maryland State Bar Association, Inc. (Board of Governors 1995-97) and Baltimore County Bar Association.
Office: Courts of Appeal Building, 361 Rowe Boulevard, Annapolis 21401.
Telephone: (410) 260-1485.

EYLER, James R. *(Associate Judge, Court of Special Appeals of Maryland)* Appointed by Governor Parris N. Glendening to term beginning Jan 9, 1996. Retained by election Nov 1996, current term expires 2006. Born Maryland July 13, 1942. Educated at University of Maryland B.A. with high honors 1964 LL.B. with honors 1967. Research Editor Maryland Law Review 1967. Law Clerk to Hon. William R. Horney, Court of Appeals of Maryland 1967-68. Member Order of the Coif. Admitted to practice Maryland 1967, District of Columbia and U.S. Supreme Court. In legal practice Baltimore Maryland 1968-96.
Author "Maryland Tort Damages" by George W. Shadoan et al. eds. Maryland Institute for Continuing Professional Education of Lawyers, Inc. 1994. Important Decisions: Conaway v. State 108 Md. App. 475, 1996; Brown v. Wheeler 109 Md. App. 710, 1996; Pettit v. Erie 117 Md. App. 212, 1997; and Hercules v. Comptroller 117 Md. App. 29, 1997. Instructor in Trial Advocacy University of Maryland School of Law 1997-98. Member J. Dudley Digges Inn of Court, Wednesday Law Club, Barristers Law Club, Judicial Conference of the Fourth Circuit, The Bar Association of Baltimore City, Maryland State Bar Association, Inc., Baltimore County and American Bar Associations. Attended Maryland Judicial Conferences 1996-97. Member Parents Anonymous, Genesis Jobs, Leadership Maryland, Everyman Theatre, Maryland General Hospital, Public Justice Center, Severn School, U.S. Olympic Committee and Maryland Science Center. Enjoys water gardening.
Office: County Courts Building, 401 Bosley Avenue, Towson 21204.
Telephone: (410) 887-3286.

FADER, John F., II *(Associate Judge, Circuit Court for Baltimore County, Third Judicial Circuit)* Appointed by Governor Harry Roe Hughes to term beginning Feb 10, 1982. Elected to subsequent terms. Born Baltimore Maryland Feb 12, 1941. Educated at University of Maryland B.S. 1963 LL.B. 1968. Member Phi Alpha Delta. Admitted to practice Maryland 1968. Judge, Maryland District Court District Eight Nov 23, 1977 to Feb 9, 1982, appointed by Acting Governor Blair Lee III.
Office: County Courts Building, 401 Bosley Avenue, Towson 21204.
Telephone: (410) 887-2916.

FINAN, W. Timothy *(Associate Judge, Circuit Court for Allegany County, Fourth Judicial Circuit)* Former

FINAN, W. TIMOTHY—*Continued*

Associate Judge, Maryland District Court District Twelve.

Office: Court House, 30 Washington Street, Cumberland 21502.

Telephone: (301) 777-5929.

FINIFTER, Michael J. *(Associate Judge, Circuit Court for Baltimore County, Third Judicial Circuit)*

Office: County Courts Building, 401 Bosley Avenue, Towson 21204.

Telephone: (410) 887-2642.

FLETCHER, Darryl G. *(Associate Judge, Maryland District Court District Eight)* Appointed by governor.

Office: 8914 Kelso Drive, Essex 21221-3135.

Telephone: (410) 512-2325.

FRANCE, Ralph H., II *(Associate Judge, Maryland District Court District Eleven)* Appointed by governor.

Office: 36 West Antietam Street, Hagerstown 21740.

Telephone: (240) 420-4665.

GALLOWAY, Michael M. *(Associate Judge, Circuit Court for Carroll County, Fifth Judicial Circuit)* Appointed by Governor Parris N. Glendening.

Office: 55 North Court Street, Westminster 21157.

Telephone: (410) 386-2650.

GARBIS, Marvin J. *(Senior Judge, United States District Court District of Maryland)* Appointed for life by President George Bush to term beginning Dec 8, 1989. Assumed Senior status, serves by assignment. Born Baltimore Maryland June 14, 1936. Jewish. Educated at Johns Hopkins University B.E.S. 1958, Harvard Law School J.D. 1961 and Georgetown University Law Center LL.M. 1962. Admitted to practice District of Columbia 1961, Maryland 1962 and U.S. Supreme Court 1967. In legal practice Baltimore Maryland 1967-88 and Washington D.C. 1988-89.

Author *Cases and Materials on Tax Procedure and Tax Fraud* West Publishing Co. 1982 and 1990 and *Federal Tax Litigation* Warren, Gorham & Lamont 1985. Important Decisions: Adams v. Blue Cross (breast cancer treatment ordered) 757 F. Supp. 318, 1991; Maryshow v. Bladensburg (severance procedure) 139 F.R.D. 318, 1991; and Reusch v. Fountain (special education) F. Supp. 1994. Instructor in Tax Procedure University of Maryland School of Law and University of Baltimore School of Law. Member American Bar Association (Committee on Civil and Criminal Tax Penalties Section of Taxation). Honorary Justice Federal Court of Australia 1998.

Office: 5C U.S. Courthouse, 101 West Lombard Street, Baltimore 21201-2690.

Telephone: (410) 962-7700.

GASPAROVIC, Gary S. *(Associate Judge, Maryland District Court District Four)* Appointed by governor.

Mailing address: P.O. Box 3070, La Plata 20646-3070.

Office: 200 Charles Street, La Plata 20646.

Telephone: (301) 932-3280.

GATEWOOD, Askew W., Jr. *(Associate Judge, Maryland District Court District One)* Appointed by governor.

Office: 5800 Wabash Avenue, Baltimore 21215-3330.

Telephone: (410) 878-8107.

GAUVEY, Susan K. *(Magistrate Judge, United States District Court District of Maryland)* Appointed by U.S. District Court judges Feb 26, 1996. Term expires Feb 2004. Born Van Wert Ohio March 1, 1948. Educated at Georgetown University School of Foreign Service 1968-69, Rosary College B.A. cum laude 1970, Northwestern University School of Law J.D. 1973 and Johns Hopkins University 1976-77. Law Clerk to Hon. Morell E. Sharp, U.S. District Court Western District of Washington 1973-74. Admitted to practice Washington 1974, Maryland 1976, U.S. District Court District of Maryland and U.S. Court of Appeals Fourth Circuit. In legal practice Baltimore Maryland 1986-96.

Staff Attorney Aug 1975 to Jan 1977 and Chief Jan 1977 to April 1979 Mental Health Law Project Legal Aid Bureau. Assistant Attorney General Department of Health and Mental Hygiene April 1979 to June 1981 and Civil Division June 1981 to April 1986 and Principal Counsel for Trial Litigation June 1984 to April 1986 Office of the Attorney General Maryland. Co-author "In Their Own Words: Addicts' Reasons for Initiating and Withdrawing from Heroin" 6 No. 4 The International Journal of the Addictions 635-645, 1971; "Staff and Client Attitudes Towards Methadone Maintenance" 7 No. 2 The International Journal of the Addictions 247-255, 1972; "The Permissibility of Involuntary Sterilization Under the Parens Patriae and Police Power Authority of the State: In Re Sterilization of Moore" 6 University of Maryland Law Forum 109, 1976; "Informed and Substitute Consent to Health Care Procedures: A Proposal for State Legislation" 15 Harvard Journal on Legislation 431 April 1978; "Alternative Dispute Resolution in Multiple Product Liability Cases" Product Safety & Liability Reporter 549-556 Bureau of National Affairs June 10, 1988; and "The Perils of Document Production: Inadvertent Waiver of Privileged Documents" XXVI No. 3 Maryland B. Jour. May/June 1993. Author "Local Counsel Beware" XXI No. 2 Maryland B. Jour. March/April 1988; "ADR: The Growing Recognition of the Need for Private Bar's Responsibility and Role in ADR" XXVI No. 4 Maryland B. Jour. Sept/Oct 1993; "Settlement Discussions and the Attorney-Client Privilege" XXIX No. 1 Maryland B. Jour. Jan/Feb 1996; and "ADR's Integration in the Federal Court System" *Litigation Issue* Maryland B. Jour. March 2001. Member Women's Law Center, National Association of Women Judges and Federal Magistrate Judges Association. Chair Board of Directors Marian House for Women. Member Network 2000.

Office: 820 U.S. Courthouse, 101 West Lombard Street, Baltimore 21201-2690.

Telephone: (410) 962-4953.

GELFMAN, Lenore R. *(Associate Judge, Circuit Court for Howard County, Fifth Judicial Circuit)* Former Associate Judge, Maryland District Court District Ten.

Office: Court House, Ellicott City 21043.

Telephone: (410) 313-2143.

GESNER, Beth P. *(Magistrate Judge, United States District Court District of Maryland)* Appointed by U.S. District Court judges to term beginning May 1999. Term expires May 2007. Born Pittsburgh Pennsylvania Aug 25, 1958. Educated at Indiana University of Pennsylvania 1979 and Georgetown University Law Center J.D. cum laude 1983. Associate Editor The Tax Lawyer. Law Clerk to Hon. William Benson Bryant, U.S. District Court District of Columbia 1983-84. Admitted to prac-

GESNER, BETH P.—*Continued*

tice U.S. District Courts District of Columbia and District of Maryland and U.S. Courts of Appeals Fourth and District of Columbia Circuits. In legal practice Washington D.C. Oct 1984 to March 1987.

Office: U.S. Courthouse, 101 West Lombard Street, Baltimore 21201-2691.

Telephone: (410) 962-4288.

GETER, Melanie M. Shaw *(Associate Judge, Circuit Court for Prince George's County, Seventh Judicial Circuit)* Appointed by Governor Parris N. Glendening. Former Associate Judge, Maryland District Court District Five.

Office: Court House, 14735 Main Street, Upper Marlboro 20772.

Telephone: (301) 952-3808.

GLYNN, John M. *(Associate Judge, Circuit Court for Baltimore City, Eighth Judicial Circuit)* Appointed by Governor Parris N. Glendening. Former Associate Judge, Maryland District Court District One.

Office: Courthouse, 100 North Calvert Street, Baltimore 21202.

Telephone: (410) 396-5090.

GORDY, Clifton J., Jr. *(Associate Judge, Circuit Court for Baltimore City, Eighth Judicial Circuit)* Appointed by Governor Harry Roe Hughes to term beginning May 24, 1985. Elected Nov 4, 1986 and Nov 2001. Current term expires Nov 2016. Born Delmar Maryland Nov 6, 1946. Religious affiliation: Union Baptist Church. Educated at Maryland State College B.A. 1968 and University of Maryland School of Law J.D. 1973. Member Omega Psi Phi. Admitted to practice Maryland 1973. In legal practice Baltimore April 1975 to Aug 1977.

Assistant State's Attorney 1973-75 and 1977-85. Former member Maryland State's Attorneys Association. Member State Conference of Circuit Court Judges 1988-90, Maryland State Bar Association, Inc. and Monumental City Bar Association. Attended Maryland State Judicial Conferences. Faculty member Sexual Assault Seminar. Participant Tri-State Judicial Seminar Maryland Institute for Continuing Professional Legal Education. Recipient Outstanding Alumnus Award from Maryland State College 1985. Public school teacher 1968-70. Former member Baltimore City Board of Bail Bond Licensing Commissioners. Board of Directors West Baltimore Community Health Care Corporation. Committee member Baltimore Museum of Art. Member America-Israel Society.

Office: Courthouse East, 111 North Calvert Street, Baltimore 21202.

Telephone: (410) 396-5062.

GREEN, Leo Edward, Jr. *(Associate Judge, Maryland District Court District Five)* Appointed by Governor Parris N. Glendening.

Office: 14735 Main Street, Suite 173B, Upper Marlboro 20772.

Telephone: (301) 952-4011.

GREENE, Clayton, Jr. *(Associate Judge, Court of Special Appeals of Maryland)* Appointed by Governor Parris N. Glendening to term beginning Jan 4, 2002. Born Glen Burnie Maryland Jan 22, 1951. Educated at University of Maryland B.A. 1973 J.D. 1976. Admitted to practice Maryland 1977, U.S. District Court District of Maryland and U.S. Courts of Appeals Fourth and District of Columbia Circuits. In legal practice 1977-88. Associate Judge 1988-95 and Administrative Judge 1990-95, Maryland District Court District Seven. Associate Judge 1995-2002, Circuit Administrative Judge Nov 1996 to Jan 4, 2002 and County Administrative Judge Nov 1996 to Jan 4, 2002, Circuit Court for Anne Arundel County, Fifth Judicial Circuit.

Assistant County Solicitor Anne Arundel County 1977-78. Assistant Public Defender 1978-85 and Deputy Public Defender 1985-88 District Seven Anne Arundel County. Member Commissioner Education Committee 1988, Gender Equality Committee 1989, Court of Appeals Standing Committee on Rules of Practice and Procedure 1990-95 and Public Awareness Committee Maryland Judicial Conference since 2000. Member Maryland Trial Lawyers Association, Maryland Circuit Judges Association, The District of Columbia Bar, Maryland State Bar Association, Inc. and Anne Arundel County Bar Association. Legal Consultant Wiley H. Bates Foundation 1985-88.

Office: Courts of Appeal Building, 361 Rowe Boulevard, Annapolis 21401.

Telephone: (410) 260-1520.

GRIMM, Paul W. *(Magistrate Judge, United States District Court District of Maryland)* Appointed by U.S. District Court judges to term beginning Feb 5, 1997. Term expires Feb 4, 2005. Born Yokohama Japan Dec 26, 1951. Educated at University of California at Davis A.B. summa cum laude 1973 and University of New Mexico School of Law J.D. magna cum laude 1976. Staff member New Mexico Law Review. Member Phi Beta Kappa and Order of the Coif. In legal practice Maryland 1984-97.

Office: 810 U.S. Courthouse, 101 West Lombard Street, Baltimore 21201-2690.

Telephone: (410) 962-4560.

GROTON, Thomas C., III *(Associate Judge, Circuit Court for Worcester County, First Judicial Circuit)* Appointed by Governor William D. Schaefer to term beginning Jan 4, 1990. Elected Nov 1990, current term expires 2005. Born Baltimore Maryland Aug 6, 1947. Episcopalian. Educated at Washington and Lee University B.A. 1970 and University of Baltimore School of Law J.D. 1974. Admitted to practice Maryland 1974, U.S. District Court District of Maryland 1975, U.S. Court of Appeals Fourth Circuit 1978 and U.S. Supreme Court 1978. In legal practice Snow Hill 1974-78 and Berlin 1978-83. Associate Judge 1983-85 and Administrative Judge 1985-89, Maryland District Court District Two, appointed by Governor Harry Roe Hughes.

Deputy City Solicitor Ocean City 1978-82. Attorney Board of Zoning Appeals 1978-83 and Planning and Zoning Commission 1978-83 Ocean City and Planning Commission Snow Hill 1981-83. Assistant State's Attorney 1979-82 and Assistant Public Defender 1982-83 Worcester County. Member The Association of Trial Lawyers of America, National District Attorneys Association, Maryland State Bar Association, Inc., Worcester County and American Bar Associations. Board of Trustees Julia A. Purnell Museum 1978-86. Member Snow Hill Lions Club 1976-80, Worcester County Arts Council since 1976, Worcester County Historical Society 1976-89, Berlin/Ocean City Jaycees (Legal Counsel 1981) 1978-84, Snow Hill Charter Revision Committee 1979-84, Worcester County Commission on Aging 1979-

GROTON, THOMAS C., III—*Continued*
85, Snow Hill Recreation Committee 1979-84 and Assateague Mobile Sportsman Association 1979-86. Vestry 1982-85 and 1994-98 and Junior Warden 1997 All Hallows Episcopal Church. Executive Committee Snow Hill Elementary School 1990-94. President Snow Hill Elementary School P.T.A. 1990-94 and Nassawango Swim Team Association 1992-93. Committee Member 1994-2001 and Committee Chair since 1999 Pocomoke Boy Scout Troup 193. Board of Directors Lower Shore YMCA. Chairman Worcester County Advisory Council-Mental Health-Drug Addiction/Alcoholism.
Office: 228A Courthouse, One West Market Street, Snow Hill 21863-1080.
Telephone: (410) 632-0600.

HACKNER, Paul A. *(Associate Judge, Circuit Court for Anne Arundel County, Fifth Judicial Circuit)* Former Associate Judge, Maryland District Court District Seven, appointed by Governor Parris N. Glendening.
Office: Court House, Church Circle, Annapolis 21401.
Telephone: (410) 222-1375.

HAMILTON, Barry A. *(Associate Judge, Maryland District Court District Six)* Appointed by governor.
Office: 27 Court House Square, Rockville 20850-2325.
Telephone: (301) 279-1551.

HANDY, Althea M. *(Associate Judge, Circuit Court for Baltimore City, Eighth Judicial Circuit)*
Office: Courthouse, 100 North Calvert Street, Baltimore 21202.
Telephone: (410) 396-5054.

HANTMAN, Sue-Ellen *(Associate Judge, Maryland District Court District Ten)* Appointed by governor.
Office: 3451 Courthouse Drive, Ellicott City 21043-4377.
Telephone: (410) 480-7706.

HARGADON, Edward R. K. *(Associate Judge, Circuit Court for Baltimore City, Eighth Judicial Circuit)*
Office: Courthouse East, 111 North Calvert Street, Baltimore 21202.
Telephone: (410) 396-5070.

HARGROVE, John R., Jr. *(Associate Judge, Maryland District Court District One)* Appointed by governor.
Office: 5800 Wabash Avenue, Baltimore 21215-3330.
Telephone: (410) 878-8107.

HARRELL, Glenn T., Jr. *(Associate Judge, Court of Appeals of Maryland)* Appointed by Governor Parris N. Glendening to term beginning Sept 10, 1999. Retained by election 2000, current term expires Nov 2010. Born Ashland Kentucky June 27, 1945. Educated at University of Maryland B.A. 1967 J.D. 1970. Member Phi Alpha Delta. Admitted to practice Maryland 1970, U.S. District Court District of Maryland 1972, U.S. Supreme Court 1974 and U.S. Court of Appeals Fourth Circuit 1980. In legal practice Hillcrest Heights 1973-76 and Upper Marlboro 1977-91. Associate Judge, Court of Special Appeals of Maryland May 28, 1991 to Sept 9, 1999, appointed by Governor William D. Schaefer.
Associate County Attorney Prince George's County 1971-73. Chair Maryland Commission on Judicial Disabilities 1996-98. Member Maryland State Bar Association, Inc. and Prince George's County Bar Association.
Mailing address: P.O. Box 209, Upper Marlboro 20773-0209.
Office: Courthouse, 150B Bourne Wing, Upper Marlboro 20772.
Telephone: (301) 952-2716.
Fax: (301) 574-5282

HARRINGTON, Ann S. *(Associate Judge, Circuit Court for Montgomery County, Sixth Judicial Circuit)* Former Associate Judge, Maryland District Court District Six.
Office: 50 Maryland Avenue, Rockville 20850.
Telephone: (240) 777-9240.

HARRINGTON, Louis Draper *(Associate Judge, Maryland District Court District Six)* Appointed by Governor Harry Roe Hughes to term beginning July 30, 1982. Reappointed by Governor William D. Schaefer 1992 and Governor Parris N. Glendening 2002. Current term expires July 30, 2012. Born Philadelphia Pennsylvania Oct 16, 1939. Religious affiliation: Society of Friends (Quakers). Educated at Swarthmore College 1957-59, Earlham College B.A. 1961, University of Pennsylvania M.A. 1963 and George Washington University LL.B. 1966. Admitted to practice Maryland 1966, District of Columbia 1966 and U.S. Supreme Court 1969. Began legal practice Washington D.C. 1966. In legal practice Rockville 1970-82.
Member Judicial Ethics Committee Maryland Judicial Conference 1986-91, The District of Columbia Bar, Maryland State Bar Association, Inc. (Board of Governors 1978-80) and American Bar Association. Named Montgomery County Volunteer of the Year 1976. Democrat. Board of Trustees The Sidwell Friends School, Washington D.C. 1988-96. Member Antique Automobile Club of America, Cadillac-LaSalle Car Club and Nash Car Club. Interested in antique automobiles.
Office: 27 Courthouse Square, Rockville 20850-2325.
Telephone: (301) 279-1544.
Fax: (301) 279-1739

HARVEY, Alexander, II *(Senior Judge, United States District Court District of Maryland)* Appointed for life by President Lyndon B. Johnson to term beginning 1966. Former Chief Judge. Assumed Senior status March 1991, serves by assignment. Born Baltimore Maryland May 3, 1923. Episcopalian (Vestry 1967-70). Educated at Yale University B.A 1947 and Columbia University LL.B. 1950. Member Phi Beta Kappa. Admitted to practice Maryland 1950. In legal practice Baltimore 1950-66.
Assistant Attorney General Maryland 1957-58. Member Governor's Committee to Study Blue Sky Law of Maryland 1961. Member Coordinating Committee for Multiple Litigation 1968-75 and member 1975-83 and Chairman 1978-83 Committee on the Administration of the Criminal Law Judicial Conference of the U.S. Member Committee on District Judge Education Federal Judicial Center 1989-92. Member Character Committee Maryland Court of Appeals from Eighth Judicial Circuit, The Bar Association of Baltimore City, Maryland State Bar Association, Inc. and American Bar Association. First Lieutenant U.S. Army ETO WWII. Board of Directors Baltimore Symphony Association 1966-68 and Baltimore Council of Social Agencies 1957-63. President

HARVEY, ALEXANDER, II—*Continued*
and Director Baltimore Opera Guild 1960. Trustee Church Home and Hospital 1952-71.
Office: 5D U.S. Courthouse, 101 West Lombard Street, Baltimore 21201-2690.
Telephone: (410) 962-4655.

HAYMAN, R. Patrick *(Associate Judge, Maryland District Court District Two)* Appointed by Governor Parris N. Glendening to term beginning Feb 12, 1999. Term expires Dec 19, 2008. Born Salisbury Maryland Dec 19, 1938. Episcopalian. Educated at University of Virginia B.A. 1960 and University of Maryland J.D. 1971. Admitted to practice Maryland 1972 and U.S. District Court District of Maryland 1976. In legal practice Crisfield 1972-73 and Princess Anne 1973-99.
Public Defender Somerset County 1973-99. Member Maryland State Bar Association, Inc. and Somerset County Bar Association (President 1975). Sergeant U.S. Army 1961-64.
Office: 11559 Somerset Avenue, Princess Anne 21853.
Telephone: (410) 651-2713.

HEARD, Wanda Keyes *(Associate Judge, Circuit Court for Baltimore City, Eighth Judicial Circuit)* Appointed by Governor Parris N. Glendening to term beginning Feb 3, 1999. Elected Nov 2000, current term expires 2015. Born Long Branch New Jersey June 1957. Baptist. Educated at University of Maryland B.A. 1979 J.D. 1982. Law Clerk to Hon. Robert L. Karwacki, Circuit Court for Baltimore City, Eighth Judicial Circuit June 1981 to June 1983. Admitted to practice Maryland 1983, U.S. District Court District of Maryland 1985 and U.S. Supreme Court 1989. In legal practice June 1985 to July 1986.
Assistant State's Attorney Baltimore City June 1983 to 1985 and 1988 to Dec 1990. Assistant Attorney General Maryland 1986-87. Assistant Federal Defender District of Maryland Office of the Federal Defender June 1987 to Sept 1988. Assistant U.S. Attorney St. Croix U.S. Virgin Islands Jan 1991 to Feb 1994 and Middle District of Florida Feb 1994 to Nov 1998. Member National Association of Women Judges, The Bar Association of Baltimore City, Maryland State Bar Association, Inc. and Monumental Bar Association. Instructor OLE Basic Criminal Trial Advocacy Course 1995 and EOUSA Working Group on Child Support Enforcement 1996 and 1998. Attended EOUSA Working Group on Federal Domestic Violence 1996 and 1997. Presenter Florida Governor Domestic Violence Summit 1996 and 1997. Presenter/Organizer Weed and Seed Law Enforcement Conference 1998. Recipient Special Achievement Award from U.S. Department of Justice 1992, Exceptional Training Award from Florida Police Chiefs Association 1995, Recognition Award from U.S. Secret Service 1997 and Drug Enforcement Administration 1997, Letter of Commendation from Attorney General Janet Reno July 1997 and Oct 1997 and Community Service Award from Edmondson Community Center 2000. Co-chair Community Law in Action. Speaker C.H.I.L.D. (Children's Health Involving Law and Drugs). Board Member Hunting Ridge Committee. Enjoys jogging and reading. Participates in outreach to teen youth.
Office: Courthouse East, 111 North Calvert Street, Baltimore 21202.
Telephone: (410) 396-4918.
E-mail address: Wanda.Heard@courts.state.md.us

HEFFRON, Robert Wilson *(Associate Judge, Maryland District Court District Five)* Appointed by Governor Parris N. Glendening.
Office: 14735 Main Street, Suite 173B, Upper Marlboro 20772.
Telephone: (301) 952-4011.

HELLER, Ellen M. *(Circuit Administrative Judge, Circuit Court for Baltimore City, Eighth Judicial Circuit)* Appointed by Governor Harry R. Hughes to term beginning Dec 6, 1986. Elected Nov 1988, current term expires Nov 2003. Judge-in-Charge of Civil Docket since 1993. Educated at Syracuse University 1958-60, Johns Hopkins University B.S. with honors 1972 and University of Maryland School of Law J.D. with honors 1977. Recipient American Jurisprudence Award in Business Associations 1975. Research Assistant to Hon. Martin B. Greenfeld, Supreme Bench of Baltimore City. Admitted to practice Maryland, U.S. District Court District of Maryland, U.S. Court of Appeals Fourth Circuit and U.S. Supreme Court.
Assistant Attorney General (Deputy Chief Education Affairs Division, Principal Counsel Maryland State Department of Education) Office of the Attorney General 1977-86. Co-author with Special Committee on Law Practice Quality "Law Practice Quality Guidelines" Maryland State Bar Association, Inc. 1985 and with S. Stiller "Eleventh Amendment Abrogation Developments" XXII No. 6 The Maryland B. Jour. Nov-Dec 1989. Author "Scientific Creationism" 7 No. 40 *Science, Technology and Human Value* Summer 1982; "Overview: Framework of Elementary and Secondary Education in Maryland" Nov 1985, "The Supreme Court and Education: Reflections on Past and Future Decisions" Nov 1986 and "Recent Decisions on Education Law at the National Level" Feb 1990 *Education and the Law* MICPEL; "The Politicalization of American Education" XVIII No. 10 Dec 1985, "Mandatory CLE: The Pros and Cons" XX No. 2 Feb 1987 and "ADR Alternative in Baltimore City" XXVI No. 5 Sept/Oct 1993 The Maryland B. Jour.; "Sticks and Stones: The Ongoing Debate Over Offensive Speech" Dec 27, 1991 to Jan 3, 1992, "Trial Dates and Postponement Policy" Feb 27, 1993, "Changes in the Trial Calendar" March 27, 1993, "Ex Parte Orders" April 24, 1993, "Striking of Attorney Appearance" May 22, 1993, "Lead Paint Related Cases" June 26, 1993, "Thank You to Civil Mediators" July 14, 1993 and "Motions Docket: How to Navigate it Successfully" Sept 24, 1994 *The Daily Record;* and "Hate: Free Speech or Crime" 7 *The Barrister* Spring 1994. Adjunct Professor University of Maryland School of Law 1984-93. Fellow Maryland Bar Foundation and American Bar Foundation. President (first woman) National Council of State Board Attorneys 1984. Trustee Maryland Institute for Continuing Professional Education of Lawyers, Inc. 1985-87. Advisory Board Child Care Mediation Service 1988-89 and Director Civil Mediation Program since 1991 Circuit Court for Baltimore City. Chair Committee on Civil Law and Procedure Conference of Circuit Court Judges 1993-94. Member Maryland Women Judges Task Force on Women in Prison since 1993. Member The American Law Institute, The Serjeants' Inn Law Club, The Rule Day Club, The Lawyers' Round Table Law Club, Maryland Circuit Judges Association (Judge-to-Judge Committee), National Association of Women Jud-

HELLER, ELLEN M.—*Continued*

ges, The Bar Association of Baltimore City (Ethics Committee 1982-87, Publications Committee since 1992, Judicial Administration Committee 1994-95), Women's Bar Association of Maryland (Steering Committee Baltimore City/Baltimore County Chapter since 1987), Maryland State Bar Association, Inc. (Member 1982-94 and Chair 1989 Special Committee on Law Practice Quality, Council Member State and Local Government Section since 1983, Chair Committee on Continuing Legal Education 1986-87) and American Bar Association. President and Honorary Board Member Cross Country Improvement Association 1971-86. Board Member Epilepsy Foundation of Maryland 1981-83 and Maryland School for the Blind 1987-89. Member Executive Committee Baltimore Jewish Community Relations Council 1982-84, Commission for Students at Risk Maryland State Department of Education 1988-89 and Dean's Working Group on Women's Health Issues Johns Hopkins University School of Hygiene and Public Health since 1992. Board of Visitors since 1992 and Chair Program Development Committee University of Maryland School of Law. Advisory Council The Learning Bank since 1992. Board of Directors Cycle Across Maryland since 1993 and American Jewish Joint Distribution Committee, Inc. since 1994.

Office: Courthouse East, 111 North Calvert Street, Baltimore 21202.

Telephone: (410) 396-4916.

HENDERSON, Christopher C. *(Associate Judge, Circuit Court for Charles County, Seventh Judicial Circuit)*

Mailing address: P.O. Box 970, La Plata 20646.

Office: 200 Charles Street, La Plata 20646.

Telephone: (301) 932-3250.

HENNEGAN, John O. *(Associate Judge, Circuit Court for Baltimore County, Third Judicial Circuit)*

Office: County Courts Building, 401 Bosley Avenue, Towson 21204.

Telephone: (410) 887-3290.

HOLLAND, Marcella A. *(Associate Judge, Circuit Court for Baltimore City, Eighth Judicial Circuit)* Appointed by Governor Parris N. Glendening to term beginning Sept 18, 1997. Elected Nov 1998, current term expires 2013. Born Baltimore Maryland Aug 31, 1947. Baptist. Educated at University of Maryland B.A. 1980 J.D. with honors 1983. Law Clerk to Hon. Robert M. Bell, Circuit Court for Baltimore City, Eighth Judicial Circuit 1982-83. Member Phi Alpha Delta. Admitted to practice Maryland 1983 and U.S. Supreme Court 1992.

Assistant State's Attorney Jan 1984 to Sept 1997. Member National Association of Women Judges (President Maryland Chapter since 2000), Bar Association of Baltimore City, Maryland State Bar Association, Inc., Monumental City, National and American Bar Associations. Attended Judicial Conference National Bar Association and Judicial Division American Bar Association. Recipient Thurgood Marshall Founder's Award from Monumental City Bar Association 1993 and Outstanding Professional Achievement Award from Coalition of 100 Black Women 1997. Named Volunteer of the Year by Druid Hill YMCA 1996, Scholarship Fundraiser Honoree by Associated Managers' 1996 and one of Maryland's Top 100 Women 1998 and 2000. Board of Managers Druid Hill YMCA. Member Commission on Historical and Architectural Preservation for Baltimore City, AFRAM Committee, Courthouse and Law Museum Foundation, NAACP and Lois G. Wright Memorial Concert Series Board. Enjoys reading, photography and travel.

Office: Courthouse East, 111 North Calvert Street, Baltimore 21202.

Telephone: (410) 396-3836.

E-mail address: Marcella.Holland@courts.state.md.us

HOLLANDER, Ellen Lipton *(Associate Judge, Court of Special Appeals of Maryland)* Appointed by Governor William Donald Schaefer to term beginning Oct 3, 1994. Retained by election. Born New York New York May 24, 1949. Educated at Goucher College B.A. 1971 and Georgetown University Law Center J.D. 1974. Associate Editor 1972-73 and Editor 1973-74 American Criminal Law Review. Law Clerk to Hon. James R. Miller, Jr., U.S. District Court District of Maryland 1974-75. Admitted to practice Maryland 1974, U.S. District Court District of Maryland 1975 and U.S. Court of Appeals Fourth Circuit 1975. In legal practice Baltimore 1975-89. Associate Judge, Circuit Court for Baltimore City, Eighth Judicial Circuit, March 1, 1989 to Oct 3, 1994, appointed by Governor William Donald Schaefer.

Assistant Attorney General Maryland May 1979 to Oct 1979. Assistant U.S. Attorney District of Maryland Nov 1979 to March 1983. Contributing Author *Res Ipsa Loquitor* 1974. Author "Juvenile Court: The Guardian of Children" 27 Maryland B. Jour. 9 May/June 1994. Member U.S. Magistrate Merit Selection Panel 1983-89 and Committee to Revise the Local Rules 1988-89 U.S. District Court District of Maryland. Chair Sentencing Review Panel Circuit Court for Baltimore City, Eighth Judicial Circuit 1992-93. Member Maryland Bar Foundation, Wrangler's Law Club, Rule Day Club, J. Dudley Digges Inn of Court Chapter XIII American Inns of Court Foundation, Women's Law Center, Maryland Judicial Conference (Committee on Juvenile Law since 1992), The Bar Association of Baltimore City (Special Committee on Fee Abuse 1988), Women's Bar Association of Maryland, Maryland State Bar Association, Inc., Federal (Executive Board Maryland Chapter 1987-91) and American Bar Associations. Recipient Award for Outstanding Public Service from Northwest Citizens Patrol 1989. Member Baltimore Jewish Council (Executive Committee since 1987, Chair Holocaust Remembrance Committee 1988-92 and World Jewry and International Human Rights Committee 1992-93, Second Vice President 1993-94, Secretary since 1994). Board of Directors Advocates For Children and Youth, Inc. 1994-96 and Baltimore Bar Library since 1994. Board of Trustees Goucher College since 1996.

Office: 626 Courthouse East, 111 North Calvert Street, Baltimore 21202.

Telephone: (410) 333-6241.

HOLT-STONE, C. Yvonne *(Associate Judge, Maryland District Court District One)* Appointed by Governor William D. Schaefer.

Office: 5800 Wabash Avenue, Baltimore 21215-3330.

Telephone: (410) 878-8107.

HONG, Jeannie Jinkyung *(Associate Judge, Maryland District Court District One)* Appointed by governor.

Office: 5800 Wabash Avenue, Baltimore 21215-3330.

Telephone: (410) 878-8107.

HORNE, William S. *(Circuit Administrative Judge, Circuit Court for Talbot County, Second Judicial Circuit)* Also serves as County Administrative Judge Talbot County.
Mailing address: P.O. Box 723, Easton 21601.
Office: Court House, 11 North Washington Street, Easton 21601.
Telephone: (410) 822-4444.

HOTTEN, Michele D. *(Associate Judge, Circuit Court for Prince George's County, Seventh Judicial Circuit)* Former Associate Judge, Maryland District Court District Five.
Office: Court House, 14735 Main Street, Upper Marlboro 20772.
Telephone: (301) 952-3788.

HUTCHINS, Miriam Brown *(Associate Judge, Maryland District Court District One)* Appointed by Governor Parris N. Glendening.
Office: 5800 Wabash Avenue, Baltimore 21215-3330.
Telephone: (410) 878-8017.

JACKSON, Dwight David *(Associate Judge, Circuit Court for Prince George's County, Seventh Judicial Circuit)* Appointed by Governor Parris N. Glendening.
Office: Court House, 14735 Main Street, Upper Marlboro 20772.
Telephone: (301) 952-4342.

JACKSON, Richard Eli *(Associate Judge, Circuit Court for Cecil County, Second Judicial Circuit)*
Office: 129 East Main Street, Elkton 21921.
Telephone: (410) 996-5317.

JAKLITSCH, Michele Dane *(Associate Judge, Circuit Court for Anne Arundel County, Fifth Judicial Circuit)*
Office: Court House, Church Circle, Annapolis 21401.
Telephone: (410) 222-1455.

JAKUBOWSKI, Ruth A. *(Associate Judge, Circuit Court for Baltimore County, Third Judicial Circuit)*
Office: County Courts Building, 401 Bosley Avenue, Towson 21204.
Telephone: (410) 887-2628.

JENSEN, Karen A. Murphy *(Associate Judge, Circuit Court for Caroline County, Second Judicial Circuit)* Appointed by Governor Parris N. Glendening. Also serves as County Administrative Judge Caroline County.
Office: Court House, 109 Market Street, Denton 21629.
Telephone: (410) 479-2303.

JOHNSON, Donald F. *(Associate Judge, Circuit Court for Dorchester County, First Judicial Circuit)* Also serves as County Administrative Judge Dorchester County.
Mailing address: P.O. Box 150, Cambridge 21613.
Office: 206 High Street, Cambridge 21613.
Telephone: (410) 228-6300.

JOHNSON, Eric M. *(Associate Judge, Circuit Court for Montgomery County, Sixth Judicial Circuit)* Appointed by Governor Parris N. Glendening. Former Associate Judge, Maryland District Court District Six.
Office: 50 Maryland Avenue, Rockville 20850.
Telephone: (240) 777-9197.

JOHNSON, Megan B. *(Associate Judge, Maryland District Court District Seven)* Appointed by Governor Parris N. Glendening.
Office: 7500 Governor Ritchie Highway, Glen Burnie 21061-3756.
Telephone: (410) 260-1828.

JOHNSON, Norman E., Jr. *(Associate Judge, Maryland District Court District One)* Appointed by governor.
Office: 5800 Wabash Avenue, Baltimore 21215-3330.
Telephone: (410) 878-8107.

JOHNSON, Stephen P. *(Associate Judge, Maryland District Court District Six)* Appointed by governor.
Office: 27 Court House Square, Rockville 20850-2325.
Telephone: (301) 279-1551.

JUNG, Barbara R. *(Associate Judge, Maryland District Court District Eight)* Appointed by governor.
Office: 120 East Chesapeake Avenue, Towson 21286-5307.
Telephone: (410) 512-2050.

KAHL, Christian M. *(Associate Judge, Circuit Court for Baltimore County, Third Judicial Circuit)* Appointed by Governor William D. Schaefer to term beginning Sept 10, 1990. Elected Nov 3, 1992, current term expires Nov 3, 2007. Born Baltimore Maryland Dec 21, 1935. Protestant. Educated at Johns Hopkins University A.B. 1958 and University of Baltimore LL.B. 1963. Law Clerk to Hon. Lester L. Barrett, Circuit Court of Maryland Third Judicial Circuit 1962-64. Admitted to practice Maryland 1963 and U.S. Supreme Court 1968. In legal practice Towson 1964-84. Associate Judge, Maryland District Court District Eight 1984-90.

Instructor in Business Law Dundalk Community College 1985-96. Member Conference of Circuit Judges, Maryland Judicial Conference, Maryland State Bar Association, Inc. and Baltimore County Bar Association. Attends annual sessions of Maryland Judicial Institute. First Lieutenant USAF and Maryland Air National Guard 1959-65.
Office: County Courts Building, 401 Bosley Avenue, Towson 21204.
Telephone: (410) 887-2500.

KAMINETZ, Marvin S. *(Associate Judge, Circuit Court for St. Mary's County, Seventh Judicial Circuit)*
Office: 41605 Courthouse Drive, Leonardtown 20650.
Telephone: (301) 475-4623.

KANE, Raymond J., Jr. *(Associate Judge, Circuit Court for Howard County, Fifth Judicial Circuit)* Former County Administrative Judge Howard County. Born Baltimore Maryland June 9, 1938. Educated at Loyola College and University of Maryland LL.B. 1963. Admitted to practice Maryland 1964. Former Judge, Maryland District Court District Ten, appointed by Acting Governor Blair Lee III to term beginning Dec 8, 1977.

Former Assistant State's Attorney, Special Prosecutor and Special Assistant Attorney General. Co-editor Howard County Code 1970 and 1972. Member The Association of Trial Lawyers of America, Maryland State Bar Association, Inc., Howard County and American Bar Associations.
Office: Court House, Ellicott City 21043.
Telephone: (410) 313-2083.

KAPLAN, Joseph H. H. *(Associate Judge, Circuit Court for Baltimore City, Eighth Judicial Circuit)* Appointed by Governor Marvin Mandel to term beginning Jan 19, 1977. Elected 1978. Reappointed by Governor William Donald Schaefer Nov 1993. Reelected Nov 8, 1994, current term expires 2009. Circuit Administrative Judge Baltimore City 1984-99. Also serves as Chief Judge. Born Brooklyn New York Jan 2, 1937. Educated at Johns Hopkins University A.B. with honors 1957 and University of Chicago J.D. 1960. Editor Chicago Law Review. Research Assistant American Bar Foundation 1959-60. Law Clerk to Chief Judge Frederick W. Brune, Court of Appeals of Maryland 1960-61. Member Phi Delta Phi. Admitted to practice Maryland, U.S. Court of Appeals for the Armed Forces, U.S. District Court District of Maryland, U.S. Court of Appeals Fourth Circuit and U.S. Supreme Court. Began legal practice Baltimore 1962.

Assistant U.S. Attorney District of Maryland 1963-65. Consultant to Community Relations Service U.S. Department of Justice 1970. President 1979-83 and Board Member 1979-95 Library Company of the Baltimore Bar. Member Executive Committee Maryland Judicial Conference 1983-88. Former Member Serjeants' Inn Law Club and Barristers Law Club. Board Member since Nov 1981 and Chairman Jan 1990 to 1999 Maryland Sentencing Guidelines Project. Member since Nov 1982 and Member Emeritus since June 26, 2000 Standing Committee on Rules of Practice and Procedure Court of Appeals of Maryland. Member Commission on the Future of Maryland Courts, Commission on Criminal Sentencing Policy, Lawyers Round Table Law Club, J. Dudley Digges Inn of Court (President 1990-91), The Bar Association of Baltimore City (Former Member Committee for the Representation of Indigents in Criminal Cases, Committee on Legal Services to the Indigent and Juvenile Law Committee, Member Judicial Administration Committee, Family Law Committee, Criminal Law Committee, Alternative Dispute Resolution Committee, Historical Committee), Maryland State Bar Association, Inc. (Chairman 1975-76 and Ex-Officio Member Section of Criminal Law and Practice, Former Member and Co-chairman 1985-87 Judicial Administration Committee and Member Special Joint Committee on Alternative Methods of Settling Disputes now Alternate Dispute Resolution Section, Member Gender Issues Committee Administrative Law Section) and American Bar Association (Former Member Administration of Criminal Law and Prison Reform Committee and Sections of Litigation, Criminal Justice, National Conference of State Trial Judges Judicial Division and Senior Lawyers Division).

Former member Board of Directors Legal Aid Bureau Inc. Former Executive Secretary Mayor's Advisory Commission on Crime. Appointed by Governor Marvin Mandel as Commissioner on State Commission on Human Relations 1969-70. Appointed by Mayor William Donald Schaefer as member Expenditure Control Committee of Baltimore City 1972-77, Board of Ethics of Baltimore City 1972-77, Committee of Administrators of the Baltimore City Deferred Compensation Plan, Residency of City Employees Committee and Equal Opportunity Committee for the City of Baltimore. Former Chairman Baltimore City Executive Pay Plan Committee. President Civil Service Commission Baltimore City 1972-77. Recipient Certificate of Distinguished Citizenship from Governor Marvin Mandel 1971 and Mayor's Citation from the Hon. Thomas J. D'Alesandro III 1971. Lieutenant USNR JAGC. Former Vice President and member Board of Directors Big Brothers and Big Sisters of Central Maryland, Inc. Former member Board of Directors Woodbourne Center Inc., Quarter Way Houses, Inc. (Former President), Dismas House, Roland Park Civic League (Past Vice President) and Neighborhood Community Centers Inc. Past President Roland Park Roads and Maintenance Corporation. Chairman Alcoholism Services Advisory Committee Alcohol and Drug Abuse Program University of Maryland School of Medicine. Honorary member Board of Directors Asthma & Allergy Foundation of America Maryland Chapter since July 1986. Board of Advisors Charles McMathias, Jr. National Study Center for Trauma and EMS.

Office: 111 North Calvert Street, Baltimore 21202.
Telephone: (410) 396-5080.

KARASIC, Ronald Alan *(Associate Judge, Maryland District Court District One)* Appointed by Governor Parris N. Glendening.

Office: 5800 Wabash Avenue, Baltimore 21215-3330.
Telephone: (410) 878-8014.

KEIR, Duncan W. *(Judge, United States Bankruptcy Court District of Maryland)* Appointed by U.S. Court of Appeals Fourth Circuit judges.

Office: U.S. Courthouse, 6500 Cherrywood Lane, Greenbelt 20770-1290.
Telephone: (301) 344-3660.

KENNEY, James A., III *(Associate Judge, Court of Special Appeals of Maryland)* Appointed by Governor Parris N. Glendening to term beginning 1997. Born Salisbury Maryland March 26, 1937. Educated at Dickinson College B.A. 1959, Yale Divinity School and George Washington University National Law Center J.D. 1963. Admitted to practice Maryland 1963.

Assistant State's Attorney St. Mary's County 1964-67. Member American College of Real Property Lawyers, American Judicature Society, Maryland Bar Foundation, Maryland State Bar Association, Inc. and American Bar Association. Member Governor's Commission on Condominiums, Cooperatives and Homeowners Associations 1982-86. Chair St. Mary's County Economic Development Commission 1989-93. President St. Mary's College of Maryland Foundation 1993-99. Board of Governors Southern Maryland Higher Education Center 1993-99.

Mailing address: P.O. Box 653, Leonardtown 20650-0653.
Telephone: (301) 475-4182.

KIM, Brian G. *(Associate Judge, Maryland District Court District Six)* Appointed by governor.

Office: 27 Court House Square, Rockville 20850-2325.
Telephone: (301) 279-1551.

KRAUSER, Peter Brunswick *(Associate Judge, Court of Special Appeals of Maryland)* Appointed by Governor Parris N. Glendening to term beginning January 31, 2000. Born Philadelphia Pennsylvania May 5, 1947. Educated at Northwestern University B.A. 1969 and University of Pennsylvania Law School J.D. 1972. Law Clerk to Hon. John P. Fullam, U.S. District Court Eastern District of Pennsylvania. Admitted to practice Pennsylvania 1973, Maryland 1978 and Virginia 1997.

Former Appellate Attorney Criminal Division U.S. Department of Justice. Former Trial and Appellate Attorney Defender Association of Philadelphia. Former Gen-

KRAUSER, PETER BRUNSWICK—*Continued*

eral Counsel Prince George Center, Inc. Member Maryland State Bar Association, Inc., Prince George's County and American Bar Associations. Maryland State Chair National Jewish Democratic Council 1993-95. Chair Maryland Democratic Party 1997-2000. Board Member American Jewish Committee since 1991 and United Jewish Appeal Federation of Greater Washington since 1991. President Jewish Community Council of Greater Washington 1994-96. Founder and Chair Black-Jewish Seder of Prince George's County 1996-97.

Office: Courts of Appeal Building, 361 Rowe Boulevard, Annapolis 21401.

Telephone: (410) 260-1469.

KRAUSER, Sherrie L. *(Associate Judge, Circuit Court for Prince George's County, Seventh Judicial Circuit)* Former Associate Judge, Maryland District Court District Five.

Office: Court House, 14735 Main Street, Upper Marlboro 20772.

Telephone: (301) 952-5285.

KRUG, Warren J. *(Associate Judge, Circuit Court for Calvert County, Seventh Judicial Circuit)* Appointed by governor. Also serves as County Administrative Judge Calvert County.

Office: Calvert County Courthouse, 175 Main Street, Prince Frederick 20678.

Telephone: (410) 535-1600.

LAMASNEY, Maureen M. *(Associate Judge, Circuit Court for Prince George's County, Seventh Judicial Circuit)*

Office: Court House, 14735 Main Street, Upper Marlboro 20772.

Telephone: (301) 952-4309.

LAMDIN, Bruce Sewell *(Associate Judge, Maryland District Court District Eight)* Appointed by governor.

Office: 120 East Chesapeake Avenue, Towson 21286-5307.

Telephone: (410) 512-2050.

LAWS, Victor H., III *(Magistrate Judge, United States District Court District of Maryland)* Appointed by U.S. District Court judges to term beginning March 22, 1988. Reappointed March 22, 1992, March 22, 1996 and March 22, 2000. Current term expires March 21, 2004. Serves part time. Born Baltimore Maryland May 11, 1953. Methodist. Educated at Brown University A.B. 1975 and University of Maryland J.D. 1978. Admitted to practice Maryland 1978 and U.S. District Court District of Maryland 1979. In legal practice Salisbury since 1978.

Important Decisions: U.S. v. Biocic (constitutional validity of beach regulation against public nudity) No. 89-0064-V aff'd 730 F. Supp. 1364 D. Md. 1990, aff'd 928 F.2d 112, 4th Cir. 1991. Instructor in Constitutional Government and Civil Liberties Salisbury State University 1985-95. Member Maryland State Bar Association, Inc., Wicomico County (President 2000) and American Bar Associations. Democrat. Chair Wicomico County Task Force on Minor League Baseball 1994. Member Salisbury Area Chamber of Commerce (President 1997-98). Graduate Leadership Maryland 1999. Enjoys golf, tennis and family activities.

Mailing address: P.O. Box 75, Salisbury 21803-0075.

Telephone: (410) 749-7500.

LEASURE, Diane O. *(Circuit Administrative Judge, Circuit Court for Howard County, Fifth Judicial Circuit)* Assumed office Nov 13, 1995. Circuit Administrative Judge since Jan 4, 2002. Also serves as County Administrative Judge Howard County since Jan 4, 2002. Educated at Virginia Polytechnic Institute and State University, Glassboro State College B.A. magna cum laude, Drexel University M.A. and Rutgers University at Camden School of Law J.D. 1982. Admitted to practice Maryland 1982. Began legal practice Greenbelt.

Former Assistant Professor Rutgers University. Former Adjunct Professor Glassboro State College (now Rowan University). Past President Prince George's County Bar Association and James Macgill American Inn of Court. Former Member Board of Directors Maryland State Bar Association, Inc. Member Maryland Judicial Council, Conference of Circuit Court Judges and Howard County Bar Association. Chairperson Executive Committee Citizenship Law-Related Education Program Schools of Maryland.

Office: Courthouse, 8360 Court Avenue, Ellicott City 21043.

Telephone: (410) 313-2066.

LEASURE, Gary George *(Associate Judge, Circuit Court for Allegany County, Fourth Judicial Circuit)* Appointed by Governor Harry Roe Hughes to term beginning July 27, 1983. Elected to subsequent terms. Also serves as County Administrative Judge Allegany County. Born Cumberland Maryland July 7, 1946. Protestant. Educated at Frostburg State College B.S. 1968 and University of Maryland J.D. 1972. Law Clerk to Hon. Charles Orth, Court of Special Appeals of Maryland. Admitted to practice Maryland 1972 and U.S. Supreme Court 1978. Began legal practice Cumberland 1973.

Former County Attorney Allegany County and City Attorney Frostburg. Instructor Frostburg State College 1976-80. Member Maryland State Bar Association, Inc., Allegany County and American Bar Associations. Sergeant U.S. Army 1969-75. Democrat.

Office: Court House, 30 Washington Street, Cumberland 21502.

Telephone: (301) 777-2261.

LEGG, Benson Everett *(Chief Judge, United States District Court District of Maryland)* Appointed for life by President George Bush to term beginning 1991. Chief Judge since Jan 7, 2003. Born Baltimore Maryland June 8, 1947. Educated at Princeton University B.A. magna cum laude 1970 and University of Virginia School of Law J.D. 1973. Editorial Board Virginia Law Review 1971-73. Law Clerk to Hon. Frank Albert Kaufman, U.S. District Court District of Maryland 1973-74. Member Order of the Coif. Admitted to practice Maryland 1973. In legal practice 1975-91.

Member Serjeants' Inn, Maryland State Bar Association, Inc., Baltimore City and American Bar Associations. Advisory Board National Aquarium Baltimore since 1987. Trustee Baltimore Zoological Society since 1990.

Office: 3D U.S. Courthouse, 101 West Lombard Street, Baltimore 21201-2690.

Telephone: (410) 962-0723.

LESSER, Jack I. *(Associate Judge, Maryland District Court District One)* Appointed by governor.

Office: 5800 Wabash Avenue, Baltimore 21215-3330.

Telephone: (410) 878-8107.

LEVITZ, Dana Mark *(Associate Judge, Circuit Court for Baltimore County, Third Judicial Circuit)* Appointed by Governor Harry Roe Hughes Nov 25, 1985. Elected Nov 1988, current term expires Nov 2003. Born Baltimore Maryland Dec 8, 1948. Jewish. Educated at University of Maryland B.A. 1970 and University of Baltimore School of Law J.D. cum laude 1973. Staff member University of Baltimore Law Review 1972-73. Admitted to practice Maryland 1973. In legal practice Baltimore 1976-81.

Assistant State's Attorney Baltimore City 1973-75. Deputy Assistant State's Attorney Baltimore County 1975-85. Instructor University of Baltimore School of Law since 1985. Member National District Attorneys Association, The Association of Trial Lawyers of America, Maryland State Bar Association, Inc., Baltimore County and American Bar Associations. Member Jewish Big Brothers/Big Sisters League.

Office: County Courts Building, 401 Bosley Avenue, Towson 21204.
Telephone: (410) 887-2630.

LEWIS, Patrice E. *(Associate Judge, Maryland District Court District Five)* Appointed by governor.
Office: 14735 Main Street, Suite 173B, Upper Marlboro 20772.
Telephone: (301) 952-4011.

LIDUMS, O. Robert *(Associate Judge, Circuit Court for Cecil County, Second Judicial Circuit)*
Office: 129 East Main Street, Elkton 21921.
Telephone: (410) 996-5341.

LIPMAN, George *(Associate Judge, Maryland District Court District One)* Appointed by Governor Parris N. Glendening.
Office: 5800 Wabash Avenue, Baltimore 21215-3330.
Telephone: (410) 878-8107.

LOMBARDI, James J. *(Associate Judge, Circuit Court for Prince George's County, Seventh Judicial Circuit)*
Office: Court House, 14735 Main Street, Upper Marlboro 20772.
Telephone: (301) 952-3814.

LONEY, Michael E. *(Associate Judge, Circuit Court for Anne Arundel County, Fifth Judicial Circuit)* Former Associate Judge, Maryland District Court District Seven.
Office: Court House, Church Circle, Annapolis 21401.
Telephone: (410) 222-1290.

LONG, Daniel M. *(Circuit Administrative Judge, Circuit Court for Somerset County, First Judicial Circuit)* Also serves as County Administrative Judge Somerset County.
Office: Court House, 30512 Prince William Street, Princess Anne 21853.
Telephone: (410) 651-1630.

LOVE, Thomas J. *(Associate Judge, Maryland District Court District Five)* Appointed by Governor Parris N. Glendening.
Office: 4990 Rhode Island Avenue, Hyattsville 20871.
Telephone: (301) 699-2777.

MALLOY, Edward A., Jr. *(Associate Judge, Maryland District Court District Twelve)* Appointed by governor.
Office: 3 Pershing Street, Second Floor, Cumberland 21502-3045.
Telephone: (301) 777-2105.

MANCK, Joseph P. *(Associate Judge, Circuit Court for Anne Arundel County, Fifth Judicial Circuit)* Also serves as County Administrative Judge Anne Arundel County. Former Associate and Administrative Judge, Maryland District Court District Seven.
Office: Court House, Church Circle, Annapolis 21401.
Telephone: (410) 222-1185.

MANNES, Paul *(Judge, United States Bankruptcy Court District of Maryland)* Appointed by U.S. District Court judges to term beginning Dec 30, 1981. Reappointed by U.S. Court of Appeals Fourth Circuit judges. Current term expires Oct 1, 2014. Former Chief Judge. Born Washington D.C. Dec 25, 1933.
Office: 385A U.S. Courthouse, 6500 Cherrywood Lane, Greenbelt 20770.
Telephone: (301) 344-8040.

MARSHALL, Thomas E. *(Associate Judge, Circuit Court for Harford County, Third Judicial Circuit)*
Office: 20 West Courtland Street, Bel Air 21014.
Telephone: (410) 638-4990.

MARTIN, Larnzell, Jr. *(Associate Judge, Circuit Court for Prince George's County, Seventh Judicial Circuit)* Appointed by Governor William D. Schaefer to term beginning Dec 1990. Elected to subsequent term, current term expires Dec 2006. Born Dallas Texas Oct 4, 1950. Educated at Carleton College B.A. 1972 and Georgetown University Law Center J.D. 1975. Admitted to practice Maryland 1976, U.S. Court of Appeals District of Columbia Circuit 1979 and U.S. District Court District of Columbia 1981. In legal practice Landover 1982-84. Associate Judge May 1988 to May 1990 and Administrative Judge May 1990 to Dec 1990, Maryland District Court District Five, appointed by Governor William D. Schaefer.

Attorney Advisor Federal Highway Administration Aug 1976 to Feb 1977. Associate County Attorney Feb 1977 to July 1982. Deputy County Attorney Dec 1984 to Dec 1986 and County Attorney Dec 1986 to May 1988 Prince George's County. Former Member Character Committee Seventh Judicial Circuit. Chairman Committee on Family Law Maryland Judicial Conference since 2001. Member Marlborough Inn of Court Chapter LXII American Inns of Court Foundation, Maryland Circuit Judges' Association (Secretary Dec 1992 to June 1998), Black Judges Caucus, J. Franklyn Bourne Bar Association (Former Chair Scholarship Committee, Parliamentarian), Maryland State Bar Association, Inc. and Prince George's County Bar Association (Former Member Law Day Committee, Local Legislation Committee, Nominating Committee, CALR Committee and Public Relations Committee; Chair Follies Committee). Instructor "Review of Landlord-Tenant Law" Nov 4, 1988 and "The Domestic Violence Case" 1992, May 1993, May 1994 and May 16, 1995 Judicial Institute of Maryland; "Team Management of CD-ROM and Electronic Media in Court Libraries in the 90's" National Center for State Courts Institute for Court Management Oct 10-12, 1996; "Discrete Task Lawyering—Its Impact on the Courts, the Bar and the Low-to-Moderate Income Clients" Joint

MARTIN, LARNZELL, JR.—*Continued*
Bench Bar Conference Maryland State Bar Association, Inc. June 7-10, 2000; "Teen Courts Ideology and Application: An American Perspective" Conference on Conflict Resolution By and For Children and Young People Universiteit Leiden Oct 19-20, 2000; "Legal Responsibilities: Fatherhood is not for Babies" Second Annual Fatherhood Conference Prince George's County June 2, 2001; "Maryland Juvenile Court Proceedings for Children in Need of Assistance (CINA): From Shelter Care Through Adoption" Lorman Education's Services Jan 18, 2002; and "Working Within the Law; Working with Family Court Justices" First National Child Access/Safe Haven Training Conference Oct 5, 2002. Chairman Process Subcommittee Minority Business Enterprise Task Force 1984 and Volunteer Task Force Board of Education 1992-93 Prince George's County. Chairman Improving Community Confidence in the Courts Committee 1996 to Jan 1998. Former Member Board of Trustees Public Defender System. Former Member Board of Directors Prince George's Community College Foundation, Inc. Former Member Prince George's County Personnel Board and Prince George's Hospital Center Foundation, Inc. Member Executive Committee Citizenship Law-Related Education Program for the Schools of Maryland and National Conference of Christians and Jews.

Office: 144M Courthouse, 14735 Main Street, Upper Marlboro 20772.
Telephone: (301) 952-3489.
Fax: (301) 952-5837
E-mail address: lmartin@co.pg.md.us

MASON, Michael D. *(Associate Judge, Circuit Court for Montgomery County, Sixth Judicial Circuit)* Appointed by governor.
Office: 50 Maryland Avenue, Rockville 20850.
Telephone: (240) 777-9233.

MATHEWS, Keith E. *(Administrative Judge, Maryland District Court District One)* Appointed by governor.
Office: 5800 Wabash Avenue, Baltimore 21215-3330.
Telephone: (410) 878-8014.

MATRICCIANI, Albert J., Jr. *(Associate Judge, Circuit Court for Baltimore City, Eighth Judicial Circuit)* Appointed by Governor William D. Schaefer to term beginning Jan 20, 1995. Elected Nov 5, 1996, current term expires Nov 2011. Judge-in-Charge of Family Division 1996-2001. Born Baltimore Maryland Jan 20, 1947. Roman Catholic. Educated at Villanova University B.A. 1969, University of Maryland J.D. 1973 and Johns Hopkins University M.L.A. 1975. Admitted to practice Maryland 1974, U.S. District Court District of Maryland 1974 and District of Columbia 1976. In legal practice Baltimore 1974-95.

Board of Trustees Maryland Institute for Continuing Professional Education of Lawyers, Inc. 1993-94 and Maryland Law Review 1993-96. Member Trial Courts Nominating Commission 1983-87 and Appellate Judicial Nominating Commission 1987-95. Former Member National Conference of Bar Presidents. Director Business and Technology Case Management Program Circuit Court for Baltimore City, Eighth Judicial Circuit since 2001. Fellow Baltimore Bar Foundation, Maryland Bar Foundation and American Bar Foundation. Member Sergeant's Inn Law Club (President 1993-94), Wednesday Law Club, The Lawyers' Roundtable Law Club, The American Law Institute, Conference of Circuit Judges, Maryland Judicial Conference (Executive Committee 1998-2000, Chair Committee on Family and Domestic Relations Law 1998-2001), Maryland Circuit Judges Association, National Conference of Juvenile and Family Court Judges, American Judicature Society, American Judges Association, The Bar Association of Baltimore City (Executive Council 1984-87 and 1990-2000, President 1995-96), Maryland State Bar Association, Inc. (Board of Governors 1986-88 and 1996-98, Select Committee on Gender Equality 1991-96, Council Member Litigation Section since 1998) and American Bar Association (National Conference of State Trial Judges Judicial Division since 1995, House of Delegates 1998-2000). Recipient Cardin Pro Bono Service Award from University of Maryland Law School Alumni Association 1995, Rosalyn Bell Award in Family Law from Women's Law Center of Maryland Nov 2000 and Judge Anselm Sadaro Judicial Civility Award from Maryland State Bar Association, Inc. 2002. Maryland Air National Guard 1969-75. Democrat. Former Member The Baltimore Coalition Against Substance Abuse. Director Baltimore Courthouse and Law Museum Foundation since 1995-2000. Vice Chair Attorney General and Lieutenant Governor's Family Violence Council 1996-98. Member The Supreme Court Historical Society, Maryland American Civil Liberties Union (Board of Governors 1983-90), Council on Equal Business Opportunity (Board of Directors 1982-89), Consumer Credit Counseling Service of Maryland, Inc. (Chair Board of Directors 1982-84), Mayor's Drug Abuse Advisory Council (Chair 1983-85), Corner Theater, Inc. (Board of Directors 1982-83) and Maryland Humanities Council (Board of Directors since 1998).

Office: 330 Courthouse East, 111 North Calvert Street, Baltimore 21202.
Telephone: (410) 396-5100, 396-5101.
Fax: (410) 545-7336

McCORMICK, Mary E. *(Associate Judge, Maryland District Court District Six)* Appointed by governor.
Office: 27 Court House Square, Rockville 20850-2325.
Telephone: (301) 279-1551.

McCURDY, Joseph P., Jr. *(Associate Judge, Circuit Court for Baltimore City, Eighth Judicial Circuit)* Former Associate Judge, Maryland District Court District One.
Office: Courthouse East, 111 North Calvert Street, Baltimore 21202.
Telephone: (410) 396-5056.

McDOWELL, John H. *(Associate Judge, Circuit Court for Washington County, Fourth Judicial Circuit)* Appointed by governor. Former Magistrate Judge, U.S. District Court District of Maryland.
Office: 95 West Washington Street, Hagerstown 21740.
Telephone: (240) 313-2565.

McGUCKIAN, Paul A. *(Associate Judge, Circuit Court for Montgomery County, Sixth Judicial Circuit)* Appointed by Governor William D. Schaefer to term beginning Feb 27, 1989. Elected Nov 6, 1990, current term expires Nov 2005. Born Norwood Massachusetts May 3, 1938. Protestant. Educated at Dickinson College A.B. 1960 and George Washington University National Law Center LL.B. 1964. Admitted to practice Maryland

MCGUCKIAN, PAUL A.—*Continued*

1964, U.S. District Court District of Maryland and U.S. Supreme Court. In legal practice Rockville 1972-78. Associate Judge, Maryland District Court District Six 1987-89.

Assistant County Attorney 1966-71 and County Attorney 1979-87 Montgomery County. Member Maryland State Bar Association, Inc. and Montgomery County Bar Association. Private First Class U.S. Army 1956.

Office: Judicial Center, 50 Maryland Avenue, Rockville 20850.

Telephone: (240) 777-9247.

McHUGH, Dennis M. *(Associate Judge, Circuit Court for Montgomery County, Sixth Judicial Circuit)* Former Associate Judge, Maryland District Court District Six, appointed by Governor William D. Schaefer.

Office: 50 Maryland Avenue, Rockville 20850.

Telephone: (240) 777-9360.

McKEE, Graydon S., III *(Associate Judge, Circuit Court for Prince George's County, Seventh Judicial Circuit)* Appointed by governor. Elected Nov 8, 1988, current term expires 2003. Former Circuit Administrative Judge. Born New Brighton Pennsylvania Nov 8, 1937. Lutheran. Educated at Baldwin-Wallace College B.A. 1960 and University of Maryland J.D. 1967. Law Clerk to Hon. William B. Bowie, Maryland Circuit Court Prince George's County 1967-68. Admitted to practice Maryland 1967, U.S. District Court District of Maryland 1968 and U.S. Supreme Court 1972. In legal practice Upper Marlboro 1968-75. Juvenile Court Master Prince George's County 1975-77. Administrative Judge, Maryland District Court District Five 1977-87, appointed by Governor Marvin Mandel.

Instructor Chesapeake College 1979-80, University of Maryland 1980-84 and M.B.A. Program Florida Institute of Technology. USMC 1955-77. Attended U.S. Army Judge Advocate School 1975-76. Member Prince George's County School Board 1971-73. Chairman Correctional Advisory Board 1982-92.

Office: Court House, 14735 Main Street, Upper Marlboro 20772.

Telephone: (301) 952-3227.

McKENNA, John Peter *(Associate Judge, Maryland District Court District Seven)* Appointed by governor.

Office: 251 Rowe Boulevard, Annapolis 21401.

Telephone: (410) 260-1360.

McKINNEY, James C. *(Administrative Judge, Maryland District Court District Three)* Appointed by governor.

Office: 170 East Main Street, Elkton 21921-5943.

Telephone: (410) 996-0704.

MESSITTE, Peter J. *(Judge, United States District Court District of Maryland)* Appointed for life by President Bill Clinton Oct 20, 1993. Born Washington D.C. July 17, 1941. Jewish. Educated at Amherst College B.A. cum laude 1963 and University of Chicago Law School J.D. 1966. Recipient First Prize Karl Llewelyn Moot Court Competition University of Chicago 1965. Admitted to practice Maryland 1969, District of Columbia 1969, U.S. District Courts District of Columbia 1969, District of Maryland 1973 and Northern District of Texas 1983, U.S. Supreme Court 1977 and U.S. Courts of Appeals Fourth 1982, District of Columbia 1983 and Fifth 1983 Circuits. In legal practice Washington D.C. 1969-71 and Chevy Chase Maryland 1971-85. Associate Judge, Circuit Court for Montgomery County, Sixth Judicial Circuit Aug 2 1985 to 1993, appointed by Governor Harry Roe Hughes.

Lecturer on Comparative Law University of São Paulo Law School, Brazil 1967-68. President 1988-90 and Bencher Montgomery County Inn of Court. Chair Latin America Working Group and Member since 1997 International Judicial Relations Committee Judicial Conference of the U.S. Head of Mission U.S.-Turkey Judicial/Prosecutorial Exchange U.S. Department of State since June 2001. Honorary Member Instituto Paulista de Magistrados. Member The American Law Institute, District Judges Association of the Fourth Circuit, Federal Judges Association, American Judicature Society, Maryland State Bar Association, Inc., Montgomery County, Federal, American and Inter-American Bar Associations. Recipient Elizabeth Scull Award for Outstanding Community Service to Montgomery County from Friendship Heights Village Council 1993, Century of Service Award for Contributions to the Administration of Justice from Bar Association of Montgomery County 1999, H. Vernon Eney Endowment Fund Award for Contributions to the Administration of Justice from Maryland Bar Foundation 2001, Gran Cruz da Ordem de São José Operário for judicial merit in the field of labor from Tribunal Regional do Trabalho, Mato Grosso Brazil 2001, Medalha de Mérito Acadêmico for academic contributions to the Brazilian judiciary from Academia Pualista de Magistrados 2002 and Leadership in Law Award from *Daily Record* Maryland 2002. Peace Corps Volunteer São Paulo Brazil 1966-68. Democrat. Delegate Democratic National Convention (Chair Uncommitted Delegate Caucus) 1980. Vice President and General Counsel Community Psychiatric Clinic, Inc. 1975-85.

Office: 475A U.S. Courthouse, 6500 Cherrywood Lane, Greenbelt 20770-1294.

Telephone: (301) 344-0632.

MILLER, John Philip *(Associate Judge, Circuit Court for Baltimore City, Eighth Judicial Circuit)* Appointed by Governor Parris N. Glendening. Former Associate Judge, Maryland District Court District One.

Office: Courthouse East, 111 North Calvert Street, Baltimore 21201.

Telephone: (410) 396-5066.

MISSOURI, William D. *(Circuit Administrative Judge, Circuit Court for Prince George's County, Seventh Judicial Circuit)* Appointed by Governor William D. Schaefer Dec 21, 1987. Elected Nov 8, 1988, current term expires 2003. Also serves as County Administrative Judge Prince George's County since Oct 1992. Born Washington D.C. Sept 4, 1940. Catholic. Educated at Prince George's Community College 1972-73, Bowie State University B.S. cum laude 1975 and University of Maryland School of Law J.D. 1978. Member Phi Alpha Delta. Admitted to practice Maryland 1981, U.S. District Court District of Maryland 1981, U.S. Courts of Appeals Fourth 1982, District of Columbia 1982 and Federal 1983 Circuits, U.S. Tax Court 1983, U.S. Court of Military Appeals 1983 and U.S. Supreme Court 1984. Associate Judge July 12, 1985 to Oct 1987 and Administrative Judge Oct 1987 to Jan 1988, Maryland District Court District Five.

Assistant State's Attorney Prince George's County 1981-85. Instructor in Paralegal Studies Prince George's Community College since 1985. Fellow Maryland State

MISSOURI, WILLIAM D.—*Continued*

Bar Association, Inc. (Board of Governors since 1991). Former member Association of Criminal Defense Attorneys and National Association of District Attorneys. Member Marlborough Chapter American Inns of Court No. LXII (Master of the Bench 1988-89, President 1990-92), J. Franklyn Bourne Bar Association, Prince George's County (Board of Directors 1982-87) and American Bar Associations. Member Special Joint Committee on Gender Bias in the Courts Criminal Pattern Jury Subcommittee Judicial Administration Section Maryland State Bar Association, Inc. and Civil Law and Procedures Committee Maryland Judicial Conference 1986-89. Attended District Court Judicial Conference Oct 1985, Oct 1986 and Oct 1987, All Courts Judicial Conference May 1986 and 1988 and Mid-winter Conference Maryland State Bar Association, Inc. Jan 1987. Recipient Citation for instructing police officers from Public Safety Department Bowie State University May 1985, Citation from Prince George's County Council July 1985 and President's Citation from National Association of Equal Opportunity in Higher Education May 1986. USAF 1958. Worked for Marriott Corp. Washington National Airport 1960-61 and U.S. Postal Service 1961-69. Member Prince George's County Democratic Party 1982-85, Black Democratic Council 1983-85, Prince George's County Rainbow Coalition 1984-85 and Ploughman and Fisherman's Club. Executive Board member University of Maryland Alumni Association 1986-92. Member Jonathan Davis Consistory 33° since 1966, Shriners Mecca Temple 10 since 1966, Prince George's County Human Relations Commission 1983-85, Prince George's County Domestic Violence Coordinating Advisory Council 1985-87, Prince George's County Cocaine Task Force 1986-87, Prince Hall Masons and Prudence Lodge 27 (Worshipful Master 1971-72). Member since 1986 and Chair since Feb 1992 Saint Joseph's Catholic Church Parish Council. Enjoys reading classical literature and working with underprivileged young people.

Office: Court House, 14735 Main Street, Upper Marlboro 20772.

Telephone: (301) 952-3728.

MITCHELL, Patricia L. *(Associate Judge, Maryland District Court District Six)* Appointed by governor.

Office: 27 Court House Square, Rockville 20850-2325.

Telephone: (301) 279-1551.

MOTZ, J. Frederick *(Judge, United States District Court District of Maryland)* Appointed for life by President Ronald Reagan to term beginning July 22, 1985. Former Chief Judge. Born Baltimore Maryland Dec 30, 1942. Educated at Wesleyan University A.B. 1964 and University of Virginia School of Law LL.B. 1967. Law Clerk to Hon. Harrison L. Winter, U.S. Court of Appeals Fourth Circuit 1967-68. Admitted to practice Maryland 1968.

Member Sergeant's Inn, Wednesday Law Club, American College of Trial Lawyers, Maryland State Bar Association, Inc., Baltimore City and American Bar Associations. Board of Trustees Friends School of Baltimore 1970-77 and 1981-88 and Sheppard and Enoch Pratt Hospital since 1987.

Office: 510 U.S. Courthouse, 101 West Lombard Street, Baltimore 21201-2690.

Telephone: (410) 962-0782.

MULIERI, Vincent A. *(Associate Judge, Maryland District Court District Seven)* Appointed by Governor William D. Schaefer.

Office: 251 Rowe Boulevard, Annapolis 21401.

Telephone: (410) 260-1361.

MURDOCK, M. Brooke *(Associate Judge, Circuit Court for Baltimore City, Eighth Judicial Circuit)*

Office: Courthouse, 100 North Calvert Street, Baltimore 21202.

Telephone: (410) 545-0115.

MURPHY, Joseph F., Jr. *(Chief Judge, Court of Special Appeals of Maryland)* Appointed by Governor William D. Schaefer to term beginning 1993. Retained by election. Chief Judge since 1996. Born Fitchburg Massachusetts Jan 9, 1944. Educated at Boston College A.B. 1965 and University of Maryland School of Law J.D. 1969. Admitted to practice Maryland 1969. Associate Judge, Circuit Court for Baltimore County, Third Judicial Circuit 1984-93.

Assistant State's Attorney 1970-75 and Deputy State's Attorney 1975-76 Baltimore City. President J. Dudley Digges Inn of Court 1989-90. Former Member Maryland State's Attorneys Association and Maryland Criminal Defense Attorneys Association (President 1984). Fellow Maryland Bar Foundation. Member Maryland State Bar Association, Inc. and Baltimore County Bar Association. Board of Directors Maryland Judicial Institute 1985-93 and since 1995.

Office: County Courts Building, 401 Bosley Avenue, Towson 21204.

Telephone: (410) 887-3206.

MURPHY, Timothy D. *(Associate Judge, Maryland District Court District One)* Appointed by Governor Parris N. Glendening.

Office: 5800 Wabash Avenue, Baltimore 21215-3330.

Telephone: (410) 878-8107.

NALLEY, Robert C. *(Associate Judge, Circuit Court for Charles County, Seventh Judicial Circuit)* Appointed by governor. Also serves as County Administrative Judge Charles County. Former Administrative Judge, Maryland District Court District Four.

Mailing address: P.O. Box 970, La Plata 20646.

Office: 200 Charles Street, La Plata 20646.

Telephone: (301) 932-3270.

NANCE, Alfred *(Associate Judge, Circuit Court for Baltimore City, Eighth Judicial Circuit)*

Office: Courthouse, 100 North Calvert Street, Baltimore 21202.

Telephone: (410) 396-4020.

NICHOLS, C. Philip, Jr. *(Associate Judge, Circuit Court for Prince George's County, Seventh Judicial Circuit)* Assumed office 1992. Born Prince George's County Maryland June 23, 1947. Catholic. Educated at Georgetown University B.A. 1969 and University of Baltimore J.D. 1973. Law Clerk to Chief Judge Ernest A. Loveless, Jr., Circuit Court of Maryland Seventh Judicial Circuit 1972-73. Admitted to practice Maryland 1973, U.S. Court of Military Appeals 1973 and U.S.

NICHOLS, C. PHILIP, JR.—*Continued*

Court of Appeals Fourth Circuit 1976. Began legal practice Laurel 1973. Commissioner Maryland District Court 1971-72. Justice of the Peace 1969-72. Judge and Chief Judge, Prince George's County Orphans' Court 1977-85. Associate Judge, Maryland District Court District Five 1985-92.

Member Maryland State Bar Association, Inc. (Board of Governors 1984-85 and 1989-91), Prince George's County (Board of Directors 1980-91, President 1989-90) and American Bar Associations. Captain USNR.

Office: Court House, 14735 Main Street, Upper Marlboro 20772.

Telephone: (301) 952-3907.

NICKERSON, William M. *(Senior Judge, United States District Court District of Maryland)* Appointed for life by President George Bush to term beginning 1990. Assumed Senior status June 11, 2002, serves by assignment. Born Baltimore Maryland Dec 6, 1933. Protestant. Educated at University of Virginia B.A. 1955 and University of Maryland LL.B. 1962. Law Clerk to Hon. James K. Cullen, Supreme Bench of Baltimore City 1958-62. Admitted to practice Maryland 1962, U.S. District Court District of Maryland and U.S. Court of Appeals Fourth Circuit. In legal practice Baltimore 1962-85 and Towson 1985. Former Associate Judge, Circuit Court for Baltimore County, Third Judicial Circuit, appointed by Governor Harry Roe Hughes to term beginning May 28, 1985.

Member Attorney Grievance Commission of Maryland (Chairman Elect Review Board 1985), Maryland State Bar Association, Inc. (Chairman Ethics Committee 1984-85) and Baltimore County Bar Association. Lieutenant USCGR 1955-59.

Office: 330 U.S. Courthouse, 101 West Lombard Street, Baltimore 21201-2690.

Telephone: (410) 962-9810.

NOEL, Thomas E. *(Associate Judge, Circuit Court for Baltimore City, Eighth Judicial Circuit)*

Office: Courthouse East, 111 North Calvert Street, Baltimore 21202.

Telephone: (410) 396-5112.

NORTH, Pamela L. *(Associate Judge, Circuit Court for Anne Arundel County, Fifth Judicial Circuit)*

Office: Court House, Church Circle, Annapolis 21401.

Telephone: (410) 222-1273.

NORTHROP, Albert Willis *(Associate Judge, Maryland District Court District Five)* Appointed by governor.

Office: 14735 Main Street, Suite 173B, Upper Marlboro 20772.

Telephone: (301) 952-4023.

NORTHROP, Edward Skottowe *(Senior Judge, United States District Court District of Maryland)* Appointed for life by President John F. Kennedy to term beginning Oct 24, 1961. Chief Judge Sept 28, 1970 to June 1981. Assumed Senior status June 12, 1981, serves by assignment. Born Chevy Chase Maryland June 12, 1911. Episcopalian. Educated at George Washington University B.S. 1933 LL.B. 1937 replaced by J.D. Admitted to practice Maryland 1937, District of Columbia 1937, Virginia 1937 and U.S. Court of Appeals Fourth Circuit 1937. In legal practice Washington D.C. 1937-61 and Rockville Maryland 1937-61.

Former General Counsel Chevy Chase. Important Decisions: Berrigan Bros. 1968, New England Mafia trials 1968 and Wirtz v. Maryland 1968. Former member Steering Committee U.S. District Court Metropolitan Chief Judges Conference. Member Committee on Administration of Probation System Judicial Conference of the U.S. 1973-79 and Advisory Corrections Council of the U.S. since 1977. Chairman State Federal Judicial Council of Maryland 1973-74. Member Judicial Panel on Multidistrict Litigation since June 1979. Member The District of Columbia Bar, Maryland State Bar Association, Inc., Montgomery County and Federal Bar Associations. Recipient Special Merit Citation in recognition of outstanding service for the improvement of the administration of justice from American Judicature Society Jan 15, 1982, Distinguished Service Award from Maryland State Bar Association, Inc. and awards from State of Maryland, Federal Bar Association and George Washington University. Commander USN 1941-45. Recipient Army Commendation medal and Navy Commendation medal. Democrat. Member State Senate Maryland 1955-61 (Majority Leader 1958-61, Chairman Finance Committee). Former Village Manager Chevy Chase. President 1950-52 and Board of Trustees 1950-58 Alumni Association Woodberry Forest School. Organizer Council of Governments in the Metropolitan Area of Washington D.C.

Office: U.S. Courthouse, 101 West Lombard Street, Baltimore 21201-2903.

Telephone: (410) 962-4674.

NORTON, John L., III *(Administrative Judge, Maryland District Court District Two)* Appointed by Governor Harry R. Hughes to term beginning Aug 6, 1985. Reappointed to subsequent term. Born Boston Massachusetts Jan 18, 1951. Protestant. Educated at Yale University B.A. with departmental honors 1972 and Boston University School of Law J.D. 1975. Admitted to practice Maryland 1975, U.S. District Court District of Maryland 1976 and U.S. Supreme Court 1979. In legal practice Cambridge 1975-78 and 1983-85.

State's Attorney Dorchester County 1979-82. Attended "Alcohol and Drugs in the Courts" course The National Judicial College, Reno Nevada 1990. Past President Dorchester Democratic Club and Cambridge Lions Club. Board of Trustees Dorchester County Public Library. Enjoys golf, travel, wine and books.

Mailing address: P.O. Box 547, Cambridge 21613.

Office: 310 Gay Street, Cambridge 21613-1813.

Telephone: (410) 901-1438.

O'BRIEN, Mark Thomas *(Associate Judge, Maryland District Court District Five)* Appointed by Governor Parris N. Glendening.

Office: 4990 Rhode Island Avenue, Hyattsville 20781.

Telephone: (301) 699-2777.

O'MALLEY, Catherine J. *(Associate Judge, Maryland District Court District One)* Appointed by Governor Parris N. Glendening.

Office: 5800 Wabash Avenue, Baltimore 21215-3330.

Telephone: (410) 878-8014.

OSHRINE, Theodore B. *(Associate Judge, Maryland District Court District One)* Appointed by governor.

Office: 5800 Wabash Avenue, Baltimore 21215-3330.

Telephone: (410) 878-8107.

PALUMBO, Richard Angelo *(Associate Judge, Maryland District Court District Five)* Appointed by Governor Parris N. Glendening.

Office: 14735 Main Street, Suite 173B, Upper Marlboro 20772.

Telephone: (301) 952-4021.

PARKS, Floyd L. *(Associate Judge, Maryland District Court District Three)* Appointed by Governor Parris N. Glendening to term beginning Nov 30, 1995. Term expires Nov 30, 2005. Born Washington D.C. July 8, 1938. Presbyterian. Educated at Johns Hopkins University B.S. 1966 and University of Maryland J.D. 1970. Law Clerk to Hon. Dulaney Foster, Supreme Bench of Baltimore City 1968-69. Admitted to practice Maryland 1970, U.S. District Court District of Maryland and U.S. Supreme Court. In legal practice Chestertown 1970-95.

State's Attorney 1975-79 and Attorney Sanitary District Kent County. Member Maryland State Bar Association, Inc. and Kent County Bar Association (Past President). Attended National District Attorneys Association Seventh Annual National Conference Los Angeles California Oct 12-15, 1997. Private First Class U.S. Army 1961-63. Democrat. Member Chestertown Rotary Club, Chester River Yacht & Country Club and Maryland Ornithological Society (Former Vice President). Enjoys golfing, fishing and birding.

Office: Courthouse, Second Floor, 103 North Cross Street, Chestertown 21620-1511.

Telephone: (410) 810-3360.

PINCUS, S. Michael *(Associate Judge, Circuit Court for Montgomery County, Sixth Judicial Circuit)* Appointed by Governor William D. Schaefer to term beginning Jan 26, 1993. Elected Nov 1994, current term expires Nov 2009. Born Washington D.C. Feb 25, 1939. Educated at University of Maryland B.A. 1961 and George Washington University J.D. 1965. Admitted to practice Maryland 1967, U.S. District Courts District of Maryland 1967 and District of Columbia 1968 and U.S. Court of Appeals District of Columbia Circuit 1968. In legal practice Silver Spring 1967-91. Associate Judge, Maryland District Court District Six 1991-93, appointed by Governor William D. Schaefer.

Member The District of Columbia Bar and Montgomery County Bar Association. Enjoys reading, history, sports, skiing and long distance running.

Office: 50 Maryland Avenue, Rockville 20850.

Telephone: (240) 777-9205.

PLATT, Steven I. *(Associate Judge, Circuit Court for Prince George's County, Seventh Judicial Circuit)* Appointed by Governor William D. Schaefer to term beginning May 7, 1990. Elected to subsequent term. Supervising Judge Family Law Operations 1995-97. Born Woodstock Virginia Jan 1, 1947. Jewish. Educated at University of Virginia B.A. 1969 and American University J.D. 1973. Law Clerk to Chief Judge Ernest A. Loveless, Circuit Court of Maryland Seventh Judicial Circuit 1973-75. Member Delta Theta Phi. Admitted to practice Maryland 1975, U.S. District Court District of Maryland 1976 and District of Columbia 1982. In legal practice Oxon Hill Maryland 1976-80 and Clinton Maryland 1980-86. Associate Judge 1978-85 and Chief Judge 1985-86, Prince George's County Orphans' Court. Arbitrator Health Claims Arbitration Office 1981-86. Associate Judge 1986-88 and Administrative Judge 1988-90, Maryland District Court District Five.

Author "The Court's Futurist Direction" XXIII No. 6 Maryland B. Jour. Nov/Dec 1990; "Family Court Concept Suffers from Legislative-Judicial Clash" 209 No. 246 *The Daily Record* Oct 23, 1993; "The Role of the Courts in the Crisis of Drugs and Violence/A Judge's Perspective" VIII No. 3 *American Jails* July/Aug 1994; "Court's Role in Drug and Violence Crisis" XXVII No. 6 Maryland B. Jour. Nov/Dec 1994; "A Judicial Vote for the Slow Lane in the Drive for a Family Court" 211 No. 63 *The Daily Record* March 18, 1995; "Commentary—Women Accused of Homicide: The Use of Expert Testimony on the Effect of Battering on Women—A Trial Judge's Perspective" 25 No. 1 University of Baltimore L. Rev. Fall 1995; "Family Court. Do it Right, or Don't Do it at All" *Maryland Family Law Monthly* April 1996; and "Reinventing Maryland's Nisi Prius Courts for the Twenty-First Century" XXX No. 2 Maryland B. Jour. March/April 1997. Instructor Paralegal Institute University of Maryland 1982-92. Faculty Paralegal/Law Enforcement Program Prince George's Community College 1984-93. Consultant Special Subcommittees on Alternative Dispute Resolution 1994 and General Administration 1997 Court of Appeals Standing Committee on Rules of Practice and Procedure. Former Member The Association of Trial Lawyers of America and National Conference of Bar Presidents, Inc. Fellow Maryland Bar Foundation. Charter Fellow The Law Foundation of Prince George's County (Board of Directors 1995-97). Master of the Bench Marlborough Inns of Court since 1988 (Administrator 1990-91, Treasurer/Counselor 1991-92, President 1992-94). Chairman Strategic Planning and Total Quality Management Council Circuit Court for Prince George's County since 1995. Member Maryland Judicial Conference (Member 1987-90 and Chairman 1989-90 Judicial Administration Committee, Long-Range Planning Committee 1990-91, Mental Health, Alcoholism and Addiction Committee 1990-91, Chairman Special Committee on Collection of Child Support 1991-92, Member Criminal Law Committee 1993-95, Public Awareness Committee 1995-97), Circuit Court Judges Association, American Judicature Society, Maryland State Bar Association, Inc. (Committee on Laws since 1986, Board of Governors 1988-90; Council Member 1989-96 and Chair 1996-98 Section of Judicial Administration, Member Special Committee on Governance 1990, Co-chair Special Committee on Judicial Personnel Management Issues 1995-97, Member Litigation Section), Prince George's County (Treasurer 1985, Secretary 1986, President Elect 1987, President 1988) and American Bar Associations.

Attended Probate Court Proceedings Specialty Session for Judges 1980 and "Alcohol and Drugs and the Courts" 1989 The National Judicial College and Continuing Judicial Education Program National College of Probate Judges 1982 and "Strengthening the Executive Component of the Court" Institute for Court Management 1988 National Center for State Courts. Consultant "Family Violence and the Courts: Exploring Expert Testimony on Battered Women" Women Judges' Fund for Justice May 1995. Faculty Maryland Judicial Institute since 1995. Recipient Certificate of Appreciation from Kiwanis Club 1983, Lions Club 1983 and Business and Professional Women Prince George's Chapter 1984, Distinguished Service to Judiciary Award from Philippine Lawyers Association of Metropolitan Washington 1991 and Conflict Resolution Award from Prince George's County Chapter National Conference of Christians and Jews 1995. Listed in *Who's Who in Washington* since

PLATT, STEVEN I.—*Continued*

1982, *Who's Who in Law* since 1987 and 31 No. 12 *Washingtonian Magazine* as one of the "Best of the Bench" Sept 1996. E-4 Maryland National Guard 1970-76. Chairman Human Relations Commission Prince George's County 1977-78. Chairman Task Force on Labor Law Revision Prince George's County Council 1981. Chairman and Initial Convener Domestic Violence Coordinating Group Prince George's County 1987-89. Member Brotherhood Citation Dinner Planning Committee National Conference of Christians and Jews 1977-80, Board of Trade Prince George's County 1982-94, Board of Trustees Henson Valley Montessori School 1983-84 (Chairman 1985-86) and Attorney General's Advisory Council on the Family Law Legal Needs of Low-Income Persons 1991. Mentor, Leadership Development Forum Prince George's County since 1986. Enjoys reading, traveling, theater, tennis and the beach.

Mailing address: P.O. Box 1600, Upper Marlboro 20773.

Telephone: (301) 952-3142.

PLITT, Emory A., Jr. *(Associate Judge, Circuit Court for Harford County, Third Judicial Circuit)* Appointed by Governor Parris N. Glendening. Former Administrative Judge, Maryland District Court District Nine, appointed by Governor William D. Schaefer.

Office: 20 West Courtland Street, Bel Air 21014.

Telephone: (410) 638-4655.

PREVAS, John N. *(Associate Judge, Circuit Court for Baltimore City, Eighth Judicial Circuit)*

Office: Courthouse East, 111 North Calvert Street, Baltimore 21202.

Telephone: (410) 396-5140.

PRICE, J. Frederick *(Associate Judge, Circuit Court for Kent County, Second Judicial Circuit)* Also serves as County Administrative Judge Kent County.

Office: 103 North Cross Street, Chestertown 21620.

Telephone: (410) 778-7440.

QUARLES, William D. *(Judge, United States District Court District of Maryland)* Appointed for life by President George W. Bush to term beginning March 24, 2003. Former Associate Judge, Circuit Court for Baltimore City, Eighth Judicial Circuit.

Office: U.S. Courthouse, 101 Lombard Street, Baltimore 21201.

Telephone: (410) 962-0946.

RAKER, Irma S. *(Associate Judge, Court of Appeals of Maryland)* Appointed by governor. Born Brooklyn New York. Educated at Syracuse University B.A. 1959, Hague Academy of International Law 1959 and Washington College of Law J.D. 1972. Staff member American University Law Review. Recipient American Jurisprudence Awards in Torts and Criminal Procedure and Lura E. Turley Award from Washington College of Law. Admitted to practice Maryland 1973. Associate Judge, Maryland District Court District Six 1980-82. Former Associate Judge, Circuit Court for Montgomery County, Sixth Judicial Circuit, assumed office 1982.

Assistant State's Attorney Montgomery County 1973-79. Author "The Right of the Police to Break and Enter: No-Knock" American University L. Rev. 1970-71. Adjunct Professor Washington College of Law. Member Montgomery County Advisory Commission on Environmental Law 1979, Montgomery County Commission on Battered Spouses and Advisory Commission on Child Abuse and Neglect. Member National Association of Women Judges, Maryland State Bar Association, Inc. (Board of Governors and Chair Committee to Draft Pattern Jury Instructions), Montgomery County, District of Columbia Women's and American Bar Associations.

Office: Judicial Center, 50 Maryland Avenue, Rockville 20850.

Telephone: (240) 777-9330.

RALEY, C. Clarke *(Associate Judge, Circuit Court for St. Mary's County, Seventh Judicial Circuit)* Former Associate Judge, Maryland District Court District Four.

Office: 41605 Courthouse Drive, Leonardtown 20650.

Telephone: (301) 475-4320.

RASIN, Gale E. *(Associate Judge, Maryland District Court District One)* Appointed by Governor William D. Schaefer.

Office: 5800 Wabash Avenue, Baltimore 21215-3330.

Telephone: (410) 878-8107.

RASIN, Martha F. *(Associate Judge, Maryland District Court District Seven)* Appointed by governor. Former Chief Judge.

Office: 251 Rowe Boulevard, Annapolis 21401.

Telephone: (410) 260-1311.

RASINSKY, Marc G. *(Associate Judge, Maryland District Court District Ten)* Appointed by governor.

Office: 101 North Court Street, Westminster 21157.

Telephone: (410) 871-3500.

RHODES, Thurman Haywood, Sr. *(Administrative Judge, Maryland District Court District Five)* Appointed by Governor William D. Schaefer to term beginning 1988. Reappointed by Governor Parris N. Glendening 1998, current term expires 2008. Born Baltimore Maryland Aug 18, 1949. Educated at Morgan State College B.A. 1972 and Catholic University of America J.D. 1975. Admitted to practice Maryland 1976, U.S. District Court District of Maryland 1978, U.S. Supreme Court 1980 and U.S. Courts of Appeals Fourth 1983 and District of Columbia 1985 Circuits.

Associate General Counsel Maryland-National Capital Park and Planning Commission 1975. Assistant Attorney General Maryland 1988. Adjunct Professor Business and Management Department Prince George's County Community College and Paralegal Studies Program University of Maryland. Member Child Support Enforcement Committee and Chair Civil Law and Procedure Committee Judicial Conference of Maryland. Member Attorney Grievance Commission of Maryland Inquiry Panel. Member J. Franklyn Bourne Bar Association, Maryland State Bar Association, Inc. (Administrative Law Committee), Prince George's County (Ethics Committee), National and American Bar Associations. Instructor in Basic Computer Assisted Legal Research Judicial Institute of Maryland. Judge Miller Cup Moot Court Competition Columbus School of Law and Catholic University of America. Charter Member and President Toastmasters Club #4320-36. President The Washington Male Chorale. Member Explorers Committee National Capital Area and Scoutmaster Troop #1696 Boy Scouts of America. Board of Trustees Henson Valley Montessori School. Board of Trustees and Lay Liturgist Bethel United Methodist Church. Member Employee Advisory Committee Maryland-National Capital Park and Planning

RHODES, THURMAN HAYWOOD, SR.—*Continued*
Commission, Rosebud Musical Theater Company and Heritage Singers of Bowie Maryland.
Office: 14735 Main Street, Suite 173B, Upper Marlboro 20772.
Telephone: (301) 952-4023.

RICKS, Essom V., Jr. *(Associate Judge, Maryland District Court District Seven)* Appointed by governor.
Office: 251 Rowe Boulevard, Annapolis 21401.
Telephone: (410) 260-1360.

ROBERTS, W. Milnor *(Administrative Judge, Maryland District Court District Eleven)* Appointed by Governor William D. Schaefer.
Office: 100 West Patrick Street, Frederick 21701.
Telephone: (301) 694-2005.

ROWAN, William J., III *(Associate Judge, Circuit Court for Montgomery County, Sixth Judicial Circuit)* Appointed by Governor Parris N. Glendening.
Office: 50 Maryland Avenue, Rockville 20850.
Telephone: (240) 777-9254.

RUPP, Nelson W., Jr. *(Associate Judge, Circuit Court for Montgomery County, Sixth Judicial Circuit)* Former Associate Judge, Maryland District Court District Six.
Office: 50 Maryland Avenue, Rockville 20850.
Telephone: (240) 777-9282.

RUSSELL, G. Darrell, Jr. *(Associate Judge, Maryland District Court District Eight)* Appointed by Governor William D. Schaefer to term beginning Dec 14, 1990. Reappointed by Governor Parris N. Glendening Dec 14, 2000, current term expires Dec 14, 2010. Born Annapolis Maryland Dec 18, 1941. Catholic. Educated at Loyola College B.S. 1964, University of Baltimore J.D. 1967 and Towson University M.A. 1988. Member Gamma Eta Gamma. Admitted to practice Maryland 1969, U.S. District Court District of Maryland 1971 and U.S. Supreme Court 1975. In legal practice Towson 1969-90.
Assistant Attorney General Maryland 1970-74. Member St. Thomas More Society, Maryland State Bar Association, Inc., Baltimore County and American Bar Associations. CLE Instructor of District Court Criminal Practice and Drunk Driving Defense 1993-99. Recipient Citizens Award for Valor 1998. Member Hibernian Society, Safety First Club and Towson YMCA. Enjoys coaching youth football and lacrosse.
Office: 120 East Chesapeake Avenue, Towson 21286-5307.
Telephone: (410) 512-2060.

RYAN, James L. *(Associate Judge, Circuit Court for Montgomery County, Sixth Judicial Circuit)* Former Associate Judge, Maryland District Court District Six.
Office: 50 Maryland Avenue, Rockville 20850.
Telephone: (240) 777-9289.

SALMON, James P. *(Associate Judge, Court of Special Appeals of Maryland)* Appointed by Governor William D. Schaefer Dec 13, 1994. Retained by election. Born Feb 9, 1940. Catholic. Educated at St. Vincent College B.A. 1962 and University of Maryland J.D. magna cum laude 1965. Law Clerk to Hon. Charles C. Marbury, Court of Appeals of Maryland 1965-66. Member Phi Alpha Delta. Admitted to practice Maryland 1965, U.S. District Court District of Maryland 1970, U.S. Supreme Court 1972 and District of Columbia 1976. In legal practice Hyattsville 1966-69 and Upper Marlboro 1969-88. Former Associate Judge, Circuit Court for Prince George's County, Seventh Judicial Circuit, appointed by governor to term beginning Dec 29, 1988.
Mailing address: P.O. Box 209, Upper Marlboro 20773-0209.
Telephone: (301) 952-5855.

SAUSE, John W., Jr. *(Associate Judge, Circuit Court for Queen Anne's County, Second Judicial Circuit)* Trust Clerk 1981-84. Appointed Associate Judge by Governor William D. Schaefer to term beginning 1988. Elected 1990, current term expires 2005. County Administrative Judge Queen Anne's County since 1988. Born Baltimore Maryland Oct 14, 1933. Educated at Williams College B.A. with honors 1955 and University of Virginia J.D. 1958. Law Clerk to Hon. William L. Henderson, Court of Appeals of Maryland 1958-59. Admitted to practice Maryland 1958. In legal practice 1962-65. Trial Magistrate, Queen Anne's County 1967-71.
Assistant State's Attorney Baltimore City 1959-62. Assistant Attorney General 1964-66. District Public Defender District Three 1971-83. Attorney Planning Commission and Department of Planning and Zoning Queen Anne's County 1987-88. Reporter Commission to Revise the Testamentary Laws of Maryland 1967-68. Member State Board of Law Examiners 1983-88. Member Business Regulations Article Review Committee 1988-89 and Conference of Circuit Judges 1989. Chair Civil Law and Procedure Committee Maryland Judicial Conference 1996-99. Member Maryland State Bar Association, Inc. (Council Criminal Law Section 1985-89), Queen Anne's County, Second Circuit and American Bar Associations. President Queen Anne's County Jaycees 1965-66. Trustee 1972-85 and President 1974-75 The Gunston School. Member Queen Anne's County Historical Society.
Office: 100 Court House Square, Centreville 21617.
Telephone: (410) 758-0216.

SAVAGE, Katherine D. *(Associate Judge, Circuit Court for Montgomery County, Sixth Judicial Circuit)* Former Associate Judge, Maryland District Court District Six, appointed by Governor Parris N. Glendening.
Office: 50 Maryland Avenue, Rockville 20850.
Telephone: (240) 777-9372.

SCHIFF, Ronald D. *(Associate Judge, Circuit Court for Prince George's County, Seventh Judicial Circuit)* Appointed by Governor Parris N. Glendening. Former Associate Judge, Maryland District Court District Five.
Office: Court House, 14735 Main Street, Upper Marlboro 20772-3042.
Telephone: (301) 952-4066.

SCHNEIDER, James F. *(Chief Judge, United States Bankruptcy Court District of Maryland)* Appointed by U.S. District Court judges to term beginning Feb 1, 1982. Reappointed by U.S. Court of Appeals Fourth Circuit judges Oct 2, 1986 and 2000. Current term expires 2014. Chief Judge since Nov 2, 2001. Born Baltimore Maryland Nov 18, 1947. Presbyterian. Educated at University of Baltimore B.A. with honors 1969 J.D. with honors 1972. Recipient Merit Award University of Baltimore 1969, Merit Award University of Baltimore School of Law 1972, Silver Key Award from Student Law Division American Bar Association 1972 and Dean Joseph Curtis Award (Outstanding Law Student) 1972. Law

SCHNEIDER, JAMES F.—*Continued*
Clerk to Hon. Albert L. Sklar, Supreme Bench of Baltimore City May 1972 to Jan 1973. Member National Honor Society, Wilson Honor Society, Phi Alpha Theta and Nu Beta Epsilon. Admitted to practice Maryland 1972 and U.S. District Court District of Maryland 1973. Began legal practice Baltimore 1973. General Equity Master, Supreme Bench of Baltimore City Jan 23, 1978 to Feb 1, 1982.

Assistant State's Attorney Baltimore Jan 24, 1973 to Jan 20, 1978. Author "The History of the Library Company of the Baltimore Bar" 1979 and "Centennial of Baltimore Bar Association" *Daily Record* 1980 and *A Century of Striving for Justice—The Maryland State Bar Association 1896-1996* 1996. Co-author with H. H. Walker Lewis *A Bicentennial History of the U.S. District Court for the District of Maryland* 1990. Member National Conference of Bankruptcy Judges, The Bar Association of Baltimore City, Maryland State Bar Association, Inc. (Chairman Special Committee for the Celebration of the Bicentennial of the U.S. Constitution 1986-87) and American Bar Association. Recipient Alumnus of the Year Award from University of Baltimore 1986. Elder First and Franklin Street Presbyterian Church. Co-founder Museum of Baltimore Legal History 1984.

Office: U.S. Courthouse, 101 West Lombard Street, Baltimore 21201-2696.

Telephone: (410) 962-2820.

SCHULZE, Jillyn K. *(Magistrate Judge, United States District Court District of Maryland)* Appointed by U.S. District Court judges. Born Birmingham Alabama March 24, 1951. Educated at Western Maryland College B.A. 1973 and University of Maryland School of Law J.D. 1980. Law Clerk to Senior Judge Roszel C. Thomsen, U.S. District Court District of Maryland 1980-81. Admitted to practice Maryland 1980, U.S. Supreme Court 1987 and Massachusetts 1990.

Assistant Attorney General Attorney General's Office Maryland 1981-91. Member National Association of Women Judges and Montgomery County Bar Association. Legal Advisor to Governor of Maryland 1991-94.

Office: 335A U.S. Courthouse, 6500 Cherrywood Lane, Greenbelt 20770-1289.

Telephone: (301) 344-0630.

SCHWAIT, Allen L. *(Associate Judge, Circuit Court for Baltimore City, Eighth Judicial Circuit)*

Office: Courthouse, 100 North Calvert Street, Baltimore 21202.

Telephone: (410) 396-1776.

SCRIVENER, Louise G. *(Associate Judge, Circuit Court for Montgomery County, Sixth Judicial Circuit)* Former Associate Judge, Maryland District Court District Six, appointed by Governor William D. Schaefer.

Office: 50 Maryland Avenue, Rockville 20850.

Telephone: (240) 777-9219.

SEIDLER, I. Marshall *(Associate Judge, Maryland District Court District Eight)* Appointed by governor.

Office: 900 Walker Avenue, Catonsville 21228-5380.

Telephone: (410) 512-2523.

SHARER, J. Frederick *(Associate Judge, Court of Special Appeals of Maryland)* Appointed by Governor Parris N. Glendening to term beginning Jan 4, 2002. Born Cumberland Maryland April 12, 1938. Educated at Washington & Jefferson College A.B. 1960 and University of Maryland School of Law LL.B. 1963. Editorial Board Maryland Law Review 1962-63. Admitted to practice Maryland 1963. Associate Judge Dec 1980 to Jan 2002 and County Administrative Judge 1983 to Jan 4, 2002, Circuit Court for Allegany County, Fourth Judicial Circuit.

Deputy State's Attorney Allegany College 1965-66. City Solicitor Cumberland 1966-80. Member State Board of Law Examiners 1978-80. Chair Executive Committee 1988-89 and Member Judicial Compensation Committee Maryland Judicial Conference. Circuit Representative Conference of Circuit Judges 1996-2002. Member Maryland Judicial Commission on Pro Bono since 1998. Chair Council on Jury Use and Management 1999-2000. Founding Member Task Force on Child Abuse and Neglect and Task Force on Drug and Alcohol Abuse Allegany County. Fellow Maryland Bar Foundation. Member Maryland State Bar Association, Inc. and Allegany County Bar Association (President 1990). President Greater Cumberland Jaycees 1966-67. Chair 1970-77 and Board of Trustees 1970-80 Allegany Community College. Member Development Council Washington & Jefferson College 1977-80. Member 1986-83 and Chair 1991-93 School Board Bishop Walsh High School.

Mailing address: P.O. Box 1731, Cumberland 21502.

Telephone: (301) 722-4842.

SHEPHERD, E. Allen *(Associate Judge, Circuit Court for Prince George's County, Seventh Judicial Circuit)* Appointed by governor. Former Associate Judge, Maryland District Court District Five, appointed by Governor William D. Schaefer.

Office: Court House, 14735 Main Street, Upper Marlboro 20772.

Telephone: (301) 952-3423.

SHERBIN, James L. *(Associate Judge, Circuit Court for Garrett County, Fourth Judicial Circuit)* Also serves as County Administrative Judge Garrett County.

Mailing address: P.O. Box 447, Oakland 21550.

Office: 203 South Fourth Street, Oakland 21550.

Telephone: (301) 334-1934.

SHUGER, Nancy B. *(Associate Judge, Maryland District Court District One)* Appointed by Governor William D. Schaefer to term beginning 1993. Term expires 2003. Educated at Cornell University B.A. cum laude with distinction 1971 and University of Maryland School of Law J.D. 1974. Recipient American Jurisprudence Award in Contracts II 1972 and Joseph Bernstein Prize for most significant article published in the Maryland Law Forum 1974 and Luther Martin Prize for best brief in the National Moot Court Competition 1974 from University of Maryland School of Law. Moot Court Board 1972-74. Admitted to practice Maryland 1975, Washington 1979 (inactive since 1987), U.S. District Courts District of Maryland and Western District of Washington, U.S. Court of Appeals Fourth Circuit and U.S. Supreme Court.

Directing Attorney Evergreen Legal Services Port Angeles Washington 1978-80. Assistant Attorney General Maryland 1980-93. Author "The Legal Rights of Handicapped Persons with Regard to Procreation" 2 Journal of Sexuality and Disabilities 216, 1979 and Chapter 9 "Procreation, Marriage and Raising Children" *The Legal Rights of Handicapped Persons, Cases, Material and Text* 857-992, 1980. Co-author with S. Leviton "Maryland's Exchangeable Children: A Critique of Maryland's

SHUGER, NANCY B.—*Continued*

System of Providing Services to Mentally Handicapped Children" 42 Maryland L. Rev. 823, 1983. Supervisor Practice and Clinical Law Programs Vermont Law School since 1993. Guest Lecturer on Trial Practice Course Criminal Law Clinic University of Maryland School of Law since 1993 and on Domestic Violence Family Law Clinic and Civil Law Clinic University of Baltimore School of Law since 1994. Mentor University of Maryland School of Law since 1996. President 1996-97 J. Dudley Digges Inn of Court. Former Member National Association of Women Judges and Maryland State Bar Association, Inc. Member Governor's Commission on Judicial Disabilities since 2002, Maryland Judicial Conference (Consultant Committee on Family and Juvenile Law 1977-78, Member Committee on Family and Domestic Relations Law 1993-2001, Foster Care Grant Committee 1994-95) and The Bar Association of Baltimore City (Committee on Professional Ethics 1991-95 and Committee on Civility 1995-96). Recipient Jennifer L. Robbins Award in recognition of special achievement in human services from Attorney General of Maryland 1991 and Woman for the Nineties Award from Laurence G. Paquin School 1995. Annual Christmas Visitor Sinai Hospital since 1991. Member since 1982 and Board of Trustees since 2000 Beth Am Synagogue.

Office: Multi-Service Center, 5800 Wabash Avenue, Baltimore 21215-3330.

Telephone: (410) 878-8109.

Fax: (410) 358-7637

E-mail address: nancy.shuger@courts.state.md.us

SILKWORTH, Ronald A. *(Associate Judge, Circuit Court for Anne Arundel County, Fifth Judicial Circuit)*

Office: Court House, Church Circle, Annapolis 21401.

Telephone: (410) 222-1451.

SIMPSON, D. William *(Associate Judge, Circuit Court for Wicomico County, First Judicial Circuit)* Also serves as County Administrative Judge Wicomico County. Born New Jersey 1937. Educated at University of Delaware A.B. 1959 and University of Maryland LL.B. 1963. Member Order of the Coif. Admitted to practice Maryland 1963. Former Judge, Maryland District Court District Two, appointed by Acting Governor Blair Lee III 1978.

Member Maryland State Bar Association, Inc., Wicomico County and American Bar Associations.

Mailing address: P.O. Box 198, Salisbury 21803-0198.

Office: 105 Courthouse, 101 North Division Street, Salisbury 21801.

Telephone: (410) 548-4822.

SLADE, John F., III *(Associate Judge, Maryland District Court District Four)* Appointed by Governor Parris N. Glendening.

Office: State Office Building, 23110 Leonard Hall Drive, Leonardtown 20650.

Telephone: (301) 475-4530.

SMALKIN, Frederic N. *(Senior Judge, United States District Court District of Maryland)* Magistrate 1976-86. Appointed Judge for life by President Ronald Reagan to term beginning Sept 26, 1986. Assumed Senior status Jan 8, 2003, serves by assignment. Former Chief Judge. Born Baltimore Maryland May 21, 1946. Educated at Johns Hopkins University B.A. 1968 and University of Maryland School of Law J.D. 1971. Member Phi Beta Kappa and Order of the Coif. Admitted to practice Maryland 1972.

Member Federal Bar Association. Member 14 West Hamilton Street Club.

Office: 310 U.S. Courthouse, 101 West Lombard Street, Baltimore 21201-2690.

Telephone: (410) 962-3840.

SMITH, Carol E. *(Associate Judge, Circuit Court for Baltimore City, Eighth Judicial Circuit)* Appointed by governor. Former Associate Judge, Maryland District Court District One.

Office: Courthouse East, 111 North Calvert Street, Baltimore 21202.

Telephone: (410) 396-6826.

SMITH, Paul A. *(Associate Judge, Circuit Court for Baltimore City, Eighth Judicial Circuit)* Born Baltimore Maryland Jan 14, 1936. Baptist. Educated at Morgan State University B.A. with honors 1963 and University of Maryland School of Law J.D. 1967. Member Delta Theta Phi. Admitted to practice Maryland 1967. Began legal practice Baltimore 1968. Master in Chancery, Supreme Bench of Baltimore City 1971-83. Former Associate Judge, Maryland District Court District One, appointed by Governor Harry Roe Hughes to term beginning Aug 15, 1983.

Assistant Interim Public Defender Legal Aid Bureau 1970-71. Member The Bar Association of Baltimore City, Maryland State Bar Association, Inc., Monumental City and National Bar Associations. Attended National College of Juvenile Justice University of Nevada 1974. Sergeant USMC 1954-57. Democrat. Member Elks and Prince Hall Masons.

Office: Courthouse East, 111 North Calvert Street, Baltimore 21202.

Telephone: (410) 396-5677.

SMITH, Thomas P. *(Associate Judge, Circuit Court for Prince George's County, Seventh Judicial Circuit)* Appointed by governor.

Office: Court House, 14735 Main Street, Upper Marlboro 20772.

Telephone: (301) 952-3896.

SONNER, Andrew L. *(Associate Judge, Court of Special Appeals of Maryland)* Appointed by Governor Parris N. Glendening to term beginning 1996. Retained by election. Born Middletown Ohio July 11, 1934. Educated at American University B.A. 1957 J.D. 1963. In legal practice 1964-66.

Deputy State's Attorney 1967-71 and State's Attorney 1971-96 Montgomery County. Board of Directors 1971-96 and President 1973-76 Maryland State's Attorneys Association. Member Governor's Commission on Law Enforcement and the Administration of Justice 1979-82. Vice President National District Attorneys Association 1981-83. Member Maryland Criminal Justice Coordinating Council 1982-85 and Maryland Commission on Criminal Sentencing Policy 1996. Chair Criminal Justice Commission Montgomery County 1975-87 and Maryland Criminal Sentencing Commission since 1999. Member American Judicature Society, Maryland State Bar Association, Inc., Montgomery County and American Bar Associations. Recipient Wasserstein Public Interest Fellowship Award from Harvard Law School 1992. Member

SONNER, ANDREW L.—*Continued*

Advisory Committee on the National Consortium on Violence Research 1996.
Office: 302 Judicial Center, 50 Maryland Avenue, Rockville 20850.
Telephone: (240) 777-9320.

SOTHORON, Richard H., Jr. *(Associate Judge, Circuit Court for Prince George's County, Seventh Judicial Circuit)*
Office: Court House, 14735 Main Street, Upper Marlboro 20772.
Telephone: (301) 952-5420.

SOUDER, Susan *(Associate Judge, Circuit Court for Baltimore County, Third Judicial Circuit)*
Office: County Courts Building, 401 Bosley Avenue, Towson 21204.
Telephone: (410) 887-6504.

SPELLBRING, William B., Jr. *(Associate Judge, Circuit Court for Prince George's County, Seventh Judicial Circuit)*
Office: Court House, 14735 Main Street, Upper Marlboro 20772.
Telephone: (301) 952-3960.

SPENCE, R. Noel *(Associate Judge, Maryland District Court District Eleven)* Appointed by governor.
Office: 36 West Antietam Street, Hagerstown 21740.
Telephone: (240) 420-4600.

STAKEM, Paul J. *(Administrative Judge, Maryland District Court District Twelve)* Appointed by Governor Harry Roe Hughes to term beginning Oct 16, 1981. Reappointed by Governor William D. Schaefer Sept 15, 1991 and by Governor Parris N. Glendening Sept 15, 2001. Current term expires Sept 15, 2011. Born Cumberland Maryland Oct 10, 1939. Catholic. Educated at St. Vincent College B.A. with honors 1961 and University of Maryland LL.B. with honors 1964. Law Clerk to Chief Judge Stedman Prescott, Court of Appeals of Maryland 1964-66. Admitted to practice Maryland 1964 and U.S. Supreme Court 1971. Began legal practice Cumberland 1966.
Deputy State's Attorney Allegany County 1966-71. District Public Defender Allegany and Garrett Counties 1972-81. Member Maryland State Bar Association, Inc. and Allegany County Bar Association (President 1991-92). Democrat. Member Elks, Knights of Columbus and Order of Alhambra. Enjoys golfing, swimming and gardening.
Office: 3 Pershing Street, Second Floor, Cumberland 21502-3045.
Telephone: (301) 777-2105.

STEINBERG, Robert J. *(Associate Judge, Maryland District Court District Eight)* Appointed by governor.
Office: 120 East Chesapeake Avenue, Towson 21286-5307.
Telephone: (410) 512-2050.

STEPLER, Mary Ann *(Associate Judge, Circuit Court for Frederick County, Sixth Judicial Circuit)* Former Administrative Judge, Maryland District Court District Eleven.
Office: 100 West Patrick Street, Frederick 21701.
Telephone: (301) 694-1999.

STEVENSON, Julie R. *(Associate Judge, Circuit Court for Frederick County, Sixth Judicial Circuit)*
Office: 100 West Patrick Street, Frederick 21701.
Telephone: (301) 694-1998.

STEWART, Lynn Kellene *(Associate Judge, Circuit Court for Baltimore City, Eighth Judicial Circuit)* Appointed by Governor Parris N. Glendening.
Office: Courthouse East, 111 North Calvert Street, Baltimore 21202.
Telephone: (410) 396-5052.

STONE, Norman R., III *(Associate Judge, Maryland District Court District Eight)* Appointed by governor.
Office: 120 East Chesapeake Avenue, Towson 21286-5307.
Telephone: (410) 512-2050.

SUNDT, Ann Newman *(Associate Judge, Circuit Court for Montgomery County, Sixth Judicial Circuit)* Appointed by Governor Parris N. Glendening. Educated at Georgetown University Law Center J.D. with honors. In legal practice twelve years.
With Family Division Masters' Office for seven and one half years. Fellow American Academy of Matrimonial Lawyers. Listed in *The Best Lawyers in America* 1993-94.
Office: 710 Judicial Center, 50 Maryland Avenue, Rockville 20850.
Telephone: (240) 777-9275.
Fax: (240) 777-9279

SWEENEY, Dennis M. *(Associate Judge, Circuit Court for Howard County, Fifth Judicial Circuit)* Appointed by Governor William D. Schaefer to term beginning 1991. Elected to subsequent term. Born Louisville Kentucky July 23, 1945. Educated at Loyola College B.A. 1967 and Georgetown University Law Center J.D. 1971. Admitted to practice Maryland 1971.
Staff Attorney 1971-75 and Chief Attorney 1975-79 Baltimore Legal Aid Bureau, Inc. Assistant Federal Public Defender 1975. Assistant Attorney General and Special Assistant to Attorney General 1979-81, Chief Civil Division and Chief General Counsel 1981-84 and Deputy Attorney General 1984-91 Maryland. Chairman State Advisory Council on Administrative Hearings 1989-91. President Public Lawyers Legal Services Program, Inc. 1989-91 and James Macgill American Inn of Court 1995-96. Member Trial Experience Committee U.S. District Court District of Maryland 1984-88, Governor's Task Force on Administrative Hearings Officers 1987-88, Advisory Council to Maryland Legal Services Corporation 1987-89, Special ad hoc Committee to Implement Maryland's New Domestic Violence Law 1992-94 and Howard County Executive's ad hoc Committee on Human Rights 1993-96. Co-chair Law Clerk Orientation Program Committee since 1997 and Family and Sexual Violence Coordinating Council of Howard County since 1997. Member Maryland Coalition for Civil Justice Private Bar Task Force, Children's Justice Act Committee, Judicial Ethics Committee, Council on Jury Use and Management, Maryland Circuit Judges Association (Executive Committee 1993-94 and 1994-97), Maryland State Bar Association, Inc. (Chairman Administrative Law Section 1984, Select Committee on Improving Bench/Bar Relations since 2000), Howard County and American (Vice Chairman Committee on Health and Human Services 1978-82) Bar Associations. Co-Chair Planning Committee Maryland Family Violence Judicial

SWEENEY, DENNIS M.—*Continued*

Conference 1994. Chairman General Assembly's Task Force on Uninsured Employers 1990. Vice Chairman Governor's Prescription Drug Commission 1990-91. Member Attorney General's and Lieutenant Governor's Family Violence Council since 1995. Member Judicial Clerkship Advisory Committee University of Maryland School of Law 1995-96.

Office: Courthouse, 8360 Courthouse Drive, Ellicott City 21043.

Telephone: (410) 313-2149.

SWEENEY, Kathleen M. *(Associate Judge, Maryland District Court District One)* Appointed by governor.

Office: 5800 Wabash Avenue, Baltimore 21215-3330.

Telephone: (410) 878-8107.

THEMELIS, John C. *(Associate Judge, Circuit Court for Baltimore City, Eighth Judicial Circuit)* Appointed by Governor William Donald Schaefer Sept 15, 1988. Elected 1990, current term expires 2005. Born Baltimore Maryland Sept 23, 1947. Greek Orthodox. Educated at University of Maryland B.S. 1970 and University of Baltimore J.D. cum laude 1975. Member Heuisler Honor Society. Admitted to practice Maryland 1975, U.S. District Court District of Maryland 1975, U.S. Tax Court 1976, U.S. Supreme Court 1978 and District of Columbia 1983. Began legal practice Baltimore Maryland 1975. Associate Judge, Maryland District Court District One Sept 14, 1984 to Sept 15, 1988, appointed by Governor Harry Roe Hughes.

Assistant State's Attorney Baltimore City 1976-83. Specially appointed Assistant Public Defender 1983-84. Panel Chairman Health Claims Arbitration Board 1978-84. Author "Contempt" 1985, "Deficiency Judgments in the Commercial Law Article of the Maryland Code" 1985 and "Probation Violations" 1986 Maryland District Court. Adjunct Faculty member University of Baltimore School of Law and Loyola College 1986-89. Member Public Awareness Committee of the State Judiciary 1986-92, Committee on Public Trust and Confidence in the Justice System 1998-99, Civil Law and Procedure Committee of the State Judiciary since 1992, Public Trust and Confidence Initiatives-Implementation Committee since 1999 and Sentencing Guidelines Commission since 1999. Member Maryland Sentencing Guideline Board since 1987. Central Maryland Regional Advisory Board Member Maryland Alternative Dispute Resolution Commission since 1998. Member The Bar Association of Baltimore City (Historical and Criminal Law Committee since 1986), The District of Columbia Bar and Maryland State Bar Association, Inc. Democrat. Board of Directors St. Nicholas Greek Orthodox Church since 1996. Enjoys reading and writing.

Office: 100 North Calvert Street, Baltimore 21202.

Telephone: (410) 396-4627.

THOMPSON, Dexter M., Jr. *(Associate Judge, Circuit Court for Cecil County, Second Judicial Circuit)* Also serves as County Administrative Judge Cecil County.

Office: 129 East Main Street, Elkton 21921.

Telephone: (410) 996-5248.

THOMPSON, Durke G. *(Associate Judge, Circuit Court for Montgomery County, Sixth Judicial Circuit)* Appointed by Governor William D. Schaefer to term beginning 1994. Elected 1996, current term expires 2011. Born Washington D.C. Aug 5, 1942. Educated at University of Maryland B.A. 1964 and University of Wisconsin J.D. 1967. Law Clerk to Hon. Thomas Anderson, Court of Special Appeals of Maryland 1967-68. Admitted to practice Maryland 1968 and U.S. Supreme Court 1992. In legal practice Bethesda 1967-1994.

Member Montgomery Inns of Court (President 1997), Maryland State Bar Association, Inc. (Executive Committee 1979-80 and 1982-84) and Montgomery County Bar Association (President 1985-86).

Office: 50 Maryland Avenue, Rockville 20850.

Telephone: (240) 777-9190.

E-mail address: dthompson@mcccourt.com

TILLERSON ADAMS, Sheila R. *(Associate Judge, Circuit Court for Prince George's County, Seventh Judicial Circuit)* Former Associate Judge, Maryland District Court District Five.

Office: Court House, 14735 Main Street, Upper Marlboro 20772.

Telephone: (301) 952-3766.

TISDALE, John H. *(Associate Judge, Circuit Court for Frederick County, Sixth Judicial Circuit)* Appointed by Governor William D. Schaefer to term beginning Jan 23, 1995. Elected Nov 5, 1996, current term expires 2011. Born Washington D.C. June 21, 1945. Episcopalian. Educated at U.S. Naval Academy B.S. 1967 and Washington and Lee University J.D. 1974. Senior Editor Washington and Lee Law Review 1973-74. Admitted to practice Maryland 1974 and Virginia 1974. In legal practice Frederick Maryland 1974-95.

Member Bar Association of Frederick County (President 1998-99), Maryland State Bar Association, Inc. (Local and Specialty Bar Committee) and Virginia State Bar. USN 1967-71 and Commander USNR 1971-87 (retired). Trustee Frederick County Public Libraries 1976-84 and Frederick Community College 1987-95. Director Frederick Memorial Hospital 1987-95. Member Rotary (President 1991-92).

Office: Courthouse, 100 West Patrick Street, Frederick 21701.

Telephone: (301) 696-2943.

TURNBULL, John Grason, II *(Circuit Administrative Judge, Circuit Court for Baltimore County, Third Judicial Circuit)* Appointed by Governor Harry Roe Hughes to term beginning June 26, 1986. Elected Nov 8, 1988, current term expires Nov 8, 2003. Circuit Administrative Judge since Nov 1, 2001. Also serves as County Administrative Judge Baltimore County since Nov 1, 2001. Born Baltimore Maryland Aug 28, 1943. Episcopalian. Educated at University of Baltimore A.A. 1964 J.D. 1966. Law Clerk to Hon. John E. Raine, Jr., Circuit Court of Maryland Third Judicial Circuit 1964-66. Member Gamma Eta Gamma. Admitted to practice Maryland, U.S. District Court District of Maryland 1969 and U.S. Supreme Court 1974. In legal practice Baltimore and Towson 1969-86.

Member Maryland State Bar Association, Inc. and Baltimore County Bar Association (President 1993-94). Second Lieutenant U.S. Army Special Forces (Airborne) 1967-69.

Office: County Courts Building, 401 Bosley Avenue, Towson 21204.

Telephone: (410) 887-2647.

VAUGHAN, James N. *(Chief Judge, Maryland District Court)* Appointed by governor. Former Administrative Judge District Ten.

Office: Courts of Appeal Building, 361 Rowe Boulevard, Annapolis 21401.

Telephone: (410) 260-1525.

VAUGHEY, Cornelius J. *(Administrative Judge, Maryland District Court District Six)* Appointed by governor.

Office: 27 Court House Square, Rockville 20850-2325.

Telephone: (301) 279-1551.

WACHS, Jeffrey Michael *(Associate Judge, Maryland District Court District Seven)* Appointed by Governor Parris N. Glendening.

Office: 7500 Governor Ritchie Highway, Glen Burnie 21061-3756.

Telephone: (410) 260-1829.

WALDRON, Stephen M. *(Associate Judge, Circuit Court for Harford County, Third Judicial Circuit)*

Office: 20 West Courtland Street, Bel Air 21014.

Telephone: (410) 638-3266.

WALLACE, Sean D. *(Associate Judge, Circuit Court for Prince George's County, Seventh Judicial Circuit)*

Office: Court House, 14735 Main Street, Upper Marlboro 20772.

Telephone: (301) 952-4056.

WARREN, Rodney C. *(Associate Judge, Circuit Court for Anne Arundel County, Fifth Judicial Circuit)*

Office: Court House, Church Circle, Annapolis 21401.

Telephone: (410) 222-1440.

WATTS, Shirley Marie *(Associate Judge, Circuit Court for Baltimore City, Eighth Judicial Circuit)* Appointed by Governor Parris N. Glendening.

Office: Courthouse, 100 North Calvert Street, Baltimore 21202.

Telephone: (410) 396-5060.

WAXMAN, Barbara Baer *(Associate Judge, Maryland District Court District One)* Appointed by Governor William D. Schaefer.

Office: 5800 Wabash Avenue, Baltimore 21215-3330.

Telephone: (410) 878-8107.

WAXTER, Thomas, Jr. *(Associate Judge, Circuit Court for Baltimore City, Eighth Judicial Circuit)* Appointed by Governor Parris N. Glendening July 26, 1996 to term beginning Aug 26, 1996. Elected 1998, current term expires 2013. Born Baltimore Maryland 1934. Episcopalian. Educated at Princeton University B.A. with honors 1956 and University of Maryland School of Law LL.B. with honors 1962. Recent Decisions Editor University of Maryland Law Review 1962. Law Clerk to Hon. Harrison L. Winter, U.S. District Court District of Maryland 1962-63. Admitted to practice Maryland 1962, District of Columbia, U.S. Court of Appeals Fourth Circuit and U.S. Supreme Court. In legal practice 1962-96.

Office: 111 North Calvert Street, Baltimore 21202.

Telephone: (410) 396-5132.

WEATHERLY, Julia Beth *(Associate Judge, Circuit Court for Prince George's County, Seventh Judicial Circuit)* Appointed by Governor Parris N. Glendening.

Office: Court House, 14735 Main Street, Upper Marlboro 20772.

Telephone: (301) 952-3822.

WEINSTEIN, Halee F. *(Associate Judge, Maryland District Court District One)* Appointed by governor.

Office: 5800 Wabash Avenue, Baltimore 21215-3330.

Telephone: (410) 878-8107.

WEINSTEIN, Paul H. *(Circuit Administrative Judge, Circuit Court for Montgomery County, Sixth Judicial Circuit)* Appointed by Governor Harry Roe Hughes to term beginning Aug 8, 1986. Elected to subsequent term. Also serves as County Administrative Judge Montgomery County. Born Washington D.C. April 20, 1933. Jewish. Educated at Washington and Lee University B.S. 1955 and George Washington University LL.B. 1959. Admitted to practice District of Columbia 1959 and Maryland 1964. Began legal practice Washington D.C. 1959. In legal practice Chevy Chase 1972. Judge, Maryland District Court District Six July 19, 1983 to Aug 7, 1986, appointed by Governor Harry Roe Hughes.

Member The District of Columbia Bar, Maryland State Bar Association, Inc. and Montgomery County Bar Association.

Office: 50 Maryland Avenue, Rockville 20850.

Telephone: (240) 777-9180.

WEITZMAN, Jamey H. *(Associate Judge, Maryland District Court District One)* Appointed by Governor William D. Schaefer.

Office: 5800 Wabash Avenue, Baltimore 21215-3330.

Telephone: (410) 878-8107.

WELCH, Martin P. *(Associate Judge, Circuit Court for Baltimore City, Eighth Judicial Circuit)*

Office: Courthouse, 100 North Calvert Street, Baltimore 21202.

Telephone: (410) 396-5082.

WHALEN, Michael Patrick *(Associate Judge, Circuit Court for Prince George's County, Seventh Judicial Circuit)* Appointed by Governor Parris N. Glendening to term beginning Nov 2, 1999. Elected Nov 7, 2000, current term expires Nov 6, 2015. Born Waltham Massachusetts April 2, 1946. Catholic. Educated at University of Maryland B.A. 1969 and University of Baltimore School of Law J.D. 1973. Recipient Ray Ehrensberger Oratorical Award 1966. Admitted to practice Maryland 1974, U.S. Supreme Court 1980, District of Columbia 1981, U.S. District Court District of Maryland 1984 and U.S. Court of Appeals Fourth Circuit 1988. In legal practice Adelphi 1980 and Upper Marlboro 1986-88. Associate Judge, Maryland District Court District Five Nov 3, 1995 to Nov 2, 1999.

Assistant State's Attorney and Deputy State's Attorney Prince George's County Aug 12, 1974 to Nov 14, 1986. County Attorney Prince George's County May 31, 1988 to Nov 2, 1995. Adjunct Associate Professor of Paralegal Studies, Legal Writing and Documentation, Litigation, Criminal Law and Procedures University of Maryland/University College since 1979. Charter Fellow Law Foundation of Prince George's County. Fellow Maryland Bar Foundation. Member Maryland State Bar Association, Inc. (Board of Governors 1994-96) and Prince George's County Bar Association (Board of Di-

WHALEN, MICHAEL PATRICK—*Continued*
rectors 1987-90, Executive Committee 1989-95, President 1993-94). Recipient Arthur A. Marshall, Jr. Prosecutor of the Year Award 1986, Certificate of Appreciation from Seventh Judicial Circuit of Maryland 1986, Teaching Recognition Award 1989-90, Certificate of Appreciation 1994 and Judge William R. Robie Award 1998 from University of Maryland/University College, President's Award from Prince George's County Bar Association 1990 and Certificate of Appreciation from Maryland Coalition Against Pornography 1991.

Office: 276B Courthouse, 14735 Main Street, Upper Marlboro 20772-3042.
Telephone: (301) 952-4520.
Fax: (301) 952-3101
E-mail address: MPW@CO.PG.MD.US

WHITEHEAD, Lloyd O. *(Associate Judge, Maryland District Court District Two)* Appointed by Governor William D. Schaefer to term beginning Sept 7, 1990. Reappointed by Governor Parris N. Glendening Sept 7, 2000, current term expires Sept 7, 2010. Born Salisbury Maryland Dec 23, 1939. Protestant. Educated at University of Maryland at College Park A.B. 1961 and Washington College of Law of American University J.D. 1964. Admitted to practice Maryland 1964, U.S. District Courts District of Maryland 1964 and District of Columbia 1965 and U.S. Supreme Court 1974. In legal practice Salisbury June 1964 to Sept 7, 2000.

Former Member Maryland Trial Lawyers Association, Commercial Law League of America, The Association of Trial Lawyers of America and American Bar Association. Member Maryland State Bar Association, Inc. and Wicomico County Bar Association (President 1976). Member Pittsville Lions Club. Interests include genealogy and U.S. history. Personal Statement or Quote: "Be prepared. Be on time. Bring your trial calendar with you to court."

Office: 201 Baptist Street, Salisbury 21801.
Telephone: (410) 543-6600.

WILCOX, Robert C. *(Associate Judge, Maryland District Court District Seven)* Appointed by Governor Parris N. Glendening.

Office: 251 Rowe Boulevard, Annapolis 21401.
Telephone: (410) 260-1360.

WILLIAMS, Alexander, Jr. *(Judge, United States District Court District of Maryland)* Appointed for life by President Bill Clinton to term beginning 1994. Born Washington D.C. May 8, 1948. Educated at Howard University B.A. 1970 J.D. cum laude 1973, Howard University School of Divinity M.A.R.S. in Ethics 1991 and Temple University M.A. 1995. Honorary Doctorate Southeastern University 1995. Admitted to practice Maryland 1973 and District of Columbia 1974. In legal practice 1974-86.

Municipal Attorney Towns of Fairmont Heights and Glenarden 1975-87. Staff Attorney Office of the Public Defender 1977-78, Hearing Examiner and Special Counsel Board of Education 1978-87 and State's Attorney 1987-94 Prince George's County. Member J. Franklyn Bourne Bar Association (Founder and First President), Prince George's County and National Bar Associations.

Office: 445A U.S. Courthouse, 6500 Cherrywood Lane, Greenbelt 20770-1292.
Telephone: (301) 344-0637.

WILLIAMS, Alexandra N. *(Administrative Judge, Maryland District Court District Eight)* Appointed by governor.

Office: 120 East Chesapeake Avenue, Towson 21286-5307.
Telephone: (410) 512-2050.

WILNER, Alan M. *(Associate Judge, Court of Appeals of Maryland)* Appointed by governor. Born Baltimore Maryland Jan 26, 1937. Jewish. Educated at Johns Hopkins University A.B. with honors 1958 M.L.A. 1966 and University of Maryland J.D. with honors 1962. Member Order of the Coif. Admitted to practice Maryland 1962. Began legal practice Baltimore 1962. Former Chief Judge, Court of Special Appeals of Maryland, appointed by Acting Governor Blair Lee, III to term beginning Aug 11, 1977.

Assistant Attorney General Maryland 1965-68. Author "The Cy-Pres Doctrine Explored" Maryland L. Rev. 1963 and "Superior Orders as a Defense to Violations of International Criminal Law" Maryland L. Rev. 1966. Instructor in Commercial Law Towson State College 1968-71. Member Maryland Judicial Conference, The Bar Association of Baltimore City and Maryland State Bar Association, Inc. Chief Legislative Officer to Governor Marvin Mandel 1974-77.

Office: County Courts Building, 401 Bosley Avenue, Towson 21204.
Telephone: (410) 887-2677.

WILSON, Dorothy Jean *(Associate Judge, Maryland District Court District Eight)* Appointed by Governor Parris N. Glendening.

Office: 120 East Chesapeake Avenue, Towson 21286-5307.
Telephone: (410) 512-2050.

WOLFE, Eugene *(Associate Judge, Maryland District Court District Six)* Appointed by Governor Parris N. Glendening.

Office: 27 Court House Square, Rockville 20850-2325.
Telephone: (301) 279-1373.

WOODARD, Beverly J. *(Associate Judge, Maryland District Court District Five)* Appointed by Governor Parris N. Glendening.

Office: 14735 Main Street, Suite 173B, Upper Marlboro 20772.
Telephone: (301) 952-4021.

WOODS, Robert J. *(Associate Judge, Circuit Court for Prince George's County, Seventh Judicial Circuit)*

Office: Court House, 14735 Main Street, Upper Marlboro 20772.
Telephone: (301) 952-3132.

WOODWARD, Patrick L. *(Associate Judge, Circuit Court for Montgomery County, Sixth Judicial Circuit)* Former Associate Judge, Maryland District Court District Six, appointed by Governor William D. Schaefer.

Office: 50 Maryland Avenue, Rockville 28050.
Telephone: (240) 777-9261.

WORSHTIL, Joel D. *(Associate Judge, Maryland District Court District Five)* Appointed by Governor Parris N. Glendening.

Office: 4990 Rhode Island Avenue, Hyattsville 20781.
Telephone: (301) 699-2777.

WRIGHT, Frederick C., III *(Circuit Administrative Judge, Circuit Court for Washington County, Fourth Judicial Circuit)* Appointed by Acting Governor Blair Lee III to term beginning Jan 5, 1979. Elected to subsequent terms. Current term expires 2009. Also serves as County Administrative Judge Washington County. Born Washington County Maryland 1938. Educated at University of Virginia B.S. in Commerce 1960 LL.B. 1963. Admitted to practice Maryland 1963. Began legal practice Hagerstown. Administrative Judge, Maryland District Court District Eleven 1971-79.

Member North American Trial Judges Association, Executive Committee of Maryland Judicial Conference, American Judicature Society, Maryland State Bar Association, Inc., Washington County and American Bar Associations. Chairman Advisory Board for Public Defender. Recipient Outstanding Young Man Award from Hagerstown Jaycees 1970. U.S. Army. Member House of Delegates Maryland 1966-71 (Speaker pro tem 1971, youngest in Maryland legislative history; Chairman Committee on Rules 1969-71; member Judiciary Committee and Committee on the Constitution and Administrative Law). Member Mason-Dixon Council Boy Scouts of America, Governor's Commission on Children and Youth, Washington County Drug Abuse Advisory Committee and Washington County Mental Health Advisory Committee. President Boys' Club for Washington County. Past President Hagerstown Jaycees. Member St. John's Episcopal Church, Kiwanis Club of Hagerstown and Elks.

Office: 95 West Washington Street, Hagerstown 21740.

Telephone: (240) 313-2550.

YOUNG, David W. *(Associate Judge, Circuit Court for Baltimore City, Eighth Judicial Circuit)* Former Associate Judge, Maryland District Court District One.

Office: Courthouse East, 111 North Calvert Street, Baltimore 21202.

Telephone: (410) 396-5076.

MASSACHUSETTS

Capital BOSTON

UNITED STATES DISTRICT COURT DISTRICT OF MASSACHUSETTS

The court sits at Boston, New Bedford, Springfield and Worcester. For descriptive information refer to the United States Courts section.

Chief Judge

William G. Young

Judges

Joseph L. Tauro	Rya W. Zobel
Mark L. Wolf	Douglas P. Woodlock
Nathaniel M. Gorton	Patti B. Saris
Reginald C. Lindsay	Richard G. Stearns
Michael A. Ponsor	Nancy Gertner
George A. O'Toole, Jr.	

Senior Judges

Robert E. Keeton
Frank H. Freedman
Walter Jay Skinner
A. David Mazzone
Edward F. Harrington

Clerk

Tony Anastas
2300 U.S. Courthouse
One Courthouse Way
Boston, Massachusetts 02210-3002
(617) 748-9152

UNITED STATES MAGISTRATE JUDGES OF MASSACHUSETTS

Lawrence P. Cohen	Joyce L. Alexander
Robert B. Collings	Marianne B. Bowler
Charles Swartwood III	Kenneth P. Neiman
Judith Gail Dein	

UNITED STATES BANKRUPTCY COURT OF MASSACHUSETTS

Chief Judge

Joan N. Feeney

Judges

Carol J. Kenner
William C. Hillman
Henry Jack Boroff
Joel B. Rosenthal

Bankruptcy Clerk

James M. Lynch
1101 Federal Building
10 Causeway Street
Boston, Massachusetts 02222-1074
(617) 565-6050

MASSACHUSETTS SUPREME JUDICIAL COURT

The Supreme Judicial Court is Massachusetts' court of last resort. The court consists of a chief justice and six associate justices appointed by the governor with the consent of the Executive Council to serve until age seventy.

The court has concurrent appellate jurisdiction with the Appeals Court over civil and criminal matters in all lower courts. The court has original appellate jurisdiction in cases of first degree murder; in any case that the Supreme Judicial Court or the Appeals Court certifies for direct review or one that has broad public concern; appealed and reserved and reported cases from the single justice session of the court; and disciplinary proceedings of clerks of court, judges or attorneys. The court exercises constitutional and statutory general superintendence of the administration of all courts in the state and of the bar and has the authority to make and promulgate rules. The court may render advisory opinions to either house of the Legislature, the governor and the Executive Council.

Four to seven justices ordinarily sit to hear and decide appeals from September to May. All seven justices may sit to hear cases of particular significance. The court generally sits in Boston, but occasionally travels to other parts of the state. Single justices hear appeals throughout the year in Boston and other parts of the state.

Chief Justice

Margaret H. Marshall

Associate Justices

John M. Greaney	Roderick L. Ireland
Judith Arnold Cowin	Francis X. Spina
Martha B. Sosman	Robert J. Cordy

Clerk of the Commonwealth

Susan Mellen
Supreme Judicial Court
1412 New Courthouse
Boston, Massachusetts 02108
(617) 557-1020

Clerk for Suffolk County

Maura Sweeney Doyle
Supreme Judicial Court
1404 New Courthouse
Boston, Massachusetts 02108
(617) 557-1100

MASSACHUSETTS APPEALS COURT

The Appeals Court is Massachusetts' intermediate appellate court. The court consists of a chief justice and twenty-four associate justices appointed by the governor with the consent of the Executive Council to serve until age seventy.

MASSACHUSETTS APPEALS COURT—*Continued*

The court has concurrent appellate jurisdiction with the Supreme Judicial Court in civil and equity matters, administrative determinations and proceedings related to extraordinary writs and in criminal matters except appeals from first degree murder convictions. The court has original jurisdiction over final orders of the Labor Relations Commission and the Appellate Tax Board and hears industrial accident appeals.

The justices sit in panels of three or more as determined by the chief justice of the Appeals Court. The court usually sits at Boston and periodically at Springfield, although occasionally panels of justices may sit in other cities.

Chief Justice
Christopher J. Armstrong

Associate Justices

Frederick L. Brown
George Jacobs
Elizabeth A. Porada
Kenneth Laurence
Susan S. Beck
Andre A. Gelinas
Elspeth B. Cypher
Joseph A. Grasso, Jr.
William I. Cowin
Gordon L. Doerfer
Scott L. Kafker
David A. Mills
Joseph A. Trainor
Charlotte Anne Perretta
Mel L. Greenberg
Barbara A. Lenk
Phillip Rapoza
Fernande R. V. Duffly
John H. Mason
R. Marc Kantrowitz
Janis M. Berry
James F. McHugh
Cynthia Cohen
Mark V. Green

Appeals Court Clerk
Ashley Ahearn, Esq.
1500 New Courthouse
Boston, Massachusetts 02108
(617) 725-8106

TRIAL COURT OF MASSACHUSETTS

The Trial Court of Massachusetts, organized in 1978, consists of seven departments reflecting the preexisting trial courts of general and specialized jurisdiction. These departments are Superior Court Department, District Court Department, Boston Municipal Court Department, Probate and Family Court Department, Land Court Department, Juvenile Court Department and Housing Court Department. The Supreme Judicial Court appoints a Chief Justice for Administration and Management of the Trial Court to serve a five-year term, who is eligible to serve additional five-year terms. The Chief Justice for Administration and Management is the appointing authority for the chief justices of the seven Trial Court Departments. The chief justices are appointed to serve five-year terms and are eligible to serve additional five-year terms.

In several departments, particularly the Superior Court, District Court and Probate and Family Court Departments, justices are often appointed to certain locations and then reassigned to other locations. These assignments may also change periodically. In order to ascertain the current court address of a particular justice, the administrative offices of that Department should be contacted. These offices will be found following the listing of justices who serve each Department.

Chief Justice for Administration and Management
Barbara A. Dortch-Okara
Administrative Office of the Trial Court
Two Center Plaza, Fifth Floor
Boston, Massachusetts 02108
(617) 742-8575

SUPERIOR COURT DEPARTMENT

The Superior Court Department is Massachusetts' highest court of general jurisdiction. Justices are appointed by the governor with the consent of the Executive Council to serve until age seventy. A chief justice is appointed by the Chief Justice for Administration and Management to serve a five-year term. The chief justice is eligible to serve additional five-year terms.

The court has original jurisdiction of all criminal offenses and of all civil actions, excluding those which are under the original exclusive jurisdiction of other courts. The court has exclusive original jurisdiction in civil actions for the foreclosure of mortgages and of real and mixed actions, except when the Land Court Department or District Court Department has jurisdiction and in claims against the commonwealth. The court also has exclusive jurisdiction when injunctive relief is sought in any matter growing out of a labor dispute. The court exercises jurisdiction concurrent with the Supreme Judicial Court in matters in equity and with the Supreme Judicial Court, Probate and Family Court Department and Land Court Department over actions for declaratory judgment. The court has appellate jurisdiction over most decisions of the Industrial Accident Board and certain other governmental bodies and commissions. A case may be transferred to the District Court Department or Boston Municipal Court Department for trial if damages do not exceed $25,000. An Appellate Division is composed of a three-justice panel to review prison sentences handed down by the court.

Justices rotate throughout the state as assigned by the chief justice of the Superior Court Department. The court sits in the fourteen counties at each shire town at least once a year and in other cities as needed. In most counties the court sits year-round.

Chief Justice
Suzanne V. DelVecchio

Associate Justices

James P. Donohue
Robert A. Mulligan
Barbara J. Rouse
R. Malcolm Graham
Catherine A. White
Wendie I. Gershengorn
Robert H. Bohn, Jr.
Margot Botsford
Patrick F. Brady
Thomas E. Connolly
Richard F. Connon
Charles T. Spurlock
Regina L. Quinlan
Mary-Lou Rup
E. Susan Garsh
Howard J. Whitehead
Richard J. Chin
Richard E. Welch, III
Herman J. Smith, Jr.
Diane M. Kottmyer
Sandra L. Hamlin
Paul A. Chernoff
Charles M. Grabau
Constance M. Sweeney
John C. Cratsley
Daniel A. Ford
Elizabeth B. Donovan
Peter M. Lauriat
Julian T. Houston
Elizabeth Butler
Charles J. Hely
Stephen E. Neel
Isaac Borenstein
Maria I. Lopez
Margaret R. Hinkle
Judd J. Carhart
Christine M. McEvoy
Bertha D. Josephson
Raymond J. Brassard
Francis R. Fecteau

TRIAL COURT OF MASSACHUSETTS—*Continued*

Carol S. Ball	Lawrence B. Wernick
Judith Fabricant	Mitchell Sikora, Jr.
Nonnie S. Burnes	Allan van Gestel
Nancy Staffier	C. Brian McDonald
Ralph D. Gants	Peter A. Velis
Thomas J. Curley, Jr.	Linda E. Giles
Timothy S. Hillman	Gary A. Nickerson
S. Jane Haggerty	Tina S. Page
Elizabeth M. Fahey	David A. McLaughlin
Leila R. Kern	Joseph M. Walker, III
Peter W. Agnes, Jr.	John S. McCann
Ernest B. Murphy	Geraldine S. Hines
Christopher J. Muse	Robert J. Kane
David A. Lowy	Jeffrey A. Locke
Janet L. Sanders	Thomas P. Billings
Paul E. Troy	John A. Agostini
Bonnie H. MacLeod	John P. Connor, Jr.
Patrick J. Riley	Richard T. Moses
Kenneth J. Fishman	

Superior Court Department
Administrative Office
U.S. Post Office and Courthouse
15th Floor, 90 Devonshire Street
Boston, Massachusetts 02109
(617) 788-8130

DISTRICT COURT DEPARTMENT

The District Court Department is a court of general jurisdiction in Massachusetts. The District Court Department consists of sixty-nine divisions. Justices are appointed by the governor to serve until age seventy. A chief justice of the District Court Department is appointed by the Chief Justice for Administration and Management to serve a five-year term. The chief justice is eligible to serve additional five-year terms. In each division, a first justice is appointed by the chief justice to serve a five-year term as administrative head of the division. The first justice may serve additional five-year terms. Circuit justices rotate throughout the state as needed.

The court has original criminal jurisdiction concurrent with the Superior Court Department over ordinance violations, all misdemeanors, felonies carrying a maximum sentence of not more than five years, and many other specific felonies with greater potential penalties. In other felony cases, the court may conduct probable cause hearings and inquiries. The court has original jurisdiction concurrent with the Superior Court Department in civil claims, eviction cases, small claims suits up to $2,000, death inquests and mental health matters. The court's civil jurisdiction also includes many specialized proceedings: supplementary process (to enforce money judgments), abuse prevention restraining orders, appeals from certain administrative agencies, civil motor vehicle infractions and equitable injunctions. Judges sitting in Berkshire, Essex, Middlesex and Norfolk counties conduct both jury and jury-waived trials, and determine with finality any matter in which the recovery will not likely exceed $25,000. In other counties, judges exercise jury-waived trial jurisdiction mostly in matters involving $25,000 or less, subject to possible retrial before a Superior Court judge. Some District Court divisions continue to exercise jurisdiction in juvenile cases (delinquency, child abuse or neglect and children in need of services), particularly in Middlesex and Norfolk counties.

Appeals on questions of law arising in civil cases originating in the District Court Department are heard by an Appellate Division. This appellate tribunal with published opinions is organized in three geographical districts, and is served by fifteen of the justices sitting in three-justice panels as designated by the chief justice of the department.

Chief Justice
Samuel E. Zoll

BARNSTABLE COUNTY

BARNSTABLE DIVISION includes Barnstable, Sandwich and Yarmouth. The court sits at Barnstable.

First Justice
Joseph J. Reardon

Justices
Don L. Carpenter
Joan E. Lynch

FALMOUTH DIVISION includes Bourne, Falmouth and Mashpee. The court sits at Falmouth.

First Justice
Michael C. Creedon

Justices
Kevan J. Cunningham
vacancy

ORLEANS DIVISION includes Brewster, Chatham, Dennis, Eastham, Harwich, Orleans, Provincetown, Truro and Wellfleet. The court sits at Orleans.

First Justice
Robert A. Welsh, Jr.

Justice
Lance J. Garth

BERKSHIRE COUNTY

NORTHERN BERKSHIRE DIVISION includes Adams, Cheshire, Clarksburg, Florida, New Ashford, North Adams, Savoy and Williamstown. It exercises concurrent jurisdiction with Pittsfield Division in Hancock and Windsor. The court sits at Adams and North Adams.

First Justice
Michael J. Ripps

Justice
Paul M. Vrabel

PITTSFIELD DIVISION includes Dalton, Hinsdale, Lanesborough, Peru, Pittsfield, Richmond and Washington. It exercises concurrent jurisdiction with Northern Berkshire Division in Hancock and Windsor and with Southern Berkshire Division in Becket and Lenox. The court sits at Pittsfield.

First Justice
Alfred A. Barbalunga

Justice
Rita Koenigs

SOUTHERN BERKSHIRE DIVISION includes Alford, Egremont, Great Barrington, Lee, Monterey, Mount Washington, New Marlborough, Otis, Sandisfield, Shef-

TRIAL COURT OF MASSACHUSETTS—*Continued*

field, Stockbridge, Tyringham and West Stockbridge. It exercises concurrent jurisdiction with Pittsfield Division in Becket and Lenox. The court sits at Great Barrington.

First Justice
James B. McElroy

Justice
Fredric D. Rutberg

BRISTOL COUNTY

ATTLEBORO DIVISION includes Attleboro, Mansfield, North Attleborough and Norton. The court sits at Attleboro.

First Justice
Gregory L. Phillips

Justices
Thomas S. Barrett
Paul J. McCallum

FALL RIVER DIVISION includes Fall River, Freetown, Somerset, Swansea and Westport. The court sits at Fall River.

First Justice
Gilbert J. Nadeau, Jr.

Justices
Bernadette L. Sabra
David T. Turcotte
vacancy

NEW BEDFORD DIVISION includes Acushnet, Dartmouth, Fairhaven, Freetown, New Bedford and Westport. The court sits at New Bedford.

First Justice
Bernadette L. Sabra

Justices
Julie J. Bernard
Ronald F. Moynahan
Toby S. Mooney

TAUNTON DIVISION includes Berkley, Dighton, Easton, Raynham, Rehoboth, Seekonk and Taunton. The court sits at Taunton.

First Justice
Kevan J. Cunningham

Justices
Joseph I. Macy
James Sullivan

DUKES COUNTY

EDGARTOWN DIVISION includes Martha's Vineyard and the Elizabeth Islands. The court sits at Edgartown.

First Justice
Brian Rowe

Justice
John M. Julian

ESSEX COUNTY

GLOUCESTER DIVISION includes Essex, Gloucester and Rockport. The court sits at Gloucester.

First Justice
Richard A. Mori

Justices
Ellen Flatley
Robert A. Brennan

HAVERHILL DIVISION includes Boxford, Georgetown, Groveland, Haverhill and West Newbury. The court sits at Haverhill.

First Justice
Kevin M. Herlihy

Justices
Peter F. Doyle
Allen G. Swan

IPSWICH DIVISION includes Ipswich. The court sits at Ipswich.

First Justice
Allen G. Swan

Justices
Robert A. Cornetta
Patricia A. Dowling

LAWRENCE DIVISION includes Andover, Lawrence, Methuen and North Andover. The court sits at Lawrence.

First Justice
Michael T. Stella, Jr.

Justice
Kevin M. Herlihy

LYNN DIVISION includes Lynn, Marblehead, Nahant, Saugus and Swampscott. The court sits at Lynn.

First Justice
Joseph I. Dever

Justice
Robert N. Tochka

NEWBURYPORT DIVISION includes Amesbury, Merrimac, Newbury, Newburyport, Rowley, Salisbury and West Newbury. The court sits at Amesbury and Newburyport.

First Justice
Peter F. Doyle

Justices
William E. Melahn
James J. O'Leary
vacancy

PEABODY DIVISION includes Lynnfield and Peabody. The court sits at Peabody.

First Justice
Santo J. Ruma

Justice
J. Dennis Healey

SALEM DIVISION includes Beverly, Danvers, Danvers State Hospital, Hamilton, Manchester, Middleton, Salem, Topsfield and Wenham. The court sits at Danvers State Hospital and Salem.

Acting First Justice
Robert A. Cornetta

TRIAL COURT OF MASSACHUSETTS—*Continued*

Justices
Michael C. Lauranzano
Samuel E. Zoll

FRANKLIN COUNTY

GREENFIELD DIVISION includes Ashfield, Bernardston, Buckland, Charlemont, Colrain, Conway, Deerfield, Gill, Greenfield, Hawley, Heath, Leverett, Leyden, Monroe, Montague, Northfield, Rowe, Shelburne, Shutesbury, Sunderland and Whately. The court sits at Greenfield.

First Justice
Herbert H. Hodos

Justice
vacancy

ORANGE DIVISION includes Athol, Erving, New Salem, Orange, Warwick and Wendell. The court sits at Orange.

First Justice
David S. Ross

Justices
M. John Schubert, Jr.
vacancy

HAMPDEN COUNTY

CHICOPEE DIVISION includes Chicopee. The court sits at Chicopee.

First Justice
Mary E. Hurley-Marks

Justices
David S. Ross
John M. Payne, Jr.

HOLYOKE DIVISION includes Holyoke. The court sits at Holyoke.

First Justice
William B. McDonough

Justice
Robert F. Kumor, Jr.

PALMER DIVISION includes Brimfield, Hampden, Holland, Ludlow, Monson, Palmer, Wales and Wilbraham. The court sits at Palmer.

First Justice
Patricia T. Poehler

Justices
Robert L. Howarth
Kenneth J. Cote, Jr.

SPRINGFIELD DIVISION includes Agawam, East Longmeadow, Longmeadow, Springfield and West Springfield. The court sits at Springfield.

First Justice
Robert F. Kumor, Jr.

Justices
William J. Boyle
Robert A. Gordon
William W. Teahan, Jr.
Nancy Dusek-Gomez
Jacques C. Leroy
H. Gregory Williams

WESTFIELD DIVISION includes Blandford, Chester, Granville, Montgomery, Russell, Southwick, Tolland and Westfield. The court sits at Westfield.

First Justice
Philip A. Contant

Justice
Patricia T. Poehler

HAMPSHIRE COUNTY

NORTHAMPTON DIVISION includes Amherst, Chesterfield, Cummington, Easthampton, Goshen, Granby, Hadley, Hatfield, Huntington, Middlefield, Northampton, Pelham, Plainfield, South Hadley, Southampton, Westhampton, Williamsburg and Worthington. The court sits at Northampton.

First Justice
Richard J. Carey

Justices
W. Michael Ryan
W. Michael Goggins

WARE DIVISION includes Belchertown and Ware. The court sits at Ware.

First Justice
Nancy Dusek-Gomez

Justices
Paul A. Losapio
vacancy

MIDDLESEX COUNTY

AYER DIVISION includes Ashby, Ayer, Boxborough, Dunstable, Groton, Littleton, Pepperell, Shirley, Townsend and Westford. The court sits at Ayer.

First Justice
Peter J. Kilmartin

Justice
James M. Geary, Jr.

CAMBRIDGE DIVISION includes Arlington, Belmont and Cambridge. The court sits at East Cambridge.

First Justice
Roanne Sragow

Justices
Jonathan Brant
Marie O. Jackson-Thompson
Severlin B. Singleton III
Michele B. Hogan
Michael J. Pomarole
George R. Sprague

CONCORD DIVISION includes Acton, Bedford, Carlisle, Concord, Lexington, Lincoln, Maynard and Stow. The court sits at Concord.

First Justice
Robert J. McKenna, Jr.

Justices
Patricia G. Curtin
James H. Wexler

FRAMINGHAM DIVISION includes Ashland, Framingham, Holliston, Hopkinton, Sudbury and Wayland. The court sits at Framingham.

TRIAL COURT OF MASSACHUSETTS—*Continued*

First Justice
Robert V. Greco

Justices
Paul F. Healy, Jr.
Douglas W. Stoddart

LOWELL DIVISION includes Billerica, Chelmsford, Dracut, Lowell, Tewksbury and Tyngsborough. The court sits at Lowell.

First Justice
Neil J. Walker

Justice
Barbara S. Pearson

MALDEN DIVISION includes Everett, Malden, Melrose and Wakefield. The court sits at Malden.

First Justice
Lee G. Johnson

Justices
Maurice R. Flynn, III
Paul F. Mahoney
Richard A. Mori
Geoffrey C. Packard

MARLBOROUGH DIVISION includes Hudson and Marlborough. The court sits at Marlborough.

First Justice
Thomas F. Sullivan, Jr.

Justices
Lynda M. Connolly
Mary Hogan Sullivan

NATICK DIVISION includes Natick and Sherborn. The court sits at Natick.

First Justice
Sarah B. Singer

Justices
James H. McGuinness, Jr.
Michael J. Brooks

NEWTON DIVISION includes Newton. The court sits at East Cambridge.

First Justice
Dyanne J. Klein

Justice
Thomas M. Brennan

SOMERVILLE DIVISION includes Medford and Somerville. The court sits at Somerville.

First Justice
Paul P. Heffernan

Justice
Mark S. Coven

WALTHAM DIVISION includes Waltham, Watertown and Weston. The court sits at Waltham.

First Justice
Gregory C. Flynn

Justice
David T. Donnelly

WOBURN DIVISION includes Burlington, North Reading, Reading, Stoneham, Wilmington, Winchester and Woburn. The court sits at Woburn.

First Justice
Marie O. Jackson-Thompson

Justices
Phyllis J. Broker
Tobin N. Harvey

NANTUCKET COUNTY

NANTUCKET DIVISION includes Nantucket. The court sits at Nantucket.

First Justice
W. James O'Neill

Justice
Deborah A. Dunn

NORFOLK COUNTY

BROOKLINE DIVISION includes Brookline. The court sits at Brookline.

First Justice
Thomas J. May

Justices
Paul K. Leary
Kevin J. O'Dea

DEDHAM DIVISION includes Dedham, Dover, Medfield, Needham, Norwood, Wellesley and Westwood. The court sits at Dedham.

Acting First Justice
Diana L. Maldonado

Justice
Kevin J. Gaffney

QUINCY DIVISION includes Braintree, Cohasset, Holbrook, Milton, Quincy, Randolph and Weymouth. The court sits at Quincy.

First Justice
Mark S. Coven

Justices
Gregory R. Baler
Warren A. Powers

STOUGHTON DIVISION includes Avon, Canton, Sharon and Stoughton. The court sits at Stoughton.

First Justice
Francis T. Crimmins, Jr.

Justice
Dennis J. Curran

WRENTHAM DIVISION includes Foxborough, Franklin, Medway, Mills, Norfolk, Plainville, Walpole and Wrentham. The court sits at Wrentham.

Acting First Justice
Emogene Johnson Smith

Justice
Daniel W. O'Malley

TRIAL COURT OF MASSACHUSETTS—*Continued*

PLYMOUTH COUNTY

BROCKTON DIVISION includes Abington, Bridgewater, Brockton, East Bridgewater, West Bridgewater and Whitman. The court sits at Brockton.

First Justice
David G. Nagle, Jr.

Justices
Robert E. Baylor
Paul C. Dawley
Richard D. Savignano

HINGHAM DIVISION includes Hanover, Hingham, Hull, Norwell, Rockland and Scituate. The court sits at Hingham.

First Justice
Patrick J. Hurley

Justice
Francis L. Marini

PLYMOUTH DIVISION includes Duxbury, Halifax, Hanson, Kingston, Marshfield, Pembroke, Plymouth and Plympton. The court sits at Plymouth.

First Justice
Thomas F. Brownell

Justice
Rosemary B. Minehan

WAREHAM DIVISION includes Carver, Lakeville, Marion, Mattapoisett, Middleboro, Rochester and Wareham. The court sits at West Wareham.

First Justice
Rosemary B. Minehan

Justices
Diane E. Moriarty
John C. Wheatley

SUFFOLK COUNTY

BRIGHTON DIVISION includes Brighton. The court sits at Brighton.

First Justice
R. Peter Anderson

Justice
Paul V. Buckley

CHARLESTOWN DIVISION includes Charlestown. The court sits at Charlestown.

First Justice
Anthony P. Sullivan

Justices
James W. Coffey
Allen J. Jarasitis

CHELSEA DIVISION includes Chelsea and Revere. The court sits at Chelsea.

First Justice
Timothy H. Gailey

Justices
Kathleen E. Coffey
Diana L. Maldonado
William J. Riley

DORCHESTER DIVISION includes Dorchester. The court sits at Dorchester.

First Justice
Sydney Hanlon

Justices
Rosalind H. Miller
Emogene Johnson Smith
Roberto Ronquillo, Jr.

EAST BOSTON DIVISION includes East Boston and Winthrop. The court sits at East Boston.

First Justice
Paul F. Mahoney

Justices
Thomas J. May
vacancy

ROXBURY DIVISION includes Roxbury. The court sits at Roxbury.

First Justice
Milton L. Wright, Jr.

Justices
Gordon A. Martin, Jr.
Paul L. McGill
Gregory L. Phillips
Edward Redd

SOUTH BOSTON DIVISION includes South Boston. The court sits at South Boston.

First Justice
Robert P. Ziemian

Justices
Mary Ann Driscoll
Robert J. McKenna, Jr.

WEST ROXBURY DIVISION includes West Roxbury. The court sits at Forest Hills.

First Justice
Kathleen E. Coffey

Justices
Robert C. Rufo
Robert P. Ziemian

WORCESTER COUNTY

CLINTON DIVISION includes Berlin, Bolton, Boylston, Clinton, Harvard, Lancaster and Sterling. The court sits at Clinton.

First Justice
Martha A. Brennan

Justice
Robert W. Gardner, Jr.

DUDLEY DIVISION includes Charlton, Dudley, Oxford, Southbridge, Sturbridge and Webster. The court sits at Dudley.

First Justice
Neil G. Snider

TRIAL COURT OF MASSACHUSETTS—*Continued*

Justices
John Conrad Geenty
vacancy

EAST BROOKFIELD DIVISION includes Brookfield, East Brookfield, Hardwick, Leicester, New Braintree, North Brookfield, Spencer, Warren and West Brookfield. The court sits at East Brookfield.

First Justice
Charles A. Abdella

Justices
Patrick A. Fox
Paul F. LoConto

FITCHBURG DIVISION includes Ashburnham, Fitchburg and Lunenburg. The court sits at Fitchburg.

First Justice
Paul F. LoConto

Justices
Andrew L. Mandell
Elliott L. Zide

GARDNER DIVISION includes Gardner, Hubbardston, Petersham, Phillipston, Royalston, Templeton and Westminster. The court sits at Gardner.

First Justice
Patrick A. Fox

Justices
Austin T. Philbin
David B. Locke

LEOMINSTER DIVISION includes Leominster and Princeton. The court sits at Leominster.

First Justice
John J. Curran, Jr.

Justice
Edward J. Reynolds

MILFORD DIVISION includes Bellingham, Hopedale, Mendon, Milford and Upton. The court sits at Milford.

First Justice
Warren A. Powers

Justices
Mary A. Orfanello
Brian F. Gilligan

UXBRIDGE DIVISION includes Blackstone, Douglas, Millville, Northbridge, Sutton and Uxbridge. The court sits at Uxbridge.

First Justice
Paul A. Losapio

Justices
Sarkis Teshoian
vacancy

WESTBOROUGH DIVISION includes Grafton, Northborough, Shrewsbury, Southborough and Westborough. The court sits at Westborough.

First Justice
Paul S. Waickowski

Justice
Robert B. Calagione

WINCHENDON DIVISION includes Winchendon. The court sits at Winchendon.

First Justice
Patrick A. Fox

Justices
Vito A. Virzi
vacancy

WORCESTER DIVISION includes Auburn, Barre, Holden, Millbury, Oakham, Paxton, Rutland, West Boylston and Worcester. The court sits at Worcester.

First Justice
Elliott L. Zide

Justices

Charles A. Abdella
Neil G. Snider
David P. Despotopulos
Dennis J. Brennan
Thomas Sullivan, Jr.
vacancy

CIRCUIT JUSTICES

Philip A. Beattie
Daniel Klubock
Margaret A. Zaleski
Timothy H. Gailey
Roanne Sragow
Michael C. Creedon
Joseph W. Jennings, III
Lee G. Johnson
Brian R. Merrick
Anthony P. Sullivan
Joseph R. Welch
James F. X. Dinneen
Thomas A. Connors
Stephen S. Ostrach
Sarah B. Singer
Albert S. Conlon

District Court Department
Administrative Office
Two Center Plaza, Suite 200
Boston, Massachusetts 02108
(617) 788-8810

BOSTON MUNICIPAL COURT DEPARTMENT

A Municipal Court Department is established in the city of Boston. Justices are appointed by the governor to serve until age seventy. A chief justice is appointed by the Chief Justice for Administration and Management to serve a five-year term. The chief justice is eligible to serve additional five-year terms.

The court's criminal and civil jurisdiction is the same as that of the District Court Department. The court has criminal jurisdiction in the city of Boston and civil jurisdiction throughout Suffolk County.

The court has an Appellate Division composed of three justices which exercises the same function as the Appellate Division of the District Court Department.

Chief Justice
Charles Ray Johnson

Associate Justices

Sally A. Kelly
Raymond Dougan
Patricia E. Bernstein
Thomas C. Horgan
Michael F. Flaherty
Dermot Meagher
Mark H. Summerville
Annette Forde
John T. Lu
Michael J. Coyne

TRIAL COURT OF MASSACHUSETTS—*Continued*

Boston Municipal Court Department
Administrative Office
24 New Chardon Street
Boston, Massachusetts 02114
(617) 788-8700

PROBATE AND FAMILY COURT DEPARTMENT

The Probate and Family Court Department is a court of special jurisdiction in Massachusetts with a division established in each county of the state. Justices are appointed by the governor to serve until age seventy. A chief justice is appointed by the Chief Justice for Administration and Management to serve a five-year term. The chief justice is eligible to serve additional five-year terms. Circuit justices rotate throughout the state as needed.

The court has jurisdiction over adoption, separate support, custody of minors and mental incompetents, the probate of wills, the administration of trusts and estates and petitions for change of name. The court has exclusive jurisdiction in domestic relations matters such as divorce, and concurrent jurisdiction with other courts in paternity and abuse protection cases. Jurisdiction in equity is concurrent with the Supreme Judicial Court and the Superior Court Department. The court also has concurrent jurisdiction with the Supreme Judicial Court and the Superior and Land Court Departments of declaratory judgment proceedings.

The court sits at each shire town and as indicated.

Chief Justice
Sean M. Dunphy

BARNSTABLE COUNTY DIVISION sits at Barnstable.

First Justice
Robert E. Terry

Associate Justice
Robert A. Scandurra

BERKSHIRE COUNTY DIVISION sits at Pittsfield.

First Justice
Edward J. Lapointe

BRISTOL COUNTY DIVISION sits at Fall River, New Bedford and Taunton.

First Justice
Elizabeth O'Neill LaStaiti

Associate Justices
Prudence M. McGregor
Armand Fernandes, Jr.
Anthony R. Nesi

DUKES COUNTY DIVISION sits at Edgartown.

First Justice
Stephen C. Steinberg

ESSEX COUNTY DIVISION sits at Lawrence, Newburyport and Salem.

First Justice
John C. Stevens, III

Associate Justices
Edward J. Rockett
Mary McCauley Manzi
John P. Cronin

FRANKLIN COUNTY DIVISION sits at Greenfield.

First Justice
Geoffrey A. Wilson

HAMPDEN COUNTY DIVISION sits at Springfield.

First Justice
David G. Sacks

Associate Justices
Marie E. Lyons
David M. Fuller

HAMPSHIRE COUNTY DIVISION sits at Northampton.

First Justice
Gail L. Perlman

MIDDLESEX COUNTY DIVISION sits at Cambridge, Concord, Lowell and Marlborough.

Acting First Justice
Beverly W. Boorstein

Associate Justices
Judith Nelson Dilday
Edward F. Donnelley, Jr.
Dorothy M. Gibson
William F. McSweeny, III
Leilah A. Keamy

NANTUCKET COUNTY DIVISION sits at Nantucket.

First Justice
Angela M. Ordoñez

NORFOLK COUNTY DIVISION sits at Dedham.

First Justice
David H. Kopelman

Associate Justices
Christina L. Harms
Robert W. Langlois
Paula M. Carey

PLYMOUTH COUNTY DIVISION sits at Brockton and Plymouth.

First Justice
Catherine P. Sabaitis

Associate Justices
James V. Menno
Stephen C. Steinberg
Michael J. Livingstone

SUFFOLK COUNTY DIVISION sits at Boston.

First Justice
John M. Smoot

Associate Justices
Elaine M. Moriarty
Nancy M. Gould
Jeremy A. Stahlin

WORCESTER COUNTY DIVISION sits at Fitchburg and Worcester.

TRIAL COURT OF MASSACHUSETTS—*Continued*

First Justice
Joseph Lian, Jr.

Associate Justices
Joseph L. Hart, Jr.
Susan D. Ricci
Ronald W. King

CIRCUIT JUSTICES

Anne M. Geoffrion
Maryanne Sahagian
Lisa A. Roberts
Gregory V. Roach
E. Chouteau Merrill
Lucille A. DiLeo
Stephen M. Rainaud
Spencer M. Kagan
Peter C. DiGangi
Virginia M. Ward
Randy J. Kaplan

Probate and Family Court Department
Administrative Office
Two Center Plaza, Suite 210
Boston, Massachusetts 02108
(617) 788-6600

LAND COURT DEPARTMENT

The Land Court Department is a court of special, statewide jurisdiction in Massachusetts. Justices are appointed by the governor to serve until age seventy. A chief justice is appointed by the Chief Justice for Administration and Management.

The court has exclusive, original jurisdiction over the registration of title to real property, over all matters and disputes concerning such title subsequent to registration and over the foreclosure and redemption of real estate tax liens. The Land Court also has concurrent jurisdiction over matters dealing with right, title or interest in real property, and as to zoning and subdivision appeals.

The court sits at Boston but may sit elsewhere as needed.

Chief Justice
Karyn Faith Scheier

Justices
Leon J. Lombardi
Alexander H. Sands
Charles W. Trombly
Gordon H. Piper

Land Court Department
Administrative Office
Two Center Plaza, Suite 210
Boston, Massachusetts 02108
(617) 788-7470

JUVENILE COURT DEPARTMENT

The Juvenile Court Department is a court of statewide jurisdiction consisting of eleven divisions and forty-one judges. Justices are appointed by the governor to serve until age seventy. A chief justice is appointed by the Chief Justice for Administration and Management to serve a five-year term. The chief justice is eligible to serve additional five-year terms. Circuit justices rotate throughout the eastern and western regions of the state as needed.

The court exercises general jurisdiction over cases involving delinquency, youthful offenders, children in need of services (CHINS), care and protection petitions, adult contributing to the delinquency of a minor cases, adoption, guardianship, and termination of parental rights proceedings. The court also has equity authority over all matters concerned with the protection and care of children within its jurisdiction.

Chief Justice
Martha P. Grace

BARNSTABLE/TOWN OF PLYMOUTH sits at Barnstable, Edgartown, Falmouth, Nantucket, Orleans and Plymouth.

First Justice
Carol Gibson Smith

Associate Justice
Louis D. Coffin

BERKSHIRE COUNTY sits at Great Barrington, North Adams and Pittsfield.

First Justice
Paul E. Perachi

BRISTOL COUNTY sits at Attleboro, Fall River, New Bedford and Taunton.

First Justice
James M. Cronin

Associate Justices
Kenneth P. Nasif
Bettina Borders

ESSEX COUNTY sits at Lawrence, Lynn, Newburyport and Salem.

First Justice
Sally F. Padden

Associate Justices
Michael F. Edgerton
José Sánchez
Mark Newman

FRANKLIN/HAMPSHIRE COUNTIES sit at Greenfield, Northampton, Orange and Ware.

First Justice
Lillian Miranda

HAMPDEN COUNTY sits at Holyoke, Palmer and Springfield.

First Justice
Daniel J. Swords

Associate Justices
Rebekah J. Crampton
Joseph A. Pellegrino

MIDDLESEX COUNTY sits at Cambridge, Framingham, Lowell, Waltham and Woburn.

First Justice
Gail Garinger

Associate Justices
Jay D. Blitzman
Margaret S. Fearey
Amy L. Nechtem
Gwendolyn R. Tyre
Patricia A. Flynn

TRIAL COURT OF MASSACHUSETTS—*Continued*

NORFOLK COUNTY sits at Dedham, Quincy and Stoughton.

First Justice
Mary M. McCallum

Associate Justice
Leslie A. Donahue

PLYMOUTH COUNTY sits at Brockton, Hingham and Wareham.

First Justice
Robert F. Murray

Associate Justice
John P. Corbett

SUFFOLK COUNTY sits at Boston, Chelsea, Dorchester and West Roxbury.

First Justice
Paul D. Lewis

Associate Justices

John J. Craven, Jr.
Marjory A. C. German
Leslie E. Harris
Mark Edward Lawton
Stephen M. Limon
Terry M. Craven

WORCESTER DIVISION sits at Dudley, Fitchburg, Leominster, Milford and Worcester.

First Justice
Jan L. Najemy

Associate Justices
George F. Leary
Luis G. Perez

CIRCUIT JUSTICES

James G. Collins
Patricia A. Dunbar
Carol A. Erskine
Joseph F. Johnston
Judith A. Locke
Kathryn A. White

Juvenile Court Department
Administrative Office
Three Center Plaza, Suite 520
P.O. Box 9664
Boston, Massachusetts 02114-9664
(617) 788-6550

HOUSING COURT DEPARTMENT

The Housing Court Department is a court of special jurisdiction established in the city of Boston and in Worcester County, as well as three divisions: the Southeastern Division encompassing Bristol and Plymouth counties; the Northeastern Division which serves Essex County and the Merrimack Valley; and the Western Division covering not only Hampden County but also the counties of Franklin, Hampshire and Berkshire. Justices are appointed by the governor to serve until age seventy. A chief justice is appointed by the Chief Justice for Administration and Management to serve a five-year term. The chief justice is eligible to serve additional five-year terms.

The court has concurrent civil and criminal jurisdiction with the Superior and District Court Departments in all matters relating to housing and to the health, safety or welfare of housing occupants. Its jurisdiction is to enforce sanitary, building, fire and zoning codes and to hear appeals from decisions of the Boston Rent Equity Board.

The jurisdiction of the Housing Court of Boston extends to the city limits. The jurisdiction of the Housing Courts of Worcester County and the Southeastern and Western divisions extend to the county boundaries. The jurisdiction of the Northeastern Division is defined by statute.

Chief Justice
Manuel Kyriakakis

BOSTON DIVISION sits at Boston.

First Justice
Manuel Kyriakakis

Associate Justices
Jeffrey M. Winik
Steven D. Pierce

NORTHEASTERN DIVISION sits at Lawrence.

First Justice
David D. Kerman

SOUTHEASTERN DIVISION sits at Brockton and Fall River.

First Justice
vacancy

Associate Justice
Wilbur P. Edwards, Jr.

WESTERN DIVISION sits at Springfield.

First Justice
William H. Abrashkin

Associate Justice
Dina Fein

WORCESTER COUNTY DIVISION sits at Worcester.

First Justice
vacancy

Associate Justice
Diana Horan

CIRCUIT JUSTICE
Anne Kenney Chaplin

Housing Court Department
Administrative Office
24 New Chardon Street
Boston, Massachusetts 02114
(617) 788-8483

Massachusetts Counties and Shire Towns

Barnstable
Barnstable

Berkshire
Pittsfield

Bristol
Fall River
New Bedford
Taunton

Dukes
Edgartown

Essex
Lawrence
Newburyport
Salem

Franklin
Greenfield

Hampden
Springfield

Hampshire
Northampton

Middlesex
Cambridge
Lowell

Nantucket
Nantucket

Norfolk
Dedham

Plymouth
Brockton
Plymouth

Suffolk
Boston

Worcester
Fitchburg
Worcester

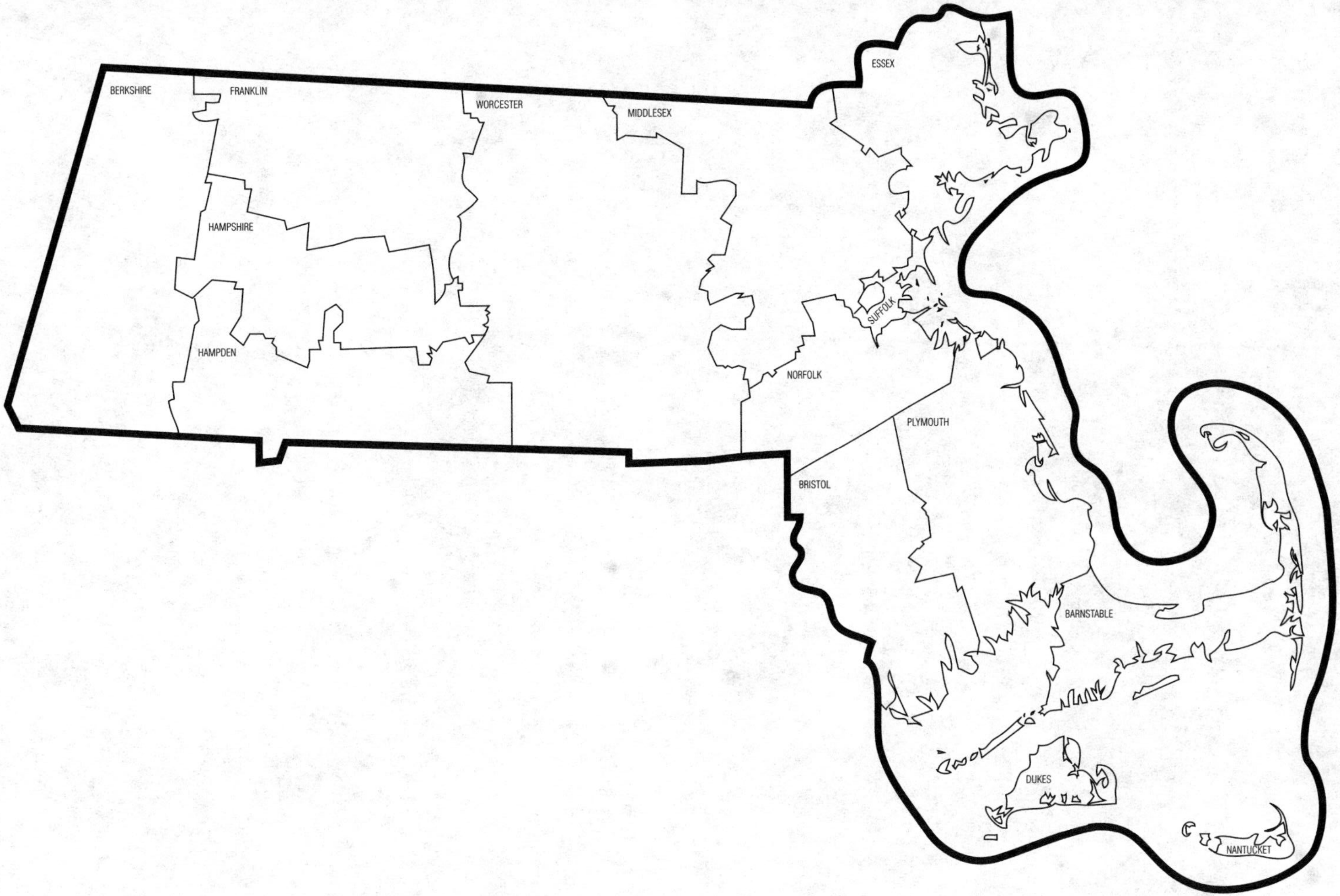
BERKSHIRE
FRANKLIN
WORCESTER
MIDDLESEX
ESSEX
HAMPSHIRE
HAMPDEN
SUFFOLK
NORFOLK
PLYMOUTH
BRISTOL
BARNSTABLE
DUKES
NANTUCKET

UNITED STATES DISTRICT COURT DISTRICT OF MASSACHUSETTS

MASSACHUSETTS

ABDELLA, Charles A. *(First Justice, Trial Court of Massachusetts District Court Department Worcester County East Brookfield Division and Justice, Worcester Division)* Appointed by Governor Argeo Paul Cellucci to term beginning 1998. First Justice since 1999. Educated at College of the Holy Cross B.S. 1964 and Boston College Law School J.D. 1967. Admitted to practice Massachusetts 1967, U.S. District Court District of Massachusetts 1968 and U.S. Supreme Court 1980. In legal practice Massachusetts 1967-98. Conciliator, Master and Arbitrator, Trial Court of Massachusetts Superior Court Department 1973-98.

Assistant City Solicitor Worcester 1970-82. Public Administrator Worcester County 1978-98. Visiting Professor Graduate Program Worcester State College 1977-78 and Institute for Paralegal Studies Assumption College 1981. Member National Panel American Arbitration Association 1978-95. Member Massachusetts Judges Conference, Worcester County and Massachusetts Bar Associations. Graduate The National Judicial College. Recipient In Hoc Signo Award from College of the Holy Cross 1989, Crusader of the Year Award from College of the Holy Cross Alumni Club of Greater Worcester 1990 and Distinguished Alumnus Award from St. John's High School 1995. Listed in *Who's Who in American Law*. USAR 1967-73. Director since 1971, Vice President 1974-76 and 1981-82, President Elect 1985-86 and President 1986-87 General Alumni Association and Life Member President's Council since 1974 College of the Holy Cross. Headmaster's Council since 1983, Parent's Council 1988-92, Counsel 1992-98 and Board of Trustees 1990-2000 St. John's High School Shrewsbury. Vice Chairman Board of Trustees Worcester City Hospital 1987-90 and Board of Trustees Anna Maria College 1989-92. Board of Directors American Lung Association of Central Massachusetts 1987-91 and WICN Public Radio 1997-98. National Corporate Member Xaverian Brothers Sponsored Schools since 2000.

Office: 544 East Main Street, East Brookfield 01515.

Telephone: (508) 885-5500.

ABRASHKIN, William H. *(First Justice, Trial Court of Massachusetts Housing Court Department Western Division)* Appointed by governor.

Office: 37 Elm Street, Springfield 01102.

Telephone: (617) 788-8483.

AGNES, Peter W., Jr. *(Associate Justice, Trial Court of Massachusetts Superior Court Department)* Appointed by governor. Former First Justice, Trial Court of Massachusetts District Court Department Suffolk County Charlestown Division.

Office: U.S. Post Office and Courthouse, 90 Devonshire Street, Fifteenth Floor, Boston 02109.

Telephone: (617) 788-8130.

AGOSTINI, John A. *(Associate Justice, Trial Court of Massachusetts Superior Court Department)* Appointed by governor.

Office: U.S. Post Office and Courthouse, 90 Devonshire Street, Fifteenth Floor, Boston 02109.

Telephone: (617) 788-8130.

ALEXANDER, Joyce London *(Magistrate Judge, United States District Court District of Massachusetts)* Appointed by U.S. District Court judges.

Office: 7410 U.S. Courthouse, One Courthouse Way, Boston 02210-3002.

Telephone: (617) 748-9236.

ANDERSON, R. Peter *(First Justice, Trial Court of Massachusetts District Court Department Suffolk County Brighton Division)* Appointed by governor.

Mailing address: Two Center Plaza, Suite 200, Boston 02108.

Telephone: (617) 788-8810.

ARMSTRONG, Christopher J. *(Chief Justice, Massachusetts Appeals Court)* Appointed by Governor Francis Williams Sargent to term beginning Oct 6, 1972. Term expires at age seventy. Chief Justice since Feb 9, 2000. Born Springfield Massachusetts July 28, 1936. Educated at Yale College A.B. cum laude 1958 LL.B. 1961. Admitted to practice Massachusetts 1961.

Member Boston and Massachusetts Bar Associations.

Office: 1500 New Courthouse, Boston 02108.

Telephone: (617) 725-8106.

BALER, Gregory R. *(Justice, Trial Court of Massachusetts District Court Department Norfolk County Quincy Division)* Appointed by governor.

Mailing address: Two Center Plaza, Suite 200, Boston 02108.

Telephone: (617) 788-8810.

BALL, Carol S. *(Associate Justice, Trial Court of Massachusetts Superior Court Department)* Appointed by governor.

Office: U.S. Post Office and Courthouse, 90 Devonshire Street, Fifteenth Floor, Boston 02109.

Telephone: (617) 788-8130.

BARBALUNGA, Alfred A. *(First Justice, Trial Court of Massachusetts District Court Department Berkshire County Pittsfield Division)* Appointed by governor.

Mailing address: Two Center Plaza, Suite 200, Boston 02108.

Telephone: (617) 788-8810.

BARRETT, Thomas S. *(Justice, Trial Court of Massachusetts District Court Department Bristol County Attleboro Division)* Appointed by governor.

Mailing address: Two Center Plaza, Suite 200, Boston 02108.

Telephone: (617) 788-8810.

BAYLOR, Robert E. *(Justice, Trial Court of Massachusetts District Court Department Plymouth County Brockton Division)* Appointed by governor.

Mailing address: Two Center Plaza, Suite 200, Boston 02108.

Telephone: (617) 788-8810.

BEATTIE, Philip A. *(Circuit Justice, Trial Court of Massachusetts District Court Department)* Appointed by governor.

Office: Two Center Plaza, Suite 200, Boston 02108.

Telephone: (617) 788-8810.

BECK, Susan S. *(Associate Justice, Massachusetts Appeals Court)* Appointed by governor.
Office: 1500 New Courthouse, Boston 02108.
Telephone: (617) 725-8106.

BERNARD, Julie J. *(Justice, Trial Court of Massachusetts District Court Department Bristol County New Bedford Division)* Appointed by governor.
Mailing address: Two Center Plaza, Suite 200, Boston 02108.
Telephone: (617) 788-8810.

BERNSTEIN, Patricia E. *(Associate Justice, Trial Court of Massachusetts Boston Municipal Court Department)* Appointed by governor.
Office: Courthouse, 90 Devonshire Street, Boston 02109.
Telephone: (617) 788-8700.

BERRY, Janis M. *(Associate Justice, Massachusetts Appeals Court)* Appointed by governor.
Office: 1500 New Courthouse, Boston 02108.
Telephone: (617) 725-8106.

BILLINGS, Thomas P. *(Associate Justice, Trial Court of Massachusetts Superior Court Department)* Appointed by Governor Jane Swift to term beginning Nov 7, 2002. Term expires at age seventy. Born Reading Pennsylvania July 2, 1953. Educated at Vassar College A.B. 1975 and Boston University School of Law J.D. summa cum laude 1980. Executive Editor Boston University Law Review 1978-80. Law Clerk to U.S. Court of Appeals First Circuit 1980-81. Admitted to practice Massachusetts 1981, U.S. District Court District of Massachusetts 1981, U.S. Courts of Appeals First 1982 and Eleventh 1984 Circuits. In legal practice Boston 1981-2002.
Office: U.S. Post Office and Courthouse, 90 Devonshire Street, Boston 02109.
Telephone: (617) 788-8130.

BLITZMAN, Jay D. *(Associate Justice, Trial Court of Massachusetts Juvenile Court Department Middlesex County Division)* Appointed by governor.
Mailing address: P.O. Box 9664, Boston 02114-9664.
Office: Three Center Plaza, Suite 520, Boston 02108.
Telephone: (617) 788-6550.

BOHN, Robert H., Jr. *(Associate Justice, Trial Court of Massachusetts Superior Court Department)* Appointed by governor. Former Justice, Trial Court of Massachusetts District Court Department Region Three Newton Division.
Office: U.S. Post Office and Courthouse, 90 Devonshire Street, Fifteenth Floor, Boston 02109.
Telephone: (617) 788-8130.

BOORSTEIN, Beverly W. *(Acting First Justice, Trial Court of Massachusetts Probate and Family Court Department Middlesex County Division)* Appointed by governor.
Mailing address: Two Center Plaza, Suite 210, Boston 02108.
Telephone: (617) 788-6600.

BORDERS, Bettina *(Associate Justice, Trial Court of Massachusetts Juvenile Court Department Bristol County Division)* Appointed by governor.
Mailing address: P.O. Box 9664, Boston 02114-9664.
Office: Three Center Plaza, Suite 520, Boston 02108.
Telephone: (617) 788-6550.

BORENSTEIN, Isaac *(Associate Justice, Trial Court of Massachusetts Superior Court Department)* Appointed by Governor William F. Weld to term beginning Oct 8, 1992. Term expires at age seventy. Born Havana Cuba Sept 10, 1950. Jewish. Educated at George Washington University B.A. with distinction 1972, Northeastern University J.D. 1975 and Harvard Law School LL.M. 1983. Admitted to practice Florida 1976 and Massachusetts 1979. Justice, Trial Court of Massachusetts District Court Department Essex County Lawrence Division Nov 14, 1986 to Oct 7, 1992, appointed by Governor Michael S. Dukakis.
With Boston Legal Assistance Project, Inc. 1975, Public Defender's Office Miami Florida 1976, Roxbury Defenders Committee, Inc. Boston Massachusetts 1977-79 and Legal Services Institute Jamaica Plain Massachusetts 1979-82. Clinical Instructor Harvard Law School 1980-82. Lecturer in Law Northeastern University Law School 1980-82 and since 1985. Associate Professor of Law New England School of Law 1983-86. Enjoys reading, sports, politics and government.
Office: U.S. Post Office and Courthouse, 90 Devonshire Street, Fifteenth Floor, Boston 02109.
Telephone: (617) 788-8130.

BOROFF, Henry Jack *(Judge, United States Bankruptcy Court District of Massachusetts)* Appointed by U.S. Court of Appeals First Circuit judges to term beginning Dec 10, 1993. Term expires Dec 10, 2007. Also Judge, Bankruptcy Appellate Panel First Circuit. Selected by the Judicial Council of the First Circuit. Born Boston Massachusetts 1951. Educated at Boston University A.B. magna cum laude 1972 J.D. 1975. Admitted to practice Massachusetts 1975, U.S. District Court District of Massachusetts 1976, U.S. Court of Appeals First Circuit 1979 and U.S. Supreme Court 1987. In legal practice Boston 1976-93.
Author "Insurance Proceeds under § 9-306: Before and After" 1974 and "The Precedential Effect of Bankruptcy Appellate Decision" 1998 Commercial L. Jour. Adjunct Professor of Bankruptcy Law and Secured Transactions Western New England College School of Law since 1996 and Northeastern University 1998-2000. Former Member Commercial Law League of America (Chair New England District 1983-84). Member Boston (Member since 1976 and Chair 1987-90 Bankruptcy Committee) and Massachusetts Bar Associations. Lecturer on bankruptcy and related topics American Bankruptcy Institute, Boston Bar Association, Hampden County Bar Association and Massachusetts Bar Association. Listed in Massachusetts Bankruptcy Listings *Best Lawyers in America* Woodward and White 1987, 1989-90, 1991-92 and 1993-94.
Office: 595 Main Street, Worcester 01608.
Telephone: (508) 770-8940.
Fax: (508) 793-0183

BOTSFORD, Margot *(Associate Justice, Trial Court of Massachusetts Superior Court Department)* Appointed by governor.
Office: U.S. Post Office and Courthouse, 90 Devonshire Street, Fifteenth Floor, Boston 02109.
Telephone: (617) 788-8130.

BOWLER, Marianne B. *(Magistrate Judge, United States District Court District of Massachusetts)* Appointed by U.S. District Court judges to term beginning May 7, 1990. Reappointed 1998, current term expires May 7, 2006. Chief Magistrate Judge since Jan 25,

BOWLER, MARIANNE B.—*Continued*

2002. Born Boston Massachusetts Feb 17, 1947. Roman Catholic. Educated at Regis College A.B. 1967 and Suffolk University Law School J.D. with honors 1976. Law Clerk to Superior Court of Massachusetts 1976-78. Admitted to practice Massachusetts 1977, U.S. District Court District of Massachusetts 1977 and U.S. Court of Appeals First Circuit 1978.

Assistant District Attorney Middlesex County 1978. Assistant U.S. Attorney District of Massachusetts 1978-90. Important Decisions: Digital v. Currie 142 F.R.D. 8, D.Mass. 1991 and Costello v. Erdlen 797 F. Supp. 1054 D.Mass. 1992. Faculty member and Judge Attorney General's Advocacy Institute U.S. Department of Justice, Washington D.C. since 1983. Frequent Lecturer Massachusetts CLE. Recipient Outstanding Alumni Award from Suffolk University Law School 1991. Previously worked as medical writer. Democrat. Chairman Board of Trustees New England Baptist Hospital. Board Member The Boston Foundation and South Cove Manor. Member Visiting Committee The Museum School, Boston Museum of Fine Arts and Save Venice. Enjoys classical French cuisine, trompe l'oeil and faux finishing.

Office: 8420 U.S. Courthouse, One Courthouse Way, Boston 02210-3002.

Telephone: (617) 748-9219.

BOYLE, William J. *(Justice, Trial Court of Massachusetts District Court Department Hampden County Springfield Division)* Appointed by governor.

Mailing address: Two Center Plaza, Suite 200, Boston 02108.

Telephone: (617) 788-8810.

BRADY, Patrick F. *(Associate Justice, Trial Court of Massachusetts Superior Court Department)* Appointed by Governor Michael S. Dukakis 1989.

Office: U.S. Post Office and Courthouse, 90 Devonshire Street, Fifteenth Floor, Boston 02109.

Telephone: (617) 788-8130.

BRANT, Jonathan *(Justice, Trial Court of Massachusetts District Court Department Middlesex County Cambridge Division)* Appointed by Governor William F. Weld March 23, 1992 to term beginning May 22, 1992. Educated at Brandeis University B.A. magna cum laude 1968 and Harvard Law School J.D. 1971. Admitted to practice Massachusetts 1971, U.S. District Court District of Massachusetts 1971, U.S. Court of Appeals First Circuit 1972, U.S. Supreme Court 1975 and U.S. Tax Court 1985. In legal practice Boston 1983-92.

Assistant Attorney General Massachusetts 1975-80. Author *Law and Mental Health Professionals: Massachusetts* American Psychological Association 1991 Supplement 1994 and Second Edition 1997. Professor New England School of Law 1980-83. Lecturer Tufts University School of Medicine since 1981. Guberman Fellow Brandeis University 1990. President Newton Schools Foundation 1990-92. Member Mental Health Legal Advisers Committee since 1989.

Mailing address: Two Center Plaza, Suite 200, Boston 02108.

Telephone: (617) 788-8810.

BRASSARD, Raymond J. *(Associate Justice, Trial Court of Massachusetts Superior Court Department)* Appointed by governor.

Office: U.S. Post Office and Courthouse, 90 Devonshire Street, Fifteenth Floor, Boston 02109.

Telephone: (617) 788-8130.

BRENNAN, Dennis J. *(Justice, Trial Court of Massachusetts District Court Department Worcester County Worcester Division)* Appointed by Governor William F. Weld to term beginning Feb 12, 1992. Term expires at age seventy. Born Lowell Massachusetts May 18, 1937. Roman Catholic. Educated at Lowell Technological Institute B.S. 1963 and University of Connecticut School of Law J.D. 1970. Admitted to practice Massachusetts 1970, U.S. District Court District of Massachusetts 1971 and U.S. Supreme Court 1980. In legal practice Gardner 1970-74 and Worcester 1974-92.

Member Hon. William J. Luby Inn of Court, The Association of Trial Lawyers of America, Northern Worcester County, Worcester County and Massachusetts Bar Associations. E-4 U.S. Army 1957-59. Member Lions Clubs International. Enjoys playing golf and reading.

Mailing address: Two Center Plaza, Suite 200, Boston 02108.

Telephone: (617) 788-8810.

BRENNAN, Martha A. *(First Justice, Trial Court of Massachusetts District Court Department Worcester County Clinton Division)* Appointed by governor.

Mailing address: Two Center Plaza, Suite 200, Boston 02108.

Telephone: (617) 788-8810.

BRENNAN, Robert A. *(Justice, Trial Court of Massachusetts District Court Department Essex County Gloucester Division)* Appointed by governor.

Mailing address: Two Center Plaza, Suite 200, Boston 02108.

Telephone: (617) 788-8810.

BRENNAN, Thomas M. *(Justice, Trial Court of Massachusetts District Court Department Middlesex County Newton Division)* Appointed by governor.

Mailing address: Two Center Plaza, Suite 200, Boston 02108.

Telephone: (617) 788-8810.

BROKER, Phyllis J. *(Justice, Trial Court of Massachusetts District Court Department Middlesex County Woburn Division)* Appointed by governor.

Mailing address: Two Center Plaza, Suite 200, Boston 02108.

Telephone: (617) 788-8810.

BROOKS, Michael J. *(Justice, Trial Court of Massachusetts District Court Department Middlesex County Natick Division)* Appointed by governor.

Mailing address: Two Center Plaza, Suite 200, Boston 02108.

Telephone: (617) 788-8810.

BROWN, Frederick L. *(Associate Justice, Massachusetts Appeals Court)* Appointed by Governor Michael S. Dukakis 1976.

Office: 1500 New Courthouse, Boston 02108.

Telephone: (617) 725-8106.

BROWNELL, Thomas F. *(First Justice, Trial Court of Massachusetts District Court Department Plymouth County Plymouth Division)* Appointed by governor.
Mailing address: Two Center Plaza, Suite 200, Boston 02108.
Telephone: (617) 788-8810.

BUCKLEY, Paul V. *(Justice, Trial Court of Massachusetts District Court Department Suffolk County Brighton Division)* Appointed by governor.
Mailing address: Two Center Plaza, Suite 200, Boston 02108.
Telephone: (617) 788-8810.

BURNES, Nonnie S. *(Associate Justice, Trial Court of Massachusetts Superior Court Department)* Appointed by governor.
Office: U.S. Post Office and Courthouse, 90 Devonshire Street, Fifteenth Floor, Boston 02109.
Telephone: (617) 788-8130.

BUTLER, Elizabeth *(Associate Justice, Trial Court of Massachusetts Superior Court Department)* Appointed by governor.
Office: U.S. Post Office and Courthouse, 90 Devonshire Street, Fifteenth Floor, Boston 02109.
Telephone: (617) 788-8130.

CALAGIONE, Robert B. *(Justice, Trial Court of Massachusetts District Court Department Worcester County Westborough Division)* Appointed by governor.
Mailing address: Two Center Plaza, Suite 200, Boston 02108.
Telephone: (617) 788-8810.

CAREY, Paula M. *(Associate Justice, Trial Court of Massachusetts Probate and Family Court Department Norfolk County Division)* Appointed by governor. Former Circuit Justice.
Mailing address: Two Center Plaza, Suite 210, Boston 02108.
Telephone: (617) 788-6600.

CAREY, Richard J. *(First Justice, Trial Court of Massachusetts District Court Department Hampshire County Northampton Division)* Appointed by governor.
Mailing address: Two Center Plaza, Suite 200, Boston 02108.
Telephone: (617) 788-8810.

CARHART, Judd J. *(Associate Justice, Trial Court of Massachusetts Superior Court Department)* Appointed by governor.
Office: U.S. Post Office and Courthouse, 90 Devonshire Street, Fifteenth Floor, Boston 02109.
Telephone: (617) 788-8130.

CARPENTER, Don L. *(Justice, Trial Court of Massachusetts District Court Department Barnstable County Barnstable Division)* Appointed by governor.
Mailing address: Two Center Plaza, Suite 200, Boston 02108.
Telephone: (617) 788-8810.

CHAPLIN, Anne Kenney *(Circuit Justice, Trial Court of Massachusetts Housing Court Department)* Appointed by governor.
Office: 24 New Chardon Street, Boston 02114.
Telephone: (617) 788-8483.

CHERNOFF, Paul A. *(Associate Justice, Trial Court of Massachusetts Superior Court Department)* Appointed by Governor Michael S. Dukakis 1985. Former Justice, Trial Court of Massachusetts District Court Department.
Office: U.S. Post Office and Courthouse, 90 Devonshire Street, Boston 02109.
Telephone: (617) 788-8130.

CHIN, Richard J. *(Associate Justice, Trial Court of Massachusetts Superior Court Department)* Appointed by governor. Former Associate Justice, Trial Court of Massachusetts Boston Municipal Court Department.
Office: U.S. Post Office and Courthouse, 90 Devonshire Street, Fifteenth Floor, Boston 02109.
Telephone: (617) 788-8130.

COFFEY, James W. *(Justice, Trial Court of Massachusetts District Court Department Suffolk County Charlestown Division)* Appointed by governor.
Mailing address: Two Center Plaza, Suite 200, Boston 02108.
Telephone: (617) 788-8810.

COFFEY, Kathleen E. *(First Justice, Trial Court of Massachusetts District Court Department Suffolk County West Roxbury Division and Justice, Chelsea Division)* Appointed by Governor William F. Weld.
Mailing address: Two Center Plaza, Suite 200, Boston 02108.
Telephone: (617) 788-8810.

COFFIN, Louis D. *(Associate Justice, Trial Court of Massachusetts Juvenile Court Department Barnstable/Town of Plymouth Division)* Appointed by governor. Former First Justice.
Mailing address: P.O. Box 9664, Boston 02114-9664.
Office: Three Center Plaza, Suite 520, Boston 02108.
Telephone: (617) 788-6550.

COHEN, Cynthia *(Associate Justice, Massachusetts Appeals Court)* Appointed by governor.
Office: 1500 New Courthouse, Boston 02108.
Telephone: (617) 725-8106.

COHEN, Lawrence P. *(Magistrate Judge, United States District Court District of Massachusetts)* Appointed by U.S. District Court judges.
Office: 7420 U.S. Courthouse, One Courthouse Way, Boston 02210-3002.
Telephone: (617) 748-9223.

COLLINGS, Robert Biddlecombe *(Magistrate Judge, United States District Court District of Massachusetts)* Appointed by U.S. District Court judges March 15, 1982. Reappointed 1990 and 1998. Current term expires March 2006. Former Chief Magistrate Judge. Born New York New York Aug 31, 1942. Roman Catholic. Educated at Hamilton College A.B. 1964 and Harvard Law School J.D. cum laude 1967. Member Emerson Literary Society and Phi Beta Kappa. Law Clerk to Massachusetts Supreme Judicial Court 1967. Admitted to practice Massachusetts 1968 and New Hampshire 1970. Began legal practice Boston Massachusetts 1971.
Assistant U.S. Attorney 1971-78 and First Assistant U.S. Attorney 1978-81 Massachusetts (Deputy Chief 1976 and Chief 1976-82 Criminal Division). Author Chapter "Magistrate Practice" *Federal Court Civil Litigation in the First Circuit* Massachusetts CLE/NELI

COLLINGS, ROBERT BIDDLECOMBE—*Continued*

Nov 1982. Instructor Attorney General Advocacy Institute 1976-81. Lieutenant USNR JAGC 1978-81.

Office: 6420 U.S. Courthouse, One Courthouse Way, Boston 02210-3002.

Telephone: (617) 748-9229.

COLLINS, James G. *(Circuit Justice, Trial Court of Massachusetts Juvenile Court Department)* Appointed by governor.

Mailing address: P.O. Box 9664, Boston 02114-9664.

Office: Three Center Plaza, Suite 520, Boston 02108.

Telephone: (617) 788-6550.

CONLON, Albert S. *(Circuit Justice, Trial Court of Massachusetts District Court Department)* Appointed by governor.

Office: Two Center Plaza, Suite 200, Boston 02108.

Telephone: (617) 788-8810.

CONNOLLY, Lynda M. *(Justice, Trial Court of Massachusetts District Court Department Middlesex County Marlborough Division)* Appointed by governor.

Mailing address: Two Center Plaza, Suite 200, Boston 02108.

Telephone: (617) 788-8810.

CONNOLLY, Thomas E. *(Associate Justice, Trial Court of Massachusetts Superior Court Department)* Appointed by governor.

Office: U.S. Post Office and Courthouse, 90 Devonshire Street, Fifteenth Floor, Boston 02109.

Telephone: (617) 788-8130.

CONNON, Richard F. *(Associate Justice, Trial Court of Massachusetts Superior Court Department)* Appointed by governor.

Office: U.S. Post Office and Courthouse, 90 Devonshire Street, Fifteenth Floor, Boston 02109.

Telephone: (617) 788-8130.

CONNOR, John P., Jr. *(Associate Justice, Trial Court of Massachusetts Superior Court Department)* Appointed by Governor Jane Swift to term beginning Dec 2002. Term expires at age seventy. Born Boston Massachusetts Oct 24, 1942. Roman Catholic. Educated at Boston College A.B. 1965 J.D. 1968. Admitted to practice Massachusetts 1968, U.S. District Court District of Massachusetts 1968, U.S. Court of Appeals First Circuit 1968 and U.S. Supreme Court 1968. In legal practice Norwood and Walpole 1968-2000. Justice, Trial Court of Massachusetts District Court Department Bristol County Attleboro Division Feb 2000 to Dec 2002, appointed by Governor Argeo Paul Cellucci.

Assistant District Attorney Norfolk County 1969-74. Member Norfolk County (President 1997-98) and Massachusetts (Board of Delegates 1999-2000) Bar Associations. Trustee Xaverian Brothers High School since 1993 and Caritas Norwood Hospital since 2001. President Boston College Alumni Association 1995-96. Former Member Second Helping Food Retrieval Program. Personal Statement or Quote: "There is no substitute for preparation and no excuse for lack of preparation."

Office: 471 High Street, Walpole 02081.

Telephone: (508) 222-5900.

CONNORS, Thomas A. *(Circuit Justice, Trial Court of Massachusetts District Court Department)* Appointed by governor.

Office: Two Center Plaza, Suite 200, Boston 02108.

Telephone: (617) 788-8810.

CONTANT, Philip A. *(First Justice, Trial Court of Massachusetts District Court Department Hampden County Westfield Division)* Appointed by governor.

Mailing address: Two Center Plaza, Suite 200, Boston 02108.

Telephone: (617) 788-8810.

CORBETT, John P. *(Associate Justice, Trial Court of Massachusetts Juvenile Court Department Plymouth County Division)* Appointed by governor.

Mailing address: P.O. Box 9664, Boston 02114-9664.

Office: Three Center Plaza, Suite 520, Boston 02108.

Telephone: (617) 788-6550.

CORDY, Robert J. *(Associate Justice, Massachusetts Supreme Judicial Court)* Appointed by Governor Argeo Paul Cellucci to term beginning Feb 2001. Term expires at age seventy. Born Manchester Connecticut May 18, 1949. Educated at Dartmouth College A.B. cum laude 1971 and Harvard Law School J.D. 1974. In legal practice Boston 1987-91.

Defense Attorney Massachusetts Defenders Committee 1974-78. Special Assistant Attorney General Department of Revenue 1978-79. Associate General Counsel in Charge of Enforcement State Ethics Commission 1979-82. Federal Prosecutor 1982-87. Lecturer Harvard Law School 1987-96. Chief Legal Counsel to Governor William F. Weld 1991-93.

Office: 1300 New Courthouse, Boston 02108.

Telephone: (617) 557-1000.

CORNETTA, Robert A. *(Acting First Justice, Trial Court of Massachusetts District Court Department Essex County Salem Division and Justice, Ipswich Division)* Appointed by Governor William F. Weld. Also serves as Regional Administrative Justice, Region II.

Mailing address: Two Center Plaza, Suite 200, Boston 02108.

Telephone: (617) 788-8810.

COTE, Kenneth J., Jr. *(Justice, Trial Court of Massachusetts District Court Department Hampden County Palmer Division)* Appointed by Governor William F. Weld to term beginning Nov 12, 1992. Term expires at age seventy. Former First Justice. Born Arecibo Puerto Rico May 27, 1945. Protestant. Educated at University of Texas at Arlington B.A. 1972 and University of Puerto Rico J.D. cum laude 1976. Contributor University of Puerto Rico Law Review 1971-72. Admitted to practice Massachusetts 1977, U.S. District Courts District of Massachusetts 1978 and District of Texas 1979. In legal practice Holyoke 1977-92.

City Solicitor Holyoke 1989-92. Member Holyoke, Hampden County and Massachusetts Bar Associations. U.S. Army 1967-70. Commissioner Massachusetts Commission Against Discrimination 1981-84. Member Lions Club of Springfield. Enjoys golf.

Mailing address: Two Center Plaza, Suite 200, Boston 02108.

Telephone: (617) 788-8810.

COVEN, Mark S. *(First Justice, Trial Court of Massachusetts District Court Department Norfolk County*

COVEN, MARK S.—*Continued*

Quincy Division and Justice, Middlesex County Somerville Division) Appointed by governor.
Mailing address: Two Center Plaza, Suite 200, Boston 02108.
Telephone: (617) 788-8810.

COWIN, Judith Arnold *(Associate Justice, Massachusetts Supreme Judicial Court)* Appointed by Governor Argeo Paul Cellucci to term beginning Oct 1999. Educated at University of Guadalajara, Mexico 1958, Wellesley College B.A. 1963, George Washington University National Law Center 1967-68 and Harvard Law School J.D. 1970. Admitted to practice Massachusetts 1970, U.S. District Court District of Massachusetts and U.S. Court of Appeals First Circuit. Associate Justice, Trial Court of Massachusetts Superior Court Department Dec 1991 to Oct 1999, appointed by Governor William F. Weld.

Assistant to Legal Counsel Massachusetts Department of Mental Health March 1971 to Jan 1972. Counsel Office of the Chief Justice District Court of Massachusetts Feb 1972 to April 1974 and Jan 1975 to July 1979. Assistant District Attorney Norfolk County Aug 1979 to Dec 1991. Author "Gone With the Wind—The Future of Attachment and Trustee Process" 16 Boston B. Jour. 5, Nov 1972; "Court Reorganization and the District Courts" 63 Massachusetts L. Rev. 191, Oct 1978; "Search and Seizure Update" 9 Massachusetts Lawyers Weekly 986, June 1, 1981; "New Developments in the Law of Search and Seizure" 25 Boston B. Jour. 32, June 1981; "Standards for Care and Protection Proceedings" 66 Massachusetts L. Rev. 77, Spring 1981; "The Spousal Abuse Law" and "Care and Protection Standards" *District Court Prosecutor's Guide* 1982; and "Wong Sun Revisited" 12 Massachusetts Lawyers Weekly 137, Oct 17, 1983. Board of Editors Massachusetts Lawyers Weekly 1983-91. Clinical Field Supervisor Criminal Prosecution Seminar Harvard Law School Jan 1980 to June 1980. Member Norfolk County and Massachusetts Bar Associations. Faculty Advisor Trial Advocacy Workshop MCLE—NELI 1983 and 1985. Faculty Member Trial Advocacy Workshop Harvard Law School 1983-89. Supervisor Urban Legal Laboratory Seminar Boston College Law School 1986 and 1987. Guest Lecturer Seminars Boston College Law School 1986 and 1989, Boston College 1990 and Criminal Prosecution Seminar Harvard Law School 1990 and 1991. Panel Member Training Session for Judges Flaschner Judicial Institute 1991. Secretary, Press Assistant and Assistant to U.S. Senator Edward M. Kennedy Oct 1963 to March 1964. Research Assistant May 1964 to July 1965. Supervisor Collections Division Department of the Attorney General Massachusetts July 1965 to Dec 1966. Alumnae Class President Class of 1963 Wellesley College 1978-83. Council Member Harvard Law School 1980-82.
Office: 1300 New Courthouse, Boston 02108.
Telephone: (617) 557-1000.

COWIN, William I. *(Associate Justice, Massachusetts Appeals Court)* Appointed by governor.
Office: 1500 New Courthouse, Boston 02108.
Telephone: (617) 725-8106.

COYNE, Michael J. *(Associate Justice, Trial Court of Massachusetts Boston Municipal Court Department)* Appointed by governor.
Office: Courthouse, 90 Devonshire Street, Boston 02109.
Telephone: (617) 788-8700.

CRAMPTON, Rebekah J. *(Associate Justice, Trial Court of Massachusetts Juvenile Court Department Hampden County Division)* Appointed by Governor Michael S. Dukakis to term beginning Oct 3, 1986. Term expires at age seventy. Former First Justice. Born New Marlborough Massachusetts Jan 26, 1938. United Church of Christ. Educated at University of Massachusetts B.S. cum laude 1959 and Western New England College of Law J.D. magna cum laude 1978. Recipient American Jurisprudence Awards in Labor and Civil Procedure. Admitted to practice Massachusetts 1978, U.S. District Court District of Massachusetts 1979, U.S. Tax Court 1979 and U.S. Court of Appeals First Circuit 1984. In legal practice Greenfield 1978-80 and Springfield 1979-86.

Special Assistant Attorney General 1982-85. Adjunct Professor Western New England College of Law 1980-85. Former member American Bar Association. Member Massachusetts Judges Conference (Board of Directors), National Association of Women Judges, National Council of Juvenile and Family Court Judges, Hampden County (Vice President 1983 and President 1984 Young Lawyers Division, Board of Directors 1984) and Massachusetts Bar Associations. Participant Juvenile Law Conference The National Judicial College Oct 1986. Recipient West Publishing Company Award 1975-76, Harley B. Goodrich Award 1977-78, Community Service Award from Child and Family Service of Pioneer Valley 1993, Volunteer Appreciation Award from Court Appointed Special Advocates (CASA) of Springfield 1994, Award for Judicial Excellence from Massachusetts Judges Conference 1999 and Appreciation Award from Dispute Resolution, Inc. 1999. Listed in *Who's Who Among American Lawyers* 1979, *Who's Who Among American Women* 1984 and Marquis' *Who's Who in American Law* 9th Edition 1996. Named Alumna of the Year by Department of Consumer Studies University of Massachusetts 1996. Teacher Lakeville 1959-61 and 1965-66 and West Springfield 1966-67. Teacher and Dean Amerikan Kiz Lisesi, Izmir Turkey 1961-65. Board of Directors Open Pantry, Inc. (Former Second Vice President, President), Western Massachusetts Legal Services, Inc. and Community United Way of Pioneer Valley. Member Gender Bias Study Commission Massachusetts Supreme Court, Court Appointed Special Advocates (CASA) of Springfield, Inc., Mayor's Task Force on Violence on Children and Youth Needs, Ad Hoc Education Subcommittee and Ad Hoc Anti-Violence Subcommittee Springfield School Committee, Alliance for Youth of Springfield, Community 2000 of Greater Springfield, Springfield Schools' Central Office Reorganization Task Force and Friends of American Schools in Turkey. Assistant Moderator and Moderator 1979-83 Foster Memorial Church. Enjoys travel, reading and Vestamayd rugs.
Office: 80 State Street, Springfield 01103.
Telephone: (413) 748-7705.
Fax: (413) 737-4383
E-mail address: crampton_r@jud.state.ma.us

CRATSLEY, John C. *(Associate Justice, Trial Court of Massachusetts Superior Court Department)* Appointed by governor.
Office: U.S. Post Office and Courthouse, 90 Devonshire Street, Fifteenth Floor, Boston 02109.
Telephone: (617) 788-8130.

CRAVEN, John J., Jr. *(Associate Justice, Trial Court of Massachusetts Juvenile Court Department Suffolk County Division)* Appointed by governor.
Mailing address: P.O. Box 9663, Boston 02114.
Office: 24 New Chardon Street, Floor 5, Boston 02114.
Telephone: (617) 788-8542.

CRAVEN, Terry M. *(Associate Justice, Trial Court of Massachusetts Juvenile Court Department Suffolk County Division)* Appointed by governor.
Mailing address: P.O. Box 9664, Boston 02114-9664.
Office: Three Center Plaza, Suite 520, Boston 02108.
Telephone: (617) 788-6550.

CREEDON, Michael C. *(Circuit Justice, Trial Court of Massachusetts District Court Department and First Justice, Barnstable County Falmouth Division)* Appointed by governor.
Office: Two Center Plaza, Suite 200, Boston 02108.
Telephone: (617) 788-8810.

CRIMMINS, Francis T., Jr. *(First Justice, Trial Court of Massachusetts District Court Department Norfolk County Stoughton Division)* Appointed by governor.
Mailing address: Two Center Plaza, Suite 200, Boston 02108.
Telephone: (617) 788-8810.

CRONIN, James M. *(First Justice, Trial Court of Massachusetts Juvenile Court Department Bristol County Division)* Appointed by Governor Michael S. Dukakis to term beginning Sept 1, 1987. Term expires at age seventy. Born Boston Massachusetts June 15, 1943. Educated at Harvard College A.B. cum laude 1965 and Boston College Law School J.D. 1969. Admitted to practice Massachusetts 1969, U.S. District Court District of Massachusetts 1970 and U.S. Court of Appeals First Circuit 1985. In legal practice New Bedford 1969-87.
Member Massachusetts Judges Conference and National Council of Juvenile and Family Court Judges. Attended Juvenile and Family Law course The National Judicial College 1987. Member Westport Historical Society, Eire Society, American Conference on Irish Studies and Fall River Country Club. Enjoys reading, attending theatre and hiking.
Mailing address: P.O. Box 9664, Boston 02114-9664.
Office: Three Center Plaza, Suite 520, Boston 02108.
Telephone: (617) 788-6550.

CRONIN, John P. *(Associate Justice, Trial Court of Massachusetts Probate and Family Court Department Essex County Division)* Appointed by Governor William F. Weld to term beginning 1992. Educated at George Washington University National Law Center J.D. with honors 1972.
Office: 36 Federal Street, Salem 01970.
Telephone: (978) 744-1020.

CUNNINGHAM, Kevan J. *(First Justice, Trial Court of Massachusetts District Court Department Bristol County Taunton Division and Justice, Barnstable County Falmouth Division)* Appointed by governor.
Mailing address: Two Center Plaza, Suite 200, Boston 02108.
Telephone: (617) 788-8810.

CURLEY, Thomas J., Jr. *(Associate Justice, Trial Court of Massachusetts Superior Court Department)* Appointed by governor.
Office: U.S. Post Office and Courthouse, 90 Devonshire Street, Fifteenth Floor, Boston 02109.
Telephone: (617) 788-8130.

CURRAN, Dennis J. *(Justice, Trial Court of Massachusetts District Court Department Norfolk County Stoughton Division)* Appointed by governor.
Mailing address: Two Center Plaza, Suite 200, Boston 02108.
Telephone: (617) 788-8810.

CURRAN, John J., Jr. *(First Justice, Trial Court of Massachusetts District Court Department Worcester County Leominster Division)* Appointed by governor. Born Worcester Massachusetts. Educated at College of the Holy Cross B.A. 1968 and Suffolk University J.D. cum laude 1975. Admitted to practice Massachusetts 1975 and U.S. District Court District of Massachusetts 1978.
Assistant Attorney General Massachusetts 1979-84. Chairman Massachusetts Parole Board 1984-89. Member Worcester County and Massachusetts Bar Associations.
Mailing address: Two Center Plaza, Suite 200, Boston 02108.
Telephone: (617) 788-8810.

CURTIN, Patricia G. *(Justice, Trial Court of Massachusetts District Court Department Middlesex County Concord Division)* Appointed by governor.
Mailing address: Two Center Plaza, Suite 200, Boston 02108.
Telephone: (617) 788-8810.

CYPHER, Elspeth B. *(Associate Justice, Massachusetts Appeals Court)* Appointed by Governor Argeo Paul Cellucci 2000.
Office: 1500 New Courthouse, Boston 02108.
Telephone: (617) 725-8106.

DAWLEY, Paul C. *(Justice, Trial Court of Massachusetts District Court Department Plymouth County Brockton Division)* Appointed by governor.
Mailing address: Two Center Plaza, Suite 200, Boston 02108.
Telephone: (617) 788-8810.

DEIN, Judith Gail *(Magistrate Judge, United States District Court District of Massachusetts)* Appointed by U.S. District Court judges to term beginning July 31, 2000.
Office: U.S. Courthouse, One Courthouse Way, Boston 02210.
Telephone: (617) 748-9040.

DelVECCHIO, Suzanne V. *(Chief Justice, Trial Court of Massachusetts Superior Court Department)* Appointed by governor.
Office: U.S. Post Office and Courthouse, 90 Devonshire Street, Fifteenth Floor, Boston 02109.
Telephone: (617) 788-8130.

DESPOTOPULOS, David P. *(Justice, Trial Court of Massachusetts District Court Department Worcester County Worcester Division)* Appointed by governor.
Mailing address: Two Center Plaza, Suite 200, Boston 02108.
Telephone: (617) 788-8810.

DEVER, Joseph I. *(First Justice, Trial Court of Massachusetts District Court Department Essex County Lynn Division)* Appointed by Governor Michael S. Dukakis to term beginning April 8, 1987. Term expires at age seventy. Born Boston Massachusetts Aug 19, 1935. Roman Catholic. Educated at Fordham University B.S. 1956 and Boston University School of Law J.D. 1960. Admitted to practice Massachusetts 1962. In legal practice Boston 1962-66.
Legal Assistant to Suffolk County District Attorney 1962-63. First Assistant Clerk Magistrate Brookline Municipal Court 1963-64. Staff Attorney 1965-68 and Regional Supervisor 1968-84 Massachusetts Defenders Committee. Regional Supervisor Committee for Public Counsel Services Essex County 1984-87. Instructor in Criminal Justice and Paralegal Skills North Shore Community College 1971-88. Member American Judges Association, Boston and Essex County Bar Associations. Lecturer Bar Advocate Training Program Massachusetts Bar Association CLE 1986-87 and "Driving Under the Influence and Search and Seizure" Massachusetts Bar Association Panel 1988. Mock Trial Judge National Institute for Trial Advocacy 1987-88. First Lieutenant Air National Guard 1963-68. Staff Judge Advocate 102nd Tactical Fighter Group. Democrat. Chairperson Parish Council Board Star of the Sea Church Marblehead 1984-88. Enjoys community theatre, music and piano.
Mailing address: Two Center Plaza, Suite 200, Boston 02108.
Telephone: (617) 788-8810.

DiGANGI, Peter C. *(Circuit Justice, Trial Court of Massachusetts Probate and Family Court Department)* Appointed by governor.
Office: Two Center Plaza, Suite 210, Boston 02108.
Telephone: (617) 788-6600.

DILDAY, Judith Nelson *(Associate Justice, Trial Court of Massachusetts Probate and Family Court Department Middlesex County Division)* Appointed by Governor William F. Weld to term beginning Nov 13, 1993. Served as Circuit Justice Nov 13, 1993 to May 12, 1998. Associate Justice since May 13, 1998. Born Pittsburgh Pennsylvania. Episcopalian. Educated at University of Pittsburgh B.A. and Boston University School of Law J.D. Member Alpha Kappa Alpha. Admitted to practice Massachusetts 1975, U.S. District Court District of Massachusetts 1975 and U.S. Supreme Court 1979. In legal practice Boston 1989-93.
Assistant District Attorney. Member Massachusetts Association of Black Judges, National Association of Women Judges, Judicial Council, Women's Bar Association of Massachusetts (Past President), Massachusetts, National and American Bar Associations. Member Coalition of 100 Black Women.
Mailing address: Two Center Plaza, Suite 210, Boston 02108.
Telephone: (617) 788-6600.

DiLEO, Lucille A. *(Circuit Justice, Trial Court of Massachusetts Probate and Family Court Department)* Appointed by governor.
Office: Two Center Plaza, Suite 210, Boston 02108.
Telephone: (617) 788-6600.

DINNEEN, James F. X. *(Circuit Justice, Trial Court of Massachusetts District Court Department)* Appointed by governor.
Office: Two Center Plaza, Suite 200, Boston 02108.
Telephone: (617) 788-8810.

DOERFER, Gordon L. *(Associate Justice, Massachusetts Appeals Court)* Appointed by Governor Argeo Paul Cellucci to term beginning 2001. Educated at Amherst College B.A. cum laude 1961 and Harvard Law School LL.B. cum laude 1966. Law Clerk to Hon. Jacob J. Spiegel, Massachusetts Supreme Judicial Court 1966-67. In legal practice Boston 1967-73 and 1981-90. Associate Justice, Trial Court of Massachusetts Boston Municipal Court Department 1973-77. Associate Justice, Trial Court of Massachusetts Superior Court Department 1977-81 and 1990-2001.
Author "Why Judicial Case Management Pays Off at Trial" 29 No. 4 *Judges Journal* Fall 1990, "Taking Pre-Trial Conferences Seriously" Boston B. Jour. Spring 1992, "Summary of Basic Law" (chapter on equitable remedies) *Massachusetts Practice Series* 1996, "The Inns of Court: Going Back to Our Roots" *Judicial Administration News* Massachusetts Bar Association June 1997 and "Vacating, Confirming or Modifying Arbitration Awards" *Effective Arbitration Advocacy* April 28, 2000. Co-author with Peter Lauriat "To Ask or Not to Ask: Questions from Jurors at Trial" MATA Journal Spring 1998. Instructor in Law Boston College Law School 1971-77 and in Business Associations, Trial Practice and Professional Ethics Suffolk University Law School 1993-97. Adjunct Instructor in Trial Practice since 2000. Member since 1990 and Chair 1995-99 Alternative Dispute Resolution Committee Superior Court. Fellow Massachusetts Bar Foundation (Trustee 1982-87 and 1992-98) and American Bar Foundation. Member American Inns of Court (Member since 1993 and Co-President 1995-96 Boston Chapter), The American Law Institute, American Judicature Society (Director 1993-99 and since 2001), Boston (Chair Administration of Justice Section 1994-86), Massachusetts (Council Member Administration of Justice Committee 1995-97) and American Bar Associations. Instructor in Trial Advocacy, Evidence, Motion Practice and Fundamentals of Civil Litigation Massachusetts Continuing Legal Education, Inc. since 1980.
Office: 1500 New Courthouse, Boston 02108.
Telephone: (617) 725-8106.

DONAHUE, Leslie A. *(Associate Justice, Trial Court of Massachusetts Juvenile Court Department Norfolk County Division)* Appointed by governor.
Mailing address: P.O. Box 9664, Boston 02114-9664.
Office: Three Center Plaza, Suite 520, Boston 02108.
Telephone: (617) 788-6550.

DONNELLEY, Edward F., Jr. *(Associate Justice, Trial Court of Massachusetts Probate and Family Court Department Middlesex County Division)* Appointed by governor.
Mailing address: Two Center Plaza, Suite 210, Boston 02108.
Telephone: (617) 788-6600.

DONNELLY, David T. *(Justice, Trial Court of Massachusetts District Court Department Middlesex County Waltham Division)* Appointed by governor.
Mailing address: Two Center Plaza, Suite 200, Boston 02108.
Telephone: (617) 788-8810.

DONOHUE, James P. *(Associate Justice, Trial Court of Massachusetts Superior Court Department)* Appointed by governor.
Office: U.S. Post Office and Courthouse, 90 Devonshire Street, Fifteenth Floor, Boston 02109.
Telephone: (617) 788-8130.

DONOVAN, Elizabeth B. *(Associate Justice, Trial Court of Massachusetts Superior Court Department)* Appointed by governor.
Office: U.S. Post Office and Courthouse, 90 Devonshire Street, Fifteenth Floor, Boston 02109.
Telephone: (617) 788-8130.

DORTCH-OKARA, Barbara A. *(Chief Justice for Administration and Management, Trial Court of Massachusetts)* Appointed by governor. Term expires at age seventy. Born Memphis Tennessee 1949. Educated at Brandeis University B.A. cum laude 1971 and Boston College Law School J.D. 1974. Admitted to practice Tennessee 1974 and Massachusetts 1975. Associate Justice, Trial Court of Massachusetts Boston Municipal Court Department 1984-89. Former Associate Justice, Trial Court of Massachusetts Superior Court Department, appointed by Governor Michael S. Dukakis to term beginning Feb 1989.
Office: Two Center Plaza, Fifth Floor, Boston 02108.
Telephone: (617) 742-8575.

DOUGAN, Raymond *(Associate Justice, Trial Court of Massachusetts Boston Municipal Court Department)* Appointed by Governor Michael S. Dukakis to term beginning Jan 3, 1991. Term expires at age seventy. Born Boston Massachusetts Dec 29, 1944. Educated at Tufts University B.A. 1966 and Boston University School of Law J.D. 1971. Admitted to practice Massachusetts 1971, U.S. District Court District of Massachusetts 1971 and Maine 1973.
Chief Environmental Protection Division Attorney General's Office Massachusetts 1989-90. Clinical Instructor Boston University School of Law 1974-79.
Office: Courthouse, 90 Devonshire Street, Boston 02109.
Telephone: (617) 788-8700.

DOWLING, Patricia A. *(Justice, Trial Court of Massachusetts District Court Department Essex County Ipswich Division)* Appointed by governor.
Mailing address: Two Center Plaza, Suite 200, Boston 02108.
Telephone: (617) 788-8810.

DOYLE, Peter F. *(First Justice, Trial Court of Massachusetts District Court Department Essex County Newburyport Division and Justice, Haverhill Division)* Appointed by governor.
Mailing address: Two Center Plaza, Suite 200, Boston 02108.
Telephone: (617) 788-8810.

DRISCOLL, Mary Ann *(Justice, Trial Court of Massachusetts District Court Department Suffolk County South Boston Division)* Appointed by governor.
Mailing address: Two Center Plaza, Suite 200, Boston 02108.
Telephone: (617) 788-8810.

DUFFLY, Fernande R. V. *(Associate Justice, Massachusetts Appeals Court)* Appointed by Governor Argeo Paul Cellucci to term beginning Feb 15, 2000. Term expires at age seventy. Born Indonesia Dec 10, 1949. Episcopalian. Educated at University of Connecticut B.S. with highest honors 1973 and Harvard University J.D. 1978. Admitted to practice Massachusetts 1978 and U.S. District Court District of Massachusetts 1979. In legal practice Boston 1978-92. Associate Justice, Trial Court of Massachusetts Probate and Family Court Department Middlesex County Division April 21, 1992 to Feb 14, 2000, appointed by Governor William F. Weld.
Office: 1500 New Courthouse, Boston 02108.
Telephone: (617) 626-7912.

DUNBAR, Patricia A. *(Circuit Justice, Trial Court of Massachusetts Juvenile Court Department)* Appointed by governor.
Mailing address: P.O. Box 9664, Boston 02114-9664.
Office: Three Center Plaza, Suite 520, Boston 02108.
Telephone: (617) 788-6550.

DUNN, Deborah A. *(Justice, Trial Court of Massachusetts District Court Department Nantucket County Nantucket Division)* Appointed by governor.
Mailing address: Two Center Plaza, Suite 200, Boston 02108.
Telephone: (617) 788-8810.

DUNPHY, Sean M. *(Chief Justice, Trial Court of Massachusetts Probate and Family Court Department)* Appointed by Governor Michael S. Dukakis to term beginning March 16, 1978. Term expires at age seventy. Former First Justice Hampshire County Division. Born Northampton Massachusetts Feb 1, 1941. Roman Catholic. Educated at Fairfield University B.S.S. 1962 and Boston University LL.B. 1965. Admitted to practice Massachusetts 1965. Began legal practice Northampton 1965.
Mayor City of Northampton 1970-75. Author Article "The Fate of Incompetent Patients, Massachusetts Medicine" July/Aug 1986, Chapter "Guardians and Conservators" *Massachusetts Family Law Manual* MCLE, Inc. 1991, 1994, 1996 and 2003 and "Probate Law and Practice" 21 and 22 *Massachusetts Practice Series* West Publishing Company 1997. Co-author Article "Medical Decisionmaking for Incompetent Persons: The Massachusetts Substituted Judgment Model" 9 Western New England L. Rev. 1987 and Chapter "Will Contestants and Compromises" *Massachusetts Probate Manual* MCLE, Inc. 1988 and 1990. Member Boston, Hampshire County and Massachusetts (Section on Family and Probate Law) Bar Associations. Named one of Outstanding Young Men of America 1973 and Outstanding Citizen of the Year by Northampton Chamber of Commerce 1973. Recipient Headliner of the Year Award from Valley Press Club 1974. Massachusetts Army National Guard. Chairman Northampton Planning Board 1968-69 and Massachusetts Appellate Tax Board 1975-78. Mayor City of Northampton 1970-75. President Massachusetts League of Cities and Towns 1973-74 and Massachusetts Mayors

DUNPHY, SEAN M.—*Continued*
Association 1975. Trustee The Clarke School for the Deaf.
Office: Two Center Plaza, Second Floor, Boston 02108.
Telephone: (617) 788-6600.

DUSEK-GOMEZ, Nancy *(First Justice, Trial Court of Massachusetts District Court Department Hampshire County Ware Division and Justice, Hampden County Springfield Division)* Appointed by Governor Michael S. Dukakis to term beginning April 15, 1986. Term expires at age seventy. Born Queens New York June 1, 1950. Catholic. Educated at State University of New York at Potsdam B.A., Harvard Graduate School of Education M.Ed. and Northeastern University School of Law J.D. Admitted to practice Massachusetts 1980.
Litigation Attorney Massachusetts Defenders Committee 1980-83. Assistant District Attorney Northwestern Division Northampton 1983-86. Member Hampden, Hampshire County and Massachusetts Bar Associations. Former Instructor Trial Advocacy Program Massachusetts Continuing Legal Education. Named Woman of the Year by Springfield area National Organization of Women 1990 and Chamber of Commerce 1993. Former teacher Cambridge School Department.
Mailing address: Two Center Plaza, Suite 200, Boston 02108.
Telephone: (617) 788-8810.

EDGERTON, Michael F. *(Associate Justice, Trial Court of Massachusetts Juvenile Court Department Essex County Division)* Appointed by governor.
Mailing address: P.O. Box 9664, Boston 02114-9664.
Office: Three Center Plaza, Suite 520, Boston 02108.
Telephone: (617) 788-6550.

EDWARDS, Wilbur P., Jr. *(Associate Justice, Trial Court of Massachusetts Housing Court Department Southeastern Division)* Appointed by governor.
Mailing address: 24 New Chardon Street, Boston 02114.
Telephone: (617) 788-8483.

ERSKINE, Carol A. *(Circuit Justice, Trial Court of Massachusetts Juvenile Court Department)* Appointed by governor.
Mailing address: P.O. Box 9664, Boston 02114-9664.
Office: Three Center Plaza, Suite 520, Boston 02108.
Telephone: (617) 788-6550.

FABRICANT, Judith *(Associate Justice, Trial Court of Massachusetts Superior Court Department)* Appointed by governor.
Office: U.S. Post Office and Courthouse, 90 Devonshire Street, Fifteenth Floor, Boston 02109.
Telephone: (617) 788-8130.

FAHEY, Elizabeth M. *(Associate Justice, Trial Court of Massachusetts Superior Court Department)* Appointed by governor.
Office: U.S. Post Office and Courthouse, 90 Devonshire Street, Fifteenth Floor, Boston 02109.
Telephone: (617) 788-8130.

FEAREY, Margaret S. *(Associate Justice, Trial Court of Massachusetts Juvenile Court Department Middlesex County Division)* Appointed by governor.
Mailing address: P.O. Box 9664, Boston 02114-9664.
Office: Three Center Plaza, Suite 520, Boston 02108.
Telephone: (617) 788-6550.

FECTEAU, Francis R. *(Associate Justice, Trial Court of Massachusetts Superior Court Department)* Appointed by governor.
Office: U.S. Post Office and Courthouse, 90 Devonshire Street, Fifteenth Floor, Boston 02109.
Telephone: (617) 788-8130.

FEENEY, Joan N. *(Chief Judge, United States Bankruptcy Court District of Massachusetts)* Appointed by U.S. Court of Appeals First Circuit judges. Chief Judge Bankruptcy Court since Dec 10, 2002. Also Judge, Bankruptcy Appellate Panel First Circuit. Selected by the Judicial Council of the First Circuit.
Office: 1101 Federal Building, 10 Causeway Street, Boston 02222-1074.
Telephone: (617) 565-6049.

FEIN, Dina *(Associate Justice, Trial Court of Massachusetts Housing Court Department Western Division)* Appointed by governor.
Office: 37 Elm Street, Springfield 01102.
Telephone: (617) 788-8483.

FERNANDES, Armand, Jr. *(Associate Justice, Trial Court of Massachusetts Probate and Family Court Department Bristol County Division)* Appointed by governor.
Mailing address: Two Center Plaza, Suite 210, Boston 02108.
Telephone: (617) 788-6600.

FISHMAN, Kenneth J. *(Associate Justice, Trial Court of Massachusetts Superior Court Department)* Appointed by governor.
Office: U.S. Post Office and Courthouse, 90 Devonshire Street, Fifteenth Floor, Boston 02109.
Telephone: (617) 788-8130.

FLAHERTY, Michael F. *(Associate Justice, Trial Court of Massachusetts Boston Municipal Court Department)* Appointed by governor.
Office: U.S. Post Office and Courthouse, 90 Devonshire Street, Boston 02109.
Telephone: (617) 788-8700.

FLATLEY, Ellen *(Justice, Trial Court of Massachusetts District Court Department Essex County Gloucester Division)* Appointed by governor.
Mailing address: Two Center Plaza, Suite 200, Boston 02108.
Telephone: (617) 788-8810.

FLYNN, Gregory C. *(First Justice, Trial Court of Massachusetts District Court Department Middlesex County Waltham Division)* Appointed by Governor William F. Weld to term beginning July 1993. Term expires at age seventy. Born Waltham Massachusetts Dec 12, 1951. Roman Catholic. Educated at College of the Holy Cross B.A. 1973, Suffolk University Law School J.D. 1977 and Boston University School of Law LL.M. in Taxation 1979. Admitted to practice Massachusetts 1977.
Assistant U.S. Attorney Massachusetts 1980-85. General Counsel Massachusetts Bay Transportation Authority 1987-92. Member Boston and Massachusetts Bar Associations. Trustee Deaconess-Waltham Hospital.
Office: 38 Linden Street, Waltham 02452.

FLYNN, Maurice R., III *(Justice, Trial Court of Massachusetts District Court Department Middlesex County Malden Division)* Appointed by governor.

Mailing address: Two Center Plaza, Suite 200, Boston 02108.

Telephone: (617) 788-8810.

FLYNN, Patricia A. *(Associate Justice, Trial Court of Massachusetts Juvenile Court Department Middlesex County Division)* Appointed by governor.

Mailing address: P.O. Box 9664, Boston 02114-9664.
Office: Three Center Plaza, Suite 520, Boston 02108.
Telephone: (617) 788-6550.

FORD, Daniel A. *(Associate Justice, Trial Court of Massachusetts Superior Court Department)* Appointed by governor.

Office: U.S. Post Office and Courthouse, 90 Devonshire Street, Fifteenth Floor, Boston 02109.

Telephone: (617) 788-8130.

FORDE, Annette *(Associate Justice, Trial Court of Massachusetts Boston Municipal Court Department)* Appointed by governor.

Office: U.S. Post Office and Courthouse, 90 Devonshire Street, Boston 02109.

Telephone: (617) 788-8700.

FOX, Patrick A. *(First Justice, Trial Court of Massachusetts District Court Department Worcester County Gardner Division, First Justice, Winchendon Division and Justice, East Brookfield Division)* Appointed by governor.

Mailing address: Two Center Plaza, Suite 200, Boston 02108.

Telephone: (617) 788-8810.

FREEDMAN, Frank H. *(Senior Judge, United States District Court District of Massachusetts)* Appointed for life by President Richard M. Nixon to term beginning 1972. Former Chief Judge. Assumed Senior status, serves by assignment. Born Springfield Massachusetts Dec 15, 1924. Jewish. Educated at Boston University LL.B. 1949 LL.M. 1950. Awarded honorary Ph.D. Western New England College 1970. In legal practice 1950-68.

Former Member Judicial Conference of the U.S. Member Lewis Marshall Club on Jurisprudence (President) and Hampden County Bar Association. Recipient National Human Relations Award from National Conference of Christians and Jews and Silver Shingle Award for Distinguished Service from Boston University. Greenaway Drive Elementary School rededicated Frank H. Freedman School 1974. USNR 1943-46. Member Springfield Republican Committee 1959-72. Delegate Republican National Convention 1964 and 1968. Member Springfield City Council 1960-67 (President 1962). Mayor City of Springfield 1968-72. Chairman fund raising drives Muscular Dystrophy Society and Leukemia Society. Member Susan Auchter Kidney Fund Raising Committee.

Office: 1550 Main Street, Room 525, Springfield 01103.

Telephone: (413) 785-0005.

FULLER, David M. *(Associate Justice, Trial Court of Massachusetts Probate and Family Court Department Hampden County Division)* Appointed by governor.

Mailing address: Two Center Plaza, Suite 210, Boston 02108.

Telephone: (617) 788-6600.

GAFFNEY, Kevin J. *(Justice, Trial Court of Massachusetts District Court Department Norfolk County Dedham Division)* Appointed by governor.

Mailing address: Two Center Plaza, Suite 200, Boston 02108.

Telephone: (617) 788-8810.

GAILEY, Timothy H. *(Circuit Justice, Trial Court of Massachusetts District Court Department and First Justice, Suffolk County Chelsea Division)* Appointed by governor.

Office: Two Center Plaza, Suite 200, Boston 02108.
Telephone: (617) 788-8810.

GANTS, Ralph D. *(Associate Justice, Trial Court of Massachusetts Superior Court Department)* Appointed by governor.

Office: U.S. Post Office and Courthouse, 90 Devonshire Street, Fifteenth Floor, Boston 02109.
Telephone: (617) 788-8130.

GARDNER, Robert W., Jr. *(Justice, Trial Court of Massachusetts District Court Department Worcester County Clinton Division)* Appointed by governor.

Mailing address: Two Center Plaza, Suite 200, Boston 02108.

Telephone: (617) 788-8810.

GARINGER, Gail *(First Justice, Trial Court of Massachusetts Juvenile Court Department Middlesex County Division)* Appointed by governor.

Mailing address: P.O. Box 9664, Boston 02114-9664.
Office: Three Center Plaza, Suite 520, Boston 02108.
Telephone: (617) 788-6550.

GARSH, E. Susan *(Associate Justice, Trial Court of Massachusetts Superior Court Department)* Appointed by governor.

Office: U.S. Post Office and Courthouse, 90 Devonshire Street, Fifteenth Floor, Boston 02109.
Telephone: (617) 788-8130.

GARTH, Lance J. *(Justice, Trial Court of Massachusetts District Court Department Barnstable County Orleans Division)* Appointed by governor.

Mailing address: Two Center Plaza, Suite 200, Boston 02108.

Telephone: (617) 788-8810.

GEARY, James M., Jr. *(Justice, Trial Court of Massachusetts District Court Department Middlesex County Ayer Division)* Appointed by governor.

Mailing address: Two Center Plaza, Suite 200, Boston 02108.

Telephone: (617) 788-8810.

GEENTY, John Conrad *(Justice, Trial Court of Massachusetts District Court Department Worcester County Dudley Division)* Appointed by Governor Francis Williams Sargent to term beginning Aug 8, 1974. Term expires at age seventy. Former First Justice. Former Circuit Justice. Born Winchester Massachusetts Oct 14, 1933. Roman Catholic. Educated at Harvard College A.B. 1955 and Boston College J.D. 1960. Admitted to

GEENTY, JOHN CONRAD—*Continued*

practice Massachusetts 1961 and U.S. District Court District of Massachusetts 1962. In legal practice Boston 1961-64, New Bedford 1962-63 and Southbridge 1964-74.

Member Boston, Southern Worcester County, Worcester County, Massachusetts and American Bar Associations. Attended The National Judicial College 1975 and 1988. Lieutenant USNR 1955-57 (retired). Member Rotary International, Harvard Club of Boston and Harvard Club of Worcester. Enjoys golf, skiing and reading.

Mailing address: Two Center Plaza, Suite 200, Boston 02108.

Telephone: (617) 788-8810.

GELINAS, Andre A. *(Associate Justice, Massachusetts Appeals Court)* Appointed by Governor Argeo Paul Cellucci 1999. Term expires at age seventy. Born Fitchburg Massachusetts Sept 11, 1938. Roman Catholic. Educated at Assumption College A.B. 1960 and University of Michigan J.D. 1963. Awarded honorary LL.D. Assumption College 1983. Member Delta Theta Phi. Admitted to practice Massachusetts 1963, U.S. District Court District of Massachusetts 1965 and U.S. Supreme Court 1969. Began legal practice Fitchburg 1963. Former First Justice, Trial Court of Massachusetts District Court Department Worcester County Fitchburg Division, appointed by Governor Francis Williams Sargent March 20, 1973.

Office: 1500 New Courthouse, Boston 02108.

Telephone: (617) 725-8085.

GEOFFRION, Anne M. *(Circuit Justice, Trial Court of Massachusetts Probate and Family Court Department)* Appointed by governor.

Office: Two Center Plaza, Suite 210, Boston 02108.

Telephone: (617) 788-6600.

GERMAN, Marjory A. C. *(Associate Justice, Trial Court of Massachusetts Juvenile Court Department Suffolk County Division)* Appointed by governor.

Mailing address: P.O. Box 9663, Boston 02114.

Office: 24 New Chardon Street, Floor 5, Boston 02114.

Telephone: (617) 788-8542.

GERSHENGORN, Wendie I. *(Associate Justice, Trial Court of Massachusetts Superior Court Department)* Appointed by governor. Former Justice, Trial Court of Massachusetts District Court Department Middlesex County Cambridge Division.

Office: U.S. Post Office and Courthouse, 90 Devonshire Street, Fifteenth Floor, Boston 02109.

Telephone: (617) 788-8130.

GERTNER, Nancy *(Judge, United States District Court District of Massachusetts)* Appointed for life by President Bill Clinton to term beginning 1994. Born New York New York May 22, 1946. Educated at Barnard College B.A. 1967 and Yale University M.A. 1971 J.D. 1971. Honorary degrees Suffolk University and Northeastern School of Law. Law Clerk to Hon. Luther M. Swygert, U.S. Court of Appeals Seventh Circuit 1971-72. In legal practice Boston 1972-94.

Instructor Boston University School of Law 1972-95, Boston College 1995-98, Yale Law School since 1998 and Northeastern University School of Law 2001. Visiting Professor Harvard Law School 1985-86. Charles R. Merriam Distinguished Professor Arizona State University College of Law since Feb 2002. Member Central and Eastern European Law Initiative Advisory Council American Bar Association since 2002. Fellow American Bar Foundation. Recipient Award for the Advancement of Civil Rights from Lawyers Committee for Civil Rights 1999, Hon. William Brennan Award from New York State Association of Criminal Defense Lawyers 2000 and Distinguished Jurist Award from Massachusetts Association of Women Lawyers.

Office: 4130 U.S. Courthouse, One Courthouse Way, Boston 02210-3002.

GIBSON, Dorothy M. *(Associate Justice, Trial Court of Massachusetts Probate and Family Court Department Middlesex County Division)* Appointed by governor.

Mailing address: Two Center Plaza, Suite 210, Boston 02108.

Telephone: (617) 788-6600.

GILES, Linda E. *(Associate Justice, Trial Court of Massachusetts Superior Court Department)* Appointed by governor. Term expires at age seventy. Born Morristown New Jersey Dec 31, 1950. Educated at McGill University B.A. 1974 and New England School of Law J.D. cum laude 1977. Case Comment Editor New England Law Review 1976-77. Member Scarlet Key Honor Society. Admitted to practice Massachusetts 1977, U.S. District Court 1978, U.S. Court of Appeals and U.S. Supreme Court. In legal practice Boston 1977-91. Former Associate Justice, Trial Court of Massachusetts Boston Municipal Court Department, appointed by Governor William F. Weld to term beginning Dec 17, 1991.

Vice President Massachusetts Judges Conference and International Lesbian and Gay Judges Association. Chair Gender Equality Advisory Board Trial Court of Massachusetts. Advisory Board Massachusetts Commission Against Discrimination 1991.

Office: U.S. Post Office and Courthouse, 90 Devonshire Street, Fifteenth Floor, Boston 02109.

Telephone: (617) 788-8130.

GILLIGAN, Brian F. *(Justice, Trial Court of Massachusetts District Court Department Worcester County Milford Division)* Appointed by governor.

Mailing address: Two Center Plaza, Suite 200, Boston 02108.

Telephone: (617) 788-8810.

GOGGINS, W. Michael *(Justice, Trial Court of Massachusetts District Court Department Hampshire County Northampton Division)* Appointed by governor.

Mailing address: Two Center Plaza, Suite 200, Boston 02108.

Telephone: (617) 788-8810.

GORDON, Robert A. *(Justice, Trial Court of Massachusetts District Court Department Hampden County Springfield Division)* Appointed by governor.

Mailing address: Two Center Plaza, Suite 200, Boston 02108.

Telephone: (617) 788-8810.

GORTON, Nathaniel M. *(Judge, United States District Court District of Massachusetts)* Appointed for life by President George Bush Sept 24, 1992 to term beginning Oct 27, 1992. Born Evanston Illinois July 25, 1938. Episcopalian. Educated at Dartmouth College B.A. 1960 and Columbia University School of Law J.D.

GORTON, NATHANIEL M.—*Continued*

1966. Admitted to practice Massachusetts 1966. In legal practice Boston 1966-92. Lieutenant j.g. USNR 1960-62.

Office: 411 Federal Bldg. & U.S. Courthouse, 595 Main Street, Worcester 01608-2076.

Telephone: (508) 929-9910.

GOULD, Nancy M. *(Associate Justice, Trial Court of Massachusetts Probate and Family Court Department Suffolk County Division)* Appointed by governor.

Mailing address: Two Center Plaza, Suite 210, Boston 02108.

Telephone: (617) 788-6600.

GRABAU, Charles M. *(Associate Justice, Trial Court of Massachusetts Superior Court Department)* Appointed by Governor Michael S. Dukakis Sept 6, 1985. Term expires at age seventy. Regional Administrative Justice Essex County Jan 1, 1995 to June 30, 1996 and for Civil and Criminal Matters Middlesex County since Dec 1999. Born Newton Massachusetts May 4, 1948. Protestant. Educated at Tufts University B.A. magna cum laude 1970 and George Washington University National Law Center J.D. with honors 1973. Washingtonian Fellow 1972-73. Member International Law Society. Volunteer Ayuda Consumer Protection Center. Admitted to practice Massachusetts 1974. Began legal practice Boston 1974. In legal practice Wellesley 1977 and Boston Jan 1978 to June 1979. Associate Justice, Trial Court of Massachusetts Boston Municipal Court Department July 1979 to Sept 1985, appointed by Governor Edward J. King.

Case analyst Equal Employment Opportunity Commission 1971-72. Worked for Boston Legal Aid Society Aug 1973 to Feb 1974. Trial attorney Massachusetts Defenders Committee April 1974 to Dec 1976. Co-author with David Ross Williamson "Language Barriers in Our Trial Courts" 70 Massachusetts L. Rev. 108, 1985 and Ross Williamson "Court Interpretation Services in the Massachusetts Trial Courts: One Step Forward, Two Steps Back" Boston B. Jour. Sept-Oct 1995 and with Llewellyn Joseph Gibbons "Protecting the Rights of Linguistic Minorities: Challenges to Court Interpretation" 30 New England L. Rev. 227, 1996. Instructor in Law and Justice Program University of Massachusetts 1980-83. Member Special Sentence of Imprisonment Committee 1979-81 and Uniform Magistrates Rules Committee 1979-81. Chairman 1980-83 and Member 1987-95 Trial Court Committee on Interpreters. Chairman Superior Court Automation Committee 1987-93. Member Gender Equality Committee Superior Court 1989-95. Former Member Massachusetts Bar Association (Spanish Affairs Committee 1974-75). Member Massachusetts Judges Conference (Co-chairman Subcommittee on Juror Communications 1994-95) and Hispanic National Bar Association (Supreme Court Committee since 1994).

Guest Lecturer Professional Education Program Massachusetts Bar Association 1980-83 and 1989-91, International Institute of Buffalo Oct 20, 1994, Lecturer Law and Justice Program University of Massachusetts 1980-89 and Massachusetts Association of Trial Attorneys Oct 21, 1994. Guest Speaker Pre-Trial Practice in White Collar Criminal Cases Criminal Justice Section Massachusetts Bar Association 1992-93. Member Ad Hoc Work Group on Court Interpretation "Court Interpretation: Challenge for the 1990's" National Center for State Courts 1992-93. Faculty Member First National Conference on Eliminating Racial and Ethnic Bias in the Courts National Center for State Courts 1994-95 and Trying Chapter 93A Cases MCLE Seminar Sept 18, 1996. Guest Panelist "Police, Lawyers and Truth Symposium" Criminal Justice Institute Harvard University Law School Nov 14, 1995; "Lanigan II, Now What? Introduction to Scientific Evidence in Massachusetts" Massachusetts School of Law April 12, 1996; "Motor Vehicle Stops, New Developments" Massachusetts Trial Court Judicial Institute March 20, 2000; "Trying Your First Criminal Case in Superior Court" June 6, 2000; and "Civil and Criminal Trial Advocacy: What Works and What Doesn't" Superior Court Judicial Forum Massachusetts CLE Dec 12, 2000. Presenter Workshop on "Everything You Wanted to Know About Interpreters But Were Afraid to Ask" All Court Conference on Racial and Ethnic Issues 1996 and on "Parallel Litigation and Simultaneous Proceedings in Juvenile and Criminal Courts" Child Abuse and Neglect, A Multidisciplinary Conference Exploring the Investigation, Prosecution and Adjudication of Child Abuse Cases Flaschner Judicial Institute June 7, 1996. Presenter Evidence Program Massachusetts Academy of Trial Attorneys Dec 10, 1996. Participant "An Evening of Mock Trials" Federal Court Public Education Project and Citizen Schools May 17, 2000.

Named one of Ten Outstanding Young Leaders by Boston Jaycees 1980. Recipient Presidential Citation from Boston Bar Association 1993, Judicial Merit Award from Massachusetts Academy of Trial Attorneys 1995 and Appreciation Award from Essex County Bar Association June 6, 1996. National Student Advisory Board American Red Cross 1969. Member College Student Work Service American National Red Cross in Nicaragua 1969. Delegate to White House Conference on Children and Youth 1970. Board of Directors Greater Boston YMCA 1979-81 and Project Commitment 1984-89. Board member Alianza Hispana, Inc. 1979-81. Member Hispanic Advisory Committee Greater Boston YMCA 1979-81 and Planning Committee Flaschner Institute Program on Minorities 1979-81. Member Tufts University Alumni Council 1994-98.

Office: U.S. Post Office & Courthouse, 90 Devonshire Street, Fifteenth Floor, Boston 02109.

Telephone: (617) 788-8130.

GRACE, Martha P. *(Chief Justice, Trial Court of Massachusetts Juvenile Court Department)* Appointed by Governor Michael S. Dukakis to term beginning Dec 27, 1990. Served Worcester Division Dec 27, 1990 to 1998. Chief Justice since 1998. Born Providence Rhode Island. Educated at Smith College B.A. 1961, Clark University M.A. 1971 and New England School of Law J.D. with honors 1981. Admitted to practice Massachusetts 1981, U.S. District Court District of Massachusetts 1985 and U.S. Supreme Court 1986. In legal practice Worcester 1981-86. Clerk Magistrate, District Court Department Worcester County Spencer Division 1986-90.

Instructor in Business Law Assumption College 1981-86. Member Massachusetts Judges Conference, National Association of Women Judges, Women Lawyers of Worcester County, Worcester County and Massachusetts Bar Associations.

Mailing address: P.O. Box 9664, Boston 02114-9664.

Office: Three Center Plaza, Suite 520, Boston 02108.

Telephone: (617) 788-6550.

GRAHAM, R. Malcolm *(Associate Justice, Trial Court of Massachusetts Superior Court Department)* Appointed by governor. Former Justice, Trial Court of Massachusetts District Court Department Suffolk County Roxbury Division.

Office: U.S. Post Office and Courthouse, 90 Devonshire Street, Fifteenth Floor, Boston 02109.

Telephone: (617) 788-8130.

GRASSO, Joseph A., Jr. *(Associate Justice, Massachusetts Appeals Court)* Appointed by governor. Former First Justice, Trial Court of Massachusetts District Court Department Middlesex County Lowell Division. Former Associate Justice, Trial Court of Massachusetts Superior Court Department.

Office: 1500 New Courthouse, Boston 02108.

Telephone: (617) 725-8106.

GREANEY, John M. *(Associate Justice, Massachusetts Supreme Judicial Court)* Appointed by governor. Term expires at age seventy. Born Westfield Massachusetts April 8, 1939. Catholic. Educated at College of the Holy Cross B.A. summa cum laude 1960 and New York University J.D. 1963. Class Valedictorian 1960. Editor-in-Chief Annual Survey of American Law New York University. Root-Tilden Scholar. Admitted to practice Massachusetts 1963, U.S. District Court District of Massachusetts and U.S. Supreme Court 1969. In legal practice Springfield 1963-73. Justice, Housing Court of the County of Hampden 1973-75. Associate Justice, Superior Court of Massachusetts 1976-78. Former Associate Justice, Massachusetts Appeals Court, appointed by Governor Michael S. Dukakis to term beginning Dec 1978.

Author "How to Probate an Estate in Massachusetts: Guardianships, Conservatorships and Adoptions" 1969, "Practice and Procedure in Housing Courts" 1974, "Recent Developments in Housing, Zoning, Consumer and Real Estate Law" 1975 and "Practical Skills Program—Housing Law and Practice" 1975, all published by Massachusetts CLE Program; "Separate Maintenance in New Hampshire" New Hampshire B. Jour. 1964; "Operation of a County Housing Court" Journal of Housing 1975; "Trial Evidence" Massachusetts CLE-New England Law Institute 1976; and "Masters-Notes on Cases and Rules" Massachusetts CLE-New England Law Institute 1977. Co-author "Citizens Advisory Committee to a Trial Court—An Idea Whose Time Has Come" American Judicature Magazine 1974. Former Professor Western New England Law School and Westfield State College. Member Hampden County (Former member Executive and Grievance Committees, former Treasurer), Massachusetts (Legal Services to the Poor Committee, former Chairman Young Lawyers Section, former member Board of Delegates Executive and Grievance Committees) and American Bar Associations. Attended National College of the State Judiciary. Selected Westfield Junior Chamber of Commerce Outstanding Young Man 1973 and Outstanding Graduate St. Mary's Alumni Association. Former Director Springfield Child Guidance Clinic. Former member Area Mental Health Board, Endowment Committee Springfield YMCA, Westfield School Study and Building Committee and Westfield Citizens Scholarship Foundation. Member Westfield YMCA Building Committee, Massachusetts Council for Public Justice and Executive Committee Reality Club. Director Westfield River Watershed Association and Blandford Golf Club. Trustee and Director Westfield Atheneum. Director and Vice President Westfield YMCA. Participant Child and Family Service Program.

Office: 1300 New Courthouse, Boston 02108.

Telephone: (617) 557-1000.

GRECO, Robert V. *(First Justice, Trial Court of Massachusetts District Court Department Middlesex County Framingham Division)* Appointed by governor.

Mailing address: Two Center Plaza, Suite 200, Boston 02108.

Telephone: (617) 788-8810.

GREEN, Mark V. *(Associate Justice, Massachusetts Appeals Court)* Appointed by Governor Jane Swift to term beginning Nov 1, 2001. Term expires at age seventy. Born Moline Illinois Sept 1, 1956. Educated at Cornell University A.B. with distinction 1978 and Harvard Law School J.D. cum laude 1982. Admitted to practice Massachusetts 1982. In legal practice Boston 1982-90. Justice, Trial Court of Massachusetts Land Court Department May 7, 1997 to Oct 31, 2001, appointed by Governor William F. Weld.

Vice President and Senior Counsel Shawmut Bank, N.A. 1990-94. General Counsel The Mortgage Acquisition Corporation 1994-95. Senior Counsel BayBank, N.A. 1995-96 and The First National Bank of Boston 1996-97. Co-author "Measures a Lender May Take Internally to Protect Itself from Environmental Liability" *The Lender's Guide to Environmental Law: Risk and Liability* Matthew Bender and Co., Inc. 1993. Contributing Writer *Carlisle Mosquito Forum* since 1996. Presenter "Life after OREO: Sales and Financings of Bank Owned Real Estate" Boston Bar Association March 28, 1991; "Environmental Liability for Lenders" Feb 27, 1992 and "Avoiding Risk Under the New Lead Paint Law" March 19, 1994 Massachusetts Bankers Association; "Land Court Judicial Forum" Boston Bar Association May 21, 1998 and Massachusetts CLE Oct 7, 1998; "Massachusetts Zoning Practice" Nov 6, 1998 and Nov 4, 1999, "Trends in Massachusetts Real Estate Law" Real Estate Law Conference '99 April 7, 1999, "Litigating Real Estate Disputes" June 1, 2000, "New Registered Land Guidelines" Oct 30, 2000 and "Zoning Practice in Massachusetts" Nov 7, 2000 Massachusetts CLE; "Judicial Forum" Young Lawyers Section Boston Bar Association Jan 20, 1999; "Land Court Guidelines and Registry of Deeds Indexing Standards" Massachusetts Conveyancers Association semi-annual meeting April 19, 2000 and Panel "Update on Massachusetts Real Estate Litigation" Real Estate Law Conference 2000 Massachusetts CLE Feb 17, 2000. Director Massachusetts Society for the Prevention of Cruelty to Children 1992-99. Trustee Hartwell Road Homeowners Association 1993-98 and Carlisle Conservation Trust and Carlisle Conservation Foundation 1994-97. Campaign Account Executive 1993-94 and Community Campaign Co-chair Carlisle-Bedford Community 1995 United Way of Massachusetts Bay. Reunion Chair Harvard Law School Class of 1982 Tenth Reunion. Member Carlisle By-Law Review Committee 1994-97 and DEP Title V Task Force 1995-96.

Office: 1500 New Courthouse, Boston 02108.

Telephone: (617) 725-8085.

GREENBERG, Mel L. *(Associate Justice, Massachusetts Appeals Court)* Appointed by Governor Michael S. Dukakis 1990. Term expires at age seventy. Born Worcester Massachusetts May 4, 1937. Jewish. Educated at Clark University B.S. magna cum laude 1958 and Boston University LL.B. 1961. Admitted to practice

GREENBERG, MEL L.—*Continued*

Massachusetts 1961, U.S. District Court District of Massachusetts 1963 and U.S. Court of Appeals First Circuit 1971. In legal practice Worcester 1961-77. Former Associate Justice, Trial Court of Massachusetts Superior Court Department, appointed by Governor Michael S. Dukakis to term beginning Sept 19, 1983.

Regional Trial Counsel Civil Liberties Union Worcester 1970-73. General Counsel to Civil Liberties Union of Massachusetts 1975-77. Author *Bench Book for Proceedings in the District Courts* Massachusetts CLE 1982 and "Double Jeopardy and Trial De Novo; The Dilemma in re State's District Courts" 68 No. 2 Massachusetts L. Rev. 1983. Co-author "Manual for District Court Defenders" Massachusetts CLE 1980. Associate Editor Massachusetts Law Review 1982-83 and 1984-85. Visiting Professor of Constitutional Law Clark University since 1972 and Principal Instructor Harvard Law School and Boston University School of Law. Member Massachusetts Trial Lawyers Association, Massachusetts District Court Justices Association, The Association of Trial Lawyers of America, North Worcester County Judges Association, American Judicature Society, Committee on Standards for Massachusetts Judiciary, District Magistrates of Massachusetts Task Force, Advisory Board Juvenile Law Reform Project of Massachusetts, Worcester County (Criminal Law Practice Committee) and Massachusetts Bar Associations.

Instructor New England Trial Advocacy Course 1980-84. Member Trial Practice Curriculum Committee Massachusetts CLE 1983-84. Co-chair Judicial Education Seminar Franklin Flaschner Institute 1983-84. Recipient Outstanding Young Leader of Worcester Award from the Greater Worcester Jaycees 1972 and Civil Libertarian Award from Worcester Civil Liberties Union 1971. Listed in *Who's Who in Massachusetts* 1974. USAR JAGC 1961-67. Democrat. Member Worcester Democratic City Committee 1972-77, Human Rights Commission of Worcester (Legal Subcommittee), Civil Liberties Union of Worcester (Chairman Legal Panel), Committee for Conscientious Objectors (Cooperating Attorney), American Friends Service Committee (Legal Advisor), Massachusetts Office for Children (Legal Consultant), Justice and Civil Rights Board of Massachusetts, Democratic Platform Committee and Legal Aid Society of Worcester (Referral Attorney). Counsel to Inter Faith Center for Draft Counseling 1972-73. Member Salisbury Heights Association (President), Worcester New School Inc. (Clerk and Director), William Snow Memorial Scholarship Fund Inc. (Clerk and Director), Board NAACP Scholarship Committee, Advisory Board Community Services of Greater Worcester 1972, Jewish Home for Aged (Director 1972), Clark University Cooperative Nursery School (President and Director 1972), Board Massachusetts Civil Liberties Union 1974-76 and Commonwealth of Massachusetts Youth Services Evaluation Board 1975. Enjoys jogging, cross-country skiing and tennis.

Office: 1500 New Courthouse, Boston 02108.
Telephone: (617) 725-8106.

HAGGERTY, S. Jane *(Associate Justice, Trial Court of Massachusetts Superior Court Department)* Appointed by governor.

Office: U.S. Post Office and Courthouse, 90 Devonshire Street, Fifteenth Floor, Boston 02109.
Telephone: (617) 788-8130.

HAMLIN, Sandra L. *(Associate Justice, Trial Court of Massachusetts Superior Court Department)* Appointed by governor.

Office: U.S. Post Office and Courthouse, 90 Devonshire Street, Fifteenth Floor, Boston 02109.
Telephone: (617) 788-8130.

HANLON, Sydney *(First Justice, Trial Court of Massachusetts District Court Department Suffolk County Dorchester Division)* Appointed by governor.

Mailing address: Two Center Plaza, Suite 200, Boston 02108.
Telephone: (617) 788-8810.

HARMS, Christina L. *(Associate Justice, Trial Court of Massachusetts Probate and Family Court Department Norfolk County Division)* Appointed by Governor Michael S. Dukakis to term beginning Dec 1989. Educated at Wellesley College B.A. 1975 and Harvard Law School J.D. 1978.

Mailing address: Two Center Plaza, Suite 210, Boston 02108.
Telephone: (617) 788-6600.

HARRINGTON, Edward F. *(Senior Judge, United States District Court District of Massachusetts)* Appointed for life by President Ronald Reagan to term beginning Feb 29, 1988. Assumed Senior status March 1, 2001, serves by assignment. Born Fall River Massachusetts Sept 16, 1933. Catholic. Educated at Holy Cross College A.B. in cursu honoris cum laude 1955 and Boston College Law School J.D. 1960. Editorial Staff Boston College Industrial and Commercial Law Review 1958-60. Law Clerk to Chief Justice Paul C. Reardon, Superior Court of Massachusetts 1960-61. Admitted to practice Massachusetts 1960, U.S. District Court District of Massachusetts 1965 and U.S. Court of Appeals First Circuit 1965. In legal practice Boston 1973-77 and Framingham 1981-88.

Attorney-in-Charge Strike Force Against Organized Crime for New England U.S. Department of Justice 1970-73. U.S. Attorney District of Massachusetts 1977-81. Ensign and Lieutenant j.g. USN 1955-57. Republican. Republican Candidate for Attorney General Massachusetts 1986.

Office: 8110 U.S. Courthouse, One Courthouse Way, Boston 02210-3002.
Telephone: (617) 748-4160.

HARRIS, Leslie E. *(Associate Justice, Trial Court of Massachusetts Juvenile Court Department Suffolk County Division)* Appointed by governor.

Mailing address: P.O. Box 9663, Boston 02114.
Office: 24 New Chardon Street, Floor 5, Boston 02114.
Telephone: (617) 788-8542.

HART, Joseph L., Jr. *(Associate Justice, Trial Court of Massachusetts Probate and Family Court Department Worcester County Division)* Appointed by governor.

Mailing address: Two Center Plaza, Suite 210, Boston 02108.
Telephone: (617) 788-6600.

HARVEY, Tobin N. *(Justice, Trial Court of Massachusetts District Court Department Middlesex County Woburn Division)* Appointed by governor.

Mailing address: Two Center Plaza, Suite 200, Boston 02108.
Telephone: (617) 788-8810.

HEALEY, J. Dennis *(Justice, Trial Court of Massachusetts District Court Department Essex County Peabody Division)* Appointed by governor.
Mailing address: Two Center Plaza, Suite 200, Boston 02108.
Telephone: (617) 788-8810.

HEALY, Paul F., Jr. *(Justice, Trial Court of Massachusetts District Court Department Middlesex County Framingham Division)* Appointed by governor.
Mailing address: Two Center Plaza, Suite 200, Boston 02108.
Telephone: (617) 788-8810.

HEFFERNAN, Paul P. *(First Justice, Trial Court of Massachusetts District Court Department Middlesex County Somerville Division)* Appointed by governor.
Mailing address: Two Center Plaza, Suite 200, Boston 02108.
Telephone: (617) 788-8810.

HELY, Charles J. *(Associate Justice, Trial Court of Massachusetts Superior Court Department)* Appointed by Governor Michael S. Dukakis to term beginning Dec 22, 1990. Educated at Colby College A.B. 1968, Boston College Law School J.D. with honors 1971 and George Washington University National Law Center LL.M. 1975. Staff member Boston College Law Review 1969-70. Admitted to practice Massachusetts 1971, U.S. Court of Military Appeals 1972, U.S. District Court District of Massachusetts 1975, U.S. Court of Appeals First Circuit 1975 and U.S. Supreme Court 1976. In legal practice Boston 1974-76. Justice, Trial Court of Massachusetts District Court Department 1989-90.
Assistant District Attorney 1976-89.
Office: U.S. Post Office and Courthouse, 90 Devonshire Street, Fifteenth Floor, Boston 02109.
Telephone: (617) 788-8130.

HERLIHY, Kevin M. *(First Justice, Trial Court of Massachusetts District Court Department Essex County Haverhill Division and Justice, Lawrence Division)* Appointed by Governor Michael S. Dukakis April 17, 1985 to term beginning July 8, 1985. Term expires at age seventy. Former First Justice Lawrence Division. Born Haverhill Massachusetts Oct 8, 1941. Educated at Boston College A.B. 1963 and Suffolk University J.D. 1971. Admitted to practice Massachusetts 1971 and U.S. District Court District of Massachusetts 1973. In legal practice Gloucester and Haverhill 1971-85.
Member Massachusetts Bar Association. Attended The National Judicial College 1986.
Mailing address: Two Center Plaza, Suite 200, Boston 02108.
Telephone: (617) 788-8810.

HILLMAN, Timothy S. *(Associate Justice, Trial Court of Massachusetts Superior Court Department)* Appointed by governor. Former First Justice, Trial Court of Massachusetts District Court Department Worcester County Gardner Division and Winchendon Division.
Office: U.S. Post Office and Courthouse, 90 Devonshire Street, Fifteenth Floor, Boston 02109.
Telephone: (617) 788-8130.

HILLMAN, William C. *(Judge, United States Bankruptcy Court District of Massachusetts)* Appointed by U.S. Court of Appeals First Circuit judges to term beginning 1991. Chief Judge Bankruptcy Court 1998-2002. Also Judge, Bankruptcy Appellate Panel First Circuit. Selected by the Judicial Council of the First Circuit to term beginning 1996. Educated at University of Chicago and Boston University School of Law J.D. cum laude LL.M. Secretary and Note Editor Boston University Law Review. Admitted to practice Massachusetts, Rhode Island, U.S. District Courts District of Connecticut, District of Massachusetts and District of Rhode Island, U.S. Courts of Appeals First, Fifth and Eleventh Circuits and U.S Supreme Court. In legal practice Providence Rhode Island 1957-91. Judge of Probate Barrington Rhode Island 1974-84. Deputy Judge of Probate West Greenwich Rhode Island 1984-91 and Hopkinton Rhode Island 1990.
Author "What's in a Name: The UCC Filing System in Court" 44 Oklahoma L. Rev. 151, 1991; "Introductory Note: Symposium on Revised Article 9 of the Uniform Commercial Code" 73 Bankruptcy L. Jour. xi Winter 1999; and "Preview of Coming Attractions: Revised Article 9 of the UCC" Norton Bankruptcy Law Advisor 7 Sept 1999. Editorial Advisory Board American Bankruptcy L. Jour. 1993-98. Co-author with Hon. Joan N. Feeney "Property of the Estate" *Chapter 11 Theory & Practice: A Guide to Reorganization* LRP Publications 1994 and with Margaret M. Crouch *Bankruptcy Deskbook* and annual supplements PLI Press 2000. Adjunct Faculty of Bankruptcy Suffolk University Law School 1996-98 and Northeastern University School of Law since 1998 and Advanced Commercial Law Seminars Boston College Law School 1996 and 2001. Secretary 1969-95 and Commissioner since 1969 Rhode Island Commission on Uniform State Laws. Member 1975-80 and Secretary 1977-80 Disciplinary Board Rhode Island Supreme Court. Chairman 1982-84 and Director 1982-88 Rhode Island Law Institute. Honorary Consultant The Law Reform Commission Australia 1984-87. Member Article 9 Review Committee Uniform Commercial Code Permanent Editorial Board 1989-92. Life Member National Conference of Commissioners on Uniform State Laws (Chairman Uniform Marital Property Act Drafting Committee 1979-83 and Uniform Franchise and Business Opportunities Act Review Committee 1983-87, Member UCC Article 6 Revision Drafting Committee 1987-88, UCC Article 5 Revision Drafting Committee 1990-95, UCC Article 2 Revision Review Committee 1991-94, UCC Article 9 Revision Drafting Committee since 1993). Fellow American College of Bankruptcy. Presenter "Remedies for Breach of Contract," "The Law of Contracts" and "Secured Transactions" U.S. Agency for International Development 1996; "Revised Article 9 of the Uniform Commercial Code" ALI-ABA 1997; "Chapter 11 Case Administration" 1997, "Leases and Licenses" 1998 and "Bankruptcy Litigation Forum" 2000 American Bankruptcy Institute; "Bankruptcy Court Jurisdiction and Venue" 1999, "The Debtor's Duties" 2000 and "Workouts and Bankruptcies in the eCommerce Economy" 2001 Practising Law Institute; "Getting Ready for an Internet Company Bankruptcy" Business Law Section American Bar Association 2000; "First Day Orders" Federal Judicial Center 2000; "Revised Article 9: Transition Rules" State Bar of Idaho 2001; and "Revised Article 9: Scope and Terminology Changes" Glasser Legal Works 2001.
Office: 1101 Federal Building, 10 Causeway Street, Boston 02222-1074.
Telephone: (617) 565-6097.

HINES, Geraldine S. *(Associate Justice, Trial Court of Massachusetts Superior Court Department)* Appointed by governor.

Office: U.S. Post Office and Courthouse, 90 Devonshire Street, Fifteenth Floor, Boston 02109.

Telephone: (617) 788-8130.

HINKLE, Margaret R. *(Associate Justice, Trial Court of Massachusetts Superior Court Department)* Appointed by governor.

Office: U.S. Post Office and Courthouse, 90 Devonshire Street, Fifteenth Floor, Boston 02109.

Telephone: (617) 788-8130.

HODOS, Herbert H. *(First Justice, Trial Court of Massachusetts District Court Department Franklin County Greenfield Division)* Appointed by Governor William F. Weld to term beginning May 1993. Term expires at age seventy. Born Cambridge Massachusetts Feb 2, 1939. Jewish. Educated at Yale University B.A. 1960 and Boston College Law School LL.B. 1963.

Mailing address: Two Center Plaza, Suite 200, Boston 02108.

Telephone: (617) 788-8810.

HOGAN, Michele B. *(Justice, Trial Court of Massachusetts District Court Department Middlesex County Cambridge Division)* Appointed by governor.

Mailing address: Two Center Plaza, Suite 200, Boston 02108.

Telephone: (617) 788-8810.

HORAN, Diana *(Associate Justice, Trial Court of Massachusetts Housing Court Department Worcester County Division)* Appointed by governor.

Office: Two Main Street, Room 101, Worcester 01608.

Telephone: (617) 788-8483.

HORGAN, Thomas C. *(Associate Justice, Trial Court of Massachusetts Boston Municipal Court Department)* Appointed by governor. Educated at Suffolk University B.S.B.A. 1970 J.D. 1974. Admitted to practice Massachusetts 1974 and U.S. Supreme Court 1975.

Member Massachusetts Judges Conference (Executive Committee).

Office: U.S. Post Office and Courthouse, 90 Devonshire Street, Boston 02109.

Telephone: (617) 788-8760.

HOUSTON, Julian T. *(Associate Justice, Trial Court of Massachusetts Superior Court Department)* Appointed by governor. Former Justice, Trial Court of Massachusetts District Court Department Suffolk County Roxbury Division, appointed by governor 1979.

Office: U.S. Post Office and Courthouse, 90 Devonshire Street, Fifteenth Floor, Boston 02109.

Telephone: (617) 788-8130.

HOWARTH, Robert L. *(Justice, Trial Court of Massachusetts District Court Department Hampden County Palmer Division)* Appointed by governor.

Mailing address: Two Center Plaza, Suite 200, Boston 02108.

Telephone: (617) 788-8810.

HURLEY, Patrick J. *(First Justice, Trial Court of Massachusetts District Court Department Plymouth County Hingham Division)* Appointed by governor.

Mailing address: Two Center Plaza, Suite 200, Boston 02108.

Telephone: (617) 788-8810.

HURLEY-MARKS, Mary E. *(First Justice, Trial Court of Massachusetts District Court Department Hampden County Chicopee Division)* Appointed by Governor William F. Weld.

Mailing address: Two Center Plaza, Suite 200, Boston 02108.

Telephone: (617) 788-8810.

IRELAND, Roderick L. *(Associate Justice, Massachusetts Supreme Judicial Court)* Appointed by governor. Term expires at age seventy. Born Springfield Massachusetts Dec 3, 1944. Educated at Lincoln University B.A. 1966, Columbia University J.D. 1969, Harvard University LL.M. 1975, Northeastern University M.P.A. Program 1971-73 and Suffolk University M.P.A. Program 1977. Clinical Fellow in Criminal Trial Advocacy 1972-73 and Teaching Fellow in Criminal Trial Advocacy and The Lawyering Process 1973-74 Harvard University. Admitted to practice Massachusetts 1971. In legal practice Boston 1975. Former Associate Justice, Trial Court of Massachusetts Juvenile Court Department Boston Division, appointed by Governor Michael S. Dukakis to term beginning Nov 1977. Former Associate Justice, Massachusetts Appeals Court.

Staff Attorney Harlem Assertion of Rights and Mobilization for Youth, Neighborhood Legal Services Offices New York City 1969-70 and The Harvard Center for Law and Education Litigation Department 1970-71. Chief Attorney 1971, Deputy Director 1972 and Director 1973 Roxbury Defenders Committee. Hearing Officer Massachusetts Civil Service Commission 1973-75. Legal Counsel Roxbury Court Clinic 1974-77. General Counsel Executive Office for Administration and Finance Massachusetts 1975-77. Author "Hyperactive Children: Process Is Due" Inequality in Education, Harvard University Center for Law and Education 1970. Lecturer on Basic Oral Advocacy University of Massachusetts 1975. Guest Lecturer on Criminal Trial Advocacy 1975 and Counsel to third-year Clinical Program in Trial Advocacy 1976-77 Harvard University. Lecturer on Criminal and Juvenile Law Boston College 1978. Adjunct Assistant Professor of Criminal Justice, Criminal Law and Criminal Procedure Northeastern University 1978. Member Massachusetts, New York State and Federal Bar Associations. Attended National Institute for Trial Advocacy 1974 and National College of Juvenile Justice 1978. Treasurer and Board of Directors Project FIRST 1972-73 (Roxbury community-based drug rehabilitation program). Appointed by Governor Francis Williams Sargent to Security and Privacy Council 1974. Board of Directors Roxbury Defenders Committee 1976-78. Chairman Massachusetts Board of Appeal on Motor Vehicles Liability Policies and Bonds 1977. Counsel to Eliot Congregational Church 1976-78, Massachusetts Minority Council on Alcoholism 1976-78 and Project AIM 1976-78.

Office: 1300 New Courthouse, Boston 02108.

Telephone: (617) 557-1000.

JACKSON-THOMPSON, Marie O. *(First Justice, Trial Court of Massachusetts District Court Department Middlesex County Woburn Division and Justice, Cam-*

JACKSON-THOMPSON, MARIE O.—*Continued*

bridge Division) Appointed by Governor Edward J. King to term beginning May 1980. Term expires at age seventy. Born Pittsburgh Pennsylvania Aug 14, 1947. Baptist. Educated at Mount Holyoke College B.A. 1969 and Harvard University J.D. 1972. Awarded honorary doctorate Notre Dame College 1991. Member Alpha Kappa Alpha. Admitted to practice Massachusetts 1973 and U.S. District Court District of Massachusetts 1973. Began legal practice Cambridge 1972. In legal practice Boston 1974-80. Administrative Judge, Division of Hearings 1975-76.

Assistant Secretary and General Counsel Governor's Executive Office of Administration & Finance 1976-1980. Member Juvenile Justice Committee Massachusetts Criminal Justice Board 1982-90. Member Massachusetts Commission to Study Racial and Ethnic Bias in Court 1992-94. Author "Use and Abuse of Certain Records in Custody Proceedings" Flaschner Judicial Institute 1984 and "They Do Not Live Happily Ever After: A Look at the Real Story of Family Violence" Mount Holyoke Alumnae Quarterly Fall 1986. Lecturer on Law and Family Urban Studies Department Brandeis University Jan 1992 to June 1992. Member Black Judges Association of Massachusetts, Massachusetts Judges Conference, National Council of Juvenile and Family Court Judges, National Association of Women Judges (Board of Directors 1982-84), National and American (Delegate Committee on Special Courts 1983) Bar Associations. Lecturer on "Practicing Under the New Rules of Adjudicatory Procedure" Massachusetts CLE, Inc.-New England Law Institute, Inc. 1979, "The Use and Abuse of Certain Records in Child Custody Proceedings" Flaschner Judicial Institute 1984, "Practice, Policy and Procedure for 209A Policy" Massachusetts CLE, Inc. 1986, "Judicial Ethics" Flaschner Judicial Institute and Massachusetts CLE, Inc. Jan 1988, "Representing Juveniles: A View From the Bench" Massachusetts CLE, Inc. 1988, "Predicting Violence" District Court Judges Conference 1988 and "Creative Dispositions & Problem Solving in Juvenile Jurisdiction Matters" District Court Judges Conference 1991. Named one of Ten Outstanding Young Leaders by Boston Jaycees 1981 and Medford ZONTA Women of the Year 1991. Recipient Boston and Vicinity Leadership Award 1981, Community Justice Award from Justice Resource Institute Feb 1985, Cambridge YWCA Tribute to Women Award Oct 1985, Mount Holyoke Sesquicentennial Alumnae Award 1988 and Pany Award from Mount Holyoke 1995. Board of Directors Greater Boston Youth Symphony Orchestra 1982-84 and Judge Baker Guidance Center 1987-92. Regional Board National Conference of Christians and Jews 1986-88. Board member Adolescent Consultation Center. Life Member National Association of Negro Business & Professional Women, Inc. and Middlesex LINKS, Inc. (inactive). Enjoys photography and collecting dolls and elephants.

Mailing address: Two Center Plaza, Suite 200, Boston 02108.

Telephone: (617) 788-8810.

JACOBS, George *(Associate Justice, Massachusetts Appeals Court)* Appointed by Governor Michael S. Dukakis to term beginning 1989. Term expires at age seventy. Born Milano Italy Sept 11, 1933. Jewish. Educated at Harvard University B.A. cum laude 1955 J.D. 1958. Admitted to practice Massachusetts 1958. In legal practice New Bedford 1958-75. Justice, Trial Court of Massachusetts Probate and Family Court Department 1975-81. Associate Justice, Trial Court of Massachusetts Superior Court Department 1981-89.

City Solicitor New Bedford 1964-70. Assistant Attorney General 1970-75. Instructor Southern New England School of Law 1988-2000 and Suffolk University Law School 1989-94.

Office: 1500 New Courthouse, Boston 02108.

Telephone: (617) 725-8106.

JARASITIS, Allen J. *(Justice, Trial Court of Massachusetts District Court Department Suffolk County Charlestown Division)* Appointed by governor.

Mailing address: Two Center Plaza, Suite 200, Boston 02108.

Telephone: (617) 788-8810.

JENNINGS, Joseph W., III *(Circuit Justice, Trial Court of Massachusetts District Court Department)* Appointed by governor.

Office: Two Center Plaza, Suite 200, Boston 02108.

Telephone: (617) 788-8810.

JOHNSON, Charles Ray *(Chief Justice, Trial Court of Massachusetts Boston Municipal Court Department)* Appointed by Governor Michael S. Dukakis 1984. Acting Chief Justice Oct 31, 2002 to March 27, 2003. Chief Justice since March 28, 2003. Educated at Tuskegee University B.S. 1971 and Harvard Law School J.D. 1975. In legal practice Roxbury.

Office: Courthouse, 90 Devonshire Street, Boston 02109.

Telephone: (617) 788-8700.

JOHNSON, Lee G. *(Circuit Justice, Trial Court of Massachusetts District Court Department and First Justice, Middlesex County Malden Division)* Appointed by governor.

Office: Two Center Plaza, Suite 200, Boston 02108.

Telephone: (617) 788-8810.

JOHNSON SMITH, Emogene *(Acting First Justice, Trial Court of Massachusetts District Court Department Norfolk County Wrentham Division and Justice, Suffolk County Dorchester Division)* Appointed by governor.

Mailing address: Two Center Plaza, Suite 200, Boston 02108.

Telephone: (617) 788-8810.

JOHNSTON, Joseph F. *(Circuit Justice, Trial Court of Massachusetts Juvenile Court Department)* Appointed by governor.

Mailing address: P.O. Box 9664, Boston 02114-9664.

Office: Three Center Plaza, Suite 520, Boston 02108.

Telephone: (617) 788-6550.

JOSEPHSON, Bertha D. *(Associate Justice, Trial Court of Massachusetts Superior Court Department)* Appointed by governor. Former Justice, Trial Court of Massachusetts District Court Department Hampden County Chicopee Division.

Office: U.S. Post Office and Courthouse, 90 Devonshire Street, Fifteenth Floor, Boston 02109.

Telephone: (617) 788-8130.

JULIAN, John M. *(Justice, Trial Court of Massachusetts District Court Department Dukes County Edgartown Division)* Appointed by governor.

Mailing address: Two Center Plaza, Suite 200, Boston 02108.

Telephone: (617) 788-8810.

KAFKER, Scott L. *(Associate Justice, Massachusetts Appeals Court)* Appointed by governor.
Office: 1500 New Courthouse, Boston 02108.
Telephone: (617) 725-8106.

KAGAN, Spencer M. *(Circuit Justice, Trial Court of Massachusetts Probate and Family Court Department)* Appointed by governor.
Office: Two Center Plaza, Suite 210, Boston 02108.
Telephone: (617) 788-6600.

KANE, Robert J. *(Associate Justice, Trial Court of Massachusetts Superior Court Department)* Appointed by governor. Former Justice, Trial Court of Massachusetts District Court Department Dukes County Edgartown Division.
Office: U.S. Post Office and Courthouse, 90 Devonshire Street, Fifteenth Floor, Boston 02109.
Telephone: (617) 788-8130.

KANTROWITZ, R. Marc *(Associate Justice, Massachusetts Appeals Court)* Appointed by Governor Argeo Paul Cellucci to term beginning 2001. Educated at Ohio University B.A. cum laude 1972, M.A. with honors 1974 and University of Toledo College of Law J.D. 1978. Staff member University of Toledo Law Review 1977-78. Moot Court Board. Participant Robert F. Wagner National Labor Law Moot Court Competition. Quarterfinalist Fornloff Intraschool Moot Court Competition. Admitted to practice Massachusetts 1978, U.S. Court of Appeals First Circuit and U.S. Supreme Court. In legal practice Boston 1985-95. Associate Justice, Trial Court of Massachusetts Juvenile Court Department Norfolk County Division 1995-2001, appointed by Governor William F. Weld.

Assistant District Attorney Suffolk County 1979-85. Program Attorney Massachusetts CLE 1988-91. Co-author "How to Prepare for the Law School Admission Test" McGraw Hill 1979; "Criminal Defense Motions, Massachusetts Practice" 42 West Publishing Company 1991 Supplement 1993, 1995 and 1996, 2nd ed. 1998 Supplement 1999-2000; "Closing Argument: What Can and Cannot Be Said" 81 Massachusetts L. Rev. 95-108, Sept 1996; "Validity of Sobriety Checkpoints Created by State or Local Police for the Purpose of Detecting Drunk Drivers" 74 American L. Rev. 319, 1999; and Part VII "Media Issues" III *Juvenile Court Benchbook* Massachusetts CLE 2000. Author *Compendium of Massachusetts Criminal Law* 1985, supp. 1988 and 1990, 2nd ed. 1993 and 3rd ed. 1995, retitled *Massachusetts Criminal Law Sourcebook* 1996, 1997, 1998, 1999, 2000, 2001 and 2002 Massachusetts CLE; Chapter "Your Direct Examination" *Fundamentals of District Court Practice* 1986, Chapter "Operating Under the Influence: An Overview" *District Court Bar Advocate Program Training Manual* 1991, Chapter 1 "Elements of Drug Offenses" *Trying Drug Cases in Massachusetts* 1992 and Chapter "Successfully Defending an OUI Case" *Massachusetts Basic Practice Manual* 1993 Massachusetts CLE; *1999 Massachusetts Juvenile Law Sourcebook* Massachusetts CLE 1999, 2001 and 2002; Chapter IV.2 "Fifth Amendment Privilege Against Self-Incrimination" III *Juvenile Court Benchbook* Massachusetts CLE 2000; and *2001 Massachusetts Juvenile Law Sourcebook* Massachusetts CLE 2000.

Author/Editor "Defending Drunk Driving Cases: The ABCs of OUIs" 1992, "Massachusetts Motor Vehicle Torts: Liability and Litigation" 1994 Massachusetts CLE and "Stranger and Nonstranger Sexual Assault: Balancing Culture and Law" Massachusetts Judicial Institute 1999. Editor "Kids in Custody: What Happens When Juveniles Are Held" Massachusetts CLE 1996. Instructor Suffolk University, Framingham State College and Quincy Junior College 1983-87. Former Chair Bar Advocate Steering Committee CLE Boston Bar Association. Chair 1993-1996 and Member 1996-99 Criminal Practice Advisory Committee Massachusetts CLE. Member Task Force on Early Court Intervention 1995 and Sub-Committee on Model Murder/Manslaughter Jury Instructions 1996-99 Supreme Judicial Court, Quincy College Criminal Law Advisory Committee 1996-98, Rape and Sexual Assault Training Advisory Group Judicial Institute 1997-99 and Settlement Practices in Criminal Cases Seminar Advisory Group Flaschner Judicial Institute 1999-2000. Captain USAR 1972-85.
Office: 1500 New Courthouse, Boston 02108.
Telephone: (617) 725-8106.

KAPLAN, Randy J. *(Circuit Justice, Trial Court of Massachusetts Probate and Family Court Department)* Appointed by governor.
Office: Two Center Plaza, Suite 210, Boston 02108.
Telephone: (617) 788-6600.

KEAMY, Leilah A. *(Associate Justice, Trial Court of Massachusetts Probate and Family Court Department Middlesex County Division)* Appointed by governor.
Mailing address: Two Center Plaza, Suite 210, Boston 02108.
Telephone: (617) 788-6600.

KEETON, Robert E. *(Senior Judge, United States District Court District of Massachusetts)* Appointed for life by President Jimmy Carter March 30, 1979. Assumed Senior status Feb 28, 2003, serves by assignment. Born Clarksville Texas Dec 16, 1919. Congregationalist. Educated at University of Texas B.B.A. 1940 LL.B. 1941 and Harvard University S.J.D. 1956. Awarded honorary LL.D. William Mitchell College 1983 and Lewis and Clark College 1988. Staff member Texas Law Review 1939-41. Admitted to practice Texas 1941 and Massachusetts 1954. Began legal practice Houston Texas 1941.

Commissioner on Uniform State Laws Massachusetts 1971-79. Author *Trial Tactics and Methods* Little, Brown and Company 2nd ed. 1973, *Legal Cause in the Law of Torts* Ohio State University Press 1963, *Venturing to Do Justice—Reforming Private Law* Harvard University Press 1969 and *Insurance Law Basic Text* West Publishing Company 1971 and co-edited with Stan Widers 2nd ed. 1988. Co-author with Prosser and Keeton *Torts* West Publishing Company 5th ed. 1984, with O'Connell *Basic Protection for the Traffic Victim* Little, Brown and Company 1965, *Judging* West Publishing Company 1990 and *Judging: The American Legal System* Lexis Law Publishing 1999. Associate Professor of Law Southern Methodist University 1951-54. Thayer Teaching Fellow 1953-54, Assistant Professor 1954-56, Professor 1956-73, Langdell Professor 1973-79 and Associate Dean 1975-79 Harvard Law School. Director National Institute of Trial Advocacy 1973-76. Fellow Massachusetts Bar Foundation and American Bar Foundation. Member The American Law Institute (Adviser on Restatements 2d of Torts and Restitution), State Bar of Texas, Massachusetts and American (Commission on Medical Professional Liability and Coordinating Committee on Legal Education) Bar Associations. Member Committees of Judicial Conference of U.S. on Admis-

KEETON, ROBERT E.—*Continued*

sion to Practice in Federal Courts (Devitt Committee 1976-79, King Committee 1979-85, Committee on Court Administration 1985-87, Member 1987-90 and Chairman 1991-93 Standing Committee on the Rules of Practice and Procedure). Recipient William B. Jones Award from National Institute of Trial Advocacy 1980, Leon Green Award from University of Texas Law Review 1981, Francis Rawle Award from ALI-ABA 1983 and Samuel E. Gates Litigation Award from American College of Trial Lawyers 1984. Lieutenant Commander USN 1942-45. Trustee College Retirement Equitees Fund 1964-68 and Flaschner Judicial Institute 1979-86. Member American Academy of Arts and Sciences.

Office: 3130 U.S. Courthouse, 1 Courthouse Way, Boston 02210-3002.

Telephone: (617) 748-9243.

KELLY, Sally A. *(Associate Justice, Trial Court of Massachusetts Boston Municipal Court Department)* Appointed by governor.

Office: Courthouse, 90 Devonshire Street, Boston 02109.

Telephone: (617) 788-8700.

KENNER, Carol J. *(Judge, United States Bankruptcy Court District of Massachusetts)* Former Chief Judge Bankruptcy Court. Also Judge, Bankruptcy Appellate Panel First Circuit. Selected by the Judicial Council of the First Circuit.

Office: 1101 Federal Building, 10 Causeway Street, Boston 02222-1074.

Telephone: (617) 565-6066.

KERMAN, David D. *(First Justice, Trial Court of Massachusetts Housing Court Department Northeastern Division)* Appointed by Governor Michael S. Dukakis to term beginning Dec 3, 1990. Term expires at age seventy. Born Durham North Carolina Jan 8, 1944. Educated at Duke University B.A. 1965 and Syracuse University J.D. 1970. Admitted to practice New York 1971, Massachusetts 1972, U.S. District Courts Northern District of New York 1971 and District of Massachusetts 1972, U.S. Courts of Appeals Second 1971 and First 1977 Circuits and U.S. Supreme Court 1977.

Executive Director Neighborhood Legal Services, Inc. 1973-90. Adjunct Faculty Hofstra University Law School since 1985. Member Lawrence, Lynn, Essex County, Massachusetts and American Bar Associations. Faculty Member National Institute for Trial Advocacy since 1985 and Massachusetts Continuing Legal Education, Inc. since 1985.

Mailing address: 24 New Chardon Street, Boston 02114.

Telephone: (617) 788-8483.

KERN, Leila R. *(Associate Justice, Trial Court of Massachusetts Superior Court Department)* Appointed by governor.

Office: U.S. Post Office and Courthouse, 90 Devonshire Street, Fifteenth Floor, Boston 02109.

Telephone: (617) 788-8130.

KILMARTIN, Peter J. *(First Justice, Trial Court of Massachusetts District Court Department Middlesex County Ayer Division)* Appointed by Governor Michael S. Dukakis Nov 1, 1989 to term beginning Jan 29, 1990. Term expires at age seventy. Born Illinois 1945. Educated at Seton Hall University B.S. with honors 1967 and Boston College Law School J.D. 1970. Admitted to practice Massachusetts 1970 and U.S. District Court District of Massachusetts. In legal practice Bedford 1974-89.

U.S. Army JAGC 1971-74. Colonel USAR JAGC (retired).

Mailing address: Two Center Plaza, Suite 200, Boston 02108.

Telephone: (617) 788-8810.

KING, Ronald W. *(Associate Justice, Trial Court of Massachusetts Probate and Family Court Department Worcester County Division)* Appointed by governor.

Mailing address: Two Center Plaza, Suite 210, Boston 02108.

Telephone: (617) 788-6600.

KLEIN, Dyanne J. *(First Justice, Trial Court of Massachusetts District Court Department Middlesex County Newton Division)* Appointed by governor.

Mailing address: Two Center Plaza, Suite 200, Boston 02108.

Telephone: (617) 788-8810.

KLUBOCK, Daniel *(Circuit Justice, Trial Court of Massachusetts District Court Department)* Appointed by governor.

Office: Two Center Plaza, Suite 200, Boston 02108.

Telephone: (617) 788-8810.

KOENIGS, Rita *(Justice, Trial Court of Massachusetts District Court Department Berkshire County Pittsfield Division)* Appointed by governor.

Mailing address: Two Center Plaza, Suite 200, Boston 02108.

Telephone: (617) 788-8810.

KOPELMAN, David H. *(First Justice, Trial Court of Massachusetts Probate and Family Court Department Norfolk County Division)* Appointed by Governor Edward S. King to term beginning Jan 31, 1981. Term expires at age seventy. Born Cambridge Massachusetts Sept 23, 1938. Educated at Harvard University A.B. 1960 J.D. 1964. Admitted to practice Massachusetts 1964. In legal practice Boston 1964-80.

Member Boston and Massachusetts Bar Associations. USAR 1961-67.

Office: 649 High Street, Dedham 02026.

Telephone: (781) 326-9255.

KOTTMYER, Diane M. *(Associate Justice, Trial Court of Massachusetts Superior Court Department)* Appointed by governor.

Office: U.S. Post Office and Courthouse, 90 Devonshire Street, Fifteenth Floor, Boston 02109.

Telephone: (617) 788-8130.

KUMOR, Robert F., Jr. *(First Justice, Trial Court of Massachusetts District Court Department Hampden County Springfield Division and Justice, Holyoke Division)* Appointed by governor.

Mailing address: Two Center Plaza, Suite 200, Boston 02108.

Telephone: (617) 788-8810.

KYRIAKAKIS, Manuel *(Chief Justice, Trial Court of Massachusetts Housing Court Department and First Justice Boston Division)* Appointed by Governor Michael S. Dukakis to term beginning Aug 30, 1990. Term expires at age seventy. Chief Justice since May 2002. Born Brooklyn New York Jan 1, 1936. Greek Orthodox.

KYRIAKAKIS, MANUEL—*Continued*

Educated at Brown University A.B. and Boston University School of Law LL.B. and LL.M. in Taxation. Admitted to practice Massachusetts 1961, Rhode Island 1961, U.S. District Court 1962 and U.S. Supreme Court 1962. In legal practice Franklin Massachusetts 1964-67.

Town Counsel Town of Somerset 1982-90. General Counsel Fall River Housing Authority 1984-90. Faculty Massachusetts Continuing Legal Education 1991-92. Member Fall River, Massachusetts, Rhode Island and American Bar Associations. Recipient Brown Cub Award. Named Outstanding Graduate from Brown University 1958. Captain USAF JAG 1961-64. Political affiliation: Independent. Enjoys reading and skiing.

Office: 24 New Chardon Street, Boston 02114.

Telephone: (617) 788-8483.

LANGLOIS, Robert W. *(Associate Justice, Trial Court of Massachusetts Probate and Family Court Department Norfolk County Division)* Appointed by governor.

Mailing address: Two Center Plaza, Suite 210, Boston 02108.

Telephone: (617) 788-6600.

LAPOINTE, Edward J. *(First Justice, Trial Court of Massachusetts Probate and Family Court Department Berkshire County Division)* Appointed by governor.

Mailing address: Two Center Plaza, Suite 210, Boston 02108.

Telephone: (617) 788-6600.

LaSTAITI, Elizabeth O'Neill *(First Justice, Trial Court of Massachusetts Probate and Family Court Department Bristol County Division)* Appointed by Governor Michael S. Dukakis to term beginning April 11, 1988. Term expires at age seventy. Born New Bedford, Massachusetts Jan 27, 1943. Roman Catholic. Educated at George Washington University B.A. with honors 1964 and Boston College Law School J.D. magna cum laude 1968. Staff member Boston College Commercial & Industrial Law Review 1966-68. Law Clerk to Hon. Andrew A. Caffrey, U.S. District Court District of Massachusetts 1968-69. Member Order of the Coif. Admitted to practice Massachusetts 1968 and U.S. District Court District of Massachusetts 1969. In legal practice New Bedford 1970-88.

Fellow Massachusetts Bar Foundation. Member Massachusetts Judges Conference, National Association of Women Judges and Massachusetts Bar Association. Chairman Board of Trustees St. Luke's Hospital 1987-90. Director I. H. Schwartz Rehabilitation Center. Trustee Southern New England School of Law.

Office: 505 Pleasant Street, New Bedford 02740.

Telephone: (508) 999-5249.

LAURANZANO, Michael C. *(Justice, Trial Court of Massachusetts District Court Department Essex County Salem Division)* Appointed by governor.

Mailing address: Two Center Plaza, Suite 200, Boston 02108.

Telephone: (617) 788-8810.

LAURENCE, Kenneth *(Associate Justice, Massachusetts Appeals Court)* Appointed by Governor Michael S. Dukakis to term beginning Dec 17, 1990. Term expires at age seventy. Born Sydney Australia April 11, 1937. Educated at Harvard University B.A. magna cum laude 1958 LL.B. cum laude 1962, London School of Economics and Political Science Certificate 1959 and Oxford University Linacre College Matr. 1962. Admitted to practice New York 1963, Maine 1964, Massachusetts 1970, U.S. District Courts District of Maine 1964, Southern District of New York 1966 and District of Massachusetts 1970, U.S. Supreme Court 1984 and U.S. Courts of Appeals First and Second Circuits. In legal practice Portland Maine 1964-65, New York New York 1965-68 and Boston Massachusetts 1969-90.

Editor *The Legal Papers of Daniel Webster* Dartmouth College 1968-70 and *Ethical Lawyering in Massachusetts* Massachusetts CLE 1992, 1997 and 2002. Co-author "Putting the Public Trust Doctrine to Work" U.S. National Oceanic and Atmospheric Administration 1990 and *The Public Trust Doctrine and the Management of America's Coasts* University of Massachusetts Press 1994. Charles Warren Fellow in American Legal History Harvard Law School 1968-70. Member The American Law Institute, Boston, Massachusetts and American Bar Associations. Instructor in Antitrust and Health Care ALI-ABA 1983-92 and Legal Ethics and Appellate Practice Boston Bar Association and Massachusetts CLE since 1987.

Office: 1500 New Courthouse, Boston 02108.

Telephone: (617) 725-8087.

LAURIAT, Peter M. *(Associate Justice, Trial Court of Massachusetts Superior Court Department)* Appointed by Governor Michael S. Dukakis to term beginning 1989. Educated at Middlebury College B.A. with honors 1968 and University of Chicago Law School J.D. 1971. In legal practice Boston for 17 years.

Co-author Volume 49 *Discovery* Massachusetts Practice Series. Editor and Contributor *Massachusetts Jury Trial Benchbook, Jury Trial Innovations in Massachusetts* and *Massachusetts Deposition Practice Manual.* Author and Lecturer on Litigation and Jury Trial Issues and Techniques. Instructor Harvard Law School and Stanford Law School. Member Jury Management Advisory Committee Massachusetts Supreme Judicial Court. Instructor The National Judicial College.

Office: U.S. Post Office and Courthouse, 90 Devonshire Street, Fifteenth Floor, Boston 02109.

Telephone: (617) 788-8130.

LAWTON, Mark Edward *(Associate Justice, Trial Court of Massachusetts Juvenile Court Department Suffolk County Division)* Appointed by Governor Edward J. King Jan 7, 1983. Term expires at age seventy. Born Boston Massachusetts July 26, 1949. Catholic. Educated at Stonehill College A.B. 1971 and New England School of Law J.D. 1974.
1975 and U.S. Dist
1976. Began legal p

Adjunct Professor
Law 1985-2002. Me
resentatives 1975-83.
Massachusetts Bar A
Award from Parents
Public Service Awar
tion 1993. Founder B
opment Council 1977
1991. Massachusetts
on Families 1980. En

Mailing address: P.

Office: 24 New
02114.

Telephone: (617) 78

LEARY, George F. *(Associate Justice, Trial Court of Massachusetts Juvenile Court Department Worcester Division)* Appointed by governor. Former First Justice.
Mailing address: P.O. Box 9664, Boston 02114-9664.
Office: Three Center Plaza, Suite 520, Boston 02108.
Telephone: (617) 788-6550.

LEARY, Paul K. *(Justice, Trial Court of Massachusetts District Court Department Norfolk County Brookline Division)* Appointed by governor.
Mailing address: Two Center Plaza, Suite 200, Boston 02108.
Telephone: (617) 788-8810.

LENK, Barbara A. *(Associate Justice, Massachusetts Appeals Court)* Appointed by Governor William F. Weld to term beginning 1995. Term expires at age seventy. Born Queens New York Dec 2, 1950. Educated at Fordham University B.A. magna cum laude 1972, Yale University Ph.D. 1978 and Harvard University J.D. 1979. In legal practice Boston 1979-93. Former Associate Justice, Trial Court of Massachusetts Superior Court Department, appointed by Governor William F. Weld.
Office: 1500 New Courthouse, Boston 02108.
Telephone: (617) 725-8085.

LEROY, Jacques C. *(Justice, Trial Court of Massachusetts District Court Department Hampden County Springfield Division)* Appointed by governor.
Mailing address: Two Center Plaza, Suite 200, Boston 02108.
Telephone: (617) 788-8810.

LEWIS, Paul D. *(First Justice, Trial Court of Massachusetts Juvenile Court Department Suffolk County Division)* Appointed by governor.
Mailing address: P.O. Box 9663, Boston 02114.
Office: 24 New Chardon Street, Floor 5, Boston 02114.
Telephone: (617) 788-8542.

LIAN, Joseph, Jr. *(First Justice, Trial Court of Massachusetts Probate and Family Court Department Worcester County Division)* Appointed by governor.
Mailing address: Two Center Plaza, Suite 210, Boston 02108.
Telephone: (617) 788-6600.

LIMON, Stephen M. *(Associate Justice, Trial Court of Massachusetts Juvenile Court Department Suffolk County Division)* Appointed by Governor William F. Weld to term beginning Aug 1994. Educated at Middlebury College A.B. 1968 and Boston College Law School J.D. 1973. Admitted to practice Massachusetts 1974, U.S. District Court District of Massachusetts 1975, U.S. Court of Appeals First Circuit 1981 and U.S. Supreme Court 1982.

Litigation Attorney Massachusetts Defenders Committee Aug 1973 to May 1976. Courts Specialist Massachusetts Committee on Criminal Justice May 1976 to March [illegible]979. Executive Secretary Commission on Judicial Con[illegible]ct March 1979 to April 1980. Assistant Attorney Gen[illegible] Department of the Attorney General April 1980 to [illegible]983. Deputy Chief Criminal Bureau Middlesex [illegible]istrict Attorney's Office Jan 1983 to Jan 1991. [illegible]sel to Attorney General Jan 1991 to 1994. [illegible]*husetts Juvenile Court Benchbook* MCLE [illegible]d *Massachusetts Juvenile Law Source-* [illegible] Adjunct Professor "Children and the [illegible]School of Law since 2001. Member Crimes and Punishments Task Force Special Study Commission on the Equal Rights Amendment 1976, District Court Special Committee on Alternative Methods of Dispute Resolution 1978-79, Mental Health Legal Advisors Committee 1979-81, Governor's Juvenile Justice Advisory Committee 1984-90, Criminal History Systems Board 1988-90, Urban District Court Committee Boston Bar Association 1989 and Judiciary/Media Committee Massachusetts Supreme Judicial Court since 2000. Member Massachusetts Bar Association (Committee on Bar Admissions 1988-90). Faculty Member Program on Juvenile Law 1977, program for prosecutors 1987 and "Hot Evidentiary Issues in Care and Protection Cases" Juvenile Law Conference Oct 1999 Massachusetts Continuing Legal Education and "Stranger and Nonstranger Sexual Assault" Judicial Institute Conference March 1999. Faculty and Student Advisor Trial Advocacy Workshop 1983-94 and Instructor "Lawyering Process: Criminal Prosecution" 1988-94 Harvard Law School. Board of Directors Boston College Legal Assistance Bureau 1971-73 and Marblehead Festival of Arts 1984. Judge/Critiquer National Mock Trial New England Regional Competition 1983-84 and Boston College Law School Competition 1983-89. Member Peabody Museum of Salem, Marblehead Arts Association, House of Seven Gables Settlement Society and Corinthian Yacht Club.
Office: Courthouse, 24 New Chardon Street, Boston 02114-4703.
Telephone: (617) 788-8542.

LINDSAY, Reginald C. *(Judge, United States District Court District of Massachusetts)* Appointed for life by President Bill Clinton to term beginning Jan 5, 1994. Born Birmingham Alabama March 19, 1945. Educated at Morehouse College A.B. magna cum laude 1967, University of Valencia, Spain Certificate 1966 and Harvard Law School J.D. 1970. Member Phi Beta Kappa and Pi Sigma Alpha. Admitted to practice Massachusetts 1970, U.S. District Court District of Massachusetts 1971 and U.S. Court of Appeals First Circuit 1971. In legal practice Boston 1970-93.

Important Decisions: Masonoff, et al. v. Dubois, et al. 899 F. Supp. 782 D. Mass. 1995; Chapin v. University of Massachusetts 977 F. Supp. 72 D. Mass. 1997; and Wampanoaq Tribe of Gay Head v. Massachusetts Commission Against Discrimination 63 F. Supp. 2d 119 D. Mass. 1999. Chair Task Force on Juvenile Justice 1992-93. Former Member Massachusetts Commission on Judicial Conduct. Member Boston, Massachusetts, National and American Bar Associations. Attended seminars The American Law Institute and American Bar Foundation. Recipient Ruffin-Fenwick Trailblazer Award from Harvard Black Law Students Association 1994, Amanda V. Houston Community Service Award from Boston College 1998, Citation of Judicial Excellence from Boston Bar Association 1999 and Frederick E. Berry Expanding Independence Award from Easter Seals 1999. Commissioner Massachusetts Department of Public Utilities 1975-77. Board of Directors Morgan Memorial Goodwill Industries, Inc. Member and President Board of Directors Partners for Youths with Disabilities, Inc. Trustee Newton-Wellesley Hospital. Board of Governors The Downtown Club.
Office: 5130 U.S. Courthouse, One Courthouse Way, Boston 02210-3002.
Telephone: (617) 748-4829.

LIVINGSTONE, Michael J. *(Associate Justice, Trial Court of Massachusetts Probate and Family Court Department Plymouth County Division)* Appointed by governor.

Mailing address: Two Center Plaza, Suite 210, Boston 02108.

Telephone: (617) 788-6600.

LOCKE, David B. *(Justice, Trial Court of Massachusetts District Court Department Worcester County Gardner Division)* Appointed by governor.

Mailing address: Two Center Plaza, Suite 200, Boston 02108.

Telephone: (617) 788-8810.

LOCKE, Jeffrey A. *(Associate Justice, Trial Court of Massachusetts Superior Court Department)* Appointed by governor.

Office: U.S. Post Office and Courthouse, 90 Devonshire Street, Fifteenth Floor, Boston 02109.

Telephone: (617) 788-8130.

LOCKE, Judith A. *(Circuit Justice, Trial Court of Massachusetts Juvenile Court Department)* Appointed by governor.

Mailing address: P.O. Box 9664, Boston 02114-9664.
Office: Three Center Plaza, Suite 520, Boston 02108.
Telephone: (617) 788-6550.

LoCONTO, Paul F. *(First Justice, Trial Court of Massachusetts District Court Department Worcester County Fitchburg Division and Justice, East Brookfield Division)* Appointed by Governor Michael S. Dukakis to term beginning Dec 20, 1985. Term expires at age seventy. Currently serves as Regional Administrative Justice Region IV. Born Worcester Massachusetts Aug 21, 1947. Roman Catholic. Educated at Boston College B.S. 1969, Suffolk University Law School J.D. 1974 and Boston University School of Law LL.M. 1980. Admitted to practice Massachusetts 1975.

Member Boston, Worcester County and Massachusetts Bar Associations. Massachusetts National Guard 1969-75.

Mailing address: Two Center Plaza, Suite 200, Boston 02108.

Telephone: (617) 788-8810.

LOMBARDI, Leon J. *(Justice, Trial Court of Massachusetts Land Court Department)* Appointed by governor.

Office: 24 New Chardon Street, Boston 02114.
Telephone: (617) 788-7470.

LOPEZ, Maria I. *(Associate Justice, Trial Court of Massachusetts Superior Court Department)* Appointed by Governor William F. Weld 1993. Justice, Trial Court of Massachusetts District Court Department Suffolk County Chelsea Division 1988-93.

Office: U.S. Post Office and Courthouse, 90 Devonshire Street, Fifteenth Floor, Boston 02109.

Telephone: (617) 788-8130.

LOSAPIO, Paul A. *(First Justice, Trial Court of Massachusetts District Court Department Worcester County Uxbridge Division and Justice, Hampshire County Ware Division)* Appointed by governor.

Mailing address: Two Center Plaza, Suite 200, Boston 02108.

Telephone: (617) 788-8810.

LOWY, David A. *(Associate Justice, Trial Court of Massachusetts Superior Court Department)* Appointed by governor. Term expires at age seventy. Born Boston Massachusetts Feb 3, 1960. Jewish. Educated at University of Massachusetts at Amherst B.A. cum laude 1983 and Boston University School of Law J.D. magna cum laude 1987. Law Clerk to Hon. Edward F. Harrington, U.S. District Court District of Massachusetts 1988-89. Member Phi Beta Kappa. Admitted to practice Massachusetts 1987 and U.S. District Court District of Massachusetts 1988. In legal practice Boston 1987 and 1989-90. Former Justice, Trial Court of Massachusetts District Court Department Essex County Ipswich Division, appointed by Governor Argeo Paul Cellucci to term beginning Sept 12, 1997.

Assistant District Attorney Essex County 1990-92 and Suffolk County 1995-97. Adjunct Professor Criminal Procedures New England School of Law since 1991 and Suffolk University Law School since 1997. Member Massachusetts Bar Association.

Office: U.S. Post Office and Courthouse, 90 Devonshire Street, Fifteenth Floor, Boston 02109.

Telephone: (617) 788-8130.

LU, John T. *(Associate Justice, Trial Court of Massachusetts Boston Municipal Court Department)* Appointed by governor. Educated at Johns Hopkins University and Boston University J.D.

Office: U.S. Post Office and Courthouse, 90 Devonshire Street, Boston 02109.

Telephone: (617) 788-8700.

LYNCH, Joan E. *(Justice, Trial Court of Massachusetts District Court Department Barnstable County Barnstable Division)* Appointed by governor.

Mailing address: Two Center Plaza, Suite 200, Boston 02108.

Telephone: (617) 788-8810.

LYONS, Marie E. *(Associate Justice, Trial Court of Massachusetts Probate and Family Court Department Hampden County Division)* Appointed by governor.

Mailing address: Two Center Plaza, Suite 210, Boston 02108.

Telephone: (617) 788-6600.

MacLEOD, Bonnie H. *(Associate Justice, Trial Court of Massachusetts Superior Court Department)* Appointed by governor. Former Justice, Trial Court of Massachusetts District Court Department Middlesex County Cambridge Division.

Office: U.S. Post Office and Courthouse, 90 Devonshire Street, Fifteenth Floor, Boston 02109.

Telephone: (617) 788-8130.

MACY, Joseph I. *(Justice, Trial Court of Massachusetts District Court Department Bristol County Taunton Division)* Appointed by governor.

Mailing address: Two Center Plaza, Suite 200, Boston 02108.

Telephone: (617) 788-8810.

MAHONEY, Paul F. *(First Justice, T Massachusetts District Court Department S East Boston Division and Justice, Midc Malden Division)* Appointed by governor.

Mailing address: Two Center Plaza, Suit 02108.

Telephone: (617) 788-8810.

MALDONADO, Diana L. *(Acting First Justice, Trial Court of Massachusetts District Court Department Norfolk County Dedham Division and Justice, Suffolk County Chelsea Division)* Appointed by governor.
Mailing address: Two Center Plaza, Suite 200, Boston 02108.
Telephone: (617) 788-8810.

MANDELL, Andrew L. *(Justice, Trial Court of Massachusetts District Court Department Worcester County Fitchburg Division)* Appointed by Governor Argeo Paul Cellucci. Educated at Suffolk University J.D. 1973.
Mailing address: Two Center Plaza, Suite 200, Boston 02108.
Telephone: (617) 788-8810.

MANZI, Mary McCauley *(Associate Justice, Trial Court of Massachusetts Probate and Family Court Department Essex County Division)* Appointed by governor.
Mailing address: Two Center Plaza, Suite 210, Boston 02108.
Telephone: (617) 788-6600.

MARINI, Francis L. *(Justice, Trial Court of Massachusetts District Court Department Plymouth County Hingham Division)* Appointed by governor.
Mailing address: Two Center Plaza, Suite 200, Boston 02108.
Telephone: (617) 788-8810.

MARSHALL, Margaret H. *(Chief Justice, Massachusetts Supreme Judicial Court)* Appointed by Governor William F. Weld to term beginning Nov 1996. Chief Justice since Oct 14, 1999. Born South Africa. Educated at University of the Witwatersrand, South Africa 1966, Harvard University Master's Degree and Yale Law School J.D.
President National Union of South African Students 1966-68. Former Vice President and General Counsel Harvard University.
Office: 1300 New Courthouse, Boston 02108.
Telephone: (617) 557-1000.

MARTIN, Gordon A., Jr. *(Justice, Trial Court of Massachusetts District Court Department Suffolk County Roxbury Division)* Appointed by governor.
Mailing address: Two Center Plaza, Suite 200, Boston 02108.
Telephone: (617) 788-8810.

MASON, John H. *(Associate Justice, Massachusetts Appeals Court)* Appointed by governor.
Office: 1500 New Courthouse, Boston 02108.
Telephone: (617) 725-8106.

MAY, Thomas J. *(First Justice, Trial Court of Massachusetts District Court Department Norfolk County Brookline Division and Justice, Suffolk County East Boston Division)* Appointed by governor.
Mailing address: Two Center Plaza, Suite 200, Boston 02108.
Telephone: (617) 788-8810.

MAZZONE, A. David *(Senior Judge, United States District Court District of Massachusetts)* Appointed for life by President Jimmy Carter to term beginning March 3, 1978. Assumed Senior status, serves by assignment. Born Everett Massachusetts June 3, 1928. Catholic. Educated at Harvard University B.A. 1950 and DePaul University J.D. 1957. Admitted to practice Illinois 1957, Massachusetts 1959, U.S. District Courts District of Massachusetts 1961 and District of Columbia 1965, U.S. Customs Court 1965, U.S. Courts of Appeals First 1961 and District of Columbia 1972 Circuits and U.S. Supreme Court 1972. Began legal practice Oak Park Illinois 1958. In legal practice Wakefield 1959-61 and Boston 1961-75 Massachusetts. Associate Justice, Superior Court of Massachusetts 1975-78.
Assistant District Attorney Middlesex County 1961. Assistant U.S. Attorney District of Massachusetts 1961-65. Instructor New England School of Law 1963-77, Suffolk University Law School 1974-77, Boston College Law School 1975-77 and Institute of Politics John F. Kennedy School of Government Harvard University since 1977. Board of Directors Federal Judicial Center Washington D.C. Member Sentencing Commission since 1990 and Federal Jurisdiction Subcommittee U.S. Courts. Member Massachusetts Trial Lawyers Association, The American Law Institute, Boston, Middlesex County, Massachusetts and Federal Bar Associations. Staff Sergeant U.S. Army 1951-52. Chairman Wakefield Democratic Town Committee. Trustee Lucius Beebe Memorial.
Office: 5730 U.S. Courthouse, One Courthouse Way, Boston 02210-3002.
Telephone: (617) 748-9107.

McCALLUM, Mary M. *(First Justice, Trial Court of Massachusetts Juvenile Court Department Norfolk County Division)* Appointed by Governor William F. Weld.
Mailing address: P.O. Box 9664, Boston 02114-9664.
Office: Three Center Plaza, Suite 520, Boston 02108.
Telephone: (617) 788-6550.

McCALLUM, Paul J. *(Justice, Trial Court of Massachusetts District Court Department Bristol County Attleboro Division)* Appointed by governor.
Mailing address: Two Center Plaza, Suite 200, Boston 02108.
Telephone: (617) 788-8810.

McCANN, John S. *(Associate Justice, Trial Court of Massachusetts Superior Court Department)* Appointed by Governor Argeo Paul Cellucci July 20, 2000. Term expires at age seventy. Born Worcester Massachusetts June 20, 1940. Roman Catholic. Educated at College of the Holy Cross B.S. 1963 and Vanderbilt University School of Law J.D. 1966. Admitted to practice Massachusetts 1966, California 1968, U.S. District Courts District of Massachusetts 1966, District of California 1969, District of Rhode Island 1979 and District of Maine 1991, U.S. Courts of Appeals First Circuit 1966 and Ninth Circuit 1968 and U.S. Supreme Court 1984. In legal practice Worcester Massachusetts 1966-67 and 1970-90 and Westborough Massachusetts 1990-93 and San Francisco California 1967-70. Justice, Trial Court of Massachusetts District Court Department Worcester County Westborough Division 1993-2000, appointed by Governor William F. Weld.
Author *Worcester County Lawyers Emergency Assistance Plan* Worcester County Bar Association 1982 and "The Attorney's Lien in Massachusetts" 69 Massachusetts L. Rev. June 1984. Instructor in Business Law Assumption College 1982-86. Member Children and the Law and the Family Committee 1992-94 and Worcester County Bench and Bar Committee 1995. Co-founder American Affiliation of Family Courts of Massachusetts 1993. Fellow American Bar Foundation. Member Worcester County Bar Foundation (Vice President 1990-

MCCANN, JOHN S.—*Continued*

91, President 1991-92), Worcester County Bar Advocates (Board of Directors), St. Thomas More Society, Massachusetts Judges Conference, World Jurist Association, State Bar of California, Worcester County (President Elect, Reduced Fee Panel Member), Massachusetts (Reduced Fee Panel Member) and American Bar Associations. Faculty Member Massachusetts CLE 1991-92. Recipient St. Thomas More Distinguished Jurist Award 2001. Trustee Worcester County Law Library since 1991. Member Massachusetts Supreme Judicial Court Historical Society. Former Member Board of Directors Holy Cross College Class of 1963 Foundation. Former Incorporator and Former Trustee The Bridge of Central Massachusetts. Former Member Parish Council Saint Luke the Evangelist Church. Former Member Westborough Chamber of Commerce, Westborough Human Rights Council, Town of Westborough Capital Expenditures Committee, Holy Cross Club of Greater Worcester, Lawyers Against Nuclear Arms and Amnesty International USA.

Office: Two Main Street, Worcester 01608.
Telephone: (508) 770-1899.
E-mail address: JohMcCn@netscape.net

McDONALD, C. Brian *(Associate Justice, Trial Court of Massachusetts Superior Court Department)* Appointed by governor.
Office: U.S. Post Office and Courthouse, 90 Devonshire Street, Fifteenth Floor, Boston 02109.
Telephone: (617) 788-8130.

McDONOUGH, William B. *(First Justice, Trial Court of Massachusetts District Court Department Hampden County Holyoke Division)* Appointed by governor.
Mailing address: Two Center Plaza, Suite 200, Boston 02108.
Telephone: (617) 788-8810.

McELROY, James B. *(First Justice, Trial Court of Massachusetts District Court Department Berkshire County Southern Berkshire Division)* Appointed by Governor William F. Weld.
Mailing address: Two Center Plaza, Suite 200, Boston 02108.
Telephone: (617) 788-8810.

McEVOY, Christine M. *(Associate Justice, Trial Court of Massachusetts Superior Court Department)* Appointed by governor. Former Justice, Trial Court of Massachusetts District Court Department Middlesex County Concord Division.
Office: U.S. Post Office and Courthouse, 90 Devonshire Street, Fifteenth Floor, Boston 02109.
Telephone: (617) 788-8130.

McGILL, Paul L. *(Justice, Trial Court of Massachusetts District Court Department Suffolk County Roxbury Division)* Appointed by Governor Michael S. Dukakis to term beginning Nov 19, 1990. Term expires at age seventy. Former Circuit Justice. Born Pittsburgh Pennsylvania May 25, 1951. Educated at Harvard College B.A. 1975 and Northeastern University School of Law J.D. 1981. Admitted to practice Massachusetts 1981, U.S. District Court District of Massachusetts, U.S. Court of Appeals First Circuit and U.S. Supreme Court. In legal practice Boston 1981-90.
Mailing address: Two Center Plaza, Suite 200, Boston 02108.
Telephone: (617) 788-8810.

McGREGOR, Prudence M. *(Associate Justice, Trial Court of Massachusetts Probate and Family Court Department Bristol County Division)* Appointed by governor.
Mailing address: Two Center Plaza, Suite 210, Boston 02108.
Telephone: (617) 788-6600.

McGUINNESS, James H., Jr. *(Justice, Trial Court of Massachusetts District Court Department Middlesex County Natick Division)* Appointed by governor.
Mailing address: Two Center Plaza, Suite 200, Boston 02108.
Telephone: (617) 788-8810.

McHUGH, James F. *(Associate Justice, Massachusetts Appeals Court)* Appointed by governor. Former Associate Justice, Trial Court of Massachusetts Superior Court Department, appointed by Governor Michael S. Dukakis to term beginning 1985.
Office: 1500 New Courthouse, Boston 02108.
Telephone: (617) 725-8106.

McKENNA, Robert J., Jr. *(First Justice, Trial Court of Massachusetts District Court Department Middlesex County Concord Division and Justice, Suffolk County South Boston Division)* Appointed by governor.
Mailing address: Two Center Plaza, Suite 200, Boston 02108.
Telephone: (617) 788-8810.

McLAUGHLIN, David A. *(Associate Justice, Trial Court of Massachusetts Superior Court Department)* Appointed by governor.
Office: U.S. Post Office and Courthouse, 90 Devonshire Street, Fifteenth Floor, Boston 02109.
Telephone: (617) 788-8130.

McSWEENY, William F., III *(Associate Justice, Trial Court of Massachusetts Probate and Family Court Department Middlesex County Division)* Appointed by governor.
Mailing address: Two Center Plaza, Suite 210, Boston 02108.
Telephone: (617) 788-6600.

MEAGHER, Dermot *(Associate Justice, Trial Court of Massachusetts Boston Municipal Court Department)* Appointed by Governor Michael S. Dukakis to term beginning May 3, 1989. Term expires at age seventy. Born Worcester Massachusetts Oct 19, 1940. Educated at Harvard University A.B. 1962 M.P.A. 1983 and Boston College Law School LL.B. 1965. Admitted Massachusetts 1966 and U.S. District Cour Massachusetts 1969.
Fellow Harvard Law School Center for tice 1971.
Office: U.S. Post Office and Courthous shire Street, Boston 02109.
Telephone: (617) 788-8700.

MELAHN, William E. *(Justice, Trial Court of Massachusetts District Court Department Essex County Newburyport Division)* Appointed by governor.
Mailing address: Two Center Plaza, Suite 200, Boston 02108.
Telephone: (617) 788-8810.

MENNO, James V. *(Associate Justice, Trial Court of Massachusetts Probate and Family Court Department Plymouth County Division)* Appointed by governor.
Mailing address: Two Center Plaza, Suite 210, Boston 02108.
Telephone: (617) 788-6600.

MERRICK, Brian R. *(Circuit Justice, Trial Court of Massachusetts District Court Department)* Appointed by governor.
Office: Two Center Plaza, Suite 200, Boston 02108.
Telephone: (617) 788-8810.

MERRILL, E. Chouteau *(Circuit Justice, Trial Court of Massachusetts Probate and Family Court Department)* Appointed by governor.
Office: Two Center Plaza, Suite 210, Boston 02108.
Telephone: (617) 788-6600.

MILLER, Rosalind H. *(Justice, Trial Court of Massachusetts District Court Department Suffolk County Dorchester Division)* Appointed by governor.
Mailing address: Two Center Plaza, Suite 200, Boston 02108.
Telephone: (617) 788-8810.

MILLS, David A. *(Associate Justice, Massachusetts Appeals Court)* Appointed by governor.
Office: 1500 New Courthouse, Boston 02108.
Telephone: (617) 725-8106.

MINEHAN, Rosemary B. *(First Justice, Trial Court of Massachusetts District Court Department Plymouth County Wareham Division and Justice, Plymouth Division)* Appointed by governor.
Mailing address: Two Center Plaza, Suite 200, Boston 02108.
Telephone: (617) 788-8810.

MIRANDA, Lillian *(First Justice, Trial Court of Massachusetts Juvenile Court Department Franklin/Hampshire Counties Division)* Appointed by governor.
Mailing address: P.O. Box 9664, Boston 02114-9664.
Office: Three Center Plaza, Suite 520, Boston 02108.
Telephone: (617) 788-6550.

MOONEY, Toby S. *(Justice, Trial Court of Massachusetts District Court Department Bristol County New Bedford Division)* Appointed by governor.
Mailing address: Two Center Plaza, Suite 200, Boston 02108.
Telephone: (617) 788-8810.

MORI, Richard A. *(First Justice, Trial Court of Massachusetts District Court Department Essex County Gloucester Division and Justice, Middlesex County Malden Division)* Appointed by governor.
Mailing address: Two Center Plaza, Suite 200, Boston 02108.
Telephone: (617) 788-8810.

MORIARTY, Diane E. *(Justice, Trial Court of Massachusetts District Court Department Plymouth County Wareham Division)* Appointed by governor.
Mailing address: Two Center Plaza, Suite 200, Boston 02108.
Telephone: (617) 788-8810.

MORIARTY, Elaine M. *(Associate Justice, Trial Court of Massachusetts Probate and Family Court Department Suffolk County Division)* Appointed by governor. Former First Justice.
Mailing address: Two Center Plaza, Suite 210, Boston 02108.
Telephone: (617) 788-6600.

MOSES, Richard T. *(Associate Justice, Trial Court of Massachusetts Superior Court Department)* Appointed by governor.
Office: U.S. Post Office and Courthouse, 90 Devonshire Street, Fifteenth Floor, Boston 02109.
Telephone: (617) 788-8130.

MOYNAHAN, Ronald F. *(Justice, Trial Court of Massachusetts District Court Department Bristol County New Bedford Division)* Appointed by governor.
Mailing address: Two Center Plaza, Suite 200, Boston 02108.
Telephone: (617) 788-8810.

MULLIGAN, Robert A. *(Associate Justice, Trial Court of Massachusetts Superior Court Department)* Appointed by governor. Former Chief Justice.
Office: U.S. Post Office and Courthouse, 90 Devonshire Street, Fifteenth Floor, Boston 02109.
Telephone: (617) 788-8130.

MURPHY, Ernest B. *(Associate Justice, Trial Court of Massachusetts Superior Court Department)* Appointed by governor.
Office: U.S. Post Office and Courthouse, 90 Devonshire Street, Fifteenth Floor, Boston 02109.
Telephone: (617) 788-8130.

MURRAY, Robert F. *(First Justice, Trial Court of Massachusetts Juvenile Court Department Plymouth County Division)* Appointed by governor.
Mailing address: P.O. Box 9664, Boston 02114-9664.
Office: Three Center Plaza, Suite 520, Boston 02108.
Telephone: (617) 788-6550.

MUSE, Christopher J. *(Associate Justice, Trial Court of Massachusetts Superior Court Department)* Appointed by governor.
Office: U.S. Post Office and Courthouse, 90 Devonshire Street, Fifteenth Floor, Boston 02109.
Telephone: (617) 788-8130.

NADEAU, Gilbert J., Jr. *(First Justice, Trial Court of Massachusetts District Court Department Bristol County Fall River Division)* Appointed by governor.
Mailing address: Two Center Plaza, Suite 200, Boston 02108.
Telephone: (617) 788-8810.

NAGLE, David G., Jr. *(First Justice, Trial Court of Massachusetts District Court Department Plymouth County Brockton Division)* Appointed by governor.
Mailing address: Two Center Plaza, Suite 200, Boston 02108.
Telephone: (617) 788-8810.

NAJEMY, Jan L. *(First Justice, Trial Court of Massachusetts Juvenile Court Department Worcester Division)* Appointed Associate Justice by governor.
Mailing address: P.O. Box 9664, Boston 02114-9664.
Office: Three Center Plaza, Suite 520, Boston 02108.
Telephone: (617) 788-6550.

NASIF, Kenneth P. *(Associate Justice, Trial Court of Massachusetts Juvenile Court Department Bristol County Division)* Appointed by Governor Edward J. King to term beginning Jan 6, 1983. Term expires at age seventy. Born Boston Massachusetts June 16, 1943. Roman Catholic. Educated at Northeastern University 1961-62 and Suffolk University B.S.B.A. 1966 J.D. 1969. Member Alpha Phi Omega. Admitted to practice Massachusetts 1969, U.S. District Court District of Massachusetts 1971, U.S. Court of Appeals First Circuit 1971, U.S. Tax Court 1974, U.S. Court of Military Appeals 1974, U.S. Court of Customs 1974, U.S. Claims Court 1974 and U.S. Supreme Court 1974. Began legal practice Boston 1969.
Constable City of Boston 1964-69. Assistant Regional Counsel U.S. Veterans Administration 1970-74. Assistant U.S. Attorney Department of Justice 1974-83. Author Land and Natural Resources Section *United States Attorneys' Manual* U.S. Department of Justice 1976. Important Decisions: Commonwealth v. William Dello Iacono (armed assault with intent to murder) 1983 and Commonwealth v. Charles J. Saia (attempted murder of police officer) 1983. Member American Judicature Society 1974-75, Massachusetts Judges Conference 1983-84, Boston, Massachusetts, Federal (Vice President 1983) and American Bar Associations. Instructor Attorney General's Advocacy Institute 1978. Previously worked as auxiliary police officer. Political affiliation: Independent. Interested in international events and improvement of judicial administration.
Mailing address: P.O. Box 9664, Boston 02114-9664.
Office: Three Center Plaza, Suite 520, Boston 02108.
Telephone: (617) 788-6550.

NECHTEM, Amy L. *(Associate Justice, Trial Court of Massachusetts Juvenile Court Department Middlesex County Division)* Appointed by governor.
Mailing address: P.O. Box 9664, Boston 02114-9664.
Office: Three Center Plaza, Suite 520, Boston 02108.
Telephone: (617) 788-6550.

NEEL, Stephen E. *(Associate Justice, Trial Court of Massachusetts Superior Court Department)* Appointed by governor.
Office: U.S. Post Office and Courthouse, 90 Devonshire Street, Fifteenth Floor, Boston 02109.
Telephone: (617) 788-8130.

NEIMAN, Kenneth P. *(Magistrate Judge, United States District Court District of Massachusetts)* Appointed by U.S. District Court judges to term beginning Jan 5, 1995. Reappointed Jan 2003, current term expires Jan 4, 2011. Born New York New York July 4, 1945. Jewish. Educated at Tufts University B.A. cum laude 1967 and Harvard Law School J.D. 1971. Admitted to practice New York 1972, Massachusetts 1974, U.S. District Court District of Massachusetts 1974, U.S. Supreme Court 1978 and U.S. Court of Appeals First Circuit 1981. In legal practice Northampton Massachusetts 1981-94.
With Center on Social Welfare Policy and Law 1971-73 and Western Massachusetts Legal Services 1973-81. Adjunct Faculty Marymount Manhattan College Spring 1973, University of Massachusetts Sept 1974 to Jan 1982, Smith College School for Social Work June 1976 to July 1981 and Western New England College School of Law Jan 1985 to June 1985 and since Jan 1998. Board Member Massachusetts Law Reform Institute Sept 1990 to Dec 1995. Member Massachusetts Bar Foundation. Member Hampshire County, Massachusetts (Access to Justice Council June 1992 to Sept 1995 and Member and Chair Committee on Public Service Responsibility Sept 1989 to Sept 1992) and American Bar Associations. Recipient Community Service Award for Outstanding Pro Bono Service from Massachusetts Bar Association March 7, 1990. Board Member Food Research and Action Center Dec 1978 to Nov 1982. Advisory Board Western Massachusetts Pro Bono Referral System April 1982 to Dec 1995.
Office: Federal Building, Fifth Floor, 1550 Main Street, Springfield 01103.
Telephone: (413) 785-0356.

NESI, Anthony R. *(Associate Justice, Trial Court of Massachusetts Probate and Family Court Department Bristol County Division)* Appointed by governor. Former Circuit Justice.
Mailing address: Two Center Plaza, Suite 210, Boston 02108.
Telephone: (617) 788-6600.

NEWMAN, Mark *(Associate Justice, Trial Court of Massachusetts Juvenile Court Department Essex County Division)* Appointed by governor.
Mailing address: P.O. Box 9664, Boston 02114-9664.
Office: Three Center Plaza, Suite 520, Boston 02108.
Telephone: (617) 788-6550.

NICKERSON, Gary A. *(Associate Justice, Trial Court of Massachusetts Superior Court Department)* Appointed by governor.
Office: U.S. Post Office and Courthouse, 90 Devonshire Street, Fifteenth Floor, Boston 02109.
Telephone: (617) 788-8130.

O'DEA, Kevin J. *(Justice, Trial Court of Massachusetts District Court Department Norfolk County Brookline Division)* Appointed by governor.
Mailing address: Two Center Plaza, Suite 200, Boston 02108.
Telephone: (617) 788-8810.

O'LEARY, James J. *(Justice, Trial Court of Massachusetts District Court Department Essex County Newburyport Division)* Appointed by governor.
Mailing address: Two Center Plaza, Suite 200, Boston 02108.
Telephone: (617) 788-8810.

O'MALLEY, Daniel W. *(Justice, Trial Court of Massachusetts District Court Department Norfolk County Wrentham Division)* Appointed by governor.
Mailing address: Two Center Plaza, Suite 200, Boston 02108.
Telephone: (617) 788-8810.

O'NEILL, W. James *(First Justice, Trial Court of Massachusetts District Court Department Nantucket*

O'NEILL, W. JAMES—*Continued*

County Nantucket Division) Appointed by Governor Michael S. Dukakis April 1987.

Mailing address: Two Center Plaza, Suite 200, Boston 02108.

Telephone: (617) 788-8810.

ORDOÑEZ, Angela M. *(First Justice, Trial Court of Massachusetts Probate and Family Court Department Nantucket County Division)* Appointed by governor.

Mailing address: P.O. Box 1116, Nantucket 02554.

Office: 16 Broad Street, Nantucket 02554.

Telephone: (508) 228-2669, 228-6852.

Fax: (508) 228-3662

ORFANELLO, Mary A. *(Justice, Trial Court of Massachusetts District Court Department Worcester County Milford Division)* Appointed by governor.

Mailing address: Two Center Plaza, Suite 200, Boston 02108.

Telephone: (617) 788-8810.

OSTRACH, Stephen S. *(Circuit Justice, Trial Court of Massachusetts District Court Department)* Appointed by Governor William F. Weld to term beginning June 5, 1997. Term expires at age seventy. Born New York New York 1947. Jewish. Educated at Massachusetts Institute of Technology S.B. 1968 and Harvard University J.D. 1974. Law Clerk to Hon. Frank Albert Kaufman, U.S. District Court District of Maryland 1974-75. Admitted to practice Ohio 1974, District of Columbia 1975 and Massachusetts 1980. In legal practice Cleveland Ohio 1974-75, Washington D.C. 1976-80 and Boston Massachusetts 1980-97.

Staff Attorney U.S. Nuclear Regulatory Commission 1976-80. Assistant Attorney General Massachusetts 1980-87. Member Massachusetts Bar Association. Specialist 5 U.S. Army 1969-71.

Office: Two Center Plaza, Suite 200, Boston 02108.

Telephone: (617) 788-8810.

O'TOOLE, George A., Jr. *(Judge, United States District Court District of Massachusetts)* Appointed for life by President Bill Clinton. Born Worcester Massachusetts Oct 7, 1947. Roman Catholic. Educated at Boston College A.B. magna cum laude 1969 and Harvard Law School J.D. 1972. Articles Editor Harvard Journal on Legislation 1971-72. Admitted to practice Massachusetts 1972, U.S. District Courts District of Massachusetts 1973 and Northern District of Texas 1978 and U.S. Court of Appeals First Circuit 1979. In legal practice Boston 1972-82. Associate Justice, Trial Court of Massachusetts Boston Municipal Court Department 1982-90. Former Associate Justice, Trial Court of Massachusetts Superior Court Department, appointed by Governor Michael S. Dukakis to term beginning Dec 7, 1990.

Member Boston and Massachusetts Bar Associations. Enjoys music, basketball and cooking.

Office: 4710 U.S. Courthouse, One Courthouse Way, Boston 02210-3002.

Telephone: (617) 748-9618.

PACKARD, Geoffrey C. *(Justice, Trial Court of Massachusetts District Court Department Middlesex County Malden Division)* Appointed by governor.

Mailing address: Two Center Plaza, Suite 200, Boston 02108.

Telephone: (617) 788-8810.

PADDEN, Sally F. *(First Justice, Trial Court of Massachusetts Juvenile Court Department Essex County Division)* Appointed by governor.

Mailing address: P.O. Box 9664, Boston 02114-9664.

Office: Three Center Plaza, Suite 520, Boston 02108.

Telephone: (617) 788-6550.

PAGE, Tina S. *(Associate Justice, Trial Court of Massachusetts Superior Court Department)* Appointed by governor.

Office: U.S. Post Office and Courthouse, 90 Devonshire Street, Fifteenth Floor, Boston 02109.

Telephone: (617) 788-8130.

PAYNE, John M., Jr. *(Justice, Trial Court of Massachusetts District Court Department Hampden County Chicopee Division)* Appointed by governor.

Mailing address: Two Center Plaza, Suite 200, Boston 02108.

Telephone: (617) 788-8810.

PEARSON, Barbara S. *(Justice, Trial Court of Massachusetts District Court Department Middlesex County Lowell Division)* Appointed by Governor William F. Weld to term beginning Jan 1994.

Mailing address: Two Center Plaza, Suite 200, Boston 02108.

Telephone: (617) 788-8810.

PELLEGRINO, Joseph A. *(Associate Justice, Trial Court of Massachusetts Juvenile Court Department Hampden County Division)* Appointed by governor. Former First Justice.

Mailing address: P.O. Box 9664, Boston 02114-9664.

Office: Three Center Plaza, Suite 520, Boston 02108.

Telephone: (617) 788-6550.

PERACHI, Paul E. *(First Justice, Trial Court of Massachusetts Juvenile Court Department Berkshire County Division)* Appointed by governor.

Mailing address: P.O. Box 9664, Boston 02114-9664.

Office: Three Center Plaza, Suite 520, Boston 02108.

Telephone: (617) 788-6550.

PEREZ, Luis G. *(Associate Justice, Trial Court of Massachusetts Juvenile Court Department Worcester Division)* Appointed by governor. Former First Justice.

Mailing address: P.O. Box 9664, Boston 02114-9664.

Office: Three Center Plaza, Suite 520, Boston 02108.

Telephone: (617) 788-6550.

PERLMAN, Gail L. *(First Justice, Trial Court of Massachusetts Probate and Family Court Department Hampshire County Division)* Appointed by governor.

Mailing address: Two Center Plaza, Suite 210, Boston 02108.

Telephone: (617) 788-6600.

PERRETTA, Charlotte Anne *(Associate Justice, Massachusetts Appeals Court)* Appointed by Governor Michael S. Dukakis 1978.

Office: 1500 New Courthouse, Boston 02108.

Telephone: (617) 725-8106.

PHILBIN, Austin T. *(Justice, Trial Court of Massachusetts District Court Department Worcester County Gardner Division)* Appointed by governor. Former First Justice.

Mailing address: Two Center Plaza, Suite 200, Boston 02108.

Telephone: (617) 788-8810.

PHILLIPS, Gregory L. *(First Justice, Trial Court of Massachusetts District Court Department Bristol County Attleboro Division and Justice, Suffolk County Roxbury Division)* Appointed by governor.
Mailing address: Two Center Plaza, Suite 200, Boston 02108.
Telephone: (617) 788-8810.

PIERCE, Steven D. *(Associate Justice, Trial Court of Massachusetts Housing Court Department Boston Division)* Appointed by governor.
Mailing address: 24 New Chardon Street, Boston 02114.
Telephone: (617) 788-8483.

PIPER, Gordon H. *(Justice, Trial Court of Massachusetts Land Court Department)* Appointed by governor.
Office: 24 New Chardon Street, Boston 02114.
Telephone: (617) 788-7470.

POEHLER, Patricia T. *(First Justice, Trial Court of Massachusetts District Court Department Hampden County Palmer Division and Justice, Westfield Division)* Appointed by governor.
Mailing address: Two Center Plaza, Suite 200, Boston 02108.
Telephone: (617) 788-8810.

POMAROLE, Michael J. *(Justice, Trial Court of Massachusetts District Court Department Middlesex County Cambridge Division)* Appointed by governor.
Mailing address: Two Center Plaza, Suite 200, Boston 02108.
Telephone: (617) 788-8810.

PONSOR, Michael A. *(Judge, United States District Court District of Massachusetts)* Appointed Magistrate Judge by U.S. District Court judges to term beginning Jan 6, 1984. Appointed Judge for life by President Bill Clinton March 14, 1994. Born Chicago Illinois Aug 13, 1946. Educated at Harvard University B.A. magna cum laude 1969, Pembroke College, Oxford University, England B.A. 1971 M.A. 1979 and Yale Law School J.D. 1975. Rhodes Scholar. Legal Assistant Public Defender's Office New Haven Connecticut 1975. Law Clerk to Hon. Joseph L. Tauro, U.S. District Court District of Massachusetts 1975-76. Admitted to practice Massachusetts 1975, U.S. District Court District of Massachusetts 1976, U.S. Court of Appeals First Circuit 1978 and U.S. Supreme Court 1980. In legal practice Boston 1976-78 and Amherst 1978-84.
Court-appointed monitor *Brewster v. Dukakis* Consent Decree Feb 1979 to Jan 1984. Adjunct Lecturer Western New England College School of Law 1988-95 and Yale Law School 1990-91. Former English teacher Kenya Institute of Administration, Nairobi Kenya.
Office: Federal Building, Fifth Floor, 1550 Main Street, Springfield 01103-1422.
Telephone: (413) 785-0217.

PORADA, Elizabeth A. *(Associate Justice, Massachusetts Appeals Court)* Appointed by Governor Michael S. Dukakis 1990. Former Justice, Trial Court of Massachusetts District Court Department. Former Associate Justice, Trial Court of Massachusetts Superior Court Department.
Office: 1500 New Courthouse, Boston 02108.
Telephone: (617) 725-8106.

POWERS, Warren A. *(First Justice, Trial Court of Massachusetts District Court Department Worcester County Milford Division and Justice, Norfolk County Quincy Division)* Appointed by governor.
Mailing address: Two Center Plaza, Suite 200, Boston 02108.
Telephone: (617) 788-8810.

QUINLAN, Regina L. *(Associate Justice, Trial Court of Massachusetts Superior Court Department)* Appointed by governor.
Office: U.S. Post Office and Courthouse, 90 Devonshire Street, Fifteenth Floor, Boston 02109.
Telephone: (617) 788-8130.

RAINAUD, Stephen M. *(Circuit Justice, Trial Court of Massachusetts Probate and Family Court Department)* Appointed by governor.
Office: Two Center Plaza, Suite 210, Boston 02108.
Telephone: (617) 788-6600.

RAPOZA, Phillip *(Associate Justice, Massachusetts Appeals Court)* Appointed by Governor Argeo Paul Cellucci to term beginning 1998. Educated at Yale College B.A. magna cum laude 1972 and Cornell Law School J.D. 1976. Justice, Trial Court of Massachusetts District Court Department Bristol County 1992-96, appointed by Governor William F. Weld. Associate Justice, Trial Court of Massachusetts Superior Court Department 1996-98, appointed by Governor William F. Weld.
Office: 1500 New Courthouse, Boston 02108.
Telephone: (617) 725-8747.

REARDON, Joseph J. *(First Justice, Trial Court of Massachusetts District Court Department Barnstable County Barnstable Division)* Appointed by Governor William F. Weld June 24, 1992 to term beginning Aug 26, 1992. Term expires at age seventy. Born Medway Massachusetts Dec 7, 1936. Catholic. Educated at College of the Holy Cross B.S. 1958 and Boston College Law School J.D. with honors 1964. Staff member Boston College Law Review 1963-64. Admitted to practice Massachusetts 1964 and U.S. District Court District of Massachusetts 1965. In legal practice Hyannis 1964-92.
Town Counsel Mashpee 1977-92. Counsel Centerville-Osterville-Marstons Mills Fire District 1987-92. Senior Lecturer Western New England College since 1995. Member Massachusetts City Solicitors and Town Counsel Association, Massachusetts Trial Lawyers Association, Massachusetts Judges Conference, National Judges Association, Barnstable County and Massachusetts Bar Associations. Lieutenant j.g. USNR 1958-61. Enjoys reading, theatre, arts and music.
Mailing address: Two Center Plaza, Suite 200, Boston 02108.
Telephone: (617) 788-8810.
E-mail address: bjudge@gis.net

REDD, Edward *(Justice, Trial Court of Massachusetts District Court Department Suffolk County Roxbury Division)* Appointed by Governor William F. Weld to term beginning 1993. Educated at Brandeis University B.A. 1971 and Boston College Law School J.D. 1974.
Mailing address: Two Center Plaza, Suite 200, Boston 02108.
Telephone: (617) 788-8810.
E-mail address: Redd4040@aol.com

REYNOLDS, Edward J. *(Justice, Trial Court of Massachusetts District Court Department Worcester County Leominster Division)* Appointed by governor.
Mailing address: Two Center Plaza, Suite 200, Boston 02108.
Telephone: (617) 788-8810.

RICCI, Susan D. *(Associate Justice, Trial Court of Massachusetts Probate and Family Court Department Worcester County Division)* Appointed by governor. Former Circuit Justice.
Mailing address: Two Center Plaza, Suite 210, Boston 02108.
Telephone: (617) 788-6600.

RILEY, Patrick J. *(Associate Justice, Trial Court of Massachusetts Superior Court Department)* Appointed by governor.
Office: U.S. Post Office and Courthouse, 90 Devonshire Street, Fifteenth Floor, Boston 02109.
Telephone: (617) 788-8130.

RILEY, William J. *(Justice, Trial Court of Massachusetts District Court Department Suffolk County Chelsea Division)* Appointed by governor.
Mailing address: Two Center Plaza, Suite 200, Boston 02108.
Telephone: (617) 788-8810.

RIPPS, Michael J. *(First Justice, Trial Court of Massachusetts District Court Department Berkshire County Northern Berkshire Division)* Appointed by governor.
Mailing address: Two Center Plaza, Suite 200, Boston 02108.
Telephone: (617) 788-8810.

ROACH, Gregory V. *(Circuit Justice, Trial Court of Massachusetts Probate and Family Court Department)* Appointed by governor.
Office: Two Center Plaza, Suite 210, Boston 02108.
Telephone: (617) 788-6600.

ROBERTS, Lisa A. *(Circuit Justice, Trial Court of Massachusetts Probate and Family Court Department)* Appointed by governor.
Office: Two Center Plaza, Suite 210, Boston 02108.
Telephone: (617) 788-6600.

ROCKETT, Edward J. *(Associate Justice, Trial Court of Massachusetts Probate and Family Court Department Essex County Division)* Appointed by governor. Former First Justice.
Mailing address: Two Center Plaza, Suite 210, Boston 02108.
Telephone: (617) 788-6600.

RONQUILLO, Roberto, Jr. *(Justice, Trial Court of Massachusetts District Court Department Suffolk County Dorchester Division)* Appointed by governor.
Mailing address: Two Center Plaza, Suite 200, Boston 02108.
Telephone: (617) 788-8810.

ROSENTHAL, Joel B. *(Judge, United States Bankruptcy Court District of Massachusetts)* Appointed by U.S. Court of Appeals First Circuit judges to term beginning Aug 10, 2000. Term expires 2014.
Office: 211 Federal Bldg. & U.S. Courthouse, 595 Main Street, Worcester 01608-2076.
Telephone: (508) 770-8901.

ROSS, David S. *(First Justice, Trial Court of Massachusetts District Court Department Franklin County Orange Division and Justice, Hampden County Chicopee Division)* Appointed by Governor Argeo Paul Cellucci to term beginning Dec 28, 1999. Term expires at age seventy. Born Northampton Massachusetts April 10, 1951. Jewish. Educated at University of Rochester B.A. with honors 1973 and Boston University School of Law J.D. 1976. Admitted to practice Massachusetts 1977 and New York 1977. In legal practice Amherst 1983-87.
Examining Attorney Department of Investigation New York City 1976-80. Assistant District Attorney Northwestern District 1980-83 and 1987-99. Named William C. O'Malley Prosecutor of the Year 1997. Representative Amherst Town Meeting 1982-99. Chairman Amherst Board of Health 1983-87.
Mailing address: Two Center Plaza, Suite 200, Boston 02108.
Telephone: (617) 788-8810.

ROUSE, Barbara J. *(Associate Justice, Trial Court of Massachusetts Superior Court Department)* Appointed by Governor Michael S. Dukakis to term beginning 1985.
Office: U.S. Post Office and Courthouse, 90 Devonshire Street, Fifteenth Floor, Boston 02109.
Telephone: (617) 788-8130.

ROWE, Brian *(First Justice, Trial Court of Massachusetts District Court Department Dukes County Edgartown Division)* Appointed by governor.
Mailing address: Two Center Plaza, Suite 200, Boston 02108.
Telephone: (617) 788-8810.

RUFO, Robert C. *(Justice, Trial Court of Massachusetts District Court Department Suffolk County West Roxbury Division)* Appointed by Governor William F. Weld.
Mailing address: Two Center Plaza, Suite 200, Boston 02108.
Telephone: (617) 788-8810.

RUMA, Santo J. *(First Justice, Trial Court of Massachusetts District Court Department Essex County Peabody Division)* Appointed by governor.
Mailing address: Two Center Plaza, Suite 200, Boston 02108.
Telephone: (617) 788-8810.

RUP, Mary-Lou *(Associate Justice, Trial Court of Massachusetts Superior Court Department)* Appointed by governor.
Office: U.S. Post Office and Courthouse, 90 Devonshire Street, Fifteenth Floor, Boston 02109.
Telephone: (617) 788-8130.

RUTBERG, Fredric D. *(Justice, Trial Court of Massachusetts District Court Department Berkshire County Southern Berkshire Division)* Appointed by governor.
Mailing address: Two Center Plaza, Suite 200, Boston 02108.
Telephone: (617) 788-8810.

RYAN, W. Michael *(Justice, Trial Court of Massachusetts District Court Department Hampshire County*

RYAN, W. MICHAEL—*Continued*

Northampton Division) Appointed by governor. Former First Justice.
Mailing address: Two Center Plaza, Suite 200, Boston 02108.
Telephone: (617) 788-8810.

SABAITIS, Catherine P. *(First Justice, Trial Court of Massachusetts Probate and Family Court Department Plymouth County Division)* Appointed by governor.
Mailing address: Two Center Plaza, Suite 210, Boston 02108.
Telephone: (617) 788-6600.

SABRA, Bernadette L. *(First Justice, Trial Court of Massachusetts District Court Department Bristol County New Bedford Division and Justice, Fall River Division)* Appointed by governor.
Mailing address: Two Center Plaza, Suite 200, Boston 02108.
Telephone: (617) 788-8810.

SACKS, David G. *(First Justice, Trial Court of Massachusetts Probate and Family Court Department Hampden County Division)* Appointed by Governor Michael S. Dukakis Oct 30, 1986. Term expires at age seventy. First Justice since June 29, 1992. Born Holyoke Massachusetts Jan 19, 1950. Jewish. Educated at American University B.A. 1971 and Suffolk University Law School J.D. 1974. Admitted to practice Massachusetts 1974, U.S. District Court District of Massachusetts 1975 and U.S. Supreme Court 1978. In legal practice Holyoke 1975-86.

Author "Trial Court Abuse Prevention Proceedings" II No. 2 Winter 1997 and "Massachusetts Becoming a Termination of Parental Rights Jurisdictional: Didn't You Always Think It Was One?" III No. 1 Winter 1998 *Association of Family and Conciliation Courts Massachusetts Chapter Newsletter;* and "Remarks on Joint Custody" pg. 16 and "Alimony Waivers When Children Are Minors" pg. 21 *Divorce Practice: A Beginner's Guide* Massachusetts Bar Association Family Law Section CLE FLG99 May 1999. Member Committee on Gender Equality and Juvenile Justice Commission Custody Task Force Massachusetts Supreme Judicial Court 1992-94, Massachusetts Trial Court Gender Equality Advisory Board since 1994, Judicial Advisory Workgroup to Director U.S. Office of Child Support Enforcement 1997-2000, Probate and Family Court Department Pro Se Litigant Committee 1997-2000 and Racial and Ethnic Access and Fairness Advisory Board Administrative Office of the Trial Court since 2001 and Member 2001 and Treasurer 2002 Board of Directors Massachusetts Judges Conference. Member Massachusetts Bar Foundation, Holyoke (Former Treasurer), Hampden County (Former Chair Young Lawyers Section, Former Member Executive Committee) and Massachusetts (Former Member Board of Delegates) Bar Associations. Instructor American Institute of Paralegal Training 1982. Participant in programs Massachusetts Bar Association, Massachusetts Academy of Trial Attorneys, Trial Court of Massachusetts, Flaschner Judicial Institute, Suffolk University Law School Advanced Legal Programs and MCLE/NELI. Recipient Anti-Prejudice Citation from Greater Holyoke Council of Human Understanding June 1982 and Friend of Education Award from Holyoke Teachers Association Sept 24, 1982. Former Chair Holyoke School Committee and Area Advisory Board Massachusetts Commission Against Discrimination.
Mailing address: P.O. Box 559, Springfield 01101.
Office: 50 State Street, Springfield 01103.
Telephone: (413) 748-7772.

SAHAGIAN, Maryanne *(Circuit Justice, Trial Court of Massachusetts Probate and Family Court Department)* Appointed by governor.
Office: Two Center Plaza, Suite 210, Boston 02108.
Telephone: (617) 788-6600.

SÁNCHEZ, José *(Associate Justice, Trial Court of Massachusetts Juvenile Court Department Essex County Division)* Appointed by Governor William F. Weld to term beginning May 3, 1995. Term expires at age seventy. Born New York New York Nov 10, 1950. Catholic. Educated at Fordham University B.A. 1984 and Northeastern University School of Law J.D. 1987. Admitted to practice Massachusetts 1988 and U.S. District Court District of Massachusetts 1990.

Public Defender Committee for Public Counsel Services 1987-95. Member Massachusetts Association of Hispanic Attorneys, Juvenile and National Hispanic Bar Associations.
Mailing address: P.O. Box 9664, Boston 02114-9664.
Office: Three Center Plaza, Suite 520, Boston 02108.
Telephone: (617) 788-6550.

SANDERS, Janet L. *(Associate Justice, Trial Court of Massachusetts Superior Court Department)* Appointed by governor. Former First Justice, Trial Court of Massachusetts District Court Department Middlesex County Concord Division and Justice, Waltham Division.
Office: U.S. Post Office and Courthouse, 90 Devonshire Street, Fifteenth Floor, Boston 02109.
Telephone: (617) 788-8130.

SANDS, Alexander H. *(Justice, Trial Court of Massachusetts Land Court Department)* Appointed by governor.
Office: 24 New Chardon Street, Boston 02114.
Telephone: (617) 788-7470.

SARIS, Patti B. *(Judge, United States District Court District of Massachusetts)* Appointed for life by President Bill Clinton. Born Boston Massachusetts July 20, 1951. Jewish. Educated at Radcliffe College B.A. magna cum laude 1973 and Harvard Law School J.D. cum laude 1976. Editor Civil Liberties Review 1975-76. Law Clerk to Hon. Robert Braucher, Massachusetts Supreme Judicial Court 1976-77. Member Phi Beta Kappa. Admitted to practice Massachusetts 1976. In legal practice Boston. Former Magistrate, U.S. District Court District of Massachusetts, appointed by U.S. District Court judges May 12, 1986. Former Associate Justice, Trial Court of Massachusetts Superior Court Department.

Staff Counsel U.S. Senate Judiciary Committee 1978-81. Assistant U.S. Attorney 1982-86. Chief, Civil Division U.S. Attorney's Office 1984-86. Co-author with Abner Mirva *Congress: The First Branch* Franklin Watts 1982. Member Women's Bar Association (Board of Directors 1982-86), Boston and Massachusetts Bar Associations.
Office: 6130 U.S. Courthouse, One Courthouse Way, Boston 02210-3002.
Telephone: (617) 748-4831.

SAVIGNANO, Richard D. *(Justice, Trial Court of Massachusetts District Court Department Plymouth County Brockton Division)* Appointed by governor.
Mailing address: Two Center Plaza, Suite 200, Boston 02108.
Telephone: (617) 788-8810.

SCANDURRA, Robert A. *(Associate Justice, Trial Court of Massachusetts Probate and Family Court Department Barnstable County Division)* Appointed by Governor William F. Weld to term beginning March 18, 1994. Term expires at age seventy. Born Queens New York July 27, 1949. Educated at Ithaca College B.A. 1971 and New England School of Law J.D. 1974. Admitted to practice Massachusetts 1974 and U.S. District Court District of Massachusetts 1976. In legal practice Hyannis 1974-79 and Barnstable 1979-94.
Instructor in paralegal studies Northeastern University since 1993. Member Massachusetts Judges Conference.
Mailing address: Two Center Plaza, Suite 210, Boston 02108.
Telephone: (617) 788-6600.
E-mail address: RASCourt@aol.com

SCHEIER, Karyn Faith *(Chief Justice, Trial Court of Massachusetts Land Court Department)* Appointed by governor.
Office: Edward W. Brooke Courthouse, 24 New Chardon Street, Boston 02114.
Telephone: (617) 788-7470.

SCHUBERT, M. John, Jr. *(Justice, Trial Court of Massachusetts District Court Department Franklin County Orange Division)* Appointed by Governor William F. Weld to term beginning Jan 8, 1993. Educated at St. Joseph's University B.S. 1968 and Georgetown University Law Center J.D. 1971. Admitted to practice Massachusetts 1972, U.S. District Court 1972 and U.S Court of Federal Claims. In legal practice West Springfield 1974-93.
Instructor in Ethics, Trial Techniques and Conveyancing Western New England College School of Law 1974-95. Member Hampden County (Board of Delegates 1980-92, President 1986) and Massachusetts (Board of Delegates 1986-93, Secretary 1991, Vice President 1992) Bar Associations. Lecturer on Evidence and Trial Techniques Massachusetts CLE. Enjoys tennis and golf.
Mailing address: Two Center Plaza, Suite 200, Boston 02108.
Telephone: (617) 788-8810.

SIKORA, Mitchell J., Jr. *(Associate Justice, Trial Court of Massachusetts Superior Court Department)* Appointed by governor.
Office: U.S. Post Office and Courthouse, 90 Devonshire Street, Fifteenth Floor, Boston 02109.
Telephone: (617) 788-8130.

SINGER, Sarah B. *(Circuit Justice, Trial Court of Massachusetts District Court Department and First Justice, Middlesex County Natick Division)* Appointed by governor.
Office: Two Center Plaza, Suite 200, Boston 02108.
Telephone: (617) 788-8810.

SINGLETON, Severlin B., III *(Justice, Trial Court of Massachusetts District Court Department Middlesex County Cambridge Division)* Appointed by governor.
Mailing address: Two Center Plaza, Suite 200, Boston 02108.
Telephone: (617) 788-8810.

SKINNER, Walter Jay *(Senior Judge, United States District Court District of Massachusetts)* Appointed for life by President Richard M. Nixon to term beginning Jan 7, 1974. Assumed Senior status, serves by assignment. Born Washington D.C. Sept 12, 1927. Educated at Harvard University A.B. 1948 J.D. 1952. Admitted to practice Massachusetts 1952. In legal practice Massachusetts 1952-57 and 1966-74.
Assistant District Attorney Plymouth County 1957-63. Scituate Town Counsel 1957-63. Assistant Attorney General Massachusetts 1963-65. Member Boston, Massachusetts and American Bar Associations.
Office: 4720 U.S. Courthouse, One Courthouse Way, Boston 02210-3002.
Telephone: (617) 748-9274.

SMITH, Carol Gibson *(First Justice, Trial Court of Massachusetts Juvenile Court Department Barnstable/Town of Plymouth Division)* Appointed by governor.
Mailing address: P.O. Box 9664, Boston 02114-9664-9664.
Office: Three Center Plaza, Suite 520, Boston 02108.
Telephone: (617) 788-6550.

SMITH, Herman J., Jr. *(Associate Justice, Trial Court of Massachusetts Superior Court Department)* Appointed by governor. Former Associate Justice, Trial Court of Massachusetts Housing Court Department Boston Division.
Office: U.S. Post Office and Courthouse, 90 Devonshire Street, Fifteenth Floor, Boston 02109.
Telephone: (617) 788-8130.

SMOOT, John M. *(First Justice, Trial Court of Massachusetts Probate and Family Court Department Suffolk County Division)* Appointed by governor.
Office: 24 New Chardon Street, Boston 02114.
Telephone: (617) 788-6600.

SNIDER, Neil G. *(First Justice, Trial Court of Massachusetts District Court Department Worcester County Dudley Division and Justice, Worcester Division)* Appointed by governor.
Mailing address: Two Center Plaza, Suite 200, Boston 02108.
Telephone: (617) 788-8810.

SOSMAN, Martha B. *(Associate Justice, Massachusetts Supreme Judicial Court)* Appointed by governor. Term expires at age seventy. Born Boston Massachusetts Oct 20, 1950. Protestant. Educated at Middlebury College B.A. cum laude 1972 and University of Michigan J.D. magna cum laude 1979. Admitted to practice Massachusetts 1979, U.S. District Court District of Massachusetts 1980 and U.S. Court of Appeals First Circuit 1985. In legal practice Boston 1979-84 and 1989-93. Associate Justice, Trial Court of Massachusetts Superior Court Department, appointed by Governor William F. Weld Dec 1992 to term beginning Jan 26, 1993.
Assistant U.S. Attorney 1984-89 and Chief Civil Divi-

SOSMAN, MARTHA B.—*Continued*
sion 1986-89 District of Massachusetts. Enjoys the piano.
Office: 1300 New Courthouse, Boston 02108.
Telephone: (617) 557-1000.

SPINA, Francis X. *(Associate Justice, Massachusetts Supreme Judicial Court)* Appointed by Governor Argeo Paul Cellucci to term beginning Oct 14, 1999. Term expires at age seventy. Born Pittsfield Massachusetts Nov 13, 1946. Educated at Amherst College B.A. and Boston College Law School J.D. In legal practice Pittsfield 1983-93. Associate Justice, Trial Court of Massachusetts Superior Court Department 1993-97, appointed by Governor William F. Weld. Associate Justice, Massachusetts Appeals Court 1997-99.
With Western Massachusetts Legal Services 1972-74. Assistant City Solicitor Pittsfield 1975-77. Second Assistant District Attorney Berkshire County 1979-83.
Office: 1300 New Courthouse, Boston 02108.
Telephone: (617) 557-1000.

SPRAGUE, George R. *(Justice, Trial Court of Massachusetts District Court Department Middlesex County Cambridge Division)* Appointed by Governor William F. Weld. Former Circuit Justice.
Mailing address: Two Center Plaza, Suite 200, Boston 02108.
Telephone: (617) 788-8810.

SPURLOCK, Charles T. *(Associate Justice, Trial Court of Massachusetts Superior Court Department)* Appointed by governor. Former Justice, Trial Court of Massachusetts District Court Department Suffolk County Roxbury Division.
Office: U.S. Post Office and Courthouse, 90 Devonshire Street, Fifteenth Floor, Boston 02109.
Telephone: (617) 788-8130.

SRAGOW, Roanne *(Circuit Justice, Trial Court of Massachusetts District Court Department and First Justice, Middlesex County Cambridge Division)* Appointed by governor.
Office: Two Center Plaza, Suite 200, Boston 02108.
Telephone: (617) 788-8810.

STAFFIER, Nancy *(Associate Justice, Trial Court of Massachusetts Superior Court Department)* Appointed by governor.
Office: U.S. Post Office and Courthouse, 90 Devonshire Street, Fifteenth Floor, Boston 02109.
Telephone: (617) 788-8130.

STAHLIN, Jeremy A. *(Associate Justice, Trial Court of Massachusetts Probate and Family Court Department Suffolk County Division)* Appointed by governor.
Mailing address: Two Center Plaza, Suite 210, Boston 02108.
Telephone: (617) 788-6600.

STEARNS, Richard G. *(Judge, United States District Court District of Massachusetts)* Appointed for life by President Bill Clinton to term beginning 1994. Born Los Angeles California June 27, 1944. Educated at American University of Beirut 1964-65, Stanford University B.A. with great distinction 1968, Oxford University, England M. Litt. 1971 and Harvard Law School J.D. 1976. Exchange Scholar 1964-65. Rhodes Scholar 1968. International Vice President U.S. National Student Association 1966-67. Member Phi Beta Kappa. Admitted to practice Massachusetts, U.S. District Court District of Massachusetts and U.S. Court of Appeals First Circuit. Associate Justice, Trial Court of Massachusetts Superior Court Department 1990-94.
Assistant District Attorney Massachusetts 1976-79 and 1980-82. Assistant U.S. Attorney (Chief General Crimes Unit, Chief Criminal Division, First Assistant U.S. Attorney and Senior Litigation Counsel) 1982-90. Author *Massachusetts Criminal Law: A Prosecutor's Guide* 22nd ed. 2002. Instructor Harvard Law School 1984-87. Member Judicial Conference Committee on Federal-State Jurisdiction 1996-2002 and Mass Torts Working Group 1998-99. Former Member Committees on Bail and Personnel Trial Court of Massachusetts Superior Court Department. Member Massachusetts and American Bar Associations. Recipient Superior Performance and Special Commendation Awards from Department of Justice. Democrat. Director Midwest Presidential Campaign of Senator Eugene J. McCarthy 1968. Deputy Manager Presidential Campaign of Senator George S. McGovern 1970-72. Director Delegate Selection Presidential Campaign of Senator Edward M. Kennedy 1979-80. Staff Member Commission on Party Reform 1969. Member Commission on the Reform of the Presidential Nominating Process 1976-78, Rules Committee Democratic National Convention 1980 and Technical Advisory Committee Presidential Nomination Commission 1981-82. Board of Trustees Vincent Memorial Hospital Boston. Interests include white-water and wilderness canoeing, cross-country skiing, Inuit carvings, U.S. Civil War history and the opera.
Office: 7130 U.S. Courthouse, One Courthouse Way, Boston 02210.
Telephone: (617) 748-9283.

STEINBERG, Stephen C. *(First Justice, Trial Court of Massachusetts Probate and Family Court Department Dukes County Division and Associate Justice, Plymouth County Division)* Appointed by governor.
Mailing address: Two Center Plaza, Suite 210, Boston 02108.
Telephone: (617) 788-6600.

STELLA, Michael T., Jr. *(First Justice, Trial Court of Massachusetts District Court Department Essex County Lawrence Division)* Appointed by Governor William F. Weld to term beginning July 8, 1993. Term expires at age seventy. Born Lawrence Massachusetts May 6, 1944. Roman Catholic. Educated at Merrimack College B.A. 1965 and Suffolk University Law School J.D. 1968. Admitted to practice Massachusetts 1968, U.S. District Court District of Massachusetts 1971, U.S. Court of Appeals First Circuit 1979 and U.S. Supreme Court 1979. In legal practice Lawrence 1968-93.
Assistant District Attorney Essex County 1971-79. Important Decision: Prosecuted William R. Horton for first degree murder of Joey Fournier. Member Massachusetts Academy of Trial Attorneys, Lawrence (Past President), Massachusetts and American Bar Associations. Named one of Outstanding Young Men in America 1970. Listed in *Who's Who in American Law* 2nd ed. 1978. Member Democratic Town Committee. Former Chairman Finance Committee and Advisory Committee and Former Acting Moderator Town of North Andover. Former Chairman and Director Lawrence Interparochial School Board. Past President, Former Vice Chairman and Director Family Service Association of Greater Lawrence, Inc. Former Director and Treasurer Greater Lawrence Junior Cham-

STELLA, MICHAEL T., JR.—*Continued*

ber of Commerce. Former Clerk and Director Greater Lawrence Chamber of Commerce. Former Director Greater Lawrence Outreach, Inc. Past President and Former Director Greater Lawrence Revolving Loan Fund, Inc. Past President and Former Treasurer and Director Lawrence Lions Club. Life Member International Association of Lions Club. Enjoys golfing, vacationing in Europe, woodworking, auto repair and reconstruction and fine dining.

Mailing address: Two Center Plaza, Suite 200, Boston 02108.

Telephone: (617) 788-8810.

STEVENS, John C., III *(First Justice, Trial Court of Massachusetts Probate and Family Court Department Essex County Division)* Appointed by governor.

Office: 36 Federal Street, Salem 01970.

Telephone: (978) 745-4559.

STODDART, Douglas W. *(Justice, Trial Court of Massachusetts District Court Department Middlesex County Framingham Division)* Appointed by governor.

Mailing address: Two Center Plaza, Suite 200, Boston 02108.

Telephone: (617) 788-8810.

SULLIVAN, Anthony P. *(Circuit Justice, Trial Court of Massachusetts District Court Department and First Justice, Suffolk County Charlestown Division)* Appointed by governor.

Office: Two Center Plaza, Suite 200, Boston 02108.

Telephone: (617) 788-8810.

SULLIVAN, James *(Justice, Trial Court of Massachusetts District Court Department Bristol County Taunton Division)* Appointed by governor.

Mailing address: Two Center Plaza, Suite 200, Boston 02108.

Telephone: (617) 788-8810.

SULLIVAN, Mary Hogan *(Justice, Trial Court of Massachusetts District Court Department Middlesex County Marlborough Division)* Appointed by governor.

Mailing address: Two Center Plaza, Suite 200, Boston 02108.

Telephone: (617) 788-8810.

SULLIVAN, Thomas F., Jr. *(First Justice, Trial Court of Massachusetts District Court Department Middlesex County Marlborough Division and Justice, Worcester County Worcester Division)* Appointed by Governor Michael S. Dukakis to term beginning Sept 4, 1984. Terms expire at age seventy. Born Worcester Massachusetts March 22, 1941. Catholic. Educated at College of the Holy Cross A.B. 1963 and Boston College Law School LL.B. 1966. Admitted to practice Massachusetts 1966 and U.S. District Court 1976. Began legal practice Boston 1966. In legal practice Worcester 1976.

Lieutenant 82nd Airborne Division Vietnam U.S. Army 1966-69.

Mailing address: Two Center Plaza, Suite 200, Boston 02108.

Telephone: (617) 788-8810.

SUMMERVILLE, Mark H. *(Associate Justice, Trial Court of Massachusetts Boston Municipal Court Department)* Appointed by governor.

Office: U.S. Post Office & Courthouse, 90 Devonshire Street, Boston 02109.

Telephone: (617) 788-8700.

SWAN, Allen G. *(First Justice, Trial Court of Massachusetts District Court Department Essex County Ipswich Division and Justice, Haverhill Division)* Appointed by Governor William F. Weld to term beginning March 7, 1997. Term expires at age seventy. Born Rochester New York April 20, 1946. Episcopalian. Educated at Williams College B.A. in History 1968 and New York University School of Law J.D. 1972. Note and Comment Editor New York University Journal of International Law and Politics 1971-72. Admitted to practice New York 1973, Massachusetts 1976, U.S. District Courts Eastern, Northern, Southern and Western Districts of New York and District of Massachusetts, U.S. Courts of Appeals First and Second Circuits and U.S. Supreme Court. In legal practice Boston Massachusetts 1976-79, Beverly Massachusetts 1979-82 and Ipswich Massachusetts 1982-97.

Assistant District Attorney New York County New York 1973-74 and Special Assistant Attorney General Special State Prosecutor New York New York 1974-76. Member Ipswich (President 1981-82 and 1995-97), Salem, Essex County (Board of Directors 1983-97) and Massachusetts Bar Associations. Specialist 6 USAR 1968-74. Member Ipswich Zoning Board of Appeals 1979-84 and Finance Committee 1984-91.

Mailing address: Two Center Plaza, Suite 200, Boston 02108.

Telephone: (617) 788-8810.

SWARTWOOD, Charles B., III *(Magistrate Judge, United States District Court District of Massachusetts)* Appointed by U.S. District Court judges.

Office: 404 Federal Bldg. & U.S. Courthouse, 595 Main Street, Worcester 01608-2076.

Telephone: (508) 929-9905.

SWEENEY, Constance M. *(Associate Justice, Trial Court of Massachusetts Superior Court Department)* Appointed by governor.

Office: U.S. Post Office and Courthouse, 90 Devonshire Street, Fifteenth Floor, Boston 02109.

Telephone: (617) 788-8130.

SWORDS, Daniel J. *(First Justice, Trial Court of Massachusetts Juvenile Court Department Hampden County Division)* Appointed Associate Justice by Governor William F. Weld to term beginning July 7, 1994. Term expires at age seventy. First Justice since 2003. Born Springfield Massachusetts Feb 4, 1948. Catholic. Educated at College of the Holy Cross B.A. 1969 and Western New England College School of Law 1976. Admitted to practice Massachusetts 1977 and U.S. District Court District of Massachusetts 1978. In legal practice Massachusetts 1982-94.

With District Attorney's Office 1980-82. Instructor in Juvenile Law Bay Path College 1999. Naval Security Group USN 1969-72. Board of Trustees Willie Ross School for Deaf and Western New England College. Enjoys golfing and fishing.

Mailing address: 80 State Street, Springfield 01103.

Telephone: (413) 748-7704.

TAURO, Joseph L. *(Judge, United States District Court District of Massachusetts)* Appointed for life by President Richard M. Nixon to term beginning Nov 2, 1972. Former Chief Judge. Born Sept 26, 1931. Educated at Brown University A.B. 1953 and Cornell University LL.B. 1956. Admitted to practice Massachusetts 1956 and District of Columbia 1961. In legal practice Boston and Lynn 1960-71.

Assistant U.S. Attorney to Elliot L. Richardson 1959-60. Chief Legal Counsel to Governor John Anthony Volpe 1965-69. U.S. Attorney District of Massachusetts 1972. Lecturer Boston University Law School since 1977. Fellow American Bar Foundation. Member Boston (Advisory Council 1968-71), Massachusetts and American Bar Associations. Selected one of Greater Boston's Ten Outstanding Young Men 1966. First Lieutenant U.S. Army (NIKE Launching Control Officer) 1956-58. Director Security National Bank 1961-72. Trustee Massachusetts General Hospital 1968-72 and Brown University since 1978. Member Executive Committee Cornell Law Association. Advisory Council Cornell Law School since 1976. Member Brown Club of Boston, North Shore Brown Club (Past President) and Corinthian Yacht Club Marblehead.

Office: 7110 U.S. Courthouse, One Courthouse Way, Boston 02210-3002.

Telephone: (617) 748-9288.

TEAHAN, William W., Jr. *(Justice, Trial Court of Massachusetts District Court Department Hampden County Springfield Division)* Appointed by Governor Michael S. Dukakis to term beginning Dec 17, 1987. Term expires at age seventy. Regional Administrative Judge Region V since 1999. Born Holyoke Massachusetts Nov 12, 1942. Educated at Dartmouth College A.B. 1964 and Boston College Law School 1970. Admitted to practice Massachusetts 1970, U.S. District Court District of Massachusetts 1971 and U.S. Tax Court 1972. In legal practice Springfield 1970-79.

First Assistant District Attorney Hampden County 1983-87. Co-author "Representing a Mentally Retarded Criminal Defendant" 64 Massachusetts L. Rev. 103, 1979. Adjunct Professor of Criminal Law 1975 and Criminal Procedure 1986 Western New England College School of Law. Member Commission on Judicial Conduct since 2000. Faculty member and Instructor in multiple programs for lawyers on civil and criminal topics Massachusetts CLE since 1978. First Lieutenant U.S. Army Intelligence Corps 1965-67. Member 1976-79 and Chair 1979 School Committee Longmeadow Massachusetts.

Mailing address: Two Center Plaza, Suite 200, Boston 02108.

Telephone: (617) 788-8810.

TERRY, Robert E. *(First Justice, Trial Court of Massachusetts Probate and Family Court Department Barnstable County Division)* Appointed by Governor Michael S. Dukakis to term beginning 1989. First Justice since 1993. Educated at College of the Holy Cross and Boston University School of Law.

Former Special Counsel Executive Office of Human Services. Former Executive Director of Legal Services for Cape Cod and the Islands. Former Associate Counsel Northern Worcester County Legal Aid Society. Former Chairman Family Law Section Barnstable County Bar Association. Participant CLE programs MCLE, Boston Bar Association and Massachusetts Bar Association. Founder and Past President Mashpee Business Association. Founder and Former Member Board of Directors Housing Assistance Corporation and Cape Cod and the Islands Child Development Council.

Mailing address: Two Center Plaza, Suite 210, Boston 02108.

Telephone: (617) 788-6600.

TESHOIAN, Sarkis *(Justice, Trial Court of Massachusetts District Court Department Worcester County Uxbridge Division)* Appointed by governor. Former First Justice.

Mailing address: Two Center Plaza, Suite 200, Boston 02108.

Telephone: (617) 788-8810.

TOCHKA, Robert N. *(Justice, Trial Court of Massachusetts District Court Department Essex County Lynn Division)* Appointed by governor.

Mailing address: Two Center Plaza, Suite 200, Boston 02108.

Telephone: (617) 788-8810.

TRAINOR, Joseph A. *(Associate Justice, Massachusetts Appeals Court)* Appointed by governor. Former First Justice, Trial Court of Massachusetts Juvenile Court Department Middlesex County Division.

Office: 1500 New Courthouse, Boston 02108.

Telephone: (617) 725-8106.

TROMBLY, Charles W. *(Justice, Trial Court of Massachusetts Land Court Department)* Appointed by governor.

Office: 24 New Chardon Street, Boston 02114.

Telephone: (617) 788-7470.

TROY, Paul E. *(Associate Justice, Trial Court of Massachusetts Superior Court Department)* Appointed by governor.

Office: U.S. Post Office and Courthouse, 90 Devonshire Street, Fifteenth Floor, Boston 02109.

Telephone: (617) 788-8130.

TURCOTTE, David T. *(Justice, Trial Court of Massachusetts District Court Department Bristol County Fall River Division)* Appointed by governor.

Mailing address: Two Center Plaza, Suite 200, Boston 02108.

Telephone: (617) 788-8810.

TYRE, Gwendolyn R. *(Associate Justice, Trial Court of Massachusetts Juvenile Court Department Middlesex County Division)* Appointed by governor.

Mailing address: P.O. Box 9664, Boston 02114-9664.

Office: Three Center Plaza, Suite 520, Boston 02108.

Telephone: (617) 788-6550.

van GESTEL, Allan *(Associate Justice, Trial Court of Massachusetts Superior Court Department)* Appointed by Governor William F. Weld Aug 1996 to term beginning Oct 8, 1996. Term expires at age seventy. Born Boston Massachusetts Dec 3, 1935. Protestant. Educated at Colby College B.A. 1957 and Boston University School of Law LL.B. with honors 1961. Editor Boston University Law Review 1959-61. Admitted to practice Massachusetts 1961, U.S. District Courts District of Massachusetts and Northern and Western Districts of New York, U.S. Courts of Appeals First, Second, Third and Fifth Circuits and U.S. Supreme Court. In legal practice Boston 1961-96.

Fellow American College of Trial Lawyers. Member

VAN GESTEL, ALLAN—*Continued*

Boston, Massachusetts and American Bar Associations. Trustee Colby College. Enjoys writing and travel.

Office: U.S. Post Office and Courthouse, 90 Devonshire Street, Fifteenth Floor, Boston 02109.

Telephone: (617) 788-8130.

VELIS, Peter A. *(Associate Justice, Trial Court of Massachusetts Superior Court Department)* Appointed by governor.

Office: U.S. Post Office and Courthouse, 90 Devonshire Street, Fifteenth Floor, Boston 02109.

Telephone: (617) 788-8130.

VIRZI, Vito A. *(Justice, Trial Court of Massachusetts District Court Department Worcester County Winchendon Division)* Appointed by Governor William F. Weld.

Mailing address: Two Center Plaza, Suite 200, Boston 02108.

Telephone: (617) 788-8810.

VRABEL, Paul M. *(Justice, Trial Court of Massachusetts District Court Department Berkshire County Northern Berkshire Division)* Appointed by governor.

Mailing address: Two Center Plaza, Suite 200, Boston 02108.

Telephone: (617) 788-8810.

WAICKOWSKI, Paul S. *(First Justice, Trial Court of Massachusetts District Court Department Worcester County Westborough Division)* Appointed by governor.

Mailing address: Two Center Plaza, Suite 200, Boston 02108.

Telephone: (617) 788-8810.

WALKER, Joseph M., III *(Associate Justice, Trial Court of Massachusetts Superior Court Department)* Appointed by governor. Former Justice, Trial Court of Massachusetts District Court Department Suffolk County Dorchester Division.

Office: U.S. Post Office and Courthouse, 90 Devonshire Street, Fifteenth Floor, Boston 02109.

Telephone: (617) 788-8130.

WALKER, Neil J. *(First Justice, Trial Court of Massachusetts District Court Department Middlesex County Lowell Division)* Appointed by governor.

Mailing address: Two Center Plaza, Suite 200, Boston 02108.

Telephone: (617) 788-8810.

WARD, Virginia M. *(Circuit Justice, Trial Court of Massachusetts Probate and Family Court Department)* Appointed by governor.

Office: Two Center Plaza, Suite 210, Boston 02108.

Telephone: (617) 788-6600.

WELCH, Joseph R. *(Circuit Justice, Trial Court of Massachusetts District Court Department)* Appointed by Governor Michael Dukakis 1990. Term expires at age seventy. Born Boston Massachusetts Dec 10, 1934. Educated at Bates College A.B. and Boston College Law School J.D. 1964. Member Lambda Delta. Admitted to practice Massachusetts 1964 and U.S. Court of Appeals First Circuit 1964. In legal practice Randolph 1964-68 and 1975-90.

Special Counsel Town of Randolph. Assistant District Attorney Norfolk County 1968-75. Founder and Past President Norfolk County Bar Advocates, Inc. Member Norfolk County (President 1979) and Massachusetts (Board of Delegates 1979) Bar Associations. Recipient Distinguished Citizenship Award from South Shore Mental Health Association 1978 and Distinguished Leadership Award from Massachusetts Heart Association 1983. Lieutenant USN 1957-60. Commander USNR 1960-77 (retired). Town Moderator Town of Randolph 1968-74. Past President South Shore Mental Health Association. Former Vice President New England Region American Heart Association. Former Chairman of the Board Massachusetts Heart Association. Former Chairman Randolph Conservation Study Committee. Former Secretary Duxbury Youth Hockey Association and Randolph Lions Club. Chairman Randolph Government Study Committee 1960-64. Member Duxbury Police Department Study Committee 1984 and Duxbury Police Chief Selection Committee 1986.

Office: Two Center Plaza, Suite 200, Boston 02108.

Telephone: (617) 788-8810.

WELCH, Richard E., III *(Associate Justice, Trial Court of Massachusetts Superior Court Department)* Appointed by Governor William F. Weld June 1994. Term expires at age seventy. Born Hamilton New York Nov 27, 1952. Unitarian. Educated at Lake Forest College B.A. summa cum laude 1974 and Boston University J.D. summa cum laude 1978. Executive Editor Boston University Law Review 1977-78. Law Clerk to Hon. Raymond Pettine, U.S. District Court District of Rhode Island 1978-79. Admitted to practice Massachusetts 1979 and U.S. District Courts District of Massachusetts and District of Rhode Island. In legal practice Boston 1979-83.

Assistant U.S. Attorney District of Massachusetts 1982-94. Author "At Federalism's Crossroads" Boston University L. Rev. 1978 and various articles on prosecuting white collar crime and environmental crime in local bar journals and CLE publications. Instructor on Federal Courts and the Federal System New England College School of Law since 1990. Instructor numerous CLE seminars and judges conferences. Recipient awards from Federal Bureau of Investigation, Environmental Protection Agency, U.S. Fish and Wildlife and U.S. Postal Service.

Office: U.S. Post Office and Courthouse, 90 Devonshire Street, Fifteenth Floor, Boston 02109.

Telephone: (617) 788-8130.

WELSH, Robert A., Jr. *(First Justice, Trial Court of Massachusetts District Court Department Barnstable County Orleans Division)* Appointed by Governor Francis Williams Sargent to term beginning June 28, 1973. Term expires at age seventy. Former Associate Justice, Appellate Division. Born Boston Massachusetts Feb 10, 1938. Roman Catholic. Educated at College of the Holy Cross A.B. cum laude 1959 and Boston College LL.B. 1962 replaced by J.D. Admitted to practice Massachusetts 1962. Began legal practice JAGC 1962.

Mailing address: Two Center Plaza, Suite 200, Boston 02108.

Telephone: (617) 788-8810.

WERNICK, Lawrence B. *(Associate Justice, Trial Court of Massachusetts Superior Court Department)* Appointed by governor.

Office: U.S. Post Office and Courthouse, 90 Devonshire Street, Fifteenth Floor, Boston 02109.

Telephone: (617) 788-8130.

WEXLER, James H. *(Justice, Trial Court of Massachusetts District Court Department Middlesex County Concord Division)* Appointed by Governor William F. Weld to term beginning 1994. Term expires at age seventy. Born Brooklyn New York Jan 17, 1948. Educated at Hobart College 1964-66, University of Wisconsin B.A. 1968, Columbia Law School 1969-71 and Harvard University M.A. 1972 J.D. 1973. Admitted to practice Massachusetts 1973, U.S. District Court District of Massachusetts, U.S. Court of Appeals First Circuit, U.S. Court of Federal Claims and U.S. Supreme Court.

Formerly with Vista Legal Services and Greater Boston Legal Services. Clinical Instructor Boston University School of Law. Adjunct Faculty Member New England School of Law. Interests include tennis, squash and history.

Mailing address: Two Center Plaza, Suite 200, Boston 02108.

Telephone: (617) 788-8810.

E-mail address: jhwexler@aol.com

WHEATLEY, John C. *(Justice, Trial Court of Massachusetts District Court Department Plymouth County Wareham Division)* Appointed by governor.

Mailing address: Two Center Plaza, Suite 200, Boston 02108.

Telephone: (617) 788-8810.

WHITE, Catherine A. *(Associate Justice, Trial Court of Massachusetts Superior Court Department)* Appointed by governor.

Office: U.S. Post Office and Courthouse, 90 Devonshire Street, Fifteenth Floor, Boston 02109.

Telephone: (617) 788-8130.

WHITE, Kathryn A. *(Circuit Justice, Trial Court of Massachusetts Juvenile Court Department)* Appointed by Governor Argeo Paul Cellucci.

Mailing address: P.O. Box 9664, Boston 02114-9664.

Office: Three Center Plaza, Suite 520, Boston 02108.

Telephone: (617) 788-6550.

WHITEHEAD, Howard J. *(Associate Justice, Trial Court of Massachusetts Superior Court Department)* Appointed by governor.

Office: U.S. Post Office and Courthouse, 90 Devonshire Street, Fifteenth Floor, Boston 02109.

Telephone: (617) 788-8130.

WILLIAMS, H. Gregory *(Justice, Trial Court of Massachusetts District Court Department Hampden County Springfield Division)* Appointed by Governor Argeo Paul Cellucci to term beginning Dec 28, 1999. Term expires at age seventy. Born Washington D.C. March 24, 1950. Educated at Western Maryland College B.A. 1972, Queen Mary College University of London, England M.A. 1973 and Washington and Lee University School of Law J.D. 1977. Staff member 1975-76 and Special Projects Editor 1976-77 Washington and Lee Law Review. Admitted to practice Florida 1977, Massachusetts 1978, U.S. District Court 1978, U.S. Court of Appeals First Circuit 1991 and U.S. Court of Federal Claims. In legal practice Springfield Massachusetts 1978-96.

Assistant Attorney General 1996-99 and Deputy Chief Western Massachusetts Division 1999 Massachusetts. Distinguished Adjunct Professor Bay Path College. Fellow Massachusetts Bar Foundation. Member Hampden County and Massachusetts Bar Associations.

Mailing address: Two Center Plaza, Suite 200, Boston 02108.

Telephone: (617) 788-8810.

WILSON, Geoffrey A. *(First Justice, Trial Court of Massachusetts Probate and Family Court Department Franklin County Division)* Appointed by Governor Argeo Paul Cellucci to term beginning Sept 25, 1997. Term expires at age seventy. Born White Plains New York March 8, 1949. Educated at Amherst College B.A. with honors 1972 and Boston University School of Law J.D. 1975. Admitted to practice Massachusetts 1976, U.S. District Court District of Massachusetts 1977 and U.S. Court of Appeals First Circuit 1983. In legal practice Greenfield Massachusetts 1977-97.

Member Massachusetts Judges Conference, Franklin County, Hampshire County and Massachusetts Bar Associations.

Mailing address: P.O. Box 590, Greenfield 01302-0590.

Telephone: (413) 774-7011.

Fax: (413) 774-3829

E-mail address: gawilson@crocker.com

WINIK, Jeffrey M. *(Associate Justice, Trial Court of Massachusetts Housing Court Department Boston Division)* Appointed by governor.

Office: 24 New Chardon Street, Boston 02114.

Telephone: (617) 788-8483.

WOLF, Mark L. *(Judge, United States District Court District of Massachusetts)* Appointed for life by President Ronald Reagan 1985. Born Nov 23, 1946. Educated at Yale University B.A. cum laude 1968 and Harvard University J.D. cum laude 1971. Awarded honorary degree Boston Latin School 1990. In legal practice Washington D.C. 1971-74 and Boston Massachusetts 1977-81.

Special Assistant to U.S. Deputy Attorney General Laurence Silberman Washington D.C. 1974 and to U.S. Attorney General Edward Levi Washington D.C. 1975-77. Special Counsel to Massachusetts Supreme Judicial Court in investigation and prosecution of Chief Judge of Superior Court 1977. Deputy U.S. Attorney and Chief of Public Corruption Unit Boston 1981-85. Author "Work Incentive Aspects of the Family Assistance Plan" 9 Harvard Journal on Legislation 179, 1972; "Changing of the Guard: Power and Leadership in America" 96 Political Science Quarterly 319, 1981; "Businessmen Can Play a Key Role in the War on Public Corruption" July 16, 1982 and "Tradition of Covenant Binds U.S. and Israel" Nov 5, 1982 *Boston Globe;* "Memorial Day: A Time for Remembrance and Inspiration" May 30, 1983 and "Begin Mapped Retirement" Sept 5, 1983 *The Boston Herald;* "Higgins Captures the Underworld on Beacon Hill" *Boston Globe* Jan 15, 1984; "Criminal Priorities and Policies of the United States Attorney's Office" Boston B. Jour. Nov-Dec 1984; "Remembering Schweitzer" Jan 14, 1985, "An Exemplar of Courage" Oct 10, 1985, "Judge Wyzanski's Legacy to Society" Sept 29, 1986 and "The Role of Politics and Partisanship in Law Enforcement" Feb 3, 1989 *Boston Globe;* "Few Are Chosen: The Judicial Appointments of Oliver Wendell Holmes, Jr. and Charles Edward Wyzanski, Jr." 74 Mas-

WOLF, MARK L.—*Continued*
sachusetts L. Rev. 221, 1989; "Silvio Conte's Cause: A Just and Compassionate Nation" *The Boston Herald* Feb 13, 1991; and "Administering Justice Without Fear or Favor" *Boston Globe* Nov 22, 1992. Lecturer on Law 1990 and Instructor Trial Advocacy Program Harvard Law School. Adjunct Professor Boston College Law School 1992. Lecturer U.S. Department of State and U.S. Information Agency Cyprus 1990, Egypt 1990 and Turkey 1991. Member Committee on Criminal Law and Probation Administration Judicial Conference 1987-94. Member The American Law Institute and Boston Bar Association (Council 1982-85). Recipient Army Medal of Commendation 1974, Presidential Certificate of Appreciation for Meritorious Service in Resettlement of Indochinese Refugees 1975, American Jewish Congress Award 1983 and U.S. Attorney General's Award for Distinguished Service 1984. E-5 USAR 1969-75. Chairman John William Ward Public Service Fellowship since 1986. President Albert Schweitzer Fellowship since 1989.

Office: 5110 U.S. Courthouse, One Courthouse Way, Boston 02210-3002.

Telephone: (617) 748-9271.

WOODLOCK, Douglas P. *(Judge, United States District Court District of Massachusetts)* Appointed for life by President Ronald Reagan to term beginning July 21, 1986. Born Hartford Connecticut Feb 27, 1947. Episcopalian. Educated at Yale University B.A. 1969 and Georgetown University J.D. 1975. Articles Editor and Executive Board member Georgetown Law Journal 1973-75. Law Clerk to Hon. Frank J. Murray, U.S. District Court District of Massachusetts 1975-76. Admitted to practice Massachusetts 1975. In legal practice Boston 1976-79 and 1983-86.

Assistant U.S. Attorney Boston 1979-83. Author "Petra Shattuck at the Beginning of a Path in the Law" 68 Boston University L. Rev. 267-272, 1988; "The 'Peculiar Embarrassment': An Architectural History of the Federal Courts in Massachusetts" 74 Massachusetts L. Rev. 268, 1989; Remarks at Presentation of Portrait of Hon. Frank J. Murray 762 F. Supp. XCVII, 1991; "Attending to the Nation's Business Within the Commonwealth, A Brief Historical Survey of the Anomalous Role of the United States District Court in the Massachusetts Judicial System," Annual Report of the [Massachusetts] Supreme Judicial Court Historical Society 77, 1994; Remarks at Presentation of Portrait of Hon. W. Arthur Garrity, Jr. 861 F. Supp. LXXVIII, 1994; "Judicial Responsibility in Federal Courthouse Design Review: Intentions and Aspirations for Boston" in *Federal Buildings in Context: The Role of Design Review* 55 National Gallery of Art, J. Carter Brown ed. 1995; and "Courthouses Are Worth The Cost" *ARCHITECTURE* 49 Jan 1996. Important Decisions: Strahan v. Coxe (Endangered Species Act) 939 F. Supp. 963 D.Mass. 1996; Xuncax v. Gramajo (international human rights) 886 F. Supp. 162 D.Mass. 1995; United States v. Mannarino (Jencks Act violation) 850 F. Supp. 57 D.Mass. 1994; Globe Newspaper Co. v. Fenton (media access to criminal records) 819 F. Supp. 89 D.Mass 1993; Commonwealth v. Mosbacher (federal legislative reapportionment) 785 F. Supp. 230 D.Mass. 1992 rev'd 505 U.S. 788, 1992; United States v. Osorio (Brady disclosure) 929 F.2d 753, 1st Cir. 1991; Oses v. Massachusetts (trial judge's misconduct) 775 F. Supp. 443 D.Mass. 1991; Jackson v. Harvard University (faculty sex discrimination) 721 F. Supp. 1397 D.Mass. 1989; Securities Industry Association v. Connolly (arbitration preemption) 703 F. Supp. 146 D.Mass. 1988; Smith v. Butler (reasonable doubt) 696 F. Supp. 748 D.Mass. 1988; Black Political Task Force v. Connolly (state legislative redistricting) 679 F. Supp. 109 D.Mass. 1988; Geer v. Federal Highway Admin. (environmental regulation of Boston's "Big Dig" highway and bridge project) 975 F. Supp. 47 D.Mass. 1997; Hasbro v. Clue Computing (internet domain names) 66 F. Supp. 2d 117 D.Mass. 1999; and Boulet v. Cellucci (mental retardation services) 107 F. Supp. 2d 61 D.Mass. 2000. Instructor Harvard Law School 1981 and 1982. Member Committee on Security, Space and Facilities Judicial Conference of the U.S. 1987-95. Chairman New Boston Federal Courthouse Building Committee 1987-98. Board Member Frank J. Murray Inn of Court 1990-92 and Federal Judges Association 1996-2001. Member The American Law Institute, American Judicature Society, American Bar Foundation, Boston, Massachusetts and American Bar Associations. Recipient Director's Award from U.S. Department of Justice 1983 and Thomas Jefferson Award from American Institute of Architects 1996. Previously employed as reporter with *Chicago Sun-Times* Chicago and Springfield Illinois 1969-71 and correspondent in Washington D.C. 1971-73. Staff member U.S. Securities and Exchange Commission Washington D.C. 1973-75. Republican. Chairman Board of Appeals Town of Hamilton 1978-79 and Committee for Public Counsel Services 1984-86. Member Massachusetts Historical Society.

Office: U.S. Courthouse, Suite 4110, 1 Courthouse Way, Boston 02210.

Telephone: (617) 748-9293.

WRIGHT, Milton L., Jr. *(First Justice, Trial Court of Massachusetts District Court Department Suffolk County Roxbury Division)* Appointed by governor.

Mailing address: Two Center Plaza, Suite 200, Boston 02108.

Telephone: (617) 788-8810.

YOUNG, William G. *(Chief Judge, United States District Court District of Massachusetts)* Appointed for life by President Ronald Reagan to term beginning 1985. Chief Judge since Jan 2, 1999. Born Huntington New York 1940. Educated at Harvard University A.B. 1962 LL.B. 1967. Admitted to practice Massachusetts 1967. Former Associate Justice, Trial Court of Massachusetts Superior Court Department.

Member Boston and Massachusetts Bar Associations.

Office: 5710 U.S. Courthouse, One Courthouse Way, Boston 02210-3002.

Telephone: (617) 748-9138.

ZALESKI, Margaret A. *(Circuit Justice, Trial Court of Massachusetts District Court Department)* Appointed by governor.

Office: Two Center Plaza, Suite 200, Boston 02108.

Telephone: (617) 788-8810.

ZIDE, Elliott L. *(First Justice, Trial Court of Massachusetts District Court Department Worcester County Worcester Division and Justice, Fitchburg Division)* Appointed by governor.

Mailing address: Two Center Plaza, Suite 200, Boston 02108.

Telephone: (617) 788-8810.

ZIEMIAN, Robert P. *(First Justice, Trial Court of Massachusetts District Court Department Suffolk County South Boston Division and Justice, West Roxbury Division)* Appointed by Governor Michael S. Dukakis to term beginning March 9, 1989. Born Boston Massachusetts. Educated at Dartmouth College and Suffolk University Law School. Admitted to practice Massachusetts 1975 and U.S. District Court District of Massachusetts 1976. In legal practice Boston 1978-80.

Assistant District Attorney Suffolk County 1975-78 and Essex County 1980-87. Director of Drug Enforcement Governor's Office Massachusetts 1987-89. Member Massachusetts Bar Association. Recipient Outstanding Member Award for developing Boston's first drug diversion course from Boston Coalition. Pilot USN Vietnam war and Persian Gulf war. Member American Legion. Coach high school and youth hockey.

Mailing address: Two Center Plaza, Suite 200, Boston 02108.

Telephone: (617) 788-8810.

ZOBEL, Rya W. *(Judge, United States District Court District of Massachusetts)* Appointed for life by President Jimmy Carter to term beginning April 2, 1979. Born Zwickau Germany Dec 18, 1931. Educated at Radcliffe College A.B. cum laude 1953 and Harvard Law School LL.B. 1956. Law Clerk to Chief Judge George C. Sweeney, U.S. District Court District of Massachusetts 1956-66. Admitted to practice Massachusetts 1956, U.S. District Court District of Massachusetts 1956 and U.S. Court of Appeals First Circuit 1967. In legal practice Boston March 1967 to 1979.

Important Decisions: Polaroid Corporation v. Eastman Kodak Company 1985 and 1988 and Martin F. Gaffney et al. v. United States of America 1991. Fellow American Bar Foundation. Member Boston, Massachusetts and American Bar Associations. Enjoys gardening and reading.

Office: 6110 U.S. Courthouse, One Courthouse Way, Boston 02210-3002.

ZOLL, Samuel E. *(Chief Justice, Trial Court of Massachusetts District Court Department and Justice, Essex County Salem Division)* Appointed by Governor Francis Williams Sargent to term beginning March 1973. Term expires at age seventy. Special Justice Ipswich Division March 1973 to Jan 1974. Former First Justice Salem Division. Chief Justice since Sept 11, 1976. Born June 20, 1934. Educated at Boston University B.S. in Accounting 1954 M.B. Ed. 1958 and Suffolk University J.D. 1962. Awarded honorary LL.D. Suffolk University 1977 and honorary Doctor of Humane Letters Salem State College May 1980. Admitted to practice Massachusetts and U.S. District Court District of Massachusetts. In legal practice Salem 1962-74.

Danvers High School teacher 1958-62. Salem City Councilor 1958-66 (President 1959-60). Public Accountant Salem 1962-74. Massachusetts House of Representatives 1965-69. Salem Mayor 1970-73. Faculty member Suffolk University Graduate School of Public Administration 1976. Chairman Subcommittee on Court Procedures Governor's Task Force on Alcohol Abuse and Highway Safety. Member Massachusetts Trial Lawyers Association, Salem, Essex County, Massachusetts and American Bar Associations. Recipient Award for Distinguished Public Service from Brandeis University 1991 and Dr. Edward Augustus Holyoke Award for public service from Essex Institute 1992. USN Korean War. Past President North Shore Society for the Prevention of Cruelty to Children. Former Member Governor's Anti-Crime Council. Corporator Charter Health Services Corporation. Member Ethics Committee The North Shore Medical Center Salem Hospital.

Office: 24 New Chardon Street, Boston 02114-9665.

Telephone: (617) 788-8810.

MICHIGAN

Capital LANSING

UNITED STATES DISTRICT COURTS DISTRICTS OF MICHIGAN

Within Michigan there are two United States District Courts. For descriptive information refer to the United States Courts section.

EASTERN DISTRICT consists of two divisions.

Northern Division includes Alcona, Alpena, Arenac, Bay, Cheboygan, Clare, Crawford, Gladwin, Gratiot, Huron, Iosco, Isabella, Midland, Montmorency, Ogemaw, Oscoda, Otsego, Presque Isle, Roscommon, Saginaw and Tuscola counties. The court sits at Bay City.

Southern Division includes Genesee, Jackson, Lapeer, Lenawee, Livingston, Macomb, Monroe, Oakland, St. Clair, Sanilac, Shiawassee, Washtenaw and Wayne counties. The court sits at Ann Arbor, Detroit, Flint and Port Huron.

Chief Judge

Lawrence P. Zatkoff

Judges

Bernard A. Friedman
Robert H. Cleland
Denise Page Hood
John Corbett O'Meara
George C. Steeh III
Marianne O. Battani
Gerald E. Rosen
Nancy G. Edmunds
Paul D. Borman
Arthur J. Tarnow
Victoria A. Roberts
David M. Lawson

Senior Judges

John Feikens
Julian A. Cook, Jr.
Anna Diggs Taylor
Patrick J. Duggan
Charles W. Joiner
Avern Cohn
George E. Woods
Paul V. Gadola

Clerk

David J. Weaver
814 U.S. Courthouse
231 West Lafayette Boulevard
Detroit, Michigan 48226
(313) 234-5051

WESTERN DISTRICT consists of two divisions.

Northern Division includes Alger, Baraga, Chippewa, Delta, Dickinson, Gogebic, Houghton, Iron, Keweenaw, Luce, Mackinac, Marquette, Menominee, Ontonagon and Schoolcraft counties. The court sits at Marquette and Sault Ste. Marie.

Southern Division includes Allegan, Antrim, Barry, Benzie, Berrien, Branch, Calhoun, Cass, Charlevoix, Clinton, Eaton, Emmet, Grand Traverse, Hillsdale, Ingham, Ionia, Kalamazoo, Kalkaska, Kent, Lake, Leelanau, Manistee, Mason, Mecosta, Missaukee, Montcalm, Muskegon, Newaygo, Oceana, Osceola, Ottawa, St. Joseph, Van Buren and Wexford counties. The court sits at Grand Rapids, Kalamazoo, Lansing and Traverse City.

Chief Judge

Robert Holmes Bell

Judges

Richard Alan Enslen
David W. McKeague
Gordon Jay Quist

Senior Judge

Wendell Alverson Miles

Clerk

Ronald C. Weston
399 Federal Building
110 Michigan Street N.W.
Grand Rapids, Michigan 49503
(616) 456-2381

UNITED STATES MAGISTRATE JUDGES OF MICHIGAN

EASTERN DISTRICT

Thomas A. Carlson
Charles E. Binder
Donald A. Scheer
R. Steven Whalen
Steven D. Pepe
Virginia M. Morgan
Wallace Capel, Jr.

WESTERN DISTRICT

Hugh W. Brenneman, Jr.
Joseph G. Scoville
Timothy P. Greeley
Ellen S. Carmody

Recalled Magistrate Judge

Paul J. Komives (Eastern)

UNITED STATES BANKRUPTCY COURTS OF MICHIGAN

EASTERN DISTRICT

Chief Judge

Steven W. Rhodes

Judges

Marci B. McIvor
Phillip J. Shefferly
Thomas J. Tucker

Recalled Judges

Walter Shapero
George Brody

Bankruptcy Clerk

Sheila M. Tighe
211 West Fort Street, Suite 2100
Detroit, Michigan 48226-3211
(313) 234-0065

UNITED STATES DISTRICT COURTS DISTRICTS OF MICHIGAN—*Continued*

WESTERN DISTRICT

Chief Judge
James D. Gregg

Judges
Jo Ann C. Stevenson
Jeffrey R. Hughes

Bankruptcy Clerk
Daniel M. LaVille
P.O. Box 3310
Grand Rapids, Michigan 49501-3310
(616) 456-2693

MICHIGAN SUPREME COURT

The Supreme Court is Michigan's court of last resort. The court consists of seven justices who are nominated by political parties and elected in nonpartisan elections for staggered eight-year terms. Vacancies are filled by the governor until the next general election. The chief justice is elected by peer vote every two years.

The court has discretionary review of cases from the Court of Appeals and other state courts. The court has rule-making authority and general superintending control of all courts in the state.

The court sits at Lansing.

Chief Justice
Maura D. Corrigan

Justices

Michael F. Cavanagh	Elizabeth A. Weaver
Marilyn Kelly	Clifford W. Taylor
Robert P. Young, Jr.	Stephen J. Markman

Clerk
Corbin R. Davis
Michigan Hall of Justice
925 West Ottawa Street
P.O. Box 30052
Lansing, Michigan 48909
(517) 373-0120

Court Administrator
John D. Ferry, Jr.
309 North Washington Square
P.O. Box 30048
Lansing, Michigan 48909
(517) 373-0130

MICHIGAN COURT OF APPEALS

The Court of Appeals is Michigan's intermediate appellate court and is divided into four districts for electoral purposes. The court consists of twenty-eight judges elected in nonpartisan district elections for six-year terms. Candidates must be residents of the districts in which they run for election. Vacancies are filled by the governor. A chief judge is selected by the Supreme Court to serve a two-year term. In turn, the chief judge of the Court of Appeals may select a chief judge pro tem to serve a two-year assignment. In the absence of the chief judge, duties of the position are performed by the chief judge pro tem.

The court has appellate jurisdiction in both civil and criminal cases. Criminal convictions from the Circuit Court may be appealed as a matter of right except for guilty plea matters. The decision of a Court of Appeals panel is final except in those cases reviewed by the Supreme Court.

The court sits in panels of at least three judges each. The panels are rotated throughout the state and sit alternately at Detroit, Grand Rapids, Lansing and Marquette.

DISTRICT ONE includes Calhoun, Hillsdale, Lenawee, Monroe and Wayne counties.

DISTRICT TWO includes Genesee, Macomb, Oakland and Shiawassee counties.

DISTRICT THREE includes Allegan, Barry, Berrien, Branch, Cass, Eaton, Ionia, Jackson, Kalamazoo, Kent, Muskegon, Newaygo, Ottawa, St. Joseph, Van Buren and Washtenaw counties.

DISTRICT FOUR includes Alcona, Alger, Alpena, Antrim, Arenac, Baraga, Bay, Benzie, Charlevoix, Cheboygan, Chippewa, Clare, Clinton, Crawford, Delta, Dickinson, Emmet, Gladwin, Gogebic, Grand Traverse, Gratiot, Houghton, Huron, Ingham, Iosco, Iron, Isabella, Kalkaska, Keweenaw, Lake, Lapeer, Leelanau, Livingston, Luce, Mackinac, Manistee, Marquette, Mason, Mecosta, Menominee, Midland, Missaukee, Montcalm, Montmorency, Oceana, Ogemaw, Ontonagon, Osceola, Oscoda, Otsego, Presque Isle, Roscommon, Saginaw, St. Clair, Sanilac, Schoolcraft, Tuscola and Wexford counties.

Chief Judge
William C. Whitbeck

Chief Judge pro tem
Michael R. Smolenski

Judges

Richard A. Bandstra	Stephen L. Borrello
Mark J. Cavanagh	Jessica R. Cooper
Pat M. Donofrio	E. Thomas Fitzgerald
Kirsten Frank Kelly	Hilda R. Gage
Richard Allen Griffin	Joel P. Hoekstra
Karen M. Fort Hood	Kathleen Jansen
Jane E. Markey	Patrick M. Meter
William B. Murphy	Christopher M. Murray
Janet T. Neff	Peter D. O'Connell
Donald S. Owens	Henry William Saad
David H. Sawyer	Bill Schuette
Michael J. Talbot	Helene Nita White
Kurtis T. Wilder	Brian K. Zahra

MICHIGAN CIRCUIT COURTS

The Circuit Courts are trial courts of general jurisdiction in Michigan. The state is divided into fifty-seven judicial circuits, each having a Circuit Court. Judges in the Thirtieth Judicial Circuit also sit as judges of the Court of Claims. On October 1, 1997, the former Recorder's Court of Detroit merged with the Third Judicial Circuit. Circuit judges are elected in nonpartisan elections for six-year terms. Candidates must be residents of the circuit in which they run for election. Vacancies are filled by the governor. In each circuit a chief judge is selected by the Supreme Court to serve a two-year term. In turn, the chief judge of a circuit where there is more than one judge, may select a chief judge pro tem to serve a two-year assignment. In the absence of the chief judge, duties of the position are performed by the chief

MICHIGAN CIRCUIT COURTS—*Continued*

judge pro tem. In November 2001, the Supreme Court appointed two judges to serve as co-chief judges in the Third Judicial Circuit along with a chief judge pro tem.

The courts have original jurisdiction in all civil cases involving more than $25,000 and in all criminal cases involving a felony or serious misdemeanor. The court also has a family division which consists of domestic relations cases including divorce and paternity actions, and juvenile proceedings including abuse/neglect, delinquency and adoptions. The courts have appellate jurisdiction over lower courts and some state administrative agencies. In addition, the courts have superintending control over lower courts within their circuits.

In circuits comprised of more than one county, judges travel between county seats to hold court sessions, which must be held at least four times per year in each county.

In 1996, the Michigan Supreme Court initiated a project to test the consolidation of some local circuit, probate and district courts into one trial court of general jurisdiction. Each demonstration project court has appointed a chief judge of the consolidated trial court. Demonstration project courts have been created in Barry, Berrien, Iron, Isabella, Lake and Washtenaw counties, and in the multi-county circuit that includes Crawford, Kalkaska and Otsego counties. As of January 1, 1999, the project has been extended indefinitely.

In 2001, the Supreme Court also instituted the Next Generation Model Trial Courts Project which involves the circuit, district and probate courts of Arenac, Bay, Cheboygan, Genesee, Kalamazoo, Marquette, Midland, Muskegon, Ogemaw and Roscommon counties and the circuit and probate courts of Eaton, Ingham, Livingston and Oakland counties.

FIRST JUDICIAL CIRCUIT includes Hillsdale County. The court sits at Hillsdale.

Chief Judge
Michael R. Smith

SECOND JUDICIAL CIRCUIT includes Berrien County. The court sits at St. Joseph and Niles.

Chief Judge
Paul L. Maloney

Judges
John N. Fields
Casper O. Grathwohl
John T. Hammond

THIRD JUDICIAL CIRCUIT includes Wayne County. The court sits at Detroit.

Co-Chief Judges
Mary Beth Kelly
Timothy Michael Kenny

Judges

Wendy M. Baxter	Annette J. Berry
Gregory D. Bill	Susan D. Borman
Ulysses W. Boykin	Margie R. Braxton
Helen E. Brown	William Leo Cahalan
Bill Callahan	Michael James Callahan
James R. Chylinski	Sean F. Cox
Robert J. Colombo, Jr.	Daphne Means Curtis
George William Crockett, III	Christopher D. Dingell
Gershwin Allen Drain	Maggie Drake
Prentis Edwards	Vonda R. Evans
Patricia Susan Fresard	John H. Gillis, Jr.
William J. Giovan	David Alan Groner
Richard B. Halloran, Jr.	Pamela R. Harwood
Amy Patricia Hathaway	Cynthia Gray Hathaway
Diane Marie Hathaway	Michael M. Hathaway
Richard P. Hathaway	Thomas Edward Jackson
Vera Massey Jones	Arthur J. Lombard
Kathleen I. Macdonald	Sheila Gibson Manning
Kathleen M. McCarthy	Warfield Moore, Jr.
Bruce U. Morrow	John A. Murphy
Susan Bieke Neilson	Maria L. Oxholm
Lita Masini Popke	James J. Rashid
Daniel P. Ryan	Michael F. Sapala
Louis F. Simmons, Jr.	Leslie Kim Smith
Jeanne Stempien	Cynthia D. Stephens
Craig S. Strong	Brian R. Sullivan
Kaye Tertzag	Deborah A. Thomas
Edward M. Thomas	Isidore B. Torres
Leonard Townsend	Mary M. Waterstone
Kym L. Worthy	Carole F. Youngblood
Robert L. Ziolkowski	

FOURTH JUDICIAL CIRCUIT includes Jackson County. The court sits at Jackson.

Chief Judge
Charles A. Nelson

Judges
Edward J. Grant
John G. McBain, Jr.
Chad C. Schmucker

FIFTH JUDICIAL CIRCUIT includes Barry County. The court sits at Hastings.

Chief Judge
James H. Fisher

SIXTH JUDICIAL CIRCUIT includes Oakland County. The court sits at Pontiac.

Chief Judge
Joan E. Young

Judges

James M. Alexander	Martha Anderson
Steven N. Andrews	Patrick J. Brennan
Rae Lee Chabot	Nanci J. Grant
Richard D. Kuhn	Denise Langford-Morris
John J. McDonald	Fred M. Mester
Rudy J. Nichols	Colleen A. O'Brien
Daniel Patrick O'Brien	Wendy Lynn Potts
Gene Schnelz	Edward Sosnick
Deborah G. Tyner	Michael D. Warren, Jr.

SEVENTH JUDICIAL CIRCUIT includes Genesee County. The court sits at Flint.

Chief Judge
Robert M. Ransom

Judges

Duncan M. Beagle	Joseph J. Farah
Judith A. Fullerton	John A. Gadola
Archie L. Hayman	Geoffrey L. Neithercut
Richard B. Yuille	

MICHIGAN CIRCUIT COURTS—*Continued*

EIGHTH JUDICIAL CIRCUIT includes Ionia and Montcalm counties. The court sits at Ionia and Stanton.

Chief Judge
Charles H. Miel

Judge
David A. Hoort

NINTH JUDICIAL CIRCUIT includes Kalamazoo County. The court sits at Kalamazoo.

Chief Judge
J. Richardson Johnson

Judges
Stephen D. Gorsalitz
Richard Ryan Lamb
Philip D. Schaefer
William G. Schma

TENTH JUDICIAL CIRCUIT includes Saginaw County. The court sits at Saginaw.

Chief Judge
Leopold P. Borrello

Judges
Fred L. Borchard
William A. Crane
Lynda L. Heathscott
Robert L. Kaczmarek

ELEVENTH JUDICIAL CIRCUIT includes Alger, Luce, Mackinac and Schoolcraft counties. The court sits at Munising, Newberry, St. Ignace and Manistique.

Chief Judge
Charles H. Stark

TWELFTH JUDICIAL CIRCUIT includes Baraga, Houghton and Keweenaw counties. The court sits at L'Anse, Houghton and Eagle River.

Chief Judge
Garfield W. Hood

THIRTEENTH JUDICIAL CIRCUIT includes Antrim, Grand Traverse and Leelanau counties. The court sits at Bellaire, Traverse City and Leland.

Chief Judge
Philip E. Rodgers, Jr.

Judge
Thomas G. Power

FOURTEENTH JUDICIAL CIRCUIT includes Muskegon County. The court sits at Muskegon.

Chief Judge
Timothy G. Hicks

Judges
James M. Graves, Jr.
William C. Marietti
John C. Ruck

FIFTEENTH JUDICIAL CIRCUIT includes Branch County. The court sits at Coldwater.

Chief Judge
Michael H. Cherry

SIXTEENTH JUDICIAL CIRCUIT includes Macomb County. The court sits at Mount Clemens.

Chief Judge
Peter J. Maceroni

Judges
James M. Biernat, Sr.
Richard L. Caretti
Mary A. Chrzanowski
Diane M. Druzinski
Donald G. Miller
Deborah A. Servitto
Edward A. Servitto, Jr.
Mark S. Switalski
Matthew S. Switalski
Antonio P. Viviano

SEVENTEENTH JUDICIAL CIRCUIT includes Kent County. The court sits at Grand Rapids.

Chief Judge
George S. Buth

Judges
Kathleen A. Feeney
Donald A. Johnston, III
Dennis C. Kolenda
Dennis B. Leiber
James Robert Redford
Paul J. Sullivan
Daniel V. Zemaitis

EIGHTEENTH JUDICIAL CIRCUIT includes Bay County. The court sits at Bay City.

Chief Judge
Lawrence M. Bielawski

Judges
William Joseph Caprathe
Kenneth W. Schmidt

NINETEENTH JUDICIAL CIRCUIT includes Benzie and Manistee counties. The court sits at Beulah and Manistee.

Chief Judge
James M. Batzer

TWENTIETH JUDICIAL CIRCUIT includes Ottawa County. The court sits at Grand Haven.

Chief Judge
Edward R. Post

Judges
Calvin L. Bosman
Wesley J. Nykamp

TWENTY-FIRST JUDICIAL CIRCUIT includes Isabella County. The court sits at Mount Pleasant.

Chief Judge
Paul H. Chamberlain

TWENTY-SECOND JUDICIAL CIRCUIT includes Washtenaw County. The court sits at Ann Arbor.

Chief Judge
Archie Cameron Brown

Judges
Timothy P. Connors
Melinda Morris
Donald E. Shelton
David Scott Swartz

TWENTY-THIRD JUDICIAL CIRCUIT includes Alcona, Arenac, Iosco and Oscoda counties. The court sits at Harrisville, Standish, Tawas City and Mio.

Chief Judge
Ronald M. Bergeron

MICHIGAN CIRCUIT COURTS—*Continued*

Judge
William F. Myles

TWENTY-FOURTH JUDICIAL CIRCUIT includes Sanilac County. The court sits at Sandusky.

Chief Judge
Donald A. Teeple

TWENTY-FIFTH JUDICIAL CIRCUIT includes Marquette County. The court sits at Marquette.

Chief Judge
Thomas L. Solka

Judge
John R. Weber

TWENTY-SIXTH JUDICIAL CIRCUIT includes Alpena and Montmorency counties. The court sits at Alpena and Atlanta.

Chief Judge
Joseph P. Swallow

Judge
John F. Kowalski

TWENTY-SEVENTH JUDICIAL CIRCUIT includes Newaygo and Oceana counties. The court sits at White Cloud and Hart.

Chief Judge
Anthony A. Monton

Judge
Terrence R. Thomas

TWENTY-EIGHTH JUDICIAL CIRCUIT includes Missaukee and Wexford counties. The court sits at Lake City and Cadillac.

Chief Judge
Charles D. Corwin

TWENTY-NINTH JUDICIAL CIRCUIT includes Clinton and Gratiot counties. The court sits at St. Johns and Ithaca.

Chief Judge
Jeffrey L. Martlew

Judge
Randy L. Tahvonen

THIRTIETH JUDICIAL CIRCUIT includes Ingham County. The court sits at Mason and Lansing.

Chief Judge
William E. Collette

Judges
Laura Baird
James R. Giddings
Paula J. Manderfield
Thomas Leo Brown
Janelle A. Lawless
Beverley Nettles-Nickerson

THIRTY-FIRST JUDICIAL CIRCUIT includes St. Clair County. The court sits at Port Huron.

Chief Judge
Peter E. Deegan

Judges
James P. Adair
Daniel J. Kelly

THIRTY-SECOND JUDICIAL CIRCUIT includes Gogebic and Ontonagon counties. The court sits at Bessemer and Ontonagon.

Chief Judge
Roy D. Gotham

THIRTY-THIRD JUDICIAL CIRCUIT includes Charlevoix County. The court sits at Charlevoix.

Chief Judge
Richard M. Pajtas

THIRTY-FOURTH JUDICIAL CIRCUIT includes Ogemaw and Roscommon counties. The court sits at West Branch and Roscommon.

Chief Judge
Michael J. Baumgartner

THIRTY-FIFTH JUDICIAL CIRCUIT includes Shiawassee County. The court sits at Corunna.

Chief Judge
Gerald D. Lostracco

THIRTY-SIXTH JUDICIAL CIRCUIT includes Van Buren County. The court sits at Paw Paw.

Chief Judge
Paul E. Hamre

Judge
William C. Buhl

THIRTY-SEVENTH JUDICIAL CIRCUIT includes Calhoun County. The court sits at Marshall and Battle Creek.

Chief Judge
Allen L. Garbrecht

Judges
James C. Kingsley
Stephen Barry Miller
Conrad J. Sindt

THIRTY-EIGHTH JUDICIAL CIRCUIT includes Monroe County. The court sits at Monroe.

Chief Judge
Joseph Anthony Costello, Jr.

Judges
Michael W. LaBeau
William F. LaVoy

THIRTY-NINTH JUDICIAL CIRCUIT includes Lenawee County. The court sits at Adrian.

Chief Judge
Harvey A. Koselka

Judge
Timothy P. Pickard

FORTIETH JUDICIAL CIRCUIT includes Lapeer County. The court sits at Lapeer.

Chief Judge
Nick O. Holowka

MICHIGAN CIRCUIT COURTS—*Continued*

Judge
Michael P. Higgins

FORTY-FIRST JUDICIAL CIRCUIT includes Dickinson, Iron and Menominee counties. The court sits at Iron Mountain, Crystal Falls and Menominee.

Chief Judge
Mary Brouillette Barglind

Judge
Richard J. Celello

FORTY-SECOND JUDICIAL CIRCUIT includes Midland County. The court sits at Midland.

Chief Judge
Thomas L. Ludington

Judge
Paul J. Clulo

FORTY-THIRD JUDICIAL CIRCUIT includes Cass County. The court sits at Cassopolis.

Chief Judge
Michael E. Dodge

FORTY-FOURTH JUDICIAL CIRCUIT includes Livingston County. The court sits at Howell.

Judges
Daniel A. Burress
Stanley J. Latreille

FORTY-FIFTH JUDICIAL CIRCUIT includes St. Joseph County. The court sits at Centreville.

Chief Judge
James P. Noecker

FORTY-SIXTH JUDICIAL CIRCUIT includes Crawford, Kalkaska and Otsego counties. The court sits at Grayling, Kalkaska and Gaylord.

Chief Judge
Alton T. Davis, Jr.

Judge
Dennis F. Murphy

FORTY-SEVENTH JUDICIAL CIRCUIT includes Delta County. The court sits at Escanaba.

Chief Judge
Stephen T. Davis

FORTY-EIGHTH JUDICIAL CIRCUIT includes Allegan County. The court sits at Allegan.

Chief Judge
George R. Corsiglia

Judge
Harry A. Beach

FORTY-NINTH JUDICIAL CIRCUIT includes Mecosta and Osceola counties. The court sits at Big Rapids and Reed City.

Chief Judge
Lawrence C. Root

FIFTIETH JUDICIAL CIRCUIT includes Chippewa County. The court sits at Sault Ste. Marie.

Chief Judge
Nicholas J. Lambros

FIFTY-FIRST JUDICIAL CIRCUIT includes Lake and Mason counties. The court sits at Baldwin and Ludington.

Chief Judge
Richard I. Cooper

FIFTY-SECOND JUDICIAL CIRCUIT includes Huron County. The court sits at Bad Axe.

Chief Judge
M. Richard Knoblock

FIFTY-THIRD JUDICIAL CIRCUIT includes Cheboygan and Presque Isle counties. The court sits at Cheboygan and Rogers City.

Chief Judge
Scott L. Pavlich

FIFTY-FOURTH JUDICIAL CIRCUIT includes Tuscola County. The court sits at Caro.

Judge
Patrick Reed Joslyn

FIFTY-FIFTH JUDICIAL CIRCUIT includes Clare and Gladwin counties. The court sits at Harrison and Gladwin.

Chief Judge
Kurt N. Hansen

FIFTY-SIXTH JUDICIAL CIRCUIT includes Eaton County. The court sits at Charlotte.

Chief Judge
Thomas S. Eveland

Judge
Calvin E. Osterhaven

FIFTY-SEVENTH JUDICIAL CIRCUIT includes Emmet County. The court sits at Petoskey.

Chief Judge
Charles W. Johnson

MICHIGAN COURT OF CLAIMS

The Court of Claims is a court of special jurisdiction in Michigan. Judges of Michigan Circuit Court Thirtieth Judicial Circuit sit as judges of the Court of Claims. The court has jurisdiction limited to claims over $1,000 against the State of Michigan, except where Circuit Courts have jurisdiction.

MICHIGAN PROBATE COURT

The Probate Court is a court of limited jurisdiction in Michigan. With the exception of ten counties which have joined to form five Probate Court districts, there is a Probate Court in each county of Michigan. Judges are elected in nonpartisan elections for six-year terms. Vacancies are filled by the governor. In each county a chief judge is selected by the Supreme Court to serve a two-year term. In turn, the chief judge of a county where there is more than one judge may select a chief judge pro tem to serve a two-year assignment. In the absence of the chief judge, the duties of the position are performed by the chief judge pro tem.

MICHIGAN

MICHIGAN PROBATE COURT—*Continued*

The court has jurisdiction in supervision of probating of wills and administration of estates and trusts, guardianships, commitment for hospital care of mentally ill, mentally handicapped and addicted persons and condemnation of land.

The court sits at each county seat and at other locations as specified.

In 1996, the Michigan Supreme Court initiated a project to test the consolidation of some local circuit, probate and district courts into one trial court of general jurisdiction. Each demonstration project court has appointed a chief judge of the consolidated trial court. Demonstration project courts have been created in Barry, Berrien, Iron, Isabella, Lake and Washtenaw counties, and in the multi-county circuit that includes Crawford, Kalkaska and Otsego counties. As of January 1, 1999, the project has been extended indefinitely.

In 2001, the Supreme Court also instituted the Next Generation Model Trial Courts Project which involves the circuit, district and probate courts of Arenac, Bay, Cheboygan, Genesee, Kalamazoo, Marquette, Midland, Muskegon, Ogemaw and Roscommon counties and the circuit and probate courts of Eaton, Ingham, Livingston and Oakland counties.

---

*Chief Judge

County	Judge
Alcona	James H. Cook*
Alger-Schoolcraft	William W. Carmody*
Allegan	Michael L. Buck*
Alpena	Douglas A. Pugh*
Antrim	Norman R. Hayes*
Arenac	Jack William Scully*
Baraga	Timothy S. Brennan*
Barry	Richard H. Shaw
Bay	Karen A. Tighe*
Benzie	Nancy A. Kida*
Berrien	Mabel Johnson Mayfield
	Thomas E. Nelson
Branch	Frederick L. Wood*
Calhoun	Phillip E. Harter
Court also sits at Battle Creek	Gary K. Reed*
Cass	Susan L. Dobrich*
Charlevoix	See Emmet-Charlevoix
Cheboygan	Robert John Butts*
Chippewa	Lowell R. Ulrich*
Clare-Gladwin	Thomas P. McLaughlin*
Clinton	Marvin E. Robertson*
Crawford	John G. Hunter
Delta	Robert E. Goebel, Jr.*
Dickinson	John A. Torreano*
Eaton	Michael F. Skinner
Emmet-Charlevoix	Frederick R. Mulhauser*
Genesee	Thomas L. Gadola
	Allen J. Nelson*
	Robert E. Weiss
Gladwin	See Clare-Gladwin
Gogebic	Joel L. Massie*
Grand Traverse	David L. Stowe*
Gratiot	Jack T. Arnold*
Hillsdale	Michael E. Nye*
Houghton	vacancy
Huron	David L. Clabuesch*
Ingham	R. George Economy*
Court also sits at Lansing	Richard Joseph Garcia
Ionia	Gerald Joseph Supina*
Iosco	John D. Hamilton*
Iron	C. Joseph Schwedler*
Isabella	William T. Ervin
Jackson	Susan E. Vandercook*
Kalamazoo	Patricia Nedwicki Conlon
	Donald R. Halstead*
	Carolyn H. Williams
Kalkaska	Lynne Marie Buday
Kent	Nanaruth H. Carpenter
	Patricia D. Gardner
	Janet A. Haynes*
	G. Patrick Hillary
Keweenaw	James George Jaaskelainen*
Lake	Mark S. Wickens*
Lapeer	Justus C. Scott*
Leelanau	Joseph E. Deegan*
Lenawee	Charles W. Jameson*
Livingston	Susan L. Reck*
Luce-Mackinac	Thomas B. North*
Mackinac	See Luce-Mackinac
Macomb	Kathryn A. George
	Pamela Gilbert O'Sullivan*
	vacancy
Manistee	John R. DeVries*
Marquette	Michael John Anderegg*
Mason	Mark D. Raven*
Mecosta-Osceola	LaVail Earl Hull*
Menominee	William A. Hupy*
Midland	Dorene S. Allen*
Missaukee	Charles Parsons*
Monroe	John A. Hohman, Jr.
	Pamela A. Moskwa*
Montcalm	Edward L. Skinner*
Montmorency	Robert P. M. Nordstrom*
Muskegon	Neil G. Mullally*
	Gregory C. Pittman
Newaygo	Graydon W. Dimkoff*
Oakland	Barry M. Grant
	Linda S. Hallmark*
	Eugene Arthur Moore
	Elizabeth M. Pezzetti
Oceana	Walter Aleksy Urick*
Ogemaw	Eugene I. Turkelson*
Ontonagon	Joseph D. Zeleznik*
Osceola	See Mecosta-Osceola
Oscoda	Kathryn Joan Root*
Otsego	Michael K. Cooper
Ottawa	Mark A. Feyen*
Presque Isle	Kenneth A. Radzibon*
Roscommon	Douglas C. Dosson*
Saginaw	Faye M. Harrison*
	Patrick J. McGraw
St. Clair	Elwood L. Brown
	John R. Monaghan*
St. Joseph	Thomas E. Shumaker*
Sanilac	R. Terry Maltby*
Schoolcraft	See Alger-Schoolcraft
Shiawassee	James R. Clatterbaugh*
Tuscola	W. Wallace Kent, Jr.*
Van Buren	Frank D. Willis*

MICHIGAN PROBATE COURT—*Continued*

Washtenaw	Nancy C. Francis
	John N. Kirkendall*
Wayne	June E. Blackwell-Hatcher
	Freddie G. Burton, Jr.
	Patricia B. Campbell
	James E. Lacey
	Milton L. Mack, Jr.*
	Cathie B. Maher
	Martin T. Maher
	Frances Pitts
	David J. Szymanski
Wexford	Kenneth L. Tacoma*

MICHIGAN DISTRICT COURTS

The District Courts are courts of limited jurisdiction established in one hundred three judicial districts throughout Michigan. All District Court judges are elected in nonpartisan elections for six-year terms. Vacancies are filled by the governor. In each district, except District Seventy-one A, a chief judge is selected by the Supreme Court to serve a two-year term. In District Seventy-one A, the chief judge duties for the District Court are handled by a Circuit Court judge. The chief judge of the district may select a chief judge pro tem to serve a two-year assignment. In the absence of the chief judge, the duties of the position are performed by the chief judge pro tem. In District Seventy-one A, the chief judge duties are handled by a Circuit Court judge. In single-judge districts, the chief judge may appoint one magistrate for each county in the district.

On September 1, 1981 the functions of Michigan's abolished Common Pleas Court were transferred to District Court Thirty-six in Detroit. The previously held jurisdiction of traffic and ordinance divisions of the Recorder's Court was also transferred at that time to District Thirty-six. In Districts Thirty-eight and Thirty-two B, Municipal Courts serve the purpose of District Courts.

The courts have exclusive jurisdiction in all civil cases up to $25,000 and in criminal misdemeanors when punishment does not exceed one year imprisonment. The courts also handle arraignments, setting and acceptance of bail, preliminary examinations in felony cases, eviction proceedings, land contract and mortgage foreclosures. A small claims division is provided for civil cases involving less than $3,000. District Courts may also establish traffic bureaus to handle traffic violations.

In 1996, the Michigan Supreme Court initiated a project to test the consolidation of some local circuit, probate and district courts into one trial court of general jurisdiction. Each demonstration project court has appointed a chief judge of the consolidated trial court. Demonstration project courts have been created in Barry, Berrien, Iron, Isabella, Lake and Washtenaw counties, and in the multi-county circuit that includes Crawford, Kalkaska and Otsego counties. As of January 1, 1999, the project has been extended indefinitely.

In 2001, the Supreme Court also instituted the Next Generation Model Trial Courts Project which involves the circuit, district and probate courts of Arenac, Bay, Cheboygan, Genesee, Kalamazoo, Marquette, Midland, Muskegon, Ogemaw and Roscommon counties and the circuit and probate courts of Eaton, Ingham, Livingston and Oakland counties.

DISTRICT ONE includes Monroe County. The court sits at Monroe.

Chief Judge
Jack Vitale

Judges
Mark S. Braunlich
Terrence P. Bronson

DISTRICT TWO A includes Lenawee County. The court sits at Adrian.

Chief Judge
James E. Sheridan

Judge
Natalia M. Koselka

DISTRICT TWO B includes Hillsdale County. The court sits at Hillsdale.

Chief Judge
Donald L. Sanderson

DISTRICT THREE A includes Branch County. The court sits at Coldwater.

Chief Judge
David T. Coyle

DISTRICT THREE B includes St. Joseph County. The court sits at Centreville.

Chief Judge
William D. Welty

Judge
Jeffrey C. Middleton

DISTRICT FOUR includes Cass County. The court sits at Cassopolis.

Chief Judge
Paul E. Deats

DISTRICT FIVE includes Berrien County. The court sits at St. Joseph and Niles.

Judges
Gary J. Bruce
Angela Pasula
C. F. Scott Schofield
Lynda A. Tolen
Dennis M. Wiley

DISTRICT SIX is combined with District Five.

DISTRICT SEVEN includes Van Buren County. The court sits at Paw Paw and South Haven.

Chief Judge
Robert T. Hentchel

Judge
Arthur H. Clarke III

DISTRICT EIGHT consists of three divisions.

Chief Judge
Vincent Castelli Westra

Division One includes the city of Kalamazoo in Kalamazoo County.

MICHIGAN DISTRICT COURTS—*Continued*

Judges
Quinn E. Benson
Ann L. Hannon
Carol A. Husum

Division Two includes the city of Portage in Kalamazoo County.

Judge
Robert C. Kropf

Division Three includes Kalamazoo County except the cities of Kalamazoo and Portage. The court sits at Kalamazoo.

Judges
Paul J. Bridenstine
Richard A. Santoni
Vincent Castelli Westra

DISTRICT NINE is combined with District Eight.

DISTRICT TEN includes Calhoun County. The court sits at Marshall, Albion and Battle Creek.

Chief Judge
John R. Holmes

Judges
Samuel I. Durham, Jr.
Franklin K. Line, Jr.
Marvin Ratner

DISTRICT ELEVEN is combined with District Ten.

DISTRICT TWELVE includes Jackson County. The court sits at Jackson.

Chief Judge
Charles J. Falahee, Jr.

Judges
Lysle G. Hall, Jr.
James M. Justin
R. Darryl Mazur

DISTRICT THIRTEEN is combined with District Twelve.

DISTRICT FOURTEEN A includes Washtenaw County except the city of Ann Arbor and the township of Ypsilanti. The court sits at Ann Arbor, Chelsea and Saline.

Chief Judge
J. Cedric Simpson

Judges
Richard E. Conlin
Kirk W. Tabbey

DISTRICT FOURTEEN B includes the township of Ypsilanti in Washtenaw County.

Chief Judge
John B. Collins

DISTRICT FIFTEEN includes the city of Ann Arbor in Washtenaw County.

Chief Judge
Ann E. Mattson

Judges
Julie Creal Goodridge
Elizabeth Pollard Hines

DISTRICT SIXTEEN includes the city of Livonia in Wayne County.

Chief Judge
Robert B. Brzezinski

Judge
Kathleen J. McCann

DISTRICT SEVENTEEN includes the township of Redford in Wayne County.

Chief Judge
Charlotte L. Wirth

Judge
Karen Khalil

DISTRICT EIGHTEEN includes the city of Westland in Wayne County.

Chief Judge
C. Charles Bokos

Judge
Gail McKnight

DISTRICT NINETEEN includes the city of Dearborn in Wayne County.

Chief Judge
Virginia A. Sobotka

Judges
William C. Hultgren
Mark W. Somers

DISTRICT TWENTY includes the city of Dearborn Heights in Wayne County.

Chief Judge
Leo K. Foran

Judge
Mark J. Plawecki

DISTRICT TWENTY-ONE includes the city of Garden City in Wayne County.

Chief Judge
Richard L. Hammer, Jr.

DISTRICT TWENTY-TWO includes the city of Inkster in Wayne County.

Chief Judge
Sylvia A. James

DISTRICT TWENTY-THREE includes the city of Taylor in Wayne County.

Chief Judge
William J. Sutherland

Judge
Geno Salomone

DISTRICT TWENTY-FOUR includes the cities of Allen Park and Melvindale in Wayne County. The court sits at Allen Park.

Chief Judge
John T. Courtright

MICHIGAN DISTRICT COURTS—*Continued*

Judge
vacancy

DISTRICT TWENTY-FIVE includes the city of Lincoln Park in Wayne County.

Chief Judge
David A. Bajorek

Judge
Joseph H. DeLaurentiis

DISTRICT TWENTY-SIX consists of two divisions.

Chief Judge
Raymond A. Charron

Division One includes the city of River Rouge in Wayne County.

Judge
Raymond A. Charron

Division Two includes the city of Ecorse in Wayne County.

Judge
Michael F. Ciungan

DISTRICT TWENTY-SEVEN consists of two divisions.

Chief Judge
Randy L. Kalmbach

Division One includes the city of Wyandotte in Wayne County.

Judge
Randy L. Kalmbach

Division Two includes the city of Riverview in Wayne County.

Judge
vacancy

DISTRICT TWENTY-EIGHT includes the city of Southgate in Wayne County.

Chief Judge
James A. Kandrevas

DISTRICT TWENTY-NINE includes the city of Wayne in Wayne County.

Chief Judge
Carolyn A. Archbold

DISTRICT THIRTY includes the city of Highland Park in Wayne County.

Chief Judge
vacancy

DISTRICT THIRTY-ONE includes the city of Hamtramck in Wayne County.

Chief Judge
Paul J. Paruk

DISTRICT THIRTY-TWO A includes the city of Harper Woods in Wayne County.

Chief Judge
Roger J. La Rose

DISTRICT THIRTY-THREE includes the cities of Flat Rock, Gibraltar, Rockwood, Trenton and Woodhaven and the townships of Brownstown and Grosse Ile in Wayne County. The court sits at Woodhaven.

Chief Judge
James Kurt Kersten

Judges
Michael K. McNally
Donald L. Swank

DISTRICT THIRTY-FOUR includes the cities of Belleville and Romulus and the townships of Huron, Sumpter and Van Buren in Wayne County. The court sits at Romulus.

Chief Judge
Tina Brooks Green

Judges
Brian A. Oakley
David M. Parrott

DISTRICT THIRTY-FIVE includes the cities of Northville and Plymouth and the townships of Canton, Northville and Plymouth in Wayne County. The court sits at Plymouth.

Chief Judge
John E. MacDonald

Judges
Michael J. Gerou
Ronald W. Lowe

DISTRICT THIRTY-SIX includes the city of Detroit in Wayne County.

Chief Judge
Marylin E. Atkins

Judges

Deborah Ross Adams	Trudy DunCombe Archer
Joseph N. Baltimore	Nancy McCaughan Blount
David Martin Bradfield	Donald Coleman
Izetta F. Bright	Nancy A. Farmer
Theresa Doss	Jimmylee Gray
Ruth Ann Garrett	Paula G. Humphries
Beverly J. Hayes-Sipes	Vanesa F. Jones-Bradley
Patricia L. Jefferson	Leonia J. Lloyd
Deborah L. Langston	Wade H. McCree
Willie G. Lipscomb Jr.	Donna R. Milhouse
Miriam B. Martin-Clark	Lydia Nance Adams
Marion A. Moore	John R. Perry
Jeanette O'Banner-Owens	Mark A. Randon
Kevin F. Robbins	David S. Robinson, Jr.
C. Lorene Royster	Ted Wallace

DISTRICT THIRTY-SEVEN includes the cities of Center Line and Warren in Macomb County. The court sits at Warren.

Chief Judge
Walter A. Jakubowski, Jr.

Judges
John M. Chmura
Jennifer Faunce
Dawnn M. Gruenburg

DISTRICT THIRTY-EIGHT: See Eastpointe Municipal Court.

DISTRICT THIRTY-NINE includes the cities of Fraser and Roseville in Macomb County. The court sits at Roseville.

Chief Judge
Joseph F. Boedeker

Judges
Marco A. Santia
Catherine B. Steenland

DISTRICT FORTY includes the city of St. Clair Shores in Macomb County.

Chief Judge
J. Craigen Oster

Judge
Mark A. Fratarcangeli

DISTRICT FORTY-ONE A includes the cities of Sterling Heights and Utica and the townships of Macomb and Shelby in Macomb County. The court sits at Shelby Township, Sterling Heights and Utica.

Chief Judge
Stephen S. Sierawski

Judges
Michael S. Maceroni
Douglas P. Shepherd

DISTRICT FORTY-ONE B includes the city of Mount Clemens and the townships of Clinton and Harrison in Macomb County. The court sits at Mount Clemens and Clinton Township.

Chief Judge
Linda Davis

Judges
William H. Cannon
John C. Foster

DISTRICT FORTY-TWO consists of two divisions.

Chief Judge
Paul A. Cassidy

Division One includes the cities of Memphis and Richmond, the townships of Armada, Bruce, Ray, Richmond and Washington and the villages of Armada and Romeo in Macomb County. The court sits at Romeo.

Judge
Denis R. LeDuc

Division Two includes the city of New Baltimore, the townships of Chesterfield and Lenox and the village of New Haven in Macomb County. The court sits at New Baltimore.

Judge
Paul A. Cassidy

DISTRICT FORTY-THREE includes the cities of Ferndale, Hazel Park and Madison Heights in Oakland County. The court sits at Ferndale, Hazel Park and Madison Heights.

Chief Judge
Keith P. Hunt

Judges
Joseph Longo
Robert J. Turner

DISTRICT FORTY-FOUR includes the city of Royal Oak in Oakland County.

Chief Judge
Daniel Sawicki

Judge
Terrence H. Brennan

DISTRICT FORTY-FIVE A includes the city of Berkley in Oakland County.

Chief Judge
William R. Sauer

DISTRICT FORTY-FIVE B includes the cities of Huntington Woods, Oak Park and Pleasant Ridge and the township of Royal Oak in Oakland County. The court sits at Oak Park.

Chief Judge
David M. Gubow

Judge
Michelle Friedman Appel

DISTRICT FORTY-SIX includes the cities of Lathrup Village and Southfield, the township of Southfield and the villages of Beverly Hills, Bingham Farms and Franklin in Oakland County. The court sits at Southfield.

Chief Judge
Stephen C. Cooper

Judges
Shelia R. Johnson
Susan M. Moiseev

DISTRICT FORTY-SEVEN includes the cities of Farmington and Farmington Hills in Oakland County. The court sits at Farmington.

Chief Judge
Marla E. Parker

Judge
James Brady

DISTRICT FORTY-EIGHT includes the cities of Birmingham, Bloomfield Hills, Keego Harbor, Orchard Lake Village and Sylvan Lake and the townships of Bloomfield and West Bloomfield in Oakland County. The court sits at Bloomfield Hills.

Chief Judge
Kimberly Small

Judges
Edward Avadenka
Diane D'Agostini

DISTRICT FORTY-NINE is covered by District Fifty-Two Division Four.

DISTRICT FIFTY includes the city of Pontiac in Oakland County.

MICHIGAN DISTRICT COURTS—*Continued*

Chief Judge
Leo Bowman

Judges
Christopher C. Brown
Preston G. Thomas
vacancy

DISTRICT FIFTY-ONE includes the township of Waterford in Oakland County.

Chief Judge
Phyllis C. McMillen

Judge
Richard D. Kuhn, Jr.

DISTRICT FIFTY-TWO consists of four divisions.

Chief Judge
Julie A. Nicholson

Division One includes the cities of Novi, South Lyon, Walled Lake and Wixom, the townships of Commerce, Highland, Lyon, Milford, Novi, Rose and White Lake and the villages of Milford and Wolverine Lake in Oakland County. The court sits at Novi.

Judges
Michael Batchik
Robert Bondy
Brian W. MacKenzie
Dennis N. Powers

Division Two includes the townships of Brandon, Groveland, Holly, Independence and Springfield and the villages of Clarkston, Davisburg, Holly and Ortonville in Oakland County. The court sits at Clarkston.

Judge
Dana Fortinberry

Division Three includes the cities of Auburn Hills, Lake Angelus, Rochester and Rochester Hills and the townships of Addison, Oakland, Orion and Oxford in Oakland County. The courts sits at Rochester Hills.

Judges
Lisa L. Asadoorian
Nancy Tolwin Carniak
Julie A. Nicholson

Division Four includes the cities of Clawson and Troy in Oakland County. The court sits at Troy.

Judges
William E. Bolle
Dennis C. Drury
Michael A. Martone

DISTRICT FIFTY-THREE includes Livingston County. The court sits at Howell and Brighton.

Chief Judge
A. John Pikkarainen

Judges
Frank R. Del Vero
Michael K. Hegarty

DISTRICT FIFTY-FOUR A includes the city of Lansing in Ingham County.

Chief Judge
Patrick F. Cherry

Judges
Louise Alderson
Frank J. DeLuca
Charles F. Filice
Amy Ronayne Krause

DISTRICT FIFTY-FOUR B includes the city of East Lansing in Ingham County.

Chief Judge
Richard D. Ball

Judge
David L. Jordon

DISTRICT FIFTY-FIVE includes Ingham County except the cities of Lansing and East Lansing. The court sits at Mason.

Chief Judge
Thomas Emmett Brennan, Jr.

Judge
Pamela J. McCabe

DISTRICT FIFTY-SIX A includes Eaton County. The court sits at Charlotte.

Chief Judge
Paul F. Berger

Judge
Harvey J. Hoffman

DISTRICT FIFTY-SIX B includes Barry County. The court sits at Hastings.

Judge
Gary R. Holman

DISTRICT FIFTY-SEVEN includes Allegan County. The court sits at Allegan.

Chief Judge
Stephen E. Sheridan

Judge
Gary A. Stewart

DISTRICT FIFTY-EIGHT includes Ottawa County. The court sits at Grand Haven, Holland and Hudsonville.

Chief Judge
Susan A. Jonas

Judges
Richard J. Kloote
Bradley S. Knoll
Kenneth David Post

DISTRICT FIFTY-NINE includes the cities of Grandville and Walker in Kent County. The court sits at Grandville and Walker.

Chief Judge
Peter P. Versluis

DISTRICT SIXTY includes Muskegon County. The court sits at Muskegon.

Chief Judge
Andrew Wierengo

MICHIGAN DISTRICT COURTS—*Continued*

Judges
Harold F. Closz III
Fredric A. Grimm, Jr.
Michael Jeffrey Nolan

DISTRICT SIXTY-ONE includes the city of Grand Rapids in Kent County.

Chief Judge
David J. Buter

Judges
Patrick C. Bowler
J. Michael Christensen
Jeanine Nemesi LaVille
Ben H. Logan, II
Don Passenger

DISTRICT SIXTY-TWO A includes the city of Wyoming in Kent County.

Chief Judge
Steven M. Timmers

DISTRICT SIXTY-TWO B includes the city of Kentwood in Kent County.

Chief Judge
William G. Kelly

DISTRICT SIXTY-THREE consists of two divisions.

Chief Judge
Sara J. Smolenski

Division One includes the cities of Cedar Springs and Rockford and the townships of Algoma, Alpine, Cannon, Courtland, Grattan, Nelson, Oakfield, Plainfield, Solon, Sparta, Spencer and Tyrone in Kent County. The court sits at Rockford.

Judge
Steven Richard Servaas

Division Two includes the cities of East Grand Rapids and Lowell and the townships of Ada, Browne, Byron, Caledonia, Cascade, Gaines, Grand Rapids, Lowell and Vergennes in Kent County. The court sits at Grand Rapids.

Judge
Sara J. Smolenski

DISTRICT SIXTY-FOUR A includes Ionia County. The court sits at Belding, Ionia and Portland.

Chief Judge
Raymond P. Voet

DISTRICT SIXTY-FOUR B includes Montcalm County. The court sits at Stanton.

Chief Judge
Donald R. Hemingsen

DISTRICT SIXTY-FIVE A includes Clinton County. The court sits at St. Johns.

Chief Judge
Richard D. Wells

DISTRICT SIXTY-FIVE B includes Gratiot County. The court sits at Ithaca and Alma.

Chief Judge
James B. Mackie

DISTRICT SIXTY-SIX includes Shiawassee County. The court sits at Corunna.

Chief Judge
Ward L. Clarkson

Judge
Terrance P. Dignan

DISTRICT SIXTY-SEVEN consists of four divisions.

Chief Judge
Christopher Odette

Division One includes the cities of Clio and Flushing and the townships of Flint, Flushing, Montrose, Thetford and Vienna in Genesee County. The court sits at Flushing.

Judge
David J. Goggins

Division Two includes the cities of Burton and Davison and the townships of Atlas, Davison, Forest and Richfield in Genesee County. The court sits at Burton and Davison.

Judges
John L. Conover
Richard L. Hughes

Division Three includes the city of Mount Morris and the townships of Genesee and Mount Morris in Genesee County. The court sits at Mount Morris.

Judge
Larry Stecco

Division Four includes the cities of Fenton, Grand Blanc and Swartz Creek and the townships of Argentine, Clayton, Fenton, Gaines, Grand Blanc and Mundy in Genesee County. The court sits at Fenton and Grand Blanc.

Judges
Mark C. McCabe
Christopher Odette

DISTRICT SIXTY-EIGHT includes the city of Flint in Genesee County.

Chief Judge
Nathaniel C. Perry, III

Judges
Peter Anastor
William H. Crawford, II
Herman Marable, Jr.
Michael D. McAra
Ramona M. Roberts

DISTRICT SIXTY-NINE is combined with District Seventy.

DISTRICT SEVENTY consists of two divisions.

Chief Judge
Terry L. Clark

Division One includes the cities of Saginaw and Zilwaukee and the townships of Bridgeport, Buena Vista, Carrollton and Zilwaukee in Saginaw County. The court sits at Saginaw.

MICHIGAN DISTRICT COURTS—*Continued*

Judges
Terry L. Clark
M. Randall Jurrens
M. T. Thompson, Jr.

Division Two includes Saginaw County except the cities of Saginaw and Zilwaukee and the townships of Bridgeport, Buena Vista, Carrollton and Zilwaukee. The court sits at Saginaw.

Judges
Christopher S. Boyd
Darnell Jackson
Kyle Higgs Tarrant

DISTRICT SEVENTY-ONE A includes Lapeer County. The court sits at Lapeer.

Judges
Laura Cheger Barnard
John T. Connolly

DISTRICT SEVENTY-ONE B includes Tuscola County. The court sits at Caro.

Chief Judge
Kim David Glaspie

DISTRICT SEVENTY-TWO includes St. Clair County. The court sits at Port Huron and Marine City.

Chief Judge
David C. Nicholson

Judges
Richard A. Cooley, Jr.
Cynthia Siemen Platzer

DISTRICT SEVENTY-THREE A includes Sanilac County. The court sits at Sandusky.

Chief Judge
James A. Marcus

DISTRICT SEVENTY-THREE B includes Huron County. The court sits at Bad Axe.

Chief Judge
Karl E. Kraus

DISTRICT SEVENTY-FOUR includes Bay County. The court sits at Bay City.

Chief Judge
Craig D. Alston

Judges
Timothy J. Kelly
Scott J. Newcombe

DISTRICT SEVENTY-FIVE includes Midland County. The court sits at Midland.

Chief Judge
Philip M. Van Dam

Judge
John Henry Hart

DISTRICT SEVENTY-SIX includes Isabella County. The court sits at Mount Pleasant.

Judge
William R. Rush

DISTRICT SEVENTY-SEVEN includes Mecosta and Osceola counties. The court sits at Big Rapids and Reed City.

Chief Judge
Susan H. Grant

DISTRICT SEVENTY-EIGHT includes Newaygo and Oceana counties. The court sits at White Cloud, Fremont and Hart.

Chief Judge
H. Kevin Drake

DISTRICT SEVENTY-NINE includes Lake and Mason counties. The court sits at Baldwin and Ludington.

Chief Judge
Peter J. Wadel

DISTRICT EIGHTY includes Clare and Gladwin counties. The court sits at Harrison and Gladwin.

Chief Judge
Gary J. Allen

DISTRICT EIGHTY-ONE includes Alcona, Arenac, Iosco and Oscoda counties. The court sits at Harrisville, Standish, Tawas City and Mio.

Chief Judge
Allen C. Yenior

DISTRICT EIGHTY-TWO includes Ogemaw County. The court sits at West Branch.

Chief Judge
Richard E. Noble

DISTRICT EIGHTY-THREE includes Roscommon County. The court sits at Roscommon.

Chief Judge
Daniel L. Sutton

DISTRICT EIGHTY-FOUR includes Missaukee and Wexford counties. The court sits at Lake City and Cadillac.

Chief Judge
David A. Hogg

DISTRICT EIGHTY-FIVE includes Benzie and Manistee counties. The court sits at Beulah and Manistee.

Chief Judge
Brent V. Danielson

DISTRICT EIGHTY-SIX includes Antrim, Grand Traverse and Leelanau counties. The court sits at Bellaire, Traverse City and Leland.

Chief Judge
Michael J. Haley

Judges
Thomas S. Gilbert
Thomas J. Phillips

DISTRICT EIGHTY-SEVEN includes Crawford, Kalkaska and Otsego counties. The court sits at Grayling, Kalkaska and Gaylord.

Judge
Patricia A. Morse

MICHIGAN DISTRICT COURTS—*Continued*

DISTRICT EIGHTY-EIGHT includes Alpena and Montmorency counties. The court sits at Alpena and Atlanta.

Chief Judge
Theodore O. Johnson

DISTRICT EIGHTY-NINE includes Cheboygan and Presque Isle counties. The court sits at Cheboygan and Rogers City.

Chief Judge
Harold A. Johnson, Jr.

DISTRICT NINETY includes Charlevoix and Emmet counties. The court sits at Charlevoix and Petoskey.

Chief Judge
Richard W. May

DISTRICT NINETY-ONE includes Chippewa County. The court sits at Sault Ste. Marie.

Chief Judge
Michael W. MacDonald

DISTRICT NINETY-TWO includes Luce and Mackinac counties. The court sits at Newberry, St. Ignace and Engadine.

Chief Judge
Steven E. Ford

DISTRICT NINETY-THREE includes Alger and Schoolcraft counties. The court sits at Munising and Manistique.

Chief Judge
Mark E. Luoma

DISTRICT NINETY-FOUR includes Delta County. The court sits at Escanaba.

Chief Judge
Glenn A. Pearson

DISTRICT NINETY-FIVE A includes Menominee County. The court sits at Menominee.

Chief Judge
Jeffrey G. Barstow

DISTRICT NINETY-FIVE B includes Dickinson and Iron counties. The court sits at Iron Mountain and Crystal Falls.

Chief Judge
Michael J. Kusz

DISTRICT NINETY-SIX includes Marquette County. The court sits at Marquette and Ishpeming.

Chief Judge
Dennis H. Girard

Judge
Roger W. Kangas

DISTRICT NINETY-SEVEN includes Baraga, Houghton and Keweenaw counties. The court sits at L'Anse, Houghton and Eagle River.

Chief Judge
Phillip L. Kukkonen

DISTRICT NINETY-EIGHT includes Gogebic and Ontonagon counties. The court sits at Bessemer and Ontonagon.

Chief Judge
Anders B. Tingstad, Jr.

MICHIGAN MUNICIPAL COURTS

Municipal Courts are courts of limited jurisdiction and serve only the few cities which in 1968 chose to retain the Municipal Court rather than change to a District Court. Judges are elected for four-year terms. Vacancies are filled as directed by city charter. A chief judge is selected by the Supreme Court to serve a two-year term. In turn, the chief judge of a city where there is more than one judge selects a chief judge pro tem to serve a two-year assignment. In the absence of the chief judge, the duties of the position are performed by the chief judge pro tem.

Civil jurisdiction is limited to $1,500. The courts have criminal jurisdiction over statute violations and misdemeanors punishable by fine and/or imprisonment for not more than one year that are committed within the corporate limits of those cities with Municipal Courts.

*Chief Judge

City (County)	Judge
Eastpointe (Macomb)	Norene S. Redmond Martin J. Smith*
Grosse Pointe (Wayne)	Russell F. Ethridge*
Grosse Pointe Farms (Wayne)	Matthew R. Rumora*
Grosse Pointe Park (Wayne)	Carl F. Jarboe*
Grosse Pointe Shores and Grosse Pointe Woods (Wayne)	Lynne A. Pierce*

Michigan Counties and County Seats

Alcona Harrisville	**Alpena** Alpena	**Baraga** L'Anse	**Benzie** Beulah
Alger Munising	**Antrim** Bellaire	**Barry** Hastings	**Berrien** St. Joseph
Allegan Allegan	**Arenac** Standish	**Bay** Bay City	**Branch** Coldwater

MICHIGAN

COUNTIES AND COUNTY SEATS—*Continued*

Calhoun
Marshall
Cass
Cassopolis
Charlevoix
Charlevoix
Cheboygan
Cheboygan
Chippewa
Sault Ste. Marie
Clare
Harrison
Clinton
St. Johns
Crawford
Grayling
Delta
Escanaba
Dickinson
Iron Mountain
Eaton
Charlotte
Emmet
Petoskey
Genesee
Flint
Gladwin
Gladwin
Gogebic
Bessemer
Grand Traverse
Traverse City
Gratiot
Ithaca
Hillsdale
Hillsdale
Houghton
Houghton
Huron
Bad Axe
Ingham
Mason
Ionia
Ionia
Iosco
Tawas City
Iron
Crystal Falls
Isabella
Mount Pleasant
Jackson
Jackson
Kalamazoo
Kalamazoo
Kalkaska
Kalkaska
Kent
Grand Rapids
Keweenaw
Eagle River
Lake
Baldwin
Lapeer
Lapeer
Leelanau
Leland
Lenawee
Adrian
Livingston
Howell
Luce
Newberry
Mackinac
St. Ignace
Macomb
Mount Clemens
Manistee
Manistee
Marquette
Marquette
Mason
Ludington
Mecosta
Big Rapids
Menominee
Menominee
Midland
Midland
Missaukee
Lake City
Monroe
Monroe
Montcalm
Stanton
Montmorency
Atlanta
Muskegon
Muskegon
Newaygo
White Cloud
Oakland
Pontiac
Oceana
Hart
Ogemaw
West Branch
Ontonagon
Ontonagon
Osceola
Reed City
Oscoda
Mio
Otsego
Gaylord
Ottawa
Grand Haven
Presque Isle
Rogers City
Roscommon
Roscommon
Saginaw
Saginaw
St. Clair
Port Huron
St. Joseph
Centreville
Sanilac
Sandusky
Schoolcraft
Manistique
Shiawassee
Corunna
Tuscola
Caro
Van Buren
Paw Paw
Washtenaw
Ann Arbor
Wayne
Detroit
Wexford
Cadillac

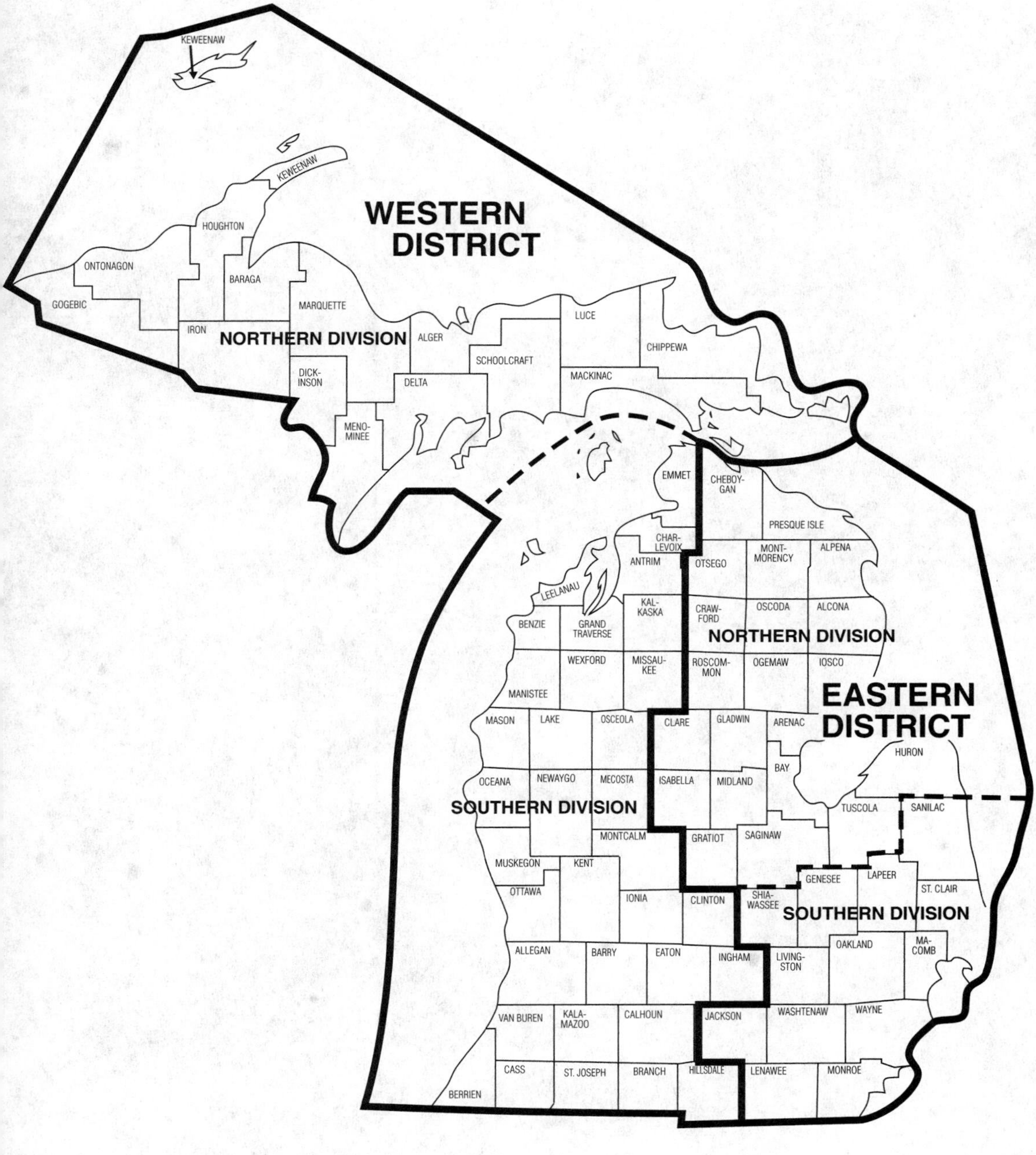
WESTERN DISTRICT
NORTHERN DIVISION
SOUTHERN DIVISION
EASTERN DISTRICT
NORTHERN DIVISION
SOUTHERN DIVISION
KEWEENAW
KEWEENAW
HOUGHTON
ONTONAGON
GOGEBIC
BARAGA
IRON
MARQUETTE
ALGER
LUCE
CHIPPEWA
SCHOOLCRAFT
MACKINAC
DICK-INSON
DELTA
MENO-MINEE
EMMET
CHEBOY-GAN
PRESQUE ISLE
CHAR-LEVOIX
ANTRIM
OTSEGO
MONT-MORENCY
ALPENA
LEELANAU
BENZIE
GRAND TRAVERSE
KAL-KASKA
CRAW-FORD
OSCODA
ALCONA
WEXFORD
MISSAU-KEE
ROSCOM-MON
OGEMAW
IOSCO
MANISTEE
MASON
LAKE
OSCEOLA
CLARE
GLADWIN
ARENAC
HURON
BAY
OCEANA
NEWAYGO
MECOSTA
ISABELLA
MIDLAND
TUSCOLA
SANILAC
MONTCALM
GRATIOT
SAGINAW
MUSKEGON
KENT
GENESEE
LAPEER
ST. CLAIR
OTTAWA
IONIA
CLINTON
SHIA-WASSEE
OAKLAND
MA-COMB
ALLEGAN
BARRY
EATON
INGHAM
LIVING-STON
VAN BUREN
KALA-MAZOO
CALHOUN
JACKSON
WASHTENAW
WAYNE
CASS
ST. JOSEPH
BRANCH
HILLSDALE
LENAWEE
MONROE
BERRIEN

UNITED STATES DISTRICT COURTS
DISTRICTS OF MICHIGAN

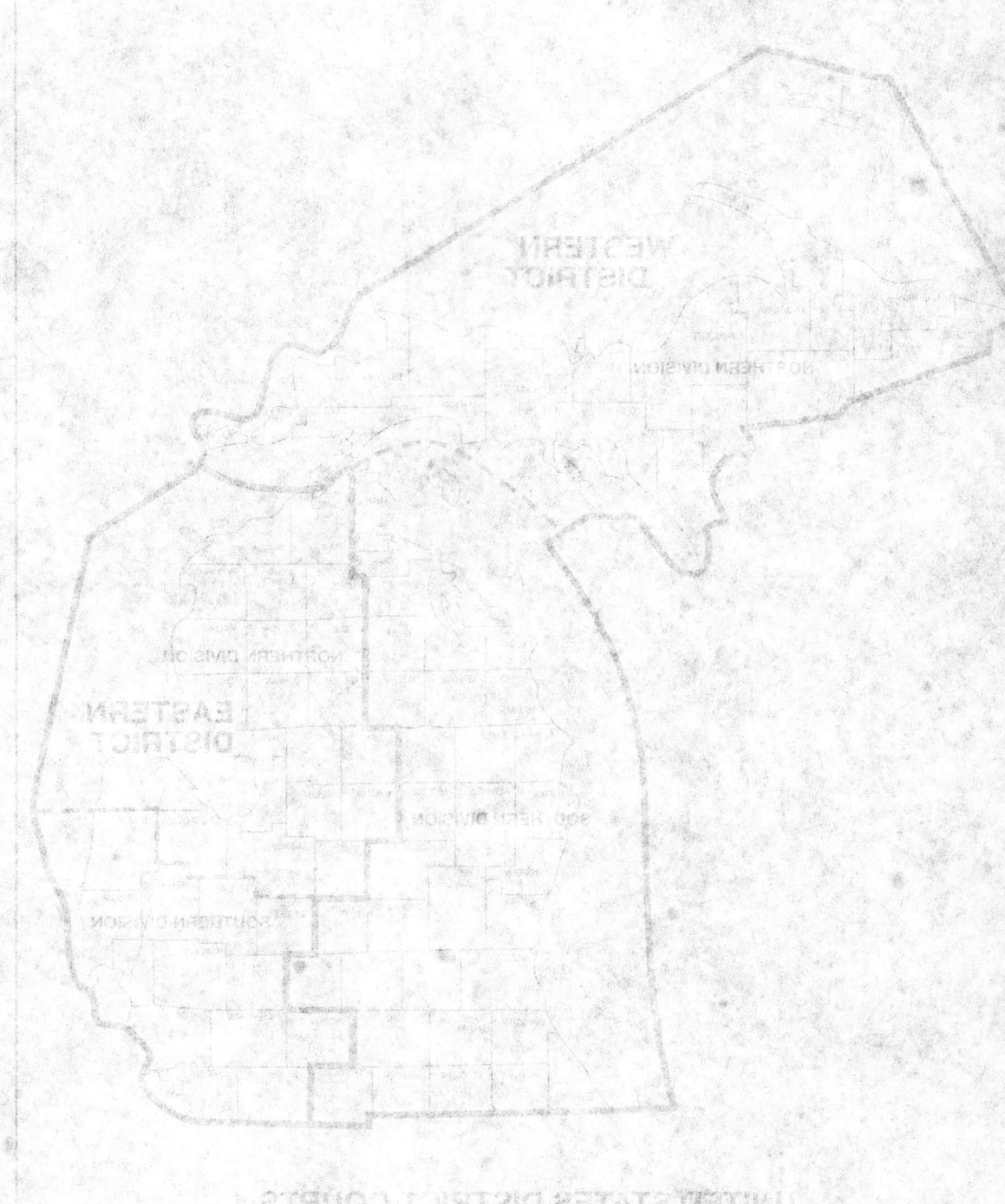

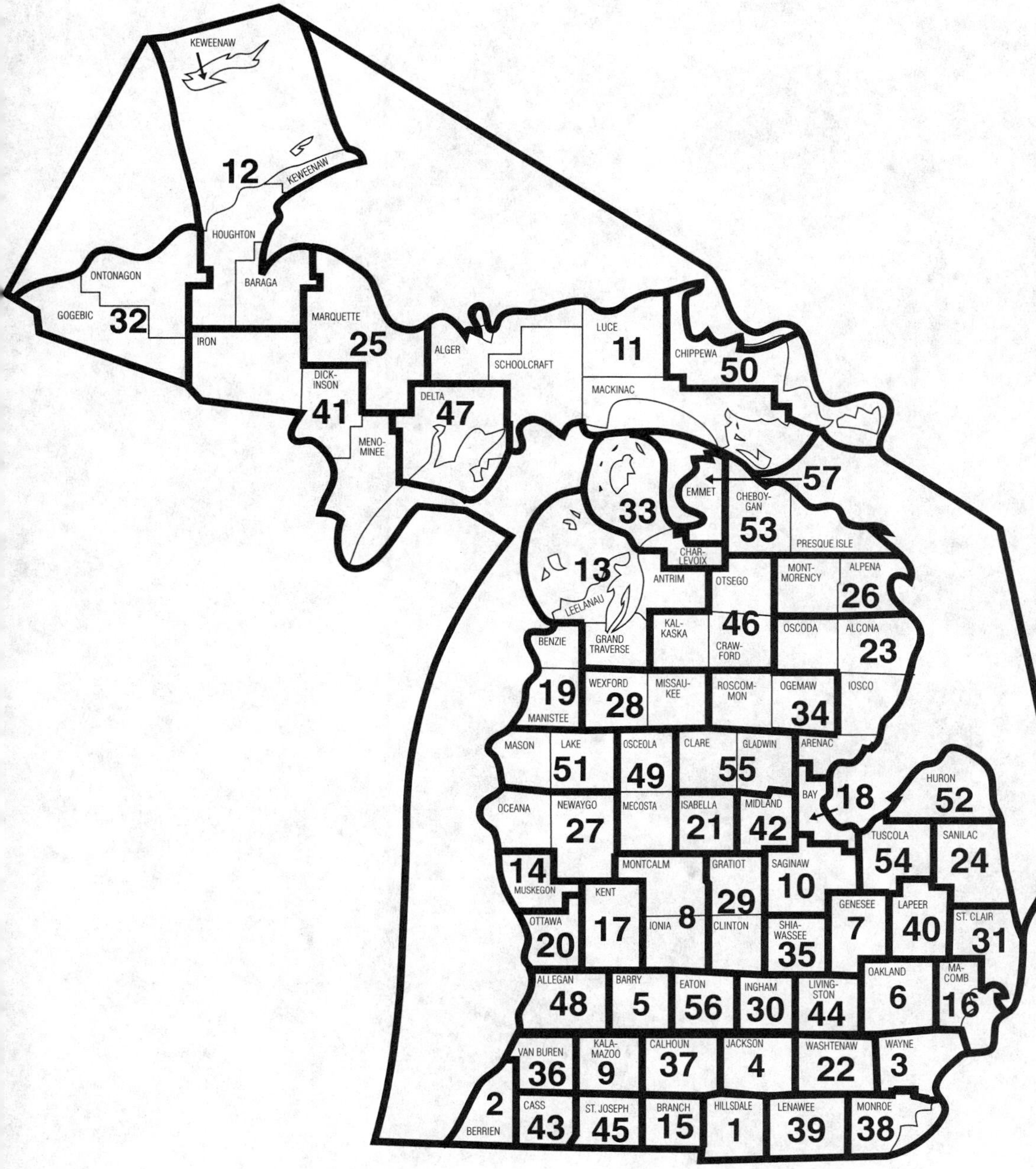
KEWEENAW
12
KEWEENAW
HOUGHTON
ONTONAGON
BARAGA
GOGEBIC
32
IRON
MARQUETTE
25
ALGER
SCHOOLCRAFT
LUCE
11
CHIPPEWA
50
DICK-
INSON
41
DELTA
47
MENO-
MINEE
MACKINAC
57
EMMET
CHEBOY-
GAN
53
33
PRESQUE ISLE
CHAR-
LEVOIX
13
ANTRIM
OTSEGO
MONT-
MORENCY
ALPENA
26
LEELANAU
46
KAL-
KASKA
OSCODA
ALCONA
23
BENZIE
GRAND
TRAVERSE
CRAW-
FORD
19
WEXFORD
28
MISSAU-
KEE
ROSCOM-
MON
OGEMAW
34
IOSCO
MANISTEE
MASON
LAKE
51
OSCEOLA
49
CLARE
GLADWIN
55
ARENAC
HURON
52
OCEANA
NEWAYGO
27
MECOSTA
ISABELLA
21
MIDLAND
42
BAY
18
TUSCOLA
54
SANILAC
24
14
MUSKEGON
MONTCALM
GRATIOT
29
SAGINAW
10
KENT
17
OTTAWA
20
IONIA
8
CLINTON
SHIA-
WASSEE
35
GENESEE
7
LAPEER
40
ST. CLAIR
31
ALLEGAN
48
BARRY
5
EATON
56
INGHAM
30
LIVING-
STON
44
OAKLAND
6
MA-
COMB
16
VAN BUREN
36
KALA-
MAZOO
9
CALHOUN
37
JACKSON
4
WASHTENAW
22
WAYNE
3
2
BERRIEN
CASS
43
ST. JOSEPH
45
BRANCH
15
HILLSDALE
1
LENAWEE
39
MONROE
38

JUDICIAL CIRCUITS OF MICHIGAN CIRCUIT COURTS

MICHIGAN

ADAIR, James P. *(Judge, Michigan Circuit Court Thirty-first Judicial Circuit)*
Office: County Building, 201 McMorran Boulevard, Port Huron 48060.
Telephone: (810) 985-2031.

ADAMS, Deborah Ross *(Judge, Michigan District Court District Thirty-six)*
Office: 421 Madison Avenue, Suite 3075, Detroit 48226.
Telephone: (313) 965-2200.

ALDERSON, Louise *(Judge, Michigan District Court District Fifty-four A)*
Office: City Hall, Sixth Floor, 124 West Michigan Avenue, Lansing 48933-1690.
Telephone: (517) 483-4421.

ALEXANDER, James M. *(Judge, Michigan Circuit Court Sixth Judicial Circuit)*
Office: 404 Courthouse Tower, 1200 North Telegraph Road, Pontiac 48341-0404.
Telephone: (248) 858-0344.

ALLEN, Dorene S. *(Chief Judge, Midland County Probate Court)*
Office: Courthouse, 301 West Main Street, Midland 48640-5183.
Telephone: (989) 832-6880.

ALLEN, Gary J. *(Chief Judge, Michigan District Court District Eighty)* Elected to term beginning Jan 1, 1985. Reelected 1990, 1996 and 2002. Current term expires Dec 31, 2008. Born Pontiac Michigan Aug 16, 1942. Protestant. Educated at Oakland University B.A. 1964 and Detroit College of Law J.D. 1970. Law Clerk to Hon. Robert Templim, Michigan Circuit Court Sixth Judicial Circuit 1967-70. Member Delta Theta Phi. Admitted to practice Michigan 1970. Began legal practice Walled Lake 1970. In legal practice Bay City 1980 and Gladwin 1981.

Elementary school teacher Clarkston 1964-65. Circuit Court Probation Officer Oakland County 1965-67. City Attorney Wolverine Lake, Township of Milford and Village of Milford 1975-80. Assistant Public Defender Bay County 1980-81. Former Member Clare/Gladwin Trial Attorneys Association and Oakland County Bar Association. Member Clare/Gladwin Trial Judges Association, Michigan District Judges Association (Chairman Government Liaison Committee) and State Bar of Michigan. Faculty Member Michigan Judicial Institute 1985. Graduate General Jurisdiction Course The National Judicial College 1986. Member Substance Abuse Advisory Committee Department of Health, Lions, Chamber of Commerce and Rotary. Enjoys archery, fishing, hunting and music.
Office: Gladwin County Building, 401 West Cedar, Gladwin 48624-2085.
Telephone: (989) 426-9207.

ALSTON, Craig D. *(Chief Judge, Michigan District Court District Seventy-four)* Elected to term beginning Jan 1, 1985. Reelected 1990, 1996 and 2002. Current term expires Dec 31, 2008. Born Bay City Michigan May 20, 1954. Educated at Michigan State University B.A. in Economics with honors 1975, Wayne State University and University of Illinois J.D. 1979. Admitted to practice Michigan 1979. In legal practice Bay City Dec 1979 to Dec 1984.

Author "Calculating Interest on Judgements" Colleague Oct 1988. Member Michigan District Judges Association, State Bar of Michigan and Bay County Bar Association. Instructor in Small Claims and Landlord/Tenant Law New Judges Seminar annually since 1987 and Discussion Group Facilitator Residence Evidence Seminars Michigan Judicial Institute. President Bay City Lions Club 1991-92. Enjoys computer science.
Office: 1230 Washington Avenue, Bay City 48708.
Telephone: (989) 895-4237.

ANASTOR, Peter *(Judge, Michigan District Court District Sixty-eight)* Elected to term beginning Jan 1, 1987. Reelected Nov 3, 1992 and 1998. Current term expires Dec 31, 2004. Former Chief Judge and Chief Judge pro tem. Born Flint Michigan Feb 17, 1941. Religious affiliation: Greek Orthodox. Educated at Flint Junior College 1959-61 and Wayne State University B.A. 1963 J.D. 1966. Admitted to practice Michigan 1967 and U.S. District Court Eastern District of Michigan 1967. In legal practice Flint 1969-86.

Assistant Prosecuting Attorney Genesee County 1967-69. Former Member Criminal Defense Committee, Family Law Committee, Law Day Committee, Pre-paid Legal Services Committee and Committee for Continuing Legal Education. Member Michigan District Judges Association, State Bar of Michigan, Hellenic and Genesee County (Board of Directors 1975-78, District Court Committee, Bench and Bar Committee) Bar Associations. Attended numerous seminars Michigan Judicial Institute 1987-2002. Previously worked as store clerk Hamady Brothers 1957-66. Former Member Parents Advisory Committee Boy Scout Troop 183. Board of Directors Shelter of Flint, Inc., The Urban League of Flint (First Vice Chairman), Assumption Greek Orthodox Church, The Community Coalition and Flint Neighborhood Coalition. Youth Advisor NAACP. Board of Directors 1972-84 and Chairman Mass Transportation Authority. Member Advisory Committee Mott Community College, The International Institute of Flint, Flint Institute of Arts, Flint Institute of Music, New Paths Advisory Council and Urban Scouting Committee Boy Scouts of America. Interests include sports, travel, cooking and photography.
Office: McCree Center, 630 South Saginaw Street, Flint 48502-1526.
Telephone: (810) 766-8983.

ANDEREGG, Michael John *(Chief Judge, Marquette County Probate Court)* Elected to term beginning Jan 1, 1977. Reelected 1982, 1988, 1994 and 2000. Current term expires Dec 31, 2006. Former Presiding Judge Family Division Michigan Circuit Court Twenty-fifth Judicial Circuit. Born Antigo Wisconsin June 6, 1945. Presbyterian. Educated at Harvard University A.B. cum laude 1967 and University of Michigan J.D. 1972.

ANDEREGG, MICHAEL JOHN—*Continued*

Member Hasty Pudding Institute. Admitted to practice Michigan 1972. Began legal practice Marquette 1972.

Staff Attorney Upper Peninsula Legal Services 1972-74. Assistant Prosecutor 1974-75 and Chief Assistant Prosecutor 1976 Marquette County. Author "Jury Debriefing Makes Sense" 1 No. 3 *Colleague Magazine* July 1988. Adjunct Assistant Professor of Business Law Northern Michigan University 1974-79. Instructor on Juvenile Law Regional Police Academy Northern Michigan University 1976-90 and since 1997. Member Probate Court Academic Advisory Committee since 1982 and Juvenile Rules Committee since 1984 Michigan Supreme Court and Michigan Juvenile Justice Committee since 1994. Member Upper Peninsula Probate Judges Association (President 1982-85), Michigan Probate Judges Association (President 1991-92), National Council of Juvenile and Family Court Judges (Board of Trustees 1988-96, Chairman Technical Assistance Advisory Committee 1993-94, Chairman President's Advisory Committee on Serious/Violent Juvenile Offenders 1996-97, Chairman Legislative Committee 1997-98, Chairman Training and Technical Assistance Committee 1997-98), State Bar of Michigan and Marquette County Bar Association (President 1987). Upper Peninsula Bar Representative Michigan Institute CLE since 1975. Instructor Michigan Judicial Institute 1979-84. Lecturer on Probate Specialty Seminars 1982 and 1984, Juvenile Court Rules Training for judges, court administrators and referees 1987 and 1988 and New Judges Training 1988 and 1989 Michigan Supreme Court; Interstate Compact 1985, Victim's Rights 1989 and Indian Child Welfare Act 1997 Michigan Probate Judges Association; Annual Conference Nebraska Juvenile Justice Association 1989; New Statutes and Court Rules Northern Michigan Legal Institute 1989; and National Council of Juvenile and Family Court Judges Annual Conference 1997. Keynote Speaker "Beyond the Bench VI" California Juvenile Justice Association 1994. Attended Faculty Training Workshop National Council of Juvenile and Family Court Judges 1996. Management Consultant National Center for Juvenile Justice 1984, 1989 and 1995. President Children's Charter of the Courts of Michigan 1986-89. Member Steering Committee Upper Peninsula Children's Coalition since 1987, W. K. Kellogg Foundation Youth Development Seminars 1988-89, Mental Health Advisory Committee Marquette General Hospital since 1990, Dean's Advisory Council Department of Behavioral Sciences, Human Services and Education Northern Michigan University since 1991, Marquette Area Public Schools Education Foundation since 1995, Marquette-Alger Human Services Coordinating Body (Secretary 1995) and W. K. Kellogg Foundation Youth Improvement Program Site Advisory Council since 1996. Enjoys fly fishing, fly tying, competitive shooting and hunting.

Office: Courthouse Annex, 234 West Baraga, Marquette 49855.

Telephone: (906) 225-8300.

ANDERSON, Martha *(Judge, Michigan Circuit Court Sixth Judicial Circuit)*

Office: Courthouse Tower, 1200 North Telegraph Road, Pontiac 48341-0404.

Telephone: (248) 858-0344.

ANDREWS, Steven N. *(Judge, Michigan Circuit Court Sixth Judicial Circuit)* Appointed by Governor William G. Milliken to term beginning April 5, 1976. Elected Nov 1976, 1978, 1984, 1990, 1996 and 2002. Current term expires Dec 31, 2008. Chief Judge 1978, 1982-83 and 1990-91. One Man Grand Juror 1979-80. Chief Judge pro tem 1988-89. Supervising Judge Citizens Grand Jury 1990. Born Detroit Michigan Dec 4, 1932. Greek Orthodox. Educated at Adrian College B.A. 1955 and Cumberland School of Law J.D. 1959. Awarded honorary LL.D. New England School of Law 1983. Member Delta Theta Phi and Alpha Tau Omega. Admitted to practice Michigan 1960 and U.S. Supreme Court. Began legal practice Clawson 1960.

City Attorney Clawson 1966-76. Former Union Attorney Troy Police Officers Association and Clawson Police Officers Association. Instructor Great Lakes College 1962 and Michigan Lutheran College 1963. Visiting Instructor in Domestic Relations Detroit College of Law at Michigan State University. Former Member The Association of Trial Lawyers of America. Member Federalist Society, American Judicature Society, Michigan Judges Association, American Judges Association, Michigan Trial Lawyers Association, American Inns of Court (Past President Oakland County Chapter), State Bar of Michigan (Representative Assembly 1972-75, Scope and Correlation Committee, Former Member Character and Fitness Committee and Advertising, Certification and Specialization Committee), Hellenic, South Oakland County (President 1971) and Oakland County (Board of Directors 1970-76, President 1976) Bar Associations. Attended National College of the State Judiciary 1977. Recipient Adrian College Outstanding Alumni Award 1980. Named one of Michigan's most respected judges by *Lawyers Weekly* 1990. Board of Directors Oakland County Legal Aid Society 1970-76. President Alumni Association 1975-76 and Member Board of Trustees 1978-86 Adrian College. Former Member Board of Directors YMCA Camp Manh-Go-Tah-See and Clawson Lions Club. Chairman Oakland County Library Board. Member Advisory Board Providence Hospital (Chairman Government Relations Committee, Member Nominating Committee). Enjoys skiing, tennis and sailing.

Office: Courthouse Tower Dept. 404, 1200 North Telegraph Road, Pontiac 48341-0404.

Telephone: (248) 858-0360.

APPEL, Michelle Friedman *(Judge, Michigan District Court District Forty-five B)*

Office: 13600 Oak Park Boulevard, Oak Park 48237.

Telephone: (248) 542-7042.

ARCHBOLD, Carolyn A. *(Chief Judge, Michigan District Court District Twenty-nine)*

Office: 34808 Sims Avenue, Wayne 48184.

Telephone: (734) 722-5220.

ARCHER, Trudy DunCombe *(Judge, Michigan District Court District Thirty-six)* Appointed by Governor James J. Blanchard to term beginning March 6, 1989.

Office: 421 Madison Avenue, Suite 3074, Detroit 48226.

Telephone: (313) 965-2200.

ARNOLD, Jack T. *(Chief Judge, Gratiot County Probate Court)* Appointed by Governor James J. Blanchard to term beginning Jan 1, 1989. Born Alma Michigan April 17, 1937. Methodist. Educated at Central Michigan University B.S. 1959 and Detroit College of Law J.D. 1962. Law Clerk to Hon. Paul Adams Michigan Supreme Court 1962. Member Delta Theta Phi. Ad-

ARNOLD, JACK T.—*Continued*
mitted to practice Michigan 1963. In legal practice Ithaca 1963-88 and Alma 1987-88.
Prosecuting Attorney Gratiot County 1964-68. Member State Bar of Michigan, Gratiot County and American Bar Associations. Member Rotary Club. 32° Mason. Enjoys hunting, fishing, golfing and skiing.
Mailing address: P.O. Box 217, Ithaca 48847.
Office: Courthouse, 214 East Center Street, Ithaca 48847.
Telephone: (989) 875-5231.

ASADOORIAN, Lisa L. *(Judge, Michigan District Court District Fifty-two Division Three)*
Office: 135 Barclay Circle, Rochester Hills 48307-5800.
Telephone: (248) 853-5553.

ATKINS, Marylin E. *(Chief Judge, Michigan District Court District Thirty-six)*
Office: 421 Madison Avenue, Suite 5028, Detroit 48226.
Telephone: (313) 965-2200.

AVADENKA, Edward *(Judge, Michigan District Court District Forty-eight)* Former Chief Judge.
Mailing address: P.O. Box 3200, Bloomfield Hills 48302-3200.
Office: 4280 Telegraph Road, Bloomfield Hills 48302.
Telephone: (248) 647-1141.

BAIRD, Laura *(Judge, Michigan Circuit Court Thirtieth Judicial Circuit)* Serves Family Division. Also Judge, Michigan Court of Claims.
Mailing address: P.O. Box 19304, Lansing 48901-7971.
Office: Veteran's Memorial Courthouse, 313 West Kalamazoo Street, Lansing 48933.
Telephone: (517) 483-6500.

BAJOREK, David A. *(Chief Judge, Michigan District Court District Twenty-five)* Former Chief Judge pro tem.
Office: 1475 Cleophus, Lincoln Park 48146-2301.
Telephone: (313) 382-8652.

BALL, Richard D. *(Chief Judge, Michigan District Court District Fifty-four B)* Elected Nov 3, 1992 to term beginning Jan 1, 1993. Reelected 1998, current term expires Dec 31, 2004. Former Chief Judge pro tem. Born Grand Rapids Michigan Aug 29, 1949. Religious affiliation: Christian Reformed (Protestant). Educated at Michigan State University B.A. 1971 and Thomas M. Cooley Law School J.D. 1976. Admitted to practice Michigan 1976. In legal practice Lansing 1976-92.
Member Michigan District Judges Association (Legislative Committee since 1993), State Bar of Michigan and Ingham County Bar Association. Major and Judge Advocate Army National Guard 1971-90. Member East Lansing Board of Education 1988-92.
Office: 101 Linden Street, East Lansing 48823.
Telephone: (517) 351-7000.

BALTIMORE, Joseph N. *(Judge, Michigan District Court District Thirty-six)* Appointed by Governor James J. Blanchard to term beginning March 30, 1988. Current term expires Dec 31, 2008. Former Chief Judge and Chief Judge pro tem. Born Markham Virginia Sept 24, 1940. Baptist. Educated at Howard University B.A. 1963 and University of Detroit J.D. 1967. Member Alpha Phi Alpha. Admitted to practice Michigan 1969, U.S. Supreme Court 1974 and U.S. Court of Appeals Sixth Circuit 1978. In legal practice Detroit 1969-79.
Supervising Assistant Corporation Counsel Detroit 1979-88. Member Michigan District Judges Association, State Bar of Michigan and Wolverine Bar Association. Life Member NAACP. Board of Trustees Franklin Wright Settlements. Member Howard University Alumni Association. Enjoys golfing and reading.
Office: 421 Madison Avenue, Suite 3073, Detroit 48226.
Telephone: (313) 965-2200.

BANDSTRA, Richard A. *(Judge, Michigan Court of Appeals)* Elected to term beginning 1994. Reelected 2002, current term expires Dec 31, 2008. Chief Judge pro tem 1997 to Jan 1999. Chief Judge Jan 22, 1999 to Dec 31, 2001. Born April 2, 1950. Educated at Calvin College B.A. 1972 and University of Chicago M.A. 1974 J.D. 1980. Associate Editor University of Chicago Law Review. In legal practice Grand Rapids 1980-85.
Speaker Michigan Judicial Conference July 1995. Participant Michigan Appellate Bench Bar Conference 1995 and 1998. Recipient Distinguished Service Award from Grand Rapids Jaycees 1988. Instructor in Sociology Trinity Christian College 1975-77. Member House of Representatives Michigan 1985-94. Member House Judiciary Committee 1987-94, 21st Century Commission on the Courts 1990 and National Conference of Commissioners on Uniform State Laws 1993-94. National Legislative Chairperson Task Force on Civil Justice Reform 1992. Floor Leader 1993-94. Board Member Eastown Community Association 1981-82, Dispute Resolution Center 1985-97, Grand Rapids Chapter Association for Public Justice 1987-94, Habitat for Humanity 1988-93, Advisory Center for Teens 1995-96, Alternative Directions since 1995 (President 1998-99), World Affairs Council of West Michigan since 1995 and Board of Publications Christian Reformed Church in North America since 1999. Member Christian Reformed Church since 1980 (Deacon 1982-85, Elder 1996-99). Interests include singing (tenor) with Grand Rapids Symphony Choir, European travel, reading, collecting first edition books, golf, tennis, basketball and wind surfing.
Office: 201 The Law Building, 330 Ionia N.W., Grand Rapids 49503.
Telephone: (616) 458-3272, 458-3297.

BARGLIND, Mary Brouillette *(Chief Judge, Michigan Circuit Court Forty-first Judicial Circuit)* Former Chief Judge pro tem.
Mailing address: P.O. Box 609, Iron Mountain 49801.
Office: Courthouse, 705 South Stephenson Street, Iron Mountain 49801.
Telephone: (906) 774-2266.

BARNARD, Laura Cheger *(Judge, Michigan District Court District Seventy-one A)* Former Chief Judge and Chief Judge pro tem.
Office: Lapeer County Complex Building, 255 Clay Street, Lapeer 48446.
Telephone: (810) 667-0314.

BARSTOW, Jeffrey G. *(Chief Judge, Michigan District Court District Ninety-five A)*
Office: Menominee County Courthouse, 839 Tenth Avenue, Menominee 49858.
Telephone: (906) 863-8532.

BATCHIK, Michael *(Judge, Michigan District Court District Fifty-two Division One)* Assumed office 1979. Elected to subsequent terms. Current term expires 2004. Currently serves as Presiding Judge Division One.
Office: 48150 Grand River Avenue, Novi 48374-1222.
Telephone: (248) 305-6080.
E-mail address: batchikm@co.oakland.mi.us

BATTANI, Marianne O. *(Judge, United States District Court Eastern District of Michigan)* Appointed for life by President Bill Clinton to term beginning June 9, 2000. Born Detroit Michigan. Roman Catholic. Educated at University of Detroit B.A. cum laude 1966 and Detroit College of Law J.D. cum laude 1972. Admitted to practice Michigan 1972. Judge, Common Pleas Court of Detroit 1981. Judge, Michigan District Court District Thirty-six 1981-82. Judge Dec 19, 1982 to June 8, 2000 and Former Chief Judge pro tem, Michigan Circuit Court Third Judicial Circuit, appointed by Governor William Grawn Milliken.
Office: 200 East Liberty Street, Suite 400, Ann Arbor 48104.
Telephone: (734) 741-2106.

BATZER, James M. *(Chief Judge, Michigan Circuit Court Nineteenth Judicial Circuit)* Elected to term beginning Jan 1, 1985. Reelected Nov 1990, 1996 and 2002. Current term expires Dec 31, 2008. Born Manistee Michigan Dec 14, 1943. Educated at Albion College 1961-63, University of Michigan B.A. 1968, Michigan State University School of Criminal Justice M.S. 1976 and Wayne State University Law School J.D. with honors 1978. Law Clerk to U.S. District Court Eastern District of Michigan 1978-79. Admitted to practice Michigan 1978, U.S. District Courts Eastern 1979 and Western 1983 Districts of Michigan and U.S. Court of Appeals Sixth Circuit 1979. Visiting Judge, Michigan Court of Appeals 1986-88.
Children's Protective Services and Juvenile Delinquency worker Michigan Department of Social Services 1968-75. Investigator Michigan Employment Security Commission 1975-78. Assistant Attorney General State of Michigan 1979-84. Author "Direct Appeals from Michigan Juvenile Delinquency Adjudications and Dispositions" 24 Wayne L. Rev. 1239, 1978. Teaching Fellow in Legal Research and Writing Detroit College of Law 1979-81. Member Michigan Judges Association since 1985 (Rules Committee since 1985, Executive Board since 1990), State Bar of Michigan since 1979 (Criminal Jury Instructions Committee since 1989, Committee on Professional and Judicial Ethics since 1990) and American Bar Association. Enjoys skiing, trout fishing, literature and history.
Mailing address: P.O. Box 484, Manistee 49660.
Office: 415 Third Street, Manistee 49660.
Telephone: (231) 723-6664.

BAUMGARTNER, Michael J. *(Chief Judge, Michigan Circuit Court Thirty-fourth Judicial Circuit)* Born Detroit Michigan April 7, 1946. Roman Catholic. Educated at Xavier University B.S. cum laude 1968 and University of Notre Dame J.D. 1974. Admitted to practice Michigan 1974. In legal practice Prudenville 1974-86. Former Judge, Roscommon County Probate Court, appointed by Governor James J. Blanchard to term beginning Oct 14, 1986.
Prosecuting Attorney Roscommon County Jan 1, 1977 to Dec 31, 1980 and Jan 1, 1985 to Oct 14, 1986. Member State Bar of Michigan, Roscommon County, Thirty-fourth Judicial Circuit and American Bar Associations. Systems Engineer IBM 1968-70. Salesman and Systems Engineer CMC 1970-71. Democrat. Member COOR Intermediate School Board 1982-86 (Former Vice President), Knights of Columbus, Elks, Moose and A.R.C. Enjoys hunting, fishing and farming.
Mailing address: P.O. Box 185, Roscommon 48653.
Office: Courthouse, 500 Lake Street, Roscommon 48653.
Telephone: (989) 275-4776.

BAXTER, Wendy M. *(Judge, Michigan Circuit Court Third Judicial Circuit)* Assumed office Oct 1, 1997. Former Judge, Recorder's Court of Detroit.
Office: 1719 Municipal Center, Two Woodward Avenue, Detroit 48226.
Telephone: (313) 224-5261.

BEACH, Harry A. *(Judge, Michigan Circuit Court Forty-eighth Judicial Circuit)* Elected to term beginning Jan 1, 1991. Reelected to subsequent terms. Former Chief Judge. Former Judge, Michigan District Court District Fifty-seven.
Office: County Building, 113 Chestnut Street, Allegan 49010.
Telephone: (269) 673-0300.

BEAGLE, Duncan M. *(Judge, Michigan Circuit Court Seventh Judicial Circuit)* Former Chief Judge pro tem. Currently serves as Presiding Judge Drug Court Planning.
Office: Genesee County Courthouse, 900 South Saginaw Street, Flint 48502.
Telephone: (810) 257-3252.

BELL, Robert Holmes *(Chief Judge, United States District Court Western District of Michigan)* Appointed for life by President Ronald Reagan to term beginning 1987. Chief Judge since May 29, 2001. Born Lansing Michigan April 19, 1944. Religious affiliation: Nondenominational (Protestant). Educated at Wheaton College B.A. 1966 and Wayne State University J.D. 1969. Admitted to practice Michigan 1970, U.S. District Court Western District of Michigan 1970 and U.S. Supreme Court 1976. In legal practice Lansing 1970-73. Judge, Michigan District Court District Fifty-five 1973-78. Judge, Michigan Circuit Court Thirtieth Judicial Circuit, 1979-87. Visiting Judge, Michigan Court of Appeals 1982-87.
Assistant Prosecutor Ingham County 1970-73. Adjunct Professor of Law Thomas M. Cooley Law School since 1978. Member American Judicature Society, Christian Legal Society, Federalist Society for Law and Public Policy, State Bar of Michigan, Ingham County, Marquette County and Federal (Western District of Michigan Chapter) Bar Associations. Board of Directors Cornerstone University.
Office: 402 Federal Building, 110 Michigan Street N.W., Grand Rapids 49503.
Telephone: (616) 456-2021.

BENSON, Quinn E. *(Judge, Michigan District Court District Eight Division One)* Appointed by Governor James J. Blanchard to term beginning May 5, 1989.
Office: 416 South Rose Street, Kalamazoo 49007-5272.
Telephone: (269) 384-8020.

BERGER, Paul F. *(Chief Judge, Michigan District Court District Fifty-six A)* Elected Judge to term begin-

BERGER, PAUL F.—*Continued*

ning Jan 1, 1985. Reelected 1990, 1996 and 2002. Current term expires Dec 31, 2008. Former Chief Judge pro tem. Born Manistique Michigan March 6, 1945. Roman Catholic. Educated at University of Michigan B.A. in Economics 1967 and Wayne State University Law School J.D. Member Sigma Chi. Admitted to practice Michigan 1972. Began legal practice Charlotte 1973.

Assistant Prosecuting Attorney 1973-75 and Prosecuting Attorney 1975-84. Member State Bar of Michigan and Eaton County Bar Association (President 1975-76). Specialist Five U.S. Army 1968-70.

Office: Eaton County Courthouse, 1045 Independence Boulevard, Charlotte 48813.

Telephone: (517) 485-6444.

BERGERON, Ronald M. *(Chief Judge, Michigan Circuit Court Twenty-third Judicial Circuit)* Former Chief Judge pro tem. Born Saginaw Michigan March 4, 1948. Educated at Michigan Technological University B.S.M.E. with honors 1970 and Wayne State University J.D. 1974. Admitted to practice Michigan 1974. Began legal practice Detroit 1974. In legal practice Standish 1975. Former Judge, Arenac County Probate Court, elected to term beginning Jan 1, 1983.

Senior Assistant Mechanical Engineer Detroit Water Department 1971-75. Registered Professional Engineer Michigan since 1976. Member Thirty-fourth Judicial District Bar Association. Member Standish Lions Club.

Mailing address: P.O. Box 609, Standish 48658.

Office: Courthouse, 120 North Grove, Standish 48658.

Telephone: (989) 846-6131.

BERRY, Annette J. *(Judge, Michigan Circuit Court Third Judicial Circuit)*

Office: 610 Hall of Justice, 1441 St. Antoine Street, Detroit 48226.

Telephone: (313) 224-4679.

BIELAWSKI, Lawrence M. *(Chief Judge, Michigan Circuit Court Eighteenth Judicial Circuit)* Appointed by Governor James J. Blanchard to term beginning Sept 1988. Elected Nov 1990, 1996 and 2002. Current term expires Dec 31, 2008. Former Chief Judge pro tem. Born Bay City Michigan May 11, 1946. Catholic. Educated at Central Michigan University B.S. 1969 and Detroit College of Law J.D. 1972. Admitted to practice Michigan 1972 and U.S. District Court Eastern District of Michigan 1973. In legal practice Bay City 1975-84. Administrative Law Judge 1984-86 and Magistrate, Workers' Compensation Bureau 1987-88.

Member Northern Michigan Judges Association, Michigan Judges Association, State Bar of Michigan and Bay County Bar Association.

Office: 1230 Washington Avenue, Bay City 48708.

Telephone: (989) 895-4265.

BIERNAT, James M., Sr. *(Judge, Michigan Circuit Court Sixteenth Judicial Circuit)*

Office: Macomb County Court Building, 40 North Main, Mount Clemens 48043-5654.

Telephone: (586) 469-5139.

BILL, Gregory D. *(Judge, Michigan Circuit Court Third Judicial Circuit)*

Office: 701 Hall of Justice, 1441 St. Antoine Street, Detroit 48226.

Telephone: (313) 224-2491.

BINDER, Charles E. *(Magistrate Judge, United States District Court Eastern District of Michigan)* Appointed by U.S. District Court judges. Current term expires Oct 2008. Born Kalamazoo Michigan April 23, 1949. Educated at Western Michigan University B.A. cum laude 1971 and Duke University School of Law J.D. 1974. Law Clerk to Hon. Wendell A. Miles, U.S. District Court Western District of Michigan 1974-76. Admitted to practice Michigan 1975.

Member Federal Magistrate Judges Association, State Bar of Michigan, Bay County and Federal (Detroit Chapter) Bar Associations.

Office: 323 Federal Building, 1000 Washington Avenue, Bay City 48708-5749.

Telephone: (989) 894-8820.

BLACKWELL-HATCHER, June E. *(Judge, Wayne County Probate Court)*

Office: 1399 Municipal Center, Two Woodward Avenue, Detroit 48226.

Telephone: (313) 224-5686.

BLOUNT, Nancy McCaughan *(Judge, Michigan District Court District Thirty-six)*

Office: 421 Madison Avenue, Suite 4070, Detroit 48226.

Telephone: (313) 965-2200.

BOEDEKER, Joseph F. *(Chief Judge, Michigan District Court District Thirty-nine)* Elected Nov 1996 to term beginning Jan 1, 1997. Reelected Nov 2002, current term expires Dec 31, 2008. Born Detroit Michigan Aug 7, 1952. Catholic. Educated at Oakland University B.A. 1975 and Detroit College of Law J.D. 1981. Admitted to practice Michigan 1981, U.S. District Court Eastern District of Michigan 1981, U.S. Supreme Court 1985 and U.S. Court of Appeals Sixth Circuit 1986. In legal practice Roseville 1981-90 and Mount Clemens 1990-96.

Assistant City Attorney Roseville and Harper Woods 1981-90. Assistant Corporation Counsel Macomb County 1990-96. Instructor Macomb Community College 1987-91. Member Michigan District Judges Association, American Judges Association, State Bar of Michigan and Macomb County Bar Association. Member Optimist Club and Knights of Columbus. Enjoys family and golf.

Office: 29733 Gratiot Avenue, Roseville 48066.

Telephone: (586) 447-4450.

Fax: (586) 445-5070

BOKOS, C. Charles *(Chief Judge, Michigan District Court District Eighteen)* Former Chief Judge pro tem.

Office: 36675 Ford Road, Westland 48185-2297.

Telephone: (734) 595-8720.

BOLLE, William E. *(Judge, Michigan District Court District Fifty-two Division Four)* Elected to term beginning July 1, 1969. Reelected to subsequent terms. Current term expires Dec 31, 2008. Former Chief Judge. Currently serves as Presiding Judge Division Four. Born Menomonie Wisconsin March 1, 1939. Educated at University of Michigan B.B.A. 1960 and University of Wisconsin J.D. 1963. Admitted to practice Michigan 1964. Former Judge, Troy Municipal Court.

Office: 520 West Big Beaver Road, Troy 48084.

Telephone: (248) 528-0400.

BONDY, Robert *(Judge, Michigan District Court District Fifty-two Division One)*

Office: 48150 Grand River Avenue, Novi 48374-1222.

Telephone: (248) 305-6080.

BORCHARD, Fred L. *(Judge, Michigan Circuit Court Tenth Judicial Circuit)* Former Judge, Saginaw County Probate Court.

Office: Courthouse, 111 South Michigan Avenue, Saginaw 48602.

Telephone: (989) 790-5471.

BORMAN, Paul D. *(Judge, United States District Court Eastern District of Michigan)* Appointed for life by President Bill Clinton to term beginning 1994. Born Detroit Michigan Jan 7, 1939. Educated at University of Michigan B.A. 1959 J.D. 1962 and Yale Law School LL.M. 1964.

Staff Attorney U.S. Commission on Civil Rights 1962-63. Assistant U.S. Attorney 1964-65. Assistant County Prosecutor Wayne County 1974-75. Chief Federal Defender Legal Aid and Defender Association of Detroit 1979-94. Special Counsel Mayor's Development Team Detroit 1967. Special Counsel to Mayor of Detroit 1967-68.

Office: 740 U.S. Courthouse, 231 West Lafayette Boulevard, Detroit 48226.

Telephone: (313) 234-5120.

BORMAN, Susan D. *(Judge, Michigan Circuit Court Third Judicial Circuit)* Elected to term beginning Jan 1, 1979. Reelected 1984, 1990, 1996 and 2002. Current term expires Dec 31, 2008. Born Elizabeth New Jersey. Jewish. Educated at Smith College A.B. 1963, Columbia University 1963-64 and University of Detroit J.D. magna cum laude 1969. Admitted to practice Michigan 1969 and U.S. District Court Eastern District of Michigan 1969. Judge, Recorder's Court of Detroit 1973-78.

Important Decision: People v. McCleod (declared statute creating new verdict of guilty but mentally ill unconstitutional) 1977.

Office: 1707 Municipal Center, Two Woodward Avenue, Detroit 48226.

Telephone: (313) 224-5261.

BORRELLO, Leopold P. *(Chief Judge, Michigan Circuit Court Tenth Judicial Circuit)* Appointed by Governor James J. Blanchard to term beginning April 30, 1987. Elected Nov 8, 1988, 1994 and 2000. Current term expires Dec 31, 2006. Born Saginaw Michigan Nov 15, 1932. Episcopalian. Educated at Albion College B.A. 1955 and University of Michigan J.D. 1958. Member Omicron Delta Kappa. Admitted to practice Michigan 1958 and U.S. Court of Appeals Sixth Circuit 1970. In legal practice Saginaw 1958-87.

Member Michigan Judges Association, American Judges Association, State Bar of Michigan, Saginaw County and American Bar Associations. Former President Saginaw Cooperative Hospitals. Former Member St. Mary's Hospital Lay Board. Member Michigan Historical Society. Enjoys judging dog shows and raising and showing Irish Wolfhounds.

Office: Courthouse, 111 South Michigan Avenue, Saginaw 48602.

Telephone: (989) 790-5488.

BORRELLO, Stephen L. *(Judge, Michigan Court of Appeals)* Appointed by Governor Jennifer Granholm to term beginning 2003. Term expires Jan 1, 2007.

Mailing address: P.O. Box 30022, Lansing 48909-7522.

Office: Hall of Justice, 925 Ottawa Street, Lansing 48915.

Telephone: (517) 373-0786.

BOSMAN, Calvin L. *(Judge, Michigan Circuit Court Twentieth Judicial Circuit)* Elected to term beginning Jan 1, 1975. Reelected 1980, 1986, 1992 and 1998. Current term expires Dec 31, 2004. Former Chief Judge and Chief Judge pro tem. Born Holland Michigan Aug 29, 1935. Presbyterian. Educated at Hope College B.A. 1959 and Detroit College of Law LL.B. 1963. Admitted to practice Michigan 1964. In legal practice Grand Haven 1964-69. Associate Judge, Grand Haven Municipal Court 1965-69. Commissioner, Michigan Circuit Court 1965-69.

Prosecuting Attorney Ottawa County 1969-74. Member State Bar of Michigan, Ottawa County and American Bar Associations. E-3 USAS 1954-56. Enjoys snow skiing.

Office: Ottawa County Building, 414 North Washington Street, Grand Haven 49417.

Telephone: (616) 846-8320.

BOWLER, Patrick C. *(Judge, Michigan District Court District Sixty-one)* Former Chief Judge.

Office: 8A Kent County Courthouse, 180 Ottawa Avenue N.W., Grand Rapids 49503-2751.

Telephone: (616) 632-5700.

BOWMAN, Leo *(Chief Judge, Michigan District Court District Fifty)*

Office: 70 North Saginaw, Pontiac 48342.

Telephone: (248) 857-8000.

BOYD, Christopher S. *(Judge, Michigan District Court District Seventy Division Two)* Appointed Judge by Governor James J. Blanchard to term beginning April 7, 1989. Former Chief Judge and Chief Judge pro tem.

Office: 111 South Michigan Avenue, Saginaw 48602.

Telephone: (989) 790-5368.

BOYKIN, Ulysses W. *(Judge, Michigan Circuit Court Third Judicial Circuit)*

Office: 603 Hall of Justice, 1441 St. Antoine Street, Detroit 48226.

Telephone: (313) 224-2275.

BRADFIELD, David Martin *(Judge, Michigan District Court District Thirty-six)*

Office: 421 Madison Avenue, Suite 4072, Detroit 48226.

Telephone: (313) 965-2200.

BRADY, James *(Judge, Michigan District Court District Forty-seven)*

Office: 32795 West Ten Mile Road, Farmington 48336-2364.

Telephone: (248) 477-5630.

BRAUNLICH, Mark S. *(Judge, Michigan District Court District One)*

Office: 106 East First Street, Monroe 48161-2143.

Telephone: (734) 240-7075.

BRAXTON, Margie R. *(Judge, Michigan Circuit Court Third Judicial Circuit)* Assumed office Oct 1, 1997. Former Judge, Recorder's Court of Detroit.
Office: 304 Hall of Justice, 1441 St. Antoine Street, Detroit 48226.
Telephone: (313) 224-2477.

BRENNAN, Patrick J. *(Judge, Michigan Circuit Court Sixth Judicial Circuit)* Elected Nov 2000 to term beginning Jan 1, 2001. Term expires Dec 31, 2006. Born Detroit Michigan July 20, 1949. Educated at Oakland University B.A. 1971, University of Detroit M.A. 1973 and Wayne State University J.D. cum laude 1977. Law Clerk to Hon. James L. Ryan, Michigan Supreme Court 1979-80. Admitted to practice Michigan 1977, U.S. District Court Eastern District of Michigan and U.S. Court of Appeals Sixth Circuit. In legal practice Pontiac 1980-96 and Bloomfield Hills 1996-2000.
Staff Attorney Oakland County Circuit Court 1978-79. Member Michigan Trial Lawyers Association and Michigan Judges Association. Board of Advisors Crossroads For Youth.
Office: Courthouse Tower, 1200 North Telegraph Road, Pontiac 48341-0404.
Telephone: (248) 858-0337.

BRENNAN, Terrence H. *(Judge, Michigan District Court District Forty-four)* Former Chief Judge.
Office: 400 East Eleven Mile Road, Royal Oak 48068.
Telephone: (248) 246-3600.

BRENNAN, Thomas Emmett, Jr. *(Chief Judge, Michigan District Court District Fifty-five)* Elected to term beginning Jan 1, 1981. Reelected 1986, 1992 and 1998. Current term expires Dec 31, 2004. Former Chief Judge pro tem. Born Detroit Michigan March 20, 1952. Roman Catholic. Educated at Michigan State University B.S. 1974 and Thomas M. Cooley Law School J.D. 1978. Law Clerk to Hon. Thomas E. Brennan, Michigan Supreme Court. Member Phi Gamma Delta. Admitted to practice Michigan 1978. In legal practice East Lansing 1978-80.
Board of Commissioners Ingham County 1979-80. Adjunct Professor Michigan State University 1982-89 and Thomas M. Cooley Law School 1983-85. Member Ingham County Trial Judges Association, Michigan District Judges Association, American Judges Association, State Bar of Michigan, Ingham County and American Bar Associations. Completed Search and Seizure Course Dec 1981, Special Court Jurisdiction Course Nov 1983, Alcohol, Drugs and the Courts Feb 1988 and Ethics for Judges Course Oct 1993 The National Judicial College, Reno Nevada and Trial Judges Academy American Academy of Judicial Education University of Virginia School of Law July 1985. Recipient Distinguished Alumnus Award from Thomas M. Cooley Law School Alumni Association Oct 15, 1983. Member State Community Corrections Board. Board of Directors Thomas M. Cooley Law School (Secretary 1979-89). Member East Lansing Rotary Club, Knights of Columbus, Catholic Lawyers Guild, Incorporated Society of Irish/American Lawyers, The Irish American Club of Lansing, Michigan State University Blue Line Club, Rebounders Club and Downtown Coaches Club. Enjoys sports.
Office: 700 Buhl Drive, Mason 48854.
Telephone: (517) 676-8414.

BRENNAN, Timothy S. *(Chief Judge, Baraga County Probate Court)* Appointed by governor to term beginning 1991. Elected 1992, 1994 and 2000. Current term expires Dec 31, 2006. Educated at Indiana University B.S. 1980 and Ohio Northern University J.D. 1983. Admitted to practice Indiana 1983, U.S. District Courts Northern 1983 and Southern 1983 Districts of Indiana and Western District of Michigan 1988, U.S. Courts of Appeals Sixth 1983 and Seventh 1988 Circuits, Michigan 1988 and U.S. Supreme Court 1988. In legal practice South Bend Indiana 1983-88 and L'Anse Michigan since 1988.
Prosecuting Attorney Baraga County 1989-91. Instructor in Legal Issues in Corrections and Business Law Soumi College 1991-93 and Legal Issues in Corrections and Criminal Justice Gogebic Community College since 1994.
Office: Courthouse, 16 North Third, L'Anse 49946.
Telephone: (906) 524-6390.

BRENNEMAN, Hugh W., Jr. *(Magistrate Judge, United States District Court Western District of Michigan)* Appointed by U.S. District Court judges to term beginning April 1, 1980. Reappointed 1988 and 1996. Current term expires 2004. Born Lansing Michigan July 4, 1945. Member Mayflower Congregational Church. Educated at Alma College B.A. with honors 1967 and University of Michigan School of Law J.D. 1970. Law Clerk to Hon. Marvin Salmon, Michigan Circuit Court Thirtieth Judicial Circuit 1970-71. Member Phi Delta Phi and Delta Sigma Phi. Admitted to practice Michigan 1970, U.S. Court of Military Appeals 1971 and District of Columbia 1975. Began legal practice Lansing 1970. In legal practice Baltimore Maryland 1971-73, Washington D.C. 1973-74 and Grand Rapids 1974-80.
Assistant U.S. Attorney 1974-78. Co-author with Edward Wesoloski "Blueprint for a Summary Jury Trial" 65 No. 9 Michigan B. Jour. Sept 1986. Instructor Western Michigan University and Grand Valley State University. Fellow State Bar of Michigan Foundation. Member Grand Rapids Chapter American Inns of Court (Past President, Master of the Bench), Federal Magistrate Judges Association, The District of Columbia Bar, State Bar of Michigan (Representative Assembly 1984-90), Grand Rapids (Chairman Committee on Bicentennial of U.S. Constitution, Co-chairman Law Day 1991) and Federal (President Western Michigan Chapter 1979-80, National Delegate 1979-84) Bar Associations. Captain U.S. Army JAGC 1971-74. Past President Grand Rapids Historical Commission. Member Boy Scouts of America (Executive Board West Michigan Shores Council) and Rotary Club (Past President, Vice President Charities Foundation).
Office: 580 Federal Building, 110 Michigan Street N.W., Grand Rapids 49503.
Telephone: (616) 456-2568.

BRIDENSTINE, Paul J. *(Judge, Michigan District Court District Eight Division Three)* Appointed by Governor John Engler to term beginning March 1, 2000. Elected 2000, current term expires Dec 31, 2006. Currently serves as Chief Judge pro tem. Formerly served Division One. Born Southfield Michigan Sept 8, 1965. Educated at University of Notre Dame B.A. 1987 and University of Detroit J.D. 1991. Law Clerk to Hon. George E. Woods, U.S. District Court Eastern District of Michigan 1992. Admitted to practice Michigan 1992, U.S. District Court Eastern District of Michigan 1992,

BRIDENSTINE, PAUL J.—*Continued*
U.S. Court of Appeals Sixth Circuit 1992 and Florida 1996.

Assistant Prosecuting Attorney Kalamazoo Sept 1992 to March 2000. Member State Bar of Michigan and Kalamazoo County Bar Association.

Office: 227 West Michigan, Kalamazoo 49007.
Telephone: (269) 384-8103.
Fax: (269) 383-8642
E-mail address: pjbrid@kalcounty.com

BRIGHT, Izetta F. *(Judge, Michigan District Court District Thirty-six)*

Office: 421 Madison Avenue, Suite 5069, Detroit 48226.
Telephone: (313) 965-2200.

BRODY, George *(Recalled Judge, United States Bankruptcy Court Eastern District of Michigan)* Appointed by the Judicial Council of the Sixth Circuit. Born Brooklyn New York. Jewish. Educated at City College of the City University of New York 1941, University of Michigan J.D. 1947 and New York University LL.M. 1957. Member Order of the Coif. Admitted to practice Michigan 1947, California 1951 and New York 1956. Former Judge and Chief Judge, U.S. Bankruptcy Court Eastern District of Michigan, appointed by U.S. District Court judges to term beginning April 14, 1960. Former Recalled Judge, U.S. Bankruptcy Court Southern District of California, appointed by the Judicial Council of the Ninth Circuit.

Office: 4400 U.S. Courthouse, 333 Constitution Avenue N.W., Washington, D.C. 20001-2802.
Telephone: (202) 273-0708.

BRONSON, Terrence P. *(Judge, Michigan District Court District One)* Elected to term beginning Jan 1, 1989. Reelected 1994 and 2000. Current term expires Dec 31, 2006. Former Chief Judge. Born Toledo Ohio Oct 12, 1949. Roman Catholic. Educated at Villanova University B.A. 1971 and Cooley Law School J.D. 1976. Law Clerk to Hon. Leo W. Corkin, Michigan Circuit Court Twenty-ninth Judicial Circuit 1975-76. Admitted to practice Michigan 1976, U.S. District Court Eastern District of Michigan 1978 and District of Columbia 1979. In legal practice Monroe 1980-88.

Assistant City Attorney Monroe 1985-88. Member Michigan District Judges Association since 1989. Attended regional seminars 1989-2000. Faculty Michigan Judicial Institute 1991. USN (active duty) 1971-73 and Captain USNR 1992 (retired). Former Member St. Mary Catholic Central School Board. Amateur radio general class license since 1964. Coach of grade school soccer team.

Office: 106 East First Street, Monroe 48161.
Telephone: (734) 240-7135.

BROWN, Archie Cameron *(Chief Judge, Michigan Circuit Court Twenty-second Judicial Circuit)* Appointed by Governor John Engler March 1999. Currently serves as Presiding Judge Family Division. Also serves as Chief Judge Trial Court. Judge, Michigan District Court District Fifteen March 1997 to March 1999.

Mailing address: P.O. Box 8645, Ann Arbor 48107-8645.
Office: Courthouse, 101 East Huron, Ann Arbor 48104.
Telephone: (734) 222-3376.

BROWN, Christopher C. *(Judge, Michigan District Court District Fifty)* Former Chief Judge pro tem.

Office: 70 North Saginaw, Pontiac 48342.
Telephone: (248) 857-8000.

BROWN, Elwood L. *(Judge, St. Clair County Probate Court)*

Office: County Building, 201 McMorran Boulevard, Port Huron 48060.
Telephone: (810) 985-2066.

BROWN, Helen E. *(Judge, Michigan Circuit Court Third Judicial Circuit)* Assumed office Oct 1, 1997. Former Judge, Recorder's Court of Detroit.

Office: 1821 Municipal Center, Two Woodward Avenue, Detroit 48226.
Telephone: (313) 224-5261.

BROWN, Thomas Leo *(Judge, Michigan Circuit Court Thirtieth Judicial Circuit)* Appointed by Governor William G. Milliken to term beginning Jan 1, 1974. Elected Nov 1974, 1980, 1986, 1992 and 1998. Current term expires Dec 31, 2004. Serves General Trial Division. Former Chief Judge pro tem. Also Judge, Michigan Court of Claims. Born Hillsdale Michigan Nov 10, 1931. Roman Catholic. Educated at Michigan State University B.A. 1957 and University of Detroit LL.B. 1961. Member Gamma Eta Gamma. Admitted to practice Michigan 1961 and U.S. District Court District of Michigan 1966. Began legal practice Lansing 1962. In legal practice Leslie 1964. Judge, Ingham County Probate Court 1971-74.

Michigan State Representative Fifty-seventh District 1967-71. Important Decisions: Western Michigan Environmental Action Council v. DNR (environmental) and Macma Comm. v. State of Michigan (agricultural cooperatives). Former Adjunct Professor Thomas M. Cooley Law School. Member Michigan Judges Association (Executive Committee 1978-92, President 1990), American Judicature Society, State Bar of Michigan, Ingham County (Executive Committee 1968) and American Bar Associations. E-4 USN 1950-54. Republican. Precinct and State Delegate. Former Member Greater Lansing Amateur Hockey Association (President 1979) and Cristo Rey Community Center (Legal Assistance Bureau). Enjoys golfing, fishing, hunting and boating.

Mailing address: P.O. Box 40771, Lansing 48901-7971.
Office: Veteran's Memorial Courthouse, 313 West Kalamazoo Street, Lansing 48933.
Telephone: (517) 483-6432.

BRUCE, Gary J. *(Judge, Michigan District Court District Five)*

Office: Berrien County Courthouse, 811 Port Street, St. Joseph 49085-1188.
Telephone: (269) 983-7111.

BRZEZINSKI, Robert B. *(Chief Judge, Michigan District Court District Sixteen)* Elected to term beginning Jan 1, 1982. Reelected 1990, 1996 and 2002. Current term expires Dec 31, 2008. Former Chief Judge pro tem. Born Detroit Michigan Nov 25, 1936. Roman Catholic. Educated at University of Notre Dame B.A. 1958 and University of Michigan J.D. 1961. Admitted to practice Michigan 1962. Began legal practice Detroit 1962. In legal practice Harper Woods 1969.

Assistant Attorney City of Livonia 1971-83. Member Wayne County District Judges Association, Michigan

BRZEZINSKI, ROBERT B.—*Continued*

District Judges Association, American Judges Association, State Bar of Michigan, Livonia and Detroit Bar Associations. Member Knights of Columbus, Elks and Lions. Enjoys golf.

Office: 15140 Farmington Road, Livonia 48154-5498.

Telephone: (734) 466-2500.

BUCK, Michael L. *(Chief Judge, Allegan County Probate Court)* Elected to term beginning Jan 1, 2001. Term expires Jan 1, 2007. Born Benton Harbor Michigan Dec 11, 1951. Educated at University of Michigan B.A. 1974 and Thomas M. Cooley Law School J.D. 1977. Admitted to practice Michigan 1977.

Assistant Prosecutor Tuscola County 1977-79 and Allegan County 1979-2000.

Office: County Building, 113 Chestnut Street, Allegan 49010.

Telephone: (269) 673-0250.

Fax: (269) 686-4603

E-mail address: mbuck@allegancounty.org

BUDAY, Lynne Marie *(Judge, Kalkaska County Probate Court)* Former Chief Judge.

Office: Kalkaska County Government Center, 605 North Birch Street, Kalkaska 49646.

Telephone: (231) 258-3330.

BUHL, William C. *(Judge, Michigan Circuit Court Thirty-sixth Judicial Circuit)* Elected to term beginning Jan 1, 1989. Reelected 1994 and 2000. Current term expires Dec 31, 2006. Former Chief Judge pro tem and Chief Judge. Born Port Huron Michigan Sept 8, 1942. Presbyterian. Educated at University of Michigan B.A. 1964 J.D. 1967. Admitted to practice Michigan 1968. In legal practice Paw Paw 1968-71. Judge, Michigan District Court District Seven 1974-88.

Assistant Prosecuting Attorney 1968 and Prosecuting Attorney 1969-74 Van Buren County. Chairman Michigan Forms Committee since 1991. Member State Bar of Michigan and Van Buren County Bar Association. Republican. Member Boy Scouts sustaining membership drive and church choir. Enjoys painting, singing, instrumental music, gardening and athletics.

Office: Courthouse, 212 Paw Paw Street, Paw Paw 49079-1492.

Telephone: (269) 657-8218.

BURRESS, Daniel A. *(Judge, Michigan Circuit Court Forty-fourth Judicial Circuit)* Former Chief Judge pro tem.

Office: 204 South Highlander Way, Suite 5, Howell 48843.

Telephone: (517) 548-1120.

BURTON, Freddie G., Jr. *(Judge, Wayne County Probate Court)* Former Chief Judge.

Office: 1269 Municipal Center, Two Woodward Avenue, Detroit 48226.

Telephone: (313) 224-5686.

BUTER, David J. *(Chief Judge, Michigan District Court District Sixty-one)*

Office: 7A Kent County Courthouse, 180 Ottawa Avenue N.W., Grand Rapids 49503-2751.

Telephone: (616) 632-5700.

BUTH, George S. *(Chief Judge, Michigan Circuit Court Seventeenth Judicial Circuit)* Former Chief Judge pro tem.

Office: 11200A Kent County Courthouse, 180 Ottawa Avenue N.W., Grand Rapids 49503-2751.

Telephone: (616) 632-5480.

E-mail address: george.buth@kentcounty.org

BUTTS, Robert John *(Chief Judge, Cheboygan County Probate Court)* Elected Nov 7, 2000 to term beginning Jan 1, 2001. Term expires Dec 31, 2006. Born Lansing Michigan Dec 20, 1951. Catholic. Educated at Central Michigan University B.S.B.A. 1975 and Thomas M. Cooley Law School J.D. 1981. Admitted to practice Michigan 1982. In legal practice Cheboygan 1982-2000.

Assistant Prosecutor Cheboygan County 1982-86. Member State Bar of Michigan (Board Member Children's Law Section) and Cheboygan County Bar Association.

Mailing address: P.O. Box 70, Cheboygan 49721.

Office: Courthouse, 807 South Main Street, Cheboygan 49721.

Telephone: (231) 627-8823.

Fax: (231) 627-8868

E-mail address: jrjb@cheboygancounty.net

CAHALAN, William Leo *(Judge, Michigan Circuit Court Third Judicial Circuit)* Elected to term beginning Jan 1, 1975. Reelected 1982, 1988, 1994 and 2000. Current term expires Dec 31, 2006. Former Judge pro tem Criminal Division. Born April 24, 1931. Catholic. Educated at University of Notre Dame A.B. cum laude 1953 and University of Michigan J.D. 1956. Admitted to practice Michigan 1956. In legal practice Detroit 1960-70.

With Wayne County Prosecutor's Office 1970-74. Instructor American Institute of Banking 1963. Former Member American Bar Association. Member State Bar of Michigan and Detroit Bar Association. Captain USAR 1957-60. Enjoys sailing down the Hudson from Schenectady to Chesapeake Bay.

Office: 203 Hall of Justice, 1441 St. Antoine Street, Detroit 48226.

Telephone: (313) 224-7001.

CALLAHAN, Bill *(Judge, Michigan Circuit Court Third Judicial Circuit)* Elected Nov 1996 to term beginning Jan 1, 1997. Reelected Nov 2002, current term expires Dec 31, 2008. Serves Family Division. Born Rockville Centre New York Feb 8, 1947. Educated at Michigan State University B.A. 1971 and Detroit College of Law J.D. cum laude 1974. Board member Detroit College of Law Review. Member Delta Theta Phi. Admitted to practice Michigan 1974. In legal practice Michigan 1976-97.

Important Decision: Alexander v. Alexander (tort claim decided in conjunction with divorce) 2000. Certified in Business Bankruptcy by the Commercial Law League of America 1996. USMC 1967-69. Director Viet Nam Veterans of America 1980-86. Commissioner Detroit Housing Commission 1993-95. Life Member Sierra Club, VFW and Disabled American Veterans. Member Detroit Institute of Arts Founders Society, Trade Union Leadership Council and Detroit Zoological Society.

Office: 1813 Municipal Center, Two Woodward Avenue, Detroit 48226.

Telephone: (313) 224-5261.

E-mail address: Bill.Callahan@3cc.co.wayne.mi.us

CALLAHAN, Michael James *(Judge, Michigan Circuit Court Third Judicial Circuit)* Elected to term beginning Jan 1, 1991. Reelected 1996 and 2002. Current term expires Dec 31, 2008. Born March 1, 1943. Catholic. Educated at Sacred Heart Seminary B.A. 1965, Catholic University of Louvain M.A. 1969, Wayne State University Law School J.D. 1975 and Catholic University of America J.C.L. 1979.

Assistant Prosecuting Attorney St. Clair County 1979-81 and Wayne County 1987-90. Board of Directors Southeast Michigan Red Cross 1984-94. Judge, Michigan High School Court Competition 1991-2003.

Office: 1619 Municipal Center, Two Woodward Avenue, Detroit 48226.

Telephone: (313) 224-5237.

CAMPBELL, Patricia B. *(Judge, Wayne County Probate Court)*

Office: 2A Lincoln Hall of Justice, 1025 East Forest Avenue, Detroit 48207.

Telephone: (313) 833-0738.

CANNON, William H. *(Judge, Michigan District Court District Forty-one B)* Elected to term beginning Jan 1, 1977. Reelected 1982, 1988, 1994 and 2000. Current term expires Dec 31, 2006. Former Chief Judge pro tem. Currently serves as Presiding Judge Clinton Township Division. Born Detroit Michigan July 24, 1934. Catholic. Educated at Catholic seminary 1957 and Detroit College of Law LL.B. 1961. Admitted to practice Michigan 1961. Began legal practice Detroit 1961. In legal practice St. Clair Shores and Fraser.

Member State Bar of Michigan, Macomb County and American Bar Associations. Member Civil Service Commission 1975 and Knights of Columbus. Enjoys boating, fishing and hunting.

Office: 40700 Romeo Plank Road, Clinton Township 48038-2951.

Telephone: (586) 286-8010.

CAPEL, Wallace, Jr. *(Magistrate Judge, United States District Court Eastern District of Michigan)* Appointed by U.S. District Court judges.

Office: 112 Federal Building, 600 Church Street, Flint 48502.

Telephone: (810) 341-7850.

CAPRATHE, William Joseph *(Judge, Michigan Circuit Court Eighteenth Judicial Circuit)* Elected to term beginning Jan 1, 1981. Reelected 1986, 1992 and 1998. Current term expires Dec 31, 2004. Former Chief Judge. Currently serves as Presiding Judge. Born Jan 5, 1939. Educated at Michigan State University B.A. 1962 and Detroit College of Law J.D. 1965. Member Sigma Nu Phi. Admitted to practice Michigan 1966. Began legal practice Detroit 1966.

Member Michigan Judges Association (Past President Executive Board, Former Chair Rules Committee), State Bar of Michigan (Former Chair Criminal Jury Instruction Committee, Former Member Lawyers and Judges Assistance Committee, Former Chair Executive Committee and Member Judicial Conference) Bay County and American (State Delegate Executive Board and Chair Jury Management Committee National Conference of State Trial Judges Judicial Division) Bar Associations. Faculty Member Michigan Judicial Institute.

Office: 1230 Washington Avenue, Suite 251, Bay City 48708-5742.

Telephone: (989) 895-4267.

Fax: (989) 895-2090

CARETTI, Richard L. *(Judge, Michigan Circuit Court Sixteenth Judicial Circuit)*

Office: Macomb County Court Building, 40 North Main, Mount Clemens 48043-5654.

CARLSON, Thomas A. *(Magistrate Judge, United States District Court Eastern District of Michigan)* Appointed by U.S. District Court judges to term beginning Oct 1979. Reappointed Oct 1987 and Oct 1995. Current term expires Oct 2003. Born Muskegon Michigan May 12, 1942. Catholic. Educated at University of Notre Dame B.A. summa cum laude 1964 and University of Michigan J.D. cum laude 1967. Admitted to practice Michigan 1967. Began legal practice Lansing 1969. Former Commissioner, Michigan Supreme Court.

Former Assistant Attorney General. Member State Bar of Michigan and American Bar Association. E-5 U.S. Army 1967-69.

Office: 673 U.S. Courthouse, 231 West Lafayette Boulevard, Detroit 48226.

Telephone: (313) 234-5205.

CARMODY, Ellen S. *(Magistrate Judge, United States District Court Western District of Michigan)* Appointed by U.S. District Court judges to term beginning Oct 10, 2000.

Office: 666 Federal Building, 110 Michigan Street N.W., Grand Rapids 49503.

Telephone: (616) 456-2528.

CARMODY, William W. *(Chief Judge, Alger-Schoolcraft Counties Probate Court District)*

Office: Courthouse Complex, 101 Court Street, Munising 49862.

Telephone: (906) 387-2080.

CARNIAK, Nancy Tolwin *(Judge, Michigan District Court District Fifty-two Division Three)*

Office: 135 Barclay Circle, Rochester Hills 48307-5800.

Telephone: (248) 853-5553.

CARPENTER, Nanaruth H. *(Judge, Kent County Probate Court)* Appointed by Governor James J. Blanchard to term beginning April 20, 1990.

Office: 9200A Kent County Courthouse, 180 Ottawa Avenue N.W., Grand Rapids 49503-2751.

Telephone: (616) 774-3703.

CASSIDY, Paul A. *(Chief Judge, Michigan District Court District Forty-two and Judge, Michigan District Court District Forty-two Division Two)* Elected Nov 8, 1994 to term beginning Jan 1, 1995. Reelected 2000, current term expires Dec 31, 2006. Former Chief Judge pro tem. Born Mount Clemens Michigan Feb 19, 1953. Educated at Central Michigan University B.A. 1975 and Ohio Northern University J.D. 1978. Admitted to practice Michigan 1978 and U.S. Supreme Court 1987. In legal practice Utica 1978-80.

Assistant Prosecuting Attorney Macomb County 1980-95. Enjoys basketball, hunting, fishing and boating.

Office: 43565 Elizabeth, Mt. Clemens 48043.

Telephone: (586) 469-5046.

CAVANAGH, Mark J. *(Judge, Michigan Court of Appeals)* Elected 1988. Reelected to subsequent terms. Current term expires Jan 1, 2009. Educated at University of Michigan and Detroit College of Law J.D.

CAVANAGH, MARK J.—*Continued*

Former Special Assistant Attorney General. Former Assistant Prosecutor Wayne County.

Office: 760 American Center Building, 27777 Franklin Road, Southfield 48034-8257.

Telephone: (248) 358-5920.

CAVANAGH, Michael F. *(Justice, Michigan Supreme Court)* Elected to term beginning Jan 1, 1983. Reelected 1990 and 1998. Current term expires Dec 31, 2006. Former Chief Justice. Born Detroit Michigan Oct 21, 1940. Roman Catholic. Educated at University of Detroit B.A. 1962 J.D. 1966. Law Clerk to Michigan Court of Appeals 1966. Member Blue Key. Admitted to practice Michigan 1966. In legal practice Lansing 1969-73. Judge, Michigan District Court District Fifty-four A 1973-75. Judge, Michigan Court of Appeals Jan 1, 1975 to Dec 31, 1982.

Lansing City Attorney 1967-69. Michigan Supreme Court Liaison Michigan Indian Tribal Courts/Michigan State Courts since 1990. Member American Judicature Society, Incorporated Society of Irish/American Lawyers (President 1987-88), State Bar of Michigan, Ingham County and American Bar Associations. Chairman Judicial Planning Committee 1977-78. Supervising Justice Supreme Court Sentencing Guidelines Committee 1983-94, Michigan Judicial Institute 1986-94 and 2001-03 and Michigan Hall of Justice Project 2001-03. Chair National Interbranch Conference of Funding the State Courts 1994-95. Member Court Improvement Program National Center for State Courts 1994-95. Honorary Member Institute of Judicial Administration New York University. Participant Michigan Justice Conference 1994-95, Michigan Justice Project 1994-95 and Commission of the Future University of Detroit 1995-96. Member County Board of Commissioners 1973-75. Member American Heart Association of Michigan (Tri-County Unit President 1976-77 and Chairman Board of Trustees 1984-85). Board of Directors Lansing YMCA 1977-78 and Thomas M. Cooley Law School 1979-88. Enjoys fishing and hunting.

Mailing address: P.O. Box 30052, Lansing 48909.

Office: Michigan Hall of Justice, Lansing 48915.

Telephone: (517) 373-8683.

CELELLO, Richard J. *(Judge, Michigan Circuit Court Forty-first Judicial Circuit)*

Mailing address: P.O. Box 609, Iron Mountain 49801.

Office: Courthouse, 705 South Stephenson Street, Iron Mountain 49801.

Telephone: (906) 774-2266.

CHABOT, Rae Lee *(Judge, Michigan Circuit Court Sixth Judicial Circuit)*

Office: Courthouse Tower, 1200 North Telegraph Road, Pontiac 48341-0404.

Telephone: (248) 858-0344.

CHAMBERLAIN, Paul H. *(Chief Judge, Michigan Circuit Court Twenty-first Judicial Circuit)* Elected Nov 1992 to term beginning Jan 1, 1993. Reelected 1998, current term expires Dec 31, 2004. Also serves as Chief Judge Trial Court. Born Mount Pleasant Michigan May 8, 1954. Educated at Central Michigan University B.S. 1976 and Thomas M. Cooley Law School J.D. 1980. Admitted to practice Michigan 1980 and U.S. District Court Eastern District of Michigan. In legal practice Mount Pleasant 1980-92.

Office: Isabella County Courthouse, 300 North Main Street, Mount Pleasant 48858.

Telephone: (989) 772-0911.

CHARRON, Raymond A. *(Chief Judge, Michigan District Court District Twenty-six and Judge, Michigan District Court District Twenty-six Division One)* Former Chief Judge pro tem.

Office: 10600 West Jefferson, River Rouge 48218.

Telephone: (313) 842-7819.

CHERRY, Michael H. *(Chief Judge, Michigan Circuit Court Fifteenth Judicial Circuit)*

Office: Branch County Courthouse, 31 Division Street, Coldwater 49036.

Telephone: (517) 279-4304.

CHERRY, Patrick F. *(Chief Judge, Michigan District Court District Fifty-four A)* Appointed to term beginning Jan 1975. Reelected 1976, 1978, 1984, 1990, 1996 and 2002. Current term expires Dec 31, 2008. Former Chief Judge pro tem. Born Lansing Michigan Jan 3, 1946. Roman Catholic. Educated at University of Michigan B.A. 1966 and Wayne State University J.D. 1969. Admitted to practice Michigan 1969.

With Ingham County Prosecuting Attorney's Office Lansing 1970-75. Instructor Lansing Business University 1969-70 and Lansing Community College. Member National College of Special Court Judges and State Bar of Michigan. Former Member Board of Directors Catholic Social Services of Ingham County and National Council on Alcoholism Lansing Regional Area. Enjoys fly fishing, bridge and athletics.

Office: City Hall, Sixth Floor, 124 West Michigan Avenue, Lansing 48933-1690.

Telephone: (517) 487-1350.

CHMURA, John M. *(Judge, Michigan District Court District Thirty-seven)* Appointed by Governor John Engler to term beginning May 9, 1996. Elected Nov 5, 1996 and Nov 7, 2000. Current term expires Dec 31, 2006. Currently serves as Chief Judge pro tem. Born Detroit Michigan Dec 28, 1962. Roman Catholic. Educated at Michigan State University B.A. 1985 and University of Wisconsin Law School J.D. 1988. Business Manager University of Wisconsin International Law Journal 1987-88. Admitted to practice Michigan 1988, Wisconsin 1988 and U.S. District Court Eastern District of Michigan 1988. In legal practice Royal Oak Michigan, Warren Michigan, Mount Clemens Michigan and Roseville Michigan 1988-96.

Macomb County Public Administrator 1991-96. Contributor *Bar Briefs* Macomb County Bar Association 1997. Member Michigan District Judges Association, Advocates Bar Association (Treasurer 1994-98, President 1998-2000), Macomb County Probate Bar Association (Treasurer since 1996), State Bar of Michigan, State Bar of Wisconsin, Macomb County (President Young Lawyers Division 1995-96) and American Bar Associations. Recipient pro bono Service Award 1995 and Outstanding Leadership Award 1996 from Macomb County Bar Association. Republican. Chairman Polish Day Parade Committee since 1997. Board Member Warren Family YMCA and Warren Symphony Orchestra. Member Polish Century Club of Detroit, Polish American Congress, Polish National Alliance, American Polish Century Club of Sterling Heights, American Polish Cultural Center,

CHMURA, JOHN M.—*Continued*

Order of the Alhambra, Friends of Polish Art, National Rifle Association, Federalist Society, Knights of Columbus, Detroit Athletic Club, Economic Club of Detroit and Warren Kiwanis Club. Enjoys classical music, opera, wine tasting and Michigan State University basketball and football.
Office: 8300 Common Road, Warren 48093-2380.
Telephone: (586) 574-4925.
Fax: (586) 574-4932

CHRISTENSEN, J. Michael *(Judge, Michigan District Court District Sixty-one)* Former Chief Judge pro tem.
Office: 7C Kent County Courthouse, 180 Ottawa Avenue N.W., Grand Rapids 49503-2751.
Telephone: (616) 632-5700.

CHRZANOWSKI, Mary A. *(Judge, Michigan Circuit Court Sixteenth Judicial Circuit)* Elected to term beginning Jan 1, 1993. Reelected 1998, current term expires Dec 31, 2004. Born Detroit Michigan Dec 9, 1961. Catholic. Educated at Wayne State University B.S. with honors 1982 and University of Detroit School of Law J.D. 1985. Admitted to practice Michigan 1987 and U.S. District Court Eastern District of Michigan 1987. In legal practice Center Line 1987-91 and Sterling Heights 1991-92.
Member State Bar of Michigan and Macomb County Bar Association. Enjoys weight lifting, travel, psychology and roller blading.
Office: Macomb County Court Building, 40 North Main, Mount Clemens 48043-5654.
Telephone: (586) 469-5149.

CHYLINSKI, James R. *(Judge, Michigan Circuit Court Third Judicial Circuit)* Appointed by Governor James J. Blanchard to term beginning May 9, 1990. Elected to term beginning Jan 1, 1991. Reelected 1992 and 1998. Current term expires Dec 31, 2004. Born Detroit Michigan Nov 25, 1948. Educated at University of Detroit A.B. 1970 J.D. 1974. Admitted to practice Michigan 1974 and U.S. District Court Eastern District of Michigan 1974. Began legal practice Warren 1974. In legal practice Detroit 1975. Judge, Michigan District Court District Thirty-six 1981-83. Judge, Recorder's Court of Detroit 1983-90.
Prosecuting Attorney Wayne County 1975-80. Member State Bar of Michigan, Detroit and Advocates Bar Associations. E-4 USAR 1969-75.
Office: 202 Hall of Justice, 1441 St. Antoine Street, Detroit 48226.
Telephone: (313) 224-5501.

CIUNGAN, Michael F. *(Judge, Michigan District Court District Twenty-six Division Two)* Former Chief Judge.
Office: 3869 West Jefferson, Ecorse 48229.
Telephone: (313) 386-7900.

CLABUESCH, David L. *(Chief Judge, Huron County Probate Court)* Appointed to term beginning May 4, 1987.
Office: County Building, 250 East Huron Avenue, Bad Axe 48413.
Telephone: (989) 269-9944.

CLARK, Terry L. *(Chief Judge, Michigan District Court District Seventy and Judge, Michigan District Court District Seventy Division One)* Appointed Judge by Governor James J. Blanchard to term beginning Aug 10, 1990. Elected Nov 1992, Nov 1994 and 2000. Current term expires Dec 31, 2006. Former Chief Judge pro tem. First African American Judge to serve Saginaw County. Born Saginaw Michigan Sept 19, 1955. Baptist. Educated at University of Michigan B.A. with honors 1977 and Texas Southern University Thurgood Marshall School of Law J.D. 1980. Member Phi Alpha Delta. Admitted to practice Michigan 1981, U.S. District Court Eastern District of Michigan 1981 and U.S. Court of Appeals Sixth Circuit 1987. In legal practice Saginaw 1985-90.
Former Assistant Prosecutor Saginaw County. Instructor "Introduction to Criminal Justice" Saginaw Valley State University 1994. Member Association of Black Judges of Michigan, Michigan District Judges Association, State Bar of Michigan (Clerk 1988-89 and Chairperson 1989-90 Representative Assembly) and Saginaw County Bar Association. Recipient numerous community service awards and certificates of appreciation. Trustee Board of Control Saginaw Valley State University 1989-92. Member New Mount Calvary Missionary Baptist Church (Trustee Board) and Rotary Club.
Office: 302 Saginaw County Courthouse, 111 South Michigan Avenue, Saginaw 48602.
Telephone: (989) 790-5371.

CLARKE, Arthur H., III *(Judge, Michigan District Court District Seven)*
Mailing address: P.O. Box 311, South Haven 49090-0311.
Office: 1007 East Wells Street, South Haven 49090.

CLARKSON, Ward L. *(Chief Judge, Michigan District Court District Sixty-six)* Former Chief Judge pro tem.
Office: Shiawassee County Courts Building, 110 East Mack Street, Corunna 48817.
Telephone: (989) 743-2395.

CLATTERBAUGH, James R. *(Chief Judge, Shiawassee County Probate Court)* Appointed by Governor James J. Blanchard to term beginning Feb 10, 1986. Elected 1986, 1988, 1994 and 2000. Current term expires Dec 31, 2006. Born Waverly Iowa June 5, 1943. Educated at University of Wisconsin B.S. 1966 and University of Iowa J.D. 1969. Admitted to practice Iowa 1969 and Michigan 1970. In legal practice Owosso Michigan March 1974 to Feb 1986.
Member Michigan Probate Judges Association, American Judges Association, State Bar of Michigan and Shiawassee County Bar Association. Bank Trust Officer Aug 1969 to March 1974. Former Board Member American Cancer Society. Former Board Chairman Salvation Army. Treasurer Owosso Sports Boosters. Member Friends of Senior Citizens and Agriculture Society. Enjoys golf, family activities and following Big Ten sports.
Office: County Courts Building, 110 East Mack Street, Corunna 48817.
Telephone: (989) 743-2211.

CLELAND, Robert H. *(Judge, United States District Court Eastern District of Michigan)* Appointed for life by President George Bush to term beginning June 19, 1990. Born St. Clair Michigan April 26, 1947. Educated at Michigan State University B.A. 1969 and University of North Carolina at Chapel Hill J.D. 1972. Admitted to

CLELAND, ROBERT H.—*Continued*
practice Michigan 1972. In legal practice Port Huron 1972-90.

Assistant Prosecuting Attorney 1972-81 and Prosecutor 1981-90 St. Clair County.

Office: 707 U.S. Courthouse, 231 West Lafayette Boulevard, Detroit 48226.

Telephone: (313) 234-5525.

CLOSZ, Harold F., III *(Judge, Michigan District Court District Sixty)*

Office: Hall of Justice, 990 Terrace Street, Muskegon 49442-3377.

Telephone: (231) 724-6283.

CLULO, Paul J. *(Judge, Michigan Circuit Court Forty-second Judicial Circuit)* Elected to term beginning Jan 1, 1985. Reelected 1990, 1996 and 2002. Current term expires Dec 31, 2008. Currently serves as Chief Judge pro tem. Former Chief Judge. Born Marquette Michigan Dec 12, 1939. Educated at University of Notre Dame B.S. in Chemistry 1962 and Marquette University LL.B. 1965. Staff member and writer Marquette Law Review 1964-65. Admitted to practice Michigan 1965 and Wisconsin 1965. Began legal practice Midland Michigan 1965.

Instructor in Business Law Northwood Institute 1965-67. Member Michigan Judges Association (Executive Committee since 1989, Chairman Domestic Relations Committee 1989-92, Chairman Annual Meeting 1993, President 1999), State Bar of Michigan, Midland County (President 1975) and American Bar Associations. Lecturer Michigan Judicial Institute since 1985. Attended courses on General Jurisdiction 1986, Judicial Writing 1988, Advanced Evidence 1992 and Computer Training for Judges 1997 The National Judicial College. Named Judge of the Year by National Child Support Enforcement Association 1990. Enjoys music, reading and backpacking.

Office: Midland County Courthouse, 301 West Main Street, Midland 48640.

Telephone: (989) 832-6830.

E-mail address: pclulo@voyager.net

COHN, Avern *(Senior Judge, United States District Court Eastern District of Michigan)* Appointed for life by President Jimmy Carter to term beginning Oct 9, 1979. Assumed Senior status Oct 9, 1999, serves by assignment. Born Detroit Michigan July 23, 1924. Jewish. Educated at University of Michigan 1942-43, John Tarleton Agricultural College 1943, Stanford University 1944, Loyola University School of Medicine 1945-46 and University of Michigan J.D. 1949. Admitted to practice Michigan 1949. In legal practice Detroit 1949-79.

Author "Effective Trial Practice: One Judge's View" Dec 1982, "Effective Brief Writing: One Judge's View" Nov 1983, "Effective Advocacy in My Court" 69 No. 10 Oct 1990, "Fair Trial—Free Press: A Trial Judge's View" 71, 190, 1992, "A Footnote to a Footnote" 75, 494, 1996 and "Judicial Review of Legislation: The Role of the Judge" 77, 32, 1998 Michigan B. Jour.; "Sentencing Federal Offenders: Some Thoughts on the Present and the Future" 4, 1983 and "Constitutional Interpretation and Judicial Treatment of Blacks in Michigan Before 1870" Winter 1986 Detroit College of Law Review; "*Doe v. University of Michigan:* A Somewhat Personal View" 37 No. 3 Wayne L. Rev. Spring 1991; "The General Accounting Office Report to Congressional Committees on Sentencing Guidelines—A Reaction" 5, 156, 1992, "The Sentencing Commission's 1993 Annual Report" 7, 137, 1994 and "Advice to the Commission—A Sentencer's View" 8, 14, 1995 Fed. Sent. R. Vera Institute of Justice; "The Unfairness of Substantial Assistance" 78, 186, 1995 and "Judicial Review is Exercised Properly" 82, 29, 1998 Judicature; "Summary of a Jury Trial—A Caution" Journal of Dispute Resolution 2999, 1995; Book Review "The Shadow University: The Betrayal of Liberty on America's Campuses" by Klor and Silvergate 98 Michigan L. Rev. 1549, 2000; Book Review "The Vote: Bush, Gore & The Supreme Court" by Sunstein and Epstein 3 Judge's Jour. 37 Summer 2002; Book Review "Sovereignty and Liberty" by Kammen 9 No. 3 Journal of the Early Republic; and "Comment: A Judge's View of Congressional Action Affecting the Courts" Journal of Law and Contemporary Problems No. 3. Co-author "The Rise and Fall of Affirmative Action in Jury Selection" 32 University of Michigan Journal of Law Reform 323, 1999 and "The Calculation of Criminal History by AUSAS and Defendants: A Study of the Inefficiency in the Eastern District of Michigan" 13 Vera Institute of Justice Fed. Sent. R. 327, 2001. Author and Presenter "A Federal Court Perspective on Extraterritorial Enforcement of Intellectual Property" 31 No. 6 CASRIP Publication Series 2000 delivered at High Technology Summit Conference University of Washington 2000. Member Michigan Social Welfare Commission 1963, Michigan Civil Rights Commission 1972-75 (Chairman 1974-75) and Detroit Board of Police Commissioners 1975-79 (Chairman 1979). Director American Judicature Society. Member State Bar of Michigan (Representative Assembly 1973-79, Chairman Special Committee on Court Congestion 1977-78), Detroit (Former Foundation Trustee, former Director), Federal and American Bar Associations. U.S. Army 1943-46. Past President Jewish Welfare Federation of Detroit.

Office: 219 U.S. Courthouse, 231 West Lafayette Boulevard, Detroit 48226.

Telephone: (313) 234-5160.

Fax: (313) 234-5351

Website address: www.judgeaverncohn.com *or* www.mied.uscourts.gov/—practices/cohn/bio.htm

COLEMAN, Donald *(Judge, Michigan District Court District Thirty-six)*

Office: 421 Madison Avenue, Suite 4066, Detroit 48226.

Telephone: (313) 965-2200.

COLLETTE, William E. *(Chief Judge, Michigan Circuit Court Thirtieth Judicial Circuit)* Appointed by Governor James J. Blanchard to term beginning Dec 10, 1990. Elected to subsequent terms. Chief Judge since Jan 1, 2003. Also Judge, Michigan Court of Claims. Judge, Michigan District Court District Fifty-four A 1979-90.

Office: 315 North Jefferson, Third Floor, Mason 48854.

COLLINS, John B. *(Chief Judge, Michigan District Court District Fourteen B)*

Office: Ypsilanti Township Civic Center, 7200 South Huron River Drive, Ypsilanti 48198.

Telephone: (734) 483-2330.

COLOMBO, Robert J., Jr. *(Judge, Michigan Circuit Court Third Judicial Circuit)* Elected to term beginning

COLOMBO, ROBERT J., JR.—*Continued*

Jan 1, 1983. Reelected 1988, 1994 and 2000. Current term expires Dec 31, 2006. Former Presiding Judge Civil Division. Born Detroit Michigan April 3, 1950. Roman Catholic. Educated at University of Miami B.B.A. cum laude 1972 and Detroit College of Law J.D. cum laude 1975. Law Clerk to Hon. George N. Bashara, Jr., Michigan Court of Appeals 1975-77. Admitted to practice Michigan 1975. Began legal practice Detroit 1977.

Author Chapter 13 "Risk Management" *Michigan Court Administration Reference Guide* 1990 and "The Computer Integrated Courtroom" The Advocates' Society Lecturer 1986. Important Decisions: UAW, et al. v. David Adamany, et al. (picketers illegally arrested in violation of first amendment) 88, 824-437 CL 1990 and City of Grosse Pointe Park v. Esquire Theater, Inc., et al. (city's condemnation of only movie theater did not violate first amendment) 88, 816-061 CC 1988. Instructor Advocacy Program Thomas M. Cooley Law School 1983-86 and 1988-90. Guest Lecturer Detroit College of Law 1984-85. Member Wayne County Judges Association, Michigan Judges Association, State Bar of Michigan and The Detroit Metropolitan Bar Association. Lecturer on Computer Aided Transcription Kansas State Judges Annual Meeting 1985, Ontario Supreme Court June 1986, The Florida Bar Annual Meeting 1986, North Carolina Superior Court Conference 1987, Ohio Judicial Conference 1987 and Annual Meeting of Louisiana State Judges 1988 and Caseflow Management California Court Management Conference 1989 and San Diego Judicial Conference 1989. Recipient Commendations from National Shorthand Reporters Association Nov 11, 1984 and Michigan Non-Partisan Alliance Dec 20, 1990. Committee Member "Sharin of the Green" Most Holy Trinity Church, Detroit 1983-87. Co-chairperson Catholic Services Appeal St. Philomena Church, Detroit 1986-91.

Office: 1101 Municipal Center, Two Woodward Avenue, Detroit 48226.

Telephone: (313) 224-5195.

CONLIN, Richard E. *(Judge, Michigan District Court District Fourteen A)* Former Chief Judge.

Office: 122 South Main Street, Chelsea 48118.

Telephone: (734) 475-8606.

CONLON, Patricia Nedwicki *(Judge, Kalamazoo County Probate Court)* Elected Nov 1996 to term beginning Jan 1, 1997. Reelected 2002, current term expires Dec 31, 2008. Currently serves as Chief Judge pro tem. Also serves Family Division Michigan Circuit Court Ninth Judicial Circuit. Born Detroit Michigan Oct 16, 1944. Educated at University of Dayton B.A. 1966 and Wayne State University J.D. 1978. Admitted to practice Michigan 1979, U.S. District Courts Eastern 1979 and Western 1990 District of Michigan and U.S. Court of Appeals Sixth Circuit 1995. In legal practice Kalamazoo 1979-83 and 1989-96.

Assistant Prosecuting Attorney 1983-89. Author *West Michigan Lawyers Manual* 1991. Instructor Paralegal and Business Programs Davenport College 1989-95. President Southwest Michigan Probate Judges Association. Member Probate Judges Association, State Bar of Michigan and Kalamazoo Bar Association. Attended Advanced Trial 1986 and Teaching Trial Advocacy 1995 National Institute for Trial Advocacy and The National Judicial College 1998, 1999, 2000 and 2001.

Office: 1400 Gull Road, Kalamazoo 49048.

Telephone: (269) 385-6003.

CONNOLLY, John T. *(Judge, Michigan District Court District Seventy-one A)* Elected to term beginning Jan 1, 1983. Reelected 1988, 1994 and 2000. Current term expires Dec 31, 2006. Former Chief Judge and Chief Judge pro tem. Born Flint Michigan Feb 22, 1942. Educated at Michigan State University B.A. 1965 and Wayne State University J.D. 1968. Member Sigma Alpha Epsilon. Admitted to practice Michigan 1969. Began legal practice Flint 1969. In legal practice Lapeer 1970.

Recipient Young Man of the Year Award from Lapeer County Jaycees 1972 and Distinguished Service Award from March of Dimes 1976 and 1977. Democrat. Lapeer County Democratic Party Chairman 1970-80. Eighth District Democratic Party Chairman 1974-80. Board of Directors Growth and Opportunity since 1984 and Council for Children 1992. Member Big Brothers/ Big Sisters (Board of Directors since 1982, President 1984), Lapeer County School Board (Vice President) and Elba Township Planning Committee. Enjoys golf, fishing and hunting.

Office: Lapeer County Complex Building, 255 Clay Street, Lapeer 48446.

Telephone: (810) 667-0314.

CONNORS, Timothy P. *(Judge, Michigan Circuit Court Twenty-second Judicial Circuit)* Former Chief Judge and Chief Judge Trial Court. Former Chief Judge, Michigan District Court District Fifteen.

Mailing address: P.O. Box 8645, Ann Arbor 48107-8645.

Office: Courthouse, 101 East Huron, Ann Arbor 48104.

Telephone: (734) 222-3001.

CONOVER, John L. *(Judge, Michigan District Court District Sixty-seven Division Two)* Former Chief Judge pro tem.

Office: 200 East Flint Street, Davison 48423.

Telephone: (810) 653-4126.

COOK, James H. *(Chief Judge, Alcona County Probate Court)* Appointed by Governor John Engler July 1991. Elected Nov 7, 1994 and 2000. Current term expires Dec 31, 2006. Born Haynes Township Michigan Sept 23, 1934. Educated at Michigan Technological University B.S.Ch.Eng. with honors 1956, Wayne State University M.B.A. 1963 and Detroit College of Law J.D. with honors 1963. Admitted to practice Michigan 1964.

Prosecuting Attorney 1964-76, Friend of the Court 1976-77 and Corporate Council 1991-94 Alcona County. Captain U.S. Army Corps of Engineers. Republican. Chairman Alcona County Republican Party. Member Lions Club.

Mailing address: P.O. Box 328, Harrisville 48740.

Office: County Building, 106 Fifth Street, Harrisville 48740.

Telephone: (989) 724-6880.

COOK, Julian Abele, Jr. *(Senior Judge, United States District Court Eastern District of Michigan)* Appointed for life by President Jimmy Carter to term beginning Sept 23, 1978. Chief Judge Dec 31, 1989 to Dec 30, 1996. Assumed Senior status Dec 31, 1996, serves by assignment. Born June 22, 1930. Educated at

COOK, JULIAN ABELE, JR.—*Continued*

Pennsylvania State University B.A. 1952, Georgetown University J.D. 1957 and University of Virginia LL.M. 1988. Awarded honorary LL.D. Georgetown University 1992, University of Detroit-Mercy May 1996 and Wayne State University 1997. Law Clerk to Hon. Arthur E. Moore, 1957-58. In legal practice 1958-78.

Special Assistant Attorney General Michigan 1968-78. General Counsel Public Television Station WTVS 1973-78. Co-author with Allen Sultan "Some Current Problems of Human Relations Administration" 49 University of Detroit Journal of Urban Law 163, 1971, with Mark S. Kende "Jurisprudence of Original Intention: A Critical Evaluation" 4 Detroit College of Law L. Rev. 1003, 1986, *Federal Civil Procedure Before Trial: Sixth Circuit* 1996, with Tracy D. Weaver, "Closing Their Eyes to the Constitution: The Declining Role of the Supreme Court in the Protection of Civil Rights" Detroit College of Law L. Rev. 541, 1996 and with Mark S. Kende "Death Penalty" 13 Cooley L. Rev. 815, 1996. Author "A Quest for Justice: Effective and Efficient Alternative Dispute Resolution Process" 4 Detroit College of Law L. Rev. 163, 1983, "Rule 11: A Judicial Approach to an Effective Administration of Justice in the United States Courts" 15 Ohio Northern University L. Rev. 397, 1988, "An Overview of the United States District Court for the Eastern District of Michigan" 28 No. 1 *Inter Alia* Winter 1990, "The Changing Role of the Probation Officer in the Federal Court" 4 No. 2 Federal Sentencing Reporter 112, 1991, "George A. Googasian—58th President of the State Bar of Michigan" 71 No. 10 Michigan B. Jour. Oct 1992, "Thurgood Marshall and Clarence Thomas: A Glance at Their Philosophies" 73 No. 3. Michigan B. Jour. 298, 1994, "ADR in the United States Court for Eastern District of Michigan" §§ 62A.405-62A.415 *Michigan Pleading and Practice—ADR* 1994, "Family Responsibility" 8 No. 3 Federal Sentencing Reporter 145, 1995 and "Dream Makers: Black Judges on Justice" 94 Michigan L. Rev. 1479, 1996. Columnist Wolverine Bar Association Newsletter 1987-90 and 1994-96. Adjunct Professor of Constitutional Law, Civil Rights and Evidence University of Detroit School of Law 1971-74. Chairman Michigan Civil Rights Commission 1968-71 and Sixth Circuit Committee on Standard Jury Instructions for District Courts Within the Sixth Circuit since 1986. Labor Arbitrator American Arbitration Association and Michigan Employment Relations Commission 1975-78. Member Michigan Supreme Court Defense Service Committee 1977. Honorary Member Federal Bar Association 1978. Member 1988-93 and Chairman 1990-93 Committee of Financial Disclosure Judicial Conference of the U.S. Member Executive Committee 1991-96 and Senior Judge Personnel Committee since 1996 Judicial Council of the Sixth Circuit. Member Judicial Advisory Group U.S. Sentencing Commission since 1996. Fellow American Bar Foundation, Michigan State Bar Foundation (Vice Chairman 1992-93, Chairman since 1993) and American Bar Association. Member The American Law Institute, Mediation Tribunal Association, Third Judicial Circuit of Michigan (Board of Directors since 1992), Industrial Relations Research Association 1978, American Inn of Courts (President 1984-95 and Master Bencher 1984-95 Chapter XI, Chairman National Nominations and Election Committee 1994-95, Member National Publications Advisory Committee 1994-96, National Board of Trustees since 1996), State Bar of Michigan (Chairman Constitutional Law Committee 1969, Vice Chairman Civil Liberties Committee 1970, Co-chairman Professional Development Task Force 1984-87, Member U.S. Courts Committee 1988-95, Committee on Professionalism since 1991), Oakland County (Chairman 1968-69 and Member 1977 CLE Committee, Vice Chairman Judicial Liaison-District Court Committee 1977, Unauthorized Practice of Law Committee 1977) and American Bar Associations. Lecturer Federal and State Court Practice Seminar Federal Bar Association since 1981. Instructor Trial Advocacy Workshop Harvard University since 1988 and Trial Advocacy Program U.S. Department of Justice 1989-90.

Recipient Distinguished Citizen of the Year Award from Oakland County NAACP 1970, Citation of Merit from Pontiac Area Urban League 1971, Resolution of Tribute as Chairman Michigan Civil Rights Commission from Michigan House of Representatives 1971, Boss of the Year Award from Oakland County Legal Secretaries Association 1974, Pathfinders Award from Oakland University 1977, Service Award from Todd-Phillips Children's Home, Inc. 1978, Focus and Impact Award Oakland University 1985, Distinguished Alumnus Award from Pennsylvania State University 1987, Bench-Bar Award from Wolverine and The Detroit Metropolitan Bar Associations 1987, Presidential Award from North Oakland County NAACP 1987, Augustus Straker Award from Wolverine Bar Association 1988, Absalom Jones Award from Union of Black Episcopalians Detroit Chapter 1988, John Carroll Distinguished Alumnus Award from Georgetown University 1989, Outstanding Community Service Award from Virginia Park Community Investment Associates Oct 16, 1992, State Senate Resolution No. 179 from Michigan State Senate 1993, State House Resolution No. 276 from Michigan State House 1993, First Annual Trailblazers Award from D. Augustus Straker Bar Association June 24, 1993, Renowned Jurist Award from Friends of Africa Art 1993, Brotherhood Award from Jewish War Veterans of the United States of America Feb 15, 1994, Champion of Justice Award from State Bar of Michigan Sept 22, 1994 and Paul R. Dean Award from Georgetown University 1997. Named one of twenty-five Most Respected Judges in Michigan by Subscribers *Michigan Lawyers Weekly* April 23, 1990 and April 29, 1991. Voted one of the Best Judges in the Metropolitan Detroit Area "Judging Our Judges" *Detroit Monthly* Nov 1991. First Lieutenant U.S. Army Signal Corps 1952-54. Board of Directors Pontiac Area Urban League 1962-68 (President), Camp Oakland, Inc. 1971-83, Michigan United Way 1973-74, Franklin-Wright Settlement, Inc. 1973-76, East Michigan Environmental Action Council 1975-77, Detroit and Michigan chapters American Civil Liberties Union 1976-78, Pontiac Opportunities Industrialization Center 1976-78, Oak Park Compensation Commission 1976-78, Oakland Youth Symphony 1976-78, Oakland-Livingston Economic Development Corporation 1977-78 (Treasurer) and Hutzel Hospital 1984-95. Member Oakland University Project Twenty Committee 1966-68 (Chairman Citizens Committee). Executive Board of Directors 1968-89 and President 1975-76 Child and Family Services of Michigan. Board of Governors Georgetown University Alumni Association 1984-90 and Georgetown University National Law Alumni Association 1986-91. Advisory Council Ashland Theological Seminary. Board of Trustees Brighton Health Services Corporation 1985-92. Member Alumni Council Pennsylvania State University

COOK, JULIAN ABELE, JR.—*Continued*

Alumni Association 1986-92 (Life Member). Board of Visitors Georgetown University Law Center since 1992. Member New York University Root-Tilden-Snow Scholarship Program Screening Panel 1991, 1995 and 1996. Life Member NAACP (Former Member State Constitutional Revision Committee and Legal Redress Committee). Honorary Member Oak Park Kiwanis Club 1980, B'nai B'rith Barristers 1980 and Justice Frank Murphy Honor Society University of Detroit School of Law 1981.

Office: 730 U.S. Courthouse, 231 West Lafayette Boulevard, Detroit 48226-2795.

Telephone: (313) 234-5100.

COOLEY, Richard A., Jr. *(Judge, Michigan District Court District Seventy-two)* Elected to term beginning Jan 1, 1981. Reelected 1986, 1992 and 1998. Current term expires Dec 31, 2004. Former Chief Judge. Born Port Huron Michigan Oct 4, 1941. Protestant. Educated at Port Huron Junior College A.A. 1961, Eastern Michigan University B.S. 1964 and Detroit College of Law J.D. 1971. Admitted to practice Michigan 1971.

Chief Trial Attorney Jackson County Prosecutor's Office 1971-73. Chief Assistant Prosecuting Attorney St. Clair County 1973-79.

Office: 201 McMorran Boulevard, Port Huron 48060.

Telephone: (810) 985-2215.

COOPER, Jessica R. *(Judge, Michigan Court of Appeals)* Born Los Angeles California Jan 18, 1946. Educated at Wayne State University B.A. with honors 1970 J.D. 1973. Student/Faculty Curriculum Committee 1970-72. Student Board of Governors 1970-73 (Treasurer 1971-72). Recipient Law School Fund Scholarship 1971-73. Admitted to practice Michigan 1973, U.S. District Court Eastern District of Michigan 1973 and U.S. Supreme Court 1980. Began legal practice Detroit 1973. In legal practice Southfield 1975-78. Former Judge and Chief Judge pro tem 1982, Michigan District Court District Forty-six, elected to term beginning Jan 1, 1979. Former Judge, Michigan Circuit Court Sixth Judicial Circuit.

Assistant Defender Michigan Appellate Defender's Office May 1973 to July 1975. Founding Member National Association of Women Judges 1979 (National Conference Planning Committee 1980-81, Newsletter and Publicity Committee since 1982, Publication Editor 1983). Member Oakland County District Judges Association (Secretary/Treasurer 1985), Michigan District Judges Association (Program Committee 1980-81, Vice Chair Committee on Recommended Fines and Costs 1982, Vice Chair 1982 and Chairperson 1983 Committee on Standard Jury Instructions), Women Lawyers Association of Michigan (Public Advisory Committee 1974-77, Recording Secretary 1975-76, Chairperson Program Committee 1976-77, Member By-Laws Committee), National Panel of Arbitrators American Arbitration Association 1977-78, Women's Bar Association of Oakland County (Chairperson Program Committee 1977-78), State Bar of Michigan (Committee on Court of Appeals 1974-79, Grievance Board 1977-78, Representative Assembly 1978-81, Committee on Standard Criminal Jury Instructions since 1981), Birmingham/Bloomfield, Southfield, Detroit 1973-77 (Criminal Jurisprudence Committee 1975-77, Public Advisory Committee 1977), Oakland County (Committee on Defense of Criminal Indigents, Speaker's Bureau) and American (Judicial Administration Division 1979 and Sections on Criminal Justice since 1974, Individual Rights and Responsibilities since 1974 and Litigation 1982) Bar Associations.

Instructor in Family Law Birmingham Community House 1977-78. Speaker First National Institute on State and Local Judicial Appointments and Election Strategies for Women sponsored by National Women's Education Fund Washington D.C. Oct 1980. Instructor New Judges Seminar Michigan Judicial Institute Jan 7, 1983 and Jan 11, 1985. Democrat. Member Southfield Democratic Club 1978-80, Birmingham/Bloomfield Democratic Club since 1980, Michigan Democratic Party Century Fund since 1981 and The One Hundred Club-Oakland County Democratic Party since 1982. Member Oakland County Task Force on Child Abuse, Haven House Board of Trustees since 1983, Jewish Family Services Board of Directors since 1983, Wolverine Chapter Sierra Club, Women's Equity Action League 1974-78 (Treasurer Michigan Region 1974-75, Chairperson Legal Committee 1975-78), Jewish Welfare Federation (Lawyers Section since 1980, Culture and Education Division 1982, Chairperson Networking Subcommittee Business and Professional Women's Section), Anti-Defamation League Michigan Region (Board Member, Cabinet Member since 1979, Co-chair Leadership Development Committee 1980-82, Vice President 1981-82), B'nai B'rith Barristers (Vice President 1980 and 1984-85), Business and Professional Chapter National Council of Jewish Women 1983-84, Liberty Chapter O.R.T. 1981-84, Jewish Community Council (Community Relations Committee since 1978, Delegate 1984-85), American Jewish Congress (Lawyers Committee since 1978), Temple Emanu-el (Board of Trustees and choir member since 1980, Member Religious Committee 1980-82) and Founders Society Detroit Institute of Arts (Friends of Modern Art 1973-77).

Office: 760 American Center Building, 27777 Franklin Road, Southfield 48034-8257.

Telephone: (248) 353-6763.

COOPER, Michael K. *(Judge, Otsego County Probate Court)*

Office: 1C Alpine Center, 800 Livingston Boulevard, Gaylord 49735.

Telephone: (989) 731-1586.

COOPER, Richard I. *(Chief Judge, Michigan Circuit Court Fifty-first Judicial Circuit)* Elected to term beginning Jan 1, 1979. Reelected 1984, 1990, 1996 and 2002. Current term expires Dec 31, 2008. Born Reed City Michigan Dec 28, 1940. Congregationalist. Educated at Central Michigan University B.A. 1963, University of Vienna, Austria 1965 (Rotary Fellowship), Indiana University M.A. 1970 and Detroit College of Law J.D. 1973. Recipient Central Michigan University Campus Leadership Award 1963. Admitted to practice Michigan 1973. Began legal practice Reed City 1973. Judge, Lake County Probate Court 1977-78.

Instructor British School of Milan, Italy 1964-65. English teacher Greenville 1967-68. Intern NASA Summer 1969 (during U.S. moon landing). Detroit Neighborhood Youth Corps Summer 1972. Reed City Prosecutor 1973-76. Important Decisions: McFetridge v. Chiado (paternity statute of limitation) Michigan Court of Appeals, dissent May 21, 1982, People v. Lange and Marland (criminal stop and search) Michigan Court of Appeals June 1984 and In re Rankin (termination of limit-

COOPER, RICHARD I.—*Continued*

ed guardianship) Michigan Court of Appeals dissent 1989, dissent adopted in part by Michigan Supreme Court in the Matter of Rankin 433 Mich. 592, Nov. 1989. Instructor in Business Law Ferris State College 1974-75. Member Michigan Judges Association, American Judicature Society, State Bar of Michigan and Mason/Lake Counties Bar Association. Judge Member Caseflow Management Seminar Michigan Judicial Institute 1987 and 1988. Recipient Annual Gideon Bible Award 1983. Former Member Central Michigan Alumni Board, Lake County Mental Health Board, Reed City Rotary Club, Probation Enhancement Board, Great Books Discussion Group, West Shore Community College Concert Band and Alternative to Incarceration Board. Life Member Scottville Clown Band. Completed two year Stephen Ministry training program Sept 1992. Enjoys skiing and canoeing.

Office: Mason County Courthouse, 304 East Ludington Avenue, Ludington 49431.

Telephone: (231) 845-0516.

Fax: (231) 845-7779

E-mail address: rcooper@masoncounty.net

COOPER, Stephen C. *(Chief Judge, Michigan District Court District Forty-six)* Elected Nov 1986 to term beginning Jan 1, 1987. Reelected 1992 and 1998. Current term expires Dec 31, 2004. Chief Judge since Jan 1, 2003. Born Detroit Michigan Aug 27, 1944. Jewish. Educated at Brandeis University 1962-64 and Wayne State University B.A. 1968 J.D. 1969. Member Tau Epsilon Rho. Admitted to practice Michigan 1969, U.S. District Courts Eastern 1969 and Western 1969 Districts of Michigan, U.S. Courts of Appeals Sixth 1973 and Federal 1983 Circuits and U.S. Supreme Court 1975. In legal practice Detroit and Southfield.

Fellow Michigan Bar Foundation. Member Michigan District Judges Association (Board of Directors, President 1995), State Bar of Michigan (Elected Member Representative Assembly) and Southfield Bar Association (Past President). Past President B'nai B'rith Barristers. Recipient Distinguished Service Award Oakland County Bar Association, Martin Luther King, Jr. Award, National Award for Legal Scholarship from Tau Epsilon Rho and Michigan Governor's Award for Volunteerism. Named "Honoree of the Year" by Women's Bar Association, Triple Distinguished Optimist President and Optimist of the Year.

Mailing address: P.O. Box 2055, Southfield 48037-2055.

Office: 26000 Evergreen Road, Southfield 48076.

Telephone: (248) 796-5800.

CORRIGAN, Maura D. *(Chief Justice, Michigan Supreme Court)* Educated at Marygrove College B.A. magna cum laude 1969 and University of Detroit School of Law J.D. cum laude 1973. Honorary Doctorate Northern Michigan University 1999 and University of Detroit-Mercy 2002. Law Clerk to Michigan Court of Appeals 1972-74. In legal practice Detroit 1989-92. Former Judge and Chief Judge, Michigan Court of Appeals, appointed March 1992.

Assistant Prosecutor Wayne County 1974-79. Assistant U.S. Attorney 1979-85 and First Assistant U.S. Attorney 1986-89 Eastern District of Michigan. Author "State Law" and "Criminal Prosecution" Wayne L. Rev. and "Appellate Advocacy" University of Toledo L. Rev. Vice Chair Committee on Formulating Rules of Criminal Procedure Michigan Supreme Court 1982-89. Member Advisory Committee on Rules Sixth Circuit 1983-90 and Local Rules Committee U.S. District Court Eastern District of Michigan 1989-92. Member Incorporated Society of Irish American Lawyers (Vice President 1989, President 1991), State Bar of Michigan (Chair U.S. District Court Committee 1989-90) and Federal Bar Association (President Detroit Chapter 1990-91). Lecturer Appellate Practice Institute American Bar Association, Institute of Continuing Legal Education, Michigan Judicial Institute, Prosecuting Attorneys Association of Michigan, Workshop on Sixth Circuit Advocacy American Bar Association-Cincinnati Bar, Attorney General's Advocacy Institute and Sixth Circuit Judges' Workshop on Sentencing Guidelines. Recipient Director's Award for Outstanding Performance as an Assistant U.S. Attorney from U.S. Department of Justice 1985, George Herman Derry Award from Marygrove College 1986 and Leonard Gilman Award from Federal Bar Association 1989. Past President Republican Women's Forum—Business and Professional. Board of Directors Lafayette Clinic 1976-88 and Boysville of Michigan 1994-99. Member Project Transition 1976-92.

Office: 8-500 Cadillac Place, 3034 West Grand Boulevard, Detroit 48202-6034.

Telephone: (313) 972-3232.

CORSIGLIA, George R. *(Chief Judge, Michigan Circuit Court Forty-eighth Judicial Circuit)* Appointed by Governor William G. Milliken May 1974. Elected Nov 1974, 1980, 1986, 1992 and 1998. Current term expires Dec 31, 2004. Former Chief Judge pro tem. Born Kalamazoo Michigan Sept 9, 1935. Educated at St. John's University 1953-55, University of Michigan A.B. 1957, Detroit College of Law LL.B. 1960 and Wayne State University Law School 1970-71. Admitted to practice Michigan 1960. Began legal practice Kalamazoo 1962. Judge, Michigan District Court District Fifty-seven 1972-74.

Assistant City Attorney Kalamazoo, Otsego and Plainwell 1962-72 and Fennville 1970-72. City Attorney Galesburg 1967-72 and Allegan 1969-72. Member American Judicature Society, Michigan Judges Association, Michigan Bar Foundation, State Bar of Michigan, Allegan County and American Bar Associations. U.S. Army 1960-62. Member Elks Club. Enjoys hunting, boating and reading.

Office: County Building, 113 Chestnut Street, Allegan 49010.

Telephone: (269) 673-0300.

CORWIN, Charles D. *(Chief Judge, Michigan Circuit Court Twenty-eighth Judicial Circuit)* Elected to term beginning Jan 1, 1991. Reelected 1996 and 2002. Current term expires Dec 31, 2008. Judge, Michigan District Court District Eighty-four Aug 1984 to Dec 1990.

Office: 437 East Division, Cadillac 49601.

Telephone: (231) 779-9490.

COSTELLO, Joseph Anthony, Jr. *(Chief Judge, Michigan Circuit Court Thirty-eighth Judicial Circuit)* Elected to term beginning Jan 1, 1997. Reelected 2002, current term expires Dec 31, 2008. Presiding Judge Family Division Jan 1, 1998 to Dec 31, 2000. Chief Judge pro tem Jan 1, 2000 to 2001. Chief Judge since 2002. Born Monroe Michigan Aug 27, 1956. Roman Catholic. Educated at Monroe County Community Col-

COSTELLO, JOSEPH ANTHONY, JR.—*Continued*

lege A.A. with honors 1976, University of Michigan B.A. with honors 1978 and Detroit College of Law J.D. 1982. Admitted to practice Michigan 1982 and U.S. District Court Eastern District of Michigan 1982. In legal practice Monroe 1982-85. Judge Dec 13, 1985 to Dec 31, 1996 and Chief Judge Feb 1988 to Dec 1989 and Jan 1, 1994 to Dec 1995, Monroe County Probate Court.

Adjunct Instructor in Political Science Monroe County Community College since Sept 1994. Former Member Michigan Probate Judges Association and National Council of Juvenile and Family Court Judges. Member State Bar of Michigan (Former Member Law Related Education Committee, Former Member Professional and Judicial Ethics Committee), Monroe County and Italian-American Bar Associations. One of ten county representatives selected nationwide to attend Federal Drug Abuse Program National Council of Juvenile and Family Court Judges 1988. Recipient Youth Services Award from Kiwanis Club of Monroe 1984, Michigan Minuteman Award 1986, Distinguished President of Kiwanis Award 1987-88, Child Advocacy Network Distinguished Service Award 1989, Spes Unica (One Hope) Award from Boysville of Michigan Aug 1994 and Alumnus of the Year Award from Monroe Catholic Central High School 1995. Named Boss of the Year by Monroe County Legal Secretaries Association 1987 and First Alumnus of the Year Monroe County Community College 1997. Listed in *Who's Who in Law Enforcement* 1990. Previously employed as factory worker for Chrysler Corporation and substitute teacher for Monroe, Airport and Dundee public school systems. Former Member Board of Directors Monroe County Chapter American Red Cross, St. Joseph's Cemetery Association, Inc., United Way of Monroe and St. Mary's Parish Ushers Club. Former officer Monroe Catholic Central Alumni Association and Monroe County Civic Awareness Committee. Former Reviewer for community grants on substance abuse and prevention OSAP. President Kiwanis Club of Monroe 1987-88. Chairman Monroe County Probate Court Citizen's Advisory Committee 1987-91. Advisory Board DARE. Judicial Representative Legal Services of Southeastern Michigan. Member Floral City Festival Committee, Ida Civic Club, Monroe Council Knights of Columbus, Monroe County Chapter NAACP, Monroe County Traffic and Safety Committee and Children's Charter of the Courts of Michigan. Enjoys golf and traveling.

Office: 106 East First Street, Monroe 48161.
Telephone: (734) 240-7160.

COURTRIGHT, John T. *(Chief Judge, Michigan District Court District Twenty-four)* Appointed by Governor John Engler to term beginning Sept 1, 2000. Elected to term beginning Jan 2003, current term expires Dec 2008. Former Chief Judge pro tem. Born Lincoln Park Michigan Aug 17, 1959. Catholic. Educated at University of San Francisco B.A. 1982 and Creighton University J.D. 1986. Admitted to practice Michigan 1987. In legal practice Allen Park 1987-2000.

Assistant Prosecutor City of Allen Park 1995-2000. Member Wayne County District Judges Association (Treasurer 2002-03) and Downriver Bar Association.

Office: 6515 Roosevelt Road, Allen Park 48101.
Telephone: (313) 928-1129.
Fax: (313) 928-1860
E-mail address: jtcourtright@24thdiscourt.org

COX, Sean F. *(Judge, Michigan Circuit Court Third Judicial Circuit)*

Office: 604 Hall of Justice, 1441 St. Antoine Street, Detroit 48226.
Telephone: (313) 224-6889.

COYLE, David T. *(Chief Judge, Michigan District Court District Three A)* Elected to term beginning Jan 1, 1979. Reelected 1984, 1990, 1996 and 2002. Current term expires Dec 31, 2008. Born Chester England Feb 1, 1944. Catholic. Educated at University of Dayton B.A. 1966 and University of Detroit J.D. 1969. Admitted to practice Michigan 1969, U.S. Court of Military Appeals 1970 and U.S. District Court District of Michigan.

Assistant Prosecuting Attorney Branch County 1976-78. Member Michigan District Court Judges Association, State Bar of Michigan, Branch County and American Bar Associations. Captain U.S. Army JAGC 1970-76. Enjoys volleyball, basketball, tennis and swimming.

Office: Branch County Courthouse, 31 Division Street, Coldwater 49036.
Telephone: (517) 279-4308.

CRANE, William A. *(Judge, Michigan Circuit Court Tenth Judicial Circuit)*

Office: Courthouse, 111 South Michigan Avenue, Saginaw 48602.
Telephone: (989) 790-5471.

CRAWFORD, William H., II *(Judge, Michigan District Court District Sixty-eight)* Former Chief Judge.

Office: 630 South Saginaw Street, Flint 48502-1526.
Telephone: (810) 766-8968.

CROCKETT, George William, III *(Judge, Michigan Circuit Court Third Judicial Circuit)* Assumed office Oct 1, 1997. Born Fairmont West Virginia Dec 23, 1938. Baptist. Educated at Wayne State University 1958-59, University of Vera Cruz 1959, Morehouse College B.A. 1961 and Detroit College of Law J.D. 1964. Admitted to practice Michigan 1964. Began legal practice Detroit 1965. In legal practice Grand Rapids 1965-67 and Detroit 1967-76. Judge, Recorder's Court of Detroit Jan 1, 1977 to Sept 30, 1997.

Supervising Attorney Neighborhood Legal Services Centers 1967 and 1970. Defender 1970-76 and Chief Deputy Defender 1976 Legal Aid and Defender Association of Detroit. Alternate Member Detroit-Wayne County Criminal Justice Systems Coordinating Council. Member Association of Black Judges of Michigan, State Bar of Michigan (Criminal Jurisprudence, Defender Systems and Services and Prisons and Corrections Committees, Alternate Member Revise Code of Criminal Procedure Committee, Council Member Criminal Law Section and Counsel Grievance Board Hearing Panel 10), Wolverine, National and American (Gavel Awards Committee) Bar Associations. Attended National Institute for Trial Advocacy 1972. Vice Chairman Proper Utilization of the Private Bar in Legal Services to the Poor. Trustee Black Law Students Scholarship Fund. Board Member Homes for Black Children and Lula Belle Stewart Center. Member ACLU and NAACP. Enjoys swimming, reading, photography, carpentry and computers.

Office: 402 Hall of Justice, 1441 St. Antoine Street, Detroit 48226.
Telephone: (313) 224-2467.

CURTIS, Daphne Means *(Judge, Michigan Circuit Court Third Judicial Circuit)* Assumed office Oct 1, 1997. Former Judge, Michigan District Court District Thirty-six. Judge, Recorder's Court of Detroit March 27, 1990 to Sept 30, 1997.

Office: 1007 Municipal Center, Two Woodward Avenue, Detroit 48226.

Telephone: (313) 224-5261.

D'AGOSTINI, Diane *(Judge, Michigan District Court District Forty-eight)*

Mailing address: P.O. Box 3200, Bloomfield Hills 48302-3200.

Office: 4280 Telegraph Road, Bloomfield Hills 48302.

Telephone: (248) 647-1141.

DANIELSON, Brent V. *(Chief Judge, Michigan District Court District Eighty-five)*

Office: Manistee County Courthouse, 415 Third Street, Manistee 49660.

Telephone: (231) 723-5010.

DAVIS, Alton T., Jr. *(Chief Judge, Michigan Circuit Court Forty-sixth Judicial Circuit)* Elected to term beginning Jan 1, 1985. Reelected Nov 1992 and 1998. Current term expires Dec 31, 2004. Also serves as Chief Judge Trial Court and Michigan District Court District Eighty-seven. Born Petoskey Michigan July 23, 1947. Episcopalian. Educated at North Central Michigan College A.A. 1967, Western Michigan University B.S. 1969 and Detroit College of Law J.D. 1974. Law Clerk to Hon. John Feikens, U.S. District Court Eastern District of Michigan 1972-74. Member Sigma Nu Phi. Admitted to practice Michigan, U.S. District Court Eastern District of Michigan and U.S. Court of Appeals Sixth Circuit 1974. Began legal practice Houghton Lake 1975. In legal practice Grayling 1975-84. Visiting Judge, Michigan Court of Appeals 1985, 1986, 1987, 1995 and 1996.

Prosecuting Attorney Crawford County 1976-80. President Elect Michigan Judges Association. Chairman Committee on Criminal Jury Instructions State Bar of Michigan. Member Michigan Trial Lawyers Association and Forty-sixth Judicial Circuit Bar Association (President 1982-83). Previously worked as high school English and debate teacher and radio announcer. Democrat. Democratic Party Chairman Crawford County 1978-84. Member Michigan State Building Authority 1984. Director Crawford County Fair Board and Au Sable Marathon. Past President and Paul Harris Fellow Rotary. Member Elks. Enjoys gardening, reading, fishing and hunting.

Office: Crawford County Building, 200 West Michigan Avenue, Grayling 49738.

Telephone: (989) 344-3201.

DAVIS, Linda *(Chief Judge, Michigan District Court District Forty-one B)* Former Chief Judge pro tem.

Office: One Crocker Boulevard, Mount Clemens 48043-2565.

Telephone: (586) 469-6870.

DAVIS, Stephen T. *(Chief Judge, Michigan Circuit Court Forty-seventh Judicial Circuit)*

Office: Delta County Building, 310 Ludington Street, Escanaba 49829.

Telephone: (906) 789-5103.

DEATS, Paul E. *(Chief Judge, Michigan District Court District Four)* Appointed by Governor William G. Milliken to term beginning Dec 17, 1979. Elected 1980, 1984, 1990, 1996 and 2002. Current term expires Dec 31, 2008. Born Los Angeles California Aug 20, 1946. Presbyterian. Educated at Whittier College B.A. 1968 M.A.T. 1971 and University of Notre Dame J.D. 1974. Admitted to practice Michigan 1974, Indiana 1974, U.S. District Courts Western District of Michigan 1974 and Southern District of Indiana 1974 and U.S. Supreme Court 1977.

Assistant Prosecuting Attorney 1974. Member Michigan District Judges Association (Regional Director, Member Legislative Committee), American Judges Association, Cass County (President 1977), Indiana and American Bar Associations. Participant 1974-79 and Guest Judge since 1980 University of Notre Dame Practice Court. Member Southwest Michigan Law Enforcement Advisory Council, Southwestern Michigan College Foundation, Edwardsburg Athletic Boosters and Edwardsburg Masonic Lodge. Enjoys sports and reading.

Office: Cass County Courthouse, 110 North Broadway, Cassopolis 49031-1396.

Telephone: (269) 445-4424.

DEEGAN, Joseph E. *(Chief Judge, Leelanau County Probate Court)*

Mailing address: P.O. Box 595, Leland 49654-0595.

Office: Courthouse, Leland 49654.

Telephone: (231) 256-9803.

DEEGAN, Peter E. *(Chief Judge, Michigan Circuit Court Thirty-first Judicial Circuit)*

Office: 306 County Building, 201 McMorran Boulevard, Port Huron 48060.

Telephone: (810) 985-2031.

DeLAURENTIIS, Joseph H. *(Judge, Michigan District Court District Twenty-five)* Elected to term beginning Jan 1, 1987. Reelected 1992 and 1998. Current term expires Dec 31, 2004. Currently serves as Chief Judge pro tem. Former Chief Judge. Born Dearborn Michigan Jan 12, 1948. Catholic. Educated at University of Michigan B.A. 1969 and Wayne State University J.D. 1972. Admitted to practice Michigan 1972. In legal practice Lincoln Park 1972-77 and Wyandotte 1977-87.

Assistant City Attorney Lincoln Park 1976-79. Former Member Detroit Bar Association. Member State Bar of Michigan and Downriver Bar Association. Attended New Judges Seminar Jan 1987 and "Decision Making" seminar March 1987. Member Lincoln Park Democratic Club (First Vice President 1980-81). Member Lincoln Park Central Kiwanis Club since 1986 (President 1990-91), Knights of Columbus since 1986 and Downriver Italian Club since 1986. Enjoys boating, music and reading.

Office: 1475 Cleophus, Lincoln Park 48146-2301.

Telephone: (313) 382-8648.

DeLUCA, Frank J. *(Judge, Michigan District Court District Fifty-four A)*

Office: City Hall, Sixth Floor, 124 West Michigan Avenue, Lansing 48933-1690.

Telephone: (517) 487-1350.

Del VERO, Frank R. *(Judge, Michigan District Court District Fifty-three)* Former Chief Judge.

Office: 204 South Highlander Way, Suite 1, Howell 48843.

Telephone: (517) 548-1000.

DeVRIES, John R. *(Chief Judge, Manistee County Probate Court)* Appointed by Governor William Grawn Milliken April 10, 1978. Elected to subsequent terms.

Office: Courthouse, 415 Third Street, Manistee 49660.

Telephone: (231) 723-3261.

DIGNAN, Terrance P. *(Judge, Michigan District Court District Sixty-six)*

Office: Shiawassee County Courts Building, 110 East Mack Street, Corunna 48817.

Telephone: (989) 743-2395.

DIMKOFF, Graydon W. *(Chief Judge, Newaygo County Probate Court)* Appointed by Governor John Engler to term beginning April 2, 1998. Elected Jan 1999 and Jan 2001. Current term expires Dec 31, 2006. Born Durand Michigan June 13, 1947. Protestant. Educated at University of Michigan B.A. 1969 and Wayne State University J.D. 1972. Admitted to practice Michigan 1972 and U.S. District Courts Western District of Michigan 1973 and Western District of Louisiana 1973. In legal practice Fremont Michigan 1976-98.

Adjunct Professor Jordan College 1983-88. Member State Bar of Michigan and Newaygo County Bar Association (Former Secretary, Treasurer, Vice President and President). Attorney U.S. Army 1973-76. Attorney USAFR 1977-93. Former Chairman Newaygo County Republican Party. Member Rotary Club of Freemont, Rotary Club of White Cloud, Fremont School Board and Fremont Downtown Development Authority. Enjoys woodworking and traveling.

Mailing address: P.O. Box 885, White Cloud 49349.

Office: 1092 Newell Street, White Cloud 49349.

Telephone: (231) 689-7270.

E-mail address: P62@voyager.net

DINGELL, Christopher D. *(Judge, Michigan Circuit Court Third Judicial Circuit)*

Office: 204 Hall of Justice, 1441 St. Antoine Street, Detroit 48226.

DOBRICH, Susan L. *(Chief Judge, Cass County Probate Court)*

Office: Courthouse, 110 North Broadway, Cassopolis 49031.

Telephone: (269) 445-4454.

DODGE, Michael E. *(Chief Judge, Michigan Circuit Court Forty-third Judicial Circuit)* Appointed to term beginning Feb 1982. Elected 1982, 1986, 1992 and 1998. Current term expires Dec 31, 2004. Born Detroit Michigan Oct 1, 1944. Catholic. Educated at University of Detroit B.A. 1966 and University of Notre Dame J.D. 1969. Admitted to practice Michigan 1969. Began legal practice Detroit 1969. In legal practice Cassopolis 1971-72. Former Judge, Cass County Probate Court, elected to term beginning Jan 1, 1977.

Prosecuting Attorney Cassopolis 1972-76. U.S. Army 1969-71.

Office: Cass County Courthouse, 110 North Broadway, Cassopolis 49031.

Telephone: (269) 445-4412.

DONOFRIO, Pat M. *(Judge, Michigan Court of Appeals)* Appointed by Governor John Engler 2002. Term expires Jan 1, 2005. Educated at Wayne State University B.S. 1967 J.D. 1970. In legal practice Oakland County 1970-97. Judge 1997-2002 and Presiding Judge Civil/Criminal Division 1998-2002, Michigan Circuit Court Sixteenth Judicial Circuit.

Office: 15161 Cadillac Place, 3020 West Grand Boulevard, Southfield, 48202-6020.

Telephone: (248) 353-6763.

DOSS, Theresa *(Judge, Michigan District Court District Thirty-six)* Assumed office Sept 1, 1981. Educated at Ohio University A.B. cum laude 1961, The Ohio State University J.D. 1964 and Wayne State University M.A. 2000. Admitted to practice Ohio 1964 and Michigan 1966. Judge, Common Pleas Court of Detroit Jan 19, 1976 to Aug 31, 1981, appointed by Governor William G. Milliken.

Commissioner Michigan Judicial Tenure Commission since 1995. Member Women Lawyers Association of Michigan (Vice President 1972-73, President 1973-74), Michigan District Judges Association (President 1991), State Bar of Michigan (State Bar Journal Advisory Committee and Representative Assembly), Detroit (Past Member Public Advisory Committee), Wolverine (Past Director and Secretary), American (Committee on Workers' Compensation and Employers' Liability Law) and National (Past President Women Section and Member Executive Committee) Bar Associations. Member Public Lighting Commission 1974-76. Life Member National Council of Negro Women and NAACP.

Office: 421 Madison Avenue, Suite 4069, Detroit 48226.

Telephone: (313) 965-2200.

DOSSON, Douglas C. *(Chief Judge, Roscommon County Probate Court)*

Mailing address: P.O. Box 607, Roscommon 48653.

Office: County Building, 500 Lake Street, Roscommon 48653.

Telephone: (989) 275-5513.

DRAIN, Gershwin Allen *(Judge, Michigan Circuit Court Third Judicial Circuit)* Assumed office Oct 1, 1997. Former Judge, Michigan District Court District Thirty-six. Judge, Recorder's Court of Detroit April 28, 1987 to Sept 30, 1997.

Office: 1519 Municipal Center, Two Woodward Avenue, Detroit 48226.

Telephone: (313) 224-5261.

DRAKE, H. Kevin *(Chief Judge, Michigan District Court District Seventy-eight)*

Mailing address: P.O. Box 129, White Cloud 49349.

Office: Newaygo County Courthouse, 1092 Newell, White Cloud 49349.

Telephone: (231) 689-7228.

DRAKE, Maggie *(Judge, Michigan Circuit Court Third Judicial Circuit)* Assumed office Oct 1, 1997. Former Judge, Recorder's Court of Detroit.

Office: 703 Hall of Justice, 1441 St. Antoine Street, Detroit 48226.

Telephone: (313) 224-2481.

DRURY, Dennis C. *(Judge, Michigan District Court District Fifty-two Division Four)* Appointed by Governor James J. Blanchard to term beginning April 10, 1984. Elected 1984, 1988, 1994 and 2000. Current term expires Dec 31, 2006. Former Chief Judge and Chief Judge pro tem. Born Lansing Michigan Sept 10, 1941. Educated at DePauw University B.A. 1963, Michigan State University B.A. with honors 1964 and University of Michigan J.D. 1966. Member Phi Alpha Theta. Ad-

DRURY, DENNIS C.—*Continued*

mitted to practice Michigan 1966. In legal practice Clawson 1967-74 and Troy 1974-84.

Associate Professor of Business Law Walsh College since 1986. Member Michigan District Judges Association, American Judges Association, State Bar of Michigan (Representative Assembly 1978-84 and 1985-90, Ethics and Judicial Conduct Committee 1983-85), South Oakland County (President 1983-84) and Oakland County (Chair Young Lawyers Section 1977-78, Board of Directors 1984-94) Bar Associations. Instructor Michigan Judicial Institute 1987 and 1990. First Lieutenant U.S. Army 1966-69. President YMCA of Michigan 1985-87. Board of Directors Troy Girls/Boys Club since 1985. Member Troy Chamber of Commerce.

Office: 520 West Big Beaver Road, Troy 48084.

Telephone: (248) 528-0400.

DRUZINSKI, Diane M. *(Judge, Michigan Circuit Court Sixteenth Judicial Circuit)*

Office: Macomb County Court Building, 40 North Main, Mount Clemens 48043-5654.

DUGGAN, Patrick J. *(Senior Judge, United States District Court Eastern District of Michigan)* Appointed for life by President Ronald Reagan to term beginning 1987. Assumed Senior status Sept 29, 2000. Educated at Xavier University 1955 and University of Detroit School of Law J.D. 1958. Admitted to practice Michigan 1958. In legal practice Livonia 1959-76. Judge, Michigan Circuit Court Third Judicial Circuit 1977-87, appointed by Governor William Grawn Milliken.

Office: 867 U.S. Courthouse, 231 West Lafayette Boulevard, Detroit 48226.

Telephone: (313) 234-5145.

DURHAM, Samuel I., Jr. *(Judge, Michigan District Court District Ten)* Appointed by Governor James J. Blanchard to term beginning Aug 9, 1989. Former Chief Judge and Presiding Judge.

Office: Calhoun County Justice Center, 161 East Michigan Avenue, Battle Creek 49014-4066.

Telephone: (269) 969-6666.

ECONOMY, R. George *(Chief Judge, Ingham County Probate Court)* Former Chief Judge pro tem. Former Presiding Judge Mental Health Division.

Office: Veteran's Memorial Courthouse, 313 West Kalamazoo Street, Lansing 48933.

Telephone: (517) 483-6500.

EDMUNDS, Nancy G. *(Judge, United States District Court Eastern District of Michigan)* Appointed for life by President George Bush Feb 10, 1992. Educated at Cornell University B.A. cum laude 1969, University of Chicago M.A. 1971 and Wayne State University Law School J.D. summa cum laude 1976. Editor-in-Chief Wayne Law Review. Law Clerk to Hon. Ralph Freeman, U.S. District Court Eastern District of Michigan. Member Phi Beta Kappa. In legal practice Detroit 1978-92.

Important Decisions: Margolis v. United Airlines, Inc. (personal injury due to an airline's negligence) 811 F. Supp. 318 E.D. Mich. 1993; Mother Waddles Perpetual Mission, Inc. v. Frazier (Lanham Act) 904 F. Supp. 603, 1995; Aetna Casualty & Surety Co. v. Dow Chemical Co. (complex environmental insurance dispute) 883 F. Supp. 1101 E.D. Mich. 1995, 44 F. Supp. 2d 847 E.D. Mich. 1997, 28 F. Supp. 2d 448 E.D. Mich. 1998, 28 F. Supp. 2d 421 E.D. Mich. 1998, 10 F. Supp. 2d 800 E.D. Mich. 1998 and 10 F. Supp. 2d 771 E.D. Mich. 1998; General Motors Corp. v. Lopez de Arriortua (federal RICO law) 948 F. Supp. 670 E.D. Mich. 1996; General Motors Corp. v. Lopez de Arriortua (Lanham Act) 948 F. Supp. 684 E.D. Mich. 1996; Wright v. Bond-Air, Ltd. (wrongful death, product liability action) 930 F. Supp. 300 E.D. Mich. 1996; Michigan Association of Homes and Services for Aging, Inc. v. Shalala (nursing home association seeking injunctive relief and declaration that federal regulations governing nursing homes were unconstitutional) 931 F. Supp. 1338 E.D. Mich. 1996; Sluiter v. Blue Cross and Blue Shield of Michigan (breast cancer patients seeking coverage for high dose chemotherapy) 979 F. Supp. 1131 E.D. Mich. 1997; MCI Telecommunications Corp. v. Michigan Bell Telephone Co. (interpretation of Telecommunications Act of 1996 and the FCC implementing regulations) Sept 29, 1999; Ford Motor Co. v. Lane 67 F. Supp. 2d 745 E.D. Mich. 1999; United States v. Efraim Garcia 68 F. Supp. 2d 802 E.D. Mich. 1999; Moore v. School Reform Board of the City of Detroit (replacing elected Detroit school board with mayoral appointees does not violate Michigan Constitution Local Acts) Oct 2000; and Cooley v. Granholm (no right to physician-assisted suicide even to alleviate suffering which cannot be remediated) Dec 2000.

Commissioner 21st Century Commission on the Courts 1990. Member Committee on Defender Services National Judicial Conference 1994-2000. Member Federal Judges Association, American Judicature Society, State Bar of Michigan (Chair United States Courts Committee 1990-91), Federal (Executive Board Eastern District of Michigan 1989-92 and since 1995) and American Bar Associations. Faculty and Board Member Federal Advocacy Institute 1983-91. Program Chair Federal Bench/Bar Conference 1990. Board of Trustees Historical Society for the U.S. District Court Eastern District of Michigan 1993-98, Temple Beth El 1990-97 and Stratford Shakespearean Festival of America. Board of Governors Cranbrook Schools. Board of Directors Michigan Members of the Stratford Festival. Member Committee of Visitors Wayne State Law School and National Council of Jewish Women.

Office: 211 U.S. Courthouse, 231 West Lafayette Boulevard, Detroit 48226.

Telephone: (313) 234-5155.

EDWARDS, Prentis *(Judge, Michigan Circuit Court Third Judicial Circuit)* Assumed office Oct 1, 1997. Former Judge, Michigan District Court District Thirty-six. Former Judge, Recorder's Court of Detroit.

Office: 503 Hall of Justice, 1441 St. Antoine Street, Detroit 48226.

Telephone: (313) 224-0250.

ENSLEN, Richard Alan *(Judge, United States District Court Western District of Michigan)* Appointed for life by President Jimmy Carter to term beginning Dec 21, 1979. Former Chief Judge. Born Kalamazoo Michigan May 28, 1931. Educated at Kalamazoo College 1949-51, Western Michigan University 1954-55, Wayne State University Law School LL.B. 1958 and University of Virginia LL.M. 1986. Member Tau Epsilon Rho. Admitted to practice Michigan 1958, U.S. District Court Western District of Michigan 1960, U.S. Courts of Appeals Sixth 1971 and Fourth 1975 Circuits and U.S. Supreme Court 1975. In legal practice Kalamazoo 1958-65

ENSLEN, RICHARD ALAN—*Continued*
and 1970-79. Judge, Michigan District Court District Nine 1968-70.

Director U.S. Peace Corps Costa Rica 1965-67. Author *Constitutional Law Dictionary: Individual Rights* Clio Press 1984, *Constitutional Law Deskbook—Individual Rights* Lawyers Co-Operative Publishing Co. 1987 and *Constitutional Law Dictionary—Governmental Powers* ABC-CLIO 1987. Adjunct Professor of Political Science Western Michigan University since 1982. Member The American Law Institute, American Judicature Society (Board of Directors since 1982), State Bar of Michigan and American Bar Association (Special Committee on Dispute Resolution since 1982). Recipient Distinguished Alumni Award from Wayne State University 1980 and Western Michigan University 1982, Award for Outstanding Practical Achievement in Dispute Resolution from the Center for Public Resources New York New York 1984 and Award for One of Most Outstanding Academic Books by *Choice Magazine* American Library Association 1985. Staff Sergeant USAF 1951-54.

Office: Federal Building, 410 West Michigan Avenue, Kalamazoo 49007.

Telephone: (269) 343-7542.

ERVIN, William T. *(Judge, Isabella County Probate Court)* Former Chief Judge and Chief Judge pro tem Isabella County Trial Court.

Office: County Building, 300 North Main Street, Mount Pleasant 48858.

Telephone: (989) 772-0911.

ETHRIDGE, Russell F. *(Chief Judge, Grosse Pointe Municipal Court)*

Office: 17145 Maumee, Grosse Pointe 48230.

Telephone: (313) 343-5262.

EVANS, Vonda R. *(Judge, Michigan Circuit Court Third Judicial Circuit)* Assumed office Oct 1, 1997. Former Judge, Recorder's Court of Detroit.

Office: 602 Hall of Justice, 1441 St. Antoine Street, Detroit 48226.

Telephone: (313) 224-5440.

EVELAND, Thomas S. *(Chief Judge, Michigan Circuit Court Fifty-sixth Judicial Circuit)* Elected to term beginning Jan 1989. Reelected 1994 and 2000. Current term expires Dec 31, 2006. Also serves as Chief Judge, Eaton County Probate Court. Born Detroit Michigan Nov 24, 1941. Presbyterian. Educated at University of Michigan B.A. 1963 J.D. 1966. Admitted to practice Michigan 1967. In legal practice Lansing 1969-88.

Instructor Thomas M. Cooley Law School 1989-93. Member Southwest Judges Association, Michigan Judges Association (Domestic Relations Committee), American Judges Association, State Bar of Michigan (Prison and Correction Committee, Michigan Criminal Council, Task Force on Assigned Counsel), Eaton County (Past President) and American Bar Associations. Attended National Conference on Family Courts American Judges Association and numerous seminars Michigan Judges Institute. Recipient Honorarium Boys and Girls Club of Lansing. Chairperson Eaton Count Community Corrections Board. Member Committee on Eaton County Shelter. Active in Meals on Wheels Delivery. Elder in church. Enjoys gardening and writing.

Office: Eaton County Courthouse, 1045 Independence Boulevard, Charlotte 48813.

Telephone: (517) 543-7500.

FALAHEE, Charles J., Jr. *(Chief Judge, Michigan District Court District Twelve)* Appointed by Governor James J. Blanchard to term beginning April 25, 1988. Elected 1988, 1990, 1996 and 2002. Current term expires Dec 31, 2008. Born Jackson Michigan April 24, 1952. Roman Catholic. Educated at University of Michigan B.B.A. 1974 and Wayne State University J.D. 1977. Admitted to practice Michigan 1977.

Office: Jackson County Courthouse, 312 South Jackson Street, Jackson 49201.

Telephone: (517) 788-4260.

FARAH, Joseph J. *(Judge, Michigan Circuit Court Seventh Judicial Circuit)* Currently serves as Presiding Judge Jury Management.

Office: Genesee County Courthouse, 900 South Saginaw Street, Flint 48502.

Telephone: (810) 257-3252.

FARMER, Nancy A. *(Judge, Michigan District Court District Thirty-six)* Appointed by Governor James J. Blanchard to term beginning March 30, 1990. Former Chief Judge pro tem.

Office: 421 Madison Avenue, Suite 4071, Detroit 48226.

Telephone: (313) 965-2200.

FAUNCE, Jennifer *(Judge, Michigan District Court District Thirty-seven)*

Office: Judicial Building, 8300 Common Road, Warren 48093-2380.

Telephone: (586) 574-4900.

FEENEY, Kathleen A. *(Judge, Michigan Circuit Court Seventeenth Judicial Circuit)*

Office: 10200B Kent County Courthouse, 180 Ottawa Avenue N.W., Grand Rapids 49503-2751.

Telephone: (616) 632-5480.

FEIKENS, John *(Senior Judge, United States District Court Eastern District of Michigan)* Appointed for life by President Richard M. Nixon to term beginning 1970. Former Chief Judge. Assumed Senior status, serves by assignment. Born Clifton New Jersey Dec 3, 1917. Educated at Calvin College A.B. 1939 and University of Michigan J.D. 1941. Admitted to practice Michigan 1942. In legal practice Detroit. Judge, U.S. District Court for Eastern District of Michigan 1960-61.

Fellow American College of Trial Lawyers. Member State Bar of Michigan (Commissioner 1965-71), Detroit (Director 1962 and Past President) and American Bar Associations. Former Chairman Republican State Central Committee. Former Member Republican National Committee. Former Co-chairman Michigan Civil Rights Commission. Member University of Michigan Club. Former Member Calvin College Board of Trustees.

Office: 851 U.S. Courthouse, 231 West Lafayette Boulevard, Detroit 48226.

Telephone: (313) 234-5125.

FEYEN, Mark A. *(Chief Judge, Ottawa County Probate Court)* Elected Nov 8, 1988 to term beginning Jan 1, 1989. Reelected Nov 8, 1994 and 2000. Current term expires Dec 31, 2006. Born Grand Rapids Michigan

FEYEN, MARK A.—*Continued*

May 20, 1956. Religious affiliation: Christian Reformed. Educated at Calvin College B.A. with honors 1978 and University of Illinois J.D. 1980. Admitted to practice Michigan 1981. In legal practice Grand Haven 1981-84.

County Prosecutor's Office Ottawa County 1984-88. Member State Bar of Michigan and Ottawa County Bar Association.

Office: 12120 Fillmore Street, West Olive 49460-9672.

Telephone: (616) 786-4110.

FIELDS, John N. *(Judge, Michigan Circuit Court Second Judicial Circuit)* Elected to term beginning Jan 1, 1995. Elected to subsequent term. Currently serves as Presiding Judge Criminal Division. Born Niles Michigan July 21, 1950. First Church of God. Educated at Michigan State University B.S. 1972 and Thomas M. Cooley Law School J.D. 1976. Admitted to practice Michigan 1976, U.S. District Court Western District of Michigan 1979 and U.S. Supreme Court 1993. Former Judge, Michigan District Court District Five, elected to term beginning Jan 1, 1981.

Assistant Prosecuting Attorney Berrien County Prosecutor's Office 1976-80. Adjunct Professor University of Notre Dame since 1990. Member Michigan Judges Association, State Bar of Michigan, Berrien County and American Bar Associations. Former Faculty Member Michigan Judicial Institute and The National Judicial College. Recipient Distinguished Alumni Award from Thomas M. Cooley Law School Alumni Association 1991. Member Berrien County 4-H Foundation (Director), National Association of Eagle Scouts and Economic Club of Southwest Michigan. Interests include travel, reading, golf, gardening and outdoor activities.

Office: Berrien County Courthouse, 811 Port Street, St. Joseph 49085-1187.

Telephone: (269) 983-7111.

FILICE, Charles F. *(Judge, Michigan District Court District Fifty-four A)* Appointed by Governor William Grawn Milliken to term beginning July 1971. Elected to subsequent terms. Former Chief Judge. Born Lansing Michigan Feb 9, 1944. Roman Catholic. Educated at Western Michigan University B.B.A. 1965 and Wayne State University J.D. 1968. Admitted to practice Michigan 1968. Began legal practice Lansing 1968.

Assistant Prosecutor Ingham County 1968-71. Member State Bar of Michigan, Italian-American Bar Association of Michigan and Ingham County Bar Association. Charter Member Girls' and Boys' Club of Lansing (recipient Man and Boy Award 1978).

Office: City Hall, Sixth Floor, 124 West Michigan Avenue, Lansing 48933-1690.

Telephone: (517) 487-1350.

FISHER, James H. *(Chief Judge, Michigan Circuit Court Fifth Judicial Circuit)* Also serves as Chief Judge Trial Court.

Office: Courthouse, 220 West State Street, Hastings 49058.

Telephone: (269) 948-4814.

FITZGERALD, E. Thomas *(Judge, Michigan Court of Appeals)* Elected Nov 1990 to term beginning Jan 1, 1991. Reelected Nov 5, 1996 and Nov 5, 2002. Current term expires Dec 31, 2008. Born Detroit Michigan Nov 29, 1939. Catholic. Educated at University of Detroit B.A. with honors 1963 and University of Detroit School of Law J.D. 1966. Admitted to practice Michigan 1967 and U.S. District Court Eastern District of Michigan 1967. In legal practice Detroit 1967-68 and Owosso 1969-91.

City Attorney Durand 1968-69. Important Decisions: People v. Kevorkian (assisted suicide issue) 205 MA 180 May 1984 and 205 MA 194 May 1994; and Hobbins v. Attorney General (assisted suicide) 205 MA 194 May 1994. Adjunct Professor of Family Law Thomas M. Cooley Law School 1991-97. Member Appellate Court Administration Committee, The Association of Trial Lawyers of America, Michigan Judges Association, American Judges Association, American Judicature Society, State Bar of Michigan, Shiawassee and Genesee County Bar Associations. USMC. Honorary Chairman March of Dimes Walk America. Member Jaycees, American Heart Association and Boy Scouts. Enjoys golf, jogging and reading.

Mailing address: P.O. Box 30022, Lansing 48909.

Office: 925 West Ottawa Street, Lansing 48915.

Telephone: (517) 373-2195.

FORAN, Leo K. *(Chief Judge, Michigan District Court District Twenty)* Former Chief Judge pro tem.

Office: 6045 Fenton, Dearborn Heights 48127.

Telephone: (313) 277-7480.

FORD, Steven E. *(Chief Judge, Michigan District Court District Ninety-two)* Elected to term beginning Jan 1, 1991. Reelected 1996 and 2002. Current term expires Dec 31, 2008. Born Newberry Michigan April 12, 1949. Educated at Central Michigan University B.S. summa cum laude 1970 and University of Michigan J.D. 1975. Began legal practice Jackson 1975. In legal practice Newberry 1976. Judge, Luce County Probate Court July 20, 1981 to Dec 31, 1990.

Member State Bar of Michigan and American Bar Association.

Office: 407 West Harrie Street, Newberry 49868.

Telephone: (906) 293-5531.

FORTINBERRY, Dana *(Judge, Michigan District Court District Fifty-two Division Two)*

Office: 5850 Lorac, Clarkston 48346.

Telephone: (248) 625-4888.

FOSTER, John C. *(Judge, Michigan District Court District Forty-one B)* Appointed by Governor James J. Blanchard to term beginning Nov 16, 1990. Elected to subsequent term. Reelected to term beginning Jan 1, 1999, current term expires Jan 1, 2005. Currently serves as Chief Judge pro tem. Former Chief Judge. Born Highland Park Michigan Dec 21, 1945. Presbyterian. Educated at Alma College B.A. 1967, Pittsburgh Theological Seminary M.Div. 1970 and Detroit College of Law J.D. cum laude 1977. Admitted to practice Michigan 1977. In legal practice St. Claire Shores 1977-83.

Corporation Counsel Macomb County 1983-90. Member Macomb County District Judges Association, Michigan District Judges Association, National Association of Special Court Judges, State Bar of Michigan, Macomb County and American Bar Associations. Board of Trustees Alma College. Advisory Board Salvation Army. Board Member Peace Presbyterian Village. Member

FOSTER, JOHN C.—*Continued*

Clinton Township Optimists. Enjoys golf, scuba, travel and reading.
Office: One Crocker Boulevard, Mount Clemens 48043-2565.
Telephone: (586) 469-6870.
E-mail address: jcfoster@flash.net

FRANCIS, Nancy C. *(Judge, Washtenaw County Probate Court)* Appointed by Governor James J. Blanchard to term beginning March 19, 1990. Elected Nov 1990. Former Chief Judge and Chief Judge pro tem.
Mailing address: P.O. Box 8645, Ann Arbor 48107-8645.
Office: Courthouse, 101 East Huron Street, Ann Arbor 48104.
Telephone: (734) 222-6340.

FRANK KELLY, Kirsten *(Judge, Michigan Court of Appeals)* Elected 2000. Term expires Jan 1, 2007. Educated at Michigan State University B.A. 1978 and University of Detroit School of Law J.D. 1981. Former Judge, Grosse Pointe Park Municipal Court. Former Presiding Judge Family Division and Judge, Michigan Circuit Court Third Judicial Circuit.
Office: 14-300 Cadillac Place, 3020 West Grand Boulevard, Detroit 48202-6020.
Telephone: (313) 972-5733.
Fax: (313) 972-5717
E-mail address: KKELLY@courts.mi.gov

FRATARCANGELI, Mark A. *(Judge, Michigan District Court District Forty)* Elected Nov 8, 2000. Currently serves as Chief Judge pro tem. Born Detroit Michigan Feb 11, 1967. Catholic. Educated at Kalamazoo College B.A. 1989 and University of Detroit J.D. Admitted to practice Michigan 1991. In legal practice Macomb County 1991-2000.
Member Macomb County and Italian American Bar Associations.
Office: 27701 Jefferson Avenue, St. Clair Shores 48081.
Telephone: (586) 445-5280, 445-5383.
Fax: (586) 445-4003

FRESARD, Patricia Susan *(Judge, Michigan Circuit Court Third Judicial Circuit)*
Office: 804 Hall of Justice, 1441 St. Antoine Street, Detroit 48226.
Telephone: (313) 224-2461.

FRIEDMAN, Bernard A. *(Judge, United States District Court Eastern District of Michigan)* Appointed for life by President Ronald Reagan to term beginning March 1988. Born Detroit Michigan Sept 23, 1943. Jewish. Educated at Detroit Institute of Technology and Detroit College of Law J.D. 1968. Member Tau Epsilon Rho. Admitted to practice Michigan 1968 and Florida 1968. Began legal practice Detroit 1970. In legal practice Southfield 1970-82. Judge, Michigan District Court District Forty-eight May 27, 1982 to March 1988.
Attorney City of Inkster 1970-82. Referee Michigan Civil Rights Commission 1973-82. Labor Arbitrator National Panel of Arbitrators American Arbitration Association 1980-82. Member State Bar of Michigan. Graduate The National Judicial College 1984. Recipient Distinguished Service Award from Oakland County Bar Association 1985. Named Eccentric Newspaper's Person of the Year 1986. Lieutenant USAR 1968-74. Board Member Children's Hospital of Michigan. Enjoys antiques and running.
Office: 238 U.S. Courthouse, 231 West Lafayette Boulevard, Detroit 48226.
Telephone: (313) 234-5170.

FULLERTON, Judith A. *(Judge, Michigan Circuit Court Seventh Judicial Circuit)* Elected to term beginning Jan 1, 1983. Reelected 1988, 1994 and 2000. Current term expires Dec 31, 2006. Currently serves as Presiding Judge Civil Division. Born Tulsa Oklahoma April 30, 1944. Educated at Vassar College B.A. 1966 and George Washington University Law School J.D. 1970. Admitted to practice District of Columbia 1970 and Michigan 1972. Began legal practice Washington D.C. 1970. In legal practice Flint 1972-80. Judge, Michigan District Court District Sixty-eight 1981-83.
With Securities and Exchange Commission Washington D.C. 1970-71. Assistant Prosecutor Genesee County 1972-78. Chief Assistant Attorney City of Flint 1978-81. Member Women Lawyers of Michigan, National Association of Women Judges, American Judicature Society, The District of Columbia Bar, State Bar of Michigan, Genesee County and American Bar Associations. Enjoys pets, children, travel, photography and cross-country skiing.
Office: Genesee County Courthouse, 900 South Saginaw Street, Flint 48502.
Telephone: (810) 257-3252.

GADOLA, John A. *(Judge, Michigan Circuit Court Seventh Judicial Circuit)* Elected to term beginning Jan 1, 2003. Educated at Michigan State University B.A. 1988 and University of Toledo J.D. 1991.
Office: Genesee County Courthouse, 900 South Saginaw Street, Flint 48502.
Telephone: (810) 257-3252.

GADOLA, Paul V. *(Senior Judge, United States District Court Eastern District of Michigan)* Appointed for life by President Ronald Reagan to term beginning Jan 6, 1989. Assumed Senior status Jan 31, 2001, serves by assignment. Born Flint Michigan July 21, 1929. Roman Catholic. Educated at Michigan State University A.B. with honors 1951 and University of Michigan Law School J.D. 1953. Member Phi Kappa Phi and Delta Theta Phi. Admitted to practice Michigan 1953, U.S. District Courts Eastern 1953 and Western 1988 Districts of Michigan, U.S. Court of Appeals Sixth Circuit 1983 and U.S. Supreme Court 1984. In legal practice Flint 1955-89.
Important Decisions: Ferlito v. Johnson & Johnson Products, Inc. (defendant not liable for burns suffered when cotton batting Halloween costume ignited when victim attempted to light cigarette) 771 F. Supp. 196 E.D. Mich. 1991; Kirk v. Hanes Corporation and BIC Corporation (cigarette lighter manufacturer not liable for injuries to child for failure to warn of open and obvious danger of disposable butane lighter) 771 F. Supp. 856 E.D. Mich. 1991; France Stone Co. v. Charter Township of Monroe (township impermissibly used its zoning power to prevent a lawful type of land use within its borders) 802 F. Supp. 90 E.D. Mich. 1992; United States v. Hart (court departed upward in sentence to statutory maximum, despite sentencing guidelines providing for substantially lesser sentencing of Detroit Police Chief convicted of embezzlement of public funds) 803 F. Supp. 53 E.D. Mich. 1992; Michigan Protective & Advocacy Service v. Kirkendall (irrevocable sterilization

GADOLA, PAUL V.—*Continued*
of mentally ill patient without her consent, constitutes deprivation of fundamental constitutional right of procreation) 841 F. Supp. 796 E.D. Mich. 1993; Buletini v. Immigration & Naturalization Service (INS abused its discretion in denying Albanian physician's visa petition) 860 F. Supp. 1222 E.D. Mich. 1994; Spearman v. United States (conviction of defendant set aside on finding that he had been denied effective assistance of counsel during plea stage, sentencing stage and appeal stage) 860 F. Supp. 1234 E.D. Mich. 1994; County of Oakland v. Vista Disposal, Inc. and United States Government (plaintiff county defrauded by conspirators, entailed to recover funds collected by U.S. Government from RICO conspirators pursuant to forfeiture orders) 900 F. Supp. 879 E.D. Mich. 1995 modified 917 F. Supp. 515 E.D. Mich. 1996; Joel Price v. Charter Township of Fenton (local ordinance limiting frequency of flights preempted by Federal Aviation Act) 909 F. Supp. 498 E.D. Mich. 1995; Drankchak v. Akzo Nobel, Inc. (employees' state law contractual claims preempted by ERISA; employer did not retaliate against employee by refusing to write favorable letter of recommendation, where employee had obtained his job by lying about his career and had been fired for violating his fiduciary duties) N.D. Ill. 1995 aff'd 88 F.3d 457, 7th Cir. 1996; Joseph Golden et al. v. Kelsey-Hayes Co., et al. (summary judgment to the retirees, finding that the language of the summary plan description was binding upon defendants and thus they could not diminish retirees' benefits which were in force at the time of their retirement) 1997 W.L. 50514 E.D. Mich. 1997; Renishaw v. Marposs Societá Per Azioni (civil action against competitor for infringement of patents) 974 F. Supp. 1056, E.D. Mich. 1997, aff'd 158 F.3d 1243, Fed. Cir. 1998; Cavalier v. Werner Co. (design and manufacturing defect) 976 F. Supp. 672, E.D. Mich. 1998; Terwilliger v. GMRI, Inc. (sex discrimination claims) 952 F. Supp. 1224, E.D. Mich. 1997, aff'd 142 F.3d 436, 6th Cir. 1998; Krear v. Malek 961 F. Supp. 1065, E.D. Mich. 1997; Taylor v. American Tobacco Company, Inc. 983 F. Supp. 686, E.D. Mich. 1997; IA, Inc. v. Thermacell Technologies, Inc. (alleged violations of the Lanham Act) 983 F. Supp. 697, E.D. Mich. 1997; Friedman v. Freidberg Law Corp. 6 F. Supp. 2d 656, 41 Fed. R. Serv. 3d 972, E.D. Mich. 1998; Holland v. Earl G. Graves Publishing Co., Inc. (breach of a compensation agreement) 46 F. Supp. 2d 681, E.D. Mich. 1998; Zach v. U.S. 224 B.R. 601, 62 A.F.T.R.2d 98-6477, 98-2 USTC P 50, 756, E.D. Mich. 1998; Quinn v. City of Detroit 23 F. Supp. 2d 741, E.D. Mich. 1998; Meyers v. Wal-Mart Stores, East, Inc. (negligence action against defendant-warehouse store) 29 F. Supp. 2d 760, E.D. Mich. 1998; Wonsey v. Life Ins. Co. of North America, 32 F. Supp. 2d 939, 38 UCC Rep. Serv. 2d 619, E.D. Mich. 1998; Peerenboom v. Yukins E.D. Mich. Nov 16, 1999; Racknor v. First Allmerica Financial Life Insurance Co. E.D. Mich. Nov 5, 1999; Columbia Pictures Industries, Inc. v. T & F Enterprises, Inc. 68 F. Supp. 2d 833, E.D. Mich. 1999; Archer v. Arms Technology, Inc. 1999 WL 993306, E.D. Mich. Oct 14, 1999; U.S. v. Hardeman 36 F. Supp. 2d 770, E.D. Mich. 1999; Friedman v. Freidberg Law Corp. 44 F. Supp. 2d 902, E.D. Mich. 1999; Wayne County Regional Educational Service Agency v. Pappas 56 F. Supp. 2d 807, 137 Ed. Law Rep. 676, E.D. Mich. 1999; Freeport-McMoran Resource Partners Ltd. Partnership v. B-B Paint Corp. 56 F. Supp. 2d 823, E.D. Mich. 1999; Phillips v. Langston Corp. (products liability) 59 F. Supp. 2d 696, E.D. Mich. 1999; and Rudder v. Rashid 1999 WL 993144, E.D. Mich. Sept 30, 1999.

Lifetime Fellow Roscoe Pound American Trial Lawyers Foundation. Fellow Michigan State Bar Foundation. Member Incorporated Society of Irish American Lawyers (President), Federalist Society for Law and Public Policy Studies, National Board of Trial Advocacy (Diplomate Civil Trial Advocacy), Federal Judges Association, State Bar of Michigan and Federal Bar Association (Executive Board Detroit Chapter). Attended numerous legal seminars sponsored by the Federal Judicial Center, Federal Judge's Association, George Mason University Law School, Foundation for Research on Economics and the Environment and Claremont Institute. Recipient Distinguished Service Award from United States Jaycees 1964 and Association of Governing Boards of Universities and Colleges 1988 and Civic Service Award from Mott Community College 1989. U.S. Army 1953-55. Past President Cystic Fibrosis Research Foundation of Genesee County and Urban League of Flint. Past Vice President Genesee County Legal Aid Society. Former Chairman March of Dimes of Genesee County. Former Director Michigan Community College Association. Former Board of Directors Foundation for Mott College. Board of Directors Historical Society for U.S. District Court Eastern District of Michigan, Detroit Alumni Senate Delta Theta Phi and Michigan State University Alumni Association. Member 1969-89 and Chairman 1983-89 Board of Trustees Mott Community College. Member Historical Society of Michigan Supreme Court, Economic Club of Detroit, University Club of Flint, University of Michigan Alumni Association, Committee of Sponsors Flint College and Cultural Development, The Philadelphia Society, Ancient Order of Hibernians and National Railway Historical Society. Interests include reading, American history, Irish/American activities, railroad history and activities, inter-collegiate athletics and college alumni activities.

Office: Federal Building, 600 Church Street, Flint 48502.

Telephone: (810) 341-7845.

GADOLA, Thomas L. *(Judge, Genesee County Probate Court)* Appointed by Governor William Grawn Milliken to term beginning Jan 20, 1977. Elected 1978, 1980, 1986, 1992 and 1998. Current term expires Dec 31, 2004. Former Chief Judge. Born Flint Michigan Jan 6, 1933. Roman Catholic. Educated at University of Michigan B.B.A. 1954 J.D. 1957. Member Delta Theta Phi. Admitted to practice Michigan 1957 and U.S. District Court Eastern District of Michigan 1958. In legal practice Flint 1957-77. Commissioner, Michigan Circuit Court 1962-64.

Board of Commissioners Genesee County 1973-77. Member Michigan Probate and Juvenile Court Judges Association, National College of Probate Judges, State Bar of Michigan and Genesee County Bar Association.

Office: 919 Beach Street, Flint 48502.

Telephone: (810) 257-3080, 257-3533.

GAGE, Hilda R. *(Judge, Michigan Court of Appeals)* Appointed by Governor John Engler to term beginning Jan 1, 1997. Elected Nov 1998 and Nov 2000. Current term expires Dec 31, 2006. Born Detroit Michigan June 16, 1939. Jewish. Educated at University of Michigan B.A. with distinction 1960 M.A. with distinction 1962

GAGE, HILDA R.—*Continued*

and Wayne State University J.D. magna cum laude 1971. Recipient Gold and Bronze Keys for Academic Achievement Wayne State University and American Jurisprudence Awards in Secured Transactions and Evidence. Law Clerk to Hon. Edward F. Bell, Michigan Circuit Court Third Judicial Circuit 1969-70. Member Phi Delta Delta and Tau Epsilon Rho. Admitted to practice Michigan 1971. In legal practice Detroit 1971-78. Judge Jan 1, 1979 to Dec 31, 1996, Chief Judge pro tem Jan 1, 1993 to Jan 1, 1994 and Chief Judge Jan 1, 1994 to Jan 1, 1996, Michigan Circuit Court Sixth Judicial Circuit. Visiting Judge, Michigan Court of Appeals June 1981, July 1983, Dec 1984, May 1988 and July 1993.

Commissioner Oct 1975 to Dec 1978 and Secretary-Treasurer 1977-78 Michigan Civil Rights Commission. Co-author "Mobile Homes: Zoning and Taxation" 55 Cornell L. Rev. 491, 1970 and *The Judge's Book* National Conference of State Trial Judges American Bar Association 1989. Author "View from the Bench: A Judge Outlines Attorney Errors in Products Litigation" *Trial Magazine* 25 Nov 1984 reprinted 7 *Journal of Products Liability* and "Delay: How to Reduce the Docket" 12 No. 1, Winter 1984, "Getting Our Message Across" 21 Fall 1986, "A Higher Standard of Conduct" 19 Spring 1987 and "Blaming the Judge?" 23 Winter 1987 The Judge's Journal. Editorial Board *The Justice System Journal* 1988 and Project Review Board *Caseflow Management Principles and Practices* 1991 Institute for Court Management National Center for State Courts. Teacher Cherry Hill School District 1960-62. Substitute teacher Detroit and Oak Park School Districts 1962-64. Instructor in Legal Research Wayne State University Law School 1971-72. Part-time Instructor in "Contemporary Issues Affecting Consumers: The Family and the Law" Wayne State University Graduate School Summer 1977. Member Sentencing Guidelines Advisory Committee since 1982, Caseflow Management Coordinating Committee since Jan 1986 and Rules Committee since Aug 1989 Michigan Sentencing Guidelines Commission. Member Oct 1985 to Jan 1991 and Chairperson Jan 1991 to Dec 1991 Michigan Judicial Tenure Commission. Board of Directors 1987-94 and Vice Chairperson 1989-94 The National Judicial College. Member Coordinating Council on Life-Sustaining Treatment Decision-Making and Advisory Committee for Assessment and Improvement of Judicial Education Faculty Development Programs and Board of Directors since July 2002 National Center for State Courts. Fellow Michigan State Bar Foundation (Secretary since 1999, Nominating Committee since 1999) and American Bar Foundation since 1979. Member Michigan Judges Association (Chairperson Domestic Relations Committee 1981 and Rules Committee 1981-83, Executive Board 1981-86, Treasurer 1983-84, Vice President 1984-85, President 1986-87), The American Law Institute, State Bar of Michigan (Standing Committee on Grievance 1977-83, Standing Committee on Scope and Correlation 1977-84, Lawyers and Judges Assistance Committee 1977-84, Representative Assembly 1978-81, Special Committee on Judicial Selection 1979, Chairperson Judicial Conference 1982-84, Committee on State Trial Courts Administration since 1985, Committee on Professional and Judicial Ethics 1988-91), Southfield (Board of Directors 1976-79, Treasurer 1978-79) and American (Chairperson Committee on Court Delay Reduction 1979-88; House of Delegates 1982-96; Chairperson 1986-87, Secretary Executive Board 1979-97 and House of Delegates 1986-92 National Conference of State Trial Judges; Task Force on Reduction of Litigation Costs and Delay 1985-94 Judicial Administration Division) Bar Associations.

Lecturer on The Michigan Civil Rights Act Western Michigan University, Civil Procedure Josephson's Bar Review Course 1979 and Negotiation Techniques in Divorce Cases March 1982, Condemnation Law and Practice May 1983, How to Win Motions in Civil Cases and Other Pre-Trial Procedures Oct 1983, Modification and Enforcement of Judgments in Family Law March 1984, Evidentiary Objections May 1984, New Michigan Court Rules March 1985 and Divorce Trial Demonstration March 1986 Institute of Continuing Legal Education. Panel Member Intellectual Properties Litigation and Business Torts Litigation ABA Annual Meeting Section of Litigation Dallas Texas Aug 1979. Guest Lecturer Conference on the Law of Trade Secrets Bureau of National Affairs Washington D.C. Oct 1979, Action Committee Task Force American Bar Association and Georgia Judges Association. Participant and Recorder Committee on Crisis in America's Jails and Prisons National Conference of the Judiciary 1985. Participant and Section Leader Rights of Victims of Crimes National Conference of the Judiciary (sponsored by National Institute of Justice and The National Judicial College) 1986. Attended "Victims and the Courts" Dec 1986 and "Presiding in Criminal Courts" Sept 1987 National Institute of Justice. Faculty Member National Judicial College 1983-93. Instructor on Access to Justice 1999 and Evidence Course 1999 Michigan Judicial Conference.

Recipient Award of Achievement from The Detroit Metropolitan Bar Association Young Lawyers Section April 1974, Citation of Appreciation from American Business Women's Association Feb 1979 and Feb 1985, Citation of Appreciation from American Judicature Society 1982 and 1984, Award of Achievement and Leadership from National Association of Women Judges Nov 1986, Judicial Award from NAACP Sept 1988, Roberts P. Hudson Award for outstanding contributions to the bar from State Bar of Michigan Oct 1991, Ayshet Chayil Award for Dedication to Justice and Citizens of Michigan from Akiva Hebrew Day School April 5, 1992, Distinguished Service Award Delta Kappa Gamma May 16, 1992, Distinguished Service Award from National Center for State Courts Jan 1993, Women of Distinction Award from North Oakland County Girl Scout Council Aug 1993, John N. O'Brien Memorial Award for Distinguished Community Activities Outside Courthouse June 1994 and the first Award of Judicial Excellence from National Conference of State Trial Judges American Bar Association Aug 1994, Michiganian of the Year Award from *The Detroit News* 1996, Sunshine Award from Child Abuse and Neglect Council of Oakland County April 1998 and Q2 Award Quality People, Quality County for Meritorious Community Service Sept 13, 1999. Named Disabled Professional Woman of the Year by The Pilot Club of Greater Birmingham 1990-91 and Public Official of the Year by National Multiple Sclerosis Society Michigan Chapter, Inc. Oct 16, 1999. Listed in *Who's Who in American Law* 3rd ed. 1983, 4th ed. 1985, 6th ed. 1989, 7th ed. 1991 and 9th ed. 1995, *Who's Who of American Women* 14th ed. 1984, *The World Who's Who of Women* 9th ed. 1987, *Oxford's Who's Who* 1992 and *Who's Who in the Midwest.* Hon-

GAGE, HILDA R.—*Continued*

ored by Women's Bar Association for contributions to women in practice of law, improving legal system and dedication to community Dec 18, 2000. Lecturer Ms. Michigan Wheelchair Beauty Pageant (co-sponsored by Mobility Awareness Team and Livonia Jaycees) July 1976 and July 1977. Participant in television series *Law in Your Life* WXYZ-TV March 1975 and *Ask the Lawyers* Channel 56 Jan 1977 to June 1978. Advisory Panel Civil Education Center Oakland County Schools since Feb 1979. Board of Directors American Committee for the Weizmann Institute of Science, Dysautonomia Foundation, Inc. since 1975 and National Multiple Sclerosis Society of Michigan since 1987. Executive Committee Wayne State University Law School Alumni Association since 1983. Board of Trustees Children's Hospital of Michigan and Congregation Shaarey Zedek. Life Member Children's Hospital Auxiliary. Member Offender Aid and Restoration of Oakland County since 1980 and Community Corrections Advisory Committee Michigan Corrections Commission 1987.

Office: 760 American Center Building, 27777 Franklin Road, Southfield 48034-2055.

Telephone: (248) 358-5923.

GARBRECHT, Allen L. *(Chief Judge, Michigan Circuit Court Thirty-seventh Judicial Circuit)* Chief Judge since May 1, 2001. Born Grand Haven Michigan Nov 7, 1949. Protestant. Educated at Hope College B.S. 1971 and University of Toledo J.D. 1976. Admitted to practice Michigan 1976. Began legal practice Marshall 1977. In legal practice Battle Creek 1978. Former Judge, Michigan District Court District Ten.

Assistant Prosecuting Attorney Calhoun County 1977-78. Member State Bar of Michigan and Calhoun County Bar Association (Treasurer 1981). E-4 U.S. Army 1971-73. Enjoys baseball, football, reading and gardening.

Office: Calhoun County Justice Center, 161 East Michigan Avenue, Battle Creek 49014-4066.

Telephone: (269) 969-6506.

GARCIA, Richard Joseph *(Judge, Ingham County Probate Court)*

Mailing address: P.O. Box 19304, Lansing 48901.

Office: Veteran's Memorial Courthouse, 313 West Kalamazoo Street, Lansing 48933.

Telephone: (517) 483-6500.

GARDNER, Patricia D. *(Judge, Kent County Probate Court)*

Office: 9500D Kent County Courthouse, 180 Ottawa Avenue N.W., Grand Rapids 49503-2751.

Telephone: (616) 774-3703.

GARRETT, Ruth Ann *(Judge, Michigan District Court District Thirty-six)*

Office: 421 Madison Avenue, Detroit 48226.

Telephone: (313) 965-2200.

GEORGE, Kathryn A. *(Judge, Macomb County Probate Court)*

Office: Macomb County Building, 40 North Main, Mount Clemens 48043-5654.

GEROU, Michael J. *(Judge, Michigan District Court District Thirty-five)*

Office: 660 Plymouth Road, Plymouth 48170.

Telephone: (734) 459-4740.

GIDDINGS, James R. *(Judge, Michigan Circuit Court Thirtieth Judicial Circuit)* Elected 1998, current term expires Dec 31, 2004. Serves General Trial Division. Also Judge, Michigan Court of Claims. Born Lansing Michigan Jan 10, 1940. Methodist. Educated at Albion College 1957-58, Michigan State University B.S. 1963 and Wayne State University J.D. 1966. Note and Comment Editor Wayne Law Review. Member Omicron Delta Kappa. Recipient Traitel and Burton Scholarships 1964-66. Admitted to practice Michigan 1967 and U.S. District Courts Western 1969 and Eastern 1972 Districts of Michigan. Judge, Michigan District Court District Fifty-four A 1972-78.

Assistant City Attorney 1969-72 and City Attorney 1972 Lansing. Author Case Note "People vs Hernandes" Vol. 11 Wayne L. Rev. 1965. Member Michigan Judges Association, State Bar of Michigan, Ingham County and American Bar Associations. Enjoys skiing and jogging.

Mailing address: P.O. Box 40771, Lansing 48901-7971.

Office: Veteran's Memorial Courthouse, 313 West Kalamazoo Street, Lansing 48933.

Telephone: (517) 483-6500.

GILBERT, Thomas S. *(Judge, Michigan District Court District Eighty-six)*

Office: Courthouse, 328 Washington Street, Traverse City 49684.

Telephone: (231) 922-4580.

GILLIS, John H., Jr. *(Judge, Michigan Circuit Court Third Judicial Circuit)* Elected to term beginning Jan 1, 1985. Reelected 1990, 1996 and 2002. Current term expires Dec 31, 2008. Born Detroit Michigan Dec 28, 1951. Catholic. Educated at Michigan State University B.A. 1974 and University of Detroit J.D. 1977. Member Lambda Chi Alpha and Gamma Eta Gamma. Admitted to practice Michigan 1978. In legal practice Detroit 1978-80 and Grosse Pointe Park 1980. Judge, Recorder's Court of Detroit Jan 1, 1981 to Dec 31, 1984.

Deputy Assistant Prosecutor Wayne County Juvenile Court 1977-78. Special Assistant Attorney General State of Michigan Aug 1978 to Dec 1980. Important Decision: Doe v. Attorney General of Michigan (upheld law banning surrogate parenting for pay) Nov 9, 1988. Member Michigan Judges Association and State Bar of Michigan. Enjoys sailing, skiing and golfing.

Office: 1901 Municipal Center, Two Woodward Avenue, Detroit 48226.

Telephone: (313) 224-5261.

GIOVAN, William J. *(Judge, Michigan Circuit Court Third Judicial Circuit)* Appointed by Governor William G. Milliken to term beginning Jan 17, 1976. Elected 1978, 1984, 1990, 1996 and 2002. Current term expires Jan 1, 2009. Currently serves as Presiding Judge Civil Division. Born Detroit Michigan March 19, 1936. Catholic. Educated at University of Detroit Ph.B. cum laude 1958 and University of Michigan J.D. 1961. Recipient Dean's Key and American Jurisprudence Award. All-American Fencing Team 1958. Admitted to practice Michigan 1962. Began legal practice Detroit 1962. Judge, Recorder's Court of Detroit 1966 and 1970-72. Judge, Common Pleas Court of Detroit 1973-76.

Author "On the Nature of Being a Judge" 41 No. 7 The Detroit Lawyer Aug 1973; "Pretrial and Trial Procedures Under the Michigan Court Rules" Oct 1984, "The Neglected Defense to the Hearsay Objection" Nov 1984 and "Hearsay—The Rest of the Definition" Jan

GIOVAN, WILLIAM J.—*Continued*
1992 Michigan B. Jour.; and Chapter 19 "Jury Instructions and Special Verdicts" *Michigan Civil Procedure* Institute of Continuing Legal Education. Chairman Supreme Court Advisory Committee on Rules of Evidence. Chair Supreme Court Committee on Model Civil Jury Instructions. Member City of Detroit Election Commission 1966, Supreme Court Committee to Draft Rules of Evidence, Committee to Review and Consolidate Michigan Court Rules, Committee to Revise Landlord-Tenant Court Rules and Committee to Evaluate Mediation (Chairman). Member Michigan Judges Association, American Justinian Society of Jurists, State Bar of Michigan (Representative Assembly 1973-77, Civil Procedure Committee 1963-70) Detroit (Circuit Court Committee 1963-70, Chairman Recorder's Court Committee 1968-70, Board of Directors 1985-2000, Chair President's Task Force 1991-92, Chair Library Committee) and Italian-American Bar Associations. Lecturer Michigan Judicial Institute, The National Judicial College, ICLE and American Academy of Judicial Education. Inducted into University of Detroit Sports Hall of Fame 1980. Former Treasurer Southeast Michigan Chapter March of Dimes. Member Grosse Pointe Theatre, MENSA and Sons of Italy. Enjoys photography, theatre, tennis and rowing.
Office: 1511 Municipal Center, Two Woodward Avenue, Detroit 48226.
Telephone: (313) 224-5430.

GIRARD, Dennis H. *(Chief Judge, Michigan District Court District Ninety-six)* Former Chief Judge pro tem.
Office: Courthouse, 234 West Baraga Avenue, Marquette 49855.
Telephone: (906) 225-8235.

GLASPIE, Kim David *(Chief Judge, Michigan District Court District Seventy-one B)* Appointed by Governor James J. Blanchard to term beginning April 9, 1990. Also serves as Chief Judge, Michigan Circuit Court Fifty-fourth Judicial Circuit.
Office: Tuscola County Courthouse, 440 North State Street, Caro 48723.
Telephone: (989) 672-3800.

GOEBEL, Robert E., Jr. *(Chief Judge, Delta County Probate Court)* Appointed by Governor William Grawn Milliken to term beginning Feb 20, 1979. Elected to subsequent terms. Born Pontiac Michigan May 10, 1944. Lutheran. Educated at Michigan State University B.A. 1968 and University of Detroit J.D. 1973. Admitted to practice Michigan 1973. Began legal practice Escanaba 1974.
Prosecuting Attorney Delta County Aug 1, 1976 to Feb 16, 1979. Member Michigan Prosecuting Attorneys Association, National District Attorneys Association and Delta County Bar Association. E-5 U.S. Army 1969-70. Member Escanaba Kiwanis Club. Enjoys hunting and fishing.
Office: Delta County Building, 310 Ludington Street, Escanaba 49829.
Telephone: (906) 789-5114.

GOGGINS, David J. *(Judge, Michigan District Court District Sixty-seven Division One)*
Office: 1415 Flushing Road, Flushing 48433.

GOODRIDGE, Julie Creal *(Judge, Michigan District Court District Fifteen)* Appointed by Governor John Engler to term beginning March 26, 1999. Born Baltimore Maryland Sept 8, 1964. Episcopalian. Educated at Kenyon College B.A. 1986 and University of Michigan J.D. 1988. Admitted to practice Michigan 1989 and District of Columbia 1989. In legal practice Washington D.C. 1989-90 and Milan Michigan 1990-99.
Mailing address: P.O. Box 8650, Ann Arbor 48107-8650.
Office: Courthouse, 101 East Huron, Ann Arbor 48107.
Telephone: (734) 222-3276.
E-mail address: goodridj@washtenaw.mi.us

GORSALITZ, Stephen D. *(Judge, Michigan Circuit Court Ninth Judicial Circuit)* Serves Family Division.
Office: 1400 Gull Road, Kalamazoo 49048.
Telephone: (269) 383-8950.

GOTHAM, Roy D. *(Chief Judge, Michigan Circuit Court Thirty-second Judicial Circuit)* Elected to term beginning Jan 1, 1991. Judge, Ontonagon County Probate Court 1983-90.
Office: Courthouse, 200 North Moore Street, Bessemer 49911-1099.
Telephone: (906) 663-4211.

GRANT, Barry M. *(Judge, Oakland County Probate Court)* Appointed by Governor William G. Milliken to term beginning Sept 7, 1977. Elected 1978, 1984, 1990, 1996 and 2002. Current term expires Dec 31, 2008. Former Chief Judge and Chief Judge pro tem. Born Detroit Michigan Jan 16, 1936. Educated at Michigan State University B.A. 1957, Wayne State University J.D. 1960, Harvard University and Northwestern University 1964. Law Clerk to Hon. Arthur E. Moore, County Probate Court and Michigan Circuit Court 1960. Admitted to practice Michigan 1960, U.S. Supreme Court 1963, U.S. District Court Eastern District of Michigan 1964 and U.S. Court of Appeals 1970. Began legal practice Pontiac 1961. In legal practice Southfield 1961-77. Legal Investigator 1960, Clerk 1960-61 and Referee 1968 and 1971, Probate Court. Former Visiting Circuit Judge, Oakland County.
Assistant Prosecuting Attorney Oakland County 1961-64. Author weekly articles for *Detroit Free Press* and *Detroit News* for eight years. Visiting Lecturer Wayne State University Law School and Oakland University. Former Secretary Michigan Court Reorganization Committee. Member Michigan Judicial Tenure Commission (Probate Court Representative since 1989, Chairperson 1992), Michigan Probate and Juvenile Judges Association (Past President, Secretary, Treasurer, Member Executive Board), Oakland County Criminal Justice Council, National Council of Juvenile and Family Court Judges, American Judicature Society, American Judges Association, State Bar of Michigan (Member since 1972 and Charter Member 1972 Representative Assembly, Council Member Judicial Conference), Oakland County (Membership Chairman 1968-72) and American Bar Associations. Executive Board National College of Probate Judges since 1989. Panel Member Institute of Continuing Education. Recipient Citation of Appreciation Award Michigan Society for the Mentally Disabled. Member Governor's Traffic Safety Commission 1964-66, Oakland County School Board 1966 and Parent-Youth Guidance Commission Southfield 1963. Secretary Southfield Beautification Committee 1964. Trustee and Secretary Southfield Board of Education 1964-68. Board of Trustees William Beaumont Hospital since 1978. Chairman Wil-

GRANT, BARRY M.—*Continued*

liam Beaumont Hospital Research Institute. Board of Directors Oakland County Chapter Michigan Heart Foundation, Oakland County Chapter YMCA, Oakland County Chapter Boy Scouts of America, Oakland County Mental Health Board 1965 and Michigan Cancer Foundation. Participant "John Kelly and Co." and "Ask the Lawyer" television programs. Enjoys athletics.

Office: Courthouse Tower Dept. 449, 1200 North Telegraph Road, Pontiac 48341-0457.

Telephone: (248) 858-0290.

GRANT, Edward J. *(Judge, Michigan Circuit Court Fourth Judicial Circuit)* Former Chief Judge pro tem.

Office: Jackson County Courthouse, 312 South Jackson Street, Jackson 49201.

Telephone: (517) 788-4268.

GRANT, Nanci J. *(Judge, Michigan Circuit Court Sixth Judicial Circuit)* Elected Nov 1996 to term beginning Jan 1, 1997. Reelected 2002, current term expires Dec 31, 2008. Former Presiding Judge General Jurisdiction. Born Detroit Michigan March 28, 1964. Educated at University of Michigan B.A. with honors 1986 and Wayne State University Law School J.D. 1989. Admitted to practice Michigan 1989, U.S. District Court Eastern 1989 and Western 1994 Districts of Michigan and U.S. Supreme Court 1997. In legal practice Bloomfield Hills 1989-96.

Member Executive Committee 1991-96 and Co-chairperson 1992 Salute to Justice. Member Citizens Alliance to the Probate Court (Chairperson Information and Advocacy), Michigan Judges Association (Treasurer, Member Rules Committee), National Association of Women Judges, National Judges Association, American Judges Association, Women's Bar Association, State Bar of Michigan (Member and Chairperson Nominating Committee, Member Rules and Calendar Committee, Representative Assembly since 1990, Young Lawyers Executive Council 1992-93, Executive Committee Judicial Conference), Oakland County (Health and Welfare Committee, Young Lawyers Committee, Membership Committee) and American Bar Associations. Chairperson Bankruptcy Seminar People's Law School. Recipient Merit Award from the Citizens Alliance for the Probate Court of Oakland County. Named one of the "40 under 40" (forty of Metro Detroit's best and brightest under the age of 40) by Crain's Detroit Business and Outstanding Young Woman of America and one of the "Top Ten Women to Watch" by National Magazine 2002. Member Rotary Club of Birmingham 1990-95, Bloomfield Youth Assistance 1991-93, Common Ground Advisory Board 1993-96, Women's Survival Center (Board Member), Michigan Cancer Foundation (Partners Executive Committee since Feb 1996), University of Michigan Alumni Association and University of Michigan Alumnae Club of Oakland County.

Office: Courthouse Tower, 1200 North Telegraph Road, Pontiac 48341-0404.

Telephone: (248) 858-0344.

GRANT, Susan H. *(Chief Judge, Michigan District Court District Seventy-seven)*

Office: Mecosta County Building, 400 Elm Street, Big Rapids 49307.

Telephone: (231) 592-0799, 832-6155.

GRATHWOHL, Casper O. *(Judge, Michigan Circuit Court Second Judicial Circuit)* Former Chief Judge and Chief Judge pro tem.

Office: Berrien County Courthouse, 811 Port Street, St. Joseph 49085-1187.

Telephone: (269) 983-7111.

GRAVES, James M., Jr. *(Judge, Michigan Circuit Court Fourteenth Judicial Circuit)* Elected to term beginning Jan 1, 1981. Reelected Nov 1988, 1994 and 2000. Current term expires Dec 31, 2006. Former Chief Judge and Chief Judge pro tem. Born Muskegon Michigan Nov 8, 1941. Member Christian Reformed Church. Educated at Northwestern University B.S. with honors 1964, University of Michigan M.P.A. with honors 1966 and Detroit College of Law J.D. with honors 1974. Admitted to practice Michigan 1974. Began legal practice Muskegon 1974. Judge, Michigan District Court District Sixty Jan 1, 1977 to Dec 31, 1980.

Member State Bar of Michigan.

Office: Hall of Justice, 990 Terrace, Muskegon 49442-3357.

Telephone: (231) 724-6316.

GRAY, Jimmylee *(Judge, Michigan District Court District Thirty-six)* Appointed to term beginning May 1, 1987.

Office: 421 Madison Avenue, Suite 5067, Detroit 48226.

Telephone: (313) 965-2200.

GREELEY, Timothy P. *(Magistrate Judge, United States District Court Western District of Michigan)* Appointed by U.S. District Court judges Jan 11, 1988. Reappointed Dec 1989 and 1997. Current term expires Dec 2005. Born Battle Creek Michigan March 13, 1954. Educated at Western Michigan University B.S. with honors 1976 and Wayne State University J.D. with honors 1980. Articles Editor Wayne Law Review 1978-80. Law Clerk to Hon. Philip Pratt, U.S. District Court Eastern District of Michigan 1980-82. Admitted to practice Michigan 1982. In legal practice Lansing 1982-87.

Instructor in Criminal Justice Northern Michigan University since 1994.

Mailing address: P.O. Box 698, Marquette 49855.

Telephone: (906) 226-3854.

GREEN, Tina Brooks *(Chief Judge, Michigan District Court District Thirty-four)* Former Chief Judge pro tem.

Office: 11131 Wayne Road, Romulus 48174.

Telephone: (734) 941-4462.

GREGG, James D. *(Chief Judge, United States Bankruptcy Court Western District of Michigan)* Appointed by U.S. Court of Appeals Sixth Circuit judges. Chief Judge since March 4, 1998.

Mailing address: P.O. Box 3310, Grand Rapids 49501-3310.

Telephone: (616) 456-2264.

GRIFFIN, Richard Allen *(Judge, Michigan Court of Appeals)* Elected to term beginning Jan 1, 1989. Reelected 1996 and 2002. Current term expires Dec 31, 2008. Born Traverse City Michigan April 15, 1952. Educated at Western Michigan University Honors College B.A. magna cum laude 1973 and University of Michigan Law School J.D. 1977. Law Clerk to Hon. Ross W. Campbell, Jr., Michigan Circuit Court Circuit Twenty-two 1975-77. Admitted to practice Michigan 1977, Flori-

GRIFFIN, RICHARD ALLEN—*Continued*

da 1978, U.S. District Court Eastern and Western Districts of Michigan and U.S. Court of Appeals Sixth Circuit. In legal practice Traverse City 1977-89.

Member American Judicature Society and State Bar of Michigan (Negligence Law Section). President Grand Traverse Zoological Society and Long Lake Township Building Authority. Ambassador National Cherry Festival.

Office: 3310 Grandview Plaza, 10850 Traverse Highway, Traverse City 49684.

Telephone: (517) 373-0786.

GRIMM, Fredric A., Jr. *(Judge, Michigan District Court District Sixty)* Elected to term beginning Jan 1, 1973. Reelected 1978, 1984, 1990, 1996 and 2002. Current term expires Dec 31, 2008. Chief Judge 1975-77. Former Chief Judge pro tem. Born Chicago Illinois April 2, 1938. Roman Catholic. Educated at Muskegon Community College A.A. 1961, Wayne State University A.B. 1963 and University of Detroit J.D. 1967. Admitted to practice Michigan 1968 and U.S. Supreme Court 1971. Began legal practice Detroit 1968 and Muskegon 1968.

Assistant Prosecuting Attorney 1968, Chief Trial Attorney 1969 and Chief Assistant Prosecuting Attorney 1970-73 Muskegon County. Former Member The Association of Trial Lawyers of America, American Judges Association, Prosecuting Attorneys Association of America and National District Attorneys Association. Member American Judicature Society, Michigan District Judges Association, State Bar of Michigan, Muskegon County and American (Former Board Member Judicial Administration Division, Former Member House of Delegates) Bar Associations. Attended National College of the State Judiciary 1973. Chairman National Conference of Special Court Judges 1985-86. Participant Second National Conference on the Judiciary 1978. Recipient Commendation for Meritorious Service in the Cause of Victim's Rights at Local, State and National Level from National Institute of Justice and U.S. Department of Justice Sept 1986. USN 1959-61. Member Muskegon Community Foundation.

Office: Hall of Justice, 990 Terrace Street, Muskegon 49442-3377.

Telephone: (231) 724-6283.

GRONER, David Alan *(Judge, Michigan Circuit Court Third Judicial Circuit)*

Office: 303 Hall of Justice, 1441 St. Antoine Street, Detroit 48226.

GRUENBURG, Dawnn M. *(Judge, Michigan District Court District Thirty-seven)* Appointed by Governor James J. Blanchard to term beginning April 23, 1990. Former Chief Judge.

Office: Judicial Building, 8300 Common Road, Warren 48093-2380.

Telephone: (586) 574-4900.

GUBOW, David M. *(Chief Judge, Michigan District Court District Forty-five B)* Chief Judge since Jan 1, 2003.

Office: 13600 Oak Park Boulevard, Oak Park 48237.

Telephone: (248) 542-7042.

HALEY, Michael J. *(Chief Judge, Michigan District Court District Eighty-six)* Former Chief Judge pro tem.

Office: Courthouse, 328 Washington Street, Traverse City 49684.

Telephone: (231) 922-4580.

HALL, Lysle G., Jr. *(Judge, Michigan District Court District Twelve)* Elected to term beginning Jan 1, 1969. Reelected 1974, 1980, 1986, 1992 and 1998. Current term expires Dec 31, 2004. Born Jackson Michigan Dec 7, 1930. Methodist. Educated at Albion College B.A. 1952 and Wayne State University J.D. with honors 1958. Admitted to practice Michigan 1958. Began legal practice Jackson 1958. Justice of the Peace 1965-68.

Chief Assistant Prosecuting Attorney Jackson County 1960-65. Instructor Spring Arbor College 1974-75. Member Michigan District Judges Association (Treasurer 1976, Secretary 1977, Vice President 1978, President 1979), American Judges Association, American Judicature Society, State Bar of Michigan (Chairperson Judicial Conference 1979) and American Bar Association. Presenter Michigan Judicial Institute. Participant 1971 and 1978 and Faculty Advisor 1988 and 1990 The National Judicial College.

Office: Jackson Court Building, 312 South Jackson Street, Jackson 49201.

Telephone: (517) 788-4260.

E-mail address: lghall@co.jackson.mi.us

HALLMARK, Linda S. *(Chief Judge, Oakland County Probate Court)*

Office: Courthouse Tower, 1200 North Telegraph Road, Pontiac 48341-0457.

Telephone: (248) 858-0290.

HALLORAN, Richard B., Jr. *(Judge, Michigan Circuit Court Third Judicial Circuit)*

Office: 1807 Municipal Center, Two Woodward Avenue, Detroit 48226.

Telephone: (313) 224-5261.

HALSTEAD, Donald R. *(Chief Judge, Kalamazoo County Probate Court)* Elected to term beginning Jan 1, 1981. Reelected 1986, 1992 and 1998. Current term expires Dec 31, 2004. Former Chief Judge pro tem. Born Chicago Illinois Sept 10, 1942. Catholic. Educated at University of Detroit B.S. 1964 J.D. 1967. Admitted to practice Michigan 1968.

Office: 150 East Crosstown Parkway, Kalamazoo 49001.

Telephone: (269) 383-8666.

HAMILTON, John D. *(Chief Judge, Iosco County Probate Court)*

Mailing address: P.O. Box 421, Tawas City 48764-0421.

Office: Iosco County Building, 422 Lake, Tawas City 48763.

Telephone: (989) 362-3991.

HAMMER, Richard L., Jr. *(Chief Judge, Michigan District Court District Twenty-one)* Appointed by Governor James J. Blanchard to term beginning March 12, 1990.

Former Assistant Attorney General.

Office: 6000 North Middlebelt Road, Garden City 48135.

Telephone: (734) 525-8805.

HAMMOND, John T. *(Judge, Michigan Circuit Court Second Judicial Circuit)* Former Chief Judge pro tem. Former Judge, Michigan District Court District Five.
Office: Berrien County Courthouse, 811 Port Street, St. Joseph 49085-1187.
Telephone: (269) 983-7111.

HAMRE, Paul E. *(Chief Judge, Michigan Circuit Court Thirty-sixth Judicial Circuit)* Former Chief Judge pro tem.
Office: Courthouse, 212 Paw Paw Street, Paw Paw 49079-1492.
Telephone: (269) 657-8218.

HANNON, Ann L. *(Judge, Michigan District Court District Eight Division One)* Former Chief Judge pro tem and Chief Judge.
Office: 416 South Rose Street, Kalamazoo 49007-5272.
Telephone: (269) 384-8020.

HANSEN, Kurt N. *(Chief Judge, Michigan Circuit Court Fifty-fifth Judicial Circuit)*
Office: Courthouse, 401 West Cedar Avenue, Gladwin 48624.
Telephone: (989) 426-9237.

HARRISON, Faye M. *(Chief Judge, Saginaw County Probate Court)*
Office: Juvenile Center, 3360 Hospital Road, Saginaw 48603-9699.
Telephone: (989) 799-2821.

HART, John Henry *(Judge, Michigan District Court District Seventy-five)*
Office: Courthouse, 301 West Main Street, Midland 48640.
Telephone: (989) 832-6709.

HARTER, Phillip E. *(Judge, Calhoun County Probate Court)* Former Chief Judge.
Office: Justice Center, 161 East Michigan Avenue, Battle Creek 49014-4066.
Telephone: (269) 969-6820.

HARWOOD, Pamela R. *(Judge, Michigan Circuit Court Third Judicial Circuit)* Appointed by Governor James J. Blanchard to term beginning Feb 17, 1989. Judge, Michigan District Court District Thirty-six 1985-89.
Office: 1401 Municipal Center, Two Woodward Avenue, Detroit 48226.
Telephone: (313) 224-5261.

HATHAWAY, Amy Patricia *(Judge, Michigan Circuit Court Third Judicial Circuit)*
Office: 1001 Municipal Center, Two Woodward Avenue, Detroit 48226.
Telephone: (313) 224-5261.

HATHAWAY, Cynthia Gray *(Judge, Michigan Circuit Court Third Judicial Circuit)* Assumed office Oct 1, 1997. Former Judge, Recorder's Court of Detroit.
Office: 801 Hall of Justice, 1441 St. Antoine Street, Detroit 48226.
Telephone: (313) 224-2120.

HATHAWAY, Diane Marie *(Judge, Michigan Circuit Court Third Judicial Circuit)* Elected to term beginning Jan 1993. Reelected to subsequent term. Serves Criminal Division since 1998. Born Michigan Feb 28, 1954. Catholic. Educated at Wayne State University 1980-81, Madonna College B.S. 1983 and Detroit College of Law J.D. 1987. Admitted to practice Michigan 1987.
Clerk Recorder's Court of Detroit 1985 and Michigan Circuit Court Third Judicial Circuit 1986. Assistant Prosecuting Attorney 1987-93. Member Prosecuting Attorneys Association of Michigan, Women Lawyers Association, Irish/American Lawyers Association, State Bar of Michigan, Detroit Metropolitan, Wolverine and Macomb County Bar Associations. Radiologic Technologist 1974-84. Real Estate Broker since 1986. Member B'Nai Brith. Personal Statement or Quote: "There is no substitute for preparation."
Office: 401 Hall of Justice, 1441 St. Antoine Street, Detroit 48226-2384.
Telephone: (313) 224-5176.

HATHAWAY, Michael M. *(Judge, Michigan Circuit Court Third Judicial Circuit)*
Office: 3E Lincoln Hall of Justice, 1025 East Forest Avenue, Detroit 48207.

HATHAWAY, Richard P. *(Judge, Michigan Circuit Court Third Judicial Circuit)* Term expires Dec 31, 2008. Former Judge, Recorder's Court of Detroit.
Office: 201 Hall of Justice, 1441 St. Antoine Street, Detroit 48226.
Telephone: (313) 224-5487.

HAYES, Norman R. *(Chief Judge, Antrim County Probate Court)* Former Judge, Chief Judge and Chief Judge pro tem, Michigan District Court District Eighty-seven.
Mailing address: P.O. Box 130, Bellaire 49615.
Office: Antrim County Building, 205 Cayuga, Bellaire 49615.
Telephone: (231) 533-6681.

HAYES-SIPES, Beverly J. *(Judge, Michigan District Court District Thirty-six)*
Office: 421 Madison Avenue, Suite 3070, Detroit 48226.
Telephone: (313) 965-2200.

HAYMAN, Archie L. *(Judge, Michigan Circuit Court Seventh Judicial Circuit)* Currently serves as Presiding Judge Criminal Division. Former Judge, Michigan District Court District Sixty-eight.
Office: Genesee County Courthouse, 900 South Saginaw Street, Flint 48502.
Telephone: (810) 257-3252.

HAYNES, Janet A. *(Chief Judge, Kent County Probate Court)*
Office: 180 Ottawa Avenue N.W., Suite 9500, Grand Rapids 49503.
Telephone: (616) 632-5429.
Fax: (616) 632-5074
E-mail address: jnthaynes@aol.com

HEATHSCOTT, Lynda L. *(Judge, Michigan Circuit Court Tenth Judicial Circuit)*
Office: Courthouse, 111 South Michigan Avenue, Saginaw 48602.
Telephone: (989) 790-5471.

HEGARTY, Michael K. *(Judge, Michigan District Court District Fifty-three)*
Office: 224 North First Street, Brighton 48116.
Telephone: (810) 229-6615.

HEMINGSEN, Donald R. *(Chief Judge, Michigan District Court District Sixty-four B)*
Office: 617 North State, Suite D, Stanton 48888.
Telephone: (989) 831-7450.

HENTCHEL, Robert T. *(Chief Judge, Michigan District Court District Seven)* Chief Judge since Jan 1, 2003. Former Chief Judge pro tem.
Office: Courthouse, 212 Paw Paw Street, Paw Paw 49079.
Telephone: (269) 657-8222.

HICKS, Timothy G. *(Chief Judge, Michigan Circuit Court Fourteenth Judicial Circuit)* Assumed office 1996. Chief Judge since 1998. Educated at Central Michigan University B.A. cum laude 1974 M.A. 1977, Michigan State University 1979-80 and Thomas M. Cooley Law School J.D. 1983. In legal practice Cheboygan 1983-85 and Muskegon 1985-96.
Special Assistant Attorney General Michigan 1991-96. Adjunct Professor of Business Law I Muskegon Community College 1987-95. Member Executive Committee Michigan Judges' Association 1999-2001.
Office: Hall of Justice, 990 Terrace Street, Muskegon 49442-3357.
Telephone: (231) 724-6337.
Fax: (231) 724-4587
E-mail address: hicks@co.muskegon.mi.us

HIGGINS, Michael P. *(Judge, Michigan Circuit Court Fortieth Judicial Circuit)*
Office: Lapeer County Complex, 255 Clay Street, Lapeer 48446.
Telephone: (810) 667-0320.

HILLARY, G. Patrick *(Judge, Kent County Probate Court)*
Office: 9200B Kent County Courthouse, 180 Ottawa Avenue N.W., Grand Rapids 49503-2751.
Telephone: (616) 774-3703.

HINES, Elizabeth Pollard *(Judge, Michigan District Court District Fifteen)* Former Chief Judge. Currently serves as Presiding Judge District Division.
Office: Courthouse, 101 East Huron, Ann Arbor 48107-8650.
Telephone: (734) 222-3266.

HOEKSTRA, Joel P. *(Judge, Michigan Court of Appeals)* Elected Nov 1994 to term beginning Jan 1, 1995. Term expires Dec 31, 2004. Born Grand Rapids Michigan May 10, 1947. Christian Reformed. Educated at Calvin College A.B. 1970 and Valparaiso University J.D. 1973. Admitted to practice Michigan 1973. Began legal practice Grand Rapids 1973. Judge, Michigan District Court District Sixty-one Jan 1, 1985 to Dec 31, 1994.
Assistant Prosecuting Attorney Kent County 1973-84. Member State Bar of Michigan and Grand Rapids Bar Association.
Office: 201 The Law Building, 330 Ionia N.W., Grand Rapids 49503.
Telephone: (616) 456-1167.

HOFFMAN, Harvey J. *(Judge, Michigan District Court District Fifty-six A)*
Office: Eaton County Courthouse, 1045 Independence Boulevard, Charlotte 48813.
Telephone: (517) 485-6444.

HOGG, David A. *(Chief Judge, Michigan District Court District Eighty-four)*
Office: Wexford County Courthouse, 501 South Garfield, Cadillac 49601.
Telephone: (231) 779-9515.

HOHMAN, John A., Jr. *(Judge, Monroe County Probate Court)* Appointed by Governor John Engler to term beginning Feb 10, 1997. Elected 2000, current term expires Dec 31, 2007. Former Chief Judge pro tem and Chief Judge. Born Hillsdale Michigan July 27, 1956. Educated at Central Michigan University B.S. with honors 1978 and Wayne State University Law School J.D.. Member Order of Barristers. Admitted to practice Michigan 1981, U.S. District Court Eastern District of Michigan 1981 and U.S. Court of Appeals Sixth Circuit 1996. In legal practice Monroe 1981-97.
Township Attorney Frenchtown 1983-97 and Berlin 1986-97. Chair Professional Division United Way. Senior Warden Trinity Episcopal Church. Member Monroe County Chamber of Commerce. Enjoys family and golf.
Office: 307 Courthouse, 106 East First Street, Monroe 48161.
Telephone: (734) 240-7160.

HOLMAN, Gary R. *(Judge, Michigan District Court District Fifty-six B)* Elected 1978 to term beginning Jan 1, 1979. Reelected 1984, 1990, 1996 and 2002. Current term expires Dec 31, 2008. Former Chief Judge.
Office: 202 Courts and Law Building, 220 West Court Street, Hastings 49058.
Telephone: (269) 948-4835.

HOLMES, John R. *(Chief Judge, Michigan District Court District Ten)*
Office: Calhoun County Justice Center, 161 East Michigan Avenue, Battle Creek 49014-4066.
Telephone: (269) 969-6666.

HOLOWKA, Nick O. *(Chief Judge, Michigan Circuit Court Fortieth Judicial Circuit)* Former Chief Judge pro tem. Also serves as Chief Judge, Michigan District Court District Seventy-one A.
Office: Lapeer County Complex, 255 Clay Street, Lapeer 48446.
Telephone: (810) 667-0320.

HOOD, Denise Page *(Judge, United States District Court Eastern District of Michigan)* Appointed for life by President Bill Clinton. Born Columbus Ohio Feb 21, 1952. United Church of Christ (Nominating Committee). Educated at Yale University B.A. and Columbia University J.D. Admitted to practice Michigan 1977, U.S. District Court Eastern District of Michigan and U.S. Court of Appeals Sixth Circuit. Began legal practice Detroit. Judge, Michigan District Court District Thirty-six 1983-89. Former Judge, Recorder's Court of Detroit, appointed by Governor James J. Blanchard to term beginning May 24, 1989. Judge, Michigan Circuit Court Third Judicial Circuit 1993-94.
Member Wayne County Neighborhood Legal Services (Former Member Board of Directors), Women Lawyers Association (Former Member Board of Directors), National Association of Women Judges (Membership Committee 1985), Association of Black Judges of Michigan, Detroit Barristers Association (President 1984-85), State Bar of Michigan (Judicial Conference since 1984), Wolverine (Former Member Board of Directors) and Detroit (Board of Directors 1984-85) Bar Associations. Demo-

HOOD, DENISE PAGE—*Continued*

crat. Member National Organization for Women (Former Vice President Political Action, Recording Secretary). Board of Directors Interim House and Cyprian Center. Enjoys swimming and Afro-American literature.

Office: 235 U.S. Courthouse, 231 West Lafayette Boulevard, Detroit 48226.

Telephone: (313) 234-5165.

HOOD, Garfield W. *(Chief Judge, Michigan Circuit Court Twelfth Judicial Circuit)* Elected to term beginning Jan 1, 1991. Reelected 1996 and 2002. Current term expires Dec 31, 2008. Judge, Baraga County Probate Court April 1973 to Dec 1990.

Office: Houghton County Courthouse, 401 East Houghton Avenue, Houghton 49931.

Telephone: (906) 482-5420.

HOOD, Karen M. Fort *(Judge, Michigan Court of Appeals)* Born Detroit Michigan Aug 26, 1953. United Church of Christ. Educated at State University of New York B.A. 1979 and Detroit College of Law J.D. 1989. Admitted to practice Michigan 1989. Judge, Recorder's Court of Detroit Jan 1, 1993 to Sept 30, 1997. Former Judge and Former Presiding Judge Criminal Division, Michigan Circuit Court Third Judicial Circuit, assumed office Oct 1, 1997.

With Wayne County Prosecutor's Office 1985-92. Member Association of Black Judges of Michigan, State Bar of Michigan and Wolverine Bar Association. Member NAACP, National Council on Alcohol, Detroit East Community Mental Health and Fellowship Chapel.

Office: 14-300 Cadillac Place, 3020 West Grand Boulevard, Detroit 48202-6020.

Telephone: (313) 972-5678.

HOORT, David A. *(Judge, Michigan Circuit Court Eighth Judicial Circuit)* Born Lansing Michigan Dec 9, 1952. Protestant. Educated at Western Michigan University B.S. 1974 and Thomas M. Cooley Law School J.D. 1977. Admitted to practice Michigan 1978. In legal practice Ionia County 1983-90. Former Judge, Michigan District Court District Sixty-four A, elected to term beginning Jan 1, 1991.

Assistant Prosecutor Bay County 1978-83. Member State Bar of Michigan and Ionia County Bar Association. Attended Short Course for Prosecuting Attorneys Northwestern University. Named Best Judge in Ionia County. Recipient Domestic Violence Award. Enjoys running.

Office: Ionia County Courthouse, 100 Main Street, Ionia 48846.

Telephone: (616) 527-5315.

E-mail address: dhoort@ioniacounty.org

HUGHES, Jeffrey R. *(Judge, United States Bankruptcy Court Western District of Michigan)* Appointed by U.S. Court of Appeals Sixth Circuit judges Jan 6, 2000. Term expires Jan 2014. Born St. Joseph Michigan Nov 16, 1954. Religious affiliation: Disciples of Christ. Educated at University of Michigan B.A. with high distinction 1977 J.D. cum laude 1980. Member Phi Beta Kappa. Admitted to practice Michigan 1980. In legal practice Grand Rapids 1980-99.

Member American Bankruptcy Institute, National Conference of Bankruptcy Judges and State Bar of Michigan. Political affiliation: Independent. Enjoys exercising, camping and downhill skiing.

Mailing address: P.O. Box 3310, Grand Rapids 49501.

Office: Federal Building, 110 Michigan N.W., Grand Rapids 49504.

Telephone: (616) 456-2233.

Fax: (616) 456-2425

E-mail address: Jeff_Hughes@miwb.uscourts.gov

HUGHES, Richard L. *(Judge, Michigan District Court District Sixty-seven Division Two)* Appointed by Governor John Engler Sept 14, 1994 to term beginning Nov 30, 1994. Elected Nov 1996 and Nov 1998. Current term expires Dec 31, 2004. Born Flint Michigan July 31, 1940. Presbyterian. Educated at Olivet College B.A. and Detroit College of Law J.D. Admitted to practice Michigan 1968. In legal practice Detroit 1968-73 and Genesee County 1973-94.

Member State Bar of Michigan and Genesee County Bar Association. Member Davison Rotary, Burton Rotary and Davison Country Club. Enjoys golf, traveling and politics.

Office: 4094 Manor Drive, Burton 48529.

Telephone: (810) 743-5600.

HULL, LaVail Earl *(Chief Judge, Mecosta-Osceola Counties Probate Court District)* Elected to term beginning Jan 1, 1983. Reelected 1988, 1994 and 2000. Current term expires Dec 31, 2006. Born Big Rapids Michigan Oct 8, 1949. United Methodist. Educated at Grand Valley State College B.A. 1972 and University of Detroit Law School J.D. 1975. Admitted to practice Michigan 1975, Trust Territory of the Pacific 1980 and Federated States of Micronesia 1981. In legal practice Ann Arbor, Grand Rapids, Micronesia (Ponape) and Chippewa Lake.

Member Probate Judges Committee on Mental Health and Michigan Legal Form Committee. Den Leader Cub Scouts of America. Lay Speaker for church. Volunteer Fireman. Ham radio license KA8-MOM. Enjoys hunting, fishing and gardening.

Mailing address: P.O. Box 820, Big Rapids 49307.

Office: Mecosta County Courthouse, 400 Elm Street, Big Rapids 49307.

Telephone: (231) 592-0136.

HULTGREN, William C. *(Judge, Michigan District Court District Nineteen)* Elected 1992. Reelected 1998, current term expires Dec 31, 2004. Former Chief Judge pro tem and Chief Judge. Educated at Hope College B.A. 1966 and Wayne State University J.D. 1969.

Office: 16077 Michigan Avenue, Dearborn 48126.

Telephone: (313) 943-4223.

Fax: (313) 943-3039

HUMPHRIES, Paula G. *(Judge, Michigan District Court District Thirty-six)* Currently serves as Executive Presiding Judge Criminal Division.

Office: 421 Madison Avenue, Suite 5070, Detroit 48226.

Telephone: (313) 965-2200.

HUNT, Keith P. *(Chief Judge, Michigan District Court District Forty-three)* Former Chief Judge pro tem.

Office: 43 East Nine Mile Road, Hazel Park 48030.

Telephone: (248) 547-3034.

HUNTER, John G. *(Judge, Crawford County Probate Court)* Elected to term beginning Jan 1, 1989. Reelected 1994 and 2000. Current term expires Dec 31,

HUNTER, JOHN G.—*Continued*

2006. Former Chief Judge. Also serves as Chief Judge pro tem Trial Court. Born Grayling Michigan Feb 6, 1951. Catholic. Educated at Hillsdale College B.A. magna cum laude 1973 and Wayne State University J.D. 1976. Staff member Wayne Law Review 1974. Law Clerk to Hon. Damon J. Keith, U.S. District Court Eastern District of Michigan 1977-78. Member Phi Sigma Epsilon, Omicron Delta Kappa and Lambda Iota Tau. Admitted to practice Michigan 1977. In legal practice Grayling 1978-88.

Member State Bar of Michigan and American Bar Association. Board of Directors George Mason Chapter Trout Unlimited, Grayling Youth Booster Club, 4-H Leader Council, Crawford County Fair Association and Ansable Property Owners Association. Member Knights of Columbus, Eagles and Rotary Club. Enjoys fly fishing, grouse hunting and backpacking.

Office: Courthouse, 200 North Michigan Avenue, Grayling 49738.

Telephone: (989) 348-2841.

HUPY, William A. *(Chief Judge, Menominee County Probate Court)* Elected to term beginning Jan 1, 1989. Reelected 1994 and 2000. Current term expires Dec 31, 2006. Born Menominee Michigan July 12, 1950. Roman Catholic. Educated at Michigan State University B.A. with honors 1972 and Marquette University Law School J.D. 1975. Admitted to practice Wisconsin 1975, Michigan 1981, U.S. District Courts Eastern 1975 and Western 1975 Districts of Wisconsin and Western District of Michigan 1985 and U.S. Supreme Court 1983. In legal practice Seymour 1975-77 and Marinette 1977-81 Wisconsin and Menominee Michigan 1981-88.

District Attorney Marinette County Wisconsin 1977-81. Author "Guidelines for Guardianships" *Colleague* Michigan Judicial Institute 1990. Important Decision: In re Vanidestine (decision to allow two-way closed circuit television for testimony of minor victim in sexual assault case) 463 N.W.2d 225, 1990. Instructor in Police Ethics Mount Senario College 1988. Member Michigan Probate Judges Association, National College of Juvenile and Family Court Judges, State Bar of Michigan, State Bar of Wisconsin and Marinette County Bar Association (Past President). Attended New Judges Seminar 1989, Probate Judges Association conferences, Systems Approach to Substance Abuse Issues in Juvenile Court 1992 and Substance Abuse Seminar The National Judicial College 1992. Recipient Elk of the Month Award Jan 1991. Previously employed at Michigan State University. Member D.A.R.E. Committee, Special Olympics (coach), Lions Club, Elks Club and Children's Charter of Michigan. Enjoys woodworking, gardening and exercising.

Office: Courthouse, 839 Tenth Avenue, Menominee 49858.

Telephone: (906) 863-2634.

HUSUM, Carol A. *(Judge, Michigan District Court District Eight Division One)*

Office: 416 South Rose Street, Kalamazoo 49007-5272.

Telephone: (269) 384-8020.

JAASKELAINEN, James George *(Chief Judge, Keweenaw County Probate Court)* Appointed by Governor William Grawn Milliken to term beginning July 21, 1977. Elected to subsequent terms. Born Laurium Michigan July 24, 1947. Lutheran. Educated at Northern Michigan University B.S. 1972 and Detroit College of Law J.D. 1975. Admitted to practice Michigan 1976. Began legal practice Hancock 1976.

Member Michigan Probate and Juvenile Court Judges Association and State Bar of Michigan. E-5 U.S. Army 1968-70. Adjutant Clyde Johnston Post 230 American Legion. Enjoys hunting and fishing.

Mailing address: HC1 Box 607, Eagle River 49950.

Office: Courthouse, One Fourth Street, Eagle River 49950.

Telephone: (906) 337-1927.

JACKSON, Darnell *(Judge, Michigan District Court District Seventy Division Two)*

Office: 111 South Michigan Avenue, Saginaw 48602.

Telephone: (989) 790-5368.

JACKSON, Thomas Edward *(Judge, Michigan Circuit Court Third Judicial Circuit)* Assumed office Oct 1, 1997. Born Oct 16, 1942. Baptist. Educated at Wayne State University B.A. 1968 J.D. 1972. Admitted to practice Michigan 1973, U.S. District Court 1973 and U.S. Court of Appeals Sixth Circuit 1975. Judge and Chief Judge pro tem, Recorder's Court of Detroit Nov 1982 to Sept 30, 1997.

Attorney Federal Defender's Office 1973-82. Member Judicial Council and National Bar Association (Board of Directors 1991-94). Attended The National Judicial College Sept/Oct 1984. Instructor Michigan Judicial Institute since 1990. Recipient Distinguished Service Award from Detroit/Wayne County Criminal Advocacy Program 1989. E-5 U.S. Army 1966-68.

Office: G-1 Hall of Justice, 1441 St. Antoine Street, Detroit 48226-2384.

Telephone: (313) 224-5435.

JAKUBOWSKI, Walter A., Jr. *(Chief Judge, Michigan District Court District Thirty-seven)* Former Chief Judge pro tem.

Office: Judicial Building, 8300 Common Road, Warren 48093-2380.

Telephone: (586) 574-4900.

JAMES, Sylvia A. *(Chief Judge, Michigan District Court District Twenty-two)*

Office: 27331 South River Park Drive, Inkster 48141.

Telephone: (313) 277-8200.

JAMESON, Charles W. *(Chief Judge, Lenawee County Probate Court)*

Office: Judicial Building, 425 North Main Street, Adrian 49221.

Telephone: (517) 264-4614.

JANSEN, Kathleen *(Judge, Michigan Court of Appeals)* Appointed by Governor James J. Blanchard to term beginning Jan 1, 1990. Elected 2000, current term expires Jan 1, 2007. Educated at Michigan State University and University of Detroit School of Law J.D. Judge, Macomb County Probate Court 1983-84. Judge, Michigan Circuit Court Sixteenth Judicial Circuit 1985-89.

Office: 14-300 Cadillac Place, 3020 West Grand Boulevard, Detroit 48202-6020.

Telephone: (313) 972-5726.

JARBOE, Carl F. *(Chief Judge, Grosse Pointe Park Municipal Court)*
Office: 15115 East Jefferson Avenue, Grosse Pointe Park 48230-1394.
Telephone: (313) 822-3535.

JEFFERSON, Patricia L. *(Judge, Michigan District Court District Thirty-six)*
Office: 421 Madison Avenue, Suite 4075, Detroit 48226.
Telephone: (313) 965-2200.

JOHNSON, Charles W. *(Chief Judge, Michigan Circuit Court Fifty-seventh Judicial Circuit)*
Office: County Building, 200 Division, Petoskey 49770.
Telephone: (231) 348-1748.

JOHNSON, Harold A., Jr. *(Chief Judge, Michigan District Court District Eighty-nine)*
Mailing address: P.O. Box 70, Cheboygan 49721.
Office: Cheboygan County Courthouse, 870 South Main, Cheboygan 49721.
Telephone: (231) 627-8809.

JOHNSON, J. Richardson *(Chief Judge, Michigan Circuit Court Ninth Judicial Circuit)* Appointed by Governor John Engler Oct 13, 1993. Elected 1994 and 2000. Current term expires Dec 31, 2006. Chief Judge since Jan 2000. Chief Judge pro tem 1997-99. Presiding Judge Trial Division 1998-99. Born Dayton Ohio Oct 12, 1945. United Church of Christ. Educated at Miami University, Ohio B.A. 1966 and University of Michigan J.D. 1969. Admitted to practice Michigan 1969, Ohio 1969, U.S. District Court Western District of Michigan 1969 and U.S. Court of Appeals Sixth Circuit 1971. In legal practice Kalamazoo Michigan 1969-93.
Member Michigan Judges Association, State Bar of Michigan, Kalamazoo County and American Bar Associations.
Office: Kalamazoo County Building, 227 West Michigan Avenue, Kalamazoo 49007-3757.
Telephone: (269) 383-8950.

JOHNSON, Shelia R. *(Judge, Michigan District Court District Forty-six)*
Mailing address: P.O. Box 2055, Southfield 48037-2055.
Office: 26000 Evergreen Road, Southfield 48076.
Telephone: (248) 796-5800.

JOHNSON, Theodore O. *(Chief Judge, Michigan District Court District Eighty-eight)* Appointed by Governor James J. Blanchard to term beginning July 1, 1984. Elected Nov 1984, 1990, 1996 and 2002. Current term expires Dec 31, 2008. Born Pontiac Michigan Oct 26, 1943. Lutheran. Educated at Wayne State University B.A. 1965 and Detroit College of Law J.D. 1973. Admitted to practice Michigan 1974. Began legal practice Alpena 1974.
U.S. Peace Corps Volunteer 1965-68. Assistant Prosecuting Attorney May 1976 to Dec 1976 and Prosecuting Attorney Jan 1977 to June 1984 Alpena County. Member Michigan District Judges Association, State Bar of Michigan and Twenty-sixth Judicial Circuit Bar Association. Chorus Director Alpena Chapter Society for the Preservation and Encouragement of Barbershop Quartet Singing in America (SPEBQSA).
Office: 3 Alpena County Office Building, 719 Chisholm Street, Alpena 49707.
Telephone: (989) 354-9680.

JOHNSTON, Donald A., III *(Judge, Michigan Circuit Court Seventeenth Judicial Circuit)* Elected 1988 to term beginning Jan 1, 1989. Reelected 1994 and 2000. Current term expires Dec 31, 2006. Born Norfolk Virginia Feb 25, 1944. Member Mayflower Congregational Church (Former Moderator). Educated at University of Virginia B.A. 1966 and Wayne State University J.D. cum laude 1969. Recipient Silver Key Award. Admitted to practice Michigan 1969 and U.S. District Court Western District of Michigan 1969. Began legal practice Grand Rapids 1969. Judge 1979-88 and Chief Judge 1981-88, Michigan District Court District Sixty-one.
Assistant Prosecuting Attorney, Chief Appellate Attorney and Chief Assistant Prosecuting Attorney Kent County 1969-79. Adjunct Professor Thomas M. Cooley Law School 1977-78. Former Member National District Attorneys Association, Prosecuting Attorneys Association of Michigan and Michigan District Judges Association. Member Michigan Judges Association, State Bar of Michigan and Grand Rapids Bar Association. Former Member and Board Chairman West Michigan Health Systems Agency. Board of Directors Downtown Grand Rapids Kiwanis Club (President 1982-83), Grand Rapids Yacht Club, The Peninsular Club of Grand Rapids, White Lake Yacht Club, Farmington Country Club of Charlottesville Virginia, Sons of the American Revolution and Society of Colonial Wars. Enjoys sailing and downhill skiing.
Office: 11500D Kent County Courthouse, 180 Ottawa Avenue N.W., Grand Rapids 49503-2751.
Telephone: (616) 632-5032.

JOINER, Charles W. *(Senior Judge, United States District Court Eastern District of Michigan)* Appointed for life by President Richard M. Nixon to term beginning July 1, 1972. Assumed Senior status, serves by assignment. Born Maquoketa Iowa Feb 14, 1916. Congregationalist. Educated at Maquoketa Junior College 1933-35 and University of Iowa B.A. 1937 J.D. 1939. Admitted to practice Iowa 1939 and Michigan 1947. In legal practice Des Moines Iowa 1939-47.
Author *Trials and Appeals* 1957 and *Civil Justice and the Jury* 1962 Prentice-Hall and *Standards for Publication of Judicial Opinions—A Report of the Committee on Use of Appellate Court Energies of the Advisory Council on Appellate Justice* FJC Research Series No. 73-2 Aug 1973. Co-author with William W. Blume and E. B. Stason *Introduction to Civil Procedure* Overbeck Company 1949, with William W. Blume *Jurisdiction and Judgments* Prentice-Hall 1953 and with Delmar Karlen *Trials and Appeals* West Publishing Company 1971. Assistant Professor of Law University of Michigan 1947-50. Associate Professor of Law 1950-53 and Professor of Law 1953-68 University of Michigan. Associate Dean 1960-68 and Acting Dean 1965-66 University of Michigan Law School. Professor of Law and Dean Wayne State University Law School 1968-72. Fellow American Bar Foundation (Secretary 1977-78 and Chairman Fellows 1978-79, Committee on Federal Tax Procedure 1961-68, Committee Research Proposal Review 1971 and Research Committee 1973-77). Member State Bar of Michigan (Chairman Civil Procedure Committee 1954-56;

JOINER, CHARLES W.—*Continued*

Commissioner Member Fiscal Committee, Legislative Drafting Committee and Drafting Committee for Revision of Criminal Code 1964; Commissioner-Advisor Specialization in Legal Practice, Legal Education Committee and Professional and Judicial Ethics Committee; Board of Commissioners 1964-71; First Vice President 1969-70; President 1970-71), Washtenaw County, Iowa State and American (Standing Committee on Ethics and Professional Responsibility 1961-70; Special Committee on Specialization 1967-73; Advisory Committee Law Notes Section of General Practice 1971-76; Section of Individual Rights and Responsibilities, Council Member 1966-71, Membership Chairman 1967-68, Ford Foundation Grant Subcommittee 1970-71, Vice Chairman 1974-75, Chairman Elect 1975-76, Chairman 1976-77; Chairman Committee on Privacy since 1977; Transnational Procedure Committee 1970; Section of Legal Education and Admissions to the Bar 1974-75; Committee on Materials for Teaching Judicial Administration 1961-67; Committee on Court Design 1967-72; American Law Student Association Board of Governors 1949-65; Special Committee on Uniform Evidence Rules for Federal Courts 1957-64, Chairman 1959-64; Committee on Lawyer Placement Information Service 1961-62; Special Committee on Recognition and Regulation of Specialization in Law Practice 1952-56 and 1960-52, Chairman 1953-56; Committee on Metropolitan Court Survey of Section on Judicial Administration 1959-62; Advisory Board ABA Journal 1961-64) Bar Associations.

Member Executive Committee ICLE Wayne State University 1959-72. Chairman and Reporter Joint Committee on Michigan Procedural Revision 1956-62. Chairman Michigan Commissioners on Uniform State Laws since 1963. Member Michigan State Bar Foundation, Michigan Association of the Professions, National Conference of Commissioners on Uniform State Laws, Standing Committee on Rules, Advisory Committee on Civil Rules 1959-70 and Advisory Committee on Rules of Evidence 1965-75 Judicial Conference of the U.S., Judicial Conference of the Sixth Circuit (Chairman of Life Members 1966), The American Law Institute (Joint Committee on Continuing Legal Education 1949-63), American Judicature Society (Board of Directors 1962-65 and Chairman Publications Committee 1961-62), The Association of Trial Lawyers of America (Advocacy College Committee 1970-71 and Federal Judicial Selection 1970-71), Scribes (President 1963-64), Association of American Law Schools (Advisory Committee on the Journal of Legal Education for Volumes 22 and 23 1969-70, Chairman Civil Procedure Round Table 1953, Chairman Audio-Visual Aids Round Table 1962-64, Chairman Continuing Legal Education Committee 1961-62 and Member Editorial Committee on Journal of Legal Education 1970-72), Council National Conference of Bar Presidents 1971-73, National Conference of Commissioners on Uniform State Laws (Executive Committee 1969-74, Chairman Committee on Scope and Program 1969-74, Committee on Cooperation with Council of State Governments, Committee on Law School Research 1969-74, Chairman Section C 1967-69, Special Committee on Uniform Certification of Questions of Law Act 1967-69, Special Committee on Model Land Sales Practices Act 1965-67, Chairman Michigan Commissioners, Chairman Public Information Committee 1967-69, Past Chairman Committee on Uniformity of Judicial Decisions, Chairman Special Committee on Uniform Act Relating to Appeals in Federal Diversity Cases 1965-67, Special Committee on Education and Student Problems 1970-73 and Chairman Federal-State Relations Committee 1971-72) and Board of Advisors Comparative Study of the Administration of Justice 1962-65. Associate Director Constitutional Convention Preparatory Commission of Michigan 1961. Co-director Research & Drafting Michigan Constitutional Convention 1961-62. Member Attorney General's Advisory Board under Federal Justice Research Program project to test feasibility of performing justice resource evaluations since 1979. Appointed to Committee to review Circuit Council Conduct and Disability Orders by Chief Justice Rehnquist since 1988. First Lieutenant USAAC 1942-45. Recipient two battle stars. Alderman Ann Arbor City Council 1955-59. Member Ann Arbor City Citizens Council Charter Review Committee 1959-61. Member University of Michigan Central Sesquicentennial Committee (Chairman 1963-68), Senate Advisory Committee of Public Relations 1959-68, Audio-Visual Education Center (Executive Committee) 1963-68, Broadcasting Committee 1959-65 and Subcommittee on Faculty Club of the Senate Advisory Committee 1958-65. Board of Directors Michigan Blue Shield 1971-73.

Mailing address: P.O. Box 7880, Ann Arbor 48107-7880.

Telephone: (734) 741-2377.

JONAS, Susan A. *(Chief Judge, Michigan District Court District Fifty-eight)*

Office: 57 West Eighth Street, Holland 49423.

Telephone: (616) 392-6991.

JONES, Vera Massey *(Judge, Michigan Circuit Court Third Judicial Circuit)* Assumed office Oct 1, 1997. Term expires Dec 31, 2008. Judge, Chief Judge pro tem and Chief Judge, Recorder's Court of Detroit Jan 1, 1979 to Sept 30, 1997.

Office: G-2 Hall of Justice, 1441 St. Antoine Street, Detroit 48226.

Telephone: (313) 224-2487.

JONES-BRADLEY, Vanesa F. *(Judge, Michigan District Court District Thirty-six)*

Office: 421 Madison Avenue, Suite 5066, Detroit 48226.

Telephone: (313) 965-2200.

JORDON, David L. *(Judge, Michigan District Court District Fifty-four B)* Elected to term beginning Jan 1, 1990. Reelected 1994 and 2000. Current term expires Dec 31, 2006. Former Chief Judge and Chief Judge pro tem.

Office: 101 Linden Street, East Lansing 48823.

Telephone: (517) 351-7000.

JOSLYN, Patrick Reed *(Judge, Michigan Circuit Court Fifty-fourth Judicial Circuit)* Elected to term beginning Jan 1, 1979. Reelected Nov 1988, 1994 and 2000. Current term expires Dec 31, 2006. Former Chief Judge. Born Lansing Michigan July 24, 1941. Catholic. Educated at Michigan State University B.A. 1963 and Detroit College of Law J.D. 1972. Member Delta Theta Phi. Admitted to practice Michigan 1971. In legal practice St. Johns 1971-75. Judge, Michigan Circuit Court Fortieth Judicial Circuit 1978-81.

Prosecuting Attorney Tuscola County 1976-78. Member Northern Michigan Circuit Judges Association (Pres-

JOSLYN, PATRICK REED—*Continued*

ident 1989-90), Michigan Judges Association since 1979 (Rules Committee 1981-91, Executive Board since 1982), Prosecuting Attorneys Association (Executive Board 1976-78), State Bar of Michigan and Tuscola County Bar Association (President 1977-78). Graduate Summer General Session The National Judicial College 1981. Attended numerous courses Michigan Judicial Institute and American Judicial Academy 1989. Recipient Outstanding Contribution to Student Government Award Lansing Community College 1964 and Outstanding Employer Award Caro Business and Professional Women's Association 1990. Quartermaster Second Class USN 1959-63. Good Conduct Medal USN 1963. Former Assistant Branch Manager and Skip Tracer HFC. Republican. Executive Board Member Tuscola County Republican Party 1976-78. Member Knights of Columbus, VFW, American Legion, Caro Rotary Club (President) and Sacred Heart Handbell Choir. Enjoys water skiing, fishing, woodworking, auto body repair, auto mechanics, plumbing, electrical work and painting.

Office: Tuscola County Courthouse, 440 North State Street, Caro 48723.

Telephone: (989) 673-3330.

JURRENS, M. Randall *(Judge, Michigan District Court District Seventy Division One)*

Office: 111 South Michigan Avenue, Saginaw 48602.

Telephone: (989) 790-5368.

JUSTIN, James M. *(Judge, Michigan District Court District Twelve)* Former Presiding Judge Traffic Division.

Office: Jackson County Courthouse, 312 South Jackson Street, Jackson 49201.

Telephone: (517) 788-4260.

KACZMAREK, Robert L. *(Judge, Michigan Circuit Court Tenth Judicial Circuit)* Elected to term beginning Jan 1, 1985. Reelected 1990, 1996 and 2002. Current term expires Dec 31, 2008. Born Saginaw Michigan Nov 10, 1944. Lutheran. Educated at Delta College A.A. 1964 and University of Michigan B.A. 1966 J.D. 1970. Admitted to practice Michigan 1970. Began legal practice Saginaw 1970.

Former Legal Services Attorney, Assistant City Attorney, Assistant Prosecuting Attorney and Prosecuting Attorney. Member State Bar of Michigan and Saginaw County Bar Association. Recipient Outstanding Prosecutor Award from Michigan Humane Society 1982. Worked for Saginaw Steering Gear 1963-67 and Chevrolet Foundry 1968-70. Republican. Enjoys sporting events, old movies and reading.

Office: Courthouse, 111 South Michigan Avenue, Saginaw 48602.

Telephone: (989) 790-5471.

KALMBACH, Randy L. *(Chief Judge, Michigan District Court District Twenty-seven and Judge, Michigan District Court District Twenty-seven Division One)*

Office: 2015 Biddle Avenue, Wyandotte 48192.

Telephone: (734) 324-4475.

KANDREVAS, James A. *(Chief Judge, Michigan District Court District Twenty-eight)*

Office: 14720 Reaume Parkway, Southgate 48195-1852.

Telephone: (734) 246-1360.

KANGAS, Roger W. *(Judge, Michigan District Court District Ninety-six)*

Office: Courthouse, 234 West Baraga Avenue, Marquette 49855.

Telephone: (906) 225-8235.

KELLY, Daniel J. *(Judge, Michigan Circuit Court Thirty-first Judicial Circuit)* Appointed by Governor John Engler Sept 9, 1994. Elected 1996 and 2002. Current term expires Dec 31, 2008. Currently serves as Chief Judge pro tem. Born Port Huron Michigan. Catholic. Educated at Port Huron Jr. College A.A. 1967 and Wayne State University B.A. 1969 J.D. 1974. Admitted to practice Michigan 1974. In legal practice Port Huron 1974-82. Former Judge, Michigan District Court District Seventy-two, elected Nov 3, 1982.

Member State Bar of Michigan and St. Clair County Bar Association. Specialist Five U.S. Army 1970-72.

Office: 3100 County Building, 201 McMorran Boulevard, Port Huron 48060.

Telephone: (810) 985-2060.

KELLY, Marilyn *(Justice, Michigan Supreme Court)* Elected to term beginning 1997. Term expires Jan 1, 2005. Educated at Eastern Michigan University B.A., University of Paris, France, Middlebury College M.A. and Wayne State University J.D. with honors 1971. Awarded honorary LL.D. Eastern Michigan University. In legal practice Oakland County and Wayne County. Judge, Michigan Court of Appeals 1988-97.

Member Women's Bar Association of Oakland County (Past President), Women Lawyers Association of Michigan (Past President), State Bar of Michigan and Oakland County Bar Association. Former Chair President's Task Force on Improved Dispute Resolution. President Michigan State Board of Education 1965-77. Co-chair Open Justice Commission since 1998.

Office: 3034 West Grand Boulevard, Suite 8-500, Detroit 48202-6034.

Telephone: (313) 972-3222.

KELLY, Mary Beth *(Co-Chief Judge, Michigan Circuit Court Third Judicial Circuit)* Appointed by Governor John Engler April 30, 1999. Co-Chief Judge since Jan 1, 2002. Former Presiding Judge Family Division. Educated at University of Michigan B.A. with distinction 1984 and Notre Dame Law School J.D. 1987. Managing Editor Journal of Law, Ethics & Public Policy 1986-87. In legal practice Detroit 1987-99.

Member Civil Litigation Committee State Bar of Michigan 1997-2000. Member Catholic Lawyers Society, Detroit, Downriver and Federal (Executive Board Member 1996-99) Bar Associations. Member Academic Advisory Committee Family Division Michigan Judicial Institute. Co-chair Child Leadership Council of Michigan.

Office: 701 Municipal Center, Two Woodward Avenue, Detroit 48226-3413.

Telephone: (313) 224-8220.

KELLY, Timothy J. *(Judge, Michigan District Court District Seventy-four)*

Office: 1230 Washington Avenue, Bay City 48708.

Telephone: (989) 895-4230.

KELLY, William G. *(Chief Judge, Michigan District Court District Sixty-two B)* Elected to term beginning Jan 1, 1979. Reelected 1984, 1990, 1996 and 2002. Current term expires Dec 31, 2008. Born Grand Rapids Michigan Nov 30, 1947. Catholic. Educated at Aquinas

KELLY, WILLIAM G.—*Continued*

College, University College Dublin Ireland and University of Detroit B.A. 1970 J.D. 1975. Member Sigma Phi Epsilon. Admitted to practice Michigan 1975. In legal practice Kalamazoo 1975-77 and Grand Rapids 1977-79.

Peace Corps Volunteer Ghana 1970-72. Assistant Prosecutor Kalamazoo County 1975-77. Public Defender Kent County 1977-78. Author "The Judge with the Fax and Other Telecommunications" *Court Review* 1990. Instructor Davenport College 1977-78. Member Catholic Lawyers Association (President 1986-88), Michigan District Judges Association (President 1989), National Center for State Courts (Board of Directors 1994-2000), Grand Rapids and American (Executive Committee 1986-94 and Chair 1992-93 National Conference of Special Court Judges, Member Traffic Committee Judicial Division since 2001) Bar Associations. Faculty Member Michigan Court Rules Seminar 1984-85 and New Judges School Michigan Judicial Institute since 1986. Recipient Distinguished Service Award from Kentwood Jaycees 1981. Named one of Five Outstanding Young Men by Michigan Jaycees 1982. Member Kentwood Jaycees (President since 1979, State Chairman Governmental Affairs 1982-83, International Senate 1984) and University of Detroit Law School Alumni (Director 1984-99). Chairman Grand Rapids Red Mass Committee 1983-84. Enjoys racquetball and golf.

Mailing address: P.O. Box 8848, Kentwood 49518-8848.

Office: 4900 Breton Road S.E., Kentwood 49508.

Telephone: (616) 554-0717.

KENNY, Timothy Michael *(Co-Chief Judge, Michigan Circuit Court Third Judicial Circuit)*

Office: 302 Hall of Justice, 1441 St. Antoine Street, Detroit 48226.

Telephone: (313) 224-5170.

KENT, W. Wallace, Jr. *(Chief Judge, Tuscola County Probate Court)* Elected to term beginning Jan 1, 1977. Reelected 1982, 1988, 1994 and 2000. Current term expires Dec 31, 2006. Born Kalamazoo Michigan Sept 6, 1941. Roman Catholic. Educated at University of Colorado at Denver 1962-64, Kalamazoo College B.A. 1965 and University of Michigan J.D. 1967. Semifinalist Campbell Moot Court Competition University of Michigan. Member Century Forum. Admitted to practice Michigan 1968, U.S. District Court Eastern District of Michigan 1970 and U.S. Court of Appeals Sixth Circuit 1970. Began legal practice Caro 1968.

Editorial Board *Colleague* magazine. Life Member Sixth Circuit Judicial Conference. Executive Member Michigan Judicial Conference (Secretary 1993, Treasurer 1993-94, Chairperson 1995-96). Member Michigan Probate Judges Association (President 1994-95), National Council of Juvenile and Family Court Judges, National College of Probate Judges, State Bar of Michigan (Grievance Board Counsel 1974-76, Representative Assembly 1988-94) and Tuscola County Bar Association (Treasurer 1972, Vice President 1973, President 1974). Instructor Michigan Judicial Institute since 1978. Sergeant U.S. Army 1961-64. Member Caro Arts Society (Vice President 1983-84), Caro Rotary Club (President 1987-88) and Knights of Columbus. Enjoys vocal music, English and American history, skiing and community theater.

Office: Courthouse, 440 North State Street, Caro 48723.

Telephone: (989) 672-3850.

Fax: (989) 672-4266

E-mail address: p79@voyager.net

KERSTEN, James Kurt *(Chief Judge, Michigan District Court District Thirty-three)* Elected to term beginning Jan 1, 1997. Reelected 2002, current term expires Dec 31, 2008. Former Chief Judge pro tem.

Office: 19000 Van Horn, Woodhaven 48183.

Telephone: (734) 671-0201.

KHALIL, Karen *(Judge, Michigan District Court District Seventeen)* Former Chief Judge.

Office: 15111 Beech-Daly Road, Redford 48239.

Telephone: (313) 387-2790.

KIDA, Nancy A. *(Chief Judge, Benzie County Probate Court)*

Mailing address: P.O. Box 377, Beulah 49617.

Office: Benzie County Government Center, Beulah 49617.

Telephone: (231) 882-0006.

KINGSLEY, James C. *(Judge, Michigan Circuit Court Thirty-seventh Judicial Circuit)* Appointed by Governor William G. Milliken to term beginning April 5, 1982. Elected to subsequent terms. Chief Judge 1984-94. Born Battle Creek Michigan June 19, 1941. Protestant. Educated at Albion College B.A. with high honors 1963 and Northwestern University Law School J.D. 1966. Admitted to practice Michigan 1966 and U.S. Supreme Court 1971. Began legal practice Albion 1966.

Assistant Prosecuting Attorney Calhoun County 1967-68. Union City Village Attorney 1968-82 and Albion City Attorney 1973-82. Member State Bar of Michigan (Representative Assembly 1978-84) and Calhoun County Bar Association (President and Director 1974-75). Recipient Distinguished Alumni Award from Albion College 1982.

Office: Calhoun County Justice Center, 161 East Michigan Avenue, Battle Creek 49014-4066.

Telephone: (269) 969-6502.

KIRKENDALL, John N. *(Chief Judge, Washtenaw County Probate Court)* Appointed by Governor James J. Blanchard to term beginning May 14, 1986. Elected Nov 1986, 1988, 1994 and 2000. Current term expires Dec 31, 2006. Currently serves as Presiding Judge Family Division Trial Court. Born Burlington Indiana April 24, 1938. Presbyterian. Educated at University of Michigan B.A. 1960 J.D. 1963. Admitted to practice Michigan 1963. In legal practice Ypsilanti 1963-86.

Fellow Michigan State Bar Foundation. Member National College of Probate Judges (Chair Technology Committee since 1999), Washtenaw County (President 1974-75) and American (Chair National Conference of Special Court Judges since 1999) Bar Associations. Faculty Member University of Michigan Institute of Continuing Legal Education, Michigan Judicial Institute and The National Judicial College. Frequent author and lec-

KIRKENDALL, JOHN N.—*Continued*

turer on guardianship and aging issues. Chairman National Kidney Foundation of Michigan 1986-88.

Mailing address: P.O. Box 8645, Ann Arbor 48107-8645.

Office: Courthouse, 101 East Huron Street, Ann Arbor 48104.

Telephone: (734) 222-6340.

E-mail address: kirkendj@co.washtenaw.mi.us

KLOOTE, Richard J. *(Judge, Michigan District Court District Fifty-eight)* Former Chief Judge and Chief Judge pro tem.

Office: Ottawa County Building, 414 Washington Avenue, Grand Haven 49417.

Telephone: (616) 846-8280.

KNOBLOCK, M. Richard *(Chief Judge, Michigan Circuit Court Fifty-second Judicial Circuit)* Elected to term beginning Jan 1, 1979. Reelected 1984, 1990, 1996 and 2002. Current term expires Dec 31, 2008. Born Detroit Michigan March 13, 1943. Catholic. Educated at Michigan State University B.A. 1970 and Wayne State University J.D. 1974. Admitted to practice Oregon 1974 and Michigan 1975. In legal practice Salem Oregon 1974-75 and Bad Axe Michigan 1976-78.

Chairperson Michigan Judicial Tenure Commission. Member Michigan Judges Association (Past President), Oregon State Bar, State Bar of Michigan and American Bar Association. E-4 U.S. Army 1961-63. Enjoys sailing, flying and golfing.

Mailing address: P.O. Box 188, Bad Axe 48413.

Office: Huron County Building, 250 East Huron, Bad Axe 48413.

Telephone: (989) 269-7112.

KNOLL, Bradley S. *(Judge, Michigan District Court District Fifty-eight)*

Office: 57 West Eighth Street, Holland 49423.

Telephone: (616) 392-6991.

KOLENDA, Dennis C. *(Judge, Michigan Circuit Court Seventeenth Judicial Circuit)* Former Chief Judge.

Office: 12200A Kent County Courthouse, 180 Ottawa Avenue N.W., Grand Rapids 49503-2751.

Telephone: (616) 632-5480.

KOMIVES, Paul J. *(Recalled Magistrate Judge, United States District Court Eastern District of Michigan)* Magistrate Judge Feb 12, 1971 to July 12, 1997. Appointed Recalled Magistrate Judge by the Judicial Council of the Sixth Circuit. Born Detroit Michigan July 12, 1932. Catholic. Educated at University of Detroit A.B. magna cum laude 1954 and University of Michigan J.D. 1958. Associate Editor Michigan Law Review 1956-57. Admitted to practice Michigan 1958, District of Columbia 1958, U.S. Court of Appeals Sixth Circuit 1961 and U.S. Supreme Court 1963. In legal practice Detroit Michigan 1967-71.

Attorney Criminal Division U.S. Department of Justice 1958-61. Assistant U.S. Attorney Eastern District of Michigan 1961-66. Special Prosecutor Wayne County 1966-67. Adjunct Professor Detroit College of Law since 1972 and Wayne State University Law School since 1998.

Office: 629 U.S. Courthouse, 231 West Lafayette Boulevard, Detroit 48226.

Telephone: (313) 234-5200.

KOSELKA, Harvey A. *(Chief Judge, Michigan Circuit Court Thirty-ninth Judicial Circuit)* Former Chief Judge pro tem.

Office: Judicial Building, 425 North Main Street, Adrian 49221.

Telephone: (517) 264-4597.

KOSELKA, Natalia M. *(Judge, Michigan District Court District Two A)* Appointed Judge by Governor William Grawn Milliken to term beginning Nov 22, 1982. Elected 1986, 1992 and 1998. Current term expires Dec 31, 2004. Former Chief Judge and Chief Judge pro tem. Born Hamilton Ohio June 3, 1936. Member St. Joseph Catholic Church. Educated at Marquette University B.S. 1958 J.D. 1960. Named Outstanding Female Law Student 1959 and 1960. Member Theta Phi Alpha. Admitted to practice Michigan 1960 and Wisconsin 1960. In legal practice Adrian Michigan 1960-82. Commissioner, Michigan Circuit Court Thirty-ninth Judicial Circuit 1963-68.

Chairperson Board of Directors Lenawee County Department of Social Services 1969-82 and Lenawee County Medical Care Facility 1969-82. Instructor Siena Heights College. Member Michigan District Judges Association, State Bar of Michigan (Probate Law and Family Law Sections) and Lenawee County Bar Association. Listed in *Outstanding Young Women of America* 1967. Board of Trustees Charlotte Stephenson Home since 1972 and Siena Heights College since 1975 (Chairperson 1984). Member Adrian YMCA (First woman elected to Board of Directors 1966), Associated Charities (Past President and Board Member) and Catholic Social Services (Former Member Board of Directors). Enjoys sewing, camping, skiing and gardening.

Office: Judicial Building, 425 North Main Street, Adrian 49221.

Telephone: (517) 264-4673.

KOWALSKI, John F. *(Judge, Michigan Circuit Court Twenty-sixth Judicial Circuit)* Former Chief Judge.

Office: Courthouse, 720 West Chisholm Street, Alpena 49707.

Telephone: (989) 354-9573.

KRAUS, Karl E. *(Chief Judge, Michigan District Court District Seventy-three B)* Appointed Judge by Governor James J. Blanchard to term beginning Oct 10, 1989. Elected to subsequent terms. Former Chief Judge pro tem.

Office: 105 Huron County Building, 250 East Huron Avenue, Bad Axe 48413.

Telephone: (989) 269-9987.

KRAUSE, Amy Ronayne *(Judge, Michigan District Court District Fifty-four A)*

Office: City Hall, Sixth Floor, 124 West Michigan Avenue, Lansing 48933-1690.

Telephone: (517) 487-1350.

KROPF, Robert C. *(Judge, Michigan District Court District Eight Division Two)* Former Chief Judge pro tem.

Office: 7810 Shaver Road, Portage 49024-5193.

Telephone: (269) 383-6460.

KUHN, Richard D. *(Judge, Michigan Circuit Court Sixth Judicial Circuit)* Former Chief Judge.

Office: Courthouse Tower Dept. 404, 1200 North Telegraph Road, Pontiac 48341-0404.

Telephone: (248) 858-0344.

KUHN, Richard D., Jr. *(Judge, Michigan District Court District Fifty-one)*

Office: 5100 Civic Center Drive, Waterford 48329.
Telephone: (248) 674-4655.

KUKKONEN, Phillip L. *(Chief Judge, Michigan District Court District Ninety-seven)*

Office: Houghton County Courthouse, 401 East Houghton Street, Houghton 49931.
Telephone: (906) 482-4980.

KUSZ, Michael J. *(Chief Judge, Michigan District Court District Ninety-five B)* Elected to term beginning Jan 1, 1991. Reelected 1996 and 2002. Current term expires Dec 31, 2008. Born Ironwood Michigan May 17, 1953. Roman Catholic. Educated at University of Minnesota B.A. with high honors 1975 J.D. 1978. Admitted to practice Michigan 1978, Wisconsin 1980 and U.S. District Courts Western District of Michigan 1980 and Eastern 1980 and Western 1980 Districts of Wisconsin. In legal practice Iron Mountain Michigan 1978-82.

Prosecuting Attorney and Corporation Counsel Dickinson County 1982-90. Member Michigan District Judges Association and American Judges Association. Attended The National Judicial College 1993.

Mailing address: P.O. Box 609, Iron Mountain 49801.
Office: Dickinson County Courthouse, Iron Mountain 49801.
Telephone: (906) 774-0506, 875-0619.

LaBEAU, Michael W. *(Judge, Michigan Circuit Court Thirty-eighth Judicial Circuit)* Elected 1984 to term beginning Jan 1, 1985. Reelected 1988, 1994 and 2000. Current term expires Dec 31, 2006. Former Chief Judge pro tem and Chief Judge. Born Monroe Michigan Sept 1, 1947. Catholic. Educated at Western Michigan University B.B.A. 1969 and Detroit College of Law J.D. 1974. Admitted to practice Michigan 1974 and U.S. District Court Eastern District of Michigan 1974. Judge, Michigan District Court District One 1985-88.

Prosecuting Attorney Monroe County 1977-84. Fellow The Association of Trial Lawyers of America. Member Michigan Judges Association, State Bar of Michigan and Monroe County Bar Association. Member Fraternal Order of Police, Knights of Columbus and NAACP. Enjoys golf.

Office: 106 East First Street, Monroe 48161.
Telephone: (734) 240-7060.

LACEY, James E. *(Judge, Wayne County Probate Court)* Appointed by Governor William Grawn Milliken to term beginning Jan 16, 1978. Elected 1982, 1988, 1994 and 2000. Current term expires Dec 31, 2006. Born Detroit Michigan June 8, 1934. Catholic. Educated at John Carroll University B.S. 1956 and Detroit College of Law LL.B. 1961. Admitted to practice Michigan 1961. Began legal practice Detroit 1962. Judge, Common Pleas Court of Detroit 1975-78.

Member State Bar of Michigan. Second Lieutenant U.S. Army 1956-57.

Office: 3A Lincoln Hall of Justice, 1025 East Forest Avenue, Detroit 48207.
Telephone: (313) 833-0662.

LAMB, Richard Ryan *(Judge, Michigan Circuit Court Ninth Judicial Circuit)* Former Chief Judge pro tem.

Office: Kalamazoo County Building, 227 West Michigan Avenue, Kalamazoo 49007-3757.
Telephone: (269) 383-8950.

LAMBROS, Nicholas J. *(Chief Judge, Michigan Circuit Court Fiftieth Judicial Circuit)* Elected to term beginning Jan 1, 1977. Reelected 1982, 1988, 1994 and 2000. Current term expires Dec 31, 2006. Born Sault Ste. Marie Michigan May 14, 1939. Eastern Orthodox (Greek). Educated at University of Michigan B.A. 1961 J.D. 1964. Admitted to practice Michigan 1965. Began legal practice Sault Ste. Marie 1965. Judge, Michigan District Court District Ninety-one 1969-73.

Important Decision: Michigan v. Albert LeBlanc 1972. Instructor Lake Superior State College 1970-71. Member American Judicature Society, Michigan Judges Association, State Bar of Michigan, Chippewa County (President 1974) and Eastern Upper Peninsula Bar Associations. Director Community Action Agency.

Office: Courthouse, 319 Court Street, Sault Ste. Marie 49783.
Telephone: (906) 635-6338.

LANGFORD-MORRIS, Denise *(Judge, Michigan Circuit Court Sixth Judicial Circuit)*

Office: Courthouse Tower Dept. 404, 1200 North Telegraph Road, Pontiac 48341-0404.
Telephone: (248) 858-0344.

LANGSTON, Deborah L. *(Judge, Michigan District Court District Thirty-six)*

Office: 421 Madison Avenue, Suite 5068, Detroit 48226.
Telephone: (313) 965-2200.

La ROSE, Roger J. *(Chief Judge, Michigan District Court District Thirty-two A)* Elected to term beginning Jan 1, 1979. Reelected 1984, 1990, 1996 and 2002. Current term expires Dec 31, 2008. Born Cleveland Ohio June 2, 1943. Roman Catholic. Educated at University of Detroit A.B. 1967 and Detroit College of Law J.D. 1973. Member Delta Phi Epsilon. Admitted to practice Michigan 1973, U.S. District Court Eastern District of Michigan 1973, U.S. Court of Appeals Sixth Circuit 1976 and U.S. Supreme Court 1977. In legal practice Detroit 1973-77 and St. Clair Shores 1977-78. Referee, Wayne County Juvenile Court 1976-78. Judge, Harper Woods Municipal Court 1978-79.

Member Michigan District Judges Association (Treasurer 1983-84, Secretary 1985, Vice President 1986, President 1987) and State Bar of Michigan (Chairperson Judicial Conference 1988-89). Interests include computers, sailing and woodworking.

Office: 19617 Harper Avenue, Harper Woods 48225-2095.
Telephone: (313) 343-2590.

LATREILLE, Stanley J. *(Judge, Michigan Circuit Court Forty-fourth Judicial Circuit)* Elected to term beginning Jan 1, 1983. Reelected 1988, 1994 and 2000. Current term expires Dec 31, 2006. Currently serves as Chief Judge pro tem. Former Chief Judge.

Office: 204 South Highlander Way, Suite 5, Howell 48843.
Telephone: (517) 546-3060.

LaVILLE, Jeanine Nemesi *(Judge, Michigan District Court District Sixty-one)*

Office: 8B Kent County Courthouse, 180 Ottawa Avenue N.W., Grand Rapids 49503-2751.

Telephone: (616) 632-5700.

LaVOY, William F. *(Judge, Michigan Circuit Court Thirty-eighth Judicial Circuit)* Appointed by Governor James J. Blanchard to term beginning June 12, 1986. Elected Nov 1986, 1992 and 1998. Current term expires Dec 31, 2004. Currently serves as Chief Judge pro tem. Former Chief Judge. Born Monroe Michigan May 23, 1934. Roman Catholic. Educated at University of Detroit B.S.Ed. 1956, University of Toledo M.Ed. 1957 and Wayne State University J.D. 1960. Admitted to practice Michigan 1961, U.S. Court of Appeals Sixth Circuit 1967 and U.S. District Court Eastern District of Michigan 1984. Began legal practice Monroe.

Assistant Prosecutor and Chief Assistant Prosecutor March 22, 1976 to Dec 31, 1984. Prosecutor Jan 1, 1985 to June 11, 1986. Instructor in Business Law Monroe County Community College 1966-68. Arbitrator National Panel of Arbitrators American Arbitration Association. Chairman Subcommittee on Education on Communism. Member State Bar of Michigan (Subcommittee on Title Standards Real Estate Section) and Monroe County Bar Association (Past President). Attended Michigan Judges Association Conference and New Judges Seminar Michigan Judicial Institute. High school teacher Airport Community Schools and Flat Rock Schools 1959-62. Former Member or Member Elks, Knights of Columbus, Fraternal Order of Police, National Rifle Association, Child Abuse and Neglect Council of Monroe, Monroe County Traffic Committee, Monroe County Historical Society and St. Michael's Parish (Usher Club, Past President School Board).

Office: 106 East First Street, Monroe 48161.

Telephone: (734) 240-7070.

LAWLESS, Janelle A. *(Judge, Michigan Circuit Court Thirtieth Judicial Circuit)* Also Judge, Michigan Court of Claims.

Mailing address: P.O. Box 40771, Lansing 48901-7971.

Office: Veteran's Memorial Courthouse, 313 West Kalamazoo Street, Lansing 48933.

Telephone: (517) 483-6500.

LAWSON, David M. *(Judge, United States District Court Eastern District of Michigan)* Appointed for life by President Bill Clinton to term beginning Aug 4, 2000. Born Detroit Michigan Jan 11, 1951. Educated at University of Notre Dame B.A. 1973 and Wayne State University J.D. 1976. Law Clerk to Hon. James L. Ryan, Michigan Supreme Court 1976-77. In legal practice 1977-94 and Birmingham 1994-2000.

Special Assistant Attorney General and Special Prosecutor Oakland County One-Man Grand Jury 1978-80. Special Prosecuting Attorney Livingston County 1991-93.

Mailing address: P.O. Box 913, Bay City 48707.

Office: 1000 Washington Avenue, Room 214, Bay City 48708.

Telephone: (989) 894-8810.

LeDUC, Denis R. *(Judge, Michigan District Court District Forty-two Division One)*

Mailing address: P.O. Box 6, Romeo 48065-0006.

Office: 14713 33 Mile Road, Romeo 48065.

Telephone: (586) 469-7370.

LEIBER, Dennis B. *(Judge, Michigan Circuit Court Seventeenth Judicial Circuit)* Elected to term beginning Jan 1, 1989. Reelected 1994 and 2000. Current term expires Dec 31, 2006. Born Chicago Illinois Feb 21, 1947. Roman Catholic. Educated at Aquinas College B.A. 1969 and Wayne State University J.D. 1972. Member Phi Alpha Delta and Order of Barristers. Admitted to practice Michigan 1973. In legal practice Grand Rapids 1975-77.

Assistant City Attorney Grand Rapids 1973-75. Assistant Prosecutor Kent County 1977-88. Instructor in Criminal Law Grand Valley State University 1985-87. Member State Bar of Michigan and Grand Rapids Bar Association. Participant General Jurisdiction course The National Judicial College 1990.

Office: 10500D Kent County Courthouse, 180 Ottawa Avenue N.W., Grand Rapids 49503-2751.

Telephone: (616) 632-5480.

LINE, Franklin K., Jr. *(Judge, Michigan District Court District Ten)* Former Chief Judge pro tem. Former Presiding Judge.

Office: Calhoun County Justice Center, 161 East Michigan Avenue, Battle Creek 49014-4066.

Telephone: (269) 969-6666.

LIPSCOMB, Willie G., Jr. *(Judge, Michigan District Court District Thirty-six)* Former Magistrate. Born Knoxville Tennessee 1943. Educated at Wayne State University B.A. 1970 and University of Notre Dame Law School J.D. 1975. Member Kappa Alpha Psi. In legal practice 1979-83.

Assistant Prosecuting Attorney Wayne County 1975-79. Executive Director Notre Dame Legal Aid and Defenders Association 1974-75. Member State Bar of Michigan. Recipient WWJ Citizen of the Week 1995, Keep the Dream Alive Award from St. Anthony Church Detroit 1995, Michiganian of the Year 1995, Alumni of the Year Award 1996, William D. Reynolds Alumni Association Award 1997 and Distinguished Black Exemplar Award 1997 from University of Notre Dame and Outstanding Service Award from National State Courts Association 1997. Founder and Administrator Handgun Intervention Program 1993. Life Member NAACP. Member Northwest Guidance Center (Board Member), Detroit Midnight Basketball (Board Member) and American Heart Association (Divisional Board Member).

Office: 421 Madison Avenue, Suite 3069, Detroit 48226.

Telephone: (313) 965-2200.

LLOYD, Leonia J. *(Judge, Michigan District Court District Thirty-six)*

Office: 421 Madison Avenue, Suite 3075, Detroit 48226.

Telephone: (313) 965-2200.

LOGAN, Ben H., II *(Judge, Michigan District Court District Sixty-one)*

Office: 8C Kent County Courthouse, 180 Ottawa Avenue N.W., Grand Rapids 49503-2751.

Telephone: (616) 632-5700.

LOMBARD, Arthur J. *(Judge, Michigan Circuit Court Third Judicial Circuit)*
Office: 1913 Municipal Center, Two Woodward Avenue, Detroit 48226.
Telephone: (313) 224-5261.

LONGO, Joseph *(Judge, Michigan District Court District Forty-three)* Former Chief Judge.
Office: 305 East Nine Mile Road, Ferndale 48220.
Telephone: (248) 547-8700.

LOSTRACCO, Gerald D. *(Chief Judge, Michigan Circuit Court Thirty-fifth Judicial Circuit)*
Office: 208 North Shiawassee Street, Corunna 48817.
Telephone: (989) 743-2239.

LOWE, Ronald W. *(Judge, Michigan District Court District Thirty-five)*
Office: 660 Plymouth Road, Plymouth 48170.
Telephone: (734) 459-4740.

LUDINGTON, Thomas L. *(Chief Judge, Michigan Circuit Court Forty-second Judicial Circuit)* Elected Nov 7, 1994 to term beginning Jan 1, 1995. Reelected 2000, current term expires Dec 31, 2006. Former Chief Judge pro tem. Born Midland Michigan Dec 28, 1953. Educated at Albion College B.A. cum laude 1976 and University of San Diego J.D. 1979. Admitted to practice California 1979, Michigan 1979 and U.S. District Court Eastern District of Michigan 1980. In legal practice Midland Michigan 1979-95.
Member State Bar of Michigan, Midland County and American Bar Associations. Attended General Jurisdiction course The National Judicial College 1995.
Office: Midland County Courthouse, 301 West Main Street, Midland 48640.
Telephone: (989) 832-6825.

LUOMA, Mark E. *(Chief Judge, Michigan District Court District Ninety-three)* Chief Judge since Jan 1, 2003.
Mailing address: P.O. Box 186, Munising 49862.
Office: Courthouse Complex, Munising 49862.
Telephone: (906) 387-3879.

MacDONALD, John E. *(Chief Judge, Michigan District Court District Thirty-five)* Former Chief Judge pro tem.
Office: 660 Plymouth Road, Plymouth 48170.
Telephone: (734) 459-4740.

MACDONALD, Kathleen I. *(Judge, Michigan Circuit Court Third Judicial Circuit)*
Office: 1107 Municipal Center, Two Woodward Avenue, Detroit 48226.
Telephone: (313) 224-5261.

MacDONALD, Michael W. *(Chief Judge, Michigan District Court District Ninety-one)* Also serves as Visiting Judge Clerk.
Office: City-County Building, 325 Court Street, Sault Ste. Marie 49783.
Telephone: (906) 635-6320.

MACERONI, Michael S. *(Judge, Michigan District Court District Forty-one A)*
Office: 40111 Dodge Park Road, Sterling Heights 48313-4138.
Telephone: (586) 446-2500.

MACERONI, Peter J. *(Chief Judge, Michigan Circuit Court Sixteenth Judicial Circuit)* Elected Nov 1990 to term beginning Jan 1, 1991. Reelected 1996 and 2002. Current term expires Dec 31, 2008. Born Detroit Michigan Aug 11, 1940. Catholic. Educated at Hillsdale College B.A. 1962 and Wayne State University J.D. 1965. Member Omicron Delta Kappa and Delta Theta Phi. Admitted to practice Michigan 1966. In legal practice Detroit 1966-70, Warren 1970-90 and Sterling Heights 1970-90.
Member Macomb Trial Lawyers Association, The Association of Trial Lawyers of America, American Arbitration Association, Michigan Judicial Association (Executive Committee), American Judges Foundation, American Judges Association, State Bar of Michigan (Judicial Council), Macomb County and Italian-American Bar Associations. Attended The National Judicial College. Named Man of the Year by the Columbus Day Committee 1993. Member Italian American Cultural Society and Italian American Chamber of Commerce. Enjoys golf and fishing.
Office: Macomb County Court Building, 40 North Main, Mount Clemens 48043-5654.
Telephone: (586) 469-5822.

MACK, Milton L., Jr. *(Chief Judge, Wayne County Probate Court)* Appointed by Governor James J. Blanchard to term beginning Dec 10, 1990. Former Chief Judge pro tem.
Office: 1219 Municipal Center, Two Woodward Avenue, Detroit 48226.
Telephone: (313) 224-5686.

MacKENZIE, Brian W. *(Judge, Michigan District Court District Fifty-two Division One)* Former Presiding Judge Division One.
Office: 48150 Grand River Avenue, Novi 48374-1222.
Telephone: (248) 305-6080.

MACKIE, James B. *(Chief Judge, Michigan District Court District Sixty-five B)* Appointed Judge by Governor James J. Blanchard to term beginning June 1986. Elected to subsequent terms. Current term expires Dec 31, 2008. Former Chief Judge pro tem. Born Edmore Michigan July 1, 1938. Protestant. Educated at Ferris Stole University B.S. with honors 1962 and Detroit College of Law J.D. with honors 1970. Admitted to practice Michigan 1970. In legal practice Alma 1970-86.
Office: 245 East Newark Street, Ithaca 48847.
Telephone: (989) 875-5240.

MAHER, Cathie B. *(Judge, Wayne County Probate Court)*
Office: A Building, Second Floor, 41001 West Seven Mile Road, Northville 48167.
Telephone: (248) 348-7794.

MAHER, Martin T. *(Judge, Wayne County Probate Court)* Former Chief Judge pro tem.
Office: 1379 Municipal Center, Two Woodward Avenue, Detroit 48226.
Telephone: (313) 224-5686.

MALONEY, Paul L. *(Chief Judge, Michigan Circuit Court Second Judicial Circuit)* Appointed by Governor John Engler to term beginning Dec 1996. Elected 1998 and 2002. Current term expires Jan 1, 2009. Also serves as Chief Judge Trial Court. Born Cleveland Ohio Dec 15, 1949. Roman Catholic. Educated at Lehigh University B.A. cum laude 1972 and University of Detroit J.D. 1975. Admitted to practice Michigan 1975. Judge, Mich-

MALONEY, PAUL L.—*Continued*

igan District Court District Five Feb 1995 to Dec 1996, appointed by Governor John Engler.

Prosecuting Attorney Berrien County 1981-89. Deputy Assistant Attorney General Criminal Division U.S. Department of Justice 1989-92. Chairman Michigan Sentencing Commission 1995-98.

Office: 811 Port Street, St. Joseph 49085-1187.
Telephone: (269) 983-7111.
Fax: (269) 982-8634
E-mail address: pmaloney@berriencounty.org

MALTBY, R. Terry *(Chief Judge, Sanilac County Probate Court)*

Office: 106 Courthouse, 60 West Sanilac Avenue, Sandusky 48471-1096.
Telephone: (810) 648-3221.

MANDERFIELD, Paula J. *(Judge, Michigan Circuit Court Thirtieth Judicial Circuit)* Elected to term beginning Jan 1, 2001. Term expires Dec 30, 2006. Currently serves as Presiding Judge Family Division. Also Judge, Michigan Court of Claims. Born Hancock Michigan. Educated at Michigan Technological University A.D. 1975, Michigan State University B.S. 1979 and Thomas M. Cooley Law School J.D. 1982. Admitted to practice Michigan 1982. In legal practice Lansing 1982-92. Former Judge and Chief Judge, Michigan District Court District Fifty-four A.

Mailing address: P.O. Box 19304, Lansing 48901-9304.
Office: Veteran's Memorial Courthouse, 313 West Kalamazoo Street, Lansing 48933.
Telephone: (517) 483-6500.
E-mail address: cc_manderfield@ingham.org

MANNING, Sheila Gibson *(Judge, Michigan Circuit Court Third Judicial Circuit)*

Office: 2A Lincoln Hall of Justice, 1025 East Forest Avenue, Detroit 48207.

MARABLE, Herman, Jr. *(Judge, Michigan District Court District Sixty-eight)* Elected Nov 7, 2000 to term beginning Jan 1, 2001. Term expires Jan 1, 2007. Born Flint Michigan Oct 4, 1962. Educated at Michigan State University James Madison College B.A. 1984 and The Ohio State University J.D. 1987.

Assistant District Attorney Allegheny County Pennsylvania 1991-93. Assistant Prosecuting Attorney Genesee County Michigan 1993-2000. Member Michigan District Judges Association, Association of Black Judges of Michigan, American Judges Association, State Bar of Michigan, Mallory-Scott-Vandyne, Genesee County and National (Judicial Council) Bar Associations. Vice President and Legal Redress Co-chair Michigan NAACP. Member Flint Neighborhood Coalition, Central Flint Optimist Club and Urban League of Flint. Interests include whitewater rafting, record collecting, map collecting, model railroading, cross country skiing, karaoke, golf, radio DXing and cable TV production.

Office: 630 South Saginaw Street, Flint 48502-1526.
Telephone: (810) 766-8985.
Fax: (810) 766-8967

MARCUS, James A. *(Chief Judge, Michigan District Court District Seventy-three A)* Former Chief Judge pro tem.

Office: Sanilac County Courthouse, 60 West Sanilac Avenue, Sandusky 48471.
Telephone: (810) 648-3250.

MARIETTI, William C. *(Judge, Michigan Circuit Court Fourteenth Judicial Circuit)* Former Judge and Chief Judge, Michigan District Court District Sixty. Former Judge and Chief Judge pro tem, Muskegon County Probate Court.

Office: Hall of Justice, 990 Terrace, Muskegon 49442-3357.
Telephone: (231) 724-6316.

MARKEY, Jane E. *(Judge, Michigan Court of Appeals)* Born Saginaw Michigan. Protestant. Educated at Michigan State University B.A. with high honors 1973 and Thomas M. Cooley Law School J.D. with honors 1981. Editor-in-Chief Thomas M. Cooley Law Review 1979-80. Law Clerk to Michigan Court of Appeals 1981-82. Admitted to practice Michigan 1981 and U.S. District Courts Western 1981 and Eastern 1990 Districts of Michigan. In legal practice Grand Rapids 1982-91. Former Judge, Michigan District Court District Sixty-one, elected to term beginning Jan 1, 1991.

Hearing Panelist Attorney Discipline Board since 1989. Member State Bar of Michigan, Grand Rapids, Federal and American Bar Associations. Instructor in Expert Witnesses 1989 and Tort Update 1990 Institute of Continuing Legal Education. Attended New Judge Seminar Michigan Judicial Institute. Recipient Award for service to Spanish speaking Americans SER Jobs for Progress 1974. Employed at Tri-City SER 1974-76 and Saginaw County Department of Social Services 1976-78.

Office: 201 The Law Building, 330 Ionia N.W., Grand Rapids 49503.
Telephone: (616) 456-1167.

MARKMAN, Stephen J. *(Justice, Michigan Supreme Court)* Appointed by Governor John Engler Sept 1999. Elected 2000, current term expires Dec 31, 2004. Born Detroit Michigan June 4, 1949. Educated at Duke University B.A. 1971 and University of Cincinnati J.D. 1974. Admitted to practice Michigan 1974, U.S. District Court Eastern District of Michigan 1985, U.S. Supreme Court 1986 and U.S. Court of Federal Claims 1987. In legal practice Detroit 1993-95. Judge, Michigan Court of Appeals Jan 23, 1995 to Sept 1999, appointed by Governor John Engler.

Assistant Attorney General U.S. Department of Justice 1985-89. U.S. Attorney Eastern District of Michigan 1989-93. Professor of Constitutional Law Hillsdale College since 1993. Fellow Michigan Bar Foundation. Member American Inns of Court. Chief Counsel Subcommittee on Constitution U.S. Senate 1978-85.

Mailing address: P.O. Box 30052, Lansing 48909.
Office: 525 West Ottawa Street, Lansing 48933.
Telephone: (517) 373-9449, 373-8160.

MARTIN-CLARK, Miriam B. *(Judge, Michigan District Court District Thirty-six)*

Office: 421 Madison Avenue, Suite 5072, Detroit 48226.
Telephone: (313) 965-2200.

MARTLEW, Jeffrey L. *(Chief Judge, Michigan Circuit Court Twenty-ninth Judicial Circuit)* Former Chief

MARTLEW, JEFFREY L.—*Continued*

Judge pro tem. Born Flint Michigan June 19, 1950. Protestant. Educated at University of Michigan B.A. 1972 and Thomas Cooley Law School J.D. 1976. Admitted to practice Michigan 1976 and U.S. District Court Eastern 1976 and Western 1979 Districts of Michigan. In legal practice Mount Morris 1976-78 and Dewitt 1979-84. Former Presiding Judge and Judge, Michigan District Court District Sixty-five Division Two, elected to term beginning Jan 1, 1985.

Member Michigan District Judges Association (Board of Directors, Chairman Government Liaison Committee since 1990), State Bar of Michigan, Ingham, Clinton County and American Bar Associations. Board of Education Flint 1972-73. Republican. Member Lions Club and Rotary Club.

Office: 4300 Courthouse, 100 East State Street, St. Johns 48879.

Telephone: (989) 224-5132.

MARTONE, Michael A. *(Judge, Michigan District Court District Fifty-two Division Four)*

Office: 520 West Big Beaver Road, Troy 48084.

Telephone: (248) 528-0400.

MASSIE, Joel L. *(Chief Judge, Gogebic County Probate Court)* Appointed by Governor John Engler to term beginning April 6, 1992. Elected Nov 3, 1992, Nov 8, 1994 and 2000. Current term expires Dec 31, 2006. Born Bessemer Michigan March 6, 1954. Lutheran. Educated at Western Michigan University B.S. with honors 1976 and Marquette University J.D. 1979. Staff member and Staff Editor Marquette Law Review 1977-79. Admitted to practice Michigan 1979, Wisconsin 1979 and U.S. District Courts Eastern 1979 and Western 1979 Districts of Wisconsin and Western District of Michigan 1985. In legal practice Hurley Wisconsin 1979-80 and Bessemer Michigan 1980-92.

City Attorney Bessemer Michigan 1981-92. Author Comment *State v. Stark* Marquette L. Rev. 1979. Instructor in Insurance Law Paralegal Program Gogebic Community College 1993-94. Member Michigan Probate Judges Association, State Bar of Michigan and Gogebic-Ontonagon Bar Association. Attended Annual Probate Judges Meetings and Michigan New Judges School Jan 1993. Recipient Distinguished Alumni Award from Bessemer Schools Football Program April 1992. President Bessemer Lions Club and Bessemer Centennial Committee. Member Sharon Lutheran Church Council, Bessemer Schools Advisory Committee and Gogebic County Economic Development Corporation. Enjoys coaching Boys Little League and Girls Grade School Basketball, fishing, grouse hunting, reading and watching competitive sports.

Office: Courthouse, 200 North Moore Street, Bessemer 49911.

Telephone: (906) 667-0421.

MATTSON, Ann E. *(Chief Judge, Michigan District Court District Fifteen)* Former Chief Judge pro tem.

Mailing address: P.O. Box 8650, Ann Arbor 48107-8650.

Office: Courthouse, 101 East Huron, Ann Arbor 48107.

Telephone: (734) 222-3276.

MAY, Richard W. *(Chief Judge, Michigan District Court District Ninety)*

Office: Charlevoix County Building, 301 State Street, Charlevoix 49720.

Telephone: (231) 547-7227.

MAYFIELD, Mabel Johnson *(Judge, Berrien County Probate Court)*

Office: Courthouse, 811 Port Street, St. Joseph 49085-1189.

Telephone: (269) 983-7111.

MAZUR, R. Darryl *(Judge, Michigan District Court District Twelve)*

Office: Jackson County Courthouse, 312 South Jackson Street, Jackson 49201.

Telephone: (517) 788-4260.

McARA, Michael D. *(Judge, Michigan District Court District Sixty-eight)*

Office: 630 South Saginaw Street, Flint 48502-1526.

Telephone: (810) 766-8968.

McBAIN, John G., Jr. *(Judge, Michigan Circuit Court Fourth Judicial Circuit)*

Office: Jackson County Courthouse, 312 South Jackson Street, Jackson 49201.

Telephone: (517) 788-4268.

McCABE, Mark C. *(Judge, Michigan District Court District Sixty-seven Division Four)* Former Chief Judge.

Office: 17100 Silver Parkway, Suite C, Fenton 48430.

Telephone: (810) 629-5318.

McCABE, Pamela J. *(Judge, Michigan District Court District Fifty-five)* Former Chief Judge and Chief Judge pro tem.

Office: 700 Buhl Drive, Mason 48854.

Telephone: (517) 676-8414.

McCANN, Kathleen J. *(Judge, Michigan District Court District Sixteen)* Elected Nov 7, 1994 to term beginning Jan 1, 1995. Reelected Nov 2000, current term expires Dec 31, 2006. Former Chief Judge. Born Highland Park Michigan July 26, 1950. Catholic. Educated at Hillsdale College B.A. 1973 and Detroit College of Law J.D. 1978. Admitted to practice Michigan 1979 and U.S. District Court Eastern District of Michigan 1986. In legal practice Livonia 1981-84 and Birmingham 1984-94.

Special Assistant Prosecutor Wayne County 1979-81. Member Wayne County District Judges Association, Michigan Judges Association, National Association of Women Judges and State Bar of Michigan (Legislative Committee since 1995, Judicial Response Committee since 1996). Member Mayor's Task Force on Families and Youth.

Office: 15140 Farmington Road, Livonia 48154-5498.

Telephone: (734) 466-2500.

McCARTHY, Kathleen M. *(Judge, Michigan Circuit Court Third Judicial Circuit)*

Office: 1507 Municipal Center, Two Woodward Avenue, Detroit 48226.

Telephone: (313) 224-5261.

McCREE, Wade H. *(Judge, Michigan District Court District Thirty-six)*

Office: 421 Madison Avenue, Suite 5071, Detroit 48226.

Telephone: (313) 965-2200.

McDONALD, John J. *(Judge, Michigan Circuit Court Sixth Judicial Circuit)* Appointed by Governor John Engler to term beginning Sept 3, 1993. Elected Nov 1994. Reelected to subsequent term. Current term expires Dec 2004. Currently serves as Presiding Judge General Jurisdiction. Born New Philadelphia Pennsylvania Aug 25, 1939. Catholic. Educated at University of Detroit 1961, Wayne State University 1965 and Detroit College of Law 1970. Admitted to practice Michigan 1970. In legal practice Farmington Hills 1970-93.

Assistant Prosecutor 1970-73. Member National Council of Juvenile and Family Court Judges, Michigan Judges Association, American Judges Association, Michigan State Bar and Oakland County Bar Association. Attended Annual Judicial Conference, Judicial Conference of Court of Appeals, Circuit and Probate Court Judges, Family Division Training Transition Seminar and Evidence Seminar. Enjoys golf, tennis, walking.

Office: Courthouse Tower Dept. 404, 1200 North Telegraph Road, Pontiac 48341-0404.

Telephone: (248) 858-0344.

McGRAW, Patrick J. *(Judge, Saginaw County Probate Court)* Appointed by Governor John Engler to term beginning Dec 6, 1999. Elected Nov 2000, current term expires Jan 2006. Currently serves as Chief Judge pro tem. Also serves Family Division Michigan Circuit Court Tenth Judicial Circuit. Born Detroit Michigan Feb 3, 1956. Catholic. Educated at Central Michigan University B.S. 1979 and Thomas M. Cooley Law School J.D. 1982. Member Phi Alpha Delta. Admitted to practice Michigan 1982, U.S. District Courts Eastern and Western Districts of Michigan and U.S. Court of Appeals Sixth Circuit. In legal practice Saginaw 1982-99.

Adjunct Instructor Legal Aspects of Health Care Administration Central Michigan University 1986-91. Member Michigan Defense Trial Counsel, Inc., Michigan Society of Hospital Attorneys, The Association of Trial Lawyers of America, Michigan Probate Judges Association, National Council of Juvenile and Family Court Judges, State Bar of Michigan (Family Law Section, Probate and Estate Planning Section, Bench and Bar Committee), Saginaw County (Bench and Bar Committee) and American Bar Associations. Named Local Legislator of the Year by Police Officers Association of Michigan 1994. Board of Trustees and Member Police Millage Committees Saginaw Township. Volunteer American Diabetes Association. Member Saginaw Township Little League, One Hundred Club of Saginaw, Knights of Columbus and Sons of the American Legion.

Office: County Governmental Building, 111 South Michigan Avenue, Saginaw 48602.

Telephone: (989) 790-5325.

Fax: (989) 790-5510

E-mail address: pmcgraw@saginawcounty.com

McIVOR, Marci B. *(Judge, United States Bankruptcy Court Eastern District of Michigan)* Appointed by U.S. Court of Appeals Sixth Circuit judges.

Office: 211 West Fort Street, Eighteenth Floor, Detroit 48226-3211.

Telephone: (313) 234-0010.

McKEAGUE, David W. *(Judge, United States District Court Western District of Michigan)* Appointed for life by President George Bush to term beginning Feb 28, 1992. Born Pittsburgh Pennsylvania Nov 5, 1946. Roman Catholic. Educated at University of Michigan B.B.A. 1968 J.D. 1971. Admitted to practice Michigan 1971, U.S. District Courts Western 1972 and Eastern 1978 Districts of Michigan, U.S. Court of Appeals Sixth Circuit 1988 and District of Columbia 1991. In legal practice Lansing Michigan 1971-92.

Adjunct Professor of Federal Courts Thomas M. Cooley Law School 1995-96 and 1998 and of Federal Jurisdiction Detroit College of Law since 1998. Chairman Committees on Alternate Dispute Resolution and Automation Western District of Michigan. President Detroit College of Law Chapter American Inns of Court. Member Defender Services Committee U.S. Judicial Conference. Fellow Michigan Bar Foundation. Member The Federalist Society, Bar Association of the District of Columbia, State Bar of Michigan and Federal Bar Association (Western Michigan Chapter). Chair District Judges Education Committee Federal Judicial Center. Named Boss of the Year Lansing Legal Secretaries Association 1977. Listed in *Who's Who in America, Who's Who in American Law, Who's Who of Emerging Leaders in America* and *The Best Lawyers in America.* Board of Governors Country Club of Lansing 1995-2001. President Wharton Center for the Performing Arts Michigan State University. Interests include golf, skiing, woodworking and renovation projects.

Office: 119 Federal Building, 315 West Allegan Street, Lansing 48933.

Telephone: (517) 377-1563.

E-mail address: mckeague@miwd.uscourts.gov

McKNIGHT, Gail *(Judge, Michigan District Court District Eighteen)* Appointed by Governor James J. Blanchard to term beginning Jan 1, 1985. Elected 1986, 1988, 1994 and 2000. Current term expires Dec 31, 2006. Former Chief Judge. Born Detroit Michigan July 31, 1945. Catholic. Educated at University of Detroit B.A. with honors 1967 and Wayne State University J.D. 1976. Admitted to practice Michigan 1977. Began legal practice Detroit 1977. Referee, Wayne County Probate Court 1981-84.

Assistant Prosecuting Attorney 1977-81. Member Zoning Board of Appeals 1974-78 and Westland City Council 1976-82. Member Society of Irish-American Lawyers, Wayne County District Judges Association (President), Michigan District Judges Association, National Association of Women Judges and Suburban Bar Association. Faculty Member and Instructor in "Child as a Witness," "Handling Child Sex Abuse Cases," "Landlord/Tenant," and "Traffic" Michigan Judicial Institute since 1982. Named Irishwoman of the Year 1981 and Westland Woman of the Year 1982. Previously worked as journalist. Democrat. Past President Board of Directors First Step (domestic violence agency). Board of Directors YMCA.

Office: 36675 Ford Road, Westland 48185-2297.

Telephone: (734) 595-8720.

McLAUGHLIN, Thomas P. *(Chief Judge, Clare-Gladwin Counties Probate Court District)* Appointed by Governor James J. Blanchard to term beginning Aug 20, 1990. Elected to subsequent term.

Mailing address: P.O. Box 96, Harrison 48625.

Office: Clare County Courthouse, 225 West Main Street, Harrison 48625.

Telephone: (989) 539-7109.

McMILLEN, Phyllis C. *(Chief Judge, Michigan District Court District Fifty-one)* Former Chief Judge pro tem.
Office: 5100 Civic Center Drive, Waterford 48329.
Telephone: (248) 674-4655.

McNALLY, Michael K. *(Judge, Michigan District Court District Thirty-three)* Former Chief Judge.
Office: 19000 Van Horn, Woodhaven 48183.
Telephone: (734) 671-0201.

MESTER, Fred M. *(Judge, Michigan Circuit Court Sixth Judicial Circuit)* Court Administrator/Judicial Assistant 1975-82. Appointed Judge by Governor William Grawn Milliken to term beginning June 1982. Elected 1984, 1990, 1996 and 2002. Current term expires Dec 31, 2008. Born Pontiac Michigan April 15, 1937. Presbyterian. Educated at Central Michigan University B.A. 1959 and Wayne State University Law School J.D. 1967. Honorary Doctor of Laws. Admitted to practice Michigan 1968 and U.S. District Court Eastern District of Michigan 1969.
Assistant U.S. Attorney and Chief Civil Division U.S. Attorney's Office 1969-75. Important Decision: People v. Michael Conat (declares statute regarding prosecutor discretion in charging juveniles). Instructor Oakland University, Madonna University and Oakland Community College 1983-2000. Member Michigan Judges Association, State Bar of Michigan, Oakland and Federal (President Detroit Chapter 1980) Bar Associations. Recipient Michigan Corrections Judicial Award for extraordinary contribution to enhancement of the judicial system 1990, Centennial Award from Central Michigan University and Earl W. Kintner Award from Federal Bar Association. Captain U.S. Army. Republican. Founder Reading to Reduce Recidivism. President Central Michigan University Alumni Association. Chairperson Oakland County NAACP 75th Anniversary Dinner.
Office: 404 Courthouse Tower, 1200 North Telegraph, Pontiac 48341-0404.
Telephone: (248) 858-0344.

METER, Patrick M. *(Judge, Michigan Court of Appeals)* Appointed by Governor John Engler 1999. Elected 2000 and 2002. Current term expires Jan 1, 2009. Educated at University of Notre Dame B.A. J.D. Former Judge, Michigan Circuit Court Tenth Judicial Circuit.
Prosecutor and Chief Assistant Prosecutor Saginaw County.
Mailing address: P.O. Box 30022, Lansing 48909-7522.
Office: 925 West Ottawa Street, Lansing 48915.
Telephone: (517) 373-6787.
Fax: (517) 373-6897

MIDDLETON, Jeffrey C. *(Judge, Michigan District Court District Three B)*
Mailing address: P.O. Box 67, Centreville 49032.
Office: Courthouse, 125 Main, Centreville 49032.
Telephone: (269) 467-5500.

MIEL, Charles H. *(Chief Judge, Michigan Circuit Court Eighth Judicial Circuit)* Former Chief Judge pro tem.
Office: Ionia County Courthouse, 100 Main Street, Ionia 48846.
Telephone: (616) 527-5315.

MILES, Wendell Alverson *(Senior Judge, United States District Court Western District of Michigan)* Appointed for life by President Richard M. Nixon to term beginning May 9, 1974. Former Chief Judge. Assumed Senior status 1986, serves by assignment. Born Holland Michigan April 17, 1916. United Methodist. Educated at Hope College A.B. 1938, University of Wyoming M.A. 1939 University of Michigan J.D. 1942, University of Paris, Sorbonne France 1945 and University of Heidelberg, Germany 1946. Awarded honorary LL.D. Hope College 1979 and Detroit College of Law 1980. Admitted to practice Michigan 1942, U.S. District Court Western District of Michigan 1953, U.S. Supreme Court 1954 and U.S. Courts of Appeals Sixth 1955 and Seventh 1963 Circuits. In legal practice Holland 1948-53 and Grand Rapids 1961-70. Judge, Michigan Circuit Court Twentieth Judicial Circuit June 1970 to May 1974. Acting Judge, Michigan Court of Appeals May 1973.
Prosecuting Attorney Ottawa County 1949-53. U.S. Attorney Western District of Michigan 1953-60. Special Counsel Grand Rapids School Board 1961-70 and City of Grand Rapids 1961-70. Special Trial Counsel Michigan Consolidated 1962-70. Ferris State College General Counsel 1965-70. Instructor in Business Law 1949-53 and American and English Constitutional History 1981-86 Hope College and American Institute of Banking 1953-60. Member American Trial Lawyers Association 1962-70 and Twentieth Judicial District Bar Association 1948-60 (President 1952). Fellow Michigan Bar Foundation and American Bar Foundation. Member American Judicature Society, State Bar of Michigan, Ottawa County (President 1950), Grand Rapids (Board of Directors 1963), Federal and American Bar Associations. Captain U.S. Army 1942-47. Trial Judge Advocate 1946-47. Employed by Michigan Department of Corrections summers 1938-1942. Republican. Vice Chair Michigan Higher Education Facilities Commission 1974-85. Chairman County Red Cross (Vice Chairman 1951-52, Fund Chairman 1951-52). Vice Chairman Chippewa District Boy Scouts 1951-52. Holland Board of Education 1951-63 (President 1961-63). Member Peninsular Club, Macatawa Bay Yacht Club, Junior Chamber of Commerce 1948-52, Western Michigan Law Enforcement Association 1953-65, Grand Rapids Chamber of Commerce 1954-62, Holland Chamber of Commerce 1954-70, Grand Rapids YMCA 1955-67, Grand Rapids University of Michigan Club 1955-70 and Holland Area Schools Study Committee 1956-57. Holland Board of Governors University of Michigan Club 1957-64. Department Judge Advocate American Legion 1959-60. Enjoys golf, tennis, skiing, travel and history.
Office: 236 Federal Building, 110 Michigan Street N.W., Grand Rapids 49503.
Telephone: (616) 456-2314.

MILHOUSE, Donna R. *(Judge, Michigan District Court District Thirty-six)*
Office: 421 Madison Avenue, Suite 3072, Detroit 48226.
Telephone: (313) 965-2200.

MILLER, Donald G. *(Judge, Michigan Circuit Court Sixteenth Judicial Circuit)*
Office: Macomb County Court Building, 40 North Main, Mount Clemens 48043-5654.
Telephone: (586) 469-5143.

MILLER, Stephen Barry *(Judge, Michigan Circuit Court Thirty-seventh Judicial Circuit)* Currently serves as Chief Judge pro tem. Born London England Oct 8, 1945. Member St. Philip's Catholic Church. Educated at Kellogg Community College 1963-66, Michigan State University B.A. in History 1967, Michigan State University Graduate School of Education 1968-69 and Wayne State University J.D. 1973. Admitted to practice Michigan 1973. In legal practice Battle Creek 1975-77. Judge 1977-86 and Chief Judge Jan 1, 1980 to Dec 31, 1983, Michigan District Court District Ten, appointed by Governor William G. Milliken.

Staff Attorney Calhoun County Legal Aid Society 1973-74. Assistant Prosecuting Attorney Calhoun County 1974-75. Member The Association of Trial Lawyers of America, Michigan Trial Lawyers Association, State Bar of Michigan (Criminal Law and Negligence Law Sections), Calhoun County (Past Treasurer) and American (Judicial Administration Division) Bar Associations. Former Member National District Attorneys Association and Michigan Prosecuting Attorneys Association. First Lieutenant Michigan Air National Guard 1969-75. Coordinated Teacher Education Project of Legal Aid Society for Battle Creek Public Schools. Former Member National Catholic Education Association and Christian Education Association.

Office: Calhoun County Justice Center, 161 East Michigan Avenue, Battle Creek 49014-4066.

Telephone: (269) 969-6510.

MOISEEV, Susan M. *(Judge, Michigan District Court District Forty-six)* Appointed by Governor James J. Blanchard to term beginning May 27, 1986. Elected Nov 1986, 1988, 1994 and 2000. Current term expires Dec 31, 2006. Former Chief Judge and Chief Judge pro tem. Born Detroit Michigan Feb 18, 1950. Educated at University of Michigan B.A. 1971 and University of Detroit J.D. 1976. Admitted to practice Michigan 1977. In legal practice Detroit 1977-81 and Southfield 1981-86.

Former Chief Counsel Civil Division Legal Aid and Defenders Association Detroit. Instructor in Legal Assistants Program Mercy College of Detroit 1981-82. Member B'nai B'rith Barristers, Women Lawyers Association of Michigan (Secretary 1984-85, Second Vice President 1985-86), Michigan District Judges Association, Oakland County District Judges Association, National Association of Women Judges (District Director), State Bar of Michigan, Southfield, Oakland County and American Bar Associations. Attended New Judges Seminar 1987, Regional Judicial Seminar 1987 and 1988, Judicial Leadership Seminar 1988 and District Court Caseflow/Project Management Seminar 1988 Michigan Judicial Institute; Civil Evidence Seminar The National Judicial College May 1987; and Annual Meetings Michigan District Judges Association and National Association of Women Judges. Board Member Jewish Federation Apartments, Jewish Vocational Service, Women's Division Jewish Welfare Federation, Anti-Defamation League and Women Lawyer's Association Foundation.

Mailing address: P.O. Box 2055, Southfield 48037-2055.

Office: 26000 Evergreen Road, Southfield 48076.

Telephone: (248) 796-5800.

MONAGHAN, John R. *(Chief Judge, St. Clair County Probate Court)* Former Chief Judge pro tem.

Office: 216 County Building, 201 McMorran Boulevard, Port Huron 48060.

Telephone: (810) 985-2066.

MONTON, Anthony A. *(Chief Judge, Michigan Circuit Court Twenty-seventh Judicial Circuit)* Chief Judge since Jan 1, 2003.

Office: M-34 Oceana County Building, 100 South State Street, Hart 49420.

Telephone: (231) 873-3977.

MOORE, Eugene Arthur *(Judge, Oakland County Probate Court)* Elected to term beginning Jan 1967. Reelected Nov 1974, 1980, 1986, 1992 and 1998. Current term expires Dec 31, 2004. Former Chief Judge and Chief Judge pro tem. Former Presiding Judge Family Division. Born Royal Oak Michigan Oct 12, 1935. Member Christ Church of Cranbrook (Senior Warden). Educated at University of Michigan B.B.A. 1957 LL.B. 1960.

Author "Delinquency Prevention Sourcebook" and "Youth Service Bureaus" American Judicature Society; "Supplement to the New Justice for Children and Families"; "The Story of Camp Oakland, Inc."; "1984 Michigan Court Rules—Probate and Juvenile"; and "Waiver to Adult Court" Michigan Bar Journal. Co-author "Marriage, Divorce and Separation" and "Probate Practice" Pocket Supplements. Former Assistant Professor of Juvenile Law and Probate Procedure Detroit College of Law. Former Member Governor's Crime Commission and State of Michigan Youth Advisory Commission. Member Governor's Committee of Children's Justice. Board of Fellows National Center for Juvenile Justice. Member National Council of Juvenile and Family Court Judges (Past President), Michigan Probate Judges Association (Past President), National College of Probate Judges, State Bar of Michigan (Former Chairman Juvenile Law Committee, Criminal Law Section Council and Crime Prevention Center Committee), Oakland County and American Bar Associations. Faculty Member National College for Juvenile and Family Court Judges and Michigan Judicial Institute. Former Chairman Birmingham Youth Assistance Committee. Past President and Former Chairman Children's Charter of the Courts of Michigan, Inc. Former Member Board of Directors Big Brothers of Oakland County. Former Director STARR Commonwealth. Board of Governors Cranbrook Schools. Director Camp Oakland, Inc. (Executive Committee), Youth Assistance Advisory Council, Boys' Club of Pontiac (Past President) and Cranbrook Educational Community.

Office: Courthouse Tower Dept. 449, 1200 North Telegraph Road, Pontiac 48341-0457.

Telephone: (248) 858-0290.

MOORE, Marion A. *(Judge, Michigan District Court District Thirty-six)*

Office: 421 Madison Avenue, Suite 3071, Detroit 48226.

Telephone: (313) 965-2200.

MOORE, Warfield, Jr. *(Judge, Michigan Circuit Court Third Judicial Circuit)* Assumed office Oct 1, 1997. Term expires Dec 31, 2008. Born Chicago Illinois March 5, 1934. Protestant. Educated at University of Michigan A.B. 1957 and Wayne State University LL.B. with honors 1960. Recipient Graduate and Professional Scholarship 1959-60. Editor Wayne Law Review 1958-

MOORE, WARFIELD, JR.—*Continued*

60. Member Tau Epsilon Rho and Kappa Alpha Psi. Admitted to practice Michigan 1961. Began legal practice Detroit 1961. Judge, Recorder's Court of Detroit Jan 1, 1979 to Sept 30, 1997.

Member State Bar of Michigan, Wolverine and National Bar Associations. Graduate Search and Seizure Course The National Judicial College, Reno Nevada.

Office: 921 Municipal Center, Two Woodward Avenue, Detroit 48226.

Telephone: (313) 224-5261.

MORGAN, Virginia M. *(Magistrate Judge, United States District Court Eastern District of Michigan)* Appointed by U.S. District Court judges to term beginning 1985. Reappointed 1993 and May 1, 2001. Current term expires 2009. Educated at University of Michigan B.S. 1968 and University of Toledo J.D. 1975. Salutatorian. Admitted to practice Michigan 1975, U.S. District Court Eastern District of Michigan 1975 and U.S. Court of Appeals Sixth Circuit 1979.

Assistant Prosecuting Attorney 1976-79. Assistant U.S. Attorney 1979-85. Honorary Member Michigan Patent Law Association. Member Michigan Women Lawyers, National Association of Women Judges, State Bar of Michigan and Federal Bar Association. Instructor Attorney General Trial Advocacy Institute, Washington D.C. 1982-84 and Michigan ICLE 1985. Attended Criminal Tax Seminar, Labor Law seminars American Bar Association and various civil practice seminars Attorney General Advocacy Institute.

Office: 651 U.S. Courthouse, 231 West Lafayette Boulevard, Detroit 48226.

Telephone: (313) 234-5210.

MORRIS, Melinda *(Judge, Michigan Circuit Court Twenty-second Judicial Circuit)* Former Chief Judge.

Mailing address: P.O. Box 8645, Ann Arbor 48107-8645.

Office: Courthouse, 101 East Huron, Ann Arbor 48104.

Telephone: (734) 222-3386.

MORROW, Bruce U. *(Judge, Michigan Circuit Court Third Judicial Circuit)* Assumed office Oct 1, 1997. Former Judge, Recorder's Court of Detroit.

Office: 404 Hall of Justice, 1441 St. Antoine Street, Detroit 48226.

Telephone: (313) 224-0415.

MORSE, Patricia A. *(Judge, Michigan District Court District Eighty-seven)* Elected to term beginning Jan 1, 1991. Reelected 1996 and 2002. Current term expires Dec 31, 2008. Former Chief Judge and Chief Judge pro tem. Born Trenton Michigan Aug 29, 1948. Catholic. Educated at Jacksonville University B.A. 1970 and Wayne State University J.D. 1982. Admitted to practice Michigan 1982 and U.S. Court of Appeals Sixth Circuit 1983. In legal practice Detroit 1982-83 and Gaylord 1983-90.

Member Forty-sixth Circuit Bar Association (Family Support Council 1986-90, Law and Education Partnership 1990-93 and President 1991-93). Seminar Instructor in sentencing and strategic planning Michigan Judicial Institute. Seminar Instructor in enforcement of child support orders Family Support Council. Board of Directors D.A.R.E. Member Kalkaska Domestic Violence Task Force.

Office: Alpine Center, Suite 1C, 800 Livingston Boulevard, Gaylord 49735.

Telephone: (989) 731-0205.

MOSKWA, Pamela A. *(Chief Judge, Monroe County Probate Court)* Former Chief Judge pro tem.

Office: Courthouse, 106 East First Street, Monroe 48161.

Telephone: (734) 240-7160.

MULHAUSER, Frederick R. *(Chief Judge, Emmet-Charlevoix Counties Probate Court District)*

Office: Emmet County Courthouse, 200 Division Street, Petoskey 49770.

Telephone: (231) 348-1765.

MULLALLY, Neil G. *(Chief Judge, Muskegon County Probate Court)* Also serves as Presiding Judge Family Division Michigan Circuit Court Fourteenth Judicial Circuit.

Office: Hall of Justice, 990 Terrace Street, Muskegon 49442.

Telephone: (231) 724-6241.

MURPHY, Dennis F. *(Judge, Michigan Circuit Court Forty-sixth Judicial Circuit)* Former Chief Judge pro tem.

Office: City-County Bldg., 225 West Main Street, Gaylord 49735.

Telephone: (989) 732-6484.

MURPHY, John A. *(Judge, Michigan Circuit Court Third Judicial Circuit)* Judge, Common Pleas Court of Detroit 1979 to Aug 31, 1981. Former Judge, Michigan District Court District Thirty-six, assumed office Sept 1, 1981.

Office: 1411 Municipal Center, Two Woodward Avenue, Detroit 48226.

Telephone: (313) 224-5261.

MURPHY, William B. *(Judge, Michigan Court of Appeals)* Appointed by Governor James J. Blanchard 1988. Elected to subsequent terms. Current term expires Jan 1, 2007. Former Chief Judge pro tem. Educated at Michigan State University and Wayne State University J.D. Law Clerk to Michigan Court of Appeals.

Chairman Judicial Tenure Commission.

Office: State Office Building, 350 Ottawa N.W., Grand Rapids 49503.

Telephone: (616) 456-1167.

MURRAY, Christopher M. *(Judge, Michigan Court of Appeals)* Born Newton Massachusetts Feb 14, 1964. Catholic. Educated at Hillsdale College B.A. 1985 and University of Detroit School of Law J.D. 1990. Member Federalist Society. Admitted to practice Michigan 1990, U.S. District Court Eastern District of Michigan 1990, U.S. Court of Appeals Sixth Circuit 1991 and U.S. Supreme Court 1994. In legal practice Detroit 1990-2000. Former Judge, Michigan Circuit Court Third Judicial Circuit, appointed by Governor John Engler to term beginning Jan 10, 2000.

Deputy Legal Counsel to Governor John Engler 1995-97. Author "Privatization and Collective Bargaining" *Michigan Public Employment and Labor Relations* 1994 and "State—Tribal Relations: A Legal Perspective" Michigan B. Jour. 1996. Member State Bar of Michigan and The Detroit Metropolitan Bar Association. Chair

MURRAY, CHRISTOPHER M.—*Continued*

State Board of Ethics 1997-2000. Member Local Government Claims Review Board 1998-2000.

Office: 14-300 Cadillac Place, 3020 West Grand Boulevard, Detroit 48202-6020.

Telephone: (313) 972-5720.

MYLES, William F. *(Judge, Michigan Circuit Court Twenty-third Judicial Circuit)*

Mailing address: P.O. Box 658, Tawas City 48764-0658.

Office: County Building, 422 Lake, Tawas City 48763.

Telephone: (989) 362-3485.

NANCE ADAMS, Lydia *(Judge, Michigan District Court District Thirty-six)*

Office: 421 Madison Avenue, Suite 4074, Detroit 48226.

Telephone: (313) 965-2200.

NEFF, Janet T. *(Judge, Michigan Court of Appeals)* Elected 1988. Reelected to subsequent terms. Current term expires Jan 1, 2007. Educated at University of Pittsburgh and Wayne State University J.D. Law Clerk to Michigan Court of Appeals.

Commissioner Michigan Supreme Court. Assistant U.S. Attorney. Assistant City Attorney Grand Rapids. Special Assistant Attorney General.

Office: Five Lyon Street N.W., Suite 624, Grand Rapids 49503.

Telephone: (616) 456-1167.

NEILSON, Susan Bieke *(Judge, Michigan Circuit Court Third Judicial Circuit)* Appointed by Governor John Engler to term beginning July 10, 1991. Elected Nov 1992, 1996 and 2002. Current term expires Dec 31, 2008. Born Ann Arbor Michigan Aug 27, 1956. Roman Catholic. Educated at University of Michigan B.A. with high honors 1977 and Wayne State University J.D. cum laude 1980. Member Wayne Law Review 1978-79. Member Phi Beta Kappa. Admitted to practice Michigan 1980. In legal practice Detroit 1980-91.

Member Women Lawyers Association of Michigan, Catholic Lawyers Society, Irish American Lawyers Society and State Bar of Michigan. Named International Woman of Distinction by Soroptimists 1994. Member Soroptimist International Service Organization and Explorer Scouts of Detroit.

Office: 1607 Municipal Center, Two Woodward Avenue, Detroit 48226.

Telephone: (313) 224-5261.

NEITHERCUT, Geoffrey L. *(Judge, Michigan Circuit Court Seventh Judicial Circuit)* Currently serves as Presiding Judge Research and Technology. Born Ann Arbor Michigan Feb 11, 1948. Interdenominational. Educated at Albion College B.A. 1970, Colgate Rochester Divinity School 1971-73 and University of Detroit Law School 1975. Former Judge and Former Chief Judge, Michigan District Court District Sixty-eight, appointed by Governor James J. Blanchard to term beginning April 7, 1986.

Office: Genesee County Courthouse, 900 South Saginaw Street, Flint 48502.

Telephone: (810) 257-3252.

NELSON, Allen J. *(Chief Judge, Genesee County Probate Court)* Former Chief Judge pro tem.

Office: 900 South Saginaw Street, Flint 48502.

Telephone: (810) 257-3533.

NELSON, Charles A. *(Chief Judge, Michigan Circuit Court Fourth Judicial Circuit)* Appointed by Governor John Engler 1992. Elected 1994 and 2000. Current term expires 2006. Former Chief Judge pro tem. Born Blue Island Illinois Dec 23, 1931. Educated at Carleton College B.A. 1953 and University of Michigan J.D. 1956. Admitted to practice Michigan 1956. In legal practice Jackson 1959-1992.

U.S. Army JAGC 1957-59.

Office: 312 South Jackson Street, Jackson 49201.

Telephone: (517) 768-8521.

Fax: (517) 788-4361

E-mail address: cnelson@co.jackson.mi.us

NELSON, Thomas E. *(Judge, Berrien County Probate Court)*

Office: Courthouse, 811 Port Street, St. Joseph 49085-1189.

Telephone: (269) 983-7111.

NETTLES-NICKERSON, Beverley *(Judge, Michigan Circuit Court Thirtieth Judicial Circuit)* Elected Nov 5, 2003 to term beginning Jan 3, 2003. Term expires Dec 31, 2008. Also Judge, Michigan Court of Claims. First black female judge in Ingham County. Born Detroit Michigan. Baptist. Educated at Michigan State University B.A. 1979, Bowling Green State University M.A. 1981 and Thomas M. Cooley Law School J.D. 1983. Finalist Client Counseling Competition 1982. Recipient Martin Luther King Scholarship and American Jurisprudence Award in Administrative Law. Listed in *Who's Who of American Law Students.* Law Clerk to Hon. Michael F. Cavanagh, Michigan Supreme Court Dec 1983 to Aug 1985. Member Alpha Kappa Alpha. Admitted to practice Michigan 1984. In legal practice Lansing Aug 1985 to Jan 1986. Administrative Law Examiner, Michigan Department of Corrections Jan 1986 to March 1987. Judge, Michigan District Court District Fifty-four A 1991-2002.

Legal Methods Instructor Thomas M. Cooley Law School 1983 and 1984 and Criminal Justice Instructor Davenport College since Sept 1987 and Lansing Community College since June 1988. Fellow Michigan State Bar Foundation. Member Justice Advisory Committee Ingham County Circuit Court, Community Corrections Board Ingham County, Lansing Black Lawyers Association, Women Lawyers Association of Mid-Michigan (President 1995), Association of Black Judges, State Bar of Michigan (Communications Committee, Committee on Criminal Justice), Wolverine and Ingham County (President 1996-97, Chair Public Relations Committee) Bar Associations. Research Analyst Michigan House of Representatives March 1987 to Nov 1987. Assistant Legal Advisor to Governor James J. Blanchard Nov 1987 to Dec 1990. Board of Directors Central Branch YMCA, Cooley Law School Alumni Association and Legal Aid of Central Michigan. Honorary Board Member American Cancer Society. Advisory Board Pro Bono Lawyers Service. Sponsor Boy Scouts of America. Mentor City of Lansing Schools. Member United Negro College Fund, NAACP, Site Committee Ronald McDonald House, LINKS, Inc., Police Athletic League, Ingham

NETTLES-NICKERSON, BEVERLEY—*Continued*

County Community Corrections Board and UNCF. Interests include golfing, reading and aerobics.

Office: Veteran's Memorial Courthouse, 313 West Kalamazoo Street, Lansing 48933.

Telephone: (517) 483-6500.

NEWCOMBE, Scott J. *(Judge, Michigan District Court District Seventy-four)* Appointed by Governor William Grawn Milliken to term beginning April 4, 1979. Elected 1980, 1986, 1992 and 1998. Current term expires Dec 31, 2004. Former Chief Judge. Born Bay City Michigan Nov 16, 1941. Presbyterian. Educated at Bay City Junior College 1961, Central Michigan University B.S.Ed. 1964 and Wayne State University J.D. 1967. Admitted to practice Michigan 1968. Began legal practice Bay City 1968.

Member Bay City Board of Education 1970-74. Former Member Delta College Board of Trustees.

Office: 1230 Washington Avenue, Bay City 48708.

Telephone: (989) 895-4230.

NICHOLS, Rudy J. *(Judge, Michigan Circuit Court Sixth Judicial Circuit)*

Office: Courthouse Tower Dept. 404, 1200 North Telegraph Road, Pontiac 48341-0404.

Telephone: (248) 858-0344.

NICHOLSON, David C. *(Chief Judge, Michigan District Court District Seventy-two)* Former Chief Judge pro tem.

Office: 201 McMorran Boulevard, Port Huron 48060.

Telephone: (810) 985-2072.

NICHOLSON, Julie A. *(Chief Judge, Michigan District Court District Fifty-two and Judge, Michigan District Court District Fifty-two Division Three)* Elected Judge Nov 1996 to term beginning Jan 2, 1997. Reelected 2002, current term expires Dec 31, 2008. Currently serves as Presiding Judge Division Three. Born Detroit Michigan Dec 27, 1960. Catholic. Educated at Michigan State University B.A. 1983 and Detroit College of Law J.D. cum laude 1987. Member Phi Alpha Delta. Staff member Detroit College of Law Review. Admitted to practice Michigan 1987 and U.S. District Court Eastern District of Michigan 1987. In legal practice Birmingham, Troy and Auburn Hills 1987-97.

Fellow Oakland Bar Foundation and Michigan State Bar Foundation. Member Local Intergovernmental Advisory Council Michigan Supreme Court. Member Michigan District Judges Association, American Judicial Association, Women Lawyers Bar Association, State Bar of Michigan, Oakland County (Alternative Dispute Resolution Committee, Bench/Bar Organizational Committee, Blue Ribbon Committee for the Public Advisory Committee), Rochester County and American Bar Associations. Guest Lecturer Walsh College of Business and on Environmental Law Issues Detroit Edison Company. Instituted Court in the Schools/Critical Life Choices Program. Member Rochester Community Coalition, Auburn Hills Coalition for the Prevention of Substance Abuse and Oakland County Coordinating Council Against Domestic Violence. Volunteer American Cancer Association and Rainbow Connection. Enjoys skiing, rollerblading, reading and traveling.

Office: 135 Barclay Circle, Rochester Hills 48307-5800.

Telephone: (248) 853-5553.

NOBLE, Richard E. *(Chief Judge, Michigan District Court District Eighty-two)*

Mailing address: P.O. Box 365, West Branch 48661.

Office: Ogemaw County Building, West Branch 48661.

Telephone: (989) 345-5040.

NOECKER, James P. *(Chief Judge, Michigan Circuit Court Forty-fifth Judicial Circuit)*

Mailing address: P.O. Box 189, Centreville 49032.

Office: Courthouse, 125 Main, Centreville 49032.

Telephone: (269) 467-5500.

NOLAN, Michael Jeffrey *(Judge, Michigan District Court District Sixty)* Former Chief Judge.

Office: Hall of Justice, 990 Terrace Street, Muskegon 49442-3377.

Telephone: (231) 724-6283.

NORDSTROM, Robert P. M. *(Chief Judge, Montmorency County Probate Court)* Elected to term beginning Jan 1, 1977. Reelected 1982, 1988, 1994 and 2000. Current term expires Dec 31, 2006. Born Detroit Michigan Sept 4, 1946. Member United Church of Christ. Educated at Michigan State University B.A. in Political Science 1968 and Detroit College of Law J.D. 1971. Admitted to practice Michigan 1971. Began legal practice Detroit 1971.

Member Michigan Probate Judges Association and State Bar of Michigan. Member Lewiston Lions Club. Enjoys golf, bowling and softball.

Mailing address: P.O. Box 789, Atlanta 49709.

Office: M-32 Courthouse, Atlanta 49709.

Telephone: (989) 785-8064.

NORTH, Thomas B. *(Chief Judge, Luce-Mackinac Counties Probate Court District)* Appointed by Governor John Engler to term beginning Nov 20, 1992. Elected 1994 and 2000. Current term expires Dec 31, 2006. Born Battle Creek Michigan March 2, 1956. Methodist. Educated at Western Michigan University B.B.A. 1977 and Thomas M. Cooley Law School J.D. 1981. Admitted to practice Michigan 1982, U.S. District Courts Western 1982 and Eastern 1983 Districts of Michigan and U.S. Courts of Appeals Federal 1986, Sixth 1991 and District of Columbia 1992 Circuits. In legal practice St. Ignace and Cheboygan 1981-92.

Fellow Michigan State Bar Foundation. Member State Bar of Michigan (Law Day Committee 1990-92) and American Bar Association. Enjoys downhill skiing, basketball and bicycling.

Office: 15 Mackinac County Courthouse, 100 South Marley Street, St. Ignace 49781.

Telephone: (906) 643-7303.

NYE, Michael E. *(Chief Judge, Hillsdale County Probate Court)* Appointed by Governor John Engler to term beginning July 26, 2002. Chief Judge since Jan 1, 2003.

Office: Courthouse, 29 North Howell, Hillsdale 49242.

Telephone: (517) 437-4643.

NYKAMP, Wesley J. *(Judge, Michigan Circuit Court Twentieth Judicial Circuit)* Elected to term beginning Jan 1, 1991. Reelected 1996 and 2002. Current term expires Dec 31, 2008. Former Chief Judge pro tem and Chief Judge. Born Grand Rapids Michigan Sept 30, 1940. Christian. Educated at Hope College B.A. 1962 and Wayne State University J.D. cum laude 1967. Admitted to practice Michigan 1968.

NYKAMP, WESLEY J.—*Continued*

Chief Assistant Prosecutor Kent County May 1966 to Dec 31, 1974. Prosecutor Ottawa County Jan 1, 1975 to Dec 31, 1990.

Office: Ottawa County Building, 414 North Washington Street, Grand Haven 49417.

Telephone: (616) 846-8320.

OAKLEY, Brian A. *(Judge, Michigan District Court District Thirty-four)*

Office: 11131 Wayne Road, Romulus 48174.

Telephone: (734) 941-4462.

O'BANNER-OWENS, Jeanette *(Judge, Michigan District Court District Thirty-six)* Appointed by Governor James J. Blanchard to term beginning 1988. Presiding Judge Civil Division Feb 1990 to Feb 1993. Educated at Wayne State University B.Ph. 1976 J.D. 1979. Moot Court. Law Clerk to U.S. Attorney's Office, Detroit June 1978 to Jan 1979. Member Phi Alpha Delta.

Deputy Defender Criminal Division and Chief Counsel Civil Division Legal Aid and Defender Association, Inc. Sept 1979 to May 1988. Contributor documentary film "No Law Without Lawyers" State Bar of Michigan. Member Judicial Conference (Treasurer, Board Member), Michigan District Judges Association (Past President, Board Member), American Judges Association, State Bar of Michigan, Detroit, Wolverine, National, Federal and American Bar Associations. Attended Anglo-American Law and England Studies courses Cambridge University, England and Master of Judicial Studies Program The National Judicial College and Supreme Court Update course John F. Kennedy School of Government Harvard Law School. Faculty Advisor The National Judicial College. Mediator Negotiation Competition Wayne State University. Moot Court Judge Wayne State University and University of Detroit. Listed in *Who's Who in America* Silver Edition since 1977, *Who's Who in Law Enforcement, International Who's Who of Professionals, Marquis' Who's Who, Who's Who Sterling* and *Who's Who International.* Organizer Michigan District Court District Thirty-six Law Day. Participant Wayne County Criminal Advocacy Program. Member Friends of Wayne Medical School, Founders Society Detroit Institute of the Arts, Downtown Detroit Lions Club and Beaulahland Temple No. 569 Elks.

Office: 421 Madison Avenue, Suite 3068, Detroit 48226.

Telephone: (313) 965-2200.

O'BRIEN, Colleen A. *(Judge, Michigan Circuit Court Sixth Judicial Circuit)*

Office: Courthouse Tower, 1200 North Telegraph Road, Pontiac 48341-0404.

Telephone: (248) 858-0344.

O'BRIEN, Daniel Patrick *(Judge, Michigan Circuit Court Sixth Judicial Circuit)*

Office: Courthouse Tower, 1200 North Telegraph Road, Pontiac 48341-0404.

Telephone: (248) 858-0344.

O'CONNELL, Peter D. *(Judge, Michigan Court of Appeals)* Elected 1994. Reelected 2000, current term expires Jan 1, 2007. Educated at Western Michigan University, Detroit College of Law J.D. and University of Nevada Reno M.J.S. Former Judge, Michigan District Court District Seventy-six, elected to term beginning Jan 1, 1979.

Former Chief Assistant Prosecutor Isabella County.

Mailing address: P.O. Box 30022, Lansing 48909-7522.

Office: Hall of Justice, Second Floor, 925 West Ottawa Street, Lansing 48915.

Telephone: (517) 373-0786.

ODETTE, Christopher *(Chief Judge, Michigan District Court District Sixty-seven and Judge, Michigan District Court District Sixty-seven Division Four)*

Office: 8173 South Saginaw Street, Suite 4B, Grand Blanc 48439.

Telephone: (810) 694-2552.

O'MEARA, John Corbett *(Judge, United States District Court Eastern District of Michigan)* Appointed for life by President Bill Clinton to term beginning Oct 4, 1994. Born Hillsdale Michigan Nov 4, 1994. Educated at University of Notre Dame A.B. with honors 1955 and Harvard Law School LL.B. 1962. Chairman Blue Circle Honor Society. Admitted to practice Michigan 1963, U.S. District Court Eastern District of Michigan 1963, U.S. Court of Appeals Sixth Circuit 1964 and U.S. Supreme Court 1965. In legal practice Detroit 1962-94.

Instructor University of Detroit School of Law 1965-70. Fellow American College of Trial Lawyers. Life Member Sixth Circuit Judicial Conference, Michigan Bar Foundation and American Bar Foundation. Member State Bar of Michigan, Detroit Metropolitan and American Bar Associations. USN Submarine Service 1955-59. Commander USNR 1959-70.

Office: 257 U.S. Courthouse, 231 West Lafeyette Boulevard, Detroit 48226.

Telephone: (313) 234-5140.

OSTER, J. Craigen *(Chief Judge, Michigan District Court District Forty)* Assumed office 1978. Elected to subsequent terms. Former Chief Judge pro tem. Born Stratton Ontario Canada Sept 9, 1924. Roman Catholic. Educated at University of Western Ontario B.A. with honors in Philosophy 1947 and University of Detroit LL.B. 1957. Admitted to practice Michigan 1958. Began legal practice Detroit 1958. In legal practice Mount Clemens 1967. Judge, St. Clair Shores Municipal Court 1970-78.

Member Macon County Bar Association. Canadian Officers Training Corps 1943-44. Member Macomb County Board of Commissioners 1968-70, Macomb County Democratic Party and St. Clair Shores Democratic Voters League.

Office: 27701 Jefferson Avenue, St. Clair Shores 48081.

Telephone: (586) 445-5280.

OSTERHAVEN, Calvin E. *(Judge, Michigan Circuit Court Fifty-sixth Judicial Circuit)*

Office: Eaton County Courthouse, 1045 Independence Boulevard, Charlotte 48813.

Telephone: (517) 543-7500.

O'SULLIVAN, Pamela Gilbert *(Chief Judge, Macomb County Probate Court)* Elected to term beginning Jan 1, 1995. Reelected 2000, current term expires Jan 1, 2007. Former Chief Judge pro tem. Former Presiding Judge Juvenile Division. Educated at University of Detroit B.S. cum laude 1980, Thomas M. Cooley Law School J.D. 1983 and Boston University School of Law

O'SULLIVAN, PAMELA GILBERT—*Continued*

LL.M. in Taxation 1984. Moot Court Quarter Finalist 1982. National Appellate Advocacy Team 1982-83. Member Delta Theta Phi and Order of Barristers. Admitted to practice U.S. District Court District of Michigan and U.S. Tax Court. In legal practice Mt. Clemens 1986-88 and 1990-95 and Port Huron 1989-90.

Instructor in Real Estate Law and Business Law Macomb County Community College 1990-95. Member Michigan Probate Judges Association, National Probate Judges Association, State Bar of Michigan (Taxation Section), Macomb County and American Bar Associations. Member Juvenile Law and Adoptions Committee Macomb County Child Advocacy Center.

Office: 21850 Dunham Road, Mount Clemens 48043.
Telephone: (586) 469-7149.
Fax: (586) 783-0971

OWENS, Donald S. *(Judge, Michigan Court of Appeals)* Appointed by Governor John Engler to term beginning Dec 1, 1999. Elected Nov 2000, current term expires Dec 31, 2004. Born Ann Arbor Michigan Dec 25, 1943. Educated at Oberlin College and University of Michigan A.B. with distinction 1966 M.B.A. with distinction 1967 J.D. 1969. Admitted to practice Michigan 1969 and U.S. District Court Western District of Michigan 1969. Began legal practice Lansing 1969. Judge Feb 8, 1974 to Nov 30, 1999, Former Chief Judge pro tem and Chief Judge, Ingham County Probate Court, appointed by Governor William G. Milliken.

Past President Ingham County Trial Judges Association and Michigan Probate Judges Association. Former Chair Judicial Conference State Bar of Michigan. Lecturer Michigan Judicial Institute since 1978. Considered authority on law of child abuse and neglect in Michigan.

Mailing address: P.O. Box 30022, Lansing 48909.
Office: 925 West Ottawa Street, Lansing 48915.
Telephone: (517) 373-9854.

OXHOLM, Maria L. *(Judge, Michigan Circuit Court Third Judicial Circuit)* Serves Civil Division. Former Judge, Michigan District Court District Thirty-six.

Office: 901 Municipal Center, Two Woodward Avenue, Detroit 48226.
Telephone: (313) 224-5261.

PAJTAS, Richard M. *(Chief Judge, Michigan Circuit Court Thirty-third Judicial Circuit)*

Office: Charlevoix County Building, 301 State Street, Charlevoix 49720.
Telephone: (231) 547-7243.

PARKER, Marla E. *(Chief Judge, Michigan District Court District Forty-seven)* Former Chief Judge pro tem.

Office: 32795 West Ten Mile Road, Farmington 48336-2364.
Telephone: (248) 477-5630.

PARROTT, David M. *(Judge, Michigan District Court District Thirty-four)*

Office: 11131 Wayne Road, Romulus 48174.
Telephone: (734) 941-4462.

PARSONS, Charles *(Chief Judge, Missaukee County Probate Court)* Elected Nov 7, 2000 to term beginning Jan 1, 2001. Term expires Dec 31, 2006.

Mailing address: P.O. Box 800, Lake City 49651.
Office: 111 South Canal Street, Lake City 49651.
Telephone: (231) 839-2266.

PARUK, Paul J. *(Chief Judge, Michigan District Court District Thirty-one)* Former Chief Judge pro tem.

Office: 3401 Evaline Avenue, Hamtramck 48212.
Telephone: (313) 876-7710.

PASSENGER, Don *(Judge, Michigan District Court District Sixty-one)* Appointed by Governor John Engler to term beginning April 1, 1995. Elected Nov 6, 1996 and 1998. Current term expires Dec 31, 2004. Born Morristown New Jersey April 2, 1960. Educated at University of Michigan B.S. 1983 and University of Notre Dame J.D. cum laude 1986. Admitted to practice Michigan 1986. In legal practice Grand Rapids 1986-95.

Member State Bar of Michigan, Grand Rapids and American Bar Associations. Hobbies include computers and water sports.

Office: 8D Kent County Courthouse, 180 Ottawa Avenue N.W., Grand Rapids 49503-2751.
Telephone: (616) 632-5700.

PASULA, Angela *(Judge, Michigan District Court District Five)*

Office: Berrien County Courthouse, 811 Port Street, St. Joseph 49085-1188.
Telephone: (269) 983-7111.

PAVLICH, Scott L. *(Chief Judge, Michigan Circuit Court Fifty-third Judicial Circuit)* Appointed by Governor John Engler to term beginning March 31, 1998. Elected Nov 1998, current term expires Jan 1, 2005. Born Flint Michigan June 14, 1951. Methodist. Educated at Michigan State University B.S. 1973 and Detroit College of Law J.D. 1978. Admitted to practice Michigan 1978, U.S. District Courts Eastern 1978 and Western 1979 Districts of Michigan and U.S. Court of Appeals Sixth Circuit 1981. In legal practice Detroit 1978-80 and Cheboygan 1981-98.

Member State Bar of Michigan and Cheboygan Bar Association (President 1982-84). Former Chairman Administrative Board St. Paul's United Methodist Church. President Cheboygan Soccer Association. Enjoys family, sports and outdoor activities.

Mailing address: P.O. Box 70, Cheboygan 49721.
Office: 870 South Main Street, Cheboygan 49721.
Telephone: (231) 627-8818.

PEARSON, Glenn A. *(Chief Judge, Michigan District Court District Ninety-four)* Chief Judge since Jan 1, 2003.

Office: 310 Ludington Street, Escanaba 49829.
Telephone: (906) 789-5106.

PEPE, Steven D. *(Magistrate Judge, United States District Court Eastern District of Michigan)* Appointed by U.S. District Court judges to term beginning Dec 2, 1983. Reappointed Dec 1991 and Dec 1999. Current term expires Dec 2007. Born Indianapolis Indiana Jan 29, 1943. Educated at University of Notre Dame B.A. cum laude in Government and Political Science 1965, University of Michigan Law School J.D. magna cum laude 1968, London School of Economics and Political Science 1970-72 and Harvard Law School LL.M. 1974. Assistant Editor Michigan Law Review 1967-68. Law Clerk to Hon. Harold Leventhal, U.S. Court of Appeals District of Columbia Circuit 1968-69. Recipient Reginald Heber Smith Community Lawyer Fellowship 1969-70, Michigan-Ford International Studies Fellowship 1970-72 and Harvard Law School Clinical Teaching Fellowship 1972-73. Member Order of the Coif.

PEPE, STEVEN D.—*Continued*

Staff Attorney Neighborhood Legal Services Program Washington D.C. 1969-70. Consultant to Office of Services to the Aging Lansing 1976-77, Administration on Aging Department of Health and Human Services Washington D.C. 1976-78, Legal Services Corporation Office of Program Support 1978-79, Educational Testing Service Princeton New Jersey 1979-80, Administration on Aging Biregional Older American Advocacy Assistance Resource and Support Center Ann Arbor 1979-81 and Board of Directors Center of Social Gerontology 1988-93. Author "Compensation for Curtailment of Life Expectancy as a Separate Element of Damages" 65 Michigan L. Rev. 786, 1967, "A Security Interest in the 'Proceeds' Does Not Include Insurance Proceeds" 65 Michigan L. Rev. 1514, 1967, "Lay Control and Organizational Complexity Render Legal Service Corporation Unacceptable to New York Court" 65 Michigan L. Rev. 389, 1967, "Is There a Doctor in the House? Opening Reflections on the Involvement of Psychiatrists in Michigan's Legal Clinic" VII Newsletter of the Council on Legal Education for Professional Responsibility, Inc. Dec 1974, "The Clinical Law Experiment, Michigan's First Five Years" 20 Law Quad Notes 10, 1975, "British Housing Law" Master's Thesis Harvard Law School 1976, "The Clinical Law Experiment, Goals, Methods and Problems" 20 Law Quad Notes 13, 1976, "Reassessing Law Schooling" 53 New York University L. Rev. 586, 1978, "Interim Report and Preliminary Findings to the American Bar Association on the Study on the Standards of Legal Negotiations" Feb 1983, "Professional Responsibility in Pretrial Discovery: A Tale of Two Cities" 64 No. 3 Michigan B. Jour. March 1985, "Clinical Legal Education: Is Taking Rites Seriously a Fantasy, Folly or Failure?" 18 Michigan Journal of Law Reform 307, 1985, "Social Security Disability Law in the Ninth and Tenth Circuits: A Compendium for Training and Practice" Sept 1986, "Social Security Disability Law in the First, Second, Third and District of Columbia Circuits: A Compendium for Training and Practice" Sept 1986, "Social Security Disability Law in the Fourth, Fifth and Eleventh Circuits: A Compendium for Training and Practice" Sept 1986, "Social Security Disability Law in the Sixth, Seventh and Eighth Circuits" Jan 1987 and update May 1988 and "Working With Questionably Competent Clients: Ethical Dilemmas in Lawyering with Anne Burns and Cecille Lindgren of The Center for Social Gerontology" 4 Nos. 2 and 3 Dec 1990 and 5 No. 1 April 1991 *Best Practice Notes*, reprinted in II No. 10 May 1991, II No. 11 June 1991 and III No. 7 Feb 1992 *The ElderLaw Report* Little Brown & Co.

Co-author with Professor C. C. Brown "Landlord and Tenant Law for the District of Columbia" Legal Services Corporation 1970, with Professor Donald G. Hagman "English Planning Law" 11 Harvard Jour. of Legislation 557, 1974 and "On Delivery of Legal Assistance to Older Persons" 4 Nos. 2 and 3 Best Practice Notes Dec 1990. Author course materials on "Legal Problems of the Aging" ICLE 1976, "Income Maintenance for the Elderly and Disabled" 1977, "Welfare System" 1977, "Legal Profession and Professional Responsibility" 1978-83, "Legal Services Training Materials on Negotiation" Legal Services Corporation 1979, "Introduction to Legal Negotiation" 1981, "Judicial Conduct for the 80's" Michigan Judicial Institute 1982 and "Social Security Disability" Federal Judicial Center 1994. Clinical Teaching Fellow Harvard Law School 1972-74. Professor of Law and Director Michigan Clinical Law Program University of Michigan Law School 1974-83. Adjunct Professor of Law Detroit Mercy School of Law 1985. Lecturer University of Michigan Law School 1985-97. Lecturer and Instructor in legal ethics, legal rights of the elderly, social security disability, trial advocacy and legal negotiations for Michigan Judicial Institute, Michigan ICLE, State Bar of Michigan, National Institute for Trial Advocacy, American Inns of Court XI, The National Conference on Law and Aging and The Center for Social Gerontology.

Mailing address: P.O. Box 7150, Ann Arbor 48107-7150.

Telephone: (734) 741-2298.

PERRY, John R. *(Judge, Michigan District Court District Thirty-six)* Appointed by Governor William G. Milliken to term beginning Feb 1, 1982. Elected 1986, 1992 and 1998. Current term expires Dec 31, 2004. Born Wyandotte Michigan Jan 11, 1931. Educated at University of Detroit LL.B. 1958. Member Gamma Eta Gamma. Admitted to practice Michigan 1958. Began legal practice Detroit 1958.

Special Assistant Attorney General 1969-82. Member State Bar of Michigan, Detroit and American Bar Associations. Airman USAF 1952-54.

Office: 421 Madison, Suite 4067, Detroit 48226.

Telephone: (313) 965-8735.

PERRY, Nathaniel C., III *(Chief Judge, Michigan District Court District Sixty-eight)* Elected to term beginning Jan 1, 1991. Reelected 1996 and 2002. Current term expires Dec 31, 2008. Born Memphis Tennessee March 14, 1947. Baptist. Educated at Fisk University B.A. 1969, Eastern Michigan University M.A. with honors 1978 and Texas Southern University J.D. 1982. Member Phi Delta Kappa. Admitted to practice Michigan 1985 and U.S. District Court Eastern District of Michigan 1988. In legal practice Flint 1988-90.

Office: 630 South Saginaw Street, Flint 48502-1526.

Telephone: (810) 766-8968.

PEZZETTI, Elizabeth M. *(Judge, Oakland County Probate Court)*

Office: Courthouse Tower Dept. 449, 1200 North Telegraph Road, Pontiac 48341-0457.

Telephone: (248) 858-0290.

PHILLIPS, Thomas J. *(Judge, Michigan District Court District Eighty-six)*

Office: Courthouse, 328 Washington Street, Traverse City 49684.

Telephone: (231) 922-4580.

PICKARD, Timothy P. *(Judge, Michigan Circuit Court Thirty-ninth Judicial Circuit)*

Office: Judicial Building, 425 North Main Street, Adrian 49221.

Telephone: (517) 264-4597.

PIERCE, Lynne A. *(Chief Judge, Grosse Pointe Shores and Grosse Pointe Woods Municipal Courts)*

Office: 20025 Mack Avenue, Grosse Pointe Woods 48236.

Telephone: (313) 343-2455.

PIKKARAINEN, A. John *(Chief Judge, Michigan District Court District Fifty-three)* Elected to term beginning Jan 1, 1989. Reelected 1994 and 2000. Current

PIKKARAINEN, A. JOHN—*Continued*

term expires Dec 31, 2006. Chief Judge 1990-91 and since Jan 1, 1994. Former Chief Judge pro tem. Born Detroit Michigan April 30, 1944. Lutheran. Educated at Michigan State University B.A. 1966 and Wayne State University J.D. 1969. Admitted to practice Michigan 1969 and U.S. District Courts Eastern and Western Districts of Michigan. In legal practice Howell 1971-88.

Chief Assistant Prosecutor and Special Assistant Prosecutor Livingston County. Member Michigan District Judges Association, American Judges Association, State Bar of Michigan (Fellow) and Livingston County Bar Association (Treasurer). President, Vice President and Member Fowlerville Community School Board. Past President and Past Vice President Howell Chamber of Commerce. Committee Chair American Cancer Society. Enjoys golf and hunting.

Office: 204 South Highlander Way, Suite 1, Howell 48843.

Telephone: (517) 548-1000.

PITTMAN, Gregory Christopher *(Judge, Muskegon County Probate Court)*

Office: Hall of Justice, 990 Terrace Street, Muskegon 49442.

Telephone: (231) 724-6241.

PITTS, Frances *(Judge, Wayne County Probate Court)* Former Presiding Judge Juvenile Division.

Office: 3B Lincoln Hall of Justice, 1025 East Forest Avenue, Detroit 48207.

Telephone: (313) 833-0667.

PLATZER, Cynthia Siemen *(Judge, Michigan District Court District Seventy-two)*

Office: 201 McMorran Boulevard, Port Huron 48060.

Telephone: (810) 985-2072.

PLAWECKI, Mark J. *(Judge, Michigan District Court District Twenty)* Former Chief Judge.

Office: 6045 Fenton, Dearborn Heights 48127.

Telephone: (313) 277-7480.

POPKE, Lita Masini *(Judge, Michigan Circuit Court Third Judicial Circuit)*

Office: 907 Municipal Center, Two Woodward Avenue, Detroit 48226.

Telephone: (313) 224-5261.

POST, Edward R. *(Chief Judge, Michigan Circuit Court Twentieth Judicial Circuit)* Former Chief Judge pro tem. Former Judge, Michigan District Court District Fifty-eight.

Office: Ottawa County Building, 414 North Washington Street, Grand Haven 49417.

Telephone: (616) 846-8320.

POST, Kenneth David *(Judge, Michigan District Court District Fifty-eight)* Elected to term beginning Jan 1, 1981. Reelected 1986, 1992 and 1998. Current term expires Dec 31, 2004. Former Chief Judge pro tem. Born Cincinnati Ohio March 29, 1944. Protestant. Educated at Dordt College B.A. 1967 and University of Arkansas J.D. 1971. Member Delta Theta Phi. Admitted to practice Michigan 1971.

City Attorney Grand Rapids April 1971 to Nov 1971. Assistant Prosecuting Attorney Kent County Nov 1971 to March 1975 and Ottawa County March 1975 to Dec 1980. Member Michigan District Judges Association (Board Member, Treasurer 1986, Secretary 1987, Vice President 1988), National Judges Association, State Bar of Michigan (Treasurer and Secretary since 1985 Judicial Section), Kent County and Ottawa County Bar Associations. Student Michigan Judicial Institute 1981 and Courts of Limited Jurisdiction Seminar The National Judicial College Nov 1983. Recipient Milwe Award in Judicial Ethics 1970. E-4 U.S. Army 1967-69. Previously employed as construction work laborer, insurance policy rater and postal service worker during the Army. Member Navigators, Zeeland Chamber of Commerce, Hudsonville City Chamber of Commerce, Central Wesleyan Church, Holland Arts Counsel, Holland Area Counsel on Alcohol and Zeeland Historical Society. Interests include woodworking, fishing, dancing, hunting, classical music, reading and gardening.

Office: 3100 Port Sheldon Road, Hudsonville 49426.

Telephone: (616) 662-3100.

POTTS, Wendy Lynn *(Judge, Michigan Circuit Court Sixth Judicial Circuit)*

Office: Courthouse Tower, 1200 North Telegraph Road, Pontiac 48341-0404.

Telephone: (248) 858-0344.

POWER, Thomas G. *(Judge, Michigan Circuit Court Thirteenth Judicial Circuit)* Former Chief Judge.

Office: Courthouse, 328 Washington Street, Traverse City 49684.

Telephone: (231) 922-4701.

POWERS, Dennis N. *(Judge, Michigan District Court District Fifty-two Division One)* Appointed by Governor John Engler to term beginning May 21, 1998. Elected 2000, current term expires Dec 31, 2006. Presiding Judge Division One since Jan 2000. Born Detroit Michigan 1942. Christian. Educated at University of Detroit A.B. 1964 M.A. 1968 and Detroit College of Law J.D. 1974. Admitted to practice Michigan 1975, U.S. Supreme Court 1981 and U.S. Courts of Appeals Sixth 1984 and Eleventh 1990 Circuits. In legal practice 1975 to May 1998.

Legal Counsel Royal Oak School Administrators 1975-79 and Michigan Association of School Placement Personnel 1975-81. Oakland County Commissioner 1993 to May 1998. Member Michigan District Judges Association, State Bar of Michigan, Oakland County (Chair District Court Committee 1995-96 and Diversity Committee 1996-97, Member Committee for the Unauthorized Practice of Law, Committee to Evaluate Judicial Candidates and Committee to Review Proposed Court Rules) and Federal Bar Associations. Attended "Advanced Evidence" National Judicial College Oct 25-30, 1998 and Judicial Workshop Michigan Judicial Institute Jan 1-7, 1999. Recipient Keep Michigan Beautiful Award from Governor John Engler 1992. USMCR Jan 19, 1961 to Dec 23, 1963. Teacher and Coach 1964-68. With General Motors 1968-71. Member 1993 to May 1998 Oakland County Republican Executive Committee (1998 Finance Team 1997 to May 1998). Precinct Delegate 1986-97. Trustee Highland Township Library Board 1981-92 and Charter Township of Highland since 1987 (Chair Solid Waste Committee since 1987, Member The Zoning Board of Appeals). Former Member Michigan Township Associations and National Association of Counties (Transportation and Aviation Committee, Criminal Justice Committee). Member Environmental Committee Michigan Association of Counties 1993 to May 1998, Highland Business Association, Huron Valley Chamber of Commerce since 1990 (Second Vice Presi-

POWERS, DENNIS N.—*Continued*

dent 1996, President since 1998) and Federalist Society. Private Pilot with multi-engine and instrument ratings. Avid camper and outdoorsman.

Office: 48150 Grand River Avenue, Novi 48374.
Telephone: (248) 305-6504.
Fax: (248) 305-9968
E-mail address: powersd@co.oakland.mi.us

PUGH, Douglas A. *(Chief Judge, Alpena County Probate Court)*

Office: 4 Alpena County Office Building, 719 West Chisholm Street, Alpena 49707.
Telephone: (989) 354-8827.

QUIST, Gordon Jay *(Judge, United States District Court Western District of Michigan)* Appointed for life by President George Bush to term beginning Aug 29, 1992. Born Grand Rapids Michigan Nov 12, 1937. Religious affiliation: Christian Reformed. Educated at Michigan State University B.A. 1959 and George Washington University National Law Center J.D. with honors 1962. Research Editor George Washington Law Review 1961-62. Member Phi Delta Phi and Order of the Coif. Admitted to practice District of Columbia 1962, Illinois 1964, U.S. District Courts Northern District of Illinois 1964 and Western District of Michigan 1967, U.S. Supreme Court 1965, Michigan 1967 and U.S. Court of Appeals Sixth Circuit 1967. In legal practice Washington D.C. 1962-64, Chicago Illinois 1964-66 and Grand Rapids Michigan 1966-92.

Vice Chairperson Business Law Section State Bar of Michigan 1991-92. Former Member American Bar Association. Member Code of Conduct Committee for U.S. Courts. Fellow Michigan State Bar Foundation. Member American Judicature Society and Federal Bar Association. Recipient Distinguished Alumnus Award from George Washington University Law School 1998. Former Board of Directors Wedgewood Acres Christian Youth Home 1968-74. Board of Directors Christian Reformed Publications 1968-78 and 1982-88, Indian Trails Camp 1970-78 and 1982-88 (President 1978, 1988), Better Business Bureau 1972-80, Mary Free Bed Hospital 1979-88, Opera Grand Rapids 1986-92, Mary Free Bed Brace Shop 1988-92 and Calvin Theological Seminary 1992-93. Enjoys travel and reading.

Office: 482 Federal Building, 110 Michigan Street N.W., Grand Rapids 49503.
Telephone: (616) 456-2253.

RADZIBON, Kenneth A. *(Chief Judge, Presque Isle County Probate Court)*

Mailing address: P.O. Box 110, Rogers City 49779.
Office: Courthouse, 151 East Huron Avenue, Rogers City 49779.
Telephone: (989) 734-3268.

RANDON, Mark A. *(Judge, Michigan District Court District Thirty-six)*

Office: 421 Madison Avenue, Suite 5072, Detroit 48226.
Telephone: (313) 965-2200.

RANSOM, Robert M. *(Chief Judge, Michigan Circuit Court Seventh Judicial Circuit)* Appointed by Governor William Grawn Milliken to term beginning April 26, 1977. Elected 1978, 1984, 1990, 1996 and 2002. Current term expires Dec 31, 2008. Born Flint Michigan May 26, 1938. Episcopalian. Educated at Flint Junior College Associate General Education degree with honors 1958, Adrian College B.A. cum laude 1959 and Detroit College of Law J.D. cum laude 1962. Highest scholastic average each year of law school. Admitted to practice Michigan 1962. Began legal practice Flint 1962.

Flushing City Attorney 1964-77. Author "Selected Materials for Civil Trial Practice" 1975 and "Opinion re: Plat Requirements" Municipal L. Jour. 1973. Instructor Thomas M. Cooley Law School 1973. Member State Bar of Michigan, Genesee County and American Bar Associations. Member Flushing Board of Education 1967-73 (President 1971-72) and Flushing Charter Commission.

Office: Genesee County Courthouse, 900 South Saginaw Street, Flint 48502.
Telephone: (810) 257-3252.

RASHID, James J. *(Judge, Michigan Circuit Court Third Judicial Circuit)* Elected to term beginning Jan 1, 1987. Reelected 1992 and 1998. Current term expires Dec 31, 2004. Former Chief Judge. Born Detroit Michigan March 5, 1954. Catholic. Educated at University of Notre Dame B.A. in Government 1976 and Detroit College of Law J.D. cum laude 1980. Admitted to practice Michigan 1980 and U.S. District Court Eastern District of Michigan 1980.

Commissioner Wayne County Jan 1979 to Dec 1982. Board of Commissioners Wayne County (Vice Chairman 1982, Member Public Safety and Judiciary Committee, Ways and Means Committee and Southeast Michigan Council of Governments). Member Michigan Judges Association, State Bar of Michigan (Sections: Public Corporation Law and Family Law), Dearborn and Detroit Bar Associations. Lecturer Annual Scientific Meeting Michigan Medical Society 1985.

Office: 1111 Municipal Center, Two Woodward Avenue, Detroit 48226.
Telephone: (313) 224-5261.

RATNER, Marvin *(Judge, Michigan District Court District Ten)* Former Chief Judge pro tem.

Office: Calhoun County Justice Center, 161 East Michigan Avenue, Battle Creek 49014-4066.
Telephone: (269) 969-6666.

RAVEN, Mark D. *(Chief Judge, Mason County Probate Court)*

Office: Mason County Courthouse, 304 East Ludington Avenue, Ludington 49431-0186.
Telephone: (231) 843-8666.

RECK, Susan L. *(Chief Judge, Livingston County Probate Court)* Also serves as Chief Judge, Michigan Circuit Court Forty-fourth Judicial Circuit.

Office: 5 Courthouse, 204 South Highlander Way, Howell 48843.
Telephone: (517) 546-3750.

REDFORD, James Robert *(Judge, Michigan Circuit Court Seventeenth Judicial Circuit)*

Office: Kent County Courthouse, 180 Ottawa Avenue N.W., Grand Rapids 49503-2751.
Telephone: (616) 632-5480.

REDMOND, Norene S. *(Judge, Eastpointe Municipal Court)*

Office: 16101 Nine Mile Road, Eastpointe 48021.
Telephone: (586) 445-5020.

REED, Gary K. *(Chief Judge, Calhoun County Probate Court)* Former Chief Judge pro tem.

Office: Justice Center, 161 East Michigan Avenue, Battle Creek 49014-4066.

Telephone: (269) 969-6794.

RHODES, Steven W. *(Chief Judge, United States Bankruptcy Court Eastern District of Michigan)* Also Chief Judge, Bankruptcy Appellate Panel Sixth Circuit. Selected by the Judicial Council of the Sixth Circuit. Born New York New York Dec 27, 1948. Jewish. Educated at Purdue University B.S.M.E. 1970 and University of Michigan J.D. 1972. Law Clerk to Hon. John Feikens, U.S. District Court Eastern District of Michigan 1973. Admitted to practice Michigan 1973. Began legal practice Detroit 1974. In legal practice Ann Arbor 1977-81. Former Magistrate Judge, U.S. District Court Eastern District of Michigan.

Member State Bar of Michigan and Federal Bar Association.

Office: 211 West Fort Street, Suite 1800, Detroit 48226-3211.

Telephone: (313) 234-0020.

ROBBINS, Kevin F. *(Judge, Michigan District Court District Thirty-six)*

Office: 421 Madison Avenue, Detroit 48226.

Telephone: (313) 965-2200.

ROBERTS, Ramona M. *(Judge, Michigan District Court District Sixty-eight)* Former Chief Judge and Chief Judge pro tem.

Office: 630 South Saginaw Street, Flint 48502-1526.

Telephone: (810) 766-8968.

ROBERTS, Victoria A. *(Judge, United States District Court Eastern District of Michigan)* Appointed for life by President Bill Clinton to term beginning Aug 11, 1998. Born Detroit Michigan Nov 25, 1951. Educated at University of Michigan B.A. 1973 and Northeastern University J.D. 1977. In legal practice Michigan 1977-85 and Detroit 1988-98.

Assistant U.S. Attorney Eastern District of Michigan 1985-88.

Office: 123 U.S. Courthouse, 231 West Lafayette Boulevard, Detroit 48226.

Telephone: (313) 234-5230.

ROBERTSON, Marvin E. *(Chief Judge, Clinton County Probate Court)* Appointed by Governor William G. Milliken March 5, 1979. Elected to subsequent terms. Also serves as Presiding Judge Family Division Michigan Circuit Court Twenty-ninth Judicial Circuit since 1998. Born Anderson Indiana Aug 13, 1942. Roman Catholic. Member St. Joseph's Catholic Church (Deacon). Educated at College of St. Francis B.A. 1965 and Detroit College of Law J.D. 1976. Admitted to practice Michigan 1976. Began legal practice St. Johns 1976. In legal practice Lansing 1976-79.

Assistant Prosecutor Clinton County May 1976 to Nov 1976. With Office of Attorney General Medicaid Fraud Unit Nov 1976 to Feb 1977. Chief Attorney Ingham County Prosecutor Family Support Unit Feb 1977 to March 1979. Instructor in Juvenile Law Michigan State Police Academy Aug 1980. Adjunct Professor of Juvenile Law 1981-90 and Chaplain Thomas More Society since 1994 Thomas M. Cooley Law School. Adjunct Professor of Law and Faculty Advisor Thomas More Society Detroit College of Law. President Central Michigan Probate Judges Association 1985-86. Member State Courthouse Evaluation Advisory Committee 1981, Advisory Committee Michigan Court Facilities Survey and Evaluation Project 1981, Executive Committee Michigan Coalition to Prevent Shoplifting 1982, Task Force on Reporting Traffic-Related Offenses 1987 and Children's Charter of the Courts of Michigan (Treasurer 1982-84). Fellow Michigan State Bar Foundation. Member Michigan Probate Court Judges Association (Chairman Legislative Committee 1983, Chairman ad hoc DSS Licensing Committee 1983, Member Permanency Planning Committee 1983, Juvenile Affairs Committee 1983, Salary and Retirement Committee 1983, Foster Care Rules Committee 1983, Children in Placement Committee 1983, Program of Education Committee 1983, Estate Code Revision Committee 1983, Juvenile Court Forms Revision Committee 1983-84, Juvenile Court Rules Committee 1984-87, Executive Board 1990-97, President 1995-96), State Bar of Michigan (Editor "Intercom" Probate Court Committee Newsletter 1983-90, Member Probate and Trust Law, Judicial and Family Law Sections, Executive Committee Judicial Conference) and Clinton County Bar Association (President 1985).

Instructor Annual Training Seminar Michigan Friend of the Court 1977. Faculty Member Office of Inspector General Training Programs 1977, Advanced Prosecutor Training Prosecuting Attorneys Association of Michigan 1978 and Michigan Judicial Institute 1983-92. Moot Court Advisor Thomas M. Cooley Law School 1987. Recipient Thomas More Award from Catholic Lawyers Guild 2000. Assistant Manager Buckner Finance Company Dec 1966 to Oct 1967 and Sun Finance Company Oct 1967 to Feb 1968. Counselor Credit Counseling Centers March 1968 to May 1969. Caseworker and Supervisor Oakland County Department of Social Services Aug 1969 to May 1976. Michigan Social Worker Certificate 1974. Investigator Certificate from Criminal Justice Institute April 1975. Assistant Area Chairman Clinton County Care Center Fund Drive 1979. Board of Directors Big Brothers/Big Sisters of Clinton County 1980, Michigan Chapter National Conference for the Prevention of Child Abuse and Neglect 1981-82 and Clinton County Council for the Prevention of Child Abuse and Neglect. President Catholic Lawyers Guild 1989-90. Foster Care Review Board 1982. Panelist Annual Meeting Michigan Association for Emotionally Disturbed Children 1986. Chairman Community Dispute Resolution Advisory Committee 1988-92. Board of Visitors Ave Maria Law School. Member Paine-Gillam-Scott Museum Advisory Board 1979-82, St. Johns Rotary Club (President 1984-85) and St. Johns Council Knights of Columbus. Enjoys travel, reading, music, swimming and grandchildren.

Office: Clinton County Courthouse, 101 East State Street, St. Johns 48879.

Telephone: (989) 224-5190.

ROBINSON, David S., Jr. *(Judge, Michigan District Court District Thirty-six)*

Office: 421 Madison Avenue, Suite 4074, Detroit 48226.

Telephone: (313) 965-2200.

RODGERS, Philip E., Jr. *(Chief Judge, Michigan Circuit Court Thirteenth Judicial Circuit)* Former Chief Judge pro tem.

Office: Courthouse, 328 Washington Street, Traverse City 49684.

Telephone: (231) 922-4701.

ROOT, Kathryn Joan *(Chief Judge, Oscoda County Probate Court)* Appointed by Governor James J. Blanchard Feb 23, 1987. Elected to term beginning Jan 1, 1989. Reelected 1994 and 2000. Current term expires Dec 31, 2006. Born Flint Michigan Aug 20, 1950. Catholic. Educated at University of Kansas 1968-69, University of Michigan B.A. 1973 and Thomas M. Cooley Law School J.D. 1977. Admitted to practice Michigan 1977. Began legal practice West Branch 1977.

Member Part-Time Probate Judges Ad Hoc Committee Michigan Supreme Court Nov 21, 1983 to July 5, 1984. Member Court Administration/Chief Judge Manual Committee June 30, 1987 to 1989, Michigan Court Forms Committee 1989 and Chair Juvenile Court Forms Committee 1989 State Court Administrator's Office. Member Judicial Assistance Committee 1990, Upper Michigan Lawyers Committee 1991-98, Children's Charter of the Courts of Michigan, Inc., Michigan Probate Judges Association (Member Child Care Fund Task Force 1992, Member Executive Board since 1993), Top of Michigan Probate Judges Association (Secretary-Treasurer 1990-91, Vice President 1992-93, President 1993-95) State Bar of Michigan (Assembly Representative 1980-85, Member 1981-85, Vice Chairperson 1982, Chairperson Committee on Rules and Calendar 1983-85; Member since 1997, Treasurer 2001-02 and Vice Chairperson 2002-03 Judicial Conference), Twenty-third Judicial Circuit and Thirty-fourth Judicial Circuit (Secretary-Treasurer 1980-81, Vice President 1981-82, President 1982-83) Bar Associations. Director Mitten Bay Girl Scout Council Saginaw 1977-84 (First Vice President 1982-84, Chairperson Program Facilities Committee 1984-85, Trustee Endowment Board since 1986), Contemplatives of St. Mary's on Mount Carmel Prescott since 1981 (Vice President since 1983), Upper Peninsula Legal Services Inc. since 1984 (Member Executive Committee since 1985, Vice President 1987-89, President since 1989) and River House Shelter since 1993. Chairperson Parish Financial Policies and Procedures Committee 1984-86 and Member 1984-94 Finance Council Gaylord Diocese. Member Timber Top Food Cooperative 1988-2002 (Secretary 1989-94, Chair), NEMCOG Regional Community Corrections Advisory Board 1989-93, Fairview Commons Lions since 1999, Friends of Steiner's Museum (Director since 1992, Secretary since 1992), Eagles Auxiliary, Kiwanis (Member 1990-97, Chair Program Committee 1990-91, Community Service 1992-93, Major Emphasis/Priority One 1993-94) and St. Mary's Catholic Church (Lector, Commentator and Eucharistic Minister 1977-92, Catechist 1977-92, Member Parish Finance Council since 1992). Enjoys gardening, spinning, hunting, reading, bowling and horseback riding.

Mailing address: P.O. Box 399, Mio 48647.

Office: Courthouse Annex, Court Street, Mio 48647.

Telephone: (989) 826-1107.

ROOT, Lawrence C. *(Chief Judge, Michigan Circuit Court Forty-ninth Judicial Circuit)* Elected to term beginning Jan 1, 1977. Reelected 1982, 1988, 1994 and 2000. Current term expires Dec 31, 2006. Born Hinsdale Illinois Dec 26, 1947. Educated at Ferris State College B.S. 1971 and University of Detroit J.D. 1975. Member Delta Sigma Pi. Admitted to practice Michigan 1975 and U.S. District Courts Eastern 1975 and Western 1975 Districts of Michigan. Began legal practice Big Rapids 1975.

Former Vice President Root Archery Company. Instructor in Business Law Ferris State College 1975-76. Important Decisions: Many cases involving labor law, the insanity defense, environmental law, oil and gas and complex commercial contracts. Member Michigan Judges Association (Executive Board since 1992, President 2002), State Bar of Michigan and American Bar Association. Enjoys fly-fishing and tying, photography, scuba diving, canoeing, skiing, snow-shoeing, hiking, shooting and other outdoor activities.

Mailing address: P.O. Box 822, Big Rapids 49307.

Office: Mecosta County Courthouse, 400 Elm Street, Big Rapids 49307.

Telephone: (231) 592-0780, 832-6155.

ROSEN, Gerald E. *(Judge, United States District Court Eastern District of Michigan)* Appointed for life by President George Bush to term beginning March 14, 1990. Born October 26, 1951. Educated at University of Stockholm, Sweden, Kalamazoo College B.A. 1973 and George Washington University National Law Center J.D. 1979. In legal practice Detroit May 1979 to March 1990. Sat by designation U.S. Court of Appeals Sixth Circuit 1991-2000, U.S. District Court Eastern District of New York 1992 and 1993, U.S. District Court Western District of Tennessee 1993 and U.S. District Court Northern District of Illinois.

Co-author "Lawyer's Advertising and Warranties: Caveat Advocatus" 64 American Bar Association Journal 867 June 1978, "Legal Advertising and Warranty Liability: Let the Lawyer Beware" Washington University Law Quarterly 443 Summer 1978 and "1983 Civil Procedure, Annual Survey of Michigan Law" 30 Wayne L. Rev. 273, 1984. Author "Labor Law Reform: Dead or Alive?" 57 University of Detroit Journal of Urban Law 1979 and "Title VII Classes and Due Process: To (b)(2) or Not to (b)(3)" 26 Wayne L. Rev. 919, 1980. Adjunct Professor of Evidence Law Wayne State University Law School since 1992 and University of Detroit School of Law 1994-98. Co-Chairman Judicial Evaluation Committee U.S. District Court Eastern District of Michigan May 1983 to 1988. Member Michigan Criminal Justice Commission 1985-87 and U.S. Judicial Conference on Criminal Law since 1995. Participant in Rule of Law Program U.S. State Department conferences Moscow Russia 1991 and T'Bilisi Georgia 1992. Lecturer on Evidence Workshop for Judges of the Sixth and Eighth Circuits Federal Judicial Center Jan 1994. Frequent Lecturer at CLE programs on variety of topics. Republican Candidate for U.S. Congress 1982. Chairman Republican Committee 17th Congressional District Feb 1983 to Feb 1985. Enjoys playing tournament tennis and squash.

Office: 802 U.S. Courthouse, 231 West Lafayette Boulevard, Detroit 48226.

Telephone: (313) 234-5135.

ROYSTER, C. Lorene *(Judge, Michigan District Court District Thirty-six)* Appointed by Governor James J. Blanchard to term beginning March 23, 1990. Elected to subsequent terms.

Office: 421 Madison Avenue, Suite 5073, Detroit 48226.

Telephone: (313) 965-2200.

RUCK, John C. *(Judge, Michigan Circuit Court Fourteenth Judicial Circuit)*
Office: Hall of Justice, 990 Terrace, Muskegon 49442-3357.
Telephone: (231) 724-6316.

RUMORA, Matthew R. *(Chief Judge, Grosse Pointe Farms Municipal Court)* Appointed by City Council to term beginning May 25, 1988. Elected Nov 1989, Nov 1993, Nov 1997 and 2001. Current term expires Dec 31, 2005. Born Detroit Michigan Dec 10, 1948. Catholic. Educated at Michigan State University B.A. with honors 1970 and University of Kentucky J.D. 1974. Law Clerk to Judge Charles M. Tackett, Kentucky Circuit Court Twenty-second Judicial Circuit 1973-74. Admitted to practice Michigan 1974 and U.S. District Court Eastern District of Michigan 1974. In legal practice St. Clair Shores 1975-2000.
Prosecuting Attorney Grosse Pointe Farms 1986-88. Instructor in Business Law Oakland County Community College 1976-78. Member Michigan Trial Lawyers Association, Michigan Association of Municipal Judges, American Judges Association, State Bar of Michigan and Macomb County Bar Association. USAR (honorable discharge 1976).
Office: 90 Kerby Road, Grosse Pointe Farms 48236.
Telephone: (313) 885-2104.

RUSH, William R. *(Judge, Michigan District Court District Seventy-six)* Former Chief Judge.
Office: 300 North Main Street, Mount Pleasant 48858.
Telephone: (989) 772-0911.

RYAN, Daniel P. *(Judge, Michigan Circuit Court Third Judicial Circuit)* Appointed by Governor John Engler to term beginning Dec 1998. Elected 2000, current term expires Jan 1, 2007. Educated at University of Detroit B.A. 1984, University of Notre Dame J.D. 1987 and University of Nevada M.J.S. 2000. Admitted to practice Indiana 1987 and Michigan 1989. Judge, Chief Judge pro tem and Chief Judge, Michigan District Court District Seventeen Aug 1994 to Dec 1998, appointed by Governor John Engler.
Office: 504 Hall of Justice, 1441 St. Antoine Street, Detroit 48226.
Telephone: (313) 224-5231.

SAAD, Henry William *(Judge, Michigan Court of Appeals)* Appointed by Governor John Engler 1994. Elected 1996 and 2002. Current term expires Dec 31, 2008. Educated at Wayne State University J.D. magna cum laude. In legal practice for 20 years.
Arbitrator Michigan Employment Relations Commission. Hearing Referee Michigan Department of Civil Rights. Member Governor's Task Force on Children's Justice. Board Member Detroit Public Television and American Heart Association.
Office: 760 American Center Building, 27777 Franklin Road, Southfield 48034-2055.
Telephone: (248) 353-6763.

SALOMONE, Geno *(Judge, Michigan District Court District Twenty-three)*
Office: 23511 Goddard Road, Taylor 48180-4197.
Telephone: (734) 374-1334.

SANDERSON, Donald L. *(Chief Judge, Michigan District Court District Two B)* Appointed by Governor William G. Milliken to term beginning Feb 21, 1978. Elected Nov 1978, 1984, 1990, 1996 and 2002. Current term expires Dec 31, 2008. Currently serves as Presiding Judge. Born East Chicago Indiana Aug 4, 1945. Educated at University of Michigan B.B.A. 1968 and Wayne State University J.D. 1974. Admitted to practice Michigan 1974. Began legal practice Hillsdale 1974.
Assistant Prosecuting Attorney Hillsdale County 1974-76. Instructor in Business Law Hillsdale College 1977. Member State Bar of Michigan and Hillsdale County Bar Association (President 1982-84). Lieutenant USN 1968-74. Member Hillsdale County Exchange Club (President 1985-86) and Hillsdale Arts Chorale (Business Manager 1976-78, Treasurer 1978-88, President 1988-92).
Office: 49 North Howell, Hillsdale 49242.
Telephone: (517) 437-7329.

SANTIA, Marco A. *(Judge, Michigan District Court District Thirty-nine)* Former Chief Judge pro tem and Chief Judge.
Office: 29733 Gratiot Avenue, Roseville 48066.
Telephone: (586) 773-2010.

SANTONI, Richard A. *(Judge, Michigan District Court District Eight Division Three)* Former Chief Judge pro tem.
Office: 227 West Michigan Avenue, Kalamazoo 49007-3757.
Telephone: (269) 384-8171.

SAPALA, Michael F. *(Judge, Michigan Circuit Court Third Judicial Circuit)* Assumed office Oct 1, 1997. Former Chief Judge. Serves Criminal Division. Born Portland Oregon Sept 26, 1942. Protestant. Educated at Wayne State University B.A. 1964 J.D. 1967 and New York University School of Law LL.M. 1968. Admitted to practice Michigan 1968, U.S. District Court Eastern District of Michigan 1968 and U.S. Court of Appeals Sixth Circuit. In legal practice Detroit 1969-78. Judge, Recorder's Court of Detroit Dec 12, 1978 to Sept 31, 1997.
President Detroit/Wayne County Criminal Advocacy Program 1985-87. Member Michigan Judges Association and National Association of Women Judges.
Office: Municipal Center, Two Woodward Avenue, Detroit 48226.
Telephone: (313) 224-5261.

SAUER, William R. *(Chief Judge, Michigan District Court District Forty-five A)*
Office: 3338 Coolidge, Berkley 48072.
Telephone: (248) 544-3300.

SAWICKI, Daniel *(Chief Judge, Michigan District Court District Forty-four)* Appointed by Governor William G. Milliken to term beginning Nov 3, 1980. Elected 1982, 1988, 1994 and 2000. Current term expires Dec 31, 2006. Former Chief Judge pro tem. Born Dearborn Michigan Nov 30, 1938. Catholic. Educated at University of Detroit B.S. 1962 J.D. 1968. Member Gamma Eta Gamma. Admitted to practice Michigan 1969, U.S. District Court Eastern District of Michigan 1976 and U.S. Court of Appeals Sixth Circuit 1977. Began legal practice Royal Oak 1969.
City Attorney Royal Oak Jan 1973 to Nov 1980. Member Oakland County District Judges Association (President 1986), Michigan District Judges Association, American Judges Association, State Bar of Michigan, South Oakland (Past President), Oakland County and Advocates Bar Associations. Named Royal Oak Citizen

SAWICKI, DANIEL—*Continued*

of the Year 1976. President Royal Oak Kiwanis Club 1978-79. Former Member Salvation Army Advisory Board. Board of Directors Royal Oak Boys Club. Member Elks and Knights of Columbus. Enjoys reading and golf.

Mailing address: P.O. Box 20, Royal Oak 48068-0020.

Office: 400 East Eleven Mile Road, Royal Oak 48068.

Telephone: (248) 246-3652.

SAWYER, David H. *(Judge, Michigan Court of Appeals)* Elected to term beginning Jan 1, 1987. Reelected 1992 and 1998. Current term expires Dec 2004. Born Grand Rapids Michigan July 14, 1947. Episcopalian. Educated at University of Arizona B.S. 1970 and Valparaiso University Law School J.D. 1973. Admitted to practice Michigan 1973, U.S. District Court Western District of Michigan and U.S. Supreme Court.

Assistant Prosecuting Attorney 1973-76 and Prosecuting Attorney Kent County 1977-86. Instructor in Criminal Justice Grand Rapids Junior College 1975-85. Chair Justice Center Task Force of Kent County 1997. Member Sentence Review Committee 1981 and Committee on Rules of Criminal Procedure since 1982 Michigan Supreme Court, Michigan United County Officers Association, Prosecuting Attorneys Association of Michigan (Former Vice President, Treasurer, Board Member and President 1985-86), National District Attorneys Association (Metro Prosecutors Committee, Curriculum Committee 1985), State Bar of Michigan (Council Member Criminal Law Section since 1982, Committees on Criminal Jury Instructions since 1983 and Prisons and Corrections since 1985) and Grand Rapids Bar Association. Presenter National Organization for Victim Assistance 1985. Faculty Member National Conference on Juvenile Justice 1986. Co-Day Chair "Leadership—Criminal Justice" Grand Rapids. Republican. Delegate State Republican Convention since 1974. Member Kent County Republican Executive Committee since 1977 (Co-chairman Lincoln Day Dinner 1977). Delegate to Mexico 1978 and Advisory Board since 1980 American Conference of Young Political Leaders. Board Member Switchboard 1977-79, Camp Manitou-Lin YMCA and Project Rehab. President Highland Park Association. Government Chairperson United Way Kent County 1978-80. Member Kiwanis Club 1978-86, YMCA (Capital Fund Campaign Committee 1983), Advisory Committee on Criminal Justice Grand Rapids Junior College, Kent County Domestic Violence Task Force, Kent County Area Law Enforcement Association, Grand Rapids Chamber of Commerce and Grand Rapids Rotary.

Office: State Office Building, 350 Ottawa N.W., Grand Rapids 49503.

Telephone: (616) 456-1167.

SCHAEFER, Philip D. *(Judge, Michigan Circuit Court Ninth Judicial Circuit)* Elected to term beginning Jan 1, 1987. Reelected Nov 1992 and 1998. Current term expires Dec 31, 2004. Former Chief Judge. Currently serves as Presiding Judge Trial Division. Born York Pennsylvania Dec 21, 1945. Lutheran. Educated at Valparaiso University B.A. 1967 J.D. 1970. Editorial Board Valparaiso University Law Review 1969-70. Admitted to practice Michigan 1970. In legal practice Kalamazoo 1970-86.

Contributing author *Michigan Municipal Law* Institute of Continuing Legal Education 1980. Member Michigan Trial Lawyers Association, The Association of Trial Lawyers of America, American Judicature Society, State Bar of Michigan, Kalamazoo County (President 1985-86) and American Bar Associations. Member Kalamazoo Rotary Club and Trout Unlimited. Enjoys trout fishing, hunting, gardening and boating.

Office: Kalamazoo County Building, 227 West Michigan Avenue, Kalamazoo 49007-3757.

Telephone: (269) 383-8950.

SCHEER, Donald A. *(Magistrate Judge, United States District Court Eastern District of Michigan)* Appointed by U.S. District Court judges.

Office: 648 U.S. Courthouse, 231 West Lafayette Boulevard, Detroit 48226.

Telephone: (313) 234-5215.

SCHMA, William G. *(Judge, Michigan Circuit Court Ninth Judicial Circuit)* Appointed by Governor James J. Blanchard to term beginning Aug 1987. Elected 1988, 1990, 1996 and 2002. Current term expires Dec 31, 2008. Former Chief Judge pro tem.

Office: Kalamazoo County Building, 227 West Michigan Avenue, Kalamazoo 49007-3757.

Telephone: (269) 383-8950.

SCHMIDT, Kenneth W. *(Judge, Michigan Circuit Court Eighteenth Judicial Circuit)* Appointed by Governor John Engler to term beginning March 22, 1996. Elected Nov 5, 1996 and 2000. Current term expires Jan 1, 2007. Born Mount Pleasant Michigan May 15, 1949. Roman Catholic. Educated at Michigan State University B.S.M.E. 1971 and University of Detroit J.D. cum laude 1975. Admitted to practice Michigan 1975, U.S. District Court Eastern District of Michigan 1975 and U.S. Court of Appeals Sixth Circuit 1986. In legal practice Redford Township 1975-78 and Bay City 1978-96.

Member State Bar of Michigan and Bay County Bar Association.

Office: 1230 Washington Avenue, Bay City 48708.

Telephone: (989) 895-4265.

SCHMUCKER, Chad C. *(Judge, Michigan Circuit Court Fourth Judicial Circuit)* Former Chief Judge.

Office: Jackson County Courthouse, 312 South Jackson Street, Jackson 49201.

Telephone: (517) 788-4268.

SCHNELZ, Gene *(Judge, Michigan Circuit Court Sixth Judicial Circuit)* Elected to term beginning Jan 1, 1979. Reelected 1984, 1990, 1996 and 2002. Current term expires Dec 31, 2008. Formerly served Family Court Division. Serves General Jurisdiction. Lutheran. Educated at Alma College B.A. 1954 and Detroit College of Law LL.B. 1957 replaced by J.D. 1968. Judge, Michigan District Court District Fifty-two 1975-78. Former Judge, Walled Lake Municipal Court.

Former Associate Professor Paralegal Program Madonna College. Past President Oakland County Chapter American Inns of Court. Member Supreme Court Committee on Remands and Mediation, Michigan Judges Association (Former Chairman Domestic Relations Committee), American Judges Association, American Judicature Society, Women Lawyers Association, State Bar of Michigan (Former Chairperson Task Force on Legal Assistants and Law Office Administrators, Future Technology in the Courts and Certification of Attorneys, Com-

SCHNELZ, GENE—*Continued*

missioner, Secretary), Oakland County (Past President) and American Bar Associations. Graduate The National Judicial College 1980. Lecturer Michigan Judicial Institute, ICLE and The National Judicial College. Honored with Resolution by Michigan State Legislature for community and civic activities June 1980. Recipient Distinguished Service Award from Walled Lake PTA Council, Walled Lake Jaycees and Alma College Alumni, Distinguished Alumni Award from Alma College, Boss of the Year Award from Oakland County Legal Secretaries Association, National Award for work on criminal justice from American Legion Auxiliary, Clarity Award for plain English writing, Michael Franck Award for Outstanding Contributions to the Legal Profession and Hudson Award for outstanding service from State Bar of Michigan, Frances Avadenka Award for public service from Oakland County Bar Association, award for outstanding contributions to the judicial system and encouragement of women in the practice of law from Women's Bar Association, Michigan Minute Award, Sunshine Award from Child Abuse and Neglect Council, Civil Rights Award from Oakland County Chapter of NAACP, First Civil Rights Award from Jewish Association for Residential Care, First Mentor Award from Legal Assistant Section of the State Bar, John N. O'Brien Award for distinguished community activities 1996 and First Award for positive leadership in the church and community from Lutheran Attorneys in Witness. Named one of Outstanding Young Men of America by National Jaycees. Past President Alma College Alumni Association, Detroit College of Law Alumni Association and Walled Lake Rotary Club. Former Trustee Alma College. Former Director Commerce Township United Fund. Board of Directors Central Scholarship Funds, Inc. President PTA. Trustee Advisory Board Henry Ford Hospital. Life Member Fraternal Order of Police. Association Board Member Area Service Association. Member Walled Lake School District Task Force Committee, Lutheran Church Missouri Synod (Commission on Theology and Church for nine years, Former Chairman National Commission on Constitutional Matters and Michigan District Constitutional Committee, Parliamentarian Michigan District), Lakes Area Chamber of Commerce, Multi-Lakes Conservation Association and Lakes Athletic Association (coached youth football, baseball and softball).

Office: Courthouse Tower Dept. 404, 1200 North Telegraph Road, Pontiac 48341-0404.

Telephone: (248) 858-5280.

Fax: (248) 975-9784

SCHOFIELD, C. F. Scott *(Judge, Michigan District Court District Five)* Appointed by Governor John Engler July 22, 1997 to term beginning Aug 29, 1997. Elected Nov 3, 1998 and 2002. Current term expires Dec 31, 2008. Born Pittsburgh Pennsylvania Nov 1, 1951. United Methodist. Educated at Alma College B.A. with high honors 1973 and University of Michigan J.D. with honors 1976. Admitted to practice Michigan 1976 and U.S. District Court Western District of Michigan 1977. In legal practice Niles 1976-97.

Member Michigan District Judges Association, State Bar of Michigan and Berrien County Bar Association. Attended General Jurisdiction The National Judicial College 1998, Domestic Violence Conference National College of District Attorneys 1999 and National Association of Drug Court Professionals Conference 2000. Member Michigan Sexual Assault Systems Response Task Force 1999-2000.

Office: Berrien County Courthouse, 811 Port Street, St. Joseph 49085-1188.

Telephone: (269) 983-7111.

E-mail address: sschofie@berriencounty.org

SCHUETTE, Bill *(Judge, Michigan Court of Appeals)* Elected Nov 2002 to term beginning Jan 2003. Term expires Jan 1, 2009. Born Midland Michigan. Educated at Georgetown University B.S.F.S. cum laude 1976, University of Aberdeen, Scotland and University of San Francisco J.D. 1979.

Mailing address: P.O. Box 30022, Lansing 48909.

Office: Hall of Justice, Second Floor, 925 West Ottawa Street, Lansing 48915.

Telephone: (517) 373-0786.

SCHWEDLER, C. Joseph *(Chief Judge, Iron County Probate Court)* Appointed by Governor James J. Blanchard to term beginning Dec 28, 1990. Elected Nov 1992, 1994 and 2000. Current term expires Dec 31, 2006. Currently serves as Administrative Chief Judge Trial Court. Born Port Austin Michigan Oct 15, 1948. Catholic. Educated at University of Detroit B.A. 1973 and Thomas M. Cooley Law School J.D. 1976. Admitted to practice Michigan 1976 and Wisconsin 1983. In legal practice Crystal Falls Michigan 1976-90 and Iron Mountain Michigan 1983-90. Judge, Michigan District Court District Ninety-five B May 24, 1990 to Dec 27, 1990.

City Attorney Crystal Falls 1980-90. Member National Council of Juvenile and Family Court Judges, State Bar of Michigan (Assembly Representative 1981-88), State Bar of Wisconsin and American Bar Association. E-5 U.S. Army 1968-70. President Iron County Little League and Lions Club. Enjoys skiing and fishing.

Office: 10 Courthouse, Two South Sixth Street, Crystal Falls 49920-1413.

Telephone: (906) 875-0659.

SCOTT, Justus C. *(Chief Judge, Lapeer County Probate Court)*

Office: Lapeer County Complex, 255 Clay Street, Lapeer 48446.

Telephone: (810) 667-0261.

SCOVILLE, Joseph G. *(Magistrate Judge, United States District Court Western District of Michigan)* Appointed by U.S. District Court judges to term beginning 1988. Reappointed 1996, current term expires 2004.

Office: 666 Federal Building, 110 Michigan Street N.W., Grand Rapids 49503.

Telephone: (616) 456-2309.

SCULLY, Jack William *(Chief Judge, Arenac County Probate Court)*

Mailing address: P.O. Box 666, Standish 48658.

Office: Courthouse, 120 North Grove, Standish 48658.

Telephone: (989) 846-6941.

SERVAAS, Steven Richard *(Judge, Michigan District Court District Sixty-three Division One)* Elected to term beginning Jan 1, 1973. Reelected 1978, 1984, 1990, 1996 and 2002. Current term expires Dec 31, 2008. Former Chief Judge. Born Pyote Texas April 20, 1945. Educated at Trinity University B.A. 1967 and University of Michigan J.D. 1970. Admitted to practice Michigan 1970 and District of Columbia 1971.

SERVAAS, STEVEN RICHARD—*Continued*

Assistant Prosecuting Attorney Kent County 1970-73. Professor in Business and Criminal Law Grand Valley State College since 1972. Member Grand Rapids Bar Association and State Bar of Michigan. Enjoys tennis, weight lifting and ice hockey.

Office: 105 Maple Street, Rockford 49341-9321.

Telephone: (616) 866-1576.

SERVITTO, Deborah A. *(Judge, Michigan Circuit Court Sixteenth Judicial Circuit)* Appointed by Governor James J. Blanchard to term beginning March 13, 1990. Elected to subsequent terms. Former Judge, Michigan District Court District Thirty-seven.

Office: Macomb County Court Building, 40 North Main, Mount Clemens 48043-5654.

Telephone: (586) 469-5147.

SERVITTO, Edward A., Jr. *(Judge, Michigan Circuit Court Sixteenth Judicial Circuit)*

Office: Macomb County Court Building, 40 North Main, Mount Clemens 48043-5654.

Telephone: (586) 469-5145.

SHAPERO, Walter *(Recalled Judge, United States Bankruptcy Court Eastern District of Michigan)* Appointed by U.S. Court of Appeals Sixth Circuit judges. Retired July 14, 2002. Appointed Recalled Judge by the Judicial Council of the Sixth Circuit.

Office: 211 West Fort Street, Suite 1950, Detroit 48226-3211.

Telephone: (313) 234-0040.

SHAW, Richard H. *(Judge, Barry County Probate Court)* Former Chief Judge.

Office: 302 Courts & Law Building, 220 West Court Street, Hastings 49058.

Telephone: (269) 948-4842.

SHEFFERLY, Phillip J. *(Judge, United States Bankruptcy Court Eastern District of Michigan)* Appointed by U.S. Court of Appeals Sixth Circuit judges.

Office: 211 West Fort Street, Nineteenth Floor, Detroit 48226-3211.

Telephone: (313) 234-0040.

SHELTON, Donald E. *(Judge, Michigan Circuit Court Twenty-second Judicial Circuit)* Appointed by Governor James J. Blanchard to term beginning Feb 27, 1990. Elected Nov 1990, 1996 and 2002. Current term expires Dec 31, 2008. Former Chief Judge pro tem. Currently serves as Presiding Judge Civil/Criminal Division. Born Jackson Michigan June 28, 1944. Educated at Western Michigan University B.A. 1966 and University of Michigan J.D. 1969. Senior Editor University of Michigan Journal of Law Reform 1968-69. Captain University of Michigan National Moot Court Team 1968. Co-winner Jessup International Law Moot Court 1969. Admitted to practice Illinois 1969 and Michigan 1974. In legal practice Ann Arbor Michigan 1974-90.

Author "The Use of Legal Assistants in Civil Litigation—Automobile Negligence" 1974 revised 1976, "The Use of Legal Assistants in Domestic Relations Cases" 1975 revised 1980, "Manual for Lawyers and Legal Assistants—Wrongful Death" 1977, "Motion Practice" *Michigan Basic Trial Practice Handbook* 1981, "Medical Malpractice—A Systems Approach" 1982, "Handling the Automobile Negligence Case: A Systems Approach" 2nd ed. 1983 revised 1988, "Michigan Wrongful Death" 1986 Institute for Continuing Legal Education and "1986 Tort Reform Legislation in Michigan" DTR Associates 1986. Lecturer in Business Law University of Maryland 1971-73 and Legal Assistant Program Washtenaw Community College 1976-79 and Oakland University 1977-79. Member Legal Assistant Advisory Committee Washtenaw Community College 1976-79, Ferris State College 1977-90 and Eastern Michigan University since 1990. Mediator Washtenaw County Circuit Court 1981-90. Member Washtenaw Trial Lawyers Association (Secretary 1982, President 1983-84), Michigan Trial Lawyers Association (Legislation Committee 1981-90, Executive Board 1984-90), The Association of Trial Lawyers of America, State Bar of Michigan (Executive Committee Economics Section 1984-88), Washtenaw County (Judiciary Committee 1981-84, Mediation Committee 1988-90) and American (Sections: Litigation, Economics) Bar Associations. Lecturer "The Use of Legal Assistants in Domestic Relations Cases" 1975, "Legal Malpractice in Michigan—The Standard of Care" 1977, "Wrongful Death Damages" 1981, and "Proving Damages in Cases Less than $50,000" 1984 Institute for Continuing Legal Education seminars and "Academics and Pragmatics of Medical Malpractice Trial Practice" Michigan Trial Lawyers Association 1990. Faculty and Speaker Basic Trial Advocacy Workshop Institute for Continuing Legal Education 1980, 1982 and 1988.

Recipient Scholar-Athlete of the Year Award from Western Michigan University 1966, Outstanding Young Man of the Year Award 1976 and Distinguished Service Award 1985 from Saline Jaycees and Attorney of the Year Award 1986 and Justice Blair Moody Judge of the Year Award 1992 from Washtenaw County Trial Lawyers Association. Captain JAGC U.S. Army 1969-74. Honor Graduate Judge Advocate General's School 1969, Recipient Meritorius Service Award from U.S. Army 1974. Member Executive Committee Washtenaw County Democratic Party 1983-88. Member Michigan Democratic State Central Committee 1986-88. Member Business Forum Michigan Democratic Party since 1986. Washtenaw County Cities and Villages Representative Executive Committee 1977-85, Vice Chair 1980-83 and Chair 1983-85 Southeast Michigan Council of Governments. Mayor pro tem 1977-78 and Mayor 1978-86 Saline. Member Governor's Small Cities Advisory Council 1983-86. Board of Directors National Association of Regional Councils 1985-86. Planning Commission 1976-87 and Urban Design Commission 1978-86 Saline. Member Saline Economic Development Corporation 1980-90, Saline Tax Increment Finance Authority 1982-87 and Saline Local Development Finance Authority 1987-90. Board of Regents Eastern Michigan University 1987-90. Chair "Golden Mile" and "Walk America" Washtenaw County March of Dimes 1988-90. Board of Directors Domestic Violence Project 1991-99.

Mailing address: P.O. Box 8645, Ann Arbor 48107-8645.

Office: Courthouse, 101 East Huron, Ann Arbor 48104.

Telephone: (734) 222-3399.

SHEPHERD, Douglas P. *(Judge, Michigan District Court District Forty-one A)*

Office: 51660 Van Dyke, Shelby Township 48316.

Telephone: (586) 739-7325.

SHERIDAN, James E. *(Chief Judge, Michigan District Court District Two A)* Elected Judge 1978. Former Chief Judge pro tem.
Office: Judicial Building, 425 North Main Street, Adrian 49221.
Telephone: (517) 264-4673.

SHERIDAN, Stephen E. *(Chief Judge, Michigan District Court District Fifty-seven)* Former Chief Judge pro tem.
Office: Allegan County Building, 113 Chestnut Street, Allegan 49010.
Telephone: (269) 673-0400.

SHUMAKER, Thomas E. *(Chief Judge, St. Joseph County Probate Court)*
Mailing address: P.O. Box 190, Centreville 49032.
Office: Courthouse, 125 Main, Centreville 49032.
Telephone: (269) 467-5500.

SIERAWSKI, Stephen S. *(Chief Judge, Michigan District Court District Forty-one A)* Chief Judge since Jan 1, 2003.
Office: 40111 Dodge Park Road, Sterling Heights 48313-4138.
Telephone: (586) 446-2500.

SIMMONS, Louis F., Jr. *(Judge, Michigan Circuit Court Third Judicial Circuit)*
Office: 1921 Municipal Center, Two Woodward Avenue, Detroit 48226.
Telephone: (313) 224-5261.

SIMPSON, J. Cedric *(Chief Judge, Michigan District Court District Fourteen A)*
Mailing address: P.O. Box 8645, Ann Arbor 48107-8645.
Office: 4133 Washtenaw Road, Ann Arbor 48108.
Telephone: (248) 971-6050.

SINDT, Conrad J. *(Judge, Michigan Circuit Court Thirty-seventh Judicial Circuit)* Former Chief Judge.
Office: Calhoun County Justice Center, 161 East Michigan Avenue, Battle Creek 49014-4066.
Telephone: (269) 969-6514.

SKINNER, Edward L. *(Chief Judge, Montcalm County Probate Court)* Also serves as Presiding Judge Family Division Michigan Circuit Court Eighth Judicial Circuit.
Mailing address: P.O. Box 309, Stanton 48888.
Office: Courthouse, 625 North State Road, Stanton 48888-0368.
Telephone: (989) 831-7316.

SKINNER, Michael F. *(Judge, Eaton County Probate Court)* Elected to term beginning Jan 1, 2001. Term expires Dec 31, 2006. Currently serves as Chief Judge pro tem. Born Cadillac Michigan Oct 21, 1951. Educated at Central Michigan University B.A. 1973 and Thomas M. Cooley Law School J.D. 1984. Law Clerk to Hon. Michael Ford Merritt, Michigan District Court District Fifty-six 1982-83. Moot Court. Member Delta Theta Phi. Admitted to practice Michigan 1984 and U.S. District Courts Eastern and Western Districts of Michigan. In legal practice Jackson May 1984 to Dec 1985 and Lansing Dec 1985 to Aug 1990.
Assistant General Counsel Blue Cross/Blue Shield of Michigan 1990-2000. Circuit Court Mediator Eaton County 1991-2000. Author "*FMC v Holliday:* Does ERISA Preempt Michigan's Anti-Subrogation Statute?" Michigan B. Jour. Nov 1992, "*Auto Club v Frederick & Herrud,* The Michigan Supreme Court Overrules Part of Federal Kemper: Should the Legislature Finish the Job?" Detroit College of Law Review Spring 1994, "Liability of Independent Insurance Agents for Placing Coverage with an Insolvent Insurance Company" 42 American Law Reports 5th 199 and "Products Liability: Liability for Injury or Death Allegedly Caused by Defect in Mobile Home or Trailer" 61 American Law Reports 5th 473. Adjunct Professor Michigan State University Detroit College of Law. Instructor Aquinas College. Member State Bar of Michigan (Insurance Law Committee 1991-98) and Eaton County Bar Association. Listed in *Who's Who in American Law* since 1996. Board of Directors Child and Family Services of Lansing 1990-93. Member Zoning Board of Appeals Delta Township 1993-96 and Michigan Crime Victims Services Commission May 2000 to Dec 2000. President Lansing Sunrise Rotary 1994-95. Board of Trustees Delta Township 1996-2000. Member Rotary. Interests include aviation and golf. Personal Statement or Quote: "Tell the truth and be done with it!"
Office: Courthouse, 1045 Independence Boulevard, Charlotte 48813.
Telephone: (517) 543-7500.
E-mail address: mskinner@co.eaton.mi.us

SMALL, Kimberly *(Chief Judge, Michigan District Court District Forty-eight)*
Mailing address: P.O. Box 3200, Bloomfield Hills 48302-3200.
Office: 4280 Telegraph Road, Bloomfield Hills 48302.
Telephone: (248) 647-1141.

SMITH, Leslie Kim *(Judge, Michigan Circuit Court Third Judicial Circuit)* Appointed by Governor Jennifer Granholm Mar 28, 2003. Former Chief Judge and Chief Judge pro tem, Michigan District Court District Thirty.
Office: 3E Lincoln Hall of Justice, 1025 East Forest Avenue, Detroit 48207.

SMITH, Martin J. *(Chief Judge, Eastpointe Municipal Court)* Former Chief Judge pro tem.
Office: 16101 Nine Mile Road, Eastpointe 48021.
Telephone: (586) 445-5020.

SMITH, Michael R. *(Chief Judge, Michigan Circuit Court First Judicial Circuit)*
Office: Courthouse, 29 North Howell, Hillsdale 49242.
Telephone: (517) 437-4321.

SMOLENSKI, Michael R. *(Chief Judge pro tem, Michigan Court of Appeals)* Elected 1994. Reelected 2000, current term expires Jan 1, 2007. Chief Judge pro tem since Jan 7, 2003. Educated at University of Michigan. Judge, Michigan District Court District Sixty-one 1984-90. Former Judge, Michigan Circuit Court Seventeenth Judicial Circuit, elected to term beginning Jan 1, 1991.
Former City Attorney Grand Rapids. Former Commissioner Kent County.
Office: 201 The Law Building, 330 Ionia N.W., Grand Rapids 49503.
Telephone: (616) 456-1167.

SMOLENSKI, Sara J. *(Chief Judge, Michigan District Court District Sixty-three and Judge, Michigan District Court District Sixty-three Division Two)* Elected Judge Nov 1990 to term beginning Jan 1, 1991. Reelected 1996 and 2002. Current term expires Dec 31, 2008.

SMOLENSKI, SARA J.—*Continued*

Former Chief Judge pro tem. Born Grand Rapids Michigan Oct 17, 1957. Catholic. Educated at University of Michigan B.A. 1979 and Thomas M. Cooley Law School J.D. 1982. Admitted to practice Michigan 1983 and U.S. District Court Western District of Michigan 1983. In legal practice Grand Rapids 1983-89.

Member Women Lawyers Association of Michigan, Michigan District Judges Association, National Association of Women Judges, State Bar of Michigan and Grand Rapids Bar Association. Board of Directors American Cancer Society.

Office: 649 Kenmoor Street, Grand Rapids 49546.

Telephone: (616) 336-3570.

SOBOTKA, Virginia A. *(Chief Judge, Michigan District Court District Nineteen)* Former Chief Judge pro tem.

Office: 16077 Michigan Avenue, Dearborn 48126.

Telephone: (313) 943-2060.

SOLKA, Thomas L. *(Chief Judge, Michigan Circuit Court Twenty-fifth Judicial Circuit)* Former Chief Judge pro tem.

Office: Courthouse, 234 West Baraga Avenue, Marquette 49855.

Telephone: (906) 225-8205.

SOMERS, Mark W. *(Judge, Michigan District Court District Nineteen)*

Office: 16077 Michigan Avenue, Dearborn 48126.

Telephone: (313) 943-2060.

SOSNICK, Edward *(Judge, Michigan Circuit Court Sixth Judicial Circuit)* Elected to term beginning Jan 1989. Reelected Nov 1994 and 2000. Current term expires Dec 31, 2006. Chief Judge Jan 1, 1996 to Jan 1, 2000. Former Chief Judge pro tem. Born Detroit Michigan Dec 24, 1940. Jewish. Educated at University of Michigan 1959-61 and Wayne State University B.A. 1963 J.D. 1967. Admitted to practice Michigan 1968. Judge, Michigan District Court District Forty-eight 1985-88.

Senior Trial Attorney Oakland County. Fellow Michigan State Bar Foundation. Member Oakland County Judges Association, Michigan Judges Association, National Council of Juvenile and Family Court Judges, State Bar of Michigan, D. Augustus Straker and Oakland County Bar Associations. Participant "Identifying and Understanding Chemical Dependency in District Court Cases" and "Domestic Violence Issues For All Judges" Michigan Judicial Institute Regional Seminars; Significant Other Awareness Program (a court sponsored program for families of alcoholics and other addictions); People's Law School (a public education program); S.M.I.L.E. Start Making It Livable for Everyone (a court sponsored program for divorcing couples on the impact of divorce on children); and Forget Me Not (a court sponsored program for parents living separately and raising children). Recipient Champion of Justice Award from State Bar of Michigan, Award for Meritorious Service to the Children of America from National Council of Juvenile and Family Court Judges, Superintendent's Vision of Youth Award from Bloomfield Hills Schools, Eleanor Roosevelt's Humanities Award, Judicial Action Award from Parents of Murdered Children, Inc., Certificate of Appreciation Award for Outstanding Victim Advocacy from HAVEN, Award of Merit for Contribution Toward Improving the Lives of Women from Women's Survival Center of Oakland County and Josephine S. Weiner Award for Community Service. Project Director "A Prosecutor's Handbook for School Administrators" and "Child Molesting, A Prosecutor's Advisory." Regional Advisory Board Anti-Defamation League. Board of Directors Cranbrook Schools Horizons-Upward Bound. Advisory Board Academy of Sacred Heart. Co-chair Oakland County Coordinating Council to Prevent Domestic Violence. Member Michigan Domestic Violence Prevention and Treatment Board (Former Chair), Michigan Psychoanalytic Foundation and Oakland County Human Services Coordinating Council.

Office: Courthouse Tower Dept. 404, 1200 North Telegraph Road, Pontiac 48341-0404.

Telephone: (248) 858-0344.

E-mail address: sosnicke@co.oakland.mi.us

STARK, Charles H. *(Chief Judge, Michigan Circuit Court Eleventh Judicial Circuit)* Former Judge, Michigan District Court District Ninety-three.

Mailing address: P.O. Box 186, Manistique 49854.

Office: Schoolcraft County Courthouse, 300 Walnut, Manistique 49854.

Telephone: (906) 341-3655.

STECCO, Larry *(Judge, Michigan District Court District Sixty-seven Division Three)*

Office: 11820 North Saginaw Street, Mount Morris 48458.

Telephone: (810) 686-7140.

STEEH, George C., III *(Judge, United States District Court Eastern District of Michigan)* Appointed for life by President Bill Clinton to term beginning 1998. Born Ann Arbor Michigan Jan 29, 1947. Educated at University of Michigan B.A. 1969 J.D. 1973. In legal practice 1980-88. Judge, Michigan District Court District Forty-one B 1989-90. Judge, Michigan Circuit Court Sixteenth Judicial Circuit 1990-98.

Assistant Prosecuting Attorney 1973-78 and First Assistant Prosecuting Attorney 1978-80 Genesee County.

Office: 235 U.S. Courthouse, 231 West Lafayette Boulevard, Detroit 48226.

Telephone: (313) 234-5175.

STEENLAND, Catherine B. *(Judge, Michigan District Court District Thirty-nine)*

Office: 29733 Gratiot Avenue, Roseville 48066.

Telephone: (586) 773-2010.

STEMPIEN, Jeanne *(Judge, Michigan Circuit Court Third Judicial Circuit)*

Office: 1601 Municipal Center, Two Woodward Avenue, Detroit 48226.

Telephone: (313) 224-5261.

STEPHENS, Cynthia D. *(Judge, Michigan Circuit Court Third Judicial Circuit)* Appointed to term beginning 1985. Elected Nov 1988, 1994 and 2000. Current term expires Dec 31, 2006. Former Chief Judge pro tem. Educated at University of Michigan B.A. 1971, Atlanta University 1971-72 and Emory University J.D. 1976. Member Delta Sigma Theta. Admitted to practice Georgia 1976, Michigan 1977, U.S. District Courts Northern District of Georgia 1976 and Eastern District of Michigan 1977 and Texas 1978. In legal practice Detroit Michigan 1981-82. Judge, Michigan District Court District Thirty-six 1982-85.

Coordinator National Conference of Black Lawyers.

STEPHENS, CYNTHIA D.—*Continued*

Consultant Coordinator National League of Cities/U.S. Conference of Mayors V.E.T.S. Project Washington D.C. 1978-79. Associate General Counsel Michigan Senate 1979-81. Elected Vice Chairperson Wayne County Charter Commission Eighth District 1981. Adjunct Instructor in Communications Law Clark College 1977-78. Former Board Member Houston Black Women Lawyers. Member Association of Black Judges of Michigan (Board Member), National Conference of Black Lawyers (Former Board Member), State Bar of Michigan (Advisory Board Michigan Bar Journal), Wolverine (Former Board Member), National and American (Committee on Judicial Evaluation) Bar Associations. Recipient Outstanding Woman Award from Woodward Avenue Presbyterian Church 1982, Distinguished Service Award from Detroit Public Schools Region Five 1983, Golden Heritage Award for Judicial Excellence from Little Rock Baptist Church 1984 and B.A.L.S.A. Special Recognition Award 1985. Named Member of the Year by Wolverine Bar Association 1984 and Outstanding Woman in Law by Hartford Baptist Church 1985. Board Member African Diaspora Project of the Delta Institute, Delta Manor L.H.D.A., Detroit Alumni Delta Sigma Theta, Wayne County Neighborhood Legal Services, Greater Detroit Health Care Council and New Detroit, Incorporated.

Office: 1421 Municipal Center, Two Woodward Avenue, Detroit 48226.

Telephone: (313) 224-5261.

STEVENSON, Jo Ann C. *(Judge, United States Bankruptcy Court Western District of Michigan)*

Mailing address: P.O. Box 3310, Grand Rapids 49501-3310.

Telephone: (616) 456-2949.

STEWART, Gary A. *(Judge, Michigan District Court District Fifty-seven)* Appointed by Governor William Grawn Milliken June 1974. Elected to term beginning Jan 1, 1975. Reelected 1978, 1984, 1990, 1996 and 2002. Current term expires Dec 31, 2008. Former Chief Judge. Born Parkersburg West Virginia Aug 22, 1942. Educated at Columbia Union College B.S. 1965 and Wayne State University J.D. 1968. Admitted to practice Michigan 1968. Began legal practice Kalamazoo.

Prosecuting Attorney Allegan County 1972-74. Instructor Kalamazoo Valley Community College. Member National Conference of Special Court Judges, State Bar of Michigan, Detroit, Kalamazoo, Allegan and American Bar Associations. Enjoys golf and fishing.

Office: Allegan County Building, 113 Chestnut Street, Allegan 49010.

Telephone: (269) 673-0400.

E-mail address: D57@voyager.net

STOWE, David L. *(Chief Judge, Grand Traverse County Probate Court)*

Office: 400 Boardman Street, Traverse City 49684.

Telephone: (231) 922-4640.

STRONG, Craig S. *(Judge, Michigan Circuit Court Third Judicial Circuit)* Assumed office Oct 1, 1997. Term expires Dec 31, 2008. Born Detroit Michigan Sept 5, 1947. Episcopalian. Educated at Howard University B.A. 1969 and Detroit College of Law J.D. 1973. Member Alpha Phi Alpha. Admitted to practice Michigan 1973 and U.S. Court of Military Appeals 1985. Began legal practice Detroit 1973. Referee, Traffic and Ordinance Division 1978 and Judge Jan 1, 1979 to Sept 30, 1997, Recorder's Court of Detroit.

Member Association of Black Judges of Michigan (Past President, Board of Directors), State Bar of Michigan (Representative Assembly since 1978), Detroit (Chairman Recorder's Court Committee 1976-77), Wolverine (President 1978-79, Board of Directors) and National (Former Regional Director, Executive Committee Judicial Council, Life Member) Bar Associations. Participated in Criminal Law and Recorder's Court Workshop sponsored by Michigan Association of Black Social Workers. Panelist Juvenile Law Black Nurses Association. Member Subcommittees on Criminal Law and Federal Judiciary Congressional Black Caucus. Speaker BALSA Third Annual Black Emphasis Day University of Detroit Law School 1979 and Wayne State University School of Law 1979. Co-Chair Wiley A. Branton Symposium National Bar Association 1994. Recipient Award of Appreciation from Wolverine Bar Association 1978, Wayne County Neighborhood Legal Services 1979 and Boy Scouts of America (Renaissance District) 1986, City of Highland Park Proclamation 1978, Special Tribute and Senate Resolution of Tribute from State of Michigan 1979, Senate Concurrent Resolution Michigan Legislature 1980, Civic Citation from Detroit City Clerk's Office and Citizens of Detroit Committee 1980, Honorary Citizen of Atlanta Georgia from Mayor Maynard Jackson 1982, Certificate of Appreciation from Wayne County Board of Commissioners 1982, Renaissance Award from 13th District Democratic Party 1982, Outstanding Museum Service Award Afro-American Museum of Detroit 1983, Humanitarian Award of Excellence from Mother Waddles Mission 1983, Man of the Year Award North End Youth Improvement Council 1985, Spirit of Detroit Award Detroit City Council 1987, Excellence in Judicial Commitment Little Rock Baptist Church 1987, Judicial Accomplishment Recognition Award from Wolverine Student Bar Association 1990, Judge of the Year from Gamma Phi Delta (Alpha Theta Chapter) 1990, Community Service Recognition Award from Native Detroiter Magazine 1990, Distinguished Alumni Award from Wolverine Bar Association 1994, Testimonial Resolution from Detroit City Council, Key to the City of Detroit from Mayor's Office, Certificate of Outstanding Citizenship from Detroit Public School System, Man of the Year Award from Detroit Urban Center, Member of the Year Award from Wolverine Bar Association, Judge of the Year Award from National Black Women Political Leadership Caucus, Outstanding Civic and Community Leadership Award, Founder's Award from Neighborhood Foundation, Distinguished Service Award from Hollywood and Vine Recovery Center Los Angeles California, Whitney M. Young, Jr. Award from Boy Scouts of America, D. Augustus Straker Award from Wolverine Bar Association, President's Award from Association of Black Judges, Distinguished Alumnus Award from Detroit College of Law and Street Law Project Award from Neighborhood Legal Services. Named "Detroit Howardite of the Year" by Howard University Alumni Club 1979.

Commander USNR VTU Law Unit. Naval Academy Information Officer. Board of Directors Westside Citizens for the Retarded 1977-80, Wayne County Neighborhood Legal Services 1975-80, Optimist Club 1986-91, Howard University Alumni Club, Michigan Cancer Foundation and Orchestra Hall, Inc. International Observer first all race election South Africa 1994. Chair-

STRONG, CRAIG S.—*Continued*
person Adopt-A-Child for Christmas Program Northend Improvement Council. District Director Boy Scouts of America. 32° Prince Hall Mason. Life Member NAACP (Former Board of Directors Detroit Chapter), Museum of African American History (Former Member Board of Directors) and Naval Reserve Association. Panelist "Programs in Media" Women's Conference of Concerns and *Ask the Lawyer* WJR Radio Program. Participant Million Man March. Enjoys restoring home and its furnishings and collecting old coins, letters, postcards and photographs.
Office: 803 Hall of Justice, 1441 St. Antoine Street, Detroit 48226.
Telephone: (313) 224-2484.

SULLIVAN, Brian R. *(Judge, Michigan Circuit Court Third Judicial Circuit)*
Office: 601 Hall of Justice, 1441 St. Antoine Street, Detroit 48226.
Telephone: (313) 224-2789.

SULLIVAN, Paul J. *(Judge, Michigan Circuit Court Seventeenth Judicial Circuit)* Appointed by Governor John Engler March 2, 1995. Elected 1996 and 2002. Current term expires Dec 31, 2008. Currently serves as Chief Judge pro tem. Born Rochester New Hampshire May 3, 1947. Roman Catholic. Educated at Georgetown University A.B. 1969 and Catholic University of America J.D. 1972. Associate Editor Catholic University Law Review 1971-72. Admitted to practice Pennsylvania 1972, Michigan 1974 and U.S. District Courts Eastern District of Pennsylvania 1972 and Western District of Michigan 1974. In legal practice Grand Rapids Michigan 1974-88. Former Judge, Michigan District Court District Sixty-one, elected to term beginning Jan 1, 1989.
Staff Assistant to U.S. Senator Norris Cotton New Hampshire 1969-72. Assistant District Attorney Philadelphia 1972-74. Member National Highway Safety Advisory Committee 1972-75. Member Grand Rapids Bar Association (Secretary, Chair Young Lawyers Section). Captain USAR (railroad officer). Former Member Kent County Republican Executive Committee. Former President Grand Rapids Lions Club. Former Director Grand Rapids Jaycee's. Former Chair Annual Catholic Services Appeal Fund Drive and Secretary Parish Education Commission St. Stephen's Church. Former Chairperson Alliance for Health Planning Board. Former Board of Directors Dispute Resolution Center of Kent County. Former Member Commission for Future Directions in Health Care Alliance for Health. Member Advisory Board Salvation Army Day Reporting Center. Private pilot.
Office: 10500C Kent County Courthouse, 180 Ottawa Avenue N.W., Grand Rapids 49503-2751.
Telephone: (616) 632-5099.

SUPINA, Gerald Joseph *(Chief Judge, Ionia County Probate Court)* Appointed by Governor William G. Milliken to term beginning April 20, 1981. Elected 1982, 1988, 1994 and 2000. Current term expires Dec 31, 2006. Born Ionia Michigan July 1, 1941. Roman Catholic. Educated at University of Detroit Bachelor of Architecture 1965 and Detroit College of Law J.D. 1970. Member Phi Kappa Theta. Admitted to practice Michigan 1970. Began legal practice Portland 1971.
City Attorney Portland 1974-81. Former Member American Judges Association. Chairman Chief Justice's Select Committee to Review Proposed Juvenile Court Rules 1987. Member Probate Court Time Standard Subcommittee 1986-87 and Probate Rules Committee since 1989. Member since 1985 and Chairman since 1987 Probate Forms Committee of State Court Administrator. Member Committee to Revise Juvenile Court Rules 1985-2000 and Caseflow Management Coordinating Committee Michigan Supreme Court 1986-87, Southwest Michigan Probate and Juvenile Judges Association (President 1984), Michigan Probate and Juvenile Judges Association since 1981 (Committees on Juvenile Law and Adoptions and Juvenile Employees Standardization, Chairman Resolutions Committee 1986-87 and since 1989, former Vice Chairman Mental Health Committee), State Bar of Michigan (Probate and Estate Planning Council since 1992) and Ionia-Montcalm Bar Association. Instructor Michigan Probate and Juvenile Judges Conference 1983 and Michigan Judicial Institute since 1984. Architectural Co-op Student Argonaut Realty (Division of General Motors) 1962-64. Previously worked as laborer for Ionia County Road Commission and retail clerk for J. C. Penney Co. Former Member Jaycees (Secretary, Vice President, President), Kiwanis International and St. Patrick's School Board (President 1987-88). Chairman Tri-County Committee on Depression and Suicide 1986-90. Member Knights of Columbus, Rotary International and Ionia County Council for the Prevention of Child Abuse and Neglect (Treasurer since 1992). Enjoys reading, fishing and family activities.
Office: Ionia County Courthouse, 100 Main Street, Ionia 48846-1695.
Telephone: (616) 527-5326.

SUTHERLAND, William J. *(Chief Judge, Michigan District Court District Twenty-three)* Former Chief Judge pro tem. Born Detroit Michigan Feb 28, 1940. Educated at Henry Ford Community College A.S. 1961, Eastern Michigan University B.S. 1963 and University of Detroit J.D. 1967. Admitted to practice Michigan 1968 and Florida 1973. Former Judge, Taylor Municipal Court, elected to term beginning May 1968.
Member Michigan Judges Association, Michigan Municipal Judges Association, American Judges Association and Downriver Bar Association.
Office: 23511 Goddard Road, Taylor 48180-4197.
Telephone: (734) 374-1334.

SUTTON, Daniel L. *(Chief Judge, Michigan District Court District Eighty-three)* Chief Judge since Jan 1, 2003.
Mailing address: P.O. Box 189, Roscommon 48653.
Office: Roscommon County Building, 500 Lake Street, Roscommon 48653.
Telephone: (989) 275-5312.

SWALLOW, Joseph P. *(Chief Judge, Michigan Circuit Court Twenty-sixth Judicial Circuit)* Former Chief Judge pro tem.
Office: Courthouse, 720 West Chisholm Street, Alpena 49707.
Telephone: (989) 354-9573.

SWANK, Donald L. *(Judge, Michigan District Court District Thirty-three)* Former Chief Judge.
Office: 19000 Van Horn, Woodhaven 48183.
Telephone: (734) 671-0201.

SWARTZ, David Scott *(Judge, Michigan Circuit Court Twenty-second Judicial Circuit)* Appointed by

SWARTZ, DAVID SCOTT—*Continued*

Governor John Engler April 14, 1997. Currently serves as Chief Judge pro tem. Also serves as Chief Judge pro tem Trial Court. Born Ann Arbor Michigan June 7, 1947. Methodist. Educated at Central Michigan University B.S. 1969 and Case Western Reserve University J.D. 1972. Member Phi Delta Phi. Admitted to practice Michigan 1972. In private practice Ann Arbor 1982-95. Judge 1995-97 and Former Chief Judge pro tem, Michigan District Court District Fourteen A.

Assistant Prosecuting Attorney 1973-82. Fellow Michigan State Bar Foundation. Member American Judges Association, American Judicature Society, State Bar of Michigan, Washtenaw County (President 1988-89) and American Bar Associations. Captain USAR Infantry 1969-75. Enjoys golfing, skiing and cooking.

Mailing address: P.O. Box 8645, Ann Arbor 48107-8645.

Office: Courthouse, 101 East Huron Street, Ann Arbor 48104.

Telephone: (734) 222-3392.

SWITALSKI, Mark S. *(Judge, Michigan Circuit Court Sixteenth Judicial Circuit)* Former Chief Judge, Michigan District Court District Thirty-nine.

Office: Macomb County Court Building, 40 North Main, Mount Clemens 48043-5654.

Telephone: (586) 469-5135.

SWITALSKI, Matthew S. *(Judge, Michigan Circuit Court Sixteenth Judicial Circuit)*

Office: Macomb County Court Building, 40 North Main, Mount Clemens 48043-5654.

SZYMANSKI, David J. *(Judge, Wayne County Probate Court)* Elected Judge to term beginning Jan 1, 1991. Reelected 1996 and 2002. Current term expires Dec 31, 2008. Born Detroit Michigan June 12, 1954. Christian. Educated at University of Notre Dame B.A. 1976 and Wayne State University J.D. 1982. Law Clerk to Hon. Gus Cifelli, Michigan District Court District Forty-eight 1980-82. Admitted to practice Michigan 1982 and Florida 1983. In legal practice Southfield Michigan 1982-86 and Birmingham Michigan 1986-90.

Member Michigan Probate Judges Association, National Probate Judges Association and Advocates Bar Association. Recipient Citizenship Award from Central Citizens Committee. Teacher and Coach Detroit public schools 1979-80. Member John W. Smith Old Timers, Polish American Congress and Fellowship of Christian Athletes. Enjoys racquetball, windsurfing, running and hockey.

Office: 1301 Municipal Center, Two Woodward Avenue, Detroit 48226.

Telephone: (313) 224-5686.

TABBEY, Kirk W. *(Judge, Michigan District Court District Fourteen A)* Appointed by Governor John Engler April 1997. Elected Nov 1998, current term expires Jan 2005. Born June 28, 1956. Catholic. Educated at Michigan State University B.A. 1978 and Wayne State University J.D. 1981. Admitted to practice Michigan 1981, U.S. District Court Eastern District of Michigan 1981 and U.S. Court of Appeals Sixth Circuit 1982. In legal practice Dearborn Oct 1981 to July 1983.

Assistant Prosecuting Attorney Washtenaw County July 1983 to Dec 1992. Special Assistant Public Defender Independent Counsel Washtenaw County Jan 1993 to Oct 1993. Senior Assistant Prosecuting Attorney Oct 1993 to Jan 1995, Chief Trial Attorney Jan 1995 to Jan 1997 and Chief Assistant Prosecuting Attorney Jan 1997 to April 1997 Jackson County. Author "Preparing a Warrant for a Computer Crime Search" Fall 1989 and "Michigan's Computer Crime Task Force" Fall 1990 *Communicator* CFCA and "Computer Crime: Preparing the Computer Specific Search Warrant" 9 No. 2 *Computers & Security* April 1990 and No. 17 *The Computer Law and Security Report* Fall 1990. Advisor and Consultant "MCI Law Enforcement Video" MCI Corporation 1991. Consultant and Participant "Crime Check" Video on Computer Viruses KDN Videoworks, Inc. 1992. Advisor, Consultant and Participant "Cell Phone Fraud" Video on Telecommunications Fraud Michigan Department of State Police 1997. Guest Instructor in Public Service Training Washtenaw Community College since 1989, in Criminal Justice Michigan State University since 1992 and in Criminal Justice University of Detroit since 1994. Legal Consultant Michigan Computer Crime Task Force since 1990. Vice Chairman Communications Subcommittee International Working Group on Computer Evidence. Vice President International Institute for the Investigation and Study of Organized Insurance Frauds and Related Crimes, Inc. Treasurer Michigan District Judges Association. Member Criminal Justice Task Force subcommittee. Liaison National Law Institute/Federal Bureau of Investigation. Member Communications Fraud Control Association, High Technology Crime Investigation Association, Information Systems Security Association, Inc., Law Enforcement and Industrial Security Association, Prosecuting Attorneys Association of Michigan, State Bar of Michigan, Jackson County and Washtenaw County Bar Associations. Graduated FBI Academy National Law Institute 1990. Instructor on Computer Crime Prosecution/Investigation Department of Justice, Department of Treasury, Financial Fraud Institute, Federal Law Enforcement Training Center and Southwestern Legal Foundation since 1990. Faculty National College of District Attorneys 1993. Guest Instructor Michigan State Police Training Academy since 1993. Eagle Scout 1970 Boy Scouts of America. Recipient Crime Prevention Citation from Detroit Police 1990, Certificate of Appreciation for Crime Prevention from West Michigan Crime Prevention Association 1990, Community Service Awards from Washtenaw County Sheriff's Department 1991 and 1992, Certificate of Appreciation from Washtenaw County Public Defender 1992 and Certificate of Appreciation for continuing contributions to the Telecommunications Fraud and Criminal Investigations Training Programs from Department of Treasury 1995. Partner Solidarity Investment Club. Past President Wayne State University National Alumni Association. Member Dearborn Security Network, Michigan State University Alumni Association and School of Criminal Justice Alumni Association, NAACP Ypsilanti/Willow Run Branch, National Eagle Scout Association, Southeast Michigan Computer Security Special Interest Group, 21st Century Club and St. Andrew's Catholic Church. Enjoys fishing, boating and traveling.

Office: 415 West Michigan Avenue, Ypsilanti 48197-5326.

Telephone: (734) 484-6690.

E-mail address: tabbeyk@washtenaw.org

TACOMA, Kenneth L. *(Chief Judge, Wexford County Probate Court)* Appointed by Governor John Engler to term beginning May 23, 1994. Elected Nov 1994 and

TACOMA, KENNETH L.—*Continued*

2000. Current term expires Dec 31, 2006. Also serves as Presiding Judge Family Division Michigan Circuit Court Twenty-eighth Judicial Circuit. Born Cadillac Michigan Aug 11, 1953. Religious affiliation: Christian Reformed. Educated at Grand Valley State College B.S. with honors 1976 and Indiana University School of Law J.D. cum laude 1980. National Honor Scholar. Recipient American Jurisprudence Awards. Member Order of the Coif. Admitted to practice Michigan 1980 and Indiana 1980. In legal practice Cadillac Michigan 1980-86. Domestic Relations Referee, Michigan Circuit Court Twenty-eighth Judicial Circuit 1986-90.

Prosecuting Attorney Wexford County 1991-94. Instructor in Business and Criminal Law Kirtland Community College and Muskegon Business College 1982-90. Former Member Prosecuting Attorneys Association of Michigan. Member Michigan Probate Judges Association, State Bar of Michigan (Representative Assembly 1980-81) and Wexford-Missaukee Counties Bar Association (President 1991-92). Presenter at various specialized training programs throughout Michigan on law enforcement domestic violence response training, Michigan Judicial Institute programs for training of probate court support staff and the role of the juvenile justice system for parent support groups.

Office: Courthouse, 503 South Garfield Street, Cadillac 49601.

Telephone: (231) 779-9510.

E-mail address: p83@voyager.net

TAHVONEN, Randy L. *(Judge, Michigan Circuit Court Twenty-ninth Judicial Circuit)* Elected to term beginning Jan 1, 1979. Reelected 1984, 1990, 1996 and 2002. Current term expires Dec 31, 2008. Currently serves as Chief Judge pro tem. Former Chief Judge. Born Grayling Michigan Feb 24, 1949. Baptist. Educated at Michigan State University B.S. 1970 and Detroit College of Law J.D. with honors 1973. Admitted to practice Michigan 1974. Began legal practice St. Johns 1974.

Member Michigan Judges Association, State Bar of Michigan, Clinton-Gratiot Counties and American Bar Associations. Faculty Member Michigan Judicial Institute.

Office: Courthouse, 100 East State Street, St. Johns 48879.

Telephone: (989) 224-5132, 875-5224.

TALBOT, Michael J. *(Judge, Michigan Court of Appeals)* Appointed by Governor John Engler 1998. Elected 2002, current term expires Jan 1, 2009. Educated at Georgetown University and University of Detroit J.D. Former Judge, Common Pleas Court of Detroit. Former Judge, Recorder's Court of Detroit. Former Judge, Michigan Circuit Court Third Judicial Circuit.

Housing Commissioner Detroit 1975-78.

Office: 14-300 Cadillac Place, 3020 West Grand Boulevard, Detroit 48202-6020.

Telephone: (313) 972-5736.

TARNOW, Arthur J. *(Judge, United States District Court Eastern District of Michigan)* Appointed for life by President Bill Clinton to term beginning 1998. Born Detroit Michigan Feb 3, 1942. Educated at Wayne State University B.A. 1963 J.D. 1965. Law Clerk to Hon. John Fitzgerald, Hon. Louis McGregor and Hon. Timothy C. Quinn, Michigan Court of Appeals 1967. In legal practice 1973-98.

Chief Deputy Defender Legal Aid and Defenders 1969-70. Attorney Foundation Appellate Defender for State of Michigan 1970-72.

Office: 124 U.S. Courthouse, 231 West Lafayette Boulevard, Detroit 48226.

Telephone: (313) 234-5180.

TARRANT, Kyle Higgs *(Judge, Michigan District Court District Seventy Division Two)* Elected to term beginning Jan 1, 1983. Reelected 1988, 1994 and 2000. Current term expires Dec 31, 2006. Former Presiding Judge Criminal Division. Born Ann Arbor Michigan Sept 8, 1949. Educated at Michigan State University B.S. with honors 1971 and Wayne State University J.D. 1974. Admitted to practice Michigan 1974. Began legal practice Saginaw 1974.

Former Prosecutor. Member Michigan District Judges Association (Legislative Committee) and Saginaw County Bar Association. Recipient Award of Professional Excellence from Michigan State Police 1981. Member Zonta Club, Lawyers' Wives and Saginaw County Child and Family Services. Interests include biking, racquetball, crafts, swimming and tennis.

Office: 111 South Michigan Avenue, Saginaw 48602.

Telephone: (989) 790-5368.

TAYLOR, Anna Diggs *(Senior Judge, United States District Court Eastern District of Michigan)* Appointed for life by President Jimmy Carter to term beginning Nov 11, 1979. Former Chief Judge. Assumed Senior status Dec 31, 1998, serves by assignment. Born Washington D.C. Dec 9, 1932. Episcopalian. Educated at Barnard College B.A. 1954 and Yale Law School LL.B. 1957. Admitted to practice District of Columbia 1957, Michigan 1961 and U.S. Court of Appeals Sixth Circuit 1973. In legal practice District of Columbia 1957-60 and Detroit 1961-79.

Assistant Solicitor of Labor 1957-60. Assistant County Prosecutor Wayne County 1962-64. Assistant U.S. Attorney 1965-66. Assistant Corporation Counsel City of Detroit 1975-79. Important Decisions: American Civil Liberties Union v. Birmingham 588 F. Supp. 1337, 1984; Plaza Securities v. Fruehauf 643 F. Supp. 1535, 1986; Central States v. Central Transport 522 F. Supp. 658; and Jackson v. Democratic Party 588 F. Supp. 1033. Adjunct Professor of Law Wayne State University Law School 1976-77. Member Michigan Association of Black Judges, Women Judges Association, Federal Judges Association, State Bar of Michigan, Wolverine, Detroit and Federal Bar Associations. Recipient Women Lawyers Division Award from National Bar Association 1981, Michigan SCLC Millender Award 1984, Bridge Builder's Award from Calvary Church of Detroit 1984, Alpha Phi Alpha Award from Epsilon Chapter 1984, Sojourner Truth Award from National Association of Black Business and Professional Women 1986, Absalom Jones Award from Michigan Black Episcopalians 1986, Detroit and Wolverine Bar Association Bench-Bar Award 1990, Menorah Award of Histadrut 1991 and Dynamic Women Award from Women's Economic Club 1992. Inducted into International Institute Hall of Fame 1997. Trustee Henry Ford Hospital System, United Foundation, Community Foundation of Southeastern Michigan, Episcopal Diocese of Michigan, Founders Society Detroit Institute of Arts, Yale Law School Alumni Association (Vice President) and Michigan Commission on Bicentennial of

TAYLOR, ANNA DIGGS—*Continued*
the U.S. Constitution. Enjoys gardening, cooking, golf, music and reading.
Office: 1035 U.S. Courthouse, 231 West Lafayette Boulevard, Detroit 48226.
Telephone: (313) 234-5105.

TAYLOR, Clifford W. *(Justice, Michigan Supreme Court)* Appointed by Governor John Engler to term beginning Sept 1, 1997. Elected 1998, current term expires Dec 2006. Born Delaware Ohio Nov 9, 1942. Catholic. Educated at University of Michigan B.A. 1964 and George Washington University National Law Center J.D. 1967. Admitted to practice Michigan 1968 and U.S. District Courts Western 1975 and Eastern 1981 Districts of Michigan. In legal practice Lansing. Judge, Michigan Court of Appeals March 2, 1992 to Aug 30, 1997, appointed by Governor John Engler.
Adjunct Professor Thomas M. Cooley Law School 1975-77. Member State Bar of Michigan. Served to Lieutenant USNR Sept 1967 to April 1971. Member Michigan State Board of Law Examiners 1991-1997. Member Michigan Supreme Court Historical Society and U.S. Supreme Court Historical Society.
Mailing address: P.O. Box 30052, Lansing 48909.
Office: Michigan Hall of Justice, 925 West Ottawa Street, Lansing 48915.
Telephone: (517) 373-0120.

TEEPLE, Donald A. *(Chief Judge, Michigan Circuit Court Twenty-fourth Judicial Circuit)*
Office: Courthouse Building, 60 West Sanilac, Sandusky 48471.
Telephone: (810) 648-2120.

TERTZAG, Kaye *(Judge, Michigan Circuit Court Third Judicial Circuit)* Appointed by Governor James J. Blanchard to term beginning March 25, 1986. Elected 1988, 1994 and 2000. Current term expires Dec 31, 2006. Born Detroit Michigan Jan 1, 1939. Armenian Orthodox. Educated at Wayne State University B.S. in Education 1961 and Detroit College of Law J.D. 1969. Member Tau Kappa Epsilon. Admitted to practice Michigan 1969. In legal practice Detroit 1969-78 and Allen Park 1978-86.
City Attorney Melvindale and River Rouge. Member Wayne County Judges Association, Michigan Judges Association, Downriver and Armenian-American Bar Associations. Attended General Jurisdiction Seminar The National Judicial College 1987. Instructor in Government and History Secondary School River Rouge. Member Charter Commission and Community College Board of Trustees Wayne County. Enjoys reading, boating and basketball.
Office: 1019 Municipal Center, Two Woodward Avenue, Detroit 48226.
Telephone: (313) 224-5261.

THOMAS, Deborah A. *(Judge, Michigan Circuit Court Third Judicial Circuit)*
Office: 802 Hall of Justice, 1441 St. Antoine Street, Detroit 48226.
Telephone: (313) 224-5210.

THOMAS, Edward M. *(Judge, Michigan Circuit Court Third Judicial Circuit)* Appointed by Governor James J. Blanchard to term beginning March 22, 1990. Born Detroit Michigan July 2, 1943. Congregationalist. Educated at Lafayette College A.B. 1966 and Detroit College of Law J.D. 1972. Member Pi Lambda Phi, Delta Theta Phi and Sigma Pi Phi. Admitted to practice Michigan 1972. Began legal practice Detroit 1973. Judge, Recorder's Court of Detroit 1979-90.
Former Assistant Prosecutor Wayne County. Member Association of Black Judges of Michigan, Michigan Judges Association, State Bar of Michigan, Wolverine and National Bar Associations. Previously worked for Chrysler Corporation and Ford Motor Company. Democrat. Chairman Salvation Army Harbor Light Advisory Council. Member Detroit Council for Political Education, Detroit Renaissance Lions Club, Cranbrook School Alumni Council, Michigan Prison Overcrowding Project Policy Team and The Cabinet (Social club). Interests include fishing, photography, music, golf and model aircraft.
Office: 913 Municipal Center, Two Woodward Avenue, Detroit 48226.
Telephone: (313) 224-5246.

THOMAS, Preston G. *(Judge, Michigan District Court District Fifty)* Former Chief Judge pro tem.
Office: 70 North Saginaw, Pontiac 48342.
Telephone: (248) 857-8000.

THOMAS, Terrence R. *(Judge, Michigan Circuit Court Twenty-seventh Judicial Circuit)* Elected to term beginning Jan 1, 1979. Reelected 1984, 1990, 1996 and 2002. Current term expires Dec 31, 2008. Former Chief Judge. Born Sept 4, 1940.
Mailing address: P.O. Box 885, White Cloud 49349.
Office: Courthouse, 1092 Newell, White Cloud 49349.
Telephone: (231) 689-7269.

THOMPSON, M. T., Jr. *(Judge, Michigan District Court District Seventy Division One)* Former Presiding Judge Traffic Division.
Office: 111 South Michigan Avenue, Saginaw 48602.
Telephone: (989) 790-5368.

TIGHE, Karen A. *(Chief Judge, Bay County Probate Court)* Elected Nov 8, 1994 to term beginning Jan 1, 1995. Reelected 2000, current term expires Dec 31, 2006. Born Detroit Michigan Feb 19, 1950. Catholic. Educated at University of Michigan B.A. 1972 and Detroit College of Law J.D. 1976. Admitted to practice Michigan 1976. Referee 1977-94 and Administrator 1990-94 Michigan Circuit Court Eighteenth Judicial Circuit.
Member State Bar of Michigan and Bay County Bar Association.
Office: 1230 Washington Avenue, Suite 715, Bay City 48708.
Telephone: (989) 895-4205.

TIMMERS, Steven M. *(Chief Judge, Michigan District Court District Sixty-two A)*
Office: Police Justice Building, 2650 DeHoop Avenue S.W., Wyoming 49509.
Telephone: (616) 530-7385.

TINGSTAD, Anders B., Jr. *(Chief Judge, Michigan District Court District Ninety-eight)*
Office: Gogebic County Courthouse, 200 North Moore Street, Bessemer 49911.
Telephone: (906) 663-4611.

TOLEN, Lynda A. *(Judge, Michigan District Court District Five)* Former Chief Judge and Chief Judge pro

TOLEN, LYNDA A.—*Continued*

tem. Former Presiding Judge Probation Division. Also serves as Presiding Judge Trial Court Civil Division.

Office: Berrien County Courthouse, 811 Port Street, St. Joseph 49085-1188.

Telephone: (269) 983-7111.

TORREANO, John A. *(Chief Judge, Dickinson County Probate Court)*

Mailing address: P.O. Box 609, Iron Mountain 49801.

Office: Courthouse, Iron Mountain 49801.

Telephone: (906) 774-1555.

TORRES, Isidore B. *(Judge, Michigan Circuit Court Third Judicial Circuit)* Assumed office Oct 1, 1997. Former Judge, Michigan District Court District Thirty-six. Former Judge, Recorder's Court of Detroit.

Office: 1011 Municipal Center, Two Woodward Avenue, Detroit 48226.

Telephone: (313) 224-5261.

TOWNSEND, Leonard *(Judge, Michigan Circuit Court Third Judicial Circuit)* Assumed office Oct 1, 1997. Term expires Dec 31, 2008. Former Judge, Recorder's Court of Detroit Jan 1, 1979 to Sept 30, 1997.

Office: 702 Hall of Justice, 1441 St. Antoine Street, Detroit 48226.

Telephone: (313) 224-2437.

TUCKER, Thomas J. *(Judge, United States Bankruptcy Court Eastern District of Michigan)* Appointed by U.S. Court of Appeals Sixth Circuit judges.

Office: 211 West Fort Street, Nineteenth Floor, Detroit 48226-3211.

Telephone: (313) 234-0030.

TURKELSON, Eugene I. *(Chief Judge, Ogemaw County Probate Court)*

Office: Ogemaw County Building, 806 West Houghton Avenue, West Branch 48661.

Telephone: (989) 345-0145.

TURNER, Robert J. *(Judge, Michigan District Court District Forty-three)* Appointed by Governor James J. Blanchard to term beginning Aug 14, 1989. Elected 1990. Reelected to subsequent terms. Former Chief Judge and Chief Judge pro tem. Currently serves as Presiding Judge Madison Heights Division.

Office: 200 West Thirteen Mile Road, Madison Heights 48071.

Telephone: (248) 583-1800.

TYNER, Deborah G. *(Judge, Michigan Circuit Court Sixth Judicial Circuit)* Elected to term beginning Jan 1, 1991. Reelected 2000, current term expires Dec 31, 2006. Born Michigan June 28, 1956. Educated at University of Michigan B.A. 1977 and Wayne State University J.D. 1981. Admitted to practice Michigan 1981 and U.S. District Court Eastern District of Michigan 1982. In legal practice Southfield and Birmingham 1985-90.

Assistant Prosecutor Wayne County 1980-85. Fellow Adams Pratt Foundation. Co-chair Committee on Criminal Attorney Appointment System Bench-Bar Conference 1997. Member Michigan Judges Association (Executive and Legislative Committee), State Bar of Michigan (Representative Assembly) and Oakland County Bar Association. Graduate The National Judicial College 1991. Attended Michigan Judicial Institute 1991-93. Recipient Brotherhood Award from Jewish War Veterans Feb 16, 1991 and B'nai B'rith Barristers Award May 7, 1991. Board of Trustees MS Society. Enjoys skiing, reading and aerobics.

Office: Courthouse Tower Dept. 404, 1200 North Telegraph Road, Pontiac 48341-0404.

Telephone: (248) 858-0344.

ULRICH, Lowell R. *(Chief Judge, Chippewa County Probate Court)*

Office: Chippewa County Courthouse, 319 Court Street, Sault Ste. Marie 49783.

Telephone: (906) 635-6316.

URICK, Walter Aleksy *(Chief Judge, Oceana County Probate Court)* Assumed office Jan 1, 1989. Elected 1994 and 2000. Current term expires Dec 31, 2006. Also serves as Presiding Judge Family Division Michigan Circuit Court Twenty-seventh Judicial Circuit. Born Evanston Illinois June 3, 1939. Methodist. Educated at Albion College A.B. magna cum laude 1961 and University of Michigan J.D. with distinction 1964. Assistant Editor Michigan Law Review 1963. Admitted to practice Michigan 1964 and U.S. Supreme Court 1970. In legal practice Hart 1965-88.

Prosecuting Attorney Oceana County 1965-70. President Top of Michigan Probate Judges Association 1995-97. Board of Directors Michigan Probate Judges Association 1995-97. Member State Bar of Michigan, Oceana County (President 1975-83) and 27th Judicial Circuit (Past President) Bar Associations. Attended The National Judicial College May 1992. Recipient Paul Harris Award from Hart Rotary Club 1991. Chairman Oceana County Republicans 1972-74 and Oceana County Michigan Week Program 1966. Member Hart Jaycees (President 1969-70), Hart Rotary Club (Secretary 1971-76, President 1976-77). President Oceana-Muskegon Legal Aid, Inc. 1971-72. Chairman Administrative Board Hart United Methodist Church 1983-86 and 2002.

Office: M-10 Oceana County Building, 100 South State Street, Hart 49420.

Telephone: (231) 873-3666.

VAN DAM, Philip M. *(Chief Judge, Michigan District Court District Seventy-five)* Chief Judge since Jan 1, 2003.

Office: Courthouse, 301 West Main Street, Midland 48640.

Telephone: (989) 832-6709.

VANDERCOOK, Susan E. *(Chief Judge, Jackson County Probate Court)* Elected to term beginning Jan 1, 1989. Reelected 1994 and 2000. Current term expires Dec 31, 2006. Also serves as Presiding Judge Family Division Michigan Circuit Court Fourth Judicial Circuit. Former Chief Judge pro tem. Born Tucson Arizona Oct 6, 1949. Episcopalian. Educated at Michigan State University B.A. with honors 1970 and Wayne State University J.D. 1975. Admitted to practice Michigan 1975.

Assistant Prosecutor Jackson County 1975-88. Instructor in Business Law Jackson Community College 1976-77. Former Member Michigan Court Reporters and Recorders Board of Review and Michigan Trial Court Assessment Commission. Member Family Court Rules Committee, Court Improvement Advisory Committee, Michigan Probate Judges Association, Southwest Probate Judges Association (President 1995-96), State Bar of Michigan (Former Member Judicial Ethics Subcommittee) and Jackson County Bar Association (Secretary 1976-77). Recipient Susan B. Anthony Award from Jackson Y-Center 1988. Finalist for Citizen of the Year

VANDERCOOK, SUSAN E.—*Continued*

Award from Jackson Citizen Patriot newspaper 1990. Elementary Teacher St. Philip's Battle Creek 1970-71. Former Board President Y-Center. Past President and Board Member Family Service and Children's Aid of Jackson County. Former Council Member Prevention of Child Abuse and Neglect Board. Former Board of Directors United Way. Former Member Advisory Committee Michigan Foster Care Review Board. Member Human Services Coordinating Alliance. Enjoys golf, walking, skiing and needlecrafts.

Office: Jackson County Courthouse, Fourth Floor, 312 South Jackson Street, Jackson 49201.

Telephone: (517) 768-2783.

VERSLUIS, Peter P. *(Chief Judge, Michigan District Court District Fifty-nine)*

Office: 3161 Wilson Avenue S.W., Grandville 49418.

Telephone: (616) 538-9660.

VITALE, Jack *(Chief Judge, Michigan District Court District One)* Elected to term beginning Jan 1, 1999. Term expires Dec 31, 2004. Chief Judge since Jan 1, 2003. Born Hamilton Ohio Nov 21, 1946. Roman Catholic. Educated at Miami University B.A. 1968 and University of Toledo College of Law J.D. 1972. Admitted to practice Michigan 1972, Ohio 1973, U.S. District Court Southern District of Michigan 1973 and U.S. Court of Appeals Seventh Circuit 1995. In legal practice Monroe Michigan 1972-98.

Assistant City Attorney Monroe 1972-76. Chief Assistant Prosecutor Monroe County 1977-79. Member Michigan District Judges Association, American Judges Association, State Bar of Michigan, Monroe County, Michigan Italian American and National Italian American Bar Associations.

Office: 106 East First Street, Monroe 48161-2143.

Telephone: (734) 240-7145.

E-mail address: jvitale@monroe.mi.org

VIVIANO, Antonio P. *(Judge, Michigan Circuit Court Sixteenth Judicial Circuit)* Former Judge and Presiding Judge Mental Health Division, Macomb County Probate Court.

Office: Macomb County Building, 40 North Main, Mount Clemens 48043-5654.

VOET, Raymond P. *(Chief Judge, Michigan District Court District Sixty-four A)*

Office: 101 West Main Street, Ionia 48846.

Telephone: (616) 527-5344.

WADEL, Peter J. *(Chief Judge, Michigan District Court District Seventy-nine)* Chief Judge since Jan 1, 2003.

Office: Mason County Courthouse, 304 East Ludington Avenue, Ludington 49431.

Telephone: (231) 843-4130.

WALLACE, Ted *(Judge, Michigan District Court District Thirty-six)*

Office: 421 Madison Avenue, Suite 4073, Detroit 48226.

Telephone: (313) 965-2200.

WARREN, Michael D., Jr. *(Judge, Michigan Circuit Court Sixth Judicial Circuit)*

Office: Courthouse Tower, 1200 North Telegraph Road, Pontiac 48341-0404.

Telephone: (248) 858-0344.

WATERSTONE, Mary M. *(Judge, Michigan Circuit Court Third Judicial Circuit)* Former Judge, Michigan District Court District Thirty-six.

Office: 403 Hall of Justice, 1441 St. Antoine Street, Detroit 48226.

Telephone: (313) 224-2415.

WEAVER, Elizabeth A. *(Justice, Michigan Supreme Court)* Elected to term beginning Jan 1, 1995. Reelected 2002, current term expires Dec 31, 2010. Former Chief Justice. Born New Orleans Louisiana. Educated at H. Sophie Newcomb College B.A. 1962 and Tulane University J.D. with honors 1965. Mortar Board. Listed in *Who's Who in American Colleges and Universities.* Recipient French Government's Excellence in French Award. Editor Tulane Law Review 1963-65. Law Clerk to Hon. Oliver P. Carriere, Civil District Court of Louisiana 1963. Member Phi Beta Kappa, Order of the Coif and Phi Mu. Honorary member Delta Kappa Gamma. Admitted to practice Louisiana 1965 and Michigan 1973. In legal practice New Orleans Louisiana 1965 and Glen Arbor Michigan 1973. Judge, Leelanau County Probate Court Jan 1, 1975 to Dec 31, 1986. Judge, Michigan Court of Appeals Jan 1, 1987 to Dec 31, 1994.

Former Attorney Title Specialist Chevron Oil Company Louisiana. Instructor and course originator "What Everyone Should Know About The Law" Central Michigan University Off-Campus Education Department. Member Michigan Commission on Criminal Justice, Michigan Committee on Juvenile Justice, Michigan Supreme Court Judicial Coordination Council, Michigan Supreme Court Docket Case Tracking Committee for Probate Courts, Special ad hoc Committee to Study and Report on Part-time Probate Judges Problem, Michigan Supreme Court Education Advisory Committee for Probate and Juvenile Judges, Michigan Advisory Committee on Juvenile Justice and Committee on Juvenile Justice (representing probate judges) since July 1984. Chair Michigan Task Force for Children's Justice since 1992 and Chair Trial Court Assessment Commission since Aug 1996. Member Law and Organizational Economics Center Judicial Advisory Board University of Kansas 1997. Treasurer Children's Charter of the Courts of Michigan, Inc. Representative Michigan Committee on Juvenile Justice National Convention of State Advisory Groups on Juvenile Justice U.S. Office of Juvenile Justice and Delinquency Prevention. Member Michigan Probate and Juvenile Judges Association (Secretary), Top of Michigan Probate Judges Association (Past President), National Council of Juvenile and Family Court Judges, National Probate Judges Association, State Bar of Michigan (Chairperson Juvenile Law Committee and Crime Prevention Center), Grand Traverse-Leelanau-Antrim Counties, Louisiana State and American Bar Associations. Advisory Board Chairperson Western Michigan University CLE. Recipient Lifetime Dedication to Children Award from Michigan Champions in Childhood Injury Prevention Jan 2000, recognition award for outstanding service to children and families of Michigan from Governor John Engler and Family Independence Agency Aug 2000, award for exceptional service and support to the drug courts of Michigan from Michigan Association of Drug Court Professionals Feb 2002 and Mary S. Coleman Award from Civic Education Through Law Dec 2002. Featured in *People* magazine and appeared on *Good Morning America* for position on juvenile justice. Named one of Five Outstanding Young Women in Michigan by Michigan Jaycees. Former Dean of

WEAVER, ELIZABETH A.—*Continued*

Girls and first grade teacher Leelanau County schools. Former elementary teacher Glen Lake Community School. Developed "Children and the Law" Project for elementary schools in Michigan. Community Advisory Committee Pathfinder School Treaty Law Demonstration Project. Member Citizen's Advisory Council Arnell Engstrom Children's Center, Northwest Michigan Regional Planning Commission (Criminal Justice Advisory Council and Economic Advisory Council), Leelanau Center for Education (Board of Trustees), Chamber Arts North (Board of Directors Leelanau County), Glen Arbor Township Zoning Board, Traverse Bay Area Traffic and Safety Committee and Zonta. Church activities include committee membership, Chairman of the Board, Sunday School teacher and clerk. Enjoys tennis, gardening and outdoor activity.

Office: 3300 Grandview Plaza, 10850 Traverse Highway, Traverse City 49684.

Telephone: (231) 929-3700.

WEBER, John R. *(Judge, Michigan Circuit Court Twenty-fifth Judicial Circuit)* Currently serves as Chief Judge pro tem. Former Chief Judge.

Office: Courthouse, 234 West Baraga Avenue, Marquette 49855.

Telephone: (906) 225-8217.

WEISS, Robert E. *(Judge, Genesee County Probate Court)*

Office: 919 Beach Street, Flint 48502.

Telephone: (810) 257-3533.

WELLS, Richard D. *(Chief Judge, Michigan District Court District Sixty-five A)*

Office: 100 East State Street, Suite 3400, St. Johns 48879.

Telephone: (989) 224-5150.

WELTY, William D. *(Chief Judge, Michigan District Court District Three B)* Former Chief Judge pro tem.

Mailing address: P.O. Box 67, Centreville 49032.

Office: Courthouse, 125 Main, Centreville 49032.

Telephone: (269) 467-5500.

WESTRA, Vincent Castelli *(Chief Judge, Michigan District Court District Eight and Judge, Michigan District Court District Eight Division Three)* Former Chief Judge pro tem. Elected Nov 1992 to term beginning Jan 1, 1993. Reelected Nov 1998, current term expires Jan 1, 2005. Born Kalamazoo Michigan April 27, 1952. Lutheran. Educated at Western Michigan University B.A. with honors 1974 and University of Toledo J.D. 1982. Law Clerk to Hon. Donald T. Anderson 1982-83 and Hon. Richard Ryan Lamb 1982-83, Michigan Circuit Court Ninth Judicial Circuit. Admitted to practice Michigan 1983. In legal practice Kalamazoo 1983-89.

Assistant City Attorney Kalamazoo 1989-92. Special Prosecuting Attorney Kalamazoo County 1989-92. Member Michigan District Judges Association, State Bar of Michigan and Kalamazoo County Bar Association. Board of Directors Kalamazoo Probation Enhancement Program. Member Community Corrections Advisory Board and Order of Sons of Italy. Enjoys golf, music and movies.

Office: 227 West Michigan Avenue, Kalamazoo 49007.

Telephone: (269) 383-8903.

Fax: (269) 383-8047

E-mail address: vcwest@kalcounty.com

WHALEN, R. Steven *(Magistrate Judge, United States District Court Eastern District of Michigan)* Appointed by U.S. District Court judges to term beginning Sept 11, 2002.

Office: 704 U.S. Courthouse, 231 West Lafayette Boulevard, Detroit 48226.

Telephone: (313) 234-5115.

WHITBECK, William C. *(Chief Judge, Michigan Court of Appeals)* Appointed by Governor John Engler to term beginning Oct 23, 1987. Elected Nov 1998, current term expires Dec 31, 2004. Former Chief Judge pro tem. Born Holland Michigan Jan 17, 1941. Roman Catholic. Educated at Northwestern University B.S. 1963 and University of Michigan Law School LL.B. 1966. Recipient McCormick Scholarship in Journalism 1959-63. Member Scribes Michigan. Admitted to practice Michigan 1969, U.S. Supreme Court 1979 and U.S. District Courts Eastern and Western Districts of Michigan. Began legal practice Lansing.

General Counsel Land Equities Group 1987-89 and Action Auto Stores, Inc. 1989-90. Author "Should Hospitals Be Regulated as Public Utilities?" 12 No. 3 *Michigan Hospitals* March 1976 and "How Much Government Is Enough?" *Michigan Forward* July 1992. Coauthor with Robert A. F. Reisner and M. Angela Hogan "Regulatory Barriers to Economic Development in Michigan" 1977 and with Frederick J. Hood "The Birth and Mid-Life Crisis of the Administrative Procedures Act of 1969" 64 No. 8A Michigan B. Jour. Aug 1985. Important Decisions: People v. Michael Alan Asquini 227 Mich. App. 702, 1998; People v. Charles L. Whitney 228 Mich. App. 230, 1998; People v. Brian Andre Warren 228 Mich. App. 336, 1998; Pioneer State Mutual Ins. Co. v. TIG Insurance Company 229 Mich. App. 406, 1998; Brian Salesin v. State Farm Fire & Casualty Co. 229 Mich. App. 346, 1998; Herald Company, Inc. v. City of Kalamazoo 229 Mich. App. 376, 1998; Bonita Hawkins v. Mercy Health Services 230 Mich. App. 315, 1998; Arthur Lincoln v. General Motors (concurring opinion) 231 Mich. App. 262, 1998; Kenneth C. Bracco v. Michigan Tech. Univ. 231 Mich. App. 578, 1998; Phyllis R. Crego v. Kermit L. Coleman 232 Mich. App. 284, 1998; Deborah L. Connaway v. Welded Construction Co. 233 Mich. App. 150, 1998; Estate of Steven Krass v. Joliet, Inc. 233 Mich. App. 661, 593 N.W.2d 578, 1999; Dallias E. Wilcoxon v. Minnesota Mining & Mfg. Co. 235 Mich. App. 347, 597 N.W.2d 250, 1999; People v. James Arthur Sabin 236 Mich. App. 1, 600 N.W.2d 98, 1999; Brandy Taylor v. Surender Kurapati M.D. 236 Mich. App. 315, 600 N.W.2d 670, 1999; Diane Zurcher v. Barbara Herveat 238 Mich. App. 267, 605 N.W.2d 329, 1999; People v. Lamphone Thenghkam 240 Mich. App. 29, 610 N.W.2d 571, 2000; PM One Ltd. v. Dept. of Treasury 240 Mich. App. 255, 611 N.W.2d 318, 2000; People v. Lawrence Antkoviak 242 Mich. App. 424, 2000; Hawra Algarawi v. Auto Club Insurance Association Docket No. 201920 Dec 15, 2000; and Jo-Dan Ltd. v. Detroit Board of Education Mich. Ct. App. Docket No. 201406.

Fellow State Bar of Michigan Foundation and American Bar Foundation. Member Michigan Law Revision Commission, Ingham County American Inns of Court, State Bar of Michigan (Administrative Law Section since 1976, Committee on Appellate Court Administra-

WHITBECK, WILLIAM C.—*Continued*

tion 1999, Michigan Appellate Bench Bar Conference Planning Group 1999), Ingham County and American Bar Associations. Attended Essential Skills for Appellate Judge Course The National Judicial College Aug 1998. Second Lieutenant USAR 1966-72. Republican. Board Member Michigan Historical Center Foundation. Member Lansing Downtown Neighborhood Association, Castle Park Association, Michigan Historical Commission (President), Michigan Political History Society, Michigan Supreme Court Historical Society and Knights of Columbus. Enjoys reading, skiing and old house restoration.

Mailing address: P.O. Box 30022, Lansing 48909-7522.

Office: Hall of Justice, Second Floor, 925 West Ottawa Street, Lansing 48915.

Telephone: (517) 373-0786.

E-mail address: wwhitbeck@jud.state.mi.us

WHITE, Helene Nita *(Judge, Michigan Court of Appeals)* Elected to term beginning Jan 1, 1993. Reelected 1998, current term expires Dec 2004. Born New York Dec 2, 1954. Jewish. Educated at Barnard College A.B. cum laude 1975 and University of Pennsylvania Law School J.D. 1978. Law Clerk to Hon. Charles L. Levin, Michigan Supreme Court 1978-80. Admitted to practice Michigan 1979 and Pennsylvania 1979. Judge, Common Pleas Court of Detroit Jan 1, 1981 to Aug 31, 1981. Judge, Michigan District Court District Thirty-six Sept 1, 1981 to Jan 1, 1983. Judge, Michigan Circuit Court Third Judicial Circuit Jan 1, 1983 to Dec 31, 1992.

Member Michigan Judges Association, National Association of Women Judges (Chairperson Publicity Committee 1983-84), American Judicature Society, Women Lawyers Association of Michigan, State Bar of Michigan, Detroit, Pennsylvania and American Bar Associations. Board of Directors Metropolitan Detroit YMCA 1985-87 (Executive Committee, Chair By-laws Committee 1990-93), Coalition on Temporary Shelter (President 1992-94) and Founders Junior Council Detroit Institute of Arts (Chair Nominating Committee since 1991). Advisory Board Detroit Women's Forum since 1987 and Sojourner Foundation since 1988. Member National Executive Council American Jewish Committee (Vice President Detroit Chapter since 1991) and National Young Leadership Cabinet United Jewish Appeal since 1994.

Office: 14-300 Cadillac Place, 3020 West Grand Boulevard, Detroit 48202-6020.

Telephone: (313) 972-5678.

WICKENS, Mark S. *(Chief Judge, Lake County Probate Court)* Elected Nov 5, 1982 to term beginning Jan 1, 1983. Reelected Nov 5, 1987, 1994 and 2000. Current term expires Dec 31, 2006. Also serves as Chief Judge Trial Court.

Office: 800 Tenth Street, Suite 300, Baldwin 49304.

Telephone: (231) 745-4614.

WIERENGO, Andrew *(Chief Judge, Michigan District Court District Sixty)*

Office: Hall of Justice, 990 Terrace Street, Muskegon 49442-3377.

Telephone: (231) 724-6283.

WILDER, Kurtis T. *(Judge, Michigan Court of Appeals)* Appointed by Governor John Engler 1998. Term expires Jan 1, 2005. Educated at University of Michigan J.D. Former Chief Judge and Chief Judge Trial Court, Michigan Circuit Court Twenty-second Judicial Circuit.

Office: 14-300 Cadillac Place, 3020 West Grand Boulevard, Detroit 48202-6020.

Telephone: (313) 972-5678.

WILEY, Dennis M. *(Judge, Michigan District Court District Five)* Appointed by Governor John Engler to term beginning Dec 6, 1996. Elected Nov 1998, current term expires Dec 31, 2004. Born Syracuse New York Feb 25, 1948. Educated at Spring Hill College B.A. 1970 and University of Notre Dame J.D. 1973. Admitted to practice Michigan 1973, Wisconsin 1973 and Missouri 1978. In legal practice St. Louis Missouri 1978-79 and St. Joseph Michigan 1979-81.

Assistant Prosecuting Attorney 1981-89 and Prosecuting Attorney 1989-96 Berrien County. Instructor in Criminal Law and Procedure Lake Michigan College since 1981 and Kalamazoo Valley Community College since 1991. Member State Bar of Michigan. Captain U.S. Army JAGC 1974-77. Member Rotary. Enjoys sailing and jogging.

Office: Courthouse, 811 Port Street, St. Joseph 49085.

Telephone: (269) 983-7111.

E-mail address: DWILEY@BERRIENCOUNTY.ORG

WILLIAMS, Carolyn H. *(Judge, Kalamazoo County Probate Court)* Appointed by Governor James J. Blanchard to term beginning Oct 31, 1986. Elected 1988, 1994 and 2000. Current term expires Dec 31, 2006. Also serves as Presiding Judge Family Division Michigan Circuit Court Ninth Judicial Circuit since 1998. Chief Judge 1994-2000. Former Chief Judge pro tem. Born Washington D.C. Nov 22, 1943. Religious affiliation: Protestant Non-Preference. Educated at George Washington University B.A. 1964 J.D. with honors 1968. Admitted to practice Michigan 1968. In legal practice Kalamazoo 1968-71 and 1984-86. Administrative Law Judge, Michigan Department of Social Services Lansing 1972-83.

Instructor Nazareth College Kalamazoo 1974 and Western Michigan University 1975-77. Member Task Force on Gender Issues in the Courts Michigan Supreme Court 1987-89. Member Southwest Michigan Women Lawyers Association, Southwest Michigan Probate Judges Association (President 1990-92), Michigan Probate Judges Association (Secretary 1992-93, Treasurer 1993-94, Vice President 1994-95, President 1996-97), National Association of Women Judges, State Bar of Michigan (Open Justice Commission 1997-2001), Kalamazoo County, National and American Bar Associations. Participant 1976 and Faculty Advisor Dec 1983 The National Judicial College. Faculty Member Michigan Judicial Institute since 1988 and Michigan Institute of CLE 1991. Recipient Red Rose Citation from Downtown Kalamazoo Kiwanis 1997, Woman of Achievement Award from YWCA 1998 and Glass Ceiling Award 1998. Named Influential Woman of West Michigan 2000. Social Science Research Analyst U.S. Department of Labor 1964-68. Co-chair Kalamazoo Healthy Futures 1994-96. Member Gilmore Piano Festival since 1997 and Child Support Coordinating Council 1998-2000. Chair Kalamazoo County Children and Family Consortium 2000-02. Charter Member Kalamazoo Chapter Links, Inc. since 2000. Member Board of Directors Greater Kalamazoo United Way, Glowing Embers Girl Scout Council, Kalamazoo Forum, Jobs for Michigan Graduates, Fidelity Federal

WILLIAMS, CAROLYN H.—*Continued*
Savings and Loan Association and Greater Kalamazoo YMCA. Enjoys tennis, walking and reading.
Office: Family Division Admin. Bldg., 1400 Gull Road, Kalamazoo 49048.
Telephone: (269) 385-6001.

WILLIS, Frank D. *(Chief Judge, Van Buren County Probate Court)* Appointed by Governor William G. Milliken June 7, 1976. Elected 1976, 1982, 1988, 1994 and 2000. Current term expires Dec 31, 2006. Born Marshall Michigan Oct 18, 1945. Religious affiliation: First Assembly of God. Educated at Albion College 1964-65, Western Michigan University B.B.A. in Accounting 1968 and University of Florida J.D. 1973. University of Florida Law Review. Moot Court. Member Phi Alpha Delta. Admitted to practice Michigan 1973 and Florida 1973.
Assistant Prosecuting Attorney 1973 and Prosecuting Attorney 1974-76 Van Buren County. Instructor Kalamazoo Valley Community College and Central Michigan University. Member Prosecuting Attorneys Association of Michigan, Southwestern Michigan Judges Association (President 1978-80), National District Attorneys Association, United County Officers Association, Probate Judges Association of Michigan, The Florida Bar, State Bar of Michigan and Van Buren County Bar Association. Speaker Michigan Judicial Institute and National Council of Juvenile and Family Court Judges. Enjoys camping, golf, reading, tennis, basketball, football and water and snow skiing.
Office: 202A Courthouse Annex, Second Floor, 212 Paw Paw Street, Paw Paw 49079-1495.
Telephone: (269) 657-8225.

WIRTH, Charlotte L. *(Chief Judge, Michigan District Court District Seventeen)* Former Chief Judge pro tem.
Office: 15111 Beech-Daly Road, Redford 48239.
Telephone: (313) 387-2790.

WOOD, Frederick L. *(Chief Judge, Branch County Probate Court)*
Office: Courthouse, 31 Division Street, Coldwater 49036.
Telephone: (517) 279-4318.

WOODS, George E. *(Senior Judge, United States District Court Eastern District of Michigan)* Appointed for life by President Ronald Reagan to term beginning Nov 16, 1983. Assumed Senior status, serves by assignment. Born Cleveland Ohio Oct 10, 1923. Episcopalian. Educated at Ohio Northern University, Texas A&M University and Detroit College of Law J.D. 1949. Member Sigma Pi and Sigma Nu Phi. Admitted to practice Michigan 1949. Began legal practice Pontiac 1949. In legal practice Detroit 1953-81. Judge, United States Bankruptcy Court Eastern District of Michigan 1981-83.
Chief Assistant U.S. Attorney 1953-60 and U.S. Attorney 1960-61 Eastern District of Michigan. Instructor in Trial Practice and Procedure Oakland University 1982-83. Fellow American College of Trial Lawyers and International Academy of Trial Lawyers. Member State Bar of Michigan, Federal (President Detroit Chapter 1968) and American Bar Associations.
Office: 277 U.S. Courthouse, 231 West Lafayette Boulevard, Detroit 48226.
Telephone: (313) 234-5150.

WORTHY, Kym L. *(Judge, Michigan Circuit Court Third Judicial Circuit)* Assumed office Oct 1, 1997. Former Judge, Recorder's Court of Detroit.
Office: 502 Hall of Justice, 1441 St. Antoine Street, Detroit 48226.
Telephone: (313) 224-2520.

YENIOR, Allen C. *(Chief Judge, Michigan District Court District Eighty-one)*
Mailing address: P.O. Box 129, Tawas City 48764.
Office: Iosco County Building, 422 Lake, Tawas City 48764.
Telephone: (989) 362-4441.

YOUNG, Joan E. *(Chief Judge, Michigan Circuit Court Sixth Judicial Circuit)* Assumed office 1997. Former Chief Judge pro tem. Chief Judge since April 16, 2001. Serves Family Division. Born Kalamazoo Michigan Oct 31, 1947. Protestant. Educated at Michigan State University B.A. 1969 and Wayne State University Law School J.D. 1974. Admitted to practice Michigan 1974 and U.S. District Court Eastern District of Michigan 1979. In legal practice Troy 1974-79. Deputy Court Administrator 1979-82 and Court Administrator/Judicial Assistant 1982-88, Michigan Circuit Court Sixth Judicial Circuit. Hearing Officer, Delta Dental Plan of Michigan 1985-88. Judge Jan 1, 1989 to 1997, Chief Judge pro tem Jan 1994 to Aug 1994 and Chief Judge Aug 1994 to 1997, Oakland County Probate Court.
Author monthly column in *LACHES* Oakland County Bar Association April 1983 to June 1988, "In Defense of the Court" *News Briefs* Michigan Defense Trial Counsel Inc. 3-6 March 1987, "Adoption: A View from the Bench" Special Issue on Adoption Michigan Family L. Jour. 34-37 1993, "Concurrent Jurisdiction Between Circuit and Probate Courts: Is it Responsive, Conflicting, or Just Plain Confusing?" *LACHES* Oct 1993 and "Litigation Involving Children: Which Court Has Jurisdiction? When? And, for What?" Michigan Family L. Jour. 654-657 July 1994. Co-Associate Editor Juvenile Affairs *Inter-Com* Michigan Probate Judges Association Quarterly. Member Jail Study Subcommittee 1980-84, Salary Administration Subcommittee 1983-85, Chair Salary Review Panel 1986-88 and Member Community Corrections Advisory Board 1990-94 Oakland County Board of Commissioners. Member 1983-88, Co-chair 1984-86 and Chair 1987-88 Circuit Court Forms Committee, Member Circuit Court Statistics Advisory Committee 1985-86 and Michigan Court Forms Committee 1988 State Court Administrator's Office. Member Supreme Court Task Force on Gender Bias Issues 1987-89. Chair Legal Subcommittee Lieutenant Governor's Special Commission on Adoption 1991-92. Member State Consortium on Post Adoption Services Michigan Department of Mental Health since 1992. Fellow Michigan State Bar Foundation. Member Women Lawyers Association of Michigan, Michigan Inter-Professional Association on Marriage, Divorce and the Family, Inc., Joint Circuit and Probate Court Committee on Proceedings Involving Children, Southeast Michigan Probate Judges Association, Michigan Probate Judges Association (Member since 1989 and Chair 1994-95 Juvenile and Adoption Committee, Member Adoption Fee Subcommittee 1992-93 and Special Committee on Technology), Oakland County Judges Association (Treasurer 1993-94), Michigan Judicial Institute (Faculty Advisory Committee since 1991, Hypertext Benchbook Advisory Committee since 1992), American Judicature Society, Women's Bar Association of Oak-

YOUNG, JOAN E.—*Continued*

land County (Co-founder 1976, Program Chair 1982-83), State Bar of Michigan (Traffic Law Committee 1978-79, Expansion of Legal Practice Committee 1978-82, Vice Chair Energy Conservation Task Force 1980-84, Member 1983-91 and Chair 1988-91 Committee on State Trial Courts Administration, Governmental Organization and Intergovernmental Relations Committee 1985-86, Plain English Committee since 1985, Task Force on Technology 1986-93, ad hoc Committee on Third Party Custody 1992-93 Family Law Section, Council Member 1994 Juvenile Law Section, Sections: Criminal Law, Law, Probate and Estate Planning), South Oakland, Oakland County (Member 1975-79 and Chairperson 1978-79 Membership and New Lawyer Admissions Committee, Member 1979-83 and Chairperson 1979-81 and 1982-84 Tel-law Committee, Program Committee 1983-84, Cable Television Committee 1984-85, Member 1985-86 and Co-chair President's Task Force on Improved Dispute Resolution, Member 1986-88 and Co-chair President's Commission to Implement Improved Dispute Resolution) and American (Committee on Probate and Surrogate's Courts 1989-93 National Conference of Special Court Judges Judicial Administration Division, Liaison to Section of Real Property, Probate and Trust Law 1989-93) Bar Associations.

Faculty Member "Michigan Court Rules for Clerks and Administrators" Dec 1984, Domestic Violence Seminar 1991, "Evidence Issues in Child Custody Proceedings" Feb 2002 and "Evidence & Evidentiary Issues" Dec 2002 Michigan Judicial Institute; "Don't Ask . . . Do Tell! On Camera Interviews in Child Custody Cases" Michigan Probate Judges Association May 2002; and "View from the Bench—Deciding Attorney Fee and Support Issues: A Case Study Approach: Four Judges Reveal How They Do It" First Annual Family Law Institute Oct 2002. Speaker on "Juvenile Court System" Sept 1988, "Probate Court" Sept 1989, "Living Wills" Sept 1990 and "Adoption" March 1993 Due Process Oakland County Bar Association; "Minor Guardianships" Michigan Probate Judges Association Jan 1990 and Family Law Committee State Bar of Michigan Nov 1990; "Youth Crime" Leadership Oakland Feb 1991, 1992, 1993 and 1994; "Termination of Parental Rights" Michigan Foster and Adoptive Parent Association, Inc. March 1991, National Foster Parents Association May 1991, Children's Charter of the Courts of Michigan, Inc. Nov 1992, Juvenile Law Committee Oakland County Bar Association April 1993 and Michigan Inter-Professional Association April 1993; "Do the Guarantees of the Bill of Rights End at Old Age: Guardianships, Conservatorships, Bankruptcy—Why, When & How?" American Bar Association Aug 1991; "Representing the Older Client: Law and Decision Making" Senior Justice Committee State Bar of Michigan Nov 1991; "Mental Health Commitments" Mental Health Committee Oakland County Bar Association Feb 1992; "Probate Court/Foster Care" 10th Annual Conference Michigan Family Support Council Oct 1992; "Fairness in the Courts" Michigan Judicial Institute Jan 1993; "Termination of Parental Rights—Divorcing Your Parents" Family Law Seminar State Bar of Michigan Feb 1993; "Domestic Violence" Oakland County Probate Court Sept 1993; and "Adoption Law" Family Law Section State Bar of Michigan Nov 1994. Recipient Distinguished Service Award from Oakland County Bar Association Dec 9, 1986, Wonder Woman Award from Women's Survival Center 1994, Child Advocate Award—Honorable Mention Child Abuse and Neglect Council County of Oakland, Inc. 1994, John N. O'Brien Award from Republican Committee of Oakland County 1999, Sustained Community Leadership Award from HAVEN 2000, Angels in Adoption Award from Congressional Coalition on Adoption 2000 and Judicial Advocate Award from Metro Detroit Chapter Parents of Murdered Children, Inc. 2001. Honored by Oakland County Women's Bar Association 1993. Social Worker Protective Services and Child Welfare Department of Social Services 1969-71 and Job's 70 Program Hope College 1971. Republican. Member Republican Leadership Committee Republican Women's Clubs and Republican Business Women's Forum. Chairperson Michigan State Teacher Tenure Commission 1979-83. Board of Directors Family Focus May 1987 to March 1990 and Goodwill Industries of Greater Detroit 1990 to Oct 1994 and since 1998. Director Emeritus of HAVEN. Board of Trustees Michigan Opera Theatre. Member Children's Services Advisory Council Oakland County Community Mental Health Services 1989-92. Advisory Board Metro Detroit Chapter Parents of Murdered Children, Inc.

Office: Courthouse Tower, 1200 North Telegraph Road, Pontiac 48341-0404.

Telephone: (248) 858-5282.

YOUNG, Robert P., Jr. *(Justice, Michigan Supreme Court)* Appointed by Governor John Engler to term beginning Jan 3, 1999. Elected 2000 and 2002. Current term expires Dec 31, 2010. Educated at Harvard College B.A. cum laude 1974 J.D. 1977. In legal practice for 15 years. Former Judge, Michigan Court of Appeals, elected to term beginning 1994.

Former General Counsel AAA Michigan. Board of Trustees Central Michigan University. Member Michigan Civil Service Commission.

Mailing address: P.O. Box 30052, Lansing 48909.

Office: Michigan Hall of Justice, 925 West Ottawa Street, Lansing 48915.

Telephone: (517) 373-0120.

YOUNGBLOOD, Carole F. *(Judge, Michigan Circuit Court Third Judicial Circuit)* Elected Nov 1994 to term beginning Jan 1, 1995. Reelected Nov 2000, current term expires Dec 31, 2006. Born Highland Park Michigan. Educated at Wayne State University B.S. 1982 and Detroit College of Law J.D. cum laude 1986. Admitted to practice Michigan 1987 and U.S. District Court Eastern District of Michigan 1987. In legal practice Detroit 1987-94. Visiting Judge Michigan Court of Appeals 1996 and 1997.

Member Black Judges Association, Women Judges Association, Michigan Judges Association, American Judges Association, Women Lawyers Bar Association, Wolverine and The Detroit Metropolitan Bar Associations.

Office: 1607 Municipal Center, Two Woodward Avenue, Detroit 48226.

Telephone: (313) 224-0391.

YUILLE, Richard B. *(Judge, Michigan Circuit Court Seventh Judicial Circuit)* Former Chief Judge pro tem.

Office: Genesee County Courthouse, 900 South Saginaw Street, Flint 48502.

Telephone: (810) 257-3252.

ZAHRA, Brian K. *(Judge, Michigan Court of Appeals)* Appointed by Governor John Engler 1999. Term expires Jan 1, 2007. Educated at Wayne State University B.A. and University of Detroit School of Law J.D. Law Clerk to Hon. Lawrence P. Zatkoff, U.S. District Court Eastern District of Michigan. Former Judge, Michigan Circuit Court Third Judicial Circuit.

Office: 14-300 Cadillac Place, 3020 West Grand Boulevard, Detroit 48202-6020.

Telephone: (313) 972-5678.

ZATKOFF, Lawrence P. *(Chief Judge, United States District Court Eastern District of Michigan)* Appointed for life by President Ronald Reagan to term beginning 1986. Born Detroit Michigan June 16, 1939. Catholic. Educated at University of Detroit B.S. in Business Administration with honors 1962 and Detroit College of Law J.D. cum laude 1966. Recipient Clarence M. Burton Memorial Scholarship for Excellence 1961-62, Alumni Scholarship for Excellence 1962-63 and 1963-64 and Lawyers Title Award for Excellence 1965-66. Admitted to practice Michigan 1966 and U.S. Supreme Court. Began legal practice Detroit 1966. In legal practice Mount Clemens 1967 and Roseville 1968-78. Judge, Macomb County Probate Court June 1978 to March 1982. Judge, Michigan Circuit Court Sixteenth Judicial Circuit 1982-86, appointed by Governor William Grawn Milliken.

Corporate Personnel Staff Chrysler Corporation 1962-66. Assistant Prosecuting Attorney Macomb County 1967. Associate Government Appeal Agent Selective Service Administration 1969-72. Part-time Faculty Member Detroit College of Law. Guest lecturer Macomb County Community College. Member American Judicature Society, National Panel of Arbitrators American Arbitration Association, National Organization on Legal Problems of Education, National Council of Juvenile and Family Court Judges, Michigan Probate and Juvenile Court Judges Association (Mental Health Committee), National College of Probate Judges (inactive member), Michigan Judges Association, State Bar of Michigan (Representative Assembly two terms, Special Committee on Grievances), Macomb County (Member-at-large Board of Directors, Probate Court Liaison, Director and Treasurer Young Lawyers Section), Detroit and American Bar Associations. Recipient Voice of Democracy Awards 1975 and 1976, Americanism Award 1976 and Special Recognition Award 1978 from VFW. Former Republican County Chairman Macomb County. Member VFW (Legal Representative and Ad Hoc Committee, Mediator and spokesman for Robert Tucci Missing in Action Committee 1976, spokesman for VFW at Vietnamese Embassy Paris June 1976, judged two Voice of Democracy Programs and State-wide Judge for VFW Scholarships), Macomb-Oakland County Regional Center (Citizens Advisory Board 1978-79), Macomb County Youthscope (ex officio member), Juvenile Employment Education Program (Originator and Project Director), March of Dimes Metropolitan Detroit Chapter (Advisory Board), Selfridge Air National Guard Base Community Council and Michigan Committee for Prevention of Child Abuse. Board of Trustees St. Joseph Hospital of Mount Clemens. Addressed National League of Families Annual Meeting July 1976 and National VFW Convention New York Aug 1976 on issue of M.I.A.'s in Southeast Asia. Enjoys fishing and reading.

Office: 730 U.S. Courthouse, 231 West Lafayette Boulevard, Detroit 48226.

Telephone: (313) 234-5110.

ZELEZNIK, Joseph D. *(Chief Judge, Ontonagon County Probate Court)*

Office: Ontonagon County Courthouse, 725 Greenland Road, Ontonagon 49953-1492.

Telephone: (906) 884-4117.

ZEMAITIS, Daniel V. *(Judge, Michigan Circuit Court Seventeenth Judicial Circuit)*

Office: Kent County Courthouse, 180 Ottawa Avenue N.W., Grand Rapids 49503-2751.

Telephone: (616) 632-5480.

ZIOLKOWSKI, Robert L. *(Judge, Michigan Circuit Court Third Judicial Circuit)* Assumed office Oct 1, 1997. Term expires Dec 31, 2008. Born Detroit Michigan July 17, 1944. Educated at University of Iowa B.B.A. 1967 and Detroit College of Law J.D. 1970. Admitted to practice Michigan 1970. Judge, Michigan District Court District Thirty-six 1988-90. Judge, Recorder's Court of Detroit March 27, 1990 to Sept 30, 1997.

Office: 1611 Municipal Center, Two Woodward Avenue, Detroit 48226.

Telephone: (313) 224-5261.

MINNESOTA

Capital ST. PAUL

UNITED STATES DISTRICT COURT DISTRICT OF MINNESOTA

United States District Court District of Minnesota consists of six divisions. For descriptive information refer to the United States Courts section.

First Division includes Dodge, Fillmore, Houston, Mower, Olmsted, Steele, Wabasha and Winona counties. The court sits at Winona.

Second Division includes Blue Earth, Brown, Cottonwood, Faribault, Freeborn, Jackson, Lac qui Parle, Le Sueur, Lincoln, Lyon, Martin, Murray, Nicollet, Nobles, Pipestone, Redwood, Rock, Sibley, Waseca, Watonwan and Yellow Medicine counties. The court sits at Mankato.

Third Division includes Chisago, Dakota, Goodhue, Ramsey, Rice, Scott and Washington counties. The court sits at St. Paul.

Fourth Division includes Anoka, Carver, Chippewa, Hennepin, Isanti, Kandiyohi, McLeod, Meeker, Renville, Sherburne, Swift and Wright counties. The court sits at Minneapolis.

Fifth Division includes Aitkin, Benton, Carlton, Cass, Cook, Crow Wing, Itasca, Kanabec, Koochiching, Lake, Mille Lacs, Morrison, Pine and St. Louis counties. The court sits at Duluth.

Sixth Division includes Becker, Beltrami, Big Stone, Clay, Clearwater, Douglas, Grant, Hubbard, Kittson, Lake of the Woods, Mahnomen, Marshall, Norman, Otter Tail, Pennington, Polk, Pope, Red Lake, Roseau, Stearns, Stevens, Todd, Traverse, Wadena and Wilkin counties. The court sits at Fergus Falls.

Chief Judge
James M. Rosenbaum

Judges
Richard H. Kyle
Michael J. Davis
John R. Tunheim
Ann D. Montgomery
Donovan W. Frank

Senior Judges
Donald D. Alsop
Harry H. MacLaughlin
Paul A. Magnuson
David S. Doty

Clerk
Richard Sletten
202 U.S. Courthouse
300 South Fourth Street
Minneapolis, Minnesota 55415
(612) 664-5000

UNITED STATES MAGISTRATE JUDGES OF MINNESOTA

Franklin L. Noel
Raymond L. Erickson
Susan Richard Nelson
Janie S. Mayeron
Jonathan G. Lebedoff
Arthur J. Boylan
Mary Kay Klein

Recalled Magistrate Judge
J. Earl Cudd

UNITED STATES BANKRUPTCY COURT OF MINNESOTA

Chief Judge
Gregory F. Kishel

Judges
Robert J. Kressel
Dennis D. O'Brien
Nancy C. Dreher

Bankruptcy Clerk
Patrick G. De Wane
301 U.S. Courthouse
300 South Fourth Street
Minneapolis, Minnesota 55415
(612) 664-5200

MINNESOTA SUPREME COURT

The Supreme Court is Minnesota's court of last resort. The court consists of a chief justice and six associate justices elected in statewide nonpartisan elections for six-year terms. Vacancies are filled by the governor from a list provided by a nominating commission. Newly appointed justices serve until the next general election occurring at least one year after appointment, at which time they run for election. Retirement is mandatory at age seventy; however, the chief justice may assign retired justices to serve in any court.

The court has original appellate jurisdiction over first degree murder convictions, legislative contest appeals and appeals from the Tax Court and Workers' Compensation Court of Appeals. The court has discretionary review of decisions of the Court of Appeals and may issue all writs and processes necessary to the exercise of proper jurisdiction. The court has supervisory control over the lower courts and authority to regulate admission to the bar and review grievance complaints against attorneys. The court may answer any question of law certified to it by a federal court.

The court sits en banc at St. Paul but may sit in three-member panels for certain Workers' Compensation and Tax Court appeals.

Chief Justice
Kathleen A. Blatz

MINNESOTA SUPREME COURT—*Continued*

Associate Justices

Alan C. Page	Paul H. Anderson
James H. Gilbert	Russell A. Anderson
Sam Hanson	Helen M. Meyer

Clerk

Frederick K. Grittner
Minnesota Judicial Center
25 Rev. Dr. Martin Luther King, Jr. Blvd.
St. Paul, Minnesota 55155
(651) 297-5529

State Court Administrator

Sue K. Dosal
Minnesota Judicial Center
25 Rev. Dr. Martin Luther King, Jr. Blvd.
St. Paul, Minnesota 55155
(651) 296-2474

MINNESOTA COURT OF APPEALS

The Court of Appeals, established by constitutional amendment effective August 1, 1983, is Minnesota's court of intermediate appellate jurisdiction. Judges are elected in statewide nonpartisan elections to six-year terms. Vacancies are filled by the governor from a list provided by a nominating commission. The chief judge is appointed by the governor to serve a three-year term. Retirement is mandatory at age seventy; however, the chief justice may assign retired judges to serve any court except the Supreme Court.

The court has appellate jurisdiction over final decisions of the trial courts except decisions of conciliation courts and first degree murder convictions, appeals from administrative agency decisions and appeals from the Commissioner of Jobs and Training. The Supreme Court has discretionary review of the court's decisions. The court may issue all writs and processes necessary to the exercise of proper jurisdiction.

The court sits in rotating panels of three. Permanent chambers are maintained at St. Paul, but the court may sit in any of the ten judicial districts.

Chief Judge

Edward J. Toussaint, Jr.

Judges

Harriet Lansing	R. A. "Jim" Randall
Thomas J. Kalitowski	Robert H. Schumacher
Roger M. Klaphake	Randolph W. Peterson
James C. Harten	Bruce Donald Willis
Gordon W. Shumaker	G. Barry Anderson
Jill Flaskamp Halbrooks	Terri Stoneburner
David Minge	Natalie Hudson
Wilhelmina M. Wright	

MINNESOTA DISTRICT COURT

The District Court is Minnesota's court of general jurisdiction and consists of ten judicial districts. In 1982, the Legislature enacted a court organization act permitting each judicial district, with the majority vote of the judges in the district, to voluntarily merge the District, County and Municipal Courts into one unified court of general jurisdiction. As of September 1987, all judicial districts have so unified, thus eliminating all County and Municipal Courts. Judges are elected in district-wide nonpartisan elections to six-year terms. Vacancies are filled by the governor from a list provided by a nominating commission. Newly appointed judges serve until the next general election occurring at least one year after appointment, at which time they run for election. A chief judge is elected in each district by peer vote to serve a two-year term. Retirement is mandatory at age seventy; however, the chief justice may assign retired judges to serve any court except the Supreme Court.

The court has original jurisdiction in all civil and criminal actions including jurisdiction previously exercised by the County and Municipal Courts. The court may issue all writs, processes and orders necessary to the exercise of proper jurisdiction. Appeals are to the Court of Appeals except where the Supreme Court has original appellate jurisdiction.

The court sits at the county seats and as specified.

FIRST JUDICIAL DISTRICT includes Carver, Dakota, Goodhue, Le Sueur, McLeod, Scott and Sibley counties. The court sits at Chaska, Hastings, South St. Paul, Red Wing, Le Center, Glencoe, Shakopee and Gaylord.

Judges

Karen Asphaug	Thomas Bibus
Timothy L. Blakely	Robert F. Carolan
Joseph T. Carter	Terrence E. Conkel
Jean A. Davies	Kevin W. Eide
Duane R. Harves	Carol Hooten
Thomas R. Howe	Philip T. Kanning
Robert R. King, Jr.	Thomas R. Lacy
Edward I. Lynch	William E. Macklin
Kevin F. Mark	Thomas G. McCarthy
Timothy J. McManus	Leslie M. Metzen
Thomas M. Murphy	Mary E. Pawlenty
Richard C. Perkins	Thomas B. Poch
Martha M. Simonett	Michael V. Sovis
Richard G. Spicer	Rex D. Stacey
Patrice K. Sutherland	Mary Theisen
William F. Thuet	LeRoy W. Yost
Michael A. Young	

SECOND JUDICIAL DISTRICT includes Ramsey County. The court sits at St. Paul.

Judges

Gary W. Bastian	Louise Dovre Bjorkman
James H. Clark, Jr.	Edward J. Cleary
Michael T. DeCourcy	A. James Dickinson
Marybeth Dorn	Michael F. Fetsch
John T. Finley	Paulette K. Flynn
Kathleen R. Gearin	David C. Higgs
Gregg E. Johnson	William H. Leary
Dale B. Lindman	Margaret M. Marrinan
M. Michael Monahan	J. Thomas Mott
Rosanne Nathanson	Salvador M. Rosas
Joanne M. Smith	George T. Stephenson
Judith M. Tilsen	John Van de North, Jr.
Teresa R. Warner	Steven D. Wheeler
Edward S. Wilson	

THIRD JUDICIAL DISTRICT includes Dodge, Fillmore, Freeborn, Houston, Mower, Olmsted, Rice, Steele, Wabasha, Waseca and Winona counties. The court sits at Mantorville, Preston, Albert Lea, Caledonia, Austin, Rochester, Faribault, Owatonna, Wabasha, Waseca and Winona.

MINNESOTA DISTRICT COURT—*Continued*

Judges

Lawrence E. Agerter	Robert R. Benson
Robert Birnbaum	Bernard E. Borene
James E. Broberg	Joseph A. Bueltel
Joseph F. Chase	John A. Chesterman
Casey J. Christian	Lawrence T. Collins
James Fabian	Debra A. Jacobson
Margaret Shaw Johnson	William A. Johnson
Kevin Lund	Donald E. Rysavy
Jeffrey D. Thompson	Fred W. Wellmann
Joseph F. Wieners	Jodi Williamson
Gerald J. Wolf	Renee L. Worke

FOURTH JUDICIAL DISTRICT includes Hennepin County. The court sits at Minneapolis.

Judges

H. Peter Albrecht	Stephen C. Aldrich
Pamela G. Alexander	Ann L. Alton
Catherine L. Anderson	Thor Anderson
Patricia L. Belois	Robert A. Blaeser
Tanya M. Bransford	Kevin S. Burke
Philip D. Bush	Regina M. Chu
Francis J. Connolly	Harry Seymour Crump
Margaret A. Daly	Mel I. Dickstein
David M. Duffy	Mary Steenson DuFresne
Diana Eagon	Harvey C. Ginsberg
Isabel Gomez	Jeanne J. Graham
Myron S. Greenberg	Deborah Hedlund
John L. Holahan, Jr.	William R. Howard
Marilyn J. Kaman	Patricia Kerr Karasov
LaJune Thomas Lange	Steven Z. Lange
Gary R. Larson	Herbert P. Lefler, III
Tony N. Leung	Robert H. Lynn
Daniel H. Mabley	Tanja K. Manrique
George F. McGunnigle	E. Anne McKinsey
John Q. McShane	Cara Lee Neville
Beryl A. Nord	Jack S. Nordby
Allen Oleisky	Bruce A. Peterson
Steven A. Pihlaja	Charles A. Porter, Jr.
Janet Nordell Poston	Kathryn Quaintance
Denise D. Reilly	Katherian D. Roe
Marilyn Brown Rosenbaum	Warren R. Sagstuen
	Heidi S. Schellhas
Richard S. Scherer	John J. Sommerville
Stephen D. Swanson	James T. Swenson
Mark S. Wernick	Thomas Wexler
Lucy Ann Wieland	Lloyd B. Zimmerman

FIFTH JUDICIAL DISTRICT includes Blue Earth, Brown, Cottonwood, Faribault, Jackson, Lincoln, Lyon, Martin, Murray, Nicollet, Nobles, Pipestone, Redwood, Rock and Watonwan counties. The court sits at Mankato, New Ulm, Windom, Blue Earth, Jackson, Ivanhoe, Marshall, Fairmont, Slayton, St. Peter, Worthington, Pipestone, Redwood Falls, Luverne and St. James.

Judges

Allison Krehbiel Baskfield	Leland O. Bush
	David E. Christensen
Timothy K. Connell	Jeffrey L. Flynn
Bruce F. Gross	George I. Harrelson
Kurt D. Johnson	Warren E. Litynski
David W. Peterson	Douglas L. Richards
John R. Rodenberg	Norbert P. Smith
Linda S. Titus	Bradley C. Walker
Robert D. Walker	

SIXTH JUDICIAL DISTRICT includes Carlton, Cook, Lake and St. Louis counties. The court sits at Carlton, Grand Marais, Two Harbors, Duluth, Virginia and Hibbing.

Judges

David E. Ackerson	Terrence M. Aronson
James B. Florey	Terry C. Hallenbeck
Robert E. Macaulay	Gerald C. Martin
Mark A. Munger	John T. Oswald
Gary J. Pagliaccetti	Carol M. Person
Jeffry S. Rantala	Kenneth A. Sandvik
David P. Sullivan	Heather L. Sweetland
Dale A. Wolf	

SEVENTH JUDICIAL DISTRICT includes Becker, Benton, Clay, Douglas, Mille Lacs, Morrison, Otter Tail, Stearns, Todd and Wadena counties. The court sits at Detroit Lakes, Foley, Moorhead, Alexandria, Milaca, Little Falls, Fergus Falls, St. Cloud, Long Prairie and Wadena.

Judges

Richard J. Ahles	Timothy James Baland
David R. Battey	Bernard E. Boland
Thomas A. Godzala	Elizabeth A. Hayden
James W. Hoolihan	Peter Irvine
Michael S. Jesse	Richard T. Jessen
Michael L. Kirk	Thomas Knapp
Vicki E. Landwehr	John E. Pearson
Skipper J. Pearson	Sally Ireland Robertson
Steven Ruble	John H. Scherer
Thomas P. Schroeder	Waldemar B. Senyk
Thomas M. Stringer	Galen J. Vaa
William E. Walker	Kathleen A. Weir
Paul E. Widick	

EIGHTH JUDICIAL DISTRICT includes Big Stone, Chippewa, Grant, Kandiyohi, Lac qui Parle, Meeker, Pope, Renville, Stevens, Swift, Traverse, Wilkin and Yellow Medicine counties. The court sits at Ortonville, Montevideo, Elbow Lake, Willmar, Madison, Litchfield, Glenwood, Olivia, Morris, Benson, Wheaton, Breckenridge and Granite Falls.

Judges

Bruce W. Christopherson	Steven E. Drange
	Peter A. Hoff
John C. Lindstrom	David L. Mennis
Paul A. Nelson	Gerald J. Seibel
Randall J. Slieter	Kathryn N. Smith
Donald M. Spilseth	Jon E. Stafsholt

NINTH JUDICIAL DISTRICT includes Aitkin, Beltrami, Cass, Clearwater, Crow Wing, Hubbard, Itasca, Kittson, Koochiching, Lake of the Woods, Mahnomen, Marshall, Norman, Pennington, Polk, Red Lake and Roseau counties. The court sits at Aitkin, Bemidji, Walker, Bagley, Brainerd, Park Rapids, Grand Rapids, Hallock, International Falls, Baudette, Mahnomen, Warren, Ada, Thief River Falls, Crookston, Red Lake Falls and Roseau.

Judges

Donald J. Aandal	Paul T. Benshoof
Frederick J. Casey	Donna K. Dixon
David F. Harrington	John Hawkinson
Terrance C. Holter	Michael J. Kraker
Lois J. Lang	Charles H. LeDuc, II
John R. Leitner	Kurt J. Marben

MINNESOTA DISTRICT COURT—*Continued*

Jon A. Maturi	Jay D. Mondry
Dennis J. Murphy	Paul E. Rasmussen
John M. Roue	John P. Smith
John R. Solien	Richard C. Taylor
David TenEyck	Richard A. Zimmerman

TENTH JUDICIAL DISTRICT includes Anoka, Chisago, Isanti, Kanabec, Pine, Sherburne, Washington and Wright counties. The court sits at Anoka, Center City, Cambridge, Mora, Pine City, Elk River, Stillwater and Buffalo.

Judges

P. Hunter Anderson	Thomas G. Armstrong
Stephen J. Askew	Edward W. Bearse
Timothy R. Bloomquist	Mary E. Carlson
John E. Cass	James E. Dehn
Bruce Rodger Douglas	David E. Doyscher
Gregory G. Galler	Sharon L. Hall
Stephen M. Halsey	Karla Hancock
Mary E. Hannon	Thomas Hayes
John C. Hoffman	Jenny Walker Jasper
Kim Robert Johnson	Lawrence R. Johnson
Daniel M. Kammeyer	Nancy Logering
Ellen L. Maas	Elizabeth H. Martin
Krista K. Martin	John R. McBride
Gary J. Meyer	Susan R. Miles
James A. Morrow	Dale E. Mossey
Stephen L. Muehlberg	Lynn C. Olson
Alan Frank Pendleton	R. Joseph Quinn
Robert G. Rancourt	James Reuter
Michael J. Roith	Gary R. Schurrer
Douglas G. Swenson	Robert B. Varco
Donald J. Venne	

MINNESOTA TAX COURT

The Tax Court is a quasi-judicial court of special jurisdiction in Minnesota that is part of the executive branch. Judges are appointed by the governor with approval of the Senate for staggered six-year terms. The chief judge is elected by peer vote for a two-year term.

The court has jurisdiction over tax cases and consists of two divisions. A small claims division handles cases in which the amount in controversy does not exceed $2,500, and a regular division handles all other cases.

The court is based in St. Paul, but the judges may travel to the district or county where the controversy arises.

Chief Judge

George W. Perez

Judges

Kathleen H. Sanberg
Sheryl A. Ramstad

MINNESOTA WORKERS' COMPENSATION COURT OF APPEALS

The Workers' Compensation Court of Appeals is a quasi-judicial court of special jurisdiction in Minnesota that is part of the executive branch. The court consists of a chief judge and four judges appointed by the governor with approval of the Senate for staggered six-year terms. The chief judge is designated by the governor for an unspecified term.

The court has statewide jurisdiction over all questions of law and fact in workers' compensation appeals from the Workers' Compensation Divisions of the Department of Labor and the Office of Administrative Hearings. Appeals are to the Supreme Court.

The court sits in rotating panels of three, or en banc for cases involving important workers' compensation issues, at St. Paul.

Chief Judge

Thomas L. Johnson

Judges

Debra A. Wilson
William R. Pederson
Miriam P. Rykken
David A. Stofferahn

Minnesota Counties and County Seats

County	County Seat
Aitkin	Aitkin
Anoka	Anoka
Becker	Detroit Lakes
Beltrami	Bemidji
Benton	Foley
Big Stone	Ortonville
Blue Earth	Mankato
Brown	New Ulm
Carlton	Carlton
Carver	Chaska
Cass	Walker
Chippewa	Montevideo
Chisago	Center City
Clay	Moorhead
Clearwater	Bagley
Cook	Grand Marais
Cottonwood	Windom
Crow Wing	Brainerd
Dakota	Hastings
Dodge	Mantorville
Douglas	Alexandria
Faribault	Blue Earth
Fillmore	Preston
Freeborn	Albert Lea
Goodhue	Red Wing
Grant	Elbow Lake
Hennepin	Minneapolis
Houston	Caledonia

COUNTIES AND COUNTY SEATS—*Continued*

Hubbard
Park Rapids

Isanti
Cambridge

Itasca
Grand Rapids

Jackson
Jackson

Kanabec
Mora

Kandiyohi
Willmar

Kittson
Hallock

Koochiching
International Falls

Lac qui Parle
Madison

Lake
Two Harbors

Lake of the Woods
Baudette

Le Sueur
Le Center

Lincoln
Ivanhoe

Lyon
Marshall

Mahnomen
Mahnomen

Marshall
Warren

Martin
Fairmont

McLeod
Glencoe

Meeker
Litchfield

Mille Lacs
Milaca

Morrison
Little Falls

Mower
Austin

Murray
Slayton

Nicollet
St. Peter

Nobles
Worthington

Norman
Ada

Olmsted
Rochester

Otter Tail
Fergus Falls

Pennington
Thief River Falls

Pine
Pine City

Pipestone
Pipestone

Polk
Crookston

Pope
Glenwood

Ramsey
St. Paul

Red Lake
Red Lake Falls

Redwood
Redwood Falls

Renville
Olivia

Rice
Faribault

Rock
Luverne

Roseau
Roseau

St. Louis
Duluth

Scott
Shakopee

Sherburne
Elk River

Sibley
Gaylord

Stearns
St. Cloud

Steele
Owatonna

Stevens
Morris

Swift
Benson

Todd
Long Prairie

Traverse
Wheaton

Wabasha
Wabasha

Wadena
Wadena

Waseca
Waseca

Washington
Stillwater

Watonwan
St. James

Wilkin
Breckenridge

Winona
Winona

Wright
Buffalo

Yellow Medicine
Granite Falls

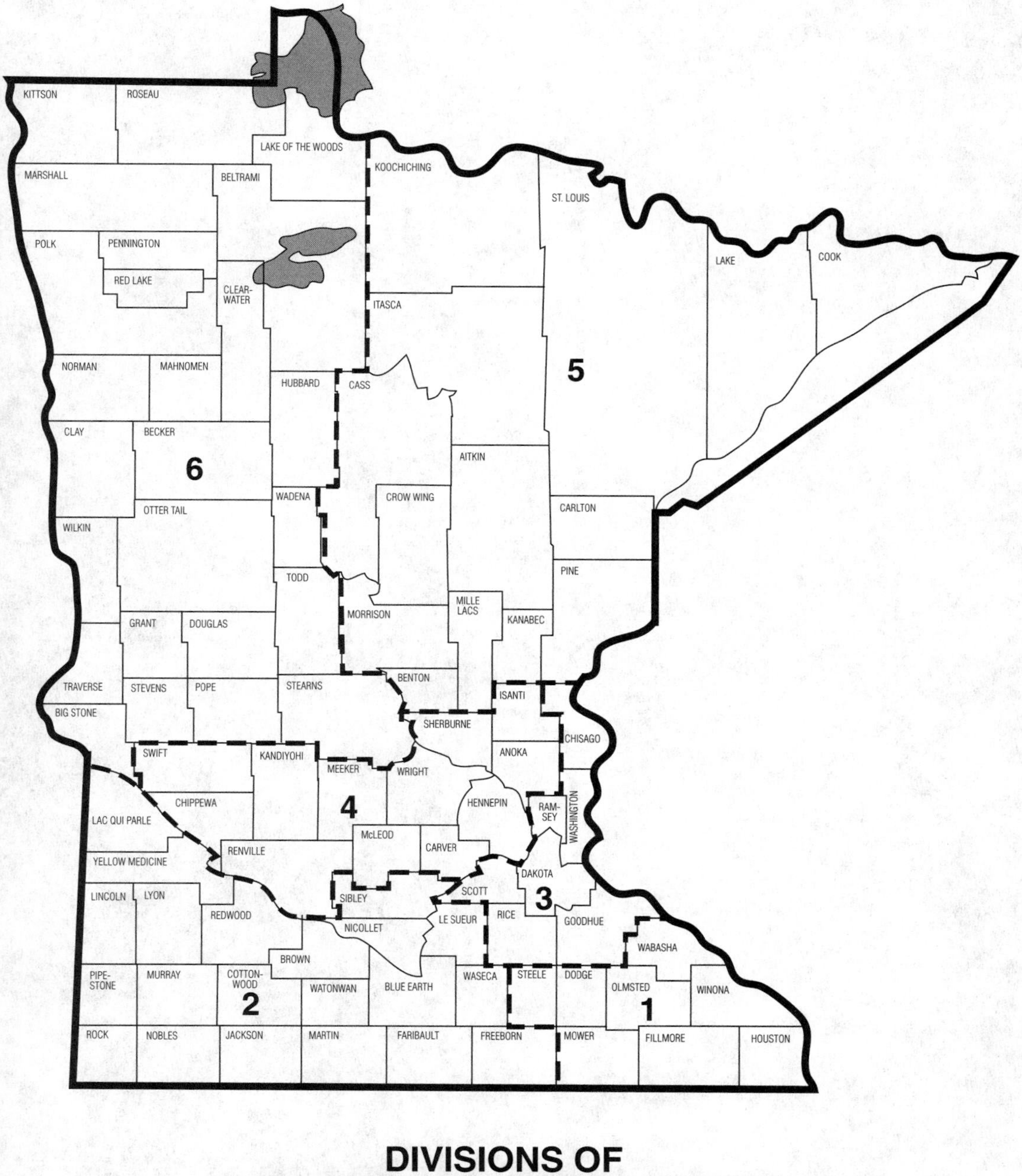
KITTSON
ROSEAU
LAKE OF THE WOODS
MARSHALL
BELTRAMI
KOOCHICHING
ST. LOUIS
POLK
PENNINGTON
RED LAKE
CLEAR-
WATER
ITASCA
LAKE
COOK
NORMAN
MAHNOMEN
HUBBARD
CASS
5
CLAY
BECKER
6
AITKIN
WADENA
CROW WING
CARLTON
OTTER TAIL
WILKIN
PINE
TODD
MILLE
LACS
KANABEC
MORRISON
GRANT
DOUGLAS
TRAVERSE
STEVENS
POPE
STEARNS
BENTON
ISANTI
BIG STONE
SHERBURNE
CHISAGO
SWIFT
KANDIYOHI
MEEKER
WRIGHT
ANOKA
CHIPPEWA
HENNEPIN
RAM-
SEY
WASHINGTON
LAC QUI PARLE
4
McLEOD
CARVER
RENVILLE
YELLOW MEDICINE
DAKOTA
SIBLEY
SCOTT
3
LINCOLN
LYON
REDWOOD
LE SUEUR
RICE
GOODHUE
NICOLLET
WABASHA
BROWN
PIPE-
STONE
MURRAY
COTTON-
WOOD
WATONWAN
BLUE EARTH
WASECA
STEELE
DODGE
OLMSTED
WINONA
2
1
ROCK
NOBLES
JACKSON
MARTIN
FARIBAULT
FREEBORN
MOWER
FILLMORE
HOUSTON

DIVISIONS OF UNITED STATES DISTRICT COURT DISTRICT OF MINNESOTA

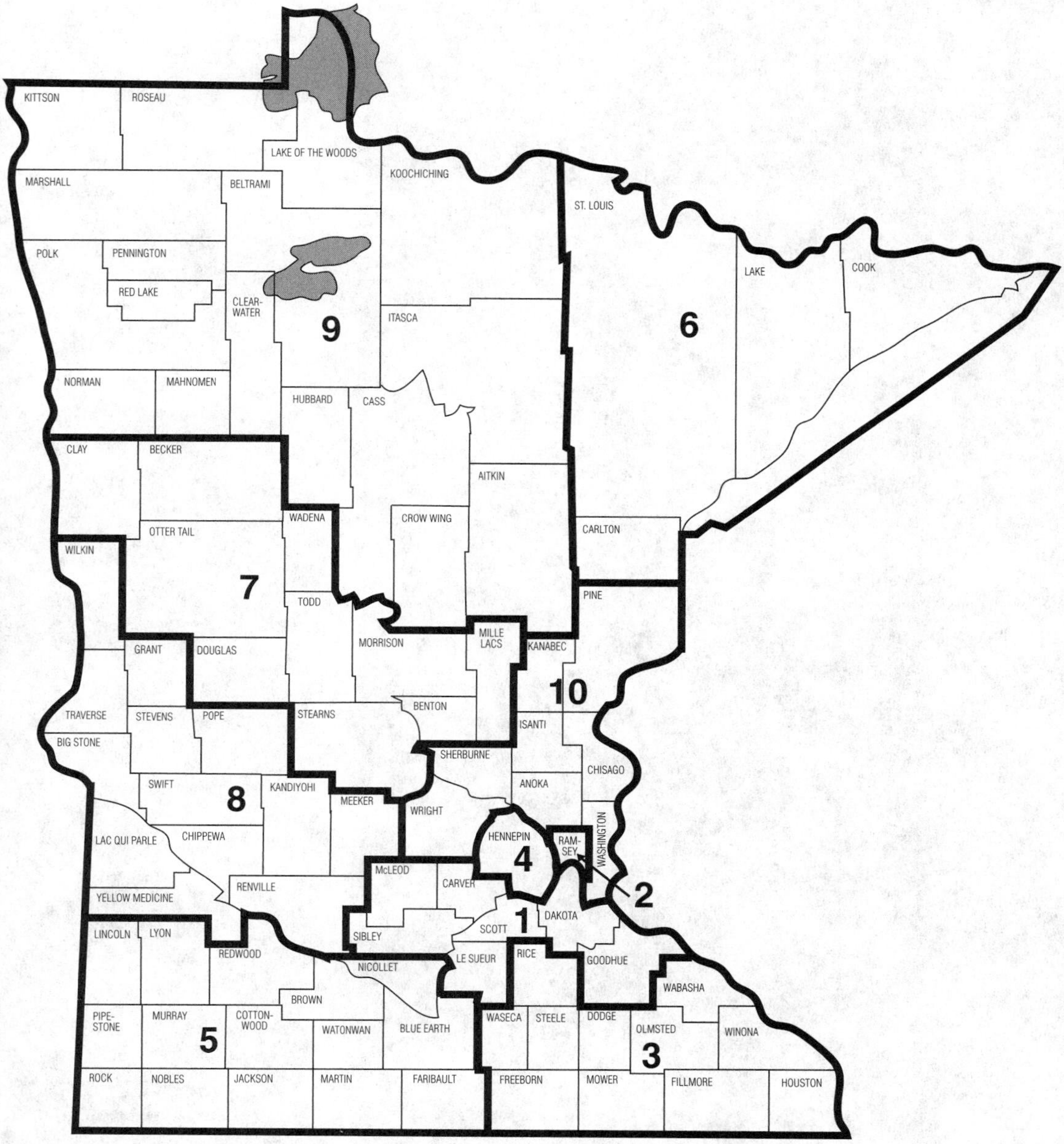
KITTSON
ROSEAU
LAKE OF THE WOODS
MARSHALL
BELTRAMI
KOOCHICHING
ST. LOUIS
POLK
PENNINGTON
RED LAKE
CLEAR-WATER
LAKE
COOK
9
ITASCA
6
NORMAN
MAHNOMEN
HUBBARD
CASS
CLAY
BECKER
AITKIN
WADENA
CROW WING
CARLTON
OTTER TAIL
WILKIN
7
PINE
TODD
MILLE LACS
GRANT
DOUGLAS
MORRISON
KANABEC
10
TRAVERSE
STEVENS
POPE
STEARNS
BENTON
ISANTI
BIG STONE
SHERBURNE
CHISAGO
SWIFT
8
KANDIYOHI
ANOKA
MEEKER
WRIGHT
WASHINGTON
HENNEPIN
RAM-SEY
LAC QUI PARLE
CHIPPEWA
4
McLEOD
CARVER
RENVILLE
2
YELLOW MEDICINE
1
DAKOTA
SCOTT
LINCOLN
LYON
SIBLEY
REDWOOD
LE SUEUR
RICE
GOODHUE
NICOLLET
WABASHA
BROWN
PIPE-STONE
MURRAY
COTTON-WOOD
WASECA
STEELE
DODGE
OLMSTED
WINONA
WATONWAN
BLUE EARTH
5
3
ROCK
NOBLES
JACKSON
MARTIN
FARIBAULT
FREEBORN
MOWER
FILLMORE
HOUSTON

JUDICIAL DISTRICTS OF MINNESOTA DISTRICT COURT

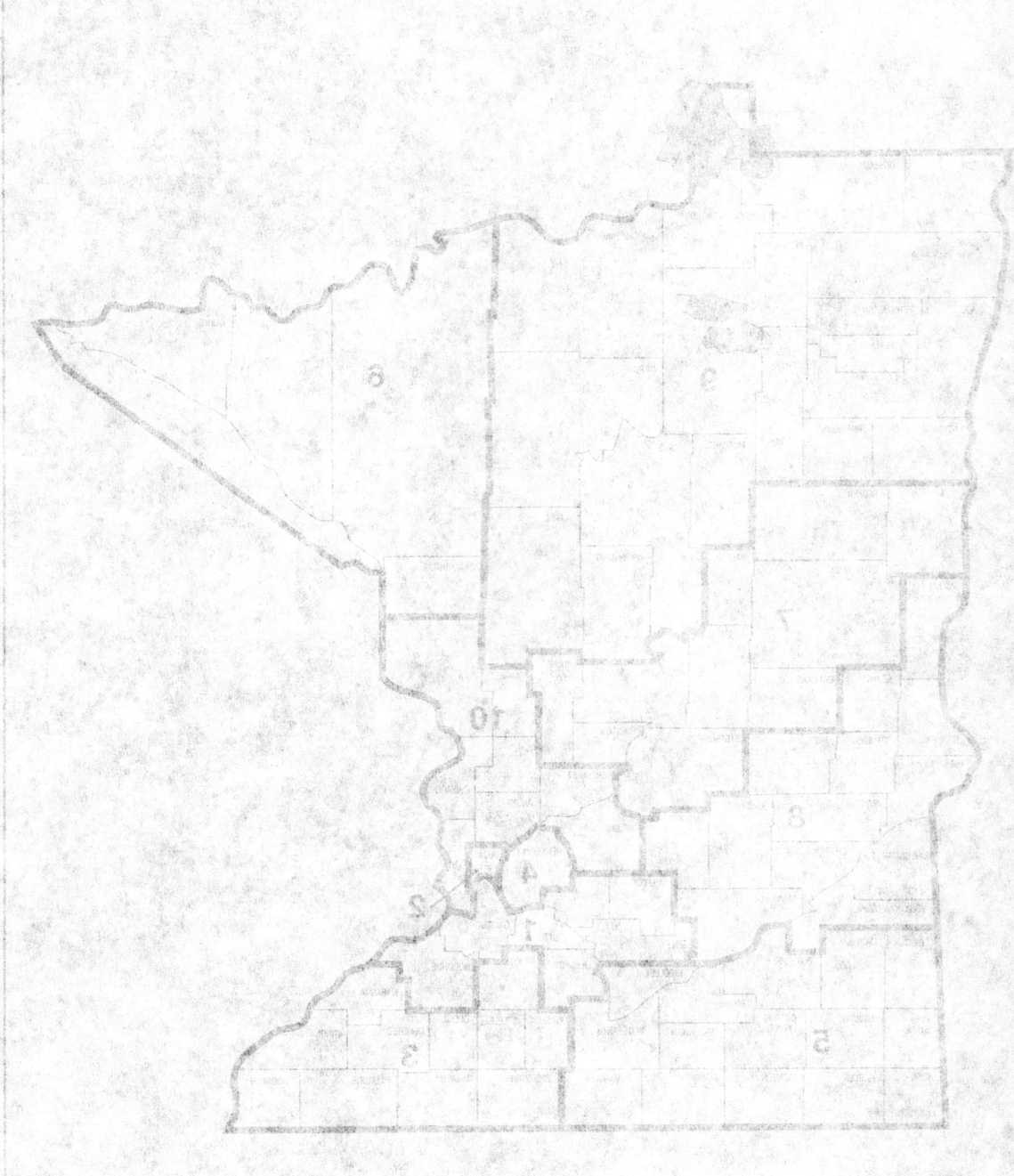

MINNESOTA

AANDAL, Donald J. *(Judge, Minnesota District Court Ninth Judicial District)*

Office: Marshall County Courthouse, 200 East Colvin Avenue, Warren 56762.

Telephone: (218) 745-4921.

ACKERSON, David E. *(Judge, Minnesota District Court Sixth Judicial District)* Assumed office July 24, 1986. Elected to subsequent terms. Former Judge, St. Louis County Court.

Office: St. Louis County Courthouse, 1810 Twelfth Avenue East, Hibbing 55746.

Telephone: (218) 262-0100.

AGERTER, Lawrence E. *(Judge, Minnesota District Court Third Judicial District)* Assumed office June 1984. Elected 1984, 1990, 1996 and 2002. Current term expires Jan 2009. Born Kasson Minnesota May 7, 1940. Lutheran. Educated at University of Minnesota, Mankato State University B.A. 1963 and William Mitchell College of Law J.D. 1968. Admitted to practice Minnesota 1968 and U.S. District Court District of Minnesota 1974. Began legal practice Owatonna 1968. In legal practice Kasson 1969-76. Judge, Dodge-Olmsted County Court 1976-84, appointed by Governor Wendell Anderson.

County Attorney Dodge County 1971-76. Member Olmsted County and Minnesota State Bar Associations. Instructor The National Judicial College 1982 and 1987.

Office: 22 Sixth Street East, #12, Mantorville 55955-2220.

Telephone: (507) 635-6260.

AHLES, Richard J. *(Judge, Minnesota District Court Seventh Judicial District)* Assumed office March 1984. Elected 1984, 1990, 1996 and 2002. Current term expires Jan 2009. Born St. Cloud Minnesota Feb 14, 1942. Educated at St. John's University B.A. 1964 and University of Minnesota J.D. 1967. Admitted to practice Minnesota 1967. In legal practice St. Cloud 1967-71. Judge, Sherburne-Benton-Stearns County Court 1976-84, appointed by Governor Wendell Anderson.

City Attorney St. Cloud 1971-76. Member Minnesota District Judges Association, Stearns-Benton (Past President) and Minnesota State Bar Associations. Past President Sertoma Club.

Office: Stearns County Courthouse, 725 Courthouse Square, St. Cloud 56303-4781.

Telephone: (320) 656-3664.

ALBRECHT, H. Peter *(Judge, Minnesota District Court Fourth Judicial District)* Born Minneapolis Minnesota Nov 27, 1944. Educated at American University 1963-65 and University of Minnesota B.A. 1967 J.D. 1971. Admitted to practice Minnesota 1971. In legal practice Minneapolis 1973-76. Former Judge, Hennepin County Municipal Court, elected to term beginning Jan 1, 1977.

With Minnesota Public Defender's Office at Minneapolis 1971. Member Hennepin County and Minnesota State Bar Associations.

Office: 12C Government Center, 300 South Sixth Street, Minneapolis 55487.

Telephone: (612) 348-2560.

ALDRICH, Stephen C. *(Judge, Minnesota District Court Fourth Judicial District)* Elected Nov 1996 to term beginning Jan 6, 1997. Reelected Nov 2002, current term expires Jan 2009. Born Minneapolis Minnesota Oct 28, 1941. Educated at Grinnell College B.A. 1963, Union Theological Seminary 1963-65 and University of Minnesota J.D. 1971. Staff member Minnesota Law Review 1969-71. Law Clerk to Hon. Philip Neville, U.S. District Court District of Minnesota 1971-72. Admitted to practice Minnesota 1972. In legal practice Minnesota 1975-97.

Assistant Senate Counsel Minnesota 1972-73. Assistant City Attorney St. Paul 1973-75. Member Hennepin County and Minnesota State Bar Associations.

Office: 12C Government Center, 300 South Sixth Street, Minneapolis 55487.

Telephone: (612) 348-7433.

E-mail address: Stephen.Aldrich@co.hennepin.mn.us

ALEXANDER, Pamela Gayle *(Judge, Minnesota District Court Fourth Judicial District)* Assumed office June 19, 1986. Born Minneapolis Minnesota Sept 25, 1952. Baptist. Educated at Augsburg College B.A. cum laude 1974 and University of Minnesota School of Law J.D. 1977. Listed in *Who's Who Among Students in American Colleges and Universities* 1972-74. Board of Directors Student Legal Services. Admitted to practice Minnesota 1977. Began legal practice Minneapolis 1977. Judge, Hennepin County Municipal Court Feb 2, 1983 to June 18, 1986.

Assistant Attorney Criminal Division Hennepin County 1981-83. Member Minnesota Minority Lawyers Association, National College of District Attorneys, National College of Criminal Defense, National Black Prosecutors Association and Hennepin County Bar Association. Recipient The Constance B. Motley Award 1982 and 1983, Phi Beta Sigma Fraternity Special Recognition Award 1982, Distinguished Service Award from Hennepin County Attorney's Office 1983, Community Service Award from Loft Teen Center 1983 and Community Service Award from Inner City Youth League 1983. Trust Administrator Corporate Trust Division First Bank of Minneapolis 1977-78. Former member Minneapolis Civil Rights Commission and Mid-Minnesota Legal Aid Board of Directors. Member Lux Alumni Association since 1977. Board member Sexual Assault Center since 1983.

Office: 12C Government Center, 300 South Sixth Street, Minneapolis 55487.

Telephone: (612) 348-5558.

ALSOP, Donald D. *(Senior Judge, United States District Court District of Minnesota)* Appointed for life by President Richard M. Nixon to term beginning Jan 17, 1975. Former Chief Judge. Assumed Senior status, serves by assignment. Born Duluth Minnesota Aug 28,

ALSOP, DONALD D.—*Continued*

1927. Lutheran. Educated at University of Minnesota-Duluth B.S.L. 1950 and University of Minnesota-Minneapolis LL.B. 1952. Student Editorial Board and staff member Minnesota Law Review 1950-51. Member Order of the Coif. Admitted to practice Minnesota 1952. In legal practice St. Paul 1952-54 and New Ulm 1954-75.

Author "Punitive Damages in Minnesota Products Liability Cases: A Judicial Perspective" 11 William Mitchell L. Rev. 319, 1985. President Ninth Judicial District Bar Association 1967-68 and Eighth Circuit Judges Association 1982-84. Director Minnesota Defense Lawyers Association 1969-71 and Minnesota Council of School Attorneys 1971-75. Member Committee to Implement the Criminal Justice Act 1979-87. Executive Committee National Conference of Federal Trial Judges American Bar Association 1990-94. Recipient New Ulm Junior Chamber of Commerce Distinguished Service Award. Private First Class U.S. Army 1945-46. Republican. Chairman Brown County Republican Committee 1961-63 and Minnesota Second Congressional District. Member District Republican Committee 1964-65 and 1967-71. Delegate Minnesota State and District Republican Conventions 1964 and Republican National Convention 1968. Co-chairman Minnesota Republican Party Convention 1968. Director New Ulm Chamber of Commerce 1964-67 and 1970-75 and University of Minnesota Law School Alumni Association 1973-77. Chairman American National Red Cross Brown-West Nicollet Chapter 1967-75. Past President New Ulm Toastmasters Club. Enjoys golf.

Office: 754 Federal Building, 316 North Robert Street, St. Paul 55101.

Telephone: (651) 848-1170.

ALTON, Ann L. *(Judge, Minnesota District Court Fourth Judicial District)*

Office: 12C Government Center, 300 South Sixth Street, Minneapolis 55487.

Telephone: (612) 348-8105.

ANDERSON, Catherine L. *(Judge, Minnesota District Court Fourth Judicial District)*

Office: 12C Government Center, 300 South Sixth Street, Minneapolis 55487.

Telephone: (612) 348-2050.

ANDERSON, G. Barry *(Judge, Minnesota Court of Appeals)* Appointed by Governor Arne H. Carlson May 21, 1998 to term beginning Aug 7, 1998. Educated at Gustavus Adolphus College and University of Minnesota Law School. Civil Trial Practice Specialist, Certified by Minnesota State Bar Association.

Office: 311 Minnesota Judicial Center, 25 Martin Luther King Jr. Blvd., St. Paul 55155.

Telephone: (651) 297-1007.

ANDERSON, P. Hunter *(Judge, Minnesota District Court Tenth Judicial District)* Appointed by Governor Rudy Perpich to term beginning Jan 13, 1986. Elected to subsequent terms.

Office: Isanti County Courthouse, 555 S.W. Eighteenth Avenue, Cambridge 55008-9386.

Telephone: (763) 689-2292.

ANDERSON, Paul H. *(Associate Justice, Minnesota Supreme Court)* Appointed by Governor Arne H. Carlson to term beginning July 1, 1994. Elected Nov 1996 and 2002. Current term expires January 2009. Born Eden Prairie Minnesota May 14, 1943. Presbyterian. Educated at Macalester College B.S. cum laude 1965 and University of Minnesota Law School J.D. 1968. Admitted to practice Minnesota 1968 and U.S. District Court District of Minnesota 1970. In legal practice South St. Paul 1971-92. Chief Judge, Minnesota Court of Appeals 1992-94.

Attorney VISTA 1968-69. Important Decisions: In the Matter of Leona Carlisle Trust Created Under the Trust Agreement dated February 9, 1985 (availability of trust assets for determining eligibility for medical assistance) 498 N.W.2d 260 Minn. Ct. App. 1993; State v. Alt (exclusion of statistical evidence and nonstatistical opinion testimony on significance of DNA "match" and cross-appeal challenging admission of DNA test results) 504 N.W.2d 38 Minn. Ct. App. 1993; and In the Matter of the Trust Created by Louis W. Hill on December 31, 1917 (challenge of beneficiary's attempt to remove and replace trustee) 499 N.W.2d 475 Minn. Ct. App. 1993. Member Dakota County, Ramsey County, Minnesota State and American (Committee on Education Council of Chief Judges Appellate Judges Conference Judicial Administration Division 1994) Bar Associations. Presenter "Court of Appeals Update" Ramsey County Bar Association Dec 9, 1992 and Dec 9, 1993, "Interlocutory Relief on Discovery Issues" May 7, 1993 and "A View from the Bench" Oct 21, 1994 Minnesota Trial Lawyers Association, "Real Estate Foreclosures in Minnesota" Minnesota State Bar Association CLE Sept 9, 1993 and Conference of Chief Judges Council of Chief Judges of Courts of Appeals Oct 1994. Participant Conference of Judges Minnesota Supreme Court Dec 1993 and Dec 1994 and "Civil Justice Consultation" Humphrey Institute Feb 1994. Instructor Family Law Institute Minnesota State Bar Association CLE April 19, 1994. Member and Chair Minnesota Judicial Selection Committee 1991-92. Board Member and Chair ISD 199 (PER Committees 1982-84). Member and Chair Community Services Advisory Committee. Board Member and Executive Committee Member South St. Paul/Inver Grove Heights Chamber of Commerce. Deacon and Ruling Elder House of Hope Presbyterian Church. Coaches girls' basketball. Enjoys tennis, gourmet cooking and bike riding (participated in The Ride Across Minnesota 1993 and 1994).

Office: 425 Minnesota Judicial Center, 25 Martin Luther King Jr. Blvd., St. Paul 55155.

Telephone: (651) 296-3314.

ANDERSON, Russell A. *(Associate Justice, Minnesota Supreme Court)* Assumed office 1998. Born Bemidji Minnesota May 28, 1942. Educated at St. Olaf College B.A. 1964, University of Minnesota Law School J.D. 1968 and George Washington University LL.M. 1977. In legal practice 1976-82. Judge, Minnesota District Court Ninth Judicial District 1982-98.

County Attorney Beltrami 1978-82. Chair Gender Fairness Implementation Committee and Liaison Advisory Committee on Rules of Criminal Procedure Minnesota Supreme Court. Member Minnesota District Judges Association, Hennepin County and Minnesota State Bar Associations.

Office: 426 Minnesota Judicial Center, 25 Martin Luther King Jr. Blvd., St. Paul 55155.

Telephone: (651) 296-2484.

ANDERSON, Thor *(Judge, Minnesota District Court Fourth Judicial District)* Appointed by Governor Arne

ANDERSON, THOR—*Continued*

H. Carlson to term beginning Feb 21, 1996. Elected Nov 1998, current term expires Jan 3, 2005. Born Kansas City Missouri Jan 6, 1937. Episcopalian. Educated at University of Mississippi B.A. 1958 and University of Minnesota LL.B. cum laude 1964. Admitted to practice Minnesota 1964, U.S. District Court District of Minnesota and U.S. Court of Appeals Eighth Circuit.

Assistant U.S. Attorney Minnesota 1969-96. Instructor in Criminal Procedure Hamline University School of Law 1980-82. Lieutenant j.g. USN 1958-61. Member House of Representatives Minnesota 1963-69. Enjoys opera.

Office: 12C Government Center, 300 South Sixth Street, Minneapolis 55487.
Telephone: (612) 348-6405.
Fax: (612) 348-2131
E-mail address: thorwald.anderson@co.hennepin.mn.us

ARMSTRONG, Thomas George *(Judge, Minnesota District Court Tenth Judicial District)* Assumed office Jan 11, 1984. Elected Nov 1986, Nov 1992 and Nov 1998. Current term expires Jan 2005. Born St. Paul Minnesota Jan 1, 1947. Catholic. Educated at University of Minnesota B.A. 1967 J.D. 1970. Admitted to practice Minnesota 1970, U.S. Court of Military Appeals 1971, Wisconsin 1973, U.S. Courts of Appeals Seventh 1973 and Eighth 1973 Circuits and U.S. Supreme Court 1973. In legal practice Lake Elmo Minnesota 1974-80. Judge, Washington County Court Jan 4, 1981 to Jan 10, 1984.

Instructor National College of Business 1976-77. Named Washington County Conservation Landowner of the Year 1992. Colonel USAR JAGC (retired) 1967-98 (active duty 1971-74). Mayor City of Lake Elmo 1977-81. Enjoys tree farming.

Mailing address: P.O. Box 3802, Stillwater 55082-3802.
Office: Washington County Government Center, Stillwater 55082-0006.
Telephone: (651) 430-6336.

ARONSON, Terrence M. *(Judge, Minnesota District Court Sixth Judicial District)*
Office: St. Louis County Courthouse, 300 South Fifth Avenue, Virginia 55792.
Telephone: (218) 749-7100.

ASKEW, Stephen J. *(Judge, Minnesota District Court Tenth Judicial District)*
Office: Anoka County Courthouse, 325 East Main Street, Anoka 55303-2489.
Telephone: (763) 422-7440.

ASPHAUG, Karen *(Judge, Minnesota District Court First Judicial District)*
Office: Dakota County Judicial Center, 1560 West Highway 55, Hastings 55033.
Telephone: (651) 438-4325.

BALAND, Timothy James *(Judge, Minnesota District Court Seventh Judicial District)* Appointed by Governor Rudy Perpich to term beginning March 2, 1984. Elected 1986, 1992 and 1998. Current term expires Jan 2005. Born Amery Wisconsin Nov 22, 1944. Educated at St. John's University B.A. in English cum laude 1966 and Cornell Law School J.D. 1975. Editor *Sagatagan* yearbook 1964 and 1965 and "Sketchbook" literary magazine 1966. Recipient Rotary Foundation Scholarship to Spain 1966-67. Law Clerk to Chief Justice Robert J. Sheran, Minnesota Supreme Court 1975-76. In legal practice Long Prairie 1976-84.

Assistant Public Defender Seventh Judicial District 1976-77. Co-author with Harrop Freeman "The Rich Get Richer and the Poor Get Taxes—Toward a Democratic Theory of Tax Reform" 2 No. 3 Hastings Constitutional L. Quar. 1975 and with Hon. Robert J. Sheran "The Law, Courts, and Lawyers in the Frontier Days of Minnesota: An Informal Legal History of the Years 1835-1865" 2 William Mitchell L. Rev. 1, 1976. Co-editor *Selected Poems of Miguel Hernandez and Blas de Otero* Beacon Press 1972. Author book review Cornell International L. Jour. Fall 1974. Member Minnesota State Bar Association (Founding member and President 1979-82 Section of General Practice). Facilitator Law and Literature Discussion Groups for Minnesota Judges and Attorneys. Editorial assistant to Mr. Robert Bly (Minnesota poet) summers of 1966 and 1967. Farmer 1967-72.

Office: Courthouse, 415 South Jefferson, Wadena 56482.
Telephone: (218) 631-7633.

BASKFIELD, Allison Krehbiel *(Judge, Minnesota District Court Fifth Judicial District)*
Mailing address: P.O. Box 518, St. James 56081.
Office: Watonwan County Courthouse, St. James 56081.
Telephone: (507) 375-1236.

BASTIAN, Gary W. *(Judge, Minnesota District Court Second Judicial District)* Appointed by Governor Arne H. Carlson Nov 26, 1997. Reelected Nov 7, 2000, current term expires Dec 31, 2006. Born St. Paul Minnesota Nov 7. Catholic. Educated at University of Wisconsin-River Falls B.S. 1970 and William Mitchell College of Law J.D. 1974. Admitted to practice Minnesota 1975, U.S. District Court District of Minnesota and U.S. Court of Appeals Eighth Circuit. In legal practice Minneapolis 1987-91.

General Counsel Teamster Local No. 320, 1987-91. Member Ramsey County and Minnesota State Bar Associations. Member Maplewood City Council 1980-90. Mayor City of Maplewood 1990-97. Commissioner Department of Labor and Industry 1995-97. Enjoys sculpting, watercolor painting and garden design.

Office: 1310 Ramsey County Courthouse, 15 West Kellogg Boulevard, St. Paul 55102.
Telephone: (651) 266-8226.
E-mail address: gary.bastian@courts.state.mn.us

BATTEY, David R. *(Judge, Minnesota District Court Seventh Judicial District)*
Office: Douglas County Courthouse, 305 West Eighth Avenue, Alexandria 56308.
Telephone: (320) 762-3033.

BEARSE, Edward W. *(Judge, Minnesota District Court Tenth Judicial District)* Appointed by Governor Rudy Perpich to term beginning April 6, 1983. Elected 1984, 1990, 1996 and 2002. Current term expires Jan 2009. Born Williamston Michigan Dec 12, 1941. Religious affiliation: Evangelical Covenant Church. Educated at Michigan State University B.A. with honors 1967 and University of Minnesota J.D. 1970. Admitted to practice Minnesota 1970 and Indiana 1971. Began legal practice Fort Wayne Indiana 1970. In legal practice St. Paul and Anoka Minnesota 1971-72 and 1975-83.

With Anoka County Attorney's Office 1971-74. Author "The Grand Jury" Minnesota County Attorneys As-

BEARSE, EDWARD W.—*Continued*

sociation 1975 and "Spousal Maintenance in Minnesota" Hennepin Lawyer April 1990. Co-author "Accommodating the Competing Goals in Minnesota's Third Party Worker's Compensation Claims" Hamline L. Rev. Feb 1987. Member Eighteenth Judicial District, Nineteenth Judicial District, Anoka County and Minnesota State Bar Associations. Specialist Five U.S. Army 1960-63. Enjoys running, hunting and fishing.

Office: Anoka County Courthouse, 325 East Main Street, Anoka 55303-2489.

Telephone: (763) 422-7440.

BELOIS, Patricia L. *(Judge, Minnesota District Court Fourth Judicial District)* Appointed by Governor Rudy Perpich to term beginning June 16, 1987. Elected Nov 8, 1988, 1994 and 2000. Current term expires Jan 2007. Born Minneapolis Minnesota May 31, 1945. Roman Catholic. Educated at University of Minnesota B.A. 1967 J.D. 1970. Law Clerk to Special Term Judge, Fourth Judicial District Minnesota 1970-71. Member Alpha Omicron Pi. Admitted to practice Minnesota 1970, U.S. District Court District of Minnesota 1972 and U.S. Supreme Court 1979. In legal practice Minneapolis 1970-73. Referee Fourth Judicial District 1976-87.

Supervisor Juvenile Division Public Defenders Office Hennepin County 1973-76. Member Minnesota Women Lawyers (President 1973-74), National Association of Women Judges, Hennepin County, Minnesota State and American Bar Associations. Participates in alumni activities of University of Minnesota. Travels internationally with University of Minnesota Law School. Enjoys doing handwork, sewing and gardening.

Office: 12C Government Center, 300 South Sixth Street, Minneapolis 55487.

Telephone: (612) 348-3534.

BENSHOOF, Paul T. *(Judge, Minnesota District Court Ninth Judicial District)* Appointed by Governor Arne H. Carlson to term beginning April 7, 1997. Elected 1998, current term expires Jan 2005. Born Detroit Lakes Minnesota Oct 13, 1951. Protestant. Educated at Carleton College B.A. magna cum laude 1974 and University of Minnesota J.D. cum laude 1978. Admitted to practice Minnesota 1978, California 1980 and U.S. Court of Appeals Eighth Circuit 1981. In legal practice Bemidji Minnesota 1978-97.

Co-author "Estimating Economic Loss for a Facially Disfigured Minor: A Case Study" Journal of Legal Economics July 1993.

Office: Beltrami County Courthouse, 619 Beltrami Avenue N.W., Bemidji 56601.

Telephone: (218) 759-6658.

BENSON, Robert R. *(Judge, Minnesota District Court Third Judicial District)*

Mailing address: P.O. Box 436, Preston 55965.

Office: Fillmore County Courthouse, Preston 55965.

Telephone: (507) 765-4483.

BIBUS, Thomas *(Judge, Minnesota District Court First Judicial District)*

Office: Goodhue County Justice Center, 454 West Sixth Street, Red Wing 55066.

Telephone: (651) 267-4800.

BIRNBAUM, Robert *(Judge, Minnesota District Court Third Judicial District)*

Office: Olmsted County Government Center, 151 Fourth Street S.E., Rochester 55904-3712.

Telephone: (507) 285-8181.

BJORKMAN, Louise Dovre *(Judge, Minnesota District Court Second Judicial District)*

Office: Juvenile & Family Justice Center, 25 West Seventh Street, St. Paul 55102.

Telephone: (651) 266-5163.

BLAESER, Robert A. *(Judge, Minnesota District Court Fourth Judicial District)*

Office: 12C Government Center, 300 South Sixth Street, Minneapolis 55487.

Telephone: (612) 348-4964.

BLAKELY, Timothy L. *(Judge, Minnesota District Court First Judicial District)*

Office: Goodhue County Justice Center, 454 West Sixth Street, Red Wing 55066.

Telephone: (651) 267-4800.

BLATZ, Kathleen A. *(Chief Justice, Minnesota Supreme Court)* Appointed by Governor Arne H. Carlson to term beginning Nov 1996. Chief Justice since Jan 1998. Educated at University of Notre Dame B.A. summa cum laude 1976 and University of Minnesota M.S.W. 1978 J.D. cum laude 1984. Member Phi Beta Kappa. In legal practice Minneapolis 1984-88. Judge, Minnesota District Court Fourth Judicial District Jan 1994 to Oct 1996.

Assistant County Attorney Hennepin County 1992-93. Chair Research Advisory Council National Center for State Courts. Board of Directors Conference of Chief Justices. Member Hennepin County and Minnesota State Bar Associations. State Representative Minnesota House of Representatives Jan 1979 to Jan 1994. Assistant Minority Leader 1987-90. Director Employee Assistance Program Fairview Community Hospital 1979-81. Board of Directors Big Brothers Big Sisters of Greater Minneapolis. Board of Visitors University of Minnesota Law School.

Office: 424 Minnesota Judicial Center, 25 Martin Luther King Jr. Blvd., St. Paul 55155.

Telephone: (651) 296-3380.

BLOOMQUIST, Timothy R. *(Judge, Minnesota District Court Tenth Judicial District)*

Office: Kanabec County Courthouse, 18 North Vine Street, Mora 55051.

Telephone: (320) 679-6400.

BOLAND, Bernard E. *(Judge, Minnesota District Court Seventh Judicial District)* Appointed by Governor Rudy Perpich to term beginning June 15, 1983. Elected 1984, 1990, 1996 and 2002. Current term expires Jan 2009. Born Minneapolis Minnesota Nov 14, 1943. Roman Catholic. Educated at University of Minnesota B.A. 1968 and William Mitchell College of Law J.D. 1973. Law Clerk to Hon. Lawrence Yetka, Minnesota Supreme Court 1973. Admitted to practice Minnesota 1973, U.S. District Court District of Minnesota 1973 and U.S. Court of Appeals Eighth Circuit 1982. Began legal practice Minneapolis 1974. In legal practice St. Cloud 1975.

City Attorney St. Cloud 1976-79. Member Minnesota State Judges Association and Minnesota State Bar Asso-

BOLAND, BERNARD E.—*Continued*

ciation. U.S. Army 1961-64. Probation Officer Hennepin County Municipal and District Courts 1969-72.

Office: Stearns County Courthouse, 725 Courthouse Square, St. Cloud 56303-4781.

Telephone: (320) 656-3672.

BORENE, Bernard E. *(Judge, Minnesota District Court Third Judicial District)* Appointed by Governor Rudy Perpich to term beginning April 2, 1984. Elected 1986, 1992 and 1998. Current term expires Jan 2005. Born Montevideo Minnesota March 8, 1945. Catholic. Educated at University of Minnesota B.A. 1967 J.D. 1970. Law Clerk to Hon. Urban J. Steimann, Minnesota District Court Third Judicial District 1970-71. Admitted to practice Minnesota 1970. Began legal practice Northfield 1971.

Member Minnesota State Bar Association. Past member and Director Northfield Jaycees and Northfield Lions Club.

Office: Rice County Courthouse, 218 N.W. Third Street, Faribault 55021.

Telephone: (507) 332-6185.

BOYLAN, Arthur J. *(Magistrate Judge, United States District Court District of Minnesota)* Appointed by U.S. District Court judges. Former Judge, Minnesota District Court Eighth Judicial District.

Office: 638 Federal Building, 316 North Robert Street, St. Paul 55101.

Telephone: (651) 848-1210.

BRANSFORD, Tanya M. *(Judge, Minnesota District Court Fourth Judicial District)*

Office: 12C Government Center, 300 South Sixth Street, Minneapolis 55487.

Telephone: (612) 348-3771.

BROBERG, James E. *(Judge, Minnesota District Court Third Judicial District)* Appointed by Governor Arne H. Carlson to term beginning Nov 7, 1997. Elected Nov 2000, current term expires Dec 31, 2006. Born Minneapolis Minnesota April 29, 1938. Catholic. Educated at University of Minnesota B.S. 1963 and University of Minnesota Law School J.D. 1965. Member Phi Alpha Delta. Admitted to practice Minnesota 1965, U.S. District Court District of Minnesota 1968 and U.S. Tax Court 1984. In legal practice Albert Lea 1965-97.

Assistant County Attorney Freeborn County 1965-68. City Attorney Albert Lea 1969-80. Member Minnesota District Judges Association and Minnesota State Bar Association. Attended Minnesota District Judges CLE, Minnesota Supreme Court CLE and Minnesota Bar Association CLE. Member Albert Lea Civic Music Board, Freeborn County Chamber of Commerce and Lions International (Melvin Jones Fellow 1992). Enjoys fishing, skiing, barbershop singing and amateur theater.

Office: Freeborn County Courthouse, 411 South Broadway, Albert Lea 56007.

Telephone: (507) 377-5153.

Fax: (507) 377-5162

E-mail address: james.broberg@courts.state.mn.us

BUELTEL, Joseph A. *(Judge, Minnesota District Court Third Judicial District)*

Office: Steele County Courthouse, 111 East Main, Owatonna 55060.

Telephone: (507) 444-7700.

BURKE, Kevin S. *(Judge, Minnesota District Court Fourth Judicial District)* Assumed office June 19, 1986. Elected to subsequent terms. Born Chicago Illinois Sept 17, 1950. Educated at University of Minnesota B.A. with honors 1972 J.D. with honors 1975. Admitted to practice Minnesota 1975, U.S. District Court District of Minnesota 1975, U.S. Court of Appeals Eighth Circuit 1975 and U.S. Supreme Court 1980. Began legal practice Minneapolis 1975. Judge, Hennepin County Municipal Court July 26, 1984 to June 18, 1986, appointed by Governor Rudy Perpich.

Author "DWI—A New Law—An Old Approach" 48 No. 2 The Hennepin Lawyer Nov-Dec 1978, "Public Defenders Trial Lawyers Manual" Minnesota Public Defenders Association and Hennepin County Public Defenders Office Oct 1979, "State on New Course for Sentencing: 'Just Desserts'" 6 No. 6 Minnesota Trial Lawyer Sept-Oct 1981 and "The Art of Cross Examination" William Mitchell Law Forum Aug 24, 1984. Adjunct Professor University of Minnesota Law School and William Mitchell College of Law. President Minnesota Public Defenders Association 1977-80. Chairman 1977-81 and Member 1977-83 Metropolitan Council Criminal Justice Committee. Chair State Board of Public Defense 1983-92. Chair Conference of Chief Judges 1991-96. Member Metropolitan Health Board 1975-76 and Minneapolis Employment Task Force 1981. Board member Legal Rights Center, Inc. 1978-84. Enjoys golfing and swimming.

Office: 12C Government Center, 300 South Sixth Street, Minneapolis 55487.

Telephone: (612) 348-4389.

BUSH, Leland O. *(Judge, Minnesota District Court Fifth Judicial District)*

Office: Lyon County Government Center, 607 West Main, Marshall 56258.

Telephone: (507) 537-6734.

BUSH, Philip D. *(Judge, Minnesota District Court Fourth Judicial District)* Appointed by Governor Rudy Perpich to term beginning July 9, 1989. Elected 1990, 1996 and 2002. Current term expires Jan 2009. Born Minneapolis Minnesota May 16, 1951. Educated at University of Minnesota B.E.S. 1975 J.D. cum laude 1980 and Sheffield University M.A. 1977. Admitted to practice Minnesota 1980 and U.S. District Court District of Minnesota 1980.

Co-author with John Stewart "Future of Voir Dire in Minnesota: Fair Juries or False Expedience" Minnesota Bench and Bar Dec 1981. Author "Court Rulemaking by the Legislature—Who Gets the Last Word" Minnesota Trial Lawyers Summer 1987.

Office: 12C Government Center, 300 South Sixth Street, Minneapolis 55487.

Telephone: (612) 348-6360.

CARLSON, Mary E. *(Judge, Minnesota District Court Tenth Judicial District)* Appointed by Governor Arne H. Carlson to term beginning Sept 1995. Elected Nov 1996 and 2002. Current term expires Jan 2009. Educated at University of Minnesota B.A. 1967 and William Mitchell College of Law J.D. 1978. Admitted to practice Minnesota 1978, U.S. District Court District of Minnesota and U.S. Court of Appeals Eighth Circuit.

Assistant Attorney Washington County 1978-81. Assistant U.S. Attorney Chief Civil Division 1981-94. Member Minnesota Women Lawyers, Minnesota District Judges Association, National Women Judges Association,

CARLSON, MARY E.—*Continued*

Washington County, Nineteenth District, Minnesota State, Federal and American Bar Associations.

Mailing address: P.O. Box 3802, Stillwater 55082-3802.

Office: Washington County Government Center, Stillwater 55082.

Telephone: (651) 430-6326.

CAROLAN, Robert F. *(Judge, Minnesota District Court First Judicial District)*

Office: Dakota County Judicial Center, 1560 West Highway 55, Hastings 55033.

Telephone: (651) 438-4325.

CARTER, Joseph T. *(Judge, Minnesota District Court First Judicial District)*

Office: Dakota County Judicial Center, 1560 West Highway 55, Hastings 55033.

Telephone: (651) 438-4325.

CASEY, Frederick J. *(Judge, Minnesota District Court Ninth Judicial District)* Elected Nov 1992 to term beginning Jan 4, 1993. Reelected Nov 1998, current term expires Jan 2005. Born Brainerd Minnesota April 30, 1942. Lutheran. Educated at Concordia College B.A. 1964 and University of Minnesota J.D. 1967. Admitted to practice Minnesota 1967 and U.S. District Court District of Minnesota. In legal practice Brainerd 1967-92.

Assistant Attorney Crow Wing County 1967-74. Assistant District Public Defender 1978-85. Member Crow Wing/Aitkin County, Minnesota State and American Bar Associations.

Office: Crow Wing County Courthouse, 326 Laurel Street, Brainerd 56401.

Telephone: (218) 824-1310.

CASS, John E. *(Judge, Minnesota District Court Tenth Judicial District)*

Mailing address: P.O. Box 3802, Stillwater 55082-3802.

Office: Washington County Government Center, Stillwater 55082.

Telephone: (651) 430-6339.

CHASE, Joseph F. *(Judge, Minnesota District Court Third Judicial District)*

Office: Olmsted Government Center, 151 Fourth Street S.E., Rochester 55904-3712.

Telephone: (507) 285-8154.

CHESTERMAN, John A. *(Judge, Minnesota District Court Third Judicial District)*

Office: Freeborn County Courthouse, 411 South Broadway, Albert Lea 56007.

Telephone: (507) 377-5153.

CHRISTENSEN, David E. *(Judge, Minnesota District Court Fifth Judicial District)* Assumed office Sept 1987. Elected 1990, 1996 and 2002. Current term expires Jan 2009. Born Tracy Minnesota Feb 12, 1940. Educated at University of Minnesota B.A. 1962 J.D. 1968. Admitted to practice Minnesota 1968. Began legal practice Pipestone 1968. Judge, Pipestone County Court Feb 26, 1979 to Sept 1987.

Member Thirteenth Judicial District and Minnesota State Bar Association. First Lieutenant USAF 1962-65.

Mailing address: P.O. Box 337, Pipestone 56164.

Office: Pipestone County Courthouse, 416 South Hiawatha Avenue, Pipestone 56164.

Telephone: (507) 825-6732.

CHRISTIAN, Casey J. *(Judge, Minnesota District Court Third Judicial District)*

Office: Steele County Courthouse, 111 East Main, Owatonna 55060.

Telephone: (507) 444-7700.

CHRISTOPHERSON, Bruce W. *(Judge, Minnesota District Court Eighth Judicial District)*

Office: Yellow Medicine County Courthouse, 415 Ninth Avenue, Granite Falls 56241.

Telephone: (320) 564-3325.

CHU, Regina M. *(Judge, Minnesota District Court Fourth Judicial District)*

Office: 12C Government Center, 300 South Sixth Street, Minneapolis 55487.

Telephone: (612) 348-7788.

CLARK, James H., Jr. *(Judge, Minnesota District Court Second Judicial District)*

Office: 1450 Ramsey County Courthouse, 15 West Kellogg Boulevard, St. Paul 55102.

Telephone: (651) 266-8207.

CLEARY, Edward J. *(Judge, Minnesota District Court Second Judicial District)*

Office: 1550 Ramsey County Courthouse, 15 West Kellogg Boulevard, St. Paul 55102.

Telephone: (651) 266-8468.

COLLINS, Lawrence T. *(Judge, Minnesota District Court Third Judicial District)* Appointed by Governor Albert H. Quie to term beginning Feb 8, 1982. Elected 1984, 1990, 1996 and 2002. Current term expires Jan 2009. Former Chief Judge.

Former Chair Conference of Chief Judges.

Office: Winona County Courthouse, 171 West Third Street, Winona 55987.

Telephone: (507) 457-6480.

CONKEL, Terrence E. *(Judge, Minnesota District Court First Judicial District)* Appointed by Governor Arne H. Carlson Aug 28, 1998. Elected Nov 2000, current term expires Jan 2007. Educated at University of Minnesota B.A. 1973 and Creighton University J.D. 1976. Admitted to practice Minnesota 1977 and U.S. District Court District of Minnesota 1982. In legal practice Glencoe 1977-98.

Member Minnesota District Judges Association and Minnesota State Bar Association.

Office: McLeod County Courthouse, 830 Eleventh Street East, Glencoe 55336.

Telephone: (320) 864-5551.

E-mail address: terrence.conkel@courts.state.mn.us

CONNELL, Timothy K. *(Judge, Minnesota District Court Fifth Judicial District)* Appointed by Governor Rudy Perpich to term beginning June 30, 1987. Elected 1988, 1994 and 2000. Current term expires Jan 2007. Born June 9, 1949. Educated at St. John's University B.A. 1971 and William Mitchell College of Law J.D. 1976. Admitted to practice Minnesota 1976. In legal practice Luverne 1976-87.

CONNELL, TIMOTHY K.—*Continued*

County Attorney Rock County 1976-87. President Minnesota District Judges Association 2001-02.
Mailing address: P.O. Box 745, Luverne 56156.
Office: Rock County Courthouse, 204 East Brown, Luverne 56156.
Telephone: (507) 283-5020.
Fax: (507) 283-5017

CONNOLLY, Francis J. *(Judge, Minnesota District Court Fourth Judicial District)*
Office: 12C Government Center, 300 South Sixth Street, Minneapolis 55487.
Telephone: (612) 596-6835.

CRUMP, Harry Seymour *(Judge, Minnesota District Court Fourth Judicial District)* Appointed by Governor Rudy Perpich to term beginning Dec 1987. Elected 1991 and 1997. Current term expires Jan 2004. Educated at Wilson Junior College of Chicago A.A. 1962, University of Illinois B.S. in Pharmacy 1967 and DePaul University College of Law J.D. 1974. Recipient American Jurisprudence Award in Criminal Law and Criminal Procedure. Administrative Law Judge, Minnesota Office of Administrative Hearings March 1979 to Dec 1983.

Field Attorney and Hearing Officer National Labor Relations Board Sept 1974 to Sept 1975. Assistant Director and Equal Employment Opportunity Commission and Compliance Officer St. Paul Department of Human Rights and Civil Rights Sept 1975 to March 1978. Commissioner Minnesota Public Utilities Commission Jan 1984 to Dec 1987 (Chairman Jan 1986 to March 1987). Faculty Member and Consultant Washington Universities. Adjunct Professor Clinical Administrative Law Program William Mitchell College of Law. Adjunct Lecturer on Jurisprudence University of Minnesota College of Pharmacy. Chair Security Committee Hennepin County District Court, Committee on Probate Minnesota District Judges and Committee on Interactive Audio-Video Communications Minnesota Supreme Court. Attorney, Executive Committee and Board of Directors Hennepin County Bar Association Legal Advice Clinics. Liaison to Administrative Law Judges Subcommittee and Member Administration Committee and Governor's Telecommunications Tax Policy Team 1987 National Association of Regulatory Utility Commissioners. Minnesota Representative U.S. Transportation Commission Conference. Co-initiator, Co-founder and First Secretary Minnesota Minority Lawyers Association. Board Director and Chair Criminal Law Committee and Events and Activities Committee. Attended "Administrative Law Procedure" Dec 18, 1982 and "Administrative Law Complex Adjudicatory Proceedings" June 24, 1983 The National Judicial College. Faculty Member National Center for State Courts. Previously worked as carpenter and automobile mechanic and teacher. Registered Pharmacist and Manager Frank's Stineway Drugs June 1962 to Jan 1968. Hospital Sales Representative Eli Lilly and Company Jan 1968 to Jan 1974. Arbitrator St. Paul Better Business Bureau. Former Vice President, Board of Directors, Attorney and Chair Legal Redress Committee St. Paul Chapter and former Vice President Minnesota/Dakota State Conferences NAACP. Past President, Cabinet Member District Governors, Zone Chairman and Telethon Chairman Burnsville Lions Club. Former Member and Vice Chairman Burnsville School Board Advisory Council. Member Integration Review Committee St. Paul School Board. Chair and Board of Directors St. Paul Urban League. Director Institute on Black Chemical Abuse. Member and Chair Health Services Committee and Chair Health and Safety Committee and Transportation Committee St. Paul Chapter American Red Cross. Director National Brotherhood of Skiers Safety Patrol. Member National Alpine Ski Patrol. Private pilot. Ski and sailboard instructor. Enjoys golf, tennis, racquetball, camping, scuba diving, sailing, chess, backgammon, mountain climbing and other sports.
Office: 12C Government Center, 300 South Sixth Street, Minneapolis 55487.
Telephone: (612) 348-5137.

CUDD, J. Earl *(Recalled Magistrate Judge, United States District Court District of Minnesota)* Appointed Magistrate by U.S. District Court judges. Appointed Recalled Magistrate Judge by the Judicial Council of the Eighth Circuit.
Office: 8E U.S. Courthouse, 300 South Fourth Street, Minneapolis 55415.
Telephone: (612) 664-5140.

DALY, Margaret A. *(Judge, Minnesota District Court Fourth Judicial District)*
Office: 12C Government Center, 300 South Sixth Street, Minneapolis 55487.
Telephone: (612) 348-6952.

DAVIES, Jean A. *(Judge, Minnesota District Court First Judicial District)*
Office: Carver County Justice Center, 600 East Fourth Street, Chaska 55318.
Telephone: (952) 361-1420.

DAVIS, Michael J. *(Judge, United States District Court District of Minnesota)* Appointed for life by President Bill Clinton to term beginning March 30, 1994. Born Cincinnati Ohio July 21, 1947. Methodist. Educated at Macalester College B.A. 1969 and University of Minnesota Law School J.D. 1972. Honorary Doctor of Law Macalester College 2001. Recipient Ralph L. Smith Freedom Scholarship. Chairman Black American Law Students Association 1971. Admitted to practice Minnesota 1974, U.S. District Court District of Minnesota, U.S. Court of Appeals Eighth Circuit and U.S. Supreme Court. Began legal practice Minneapolis 1974. Judge, Hennepin County Municipal Court 1983-84. Judge, Minnesota District Court Fourth Judicial District April 3, 1984 to March 29, 1994.

Office of General Counsel Litigation Division U.S. Department of Health, Education and Welfare 1973. Criminal Defense Lawyer Neighborhood Justice Center, Inc. St. Paul 1974, Legal Rights Center, Inc. Minneapolis 1975-78 and Public Defender's Office Hennepin County 1978-83. Instructor in Criminal Defense Trial Skills National Lawyers Guild Seminar 1977 and Trial Skills William Mitchell College of Law 1977-81. Adjunct Professor University of Minnesota Law School since 1982 and Hubert H. Humphrey School of Public Affairs Fall 1990. Lecturer on "Evidence in the Courtroom" Minnesota Continuing Legal Education 1990 and on "Forensic DNA Technology and the Courtroom" Federal Bureau of Investigation Academy Quantico Virginia Fall 1991 and Spring 1992. Lecturer Civil Trial Practice Institute Minnesota Institute of Legal Education 1991 and 1992 and National Conference National Association of Pretrial Services Agencies Oct 1992. Faculty member Bemidji Trial Advocacy Course June 1991 and 1992.

DAVIS, MICHAEL J.—*Continued*

Member Attorney General's Task Force on the Prevention of Sexual Violence Against Women 1988-89 and Closed-Circuit Television Task Force 1991 and Racial Bias Task Force (Co-chair Criminal Process Committee, Chair Editorial Committee, Member Executive Committee and Data Collection Committee since 1990) Minnesota Supreme Court. Chair Pretrial Release and Bail Evaluation Committee U.S. District Court District of Minnesota since 1997. Member Eighth Circuit Jury Instruction Committee, Federal Judges Association, International Academy of Trial Judges and National Bar Association. Attended Hague Academy of International Law Hague, Netherlands Summer 1973; National Institute for Trial Advocacy Reno, Nevada Summer 1974; National College of Criminal Defense and Public Defenders Houston, Texas Summer 1975; "General Jurisdiction" 1983 and "Civil Litigation" 1984 The National Judicial College; and "Evidence" 1986, "Criminal Trial Skills" 1987 and "Advanced Evidence" 1991 American Academy of Judicial Education. Recipient Macalester College Outstanding Alumni Award 1989, Distinguished Service Award 2000 and WCCO Radio Good Neighbor Award for efforts in masterminding the criminal caseload reduction program in Hennepin County. Member National Association for Public Interest Law Fellowships for Equal Justice 1996-2001. Board of Directors Legal Rights Center since 2000. Former Member Board of Directors Try Us Meyerhoff Fund.

Office: 14E U.S. Courthouse, 300 South Fourth Street, Minneapolis 55415.

Telephone: (612) 664-5070.

DeCOURCY, Michael T. *(Judge, Minnesota District Court Second Judicial District)*

Office: Juvenile & Family Justice Center, 25 West Seventh Street, St. Paul 55102.

Telephone: (651) 266-5166.

DEHN, James E. *(Judge, Minnesota District Court Tenth Judicial District)* Appointed by Governor Rudy Perpich to term beginning June 26, 1987. Elected Nov 5, 1988, 1994 and 2000. Current term expires Jan 2007. Born Minneapolis Minnesota Sept 25, 1949. Methodist. Educated at University of Minnesota B.A. 1971 and William Mitchell College of Law J.D. 1975. Admitted to practice Minnesota 1976. In legal practice Cambridge 1980-87.

Member Minnesota State Bar Association. Attended General Jurisdiction Course The National Judicial College Reno April 1988. Instructor in Sentencing Alternatives New Judges Seminar 1989-90 and Minnesota Sentencing Institute 1989-91. Enjoys hiking, canoeing, family biking and winter camping.

Office: Isanti County Government Center, 555 S.W. Eighteenth Avenue, Cambridge 55008-9386.

Telephone: (763) 689-2292.

DICKINSON, A. James *(Judge, Minnesota District Court Second Judicial District)* Appointed by Governor Arne H. Carlson to term beginning April 17, 1997.

Office: 1680 Ramsey County Courthouse, 15 West Kellogg Boulevard, St. Paul 55102.

Telephone: (651) 266-8282.

DICKSTEIN, Mel I. *(Judge, Minnesota District Court Fourth Judicial District)*

Office: 12C Government Center, 300 South Sixth Street, Minneapolis 55487.

Telephone: (612) 596-8825.

DIXON, Donna K. *(Judge, Minnesota District Court Ninth Judicial District)*

Office: Roseau County Courthouse, 606 Fifth Avenue S.W., Roseau 56751.

Telephone: (218) 463-2541.

DORN, Marybeth *(Judge, Minnesota District Court Second Judicial District)*

Office: 1640 Ramsey County Courthouse, 15 West Kellogg Boulevard, St. Paul 55102.

Telephone: (651) 266-8211.

DOTY, David S. *(Senior Judge, United States District Court District of Minnesota)* Appointed for life by President Ronald Reagan to term beginning May 7, 1987. Assumed Senior status June 30, 1998, serves by assignment. Born Anoka Minnesota June 30, 1929. Educated at University of Minnesota cum laude 1961. Editor Minnesota Law Review. Admitted to practice Minnesota, U.S. District Court District of Minnesota, U.S. Courts of Appeals Eighth and Ninth Circuits and U.S. Supreme Court. In legal practice Minneapolis 1962-87.

Special Attorney General 1968-69. Instructor in Labor Law William Mitchell College of Law 1965-66. Former member National Panel of Arbitrators American Arbitration Association. Fellow American Bar Foundation. Member American Law Institute, American Judicature Society, Federal Judges Association, Hennepin County (President 1975-76), Minnesota State (Board of Governors 1976-87, Secretary 1980-83, President 1984-85), Federal and American Bar Associations. Member Supreme Court Committee on Public Education and Information 1978-81. Chairman Judicial Nominating Committee Hennepin County 1980-82 and Supreme Court Nominating Committee 1981. Served to Captain USMC 1952-58. Trustee Minneapolis Library Board 1970-80 and Minneapolis Foundation 1976-82. Board member Minnesota Hearing Society 1983-87. Board of Visitors University of Minnesota Law School 1983-88. Member Citizens League, Friends of the Library, Six O'Clock Club, Minneapolis Club, Minikahda Club and St. Mark's Episcopal Church.

Office: 14W U.S. Courthouse, 300 South Fourth Street, Minneapolis 55415.

Telephone: (612) 664-5060.

DOUGLAS, Bruce Rodger *(Judge, Minnesota District Court Tenth Judicial District)* Appointed by Governor Albert H. Quie to term beginning Dec 31, 1982. Elected 1984, 1990, 1996 and 2002. Current term expires Jan 2009. Born Minneapolis Minnesota Aug 14, 1945. Educated at Carleton College B.A. 1967 and University of Minnesota J.D. 1970. Admitted to practice Minnesota 1970, U.S. District Court District of Minnesota 1970, U.S. Court of Military Appeals 1973 and Washington 1979. In legal practice Buffalo Minnesota 1975-82.

Assistant Public Defender Tenth Judicial District 1975-82. Member Minnesota State and American Bar

DOUGLAS, BRUCE RODGER—*Continued*
Associations. Lieutenant USNR JAGC 1968-79 (active duty 1970-74).

Office: 201 Wright County Government Center, 10 Second Street N.W., Buffalo 55313-1192.

Telephone: (763) 682-7539.

DOYSCHER, David E. *(Judge, Minnesota District Court Tenth Judicial District)* Appointed by Governor Rudy Perpich Dec 13, 1985 to term beginning Feb 3, 1986. Elected Nov 8, 1988, Nov 8, 1994 and 2000. Current term expires Jan 2007. Chief Judge since 1994. Born Jackson Minnesota Aug 30, 1939. Lutheran. Educated at Maryville College (Tennessee) B.A. with honors 1961 and University of Minnesota J.D. with honors 1971. Member Gamma Eta Gamma. Admitted to practice Minnesota 1971 and U.S. District Court District of Minnesota 1971. In legal practice St. Paul 1971-77 and Forest Lake 1977-86.

Member Nineteenth District (Past President), Washington County and Minnesota State Bar Associations. U.S. Army 1961-64.

Mailing address: P.O. Box 3802, Stillwater 55082-3802.

Office: Washington County Government Center, Stillwater 55082.

Telephone: (651) 430-6342.

DRANGE, Steven E. *(Judge, Minnesota District Court Eighth Judicial District)*

Office: Meeker County Courthouse, 325 Sibley Avenue North, Litchfield 55355.

Telephone: (320) 693-5230.

DREHER, Nancy C. *(Judge, United States Bankruptcy Court District of Minnesota)* Appointed by U.S. Court of Appeals Eighth Circuit judges to term beginning 1988. Reappointed Jan 2002, current term expires Jan 2016. Also Judge, Bankruptcy Appellate Panel Eighth Circuit. Selected by the Judicial Council of the Eighth Circuit to term beginning 1996. Educated at University of Wisconsin B.A. 1964 J.D. 1967. Articles Editor Wisconsin Law Review. In legal practice 1968-88.

Adjunct Professor of Civil Trial Practice William Mitchell College of Law 1981-82. Adjunct Professor University of Minnesota 1992-94.

Office: 7W U.S. Courthouse, 300 South Fourth Street, Minneapolis 55415.

Telephone: (612) 664-5260.

DUFFY, David M. *(Judge, Minnesota District Court Fourth Judicial District)*

Office: 12C Government Center, 300 South Sixth Street, Minneapolis 55487.

Telephone: (612) 348-6251.

DuFRESNE, Mary Steenson *(Judge, Minnesota District Court Fourth Judicial District)*

Office: 12C Government Center, 300 South Sixth Street, Minneapolis 55487.

Telephone: (612) 348-7174.

EAGON, Diana *(Judge, Minnesota District Court Fourth Judicial District)*

Office: 12C Government Center, 300 South Sixth Street, Minneapolis 55487.

Telephone: (612) 348-7577.

EIDE, Kevin W. *(Judge, Minnesota District Court First Judicial District)*

Office: Carver County Justice Center, 600 East Fourth Street, Chaska 55318.

Telephone: (952) 361-1440.

ERICKSON, Raymond L. *(Magistrate Judge, United States District Court District of Minnesota)* Appointed by U.S. District Court judges.

Office: 412 U.S. Courthouse, 515 West First Street, Duluth 55802.

Telephone: (218) 529-3520.

FABIAN, James *(Judge, Minnesota District Court Third Judicial District)*

Office: Houston County Courthouse, 304 South Marshall Street, Calendonia 55921.

Telephone: (507) 725-5806.

FETSCH, Michael F. *(Judge, Minnesota District Court Second Judicial District)*

Office: Juvenile & Family Justice Center, 25 West Seventh Street, St. Paul 55102.

Telephone: (651) 266-5172.

FINLEY, John T. *(Judge, Minnesota District Court Second Judicial District)* Elected Nov 1996 to term beginning Jan 1997. Reelected 2002, current term expires Dec 31, 2008. Born St. Paul Minnesota May 20, 1940. Catholic. Educated at University of St. Thomas B.A. 1962, University of Minnesota and William Mitchell College of Law J.D. 1969. Admitted to practice Minnesota 1969 and U.S. District Court District of Minnesota 1970. In legal practice St. Paul 1969-96.

Member Minnesota Trial Lawyers Association, The Association of Trial Lawyers of America, Ramsey County, Minnesota State and American Bar Associations. Commissioner Ramsey County 1970-96. Enjoys golf, cross-country skiing and racquetball.

Office: 1110 Ramsey County Courthouse, 15 West Kellogg Boulevard, St. Paul 55102.

Telephone: (651) 266-8330.

FLOREY, James B. *(Judge, Minnesota District Court Sixth Judicial District)*

Office: St. Louis County Courthouse, 300 South Fifth Avenue, Virginia 55792.

Telephone: (218) 749-7100.

FLYNN, Jeffrey L. *(Judge, Minnesota District Court Fifth Judicial District)* Assumed office Sept 1987. Former Judge, Nobles County Court.

Mailing address: P.O. Box 547, Worthington 56187-0547.

Office: Nobles County Courthouse, Worthington 56187.

Telephone: (507) 372-8263.

FLYNN, Paulette K. *(Judge, Minnesota District Court Second Judicial District)*

Office: 1130 Ramsey County Courthouse, 15 West Kellogg Boulevard, St. Paul 55102.

Telephone: (651) 266-9175.

FRANK, Donovan W. *(Judge, United States District Court District of Minnesota)* Appointed for life by President Bill Clinton to term beginning Nov 2, 1998. Born Rochester Minnesota June 24, 1951. Educated at Luther College B.A. magna cum laude 1973, University of Durham, England 1971-72 and Hamline University School of Law J.D. magna cum laude 1977. Recipient Regent's

FRANK, DONOVAN W.—*Continued*

Scholarship and American Jurisprudence Award in Evidence. Admitted to practice Minnesota 1977, U.S. District Court District of Minnesota 1978 and U.S. Court of Appeals Eighth Circuit 1981. Judge 1985-98, Assistant Chief Judge 1991-96 and Former Chief Judge, Minnesota District Court Sixth Judicial District.

Assistant Attorney St. Louis County 1977-85. Important Decisions: Keith v. Keith 429 N.W.2d 276 Minn. Ct. App. 1988, State v. Hannuksela 452 N.W.2d 668 Minn. 1990, State v. Justin Bauer 471 N.W.2d 363 Minn. Ct. App. 1991 and State v. Gary Lee Graff 510 N.W.2d 212 Minn. Ct. App. 1993. Member Criminal Rules Advisory Committee 1986-98, Racial Bias Task Force 1991-93, Racial Fairness Implementation Committee 1993-98 and Advisory Committee on Open Juvenile Protection Hearings 1998 Minnesota Supreme Court and Conference of Chief Judges Community Outreach Planning Committee 1997-98. Chair Sixth Judicial District Community Outreach Committee 1997-98. Member Minnesota District Judges Association, Federal Judges Association, Range, Minnesota State and Federal (Board of Directors since 1999) Bar Associations. Recipient Alumni Association Distinguished Achievement Award 1986 and Distinguished Alumnus Award 2000 from Hamline University School of Law and Annual Recognition Award Range Women's Advocates 1995. Named Minnesota Trial Judge of the Year by Conference of Chief Judges 1996. Board of Directors East Range Developmental Achievement Center 1978-80 and Arrowhead Center, Inc. 1983-85. Member Virginia Rotary Club 1996-98.

Office: 738 Federal Building, 316 North Robert Street, St. Paul 55101.

Telephone: (651) 848-1290.

GALLER, Gregory G. *(Judge, Minnesota District Court Tenth Judicial District)*

Office: Sherburne County Government Center, 13880 Highway 10, Elk River 55330-4608.

Telephone: (763) 241-2800.

GEARIN, Kathleen R. *(Judge, Minnesota District Court Second Judicial District)*

Office: 1210 Ramsey County Courthouse, 15 West Kellogg Boulevard, St. Paul 55102.

Telephone: (651) 266-5172.

GILBERT, James H. *(Associate Justice, Minnesota Supreme Court)* Appointed by Governor Arne H. Carlson to term beginning Jan 29, 1998. Born Minneapolis Minnesota March 11, 1947. Educated at University of Minnesota B.A. 1969 J.D. 1972. Admitted to practice Minnesota, Wisconsin, U.S. District Court District of Arizona, U.S. Courts of Appeals Eighth and Tenth Circuits, U.S. Tax Court and U.S. Supreme Court. Civil Trial Practice Specialist, Certified by Minnesota State Bar Association.

Member 1991 and Chair 1992-97 Judicial Merit Selection Commission. Member Minnesota Courts Strategic Plan 1996-97. Member Minnesota State Bar Association. Member Orono City Park Commission 1988-91. Orono Fast Pitch Softball Coach 1991-98. Board of Directors Minnesota D.A.R.E., Inc. since Sept 1998.

Office: 422 Minnesota Judicial Center, 25 Martin Luther King Jr. Blvd., St. Paul 55155.

Telephone: (651) 297-5454.

GINSBERG, Harvey C. *(Judge, Minnesota District Court Fourth Judicial District)*

Office: 12C Government Center, 300 South Sixth Street, Minneapolis 55487.

Telephone: (612) 348-3317.

GODZALA, Thomas A. *(Judge, Minnesota District Court Seventh Judicial District)*

Office: Morrison County Courthouse, 213 First Avenue S.E., Little Falls 56345.

Telephone: (320) 632-0325.

GOMEZ, Isabel *(Judge, Minnesota District Court Fourth Judicial District)* Assumed office June 19, 1986. Elected 1986, 1992 and 1998. Current term expires Jan 2005. Born Montpelier Vermont April 17, 1941. Congregationalist. Educated at Middlebury College B.A. cum laude 1963, University of Minnesota M.A. 1970 and Arizona State University J.D. 1979. Recipient Woodrow Wilson Fellowship 1965-66. Articles Editor Arizona State University Law Review 1978-79. Law Clerk to Arizona Supreme Court 1979-80. Admitted to practice Arizona 1979 and Minnesota 1981. Began legal practice St. Paul Minnesota 1981. Judge, Hennepin County Municipal Court April 4, 1984 to June 18, 1986, appointed by Governor Rudy Perpich.

Member Minnesota Lawyers for International Human Rights, Minnesota Minority Lawyers' Association, Minnesota Board of Law Examiners, Minnesota Judges Association, National Association of Women Judges and State Bar of Arizona. Teacher 1963-65. Recipient McKnight Foundation Fellowship to the Salzburg Seminar 1986. Board member Centro Legal 1982-84 and Minnesota Lawyers International Human Rights Committee. Member Minneapolis Police Review Board 1983-88, Minnesota Crime Victim Advisory Council 1986-88, Hennepin Crime Victim Council and Midwest Conference Elected/Appointed Hispanic Officials. Enjoys reading and reviewing books, travel, theater and volunteer work regarding women's and children's issues.

Office: 12C Government Center, 300 South Sixth Street, Minneapolis 55487.

Telephone: (612) 348-8284.

GRAHAM, Jeanne J. *(Judge, Minnesota District Court Fourth Judicial District)*

Office: 12C Government Center, 300 South Sixth Street, Minneapolis 55487.

Telephone: (612) 596-7751.

GREENBERG, Myron S. *(Judge, Minnesota District Court Fourth Judicial District)* Appointed by Governor Rudy Perpich to term beginning July 3, 1987. Elected 1988, 1994 and 2000. Current term expires Jan 2007. Born Minot North Dakota Sept 13, 1943. Jewish. Educated at University of Minnesota B.A. 1966 J.D. 1969. Member Gamma Eta Gamma. Admitted to practice Minnesota 1971. Administrative Law Judge 1976-84 and Assistant Chief Administrative Law Judge 1984-87, Office of Administrative Hearings Minnesota.

Corporate Attorney, Fingerhut Corporation 1971-74. Member Minnesota Supreme Court Committee on Alternative Dispute Resolution since 1994. Member American Judges Association. Purchasing Manager Elscint, Ltd., Haifa Israel 1974-75. Board of Directors Herzl Camp

GREENBERG, MYRON S.—*Continued*

and Keshet Dance Company. Chairman Genesis Community Theater. Enjoys theater, golf and gin rummy.

Office: 12C Government Center, 300 South Sixth Street, Minneapolis 55487.

Telephone: (612) 348-6252.

GROSS, Bruce F. *(Judge, Minnesota District Court Fifth Judicial District)*

Mailing address: P.O. Box 97, Windom 56101.

Office: Cottonwood County Courthouse, Windom 56101.

Telephone: (507) 831-4551.

HALBROOKS, Jill Flaskamp *(Judge, Minnesota Court of Appeals)* Appointed by Governor Arne H. Carlson to term beginning Nov 1998. Elected Nov 2000, current term expires Jan 2007. Born Ann Arbor Michigan Nov 4, 1949. Educated at University of Colorado at Boulder B.A. 1971 M.A. 1976, University of California at Davis Counseling Practicum 1975-76 and William Mitchell College of Law J.D. cum laude 1985. In legal practice Minneapolis Sept 1985 to Nov 1998.

Co-chair Program Committee Minnesota Women Lawyers 1995-97. President Minnesota Chapter American Board of Trial Advocates 2000. President Elect 2002-03 and Group Leader Warren E. Burger Inn of Court. Fellow International Society of Barristers. Member National Association of Women Judges and Minnesota State Bar Association. Volunteer Grief Counseling Team Hospice Boulder Colorado 1977-81. Alumni Board of Directors William Mitchell College of Law 1990-96. Career Day Parent Coordinator South View Middle School Edina 1999-2000. Volunteer Everybody Wins Reading Program.

Office: 229 Minnesota Judicial Center, 25 Martin Luther King Jr. Blvd., St. Paul 55155.

Telephone: (651) 297-1002.

HALL, Sharon L. *(Judge, Minnesota District Court Tenth Judicial District)* Appointed by Governor Arne H. Carlson. Elected 2000, current term expires 2006. Born St. Cloud Minnesota July 23, 1954. Educated at College of St. Benedict B.A. 1976 and Hamline University School of Law J.D. 1979. Admitted to practice Minnesota 1980 and U.S. District Court District of Minnesota 1981. In legal practice Coon Rapids 1983-93.

Member John Simonette Inns of Court, National Association of Women Judges and Minnesota State Bar Association.

Office: Anoka County Courthouse, 325 East Main Street, Anoka 55303-2489.

Telephone: (763) 422-7350.

HALLENBECK, Terry C. *(Judge, Minnesota District Court Sixth Judicial District)*

Office: St. Louis County Courthouse, 100 North Fifth Avenue West, Duluth 55802-1212.

Telephone: (218) 726-2460.

HALSEY, Stephen M. *(Judge, Minnesota District Court Tenth Judicial District)*

Office: 201 Wright County Government Center, 10 Second Street N.W., Buffalo 55313-1192.

Telephone: (763) 682-7539.

HANCOCK, Karla *(Judge, Minnesota District Court Tenth Judicial District)*

Office: Sherburne County Government Center, 13880 Highway 10, Elk River 55330-4608.

Telephone: (763) 241-2800.

HANNON, Mary E. *(Judge, Minnesota District Court Tenth Judicial District)*

Mailing address: P.O. Box 3802, Stillwater 55082-3802.

Office: Washington County Government Center, Stillwater 55082.

Telephone: (651) 430-4427.

HANSON, Sam *(Associate Justice, Minnesota Supreme Court)* Appointed by Governor Jesse Ventura to term beginning Sept 3, 2002. Born Mankato Minnesota Aug 26, 1939. Lutheran. Educated at St. Olaf College B.A. 1961 and William Mitchell College of Law LL.B. with honors 1965. Law Clerk to Hon. Douglas K. Amdahl, Hennepin County District Court Aug 1, 1964 to Aug 1, 1965 and Hon. Robert J. Sheran, Minnesota Supreme Court Aug 1, 1965 to Aug 1, 1966. Admitted to practice Minnesota 1965, U.S. District Court District of Minnesota 1966, U.S. Court of Appeals Eighth Circuit 1966 and U.S. Supreme Court 1970. In legal practice St. Paul and Minneapolis Aug 1966 to Nov 2000. Judge, Minnesota Court of Appeals Nov 27, 2000 to Aug 31, 2002, appointed by Governor Jesse Ventura.

Member Advisory Committee Rules of Civil Appellate Procedure Minnesota Supreme Court 1984-90 and since 1997 and Civil Justice Reform Act Advisory Committee U.S. District Court District of Minnesota 1995-98. Member Minnesota Board of Law Examiners 1995-2002. Director National Conference of Bar Examiners since 2002. Advocate American Board of Trial Advocates. Fellow American College of Trial Lawyers (Minnesota Chairman 1991-92). Member Minnesota State (Co-chair Women and the Law Committee 1994-97 and Public Utilities Committee 1994-98) and American Bar Associations. Named One of Minnesota's Leading Trial Lawyers Sept 1991 and One of Most Courteous, Most Well Prepared and Wins the Most Cases Oct 1991 and Nov 1991 by *The Minnesota Lawyer.* Recipient Distinguished Alumni/ae Award from William Mitchell College of Law Oct 6, 1995. Listed in *The Best Lawyers in America.* Director Minneapolis Regional Office 1976-82 and National Board of Directors 1988-96 Institute of Cultural Affairs. Director Rural Ventures, Inc. 1981-87, Crossroads Adoption Services 1984-2000 and Rural Technology Partnership 1987-97. Member National Steering Committee International Exposition on Rural Development 1982-85. Co-founder, Director and Member Executive Committee Global Volunteers since 1984. Member since 1997, Secretary 1998-2000, Vice Chair 2000-02 and Chair since 2002 Board of Trustees William Mitchell College of Law. Board of Directors since 1999 and Member Executive Committee since 2000 Minnesota Advocates for Human Rights. Interests include golf, basketball, racquetball, pottery and photography.

Office: 421 Minnesota Judicial Center, 25 Martin Luther King Jr. Blvd., St. Paul 55155.

Telephone: (651) 297-7676.

HARRELSON, George I. *(Judge, Minnesota District Court Fifth Judicial District)* Assumed office Sept 1987. Elected 1990, 1996 and 2002. Current term expires Jan 2009. Born St. Paul Minnesota May 17, 1944. Educated at University of Minnesota B.A. 1971 and William

HARRELSON, GEORGE I.—*Continued*

Mitchell College of Law J.D. 1975. Law Clerk to Minnesota District Court 1976. Admitted to practice Minnesota 1975. Began legal practice Marshall 1977. Judge, Lincoln-Lyon-Redwood County Court May 23, 1983 to Sept 1987, appointed by Governor Rudy Perpich.

Former Public Defender and County Attorney.

Office: Lyon County Courthouse, 607 West Main, Marshall 56258.

Telephone: (507) 537-6741.

HARRINGTON, David F. *(Judge, Minnesota District Court Ninth Judicial District)*

Mailing address: P.O. Box 3000, Walker 56484.

Office: Cass County Courthouse, Walker 56484.

Telephone: (218) 547-7214.

HARTEN, James C. *(Judge, Minnesota Court of Appeals)* Appointed by Governor Arne H. Carlson to term beginning Feb 1992. Elected 1994 and 2000. Current term expires Jan 2007. Born Mankato Minnesota March 24, 1935. Protestant. Educated at St. Olaf College B.A. magna cum laude 1957, West Texas State College 1958-59 and Northwestern University J.D. 1964. Member Phi Beta Kappa. Admitted to practice Minnesota 1964, U.S. District Court District of Minnesota 1964 and U.S. Supreme Court 1971. Began legal practice Minneapolis 1964. Judicial Officer Blue Earth County Jan 1976 to Dec 1976. Judge, Blue Earth County Court Dec 6, 1976 to Sept 1987, appointed by Governor Wendell Anderson. Former Judge, Minnesota District Court Fifth Judicial District, assumed office Sept 1987.

Assistant County Attorney 1965-67 and County Attorney 1967-71 Blue Earth County. Instructor in Criminal Law Mankato State University 1972-77. Member Blue Earth County (President 1967), Minnesota State and American Bar Associations. First Lieutenant USAF 1957-60. Member 1968-75 and Secretary 1968-74 Governor's Area F Crime Commission. Member 1972-76 and Chairman 1975 Minnesota Valley Mental Health Board. Enjoys literature, music and sports.

Office: 332 Minnesota Judicial Center, 25 Martin Luther King Jr. Blvd., St. Paul 55155.

Telephone: (651) 297-1011.

HARVES, Duane R. *(Judge, Minnesota District Court First Judicial District)*

Office: Dakota County Judicial Center, 1560 West Highway 55, Hastings 55033.

Telephone: (651) 438-4325.

HAWKINSON, John *(Judge, Minnesota District Court Ninth Judicial District)*

Office: Itasca County Courthouse, 123 Fourth Street N.E., Grand Rapids 55744.

Telephone: (218) 327-2892.

HAYDEN, Elizabeth A. *(Judge, Minnesota District Court Seventh Judicial District)* Appointed by Governor Rudy Perpich Oct 1986. Elected Nov 1988, 1994 and 2000. Current term expires Jan 2007. Born Le Sueur Minnesota April 10, 1946. Catholic. Educated at College of St. Benedict B.A. 1968 and Oklahoma City University School of Law J.D. 1978. Member Phi Alpha Delta. Admitted to practice Minnesota 1979. In legal practice St. Paul 1980.

Assistant County Attorney Stearns County 1980-86. Adjunct Instructor Criminal Justice Department St. Cloud State University since 1983. Member Minnesota Women Lawyers Association, Minnesota District Judges Association (Past President), National Women Judges Association, Stearns-Benton and Minnesota State Bar Associations. Member Curriculum Committee Minnesota Judicial College since 1990. Past President Exchange Club. Board Member St. Cloud Area Big Brothers/Big Sisters Organization. Board of Trustees College of St. Benedict. Member Christ Church Newman Center St. Cloud State University.

Office: Stearns County Courthouse, 725 Courthouse Square, St. Cloud 56303-4781.

Telephone: (320) 656-3620.

HAYES, Thomas *(Judge, Minnesota District Court Tenth Judicial District)*

Office: Anoka County Courthouse, 325 East Main Street, Anoka 55303-2489.

Telephone: (763) 422-7440.

HEDLUND, Deborah *(Judge, Minnesota District Court Fourth Judicial District)* Assumed office June 19, 1986. Elected to subsequent terms. Former Judge, Hennepin County Municipal Court.

Office: 12C Government Center, 300 South Sixth Street, Minneapolis 55487.

Telephone: (612) 348-6401.

HIGGS, David C. *(Judge, Minnesota District Court Second Judicial District)*

Office: 1150 Ramsey County Courthouse, 15 West Kellogg Boulevard, St. Paul 55102.

Telephone: (651) 266-8215.

HOFF, Peter A. *(Judge, Minnesota District Court Eighth Judicial District)*

Mailing address: P.O. Box 219, Breckenridge 56520.

Office: Wilkin County Courthouse, Breckenridge 56520.

Telephone: (218) 643-7172.

HOFFMAN, John C. *(Judge, Minnesota District Court Tenth Judicial District)*

Office: Anoka County Courthouse, 325 East Main Street, Anoka 55303-2489.

Telephone: (763) 422-7440.

HOLAHAN, John L., Jr. *(Judge, Minnesota District Court Fourth Judicial District)*

Office: 12C Government Center, 300 South Sixth Street, Minneapolis 55487.

Telephone: (612) 348-9772.

HOLTER, Terrance C. *(Judge, Minnesota District Court Ninth Judicial District)* Assumed office July 1, 1985. Former Judge, Beltrami County Court.

Office: Beltrami County Courthouse, 619 Beltrami Avenue N.W., Bemidji 56601.

Telephone: (218) 759-4122.

HOOLIHAN, James W. *(Judge, Minnesota District Court Seventh Judicial District)* Appointed by Governor Arne H. Carlson to term beginning April 1, 1997.

Mailing address: P.O. Box 189, Foley 56329.

Office: Benton County Courts Facility, 615 Highway 23, Foley 56329.

Telephone: (320) 968-5205.

HOOTEN, Carol *(Judge, Minnesota District Court First Judicial District)*
Office: Scott County Government Center, 200 Fourth Avenue West, Shakopee 55379.
Telephone: (952) 496-8200.

HOWARD, William R. *(Judge, Minnesota District Court Fourth Judicial District)*
Office: 12C Government Center, 300 South Sixth Street, Minneapolis 55487.
Telephone: (612) 348-9845.

HOWE, Thomas R. *(Judge, Minnesota District Court First Judicial District)*
Office: Scott County Government Center, 200 Fourth Avenue West, Shakopee 55379.
Telephone: (952) 496-8200.

HUDSON, Natalie *(Judge, Minnesota Court of Appeals)* Appointed by Governor Jesse Ventura to term beginning 2002.
Office: Minnesota Judicial Center, 25 Martin Luther King Jr. Blvd., St. Paul 55155.

IRVINE, Peter *(Judge, Minnesota District Court Seventh Judicial District)*
Office: Douglas County Courthouse, 305 Eighth Avenue West, Alexandria 56308.
Telephone: (320) 762-3033.

JACOBSON, Debra A. *(Judge, Minnesota District Court Third Judicial District)*
Office: Olmsted Government Center, 151 Fourth Street S.E., Rochester 55904-3712.
Telephone: (507) 287-1635.

JASPER, Jenny Walker *(Judge, Minnesota District Court Tenth Judicial District)*
Office: Anoka County Courthouse, 325 East Main Street, Anoka 55303-2489.
Telephone: (763) 422-7440.

JESSE, Michael S. *(Judge, Minnesota District Court Seventh Judicial District)*
Office: Mille Lacs County Courthouse, 635 Second Street S.E., Milaca 56353.
Telephone: (320) 983-8313.

JESSEN, Richard T. *(Judge, Minnesota District Court Seventh Judicial District)*
Office: Stearns County Courthouse, 725 Courthouse Square, St. Cloud 56303-4781.
Telephone: (320) 656-3620.

JOHNSON, Gregg E. *(Judge, Minnesota District Court Second Judicial District)*
Office: 1230 Ramsey County Courthouse, 15 West Kellogg Boulevard, St. Paul 55102.
Telephone: (651) 266-8203.

JOHNSON, Kim Robert *(Judge, Minnesota District Court Tenth Judicial District)* Appointed by Governor Rudy Perpich to term beginning Sept 1, 1983. Elected 1984, 1990, 1996 and 2002. Current term expires Jan 2009. Born Buffalo Minnesota Nov 12, 1941. Roman Catholic. Educated at St. John's University B.A. cum laude 1953 and University of Minnesota LL.B. cum laude 1966. Member Order of the Coif. Admitted to practice Minnesota 1966. Captain USAR Signal Corps 1966-68.
Office: 201 Wright County Government Center, 10 Second Street N.W., Buffalo 55313-1192.
Telephone: (763) 682-7539.

JOHNSON, Kurt D. *(Judge, Minnesota District Court Fifth Judicial District)*
Mailing address: P.O. Box 0347, Mankato 56002-0347.
Office: Blue Earth County Courthouse, Mankato 56001.
Telephone: (507) 389-8667.

JOHNSON, Lawrence R. *(Judge, Minnesota District Court Tenth Judicial District)*
Office: Anoka County Courthouse, 325 East Main Street, Anoka 55303-2489.
Telephone: (763) 422-7440.

JOHNSON, Margaret Shaw *(Judge, Minnesota District Court Third Judicial District)* Appointed by Governor Rudy Perpich to term beginning May 1987. Elected Nov 1988, 1994 and 2000. Current term expires Jan 2007. Born Leavenworth Kansas Jan 26, 1946. Catholic. Educated at University of Minnesota 1968 and William Mitchell College of Law J.D. with honors 1980. Law Clerk to Hon. Glenn E. Kelley, Minnesota District Court Third Judicial District and Hon. Lawrence T. Collins, Minnesota District Court Third Judicial District 1982-83. Admitted to practice Minnesota 1980. In legal practice Minneapolis, St. Paul, Winona, Houston and Rochester 1980-87.
Associate Professor of Legal Writing Winona State University 1984. Attended The National Judicial College 1988.
Office: Winona County Courthouse, 171 West Third Street, Winona 55987.
Telephone: (507) 457-6375.

JOHNSON, Thomas L. *(Chief Judge, Minnesota Workers' Compensation Court of Appeals)* Appointed by governor. Former Administrative Judge.
Office: Minnesota Judicial Center, 25 Martin Luther King Jr. Blvd., St. Paul 55155.
Telephone: (651) 296-6526.

JOHNSON, William A. *(Judge, Minnesota District Court Third Judicial District)* Assumed office June 1984. Elected to subsequent terms. Born Minneapolis Minnesota Nov 29, 1945. Educated at Michigan State University B.A. with high honors 1967 and Harvard University J.D. cum laude 1972. Admitted to practice Minnesota 1972. Began legal practice Northfield 1973. Judge, Rice County Court Jan 1977 to June 1984, appointed by Governor Wendell Anderson.
Member Rice County, Fifth Judicial District, Minnesota State and American Bar Associations.
Office: Rice County Courthouse, 218 N.W. Third Street, Faribault 55021.
Telephone: (507) 332-6180.

KALITOWSKI, Thomas J. *(Judge, Minnesota Court of Appeals)* Assumed office Nov 1987. Born Robbinsdale Minnesota March 26, 1948. Educated at University of Minnesota B.A. 1970 J.D. 1973. Law Clerk to Hon. Lindsay G. Arthur, Hennepin County District Court May 1972 to June 1973.
Special Assistant Attorney General Department of Agriculture, Livestock Sanitary Board, Veterinary Examin-

KALITOWSKI, THOMAS J.—*Continued*

ing Board and Horticultural Society Sept 1973 to Jan 1975. Assistant Commissioner Minnesota Department of Agriculture Jan 1975 to Aug 1977. Commissioner Minnesota Pollution Control Agency May 1984 to Nov 1987. Chairman Minnesota Water Planning Board, Upper Mississippi River Basin Association and Red River Water Resources Council Aug 1977 to June 1983. Chairman Minnesota Environmental Quality Board and Director Environmental Division State Planning Agency June 1983 to May 1984.

Office: 318 Minnesota Judicial Center, 25 Martin Luther King Jr. Blvd., St. Paul 55155.

Telephone: (651) 297-3530.

KAMAN, Marilyn J. *(Judge, Minnesota District Court Fourth Judicial District)*

Office: 12C Government Center, 300 South Sixth Street, Minneapolis 55487.

Telephone: (612) 348-8224.

KAMMEYER, Daniel M. *(Judge, Minnesota District Court Tenth Judicial District)*

Office: Anoka County Courthouse, 325 East Main Street, Anoka 55303-2489.

Telephone: (763) 422-7440.

KANNING, Philip T. *(Judge, Minnesota District Court First Judicial District)* Assumed office Aug 1987. Elected 1992 and 1998. Current term expires Jan 1, 2005. Born Truman Minnesota Aug 14, 1946. Protestant. Educated at Valparaiso University B.S. 1968, William Mitchell College of Law J.D. 1974 and Harvard University M.P.A. 1996. Admitted to practice Minnesota 1974 and U.S. Court of Appeals Eighth Circuit 1974. In legal practice St. Paul 1974-75 and Shakopee 1975-84. Judge, Scott-Carver County Court 1984-87, appointed by Governor Rudy Perpich.

Important Decisions: Kelzer v. Wachholz (in appeal of civil action to recover compensatory and punitive damages from alleged intruder for trespass and intentional tort, Minnesota Court of Appeals held that no error was committed by omitting a jury instruction on comparative negligence since intentional tort actions are not subject to Minnesota's comparative fault statute) 381 N.W.2d 852, 1986; State v. Morrow (revoked probation of convicted sex offender in lieu of treatment program for which neither county nor offender had funds, affirmed by Minnesota Court of Appeals that right to equal protection and due process was not violated) 492 N.W.2d 539, 1992; State v. Krotzer (stayed adjudication on charge of third-degree criminal sexual conduct and placed accused on probation including 60 days in jail, upheld by Minnesota Supreme Court 1996) 548 N.W.2d 252, 1994.

Office: Carver County Justice Center, 600 East Fourth Street, Chaska 55318.

Telephone: (952) 361-1445.

KARASOV, Patricia Kerr *(Judge, Minnesota District Court Fourth Judicial District)*

Office: 12C Government Center, 300 South Sixth Street, Minneapolis 55487.

Telephone: (612) 348-6585.

KING, Robert R., Jr. *(Judge, Minnesota District Court First Judicial District)*

Office: Dakota County Courthouse, 1560 West Highway 55, Hastings 55033.

Telephone: (651) 438-4325.

KIRK, Michael L. *(Judge, Minnesota District Court Seventh Judicial District)*

Office: Clay County Courthouse, 807 North Eleventh Street, Moorhead 56560.

Telephone: (218) 299-5065.

KISHEL, Gregory F. *(Chief Judge, United States Bankruptcy Court District of Minnesota)* Appointed by U.S. District Court judges to term beginning May 25, 1984. Reappointed by U.S. Court of Appeals Eighth Circuit judges Oct 1, 1986 and Oct 1, 2000. Current term expires Oct 2014. Chief Judge since Oct 1, 2000. Also Judge pro tem, Bankruptcy Appellate Panel for the Eighth Circuit. Selected by the Judicial Council of the Eighth Circuit 1996-2003. Born Virginia Minnesota Jan 26, 1951. Educated at Cornell University A.B. 1973 and Boston College Law School J.D. 1977. Admitted to practice Minnesota 1978, Wisconsin 1985, U.S. District Courts District of Minnesota 1978 and Western District of Wisconsin 1985 and U.S. Court of Appeals Eighth Circuit 1978. Began legal practice Virginia Minnesota 1978. In legal practice Duluth 1979-86.

Staff Attorney 1978-81, Board member 1981-82, Vice President 1982-83 and President 1983-84 Legal Aid Service of Northeastern Minnesota. Member National Conference of Bankruptcy Judges and Minnesota State Bar Association. Speaker at numerous Minnesota CLE seminars. Chair Committee No. 535 Cornell University Alumni Admissions Ambassador Network 1978-2003. Member Lawyers Section Urgent Action Network Amnesty International 1979-84. Secretary 1993-95 and President 1996-2000 Polish Genealogical Society of Minnesota.

Office: 210 Federal Building, 316 North Robert Street, St. Paul 55101.

Telephone: (651) 848-1060.

KLAPHAKE, Roger M. *(Judge, Minnesota Court of Appeals)* Appointed by Governor Rudy Perpich to term beginning Aug 8, 1989. Elected to subsequent terms. Educated at University of Minnesota J.D. Judge, Sherburne-Benton-Stearns County Court 1975-83. Judge and Assistant Chief Judge, Minnesota District Court Seventh Judicial District 1983-89. Former Judicial Officer.

Office: 315 Minnesota Judicial Center, 25 Martin Luther King Jr. Blvd., St. Paul 55155.

Telephone: (651) 297-1026.

KLEIN, Mary Kay *(Magistrate Judge, United States District Court District of Minnesota)* Appointed by U.S. District Court judges. Serves part time.

Mailing address: P.O. Box 1390, Bemidji 56619-1390.

Office: 323 Beltrami Avenue N.W., Bemidji 56601.

Telephone: (218) 751-0399.

KNAPP, Thomas *(Judge, Minnesota District Court Seventh Judicial District)*

Mailing address: P.O. Box 189, Foley 56329.

Office: Benton County Courts Facility, 615 Highway 23, Foley 56329.

Telephone: (320) 968-5205.

KRAKER, Michael J. *(Judge, Minnesota District Court Ninth Judicial District)*
Mailing address: P.O. Box 435, Mahnomen 56557.
Office: Mahnomen County Courthouse, Mahnomen 56557.
Telephone: (218) 784-7404.

KRESSEL, Robert J. *(Judge, United States Bankruptcy Court District of Minnesota)* Appointed by U.S. District Court judges Dec 6, 1982. Reappointed by U.S. Court of Appeals Eighth Circuit judges Dec 5, 1986 and Dec 5, 2000. Current term expires Dec 4, 2014. Former Chief Judge Bankruptcy Court. Also Chief Judge, Bankruptcy Appellate Panel Eighth Circuit. Selected by the Judicial Council of the Eighth Circuit to term beginning Sept 10, 1996. Educated at University of Notre Dame A.B. in Mathematics cum laude 1969 and Harvard Law School J.D. 1972. In legal practice Minneapolis 1972-79. Referee, Hennepin County Conciliation Court 1979.
Bankruptcy Analyst U.S. Trustee's Office Minneapolis 1979-81. Assistant U.S. Trustee Districts of Minnesota, North Dakota and South Dakota July 26, 1981 to Dec 4, 1982. Author "Ethical Considerations in Representing Creditors and Debtors" *Hennepin Lawyer* March-April 1982, "Tardy Claims: The Congressional Solution to the Hausladen Problem" *Norton Bankruptcy Law Advisor* Jan 1995 and "Calculating the Present Value of Deferred Payment Under a Chapter 12 Plan: A New Twist to an Old Problem" 62 American Bankruptcy L. Jour. 313. Adjunct Professor of Law Hamline University School of Law 1983-84 and William Mitchell College of Law 1986-95. Member National Conference of Bankruptcy Judges (Board of Governors 1987-90), Hennepin County (Secretary 1979-80 and Chairman 1980-82 Debtor-Creditor Remedies Committee, Member Governing Council 1980-82 and Ethics Committee 1982-83), Minnesota State (Bankruptcy Section), Federal (President Minnesota Chapter 1989-90) and American Bar Associations.
Lecturer "Ten Most Common Mistakes Made in Bankruptcy Court" March 10, 1981 and "Effect of Bankruptcy on Real Estate Mortgage Foreclosures" Dec 1, 1992 Debtor-Creditor Remedies Committee Hennepin County Bar Association; "Selected Problems and Practical Considerations in Bankruptcy Practice" Dec 2-3, 1982 and "Bankruptcy Practice 1985" March 22, 1985 Advanced Legal Education Hamline University School of Law; "Divorce" Minnesota Trial Lawyers Association and American Academy of Matrimonial Lawyers Oct 11-13, 1984; "Continuing Education for Revenue Officers" March 28, 1985 and "Treatment of Creditors Who Tardily File Claims" April 19, 1994 Internal Revenue Service; "Debtors' and Creditors' Practice and Procedure" March 29, 1985, "Successfully Representing Financial Institutions" Nov 4, 1988, "Practicing Under the New Local and National Bankruptcy Rules" June 13, 1991 and "Family Law Institute" 1993, 1995 and 1996 Minnesota CLE; "What You Should Know About the United States Bankruptcy Court" Minnesota Association for Court Administration June 12, 1985; "Bankruptcy's Impact on Consumer Lending" Minneapolis Consumer Credit Association Oct 16, 1985; "Bankruptcy Institute" 1985-89 and 1991-96 and "Bankruptcy Practice and Appeals Under the New Local Rules" Feb 7, 1986 Minnesota CLE and Bankruptcy Section Minnesota State Bar Association; "Foreclosure and Repossession" May 9, 1986 and "Farm and Small Business Reorganization" July 21, 1986 National Business Institute; "Environmental Issues in Bankruptcy" June 16, 1987 and "Trustee's Liability for Environmental Cleanup and Abandonment of Property" Jan 17, 1989 Environmental Law Committee Hennepin County Bar Association; "Chapter 12 Review and Assessment Workshop for Bankruptcy Judges" Sept 20-22, 1987, "Bankruptcy Case Management Workshop" March 13-15, 1988, "Seminar for Bankruptcy Judges" Feb 22-24, 1989, "Workshop for Chief Bankruptcy Judges" Sept 18-20, 1989 and "Workshop for Bankruptcy Judges of the Eighth, Ninth and Tenth Circuits" Dec 4-6, 1989 Federal Judicial Center; "Federal Court Practice Seminar" Minnesota Chapter Federal Bar Association April 8, 1988; "The Bankruptcy Rules" Commercial Law League of America July 10, 1988; "Drafting and Confirming Reorganization Plans" Aug 12, 1988 and "Bankruptcy Litigation and Practice in Minnesota" Feb 17, 1989 Professional Education Systems, Inc.; "Strategic Uses of Chapter 11" Advanced Legal Education Sept 9, 1988; "Environmental Liability in Bankruptcy Cases" Hennepin County Bar Association March 8, 1990; "New Value on Cramdown" National Conference of Bankruptcy Judges Nov 10, 1990; "Cramdown After *Ahlers*" National Real Estate Development Center March 7, 1991; "Welcome to the Nineties: Bankruptcy Law and Practice for Everyone" University of Minnesota Law School March 25, 1992; "Bankruptcy Reform Act of 1994" Minnesota Institute for Legal Education Nov 30, 1994; "Child Support Seminar" Office of Administrative Hearings Oct 27, 1995; and "A Bankruptcy Primer for State Court Judges" Annual Conference of Judges Minnesota Supreme Court Dec 6, 1995.
Director 1975-81, Secretary 1977-79, Vice Chairman 1979-80 and Chairman Nominating Committee and Bylaws Committee Kidney Foundation of the Upper Midwest. Trustee National Kidney Foundation 1976-81. Member 1980-86 and Chairman 1982-83 Board of Trustees and Member Management Committee, Children's Center Advisory Committee and Program Council YWCA of Minneapolis.
Office: 8W U.S. Courthouse, 300 South Fourth Street, Minneapolis 55415.
Telephone: (612) 664-5250.

KYLE, Richard H. *(Judge, United States District Court District of Minnesota)* Appointed for life by President George Bush to term beginning May 15, 1992. Born St. Paul Minnesota April 30, 1937. Episcopalian. Educated at University of Minnesota B.A. 1959 LL.B. 1962. President Minnesota Law Review 1960-62. Law Clerk to Hon. Edward J. Devitt, U.S. District Court District of Minnesota 1962-63. Member Order of the Coif. Admitted to practice Minnesota 1962, U.S. District Court District of Minnesota, U.S. Court of Appeals Eighth Circuit and U.S. Supreme Court. In legal practice St. Paul 1963-92.
Solicitor General Minnesota 1968-70.
Office: 764 Federal Building, 316 North Robert Street, St. Paul 55101.
Telephone: (651) 848-1160.

LACY, Thomas R. *(Judge, Minnesota District Court First Judicial District)* Assumed office Aug 1987. Former Judge, Dakota County Court.
Office: Dakota County Judicial Center, 1560 West Highway 55, Hastings 55033.
Telephone: (651) 438-4295.

LANDWEHR, Vicki E. *(Judge, Minnesota District Court Seventh Judicial District)* Appointed by Governor

LANDWEHR, VICKI E.—*Continued*

Arne H. Carlson to term beginning July 28, 1993. Elected Nov 1994 and 2000. Current term expires Jan 1, 2007. Born Alexandria Minnesota March 13, 1955. Educated at St. Cloud State University B.A. with honors 1975 and University of Minnesota School of Law J.D. with honors 1978. Member Phi Kappa Phi. Admitted to practice Minnesota 1978 and U.S. District Court District of Minnesota 1980. In legal practice St. Cloud 1979-93.

Member John E. Simonett American Inn of Court, National Association of Women Judges, Stearns-Benton and Minnesota State Bar Associations.

Office: Stearns County Courthouse, 725 Courthouse Square, St. Cloud 56303-4781.

Telephone: (320) 656-3620.

LANG, Lois J. *(Judge, Minnesota District Court Ninth Judicial District)*

Office: Itasca County Courthouse, 123 Fourth Street N.E., Grand Rapids 55744.

Telephone: (218) 327-2892.

LANGE, LaJune Thomas *(Judge, Minnesota District Court Fourth Judicial District)* Assumed office June 19, 1986. Elected Nov 1986, Nov 1992 and Nov 1998. Current term expires Jan 2005. Educated at Augsburg College B.A. in Psychology 1975 and University of Minnesota Law School J.D. 1978. Admitted to practice Minnesota 1978, U.S. District Court District of Minnesota 1978, U.S. Court of Appeals Eighth Circuit 1978 and U.S. Supreme Court 1983. Judge, Hennepin County Municipal Court Jan 1985 to June 18, 1986, appointed by Governor Rudy Perpich.

Assistant Public Defender Hennepin County 1978-85. Guest Lecturer Department of Psychology Augsburg College 1979 and 1980 and University of Minnesota 1980, 1981 and 1982. Adjunct Professor of Advanced Trial Advocacy, Trial Advocacy and Civil Rights since 1983 William Mitchell College of Law. Member Minnesota Minority Lawyers Association (Founding member), Minnesota Women Lawyers, Hennepin County (Chairperson Criminal Law Committee and Nominating Committee, member Governing Council, Bench and Bar Committee, Public Relations Committee and Bar Benefit Committee), Minnesota State (Board of Governors, Committees on Real Property Law, Organization and Governance, Long Range Planning), American and National Bar Associations. Attended Minnesota Institute of Criminal Justice 1979, Advanced Training Program for Trial Advocacy Instructors and Employment Discrimination 1984 and 1985 and Advanced General Jurisdiction course The National Judicial College 1985. Faculty member National Institute of Trial Advocacy 1980. Frequent Lecturer CLE. International Lecturer U.S. Speakers Bureau U.S.I.S.-U.S.I.A. Formerly worked as legal assistant, Field Representative Minneapolis Department of Civil Rights and Counselor Twin Cities Opportunities Industrialization Center. Former Member Minnesota Women's Consortium, YWCA National Council of Negro Women and NAACP. Member Board of Directors Minnesota Public Interest Research Foundation 1978-82, Minneapolis Civil Rights Commission 1979-85 and St. Peter's A.M.E. Church Board of Regents Augsburg College. Board of Directors Minnesota International Center, Girl Scouts and Council of Churches.

Office: 12C Government Center, 300 South Sixth Street, Minneapolis 55487.

Telephone: (612) 348-5474.

LANGE, Steven Z. *(Judge, Minnesota District Court Fourth Judicial District)* Appointed by Governor Rudy Perpich to term beginning May 12, 1986. Elected Nov 8, 1994 and Nov 7, 2000. Current term expires Jan 1, 2007. Born Hadera Israel April 12, 1938. Jewish. Educated at University of Minnesota B.A. magna cum laude 1960 J.D. 1963. Member Phi Delta Phi and Phi Beta Kappa. Admitted to practice Minnesota 1963, U.S. District Court District of Minnesota 1964 and U.S. Court of Appeals Eighth Circuit 1964. In legal practice Minneapolis 1967-86.

Assistant County Attorney Hennepin County 1964-66. Assistant U.S. Attorney District of Minnesota 1966-67. Special Assistant State Public Defender 1967-70. U.S. Army 1956-60.

Office: 12C Government Center, 300 South Sixth Street, Minneapolis 55487.

Telephone: (612) 348-2554.

LANSING, Harriet *(Judge, Minnesota Court of Appeals)* Appointed to term beginning Nov 1, 1983. Elected 1984, 1990, 1996 and 2002. Current term expires Jan 2009. Born Waverly Wisconsin May 19, 1945. Educated at Macalester College B.A. 1967 and University of Minnesota J.D. 1970. Admitted to practice Minnesota 1970, U.S. District Court District of Minnesota 1971, U.S. Court of Appeals Eighth Circuit 1976 and U.S. Supreme Court 1987. In legal practice St. Paul 1973-76. Judge, Ramsey County Municipal Court 1978-83.

Staff Counsel St. Paul Housing and Redevelopment Authority 1970-72. Assistant City Attorney 1972-73. City Attorney St. Paul 1976-78. Co-author "Gender Fairness Task Force Report" 15 William Mitchell L. Rev. 827, 1989 and *The Preparation and Presentation of a Claim Based on the Minnesota Constitution* Government Liability Institute Minnesota State Bar Association 1993. Author "Rosalie E. Wahl and the Jurisprudence of Inclusivity" 21 William Mitchell L. Rev. 11 Fall 1995. Important Decisions: Rostad v. On-Deck, Inc. (extending long-arm jurisdiction to nationwide distributorships operating within Minnesota) 354 N.W.2d 95 (Minn. App.) 1984, Phipps v. Clark Oil and Refining Corp. (exception to employment-at-will doctrine for employees discharged for reasons that contravene clear mandate of public policy) 396 N.W.2d 588 (Minn. App.) 1986, Yunker v. Honeywell, Inc. (applying and distinguishing employment doctrines of negligent hiring and negligent supervision in a case in which co-employee was fatally shot) 496 N.W.2d 419 (Minn. App.) 1993, Dorn v. Peterson (Minnesota Human Rights Act has no upper age limit for purposes of protection from age discrimination) No. C8-93-1431 (Minn. App.) March 8, 1994, Dayton Hudson Corp. v. Johnson (corporations are persons for purposes of seeking a restraining order) No. C1-94-1961 (Minn. App.) Feb 28, 1995, Wenzel v. Mathies, et al. (fiduciary duties of shareholders in small, closely held corporation) 542 N.W.2d 634 (Minn. App.) 1996, Heller v. Schwan's Sales Enterprises, Inc. (basis for approval of class-action settlement) 548 N.W.2d 287 (Minn. App.) 1996, Molenaar v. United Cattle Co. (upholding the application of punitive damages to conversion ac-

LANSING, HARRIET—*Continued*

tions) 553 N.W.2d 424 (Minn. App.) 1996, In re Trusts by Hormel (effects of res judicata on continuing fiduciary duty to diversify trusts) N.W.2d (Minn. App.) 1996, Potter v. Pohlad (fiduciary obligation of corporate officers and directors and applying business judgment rule) 560 N.W.2d 389 (Minn. App.) 1997, Jussila v. U.S. Snowmobile Assoc. (doctrine of primary risk did not apply to snowmobile racing because it was an inherently dangerous act) 556 N.W.2d (Minn. App.) 1997, Bast v. Capitol Indemnity Corp. (loss payee in an insurance contract with a standard-form mortgage clause is entitled to notice of material changes in the policy that result in a substantial reduction in coverage) No. C9-96-1906 (Minn. App.) April 15, 1997 and Bauer v. Gannett Co., Inc. (KARE 11) (defining factors to be considered in media's qualified constitutional privilege when compelling disclosure of reporter's confidential source) 557 N.W.2d 608 (Minn. App.) 1997.

Adjunct Professor William Mitchell College of Law 1978-81 and Hamline University School of Law 1990-92. Fellow 1978-81 and Secretary Treasurer 1979-81 Minnesota Bar Foundation. Member Supreme Court Continuing Education for Judges 1983-88, Advisory Committee Minnesota Institute for Legal Education 1985-89, Committee to Reduce Appellate Delay National Center for State Courts 1987-89 and Warren Burger Inns of Court 1992-93. Vice Chair Supreme Court Gender Fairness Task Force 1986-89. Fellow American Bar Foundation. Member American Interprofessional Institute, National Conference of Commissioners on Uniform State Laws (Committees to Redraft Limited Partnership Act and Uniform Certification of Questions of Law), National Association of Women Judges (Board of Directors 1981-83, Education Chair National Conference 1987), Ramsey County Judges Association, American Judges Association, Ramsey County, Minnesota State (Chair Long-Range Planning Committee 1979-83) and American (National Conference of Special Court Judges Judicial Administration Division 1971-83) Bar Associations. Attended Law and Literature Seminar 1989-2001, Minority Diversity Program 1990 and Employment Program 1991 William Mitchell College of Law. Faculty Member Appellate Judges Seminar Institute of Judicial Administration New York University 1999-2000. Lecturer Robert A. Taft Institute of Government Seminar, National Practice Institute, American Judicature Society, Minnesota Administrators Academy and Center for International Leadership. Recipient Distinguished Service Awards from Macalester College, University of Minnesota Law School, St. Paul Jaycees and YWCA. Chair 1990-92 and Member Board of Visitors University of Minnesota Law School. Board of Directors YMCA Camp Widjiwagan. Member Committee to Determine Class Size University of Minnesota Law School 1985, Endowed Chair Selection Committee 1988-91 University of Minnesota, Rhodes Scholar Selection Committee (Minnesota Chair 1986-87), Crime Victims Center Advisory Board, Corrections Advisory Board, Ramsey County Juvenile Center Building Committee, Warren Burger Scholarship Committee, St. Paul Chamber Orchestra (Vice President, Executive Committee) and Family Service of St. Paul.

Office: 313 Minnesota Judicial Center, 25 Martin Luther King Jr. Blvd., St. Paul 55155.

Telephone: (651) 297-1010.

LARSON, Gary R. *(Judge, Minnesota District Court Fourth Judicial District)* Assumed office June 19, 1986. Elected Nov 1986, Nov 1992 and Nov 1998. Current term expires Jan 2005. Born Covington Virginia May 23, 1943. Educated at University of Minnesota B.A. 1964 J.D. with honors 1967. Law Clerk to Cahill District Court 1967. Member Delta Tau Delta. Admitted to practice Minnesota 1967. In legal practice Excelsior 1967-85. Former Judge, Hennepin County Municipal Court.

City Attorney Tonka Bay 1970-85, Excelsior 1980-82 and Shorewood 1980-85.

Office: 12C Government Center, 300 South Sixth Street, Minneapolis 55487.

Telephone: (612) 348-6102.

LEARY, William H. *(Judge, Minnesota District Court Second Judicial District)*

Office: 1410 Ramsey County Courthouse, 15 West Kellogg Boulevard, St. Paul 55102.

Telephone: (651) 266-9262.

LEBEDOFF, Jonathan G. *(Magistrate Judge, United States District Court District of Minnesota)* Appointed by U.S. District Court judges to term beginning Sept 20, 1991. Reappointed Sept 1999, current term expires Sept 2007. Currently serves as Chief Magistrate Judge. Born Minneapolis Minnesota April 29, 1938. Educated at University of Minnesota B.A. 1960 LL.B. 1963. Admitted to practice Minnesota 1963. In legal practice Minneapolis 1963-71. Judge, Hennepin County Municipal Court Dec 1971 to April 1974. Judge, Minnesota District Court Fourth Judicial District April 1974 to Sept 19, 1991, appointed by Governor Wendell Anderson.

Member Hennepin County, Minnesota State and American Bar Associations. Former member State Judicial Council and Governor's Commission on Crime Prevention and Control.

Office: 9E U.S. Courthouse, 300 South Fourth Street, Minneapolis 55415.

Telephone: (612) 664-5120.

LeDUC, Charles H., II *(Judge, Minnesota District Court Ninth Judicial District)*

Office: Koochiching County Courthouse, 715 Fourth Street, International Falls 56649.

Telephone: (218) 283-1166.

LEFLER, Herbert P., III *(Judge, Minnesota District Court Fourth Judicial District)*

Office: 12C Government Center, 300 South Sixth Street, Minneapolis 55487.

Telephone: (612) 348-8302.

LEITNER, John R. *(Judge, Minnesota District Court Ninth Judicial District)*

Office: Crow Wing County Courthouse, 326 Laurel Street, Brainerd 56401.

Telephone: (218) 824-1310.

LEUNG, Tony N. *(Judge, Minnesota District Court Fourth Judicial District)* Appointed by Governor Arne H. Carlson July 29, 1994. Elected to term beginning Jan 1, 1997. Reelected 2002, current term expires Jan 1, 2009. Born Hong Kong Aug 16, 1959. Roman Catholic. Educated at Yale University B.A. 1985 and New York University School of Law J.D. 1992.

Office: 12C Government Center, 300 South Sixth Street, Minneapolis 55487.

Telephone: (612) 348-3802.

LINDMAN, Dale B. *(Judge, Minnesota District Court Second Judicial District)* Appointed by Governor Arne H. Carlson Sept 3, 1998 to term beginning Oct 5, 1998. Elected Nov 7, 2000, current term expires Dec 31, 2006. Born Minneapolis Minnesota May 17, 1944. Educated at University of Minnesota B.S.B. 1967 and William Mitchell College of Law LL.B. 1972. Admitted to practice Minnesota 1972, U.S. District Court District of Minnesota 1972, U.S. Court of Appeals Eighth Circuit 1974 and Wisconsin 1996. In legal practice Minneapolis Minnesota 1972-98.

Member Minnesota Defense Lawyers Association (President 1993-94), Federation of Insurance and Corporate Counsel, The Defense Research Institute, Inc. (Minnesota State Representative 1993-98), Hennepin County, Ramsey County, Minnesota State and American Bar Associations.

Office: 1030 Ramsey County Courthouse, 15 West Kellogg Boulevard, St. Paul 55102.

Telephone: (651) 266-8342.

LINDSTROM, John C. *(Judge, Minnesota District Court Eighth Judicial District)*

Office: Kandiyohi County Courthouse, 505 West Becker Avenue, Willmar 56201.

Telephone: (320) 231-6206.

LITYNSKI, Warren E. *(Judge, Minnesota District Court Fifth Judicial District)* Assumed office Sept 1987. Former Judge, Nicollet County Court.

Mailing address: P.O. Box 496, St. Peter 56082.

Office: Nicollet County Courthouse, 501 South Minnesota Avenue, St. Peter 56082.

Telephone: (507) 931-6800.

LOGERING, Nancy *(Judge, Minnesota District Court Tenth Judicial District)* Appointed by Governor Jesse Ventura to term beginning Aug 9, 2000. Elected 2002, current term expires Jan 2009. Admitted to practice Minnesota 1985, U.S. District Court District of Minnesota 1985, U.S. Court of Appeals Eighth Circuit 1985 and U.S. Supreme Court 1993.

Office: Anoka County Courthouse, 325 East Main Street, Anoka 55303-2489.

Telephone: (763) 422-7440.

LUND, Kevin *(Judge, Minnesota District Court Third Judicial District)*

Office: Olmsted Government Center, 151 Fourth Street S.E., Rochester 55904-3712.

Telephone: (507) 285-8161.

LYNCH, Edward I. *(Judge, Minnesota District Court First Judicial District)*

Office: Dakota County Judicial Center, 1560 West Highway 55, Hastings 55033.

Telephone: (651) 438-4325.

LYNN, Robert H. *(Judge, Minnesota District Court Fourth Judicial District)*

Office: 12C Government Center, 300 South Sixth Street, Minneapolis 55487.

Telephone: (612) 348-7683.

MAAS, Ellen L. *(Judge, Minnesota District Court Tenth Judicial District)*

Office: Anoka County Courthouse, 325 East Main Street, Anoka 55303-2489.

Telephone: (763) 422-7440.

MABLEY, Daniel H. *(Judge, Minnesota District Court Fourth Judicial District)*

Office: 12C Government Center, 300 South Sixth Street, Minneapolis 55487.

Telephone: (612) 348-3116.

MACAULAY, Robert E. *(Judge, Minnesota District Court Sixth Judicial District)*

Mailing address: P.O. Box 190, Carlton 55718.

Office: Carlton County Courthouse, Carlton 55718.

Telephone: (218) 384-4281.

MACKLIN, William E. *(Judge, Minnesota District Court First Judicial District)*

Office: Scott County Government Center, 200 Fourth Avenue West, Shakopee 55379.

Telephone: (952) 496-8224.

MacLAUGHLIN, Harry H. *(Senior Judge, United States District Court District of Minnesota)* Appointed for life by President Jimmy Carter to term beginning Sept 1977. Assumed Senior status Oct 1992, serves by assignment. Born Breckenridge Minnesota Aug 9, 1927. Educated at University of Minnesota B.B.A. with distinction 1949 LL.B. 1956 J.D. 1956. Board of Editors Minnesota Law Review 1954-55. Member Beta Gamma Sigma and Phi Delta Phi. Law Clerk to Hon. Frank Gallagher, Minnesota Supreme Court 1955-56. Admitted to practice Minnesota 1956. In legal practice Minneapolis 1956-72. Associate Justice, Minnesota Supreme Court 1972-77.

Instructor William Mitchell College of Law 1958-63 and University of Minnesota 1973-86. USNR 1945-46. Member National Advisory Council Small Business Administration 1968-70, State College Board 1971-72 and Minneapolis Charter Commission 1966-72.

Office: 12W U.S. Courthouse, 300 South Fourth Street, Minneapolis 55415.

Telephone: (612) 664-5130.

MAGNUSON, Paul A. *(Senior Judge, United States District Court District of Minnesota)* Appointed for life by President Ronald Reagan to term beginning Nov 16, 1981. Chief Judge 1994-2001. Assumed Senior status Feb 9, 2002, serves by assignment. Born Carthage South Dakota Feb 9, 1937. Educated at Gustavus Adolphus College B.A. 1959 and William Mitchell College of Law J.D. 1963. Honorary Doctor of Laws William Mitchell College of Law 1991. Member Alpha Kappa Psi and Delta Theta Phi. Admitted to practice Minnesota 1963 and U.S. District Court District of Minnesota 1963. In legal practice South St. Paul 1963-81.

Important Decisions: Masepohl v. American Tobacco Co., Inc. 974 F. Supp. 1245 D. Minn. 1997; In re Grain Land Coop Cases 987 F. Supp. 1267 D. Minn. 1997; Gold Star Taxi and Transp. Serv. v. Mall of America Co. 987 F. Supp. 741 D. Minn. 1997; Malt-O-Meal Co. v. MRM Communications, Inc. Civ. File No. 3-96-1014 slip op. D. Minn. Jan 13, 1999; Randy's Sanitation, Inc. v. Wright County 65 F. Supp. 2d 1017 D. Minn 1999; Thompson v. American Tobacco Co., Inc. 189 F.R.D. 544 D. Minn. 1999; United States v. Langmade 125 F. Supp. 2d 373 D. Minn. 2001; In re Lutheran Brotherhood Variable Insurance Products Sales Practices Litigation 201 F.R.D. 456 D. Minn. 2001; United States v. Wadlington 233 F.3d 1067, 8th Cir. 2001; EEOC v. United Parcel Service 141 F. Supp. 2d 1216 D. Minn. 2001; AT&T Equipment Lease Contract Litigation MDL-781; and In re Lutheran Brotherhood Variable In-

MAGNUSON, PAUL A.—*Continued*

surance Products Sales Practices Litigation WL 1023150 D. Minn. May 17, 2002. Legal Counsel Minnesota Republican Party. Member 1987-96 and Chairman 1993-96 Judicial Conference Committee on the Administration of the Bankruptcy System. Member 1992-97 and Chairman 1994-97 Eighth Circuit Education Committee. Member since 1997 and Chairman since 1997 Judicial Conference Committee on International Judicial Relations. Member Federal Judges Association (Board of Directors since 1995, Treasurer 1997-2001, Vice President since 2001), American Judicature Society, Tenth Judicial District, Dakota County, Minnesota State, Federal and American Bar Associations. Named Distinguished Alumnus of Gustavus Adolphus College 1982. Former Chairman and National Committeeman Minnesota Young Republicans. Former Chairman First District Young Republicans, Dakota County Republicans and Durenberger Senate Volunteer Committee. Board of Directors Minnesota Prayer Breakfast Committee. Member St. Paul Chamber of Commerce, South St. Paul Chamber of Commerce and Southeast Metro Chamber of Commerce, Citizens League, Metropolitan Health Board and St. Lucas Community Church. Enjoys fishing, canoeing and camping.

Office: 730 Federal Building, 316 North Robert Street, St. Paul 55101.

Telephone: (651) 848-1150.

MANRIQUE, Tanja K. *(Judge, Minnesota District Court Fourth Judicial District)*

Office: 12C Government Center, 300 South Sixth Street, Minneapolis 55487.

Telephone: (612) 596-6986.

MARBEN, Kurt J. *(Judge, Minnesota District Court Ninth Judicial District)*

Office: Polk County Courthouse, 612 North Broadway, Crookston 56716.

Telephone: (218) 281-2332.

MARK, Kevin F. *(Judge, Minnesota District Court First Judicial District)*

Office: Goodhue County Justice Center, 454 West Sixth Street, Red Wing 55066.

Telephone: (651) 267-4800.

MARRINAN, Margaret M. *(Judge, Minnesota District Court Second Judicial District)* Assumed office Sept 13, 1986. Judge, Ramsey County Municipal Court Jan 1985 to Sept 1986.

Office: 1430 Ramsey County Courthouse, 15 West Kellogg Boulevard, St. Paul 55102.

Telephone: (651) 266-9181.

MARTIN, Elizabeth H. *(Judge, Minnesota District Court Tenth Judicial District)*

Mailing address: P.O. Box 3802, Stillwater 55082-3802.

Office: Washington County Government Center, Stillwater 55082.

Telephone: (651) 430-6345.

MARTIN, Gerald C. *(Judge, Minnesota District Court Sixth Judicial District)* Assumed office July 24, 1986. Judge, St. Louis County Court Dec 1978 to July 23, 1986, appointed by Governor Rudy Perpich.

Office: St. Louis County Courthouse, 100 North Fifth Avenue West, Duluth 55802-1212.

Telephone: (218) 726-2500.

MARTIN, Krista K. *(Judge, Minnesota District Court Tenth Judicial District)*

Office: Pine County Courthouse, 315 Sixth Street, Pine City 55063-1693.

Telephone: (320) 629-5646.

MATURI, Jon A. *(Judge, Minnesota District Court Ninth Judicial District)* Appointed by Governor Arne H. Carlson to term beginning July 1, 1996. Elected Nov 1998, current term expires 2005. Born Hibbing Minnesota April 16, 1947. Educated at University of Notre Dame B.A. 1969 and DePaul University College of Law J.D. cum laude 1977. Admitted to practice Minnesota 1977 and U.S. District Court District of Minnesota 1978. In legal practice Grand Rapids 1977-96.

Assistant County Attorney St. Louis County April 1977 to July 1977. Assistant District Public Defender July 1977 to July 1996. Member Minnesota District Judges Association and American Judges Association. USAF 1969-74. Board of Directors Grand Rapids Area Basketball Association, Grand Rapids Football Association and Grand Rapids Area Baseball Association. Enjoys canoeing, snow shoeing, basketball and athletics.

Office: Itasca County Courthouse, 123 N.E. Fourth Street, Grand Rapids 55744.

Telephone: (218) 327-2870.

E-mail address: jon.maturi@courts.state.mn.us

MAYERON, Janie S. *(Magistrate Judge, United States District Court District of Minnesota)* Appointed by U.S. District Court judges to term beginning Feb 7, 2003.

Office: Federal Building, 316 North Robert Street, St. Paul 55101.

Telephone: (651) 848-1190.

McBRIDE, John R. *(Judge, Minnesota District Court Tenth Judicial District)*

Office: Chisago County Courthouse, 313 North Main Street, Center City 55012.

Telephone: (651) 213-0485.

McCARTHY, Thomas G. *(Judge, Minnesota District Court First Judicial District)*

Mailing address: P.O. Box 867, Gaylord 55334.

Office: Sibley County Courthouse, Gaylord 55334.

Telephone: (507) 237-4051.

McGUNNIGLE, George F. *(Judge, Minnesota District Court Fourth Judicial District)*

Office: 12C Government Center, 300 South Sixth Street, Minneapolis 55487.

Telephone: (612) 596-7730.

McKINSEY, E. Anne *(Judge, Minnesota District Court Fourth Judicial District)* Appointed by Governor Rudy Perpich to term beginning Aug 6, 1990. Elected Nov 1992 and Nov 1998. Current term expires Jan 2005. Born Tulsa Oklahoma Sept 28, 1946. Educated at University of Minnesota B.A. 1971 and Washington College of Law of American University J.D. 1976. Associate Editor American University Law Review. Law Clerk to Hon. Joyce Hens Green, Superior Court of the District of Columbia. Admitted to practice District of

MCKINSEY, E. ANNE—*Continued*

Columbia 1976, U.S. Courts of Appeals District of Columbia 1977, Tenth 1983, Eighth 1985, Fourth 1986, Fifth 1988 and Ninth 1989 Circuits, U.S. District Courts District of Columbia 1981 and District of Minnesota 1983, U.S. Supreme Court 1980 and Minnesota 1983. In legal practice Minneapolis 1983-90.

Assistant U.S. Attorney District of Columbia 1977-82. Instructor in Legal Writing University of Minnesota 1990-92 and Trial Practice William Mitchell College of Law since 1992. Member Minnesota Women Lawyers, Hennepin County and Minnesota State Bar Associations. Instructor National Institute for Trial Advocacy since 1991. Faculty Member Evidence Seminar Minnesota Institute of Legal Education 1991 and 1993 and Minnesota Judicial College since 1994. Political affiliation: DFL (Precinct Chair 1984-90, State Central Committee). Member Superior Hiking Trail Association.

Office: 12C Government Center, 300 South Sixth Street, Minneapolis 55487.

Telephone: (612) 348-9850.

McMANUS, Timothy J. *(Judge, Minnesota District Court First Judicial District)*

Office: Dakota County Judicial Center, 1560 West Highway 55, Hastings 55033.

Telephone: (651) 438-8037.

McSHANE, John Q. *(Judge, Minnesota District Court Fourth Judicial District)*

Office: 12C Government Center, 300 South Sixth Street, Minneapolis 55487.

Telephone: (612) 596-6830.

MENNIS, David L. *(Judge, Minnesota District Court Eighth Judicial District)*

Office: Swift County Courthouse, 301 Fourteenth Street North, Benson 56215.

Telephone: (320) 843-2744.

METZEN, Leslie M. *(Judge, Minnesota District Court First Judicial District)* Assumed office Aug 1987. Former Judge, Dakota County Court.

Office: Dakota County Judicial Center, 1560 West Highway 55, Hastings 55033.

Telephone: (651) 438-4338.

MEYER, Gary J. *(Judge, Minnesota District Court Tenth Judicial District)* Appointed by Governor Rudy Perpich to term beginning July 1, 1987. Elected Nov 1988, 1994 and 2000. Current term expires Jan 2007. Born Chicago Illinois Oct 30, 1935. Educated at University of Minnesota B.S.L. 1957 LL.B. cum laude 1959. Editor Minnesota Law Review 1956-58. Member Phi Delta Phi and Order of the Coif. Admitted to practice Minnesota 1959. In legal practice Minneapolis 1959-63 and Robbinsdale and New Hope 1963-87.

Member Minnesota State and American (Committee on Family Law) Bar Associations.

Mailing address: P.O. Box 3802, Stillwater 55082-3802.

Office: Washington County Government Center, Stillwater 55082.

Telephone: (651) 430-6348.

MEYER, Helen M. *(Associate Justice, Minnesota Supreme Court)* Appointed by Governor Jesse Ventura to term beginning 2002.

Office: 427 Minnesota Judicial Center, 25 Martin Luther King Jr. Blvd., St. Paul 55155.

Telephone: (651) 296-2285.

MILES, Susan R. *(Judge, Minnesota District Court Tenth Judicial District)*

Mailing address: P.O. Box 3802, Stillwater 55082-3802.

Office: Washington County Government Center, Stillwater 55082.

Telephone: (651) 430-6333.

MINGE, David *(Judge, Minnesota Court of Appeals)* Appointed by Governor Jesse Ventura to term beginning May 2002. Born Clarkfield Minnesota March 19, 1942. Educated at St. Olaf College B.A. magna cum laude 1964 and University of Chicago Law School J.D. 1967. Member Phi Beta Kappa. In legal practice Minneapolis 1967-70 and Montevideo 1977-92.

Professor University of Wyoming College of Law 1970-77. Fulbright Lecturer University of Helsinki, Finland 1976. Lecturer University of Minnesota at Morris 2001-02. Co-founder and Former Chair Agricultural Law Section Minnesota State Bar Association. Member U.S. House of Representatives 1992-2000. Board Member and Participant Legal Advice Clinics Ltd. 1968-70. Fellow WW Kellogg Foundation Food and Society Policy Program 2001-2003. Scholar Woodrow Wilson Center, Washington D.C. Jan 2002 to April 2002. Past President Kinder Kare Board. Former Chair and Former Board Member Western Minnesota Legal Services. Former Member Montevideo School Board, Montevideo Chamber of Commerce Board, Montevideo Community Development Board and Salem Lutheran Church Council. Former Participant Volunteer Attorney Program. Co-founder and Former Board Member Clean Up the River Environment. Director Research Project on Medicare Payment Disparities. Consultant Conservation Initiatives in Federal Farm Programs.

Office: 232 Minnesota Judicial Center, 25 Martin Luther King Jr. Blvd., St. Paul 55155.

Telephone: (651) 297-1003.

E-mail address: david.minge@courts.state.mn.us

MONAHAN, M. Michael *(Judge, Minnesota District Court Second Judicial District)* Appointed by Governor Arne H. Carlson to term beginning May 3, 1991. Elected Nov 1992 and Nov 1998. Current term expires Jan 2005. Born Buenos Aires Argentina Oct 26, 1941. Educated at Georgetown University A.B. 1964 and University of Minnesota J.D. 1967. Admitted to practice Minnesota 1967, U.S. District Court District of Minnesota 1972, U.S. Supreme Court 1982 and U.S. Court of Appeals Eighth Circuit 1984. In legal practice St. Paul 1969-91. Captain (Armor) U.S. Army 1967-69.

Office: 1510 Ramsey County Courthouse, 15 West Kellogg Boulevard, St. Paul 55102.

Telephone: (651) 266-9184.

MONDRY, Jay D. *(Judge, Minnesota District Court Ninth Judicial District)* Elected 1990 to term beginning Jan 7, 1991. Reelected 1996 and 2002. Current term expires Jan 2009. Born Grand Forks North Dakota May 4, 1939. Roman Catholic. Educated at University of Notre Dame B.A. 1961 and University of North Dakota LL.B. 1964. Admitted to practice North Dakota 1964 and Min-

MONDRY, JAY D.—*Continued*
nesota 1964. In legal practice Wadena 1965-70 and Park Rapids 1970-90 Minnesota.

County Attorney Hubbard County Minnesota 1971-78. Member Minnesota State Bar Association.

Office: Hubbard County Courthouse, 301 Court Avenue, Park Rapids 56470.

Telephone: (218) 732-3573.

MONTGOMERY, Ann D. *(Judge, United States District Court District of Minnesota)* Magistrate Judge Nov 17, 1994 to Aug 1996. Appointed Judge for life by President Bill Clinton to term beginning Aug 6, 1996. Educated at Kansas University and University of Minnesota J.D. Judge, Minnesota District Court Fourth Judicial District 1983-94.

Assistant U.S. Attorney Minnesota 1976-83. Co-author with Myron Bright and Ronald Carlson *Objections At Trial* Minnesota ed. Instructor of Trial Practice University of Minnesota. Lecturer William Mitchell College of Law and Hamline University School of Law. Past President Federal Bar Association of Minnesota. Former Member Supreme Court Advisory Committees and Civil Jury Instruction Guide Committee Minnesota Judges Association. Recipient Professionalism Award from Hennepin County Bar Association 1993, Trial Judge of the Year Award from American Board of Trial Advocates 1996 and Myra Bradwell Award form Minnesota Women Lawyers Association 2000.

Office: 13W U.S. Courthouse, 300 South Fourth Street, Minneapolis 55415.

Telephone: (612) 664-5090.

MORROW, James A. *(Judge, Minnesota District Court Tenth Judicial District)* Appointed by Governor Rudy Perpich to term beginning Feb 18, 1983. Elected 1984, 1990, 1996 and 2002. Current term expires Jan 2009. Born Des Moines Iowa May 11, 1945. Lutheran. Educated at University of Minnesota B.A. 1972 and William Mitchell College of Law J.D. magna cum laude 1978. Law Clerk to Hon. Douglas K. Amdahl, Minnesota District Court Fourth Judicial District July 1976 to July 1978. Admitted to practice Minnesota 1978, U.S. District Court District of Minnesota 1978 and U.S. Court of Appeals Eighth Circuit 1978.

Assistant U.S. Attorney District of Minnesota Aug 1978 to Feb 1983. Member Minnesota Supreme Court Criminal Courts Study Commission 1990. Former Chair Judicial Evaluation Drafting Committee. Member Supreme Court Judicial Evaluation Drafting Committee. Adjunct Instructor in Trial Advocacy and Criminal Law William Mitchell College since 1980. Member Committee to Update Minnesota Judges Criminal Benchbook. Former member American Trial Lawyers Association. Member Anoka, Minnesota State (Secretary of the Governing Council Civil Litigation Section, Women in the Legal Profession Committee, Former Chairman-Elect Young Lawyers Section) and American Bar Associations. Faculty Advisor The National Judicial College Spring 1985. Judicial Ethics Panel Minnesota Judges Conference. Adjunct Faculty Minnesota Judicial Training Skills Program, Minnesota School for Prosecutors and Defense Attorneys, Minnesota Trial Lawyers Evidence Seminar, Minnesota Evidence Seminar for Attorneys and Judges, Minnesota Civil Trial Practice Institute, Minnesota New Judges Orientation, Minnesota Judicial Advocacy Institute, National Conference on Judicial Evaluation and National Institute for Trial Advocacy. Group Leader Minnesota Evidence Seminars and Minnesota Institute for Criminal Justice. Member 1990 and 1991 and Faculty member 1992 National Leadership Institute on Judicial Education. Staff Sergeant Air National Guard 1963-70. Chemical Dependency Counselor Hastings State Hospital Dec 1970 to Dec 1972. DFL Research Analyst Minnesota House of Representatives Dec 1972 to June 1976. Past President Warren E. Burger Inn of Court. Former Big Brother. Former member Anoka County Children's Mental Health Council. Former Advisory Board member of Freedom House. Former Den Leader for Cub Scouts. Former Volunteer Crisis Intervention Counselor. Former Volunteer Legal Aid Attorney. Board member Advisory Committee to Establish a Counseling Program at William Mitchell College of Law. Member Anoka County DWI Repeat Offender Task Force, Minnesota Lawyers Concerned for Lawyers and Coon Rapids Human Services Advisory Commission. Enjoys family activities, reading and jogging.

Office: Anoka County Courthouse, 325 East Main Street, Anoka 55303-2489.

Telephone: (763) 422-7440.

MOSSEY, Dale E. *(Judge, Minnesota District Court Tenth Judicial District)*

Office: 201 Wright County Government Center, 10 Second Street N.W., Buffalo 55313-1192.

Telephone: (763) 682-7539.

MOTT, J. Thomas *(Judge, Minnesota District Court Second Judicial District)* Appointed by Governor Rudy Perpich to term beginning March 18, 1988. Elected 1990, 1996 and 2002. Current term expires Jan 2009. Currently serves as Assistant Chief Judge. Born Rochelle Illinois Nov 9, 1949. Episcopalian. Educated at Austin State Junior College A.A. 1970, University of Minnesota B.A. 1972 and William Mitchell College of Law J.D. 1976. Admitted to practice Minnesota 1976, U.S. District Court District of Minnesota 1976 and U.S. Court of Appeals Eighth Circuit 1979. In legal practice St. Paul 1976-88.

Part-time Assistant Public Defender Ramsey County 1976-88. Part-time Instructor Criminal Law Clinic William Mitchell College of Law 1976-81 and Law Enforcement Program Lakewood Community College 1980-81. Member Minnesota District Judges Association, Ramsey County and Minnesota State Bar Associations. Recipient Outstanding Service Award for Improvement of the Judicial System from Minnesota District Judges Association 2000. Previously worked as Field Representative Minnesota Esthetic Environment Program, Customer Service Representative Mail Marketing Co., clothing salesman Gildners Menswear and Engineering Aide City of Albert Lea. Former Assistant Scheduling Director Minnesota Campaign McGovern for President. Chair Senate District 31 Freeborn County 1972-74, Member State Central Committee 1972-80, Rosalie Wahl Citizens Committee 1978 and State Secretary 1974-80 Democratic Farm Labor Party. Board of Directors Summit-University Teen Center and Canabury Square Condominium Association. Enjoys traveling, biking and playing tennis.

Office: 1010 Ramsey County Courthouse, 15 West Kellogg Boulevard, St. Paul 55102.

Telephone: (651) 266-9187.

MUEHLBERG, Stephen L. *(Judge, Minnesota District Court Tenth Judicial District)*

MUEHLBERG, STEPHEN L.—*Continued*

Mailing address: P.O. Box 3802, Stillwater 55082-3802.

Office: Washington County Government Center, Stillwater 55082.

Telephone: (651) 430-4426.

MUNGER, Mark A. *(Judge, Minnesota District Court Sixth Judicial District)*

Office: St. Louis County Courthouse, 100 North Fifth Avenue West, Duluth 55802-1212.

Telephone: (218) 726-2554.

MURPHY, Dennis J. *(Judge, Minnesota District Court Ninth Judicial District)* Elected Nov 8, 1988 to term beginning January 2, 1989. Reelected Nov 8, 1994 and 2000. Current term expires Jan 2007. Born Grand Rapids Minnesota July 25, 1938. Catholic. Educated at University of Notre Dame B.B.A. with honors 1960 and University of Minnesota J.D. 1963. Admitted to practice Minnesota 1963. In legal practice Grand Rapids 1963-81 and Thief River Falls 1981-89.

Mailing address: P.O. Box 366, Thief River Falls 56701.

Office: Pennington County Courthouse, 101 North Main, Thief River Falls 56701.

Telephone: (218) 681-0905.

MURPHY, Thomas M. *(Judge, Minnesota District Court First Judicial District)* Assumed office Aug 1987. Former Judge, Dakota County Court.

Office: Dakota County Judicial Center, 1560 West Highway 55, Hastings 55033.

Telephone: (651) 438-4325.

NATHANSON, Rosanne *(Judge, Minnesota District Court Second Judicial District)*

Office: 1470 Ramsey County Courthouse, 15 West Kellogg Boulevard, St. Paul 55102.

Telephone: (651) 266-8346.

NELSON, Paul A. *(Judge, Minnesota District Court Eighth Judicial District)* Appointed by Governor Arne H. Carlson March 3, 1997 to term beginning April 11, 1997. Elected Nov 3, 1998, current term expires Dec 31, 2004. Born Sibley Illinois Aug 18, 1947. Educated at Wartburg College B.A. 1969 and University of Minnesota Law School J.D. cum laude 1975. Admitted to practice Minnesota 1975 and U.S. District Court District of Minnesota 1978. In legal practice Olivia 1975-97.

Member Twelfth District and Minnesota State Bar Associations. Sergeant U.S. Army 1970-72.

Mailing address: P.O. Box 697, Montevideo 56265-0697.

Office: Chippewa County Courthouse, Montevideo 56265.

Telephone: (320) 269-7774.

E-mail address: paul.nelson@courts.state.mn.us

NELSON, Susan Richard *(Magistrate Judge, United States District Court District of Minnesota)* Appointed by U.S. District Court judges to term beginning June 1, 2000. Term expires May 31, 2008.

Office: Federal Building, 316 North Robert Street, St. Paul 55101.

Telephone: (651) 848-1200.

NEVILLE, Cara Lee *(Judge, Minnesota District Court Fourth Judicial District)* Assumed office June 19, 1986. Elected to subsequent terms. Educated at William Mitchell College of Law J.D. 1975. Recipient Hornbook Award for Scholastic Achievement as first in senior class from West Publishing Company 1975. Student Board of Governors 1973-75. President Student Bar Association 1974-75. Staff Writer "Opinion" 1974-75. Member Phi Alpha Delta (Recipient Certificate of Appreciation 1973, Treasurer 1974-75). Admitted to practice Minnesota 1975, U.S. District Court District of Minnesota 1976, U.S. Court of Appeals Eighth Circuit 1976 and U.S. Supreme Court 1980. Judge, Hennepin County Municipal Court Sept 1, 1983 to June 18, 1986, appointed by Governor Rudy Perpich.

Assistant Attorney Criminal Division 1975-78 and Assistant Public Defender 1978-83 Hennepin County. Adjunct Professor of Clinical Programs, Moot Court and National Trial Practice William Mitchell College of Law 1979-82. Fellow American Bar Foundation. Board of Directors Women Judges Fund for Justice (Secretary 1987-88). Member Minnesota Women Lawyers Association (Treasurer 1980-81, Secretary 1981-82), Minnesota Trial Lawyers Association (Executive Director 1974-75, Co-chair Criminal Law Committee 1977-78, Board of Governors 1978-83, Chairperson Legislature Committee 1980-81 and Education Committee 1981-82, Treasurer 1980-81, Secretary 1981-82, Vice President 1982, President 1983), Minnesota County Attorneys Council 1975-78, Minnesota Association of Women in Criminal Justice (Executive Committee 1979-80), The Association of Trial Lawyers of America 1975-84, National District Attorneys Association 1975-78, National Association of Women Judges (Board of Directors, Secretary 1988-89), Hennepin County (Governing Council since 1981), Minnesota State (Chairperson 1978-79 Criminal Law Section, Alternate to Board of Governors 1979-81, Board of Governors since 1981, Liaison to ABA Section of Criminal Justice) and American (Judicial Administration Division, Section of Criminal Justice since 1979, Vice Chair Committee on Specialization Section of Criminal Justice 1981-82, Special Advisor to Chair of Criminal Justice Section on Attorney Specialization 1982, Vice Chair Economics of Law Practice Committee Section of Criminal Justice 1982, Vice Chair Providing Defense Services 1983-84, Governing Council 1985-86 and since 1988, House of Delegates) Bar Associations. Faculty Advisor The National Judicial College. Named Outstanding Young Woman of Minnesota 1977 and one of the Outstanding Young Women of America 1977.

Office: 12C Government Center, 300 South Sixth Street, Minneapolis 55487.

Telephone: (612) 348-8901.

NOEL, Franklin L. *(Magistrate Judge, United States District Court District of Minnesota)* Appointed by U.S. District Court judges to term beginning Nov 1989. Reappointed Nov 1997, current term expires Nov 2005. Born New York New York Dec 7, 1951. Episcopalian. Educated at State University of New York at Binghamton B.A. with high honors 1974 and Georgetown University Law Center J.D. with honors 1977. Circuits Note Editor Georgetown Law Journal 1976-77. Admitted to practice District of Columbia 1977, U.S. District Courts District of Columbia 1977 and District of Minnesota 1983, U.S. Courts of Appeals District of Columbia 1977 and Eighth 1983 Circuits, Pennsylvania 1979 and Minnesota 1983. In legal practice Washington D.C. 1977-79.

Assistant District Attorney Philadelphia Pennsylvania 1979-83. Assistant U.S. Attorney Minneapolis 1983-89. Instructor in Legal Writing University of Minnesota Law

NOEL, FRANKLIN L.—*Continued*

School 1989-92. Adjunct Faculty University of Minnesota Law School since 1996. Member Hennepin County and Minnesota State Bar Associations.

Office: 9W U.S. Courthouse, 300 South Fourth Street, Minneapolis 55415.

Telephone: (612) 664-5110.

NORD, Beryl A. *(Judge, Minnesota District Court Fourth Judicial District)* Assumed office June 19, 1986. Elected Nov 1990, Nov 1996 and 2002. Current term expires Jan 2009. Born Frederic Wisconsin Oct 12, 1948. Educated at Macalester College 1966-67 and University of Minnesota B.A. cum laude 1970 J.D. cum laude 1973. Staff member University of Minnesota Law Review 1972-73. Law Clerk to Hon. James C. Otis, Minnesota Supreme Court 1973-74. Student Director Legal Assistance to Minnesota Prisoners 1972-73. Member Law Council 1970-71 and Women's Caucus 1971-73. Member Intercollegiate Debate Team and Pi Kappa Delta. Admitted to practice Minnesota 1973, U.S. District Court District of Minnesota 1973 and U.S. Court of Appeals Eighth Circuit 1977. Began legal practice St. Paul 1974. Judge, Hennepin County Municipal Court April 1, 1983 to June 18, 1986.

Assistant City Attorney City of St. Paul 1974-83. Adjunct Professor of Trial Practice University of Minnesota Law School 1983-87. Former member Ramsey County Bar Association (Criminal Law Committee 1978-80, Ethics Committee 1981-83, Delegate to State Bar Convention 1980 and 1982). Member National Association of Women Judges (Director 1987-89), Minnesota Judges Association (Board member since 1989), Minnesota Women Lawyers (Appointments Committee since 1979, President 1989-90), Hennepin County (Hennepin Lawyer Committee 1984-89, Delegate to State Bar Convention 1983, 1984, 1988, 1989 and 1990), Minnesota State (Board of Governors 1989-91) and American Bar Associations. Instructor Update for City Attorneys Government Training Service Jan 1978. Lecturer on Criminal law and procedure and training bulletins for St. Paul Police Department 1978-80. Former member Minnesota Women's Political Caucus. Member 1974-83 and Board Member 1976-78 DFL Feminist Caucus. Director 1976-80 and Chairperson 1980-82 58th District DFL. Board Member Criminal Justice Coordinating Council 1978-80. Member DFL State Central Committee 1980-83. Member YWCA Big Sister Program St. Paul 1973-76. Enjoys sailing and card playing.

Office: 12C Government Center, 300 South Sixth Street, Minneapolis 55487.

Telephone: (612) 348-8248.

NORDBY, Jack S. *(Judge, Minnesota District Court Fourth Judicial District)*

Office: 12C Government Center, 300 South Sixth Street, Minneapolis 55487.

Telephone: (612) 348-3502.

O'BRIEN, Dennis D. *(Judge, United States Bankruptcy Court District of Minnesota)* Appointed by U.S. Court of Appeals Eighth Circuit judges. Former Chief Judge.

Office: 238 Federal Building, 316 North Robert Street, St. Paul 55101.

Telephone: (651) 848-1050.

OLEISKY, Allen *(Judge, Minnesota District Court Fourth Judicial District)* Appointed by Governor Wendell R. Anderson to term beginning 1974. Elected 1976, 1982, 1988, 1994 and 2000. Current term expires Jan 2007. Born Pierre South Dakota March 31, 1938. Educated at University of Minnesota B.A. 1960 LL.B. 1962. In legal practice Minneapolis 1962-72. Judge, Hennepin County Municipal Court 1972-74.

Office: 12C Government Center, 300 South Sixth Street, Minneapolis 55487.

Telephone: (612) 348-6634.

OLSON, Lynn C. *(Judge, Minnesota District Court Tenth Judicial District)* Appointed by Governor Rudy Perpich to term beginning Feb 1, 1983. Elected 1984, 1990, 1996 and 2002. Current term expires Jan 2009. Born Pittsburgh Pennsylvania Oct 14, 1941. Educated at Michigan State University B.A. 1963 and William Mitchell College of Law J.D. 1977. Student Director Legal Aid to Minnesota Prisoners William Mitchell College of Law May 1976 to Jan 1977. Admitted to practice Minnesota 1977, U.S. District Court District of Minnesota 1977 and U.S. Court of Appeals Eighth Circuit 1977. Began legal practice Minneapolis 1977. In legal practice Anoka 1979-82. Judge, Anoka County Court 1982-83.

Attorney Public Defender's Office Hennepin County 1977-79 and Assistant County Attorney Criminal Division Anoka County 1979. Member Minnesota Judicial Appeal Panel Mentally Ill and Dangerous Commitments 1985-90. Author "Bail: A Primer" 6 No. 3 Minnesota Trial Lawyer April 1981, "Eighth Amendment Issues" CLE 17th Annual Criminal Justice Institute Aug 1982, "Views From the Bench" CLE Fourth Annual Family Law Institute April 1983, "The Commission to Investigate the Possible Removal of Scott County Attorney, R. Kathleen Morris" North Dakota L. Rev. 1987 and "Two Roads Diverged: Reflections on a Study of Career Paths" 46 No. 9 *Bench and Bar of Minnesota* Oct 1989. Member Minnesota Trial Lawyers Association 1980-82 (Co-chair Criminal Law Committee 1981-82), Minnesota Women Lawyers Association, Minnesota County Judges Association 1982-83, Minnesota District Judges Association (President 1988), National Council of Juvenile and Family Court Judges, Anoka County, Minnesota State (Delegate to State Convention 1979-84, Vice Chair Criminal Law Section 1980-82, Board of Governors 1989-92) and American Bar Associations. Faculty National Institute Trial Advocacy since 1983. Recipient Susan B. Anthony Award Minnesota Center for Women in Government 1992 and Myra P. Bradwell Award Minnesota Women Lawyers 1992. Teacher U.S. Peace Corps, Nigeria West Africa 1964-66, Jefferson Junior High School, Champaign Illinois 1966-67, Pennsylvania Valley Area High School, Spring Mills Pennsylvania 1967-68 and Presbyterian Ladies College, Melbourne Australia 1969-70. Social Worker Welfare Department Hennepin County 1971-76. Executive Board Anoka County Sexual Assault Committee since 1980. Member Anoka County DWI Task Force since 1982. Chair Board of Directors Alexandra House (Anoka County shelter for battered women) since 1983. Advisory Board Anoka County Community Corrections Board 1984. Minnesota Board Medical Examiner Task Force HIV Positive Physicians 1991. Member State Bicentennial Commission 1990-92. Chair Anoka County Public Defender Board 1992-93.

OLSON, LYNN C.—*Continued*

Chair Mercy Hospital Foundation Board 1992-93. Member Hospital Medical Ethics Committee.

Office: Anoka County Courthouse, 325 East Main Street, Anoka 55303-2489.

Telephone: (763) 422-7430.

OSWALD, John T. *(Judge, Minnesota District Court Sixth Judicial District)* Appointed by Governor Rudy Perpich to term beginning March 11, 1985. Elected 1986, Nov 1992 and Nov 1998. Current term expires Jan 2005. Chief Judge July 1, 1989 to June 30, 1991 and since 1996. Born Duluth Minnesota Dec 2, 1941. Catholic. Educated at Marquette University B.S. 1964 J.D. 1968. Staff member Marquette Law Review. Member Delta Theta Phi. Admitted to practice Minnesota 1968 and Wisconsin 1968. In legal practice Duluth Minnesota 1968-83. Judicial Officer, St. Louis County Court 1983-85.

Member District Court General Rules of Practice Committee. Member Minnesota Judges Association, Minnesota Conference of Chief Judges, State Bar of Wisconsin, Minnesota State and American Bar Associations. Attended National Conference of Juvenile Justice 1978, 1979 and 1980 and American Academy of Trial Judges 1985.

Office: St. Louis County Courthouse, 100 North Fifth Avenue West, Duluth 55802-1212.

Telephone: (218) 726-2460.

PAGE, Alan C. *(Associate Justice, Minnesota Supreme Court)* Assumed office 1993. Born Aug 7, 1945. Educated at University of Notre Dame B.A. 1967 and University of Minnesota Law School J.D. 1978. Honorary Doctor of Law University of Notre Dame 1993, St. John's University 1994, Westfield State College 1994 and Luther College 1995. In legal practice 1979-84.

Special Assistant Attorney General Employment Law Division 1985-87. Assistant Attorney General Minnesota 1987-93. Member Minnesota Minority Lawyers' Association, The American Law Institute, Minnesota State, National and American Bar Associations. Advisory Board Member Mixed Blood Theatre since 1984. Board of Directors Minneapolis Urban League 1987-90. Founder Page Education Foundation 1988. Board of Regents University of Minnesota 1989-92.

Office: 423 Minnesota Judicial Center, 25 Martin Luther King Jr. Blvd., St. Paul 55155.

Telephone: (651) 296-6615.

PAGLIACCETTI, Gary J. *(Judge, Minnesota District Court Sixth Judicial District)* Appointed by Governor Rudy Perpich to term beginning June 30, 1989. Elected 1990, 1996 and 2002. Current term expires Jan 1, 2009. Born St. Cloud Minnesota Oct 3, 1954. Catholic. Educated at St. John's University B.A. 1976 and Hamline University School of Law J.D. cum laude 1979. Member Silver Gavel Honor Society. Admitted to practice Minnesota 1979, U.S. District Court District of Minnesota 1980 and U.S. Court of Appeals 1980. In legal practice Virginia Minnesota 1980-89.

Member Minnesota State Bar Association.

Office: St. Louis County Courthouse, 300 South Fifth Avenue, Virginia 55792.

Telephone: (218) 749-7106.

PAWLENTY, Mary E. *(Judge, Minnesota District Court First Judicial District)*

Office: Dakota County Judicial Center, 1560 West Highway 55, Hastings 55033.

Telephone: (651) 438-4325.

PEARSON, John E. *(Judge, Minnesota District Court Seventh Judicial District)*

Office: Clay County Courthouse, 807 North Eleventh Street, Moorhead 56560.

Telephone: (218) 299-5065.

PEARSON, Skipper J. *(Judge, Minnesota District Court Seventh Judicial District)*

Office: Stearns County Courthouse, 725 Courthouse Square, St. Cloud 56303-4781.

Telephone: (320) 656-3620.

PEDERSON, William R. *(Judge, Minnesota Workers' Compensation Court of Appeals)* Appointed by Governor Arne H. Carlson to term beginning Aug 1998.

Office: Minnesota Judicial Center, 25 Martin Luther King Jr. Blvd., St. Paul 55155.

Telephone: (651) 296-6526.

PENDLETON, Alan Frank *(Judge, Minnesota District Court Tenth Judicial District)* Appointed by Governor Jesse Ventura Sept 14, 1999 to term beginning Nov 10, 1999. Elected 2002, current term expires Nov 2008. Born Kansas City Missouri Dec 8, 1954. Lutheran. Educated at Bemidji State University B.S. cum laude 1977 and Drake University Law School J.D. cum laude 1980. Staff Writer Drake Law Review 1978-80. Admitted to practice Minnesota 1980 and U.S. District Court District of Minnesota 1981. In legal practice Minneapolis Minnesota 1985-88.

Assistant County Attorney Winona County 1981-85 and Anoka County 1988-99. Author Anoka County Attorney Training Update Newsletter 1991-99 and *Minnesota Handbook on Motor Vehicle Stops, Warrantless Searches & Seizures* 1994 Anoka County Attorneys Office and *Minnesota Criminal Elements Handbook* Minnesota County Attorneys Association 1992-98. Adjunct Professor Century College and William Mitchell College of Law. Former Member Minnesota County Attorneys Association. Member Minnesota District Judges Association, Minnesota State and American Bar Associations. Faculty Member National Institute for Trial Advocacy. Attended Minnesota Judicial Winter Conference 1999 and 2000 and Minnesota Judicial Orientation Program May 2000 Minnesota District Judges Association. Recipient Certificate of Appreciation from Minnesota Chiefs of Police Association April 26, 1995. Named one of 14 Minnesota Public Sector Lawyers of Distinction by Minnesota Journal of Law and Politics Aug 1996. Guest speaker DARE graduation ceremonies. Enjoys reading, computer technology and spending time with family.

Office: Sherburne County Government Center, 13880 Highway 10, Elk River 55330-4608.

Telephone: (763) 241-2800.

E-mail address: alan.pendleton@courts.state.mn.us

PEREZ, George W. *(Chief Judge, Minnesota Tax Court)* Appointed by governor.

Office: 245 Minnesota Judicial Center, 25 Martin Luther King Jr. Blvd., St. Paul 55155.

Telephone: (651) 296-2806.

PERKINS, Richard C. *(Judge, Minnesota District Court First Judicial District)*
Office: LeSueur County Courthouse, 88 South Park Avenue, LeCenter 56057-1620.
Telephone: (507) 357-2251.

PERSON, Carol M. *(Judge, Minnesota District Court Sixth Judicial District)*
Office: St. Louis County Courthouse, 100 North Fifth Avenue West, Duluth 55802-1212.
Telephone: (218) 726-2460.

PETERSON, Bruce A. *(Judge, Minnesota District Court Fourth Judicial District)*
Office: 12C Government Center, 300 South Sixth Street, Minneapolis 55487.
Telephone: (612) 596-7126.

PETERSON, David W. *(Judge, Minnesota District Court Fifth Judicial District)*
Mailing address: P.O. Box 130, Redwood Falls 56283.
Office: Redwood County Courthouse, Redwood Falls 56283.
Telephone: (507) 637-4020.

PETERSON, Randolph W. *(Judge, Minnesota Court of Appeals)* Appointed by Governor Rudy Perpich to term beginning Dec 4, 1990. Elected 1992 and 1998. Current term expires 2004. Educated at University of Minnesota B.A. J.D.
Former Special Assistant County Attorney Anoka County. Senator Minnesota State Senate 1980-86.
Office: 316 Minnesota Judicial Center, 25 Martin Luther King Jr. Blvd., St. Paul 55155.
Telephone: (651) 297-7807.

PIHLAJA, Steven A. *(Judge, Minnesota District Court Fourth Judicial District)*
Office: 12C Government Center, 300 South Sixth Street, Minneapolis 55487.
Telephone: (612) 348-5693.

POCH, Thomas B. *(Judge, Minnesota District Court First Judicial District)*
Office: Dakota County Judicial Center, 1560 West Highway 55, Hastings 55033.
Telephone: (651) 438-4325.

PORTER, Charles A., Jr. *(Judge, Minnesota District Court Fourth Judicial District)*
Office: 1801C Government Center, 300 South Sixth Street, Minneapolis 55487.
Telephone: (612) 348-8150.

POSTON, Janet Nordell *(Judge, Minnesota District Court Fourth Judicial District)*
Office: 12C Government Center, 300 South Sixth Street, Minneapolis 55487.
Telephone: (612) 348-7199.

QUAINTANCE, Kathryn *(Judge, Minnesota District Court Fourth Judicial District)*
Office: 12C Government Center, 300 South Sixth Street, Minneapolis 55487.
Telephone: (612) 348-5434.

QUINN, R. Joseph *(Judge, Minnesota District Court Tenth Judicial District)* Currently serves as Chief Judge.
Office: Anoka County Courthouse, 325 East Main Street, Anoka 55303.
Telephone: (763) 422-7440.

RAMSTAD, Sheryl A. *(Judge, Minnesota Tax Court)* Appointed by governor.
Office: 245 Minnesota Judicial Center, 25 Martin Luther King Jr. Blvd., St. Paul 55155.
Telephone: (651) 296-2806.

RANCOURT, Robert G. *(Judge, Minnesota District Court Tenth Judicial District)*
Office: Chisago County Courthouse, 313 North Main Street, Center City 55012.
Telephone: (651) 213-0485.

RANDALL, R. A. "Jim" *(Judge, Minnesota Court of Appeals)* Appointed by Governor Rudy Perpich April 2, 1984. Elected 1986, 1992 and 1998. Current term expires Jan 2005. Born Little Falls Minnesota Aug 31, 1940. Catholic. Educated at Gonzaga University B.A. cum laude 1962 and University of Minnesota J.D. 1967. Participant General Electric College Bowl 1960. Law Clerk to Hennepin County District Court 1967. Member Gamma Eta Gamma. Admitted to practice Minnesota 1967, U.S. District Court District of Minnesota 1967 and U.S. Supreme Court 1981. In legal practice Hibbing 1967-84.
Instructor in Judicial Philosophy University of Hamline Law School since 1990. Member Iron Range, Minnesota State and American Bar Associations. Second Lieutenant USMC 1962-65. Active with Native American and minority issues and with groups working in the inner city of St. Paul and Minneapolis. Provides auxiliary support on a voluntary basis to inmates in state institutions. Enjoys long distance running, all sports, reading, chess and antiques.
Office: 317 Minnesota Judicial Center, 25 Martin Luther King Jr. Blvd., St. Paul 55155.
Telephone: (651) 297-1004.

RANTALA, Jeffry S. *(Judge, Minnesota District Court Sixth Judicial District)*
Office: St. Louis County Courthouse, 1810 East Twelfth Avenue, Hibbing 55746.
Telephone: (218) 262-0100.

RASMUSSEN, Paul E. *(Judge, Minnesota District Court Ninth Judicial District)*
Office: Clearwater County Courthouse, Department 303, 213 Main Avenue North, Bagley 56621-8304.
Telephone: (218) 694-6177.

REILLY, Denise D. *(Judge, Minnesota District Court Fourth Judicial District)*
Office: 12C Government Center, 300 South Sixth Street, Minneapolis 55487.
Telephone: (612) 348-0112.

REUTER, James *(Judge, Minnesota District Court Tenth Judicial District)*
Office: Pine County Courthouse, 315 Sixth Street, Pine City 55063-1693.
Telephone: (320) 629-5634.

RICHARDS, Douglas L. *(Judge, Minnesota District Court Fifth Judicial District)*
Mailing address: P.O. Box 130, Blue Earth 56013.
Office: Faribault County Courthouse, Blue Earth 56013.
Telephone: (507) 526-6273.

ROBERTSON, Sally Ireland *(Judge, Minnesota District Court Seventh Judicial District)*
Office: Todd County Courthouse, 221 First Avenue South, Long Prairie 56347.
Telephone: (320) 732-7800.

RODENBERG, John R. *(Judge, Minnesota District Court Fifth Judicial District)* Appointed by Governor Jesse Ventura Sept 11, 2000 to term beginning Oct 27, 2000. Elected Nov 5, 2002, current term expires Jan 1, 2009. Born New Ulm Minnesota June 8, 1956. Educated at St. Olaf College B.A. cum laude 1978 and Hamline University J.D. cum laude 1981. Staff member Hamline University Law Review 1979-81. Member Silver Gavel Honor Society. Admitted to practice Minnesota 1981 and U.S. District Court District of Minnesota 1984. Civil Trial Practice Specialist, Certified by Minnesota State Bar Association. In legal practice New Ulm 1982-2000.
Staff Attorney Social Security Administration 1981-82. Assistant County Attorney Brown County 1982-2000. Former Member American Veterinary Medical Law Association. Member Minnesota Defense Lawyers Association, The Defense Research Institute, Inc., Minnesota District Judges Association, Ninth District Bar Association, Brown County, Minnesota State (Civil Juries Subcommittee 1996) and American Bar Associations. Participant and Presenter Continuing Legal Education seminars Minnesota State Bar Association. Named one of Minnesota's top twenty-five "Superlawyers" by Minnesota Journal of Law and Politics 2000. Member and Chairman New Ulm Police Commission 1991-97. Past President and Council Member Christ the King Lutheran Church. Past President, Director, Board Member, League and Tournament Coordinator and Coach New Ulm Baseball Association. Former Volunteer Attorney Southern Minnesota Regional Legal Services. Former Member Brown County Child Protection Team. Coach and Active Member New Ulm Hockey Association. Certified Referee USA Hockey. Mock Trial Coach New Ulm Public High School.
Mailing address: P.O. Box 248, New Ulm 56073-0248.
Office: Brown County Courthouse, 12 South State Street, New Ulm 56073-3154.
Telephone: (507) 233-6670.
Fax: (507) 359-9562
E-mail address: john.rodenberg@courts.state.mn.us

ROE, Katherian D. *(Judge, Minnesota District Court Fourth Judicial District)*
Office: 12C Government Center, 300 South Sixth Street, Minneapolis 55487.
Telephone: (612) 596-8733.

ROITH, Michael J. *(Judge, Minnesota District Court Tenth Judicial District)*
Office: Anoka County Courthouse, 325 East Main Street, Anoka 55303-2489.
Telephone: (763) 422-7440.

ROSAS, Salvador M. *(Judge, Minnesota District Court Second Judicial District)*
Office: 870 Ramsey County Courthouse, 15 West Kellogg Boulevard, St. Paul 55102.
Telephone: (651) 266-8157.

ROSENBAUM, James M. *(Chief Judge, United States District Court District of Minnesota)* Appointed for life by President Ronald Reagan to term beginning 1985. Chief Judge since July 1, 2001. Born Fort Snelling Minnesota Oct 12, 1944. Educated at University of Minnesota B.A. 1966 J.D. 1969. In legal practice Minneapolis 1973-81.
Attorney VISTA 1969-70. Staff Attorney Leadership Council 1970-72. U.S. Attorney District of Minnesota 1981-85. Instructor University of Minnesota and William Mitchell College of Law. Member U.S. Courts Design Guide Committee. President Minnesota Chapter Federal Bar Association. Instructor National Institute for Trial Advocacy, Federal Judicial Conference and National Convention and Committee Conference American Bar Association. Board of Visitors University of Minnesota Law School. Enjoys reading, baking, travel and baseball.
Office: 15E U.S. Courthouse, 300 South Fourth Street, Minneapolis 55415.
Telephone: (612) 664-5050.

ROSENBAUM, Marilyn Brown *(Judge, Minnesota District Court Fourth Judicial District)* Appointed by Governor Arne H. Carlson to term beginning July 21, 1992. Elected 1994 and 2000. Current term expires Jan 2007. Born Chicago Illinois Sept 2, 1944. Educated at University of Illinois at Champaign-Urbana B.S. with honors 1966 and Georgetown University Law Center J.D. 1969. Admitted Illinois 1970, Minnesota 1973, U.S. Court of Appeals Seventh Circuit 1970, U.S. District Courts Northern District of Illinois 1970 and District of Minnesota 1974 and U.S. Supreme Court 1979. In legal practice Chicago Illinois 1970-72 and Minneapolis Minnesota 1973-92. Hearing Examiner, Minneapolis Civil Rights Commission 1979.
Staff Attorney Leadership Council for Metropolitan Open Communities 1970-71. Internal Revenue Service U.S. Department of the Treasury 1972-77. Author *Open Housing: A Guide to Practice* 1971. Instructor International Law and Practice Masters Program University of Nottingham Law School, England 1998 and in Trial and Motion Practice William Mitchell College of Law. Guest Lecturer on Sentencing Guidelines University of Minnesota Law School. Member Executive Committee 1994-98, Civil Committee, Criminal Committee and Bench Resource Committee Fourth Judicial District, Gender Fairness Implementation Committee 1995-98 and Joint Committee Gender Fairness and Racial Bias Task Force 1994-98 Minnesota Supreme Court and ad hoc Committee State Board of Public Defense 1996-1997. Member Minnesota Women Lawyers, Minnesota District Judges Association, Hennepin County and Minnesota State Bar Associations. Co-chair Program Committee and Organizer "The Year 2001: The Law and Women" co-sponsored by Minnesota Defense Lawyers, Minnesota Trial Lawyers and Minnesota Women Lawyers. Instructor in Lost Profits CLE Minnesota State Bar Association and in Chronic Pain Minnesota Institute of Legal Education. Discussion Leader "Managing the Complex Civil Case" The National Judicial College.
Office: 12C Government Center, 300 South Sixth Street, Minneapolis 55487.
Telephone: (612) 348-8777.

ROUE, John M. *(Judge, Minnesota District Court Ninth Judicial District)* Assumed office July 1, 1985. Former Judge, Polk County Court.
Office: Polk County Courthouse, 612 North Broadway, Crookston 56716.
Telephone: (218) 281-5243.

RUBLE, Steven *(Judge, Minnesota District Court Seventh Judicial District)*
Office: Mille Lacs County Courthouse, 635 Second Street S.E., Milaca 56353.
Telephone: (320) 983-8313.

RYKKEN, Miriam P. *(Judge, Minnesota Workers' Compensation Court of Appeals)* Appointed by Governor Jesse Ventura to term beginning June 17, 1999.
Office: 405 Minnesota Judicial Center, 25 Martin Luther King Jr. Blvd., St. Paul 55155.
Telephone: (651) 296-2454.

RYSAVY, Donald E. *(Judge, Minnesota District Court Third Judicial District)*
Office: Mower County Courthouse, 201 First Street N.E., Austin 55912.
Telephone: (507) 437-9475.

SAGSTUEN, Warren R. *(Judge, Minnesota District Court Fourth Judicial District)*
Office: 12C Government Center, 300 South Sixth Street, Minneapolis 55487.
Telephone: (612) 348-8276.

SANBERG, Kathleen H. *(Judge, Minnesota Tax Court)* Appointed by Governor Jesse Ventura.
Office: 245 Minnesota Judicial Center, 25 Martin Luther King Jr. Blvd., St. Paul 55155.
Telephone: (651) 296-2806.

SANDVIK, Kenneth A. *(Judge, Minnesota District Court Sixth Judicial District)* Assumed office July 24, 1986. Elected Nov 1986, 1992 and 1998. Current term expires Jan 2005. Judge, Cook-Lake County Court Nov 1984 to July 23, 1986.
Office: Lake County Courthouse, 601 Third Avenue, Two Harbors 55616.
Telephone: (218) 834-8333.

SCHELLHAS, Heidi S. *(Judge, Minnesota District Court Fourth Judicial District)*
Office: 12C Government Center, 300 South Sixth Street, Minneapolis 55487.
Telephone: (612) 348-6113.

SCHERER, John H. *(Judge, Minnesota District Court Seventh Judicial District)*
Office: Morrison County Courthouse, 213 First Avenue S.E., Little Falls 56345.
Telephone: (320) 632-0325.

SCHERER, Richard S. *(Judge, Minnesota District Court Fourth Judicial District)* Appointed by Governor Arne H. Carlson to term beginning July 5, 1994. Elected to term beginning Jan 6, 1997. Reelected 2002, current term expires Jan 1, 2009. Born Minneapolis Minnesota Aug 13, 1946. Congregationalist. Educated at Gustavus Adolphus College B.A. cum laude 1968 and University of Minnesota Law School J.D. cum laude 1975. Admitted to practice Minnesota 1975, U.S. District Court District of Minnesota 1975 and U.S. Court of Appeals Eighth Circuit 1975. In legal practice Minneapolis 1975-94.
Member Hennepin County, Minnesota State and American Bar Associations. E-5 U.S. Army July 1, 1970 to Jan 6, 1972.
Office: 12C Government Center, 300 South Sixth Street, Minneapolis 55487.
Telephone: (612) 348-3750.

SCHROEDER, Thomas P. *(Judge, Minnesota District Court Seventh Judicial District)*
Office: Becker County Courthouse, 915 Lake Avenue, Detroit Lakes 56501.
Telephone: (218) 846-7305.

SCHUMACHER, Robert H. *(Judge, Minnesota Court of Appeals)* Appointed by Governor Rudy Perpich Dec 1, 1987. Elected to subsequent terms. Born Minneapolis Minnesota Jan 21, 1936. Educated at College of St. Thomas B.A. and William Mitchell College of Law J.D. Admitted to practice Minnesota 1962. Began legal practice Minneapolis 1962. Judge, Hennepin County Municipal Court Oct 9, 1974 to June 30, 1984, appointed by Governor Wendell Anderson. Former Judge, Minnesota District Court Fourth Judicial District, appointed by Governor Rudy Perpich to term beginning July 1, 1984.
Member Hennepin County, Minnesota State and American Bar Associations. USNR 1953-61.
Office: 330 Minnesota Judicial Center, 25 Martin Luther King Jr. Blvd., St. Paul 55155.
Telephone: (651) 297-1009.

SCHURRER, Gary R. *(Judge, Minnesota District Court Tenth Judicial District)*
Mailing address: P.O. Box 3802, Stillwater 55082-3802.
Office: Washington County Government Center, Stillwater 55082.
Telephone: (651) 430-6350.

SEIBEL, Gerald J. *(Judge, Minnesota District Court Eighth Judicial District)*
Mailing address: P.O. Box 530, Morris 56267.
Office: Stevens County Courthouse, Morris 56267.
Telephone: (320) 589-7286.

SENYK, Waldemar B. *(Judge, Minnesota District Court Seventh Judicial District)*
Mailing address: P.O. Box 417, Fergus Falls 56538-0417.
Office: Otter Tail County Courthouse, Fergus Falls 56537.
Telephone: (218) 998-8420.

SHUMAKER, Gordon W. *(Judge, Minnesota Court of Appeals)* Appointed by Governor Arne H. Carlson to term beginning Jan 6, 1998. Educated at University of St. Thomas B.A. 1964 M.A. 1965 and William Mitchell College of Law J.D. 1971. Recipient Harvey T. Reid Scholarship 1968, American Jurisprudence Award in Tort Law 1968, State Public Defender Summer Intern Scholarship 1970 and Judge Dell Trust Scholarship 1971. First Place Award William Mitchell Appellate Moot Court 1971. Admitted to practice Minnesota 1971, U.S. District Court District of Minnesota 1972, U.S. Supreme Court 1977 and U.S. Court of Appeals Eighth Circuit 1979. In legal practice Oct 15, 1971 to March 1, 1982. Judge March 10, 1982 to Dec 31, 1997 and Chief Judge July 1, 1996 to Dec 31, 1997, Minnesota District Court Second Judicial District, appointed by Governor Albert H. Quie.
Chair Second Judicial District Race Bias Task Force Committee 1994 to Dec 1997. Former Member Minnesota District Judges Association (Treasurer 1989 to Dec 1997) and International Academy of Trial Judges. Member Ramsey County (President 1981-82) and Minnesota State Bar Associations. Member since 1971 and President 1974-75 William Mitchell Alumni Association.

SHUMAKER, GORDON W.—*Continued*

Board of Directors Merriam Park Community Center 1986-91. Board of Trustees 1986-91 and Participant Student Mentorship Program since 1997 William Mitchell College of Law.
Office: 327 Minnesota Judicial Center, 25 Martin Luther King Jr. Blvd., St. Paul 55155.
Telephone: (651) 297-1068.

SIMONETT, Martha M. *(Judge, Minnesota District Court First Judicial District)*
Office: Dakota County Judicial Center, 1560 West Highway 55, Hastings 55033.
Telephone: (651) 438-4325.

SLIETER, Randall J. *(Judge, Minnesota District Court Eighth Judicial District)*
Office: Renville County Courthouse, 500 East DePue, Olivia 56277.
Telephone: (320) 523-3680.

SMITH, Joanne M. *(Judge, Minnesota District Court Second Judicial District)* Assumed office Sept 13, 1986. Elected Nov 9, 1986, Nov 1992 and Nov 1998. Current term expires Jan 2005. Born Winnipeg Manitoba Aug 22, 1946. Protestant. Educated at University of Minnesota-Duluth B.A. cum laude 1968 M.A. with highest honors 1972 and Hamline University J.D. with honors 1977. Law Clerk to Hon. Allen Oleisky, Hennepin County Court 1978-79. Member Phi Alpha Delta. Admitted to practice Minnesota 1978 and U.S. District Court District of Minnesota 1978. Began legal practice St. Paul 1979. Judge, Ramsey County Municipal Court Nov 10, 1983 to Sept 12, 1986.
Adjunct Professor William Mitchell College of Law 1979-81. Member Minnesota Women Elected Officials, Minnesota Judges Association, National Association of Women Judges, Ramsey County and Minnesota State Bar Associations. Former Vocational Rehabilitation Counselor and Counselor and Assistant Director Dayton Halfway House. Guest Lecturer on judicial system, legal process and women in law at local high schools. Volunteer attorney advisor on domestic abuse cases. Board member St. Paul Domestic Abuse Project and Crime Victim-Witness Advisory Board. Enjoys water skiing, snow skiing, tennis, golfing, reading, gardening and biking.
Office: 1530 Ramsey County Courthouse, 15 West Kellogg Boulevard, St. Paul 55102.
Telephone: (651) 266-9190.

SMITH, John P. *(Judge, Minnesota District Court Ninth Judicial District)* Appointed by Governor Arne H. Carlson to term beginning Sept 16, 1991. Elected Nov 1992 and Nov 1998. Current term expires Jan 2005. Currently serves as Assistant Chief Judge. Born Park Rapids Minnesota Oct 3, 1950. Protestant. Educated at Concordia College B.A. with honors 1971, William Mitchell College of Law J.D. 1975 and Emory University LL.M. 1987. Admitted to practice Minnesota 1975, Georgia 1987 and U.S. Supreme Court. In legal practice Park Rapids Minnesota 1976-91.
Member Minnesota District Court Judges Association (Former Member Board of Governors) and Cass-Hubbard County Bar Association. Recipient Bush Fellowship 1986, Northwest Minnesota Outstanding Community Leader Award and Jaycee Key Man Award. Supervisor Crow Wing Township 1976-78. Member Nevis School Board. Scout Master Troop 56 Boy Scouts of America. Past President Fraternal Order of Eagles, Jaycees and Rotary Club.
Mailing address: P.O. Box 3000, Walker 56484.
Office: Cass County Courthouse, Walker 56484.
Telephone: (218) 547-7245.
E-mail address: john.smith@courts.state.mn.us

SMITH, Kathryn N. *(Judge, Minnesota District Court Eighth Judicial District)* Appointed by Governor Arne H. Carlson to term beginning May 5, 1997.
Office: Kandiyohi County Courthouse, 505 West Becker Avenue, Willmar 56201.
Telephone: (320) 231-6206.

SMITH, Norbert P. *(Judge, Minnesota District Court Fifth Judicial District)*
Mailing address: P.O. Box 0347, Mankato 56002-0347.
Office: Blue Earth County Courthouse, Mankato 56001.
Telephone: (507) 389-8233.

SOLIEN, John R. *(Judge, Minnesota District Court Ninth Judicial District)*
Office: Aitkin County Courthouse, 209 Second Street N.W., Aitkin 56431.
Telephone: (218) 927-7350.

SOMMERVILLE, John J. *(Judge, Minnesota District Court Fourth Judicial District)* Assumed office June 19, 1986. Born Bemidji Minnesota Jan 12, 1946. Roman Catholic. Educated at University of Minnesota B.A. summa cum laude 1968 J.D. cum laude 1972. Law Clerk to Hon. Gerald W. Heaney, U.S. Court of Appeals Eighth Circuit 1972-74. Member Phi Beta Kappa and Phi Gamma Delta. Admitted to practice Minnesota 1972 and U.S. Court of Appeals Eighth Circuit 1973. Began legal practice Minneapolis 1974. Judge, Hennepin County Municipal Court Nov 23, 1983 to June 18, 1986, appointed by Governor Rudy Perpich. USAR 1968-74.
Office: 12C Government Center, 300 South Sixth Street, Minneapolis 55487.
Telephone: (612) 348-2371.

SOVIS, Michael V. *(Judge, Minnesota District Court First Judicial District)*
Office: Dakota County Judicial Center, 1560 West Highway 55, Hastings 55033.
Telephone: (651) 438-4325.

SPICER, Richard G. *(Judge, Minnesota District Court First Judicial District)*
Office: Dakota County Judicial Center, 1560 West Highway 55, Hastings 55033.
Telephone: (651) 438-4325.

SPILSETH, Donald M. *(Judge, Minnesota District Court Eighth Judicial District)*
Office: Kandiyohi County Courthouse, 505 West Becker Avenue, Willmar 56201.
Telephone: (320) 231-6206.

STACEY, Rex D. *(Judge, Minnesota District Court First Judicial District)*
Office: Dakota County Judicial Center, 1560 West Highway 55, Hastings 55033.
Telephone: (651) 438-8042.

STAFSHOLT, Jon E. *(Judge, Minnesota District Court Eighth Judicial District)* Assumed office July

STAFSHOLT, JON E.—*Continued*

1987. Elected 1990, 1996 and 2002. Current term expires Jan 2009. Born St. Paul Minnesota April 17, 1943. Lutheran. Educated at California Lutheran University A.A. 1963, University of Missouri B.A. 1965 B.J. 1965 and University of Minnesota J.D. 1972. Admitted to practice Minnesota 1972 and U.S. District Court District of Minnesota 1972. In legal practice Elbow Lake 1972-83. Judge, Grant County Court June 20, 1983 to July 1987.

Part-time County Attorney Grant County 1979-83. Author "Beginning of the End to Farm Wife Discrimination" 1976 and "Bionic Lawyer" 1980 Bench and Bar and "Making Courthouses Safe for Domestic Abuse Victims" State Court News 1992. Part-time Instructor University of Minnesota 1975-84 and Fergus Falls Community College 1978-87. Member Lawyer Professional Responsibility Board 1980-83. Member Sixteenth District (President 1974-75), Minnesota State (Board of Governors 1975-77, 1983-89 and 1996-2002, Chairman General Practice Section 1978-80, Chairman Agricultural Law Section 1989-90, Member Executive Committee 1998-2000, Delegate to American Bar Association 1997, 1999 and 2001) and American (Executive Committee National Conference of State Trial Judges 2001 Judicial Division, Committee on Court Delay Reduction Judicial Administration Division, POW-MIA Task Force, Probate Committee) Bar Associations. Graduate The National Judicial College 1983 and National Academy of Judicial Education 1984. Lecturer on Inheritance Tax Law Reform, General Practice Issues and Alternative Dispute Resolution Techniques CLE. Recipient Outstanding Service Award from Domestic Violence Council 1992, Access to Justice Award 1994 and Partner in Justice Award 1997 from Legal Services of Northwest Minnesota and Community Service Award from Conference of Chief Judges 1999. First Lieutenant U.S. Army 1967-70 Vietnam. Recipient Bronze Star for Meritorious Service. Previously worked as assistant editor Bruce Publishing Company, St. Paul Minnesota. Board of Directors Northwest Minnesota Legal Services Corporation and Lakeland Mental Health Center.

Office: Pope County Courthouse, 130 East Minnesota Avenue, Glenwood 56334.

Telephone: (320) 634-5222.

STEPHENSON, George T. *(Judge, Minnesota District Court Second Judicial District)*

Office: 1170 Ramsey County Courthouse, 15 West Kellogg Boulevard, St. Paul 55102.

Telephone: (651) 266-8326.

STOFFERAHN, David A. *(Judge, Minnesota Workers' Compensation Court of Appeals)* Appointed by Governor Jesse Ventura to term beginning 2002.

Office: Minnesota Judicial Center, 25 Martin Luther King Jr. Blvd., St. Paul 55155.

Telephone: (651) 296-6526.

STONEBURNER, Terri *(Judge, Minnesota Court of Appeals)* Appointed by Governor Jesse Ventura to term beginning April 28, 2000. Educated at University of Geneva, Switzerland 1965-66, Hanover College B.A. cum laude 1967 and University of Washington School of Law 1975. In legal practice Mankato March 1980 to March 1990. Former Judge and Assistant Chief Judge, Minnesota District Court Fifth Judicial District.

Staff Attorney State of Alaska Commission for Human Rights Nov 1977 to March 1979. Board of Directors Minnesota State Bar Foundation 1988-93. Member Board of Continuing Legal Education 1988 to June 1994, Alternative Dispute Resolution Board 1995-99 and Open Hearings Advisory Board since 1998 Minnesota Supreme Court. Member Minnesota Women Lawyers Association and Minnesota State Bar Association. Board of Trustees YWCA Mankato 1988-90. Member 1991 to April 2000 and Board of Directors 1996-99 Women League of Voters New Ulm. Member American Association of University Women 1992 to April 2000, Judicial Advisory Council on Families 1995 to April 2000 and Teen Court Advisory Board 1997 to April 2000 Brown County. Enjoys backpacking, quilting, reading, motorcycling and hunting.

Office: 231 Minnesota Judicial Center, 25 Martin Luther King Jr. Blvd., St. Paul 55155.

Telephone: (651) 297-1008.

STRINGER, Thomas M. *(Judge, Minnesota District Court Seventh Judicial District)* Appointed by Governor Rudy Perpich to term beginning July 28, 1989. Elected 1990, 1996 and 2002. Current term expires Jan 2009. Born Canby Minnesota Jan 24, 1943. Educated at University of Minnesota B.A. 1969 J.D. 1972. Admitted to practice Minnesota 1972, U.S. District Court District of Minnesota 1972, U.S. Court of Appeals Eighth Circuit 1972 and U.S. Supreme Court 1977. In legal practice Minneapolis 1972-78 and Fergus Falls 1978-89.

President Minnesota District Judges Association 2000-01. Sergeant U.S. Army 1964-66.

Mailing address: P.O. Box 417, Fergus Falls 56538-0417.

Office: Otter Tail County Courthouse, Fergus Falls 56537.

Telephone: (218) 998-8400.

SULLIVAN, David P. *(Judge, Minnesota District Court Sixth Judicial District)*

Office: St. Louis County Courthouse, 100 North Fifth Avenue West, Duluth 55802-1212.

Telephone: (218) 726-2460.

SUTHERLAND, Patrice K. *(Judge, Minnesota District Court First Judicial District)*

Office: Dakota County Judicial Center, 1560 West Highway 55, Hastings 55033.

Telephone: (651) 438-4325.

SWANSON, Stephen D. *(Judge, Minnesota District Court Fourth Judicial District)*

Office: 12C Government Center, 300 South Sixth Street, Minneapolis 55487.

Telephone: (612) 348-8441.

SWEETLAND, Heather L. *(Judge, Minnesota District Court Sixth Judicial District)* Appointed by Governor Arne H. Carlson Dec 21, 1995 to term beginning Feb 2, 1996. Elected Nov 1998, current term expires Jan 1, 2005. Born St. Paul Minnesota Oct 11, 1952. Lutheran. Educated at Mankato State University B.S. cum laude 1974 and William Mitchell College of Law J.D. 1982. Admitted to practice Minnesota 1982 and U.S. District Court District of Minnesota 1982.

Assistant Public Defender Sixth Judicial District 1982-96. Member Eleventh District (Secretary 1989-90, Vice President 1990-91, President 1991-92), Minnesota State (Board of Governors 1992-97) and American Bar Associations. Named Volunteer Attorney of the Year by

SWEETLAND, HEATHER L.—*Continued*

Eleventh District Bar Association 1987. Former Member Board of Directors YWCA. Former Member Foster Parent Advisory Board. Member various church boards.

Office: St. Louis County Courthouse, 100 North Fifth Avenue West, Duluth 55802-1212.

Telephone: (218) 726-2460.

SWENSON, Douglas G. *(Judge, Minnesota District Court Tenth Judicial District)* Appointed by Governor Arne H. Carlson to term beginning Jan 16, 1998. Elected 2000, current term expires Jan 2007. Born St. Peter Minnesota Aug 16, 1945. Lutheran. Educated at Gustavus Adolphus College B.S.B.A. 1967 and William Mitchell College of Law J.D. 1971. Admitted to practice Minnesota 1971 and U.S. District Court District of Minnesota 1976. In legal practice Forest Lake 1972-75.

Assistant County Attorney Washington County 1975-97. Member Nineteenth District Bar Association (President 1978), Washington County and Minnesota State Bar Associations. State Representative 1987-98.

Office: Chisago County Courthouse, 313 North Main Street, Center City 55012.

Telephone: (651) 213-0485.

E-mail address: douglas.swenson@courts.state.mn.us

SWENSON, James T. *(Judge, Minnesota District Court Fourth Judicial District)*

Office: 12C Government Center, 300 South Sixth Street, Minneapolis 55487.

Telephone: (612) 348-2122.

TAYLOR, Richard C. *(Judge, Minnesota District Court Ninth Judicial District)*

Office: Polk County Courthouse, 612 North Broadway, Crookston 56716.

Telephone: (218) 281-2332.

TenEYCK, David *(Judge, Minnesota District Court Ninth Judicial District)*

Office: Crow Wing County Courthouse, 326 Laurel Street, Brainerd 56401.

Telephone: (218) 824-1310.

THEISEN, Mary *(Judge, Minnesota District Court First Judicial District)*

Office: Scott County Government Center, 200 Fourth Avenue West, Shakopee 55379.

Telephone: (952) 496-8200.

THOMPSON, Jeffrey D. *(Judge, Minnesota District Court Third Judicial District)* Appointed by Governor Arne H. Carlson. Elected 2000, current term expires Jan 1, 2007. Born St. Paul Minnesota June 20, 1949. Educated at Carleton College B.A. 1971 and William Mitchell College of Law J.D. cum laude 1975. Admitted to practice Minnesota 1975. In legal practice Winona Sept 1979 to Jan 1986.

Assistant County Attorney Winona County Sept 1976 to Sept 1979 and Feb 1986 to July 1989. County Attorney Rice County Aug 1989 to Feb 1999. Participant T'ai Chi Ch'uan seven years.

Office: Winona County Courthouse, 171 West Third Street, Winona 55987.

Telephone: (507) 457-6375.

THUET, William F. *(Judge, Minnesota District Court First Judicial District)* Appointed by Governor Rudy Perpich to term beginning June 1, 1983. Elected 1984, 1990, 1996 and 2002. Current term expires Jan 1, 2009. Born St. Paul Minnesota June 26, 1947. Educated at University of Minnesota-Duluth B.A. 1969 and University of Minnesota-Minneapolis J.D. 1972. Admitted to practice Minnesota 1972, U.S. District Court District of Minnesota 1972 and U.S. Supreme Court 1976. In legal practice South St. Paul 1972-75 and Hastings 1975-83. Former Judge, Dakota County Court.

Office: Dakota County Judicial Center, 1560 West Highway 55, Hastings 55033.

Telephone: (651) 438-8027.

TILSEN, Judith M. *(Judge, Minnesota District Court Second Judicial District)*

Office: 1650 Ramsey County Courthouse, 15 West Kellogg Boulevard, St. Paul 55102.

Telephone: (651) 266-9215.

TITUS, Linda S. *(Judge, Minnesota District Court Fifth Judicial District)*

Mailing address: P.O. Box 177, Jackson 56143.

Office: Jackson County Courthouse, Jackson 56143.

Telephone: (507) 847-4695.

TOUSSAINT, Edward J., Jr. *(Chief Judge, Minnesota Court of Appeals)* Appointed by Governor Arne H. Carlson to term beginning 1995. Chief Judge since 1995. Educated at DePaul University College of Law J.D. Judge, Minnesota Worker's Compensation Court of Appeals 1987-92. Former Judge, Minnesota District Court Fourth Judicial District, appointed by Governor Arne H. Carlson to term beginning 1992.

Claim Counsel American Family Insurance 1975-81. Member Executive Committee since 1996 and President 1998 Council of Chief Judges. Member Hennepin County and Minnesota State (Board of Governors since 1998) Bar Associations.

Office: 314 Minnesota Judicial Center, 25 Martin Luther King Jr. Blvd., St. Paul 55155.

Telephone: (651) 297-1006.

TUNHEIM, John R. *(Judge, United States District Court District of Minnesota)* Appointed for life by President Bill Clinton.

Office: 13E U.S. Courthouse, 300 South Fourth Street, Minneapolis 55415.

Telephone: (612) 664-5080.

VAA, Galen J. *(Judge, Minnesota District Court Seventh Judicial District)* Appointed by Governor Jesse Ventura to term beginning Jan 18, 2000. Born Elbow Lake Minnesota March 5, 1948. Roman Catholic. Educated at Moorhead State University B.A. 1970 and University of South Dakota J.D. 1974. Member Delta Theta Phi. Admitted to practice South Dakota 1974, Minnesota 1975, U.S. District Court District of Minnesota 1976 and North Dakota 1980. In legal practice Moorhead Minnesota 1975-2000.

Assistant Attorney General South Dakota 1974-75. Instructor in "Innkeeper's Law" Moorhead State University 1981. Civil Trial Practice Specialist, Certified by Minnesota State Bar Association and National Board of Trial Advocacy 1990-2000. Member Minnesota Trial Lawyers Association, North Dakota Trial Lawyers Association, American Board of Trial Advocates, Minnesota State, Federal and American Bar Associations.

Mailing address: P.O. Box 417, Fergus Falls 56538-0417.

VAA, GALEN J.—*Continued*

Office: Otter Tail County Courthouse, Fergus Falls 56538.
Telephone: (218) 998-2435.
E-mail address: galen.vaa@courts.state.mn.us

Van de NORTH, John B. "Jack", Jr. *(Judge, Minnesota District Court Second Judicial District)* Appointed by Governor Arne H. Carlson to term beginning Oct 21, 1998. Elected 2000, current term expires Dec 31, 2006. Born Oak Park Illinois March 7, 1945. Roman Catholic. Educated at St. John's University, Collegeville Minnesota B.S. 1967 and University of Notre Dame J.D. 1970. Notre Dame Moot Court. Admitted to practice Minnesota 1971, U.S. District Courts District of Minnesota 1972 and District of Wisconsin 1985, U.S. Court of Appeals Eighth Circuit 1992 and U.S. Supreme Court 1994. In legal practice St. Paul and Minneapolis 1975-98.

Special Assistant Attorney General Minnesota 1970-71 and 1973-75. Former Member Warren Burger Inn of Court. Member Ramsey County (Youth and Law Committee), Minnesota State and American Bar Associations. Attended Minnesota Judges Conference and Training 1998 and The National Judicial College Reno 2000. First Lieutenant U.S. Army and USAR 1970-75. Enjoys tennis and skiing.

Office: Juvenile & Family Justice Center, 25 West Seventh Street, St. Paul 55102.
Telephone: (651) 266-5154.
E-mail address: johnvandenorth@courts.state.mn.us

VARCO, Robert B. *(Judge, Minnesota District Court Tenth Judicial District)*
Office: Sherburne County Government Center, 13880 Highway 10, Elk River 55330-4608.
Telephone: (763) 241-2800.

VENNE, Donald J. *(Judge, Minnesota District Court Tenth Judicial District)*
Office: Anoka County Courthouse, 325 East Main Street, Anoka 55303-2489.
Telephone: (763) 422-7440.

WALKER, Bradley C. *(Judge, Minnesota District Court Fifth Judicial District)*
Mailing address: P.O. Box 0347, Mankato 56002-0347.
Office: Blue Earth County Courthouse, 204 South Fifth Street, Mankato 56001.
Telephone: (507) 389-8801.

WALKER, Robert D. *(Judge, Minnesota District Court Fifth Judicial District)*
Office: Martin County Courthouse, 201 Lake Avenue, Fairmont 56031.
Telephone: (507) 238-3249.

WALKER, William E. *(Judge, Minnesota District Court Seventh Judicial District)*
Office: Becker County Courthouse, 915 Lake Avenue, Detroit Lakes 56501.
Telephone: (218) 846-7305.

WARNER, Teresa R. *(Judge, Minnesota District Court Second Judicial District)*
Office: 1070 Ramsey County Courthouse, 15 West Kellogg Boulevard, St. Paul 55102.
Telephone: (651) 266-8233.

WEIR, Kathleen A. *(Judge, Minnesota District Court Seventh Judicial District)*
Office: Clay County Courthouse, 807 North Eleventh Street, Moorhead 56560.
Telephone: (218) 299-5065.

WELLMANN, Fred W. *(Judge, Minnesota District Court Third Judicial District)*
Office: Mower County Courthouse, 201 First Street N.E., Austin 55912.
Telephone: (507) 437-9478.

WERNICK, Mark S. *(Judge, Minnesota District Court Fourth Judicial District)*
Office: 2520 Park Avenue, Minnesota 55404.

WEXLER, Thomas *(Judge, Minnesota District Court Fourth Judicial District)*
Office: 12C Government Center, 300 South Sixth Street, Minneapolis 55487.
Telephone: (612) 348-9940.

WHEELER, Steven D. *(Judge, Minnesota District Court Second Judicial District)* Former Chief Judge, Minnesota Workers' Compensation Court of Appeals.
Office: 1350 Ramsey County Courthouse, 15 West Kellogg Boulevard, St. Paul 55102.
Telephone: (651) 266-8349.

WIDICK, Paul E. *(Judge, Minnesota District Court Seventh Judicial District)*
Office: Stearns County Courthouse, 725 Courthouse Square, St. Cloud 56303-4781.
Telephone: (320) 656-3620.

WIELAND, Lucy Ann *(Judge, Minnesota District Court Fourth Judicial District)*
Office: 12C Government Center, 300 South Sixth Street, Minneapolis 55487.
Telephone: (612) 348-9808.

WIENERS, Joseph F. *(Judge, Minnesota District Court Third Judicial District)* Appointed by Governor Rudy Perpich Aug 1, 1989 to term beginning Sept 4, 1989. Elected Nov 1990, Nov 1996 and 2002. Current term expires Jan 2009. Born Hastings Minnesota Aug 10, 1947. Roman Catholic. Educated at College of St. Thomas B.A. 1969 and University of Minnesota J.D. 1973. Law Clerk to Hon. John Bartholomew, Wisconsin Circuit Court Eighth Circuit 1973-74. Admitted to practice Wisconsin 1974 and Minnesota 1976. In legal practice Menomonie Wisconsin 1974-76 and Kasson and Rochester Minnesota 1976-89.

Attorney Dodge County 1976-79 and 1982-89. Instructor in Labor Law and Hotel-Restaurant Law University of Wisconsin 1974-76 and Hotel-Restaurant Law, Criminal Law and Constitutional Law Rochester Community College 1979-80 and 1995-96. Former Member Minnesota Trial Lawyers Association, The Association of Trial Lawyers of America, State Bar of Wisconsin

WIENERS, JOSEPH F.—*Continued*

and Dodge County (Minnesota) Bar Association. Member Minnesota State Bar Association.

Office: Olmsted Government Center, 151 Fourth Street S.E., Rochester 55904-3712.

Telephone: (507) 287-2065.

WILLIAMSON, Jodi *(Judge, Minnesota District Court Third Judicial District)*

Office: Olmsted Government Center, 151 Fourth Street S.E., Rochester 55904-3712.

Telephone: (507) 285-8243.

WILLIS, Bruce Donald *(Judge, Minnesota Court of Appeals)* Appointed by Governor Arne H. Carlson to term beginning 1995. Elected 1996 and 2002. Current term expires Jan 2009. Born Minneapolis Minnesota Jan 29, 1941. Educated at Yale University B.A. 1962 and Harvard Law School LL.B. 1965. Admitted to practice Minnesota 1965, U.S. District Court District of Minnesota 1965, U.S. Court of Federal Claims 1989, U.S. Court of Appeals Eighth Circuit 1991 and U.S. Supreme Court 1992. In legal practice Minneapolis 1965-95.

Author "Campaign Finance in Minnesota: Tune-up or Overhaul?" The Hennepin Lawyer July-Aug 1992. Member Minnesota Commission on Judicial Selection 1991-94, Minnesota Board on Judicial Standards since 1997 and Advisory Committee on Civil Appellate Rules Minnesota Supreme Court since 1997. Member Hennepin County (Member 1981-86 and Chair 1983-86 Legal Fee Arbitration Board, Member Ethics Committee 1981-88), Minnesota State (Public Law Section) and American (Section of Appellate Judges) Bar Associations. Advisory Board Minnesota Institute of Legal Education since 1986. Chair and Lecturer "Election Law 1990" 1990, "Campaigns, Elections, and Lobbying in Minnesota" 1992 and "Election Law 1994" 1994 Minnesota Institute of Legal Education. Lecturer on Election Law Minnesota Institute of Legal Education 1996, 1998, 2000 and 2002. Lecturer "How to Run a Judicial Campaign" 1996 and "Judicial Campaign Law and Ethics" 1998 and 2000 Continuing Legal Education Minnesota State Bar Association. Named one of 1990's Lawyers of the Year by Minnesota's Journal of Law and Politics 1991, one of Minnesota's Best Trial Lawyers by Minnesota Lawyer 1991 and Alumnus of the Year by Orono High School 1998. Listed in various *Who's Who* publications including *Who's Who in America.* USAR 1965-68. Final Rank Lieutenant USNR 1968-74. Member Federal Commission on Voter Participation and Ballot Integrity 1987, Advisory Committee for Contested Elections and Recounts Project Federal Election Commission 1989-90, Common Cause Task Force on Election Law Reform 1992-93 and Judicial Advisory Board Law and Organizational Economics Center University of Kansas 1997-2001. Chair Commissioner Search Committee Minnesota Pollution Control Agency 1990-91. Board Member Minnesota Ethical Practices Board 1990-95. Member Wayzata Community Church.

Office: 231 Minnesota Judicial Center, 25 Martin Luther King Jr. Blvd., St. Paul 55155.

Telephone: (651) 297-1001.

WILSON, Debra A. *(Judge, Minnesota Workers' Compensation Court of Appeals)* Appointed by Governor Arne H. Carlson to term beginning March 20, 1991. Reappointed to subsequent terms. Current term expires Jan 2009. Born Cedar Rapids Iowa July 26, 1949. Educated at Luther College B.A. 1971, University of Minnesota M.A. 1973 and William Mitchell College of Law J.D. 1981. Admitted to practice Minnesota 1981. In legal practice Minneapolis 1981-85. Compensation Judge, Office of Administrative Hearings 1985-91.

Member Minnesota Women Lawyers, National Association of Women Judges and Minnesota State Bar Association.

Office: Minnesota Judicial Center, 25 Martin Luther King Jr. Blvd., St. Paul 55155.

Telephone: (651) 296-6526.

WILSON, Edward S. *(Judge, Minnesota District Court Second Judicial District)*

Office: 1570 Ramsey County Courthouse, 15 West Kellogg Boulevard, St. Paul 55102.

Telephone: (651) 266-8297.

WOLF, Dale A. *(Judge, Minnesota District Court Sixth Judicial District)* Assumed office July 24, 1986. Former Judge, Carlton County Court.

Mailing address: P.O. Box 190, Carlton 55718.

Office: Carlton County Courthouse, Carlton 55718.

Telephone: (218) 384-4281.

WOLF, Gerald J. *(Judge, Minnesota District Court Third Judicial District)* Assumed office June 1984. Born Esmond North Dakota Aug 14, 1939. Catholic. Educated at North Dakota State University 1961-63, Moorhead State University B.A. 1967 and University of North Dakota J.D. 1970. Admitted to practice Minnesota 1970 and North Dakota 1970. Began legal practice Faribault Minnesota 1970. Judge, Rice County Court 1975-84.

Member Minnesota State and American Bar Associations. Private First Class USAS. Democrat.

Office: Rice County Courthouse, 218 N.W. Third Street, Faribault 55021.

Telephone: (507) 332-6182.

WORKE, Renee L. *(Judge, Minnesota District Court Third Judicial District)*

Office: Waseca County Courthouse, 307 North State Street, Waseca 56093.

Telephone: (507) 835-0530.

WRIGHT, Wilhelmina M. *(Judge, Minnesota Court of Appeals)* Appointed by Governor Jesse Ventura to term beginning 2002. Former Judge, Minnesota District Court Second Judicial District.

Office: 310 Minnesota Judicial Center, 25 Martin Luther King Jr. Blvd., St. Paul 55155.

Telephone: (651) 296-4033.

YOST, LeRoy W. *(Judge, Minnesota District Court First Judicial District)* Assumed office Aug 1987. Former Judge, Le Sueur-McLeod-Sibley County Court.

Office: McLeod County Courthouse, 830 Eleventh Street East, Glencoe 55336.

Telephone: (612) 864-5551.

YOUNG, Michael A. *(Judge, Minnesota District Court First Judicial District)* Assumed office Aug 1987. Former Judge, Carver-Scott County Court.

Office: Scott County Government Center, 200 Fourth Avenue West, Shakopee 55379.

Telephone: (952) 496-8200.

ZIMMERMAN, Lloyd B. *(Judge, Minnesota District Court Fourth Judicial District)* Appointed by Governor Jesse Ventura to term beginning Dec 1, 2000. Elected to subsequent term. Born Chicago Illinois April 17, 1954. Educated at University of Illinois B.A. summa cum laude 1975 and New York University School of Law 1978. Root-Tilden Scholar. Admitted to practice Minnesota 1978 and U.S. District Court District of Minnesota.

Senior Trial Attorney U.S. Equal Employment Opportunity Commission Nov 1979 to Dec 2000. Contributing Author *Age Discrimination* The Bureau of National Affairs, Inc. Dec 2001. Adjunct Professor of Law University of Minnesota Law School. Member Minnesota State Bar Association (Chair Labor and Employment Section 2000-01, Member Legal Assistance to the Disadvantaged, Human Rights Committee). Speaker on litigation and employment discrimination at numerous CLE seminars. Member CLE Committee Hennepin County. Volunteer Alzheimer's Ward Nursing Home. Interests include distance running, playing guitar and family.

Office: 12C Government Center, 300 South Sixth Street, Minneapolis 55487.

Telephone: (612) 596-7745.

Fax: (612) 348-2131

E-mail address: lloyd.zimmerman@co.hennepin.mn.us

ZIMMERMAN, Richard A. *(Judge, Minnesota District Court Ninth Judicial District)*

Office: Crow Wing County Courthouse, 326 Laurel Street, Brainerd 56401.

Telephone: (218) 824-1310.

MISSISSIPPI

Capital JACKSON

UNITED STATES DISTRICT COURTS DISTRICTS OF MISSISSIPPI

Within Mississippi there are two United States District Courts. For descriptive information refer to the United States Courts section.

NORTHERN DISTRICT consists of four divisions.

Delta Division includes Bolivar, Coahoma, DeSoto, Panola, Quitman, Tallahatchie, Tate and Tunica counties. The court sits at Clarksdale.

Eastern Division includes Alcorn, Attala, Chickasaw, Choctaw, Clay, Itawamba, Lee, Lowndes, Monroe, Oktibbeha, Prentiss, Tishomingo and Winston counties. The court sits at Aberdeen, Ackerman and Corinth.

Greenville Division includes Carroll, Humphreys, Leflore, Sunflower and Washington counties. The court sits at Greenville.

Western Division includes Benton, Calhoun, Grenada, Lafayette, Marshall, Montgomery, Pontotoc, Tippah, Union, Webster and Yalobusha counties. The court sits at Oxford.

Chief Judge
Glen H. Davidson

Judges
W. Allen Pepper, Jr.
Michael P. Mills

Senior Judges
L. T. Senter, Jr.
Neal B. Biggers, Jr.

Clerk
Arlen B. Coyle
369 U.S. Courthouse
911 Jackson Avenue West
Oxford, Mississippi 38655-3622
(662) 234-1971

SOUTHERN DISTRICT consists of five divisions.

Eastern Division includes Clarke, Jasper, Kemper, Lauderdale, Neshoba, Newton, Noxubee and Wayne counties. The court sits at Meridian.

Hattiesburg Division includes Covington, Forrest, Greene, Jefferson Davis, Jones, Lamar, Lawrence, Marion, Perry and Walthall counties. The court sits at Hattiesburg.

Jackson Division includes Amite, Copiah, Franklin, Hinds, Holmes, Leake, Lincoln, Madison, Pike, Rankin, Scott, Simpson and Smith counties. The court sits at Jackson.

Southern Division includes George, Hancock, Harrison, Jackson, Pearl River and Stone counties. The court sits at Biloxi and Gulfport.

Western Division includes Adams, Claiborne, Issaquena, Jefferson, Sharkey, Warren, Wilkinson and Yazoo counties. The court sits at Natchez and Vicksburg.

Chief Judge
Tom Stewart Lee

Judges
William H. Barbour, Jr.
Henry T. Wingate
Walter J. Gex, III
Charles W. Pickering, Sr.
David C. Bramlette

Senior Judge
Dan Monroe Russell, Jr.

Clerk
J. T. Noblin
316 U.S. Courthouse
245 East Capitol Street
Jackson, Mississippi 39201
(601) 965-4439

UNITED STATES MAGISTRATE JUDGES OF MISSISSIPPI

NORTHERN DISTRICT
Jerry A. Davis
S. Allan Alexander
Eugene M. Bogen

SOUTHERN DISTRICT
John M. Roper, Sr.
Alfred G. Nicols, Jr.
James C. Sumner, Jr.
Louis Guirola, Jr.

UNITED STATES BANKRUPTCY COURTS OF MISSISSIPPI

NORTHERN DISTRICT

Judge
David W. Houston, III

Bankruptcy Clerk
Joseph E. Wroten
P.O. Drawer 867
Aberdeen, Mississippi 39730-0867
(662) 369-2596

SOUTHERN DISTRICT

Chief Judge
Edward Ellington

Judge
Edward R. Gaines

UNITED STATES DISTRICT COURTS DISTRICTS OF MISSISSIPPI—*Continued*

Bankruptcy Clerk
Charlene J. Kennedy
P.O. Drawer 2448
Jackson, Mississippi 39225-2448
(601) 965-5301

Clerk
Betty Sephton
P.O. Box 249
Jackson, Mississippi 39205
(601) 359-3694

Court Administrator
Stephen J. Kirchmayr
P.O. Box 117
Jackson, Mississippi 39205
(601) 359-3697

MISSISSIPPI SUPREME COURT

The Supreme Court is Mississippi's court of last resort. The state is divided into three Supreme Court districts for election purposes. Three justices represent each district and are elected from their respective districts for eight-year terms. Vacancies are filled by the governor. Newly appointed justices serve until the first state election occurring more than nine months after the initial appointment. The justice serving the longest continuous term is the chief justice; the two justices serving the next longest terms are presiding justices. Retired justices may continue to serve in a limited capacity at the request of the court.

The court exercises appellate jurisdiction as to law and fact over the lower courts and may issue writs necessary to the exercise of proper jurisdiction. The court also exercises jurisdiction over all matters relating to the state bar.

The court sits in divisions of three justices each but may sit en banc as needed. The court sits at Jackson and recesses during March, June and October.

DISTRICT ONE includes Attala, Bolivar, Hinds, Holmes, Humphreys, Issaquena, Kemper, Lauderdale, Leake, Madison, Neshoba, Newton, Noxubee, Rankin, Scott, Sharkey, Sunflower, Warren, Washington, Winston and Yazoo counties.

DISTRICT TWO includes Adams, Amite, Claiborne, Clarke, Copiah, Covington, Forrest, Franklin, George, Greene, Hancock, Harrison, Jackson, Jasper, Jefferson, Jefferson Davis, Jones, Lamar, Lawrence, Lincoln, Marion, Pearl River, Perry, Pike, Simpson, Smith, Stone, Walthall, Wayne and Wilkinson counties.

DISTRICT THREE includes Alcorn, Benton, Calhoun, Carroll, Chickasaw, Choctaw, Clay, Coahoma, DeSoto, Grenada, Itawamba, Lafayette, Lee, Leflore, Lowndes, Marshall, Monroe, Montgomery, Oktibbeha, Panola, Pontotoc, Prentiss, Quitman, Tallahatchie, Tate, Tippah, Tishomingo, Tunica, Union, Webster and Yalobusha counties.

Chief Justice
Edwin Lloyd Pittman

Presiding Justices
Chuck McRae
James W. Smith, Jr.

Justices
William L. Waller, Jr.
Kay B. Cobb
Oliver E. Diaz, Jr.
Charles D. Easley, Jr.
George C. Carlson, Jr.
James E. Graves, Jr.

COURT OF APPEALS OF MISSISSIPPI

The Court of Appeals, established in 1993, is a court of limited appellate jurisdiction in Mississippi. It consists of ten judges elected in nonpartisan elections for eight-year terms. Vacancies are filled by the governor. A chief judge and two presiding judges are appointed by the chief justice of the Supreme Court to serve a four-year term and are eligible for reappointment at the discretion of the chief justice.

The court exercises appellate jurisdiction limited to matters which have been assigned to it by the Supreme Court and may issue writs necessary to the exercise of proper jurisdiction. Decisions of the Court of Appeals are final and not subject to review by the Supreme Court except by writ of certiorari.

The court sits at Jackson, but the court en banc, or any panel thereof, may sit at other locations in the state as determined by rule.

Chief Judge
Roger H. McMillin, Jr.

Presiding Judges
Leslie D. King
Leslie H. Southwick

Judges
Billy G. Bridges
L. Joseph Lee
William H. Myers
T. Kenneth Griffis
James E. Thomas
Tyree Irving
David A. Chandler

MISSISSIPPI CHANCERY COURT

The Chancery Court is a Mississippi trial court of general jurisdiction. Judges are elected in nonpartisan elections in each chancery district for four-year terms. Vacancies may be filled by the governor or by special election.

The court has original jurisdiction over matters in equity, alimony and divorce, probate, mental competency, controversies involving real estate titles and administration of estates. The court has concurrent jurisdiction with the Circuit Court over bonding offenses of fiduciaries and public officers and in matters relating to mutual funds. The court also has concurrent jurisdiction with the Circuit and County Courts in equity cases involving less than $75,000 and with the Circuit and County Courts in bastardy proceedings. In counties with no County Court, a Youth Court may be established as a division of the Chancery Court to exercise exclusive jurisdiction over delinquent, neglected and battered children. The court has appellate jurisdiction over the Equity and Youth Divisions of the County Court, Boards of Supervisors, municipal authorities and certain state agen-

MISSISSIPPI CHANCERY COURT—*Continued*

cies as provided by law. The court may issue writs necessary to the exercise of proper jurisdiction.

The court sits at the county seats on a rotating basis within each chancery district.

FIRST JUDICIAL DISTRICT includes Alcorn, Itawamba, Lee, Monroe, Pontotoc, Prentiss, Tishomingo and Union counties. The court sits at Corinth, Fulton, Tupelo, Aberdeen, Pontotoc, Booneville, Iuka and New Albany.

Judges

Jacqueline Estes Mask
Rodney E. Shands
Talmadge D. Littlejohn, Jr.

SECOND JUDICIAL DISTRICT includes Jasper, Newton and Scott counties. The court sits at Bay Springs, Paulding, Decatur and Forest.

Judge

H. David Clark, II

THIRD JUDICIAL DISTRICT includes DeSoto, Grenada, Montgomery, Panola, Tate and Yalobusha counties. The court sits at Hernando, Grenada, Winona, Batesville, Sardis, Senatobia, Coffeeville and Water Valley.

Judges

Percy L. Lynchard
Mitchell M. Lundy, Jr.
Melvin McClure, Jr.

FOURTH JUDICIAL DISTRICT includes Amite, Franklin, Pike and Walthall counties. The court sits at Liberty, Meadville, Magnolia and Tylertown.

Judge

W. Hollis McGehee

FIFTH JUDICIAL DISTRICT includes Hinds County. The court sits at Jackson and Raymond.

Judges

Stuart Robinson
Denise Owens
Patricia D. Wise
William H. Singletary

SIXTH JUDICIAL DISTRICT includes Attala, Carroll, Choctaw, Kemper, Neshoba and Winston counties. The court sits at Kosciusko, Carrollton, Vaiden, Ackerman, DeKalb, Philadelphia and Louisville.

Judges

John C. Love, Jr.
Edward C. Prisock

SEVENTH JUDICIAL DISTRICT includes Bolivar, Coahoma, Leflore, Quitman, Tallahatchie and Tunica counties. The court sits at Cleveland, Rosedale, Clarksdale, Greenwood, Marks, Charleston, Sumner and Tunica.

Judges

William Willard
Jon M. Barnwell

EIGHTH JUDICIAL DISTRICT includes Hancock, Harrison and Stone counties. The court sits at Bay St. Louis, Gulfport, Biloxi and Wiggins.

Judges

Jim Persons
Margaret Alfonso
Sanford R. Steckler
Carter Bise

NINTH JUDICIAL DISTRICT includes Humphreys, Issaquena, Sharkey, Sunflower, Warren and Washington counties. The court sits at Belzoni, Mayersville, Rolling Fork, Indianola, Vicksburg and Greenville.

Judges

Vicki Barnes
Jane R. Weathersby
Marie Wilson

TENTH JUDICIAL DISTRICT includes Forrest, Lamar, Marion, Pearl River and Perry counties. The court sits at Hattiesburg, Purvis, Columbia, Poplarville and New Augusta.

Judges

Sebe Dale, Jr.
James H. C. Thomas, Jr.
Johnny Lee Williams

ELEVENTH JUDICIAL DISTRICT includes Holmes, Leake, Madison and Yazoo counties. The court sits at Lexington, Carthage, Canton and Yazoo City.

Judges

William J. Lutz
Janace Harvey Goree

TWELFTH JUDICIAL DISTRICT includes Clarke and Lauderdale counties. The court sits at Quitman and Meridian.

Judges

Jerry G. Mason
Sarah P. Springer

THIRTEENTH JUDICIAL DISTRICT includes Covington, Jefferson Davis, Lawrence, Simpson and Smith counties. The court sits at Collins, Prentiss, Monticello, Mendenhall and Raleigh.

Judge

Larry Buffington

FOURTEENTH JUDICIAL DISTRICT includes Chickasaw, Clay, Lowndes, Noxubee, Oktibbeha and Webster counties. The court sits at Houston, Okolona, West Point, Columbus, Macon, Starkville and Walthall.

Judges

Robert L. Lancaster
Dorothy W. Colom
Kenneth M. Burns

FIFTEENTH JUDICIAL DISTRICT includes Copiah and Lincoln counties. The court sits at Hazlehurst and Brookhaven.

Judge

Edward E. Patten, Jr.

SIXTEENTH JUDICIAL DISTRICT includes George, Greene and Jackson counties. The court sits at Lucedale, Leakesville and Pascagoula.

Judges

Glenn Barlow
Pat H. Watts, Jr.
Jaye Bradley

MISSISSIPPI CHANCERY COURT—*Continued*

SEVENTEENTH JUDICIAL DISTRICT includes Adams, Claiborne, Jefferson and Wilkinson counties. The court sits at Natchez, Port Gibson, Fayette and Woodville.

Judges
Kennie E. Middleton
George Ward

EIGHTEENTH JUDICIAL DISTRICT includes Benton, Calhoun, Lafayette, Marshall and Tippah counties. The court sits at Ashland, Pittsboro, Oxford, Holly Springs and Ripley.

Judges
Glenn Alderson
Edwin H. Roberts, Jr.

NINETEENTH JUDICIAL DISTRICT includes Jones and Wayne counties. The court sits at Ellisville, Laurel and Waynesboro.

Judge
Franklin C. McKenzie, Jr.

TWENTIETH JUDICIAL DISTRICT includes Rankin County. The court sits at Brandon.

Judges
Thomas L. Zebert
John S. Grant, III

MISSISSIPPI CIRCUIT COURT

The Circuit Court is a Mississippi trial court of general jurisdiction. Judges are elected in nonpartisan elections in each district for four-year terms. Vacancies may be filled by the governor or by special election.

The court has original jurisdiction of all civil cases involving more than $2,500 and of all criminal cases. The court has concurrent jurisdiction with the Chancery Court over bonding offenses of fiduciaries and public officers and in matters relating to mutual funds and with the County Courts in civil matters not exceeding $75,000. The court also exercises concurrent jurisdiction with the Chancery and County Courts over bastardy proceedings and with the Justice Courts in criminal cases when the punishment does not exceed a fine and imprisonment in the county jail. Except as provided by law, the court has appellate jurisdiction over cases from the Law Division of the County Courts, and from the Justice and Municipal Courts as well as over decisions of certain local administrative bodies and state agencies. The court may issue writs necessary to the exercise of proper jurisdiction.

The court sits at the county seats within each district.

FIRST JUDICIAL DISTRICT includes Alcorn, Itawamba, Lee, Monroe, Pontotoc, Prentiss and Tishomingo counties. The court sits at Corinth, Fulton, Tupelo, Aberdeen, Pontotoc, Booneville and Iuka.

Judges
Thomas J. Gardner, III
Sharion Aycock
Paul S. Funderburk

SECOND JUDICIAL DISTRICT includes Hancock, Harrison and Stone counties. The court sits at Bay St. Louis, Gulfport, Biloxi and Wiggins.

Judges
Kosta N. Vlahos
Jerry O. Terry
Robert H. Walker
Steve Simpson

THIRD JUDICIAL DISTRICT includes Benton, Calhoun, Chickasaw, Lafayette, Marshall, Tippah and Union counties. The court sits at Ashland, Pittsboro, Houston, Okolona, Oxford, Holly Springs, Ripley and New Albany.

Judges
Henry L. Lackey
Andrew K. Howorth

FOURTH JUDICIAL DISTRICT includes Leflore, Sunflower and Washington counties. The court sits at Greenwood, Indianola and Greenville.

Judges
Betty W. Sanders
W. Ashley Hines
Margaret Carey McCray
Richard Smith

FIFTH JUDICIAL DISTRICT includes Attala, Carroll, Choctaw, Grenada, Montgomery, Webster and Winston counties. The court sits at Kosciusko, Carrollton, Vaiden, Ackerman, Grenada, Winona, Walthall and Louisville.

Judges
Joseph H. Loper
Clarence E. "Cem" Morgan, III

SIXTH JUDICIAL DISTRICT includes Adams, Amite, Franklin and Wilkinson counties. The court sits at Natchez, Liberty, Meadville and Woodville.

Judges
Forrest Al Johnson
Lillie Blackmon Sanders

SEVENTH JUDICIAL DISTRICT includes Hinds County. The court sits at Jackson and Raymond.

Judges
W. Swan Yerger
Tomie T. Green
Winston L. Kidd
Bobby B. DeLaughter

EIGHTH JUDICIAL DISTRICT includes Leake, Neshoba, Newton and Scott counties. The court sits at Carthage, Philadelphia, Decatur and Forest.

Judges
Marcus D. Gordon
Vernon Cotten

NINTH JUDICIAL DISTRICT includes Issaquena, Sharkey and Warren counties. The court sits at Mayersville, Rolling Fork and Vicksburg.

Judges
Frank Vollor
Isadore W. Patrick

TENTH JUDICIAL DISTRICT includes Clarke, Kemper, Lauderdale and Wayne counties. The court sits at Quitman, DeKalb, Meridian and Waynesboro.

MISSISSIPPI CIRCUIT COURT—*Continued*

Judges
Larry E. Roberts
Robert Bailey

ELEVENTH JUDICIAL DISTRICT includes Bolivar, Coahoma, Quitman and Tunica counties. The court sits at Rosedale, Cleveland, Clarksdale, Marks and Tunica.

Judges
Kenneth Thomas
Al Smith
Larry Lewis

TWELFTH JUDICIAL DISTRICT includes Forrest and Perry counties. The court sits at Hattiesburg and New Augusta.

Judge
Robert Helfrich

THIRTEENTH JUDICIAL DISTRICT includes Covington, Jasper, Simpson and Smith counties. The court sits at Collins, Bay Springs, Paulding, Mendenhall and Raleigh.

Judge
Robert G. Evans

FOURTEENTH JUDICIAL DISTRICT includes Lincoln, Pike and Walthall counties. The court sits at Brookhaven, Magnolia and Tylertown.

Judges
Keith Starrett
Mike Smith

FIFTEENTH JUDICIAL DISTRICT includes Jefferson Davis, Lamar, Lawrence, Marion and Pearl River counties. The court sits at Prentiss, Purvis, Monticello, Columbia and Poplarville.

Judges
R. I. Prichard, III
Michael R. Eubanks

SIXTEENTH JUDICIAL DISTRICT includes Clay, Lowndes, Noxubee and Oktibbeha counties. The court sits at West Point, Columbus, Macon and Starkville.

Judges
Lee J. Howard
James T. Kitchens, Jr.

SEVENTEENTH JUDICIAL DISTRICT includes DeSoto, Panola, Tallahatchie, Tate and Yalobusha counties. The court sits at Hernando, Batesville, Sardis, Charleston, Sumner, Senatobia, Coffeeville and Water Valley.

Judges
Andrew C. Baker
George B. Ready
Ann Lamar

EIGHTEENTH JUDICIAL DISTRICT includes Jones County. The court sits at Ellisville and Laurel.

Judge
Billy Joe Landrum

NINETEENTH JUDICIAL DISTRICT includes George, Greene and Jackson counties. The court sits at Lucedale, Leakesville and Pascagoula.

Judges
Robert P. Krebs
Kathy King Jackson
Dale Harkey

TWENTIETH JUDICIAL DISTRICT includes Madison and Rankin counties. The court sits at Canton and Brandon.

Judges
Samac S. Richardson
William E. Chapman, III

TWENTY-FIRST JUDICIAL DISTRICT includes Holmes, Humphreys and Yazoo counties. The court sits at Lexington, Belzoni and Yazoo City.

Judge
Jannie M. Lewis

TWENTY-SECOND JUDICIAL DISTRICT includes Claiborne, Copiah and Jefferson counties. The court sits at Port Gibson, Hazlehurst and Fayette.

Judge
Lamar Pickard

MISSISSIPPI COUNTY COURTS

County Courts are courts of limited jurisdiction established in counties meeting statutory requirements. Judges are elected in nonpartisan elections in their respective counties for four-year terms. Vacancies may be filled by the governor or by special election.

The courts have concurrent jurisdiction with the Circuit and Chancery Courts in matters of law and equity not exceeding $75,000 and with the Circuit and Chancery Courts in bastardy proceedings. The courts also exercise concurrent jurisdiction with the Circuit Court in all misdemeanors and with the Justice Courts in all civil and criminal cases in which the Justice Courts have jurisdiction. The courts have exclusive jurisdiction over matters relating to eminent domain, partition of personal property and actions of unlawful entry and detainer. The courts exercise concurrent appellate jurisdiction with the Circuit Courts over Justice and Municipal Courts. Youth Courts are established as a division of County Courts and have exclusive original jurisdiction over delinquent or neglected children within the county.

The courts sit at the county seats.

County	Judge
Adams	John N. Hudson
Bolivar	Gwendolyn J. Thomas
Coahoma	Tommy Allen
DeSoto	Mills Barbee
Forrest	Michael W. McPhail
Harrison	Gaston Henderson Hewes
	Robin Alfred Midcalf
	Michael H. Ward
Hinds	Houston J. Patton
	Bill Barnett
	Mike T. Parker
Jackson	Sharon W. Sigalas
	T. Larry Wilson
Jones	Gaylon K. Harper
Lauderdale	Frank M. Coleman
Lee	Charlie Brett
Leflore	Solomon C. Osborne
Lowndes	Beverly M. Franklin

MISSISSIPPI COUNTY COURTS—*Continued*

Madison	William Agin
	Cynthia Lee Brewer
Pike	John Price
Rankin	Kent McDaniel
	Thomas H. Broome
Warren	John S. Price, Jr.
Washington	Vernita King Johnson
Yazoo	Hudson L. Thomas

MISSISSIPPI JUSTICE COURTS

Justice Courts are courts of limited jurisdiction in Mississippi. Justices are elected in partisan elections by the voters of their respective districts for four-year terms.

The courts exercise civil jurisdiction over cases when the amount in controversy does not exceed $2,500 and concurrent jurisdiction with the Circuit Court in criminal matters when punishment does not exceed a fine and imprisonment in the county jail. The courts have concurrent jurisdiction with the County Courts in all civil and criminal cases in which Justice Courts have jurisdiction. Justice Courts may also handle preliminary matters such as initial appearances and preliminary hearings in felony cases arising in the county.

The courts sit in their respective districts within each county.

MISSISSIPPI MUNICIPAL COURTS

Municipal Courts, also known as Police Courts, are courts of limited jurisdiction established in all municipalities. Judges are appointed by the governing authorities in cities having populations of 10,000 or more and must be attorneys at law. In cities with a population of less than 10,000, a justice court judge of the county may serve as municipal judge. The judges' terms are locally determined but are usually for four years.

The courts exercise jurisdiction over all violations of municipal ordinances and conduct hearings on violations of criminal laws within the county and on felonies within the municipality. In counties with no County Court, a Youth Court may be established as part of the Municipal Court with exclusive original jurisdiction over delinquent, neglected or battered children.

Mississippi Counties and County Seats

Adams
Natchez

Alcorn
Corinth

Amite
Liberty

Attala
Kosciusko

Benton
Ashland

Bolivar
Cleveland
Rosedale

Calhoun
Pittsboro

Carroll
Carrollton
Vaiden

Chickasaw
Houston
Okolona

Choctaw
Ackerman

Claiborne
Port Gibson

Clarke
Quitman

Clay
West Point

Coahoma
Clarksdale

Copiah
Hazlehurst

Covington
Collins

DeSoto
Hernando

Forrest
Hattiesburg

Franklin
Meadville

George
Lucedale

Greene
Leakesville

Grenada
Grenada

Hancock
Bay St. Louis

Harrison
Biloxi
Gulfport

Hinds
Jackson
Raymond

Holmes
Lexington

Humphreys
Belzoni

Issaquena
Mayersville

Itawamba
Fulton

Jackson
Pascagoula

Jasper
Bay Springs
Paulding

Jefferson
Fayette

Jefferson Davis
Prentiss

Jones
Ellisville
Laurel

Kemper
DeKalb

Lafayette
Oxford

Lamar
Purvis

Lauderdale
Meridian

Lawrence
Monticello

Leake
Carthage

Lee
Tupelo

Leflore
Greenwood

Lincoln
Brookhaven

Lowndes
Columbus

Madison
Canton

Marion
Columbia

Marshall
Holly Springs

Monroe
Aberdeen

Montgomery
Winona

Neshoba
Philadelphia

Newton
Decatur

Noxubee
Macon

Oktibbeha
Starkville

Panola
Batesville
Sardis

Pearl River
Poplarville

Perry
New Augusta

Pike
Magnolia

Pontotoc
Pontotoc

Prentiss
Booneville

COUNTIES AND COUNTY SEATS—*Continued*

Quitman
Marks

Rankin
Brandon

Scott
Forest

Sharkey
Rolling Fork

Simpson
Mendenhall

Smith
Raleigh

Stone
Wiggins

Sunflower
Indianola

Tallahatchie
Charleston
Sumner

Tate
Senatobia

Tippah
Ripley

Tishomingo
Iuka

Tunica
Tunica

Union
New Albany

Walthall
Tylertown

Warren
Vicksburg

Washington
Greenville

Wayne
Waynesboro

Webster
Walthall

Wilkinson
Woodville

Winston
Louisville

Yalobusha
Coffeeville
Water Valley

Yazoo
Yazoo City

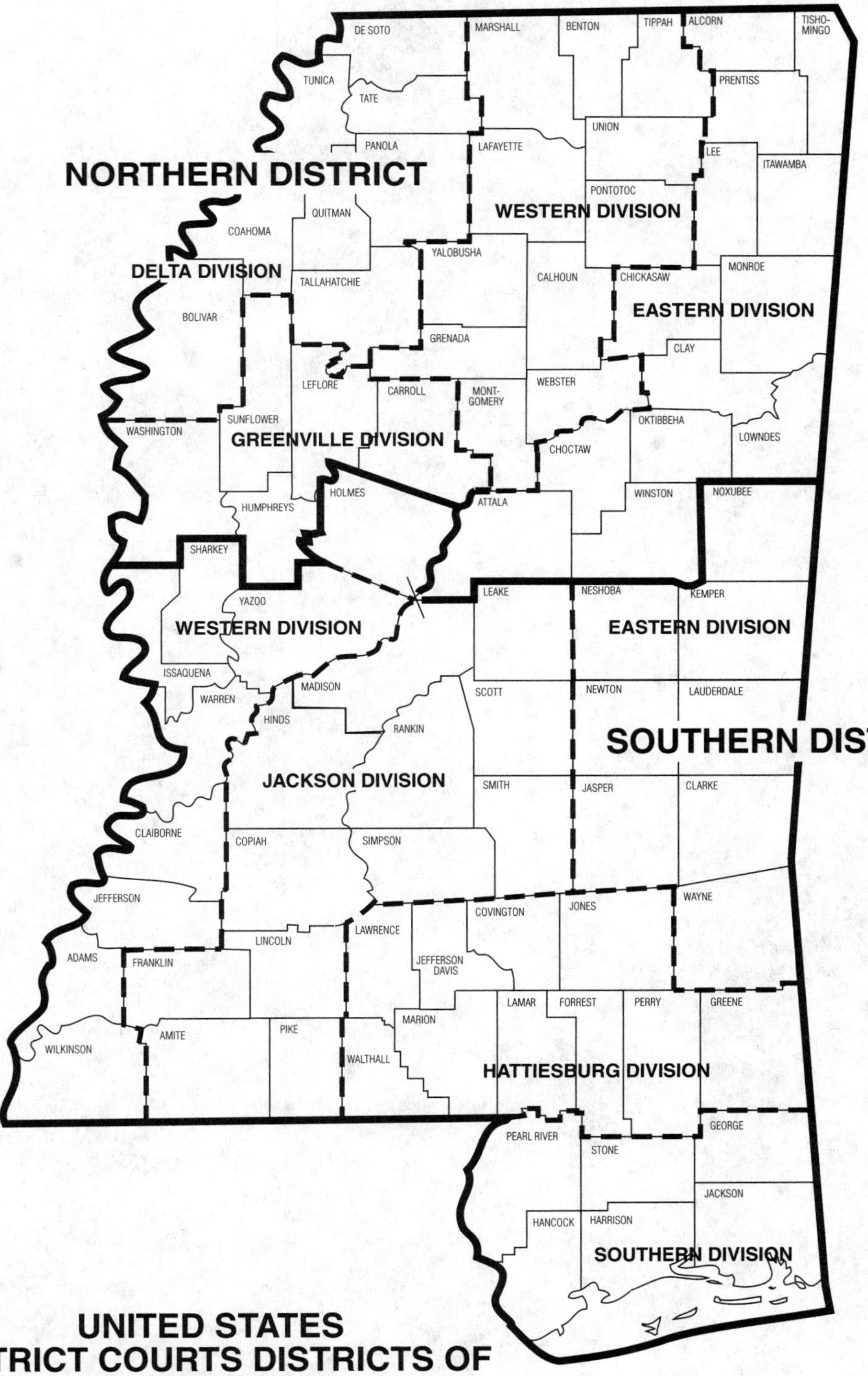
NORTHERN DISTRICT
DELTA DIVISION
WESTERN DIVISION
EASTERN DIVISION
GREENVILLE DIVISION
DE SOTO
MARSHALL
BENTON
TIPPAH
ALCORN
TISHO-MINGO
TUNICA
TATE
PRENTISS
UNION
PANOLA
LAFAYETTE
LEE
ITAWAMBA
PONTOTOC
QUITMAN
COAHOMA
YALOBUSHA
CALHOUN
CHICKASAW
MONROE
TALLAHATCHIE
BOLIVAR
GRENADA
CLAY
LEFLORE
CARROLL
MONT-GOMERY
WEBSTER
SUNFLOWER
WASHINGTON
OKTIBBEHA
LOWNDES
CHOCTAW
HOLMES
HUMPHREYS
ATTALA
WINSTON
NOXUBEE
SHARKEY
SOUTHERN DISTRICT
WESTERN DIVISION
EASTERN DIVISION
JACKSON DIVISION
HATTIESBURG DIVISION
SOUTHERN DIVISION
LEAKE
NESHOBA
KEMPER
YAZOO
ISSAQUENA
MADISON
SCOTT
NEWTON
LAUDERDALE
WARREN
HINDS
RANKIN
SMITH
JASPER
CLARKE
CLAIBORNE
COPIAH
SIMPSON
JEFFERSON
COVINGTON
JONES
WAYNE
LAWRENCE
ADAMS
LINCOLN
FRANKLIN
JEFFERSON DAVIS
LAMAR
FORREST
PERRY
GREENE
MARION
AMITE
PIKE
WILKINSON
WALTHALL
PEARL RIVER
GEORGE
STONE
JACKSON
HANCOCK
HARRISON

UNITED STATES DISTRICT COURTS DISTRICTS OF MISSISSIPPI

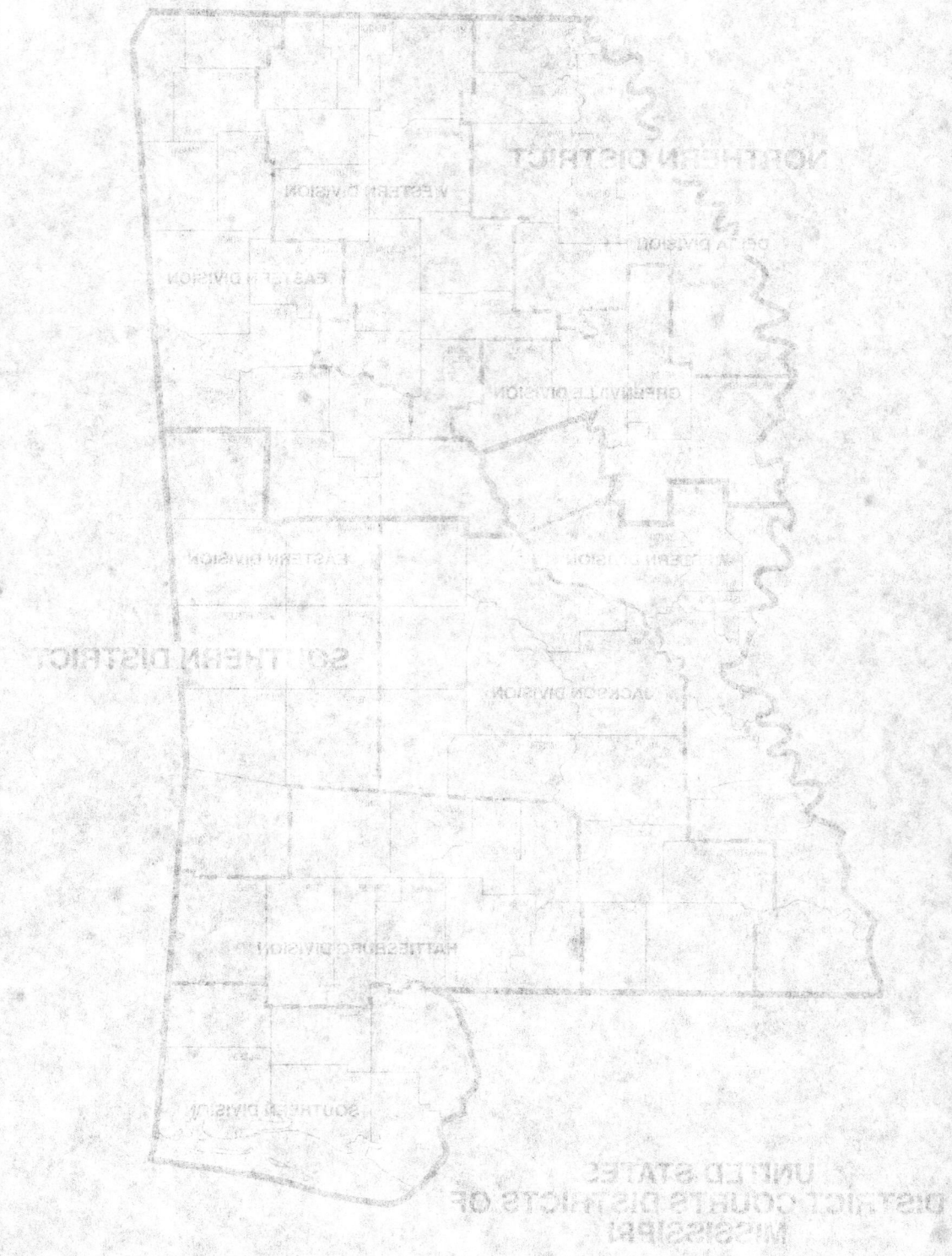

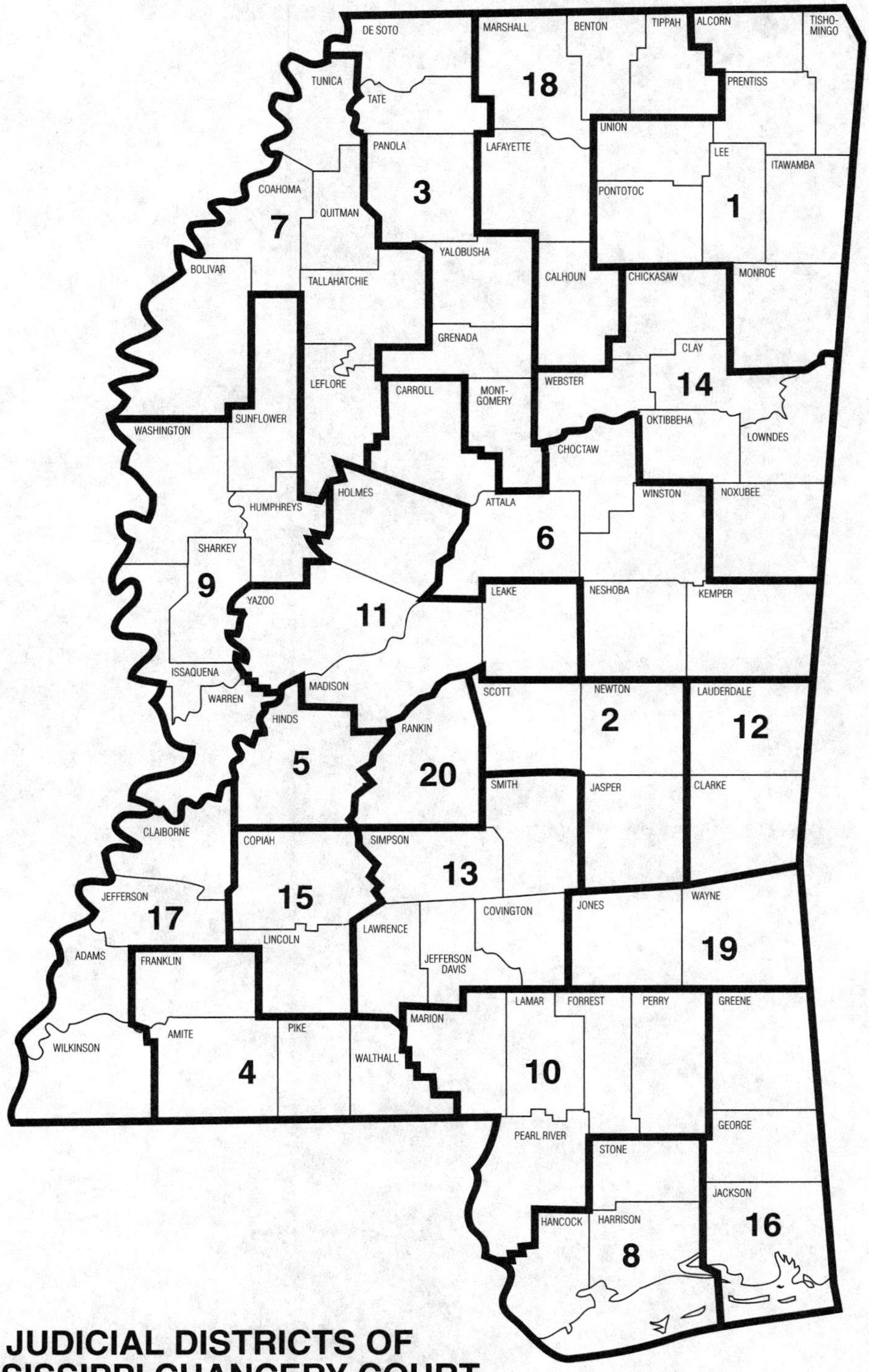
DE SOTO
MARSHALL
BENTON
TIPPAH
ALCORN
TISHO-
MINGO
TUNICA
TATE
18
PRENTISS
UNION
PANOLA
LAFAYETTE
LEE
ITAWAMBA
COAHOMA
3
PONTOTOC
1
QUITMAN
7
YALOBUSHA
BOLIVAR
CALHOUN
CHICKASAW
MONROE
TALLAHATCHIE
GRENADA
CLAY
LEFLORE
CARROLL
MONT-
GOMERY
WEBSTER
14
SUNFLOWER
WASHINGTON
OKTIBBEHA
LOWNDES
CHOCTAW
HOLMES
WINSTON
NOXUBEE
HUMPHREYS
ATTALA
6
SHARKEY
9
YAZOO
11
LEAKE
NESHOBA
KEMPER
ISSAQUENA
MADISON
WARREN
SCOTT
NEWTON
LAUDERDALE
HINDS
RANKIN
2
12
5
20
SMITH
JASPER
CLARKE
CLAIBORNE
COPIAH
SIMPSON
13
JEFFERSON
15
JONES
WAYNE
17
COVINGTON
LAWRENCE
LINCOLN
19
ADAMS
FRANKLIN
JEFFERSON
DAVIS
LAMAR
FORREST
PERRY
GREENE
MARION
AMITE
PIKE
WILKINSON
WALTHALL
4
10
PEARL RIVER
GEORGE
STONE
JACKSON
HANCOCK
HARRISON
16
8

JUDICIAL DISTRICTS OF MISSISSIPPI CHANCERY COURT

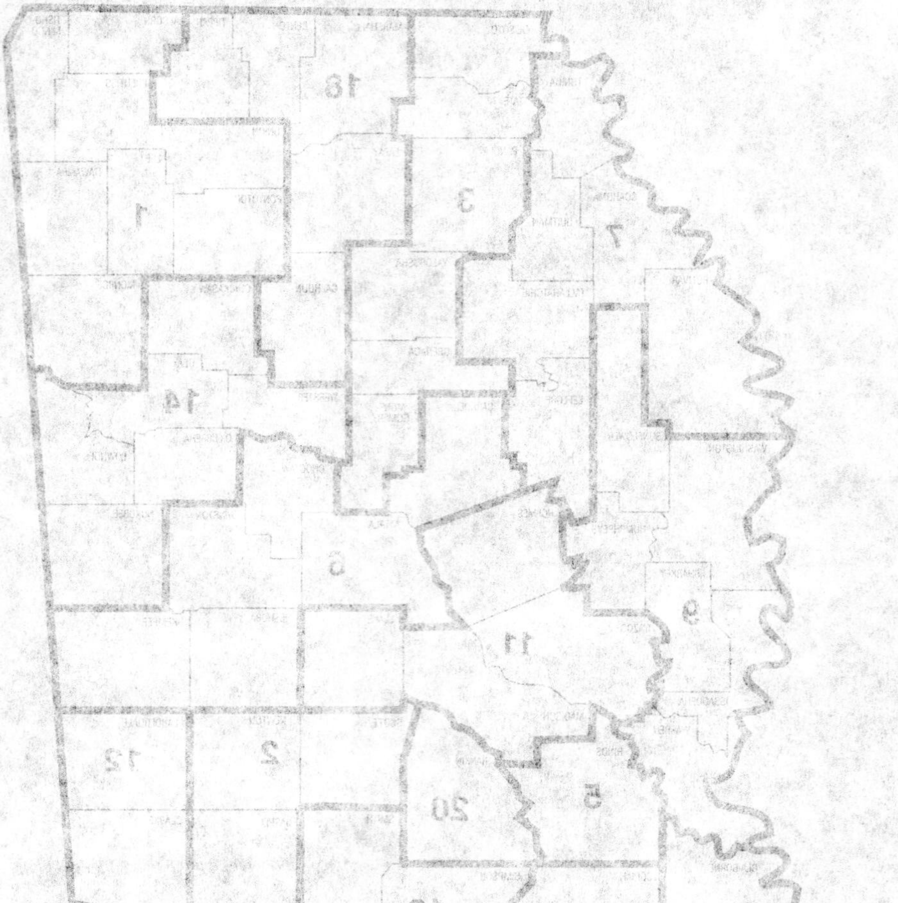
JUDICIAL DISTRICTS OF
MISSISSIPPI CHANCERY COURT

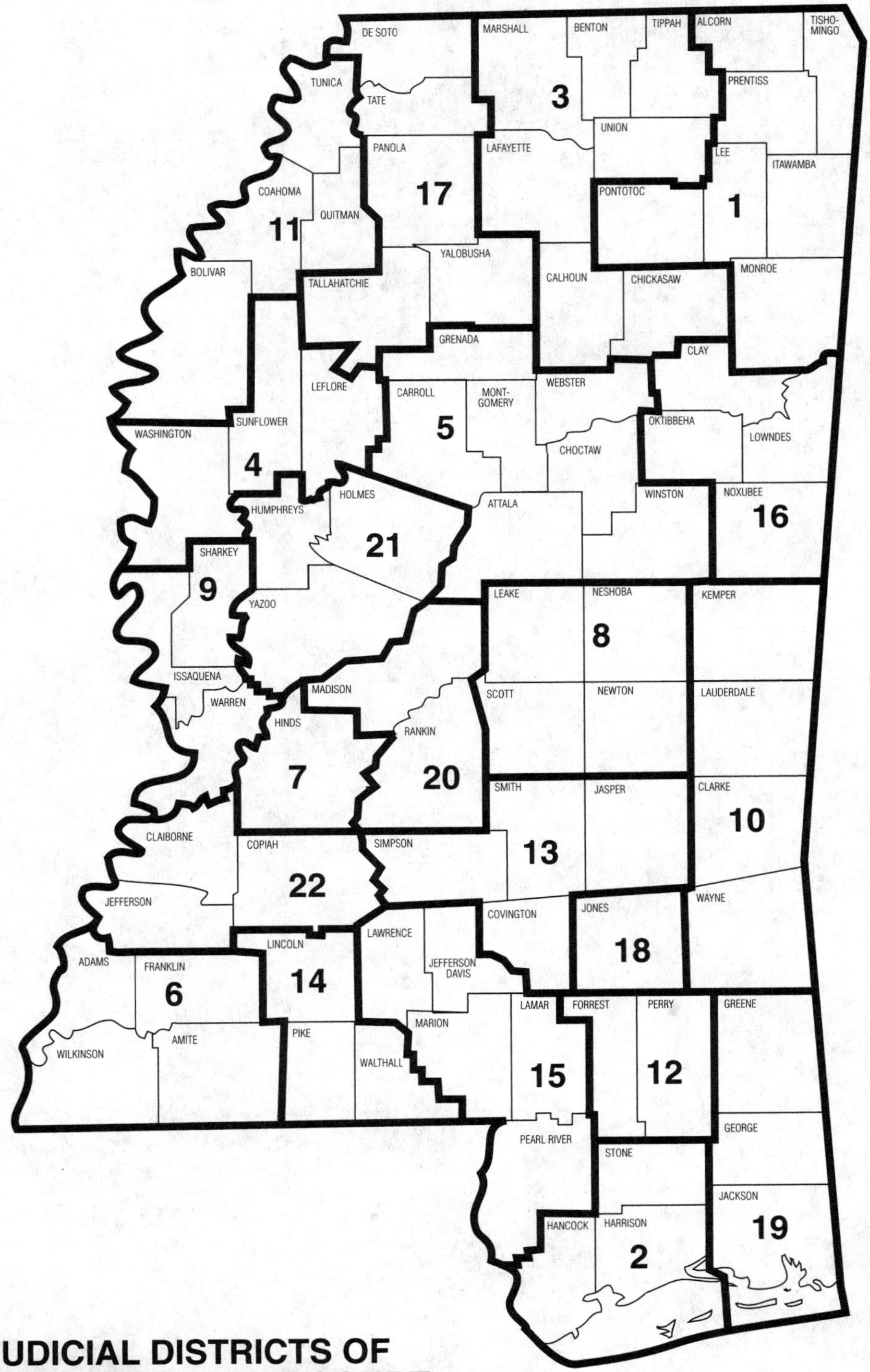
DE SOTO
MARSHALL
BENTON
TIPPAH
ALCORN
TISHO-
MINGO
TUNICA
TATE
3
PRENTISS
UNION
PANOLA
LAFAYETTE
LEE
ITAWAMBA
COAHOMA
17
PONTOTOC
1
QUITMAN
11
YALOBUSHA
BOLIVAR
MONROE
TALLAHATCHIE
CALHOUN
CHICKASAW
GRENADA
CLAY
LEFLORE
CARROLL
MONT-
GOMERY
WEBSTER
5
OKTIBBEHA
WASHINGTON
SUNFLOWER
LOWNDES
CHOCTAW
4
HOLMES
HUMPHREYS
ATTALA
WINSTON
NOXUBEE
16
21
SHARKEY
9
LEAKE
NESHOBA
KEMPER
YAZOO
8
ISSAQUENA
MADISON
SCOTT
NEWTON
LAUDERDALE
WARREN
HINDS
RANKIN
7
20
SMITH
JASPER
CLARKE
10
CLAIBORNE
COPIAH
SIMPSON
13
22
JEFFERSON
WAYNE
COVINGTON
JONES
LINCOLN
LAWRENCE
18
ADAMS
FRANKLIN
JEFFERSON
DAVIS
14
6
LAMAR
FORREST
PERRY
GREENE
AMITE
PIKE
MARION
WILKINSON
WALTHALL
15
12
GEORGE
PEARL RIVER
STONE
JACKSON
19
HANCOCK
HARRISON
2

JUDICIAL DISTRICTS OF MISSISSIPPI CIRCUIT COURT

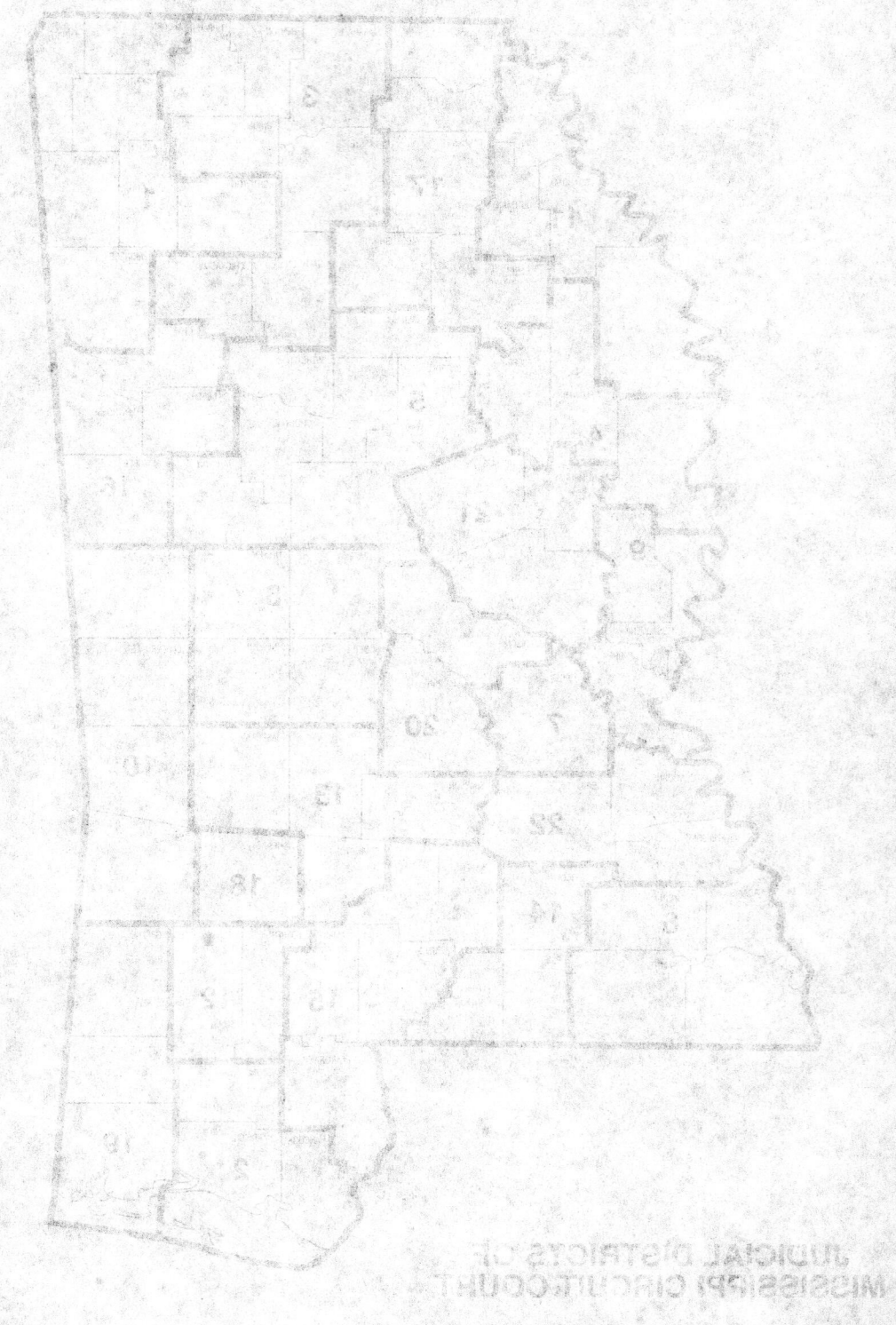

MISSISSIPPI

AGIN, William *(Judge, Madison County Court)*
Mailing address: P.O. Box 343, Canton 39046.
Telephone: (601) 859-5211.
Fax: (601) 859-8555

ALDERSON, Glenn *(Judge, Mississippi Chancery Court Eighteenth Judicial District)*
Mailing address: P.O. Drawer 70, Oxford 38655.
Telephone: (662) 236-0232.
Fax: (662) 234-8057

ALEXANDER, S. Allan *(Magistrate Judge, United States District Court Northern District of Mississippi)* Appointed by U.S. District Court judges.
Office: 242 U.S. Courthouse, 911 Jackson Avenue West, Oxford 38655-3621.
Telephone: (662) 234-3114.

ALFONSO, Margaret *(Judge, Mississippi Chancery Court Eighth Judicial District)*
Mailing address: P.O. Box 986, Gulfport 39502.
Telephone: (228) 868-3680.
Fax: (228) 865-1646

ALLEN, Tommy *(Judge, Coahoma County Court)*
Mailing address: P.O. Box 756, Clarksdale 38614.
Telephone: (662) 624-3046.
Fax: (662) 624-3075

AYCOCK, Sharion *(Judge, Mississippi Circuit Court First Judicial District)* Elected Nov 2002 to term beginning Jan 2003. Term expires Dec 2006.
Mailing address: P.O. Drawer 1100, Tupelo 38802.
Telephone: (662) 680-6075.
Fax: (662) 680-6078

BAILEY, Robert *(Judge, Mississippi Circuit Court Tenth Judicial District)*
Mailing address: P.O. Box 1167, Meridian 39302.
Telephone: (601) 482-9741.
Fax: (601) 484-3970

BAKER, Andrew C. *(Judge, Mississippi Circuit Court Seventeenth Judicial District)*
Mailing address: P.O. Drawer 368, Charleston 38921.
Telephone: (662) 647-3586.
Fax: (662) 647-8490

BARBEE, Mills *(Judge, DeSoto County Court)*
Office: 2535 Highway 51 South, Hernando 38632.
Telephone: (662) 429-5011.
Fax: (662) 429-1311

BARBOUR, William H., Jr. *(Judge, United States District Court Southern District of Mississippi)* Appointed for life by President Ronald Reagan to term beginning April 25, 1983. Former Chief Judge. Born Yazoo City Mississippi Feb 4, 1941. Presbyterian. Educated at Princeton University B.A. 1963, University of Mississippi J.D. 1966 and New York University 1966. Member Phi Delta Phi. Admitted to practice Mississippi 1966. In legal practice Yazoo City 1966-82.
Member American Bar Association.
Office: 430 U.S. Courthouse, 245 East Capitol Street, Jackson 39201.
Telephone: (601) 965-4545.

BARLOW, Glenn *(Judge, Mississippi Chancery Court Sixteenth Judicial District)*
Mailing address: P.O. Box 998, Pascagoula 39568.
Telephone: (228) 769-3035.
Fax: (228) 769-3424

BARNES, Vicki *(Judge, Mississippi Chancery Court Ninth Judicial District)*
Mailing address: P.O. Box 351, Vicksburg 39181.
Telephone: (601) 636-8327.
Fax: (601) 630-8021

BARNETT, Bill *(Judge, Hinds County Court)*
Mailing address: P.O. Box 327, Jackson 39205.
Telephone: (601) 968-6670.
Fax: (601) 973-5575

BARNWELL, Jon M. *(Judge, Mississippi Chancery Court Seventh Judicial District)* Elected May 1989 to term beginning July 1, 1989. Reelected Nov 1990, Nov 1994, Nov 1998 and 2002. Current term expires Dec 31, 2006. Born Greenwood Mississippi Oct 3, 1943. Episcopalian. Educated at Mississippi State University B.S. 1966 and University of Mississippi J.D. 1971. Member Phi Delta Phi. Admitted to practice Mississippi 1971 and U.S. District Court Northern District of Mississippi 1971. In legal practice Clarksdale 1971-76 and Greenwood 1976-89. Judge pro tem, Clarksdale Municipal Court 1972-74.
Member The American Law Institute, Mississippi State Bar, Leflore County and American Bar Associations. U.S. Army 1966-68. Member Lions Club. Enjoys golf.
Mailing address: P.O. Box 1579, Greenwood 38930.
Telephone: (662) 453-1432.
Fax: (662) 455-7959

BIGGERS, Neal B., Jr. *(Senior Judge, United States District Court Northern District of Mississippi)* Appointed for life by President Ronald Reagan April 2, 1984. Assumed Senior status Oct 1, 2000, serves by assignment. Chief Judge July 31, 1998 to Oct 1, 2000. Born Corinth Mississippi July 1, 1935. Presbyterian. Educated at Millsaps College B.A. 1956, Union Theological Seminary 1961 and University of Mississippi J.D. 1963. Assistant Editor Law Journal. Admitted to practice Mississippi 1963. Began legal practice Corinth 1963. Judge, Mississippi Circuit Court Jan 1, 1975 to April 1, 1984.
Alcorn County Attorney 1963-67. District Attorney 1968-74. Author "Criminal Discovery" Mississippi L. Jour. 1969. Assistant Instructor University of Mississippi 1974. Member Mississippi State Bar and American Bar

BIGGERS, NEAL B., JR.—*Continued*

Association. Lieutenant Commander USNR 1956-60. Democrat.

Office: 388 U.S. Courthouse, 911 Jackson Avenue West, Oxford 38655-3622.

Telephone: (662) 234-3401.

BISE, Carter *(Judge, Mississippi Chancery Court Eighth Judicial District)*

Mailing address: P.O. Box 3385, Gulfport 39505.

Telephone: (228) 868-3379.

Fax: (228) 865-1646

BOGEN, Eugene M. *(Magistrate Judge, United States District Court Northern District of Mississippi)* Appointed by U.S. District Court judges. Born Greenville Mississippi May 30, 1943. Episcopalian. Educated at University of Virginia B.A. 1965 and University of Mississippi J.D. 1968. Staff member University of Mississippi Law Journal 1966-68. Member Phi Delta Phi. Admitted to practice Mississippi 1968, U.S. District Court Northern District of Mississippi 1968 and U.S. Supreme Court 1976. In legal practice Greenville 1968-87. Former Judge, Mississippi Circuit Court Fourth Judicial District, appointed by Governor William A. Allain to term beginning Jan 1, 1987.

Member American Judicature Society, Mississippi State Bar and American Bar Association. Attended "Fact Finding and Decision Making" Harvard University 1987 and "Judicial Independence . . . Liability" Stanford University 1989 American Academy of Judicial Education. Delegate from Mississippi Circuit Judges Conference to National Conference of State Trial Judges (Executive Committee since 1993) Judicial Administration Division American Bar Association since 1990.

Mailing address: P.O. Box 1353, Greenville 38702.

Telephone: (662) 335-9214.

BRADLEY, Jaye *(Judge, Mississippi Chancery Court Sixteenth Judicial District)*

Mailing address: P.O. Box 998, Pascagoula 39568-0998.

Telephone: (228) 769-3036.

Fax: (228) 769-3189

BRAMLETTE, David C. *(Judge, United States District Court Southern District of Mississippi)* Appointed for life by President George Bush July 26, 1991 to term beginning Dec 1991. Born Woodville Mississippi Nov 27, 1939. Episcopalian. Educated at Princeton University B.A. 1962 and University of Mississippi School of Law J.D. 1965. Admitted to practice Mississippi 1965. In legal practice Natchez 1975-91. Special Judge, Mississippi Circuit Court Sixth Judicial District 1977. Special Judge, Mississippi Chancery Court Seventeenth Judicial District 1979.

Member Adams County Bar, The Mississippi Bar and Federal Bar Association.

Office: 216 Federal Building, 725 Martin Luther King Jr. Blvd., Biloxi 39530.

Telephone: (228) 436-4317.

BRETT, Charlie *(Judge, Lee County Court)*

Mailing address: P.O. Box 736, Tupelo 38802.

Telephone: (662) 841-9730.

Fax: (662) 841-9732

BREWER, Cynthia Lee *(Judge, Madison County Court)*

Mailing address: P.O. Box 1678, Canton 39046.

BRIDGES, Billy G. *(Judge, Court of Appeals of Mississippi)* Elected Nov 8, 1994 to term beginning Jan 1, 1995. Reelected 2000, current term expires Jan 1, 2009. Former Chief Judge. Born Simpson County Mississippi May 5, 1934. Baptist. Educated at University of Mississippi B.B.A. 1958 LL.B. 1961 J.D. 1968. Admitted to practice Mississippi 1961, U.S. District Court Southern District of Mississippi 1974, U.S. Court of Appeals Fifth Circuit and U.S. Supreme Court. In legal practice Brandon 1961-77 and Pearl 1991-95. Judge, Mississippi Chancery Court Twentieth Judicial District 1977-91.

County Prosecutor Rankin County 1971-75. District Attorney Twentieth Judicial District 1975-77. Member Mississippi State Bar and Magnolia Bar Association. USMC and USMCR 1952-56. Member Rotary Club and Gideons International. Enjoys hunting and fishing.

Mailing address: P.O. Box 22847, Jackson 39225-2847.

Telephone: (601) 354-7410.

E-mail address: jbridges@mssc.state.ms.us

BROOME, Thomas H. *(Judge, Rankin County Court)*

Mailing address: P.O. Drawer 1599, Brandon 39043.

Telephone: (601) 825-1474.

Fax: (601) 825-1465

BUFFINGTON, Larry *(Judge, Mississippi Chancery Court Thirteenth Judicial District)* Elected Nov 8, 1994 to term beginning Jan 1, 1995. Reelected Nov 1998 and 2002. Current term expires Dec 31, 2006. Born Kosciusko Mississippi Aug 3, 1953. Episcopalian. Educated at Louisiana State University B.A. 1974 and Mississippi College School of Law J.D. 1978. Admitted to practice Mississippi 1980. In legal practice Collins 1980-94.

Public Defender Covington County 1985-93. City Attorney Collins. Member Mississippi State Bar and Covington County Bar Association. Political affiliation: Nonpartisan.

Mailing address: P.O. Box 924, Collins 39428.

Telephone: (601) 765-8267.

Fax: (601) 765-4564

BURNS, Kenneth M. *(Judge, Mississippi Chancery Court Fourteenth Judicial District)* Elected Nov 2002 to term beginning Jan 2003. Term expires Dec 2006.

Mailing address: P.O. Box 110, Okolona 38860.

Telephone: (662) 447-3486.

Fax: (662) 447-2512

CAREY McCRAY, Margaret *(Judge, Mississippi Circuit Court Fourth Judicial District)*

Mailing address: P.O. Box 1775, Greenville 38792.

Telephone: (662) 334-2797.

Fax: (662) 334-2716

CARLSON, George C., Jr. *(Justice, Mississippi Supreme Court)* Born Greenwood Mississippi May 23, 1946. Presbyterian. Educated at Mississippi State University B.S. 1969 and University of Mississippi J.D. 1972. Member Sigma Chi. Admitted to practice Mississippi 1972. Began legal practice Sardis 1972. In legal practice Batesville 1978-82. Judge pro tempore, Municipal Court of the City of Batesville 1980-82. Former Judge, Mississippi Circuit Court Seventeenth Judicial District, elected to term beginning Jan 1, 1983.

CARLSON, GEORGE C., JR.—*Continued*

School Board Attorney South Panola Consolidated School District 1972-82. Attorney Second Court District Industrial Development Authority of Panola County 1980-82. Member Governor's Criminal Justice Task Force 1991. Member and Past President William C. Keady American Inns of Court. Fellow Mississippi Bar Foundation. Member American Judges Association, Mississippi State Bar (Board of Directors Young Lawyers Section 1975-78, State Chairman MSB Council of School Board Attorneys 1980-81, Member Commission on the Courts in the 21st Century 1992-93), Panola County (President 1975-76) and American Bar Associations. Participant National Judicial College University of Nevada Reno. Named Boss of the Year Panola County Legal Secretaries Association 1981. Sergeant Army National Guard 1968-74. Member 1976-82 and Secretary-Treasurer 1976-80 Panola County Democratic Executive Committee. Member Panola Partnership, Inc. Enjoys snow skiing and golf.

Mailing address: P.O. Box 117, Jackson 39205.
Office: Justice Building, 450 High Street, Jackson 39205.
Telephone: (601) 359-3697.
E-mail address: jcarlson@mssc.state.ms.us

CHANDLER, David A. *(Judge, Court of Appeals of Mississippi)* Presbyterian. Educated at Mississippi State University B.A. M.A. Ph.D. and University of Mississippi J.D. Judge, Weir Municipal Court 1999-2000.

Mailing address: P.O. Box 22847, Jackson 39225-2847.
Office: 656 North State Street, Jackson 39202.
Telephone: (601) 354-7410.
E-mail address: jchandler@mssc.state.ms.us

CHAPMAN, William E., III *(Judge, Mississippi Circuit Court Twentieth Judicial District)*

Mailing address: P.O. Box 1626, Canton 39046.
Telephone: (601) 855-5555.
Fax: (601) 855-5704

CLARK, H. David, II *(Judge, Mississippi Chancery Court Second Judicial District)* Elected April 1989 to term beginning July 3, 1989. Reelected Nov 1990, Nov 1994, Nov 1998 and 2002. Current term expires Dec 31, 2006. Born New Orleans Louisiana Aug 17, 1954. Southern Baptist. Educated at Mississippi College J.D. cum laude 1978. Admitted to practice Mississippi 1978 and U.S. District Court Southern District of Mississippi 1980. In legal practice Forest 1980-89. Former Youth Court Referee Scott County.

County Attorney Scott County 1984-89. Former Chairman Programs Committee, Former Secretary, Former Vice Chairman and Chairman since Oct 1993 Mississippi Conference of Chancery Court Judges. Member Mississippi State Bar, Scott County and American Bar Associations. Attended General Jurisdiction courses I and II The National Judicial College and National Judicial Child Support Curriculum Training sponsored by American Bar Association Child Support Project and National Council of Juvenile and Family Court Judges. Previously employed at Mississippi Department of Public Welfare.

Mailing address: P.O. Box 434, Forest 39074.
Telephone: (601) 469-2447.
Fax: (601) 469-3116

COBB, Kay B. *(Justice, Mississippi Supreme Court)* Appointed by Governor Kirk Fordice to term beginning April 1, 1999. Elected 2000, current term expires Dec 31, 2008. Born Mississippi Feb 28, 1942. Baptist. Educated at Mississippi University for Women 1963 and University of Mississippi School of Law J.D. 1978. Listed in *Who's Who in American Universities and Colleges.* Editor-in-Chief Journal of Space Law. National Moot Court Team. Member Phi Alpha Delta and Phi Delta Phi. In legal practice Oxford 1978-84 and 1996-99.

Attorney Mississippi Bureau of Narcotics 1984-88. Special Assistant Attorney General 1988-92. Former Director Mississippi Prosecutor's Association. State Senator Mississippi 1992-96. Member President's Commission United States' Model State Drug Laws and the National Alliance for Model State Drug Laws. President Alumnae Board Mississippi University for Women. Chairman Inter-Alumni Council for State Institutions of Higher Learning. Sunday School teacher.

Mailing address: P.O. Box 117, Jackson 39205.
Office: Justice Building, 450 High Street, Jackson 39205.
Telephone: (601) 359-2099.
E-mail address: jcobb@mssc.state.ms.us

COLEMAN, Frank M. *(Judge, Lauderdale County Court)*

Mailing address: P.O. Box 5822, Meridian 39302.
Telephone: (601) 482-9756.
Fax: (601) 484-3970

COLOM, Dorothy W. *(Judge, Mississippi Chancery Court Fourteenth Judicial District)*

Mailing address: P.O. Box 708, Columbus 39703-0708.
Telephone: (662) 329-5844.
Fax: (662) 241-1913

COTTEN, Vernon *(Judge, Mississippi Circuit Court Eighth Judicial District)*

Office: 205 Main Street, Carthage 39051-4117.
Telephone: (601) 267-5615.
Fax: (601) 267-5616

DALE, Sebe, Jr. *(Judge, Mississippi Chancery Court Tenth Judicial District)* Elected to term beginning Jan 1, 1979. Reelected 1982. Elected at special election 1989. Reelected 1990, 1994, 1998 and 2002. Current term expires Dec 31, 2006. Born Hathorn Mississippi May 2, 1921. Baptist. Educated at Mississippi College 1939-41 and University of Mississippi J.D. 1948. Member Phi Alpha Delta, Beta Theta Pi and Pi Tau Chi. Admitted to practice Mississippi 1948, U.S. District Court Southern District of Mississippi 1948, U.S. Supreme Court 1954 and U.S. Court of Military Appeals 1954. Began legal practice Columbia 1948. Youth Court Referee 1958-68.

Columbia City Attorney 1954. Chairman Mississippi Children's Code Commission 1954-64. Mississippi State Penitentiary Board 1968-72. Member Chancery Judges Conference of Mississippi (Former Chairman), Conference of Mississippi Judges, Mississippi State Bar (Former Commissioner Fifteenth Circuit Court District), Marion County (Past President) and American Bar Associations. Member and Chairman Board of Governors Mississippi Judicial College. Colonel U.S. Army Air Corps WWII and USAFR 1942-73 (retired). Graduate Air War College Maxwell Air Force Base. Member Masons, Shriners, American Legion (Former Post Com-

DALE, SEBE, JR.—*Continued*
mander) and Lions Club (Past President). Enjoys flying, hunting and fishing.
Mailing address: P.O. Box 1248, Columbia 39429.
Telephone: (601) 736-2220.
Fax: (601) 736-4166

DAVIDSON, Glen H. *(Chief Judge, United States District Court Northern District of Mississippi)* Appointed for life by President Ronald Reagan to term beginning Oct 27, 1985. Chief Judge since Oct 1, 2000. Born Pontotoc Mississippi Nov 20, 1941. Presbyterian. Educated at University of Mississippi B.A. 1962 J.D. 1965. Member Phi Alpha Delta and Pi Kappa Alpha. Admitted to practice Mississippi 1965, U.S. District Court District of Mississippi 1965, U.S. Court of Appeals Fifth Circuit 1968 and U.S. Supreme Court 1971. In legal practice Tupelo 1969-81.
District Attorney First Judicial District 1972-75. U.S. Attorney Northern District of Mississippi 1981-85. Member American Judicature Society, Federal Judges Association, Mississippi Bar Foundation, Mississippi State Bar and American Bar Association. Major USAF JAGC 1966-69. Member Kiwanis International.
Mailing address: P.O. Box 767, Aberdeen 39730-0767.
Telephone: (662) 369-6486.

DAVIS, Jerry A. *(Magistrate Judge, United States District Court Northern District of Mississippi)* Appointed by U.S. District Court judges to term beginning June 4, 1984. Reappointed June 4, 1992 and 2000. Current term expires June 2008. Born Waukegan Illinois July 1, 1946. Episcopalian. Educated at Mississippi State University B.A. 1968 and University of Virginia J.D. 1971. Member Sigma Alpha Epsilon and Delta Theta Phi. Admitted to practice Mississippi 1971, U.S. Court of Military Appeals 1972, U.S. Supreme Court 1975, U.S. District Courts Southern 1980 and Northern 1984 Districts of Mississippi and U.S. Courts of Appeals Fifth 1980 and Eleventh 1982 Circuits. Began legal practice Fort Hood Texas 1972.
With Department of Justice Washington D.C. 1973-80. Assistant U.S. Attorney Jackson Mississippi 1980-84. Member Court Administration and Case Management Committee Judicial Conference of the U.S., Magistrate Judges Education Committee Federal Judicial Center, American Inns of Court, American Judicature Society, Mississippi State Bar, Federal and American Bar Associations. Attended Fifth Circuit Judicial Conference 1985-2002. Captain U.S. Army 1972-75. Enjoys reading, fishing and baseball.
Mailing address: P.O. Box 726, Aberdeen 39730-0726.
Telephone: (662) 369-2138.
Fax: (662) 369-1039

DeLAUGHTER, Bobby B. *(Judge, Mississippi Circuit Court Seventh Judicial District)* Elected Nov 2002 to term beginning Jan 2003. Term expires Dec 2006. Born Vicksburg Mississippi Feb 28, 1954. Baptist. Educated at University of Mississippi B.A. with honors 1975 J.D. 1977. Member Phi Alpha Delta. Admitted to practice Mississippi 1978, U.S. District Courts Northern 1978 and Southern 1978 Districts of Mississippi and U.S. Court of Appeals Fifth Circuit 1978. In legal practice Jackson 1978-87. Judge, Hinds County Court Dec 10, 1999 to 2002.
Assistant District Attorney Hinds County 1987-99. Author *Never Too Late: A Prosecutor's Story of Justice in the Medgar Evers Murder Case* Scribner Publishing Co. 2001. Member 1987-99 and President 1993-94 Mississippi Prosecutors Association. Member The Mississippi Bar. Attended "Evidence" American Judicial Academy Dec 2000. Annual Speaker Williams Homicide Seminar New York State Police. Recipient Faculty Alumni Public Service Award from University of Mississippi 1999. Portrayed in movie "Ghosts of Mississippi" Castle Rock Pictures 1996 (for prosecution of Byron De La Beckwith for 1963 murder of Medgar Evers). Former Member Executive Committee Hinds County Republican Party. Member Exchange Club. Enjoys writing and horseback riding.
Mailing address: P.O. Box 327, Jackson 39205.
Telephone: (601) 968-6650.
Fax: (601) 948-2689
E-mail address: bdelaughter@co.hinds.ms.us

DIAZ, Oliver E., Jr. *(Justice, Mississippi Supreme Court)* Born Biloxi Mississippi Dec 16, 1959. Catholic. Educated at Mississippi Gulf Coast Junior College A.A. 1979, University of South Alabama B.A. 1982 and University of Mississippi School of Law J.D. 1985. Admitted to practice Mississippi 1985. In legal practice Gulfport 1985-90 and D'Iberville April 1990 to 1995. Former Judge, Court of Appeals of Mississippi, elected to term beginning Jan 1, 1995.
City Attorney D'Iberville four years. Member House of Representatives Mississippi (Secretary Constitution Committee, Chairman Insurance Subcommittee and Judiciary Subcommittee, Member Ways and Means Committee) seven years. Member Mississippi State Bar (Advertising Committee). Member Gulfport School District Mentor Program, Leadership Gulf Coast, Harrison County Council of Governments, Biloxi Bay Chamber of Commerce, North Bay Chamber of Commerce and American Legislative Exchange Council. Host Family Foreign Student Exchange Program.
Mailing address: P.O. Box 117, Jackson 39205.
Office: Justice Building, 450 High Street, Jackson 39205.
Telephone: (601) 359-3697.
Fax: (601) 359-2443
E-mail address: jdiaz@mssc.state.ms.us

EASLEY, Charles D., Jr. *(Justice, Mississippi Supreme Court)* Elected to term beginning Jan 2001. Term expires Dec 2008. Born Port of Spain Trinidad April 8, 1949. Educated at University of Mississippi B.B.A 1972 J.D. 1979 and Mississippi State University M.B.A. 1976. In legal practice Columbus 1983-2000.
Assistant District Attorney Third Judicial Circuit 1980-83. Former Prosecutor Town of Caledonia. Member Mississippi Municipal Judges Association, Mississippi Trial Lawyers Association, The Association of Trial Lawyers of America, Lowndes County and American Bar Associations. Graduate Career Prosecutor's Course National District Attorneys College 1980. Member Kolola Springs Baptist Church, National Rifle Association, Shriner, York Rite and Scottish Rite Mason.
Mailing address: P.O. Box 117, Jackson 39205.
Office: Justice Building, 450 High Street, Jackson 39205.
Telephone: (601) 359-2107.
Fax: (601) 359-2443
E-mail address: jeasley@mssc.state.ms.us

ELLINGTON, Edward *(Chief Judge, United States Bankruptcy Court Southern District of Mississippi)*
Mailing address: P.O. Drawer 2448, Jackson 39225-2448.
Telephone: (601) 965-5304.

EUBANKS, Michael R. *(Judge, Mississippi Circuit Court Fifteenth Judicial District)* Elected to term beginning Jan 1, 1983. Elected at special election 1989. Reelected 1990, 1994, 1998 and 2002. Current term expires Dec 31, 2006. Born Lumberton Mississippi Sept 21, 1940. Methodist. Educated at Tulane University B.B.A. 1962 J.D. 1965. Admitted to practice Louisiana 1965 and Mississippi 1966. Began legal practice Lumberton Mississippi 1966. In legal practice Purvis Mississippi 1971-82.
Member Mississippi State Bar, Louisiana State and American Bar Associations. Enjoys boating.
Mailing address: P.O. Box 488, Purvis 39475.
Telephone: (601) 794-6035.
Fax: (601) 794-2801

EVANS, Robert G. "Bob" *(Judge, Mississippi Circuit Court Thirteenth Judicial District)* Appointed by Governor Ray Mabus to term beginning Feb 12, 1991. Elected at special election Sept 17, 1991. Reelected Nov 7, 1994, Nov 1998 and 2002. Current term expires Dec 31, 2006. Born Morton Mississippi Jan 11, 1949. Baptist. Educated at University of Mississippi B.S. 1972 and University of Mississippi School of Law J.D. 1974. Admitted to practice Mississippi 1974, U.S. District Court Southern District of Mississippi 1974 and U.S. Supreme Court 1988. In legal practice Mendenhall 1974-80.
District Attorney Mississippi Circuit Court Thirteenth Judicial District 1980-91. Author "*Batson v. Kentucky:* Its Progeny and Applications in Mississippi State Courts" *Mississippi Public Defenders' Association Handbook* 1998; "The Defenders Depart," "Anselm McLaurin" and "The Yankees is Coming!" *Smith County Memoirs* Smith County Genealogical Society 1998; *The Seven Messianic Festivals* 2001; and *The 16th Mississippi Infantry: Civil War Letters and Reminiscenes* University Press of Mississippi Nov 2002. Editor *The Civil War Letters of William Harris Hardy to Sallie Johnson Hardy* 1999, *Letters of Hugh Carroll Dickson, Company C, Sixteenth Mississippi Infantry* 1999 and *Letters of P. H. Craven, Company B, Nineteenth Virginia Volunteers* 1999 University of Southern Mississippi. Member The American Law Institute, Mississippi Conference of Circuit Court Judges (Chairman 2001-02) and The Mississippi Bar. Attended General Jurisdiction, Settlement Techniques and Search and Seizure seminars The National Judicial College Reno Nevada. Vice Chairman Mississippi Young Democrats 1976. Member Mensa Society. Enjoys gardening, golfing, reading and traveling.
Mailing address: P.O. Box 545, Raleigh 39153.
Telephone: (601) 782-4413.
Fax: (601) 782-9481

FRANKLIN, Beverly Mitchell *(Judge, Lowndes County Court)*
Mailing address: P.O. Box 1829, Columbus 39703.
Telephone: (662) 329-5940.
Fax: (662) 329-5870

FUNDERBURK, Paul S. *(Judge, Mississippi Circuit Court First Judicial District)*
Mailing address: P.O. Drawer 1100, Tupelo 38802-1398.
Telephone: (662) 680-6013.
Fax: (662) 680-6078

GAINES, Edward R. *(Judge, United States Bankruptcy Court Southern District of Mississippi)*
Office: 117 Federal Building, 725 Martin Luther King Jr. Blvd., Biloxi 39530-2267.
Telephone: (228) 432-5544.

GARDNER, Thomas J., III *(Judge, Mississippi Circuit Court First Judicial District)* Elected at special election to term beginning Jan 1, 1981. Reelected 1982. Elected at special election 1989. Reelected 1990, 1994, 1998 and 2002. Current term expires Dec 31, 2006. Born Jackson Mississippi Feb 12, 1936. Methodist. Educated at Millsaps College B.A. 1960 and University of Mississippi School of Law J.D. 1966. Admitted to practice Mississippi 1966. Began legal practice Tupelo 1966.
Assistant District Attorney First Judicial District 1976-79. Member Mississippi State Bar, Lee County and First District Bar Associations. E-5 U.S. Army 1956-58. Enjoys hunting and fishing.
Mailing address: P.O. Drawer 1100, Tupelo 38802.
Telephone: (662) 680-6013.
Fax: (662) 680-6078

GEX, Walter J., III *(Judge, United States District Court Southern District of Mississippi)* Appointed for life by President Ronald Reagan to term beginning Feb 27, 1986. Catholic. Educated at University of Mississippi B.B.A. 1961 LL.B. 1963. Admitted to practice Mississippi 1963 and U.S. District Court District of Mississippi 1963. In legal practice Jackson 1963-72 and Bay St. Louis 1972-86.
Instructor Jackson School of Law (now Mississippi College School of Law) 1963-72. Former Vice President Mississippi Association of County Board Attorneys. Former President Hancock County Bar Association. Former Member Mississippi State Bar Commission. Fellow Mississippi Bar Foundation. Member Fifth Circuit Judges Association, Federal Judges Association, Mississippi State Bar, Federal and American Bar Associations.
Office: 238 Federal Building, 725 Martin Luther King Jr. Blvd., Biloxi 39530.
Telephone: (228) 374-2807.

GORDON, Marcus D. *(Judge, Mississippi Circuit Court Eighth Judicial District)*
Mailing address: P.O. Box 220, Decatur 39327.
Telephone: (601) 635-3540.
Fax: (601) 635-2893

GOREE, Janace Harvey *(Judge, Mississippi Chancery Court Eleventh Judicial District)* Elected Nov 2002 to term beginning Jan 2003. Term expires Dec 2006.
Mailing address: P.O. Box 39, Lexington 39095.
Telephone: (662) 834-2599.
Fax: (662) 834-0438

GRANT, John S., III *(Judge, Mississippi Chancery Court Twentieth Judicial District)*
Mailing address: P.O. Box 1437, Brandon 39043.
Telephone (601) 825-1477.

GRAVES, James E., Jr. *(Justice, Mississippi Supreme Court)* Appointed by Governor Ronnie Musgrove

GRAVES, JAMES E., JR.—*Continued*

to term beginning Nov 1, 2001. Born Hinds County Mississippi. Educated at Millsaps College B.A. 1975 and Syracuse University M.P.A. 1980 J.D. 1980. Admitted to practice Mississippi 1980. In legal practice Jackson 1983-86. Judge, Mississippi Circuit Court Seventh Judicial District Feb 11, 1991 to 2001, appointed by Governor Ray Mabus.

Staff Attorney Central Mississippi Legal Services June 1980 to Aug 1983. Legal Counsel Health Law Division Nov 1986 to Jan 1989, Special Assistant Nov 1986 to June 1990, Civil Litigation Division Jan 1989 to Aug 1989 and Chief Legal Counsel Human Services Division Aug 1989 to June 1990 Attorney General's Office Mississippi. Director Division of Child Support Enforcement Mississippi Department of Human Services July 1990 to Feb 1991. Author "The Big Case: A Perspective from the Bench" May/June 1999 and "Technology in the Courtroom—Changes in Hinds County" Oct 2001 *The Mississippi Lawyer* and "Technological Changes in Hinds County" *The Judges' Journal* American Bar Association Summer 2001. Adjunct Professor of Media Law and Ethics 1980-82 and 1995 to 1997, Civil Rights Law 1990 and Correctional Systems and Black Perspectives in Public Administration 1995-96 Jackson State University. Delegate on behalf of Mississippi Conference of Circuit Judges 1993-2001, Vice Chairman 2000, Chair Elect 2001, Chairman Law and Technology Committee and Member Executive Committee 1994-2001 National Conference of State Trial Judges Judicial Division American Bar Association. Chair Courts and the Media Committee Mississippi Supreme Court since 2001.

Presenter Violence Prevention Workshop National Conference on Strategies by Historically Black Colleges and Universities to Prevent Violence in African-American Communities 1994; Workshop on Violence Prevention Strategies 100 Black Men of American Annual Convention 1994; Workshop on Violence Prevention Strategies Congressional Black Caucus Foundation Annual Convention 1994, 1995, 1996 and 1997; "Views from the Bench" 1994 and "Ethics for Lawyers" 1996 Magnolia Bar Association; Mississippi Youth Summit on Violence The Mississippi Bar 1995; Youth Crime Summit City of Jackson 1995; "Ethics for Lawyers" 1995 and "Improving the Effectiveness of Counsel: A Perspective from the Bench" 1995 American Trial Lawyers Association; "Ethics for Lawyers" Mississippi Trial Lawyers Association 1995; Workshop on Domestic Violence Mississippi Department of Public Safety 1996; Workshop on Re-Inventing Government 100 Black Men of America Annual Convention 1998; and "Technology in the Courtroom" Hinds County Bar Association 1999, The Association of Trial Lawyers of America 2000, Mississippi Judicial College 2000, Mississippi Trial Lawyers Association Nov 2000 and Mississippi Judicial College 2001. Panelist "Litigation Survival Tactics in the Courtroom" Summer School for Lawyers The Mississippi Bar 2001 and "Courtroom Etiquette and Decorum" Magnolia Bar Association 2002 and Jackson Young Lawyers 2002. Named Champion Adopter by Mentor Lake Elementary Schools Boys for a Brighter Tomorrow Program 1991, Judge of the Year by National Conference of Black Lawyers 1992, Alumnus of the Year by Millsaps College Black Students Association 1993 and Parent of the Year by Jackson Public School District 2000-01. Recipient Government Service Award 1993 and 1998 and R. Jess Brown Award 1994 from Magnolia Bar Association, Thurgood Marshall Award from The City of Jackson's Martin Luther King Celebration 1994 and 2002, Distinguished Jurist Award from National Bar Association Inc. 1996, Innovation Award from Hinds County Bar Association 2000, Commissioner's Award from U.S. Department of Health and Human Services 2001, Special Achievement Award from Jackson Federal Executive Association 2002 and Humanized Education Award from Mississippi Association of Educators 2002. Coached high school Mock Trial Teams since 1990. Chairman Anti-Violence Committee 100 Black Men of America 1994-96. President Wingfield Place Neighborhood Association 2000-02. Advisory Council Millsaps College Alumni since 2000.

Mailing address: P.O. Box 117, Jackson 39205.

Office: Justice Building, 450 High Street, Jackson 39205.

Telephone: (601) 359-3697.

E-mail address: jgraves@mssc.state.ms.us

GREEN, Tomie T. *(Judge, Mississippi Circuit Court Seventh Judicial District)* Elected Nov 1998 to term beginning Jan 1999. Reelected 2002, current term expires Dec 2006. Born Hinds County Mississippi. African Methodist Episcopal. Educated at Tougaloo College B.A. cum laude 1973, Jackson State University M.S.Ed. summa cum laude 1976 and Mississippi College School of Law J.D. 1983. Law Clerk to Hon. Henry T. Wingate, U.S. District Court Southern District of Mississippi 1984-86. Member Phi Alpha Delta. Admitted to practice Mississippi 1984, U.S. District Courts Northern 1984 and Southern 1984 Districts of Mississippi and U.S. Court of Appeals Fifth Circuit 1986. In legal practice July 1984 to Dec 1985 and Oct 1988 to 1998.

Assistant District Attorney Hinds County and Yazoo County 1986-88. Co-author with J. Walker "Pretrial Motions" *Excellence in Advocacy: Trial Expertise and Wisdom from the National College of Advocacy* The Association of Trial Lawyers of America Press 1992 and with W. Kidd "Prognosis of the Physician-Patient Privilege: Guarded or Fatal" 15 Trial Diplomacy Journal 243, 1992. Adjunct Professor of Pre-Trial Procedure Mississippi College School of Law since 1994. Certified Mediator/Arbitrator American Arbitration Association. Member Mississippi Trial Lawyers Association, The Association of Trial Lawyers of America, The Mississippi Bar, Magnolia, Hinds County, National and Federal Bar Associations. Lecturer on "Structured Settlement in Minor Claims" Mississippi Judicial College and Mississippi Chancery Judges Conference, "Handling Minors' Personal Injury Claims—From Start to Finish" Magnolia Bar Association, "Building Bridges: Multiculturalism in the Profession—Is the Courtroom Ready for a Multicultural Society?" The Association of Trial Lawyers of America Annual Convention Washington D.C., "Products Liability: What to Expect in Discovery" The Association of Trial Lawyers of America Annual Convention San Francisco, "Health Care and Culture: Representing People of Color—Examination of the Client" The Association of Trial Lawyers of America Annual Convention Chicago and "What to Expect in Discovery" Mississippi Trial Lawyers Association. Recipient Recognition of Excellence Award from South Central Region Zeta Phi Beta, Inc. 1993, Outstanding Service Award from Department of Health Education Jackson State University 1993,

GREEN, TOMIE T.—*Continued*

Achievement Award from Women in Trade & Technology 1993, Woman of the Year Award from 100 Black Women 1993, Government Service Award from Magnolia Bar Association 1994, Fannie Lou Hamer Award from Mississippi Democratic Party 1995, Jack Young Legal Award from NAACP 1996, Distinguished Service Award from Southeastern Community Services Agencies 1996 and National Trio Achiever Award from National Council Educational Opportunity Association. Member House of Representatives Mississippi 1992-98. Health educator/counselor Jackson Hinds Comprehensive Health Center June 1975 to May 1977. Program Coordinator Division of Mental Retardation Mississippi Department of Mental Health June 1997 to July 1978. Formerly worked as social worker Hudspeth Retardation Center. Member Mississippi House of Representatives 1992-98. Member Mississippi Legislative Black Caucus, Mississippi Federation of Democratic Women, Mississippi League of Women Voters, National Coalition of 100 Black Women, American Association of University Women, NAACP and SCLC. Enjoys golf, writing and travel.

Mailing address: P.O. Box 327, Jackson 39205-0327.
Telephone: (601) 968-6658.
Fax: (601) 366-1553
E-mail address: tgreen@co.hinds.ms.us

GRIFFIS, T. Kenneth *(Judge, Court of Appeals of Mississippi)*
Mailing address: P.O. Box 22847, Jackson 39225-2847.
Office: 656 North State Street, Jackson 39202.
Telephone: (601) 354-7410.
E-mail address: jgriffis@mssc.state.ms.us

GUIROLA, Louis, Jr. *(Magistrate Judge, United States District Court Southern District of Mississippi)* Appointed by U.S. District Court judges.
Office: 214 Bancorp South Building, 2909 Thirteenth Street, Gulfport 39501-1950.
Telephone: (228) 863-1583.

HARKEY, Dale *(Judge, Mississippi Circuit Court Nineteenth Judicial District)* Assumed office 1999. Educated at Spring Hill College B.S. 1974 and University of Mississippi School of Law J.D. 1978.

Assistant District Attorney 1984-88 and District Attorney 1992-98 Nineteenth Circuit Court District. Assistant District Attorney Second Circuit Court District 1990-91. Board of Directors Mississippi Prosecutors Association 1992-97. Former Member The Mississippi Bar. Member Russell-Blass-Walker Chapter American Inns of Court and Jackson County Bar Association. Graduate General Jurisdiction Course The National Judicial College 1999. Graduate Leadership Jackson County 1995. Vestry Member St. John's Episcopal Church since 2002. Past President Pascagoula Kiwanis Club. Board of Directors Southeast Mississippi Chapter American Red Cross. Master Mason F&AM Lodge 419. 32° Scottish Rite Mason. Member Grand York Rite Bodies of Mississippi.

Mailing address: P.O. Box 998, Pascagoula 39568-0998.
Telephone: (228) 769-3042.
Fax: (228) 769-3262

HARPER, Gaylon K. *(Judge, Jones County Court)*
Mailing address: P.O. Box 764, Laurel 39441.
Telephone: (601) 649-7500.
Fax: (601) 428-3620

HELFRICH, Robert *(Judge, Mississippi Circuit Court Twelfth Judicial District)* Elected Nov 2002 to term beginning Jan 2003. Term expires Dec 2006.
Mailing address: P.O. Box 309, Hattiesburg 39403.
Telephone: (601) 544-5495.
Fax: (601) 545-6179

HEWES, Gaston Henderson *(Judge, Harrison County Court)* Appointed by Governor William Waller 1968. Elected 1970, 1974, 1978 and 1982. Elected at special election 1989. Reelected 1990, 1994, 1998 and 2002. Current term expires Dec 31, 2006. Born Gulfport Mississippi March 19, 1903. Episcopalian. Educated at University of Mississippi B.S. 1925 LL.B. 1926. Admitted to practice Mississippi 1926. Member Sigma Alpha Epsilon. In legal practice Gulfport 1926-68.

Harrison County Prosecuting Attorney 1932-68. Member Mississippi State Bar (Past Vice President, Secretary, Treasurer) and Harrison County Bar Association (Past President). Inducted into University of Mississippi Athletic Hall of Fame 1986. Democrat. Former President Young Men's Business Club, Great Southern Country Club, Gulfport Gridiron Club, Cotillion Club and Century Club. Chairman Gulfport Recreational Board 1981-86. Member Masons, Elks Club, Mississippi Gulf Coast Chapter National Football Foundation and Hardwood Club (Vice President). Recreational Center in Gulfport bears his name (Gaston Hewes Recreational Center). Enjoys golf, children and athletics.

Mailing address: P.O. Box 973, Gulfport 39502.
Telephone: (228) 865-4025.
Fax: (228) 867-6523

HINES, W. Ashley *(Judge, Mississippi Circuit Court Fourth Judicial District)*
Mailing address: P.O. Box 1315, Greenville 38702.
Telephone: (662) 334-2652.
Fax: (662) 335-2381

HOUSTON, David W., III *(Judge, United States Bankruptcy Court Northern District of Mississippi)* Appointed by U.S. Court of Appeals Fifth Circuit judges Dec 31, 1984. Reappointed 1998, current term expires Dec 31, 2012. Born Gloversville New York March 11, 1944. Educated at University of Mississippi B.B.A. cum laude 1966 J.D. 1969. Admitted to practice Mississippi 1969, U.S. District Court Northern District of Mississippi 1969, U.S. Tax Court 1972 and U.S. Supreme Court 1972. In legal practice Aberdeen 1972-83. Judge, Aberdeen Municipal Court 1974-76.

President National Conference of Bankruptcy Court Judges 1993-94. Fellow Mississippi Bar Foundation and American College of Bankruptcy. Member William C. Keady American Inn of Court, American Bankruptcy Institute (Board of Directors 1993-99), Mississippi State Bar (Board of Bar Commissioners 1983-86), Monroe County and First Judicial District (Former Secretary-Treasurer, Vice President and President) Bar Associations. Special Agent FBI 1969-72.

Mailing address: P.O. Drawer 867, Aberdeen 39730-0867.
Telephone: (662) 369-2624.

HOWARD, Lee J. *(Judge, Mississippi Circuit Court Sixteenth Judicial District)*
Mailing address: P.O. Box 1344, Starkville 39760.
Telephone: (662) 329-5919.

HOWORTH, Andrew K. *(Judge, Mississippi Circuit Court Third Judicial District)* Appointed by Governor Ronnie Musgrove to term beginning Jan 1, 2002. Elected 2002, current term expires Jan 1, 2007.
Office: One Courthouse Square, Suite 201, Oxford 38655.
Telephone: (662) 234-4951.
Fax: (662) 236-0238

HUDSON, John N. *(Judge, Adams County Court)*
Mailing address: P.O. Box 1371, Natchez 39121.
Telephone: (601) 445-7933.
Fax: (601) 445-2369

IRVING, Tyree *(Judge, Court of Appeals of Mississippi)* Elected to term beginning Jan 1, 1999. Term expires Dec 31, 2006. Born Greenwood Mississippi July 12, 1946. Methodist. Educated at Jackson State College 1968 and University of Mississippi School of Law J.D. 1974. Law Clerk to Chief Justice Robert G. Gillespie, Mississippi Supreme Court 1975. Member Alpha Phi Alpha. In legal practice Greenwood.
Assistant U.S. Attorney Northern District of Mississippi 1978. Board Attorney Board of Supervisors Humphreys County 1988. Former Attorney City of Mound Bayou, Mound Bayou School District and town of Winstonville. Former Member National Council of School Attorneys and The Association of Trial Lawyers of America. Member The Mississippi Bar, LeFlore County and Magnolia Bar Associations. Member Wesley United Methodist Church in Greenwood and NAACP.
Mailing address: P.O. Box 22847, Jackson 39225-2847.
Office: 656 North State Street, Jackson 39202.
Telephone: (601) 354-7410.
E-mail address: jirving@mssc.state.ms.us

JACKSON, Kathy King *(Judge, Mississippi Circuit Court Nineteenth Judicial District)*
Mailing address: P.O. Box 998, Pascagoula 39568.
Telephone: (228) 769-3196.
Fax: (228) 769-3262

JOHNSON, Forrest Al *(Judge, Mississippi Circuit Court Sixth Judicial District)* Elected Nov 1994 to term beginning Jan 1, 1995. Reelected Nov 1998 and 2002. Current term expires Dec 31, 2006. Born Natchez Mississippi June 8, 1955. Church of Christ. Educated at University of Mississippi B.A. 1976 J.D. 1979. Admitted to practice Mississippi 1979, U.S. District Courts Northern 1979 and Southern 1979 Districts of Mississippi and U.S. Supreme Court. In legal practice Natchez 1979-88.
Assistant District Attorney Sixth Judicial District 1988-94. Member The Mississippi Bar.
Mailing address: P.O. Box 1372, Natchez 39121.
Office: Adams County Courthouse, Third Floor, 300 Market Street, Natchez 39120.
Telephone: (601) 442-8363.
Fax: (601) 445-7954
E-mail address: johnson@telapex.com

JOHNSON, Vernita King *(Judge, Washington County Court)* Elected Nov 1998 to term beginning Jan 1, 1999. Reelected 2002, current term expires Dec 31, 2006. Born Holly Springs Mississippi Aug 13, 1956. Baptist. Educated at University of Mississippi B.A. 1979 J.D. 1981. Moot Court Board 1981. Admitted to practice Mississippi 1981. In legal practice Greenville 1981-98. Judge, Hollandale Municipal Court 1987-93, Arcola Municipal Court 1992-98 and Greenville Municipal Court 1995-98.
Member The Mississippi Bar and Magnolia Bar Association. Attended Trial Judges Conferences Mississippi Judicial College April 1999, Oct 1999, April 2000 and Oct 2000; "Enhancing Judicial Skills in Domestic Violence Cases" National Judicial Institute on Domestic Violence May 1999; and General Jurisdiction The National Judicial College July 1999. Volunteer Chamber of Commerce, Greenville Daycare Center and Moderne Art & Civil Club. Enjoys music and reading.
Mailing address: P.O. Box 816, Greenville 38702.
Telephone: (662) 334-2657.
Fax: (662) 334-2796

KIDD, Winston L. *(Judge, Mississippi Circuit Court Seventh Judicial District)*
Mailing address: P.O. Box 327, Jackson 39205.
Telephone: (601) 968-6677.
Fax: (601) 714-6305

KING, Leslie D. *(Presiding Judge, Court of Appeals of Mississippi)* Elected 1994 to term beginning Jan 1, 1995. Reelected 2000, current term expires Jan 1, 2009. Born Greenville Mississippi Jan 17, 1949. Religious affiliation: African Methodist Episcopal. Educated at University of Mississippi B.A. 1970 and Texas Southern University J.D. 1973. Articles Editor Texas Southern Law Review. Member Phi Alpha Delta. Admitted to practice Mississippi 1973, Texas 1973, U.S. District Courts Northern and Southern Districts of Mississippi and U.S. Court of Appeals Fifth Circuit. In legal practice Greenville 1973-95.
Member Mississippi House of Representatives 1980-94. Enjoys reading and cooking.
Mailing address: P.O. Box 22847, Jackson 39225-2847.
Office: 656 North State Street, Jackson 39202.
Telephone: (601) 354-7410.
E-mail address: jking@mssc.state.ms.us

KITCHENS, James T., Jr. *(Judge, Mississippi Circuit Court Sixteenth Judicial District)* Elected Nov 2002 to term beginning Jan 2003. Term expires Dec 2006.
Mailing address: P.O. Box 1387, Columbus 39703.
Telephone: (662) 329-5919.

KREBS, Robert P. *(Judge, Mississippi Circuit Court Nineteenth Judicial District)* Elected Nov 2002 to term beginning Jan 2003. Term expires Dec 2006.
Mailing address: P.O. Box 998, Pascagoula 39568.
Telephone: (228) 769-3244.
Fax: (228) 769-3262

LACKEY, Henry L. *(Judge, Mississippi Circuit Court Third Judicial District)*
Mailing address: P.O. Drawer T, Calhoun City 38916.
Telephone: (662) 628-5131.
Fax: (662) 628-5131

LAMAR, Ann *(Judge, Mississippi Circuit Court Seventeenth Judicial District)*
Mailing address: P.O. Box 707, Senatobia 38668.
Telephone: (662) 560-6201.
Fax: (662) 562-0491

LANCASTER, Robert L. *(Judge, Mississippi Chancery Court Fourteenth Judicial District)*
Mailing address: P.O. Box 884, Columbus 38703-0884.
Telephone: (662) 329-5844.
Fax: (662) 241-1913

LANDRUM, Billy Joe *(Judge, Mississippi Circuit Court Eighteenth Judicial District)* Former Judge, Jones County Court.
Mailing address: P.O. Box 685, Laurel 39441.
Telephone: (601) 428-4572.
Fax: (601) 428-3189

LEE, L. Joseph *(Judge, Court of Appeals of Mississippi)* Elected Nov 1998 to term beginning Jan 1999. Reelected 2002, current term expires 2011. Born 1945. Educated at University of Southern Mississippi, William Carey College B.A. and Mississippi College School of Law J.D. In legal practice Mississippi 1973-98.
Member Mississippi Trial Lawyers Association, The Mississippi Bar, State Bar of Texas and American Bar Association. Former owner and operator Baldwin-Lee Funeral Homes Jackson.
Mailing address: P.O. Box 22847, Jackson 39225-2847.
Office: 656 North State Street, Jackson 39202.
Telephone: (601) 354-7410.
E-mail address: jlee@mssc.state.ms.us

LEE, Tom Stewart *(Chief Judge, United States District Court Southern District of Mississippi)* Appointed for life by President Ronald Reagan to term beginning June 14, 1984. Chief Judge since Nov 4, 1996. Born Jackson Mississippi April 8, 1941. Baptist. Educated at Mississippi College B.A. with honors 1963 and University of Mississippi J.D. with honors 1965. Recipient D. M. Nelson, Jr. Memorial Scholarship Trophy for graduating first in class and Frederick P. Hamel Award for academic achievement in first year law class. Chief Justice Student Body Judicial Council. Listed in *Who's Who in American Colleges and Universities.* Assistant Editor Mississippi Law Journal. Member Phi Delta Phi and Omicron Delta Kappa (President). Admitted to practice Mississippi 1965, U.S. District Court Southern District of Mississippi, U.S. Court of Appeals Fifth Circuit and U.S. Court of Military Appeals. Began legal practice Forest 1965. Judge, Scott County Youth Court 1972-83. Judge, Forest Municipal Court 1982.
Prosecuting Attorney Scott County 1968-71. Former Attorney Scott County Board of Supervisors, Scott County Board of Education and City of Morton. Spell Lecturer Mississippi College 1993. Former Mississippi State Bar Commissioner. Member Court Administration and Case Management Committee Judicial Conference of The U.S., Mississippi State Bar, Scott County and Federal Bar Associations. Captain U.S. Army JAGC 1965-73. School Board President Forest Public Schools. President Forest Jaycees, Scott County Heart Association and Scott County Ole Miss Alumni Association. Director Forest Chamber of Commerce. Enjoys sports (baseball, basketball, tennis).
Office: 110 U.S. Courthouse, 245 East Capitol Street, Jackson 39201.
Telephone: (601) 965-4963.

LEWIS, Jannie M. *(Judge, Mississippi Circuit Court Twenty-first Judicial District)* Elected Nov 4, 1994 to term beginning Jan 1, 1995. Reelected 1998 and 2002. Current term expires Dec 31, 2006. Born Cruger Mississippi Oct 4, 1958. Baptist. Educated at Jackson State University B.A. 1980 and University of Iowa J.D. 1983. Admitted to practice Mississippi 1984 and U.S. District Courts Northern and Southern Districts of Mississippi. In legal practice Lexington 1987-94. Municipal Judge, Town of Tchula 1992-94.
Public Defender 1988-94 and Prosecuting Attorney 1992-94. Member Mississippi State Bar and Magnolia Bar Association. Attended The National Judicial College. Enjoys reading, tennis, jogging and aerobics.
Mailing address: P.O. Box 605, Lexington 39095.
Telephone: (662) 834-1452.
Fax: (662) 834-1481

LEWIS, Larry *(Judge, Mississippi Circuit Court Eleventh Judicial District)*
Mailing address: P.O. Drawer 998, Clarksdale 38614-0998.
Telephone: (662) 624-3017.
Fax: (662) 624-2515

LITTLEJOHN, Talmadge D., Jr. *(Judge, Mississippi Chancery Court First Judicial District)* Elected Nov 2002 to term beginning Jan 2003. Term expires Dec 2006.
Mailing address: P.O. Box 869, New Albany 38652.
Telephone: (662) 534-6835.
Fax: (662) 534-6215

LOPER, Joseph H. *(Judge, Mississippi Circuit Court Fifth Judicial District)*
Mailing address: P.O. Box 616, Ackerman 39735.
Telephone: (662) 285-3818.
Fax: (662) 285-3160

LOVE, John C., Jr. *(Judge, Mississippi Chancery Court Sixth Judicial District)* Elected to term beginning Jan 1, 1975. Reelected 1978, 1982 and 1986. Elected at special election 1989. Reelected 1990, 1994, 1998 and 2002. Current term expires Dec 31, 2006. Born Jackson Mississippi July 3, 1938. Presbyterian. Educated at University of Mississippi B.A. 1960 LL.B. 1961. Admitted to practice Mississippi 1961. Began legal practice Kosciusko 1961.
Member Mississippi State Bar. Captain Mississippi National Guard 1961-68. Past President Kosciusko Jaycees and Kosciusko-Attala Chamber of Commerce. Enjoys hunting.
Mailing address: P.O. Box 673, Kosciusko 39090.
Telephone: (662) 289-3862.
Fax: (662) 289-7662

LUNDY, Mitchell M., Jr. *(Judge, Mississippi Chancery Court Third Judicial District)* Elected Nov 2002 to term beginning Jan 2003. Term expires Dec 2006.
Mailing address: P.O. Drawer 471, Grenada 38901.
Telephone: (662) 226-1343.
Fax: (662) 226-1347

LUTZ, William J. *(Judge, Mississippi Chancery Court Eleventh Judicial District)*
Mailing address: P.O. Box 404, Canton 39046.
Telephone: (601) 859-5783.
Fax: (601) 859-0795

LYNCHARD, Percy L. *(Judge, Mississippi Chancery Court Third Judicial District)*
Mailing address: P.O. Box 340, Hernando 38632.

LYNCHARD, PERCY L.—*Continued*
Telephone: (662) 429-5580.
Fax: (662) 429-1395

MASK, Jacqueline Estes *(Judge, Mississippi Chancery Court First Judicial District)* Elected Nov 1998 to term beginning Jan 4, 1999. Reelected Nov 5, 2002, current term expires Dec 31, 2006. Born Tupelo Mississippi May 12, 1958. Methodist. Educated at Mississippi State University for Women B.S. cum laude 1979 and University of Mississippi J.D. 1982. Index and Review Editor Mississippi Law Journal 1981-82. Admitted to practice Mississippi 1982, U.S. District Court District of Mississippi 1982 and U.S. Court of Appeals Fifth Circuit 1982. In legal practice Tupelo 1982-98.

Public Defender Lee County Youth Court 1983-98 and City of Tupelo 1987-92. Member National Association of Women Judges, The Mississippi Bar, Lee County and First District Bar Associations. Teacher Sunday School. Member Business and Professional Womens Club and Civitans.

Mailing address: P.O. Box 787, Tupelo 38802.
Telephone: (662) 680-6055.
Fax: (662) 680-6057

MASON, Jerry G. *(Judge, Mississippi Chancery Court Twelfth Judicial District)* Appointed by Governor William Winter Dec 1981 to term beginning Feb 1, 1982. Elected 1982 and 1986. Elected at special election 1989. Reelected 1990, 1994, 1998 and 2002. Current term expires Dec 31, 2006. Born Greenville Mississippi July 6, 1942. United Methodist. Educated at University of Mississippi B.A. 1964 J.D. 1969. Admitted to practice Mississippi 1969. In legal practice Meridian 1969-82.

Mailing address: P.O. Box 5681, Meridian 39302.
Telephone: (601) 482-9729.
Fax: (601) 486-4921

McCLURE, Melvin, Jr. *(Judge, Mississippi Chancery Court Third Judicial District)*
Mailing address: P.O. Box 248, Senatobia 38668.
Telephone: (662) 562-4809.
Fax: (662) 562-7731

McDANIEL, Kent *(Judge, Rankin County Court)* Appointed by Governor Kirk Fordice to term beginning Sept 1, 1997. Elected Nov 1998 and 2002. Current term expires Dec 31, 2006. Born Panama City Florida Sept 22, 1947. Presbyterian. Educated at Belhaven College B.S. cum laude 1969, University of Southern Mississippi M.S. with honors 1978 and Mississippi College School of Law J.D. with honors 1986. Research Editor Mississippi College Law Review 1984-85. Admitted to practice Mississippi 1986, U.S. District Courts Northern 1986 and Southern 1986 Districts of Mississippi and U.S. Court of Appeals Fifth Circuit 1986. In legal practice Jackson 1986-89 and Flowood 1995-97. Judge, Flowood Municipal Court 1995-97.

First Assistant U.S. Attorney Southern District of Mississippi 1989-95. Adjunct Faculty Mississippi College School of Law 1991-2003. 20th Special Forces Group 1968-73 and Military Police 1973-78 Mississippi National Guard.

Mailing address: P.O. Drawer 1599, Brandon 39043.
Telephone: (601) 825-1474.
Fax: (601) 825-1465

McGEHEE, W. Hollis *(Judge, Mississippi Chancery Court Fourth Judicial District)*
Mailing address: P.O. Box 279, Meadville 39653.
Telephone: (601) 384-3833.
Fax: (601) 384-4349

McKENZIE, Franklin C., Jr. *(Judge, Mississippi Chancery Court Nineteenth Judicial District)* Elected Nov 1994 to term beginning Jan 1995. Reelected Nov 1998 and 2002. Current term expires Dec 31, 2006. Born Laurel Mississippi Dec 19, 1946. United Methodist. Educated at University of Southern Mississippi B.A. 1968 and University of Mississippi J.D. 1972. Research Editor Mississippi Law Journal 1971-72. Member Phi Kappa Phi. Admitted to practice Mississippi 1970, U.S. District Courts Northern 1970 and Southern 1970 Districts of Mississippi and U.S. Court of Appeals Fifth Circuit 1970. In legal practice Laurel 1970-95.

City Attorney Laurel 1972-94. Corporate Counsel South Central Regional Medical Center 1984-95. Author "Search Incident to Arrest and the Automobile" Mississippi L. Jour. 1972. Attended General Jurisdiction The National Judicial College 1995. Mississippi Army National Guard 1968-78.

Mailing address: P.O. Box 1961, Laurel 39441.
Telephone: (601) 428-7625.
Fax: (601) 428-3119

McMILLIN, Roger H., Jr. *(Chief Judge, Court of Appeals of Mississippi)* Elected Nov 8, 1994 to term beginning Jan 1, 1995. Reelected 2002, current term expires Jan 1, 2011. Born New Albany Mississippi May 28, 1945. Presbyterian. Educated at Mississippi State University B.A. with honors 1967 and Memphis State University J.D. 1972. Admitted to practice Tennessee 1973, Georgia 1976 and Mississippi 1977. In legal practice New Albany Mississippi 1977-94. Lieutenant j.g. USN 1967-69.

Mailing address: P.O. Box 22847, Jackson 39225-2847.
Office: 656 North State Street, Jackson 39202.
Telephone: (601) 354-7410.
E-mail address: jmcmillin@mssc.state.ms.us

McPHAIL, Michael W. *(Judge, Forrest County Court)* Appointed by Governor William A. Allain to term beginning May 25, 1984. Reappointed 1987. Elected 1990, 1994, 1998 and 2002. Current term expires Dec 31, 2006. Also serves as Youth Court Judge. Born Hattiesburg Mississippi. Educated at University of Southern Mississippi B.S. 1974 and Mississippi College School of Law J.D. with honors 1978. Law Clerk to Hon. Harry Grey Walker, Mississippi Supreme Court 1978-79 and Magistrate Judge John M. Roper, U.S. District Court Southern District of Mississippi 1979-80. Admitted to practice Mississippi 1978 and U.S. District Court Southern District of Mississippi 1978. In legal practice Hattiesburg 1980-84. Judge, City Court of Lumberton 1980-83.

Assistant District Attorney Forrest and Perry Counties Jan 1, 1984 to May 24, 1984. Instructor in Legal Research and Circuit Court Practice University of Southern Mississippi. Member National Council of Juvenile and Family Court Judges, Mississippi State Bar and South Central Mississippi Bar Association. Recipient Most Dis-

MCPHAIL, MICHAEL W.—*Continued*
tinguished Juvenile Justice Advocate Award from Juvenile Justice Advisory Group 1989.
Mailing address: P.O. Box 190, Hattiesburg 39403-0190.
Telephone: (601) 545-6075.
Fax: (601) 545-6105

McRAE, Chuck *(Presiding Justice, Mississippi Supreme Court)* Elected Nov 1990 to term beginning Jan 1, 1991. Reelected 1998, current term expires Dec 31, 2006. Educated at Marietta College B.A. 1962 and Mississippi College School of Law J.D. cum laude 1970. In legal practice Pascagoula 1970-90. Special Chancellor, Mississippi Chancery Courts Twelfth, Fourteenth and Nineteenth Judicial Districts 1990. Special Judge, Mississippi Circuit Courts Twelfth, Fourteenth and Nineteenth Judicial Districts 1990.
Former Attorney Jackson County School Board and Pascagoula Police Association. Lifetime Member Mississippi Trial Lawyers Association. Member The Association of Trial Lawyers of America, American Judicature Society, Magnolia, Fifth Circuit, Eleventh Circuit, Federal and American Bar Associations. Taught and coached in high schools Moss Point Mississippi and Panama City Florida. Member Marietta College Athletic Founders Board and First United Methodist Church Pascagoula.
Mailing address: P.O. Box 117, Jackson 39205.
Office: Justice Building, 450 High Street, Jackson 39205.
Telephone: (601) 359-3697.
E-mail address: mcraecr@mssc.state.ms.us

MIDCALF, Robin Alfred *(Judge, Harrison County Court)* Elected Nov 1998 to term beginning Jan 4, 1999. Reelected Nov 2002, current term expires Dec 31, 2006. Born Gulfport Mississippi Nov 13, 1961. Catholic. Educated at William Carey College B.S. with honors 1985 and University of Mississippi J.D. 1988. Law Clerk to Hon. James E. Thomas, Mississippi Circuit Court Second Judicial District. Member Delta Theta Phi. Admitted to practice Mississippi 1988. In legal practice Gulfport 1988-98.
Attorney Mississippi Contract Criminal Defense Harrison County April 1989 to Aug 1992. Supervisor Harrison County Board of Supervisors Jan 1993 to Jan 1999. Member The Mississippi Bar, Harrison County and American Bar Associations. Named Citizen of the Year by Omega Psi Phi Fraternity 1994 and Career Woman 1998 from Lighthouse Business and Professional Women. Recipient President's Award from Local Brotherhood Union 1996. Listed in *Outstanding Young Women of America* 1997. Democrat. Member Mississippi Democratic Executive Committee 1995-96. Secretary Democratic County Conventions 1996. Delegate State Democratic Convention 1996. Board of Trustees Leadership Gulf Coast 1993-96. Board of Directors 1994-96 and Vice President of Operations 1995-96 United Way of South Mississippi. Board of Directors Gulf Pines Council Girl Scouts 1997. Board of Directors and Co-founder "Values + Education = Success" Mentoring Program. Lector, Reader, Eucharistic Minister and Member St. Therese's Catholic Church. Volunteer Christmas in April. Member Gulfport Branch NAACP, Mississippi Association of Supervisors (Education Committee), Mississippi Gulf Coast Area Chamber of Commerce and National Association of County Officials.
Mailing address: P.O. Box 1889, Gulfport 39502.
Telephone: (228) 865-4109.
Fax: (228) 865-4485
E-mail address: RAlfred@co.harrison.ms.us

MIDDLETON, Kennie E. *(Judge, Mississippi Chancery Court Seventeenth Judicial District)*
Mailing address: P.O. Box 10, Fayette 39069.
Telephone: (601) 786-6123.
Fax: (601) 786-6130

MILLS, Michael P. *(Judge, United States District Court Northern District of Mississippi)* Appointed for life by President George W. Bush to term beginning Nov 1, 2001. Born Itawamba County Mississippi. Educated at Itawamba Community College, University of Mississippi B.S. 1978 J.D. 1980 and University of Virginia School of Law LL.M. 2001. Admitted to practice Mississippi, U.S. Court of Appeals Fifth Circuit and U.S. Supreme Court. In legal practice Monroe County and Itawamba County 1980-95. Justice, Mississippi Supreme Court 1995 to Oct 31, 2001, appointed by Governor Kirk Fordice.
Commissioner National Conference of Commissioners on Uniform State Laws. Member The Federalist Society and The Mississippi Bar. Served twelve years in Mississippi Legislature. Director Mississippi Institute for Racial Reconciliation. Member Scottish Rite.
Office: 335 U.S. Courthouse, 911 Jackson Avenue West, Oxford 38655.
Telephone: (662) 234-1538.

MORGAN, Clarence E. "Cem", III *(Judge, Mississippi Circuit Court Fifth Judicial District)* Elected Nov 1994 to term beginning Jan 2, 1995. Reelected 1998 and 2002. Current term expires Dec 31, 2006. Born Kosciusko Mississippi Dec 19, 1945. Episcopalian. Educated at University of Mississippi B.A. 1968 J.D. 1970. Law Clerk to Hon. James P. Coleman, U.S. Court of Appeals Fifth Circuit 1970-71. Member Phi Alpha Delta. Admitted to practice Mississippi 1970. In legal practice Kosciusko 1970-94. Municipal Judge, City of Kosciusko 1980-94.
Attorney Attala County 1972-78. Member Mississippi State Bar. Attended general jurisdiction course The National Judicial College. Enjoys golf, hunting, fishing, travel and reading.
Mailing address: P.O. Box 721, Kosciusko 39090.
Telephone: (662) 289-2033.
Fax: (662) 289-1001

MYERS, William H. *(Judge, Court of Appeals of Mississippi)* Appointed by Governor Ronnie Musgrove to term beginning June 30, 2000. Educated at Mississippi State University and University of Mississippi School of Law J.D. Former Judge, Mississippi Chancery Court Sixteenth Judicial District.
Former Secretary, Vice Chairman and Chairman Chancery Judges Conference. Former Board Member and Past President Mississippi Gulf Coast YMCA. Member American Legion and Masons.
Mailing address: P.O. Box 22847, Jackson 39225-2847.
Office: 656 North State Street, Jackson 39202.
Telephone: (601) 354-7410.
E-mail address: jmyers@mssc.state.ms.us

NICOLS, Alfred G., Jr. *(Magistrate Judge, United States District Court Southern District of Mississippi)* Appointed by U.S. District Court judges to term beginning July 5, 1991. Born Morton Mississippi Feb 18, 1941. Member First Presbyterian Church of Jackson. Educated at University of Mississippi B.A. 1963 J.D. 1965. Associate Editor Mississippi Law Journal 1965. Member Sigma Chi. Admitted to practice Mississippi 1965. Began legal practice Jackson 1967. In legal practice Brandon 1970-78 and Pearl 1978-80. Former Judge, Mississippi Circuit Court Twentieth Judicial District, appointed by Governor William Winter to term beginning Sept 10, 1980.

Member Mississippi State Bar, Rankin County and American Bar Associations. Captain U.S. Army 1965-67.

Office: U.S. Courthouse, 245 East Capitol Street, Room 502, Jackson 39201.

Telephone: (601) 965-4525.

OSBORNE, Solomon C. *(Judge, Leflore County Court)*

Mailing address: P.O. Box 452, Greenwood 38935-0452.

Telephone: (662) 445-7945.

Fax: (662) 445-7959

OWENS, Denise *(Judge, Mississippi Chancery Court Fifth Judicial District)* Elected at special election 1989. Reelected 1990, 1994, 1998 and 2002. Current term expires Dec 31, 2006. Born Jackson Mississippi Aug 11, 1954. Educated at Tougaloo College B.A. in Political Science cum laude 1976 and George Washington University J.D. 1979. Admitted to practice Mississippi 1979 and U.S. Court of Appeals Fifth Circuit. In legal practice Jackson 1983-89.

Staff Attorney Central Mississippi Legal Services 1979-82. Assistant City Prosecutor Jackson 1983. Author "Custodial Considerations in Trial Custody Cases" 1993. Instructor in Legal Writing, Criminology and Constitutional Law Tougaloo College since 1979, Legal Writing and Real Property, Wills and Estates Hinds Community College since 1979 and Business Law Jackson State University. Member Mississippi Supreme Court Pro Se Task Force, Mississippi Conference of Chancery Court Judges (Secretary 1996-98, Program Chairperson/Vice Chair 1998-2000, President 2000-02), The Association of Trial Lawyers of America (Judicial Division), The Mississippi Bar (Gender Bias Task Force, Race and Ethics Bias Task Force, Family Law Section, Vice Chair Delivery of Legal Services Committee, Facilitator Law School Professionalism Orientation Program 1999-2000), Magnolia (President Judicial Council), Hinds County, National (Judicial Division) and American (Judicial Division) Bar Associations. Attended Court Practice Institute 1981 and seminars on General Jurisdiction I, General Jurisdiction II, Advanced Evidence, Legal Writing, Essential Judicial Skills and Trial Management The National Judicial College 1989-98. Board member Catholic Charities 1990-92.

Mailing address: P.O. Box 686, Jackson 39205.

Telephone: (601) 968-6545.

Fax: (601) 968-6794

PARKER, Mike T. *(Judge, Hinds County Court)*

Mailing address: P.O. Box 327, Jackson 39205.

Telephone: (601) 968-6671.

Fax: (601) 973-5575

PATRICK, Isadore W. *(Judge, Mississippi Circuit Court Ninth Judicial District)* Elected April 14, 1989 to term beginning June 6, 1989. Reelected Nov 6, 1994, Nov 1998 and 2002. Current term expires Dec 31, 2006. Born Jackson Mississippi. Catholic. Educated at Jackson State University B.S. with honors 1973 and University of Mississippi J.D. 1981. Admitted to practice Mississippi 1981 and U.S. District Courts Northern 1981 and Southern 1987 Districts of Mississippi.

Assistant District Attorney Vicksburg 1981-89. Member National Bar Judicial Council, American Judges Association, American Judicature Society, Magnolia and American Bar Associations. Advisor Dispute Resolution Conference The National Judicial College San Diego California 1996. Board Member Salvation Army. Member Jackson State Alumni. Enjoys tennis, golf and reading novels.

Mailing address: P.O. Box 351, Vicksburg 39180.

Telephone: (601) 634-8042.

Fax: (601) 634-8049

PATTEN, Edward E., Jr. *(Judge, Mississippi Chancery Court Fifteenth Judicial District)* Elected to term beginning Jan 1, 1999. Reelected 2002, current term expires Dec 31, 2006. Born Columbia South Carolina Nov 3, 1952. Baptist. Educated at University of Mississippi B.S. 1975 J.D. 1977. Member Rho Chi and Phi Delta Phi. Admitted to practice Mississippi 1978, U.S. District Courts Northern and Southern Districts of Mississippi and U.S. Supreme Court. In legal practice Hazlehurst 1978-1999.

Member The Mississippi Bar and American Bar Association. Enjoys golfing and fishing. Personal Statement or Quote: "A judge is more learned than witty, more reverent than plausible, and more advised than confident. Above all things, integrity is their portion and proper value" (Francis Bacon).

Mailing address: P.O. Drawer 707, Hazlehurst 39083.

Telephone: (601) 894-6196.

Fax: (601) 894-4792

E-mail address: e.patten.jr@att.net

PATTON, Houston J. *(Judge, Hinds County Court)*

Mailing address: P.O. Box 327, Jackson 39205.

Telephone: (601) 968-6663.

Fax: (601) 973-5575

PEPPER, W. Allen, Jr. *(Judge, United States District Court Northern District of Mississippi)* Appointed for life by President Bill Clinton to term beginning July 7, 1999. Born Greenwood Mississippi July 20, 1941. Educated at University of Mississippi B.A. 1963 J.D. 1968. In legal practice Cleveland 1968-1999.

Mailing address: P.O. Box 370, Greenville 38702-0370.

Telephone: (662) 335-4416.

PERSONS, Jim *(Judge, Mississippi Chancery Court Eighth Judicial District)* Elected Nov 2002 to term beginning Jan 2003. Term expires Dec 2006.

Mailing address: P.O. Box 457, Gulfport 39502.

Telephone: (228) 868-3680.

PICKARD, Lamar *(Judge, Mississippi Circuit Court Twenty-second Judicial District)*

Mailing address: P.O. Box 310, Hazlehurst 39083.

Telephone: (601) 894-3311.

Fax: (601) 894-3315

PICKERING, Charles W., Sr. *(Judge, United States District Court Southern District of Mississippi)* Appointed for life by President George Bush to term beginning Oct 1, 1990. Born Jones County Mississippi May 29, 1937. Educated at University of Mississippi B.A. 1959 J.D. 1961. In legal practice Laurel 1961-90. Judge, Mississippi Municipal Court 1968.

Prosecuting Attorney Laurel 1963-64. County Attorney Jones County 1964-68.

Office: 228 U.S. Courthouse, 701 North Main Street, Hattiesburg 39401.

Telephone: (601) 583-4422.

PITTMAN, Edwin Lloyd *(Chief Justice, Mississippi Supreme Court)* Elected to term beginning Jan 1, 1989. Reelected 1996, current term expires Dec 31, 2004. Former Presiding Justice. Born Hattiesburg Mississippi Jan 2, 1935. Baptist. Educated at University of Southern Mississippi B.S. and University of Mississippi J.D. Admitted to practice Mississippi 1960, U.S. District Courts Northern and Southern Districts of Mississippi, U.S. Court of Appeals Fifth Circuit and U.S. Supreme Court. In legal practice Hattiesburg 1960-76.

Senator 1964-72, State Treasurer 1976-80, Secretary of State 1980-84 and Attorney General 1984-88 Mississippi. Member Executive Committee National Association of Attorneys General 1985-87. Chairman Southern Conference of Attorneys General 1987. Attended Institute for Advanced Judicial Studies June 11-24, 1989 and Spring Conference March 21-23, 1991 Mississippi Judicial College, Harvard School for Lawyers/Judges Aug 28, 1989 to Sept 1, 1989 and Appellate Judges Seminar American Bar Association Aug 19-23, 1990. Recipient Humanized Education Award for 1989 from Mississippi Association of Educators and HUB City Award 1989. Brigadier General Mississippi National Guard (retired). Charter member University of Southern Mississippi Alumni Hall of Fame.

Mailing address: P.O. Box 117, Jackson 39205.

Office: Justice Building, 450 High Street, Jackson 39205.

Telephone: (601) 359-3697.

E-mail address: jpittman@mssc.state.ms.us

PRICE, John *(Judge, Pike County Court)*
Office: 294 East Laurel Street, Magnolia 39652.
Telephone: (601) 783-2262.
Fax: (601) 783-5185

PRICE, John S., Jr. *(Judge, Warren County Court)*
Mailing address: P.O. Box 351, Vicksburg 39181.
Telephone: (601) 638-8026.
Fax: (601) 631-8816

PRICHARD, R. I., III *(Judge, Mississippi Circuit Court Fifteenth Judicial District)* Elected to term beginning Oct 1972. Reelected 1974, 1978 and 1982. Elected at special election 1989. Reelected 1990, 1994, 1998 and 2002. Current term expires Dec 31, 2006. Born Atlanta Georgia Dec 4, 1938. Baptist. Educated at University of Alabama B.S. 1960 J.D. 1963. Admitted to practice Mississippi 1963 and Alabama 1963. Began legal practice Picayune Mississippi 1963. Judge, Picayune City Court 1969-72. Referee, Pearl River County Youth Court 1969-72.

Adjunct Instructor University of Southern Mississippi. Member American Judicature Society, Alabama State Bar, Mississippi State Bar and American Bar Association. Recipient Jurist of the Year Award from Lamar County 2001 and Judicial Excellence Award from The Mississippi Bar 2002. Member Picayune Rotary Club (Past President, Vice President and Board of Directors) and Pine Burr Area Council Boy Scouts of America (Executive Board, Eagle Scout). Former member Picayune Jaycees (Board of Directors), YMCA (Board of Directors) and Chamber of Commerce.

Mailing address: P.O. Box 1075, Picayune 39466.
Telephone: (601) 794-6035.
Fax: (601) 794-2801

PRISOCK, Edward C. *(Judge, Mississippi Chancery Court Sixth Judicial District)*
Office: 201 North Hudson Avenue, Louisville 39339.
Telephone: (662) 773-5811.
Fax: (662) 773-4746

READY, George B. *(Judge, Mississippi Circuit Court Seventeenth Judicial District)* Elected Nov 4, 1994 to term beginning Jan 2, 1995. Reelected 1998 and 2002. Current term expires Dec 31, 2006. Catholic. Educated at University of Mississippi B.B.A. with honors 1977 J.D. 1980. Admitted to practice Mississippi 1980, U.S. District Courts Northern 1980 and Southern 1980 Districts of Mississippi, U.S. Court of Appeals Fifth Circuit 1983 and U.S. Supreme Court 1989. In legal practice DeSoto County 1981-94. Judge, City of Southaven 1985-91.

Member Mississippi State Bar and American Bar Associations. Attended The National Judicial College 1995. State Senator 1992-94.

Mailing address: P.O. Box 127, Hernando 38632.
Telephone: (662) 429-4110.
Fax: (662) 429-4111

RICHARDSON, Samac S. *(Judge, Mississippi Circuit Court Twentieth Judicial District)* Born Union Mississippi May 1, 1947. Baptist. Educated at Mississippi State University B.S. in Accounting 1970 and Jackson School of Law J.D. 1975. Member Sigma Delta Kappa. Admitted to practice Mississippi 1978. In legal practice Brandon 1979-82 and 1988-93. Hearings Officer Rankin County School Board 1988-93. Former Judge, Rankin County Court, appointed by Governor Kirk Fordice to term beginning Jan 1993.

Assistant District Attorney Twentieth Judicial District 1982-88. Public Defender City of Brandon and Rankin County 1988-93. Board Attorney City of Pearl 1990-93. Bar Commissioner Twentieth Circuit Court District July 1990 to Jan 1993. Member Mississippi Supreme Court Bar Complaint Tribunal Aug 1995 to Aug 2001. Former Member and Chair Conference of County Court Judges. Member Advisory Committee on Rules Mississippi Supreme Court, Conference of Circuit Court Judges, The Mississippi Bar, Madison County and Rankin County Bar Associations. Sergeant E-5 367th Mnt. Co. Mississippi National Guard July 1967 to July 1973. Non-Partisan. Member Masonic Lodge, York Rite Bodies, Scottish Rite Bodies, Shrine, Gideons and Eastern Star.

Mailing address: P.O. Box 1885, Brandon 39043.
Telephone: (601) 825-1476.
Fax: (601) 824-2441

ROBERTS, Edwin H., Jr. *(Judge, Mississippi Chancery Court Eighteenth Judicial District)* Elected Nov 2002 to term beginning Jan 2003. Term expires Dec 2006.

Mailing address: P.O. Box 49, Oxford 38655.

ROBERTS, EDWIN H., JR.—*Continued*
Telephone: (662) 236-0233.
Fax: (662) 236-3590

ROBERTS, Larry E. *(Judge, Mississippi Circuit Court Tenth Judicial District)* Appointed by Governor William A. Allain to term beginning Dec 31, 1986. Elected at special election 1989. Reelected 1990, 1994, 1998 and 2002. Current term expires Dec 31, 2006. Born Cleveland Mississippi June 27, 1949. Baptist. Educated at Mississippi State University 1966 and University of Mississippi B.B.A. 1970 J.D. 1973. Admitted to practice Mississippi 1973. In legal practice Meridian 1973-78. Judge, Lauderdale County Court 1979-86.

Member Mississippi State Bar, Lauderdale County and American Bar Associations. Lieutenant Colonel USAR 1971-95.
Mailing address: P.O. Box 1002, Meridian 39302.
Telephone: (601) 482-9742.
Fax: (601) 484-3970

ROBINSON, Stuart *(Judge, Mississippi Chancery Court Fifth Judicial District)*
Mailing address: P.O. Box 686, Jackson 39205.
Telephone: (601) 968-6551.
Fax: (601) 973-5554

ROPER, John M., Sr. *(Magistrate Judge, United States District Court Southern District of Mississippi)* Appointed by U.S. District Court judges to term beginning July 1, 1975. Reappointed July 1, 1983, 1991 and 1999. Current term expires July 1, 2007. Born Greenville Alabama Dec 11, 1942. Educated at Auburn University B.S. 1964 and Tulane University of Louisiana J.D. 1968.

Member Security Committee 1987-88 and Budget Committee 1988-97 Judicial Conference. Member Federal Magistrates Judges Association (Officer or Director 1976-86, President 1986-87), Alabama State Bar, Mississippi State Bar and Federal Bar Association.
Office: 150 Federal Building, 725 Martin Luther King Jr. Blvd., Biloxi 39530.
Telephone: (228) 432-8612.

RUSSELL, Dan Monroe, Jr. *(Senior Judge, United States District Court Southern District of Mississippi)* Appointed for life by President Lyndon B. Johnson to term beginning Oct 25, 1965. Assumed Senior status Oct 25, 1983, serves by assignment. Born Magee Mississippi March 15, 1913. Baptist. Educated at University of Mississippi B.A. in Law 1935 LL.B. 1937. Member Tau Kappa Alpha, Scribblers and Omicron Delta Kappa. Admitted to practice Mississippi 1938. Began legal practice Bay St. Louis 1938.

Important Decision: Joseph Zuccaro v. Humble Oil Company 1969. Advisory Board Mississippi Chapter The Federalist Society. Honorary Member Russell-Blass-Walker American Inns of Court. Lieutenant Commander USAS 1941-45. Democrat. Honorary Member Bay St. Louis and Gulfport Rotary Clubs.
Mailing address: P.O. Box 1930, Gulfport 39502-1930.
Telephone: (228) 863-2762.

SANDERS, Betty W. *(Judge, Mississippi Circuit Court Fourth Judicial District)*
Mailing address: P.O. Box 244, Greenwood 38935-0244.
Telephone: (662) 455-7946.
Fax: (662) 455-7959

SANDERS, Lillie Blackmon *(Judge, Mississippi Circuit Court Sixth Judicial District)*
Mailing address: P.O. Box 1384, Natchez 39121.
Telephone: (601) 445-7933.
Fax: (601) 445-2369

SENTER, L. T., Jr. *(Senior Judge, United States District Court Northern District of Mississippi)* Appointed for life by President Jimmy Carter 1979. Former Chief Judge. Assumed Senior status July 31, 1998, serves U.S. District Court Southern District of Mississippi by assignment. Born Fulton Mississippi July 30, 1933. Presbyterian. Educated at University of Southern Mississippi B.S. 1956 and University of Mississippi LL.B. 1959. Admitted to practice Mississippi 1959. Judge, Mississippi Circuit Court First Judicial District 1968-80.

County Prosecuting Attorney 1960-64. U.S. Commissioner 1966-68. Member Mississippi State Bar.
Office: 725 Dr. Martin Luther King Jr. Boulevard, Suite 229, Biloxi 39530.
Telephone: (228) 432-5833.

SHANDS, Rodney E. *(Judge, Mississippi Chancery Court First Judicial District)* Elected Nov 2002 to term beginning Jan 2003. Term expires Dec 2006.
Mailing address: P.O. Box 30, New Albany 38652.
Telephone: (662) 534-7603.
Fax: (662) 534-7881

SIGALAS, Sharon W. *(Judge, Jackson County Court)*
Office: 4903 Telephone Road, Pascagoula 39567.
Telephone: (228) 762-7370.
Fax: (228) 769-3411

SIMPSON, Steve *(Judge, Mississippi Circuit Court Second Judicial District)*
Mailing address: P.O. Box 1570, Gulfport 39502.
Telephone: (228) 865-4220.
Fax: (228) 865-4376

SINGLETARY, William H. *(Judge, Mississippi Chancery Court Fifth Judicial District)*
Mailing address: P.O. Box 686, Jackson 39205.
Telephone: (601) 968-6548.
Fax: (601) 973-5554

SMITH, Al *(Judge, Mississippi Circuit Court Eleventh Judicial District)* Appointed by Governor David Ronald Musgrove to term beginning July 1, 2000. Elected Nov 2002, current term expires Dec 31, 2006.
Mailing address: P.O. Box 478, Cleveland 38732.
Telephone: (662) 843-3346.
Fax: (662) 846-2930

SMITH, James W., Jr. *(Presiding Justice, Mississippi Supreme Court)* Born Louisville Mississippi Oct 28, 1943. Protestant. Educated at Hinds Junior College 1963, University of Southern Mississippi B.S. 1965, Jackson School of Law J.D. 1972 and Mississippi College M.Ed. with honors 1973. Member Sigma Delta Kappa. Admitted to practice Mississippi 1972, U.S. District Courts Northern 1973 and Southern 1973 Districts of Mississippi and U.S. Court of Appeals Fifth Circuit 1974. In legal practice Pearl 1972-78 and Brandon 1979-80. Former Judge, Rankin County Court, appointed by Governor William Winter to term beginning May 15, 1982.

SMITH, JAMES W., JR.—*Continued*

Prosecuting Attorney City of Pearl 1973-80. Rankin County Attorney 1976-77. District Attorney Twentieth Judicial District 1977-82. Instructor in Courtroom Procedure and Testifying Mississippi Law Enforcement Training Academy 1980-91. Member Mississippi Youth Court Judges, Mississippi State Bar, Rankin County and American Bar Associations. Attended Mississippi Judicial College. Recipient Outstanding Young Educator of the Year Award from Pearl Jaycees 1969. Named Wildlife Conservationist of the Year Rankin County 1988. Listed in *Who's Who in American Law.* Sergeant E-5 U.S. Army 1966-69. Previously employed as teacher and principal Rankin County Schools 1969-72. Republican. Member Rankin County Republican Executive Committee. Member National Wildlife Federation, National Rifle Association, National Wild Turkey Federation and Masons. Enjoys hunting and fishing.

Mailing address: P.O. Box 117, Jackson 39205.

Office: Justice Building, 450 High Street, Jackson 39205.

Telephone: (601) 359-3697.

E-mail address: jsmith@mssc.state.ms.us

SMITH, Mike *(Judge, Mississippi Circuit Court Fourteenth Judicial District)*

Mailing address: P.O. Box 549, McComb 39649.

Telephone: (601) 684-3400.

Fax: (601) 684-2700

SMITH, Richard *(Judge, Mississippi Circuit Court Fourth Judicial District)* Appointed by Governor Ronnie Musgrove to term beginning June 2001. Former Judge, Leflore County Court.

Mailing address: P.O. Box 1953, Greenwood 38930.

Telephone: (662) 453-1429.

Fax: (662) 455-9056

SOUTHWICK, Leslie H. *(Presiding Judge, Court of Appeals of Mississippi)* Elected Nov 1994 to term beginning Jan 1, 1995. Reelected Nov 1998, current term expires Dec 31, 2006. Born Edinburg Texas Feb 10, 1950. Catholic. Educated at Rice University B.A. cum laude 1972 and University of Texas J.D. 1975. Law Clerk to Chief Judge John F. Onion, Jr., Texas Court of Criminal Appeals 1975-76 and Hon. Charles Clark, U.S. Court of Appeals Fifth Circuit 1976-77. Admitted to practice Texas 1975 (inactive) and Mississippi 1977. In legal practice Jackson Mississippi 1977-89.

Deputy Assistant Attorney General Civil Division U.S. Department of Justice Aug 1, 1989 to Jan 20, 1993. Member Mississippi Constitution Study Commission 1985-86. Author *Presidential Also-Rans and Running Mates, 1788-1996* McFarland 1984 2nd edition 1998; "State Constitution Revision: Mississippi & the South" Mississippi Lawyer 21, 1985; "Methods of Constitutional Revision: Which Way Mississippi?" 56 Mississippi L. Jour. 17, 1986; "A Tribute to Chief Judge Charles Clark" 12 Mississippi College L. Rev. 355, 1992; "The Mississippi Court of Appeals: History, Procedures, & First Year's Jurisprudence" 65 Mississippi L. Jour. 593, 1996; "Mississippi Supreme Court Elections: A Historical Perspective 1916-1996" 18 Mississippi College L. Rev. 115, 1998; and numerous legal and historical articles for Mississippi Law Journal, Mississippi College Law Review and *The Wall Street Journal.* Important Opinions: Hynson v. Jeffries ("open mines" doctrine for producing wells, first published opinion of Court of Appeals) 667 So. 2d 639 Miss. Ct. App. 1997; Pearson v. Columbus & Greenville Railway (federal preemption regarding railroad crossing accidents) 737 So. 2d 390 Miss. Ct. App. 1998; Dawson v. Townsend & Sons, Inc. (joinder of intentional and negligent tortfeasors in same suit) 735 So. 2d 1131 Miss. Ct. App. 1999; McMillan v. Aru (homestead exemption) 773 So. 2d 355 Miss. Ct. App. 2000; Myers v. State (State's violation of plea agreement) 770 So. 2d 542 Miss. Ct. App. 2000; Wolf v. Stanley Works (Mississippi Products Liability Act) 757 So. 2d 316 Miss. Ct. App. 2000; and Mills v. State (dissent, present sense impression hearsay) 763 So. 2d 924, 930 Miss Ct. App. 2000. Adjunct Professor of Legislation and Administrative Law Mississippi College School of Law 1985-89 and since 1998. Speaker on civil rules, financial fraud, school law and energy seminars. Bencher Charles Clark American Inns of Court since 1995. Named Volunteer of the Year by Hinds County Mental Health Association 1981 and 1985. Recipient Best Reference Work of the Year Award from American Library Association 1985. Major Mississippi National Guard JAGC. Member Hinds County and State Executive Committees Republican Party. Campaign Manager Mississippi 1980 and Chairman Mississippi Steering Committee 1988 George Bush Presidential Campaigns. Alternate Delegate 1984 and Delegate 1988 Republican National Conventions. Member Hinds County Mental Health Association (President 1981-82) and Mississippi Economic Council (Councils on Government and Business 1987-89). Volunteer Habitat for Humanity. Interested in reading and writing about American history and law. Enjoys jogging.

Mailing address: P.O. Box 22847, Jackson 39225-2847.

Office: 656 North State Street, Jackson 39202.

Telephone: (601) 354-7410.

E-mail address: jsouthwick@mssc.state.ms.us

SPRINGER, Sarah P. *(Judge, Mississippi Chancery Court Twelfth Judicial District)* Elected Nov 8, 1994 to term beginning Jan 1, 1995. Reelected 1998 and 2002. Current term expires Dec 31, 2006. Born Leesburg Virginia Aug 25, 1956. Episcopalian. Educated at University of South Carolina B.A. with honors 1977 J.D. 1980. Admitted to practice Texas 1980 and Mississippi 1981. In legal practice Austin Texas 1980-81 and Meridian Mississippi 1981-94.

Delegate Chancery Judges Conference since 1997. Member National Association of Women Judges and American Bar Associations. Attended general jurisdiction course The National Judicial College Sept 1995. Named Woman of the Year Meridian Star 1993 and Pro Bono Lawyer of the Year Mississippi State Bar 1994. Recipient People's Choice Award Meridian Star 1993 and President's Award Mississippi State Bar 1994. Member Earnest Workers Circle, Kings Daughters and Sons Board, Key Chapter and Red Cross. Interests include travel and computers.

Mailing address: P.O. Box 5165, Meridian 39302.

Telephone: (601) 482-9729.

Fax: (601) 486-4921

STARRETT, Keith *(Judge, Mississippi Circuit Court Fourteenth Judicial District)* Appointed by Governor Kirk Fordice to term beginning July 1, 1992. Elected Nov 8, 1994, Nov 1998 and Nov 2002. Current term expires Dec 31, 2006. Born McComb Mississippi. Baptist. Educated at Mississippi State University B.S. 1972

STARRETT, KEITH—*Continued*
and University of Mississippi J.D. 1974. Admitted to practice Mississippi 1974 and U.S. District Courts Northern 1974 and Southern 1979 Districts of Mississippi. In legal practice Magnolia 1975-89 and McComb 1989-92.

Member Mississippi State Bar.

Mailing address: P.O. Box 1913, McComb 39649.
Office: 299 Apache Drive, McComb 39649.
Telephone: (601) 684-0603.
Fax: (601) 684-6482

STECKLER, Sanford R. *(Judge, Mississippi Chancery Court Eighth Judicial District)*
Mailing address: P.O. Box 1719, Gulfport 39502.
Telephone: (228) 868-3379.
Fax: (228) 865-1646

SUMNER, James C., Jr. *(Magistrate Judge, United States District Court Southern District of Mississippi)* Appointed by U.S. District Court judges. Former Judge, Mississippi Circuit Court Fifth Judicial District.

Office: 400 U.S. Courthouse, 245 East Capitol Street, Jackson 39201.
Telephone: (601) 965-4292.

TERRY, Jerry O. *(Judge, Mississippi Circuit Court Second Judicial District)*
Mailing address: P.O. Box 1461, Gulfport 39502.
Telephone: (228) 865-4104.
Fax: (228) 867-6536

THOMAS, Gwendolyn J. *(Judge, Bolivar County Court)* Elected to term beginning Jan 2, 2003. Term expires Dec 2006. Born Selma Alabama Nov 24, 1947. Catholic. Educated at Cleveland State University B.A. 1972 and Howard University School of Law J.D. 1976. Recipient American Jurisprudence Award. Member Phi Alpha Delta. Admitted to practice Mississippi 1979. In legal practice Cleveland 1988-2002. Judge, Rosedale Municipal Court 1980-93. Judge, Cleveland Municipal Court 1989-2002.

Family Master Bolivar County 1991-2003. Member The Mississippi Bar, Magnolia, Bolivar County and National Bar Associations. Board of Directors Bolivar County Chamber of Commerce. Member Alpha Kappa Alpha Sorority, United Way and NAACP. Enjoys cooking, reading, traveling, tours and antiques. Personal Statement or Quote: "Act with respect and dignity before the court."

Mailing address: P.O. Box 188, Cleveland 38732-0188.
Office: 200 Court Street, Cleveland 38732.
Telephone: (662) 843-7175.
Fax: (662) 843-5337
E-mail address: judgegjt@tecinfo.com

THOMAS, Hudson L. *(Judge, Yazoo County Court)*
Mailing address: P.O. Box 296, Yazoo City 39194.
Telephone: (662) 746-5214.
Fax: (662) 746-9685

THOMAS, James E. *(Judge, Court of Appeals of Mississippi)* Elected to term beginning Jan 1, 1995. Reelected 2000, current term expires Jan 1, 2009. Born Columbia Mississippi March 1, 1950. Educated at University of Southern Mississippi M.S. 1971 and University of Mississippi School of Law J.D. 1973. Admitted to practice Mississippi 1973 and U.S. District Court Northern District of Mississippi 1973. In legal practice Biloxi 1973-74. Judge, Mississippi Circuit Court Second Judicial District Jan 1, 1983 to Dec 31, 1994.

Assistant District Attorney Second Judicial District 1974-82. Member American Judges Association, Mississippi State Bar and American Bar Association.

Mailing address: P.O. Box 22847, Jackson 39225-2847.
Office: 656 North State Street, Jackson 39202.
Telephone: (601) 354-7410.
E-mail address: jthomas@mssc.state.ms.us

THOMAS, James H. C., Jr. *(Judge, Mississippi Chancery Court Tenth Judicial District)*
Mailing address: P.O. Box 807, Hattiesburg 39403-0808.
Telephone: (601) 545-6028.
Fax: (601) 545-6080

THOMAS, Kenneth *(Judge, Mississippi Circuit Court Eleventh Judicial District)* Former Judge, Bolivar County Court.

Mailing address: P.O. Box 548, Cleveland 38732.
Telephone: (662) 846-2939.
Fax: (662) 846-2937

VLAHOS, Kosta N. *(Judge, Mississippi Circuit Court Second Judicial District)*
Mailing address: P.O. Box 7575, Gulfport 39506.
Telephone: (228) 865-4220.
Fax: (228) 865-4376

VOLLOR, Frank *(Judge, Mississippi Circuit Court Ninth Judicial District)*
Mailing address: P.O. Box 351, Vicksburg 39180.
Telephone: (601) 638-8981.
Fax: (601) 630-8033
E-mail address: circuitjudgefv@co.warren.ms.us

WALKER, Robert H. *(Judge, Mississippi Circuit Court Second Judicial District)*
Mailing address: P.O. Box 695, Gulfport 39502.
Telephone: (228) 865-4165.
Fax: (228) 865-1636

WALLER, William L., Jr. *(Justice, Mississippi Supreme Court)* Elected Nov 1996 to term beginning Jan 1998. Term expires Dec 31, 2005. Born Jackson Mississippi Feb 9, 1952. Baptist. Educated at Mississippi State University B.S. in General Business 1974 and University of Mississippi School of Law J.D. 1977. Member Phi Alpha Delta. In legal practice 1977-97. Judge, Jackson Municipal Court Jan 1995 to July 1996.

Barrister Charles Clark American Inn of Court 1989-91. Member Christian Legal Society, The Mississippi Bar, Hinds County and American Bar Associations. Brigadier General Mississippi National Guard (Commander 66th Troop Command). Former General Counsel Central Mississippi Chapter of the Lupus Foundation of America. Former Board Member and Chairman Jackson Council of Neighborhoods. Sunday school teacher and deacon First Baptist Church Jackson.

Mailing address: P.O. Box 117, Jackson 39205.
Telephone: (601) 359-3697.
Fax: (601) 359-2443

WARD, George *(Judge, Mississippi Chancery Court Seventeenth Judicial District)*
Mailing address: P.O. Box 1144, Natchez 39121.

WARD, GEORGE—*Continued*

Telephone: (601) 442-7454.
Fax: (601) 445-7913

WARD, Michael H. *(Judge, Harrison County Court)* Former Judge, Harrison County Family Court.
Mailing address: P.O. Box 7017, Gulfport 39506-7017.
Telephone: (228) 865-7000.
Fax: (228) 865-7012

WATTS, Pat H., Jr. *(Judge, Mississippi Chancery Court Sixteenth Judicial District)*
Mailing address: P.O. Box 998, Pascagoula 39568-0998.
Telephone: (228) 769-3193.
Fax: (228) 769-3397

WEATHERSBY, Jane R. *(Judge, Mississippi Chancery Court Ninth Judicial District)*
Mailing address: P.O. Box 1380, Indianola 38751.
Telephone: (662) 887-7070.
Fax: (662) 887-7071

WILLARD, William *(Judge, Mississippi Chancery Court Seventh Judicial District)*
Mailing address: P.O. Box 22, Clarksdale 38614.
Telephone: (662) 624-3003.
Fax: (662) 624-3078

WILLIAMS, Johnny Lee *(Judge, Mississippi Chancery Court Tenth Judicial District)*
Mailing address: P.O. Box 1664, Hattiesburg 39403.
Telephone: (601) 545-6037.
Fax: (601) 545-6038

WILSON, Marie *(Judge, Mississippi Chancery Court Ninth Judicial District)* Elected Nov 2002 to term beginning Jan 2003. Term expires Dec 2006.
Mailing address: P.O. Box 1762, Greeneville 38702-1762.
Telephone: (662) 334-2685.
Fax: (662) 334-2782

WILSON, T. Larry *(Judge, Jackson County Court)*
Mailing address: P.O. Box 998, Pascagoula 39568.
Telephone: (228) 769-3037.
Fax: (228) 762-7385

WINGATE, Henry T. *(Judge, United States District Court Southern District of Mississippi)* Appointed for life by President Ronald Reagan to term beginning Oct 17, 1985. Born Jackson Mississippi Jan 6, 1947. Educated at Grinnell College B.A. 1969 and Yale Law School J.D. 1972. Law Clerk to Community Legal Aid 1972-73. In legal practice Jackson 1973.

Special Assistant Attorney General Mississippi 1976-80. Assistant District Attorney Seventh Circuit Court District 1980-84. Assistant U.S. Attorney Southern District of Mississippi 1984-85.

Office: 109 U.S. Courthouse, 245 East Capitol Street, Jackson 39201.
Telephone: (601) 965-4042.

WISE, Patricia D. *(Judge, Mississippi Chancery Court Fifth Judicial District)* Elected at special election June 1989. Reelected 1990, 1994, 1998 and 2002. Current term expires Dec 31, 2006. Born Memphis Tennessee Aug 3, 1951. Baptist. Educated at University of Mississippi B.S. 1971 M.C.D. 1976 J.D. 1984. Law Clerk to Hon. Reuben V. Anderson, Mississippi Circuit Court Seventh Judicial District 1984. Admitted to practice Mississippi 1984. In legal practice Jackson 1984-89.

Member Mississippi Women Lawyers Association, Conference of Chancery Court Judges, Mississippi State Bar, Magnolia, Hinds County and National Bar Associations. Faculty Seminar Speaker The National Judicial College, Mississippi Judicial College, Mississippi Women Lawyers Association, Mississippi Pro Bono Project and Magnolia Bar Association. Recipient Black Women's Political Action Forum Award of Distinction University of Mississippi. Previously employed as public school educator and speech pathologist. Democrat. Former member Hinds County Democratic Executive Committee. Member Zeta Phi Beta, Inc., Links, Inc. and NAACP. Enjoys reading and collecting coffee mugs.

Mailing address: P.O. Box 686, Jackson 39205.
Telephone: (601) 968-6549.
Fax: (601) 968-6794

YERGER, W. Swan *(Judge, Mississippi Circuit Court Seventh Judicial District)* Appointed by Governor Kirk Fordice to term beginning Jan 1, 1997. Elected Nov 1998. Reelected Nov 2002, current term expires Dec 31, 2006. Born Jackson Mississippi June 11, 1932. Episcopalian. Educated at Virginia Military Institute 1950-52, University of Mississippi B.A. 1954 and University of Virginia LL.B. 1958. Member Phi Delta Phi. Admitted to practice Mississippi 1958, U.S. District Courts Northern 1959 and Southern 1959 Districts of Mississippi, U.S. Court of Appeals Fifth Circuit 1961 and U.S. Supreme Court 1980. In legal practice Jackson 1958-96.

Treasurer Mississippi Conference of Circuit Judges 2000-02. Former President Mississippi Chapter Federal Bar Association. Former Board Member Hinds County Bar Association. Judicial Fellow and Former Fellow American College of Trial Lawyers. Member The Mississippi Bar (Former Chairman Ethics Committee). Attended The National Judicial College 1997. Lieutenant USAF 1954-56 and Captain USAFR 1957-62. Former Chairman of the Board Jackson Metropolitan YMCA. Charter President North Jackson Rotary Club. Enjoys spectator sports, history and travel.

Mailing address: P.O. Box 327, Jackson 39205.
Telephone: (601) 968-6661.
Fax: (601) 948-2689

ZEBERT, Thomas L. *(Judge, Mississippi Chancery Court Twentieth Judicial District)* Elected Nov 1994 to term beginning Jan 3, 1995. Reelected Nov 1998 and 2002. Current term expires Dec 31, 2006. Born Winchester Indiana. Protestant. Educated at Hinds Junior College A.A. and Mississippi College School of Law LL.B. Admitted to practice Mississippi 1963, U.S. District Courts Northern 1963 and Southern 1963 Districts of Mississippi, U.S. Court of Appeals Fifth Circuit 1965 and U.S. Supreme Court 1968. In legal practice Pearl 1963-95. Judge, Rankin County Youth Court 1993-95 (part time).

Rankin County Attorney 1968-72. Recipient Justice Achievement Award 1995. Sergeant USAF Strategic Air Command. Enjoys wood working, lawn work and golf.

Mailing address: P.O. Box 1437, Brandon 39043.
Telephone: (601) 824-1473.
Fax: (601) 824-2437

MISSOURI

Capital JEFFERSON CITY

UNITED STATES DISTRICT COURTS DISTRICTS OF MISSOURI

Within Missouri there are two United States District Courts. For descriptive information refer to the United States Courts section.

EASTERN DISTRICT consists of three divisions.

Eastern Division includes Crawford, Dent, Franklin, Gasconade, Iron, Jefferson, Lincoln, Maries, Phelps, St. Charles, St. Francois, St. Louis, Ste. Genevieve, Warren and Washington counties and the city of St. Louis. The court sits at St. Louis.

Northern Division includes Adair, Audrain, Chariton, Clark, Knox, Lewis, Linn, Macon, Marion, Monroe, Montgomery, Pike, Ralls, Randolph, Schuyler, Scotland and Shelby counties. The court sits at Hannibal.

Southeastern Division includes Bollinger, Butler, Cape Girardeau, Carter, Dunklin, Madison, Mississippi, New Madrid, Pemiscot, Perry, Reynolds, Ripley, Scott, Shannon, Stoddard and Wayne counties. The court sits at Cape Girardeau.

Chief Judge

Carol E. Jackson

Judges

Jean C. Hamilton
Charles A. Shaw
E. Richard Webber
Henry Edward Autrey
Donald J. Stohr
Catherine D. Perry
Rodney W. Sippel

Senior Judges

Edward L. Filippine
Stephen N. Limbaugh

Clerk

James Woodward
3.300 U.S. Courthouse
111 South Tenth Street
St. Louis, Missouri 63102
(314) 244-7900

WESTERN DISTRICT consists of five divisions.

Central Division includes Benton, Boone, Callaway, Camden, Cole, Cooper, Hickory, Howard, Miller, Moniteau, Morgan, Osage and Pettis counties. The court sits at Jefferson City.

St. Joseph Division includes Andrew, Atchison, Buchanan, Caldwell, Clinton, Daviess, De Kalb, Gentry, Grundy, Harrison, Holt, Livingston, Mercer, Nodaway, Platte, Putnam, Sullivan and Worth counties. The court sits at St. Joseph.

Southern Division includes Cedar, Christian, Dade, Dallas, Douglas, Greene, Howell, Laclede, Oregon, Ozark, Polk, Pulaski, Taney, Texas, Webster and Wright counties. The court sits at Springfield.

Southwestern Division includes Barry, Barton, Jasper, Lawrence, McDonald, Newton, Stone and Vernon counties. The court sits at Joplin.

Western Division includes Bates, Carroll, Cass, Clay, Henry, Jackson, Johnson, Lafayette, Ray, St. Clair and Saline counties. The court sits at Kansas City.

Chief Judge

Dean Whipple

Judges

Fernando J. Gaitan, Jr.
Ortrie D. Smith
Gary A. Fenner
Nanette K. Laughrey
Richard E. Dorr

Senior Judges

Scott O. Wright
Howard F. Sachs

Clerk

Patricia L. Brune
2710 U.S. Courthouse
400 East Ninth Street
Kansas City, Missouri 64106
(816) 512-5000

UNITED STATES MAGISTRATE JUDGES OF MISSOURI

EASTERN DISTRICT

David D. Noce
Lewis M. Blanton
Mary Ann L. Medler
Audrey G. Fleissig
Frederick R. Buckles
Terry I. Adelman
Thomas Mummert, III

WESTERN DISTRICT

James C. England
William A. Knox
John T. Maughmer
Robert E. Larsen
Sarah W. Hays

UNITED STATES BANKRUPTCY COURTS OF MISSOURI

EASTERN DISTRICT

Chief Judge

James J. Barta

Judges

David P. McDonald
Barry S. Schermer

Bankruptcy Clerk

Dana McWay
U.S. Courthouse, Fourth Floor
111 South Tenth Street

UNITED STATES DISTRICT COURTS DISTRICTS OF MISSOURI—*Continued*

St. Louis, Missouri 63102-1125
(314) 244-4600

WESTERN DISTRICT

Chief Judge
Arthur B. Federman

Judge
Jerry W. Venters

Bankruptcy Clerk
Patricia L. Brune
2710 U.S. Courthouse
400 East Ninth Street
Kansas City, Missouri 64106
(816) 512-5000

SUPREME COURT OF MISSOURI

The Supreme Court is Missouri's court of last resort. The court consists of a chief justice and six judges appointed by the governor from a list of candidates submitted by a nonpartisan appellate judicial commission. Judges must stand for retention at the next general election occurring after one year in office. Retention elections are held every twelve years. The chief justice is elected by peer vote for a two-year term. Retirement is mandatory at age seventy; however, retired judges may accept judicial assignments from the Supreme Court to serve as senior judges in any Missouri court. Senior judges have the same authority as active judges.

The court has exclusive appellate jurisdiction in all cases involving federal or Missouri constitutional law, federal treaties or statutes, Missouri revenue laws and in any case involving the death penalty or life imprisonment. The court exercises appellate jurisdiction over cases transferred from the Court of Appeals. The court has rule-making authority over the lower courts, regulates admission to the bar and may issue writs necessary to the exercise of proper jurisdiction.

The court sits en banc or may sit in two divisions of at least three judges. The court sits at Jefferson City.

Chief Justice
Stephen N. Limbaugh, Jr.

Judges

Duane Benton
Laura Denvir Stith
Ronnie L. White
William Ray Price, Jr.
Richard Teitelman
Michael A. Wolff

Clerk
Thomas F. Simon
Supreme Court Building
P.O. Box 150
Jefferson City, Missouri 65102
(573) 751-4144
Fax: (573) 751-7514

State Courts Administrator
Michael L. Buenger
P.O. Box 104480
Jefferson City, Missouri 65110
(573) 751-4377, 751-3585
Fax: (573) 751-5540

MISSOURI COURT OF APPEALS

The Court of Appeals is Missouri's court of intermediate appellate jurisdiction. The court consists of three districts, and judges must be residents of the district they serve. Judges are appointed by the governor from a list of candidates submitted by a nonpartisan appellate judicial commission. Judges must stand for retention at the next general election occurring after one year in office. Retention elections are held every twelve years. A chief judge is elected by peer vote in each district for a term determined by the district. A presiding judge is chosen for each division within the three court districts. Methods of selection and lengths of terms for the presiding judges vary by district. Retirement is mandatory at age seventy; however, retired judges may accept judicial assignments from the Supreme Court to serve as senior judges in any Missouri court. Senior judges have the same authority as active judges.

The court has appellate jurisdiction over all cases except those within the exclusive jurisdiction of the Supreme Court. The court has superintending control over lower courts and may issue and determine original remedial writs.

EASTERN DISTRICT includes Audrain, Cape Girardeau, Clark, Franklin, Gasconade, Jefferson, Knox, Lewis, Lincoln, Madison, Marion, Monroe, Montgomery, Osage, Perry, Pike, Ralls, St. Charles, St. Francois, St. Louis, Ste. Genevieve, Scotland, Shelby, Warren and Washington counties and the city of St. Louis. The court sits at Clayton and St. Louis.

Chief Judge
Lawrence E. Mooney

Judges

Clifford H. Ahrens
William H. Crandall, Jr.
George W. Draper III
Mary K. Hoff
Mary Rhodes Russell
Paul J. Simon
Lawrence G. Crahan
Kathianne Knaup Crane
Robert G. Dowd, Jr.
Gary M. Gaertner, Sr.
Glenn Norton
Booker T. Shaw
Sherri B. Sullivan

SOUTHERN DISTRICT includes Barry, Barton, Bollinger, Butler, Camden, Carter, Cedar, Christian, Crawford, Dade, Dallas, Dent, Douglas, Dunklin, Greene, Hickory, Howell, Iron, Jasper, Laclede, Lawrence, Maries, McDonald, Mississippi, New Madrid, Newton, Oregon, Ozark, Pemiscot, Phelps, Polk, Pulaski, Reynolds, Ripley, St. Clair, Scott, Shannon, Stoddard, Stone, Taney, Texas, Wayne, Webster and Wright counties. The court sits at Poplar Bluff and Springfield.

Chief Judge
Nancy Steffen Rahmeyer

Judges

Robert S. Barney
Kerry L. Montgomery
James K. Prewitt
Phillip R. Garrison
John Edward Parrish
Kenneth W. Shrum

WESTERN DISTRICT includes Adair, Andrew, Atchison, Bates, Benton, Boone, Buchanan, Caldwell, Callaway, Carroll, Cass, Chariton, Clay, Clinton, Cole, Cooper, Daviess, De Kalb, Gentry, Grundy, Harrison, Henry, Holt, Howard, Jackson, Johnson, Lafayette, Linn, Livingston, Macon, Mercer, Miller, Moniteau, Morgan, Nodaway, Pettis, Platte, Putnam, Randolph, Ray, Saline,

MISSOURI COURT OF APPEALS—*Continued*

Schuyler, Sullivan, Vernon and Worth counties. The court sits at Kansas City.

Chief Judge
Joseph M. Ellis

Judges

Patricia Breckenridge	Lisa White Hardwick
Ronald R. Holliger	Victor C. Howard
Harold L. Lowenstein	Thomas H. Newton
James M. Smart, Jr.	Edwin H. Smith
Paul M. Spinden	Robert G. Ulrich

MISSOURI CIRCUIT COURTS

Missouri Circuit Courts were reorganized effective January 1979, eliminating the Magistrate Court, Probate Court, Municipal Court and Hannibal and Cape Girardeau Courts of Common Pleas. The Circuit Courts are divided into forty-five judicial circuits and are served by circuit judges, associate circuit judges, municipal court judges and commissioners.

Circuit judges are elected at partisan elections except in the Sixth, Seventh, Sixteenth, Twenty-first and Twenty-second Judicial Circuits, where they are appointed by the governor from a list of candidates supplied by a nonpartisan judicial commission and then stand for retention after one year in office. All circuit judges serve six-year terms. Associate circuit judges are elected and appointed in the same manner and serve four-year terms. Municipal judges are elected or appointed according to individual city ordinance or charter and serve terms of at least two years. Commissioners are appointed by a majority of the circuit judges in a circuit, usually to terms of four years, and are utilized in circuits with heavy caseloads. In each circuit a presiding judge is elected for a two-year term by the circuit and associate circuit judges from among the circuit judges. In circuits with only one circuit judge, the circuit judge automatically becomes the presiding judge. Retirement is mandatory at age seventy; however, retired circuit judges, associate circuit judges and commissioners may accept judicial assignments from the Supreme Court to serve as senior judges in any Missouri court.

The courts consist of five divisions. The Circuit Division exercises original jurisdiction over all civil and criminal cases and is served by circuit judges. The Juvenile Division handles all juvenile matters and is served by circuit judges, associate circuit judges and commissioners. In some circuits, a Family Court Division may be established which exercises exclusive original jurisdiction over dissolution of marriage, legal separation, separate maintenance, child custody, adoptions and other domestic relations and juvenile cases as provided by law; this division is presided over by circuit judges, associate circuit judges and commissioners. The Associate Division exercises jurisdiction over all civil cases in which the amount in controversy does not exceed $25,000, small claims cases, felony preliminary hearings, misdemeanors, infractions and traffic cases and is served by associate circuit judges. The Probate Division exercises jurisdiction over the estates of decedents, minors and incompetents and over mental health proceedings and is served by circuit judges, associate circuit judges and commissioners. The Municipal Division handles municipal traffic and ordinance violations and is served by municipal judges.

The courts sit at each county seat and as specified.

FIRST JUDICIAL CIRCUIT includes Clark, Schuyler and Scotland counties. The court sits at Kahoka, Lancaster and Memphis.

Presiding Judge
Gary Dial

Associate Circuit Judges
John Moon
Stephen K. Willcox
Karl A. W. DeMarce

SECOND JUDICIAL CIRCUIT includes Adair, Knox and Lewis counties. The court sits at Kirksville, Edina, Monticello and Canton.

Presiding Judge
Russell E. Steele

Associate Circuit Judges
Kristie Swaim
Garry D. Lewis
Fred Westhoff

THIRD JUDICIAL CIRCUIT includes Grundy, Harrison, Mercer and Putnam counties. The court sits at Trenton, Bethany, Princeton and Unionville.

Presiding Judge
Andrew A. Krohn

Associate Circuit Judges
Steven D. Hudson
Thomas R. Alley
J. Brad Funk
Jerri Bush

FOURTH JUDICIAL CIRCUIT includes Atchison, Gentry, Holt, Nodaway and Worth counties. The court sits at Rock Port, Albany, Oregon, Maryville and Grant City.

Presiding Judge
Roger M. Prokes

Associate Circuit Judges
Kay F. Graves Rosenbohm
Roger E. Combs
Wm. S. Richards
Glen Dietrich
Wm. Rex Beavers

FIFTH JUDICIAL CIRCUIT includes Andrew and Buchanan counties. The court sits at Savannah and St. Joseph.

Presiding Judge
Patrick K. Robb

Circuit Judges
Randall R. Jackson
Weldon C. Judah
Daniel F. Kellogg

Associate Circuit Judges
Michael J. Ordnung
Keith Marquart
Ronald E. Taylor

SIXTH JUDICIAL CIRCUIT includes Platte County. The court sits at Platte City.

MISSOURI CIRCUIT COURTS—*Continued*

Presiding Judge
Owens Lee Hull, Jr.

Circuit Judge
Abe Shafer

Associate Circuit Judges
Daniel M. Czamanske
James W. Van Amburg
Gary D. Witt

SEVENTH JUDICIAL CIRCUIT includes Clay County. The court sits at Liberty.

Presiding Judge
James E. Welsh

Circuit Judges
Michael J. Maloney
David W. Russell
Larry D. Harman

Associate Circuit Judges
K. Elizabeth Davis
A. Rex Gabbert
Janet Sutton

EIGHTH JUDICIAL CIRCUIT includes Carroll and Ray counties. The court sits at Carrollton and Richmond.

Presiding Judge
Werner A. Moentmann

Associate Circuit Judges
Robert A. Bryant
David L. Busch

NINTH JUDICIAL CIRCUIT includes Chariton, Linn and Sullivan counties. The court sits at Keytesville, Linneus, Brookfield and Milan.

Presiding Judge
Gary E. Ravens

Associate Circuit Judges
Michael L. Midyett
James P. Williams
Jeffrey D. Sayre

TENTH JUDICIAL CIRCUIT includes Marion, Monroe and Ralls counties. The court sits at Palmyra, Paris and New London.

Presiding Judge
Robert M. Clayton, II

Associate Circuit Judges
John J. Jackson
Carroll M. Blackwell
David C. Mobley

ELEVENTH JUDICIAL CIRCUIT includes St. Charles County. The court sits at St. Charles.

Presiding Judge
Lucy D. Rauch

Circuit Judges
Steve Ehlmann
Nancy L. Schneider
Joseph R. Briscoe, Jr.

Associate Circuit Judges
Jon Alan Cunningham
Terry R. Cundiff
Daniel Pelikan
Ted House

TWELFTH JUDICIAL CIRCUIT includes Audrain, Montgomery and Warren counties. The court sits at Mexico, Montgomery City and Warrenton.

Presiding Judge
Keith M. Sutherland

Associate Circuit Judges
Linda R. Hamlett
Roy L. Richter
Wesley C. Dalton

THIRTEENTH JUDICIAL CIRCUIT includes Boone and Callaway counties. The court sits at Columbia and Fulton.

Presiding Judge
Gene Hamilton

Circuit Judges
Gary Oxenhandler
Ellen S. Roper

Associate Circuit Judges
Jodie Capshaw Asel
Christopher S. Kelly
Joe D. Holt
Larry A. Bryson
Christine Carpenter
Cary Augustine

FOURTEENTH JUDICIAL CIRCUIT includes Howard and Randolph counties. The court sits at Fayette, Huntsville and Moberly.

Presiding Judge
Ralph H. Jaynes

Associate Circuit Judges
Gary G. Sprick
Scott Hayes

FIFTEENTH JUDICIAL CIRCUIT includes Lafayette and Saline counties. The court sits at Lexington, Higginsville and Marshall.

Presiding Judge
Dennis A. Rolf

Associate Circuit Judges
John G. Miller
John Frerking
Hugh C. Harvey
James T. Bellamy

SIXTEENTH JUDICIAL CIRCUIT includes Jackson County. The court sits at Independence and Kansas City.

Presiding Judge
Jay A. Daugherty

Circuit Judges
Sandra C. Midkiff
Thomas C. Clark
W. Stephen Nixon
Catharine A. Mesle
Kelly Moorhouse
J. D. Williamson
John M. Torrence
Michael W. Manners
Justine E. Del Muro
John R. O'Malley
Peggy Stevens McGraw
Charles E. Atwell
Edith Louise Messina
K. Preston Dean

MISSOURI CIRCUIT COURTS—*Continued*

Marco Roldan
Jon R. Gray
C. William Kramer
John A. Borron, Jr.

Associate Circuit Judges

Richard E. Standridge
Gregory B. Gillis
Margaret L. Sauer
Christine T. Sill-Rogers
Robert Beaird
Vernon Scoville III
Twila K. Rigby
Robert L. Trout
Jeffrey L. Bushur

SEVENTEENTH JUDICIAL CIRCUIT includes Cass and Johnson counties. The court sits at Harrisonville and Warrensburg.

Presiding Judge
Joseph Dandurand

Circuit Judge
Jacqueline Cook

Associate Circuit Judges
Thomas Campbell
William B. Collins
Garrett R. Crouch II
Stephen Angle

EIGHTEENTH JUDICIAL CIRCUIT includes Cooper and Pettis counties. The court sits at Boonville and Sedalia.

Presiding Judge
Donald Barnes

Associate Circuit Judges
Kenton G. Askren
Robert Liston
Robert L. Koffman

NINETEENTH JUDICIAL CIRCUIT includes Cole County. The court sits at Jefferson City.

Presiding Judge
Thomas Brown III

Circuit Judges
Richard Callahan
Patricia S. Joyce

Associate Circuit Judge
Thomas Sodergren

TWENTIETH JUDICIAL CIRCUIT includes Franklin, Gasconade and Osage counties. The court sits at Union, Hermann and Linn.

Presiding Judge
Gael D. Wood

Circuit Judge
Jeff W. Schaeperkoetter

Associate Circuit Judges
Walter A. Murray, Jr.
Cindy Eckelkamp
Stanley D. Williams
John B. Berkemeyer
Robert Schollmeyer

TWENTY-FIRST JUDICIAL CIRCUIT includes St. Louis County. The court sits at Clayton.

Presiding Judge
Barbara W. Wallace

Circuit Judges

Robert S. Cohen
Mark D. Seigel
John F. Kintz
Carolyn C. Whittington
David Lee Vincent III
Emmett M. O'Brien
James R. Hartenbach
Susan Block
Philip J. Sweeney
Colleen Dolan
Maura McShane
Bernhardt Drumm, Jr.
Gary M. Gaertner, Jr.
Tommy W. DePriest, Jr.
Kenneth M. Romines
Steven H. Goldman
John A. Ross
Larry L. Kendrick
Melvyn Wade Wiesman

Associate Circuit Judges

Barbara A. Crancer
Brenda Stith Loftin
Joseph A. Goeke, III
Gloria Jean Clark Reno
Ellen Levy-Siwak
Dennis Smith
Sandra Farragut-Hemphill
Mary Bruntrager Schroeder
Thea A. Sherry
John R. Essner
Patrick Clifford
Michael D. Burton
Michael T. Jamison

TWENTY-SECOND JUDICIAL CIRCUIT includes the city of St. Louis. The court sits at St. Louis.

Presiding Judge
Michael P. David

Circuit Judges

Steven R. Ohmer
Julian L. Bush
John J. Riley
Margaret M. Neill
Donald L. McCullin
Joan M. Burger
Patricia L. Cohen
Robert H. Dierker, Jr.
Angela Turner Quigless
Michael B. Calvin
Thomas J. Frawley
vacancy
Thomas C. Grady
David L. Dowd
Nannette A. Baker
Philip D. Heagney
Dennis M. Schaumann
Mark H. Neill
David C. Mason
Jimmie M. Edwards
Evelyn M. Baker
Timothy J. Wilson
Joan L. Moriarty

Associate Circuit Judges

Michael Mullen
Barbara T. Peebles
Iris Golliday Ferguson
vacancy
Edward Sweeney
Thad F. Niemira
John F. Garvey

TWENTY-THIRD JUDICIAL CIRCUIT includes Jefferson County. The court sits at Hillsboro.

Presiding Judge
Timothy J. Patterson

Circuit Judges
Gary P. Kramer
M. Edward Williams
Dennis J. Kehm

Associate Circuit Judges
William J. Wegge, Jr.
Mark T. Stoll
Darrell Missey

TWENTY-FOURTH JUDICIAL CIRCUIT includes Madison, St. Francois, Ste. Genevieve and Washington counties. The court sits at Fredericktown, Farmington, Ste. Genevieve and Potosi.

Presiding Judge
Kenneth W. Pratte

MISSOURI CIRCUIT COURTS—*Continued*

Circuit Judge
Sandy Martinez

Associate Circuit Judges
Robert C. Stillwell
Thomas L. Ray
James H. Kelly
Raymond M. Weber
Troy K. Hyde

TWENTY-FIFTH JUDICIAL CIRCUIT includes Maries, Phelps, Pulaski and Texas counties. The court sits at Vienna, Rolla, Waynesville and Houston.

Presiding Judge
Douglas E. Long, Jr.

Circuit Judge
John D. Wiggins

Associate Circuit Judges
John Clayton
Ralph J. Haslag
David Gregory Warren
Mary W. Sheffield
Tracy Lee Storie
Brad Ellsworth

TWENTY-SIXTH JUDICIAL CIRCUIT includes Camden, Laclede, Miller, Moniteau and Morgan counties. The court sits at Camdenton, Lebanon, Tuscumbia, California and Versailles.

Presiding Judge
James A. Franklin, Jr.

Circuit Judge
Mary Dickerson

Associate Circuit Judges
Jack A. Bennett
Greg Kays
Kenneth L. Oswald
Kevin Schehr
Bruce Coyler
Larry Winfrey
Peggy Richardson

TWENTY-SEVENTH JUDICIAL CIRCUIT includes Bates, Henry and St. Clair counties. The court sits at Butler, Clinton and Osceola.

Presiding Judge
William J. Roberts

Associate Circuit Judges
John M. O'Bannon
Wayne P. Strothmann
Michael Dawson

TWENTY-EIGHTH JUDICIAL CIRCUIT includes Barton, Cedar, Dade and Vernon counties. The court sits at Lamar, Stockton, Greenfield and Nevada.

Presiding Judge
James R. Bickel

Associate Circuit Judges
Charles Curless
Joseph B. Phillips
David R. Munton
Gerald D. McBeth

TWENTY-NINTH JUDICIAL CIRCUIT includes Jasper County. The court sits at Carthage and Joplin.

Presiding Judge
David C. Dally

Circuit Judges
William C. Crawford
Jon A. Dermott

Associate Circuit Judges
Joseph Schoeberl
Richard Dennis Copeland
Stephen P. Carlton

THIRTIETH JUDICIAL CIRCUIT includes Benton, Dallas, Hickory, Polk and Webster counties. The court sits at Warsaw, Buffalo, Hermitage, Bolivar and Marshfield.

Presiding Judge
John W. Sims

Associate Circuit Judges
Larry M. Burditt
James P. Anderton
Daniel Max Knust
Cody A. Hanna
Gary Lynch
Kenneth F. Thompson

THIRTY-FIRST JUDICIAL CIRCUIT includes Greene County. The court sits at Springfield.

Presiding Judge
J. Miles Sweeney

Circuit Judges
Don E. Burrell, Jr.
Henry W. Westbrooke, Jr.
Thomas E. Mountjoy
Calvin Holden

Associate Circuit Judges
Max E. Bacon
J. Dan Conklin
Mark E. Fitzsimmons
Mark A. Powell

THIRTY-SECOND JUDICIAL CIRCUIT includes Bollinger, Cape Girardeau and Perry counties. The court sits at Marble Hill, Cape Girardeau, Jackson and Perryville.

Presiding Judge
William L. Syler

Circuit Judge
John W. Grimm

Associate Circuit Judges
Scott Thomsen
Peter Statler
Gary A. Kamp
Michael Bullerdieck

THIRTY-THIRD JUDICIAL CIRCUIT includes Mississippi and Scott counties. The court sits at Charleston and Benton.

Presiding Judge
David A. Dolan

Associate Circuit Judges
T. Lynn Brown
W. H. Winchester, III
David C. Mann

MISSOURI CIRCUIT COURTS—*Continued*

THIRTY-FOURTH JUDICIAL CIRCUIT includes New Madrid and Pemiscot counties. The court sits at New Madrid and Caruthersville.

Presiding Judge
Fred W. Copeland

Associate Circuit Judges
Charles L. Spitler
W. Keith Currie
Byron D. Luber

THIRTY-FIFTH JUDICIAL CIRCUIT includes Dunklin and Stoddard counties. The court sits at Kennett and Bloomfield.

Presiding Judge
Stephen R. Sharp

Associate Circuit Judges
John M. Beaton
Dan J. Crawford
Joe Z. Satterfield
Stephen R. Mitchell

THIRTY-SIXTH JUDICIAL CIRCUIT includes Butler and Ripley counties. The court sits at Poplar Bluff and Doniphan.

Presiding Judge
Mark L. Richardson

Associate Circuit Judges
William J. Clarkson
John Bloodworth
James R. Hall

THIRTY-SEVENTH JUDICIAL CIRCUIT includes Carter, Howell, Oregon and Shannon counties. The court sits at Van Buren, West Plains, Alton and Eminence.

Presiding Judge
R. Jack Garrett

Associate Circuit Judges
David J. Hedspeth
Donald M. Henry
David Evans
Jo Beth Prewitt
Robert M. Heller

THIRTY-EIGHTH JUDICIAL CIRCUIT includes Christian and Taney counties. The court sits at Ozark and Forsyth.

Presiding Judge
James Eiffert

Associate Circuit Judges
Mark Orr
John S. Waters
Tony Williams
James Justus

THIRTY-NINTH JUDICIAL CIRCUIT includes Barry, Lawrence and Stone counties. The court sits at Cassville, Mount Vernon and Galena.

Presiding Judge
J. Edward Sweeney

Associate Circuit Judges
Michael Garrett
Carr Woods
Scott S. Sifferman
Larry W. Meyer
Alan Blankenship

FORTIETH JUDICIAL CIRCUIT includes McDonald and Newton counties. The court sits at Pineville and Neosho.

Presiding Judge
Timothy W. Perigo

Associate Circuit Judges
John LePage
Kevin Selby
Gregory Stremel

FORTY-FIRST JUDICIAL CIRCUIT includes Macon and Shelby counties. The court sits at Macon and Shelbyville.

Presiding Judge
Hadley E. Grimm

Associate Circuit Judges
Paul K. Parkinson
Gary G. Wallace

FORTY-SECOND JUDICIAL CIRCUIT includes Crawford, Dent, Iron, Reynolds and Wayne counties. The court sits at Steelville, Salem, Ironton, Centerville and Greenville.

Presiding Judge
J. Max Price

Circuit Judge
William C. Seay

Associate Circuit Judges
J. Kent Howald
Sanborn N. Ball
Kelly W. Parker
Edith R. Rutter
Randy P. Schuller

FORTY-THIRD JUDICIAL CIRCUIT includes Caldwell, Clinton, Daviess, De Kalb and Livingston counties. The court sits at Kingston, Plattsburg, Gallatin, Maysville and Chillicothe.

Presiding Judge
Stephen K. Griffin

Circuit Judge
Warren L. McElwain

Associate Circuit Judges
Daniel L. Chadwick
Paul T. Luckenbill, Jr.
Daren L. Adkins
R. Brent Elliott
Barbara Gale Lame

FORTY-FOURTH JUDICIAL CIRCUIT includes Douglas, Ozark and Wright counties. The court sits at Ava, Gainesville and Hartville.

MISSOURI CIRCUIT COURTS—*Continued*

Presiding Judge

John Moody

Associate Circuit Judges

Roger Wall

John Jacobs

Lynette Veenstra

FORTY-FIFTH JUDICIAL CIRCUIT includes Lincoln and Pike counties. The court sits at Troy and Bowling Green.

Presiding Judge

Dan Dildine

Associate Circuit Judges

Amy Kinker

T. Bennett Burkemper

David Ash

Missouri Counties and County Seats

Adair
Kirksville

Andrew
Savannah

Atchison
Rock Port

Audrain
Mexico

Barry
Cassville

Barton
Lamar

Bates
Butler

Benton
Warsaw

Bollinger
Marble Hill

Boone
Columbia

Buchanan
St. Joseph

Butler
Poplar Bluff

Caldwell
Kingston

Callaway
Fulton

Camden
Camdenton

Cape Girardeau
Jackson

Carroll
Carrollton

Carter
Van Buren

Cass
Harrisonville

Cedar
Stockton

Chariton
Keytesville

Christian
Ozark

Clark
Kahoka

Clay
Liberty

Clinton
Plattsburg

Cole
Jefferson City

Cooper
Boonville

Crawford
Steelville

Dade
Greenfield

Dallas
Buffalo

Daviess
Gallatin

De Kalb
Maysville

Dent
Salem

Douglas
Ava

Dunklin
Kennett

Franklin
Union

Gasconade
Hermann

Gentry
Albany

Greene
Springfield

Grundy
Trenton

Harrison
Bethany

Henry
Clinton

Hickory
Hermitage

Holt
Oregon

Howard
Fayette

Howell
West Plains

Iron
Ironton

Jackson
Independence

Jasper
Carthage

Jefferson
Hillsboro

Johnson
Warrensburg

Knox
Edina

Laclede
Lebanon

Lafayette
Lexington

Lawrence
Mount Vernon

Lewis
Monticello

Lincoln
Troy

Linn
Linneus

Livingston
Chillicothe

Macon
Macon

Madison
Fredericktown

Maries
Vienna

Marion
Palmyra

McDonald
Pineville

Mercer
Princeton

Miller
Tuscumbia

Mississippi
Charleston

Moniteau
California

Monroe
Paris

Montgomery
Montgomery City

Morgan
Versailles

New Madrid
New Madrid

Newton
Neosho

Nodaway
Maryville

Oregon
Alton

Osage
Linn

Ozark
Gainesville

Pemiscot
Caruthersville

Perry
Perryville

Pettis
Sedalia

Phelps
Rolla

Pike
Bowling Green

Platte
Platte City

Polk
Bolivar

COUNTIES AND COUNTY SEATS—*Continued*

Pulaski
Waynesville

Putnam
Unionville

Ralls
New London

Randolph
Huntsville

Ray
Richmond

Reynolds
Centerville

Ripley
Doniphan

St. Charles
St. Charles

St. Clair
Osceola

St. Francois
Farmington

St. Louis
Clayton

St. Louis City
(Independent City)

Ste. Genevieve
Ste. Genevieve

Saline
Marshall

Schuyler
Lancaster

Scotland
Memphis

Scott
Benton

Shannon
Eminence

Shelby
Shelbyville

Stoddard
Bloomfield

Stone
Galena

Sullivan
Milan

Taney
Forsyth

Texas
Houston

Vernon
Nevada

Warren
Warrenton

Washington
Potosi

Wayne
Greenville

Webster
Marshfield

Worth
Grant City

Wright
Hartville

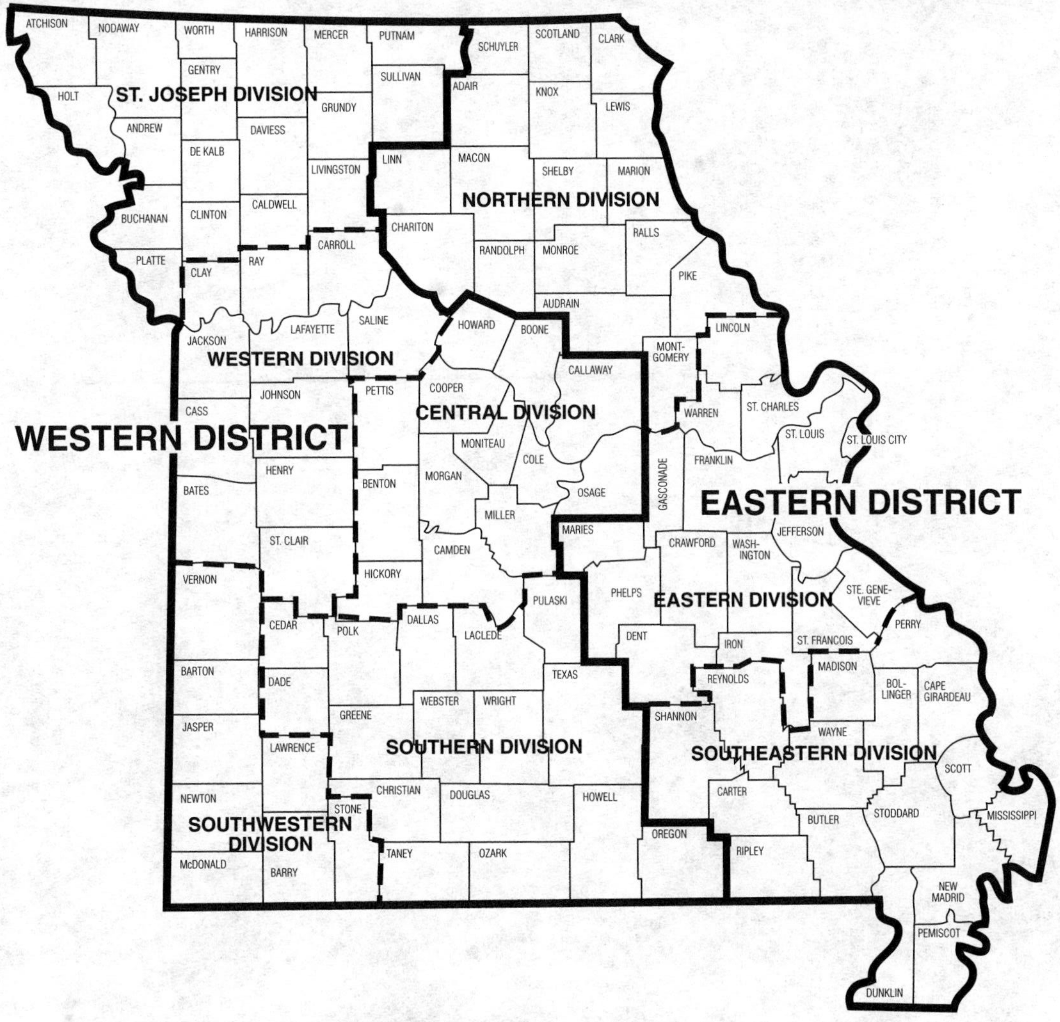
WESTERN DISTRICT
EASTERN DISTRICT
ST. JOSEPH DIVISION
NORTHERN DIVISION
WESTERN DIVISION
CENTRAL DIVISION
SOUTHERN DIVISION
SOUTHWESTERN DIVISION
EASTERN DIVISION
SOUTHEASTERN DIVISION
ATCHISON
NODAWAY
WORTH
HARRISON
MERCER
PUTNAM
SCHUYLER
SCOTLAND
CLARK
HOLT
GENTRY
SULLIVAN
ADAIR
KNOX
LEWIS
ANDREW
GRUNDY
DAVIESS
DE KALB
LIVINGSTON
LINN
MACON
SHELBY
MARION
BUCHANAN
CLINTON
CALDWELL
CHARITON
RANDOLPH
MONROE
RALLS
PLATTE
CLAY
RAY
CARROLL
PIKE
AUDRAIN
LAFAYETTE
SALINE
HOWARD
BOONE
LINCOLN
JACKSON
MONT-GOMERY
CALLAWAY
JOHNSON
PETTIS
COOPER
WARREN
ST. CHARLES
CASS
MONITEAU
COLE
ST. LOUIS
ST. LOUIS CITY
FRANKLIN
HENRY
BENTON
MORGAN
GASCONADE
OSAGE
BATES
MILLER
MARIES
JEFFERSON
ST. CLAIR
CAMDEN
CRAWFORD
WASH-INGTON
VERNON
HICKORY
PULASKI
PHELPS
STE. GENE-VIEVE
PERRY
CEDAR
POLK
DALLAS
LACLEDE
DENT
IRON
ST. FRANCOIS
TEXAS
REYNOLDS
MADISON
BARTON
DADE
BOL-LINGER
CAPE GIRARDEAU
GREENE
WEBSTER
WRIGHT
SHANNON
WAYNE
JASPER
LAWRENCE
SCOTT
CHRISTIAN
DOUGLAS
HOWELL
CARTER
NEWTON
STONE
STODDARD
MISSISSIPPI
BUTLER
OREGON
TANEY
OZARK
RIPLEY
McDONALD
BARRY
NEW MADRID
PEMISCOT
DUNKLIN

UNITED STATES DISTRICT COURTS DISTRICTS OF MISSOURI

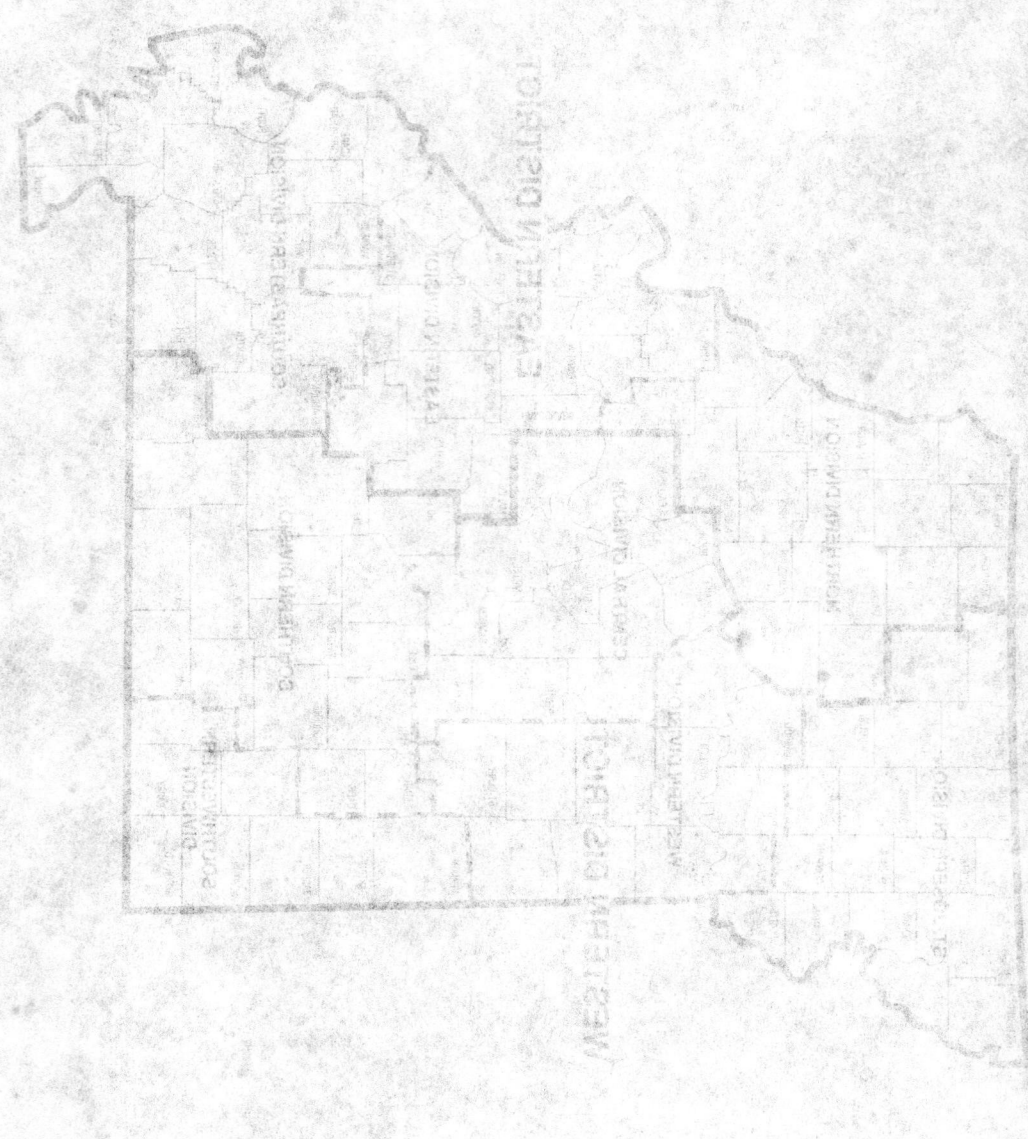

WESTERN DISTRICT
EASTERN DISTRICT
SOUTHERN DISTRICT
ATCHISON
NODAWAY
WORTH
HARRISON
MERCER
PUTNAM
SCHUYLER
SCOTLAND
CLARK
HOLT
GENTRY
SULLIVAN
ADAIR
KNOX
LEWIS
ANDREW
DAVIESS
GRUNDY
DE KALB
LIVINGSTON
LINN
MACON
SHELBY
MARION
BUCHANAN
CLINTON
CALDWELL
CHARITON
RALLS
PLATTE
RAY
CARROLL
RANDOLPH
MONROE
CLAY
PIKE
SALINE
HOWARD
AUDRAIN
LINCOLN
BOONE
JACKSON
LAFAYETTE
MONT-
GOMERY
CALLAWAY
JOHNSON
PETTIS
COOPER
CASS
WARREN
ST. CHARLES
ST. LOUIS
ST. LOUIS CITY
MONITEAU
COLE
FRANKLIN
HENRY
GASCONADE
MORGAN
BENTON
BATES
OSAGE
MILLER
JEFFERSON
MARIES
CRAWFORD
WASH-
INGTON
ST. CLAIR
CAMDEN
HICKORY
VERNON
STE. GENE-
VIEVE
PULASKI
PHELPS
DALLAS
CEDAR
POLK
LACLEDE
PERRY
DENT
ST. FRANCOIS
IRON
BARTON
MADISON
TEXAS
REYNOLDS
DADE
CAPE
GIRARDEAU
WEBSTER
WRIGHT
GREENE
SHANNON
JASPER
BOL-
LINGER
WAYNE
LAWRENCE
SCOTT
CHRISTIAN
DOUGLAS
HOWELL
CARTER
NEWTON
STODDARD
STONE
BUTLER
MISSISSIPPI
OREGON
BARRY
RIPLEY
TANEY
OZARK
McDONALD
NEW
MADRID
PEMISCOT
DUNKLIN

DISTRICTS OF MISSOURI COURT OF APPEALS

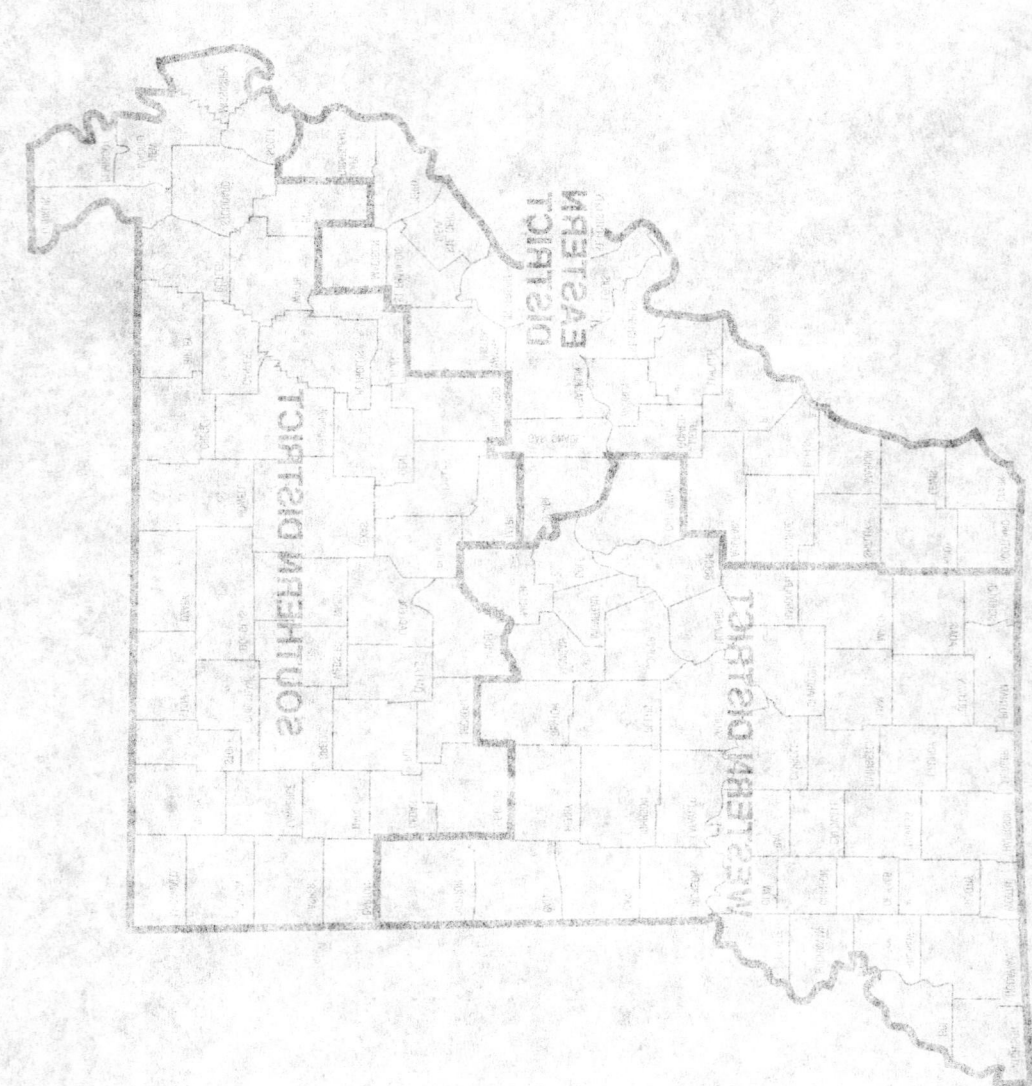

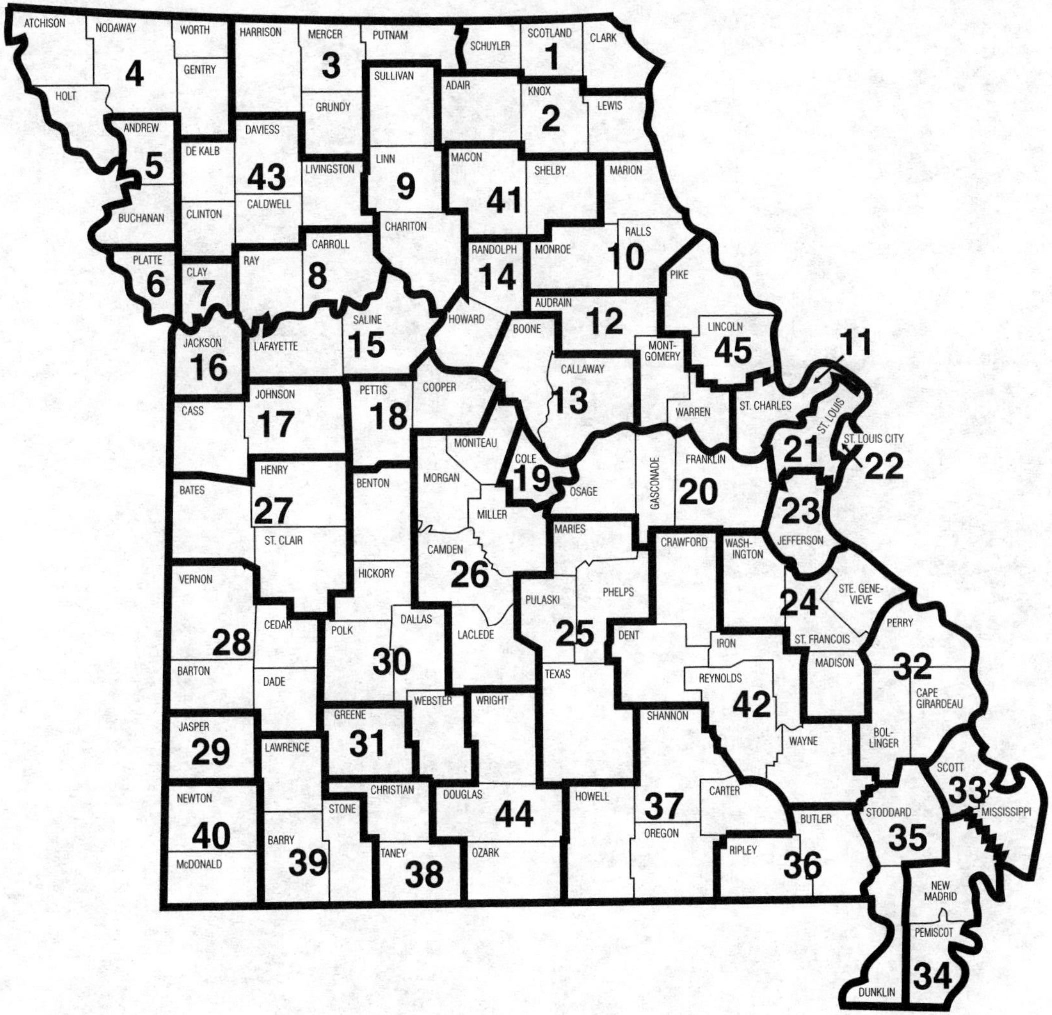
ATCHISON
NODAWAY
WORTH
HARRISON
MERCER
PUTNAM
SCHUYLER
SCOTLAND
CLARK
HOLT
GENTRY
GRUNDY
SULLIVAN
ADAIR
KNOX
LEWIS
ANDREW
DE KALB
DAVIESS
LIVINGSTON
LINN
MACON
SHELBY
MARION
BUCHANAN
CLINTON
CALDWELL
CHARITON
RALLS
MONROE
RANDOLPH
PLATTE
CLAY
RAY
CARROLL
PIKE
AUDRAIN
SALINE
HOWARD
BOONE
LINCOLN
MONT-
GOMERY
JACKSON
LAFAYETTE
CALLAWAY
ST. CHARLES
WARREN
JOHNSON
PETTIS
COOPER
CASS
MONITEAU
COLE
ST. LOUIS
ST. LOUIS CITY
HENRY
BENTON
MORGAN
OSAGE
GASCONADE
FRANKLIN
BATES
MILLER
MARIES
ST. CLAIR
CRAWFORD
WASH-
INGTON
JEFFERSON
CAMDEN
HICKORY
VERNON
PULASKI
PHELPS
STE. GENE-
VIEVE
CEDAR
DALLAS
POLK
LACLEDE
DENT
IRON
ST. FRANCOIS
PERRY
BARTON
DADE
TEXAS
REYNOLDS
MADISON
CAPE
GIRARDEAU
WEBSTER
WRIGHT
GREENE
JASPER
SHANNON
BOL-
LINGER
WAYNE
LAWRENCE
SCOTT
CHRISTIAN
NEWTON
DOUGLAS
HOWELL
CARTER
STONE
BUTLER
STODDARD
MISSISSIPPI
BARRY
OREGON
RIPLEY
TANEY
OZARK
McDONALD
NEW
MADRID
PEMISCOT
DUNKLIN
1
2
3
4
5
6
7
8
9
10
11
12
13
14
15
16
17
18
19
20
21
22
23
24
25
26
27
28
29
30
31
32
33
34
35
36
37
38
39
40
41
42
43
44
45

JUDICIAL CIRCUITS OF MISSOURI CIRCUIT COURTS

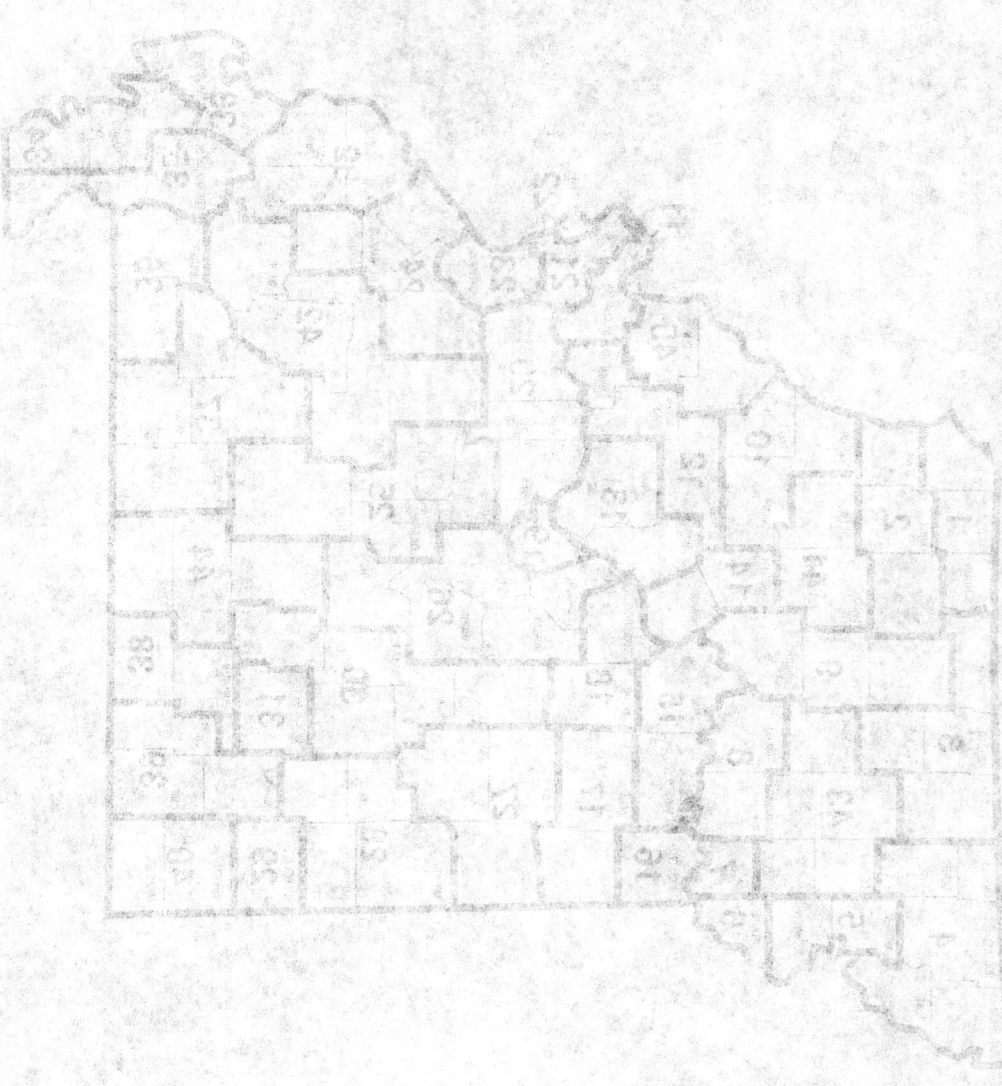

MISSOURI

ADELMAN, Terry I. *(Magistrate Judge, United States District Court Eastern District of Missouri)* Appointed by U.S. District Court judges.

Office: U.S. Courthouse, 111 South Tenth Street, St. Louis 63102.

Telephone: (314) 244-7550.

ADKINS, Daren L. *(Associate Circuit Judge, Missouri Circuit Court Forty-third Judicial Circuit)* Serves Probate Division.

Office: 102 South Main, Gallatin 64640.

Telephone: (660) 663-2532.

Fax: (660) 663-3376.

AHRENS, Clifford H. *(Judge, Missouri Court of Appeals Eastern District)* Appointed by Governor John D. Ashcroft to term beginning March 6, 1991. Retained by election Nov 3, 1992, current term expires Dec 31, 2004. Chief Judge 1996-97. Born Hannibal Missouri Dec 19, 1945. Catholic. Educated at University of Missouri-Columbia B.S. cum laude 1967 J.D. 1969. Staff member Missouri Law Review 1968-69. Member Phi Delta Phi. Admitted to practice Missouri 1969, U.S. District Court Eastern District of Missouri 1969, U.S. Court of Appeals Eighth Circuit 1984 and U.S. Supreme Court 1991. In legal practice Hannibal 1969-91.

Author Comment "Planned Unit Development" 35 Missouri L. Rev. 27, 1970 and Chapter 7 *Equitable Proceedings, Missouri Creditors'-Debtors' Remedies* The Missouri Bar Continuing Legal Education 4th ed. 1985. Instructor in Business Law Hannibal LaGrange College 1971. Chairman Missouri Court Automation Committee. Member American Judicature Society, The Bar Association of Metropolitan St. Louis, The Missouri Bar (Division of Judicial Administration), Tenth Judicial Circuit (President 1981-82) and American Bar Associations. Speaker "New Farm Legislation—Ag Seminar" Bank Administrative Institute Illiamo Chapter 1987. Speaker and Author course materials "Workouts, Creditors' Perspective" Farm Crisis Seminar The Missouri Bar Continuing Legal Education 1987 and Chapter 12 "Bankruptcy & Reorganization" Year in Review Seminar University of Missouri Continuing Legal Education 1990. Commentator Bankruptcy Practice Program The Missouri Bar 1989. Named Outstanding Attorney by Legal Services of Northeastern Missouri 1982 and Kiwanian of the Year by Kiwanis Club of Hannibal 1983-84. Member 1979-83 and Chairman 1983-86 Hannibal Missouri Planning Commission. Board of Directors Children's Trust Fund of Missouri 1987-91. Board of Electors St. Louis City-St. Louis County 1990-91. Member YMCA of Hannibal (President 1981-83), Kiwanis Club of Hannibal (President 1978-79), United Way of Hannibal (President 1977-78) and Hannibal Chamber of Commerce (President 1979). Enjoys amateur radio, reading and computers.

Office: 121 South Meramec, Suite 500, St. Louis 63105.

Telephone: (314) 512-7704.

Fax: (314) 512-7707

Office: 65 Pioneer Trail, Hannibal 63401.

Telephone: (573) 248-2504.

ALLEY, Thomas R. *(Associate Circuit Judge, Missouri Circuit Court Third Judicial Circuit)* Serves Probate Division.

Mailing address: P.O. Box 189, Bethany 64424.

Telephone: (660) 425-6432.

Fax: (660) 425-6390

ANDERTON, James P. *(Associate Circuit Judge, Missouri Circuit Court Thirtieth Judicial Circuit)* Serves Probate Division.

Mailing address: P.O. Box 75, Hermitage 65668.

Telephone: (417) 745-6822.

Fax: (417) 745-6670

ANGLE, Stephen *(Associate Circuit Judge, Missouri Circuit Court Seventeenth Judicial Circuit)*

Office: 300 North Holden, Warrensburg 64093.

Telephone: (660) 422-7410.

Fax: (660) 422-7412

ASEL, Jodie Capshaw *(Associate Circuit Judge, Missouri Circuit Court Thirteenth Judicial Circuit)*

Office: 705 East Walnut Street, Columbia 65201.

Telephone: (573) 886-4050.

Fax: (573) 886-4070

ASH, David *(Associate Circuit Judge, Missouri Circuit Court Forty-fifth Judicial Circuit)* Serves Probate Division.

Office: 115 West Main, Bowling Green 63334.

Telephone: (573) 324-5582.

Fax: (573) 324-6297

ASKREN, Kenton G. *(Associate Circuit Judge, Missouri Circuit Court Eighteenth Judicial Circuit)* Elected to term beginning Jan 1, 1979. Reelected 1982, 1986, 1990, 1994, 1998 and 2002. Current term expires Dec 31, 2006. Serves Probate Division. Born Kansas City Missouri Nov 11, 1948. Christian. Educated at Central Missouri State University B.S. 1971 and University of Missouri at Columbia J.D. 1974. Admitted to practice Missouri 1974. Began legal practice Boonville 1974. In legal practice Pilot Grove 1974. Judge, Cooper County Probate and Magistrate Courts Jan 1, 1975 to Dec 31, 1978.

Secretary Boonville Planning and Zoning Commission. Instructor Missouri University Extension Program 1977-78. Member Missouri Association of Probate and Associate Circuit Court Judges (Board of Directors), The Missouri Bar, Cooper County and American Bar Associations. Second Lieutenant USAF 1973-75. Democrat. Subchairman Missouri State Advisory Council to Division of Alcohol and Drug Abuse. Chairman CARE Inc. Board of Directors Cooper County Mental Health Association, Boonville Jaycees and Boonville Kiwanis. President Boonslick Habitat for Humanity, Inc. Member Region IV Department of Mental Health Alcohol and Drug Abuse Advisory Council. Enjoys tennis and volleyball.

Office: 200 Main, Room 31, Boonville 65233.

Telephone: (660) 882-5604.

Fax: (660) 882-8747

ATWELL, Charles E. *(Circuit Judge, Missouri Circuit Court Sixteenth Judicial Circuit)* Appointed by governor. Retained by election.
Office: Courthouse, 415 East Twelfth Street, Kansas City 64106.
Telephone: (816) 881-3610.
Fax: (816) 881-3893

AUGUSTINE, Cary *(Associate Circuit Judge, Missouri Circuit Court Thirteenth Judicial Circuit)*
Office: 10 East Fifth Street, Fulton 65251.
Telephone: (573) 642-0777.
Fax: (573) 648-0700

AUTREY, Henry Edward *(Judge, United States District Court Eastern District of Missouri)* Appointed for life by President George W. Bush to term beginning Sept 16, 2002. Born Mobile Alabama March 18, 1952. Catholic. Educated at St. Louis University B.A. with honors 1974 J.D. 1977. Admitted to practice Missouri 1978 and U.S. District Court Eastern District of Missouri 1978. Former Associate Circuit Judge, Missouri Circuit Court Twenty-second Judicial Circuit, appointed by Governor John D. Ashcroft to term beginning Feb 16, 1986. Former Circuit Judge, Missouri Circuit Court Twenty-second Judicial Circuit, appointed by Governor Mel Carnahan.

Author "Small Claims Primer" 1987 and "Professionalism: Accommodating the Disabled Under the Americans with Disabilities Act" 1992 Missouri State Judges Judicial Conference. Adjunct Professor of Law 1991-94. Member Operational Support Committee Twenty-second Judicial Circuit, Rules Committee and Ad Hoc Committee on Individualized Dockets. Member The Missouri Bar and Mound City Bar Association. Attended Missouri State Judges Judicial Conference annually since 1986. Recipient Certificate of Appreciation from Black Law Student Association Feb 26, 1986 and Grand Jury Award Dec 21, 1990. Board of Directors St. Louis Food Bank and Human Energies, Inc. Hobbies include sports cars, composing, bodybuilding, studying urban architecture and travel.
Office: 111 South Tenth Street, Suite 10.148, St. Louis 63102.
Telephone: (314) 244-7450.

BACON, Max E. *(Associate Circuit Judge, Missouri Circuit Court Thirty-first Judicial Circuit)*
Office: 1010 Boonville, Springfield 65802.
Telephone: (417) 868-4097.

BAKER, Evelyn M. *(Circuit Judge, Missouri Circuit Court Twenty-second Judicial Circuit)* Appointed by governor. Retained by election.
Office: Municipal Courts Building, 1320 Market Street, St. Louis 63103.
Telephone: (314) 622-4680.

BAKER, Nannette A. *(Circuit Judge, Missouri Circuit Court Twenty-second Judicial Circuit)* Appointed by Governor Mel Carnahan.
Office: Civil Courts Building, 10 North Tucker Street, St. Louis 63101.
Telephone: (314) 622-5604.

BALL, Sanborn N. *(Associate Circuit Judge, Missouri Circuit Court Forty-second Judicial Circuit)* Serves Probate Division.
Office: 112 East Fifth Street, Salem 65560.
Telephone: (573) 729-3134.
Fax: (573) 729-9414

BARNES, Donald *(Presiding Judge, Missouri Circuit Court Eighteenth Judicial Circuit)* Elected to term beginning Jan 1, 1977. Reelected 1982, 1988, 1994 and 2000. Current term expires Dec 31, 2006. Born Marshall Missouri March 18, 1935. Community of Christ. Educated at Central Missouri State College A.B. 1957 B.S. in Education 1957 and University of Missouri J.D. 1960. Admitted to practice Missouri 1960. In legal practice Sedalia 1960-76.

Instructor Central Missouri State College 1967 and State Fair Community College 1968-73. Staff Sergeant USAS 1960-65. Republican. Member Sedalia School Board 1973-76.
Office: 415 South Ohio Street, Sedalia 65301.
Telephone: (660) 827-0164.
Fax: (660) 827-8616

BARNEY, Robert S. *(Judge, Missouri Court of Appeals Southern District)* Appointed by Governor Mel Carnahan to term beginning Dec 1995. Retained by election. Former Chief Judge. Educated at Southeast Missouri State University B.S. and George Washington University National Law Center J.D. Associate Circuit Judge, Missouri Circuit Court Thirty-fifth Judicial Circuit 1987-95.

Member The District of Columbia Bar, The Florida Bar and The Missouri Bar. Served to Captain U.S. Army. Member House of Representatives Missouri.
Office: 300 Hammons Parkway, Springfield 65806.
Telephone: (417) 895-6818.

BARTA, James J. *(Chief Judge, United States Bankruptcy Court Eastern District of Missouri)* Chief Judge since Jan 11, 2003.
Office: U.S. Courthouse, 111 South Tenth Street, St. Louis 63102.
Telephone: (314) 244-4510.

BEAIRD, Robert *(Associate Circuit Judge, Missouri Circuit Court Sixteenth Judicial Circuit)* Appointed by Governor Bob Holden.
Office: Courthouse, 415 East Twelfth Street, Kansas City 64106.
Telephone: (816) 881-3685.

BEATON, John M. *(Associate Circuit Judge, Missouri Circuit Court Thirty-fifth Judicial Circuit)* Elected Nov 1998 to term beginning Jan 1, 1999. Reelected 2002, current term expires Dec 31, 2006. Serves Probate and Juvenile Divisions. Born Paducah Kentucky Aug 3, 1946. United Methodist. Educated at Murray State University B.S. with honors 1969 and Tulane University J.D. 1972. Tulane Moot Court. Member Delta Theta Phi. Admitted to practice Missouri 1972, U.S. District Court Eastern District of Missouri 1973 and U.S. Court of Appeals Eighth Circuit 1981. In legal practice Missouri 1972-99.

Member The Missouri Bar and Dunklin County Bar Association. Former Board Member Association for Children with Learning Disabilities. Advisory Board Missouri Center for Safe Schools. Lay Leader First United Methodist Church. Member Kennett Kiwanis. Enjoys Taekwondo, fishing and golfing.
Mailing address: P.O. Box 466, Kennett 63857.
Telephone: (573) 888-3272.

BEAVERS, Wm. Rex *(Associate Circuit Judge, Missouri Circuit Court Fourth Judicial Circuit)* Serves Probate Division.
Mailing address: P.O. Box 428, Grant City 64456.
Telephone: (660) 564-2152.

BELLAMY, James T. *(Associate Circuit Judge, Missouri Circuit Court Fifteenth Judicial Circuit)*
Mailing address: P.O. Box 751, Marshall 65340.
Telephone: (660) 886-6988.
Fax: (660) 886-2919

BENNETT, Jack A. *(Associate Circuit Judge, Missouri Circuit Court Twenty-sixth Judicial Circuit)* Serves Probate Division.
Office: One Court Circle, Suite 9, Camdenton 65020.
Telephone: (573) 346-4440.
Fax: (573) 346-5422

BENTON, Duane *(Judge, Supreme Court of Missouri)* Appointed by Governor John D. Ashcroft to term beginning Aug 1991. Retained by election 1992, current term expires Dec 31, 2004. Chief Justice July 1, 1997 to June 30, 1999. Born Springfield Missouri Sept 8, 1950. Educated at Northwestern University B.A. summa cum laude 1972, Yale University J.D. 1975, Memphis State University M.B.A. 1979 and University of Virginia LL.M. 1995. Honorary LL.D. Central Missouri State University 1994 and Westminster College 1999. Editor Yale Law Journal 1974-75. Admitted to practice Missouri 1975, U.S. Tax Court and U.S. Supreme Court. In legal practice Jefferson City 1983-89.
Adjunct Professor University of Missouri-Columbia and Westminster College. Member The Missouri Bar and American Bar Association. Presenter judicial conference "Winning Appellate Practice." Captain USNR (retired). Former Chief of Staff to Congressman Wendell Bailey. Member United Way and Rotary.
Mailing address: P.O. Box 150, Jefferson City 65102.
Office: Supreme Court Building, 210 East High Street, Jefferson City 65101.
Telephone: (573) 751-6880.
Fax: (573) 751-7361
E-mail address: Duane_Benton@osca.state.mo.us

BERKEMEYER, John B. *(Associate Circuit Judge, Missouri Circuit Court Twentieth Judicial Circuit)* Serves Probate Division.
Office: 119 East First Street, Room 3, Hermann 65041.
Telephone: (573) 486-2321.

BICKEL, James R. *(Presiding Judge, Missouri Circuit Court Twenty-eighth Judicial Circuit)*
Office: 100 West Cherry, Nevada 64772.
Telephone: (417) 667-5016.
Fax: (417) 448-2535

BLACKWELL, Carroll M. *(Associate Circuit Judge, Missouri Circuit Court Tenth Judicial Circuit)* Appointed by Governor Warren Eastman Hearnes Sept 1971. Elected to subsequent terms. Current term expires Dec 31, 2006. Serves Probate Division. Born Anniston Missouri April 14, 1936. Christian. Educated at University of Missouri B.S. 1958 J.D. 1961. Admitted to practice Missouri 1961. Former Judge, Monroe County Probate and Magistrate Courts.
Member The Missouri Bar and Monroe County Bar Association. Democrat.
Office: 300 North Main, Paris 65275.
Telephone: (660) 327-5220.
Fax: (660) 327-5781

BLANKENSHIP, Alan *(Associate Circuit Judge, Missouri Circuit Court Thirty-ninth Judicial Circuit)* Serves Probate Division.
Mailing address: P.O. Box 186, Galena 65656.
Telephone: (417) 357-6511.
Fax: (417) 357-6163

BLANTON, Lewis M. *(Magistrate Judge, United States District Court Eastern District of Missouri)* Appointed by U.S. District Court judges 1991. Reappointed 1999, current term expires 2007. Born Cape Girardeau Missouri March 5, 1934. Roman Catholic. Educated at St. Louis University A.B. 1958 M.A. 1962 and University of Missouri J.D. 1965. Editor Missouri Law Review. Recipient Guy A. Thompson Scholarship. Member Student Bar Association (Treasurer 1964) and Phi Delta Phi. Admitted to practice Missouri 1965, U.S. District Court Eastern District of Missouri 1965 and U.S. Court of Appeals Eighth Circuit 1971. In legal practice St. Louis 1965-69 and Sikeston 1969-78. Associate Circuit Judge, Missouri Circuit Court Thirty-third Judicial Circuit, Jan 1, 1979 to 1991.
City Attorney Chaffee 1973-75. Author "Torts—Public Swimming Pool—Contributory Negligence as a Matter of Law" 29 Missouri L. Rev. 115, 1964; "Reverse Condemnation" 21 Journal of the Missouri Bar 211 May 1965 and "Adult Abuse Act and Note on Child Protection Orders Act" *Bench Book for Missouri Trial Judges* 1989. Member Missouri Association of Probate and Associate Circuit Judges 1979-91 (Board of Directors 1984-88), Missouri Supreme Court Judicial Records Committee 1982-91, The Missouri Bar (Legal Education Committee 1982-87, Vice Chairman 1985-87), The Bar Association of Metropolitan St. Louis, Cape Girardeau County, Scott County and American Bar Associations. Lecturer The Missouri Bar CLE 1983-87 and 1990 and Missouri Supreme Court Judicial Education Committee 1990. Board of Directors Sikeston United Fund 1971-77, Sikeston Child Development Center (Vice Chairman) 1973-77 and Tri-County Counseling Center 1975-78. Executive Board Southeast Missouri Council Boy Scouts of America 1986-94. Past President Sikeston Rotary Club. Member Advisory Board Group Home IV Missouri Division of Youth Services 1974-76.
Office: 111 Federal Building, 339 Broadway Street, Cape Girardeau 63701.
Telephone: (573) 334-2075.

BLOCK, Susan *(Circuit Judge, Missouri Circuit Court Twenty-first Judicial Circuit)* Former Associate Circuit Judge. Appointed Circuit Judge by Governor Mel Carnahan. Retained by election. Serves Juvenile Division.
Office: 501 South Brentwood, Clayton 63105.
Telephone: (314) 615-1516.
Fax: (314) 615-4477

BLOODWORTH, John *(Associate Circuit Judge, Missouri Circuit Court Thirty-sixth Judicial Circuit)*
Office: 100 North Main, Poplar Bluff 63901.
Telephone: (573) 686-8087.
Fax: (573) 686-8093

BORRON, John A., Jr. *(Circuit Judge, Missouri Circuit Court Sixteenth Judicial Circuit)* Appointed by governor. Retained by election. Serves Probate Division.
Office: Courthouse, 415 East Twelfth Street, Kansas City 64106.
Telephone: (816) 881-3761.

BRECKENRIDGE, Patricia *(Judge, Missouri Court of Appeals Western District)* Appointed by Governor John D. Ashcroft to term beginning Dec 18, 1990. Retained by election 1992, current term expires Dec 31, 2004. Former Chief Judge. Born Nevada Oct 14, 1953. Educated at University of Arkansas at Fayetteville and University of Missouri-Columbia B.S. J.D. Associate Circuit Judge, Missouri Circuit Court Twenty-eighth Judicial Circuit Jan 22, 1982 to Dec 17, 1990.
Member Missouri Task Force on Gender and Justice 1990-93. Fellow American Bar Foundation. Member Association of Probate and Associate Circuit Judges (President 1990-91), The Missouri Bar, The Kansas City Metropolitan, Vernon County and American Bar Associations. Member United Methodist Church.
Office: 1300 Oak Street, Kansas City 64106-2970.
Telephone: (816) 889-3614.
Fax: (816) 889-3599

BRISCOE, Joseph R., Jr. *(Circuit Judge, Missouri Circuit Court Eleventh Judicial Circuit)*
Office: 300 North Second Street, Room 512, St. Charles 63301.
Telephone: (636) 949-7900.
Fax: (636) 949-3070

BROWN, T. Lynn *(Associate Circuit Judge, Missouri Circuit Court Thirty-third Judicial Circuit)* Elected Nov 1990 to term beginning Jan 1, 1991. Reelected 1994, 1998 and 2002. Current term expires Dec 31, 2006. Serves Probate Division. Born Sikeston Missouri Dec 31, 1960. United Methodist Church. Educated at University of Missouri-Columbia A.B. 1983 and Washington University J.D. 1986. Admitted to practice Missouri 1986, U.S. District Court Eastern District of Missouri 1989 and U.S. Court of Appeals Eighth Circuit 1989.
Prosecuting Attorney Mississippi County Jan 1, 1987 to Dec 31, 1990. Democrat.
Mailing address: P.O. Box 369, Charleston 63834.
Telephone: (573) 683-2146.

BROWN, Thomas, III *(Presiding Judge, Missouri Circuit Court Nineteenth Judicial Circuit)* Former Associate Circuit Judge.
Mailing address: P.O. Box 1156, Jefferson City 65102.
Telephone: (573) 634-9192.
Fax: (573) 634-2584

BRYANT, Robert A. *(Associate Circuit Judge, Missouri Circuit Court Eighth Judicial Circuit)* Elected Nov 8, 1994 to term beginning Jan 1, 1995. Reelected 1998 ad 2002. Current term expires Dec 31, 2006. Serves Criminal, Civil, Municipal and Probate Divisions. Born Carrollton Missouri Jan 29, 1934. Educated at University of Missouri B.S.B.A. 1956 and University of Missouri-Kansas City LL.B. 1964. Admitted to practice Missouri 1964. In legal practice Carrollton 1964-94.
Prosecuting Attorney Carroll County 1967-90. Member The Missouri Bar and Carroll County Bar Association. Captain USAF 1956-59 and 1961-62. Democrat.
Office: Eight South Main, Suite 1, Carrollton 64633.
Telephone: (660) 542-1818.
Fax: (660) 542-1877

BRYSON, Larry A. *(Associate Circuit Judge, Missouri Circuit Court Thirteenth Judicial Circuit)* Elected Nov 1986 to term beginning Jan 1, 1987. Reelected 1990, 1994, 1998 and 2002. Current term expires Dec 31, 2006. Born Mexico Missouri Aug 10, 1948. Christian/Baptist. Educated at University of Missouri-Columbia B.A. 1970 J.D. 1972. Admitted to practice Missouri 1972 and U.S. District Court Western District of Missouri 1973. In legal practice Centralia 1972-86.
Member The Missouri Bar. Attended General Jurisdiction course The National Judicial College 1987. Captain USAR 1979. Treasurer, Vice Chairman and Chairman Democratic Central Committee Boone County 1973-86. Member, Deacon and Sunday School Teacher First Baptist Church. Enjoys hunting, fishing, cooking and family.
Office: 705 East Walnut Street, Columbia 65201.
Telephone: (573) 886-4050.
Fax: (573) 886-4070

BUCKLES, Frederick R. *(Magistrate Judge, United States District Court Eastern District of Missouri)* Appointed by U.S. District Court judges.
Office: U.S. Courthouse, 111 South Tenth Street, St. Louis 63102-9958.
Telephone: (314) 244-7570.

BULLERDIECK, Michael *(Associate Circuit Judge, Missouri Circuit Court Thirty-second Judicial Circuit)* Serves Probate Division. Former Associate Circuit Judge, Missouri Circuit Court Twenty-fourth Judicial Circuit.
Office: 15 West Ste. Marie Street, Suite 3, Perryville 63775.
Telephone: (573) 547-7861.

BURDITT, Larry M. *(Associate Circuit Judge, Missouri Circuit Court Thirtieth Judicial Circuit)* Serves Probate Division.
Mailing address: P.O. Box 37, Warsaw 65355.
Telephone: (660) 438-6231.
Fax: (660) 438-5755

BURGER, Joan M. *(Circuit Judge, Missouri Circuit Court Twenty-second Judicial Circuit)* Appointed by governor. Retained by election.
Office: Civil Courts Building, 10 North Tucker Boulevard, St. Louis 63101.
Telephone: (314) 622-4381.

BURKEMPER, T. Bennett, Jr. *(Associate Circuit Judge, Missouri Circuit Court Forty-fifth Judicial Circuit)*
Office: 201 Main, Troy 63379.
Telephone: (636) 528-6300.
Fax: (636) 528-9168

BURRELL, Don E., Jr. *(Circuit Judge, Missouri Circuit Court Thirty-first Judicial Circuit)* Elected Nov 3, 1998 to term beginning Jan 4, 1999. Reelected Nov 7, 2000, current term expires Dec 31, 2006. Born Springfield Missouri Dec 4, 1960. Protestant. Educated at Southwest Missouri State University B.S. magna cum laude 1982 and University of Missouri-Kansas City J.D. 1991. Staff member Missouri Law Review 1989-91.

BURRELL, DON E., JR.—*Continued*

Law Clerk to Hon. Kathryn H. Vratil, U.S. District Court District of Kansas 1992-93. Member Order of Bench and Robe. Admitted to practice Missouri 1991. In legal practice Kansas City 1991-93 and Springfield 1993-98.

Member Springfield Metropolitan Bar Association. Attended General Jurisdiction Course The National Judicial College. Republican. Enjoys reading, weight lifting and snow skiing.

Office: 1010 Boonville, Springfield 65802.
Telephone: (417) 868-4078.
Fax: (417) 829-6366
E-mail address: dburrell@osca.state.mo.us

BURTON, Michael D. *(Associate Circuit Judge, Missouri Circuit Court Twenty-first Judicial Circuit)* Appointed by Governor Mel Carnahan to term beginning May 27, 1999. Retained by election 2000, current term expires Jan 2005. Born Philadelphia Pennsylvania June 20, 1960. Roman Catholic. Educated at University of Notre Dame B.A. 1982 and Washington University J.D. 1985. Admitted to practice Missouri 1985, Illinois 1986 and U.S. District Court Eastern District of Missouri 1989. In legal practice St. Louis 1985-89 and Clayton 1989-99 Missouri.

Assistant Public Defender Special Public Defender's Office 1985-89. Instructor in Pre-Trial Procedure St. Louis University School of Law since 1992 and Trial Advocacy Washington University School of Law since 1995. Named Outstanding Young Lawyer of St. Louis County by St. Louis County Bar Association 1996. President Boys Club and Project Kids East St. Louis since 1991. Chairman Alumni Association Big Brothers/Big Sisters of St. Louis. Volunteer Judge St. Louis County Truancy Court Program.

Office: St. Louis County Courthouse, Division 41, 7900 Carondelet Avenue, Clayton 63105.
Telephone: (314) 615-1541.
Fax: (314) 615-2689
E-mail address: michael_burton@osca.state.mo.us

BUSCH, David L. *(Associate Circuit Judge, Missouri Circuit Court Eighth Judicial Circuit)* Serves Probate Division.

Office: 100 Main, Second Floor, Richmond 64085.
Telephone: (816) 776-2335.
Fax: (816) 776-2183

BUSH, Jerri *(Associate Circuit Judge, Missouri Circuit Court Third Judicial Circuit)* Serves Probate Division.

Office: 1601 West Main, Room 101, Unionville 63565.
Telephone: (660) 947-2117.
Fax: (660) 947-7348

BUSH, Julian L. *(Circuit Judge, Missouri Circuit Court Twenty-second Judicial Circuit)* Appointed by Governor Mel Carnahan June 15, 1995. Retained by election Nov 5, 1996 and Nov 5, 2002. Current term expires Dec 31, 2008. Born Beaver Falls Pennsylvania Nov 7, 1949. Educated at George Washington University B.A. 1971 and Washington University at St. Louis J.D. 1976. Admitted to practice Missouri 1976, U.S. District Court Eastern District of Missouri 1978, U.S. Court of Appeals Eighth Circuit and U.S. Supreme Court. In legal practice St. Louis 1976-95.

Associate City Counselor St. Louis 1982-95. Member The Bar Association of Metropolitan St. Louis and The Missouri Bar.

Office: Civil Courts Building, 10 North Tucker Street, St. Louis 63101.
Telephone: (314) 622-3668.

BUSHUR, Jeffrey L. *(Associate Circuit Judge, Missouri Circuit Court Sixteenth Judicial Circuit)* Appointed by governor.

Office: Courthouse Annex, 308 West Kansas, Independence 64050.
Telephone: (816) 881-1783.

CALLAHAN, Richard *(Circuit Judge, Missouri Circuit Court Nineteenth Judicial Circuit)*

Mailing address: P.O. Box 124, Jefferson City 65102.
Telephone: (573) 634-9190.
Fax: (573) 634-7676

CALVIN, Michael B. *(Circuit Judge, Missouri Circuit Court Twenty-second Judicial Circuit)* Appointed by governor. Retained by election. Former Presiding Judge.

Office: Municipal Courts Building, 1320 Market Street, St. Louis 63103.
Telephone: (314) 622-4929.

CAMPBELL, Thomas *(Associate Circuit Judge, Missouri Circuit Court Seventeenth Judicial Circuit)* Serves Probate Division.

Office: 102 East Wall, Harrisonville 64701.
Telephone: (816) 380-8217.
Fax: (816) 380-8215

CARLTON, Stephen P. *(Associate Circuit Judge, Missouri Circuit Court Twenty-ninth Judicial Circuit)*

Office: 302 South Main, Carthage 64836.
Telephone: (417) 237-1096.

CARPENTER, Christine *(Associate Circuit Judge, Missouri Circuit Court Thirteenth Judicial Circuit)*

Office: 705 East Walnut Street, Columbia 65201.
Telephone: (573) 886-4050.
Fax: (573) 886-4070

CHADWICK, Daniel L. *(Associate Circuit Judge, Missouri Circuit Court Forty-third Judicial Circuit)* Serves Probate Division.

Mailing address: P.O. Box 5, Kingston 64650.
Telephone: (816) 586-2771.
Fax: (816) 586-2333

CLARK, Thomas C. *(Circuit Judge, Missouri Circuit Court Sixteenth Judicial Circuit)* Appointed by governor. Retained by election.

Office: Courthouse, 415 East Twelfth Street, Kansas City 64106.
Telephone: (816) 881-3603.

CLARKSON, William J. *(Associate Circuit Judge, Missouri Circuit Court Thirty-sixth Judicial Circuit)* Serves Probate Division.

Office: 100 North Main, Poplar Bluff 63901.
Telephone: (573) 686-8073.
Fax: (573) 686-0056

CLAYTON, John *(Associate Circuit Judge, Missouri Circuit Court Twenty-fifth Judicial Circuit)* Serves Probate Division.

Mailing address: P.O. Box 490, Vienna 65582.
Telephone: (573) 422-3303.
Fax: (573) 422-3976

CLAYTON, Robert M., II *(Presiding Judge, Missouri Circuit Court Tenth Judicial Circuit)*
Office: 906 Broadway, Hannibal 63401.
Telephone: (573) 221-0579.
Fax: (573) 221-0366
E-mail address: Robert_Clayton_II@osca.state.mo.us

CLIFFORD, Patrick *(Associate Circuit Judge, Missouri Circuit Court Twenty-first Judicial Circuit)* Appointed by governor. Retained by election.
Office: St. Louis County Court Building, 7900 Carondelet, Clayton 63105.
Telephone: (314) 615-1539.

COHEN, Patricia L. *(Circuit Judge, Missouri Circuit Court Twenty-second Judicial Circuit)* Appointed by Governor Mel Carnahan.
Office: Municipal Courts Building, 1320 Market Street, St. Louis 63103.
Telephone: (314) 622-4444.

COHEN, Robert S. *(Circuit Judge, Missouri Circuit Court Twenty-first Judicial Circuit)* Former Associate Circuit Judge, assumed office Jan 1979. Appointed Circuit Judge by governor. Retained by election. Former Presiding Judge. Born St. Louis Missouri July 4, 1946. Jewish. Educated at University of Missouri 1964-65, Washington University at St. Louis A.B. 1968 and St. Louis University J.D. 1971. Admitted to practice Missouri 1971 and U.S. District Court Eastern District of Missouri 1971. Began legal practice St. Louis 1971. Judge, St. Louis County Magistrate Court Jan 1, 1975 to Dec 31, 1978.
Author "Actions Before Associate Circuit Judges" Missouri Bar CLE Desk Book *Civil Actions II* 1981, "Civil Practice Before Associate Circuit Judges Since the Court Reform" Journal of The Missouri Bar June 1981 and "Continuing the Court Reform: Eliminating the Trial De Novo from the Associate Circuit Judge" Journal of The Missouri Bar April/May 1983. Instructor Practice Court St. Louis University School of Law 1975-77. Member The Bar Association of Metropolitan St. Louis, The Missouri Bar and St. Louis County Bar Association (President Elect). Former member Committee to Revise the Mental Health Laws of Missouri.
Office: St. Louis County Court Building, 7900 Carondelet, Clayton 63105.
Telephone: (314) 615-1501.
Fax: (314) 615-8280

COLLINS, William B. *(Associate Circuit Judge, Missouri Circuit Court Seventeenth Judicial Circuit)*
Mailing address: P.O. Box 384, Harrisonville 64701.
Telephone: (816) 380-8196.
Fax: (816) 380-8195

COMBS, Roger E. *(Associate Circuit Judge, Missouri Circuit Court Fourth Judicial Circuit)* Serves Probate Division.
Office: 200 West Clay, Albany 64402.
Telephone: (660) 726-3411.
Fax: (660) 726-3130

CONKLIN, J. Dan *(Associate Circuit Judge, Missouri Circuit Court Thirty-first Judicial Circuit)*
Office: 1010 Boonville, Springfield 65802.
Telephone: (417) 868-4105.

COOK, Jacqueline *(Circuit Judge, Missouri Circuit Court Seventeenth Judicial Circuit)*
Office: 102 East Wall, Harrisonville 64701.
Telephone: (816) 422-7407.
Fax: (816) 422-7417

COPELAND, Fred W. *(Presiding Judge, Missouri Circuit Court Thirty-fourth Judicial Circuit)*
Mailing address: P.O. Box 34, Caruthersville 63830.
Telephone: (573) 333-4156.
Fax: (573) 333-4157

COPELAND, Richard Dennis *(Associate Circuit Judge, Missouri Circuit Court Twenty-ninth Judicial Circuit)* Appointed by governor to term beginning Jan 6, 1981. Elected 1982, 1986, 1990, 1994, 1998 and 2002. Current term expires Dec 31, 2006. Born St. Louis Missouri April 17, 1945. Methodist. Educated at University of Missouri B.A. 1967 J.D. 1972. Admitted to practice Missouri 1972. In legal practice Webb City 1972-77 and Joplin 1977-81.
City Attorney Webb City 1972-76. Member The Missouri Bar and Jasper County Bar Association. Attended The National Judicial College 1984 and 1985. E-5 U.S. Army 1969-71.
Office: Courts Building, 601 South Pearl, Joplin 64801.
Telephone: (417) 625-4316.

COYLER, Bruce *(Associate Circuit Judge, Missouri Circuit Court Twenty-sixth Judicial Circuit)*
Office: One Court Circle, Suite 9, Camdenton 65020.
Telephone: (573) 346-5160.
Fax: (573) 346-0369

CRAHAN, Lawrence G. *(Judge, Missouri Court of Appeals Eastern District)* Appointed by Governor John D. Ashcroft to term beginning Oct 13, 1992. Retained by election 1994, current term expires Dec 31, 2006. Chief Judge 1997-98. Born Guam. Educated at University of Missouri-Columbia B.A. 1971 J.D. cum laude 1977. Editor-in-Chief Missouri Law Review. Law Clerk to Presiding Justice James A. Finch, Jr., Missouri Supreme Court Division Two 1977-78. Member Order of the Coif.
Member St. Louis Bar Foundation, American Judicature Society, The Bar Association of Metropolitan St. Louis and The Missouri Bar. Member University of Missouri-Columbia School of Law Foundation (Trustee 1989-92), University of Missouri-Columbia Law Society and Missouri Supreme Court Historical Society.
Office: Wainwright State Office Building, 111 North Seventh Street, St. Louis 63101.
Telephone: (314) 340-6926.
Fax: (314) 340-7703

CRANCER, Barbara A. *(Associate Circuit Judge, Missouri Circuit Court Twenty-first Judicial Circuit)* Appointed by governor. Retained by election.
Office: St. Louis County Court Building, 7900 Carondelet, Clayton 63105.
Telephone: (314) 615-1531.
Fax: (314) 615-2689

CRANDALL, William H., Jr. *(Judge, Missouri Court of Appeals Eastern District)* Appointed by Governor Christopher S. Bond to term beginning Jan 1, 1982. Retained by election. Current term expires Dec 31, 2008. Former Chief Judge. Born Urbana Illinois Sept 27, 1939. Educated at Washington University at St.

CRANDALL, WILLIAM H., JR.—*Continued*

Louis B.S.B.A. 1961 J.D. 1963. Member Phi Delta Phi. Admitted to practice Missouri 1963, U.S. District Court Eastern District of Missouri and U.S. Court of Appeals Eighth Circuit. In legal practice 1963-66. Judge, Eighth District Magistrate Court 1968-75. Acting Judge, Seventh District Magistrate Court 1971. Judge, Missouri Circuit Court Twenty-first Judicial Circuit July 9, 1975 to Dec 8, 1981, appointed by Governor Christopher S. Bond.

Assistant Public Defender 1966-68. Lecturer St. Louis University Law School 1973-75. Member The Bar Association of Metropolitan St. Louis, The Missouri Bar and St. Louis County Bar Association (Chairman Criminal Law Committee 1970-71). Lecturer Missouri Bar Practical Skills 1969-75 and Missouri Trial Judges Seminar 1972-73. Private First Class USAR 1963-66 and Lieutenant USNR 1966-75.

Office: 121 South Meramec, Suite 500, Clayton 63105.

Telephone: (314) 512-7705.

Fax: (314) 340-7703

CRANE, Kathianne Knaup *(Judge, Missouri Court of Appeals Eastern District)* Appointed by Governor John D. Ashcroft to term beginning July 9, 1990. Retained by election Nov 4, 1992, current term expires Dec 31, 2004. Educated at Washington University A.B. 1967 and St. Louis University J.D. cum laude 1971. Associate Editor of Student Writings St. Louis University Law Journal 1969-71. Admitted to practice Missouri 1972, U.S. District Court Eastern District of Missouri 1972, U.S. Court of Appeals Eighth Circuit 1972 and U.S. Supreme Court 1975. In legal practice St. Louis 1972-80.

Assistant U.S. Attorney Eastern District of Missouri 1980-90. Co-author "Tips and Suggestions from the Perspective of the Appellate Bench" St. Louis B. Jour. Winter 1993. Instructor in Legal Research and Writing 1974 and Business Associations 1975 St. Louis University. Fellow Missouri Bar Foundation and American Bar Foundation. Member The American Law Institute, American Judicature Society, The Bar Association of Metropolitan St. Louis and American Bar Association. Speaker at numerous seminars and continuing legal education programs. Recipient Robert Walston Chubb Award from Legal Services of Eastern Missouri, Vincent Immel Alumni Merit Award from St. Louis University School of Law and Chief Justice's Award from Chief Justice, Supreme Court of Missouri. Member Peace Corps 1967-68.

Office: 121 South Meramec, Suite 500, Clayton 63105.

Telephone: (314) 512-7706.

CRAWFORD, Dan J. *(Associate Circuit Judge, Missouri Circuit Court Thirty-fifth Judicial Circuit)* Elected Nov 6, 1994 to term beginning Jan 1, 1995. Reelected Nov 1998 and 2002. Current term expires Dec 31, 2006. Born Sikeston Missouri. Methodist. Educated at Southeast Missouri State University B.S. 1976 and University of Missouri-Columbia J.D. 1982. Member Phi Delta Phi. Admitted to practice Missouri 1982.

Assistant Attorney General Missouri 1983-86. Assistant Prosecuting Attorney Dunklin County 1986-94. Member The Missouri Bar.

Office: Courthouse, Room 103, Kennett 63857.

Telephone: (573) 888-3378.

Fax: (573) 888-0754

CRAWFORD, William C. *(Circuit Judge, Missouri Circuit Court Twenty-ninth Judicial Circuit)* Former Presiding Judge.

Office: 320 Courts Building, 601 South Pearl, Joplin 64801.

Telephone: (417) 625-4318.

Fax: (417) 625-4396

CROUCH, Garrett R., II *(Associate Circuit Judge, Missouri Circuit Court Seventeenth Judicial Circuit)* Serves Probate Division.

Office: 300 North Holden, Warrensburg 64093.

Telephone: (660) 422-7405.

Fax: (660) 422-7412

CUNDIFF, Terry R. *(Associate Circuit Judge, Missouri Circuit Court Eleventh Judicial Circuit)*

Office: 300 North Second Street, Room 436, St. Charles 63301.

Telephone: (636) 949-7900.

Fax: (636) 949-3072

CUNNINGHAM, Jon Alan *(Associate Circuit Judge, Missouri Circuit Court Eleventh Judicial Circuit)* Elected Nov 6, 1990 to term beginning Jan 1, 1991. Reelected Nov 8, 1994, Nov 1998 and 2002. Current term expires Dec 31, 2006. Serves Probate Division. Born Louisiana Missouri Nov 8, 1955. Methodist. Educated at Northeast Missouri State University B.S.E. magna cum laude 1978 and University of Missouri-Columbia J.D. 1982. Member Phi Delta Phi. Admitted to practice Missouri 1982 and U.S. District Court Eastern District of Missouri 1984. In legal practice St. Charles 1982-90.

Member Missouri Association of Probate and Associate Judges, American Judges Association, The Missouri Bar and St. Charles County Bar Association (President 1996). Republican. Member Rotary International. Hobbies include tennis, remodeling, scuba diving and whaling.

Office: 300 North Second Street, Room 333, St. Charles 63301.

Telephone: (636) 949-7900.

Fax: (636) 949-7457

CURLESS, Charles *(Associate Circuit Judge, Missouri Circuit Court Twenty-eighth Judicial Circuit)* Elected Nov 8, 1994 to term beginning Jan 1, 1995. Reelected Nov 1998 and 2002. Current term expires Dec 31, 2006. Serves Probate Division. Born Lamar Missouri Aug 30, 1951. United Methodist. Educated at Southwest Missouri State University B.S. 1973 and Oklahoma City University J.D. 1980. Member Phi Alpha Delta (Former District Justice). Admitted to practice Missouri 1981 and U.S. District Court Western District of Missouri 1981. In legal practice Springfield 1981-83 and Lamar 1983-95.

Member Missouri Association of Probate and Associate Circuit Judges (Executive Board), Missouri Municipal and Associate Circuit Judges Association, The Missouri Bar and Barton County Bar Association (Past President). Attends various judicial conferences and seminars annually. Past President Lamar Country Club. Former Chairman Barton County United Fund. Former Member

CURLESS, CHARLES—*Continued*

Lamar R-1 School Board. President Mark IV Industries, Inc. Board of Directors Helping Hearts, Inc. Life Member Barton County Historical Society. Member Lamar Masonic Lodge, Scottish Rite, Abou Ben Adhem Shrine, Metro Club, Rotary International (Board of Directors), Lamar High School Booster Club, Chamber of Commerce, Lamar Community Theatre, Barton County Arts Council and Elks. Interests include guitar, harmonica, saxophone, hunting and fishing.
Office: 1007 Broadway, Lamar 64759.
Telephone: (417) 682-5754.
Fax: (417) 682-2960

CURRIE, W. Keith *(Associate Circuit Judge, Missouri Circuit Court Thirty-fourth Judicial Circuit)* Serves Probate Division.
Office: Seventh and Ward Avenue, Caruthersville 63830.
Telephone: (573) 333-0152.

CZAMANSKE, Daniel M. *(Associate Circuit Judge, Missouri Circuit Court Sixth Judicial Circuit)* Appointed by Governor John Ashcroft to term beginning April 20, 1992. Retained by election 1994, 1998 and 2002. Current term expires Dec 31, 2006. Born Royal Oak Michigan May 24, 1940. Educated at University of Missouri B.S. 1966 and University of Missouri-Columbia J.D. 1969. In legal practice Aug 1969 to April 1992. Judge, Riverside Municipal Court Aug 1987 to April 19, 1992.
Member Clay-Platte Municipal and Associate Circuit Judges Association, Missouri Probate and Associate Circuit Judges Association, The Missouri Bar (Board of Governors 1986-92) and Platte County Bar Association (Courthouse Committee 1976, Secretary, Treasurer, Vice President and President 1978-81). U.S. Army Security Agency Feb 1960 to Feb 1963. Mayor City of Riverside April 1972 to April 1976. Member Riverside Planning Commission 1970 to April 1972 and Riverside Board of Zoning Adjustment 1978 to Aug 1987. Member Christ Lutheran Church. Enjoys bass fishing and golf.
Office: 328 Main, Box 50 CH, Platte City 64079.
Telephone: (816) 858-3434.
Fax: (816) 858-3392

DALLY, David C. *(Presiding Judge, Missouri Circuit Court Twenty-ninth Judicial Circuit)* Elected Nov 1998 to term beginning Jan 1, 1999. Term expires Dec 31, 2004. Born Ishpeming Michigan March 15, 1948. Presbyterian. Educated at University of Missouri B.A. 1970 and University of Missouri-Columbia J.D. 1973. Admitted to practice Missouri 1973 and U.S. District Court Western District of Missouri 1974. In legal practice Carthage 1973.
City Attorney Carthage 1974-99. Prosecuting Attorney Jasper County 1987-99. Past President Missouri Association of Prosecuting Attorneys and Missouri Association of Municipal Attorneys. Member The Missouri Bar and Jasper County Bar Association.
Office: Courts Building, 601 South Pearl, Joplin 64801.
Telephone: (417) 625-4320.
Fax: (417) 625-4321

DALTON, Wesley C. *(Associate Circuit Judge, Missouri Circuit Court Twelfth Judicial Circuit)* Appointed by Governor Roger B. Wilson to term beginning Jan 1, 2001. Serves Probate Division. Born St. Charles Missouri Oct 10, 1958. Methodist. Educated at University of Missouri 1982 J.D. 1988. Admitted to practice Missouri 1988. In legal practice Warrenton Oct 1, 1988 to Dec 31, 2000. Interests include family and golf.
Office: 104 West Main Street, Warrenton 63383.
Telephone: (636) 456-3375.
Fax: (636) 456-2422

DANDURAND, Joseph *(Presiding Judge, Missouri Circuit Court Seventeenth Judicial Circuit)*
Office: Johnson County Justice Center, 101 West Market, Warrensburg 64093.
Telephone: (660) 422-7407.
Fax: (816) 422-7417

DAUGHERTY, Jay A. *(Presiding Judge, Missouri Circuit Court Sixteenth Judicial Circuit)* Appointed by governor. Retained by election.
Office: Courthouse Annex, 308 West Kansas, Independence 64050.
Telephone: (816) 881-3613.

DAVID, Michael P. *(Presiding Judge, Missouri Circuit Court Twenty-second Judicial Circuit)* Former Associate Circuit Judge. Appointed Circuit Judge by governor. Retained by election.
Office: Civil Courts Building, 10 North Tucker Street, St. Louis 63101.
Telephone: (314) 622-4311.
Fax: (314) 589-6599

DAVIS, K. Elizabeth *(Associate Circuit Judge, Missouri Circuit Court Seventh Judicial Circuit)* Appointed by governor. Retained by election.
Office: 11 South Water, Liberty 64068.
Telephone: (816) 792-7715.
Fax: (816) 792-7795

DAWSON, Michael *(Associate Circuit Judge, Missouri Circuit Court Twenty-seventh Judicial Circuit)* Serves Probate Division.
Office: 655 Second Street, Osceola 64776.
Telephone: (417) 646-2421.

DEAN, K. Preston *(Circuit Judge, Missouri Circuit Court Sixteenth Judicial Circuit)* Appointed by Governor John D. Ashcroft to term beginning Sept 25, 1989. Retained by election Nov 1990, Nov 1996 and Nov 2002. Current term expires Dec 31, 2008. Born Mexico Missouri Nov 9, 1946. Educated at University of Missouri-Columbia B.A. 1968 J.D. 1971. Admitted to practice Missouri 1971, U.S. District Court Western District of Missouri 1971, U.S. Court of Appeals Eighth Circuit 1974 and U.S. Supreme Court 1975. In legal practice Kansas City 1985-87.
Assistant Attorney General Missouri 1971-82. Company Counsel Missouri Public Service Company 1982-84. Assistant U.S. Attorney Western District of Missouri 1987-89.
Office: Courthouse, 415 East Twelfth Street, Kansas City 64106.
Telephone: (816) 881-3615.

DEL MURO, Justine E. *(Circuit Judge, Missouri Circuit Court Sixteenth Judicial Circuit)* Appointed by governor. Retained by election.
Office: Courthouse, 415 East Twelfth Street, Kansas City 64106.
Telephone: (816) 881-3604.

DeMARCE, Karl A. W. *(Associate Circuit Judge, Missouri Circuit Court First Judicial Circuit)* Elected 1998 to term beginning Jan 1, 1999. Reelected 2002, current term expires Dec 31, 2006. Serves Probate Division. Born Maryville Missouri Aug 18, 1968. Lutheran. Educated at University of Missouri-Columbia B.S. with honors 1989 M.S. 1992 J.D. with honors 1997. Editor-in-Chief Missouri Law Review 1996-97. Member Order of the Coif. Admitted to practice Missouri 1997. In legal practice Memphis 1997-98.

Member Missouri Association of Probate and Associate Circuit Judges, National College of Probate Judges, The Missouri Bar (Legislative Committee, Probate and Trust Law Committee) and First Judicial Circuit Bar Association. Recipient Community Service Award from Scotland County Rotary Club 1994 and Friend of Agriculture Award from Missouri Farm Bureau 1998. Democrat. State Representative First District of Missouri 1997-98. Member Scotland County Rotary Club, Masons Memphis Lodge No. 16, Scotland County Business and Professional Association and Scotland County Historical Society.

Office: 102 Scotland County Courthouse, 117 South Market Street, Memphis 63555.
Telephone: (660) 465-2404.
Fax: (660) 465-8673
E-mail address: kdemarce@osca.state.mo.us

DePRIEST, Tommy W., Jr. *(Circuit Judge, Missouri Circuit Court Twenty-first Judicial Circuit)* Appointed by governor.

Office: St. Louis County Court Building, 7900 Carondelet, Clayton 63105.
Telephone: (314) 615-1508.
Fax: (314) 615-8280

DERMOTT, Jon A. *(Circuit Judge, Missouri Circuit Court Twenty-ninth Judicial Circuit)* Elected 1995. Former Presiding Judge. Serves Circuit and Probate Divisions. Born Lamar Missouri. Episcopalian. Educated at University of Arkansas LL.B. 1963. Admitted to practice Arkansas 1963, Texas 1964, Missouri 1967, U.S. District Court Southern District of Missouri and U.S. Court of Appeals Eighth Circuit. In legal practice Little Rock Arkansas 1965-67 and Joplin Missouri 1967-94.

Editor *Courts and CLE Bulletin* 1985-94. Member The Missouri Bar (Professionalism Committee and Judicial Redistricting Committee 1992), State Bar of Texas, Jasper County, Arkansas and American Bar Associations. Named Outstanding Alumnus by University of Arkansas School of Law 1990. USMCR 1956-63. Republican. President United Way of Joplin 1973-74. President Board of Directors 1982-83 and Member Advisory Board since 1991 Freeman Hospital. Board Member University of Arkansas Alumni Association 1987-89.

Office: Courts Building, 601 South Pearl, Joplin 64801.
Telephone: (417) 625-4325.
Fax: (417) 625-4326

DIAL, Gary *(Presiding Judge, Missouri Circuit Court First Judicial Circuit)*

Office: 117 South Market, Room 205, Memphis 63555.
Telephone: (660) 465-7012.
Fax: (660) 465-7079

DICKERSON, Mary *(Circuit Judge, Missouri Circuit Court Twenty-sixth Judicial Circuit)* Associate Circuit Judge May 12, 1981 to 1988, appointed by Governor Christopher S. Bond. Elected Circuit Judge 1988. Reelected 1992 and 1998. Current term expires Dec 31, 2004. Former Presiding Judge. Born Tuscumbia Missouri. Southern Baptist. Educated at University of Missouri-Columbia B.A. 1974 J.D. 1977. Admitted to practice Missouri 1978.

Member Circuit Court Budget Committee, The Missouri Bar (Judicial Administration Committee), Camden County and Twenty-sixth Judicial Circuit Bar Associations. Republican.

Office: One Court Circle, Suite 9, Camdenton 65020.
Telephone: (573) 346-5160.

DIERKER, Robert H., Jr. *(Circuit Judge, Missouri Circuit Court Twenty-second Judicial Circuit)* Appointed by Governor John D. Ashcroft to term beginning March 6, 1986. Retained by election. Former Presiding Judge. Born St. Louis Missouri Feb 24, 1949. Roman Catholic. Educated at St. Louis University A.B. summa cum laude 1971, University of Missouri-Kansas City J.D. with distinction 1974 and Harvard University LL.M. 1975. Recipient scholarship to St. Louis University 1967-71 and University of Missouri-Kansas City 1971-74 from Stinson Mag. Articles Editor University of Missouri-Kansas City Law Review 1973-74. Law Clerk to Hon. Joseph J. Simeone, Missouri Court of Appeals Eastern District 1974-75. Member Phi Beta Kappa. Admitted to practice Missouri 1974, U.S. District Court Eastern District of Missouri 1975, U.S. Court of Appeals Eighth Circuit 1977 and U.S. Supreme Court 1979. In legal practice St. Louis 1975-86.

Assistant and Associate City Counselor City of St. Louis 1979-86. Author "Sub Deo Et Lege: Toward Limitation of Federal Judicial Power" St. Louis University Public Law Forum 1985, *Missouri Criminal Practice Handbook* 1996 and *Missouri Criminal Law* West 1999. Co-author *Missouri Personal Injury and Torts* Lawyers Co-op 1996 and *Missouri Contracts Litigation* Lawyers Co-op 1996. Member Lawyers Association of St. Louis, Missouri Association of Trial Attorneys, American Judicature Society, The Bar Association of Metropolitan St. Louis and The Missouri Bar. Attended General Jurisdiction Course The National Judicial College 1986. Republican. Candidate for Missouri House of Representatives 1978. Campaign Treasurer Republican candidate for Missouri Senate 1978. Former member various Republican clubs. Member Selden Society and Federalist Society. Enjoys trapshooting.

Office: Municipal Courts Building, 1320 Market Street, St. Louis 63103.
Telephone: (314) 622-4331.

DIETRICH, Glen *(Associate Circuit Judge, Missouri Circuit Court Fourth Judicial Circuit)* Serves Probate Division.

Office: 303 North Market, Maryville 64468.
Telephone: (660) 582-2531.
Fax: (660) 582-2047

DILDINE, Dan *(Presiding Judge, Missouri Circuit Court Forty-fifth Judicial Circuit)* Elected to term beginning Jan 1, 2001.

Office: 201 Main, Troy 63379.
Telephone: (636) 528-6300.
Fax: (636) 528-9168

DOLAN, Colleen *(Circuit Judge, Missouri Circuit Court Twenty-first Judicial Circuit)* Former Associate

DOLAN, COLLEEN—*Continued*
Circuit Judge. Appointed Circuit Judge by Governor Mel Carnahan.
Office: St. Louis County Court Building, 7900 Carondelet, Clayton 63105.
Telephone: (314) 615-1520.
Fax: (314) 615-7658

DOLAN, David A. *(Presiding Judge, Missouri Circuit Court Thirty-third Judicial Circuit)* Former Associate Circuit Judge.
Mailing address: P.O. Box 256, Benton 63736.
Telephone: (573) 545-3141.
Fax: (573) 545-3000

DORR, Richard E. *(Judge, United States District Court Western District of Missouri)* Appointed for life by President George W. Bush to term beginning Aug 9, 2002.
Office: 3100 U.S. Courthouse, 222 North John Q. Hammons Parkway, Springfield 65808.
Telephone: (417) 865-3741.

DOWD, David L. *(Circuit Judge, Missouri Circuit Court Twenty-second Judicial Circuit)* Appointed by governor.
Office: Civil Courts Building, 10 North Tucker Street, St. Louis 63101.
Telephone: (314) 622-4233.

DOWD, Robert G., Jr. *(Judge, Missouri Court of Appeals Eastern District)* Appointed by Governor Mel Carnahan. Former Chief Judge. Born St. Louis Missouri March 6, 1951. Catholic. Educated at University of Missouri-St. Louis, Quincy College B.A. 1973 and St. Mary's University School of Law J.D. 1977. Admitted to practice Missouri 1978. In legal practice St. Louis 1978-79. Former Juvenile Officer Juvenile Court. Former Circuit Judge, Missouri Circuit Court Twenty-second Judicial Circuit, appointed by Governor John D. Ashcroft to term beginning July 17, 1985.
Member The Bar Association of Metropolitan St. Louis, The Missouri Bar and American Bar Association. Attended annual judicial seminars since 1979. Graduate The National Judicial College, Reno Nevada. Member Catholic Youth Council.
Office: Wainwright State Office Building, 111 North Seventh Street, St. Louis 63101.
Telephone: (314) 340-6938.
Fax: (314) 340-7703

DRAPER, George W., III *(Judge, Missouri Court of Appeals Eastern District)* Appointed by Governor Mel Carnahan May 16, 2000. Born St. Louis Missouri Aug 5, 1953. Educated at Morehouse College B.A. and Howard University School of Law J.D. Associate Circuit Judge, Missouri Circuit Court Twenty-first Judicial Circuit, appointed by Governor Mel Carnahan July 1994. Circuit Judge, Missouri Circuit Court Twenty-first Judicial Circuit, appointed by Governor Mel Carnahan June 1998.
With Office of the Circuit Attorney St. Louis 1984-94. Former General Counsel State of Missouri Department of Corrections. Adjunct Professor of Trial Advocacy St. Louis University School of Law since 1996. Member Lawyers Association of St. Louis and Mound City Bar Association. Member Northside Family Worship Center.
Office: Wainwright State Office Building, 111 North Seventh Street, St. Louis 63101.
Telephone: (314) 340-6932.
Fax: (314) 340-7703

DRUMM, Bernhardt C., Jr. *(Circuit Judge, Missouri Circuit Court Twenty-first Judicial Circuit)* Appointed by Governor Christopher S. Bond to term beginning Jan 28, 1983. Retained by election 1984, 1990, 1996 and 2002. Current term expires Dec 31, 2008. Presiding Judge 1987-88. Serves Probate Division. Born St. Louis Missouri Aug 29, 1941. Presbyterian. Educated at Amherst College B.A. in Economics cum laude 1963 and Washington University J.D. 1966. Member Beta Theta Pi, Harlan Fiske Stone Society and Phi Delta Phi. Admitted to practice Missouri 1966, U.S. District Courts Eastern District of Missouri 1969 and Eastern District of Wisconsin 1969, U.S. Court of Appeals Eighth Circuit 1970 and U.S. Supreme Court 1976. In legal practice St. Louis 1969-83. Special Judge, Missouri Court of Appeals Eastern District 1985.
Special Agent FBI 1966-69. Assistant U.S. Attorney Eastern District of Wisconsin 1969. Member Circuit Court Budget Committee 1984-93, ad hoc Committee to Study the Revision of Rule 74 Relating to Judgments 1986, Legislative Steering Committee 1987-88, Presiding Judges Executive Committee 1987-88 and Executive Council 1990-93 Missouri Supreme Court. Member Lawyers Association of St. Louis (Gridiron Show 1969-73), Missouri State Trial Judges Association (Secretary-Treasurer 1985, Vice President 1986, President 1987), The Bar Association of Metropolitan St. Louis (Vice Chairman 1974, Chairman Elect 1975 and Chairman 1976 Young Lawyers Section and Chairman County Section 1982), The Missouri Bar (Chairman Judicial Administration Division 1990-91 and Professionalism Committee 1992-93) and St. Louis County Bar Association. Instructor Missouri Judicial College 1985. Listed in *Who's Who in American Law*. Recipient Outstanding Young Man of America Award from U.S. Jaycees 1977, KMOX Radio Call for Action Community Service Award 1977 and American Bar Association First Place Awards to Young Lawyers Section of The Bar Association of Metropolitan St. Louis in Comprehensive Program and Single Project category in the Award of Achievement competition 1977. Member 1972-83 and Chairman 1976-83 St. Louis County Air Pollution Appeals Board. Secretary 1975, Chairman Elect 1976, Chairman 1977 and Chairman South Central Region Conference 1978 St. Louis Chapter Society of Former FBI Agents. Member Jefferson Township Republican Club (Director) and Queeny Township Republican Club (Director and President 1978-82). Member Bonhomme Presbyterian Church (Elder), Amherst Association of St. Louis (President 1978-83), Missouri Athletic Club (Nominating Committee 1977), Arc House, Inc. (Board of Directors and Legal Counsel 1973 and 1974) and St. Louis Jaycees Inc. (Board of Directors and Legal Counsel 1974).
Office: St. Louis County Court Building, 7900 Carondelet, Clayton 63105.
Telephone: (314) 615-1504.
Fax: (314) 615-8293

ECKELKAMP, Cindy *(Associate Circuit Judge, Missouri Circuit Court Twentieth Judicial Circuit)*
Office: 120 South Church Street, Union 63084.
Telephone: (636) 583-6318.

EDWARDS, Jimmie M. *(Circuit Judge, Missouri Circuit Court Twenty-second Judicial Circuit)* Appointed by governor. Retained by election.
Office: Municipal Courts Building, 1320 Market Street, St. Louis 63103.
Telephone: (314) 622-4376.

EHLMANN, Steve *(Circuit Judge, Missouri Circuit Court Eleventh Judicial Circuit)* Former Associate Circuit Judge.
Office: 300 North Second Street, Room 539, St. Charles 63301.
Telephone: (636) 949-7900.
Fax: (636) 949-3099

EIFFERT, James *(Presiding Judge, Missouri Circuit Court Thirty-eighth Judicial Circuit)*
Office: 110 West Elm Street, Room 205, Ozark 65721.
Telephone: (417) 581-2727.
Fax: (417) 581-0091

ELLIOTT, R. Brent *(Associate Circuit Judge, Missouri Circuit Court Forty-third Judicial Circuit)* Serves Probate Division.
Mailing address: P.O. Box 248, Maysville 64469.
Telephone: (816) 449-5400.
Fax: (816) 449-2440

ELLIS, Joseph M. *(Chief Judge, Missouri Court of Appeals Western District)* Appointed by Governor Mel Carnahan to term beginning Aug 4, 1993. Retained by election. Born St. Louis Missouri Oct 25, 1946. Educated at University of Missouri-St. Louis and Washington University B.A. J.D. In legal practice Macon. Former Municipal Judge, City of Macon.
Member The Missouri Bar (Board of Governors, Young Lawyers Section). USAF. Past Chair Immaculate Conception Church.
Mailing address: P.O. Box 583, Macon 63552.
Office: 1300 Oak Street, Kansas City 64106-2970.
Telephone: (816) 889-3622, (660) 385-3144.
Fax: (816) 889-3599

ELLSWORTH, Brad *(Associate Circuit Judge, Missouri Circuit Court Twenty-fifth Judicial Circuit)*
Office: 210 North Grand, Houston 65483.
Telephone: (417) 967-3663.
Fax: (417) 967-2798

ENGLAND, James C. *(Magistrate Judge, United States District Court Western District of Missouri)* Appointed by U.S. District Court judges.
Office: 2200 U.S. Courthouse, 222 North John Q. Hammons Parkway, Springfield 65806.
Telephone: (417) 865-3761.

ESSNER, John R. *(Associate Circuit Judge, Missouri Circuit Court Twenty-first Judicial Circuit)* Appointed by Governor Mel Carnahan.
Office: St. Louis County Court Building, 7900 Carondelet, Clayton 63105.
Telephone: (314) 615-1537.

EVANS, David *(Associate Circuit Judge, Missouri Circuit Court Thirty-seventh Judicial Circuit)*
Office: 222 Courthouse, West Plains 65775.
Telephone: (417) 256-4050.
Fax: (417) 256-5826

FARRAGUT-HEMPHILL, Sandra *(Associate Circuit Judge, Missouri Circuit Court Twenty-first Judicial Circuit)* Appointed by Governor John D. Ashcroft to term beginning April 1991. Retained by election Nov 1992, Nov 1996 and Nov 2000. Current term expires Dec 31, 2004. Born Tampa Florida Dec 9, 1953. Educated at Spelman College B.S. cum laude 1975 and University of Florida School of Law J.D. 1979. Admitted to practice Missouri 1982 and U.S. District Court Eastern District of Missouri 1982. Began legal practice St. Louis.
Instructor St. Louis University School of Law 1983-85 and Washington University School of Law since 1990.
Office: St. Louis County Court Building, 7900 Carondelet, Clayton 63105.
Telephone: (314) 615-1542.
Fax: (314) 615-2689

FEDERMAN, Arthur B. *(Chief Judge, United States Bankruptcy Court Western District of Missouri)* Appointed by U.S. Court of Appeals Eighth Circuit judges. Chief Judge since Jan 1, 2000. Also Judge, Bankruptcy Appellate Panel Eighth Circuit. Selected by the Judicial Council of the Eighth Circuit.
Office: 6552 U.S. Courthouse, 400 East Ninth Street, Kansas City 64106.
Telephone: (816) 512-1910.

FENNER, Gary A. *(Judge, United States District Court Western District of Missouri)* Appointed for life by President Bill Clinton to term beginning 1996. Born St. Joseph Missouri Jan 31, 1947. Educated at University of Kansas B.A. 1970 and University of Missouri-Kansas City School of Law J.D. 1973. In legal practice Platte City 1973 and St. Joseph 1977-79. Circuit Judge, Missouri Circuit Court Fifth Judicial Circuit 1979-87. Judge 1988-94 and Chief Judge 1994-96, Missouri Court of Appeals Western District.
Assistant City Attorney St. Joseph 1973-77. Business Law Instructor Webster College 1976-77.
Office: 8452 U.S. Courthouse, 400 East Ninth Street, Kansas City 64106.
Telephone: (816) 512-5660.

FERGUSON, Iris Golliday *(Associate Circuit Judge, Missouri Circuit Court Twenty-second Judicial Circuit)* Appointed by Governor Mel Carnahan to term beginning April 1993. Retained by election 1995 and 1999. Current term expires Dec 31, 2003. Born St. Louis Missouri. Educated at Lincoln University B.A. 1966 and St. Louis University M.A. 1978 J.D. 1978. Staff member St. Louis University Law Journal 1977-78. Admitted to practice Missouri 1978. Municipal Judge, City of Pagedale 1989-93. Municipal Judge, City of Kinloch 1992-93.
Member Mound City and National Bar Associations.
Office: Civil Courts Building, 10 North Tucker Street, St. Louis 63101.
Telephone: (314) 622-4282.

FILIPPINE, Edward L. *(Senior Judge, United States District Court Eastern District of Missouri)* Appointed for life by President Jimmy Carter to term beginning

FILIPPINE, EDWARD L.—*Continued*

Aug 26, 1977. Former Chief Judge. Assumed Senior status, serves by assignment. Born St. Louis Missouri June 11, 1930. Roman Catholic. Educated at St. Louis University A.B. 1951 J.D. replaced LL.B. conferred cum laude 1957. Associate Editor St. Louis University Law Journal 1956-57. Member Order of the Woolsack, Phi Delta Phi and Phi Kappa Theta (formerly Theta Kappa Phi). Admitted to practice Missouri 1957, U.S. District Court Eastern District of Missouri 1957 and District of Columbia 1962. Began legal practice St. Louis 1957.

Staff Assistant to U.S. Senator Thomas F. Eagleton 1969-74. Special Assistant Attorney General Missouri 1963-64. Member The Missouri Bar, The Bar Association of Metropolitan St. Louis, St. Louis County and American Bar Associations. First Lieutenant USAF 1951-53 and Captain USAFR 1953-65. Enjoys golf and sailing.

Office: Thomas F. Eagleton U.S. Courthouse, Tenth Floor, 111 South Tenth Street, St. Louis 63102-9958.
Telephone: (314) 244-7640.

FITZSIMMONS, Mark E. *(Associate Circuit Judge, Missouri Circuit Court Thirty-first Judicial Circuit)* Elected Nov 3, 1998 to term beginning Jan 1, 1999. Reelected 2002, current term expires Dec 31, 2006. Born St. Louis Missouri Dec 13, 1952. Educated at Illinois College A.B. with honors 1975, Western Illinois University M.A. 1976 and University of Missouri-Kansas City J.D. 1981. Admitted to practice Missouri 1981, U.S. District Court Western District of Missouri and U.S. Courts of Appeals Eighth and Ninth Circuits. In legal practice Springfield 1981-98.

Member Missouri Association of Trial Attorneys, Missouri Association of Probate and Associate Circuit Judges, The Missouri Bar and American Bar Association.

Office: 1010 Boonville, Springfield 65802.
Telephone: (417) 868-4095.

FLEISSIG, Audrey G. *(Magistrate Judge, United States District Court Eastern District of Missouri)* Appointed by U.S. District Court judges to term beginning Aug 3, 2001.

Office: 111 South Tenth Street, Suite 9.152, St. Louis 63102.
Telephone: (314) 244-7420.

FRANKLIN, James A., Jr. *(Presiding Judge, Missouri Circuit Court Twenty-sixth Judicial Circuit)*

Office: One Court Circle, Suite 9, Camdenton 65020.
Telephone: (573) 346-5160.
Fax: (573) 346-0369

FRAWLEY, Thomas J. *(Circuit Judge, Missouri Circuit Court Twenty-second Judicial Circuit)* Appointed by governor. Retained by election. Serves Juvenile Division.

Office: 920 North Vandeventer, St. Louis 63108.
Telephone: (314) 552-2025.
Fax: (314) 552-2361

FRERKING, John *(Associate Circuit Judge, Missouri Circuit Court Fifteenth Judicial Circuit)* Serves Probate Division.

Mailing address: P.O. Box 557, Lexington 64067.
Telephone: (660) 259-2324.
Fax: (660) 259-4997

FUNK, J. Brad *(Associate Circuit Judge, Missouri Circuit Court Third Judicial Circuit)* Serves Probate Division.

Office: 802 East Main, Princeton 64673.
Telephone: (660) 748-4232.
Fax: (660) 748-4292

GABBERT, A. Rex *(Associate Circuit Judge, Missouri Circuit Court Seventh Judicial Circuit)* Appointed by Governor Mel Carnahan to term beginning July 16, 1994. Retained by election 1996 and 2000. Current term expires Dec 31, 2004. Born Kansas City Missouri Sept 25, 1956. Episcopalian. Educated at University of Missouri-Kansas City B.A. 1980 and Mississippi College School of Law J.D. 1985. Moot Court Board. Member Phi Alpha Delta. Admitted to practice Missouri 1986, U.S. District Courts Western District of Missouri 1986 and District of Kansas 1991, U.S. Supreme Court 1990 and Kansas 1991. In legal practice 1986 and 1991-94. Judge, North Kansas City Municipal Court 1993-94. Judge pro tem, Kansas City Municipal Court 1993-94.

Assistant Prosecuting Attorney Clay County 1987-91. Prosecuting Attorney Gladstone 1991-92. Representative Sixth Congressional District U.S. Attorney and U.S. Marshall Selection Commission 1993. Board Member Legislative Steering Committee Missouri Supreme Court. Board of Directors Missouri Associate and Probate Judges. Member Clay-Platte Municipal and Associate Circuit Judges Association, Missouri Municipal and Associate Circuit Judges Association (Board of Directors 1995-2000), American Judicature Society, The Missouri Bar, The Kansas City Metropolitan, Clay County (Secretary-Treasurer 1988-90) and Kansas Bar Associations. Former Member Board of Trustees Clay-Platte Ray Mental Health Tax Levy Board and North Kansas City Hospital. Member Harry S. Truman Library Institute and U.S. Supreme Court Historical Society.

Office: 11 South Water, Liberty 64068.
Telephone: (816) 792-7716.
Fax: (816) 792-7795

GAERTNER, Gary M., Jr. *(Circuit Judge, Missouri Circuit Court Twenty-first Judicial Circuit)* Appointed by Governor Mel Carnahan to term beginning July 14, 2000. Retained by election 2002, current term expires Dec 31, 2008. Born St. Louis Missouri. Catholic. Educated at St. Louis University B.S. magna cum laude J.D. cum laude. Staff member St. Louis University Law Journal. Member Alpha Sigma Nu.

Assistant Circuit Attorney St. Louis. Assistant U.S. Attorney Eastern District of Missouri. Former Council Member Young Lawyers' Section The Missouri Bar. Chair Insurance Fraud Task Force Eastern District of Missouri U.S. Department of Justice. Member Women Lawyers' Association, The Bar Association of Metropolitan St. Louis, Mound City and St. Louis County Bar Associations. Recipient The John C. Shepherd Professionalism Award from The Bar Association of Metropolitan St. Louis.

Office: St. Louis County Court Building, 7900 Carondelet, Clayton 63105.
Telephone: (314) 615-1506.
Fax: (314) 615-7658

GAERTNER, Gary M., Sr. *(Judge, Missouri Court of Appeals Eastern District)* Appointed by governor 1985. Retained by election. Born St. Louis Missouri Aug 11, 1937. Catholic. Educated at St. Louis University J.D. Member Phi Delta Phi. Admitted to practice

GAERTNER, GARY M., SR.—*Continued*

Missouri 1961, Illinois, U.S. District Court Eastern District of Missouri 1962, U.S. Court of Appeals Eighth Circuit 1962 and U.S. Supreme Court 1966. Circuit Judge and former Presiding Judge, Missouri Circuit Court Twenty-second Judicial Circuit July 14, 1969 to 1985.

Assistant City Counselor 1961-64, Associate City Counselor 1964-67 and City Counselor 1967-69 St. Louis. Member American Judicature Society, Missouri Council on Criminal Justice Region Five (Former Chairman and Vice Chairman), Lawyers Association of St. Louis, The Bar Association of Metropolitan St. Louis, The Missouri Bar and American Bar Association. Past President Missouri State Council of Juvenile Court Judges. Former member St. Louis Commission on Crime and Law Enforcement. Attended The National Judicial College, Missouri Trial Judges College, American Academy of Judicial Education University of New Hampshire, University of Virginia and Stanford University. Recipient Judiciary Award from St. Louis Grand Jury Association, Man of the Year Award from George Khoury International Association and Special Act Award from U.S. Association of Federal Investigators. Named An Outstanding Young St. Louisian by St. Louis Junior Chamber of Commerce. Listed in *Who's Who in American Law* and *The International Biography.* Served USCG. Former District Chairman and Vice Chairman Tomahawk District Boy Scouts of America. Former Board of Directors Boys and Girls Town of Missouri and The St. Louis Backstoppers. Vice President Khoury International Leagues and Shared Resource Enterprises, Inc. Executive Board St. Louis Area Council Boy Scouts of America.

Office: Wainwright State Office Building, 111 North Seventh Street, St. Louis 63101.
Telephone: (314) 340-6916.
Fax: (314) 340-7703

GAITAN, Fernando J., Jr. *(Judge, United States District Court Western District of Missouri)* Appointed for life by President George Bush to term beginning 1991. Born Kansas City Kansas Aug 22, 1948. Educated at Pittsburg State University B.S. 1970 and University of Missouri-Kansas City School of Law J.D. 1974. Circuit Judge, Missouri Circuit Court Sixteenth Judicial Circuit 1980-86. Judge, Missouri Court of Appeals Western District 1986-91.

Attorney Southwestern Bell Telephone Company 1974-80.

Office: 7552 U.S. Courthouse, 400 East Ninth Street, Kansas City 64106.
Telephone: (816) 512-5630.

GARRETT, Michael *(Associate Circuit Judge, Missouri Circuit Court Thirty-ninth Judicial Circuit)* Serves Probate Division.

Office: 700 Main, Cassville 65625.
Telephone: (417) 847-2127.
Fax: (417) 847-5760

GARRETT, R. Jack *(Presiding Judge, Missouri Circuit Court Thirty-seventh Judicial Circuit)*

Office: 225 Courthouse, West Plains 65775.
Telephone: (417) 256-4383.
Fax: (417) 256-6591

GARRISON, Phillip R. *(Judge, Missouri Court of Appeals Southern District)* Appointed by Governor John D. Ashcroft to term beginning Dec 30, 1992. Retained by election 1994, current term expires Dec 31, 2006. Former Chief Judge. Born Springfield Missouri May 7, 1942. Educated at Drury College B.A. 1964 and University of Missouri-Columbia J.D. 1966. In legal practice Ozark and Springfield.

Prosecuting Attorney Christian County 1971-72. Fellow American College of Trial Lawyers. Member The Missouri Bar, Greene County and American Bar Associations.

Office: 300 Hammons Parkway, Springfield 65806.
Telephone: (417) 895-6826.

GARVEY, John F. *(Associate Circuit Judge, Missouri Circuit Court Twenty-second Judicial Circuit)* Appointed by Governor Mel Carnahan.

Office: Civil Courts Building, 10 North Tucker Street, St. Louis 63101.
Telephone: (314) 622-4841.

GILLIS, Gregory B. *(Associate Circuit Judge, Missouri Circuit Court Sixteenth Judicial Circuit)* Appointed by Governor Bob Holden to term beginning April 2001. Educated at University of Missouri-Columbia B.A. 1981 J.D. 1984.

Human Rights Officer Missouri Commission on Human Rights 1985. With Jackson County Prosecutor's Office 1987-2001. Drug Court Commissioner Jackson County Nov 1999 to 2001.

Office: Courthouse, 415 East Twelfth Street, Kansas City 64106.
Telephone: (816) 881-3691.
Fax: (816) 881-3894

GOEKE, Joseph A., III *(Associate Circuit Judge, Missouri Circuit Court Twenty-first Judicial Circuit)* Assumed office Jan 1979. Retained by election Nov 1982, Nov 1986, Nov 1990, Nov 1994, Nov 1998 and Nov 2002. Current term expires Dec 31, 2006. Born St. Louis Missouri July 19, 1945. Roman Catholic. Educated at St. Louis University B.S. in Commerce 1967 J.D. 1972 and Loyola University Law School of New Orleans 1969-71. Admitted to practice Missouri 1973 and U.S. District Courts Western 1973 and Eastern 1974 Districts of Missouri. In legal practice St. Louis and Fenton 1973-75. Judge, St. Louis County Magistrate Court Oct 16, 1975 to Dec 31, 1978.

Assistant Prosecuting Attorney St. Louis County 1973. Executive Council Judicial Conference of Missouri since 1986. Board of Directors 1988-93 and since 1999 and President 1992-93 Missouri Association of Probate and Associate Circuit Judges. Member The Bar Association of Metropolitan St. Louis, The Missouri Bar and St. Louis County Bar Association. Captain USCGR since 1968. Enjoys refereeing and coaching basketball.

Office: St. Louis County Court Building, 7900 Carondelet, Clayton 63105.
Telephone: (314) 615-1534.

GOLDMAN, Steven H. *(Circuit Judge, Missouri Circuit Court Twenty-first Judicial Circuit)* Appointed by Governor John D. Ashcroft to term beginning March 18, 1988. Retained by election Nov 1990, Nov 1996 and Nov 2002. Current term expires Dec 31, 2008. Born St. Louis Missouri 1946. Jewish. Educated at Washington University A.B. 1968 and St. Louis University J.D. cum laude 1972. Member Phi Delta Phi. Admitted to practice

GOLDMAN, STEVEN H.—*Continued*
Missouri 1972, U.S. District Courts Eastern 1972 and Western 1972 Districts of Missouri and U.S. Supreme Court 1976.

Chief Trial Attorney and Assistant Prosecutor St. Louis County 1972-88. Drafted legislation of homicide and assault statutes Missouri 1983. Chair Ad Hoc Committee for Revision of Court Rules Governing Arrest Warrants Missouri Supreme Court 1999. Member Lawyers Association of St. Louis and St. Louis County Bar Association. USAR 1968-72. Lay Advisor Grievance Committee St. Louis Society for Medical and Scientific Education 2000. Member United Hebrew Temple. Enjoys handball and fountain pens.

Office: St. Louis County Court Building, 7900 Carondelet, Clayton 63105.
Telephone: (314) 615-1512.

GRADY, Thomas Christian *(Circuit Judge, Missouri Circuit Court Twenty-second Judicial Circuit)* Associate Circuit Judge Jan 1979 to Feb 23, 1994. Appointed Circuit Judge by Governor Mel Carnahan to term beginning Feb 24, 1994. Retained by election. Born St. Louis Missouri Feb 4, 1945. Roman Catholic. Educated at St. Louis University A.B. 1966 J.D. 1970. Admitted to practice Missouri 1970. Began legal practice St. Louis 1970. Judge, St. Louis City Magistrate Court Dec 27, 1976 to Dec 31, 1978.

Member Lawyers Association of St. Louis, The Bar Association of Metropolitan St. Louis and The Missouri Bar. Member and Former Chair Herman T. Pott Inland Waterways Library. Past Commodore Harbor Point Yacht Club. Member Society of Architectural Historians, Landmarks Association of St. Louis, Inc. and St. Louis Mercantile Library Association. Active in architectural and urban neighborhood preservation.

Office: Civil Courts Building, 10 North Tucker Street, St. Louis 63101.
Telephone: (314) 622-3706.

GRAY, Jon R. *(Circuit Judge, Missouri Circuit Court Sixteenth Judicial Circuit)* Appointed by Governor John D. Ashcroft to term beginning Jan 1, 1987. Retained by election 1988, 1994 and 2000. Current term expires Dec 31, 2006. Born Little Rock Arkansas Nov 16, 1951. United Methodist. Educated at Grinnell College B.A. 1973 and University of Missouri-Kansas City J.D. 1976. Member Sigma Pi Phi. Admitted to practice Missouri 1977, U.S. District Court Western District of Missouri 1977 and U.S. Court of Appeals Eighth Circuit 1977.

Member The Missouri Bar, Kansas City Metropolitan, Jackson County and National Bar Associations. Board of Trustees Southern Methodist University 1988-2000. Life Member University of Missouri-Kansas City Alumni Association and NAACP. Member Mount Oread Lodge 76 Masons PHA and Kansas City Consistory 7, 32° Scottish Rite PHA.

Office: Courthouse, 415 East Twelfth Street, Kansas City 64106.
Telephone: (816) 881-3618.
Fax: (816) 881-3950

GRIFFIN, Stephen K. *(Presiding Judge, Missouri Circuit Court Forty-third Judicial Circuit)*
Mailing address: P.O. Box 275, Plattsburg 64477.
Telephone: (816) 539-3732.

GRIMM, Hadley E. *(Presiding Judge, Missouri Circuit Court Forty-first Judicial Circuit)* Former Associate Circuit Judge.
Mailing address: P.O. Box 368, Macon 63552.
Telephone: (660) 385-3713.
Fax: (660) 385-4235

GRIMM, John W. *(Circuit Judge, Missouri Circuit Court Thirty-second Judicial Circuit)* Appointed by Governor Mel Carnahan to term beginning Dec 1, 1993. Elected Nov 1994 and Nov 2000. Current term expires Dec 31, 2006. Former Presiding Judge. Born Cape Girardeau Missouri July 28, 1962. Lutheran. Educated at Southeast Missouri State University B.S. 1984 and University of Missouri-Kansas City J.D. 1987. Topics Editor Missouri Law Review 1985-87. Law Clerk to Hon. Stephen N. Limbaugh, U.S. District Court Eastern District of Missouri 1987-89. Member Delta Theta Phi. Admitted to practice Missouri 1987 and Illinois 1988. In legal practice Cape Girardeau Missouri 1989-93.

Member The Missouri Bar, Cape Girardeau County (President Young Lawyers Section 1993) and American (Executive Council Young Lawyers Division 1995-97, Executive Committee National Conference of State Trial Judges 1999-2001) Bar Associations. Recipient Young Alumni Merit Award from Southeast Missouri State University 1994 and Outstanding Young Missourian Award from Missouri Jaycees 2000. Democrat.

Office: 44 North Lorimier, Cape Girardeau 63701.
Telephone: (573) 335-2802.
Fax: (573) 331-2349
E-mail address: jgrimm@osca.state.mo.us

HALL, James R. *(Associate Circuit Judge, Missouri Circuit Court Thirty-sixth Judicial Circuit)* Serves Probate Division.
Office: 100 Court Square, Doniphan 63935.
Telephone: (573) 996-2013.
Fax: (573) 996-5014

HAMILTON, Gene *(Presiding Judge, Missouri Circuit Court Thirteenth Judicial Circuit)* Elected to term beginning Jan 1, 1983. Reelected 1988, 1994 and 2000. Current term expires Dec 31, 2006. Born Bachelor Missouri Oct 31, 1942. Presbyterian. Educated at Westminster College B.S. 1964 and University of Missouri School of Law J.D. 1967. Member Delta Tau Delta and Phi Delta Phi. Admitted to practice Missouri 1967. Began legal practice Jefferson City 1967. In legal practice Fulton 1970.

Prosecuting Attorney Callaway County 1970-80. Instructor William Woods College 1974-82 and Department of Public Safety University of Missouri 1976-82. Member The Missouri Bar, Boone County and Callaway County Bar Associations. Captain U.S. Army Signal Corps 1968-69. Democrat. Board of Trustees William Woods College. Chairman Callaway County United Way. Enjoys fox hunting.

Office: 705 East Walnut Street, Columbia 65201.
Telephone: (573) 886-4050.
Fax: (573) 886-4070

HAMILTON, Jean C. *(Judge, United States District Court Eastern District of Missouri)* Appointed for life by President George Bush Oct 1, 1990 to term beginning Nov 5, 1990. Chief Judge 1995-2002. Born St. Louis Missouri Nov 12, 1945. Episcopalian. Educated at Wellesley College A.B. 1968, Washington University School of Law J.D. 1971 and Yale Law School LL.M.

HAMILTON, JEAN C.—*Continued*

1982. Articles Editor Washington University Law Quarterly 1969-70. Member Phi Delta Phi. Honorary member Order of the Coif. Admitted to practice Missouri 1971, U.S. Court of Appeals Eighth Circuit 1974, U.S. District Court Eastern District of Missouri 1978 and U.S. Supreme Court 1989. In legal practice Washington D.C. 1971-73 and St. Louis 1973-81. Circuit Judge, Missouri Circuit Court Twenty-second Judicial Circuit 1982-88. Judge, Missouri Court of Appeals Eastern District 1988-90.

Attorney U.S. Department of Justice Washington D.C. 1971-73 and Southwestern Bell Telephone Company 1978-81. Assistant U.S. Attorney Eastern District of Missouri 1973-78. Member Women Lawyers Association of St. Louis, The American Law Institute, National Association of Women Judges, The Bar Association of Metropolitan St. Louis, The Missouri Bar and American Bar Association.

Office: 16-148 U.S. Courthouse, 111 South Tenth Street, St. Louis 63102.
Telephone: (314) 244-7601.

HAMLETT, Linda R. *(Associate Circuit Judge, Missouri Circuit Court Twelfth Judicial Circuit)* Serves Probate Division.

Office: 101 North Jefferson, Room 205, Mexico 65265.
Telephone: (573) 473-5850.
Fax: (573) 581-3364

HANNA, Cody A. *(Associate Circuit Judge, Missouri Circuit Court Thirtieth Judicial Circuit)* Appointed by Governor John D. Ashcroft to term beginning Jan 20, 1989. Elected 1990, 1994, 1998 and 2002. Current term expires Dec 31, 2006. Serves Probate Division. Born Pittsburg Kansas Aug 13, 1944. Educated at Southwest Missouri State University B.S. 1971 and University of Missouri-Columbia J.D. 1974. Admitted to practice Missouri 1974, U.S. District Court Western District of Missouri 1974 and U.S. Supreme Court 1978. In legal practice Buffalo 1974-89.

Member The Missouri Bar and Thirtieth Judicial Circuit Bar Association (Past President). Attended General Jurisdiction course The National Judicial College May 1992. Attends Missouri Judicial College annually. Commander USNR (retired). Past Master Masonic Lodge. Private pilot.

Mailing address: P.O. Box 1150, Buffalo 65622.
Telephone: (417) 345-7641.

HARDWICK, Lisa White *(Judge, Missouri Court of Appeals Western District)* Appointed by Governor Bob Holden to term beginning May 2, 2001. Born Kansas City Missouri Oct 5, 1960. Educated at University of Missouri-Columbia B.J. 1982 and Harvard University Law School J.D. 1985. Admitted to practice Missouri 1985. In legal practice Kansas City. Judge, Missouri Circuit Court Sixteenth Judicial Circuit Jan 20, 2000 to May 1, 2001, appointed by Governor Mel Carnahan.

Office: 1300 Oak Street, Kansas City 64106-2970.
Telephone: (816) 889-3611.

HARMAN, Larry D. *(Circuit Judge, Missouri Circuit Court Seventh Judicial Circuit)* Appointed by governor. Retained by election. Former Presiding Judge. Serves Probate Division.

Office: 11 South Water, Liberty 64068.
Telephone: (816) 792-7714.
Fax: (816) 792-7144

HARTENBACH, James R. *(Circuit Judge, Missouri Circuit Court Twenty-first Judicial Circuit)* Appointed by governor. Retained by election. Former Presiding Judge.

Office: St. Louis County Court Building, 7900 Carondelet, Clayton 63105.
Telephone: (314) 615-1514.
Fax: (314) 615-7658

HARVEY, Hugh C. *(Associate Circuit Judge, Missouri Circuit Court Fifteenth Judicial Circuit)* Serves Probate Division.

Office: 101 East Arrow, Room 302, Marshall 65340.
Telephone: (660) 886-8808.
Fax: (660) 886-3114

HASLAG, Ralph J. *(Associate Circuit Judge, Missouri Circuit Court Twenty-fifth Judicial Circuit)* Elected Nov 1990 to term beginning Jan 1, 1991. Reelected 1994, 1998 and 2002. Current term expires Dec 31, 2006. Born Jefferson City Missouri May 17, 1954. Admitted to practice Missouri 1980.

Office: 200 North Main, Rolla 65401.
Telephone: (573) 364-1891.

HAYES, Scott *(Associate Circuit Judge, Missouri Circuit Court Fourteenth Judicial Circuit)* Serves Probate Division.

Office: 223 North Williams, Moberly 65270.
Telephone: (660) 263-4450.
Fax: (660) 263-1007

HAYS, Sarah W. *(Magistrate Judge, United States District Court Western District of Missouri)* Appointed by U.S. District Court judges.

Office: 6672 U.S. Courthouse, 400 East Ninth Street, Kansas City 64106.
Telephone: (816) 512-5775.

HEAGNEY, Philip Daniel *(Circuit Judge, Missouri Circuit Court Twenty-second Judicial Circuit)* Appointed by Governor Mel Carnahan Feb 28, 1996 to term beginning April 1, 1996. Retained by election 1998, current term expires Dec 31, 2004. Born Spokane Washington Nov 24, 1947. Catholic. Educated at Johns Hopkins University B.A. 1970 and Harvard Law School J.D. 1976. Admitted to practice Missouri 1976. In legal practice St. Louis 1976-96.

Instructor in Pretrial Practice Washington University School of Law 1982-86. Member Lawyers Association of St. Louis and The Missouri Bar. Attended General Program Aug 1996 and General Jurisdiction Course Oct 1996 The National Judicial College. Patrolman Metropolitan Police Department of St. Louis 1970-73. Member Landmarks Association of St. Louis, Forest Park Southeast Neighborhood Association and St. Cronan Catholic Church. Enjoys National Public Radio, reading, architecture, conservation, city life, urban history and outdoor activities such as canoeing, hiking, basketball, baseball and lacrosse.

Office: Civil Courts Building, 10 North Tucker Street, St. Louis 63101.
Telephone: (314) 622-4491.
Fax: (314) 622-4524

HEDSPETH, David J. *(Associate Circuit Judge, Missouri Circuit Court Thirty-seventh Judicial Circuit)* Elected to term beginning Jan 1, 1979. Reelected 1982, 1986, 1990, 1994, 1998 and 2002. Current term expires Dec 31, 2006. Serves Probate, Civil and Criminal Divisions. Born Poplar Bluff Missouri Feb 10, 1947. Baptist. Educated at Southern Baptist College A.A. 1966, University of Missouri B.S. in Agriculture 1969, Blackstone School of Law LL.B. 1971 and Cumberland School of Law of Samford University J.D. 1975. Admitted to practice Missouri 1975. Began legal practice Van Buren 1975. Judge, Carter County Probate and Magistrate Courts Jan 1, 1977 to Dec 31, 1978.

Author "A Tribute to Cumberland School of Law" 27 No. 3 Cumberland L. Rev. 1996-97. Member Carter County Jury Commission, The Missouri Bar, Carter County and Thirty-seventh Judicial Circuit Bar Associations. Specialist Fourth Class U.S. Army 1969-71. Member Carter County Democratic Party. Deacon First Baptist Church. Advisory Board Three Rivers Community College. Member South Missouri Baptist Assembly (Treasurer), Carter County Farm Bureau and Carter County Law Library. Owner Hedspeth Farms. Interests include international short wave listening, land surveying and farming.

Mailing address: P.O. Box 328, Van Buren 63965.
Telephone: (573) 323-4344.

HELLER, Robert M. *(Associate Circuit Judge, Missouri Circuit Court Thirty-seventh Judicial Circuit)* Elected to term beginning Jan 1, 1979. Reelected 1982, 1986, 1990, 1994, 1998 and 2002. Current term expires Dec 31, 2006. Serves Probate Division. Born St. Louis Missouri Aug 12, 1952. Educated at Northwestern University B.A. 1973 and University of Missouri J.D. 1976. Admitted to practice Missouri 1976.

Mailing address: P.O. Box 845, Eminence 65466.
Telephone: (573) 226-5515.
Fax: (573) 226-3239

HENRY, Donald M. *(Associate Circuit Judge, Missouri Circuit Court Thirty-seventh Judicial Circuit)* Serves Probate Division.

Office: 222 Courthouse, West Plains 65775.
Telephone: (417) 256-4050.
Fax: (417) 256-5826

HOFF, Mary K. *(Judge, Missouri Court of Appeals Eastern District)* Appointed by Governor Mel Carnahan to term beginning Jan 9, 1996. Retained by election 1998. Term expires Dec 31, 2010. Former Chief Judge. Born St. Louis Missouri Jan 5, 1953. Educated at University of Missouri-Columbia B.S. 1974 and St. Louis University School of Law J.D. 1978. Admitted to practice Missouri 1978. In legal practice St. Louis 1982-89. Circuit Judge, Missouri Circuit Court Twenty-second Judicial Circuit June 9, 1989 to Jan 8, 1996, appointed by Governor John D. Ashcroft.

Member Women Lawyers Association of Greater St. Louis, National Association of Women Judges, The Bar Association of Metropolitan St. Louis and The Missouri Bar.

Office: Wainwright State Office Building, 111 North Seventh Street, St. Louis 63101.
Telephone: (314) 340-6912.
Fax: (314) 340-7703

HOLDEN, Calvin *(Circuit Judge, Missouri Circuit Court Thirty-first Judicial Circuit)* Serves Probate Division.

Office: 1010 Boonville, Springfield 65802.
Telephone: (417) 868-4838.
Fax: (417) 868-4809

HOLLIGER, Ronald R. *(Judge, Missouri Court of Appeals Western District)* Appointed by Governor Mel Carnahan to term beginning Jan 4, 2000. Educated at University of Missouri-Kansas City J.D. 1973. Law Clerk to Hon. Charles Shangler, Missouri Court of Appeals 1973-74. In legal practice 1974-95. Circuit Judge, Missouri Circuit Court Sixteenth Judicial Circuit March 1, 1995 to Jan 3, 2000, appointed by Governor Mel Carnahan.

Office: 1300 Oak Street, Kansas City 64106-2970.
Telephone: (816) 889-3608.
Fax: (318) 889-3599

HOLT, Joe D. *(Associate Circuit Judge, Missouri Circuit Court Thirteenth Judicial Circuit)* Serves Probate Division.

Office: 10 East Fifth Street, Fulton 65251.
Telephone: (573) 642-0777.
Fax: (573) 648-0700

HOUSE, Ted *(Associate Circuit Judge, Missouri Circuit Court Eleventh Judicial Circuit)*

Office: 300 North Second Street, Room 431, St. Charles 63301.
Telephone: (636) 949-7900.

HOWALD, J. Kent *(Associate Circuit Judge, Missouri Circuit Court Forty-second Judicial Circuit)* Serves Probate Division.

Mailing address: P.O. Box BC, Steelville 65565.
Telephone: (573) 775-2149.

HOWARD, Victor C. *(Judge, Missouri Court of Appeals Western District)* Appointed by Governor Mel Carnahan to term beginning Sept 30, 1996. Retained by election 1998, current term expires Dec 31, 2010. Born Kansas City Missouri July 9, 1952. Educated at Central Missouri State University B.S. 1973 and University of Missouri-Kansas City J.D. 1976. Law Clerk to Hon. William J. Marsh, Missouri Circuit Court Circuit Sixteen 1977. Circuit Judge, Missouri Circuit Court Seventh Judicial Circuit 1993-96.

Deputy County Counselor Clay County 1977-91. President Clay County Bar Association 1992-93. Secretary North Kansas City Board of Education 1977-93. Member Kansas City Board of Zoning Adjustment 1991-93. Chairman Youth Friends Advisory Board. Board Member Domestic Violence Community Response Team. Member Tri-County Mental Health Supportive Employment Task Force.

Office: 1300 Oak Street, Kansas City 64106-2970.
Telephone: (816) 889-3626.
Fax: (816) 889-3599

HUDSON, Steven D. *(Associate Circuit Judge, Missouri Circuit Court Third Judicial Circuit)* Serves Probate Division.

Mailing address: P.O. Box 26, Trenton 64683.
Telephone: (660) 359-6909.
Fax: (660) 395-6604

HULL, Owens Lee, Jr. *(Presiding Judge, Missouri Circuit Court Sixth Judicial Circuit)* Former Associate

HULL, OWENS LEE, JR.—*Continued*

Circuit Judge. Appointed Circuit Judge by Governor Mel Carnahan.
Office: 415 Third Street, Suite 65, Platte City 64079.
Telephone: (816) 858-2232.
Fax: (816) 858-3392

HYDE, Troy K. *(Associate Circuit Judge, Missouri Circuit Court Twenty-fourth Judicial Circuit)* Elected Nov 5, 1996 to term beginning Jan 1, 1997. Reelected 1998 and 2002. Current term expires Dec 31, 2006. Serves Probate Division. Born St. Louis Missouri Nov 2, 1962. Lutheran. Educated at University of Missouri-St. Louis B.A. 1986 and Ohio Northern University J.D. 1990. Lead Research Editor Ohio Northern Law Review 1989-90. Member Delta Theta Phi. Admitted to practice Missouri 1990. In legal practice Farmington, Potosi, Ironton and Fredricktown.
Assistant Public Defender 1991-93. Assistant Prosecuting Attorney Washington County. Member The Missouri Bar.
Office: 102 North Missouri Street, Potosi 63664.
Telephone: (573) 438-3691.
Fax: (573) 438-7900

JACKSON, Carol E. *(Chief Judge, United States District Court Eastern District of Missouri)* Magistrate Judge 1986-92. Appointed Judge for life by President George Bush to term beginning 1992. Chief Judge since June 11, 2002. Born St. Louis Missouri Aug 9, 1952. Educated at Wellesley College B.A. 1973 and University of Michigan Law School J.D. 1976. In legal practice St. Louis 1976-83.
Senior Attorney Mallinckrodt, Inc. 1983-85. Adjunct Professor Washington University School of Law 1989-92.
Office: U.S. Courthouse, Fourteenth Floor, 111 South Tenth Street, St. Louis 63102-9958.
Telephone: (314) 244-7540.

JACKSON, John J. *(Associate Circuit Judge, Missouri Circuit Court Tenth Judicial Circuit)* Serves Probate Division.
Office: 906 Broadway, Hannibal 63401.
Telephone: (573) 221-0288.
Fax: (573) 221-0945

JACKSON, Randall R. *(Circuit Judge, Missouri Circuit Court Fifth Judicial Circuit)* Magistrate Judge 1977-78. Associate Circuit Judge 1978-88. Appointed Circuit Judge by Governor John D. Ashcroft Feb 1988. Elected 1988, 1994 and 2000. Current term expires Dec 31, 2006. Born St. Joseph Missouri July 19, 1949. Member Green Valley Baptist Church. Educated at Missouri Western College 1967-69 and University of Missouri-Columbia B.A. 1971 J.D. 1974. Admitted to practice Missouri 1974 and U.S. District Court Western District of Missouri 1974. Began legal practice St. Joseph 1974. Judge, Buchanan County Magistrate Court 1977-78.
Assistant City Attorney and City Prosecutor St. Joseph 1974-76. Member The Missouri Bar and St. Joseph Bar Association. Member Advisory Committee Department of Criminal Justice Missouri Western State College. Recipient Appreciation Award from Fraternal Order of Police 1977 and Rasch Award for Outstanding Article of 1999 from Journal of the Missouri Bar. Republican. Enjoys hunting, fishing, photography and sports.
Office: 411 Jules, St. Joseph 64501.
Telephone: (816) 271-1447.
Fax: (816) 271-1575

JACOBS, John *(Associate Circuit Judge, Missouri Circuit Court Forty-fourth Judicial Circuit)* Serves Probate Division.
Mailing address: P.O. Box 278, Gainesville 65655.
Telephone: (417) 679-4611.
Fax: (417) 679-2099

JAMISON, Michael T. *(Associate Circuit Judge, Missouri Circuit Court Twenty-first Judicial Circuit)* Appointed by Governor Mel Carnahan May 1997. Retained by election. Educated at Washington University A.B. 1973 and St. Louis University School of Law J.D. 1976. Member Phi Alpha Delta. In legal practice 1992-94.
Field Attorney and Trial Specialist National Labor Relations Board 1976-92. Associate General Counsel Labor Section Anheuser-Busch Companies, Inc. July 1994 to May 1997. Past President Mound City Bar Association. Member The Bar Association of Metropolitan St. Louis, The Missouri Bar and American Bar Association (Section of Labor and Employment Law). Board Member Northside Community Center and People's Health Center. Trustee Trailwoods Subdivision North County. Member Downtown St. Louis, Inc.
Office: St. Louis County Court Building, 7900 Carondelet, Clayton 63105.
Telephone: (314) 615-1543.

JAYNES, Ralph H. *(Presiding Judge, Missouri Circuit Court Fourteenth Judicial Circuit)*
Office: 223 North Williams, Moberly 65270.
Telephone: (660) 263-5105.
Fax: (660) 263-9008

JOYCE, Patricia S. *(Circuit Judge, Missouri Circuit Court Nineteenth Judicial Circuit)* Associate Circuit Judge Jan 1, 1995 to Dec 31, 2002. Elected Circuit Judge Nov 2002 to term beginning Jan 2003. Term expires Dec 31, 2008. Serves Probate Division. Born Cape Girardeau Missouri Sept 6, 1955. Catholic. Educated at Southeast Missouri State University B.S. summa cum laude 1976 and St. Louis University J.D. cum laude 1979. Admitted to practice Missouri 1979.
Assistant Prosecuting Attorney Cole County 1983-94.
Office: 301 East High Street, Jefferson City 65101.
Telephone: (573) 634-9177.
Fax: (573) 634-9208

JUDAH, Weldon C. *(Circuit Judge, Missouri Circuit Court Fifth Judicial Circuit)* Former Associate Circuit Judge.
Office: 411 Jules, St. Joseph 64501.
Telephone: (816) 271-1441.
Fax: (816) 271-1575

JUSTUS, James *(Associate Circuit Judge, Missouri Circuit Court Thirty-eighth Judicial Circuit)*
Mailing address: P.O. Box 129, Forsyth 65653.
Telephone: (417) 546-7206.
Fax: (417) 546-5821

KAMP, Gary A. *(Associate Circuit Judge, Missouri Circuit Court Thirty-second Judicial Circuit)* Elected Nov 8, 1994 to term beginning Jan 1, 1995. Reelected Nov 1998 and 2002. Current term expires Dec 31, 2006.

KAMP, GARY A.—*Continued*

Born Cape Girardeau Missouri April 9, 1952. Lutheran-Missouri Synod. Educated at Southeast Missouri State University B.A. with honors 1975 and University of Missouri-Columbia J.D. 1978. Admitted to practice Missouri 1978 and U.S. District Court Eastern District of Missouri 1979. In legal practice Marble Hill 1978-94.

Assistant Prosecuting Attorney Bollinger County 1978-86 and Cape Girardeau 1987-88. Member Missouri Municipal Attorneys Association (Young Lawyers Section), The Missouri Bar and Thirty-second Circuit Bar Association. Recipient Jaycee International Senatorship and United States Ambassadorship. U.S. Army National Guard. Republican. Member National Rifle Association and United States Jaycees. Hobbies include American Civil War activities and pistol and rifle shoots.

Office: 100 Court Street, Jackson 63755.
Telephone: (573) 243-8446.
Fax: (573) 204-2367

KAYS, Greg *(Associate Circuit Judge, Missouri Circuit Court Twenty-sixth Judicial Circuit)* Serves Probate Division.

Office: 200 North Adams, Lebanon 65536.
Telephone: (417) 532-9196.
Fax: (417) 532-5917

KEHM, Dennis J. *(Circuit Judge, Missouri Circuit Court Twenty-third Judicial Circuit)* Elected Nov 1986 to term beginning Jan 1, 1987. Reelected 1988, 1994 and 2000. Current term expires Dec 31, 2006. Former Presiding Judge. Born St. Louis Missouri Oct 30, 1942. Roman Catholic. Educated at Southeast Missouri State University B.S. 1965, Washington University and University of Missouri-Kansas City J.D. 1972. Member Delta Theta Phi. Admitted to practice Missouri 1972 and U.S. District Court Western District of Missouri. In legal practice Kansas City 1972-75.

First Assistant Prosecuting Attorney 1975-80 and Prosecuting Attorney 1980-87 Jefferson County. Member Missouri Council of Juvenile and Family Court Judges, National Council of Juvenile and Family Court Judges, The Missouri Bar and Jefferson County Bar Association. Attended Missouri Judicial College Judicial Education Committee Missouri Supreme Court 1989-90. Lecturer on Juvenile Law Missouri Judicial Orientation Conference Judicial Education Committee Missouri Supreme Court 1991. Named Alumni of the Year by Kansas City Senate Delta Theta Phi 1977. Recipient Equal Justice Award from Legal Services of Eastern Missouri 1989. History and social studies teacher Hillsboro R3 School District 1966-68. Missouri History teacher Pattonville School District 1968-69. Democrat. President Central Township Jefferson County Democrat Club 1980-85. Member Jefferson County Democrat Club and various township clubs. Former Director Jefferson County Law Enforcement Academy. Member Hillsboro Civic Club, Jefferson County Model Railroad Club, Southern Model Railroad Club, Crystal City Rotary and DeSoto Kiwanis. Enjoys model railroading.

Mailing address: P.O. Box 100, Hillsboro 63050.
Telephone: (636) 797-5443.

KELLOGG, Daniel F. *(Circuit Judge, Missouri Circuit Court Fifth Judicial Circuit)* Former Associate Circuit Judge. Serves Probate Division.

Office: 411 Jules, St. Joseph 64501.
Telephone: (816) 271-1477.
Fax: (816) 271-1575

KELLY, Christopher S. *(Associate Circuit Judge, Missouri Circuit Court Thirteenth Judicial Circuit)*

Office: 705 East Walnut Street, Columbia 65201.
Telephone: (573) 886-4050.
Fax: (573) 886-4070

KELLY, James H. *(Associate Circuit Judge, Missouri Circuit Court Twenty-fourth Judicial Circuit)* Elected to term beginning Jan 1, 1975. Reelected 1978, 1982, 1986, 1990, 1994, 1998 and 2002. Current term expires Dec 31, 2006. Serves Probate Division. Born St. Louis Missouri Dec 25, 1947. Catholic. Educated at Meramec Community College A.S. 1967 and University of Missouri B.S. in Business 1969 J.D. 1974. Admitted to practice Missouri 1974. Former Judge, St. Francois County Probate Court.

Member The Missouri Bar and St. Francois County Bar Association. Sergeant U.S. Army 1969-71. Democrat. Enjoys outdoor recreation.

Office: One North Washington, Farmington 63640.
Telephone: (573) 756-6601.
Fax: (573) 756-6602

KENDRICK, Larry L. *(Circuit Judge, Missouri Circuit Court Twenty-first Judicial Circuit)* Former Associate Circuit Judge. Appointed Circuit Judge by governor. Retained by election.

Office: St. Louis County Court Building, 7900 Carondelet, Clayton 63105.
Telephone: (314) 615-1517.
Fax: (314) 615-8739

KINKER, Amy *(Associate Circuit Judge, Missouri Circuit Court Forty-fifth Judicial Circuit)* Serves Probate Division.

Office: 201 Main, Troy 63379.
Telephone: (636) 528-6300.
Fax: (636) 528-3787

KINTZ, John F. *(Circuit Judge, Missouri Circuit Court Twenty-first Judicial Circuit)* Associate Circuit Judge 1979-93. Appointed Circuit Judge by governor to term beginning Jan 10, 1993. Retained by election. Born St. Louis Missouri Sept 18, 1940. Catholic. Educated at St. Louis University B.S. 1963 J.D. 1966. Admitted to practice Missouri 1966. Began legal practice St. Louis 1966. Judge, Brentwood Municipal Court 1975-78.

Public Defender Brentwood 1971-75. Member Missouri Association of Probate and Associate Circuit Judges, The Missouri Bar, The Bar Association of Metropolitan St. Louis, St. Louis County and American Bar Associations. Republican. Member Brentwood Lions Club. Enjoys racquetball and water skiing.

Office: St. Louis County Court Building, 7900 Carondelet, Clayton 63105.
Telephone: (314) 615-1505.

KNOX, William A. *(Magistrate Judge, United States District Court Western District of Missouri)* Appointed by U.S. District Court judges to term beginning Dec 15, 1985. Reappointed Dec 1993 and Dec 2001. Current term expires Dec 2009. Born Fargo North Dakota Jan 8, 1945. Educated at North Dakota State University B.S. 1966 and University of Minnesota J.D. cum laude 1968. Staff member Minnesota Law Review 1967-68. Admitted to practice Minnesota 1968 and Missouri 1977. In legal practice Columbia Missouri 1977-85.

KNOX, WILLIAM A.—*Continued*

Assistant Prosecuting Attorney Jackson County Missouri 1984. Author *Missouri Practice—Criminal Practice and Procedure* 19 and *West's Federal Forms—Criminal* 5 and 5A West Publishing Co. Professor University of Missouri-Columbia School of Law 1972-85. Officer U.S. Coast Guard 1968-72.

Office: 204 U.S. Courthouse, 131 West High Street, Jefferson City 65101.
Telephone: (573) 634-3418.

KNUST, Daniel Max *(Associate Circuit Judge, Missouri Circuit Court Thirtieth Judicial Circuit)* Elected to term beginning Jan 1, 1979. Reelected 1982, 1986, 1990, 1994, 1998 and 2002. Current term expires Dec 31, 2006. Born Brazil Indiana Oct 18, 1947. Educated at Trinity University, Earlham College A.B. 1969 and Indiana University J.D. 1972. Admitted to practice Missouri 1972 and Indiana 1974. Began legal practice Springfield Missouri 1972.

City Attorney Rogersville 1972-76. Adjunct Instructor Drury University 1977-78. Member Missouri Association of Probate and Associate Circuit Judges and The Missouri Bar. Republican. Member Masons and Scottish Rite. Enjoys raising cattle.

Office: Courthouse, Marshfield 65706.
Telephone: (417) 859-2041.
Fax: (417) 859-6265

KOFFMAN, Robert L. *(Associate Circuit Judge, Missouri Circuit Court Eighteenth Judicial Circuit)* Appointed by Governor Christopher S. Bond to term beginning July 1, 1981. Elected 1982, 1986, 1990, Nov 8, 1994, Nov 1998 and 2002. Current term expires Dec 31, 2006. Serves Probate Division. Born Maryville Missouri Dec 24, 1953. Methodist. Educated at Central Missouri State University B.S.B.A. 1977 and St. Mary's University School of Law J.D. 1980. Member St. Thomas More Society, Mace and Torch Honor Society and Delta Theta Phi. Admitted to practice Missouri 1980. Began legal practice Springfield 1980. In legal practice Moberly 1980.

Member Judicial Conference of Missouri, Missouri Association of Probate and Associate Circuit Judges, The Missouri Bar, Pettis County and Randolph County Bar Associations. Named one of Outstanding Young Men of America 1984. Listed in *Who's Who in American Law* and *Who's Who in Society*. Republican. Member Granite Masons Lodge 272 and Sedalia Rotary Club. Enjoys politics.

Office: 415 South Ohio, Sedalia 65301.
Telephone: (660) 826-0368.
Fax: (660) 827-8637

KRAMER, C. William *(Circuit Judge, Missouri Circuit Court Sixteenth Judicial Circuit)* Appointed by governor. Retained by election. Former Presiding Judge.

Office: Courthouse, 415 East Twelfth Street, Kansas City 64102.
Telephone: (816) 881-4417.
Fax: (816) 881-3378

KRAMER, Gary P. *(Circuit Judge, Missouri Circuit Court Twenty-third Judicial Circuit)* Associate Circuit Judge Jan 1983 to Dec 1990. Elected Circuit Judge Nov 1990 to term beginning Jan 1991. Reelected 1996 and 2002. Current term expires Dec 31, 2008. Presiding Judge Jan 1, 1997 to Dec 31, 1998. Serves Probate Division. Born Pontiac Illinois Aug 14, 1947. Methodist. Educated at Carleton College B.A. 1969 and Washington University J.D. 1972. Member Delta Theta Phi. Admitted to practice Missouri 1972, U.S. District Courts Eastern 1972 and Western 1972 Districts of Missouri and U.S. Supreme Court 1977. Began legal practice Clayton 1971. In legal practice St. Louis 1972-74 and Hillsboro 1974-82.

Part-time Assistant Prosecuting Attorney Jefferson County 1972-74. Instructor Jefferson County Police Academy 1976. Chairman Twenty-third Circuit Computer Committee since 1984. Member Missouri Association of Probate and Associate Circuit Judges (Board of Directors 1989-93), Missouri Trial Judges Association, The Bar Association of Metropolitan St. Louis, The Missouri Bar and Jefferson County Bar Association. Attended General Jurisdiction Course Spring 1984, Advanced Computers in Courts Winter 1987, Domestic Violence 1991 and Judicial Writing 1993 The National Judicial College. Faculty Advisor and Discussion Group Leader General Jurisdiction Course 1992 and Faculty Member Introduction to Computers Fall 1993 The National Judicial College. Recipient Equal Justice Award from Legal Services of Eastern Missouri, Inc. 1990. Worked in construction 1966-72. Member Elks Lodge 1721. Active in youth and adult athletics (baseball, softball and basketball). Interests include woodworking and stone masonry.

Mailing address: P.O. Box 100, Hillsboro 63050.
Telephone: (636) 797-5443.

KROHN, Andrew A. *(Presiding Judge, Missouri Circuit Court Third Judicial Circuit)* Former Associate Circuit Judge.

Office: 802 East Main, Princeton 64673.
Telephone: (660) 748-3430.
Fax: (660) 748-3442

LAME, Barbara Gale *(Associate Circuit Judge, Missouri Circuit Court Forty-third Judicial Circuit)* Appointed by Governor Christopher S. Bond to term beginning Feb 23, 1976. Elected Nov 1976, 1978, 1982, 1986, 1990, 1994, 1998 and 2002. Current term expires Dec 31, 2006. Also serves Probate Division. Born Chillicothe Missouri Nov 21, 1946. Member United Methodist Church. Educated at University of Missouri-Columbia B.S.Ed. 1968, University of Hawaii 1967 and University of Missouri-Kansas City J.D. 1972. Member Phi Delta Phi. Admitted to practice Missouri 1972. In legal practice Chillicothe 1973-76.

City Attorney Chillicothe 1973-76. Associate Professor of Business Law Central Missouri State College 1972. Member Associate Circuit Judges Association, Missouri Municipal Attorneys Association, Missouri Judicial Conference, The Missouri Bar, Livingston County (President 1973) and Forty-third Judicial Circuit (President 1973-74) Bar Associations. Member Supreme Court Committee to Establish Uniform Record Keeping Procedures in Missouri Courts. Attended Missouri Judicial Conference, Missouri College for Trial Judges 1977-79, 1981-92 and 1994-2002 and "Victim Rights" The National Judicial College 1977. Named Outstanding Young Woman of America 1973 and 1976. Recipient Bell Volunteer of the Year Award from Southwestern Bell Telephone 1990. Life member Grand River Historical Society (Former Director). Board of Directors R.S.V.P. (Former Chairman) and VISTA. Hosted Foreign Exchange Student from Brazil 1993-94. Member Chapter T, P.E.O. and Rotary (Vice President). Founder Just Say No Basketball

LAME, BARBARA GALE—*Continued*

Tournament and Annual Bicycle Safety Rodeo. Created Mediation Program for dispute resolution Livingston County RII school system. Enjoys sports.
Office: 700 Webster, Suite 8, Chillicothe 64601.
Telephone: (660) 646-2055.
Fax: (660) 646-8014

LARSEN, Robert E. *(Magistrate Judge, United States District Court Western District of Missouri)* Appointed by U.S. District Court judges.
Office: 6652 U.S. Courthouse, 400 East Ninth Street, Kansas City 64106.
Telephone: (816) 512-5760.

LAUGHREY, Nanette K. *(Judge, United States District Court Western District of Missouri)* Appointed for life by President Bill Clinton to term beginning 1996. Born Cheyenne Wyoming Feb 11, 1946. Educated at University of California at Los Angeles B.A. 1967 and University of Missouri-Columbia School of Law J.D. 1975. In legal practice Columbia 1980-83. Municipal Judge, City of Columbia 1979-83.
Assistant State Attorney General 1975-79 and Deputy State Attorney General 1992-93 Missouri.
Office: 7452 U.S. Courthouse, 400 East Ninth Street, Kansas City 64106.
Telephone: (816) 512-5675.

LePAGE, John *(Associate Circuit Judge, Missouri Circuit Court Fortieth Judicial Circuit)* Serves Probate Division.
Mailing address: P.O. Box 157, Pineville 64856.
Telephone: (417) 223-4717.
Fax: (417) 223-4125

LEVY-SIWAK, Ellen *(Associate Circuit Judge, Missouri Circuit Court Twenty-first Judicial Circuit)* Appointed by Governor Bob Holden.
Office: St. Louis County Court Building, 7900 Carondelet, Clayton 63105.
Telephone: (314) 615-1538.

LEWIS, Garry D. *(Associate Circuit Judge, Missouri Circuit Court Second Judicial Circuit)* Serves Probate Division.
Mailing address: P.O. Box 126, Edina 63537.
Telephone: (660) 397-3146.
Fax: (660) 397-3331

LIMBAUGH, Stephen N. *(Senior Judge, United States District Court Eastern District of Missouri)* Appointed for life by President Ronald Reagan to term beginning July 19, 1983. Assumed Senior status, serves by assignment. Born Cape Girardeau Missouri Nov 17, 1927. Methodist. Educated at Southeast Missouri State University A.B. 1950 and University of Missouri-Columbia J.D. 1951. Member Pi Kappa Delta, Phi Alpha Theta, Phi Delta Phi and Beta Theta Pi. Admitted to practice Missouri 1951, U.S. District Court Eastern District of Missouri 1951 and U.S. Tax Court 1964. Began legal practice Cape Girardeau 1951.
Prosecuting Attorney Cape Girardeau County 1954-58. City Attorney Cape Girardeau 1968-72. Member The Missouri Bar (Board of Governors 1976-84, President 1982-83). Recipient Award of Merit for Outstanding Service in the Law from University of Missouri-Columbia 1982. Seaman First Class USN 1945-46. Republican.
Office: U.S. Courthouse, 111 South Tenth Street, St. Louis 63102.
Telephone: (314) 244-7400.

LIMBAUGH, Stephen N., Jr. *(Chief Justice, Supreme Court of Missouri)* Appointed by Governor John D. Ashcroft to term beginning Aug 19, 1992. Retained by election Nov 8, 1994, current term expires Dec 31, 2006. Born Cape Girardeau Missouri Jan 25, 1952. Methodist. Educated at Southern Methodist University B.A. 1973 J.D. 1976. Admitted to practice Missouri 1977, Texas 1977, U.S. District Court Eastern District of Missouri 1977 and U.S. Court of Appeals Eighth Circuit 1985. In legal practice Cape Girardeau Missouri 1977-78 and 1983-87. Former Circuit Judge and Presiding Judge, Missouri Circuit Court Thirty-second Judicial Circuit 1987-92.
Prosecuting Attorney Cape Girardeau 1979-82. Fellow American Bar Foundation. Member The Missouri Bar, State Bar of Texas and American Bar Association. Member Missouri Division Youth Services Advisory Board, Governing Boards of Southeast Missouri Hospital, Cape Girardeau United Way, SEMO Council Boy Scouts of America, Cape Girardeau Civic Center, Cape Girardeau Rotary Club and Cape Girardeau Jaycees.
Mailing address: P.O. Box 150, Jefferson City 65102.
Office: Supreme Court Building, Jefferson City 65101.
Telephone: (573) 751-4375.
Fax: (573) 751-7362

LISTON, Robert *(Associate Circuit Judge, Missouri Circuit Court Eighteenth Judicial Circuit)*
Office: 415 South Ohio, Sedalia 65301.
Telephone: (660) 826-4699.
Fax: (660) 827-8613

LOFTIN, Brenda Stith *(Associate Circuit Judge, Missouri Circuit Court Twenty-first Judicial Circuit)* Appointed by governor. Retained by election.
Office: St. Louis County Court Building, 7900 Carondelet, Clayton 63105.
Telephone: (314) 615-8717.
Fax: (314) 615-2689

LONG, Douglas E., Jr. *(Presiding Judge, Missouri Circuit Court Twenty-fifth Judicial Circuit)* Former Judge, Pulaski County Probate Court.
Office: 301 Historic Route 66 East, Suite 318, Waynesville 65583.
Telephone: (573) 774-4789.
Fax: (573) 774-6032

LOWENSTEIN, Harold L. *(Judge, Missouri Court of Appeals Western District)* Appointed by Governor Christopher S. Bond to term beginning July 31, 1981. Retained by election 1982 and 1994. Current term expires Dec 31, 2006. Former Chief Judge. Born Marshall Missouri Aug 18, 1939. Educated at University of Missouri-Columbia B.S. 1961 J.D. 1965. Admitted to practice Missouri 1965. Began legal practice Kansas City 1965.
Former Member Missouri House of Representatives. Member Big Brothers. Enjoys sports and reading.
Office: 1300 Oak Street, Kansas City 64106-2970.
Telephone: (816) 889-3617.
Fax: (816) 889-3599

LUBER, Byron D. *(Associate Circuit Judge, Missouri Circuit Court Thirty-fourth Judicial Circuit)* Appointed by Governor John D. Ashcroft to term beginning Oct 7, 1985. Elected Nov 4, 1986, Nov 6, 1990, Nov 8, 1994, Nov 1998 and 2002. Current term expires Dec 31, 2006. Born Cape Girardeau Missouri Aug 15, 1944. Catholic. Educated at Southeastern Missouri State University B.S. 1966 and University of Memphis J.D. 1970. Member Phi Alpha Delta. Admitted to practice Missouri 1970, Tennessee 1970, U.S. District Courts Eastern 1970 and Western 1970 Districts of Missouri and U.S. Court of Appeals Eighth Circuit 1972. In legal practice Caruthersville 1970-85.

City Attorney Caruthersville 1972-85 and Hayti 1974-85. Author Chapter "Municipal Corporations" *Practical Skills Handbook* 1978. Member Committee on Rules of Criminal Procedure Supreme Court of Missouri. Member The Missouri Bar and American Bar Association. Chairman Practical Skills course The Missouri Bar 1976-78. Attended General Jurisdiction course The National Judicial College 1991. Recipient Distinguished Service Award from The Missouri Bar 1978. Democrat.

Mailing address: P.O. Box 228, Caruthersville 63830.
Telephone: (573) 333-2784.
Fax: (573) 333-4722

LUCKENBILL, Paul T., Jr. *(Associate Circuit Judge, Missouri Circuit Court Forty-third Judicial Circuit)* Elected to term beginning Jan 1, 1983. Reelected 1986, 1990, 1994, 1998 and 2002. Current term expires Dec 31, 2006. Serves Probate Division. Born Kansas City Kansas March 21, 1949. Protestant. Educated at University of Kansas B.A. 1971 and University of Missouri-Columbia J.D. cum laude 1974. Note and Comment Editor Missouri Law Review. Member Order of the Coif and Phi Kappa Phi. Admitted to practice Missouri 1974. Began legal practice Cameron 1974.

Member The Missouri Bar and Clinton County Bar Association. Previously worked in Trust Department American National Bank. Democrat. Board member Clinco Sheltered Industries, Inc. Interests include golf and tropical fish.

Mailing address: P.O. Box 383, Plattsburg 64477.
Telephone: (816) 539-3755.

LYNCH, Gary *(Associate Circuit Judge, Missouri Circuit Court Thirtieth Judicial Circuit)* Serves Probate Division.

Office: 102 East Broadway, Room 7, Bolivar 65613.
Telephone: (417) 326-4921.
Fax: (417) 326-5238

MALONEY, Michael J. *(Circuit Judge, Missouri Circuit Court Seventh Judicial Circuit)* Former Associate Circuit Judge. Appointed Circuit Judge by Governor Mel Carnahan. Retained by election. Former Presiding Judge.

Office: 11 South Water, Liberty 64068.
Telephone: (816) 792-7711.

MANN, David C. *(Associate Circuit Judge, Missouri Circuit Court Thirty-third Judicial Circuit)* Elected to term beginning Jan 1, 1979. Reelected 1982, 1986, 1990, 1994, 1998 and 2002. Current term expires Dec 31, 2006.

Mailing address: P.O. Box 249, Benton 63736.
Telephone: (573) 545-3576.
Fax: (573) 545-4231

MANNERS, Michael W. *(Circuit Judge, Missouri Circuit Court Sixteenth Judicial Circuit)* Appointed by governor to term beginning Dec 15, 2000. Retained by election Nov 5, 2002, current term expires Dec 31, 2008. Born Independence Missouri Sept 25, 1950. Educated at Central Missouri State University B.A. summa cum laude 1972 and University of Missouri-Kansas City School of Law J.D. 1976. Admitted to practice Missouri 1976, U.S. District Court Western District of Missouri 1976, U.S. Court of Appeals Eighth Circuit 1980 and U.S. Supreme Court 1983. In legal practice Independence 1976-2000.

Prosecuting Attorney Smithville 1982-2000. Member Missouri Association of Trial Attorneys (President 1998-99), American Board of Trial Advocates, American Judges Association and Eastern Jackson County Bar Association (President 1987-88). Personal Statement or Quote: "I believe in allowing the attorneys to try their cases."

Office: 310 West Kansas, Suite 214, Independence 64050.
Telephone: (816) 881-4402.
Fax: (816) 881-4693
E-mail address: mmanners@osca.state.mo.us

MARQUART, Keith *(Associate Circuit Judge, Missouri Circuit Court Fifth Judicial Circuit)*

Office: 411 Jules, St. Joseph 64501.
Telephone: (816) 271-1454.
Fax: (816) 271-1538

MARTINEZ, Sandy *(Circuit Judge, Missouri Circuit Court Twenty-fourth Judicial Circuit)*

Office: One North Washington, Third Floor, Farmington 63640.
Telephone: (573) 756-5144.
Fax: (573) 757-3733

MASON, David C. *(Circuit Judge, Missouri Circuit Court Twenty-second Judicial Circuit)* Appointed by governor. Retained by election.

Office: Municipal Courts Building, 1320 Market Street, St. Louis 63103.
Telephone: (314) 622-4421.

MAUGHMER, John T. *(Magistrate Judge, United States District Court Western District of Missouri)* Appointed by U.S. District Court judges to term beginning Sept 29, 1988. Reappointed 1996, current term expires 2004. Born St. Joseph Missouri Nov 26, 1954. Educated at University of Missouri-Columbia B.S. magna cum laude 1977 and University of Missouri-Kansas City J.D. with honors 1980. Staff member Missouri Law Review 1978-80. Law Clerk to Hon. Elmo B. Hunter, U.S. District Court Western District of Missouri 1980-82. Member Beta Theta Pi and Order of Bench and Robe. Admitted to practice Missouri 1980, U.S. District Court Western District of Missouri 1980, U.S. Court of Appeals Eighth Circuit 1983 and U.S. Supreme Court 1983. In legal practice Kansas City 1982-88.

Author Note "In re Westinghouse: Commercial Impracticability as a Contractual Defense" 47 Missouri L. Rev. 650, 1979. Member The Kansas City Metropolitan Bar Association.

Office: 7662 U.S. Courthouse, 400 East Ninth Street, Kansas City 64106.
Telephone: (816) 512-5745.

McBETH, Gerald D. *(Associate Circuit Judge, Missouri Circuit Court Twenty-eighth Judicial Circuit)* Ap-

MCBETH, GERALD D.—*Continued*

pointed by Governor John D. Ashcroft to term beginning Feb 1, 1991. Elected 1992, 1994, 1998 and Nov 7, 2002. Current term expires Dec 31, 2006. Serves Probate Division. Born Macon Missouri Oct 28, 1941. Protestant. Educated at William Jewell College B.A. 1963 and University of Missouri-Columbia J.D. 1971. Staff member Missouri Law Review 1969-71. Member Phi Delta Phi and Order of the Coif. Admitted to practice Missouri 1971, U.S. District Courts Eastern 1971 and Western 1971 Districts of Missouri and Texas 1988. In legal practice Nevada Missouri 1971-91.

Author Articles in Missouri L. Rev. 1968-71. Member The Association of Trial Lawyers of America, The Missouri Bar, State Bar of Texas, Vernon County and American Bar Associations. Author various Articles and Chapters for continuing legal education The Missouri Bar.

Office: 100 West Cherry, Nevada 64772.
Telephone: (417) 448-2550.
Fax: (417) 448-2512

McCULLIN, Donald L. *(Circuit Judge, Missouri Circuit Court Twenty-second Judicial Circuit)* Appointed by Governor Mel Carnahan.

Office: Civil Courts Building, 10 North Tucker Street, St. Louis 63101.
Telephone: (314) 622-4412.

McDONALD, David P. *(Judge, United States Bankruptcy Court Eastern District of Missouri)* Appointed by U.S. District Court judges to term beginning Dec 3, 1982. Reappointed by U.S. Court of Appeals Eighth Circuit judges Dec 2, 1986 and Dec 2, 2000. Current term expires Dec 2, 2014. Chief Judge Oct 1, 1999 to Jan 10, 2003. Born St. Louis Missouri Jan 10, 1938. Educated at Washington University B.A. 1960 J.D. 1962. Admitted to practice Missouri 1962. Began legal practice St. Louis. Administrative Law Judge, Hearings of Appeals Social Security Administration 1975-79 and National Labor Relations Board 1979-82.

Member National Conference of Bankruptcy Judges, The Bar Association of Metropolitan St. Louis and The Missouri Bar. First Lieutenant U.S. Army Artillery 1962-64.

Office: U.S. Courthouse, 111 South Tenth Street, Seven North, St. Louis 63102.
Telephone: (314) 244-4520.

McELWAIN, Warren L. *(Circuit Judge, Missouri Circuit Court Forty-third Judicial Circuit)* Associate Circuit Judge Jan 1, 1979 to Dec 31, 2000. Elected Circuit Judge Nov 2000 to term beginning Jan 1, 2001. Born Kansas City Missouri Nov 7, 1947. Educated at University of Missouri-Columbia B.S. with honors 1969 J.D. 1972. Admitted to practice Missouri 1972. Began legal practice Maysville 1972.

Prosecuting Attorney De Kalb County 1975-78. Member The Missouri Bar. Republican. Delegate to GOP State Convention 1976. President Board of Directors Cameron Community Hospital 1993, 1994 and 1995. Secretary Crestview Estates, Inc. Member Maysville United Methodist Church, Maysville Area Chamber of Commerce (Former Member Board of Directors) and De Kalb County Health Services Inc. (President). Enjoys swimming, running, basketball, softball, music and spending time with wife and daughters.

Mailing address: P.O. Box 512, Maysville 64469.
Telephone: (816) 449-2602, (660) 646-6664.
Fax: (816) 449-2440, (660) 646-8007

McGRAW, Peggy Stevens *(Circuit Judge, Missouri Circuit Court Sixteenth Judicial Circuit)* Former Associate Circuit Judge. Appointed Circuit Judge by governor.

Office: Courthouse, 415 East Twelfth Street, Kansas City 64106.
Telephone: (816) 881-3608.
Fax: (816) 881-3390

McSHANE, Maura *(Circuit Judge, Missouri Circuit Court Twenty-first Judicial Circuit)* Appointed by governor. Retained by election.

Office: 501 South Brentwood, Clayton 63105.
Telephone: (314) 615-1502.
Fax: (314) 615-8280

MEDLER, Mary Ann L. *(Magistrate Judge, United States District Court Eastern District of Missouri)* Appointed by U.S. District Court judges.

Office: U.S. Courthouse, 111 South Tenth Street, St. Louis 63102-9958.
Telephone: (314) 244-7490.

MESLE, Catharine A. *(Circuit Judge, Missouri Circuit Court Sixteenth Judicial Circuit)* Appointed by governor.

Office: Courthouse, 415 East Twelfth Street, Kansas City 64106.
Telephone: (816) 881-3607.

MESSINA, Edith Louise *(Circuit Judge, Missouri Circuit Court Sixteenth Judicial Circuit)* Appointed by governor. Retained by election. Former Presiding Judge.

Office: Courthouse, 415 East Twelfth Street, Kansas City 64106.
Telephone: (816) 881-3612.
Fax: (816) 881-3233

MEYER, Larry W. *(Associate Circuit Judge, Missouri Circuit Court Thirty-ninth Judicial Circuit)* Serves Probate Division.

Office: One Courthouse Square, Mount Vernon 65712.
Telephone: (417) 466-2463.
Fax: (417) 466-0463

MIDKIFF, Sandra C. *(Circuit Judge, Missouri Circuit Court Sixteenth Judicial Circuit)* Appointed by Governor Bob Holden.

Office: Courthouse, 415 East Twelfth Street, Kansas City 64106.
Telephone: (816) 881-3601.

MIDYETT, Michael L. *(Associate Circuit Judge, Missouri Circuit Court Ninth Judicial Circuit)* Serves Probate Division.

Office: 306 South Cherry, Keytesville 65261.
Telephone: (660) 288-3271.
Fax: (660) 288-1511

MILLER, John G. *(Associate Circuit Judge, Missouri Circuit Court Fifteenth Judicial Circuit)*

Mailing address: P.O. Box 236, Lexington 64067.
Telephone: (660) 259-6151.
Fax: (660) 259-4997

MISSEY, Darrell *(Associate Circuit Judge, Missouri Circuit Court Twenty-third Judicial Circuit)*
Mailing address: P.O. Box 100, Hillsboro 63050.
Telephone: (636) 797-5424.
Fax: (636) 797-5073

MITCHELL, Stephen R. *(Associate Circuit Judge, Missouri Circuit Court Thirty-fifth Judicial Circuit)* Serves Probate Division.
Mailing address: P.O. Box 518, Bloomfield 63825.
Telephone: (573) 568-2181.
Fax: (573) 568-3229

MOBLEY, David C. *(Associate Circuit Judge, Missouri Circuit Court Tenth Judicial Circuit)* Serves Probate Division.
Mailing address: P.O. Box 466, New London 63459.
Telephone: (573) 985-5641.
Fax: (573) 985-5241

MOENTMANN, Werner A. *(Presiding Judge, Missouri Circuit Court Eighth Judicial Circuit)*
Mailing address: P.O. Box 346, Richmond 64085.
Telephone: (816) 776-3525.
Fax: (816) 776-6016

MONTGOMERY, Kerry L. *(Judge, Missouri Court of Appeals Southern District)* Appointed by Governor John D. Ashcroft to term beginning Aug 30, 1991. Retained by election 1992, current term expires Dec 31, 2004. Former Chief Judge. Born Greenfield Missouri July 23, 1936. Educated at Southwest Missouri State University B.S. and University of Missouri-Columbia M.A. J.D. Staff member Missouri Law Review. Member Phi Delta Phi. Former part-time Municipal Judge, City of Springfield.
Assistant Prosecuting Attorney and Chief Trial Assistant Greene County 1967-71. Member The Missouri Bar and Greene County Bar Association (Former Treasurer). USMC.
Office: 300 Hammons Parkway, Springfield 65806.
Telephone: (417) 895-6824.

MOODY, John *(Presiding Judge, Missouri Circuit Court Forty-fourth Judicial Circuit)* Former Associate Circuit Judge.
Mailing address: P.O. Box 439, Mansfield 65704.
Telephone: (417) 924-3246.
Fax: (417) 924-3325

MOON, John *(Associate Circuit Judge, Missouri Circuit Court First Judicial Circuit)* Serves Probate Division.
Office: 113 West Court Street, Kahoka 63445.
Telephone: (660) 727-3628.
Fax: (660) 727-2544

MOONEY, Lawrence E. *(Chief Judge, Missouri Court of Appeals Eastern District)* Appointed by Governor Mel Carnahan to term beginning Aug 14, 1998. Retained by election Nov 7, 2000, current term expires Dec 31, 2012. Born St. Louis Missouri. Educated at St. Louis University A.B. J.D. and Harvard University Program for Senior Executives. In legal practice 1974-75 and 1977-78.
Assistant Prosecuting Attorney 1975-77, First Assistant Prosecuting Attorney 1979-90 and Executive Assistant to the County Executive 1991-98 St. Louis County. Member International Association of Lesbian and Gay Judges, The Bar Association of Metropolitan St. Louis, The Missouri Bar and American Bar Association. Board Member Metropolitan Education and Training Center, Laumeier Sculpture Park and National Conference for Community and Justice.
Office: Wainwright State Office Building, 111 North Seventh Street, St. Louis 63101.
Telephone: (314) 340-6936.
Fax: (314) 340-7703

MOORHOUSE, Kelly *(Circuit Judge, Missouri Circuit Court Sixteenth Judicial Circuit)* Appointed by governor.
Office: 415 East Twelfth Street, Kansas City 64106.
Telephone: (816) 881-3609.
Fax: (816) 881-3227

MORIARTY, Joan L. *(Circuit Judge, Missouri Circuit Court Twenty-second Judicial Circuit)* Appointed by governor. Serves Probate Division.
Office: Civil Courts Building, 10 North Tucker Street, St. Louis 63101.
Telephone: (314) 622-4927.

MOUNTJOY, Thomas E. *(Circuit Judge, Missouri Circuit Court Thirty-first Judicial Circuit)*
Office: 1010 Boonville, Springfield 65802.
Telephone: (417) 868-4089.
Fax: (417) 868-4119

MULLEN, Michael *(Associate Circuit Judge, Missouri Circuit Court Twenty-second Judicial Circuit)* Appointed by Governor Bob Holden.
Office: Civil Courts Building, 10 North Tucker Street, St. Louis 63101.
Telephone: (314) 622-4277.

MUMMERT, Thomas C., III *(Magistrate Judge, United States District Court Eastern District of Missouri)* Appointed by U.S. District Court judges to term beginning 1995. Born St. Louis Missouri Dec 11, 1950. Catholic. Educated at University of Dayton B.A. 1973 and St. Mary's University School of Law J.D. 1976. Admitted to practice Missouri 1976. Began legal practice St. Louis. Judge, St. Louis Municipal Court 1981-84. Circuit Judge June 8, 1984 to 1995 and Presiding Judge Jan 1, 1993 to Jan 1, 1995, Missouri Circuit Court Twenty-second Judicial Circuit.
Member The Bar Association of Metropolitan St. Louis and The Missouri Bar. Attended The National Judicial College.
Office: U.S. Courthouse, 111 South Tenth Street, St. Louis 63102-9958.
Telephone: (314) 244-7510.

MUNTON, David R. *(Associate Circuit Judge, Missouri Circuit Court Twenty-eighth Judicial Circuit)* Elected to term beginning Jan 1, 1995. Reelected Nov 1998 and 2002. Current term expires 2006. Serves Probate Division. Born Kirkwood Missouri March 18, 1958. Southern Baptist. Educated at Southwest Baptist College B.S. 1979 and University of Missouri-Columbia J.D. 1982. Admitted to practice Missouri 1982.
Office: 300 West Water, Greenfield 65661.
Telephone: (417) 637-2741.

MURRAY, Walter A., Jr. *(Associate Circuit Judge, Missouri Circuit Court Twentieth Judicial Circuit)* Serves Probate Division.
Office: 401 East Springfield, Union 63084.
Telephone: (636) 583-6312.

NEILL, Margaret M. *(Circuit Judge, Missouri Circuit Court Twenty-second Judicial Circuit)* Appointed by governor. Retained by election. Former Presiding Judge.
Office: Civil Courts Building, 10 North Tucker Street, St. Louis 63101.
Telephone: (314) 622-4682.
Fax: (314) 622-4524

NEILL, Mark H. *(Circuit Judge, Missouri Circuit Court Twenty-second Judicial Circuit)* Appointed by Governor Bob Holden.
Office: Civil Courts Building, 10 North Tucker Boulevard, St. Louis 63101.
Telephone: (314) 622-4802.

NEWTON, Thomas H. *(Judge, Missouri Court of Appeals Western District)* Appointed by Governor Mel Carnahan to term beginning Nov 1, 1999. Retained by election 2000, current term expires Dec 2012. Born Washington D.C. April 23, 1952. Educated at Howard University B.A. J.D. Circuit Judge, Missouri Circuit Court Sixteenth Judicial Circuit Sept 7, 1993 to Oct 31, 1999, appointed by Governor Mel Carnahan.
Assistant Prosecuting Attorney Jackson County 1984-87. Assistant U.S. Attorney Western District of Missouri 1987-93. Member Swope Parkway United Christian Church.
Office: 1300 Oak Street, Kansas City 64106-2970.
Telephone: (816) 889-3629.
Fax: (816) 889-3599

NIEMIRA, Thad F. *(Associate Circuit Judge, Missouri Circuit Court Twenty-second Judicial Circuit)* Appointed by governor. Retained by election.
Office: Civil Courts Building, 10 North Tucker Street, St. Louis 63101.
Telephone: (314) 622-4765.

NIXON, W. Stephen *(Circuit Judge, Missouri Circuit Court Sixteenth Judicial Circuit)* Appointed by Governor Mel Carnahan to term beginning March 1998. Retained by election to term beginning Jan 1, 2001, current term expires Dec 31, 2006. Currently serves as Family Court Administrative Judge. Born Kentucky Sept 5, 1951. Educated at University of Missouri-Kansas City B.A. 1973 J.D. 1975. Admitted to practice Missouri 1975.
Office: 625 East 26th Street, Kansas City 64108.
Telephone: (816) 435-4711.
Fax: (816) 435-8016
E-mail address: snixon@osca.state.mo.us

NOCE, David D. *(Magistrate Judge, United States District Court Eastern District of Missouri)* Appointed by U.S. District Court judges to term beginning Oct 1, 1976. Reappointed 1984, 1992 and 2000. Current term expires Sept 2008. Born St. Louis Missouri Feb 29, 1944. Roman Catholic. Educated at Cardinal Glennon College, St. Louis University A.B. 1966 and University of Missouri J.D. 1969. Admitted to practice Missouri 1969.
Law Clerk to U.S. District Court Eastern District of Missouri 1972-75. Assistant U.S. Attorney 1975-76. Author *Jury Instructions Drafting Workbook Supplement Material for Trial Advocacy Courses* West Group 1999. Instructor in Business Law Northwest Missouri State University 1970. Adjunct Professor of Law (jury instructions course) St. Louis University School of Law and Washington University School of Law. Member Federal Magistrate Judges Association, The Bar Association of Metropolitan St. Louis, The Missouri Bar and American Bar Association. First Lieutenant (legal officer) U.S. Army 1970-72. Enjoys athletics and reading.
Office: U.S. Courthouse, 111 South Tenth Street, St. Louis 63102-9958.
Telephone: (314) 244-7630.

NORTON, Glenn *(Judge, Missouri Court of Appeals Eastern District)* Appointed by Governor Bob Holden.
Office: Wainwright State Office Building, 111 North Seventh Street, St. Louis 63101.
Telephone: (314) 340-6934.
Fax: (314) 340-7703

O'BANNON, John M. *(Associate Circuit Judge, Missouri Circuit Court Twenty-seventh Judicial Circuit)* Serves Probate Division.
Office: One North Delaware, Butler 64730.
Telephone: (660) 679-3311.

O'BRIEN, Emmett M. *(Circuit Judge, Missouri Circuit Court Twenty-first Judicial Circuit)* Appointed by governor. Retained by election.
Office: St. Louis County Court Building, 7900 Carondelet, Clayton 63105.
Telephone: (314) 615-1511.
Fax: (314) 615-8280

OHMER, Steven R. *(Circuit Judge, Missouri Circuit Court Twenty-second Judicial Circuit)* Former Associate Circuit Judge, appointed by Governor Mel Carnahan to term beginning June 16, 1994. Appointed Circuit Judge by Governor Mel Carnahan to term beginning Aug 1, 2000. Retained by election Nov 5, 2002, current term expires Dec 31, 2008. Born St. Louis Missouri April 18, 1954. Catholic. Educated at Florida State University B.S. 1975 and Creighton University J.D. 1979. Admitted to practice Missouri 1979, U.S. District Court Eastern District of Missouri 1979, Illinois 1980 and U.S. Supreme Court 1988. In legal practice St. Louis Missouri 1983-87.
Assistant Circuit Attorney St. Louis 1979-83 and 1987-92. Chief Warrant Officer for Circuit Attorney 1992-94. Author Casenote "Bankruptcy" 12 Creighton L. Rev. Spring 1979 and "The Role of the Guardian Ad Litem in Domestic Violence" St. Louis B. Jour. Spring 1996 and Chapters "Landlord/Tenant" and "Jury Call and Management" *Bench Book* Missouri Trial Judges 2001. Member American Judges Association, Lawyers Association of St. Louis, The Bar Association of Metropolitan St. Louis and The Missouri Bar. Attended Annual Meeting and Orientation Conference Missouri Judicial College 1994, 1995, 1996, 1997, 1998, 1999, 2000, 2001 and 2002 and General Jurisdiction Course The National Judicial College 1995. Former Athletic Director Youth Sports Program and Member St. Pius V Church. Enjoys golf, gardening and reading.
Office: Civil Courts Building, 10 North Tucker Street, St. Louis 63101.
Telephone: (314) 622-5606.
Fax: (314) 622-4524

O'MALLEY, John R. *(Circuit Judge, Missouri Circuit Court Sixteenth Judicial Circuit)* Appointed by Governor John D. Ashcroft to term beginning April 19, 1989. Retained by election Jan 1, 1990, Jan 1, 1996 and Nov 2002. Current term expires Dec 31, 2008. Former

O'MALLEY, JOHN R.—*Continued*

Presiding Judge. Born Kansas City Missouri April 9, 1948. Roman Catholic. Educated at St. Louis University A.B. 1970 J.D. 1973. Admitted to practice Missouri 1973 and U.S. District Courts Eastern 1973 and Western 1973 Districts of Missouri. In legal practice Kansas City 1975-79 and Grandview 1979-89.

Assistant City Counselor St. Louis June 1973 to April 1975. City Prosecutor Grandview March 1979 to April 1989. Instructor in Business Law, Philosophy and Paralegal subjects in Kansas City area colleges since 1975. Chairman Missouri Commission on Retirement, Removal and Discipline of Judges 2000-01. Member The Missouri Bar and Kansas City Metropolitan Bar Association. Lieutenant Colonel USAR JAGC. Member Mayor's Task Force on Race Relations 1997. Enjoys his three children, fishing and music.

Office: Courthouse, 415 East Twelfth Street, Kansas City 64106.
Telephone: (816) 881-3606.
Fax: (816) 881-3390
E-mail address: John_R_O'Malley@OSCA.state.mo

ORDNUNG, Michael J. *(Associate Circuit Judge, Missouri Circuit Court Fifth Judicial Circuit)* Serves Probate Division.

Mailing address: P.O. Box 49, Savannah 64485.
Telephone: (816) 324-3921.
Fax: (816) 324-3191

ORR, Mark *(Associate Circuit Judge, Missouri Circuit Court Thirty-eighth Judicial Circuit)*

Office: 110 West Elm Street, Room 203, Ozark 65721.
Telephone: (417) 581-2425.

OSWALD, Kenneth L. *(Associate Circuit Judge, Missouri Circuit Court Twenty-sixth Judicial Circuit)* Serves Probate Division.

Office: Courthouse Square, Tuscumbia 65082.
Telephone: (573) 369-2330.
Fax: (573) 369-0077

OXENHANDLER, Gary *(Circuit Judge, Missouri Circuit Court Thirteenth Judicial Circuit)*

Office: 705 East Walnut Street, Columbia 65201.
Telephone: (573) 886-4050.
Fax: (573) 886-4070

PARKER, Kelly W. *(Associate Circuit Judge, Missouri Circuit Court Forty-second Judicial Circuit)* Serves Probate Division.

Mailing address: P.O. Box 325, Ironton 63650.
Telephone: (573) 546-2511.
Fax: (573) 546-6006

PARKINSON, Paul K. *(Associate Circuit Judge, Missouri Circuit Court Forty-first Judicial Circuit)* Appointed by Governor Roger B. Wilson to term beginning Jan 1, 2001. Elected Nov 5, 2002, current term expires Dec 31, 2006. Serves Probate Division. Born Durango Colorado Feb 8, 1952. Educated at Truman State University B.S.E. magna cum laude 1997, University of Missouri-Kansas City J.D. 1980 and University of Miami LL.M. 1981. Admitted to practice Missouri 1980 and Kansas 1988. In legal practice Kansas City Missouri 1980-90 and Macon Missouri 1990-2000.

Assistant Prosecuting Attorney Macon County Jan 1, 1999 to Dec 31, 2000.

Mailing address: P.O. Box 491, Macon 63552.
Office: Building Two, 101 East Washington, Macon 63552.
Telephone: (660) 385-3531.
Fax: (660) 385-3132
E-mail address: Paul_Parkinson@osca.state.mo.us

PARRISH, John Edward *(Judge, Missouri Court of Appeals Southern District)* Appointed by Governor John D. Ashcroft to term beginning Jan 1990. Retained by election Nov 3, 1992, current term expires Dec 31, 2004. Chief Judge 1992-94. Born Lebanon Missouri June 10, 1940. Educated at University of Missouri-Columbia B.S. 1962 J.D. 1965. Staff member and Revising Editor Missouri Law Review 1963-65. Member Phi Delta Phi and Beta Gamma Sigma. Admitted to practice Missouri 1965. In legal practice Camdenton 1968-73. Circuit Judge and Presiding Judge, Missouri Circuit Court Twenty-sixth Judicial Circuit 1973-90.

Prosecuting Attorney Camden County 1969-73. Member The Missouri Bar, Camden County, Greene County and American Bar Associations. Graduate 1974 and Faculty Advisor 1982 The National Judicial College. Captain U.S. Army 1966-68. Board of Education Camdenton R-3 School District 1973-76. Board of Directors Lake Regional Health System since 1978. Member Community Christian Church (Disciples of Christ).

Office: 300 Hammons Parkway, Springfield 65806.
Telephone: (417) 895-6820.

PATTERSON, Timothy J. *(Presiding Judge, Missouri Circuit Court Twenty-third Judicial Circuit)* Elected Circuit Judge to term beginning Jan 1, 1983. Reelected 1988, 1994 and 2000. Current term expires Dec 31, 2006. Born St. Louis Missouri Aug 6, 1941. Roman Catholic. Educated at Southeast Missouri State University B.S. 1963 and University of Missouri-Kansas City J.D. 1972. Law Clerk to Hon. George C. Berry, Kansas City Probate Court 1970-73. Member Sigma Chi and Phi Delta Phi. Admitted to practice Missouri 1972. Began legal practice Hillsboro 1973.

High school teacher Hillsboro 1963-65. Prosecuting Attorney Jefferson County 1975-78. Part-time Instructor in Police Training University of Missouri-Columbia 1977-82. Part-time Instructor Jefferson Junior College 1978-82. Former Member The Missouri Bar (CLE Committee) and Executive Council Missouri Judicial Conference. Member Commission for Alternative Dispute Resolution and Missouri Circuit Judges Association (Secretary-Treasurer, Past Vice President, President). Recipient Equal Justice Award from Legal Services of Eastern Missouri 2000. Staff Sergeant USAF 1966-70. Democrat. Board of Directors Community Treatment, Inc. Member Boy Scouts of America (Assistant Scoutmaster and Merit Badge Counselor), Knights of Columbus (Former State Advocate), Rotary Club and St. Louis Archdiocesan Pastoral Council. Enjoys swimming, canoeing and camping.

Mailing address: P.O. Box 100, Hillsboro 63050.
Telephone: (636) 797-5410.

PEEBLES, Barbara T. *(Associate Circuit Judge, Missouri Circuit Court Twenty-second Judicial Circuit)* Appointed by governor.
Office: Municipal Courts Building, 1320 Market Street, St. Louis 63103.
Telephone: (314) 622-4536.

PELIKAN, Daniel *(Associate Circuit Judge, Missouri Circuit Court Eleventh Judicial Circuit)*
Office: 300 North Second Street, Room 336, St. Charles 63301.
Telephone: (636) 949-7900.

PERIGO, Timothy W. *(Presiding Judge, Missouri Circuit Court Fortieth Judicial Circuit)* Former Associate Circuit Judge.
Office: 101 South Wood, Neosho 64850.
Telephone: (417) 451-8234.
Fax: (417) 451-8282

PERRY, Catherine D. *(Judge, United States District Court Eastern District of Missouri)* Magistrate Judge 1990-94. Appointed Judge for life by President Bill Clinton to term beginning Oct 21, 1994. Born Hobart Oklahoma Sept 6, 1952. Educated at University of Oklahoma B.A. 1977 and Washington University J.D. with honors 1980. Managing Editor Washington University Law Quarterly 1979-80. Admitted to practice Missouri 1980 and Illinois 1981. In legal practice St. Louis Missouri 1980-90.
Adjunct Professor Washington University School of Law 1982-87 and 1991-95. Member Women Lawyers Association of Greater St. Louis, Federal Judges Association, Federal Magistrate Judges Association, National Association of Women Judges, The Bar Association of Metropolitan St. Louis, The Missouri Bar and American Bar Association.
Office: U.S. Courthouse, Fourteenth Floor, 111 South Tenth Street, St. Louis 63102-9958.
Telephone: (314) 244-7520.

PHILLIPS, Joseph B. *(Associate Circuit Judge, Missouri Circuit Court Twenty-eighth Judicial Circuit)* Serves Probate Division.
Mailing address: P.O. Box 665, Stockton 65785.
Telephone: (417) 276-6700.
Fax: (417) 276-5001

POWELL, Mark A. *(Associate Circuit Judge, Missouri Circuit Court Thirty-first Judicial Circuit)*
Office: 1010 Boonville, Springfield 65802.
Telephone: (417) 829-6546.
Fax: (417) 868-4809

PRATTE, Kenneth W. *(Presiding Judge, Missouri Circuit Court Twenty-fourth Judicial Circuit)*
Office: One North Washington, Third Floor, Farmington 63640.
Telephone: (573) 756-5144.
Fax: (573) 757-3733

PREWITT, James K. *(Judge, Missouri Court of Appeals Southern District)* Appointed by Governor Joseph P. Teasdale May 30, 1979 to term beginning July 1, 1979. Retained by election 1980 and 1992. Current term expires Dec 31, 2004. Former Chief Judge. Born California Missouri Jan 13, 1936. Educated at University of Missouri-Columbia LL.B. Staff member Missouri Law Review. Member Phi Delta Phi, Alpha Tau Omega and Order of the Coif. In legal practice Kansas City and Springfield.
Member The Missouri Bar, Greene County and American Bar Associations.
Office: 300 Hammons Parkway, Springfield 65806.
Telephone: (417) 895-6825.

PREWITT, Jo Beth *(Associate Circuit Judge, Missouri Circuit Court Thirty-seventh Judicial Circuit)* Serves Probate Division.
Mailing address: P.O. Box 211, Alton 65606.
Telephone: (417) 778-7461.

PRICE, J. Max *(Presiding Judge, Missouri Circuit Court Forty-second Judicial Circuit)*
Mailing address: P.O. Box 551, Salem 65560.
Telephone: (573) 729-6816.
Fax: (573) 729-5146

PRICE, William Ray, Jr. *(Judge, Supreme Court of Missouri)* Appointed by Governor John D. Ashcroft to term beginning 1992. Retained by election. Chief Justice July 1, 1999 to June 31, 2001. Educated at University of Iowa, Yale University and Washington and Lee University School of Law J.D. cum laude 1978. Recipient Rockefeller Fellowship. Member Phi Beta Kappa. In legal practice Kansas City.
President Kansas City Police Commissioners. Director Truman Medical Center.
Mailing address: P.O. Box 150, Jefferson City 65102.
Office: Supreme Court Building, Jefferson City 65101.
Telephone: (573) 751-4513.
Fax: (573) 751-7365

PROKES, Roger M. *(Presiding Judge, Missouri Circuit Court Fourth Judicial Circuit)*
Mailing address: P.O. Box 218, Maryville 64468.
Telephone: (660) 582-4231.
Fax: (660) 582-5499

QUIGLESS, Angela Turner *(Circuit Judge, Missouri Circuit Court Twenty-second Judicial Circuit)* Former Associate Circuit Judge, appointed by Governor Mel Carnahan to term beginning 1995. Appointed Circuit Judge by Governor Bob Holden.
Office: Municipal Courts Building, 1320 Market Street, St. Louis 63103.
Telephone: (314) 622-4786.

RAHMEYER, Nancy Steffen *(Chief Judge, Missouri Court of Appeals Southern District)* Appointed by Governor Bob Holden to term beginning Feb 1, 2001. Born Spencer Iowa Oct 10, 1951. Educated at Iowa State University B.S., Southwest Missouri State University M.S.Ed. and University of Arkansas J.D. Law Clerk to Federal District Court 1987-89. In legal practice Springfield 1989-2001. Part-time Municipal Judge, Springfield 1993-2001.
Member The Missouri Bar and Springfield Metropolitan Bar Association.
Office: 300 Hammons Parkway, Springfield 65806.
Telephone: (417) 895-6823.

RAUCH, Lucy D. *(Presiding Judge, Missouri Circuit Court Eleventh Judicial Circuit)* Associate Circuit Judge 1982-91. Appointed Circuit Judge Oct 1, 1991. Elected 1992, 1994 and 2000. Current term expires Dec 31, 2006. Educated at Duke University B.A. 1972, University of North Carolina at Chapel Hill M.S.L.S. 1973 and St. Louis University School of Law J.D. 1979. Admitted

RAUCH, LUCY D.—*Continued*

to practice Missouri 1979. Assistant Prosecuting Attorney St. Charles County 1979-82.
Office: 300 North Second Street, St. Charles 63301.
Telephone: (636) 949-7900.

RAVENS, Gary E. *(Presiding Judge, Missouri Circuit Court Ninth Judicial Circuit)*
Mailing address: P.O. Box 84, Linneus 64653.
Office: 108 North High, Linneus 64653.
Telephone: (660) 895-5523.
Fax: (660) 895-5277

RAY, Thomas L. *(Associate Circuit Judge, Missouri Circuit Court Twenty-fourth Judicial Circuit)*
Office: One North Washington, Farmington 63640.
Telephone: (573) 756-5755.
Fax: (573) 756-8173

RENO, Gloria Jean Clark *(Associate Circuit Judge, Missouri Circuit Court Twenty-first Judicial Circuit)* Appointed by Governor Bob Holden.
Office: St. Louis County Court Building, 7900 Carondelet, Clayton 63105.
Telephone: (314) 615-1536.

RICHARDS, Wm. S. *(Associate Circuit Judge, Missouri Circuit Court Fourth Judicial Circuit)* Serves Probate Division.
Mailing address: P.O. Box 173, Oregon 64473.
Telephone: (660) 446-3380.
Fax: (660) 446-3588

RICHARDSON, Mark L. *(Presiding Judge, Missouri Circuit Court Thirty-sixth Judicial Circuit)*
Office: 100 North Main, Poplar Bluff 63901.
Telephone: (573) 686-8080.
Fax: (573) 778-8034

RICHARDSON, Peggy *(Associate Circuit Judge, Missouri Circuit Court Twenty-sixth Judicial Circuit)* Serves Probate Division.
Office: 200 East Main, California 65018.
Telephone: (573) 796-4671.

RICHTER, Roy L. *(Associate Circuit Judge, Missouri Circuit Court Twelfth Judicial Circuit)* Elected to term beginning Jan 1, 1979. Reelected 1982, 1986, 1990, 1994, 1998 and 2002. Current term expires Dec 31, 2006. Serves Probate Division. Born St. Louis Missouri July 14, 1950. Religious affiliation: Congregational Church. Educated at Drury College B.A. 1972 and University of Missouri-Columbia J.D. 1976. Admitted to practice Missouri 1976. Began legal practice Montgomery City 1976.

Prosecuting Attorney Montgomery County 1977-78. Board member Missouri Association of Probate and Associate Circuit Judges (Vice President 1987-88, President 1988-89). Member Circuit Court Budget Committee, Legislative Steering Committee, Executive Council Judicial Conference, The Missouri Bar (Judicial Article Review Commission), Twelfth Judicial Circuit and Montgomery County Bar Associations. Republican. Member Montgomery City Kiwanis Club.
Office: 211 East Third Street, Montgomery City 63361.
Telephone: (573) 564-3348.
Fax: (573) 564-8081

RIGBY, Twila K. *(Associate Circuit Judge, Missouri Circuit Court Sixteenth Judicial Circuit)* Appointed by Governor Mel Carnahan.
Office: Courthouse Annex, 308 West Kansas, Independence 64050.
Telephone: (816) 881-4506.
Fax: (816) 881-1647

RILEY, John J. *(Circuit Judge, Missouri Circuit Court Twenty-second Judicial Circuit)* Appointed by Governor Mel Carnahan to term beginning 1995. Retained by election.
Office: Civil Courts Building, 10 North Tucker Street, St. Louis 63101.
Telephone: (314) 613-7187.

ROBB, Patrick K. *(Presiding Judge, Missouri Circuit Court Fifth Judicial Circuit)* Associate Circuit Judge 1987-88. Elected Circuit Judge to term beginning Jan 1, 1989. Reelected 1994 and 2000. Current term expires Dec 31, 2006. Born Quincy Illinois Nov 6, 1955. Presbyterian. Educated at Southeast Missouri State University B.A. magna cum laude 1977 and University of Missouri-Kansas City J.D. 1979. Staff member University of Missouri-Kansas City Law Review 1977-79. Member Delta Theta Phi. Admitted to practice Missouri 1980. In legal practice St. Joseph 1980-86.

Assistant Prosecuting Attorney Buchanan County 1980-86. Recipient Award for Distinguished Service as a Prosecutor in the State of Missouri Dec 1985. Democrat. Member Independent Democratic Club. Enjoys sports, camping, canoeing, sailing and bike riding.
Office: 411 Jules, St. Joseph 64501.
Telephone: (816) 271-1444.
Fax: (816) 271-1575

ROBERTS, William J. *(Presiding Judge, Missouri Circuit Court Twenty-seventh Judicial Circuit)*
Mailing address: P.O. Box 83, Clinton 64735.
Telephone: (660) 885-6963.
Fax: (660) 885-8456

ROLDAN, Marco *(Circuit Judge, Missouri Circuit Court Sixteenth Judicial Circuit)* Appointed by Governor Mel Carnahan.
Office: Courthouse, 415 East Twelfth Street, Kansas City 64106.
Telephone: (816) 881-4416.
Fax: (816) 881-4692.

ROLF, Dennis A. *(Presiding Judge, Missouri Circuit Court Fifteenth Judicial Circuit)* Elected. Term expires Dec 31, 2006. Born Warrensburg Missouri Dec 7, 1958. Lutheran. Educated at University of Missouri B.S. magna cum laude 1980 J.D. 1983. Admitted to practice Missouri 1983. In legal practice Carrolton Aug 1, 1983 to July 31, 1984 and Concordia Aug 1, 1984 to Jan 1, 2001.

Assistant Prosecutor Lafayette County June 1, 1983 to July 31, 1984. Public Defender Missouri Aug 1, 1984 to June 30, 1988. Member The Missouri Bar, Lafayette County and Saline County Bar Associations. Member Trinity Lutheran Church. Enjoys sports.
Mailing address: P.O. Box 751, Concordia 64020.
Office: 548 Main, Concordia 64020.
Telephone: (660) 463-5834.
Fax: (660) 463-5835
E-mail address: Dennis_Rolf@osca.state.mo.us

ROMINES, Kenneth M. *(Circuit Judge, Missouri Circuit Court Twenty-first Judicial Circuit)* Appointed by governor. Retained by election. Former Presiding Judge.
Office: St. Louis County Court Building, 7900 Carondelet, Clayton 63105.
Telephone: (314) 615-1510.

ROPER, Ellen S. *(Circuit Judge, Missouri Circuit Court Thirteenth Judicial Circuit)* Elected to term beginning Jan 1, 1979. Reelected 1982, 1988, 1994 and 2000. Current term expires Dec 31, 2006. Serves Probate, Criminal and Civil Divisions. Born Dallas Texas Sept 15, 1940. Educated at Brandeis University A.B. 1963 and University of Missouri-Columbia J.D. 1973. Staff member Missouri Law Review. Admitted to practice Missouri 1973. Began legal practice Jefferson City 1973. Judge, Boone County Probate Court Jan 1, 1976 to Dec 31, 1978. Special Judge, Missouri Supreme Court Sept 1981. Special Judge, Missouri Court of Appeals Western District April 1986.
Assistant Attorney General Missouri 1973-74. Important Decisions: State v. Moland 626 S.W.2d 368 Mo. 1982; State v. Bradford 627 S.W.2d 281 Mo. 1982; and Goldberg v. Mo 631 S.W.2d 342 Mo. 1982. Member Missouri Judicial Conference, Missouri Association of Trial Judges, The Missouri Bar, Boone County and Callaway County (Honorary) Bar Associations. Instructor in General Jurisdiction and Criminal Law courses The National Judicial College Oct 1982, July 1984, July 1985, July 1986, July 1987, July 1988, July 1989, July 1990, July 1991, July 1992, July 1993, July 1994 and July 1995. Republican. Executive Director Missouri Committee on Human Rights 1974-75.
Office: 705 East Walnut Street, Columbia 65201.
Telephone: (573) 886-4050.
Fax: (573) 886-4070

ROSENBOHM, Kay F. Graves *(Associate Circuit Judge, Missouri Circuit Court Fourth Judicial Circuit)* Serves Probate Division.
Mailing address: P.O. Box 187, Rock Port 64482.
Telephone: (660) 744-2700.
Fax: (660) 744-5705

ROSS, John A. *(Circuit Judge, Missouri Circuit Court Twenty-first Judicial Circuit)* Appointed by Governor Mel Carnahan to term beginning Jan 1, 2000. Retained by election Nov 7, 2002, current term expires Dec 31, 2008. Born St. Louis Missouri. Educated at Emory University B.A. 1976 J.D. 1979. Admitted to practice Missouri 1979 and Georgia 1979.
Prosecuting Attorney and Chief Trial Attorney 1979-91 and County Counselor 1991-2000 St. Louis County.
Office: St. Louis County Court Building, 7900 Carondelet, Clayton 63105.
Telephone: (314) 615-1515.
Fax: (314) 615-8280

RUSSELL, David W. *(Circuit Judge, Missouri Circuit Court Seventh Judicial Circuit)* Former Associate Circuit Judge, appointed by Governor John D. Ashcroft. Former Presiding Judge.
Office: 11 South Water, Liberty 64068.
Telephone: (816) 792-7712.
Fax: (816) 792-7795

RUSSELL, Mary Rhodes *(Judge, Missouri Court of Appeals Eastern District)* Appointed by Governor Mel Carnahan to term beginning June 14, 1995. Retained by election 1996, current term expires Dec 31, 2008. Former Chief Judge. Born Hannibal Missouri July 28, 1958. Episcopalian. Educated at Truman State University B.S. summa cum laude 1980 B.A. summa cum laude 1980 and University of Missouri-Columbia J.D. 1983. Dean's List. Law Clerk to Hon. George F. Gunn, Jr., Missouri Supreme Court 1983-84. Member Phi Delta Phi. Admitted to practice Missouri 1983, U.S. District Courts Eastern 1983 and Western 1983 Districts of Missouri, Illinois 1984 and U.S. Supreme Court 1992. In legal practice Hannibal Missouri 1984-95.
Author Rule 61 "Enforcement of Discovery Sanctions" *Civil Procedure Deskbook* 1994-95 and Supplement 2001 The Missouri Bar. Editor pamphlet on rights and responsibilities of 18-year-olds "Stepping Out" The Missouri Bar. Member National Association of Women Judges, Women's Lawyer Association of St. Louis, Lawyers Association of St. Louis, Bar Association of Metropolitan St. Louis, The Missouri Bar and Tenth Circuit Bar Association. Speaker on Civil Procedure and Appellate Practice. Recipient Young Lawyers Chairpersons Award 1992 and 1993, Equal Justice Award 1994, Citation of Merit Award from University of Missouri-Columbia School of Law 1997, Henry Toll Fellowship 1997, Appreciation Award from Matthews Dickey Boys/Girls Club 2001 and Faculty Alumni Award from University of Missouri 2002. Named Kirkwood Citizen of the Year 2003. Political affiliation: Nonpartisan. Member St. Louis Leadership Class 2001, Missouri Academy of Squires, Rotary, PEO, Episcopal Church, St. Joseph Hospital Board and Sue Shear Institute for Women in Public Life. Enjoys Cardinal baseball and travel.
Office: Wainwright State Office Building, 111 North Seventh Street, St. Louis 63101.
Telephone: (314) 340-6928.
Fax: (314) 340-7703

RUTTER, Edith R. *(Associate Circuit Judge, Missouri Circuit Court Forty-second Judicial Circuit)* Serves Probate Division.
Mailing address: P.O. Box 39, Centerville 63633.
Telephone: (573) 648-2494.

SACHS, Howard F. *(Senior Judge, United States District Court Western District of Missouri)* Appointed for life by President Jimmy Carter to term beginning Oct 5, 1979. Former Chief Judge. Assumed Senior status, serves by assignment. Born Kansas City Missouri Sept 13, 1925. Jewish. Educated at Williams College B.A. summa cum laude 1947 and Harvard University J.D. 1950. Law Clerk to Hon. Albert A. Ridge, U.S. District Court Western District of Missouri 1950-51. Member Phi Beta Kappa. Admitted to practice Missouri 1950. Began legal practice Kansas City 1951.
Important Decisions: Meyers v. Ford Motor Co. 480 F. Supp. 894 W.D. Mo. 1979; Heitman v. Gabriel 524 F. Supp. 622 W.D. Mo. 1981; Valente v. Larson 637 F.2d 562 8th Cir. 1981; MRI v. U.S. 554 F. Supp. 1379 W.D. Mo. 1983; Safley v. Turner 586 F. Supp. 589 W.D. Mo. 1984; In re Long 774 F.2d 875, 8th Cir. 1985; and Beech v. Harris 631 F. Supp. 1449 W.D. Mo. 1986. Member Kansas City School Desegregation Task Force 1976-77, Kansas City Human Relations Commission 1967-73, American Judicature Society, Lawyers Association of Kansas City, The Missouri Bar, Kansas City and American Bar Associations. ETM Second Class USN 1944-46. Democrat. President Jackson County

SACHS, HOWARD F.—*Continued*

Young Democrats 1958-59. Treasurer Kennedy-Johnson Club of Jackson County 1960. Interests include biographies and history.

Office: 7462 U.S. Courthouse, 400 East Ninth Street, Kansas City 64106.

Telephone: (816) 512-5715.

SATTERFIELD, Joe Z. *(Associate Circuit Judge, Missouri Circuit Court Thirty-fifth Judicial Circuit)*

Mailing address: P.O. Box 218, Bloomfield 63825.

Telephone: (573) 568-4671.

Fax: (573) 568-2299

SAUER, Margaret L. *(Associate Circuit Judge, Missouri Circuit Court Sixteenth Judicial Circuit)* Appointed by governor.

Office: Courthouse, 415 East Twelfth Street, Kansas City 64106.

Telephone: (816) 881-3734.

SAYRE, Jeffrey D. *(Associate Circuit Judge, Missouri Circuit Court Ninth Judicial Circuit)* Serves Probate Division.

Office: 109 North Main, Milan 63556.

Telephone: (660) 265-3303.

Fax: (660) 265-5071

SCHAEPERKOETTER, Jeff W. *(Circuit Judge, Missouri Circuit Court Twentieth Judicial Circuit)* Former Presiding Judge.

Office: 811 Oakbrook Drive, Owensville 65066.

Telephone: (636) 583-6309.

Fax: (636) 583-7390

SCHAUMANN, Dennis M. *(Circuit Judge, Missouri Circuit Court Twenty-second Judicial Circuit)* Former Associate Circuit Judge. Appointed Circuit Judge by Governor Mel Carnahan.

Office: Civil Courts Building, 10 North Tucker Street, St. Louis 63101.

Telephone: (314) 622-4420.

SCHEHR, Kevin *(Associate Circuit Judge, Missouri Circuit Court Twenty-sixth Judicial Circuit)* Serves Probate Division.

Office: 211 East Newton, Versailles 65084.

Telephone: (573) 378-4235.

Fax: (573) 378-6847

SCHERMER, Barry S. *(Judge, United States Bankruptcy Court Eastern District of Missouri)* Appointed by U.S. Court of Appeals Eighth Circuit judges to term beginning 1986. Reappointed 2000, current term expires 2014. Former Chief Judge Bankruptcy Court. Also Judge, Bankruptcy Appellate Panel Eighth Circuit. Selected by the Judicial Council of the Eighth Circuit to term beginning 1996. Educated at Washington University J.D. 1973.

Adjunct Professor Washington University School of Law.

Office: U.S. Courthouse, 111 South Tenth Street, St. Louis 63102.

Telephone: (314) 244-4531.

SCHNEIDER, Nancy L. *(Circuit Judge, Missouri Circuit Court Eleventh Judicial Circuit)* Associate Circuit Judge July 1, 1991 to Dec 31, 1998. Elected Circuit Judge Nov 1998 to term beginning Jan 1, 1999. Term expires Dec 31, 2004. Former Presiding Judge. Born St. Louis Missouri June 28, 1948. Catholic. Educated at Lindenwood University B.S.B.A. cum laude 1978 and St. Louis University J.D. cum laude 1981. Admitted to practice Missouri 1981 and U.S. District Court Eastern District of Missouri 1984. In legal practice St. Charles 1981-91.

Prosecuting Attorney Juvenile Court St. Charles County 1984-87. Special Assistant Attorney General 1989-91. Member The Missouri Bar and St. Charles County Bar Association. Attended The National Judicial College 1997. Republican.

Office: 300 North Second Street, Room 439, St. Charles 63301.

Telephone: (636) 949-7900.

Fax: (636) 949-7343

SCHOEBERL, Joseph *(Associate Circuit Judge, Missouri Circuit Court Twenty-ninth Judicial Circuit)*

Office: 302 South Main, Room 304, Carthage 64836.

Telephone: (417) 358-0450.

Fax: (417) 358-0460

SCHOLLMEYER, Robert *(Associate Circuit Judge, Missouri Circuit Court Twentieth Judicial Circuit)* Serves Probate Division.

Mailing address: P.O. Box 470, Linn 65051.

Telephone: (573) 897-2136.

SCHROEDER, Mary Bruntrager *(Associate Circuit Judge, Missouri Circuit Court Twenty-first Judicial Circuit)* Appointed by Governor Mel Carnahan.

Office: St. Louis County Court Building, 7900 Carondelet, Clayton 63105.

Telephone: (314) 615-1532.

SCHULLER, Randy P. *(Associate Circuit Judge, Missouri Circuit Court Forty-second Judicial Circuit)* Elected Nov 6, 1990 to term beginning Jan 1, 1991. Reelected Nov 8, 1994, Nov 1998 and 2002. Current term expires Dec 31, 2006. Serves Probate Division. Born St. Louis Missouri May 23, 1955. Methodist. Educated at Drake University B.S.B.A. with honors 1977 and University of Missouri-Columbia J.D. 1980. Admitted to practice Missouri 1980, U.S. District Courts Western 1980 and Eastern 1982 Districts of Missouri and U.S. Court of Appeals Eighth Circuit 1989. In legal practice Piedmont 1980-91.

Prosecuting Attorney Wayne County 1983-87. Member Missouri Association of Probate and Associate Circuit Judges, The Missouri Bar and Forty-second Judicial Circuit Bar Association.

Mailing address: P.O. Box 188, Greenville 63944.

Telephone: (573) 224-3052.

Fax: (573) 224-3225

SCOVILLE, Vernon E., III *(Associate Circuit Judge, Missouri Circuit Court Sixteenth Judicial Circuit)* Appointed by governor. Retained by election.

Office: 308 West Kansas, Independence 64050.

Telephone: (816) 881-4606.

SEAY, William C. *(Circuit Judge, Missouri Circuit Court Forty-second Judicial Circuit)* Former Presiding Judge.

Mailing address: P.O. Box 551, Salem 65560.

Telephone: (573) 729-6816.

Fax: (573) 729-5146

SEIGEL, Mark D. *(Circuit Judge, Missouri Circuit Court Twenty-first Judicial Circuit)* Appointed by gover-

SEIGEL, MARK D.—*Continued*
nor. Retained by election. Serves Civil and Criminal Divisions.
Office: St. Louis County Court Building, 7900 Carondelet, Clayton 63105.
Telephone: (314) 615-1503.
Fax: (314) 615-8280

SELBY, Kevin *(Associate Circuit Judge, Missouri Circuit Court Fortieth Judicial Circuit)* Serves Probate Division.
Office: 101 South Wood, Neosho 64850.
Telephone: (417) 451-8231.
Fax: (417) 451-8265

SHAFER, Abe *(Circuit Judge, Missouri Circuit Court Sixth Judicial Circuit)* Appointed by Governor Mel Carnahan.
Office: 415 Third Street, Suite 65, Platte City 64079.
Telephone: (816) 858-2232.
Fax: (816) 858-3392

SHARP, Stephen R. *(Presiding Judge, Missouri Circuit Court Thirty-fifth Judicial Circuit)*
Mailing address: P.O. Box 507, Kennett 63857.
Telephone: (573) 888-9133.
Fax: (573) 888-9140

SHAW, Booker T. *(Judge, Missouri Court of Appeals Eastern District)* Appointed by Governor Bob Holden. Former Associate Circuit Judge and Circuit Judge, Missouri Circuit Court Twenty-second Judicial Circuit.
Office: Wainwright State Office Building, 111 North Seventh Street, St. Louis 63101.
Telephone: (314) 340-6918.
Fax: (314) 340-7703

SHAW, Charles A. *(Judge, United States District Court Eastern District of Missouri)* Appointed for life by President Bill Clinton to term beginning 1993. Born Jackson Tennessee Dec 31, 1944. Educated at Harris-Stowe State College B.A. 1966, University of Missouri-Columbia M.B.A. 1971 and Catholic University of America School of Law J.D. 1974. In legal practice St. Louis 1976-80. Circuit Judge, Missouri Circuit Court Twenty-second Judicial Circuit 1987-93.
Attorney Division of Enforcement Appellate Branch National Labor Relations Board 1974-76. Assistant U.S. Attorney Eastern District of Missouri 1980-87.
Office: U.S. Courthouse, Twelfth Floor, 111 South Tenth Street, St. Louis 63102-9958.
Telephone: (314) 244-7480.

SHEFFIELD, Mary W. *(Associate Circuit Judge, Missouri Circuit Court Twenty-fifth Judicial Circuit)* Elected to term beginning Jan 1, 1983. Reelected 1986, 1990, 1994, 1998 and 2002. Current term expires Dec 31, 2006. Serves Probate Division. Born Durham North Carolina Jan 26, 1955. Methodist. Educated at North Carolina State University B.A. with honors 1977 and University of Miami J.D. 1980. Executive Editor International Lawyer of the Americas 1979-80. Admitted to practice Missouri 1980. Began legal practice Salem 1980. In legal practice Rolla 1982.
President Blue Ridge Institute for Juvenile and Family Court Judges 1995 and National College of Probate Judges 2001.
Office: 200 North Main, Rolla 65401.
Telephone: (573) 364-1891.

SHERRY, Thea A. *(Associate Circuit Judge, Missouri Circuit Court Twenty-first Judicial Circuit)* Appointed by Governor Mel Carnahan to term beginning July 31, 1998. Reappointed by Governor Roger Wilson Dec 20, 2000. Retained by election Nov 7, 2000, current term expires Dec 31, 2004. Born London England. Episcopalian. Educated at University of California at Riverside B.A. and Washington University J.D. Associate Articles Editor Urban Law Annual. Law Clerk to Hon. Gerald M. Smith, Missouri Court of Appeals St. Louis District Feb 1977 to Sept 1978. Admitted to practice Missouri 1976 and U.S. District Courts Eastern 1976 and Western 1976 Districts of Missouri. In legal practice Clayton June 1981 to July 1998.
Assistant Public Defender St. Louis County Sept 1978 to June 1981. Member Women Lawyers Association, National Association of Women Judges, The Missouri Bar and American Bar Association.
Office: St. Louis County Court Building, 7900 Carondelet, Clayton 63105.
Telephone: (314) 615-1535.
Fax: (314) 615-2689

SHRUM, Kenneth W. *(Judge, Missouri Court of Appeals Southern District)* Appointed by Governor John D. Ashcroft to term beginning May 19, 1990. Retained by election 1992, current term expires Dec 31, 2004. Former Chief Judge. Born Cape Girardeau Missouri March 22, 1938. Educated at University of Missouri-Rolla B.Ch.E. and University of Missouri-Columbia LL.B. Staff member Missouri Law Review. Member Tau Beta Pi, Alpha Chi Epsilon and Order of the Coif. In legal practice Jefferson City and Marble Hill.
Prosecuting Attorney Bollinger County 1964-86. City Attorney Frederickton 1967-89. Member The Missouri Bar, Bollinger County, Cape Girardeau County and Greene County Bar Associations. Member Marble Hill United Methodist Church.
Office: 300 Hammons Parkway, Springfield 65806.
Telephone: (417) 895-6822.

SIFFERMAN, Scott S. *(Associate Circuit Judge, Missouri Circuit Court Thirty-ninth Judicial Circuit)* Appointed by Governor John D. Ashcroft to term beginning Aug 28, 1989. Elected Nov 6, 1990, 1994, 1998 and 2002. Current term expires Dec 31, 2006. Born Aurora Missouri Feb 22, 1954. Baptist. Educated at University of Missouri-Columbia B.S. 1976 M.S. 1977 J.D. 1980. Honors Scholar. Student body representative 1980. Member Phi Alpha Delta. Admitted to practice Missouri 1980 and U.S. District Court Western District of Missouri 1980. In legal practice Springfield 1980-82 and Mt. Vernon 1982-89.
Prosecuting Attorney Lawrence County 1983-89. Member Missouri Association of Probate and Associate Circuit Judges, The Missouri Bar and Thirty-ninth Judicial Circuit Bar Association (President 1986-87). Participant Missouri Supreme Court programs Missouri Trial Judges College 1989, 1990, 1991, 1992, 1993 and 1994. Listed in *Who's Who in American Law* 1992-93. Republican. President Mount Vernon Chamber of Commerce 1986-87 and Missouri Veteran's Assistance League since 1991. Member Mount Vernon Drug Advisory Council since 1989. President Corporate Board Covenant Baptist Church. Enjoys golf.
Office: One Courthouse Square, Mount Vernon 65712.
Telephone: (417) 466-2463.
Fax: (417) 466-0463

SILL-ROGERS, Christine T. *(Associate Circuit Judge, Missouri Circuit Court Sixteenth Judicial Circuit)* Appointed by governor. Retained by election.
Office: Courthouse, 415 East Twelfth Street, Kansas City 64106.
Telephone: (816) 881-3281.

SIMON, Paul J. *(Judge, Missouri Court of Appeals Eastern District)* Appointed by Governor Joseph P. Teasdale to term beginning Oct 15, 1979. Retained by election 1980 and 1992. Current term expires Dec 31, 2004. Born St. Louis Missouri. Educated at Washington University B.S. and St. Louis University J.D. cum laude. Member Alpha Sigma Nu. Former Chief Deputy Clerk, Magistrate Court.
Former Special Assistant Attorney General. State Representative Missouri 1967-73. President Board of Aldermen City of St. Louis 1975-79, Member St. Raymond's Maronite Catholic Church (Board of Directors), St. Raphael's Church, Daughters of St. Paul and Boys Club of St. Louis.
Office: Wainwright State Office Building, 111 North Seventh Street, St. Louis 63101.
Telephone: (314) 340-6922.
Fax: (314) 340-7703

SIMS, John W. *(Presiding Judge, Missouri Circuit Court Thirtieth Judicial Circuit)* Elected Nov 7, 2000 to term beginning Jan 1, 2001. Term expires Dec 31, 2006. Methodist. Educated at University of Kansas B.A. 1965 J.D. 1969. Editor Kansas Law Review 1968-69. Member Order of the Coif. Admitted to practice Kansas 1969 and Missouri 1970. In legal practice Marshfield Missouri 1970-2000.
Prosecuting Attorney Webster County 1972-74. City Attorney Marshfield 1974-2000. Former Member Missouri Municipal Attorneys Association (President 1999).
Mailing address: P.O. Box 679, Buffalo 65622.
Office: Dallas County Courthouse, Buffalo 65622.
Telephone: (417) 345-6822.
Fax: (417) 345-6829

SIPPEL, Rodney W. *(Judge, United States District Court Eastern District of Missouri)* Appointed for life by President Bill Clinton to term beginning Jan 27, 1998. Born Jefferson City Missouri July 16, 1956. Educated at University of Tulsa B.S. 1978 and Washington University School of Law J.D. 1981. In legal practice St. Louis 1982-93 and 1995-97.
Administrative Assistant U.S. Representative Richard A. Gephardt 1993-95.
Office: U.S. Courthouse, Tenth Floor, 111 South Tenth Street, St. Louis 63102-9958.
Telephone: (314) 244-7430.

SMART, James M., Jr. *(Judge, Missouri Court of Appeals Western District)* Appointed by Governor John D. Ashcroft to term beginning Jan 1, 1992. Retained by election Nov 1994, current term expires Dec 31, 2006. Born Mexia Texas June 28, 1945. Christian. Educated at College of William & Mary A.B. 1966 and University of Missouri School of Law J.D. 1969. Recipient Roscoe Anderson Award for Oral Advocacy and Guy Thompson Award for Outstanding Student Law Review Article. Article Editor Missouri Law Review. Member Order of the Coif. Admitted to practice Missouri 1969, U.S. Court of Appeals Eighth Circuit 1974 and U.S. Supreme Court 1974. In legal practice Kansas City 1974-91.
Assistant Prosecuting Attorney Jackson County 1969-70 and 1981-1982. Author "The Fourteenth Amendment and University Disciplinary Procedures" 34 Missouri L. Rev. 236, 1969 and "*Widmar v. Vincent* and the Purposes of the Establishment Clause" 9 Journal of College and University Law 469, 1983. Important Decisions: State ex rel. Lichtor v. Clark 845 S.W.2d 55, 1992. Member American Judicature Society and The Missouri Bar. Captain U.S. Army JAGC 1970-74. Recipient Army Commendation Medal. Attorney Kansas City Board of Election Commissioners. Board of Directors Greater Kansas City Foundation for Citizens with Retardation. Board of Elders Westbrooke Church. Enjoys hiking, canoeing, camping and sports.
Office: 1300 Oak Street, Kansas City 64106-2970.
Telephone: (816) 889-3605.
Fax: (816) 889-3599

SMITH, Dennis *(Associate Circuit Judge, Missouri Circuit Court Twenty-first Judicial Circuit)* Appointed by Governor Mel Carnahan. Retained by election.
Office: St. Louis County Court Building, 7900 Carondelet, Clayton 63105.
Telephone: (314) 615-1540.

SMITH, Edwin H. *(Judge, Missouri Court of Appeals Western District)* Appointed by Governor Mel Carnahan to term beginning Oct 16, 1995. Retained by election Nov 5, 1996, current term expires Dec 31, 2008. Born St. Joseph Missouri Dec 8, 1951. Educated at University of Missouri-Columbia A.B. with honors 1974 J.D. 1977. Admitted to practice Missouri 1977. Began legal practice St. Joseph 1977. Associate Circuit Judge Jan 1, 1979 to Dec 31, 1988 and Presiding Judge Jan 1, 1989 to Oct 15, 1995, Missouri Circuit Court Fifth Judicial Circuit.
Member Associate Circuit Judges Association (Past President), The Missouri Bar, Andrew County, St. Joseph and Kansas City Metropolitan Bar Associations. Member Masons, Scottish Rite, Moila Shrine and Southside Lions. Enjoys breeding and showing Boxer dogs.
Office: 1300 Oak Street, Kansas City 64106-2970.
Telephone: (816) 889-3632.
Fax: (816) 889-3599

SMITH, Ortrie D. *(Judge, United States District Court Western District of Missouri)* Appointed for life by President Bill Clinton to term beginning 1995. Born Jonesboro Arkansas 1946. Educated at University of Missouri B.A. 1968 J.D. with distinction 1971. Staff member University of Missouri-Kansas City Law Review. Member Order of the Bench and Robe. Admitted to practice Missouri 1971. In legal practice Nevada Missouri 1971-95.
Adjunct Professor University of Missouri-Kansas City School of Law 1999-2001. Secretary-Treasurer Vernon County Bar Association 1972-75. Member Young Lawyers Council 1975-82, Board of Governors 1978-93, President 1991-92 and Chairman Finance Committee three terms The Missouri Bar. Member House of Delegates American Bar Association 1993-97. Master Ross T. Roberts Inn of Court since 1996. Member Edward J. Devitt Distinguished Service to Justice Award Committee American Judicature Society 2000-01 and Committee on Financial Disclosure Judicial Conference of the U.S. since 2000. Former Member The American Law Institute. Fellow Missouri Bar Foundation and American Bar Foundation. Speaker Continuing Legal Education programs The Missouri Bar, University of Missouri-Columbia School of Law, University of Missouri-Kansas

SMITH, ORTRIE D.—*Continued*

City School of Law, The Kansas City Metropolitan Bar Association, Lawyers Association of Kansas City and Kansas Bar Association. Named Honorary Editor-in-Chief by University of Missouri-Kansas City Law Review 1997, Citizen of the Year by Nevada Rotary Club and Key Man of the Year by Nevada Jaycees. Recipient Alumni Achievement Award from University of Missouri-Kansas City School of Law 1999, Tom Cochran Community Service Award from Young Lawyers Section The Missouri Bar, Distinguished Service Award from Nevada Jaycees, Award of Appreciation from Missouri Judicial Conference and Award of Merit from The Missouri Bar. Treasurer Vernon County Young Democrats 1982-95. President Nevada Jaycees 1974, Vernon County Chamber of Commerce 1975, Vernon County Chapter American Red Cross 1976, Community Council for the Performing Arts 1980 and Nevada Rotary Club 1983. Member 1983-95 and President 1985 and 1988 Board of Education Nevada R-V School District. Board of Directors 1992-2000 and Chairman of the Board since 2000 Missouri Institute for Justice, Inc. Board of Trustees University of Missouri-Kansas City School of Law Foundation since 1997.

Office: 8552 U.S. Courthouse, 400 East Ninth Street, Kansas City 64106.
Telephone: (816) 512-5645.

SODERGREN, Thomas *(Associate Circuit Judge, Missouri Circuit Court Nineteenth Judicial Circuit)*

Mailing address: P.O. Box 503, Jefferson City 65102.
Telephone: (573) 634-9170.
Fax: (573) 635-5376

SPINDEN, Paul M. *(Judge, Missouri Court of Appeals Western District)* Appointed by Governor John D. Ashcroft to term beginning Oct 1, 1991. Retained by election Nov 3, 1992, current term expires Dec 31, 2004. Former Chief Judge. Born Nov 10, 1948. Educated at Evangel College B.S., Southwest Missouri State University M.A. and University of Missouri-Kansas City J.D. Staff member Missouri Law Review. Administrative Law Judge, Division of Transportation 1985-87. Former Commissioner, Administrative Hearing Commission 1987-91.

Assistant Chief Counsel 1980-82 and Chief Counsel 1982-85 Missouri Attorney General. Adjunct Professor of Constitutional Law Westminster College 1980-91. Member American Judicature Society. Member Northland Cathedral Assembly of God of Kansas City and Kiwanis International.

Office: 1300 Oak Street, Kansas City 64106-2970.
Telephone: (816) 889-3620.
Fax: (816) 889-3599

SPITLER, Charles L. *(Associate Circuit Judge, Missouri Circuit Court Thirty-fourth Judicial Circuit)* Serves Probate Division.

Office: 450 Main Street, New Madrid 63869.
Telephone: (573) 748-5556.
Fax: (573) 748-9274

SPRICK, Gary G. *(Associate Circuit Judge, Missouri Circuit Court Fourteenth Judicial Circuit)* Serves Probate and Associate Divisions.

Mailing address: P.O. Box 370, Fayette 65248.
Telephone: (660) 248-3326.
Fax: (660) 248-1075

STANDRIDGE, Richard E. *(Associate Circuit Judge, Missouri Circuit Court Sixteenth Judicial Circuit)* Appointed by governor. Retained by election.

Office: Courthouse, 415 East Twelfth Street, Kansas City 64106.
Telephone: (816) 881-3678.

STATLER, Peter *(Associate Circuit Judge, Missouri Circuit Court Thirty-second Judicial Circuit)* Serves Probate Division.

Office: 44 North Lorimier, Cape Girardeau 63701.
Telephone: (573) 334-6249.
Fax: (573) 335-8295

STEELE, Russell E. *(Presiding Judge, Missouri Circuit Court Second Judicial Circuit)*

Office: 106 West Washington, Kirksville 63501.
Telephone: (660) 665-3145.
Fax: (660) 785-3213

STILLWELL, Robert C. *(Associate Circuit Judge, Missouri Circuit Court Twenty-fourth Judicial Circuit)* Appointed by Governor Mel Carnahan to term beginning Sept 18, 1998. Elected Nov 3, 1998 and Nov 5, 2002. Current term expires Dec 31, 2006. Serves Civil, Criminal and Probate Divisions. Educated at Cameron University B.A. 1977, Oklahoma City University J.D. 1993 and Boston University. Admitted to practice Missouri 1993.

Assistant Prosecuting Attorney St. Francois County. Major U.S. Army (retired). Enjoys golf, hiking, gardening, physical fitness and travel.

Mailing address: P.O. Box 521, Fredericktown 63645.
Telephone: (573) 783-3105.
Fax: (573) 783-5920
E-mail address: Robert_Stillwell@osca.state.mo.us

STITH, Laura Denvir *(Judge, Supreme Court of Missouri)* Appointed by Governor Bob Holden March 7, 2001. Retained by election Nov 2002, current term expires Dec 31, 2014. Born St. Louis Missouri Oct 30, 1953. Educated at Tufts University B.A. magna cum laude 1975 and Georgetown University Law Center J.D. magna cum laude 1978. Law Clerk to Hon. Robert E. Seiler, Missouri Supreme Court. In legal practice Kansas City 1979-94. Former Judge, Missouri Court of Appeals Western District, appointed by Governor Mel Carnahan to term beginning Aug 19, 1994.

Member Association for Women Lawyers of Greater Kansas City (President 1994-95), National Association of Women Judges, The Missouri Bar (Chair Civil Practice Committee 1992-94), The Kansas City Metropolitan (Former Chair Appellate Court Committee, Former Vice Chair Tort Law Committee) and American Bar Associations. Founding Director Lawyers Encouraging Academic Performance.

Mailing address: P.O. Box 150, Jefferson City 65102.
Office: Supreme Court Building, Jefferson City 65101.
Telephone: (573) 751-3570.

STOHR, Donald J. *(Judge, United States District Court Eastern District of Missouri)* Appointed for life by President George Bush to term beginning 1992. Born Sedalia Missouri March 9, 1934. Educated at St. Louis University B.S. 1956 J.D. 1958. In legal practice St. Louis 1958-62, 1966-73 and 1976-92.

First Assistant County Counselor 1963-65 and County

STOHR, DONALD J.—*Continued*

Counselor 1965-66 St. Louis County. U.S. Attorney Eastern District of Missouri 1973-76.

Office: U.S. Courthouse, 111 South Tenth Street, St. Louis 63102-9958.

Telephone: (314) 244-7580.

STOLL, Mark T. *(Associate Circuit Judge, Missouri Circuit Court Twenty-third Judicial Circuit)* Appointed by Governor Mel Carnahan to term beginning 1997. Elected 1998 and 2002. Current term expires Dec 31, 2006. Catholic. Educated at University of Missouri-Columbia B.S.B.A. cum laude 1974 J.D. 1977. Board of Student Editors Missouri Law Review 1976-77. Admitted to practice Missouri 1977, U.S. District Court Eastern District of Missouri 1981, U.S. Court of Appeals Eighth Circuit 1986 and U.S. Supreme Court 1996. In legal practice Hillsboro 1977-97.

City Attorney DeSoto 1977-97. Member Legislative Steering Committee Missouri Judicial Conference. Member Missouri Probate and Associate Circuit Judges Association (Secretary/Treasurer since 2002), Missouri Municipal and Associate Circuit Judges Association (Board Member since 1998), The Missouri Bar and Jefferson County Bar Association. Member Rotary Club of DeSoto (President), Cub Scouts Pack 484 (Treasurer) and Love Basket, Inc. adoption agency (Board Member since 1998).

Mailing address: P.O. Box 100, Hillsboro 63050.

Office: Jefferson County Courthouse, Hillsboro 63050.

Telephone: (636) 797-5375.

Fax: (636) 797-6047

E-mail address: Mark_Stoll@osca.state.mo.us

STORIE, Tracy Lee *(Associate Circuit Judge, Missouri Circuit Court Twenty-fifth Judicial Circuit)* Elected to term beginning Jan 1, 1979. Reelected 1982, 1986, 1990, 1994, 1998 and 2002. Current term expires Dec 31, 2006. Born Waynesville Missouri July 18, 1948. Southern Baptist. Educated at University of Missouri-Rolla B.A. 1970 and University of Arkansas J.D. 1973. Admitted to practice Missouri 1974. Judge, Pulaski County Magistrate Court May 1974 to Dec 1978.

Instructor Drury University since 1980. Democrat.

Office: 301 Historic Route 66 East, Suite 314, Waynesville 65583.

Telephone: (573) 774-4786.

Fax: (573) 774-6673

STREMEL, Gregory *(Associate Circuit Judge, Missouri Circuit Court Fortieth Judicial Circuit)*

Mailing address: P.O. Box 170, Neosho 64850.

Telephone: (417) 451-8212.

Fax: (417) 451-8272

STROTHMANN, Wayne P. *(Associate Circuit Judge, Missouri Circuit Court Twenty-seventh Judicial Circuit)* Elected Nov 1994 to term beginning Jan 1, 1995. Reelected Nov 1998 and 2002. Current term expires Dec 31, 2006. Serves Probate Division. Born Washington Missouri March 21, 1954. Educated at University of Missouri-Columbia B.S.B.A. with honors 1976 J.D. 1979. Admitted to practice Missouri 1979 and U.S. District Court Western District of Missouri 1979. In legal practice Clinton 1979-94.

Assistant Prosecuting Attorney 1979-80 and 1984-86 and Prosecuting Attorney 1987-90 Henry County. Member Missouri Association of Probate and Associate Circuit Judges and Missouri Municipal and Associate Circuit Judges Association. Past President Mid-Day Optimist Club. Board of Directors Clinton Area Chamber of Commerce. Enjoys flying and boating.

Office: Henry County Courthouse, Clinton 64735.

Telephone: (660) 885-6963.

Fax: (660) 885-8247

E-mail address: Wayne_Strothmann@osca.state.mo.us

SULLIVAN, Sherri B. *(Judge, Missouri Court of Appeals Eastern District)* Appointed by Governor Mel Carnahan to term beginning Aug 5, 1999. Born St. Louis Missouri Sept 20, 1953. Educated at University of Missouri-St. Louis B.S. summa cum laude 1978 and St. Louis University J.D. 1981. Admitted to practice Missouri 1981. Associate Circuit Judge 1989 to Oct 1994 and Circuit Judge Oct 1994 to Aug 4, 1999, Missouri Circuit Court Twenty-second Judicial Circuit, appointed by Governor Mel Carnahan.

Assistant Circuit Attorney St. Louis 1981-89. Member Women Lawyers Association, National Association of Women Judges and The Missouri Bar.

Office: Wainwright State Office Building, 111 North Seventh Street, St. Louis 63101.

Telephone: (314) 340-6920.

Fax: (314) 340-7703

SUTHERLAND, Keith M. *(Presiding Judge, Missouri Circuit Court Twelfth Judicial Circuit)* Associate Circuit Judge Jan 1, 1979 to Dec 31, 2000. Elected Circuit Judge to term beginning Jan 1, 2001. Born Washington D.C. June 29, 1945. United Church of Christ. Educated at Western Reserve University (now Case Western Reserve University) B.A. 1967 and University of Missouri-Columbia J.D. 1973. Admitted to practice Missouri 1973. Began legal practice Warrenton 1973.

Prosecuting Attorney Warren County 1975-78. Member 1985-2000 and Chair 1993-2000 Missouri Supreme Court Municipal Judge Education Committee. Member Coordinating Commission for Judicial Department Education 1998-2000. Member Missouri Council on Criminal Justice (Vice Chairman 1976 and Chairman 1977-78 Region XIV, Chairman Service Area C 1977-79), Missouri Association of Probate and Associate Circuit Judges, The Missouri Bar and Warren County Bar Association. E-5 U.S. Army 1969-71. Republican. Member since 1985 and Chair 1993-95 Board of Directors Crider Center for Mental Health. Member Warrenton Jaycees 1974-78 (Secretary 1976), Warrenton Chamber of Commerce (Board of Directors 1974, Treasurer 1975, Vice President 1976), Rotary Club of Warrenton (Board of Directors 1975-76, Treasurer 1976-77, Secretary 1977-78, Vice President 1978-79, President 1979-80) and Warrenton F.F.A. Alumni 1980-85 (Secretary-Treasurer 1984-85). Enjoys philately.

Office: Warren County Courthouse, 104 West Booneslick Road, Warrenton 63383.

Telephone: (636) 456-9705.

Fax: (636) 456-0605

SUTTON, Janet *(Associate Circuit Judge, Missouri Circuit Court Seventh Judicial Circuit)* Appointed by Governor Bob Holden.

Office: 11 South Water, Liberty 64068.

Telephone: (816) 792-7717.

SWAIM, Kristie *(Associate Circuit Judge, Missouri Circuit Court Second Judicial Circuit)* Serves Probate Division.
Office: 106 West Washington, Kirksville 63501.
Telephone: (660) 665-3877.

SWEENEY, Edward *(Associate Circuit Judge, Missouri Circuit Court Twenty-second Judicial Circuit)* Appointed by Governor Mel Carnahan.
Office: Municipal Courts Building, 1320 Market Street, St. Louis 63103.
Telephone: (314) 622-4687.

SWEENEY, J. Edward *(Presiding Judge, Missouri Circuit Court Thirty-ninth Judicial Circuit)* Associate Circuit Judge 1985-94. Elected Circuit Judge Nov 8, 1994 to term beginning Jan 1, 1995. Reelected Nov 7, 2000, current term expires Dec 31, 2006. Born Monett Missouri Aug 4, 1944. Catholic. Educated at Marquette University A.B. 1966 and University of Missouri-Columbia J.D. 1969. Member Phi Alpha Delta. Admitted to practice Missouri 1969 and U.S. District Court Western District of Missouri 1969. In legal practice Monett 1971-85.

Prosecuting Attorney Barry County 1973-74. Important Decision: Herndon v. Tuhey (constitutional right of grandparent visitation in Missouri) 857 S.W.2d 203, 1993. Member Time Limitations Committee since 1992, State Judges Transfer Committee since 1993, Missouri Council of Juvenile Judges, The Missouri Bar and Thirty-ninth Judicial Circuit Bar Association. Attended Judicial College for Missouri Judges since 1985. Recipient Lon O. Hocker Young Trial Lawyer Award from The Missouri Bar 1978. E-5 U.S. Army Vietnam 1969-71. Republican. Member Monett Chamber of Commerce, American Legion and VFW. Enjoys golf and spectator sports.
Mailing address: P.O. Box 400, Monett 65708.
Telephone: (417) 235-6245.
Fax: (417) 235-6254

SWEENEY, J. Miles *(Presiding Judge, Missouri Circuit Court Thirty-first Judicial Circuit)*
Office: 1010 Boonville, Springfield 65802.
Telephone: (417) 868-4086.

SWEENEY, Philip J. *(Circuit Judge, Missouri Circuit Court Twenty-first Judicial Circuit)* Appointed by governor. Retained by election.
Office: St. Louis County Court Building, 7900 Carondelet, Clayton 63105.
Telephone: (314) 615-1518.

SYLER, William L. *(Presiding Judge, Missouri Circuit Court Thirty-second Judicial Circuit)* Appointed by Governor John D. Ashcroft to term beginning Oct 1, 1992. Elected Nov 3, 1992, Nov 5, 1996 and 2002. Current term expires Dec 31, 2008. Born St. Louis Missouri Nov 28, 1948. Educated at Southeast Missouri State University B.A. cum laude 1971 and University of Missouri-Kansas City J.D. 1974. Member Phi Delta Phi. Admitted to practice Missouri 1974, U.S. District Courts Western 1974 and Eastern 1975 Districts of Missouri and U.S. Court of Appeals Eighth Circuit 1987. In legal practice Cape Girardeau 1977-92.

Assistant Prosecuting Attorney Jackson County 1974 and Cape Girardeau County 1975-76. Instructor in Criminal Law Southeast Missouri State University 1975. Member The Missouri Bar and Cape Girardeau County Bar Association (President 1997-98). Republican. President Board of Trustees Cape Girardeau Board of Health 1986-92. Board Member Southeast Missouri State University Foundation and St. Francis Medical Center Foundation.
Office: 44 North Lorimier, Cape Girardeau 63701.
Telephone: (573) 335-2802.
Fax: (573) 331-2349

TAYLOR, Ronald E. *(Associate Circuit Judge, Missouri Circuit Court Fifth Judicial Circuit)* Appointed by Governor Roger B. Wilson Jan 1, 2000. Elected to term beginning Jan 1, 2002. Born Smithville Missouri Dec 18, 1944. Educated at University of Missouri B.A. 1966 J.D. 1969. Admitted to practice Missouri 1969. In legal practice 1977-2000. Judge, Gower Municipal Court 1997-2000.

City Attorney St. Joseph 1969-77. Member The Missouri Bar (Board of Governors). Democrat. Member Lions Club and Trailwinds Flying Club. Personal Statement or Quote: "Be polite, be brief, be seated."
Office: 411 Jules, Room 331, St. Joseph 64501.
Telephone: (816) 271-1448.
Fax: (816) 271-1538

TEITELMAN, Richard B. *(Judge, Supreme Court of Missouri)* Appointed by Governor Bob Holden to term beginning Feb 2002. Term expires Dec 31, 2004. Born Philadelphia Pennsylvania Sept 25, 1947. Jewish. Educated at University of Pennsylvania B.A. and Washington University School of Law J.D. 1973. Member Order of the Coif. Admitted to practice Missouri 1973. Judge, Missouri Court of Appeals Eastern District 1998-2002, appointed by Governor Mel Carnahan.

Executive Director Legal Services of Eastern Missouri, Inc. 1975-98. Past President St. Louis Bar Foundation and St. Louis Bar Association. Former Chair Young Lawyers Section The Bar Association of Metropolitan St. Louis. Former Member Missouri Supreme Court Advisory Committee. Member Lawyers Association of Greater St. Louis, Women Lawyers Association of Greater St. Louis, American Judicature Society (Executive Committee), The Missouri Bar (Board of Governors), Mound City and American (House of Delegates, Division Chairperson) Bar Associations. Former Board Member Security Exchange Commission of the State of Missouri. Member Midwestern Board of American Foundation for the Blind, National Federation of the Blind and Board of St. Louis Public Library. Personal Statement or Quote: "Equal access to justice for all."
Mailing address: P.O. Box 150, Jefferson City 65102.
Telephone: (573) 751-1004.
Fax: (573) 751-7161

THOMPSON, Kenneth F. *(Associate Circuit Judge, Missouri Circuit Court Thirtieth Judicial Circuit)*
Office: Courthouse, Marshfield 65706.
Telephone: (417) 859-2041.

THOMSEN, Scott *(Associate Circuit Judge, Missouri Circuit Court Thirty-second Judicial Circuit)* Serves Probate Division.
Mailing address: P.O. Box 1040, Marble Hill 63764.
Telephone: (573) 238-2730.
Fax: (573) 238-4511

TORRENCE, John M. *(Circuit Judge, Missouri Circuit Court Sixteenth Judicial Circuit)* Appointed by Governor Bob Holden.
Office: Courthouse, 415 East Twelfth Street, Kansas City 64106.
Telephone: (816) 881-3614.

TROUT, Robert L. *(Associate Circuit Judge, Missouri Circuit Court Sixteenth Judicial Circuit)* Appointed by governor. Retained by election.
Office: Courthouse Annex, 308 West Kansas, Independence 64050.
Telephone: (816) 881-4518.
Fax: (816) 881-4412

ULRICH, Robert G. *(Judge, Missouri Court of Appeals Western District)* Appointed by Governor John D. Ashcroft to term beginning March 30, 1989. Retained by election. Former Chief Judge. Born St. Louis Missouri Nov 23, 1941. Educated at William Jewell College B.A. and University of Missouri-Kansas City J.D. LL.M.
Assistant U.S. Attorney and U.S. Attorney Western District of Missouri 1981-89. Member 1984 and Chair 1986-89 Attorney General's Advisory Committee of U.S. Attorneys. Former Member Advisory Committee U.S. Court of Appeals Eighth Circuit and Sentencing Guidelines Education Committee. Member Economic Crime Council and Resource Board Department of Justice, National Association of Former U.S. Attorneys, Association of Judicial Administration, American Judicature Society, The Missouri Bar and The Kansas City Metropolitan Bar Association.
Office: 1300 Oak Street, Kansas City 64106-2970.
Telephone: (816) 889-3602.
Fax: (816) 889-3599

VAN AMBURG, James W. *(Associate Circuit Judge, Missouri Circuit Court Sixth Judicial Circuit)* Appointed by governor. Retained by election. Serves Probate Division.
Office: 415 Third Street, Suite 95, Platte City 64079.
Telephone: (816) 858-1977.
Fax: (816) 858-3392

VEENSTRA, Lynette B. *(Associate Circuit Judge, Missouri Circuit Court Forty-fourth Judicial Circuit)* Appointed by Governor Bob Holden Nov 1, 2002. Elected Nov 5, 2002, current term expires Dec 31, 2006. Serves Probate Division. Educated at Southwest Missouri State University B.S. summa cum laude 1990 and Vanderbilt University School of Law J.D. 1993. Member Order of the Coif.
Mailing address: P.O. Box 58, Hartville 65667.
Telephone: (417) 741-6505.
Fax: (417) 741-7504

VENTERS, Jerry W. *(Judge, United States Bankruptcy Court Western District of Missouri)* Appointed by U.S. Court of Appeals Eighth Circuit judges to term beginning Feb 1, 1999. Term expires Jan 31, 2013. Born Bentonville Arkansas July 4, 1943. Episcopalian. Educated at University of Missouri-Columbia Journalism degree 1965 J.D. 1976. Admitted to practice Missouri 1976. In legal practice Jefferson City 1976-99.
Important Decision: In re Moss (appointment of limited guardian in Chapter 7) 239 B.R. 537, 1999. Instructor in Bankruptcy topics University of Missouri-Columbia Law School. Member National Conference of Bankruptcy Judges (Board of Governors since 2002) and The Missouri Bar. Recipient Michael R. Roser Excellence in Bankruptcy Practice Award from Commercial Law Committee The Missouri Bar 1998. Member and Paul Harris Fellow Kansas City Plaza Rotary Club. Enjoys golf, reading and travel.
Office: 6462 U.S. Courthouse, 400 East Ninth Street, Kansas City 64106.
Telephone: (816) 512-1895.
Fax: (816) 512-1908
E-mail address: jerry.venters@mow.uscourts.gov

VINCENT, David Lee, III *(Circuit Judge, Missouri Circuit Court Twenty-first Judicial Circuit)* Appointed by Governor Mel Carnahan.
Office: St. Louis County Court Building, 7900 Carondelet, Clayton 63105.
Telephone: (314) 615-1509.

WALL, Roger *(Associate Circuit Judge, Missouri Circuit Court Forty-fourth Judicial Circuit)* Serves Probate Division.
Mailing address: P.O. Box 276, Ava 65608.
Telephone: (417) 683-2114.
Fax: (417) 683-2794

WALLACE, Barbara W. *(Presiding Judge, Missouri Circuit Court Twenty-first Judicial Circuit)* Appointed by Governor Mel Carnahan. Retained by election.
Office: St. Louis County Court Building, 7900 Carondelet, Clayton 63105.
Telephone: (314) 615-1513.
Fax: (314) 615-8280

WALLACE, Gary G. *(Associate Circuit Judge, Missouri Circuit Court Forty-first Judicial Circuit)* Serves Probate Division.
Mailing address: P.O. Box 206, Shelbyville 63469.
Telephone: (573) 633-2251.
Fax: (573) 633-2142

WARREN, David Gregory *(Associate Circuit Judge, Missouri Circuit Court Twenty-fifth Judicial Circuit)* Appointed by Governor Mel Carnahan to term beginning April 10, 1994. Elected Nov 1994, Nov 1998 and 2002. Current term expires Dec 31, 2006. Serves Probate Division. Born Richland Missouri May 30, 1949. Methodist. Educated at University of Missouri-Columbia A.B. with honors 1971 and George Washington University J.D. with honors 1974. Member Phi Alpha Delta. Admitted to practice Missouri 1974. In legal practice Richland 1974-94.
Prosecuting Attorney Pulaski County 1981-94. USAR Signal Corps 1972-80. Democrat.
Office: 301 Historic Route 66 East, Suite 316, Waynesville 65583.
Telephone: (573) 774-4784.

WATERS, John S. *(Associate Circuit Judge, Missouri Circuit Court Thirty-eighth Judicial Circuit)* Serves Probate Division.
Office: 110 West Elm, Room 105, Ozark 65721.
Telephone: (417) 581-4523.
Fax: (417) 581-1443

WEBBER, E. Richard *(Judge, United States District Court Eastern District of Missouri)* Appointed for life by President Bill Clinton to term beginning 1996. Born Kahoka Missouri June 4, 1942. Educated at University of Missouri-Columbia B.S. 1964 J.D. 1967. In legal

WEBBER, E. RICHARD—*Continued*
practice Memphis 1967-79. Circuit Judge, Missouri Circuit Court First Judicial Circuit 1979-96.

Prosecuting Attorney Schuyler County 1967-75, Putnam County 1968 and Scotland County 1969-71.

Office: U.S. Courthouse, Twelfth Floor, 111 South Tenth Street, St. Louis 63102-9958.

Telephone: (314) 244-7460.

WEBER, Raymond M. *(Associate Circuit Judge, Missouri Circuit Court Twenty-fourth Judicial Circuit)* Serves Probate Division.

Office: 55 South Third Street, Suite 24, Ste. Genevieve 63670.

Telephone: (573) 883-2265.

Fax: (573) 883-9351

WEGGE, William J., Jr. *(Associate Circuit Judge, Missouri Circuit Court Twenty-third Judicial Circuit)*

Mailing address: P.O. Box 100, Hillsboro 63050.

Telephone: (636) 797-5362.

WELSH, James E. *(Presiding Judge, Missouri Circuit Court Seventh Judicial Circuit)* Associate Circuit Judge 1985-88. Appointed Circuit Judge by Governor John D. Ashcroft to term beginning Dec 5, 1988. Retained by election Nov 1990, 1996 and 2002. Current term expires Dec 31, 2008. Born Brookfield Missouri May 26, 1948. Roman Catholic. Educated at Parks College of Aeronautical Technology B.S. 1969 and St. Louis University J.D. 1975. Law Clerk to Hon. William E. Turnage, Missouri Court of Appeals Western District 1975-76. Admitted to practice Missouri 1975. In legal practice Kansas City 1976-85. Municipal Judge, Liberty Municipal Court 1983-85.

Former Member Missouri State Sentencing Commission. Member Gender Fairness Implementation Committee, Clay Platte Municipal and Associate Circuit Judges Association (Vice President 1983-84, President 1984-85), Missouri Municipal and Associate Circuit Judges Association (Treasurer 1985-86, Secretary 1986-88), Circuit Judges Association (Vice President 1995-96, President 1996-97), The Missouri Bar and Clay County Bar Association. Contract Services Engineer McDonnell Douglas Astronautics Company 1969-75.

Office: 11 South Water, Liberty 64068.

Telephone: (816) 792-7713.

WESTBROOKE, Henry W., Jr. *(Circuit Judge, Missouri Circuit Court Thirty-first Judicial Circuit)* Appointed Associate Circuit Judge by Governor John D. Ashcroft to term beginning Aug 17, 1990. Elected Circuit Judge to term beginning Jan 1, 1999. Term expires Dec 31, 2004. Former Presiding Judge. Born Memphis Tennessee Sept 20, 1936. Presbyterian. Educated at University of Missouri-Columbia B.S.B.A. J.D. Admitted to practice Missouri 1963. In legal practice Springfield 1963-90.

Member The Missouri Bar. U.S. Army 1958-60. USAR 1960-75.

Office: 1010 Boonville, Springfield 65802.

Telephone: (417) 868-4080.

WESTHOFF, Fred *(Associate Circuit Judge, Missouri Circuit Court Second Judicial Circuit)* Elected to term beginning Jan 1, 1987. Reelected 1990, 1994, 1998 and 2002. Current term expires Dec 31, 2006. Serves Probate Division. Born Quincy Illinois Dec 23, 1952. Religious affiliation: New Testament Christian. Educated at Northeast Missouri State University B.A. magna cum laude 1975 and University of Missouri-Columbia J.D. 1978. Admitted to practice Missouri 1978. In legal practice Canton Missouri 1978-86.

Prosecuting Attorney Lewis County 1981-1986. Member Association of Missouri Associate and Probate Judges, Missouri Judicial Conference and The Missouri Bar.

Mailing address: P.O. Box 36, Monticello 63457.

Telephone: (573) 767-5352.

Fax: (573) 767-5342

WHIPPLE, Dean *(Chief Judge, United States District Court Western District of Missouri)* Appointed for life by President Ronald Reagan to term beginning 1988. Chief Judge since Jan 22, 2000. Born Lebanon Missouri April 3, 1938. Methodist. Educated at Drury College B.A. 1961 and University of Missouri-Kansas City J.D. 1965. Admitted to practice Missouri 1965, U.S. District Court Western District of Missouri 1965 and U.S. Supreme Court 1970. In legal practice Lebanon 1965-75. Circuit Judge, Missouri Circuit Court Twenty-sixth Judicial Circuit 1975-87.

Office: 8652 U.S. Courthouse, 400 East Ninth Street, Kansas City 64106.

Telephone: (816) 512-5615.

WHITE, Ronnie L. *(Judge, Supreme Court of Missouri)* Appointed by Governor Mel Carnahan to term beginning 1995. Retained by election. Educated at St. Louis Community College, St. Louis University and University of Missouri-Kansas City. In legal practice St. Louis. Judge, Missouri Court of Appeals Eastern District 1994-95, appointed by Governor Mel Carnahan.

Former Public Defender and City Counselor 1993-94 St. Louis. State Representative Missouri.

Mailing address: P.O. Box 150, Jefferson City 65102.

Office: Supreme Court Building, Jefferson City 65101.

Telephone: (573) 751-9652.

Fax: (573) 751-7359

WHITTINGTON, Carolyn C. *(Circuit Judge, Missouri Circuit Court Twenty-first Judicial Circuit)* Former Associate Circuit Judge. Appointed Circuit Judge by Governor Bob Holden.

Office: St. Louis County Court Building, 7900 Carondelet, Clayton 63105.

Telephone: (314) 615-1507.

WIESMAN, Melvyn Wade *(Circuit Judge, Missouri Circuit Court Twenty-first Judicial Circuit)* Appointed by Governor Joseph P. Teasdale to term beginning Jan 2, 1979. Retained by election 1980, 1986, 1992 and 1998. Current term expires Dec 31, 2004. Served Juvenile Division 1982-84. Administrative Judge Family Court Division 1993-99. Born Granite City Illinois Feb 8, 1939. Member Congregation Shaare Emeth (Director 1968-74). Educated at Washington University at St. Louis A.B. 1960 and University of Missouri-Columbia J.D. 1963. Recipient James Lewis Parks Prize. Board of Editors Missouri Law Review. Member Phi Delta Phi. Admitted to practice Missouri 1963 and U.S. District Court Eastern District of Missouri 1964. In legal practice St. Louis 1963 and University City 1964. Judge, St. Louis County Magistrate Court 1966-78.

Author "Domestic Relations—Modification of Future Payments Under Alimony and Support Decrees—Ten Year Limitation Upon" 27 Missouri L. Rev. 527, 1962; "Conflict of Law—The Substantial Contact Test in Tort Choice of Law and The Federal Tort Claims Act" 28

WIESMAN, MELVYN WADE—*Continued*

Missouri L. Rev. 151, 1963; "Thoughts from the Bench" 12 No. 3 St. Louis B. Jour. 95 Spring 1966; "Eight Days to Oblivion—A Precedent" 26 Journal of The Missouri Bar 516, 1970; "Obscenity—The Court Tries Again" 30 Journal of The Missouri Bar 81, 1974; "Prehearing Seizures—To Be or Not to Be" 30 Journal of The Missouri Bar 474, 1974; "Prehearing Seizures—To Be or Not to Be: A Post Script" 31 Journal of The Missouri Bar 184, 1975; "The New Small Claims Court" 32 Journal of the Missouri Bar 421, 1976; "Prejudgment Remedies and Due Process" National College of the State Judiciary 1976; "Misdemeanor Trials" 19 *Missouri Criminal Practice* 1977; and Chapter 19 "Instructions" 1 *Bench Book for Missouri Trial Judges* 1990. Faculty Member Washington University 1971-94 and Law School 1982-85. Chairman Missouri Supreme Court Committee on Small Claims Procedures 1976-78. Director St. Louis Bar Foundation 1983-88. Officer 1985-89 and President 1988-89 Missouri Council of Juvenile Court Judges. Member Task Force on Cameras in the Courtroom 1991-92, Family Court Planning and Implementation Committee 1993-95, Judicial Education Committee since 1993, Task Force on Children and Families 1994-98, Family Court Committee 1995-98 and Commission on Judicial Branch Education since 1998 Missouri Supreme Court. Member Lawyers Association of St. Louis (Secretary 1974-75), Judicial Conference of Missouri (Executive Council 1978-79), The Bar Association of Metropolitan St. Louis, The Missouri Bar (Committee to propose legislation to implement constitutional judicial reform 1977, Committee to draft Continuing Legal Education handbook on Criminal Law 1977, Special Committee to draft proposed legislation to reform Magistrate Courts and create Small Claims Courts 1975, Committee Council of the Courts and Judiciary Committee 1974-75) and St. Louis County Bar Association. Lecturer on "Prehearing Seizure and Due Process" ABA annual convention in Quebec 1975 and The Missouri Bar Practical Skills Course 1976-77. Attended National College of the State Judiciary 1971, 1975-76 (Faculty Member 1975-89) and Missouri College of Trial Judges 1973, 1974, 1977, 1983-84 (Faculty Member 1975 and 1983-2001). Recipient Robert Walton Chubb Award from Legal Services of Eastern Missouri, Inc. 1994, Faith in Action Award from Lutherans Family and Children's Services of Missouri 1998 and Special Recognition Award from Missouri Judicial Conference. E-4 USAS 1963-66. Democrat. Member Superintendent's Advisory Council Pattonville R-3 School District 1975-76. President Ebn Ezra Lodge B'nai B'rith 1971-72.

Office: St. Louis County Court Building, 7900 Carondelet, Clayton 63105.
Telephone: (314) 615-1519.

WIGGINS, John D. *(Circuit Judge, Missouri Circuit Court Twenty-fifth Judicial Circuit)*
Mailing address: P.O. Box 340, Rolla 65401.
Telephone: (573) 364-1891.
Fax: (573) 364-1419

WILLCOX, Stephen K. *(Associate Circuit Judge, Missouri Circuit Court First Judicial Circuit)* Elected to term beginning Jan 1, 1979. Reelected 1982, 1986, 1990, 1994, 1998 and 2002. Current term expires Dec 31, 2006. Serves Associate and Probate Divisions. Born Columbia Missouri Dec 15, 1946. Member Christian Church. Educated at University of Missouri-Columbia B.A. 1970 J.D. 1975. Admitted to practice Missouri 1975 and U.S. District Courts Eastern 1975 and Western 1976 Districts of Missouri. Began legal practice Kirksville 1975. In legal practice Lancaster 1978.

Assistant Prosecuting Attorney 1975-78 and Prosecuting Attorney 1978 Schuyler County. Author Chapter 3 "Service of Process" *Bench Book for Missouri Trial Judges* since 1994. Member Judicial Conference of Missouri (Executive Council 1982-90 and since 2002), Missouri Association of Probate and Associate Circuit Judges (Director 1999-2002), The Missouri Bar and American Bar Association. Democrat. Peace Corps Volunteer India 1966-68. Editor Schuyler County Visitor Tourism Newspaper 1988-94. Member Schuyler County Ram Booster Club (President 1979), Lancaster Community Club, Schuyler County Historical Society, Rebels Cove Historical Society (President 1984-85), Legal Services for Elderly Committee, Northeast Missouri Area Agency of Aging (Chairman 1978-79) and Schuyler County Rotary Club (President 1982-84). Enjoys gardening, fishing and golfing.

Mailing address: P.O. Box 158, Lancaster 63548.
Telephone: (660) 457-3755.
Fax: (660) 457-3016

WILLIAMS, James P. *(Associate Circuit Judge, Missouri Circuit Court Ninth Judicial Circuit)* Serves Probate Division.
Mailing address: P.O. Box 84, Linneus 64653.
Office: 108 North High, Linneus 64653.
Telephone: (660) 895-5212.
Fax: (660) 895-5277

WILLIAMS, M. Edward *(Circuit Judge, Missouri Circuit Court Twenty-third Judicial Circuit)* Associate Circuit Judge 1994-97. Appointed Circuit Judge by Governor Mel Carnahan to term beginning Sept 3, 1997. Elected to term beginning Jan 1, 1999, current term expires Dec 31, 2004. Former Presiding Judge. Born Jerome Missouri Aug 29, 1941. Educated at University of Missouri B.A. 1964 J.D. 1966. Admitted to practice Missouri 1966, Virginia 1972, Pennsylvania 1973 and U.S. District Court Eastern District of Missouri 1974. In legal practice Rolla Missouri 1967-69 and Hillsboro Missouri 1980-94.

Public Defender 1975-78. Prosecuting Attorney 1978-80.

Mailing address: P.O. Box 100, Hillsboro 63050.
Office: Courthouse Square, 300 Second Street, Hillsboro 63050.
Telephone: (636) 797-5430.
Fax: (636) 797-5073
E-mail address: m_edward_williams@osca.state.mo.us

WILLIAMS, Stanley D. *(Associate Circuit Judge, Missouri Circuit Court Twentieth Judicial Circuit)*
Office: 120 South Church Street, Union 63084.
Telephone: (636) 583-6326.

WILLIAMS, Tony *(Associate Circuit Judge, Missouri Circuit Court Thirty-eighth Judicial Circuit)* Serves Probate Division.
Mailing address: P.O. Box 129, Forsyth 65653.
Telephone: (417) 546-7212.
Fax: (417) 546-4513

WILLIAMSON, J. D. *(Circuit Judge, Missouri Circuit Court Sixteenth Judicial Circuit)* Appointed by Governor Mel Carnahan. Retained by election.
Office: 625 East 26th Street, Kansas City 64108.
Telephone: (816) 435-4711.
Fax: (816) 435-8016

WILSON, Timothy J. *(Circuit Judge, Missouri Circuit Court Twenty-second Judicial Circuit)* Appointed by Governor John D. Ashcroft. Retained by election.
Office: Municipal Courts Building, 1320 Market Street, St. Louis 63103.
Telephone: (314) 622-4926.

WINCHESTER, W. H., III *(Associate Circuit Judge, Missouri Circuit Court Thirty-third Judicial Circuit)* Serves Probate Division.
Mailing address: P.O. Box 220, Benton 63736.
Telephone: (573) 545-3511.
Fax: (573) 545-3511

WINFREY, Larry *(Associate Circuit Judge, Missouri Circuit Court Twenty-sixth Judicial Circuit)*
Office: 200 North Adams, Lebanon 65536.
Telephone: (417) 533-7451.
Fax: (417) 532-5917

WITT, Gary D. *(Associate Circuit Judge, Missouri Circuit Court Sixth Judicial Circuit)* Appointed by Governor Mel Carnahan Oct 14, 1998. Retained by election Nov 7, 2000, current term expires Dec 31, 2004. Born Smithville Missouri 1965. Baptist. Educated at William Jewell College B.A. 1987 and University of Missouri J.D. 1990. Admitted to practice Missouri 1990 and Kansas 1992. In legal practice Platte City Missouri 1990-98.
City Attorney and Prosecutor Platte City, Weatherby Lake, Houston Lake and Crystal Lakes Missouri. Author "Accident Injury and Occupational Disease" University of Missouri 1993. Co-author with Korte "Employer Employee Relationship" The Missouri Bar 1994 and with Holloran "Reduction and Compromise of Medicaid Liens" *Missouri Trial Attorney* 1996. Member Missouri Judicial Conference, Associate and Probate Judges Association (Board of Directors), The Missouri Bar and Platte County Bar Association (President 2002). Faculty Member Missouri Judicial College 1994 and 1995. Speaker "Defending the Drinking Driver" 2000 and "Afternoon with Trial Judges" 2000. Named Walter Pope Binns Public Service Fellow by William Jewell College 1993 and one of Ten Outstanding Young Missourians by Missouri Jaycees 1993. State Representative 1991-97 (Chair Judiciary and Ethics Committee and Special Committee on Impeachment). Treasurer Platte County Historical Society.
Office: 415 Third Street, Platte City 64079.
Telephone: (816) 858-1925.

WOLFF, Michael A. *(Judge, Supreme Court of Missouri)* Appointed by Governor Mel Carnahan to term beginning Aug 1998. Retained by election. Educated at Dartmouth College 1967 and University of Minnesota School of Law J.D. 1970. In legal practice St. Louis.
Legal Services Lawyer. Co-author *Federal Jury Practice and Instructions.* Faculty St. Louis University School of Law 1975-98. Chief Counsel 1993-94 and Special Counsel 1994-98 to Governor Mel Carnahan.
Mailing address: P.O. Box 150, Jefferson City 65102.
Office: Supreme Court Building, Jefferson City 65101.
Telephone: (573) 751-6644.
Fax: (573) 751-7341

WOOD, Gael D. *(Presiding Judge, Missouri Circuit Court Twentieth Judicial Circuit)*
Office: 300 East Main, Room 302, Union 63084.
Telephone: (636) 583-6306.
Fax: (636) 583-7390

WOODS, Carr *(Associate Circuit Judge, Missouri Circuit Court Thirty-ninth Judicial Circuit)*
Office: 700 Main, Cassville 65625.
Telephone: (417) 846-1842.

WRIGHT, Scott O. *(Senior Judge, United States District Court Western District of Missouri)* Appointed for life by President Jimmy Carter Oct 5, 1979. Chief Judge Jan 1, 1985 to July 31, 1990. Assumed Senior status Oct 5, 1991, serves by assignment. Born Haigler Nebraska Jan 15, 1923. Educated at Central Methodist College 1940-42 and University of Missouri-Columbia LL.B. 1950. In legal practice Columbia 1950-54 and 1958-79.
City Attorney Columbia 1951-53. Prosecuting Attorney Boone County 1954-58. Chairman Eighth Circuit Pattern Jury Instruction Committee since 1983. Consultant Eighth Circuit Gender Bias Task Force since July 1993 Eighth Circuit. Member Judicial Conference Committee on Oversight of the Administrative Office 1988-94. Member Missouri Trial Lawyers Association (Board of Governors 1969-79), The Association of Trial Lawyers of America, Federal Judges Association, The Missouri Bar, The Kansas City Metropolitan, Boone County and American Bar Associations. Recipient Distinguished Alumnus Award from Central Methodist College 1987, Thomas F. Eagleton Award from Legal Aid of Western Missouri 1990, Achievement Award from The Kansas City Metropolitan Bar Association 1991 and Faculty-Alumni Award from University of Missouri-Columbia 1995. Named Marine of the Year by Globe & Anchor Society 1994. USN 1942-43. Aviator USMC 1943-46. President Young Democrats Boone County 1950. Chairman United Fund Columbia 1961-62 and Unitarian Forum All Souls Unitarian Church 1991-93. President Rotary Club Columbia 1969-71. Member Eighth Circuit Archives History Committee 1980-81. Board of Trustees Harry S. Truman Scholarship Foundation since May 2000. Member Western District Historical Society, Eighth Circuit Historical Society and Jefferson Club University of Missouri-Columbia School of Law. Enjoys tennis, golf and jogging.
Office: 8662 U.S. Courthouse, 400 East Ninth Street, Kansas City 64106.
Telephone: (816) 512-5700.
Fax: (816) 512-5713

MONTANA

Capital HELENA

UNITED STATES DISTRICT COURT DISTRICT OF MONTANA

Within Montana, exclusive of Yellowstone National Park (which is under the jurisdiction of the United States District Court District of Wyoming), there is one United States District Court. The court sits at Billings, Butte, Glasgow, Great Falls, Havre, Helena, Kalispell, Lewistown, Livingston, Miles City and Missoula. For descriptive information refer to the United States Courts section.

Chief Judge
Donald W. Molloy

Judges
Richard F. Cebull
Sam E. Haddon

Senior Judges
Charles C. Lovell
Jack D. Shanstrom

Clerk
Patrick E. Duffy
P.O. Box 8537
Missoula, Montana 59807-8537
(406) 542-7260

UNITED STATES MAGISTRATE JUDGES OF MONTANA

Gerard M. Schuster
Richard W. Anderson
Leif "Bart" Erickson
Carolyn Ostby

Recalled Magistrate Judge
Robert M. Holter

UNITED STATES BANKRUPTCY COURT OF MONTANA

Judge
Ralph B. Kirscher

Recalled Judge
John L. Peterson

Bankruptcy Clerk
Bernard F. McCarthy
303 Federal Building and U.S. Courthouse
400 North Main Street
Butte, Montana 59701
(406) 782-3354

MONTANA SUPREME COURT

The Supreme Court is Montana's court of last resort. The court consists of a chief justice and six justices elected at large in nonpartisan elections for eight-year terms. Vacancies are filled by appointment by the governor from a list of nominees submitted by the Judicial Nominations Commission. Senate confirmation is required for all appointees. Retired justices may serve when called by the court.

The court has appellate jurisdiction over all cases in law and equity from the District Court, supervisory control over all courts and authority to regulate admission to the bar and the conduct of its members. The court may issue writs necessary to the exercise of proper jurisdiction.

The court sits at Helena en banc or in five-judge panels and recesses during July and August.

Chief Justice
Karla M. Gray

Justices

W. William Leaphart	James C. Nelson
Jim Regnier	Patricia Cotter
James A. Rice, Jr.	John Warner

Clerk
Edwin A. Smith
Justice Building, Room 323
215 North Sanders
Helena, Montana 59620
(406) 444-3858

Court Administrator
Jim Oppedahl
Justice Building, Room 315
215 North Sanders
P.O. Box 203002
Helena, Montana 59620-3002
(406) 444-2627

MONTANA DISTRICT COURT

The District Court is Montana's court of general jurisdiction. The state is divided into twenty-two judicial districts. Judges are elected in nonpartisan elections by the voters in their district for six-year terms. Vacancies are filled by appointment by the governor from a list of nominees submitted by the Judicial Nominations Commission. Senate confirmation is required for all appointees. Each district has a chief judge who serves either by seniority or on a rotating basis for a one-year term. Retired judges may serve when called by the Supreme Court.

The court exercises exclusive jurisdiction over all felonies and juvenile matters and original jurisdiction over all cases in law and equity, all civil and probate matters, and all misdemeanors not otherwise provided for by law. The court has appellate jurisdiction over the lower courts. A Sentence Review Division, composed of three District Court judges appointed by the chief justice of the Supreme Court, is empowered to review all sentences imposed and can raise, lower or permit the sen-

MONTANA DISTRICT COURT—*Continued*

tence to stand. The court may issue writs necessary to the exercise of proper jurisdiction and has concurrent jurisdiction with the Supreme Court to issue extraordinary writs.

The court sits at each county seat.

†Also serves Water Court

FIRST JUDICIAL DISTRICT includes Broadwater and Lewis and Clark counties. The court sits at Townsend and Helena.

Judges
Thomas C. Honzel
Dorothy McCarter
Jeffrey M. Sherlock†

SECOND JUDICIAL DISTRICT includes Silver Bow County. The court sits at Butte.

Judges
Kurt Krueger
John W. Whelan

THIRD JUDICIAL DISTRICT includes Deer Lodge, Granite and Powell counties. The court sits at Anaconda, Philipsburg and Deer Lodge.

Judge
Ted L. Mizner†

FOURTH JUDICIAL DISTRICT includes Mineral and Missoula counties. The court sits at Superior and Missoula.

Judges
Douglas G. Harkin
John S. Henson
John W. Larson
Edward P. McLean

FIFTH JUDICIAL DISTRICT includes Beaverhead, Jefferson and Madison counties. The court sits at Dillon, Boulder and Virginia City.

Judge
Loren Tucker

SIXTH JUDICIAL DISTRICT includes Park and Sweet Grass counties. The court sits at Livingston and Big Timber.

Judge
William Nels Swandal

SEVENTH JUDICIAL DISTRICT includes Dawson, McCone, Prairie, Richland and Wibaux counties. The court sits at Glendive, Circle, Terry, Sidney and Wibaux.

Judges
Katherine M. Irigoin
Richard A. Simonton

EIGHTH JUDICIAL DISTRICT includes Cascade County. The court sits at Great Falls.

Judges
Julie Macek
Thomas M. McKittrick
Kenneth R. Neill
Dirk Sandefur

NINTH JUDICIAL DISTRICT includes Glacier, Pondera, Teton and Toole counties. The court sits at Cut Bank, Conrad, Choteau and Shelby.

Judge
Marc G. Buyske

TENTH JUDICIAL DISTRICT includes Fergus, Judith Basin and Petroleum counties. The court sits at Lewistown, Stanford and Winnett.

Judge
E. Wayne Phillips

ELEVENTH JUDICIAL DISTRICT includes Flathead County. The court sits at Kalispell.

Judges
Katherine R. Curtis
Ted O. Lympus
Stewart E. Stadler

TWELFTH JUDICIAL DISTRICT includes Choteau, Hill and Liberty counties. The court sits at Fort Benton, Havre and Chester.

Judge
vacancy

THIRTEENTH JUDICIAL DISTRICT includes Yellowstone county. The court sits at Billings.

Judges
Diane G. Barz
G. Todd Baugh
Gregory R. Todd
Russell C. Fagg
Susan P. Watters

FOURTEENTH JUDICIAL DISTRICT includes Golden Valley, Meagher, Musselshell and Wheatland counties. The court sits at Ryegate, White Sulphur Springs, Roundup and Harlowton.

Judge
Randal I. Spaulding

FIFTEENTH JUDICIAL DISTRICT includes Daniels, Roosevelt and Sheridan counties. The court sits at Scobey, Wolf Point and Plentywood.

Judge
David Cybulski

SIXTEENTH JUDICIAL DISTRICT includes Carter, Custer, Fallon, Garfield, Powder River, Rosebud and Treasure counties. The court sits at Ekalaka, Miles City, Baker, Jordan, Broadus, Forsyth and Hysham.

Judges
Joe L. Hegel†
Gary L. Day

SEVENTEENTH JUDICIAL DISTRICT includes Blaine, Phillips and Valley counties. The court sits at Chinook, Malta and Glasgow.

Judge
John C. McKeon

EIGHTEENTH JUDICIAL DISTRICT includes Gallatin County. The court sits at Bozeman.

Judges
Michael A. Salvagni
Mark Guenther

MONTANA DISTRICT COURT—*Continued*

NINETEENTH JUDICIAL DISTRICT includes Lincoln County. The court sits at Libby.

Judge
Michael Prezeau

TWENTIETH JUDICIAL DISTRICT includes Lake and Sanders counties. The court sits at Polson and Thompson Falls.

Judges
C. B. McNeil
Deborah Kim Christopher

TWENTY-FIRST JUDICIAL DISTRICT includes Ravalli County. The court sits at Hamilton.

Judges
Jeffrey H. Langton
Jim Haynes

TWENTY-SECOND JUDICIAL DISTRICT includes Big Horn, Carbon and Stillwater counties. The court sits at Hardin, Red Lodge and Columbus.

Judge
W. Blair Jones

MONTANA WATER COURT

The Water Court is a court of special jurisdiction in Montana. The water judges are designated for each water division by a majority vote of a committee composed of the district judge from each single-judge judicial district and the chief district judge from each multiple-judge judicial district to serve a four-year term. The water judges are usually district judges or retired district judges who also serve a district falling within the water division. A chief judge is appointed by the chief justice from a list of nominees submitted by the Judicial Nominations Commission and serves a four-year term.

The court has jurisdiction over the determination and interpretation of all water rights disputes and over all matters relating to the determination of existing water rights. Appeals are to the Supreme Court.

The court sits where required.

Chief Judge
C. Bruce Loble

YELLOWSTONE RIVER BASIN DIVISION includes those areas drained by the Yellowstone and Little Missouri rivers and any remaining areas in Carter County.

Judge
Roy C. Rodeghiero

LOWER MISSOURI RIVER BASIN DIVISION includes those areas drained by the Missouri River from below the mouth of the Marias River and any remaining areas in Glacier and Sheridan counties.

Judge
Joe L. Hegel

UPPER MISSOURI RIVER BASIN DIVISION includes those areas drained by the Missouri River to below the mouth of the Marias River.

Judge
Jeffrey M. Sherlock

CLARK FORK RIVER BASIN DIVISION includes those areas drained by the Clark Fork and Kootenai rivers and any remaining areas in Lincoln County.

Judge
Ted L. Mizner

MONTANA WORKERS' COMPENSATION COURT

The Workers' Compensation Court is a court of special jurisdiction in Montana, created to adjudicate disputes arising from the workers' compensation benefit program. The workers' compensation judge is appointed by the governor from a list of nominees submitted by the Judicial Nominations Commission and serves a six-year term.

The court has exclusive jurisdiction to make determinations concerning disputes arising under Title 39, Montana Code Annotated. The court's organization and functions are similar to the District Court, except that it is not bound by common law nor statutory rules of evidence.

The court sits at Helena.

Judge
Mike McCarter

MONTANA JUSTICE OF THE PEACE COURTS

Justice of the Peace Courts are Montana's major courts of limited jurisdiction. There is at least one court in each county, and the Board of County Commissioners in each county has authority to constitute additional courts as deemed necessary and to fill any vacancies which may occur. Justices are elected in nonpartisan elections for four-year terms. Justices may also be appointed by town councils to serve as City Court judges.

The courts have civil jurisdiction in most matters in which the amount in controversy does not exceed $7,000 and criminal jurisdiction over fish and game violations punishable by a fine not exceeding $1,000 or imprisonment not exceeding six months or both. Jurisdiction is concurrent with the Missoula Municipal Court. The courts have concurrent jurisdiction with the District Court over misdemeanors punishable by a fine not exceeding $500 or imprisonment not exceeding six months or both, over misdemeanors arising from a felony and over forcible entry and unlawful detainer. The courts also have concurrent jurisdiction with the City Courts over misdemeanors punishable by a fine not exceeding $500 or imprisonment not exceeding six months or both.

The courts sit at each county seat unless otherwise indicated.

*Also serves City Court

County	Justice
Beaverhead	Candy Hoerning
Big Horn	Natasha J. Morton
Blaine Court also sits at Harlem	Perry Miller*
Broadwater	Gary A. Olsen
Carbon	Johnny D. Seiffert

MONTANA JUSTICE OF THE PEACE COURTS—*Continued*

Carter	Tracey D. Walker*
Court also sits at Alzada	
Cascade	Samuel Harris
	Kathleen Jensen
Chouteau	Susan Spencer
Custer	Donald R. Neese
Daniels	Alvin "Bud" Kaul*
Dawson	Ed Williamson
Deer Lodge	JoAnne M. Welch*
Fallon	Anna K. Straub*
Fergus	Jack Shields*
Flathead	David Ortley
Gallatin	Gordon L. Smith*
	Scott Wyckman
Garfield	Art Gallinger*
Glacier	Robert J. Yunck*
Golden Valley	Gail Schaff*
Court sits at Lavina	
Granite	Samuel E. Brown*
Court also sits at Drummond	Melody Gessele* (Drummond)
Hill	Terry L. Stoppa
Jefferson	Dennis H. Giulio*
Judith Basin	Larry G. Carver*
Lake	Chuck Wall
Lewis and Clark	Wallace Jewell
Liberty	Neal A. Eveland*
Lincoln	Gary D. Hicks
	Terry Utter
Madison	Mary Ann O'Malley
McCone	Mary Garfield*
Meagher	Ronda Shinabarger*
Mineral	Wanda Dinius James*
Missoula	John E. Odlin
	Karen A. Orzech
Musselshell	Donna Marsh*
Park	Deanna G. Egeland
Petroleum	Donna M. Lund*
Phillips	Gayle Stahl*
Pondera	Audrey Brown
Powder River	Peggy D. Jones
Powell	Terry J. McGillis*
Prairie	Kathy Henry*
Ravalli	Jim Bailey
	Robin Clute
Richland	Gregory P. Mohr*
Roosevelt	Traci Harada*
	Bruce Waldhausen*
Rosebud	Mary O'Hara Kunst*
Court also sits at Colstrip	Gail D. Beckham (Colstrip)
Sanders	Bob L. Beitz*
Sheridan	Thomas Robertson*
Silver Bow	Robert Lee
	Debra Williams
Stillwater	Marilyn Kober*
Sweet Grass	Jessie McKenney*
Teton	John L. "Pete" Howard*
Toole	Janice Freeland*
Treasure	Willis F. Etter*
Valley	Linda Mogan-Hartsock*
Wheatland	Richard Egebakken*
Wibaux	Bill Franks*
Yellowstone	Larry D. Herman
	Pedro R. Hernandez

MONTANA CITY COURTS

City Courts are courts of limited jurisdiction in Montana. Judges are elected at general elections for four-year terms. Vacancies are filled by the local governing body of each city. Judges need not be attorneys. Justices of the Peace may also be appointed by town councils to serve as City Court judges.

The courts exercise concurrent jurisdiction with the Justice of the Peace Courts over all misdemeanors punishable by a fine not exceeding $500 or imprisonment not exceeding six months or both. The courts exercise exclusive jurisdiction over ordinance violations, recovery of city property if less than $5,000, collection of money due the city if less than $5,000 and collection of city taxes.

*Also Justice of the Peace

City	Judge
Alberton	Wanda Dinius James*
Alzada	Tracey D. Walker*
Anaconda	JoAnne M. Welch*
Baker	Anna K. Straub*
Belgrade	Michelle Snowberger
Belt	Ronald L. Bissell
Big Timber	Jessie McKenney*
Boulder	Dennis H. Giulio*
Bozeman	Gordon L. Smith*
Bridger	Carol S. Anderson
Broadus	Rebecca L. McEuen
Butte	Thomas Gallagher
Cascade	Lauri Cary
Chester	Neal A. Eveland*
Chinook	Perry Miller*
Choteau	John L. "Pete" Howard*
Circle	Mary Garfield*
Colstrip	Joyce Obland
Columbia Falls	Susan "Tina" Gordon
Columbus	Marilyn Kober*
Conrad	Shannen Rossmiller
Culbertson	Bruce Waldhausen*
Cut Bank	Robert J. Yunck*
Darby	Barbara "Skip" Kohn
Deer Lodge	Terry J. McGillis*
Dillon	Virginia Compton
Drummond	Melody Gessele*
Dutton	John L. "Pete" Howard*
East Helena	Lawrence Murphy
Ekalaka	Tracey D. Walker*
Ennis	Kathleen Humphrey
Eureka	Stephen J. Franklin
Fairfield	John L. "Pete" Howard*
Fairview	Margaret Flynn
Forsyth	Mary O'Hara Kunst*
Fort Benton	A. E. Anderson
Fort Peck	Linda Mogan-Hartsock*
Fromberg	Carol S. Anderson
Glasgow	Linda Mogan-Hartsock*
Glendive	Katherine Lee
Hamilton	Patricia Sanders
Hardin	Janice Heath

MONTANA CITY COURTS—*Continued*

Harlem	Reuben M. Kuntz
Harlowton	Richard Egebakken*
Havre	Joyce Perszyk
Helena	Myron E. Pitch
Hobson	Larry G. Carver*
Hot Springs	Bob L. Beitz*
Hysham	Willis F. Etter*
Joliet	Carol S. Anderson
Jordan	Art Gallinger*
Laurel	Jean Kerr
Lewistown	Jack Shields*
Libby	Linda Dorrington
Lima	Jean L. Huntsman
Livingston	Neil Maurice Travis
Malta	Gayle Stahl*
Manhattan	Gordon L. Smith*
Miles City	Kenneth W. Hom
Nashua	Linda Mogan-Hartsock*
Philipsburg	Samuel E. Brown*
Pinesdale	Morris T. Jessop
Plains	Bob L. Beitz*
Plentywood	Thomas Robertson*
Polson	Donald Lucas
Poplar	Bruce Waldhausen*
Red Lodge	Carol S. Anderson
Ronan	Glenn Frame
Roundup	Donna Marsh*
Ryegate	Gail Schaff*
St. Ignatius	Craig L. Hoppe
Scobey	Alvin "Bud" Kaul*
Shelby	Janice Freeland*
Sidney	Gregory P. Mohr*
Stanford	Larry G. Carver*
Stevensville	Barbara "Skip" Kohn
Superior	Wanda Dinius James*
Terry	Kathy Henry*
Thompson Falls	Bob L. Beitz*
Three Forks	Karla K. Walker
Townsend	Tori J. Marion
Troy	John H. Duehr
West Yellowstone	G. Lewis Scott
White Sulphur Springs	Ronda Shinabarger*
Whitefish	Bradley F. Johnson
Whitehall	Dennis H. Giulio*
Wibaux	Bill Franks*
Winnett	Donna M. Lund*
Wolf Point	Traci Harada*

MONTANA MUNICIPAL COURTS

The Montana Municipal Courts are courts of limited jurisdiction in Montana. Municipal Courts can be established in cities with populations of 10,000 or more. Presently, there are five Municipal Courts in operation. Judges are elected at nonpartisan elections for four-year terms. Judges must be admitted to practice in Montana.

The courts have concurrent jurisdiction with the District Court in forcible entry and detainer actions and with the Justice of the Peace Courts in the city in which the court is located. The courts have the same jurisdiction as City Courts in criminal and civil matters.

City	Judge
Billings	MaryJane McCalla Knisely
Bozeman	Patricia Carlson
Great Falls	Nancy Luth
Kalispell	Heidi J. Ulbricht
Missoula	Donald J. Louden

Montana Counties and County Seats

Beaverhead
Dillon

Big Horn
Hardin

Blaine
Chinook

Broadwater
Townsend

Carbon
Red Lodge

Carter
Ekalaka

Cascade
Great Falls

Chouteau
Fort Benton

Custer
Miles City

Daniels
Scobey

Dawson
Glendive

Deer Lodge
Anaconda

Fallon
Baker

Fergus
Lewistown

Flathead
Kalispell

Gallatin
Bozeman

Garfield
Jordan

Glacier
Cut Bank

Golden Valley
Ryegate

Granite
Philipsburg

Hill
Havre

Jefferson
Boulder

Judith Basin
Stanford

Lake
Polson

Lewis and Clark
Helena

Liberty
Chester

Lincoln
Libby

Madison
Virginia City

McCone
Circle

Meagher
White Sulphur Springs

Mineral
Superior

Missoula
Missoula

Musselshell
Roundup

Park
Livingston

Petroleum
Winnett

Phillips
Malta

Pondera
Conrad

Powder River
Broadus

Powell
Deer Lodge

Prairie
Terry

Ravalli
Hamilton

Richland
Sidney

Roosevelt
Wolf Point

Rosebud
Forsyth

COUNTIES AND COUNTY SEATS—*Continued*

County	County Seat
Sanders	Thompson Falls
Sheridan	Plentywood
Silver Bow	Butte
Stillwater	Columbus
Sweet Grass	Big Timber
Teton	Choteau
Toole	Shelby
Treasure	Hysham
Valley	Glasgow
Wheatland	Harlowton
Wibaux	Wibaux
Yellowstone	Billings

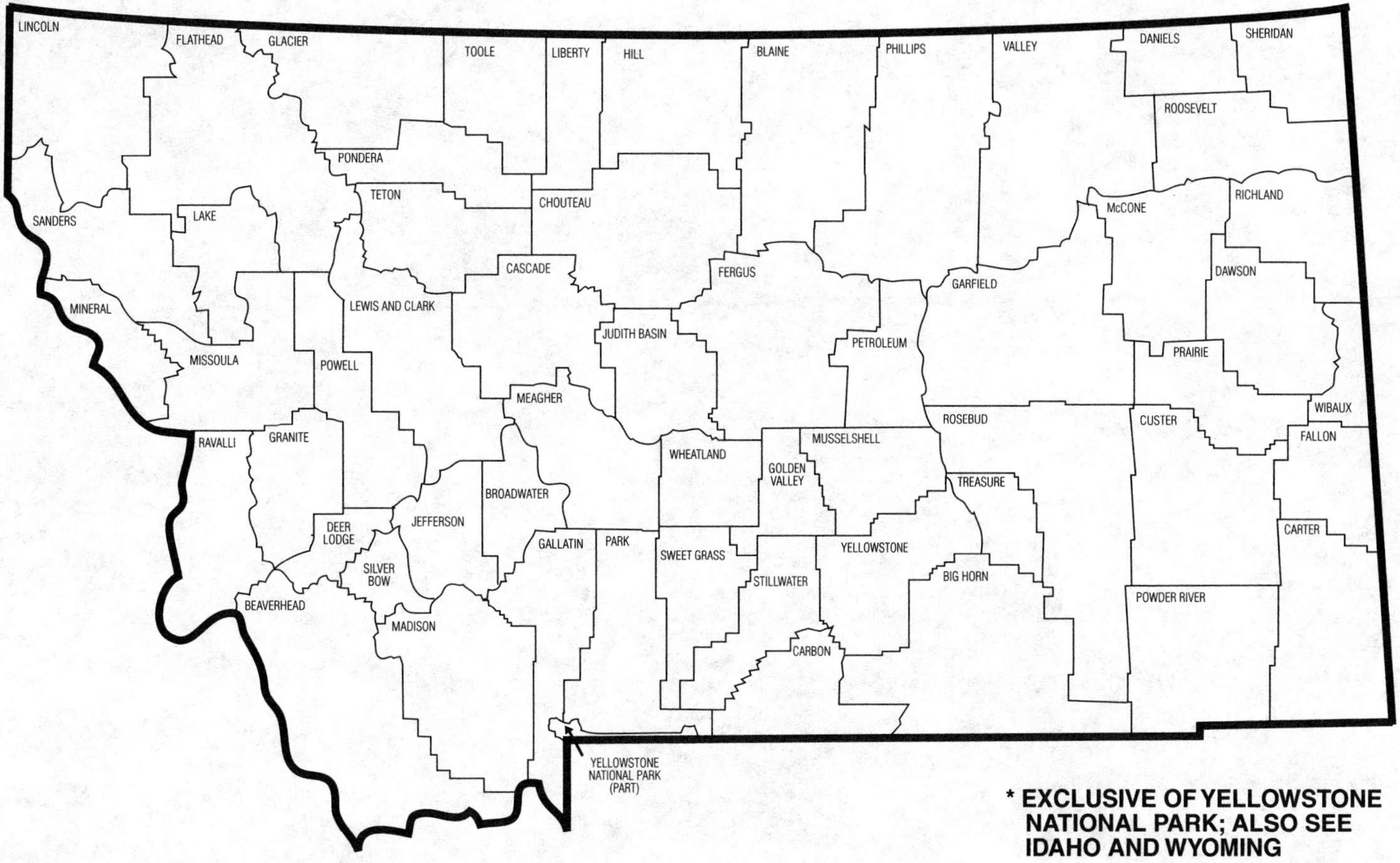
LINCOLN
FLATHEAD
GLACIER
TOOLE
LIBERTY
HILL
BLAINE
PHILLIPS
VALLEY
DANIELS
SHERIDAN
ROOSEVELT
PONDERA
TETON
CHOUTEAU
SANDERS
LAKE
RICHLAND
McCONE
CASCADE
FERGUS
GARFIELD
DAWSON
MINERAL
LEWIS AND CLARK
JUDITH BASIN
PETROLEUM
MISSOULA
POWELL
PRAIRIE
MEAGHER
ROSEBUD
CUSTER
WIBAUX
FALLON
RAVALLI
GRANITE
MUSSELSHELL
WHEATLAND
GOLDEN VALLEY
TREASURE
BROADWATER
DEER LODGE
JEFFERSON
GALLATIN
PARK
CARTER
YELLOWSTONE
SWEET GRASS
SILVER BOW
BIG HORN
STILLWATER
BEAVERHEAD
POWDER RIVER
MADISON
CARBON
YELLOWSTONE NATIONAL PARK (PART)
* EXCLUSIVE OF YELLOWSTONE NATIONAL PARK; ALSO SEE IDAHO AND WYOMING

UNITED STATES DISTRICT COURT DISTRICT OF MONTANA *

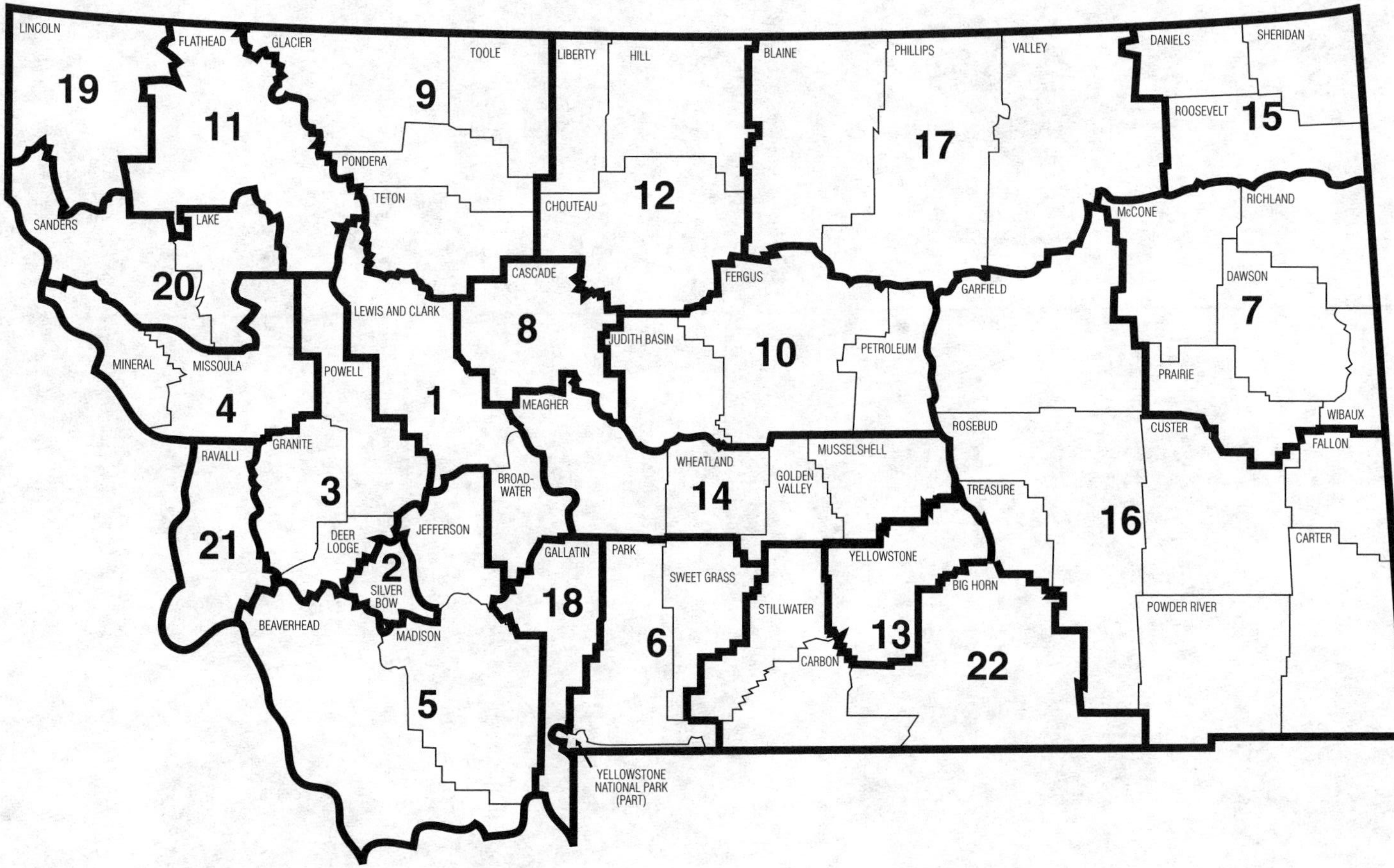
LINCOLN
FLATHEAD
GLACIER
TOOLE
LIBERTY
HILL
BLAINE
PHILLIPS
VALLEY
DANIELS
SHERIDAN
ROOSEVELT
19
11
9
12
17
15
PONDERA
TETON
CHOUTEAU
SANDERS
LAKE
20
McCONE
RICHLAND
CASCADE
FERGUS
GARFIELD
DAWSON
7
LEWIS AND CLARK
8
JUDITH BASIN
10
PETROLEUM
MINERAL
MISSOULA
POWELL
4
1
MEAGHER
PRAIRIE
WIBAUX
ROSEBUD
CUSTER
FALLON
RAVALLI
GRANITE
MUSSELSHELL
WHEATLAND
GOLDEN VALLEY
BROAD-WATER
3
14
TREASURE
16
JEFFERSON
DEER LODGE
21
2
GALLATIN
PARK
SWEET GRASS
YELLOWSTONE
CARTER
SILVER BOW
18
BIG HORN
BEAVERHEAD
STILLWATER
POWDER RIVER
MADISON
6
13
CARBON
22
5
YELLOWSTONE NATIONAL PARK (PART)

JUDICIAL DISTRICTS OF MONTANA DISTRICT COURT

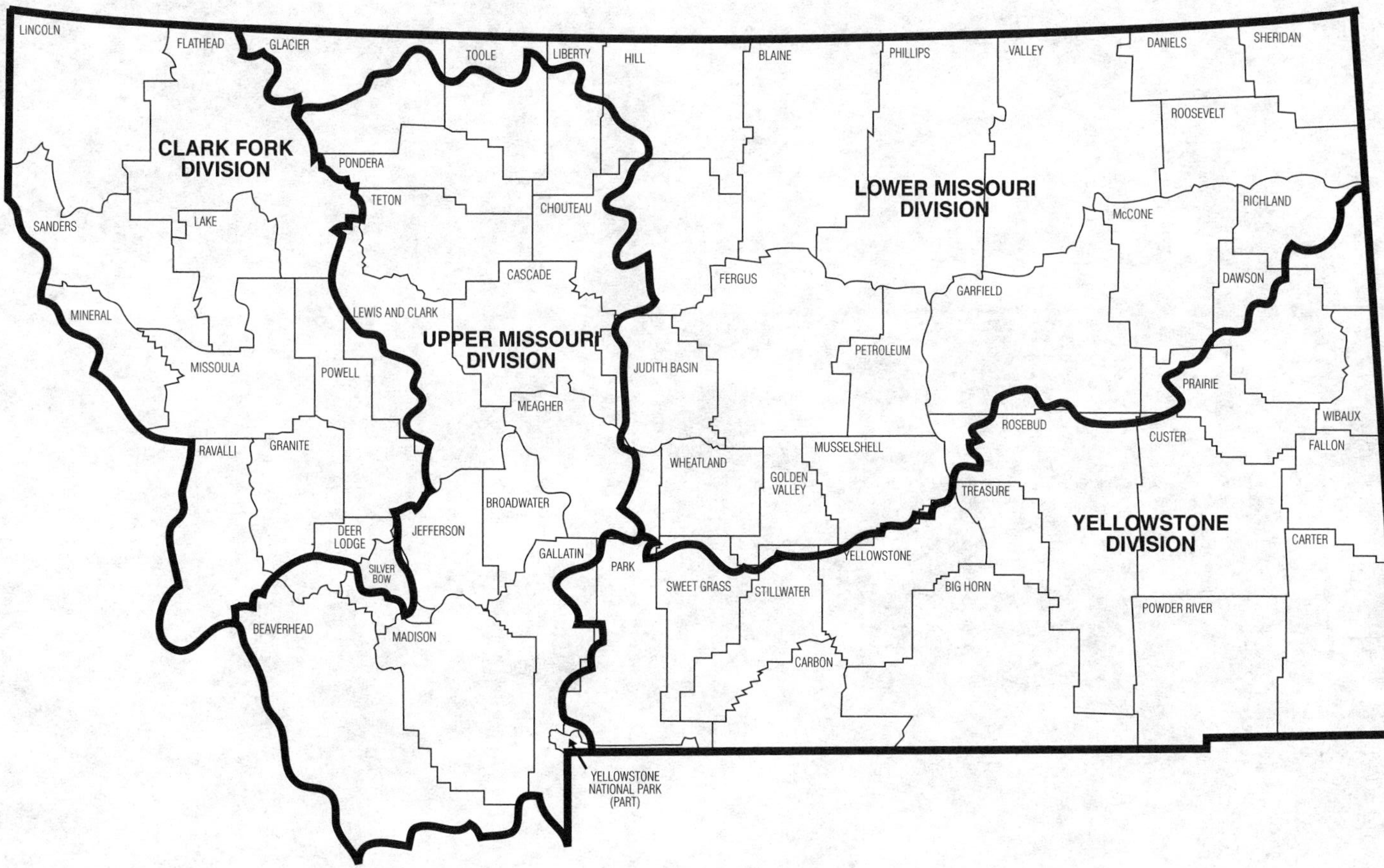
LINCOLN
FLATHEAD
GLACIER
TOOLE
LIBERTY
HILL
BLAINE
PHILLIPS
VALLEY
DANIELS
SHERIDAN
ROOSEVELT
CLARK FORK
DIVISION
PONDERA
TETON
CHOUTEAU
LOWER MISSOURI
DIVISION
McCONE
RICHLAND
SANDERS
LAKE
CASCADE
FERGUS
GARFIELD
DAWSON
MINERAL
LEWIS AND CLARK
UPPER MISSOURI
DIVISION
MISSOULA
POWELL
JUDITH BASIN
PETROLEUM
PRAIRIE
MEAGHER
ROSEBUD
WIBAUX
RAVALLI
GRANITE
MUSSELSHELL
CUSTER
FALLON
WHEATLAND
GOLDEN
VALLEY
TREASURE
BROADWATER
YELLOWSTONE
DIVISION
DEER
LODGE
JEFFERSON
CARTER
SILVER
BOW
GALLATIN
PARK
YELLOWSTONE
SWEET GRASS
STILLWATER
BIG HORN
BEAVERHEAD
MADISON
POWDER RIVER
CARBON
YELLOWSTONE
NATIONAL PARK
(PART)

RIVER BASIN DIVISIONS OF MONTANA WATER COURTS

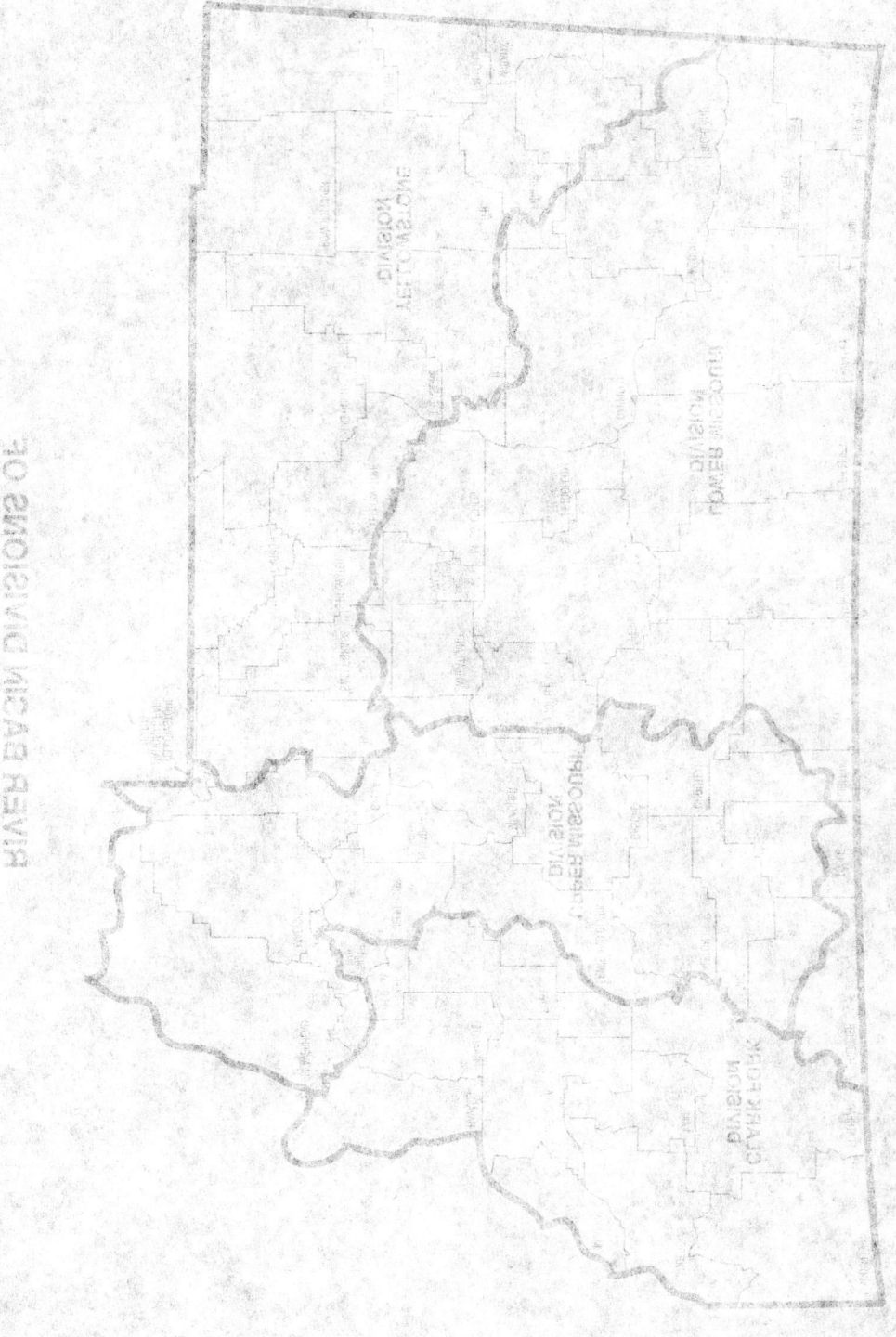

MONTANA

ANDERSON, A. E. *(Judge, Fort Benton City Court)* Appointed by Mayor George Fultz to term beginning July 1, 1990. Reappointed Jan 1, 1991, 1994, 1998 and 2002. Current term expires Dec 31, 2005. Born Fort Benton Montana Aug 26, 1935. Methodist. Educated at University of Montana B.A. 1957 LL.B. 1961. Admitted to practice Montana 1961 and U.S. District Court District of Montana 1967. In legal practice Fort Benton 1961-67 and since 1970.

County Attorney Chouteau County 1963-67 and 1971-75. Staff Attorney Montana Legal Services Association 1967-71. Member State Bar of Montana. Sergeant USAR. Member Masons, Scottish Rite and Shriners. Hobbies include playing golf, fishing and traveling.

Mailing address: P.O. Box 1227, Fort Benton 59442.
Telephone: (406) 622-5494.

ANDERSON, Carol S. *(Judge, Bridger, Fromberg, Joliet and Red Lodge City Courts)* Appointed to Red Lodge City Court by City Council to term beginning April 4, 1984. Reappointed Jan 3, 1986, Jan 2, 1990, 1994, 1998 and 2002.

Mailing address: P.O. Box 9, Red Lodge 59068.
Telephone: (406) 446-1606 (Red Lodge), 662-3116 (Bridger), 668-7382 (Fromberg).

ANDERSON, Richard W. *(Magistrate Judge, United States District Court District of Montana)* Appointed by U.S. District Court judges.

Office: 5405 U.S. Courthouse, 316 North 26th Street, Billings 59101.
Telephone: (406) 247-7025.

BAILEY, Jim *(Justice, Ravalli County Justice of the Peace Court)*

Office: 205 Bedford Street, Suite F, Hamilton 59840.
Telephone: (406) 375-6252.

BARZ, Diane G. *(Judge, Montana District Court Thirteenth Judicial District)*

Mailing address: P.O. Box 35029, Billings 59107.
Telephone: (406) 256-2916.
Fax: (406) 256-2736

BAUGH, G. Todd *(Judge, Montana District Court Thirteenth Judicial District)* Elected to term beginning Jan 1985. Reelected 1990, 1996 and 2002. Current term expires Dec 31, 2008. Born Sweetwater Texas Oct 12, 1941. Protestant. Educated at Rice University B.A. 1964 and University of Texas LL.B. 1967. Law Clerk to Hon. James F. Battin, U.S. District Court District of Montana 1969. Admitted to practice Montana 1967, Colorado 1967 and Texas 1967.

Mailing address: P.O. Box 35042, Billings 59107.
Telephone: (406) 256-2922.
Fax: (406) 256-2736

BECKHAM, Gail D. *(Justice, Rosebud County Justice of the Peace Court)*

Mailing address: P.O. Box 575, Colstrip 59323.
Telephone: (406) 748-2934.
Fax: (406) 748-4832

BEITZ, Bob L. *(Justice, Sanders County Justice of the Peace Court and Judge, Hot Springs, Plains and Thompson Falls City Courts)* Appointed Justice by County Commissioners to term beginning Oct 1979. Elected 1982, 1986, 1990, 1994, 1998 and 2002. Current term expires Dec 31, 2006. Born American Falls Idaho May 6, 1948. Educated at University of Idaho B.S. 1971. Member Alpha Tau Omega.

Member Montana Magistrates Association (District Chairman 1983-84 and Western Vice President 1985-87).

Mailing address: P.O. Box 519, Thompson Falls 59873.
Telephone: (406) 827-6941.

BISSELL, Ronald L. *(Judge, Belt City Court)*

Mailing address: P.O. Box 453, Belt 59412.
Telephone: (406) 277-3621.

BROWN, Audrey *(Justice, Pondera County Justice of the Peace Court)* Elected to term beginning Jan 1999. Reelected 2002, current term expires Dec 2006.

Member Montana Magistrates Association and National Judges Association.

Office: 20 Fourth Avenue S.W., Conrad 59425.
Telephone: (406) 271-4030.

BROWN, Samuel E. *(Justice, Granite County Justice of the Peace Court and Judge, Philipsburg City Court)* Elected Justice to term beginning Jan 1, 1995. Reelected 1998 and 2002. Current term expires Dec 31, 2006. Born Anaconda Montana July 4, 1947. Lutheran. Educated at University of Redlands B.S. 1980.

Captain USAF Nov 1966 to Sept 1991. Member Masons, Veterans of Foreign Wars and Eagles. Enjoys football, hunting, fishing, camping, riding and raising horses.

Mailing address: P.O. Box 356, Philipsburg 59858.
Telephone: (406) 859-3006.

BUYSKE, Marc G. *(Judge, Montana District Court Ninth Judicial District)*

Mailing address: P.O. Box 822, Shelby 59474.
Office: Toole County Courthouse, Shelby 59474.
Telephone: (406) 434-2451.
Fax: (406) 434-7225

CARLSON, Patricia *(Judge, Bozeman Municipal Court)* Former Judge, Bozeman City Court.

Office: 615 South 16th, Suite 123, Bozeman 59715.
Telephone: (406) 582-2040.

CARVER, Larry G. *(Justice, Judith Basin County Justice of the Peace Court and Judge, Hobson and Stanford City Courts)*

Mailing address: P.O. Box 339, Stanford 59479.
Telephone: (406) 566-2277.
E-mail address: 7carver7@3rivers.net

CARY, Lauri *(Judge, Cascade City Court)*

Office: Nine North Front Street, Cascade 59421.
Telephone: (406) 468-2802.
E-mail address: lauri@montana.com

CEBULL, Richard F. *(Judge, United States District Court District of Montana)* Magistrate Judge Feb 1, 1998 to July 26, 2001. Appointed Judge for life by

CEBULL, RICHARD F.—*Continued*

President George W. Bush to term beginning July 26, 2001.

Office: 5428 U.S. Courthouse, 316 North 26th Street, Billings 59101.

Telephone: (406) 247-7766.

CHRISTOPHER, Deborah Kim *(Judge, Montana District Court Twentieth Judicial District)* Elected to term beginning Jan 2001. Term expires Dec 2006. Born Missoula Montana Jan 8, 1960. Presbyterian. Educated at University of Montana B.A. 1982 J.D. 1988. Admitted to practice Montana 1988 and Washington 1991. In legal practice Polson Montana 1991-93.

Deputy District Attorney Cascade County and District Attorney Lake County Dec 1991 to Dec 2000. Secretary Montana County Attorneys Association 1991-2000. Member Montana District Judges Association, State Bar of Montana and Washington State Bar Association. Captain U.S. Army JAGC Sept 1988 to Dec 1991. Republican. Member Rotary, PEO and First Presbyterian Church. Enjoys children, basketball and reading. Personal Statement or Quote: "Please remember who we represent and who we serve."

Office: 106 Fourth Avenue East, Polson 59860.

Telephone: (406) 883-7360.

Fax: (406) 883-7297

CLUTE, Robin *(Justice, Ravalli County Justice of the Peace Court)*

Office: 205 Bedford Street, Suite F, Hamilton 59840.

Telephone: (406) 375-6252.

COMPTON, Virginia *(Judge, Dillon City Court)*

Office: 125 North Idaho, Dillon 59725.

Telephone: (406) 683-2333.

COTTER, Patricia *(Justice, Montana Supreme Court)* Elected November 7, 2000. Educated at Western Michigan University B.S. with honors 1972 and Notre Dame Law School J.D. 1977. In legal practice South Bend Indiana 1977-83 and Great Falls Montana.

Mailing address: P.O. Box 203001, Helena 59620-3001.

Office: 414 Justice Building, Helena 59601.

Telephone: (406) 444-5570.

CURTIS, Katherine R. *(Judge, Montana District Court Eleventh Judicial District)*

Office: 920 South Main, Kalispell 59901.

Telephone: (406) 758-5669.

CYBULSKI, David *(Judge, Montana District Court Fifteenth Judicial District)*

Mailing address: P.O. Box 187, Plentywood 59254.

Office: Roosevelt County Courthouse, Plentywood 59254.

Telephone: (406) 286-5616.

Fax: (406) 286-5616

DAY, Gary L. *(Judge, Montana District Court Sixteenth Judicial District)* Appointed by Governor Marc Racicot Nov 7, 1997. Elected 1998 and 2000. Current term expires 2006. Born Park Rapids Minnesota Jan 3, 1951. Educated at Moorhead State University B.S. in Biology and University of Montana M.S. in Wildlife Biology J.D. Editor-in-Chief Public Land Law Review 1980-81.

Member State Bar of Montana (Past President) and Badlands Bar Association. Attended The National Judicial College 1998. Enjoys hunting, backpacking, horsepacking, dog training and reading.

Office: Custer County Courthouse, 1010 Main Street, Miles City 59301.

Telephone: (406) 233-3335.

Fax: (406) 233-3450

DORRINGTON, Linda *(Judge, Libby City Court)*

Mailing address: P.O. Box 1428, Libby 59923.

Telephone: (406) 293-4440.

E-mail address: ehcaddis@libby.org

DUEHR, John H. *(Judge, Troy City Court)*

Mailing address: P.O. Box 823, Troy 59935.

Telephone: (406) 295-4151.

E-mail address: jpduehr@libby.org

EGEBAKKEN, Richard *(Justice, Wheatland County Justice of the Peace Court and Judge, Harlowton City Court)*

Mailing address: P.O. Box 618, Harlowton 59036.

Telephone: (406) 632-4821.

EGELAND, Deanna G. *(Justice, Park County Justice of the Peace Court)* Elected Justice to term beginning April 4, 1977. Reelected 1981, 1982, 1986, 1990, 1994, 1998 and 2002. Current term expires 2006. Former Judge, Livingston City Court. Born Livingston Montana July 14, 1938. Lutheran.

Former member American Judges Association. Member Montana Magistrates Association. Attended 42 State Judicial Conferences and Seminars. Attended The National Judicial College Reno. Area Manager Tupperware 1969-76. Board of Directors Treasure Trails Girl Scout Council for 46 years. Enjoys oil painting, gourmet cooking and camping.

Office: 414 East Callender, Livingston 59047.

Telephone: (406) 222-4171.

ERICKSON, Leif "Bart" *(Magistrate Judge, United States District Court District of Montana)* Appointed by U.S. District Court judges. Born Helena Montana June 10, 1942. Educated at University of Montana J.D. Former Judge, Montana District Court Eleventh Judicial District, appointed by Governor Ted Schwinden to term beginning Dec 11, 1985. Former Judge, Montana Water Court Clark Fork River Basin Division, appointed by Chief Justice.

Office: 370 Federal Building, 201 East Broadway Street, Missoula 59802.

Telephone: (406) 542-7280.

ETTER, Willis F. *(Justice, Treasure County Justice of the Peace Court and Judge, Hysham City Court)* Appointed Justice by County Commissioners to term beginning May 1, 1985. Elected Nov 4, 1986, 1990, 1994, 1998 and Nov 5, 2002. Current term expires Dec 31, 2006. Born Wimbledon North Dakota July 27, 1927. Roman Catholic. Educated at St. John's University B.A. 1948.

Attended Montana Magisterial Association Seminars. Former Roman Catholic Priest. Previously employed as music teacher, agricultural and service station manager and office manager for Hysham Community Elevator, Inc. Member Hysham Lions' Club. Enjoys music, literature, golf, travel and sports.

Mailing address: P.O. Box 267, Hysham 59038.

Telephone: (406) 342-5689.

EVELAND, Neal A. *(Justice, Liberty County Justice of the Peace Court and Judge, Chester City Court)*
Mailing address: P.O. Box K, Chester 59522.
Telephone: (406) 759-5172.

FAGG, Russell C. *(Judge, Montana District Court Thirteenth Judicial District)* Elected Nov 1994 to term beginning Jan 1, 1995. Reelected Nov 2000, current term expires Dec 31, 2006. Born Billings Montana June 26, 1960. Religious affiliation: Faith Chapel. Educated at Whitman College B.A. 1983, University of Montana J.D. 1986 and University of Nevada Reno M.J.S. 1999. Law Clerk to Hon. Fred J. Weber, Montana Supreme Court 1986-87. Admitted to practice Montana 1986 and U.S. District Court District of Montana 1986. In legal practice Billings 1987-89.
City Prosecutor City of Billings 1989-91. Deputy County Attorney Yellowstone County 1991-94. Chairman House Judiciary Committee 1993-94. Member State Bar of Montana and Yellowstone County Bar Association. Attended The National Judicial College 1995-99. Member Montana Legislature 1991-94. Enjoys reading, hiking, fishing and skiing.
Mailing address: P.O. Box 35027, Billings 59107.
Telephone: (406) 256-2906.
Fax: (406) 256-2736

FLYNN, Margaret *(Judge, Fairview City Court)* Appointed by mayor to term beginning March 1, 2001. Elected Jan 1, 2002.
Mailing address: P.O. Box 426, Fairview 59221.
Telephone: (406) 742-5616.
Fax: (406) 742-5480

FRAME, Glenn *(Judge, Ronan City Court)*
Office: 207 Main Street S.W., #A, Ronan 59864-2706.
Telephone: (406) 676-0211.

FRANKLIN, Stephen J. *(Judge, Eureka City Court)*
Mailing address: P.O. Box 313, Eureka 59917.
Telephone: (406) 296-2121.

FRANKS, Bill *(Justice, Wibaux County Justice of the Peace Court and Judge, Wibaux City Court)* Elected Nov 6, 1990 to term beginning Jan 7, 1991. Reelected 1994, 1998 and 2002. Current term expires Dec 31, 2006. Born San Francisco California Oct 8, 1952. Catholic. Educated at California State University at Chico B.A. 1975.
Member Montana Magistrates Association. Title Insurance Agent/Abstracter Wibaux County Abstract Company since 1985. Insurance Agent A.I.M., Ltd. since 1986. Member Wibaux Volunteer Fire Department, Wibaux County Recreation Board, Wibaux County Chamber of Commerce and Wibaux Civic Club. Enjoys golf, tennis, skiing, weight lifting, bowling and biking.
Mailing address: P.O. Box 445, Wibaux 59353.
Telephone: (406) 796-2484.

FREELAND, Janice *(Justice, Toole County Justice of the Peace Court and Judge, Shelby City Court)*
Mailing address: P.O. Box 748, Shelby 59474.
Telephone: (406) 434-2651, 434-2652.

GALLAGHER, Thomas *(Judge, Butte City Court)*
Office: Silver Bow County Courthouse, Butte 59701.
Telephone: (406) 497-6365.

GALLINGER, Art *(Justice, Garfield County Justice of the Peace Court and Judge, Jordan City Court)*
Mailing address: P.O. Box 482, Jordan 59337.
Telephone: (406) 557-2733.
E-mail address: judgeart@midrivers.com

GARFIELD, Mary *(Justice, McCone County Justice of the Peace Court and Judge, Circle City Court)*
Mailing address: P.O. Box 192, Circle 59215.
Telephone: (406) 485-3548.
E-mail address: clerk@midrivers.com

GESSELE, Melody *(Justice, Granite County Justice of the Peace Court and Judge, Drummond City Court)*
Mailing address: P.O. Box 159, Drummond 59832.
Telephone: (406) 288-3446.
E-mail address: Drm3050@montana.net

GIULIO, Dennis H. *(Justice, Jefferson County Justice of the Peace Court and Judge, Boulder and Whitehall City Courts)*
Mailing address: P.O. Box H, Boulder 59632.
Telephone: (406) 225-4055.

GORDON, Susan "Tina" *(Judge, Columbia Falls City Court)* Conference Chair National Judges Association 1997.
Mailing address: P.O. Box 2735, Columbia Falls 59912.
Telephone: (406) 892-4340.

GRAY, Karla M. *(Chief Justice, Montana Supreme Court)* Appointed by Governor Stanley G. Stephens to term beginning March 4, 1991. Elected Nov 3, 1992 and 1998. Current term expires 2006. First woman elected to Montana Supreme Court. Born Escanaba Michigan May 10, 1947. Educated at Western Michigan University B.A. 1969 M.A. in History 1972 and University of California Hastings College of the Law J.D. 1976. Law Clerk to Hon. W. D. Murray, U.S. District Court District of Montana 1976-77. Admitted to practice Montana 1976, U.S. District Court District of Montana 1976 and California 1977. In legal practice Butte 1981-84.
Staff Attorney Atlantic Richfield Company 1977-81. Staff Attorney and Lobbyist Montana Power Company 1984-91. Fellow American Bar Foundation. Director American Judicature Society. Member National Association of Women Judges, State Bar of Montana, State Bar of California and American Bar Association. Recipient Distinguished Service Award from State Bar of Montana 1991 and Distinguished Alumna Award from Western Michigan University 1992. Member Montana Association of Female Executives, National Association of Female Executives, Kiwanis and Holter Museum. Hobbies include cross-country skiing, fly fishing, reading, traveling, researching family genealogy and playing piano.
Mailing address: P.O. Box 203001, Helena 59620-3001.
Office: 414 Justice Building, Helena 59601.
Telephone: (406) 444-5490.

GUENTHER, Mark *(Judge, Montana District Court Eighteenth Judicial District)*
Office: Law & Justice Center, 615 South Sixteenth Avenue, Bozeman 59715.
Telephone: (406) 582-2140.

HADDON, Sam E. *(Judge, United States District Court District of Montana)* Appointed for life by President George W. Bush to term beginning July 26, 2001.

HADDON, SAM E.—*Continued*

Born West Monroe Louisiana 1937. Educated at Rice University B.S. 1959 and University of Montana J.D. 1965. Law Clerk to Hon. William J. Jameson, U.S. District Court District of Montana 1965-66. Admitted to practice Montana 1965, U.S. District Court District of Montana 1966, U.S. Court of Appeals Ninth Circuit 1966 and U.S. Supreme Court 1975.

Faculty Member University of Montana 1971-93 and 1996-2001. Member 1986 and Chairman 1996-2001 Commission on Practice Montana Supreme Court. Fellow American College of Trial Lawyers and American Bar Foundation. Advocate American Board of Trial Advocates. Member The American Law Institute, American Academy of Appellate Lawyers, American Judicature Society, State Bar of Montana, Western Montana and American Bar Associations. Faculty Member National Institute for Trial Advocacy 1982-88.

Office: U.S. Post Office Building, 215 First Avenue North, Great Falls 59401.
Telephone: (406) 727-8877.

HARADA, Traci *(Justice, Roosevelt County Justice of the Peace Court and Judge, Wolf Point City Court)* Former Judge Poplar City Court.

Office: 400 Second Avenue South, Wolf Point 59201.
Telephone: (406) 653-6261.

HARKIN, Douglas G. *(Judge, Montana District Court Fourth Judicial District)* Elected 1980. Reelected 1986, 1992 and 1998. Current term expires 2004. Born Sidney Montana May 21, 1943. Educated at University of Montana B.S. in Accounting J.D. and The National Judicial College M.J.S. Former County Attorney Ravalli County. USMC.

Office: Missoula County Courthouse, 200 West Broadway, Missoula 59802.
Telephone: (406) 523-4774.
Fax: (406) 523-4899

HARRIS, Samuel *(Justice, Cascade County Justice of the Peace Court)*

Office: Cascade County Courthouse, 415 Second Avenue North, Great Falls 59401.
Telephone: (406) 454-6873.

HAYNES, Jim *(Judge, Montana District Court Twenty-first Judicial District)* Elected Nov 2002 to term beginning Jan 6, 2003. Term expires 2009. Born Schnectady New York Feb 9, 1950. Educated at U.S. Military Academy, University of Arizona B.S. with honors 1972 and University of Montana J.D. with honors 1982. Admitted to practice Montana 1982, U.S. District Court District of Montana 1982, U.S. Court of Appeals Ninth Circuit 1985 and U.S. Supreme Court 1993. In legal practice Hamilton June 1982 to Dec 2002. Justice, Ravalli County Justice of the Peace Court 1984-87.

Deputy Attorney 1982-83 and Public Defender 1988-91 Ravalli County. City Attorney Hamilton 1992-2002. Former Member Montana Trial Lawyers Association, State Bar of Montana and American Bar Association. Previously worked as smokejumper and OTR operator.

Office: 205 Bedford Street, Suite A, Hamilton 59840.
Telephone: (406) 375-6241.
Fax: (406) 375-6382
E-mail address: haynes@bitterroot.net

HEATH, Janice *(Judge, Hardin City Court)* Appointed by City Council to term beginning May 31, 2002. Reappointed Nov 12, 2002 and 2003. Also Justice pro tem, Big Horn County Justice of the Peace Court since May 31, 2002. Born Hardin Montana.

Clerk of District Court Big Horn County 1981-2000. President Montana Association of Clerks of District Court 1986-87. Member Montana Magistrates Association.

Mailing address: P.O. Box 908 Hardin 59034-0908.
Office: 121 West Third Street, Room 210, Hardin 59034.
Telephone: (406) 665-9760.
Fax: (406) 665-9764
E-mail address: Heath65@msn.com

HEGEL, Joe L. *(Judge, Montana District Court Sixteenth Judicial District and Judge, Montana Water Court Lower Missouri River Basin Division)* Elected to District Court Nov 1988. Reelected to subsequent terms. Elected to Water Court by judicial committee. Born Forsyth Montana April 10, 1951. Educated at St. John's University B.A. in Government 1973, University of Montana J.D. 1977 and Boston University LL.M. in Taxation 1978.

Mailing address: P.O. Box 1260, Forsyth 59327.
Telephone: (406) 356-7310.
Fax: (406) 356-2457

HENRY, Kathy *(Justice, Prairie County Justice of the Peace Court and Judge, Terry City Court)*

Mailing address: P.O. Box 40, Terry 59349.
Telephone: (406) 635-4466.

HENSON, John S. *(Judge, Montana District Court Fourth Judicial District)* Appointed by Governor Thomas Lee Judge to term beginning May 1979. Elected to subsequent terms. Born Wadsworth Ohio Sept 29, 1940. Educated at Arizona State University B.S. and University of Kentucky J.D. Former County Attorney Mineral County.

Office: Missoula County Courthouse, 200 West Broadway, Missoula 59802.
Telephone: (406) 523-4771.

HERMAN, Larry D. *(Justice, Yellowstone County Justice of the Peace Court)* Elected to term beginning Jan 1, 1982. Reelected 1986, 1990, 1994, 1998 and 2002. Current term expires Dec 31, 2006. Born Billings Montana Oct 15, 1940. Methodist. Educated at Eastern Montana College B.S. 1965 and University of Montana J.D. 1970. Admitted to practice Montana 1970. Began legal practice Havre 1970. In legal practice Great Falls 1971 and Laurel 1972. Former Judge, Laurel City Court.

City Prosecutor Great Falls 1971-72. Alderman 1974-75, City Attorney 1975-77 and Mayor 1977-82 City of Laurel. Member and Chairman METRA Yellowstone County 1976-79. Member Commission on Courts of Limited Jurisdiction since 1985, American Judicature Society, Montana Magistrates Association, American Judges Association, State Bar of Montana, Yellowstone and American Bar Associations. Named Official of the Year by Laurel Chamber of Commerce 1980. Recipient Certificate of Recognition from City of Laurel 1981 and Certificate of Appreciation from Laurel Public Schools 1981. Petty Officer Third Class (neuropsychiatric technician) USN 1960-64. Member Rotary, Masonic bodies (Blue Lodge, Shrine, Scottish Rite, York Rite), Chamber

HERMAN, LARRY D.—*Continued*

of Commerce and Elks. Interests include history, music, fine arts, chess and skiing.

Mailing address: P.O. Box 35032, Billings 59107.
Telephone: (406) 256-2985.
E-mail address: precipe@AOL.com

HERNANDEZ, Pedro R. *(Justice, Yellowstone County Justice of the Peace Court)*

Mailing address: P.O. Box 35032, Billings 59107.
Telephone: (406) 256-2894.
E-mail address: Juez-1@excite.com

HICKS, Gary D. *(Justice, Lincoln County Justice of the Peace Court)* Elected to term beginning Jan 1, 2003. Term expires Dec 31, 2006. Born Kansas City March 26, 1950. Lutheran.

Member Montana Magistrates Association and National Judicial Association. Enjoys hunting.

Office: 418 Mineral Avenue, Libby 59923.
Telephone: (406) 293-7781.
E-mail address: hicksgsj@frontiernet.net

HOERNING, Candy *(Justice, Beaverhead County Justice of the Peace Court)*

Office: Two South Pacific #16, Dillon 59725.
Telephone: (406) 683-3755.

HOLTER, Robert M. *(Recalled Magistrate Judge, United States District Court District of Montana)* Appointed Magistrate Judge by U.S. District Court judges. Appointed Recalled Magistrate Judge by Judicial Council of the Ninth Circuit. Born Williston North Dakota March 13, 1927. Episcopalian. Educated at University of Montana B.S. J.D. 1954. Admitted to practice Montana 1954. Began legal practice Bozeman 1956. Magistrate, U.S. District Court District of Montana 1972-77. Former Judge, Montana District Court Nineteenth Judicial District, appointed by Governor Thomas L. Judge to term beginning July 23, 1977. Former Judge, Montana Water Courts.

Gallatin County Attorney 1961-62. Chairman Montana Criminal Jury Instruction Commission 1980-91 and Montana Child Support Enforcement Commission 1985-87. Member Montana District Court Committee 1979-85. Member Montana Judges Association (President 1986-87) and State Bar of Montana. Faculty member The National Judicial College 1985-88. Recipient Distinguished Service Award from Jaycees 1965, National Patrolman Award and National Ski Patrol Award. U.S. Army 1945-46 and First Lieutenant USAF 1954-56. Member Rotary Club and Masons. Enjoys skiing, antique collecting, flying and golf.

Office: U.S. Post Office Building, 215 First Avenue North, Great Falls 59401.
Telephone: (406) 727-0028.

HOM, Kenneth W. *(Judge, City Court of Miles City)*
Mailing address: P.O. Box 910, Miles City 59301.
Telephone: (406) 232-5939.

HONZEL, Thomas C. *(Judge, Montana District Court First Judicial District)* Elected Nov 1984. Reelected to subsequent terms. Born Spokane Washington March 1, 1945. Educated at Carroll College B.A. in English and University of Montana School of Law J.D. Former Deputy County Attorney Lewis and Clark County. U.S. Army.

Office: Lewis and Clark County Courthouse, 228 Broadway, Helena 59601.
Telephone: (406) 447-8205.

HOPPE, Craig L. *(Judge, St. Ignatius City Court)* Appointed by City Council to term beginning Nov 1, 1986. Reappointed to subsequent terms. Born Havre Montana March 21, 1950. Lutheran. Educated at Concordia College and University of Montana. Former Justice, Lake County Justice of the Peace Court, appointed Dec 27, 1990.

Member Montana Magistrates Association (Board of Directors 1988, Chairman 1988 and Vice President since 1990 Western District). Recipient Outstanding Volunteer Service to the National Bison Range Award from Fish and Wildlife Service U.S. Department of the Interior 1984. Previously employed by Bureau of Indian Affairs U.S. Department of the Interior. Past President Old Town Development Corporation. Member St. Ignatius Volunteer Fire Department. Enjoys fishing, rifle and pistol target shooting and fine woodworking with emphasis on traditional joinery techniques.

Mailing address: P.O. Box 42, St. Ignatius 59865.
Telephone: (406) 745-3791.
E-mail address: clhoppe@blackfoot.net

HOWARD, John L. "Pete" *(Justice, Teton County Justice of the Peace Court and Judge, Choteau, Dutton and Fairfield City Courts)*

Mailing address: P.O. Box 337, Choteau 59422.
Telephone: (406) 466-5611.

HUMPHREY, Kathleen *(Judge, Ennis City Court)*
Mailing address: P.O. Box 147, Ennis 59729.
Telephone: (406) 682-7339.

HUNTSMAN, Jean L. *(Judge, Lima City Court)* Former Justice, Beaverhead County Justice of the Peace Court.

Mailing address: P.O. Box 107, Lima 59739.
Telephone: (406) 276-3741.

IRIGOIN, Katherine M. *(Judge, Montana District Court Seventh Judicial District)*

Office: Richland County Courthouse, 201 West Main Street, Sidney 59270.
Telephone: (406) 433-5939.
Fax: (406) 433-6879

JAMES, Wanda Dinius *(Justice, Mineral County Justice of the Peace Court and Judge, Alberton and Superior City Courts)* Elected Justice Nov 1998. Appointed to Superior City Court by Town Council to term beginning Jan 1, 1995. Reappointed 1998. Also serves as Special Magistrate Judge, Mineral County Youth Drug Court since 2001. Educated at University of Montana B.A. with high honors 1996. Scholar of the College of Arts and Sciences. Recipient Outstanding Senior in Sociology Presidential Recognition Award 1996. Member Alpha Lambda Delta, Phi Kappa Phi, Golden Key National Honor Society and Mortar Board (Officer). Substitute Justice, Mineral and Sanders County Justice of the Peace Courts 1995-96.

Vice President Western State Montana Magistrates Association. Member National Judges Association. Attended Montana Judicial Institute University of Montana School of Law. Teacher, Substitute Teacher, Tutor and Special Education Aide, Superior School District 1986-

JAMES, WANDA DINIUS—*Continued*

94. Volunteer Department of Education Missoula Community Hospital 1993 and Consortium on Rural Health Care 1995-96. Presenter Montana Gerontology Conference 1996. Enjoys hiking, biking, skiing, rafting, reading, swimming and a diversity of activities, especially those with multi-cultural emphasis.
Mailing address: P.O. Box 658, Superior 59872.
Telephone: (406) 822-3550.
E-mail address: rumble@blackfoot.net

JENSEN, Kathleen *(Justice, Cascade County Justice of the Peace Court)*
Office: Cascade County Courthouse, 415 Second Avenue North, Great Falls 59401.
Telephone: (406) 454-6873.

JESSOP, Morris T. *(Judge, Pinesdale City Court)*
Mailing address: P.O. Box 410268, Pinesdale 59841.

JEWELL, Wallace *(Justice, Lewis and Clark County Justice of the Peace Court)* Former Judge, Havre City Court.
Office: 228 Broadway, Helena 59601-4263.
Telephone: (406) 447-8202.
E-mail address: wjewell@co.lewis-clark.mt.us

JOHNSON, Bradley F. *(Judge, Whitefish City Court)* Elected to term beginning Jan 7, 1986. Reelected 1989, 1993, 1998 and 2001. Born Tulsa Oklahoma 1948. Educated at Southern Methodist University B.B.A. 1970, University of Tulsa J.D. 1973 and University of Montana School of Law 1994-95. Admitted to practice Oklahoma 1974, U.S. District Court District of Montana 1988 and Montana 1990.
Mailing address: P.O. Box 158, Whitefish 59937.
Telephone: (406) 863-2440.

JONES, W. Blair *(Judge, Montana District Court Twenty-second Judicial District)*
Mailing address: P.O. Box 1268, Columbus 59019.
Telephone: (406) 322-5406.
Fax: (406) 322-8429

JONES, Peggy D. *(Justice, Powder River County Justice of the Peace Court)* Former Judge, Broadus City Court.
Mailing address: P.O. Box 488, Broadus 59317.
Telephone: (406) 436-2503.

KAUL, Alvin "Bud" *(Justice, Daniels County Justice of the Peace Court and Judge, Scobey City Court)*
Office: Daniels County Courthouse, Scobey 59263.
Telephone: (406) 487-5432.

KERR, Jean *(Judge, Laurel City Court)*
Mailing address: P.O. Box 10, Laurel 59044.
Telephone: (406) 628-1964.

KIRSCHER, Ralph B. *(Judge, United States Bankruptcy Court District of Montana)* Appointed by U.S. District Court judges to term beginning Nov 18, 1999.
Office: 215 Federal Building & U.S. Courthouse, 400 North Main Street, Butte 59701.
Telephone: (406) 782-3338.

KNISELY, MaryJane McCalla *(Judge, Billings Municipal Court)*
Mailing address: P.O. Box 1178, Billings 59103.
Telephone: (406) 657-8314.
E-mail address: knisleym@magiccity.org

KOBER, Marilyn *(Justice, Stillwater County Justice of the Peace Court and Judge, Columbus City Court)*
Mailing address: P.O. Box 77, Columbus 59019.
Telephone: (406) 322-8040.

KOHN, Barbara "Skip" *(Judge, Darby and Stevensville City Courts)*
Mailing address: P.O. Box 37, Darby 59829.
Telephone: (406) 821-3748.

KRUEGER, Kurt *(Judge, Montana District Court Second Judicial District)* Elected Nov 7, 2000 to term beginning Jan 2, 2001. Term expires Jan 2007. Born Worthington Minnesota May 8, 1952. Educated at Montana State University B.A. and George Mason University School of Law J.D. 1978. In private legal practice Butte 1983-2000.
Staff Attorney Montana Legal Services 1980-83. State Representative District 69 Montana State Legislature 1985-87.
Office: Silver Bow County Courthouse, 155 West Granite, Butte 59701.
Telephone: (406) 723-8262.

KUNST, Mary O'Hara *(Justice, Rosebud County Justice of the Peace Court and Judge, Forsyth City Court)* Elected Justice Nov 3, 1998 to term beginning Jan 1, 1999. Reelected Nov 5, 2002, current term expires Dec 31, 2006. Born Billings Montana.
Member Montana Magistrates Association and National Judges Association.
Mailing address: P.O. Box 504, Forsyth 59327.
Telephone: (406) 356-2638.

KUNTZ, Reuben M. *(Judge, Harlem City Court)*
Mailing address: P.O. Box 579, Harlem 59526.
Telephone: (406) 353-2361.

LANGTON, Jeffrey H. *(Judge, Montana District Court Twenty-first Judicial District)* Elected Nov 3, 1992 to term beginning Jan 1, 1993. Reelected 1998, current term expires 2004. Born Hamilton Montana April 22, 1953. Presbyterian. Educated at University of Montana B.A. with high honors 1975 J.D. 1978. Member Phi Alpha Theta. Admitted to practice Montana 1978 and U.S. District Court District of Montana 1978. In legal practice Hamilton 1978-93. Acting Justice, Ravalli County Justice of the Peace Court 1987-92.
Montana Representative to National Conference of State Trial Judges since 1996. Member 1998-2001 and Chairman 2000-01 Sentence Review Commission Montana Supreme Court. Former Member State Bar of Montana. Member Montana Judges Association, American Judicature Society and American Bar Association. Discussion Leader on Court Management 1994 The National Judicial College. Named Victor Citizen of the Year 1987 and 1993. Secretary-Treasurer Ravalli Bar Library Association 1985-92. Board of Clinical Visitors University of Montana School of Law 1993-99. President Victor Cemetery Association. Vice President Daly Mansion Preservation Trust. Interests include Montana history, current affairs, environmental issues and flyfishing.
Mailing address: P.O. Box 5012, Hamilton 59840.
Office: Ravalli County Courthouse, Hamilton 59840.
Telephone: (406) 375-6241.
Fax: (406) 375-6382

LARSON, John W. *(Judge, Montana District Court Fourth Judicial District)*
Office: Missoula County Courthouse, 200 West Broadway, Missoula 59802.
Telephone: (406) 523-4771.
E-mail address: jlarson@co.missoula.mt.us

LEAPHART, W. William *(Justice, Montana Supreme Court)* Elected to term beginning Jan 3, 1995. Reelected 2002, current term expires Dec 31, 2011. Born Butte Montana Dec 3, 1946. Educated at Whitman College 1965-66 and University of Montana B.A. 1969 J.D. 1972. Associate Editor Montana Law Review 1970-72. Law Clerk to Hon. W. D. Murray, U.S. District Court District of Montana 1972-74. Admitted to practice Montana 1972 and U.S. Supreme Court 1975. In legal practice Montana 1974-95.
Judicial Fellow American Academy of Appellate Lawyers.
Mailing address: P.O. Box 203001, Helena 59620-3001.
Office: 414 Justice Building, 215 North Sanders, Helena 59601.
Telephone: (406) 444-2621.

LEE, Katherine *(Judge, Glendive City Court)*
Office: 300 South Merrill, Glendive 59330.
Telephone: (406) 377-3318.

LEE, Robert *(Justice, Silver Bow County Justice of the Peace Court)*
Office: Silver Bow County Courthouse, Butte 59701.
Telephone: (406) 497-6392.

LOBLE, C. Bruce *(Chief Judge, Montana Water Court)* Appointed by Chief Justice Jean A. Turnage May 14, 1990. Reappointed 1993, 1997 and 2001. Current term expires June 30, 2005. Born Helena Montana Feb 4, 1947. Educated at University of Montana B.A. and J.D. Admitted to practice Montana 1972 and U.S. District Court District of Montana 1972. In legal practice Helena 1973-90.
Co-author "The Rocky Road to Water for Energy" 52 North Dakota L. Rev. 529, 1976, reprinted 13 *Public Land Resources Digest* 334. Member State Bar of Montana (Chairman Section on Land and Natural Resources 1978-82), First Judicial District (President 1978-79) and American Bar Associations. Captain USAR 1969-77.
Mailing address: P.O. Box 1389, Bozeman 59771-1389.
Telephone: (406) 586-4364.

LOUDEN, Donald J. *(Judge, Missoula Municipal Court)*
Office: 435 Ryman, Missoula 59801.
Telephone: (406) 721-5700.

LOVELL, Charles C. *(Senior Judge, United States District Court District of Montana)* Appointed for life by President Ronald Reagan April 4, 1985. Assumed Senior status June 14, 2000, serves by assignment. Born Anaconda Montana Sept 10, 1929. Presbyterian. Educated at University of Montana B.S. 1952 LL.B. 1959 replaced by J.D. Staff member and Associate Editor Montana Law Review 1956-59. Member Phi Delta Phi. Admitted to practice Montana 1959, U.S. District Court District of Montana 1959, U.S. Supreme Court 1969 and U.S. Court of Appeals Ninth Circuit 1970. In legal practice Great Falls 1959-85.
Chief Counsel Attorney General's Office Montana 1969-72. Former Member Commission on Practice Montana Supreme Court. Former Regent American College of Mortgage Attorneys. Member Ninth Circuit District Judges Association, Federal Judges Association, State Bar of Montana (Former Trustee, Director) and American Bar Association. Captain USAF 1952-54.
Mailing address: P.O. Drawer 10115, Helena 59626-0115.
Telephone: (406) 441-1350.

LUCAS, Donald *(Judge, Polson City Court)*
Mailing address: P.O. Box 238, Polson 59860.
Telephone: (406) 883-8219.

LUND, Donna M. *(Justice, Petroleum County Justice of the Peace Court and Judge, Winnett City Court)*
Mailing address: P.O. Box 226, Winnett 59087.
Telephone: (406) 429-5551.

LUTH, Nancy *(Judge, Great Falls Municipal Court)* Former Judge Great Falls City Court.
Mailing address: P.O. Box 5021, Great Falls 59403.
Telephone: (406) 771-1180.
E-mail address: nluth@i.greatfalls.mt.us

LYMPUS, Ted O. *(Judge, Montana District Court Eleventh Judicial District)* Appointed by Governor Stanley G. Stephens to term beginning April 1992. Elected Nov 1994 and 2000. Current term expires Dec 31, 2006. Born Missoula Montana Dec 26, 1942. Protestant. Educated at University of Montana B.A. 1966 J.D. 1972. Law Clerk to Hon. E. Gardner Brownlee, Montana District Court Fourth Judicial District 1970-72. Member Phi Delta Phi. Admitted to practice Montana 1972, U.S. District Court District of Montana 1972 and U.S. Court of Appeals Ninth Circuit 1989. In legal practice Polson 1972-75 and Kalispell 1975-79.
Attorney Flathead County 1979-92. Member Montana County Attorneys Association (President 1989-90), Montana Judges Association, American Judicature Society, State Bar of Montana and Northwest Montana Bar Association. Attended General Jurisdiction Course The National Judicial College 1995 and numerous other CLEs and seminars. E-4 USAR 1966-72. Republican. Enjoys hiking, skiing, boating and playing golf.
Office: 920 South Main, Kalispell 59901.
Telephone: (406) 758-5669.

MACEK, Julie *(Judge, Montana District Court Eighth Judicial District)*
Office: Cascade County Courthouse, Third Floor, Great Falls 59401.
Telephone: (406) 454-6894.

MARION, Tori J. *(Judge, Townsend City Court)*
Office: 129 South Spruce, Townsend 59644.
Telephone: (406) 266-5441.
E-mail address: taratori@mt.net

MARSH, Donna *(Justice, Musselshell County Justice of the Peace Court and Judge, Roundup City Court)*
Mailing address: P.O. Box 660, Roundup 59072.
Telephone: (406) 323-1078.

McCARTER, Dorothy *(Judge, Montana District Court First Judicial District)* Appointed by Governor Stanley G. Stephens Oct 5, 1989. Elected Nov 1992, Nov 1994 and 2000. Current term expires 2006. Born Watertown New York Feb 5, 1947. Jewish. Educated at University of Colorado B.S. 1969 and New England School of Law J.D. 1977. Law Clerk to Hon. Gordon R.

MCCARTER, DOROTHY—*Continued*

Bennett, Montana District Court First Judicial District 1978-81. Admitted to practice Montana 1977, U.S. District Court District of Montana 1977, U.S. Court of Appeals Ninth Circuit 1982 and U.S. Supreme Court 1984.

Assistant Attorney General Montana 1981-89. Assistant U.S. Attorney 1984-89. Member Montana Judges Association and State Bar of Montana. Co-chair Montana Gender Fairness Commission. Board Member Friendship Center, Inc and Montana Board of Crime Control. Member Rotary Club. Enjoys fishing, reading, hiking and camping.

Office: Lewis and Clark County Courthouse, 228 Broadway, Helena 59601.

Telephone: (406) 447-8205.

McCARTER, Mike *(Judge, Montana Workers' Compensation Court)* Appointed by Governor Marc Racicot to term beginning Sept 7, 1993. Reappointed to subsequent term. Born St. Louis Missouri. Educated at University of Colorado B.A. 1970 and Harvard Law School J.D. cum laude 1973. Member Phi Beta Kappa. In legal practice 1973-77, 1982 and 1984-93.

Mailing address: P.O. Box 537, Helena 59624-0537.

Office: 1625 Eleventh Avenue, Helena 59601.

Telephone: (406) 444-7794.

Fax: (406) 444-7798

McEUEN, Rebecca L. *(Judge, Broadus City Court)*

Mailing address: P.O. Box 659, Broadus 59317.

Telephone: (406) 436-2409.

E-mail address: mceuen@mcn.net

McGILLIS, Terry J. *(Justice, Powell County Justice of the Peace Court and Judge, Deer Lodge City Court)* Appointed Justice Sept 1977. Elected 1978, 1982, 1986, 1990, 1994, 1998 and 2002. Current term expires 2006. Appointed Judge Sept 1988. Born Townsend Montana Aug 21, 1944. Catholic. Enjoys cake decorating, sewing, biking and reading.

Office: Powell County Courthouse, Deer Lodge 59722.

Telephone: (406) 846-3680.

McKENNEY, Jessie *(Justice, Sweet Grass County Justice of the Peace Court and Judge, Big Timber City Court)*

Mailing address: P.O. Box 1432, Big Timber 59011.

Telephone: (406) 932-5150.

E-mail address: sgjustice@mcn.net

McKEON, John C. *(Judge, Montana District Court Seventeenth Judicial District)* Appointed by Governor Marc Racicot to term beginning Jan 7, 1994. Elected Nov 1994 and 2000. Term expires Dec 31, 2006. Born Havre Montana Nov 1, 1950. Educated at Gonzaga University B.A. 1972 and University of Montana School of Law J.D. 1975. Admitted to practice Montana 1975 and U.S. District Court District of Montana 1975. In legal practice Malta 1975-94.

Member Montana Judges Association, American Judges Association and State Bar of Montana.

Mailing address: P.O. Box 470, Malta 59538.

Office: Phillips County Courthouse, Malta 59538.

Telephone: (406) 654-1062.

Fax: (406) 654-2363

McKITTRICK, Thomas M. *(Judge, Montana District Court Eighth Judicial District)* Appointed by Governor Ted Schwinden to term beginning Dec 1983. Elected to subsequent terms. Born Anaconda Montana Jan 7, 1944. Educated at Carroll College B.A. in Political Science 1966 and Gonzaga University J.D. Former Deputy County Attorney Cascade County.

Office: Cascade County Courthouse, Third Floor, Great Falls 59401.

Telephone: (406) 454-6894.

McLEAN, Edward P. *(Judge, Montana District Court Fourth Judicial District)* Appointed by Governor Ted Schwinden to term beginning Feb 9, 1989. Elected to subsequent terms. Born Anaconda Montana April 12, 1946. Roman Catholic. Educated at University of Washington and University of Montana B.S. in Business 1969 J.D. 1973. Admitted to practice Montana 1973, U.S. District Court District of Montana 1973 and U.S. Supreme Court 1980. In legal practice Missoula 1973-74.

Deputy County Attorney Missoula County 1973-89. Member Montana State Judges Association and State Bar of Montana. Attended courses on State and Tribal Courts and Jury Standards State Courts Institute The National Judicial College. Enjoys fishing, hunting and wood working.

Office: Missoula County Courthouse, 200 West Broadway, Missoula 59802.

Telephone: (406) 523-4771.

McNEIL, C. B. *(Judge, Montana District Court Twentieth Judicial District)* Elected 1984. Reelected to subsequent terms. Born Anaconda Montana Feb 17, 1937. Educated at Montana School of Mines B.S. in Metallurgical Engineering, University of Alaska and University of Montana J.D.

Delegate Montana Constitutional Convention 1972. Pilot U.S. Army.

Office: Lake County Courthouse, 106 Fourth Avenue East, Polson 59860.

Telephone: (406) 883-7250.

MILLER, Perry *(Justice, Blaine County Justice of the Peace Court and Judge, Chinook City Court)*

Mailing address: P.O. Box 1266, Chinook 59523.

Telephone: (406) 357-2335.

MIZNER, Ted L. *(Judge, Montana District Court Third Judicial District and Judge, Montana Water Court Clark Fork River Basin Division)* Appointed to District Court by Governor Ted Schwinden to term beginning June 1987. Elected to subsequent terms. Elected to Water Court by judicial committee. Born Deer Lodge Montana Oct 21, 1948. Educated at University of Montana B.S.B.A. in Accounting J.D. In legal practice thirteen years.

Former County Attorney Powell County. CPA Montana.

Office: 409 Missouri Avenue, Deer Lodge 59722.

Telephone: (406) 846-3680.

Fax: (406) 846-2784

MOGAN-HARTSOCK, Linda *(Justice, Valley County Justice of the Peace Court and Judge, Fort Peck, Glasgow and Nashua City Courts)*

Office: 501 Court Square, #10, Glasgow 59230.

Telephone: (406) 228-8221.

E-mail address: Chart500@nemont.tel

MOHR, Gregory P. *(Justice, Richland County Justice of the Peace Court and Judge, Sidney City Court)* Elected Justice to term beginning Jan 5, 1987. Reelected

MOHR, GREGORY P.—*Continued*

1990, 1994, 1998 and 2002. Current term expires 2006. Born Iowa City Iowa March 5, 1955. Lutheran. Educated at Iowa State University B.S. 1977.

Member Commission on Courts of Limited Jurisdiction. President Montana Magistrates Association. Completed Courts of Limited Jurisdiction course. Previously employed as field superintendent Balco, Inc. Enjoys hunting, fishing, trapping and karate.

Office: 123 West Main, Sidney 59270.

MOLLOY, Donald W. *(Chief Judge, United States District Court District of Montana)* Appointed for life by President Bill Clinton Aug 16, 1996. Chief Judge since Jan 31, 2001. Born Butte Montana July 18, 1946. Roman Catholic. Educated at University of Montana B.A. 1968 J.D. with high honors 1976. Staff member University of Montana Law Review. Law Clerk to Hon. James F. Battin, U.S. District Court District of Montana 1976-78. Admitted to practice Montana 1976, Crow Tribal Court, U.S. District Court District of Montana, U.S. Court of Appeals Ninth Circuit and U.S. Supreme Court. In legal practice Montana 1978-96.

Author "Must the Paleface Pay to Puff? *Confederated Salish and Kootenai v. Moe*" 36 No. 1 Montana L. Rev. 93, 1975; "Bad Laws Make Hard Cases: *State ex rel Angvall v. District Court,* and the Law of Annulment in Montana" 36 No. 2 Montana L. Rev. 267, 1975; "Punitive Damages" *Montana Lawyer* 1979; President's message *Trial Trends* Fall 1989, Spring 1990, Summer 1990 and Winter 1990. Co-author with Frederick W. Huszagh "Legal Malpractice: A Calculus for Reform" 37 No. 1 Montana L. Rev. 279, 1976. Lecturer on Philosophy of Law Spring 1998 and Speaker "Planning the Closing Argument from the Start of the Case" University of Montana School of Law. Chairman Speedy Trial Act Implementation Committee 1978-79, Appointed Member Civil Justice Expense and Delay Reduction Committee and Peer Review Committee and Member Uniform Rules Commission. Delegate and Lawyer Representative Judicial Conference of the Ninth Circuit 1990-91. Chairman Joint State and Federal Judicial Council Meeting and U.S. Magistrate Search Committee. Fellow Roscoe Pound Society. Member Yellowstone County Claimants Lawyers' Association, Montana Trial Lawyers Association (President 1989-90), Pennsylvania Trial Lawyers Association, Texas Trial Lawyers Association, American Board of Trial Advocates (Founding Member Montana Chapter, Member National Amicus Curiae Committee), American College of Trial Lawyers, American Judicature Society, The Association of Trial Lawyers of America (Board of Governors 1990-91, Key Person Committee 1990-91), National Institute for Trial Advocacy (Sponsor), State Bar of Montana (Ethics Committee, Chairman Federal Practice Section 1990-91, Chairman Committee to Investigate Cost and Delay in Montana Courts), Yellowstone County (President 1994-95) and American Bar Associations. Tort Liability course 1982 and Aviation course 1994 National College of Advocacy, Advanced Trial Advocacy Skills National Institute for Trial Advocacy, Judicial Conference of the Ninth Circuit Aug 19, 1986, Judicial Trial Skills Training Oct 10, 1996, Video Orientation Oct 28, 1996, National Workshop for District Court Judges May 8, 1997 and Federal Judges Association Meeting May 12, 1997.

Lecturer on "Use of Video Depositions in Montana: How to Make it Legal" 1984, "Three Perspectives on Changes in the Federal Rules of Civil Procedure" 1992, "The New Federal Rules of Civil Procedure: Can You Teach Old Dogs New Tricks?" 1994 and "Demonstration of Opening Statements" 1995 Montana Trial Lawyers Association; "Direct and Cross-Exam of a Medical Expert: Demonstration and Discussion" 1986 and "The New Federal Rules of Civil Procedure and the Local Rules of Procedure for the District of Montana" 1994 State Bar of Montana; "Can the Plaintiff Have Any Secrets? Discovery and the Lawyers-Clients Work or Privacy" Wyoming Trial Lawyers Seminar 1992; and "Masters in Trial" The Foundation of the American Board of Trial Advocates 1996. Panelist "Understanding Brain Injury" Wyoming Brain Injury Association 1993 and "Bad Faith" Insurance Adjusters Seminar. Recipient Public Service Award 1990-91 and Trial Lawyer of the Year Award 1993 Montana Trial Lawyers Association. Listed in *The Best Lawyers in America.* USN 1968-73 and Lieutenant USNR. Democratic Precinct Person Billings Heights. Member Central Committee, Democratic Finance Committee and Democratic Party Yellowstone County. Member Montana Democratic Chairman's Council and Montana Democratic Party. Counselor Montana Boy's State 1974-76. Cub Scout Den Leader 1984-85. State Membership Chair U.S. Supreme Court Historical Society 1990-92. Trustee Billings Area Catholic Educational Trust 1992-95. Lay Lector and Eucharistic Minister St. Bernard's Catholic Church. Board of Directors Medlink Corporation and Billings Campfire Girls. President's Advisory Council and Capital Campaign Steering Committee University of Montana. Board of Visitors University of Montana School of Law. Patron of Youth Billings YMCA. Little League and Little Guy Football Coach. Member Montana Pilots Association, Grizzly Athletic Association, Briarwood Club, Aircraft Owners and Pilots Association and American Legion Post 105. Interests include reading, flying, kids, sports and guitar.

Mailing address: P.O. Box 7309, Missoula 59807-7309.

Telephone: (406) 542-7286.

MORTON, Natasha J. *(Justice, Big Horn County Justice of the Peace Court)* Elected Nov 12, 2002 to term beginning Jan 1, 2003. Term expires Dec 31, 2006. Born Plentywood Montana Oct 27, 1955. Educated at University of Montana B.A. 1977 J.D. 1980. Admitted to practice Montana 1980. In legal practice Hardin since 1982.

City Attorney Hardin since 1982. Member State Bar of Montana.

Mailing address: P.O. Box 908, Hardin 59034.

Telephone: (406) 665-9760.

Fax: (406) 665-9764

MURPHY, Lawrence *(Judge, East Helena City Court)*

Mailing address: P.O. Box 1170, East Helena 59635.

Telephone: (406) 227-5321.

NEESE, Donald R. *(Justice, Custer County Justice of the Peace Court)* Elected to term beginning Jan 1, 1999. Reelected 2002, current term expires Dec 31, 2006. Born Billings Montana Oct 5, 1956.

Retired Law Enforcement (20 years). Enjoys restoring Corvettes and old planes and flying and driving anything that will go fast.

Office: 1010 Main Street, Miles City 59301.

NEESE, DONALD R.—*Continued*
Telephone: (406) 874-3408.
Fax: (406) 874-3452

NEILL, Kenneth R. *(Judge, Montana District Court Eighth Judicial District)*
Office: Cascade County Courthouse, Third Floor, Great Falls 59401.
Telephone: (406) 454-6894.

NELSON, James C. *(Justice, Montana Supreme Court)* Appointed by Governor Marc Racicot to term beginning May 10, 1993. Elected Nov 1994 and Nov 1996. Current term expires Jan 2005. Born Moscow Idaho Feb 20, 1944. Roman Catholic. Educated at University of Idaho B.S. cum laude 1966 and George Washington University J.D. cum laude 1974. Admitted to practice Montana 1974, District of Columbia 1975, U.S. District Court District of Montana 1975 and U.S. Court of Appeals Ninth Circuit 1984. In legal practice Cut Bank.
Attorney Glacier County 1979-93. Member State Bar of Montana. First Lieutenant U.S. Army 1962-69. Political affiliation: Non-partisan.
Mailing address: P.O. Box 203001, Helena 59620-3001.
Office: 414 Justice Building, Helena 59601.
Telephone: (406) 444-5570.

OBLAND, Joyce *(Judge, Colstrip City Court)*
Mailing address: P.O. Box 1902, Colstrip 59323.
Telephone: (406) 748-2300.

ODLIN, John E. *(Justice, Missoula County Justice of the Peace Court)*
Office: Missoula County Courthouse, Missoula 59802.
Telephone: (406) 721-5700.

OLSEN, Gary A. *(Justice, Broadwater County Justice of the Peace Court)*
Office: 515 Broadway, Townsend 59644.
Telephone: (406) 266-3145.
E-mail address: Gojo65oly@cs.com

O'MALLEY, Mary Ann *(Justice, Madison County Justice of the Peace Court)*
Mailing address: P.O. Box 277, Virginia City 59765.
Telephone: (406) 843-4237.
E-mail address: jpcourt@3rivers.net

ORTLEY, David *(Justice, Flathead County Justice of the Peace Court)* Appointed by Board of County Commissioners to term beginning Oct 1999. Elected Nov 2000 and Nov 2002. Current term expires Dec 2006. Born Mankato Minnesota. Educated at Mankato State University B.S. in 1980 and Hamline University School of Law J.D. 1983. Admitted to practice Minnesota 1983, U.S. District Courts District of Minnesota 1983 and District of Montana 1989 and U.S. Court of Appeals Ninth Circuit 1996. In legal practice Kalispell Montana Oct 1989 to Dec 1999.
Office: 800 South Main Street, Kalispell 59901.
Telephone: (406) 758-5642.
E-mail address: dortley@co.flathead.mt.us

ORZECH, Karen A. *(Justice, Missoula County Justice of the Peace Court)* Elected Nov 1998 to term beginning Jan 1, 1999. Term expires Dec 31, 2003. Educated at Arizona State University B.S. with honors 1980 Ph.D. with honors 1986.
Chairperson District One Montana Magistrates Association. Attended Judges Training Conference for Courts of Limited Jurisdiction Fall 1998, Spring 1999 and Fall 1999 and The Judicial Institute University of Montana Summer 1999. Named Graduate Student of the Year Arizona State University 1986. Board Member The Parent Aide Program and Children's Visitation Center. Member Kiwanis Club of Missoula.
Office: 200 West Broadway, Missoula 59802.
Telephone: (406) 721-5700.

OSTBY, Carolyn *(Magistrate Judge, United States District Court District of Montana)* Appointed by U.S. District Court judges to term beginning Feb 25, 2002.
Mailing address: P.O. Box 2386, Great Falls 59403.
Telephone: (406) 727-0028.

PERSZYK, Joyce *(Judge, Havre City Court)*
Mailing address: P.O. Box 231, Havre 59501.
Telephone: (406) 265-8575.
E-mail address: 635p@hi-line.net

PETERSON, John L. *(Recalled Judge, United States Bankruptcy Court District of Montana)* Appointed Recalled Judge by the Judicial Council of the Ninth Circuit.
Office: 215 Federal Building & U.S. Courthouse, 400 North Main Street, Butte 59701.
Telephone: (406) 782-3338.

PHILLIPS, E. Wayne *(Judge, Montana District Court Tenth Judicial District)* Elected to term beginning Jan 1, 2001. Term expires Dec 31, 2006. Born Rudyard Montana Oct 27, 1948. Educated at Colorado College B.A. 1971 and University of Montana School of Law J.D. with honors 1990. Associate and Editor Montana Law Review 1988-89. Admitted to practice Montana 1990, U.S. District Court District of Montana and U.S. Court of Appeals Ninth Circuit. In legal practice Stanford and Lewistown Jan 1998 to Dec 2000.
Agency Counsel Montana Fish, Wildlife and Parks 1993-97. Member State Bar of Montana. Deputy Chief Legal Counsel to Governor Stanley G. Stephens 1990-92. Interests include hiking in Glacier Park, history, archaeology and anthropology. Personal Statement or Quote: "Life leads its lover and betrays its rebel."
Mailing address: P.O. Box 1124, Lewistown 59457.
Office: Fergus County Courthouse, Lewistown 59457.
Telephone: (406) 538-8028.
Fax: (406) 538-6076

PITCH, Myron E. *(Judge, Helena City Court)*
Office: 228 Broadway, Helena 59601.
Telephone: (406) 447-8465.

PREZEAU, Michael *(Judge, Montana District Court Nineteenth Judicial District)*
Office: Lincoln County Courthouse, 512 California, Libby 59923.
Telephone: (406) 293-8120.
Fax: (406) 293-9816

REGNIER, Jim *(Justice, Montana Supreme Court)* Elected Nov 1996 to term beginning Jan 6, 1997. Born Aurora Illinois. Educated at Marquette University B.S. 1966 and University of Illinois College of Law J.D. 1973. In legal practice Rochelle 1973-78, Great Falls 1979-91 and Missoula 1991-97.
Contributing Author *Montana Pattern Jury Instructions for Civil Cases.* Lecturer on Alternate Dispute Res-

REGNIER, JIM—*Continued*

olution University of Montana School of Law. Lawyer Representative 1987-89 and Chair Montana Delegation 1989 Judicial Conference of the Ninth Circuit. Founder Federal Practice Section State Bar of Montana. Judicial Fellow American College of Trial Lawyers and International Society of Barristers. Member Commission on Civil Jury Instruction Montana Supreme Court since 1985. Past President Montana Chapter American Board of Trial Advocates. Frequent lecturer at continuing legal education seminars. Completed Mediator Training Attorney-Mediator Institute 1993. Listed in *The Best Lawyers in America* since 1987. USN.

Mailing address: P.O. Box 203001, Helena 59620-3001.

Office: 414 Justice Building, Helena 59601.

Telephone: (406) 444-5494.

RICE, James A., Jr. *(Justice, Montana Supreme Court)* Appointed by Governor Judy Martz to term beginning March 15, 2001. Born Ontario Canada November 15, 1957. Educated at Montana State University B.A. 1979 and University of Montana School of Law J.D. 1982. In legal practice Helena 1985-2001.

Public Defender Lewis and Clark County for four years. Member and Former Majority Whip House of Representatives Montana.

Mailing address: P.O. Box 203001, Helena 59620-3001.

Office: 414 Justice Building, Helena 59601.

Telephone: (406) 444-5573.

ROBERTSON, Thomas *(Justice, Sheridan County Justice of the Peace Court and Judge, Plentywood City Court)*

Office: 210 First Avenue West, Plentywood 59254.

Telephone: (406) 765-2310.

RODEGHIERO, Roy C. *(Judge, Montana Water Court Yellowstone River Basin Division)* Elected by judicial committee. Born Roundup Montana March 28, 1936. Educated at Montana State University B.A. in Business Administration and J.D. Former Judge, Montana District Court Fourteenth Judicial District. Former County Attorney Musselshell County.

Mailing address: P.O. Box 357, Roundup 59072.

Telephone: (406) 323-1701.

Fax: (406) 323-1710

ROSSMILLER, Shannen *(Judge, Conrad City Court)*

Office: 411 1/2 South Main Street, Conrad 59425.

Telephone: (406) 271-3623.

Fax: (406) 271-5602

E-mail address: shannenmtlaw@montana.com

SALVAGNI, Michael A. *(Judge, Montana District Court Eighteenth Judicial District)*

Office: Law & Justice Center, 615 South Sixteenth Avenue, Bozeman 59715.

Telephone: (406) 582-2140.

SANDEFUR, Dirk *(Judge, Montana District Court Eighth Judicial District)*

Office: Cascade County Courthouse, Third Floor, Great Falls 59401.

Telephone: (406) 454-6894.

SANDERS, Patricia *(Judge, Hamilton City Court)*

Office: 223 South Second Street, Hamilton 59840.

Telephone: (406) 363-6823.

SCHAFF, Gail *(Justice, Golden Valley County Justice of the Peace Court and Judge, Ryegate City Court)*

Mailing address: P.O. Box 10, Ryegate 59074.

Telephone: (406) 568-2272.

E-mail address: c-sfi@tcc-cmc.com

SCHUSTER, Gerard M. *(Magistrate Judge, United States District Court District of Montana)* Appointed by U.S. District Court judges. Serves part time. Born Glasgow Montana Aug 21, 1945. Roman Catholic. Educated at University of Montana B.A. 1967 J.D. 1972. Admitted to practice Montana 1972. Began legal practice Wolf Point 1972.

Member National District Attorneys Association, State Bar of Montana and American Bar Association. E-5 U.S. Army 1969-70.

Office: 112 Main Street, Wolf Point 59201.

Telephone: (406) 653-2201.

SCOTT, G. Lewis *(Judge, West Yellowstone City Court)*

Mailing address: P.O. Box 579, West Yellowstone 59758.

Telephone: (406) 646-7845.

E-mail address: Gscott@wyellowstone.com

SEIFFERT, Johnny D. *(Justice, Carbon County Justice of the Peace Court)* Appointed by Carbon County Commissioners April 1993 to term beginning June 1, 1993. Elected Nov 1994, 1998 and 2002. Current term expires Dec 31, 2006. Born Billings Montana Sept 16, 1961.

President Montana Magistrates Association. Attended Montana Judicial Institute University of Montana School of Law 1994 and 1995.

Mailing address: P.O. Box 2, Red Lodge 59068.

Telephone: (406) 446-1440.

SHANSTROM, Jack D. *(Senior Judge, United States District Court District of Montana)* Magistrate 1983-90. Appointed Judge for life by President George Bush to term beginning May 14, 1990. Former Chief Judge. Assumed Senior status Jan 30, 2001, serves by assignment. Born Hewitt Minnesota Nov 30, 1932. Congregationalist. Educated at University of Montana B.S. 1956 B.A. 1957 LL.B. 1957. Admitted to practice Montana 1957 and U.S. District Court District of Montana 1957. In legal practice Livingston 1960-64. Judge, Montana District Court Sixth Judicial District 1965-83.

Attorney Park County 1960-64. First Lieutenant USAF Judge Advocate.

Mailing address: P.O. Box 985, Billings 59103-0985.

Telephone: (406) 247-7011.

SHERLOCK, Jeffrey M. *(Judge, Montana District Court First Judicial District and Judge, Montana Water Court Upper Missouri River Basin Division)* Elected District Judge Nov 1988. Reelected to subsequent terms. Elected to Water Court by judicial committee. Born Great Falls Montana April 3, 1950. Educated at University of Montana B.A. and J.D. Former City Attorney Helena.

Office: Lewis and Clark County Courthouse, 228 Broadway, Helena 59601.

Telephone: (406) 447-8205.

Fax: (406) 447-8275

SHIELDS, Jack *(Justice, Fergus County Justice of the Peace Court and Judge, Lewistown City Court)*
Office: 121 Eighth Avenue South, Lewistown 59457.
Telephone: (406) 538-5418.

SHINABARGER, Ronda *(Justice, Meagher County Justice of the Peace Court and Judge, White Sulphur Springs City Court)*
Mailing address: P.O. Box 698, White Sulphur Springs 59645.
Telephone: (406) 547-3954.

SIMONTON, Richard A. *(Judge, Montana District Court Seventh Judicial District)* Born Wahpeton North Dakota 1944. Educated at Dawson College A.A. with honors 1964, North Dakota State University B.S. with honors 1966 and University of Montana J.D. 1971. Admitted to practice Montana 1971 and North Dakota 1981.
Mailing address: P.O. Box 1249, Glendive 59330-1249.
Telephone: (406) 377-2666.
Fax: (406) 377-7280

SMITH, Gordon L. *(Justice, Gallatin County Justice of the Peace Court and Judge, Bozeman and Manhattan City Courts)* Elected Justice Jan 7, 1991. Reelected 1995 and 1999. Current term expires Dec 31, 2003. Born Bryan Texas April 20, 1932. Church of Jesus Christ of Latter-day Saints. Educated at Texas A&M University B.S. 1954. Former Judge, Belgrade City Court appointed by City Council April 1, 1987. Former Judge, Three Forks City Court.
Member Montana Magistrates Association and National Judges Association. First Lieutenant U.S. Army 1954-56. Previously owned several small businesses. Member Boy Scouts of America and School Board. Enjoys fly tying and fly fishing.
Office: 615 South Sixteenth, Room 168, Bozeman 59715.
Telephone: (406) 582-2191.

SNOWBERGER, Michelle *(Judge, Belgrade City Court)*
Office: 91 East Central, Belgrade 59714.
Telephone: (406) 388-3774.

SPAULDING, Randal I. *(Judge, Montana District Court Fourteenth Judicial District)* Elected to term beginning Jan 2001. Born Fort Campbell Kentucky Nov 25, 1967. Baptist. Educated at Dawson Community College, Minot State University B.S. in Criminal Justice 1990 and University of Montana School of Law J.D. 1993. Admitted to practice Montana 1993 and U.S. District Court District of Montana 1993. In legal practice Roundup July 1994 to Jan 1998.
County Attorney Musselshell County and Golden Valley County 1998-2000. Former Member Montana County Attorneys Association. Member Montana Judges Association and State Bar of Montana. Enjoys hunting and fishing. Personal Statement or Quote: "Civility, civility, civility."
Mailing address: P.O. Box 357, Roundup 59072.
Telephone: (406) 323-1701.
Fax: (406) 323-1710
E-mail address: randalspaulding@hotmail.com

SPENCER, Susan *(Justice, Chouteau County Justice of the Peace Court)*
Mailing address: P.O. Box 459, Fort Benton 59442.
Telephone: (406) 622-5502.

STADLER, Stewart E. *(Judge, Montana District Court Eleventh Judicial District)* Former Justice, Flathead County Justice of the Peace Court.
Office: 920 South Main, Kalispell 59901.
Telephone: (406) 758-5669.

STAHL, Gayle *(Justice, Phillips County Justice of the Peace Court and Judge, Malta City Court)* Elected Judge Nov 1975 to term beginning Jan 1976. Reelected to subsequent terms. Born North Dakota 1949. Lutheran.
Mailing address: P.O. Box 1396, Malta 59538.
Telephone: (406) 654-1118.

STOPPA, Terry L. *(Justice, Hill County Justice of the Peace Court)* Elected to term beginning Jan 2, 2003. Term expires Dec 31, 2006. Born Alpena Michigan.
Office: Hill County Courthouse, Havre 59501.
Telephone: (406) 265-5481.

STRAUB, Anna K. *(Justice, Fallon County Justice of the Peace Court and Judge, Baker City Court)*
Mailing address: P.O. Box 846, Baker 59313.
Telephone: (406) 778-7128.

SWANDAL, William Nels *(Judge, Montana District Court Sixth Judicial District)*
Office: Park County Courthouse, 414 East Callender, Livingston 59047.
Telephone: (406) 222-4132.
Fax: (406) 222-4128

TODD, Gregory R. *(Judge, Montana District Court Thirteenth Judicial District)*
Mailing address: P.O. Box 35026, Billings 59107.
Telephone: (406) 256-2901.
Fax: (406) 256-2736

TRAVIS, Neil Maurice *(Judge, Livingston City Court)* Appointed Judge to term beginning Feb 1, 1983. Elected 1985, 1989, 1993, 1997 and Nov 2001. Current term expires Dec 31, 2005. Certified by Montana Supreme Court. Born Walton New York April 1, 1943. Religious affiliation: Independent Bible. Educated at New York Institute of Photography 1965 and Wayne State University. Former Justice, Park County Justice of the Peace Court.
Member Montana Magistrates Association. Attended The National Judicial College 1984: "Sentencing of Misdemeanants Graduate Session" and "Evidence in Special Courts Specialty Session." Previously worked for Farmington, Michigan Public Schools (custodial administration), First Bank of Livingston and Burlington Northern Railroad. Chief Livingston Volunteer Fire Department for twelve years. Life Member Trout Unlimited. Elder, Board Member and Former Chairman Livingston Bible Church. Enjoys fly fishing, painting with watercolors and acrylics, Christian education, bird watching and banding (Federal bird bander U.S. Fish and Wildlife Service for thirty-seven years), astronomy, photography and gardening.
Office: 414 East Callender Street, Livingston 59047.
Telephone: (406) 823-6013.

TUCKER, Loren *(Judge, Montana District Court Fifth Judicial District)* Elected to term beginning Jan 1, 2001. Term expires Dec 31, 2006. Born Iowa Aug 24,

TUCKER, LOREN—*Continued*

1946. Christian. Educated at Iowa State University B.Sc. 1969 and University of Minnesota School of Law J.D. 1972. Managing Editor Minnesota Law Review 1972. Law Clerk to Hon. Philip Neville, U.S. District Court District of Minnesota 1972-73. Admitted to practice Minnesota 1972, Montana 1976, U.S. District Courts District of Minnesota and District of Montana and U.S. Court of Appeals Ninth Circuit. In legal practice Minneapolis Minnesota 1974-75 and Red Lodge 1976-78 and Virginia City 1981-2000 Montana.

City Attorney Red Lodge 1976-78. County Attorney Madison County 1981-96. Member Montana County Attorneys Association (Board of Directors 1983-85 and 1987-89, President 1994-95, Former Vice President, Former Secretary), State Bar of Montana (Client Security Fund 1985-98, Resolution Committee 1988-94) and Fifth Judicial District Bar Association (Past President, Former Vice President, Former Secretary). Attended The National Judicial College. Republican. Chairman Madison County Republican Central Committee for two years. Former Volunteer Firefighter. Member Lions Club and Benevolent and Protective Order of Elks No. 390.

Mailing address: P.O. Box 185, Virginia City 59755.
Office: Two South Pacific Street, Dillon 59725.
Telephone: (406) 683-5841.
Fax: (406) 683-6473
E-mail address: lotucker@state.mt.us

ULBRICHT, Heidi J. *(Judge, Kalispell Municipal Court)*
Mailing address: P.O. Drawer 1997, Kalispell 59903.
Telephone: (406) 758-7705.
E-mail address: munict@digidyd.com

UTTER, Terry *(Justice, Lincoln County Justice of the Peace Court)*
Office: Highway 93 North, Eureka 59917.
Telephone: (406) 296-3139.

WALDHAUSEN, Bruce *(Justice, Roosevelt County Justice of the Peace Court and Judge, Culbertson and Poplar City Courts)* Appointed Justice to term beginning May 1, 1990. Elected Nov 6, 1990, 1994, 1998 and 2002. Current term expires Dec 31, 2006. Born Culbertson Montana Sept 27, 1940. Lutheran. Educated at Northern Montana College B.A. in Education 1966.

Attends training by Montana Commission on Courts of Limited Jurisdiction Spring and Fall annually. Former farmer for 28 years and elementary school teacher 1961-90.

Mailing address: P.O. Box 421, Culbertson 59218.
Telephone: (406) 787-6607.
Fax: (406) 787-6607

WALKER, Karla K. *(Judge, Three Forks City Court)*
Mailing address: P.O. Box 187, Three Forks 59752-0187.
Office: 106 Main, Three Forks 59752.
Telephone: (406) 285-3431.

WALKER, Tracey D. *(Justice, Carter County Justice of the Peace Court and Judge, Alzada and Ekalaka City Courts)*
Mailing address: P.O. Box 72, Ekalaka 59342.
Telephone: (406) 775-8754.

WALL, Chuck *(Justice, Lake County Justice of the Peace Court)* Elected Nov 5, 2002 to term beginning Jan 1, 2003. Term expires Jan 1, 2007. Born Greer South Carolina Jan 20, 1969. Educated at University of South Carolina 1992 and Cumberland School of Law of Samford University J.D. 1996. Admitted to practice South Carolina 1996 and Montana 1997. In legal practice Ronan and Polson Montana 1996-2003.

President Montana Twentieth Judicial District Bar Association. Member Montana Trial Lawyers Association, The Association of Trial Lawyers of America and American Bar Association. Enjoys hunting, fishing, racquetball and weightlifting. Personal Statement or Quote: "Throughout history, it has been the inaction of those who could have acted, the indifference of those who should have known better, the silence of the voice of justice when it mattered most, that has made it possible for evil to triumph" (Ethiopian Emperor Haile Selassie).

Office: 106 Fourth Avenue East, Polson 59860.
Telephone: (406) 883-7260.
Fax: (406) 883-7343
E-mail address: Chuckwall.jpcourt@lakecounty-mt.org

WARNER, John *(Justice, Montana Supreme Court)* Appointed by Governor Judy Martz to term beginning May 2, 2003. Born Great Falls Montana Jan 22, 1943. Roman Catholic. Educated at University of Montana B.A. 1965 LL.B. 1967. Law Clerk to Montana Supreme Court 1967-68. Member Phi Delta Phi. Admitted to practice Montana 1967, U.S. District Court District of Montana 1967 and U.S. Court of Appeals Ninth Circuit 1982. In legal practice Havre 1968-88. Judge, Montana District Court Twelfth Judicial District Jan 1989 to May 2003.

City Attorney Havre 1984-88. Member Montana Sentence Review Commission 1993-96 and Montana Judicial Standards Commission since 1993. Member State Bar of Montana (Trustee 1980-89, President 1988) and American Bar Association. Attended General Jurisdiction course 1989, Searches and Seizures course 1990 and Advanced Evidence course 1996 The National Judicial College. Member Lions. Enjoys fishing, hunting and skiing.

Mailing address: P.O. Box 203001, Helena 59620-3001.
Office: 414 Justice Building, Helena 59601.
Telephone: (406) 444-5494.

WATTERS, Susan P. *(Judge, Montana District Court Thirteenth Judicial District)*
Mailing address: P.O. Box 35028, Billings 59107.
Telephone: (406) 256-2911.
Fax: (406) 256-2736

WELCH, JoAnne M. *(Justice, Deer Lodge County Justice of the Peace Court and Judge, Anaconda City Court)* Elected Justice to term beginning Jan 1, 2003. Term expires Dec 31, 2006.
Office: 800 Main Street, Anaconda 59711.
Telephone: (406) 563-4025.
Fax: (406) 563-4028.

WHELAN, John W. *(Judge, Montana District Court Second Judicial District)*
Office: Silver Bow County Courthouse, 155 West Granite Street, Butte 59701.
Telephone: (406) 497-6410.

WILLIAMS, Debra *(Justice, Silver Bow County Justice of the Peace Court)*

Office: Silver Bow County Courthouse, Butte 59701.

Telephone: (406) 497-6391.

WILLIAMSON, Ed *(Justice, Dawson County Justice of the Peace Court)* Former Judge, Glendive City Court.

Office: 207 West Bell, Glendive 59330.

Telephone: (406) 377-5425.

WYCKMAN, Scott *(Justice, Gallatin County Justice of the Peace Court)*

Office: 615 South Sixteenth Avenue, Bozeman 59715.

Telephone: (406) 582-2191.

YUNCK, Robert J. *(Justice, Glacier County Justice of the Peace Court and Judge, Cut Bank City Court)*

Office: 512 East Main, Cut Bank 59427.

Telephone: (406) 873-5063.

NEBRASKA

Capital LINCOLN

UNITED STATES DISTRICT COURT DISTRICT OF NEBRASKA

The court sits at Lincoln, North Platte and Omaha. For descriptive information refer to the United States Courts section.

Chief Judge
Richard G. Kopf

Judges
Thomas M. Shanahan
Joseph F. Bataillon
Laurie Smith Camp

Senior Judges
Warren K. Urbom
Lyle E. Strom

Clerk
Gary D. McFarland
1152 U.S. Courthouse
111 South Eighteenth Plaza
Omaha, Nebraska 68102-1322
(402) 661-7350

UNITED STATES MAGISTRATE JUDGES OF NEBRASKA

David L. Piester
Thomas D. Thalken
F. A. Gossett

UNITED STATES BANKRUPTCY COURT OF NEBRASKA

Chief Judge
Timothy J. Mahoney

Clerk
Diane Zech
1125 U.S. Courthouse
111 South Eighteenth Plaza
Omaha, Nebraska 68102-1321
(402) 661-7444

NEBRASKA SUPREME COURT

The Supreme Court is Nebraska's court of last resort. The court consists of a chief justice and six associate justices appointed by the governor from a list submitted by a judicial nominating commission. Justices run for retention at the next general election occurring more than three years from the date of appointment. If retained, they serve additional six-year terms. The chief justice is selected from the state at large and one justice is selected from each of the six Supreme Court judicial districts. Retired justices may serve by Supreme Court appointment.

The court has discretionary review of cases from the Court of Appeals and hears cases regarding constitutional issues. The court has the authority to regulate admission to the bar and the conduct of its members. The court exercises administrative authority over the lower courts and may issue writs necessary to the exercise of proper jurisdiction.

The court usually sits en banc but may sit in two five-member divisions, with the assistance of district court judges or retired justices as needed. The court sits at Lincoln.

Chief Justice
John V. Hendry

Associate Justices

John F. Wright	William M. Connolly
John M. Gerrard	Kenneth C. Stephan
Michael McCormack	Lindsey Miller-Lerman

Clerk
Lanet S. Asmussen
P.O. Box 98910
2413 State Capitol
Lincoln, Nebraska 68509
(402) 471-3731
Fax: (402) 471-3480

Court Administrator
Joseph C. Steele
Office of the State Court Administrator
P.O. Box 98910
1220 State Capitol
Lincoln, Nebraska 68509-8910
(402) 471-3730
Fax: (402) 471-2197

NEBRASKA COURT OF APPEALS

The Court of Appeals is Nebraska's court of intermediate appellate jurisdiction. Created by constitutional amendment and approved by the voters in November 1990, the court began operation in September 1991. The court consists of six judges appointed by the governor from a list submitted by judicial nominating commissions. Judges run for retention at the next general election occurring more than three years from the date of appointment. If retained, they serve additional six-year terms. The chief judge is selected by the Supreme Court for a renewable one-year term.

The court has jurisdiction over all cases appealed from the District Courts except cases involving death penalty or life imprisonment and cases raising constitutionality of statute. The court has final appellate jurisdiction unless the Supreme Court issues a writ of certiorari.

The court sits at Lincoln but may sit elsewhere as required.

NEBRASKA COURT OF APPEALS—*Continued*

Judges

Theodore L. Carlson	Edward E. Hannon
Everett O. Inbody, II	John F. Irwin
Frankie J. Moore	Richard D. Sievers

NEBRASKA DISTRICT COURTS

The District Courts are Nebraska's courts of general jurisdiction. The state is divided into twelve judicial districts. Judges are initially appointed by the governor from a list submitted by a judicial nominating commission. Judges run for election to six-year terms at the next general election occurring more than three years from the date of appointment. A presiding judge is chosen in each district by peer vote to serve a one-year term. Retired judges may serve by Supreme Court appointment.

The courts have general jurisdiction in criminal cases and in all civil cases involving over $45,000. The courts have concurrent jurisdiction with the County Courts in cases involving less than $45,000. Jury trials are available in civil and criminal cases. District Courts have appellate jurisdiction over some cases from County Courts and from several administrative agencies. Most appeals are decided solely on the record; however, small claims appeals are tried de novo in the District Courts. Appeals are to the Court of Appeals.

The courts sit at each county seat.

FIRST JUDICIAL DISTRICT includes Fillmore, Gage, Jefferson, Johnson, Nemaha, Pawnee, Richardson, Saline and Thayer counties. The court sits at Geneva, Beatrice, Fairbury, Tecumseh, Auburn, Pawnee City, Falls City, Wilber and Hebron.

Judges

Daniel E. Bryan, Jr.
Orville L. Coady
Paul W. Korslund

SECOND JUDICIAL DISTRICT includes Cass, Otoe and Sarpy counties. The court sits at Plattsmouth, Nebraska City and Papillion.

Judges

Ronald E. Reagan
Randall L. Rehmeier
George A. Thompson
William B. Zastera

THIRD JUDICIAL DISTRICT includes Lancaster County. The court sits at Lincoln.

Judges

Steven D. Burns	Jeffre Cheuvront
John A. Colborn	Karen B. Flowers
Bernard J. McGinn	Paul D. Merritt, Jr.
Earl J. Witthoff	

FOURTH JUDICIAL DISTRICT includes Douglas County. The court sits at Omaha.

Judges

W. Mark Ashford	Peter C. Bataillon
Robert V. Burkhard	J. Michael Coffey
J. Russell Derr	Sandra L. Dougherty
James T. Gleason	John D. Hartigan, Jr.
Patricia A. Lamberty	Gerald E. Moran
J. Patrick Mullen	Thomas A. Otepka
Gary B. Randall	Gregory M. Schatz
Richard J. Spethman	Joseph S. Troia

FIFTH JUDICIAL DISTRICT includes Boone, Butler, Colfax, Hamilton, Merrick, Nance, Platte, Polk, Saunders, Seward and York counties. The court sits at Albion, David City, Schuyler, Aurora, Central City, Fullerton, Columbus, Osceola, Wahoo, Seward and York.

Judges

Mary C. Gilbride
Alan G. Gless
Michael J. Owens
Robert R. Steinke

SIXTH JUDICIAL DISTRICT includes Burt, Cedar, Dakota, Dixon, Dodge, Thurston and Washington counties. The court sits at Tekamah, Hartington, Dakota City, Ponca, Fremont, Pender and Blair.

Judges

Darvid D. Quist
Maurice S. Redmond

SEVENTH JUDICIAL DISTRICT includes Antelope, Cuming, Knox, Madison, Pierce, Stanton and Wayne counties. The court sits at Neligh, West Point, Center, Madison, Pierce, Stanton and Wayne.

Judges

Robert B. Ensz
Patrick G. Rogers

EIGHTH JUDICIAL DISTRICT includes Blaine, Boyd, Brown, Cherry, Custer, Garfield, Greeley, Holt, Howard, Keya Paha, Loup, Rock, Sherman, Valley and Wheeler counties. The court sits at Brewster, Butte, Ainsworth, Valentine, Broken Bow, Burwell, Greeley, O'Neill, St. Paul, Springview, Taylor, Bassett, Loup City, Ord and Bartlett.

Judges

William B. Cassel
Ronald D. Olberding

NINTH JUDICIAL DISTRICT includes Buffalo and Hall counties. The court sits at Kearney and Grand Island.

Judges

John Philip Icenogle
James D. Livingston
Teresa K. Luther

TENTH JUDICIAL DISTRICT includes Adams, Clay, Franklin, Harlan, Kearney, Nuckolls, Phelps and Webster counties. The court sits at Hastings, Clay Center, Franklin, Alma, Minden, Nelson, Holdrege and Red Cloud.

Judges

Terri S. Harder
Stephen R. Illingworth

ELEVENTH JUDICIAL DISTRICT includes Arthur, Chase, Dawson, Dundy, Frontier, Furnas, Gosper, Hayes, Hitchcock, Hooker, Keith, Lincoln, Logan, McPherson, Perkins, Red Willow and Thomas counties. The court sits at Arthur, Imperial, Lexington, Benkelman, Stockville, Beaver City, Elwood, Hayes Center, Trenton, Mullen, Ogallala, North Platte, Stapleton, Tryon, Grant, McCook and Thedford.

NEBRASKA DISTRICT COURTS—*Continued*

Judges

John J. Battershell
James E. Doyle, IV
John P. Murphy
Donald E. Rowlands

TWELFTH JUDICIAL DISTRICT includes Banner, Box Butte, Cheyenne, Dawes, Deuel, Garden, Grant, Kimball, Morrill, Scotts Bluff, Sheridan and Sioux counties. The court sits at Harrisburg, Alliance, Sidney, Chadron, Chappell, Oshkosh, Hyannis, Kimball, Bridgeport, Gering, Rushville and Harrison.

Judges

Kristine R. Cecava
Paul D. Empson
Robert Owen Hippe
Randall L. Lippstreu
Brian C. Silverman

NEBRASKA COUNTY COURTS

The County Courts are Nebraska's courts of limited jurisdiction. The County Court system was reorganized effective 1973 when the Justice of the Peace and Police Magistrate Courts were combined with the County Courts. Effective July 1, 1985, the Lincoln Municipal Court and the Omaha Municipal Court were also incorporated into the County Courts. The County Court system is composed of twelve judicial districts ranging in size from one to seventeen counties. Judges are appointed by the governor from a list submitted by a judicial nominating commission. Judges run for election to six-year terms at the next general election occurring more than three years from the date of appointment. Except in Douglas and Lancaster counties, each county has at least one clerk magistrate. Most clerk magistrates are non-lawyers and perform administrative and some routine judicial duties. In Douglas and Lancaster counties, these duties are performed by judicial administrators. Retired judges may serve by Supreme Court appointment.

The courts have concurrent jurisdiction with the District Courts in civil cases involving less than $45,000 and over most misdemeanors, including traffic offenses and violations of municipal ordinances. The courts have jurisdiction over juvenile matters, except in Douglas, Lancaster and Sarpy counties where Separate Juvenile Courts have been established. The courts also have exclusive jurisdiction over probate, guardianship, conservatorship, adoption and eminent domain matters. Each County Court has a small claims department where cases involving less than $2,100 may be tried. The courts may conduct preliminary hearings in felony cases.

FIRST JUDICIAL DISTRICT includes Gage, Jefferson, Johnson, Nemaha, Pawnee, Richardson, Saline and Thayer counties. The court sits at Beatrice, Fairbury, Tecumseh, Auburn, Pawnee City, Falls City, Wilber and Hebron.

Judges

Curtis L. Maschman
J. Patrick McArdle
Steven B. Timm

SECOND JUDICIAL DISTRICT includes Cass, Otoe and Sarpy counties. The court sits at Plattsmouth, Nebraska City and Papillion.

Judges

Larry F. Fugit
Todd J. Hutton
John F. Steinheider
Robert C. Wester

THIRD JUDICIAL DISTRICT includes Lancaster County. The court sits at Lincoln.

Judges

Mary L. Doyle	James L. Foster
Jack Burton Lindner	Jean A. Lovell
Gale Pokorny	Laurie Yardley

FOURTH JUDICIAL DISTRICT includes Douglas County. The court sits at Omaha.

Judges

Edna Atkins	Lawrence E. Barrett
Joseph P. Caniglia	Samuel V. Cooper
Marcena M. Hendrix	John E. Huber
Darryl R. Lowe	Jeffrey Marcuzzo
Thomas G. McQuade	Jane H. Prochaska
Stephen M. Swartz	Lyn V. White

FIFTH JUDICIAL DISTRICT includes Boone, Butler, Colfax, Hamilton, Merrick, Nance, Platte, Polk, Saunders, Seward and York counties. The court sits at Albion, David City, Schulyer, Aurora, Central City, Fullerton, Columbus, Osceola, Wahoo, Seward and York.

Judges

Curtis H. Evans	Gary F. Hatfield
Patrick R. McDermott	Marvin V. Miller
Gerald E. Rouse	Frank J. Skorupa

SIXTH JUDICIAL DISTRICT includes Burt, Cedar, Dakota, Dixon, Dodge, Thurston and Washington counties. The court sits at Tekamah, Hartington, Dakota City, Ponca, Fremont, Pender and Blair.

Judges

Daniel J. Beckwith
Kurt Rager
Paul R. Robinson, Sr.
C. Matthew Samuelson

SEVENTH JUDICIAL DISTRICT includes Antelope, Cuming, Knox, Madison, Pierce, Stanton and Wayne counties. The court sits at Neligh, West Point, Center, Madison, Pierce, Stanton and Wayne.

Judges

Richard W. Krepela
Philip R. Riley
Donna F. Taylor

EIGHTH JUDICIAL DISTRICT includes Blaine, Boyd, Brown, Cherry, Custer, Garfield, Greeley, Holt, Howard, Loup, Keya Paha, Rock, Sherman, Valley and Wheeler counties. The court sits at Brewster, Butte, Ainsworth, Valentine, Broken Bow, Burwell, Greeley, O'Neill, St. Paul, Taylor, Springview, Bassett, Loup City, Ord and Bartlett.

Judges

Alan L. Brodbeck
August F. Schuman
Gary G. Washburn

NEBRASKA COUNTY COURTS—*Continued*

NINTH JUDICIAL DISTRICT includes Buffalo and Hall counties. The court sits at Kearney and Grand Island.

Judges
Graten D. Beavers
David A. Bush
Gerald R. Jorgensen, Jr.
Mac Martin

TENTH JUDICIAL DISTRICT includes Adams, Clay, Fillmore, Franklin, Harlan, Kearney, Nuckolls, Phelps and Webster counties. The court sits at Hastings, Clay Center, Geneva, Franklin, Alma, Minden, Nelson, Holdrege and Red Cloud.

Judges
Robert A. Ide
Michael Offner
Jack Robert Ott

ELEVENTH JUDICIAL DISTRICT includes Arthur, Chase, Dawson, Dundy, Frontier, Furnas, Gosper, Hayes, Hitchcock, Hooker, Keith, Lincoln, Logan, McPherson, Perkins, Red Willow and Thomas counties. The court sits at Arthur, Imperial, Lexington, Benkelman, Stockville, Beaver City, Elwood, Hayes Center, Trenton, Mullen, Ogallala, North Platte, Stapleton, Tryon, Grant, McCook and Thedford.

Judges
Carlton E. Clark
Cloyd Clark
Kent E. Florom
B. Bert Leffler
Kent D. Turnbull

TWELFTH JUDICIAL DISTRICT includes Banner, Box Butte, Cheyenne, Dawes, Deuel, Garden, Grant, Kimball, Morrill, Scotts Bluff, Sheridan and Sioux counties. The court sits at Harrisburg, Alliance, Sidney, Chadron, Chappell, Oshkosh, Hyannis, Kimball, Bridgeport, Gering, Rushville and Harrison.

Judges
G. Glenn Camerer
James T. Hansen
Charles Plantz
Thomas H. Dorwart
James L. Macken
C. G. Wallace

NEBRASKA WORKERS' COMPENSATION COURT

The Workers' Compensation Court is a court of special jurisdiction in Nebraska. The court consists of a presiding judge and six judges initially appointed by the governor. Judges run for election to six-year terms at the next general election occurring more than three years from the date of appointment. The presiding judge is chosen by peer vote to serve a two-year term.

The court has original jurisdiction to determine all controversies arising under the Nebraska Workers' Compensation Act. The hearings are usually held within the county where the accident occurred. The first hearing is before a single judge. If an appeal is made, a three-person panel sits at the rehearing; any further appeal is made to the Court of Appeals.

The court has statewide jurisdiction, and the judges travel to all parts of the state to hold hearings at the county seats.

Presiding Judge
Michael K. High

Judges
Ronald L. Brown
James R. Coe
John R. Hoffert
Michael P. Cavel
J. Michael Fitzgerald
Laureen K. Van Norman

NEBRASKA SEPARATE JUVENILE COURTS

The Separate Juvenile Courts are courts of special countywide jurisdiction in Nebraska and may be established in counties with populations of more than 75,000. Currently they are established only in Douglas, Lancaster and Sarpy counties. Judges are initially appointed by the governor. Judges run for election to six-year terms at the next general election occurring more than three years from the date of appointment. A presiding judge may be chosen in each court by peer vote to serve a one-year term.

The courts have exclusive original jurisdiction over all juveniles under the age of eighteen who are dependent, neglected, or in need of special supervision, and over all juveniles under the age of sixteen who are alleged to have committed a misdemeanor. The courts have concurrent jurisdiction with the District Courts over juveniles who are alleged to have committed a felony and with the County Courts over juveniles sixteen or seventeen years of age who are alleged to have committed misdemeanors. If no Separate Juvenile Court is established, the County Court has exclusive jurisdiction. Appeals are to the Court of Appeals.

The courts sit at Omaha, Lincoln and Papillion.

DOUGLAS COUNTY

Judges
Elizabeth Crnkovich
Vernon Daniels
Douglas F. Johnson
Christopher Kelly
Wadie Thomas

LANCASTER COUNTY

Judges
Thomas B. Dawson
Linda S. Porter
Toni G. Thorson

SARPY COUNTY

Judges
Lawrence D. Gendler
Robert B. O'Neal

Nebraska Counties and County Seats

Adams
Hastings

Antelope
Neligh

Arthur
Arthur

Banner
Harrisburg

Blaine
Brewster

Boone
Albion

Box Butte
Alliance

Boyd
Butte

Brown
Ainsworth

Buffalo
Kearney

Burt
Tekamah

Butler
David City

Cass
Plattsmouth

Cedar
Hartington

Chase
Imperial

Cherry
Valentine

Cheyenne
Sidney

Clay
Clay Center

Colfax
Schuyler

Cuming
West Point

Custer
Broken Bow

Dakota
Dakota City

Dawes
Chadron

Dawson
Lexington

Deuel
Chappell

Dixon
Ponca

Dodge
Fremont

Douglas
Omaha

Dundy
Benkelman

Fillmore
Geneva

Franklin
Franklin

Frontier
Stockville

Furnas
Beaver City

Gage
Beatrice

Garden
Oshkosh

Garfield
Burwell

Gosper
Elwood

Grant
Hyannis

Greeley
Greeley

Hall
Grand Island

Hamilton
Aurora

Harlan
Alma

Hayes
Hayes Center

Hitchcock
Trenton

Holt
O'Neill

Hooker
Mullen

Howard
St. Paul

Jefferson
Fairbury

Johnson
Tecumseh

Kearney
Minden

Keith
Ogallala

Keya Paha
Springview

Kimball
Kimball

Knox
Center

Lancaster
Lincoln

Lincoln
North Platte

Logan
Stapleton

Loup
Taylor

Madison
Madison

McPherson
Tryon

Merrick
Central City

Morrill
Bridgeport

Nance
Fullerton

Nemaha
Auburn

Nuckolls
Nelson

Otoe
Nebraska City

Pawnee
Pawnee City

Perkins
Grant

Phelps
Holdrege

Pierce
Pierce

Platte
Columbus

Polk
Osceola

Red Willow
McCook

Richardson
Falls City

Rock
Bassett

Saline
Wilber

Sarpy
Papillion

Saunders
Wahoo

Scotts Bluff
Gering

Seward
Seward

Sheridan
Rushville

Sherman
Loup City

Sioux
Harrison

Stanton
Stanton

Thayer
Hebron

Thomas
Thedford

Thurston
Pender

Valley
Ord

Washington
Blair

Wayne
Wayne

Webster
Red Cloud

Wheeler
Bartlett

York
York

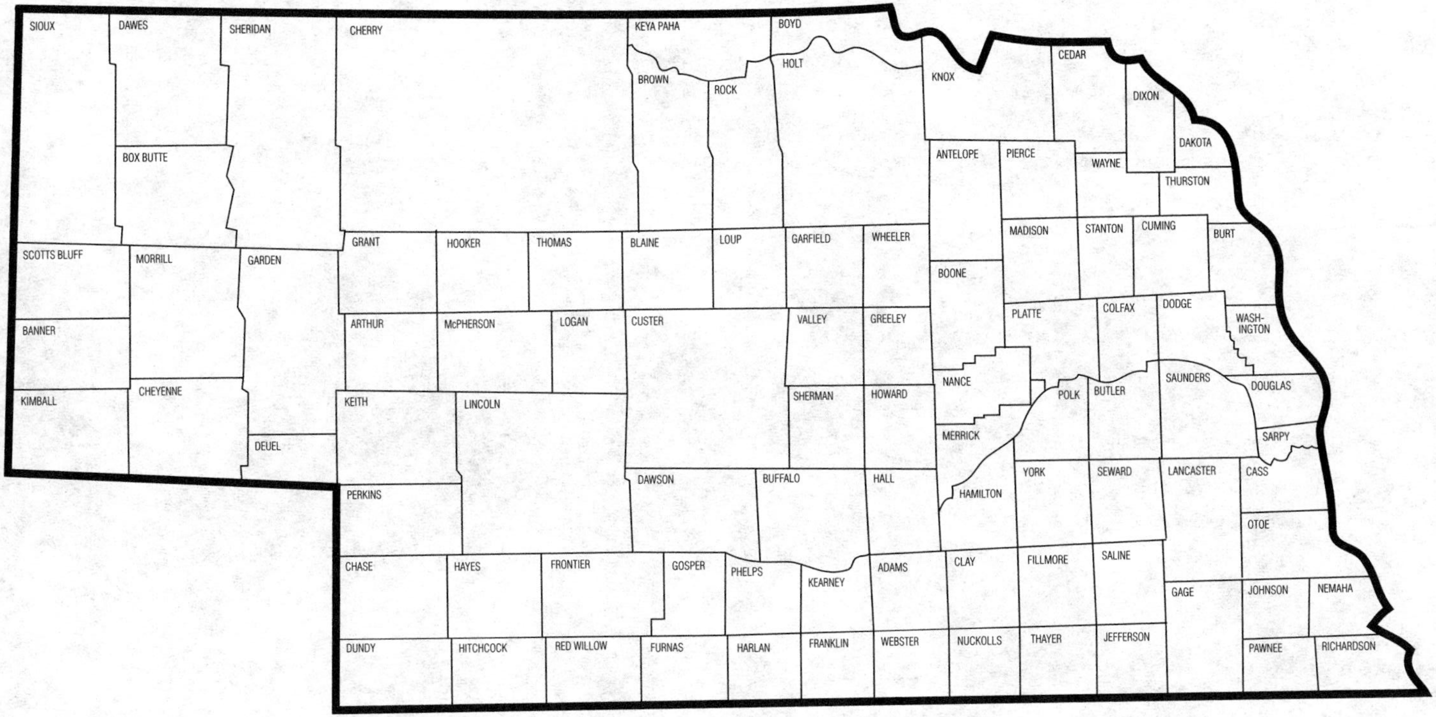
SIOUX
DAWES
SHERIDAN
CHERRY
KEYA PAHA
BOYD
BROWN
ROCK
HOLT
KNOX
CEDAR
DIXON
DAKOTA
BOX BUTTE
ANTELOPE
PIERCE
WAYNE
THURSTON
SCOTTS BLUFF
MORRILL
GARDEN
GRANT
HOOKER
THOMAS
BLAINE
LOUP
GARFIELD
WHEELER
MADISON
STANTON
CUMING
BURT
BOONE
BANNER
ARTHUR
McPHERSON
LOGAN
CUSTER
VALLEY
GREELEY
PLATTE
COLFAX
DODGE
WASH-
INGTON
KIMBALL
CHEYENNE
KEITH
LINCOLN
SHERMAN
HOWARD
NANCE
POLK
BUTLER
SAUNDERS
DOUGLAS
DEUEL
MERRICK
SARPY
PERKINS
DAWSON
BUFFALO
HALL
HAMILTON
YORK
SEWARD
LANCASTER
CASS
OTOE
CHASE
HAYES
FRONTIER
GOSPER
PHELPS
KEARNEY
ADAMS
CLAY
FILLMORE
SALINE
GAGE
JOHNSON
NEMAHA
DUNDY
HITCHCOCK
RED WILLOW
FURNAS
HARLAN
FRANKLIN
WEBSTER
NUCKOLLS
THAYER
JEFFERSON
PAWNEE
RICHARDSON

UNITED STATES DISTRICT COURT DISTRICT OF NEBRASKA

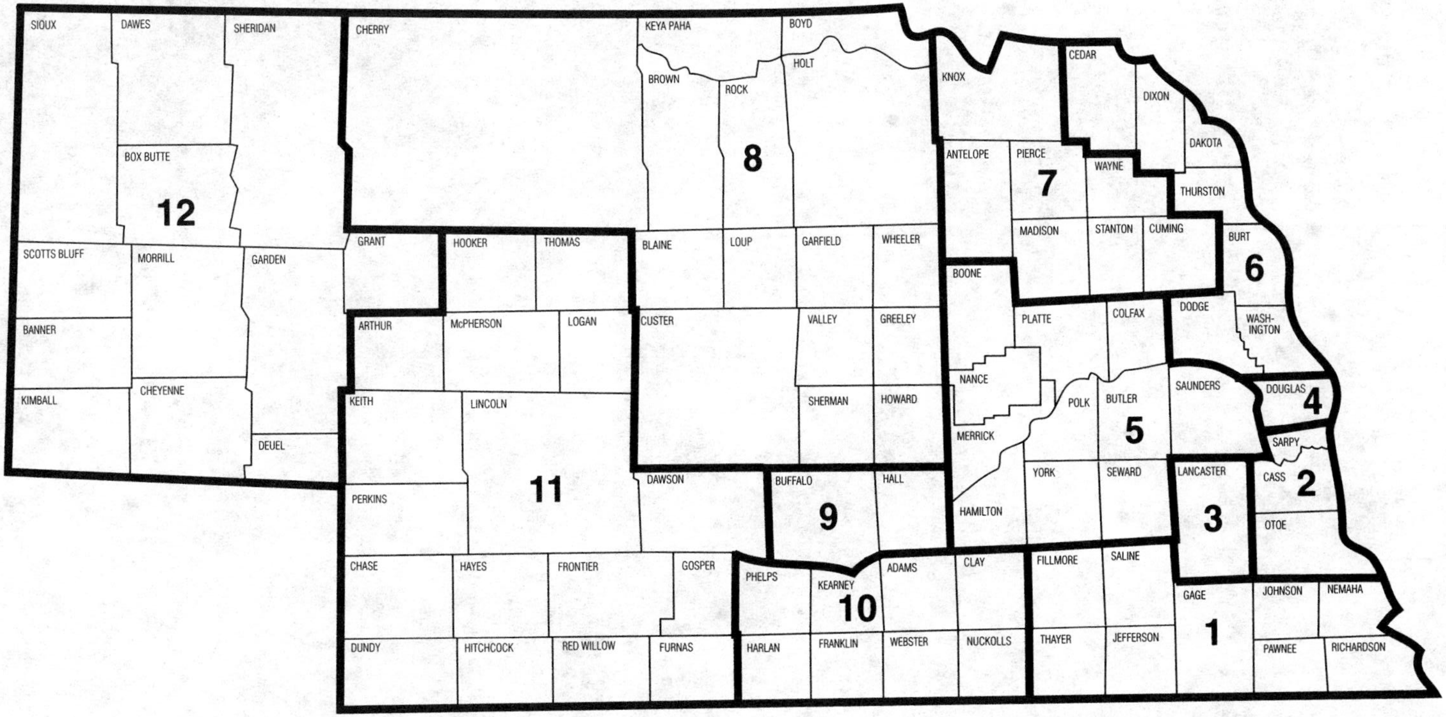
SIOUX
DAWES
SHERIDAN
CHERRY
KEYA PAHA
BOYD
BROWN
ROCK
HOLT
KNOX
CEDAR
DIXON
DAKOTA
BOX BUTTE
12
8
ANTELOPE
PIERCE
7
WAYNE
THURSTON
MADISON
STANTON
CUMING
BURT
6
SCOTTS BLUFF
MORRILL
GARDEN
GRANT
HOOKER
THOMAS
BLAINE
LOUP
GARFIELD
WHEELER
BOONE
PLATTE
COLFAX
DODGE
WASH-INGTON
BANNER
ARTHUR
McPHERSON
LOGAN
CUSTER
VALLEY
GREELEY
NANCE
SAUNDERS
DOUGLAS
4
KIMBALL
CHEYENNE
KEITH
LINCOLN
SHERMAN
HOWARD
POLK
BUTLER
5
MERRICK
SARPY
DEUEL
DAWSON
BUFFALO
HALL
YORK
SEWARD
LANCASTER
CASS
2
PERKINS
11
9
HAMILTON
3
OTOE
CHASE
HAYES
FRONTIER
GOSPER
PHELPS
KEARNEY
ADAMS
CLAY
FILLMORE
SALINE
GAGE
JOHNSON
NEMAHA
10
1
DUNDY
HITCHCOCK
RED WILLOW
FURNAS
HARLAN
FRANKLIN
WEBSTER
NUCKOLLS
THAYER
JEFFERSON
PAWNEE
RICHARDSON

JUDICIAL DISTRICTS OF NEBRASKA DISTRICT COURTS

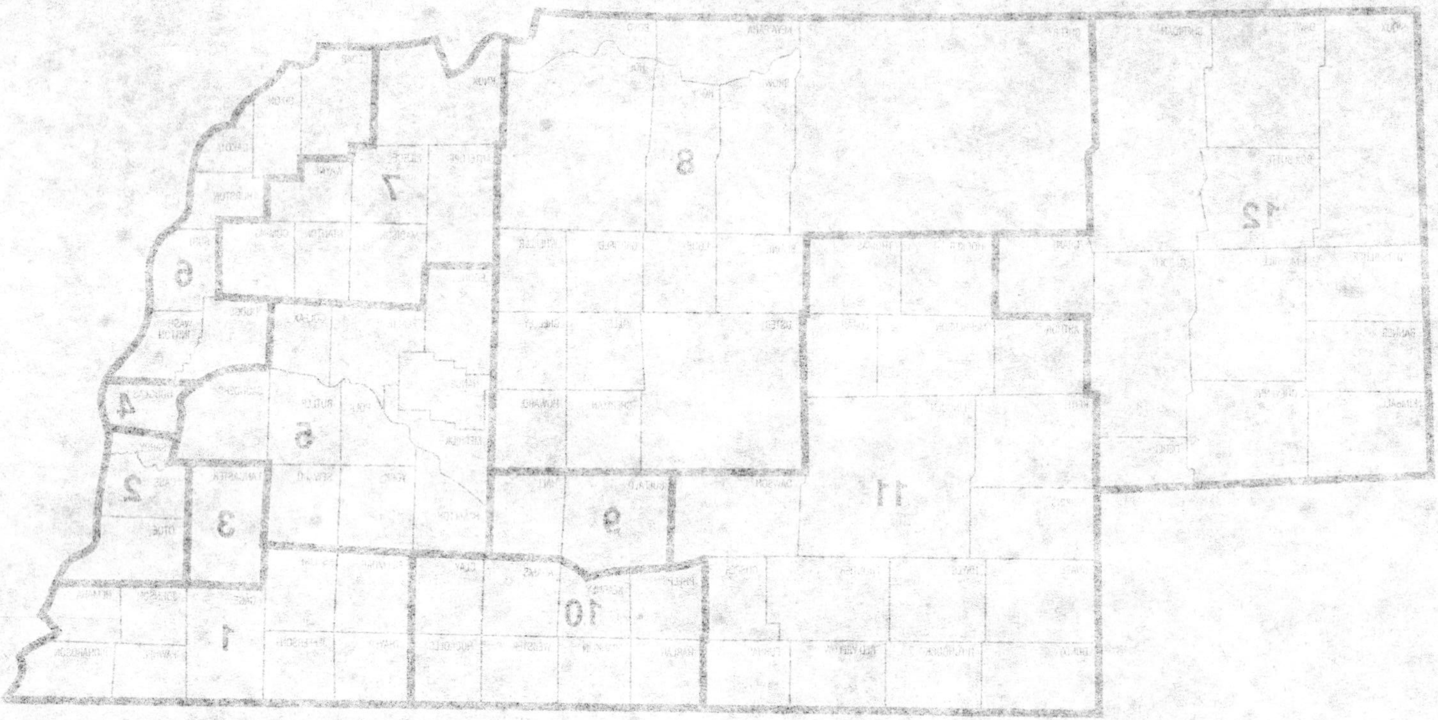
1
2
3
4
5
6
7
8
9
10
11
12

JUDICIAL DISTRICTS OF NEBRASKA DISTRICT COURTS

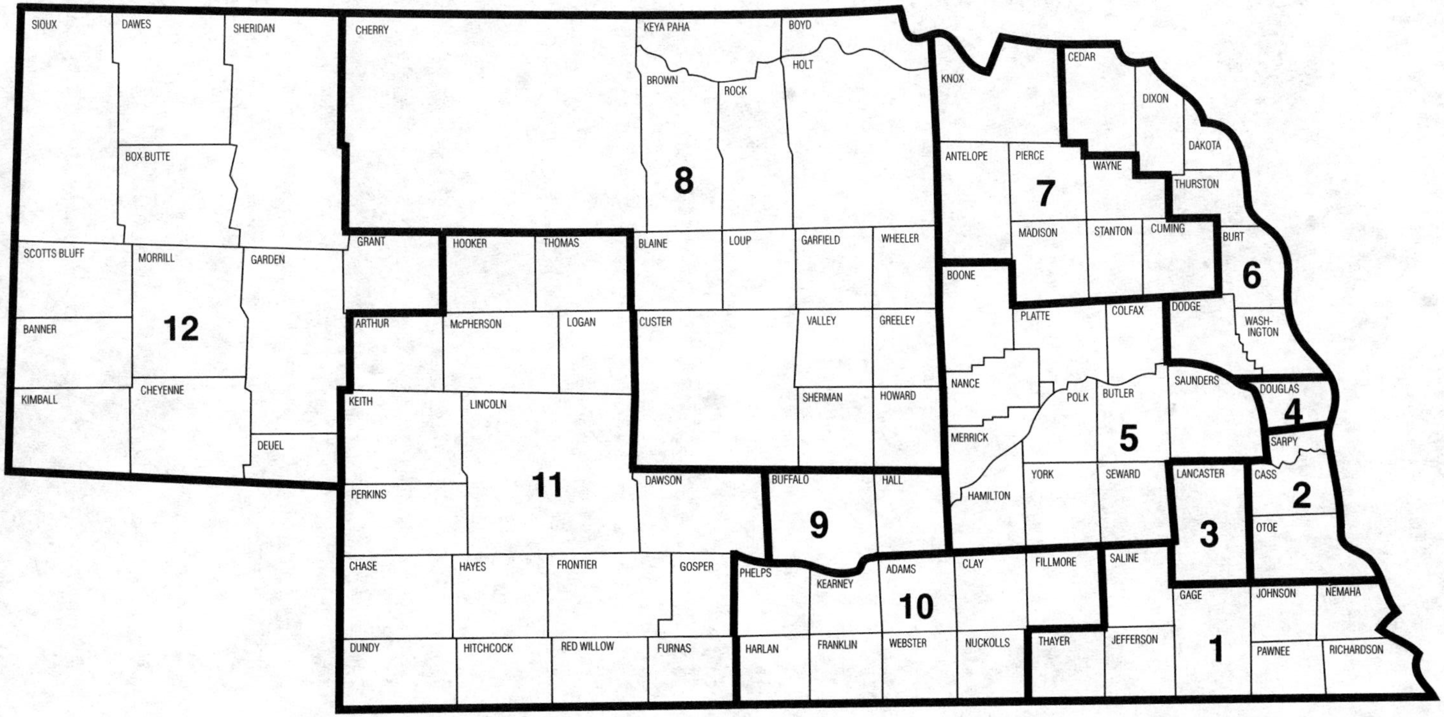
SIOUX
DAWES
SHERIDAN
CHERRY
KEYA PAHA
BOYD
BROWN
ROCK
HOLT
KNOX
CEDAR
DIXON
DAKOTA
BOX BUTTE
8
ANTELOPE
PIERCE
WAYNE
THURSTON
7
MADISON
STANTON
CUMING
BURT
SCOTTS BLUFF
MORRILL
GARDEN
GRANT
HOOKER
THOMAS
BLAINE
LOUP
GARFIELD
WHEELER
BOONE
6
BANNER
12
ARTHUR
McPHERSON
LOGAN
CUSTER
VALLEY
GREELEY
PLATTE
COLFAX
DODGE
WASH-
INGTON
KIMBALL
CHEYENNE
KEITH
LINCOLN
SHERMAN
HOWARD
NANCE
POLK
BUTLER
SAUNDERS
DOUGLAS
4
DEUEL
MERRICK
5
SARPY
PERKINS
11
DAWSON
BUFFALO
HALL
HAMILTON
YORK
SEWARD
LANCASTER
CASS
2
9
3
OTOE
CHASE
HAYES
FRONTIER
GOSPER
PHELPS
KEARNEY
ADAMS
CLAY
FILLMORE
SALINE
10
GAGE
JOHNSON
NEMAHA
DUNDY
HITCHCOCK
RED WILLOW
FURNAS
HARLAN
FRANKLIN
WEBSTER
NUCKOLLS
THAYER
JEFFERSON
1
PAWNEE
RICHARDSON

JUDICIAL DISTRICTS OF NEBRASKA COUNTY COURTS

NEBRASKA

ASHFORD, W. Mark *(Judge, Nebraska District Court Fourth Judicial District)* Appointed by Governor Mike Johanns. Former Judge, Nebraska County Court Fourth Judicial District.
Office: 1701 Farnam, Omaha 68183.
Telephone: (402) 444-7011.
Fax: (402) 996-8164

ATKINS, Edna *(Judge, Nebraska County Court Fourth Judicial District)* Appointed by governor.
Office: 1701 Farnam Street, Omaha 68183.
Telephone: (402) 444-4230.
Fax: (402) 444-6890

BARRETT, Lawrence E. *(Judge, Nebraska County Court Fourth Judicial District)* Appointed by Governor E. Benjamin Nelson.
Office: 1819 Farnam Street, Omaha 68183.
Telephone: (402) 444-5430.
Fax: (402) 444-6890

BATAILLON, Joseph F. *(Judge, United States District Court District of Nebraska)* Appointed for life by President Bill Clinton 1997. Born Omaha Nebraska Oct 3, 1949. Educated at Creighton University B.A. 1971 J.D. 1974. In legal practice Omaha 1980-97.
Deputy Public Defender Douglas County 1974-80.
Office: 3259 U.S. Courthouse, 111 South Eighteenth Plaza, Omaha 68102.
Telephone: (402) 661-7302.

BATAILLON, Peter C. *(Judge, Nebraska District Court Fourth Judicial District)* Appointed by Governor Mike Johanns.
Office: 1701 Farnam, Omaha 68183.
Telephone: (402) 444-7007.
Fax: (402) 444-8158

BATTERSHELL, John J. *(Judge, Nebraska District Court Eleventh Judicial District)* Appointed by governor.
Mailing address: P.O. Box 847, McCook 69001.
Telephone: (308) 345-4539.
Fax: (308) 345-7907

BEAVERS, Graten D. *(Judge, Nebraska County Court Ninth Judicial District)* Appointed by Governor E. Benjamin Nelson April 1991 to term beginning May 15, 1991. Retained by election Nov 1994 and 2000. Current term expires Jan 2007. Currently serves as Presiding Judge. Born Geneva Nebraska Sept 19, 1949. Methodist. Educated at University of Nebraska B.S. 1971 J.D. 1974. Admitted to practice Nebraska 1974.
Member Buffalo County (President) and Nebraska State Bar Associations. Colonel, JAGC since 1971 and Military Judge since 1993 USAR.
Mailing address: P.O. Box 520, Kearney 68848.
Telephone: (308) 236-1229.
Fax: (308) 236-1243

BECKWITH, Daniel J. *(Judge, Nebraska County Court Sixth Judicial District)* Appointed by Governor J. J. Exon to term beginning Feb 2, 1976. Retained by election. Born Dodge County Nebraska April 20, 1946. Educated at Midland Lutheran College B.A. 1968 and Creighton University J.D. 1973. Admitted to practice Nebraska 1973. Began legal practice Albion 1973. In legal practice Fremont 1974-76.
Member Boone County 1973-74, Dodge County and Nebraska State Bar Associations. Petty Officer Second Class USNR 1963-72. Member First Christian Church. Enjoys photography, backpacking and his family.
Office: 428 North Broad, Fremont 68025.
Telephone: (402) 727-2755.
Fax: (402) 727-2762

BRODBECK, Alan L. *(Judge, Nebraska County Court Eighth Judicial District)* Appointed by Governor Bob Kerrey to term beginning March 15, 1984. Retained by election. Born Orange California March 12, 1951. Methodist. Educated at Dana College B.A. 1973 and University of Nebraska J.D. 1976. Member Phi Delta Phi. Admitted to practice Nebraska 1976. Began legal practice Neligh 1976.
County Attorney Antelope County 1977-84. Member Nebraska County Judges Association and Nebraska State Bar Association. Republican. Enjoys golf.
Office: 204 North Fourth Street, O'Neill 68763.
Telephone: (402) 336-1662.
Fax: (402) 336-1663

BROWN, Ronald L. *(Judge, Nebraska Workers' Compensation Court)* Appointed by Governor E. Benjamin Nelson April 8, 1994. Retained by election. Former Presiding Judge. Educated at Dana College B.S. cum laude and Creighton University School of Law J.D. In legal practice 1979-94.
Assistant Public Defender Douglas County 1977-78. Member Nebraska Association of Trial Attorneys, The Association of Trial Lawyers of America and Nebraska State Bar Association.
Office: 1701 Farnam, Omaha 68183.
Telephone: (402) 595-3901.

BRYAN, Daniel E., Jr. *(Judge, Nebraska District Court First Judicial District)* Appointed by Governor Mike Johanns. Former Judge, Nebraska County Court Tenth Judicial District.
Office: 1824 N Street, Auburn 68305.
Telephone: (402) 274-5559.
Fax: (402) 274-4478

BURKHARD, Robert V. *(Judge, Nebraska District Court Fourth Judicial District)* Appointed by Governor Charles Thone to term beginning Feb 1, 1980. Retained by election 1984, 1990, 1996 and 2002. Current term expires Jan 2009. Born Omaha Nebraska Feb 27, 1928. Roman Catholic. Educated at Creighton University LL.B. 1952. Admitted to practice Nebraska 1952 and U.S. District Court District of Nebraska 1959.
Office: 1701 Farnam, Omaha 68183.
Telephone: (402) 444-7009.
Fax: (402) 996-8161

BURNS, Steven D. *(Judge, Nebraska District Court Third Judicial District)* Appointed by Governor E. Benjamin Nelson March 27, 1997 to term beginning May 1, 1997. Retained by election, current term expires Jan

BURNS, STEVEN D.—*Continued*

2007. Born Marshalltown Iowa March 20, 1948. Educated at University of Nebraska at Lincoln B.A. 1971 J.D. 1973. Admitted to practice Nebraska 1973, U.S. District Court District of Nebraska, U.S. Court of Appeals Eighth Circuit and U.S. Supreme Court. In legal practice Lincoln 1973-97.

Member Lincoln and Nebraska State Bar Associations. Attended The National Judicial College.

Office: 575 South Tenth Street, Lincoln 68508.
Telephone: (402) 441-7605.
Fax: (402) 441-6190
E-mail address: sburns@ci.lincoln.ne.us

BUSH, David A. *(Judge, Nebraska County Court Ninth Judicial District)* Appointed by governor.

Office: 111 West First, Suite 1, Grand Island 68802.
Telephone: (308) 385-5135.
Fax: (308) 385-5138

CAMERER, G. Glenn *(Judge, Nebraska County Court Twelfth Judicial District)* Elected to term beginning Jan 3, 1973. Retained by election, current term expires Jan 2007. Born Sergeant Bluff Iowa May 25, 1945. Episcopalian. Educated at University of South Dakota B.S. 1967 J.D. 1970. Admitted to practice Nebraska 1970. Began legal practice Gering 1970.

Member Scotts Bluff County, Nebraska State and American Bar Associations. Democrat. Enjoys hunting, skiing, camping and bridge.

Office: 1725 Tenth Street, Gering 69341.
Telephone: (308) 436-6648.
Fax: (308) 436-6782

CAMP, Laurie Smith *(Judge, United States District Court District of Nebraska)* Appointed for life by President George W. Bush to term beginning Nov 2, 2001. Born Omaha Nebraska 1953. Educated at Stanford University B.A. 1974 and University of Nebraska College of Law J.D. 1977. In legal practice 1978-80.

General Counsel Nebraska Department of Correctional Services 1980-91. Chief Civil Rights Section 1991-95 and Chief Deputy Attorney General 1995-2001 Nebraska Department of Justice.

Office: 3210 U.S. Courthouse, 111 South Eighteenth Plaza, Omaha 68102.
Telephone: (402) 661-7323.

CANIGLIA, Joseph P. *(Judge, Nebraska County Court Fourth Judicial District)* Appointed by Governor E. Benjamin Nelson.

Office: 1701 Farnam, Omaha 68183.
Telephone: (402) 444-5434.
Fax: (402) 444-6890

CARLSON, Theodore L. *(Judge, Nebraska Court of Appeals)* Appointed by governor. Born Wakefield Nebraska July 23, 1938. Educated at Omaha University B.A. 1960 and Creighton University Law School J.D. 1963. Admitted to practice Nebraska 1963. Began legal practice Omaha 1963. Judge, Omaha Municipal Court 1971-83. Former Judge, Nebraska District Court Fourth Judicial District, appointed by Governor Robert Kerrey to term beginning Oct 14, 1984.

Former Assistant Prosecutor and Assistant Attorney City of Omaha. Instructor in Criminal Law 1972-80 and Evidence and Business Law since 1983 University of Nebraska at Omaha.

Office: 709 Civic Center, 1819 Farnam Street, Omaha 68183.
Telephone: (402) 595-1112.
Fax: (402) 595-1016

CASSEL, William B. *(Judge, Nebraska District Court Eighth Judicial District)* Appointed by Governor E. Benjamin Nelson to term beginning April 22, 1992. Retained by election 1996 and 2002. Current term expires Jan 2009. Born Ainsworth Nebraska Sept 20, 1955. United Church of Christ. Educated at University of Nebraska at Lincoln B.S. cum laude 1977 J.D. cum laude 1979. Associate Editor Nebraska Law Review 1977-79. Member Order of the Coif. Admitted to practice Nebraska 1979, U.S. District Court District of Nebraska 1979 and U.S. Supreme Court 1990. In legal practice Ainsworth 1979-92.

City Attorney Ainsworth 1979-92 and Long Pine 1981-92. Village Attorney Johnstown 1981-92. Past President Fifteenth Judicial District Bar Association. Member Nebraska State and American Bar Associations. Board Member Ainsworth Airport Authority 1980-92. Licensed pilot. Enjoys golf and racquetball.

Mailing address: P.O. Box 105, Ainsworth 69210-0105.
Office: Brown County Courthouse, Ainsworth 69210.
Telephone: (402) 387-2162.
Fax: (402) 387-0918
E-mail address: cassel08@nol.org
Website address: http://www.nol.org/home/DC8

CAVEL, Michael P. *(Judge, Nebraska Workers' Compensation Court)* Appointed by Governor Bob Kerrey to term beginning Oct 5, 1983. Retained by election 1986, 1992 and 1998. Current term expires Jan 2005. Born Alamogordo New Mexico Sept 17, 1944. Educated at Creighton University B.A. 1966 J.D. 1968. Member Delta Theta Phi. Admitted to practice Nebraska 1968. Began legal practice Omaha 1971.

Author *Nebraska Workmen's Compensation Practice and Forms* Mason Publishing Company 1981. Member Omaha and Nebraska State Bar Associations. First Lieutenant U.S. Army 1968-71.

Office: 173 Hall of Justice, Omaha 68183.
Telephone: (402) 595-3903.
Fax: (402) 444-3927

CECAVA, Kristine R. *(Judge, Nebraska District Court Twelfth Judicial District)* Appointed by Governor Mike Johanns. Born North Platte Nebraska May 21, 1952. Catholic. Educated at University of Nebraska at Lincoln B.S. 1973 J.D. with honors 1976. Assistant Editor Nebraska Law Review 1976-77. Member Order of the Coif. Admitted to practice Nebraska 1977 and U.S. District Court District of Nebraska 1977. In legal practice Ogallala 1977-87. Former Judge, Nebraska County Court Eleventh Judicial District, appointed by Governor Kay Orr to term beginning Nov 6, 1987.

Attorney Keith County 1980-86.

Mailing address: P.O. Box 217, Sidney 69162.
Telephone: (308) 254-2814.
Fax: (308) 254-4293

CHEUVRONT, Jeffre *(Judge, Nebraska District Court Third Judicial District)* Appointed by governor.

Office: 575 South Tenth Street, Lincoln 68508.

CHEUVRONT, JEFFRE—*Continued*
Telephone: (402) 441-7065.
Fax: (402) 441-6190

CLARK, Carlton E. *(Judge, Nebraska County Court Eleventh Judicial District)* Appointed by Governor Mike Johanns.
Office: 700 North Washington, Lexington 68850.
Telephone: (308) 324-5606.
Fax: (308) 324-3374

CLARK, Cloyd *(Judge, Nebraska County Court Eleventh Judicial District)* Appointed by governor.
Mailing address: P.O. Box 199, McCook 69001.
Telephone: (308) 345-1904.
Fax: (308) 345-1503

COADY, Orville L. *(Judge, Nebraska District Court First Judicial District)* Appointed by Governor J. J. Exon to term beginning May 1971. Retained by election. Current term expires Jan 2005. Born Stamford Nebraska Dec 8, 1936. Educated at University of Nebraska B.S.B.A. 1958 and University of Michigan LL.B. 1963. Admitted to practice Nebraska 1964. Began legal practice Hebron 1964. Democrat.
Mailing address: P.O. Box 297, Hebron 68370.
Telephone: (402) 768-6838.
Fax: (402) 768-7232

COE, James R. *(Judge, Nebraska Workers' Compensation Court)* Appointed by Governor Kay Orr Oct 7, 1988. Retained by election. Educated at University of Nebraska at Lincoln B.S.B.A. J.D. In legal practice 1974-88.
President Dora Bingel Foundation. Member West Omaha Rotary Club.
Office: 173 Hall of Justice, Omaha 68183.
Telephone: (402) 595-3902
Fax: (402) 444-3927

COFFEY, J. Michael *(Judge, Nebraska District Court Fourth Judicial District)* Appointed by governor.
Office: 1701 Farnam, Omaha 68183.
Telephone: (402) 444-1997.
Fax: (402) 996-8160

COLBORN, John A. *(Judge, Nebraska District Court Third Judicial District)* Appointed by Governor Mike Johanns.
Office: 575 South Tenth Street, Lincoln 68508.
Telephone: (402) 441-7303.
Fax: (402) 441-6190

CONNOLLY, William M. *(Associate Justice, Nebraska Supreme Court)* Appointed by Governor E. Benjamin Nelson to term beginning Dec 15, 1994. Retained by election. Born Omaha Nebraska March 31, 1938. Educated at Creighton University J.D. 1963. In legal practice Hastings 1972-91. Judge, Nebraska Court of Appeals 1992-94.
Deputy County Attorney 1964-66 and County Attorney 1967-72 Adams County.
Mailing address: P.O. Box 98910, Lincoln 68509.
Telephone: (402) 471-3733.
Fax: (402) 471-2197

COOPER, Samuel V. *(Judge, Nebraska County Court Fourth Judicial District)* Appointed by governor.
Office: 1701 Farnam Street, Omaha 68183.
Telephone: (402) 444-7119.
Fax: (402) 444-6890

CRNKOVICH, Elizabeth *(Judge, Douglas County Separate Juvenile Court)* Appointed by Governor E. Benjamin Nelson.
Office: 1701 Farnam, Room 600, Omaha 68183.
Telephone: (402) 444-7888.
Fax: (402) 444-3960

DANIELS, Vernon *(Judge, Douglas County Separate Juvenile Court)* Appointed by Governor Mike Johanns.
Office: 1701 Farnam, Room 600, Omaha 68183.
Telephone: (402) 444-3305.
Fax: (402) 996-8005

DAWSON, Thomas B. *(Judge, Lancaster County Separate Juvenile Court)* Appointed by Governor E. Benjamin Nelson.
Office: 575 South Tenth Street, Lincoln 68508.
Telephone: (402) 441-7385.
Fax: (402) 441-6930

DERR, J. Russell *(Judge, Nebraska District Court Fourth Judicial District)* Appointed by Governor Mike Johanns.
Office: 1701 Farnam, Omaha 68183.
Telephone: (402) 444-7529.
Fax: (402) 996-8156

DORWART, Thomas H. *(Judge, Nebraska County Court Twelfth Judicial District)* Appointed by Governor J. J. Exon to term beginning Jan 1977. Retained by election. Born Lexington Nebraska Sept 10, 1929. Roman Catholic. Educated at Creighton University B.S. 1959 and University of Nebraska J.D. 1964. Admitted to practice Nebraska 1964 and U.S. Supreme Court 1968. In legal practice Sidney 1970-77.
With Attorney General's Office and Nebraska Department of Roads 1964-67. Deputy Attorney Nebraska Insurance Department 1967-70. City Attorney Sidney 1973-77. Member Western Nebraska and Nebraska State Bar Associations. Instructor Nebraska Continuing Legal Education 1976. Sergeant USMC 1950-52. Republican. Honorary member Nebraska Dental Association 1972. Enjoys reading, golf, woodworking and gardening.
Office: 1000 Tenth Avenue, Sidney 69162.
Telephone: (308) 254-4147.
Fax: (308) 254-4641
E-mail address: thdpsd@hamilton.net

DOUGHERTY, Sandra L. *(Judge, Nebraska District Court Fourth Judicial District)* Appointed by governor.
Office: 1701 Farnam, Omaha 68183.
Telephone: (402) 444-7014.
Fax: (402) 996-8157

DOYLE, James E., IV *(Judge, Nebraska District Court Eleventh Judicial District)* Appointed by Governor Mike Johanns.
Office: 700 North Washington, Lexington 68850.
Telephone: (308) 324-8412.
Fax: (308) 324-8847

DOYLE, Mary L. *(Judge, Nebraska County Court Third Judicial District)* Appointed by governor.
Office: 575 South Tenth Street, Lincoln 68508.
Telephone: (402) 441-8975.
Fax: (402) 441-6056

EMPSON, Paul D. *(Judge, Nebraska District Court Twelfth Judicial District)* Appointed by governor.
Office: Box 630, Chadron 69337.
Telephone: (308) 432-0111.
Fax: (308) 432-0110

ENSZ, Robert B. *(Judge, Nebraska District Court Seventh Judicial District)* Appointed by governor.
Mailing address: P.O. Box 306, Wayne 68787.
Telephone: (402) 375-3534.
Fax: (402) 375-4769

EVANS, Curtis H. *(Judge, Nebraska County Court Fifth Judicial District)* Appointed by governor.
Office: 510 Lincoln Avenue, York 68467.
Telephone: (402) 362-4925.
Fax: (402) 362-2577

FITZGERALD, J. Michael *(Judge, Nebraska Workers' Compensation Court)* Appointed by Governor E. Benjamin Nelson April 12, 1996. Retained by election. Educated at University of Notre Dame B.S.B.A., Georgetown University Law Center J.D. and Creighton University. Admitted to practice Nebraska, U.S. District Court District of Nebraska, U.S. Court of Appeals Eighth Circuit and U.S. Tax Court. Began legal practice 1969.
Member Omaha, Nebraska State and American Bar Associations.
Mailing address: P.O. Box 98908, Lincoln 68509-8908.
Telephone: (402) 471-3661.
Fax: (402) 679-7558

FLOROM, Kent E. *(Judge, Nebraska County Court Eleventh Judicial District)* Appointed by governor.
Mailing address: P.O. Box 519, North Platte 69103.
Telephone: (308) 534-4350.
Fax: (308) 535-3525

FLOWERS, Karen B. *(Judge, Nebraska District Court Third Judicial District)* Appointed by Governor E. Benjamin Nelson.
Office: 575 South Tenth Street, Lincoln 68508.
Telephone: (402) 441-7509.
Fax: (402) 441-6190

FOSTER, James L. *(Judge, Nebraska County Court Third Judicial District)* Appointed by Governor Bob Kerrey to term beginning Aug 12, 1983. Retained by election. Born Dubuque Iowa Feb 10, 1946. Educated at University of Iowa, Iowa Wesleyan College B.A. 1969 and University of Nebraska J.D. 1972. Member Sigma Chi. Admitted to practice Nebraska 1973 and Iowa 1973. Began legal practice Lincoln Nebraska 1973.
Office: 575 South Tenth Street, Lincoln 68508.
Telephone: (402) 441-7656.
Fax: (402) 441-6056

FUGIT, Larry F. *(Judge, Nebraska County Court Second Judicial District)* Appointed by Governor E. Benjamin Nelson.
Office: 1210 Golden Gate Drive, Papillion 68046.
Telephone: (402) 593-2254.
Fax: (402) 593-2158

GENDLER, Lawrence D. *(Judge, Sarpy County Separate Juvenile Court)* Appointed by Governor E. Benjamin Nelson 1992. Retained by election. Educated at University of Missouri-Columbia B.S. 1975 and Creighton University School of Law J.D. 1978.
Former Chief Deputy Attorney Sarpy County. Author "Nebraska Juvenile System: Still Room for Improvement" 4 No. 5, 12-13 Oct/Nov 1985 and "New Legislative Session Has Tough Act to Follow" 3 No. 2, 4-5 Jan 1991 *Speaking for Children.* Adjunct Faculty Member Bellevue College 1981-92. Member Nebraska Juvenile Court Judges Association, National Council of Juvenile and Family Court Judges, Sarpy County and Nebraska State Bar Associations. Recipient State of Nebraska Prosecution Award for Juvenile Court and Community Activity Involvement from Nebraska Crime Commission and Governor Robert Kerrey 1986, A. W. Clarke Award from Child Saving Institute 2000 and Lifetime Membership Award from Youth Emergency Services 2000. Named one of Ten Outstanding Young Omahans by Omaha Jaycees 1991. Governor's Commission for Protection of Children 1992-98. Member Drug Free Schools and Community Advisory Committee Papillion/La Vista Public Schools 1988-92, Advisory Committee River Cities Camp Fire Council Board 1991-92. Founder and President Marilyn Gendler Memorial Scholarship Foundation since 1988. Board of Directors Youth Emergency Services 1989-92, Nebraska Committee for Children and Youth 1991-92 and PRIDE OMAHA, Inc. 1995-98. Vice Chair Nebraska Child Protection Commission 1991-92. Member Omaha Community Partnership and Nebraska Coalition for Juvenile Justice.
Office: 1210 Golden Gate Drive, Papillion 68046.
Telephone: (402) 593-2217.
Fax: (402) 593-2221
E-mail address: lgendler@Sarpy.com

GERRARD, John M. *(Associate Justice, Nebraska Supreme Court)* Appointed by Governor E. Benjamin Nelson to term beginning July 6, 1995. Retained by election. Born Schuyler Nebraska Nov 2, 1953. Educated at Nebraska Wesleyan University B.S. 1976, University of Arizona M.P.A. 1977 and McGeorge School of Law University of the Pacific J.D. 1981. In legal practice Norfolk 1981-95.
City Attorney Battle Creek 1982-95.
Mailing address: P.O. Box 98910, Lincoln 68509.
Office: 2219 State Capitol, Lincoln 68509.
Telephone: (402) 471-3736.
Fax: (402) 471-3480

GILBRIDE, Mary C. *(Judge, Nebraska District Court Fifth Judicial District)* Appointed by governor. Former Judge, Nebraska County Court Fifth Judicial District.
Office: 433 North Chestnut, Wahoo 68066.
Telephone: (402) 443-8113.
Fax: (402) 443-8170

GLEASON, James T. *(Judge, Nebraska District Court Fourth Judicial District)* Appointed by Governor Mike Johanns.
Office: 1701 Farnam, Omaha 68183.
Telephone: (402) 444-7008.
Fax: (402) 996-8154

GLESS, Alan G. *(Judge, Nebraska District Court Fifth Judicial District)* Appointed by Governor E. Benjamin Nelson to term beginning July 21, 1995. Retained by election 1998, current term expires Jan 2005. Born Columbus Nebraska March 21, 1950. Roman Catholic. Educated at University of Nebraska at Lincoln B.A. 1971 J.D. 1975. Member Phi Delta Phi. Admitted to practice Nebraska 1975, U.S. District Court District of

GLESS, ALAN G.—*Continued*

Nebraska 1975 and U.S. Supreme Court 1980. In legal practice Osceola 1975-80. Judge, Nebraska County Court Fifth Judicial District Sept 2, 1980 to July 20, 1995.

City Attorney Osceola 1977-80. County Attorney Polk County 1979-80. Author "Nebraska's Corroboration Rule" 54 Nebraska L. Rev. 93, 1975; "Arrest and Citation: Definition and Analysis" 59 Nebraska L. Rev. 279, 1980; Chapter "Accepting Guilty and No Contest Pleas" *County Judges Benchbook* Nebraska Judicial College, Nebraska County Judges Association 1987, Nebraska Judicial System Benchbook 1990; "Nebraska Probation Revocation—A Primer" 68 Nebraska L. Rev. 516, 1989; "Some Post-*Daubert* Trial Tribulations of a Simple Country Judge: Behavioral Science Evidence in Trial Courts" 13 *Behavioral Sciences & the Law* 261, 1995; "Nebraska Plea-Based Convictions Practice: A Primer and Commentary" 79 Nebraska L. Rev. 293, 2000; and "Nineteenth Century Questions of Federal Privilege, Production, Immunity, and Compulsion" American Journal of Legal History Feb 2003. Member Nebraska Supreme Court Committee on Practice and Procedure 1987-92, Nebraska Judicial Ethics Advisory Committee 1988-92, Nebraska Supreme Court Gender Fairness Task Force 1991, Nebraska Indigent Defense Services Task Force 1992, Nebraska Judicial Ethics Committee 1992-95, Nebraska State Bar Foundation, Nebraska County Judges Association (President 1991-92), Nebraska State and American (Co-Chair Ethics Committee National Conference of Special Court Judges 1990-92) Bar Associations. Instructor on "Judicial Ethics for County Judges" Nebraska County Judges Association 1989 and 1992, "Probation Revocation" Nebraska County Judges Association 1989, Nebraska County Attorneys Association 1990 and Nebraska Criminal Defense Attorneys Association 1990, "Use of Advisory Opinions" American Judicature Society 1990, "Criminal Procedure" Nebraska County Judges Association 1991 and 1992, "Expert Evidence Issues" Nebraska Department of Social Services Child Abuse Seminar 1992 and "Special Ethical Problems of Rural Judges" American Judicature Society 1992. Enjoys photography and philosophy.

Mailing address: P.O. Box 36, Seward 68434.
Telephone: (402) 643-4060.
Fax: (402) 643-2950
E-mail address: ag11024@alltel.net

GOSSETT, F. A., III *(Magistrate Judge, United States District Court District of Nebraska)* Appointed by U.S. District Court judges to term beginning May 29, 2003. Born Columbus Nebraska July 29, 1944. Catholic. Educated at University of Nebraska, Midland Lutheran College B.A. 1967 and Creighton University J.D. 1972. Law Clerk to Hon. Robert Troyen, Nebraska County Court Fourth Judicial District 1971-72. Admitted to practice Nebraska 1973. Began legal practice Fremont 1973. Associate Judge 1974-75. Judge, Nebraska County Court Sixth Judicial District, March 20, 1981 to 1998, appointed by Governor Charles Thone. Judge, Nebraska District Court Sixth Judicial District 1998 to May 2003, appointed by Governor E. Benjamin Nelson.

County Attorney Dodge County 1975-81. City Prosecutor Fremont 1975-81. Author *Nebraska Evidence Handbook* revised ed. Nebraska Continuing Legal Education 2000. Instructor Metropolitan Community College 1977-81. Member Nebraska County Attorneys Association (Instructor 1975-81, Board of Directors 1980-81), Nebraska Judges Association (President 1984-85), Dodge County (President 1981), Nebraska State (Author *Nebraska Court Guide* 1980) and American (Chair Education Committee National Conference of Special Court Judges Judicial Division 1986-97) Bar Associations. Graduate 1981, Faculty member since 1985 and Chair Faculty Council 1997 The National Judicial College. Recipient Distinguished Service Award from Nebraska State Bar Foundation 1998 and Distinguished Judge Award for Improvement of the Judiciary from Nebraska Supreme Court 2000. Owner KHUB Radio 1967-71. Enjoys jogging and reading.

Office: 111 South 18th Plaza, Suite 2210, Omaha 68102.
Telephone: (402) 661-7340.

HANNON, Edward E. *(Judge, Nebraska Court of Appeals)* Appointed by governor. Born Omaha Nebraska Sept 3, 1931. Roman Catholic. Educated at University of Missouri and Creighton University LL.B. 1959. Member Delta Theta Phi. Admitted to practice Nebraska 1959. Began legal practice Grand Island 1959. In legal practice O'Neill 1960-83. Former Judge, Nebraska District Court Fifteenth Judicial District, appointed by Governor Bob Kerrey to term beginning Dec 2, 1983.

Member Nebraska State and American Bar Associations. Electronics Technician First Class USN 1950-55.

Mailing address: P.O. Box 98910, Lincoln 68509-8910.
Telephone: (402) 471-3732.
Fax: (402) 471-4148

HANSEN, James T. *(Judge, Nebraska County Court Twelfth Judicial District)* Appointed by governor.

Mailing address: P.O. Box 806, Chadron 69337.
Telephone: (308) 432-0116.
Fax: (308) 432-0110

HARDER, Terri S. *(Judge, Nebraska District Court Tenth Judicial District)* Appointed by Governor Mike Johanns.

Mailing address: P.O. Box 208, Minden 68959.
Telephone: (308) 832-1038.
Fax: (308) 832-0636

HARTIGAN, John D., Jr. *(Judge, Nebraska District Court Fourth Judicial District)* Appointed by governor. Born Rochester Minnesota 1945. Educated at Creighton University J.D. 1978. Admitted to practice Nebraska 1978.

Member Omaha, Nebraska State and American Bar Associations.

Office: 1701 Farnam, Omaha 68183.
Telephone: (402) 444-7371.
Fax: (402) 996-8165

HATFIELD, Gary F. *(Judge, Nebraska County Court Fifth Judicial District)* Elected to term beginning Jan 3, 1973. Retained by election. Current term expires Jan 2007. Born Bedford Iowa March 28, 1940. Catholic. Educated at University of Nebraska B.A. 1970 J.D. 1972. Admitted to practice Nebraska 1972. Began legal practice Central City 1972. USN 1958-62. Republican.

Mailing address: P.O. Box 27, Central City 68826.
Telephone: (308) 946-2812.
Fax: (308) 946-3838

HENDRIX, Marcena M. *(Judge, Nebraska County Court Fourth Judicial District)* Appointed by governor.
Office: 1819 Farnam, Omaha 68183.
Telephone: (402) 444-5433.
Fax: (402) 444-3677

HENDRY, John V. *(Chief Justice, Nebraska Supreme Court)* Appointed by Governor E. Benjamin Nelson to term beginning 1998. Retained by election. Chief Justice since Oct 1, 1998. Born Omaha Nebraska Aug 23, 1948. Educated at University of Nebraska B.S. 1970 J.D. 1974. In legal practice Lincoln 1974-95. Judge, Nebraska County Court Third Judicial District 1995-98, appointed by Governor E. Benjamin Nelson.
Mailing address: P.O. Box 98910, Lincoln 68509.
Telephone: (402) 471-3738.
Fax: (402) 471-2197

HIGH, Michael K. *(Presiding Judge, Nebraska Workers' Compensation Court)* Appointed by Governor E. Benjamin Nelson Jan 8, 1998. Educated at University of Nebraska at Lincoln B.S. 1972 M.A. 1986 J.D. 1986. In legal practice 1986-98.
Commissioner Gosper County 1978-82. Farmer and rancher 1972-82.
Mailing address: P.O. Box 98908, Lincoln 68509-8908.
Telephone: (402) 471-3922.
Fax: (402) 471-8231

HIPPE, Robert Owen *(Judge, Nebraska District Court Twelfth Judicial District)* Appointed by Governor J. J. Exon to term beginning Jan 1977. Retained by election. Born Gordon Nebraska Sept 28, 1941. Catholic. Educated at Kearney State College A.B. in Education 1963 and University of Nebraska J.D. 1968. Admitted to practice Nebraska 1968 and U.S. Court of Appeals Eighth Circuit 1971. Began legal practice Scottsbluff 1968. Acting Judge, Scotts Bluff County Court 1969-72.
President Nebraska District Court Judges Association 1988-89. Member Scotts Bluff County, Nebraska State and American (1968-75) Bar Associations. Democrat.
Office: 1725 Tenth Street, Gering 69341.
Telephone: (308) 436-6660.
Fax: (308) 436-6759

HOFFERT, John R. *(Judge, Nebraska Workers' Compensation Court)* Appointed by Governor Mike Johanns Oct 4, 2001. Educated at Western Illinois University B.A. with high honors and University of Nebraska College of Law J.D. with distinction. In legal practice 1980-2001.
Former Member Nebraska Association of Trial Attorneys, The Association of Trial Lawyers of America and American Judicature Society. U.S. Army 1970-72. Former Member Board of Directors Legal Services of Southeast Nebraska and Folsom Children's Zoo and Botanical Gardens.
Mailing address: P.O. Box 98908, Lincoln 68509.
Telephone: (402) 471-3512.

HUBER, John E. *(Judge, Nebraska County Court Fourth Judicial District)* Appointed by governor.
Office: 1819 Farnam Street, Omaha 68183.
Telephone: (402) 444-1928.
Fax: (402) 444-6890

HUTTON, Todd J. *(Judge, Nebraska County Court Second Judicial District)* Appointed by governor.
Office: 1210 Golden Gate Drive, Papillion 68046.
Telephone: (402) 593-2307.
Fax: (402) 593-2158

ICENOGLE, John Philip *(Judge, Nebraska District Court Ninth Judicial District)* Appointed by Governor Kay Orr to term beginning May 22, 1990. Retained by election 1994 and 2000. Current term expires Jan 2007. Born Mattoon Illinois Dec 26, 1948. Presbyterian. Educated at Columbia University B.A. 1971 and Tulane University J.D. 1974. Assistant Editor Tulane Law Review 1972-74. Admitted to practice Nebraska 1974 and U.S. District Court District of Nebraska 1974. In legal practice Kearney 1974-76. Judge, Nebraska County Court Twelfth Judicial District 1976-90.
Part-time Faculty Law Courses University of Nebraska at Kearney 1984-91. President Nebraska Juvenile Justice Association 1981 and Nebraska County Judges Association 1986-87. Member Nebraska District Judges Association (Chair Education Committee since 1996, Member Executive Committee), Buffalo County and Nebraska State Bar Associations. Republican. Member Governor's Study Group on Community Corrections. Member Study Groups Nebraska Fatherhood Initiative. Enjoys golf and reading.
Mailing address: P.O. Box 520, Kearney 68848.
Telephone: (308) 236-1246.
Fax: (308) 233-3693

IDE, Robert A. *(Judge, Nebraska County Court Tenth Judicial District)* Appointed by Governor Mike Johanns.
Mailing address: P.O. Box 255, Holdrege 68949.
Telephone: (308) 995-6561.
Fax: (308) 995-6562

ILLINGWORTH, Stephen R. *(Judge, Nebraska District Court Tenth Judicial District)* Appointed by governor.
Mailing address: P.O. Box 9, Hastings 68901.
Telephone: (402) 461-7264.
Fax: (402) 461-7269

INBODY, Everett O., II *(Judge, Nebraska Court of Appeals)* Appointed by Governor E. Benjamin Nelson to term beginning April 28, 1995. Retained by election. Born Columbus Nebraska Sept 13, 1945. Lutheran. Educated at University of Nebraska at Lincoln B.S. 1967 J.D. 1970. Admitted to practice Nebraska 1970, U.S. District Court District of Nebraska 1970 and U.S. Supreme Court 1982. In legal practice Wahoo 1970-86. Judge, Nebraska County Court Fifth Judicial District 1986-91, appointed by Governor Robert Kerrey. Judge, Nebraska District Court Fifth Judicial District Nov 15, 1991 to 1995, appointed by Governor E. Benjamin Nelson.
Former Deputy County Attorney Saunders County. Treasurer 1986-89 and President 1990-91 Nebraska County Judges Association. Former Member Nebraska District Judges Association and American Judicature Society. Member Nebraska State Bar Association (President Young Lawyers Section 1978-79, Representative House of Delegates 1979-87). Attended American Academy of Judicial Education Diploma of Judicial Skills 1990 and Diploma of Humanities and Judging 1999. Member Organizing Committee for first Nebraska Bar Bench Conference May 1992. Named Outstanding Young Person of

INBODY, EVERETT O., II—*Continued*
Saunders County 1976 and Volunteer of the Year by Wahoo Parks and Recreation 1992. Recipient Sam Crawford Award from Wahoo Chamber of Commerce 2001. Organizer of Youth Sports program in Wahoo (Wahoops). Interests include sports, sports cards, Department 56 and bridge.

Office: 112 East Seventh Street, Wahoo 68066.
Telephone: (402) 443-5180.
Fax: (402) 443-5285

IRWIN, John F. *(Judge, Nebraska Court of Appeals)* Appointed by Governor E. Benjamin Nelson to term beginning Jan 13, 1992. Retained by election. Born May 25, 1952. Educated at University of Nebraska at Omaha B.A. 1974 and Creighton University School of Law J.D. 1977. In legal practice Omaha 1977-81.

Chief Deputy Attorney Sarpy County 1981-91.
Office: 1210 Golden Gate Drive, Papillion 68046.
Telephone: (402) 593-4491.
Fax: (402) 593-4493

JOHNSON, Douglas F. *(Judge, Douglas County Separate Juvenile Court)* Appointed by Governor E. Benjamin Nelson.

Office: 1701 Farnam, Room 600, Omaha 68183.
Telephone: (402) 444-7881.
Fax: (402) 444-3961

JORGENSEN, Gerald R., Jr. *(Judge, Nebraska County Court Ninth Judicial District)* Appointed by governor.

Mailing address: P.O. Box 520, Kearney 68848.
Telephone: (308) 236-1229.
Fax: (308) 236-1243

KELLY, Christopher *(Judge, Douglas County Separate Juvenile Court)* Appointed by Governor Mike Johanns.

Office: 1701 Farnam, Room 600, Omaha 68183.
Telephone: (402) 444-6618.
Fax: (402) 444-3573

KOPF, Richard G. *(Chief Judge, United States District Court District of Nebraska)* Appointed Magistrate Judge by U.S. District Court judges 1987. Appointed Judge for life by President George Bush to term beginning May 26, 1992. Chief Judge since Nov 1, 1999. Born Toledo Ohio Dec 1, 1946. Educated at University of Nebraska at Kearney B.A. and University of Nebraska at Lincoln J.D. with distinction 1972. Law Clerk to Hon. Donald R. Ross, U.S. Court of Appeals Eighth Circuit 1972-74. Admitted to practice Nebraska 1972. In legal practice Lexington 1974-86.

Office: 586 U.S. Courthouse, 100 Centennial Mall North, Lincoln 68508.
Telephone: (402) 437-5252.

KORSLUND, Paul W. *(Judge, Nebraska District Court First Judicial District)* Appointed by governor.

Mailing address: P.O. Box 845, Beatrice 68310.
Telephone: (402) 223-1332.
Fax: (402) 223-1313

KREPELA, Richard W. *(Judge, Nebraska County Court Seventh Judicial District)* Appointed by governor.

Mailing address: P.O. Box 230, Madison 68748.
Telephone: (402) 454-3311.
Fax: (402) 454-3438

LAMBERTY, Patricia A. *(Judge, Nebraska District Court Fourth Judicial District)* Appointed by Governor E. Benjamin Nelson to term beginning July 21, 1998. Educated at University of Nebraska at Omaha B.S. summa cum laude 1976 and Creighton University School of Law J.D. cum laude 1979. Staff member Creighton Law Review 1978-79. Moot Court Board 1978-79. Admitted to practice Nebraska 1979, U.S. District Court District of Nebraska 1979 and U.S. Court of Appeals Eighth Circuit 1982. In legal practice Sept 1979 to July 1998. Hearing Examiner, Nebraska Equal Opportunity Commission.

Co-author "Can We Stop the Violence in Omaha" Oct 1995. Chairperson Governor's Child Support Enforcement Study Committee 1994. Member Governor's Visitation Interference Task Force 1995-96 and State Advisory Council Nebraska State Office of Dispute Resolution since 1998. Certified Mediator National Association of Security Dealers May 1996. Former Member Academy of Family Mediators, Nebraska Association of Trial Attorneys and National Association of Trial Attorneys. Fellow Nebraska State Bar Foundation. Member Omaha (Founding member and Chairperson 1994-96 Mediation Committee), Nebraska State (Board of Directors Family Law Committee 1995-99, Judiciary Committee since 2000) and American Bar Associations. Attended CDR Associates Certificate in Basic Mediation Feb 1993, Divorce and Family Mediation from Coast to Coast Mediation July 1993, International Meeting of Academy of Family Mediators July 1994 and July 1996, Federal Court Mediation CPR Institute for Dispute Resolution May 1995, Mediation of Claims under American Disability Act U.S. Department of Justice April 1996 and Victim-Offender Mediation Nebraska Office of Dispute Resolution March 1998. Presenter "Mediating Conflicts Between Businesses" Workshop Chamber of Commerce and Industry, Brasov Romania July 1995; "Mediating Conflicts Between Individuals" Workshop Brasov Romania County Council July 1995; "Legal Ethics and Domestic Violence" Seminar College of St. Mary 1996; "Activities of the Domestic Violence Coordinating Council" Adult Abuse Conference May 1997; "Legal Trends and Mediation Under the American Disability Act" Paralyzed Vet's Association May 1997; "Women and the Law: Legal Issues—Legal Rights" Women's Leadership Conference ICAN Feb 10, 1999; and "Domestic Violence in Omaha: Cause and Effect on Our System" Creighton University Center for Health Policy and Ethics Sept 2000. Recipient B'nai B'rith Safety Award from Health Wellness and Safety Council May 14, 1997, Woman of Distinction Award from Nebraska Commission on the Status of Women March 5, 1999, Woman of Distinction Award for Professions from YWCA May 1999, Legal Pioneer Award from Nebraska State Bar Foundation 1999 and Citation for Alumnus Achievement from University of Nebraska at Omaha 2000. Program Director Omaha YWCA Jan 1973 to Dec 1974. Board of Directors 1991-97 and Chairperson Domestic Violence Task Force 1994-98 Women's Fund of Greater Omaha. Board of Counselors 1992-2000 and Advisory Board College of Nursing 1995-99 University of Nebraska Medical Center. President 1996 and Founding Member since 1996 Metropolitan Omaha Mediation Network Association. Co-chairperson and Founding Member Domestic Violence Coordinating Council of Greater Omaha March 1996 to March 1998. Board of

LAMBERTY, PATRICIA A.—*Continued*

Directors since 1996 and Executive Board since 1999 College of St. Mary.
Office: 1701 Farnam Street, Omaha 68183.
Telephone: (402) 444-7089.
Fax: (402) 996-8155
E-mail address: plambert@co.douglas.ne.us

LEFFLER, B. Bert *(Judge, Nebraska County Court Eleventh Judicial District)* Appointed by Governor J. J. Exon to term beginning Jan 6, 1977. Retained by election Nov 1992 and 1998. Current term expires Jan 2005. Born Holdrege Nebraska Sept 18, 1940. Methodist. Educated at University of Nebraska B.A. 1970 and Creighton University J.D. 1974. Member Phi Delta Theta. Admitted to practice Nebraska 1974 and U.S. District Court District of Nebraska 1974. In legal practice Grant 1974-76.
Member Nebraska County Judges Association and Nebraska State Bar Association. E-4 U.S. Army 1962-64. Republican. Co-chairman Perkins County Republicans 1975-76. Enjoys reading, sailing, photography and hunting.
Mailing address: P.O. Box 377, Benkelman 69021.
Telephone: (308) 423-2374.
Fax: (308) 423-2325

LINDNER, Jack Burton *(Judge, Nebraska County Court Third Judicial District)* Assumed office July 1, 1986. Retained by election. Born Waterloo Iowa Jan 23, 1934. Lutheran. Educated at Morningside College 1953, University of Northern Iowa 1955 and University of Tennessee J.D. 1960. Admitted to practice Tennessee 1960, Nebraska 1964, Iowa 1971 and Minnesota 1983. Began legal practice Knoxville Tennessee 1960. In legal practice Lincoln Nebraska 1964 and Ames Iowa 1971. Acting Judge 1975-79 and Judge Sept 30, 1983 to June 30, 1985, Lincoln Municipal Court.
City Prosecutor Lincoln 1964-71. U.S. Army 1951-55.
Office: 575 South Tenth Street, Lincoln 68508-2848.
Telephone: (402) 441-7655.
Fax: (402) 441-6056

LIPPSTREU, Randall L. *(Judge, Nebraska District Court Twelfth Judicial District)* Appointed by Governor E. Benjamin Nelson.
Office: 1725 Tenth Street, Gering 69341.
Telephone: (308) 436-6660.
Fax: (308) 436-6759

LIVINGSTON, James D. *(Judge, Nebraska District Court Ninth Judicial District)* Appointed by governor.
Office: 111 West First, Grand Island 68801.
Telephone: (308) 385-5770.
Fax: (308) 385-5669

LOVELL, Jean A. *(Judge, Nebraska County Court Third Judicial District)* Appointed by governor.
Office: 575 South Tenth Street, Lincoln 68508-2848.
Telephone: (402) 441-8976.
Fax: (402) 441-6056

LOWE, Darryl R. *(Judge, Nebraska County Court Fourth Judicial District)* Appointed by governor.
Office: 1701 Farnam, Omaha 68183.
Telephone: (402) 444-6828.
Fax: (402) 444-6890

LUTHER, Teresa K. *(Judge, Nebraska District Court Ninth Judicial District)* Appointed by Governor E. Benjamin Nelson.
Office: 111 West First, Grand Island 68801.
Telephone: (308) 385-5666.
Fax: (308) 385-5669

MACKEN, James L. *(Judge, Nebraska County Court Twelfth Judicial District)* Assumed office May 1969. Retained by election. Current term expires Jan 2007. Born Alliance Nebraska Feb 17, 1929. Roman Catholic. Educated at Casper College A.A. 1948 and Creighton University J.D. 1952. Member Phi Theta Kappa. Admitted to practice Nebraska 1952 and Wyoming 1952. Former Magistrate, U.S. District Court District of Nebraska.
County Attorney Morrill County 1959-69. Instructor Nebraska Western College 1972. Member Scotts Bluff County (President 1973) and Nebraska State Bar Associations. Recipient Governor's Award for quality of Traffic Court. First Lieutenant USAS JAGC 1952-55. Democrat. Enjoys golf.
Office: 1725 Tenth Street, Gering 69341.
Telephone: (308) 436-6648.
Fax: (308) 436-6782

MAHONEY, Timothy J. *(Chief Judge, United States Bankruptcy Court District of Nebraska)*
Office: 1125 U.S. Courthouse, 111 South Eighteenth Plaza, Omaha 68102-1321.
Telephone: (402) 661-7480.

MARCUZZO, Jeffrey *(Judge, Nebraska County Court Fourth Judicial District)* Appointed by Governor Mike Johanns.
Office: 1701 Farnam, Omaha 68183.
Telephone: (402) 444-5438.
Fax: (402) 444-6890

MARTIN, Mac *(Judge, Nebraska County Court Ninth Judicial District)* Appointed by governor.
Office: 111 West First, Suite 1, Grand Island 68802.
Telephone: (308) 385-5135.
Fax: (308) 385-5138

MASCHMAN, Curtis L. *(Judge, Nebraska County Court First Judicial District)* Appointed by Governor E. Benjamin Nelson.
Office: 1700 Stone Street, Room 205, Falls City 68355.
Telephone: (402) 245-2812.
Fax: (402) 245-3352

McARDLE, J. Patrick *(Judge, Nebraska County Court First Judicial District)* Appointed by Governor Bob Kerrey to term beginning Aug 1, 1983. Retained by election. Born Omaha Nebraska Dec 8, 1945. United Church of Christ. Educated at Doane College B.A. 1968 and University of Nebraska J.D. 1972. Member Delta Theta Phi. Admitted to practice Nebraska 1972. Began legal practice Crete 1972.
Former Chairman Advisory Committee Region V Mental Retardation Services. Member National Council of Juvenile and Family Court Judges, American Judicature Society, Saline County (President 1972-74), Nebraska State and American Bar Associations. Member Crete Sertoma Club (Past President and Former District Governor).
Mailing address: P.O. Box 865, Wilber 68465.
Telephone: (402) 821-2131.
Fax: (402) 821-2132

McCORMACK, Michael *(Associate Justice, Nebraska Supreme Court)* Appointed by Governor E. Benjamin Nelson to term beginning March 19, 1997. Retained by election. Born Omaha Nebraska July 20, 1939. Educated at Creighton University J.D. 1963. In legal practice Omaha 1966-97.
Assistant Public Defender Douglas County 1963-66.
Mailing address: P.O. Box 98910, Lincoln 68509.
Office: 2218 State Capitol, Lincoln 68509.
Telephone: (402) 471-4345.
Fax: (402) 471-2197

McDERMOTT, Patrick R. *(Judge, Nebraska County Court Fifth Judicial District)* Appointed by Governor E. Benjamin Nelson.
Mailing address: P.O. Box 191, Schuyler 68661.
Telephone: (402) 352-8511.
Fax: (402) 352-8535

McGINN, Bernard J. *(Judge, Nebraska District Court Third Judicial District)* Appointed by governor.
Office: 575 South Tenth Street, Lincoln 68508.
Telephone: (402) 441-7302.
Fax: (402) 441-6190

McQUADE, Thomas G. *(Judge, Nebraska County Court Fourth Judicial District)* Appointed by governor.
Office: 1819 Farnam, Omaha 68183.
Telephone: (402) 444-5439.
Fax: (402) 444-6890

MERRITT, Paul D., Jr. *(Judge, Nebraska District Court Third Judicial District)* Appointed by governor.
Office: 575 South Tenth Street, Lincoln 68508.
Telephone: (402) 441-7301.
Fax: (402) 441-3833

MILLER, Marvin V. *(Judge, Nebraska County Court Fifth Judicial District)* Appointed by governor.
Office: 433 North Chestnut, Wahoo 68066.
Telephone: (402) 443-8117.
Fax: (402) 443-8121

MILLER-LERMAN, Lindsey *(Associate Justice, Nebraska Supreme Court)* Appointed by Governor E. Benjamin Nelson to term beginning Sept 1, 1998. Retained by election Nov 2002, current term expires Jan 2009. Born Los Angeles California July 30, 1947. Educated at Wellesley College B.A. with high honors 1968 and Columbia University School of Law J.D. 1973. Honorary doctorate College of St. Mary 1993. Board of Editors Columbia Law Review. Law Clerk to Chief Judge Constance Baker Motley, U.S. District Court Southern District of New York 1973-75. Harlan Fiske Stone Scholar. Moot Court Executive Committee and Moot Court Judge. Admitted to practice New York 1974, U.S. District Courts Southern 1974 and Eastern 1975 Districts of New York and District of Nebraska 1976, U.S. Courts of Appeals Second 1974, Eighth 1979, Sixth 1984 and Tenth 1987 Circuits, Nebraska 1976 and U.S. Supreme Court 1982. In legal practice Omaha Nebraska 1976-92. Judge 1992-96 and Chief Judge 1996-98, Nebraska Court of Appeals.
Co-author with Lerman, Lerman, Gold and Nankervis "Accuracy of Rubella History" 74 *Annals of Internal Medicine* 97, 1971; with Nejelski and Lerman "A Researcher-Subject Testimonial Privilege: What to do Before the Subpoena Arrives" Wisconsin L. Rev. 1085, 1971; and with Gerber and Lerman "Copyright Law" *The National Law Journal* 44 Aug 1, 1983. Author Note "Screening of Criminal Cases in the Federal Courts of Appeals: Practice and Proposals" Columbia L. Rev. 1973, "Timeliness of Filing for Attorney's Fees" *Litigation* 33 Winter 1985, "An Indemnification Counterclaim Asserted Against Plaintiff-Investor" *The National Law Journal* 28 April 14, 1986, "Should Part-Time Lawyers Stay on the Partnership Track: Merit is More than Billable Hours" American Bar Association Journal 36 Jan 1, 1987, "Development in Section 10(b) Statute of Limitations" March 1991, "Woodruff (Rule 11)" 1 July 1991 and "Lampf Expanded: *Brumbaugh v. Princeton Partners*" 2 Sept 1991 *News & Notes* Securities Industry Association and "The Nebraska Court of Appeals" 27 Creighton L. Rev. 146, 1993. Former Member Program Committee Judicial Conference of the Eighth Circuit. Former Chair Civil Procedure and Practice Committee U.S. District Court District of Nebraska. Former Member Securities Industry Association (Compliance and Legal Division). Member American Bar Foundation, National Association of Women Judges, The Association of the Bar of the City of New York, Omaha, Nebraska State and American (Sections: Judicial Administration Division, Litigation, Antitrust Law, Public Utility, Communications and Transportation Law) Bar Associations. Former Member Board of Directors Landmarks Preservation, Inc., Children's Museum and ArtOmaha. Board of Directors Tuesday Musical. Enjoys travel.
Mailing address: P.O. Box 98910, Lincoln 68509.
Telephone: (402) 471-3734.
Fax: (402) 435-7872

MOORE, Frankie J. *(Judge, Nebraska Court of Appeals)* Appointed by Governor Mike Johanns to term beginning Jan 28, 2000. Born Aug 13, 1958. Educated at Nebraska Wesleyan University B.A. 1980 and University of Nebraska J.D. 1983. In legal practice North Platte 1983-2000. Judge, Nebraska Commission of Industrial Relations 1989-2000.
Office: 300 East Third Street, Suite 254, North Platte 69101.
Telephone: (308) 535-8342.
Fax: (308) 535-8344

MORAN, Gerald E. *(Judge, Nebraska District Court Fourth Judicial District)* Appointed by Governor E. Benjamin Nelson.
Office: 1701 Farnam, Omaha 68183.
Telephone: (402) 444-7817.
Fax: (402) 996-8150

MULLEN, J. Patrick *(Judge, Nebraska District Court Fourth Judicial District)* Appointed by governor.
Office: 1701 Farnam, Omaha 68183.
Telephone: (402) 444-7086.
Fax: (402) 996-8153

MURPHY, John P. *(Judge, Nebraska District Court Eleventh Judicial District)* Appointed by Governor Bob Kerrey to term beginning April 2, 1983. Retained by election. Born Omaha Nebraska July 26, 1947. Roman Catholic. Educated at St. Louis University A.B. 1969 and Creighton University J.D. 1974. Admitted to practice Nebraska 1975, U.S. District Court District of Nebraska 1975 and U.S. Supreme Court 1978. Began legal practice North Platte 1975.
Deputy Attorney 1975-77 and Public Defender 1981-83 Lincoln County. Co-author "Free Press v. Fair Trial in Nebraska: A Position Paper" Nebraska L. Rev. 1976 and "*Nebraska Press Association v. Stuart*—A Prosecu-

MURPHY, JOHN P.—*Continued*

tor's View of Pre-trial Restraints on the Press" DePaul L. Rev. 1977. Instructor in Criminal Law Kearny State College 1977-83 and Mid-Plains Community College 1977-83. Member Nebraska Supreme Court Judicial Nominating Commission 1978-83 and Governor's Task Force on Sexual Assault 1984. Member Lincoln County, Western Nebraska, Nebraska State (Committee on the Judiciary 1983) and American Bar Associations. Listed in *Who's Who in the Midwest* and *Who's Who in American Politics*. First Lieutenant USAF 1969-72. Democrat. Treasurer 1976-78 and Chair 1978-82 Lincoln County Democratic Party. Arrangements Chair Nebraska State Democratic Convention 1982. Nebraska Democratic Central Committee 1982-83. Member North Platte Board of Adjustments 1978-79, Board of Directors Western Nebraska Legal Services 1978-83, Board of Directors Nebraska Advocacy Services 1979-83, North Platte Planning Commission 1979-83 (Chairman 1982-83) and Board of Directors Nebraska Center for Sentencing Alternatives 1983-84.

Mailing address: P.O. Box 1616, North Platte 69103.
Telephone: (308) 534-4350.
Fax: (308) 535-3528

OFFNER, Michael *(Judge, Nebraska County Court Tenth Judicial District)* Appointed by Governor Mike Johanns.

Office: 621 North Cedar Street, Red Cloud 68970.
Telephone: (402) 746-2777.
Fax: (402) 746-2771

OLBERDING, Ronald D. *(Judge, Nebraska District Court Eighth Judicial District)* Appointed by governor.

Mailing address: P.O. Box 280, Burwell 68823.
Telephone: (308) 346-5277.
Fax: (308) 346-5064

O'NEAL, Robert B. *(Judge, Sarpy County Separate Juvenile Court)* Appointed by Governor E. Benjamin Nelson.

Office: 1210 Golden Gate Drive, Papillion 68046.
Telephone: (402) 593-5920.
Fax: (402) 593-2221

OTEPKA, Thomas A. *(Judge, Nebraska District Court Fourth Judicial District)* Appointed by Governor Mike Johanns.

Office: 1701 Farnam, Omaha 68183.
Telephone: (402) 444-7755.
Fax: (402) 444-8163

OTT, Jack Robert *(Judge, Nebraska County Court Tenth Judicial District)* Appointed by Governor J. J. Exon to term beginning Jan 1, 1978. Retained by election. Born Holdrege Nebraska Nov 13, 1944. Presbyterian. Educated at University of Nebraska B.S. J.D. Admitted to practice Colorado 1972 and Nebraska 1972. Began legal practice Alma Nebraska 1972.

County Attorney Harlan County 1975-77. Member Tenth Judicial District (Secretary-Treasurer), Colorado and Nebraska State Bar Associations. CPA. Republican.

Mailing address: P.O. Box 95, Hastings 68902.
Telephone: (402) 461-7143.
Fax: (402) 461-7144

OWENS, Michael J. *(Judge, Nebraska District Court Fifth Judicial District)* Appointed by Governor E. Benjamin Nelson.

Mailing address: P.O. Box 201, Aurora 68818-0201.
Telephone: (402) 694-6334.
Fax: (402) 694-2250

PIESTER, David L. *(Magistrate Judge, United States District Court District of Nebraska)* Appointed by U.S. District Court judges to term beginning Jan 1981. Reappointed 1989 and 1997. Current term expires Jan 2005. Born Lincoln Nebraska Nov 18, 1947. Educated at University of Nebraska B.S.B.A. 1969 J.D. 1972. Admitted to practice Nebraska 1972, U.S. District Court District of Nebraska 1972, U.S. Court of Appeals Eighth Circuit 1976 and U.S. Supreme Court 1979. Began legal practice Lincoln 1972.

Law Clerk Office of Nebraska Secretary of State 1969-72. Staff Attorney Aug 1972 to Nov 1973 and Executive Director Nov 1973 to Sept 1979 Legal Aid Society of Lincoln, Inc. (now Nebraska Legal Services). Consultant to National Legal Aid and Defender Association 1974-76 and Legal Services Corporation 1975-77. Assistant U.S. Attorney District of Nebraska Sept 1979 to Jan 1981. Member Nebraska Committee for Children and Youth (Legislative Study Committee on Child Care Licensing) 1977-78, National Legal Aid and Defender Association 1977-79, Eighth Circuit Judicial Council Education Committee 1991-96, Federal Magistrate Judges Association, Lincoln, Nebraska State and American Bar Associations. Delegate National Conference on State-Federal Judicial Resolutions State Justice Institute 1992. Faculty presenter for numerous legal education seminars sponsored by Federal Judicial Center, Federal Bar Association, Eighth Circuit Education Committee, Nebraska State Bar Association Continuing Legal Education, Inc., Nebraska Association of Trial Attorneys, Nebraska Association of Criminal Defense Attorneys and Federal Practice Committee of Nebraska. Recipient Outstanding Young Individual Award from Lincoln Jaycees 1980. Board member Citizens for Environmental Improvement 1972-75. Member Lincoln Agency Executives Association 1973-79 (Vice President 1976-77, President 1977-78), Project Advisory Group 1974-77 (Funding Criteria Committee), Lincoln Indian Center Ex-Offender Program Advisory Board 1977-78, Beta Theta Pi Alumni Advisory Board 1977-81 and 1990-96, City of Lincoln Human Rights Commission May 1978 to Dec 1979 (Vice Chairperson 1979) and Lincoln Landmarks 1978-80.

Office: 566 U.S. Courthouse, 100 Centennial Mall North, Lincoln 68508-3803.
Telephone: (402) 437-5235.

PLANTZ, Charles *(Judge, Nebraska County Court Twelfth Judicial District)* Appointed by Governor E. Benjamin Nelson Oct 28, 1991 to term beginning Dec 12, 1991. Retained by election Nov 5, 1996 and Nov 9, 2002. Current term expires Jan 2009. Born Rushville Nebraska Nov 17, 1947. Episcopalian. Educated at Shimer College A.B. with honors 1969 and Northwestern University School of Law J.D. 1972. Admitted to practice Nebraska 1972. In legal practice Rushville 1972-91.

Public Defender 1973-79 and County Attorney 1987-91 Sheridan County. Member Nebraska State and American Bar Associations.

Mailing address: P.O. Box 430, Rushville 69360.
Telephone: (308) 327-2692.
Fax: (308) 327-2936

POKORNY, Gale *(Judge, Nebraska County Court Third Judicial District)* Appointed by governor.
Office: 575 South Tenth Street, Lincoln 68508-2848.
Telephone: (402) 441-8988.
Fax: (402) 441-6056

PORTER, Linda S. *(Judge, Lancaster County Separate Juvenile Court)* Appointed by Governor Mike Johanns July 21, 1999 to term beginning Aug 25, 1999. Retained by election Nov 2002, current term expires Jan 2009. Educated at University of Nebraska B.A. with honors 1976 and University of Cincinnati J.D. with honors 1981. Note Editor University of Cincinnati Law Review 1979-81. Law Clerk to Hon. Carl B. Rubin, U.S. District Court Southern District of Ohio 1981-83. Admitted to practice Ohio 1981 and Nebraska 1989.
Deputy County Attorney Lancaster County 1989-99. Member Nebraska State Bar Association.
Office: 555 South Tenth Street, Lincoln 68508.
Telephone: (402) 441-7406.
Fax: (402) 441-7415
E-mail address: lporter@ci.lincoln.ne.us

PROCHASKA, Jane H. *(Judge, Nebraska County Court Fourth Judicial District)* Appointed by Governor Robert Kerrey to term beginning Sept 26, 1985. Retained by election. Current term expires Jan 2007.
Office: 1701 Farnam, Omaha 68183.
Telephone: (402) 444-5411.
Fax: (402) 444-6890

QUIST, Darvid D. *(Judge, Nebraska District Court Sixth Judicial District)* Appointed by Governor Charles Thone to term beginning Jan 21, 1981. Retained by election. Born Blair Nebraska June 20, 1936. Lutheran. Educated at Dana College B.Sc. 1958 and University of Nebraska J.D. 1961. Admitted to practice 1961.
Office: 1555 Colfax Street, Blair 68008.
Telephone: (402) 426-6808.
Fax: (402) 426-6821

RAGER, Kurt *(Judge, Nebraska County Court Sixth Judicial District)* Appointed by Governor Mike Johanns.
Mailing address: P.O. Box 385, Dakota City 68731.
Telephone: (402) 987-2145.
Fax: (402) 987-2185

RANDALL, Gary B. *(Judge, Nebraska District Court Fourth Judicial District)* Appointed by governor.
Office: 1701 Farnam, Omaha 68183.
Telephone: (402) 444-7012.
Fax: (402) 996-8151

REAGAN, Ronald E. *(Judge, Nebraska District Court Second Judicial District)* Appointed by Governor J. J. Exon to term beginning July 7, 1972. Retained by election 1976, 1982, 1988, 1994 and 2000. Current term expires Jan 2007. Presiding Judge 1972-96. Born Auburn Nebraska Sept 13, 1938. Educated at University of Nebraska B.S. in Education 1960 and Creighton University J.D. with honors 1967. Recipient Regent's Scholarship 1956 and Naval Reserve Officer's Training Corps Scholarship 1957-60. Member Alpha Sigma Nu and Sigma Nu. Admitted to practice Nebraska 1967. In legal practice Omaha 1967-72.
Member Nebraska Probation Systems Committee 1978-85. Member Nebraska District Court Judges Association (Executive Committee 1976-84, Chairman Legislative Committee 1975-76 and Retirement Committee 1978, President 1979), Omaha, Nebraska State and American (Delegate 1979-88 and Conference Delegate 1985-88; Member Nominating Committee 1983-84, Committee on Judicial Immunity 1981-89 and Committee on Constitution and By-Laws 1984-85 and Member and Chairman Judicial Evaluation Committee 1983-88 National Conference of State Trial Judges; Special Committee on Evaluation of Judicial Performance 1983-89; Committee on Implementation of Jury Standards 1986-89; Member Judicial Division) Bar Associations. Participant National Conference of the Judiciary on the Rights of Victims of Crime The National Judicial College 1983 and First National Judicial State of the Art Conference "Presiding in Criminal Court" National Institute of Justice 1987. Captain USMC 1960-64. Democrat. Democratic Nominee for Lieutenant Governor State of Nebraska 1970. Delegate Democratic National Convention 1972. Member Bellevue Board of Education 1972-76, Bellevue Chapter Eagles Club, Bellevue Chapter VFW and Platteview Country Club. Enjoys hunting, fishing and golf.
Office: 1210 Golden Gate Drive, Papillion 68046.
Telephone: (402) 593-2265.
Fax: (402) 593-2158

REDMOND, Maurice S. *(Judge, Nebraska District Court Sixth Judicial District)* Appointed by Governor E. Benjamin Nelson.
Mailing address: Box 566, Dakota City 68731.
Telephone: (402) 987-2111.
Fax: (402) 987-2117

REHMEIER, Randall L. *(Judge, Nebraska District Court Second Judicial District)* Appointed by Governor Kay Orr 1990. Retained by election. Former Judge, Nebraska County Court Second Judicial District.
Office: 1021 Central Avenue, Nebraska City 68410.
Telephone: (402) 873-9595.
Fax: (402) 873-9583

RILEY, Philip R. *(Judge, Nebraska County Court Seventh Judicial District)* Appointed by governor.
Mailing address: P.O. Box 230, Madison 68748.
Telephone: (402) 454-3311.
Fax: (402) 454-3438

ROBINSON, Paul R., Sr. *(Judge, Nebraska County Court Sixth Judicial District)* Appointed by governor.
Mailing address: P.O. Box 695, Hartington 68739.
Telephone: (402) 254-7441.
Fax: (402) 254-6954

ROGERS, Patrick G. *(Judge, Nebraska District Court Seventh Judicial District)* Appointed by Governor Mike Johanns. Former Judge, Nebraska County Court Sixth Judicial District, appointed by Governor E. Benjamin Nelson.
Mailing address: P.O. Box 934, Norfolk 68702.
Telephone: (402) 379-0363.
Fax: (402) 379-2250

ROUSE, Gerald E. *(Judge, Nebraska County Court Fifth Judicial District)* Appointed by Governor J. J. Exon Nov 16, 1971. Retained by election. Current term expires Jan 2007. Born Grand Island Nebraska Jan 19, 1944. Presbyterian. Educated at Hastings College B.A. 1968 and University of Nebraska J.D. 1971. Admitted to practice Nebraska 1971. Began legal practice Columbus 1971.
Adult Education Instructor Platte Technical Community College 1974-79. Member Nebraska County Judges

ROUSE, GERALD E.—*Continued*

Association (Treasurer 1973-76), National Council of Juvenile and Family Court Judges (Board of Trustees since 1981), Nebraska Association for Juvenile Justice, Nebraska State and American Bar Associations. Attended National College of the State Judiciary 1972-76 (Faculty Advisor 1976). Mock Trial Judge Law Enforcement Training Center 1975. Recipient President's Award Nebraska Juvenile Justice Association, Founder's Day Award Epworth Village, York, George H. Turner Award Nebraska State Bar Association and Commissioner's Award for the Prevention of Child Abuse and Neglect Department of Health and Human Services, Denver Colorado. Republican. Moderator Homestead Presbytery 1984. Member Elder Commission 196th General Assembly of Presbyterian Church U.S.A. Advisory Board Member Transitional Living Center since 1982. Enjoys jogging, bicycling, tennis, weight conditioning, reading and little theatre.

Mailing address: P.O. Box 37, Seward 68434.
Telephone: (402) 643-3214.
Fax: (402) 643-2950

ROWLANDS, Donald E. *(Judge, Nebraska District Court Eleventh Judicial District)* Appointed by governor.
Mailing address: P.O. Box 1616, North Platte 69103.
Telephone: (308) 534-4350.
Fax: (308) 535-3528

SAMUELSON, C. Matthew *(Judge, Nebraska County Court Sixth Judicial District)* Appointed by governor.
Office: 1555 Colfax, Blair 68008.
Telephone: (402) 426-6833.
Fax: (402) 426-6840

SCHATZ, Gregory M. *(Judge, Nebraska District Court Fourth Judicial District)* Appointed by Governor Mike Johanns.
Office: 1701 Farnam, Omaha 68183.
Telephone: (402) 444-6936.
Fax: (402) 996-8158

SCHUMAN, August F. *(Judge, Nebraska County Court Eighth Judicial District)* Appointed by Governor J. J. Exon June 15, 1977. Retained by election. Born Anoka Nebraska Sept 2, 1938. Educated at Norfolk Junior College 1958 and University of Nebraska law degree 1962. Admitted to practice Nebraska 1963. Began legal practice Anoka 1963. In legal practice Butte 1966. County Attorney Boyd County 1967-77.
Office: 148 West Fourth, Ainsworth 69210.
Telephone: (402) 387-2864.
Fax: (402) 387-0918

SHANAHAN, Thomas M. *(Judge, United States District Court District of Nebraska)* Appointed for life by President Bill Clinton to term beginning Dec 3, 1993. Born Omaha Nebraska May 5, 1934. Educated at University of Notre Dame A.B. magna cum laude 1956 and Georgetown University J.D. 1959. In legal practice Ogallala Nebraska. Associate Justice, Nebraska Supreme Court March 24, 1983 to 1993.

Secretary-treasurer 1969-70 and President 1975-76 Western Nebraska Bar Association. Member Nebraska State Bar Association (House of Delegates Thirteenth Judicial District 1975-83 and Executive Council Sixth Supreme Court Judicial District 1979-83).
Office: 3141 U.S. Courthouse, 111 South Eighteenth Plaza, Omaha 68102-1322.
Telephone: (402) 661-7310.

SIEVERS, Richard D. *(Judge, Nebraska Court of Appeals)* Appointed by Governor E. Benjamin Nelson to term beginning Jan 7, 1992. Retained by election. Current term expires Jan 2009. Chief Judge 1992-95. Born Dec 31, 1947. Educated at Kearney State College B.A. 1970 and University of Nebraska College of Law J.D. 1972. In legal practice Lincoln for 19 years.
Mailing address: P.O. Box 98910, Lincoln 68509.
Telephone: (402) 471-3732.
Fax: (402) 471-4148

SILVERMAN, Brian C. *(Judge, Nebraska District Court Twelfth Judicial District)* Appointed by governor.
Office: 515 Box Butte Avenue, Alliance 69301.
Telephone: (308) 762-5354.
Fax: (308) 762-7703

SKORUPA, Frank J. *(Judge, Nebraska County Court Fifth Judicial District)* Appointed by Governor E. Benjamin Nelson.
Mailing address: P.O. Box 538, Columbus 68602.
Telephone: (402) 563-4942.
Fax: (402) 562-8158

SPETHMAN, Richard J. *(Judge, Nebraska District Court Fourth Judicial District)* Appointed by governor.
Office: 1701 Farnam, Omaha 68183.
Telephone: (402) 444-7015.
Fax: (402) 996-8152

STEINHEIDER, John F. *(Judge, Nebraska County Court Second Judicial District)* Appointed by Governor E. Benjamin Nelson.
Mailing address: P.O. Box 487, Nebraska City 68410.
Telephone: (402) 873-9575.
Fax: (402) 873-9030

STEINKE, Robert R. *(Judge, Nebraska District Court Fifth Judicial District)* Appointed by governor.
Mailing address: P.O. Box 1188, Columbus 68601.
Telephone: (402) 563-4956.
Fax: (402) 562-6718

STEPHAN, Kenneth C. *(Associate Justice, Nebraska Supreme Court)* Appointed by Governor E. Benjamin Nelson to term beginning March 10, 1997. Retained by election. Born Omaha Nebraska Oct 8, 1946. Educated at University of Nebraska B.A. 1968 J.D. with high distinction 1972. In legal practice Lincoln 1973-97. U.S. Army 1969-71.
Mailing address: P.O. Box 98910, Lincoln 68509.
Office: 2211 State Capitol, Lincoln 68509.
Telephone: (402) 471-3737.
Fax: (402) 471-2197

STROM, Lyle E. *(Senior Judge, United States District Court District of Nebraska)* Appointed for life by President Ronald Reagan to term beginning Nov 1, 1985. Chief Judge 1987-94. Assumed Senior status, serves by assignment. Born Omaha Nebraska Jan 6, 1925. Roman Catholic. Educated at Creighton University A.B. 1950 J.D. cum laude 1953. Member Alpha Sigma Nu. Admitted to practice Nebraska 1953, U.S. District Court District of Nebraska 1953, U.S. Courts of Appeals

STROM, LYLE E.—*Continued*

Eighth 1955 and Tenth 1974 Circuits and U.S. Supreme Court 1970. In legal practice Omaha 1953-85.

Author *Nebraska Jury Instructions* West Publishing Company 1969 and 1974, *Nebraska Rules of Evidence* 1974 and "Proposed Relevancy Rules Generally Restate Law" Nebraska L. Rev. 1974. Instructor in Municipal Corporations 1956-67 and Trial Practice 1972-96 Creighton University. Member Omaha (President 1980-81), Nebraska State (President 1989-90) and American Bar Associations. Ensign U.S. Merchant Marines 1943-46. Republican. Director Robert M. Spire Internship program Creighton University since 1996. Member Rotary International, Archbishop's Committee for Educational Development, Boy Scouts of America and Pines Country Club. Interests include golf and reading.

Office: 3190 U.S. Courthouse, 111 South Eighteenth Plaza, Omaha 68102-1322.
Telephone: (402) 661-7320.

SWARTZ, Stephen M. *(Judge, Nebraska County Court Fourth Judicial District)* Appointed by Governor Robert Kerrey to term beginning Jan 7, 1987. Retained by election 1990, 1996 and 2002. Current term expires Jan 2009. Born Des Moines Iowa Feb 18, 1946. Catholic. Educated at Creighton University B.A. 1968 J.D. 1971. Business Editor Creighton Law Review 1971. Member Phi Alpha Delta and Sigma Alpha Epsilon. Admitted to practice Nebraska 1971 and Iowa 1971. In legal practice Omaha Nebraska 1971-86. Major USAR 1976-85. Democrat.

Office: 1701 Farnam Street, Omaha 68183.
Telephone: (402) 444-5435.
Fax: (402) 444-6890

TAYLOR, Donna F. *(Judge, Nebraska County Court Seventh Judicial District)* Appointed by Governor Mike Johanns.

Mailing address: P.O. Box 230, Madison 68748.
Telephone: (402) 454-3311.
Fax: (402) 454-3438

THALKEN, Thomas D. *(Magistrate Judge, United States District Court District of Nebraska)* Appointed by U.S. District Court judges.

Office: 2271 U.S. Courthouse, 111 South Eighteenth Plaza, Omaha 68102-1322.
Telephone: (402) 661-7343.

THOMAS, Wadie *(Judge, Douglas County Separate Juvenile Court)* Appointed by Governor E. Benjamin Nelson.

Office: 1701 Farnam, Room 600, Omaha 68183.
Telephone: (402) 444-4539.
Fax: (402) 444-3444

THOMPSON, George A. *(Judge, Nebraska District Court Second Judicial District)* Appointed by governor.

Office: 1210 Golden Gate Drive, Papillion 68046.
Telephone: (402) 593-2261.
Fax: (402) 593-2158

THORSON, Toni G. *(Judge, Lancaster County Separate Juvenile Court)* Appointed by governor.

Office: 575 South Tenth Street, Lincoln 68508.
Telephone: (402) 441-8487.
Fax: (402) 441-6930

TIMM, Steven B. *(Judge, Nebraska County Court First Judicial District)* Appointed by Governor Charles Thone to term beginning April 1, 1980. Retained by election Nov 1990 and Nov 1996. Current term expires Jan 3, 2003. Born Omaha Nebraska Nov 7, 1945. Methodist. Educated at University of Nebraska at Lincoln B.S. 1971 J.D. 1974. Assistant Editor Nebraska Law Review 1973-75. Admitted to practice Nebraska 1975 and U.S. District Court District of Nebraska 1975. In legal practice Lexington 1975-76 and Beatrice 1976-80.

County Attorney Gage County 1978-80. Author Case Note "*Hawkins Construction v. Mathews,* Strict Liability in Nebraska" 1973. President Nebraska County Judges Association 1989-90. Member Gage County, Nebraska State and American Bar Associations. Speaker at Criminal Procedure seminars Fall Institute of Nebraska Law 1979-2000. USAF 1963-67.

Mailing address: P.O. Box 219, Beatrice 68310.
Telephone: (402) 223-1323.
Fax: (402) 223-1374
E-mail address: stimm@inetnebr.com

TROIA, Joseph S. *(Judge, Nebraska District Court Fourth Judicial District)* Appointed by governor. Former Judge, Nebraska County Court Fourth Judicial District. Former Judge, Omaha Municipal Court.

Office: 1701 Farnam, Omaha 68183.
Telephone: (402) 444-5410.
Fax: (402) 996-8162

TURNBULL, Kent D. *(Judge, Nebraska County Court Eleventh Judicial District)* Appointed by Governor Mike Johanns.

Mailing address: P.O. Box 519, North Platte 69103.
Telephone: (308) 534-4350.
Fax: (308) 535-3525

URBOM, Warren K. *(Senior Judge, United States District Court District of Nebraska)* Appointed for life by President Richard M. Nixon to term beginning May 5, 1970. Assumed Senior status Jan 1, 1991, serves by assignment. Born Atlanta Nebraska Dec 17, 1925. United Methodist. Educated at Nebraska Wesleyan University A.B. with highest distinction 1950 and University of Michigan J.D. with distinction 1953. Awarded honorary LL.D. Nebraska Wesleyan University 1984. Associate Editor Michigan Law Review 1951-53. Admitted to practice Nebraska 1953. Began legal practice Lincoln 1953.

Author "You Can Bury My Heart at Wounded Knee" 17 International Society of Barristers Quarterly April 1982, "Toward Better Treatment of Jurors by Judges" 61 Nebraska L. Rev. 409, 1983 and "Hauling a Lawyer's Bones" International Society of Barristers Quarterly April 1985. Important Decisions: U.S. v. Consolidated Wounded Knee Cases 389 F. Supp. 235, 1975; U.S. v. Cooper 397 F. Supp. 277, 1975; Aitken, Hazen, Hoffman, Miller v. Empire Construction Co. 542 F. Supp. 252, 1982; State of Missouri v. Andrews 586 F. Supp. 1268, 1984; Brown v. Board of Regents (civil rights) 640 F. Supp. 674, 1986; Trailer Train v. Luenberger (taxation of railroads) CV 87 L 504, 1988; and Rushton v. N.P.P.D. (drug testing) 653 F. Supp. 1510, 1988, aff'd 844 F.2d 562, 1988. Instructor in Trial Advocacy University of Nebraska College of Law 1979-90. Board of Directors 1982-86 and Chairman Committee on Education of New Federal Judges 1986-89 Federal Judicial Center. Member Judicial Conference of the U.S. (Subcommittee on Federal Jurisdiction 1976-82), Lincoln (President 1968), Nebraska State (Former Member House of Delegates) and American Bar Associations.

URBOM, WARREN K.—*Continued*
Chairman Nebraska State-Federal Judicial Council 1977-86. President Federal District Judges Association for the Eighth Circuit 1977-79. Named Outstanding Legal Educator of 1990 by Nebraska Bar Foundation. Recipient Distinguished Service Award from Kiwanis 1993 and Lewis F. Powell, Jr. Award for Professionalism and Ethics from American Inns of Court Foundation 1995. Technical Sergeant USAS 1944-46. Republican. Chairman Board of Governors Nebraska Wesleyan University 1975-80. Board of Directors St. Paul School of Theology, Kansas City Missouri 1986-90. Active in church on local, state and national levels. Enjoys public speaking.
Office: 507 U.S. Courthouse, 100 Centennial Mall North, Lincoln 68508.
Telephone: (402) 437-5231.

VAN NORMAN, Laureen K. *(Judge, Nebraska Workers' Compensation Court)* Appointed by Governor E. Benjamin Nelson July 6, 1993. Retained by election. Former Presiding Judge. Educated at University of Nebraska at Lincoln B.A. J.D.
Former Legal Counsel Nebraska Department of Labor. Member Supreme Court Gender Bias Task Force and Nebraska State Bar Association (Former Chair Government Practice Committee, Former Member Executive Board Women and the Law Section).
Mailing address: P.O. Box 98908, Lincoln 68509.
Telephone: (402) 471-3600.
Fax: (402) 471-2700

WALLACE, C. G. *(Judge, Nebraska County Court Twelfth Judicial District)* Appointed by Governor Kay Orr April 22, 1988 to term beginning May 30, 1988. Retained by election Nov 3, 1992 and 1998. Current term expires Jan 2005. Born Hastings Nebraska March 1, 1938. Educated at University of Nebraska B.A. 1961 J.D. 1964. Member Phi Delta Phi. Admitted to practice Nebraska 1964 and U.S. District Court District of Nebraska 1964. In legal practice North Platte 1967-83 and Omaha 1983-88. Police Magistrate North Platte 1967-70.
Member Judicial Qualifications Commission since 1993. Member Nebraska County Judges Association and Nebraska State Bar Association. Member St. Joseph's Catholic Church.
Office: 114 East Third Street, Kimball 69145.
Telephone: (308) 235-2831.
Fax: (308) 235-3927

WASHBURN, Gary G. *(Judge, Nebraska County Court Eighth Judicial District)* Appointed by governor.
Office: 431 South Tenth Street, Broken Bow 68822.
Telephone: (308) 872-5761.
Fax: (308) 872-6052

WESTER, Robert C. *(Judge, Nebraska County Court Second Judicial District)* Appointed by Governor E. Benjamin Nelson.
Office: 1210 Golden Gate Drive, Papillion 68046.
Telephone: (402) 593-2253.
Fax: (402) 593-2158

WHITE, Lyn V. *(Judge, Nebraska County Court Fourth Judicial District)* Appointed by governor.
Office: 1701 Farnam, Omaha 68183.
Telephone: (402) 444-5432.
Fax: (402) 444-6890

WITTHOFF, Earl J. *(Judge, Nebraska District Court Third Judicial District)* Appointed by governor.
Office: 575 South Tenth Street, Lincoln 68508.
Telephone: (402) 441-7304.
Fax: (402) 441-6190

WRIGHT, John F. *(Associate Justice, Nebraska Supreme Court)* Appointed by Governor E. Benjamin Nelson to term beginning Feb 25, 1994. Retained by election. Born Scottsbluff Nebraska Dec 24, 1945. Educated at University of Nebraska B.S. 1967 J.D. 1970. In legal practice Nebraska 1970-91. Judge, Nebraska Court of Appeals 1992-94. U.S. Army 1970. Nebraska National Guard 1970-76.
Mailing address: P.O. Box 98910, Lincoln 68509.
Telephone: (402) 471-3735.
Fax: (402) 471-3480

YARDLEY, Laurie *(Judge, Nebraska County Court Third Judicial District)* Appointed by Governor E. Benjamin Nelson.
Office: 575 South Tenth Street, Lincoln 68508.
Telephone: (402) 441-8741.
Fax: (402) 441-6056

ZASTERA, William B. *(Judge, Nebraska District Court Second Judicial District)* Appointed by Governor E. Benjamin Nelson. Former Judge, Nebraska County Court Second Judicial District.
Office: 1210 Golden Gate Drive, Papillion 68046.
Telephone: (402) 593-5950.
Fax: (402) 593-2158

NEVADA

Capital CARSON CITY

UNITED STATES DISTRICT COURT DISTRICT OF NEVADA

The court sits at Carson City, Elko, Ely, Las Vegas, Lovelock and Reno. For descriptive information refer to the United States Courts section.

Chief Judge

Philip M. Pro

Judges

Howard D. McKibben	David W. Hagen
Roger L. Hunt	Kent J. Dawson
Larry R. Hicks	James C. Mahan

Senior Judges

Edward C. Reed, Jr.
Lloyd D. George

Clerk

Lance S. Wilson
U.S. Courthouse
333 Las Vegas Boulevard South
Las Vegas, Nevada 89101
(702) 464-5400

UNITED STATES MAGISTRATE JUDGES OF NEVADA

Lawrence R. Leavitt
Robert J. Johnston
Robert A. McQuaid, Jr.
Valerie P. Cooke
Peggy A. Leen

UNITED STATES BANKRUPTCY COURT OF NEVADA

Chief Judge

Gregg W. Zive

Judges

Robert Clive Jones
Linda B. Riegle

Recalled Judge

Bert M. Goldwater

Bankruptcy Clerk

Patricia Gray
8112 U.S. Courthouse
333 Las Vegas Boulevard South
Las Vegas, Nevada 89101
(702) 388-6257

NEVADA SUPREME COURT

The Supreme Court is Nevada's court of last resort. In 1997, the Legislature increased the size of the court from five to seven justices. The justices are elected in nonpartisan elections for staggered six-year terms. Vacancies are filled by the governor from nominees of the Commission on Judicial Selection. Appointees serve until the next general election. The chief justice is selected on the basis of seniority and serves a two-year term. Retired justices may be recalled to serve as either senior justices or justices pro tem. Senior justices serve on a continuing basis, while justices pro tem serve less frequently.

The court has appellate jurisdiction over equity, cases at law over $300, all civil matters not given to a lower court and questions of law in criminal cases of the District Courts. The court may also issue remedial writs necessary to the exercise of proper jurisidiction. The court exercises administrative control over the lower courts and adopts rules governing the legal profession in the state.

Beginning in January 1999, the court sits in panels of three justices, with membership rotating every six months. The concurrence of three justices is necessary to pronounce judgment. The court sits at Carson City and Las Vegas and recesses during July and August.

Chief Justice

Deborah A. Agosti

Justices

Nancy A. Becker	Mark Gibbons
Myron E. Leavitt	A. William Maupin
Robert E. Rose	Miriam Shearing

Senior Justices

Cliff Young
David Zenoff

Clerk

Janette Bloom
Supreme Court Building
201 South Carson Street, Suite 201
Carson City, Nevada 89701-4702
(775) 684-1600

Administrative Office of the Courts

Ronald R. Titus
Director and State Court Administrator
Supreme Court Building
201 South Carson Street, Suite 250
Carson City, Nevada 89701-4702
(775) 684-1717

NEVADA DISTRICT COURTS

The District Courts are Nevada's trial courts of general jurisdiction. The state is divided into nine judicial districts. Judges are elected by the voters of their respective districts in nonpartisan elections for six-year terms. In districts with a population of 100,000 or more, a chief judge is required. In other districts, a chief judge may be selected if needed. A chief judge is chosen by peer vote to serve a two-year term. Retired judges may

NEVADA DISTRICT COURTS—*Continued*

be recalled to serve as either senior judges or judges pro tem. Senior judges serve on a continuing basis, while judges pro tem serve less frequently.

The courts have original jurisdiction in civil cases involving more than $7,500; equity, probate and guardianship matters; forcible entry and detainer; contested election cases; and cases at law involving real property, mining claims or the legality of any tax. The courts have jurisdiction in all criminal cases except where exclusive jurisdiction has been conferred upon another court. The courts also exercise exclusive original jurisdiction in juvenile matters. The courts hear appeals de novo from the Justice and Municipal Courts and may issue writs necessary to the exercise of proper jurisdiction.

The courts sit at each county seat.

FIRST JUDICIAL DISTRICT includes Carson City and Storey County. The court sits at Carson City and Virginia City.

Judges
Michael R. Griffin
William A. Maddox

SECOND JUDICIAL DISTRICT includes Washoe County. The court sits at Reno.

Chief Judge
James W. Hardesty

Judges

Janet J. Berry	Charles M. McGee
Jerome M. Polaha	Connie J. Steinheimer
Deborah E. Schumacher	Brent T. Adams
Peter I. Breen	Steven R. Kosach
Steven P. Elliott	Scott Jordan
Frances Doherty	

THIRD JUDICIAL DISTRICT includes Churchill and Lyon counties. The court sits at Fallon and Yerington.

Judges
David A. Huff
Archie E. Blake
Robert E. Estes

FOURTH JUDICIAL DISTRICT includes Elko County. The court sits at Elko.

Judges
Mike Memeo
Andrew J. Puccinelli

FIFTH JUDICIAL DISTRICT includes Esmeralda, Mineral and Nye counties. The court sits at Goldfield, Hawthorne and Tonopah.

Judges
John P. Davis
Robert W. Lane

SIXTH JUDICIAL DISTRICT includes Humboldt, Lander and Pershing counties. The court sits at Winnemucca, Battle Mountain and Lovelock.

Judges
Richard Wagner
John M. Iroz

SEVENTH JUDICIAL DISTRICT includes Eureka, Lincoln and White Pine counties. The court sits at Eureka, Pioche and Ely.

Chief Judge
Dan L. Papez

Judge
Steve L. Dobrescu

EIGHTH JUDICIAL DISTRICT includes Clark County. The court sits at Las Vegas.

Chief Judge
Gene T. Porter

Judges

Valorie Vega	Ronald D. Parraguirre
Kathy A. Hardcastle	Jackie Glass
Joseph T. Bonaventure	Stewart L. Bell
Lee A. Gates	Jennifer P. Togliatti
Jessie Walsh	Michael L. Douglas
Michelle Leavitt	Mark R. Denton
Donald M. Mosley	Sally L. Loehrer
John S. McGroarty	Michael A. Cherry
Nancy M. Saitta	Allan R. Earl
David Wall	Valerie Adair
William O. Voy	Gloria S. Sanchez
Steven E. Jones	Gerald W. Hardcastle
Robert W. Lueck	Robert E. Gaston
Cynthia Dianne Steel	T. Arthur Ritchie, Jr.
Cheryl B. Moss	Lisa Brown
Nicholas A. Del Vecchio	Jennifer Elliott

NINTH JUDICIAL DISTRICT includes Douglas County. The court sits at Minden.

Judges
David R. Gamble
Michael P. Gibbons

SENIOR DISTRICT COURT JUDGES

Jack B. Ames	John W. Barrett
James A. Brennan	Stephen L. Huffaker
Jack Lehman	Joseph S. Pavlikowski
Mario G. Recanzone	Norman C. Robison

NEVADA JUSTICES' COURTS

Justices' Courts are courts of limited jurisdiction in Nevada. Justices of the Peace are elected by the voters of their respective townships for six-year terms. Vacancies may be filled in each county by the county commissioners. In townships having more than two justices of the peace, a chief justice of the peace is designated to serve for a term specified by each township. Some justices of the peace also serve as Municipal Court judges.

The courts have civil jurisdiction in cases when the amount does not exceed $7,500 and criminal jurisdiction over misdemeanors punishable by not more than six months imprisonment and/or a fine of $1,000. The courts also have jurisdiction over small claims actions not exceeding $5,000 and may conduct preliminary examinations in all felony and gross misdemeanor cases.

*Also Municipal Court Judge

Township	Justice of the Peace
Argenta	Max W. Bunch
Austin	James W. Andersen
Baker	Valeria M. Taylor
Beatty	Bill Sullivan
Beowawe	Susan Fye

NEVADA JUSTICES' COURTS—*Continued*

Boulder	Victor L. Miller*
Bunkerville	Cecil R. Leavitt
Canal	Robert J. Bennett
Carlin	Barbara J. Nethery*
Carson City	Robey B. Willis*
	John Tatro*
Dayton	William G. Rogers
East Fork	James EnEarl
East Line	Laura Grant*
Elko	Mary E. Leddy*
Ely	Ronald J. Niman
Esmeralda	Juanita M. Colvin
Eureka	John F. Schweble
Gerlach	Phil Thomas
Goldrun	Gene Wambolt
Goodsprings	Dawn L. Haviland
Hawthorne	Victor P. Trujillo
Henderson	Rodney T. Burr
	Stephen George
Incline Village/Crystal Bay	James V. Mancuso
Jackpot	Phyllis Black
Lake	Carol Nelsen
Las Vegas	Deborah J. Lippis
	Douglas E. Smith
	Anthony L. Abbatangelo
	James M. Bixler
	William D. Jansen
	Nancy C. Oesterle
	Karen Bennett-Haron
	Ann E. Zimmerman
Laughlin	Billy R. Moma
Lund	Russel W. Peacock
Mason Valley	Dennis Milligan
McDermitt	Howard Huttman, Jr.
Meadow Valley	Sarah K. "Pete" Getker
Mesquite	Ron L. Dodd*
Mina	Morris "Moe" Fanning
Moapa	Ruth Kolhoss
Moapa Valley	D. Lanny Waite
New River	Daniel P. Ward
North Las Vegas	Stephen J. Dahl
	Natalie Tyrrell
Pahranagat Valley	Nola A. Holton*
Pahrump	Tina Brisebill
Paradise Valley	Elizabeth Chabot
Reno	Fidel Salcedo
	Ed Dannan
	Jack Schroeder
	Harold G. Albright
	Barbara K. Finley
Searchlight	Wendell Ellis Turner
Smith Valley	Frances R. Vidal*
Sparks	Susan Deriso
	Paul W. Freitag
Tahoe	Richard Glasson
Tecoma	Roberta "Bobbie" Weighall
Tonopah	Joe Maslach
Union	Gene Wambolt
Verdi	Margie I. Clark
Virginia City	Annette Daniels
Wadsworth	Terry Graham
Wells	Patricia Calton*

NEVADA MUNICIPAL COURTS

Municipal Courts are courts of limited jurisdiction in Nevada established in incorporated cities and towns. Judges may be either elected or appointed, as provided by city ordinance. Judges can hold office for up to six years as fixed in the incorporating law. Vacancies may be filled by the local governing bodies. A chief judge may be designated to serve for a term specified by local law or charter. Some judges also serve as justices of the peace.

Jurisdiction of the Municipal Courts varies in each city as provided by law. The courts generally have jurisdiction over actions or proceedings for violations of city ordinances and over misdemeanors committed in their cities which are punishable by a fine not exceeding $2,500 and/or six months imprisonment.

*Also Justice of the Peace

City	Judge
Boulder City	Victor L. Miller*
Caliente	Nola A. Holton*
Carlin	Barbara J. Nethery*
Carson City	Robey B. Willis*
	John Tatro*
Elko	Mary E. Leddy*
Ely	Ronald J. Niman
Fallon	W. E. Teurman
Fernley	Daniel J. Bauer
Henderson	Ken Proctor
	Douglas Hedger
Las Vegas	Toy R. Gregory
	Elizabeth Kolkoski
	George Assad
	Bert M. Brown
	Cedric A. Kerns
	Dayvid Figler
Lovelock	Gordon N. Richardson
Mesquite	Ron L. Dodd*
North Las Vegas	Warren R. Van Landschoot
Reno	Jay D. Dilworth
	Paul Stewart Hickman
	James Van Winkle
	Kenneth R. Howard
Sparks	Barbara S. McCarthy
	Larry Sage
Wells	Patricia Calton*
West Wendover	Laura Grant*
Yerington	Frances R. Vidal*

Nevada Counties and County Seats

Carson City
(Independent City)

Churchill
Fallon

Clark
Las Vegas

Douglas
Minden

Elko
Elko

Esmeralda
Goldfield

Eureka
Eureka

Humboldt
Winnemucca

Lander
Battle Mountain

Lincoln
Pioche

Lyon
Yerington

Mineral
Hawthorne

Nye
Tonopah

Pershing
Lovelock

Storey
Virginia City

Washoe
Reno

White Pine
Ely

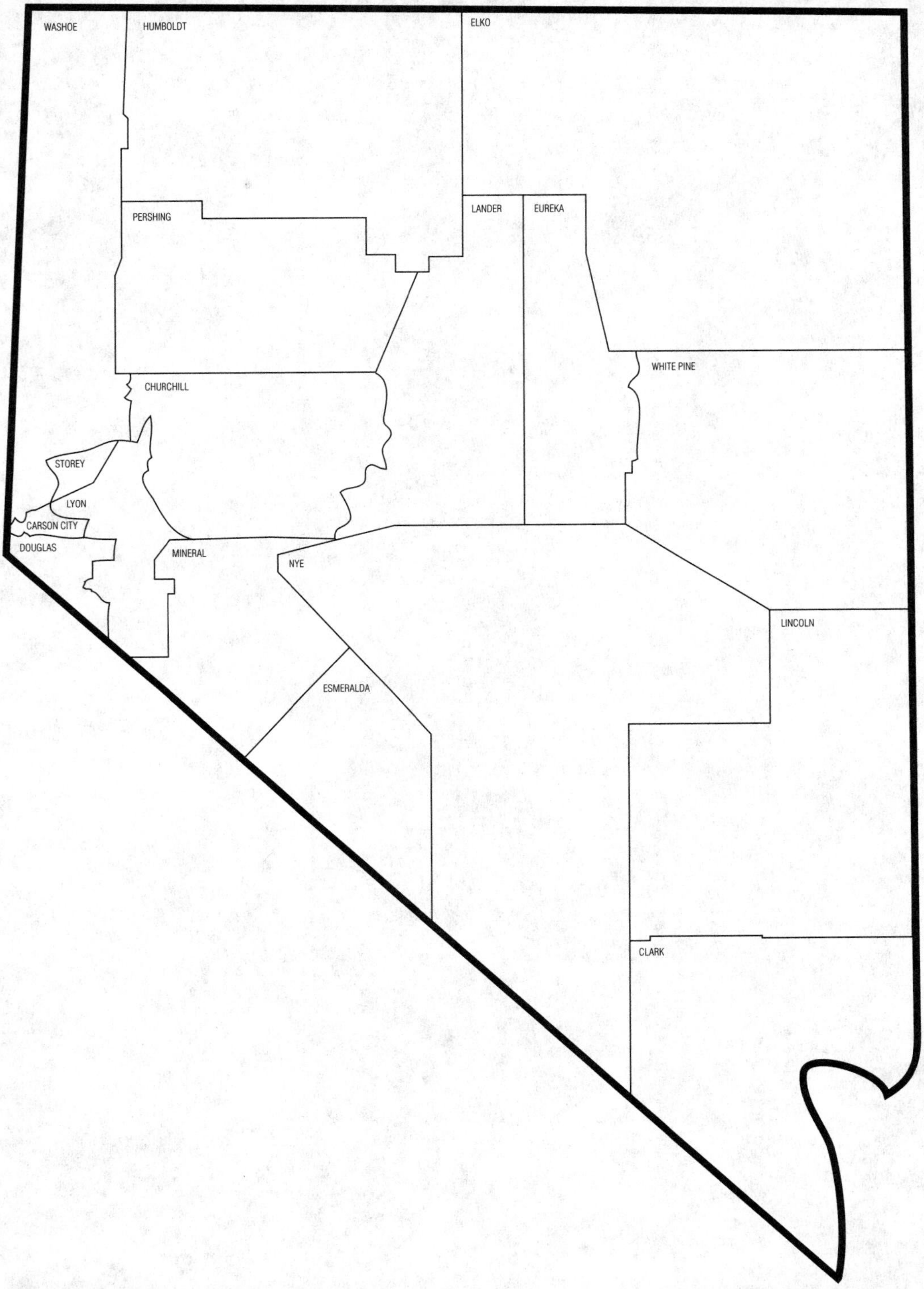
WASHOE
HUMBOLDT
ELKO
PERSHING
LANDER
EUREKA
WHITE PINE
CHURCHILL
STOREY
LYON
CARSON CITY
DOUGLAS
MINERAL
NYE
LINCOLN
ESMERALDA
CLARK

UNITED STATES DISTRICT COURT DISTRICT OF NEVADA

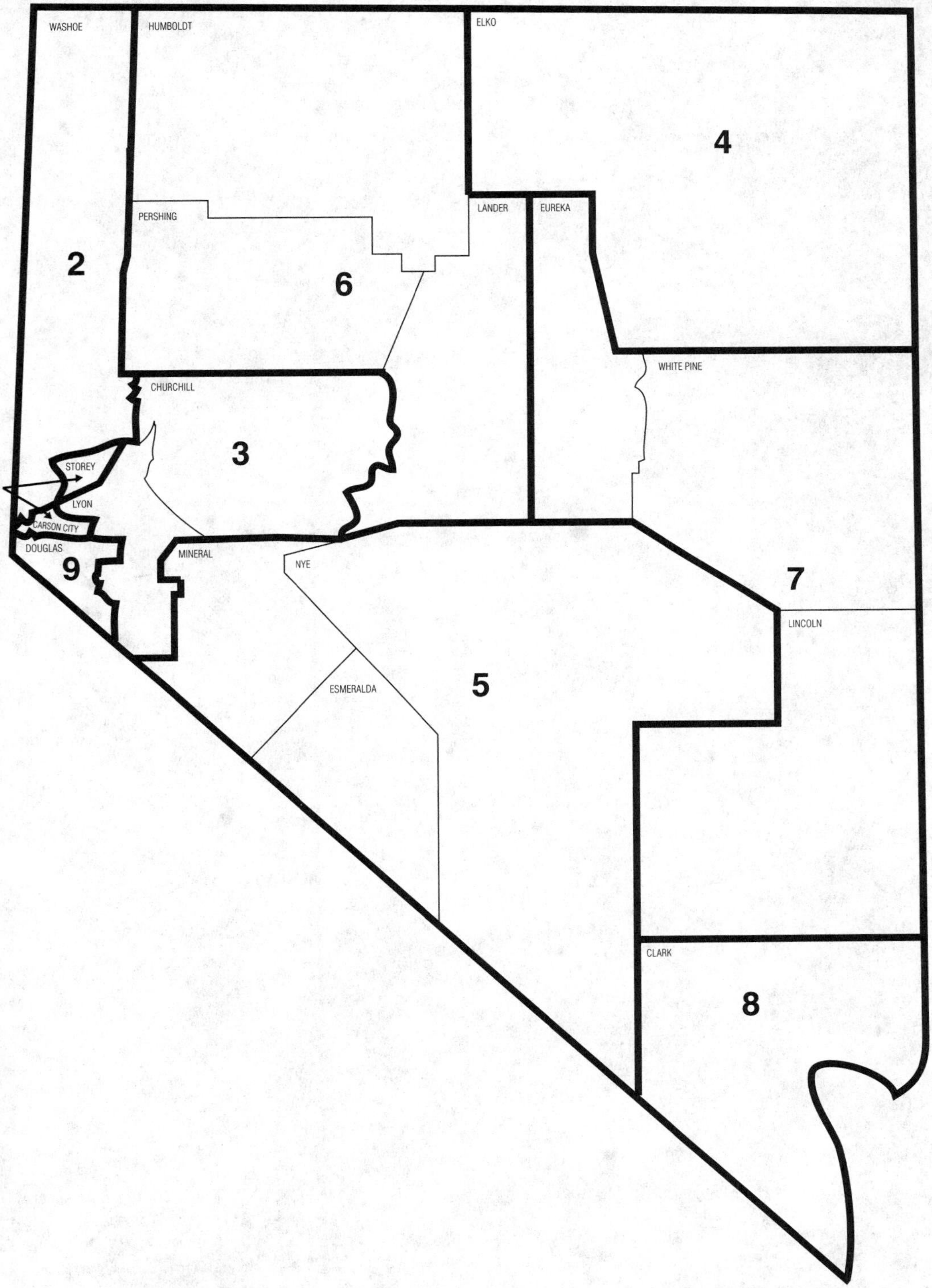
WASHOE
HUMBOLDT
ELKO
4
PERSHING
LANDER
EUREKA
2
6
CHURCHILL
WHITE PINE
3
STOREY
1
LYON
CARSON CITY
DOUGLAS
MINERAL
9
NYE
7
LINCOLN
ESMERALDA
5
CLARK
8

JUDICIAL DISTRICTS OF NEVADA DISTRICT COURTS

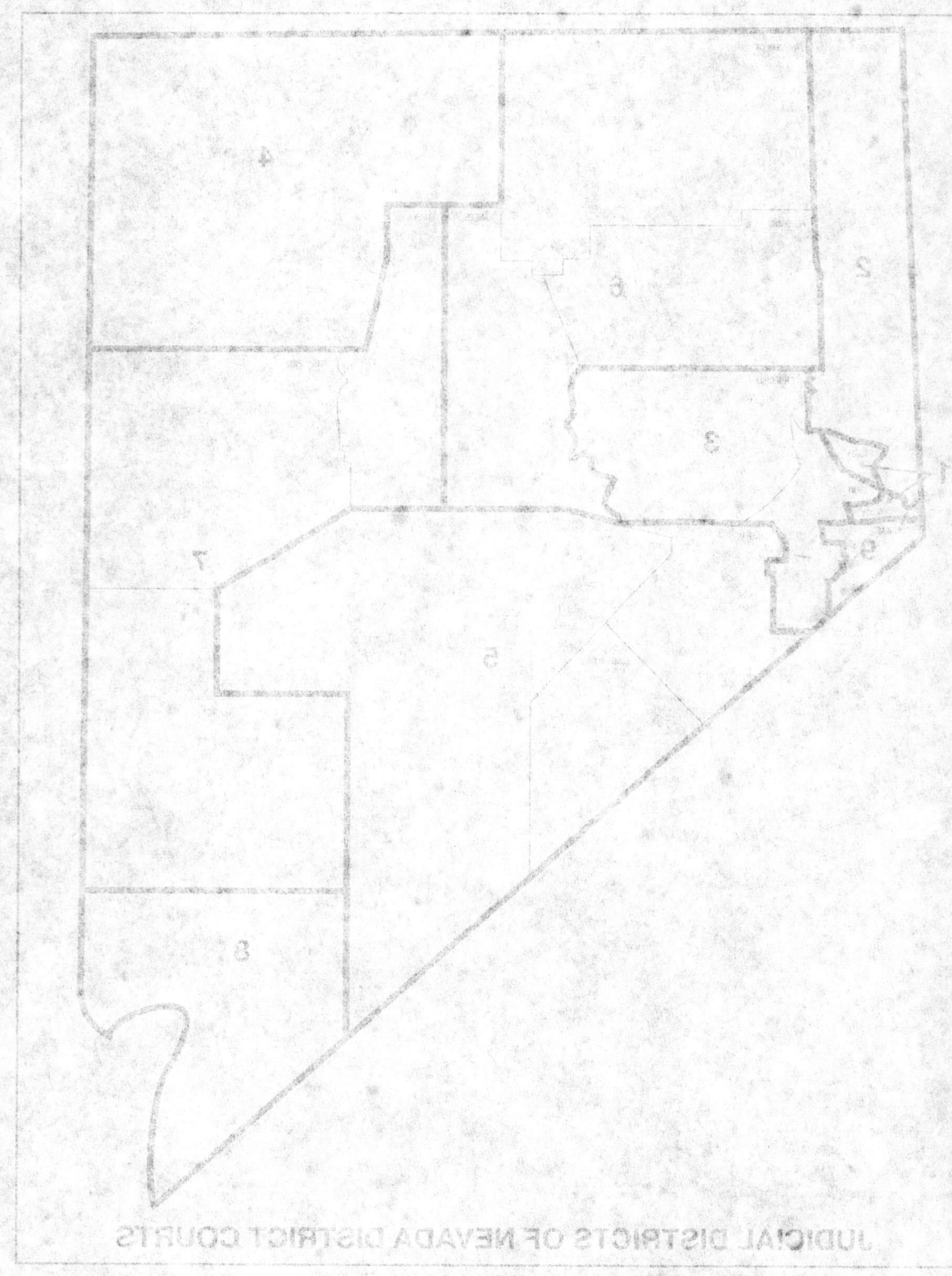

NEVADA

ABBATANGELO, Anthony L. *(Justice of the Peace, Las Vegas Justices' Court)* Elected to term beginning Sept 23, 1996. Reelected 1998, current term expires 2005. Currently serves as Vice Chief Justice of the Peace. Born Las Vegas Nevada April 29, 1965. Catholic. Educated at University of San Diego B.A. 1987 J.D. 1990 and Oxford International and Comparative Law Institute Summer 1988. Admitted to practice Nevada 1990 and U.S. District Court District of Nevada 1990. In legal practice 1990-93. Judge, Las Vegas Municipal Court May 3, 1993 to Sept 13, 1996.

Member Nevada Supreme Court Task Force for Racial and Economic Diversity, Nevada Society of American-Italian Lawyers (Secretary 1992-93, Treasurer 1993-94), Nevada Judges Association, American Judges Association, State Bar of Nevada (Executive Committee 1990, Secretary 1991 and Vice Chair 1992 Young Lawyers Section), Clark County (Public Service Committee 1995, Judicial Representative Executive Board Jan 16, 1997) and American Bar Associations. Host "Just Us" Program KCEP 88.1 FM May 1994 to May 1996. Completed more than 225 hours of judicial CLE. President Augustus Society 1999. Enjoys racquetball, swimming, reading, sporting events and movies.

Mailing address: P.O. Box 552511, Las Vegas 89155-2511.
Telephone: (702) 455-4124.
Fax: (702) 455-4223
E-mail address: ABB@co.clark.nv.us

ADAIR, Valerie *(Judge, Nevada District Court Eighth Judicial District)* Serves Civil/Criminal Division.
Office: Clark County Courthouse, 200 South Third Street, Las Vegas 89155.
Telephone: (702) 455-6809.
Fax: (702) 385-8967

ADAMS, Brent T. *(Judge, Nevada District Court Second Judicial District)* Serves Civil/Criminal Division.
Mailing address: P.O. Box 30083, Reno 89520-3083.
Office: 75 Court Street, Reno 89501.
Telephone: (775) 328-3176.
Fax: (775) 328-3532

AGOSTI, Deborah A. *(Chief Justice, Nevada Supreme Court)* Born Toledo Ohio Oct 10, 1951. Catholic. Educated at University of Toledo B.A. in Psychology cum laude 1973 J.D. 1976. Admitted to practice Ohio 1976 and Nevada 1978. Began legal practice Dayton Ohio 1977. In legal practice Reno Nevada 1977-82. Justice of the Peace, Reno Justice Court Jan 1983 to Jan 1985. Former Judge, Nevada District Court Second Judicial District, elected to term beginning Jan 7, 1985.

Assistant Public Defender Montgomery County Ohio 1977. Senior Staff Attorney Senior Citizens Legal Assistance Program Washoe County Legal Services 1977-79. District Attorney, Deputy District Attorney and Chief Deputy Juvenile Division Washoe County 1979-82. Cochair Jury Improvement Committee Nevada Supreme Court. Board of Trustees The National Judicial College and Pretrial Services Resource Center. Member Nevada Women Lawyers Association, Nevada District Judges Association (Secretary 1987-89, Vice President 1989-90, President 1990-91), National Women Judges Association, State Bar of Nevada and Washoe County Bar Association. Faculty Member The National Judicial College since 1989. Instructor in Evidence and Family Law Continuing Legal Education State Bar of Nevada 1990. Lecturer on Evidence Nevada Judges Association 1991. Named Outstanding Young Woman State of Nevada by Outstanding Young Women of America 1983. Former Instructor in Legal Consequences of Drug and Alcohol Abuse Washoe County School District. Board Member Reno Cancer Center and Reno Traffic Survival School. Member Soroptimists International of Truckee Meadows. Enjoys ethnic cooking, reading, music and cinema.

Office: 300 Supreme Court Building, 201 South Carson Street, Carson City 89701-4702.
Telephone: (775) 684-1510.

ALBRIGHT, Harold G. *(Justice of the Peace, Reno Justices' Court)* Currently serves as Chief Justice of the Peace.
Mailing address: P.O. Box 30083, Reno 89520-3083.
Telephone: (775) 325-6505.
Fax: (775) 325-6510

AMES, Jack B. *(Senior Judge, Nevada District Court)* Elected to term beginning Jan 7, 1991. Reelected 1996. Retired, serves by recall. Born Blackfoot Idaho Dec 17, 1945. Church of Jesus Christ of Latter-day Saints. Educated at Idaho State University 1964-65, Utah State University 1965-67 and University of Utah J.D. 1970. Law Clerk to Justice Thompson, Nevada Supreme Court 1970-71. Admitted to practice Nevada 1970. In legal practice Reno 1971-72 and Elko 1972-83. Magistrate, U.S. District Court District of Nevada Aug 1972 to Oct 1982. Justice of the Peace, Elko Justice Court 1983-91. Judge, Elko Municipal Court 1983-91.

Member Nevada Judges Association (President Elect 1987, President 1988), Nevada District Judges Association (Secretary 1996-97, Vice President 1997-98) and American Bar Association (Delegate National Conference of Special Court Judges Judicial Administration Division). Recipient Outstanding Judge of the Year Award from Nevada Judges Association 1986. Recognized by Nevada Supreme Court for outstanding judicial service as Elko Municipal Judge 1990. Specialist E-4 Nevada National Guard 1968-74. City Supervisor Elko 1975-83. Enjoys golf, aerobics and running.

Mailing address: 484 Hoala Drive, Kihei, Hawaii 96753.

ANDERSEN, James W. *(Justice of the Peace, Austin Justices' Court)* Elected Nov 1994 to term beginning Jan 3, 1995. Reelected 2000, current term expires Dec 31, 2006. Born Torrance California March 10, 1944. Completed high school education (no legal education).

Attended several courses The National Judicial College. Lance Corporal USMC 1962-64. Retired Deputy Sheriff.

Mailing address: P.O. Box 100, Austin 89310.
Telephone: (775) 964-2380.
Fax: (775) 964-2327

ASSAD, George *(Judge, Las Vegas Municipal Court)*
Office: 400 East Stewart Avenue, Las Vegas 89101.
Telephone: (702) 229-6584.
Fax: (702) 382-0320

BARRETT, John W. *(Senior Judge, Nevada District Court)* Serves by recall.
Mailing address: 1930 Marla Drive, Reno 89509.

BAUER, Daniel J. *(Judge, Fernley Municipal Court)*
Office: 565 East Main Street, Fernley 89408.
Telephone: (775) 575-3355.
Fax: (702) 575-3359

BECKER, Nancy A. *(Justice, Nevada Supreme Court)* Former Judge, Las Vegas Municipal Court. Former Judge and Chief Judge, Nevada District Court Eighth Judicial District.
Office: 316 Bridger Avenue, Las Vegas 89101.
Telephone: (702) 486-3205.

BELL, Stewart L. *(Judge, Nevada District Court Eighth Judicial District)* Serves Civil/Criminal Division.
Office: Clark County Courthouse, 200 South Third Street, Las Vegas 89155.
Telephone: (702) 455-4662.
Fax: (702) 455-2430

BENNETT, Robert J. *(Justice of the Peace, Canal Justices' Court)*
Office: 565 East Main Street, Fernley 89408.
Telephone: (775) 575-3355.
Fax: (775) 575-3359

BENNETT-HARON, Karen *(Justice of the Peace, Las Vegas Justices' Court)*
Mailing address: P.O. Box 552511, Las Vegas 89155-2511.
Telephone: (702) 455-4557.
Fax: (702) 382-3059

BERRY, Janet J. *(Judge, Nevada District Court Second Judicial District)* Former Chief Judge. Serves Civil/Criminal Division. Former Judge, Reno Municipal Court.
Mailing address: P.O. Box 30083, Reno 89520-3083.
Office: 75 Court Street, Reno 89501.
Telephone: (775) 328-3171.
Fax: (775) 328-3170

BIXLER, James M. *(Justice of the Peace, Las Vegas Justices' Court)* Elected Nov 4, 1980 to term beginning Jan 1981. Reelected Nov 6, 1984, Nov 8, 1988, Nov 3, 1992 and Nov 5, 1998. Current term expires 2004. Chief Justice of the Peace 1986, 1991 and 1997. Former Vice Chief Justice of the Peace. Born Nebraska 1947. Educated at Eastern New Mexico University B.B.A. 1971 and Baylor University School of Law J.D. 1973. Member Phi Alpha Delta. Admitted to practice Texas 1973, Nevada 1974 and U.S. District Court District of Nevada 1974. In legal practice Las Vegas 1974-81. Clerk Administrator North Las Vegas Municipal Court 1973-74.
Former Representative Judicial Council of the State of Nevada. Member Nevada Judges Association, State Bar of Nevada, State Bar of Texas and Clark County Bar Association (Former Member Judicial Evaluation Committee). Participant The National Judicial College since 1981. USMC two years. Former Chairman Clark County Law Library and Las Vegas Sporting House Memorial Day Olympics Annual Fundraiser. Former Board of Directors Senior Times, Opportunity Village Association and Clark County Traffic Survival School.
Mailing address: P.O. Box 552511, Las Vegas 89155-2511.
Office: Clark County Courthouse, Second Floor, 200 South Third Street, Las Vegas 89155-2511.
Telephone: (702) 455-3469.
Fax: (702) 455-4224

BLACK, Phyllis *(Justice of the Peace, Jackpot Justices' Court)*
Mailing address: P.O. Box 229, Jackpot 89825.
Telephone: (775) 755-2456.
Fax: (775) 755-2455

BLAKE, Archie E. *(Judge, Nevada District Court Third Judicial District)* Appointed by Governor Richard H. Bryan to term beginning Jan 5, 1988. Elected 1989, 1990, Nov 1996 and Nov 2002. Current term expires Jan 2009. Born Ontario Oregon Jan 26, 1943. Protestant. Educated at Southern Oregon College B.S. 1970, University of Nevada Reno M.S. in Econ. 1972 Master of Judicial Studies 1996 and University of Notre Dame J.D. 1977. Admitted to practice Nevada 1977. In legal practice Carson City 1977-79 and Yerington 1979-88.
Assistant District Attorney Lyon County 1979-88. City Attorney 1979-88 and Walker River Tribal Prosecutor 1979-88 Schurz Nevada. Instructor in Business Law 1979-80. Member American Judges Association, State Bar of Nevada, Washoe County and American Bar Associations. Attended numerous CLE courses and The National Judicial College courses. USN 1963-68. Research Economist State of Nevada 1970-74. Past President Yerington Rotary. Enjoys running, sailing and motorcycling. Personal Statement or Quote: "Live as if you will die tomorrow; learn as if you will live forever."
Office: 31 South Main, Suite B, Yerington 89447.
Telephone: (775) 463-6571.
Fax: (775) 463-6575
E-mail address: tjdc@gte.net

BONAVENTURE, Joseph T. *(Judge, Nevada District Court Eighth Judicial District)* Serves Civil/Criminal Division. Former Justice of the Peace, Las Vegas Justice Court.
Office: Clark County Courthouse, 200 South Third Street, Las Vegas 89155.
Telephone: (702) 455-4658.
Fax: (702) 455-2107

BREEN, Peter I. *(Judge, Nevada District Court Second Judicial District)* Elected to term beginning Jan 1974. Reelected to subsequent terms. Former Chief Judge. Born Reno Nevada Nov 8, 1939. Catholic. Educated at University of Nevada B.A. and University of Santa Clara LL.B. Admitted to practice Nevada 1963.
Member Washoe County Bar Association. Enjoys running, motorcycles and hunting.
Mailing address: P.O. Box 30083, Reno 89520-3083.
Office: 75 Court Street, Reno 89501.
Telephone: (775) 328-3158.
Fax: (775) 328-3851

BRENNAN, James A. *(Senior Judge, Nevada District Court)* Elected to term beginning Jan 6, 1975. Reelected to subsequent terms. Retired, serves by recall. Born Miami Florida Aug 22, 1930. Catholic. Educated at University of Nevada Reno B.A. 1954 and Hastings College of the Law J.D. 1958. Member Lambda Chi Alpha. Ad-

BRENNAN, JAMES A.—*Continued*

mitted to practice Nevada 1958. Began legal practice Las Vegas 1958. Justice of the Peace, Las Vegas Justice Court, elected to term beginning 1965.

Deputy District Attorney 1959. Clark County Commissioner 1968-72 (Chairman 1972). Legal Advisor to Clark County Health District and Colorado River Water Advisory Commission. Member State Bar of Nevada, Clark County and American Bar Associations. Republican. Board of Trustees 1960 and Chairman 1964 South Nevada Memorial Hospital. Former member Board of Directors YMCA, Red Cross and Clark County Chapter American Cancer Society. Member Variety Clubs International. Enjoys snow skiing, scuba diving and dove hunting.

Office: 330 South Third Street, Suite 1120, Las Vegas 89101.
Telephone: (702) 455-0446.

BRISEBILL, Tina *(Justice of the Peace, Pahrump Justices' Court)*
Office: Nye County Government Center, 1520 East Basin Avenue, Pahrump 89060.
Telephone: (775) 751-7050.
Fax: (775) 751-7059

BROWN, Bert M. *(Judge, Las Vegas Municipal Court)*
Office: 400 East Stewart Avenue, Las Vegas 89101.
Telephone: (702) 229-2036.
Fax: (702) 382-0320

BROWN, Lisa *(Judge, Nevada District Court Eighth Judicial District)* Serves Family Division.
Office: Courthouse, 601 North Pecos, Las Vegas 89101-2408.
Telephone: (702) 455-1882.
Fax: (702) 455-5989

BUNCH, Max W. *(Justice of the Peace, Argenta Justices' Court)*
Office: 315 South Humboldt, Battle Mountain 89820.
Telephone: (775) 635-5151.
Fax: (775) 635-0604

BURR, Rodney T. *(Justice of the Peace, Henderson Justices' Court)* Elected to term beginning Dec 4, 1990. Reelected 1994 and Jan 2001. Current term expires Jan 2007. Born Richfield Utah May 27, 1958. Educated at University of Nevada Las Vegas B.A. 1983 and McGeorge School of Law University of the Pacific J.D. 1986. Admitted to practice Nevada 1986.

Prosecutor District Attorney's Office Clark County 1986-90. Member Urban Court Workload Assessment Commission. Member Nevada Judges Association (Former First Vice President and President 1997 Board), American Judges Association, State Bar of Nevada, Clark County and American Bar Associations. Recipient Judge of the Year Award from Nevada Conference of Police and Sheriffs 1993.

Office: 243 Water Street, Henderson 89015.
Telephone: (702) 455-7962.
Fax: (702) 455-7935

CALTON, Patricia *(Justice of the Peace, Wells Justices' Court and Judge, Wells Municipal Court)*
Mailing address: P.O. Box 297, Wells 89835.
Telephone: (775) 752-3726.
Fax: (775) 752-3363

CHABOT, Elizabeth *(Justice of the Peace, Paradise Valley Justices' Court)*
Mailing address: P.O. Box 3, Paradise Valley 89426.
Telephone: (775) 578-3582.

CHERRY, Michael A. *(Judge, Nevada District Court Eighth Judicial District)* Serves Civil/Criminal Division.
Office: Clark County Courthouse, 200 South Third Street, Las Vegas 89155.
Telephone: (702) 455-5117.
Fax: (702) 382-3790

CLARK, Margie I. *(Justice of the Peace, Verdi Justices' Court)*
Mailing address: P.O. Box 740, Verdi 89439.
Telephone: (775) 345-0173.
Fax: (775) 345-0633

COLVIN, Juanita M. *(Justice of the Peace, Esmeralda Justices' Court)* Also serves as Juvenile Master, Nevada District Court Fifth Judicial District.
Mailing address: P.O. Box 370, Goldfield 89013.
Telephone: (775) 485-6359.
Fax: (775) 485-3462

COOKE, Valerie P. *(Magistrate Judge, United States District Court District of Nevada)* Appointed by U.S. District Court judges to term beginning Nov 1, 1999. Term expires 2007.
Office: U.S. Courthouse, 400 South Virginia Street, Reno 89501.
Telephone: (702) 464-5400.

DAHL, Stephen J. *(Justice of the Peace, North Las Vegas Justices' Court)*
Office: 2428 North Martin Luther King Boulevard, North Las Vegas 89032.
Telephone: (702) 455-7804.
Fax: (702) 455-7831

DANIELS, Annette *(Justice of the Peace, Virginia City Justices' Court)*
Mailing address: P.O. Box 674, Virginia City 89440.
Telephone: (775) 847-0962.
Fax: (775) 847-0915

DANNAN, Ed *(Justice of the Peace, Reno Justices' Court)* Former Chief Justice of the Peace.
Mailing address: P.O. Box 30083, Reno 89520-3083.
Telephone: (775) 325-6505.
Fax: (775) 325-6510

DAVIS, John P. *(Judge, Nevada District Court Fifth Judicial District)* Elected Nov 1990 to term beginning Jan 1991. Reelected Nov 1996 and 2002. Current term expires Jan 2009. Born New York New York April 11, 1934. Protestant. Educated at Colorado School of Mines E.M. with honors 1956 and University of California J.D. 1972. Admitted to practice California 1972, Nevada 1973, U.S. District Court District of Nevada 1973 and U.S. Supreme Court. In legal practice Minden Nevada 1972-81 and Yerington Nevada 1981-87. Justice of the Peace, Smith Valley Justices' Court 1983-87.

Attended several courses The National Judicial College. 1st Lieutenant U.S. Army Corps of Engineers 1956-58. Republican. Enjoys hunting, hiking and fishing.
Mailing address: P.O. Box 393, Tonopah 89049.
Office: One Courthouse Road, Tonopah 89049.
Telephone: (775) 482-8141 (Tonopah), 945-2446 (Hawthorne), 485-6367 (Goldfield).
Fax: (775) 482-8133

DAWSON, Kent J. *(Judge, United States District Court District of Nevada)* Appointed for life by President Bill Clinton to term beginning July 7, 2000. Born Ogden Utah June 13, 1944. Educated at Weber State College B.S. 1969 and University of Utah College of Law J.D. 1971. Law Clerk to Hon. James J. Guinan, Nevada District Court District Two 1971-72. In legal practice Las Vegas 1979-95. Judge pro tem, Henderson Municipal Court 1993-95. Justice of the Peace, Henderson Justices' Court 1995-2000.

Assistant City Attorney 1972-73 and City Attorney 1973-79 Henderson. General Counsel Nevada Public Improvement Trust Henderson 1973-95. City Manager Henderson 1977.

Office: U.S. Courthouse, 333 Las Vegas Boulevard South, Las Vegas 89101.
Telephone: (702) 464-5400.

DEL VECCHIO, Nicholas Anthony *(Judge, Nevada District Court Eighth Judicial District)* Serves Family Division.

Office: Courthouse, 601 North Pecos, Las Vegas 89101-2408.
Telephone: (702) 455-1892.
Fax: (702) 455-5989

DENTON, Mark R. *(Judge, Nevada District Court Eighth Judicial District)* Serves Civil/Criminal Division. Former Judge, Boulder City Municipal Court.

Office: Clark County Courthouse, 200 South Third Street, Las Vegas 89155.
Telephone: (702) 455-4313.
Fax: (702) 384-1515

DERISO, Susan *(Justice of the Peace, Sparks Justices' Court)*

Office: 630 Greenbrae Drive, Sparks 89431.
Telephone: (775) 352-3000.
Fax: (775) 352-3004

DILWORTH, Jay D. *(Judge, Reno Municipal Court)* Currently serves as Chief Judge.

Mailing address: P.O. Box 1900, Reno 89505.
Telephone: (775) 334-2296.
Fax: (702) 334-3859

DOBRESCU, Steve L. *(Judge, Nevada District Court Seventh Judicial District)*

Mailing address: P.O. Box 151597, Ely 89315.
Office: 801 Clark Street, Ely 89301.
Telephone: (775) 289-4813, 962-5390 (Pioche), 237-5262 (Eureka).
Fax: (775) 289-1541

DODD, Ron L. *(Justice of the Peace, Mesquite Justices' Court and Judge, Mesquite Municipal Court)* Appointed Justice of the Peace to term beginning Oct 1998. Elected 2000, current term expires Dec 2006.

Justices' Court mailing address: P.O. Box 1209, Mesquite 89024.
Telephone: (702) 346-5298.
Fax: (702) 346-7319
Municipal Court office: 500 Hillside, Mesquite 89027.
Telephone: (702) 346-5291.
Fax: (702) 346-6587

DOHERTY, Frances *(Judge, Nevada District Court Second Judicial District)* Serves Family Division.

Office: One South Sierra Street, Third Floor, Reno 89501.
Telephone: (775) 328-3470.
Fax: (775) 328-3475

DOUGLAS, Michael Lawrence *(Judge, Nevada District Court Eighth Judicial District)* Appointed by Governor Bob Miller to term beginning Jan 12, 1996. Elected 1996 and 2002. Current term expires 2008. Serves Civil/Criminal Division. Born Los Angeles California March 13, 1948. Presbyterian. Educated at California State University at Long Beach B.A. 1971 and University of California Hastings College of the Law J.D. 1974. Member Alpha Phi Alpha and Sigma Pi Phi. Admitted to practice Pennsylvania 1981, Nevada 1983, U.S. District Courts Eastern District of Pennsylvania 1981 and District of Nevada 1983 and U.S. Court of Appeals Ninth Circuit 1983. In legal practice Philadelphia Pennsylvania 1981-82.

Directing Attorney Nevada Legal Services Program 1982-84 and Deputy District Attorney Civil Division 1984-96 Clark County. Legal Instructor Los Angeles Community College District 1975-77. Secretary 1985-86 and 1986-87, President 1987-88, Member Scholarship Banquet Committee 1987-94 and Scholarship Chairman 1989-95 Las Vegas Chapter National Bar Association. Board Member Nevada Law Foundation 1991-93. Member Nevada Inns of Court 1996-98. Member Nevada Gaming Attorneys, National District Attorneys Association, State Bar of Nevada (Southern Nevada Disciplinary Board 1988-95), Philadelphia, Clark County, Pennsylvania and American Bar Associations. Recipient Community Service Award from California State Assembly 1981, Service Award from Las Vegas Chapter National Bar Association 1987 and 1991, Proclamation for Community Service Award from Clark County 1989 and Mark of Excellence Award from National Federation of Black Public Administrators 1996. Named Boss of the Year by ABWA 1984. Board Member 1983-85 and Advisory Board 1991-97 Temporary Assistance for Domestic Crisis. Coach Central Valley Little League 1991-95. Participant Spirit of Nevada Art Contest 1997-98. Member University of California Hastings College of the Law Alumni Association and California State University at Long Beach Alumni Association.

Office: Clark County Courthouse, 200 South Third Street, Las Vegas 89155.
Telephone: (702) 455-4527.
Fax: (702) 455-0058

EARL, Allan R. *(Judge, Nevada District Court Eighth Judicial District)* Serves Civil/Criminal Division.

Office: Clark County Courthouse, 200 South Third Street, Las Vegas 89155.
Telephone: (702) 455-5292.
Fax: (702) 382-3797

ELLIOTT, Jennifer *(Judge, Nevada District Court Eighth Judicial District)* Serves Family Division.

Office: Courthouse, 601 North Pecos, Las Vegas 89101-2408.
Telephone: (702) 455-0158.
Fax: (702) 382-4239

ELLIOTT, Steven P. *(Judge, Nevada District Court Second Judicial District)* Elected Nov 5, 1996 to term beginning Jan 5, 1997. Reelected Nov 5, 2002, current

ELLIOTT, STEVEN P.—*Continued*
term expires Jan 2009. Born Hawthorne California April 22, 1948. Roman Catholic. Educated at Stanford University B.A. 1971 and University of Denver J.D. 1975. Admitted to practice California 1975, Nevada 1976, U.S. Court of Appeals Ninth Circuit 1979, U.S. District Court District of Nevada 1980 and U.S. Supreme Court 1980. In legal practice Reno 1976-77.

Assistant City Attorney 1977-79 and City Attorney 1979-97 Sparks. State Chairman National Institute of Municipal Law Officers 1983 and 1989. Member State Bar of California, State Bar of Nevada and Washoe County Bar Association. Attended course for Prosecuting Attorneys Northwestern University School of Law 1977. Instructor "Proposed Amendments to Civil Rights Act 42 USC" 1983 and "Dedication of Water Rights" 1985 National Institute of Municipal Law Officers and "View from the Bench" Seminar State Bar of Nevada 1998-2000. President Pyramid Sertoma Club 1980-81 and Sparks Traffic Survival School 1986-88. Board of Directors Sparks Community Chamber of Commerce and Boys and Girls Club of Truckee Meadows. Director Western Nevada Clean Communities. Member Reno Rotary Club. Enjoys skiing, golfing and mountain climbing.

Mailing address: P.O. Box 30083, Reno 89520-3083.
Office: 75 Court Street, Reno 89501.
Telephone: (775) 328-3530.
Fax: (775) 328-3829

EnEARL, James *(Justice of the Peace, East Fork Justices' Court)* Also serves as Juvenile Master, Nevada District Court Ninth Judicial District.

Mailing address: P.O. Box 218, Minden 89423.
Telephone: (775) 782-9955.
Fax: (775) 782-9947

ESTES, Robert E. *(Judge, Nevada District Court Third Judicial District)*

Office: 31 South Main Street, Second Floor, Yerington 89447.
Telephone: (775) 463-6571.
Fax: (775) 463-6575

FANNING, Morris "Moe" *(Justice of the Peace, Mina Justices' Court)*

Mailing address: P.O. Box 415, Mina 89422.
Telephone: (775) 573-2547.
Fax: (775) 573-2663

FIGLER, Dayvid *(Judge, Las Vegas Municipal Court)*

Office: 400 East Stewart Avenue, Las Vegas 89101.
Telephone: (702) 229-2407.
Fax: (702) 384-7477

FINLEY, Barbara K. *(Justice of the Peace, Reno Justices' Court)* Elected Nov 1998 to term beginning Jan 4, 1999. Term expires Jan 2005. Born Phoenix Arizona Oct 10, 1943. Protestant. Educated at University of Nevada Las Vegas B.A. 1971 and Old College Law School J.D. cum laude 1983. Law Clerk to Hon. Peter I. Breen, Nevada District Court Second Judicial District 1988 to 1989. Member Delta Theta Phi. Admitted to practice Nevada 1987 and U.S. District Court District of Nevada 1987. In legal practice Reno Sept 1989 to Dec 1998.

Member Northern Nevada Women Lawyers, Nevada Judges Association, State Bar of Nevada and American Bar Association.

Mailing address: P.O. Box 30083, Reno 89520-3083.
Telephone: (775) 325-6505.
Fax: (775) 325-6591
E-mail address: bfinley@mail.co.washoe.nv.us

FREITAG, Paul W. *(Justice of the Peace, Sparks Justices' Court)*

Office: 630 Greenbrae Drive, Sparks 89431.
Telephone: (775) 352-3000.
Fax: (775) 352-3004

FYE, Susan *(Justice of the Peace, Beowawe Justices' Court)*

Mailing address: P.O. Box 211338, Crescent Valley 89821.
Telephone: (775) 468-0244, 237-5221.
Fax: (775) 468-0323

GAMBLE, David R. *(Judge, Nevada District Court Ninth Judicial District)* Elected to term beginning Jan 5, 1987. Reelected 1990, 1996 and 2002. Current term expires Jan 2008. Born Lovelock Nevada Dec 10, 1950. Christian. Educated at Stanford University B.A. 1972 and Willamette University College of Law J.D. 1976. Admitted to practice Nevada 1976, U.S. District Court District of Nevada 1977 and U.S. Court of Appeals Ninth Circuit 1977. In legal practice Carson City 1976-87.

Member Nevada Trial Lawyers Association (Board of Governors 1978-86, President 1984-85), The Association of Trial Lawyers of America (Delegate 1983-86) and State Bar of Nevada. Republican. Enjoys hunting and fishing.

Mailing address: P.O. Box 218, Minden 89423.
Office: Judicial & Law Enforcement Building, 1625 Eighth Street, Minden 89423.
Telephone: (775) 782-9961.
Fax: (775) 782-9964

GASTON, Robert E. *(Judge, Nevada District Court Eighth Judicial District)* Elected Nov 1992 to term beginning Jan 1993. Reelected 1997, current term expires Dec 31, 2004. Former Presiding Judge. Former Juvenile Judge Family Division. Serves Family Division. Born Sacramento California Oct 4, 1939. Methodist. Educated at Baylor University B.A. 1962, California Western University M.A. with honors 1966, University of Nevada Las Vegas Ed.D with honors 1979 and California Western School of Law J.D. with honors 1982. Editor International Law Review 1981-82. Admitted to practice Nevada 1982, U.S. District Court District of Nevada 1982 and U.S. Court of Appeals Ninth Circuit 1982. In legal practice Las Vegas 1982-93.

Important Decision: Lofgren v. Lofgren (allowed for the unequal distribution of property based on "compelling reasons") 112 Nev. Adv. Opinion 156, 1996. Instructor in Educational Law University of Nevada Las Vegas 1988. Member Standing Committee on Judicial Ethics, National Council of Juvenile and Family Court Judges, American Judges Association and American Bar Association. Instructor CLE seminars on Domestic Violence, Losing Credibility in Court, Domestic Torts, Censorship, Term Limits for the Judiciary, Court Policies and Procedures and Legislative Enactments. Recipient "Good Guy" Award from Women's Political Caucus and Volunteer Service Award from Domestic Violence Shelter. Democrat. Assemblyman Nevada Legislature 1987-

GASTON, ROBERT E.—*Continued*

1990. President Rotary Club. Board of Directors Domestic Violence Shelter. Member Attorney General's Domestic Violence Prevention Council. Boy Scout Leader. Private pilot.

Office: Courthouse, 601 North Pecos, Las Vegas 89101-2408.

Telephone: (702) 455-5995.

Fax: (702) 382-0062

GATES, Lee A. *(Judge, Nevada District Court Eighth Judicial District)* Appointed by Governor Bob Miller to term beginning Sept 9, 1991. Elected Nov 1992, 1996 and 2002. Current term expires Dec 31, 2008. Former Chief Judge. Serves Civil/Criminal Division. Born Madison Parish Louisiana Sept 4, 1952. Protestant. Educated at University of Nevada Las Vegas B.A. with honors 1974 and University of Colorado J.D. 1977. Admitted to practice Colorado 1977, Texas 1982 and Nevada 1986. In legal practice Las Vegas Nevada 1987-91.

Board of Directors YMCA.

Office: Clark County Courthouse, 200 South Third Street, Las Vegas 89155.

Telephone: (702) 455-4681.

Fax: (702) 382-1015

GEORGE, Lloyd D. *(Senior Judge, United States District Court District of Nevada)* Bankruptcy Judge March 4, 1974 to May 1, 1984. Appointed Judge for life by President Ronald Reagan to term beginning May 2, 1984. Former Chief Judge. Assumed Senior status, serves by assignment. Born Montpelier Idaho Feb 22, 1930. Church of Jesus Christ of Latter-day Saints. Educated at Brigham Young University B.S. 1955 and University of California at Berkeley J.D. 1961. Admitted to practice Nevada 1961. Began legal practice Las Vegas 1961. Justice of the Peace, Clark County Justices' Court 1962-69. Special Master, Juvenile Court Eighth Judicial District 1970-74.

Member Ninth Circuit Bankruptcy Appellate Panels 1979-84, Federal Judicial Center 1979-83 (Board member), National Bankruptcy Conference 1982, The Association of Trial Lawyers of America, State Bar of Nevada, Clark County, Washoe County and American Bar Associations. Captain USAF (pilot) 1955-58. Former Chairman State Apprenticeship Council. Former member Small Business Administration Advisory Council. Past President Brigham Young University International Alumni Association. Member Executive Committee Visiting Board J. Reuben Clark Law School Brigham Young University. Board of Directors Business and Professional Association of Southern Nevada (President) and local chapter National Conference of Christians and Jews (Executive Committee). Past President Clark County Association for Retarded Children. Enjoys golf and skiing.

Office: 6073 U.S. Courthouse, 333 Las Vegas Boulevard South, Las Vegas 89101.

Telephone: (702) 464-5500.

GEORGE, Stephen *(Justice of the Peace, Henderson Justices' Court)*

Office: 243 Water Street, Henderson 89015.

Telephone: (702) 455-7985.

Fax: (702) 455-7935

GETKER, Sarah K. "Pete" *(Justice of the Peace, Meadow Valley Justices' Court)* Appointed to term beginning Feb 5, 1982. Elected 1982, 1986, 1990, 1994 and 2000. Current term expires Jan 1, 2007. Born Cedar City Utah Dec 5, 1937. Church of Jesus Christ of Latter-day Saints. Educated at College of Southern Utah Secretarial Science degree 1958. Member Phi Rho Omega.

President Nevada Judges Association 1989-90. Graduate The National Judicial College 1985. Recipient Distinguished Jurist Award from The National Judicial College Dec 13, 1985. Interests include cat collectibles, dancing and yard work.

Mailing address: P.O. Box 36, Pioche 89043.

Telephone: (775) 962-5140, 728-4610.

Fax: (775) 962-5559

GIBBONS, Mark *(Justice, Nevada Supreme Court)* Former Judge and Chief Judge, Nevada District Court Eighth Judicial District.

Office: 300 Supreme Court Building, 201 South Carson Street, Carson City 89701-4702.

Telephone: (775) 684-1500.

GIBBONS, Michael P. *(Judge, Nevada District Court Ninth Judicial District)* Elected to term beginning 1995. Reelected to subsequent term. Born Whittier California Feb 22, 1956. Roman Catholic. Educated at Cypress College A.A. 1975, University of California at Los Angeles B.A. 1977 and University of Idaho College of Law J.D. 1980. Notes and Comments Editor Idaho Law Review 1979-80. Law Clerk to Hon. Howard D. McKibben, Nevada District Court Ninth Judicial District 1980-81. Admitted to practice Nevada 1980, California 1981, U.S. District Courts District of Nevada 1981 and Eastern, Northern and Southern Districts of California, U.S. Court of Appeals Ninth Circuit 1984 and U.S. Supreme Court 1986. In legal practice Minden Nevada 1981-92.

Deputy District Attorney 1981-84 and Chief Criminal Deputy District Attorney 1984-94 Douglas County. Special Assistant U.S. Attorney Reno 1984-85. Special Deputy Attorney General Nevada 1992-93. Author Opinion "Victims Have Rights, Too" The Record Courier April 1989. Disciplinary Board Northern District State Bar of Nevada 1990-94. Member Nevada Commission on Judicial Discipline 1995, Nevada State Judicial Council since 1998 and Nevada Committee on Judicial Ethics and Election Practice since 1998. Trustee National Council of Juvenile and Family Court Judges 2001-02. Executive Board Douglas County Juvenile Probation Advisory Committee. Member Sierra Regional Judicial Council (Chair since 1998), Nevada District Judges Association (Education Committee, Legislative Committee) and Douglas County Bar Association (President 1987-88). Recipient Certificate of Special Appreciation from Mothers Against Drunk Driving 1994, Quiet Rotarian Award 1995-96, Pride Award from Nevada State Library 1997 and Certificate of Appreciation from Court Appointed Special Advocates 1999. Republican. Head Coach AYSO Girls Soccer 2000-01. Member Douglas County School Safety Task Force, Tahoe-Douglas Rotary Club (Board of Directors 1993-95), Carson Valley Chamber of Commerce and St. Gall Church.

Mailing address: P.O. Box 218, Minden 89423.

Office: Judicial & Law Enforcement Building, 1625 Eighth Street, Minden 89423.

Telephone: (775) 782-9951.

Fax: (775) 782-9878

E-mail address: mgibbons@co.douglas.nv.us

GLASS, Jackie *(Judge, Nevada District Court Eighth Judicial District)* Serves Civil/Criminal Division.
Office: Clark County Courthouse, 200 South Third Street, Las Vegas 89155.
Telephone: (702) 455-4655.
Fax: (702) 455-0056

GLASSON, Richard *(Justice of the Peace, Tahoe Justices' Court)* Elected to term beginning Jan 2001. Term expires Jan 2007. Born San Mateo California May 1953. Jewish. Educated at University of California A.B. 1975 and University of the Pacific J.D. 1978. Member Traynor Honor Society. Admitted to practice California 1978, Nevada 1979, U.S. Court of Appeals Ninth Circuit 1980 and U.S. Supreme Court 1992. In legal practice Stateline Nevada 1978-2000.
Member American Judges Association, State Bar of California, State Bar of Nevada and Washoe County Bar Association.
Mailing address: P.O. Box 7169, Stateline 89449.
Telephone: (775) 586-7200.

GOLDWATER, Bert M. *(Recalled Judge, United States Bankruptcy Court District of Nevada)* Appointed Judge by U.S. Court of Appeals Ninth Circuit judges. Appointed Recalled Judge by the Judicial Council of the Ninth Circuit.
Office: Federal Building, 300 Booth Street, Reno 89509.
Telephone: (775) 784-5017.

GRAHAM, Terry *(Justice of the Peace, Wadsworth Justices' Court)*
Mailing address: P.O. Box 68, Wadsworth 89442.
Telephone: (775) 575-4585.
Fax: (775) 575-0253

GRANT, Laura *(Justice of the Peace, East Line Justices' Court and Judge, West Wendover Municipal Court)*
Mailing address: P.O. Box 2300, West Wendover 89883.
Telephone: (775) 664-2305.
Fax: (775) 664-2979

GREGORY, Toy R. *(Judge, Las Vegas Municipal Court)* Appointed by Las Vegas City Council Jan 1983. Elected June 1983, June 1987, 1991, 1995 and 1999. Current term expires 2005. Currently serves as Chief Judge. Born Lancaster South Carolina Oct 29, 1933. Baptist. Educated at University of North Carolina A.B. 1956 LL.B. 1958. Admitted to practice Nevada 1958. In legal practice Las Vegas 1958-83.
Past President Southern Nevada Trial Lawyers Association. Member Nevada Judges Association, American Judges Association, State Bar of Nevada and American Bar Association (National Conference of Special Court Judges Judicial Administration Division). First Lieutenant USAR 1959-62. Past President Las Vegas Jaycees and Las Vegas Host Lions Club. Former member Board of Directors Las Vegas Chamber of Commerce.
Office: 400 East Stewart Avenue, Las Vegas 89101.
Telephone: (702) 229-2059.
Fax: (702) 384-7477

GRIFFIN, Michael R. *(Judge, Nevada District Court First Judicial District)*
Office: 885 East Musser Street, Suite 3061, Carson City 89701.
Telephone: (775) 882-1996.
Fax: (775) 887-2272

HAGEN, David W. *(Judge, United States District Court District of Nevada)* Appointed for life by President Bill Clinton to term beginning Nov 22, 1993. Born Camden Arkansas Oct 2, 1931. Educated at University of Wisconsin B.B.A. 1956 and University of San Francisco School of Law LL.B. 1959. In legal practice Berkeley California 1960-62, Loyalton California 1962-63 and Reno Nevada 1963-93.
Office: 805 U.S. Courthouse, 400 South Virginia Street, Reno 89501.
Telephone: (775) 686-5888.

HARDCASTLE, Gerald W. *(Judge, Nevada District Court Eighth Judicial District)* Currently serves as Juvenile Judge Family Division.
Office: Courthouse, 601 North Pecos, Las Vegas 89101-2408.
Telephone: (702) 455-5993.
Fax: (702) 455-5989

HARDCASTLE, Kathy A. *(Judge, Nevada District Court Eighth Judicial District)* Serves Civil/Criminal Division.
Office: Clark County Courthouse, 200 South Third Street, Las Vegas 89155.
Telephone: (702) 455-4652.
Fax: (702) 455-0139

HARDESTY, James W. *(Chief Judge, Nevada District Court Second Judicial District)* Serves Civil/Criminal Division.
Mailing address: P.O. Box 30083, Reno 89520-3083.
Office: 75 Court Street, Reno 89501.
Telephone: (775) 328-3162.
Fax: (775) 328-3193

HAVILAND, Dawn L. *(Justice of the Peace, Goodsprings Justices' Court)*
Mailing address: P.O. Box 19155, Jean 89019-9155.
Telephone: (702) 874-1405.
Fax: (702) 874-1612

HEDGER, Douglas *(Judge, Henderson Municipal Court)* Elected to term beginning 2003.
Office: 243 Water Street, Henderson 89015.
Telephone: (702) 565-1580.
Fax: (702) 565-2308

HICKMAN, Paul Stewart *(Judge, Reno Municipal Court)* Chief Judge July 1996 to June 1997.
Mailing address: P.O. Box 1900, Reno 89505.
Telephone: (775) 334-2297.
Fax: (775) 334-3859

HICKS, Larry R. *(Judge, United States District Court District of Nevada)* Appointed for life by President George W. Bush to term beginning Nov 29, 2001. Born Evanston Illinois Dec 13, 1943. Episcopalian. Educated at University of Nevada at Reno B.S. 1965 and University of Colorado at Boulder J.D. 1968. Admitted to practice Nevada 1968, U.S. Supreme Court 1978 and U.S. Court of Appeals Ninth Circuit 1986. In legal practice Reno 1979-2001. Settlement Judge, Nevada Supreme Court 1997-2001.
District Attorney Washoe County 1974-78. Member American Inns of Court (President Bruce R. Thompson Chapter 1999-2000), State Bar of Nevada (President

HICKS, LARRY R.—*Continued*

1993-94) and American Bar Association (Delegate 1994-2000). Republican.

Las Vegas office: U.S. Courthouse, 333 Las Vegas Boulevard South, Las Vegas 89101.

Telephone: (702) 464-5480.

Reno office: U.S. Courthouse, 400 South Virginia Street, Reno 89501.

Telephone: (775) 686-5700.

HOLTON, Nola A. *(Justice of the Peace, Pahranagat Valley Justices' Court and Judge, Caliente Municipal Court)*

Justices' Court mailing address: P.O. Box 449, Alamo 89001.

Telephone: (775) 725-3357.

Fax: (775) 725-3566

Municipal Court mailing address: P.O. Box 158, Caliente 89008.

Telephone: (775) 726-3193.

Fax: (775) 725-3566

HOWARD, Kenneth R. *(Judge, Reno Municipal Court)* Former Chief Judge.

Mailing address: P.O. Box 1900, Reno 89505.

Telephone: (775) 326-6673.

Fax: (775) 326-6684

HUFF, David A. *(Judge, Nevada District Court Third Judicial District)*

Office: 73 North Maine Street, Suite B, Fallon 89406.

Telephone: (775) 423-6088.

Fax: (775) 423-8578

E-mail address: distct-Judge1@churchillcounty.org

HUFFAKER, Stephen L. *(Senior Judge, Nevada District Court)* Appointed by Governor Robert List to term beginning Feb 22, 1980. Elected 1980, 1984, 1990 and 1996. Retired, serves by recall. Formerly served Civil/Criminal Division. Born Salt Lake City Utah Jan 28, 1934. Church of Jesus Christ of Latter-day Saints. Educated at Utah State University B.S. 1956 and Loyola University J.D. with honors 1974. Managing Editor Loyola Law Review 1972-73. Admitted to practice Nevada 1974 and U.S. District Court District of Nevada 1974. Began legal practice Las Vegas 1974.

Assistant Public Defender 1977-80. Member State Bar of Nevada, Clark County and American Bar Associations. Captain USAF 1957-66. Previously worked as writer and editor. Republican. Board of Directors Citizens for Responsible Government 1977-83. Enjoys tennis, golf, jogging and reading.

Office: 330 South Third Street, Suite 1120, Las Vegas 89101.

Telephone: (702) 455-0446.

HUNT, Roger L. *(Judge, United States District Court District of Nevada)* Magistrate Judge 1992-2000. Appointed Judge for life by President Bill Clinton to term beginning May 25, 2000. Born Overton Nevada April 29, 1942. Educated at Brigham Young University B.A. 1966 and George Washington University J.D. 1970. In legal practice Las Vegas 1971-92.

Deputy District Attorney Clark County 1970-71.

Office: 6018 U.S. Courthouse, 333 Las Vegas Boulevard South, Las Vegas 89101.

Telephone: (702) 464-5530.

HUTTMAN, Howard, Jr. *(Justice of the Peace, McDermitt Justices' Court)*

Mailing address: P.O. Box 381, McDermitt 89421.

Telephone: (775) 532-8292.

IROZ, John M. *(Judge, Nevada District Court Sixth Judicial District)*

Office: Humboldt County Courthouse, Drawer 409, 50 West Fifth Street, Winnemucca 89446.

Telephone: (775) 623-6371, 635-5738 (Battle Mountain), 273-2105 (Lovelock).

Fax: (775) 623-6457

JANSEN, William D. *(Justice of the Peace, Las Vegas Justices' Court)* Appointed to term beginning Sept 16, 1986. Elected 1986, 1990, 1994 and 2000. Current term expires Jan 1, 2007. Former Chief Justice of the Peace and Vice Chief Justice of the Peace. Born Pekin Illinois Sept 13, 1935. Methodist. Educated at Michigan State University B.S. 1958 and Drake University J.D. 1962. Staff member Drake Law Review 1961. Admitted to practice Nevada 1972, U.S. District Court District of Nevada 1972 and U.S. Court of Appeals Ninth Circuit 1973.

Member State Bar of Nevada, Clark County and American Bar Associations. Attended The National Judicial College 1985. Former Special Agent FBI (retired). Enjoys traveling.

Mailing address: P.O. Box 552511, Las Vegas 89155-2511.

Telephone: (702) 455-4381.

Fax: (702) 455-4225

JOHNSTON, Robert J. *(Magistrate Judge, United States District Court District of Nevada)* Appointed by U.S. District Court judges to term beginning Dec 14, 1987. Reappointed 1995, current term expires Dec 2003. Born Denver Colorado Sept 30, 1947. Church of Jesus Christ of Latter-day Saints. Educated at Brigham Young University B.S. 1973 and McGeorge School of Law University of the Pacific J.D. 1977. Law Clerk to Hon. Merlyn Hoyt, Nevada District Court Seventh Judicial District 1977-78. Member Phi Delta Phi. Admitted to practice Nevada 1977, U.S. District Court District of Nevada 1978 and U.S. Court of Appeals Ninth Circuit 1984. In legal practice Ely 1978-82.

District Attorney White Pine County 1979-82. Assistant U.S. Attorney 1984-87. Member Federal Magistrate Judges Association (Director Ninth Circuit 1990-92) and Clark County Bar Association. E-5 U.S. Army 1967-70. Member Ninth Judicial Circuit Historical Society, Southwest Oral History Society, Las Vegas Track Club and Boy Scouts of America.

Office: 3005 U.S. Courthouse, 333 Las Vegas Boulevard South, Las Vegas 89101.

Telephone: (702) 464-5550.

JONES, Robert Clive *(Judge, United States Bankruptcy Court District of Nevada)* Appointed by U.S. District Court judges to term beginning Feb 11, 1983. Reappointed by U.S. Court of Appeals Ninth Circuit judges. Former Chief Judge. Born Las Vegas Nevada July 21, 1947. Church of Jesus Christ of Latter-day Saints. Educated at Brigham Young University B.S. with honors 1971 and University of California at Los Angeles J.D. with honors 1975. Associate Editor UCLA Law Review 1974-75. Law Clerk to Hon. J. Clifford Wallace, U.S. Court of Appeals Ninth Circuit 1975. Member Order of the Coif and Order of Barristers. Admitted to

JONES, ROBERT CLIVE—*Continued*

practice California 1975, Nevada 1976, U.S. District Court District of Nevada 1976 and U.S. Tax Court 1977. Began legal practice Las Vegas Nevada 1977. Former Judge, Bankruptcy Appellate Panel Ninth Circuit.

With Haskins & Sells, Certified Public Accountants 1976. Author "Estate and Income Tax: Claims Against the Estate and Events Subsequent to Date of Death" UCLA L. Rev. 1975 and "How Community Property Laws Affect Employee Benefits Plans" 3 Community Property Jour. 1975. Member Clark County, Washoe County and American Bar Associations. Staff Sergeant Army National Guard 1971-72 and Air National Guard 1972-77. Enjoys historical and biographical reading, water sports, snow skiing, horses and running.

Office: 4085 U.S. Courthouse, 333 Las Vegas Boulevard South, Las Vegas 89101.

Telephone: (702) 388-6505.

JONES, Steven E. *(Judge, Nevada District Court Eighth Judicial District)* Former Presiding Judge. Serves Family Division.

Office: Courthouse, 601 North Pecos, Las Vegas 89101-2408.

Telephone: (702) 455-5992.

Fax: (702) 455-2394

JORDAN, Scott *(Judge, Nevada District Court Second Judicial District)* Serves Family Division.

Office: One South Sierra Street, Third Floor, Reno 89501.

Telephone: (775) 328-3800.

Fax: (775) 325-6603

KERNS, Cedric A. *(Judge, Las Vegas Municipal Court)*

Office: 400 East Stewart Avenue, Las Vegas 89101.

Telephone: (702) 229-6061.

Fax: (702) 386-9674

KOLHOSS, Ruth *(Justice of the Peace, Moapa Justices' Court)*

Mailing address: P.O. Box 280, Moapa 89025.

Telephone: (702) 864-2333, 865-2833.

Fax: (702) 864-2585

KOLKOSKI, Elizabeth *(Judge, Las Vegas Municipal Court)*

Office: 400 East Stewart Avenue, Las Vegas 89101.

Telephone: (702) 229-5949.

Fax: (702) 386-9674

KOSACH, Steven R. *(Judge, Nevada District Court Second Judicial District)* Former Chief Judge. Serves Civil/Criminal Division.

Mailing address: P.O. Box 30083, Reno 89520-3083.

Office: 75 Court Street, Reno 89501.

Telephone: (775) 328-3166.

Fax: (775) 328-3120

LANE, Robert W. *(Judge, Nevada District Court Fifth Judicial District)* Elected to term beginning Jan 1, 2001. Reelected Nov 5, 2002, current term expires Jan 2009. Born Omaha March 22, 1959. Church of Jesus Christ of Latter-Day Saints. Educated at University of Nevada Las Vegas B.A. 1989 and University of Utah J.D. 1992. Admitted to practice Nevada 1992 and U.S. District Court District of Nevada 1994. In legal practice Las Vegas Jan 1, 1993 to Sept 1, 1993.

Deputy District Attorney Nye County Sept 1, 1993 to Dec 31, 2000.

Office: 105 Nye County Government Center, 1520 East Basin Avenue, Pahrump 89060.

Telephone: (775) 751-4210, 945-2446 (Hawthorne), 485-6367 (Goldfield).

Fax: (775) 751-4218

E-mail address: robert.lane@co.nye.nv.us

LEAVITT, Cecil R. *(Justice of the Peace, Bunkerville Justices' Court)*

Mailing address: P.O. Box 7185, Bunkerville 89007.

Telephone: (702) 346-5711.

Fax: (702) 346-7212

LEAVITT, Lawrence R. *(Magistrate Judge, United States District Court District of Nevada)* Appointed by U.S. District Court judges.

Office: 3014 U.S. Courthouse, 333 Las Vegas Boulevard South, Las Vegas 89101.

Telephone: (702) 464-5540.

LEAVITT, Michelle *(Judge, Nevada District Court Eighth Judicial District)* Serves Civil/Criminal Division. Former Judge, Las Vegas Municipal Court.

Office: Clark County Courthouse, 200 South Third Street, Las Vegas 89155.

Telephone: (702) 455-4793.

Fax: (702) 382-6263

LEAVITT, Myron E. *(Justice, Nevada Supreme Court)* Former Judge and Chief Judge, Nevada District Court Eighth Judicial District.

Office: 316 Bridger Avenue, Las Vegas 89101.

Telephone: (702) 486-3225.

LEDDY, Mary E. *(Justice of the Peace, Elko Justices' Court and Judge, Elko Municipal Court)*

Mailing address: P.O. Box 176, Elko 89803.

Telephone: (775) 738-8403.

Fax: (775) 738-8416

LEEN, Peggy A. *(Magistrate Judge, United States District Court District of Nevada)* Appointed by U.S. District Court judges to term beginning Jan 16, 2001. Term expires Jan 16, 2009. Educated at University of Nevada Las Vegas B.A. 1976 and University of San Diego J.D. 1979. Admitted to practice Nevada 1979, U.S. District Court District of Nevada 1979 and U.S. Court of Appeals Ninth Circuit 1983. In legal practice Las Vegas 1981-95.

Deputy Public Defender 1979-81 and Deputy District Attorney 1996-2000 Clark County. Member American College of Trial Lawyers, International Academy of Trial Lawyers and International Society of Barristers.

Office: U.S. Courthouse, 333 Las Vegas Boulevard South, Las Vegas 89101.

Telephone: (702) 464-5400.

LEHMAN, Jack *(Senior Judge, Nevada District Court)* Appointed by Governor Richard Bryan to term beginning Jan 7, 1988. Elected 1988, 1990 and 1996. Retired Jan 6, 2003, serves by recall. Chief Judge 1991-92. Organizer and Presiding Judge, Clark County Drug Court since 1992. Serves Civil/Criminal Division. Born Chemnitz Germany Jan 27, 1928. Jewish. Educated at University of California at Berkeley B.A. 1951 and University of Southern California J.D. 1967. Member Phi Alpha Delta. Admitted to practice Nevada 1967 and

LEHMAN, JACK—*Continued*

U.S. District Court District of Nevada 1967. In legal practice Las Vegas 1968-88.

Former Division Chief U.S. Department of Commerce. Former Director Nevada Department of Economic Development. Instructor University of Nevada College of Hotel Administration 1968-82. President Nevada District Judges Association 1991-92. Former member Nevada Trial Lawyers Association (Board of Governors 1974-88, President 1977-78) and The Association of Trial Lawyers of America. Member State Bar of Nevada, Clark County and American Bar Associations. Attended General Jurisdiction Seminar The National Judicial College 1988. First Lieutenant U.S. Army 1946-47 and 1951-53. Previously employed as radio and television announcer and newscaster, insurance agent, finance company worker and salesman. Democrat. Chairman Colorado River Commission of Nevada 1971-88. Member American Cancer Society, City of Hope and Toastmasters. Enjoys snow skiing, hiking, scuba diving and water skiing.

Office: 330 South Third Street, Suite 1120, Las Vegas 89101.

Telephone: (702) 455-6294.

Fax: (702) 382-9054

LIPPIS, Deborah J. *(Justice of the Peace, Las Vegas Justices' Court)* Former Chief Justice of the Peace and Vice Chief Justice of the Peace.

Mailing address: P.O. Box 552511, Las Vegas 89155-2511.

Telephone: (702) 455-4380.

Fax: (702) 455-4221

LOEHRER, Sally L. *(Judge, Nevada District Court Eighth Judicial District)* Appointed by Governor Bob Miller to term beginning Jan 18, 1993. Elected Nov 1994, 1996 and 2002. Current term expires Dec 31, 2008. Serves Civil/Criminal Division. Born Milwaukee Wisconsin Feb 25, 1947. Presbyterian. Educated at Wisconsin State University B.S. 1969 and Valparaiso University School of Law J.D. 1976. Admitted to practice Arizona 1976, Nevada 1977 and U.S. District Court District of Nevada 1977. In legal practice Las Vegas 1984-93.

Chief Deputy District Attorney Clark County 1980-84. Member CLE Committee 1980-90 and President 1985 Clark County Bar Association. Member Lawyer Referral Service Committee State Bar of Nevada.

Office: Clark County Courthouse, 200 South Third Street, Las Vegas 89155.

Telephone: (702) 455-4305.

Fax: (702) 455-0095

LUECK, Robert W. *(Judge, Nevada District Court Eighth Judicial District)* Serves Family Division.

Office: Courthouse, 601 North Pecos, Las Vegas 89101-2408.

Telephone: (702) 455-5994.

Fax: (702) 455-5559

MADDOX, William A. *(Judge, Nevada District Court First Judicial District)*

Office: 885 East Musser Street, Suite 3057, Carson City 89701.

Telephone: (775) 882-1619.

Fax: (775) 887-2296

MAHAN, James C. *(Judge, United States District Court District of Nevada)* Appointed for life by President George W. Bush to term beginning Feb 1, 2002. Born El Paso Texas. Educated at University of Charleston and Vanderbilt University School of Law. National Moot Court Team. Member Tau Kappa Epsilon. Admitted to practice Nevada 1974, U.S. District Court District of Nevada 1974, U.S. Court of Appeals Ninth Circuit 1975, U.S. Tax Court 1979 and U.S. Supreme Court 1980. In legal practice Las Vegas 1973-99. Judge, Nevada District Court Eighth Judicial District Feb 1999 to Jan 31, 2002, appointed by Governor Kenny C. Guinn.

Former Chairman Committee to Review and Revise the Eighth Judicial District Court Rules and Clark Regional Judicial Council. Former Member Judicial Council of the State of Nevada, Joint Task Force on Civil/Criminal Specialization and Study Committee to Review the Nevada Rules of Civil Procedure. USN 1966-69.

Office: 6085 U.S. Courthouse, 333 Las Vegas Boulevard South, Las Vegas 89101.

Telephone: (702) 464-5520.

Fax: (702) 464-5521

MANCUSO, James V. *(Justice of the Peace, Incline Village/Crystal Bay Justices' Court)* Appointed to term beginning Nov 26, 1980. Elected 1982, 1986, 1990, 1994 and 2000. Current term expires Jan 1, 2007. Also serves as Juvenile Master and Special Master—Juvenile Traffic and Domestic Violence, Nevada District Court Second Judicial District. Educated at University of Nevada Reno B.A. cum laude 1971 and McGeorge School of Law University of the Pacific J.D. with distinction 1975. Law Clerk to Hon. Bruce Thompson, U.S. District Court District of Nevada 1975-77. Member Traynor Society, Blue Key, Phi Kappa Phi, Pi Sigma Alpha, Phi Delta Phi and Lambda Chi Alpha. Admitted to practice Nevada 1975, U.S. District Court District of Nevada 1975, California 1976, U.S. Court of Appeals Ninth Circuit 1976, U.S. Tax Court 1976 and District of Columbia 1979. Began legal practice Reno 1975. In legal practice Lake Tahoe since 1979. Interim Justice of the Peace, Virginia City Justice Court Nov 1985 to Dec 31, 1986, served by special appointment.

Deputy District Attorney Washoe County 1977-79. Instructor Western Nevada Community College 1979-80 and Sierra Nevada College 1983-88. Member Nevada Judges Association (Director 1985), American Justinian Society of Jurists, The District of Columbia Bar, State Bar of California, State Bar of Nevada, Incline Village (President 1982 and 1993), Tahoe-Truckee and Washoe County Bar Associations. Graduate The National Judicial College (Certificate 1984, Advanced Certificate 1990, Distinguished Jurist Award 2000). Named Outstanding Justices' Court Jurist Washoe Region 1990. Republican. Board of Directors Children's Cabinet of Incline Village 1993-99. Coach and Director North Tahoe Little League since 1996. Member Optimist Club, Rotary Club, E. Clampus Vitus and National Rifle Association. Enjoys softball, desert exploration and target shooting.

Office: 865 Tahoe Boulevard, Suite 301, Incline Village 89451.

Telephone: (775) 832-4100.

Fax: (775) 832-4162

MASLACH, Joe *(Justice of the Peace, Tonopah Justices' Court)* Also serves as Juvenile Master, Nevada District Court Fifth Judicial District.

Mailing address: P.O. Box 1151, Tonopah 89049.

Telephone: (775) 482-8155.

Fax: (775) 482-7349

MAUPIN, A. William *(Justice, Nevada Supreme Court)* Former Chief Justice. Former Judge, Nevada District Court Eighth Judicial District.
Office: 300 Supreme Court Building, 201 South Carson Street, Carson City 89701-4702.
Telephone: (775) 684-1520.

McCARTHY, Barbara S. *(Judge, Sparks Municipal Court)*
Office: 1450 C Street, Sparks 89431.
Telephone: (775) 353-2374.
Fax: (775) 353-2400

McGEE, Charles M. *(Judge, Nevada District Court Second Judicial District)* Juvenile Master 1980-84. Elected Judge to term beginning Jan 7, 1985. Reelected 1990, 1996 and 2002. Current term expires Dec 31, 2008. Chief Judge 1989-90 and 1998-2000. Serves Family Division. Former Juvenile Judge. Born Salt Lake City Utah June 11, 1945. Protestant. Educated at University of the Pacific B.A. 1963, University of Denver College of Law J.D. 1969 and University of Nevada M.J.S. 1989. Symposium Editor Denver University Law Review 1968-69. Member Order of St. Ives. Admitted to practice Nevada 1969 and California 1973. In legal practice Reno 1973-80.
Author "Measured Steps Toward Clarity and Balance in the Juvenile Justice System" 40 No. 3 Juvenile & Family Court Journal 1989. Important Decision: Kelly v. Tahoe Regional Planning Agency 18325 Ninth Judicial District Court 1990. Vice Chair National Association of Drug Court Professionals. Member National Council of Family and Juvenile Court Judges, American Judicature Society and American Bar Association. Instructor in Legal Writing The National Judicial College since 1987 and Juvenile Law National College of Juvenile Justice since 1988. Attended 18th National Conference on Juvenile Justice Albuquerque New Mexico May 17-20, 1990. Recipient Associated General Contractors Skill Integrity and Responsibility Award 1988, McReynolds Psychological Services Award 1989 and Truckee Meadows Human Service Award 1990. Named Humanitarian of the Year by National Conference for Community and Justice 2000. Captain U.S. Army JAGC 1969-73 (Chief of Military Justice 101st Airborne Division Vietnam). Member Prospectors Club, United Way, Police Athletic League Children's Cabinet, Governor's Advisory Group-Youth, Parents United, CASA and Family Academy. Enjoys skiing, hunting, fishing and backpacking.
Mailing address: P.O. Box 30083, Reno 89520.
Office: One South Sierra Street, Third Floor, Reno 89501.
Telephone: (775) 328-3179.
Fax: (775) 328-3565

McGROARTY, John S. *(Judge, Nevada District Court Eighth Judicial District)* Serves Civil/Criminal Division. Born Los Angeles California Oct 23, 1941. Educated at University of Notre Dame A.B. in Communication Arts 1963 and Howard University J.D. 1969. Law Clerk to Hon. John F. Mendoza Feb to July 1969. Justice of the Peace, Las Vegas Justice Court 1978-80.
With Southern Nevada Power Company 1958-59. With Capitol Hill Police Force 1964-68. Legislative Aide to Senator Howard Cannon 1968-69. Deputy District Attorney Clark County Civil Division Sept to Dec 1970. Assistant City Attorney North Las Vegas Dec 1970. Administrative Assistant and Legal Counsel to Governor Mike O'Callaghan 1970-78. Member State Bar of Nevada, Washoe County, Clark County 1969-71 and American 1969-72 Bar Associations. Democrat. With Democratic National Committee 1968. Alternate Delegate Democratic National Convention 1968. President Clark County Young Democrats 1970. Member Knights of Columbus.
Office: Clark County Courthouse, 200 South Third Street, Las Vegas 89155.
Telephone: (702) 455-3306.
Fax: (702) 382-0353

McKIBBEN, Howard D. *(Judge, United States District Court District of Nevada)* Appointed for life by President Ronald Reagan to term beginning Oct 4, 1984. Chief Judge 1997 to Oct 12, 2002. Born Virginia Illinois April 1, 1940. Educated at Bradley University B.S. 1962, University of Pittsburgh M.P.A. 1964 and University of Michigan Law School J.D. 1967. In legal practice Minden 1967-71. Judge, Nevada District Court Ninth Judicial District 1977-84.
Deputy District Attorney 1969-71 and District Attorney 1971-77 Douglas County.
Office: 804 U.S. Courthouse, 400 South Virginia Street, Reno 89501.
Telephone: (775) 686-5880.

McQUAID, Robert A., Jr. *(Magistrate Judge, United States District Court District of Nevada)* Appointed by U.S. District Court judges.
Office: 405 U.S. Courthouse, 400 South Virginia Street, Reno 89501.
Telephone: (775) 686-5858.

MEMEO, Mike *(Judge, Nevada District Court Fourth Judicial District)*
Office: Elko County Courthouse, 571 Idaho Street, Elko 89801.
Telephone: (775) 753-4601.
Fax: (775) 753-4611

MILLER, Victor L. *(Justice of the Peace, Boulder Justices' Court and Judge, Boulder City Municipal Court)*
Office: 501 Avenue G, Boulder City 89005.
Telephone: (702) 455-8000 (Justices' Court), 293-9278 (Municipal Court).
Fax: (702) 455-8003 (Justices' Court), 293-9345 (Municipal Court)

MILLIGAN, Dennis *(Justice of the Peace, Mason Valley Justices' Court)*
Office: 30 Nevin Way, Yerington 89447.
Telephone: (775) 463-6639.
Fax: (775) 463-6638

MOMA, Billy R. *(Justice of the Peace, Laughlin Justices' Court)*
Office: 101 Civic Way, Suite 2, Laughlin 89029.
Telephone: (702) 298-4622.
Fax: (702) 386-9104

MOSLEY, Donald M. *(Judge, Nevada District Court Eighth Judicial District)* Elected to term beginning Jan 2, 1983. Reelected to subsequent terms. Current term expires Jan 2009. Former Chief Judge. Serves Civil/Criminal Division. Born Coffeyville Kansas Feb 28, 1947. Educated at Northeastern University B.A. 1970 and University of Tulsa J.D. 1976. Member Phi Delta Phi. Admitted to practice Nevada 1977. Began legal

MOSLEY, DONALD M.—*Continued*

practice 1977. Judge, Las Vegas Municipal Court 1979-83.

Former Deputy City Attorney. Attended The National Judicial College 1982.

Office: Clark County Courthouse, 200 South Third Street, Las Vegas 89155.

Telephone: (702) 455-4304.

Fax: (702) 382-6040

MOSS, Cheryl B. *(Judge, Nevada District Court Eighth Judicial District)* Elected to term beginning Nov 2000. Reelected Nov 2002, current term expires Dec 31, 2008. Serves Family Division. Born Milwaukee Wisconsin Jan 12, 1967. Educated at George Washington University B.A. cum laude 1989 and Catholic University of America J.D. 1994. Law Clerk to Hon. John H. Bayly, Jr., Superior Court of the District of Columbia 1994-95. Admitted to practice Maryland 1994, District of Columbia 1995, Nevada 1997 and U.S. District Court District of Nevada 1997. In legal practice Las Vegas Nevada 1998-2000.

Member National Council of Juvenile and Family Court Judges, American Judges Association and State Bar of Nevada.

Office: Courthouse, 601 North Pecos, Las Vegas 89101-2408.

Telephone: (702) 455-1887.

Fax: (702) 455-5989

E-mail address: mossche@co.clark.nv.us

NELSEN, Carol *(Justice of the Peace, Lake Justices' Court)*

Mailing address: P.O. Box 8, Lovelock 89419.

Telephone: (775) 273-2753.

Fax: (775) 273-0416

NETHERY, Barbara J. *(Justice of the Peace, Carlin Justices' Court and Judge, Carlin Municipal Court)*

Mailing address: P.O. Box 789, Carlin 89822.

Telephone: (775) 754-6321.

Fax: (775) 754-6893

NIMAN, Ronald J. *(Justice of the Peace, Ely Justices' Court and Judge, Ely Municipal Court)*

Mailing address: P.O. Box 151055, Ely 89315.

Office: 801 Clark Street, Suite 6, Ely 89301.

Telephone: (775) 289-2678 (Justices' Court), 289-4838 (Municipal Court).

Fax: (775) 289-3392 (Justices' Court), 289-8225 (Municipal Court)

OESTERLE, Nancy C. *(Justice of the Peace, Las Vegas Justices' Court)* Former Chief Justice of the Peace.

Mailing address: P.O. Box 552511, Las Vegas 89155-2511.

Telephone: (702) 455-5510.

Fax: (702) 455-4226

PAPEZ, Dan L. *(Chief Judge, Nevada District Court Seventh Judicial District)* Assumed office Jan 1993. Elected to subsequent term. Educated at University of Nevada Reno B.S. 1972 and McGeorge School of Law University of the Pacific J.D. 1982. Admitted to practice Nevada, U.S. District Court District of Nevada and U.S. Supreme Court. In legal practice Ely Jan 1991 to Dec 1992.

District Attorney White Pine County June 1986 to Dec 1990. Past President Nevada District Attorneys Association. President-Elect Nevada District Judges Association. Co-chair Judicial Council of the State of Nevada. Member State Bar of Nevada. Attended The National Judicial College May 1993. Military Policeman Nevada National Guard. Game Warden Nevada Department of Wildlife June 1973 to May 1978. Member Nevada Board of Wildlife Commissioners Aug 1989 to Dec 1992. Past President Ely Rotary Club. Enjoys wildlife and nature photography, fly-fishing, gardening and reading.

Mailing address: P.O. Box 151629, Ely 89315.

Office: 801 Clark Street, Ely 89301.

Telephone: (775) 289-1546, 962-5390 (Pioche), 237-5262 (Eureka).

Fax: (775) 289-1582

PARRAGUIRRE, Ronald D. *(Judge, Nevada District Court Eighth Judicial District)* Serves Civil/Criminal Division. Former Judge, Las Vegas Municipal Court.

Office: Clark County Courthouse, 200 South Third Street, Las Vegas 89155.

Telephone: (702) 455-4648.

Fax: (702) 382-0082

PAVLIKOWSKI, Joseph S. *(Senior Judge, Nevada District Court)* Serves by recall. Formerly served Civil/Criminal Division.

Office: 330 South Third Street, Suite 1120, Las Vegas 89101.

Telephone: (702) 455-0446.

PEACOCK, Russel W. *(Justice of the Peace, Lund Justices' Court)* Appointed by County Commissioners to term beginning Jan 3, 1995. Elected Nov 1996 and 2000. Current term expires Jan 2007. Born East Ely Nevada March 15, 1951. Educated at University of Nevada Reno B.S. 1973. Member Phi Kappa Phi and Alpha Zeta.

Member Nevada Judges Association. Major U.S. Army 1973-93 (retired). Member Society of American Military Engineers.

Mailing address: P.O. Box 87, Lund 89317.

Telephone: (775) 238-5400.

Fax: (775) 289-9696

POLAHA, Jerome M. *(Judge, Nevada District Court Second Judicial District)* Serves Civil/Criminal Division.

Mailing address: P.O. Box 30083, Reno 89520-3083.

Office: 75 Court Street, Reno 89501.

Telephone: (775) 328-3189.

Fax: (775) 328-3877

PORTER, Gene T. *(Chief Judge, Nevada District Court Eighth Judicial District)* Serves Civil/Criminal Division.

Office: Clark County Courthouse, 200 South Third Street, Las Vegas 89155.

Telephone: (702) 455-4641.

Fax: (702) 455-0104

PRO, Philip M. *(Chief Judge, United States District Court District of Nevada)* Magistrate 1980-87. Appointed Judge for life by President Ronald Reagan to term beginning 1987. Chief Judge since Oct 13, 2002. Born Richmond California Dec 12, 1946. Educated at San Francisco State University B.A. in Political Science 1968 and Golden Gate University School of Law J.D. 1972. Staff member 1971 and Board of Editors 1972 Golden Gate Law Review. Teaching Assistant for Legal

PRO, PHILIP M.—*Continued*

Writing and Research Program 1972. Active in Trial Advocacy Program 1972. Law Clerk to Hon. William P. Compton, Nevada District Court Eighth Judicial District 1972-73. Admitted to practice California 1972, Nevada 1973, U.S. Court of Appeals Ninth Circuit 1973, U.S. District Court District of Nevada 1973 and U.S. Supreme Court 1976. Began legal practice Las Vegas 1973. In legal practice Reno 1978-79.

Deputy Public Defender Las Vegas 1973-75. Assistant U.S. Attorney District of Nevada 1975-78. Deputy Attorney General Carson City 1979-80. Chief Assistant U.S. Attorney Reno 1980. Lecturer on Nevada Gaming Control Act sponsored by the National Conference of State Legislatures Albany New York 1979. Instructor and Presiding Judge Attorney General's Advocacy Institute U.S. Department of Justice Washington D.C. since 1980. Instructor National Institute for Trial Advocacy (NITA) National Session Boulder Colorado 1992. Member Ninth Circuit Jury Instructions Committee 1986-93. Member U.S. Judicial Conference Committee on Administration of the Magistrate Judges System (Chairman 1993-98). Member Federal Judges Association (Vice President 1997-2001), American Inns of Court Nevada Chapter (President 1988-90), State Bar of Nevada (Chairman Law Day Essay Contest since 1976, Vice Chairman CLE Committee since 1980) and American Bar Association (Ninth Circuit Delegate to Conference of Special Court Judges). Chairman Issues in Justice Forum Committee and Presiding Co-chairman Board of Directors National Conference of Christians and Jews. Member Administration of Justice Program Advisory Committee University of Nevada Las Vegas Boyd School of Law, Advisory Committee Anytown Nevada Youth Camp and Southern Nevada Arson Task Force. Insurance Claims Adjuster California State Automobile Association 1968-69.

Office: 7015 U.S. Courthouse, 333 Las Vegas Boulevard South, Las Vegas 89101.
Telephone: (702) 464-5510.

PROCTOR, Ken *(Judge, Henderson Municipal Court)*
Office: 243 Water Street, Henderson 89015.
Telephone: (702) 565-2078.
Fax: (702) 565-2308

PUCCINELLI, Andrew J. *(Judge, Nevada District Court Fourth Judicial District)*
Office: Elko County Courthouse, 571 Idaho Street, Elko 89801.
Telephone: (775) 753-4602.
Fax: (775) 753-3762

RECANZONE, Mario G. *(Senior Judge, Nevada District Court)* Appointed by Governor Robert List to term beginning May 4, 1982. Elected 1984 and 1990. Retired, serves by recall. Born Paradise Valley Nevada May 2, 1921. Catholic. Educated at University of Nevada B.A. 1943 and Hastings College of the Law J.D. 1950. Member Alpha Tau Omega. Admitted to practice Nevada 1950. Began legal practice Fallon 1950.

City Attorney Fallon 1955-82 and Yerington 1955-70. Nevada State Board of Bar Examiners 1960-73. Member State Bar of Nevada, Washoe County and American Bar Associations. Captain U.S. Army Infantry 1943-46. Republican. Interests include ranching, golf and horsemanship.

Mailing address: 1999 Rio Vista, Fallon 89406.

REED, Edward C., Jr. *(Senior Judge, United States District Court District of Nevada)* Appointed for life by President Jimmy Carter to term beginning Oct 1, 1979. Former Acting Chief Judge. Former Chief Judge. Assumed Senior status, serves by assignment. Born Mason Nevada July 8, 1924. Baptist. Educated at University of Nevada B.A. 1949 and Harvard Law School J.D. 1952. Member Alpha Tau Omega. Admitted to practice Nevada 1952, U.S. District Court District of Nevada 1958, U.S. Court of Appeals Ninth Circuit 1972 and U.S. Supreme Court 1972. Began legal practice Reno 1953.

Attorney Arthur Andersen & Company 1952-53. Special Deputy Attorney General Nevada 1967-69. Important Decisions: State of Nevada ex rel, Nevada State Board of Agriculture v. United States of America et al. (rejects contentions of state in "Sagebush Rebellion") 512 F. Supp. 166 D.Nev. 1981; Holland Livestock Ranch et al. v. United States of America et al. (Bureau of Land Management access-trespass theory) 543 F. Supp. 158 D.Nev. 1982; Cooper v. Department of Administration (racial discrimination in state hiring practices) 558 F. Supp. 244 D.Nev. 1982; Echo Morton Penrose et al. v. Margaret M. Heckler (presumptions of death and necessary evidence for payment of Social Security survivors' benefits) 566 F. Supp. 301 D.Nev. 1983; Allen B. Morrison et al. v. MGM Grand Hotel-Reno et al. (protection of patrons from third-party criminal attacks) 570 F. Supp. 1449 D.Nev. 1983; Videotronics, Inc. v. Bend Electronics (question of copyright regarding computer program for poker and keno casino gambling games) 564 F. Supp. 1471 D.Nev. 1983; Shuman v. Wolff (Nevada mandatory death penalty statute found unconstitutional) 571 F. Supp. 213 D.Nev. 1983; United States v. Lowry (YCA sentence compared to maximum adult sentence) 726 F.2d 474, 9th Cir. 1983; United States v. McClelland (terms of conviction under Hobbs Act) 731 F.2d 1438, 9th Cir. 1984; Sparks Nugget, Inc. et al. v. James S. Scott et al. (labor disputes with NLRB) CV-R-83-362-ECR 1984; Carolyn Burke Snow v. Nevada Department of Prisons et al. (sex discrimination in hiring) CV-R-78-101-ECR 1984; and John L. Falen et al. v. Cervi Livestock Company (long-arm jurisdiction over interstate transportation of livestock) CV-R-81-138-ECR 1984. Instructor in Commercial Law American Institute of Banking 1954-55. Lecturer on Water Rights University of Nevada School of Agriculture 1955-60. Chairman Governor's School Survey Committee 1958-61. Recipient Award for Patriotic Civilian Service from U.S. Army 1973. Honored by dedication of Edward C. Reed High School 1973. Staff Sergeant U.S. Army 1943-46. Democrat. Provided legal assistance to Girl Scouts of America Sierra Nevada Council, Nevada Agricultural Foundation University of Nevada, Nevada State School Administrators Association and Nevada Congress of Parents and Teachers. Member Washoe County School Board 1956-72 (President 1959, 1963 and 1969), Washoe County Board of Tax Equalization 1957-58, Washoe County Annexation Commission 1968-72, Washoe County Personnel Committee 1973-77 (Chairman 1973), Citizens Advisory Committee for Washoe County School Bond Issue 1977-78, Nevada PTA (Life member), United Way (Chairman Professional Division 1978), Sun Valley Swimming Pool Committee 1978, Reno Silver Sox baseball team (Board of Direc-

REED, EDWARD C., JR.—*Continued*

tors 1962-65) and Washoe County Blue Ribbon Task Force Committee on Growth. Interests include public education, reading, travel, symphonic music and gardening.

Office: U.S. Courthouse, 400 South Virginia Street, Reno 89501.

Telephone: (775) 686-5919.

RICHARDSON, Gordon N. *(Judge, Lovelock Municipal Court)* Former Justice of the Peace, Lake Justices' Court.

Mailing address: P.O. Box 1010, Lovelock 89419.

Telephone: (775) 273-2377.

Fax: (775) 273-7979

RIEGLE, Linda B. *(Judge, United States Bankruptcy Court District of Nevada)* Appointed by U.S. Court of Appeals Ninth Circuit judges to term beginning Jan 11, 1988. Former Chief Judge.

Office: 4073 U.S. Courthouse, 333 Las Vegas Boulevard South, Las Vegas 89101.

Telephone: (702) 388-6120.

RITCHIE, T. Arthur, Jr. *(Judge, Nevada District Court Eighth Judicial District)* Serves Family Division.

Office: Courthouse, 601 North Pecos, Las Vegas 89101-2408.

Telephone: (702) 455-6944.

Fax: (702) 382-0062

ROBISON, Norman C. *(Senior Judge, Nevada District Court)* Appointed by Governor Robert List to term beginning Feb 16, 1982. Elected 1984 and 1990. Retired, serves by recall. Born Santa Ana California May 4, 1937. Protestant. Educated at Hartnell Junior College A.A. 1961, University of Nevada Reno 1967-68 and McGeorge School of Law University of the Pacific J.D. 1971. Member Phi Alpha Delta. Admitted to practice Nevada 1971 and California 1972. In legal practice Gardnerville Nevada 1971-74.

Deputy Attorney General State of Nevada 1971-82. Instructor in Criminal Law and Procedure 1972-78 and Police Officers Standard Training 1977-78 Nevada Highway Patrol Academy. Member American Judicature Society, State Bar of Nevada and State Bar of California. Petty Officer Second Class USN 1954-58. Previously worked as Douglas County Sheriff's Deputy and Nevada Highway Patrolman. Involved with China Springs Youth Camp (juvenile facility). Enjoys hunting, fishing, gourmet cooking and working in greenhouse.

Mailing address: P.O. Box 1237, Gardnerville 89410.

ROGERS, William G. *(Justice of the Peace, Dayton Justices' Court)*

Office: 235 Main Street, Dayton 89403.

Telephone: (775) 246-6233.

Fax: (775) 246-6203

ROSE, Robert E. *(Justice, Nevada Supreme Court)* Former Chief Justice. Former Judge, Nevada District Court Eighth Judicial District.

Office: 300 Supreme Court Building, 201 South Carson Street, Carson City 89701-4702.

Telephone: (775) 684-1540.

SAGE, Larry *(Judge, Sparks Municipal Court)* Elected to term beginning June 6, 1995. Reelected June 7, 1999 and June 3, 2003. Current term expires 2006. Currently serves as Administrative Judge. Born Kansas City Kansas Feb 21, 1946. Baptist. Educated at University of California at Berkeley B.A. 1968, University of California Hastings College of the Law J.D. 1975 and Army Command and General Staff College 1987. Admitted to practice California 1975, Nevada, U.S. District Courts Central, Eastern, Northern and Southern Districts of California and District of Nevada, U.S. Courts of Appeals Ninth and Federal Circuits, U.S. Court of Federal Claims, U.S. Court of Appeals for the Armed Forces, U.S. Tax Court and U.S. Supreme Court. In legal practice Ventura California 1977-80 and Nevada City California 1983-85. Judge pro tem, Ventura County Superior Court (California) 1978-80. Judge pro tem, Reno Justices' Court 1997-98. Judge pro tem, Nevada District Court Second Judicial District 1998-99.

Deputy County Counsel Nevada County California 1980-83. Chief Deputy District Attorney Washoe County Nevada 1986-95. Author "Good Marks for a Bad Check Program" *Nevada Lawyer* 1994. Adjunct Professor of Administrative Law Golden Gate University Extension 1982-83 and Business Law 1987-90 and Legal Environment 1987-91 University of Nevada Reno. Member Judicial Collections Task Force since 1998 and Statistical Project Committee since 1998 Nevada Supreme Court. Member Nevada Judges Association, American Judicature Society, State Bar of California, State Bar of Nevada and American Bar Association (Committee on Victims 1989-93, Committee on Judicial Ethics since 1997 and Co-Chair Committee on Domestic Law Issues since 1997 National Conference of Special Court Judges Judicial Division). Recipient Certificate in Judicial Development (Special Court Trial Skills) from The National Judicial College 1998 and Advanced Achievement in Judicial Education Certificate from Nevada Supreme Court 1999. Adjunct Professor of Search and Seizure 1998-99, Instructor "Courage 2000 Project" since 1998 and Member Annual Nevada DUI Conference Steering Committee since 1998 The National Judicial College. Served to Colonel U.S. Army and USAR 1968-98 (retired). Recipient Bronze Star 1968 and 1991, Army Good Conduct Medal 1969, Army Achievement Medal 1983, Army Commendation Medals 1984, 1988, 1990, 1993 and 1994, Humanitarian Service Medal 1987 and 1997 and Meritorious Service Medal 1991 and 1996. Inducted into U.S. Army OCS Hall of Fame Fort Benning Georgia 1998. Alumni Board of Governors University of California Hastings College of the Law since 1998. Enjoys "old man softball" and his sons' athletics.

Office: Courthouse, 1450 C Street, Sparks 89431.

Telephone: (775) 353-2374.

Fax: (775) 353-2400

E-mail address: sageOO@nvbell.net

SAITTA, Nancy M. *(Judge, Nevada District Court Eighth Judicial District)* Elected to term beginning Jan 1999. Reelected 2002, current term expires Nov 2008. Serves Civil/Criminal Division. Born Detroit Michigan April 29, 1951. Educated at Wayne State University B.S. magna cum laude 1983 J.D. 1986. Admitted to practice Michigan 1986 and Nevada 1991. In legal practice Detroit Michigan, Southfield Michigan and Las Vegas Nevada March 1984 to Dec 1993. Judge, Las Vegas Municipal Court 1996-98.

Senior Deputy Attorney General Office of Attorney General Jan 1994 to Oct 1996. Associate Professor Wayne State University Jan 1987. Instructor in Litigation I and II American Institute of Paralegal Studies Jan 1987. Arbitrator New York Stock Exchange Arbitration Panel June 1985 and U.S. Arbitration and Mediation

SAITTA, NANCY M.—*Continued*

1985-1990. Member Nevada State Juvenile Justice Commission since 1993 and Child Death Review Subcommittee and Administrative-Judicial Subcommittee Nevada Children's Justice Task Force since 1993. Board of Directors Clark County Bar Association. Attended Winning the Personal Injury Case 1991 and 1993, North American Symposium of International Child Abduction and National Conference on Children and the Law American Bar Association; Basic Training for Child Abuse Prosecutors American Prosecutors Research Institute and National Center for Prosecution of Child Abuse Conference; Family Law Practice and Family Law Conference Family Law Section State Bar of Nevada; Medical Malpractice seminars; Investigation and Prosecution of Child Abduction Cases American Prosecutor Research Institute; Responding to Child Maltreatment Children's Center for Child Protection; and "Violence in the Media and its Effect on Children" General Consumer Protection Seminar National Association of Attorneys. Presenter "Bringing Our Children Home" Conference National Association of Missing Children Sept 1996 and Children and Violence National Conference on Violence Sept 1998. Keynote Speaker Western Coalition of Missing Children Clearinghouses Oct 1997. Participant Effects of Domestic Violence on Children and Families Legal Medical Conference Oct 1997 and Identification of Child Abuse in Domestic Violence Situations Domestic Violence Summit June 1999.

Recipient District Attorney's Meritorious Award 1996, Good Gal Award from Women's Lobby 1997 and For the Children Award from National Association of Attorneys General in recognition of outstanding contribution to Nevada's children. Volunteer Attorney Pro Bono Project 1990-94. Member Citizen's Committee for Victim Rights 1993-97, Planning Counsel Las Vegas Center for Children 1994-95 and Southern Nevada Domestic Violence Task Force since 1996. Board of Directors Variety Club Children's Charity 1994-97 and CASA Foundation since 1995. Judge and Legal Advisor Trial by Peers since 1996. Advisory Board Project Hope 1998. Former member West Coast Coalition of Missing Children's Clearinghouse and Michigan Society of Hospital Risk Managers. Member Council of Advocates Planned Parenthood of Southern Nevada and American Society on the Abuse of Children.

Office: Clark County Courthouse, 200 South Third Street, Las Vegas 89155.
Telephone: (702) 455-5118.
Fax: (702) 382-3799
E-mail address: saitta@co.clark.nv.us *or* momjudge-@aol.com

SALCEDO, Fidel *(Justice of the Peace, Reno Justices' Court)* Appointed to term beginning Jan 1985. Elected 1986, 1990, 1994 and 2000. Current term expires Jan 2007. Former Chief Justice of the Peace. Born Dec 10, 1944. Catholic.

Mailing address: P.O. Box 30083, Reno 89520-3083.
Telephone: (775) 325-6505.
Fax: (775) 325-6591

SANCHEZ, Gloria S. *(Judge, Nevada District Court Eighth Judicial District)* UIFSA/Paternity Hearing Master 1984-88. Domestic Relations Referee 1988-92. Elected to term beginning Jan 1993. Reelected Nov 1998, current term expires Dec 31, 2004. Formerly Presiding Judge Family Division. Serves Family Division. Born San Francisco California June 28, 1953. Educated at University of California at San Diego B.A. cum laude 1975 and University of Santa Clara School of Law J.D. 1980. Law Clerk to Hon. Thomas J. O'Donnell, Nevada District Court Eighth Judicial District 1982-83. Member Phi Alpha Delta. Admitted to practice Pennsylvania 1981, Nevada 1983 and U.S. District Court District of Nevada 1983. In legal practice Las Vegas Nevada 1983-88.

Member Southern Nevada Association of Women Attorneys, National Association of Women Judges, National Council of Juvenile and Family Court Judges, Association of Family and Conciliation Courts, American Judges Association, State Bar of Nevada, Clark County, Pennsylvania and American Bar Associations. Recipient Irvin J. Westheimer Award from Big Brothers and Big Sisters 1988, Attorney of the Year Award from Equal Rights for Divorced Fathers 1988 and Peacemaker of the Year Award from Mediators of South Nevada 1998. Finalist Legal Category Women of Achievement Award from Las Vegas Chamber of Commerce. Democrat. Past President Big Brothers and Big Sisters of Southern Nevada. Sponsor Central Little League Teams and Nevada Law Enforcement Games. Enjoys collecting pencils with colorful tops.

Office: Courthouse, 601 North Pecos Road, Las Vegas 89101-2408.
Telephone: (702) 455-5991.
Fax: (702) 455-5989

SCHROEDER, Jack *(Justice of the Peace, Reno Justices' Court)* Former Chief Justice of the Peace.

Mailing address: P.O. Box 30083, Reno 89520-3083.
Telephone: (775) 325-6505.
Fax: (775) 325-6591

SCHUMACHER, Deborah E. *(Judge, Nevada District Court Second Judicial District)* Serves Family Division.

Office: One South Sierra Street, Third Floor, Reno 89501.
Telephone: (775) 328-3186.
Fax: (775) 328-3565

SCHWEBLE, John F. *(Justice of the Peace, Eureka Justices' Court)* Elected to term beginning Jan 2, 2000. Term expires Jan 2, 2006. Born Fallon Nevada March 26, 1943. Catholic.

Member Nevada Judges Association and National Judges Association. U.S. Army and National Guard 1964-70. Republican. District Representative State Convention 1987-89. Member Eureka County School Board 1986-94. Member Lions Club, Masonic Lodge, Fire Department and Boy Scouts. Enjoys vintage automobiles, fishing, hunting and anything outdoors.

Mailing address: P.O. Box 496, Eureka 89316.
Telephone: (775) 237-5540.
Fax: (775) 237-6016
E-mail address: EUREKAJUDGE@EUREKANV.ORG

SHEARING, Miriam *(Justice, Nevada Supreme Court)* Assumed office 1993. Chief Justice 1997-98. Born Waverly New York Feb 24, 1935. Educated at Cornell University B.A. 1956 and Boston College J.D. 1964. Admitted to practice California 1965 and Nevada 1969. In legal practice San Francisco California 1966-68 and Las Vegas Nevada 1969-77. Alternate Juvenile Court Referee, Clark County 1975-76. Justice of the

SHEARING, MIRIAM—*Continued*
Peace, Las Vegas Justice Court 1977-81. Judge 1983-93 and Chief Judge 1986, Nevada District Court Eighth Judicial District.

Member Nevada Judges Association (Secretary 1978), Nevada District Judges Association (Secretary 1984-85, President 1986-87), American Judicature Society (Chair), State Bar of Nevada, State Bar of California, Clark County and American Bar Associations. Democrat.

Office: 201 South Carson Street, Carson City 89701-4702.
Telephone: (775) 684-1530.

SMITH, Douglas E. *(Justice of the Peace, Las Vegas Justices' Court)* Former Chief Justice of the Peace and Vice Chief Justice of the Peace.
Mailing address: P.O. Box 552511, Las Vegas 89155-2511.
Telephone: (702) 455-4122.
Fax: (702) 455-4222

STEEL, Cynthia Dianne *(Judge, Nevada District Court Eighth Judicial District)* Currently serves as Presiding Judge and Juvenile Judge Family Division.
Office: Courthouse, 601 North Pecos, Las Vegas 89101-2408.
Telephone: (702) 455-6940.
Fax: (702) 455-2394

STEINHEIMER, Connie J. *(Judge, Nevada District Court Second Judicial District)* Serves Civil/Criminal Division.
Mailing address: P.O. Box 30083, Reno 89520-3083.
Office: 75 Court Street, Reno 89501.
Telephone: (775) 328-3183.
Fax: (775) 328-3821

SULLIVAN, Bill *(Justice of the Peace, Beatty Justices' Court)* Also serves as Juvenile Master, Nevada District Court Fifth Judicial District.
Mailing address: P.O. Box 805, Beatty 89003.
Telephone: (775) 553-2951.
Fax: (775) 553-2136

TATRO, John *(Justice of the Peace, Carson City Justices' Court and Judge, Carson City Municipal Court)*
Office: 885 East Musser Street, Suite 2007, Carson City 89701.
Telephone: (775) 887-2121.
Fax: (775) 887-2351

TAYLOR, Valeria M. *(Justice of the Peace, Baker Justices' Court)*
Mailing address: P.O. Box 2, Baker 89311.
Telephone: (775) 234-7100.
Fax: (775) 234-7252

TEURMAN, W. E. *(Judge, Fallon Municipal Court)* Appointed to term beginning April 1975. Elected to subsequent terms. Also serves as Juvenile Master, Nevada District Court Third Judicial District. Born Perryton Texas Sept 12, 1924. Protestant. Educated at East Los Angeles Junior College 1953-54. Appointed Juvenile Court Master, Nevada District Court Third Judicial District Dec 1976. Served temporary appointment as Tribal Judge, Paiute Shoshone and Yomba Shoshone Reservations.

Attended FBI School, California Highway Patrol Academy and National College of the State Judiciary. BM2 USN 1942-48. Democrat. Life member Churchill Masonic Lodge 12 and Elks 2094 South Lake Tahoe. Enjoys building woodwork.
Office: 55 West Williams Avenue, Fallon 89406.
Telephone: (775) 423-6244.
Fax: (775) 867-2378

THOMAS, Phil *(Justice of the Peace, Gerlach Justices' Court)*
Mailing address: P.O. Box 98, Gerlach 89412.
Telephone: (775) 557-2434.

TOGLIATTI, Jennifer P. *(Judge, Nevada District Court Eighth Judicial District)* Serves Civil/Criminal Division. Former Justice of the Peace, Las Vegas Justices' Court.
Office: Clark County Courthouse, 200 South Third Street, Las Vegas 89155.
Telephone: (702) 455-4666.
Fax: (702) 455-2262

TRUJILLO, Victor P. *(Justice of the Peace, Hawthorne Justices' Court)* Also serves as Juvenile Master, Nevada District Court Fifth Judicial District.
Mailing address: P.O. Box 1660, Hawthorne 89415.
Telephone: (775) 945-3859.
Fax: (775) 945-0700

TURNER, Wendell Ellis *(Justice of the Peace, Searchlight Justices' Court)*
Mailing address: P.O. Box 815, Searchlight 89046.
Telephone: (702) 297-1252.
Fax: (702) 297-1022

TYRRELL, Natalie *(Justice of the Peace, North Las Vegas Justices' Court)* Elected to term beginning Jan 2001. Term expires Jan 2007. Born Mankato Minnesota June 20, 1964. Religious affiliation: ELCA. Educated at Mankato State University B.A. magna cum laude 1986 and University of Minnesota Law School J.D. 1989. Law Clerk to Hon. Margaret Shaw Johnson, Minnesota District Court Third Judicial District 1989-90. Admitted to practice Minnesota 1989, Nevada 1991, U.S. District Court District of Nevada 1992 and U.S. Supreme Court 1995.

District Attorney Appellate Division Clark County Nov 1990 to Oct 1991. Member Southern Nevada Association of Women Attorneys, Nevada Judges Association, National Association of Women Judges, American Judges Association, Clark County and American Bar Associations. Member Senior Citizens Law Project City of Las Vegas Feb 1992 to Dec 2000, North Las Vegas Chamber, Latin Chamber, Trial by Peers, Eighth Judicial District Pro Bono Foundation, Friends of the North Las Vegas Library District and Lee Antonello PTA. Enjoys traveling, playing piano and spending time with family. Personal Statement or Quote: "We all make a living by what we get, but we make a life by what we give" (Winston Churchill).

Office: 2428 Martin Luther King Boulevard, North Las Vegas 89032.
Telephone: (702) 455-0733.

TYRRELL, NATALIE—*Continued*

Fax: (702) 455-7831
E-mail address: TYRRELNL@co.clark.nv.us

VAN LANDSCHOOT, Warren R. *(Judge, North Las Vegas Municipal Court)*
Office: 2240 Civic Center Drive, North Las Vegas 89030.
Telephone: (702) 633-1133.
Fax: (702) 633-1565

VAN WINKLE, James *(Judge, Reno Municipal Court)* Former Chief Judge.
Mailing address: P.O. Box 1900, Reno 89505.
Telephone: (775) 334-3822.
Fax: (775) 334-2425

VEGA, Valorie *(Judge, Nevada District Court Eighth Judicial District)* Serves Civil/Criminal Division. Former Judge, Las Vegas Municipal Court.
Office: Clark County Courthouse, 200 South Third Street, Las Vegas 89155.
Telephone: (702) 455-4645.
Fax: (702) 382-0006

VIDAL, Frances R. *(Justice of the Peace, Smith Valley Justices' Court and Judge, Yerington Municipal Court)* Clerk Aug 1985 to Feb 1988. Appointed Justice of the Peace by Lyon County Board of Commissioners to term beginning Feb 4, 1988. Elected 1988, 1990, 1994 and 2000. Current term expires Jan 2007. Assumed office Yerington Municipal Court July 1989. Also serves as Judge pro tem, Mineral, Churchill, Douglas and Lyon counties, Fallon Municipal Court and Lyon County Juvenile Court since 1988. Born Orange California March 25, 1941. Protestant. Interim Justice of the Peace, Mason Valley Justices' Court May 1994 to Jan 3, 1995.

Member Nevada Judges Association (Judicial Education Committee since 1988). Attended Special Court for Non-Law Trained Judges Course 1988, Special Court-Intermediate Jurisdiction, "Sentencing Misdemeanants," "Judicial Writing," "Alcohol and Drugs and the Courts," "Traffic Court" and "Domestic Violence" The National Judicial College and Winter Seminar Nevada Judges Association Laughlin Jan 10, 1989. Recipient Certificate of Basic Achievement in Judicial Education from State of Nevada Judicial Department Supreme Court and Award for Advanced Achievement in Judicial Education from Administrative Office of the Courts. Previously employed as legal secretary. Owner/operator Artist View Stables, Inc. (summer camp for girls) 1976-89 and Nelson's News Service, Inc. 1978-92. Enjoys raising and training quarter horses.

Justices' Court mailing address: P.O. Box 141, Smith 89430.
Municipal Court office: 102 South Main, Yerington 89447.
Telephone: (775) 465-2313, 463-3511.
Fax: (775) 465-2153 (Justices' Court), 463-9691 (Municipal Court)

VOY, William O. *(Judge, Nevada District Court Eighth Judicial District)* Serves Family Division.
Office: Courthouse, 601 North Pecos, Las Vegas 89101-2408.
Telephone: (702) 455-5990.
Fax: (702) 455-5989

WAGNER, Richard *(Judge, Nevada District Court Sixth Judicial District)*
Mailing address: P.O. Box H, Lovelock 89419.
Office: Pershing County Courthouse, 400 Main Street, Lovelock 89419.
Telephone: (775) 273-2105, 635-5739 (Battle Mountain), 623-5427 (Winnemucca).
Fax: (775) 273-4921

WAITE, D. Lanny *(Justice of the Peace, Moapa Valley Justices' Court)*
Mailing address: P.O. Box 337, Overton 89040.
Telephone: (702) 397-2840, 454-8870.
Fax: (702) 397-2842

WALL, David *(Judge, Nevada District Court Eighth Judicial District)* Serves Civil/Criminal Division.
Office: Clark County Courthouse, 200 South Third Street, Las Vegas 89155.
Telephone: (702) 455-6808.
Fax: (702) 366-7071

WALSH, Jessie *(Judge, Nevada District Court Eighth Judicial District)* Serves Civil/Criminal Division. Educated at University of San Diego B.A. 1982 and University of Arizona College of Law J.D. 1992. In legal practice June 1996 to 1998. Former Judge, Las Vegas Municipal Court, appointed to term beginning Oct 1999.

Deputy City Attorney Las Vegas City Attorney's Office 1992-96. With Public Defender's Office Clark County 1998-99. Member Southern Nevada Association of Women Attorneys and Judicial Council of the State of Nevada. Named Volunteer of the Year by Clark County Bar Association 1999. Development Officer Department of Economic and Urban Development City of Las Vegas 1989-90. Volunteer Judge "We the People . . . the Citizen & the Constitution" 1999 and 2000 and Client Counseling Competition University of Nevada Las Vegas Spring 2001. Advisory Board Police Athletic League. Volunteer Judge, Committee Member and Former Co-chair Trial by Peers. Conservation Chairperson Daughters of the American Revolution.

Office: Clark County Courthouse, 200 South Third Street, Las Vegas 89155.
Telephone: (702) 455-4668.
Fax: (702) 455-0057

WAMBOLT, Gene *(Justice of the Peace, Goldrun and Union Justices' Courts)*
Mailing address: P.O. Box 3, Golconda 89414.
Telephone: (775) 623-4749, 623-6059 (Winnemucca).
Fax: (775) 623-4749, 623-6439 (Winnemucca)

WARD, Daniel P. *(Justice of the Peace, New River Justices' Court)* Elected to term beginning Jan 7, 1991. Reelected 1994 and 2000. Current term expires Jan 2007. Also serves as Juvenile Master, Nevada District Court Third Judicial District. Born Reno Nevada March 16, 1946. Catholic. Educated at University of Nevada.

USAF Feb 1966 to Aug 1969. Nevada Highway Patrol Officer 1970-91. Member Navy League, Optimists Club and National Rifle Association. Enjoys horses and hunting.

Office: 71 North Maine Street, Fallon 89406.
Telephone: (775) 423-2845.
Fax: (775) 423-0472

WEIGHALL, Roberta "Bobbie" *(Justice of the Peace, Tecoma Justices' Court)*
Mailing address: P.O. Box 8, Montello 89830.
Telephone: (775) 776-2544.
Fax: (775) 776-2405

WILLIS, Robey B. *(Justice of the Peace, Carson City Justices' Court and Judge, Carson City Municipal Court)*
Office: 885 East Musser Street, Suite 2007, Carson City 89701.
Telephone: (775) 887-2121.
Fax: (775) 887-2351

YOUNG, Cliff *(Senior Justice, Nevada Supreme Court)* Elected Nov 1984 to term beginning Jan 7, 1985. Reelected 1990 and 1996. Former Chief Justice. Retired, serves by recall. Born Lovelock Nevada Nov 7, 1922. Educated at University of Nevada B.A. 1943 and Harvard Law School LL.B. 1949.
Office: 201 Supreme Court Building, 201 South Carson Street, Carson City 89701-4702.
Telephone: (775) 684-1600.

ZENOFF, David *(Senior Justice, Nevada Supreme Court)* Serves by recall.
Office: 201 Supreme Court Building, 201 South Carson Street, Carson City 89701-4702.
Telephone: (775) 684-1600.

ZIMMERMAN, Ann E. *(Justice of the Peace, Las Vegas Justices' Court)* Currently serves as Chief Justice of the Peace.
Mailing address: P.O. Box 552511, Las Vegas 89155-2511.
Telephone: (702) 455-1575.
Fax: (702) 759-0061

ZIVE, Gregg W. *(Chief Judge, United States Bankruptcy Court District of Nevada)* Appointed by U.S. Court of Appeals Ninth Circuit judges. Chief Judge since Oct 1, 1999.
Office: 1167 U.S. Courthouse, 300 Booth Street, Reno 89509.
Telephone: (775) 784-5017.

NEW HAMPSHIRE

Capital CONCORD

UNITED STATES DISTRICT COURT DISTRICT OF NEW HAMPSHIRE

The court sits at Concord and Littleton. For descriptive information refer to the United States Courts section.

Chief Judge
Paul J. Barbadoro

Judges
Joseph Anthony DiClerico, Jr.
Steven J. McAuliffe

Clerk
James R. Starr
110 U.S. Courthouse
55 Pleasant Street
Concord, New Hampshire 03301-3941
(603) 225-1423

UNITED STATES MAGISTRATE JUDGE OF NEW HAMPSHIRE

James R. Muirhead

UNITED STATES BANKRUPTCY COURT OF NEW HAMPSHIRE

Chief Judge
Mark W. Vaughn

Judge
J. Michael Deasy

Bankruptcy Clerk
George A. Vannah
404 Federal Building
275 Chestnut Street
Manchester, New Hampshire 03101-2411
(603) 222-2600

NEW HAMPSHIRE SUPREME COURT

The Supreme Court is New Hampshire's court of last resort. The court consists of one chief justice and four associate justices appointed by the governor and Executive Council to serve until age seventy. Retired justices may serve by assignment as senior justices.

The court has final appellate jurisdiction over all questions of law and over decisions or appeals of several administrative agencies. The court may issue writs necessary to the exercise of proper jurisdiction and has general superintendence over all courts in the state.

The court sits en banc at Concord and holds session all year.

Chief Justice
David Allen Brock

Associate Justices
John T. Broderick, Jr.
Joseph P. Nadeau
Linda Stewart Dalianis
James E. Duggan

Clerk
Eileen Fox
Supreme Court Building
One Noble Drive
Concord, New Hampshire 03301-6160
(603) 271-2646

Director
Donald D. Goodnow
Administrative Office of the Courts
Two Noble Drive
Concord, New Hampshire 03301-6160
(603) 271-2521

NEW HAMPSHIRE SUPERIOR COURT

The Superior Court is New Hampshire's trial court of general jurisdiction. A chief justice and twenty-eight associate justices are appointed by the governor and Executive Council to serve until age seventy. Retired justices may serve by assignment as senior justices.

The court has exclusive jurisdiction in civil actions when the amount in controversy exceeds $25,000 and concurrent jurisdiction with the District Court when the amount in controversy is between $1,500 and $25,000 and title to real estate is not involved. The court has jurisdiction over felony matters and hears misdemeanor appeals and appeals from convictions of offenses which provide the basis for enhanced penalties for subsequent convictions of the same offenses. Appeals are heard de novo from the District and Municipal Courts. The court may issue writs necessary to the exercise of proper jurisdiction.

The court sits at Brentwood, Concord, Dover, Keene, Laconia, Lancaster, Manchester, Nashua, Newport, North Haverhill and Ossipee.

Chief Justice
Walter L. Murphy

Associate Justices

Harold W. Perkins	Peter W. Smith
Robert E. K. Morrill	Kenneth R. McHugh
William J. Groff	Philip P. Mangones
Peter Hofstra Fauver	Bruce E. Mohl
James J. Barry, Jr.	James D. O'Neill, III
Kathleen A. McGuire	Bernard Hampsey, Jr.
David B. Sullivan	Patricia C. Coffey
Larry M. Smukler	Arthur D. Brennan
Carol Ann Conboy	John P. Arnold
Edward Fitzgerald, III	Robert J. Lynn
Gillian L. Abramson	Richard E. Galway
Tina L. Nadeau	Jean K. Burling

NEW HAMPSHIRE SUPERIOR COURT—*Continued*

John M. Lewis	Steven M. Houran
Gary E. Hicks	Timothy J. Vaughn

PROBATE COURTS OF NEW HAMPSHIRE

The Probate Courts are courts of special jurisdiction in New Hampshire. Judges are appointed by the governor and Executive Council to serve on either a full-time or a part-time basis until age seventy. One judge serves each county. Retired judges may serve as referees.

The courts exercise original jurisdiction over all matters concerning the probate of wills, administration of estates, appointment and removal of conservators and guardians, adoptions, commitment of the mentally ill, termination of parental rights, partition of real estate where there is no question of title, custodianship of the property of minors, apportionment of federal estate taxes, change of names and durable power of attorney for health care. The courts have jurisdiction for the interpretation, construction and termination of testamentary and inter vivos trust, except cases involving charitable uses and trusts, which are subject to concurrent jurisdiction with the Superior Court. The Probate Court has equity jurisdiction in its subject matter jurisdiction.

A Probate Court is located in each county and sits at the county seat.

County	Judge
Belknap	Christina M. O'Neill
Carroll	James R. Patten
Cheshire	Albert H. Weeks
Coos	David D. King
Grafton	Gary W. Boyle
Hillsborough	Raymond A. Cloutier
Merrimack	Richard A. Hampe
Rockingham	John R. Maher
Strafford	Gary R. Cassavechia
Sullivan	Michael R. Feeney

NEW HAMPSHIRE DISTRICT COURTS

The District Courts are courts of limited jurisdiction in New Hampshire. The state is divided into thirty-six districts. Justices and special justices are appointed by the governor and Executive Council to serve until age seventy. In Concord, Manchester and Nashua Districts, the justices are assisted by associate justices. An administrative justice for the District Courts is appointed by the Supreme Court and serves a three-year term.

The courts have original criminal jurisdiction of all offenses which are punishable by a fine of less than $2,000 and/or imprisonment not exceeding one year. The courts may conduct preliminary examinations in felony cases, and certain District Courts have been designated by the Supreme Court as regional jury trial courts. The courts have civil jurisdiction concurrent with the Superior Court in cases involving $25,000 or less ($50,000 in the case of selected District Courts), provided the defendant or plaintiff resides within the district. The courts have original and exclusive civil jurisdiction in cases involving less than $1,500 unless a question of title to real estate is involved. The courts also have original juvenile jurisdiction.

Administrative Justice
Edwin W. Kelly

AUBURN DISTRICT includes Auburn, Candia, Deerfield, Nottingham, Raymond and Northwood in Rockingham County. The court sits at Auburn.

Justice
David G. LeFrancois

Special Justice
Bruce R. Larson

BERLIN DISTRICT includes Berlin, Milan, Dummer, Cambridge (unincorporated) and Success in Coos County. The court sits at Berlin.

Justice
Wallace J. Anctil

Special Justice
Peter H. Bornstein

CLAREMONT DISTRICT includes Claremont, Cornish, Unity, Charlestown, Acworth, Langdon and Plainfield in Sullivan County. The court sits at Claremont.

Justice
John J. Yazinski

Special Justice
vacancy

COLEBROOK DISTRICT includes Colebrook, Pittsburg, Clarksville, Wentworth's Location, Errol, Millsfield, Columbia, Stewartstown, Stratford, Dix's Grant (unincorporated), Atkinson and Gilmanton Academy Grant, Second Collect Grant, Dixville, Erving's Location and Odell in Coos County. The court sits at Colebrook.

Justice
Paul D. Desjardins

Special Justice
James E. Michalik

CONCORD DISTRICT includes Pittsfield, Chichester, Epsom, Hopkinton, Concord, Loudon, Canterbury, Dunbarton and Bow in Merrimack County. The court sits at Concord.

Justice
Arthur E. Robbins

Associate Justice
Michael F. Sullivan

Special Justice
Susan B. Carbon

DERRY DISTRICT includes Derry, Chester, Londonderry and Sandown in Rockingham County. The court sits at Derry.

Justice
Lawrence F. Warhall

Special Justice
Edward R. Thornton, Jr.

DOVER DISTRICT includes Dover, Rollinsford and Somersworth in Strafford County. The court sits at Dover.

NEW HAMPSHIRE DISTRICT COURTS—*Continued*

Justices
Robert L. Cullinane
Clyde R. Coolidge

Special Justices
Stephen M. Morrison
Stephen H. Roberts

DURHAM DISTRICT includes Durham, Lee and Madbury in Strafford County. The court sits at Durham.

Justice
Gerald Taube

Special Justice
vacancy

EXETER DISTRICT includes Exeter, Newmarket, Stratham, Newfields, Fremont, East Kingston, Kensington, Epping and Brentwood in Rockingham County. The court sits at Exeter.

Justice
R. Laurence Cullen

Special Justice
Patricia DiMeo Reardon

FRANKLIN DISTRICT includes Franklin, Northfield, Danbury, Andover, Boscawen, Salisbury, Hill, Webster, Sanbornton and Tilton in Merrimack County. The court sits at Franklin.

Justice
W. H. Dale Townley-Tilson

Special Justice
Jay C. Boynton

GOFFSTOWN DISTRICT includes Goffstown, Weare, New Boston and Francestown in Hillsborough County. The court sits at Goffstown.

Justice
Paul H. Lawrence

Special Justice
Michael J. Ryan

GORHAM DISTRICT includes Bean's Purchase (unincorporated), Martin's Location, Green's Grant, Pinkham's Grant, Sargent's Purchase, Low & Burbank's Grant, Gorham, Shelburne and Randolph in Coos County. The court sits at Gorham.

Justice
Peter H. Bornstein

Special Justice
Wallace J. Anctil

HAMPTON DISTRICT includes Hampton, Hampton Falls, North Hampton, South Hampton and Seabrook in Rockingham County. The court sits at Hampton.

Justice
Francis J. Frasier

Special Justice
Edward J. McDermott

HAVERHILL DISTRICT includes Haverhill, Bath, Landaff, Benton, Piermont, Warren and Woodsville in Grafton County. The court sits at North Haverhill.

Justice
Timothy J. McKenna

Special Justice
Jennifer B. Sobel

HENNIKER DISTRICT includes Henniker, Warner and Bradford in Merrimack County. The court sits at Henniker.

Justice
Brackett Leighton Scheffy

Special Justice
Ellen L. Arnold

HILLSBOROUGH DISTRICT includes Hillsboro, Deering, Windsor, Antrim and Bennington in Hillsborough County. The court sits at Hillsboro.

Justice
Douglas S. Hatfield, Jr.

Special Justice
Thomas T. Barry

HOOKSETT DISTRICT includes Hooksett, Pembroke and Allenstown in Merrimack County. The court sits at Hooksett.

Justice
Robert L. LaPointe, Jr.

Special Justice
Lucinda V. Sadler

JAFFREY-PETERBOROUGH DISTRICT includes Jaffrey, Dublin, Fitzwilliam, Rindge, Temple, Sharon, Greenville, Greenfield, Peterborough, Hancock and New Ipswich in Cheshire County. The court sits at Jaffrey.

Justice
L. Phillips Runyon, III

Special Justices
William N. Prigge
vacancy

KEENE DISTRICT includes Nelson, Roxbury, Marlow, Swanzey, Marlborough, Winchester, Richmond, Hinsdale, Harrisville, Walpole, Alstead, Chesterfield, Keene, Stoddard, Westmoreland, Surrey, Gilsum, Sullivan and Troy in Cheshire County. The court sits at Keene.

Justice
Richard J. Talbot

Special Justice
Howard B. Lane, Jr.

LACONIA DISTRICT includes Laconia, Meredith, New Hampton, Gilford, Belmont, Alton, Gilmanton, Center Harbor and Barnstead in Belknap County. The court sits at Laconia.

Justice
David O. Huot

Special Justice
Willard G. Martin, Jr.

LANCASTER DISTRICT includes Northumberland, Carroll, Whitefield, Dalton, Chandler's Purchase, Jefferson, Kilkenney (unincorporated), Bean's Grant, Crawford's Purchase, Lancaster, Stark and Thompson and

NEW HAMPSHIRE DISTRICT COURTS—*Continued*

Meserve's Purchase in Coos County. The court sits at Lancaster.

Justice
Peter H. Bornstein

Special Justice
Jennifer B. Sobel

LEBANON DISTRICT includes Lebanon, Enfield, Canaan, Grafton, Orange, Hanover, Orford and Lyme in Grafton County. The court sits at Lebanon.

Justice
Albert J. Cirone, Jr.

Special Justice
Lawrence A. MacLeod, Jr.

LITTLETON DISTRICT includes Littleton, Monroe, Lyman, Lisbon, Easton, Franconia, Bethlehem and Sugar Hill in Grafton County. The court sits at Littleton.

Justice
John P. Cyr

Special Justice
Jennifer B. Sobel

MANCHESTER DISTRICT includes Manchester in Hillsborough County. The court sits at Manchester.

Justice
William H. Lyons

Associate Justice
Norman E. Champagne

Special Justice
John C. Emery

MERRIMACK DISTRICT includes Merrimack, Bedford and Litchfield in Hillsborough County. The court sits at Merrimack.

Justice
Clifford R. Kinghorn, Jr.

Special Justice
Gregory E. Michael

MILFORD DISTRICT includes Milford, Brookline, Amherst, Mason, Wilton, Lyndeborough and Mont Vernon in Hillsborough County. The court sits at Milford.

Justice
Martha R. Crocker

Special Justice
Paul S. Moore

NASHUA DISTRICT includes Nashua, Hudson and Hollis in Hillsborough County. The court sits at Nashua.

Justice
H. Philip Howorth

Associate Justice
Thomas E. Bamberger

Special Justice
James H. Leary

NEW LONDON DISTRICT includes New London, Wilmot, Newbury and Sutton in Merrimack County. The court sits at New London.

Justice
F. Graham McSwiney

Special Justice
Gerald J. Carney

NEWPORT DISTRICT includes Newport, Grantham, Croydon, Springfield, Goshen, Sunapee, Lempster and Washington in Sullivan County. The court sits at Newport.

Justice
Bruce A. Cardello

Special Justice
Edward B. Tenney

NORTHERN CARROLL COUNTY DISTRICT includes Conway, Bartlett, Jackson, Eaton, Chatham, Hart's Location, Albany, Madison, Hale's Location (unincorporated), Glen, Livermore, Cutt's Grant and Hadley's Purchase in Carroll County. The court sits at Conway.

Justice
Pamela D. Albee

Special Justice
James R. Patten

PLAISTOW DISTRICT includes Plaistow, Hampstead, Kingston, Newton, Atkinson and Danville in Rockingham County. The court sits at Plaistow.

Justice
Peter G. Hurd

Special Justice
Peter H. Bronstein

PLYMOUTH DISTRICT includes Plymouth, Bristol, Dorchester, Groton, Wentworth, Rumney, Thornton, Campton, Waterville, Ashland, Hebron, Holderness, Bridgewater, Alexandria, Lincoln, Woodstock, Livermore and Ellsworth in Grafton County. The court sits at Plymouth.

Resident Justice
Edwin W. Kelly

Justice
Stephen U. Samaha

Special Justices
David L. Kent
Thomas A. Rappa, Jr.

PORTSMOUTH DISTRICT includes Portsmouth, Newington, Greenland, Rye and New Castle in Rockingham County. The court sits at Portsmouth.

Justice
Alvin E. Taylor

Special Justice
Sharon N. DeVries

ROCHESTER DISTRICT includes Rochester, Milton, New Durham, Farmington, Strafford, Middleton and Barrington in Strafford County. The court sits at Rochester.

Justice
Franklin C. Jones

Special Justice
Daniel M. Capiello

SALEM DISTRICT includes Salem, Windham and Pelham in Rockingham County. The court sits at Salem.

Justice
John A. Korbey

Special Justices
Michael E. Jones
vacancy

SOMERSWORTH DISTRICT is consolidated with Dover District.

SOUTHERN CARROLL COUNTY DISTRICT includes Wolfeboro, Tuftonboro, Moultonboro, Sandwich, Brookfield, Ossipee, Tamworth, Sanbornville, Wakefield, Freedom and Effingham in Carroll County. The court sits at Ossipee.

Justices
Robert Charles Varney
Pamela D. Albee

Special Justice
James R. Patten

New Hampshire Counties and County Seats

Belknap
Laconia

Carroll
Ossipee

Cheshire
Keene

Coos
Berlin

Grafton
Woodsville

Hillsborough
Manchester
Nashua

Merrimack
Concord

Rockingham
Exeter

Strafford
Dover

Sullivan
Newport

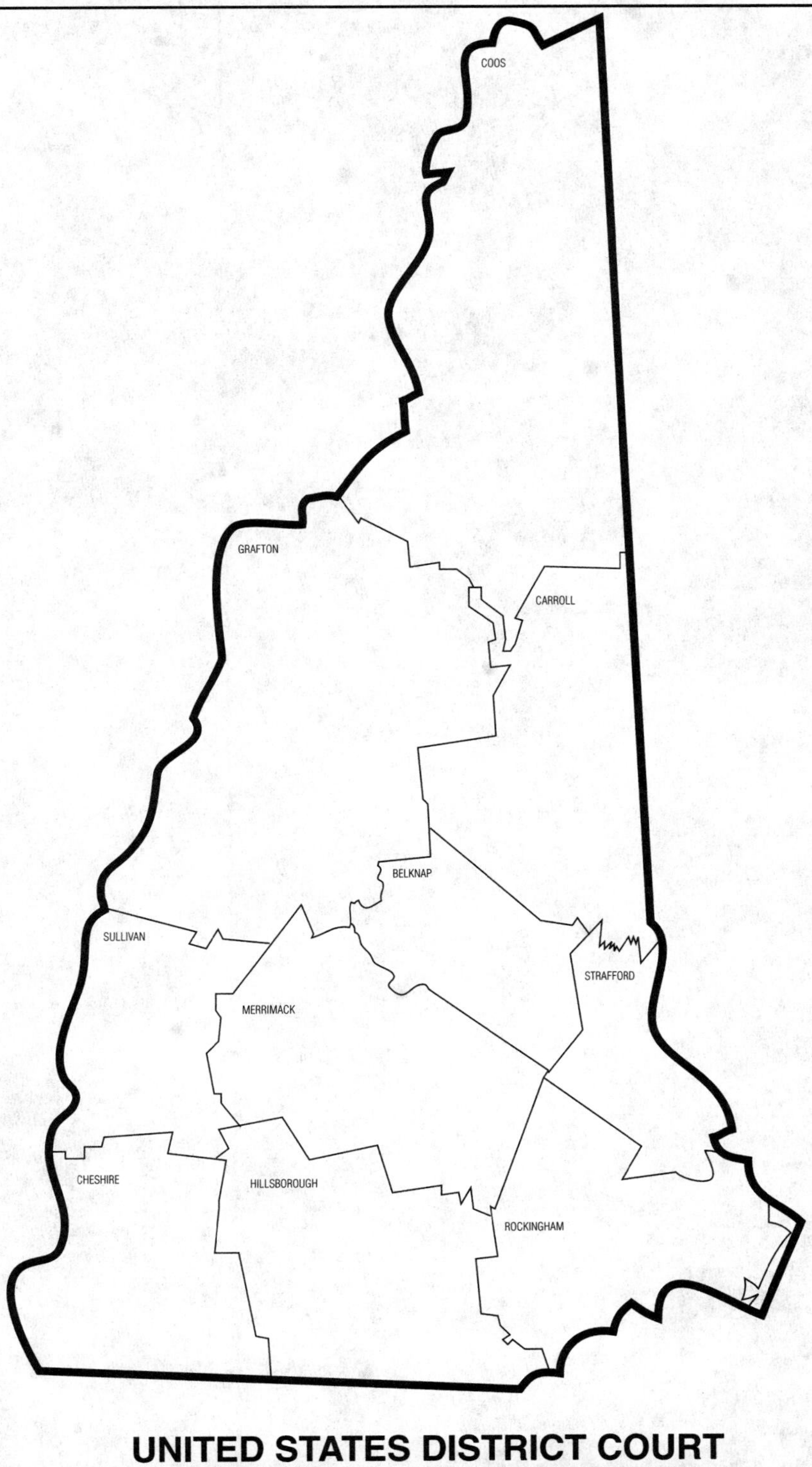
COOS
GRAFTON
CARROLL
BELKNAP
SULLIVAN
STRAFFORD
MERRIMACK
CHESHIRE
HILLSBOROUGH
ROCKINGHAM

UNITED STATES DISTRICT COURT
DISTRICT OF NEW HAMPSHIRE

NEW HAMPSHIRE

ABRAMSON, Gillian L. *(Associate Justice, New Hampshire Superior Court)* Appointed by governor.

Office: 1 Superior Court Center, 17 Chenell Drive, Concord 03301.

Telephone: (603) 271-2030.

ALBEE, Pamela D. *(Justice, Northern Carroll County District Court and Southern Carroll County District Court)* Appointed to Southern Carroll County District Court by Governor John H. Sununu to term beginning Jan 5, 1989. Appointed to Northern Carroll County District Court by Governor Jeanne Shaheen to term beginning 1997. Terms expire at age seventy. Born Wolfeboro New Hampshire Aug 7, 1948. Protestant. Educated at Wheaton College B.A. magna cum laude 1970 and University of Maine J.D. magna cum laude 1983. Articles Editor Maine Law Review 1981-83. Member Phi Beta Kappa. Admitted to practice New Hampshire 1983 and U.S. District Court District of New Hampshire 1983. In legal practice Ossipee 1987-2000.

Author "Deinstitutionalizing the Mentally Retarded in Maine: The Inevitable Face-off with Zoning" 35 No. 1 Maine L. Rev. 1983. Instructor in Civil Litigation School for Lifelong Learning University of New Hampshire 1986. Member New Hampshire District and Municipal Court Judges Association and New Hampshire Bar Association. Attends New Hampshire District and Municipal Court Judges Association conferences biannually. Enjoys painting, skiing and gardening.

Mailing address: P.O. Box 421, Ossipee 03864.

Office: Courthouse Square, Route 171, Ossipee 03864.

Telephone: (603) 539-4561.

Office: East Conway Road/Route 302, North Conway 03818.

Telephone: (603) 356-7710.

ANCTIL, Wallace J. *(Justice, Berlin District Court and Special Justice, Gorham District Court)* Appointed Special Justice Gorham District Court by Governor Meldrim Thomson, Jr. Jan 30, 1975. Appointed Justice Berlin District Court by Governor Meldrim Thomson, Jr. July 14, 1976. Terms expire at age seventy. Born Berlin New Hampshire July 5, 1939. Educated at St. Michael's College B.A. 1961 and Washington College of Law of American University J.D. 1969. Admitted to practice New Hampshire 1969. Began legal practice Berlin 1969.

Member New Hampshire Judges Association, Coos County (President 1972-74) and New Hampshire (Board of Governors 1974-77) Bar Associations. Member Berlin Board of Education 1970-74.

Mailing address: P.O. Box 176, Gorham 03581.

Office: Town Building, Park Street, Gorham 03581.

Telephone: (603) 466-2454.

Office: 220 Main Street, Berlin 03570.

Telephone: (603) 752-3160.

ARNOLD, Ellen L. *(Special Justice, Henniker District Court)* Appointed by governor. Also serves as Judge Family Division Pilot Project.

Office: 2 Depot Street, Henniker 03242.

Telephone: (603) 428-3214.

ARNOLD, John P. *(Associate Justice, New Hampshire Superior Court)* Appointed by governor.

Office: 1 Superior Court Center, 17 Chenell Drive, Concord 03301.

Telephone: (603) 271-2030.

BAMBERGER, Thomas E. *(Associate Justice, Nashua District Court)* Appointed Special Justice Concord District Court by Governor John H. Sununu to term beginning Nov 1988. Appointed Associate Justice Nashua District Court by Governor Jeanne Shaheen. Term expires at age seventy. Born Dover New Hampshire Dec 11, 1950. Congregationalist. Educated at University of New Hampshire B.A. 1972 and Franklin Pierce Law Center J.D. 1981. Admitted to practice New Hampshire 1981 and U.S. District Court District of New Hampshire 1981. In legal practice Concord 1981-93.

Member New Hampshire District and Municipal Court Judges Association, American Judges Association and New Hampshire Bar Association.

Office: 25 Walnut Street, Nashua 03060.

Telephone: (603) 880-3333, 880-3336.

BARBADORO, Paul J. *(Chief Judge, United States District Court District of New Hampshire)* Appointed for life by President George Bush to term beginning 1992. Chief Judge since Nov 1, 1997. Born Providence Rhode Island June 4, 1955. Educated at Gettysburg College B.A. 1977 and Boston College Law School J.D. 1980. In legal practice Concord 1986-92.

Assistant State Attorney General New Hampshire 1980-84. Counsel to U.S. Senator Warren B. Rudman 1984-86. Deputy Chief Counsel to Committee on Secret Military Assistance to Iran and the Nicaraguan Opposition U.S. Senate 1987.

Office: 409 U.S. Courthouse, 55 Pleasant Street, Concord 03301-3938.

Telephone: (603) 226-7303.

BARRY, James J., Jr. *(Associate Justice, New Hampshire Superior Court)* Appointed by governor.

Office: 1 Superior Court Center, 17 Chenell Drive, Concord 03301.

Telephone: (603) 271-2030.

BARRY, Thomas T. *(Special Justice, Hillsborough District Court)* Appointed by governor.

Mailing address: P.O. Box 763, Hillsboro 03244.

Office: 27 School Street, Hillsboro 03244.

Telephone: (603) 464-5811.

BORNSTEIN, Peter H. *(Justice, Gorham and Lancaster District Courts and Special Justice, Berlin District Court)* Appointed by governor.

Mailing address: P.O. Box 176, Gorham 03581.

Telephone: (603) 466-2454.

Office: 55 School Street, Suite 201, Lancaster 03584.

Telephone: (603) 788-4485.

Office: 220 Main Street, Berlin 03570.

Telephone: (603) 752-3160.

BOYLE, Gary W. *(Judge, Probate Court of New Hampshire Grafton County)* Appointed by Governor Hugh J. Gallen to term beginning Oct 4, 1982. Term

BOYLE, GARY W.—*Continued*

expires at age seventy. Serves part time. Former Judge Family Division Pilot Project. Born Whitefield New Hampshire Nov 6, 1948. Congregationalist. Educated at American University B.A. 1970 and Suffolk University J.D. 1975. Member Alpha Tau Omega. Admitted to practice New Hampshire 1975 and U.S. District Court District of New Hampshire 1975. Began legal practice Plymouth 1975. In legal practice Littleton 1976.

Chairman New Hampshire Commission of Eminent Domain 1979-82. Former member New Hampshire State Democratic Committee. Past Chairman Coos County Democratic Committee. Member Grafton County (Treasurer) and New Hampshire Bar Associations. Member New Hampshire Cancer Society. Enjoys family and sports.

Office: 3785 D.C. Highway, Box 3, North Haverhill 03774-9700.

Telephone: (603) 787-6931.

BOYNTON, Jay C. *(Special Justice, Franklin District Court)* Appointed by Governor Hugh J. Gallen to term beginning 1979. Term expires at age seventy. Born Laconia New Hampshire Oct 8, 1945. Educated at University of New Hampshire B.S. 1968 and University of Oregon J.D. 1971. Staff member Oregon Law Review 1970-71. Member Phi Delta Phi. Admitted to practice Oregon 1971, Ohio 1972 and New Hampshire 1975.

Law Instructor U.S. Coast Guard Academy 1973-75. Member American Judicature Society, Oregon State Bar, Belknap County, Ohio State, New Hampshire and American Bar Associations. Lieutenant USCG 1971-75 and Lieutenant Commander USCGR since 1976.

Office: 7 Hancock Terrace, Franklin 03235.

Telephone: (603) 934-3290.

BRENNAN, Arthur D. *(Associate Justice, New Hampshire Superior Court)* Appointed by governor.

Office: 1 Superior Court Center, 17 Chenell Drive, Concord 03301.

Telephone: (603) 271-2030.

BROCK, David Allen *(Chief Justice, New Hampshire Supreme Court)* Appointed Associate Justice by Governor Meldrim Thomson, Jr. June 9, 1978. Appointed Chief Justice by Governor John H. Sununu Oct 4, 1986. Term expires at age seventy. Born Stoneham Massachusetts July 6, 1936. Educated at Dartmouth College A.B. 1958 and University of Michigan LL.B. 1963. Admitted to practice New Hampshire 1963, U.S. District Court District of New Hampshire, U.S. Court of Appeals First Circuit and U.S. Supreme Court. In legal practice Manchester 1963-69 and Concord 1972-76. Associate Justice, New Hampshire Superior Court 1976-78.

U.S. Attorney District of New Hampshire 1969-72. Member National District Attorneys Association 1969-72, New Hampshire Judicial Council 1979-87 and Select Commission on a Unified Court System 1980-84, Judicial Education and Technical Assistance Consortium 1989-97 and Long Range Planning Committee The National Judicial College 1990. Chairman District Court Reform Subcommittee Governor's Commission for Court System Improvement 1974-75, New Hampshire Legal Services Advisory Commission 1977-79, Committee on Judicial Conduct New Hampshire Supreme Court 1981-89, Rules Advisory Committee New Hampshire Supreme Court 1985-97, Commission on Court Accreditation New Hampshire Supreme Court since 1986 and New Hampshire Interbranch Council on Substance Abuse and the Criminal Justice System 1991-95. Board of Directors 1992-98, Vice Chairman 1994-95 and Co-chair 1995-98 State Justice Institute. Board of Directors 1993-94, Vice President 1996-97, President Elect 1997-98 and President 1998-99 Conference of Chief Justices. Advisory Policy Board National Criminal Justice Information Services since 1999. Advisory Board The Reynolds National Center for Courts and Media since 2000. Member National Center for State Courts (Board of Directors 1996-2000, Chair Elect 1997-98, Chairman 1998-99), New Hampshire (Chairman Constitutional Revision Committee 1976-77) and American (Education Committee 1981-97 and Appellate Advocacy Committee 1982-84 Appellate Judges' Conference, House of Delegates representing Conference of Chief Justices 1994-96) Bar Associations. Lecturer Municipal Law Seminar 1976. Attended The National Judicial College 1977. Faculty Member Appellate Judges' Seminar Program American Bar Association 1984-89 and Leadership Institute in Judicial Education 1990-97. Recipient Distinguished Service Award from Leadership Institute for Judicial Education 1998. Lieutenant USMC 1958-60. Captain USMCR. Recipient Letter of Commendation from Commandant of the Marine Corps 1960. Vice Chairman New Hampshire Republican State Committee 1968-69. Chairman Manchester Republican City Committee 1967-69. Republican Candidate for U.S. Senate 1972. Delegate New Hampshire Constitutional Convention 1974. Special Counsel to Governor Meldrim Thomson, Jr. and Executive Council New Hampshire 1974-76. Legal Counsel to Governor Meldrim Thomson, Jr. 1976. Director 1966-72 and President 1969-72 Manchester Community Guidance Center, Inc. Trustee Manchester Boys Club 1969-72 and Holderness School, Plymouth 1972-73. Member Manchester Industrial Council 1968-76, Greater Manchester Mental Health Center Fund Raising Campaign 1971-72, New Hampshire Mental Health Advisory Commission 1976-78 and Governor's Commission for the Handicapped 1978-79.

Office: Supreme Court Building, One Noble Drive, Concord 03301.

Telephone: (603) 271-2149.

BRODERICK, John T., Jr. *(Associate Justice, New Hampshire Supreme Court)* Appointed by governor.

Office: Supreme Court Building, One Noble Drive, Concord 03301.

Telephone: (603) 271-2646.

BRONSTEIN, Peter H. *(Special Justice, Plaistow District Court)* Appointed by governor. Former Judge Family Division Pilot Project.

Mailing address: P.O. Box 129, Plaistow 03865.

Office: 14 Elm Street, Plaistow 03865.

Telephone: (603) 382-4651.

BURLING, Jean K. *(Associate Justice, New Hampshire Superior Court)* Appointed by Governor Jeanne Shaheen. Term expires at age seventy. Former Judge Family Division Pilot Project. Born Worcester Massachusetts July 7, 1946. Educated at Wellesley College B.A. 1968 and Boston University J.D. 1973. Admitted to practice New Hampshire 1973 and U.S. District Court District of New Hampshire 1975. Former Special Justice, Claremont District Court, appointed by Governor Hugh J. Gallen to term beginning April 11, 1979.

Former Member New Hampshire Police Standards and Training Council (Vice Chairman 1981-83). Fellow New Hampshire Bar Foundation (Judicial Conduct Commit-

BURLING, JEAN K.—*Continued*
tee). Chair Professional Conduct Committee and Member Character and Fitness Committee New Hampshire Supreme Court. Chair Judicial Education Committee New Hampshire District Court. Member New Hampshire Judicial Education Services Committee. Board of Governors New Hampshire District Court Association.

Office: 1 Superior Court Center, 17 Chenell Drive, Concord 03301.

Telephone: (603) 271-2030.

CAPPIELLO, Daniel M. *(Special Justice, Rochester District Court)* Appointed by governor.

Office: 76 North Main Street, Rochester 03867-1905.

Telephone: (603) 332-3516, 332-3150.

CARBON, Susan B. *(Special Justice, Concord District Court)* Appointed by Governor Judd Gregg to term beginning 1991. Supervisory Judge Grafton County Family Division Pilot Project since Mar 1996. Educated at University of Wisconsin B.A. with honors 1974 and DePaul University J.D. 1980. Staff member DePaul Law Review 1977-78.

Chair Permanency Planning Committee and Member District Court Policy Committee New Hampshire District Court. Fellow New Hampshire Bar Foundation and American Bar Foundation. Member National Council of Juvenile and Family Court Judges (Board of Trustees 1999, Chair Family Violence Committee 2001, Member Permanency Planning Committee and Juvenile and Family Drug Courts Committee), National Association of Women Judges, American Judges Association, New Hampshire (Board of Governors 1991-95, President 1993-94, Former Chair Family Violence Conference Committee) and American Bar Associations. Presenter "Dynamics of Domestic Violence" Municipal Police Academy Petrozavodsk Russia March 2000; "New Hampshire Court Improvement Project" Eighth Annual Conference New Hampshire Division for Children, Youth and Families May 2000; "Supervised Visitation Centers" New Hampshire's Sixth Annual Conference on Domestic Violence June 2000; "Advanced Domestic Violence" New Hampshire Bar Association Sept 2000; "Domestic Violence Fatality Review" STOP Conference Pennsylvania Coalition Against Domestic Violence Oct 2000; "Court Improvement Project Training" Attorney General's Conference on Child Abuse Oct 2000; "New Hampshire's Juvenile Justice/Community and the Courts Project" Juvenile Delinquency and the Courts Conference California Judicial Council Jan 25, 2001; and "Domestic Violence Fatality Review: New Hampshire's Experience" Battered Women's Justice Project Conference March 2001. Recipient Frank Rowe Kenison Award from New Hampshire Bar Foundation June 2000 and Marilla Ricker Award for Judicial Excellence from New Hampshire Women's Bar Oct 2000. Board of Directors YMCA Lakes Region 1983-87. Member Pittsfield School Board 1987-90 and New Hampshire Charitable Foundation since 1993. Chair Pittsfield Zoning Board of Adjustment 1988. Chair Domestic Violence Fatality Review Committee and Member Executive Committee New Hampshire Governor's Commission on Domestic and Sexual Violence. Member New Hampshire Children's Alliance.

Mailing address: P.O. Box 3420, Concord 03302-3420.

Office: 32 Clinton Street, Concord 03301.

Telephone: (603) 271-6400.

CARDELLO, Bruce A. *(Justice, Newport District Court)* Appointed by Governor Jeanne Shaheen. Also serves as Judge Family Division Pilot Project.

Mailing address: P.O. Box 581, Newport 03773.

Office: Main Street, Newport 03773.

Telephone: (603) 863-1832.

CARNEY, Gerald J. *(Special Justice, New London District Court)* Appointed by Governor Hugh J. Gallen to term beginning Feb 13, 1981. Term expires at age seventy. Born New York Jan 6, 1941. Educated at C. W. Post College and St. John's University. Admitted to practice New York 1969 and New Hampshire 1974. Began legal practice New York City 1969. In legal practice New Hampshire 1974.

Member Sullivan County, New Hampshire and American Bar Associations.

Mailing address: P.O. Box 1966, New London 03257.

Office: Main Street, New London 03257.

Telephone: (603) 526-6519.

CASSAVECHIA, Gary R. *(Judge, Probate Court of New Hampshire Strafford County)* Appointed by governor. Serves part time.

Mailing address: P.O. Box 799, Dover 03821.

Office: County Farm Road, Dover 03820.

Telephone: (603) 742-2550.

CHAMPAGNE, Norman E. *(Associate Justice, Manchester District Court)* Appointed by governor.

Mailing address: P.O. Box 456, Manchester 03105-0456.

Office: 35 Amherst Street, Manchester 03101.

Telephone: (603) 624-6510.

CIRONE, Albert J., Jr. *(Justice, Lebanon District Court)* Appointed by Governor John H. Sununu to term beginning June 1988. Term expires at age seventy. Currently serves as Presiding Justice. Born Adams Massachusetts May 5, 1948. Roman Catholic. Educated at Tufts University B.A. cum laude 1970, George Washington University J.D. with honors 1973 and University of New Hampshire M.B.A. 1985. Admitted to practice New Hampshire 1973 and U.S. District Court District of New Hampshire 1973. In legal practice Lebanon since 1974.

Member Grafton County and New Hampshire Bar Associations. Enjoys golf, traveling and reading.

Office: 38 Centerra Parkway, Lebanon 03766.

Telephone: (603) 643-3555.

CLOUTIER, Raymond A. *(Judge, Probate Court of New Hampshire Hillsborough County)* Appointed by Governor Hugh J. Gallen to term beginning Feb 3, 1981. Term expires at age seventy. Born Manchester New Hampshire Aug 11, 1938. Catholic. Educated at Assumption College B.A. 1960 and Boston University School of Law LL.B. 1963. Admitted to practice New Hampshire 1963. In legal practice Manchester 1963-81.

Town Moderator Goffstown 1964-65. Attorney Hillsborough County 1976-81. Member American Judicature Society, The Association of Trial Lawyers of America, Manchester, New Hampshire and American Bar Associations. Enjoys farming.

Mailing address: P.O. Box P, Nashua 03061-6015.

Office: 30 Spring Street, Nashua 03061.

Telephone: (603) 882-1231, 424-7844, 627-5609.

COFFEY, Patricia C. *(Associate Justice, New Hampshire Superior Court)* Appointed by governor. Former Special Justice, Portsmouth District Court.

Office: 1 Superior Court Center, 17 Chenell Drive, Concord 03301.

Telephone: (603) 271-2030.

CONBOY, Carol Ann *(Associate Justice, New Hampshire Superior Court)* Appointed by governor.

Office: 1 Superior Court Center, 17 Chenell Drive, Concord 03301.

Telephone: (603) 271-2030.

COOLIDGE, Clyde R. *(Justice, Dover District Court)* Appointed by Governor Meldrim Thomson, Jr. to term beginning June 24, 1975. Term expires at age seventy. Born Manchester New Hampshire Dec 9, 1938. Unitarian. Educated at University of New Hampshire B.A. magna cum laude 1960 and Boston College J.D. 1963. Member Phi Beta Kappa. Admitted to practice New Hampshire 1963. Began legal practice Somersworth 1963.

Somersworth Mayor 1967-71. Member Strafford County, New Hampshire and American Bar Associations. Captain USAF 1963-66. Enjoys running and road races.

Office: 25 St. Thomas Street, Dover 03820.

Telephone: (603) 742-7202, 749-4612.

CROCKER, Martha R. *(Justice, Milford District Court)* Special Justice Jaffrey-Peterborough District Court 1985-2002. Appointed Justice by Governor Jeanne Shaheen to term beginning Sept 1, 2002. Term expires at age seventy. Born Boston Massachusetts March 24, 1949. Educated at Vassar College A.B. 1971 and Franklin Pierce Law Center J.D. 1979. Admitted to practice New Hampshire 1979 and U.S. District Court District of New Hampshire 1979.

Assistant County Attorney Cheshire County 1980-84.

Office: 180 Elm Street, Milford 03055.

Telephone: (603) 673-2900.

E-mail address: mcrocker@courts.state.n.h

CULLEN, R. Laurence *(Justice, Exeter District Court)* Special Justice Oct 1986 to April 1989. Appointed Justice by Governor John H. Sununu to term beginning April 1989. Term expires at age seventy. Born Medford Massachusetts Nov 15, 1940. Educated at Williams College B.A. 1962 and Boston University J.D. 1970. Admitted to practice Massachusetts 1970, New Hampshire 1971 and U.S. District Court District of New Hampshire 1971.

With Office of Legislative Services. Member Barreau du Canada, New Hampshire and Massachusetts Bar Associations. USN 1962-67.

Mailing address: P.O. Box 394, Exeter 03833.

Office: 120 Water Street, Exeter 03833.

Telephone: (603) 772-2931.

CULLINANE, Robert L. *(Justice, Dover District Court)* Appointed by governor. Currently serves as Presiding Justice.

Office: 25 St. Thomas Street, Dover 03820.

Telephone: (603) 742-7202, 749-4612.

CYR, John P. *(Justice, Littleton District Court)* Appointed by governor. Also serves as Judge Family Division Pilot Project.

Office: 134 Main Street, Littleton 03561.

Telephone: (603) 444-7750, 444-5514.

DALIANIS, Linda Stewart *(Associate Justice, New Hampshire Supreme Court)* Appointed by Governor Jeanne Shaheen. Term expires at age seventy. Born Boston Massachusetts Oct 9, 1948. Catholic. Educated at Northeastern University B.A. cum laude 1970 and Suffolk University J.D. 1974. Admitted to practice New Hampshire 1974. Began legal practice Nashua 1974. Former Associate Justice and Chief Justice, New Hampshire Superior Court, appointed by Governor Hugh J. Gallen to term beginning Oct 15, 1980.

Member National Association of Women Judges, American Judges Association, American Judicature Society, Nashua, New Hampshire and American Bar Associations. Named New Hampshire Young Career Woman 1975. Member New Hampshire Association of Business and Professional Women's Clubs. Interests include skiing, horseback riding, reading and piano.

Office: Supreme Court Building, One Noble Drive, Concord 03301.

Telephone: (603) 271-2646.

DEASY, J. Michael *(Judge, United States Bankruptcy Court District of New Hampshire)* Appointed by U.S. Court of Appeals First Circuit judges to term beginning March 19, 1999. Former Judge, Bankruptcy Appellate Panel First Circuit, selected by the Judicial Council of the First Circuit to term beginning Jan 2000. Educated at Rensselaer Polytechnic Institute B.S. 1967 and Boston College J.D. cum laude 1973. Admitted to practice New Hampshire 1973 and U.S. District Court District of New Hampshire 1973. In legal practice Nashua 1973-99.

Member American Bankruptcy Institute, National Conference of Bankruptcy Judges, Nashua, New Hampshire and American Bar Associations. Presenter Seminars on Avoiding Environmental Liability 1990 and 1992, Bankruptcy and Lender Liability Law 1991, Foreclosures in New Hampshire 1991, Problem Real Estate Loans 1992, Bankruptcy Procedure in New Hampshire 1993, Bankruptcy Law for Municipalities 1994 and Bankruptcy Practice Update 1997. Presenter on Bankruptcy New Hampshire Bar Practical Skills Course 1990-98 and Northeast Bankruptcy Conference American Bankruptcy Institute 1996 and 1999-2002. Listed in *Best Lawyers in America.* Polaris Submarine Officer USN 1967-70. Member 1979-83 and Chairman 1980-81 Milford School Board. Member 1984-99, Director 1987-88 and President 1989-90 Milford Rotary Club. Director Greater Nashua Chamber of Commerce 1990-91. Director 1995-99 and President 1996-99 Milford Industrial Development Corporation. Member since 1996 and President since 1998 Wadleigh Library Development Fund. Director New Hampshire Legal Assistance 1998.

Office: 275 Chestnut Street, 4th Floor, Manchester, New Hampshire 03101.

Telephone: (603) 222-2640.

Fax: (603) 666-7922

E-mail address: michael_deasy@nhb.uscourts.gov

DESJARDINS, Paul D. *(Justice, Colebrook District Court)* Appointed Special Justice Lancaster District Court by Governor John H. Sununu 1988. Appointed Special Justice Colebrook District Court by Governor Judd Gregg 1990. Appointed Justice by Governor Stephen Merrill. Term expires at age seventy. Born Whitefield New Hampshire Oct 22, 1954. Roman Catholic. Educated at University of New Hampshire B.A. magna cum laude 1976 and University of Dayton J.D. 1979. Member Phi Alpha Delta, Phi Beta Kappa, Psi Epsilon

DESJARDINS, PAUL D.—*Continued*

and Omicron Delta Epsilon. Recipient Carroll M. Degler Scholarship. Moot Court Board. Admitted to practice New Hampshire 1979 and U.S. District Court District of New Hampshire 1979. In legal practice Whitefield 1979-83 and Lancaster since 1983.

Colonel Town Spending Committee 1988-93. Member Coos County (Past President) and New Hampshire Bar Associations. Attends all Continuing Judicial Education seminars sponsored by New Hampshire District and Municipal Court Judges Association. Former Member Lancaster Rotary Club. Enjoys golf, basketball and soccer.

Mailing address: P.O. Box 5, Colebrook 03576.
Office: 10 Bridge Street, Colebrook 03576.
Telephone: (603) 237-4229.

DeVRIES, Sharon N. *(Special Justice, Portsmouth District Court)* Appointed by governor. Also serves as Judge Family Division Pilot Project.

Office: 111 Parrott Avenue, Portsmouth 03801-4490.
Telephone: (603) 431-2192.

DiCLERICO, Joseph Anthony, Jr. *(Judge, United States District Court District of New Hampshire)* Appointed for life by President George Bush to term beginning Sept 11, 1992. Chief Judge 1992 to Oct 31, 1997. Born Lynn Massachusetts Jan 30, 1941. Roman Catholic. Educated at Williams College B.A. cum laude 1963 and Yale University LL.B. 1966. Law Clerk to Hon. Aloysius Connor, U.S. District Court District of New Hampshire 1966-67 and New Hampshire Supreme Court 1967-68. Member Phi Beta Kappa. Admitted to practice New Hampshire 1967, U.S. District Court District of New Hampshire 1967, U.S. Court of Appeals First Circuit 1973 and U.S. Supreme Court 1975. In legal practice Concord 1968-70. Chief Justice 1991-92 and Associate Justice 1977-91, New Hampshire Superior Court, appointed by Governor Meldrim Thomson, Jr.

Assistant Attorney General New Hampshire 1970-77. Author "Cy Pres: A Proposal for Change" Vol. XLVII Boston University L. Rev. 153 Spring 1967. Member 1977-87 and Chairman 1987 to Sept 1992 Sentence Review Division New Hampshire Superior Court. Member New Hampshire Supreme Court Advisory Commission on Rules Jan 1985 to Sept 1992. Former Member American Bar Association (Member 1986-92 and Co-chair 1990-91 Judicial Immunity Committee, Delegate 1987-92 National Conference of State Trial Judges Judicial Administration Division). Member Committee on Codes of Conduct 1994-2002 and District Judge Representative from the First Circuit 1997-2000 Judicial Conference of the U.S. Member New Hampshire Bar Foundation, American Bar Foundation, New London, Merrimack County (Treasurer-Secretary 1969-71) and New Hampshire (Former member Committee on Professional Conduct) Bar Associations. President 1973-75 and Director 1996-2000 Little Sunapee Protective Association. Member New London Planning Board 1975-77, Dartmouth-Hitchcock Memorial Hospital Assembly of Overseers 1988-99 and Independent Order of Odd Fellows. Enjoys gardening, tennis, hiking, skiing and bicycling.

Office: 400 U.S. Courthouse, 55 Pleasant Street, Concord 03301-3938.
Telephone: (603) 226-7746.

DUGGAN, James E. *(Associate Justice, New Hampshire Supreme Court)* Appointed by Governor Jeanne Shaheen.

Office: Supreme Court Building, One Noble Drive, Concord 03301.
Telephone: (603) 271-2646.

EMERY, John C. *(Special Justice, Manchester District Court)* Appointed by Governor Jeanne Shaheen.

Mailing address: P.O. Box 456, Manchester 03105-0456.
Office: 35 Amherst Street, Manchester 03101.
Telephone: (603) 624-6510.

FAUVER, Peter Hofstra *(Associate Justice, New Hampshire Superior Court)* Appointed by governor. Term expires at age seventy. Born Hanover New Hampshire July 18, 1947. Episcopalian. Educated at University of North Carolina A.B. 1970 and University of Tennessee J.D. 1973. Admitted to practice New Hampshire 1973. In legal practice North Conway 1973 and since 1977 and Chocorua 1974-76. Former Justice, Conway District Court and Ossipee District Court, appointed by Governor Meldrim Thomson, Jr. to term beginning 1977.

Member Carroll County, New Hampshire and American Bar Associations.

Office: 1 Superior Court Center, 17 Chenell Drive, Concord 03301.
Telephone: (603) 271-2030.

FEENEY, Michael R. *(Judge, Probate Court of New Hampshire Sullivan County)* Appointed by governor. Serves part time.

Mailing address: P.O. Box 417, Newport 03773.
Telephone: (603) 863-3150.

FITZGERALD, Edward, III *(Associate Justice, New Hampshire Superior Court)* Appointed by governor.

Office: 1 Superior Court Center, 17 Chenell Drive, Concord 03301.
Telephone: (603) 271-2030.

FRASIER, Francis J. *(Justice, Hampton District Court)* Appointed by governor.

Mailing address: P.O. Box 10, Hampton 03843-0010.
Office: 132 Winnacunnet Road, Hampton 03842.
Telephone: (603) 926-8117.

GALWAY, Richard E. *(Associate Justice, New Hampshire Superior Court)* Appointed by governor.

Office: 1 Superior Court Center, 17 Chenell Drive, Concord 03301.
Telephone: (603) 271-2030.

GROFF, William J. *(Associate Justice, New Hampshire Superior Court)* Appointed by Governor John H. Sununu to term beginning May 7, 1988. Educated at Harvard College B.A. cum laude 1967 and Boston College Law School J.D. 1972. Admitted to practice New Hampshire 1972 and U.S. District Court District of New Hampshire 1972. In legal practice Nashua 1972-87. E-5 U.S. Army Vietnam 1968-70.

Office: 1 Superior Court Center, 17 Chenell Drive, Concord 03301.
Telephone: (603) 271-2030.

HAMPE, Richard A. *(Judge, Probate Court of New Hampshire Merrimack County)* Appointed by Governor Stephen Merrill.

Office: 163 North Main Street, Concord 03301.
Telephone: (603) 224-9589.

HAMPSEY, Bernard J., Jr. *(Associate Justice, New Hampshire Superior Court)* Appointed by governor. Former Justice, Jaffrey-Peterborough District Court.

Office: 1 Superior Court Center, 17 Chenell Drive, Concord 03301.

Telephone: (603) 271-2030.

HATFIELD, Douglas S., Jr. *(Justice, Hillsborough District Court)* Appointed Special Justice by governor to term beginning 1969. Appointed Justice by Governor John H. Sununu 1984. Term expires at age seventy. Born Plainfield New Jersey Oct 29, 1935. Educated at Colby College A.B. 1958 and Boston University LL.B. 1961. Admitted to practice New Hampshire 1961.

Member New Hampshire and American Bar Associations.

Mailing address: P.O. Box 763, Hillsboro 03244.

Office: 27 School Street, Hillsboro 03244.

Telephone: (603) 464-5811.

HICKS, Gary E. *(Associate Justice, New Hampshire Superior Court)* Appointed by Governor Jeanne Shaheen.

Office: 1 Superior Court Center, 17 Chenell Drive, Concord 03301.

Telephone: (603) 271-2030.

HOURAN, Steven M. *(Associate Justice, New Hampshire Superior Court)* Appointed by Governor Jeanne Shaheen.

Office: 1 Superior Court Center, 17 Chenell Drive, Concord 03301.

Telephone: (603) 271-2030.

HOWORTH, H. Philip *(Justice, Nashua District Court)* Associate Justice April 11, 1984 to April 22, 1986. Appointed Justice by Governor John H. Sununu to term beginning April 23, 1986. Term expires at age seventy. Born Cumberland Maryland July 11, 1933. Educated at Haverford College A.B. 1954 and Harvard University LL.B. 1957. Admitted to practice New Hampshire 1958 and Massachusetts 1959. Began legal practice Concord New Hampshire 1961. In legal practice Boston Massachusetts 1962 and Nashua New Hampshire 1965.

Chairman Nashua Board of Assessors 1972. Corporation Counsel City of Nashua 1973-84. Instructor in Labor Law Rivier College 1982. Member Nashua (President Elect) and New Hampshire Bar Associations.

Office: 25 Walnut Street, Nashua 03060.

Telephone: (603) 880-3333, 880-3336.

HUOT, David O. *(Justice, Laconia District Court)* Appointed by Governor Hugh J. Gallen to term beginning May 1, 1979. Term expires at age seventy. Born Laconia New Hampshire April 4, 1942. Roman Catholic. Educated at St. Anselm's College A.B. 1964 and Georgetown University Law Center J.D. 1967. Admitted to practice New Hampshire 1967. Began legal practice Laconia 1967.

New Hampshire House of Representatives 1971-75. Member New Hampshire District and Municipal Judges Association, American Judges Association, Belknap County, New Hampshire (Board of Governors 1978-80) and American (Judicial Administration Division) Bar Associations. Member New Hampshire Air National Guard since 1967.

Mailing address: P.O. Box 1010, Laconia 03247-1010.

Office: 26 Academy Street, Laconia 03246.

Telephone: (603) 524-4128, 524-4051.

HURD, Peter G. *(Justice, Plaistow District Court)* Appointed by Governor John H. Sununu to term beginning Sept 29, 1983. Term expires at age seventy. Born Newton Massachusetts Jan 8, 1944. Protestant. Educated at University of Massachusetts-Amherst B.B.A. 1966 and Suffolk University J.D. 1973. Member Kappa Sigma. Admitted to New Hampshire 1973, U.S. District Court District of New Hampshire 1974 and U.S. Supreme Court 1978. In legal practice Salem 1974-76 and Plaistow since 1976.

Assistant Director of Personnel Avco Everett Research Laboratory, Inc. 1968-73. Member New Hampshire Trial Lawyers Association, American Judges Association, Rockingham County, New Hampshire and American Bar Associations. First Lieutenant U.S. Army Corps of Engineers 1966-68. Enjoys skiing, sailing, hiking, water skiing and golf.

Mailing address: P.O. Box 129, Plaistow 03865.

Office: 14 Elm Street, Plaistow 03865.

Telephone: (603) 382-4651.

JONES, Franklin C. *(Justice, Rochester District Court)* Former Special Justice. Appointed Justice by Governor Jeanne Shaheen.

Office: 76 North Main Street, Rochester 03867-1905.

Telephone: (603) 332-3516, 332-3150.

JONES, Michael E. *(Special Justice, Salem District Court)* Appointed by Governor Judd Gregg to term beginning 1989. Educated at Denison University B.A., Wharton School of Finance and Commerce University of Pennsylvania M.B.A. and University of Miami School of Law J.D. Admitted to practice New Hampshire 1978 and U.S. Supreme Court.

Member New Hampshire House of Representatives 1982-88. Associate Professor University of Massachusetts since 1983.

Office: 35 Geremonty Drive, Salem 03079.

Telephone: (603) 893-4483.

KELLY, Edwin W. *(Administrative Justice, New Hampshire District Court and Resident Justice, Plymouth District Court)* Appointed Resident Justice by Governor John H. Sununu to term beginning Dec 18, 1985. Term expires at age seventy. Appointed Administrative Justice Jan 2, 1991. Former Administrative Justice, New Hampshire Municipal Courts Jan 2, 1991 to 2000. Born Suffern New York Dec 11, 1951. Roman Catholic. Educated at Providence College B.A. 1973 and Western New England College J.D. cum laude 1979. Law Clerk to New Hampshire Superior Court 1979-80. Admitted to practice New Hampshire 1979.

Member American Judges Association and New Hampshire Bar Association. Previously employed as teacher Rochester Alternative School and with U.S. Civil Service Commission, Washington D.C. Democrat.

Office: 26 Green Street, Plymouth 03264.

Telephone: (603) 536-3326.

KENT, David L. *(Special Justice, Plymouth District Court)* Appointed by governor. Educated at University of New Hampshire B.S. 1964, Northeastern University M.B.A. 1968, Boston College J.D. 1971 and University of Edinburgh, Danforth and Post Doctoral Fellow 1979. Admitted to practice New Hampshire 1972, Massachusetts 1972 and U.S. District Court District of New Hampshire 1972.

Member New Hampshire District and Municipal Jud-

KENT, DAVID L.—*Continued*

ges Association, Grafton County and New Hampshire Bar Associations.

Office: 26 Green Street, Plymouth 03264.
Telephone: (603) 536-3326.

KING, David D. *(Judge, Probate Court of New Hampshire Coos County)* Appointed by governor. Serves part time.

Office: 55 School Street, Suite 104, Lancaster 03584.
Telephone: (603) 788-2001.

KINGHORN, Clifford R., Jr. *(Justice, Merrimack District Court)* Appointed by governor.

Mailing address: P.O. Box 324, Merrimack 03054.
Office: Town Hall Building, Baboosic Lake Road, Merrimack 03054.
Telephone: (603) 424-9916, 424-9917, 424-7005.

KORBEY, John A. *(Justice, Salem District Court)* Appointed by Governor Meldrim Thomson, Jr. to term beginning 1976. Term expires at age seventy. Also serves as Judge Family Division Pilot Project. Born Lawrence Massachusetts 1947. Catholic. Educated at University of Massachusetts A.B. 1969 and Boston College Law School J.D. 1972. Admitted to practice New Hampshire 1972 and U.S. District Court District of New Hampshire 1972. In legal practice Derry 1972-95.

Member National Council of Juvenile and Family Court Judges, American Judges Association and New Hampshire Bar Association.

Office: 35 Geremonty Drive, Salem 03079.
Telephone: (603) 893-4483.

LANE, Howard B., Jr. *(Special Justice, Keene District Court)* Appointed by governor.

Mailing address: P.O. Box 364, Keene 03431.
Office: 3 Washington Street, Keene 03431.
Telephone: (603) 352-2559, 352-2047.

LaPOINTE, Robert L., Jr. *(Justice, Hooksett District Court)* Appointed by governor.

Office: 101 Merrimack Street, Hooksett 03106-1416.
Telephone: (603) 485-9901, 485-9220.

LARSON, Bruce R. *(Special Justice, Auburn District Court)* Appointed by governor.

Office: 5 Priscilla Lane, Auburn 03032.
Telephone: (603) 624-2084, 624-2265.

LAWRENCE, Paul H. *(Justice, Goffstown District Court)* Appointed by governor.

Mailing address: P.O. Box 129, Goffstown 03045-0129.
Office: 16 Main Street, Goffstown 03045.
Telephone: (603) 497-2597.

LEARY, James H. *(Special Justice, Nashua District Court)* Appointed by governor.

Office: 25 Walnut Street, Nashua 03060.
Telephone: (603) 880-3333, 880-3336.

LeFRANCOIS, David G. *(Justice, Auburn District Court)* Appointed by Governor Jeanne Shaheen.

Office: 5 Priscilla Lane, Auburn 03032.
Telephone: (603) 624-2084, 624-2265.

LEWIS, John M. *(Associate Justice, New Hampshire Superior Court)* Appointed by Governor Jeanne Shaheen.

Office: 1 Superior Court Center, 17 Chenell Drive, Concord 03301.
Telephone: (603) 271-2030.

LYNN, Robert J. *(Associate Justice, New Hampshire Superior Court)* Appointed by Governor Judd Gregg to term beginning Dec 17, 1992. Term expires at age seventy. Born New Haven Connecticut Aug 26, 1949. Educated at University of New Haven B.S. magna cum laude 1971 and University of Connecticut School of Law J.D. with high honors 1975. Recipient American Jurisprudence Awards in Business Organizations, Conflict of Laws, Advanced Criminal Procedure and Trusts and Estates. Executive Editor Connecticut Law Review 1974-75. Law Clerk to Hon. J. William Ditter, Jr., U.S. District Court Eastern District of Pennsylvania June 1975 to July 1977. Member Alpha Chi. Admitted to practice Connecticut, New Hampshire and Pennsylvania (inactive). In legal practice Concord New Hampshire Sept 1984 to Feb 1989.

Special Attorney Organized Crime Strike Force Eastern District of New York July 1977 to Oct 1978. Assistant U.S. Attorney Oct 1978 to Sept 1984 and First Assistant 1982-84 District of New Hampshire. Assistant U.S. Attorney District of Connecticut Feb 1989 to May 1991. Assistant U.S. Attorney May 1991 to Dec 1992 and Chief New England Organized Crime Drug Enforcement Task Force Jan 1992 to Dec 1992 District of Massachusetts. Author Comment "Search Incident to Arrest: *United States v. Robinson*—An Analytical View" 7 Connecticut L. Rev. 346, 1975; "Declaratory Judgments in Insurance Cases: Recent Amendment Solves the 'Where to Sue' Problem But Leaves the 'When to Sue' Question Unresolved" 36 New Hampshire B. Jour. 58, 1995; and "Judicial Rule-Making and the Separation of Powers: The Need for Constitutional Reform" 42 New Hampshire B. Jour 44, 2001. Adjunct Faculty Member Massachusetts School of Law since 1996. Member New Hampshire Bar Association (Rules of Criminal Procedure Committee 1985-89, Continuing Legal Education Committee since 1994, Public Information Committee 1995-97, Cooperation with Courts Committee since 1997). Instructor Attorney General's Advocacy Institute 1989-90. Member School Board of Bow New Hampshire 1982-89 (Chairman Bow Secondary Education Study Committee 1982-83).

Office: 1 Superior Court Center, 17 Chenell Drive, Concord 03301.
Telephone: (603) 271-2030.

LYONS, William H. *(Justice, Manchester District Court)* Appointed by governor.

Mailing address: P.O. Box 456, Manchester 03105-0456.
Office: 35 Amherst Street, Manchester 03101.
Telephone: (603) 624-6510.

MacLEOD, Lawrence A., Jr. *(Special Justice, Lebanon District Court)* Appointed by Governor Jeanne Shaheen Aug 2002. Term expires at age seventy. Born Hanover New Hampshire Feb 13, 1960. Roman Catholic. Educated at Tufts University B.A. 1982, Cambridge University M.Phil. 1987 and University of Maine School of Law J.D. 1991. Admitted to practice New Hampshire 1991, U.S. District Court District of New Hampshire

MACLEOD, LAWRENCE A., JR.—*Continued*
1991 and Vermont 2000. In legal practice Lebanon New Hampshire since 1991.

Member New Hampshire Trial Lawyers Association, Grafton County and New Hampshire (Board of Governors) Bar Associations. Member New Hampshire Guardian ad litem Board. Enjoys farming and reading.

Office: 38 Centerra Parkway, Lebanon 03766.
Telephone: (603) 448-3555.

MAHER, John R. *(Judge, Probate Court of New Hampshire Rockingham County)* Appointed by Governor John H. Sununu to term beginning Aug 1983. Term expires at age seventy. Administrative Judge since Dec 1990. Former Supervisory Judge Family Division Pilot Project. Born Stratford Connecticut Dec 3, 1941. Unitarian. Educated at Fairfield University B.A. 1964 and Suffolk University Law School J.D. 1968. Admitted to practice New Hampshire 1969 and Massachusetts 1969. In legal practice Portsmouth New Hampshire 1969-90.

Member New Hampshire Judicial Council, New Hampshire Court Accreditation Commission, Supreme Court Advisory Committee on Rules, National College of Probate Judges and Charles C. Doe Inns of Court. Recipient Governor's Volunteer Recognition Award 1993. Assistant Mayor Portsmouth City Council 1973-78. Past President Portsmouth Anthanaeum, Seacoast United Way and Odyssey House. Former Director Exeter Banking Group, Portsmouth Community Foundation, Berwick Academy, Portsmouth 350th Celebration and Prescott Park Arts Festival. Volunteer Seacoast Hospice and Portsmouth Community Child Care Center. Enjoys skiing, hiking, ocean kayaking and golfing.

Mailing address: P.O. Box 789, Kingston 03848.
Office: Rockingham County Courthouse, 10 Route 125, Brentwood 03833.
Telephone: (603) 642-5437.

MANGONES, Philip P. *(Associate Justice, New Hampshire Superior Court)* Appointed by governor.

Office: 1 Superior Court Center, 17 Chenell Drive, Concord 03301.
Telephone: (603) 271-2030.

MARTIN, Willard G., Jr. *(Special Justice, Laconia District Court)* Appointed by Governor Walter Peterson to term beginning Dec 1972. Term expires at age seventy. Also serves as Judge Family Division Pilot Project. Born Boston Massachusetts Dec 12, 1937. Unitarian. Educated at Bates College A.B. cum laude 1959, Harvard Law School LL.B. 1962 and Boston University LL.M. in Taxation 1984. Member Phi Beta Kappa. Admitted to practice New Hampshire 1962 and U.S. District Court District of New Hampshire 1962. In legal practice Laconia since 1962.

Laconia City Solicitor 1963-66. Belknap County Attorney 1967-68. Member New Hampshire General Court 1969-70. New Hampshire Bar Examiner since 1972. Member New Hampshire Committee on Character and Fitness since 1975. Member New Hampshire Judicial Council 1971-75, Belknap and New Hampshire Bar Associations.

Mailing address: P.O. Box 1010, Laconia 03247-1010.
Office: 26 Academy Street, Laconia 03246.
Telephone: (603) 524-4128, 524-4051.

McAULIFFE, Steven J. *(Judge, United States District Court District of New Hampshire)* Appointed for life by President George Bush Oct 10, 1992 to term beginning Nov 17, 1992. Born Cambridge Massachusetts March 3, 1948. Educated at Virginia Military Institute B.A. with honors 1970 and Georgetown University Law Center J.D. 1973. Admitted to practice District of Columbia, New Hampshire, U.S. District Court District of New Hampshire, U.S. Courts of Appeals First and District of Columbia Circuits, U.S. Court of Appeals for the Armed Forces, U.S. Army Court of Military Review, U.S. Tax Court, U.S. Court of Federal Claims and U.S. Supreme Court. In legal practice Concord 1980-92.

Assistant Attorney General New Hampshire 1977-80. Fellow New Hampshire Bar Foundation. Member New Hampshire Trial Lawyers Association (Bar Member Supreme Court Committee on Professional Conduct 1989, Vice President 1989, President Elect 1990, President 1991-92). Captain 1973-77 and Major since 1977 JAGC U.S. Army. Captain USAR 1978-79. New Hampshire Army National Guard (inactive since 1988). Board of Directors New Hampshire Office of Public Guardian 1979-92. Trustee 1986-94, Legal Counsel to the Board since 1987 and Board Vice Chairman since 1990 University System of New Hampshire. Director Challenger Center for Space Science Education since 1986. Board Member New Hampshire Medical Malpractice Stabilization Reserve Fund Trust 1987-92 (Chairman 1991).

Office: 416 U.S. Courthouse, 55 Pleasant Street, Concord 03301-3938.
Telephone: (603) 226-7304.

McDERMOTT, Edward J. *(Special Justice, Hampton District Court)* Appointed by governor.

Mailing address: P.O. Box 10, Hampton 03843-0010.
Office: 132 Winnacunnet Road, Hampton 03842.
Telephone: (603) 926-8117.

McGUIRE, Kathleen A. *(Associate Justice, New Hampshire Superior Court)* Appointed by Governor Judd Gregg to term beginning Sept 8, 1989. Term expires at age seventy. Born Manchester New Hampshire April 4, 1948. Educated at University of New Hampshire B.A. 1970, University of Florida M.A. 1975 and Boston College J.D. cum laude 1983. Recipient Judicial Fellowship from New Hampshire Bar Association and Fellowship from American Bar Association. Law Clerk to Hon. Charles Douglas, New Hampshire Supreme Court 1984-85. Admitted to practice New Hampshire 1984, U.S. District Court District of New Hampshire 1984 and U.S. Court of Appeals First Circuit 1988.

Office: 1 Superior Court Center, 17 Chenell Drive, Concord 03301.
Telephone: (603) 271-2030.

McHUGH, Kenneth R. *(Associate Justice, New Hampshire Superior Court)* Appointed by Governor John H. Sununu to term beginning Oct 1, 1986. Term expires at age seventy. Born Manchester New Hampshire July 18, 1944. Roman Catholic. Educated at St. Anselm's College B.A. 1966 and Suffolk University J.D. 1969. Admitted to practice New Hampshire 1969. Began legal practice Manchester 1969. Justice, Hooksett District Court 1976-86.

Member Manchester, New Hampshire and American Bar Associations. Democrat. Enjoys sports.

Office: 1 Superior Court Center, 17 Chenell Drive, Concord 03301.
Telephone: (603) 271-2030.

McKENNA, Timothy J. *(Justice, Haverhill District Court)* Former Special Justice. Appointed Justice by Governor Stephen Merrill.
Office: 3785 D.C. Highway, Box 10, North Haverhill 03774.
Telephone: (603) 787-6626.

McSWINEY, F. Graham *(Justice, New London District Court)* Appointed by governor.
Mailing address: P.O. Box 1966, New London 03257.
Office: Main Street, New London 03257.
Telephone: (603) 526-6519.

MICHAEL, Gregory E. *(Special Justice, Merrimack District Court)* Appointed by Governor John H. Sununu to term beginning Dec 1, 1986. Term expires at age seventy. Born Niskayuna New York Dec 10, 1947. Episcopalian. Educated at University of New Hampshire B.S. 1969 and Suffolk University J.D. 1972. Lead Article Editor Suffolk University Law Review 1971-72. Admitted to practice New Hampshire 1972 and Massachusetts 1972. In legal practice Merrimack New Hampshire since 1977.
Author "The Unitary Theory; A Proposal for a Stable Student-School Legal Relationship" Journal of Law and Education July 1972. Instructor Daniel Webster College 1978-80. Member New Hampshire and American Bar Associations. Colonel USAFR JAGC (active duty 1973-77). Director New England Salem Children's Trust. Enjoys light plane flying, scuba diving and snow and water skiing.
Mailing address: P.O. Box 324, Merrimack 03054.
Office: Town Hall Building, Baboosic Lake Road, Merrimack 03054.
Telephone: (603) 424-9916, 424-9917, 424-7005.

MICHALIK, James E. *(Special Justice, Colebrook District Court)* Appointed by Governor Jeanne Shaheen.
Mailing address: P.O. Box 5, Colebrook 03576.
Office: 10 Bridge Street, Colebrook 03576.
Telephone: (603) 237-4229.

MOHL, Bruce E. *(Associate Justice, New Hampshire Superior Court)* Appointed by Governor John H. Sununu Dec 15, 1987 to term beginning Feb 7, 1988. Term expires at age seventy. Born Tarrytown New York May 2, 1946. Educated at Hamilton College A.B. 1968 and Boston University School of Law J.D. 1971. Admitted to practice Massachusetts 1971, New Hampshire 1981, U.S. District Courts District of Massachusetts 1971 and District of New Hampshire 1982 and U.S. Court of Appeals First Circuit 1981. In legal practice Boston Massachusetts 1971-82 and Concord New Hampshire 1982-88.
Assistant Attorney General Massachusetts 1980-82 and New Hampshire 1982-85. Deputy Attorney General New Hampshire 1985-88. Instructor Boston University School of Law 1974-76 and Boston College Law School 1980-82. Member New Hampshire Bar Association.
Office: 1 Superior Court Center, 17 Chenell Drive, Concord 03301.
Telephone: (603) 271-2030.

MOORE, Paul S. *(Special Justice, Milford District Court)* Appointed by Governor Jeanne Shaheen.
Office: 180 Elm Street, Milford 03055.
Telephone: (603) 673-2900, 673-2295.

MORRILL, Robert E. K. *(Associate Justice, New Hampshire Superior Court)* Appointed by Governor John H. Sununu to term beginning March 26, 1986. Term expires at age seventy. Former Judge Family Division Pilot Project. Born Keene New Hampshire Feb 1, 1947. Episcopalian. Educated at Harvard University B.A. cum laude 1970, Victoria University Wellington, New Zealand Honours B.A. 1971 and University of Pennsylvania J.D. 1974. Admitted to practice New Hampshire 1974 and U.S. District Court District of New Hampshire 1974. In legal practice Concord 1974-86.
Office: 1 Superior Court Center, 17 Chenell Drive, Concord 03301.
Telephone: (603) 271-2030.

MORRISON, Stephen M. *(Special Justice, Dover District Court)* Appointed by Governor John H. Sununu to term beginning Aug 27, 1986. Term expires at age seventy. Born Dover New Hampshire Oct 1, 1948. Catholic. Educated at Assumption College B.A. 1970 and Suffolk University J.D. 1973. Admitted to practice New Hampshire 1973 and U.S. District Court District of New Hampshire 1974. In legal practice Dover since 1973.
With County Attorney's Office Strafford County 1973-77. City Attorney Dover City 1977-78. Attorney New Hampshire Real Estate Commission 1977-79. Member Strafford County, New Hampshire and American Bar Associations.
Office: 25 St. Thomas Street, Dover 03820.
Telephone: (603) 742-7202, 749-4612.

MUIRHEAD, James R. *(Magistrate Judge, United States District Court District of New Hampshire)* Appointed by U.S. District Court judges.
Office: 417 U.S. Courthouse, 55 Pleasant Street, Concord 03301-3938.
Telephone: (603) 225-1493.

MURPHY, Walter L. *(Chief Justice, New Hampshire Superior Court)* Appointed Associate Justice by Governor John H. Sununu to term beginning Dec 7, 1983. Appointed Chief Justice by Governor Jeanne Shaheen to term beginning Oct 4, 2000. Term expires at age seventy. Former Supervisory Judge, Hillsborough County Superior Court. Born Boston Massachusetts Dec 11, 1937. Roman Catholic. Educated at College of the Holy Cross B.S. 1959 and Boston College Law School J.D. 1962. Admitted to practice New Hampshire 1962, U.S. District Court District of New Hampshire 1964 and U.S. Court of Appeals First Circuit 1966. Began legal practice Plymouth 1962. Special Justice, Plymouth District Court 1965-75. Clerk, Grafton County Superior Court 1975-77.
Co-author *New Hampshire Civil Jury Instructions* Michie Publishing. Adjunct Professor of Trial Advocacy Franklin Pierce Law Center since 1987. Member Supreme Court Committee on Professional Conduct 1972-83 and Supreme Court Committee on Judicial Conduct 1995-2000. Former Chairman Supreme Court Courthouse Security Commission. Past Member Superior Court Executive and Policy Committee. State Delegate National Conference of Trial Court Judges. Member Superior Court Committee relating to Media in the Courtroom, Supreme Court Committee on Corrections, Supreme Court Committee on Judicial Conduct, New Hampshire Bar Foundation, New Hampshire Trial Lawyers Association, American Judicature Society, Grafton County (President 1972-73), New Hampshire (Board of Directors 1970-72) and American Bar Associations. Lecturer Continuing Legal Education programs New Hampshire Bar Association, New Hampshire Trial Lawyers Association and State Trial Judges. Faculty Advisor The National Judicial College. Recipient Justice William A. Grimes

MURPHY, WALTER L.—*Continued*

Award for Judicial Professionalism from New Hampshire Bar Association.

Office: 1 Superior Court Center, 17 Chenell Drive, Concord 03301.

Telephone: (603) 271-2030.

NADEAU, Joseph P. *(Associate Justice, New Hampshire Supreme Court)* Appointed by Governor Jeanne Shaheen. Term expires at age seventy. Born Rochester New Hampshire June 30, 1938. Religious affiliation: Maronite. Educated at Phillips Exeter Academy 1955, Dartmouth College A.B. 1959 and Boston University J.D. 1962. Admitted to practice New Hampshire 1962. Began legal practice Dover 1962. Former Justice, Durham District Court appointed by Governor John W. King to term beginning Dec 27, 1968. Former Chief Justice, New Hampshire Superior Court.

Dover City Attorney 1967. Instructor since 1972 and member Board of Directors since 1988 American Academy of Judicial Education. Member New Hampshire Judges Association (President 1973), American Judges Association (Board of Governors since 1973), Strafford County (President 1972) and New Hampshire Bar Associations. USMC 1962. Democrat. Member New Hampshire Real Estate Commission (Chairman 1969). Enjoys tennis, poetry, antiques and boating.

Office: Supreme Court Building, One Noble Drive, Concord 03301.

Telephone: (603) 271-2646.

NADEAU, Tina L. *(Associate Justice, New Hampshire Superior Court)* Appointed by governor.

Office: 1 Superior Court Center, 17 Chenell Drive, Concord 03301.

Telephone: (603) 271-2030.

O'NEILL, Christina M. *(Judge, Probate Court of New Hampshire Belknap County)* Appointed by governor. Also serves as Judge Family Division Pilot Project.

Mailing address: P.O. Box 1343, Laconia 03247-1343.

Office: 64 Court Street, Laconia 03246.

Telephone: (603) 524-0903.

O'NEILL, James D., III *(Associate Justice, New Hampshire Superior Court)* Appointed by governor.

Office: 1 Superior Court Center, 17 Chenell Drive, Concord 03301.

Telephone: (603) 271-2030.

PATTEN, James R. *(Judge, Probate Court of New Hampshire Carroll County and Special Justice, Northern Carroll County District Court and Southern Carroll County District Court)* Appointed by governor. Serves Probate Court part time.

Probate Court mailing address: P.O. Box 419, Ossipee 03864.

Telephone: (603) 539-4123.

Northern Carroll office: East Conway Road, Route 302, North Conway 03818.

Telephone: (603) 356-7710.

Southern Carroll office: Courthouse Square, Route 171, Ossipee 03864.

Telephone: (603) 539-4561.

PERKINS, Harold W. *(Associate Justice, New Hampshire Superior Court)* Appointed by governor.

Office: 1 Superior Court Center, 17 Chenell Drive, Concord 03301.

Telephone: (603) 271-2030.

PRIGGE, William N. *(Special Justice, Jaffrey-Peterborough District Court)* Appointed by governor.

Mailing address: P.O. Box 39, Jaffrey 03452-0039.

Office: 7 Knight Street, Jaffrey 03452.

Telephone: (603) 532-8698, 532-7276.

RAPPA, Thomas A., Jr. *(Special Justice, Plymouth District Court)* Appointed by Governor John H. Sununu to term beginning Dec 1988. Term expires at age seventy. Born Wilmington Delaware Jan 18, 1953. Educated at Middlebury College B.A. 1975 and Franklin Pierce Law Center J.D. 1986. Admitted to practice New Hampshire 1986 and U.S. District Court District of New Hampshire 1986. In legal practice Woodsville since 1991.

Instructor Plymouth State College 1989-90 and College of Life Long Learning University of New Hampshire since 1995. Member New Hampshire Trial Lawyers Association, The Association of Trial Lawyers of America, Grafton County, New Hampshire and American Bar Associations. Recipient President's Award for Grafton County 1988 and 1989 and L. Jonathan Ross Award 1989. Hobbies include performing in a bluegrass band and outdoor sports.

Office: 26 Green Street, Plymouth 03264.

Telephone: (603) 536-3326.

REARDON, Patricia DiMeo *(Special Justice, Exeter District Court)* Appointed by governor. Also serves as Judge Family Division Pilot Project.

Mailing address: P.O. Box 394, Exeter 03833.

Office: 120 Water Street, Exeter 03833.

Telephone: (603) 772-2931.

ROBBINS, Arthur E. *(Justice, Concord District Court)* Appointed by governor.

Mailing address: P.O. Box 3420, Concord 03302-3420.

Office: 32 Clinton Street, Concord 03301.

Telephone: (603) 271-6400.

ROBERTS, Stephen H. *(Special Justice, Dover District Court)* Appointed by governor.

Office: 25 St. Thomas Street, Dover 03820.

Telephone: (603) 742-7202, 749-4612.

RUNYON, L. Phillips, III *(Justice, Jaffrey-Peterborough District Court)* Appointed by governor.

Mailing address: P.O. Box 39, Jaffrey 03452-0039.

Office: 7 Knight Street, Jaffrey 03452.

Telephone: (603) 532-8698, 532-7276.

RYAN, Michael J. *(Special Justice, Goffstown District Court)* Appointed by Governor Jeanne Shaheen.

Mailing address: P.O. Box 129, Goffstown 03045-0129.

Office: 16 Main Street, Goffstown 03045.

Telephone: (603) 497-2597.

SADLER, Lucinda V. *(Special Justice, Hooksett District Court)* Appointed by Governor Jeanne Shaheen.

Office: 101 Merrimack Street, Hooksett 03106-1416.

Telephone: (603) 485-9901, 485-9220.

SAMAHA, Stephen U. *(Justice, Plymouth District Court)* Appointed by governor to term beginning 1979. Term expires at age seventy. Born Ayer Massachusetts Feb 11, 1944. Educated at Dartmouth College A.B. 1966 and Boston University School of Law J.D. 1969. Admitted to practice New Hampshire 1969. In legal practice Manchester 1969-73 and Littleton 1973-95. Former Justice, Lincoln District Court. Captain U.S. Army National Guard 1969-77.
Office: 26 Green Street, Plymouth 03264.
Telephone: (603) 536-3326.

SCHEFFY, Brackett Leighton *(Justice, Henniker District Court)* Appointed by Governor John H. Sununu to term beginning Dec 23, 1985. Term expires at age seventy. Born New Rochelle New York May 31, 1943. Educated at Boston University B.A. 1967 J.D. 1970. Admitted to practice Massachusetts 1970, U.S. Court of Appeals First Circuit 1970 and New Hampshire 1973. In legal practice Boston Massachusetts 1970-75 and Bradford and Warner New Hampshire since 1973.
Member Merrimack County, New London and New Hampshire Bar Associations. DK3 USN 1963-65. Enjoys playing tennis, reading and sailing.
Office: 2 Depot Street, Henniker 03242.
Telephone: (603) 428-3214.

SMITH, Peter W. *(Associate Justice, New Hampshire Superior Court)* Appointed by governor.
Office: 1 Superior Court Center, 17 Chenell Drive, Concord 03301.
Telephone: (603) 271-2030.

SMUKLER, Larry M. *(Associate Justice, New Hampshire Superior Court)* Appointed by governor.
Office: 1 Superior Court Center, 17 Chenell Drive, Concord 03301.
Telephone: (603) 271-2030.

SOBEL, Jennifer B. *(Special Justice, Haverhill, Lancaster and Littleton District Courts)* Appointed by governor.
Office: 3785 D.C. Highway, Box 10, North Haverhill 03774.
Telephone: (603) 787-6626.
Office: 55 School Street, Suite 201, Lancaster 03584.
Telephone: (603) 788-4485.

SULLIVAN, David B. *(Associate Justice, New Hampshire Superior Court)* Appointed by Governor Judd Gregg to term beginning Aug 1991. Term expires at age seventy. Born Boston Massachusetts July 6, 1947. Educated at Wesleyan University B.A. 1969 and Boston University School of Law J.D. magna cum laude 1973. Editor Boston University Law Review 1971-73. Admitted to practice New Hampshire 1973.
Office: 17 Chenell Drive, Suite 1, Concord 03301.
Telephone: (603) 271-2030.

SULLIVAN, Michael F. *(Associate Justice, Concord District Court)* Appointed by Governor Hugh J. Gallen to term beginning Sept 9, 1981. Term expires at age seventy. Born Medford Massachusetts March 17, 1945. Roman Catholic. Educated at University of Massachusetts B.A. 1967 and Suffolk University J.D. with honors 1974. Admitted to practice Massachusetts 1974 and New Hampshire 1977. Began legal practice Concord New Hampshire 1977.
Senior Legislative Attorney 1974-78. General Counsel New Hampshire House Committees 1978-79. Executive Director New Hampshire Crime Commission 1979-81. Past President New Hampshire District Court Association. Member New Hampshire and American (Executive Committee Conference of Special Court Judges) Bar Associations. Captain USAF 1967-71. Former member Board of Directors New Hampshire Friends Program and New Hampshire Mediation Program. Vice Chairman Pro Bono Referral System 1983-84.
Mailing address: P.O. Box 3420, Concord 03302-3420.
Office: 32 Clinton Street, Concord 03301.
Telephone: (603) 271-6400.

TALBOT, Richard J. *(Justice, Keene District Court)* Appointed Special Justice by Governor Walter Peterson to term beginning May 29, 1969. Appointed Justice by Governor John H. Sununu Nov 26, 1984. Term expires at age seventy. Born Boston Massachusetts May 15, 1942. Unitarian. Educated at Brown University A.B. 1964 and Boston University J.D. 1967. Admitted to practice New Hampshire 1967. In legal practice Keene 1967-84.
Important Decision: In re Juvenile no. 1089, 1979. Instructor New Hampshire Police Standards Training Council since 1978 and Paralegal Program University of New Hampshire since 1980. Member New Hampshire Bar Association. Attended course on Special Jurisdiction The National Judicial College 1988. Moderator Monadnock Regional School District 1971-84. Trustee Trust Funds Town of Swanzey. Treasurer Elliott Institute of Fitzwilliam.
Mailing address: P.O. Box 364, Keene 03431.
Office: 3 Washington Street, Keene 03431.
Telephone: (603) 352-2559, 352-2047.

TAUBE, Gerald *(Justice, Durham District Court)* Former Special Justice. Appointed Justice by Governor Stephen Merrill. Also serves as Supervising Judge Family Division Pilot Project.
Office: Main Street, Durham 03824.
Telephone: (603) 868-2323.

TAYLOR, Alvin E. *(Justice, Portsmouth District Court)* Former Special Justice. Appointed Justice by governor.
Office: 111 Parrott Avenue, Portsmouth 03801-4490.
Telephone: (603) 431-2192.

TENNEY, Edward B. *(Special Justice, Newport District Court)* Appointed by Governor Judd Gregg to term beginning Aug 7, 1991. Term expires at age seventy. Born Claremont New Hampshire April 19, 1961. Protestant. Educated at University of New Hampshire B.A. cum laude 1983 and Franklin Pierce Law Center J.D. 1986. Admitted to practice New Hampshire 1986. In legal practice Claremont 1986-95.
Author "The Horizontal Gaze Nystagmus Test and the Admissibility of Scientific Evidence" 27 No. 3 New Hampshire B. Jour. Spring 1986. Member New Hampshire District and Municipal Court Judges Association, New Hampshire Trial Lawyers Association, New Hampshire and American Bar Associations. Republican. Enjoys golfing and coaching high school basketball.
Mailing address: P.O. Box 581, Newport 03773.
Office: Main Street, Newport 03773.
Telephone: (603) 863-1832.

THORNTON, Edward R., Jr. *(Special Justice, Derry District Court)* Appointed by Governor John H.

THORNTON, EDWARD R., JR.—*Continued*

Sununu to term beginning Dec 1987. Term expires at age seventy. Born Manchester New Hampshire July 27, 1939. Catholic. Educated at Dartmouth College A.B. 1961 and University of Maine School of Law J.D. 1965. Business Manager University of Maine Law Review 1964-65. Member Alpha Chi Rho. Admitted to practice New Hampshire 1965, U.S. District Court District of New Hampshire 1968, U.S. Supreme Court 1977 and U.S. Tax Court 1977. In legal practice Manchester since 1965 and Lincoln since 1988.

Editor-in-Chief Trial Bar News 1981-83 and since 1984. Author "Use of Experts to Determine Reliability of Dental Records" 1 Journal of Proceedings The Association of Trial Lawyers of America Aug 2, 1985. Instructor Mount St. Mary's College 1967-68. Member New Hampshire District and Municipal Court Judges Association, New Hampshire Trial Lawyers Association (Treasurer 1978-79, Board of Governors 1978-85, Executive Committee Board of Governors 1978-85, Jury Verdict Survey Committee 1980-82, Chairman Committees on Marital Masters 1980-83 and Constitution and By-Law Revision since 1980, member since 1980 and Chairman 1980-82 Legislative Committee, President Elect 1982-83, President 1983-84, CLE Committee since 1983, Immediate Past President 1984-85, Representative Citizen's Insurance Research Group since 1985, Faculty Member People's Law School 1988, 1990, 1991 and 1992), National Panel of Arbitrators American Arbitration Association, The Association of Trial Lawyers of America (Council of State Delegates 1985-91), Manchester (District Court System Improvement Committee 1978-79, Hillsborough County Law Library Committee 1983-84), New Hampshire (Chairman Junior Bar Activities 1966-68 and Lawyer Disability Committee since 1990, Member Committees on Young Lawyers 1966-70, Professional Continuity and Lawyers Assistance since 1981 and Cooperation with the Courts since 1983, Hillsborough County Joint Scheduling Committee since 1983) and American (Committee on Sole Practitioners and Small Firms 1980-85 and Subcommittees on Associates 1980-85 and Computers in Small Firms 1982-85 General Practice Section, Committee on Part-time Judicial Officers Judicial Administration Division since 1988, Sections: Tort and Insurance Practice 1986-90, Litigation since 1980) Bar Associations.

Participant Citizens Conference on the Administration of Justice Jan 1983, Superior Court Scheduling Conference April 1983, Bench/Bar Conference April 1985, Case Management and Scheduling Conference April 1987, Leadership Conference (Panelist) Sept 1987 and 1990, Pro Bono Program, Lawyer Referral Program, Association Elderly Services Program and Practical Skills Seminar for newly admitted lawyers 1990 New Hampshire Bar Association. Recipient President's Awards for Outstanding Pro Bono Service 1986 and Distinguished Service 1988 New Hampshire Bar Association and Presidential Citation New Hampshire Jaycees. Named Member of the Decade New Hampshire Trial Lawyers Association 1988. Neighborhood Commissioner 1965-69 and Merit Badge Counselor since 1965 Boy Scouts of America. Special Gifts Campaign New Hampshire Catholic Charities since 1966. State Counsel New Hampshire Jaycees 1967. Chamber of Commerce Greater Manchester since 1968. Board of Directors Greater Manchester Chapter National Council on Alcoholism since 1981. WIDIP Advisory Board The Alcohol Center Alice Peck Day Memorial Hospital 1983-84. Vice President Chestnut Title Corporation since 1984. Board of Incorporators and Board of Trustees Manchester Alcohol Rehabilitation Center The Farnum Center since 1985. Advisory Board Student Assistance Program Manchester High School West since 1987. Member United Way, Breakfast Forum Committee, United States Power Squadron (Past Assistant District Legal Officer) and Balmoral Improvement Association. Enjoys hunting, fishing, cooking, gardening and building scale model sailing ships.

Office: 10 Manning Street, Derry 03038.
Telephone: (603) 434-4676, 434-4677.

TOWNLEY-TILSON, W. H. Dale *(Justice, Franklin District Court)* Special Justice Concord District Court 1978-85. Appointed Justice Franklin District Court by Governor John H. Sununu to term beginning July 1986. Term expires at age seventy. Born Winchester Massachusetts May 17, 1937. Protestant. Educated at Boston University B.S. in Engineering and Suffolk University Law School J.D. Admitted to practice Massachusetts 1970, New Hampshire 1971, U.S. District Court District of New Hampshire 1971 and U.S. Supreme Court. In legal practice Concord 1972-73 and 1978-85.

First Assistant U.S. Attorney 1973-77. Legal Consultant New Hampshire Legislative Services 1978-82. Legislative Consultant New Hampshire Office of the Governor 1983-85. Member New Hampshire Bar Association. Recipient Sustained Service Award from the U.S. Department of Justice 1977. USAF 1957-63. Enjoys hunting, fishing and photography.

Office: 7 Hancock Terrace, Franklin 03235.
Telephone: (603) 934-3290.

VARNEY, Robert Charles *(Justice, Southern Carroll County District Court)* Appointed Special Justice by Governor Meldrim Thomson, Jr. to term beginning May 16, 1974. Term expires at age seventy. Born London England Nov 28, 1944. Educated at University of Pennsylvania A.B. 1966, Georgetown University J.D. 1972 and University of New Hampshire M.A. 1985. Editor Georgetown Law Journal 1971-72. Law Clerk to Hon. Howard F. Corcoran, U.S. District Court District of Columbia 1972-73. Admitted to practice New Hampshire 1973. In legal practice Wolfeboro since 1973.

Member Carroll County, New Hampshire and American Bar Associations. First Lieutenant USAS 1967-69. Republican. Town Moderator Wolfeboro since 1975.

Mailing address: P.O. Box 421, Ossipee 03864.
Office: Courthouse Square, Route 171, Ossipee 03864.
Telephone: (603) 539-4561.

VAUGHN, Mark W. *(Chief Judge, United States Bankruptcy Court District of New Hampshire)* Appointed by U.S. Court of Appeals First Circuit judges to term beginning Nov 12, 1993. Term expires Nov 12, 2007. Also Judge, Bankruptcy Appellate Panel First Circuit. Selected by the Judicial Council of the First Circuit. Born New York New York July 30, 1941. Educated at Franklin & Marshall College A.B. 1963 and Boston College Law School J.D. 1970. Admitted to practice New Hampshire 1970 and U.S. District Court District of New Hampshire 1970. In legal practice Manchester 1970-93.

Certified in Business Bankruptcy Law by American Board of Bankruptcy Certification. Fellow New Hampshire Bar Foundation and American College of Bankruptcy. Member American Bankruptcy Institute, National Conference of Bankruptcy Judges, Manchester, New

VAUGHN, MARK W.—*Continued*

Hampshire and American Bar Associations. USN 1963-67.
Office: Federal Building, 275 Chestnut Street, Manchester 03101-2411.
Telephone: (603) 222-2680.

VAUGHN, Timothy J. *(Associate Justice, New Hampshire Superior Court)* Appointed by governor.
Office: 1 Superior Court Center, 17 Chenell Drive, Concord 03301.
Telephone: (603) 271-2030.

WARHALL, Lawrence F. *(Justice, Derry District Court)* Appointed by Governor Hugh J. Gallen to term beginning Aug 2, 1981. Term expires at age seventy. Born Fall River Massachusetts Oct 27, 1936. Roman Catholic. Educated at Southeastern Massachusetts University B.S. 1961 and New England School of Law J.D. 1975. Admitted to practice New Hampshire 1975 and U.S. District Court District of New Hampshire 1975. Began legal practice Derry 1975. In legal practice Londonderry 1976.
Member New Hampshire Trial Lawyers Association, Rockingham County and American Bar Associations. E-3 U.S. Army 1955-57.
Office: 10 Manning Street, Derry 03038.
Telephone: (603) 434-4676, 434-4677.

WEEKS, Albert H. *(Judge, Probate Court of New Hampshire Cheshire County)* Appointed by Governor Jeanne Shaheen Jan 5, 2000 to term beginning March 28, 2000. Term expires at age seventy. Serves part time. Born New York New York April 15, 1948. Episcopalian. Educated at Princeton University A.B. 1970 and Catholic University of America J.D. 1982. Admitted to practice New Hampshire 1982. In legal practice Keene since 1982.
Member Cheshire County and New Hampshire Bar Associations.
Office: 12 Court Street, Keene 03431.
Telephone: (603) 357-7786.

YAZINSKI, John J. *(Justice, Claremont District Court)* Appointed by Governor Jeanne Shaheen. Also serves as Judge Family Division Pilot Project.
Mailing address: P.O. Box 313, Claremont 03743.
Office: Tremont Square, Claremont 03743.
Telephone: (603) 542-6064.

NEW JERSEY

Capital TRENTON

UNITED STATES DISTRICT COURT DISTRICT OF NEW JERSEY

The court sits at Camden, Newark and Trenton. For descriptive information refer to the United States Courts section.

Chief Judge

John W. Bissell

Judges

Garrett E. Brown, Jr.	William G. Bassler
Mary Little Cooper	Jerome B. Simandle
William H. Walls	Stephen M. Orlofsky
Joseph Greenaway, Jr.	Katharine S. Hayden
Faith S. Hochberg	Joel A. Pisano
Dennis M. Cavanaugh	William J. Martini
Stanley R. Chesler	Robert B. Kugler
Jose L. Linares	Freda L. Wolfson

Senior Judges

Stanley S. Brotman	Anne E. Thompson
Harold A. Ackerman	Dickinson R. Debevoise
Joseph H. Rodriguez	Alfred M. Wolin
John C. Lifland	Joseph E. Irenas

Clerk

William T. Walsh
U.S. Courthouse
Fourth Floor
50 Walnut Street
Newark, New Jersey 07102
(973) 645-3730

UNITED STATES MAGISTRATE JUDGES OF NEW JERSEY

Edward R. Knight	G. Donald Haneke
Ronald J. Hedges	Joel B. Rosen
John J. Hughes	Susan D. Wigenton
Anthony R. Mautone	Madeline Cox Arleo
Mark Falk	Patty Shwartz
Ann Marie Donio	Tonianne J. Bongiovanni

UNITED STATES BANKRUPTCY COURT OF NEW JERSEY

Chief Judge

Rosemary Gambardella

Judges

Judith H. Wizmur	Novalyn L. Winfield
Gloria M. Burns	Kathryn C. Ferguson
Raymond T. Lyons	Donald H. Steckroth
Morris Stern	

Recalled Judge

William H. Gindin

Bankruptcy Clerk

James J. Waldron
U.S. Courthouse
Third Floor
50 Walnut Street
Newark, New Jersey 07102-3550
(973) 645-3930

SUPREME COURT OF NEW JERSEY

The Supreme Court is New Jersey's court of last resort. The court consists of a chief justice and six associate justices initially appointed by the governor with consent of the Senate for seven-year terms with tenure granted upon reappointment. Retirement is mandatory at age seventy; however, retired justices may serve on a recall basis by order of the court.

The court has final appellate jurisdiction on all constitutional questions, cases involving the death penalty, cases with dissents in the Appellate Division, petitions for certification and such cases as provided by law. The court also has rule-making authority and regulates admission and discipline of attorneys and judges.

The court sits at Trenton.

Chief Justice

Deborah T. Poritz

Associate Justices

Barry T. Albin	Jaynee La Vecchia
Virginia A. Long	Peter G. Verniero
John E. Wallace, Jr.	James Zazzali

Clerk

Stephen W. Townsend, Esq.
R. J. Hughes Justice Complex
P.O. Box 970
Trenton, New Jersey 08625
(609) 984-7791

Administrative Director

Richard J. Williams
Administrative Office of the Courts
R. J. Hughes Justice Complex
P.O. Box 037
Trenton, New Jersey 08625-0037
(609) 984-0275

NEW JERSEY SUPERIOR COURT

The Superior Court is New Jersey's sole trial court of original general jurisdiction. By constitutional amendment the County Courts merged with the Superior Court effective December 7, 1978. A second merger occurred on December 31, 1983, when the Juvenile and Domestic Relations Court and the County District Courts were incorporated into the Superior Court system. The court is divided into Appellate, Law and Chancery Divisions. Law and Chancery Division judges are initially ap-

NEW JERSEY SUPERIOR COURT—*Continued*

pointed by the governor with consent of the Senate for seven-year terms with tenure granted upon reappointment. Appellate Division judges are assigned from among the Law and Chancery Division judges by the chief justice. Retirement is mandatory at age seventy; however, retired judges may serve on a recall basis by order of the Supreme Court.

The Appellate Division is the intermediate appellate court and hears appeals from the Law and Chancery Divisions, Tax Court, state administrative agencies and as provided by law. The Appellate Division is divided into eight parts of four to five judges each. Appellate Division judges sit in panels of two or three. A presiding judge for administration is selected from among the judges and presides over the entire division. A presiding judge is also designated for each part.

The state is divided into fifteen vicinages consisting of one to three counties. An assignment judge is appointed by the chief justice to serve each vicinage. Law and Chancery Division judges are assigned to specific vicinages.

The Law Division consists of Criminal and Civil Divisions and a Special Civil Part. The Criminal Division has general jurisdiction in all criminal cases. The Civil Division has general jurisdiction in all civil cases and appellate jurisdiction over the municipal courts. The Special Civil Part has jurisdiction previously exercised by the County District Courts over contract, penalty and tort actions up to $15,000, small claims and landlord-tenant actions.

The Chancery Division consists of two parts. The General Equity Part has general jurisdiction in probate, foreclosure and all equity cases. The Family Part has jurisdiction over juvenile delinquency, matrimonial, domestic relations, adoption and family crisis cases.

The Appellate Division sits at Hackensack, Morristown, Newark and Trenton. The Law and Chancery Divisions sit at the county seats and as indicated.

APPELLATE DIVISION

Presiding Judge for Administration
Sylvia B. Pressler

Administrative Director of the Courts
Richard J. Williams

Judges

Edwin R. Alley
Philip S. Carchman
Donald S. Coburn
Erminie L. Conley
Naomi G. Eichen
Jose L. Fuentes
Helen E. Hoens
Michael Patrick King
Jack L. Lintner
Richard Newman
Anthony J. Parrillo
James J. Petrella
Stephen Skillman
Barbara Byrd Wecker
Harvey Weissbard
Michael Winkelstein
Dennis J. Braithwaite
James J. Ciancia
Donald Collester, Jr.
Mary Catherine Cuff
Robert A. Fall
James M. Havey
Howard H. Kestin
Steven L. Lefelt
Joseph F. Lisa
Lorraine C. Parker
Edith K. Payne
Ariel A. Rodríguez
Edwin H. Stern
Dorothea O'C. Wefing
Harold B. Wells, III
vacancy

Retired Settlement Judges on Recall

Melvin P. Antell
Lawrence Bilder
Robert E. Gaynor
Paul Gans Levy
David S. Baime
John M. Boyle
David Landau
Thomas S. O'Brien

LAW AND CHANCERY DIVISIONS

VICINAGE ONE includes Atlantic and Cape May counties. The court sits at Atlantic City, Mays Landing and Cape May Court House.

Assignment Judge
Valerie H. Armstrong

Judges

Carmen H. Alvarez
Raymond A. Batten
Michael R. Connor
Albert J. Garofolo
John G. Himmelberger, Jr.
Susan F. Maven
William E. Nugent
John R. Rauh
George L. Seltzer
William C. Todd III
Max A. Baker
Kyran Connor
Michael A. Donio
Carol E. Higbee
James L. Jackson
Joseph E. Kane
Charles Middlesworth, Jr.
Steven P. Perskie
Vincent D. Segal
Daryl F. Todd, Sr.
Joseph C. Visalli

VICINAGE TWO includes Bergen County. The court sits at Hackensack.

Assignment Judge
Sybil R. Moses

Judges

Eugene H. Austin
Harry G. Carroll
Joseph Stephen Conte
Donald W. deCordova
William Delorenzo, Jr.
Peter E. Doyne
Patrick Fitzpatrick
Sebastian Gaeta, Jr.
Harold C. Hollenbeck
Lois Lipton
Daniel P. Mecca
Elijah L. Miller, Jr.
Patrick J. Roma
Mark M. Russello
Lawrence D. Smith
Edward V. Torack
Charles J. Walsh
Joseph L. Yannotti
Peter F. Boggia
John A. Conte
Robert P. Contillo
Estela M. De La Cruz
Richard J. Donohue
Gerald C. Escala
Bruce A. Gaeta
Jonathan N. Harris
Ellen L. Koblitz
Brian R. Martinotti
William C. Meehan
George W. Parsons, Jr.
Joseph Rosa, Jr.
Marguerite T. Simon
Isabel B. Stark
Donald R. Venezia
Robert C. Wilson

VICINAGE THREE includes Burlington County. The court sits at Mount Holly.

Assignment Judge
John A. Sweeney

Judges

John A. Almeida
Marie White Bell
Cynthia Covie-Leese
Michael J. Hogan
E. David Millard
Marvin E. Schlosser
Cornelius P. Sullivan
Craig L. Wellerson
Marc M. Baldwin
Ronald E. Bookbinder
John E. Harrington
Patricia Richmond Le Bon
Thomas S. Smith, Jr.
Karen L. Suter

VICINAGE FOUR includes Camden County. The court sits at Camden.

NEW JERSEY SUPERIOR COURT—*Continued*

Assignment Judge
Francis J. Orlando, Jr.

Judges

Linda G. Baxter
Thomas A. Brown, Jr.
Mary Eva Colalillo
William J. Cook
Theodore Z. Davis
Louise D. Donaldson
John A. Fratto
Ronald J. Freeman
Louis F. Hornstine
Michael Kassel
Frank M. Lario, Jr.
Lee B. Laskin
Charles A. Little
John T. McNeill, III
Octavia Melendez
Louis R. Meloni
Robert G. Millenky
Samuel D. Natal
Robert W. Page
Charles M. Rand
Irvin J. Snyder
Stephen W. Thompson
M. Allan Vogelson

VICINAGE FIVE includes Essex County. The court sits at Newark.

Assignment Judge
Joseph A. Falcone

Judges

Stephen J. Bernstein
Thomas C. Brown
Richard C. Camp
Michael R. Casale
Joseph C. Cassini, III
Alfonse J. Cifelli
Eugene J. Codey, Jr.
R. Benjamin Cohen
Claude M. Coleman
James B. Convery
Martin Cronin
Philip B. Cummis
Rachel N. Davidson
Hector E. DeSoto
Mahlon L. Fast
Carol A. Ferentz
Sallyanne Floria
Terence P. Flynn
Harold W. Fullilove
F. Michael Giles
Donald S. Goldman
Glenn A. Grant
Craig Randall Harris
Michelle Hollar-Gregory
Jared D. Honigfeld
Joseph V. Isabella
Mary C. Jacobson
Harriet Farber Klein
Betty Joan Lester
Kenneth S. Levy
Sebastian P. Lombardi
Thomas M. McCormack
Donald W. Merkelbach
Michael J. Nelson
Michael A. Petrolle
Michael L. Ravin
James S. Rothschild
Peter V. Ryan
Francine A. Schott
Edward R. Schwartz
Marie P. Simonelli
Nancy Sivilli
Patricia Medina Talbert
James G. Troiano
Peter J. Vazquez
Thomas R. Vena
Paul J. Vichness
Donald Volkert, Jr.
Renee Jones Weeks
Theodore A. Winard
Thomas P. Zampino

VICINAGE SIX includes Hudson County. The court sits at Jersey City.

Assignment Judge
Arthur N. D'Italia

Judges

Frances Lawrence Antonin
Mark A. Baber
Salvatore Bovino
Kevin G. Callahan
Patricia K. Costello
Barbara A. Curran
Elaine L. Davis
Lawrence P. De Bello
Paul M. DePascale
Maurice J. Gallipoli
Camille M. Kenny
Melvin S. Kracov
Severiano Lisboa III
Maureen B. Mantineo
John A. McLaughlin
Carmen Messano
Mark J. Nelson
Edward T. O'Connor, Jr.
Thomas P. Olivieri
John A. O'Shaughnessy
Francis B. Schultz
Maureen P. Sogluizzo
Frederick J. Theemling, Jr.
Shirley A. Tolentino
Hector R. Velazquez

VICINAGE SEVEN includes Mercer County. The court sits at Trenton.

Assignment Judge
Linda R. Feinberg

Judges

Maryann K. Bielamowicz
Audrey Hope Peyton Blackburn
Gerald J. Council
Charles A. Delehey
F. Lee Forrester
Jane Grall
Paul Innes
Thomas P. Kelly
Paul T. Koenig, Jr.
Laura Lewinn
Bill H. Mathesius
F. Patrick McManimon
Jack M. Sabatino
Paulette Sapp-Peterson
Neil H. Shuster
Andrew J. Smithson
Maria Marinari Sypek

VICINAGE EIGHT includes Middlesex County. The court sits at New Brunswick.

Assignment Judge
Robert A. Longhi

Judges

Glenn J. Berman
Jane B. Cantor
Amy Piro Chambers
Yolanda Ciccone
Marina Corodemus
Roger W. Daley
Harriet E. Derman
Frederick P. DeVesa
Mark B. Epstein
Bradley J. Ferencz
Travis L. Francis
Bryan D. Garruto
Melvin L. Gelade
Douglas T. Hague
Jamie D. Happas
James P. Hurley
Fred Kieser, Jr.
Vincent LeBlon
Jessica R. Mayer
Ann Graf McCormick
Joseph C. Messina
James F. Mulvihill
Dennis V. Nieves
Phillip Lewis Paley
Lorraine Pullen
Mathias E. Rodriguez
David A. Rosenberg
Edward J. Ryan
Barbara Clarke Stolte
Nicholas J. Stroumtsos, Jr.
Deborah J. Venezia
Alexander Waugh, Jr.

VICINAGE NINE includes Monmouth County. The court sits at Freehold.

Assignment Judge
Lawrence M. Lawson

Judges

Thomas Cavanagh, Jr.
Paul F. Chaiet
Patricia DelBueno Cleary
Robert A. Coogan
Francis P. De Stefano
Michael D. Farren
Clarkson Fisher, Jr.
William P. Gilroy
Eugene A. Iadanza
Paul A. Kapalko
James A. Kennedy
Ira E. Kreizman
Alexander D. Lehrer
Louis F. Locascio
James McGann
Anthony Mellaci, Jr.
E. Benn Micheletti
Robert W. O'Hagan
Norman J. Peer
Jamie S. Perri
Joseph P. Quinn
Thomas F. Scully
Mark A. Sullivan, Jr.
Bette E. Uhrmacher
Daniel M. Waldman

VICINAGE TEN includes Morris and Sussex counties. The court sits at Morristown and Newton.

NEW JERSEY SUPERIOR COURT—*Continued*

Assignment Judge
B. Theodore Bozonelis

Judges

Salem Vincent Ahto
N. Peter Conforti
David S. Cramp
Thomas J. Critchley
John B. Dangler
W. Hunt Dumont
James A. Farber
Ronald B. Graves
Stephan C. Hansbury
John J. Harper
Catherine Langlois
Kenneth C. MacKenzie
David B. Rand
Karen D. Russell
Stephen F. Smith, Jr.
Deanne M. Wilson
Barbara Zucker-Zarett

VICINAGE ELEVEN includes Passaic County. The court sits at Paterson.

Assignment Judge
Robert J. Passero

Judges

Thomas F. Brogan
Ernest M. Caposela
Marilyn C. Clark
Miguel de la Carrera
Ralph L. De Luccia, Jr.
Michael K. Diamond
Frank M. Donato
Edward V. Gannon
Anthony J. Graziano
Nestor F. Guzman
Ronald G. Marmo
Margaret Mary McVeigh
Christine L. Miniman
Susan L. Reisner
Joseph J. Riva
George F. Rohde, Jr.
Garry S. Rothstadt
George E. Sabbath
Joseph F. Scancarella
John E. Selser
Ronald B. Sokalski
Randolph M. Subryan
David Waks
Glenn R. Wenzel
Stephen H. Womack

VICINAGE TWELVE includes Union County. The court sits at Elizabeth.

Assignment Judge
Edward W. Beglin, Jr.

Judges

Roberto Alcazar
Ross R. Anzaldi
Walter R. Barisonek
Kathryn A. Brock
Karen M. Cassidy
Lisa F. Chrystal
Rudy B. Coleman
Joseph P. Donohue
Katherine R. Dupuis
Rudolph Hawkins, Jr.
James C. Heimlich
David J. Issenman
Thomas N. Lyons
John F. Malone
Frederic R. McDaniel
Scott J. Moynihan
Stuart L. Peim
Joseph P. Perfilio
John Pisansky
Miriam N. Span
Jo-Anne B. Spatola
John S. Triarsi
William Wertheimer
Melvin S. Whitken

VICINAGE THIRTEEN includes Hunterdon, Somerset and Warren counties. The court sits at Flemington, Somerville and Belvidere.

Assignment Judge
Graham T. Ross

Judges

Paul W. Armstrong
Victor Ashrafi
Ann Reynolds Bartlett
Edmund R. Bernhard
Edward M. Coleman
John J. Coyle, Jr.
Thomas H. Dilts
Francis W. Gasiorowski
Marilyn Rhyne Herr
Fred H. Kumpf
Roger F. Mahon
Amy O'Connor
John H. Pursel
Ronald Lee Reisner
Stephen B. Rubin
Harry K. Seybolt
Rosemarie R. Williams

VICINAGE FOURTEEN includes Ocean County. The court sits at Toms River.

Assignment Judge
Eugene D. Serpentelli

Judges

Frank Buczynski, Jr.
Donald F. Campbell
James N. Citta
James D. Clyne
James P. Courtney, Jr.
Wendel E. Daniels
Marlene Lynch Ford
Sheldon R. Franklin
Peter J. Giovine
Vincent J. Grasso
Ronald E. Hoffman
Thomas E. O'Brien
Edward M. Oles
Darlene J. Pereksta
John A. Peterson, Jr.
Francis P. Piscal
Alan J. Pogarsky
Edward J. Turnbach
Barbara Ann Villano

VICINAGE FIFTEEN includes Cumberland, Gloucester and Salem counties. The court sits at Bridgeton, Woodbury and Salem.

Assignment Judge
George H. Stanger, Jr.

Judges

Christine Allen-Jackson
G. Thomas Bowen
Diane B. Cohen
Georgia M. Curio
Timothy G. Farrell
Michael Brooke Fisher
William L. Forester
Robert E. Francis
Richard J. Geiger
Martin A. Herman
John S. Holston, Jr.
Harold U. Johnson, Jr.
Walter L. Marshall, Jr.
Anne McDonnell
Jean B. McMaster
Julio L. Mendez
David W. Morgan
James E. Rafferty
Donald A. Smith, Jr.
Joseph P. Testa
John Tomasello
John M. Waters, Jr.

RETIRED SUPERIOR COURT JUDGES ON RECALL

John J. Callahan
Rosalie B. Cooper
David G. Eynon
Philip M. Freedman
Martin L. Greenberg
Joseph F. Greene, Jr.
Burrell Ives Humphreys
Anthony J. Iuliani
Bernard A. Kannen
Irwin I. Kimmelman
Samuel D. Lenox, Jr.
Thomas B. Mannion
Seymour Margulies
Patrick J. McGann, Jr.
A. Donald McKenzie
Joseph M. Nardi, Jr.
Robert Neustadter
George J. Nicola
Kevin M. O'Halloran
Serena Perretti
Florence R. Peskoe
Kenneth R. Stein
June Strelecki
Timothy J. Sullivan
Samuel L. Supnick
Birger M. Sween
Norman Telsey
Charles E. Villanueva
James J. Walsh
Frederic G. Weber

NEW JERSEY TAX COURT

The Tax Court, established July 1, 1979, is a court of limited jurisdiction in New Jersey. Judges are appointed by the governor with consent of the Senate for seven-year terms with tenure granted upon reappointment. A presiding judge is appointed by the chief justice to an unspecified term. Retirement is mandatory at age seventy.

The court has jurisdiction to review the determinations of agencies and officials charged with the administration

NEW JERSEY TAX COURT—*Continued*

of state and local taxes, specifically the assessments of local property and state taxes and equalization tables issued by the Division of Taxation or the County Boards of Taxation.

The court sits at Atlantic City, Camden, Hackensack, Morristown, Newark, New Brunswick, Paterson and Trenton.

---

*Temporarily assigned to Superior Court

Presiding Judge

Joseph C. Small

Judges

Francine I. Axelrad*
Vito L. Bianco
Angelo J. Di Camillo*
Joseph L. Foster*
Raymond A. Hayser*
James E. Isman*
Roger M. Kahn
Harold A. Kuskin
Marie E. Lihotz*
Gail L. Menyuk
Peter D. Pizzuto

NEW JERSEY SURROGATE'S OFFICE

The Surrogate's Office is a court of limited jurisdiction in New Jersey. Surrogates serve as deputy clerks of the Superior Court's Chancery Division—Probate Part and handle uncontested probate matters and accept the filing of adoptions. Surrogates are elected by their respective counties for five-year terms.

NEW JERSEY MUNICIPAL COURTS

Municipal Courts are courts of limited jurisdiction in New Jersey. Any municipality or group of municipalities may establish a Municipal Court. Judges are appointed by their respective governing bodies for three-year terms. In cases of a joint Municipal Court, judges are appointed by the governor.

The courts have jurisdiction over minor criminal offenses, traffic, ordinance, fish and game and navigation violations. They may also hold probable cause hearings on indictable offenses.

New Jersey Counties and County Seats

Atlantic
Mays Landing

Bergen
Hackensack

Burlington
Mount Holly

Camden
Camden

Cape May
Cape May Court House

Cumberland
Bridgeton

Essex
Newark

Gloucester
Woodbury

Hudson
Jersey City

Hunterdon
Flemington

Mercer
Trenton

Middlesex
New Brunswick

Monmouth
Freehold

Morris
Morristown

Ocean
Toms River

Passaic
Paterson

Salem
Salem

Somerset
Somerville

Sussex
Newton

Union
Elizabeth

Warren
Belvidere

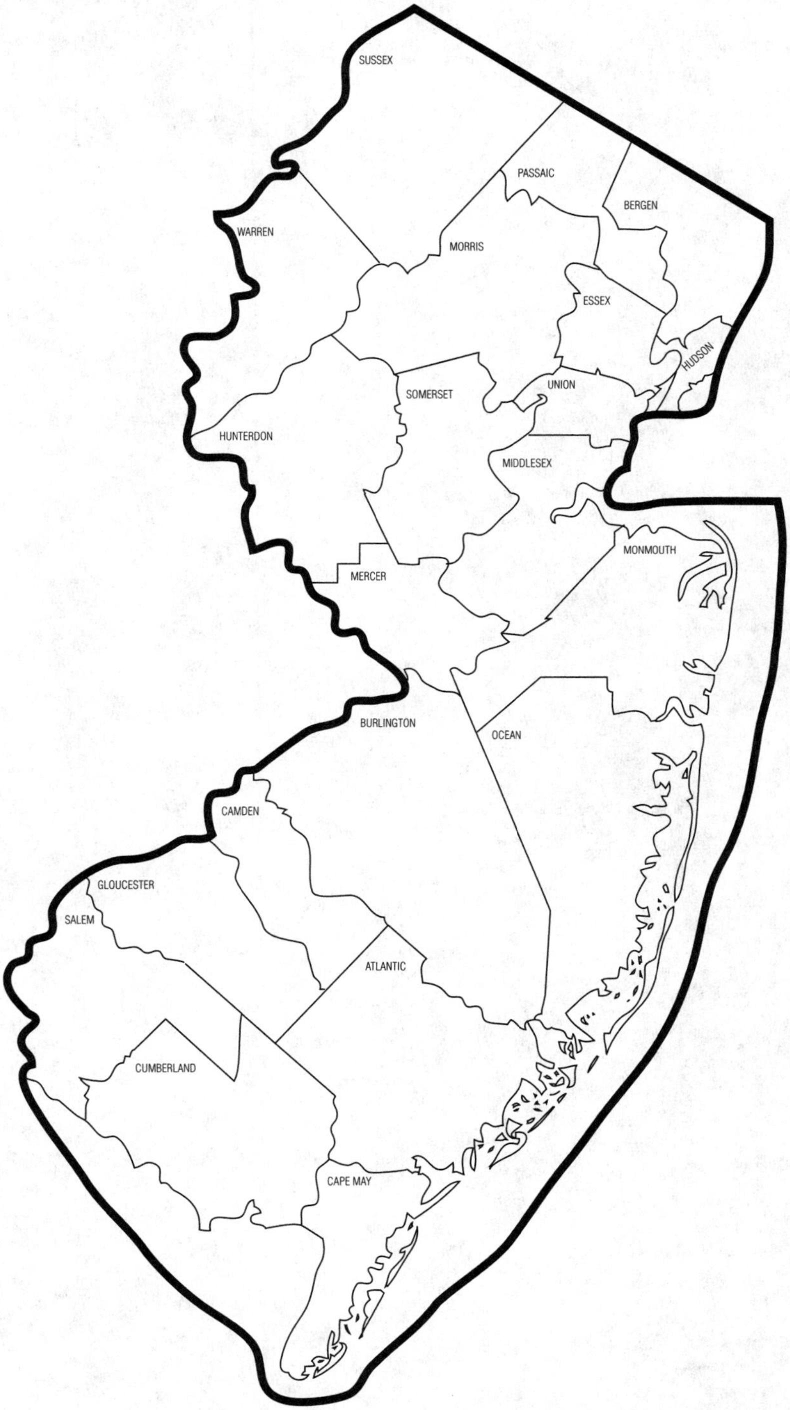
SUSSEX
PASSAIC
BERGEN
WARREN
MORRIS
ESSEX
HUDSON
UNION
SOMERSET
HUNTERDON
MIDDLESEX
MONMOUTH
MERCER
BURLINGTON
OCEAN
CAMDEN
GLOUCESTER
SALEM
ATLANTIC
CUMBERLAND
CAPE MAY

UNITED STATES DISTRICT COURT DISTRICT OF NEW JERSEY

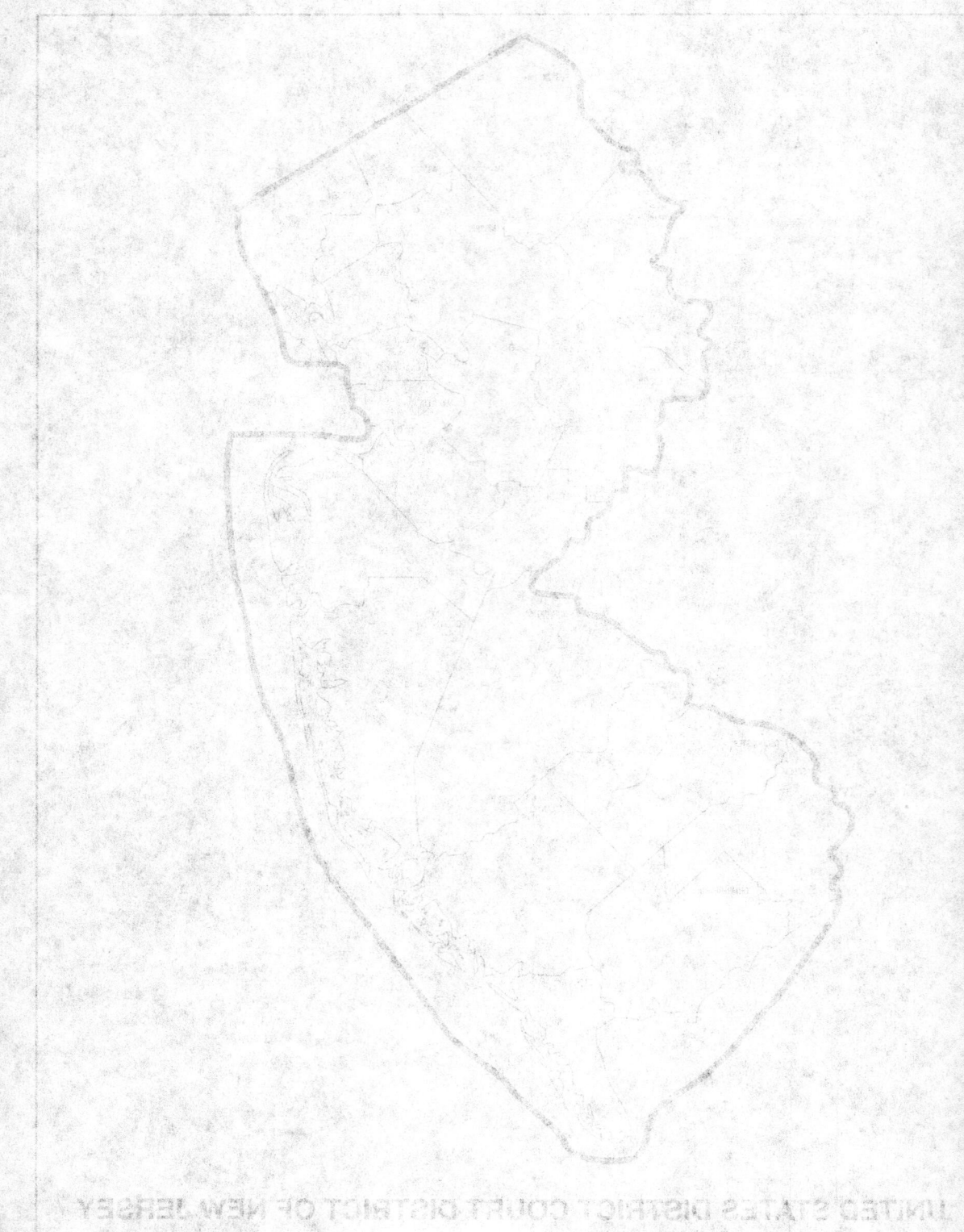

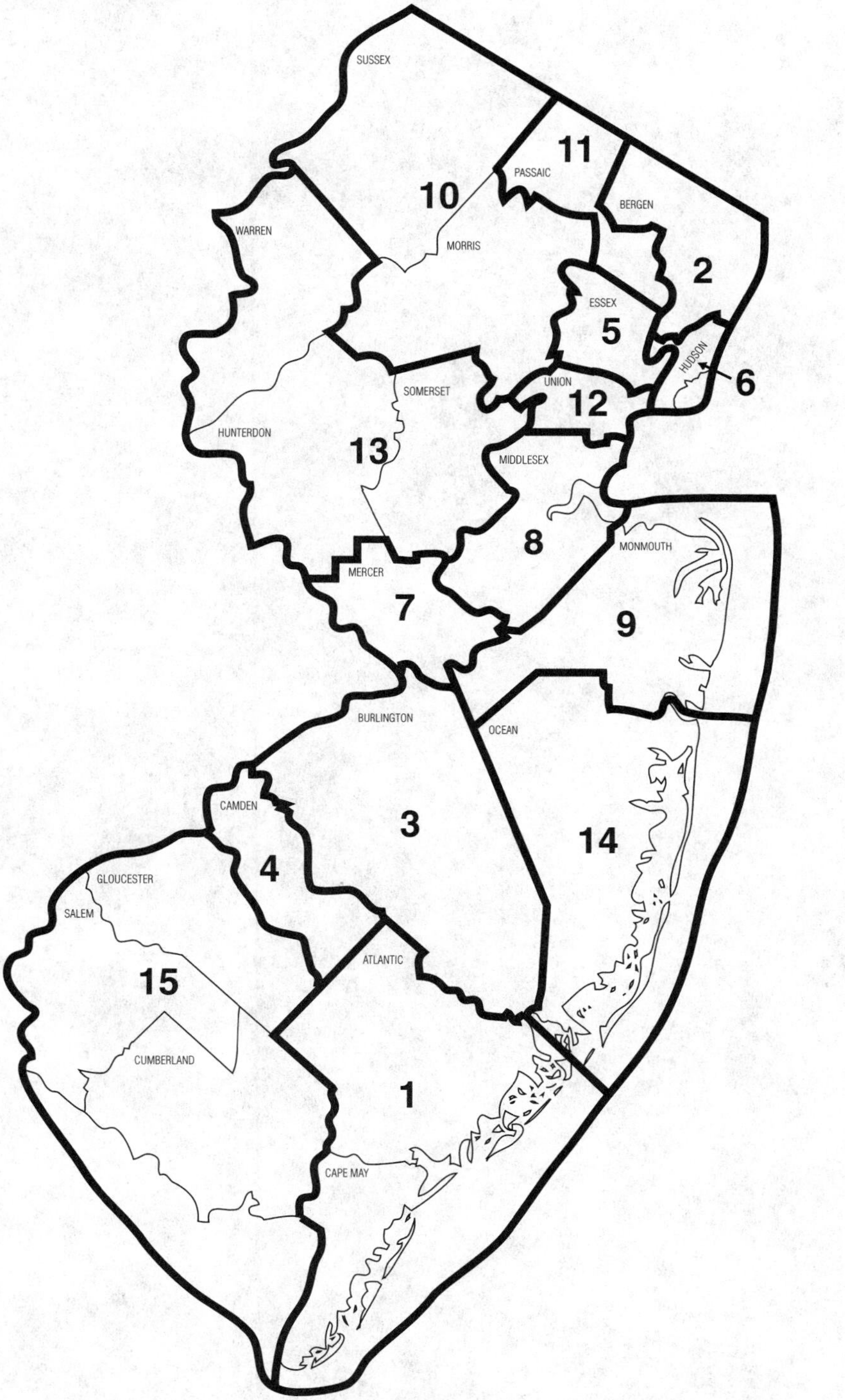
SUSSEX
11
PASSAIC
10
BERGEN
WARREN
MORRIS
2
ESSEX
5
HUDSON
6
UNION
SOMERSET
12
HUNTERDON
13
MIDDLESEX
8
MONMOUTH
MERCER
7
9
BURLINGTON
OCEAN
CAMDEN
3
14
4
GLOUCESTER
SALEM
ATLANTIC
15
CUMBERLAND
1
CAPE MAY

VICINAGES OF NEW JERSEY SUPERIOR COURT

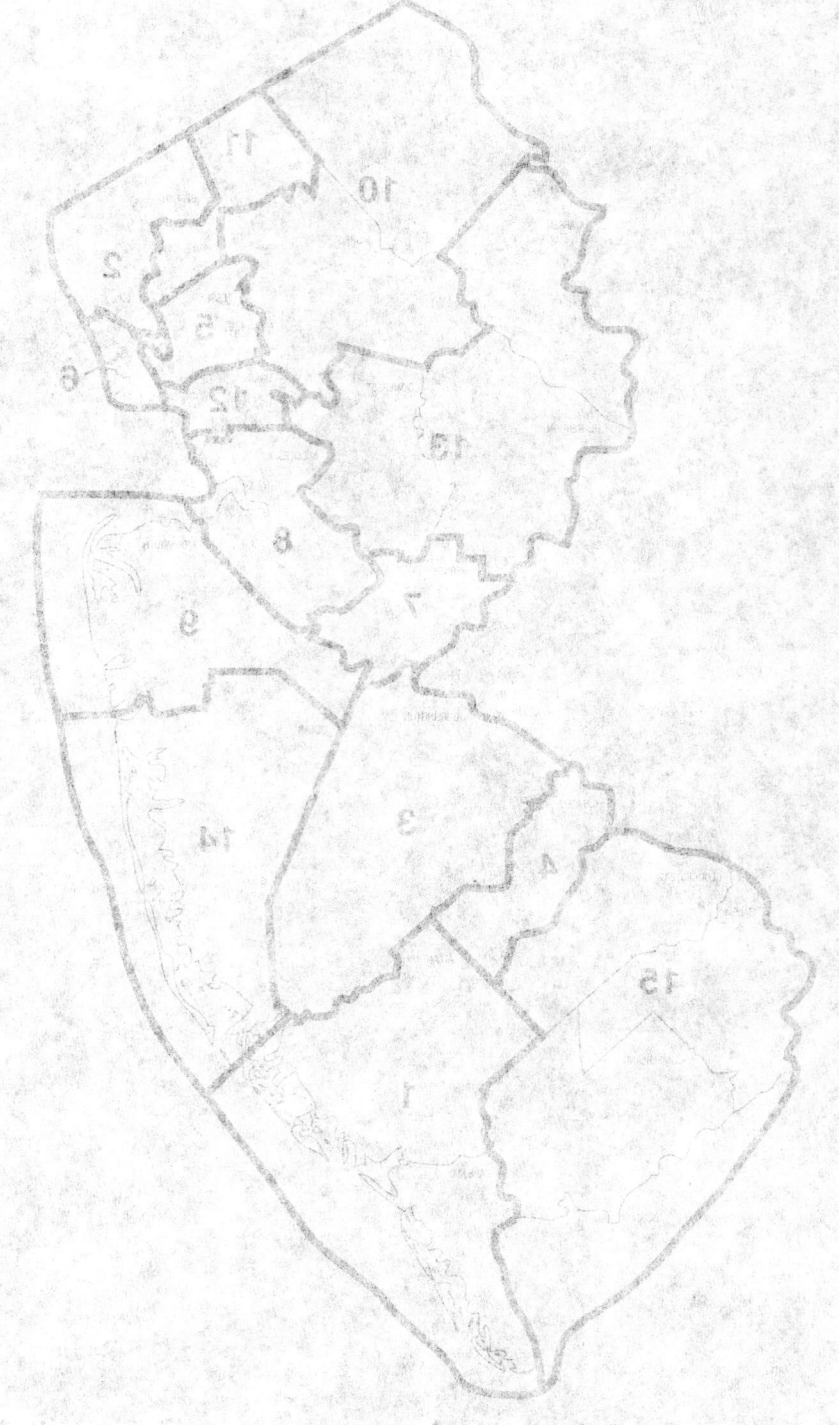

NEW JERSEY

ACKERMAN, Harold A. *(Senior Judge, United States District Court District of New Jersey)* Appointed for life by President Jimmy Carter to term beginning 1979. Assumed Senior status Feb 15, 1994, serves by assignment. Born Newark New Jersey Feb 15, 1928. Educated at Rutgers University School of Law LL.B. 1951. In legal practice 1951-54. Judge, Compensation Court of New Jersey 1955-65. Judge, Union County District Court 1965-70. Judge, New Jersey County Court Union County 1970-73. Judge, New Jersey Superior Court Law Division 1973-75. Judge, New Jersey Superior Court Chancery Division General Equity Vicinage Twelve 1975-79.

Mailing address: P.O. Box 999, Newark 07101-0999.

Office: U.S. Post Office & Courthouse, Newark 07102.

Telephone: (973) 645-3493.

AHTO, Salem Vincent *(Judge, New Jersey Superior Court Vicinage Ten)* Appointed by governor. Currently serves as Presiding Judge Family Division.

Mailing address: P.O. Box 910, Morristown 07963-0910.

Office: Morris County Courthouse, Morristown 07960.

Telephone: (973) 656-4038.

ALBIN, Barry T. *(Associate Justice, Supreme Court of New Jersey)* Appointed by Governor James E. McGreevey.

Office: 50 Division Street, Somerville 08876.

Telephone: (908) 704-8109.

ALCAZAR, Roberto *(Judge, New Jersey Superior Court Vicinage Twelve)* Appointed by governor.

Office: Union County Courthouse, Two Broad Street, Elizabeth 07207.

Telephone: (908) 659-3419.

ALLEN-JACKSON, Christine *(Judge, New Jersey Superior Court Vicinage Fifteen)* Appointed by governor. Also serves as Designated Judge Special Civil Part.

Office: Family Court Building, Two South Broad Street, Woodbury 08096.

Telephone: (856) 686-7530.

ALLEY, Edwin R. *(Judge, New Jersey Superior Court Appellate Division)* Appointed Judge Vicinage Twelve by governor. Assigned to Appellate Division by Chief Justice Deborah T. Poritz.

Office: 155 Morris Avenue, Springfield 07081-1216.

Telephone: (973) 564-9404, 564-9405.

ALMEIDA, John A. *(Judge, New Jersey Superior Court Vicinage Three)* Appointed by governor.

Office: Burlington County Court Facility, 49 Rancocas Road, Mount Holly 08060.

Telephone: (609) 518-2840.

ALVAREZ, Carmen H. *(Judge, New Jersey Superior Court Vicinage One)* Appointed by governor.

Office: Cape May County Courthouse, Main Street, Cape May Court House 08210.

Telephone: (609) 463-6588.

ANTELL, Melvin P. *(Retired Judge, New Jersey Superior Court Appellate Division)* Appointed Judge by governor. Assigned to Appellate Division by chief justice. Former Presiding Judge Part A. Retired, serves on recall.

Office: 155 Morris Avenue, Springfield 07081.

Telephone: (973) 564-9692.

ANTONIN, Frances Lawrence *(Judge, New Jersey Superior Court Vicinage Six)* Appointed by Governor Thomas H. Kean to term beginning July 7, 1989. Reappointed by Governor Christine T. Whitman June 1996. Term expires at age seventy. Born Jersey City New Jersey Feb 10, 1945. Presbyterian. Educated at Bloomfield College B.A. in Psychology 1965 and Seton Hall University School of Law J.D. 1976. Admitted to practice New Jersey 1976, U.S. District Court District of New Jersey 1976 and U.S. Supreme Court 1979. In legal practice Jersey City 1976-84. Judge, Jersey City Municipal Court 1984-89.

Assistant County Counsel Hudson County 1976-79. Assistant Corporation Counsel Jersey City 1981-84. Member National Association of Women Judges (Board Member 1996-98), American Judges Association, Association of Black Women Lawyers, Hudson County, Garden State, New Jersey National and American Bar Associations. Enjoys walking, reading and owl and angel collecting.

Office: Courthouse, 583 Newark Avenue, Jersey City 07306.

Telephone: (201) 795-6677.

ANZALDI, Ross R. *(Judge, New Jersey Superior Court Vicinage Twelve)* Appointed by governor. Served Vicinage Six.

Office: Union County Courthouse, Two Broad Street, Elizabeth 07207.

Telephone: (908) 659-3448.

ARLEO, Madeline Cox *(Magistrate Judge, United States District Court District of New Jersey)* Appointed by U.S. District Court judges to term beginning Dec 28, 2000.

Office: U.S. Courthouse, 50 Walnut Street, Newark 07102.

Telephone: (973) 297-4903.

ARMSTRONG, Paul W. *(Judge, New Jersey Superior Court Vicinage Thirteen)* Appointed by Governor Christine T. Whitman 2000. Currently serves Criminal Division. Educated at University of Dayton M.A. University of Notre Dame J.D. and New York University School of Law LL.M. In legal practice Bridgewater.

Co-author with Robert S. Olick "Advance Health Care Directives" *West's New Jersey Legal Forms.* Editorial Board *New Jersey Medicine* Medical Society of New Jersey and *New Jersey Lawyer* New Jersey State Bar Association. Principal Draughtsman and Legislative Architect New Jersey Advance Directives for Health Care and Declaration of Death Acts. Adjunct Professor Rutgers University School of Law and Robert Wood Johnson Medical School. Chairman Minority Concerns Committee New Jersey Superior Court Vicinage Thirteen.

ARMSTRONG, PAUL W.—*Continued*

Recipient Citizen's Award from Academy of Medicine of New Jersey 1989, Victoria Fellowship in Contemporary Issues from Rutgers University 1990, President's Award from New Jersey State Nurses Association 1990, John Elbridge Hines Lectureship from Episcopal Diocese of Newark 1991, American Health and Law Award from Boy Scouts of America 1996, Hospice Award from Visiting Nurses and Health Services 1997, Ezra Mundy Award for Excellence in Public Health from New Jersey Public Health Association 2000 and Founder's Award from New Jersey Health Decisions 2001. Honored by Samaritan Homeless Interim Program with the naming of its first mobile soup kitchen 2000. Past President Samaritan Homeless Interim Program. Former Chairman New Jersey Bioethics Commission, Governor's Advisory Council on AIDS and New Jersey Health Decisions. Former Co-chairman Expert Panel on Late Term Abortion Medical Society of New Jersey. Former Member Advisory Board Health Law and Public Policy Seton Hall University School of Law.

Mailing address: P.O. Box 3000, Somerville 08876-1262.

Office: Historic Courthouse, 20 North Bridge Street, Somerville 08876.

Telephone: (908) 231-7063.

ARMSTRONG, Valerie H. *(Assignment Judge, New Jersey Superior Court Vicinage One)* Appointed by governor. Former Presiding Judge Family Division and Former Acting Assignment Judge.

Office: County Civil Court Building, 1201 Bacharach Boulevard, Atlantic City 08401-4510.

Telephone: (609) 343-2234.

ASHRAFI, Victor *(Judge, New Jersey Superior Court Vicinage Thirteen)* Appointed by governor. Former Designated Judge Special Civil Part.

Mailing address: P.O. Box 3000, Somerville 08876.

Office: Somerset County Courthouse, Somerville 08876.

Telephone: (908) 231-7071.

AUSTIN, Eugene H. *(Judge, New Jersey Superior Court Vicinage Two)* Appointed by governor.

Office: Bergen County Justice Center, 10 Main Street, Hackensack 07601.

Telephone: (201) 646-3340, 646-3346.

AXELRAD, Francine I. *(Judge, New Jersey Tax Court)* Appointed by governor. Currently serves New Jersey Superior Court Appellate Division. Educated at Connecticut College magna cum laude 1974 and Rutgers University School of Law J.D. 1977. In legal practice Camden.

Office: 216 Haddon Avenue, Suite 700, Westmont 08108-2815.

Telephone: (856) 854-8590, 854-8592.

BABER, Mark A. *(Judge, New Jersey Superior Court Vicinage Six)* Appointed by governor.

Office: Administration Building, 595 Newark Avenue, Jersey City 07306.

Telephone: (201) 795-6734, 795-6735.

BAIME, David S. *(Retired Judge, New Jersey Superior Court Appellate Division)* Appointed Judge by governor. Assigned to Appellate Division by Chief Justice Robert N. Wilentz. Former Presiding Judge Part D. Retired, serves on recall. Born Newark New Jersey May 18, 1942. Educated at American University B.A. cum laude 1964 and Cornell University J.D. 1967. Editor Cornell Law Review. Admitted to practice New Jersey 1967. Began legal practice Newark 1967. Former Judge, Essex County District Court, assumed office June 1978.

Prosecutor Essex County 1968-72. Deputy Attorney General and Chief Appellate Section Criminal Justice Division 1972-77. Assistant Attorney General 1977-78. Prepared original Criminal Law Digest. Important Decisions: Parkway, Inc. v. Curry 1978 and Hill Manor Apartments v. Brome 1978. Member Somerset County, Essex County and New Jersey State Bar Associations.

Office: North Tower Suite 1101, 158 Headquarters Plaza, Morristown 07960-3965.

Telephone: (973) 631-6365, 631-6366.

BAKER, Max A. *(Judge, New Jersey Superior Court Vicinage One)* Appointed by governor.

Office: County Civil Court Building, 1201 Bacharach Boulevard, Atlantic City 08401-4510.

Telephone: (609) 343-2338.

BALDWIN, Marc M. *(Judge, New Jersey Superior Court Vicinage Three)* Appointed by governor.

Office: Burlington County Court Facility, 49 Rancocas Road, Mount Holly 08060.

Telephone: (609) 518-2828.

BARISONEK, Walter R. *(Judge, New Jersey Superior Court Vicinage Twelve)* Appointed by Governor Thomas H. Kean to term beginning July 6, 1984. Reappointed by Governor Jim Florio June 21, 1991. Term expires at age seventy. Presiding Judge Family Division 1985-87. Presiding Judge Criminal Division 1993-97. Born Bayonne New Jersey Aug 5, 1944. Catholic. Educated at Marist College B.A. in History 1965 and Seton Hall University School of Law J.D. 1968. Recipient scholarships from St. John's University School of Law, Seton Hall University School of Law and Villanova University School of Law. Admitted to practice New Jersey 1968 and U.S. District Court District of New Jersey 1968. Certified Trial Attorney New Jersey Supreme Court. Began legal practice Irvington 1968. In legal practice Linden and Roselle 1969-84.

Municipal Prosecutor Borough of Roselle 1969-73 and Township of Clark 1981-84. Important Opinions: State v. Arundell 278 N.J. Super. 202; State v. Antonio Vieira 334 N.J. Super. 681; State v. Lewis Epps 259 N.J. Super. 266; State v. Roosevelt Curry 245 N.J. Super. 278; State v. Saulo Burbano 304 N.J. Super. 215; State v. John Logan 244 N.J. Super. 137; State v. Jose Perez 331 N.J. Super. 497; Mary Johns v. Philip Johns 208 N.J. Super. 733; Walter Fulton v. Patricia Fulton 204 N.J. Super. 544; and Albert Mehalick v. Malcolm Schwartz, M.D., et al. 223 Super. 259. Associate Professor of Law and Banking Middlesex, Somerset and Union Chapter American Institute of Banking 1975-81. Chair Legislative Committee for Criminal Presiding Judges. Master Richard J. Hughes Inn of Court. Member Judicial Education Committee. Member National Council of Juvenile and Family Court Judges, Union County and New Jersey State Bar Associations. Established Alternative Sentencing Program Sheriff's Labor Assistant Program, Hearing Officer Program Union County, CASA Program Union County (for children in out of home placement), Early Settlement Program (for matrimonial cases) and Collection Enforcement Unit (for nonpayment of support in Family Court matters). Guest Lecturer on

BARISONEK, WALTER R.—*Continued*

Family Law ICLE. Graduate The National Judicial College Reno Nevada. Lecturer Young Lawyers of Union County, New Jersey Judicial College, New Jersey Skills and Methods Course, New Jersey New Judges Educational Training Program, Institute for Continuing Legal Education and American Academy of Judicial Education. Recipient Cardinal Spellman Award.

Office: Union County Courthouse, Two Broad Street, Elizabeth 07207.

Telephone: (908) 659-3438.

BARTLETT, Ann Reynolds *(Judge, New Jersey Superior Court Vicinage Thirteen)* Appointed by Acting Governor Donald DiFrancesco July 27, 2001. Born Ogdensburg New York Sept 7, 1948. Educated at Wells College 1966-68, Syracuse University B.A. magna cum laude 1972 and Catholic University of America J.D. 1975. Staff member Catholic University Law Review. Moot Court. Admitted to practice New Jersey 1975, U.S. District Court District of New Jersey 1975 and U.S. Supreme Court 1987. Certified by the Supreme Court of New Jersey as a Matrimonial Law Attorney. In legal practice New Jersey 1976-2001.

Author "Equitable Distribution of Employment Benefits: Valuing Defined Benefit Pension Plans" 5 No. 39 *New Jersey Lawyer* Sept 23, 1996 and "Flush Out All Employment Benefits" 6 *New Jersey Lawyer* 706 March 24, 1997. Trustee New Jersey State Bar Foundation since 1994. Member Committee on Family Division Practice 1988-98 and 2000, Ad Hoc Committee on Matrimonial Attorney Certification 1992-95 and Special Committee on Matrimonial Practice 1996-98 Supreme Court of New Jersey. Master Central New Jersey Family Inn of Court 1997-99. Member Magistrate Selection Committee U.S. District Court 2000. Fellow American Bar Foundation. Member Hunterdon County (Early Matrimonial Settlement Panelist since 1987, President 1992-93), New Jersey State (Member General Council 1982 and since 1988, Trustee Women in the Profession Section since 1986, Executive Committee Family Law Section since 1987, Secretary 1994-95, Treasurer 1995-96, Second Vice President 1996-97, First Vice President 1997-98, President 1999-2000) and American Bar Associations.

Faculty Member New Judges School 1997, in Family Law Judicial College 1991 and 1993, Family Court Judges Retreat 1990 and Bar Leaders Symposium on the Economic Consequences of Divorce 1990. Lecturer and Panelist New Jersey Institute for Continuing Legal Education since 1990. Panelist Bench-Bar Conference 1990. Recipient Legislative Services Award from New Jersey State Bar Association 1998, Walter N. Read Award for State Bar Association Leadership from Legal Services of New Jersey 2000, Professionalism Award for Hunterdon County from New Jersey Commission on Professionalism 2000 and Saul Tischler Award from Family Law Section New Jersey State Bar Association 2000. County Democratic Committee Woman Bethlehem Township District I 1985-95 and 2000. Deacon and Ruling Elder Flemington Presbyterian Church 1978-84. Chair Hunterdon County Library Commission 1979. Counsel Rolling Hills Girl Scout Council 1980-82. Pro Bono Lawyer/Volunteer Hunterdon County Legal Services 1980-96. Trustee Hunterdon Women's Fund 1986-94. Trustee since 1990 and Secretary since 1999 Community Care Association, Inc. Former Member New Jersey Association of Women Business Owners.

Office: Hunterdon County Justice Center, 65 Park Avenue, Flemington 08822.

Telephone: (908) 806-5144.

BASSLER, William G. *(Judge, United States District Court District of New Jersey)* Appointed for life by President George Bush to term beginning 1991. Born Butler Pennsylvania March 6, 1938. Educated at Fordham University B.A. 1960, Georgetown University J.D. 1963 and New York University LL.M. 1969. Law Clerk to Hon. Mark Sullivan, New Jersey Superior Court Appellate Division 1963-64. In legal practice 1964-88. Judge, New Jersey Superior Court Vicinage Nine 1988-91.

Office: U.S. Courthouse, 50 Walnut Street, Newark 07102.

Telephone: (973) 645-2981.

BATTEN, Raymond A. *(Judge, New Jersey Superior Court Vicinage One)* Appointed by governor.

Office: Cape May County Courthouse, Main Street, Cape May Court House 08210.

Telephone: (609) 463-6635.

BAXTER, Linda G. *(Judge, New Jersey Superior Court Vicinage Four)* Appointed by governor. Currently serves as Presiding Judge Criminal Division.

Office: 340 Camden County Hall of Justice, 101 South Fifth Street, Camden 08103-4001.

Telephone: (856) 379-2356.

BEGLIN, Edward W., Jr. *(Assignment Judge, New Jersey Superior Court Vicinage Twelve)* Assumed office Dec 7, 1978. Reappointed by Governor Thomas H. Kean March 26, 1987. Term expires at age seventy. Former Presiding Judge Civil Division. Born Elizabeth New Jersey Jan 15, 1934. Presbyterian. Educated at Wesleyan University A.B. with honors 1955 and New York University School of Law LL.B. with honors 1958. John Ben Snow Scholar New York University School of Law. Admitted to practice New Jersey 1959, U.S. District Court District of New Jersey 1959 and U.S. Supreme Court 1963. In legal practice Plainfield 1961-76. Judge, Union County District Court April 23, 1976 to Dec 6, 1978, appointed by Governor Brendan T. Byrne.

Attorney Plainfield Board of Adjustment 1968. Prosecutor Plainfield Municipal Court 1968. City Solicitor Plainfield 1969-76. Attorney Board of Adjustment Bridgewater Township 1970-76. Attorney Borough of Fanwood 1972-76. Important Decisions: F. Richard Tell v. Cambridge Mutual Insurance Company 150 N.J. Super. 246; State v. Jose Ignacio Tenriero 183 N.J. Super. 519; John N. Zamboni v. John H. Stamler et al. 194 N.J. Super. 598, 1984 aff'd 199 N.J. Super. 327 N.J. Super. Ct. App. Div. 1990; Louis J. Coletti v. Union County Board of Chosen Freeholders aff'd 217 N.J. Super. 31; State v. Howard W. Newman 218 N.J. Super. 580, aff'd 223 N.J. Super. 284 N.J. Super. Ct. App. Div. 1988; State v. Francisco Jardim et al. 226 N.J. Super 497; Wilson Coalition v. Mayor and Common Council of the City of Summit 245 N.J. Super. 616; Richard T. Brezizecki et al. v. John T. Gregorio et al. 246 N.J. Super. 634; Thomas J. Geraghty, Jr. v. The Township of Berkeley Heights et al. 259 N.J. Super. 350, 1990 aff'd 259 N.J. Super. 327 N.J. Super. Ct. App. Div. 1990; William Motley v. Neil Cohen et al. (civil) 267 N.J. Su-

BEGLIN, EDWARD W., JR.—*Continued*

per. 325; Union County Utilities Authority v. Paul Josewitch et al. (civil) 269 N.J. Super. 218; State of New Jersey v. Ishaque (criminal) 312 N.J. Super. 207; and Peter Corvelli v. Antonio Fonseca et al (civil) 323 N.J. Super 342. Instructor Plainfield Adult School and Rutgers University Extension Division. Member Plainfield (President 1972-73), Union County, New Jersey State and American Bar Associations. Instructor Civil Practice Course New Jersey Institute for Continuing Legal Education since 1991. E-5 U.S. Army 1959-61. Clerk of Session United Presbyterian Church of Plainfield 1970-74. Member Lions Club (President 1971-72).

Office: Union County Courthouse, 2 Broad Street, Elizabeth 07207.

Telephone: (908) 659-3666.

BELL, Marie White *(Judge, New Jersey Superior Court Vicinage Three)* Appointed by governor.

Office: Burlington County Court Facility, 49 Rancocas Road, Mount Holly 08060.

Telephone: (609) 518-2720.

BERMAN, Glenn J. *(Judge, New Jersey Superior Court Vicinage Eight)* Appointed by Governor James E. McGreevey.

Office: Middlesex County Courthouse, One John F. Kennedy Square, New Brunswick 08901.

Telephone: (732) 981-3024.

BERNHARD, Edmund R. *(Judge, New Jersey Superior Court Vicinage Thirteen)* Appointed by governor.

Office: Hunterdon County Justice Center, 65 Park Avenue, Flemington 08822.

Telephone: (908) 788-1242.

BERNSTEIN, Stephen J. *(Judge, New Jersey Superior Court Vicinage Five)* Appointed by governor.

Office: 227 Hall of Records, 465 Dr. Martin Luther King Jr. Blvd., Newark 07102.

Telephone: (973) 693-6749, 693-6750.

BIANCO, Vito L. *(Judge, New Jersey Tax Court)* Appointed by Acting Governor Donald DiFrancesco to term beginning Aug 15, 2001. Term expires Aug 15, 2008. Born Denville New Jersey June 12, 1958. Christian. Educated at Rutgers College B.A. 1980 and California Western School of Law J.D. 1983. Admitted to practice New York 1984, New Jersey 1986 and District of Columbia 1986. In legal practice 1986-2001.

Attorney 1986 and Chairman 1988 Rockaway Township Board of Adjustment. Attorney Denville Township Board of Adjustment 1988-89. Municipal Attorney East Hanover Township 1999-2001. Member Committee on Minority Concerns and Committee on the Tax Court Supreme Court of New Jersey. Member The District of Columbia Bar, New Jersey State and New York State Bar Associations. Councilman 1994-2001 and Council President 1997-98 Denville Township. President Denville Historical Society and Museum since 1999.

Office: Wilentz Building, Eighth Floor, 153 Halsey Street, Newark 07101.

Telephone: (973) 648-2921.

Fax: (973) 648-2149

E-mail address: vito.bianco@judiciary.state.nj.us

BIELAMOWICZ, Maryann K. *(Judge, New Jersey Superior Court Vicinage Seven)* Appointed by governor.

Mailing address: P.O. Box 8068, Trenton 08650.

Office: Mercer County Courthouse, 209 South Broad and Market Streets, Trenton 08608.

Telephone: (609) 989-6195.

BILDER, Lawrence *(Retired Judge, New Jersey Superior Court Appellate Division)* Appointed Judge Vicinage Six by governor. Assigned to Appellate Division by chief justice. Retired, serves on recall.

Office: Court Plaza North, 25 Main Street, Hackensack 07601.

Telephone: (201) 996-8049.

BISSELL, John W. *(Chief Judge, United States District Court District of New Jersey)* Appointed for life by President Ronald Reagan to term beginning 1982. Chief Judge since June 2, 2001. Born Exeter New Hampshire June 7, 1940. Educated at Princeton University A.B. 1962 and University of Virginia LL.B. 1965. Law Clerk to Hon. Arthur S. Lane, U.S. District Court District of New Jersey 1965-66. Admitted to practice New Jersey 1966, U.S. Court of Appeals Third Circuit 1967 and U.S. Supreme Court 1973. Began legal practice Newark 1966. In legal practice Newark and Morristown 1966-69 and 1972-78. Former Judge, Essex County District Court, appointed by Governor Brendan T. Byrne to term beginning Sept 15, 1978. Former Judge, New Jersey Superior Court.

Assistant U.S. Attorney 1969-71. Fellow American Bar Foundation. Former member Federal Bar Council of New York, New Jersey and Connecticut. Member Essex County, New Jersey State, Federal and American Bar Associations. Republican. Member Union Congregational Church of Upper Montclair, National Ice Hockey Officials Association and Montclair Chapter Society for the Preservation and Encouragement of Barbershop Quartet Singing in America (SPEBSQSA). Enjoys golf, tennis, ice hockey, reading, singing, camping, theatre and family activities.

Mailing address: P.O. Box 999, Newark 07101-0999.

Office: U.S. Post Office & Courthouse, Newark 07102.

Telephone: (973) 645-2517.

BLACKBURN, Audrey Hope Peyton *(Judge, New Jersey Superior Court Vicinage Seven)* Appointed by Governor Christine T. Whitman to term beginning Nov 19, 1999. Term expires 2006. Educated at Rutgers University B.A. 1961 and Rutgers University School of Law at Camden J.D. 1974. In legal practice Trenton 1974-87. Judge, Trenton Municipal Court Feb 1, 1990 to Nov 19, 1999.

Dean of Students Rutgers University School of Law at Camden 1987-90. Guest Speaker "Into the 21st Century" Rutgers University School of Law at Camden 1995. Recipient Community Service Award from Carrier Center Women's Association 1980 and Achievement Awards from La Chaperones Debutante Ball 1982, New Jersey Women Lawyers Association 1991 and 2000 and Black Network Association Douglass College 1990. Teacher of English 1960-68. Commissioner Housing Authority City of Trenton 1980-91. Leader 1969-72 and Director Community Choir 1970-72 Host Family for the Box Project since 1974. Member Mayor's Economic Development Committee 1978-87. Willingboro Girl Scouts of America. Board of Trustees Delaware Raritan Girl Scout Council, Inc. 1985-90 and Children's Home Soci-

BLACKBURN, AUDREY HOPE PEYTON—*Continued*

ety 1987. Former Member Links, Inc., American Association of University Women and Mercer County Community Chorus. Park Chairperson Helping Hands Willingboro PTA.

Mailing address: P.O. Box 8068, Trenton 08650.

Office: Mercer County Civil Courts, 175 South Broad Street, Trenton 08608.

Telephone: (609) 278-7197.

BOGGIA, Peter F. *(Judge, New Jersey Superior Court Vicinage Two)* Appointed by governor.

Office: Bergen County Justice Center, 10 Main Street, Hackensack 07601.

Telephone: (201) 646-2480, 646-2479.

BONGIOVANNI, Tonianne J. *(Magistrate Judge, United States District Court District of New Jersey)* Appointed by U.S. District Court judges to term beginning April 14, 2003.

Office: 2020 U.S. Courthouse, 402 East State Street, Trenton 08608.

Telephone: (609) 989-2040.

BOOKBINDER, Ronald E. *(Judge, New Jersey Superior Court Vicinage Three)* Appointed by governor. Former Presiding Judge Civil Division. Currently serves as Presiding Judge General Equity Division and Acting Assignment Judge.

Office: Burlington County Court Facility, 49 Rancocas Road, Mount Holly 08060.

Telephone: (609) 518-2835.

BOVINO, Salvatore *(Judge, New Jersey Superior Court Vicinage Six)* Appointed by governor. Former Presiding Judge Family Division.

Office: Administration Building, 595 Newark Avenue, Jersey City 07306.

Telephone: (201) 795-6632, 795-6633.

BOWEN, G. Thomas *(Judge, New Jersey Superior Court Vicinage Fifteen)* Appointed by governor. Also serves as Designated Judge Special Civil Part.

Office: Salem County Courthouse, 92 Market Street, Salem 08079.

Telephone: (856) 935-7510.

BOYLE, John M. *(Retired Judge, New Jersey Superior Court Appellate Division)* Appointed by Governor Thomas H. Kean to term beginning Nov 30, 1984. Reappointed by Governor Jim Florio 1991. Assigned to Appellate Division by Chief Justice Deborah T. Poritz. Former Presiding Judge General Equity Division. Served Vicinage Twelve. Retired, serves on recall. Born Elizabeth New Jersey July 5, 1929. Roman Catholic. Educated at Rutgers University A.B. in Political Science 1952 J.D. 1954. Henry Rutgers Scholar in history and political science 1951. Member Delta Sigma Phi, Phi Delta Phi and Phi Alpha Theta. Admitted to practice New Jersey 1954, U.S. District Court District of New Jersey 1954 and U.S. Supreme Court 1960. In legal practice Elizabeth 1955-78, Somerville 1978-84 and Union and Westfield 1978-84. Administrative Judge, Waterfront Commission New York Harbor 1968-84.

Assistant City Attorney 1960-62 and City Attorney and Director of Law Department 1962-64 Elizabeth. Author various articles in real estate trade journals. Important Decision: Berkeley Dev. Co. v. The Great Atlantic and Pacific (restrictive covenant in shopping center lease, slip opinion-citation pending) 1987. Fellow International Society of Barristers. Member New Jersey Judicial Conference, New Jersey Trial Lawyers Association, Union County (President 1979), New Jersey State and American Bar Associations. Instructor in Real Estate Law 1986 and Skills and Methods ICLE and The Legal Aspects of Nursing and GAR courses St. Elizabeth Hospital. Listed in *The Outstanding Young Men of America* 1965. Named Irishman of the Year by Friendly Sons of St. Patrick. T-5 U.S. Army 1946-48. Previously employed as licensed real estate and insurance broker. Chairman City Planning Board Elizabeth 1956-63. City Councilman Elizabeth 1958-60. Chairman Planning Board Union County 1967-74. Democrat. Member Union County Ethics Committee 1968-70. President Advisory Board John E. Runnells Hospital 1975-80. Advisory Council St. Elizabeth Hospital. Advisory Board Center for Hope. Enjoys music, swimming, art, literature, travel and toastmaster activities.

Office: Union County Courthouse, 2 Broad Street, Elizabeth 07207.

Telephone: (908) 659-3677.

BOZONELIS, B. Theodore *(Assignment Judge, New Jersey Superior Court Vicinage Ten)* Appointed by governor. Former Presiding Judge Family Division. Currently serves as Presiding Judge Criminal Division.

Mailing address: P.O. Box 910, Morristown 07963-0910.

Office: Morris County Courthouse, Morristown 07960.

Telephone: (973) 656-4020.

BRAITHWAITE, Dennis J. *(Judge, New Jersey Superior Court Appellate Division)* Appointed Judge Vicinage One by governor. Former Presiding Judge Criminal Division. Assigned to Appellate Division by Chief Justice Robert N. Wilentz.

Office: Civil Court Building, 1201 Bacharach Boulevard, Atlantic City 08401-4510.

Telephone: (609) 441-3330.

BROCK, Kathryn A. *(Judge, New Jersey Superior Court Vicinage Twelve)* Appointed by Governor Christine T. Whitman to term beginning June 27, 1997.

Office: Union County Courthouse, Two Broad Street, Elizabeth 07207.

Telephone: (908) 659-3855.

BROGAN, Thomas F. *(Judge, New Jersey Superior Court Vicinage Eleven)* Appointed by governor.

Office: Passaic County Admin. Bldg., 401 Grand Street, Paterson 07505.

Telephone: (973) 247-8449.

BROTMAN, Stanley S. *(Senior Judge, United States District Court District of New Jersey)* Appointed for life by President Gerald R. Ford to term beginning April 23, 1975. Assumed Senior status April 23, 1990, serves by assignment. Born Vineland New Jersey July 27, 1924. Religious affiliation: Hebrew. Educated at Yale University A.B. 1947 and Harvard University LL.B. 1950. Winner Ames Competition 1950. Admitted to practice New Jersey 1950 and District of Columbia 1951. In legal practice Vineland New Jersey 1950-75. Acting Chief Judge, U.S. District Court District of the Virgin Islands Dec 22, 1989 to Aug 14, 1992.

Important Decisions 1975-86: Delaware River Port Authority v. Tiemann 403 F. Supp. 1117, 1975; Furey v. Hyland 395 F. Supp. 1356, 1976; U.S. v. LaBrecque

BROTMAN, STANLEY S.—*Continued*

419 F. Supp. 430, 1976; Sixth Camden Corp. v. Township of Evesham 420 F. Supp. 709, 1976; Delaware River Port Authority v. Tiemann 421 F. Supp. 142, 1976; Health Corp. of America Inc. v. New Jersey Dental Association 424 F. Supp. 931, 1977; Klein v. Matthews 430 F. Supp. 1005, 1977; U.S. v. Stassi 443 F. Supp. 661, 1977; U.S. v. Callaghan 445 F. Supp. 1296, 1978; Rennie v. Klein 462 F. Supp. 1131, 1978; Rosemary Popow et al. v. City of Margate et al. Civil Action No. 78-1536 D.N.J. 476 F. Supp. 1237 Aug 31, 1979; John E. Rennie et al. v. Ann Klein et al. Civil Action No. 77-2624 D.N.J. 462 F. Supp. 1131 Nov 9, 1978, 476 F. Supp. 1237 Aug 31, 1979, 481 F. Supp. 552 Dec 21, 1979; Estate of Elvis Presley v. Rob Russen d/b/a The Big El Show Civil Action No. 80-0951 D.N.J. 513 F. Supp. 1339, 1981; Joseph P. Galda et al. v. Dr. Edward J. Bloustein et al. Civil Action No. 79-2811 D.N.J. 86 F.R.D. 561 June 12, 1980, 516 F. Supp. 1142 June 19, 1981, 589 F. Supp. 489 June 20, 1984; Hotel and Restaurant Employees and Bartenders International Union Local 54 and Frank Gerace v. Martin Danzinger, etc. et al. Civil Action No. 81-2630 D.N.J. 536 F. Supp. 317 April 12, 1982, F. Supp. Nov 5, 1984, F. Supp. Nov 26, 1984; United States of America v. Charles Price, Individually and d/b/a Price's Trucking Company et al. Civil Action No. 80-4104 D.N.J. 577 F. Supp. 1103 July 28, 1983; United States of America v. Lawrence A. Smith Criminal No. 83-39 D.N.J. 580 F. Supp. 1418 Feb 27, 1984; Holiday Inns, Inc. et al. v. Donald J. Trump et al. Civil Action No. 85-2884 D.N.J. 617 F. Supp. 1443, 1985; William Shoemaker et al. v. Hal Handel, etc. et al. Civil Action No. 85-1770 D.N.J. 619 F. Supp. 1089, 1985 aff'd 795 F.2d 1136; California Natural, Inc. v. Nestle Holdings, Inc. et al. Civil Action No. 84-2222 D.N.J. 631 F. Supp. 465, 1986; Hotel and Restaurant Employees and Bartenders International Union Local 54 et al. v. Walter N. Read, Chairman et al. Civil Action No. 81-2630 D.N.J. 641 F. Supp. 757, 1986; and In Re Data Access Systems Securities Litigation et al. Civil Action No. 81-1923 D.N.J. 103 F.R.D. 130.

Current Important Decisions 1988-92: United States of America v. Morris Levy et al. Criminal No. 86-301 D.N.J. 694 F. Supp. 1136, 1988; State of New Jersey Department of Environmental Protection v. Gloucester Environmental Management Services, Inc. et al. Civil Action No. 84-0152 D.N.J. 719 F. Supp. 325, 1989; Jeffrey B.C. Moorhead v. Alexander Farrelly et al. Civil Action No. 89-360 D.V.I. Division of St. Thomas 727 F. Supp. 193, 1989; Jane Doe, etc. et al. v. Borough of Barrington et al. Civil Action No. 88-2642 D.N.J. 729 F. Supp. 376, 1990; Leksi, Inc. v. Federal Insurance Co. et al. Civil Action No. 88-4123 D.N.J. 736 F. Supp. 1331, 1990; Dr. Kareem Abdulghani v. Virgin Island Seaplane Shuttle, Inc. Civil Action No. 1987/156 D.V.I. Division of St. Croix 749 F. Supp. 113 Oct 24, 1990; United States of America v. Louis Gatto, Sr. et al. Criminal No. 89-250 D.N.J. 750 F. Supp. 664 Oct 30, 1990; Curley v. Cumberland Farms, Inc. et al. Civil Action No. 86-5057 D.N.J. 134 F.R.D. 77 Jan 24, 1991; Robert J. Gilmore et al. v. John Gordon Berg et al. Civil Action No. 86-4694 D.N.J. 761 F. Supp. 358, 1991; Government of the Virgin Islands v. Brett A. Clark Criminal No. 91/07 D.V.I. Division of St. Croix 763 F. Supp. 1321 April 29, 1991; Government of the Virgin Islands v. Henry D. Knight Criminal No. 1990-131 D.V.I. Division of St. Croix 764 F. Supp. 1042 May 21, 1991; William W. Evans v. United Arab Shipping Company (S.A.G.) et al. Civil Action No. 89-5246 D.N.J. 767 F. Supp. 1284 July 30, 1991; United States of America v. Gaetano Vastola et al. Criminal No. 86-301 D.N.J. 772 F. Supp. 1472 Aug 15, 1991; Virdin C. Brown et al. v. Alicia Hansen et al. Civil Action No. 92-35 D.V.I. Division of St. Thomas and St. John March 19, 1992 as amended March 20, 1992; Government of the Virgin Islands v. Jesus Santiago 1992 U.S. Dist. Lexis 10467 June 26, 1992; and Atlantic Business & Community Development Corp. v. IRS Wall Street Journal Aug 4, 1992.

Current Important Decisions 1993-94: Birthright v. Birthright, Inc. and Birthright of Woodbury, Inc. Civil Action No. 92-1837 D.N.J. 827 F. Supp. 1114 July 21, 1993; United States of America v. Gaetano Vastola et al. Criminal No. 86-301 D.N.J. 830 F. Supp. 250 Aug 17, 1993; In Re Tutu Wells Contamination Litigation 846 F. Supp. 1243 D.V.I. 1993; Rhoda J. Harthman et al. v. Texaco, Inc. et al. Master Docket File No. 1989-107 Civil Action No. 89-220 Civil Action No. 89-224 D.V.I. Division of St. Thomas and St. John 846 F. Supp. 1243 Sept 2, 1993; Lesal Interiors, Inc. v. Resolution Trust Corporation as Receiver for CorEast Savings Bank, F.S.B. et al. Civil Action No. 91-2595 D.N.J. 834 F. Supp. 721 Oct 20, 1993; E.M. individually and as guardian ad litem for L.M., a minor v. Millville Board of Education Civil Action No. 93-3558 D.N.J. 849 F. Supp. 312 April 28, 1994; Chiropractic Alliance of New Jersey v. New Jersey Department of Insurance D.N.J. 854 F. Supp. 299 May 25, 1994; Virgin Islands Conservation Society, Inc. v. Virgin Islands Board of Land Use Appeals and Virgin Islands Coastal Zone Management Commission and Sugar Bay Land Development, Ltd. Civil Action No. 87/339 D.V.I. Division of St. Croix 857 F. Supp. 1112 June 13, 1994; Sunken Treasure, Inc. Government of the Virgin Islands Department of Planning and Natural Resources v. The Unidentified, Wrecked and Abandoned Vessel her tackle, etc. and United States of America Civil Action No. 1991/263 D.V.I. Division of St. Croix 857 F. Supp. 1129 July 14, 1994; and Anna Marie Ingemi, Trustee of the Joseph Ingemi Trust v. Pelino & Lentz et al. Civil Action No. 94-1246 D.N.J. 866 F. Supp. 156, 1994.

Current Important Decisions 1995-2002: D. B. v. Howard Bloom and Madison Dental Centre 896 F. Supp. 166 D.N.J. 1995; Local 56, United Food and Commercial Workers Union v. Campbell Soup Co. 898 F. Supp. 1118 D.N.J. 1995; In re Tutu Wells Contamination Litigation 1995 WL 771116 D.V.I. 1995; Hawksbill Sea Turtle v. Federal Emergency Management Agency 939 F. Supp. 1195 D.V.I. 1996 rev'd 126 F.3d 461 3rd Cir. 1997; Dirkes v. Borough of Runnemede 936 F. Supp. 235 D.N.J. 1996; In Re Tutu Wells Contamination Litigation 166 F.R.D. 331 D.V.I. 1996 modified 120 F.3d 368 3rd Cir. 1997; Arc of New Jersey, Inc. v. State of New Jersey 950 F. Supp. 637 D.N.J. 1996; Local 56 United Food and Commercial Workers Union v. Campbell Soup Co. 954 F. Supp. 1000 D.N.J. 1997; Kennedy v. CNA Insurance Co. 969 F. Supp. 931 D.N.J. 1997; Hawksbill Sea Turtle (Eretmochelys Imbricata) v. Federal Emergency Management Agency 11 F. Supp. 2d 529 D.V.I. 1998; Atlantic City Coin & Slot Service v. IGT 14 F. Supp. 2d 644 D.N.J. 1998; Martin v. Perinni Corp. 37 F. Supp. 2d 362 D.N.J. 1999; Rodin

BROTMAN, STANLEY S.—*Continued*

Properties-Shore Mall, N.V. v. Cushman & Wakefield of Pennsylvania, Inc. 49 F. Supp. 2d 728 D.N.J. 1999; In re Tutu Water Wells Contamination Litigation 78 F. Supp. 2d 423 D.V.I. 1999; Kitchnefsky v. National Rent-A-Fence of America, Inc. 88 F. Sup. 2d 360 (D.N.J.) 2000; Universal Underwriters Insurance Group v. Public Service Electric & Gas Co. 103 F. Supp. 2d 744 D.N.J. 2000; Tobin v. United States 170 F. Supp. 2d 472 D.N.J. 2001; Cooper v. Cape May County Board of Social Services 175 F. Supp. 2d 732 D.N.J. 2001; Warner v. Federal Express Corp. 174 F. Supp. 2d 215 D.N.J. 2001; Hightower v. Roman, Inc. 190 F. Supp. 2d 740 D.N.J. 2002; and Garlanger v. Verbeke 223 F. Supp. 2d 596 D.N.J. 2002.

Member New Jersey Board of Bar Examiners 1970-74. Member Space and Facilities Committee Judicial Conference of the U.S. 1988-93. Membership Chairman and Former Vice President 1992-99 Federal Judges Association. Fellow American Bar Foundation. Member American Judicature Society (Director 1995-99), Cumberland County (President 1969-70), New Jersey State (President 1974-75) and American (House of Delegates 1975-80, Nominating Committee 1982-93, New Jersey State Delegate House of Delegates 1983-93, Executive Committee 1984-87, Chairman 1987-88 National Conference of Federal Trial Judges Judicial Division, Chairman Standing Committee on Judicial Selection, Tenure and Compensation 1988-92, Member 1982-93 and Chairman Steering Committee 1992-93 Nominating Committee, Member Standing Committee on Federal Judicial Improvements since 1992, Chairman Judicial Immigration Education Project since 1996) Bar Associations. Recipient Medal of Honor from New Jersey State Bar Foundation 1990, Person of the Year Award from Virgin Islands Bar Association 1991, Herbert Harley Award from American Judicature Society 1994, William J. Brennan Jr. Award from Association of the Federal Bar of New Jersey 1995 and Special Recognition Award from Trial Attorneys of New Jersey 1995. First Lieutenant USAS O.S.S. in Burma 1943-45 and Armed Forces Security Agency 1951-52. Member Harvard Law School Association of New Jersey (President 1974-75). Trustee Newcomb Hospital 1953-68. Member American Legion, Jewish War Veterans, Yale Club, B'nai B'rith, Masons and Shriners. Enjoys photography and travel.

Office: 6040 U.S. Courthouse, One John F. Gerry Plaza, 400 Cooper Street, Camden 08102.

Telephone: (856) 757-5062.

BROWN, Garrett E., Jr. *(Judge, United States District Court District of New Jersey)* Appointed for life by President Ronald Reagan to term beginning 1985. Born Orange New Jersey March 20, 1943. Educated at Lafayette College A.B. 1965 and Duke University J.D. 1968. Law Clerk to Hon. Vincent S. Haneman, Supreme Court of New Jersey 1968-69. In legal practice Newark 1973-81.

Assistant U.S. Attorney Newark 1969-73. General Counsel U.S. Government Printing Office 1981-83. Chief Counsel U.S. Maritime Administration 1983-85.

Office: 4050 U.S. Courthouse, 402 East State Street, Trenton 08608.

Telephone: (609) 989-2009.

BROWN, Thomas A., Jr. *(Judge, New Jersey Superior Court Vicinage Four)* Appointed by governor.

Office: 370 Camden County Hall of Justice, 101 South Fifth Street, Camden 08103-4001.

Telephone: (856) 379-2537.

BROWN, Thomas C. *(Judge, New Jersey Superior Court Vicinage Five)* Appointed by governor.

Office: 918 Essex County Courts Building, 50 West Market Street, Newark 07102.

Telephone: (973) 693-5802, 693-5803.

BUCZYNSKI, Frank A., Jr. *(Judge, New Jersey Superior Court Vicinage Fourteen)* Appointed by governor. Currently serves as Presiding Judge Civil Division.

Office: Ocean County Courthouse, 100 Hooper Avenue, Toms River 08753.

Telephone: (732) 929-4789.

BURNS, Gloria M. *(Judge, United States Bankruptcy Court District of New Jersey)* Appointed by U.S. Court of Appeals Third Circuit judges to term beginning Feb 4, 1993. Born Camden New Jersey April 5, 1950. Educated at Northeastern University B.S. with honors 1973 and Rutgers University School of Law J.D. 1979. Admitted to practice New Jersey 1979, Pennsylvania 1979, U.S. District Courts District of New Jersey and Eastern District of Pennsylvania, U.S. Court of Appeals Third Circuit and U.S. Supreme Court. In legal practice 1980-93.

Member National Conference of Bankruptcy Judges and Camden County Bar Association.

Office: U.S. Courthouse, 400 Cooper Street, Camden 08101.

Telephone: (856) 757-5174.

Fax: (856) 757-5018

CALLAHAN, John J. *(Retired Judge, New Jersey Superior Court)* Assumed office Dec 31, 1983. Served Vicinage Twelve. Retired, serves on recall. Born Orange New Jersey Oct 7, 1935. Roman Catholic. Educated at College of the Holy Cross A.B. cum laude 1957 and Georgetown University J.D. 1960. Admitted to practice New Jersey 1961. Began legal practice Newark 1961. Judge, Union County District Court May 1973 to Dec 30, 1983, appointed by Governor William T. Cahill.

With Office of Prosecutor Union County 1964-72. Member New Jersey State Bar Association (Second Vice Chairman Criminal Law Section 1963-65, Secretary 1968-72, Chairman Probation Committee 1969-72 and Causes of Crime and Disorder Committee 1970). Instructor ICLE 1970-73. U.S. Army 1960-63. Democrat. Member Union County Mental Health Organization and Youth Advisory Council. Chairman Newark YMCA. Member Committee of Management Junior League. Advisor to State Public Affairs Committee. Director New Jersey Association for Mental Health. Trustee and Vice President Visiting Nurse Association Home Health Committee.

Mailing address: 15 Stony Hill Court, Summit 07901-3033.

Telephone: (908) 277-1155.

CALLAHAN, Kevin G. *(Judge, New Jersey Superior Court Vicinage Six)* Appointed by governor.

Office: Administration Building, 595 Newark Avenue, Jersey City 07306.

Telephone: (201) 795-6643, 795-6644.

CAMP, Richard C. *(Judge, New Jersey Superior Court Vicinage Five)* Appointed by governor.
Office: Gibraltar Building, Tenth Floor, 212 Washington Street, Newark 07102.
Telephone: (973) 693-5810, 693-5811.

CAMPBELL, Donald F. *(Judge, New Jersey Superior Court Vicinage Fourteen)* Appointed by Governor Brendan T. Byrne to term beginning Jan 18, 1982. Reappointed by Governor Thomas H. Kean Jan 1989. Term expires at age seventy. Served Vicinage Three. Born Temple Texas April 23, 1943. Catholic. Educated at Seton Hall University B.A. 1965 J.D. 1968. President Sigma Delta Psi. Admitted to practice New Jersey 1968 and U.S. District Court District of New Jersey 1970. Began legal practice Lakewood 1970. In legal practice Jackson 1973-82. Judge, Island Heights Municipal Court 1973.
Attorney Lacey Township MUA 1974-82. Member Ocean County and American Bar Associations. Captain U.S. Army 1968-70. Major General Active Reserve USAR since 1970. State Inheritance Tax Supervisor Ocean County 1979-82. Former representative Boards of Fire Commissioners.
Office: 213 Washington Street, First Floor, Toms River 08753.
Telephone: (732) 929-2179.

CANTOR, Jane B. *(Judge, New Jersey Superior Court Vicinage Eight)* Appointed by governor.
Mailing address: P.O. Box 964, New Brunswick 08903.
Office: Middlesex County Courthouse, One John F. Kennedy Square, New Brunswick 08901.
Telephone: (732) 981-3194.

CAPOSELA, Ernest M. *(Judge, New Jersey Superior Court Vicinage Eleven)* Appointed by governor.
Office: Passaic County Courthouse, 77 Hanilton Street, Paterson 07505.
Telephone: (973) 247-8326.

CARCHMAN, Philip S. *(Judge, New Jersey Superior Court Appellate Division)* Appointed Judge Vicinage Seven by Governor Thomas H. Kean to term beginning March 6, 1986. Reappointed by Governor Jim Florio 1993. Former Assignment Judge. Served Vicinage Five. Former Presiding Judge Chancery Division. Assigned to Appellate Division by Chief Justice Deborah T. Poritz. Term expires at age seventy. Born Bronx New York March 16, 1942. Jewish. Educated at University of Pennsylvania B.S. 1963 J.D. 1966. Law Clerk to Hon. Leon Gerofsky and Hon. John Demos, New Jersey Superior Court 1966-67. Admitted to practice New Jersey 1966, U.S. District Court District of New Jersey 1966, U.S. Court of Appeals Third Circuit 1967 and U.S. Supreme Court 1970. In legal practice Newark 1967-75 and Princeton 1970-81. Judge, Princeton Municipal Court 1973-81.
Deputy Attorney General 1967-70. County Prosecutor Mercer County 1981-86. Author "Report of the Working Group on the Prevention of Domestic Violence Act—A Summary" 84 New Jersey Family Lawyer 115, 1985. Chair Supreme Court Advisory Committee on Extrajudicial Activities and Rules of Evidence. Vice Chair Supreme Court Committee on Outside Activities of Judiciary Employees. Member Supreme Court Committees Judicial Performance and Pensions and Salaries, County Prosecutors Association of New Jersey (Vice President 1985-86), National District Attorneys Association (Assistant Treasurer 1984-86), Princeton, Mercer County, New Jersey State and American Bar Associations. Instructor ICLE. Lecturer American Academy of Judicial Education, New Jersey Judicial College and The National Judicial College.
Mailing address: P.O. Box 977, Trenton 08625-0977.
Office: Hughes Justice Complex, Trenton 08625.
Telephone: (609) 292-9055.

CARROLL, Harry G. *(Judge, New Jersey Superior Court Vicinage Two)* Appointed by governor.
Office: Bergen County Justice Center, 10 Main Street, Hackensack 07601.
Telephone: (201) 752-4203.

CASALE, Michael R. *(Judge, New Jersey Superior Court Vicinage Five)* Appointed by Governor Christine T. Whitman to term beginning Jan 2, 1996. Reappointed by Governor James E. McGreevey 2003. Term expires at age seventy. Born Newark New Jersey May 30, 1956. Catholic. Educated at University of Connecticut B.A. with honors 1978 and Seton Hall University School of Law J.D. with honors 1981. Law Clerk to Hon. Nicholas J. Scalera, New Jersey Superior Court Vicinage Five 1981-82. Admitted to practice New Jersey 1981 and U.S. District Court New Jersey 1981. In legal practice Montclair 1982-85 and Belleville 1985-95.
Assistant Township Attorney Bloomfield 1992-95. Member Essex County and New Jersey State Bar Associations. Councilman Township of Bloomfield Jan 1, 1985 to Dec 31, 1990. Enjoys coaching and sports.
Office: 702 Essex County Courts Building, 50 West Market Street, Newark 07102.
Telephone: (973) 693-5812, 693-5813.

CASSIDY, Karen M. *(Judge, New Jersey Superior Court Vicinage Twelve)* Appointed by governor.
Office: Union County Courthouse, Two Broad Street, Elizabeth 07207.
Telephone: (908) 659-3858.

CASSINI, Joseph C., III *(Judge, New Jersey Superior Court Vicinage Five)* Appointed by governor.
Office: 1004 Essex County Courts Building, 50 West Market Street, Newark 07102.
Telephone: (973) 693-6847, 693-6848.

CAVANAGH, Thomas W., Jr. *(Judge, New Jersey Superior Court Vicinage Nine)* Appointed by governor.
Mailing address: P.O. Box 1266, Freehold 07728-1266.
Office: Monmouth County Courthouse, Monument and Court Streets, Freehold 07728.
Telephone: (732) 677-4107.

CAVANAUGH, Dennis M. *(Judge, United States District Court District of New Jersey)* Magistrate Judge 1993-2000, appointed by U.S. District Court judges. Appointed Judge for life by President Bill Clinton to term beginning Sept 20, 2000. Born Orange New Jersey Jan 28, 1947. Educated at Morehead State University B.A. 1969 and Seton Hall University J.D. 1972. Law Clerk to Hon. Francis W. Hayden, New Jersey Superior Court 1972-73. In legal practice 1977-92.
Assistant Deputy Public Defender New Jersey 1973-77. Borough Prosecutor Caldwell 1988-89.
Office: U.S. Courthouse, 50 Walnut Street, Newark 07102.
Telephone: (973) 645-3574.

CHAIET, Paul F. *(Judge, New Jersey Superior Court Vicinage Nine)* Appointed by governor.
Mailing address: P.O. Box 1266, Freehold 07728-1266.
Office: Monmouth County Courthouse, Monument and Court Streets, Freehold 07728.
Telephone: (732) 677-4110.

CHAMBERS, Amy Piro *(Judge, New Jersey Superior Court Vicinage Eight)* Appointed by governor. Currently serves as Presiding Judge Civil Division.
Mailing address: P.O. Box 964, New Brunswick 08903.
Office: Middlesex County Courthouse, One John F. Kennedy Square, New Brunswick 08901.
Telephone: (732) 981-3108.

CHESLER, Stanley R. *(Judge, United States District Court District of New Jersey)* Magistrate Judge June 1987 to Dec 2002. Appointed Judge for life by President George W. Bush to term beginning Dec 4, 2002. Born Brooklyn New York June 15, 1947. Educated at State University of New York at Binghamton B.A. 1968, Brooklyn College and St. John's University School of Law J.D. 1974. Admitted to practice New York 1975, U.S. District Courts Eastern 1975 and Southern 1975 Districts of New York and District of New Jersey 1985, U.S. Court of Appeals Second Circuit 1975 and New Jersey 1985.
Assistant District Attorney 1974-80 and Chief Rackets/Narcotics Bureau 1978-80 Bronx District Attorneys Office. Special Attorney 1980-86 and Deputy Chief 1984-86 Organized Crime Strike Force U.S. Department of Justice. Assistant U.S. Attorney District of New Jersey 1986-87. Fellow American Bar Foundation. Master John J. Gibbons American Inn of Court. Member Federal Bar Association (Board of Advisors New Jersey Branch). Recipient Special Commendation Award from U.S. Department of Justice 1984.
Office: 2020 U.S. Courthouse, 402 East State Street, Trenton 08608.
Telephone: (609) 989-2182.

CHRYSTAL, Lisa F. *(Judge, New Jersey Superior Court Vicinage Twelve)* Appointed by governor.
Office: Union County Courthouse, Two Broad Street, Elizabeth 07207.
Telephone: (908) 659-3682.

CIANCIA, James J. *(Judge, New Jersey Superior Court Appellate Division)* Appointed Judge Vicinage Four by governor. Administrative Director of the Courts July 20, 1986 to July 31, 1999. Assigned to Appellate Division by Chief Justice Deborah T. Poritz August 1, 1999.
Mailing address: P.O. Box 977, Trenton 08625-0977.
Office: Hughes Justice Complex, Trenton 08625.
Telephone: (609) 777-0200.

CICCONE, Yolanda *(Judge, New Jersey Superior Court Vicinage Eight)* Appointed by governor.
Mailing address: P.O. Box 964, New Brunswick 08903.
Office: Middlesex County Courthouse, One John F. Kennedy Square, New Brunswick 08901.
Telephone: (732) 981-3185.

CIFELLI, Alfonse J. *(Judge, New Jersey Superior Court Vicinage Five)* Appointed by governor.
Office: Gibraltar Building, Eighth Floor, 212 Washington Street, Newark 07102.
Telephone: (973) 693-6653.

CITTA, James N. *(Judge, New Jersey Superior Court Vicinage Fourteen)* Appointed by governor.
Office: Ocean County Justice Complex, 120 Hooper Avenue, Toms River 08753.
Telephone: (732) 506-5012.

CLARK, Marilyn C. *(Judge, New Jersey Superior Court Vicinage Eleven)* Appointed by governor. Currently serves as Presiding Judge Criminal Division and Acting Assignment Judge.
Office: Passaic County Courthouse, 77 Hamilton Street, Paterson 07505.
Telephone: (973) 247-8314.

CLEARY, Patricia DelBueno *(Judge, New Jersey Superior Court Vicinage Nine)* Appointed by governor.
Mailing address: P.O. Box 1266, Freehold 07728-1266.
Office: Monmouth County Courthouse, Monument and Court Streets, Freehold 07728.
Telephone: (732) 677-4113.

CLYNE, James D. *(Judge, New Jersey Superior Court Vicinage Fourteen)* Appointed by Governor Thomas H. Kean to term beginning Aug 17, 1984. Reappointed by Governor James Florio 1991. Former Presiding Judge Civil Division. Currently serves as Presiding Judge General Equity Division and Acting Assignment Judge.
Office: 206 Courthouse Lane, First Floor, Toms River 08753.
Telephone: (732) 929-4702.

COBURN, Donald S. *(Judge, New Jersey Superior Court Appellate Division)* Appointed Judge Vicinage Five by Governor Brendan T. Byrne to term beginning April 8, 1981. Reappointed by Governor Thomas H. Kean April 7, 1988. Assigned to Appellate Division by chief justice. Educated at Cornell University B.A. 1961 and University of Pennsylvania J.D. cum laude 1966. Law Clerk to Chief Justice Joseph Weintraub, New Jersey Supreme Court 1966-67. Admitted to practice New Jersey 1966, U.S. Court of Appeals Third Circuit 1969 and U.S. Supreme Court 1971. Began legal practice Newark 1967. In legal practice East Orange 1972-78.
Special Deputy Attorney General 1978. Prosecutor Essex County 1978-81. Adjunct Professor Rutgers University Law School 1980. Member Essex County, New Jersey State and American Bar Associations. First Lieutenant U.S. Army 1961-63. City Councilman Livingston 1975-78.
Office: North Tower Suite 1101, 158 Headquarters Plaza, Morristown 07960-3965.
Telephone: (973) 631-6455.

CODEY, Eugene J., Jr. *(Judge, New Jersey Superior Court Vicinage Five)* Appointed by governor. Currently serves as Presiding Judge Civil Division.
Office: 606 Essex County Courts Building, 50 West Market Street, Newark 07102.
Telephone: (973) 693-5816, 693-5817.

COHEN, Diane B. *(Judge, New Jersey Superior Court Vicinage Fifteen)* Appointed by governor. Currently serves as Presiding Judge Family Division.

Office: Cumberland County Courthouse, West Broad and Fayette Streets, Bridgeton 08302.

Telephone: (856) 453-4388.

COHEN, R. Benjamin *(Judge, New Jersey Superior Court Vicinage Five)* Assumed office Dec 31, 1983. Term expires at age seventy. Currently serves as Presiding Judge General Equity Division. Born Newark New Jersey Feb 4, 1944. Jewish. Educated at Dartmouth College A.B. 1966 and Rutgers University at Newark J.D. 1969. Member Pi Lambda Phi and Phi Delta Phi. Admitted to practice New Jersey 1969, U.S. District Court District of New Jersey 1969, U.S. Supreme Court 1973 and U.S. Court of Appeals Third Circuit 1976. Began legal practice Montclair 1969. In legal practice Newark 1970-77 and Trenton 1977-81. Judge, Essex County Juvenile and Domestic Relations Court July 14, 1981 to Dec 30, 1983, appointed by Governor Brendan T. Byrne.

Assistant Prosecutor 1970-77. General Counsel New Jersey Casino Control Commission 1977-81. Member Essex County Bar Association. Democrat. Member Unity Club of Maplewood.

Office: Gibraltar Building, Eighth Floor, 212 Washington Street, Newark 07102.

Telephone: (973) 648-2021.

COLALILLO, Mary Eva *(Judge, New Jersey Superior Court Vicinage Four)* Appointed by governor. Served Vicinage Fifteen.

Office: 370 Hall of Justice, 101 South Fifth Street, Camden 08103-4001.

Telephone: (856) 379-2358.

COLEMAN, Claude M. *(Judge, New Jersey Superior Court Vicinage Five)* Appointed by governor.

Office: 201 Hall of Records, 465 Dr. Martin Luther King Jr. Blvd., Newark 07102.

Telephone: (973) 693-5800.

COLEMAN, Edward M. *(Judge, New Jersey Superior Court Vicinage Thirteen)* Appointed by governor. Currently serves as Presiding Judge Criminal Division.

Mailing address: P.O. Box 3000, Somerville 08876.

Office: Somerset County Courthouse, Somerville 08876.

Telephone: (908) 231-7066.

COLEMAN, Rudy B. *(Judge, New Jersey Superior Court Vicinage Twelve)* Appointed by governor.

Office: Union County Courthouse, Two Broad Street, Elizabeth 07207.

Telephone: (908) 659-4143.

COLLESTER, Donald G., Jr. *(Judge, New Jersey Superior Court Appellate Division)* Assumed office as Judge Vicinage Ten Dec 31, 1983. Reappointed by Governor Thomas H. Kean April 3, 1987. Presiding Judge Family Division 1983-86. Former Presiding Judge Vicinage Ten and Criminal Division. Assigned to Appellate Division by Chief Justice Deborah T. Poritz. Term expires at age seventy. Born New York New York Oct 20, 1939. Presbyterian. Educated at Colgate University A.B. magna cum laude 1961 and Harvard Law School LL.B. 1964. Member Phi Beta Kappa. Admitted to practice New Jersey 1965. In legal practice Newark 1965, Montclair 1966-67 and Morristown 1967-70. Judge, Borough of Netcong Municipal Court 1969-70. Judge, Morris County Juvenile and Domestic Relations Court April 19, 1977 to Dec 30, 1983, appointed by Governor Brendan T. Byrne.

Assistant Prosecutor 1969-71 and Prosecutor 1971-77 Morris County. Author "Forming Small Corporations in New Jersey." Adjunct Professor Seton Hall University School of Law since 1987. Instructor Rutgers University School of Law ICLE. Member National District Attorneys Association, Morris County and New Jersey State Bar Associations. Republican.

Office: North Tower Suite 1101, 158 Headquarters Plaza, Morristown 07960-3965.

Telephone: (973) 631-6370.

CONFORTI, N. Peter *(Judge, New Jersey Superior Court Vicinage Ten)* Appointed by Governor Thomas H. Kean to term beginning Feb 24, 1983. Reappointed by Governor Thomas H. Kean Dec 13, 1989. Term expires at age seventy. Served Family and Civil Divisions. Currently serves Criminal Division. Born Elizabeth New Jersey Nov 9, 1943. Roman Catholic. Educated at St. Vincent College B.A. magna cum laude 1965 and Rutgers University J.D. 1968. Member Phi Delta Phi. Admitted to practice New Jersey 1969, U.S. District Court District of New Jersey 1969, U.S. Court of Appeals Third Circuit 1970 and U.S. Supreme Court 1973. Began legal practice New Jersey 1969. In legal practice Newton 1971-73 and Sussex 1973-83. Judge, Sussex Borough Municipal Court 1972-83. Judge, Sparta Township Municipal Court 1974-83. Judge, Byram Township Municipal Court 1978-83.

Master Worrell F. Mountain American Inn of Court (President 1990-92). Member Sussex County (Trustee and Treasurer), New Jersey State and American Bar Associations. Graduate General Jurisdiction Courses 1979 and 1983, Faculty Advisor 1981 and Discussion Leader 1984 and 1986 The National Judicial College.

Office: Sussex County Judicial Center, 43-47 High Street, Newton 07860.

Telephone: (973) 579-0690.

CONLEY, Erminie L. *(Judge, New Jersey Superior Court Appellate Division)* Appointed Judge Vicinage Eight by governor. Assigned to Appellate Division by Chief Justice Robert N. Wilentz. Currently serves as Presiding Judge Part F.

Mailing address: P.O. Box 977, Trenton 08625-0977.

Office: Hughes Justice Complex, Trenton 08625.

Telephone: (609) 777-3086.

CONNOR, Kyran *(Judge, New Jersey Superior Court Vicinage One)* Appointed by governor.

Office: Cape May County Courthouse, Main Street, Cape May Court House 08210.

Telephone: (609) 463-6585.

CONNOR, Michael R. *(Judge, New Jersey Superior Court Vicinage One)* Appointed by Governor Brendan T. Byrne to term beginning March 9, 1981. Reappointed by Governor Thomas H. Kean Feb 1988. Term expires at age seventy. Former General Equity Disqualification Judge. Born Philadelphia Pennsylvania Nov 6, 1942. Educated at University of Delaware B.A. 1964 and Dickinson School of Law J.D. 1967. Staff member Dickinson Law Review. Admitted to practice New Jersey 1967, U.S. District Court District of New Jersey 1967, U.S. Supreme Court 1971 and U.S. Court of Appeals Third Circuit 1978. Began legal practice Atlantic City 1967.

CONNOR, MICHAEL R.—*Continued*

Judge, Atlantic County District Court March 2, 1979 to March 9, 1981, appointed by Governor Brendan T. Byrne.

City Solicitor Ocean City 1975-79. Member Atlantic County and New Jersey State Bar Associations. Instructor ICLE 1970-75.

Office: County Criminal Courthouse, 5909 Main Street, Mays Landing 08330.

Telephone: (609) 645-5887.

CONTE, John A. *(Judge, New Jersey Superior Court Vicinage Two)* Appointed by Governor Jim Florio to term beginning 1991. Currently serves Criminal Division. Born Jersey City New Jersey Nov 27, 1936. Educated at Seton Hall University 1961 J.D. 1967. Admitted to practice New Jersey 1967. Former Judge, Elmwood Park, Fort Lee, Rochelle Park, Saddle Brook and Wallington Municipal Courts.

Former Borough Attorney and Municipal Prosecutor Elmwood Park. Former Attorney Wallington Planning Board, Elmwood Park Board of Adjustment, Lodi Board of Adjustment and Saddle Brook Board of Adjustment. Author "N.J. Cemetery Law" *The Director* Sept/Oct 1967. Member Ethics Committee and Committee on Municipal Courts Supreme Court of New Jersey. Member Bergen County and New York State Bar Associations. U.S. Army 1961-62.

Office: 403 Bergen County Justice Center, 10 Main Street, Hackensack 07601.

Telephone: (201) 646-2164.

Fax: (201) 752-4428

CONTE, Joseph Stephen *(Judge, New Jersey Superior Court Vicinage Two)* Appointed by Governor Jim Florio to term beginning June 1993. Served Vicinage Eleven. Currently serves Criminal Division. Born Passaic New Jersey Jan 27, 1944. Catholic. Educated at University of Dayton B.S. 1965 and Cleveland-Marshall College of Law J.D. 1971. Admitted to practice Ohio 1971, New Jersey 1972 and U.S. District Court District of New Jersey 1972. Former Judge, Upper Saddle River, Rochelle Park, Ringwood and Wallington Municipal Courts.

Public Defender Borough of Paramus 1976-80. Special Attorney Borough of Ringwood 1981-82. Co-author "Major Land Use & Laws in New Jersey" 1991. Important Decision: State v. Rondinnone 291 N.J. Super. 489, 1996. Instructor Bergen Community College. President Bergen County Municipal Judges Association. Member New Jersey State and Ohio State Bar Associations. President Paramus Rotary Club, Paramus Chamber of Commerce, Garfield Rotary Club and Paramus Jaycees. Vice President New Jersey Jaycees. Chairman American Heart Association. Board of Trustees Saddle River Valley Cultural Center. Director Mid-Bergen Mental Health Center. Member American Red Cross. Enjoys skiing and playing golf.

Office: Bergen County Justice Center, 10 Main Street, Hackensack 07601.

Telephone: (201) 646-2556.

CONTILLO, Robert P. *(Judge, New Jersey Superior Court Vicinage Two)* Appointed by governor.

Office: Bergen County Justice Center, 10 Main Street, Hackensack 07601.

Telephone: (201) 646-6804.

CONVERY, James B. *(Judge, New Jersey Superior Court Vicinage Five)* Appointed by governor.

Office: Gibraltar Building, Twelfth Floor, 212 Washington Street, Newark 07102.

Telephone: (973) 693-6643, 693-6644.

COOGAN, Robert A. *(Judge, New Jersey Superior Court Vicinage Nine)* Appointed by governor.

Mailing address: P.O. Box 1266, Freehold 07728-1266.

Office: Monmouth County Courthouse, Monument and Court Streets, Freehold 07728.

Telephone: (732) 677-4116.

COOK, William J. *(Judge, New Jersey Superior Court Vicinage Four)* Appointed by governor.

Office: 340 Hall of Justice, 101 South Fifth Street, Camden 08103-4001.

Telephone: (856) 225-7142.

COOPER, Mary Little *(Judge, United States District Court District of New Jersey)* Appointed for life by President George Bush to term beginning March 13, 1992. Born Fond du Lac Wisconsin Aug 13, 1946. Episcopal. Educated at Bryn Mawr College B.A. cum laude 1968 and Villanova University School of Law J.D. with honors 1972. Honorary LL.D. Georgian Court College 1987. Associate Editor Villanova Law Review 1970-72. Member Order of the Coif. Admitted to practice New Jersey 1972, U.S. District Court District of New Jersey 1972 and U.S. Court of Appeals Third Circuit 1976. In legal practice Newark 1972-84.

Commissioner New Jersey Department of Banking July 1984 to Jan 1990. Associate Counsel and General Counsel Prudential Property and Casualty Insurance Co. 1990-92. Member Civil Practice Committee 1982-84 and District Ethics Committee 1982-84 Supreme Court of New Jersey. Fellow American Bar Foundation. Judge Master John J. Gibbons Intellectual Property Inn of Court since 1994. Member Mercer County, New Jersey State (Chairperson Committee on Rights of the Mentally Handicapped 1974-77) and American Bar Associations. Recipient Virginia Apgar Award from March of Dimes 1985, Achievement Award from Women's Political Caucus of New Jersey 1985 and Distinguished Service Award from Community Health Law Project 1986. Named Woman of the Year by Ironbound Manufacturers Association 1985 and Women of Leadership by Monmouth Council of Girl Scouts 1987. Former Chairperson Pinelands Development Credit Bank. Former Vice Chairperson Executive Commission on Ethical Standards and New Jersey Housing and Mortgage Finance Agency. Member Conference of State Bank Supervisors 1984-90.

Office: 5000 U.S. Courthouse, 402 East State Street, Trenton 08608.

Telephone: (609) 989-2105.

COOPER, Rosalie B. *(Retired Judge, New Jersey Superior Court)* Appointed by Governor Thomas H. Kean to term beginning Aug 9, 1984. Reappointed by Governor Jim Florio Aug 1991. Served Vicinage 14. Retired, serves on recall. Born New York New York June 22, 1931. Religious affiliation: Hebrew. Educated at Douglass College B.A. 1952 and Rutgers University Law School LL.B. 1953 replaced by J.D. 1968. First woman in law school to graduate first in class. Recipient Real Property Prize and Agency Prize. Associate Editor Rutgers Law Review 1952-53. Admitted to practice New

COOPER, ROSALIE B.—*Continued*

Jersey 1954. In legal practice Newark 1954-57, Lakewood 1965-84 and Toms River 1971-82.

Land Acquisition Counsel Lakewood Township 1965-84. Assistant Prosecutor Tidelands Resource Council Ocean County 1971-82. Important Decisions: Fitzgibbon v. Fitzgibbon 197 N.J. Super. 63; Mc. v. Mc. 215 N.J. Super. 132; K.-K. v. G. 219 N.J. Super. 334; Brown v. Brown 223 N.J. Super. 68; Jersey Central Power & Light Company v. John G. Weigand 234 N.J. Super 514; and Murphy v. Allstate Insurance Company 246 N.J. Super. 42. Approved Instructor New Jersey Police Training Course. Member Women Lawyers Association, National Association of Women Judges, Ocean County and New Jersey State Bar Associations. Named 1984 Honoree of the Year by Ocean County Girl Scouts Council. Inducted into The Douglass Society April 13, 1994. Founder Holocaust Memorial. Member Ocean County Handicapped Commission, League of Women Voters, Ocean County Medical Wives, Temple Beth-Am, Sisterhood Temple Beth-Am, Paul Kimball Hospital Ladies Auxiliary, Ocean County Women's Federation, Rutgers Alumni Association, Rutgers University School of Law Alumni Association, Douglass College Alumni Association, Girl Scouts, Boy Scouts, Hadassah and United Jewish Appeal.

Office: Justice Complex, 120 Hooper Avenue, Toms River 08753.

Telephone: (732) 929-2104.

CORODEMUS, Marina *(Judge, New Jersey Superior Court Vicinage Eight)* Appointed by governor.

Mailing address: P.O. Box 964, New Brunswick 08903.

Office: Middlesex County Courthouse, One John F. Kennedy Square, New Brunswick 08901.

Telephone: (732) 981-3115.

COSTELLO, Patricia K. *(Judge, New Jersey Superior Court Vicinage Six)* Appointed by governor. Currently serves as Presiding Judge Family Division.

Office: Administration Building, 595 Newark Avenue, Jersey City 07306.

Telephone: (201) 795-6666.

COUNCIL, Gerald J. *(Judge, New Jersey Superior Court Vicinage Seven)* Appointed by Governor Christine T. Whitman to term beginning February 18, 1998. Term expires Feb 2005.

Mailing address: P.O. Box 8068, Trenton 08650.

Office: Mercer County Civil Courts, 175 South Broad Street, Trenton 08608.

Telephone: (609) 989-6239.

COURTNEY, James P., Jr. *(Judge, New Jersey Superior Court Vicinage Fourteen)* Appointed by governor. Also serves as Designated Judge Special Civil Part.

Office: Ocean County Courthouse, 100 Hooper Street, Toms River 08753.

Telephone: (732) 929-4782.

COVIE-LEESE, Cynthia *(Judge, New Jersey Superior Court Vicinage Three)* Appointed by Governor Christine T. Whitman to term beginning Aug 17, 1999. Born Rockville Centre New York July 2, 1961. Educated at Franklin & Marshall College B.A. 1983 and Rutgers University School of Law at Camden J.D. 1987. Law Clerk to U.S. Court of Appeals Third Circuit 1987-89. Admitted to practice New Jersey 1987, Pennsylvania 1987, U.S. District Courts District of New Jersey 1987 and Eastern District of Pennsylvania 1988 and U.S. Court of Appeals Third Circuit 1989. In legal practice Philadelphia Pennsylvania 1989-91.

Assistant County Counsel Camden County 1991-94. Member Burlington County Bar Association. Assistant Counsel to Governor Christine T. Whitman 1994-97. Director Governor's Authorities Unit 1998-99.

Office: Olde Courthouse, Second Floor, 120 High Street, Mount Holly 08060.

Telephone: (609) 518-2880.

Fax: (609) 518-2599

COYLE, John J., Jr. *(Judge, New Jersey Superior Court Vicinage Thirteen)* Appointed by governor.

Office: Warren County Courthouse, 413 Second Street, Belvidere 07823.

Telephone: (908) 475-6191.

CRAMP, David S. *(Judge, New Jersey Superior Court Vicinage Ten)* Appointed by governor. Currently serves as Presiding Judge Civil Division. Former Designated Judge Special Civil Part.

Mailing address: P.O. Box 910, Morristown 07963-0910.

Office: Morris County Courthouse, Morristown 07960.

Telephone: (973) 656-3934.

CRITCHLEY, Thomas J. *(Judge, New Jersey Superior Court Vicinage Ten)* Appointed by governor.

Mailing address: P.O. Box 910, Morristown 07963-0910.

Office: Morris County Courthouse, Morristown 07960.

Telephone: (973) 656-3995.

CRONIN, Martin *(Judge, New Jersey Superior Court Vicinage Five)* Appointed by governor.

Office: 1114 Essex County Courts Bldg., 50 West Market Street, Newark 07102.

Telephone: (973) 693-6444.

CUFF, Mary Catherine *(Judge, New Jersey Superior Court Appellate Division)* Appointed Judge Vicinage Nine by governor. Former Presiding Judge Family Division. Assigned to Appellate Division by Chief Justice Robert N. Wilentz.

Office: 151 Bodman Place, Red Bank 07701-1014.

Telephone: (732) 576-1992, 576-1930.

CUMMIS, Philip B. *(Judge, New Jersey Superior Court Vicinage Five)* Appointed by governor.

Office: Gibraltar Building, Thirteenth Floor, 212 Washington Street, Newark 07102.

Telephone: (973) 693-6696, 973-6697.

CURIO, Georgia M. *(Judge, New Jersey Superior Court Vicinage Fifteen)* Appointed by Governor Christine T. Whitman to term beginning June 28, 1995. Reappointed by Governor James E. McGreevey June 2002. Term expires at age seventy. Presiding Judge Civil Division since July 1, 2001. Born Vineland New Jersey Aug 30, 1956. Educated at Glassboro State College B.A. 1977 and Rutgers University School of Law J.D. 1980. In legal practice Vineland Aug 1980 to June 1995.

Public Defender Vineland June 1992 to Sept 1993. Certified Civil Trial Attorney 1990. Member Cumber-

CURIO, GEORGIA M.—*Continued*

land County (Trustee 1991-94, President Elect 1994-95), New Jersey State and American Bar Associations.

Office: Cumberland County Courthouse, West Broad and Fayette Streets, Bridgeton 08302.

Telephone: (856) 453-4377.

CURRAN, Barbara A. *(Judge, New Jersey Superior Court Vicinage Six)* Appointed by Governor Jim Florio Feb 19, 1993. Reappointed by Governor Christine T. Whitman Jan 2000. Educated at St. Mary of the Woods College B.A., Syracuse University M.A. and Seton Hall University School of Law J.D. Honorary degree Caldwell College. Admitted to practice New Jersey 1977 and U.S. District Court District of New Jersey 1977. In legal practice Roseland 1989-93.

Attorney Chubb & Son Ins. Co. 1978-80. Author "Rate Cases from the BRC Perspective" *Management Quarterly* Spring 1992. Former Member National Association of Regulatory Utility Commissioners (Committee on Gas, Committee on Electricity, Nuclear Regulatory Commission Liaison). Member Governor's Commission on the Future of Independent Higher Education in New Jersey and New Jersey State Bar Association (Board of Consulters Public Utility Law Section, Environmental Law Section). Named one of New Jersey's Most Powerful Women by *New Jersey Monthly Magazine* and Woman of the Year by Newark Ironbound Manufacturer's Association and New Jersey Federation of Republican Women. Listed in *Who's Who Among American Women* and *Who's Who Among International Women.* Former television news writer and commentator. With Publications Ltd. (publisher) 1963-69. Assistant Dean for Placement Seton Hall University School of Law 1974-78. Commissioner 1980-81 and President 1982-87 New Jersey Board of Public Utilities. Corporate Vice President Drexel Burnham Lambert 1987-89. Republican. Member General Assembly New Jersey 1973-80. Trustee The Chubb Foundation and Fund for Educational Advancement. Board of Visitors Drew University. Board of Directors Irish Youth Fund, Inc. and St. Vincent Academy. Honorary Committee New Jersey Pride Awards. Former Member American Council of Young Political Leaders, Board of Directors New Jersey Girl Scouts and Board of Trustees St. Mary of the Woods College. Member Women Executives in State Government.

Office: Administration Building, 595 Newark Avenue, Jersey City 07306.

Telephone: (201) 795-6738, 795-6773.

DALEY, Roger W. *(Judge, New Jersey Superior Court Vicinage Eight)* Appointed by governor.

Mailing address: P.O. Box 2691, New Brunswick 08903-2691.

Office: Middlesex County Family Court, 120 New Street, New Brunswick 08901.

Telephone: (732) 981-3040.

DANGLER, John B. *(Judge, New Jersey Superior Court Vicinage Ten)* Appointed by governor.

Mailing address: P.O. Box 910, Morristown 07963-0910.

Office: Morris County Courthouse, Morristown 07960.

Telephone: (973) 656-4144.

DANIELS, Wendel E. *(Judge, New Jersey Superior Court Vicinage Fourteen)* Appointed by governor.

Office: Ocean County Justice Complex, 120 Hooper Avenue, Toms River 08753.

Telephone: (732) 929-2171.

DAVIDSON, Rachel N. *(Judge, New Jersey Superior Court Vicinage Five)* Appointed by governor.

Office: Gibraltar Building, Ninth Floor, 212 Washington Street, Newark 07102.

Telephone: (973) 693-6716, 693-6717.

DAVIS, Elaine L. *(Judge, New Jersey Superior Court Vicinage Six)* Appointed by governor. Currently serves as Presiding Judge Criminal Division.

Office: Administration Building, 595 Newark Avenue, Jersey City 07306.

Telephone: (201) 795-6662, 795-6663.

DAVIS, Theodore Z. *(Judge, New Jersey Superior Court Vicinage Four)* Appointed by governor. Currently serves as Presiding Judge General Equity Division and Acting Assignment Judge.

Office: 640 Camden County Hall of Justice, 101 South Fifth Street, Camden 08103-4001.

Telephone: (856) 379-2360.

De BELLO, Lawrence P. *(Judge, New Jersey Superior Court Vicinage Six)* Appointed by governor.

Office: Administration Building, 595 Newark Avenue, Jersey City 07306.

Telephone: (201) 795-6045.

DEBEVOISE, Dickinson R. *(Senior Judge, United States District Court District of New Jersey)* Appointed for life by President Jimmy Carter to term beginning Nov 16, 1979. Assumed Senior status, serves by assignment. Born Orange New Jersey April 23, 1924. United Church of Christ. Educated at Williams College B.A. 1948 and Columbia University LL.B. 1951. Board of Editors Columbia Law Review 1949-51. Law Clerk to Hon. Phillip Forman, U.S. District Court District of New Jersey 1952-53. Admitted to practice New Jersey 1953, U.S. Courts of Appeals Third 1953 and Fifth 1964 Circuits and U.S. Supreme Court 1956. Began legal practice Newark 1953.

Author "New Jersey Attorneys in the South—Summer of 1964" New Jersey L. Jour. 1964 and "American History and the Study of Constitutional Law" 45 Rutgers L. Rev. 615, 1993. Important Decisions: May v. Cooperman (school prayer and minute of silence) 572 F. Supp. 1561, 578 F. Supp. 1308, 1983; U.S. v. Kungys (deportation for alleged war crimes) 575 F. Supp. 1208, 1983; and Robinson v. New Jersey (compulsory union dues for state employees) 547 F. Supp. 1297, 559 F. Supp. 754, 565 F. Supp. 942, 1983 rev'd F. 1984. Chairman New Jersey Clients' Security Fund 1969-73, Governor's Workmen's Compensation Study Commission 1972-73 and New Jersey Disciplinary Review Board 1978-79. President 1965-70 and Trustee 1968-71 Newark Legal Services Project. Member New Jersey Supreme Court Advisory Committee on Judicial Conduct 1974-78, Lawyers Advisory Committee of Third Circuit 1975-79 (Chairman 1978), Lawyers Constitutional Defense Committee, Committee on Financial Disclosure Judicial Conference of the U.S. 1986-94, The American Law Institute, Association of Federal Bar of New Jersey, Essex County (Treasurer 1960-64), New Jersey State and American Bar Associations. Sergeant U.S. Army Combat

DEBEVOISE, DICKINSON R.—*Continued*

Engineers 1943-45 and First Lieutenant U.S. Army Security Agency 1951-52. Democrat. President Democrats for Good Government. Trustee Hospital Center Orange 1957-79, Williams College 1969-74, Ramapo College of New Jersey 1969-74 (Chairman 1978-79) and Fund for New Jersey. Former Vestryman St. Stephen's Episcopal Church. Former member Millburn-Short Hills Human Relations Council and Newark Citizens for Community Action. Enjoys sailing and playing squash and tennis. Interested in biographies and history.

Mailing address: P.O. Box 999, Newark 07101-0999.

Office: U.S. Courthouse, 50 Walnut Street, Newark 07102.

Telephone: (973) 645-6121.

deCORDOVA, Donald W. *(Judge, New Jersey Superior Court Vicinage Two)* Appointed by Governor Brendan T. Byrne to term beginning Feb 6, 1981. Reappointed by Governor Thomas H. Kean Jan 14, 1986. Term expires at age seventy. Designated Judge Special Civil Part 1982-87 and since 1999. Served Family Division 1992-98. Born New York New York June 26, 1934. Educated at Princeton University B.A. 1956, Woodrow Wilson School of Public and International Affairs 1956 and Rutgers University J.D. 1961. Admitted to practice New Jersey 1961. Began legal practice Hackensack 1961. Municipal Judge, Borough of Bogota Jan 1968 to Feb 1981.

Borough Attorney of Tenafly Jan 1963 to Feb 1981. Prosecutor Borough of Bogota Jan 1965 to Dec 1967. Planning Board Attorney Borough of Park Ridge Jan 1969 to Feb 1981. Member Bergen County and New Jersey State Bar Associations. Captain USNR June 1956 to Sept 1958 and Feb 1973 to May 1973. USNR Naval Intelligence Program (retired). Republican. Councilman Borough of Bogota Nov 1963 to Dec 1964. Trustee Bergen Community Regional Blood Center. Elder Bogart Memorial Church.

Office: Bergen County Justice Center, 10 Main Street, Hackensack 07601.

Telephone: (201) 646-3003, 646-3733.

de la CARRERA, Miguel *(Judge, New Jersey Superior Court Vicinage Eleven)* Appointed by Acting Governor Donald DiFrancesco to term beginning Jan 30, 2002. Born Havana Cuba Feb 5, 1955. Educated at Yale College B.A. cum laude 1977 and Columbia University J.D. 1982. Admitted to practice New Jersey 1983. In legal practice Paterson July 1985 to Jan 2002. Judge, Paterson Municipal Court March 1993 to Jan 2000.

Staff Attorney Essex-Newark Legal Services Aug 1982 to July 1985. Assistant County Counsel Essex County March 2000 to June 2001. Member Hispanic Bar Association of New Jersey, Passaic County and New Jersey State Bar Associations. Trustee Passaic County Community College Nov 1989 to Nov 2001.

Office: 77 Hamilton Street, Paterson 07505.

Telephone: (973) 247-8329.

Fax: (973) 247-3283

E-mail address: Miguel.delaCarrera-@judiciary.state.nj.us

De La CRUZ, Estela M. *(Judge, New Jersey Superior Court Vicinage Two)* Appointed by Governor Christine T. Whitman to term beginning June 10, 1997. Term expires June 2004. Born Cuba May 11. Educated at Seton Hall University B.A. 1979 and Rutgers University School of Law J.D. 1982. Admitted to practice New Jersey 1983. In legal practice New Jersey 1983 to June 9, 1997.

Member Fee Arbitration Committee Panel Supreme Court of New Jersey. Member Governor's Commission on Racism, Racial Violence and Religious Violence 1992-94, District VI Ethics Committee Supreme Court of New Jersey 1996 and Free Cuba Task Force 1996. President Hispanic Bar Association of New Jersey, Inc. 1993-94. New Jersey Regional President Hispanic National Bar Association 1994-96. Member State Committee Task Force on Minority Concerns Supreme Court of New Jersey, Bergen County, Essex County, Hudson County (Board of Trustees) and New Jersey State Bar Associations.

Office: Bergen County Justice Center, 10 Main Street, Hackensack 07601.

Telephone: (201) 646-3085.

DELEHEY, Charles A. *(Judge, New Jersey Superior Court Vicinage Seven)* Appointed by governor. Currently serves as Presiding Judge Criminal Division.

Mailing address: P.O. Box 8068, Trenton 08650.

Office: Mercer County Courthouse, 209 South Broad and Market Streets, Trenton 08608.

Telephone: (609) 989-6186.

DELORENZO, William R., Jr. *(Judge, New Jersey Superior Court Vicinage Two)* Appointed by governor.

Office: Bergen County Justice Center, 10 Main Street, Hackensack 07601.

Telephone: (201) 646-3665.

De LUCCIA, Ralph L., Jr. *(Judge, New Jersey Superior Court Vicinage Eleven)* Appointed by Governor Jim Florio to term beginning March 2, 1993. Reappointed by Governor Christine T. Whitman to term beginning March 2000. Term expires at age seventy. Born Washington D.C. Oct 8, 1944. Roman Catholic. Educated at Seton Hall University B.A. 1966 and University of Tennessee J.D. 1969. Member Delta Theta Phi. Admitted to practice New Jersey 1970, U.S. District Court District of New Jersey 1970, U.S. Supreme Court 1979 and U.S. Court of Appeals Third Circuit 1984. In legal practice Paterson 1970-87 and Saddle Brook 1987-93.

Assistant Corporation Counsel 1970-86 and Corporation Counsel 1986-93 Department of Law City of Paterson. Important Decisions: State v. Long (harassment of debtor by creditor) 266 N.J. Super. 716, 1993; Fireman's Fund of N.J. v. Caldwell (household member exclusion on home owners insurance policy) 270 N.J. Super. 157, 1993; R.T.C. v. Berman Industries (liability of defaulting mortgagee on deficiency sale) 271 N.J. Super. 56, 1994; Bishop v. Bishop (emancipation of West Point cadet) 287 N.J. Super. 593, 1995; State v. Jackson (pretextual warrantless search of pretrial detainee defendant's dormitory area at county jail violated search and seizure provisions and state and federal constitutions) 321 N.J. Super. 365, 1999; and State v. Burke (evidence of prior virginity of alleged victim of sexual assault excluded by evidence rule prohibiting admission of evidence of a person's character or character trait to prove that the person acted in conformity therewith on a particular occasion) 354 N.J. Super. 97, 2002. Member New Jersey Council of Juvenile and Family Court Judges and Passaic County Bar Association. Attended course on "Current Issues in Family Law" 1994, course on "Financial Statements in the Courtroom" 1994 and course on "Municipal Land Use" The National Judicial College and course

DE LUCCIA, RALPH L., JR.—*Continued*

on "No Reversals, Correct Rulings" Evidence in Action American Academy of Judicial Education 1995.

Office: Passaic County Courthouse, 77 Hamilton Street, Paterson 07505.

Telephone: (973) 247-3209.

DePASCALE, Paul M. *(Judge, New Jersey Superior Court Vicinage Six)* Appointed by governor.

Office: Administration Building, 595 Newark Avenue, Jersey City 07306.

Telephone: (201) 795-6392.

DERMAN, Harriet E. *(Judge, New Jersey Superior Court Vicinage Eight)* Appointed by Governor Christine T. Whitman to term beginning Feb 1998. Term expires Feb 2005.

Mailing address: P.O. Box 2691, New Brunswick 08903-2691.

Office: Middlesex County Family Court, 120 New Street, New Brunswick 08901.

Telephone: (732) 981-3034.

DeSOTO, Hector E. *(Judge, New Jersey Superior Court Vicinage Five)* Appointed by governor.

Office: Gibraltar Building, Tenth Floor, 212 Washington Street, Newark 07102.

Telephone: (973) 693-5849, 693-5850.

De STEFANO, Francis P. *(Judge, New Jersey Superior Court Vicinage Nine)* Appointed by governor. Served Vicinage Six.

Mailing address: P.O. Box 1266, Freehold 07728-1266.

Office: Monmouth County Courthouse, Monument and Court Streets, Freehold 07728.

Telephone: (732) 677-4120.

DeVESA, Frederick P. *(Judge, New Jersey Superior Court Vicinage Eight)* Appointed by governor.

Mailing address: P.O. Box 964, New Brunswick 08903.

Office: Middlesex County Courthouse, One John F. Kennedy Square, New Brunswick 08901.

Telephone: (732) 981-3198.

DIAMOND, Michael K. *(Judge, New Jersey Superior Court Vicinage Eleven)* Appointed by governor.

Office: Passaic County Admin. Bldg., 401 Grand Street, Paterson 07505.

Telephone: (973) 247-8435.

Di CAMILLO, Angelo J. *(Judge, New Jersey Tax Court)* Appointed by governor. Currently serves New Jersey Superior Court Vicinage Four.

Office: 220 Hall of Justice, 101 South Fifth Street, Camden 08103-4001.

Telephone: (856) 379-2361.

DILTS, Thomas H. *(Judge, New Jersey Superior Court Vicinage Thirteen)* Appointed by governor. Currently serves as Presiding Judge Family Division.

Mailing address: P.O. Box 3000, Somerville 08876.

Office: Somerset County Courthouse, Somerville 08876.

Telephone: (908) 231-7647.

D'ITALIA, Arthur N. *(Assignment Judge, New Jersey Superior Court Vicinage Six)* Appointed by governor.

Office: Administration Building, 595 Newark Avenue, Jersey City 07306.

Telephone: (201) 795-6611.

DONALDSON, Louise D. *(Judge, New Jersey Superior Court Vicinage Four)* Appointed by governor.

Office: 120 Hall of Justice, 101 South Fifth Street, Camden 08103-4001.

Telephone: (856) 379-2362.

DONATO, Frank M. *(Judge, New Jersey Superior Court Vicinage Eleven)* Appointed by Governor Brendan T. Byrne to term beginning Jan 13, 1982. Reappointed by Governor Thomas H. Kean Jan 13, 1987. Term expires at age seventy. Born Paterson New Jersey June 6, 1941. Educated at Georgetown University B.A. 1963 and Cornell Law School J.D. 1966. Law Clerk to Hon. C. Thomas Schettino, New Jersey Supreme Court 1966-67. Admitted to practice New Jersey 1966 and U.S. District Court District of New Jersey 1966. In legal practice Little Falls 1972-82.

Assistant Prosecutor Passaic County 1970-71. Important Decisions: Atamian v. Supermarkets General 147 N.J. Super. 149 (Law Div. 1976) 1976; Windmill Estates v. Borough of Totowa 147 N.J. Super. 65, 1976, rev'd 158 N.J. Super. 179, 1978; State v. Konzelmann 204 N.J. Super. 389, 1985; and Matter of Taylor 259 N.J. Super. 478, 1992. Member 1988-96 and Chair 1992-96 New Jersey Supreme Court Committee on Model Criminal Charges. Member Passaic County Bar Association. Attended The National Judicial College 1984 and American Academy of Judicial Education Stanford 1985, Harvard 1988 and San Diego 1995. Lifetime Silver Card Holder Passaic County Bar Association. Captain U.S. Army 1967-69. Administrative Assistant to Governor William T. Cahill 1971-72. President Passaic County Chapter American Cancer Society 1976. Former Member Board of Directors Valley National Bank. Enjoys playing golf.

Office: Passaic County Courthouse, 77 Hamilton Street, Paterson 07505.

Telephone: (973) 247-8135.

DONIO, Ann Marie *(Magistrate Judge, United States District Court District of New Jersey)* Appointed by U.S. District Court judges to term beginning March 24, 2003.

Office: U.S. Courthouse, One John F. Gerry Plaza, 400 Cooper Street, Camden 08102.

Telephone: (856) 757-5021.

DONIO, Michael A. *(Judge, New Jersey Superior Court Vicinage One)* Appointed by governor.

Office: County Criminal Courthouse, 5909 Main Street, Mays Landing 08330.

Telephone: (609) 645-5816.

DONOHUE, Joseph P. *(Judge, New Jersey Superior Court Vicinage Twelve)* Appointed by governor.

Office: Union County Courthouse, Two Broad Street, Elizabeth 07207.

Telephone: (908) 659-3865.

DONOHUE, Richard J. *(Judge, New Jersey Superior Court Vicinage Two)* Appointed by governor.
Office: Bergen County Justice Center, 10 Main Street, Hackensack 07601.
Telephone: (201) 752-4362.

DOYNE, Peter E. *(Judge, New Jersey Superior Court Vicinage Two)* Appointed by Governor Jim Florio to term beginning March 17, 1993. Born New York New York June 18, 1951. Educated at Lafayette College B.A. cum laude 1973 and Rutgers University School of Law J.D. 1976. Admitted to practice New Jersey 1976 and New York 1977. In legal practice Hackensack New Jersey 1989-92.
President Morris Pashman American Inn of Court since 1997. Fellow American Bar Foundation. Member Bergen County Bar Association (Judicial Selection Committee 1986-90). Frequent Lecturer ICLE. Coach Little League.
Office: 420 Bergen County Justice Center, 10 Main Street, Hackensack 07601.
Telephone: (201) 646-3553.
Fax: (201) 752-4413

DUMONT, W. Hunt *(Judge, New Jersey Superior Court Vicinage Ten)* Appointed by governor. Served Vicinage Eleven.
Mailing address: P.O. Box 910, Morristown 07963-0910.
Office: Morris County Courthouse, Morristown 07960.
Telephone: (973) 656-3946.

DUPUIS, Katherine R. *(Judge, New Jersey Superior Court Vicinage Twelve)* Appointed by governor. Served Vicinage Thirteen.
Office: Union County Courthouse, Two Broad Street, Elizabeth 07207.
Telephone: (908) 659-4138.

EICHEN, Naomi G. *(Judge, New Jersey Superior Court Appellate Division)* Appointed Judge Vicinage Two by governor. Assigned to Appellate Division by Chief Justice Robert N. Wilentz.
Office: Court Plaza North, Fifth Floor, 25 Main Street, Hackensack 07601-7015.
Telephone: (201) 996-8018, 996-8019.

EPSTEIN, Mark B. *(Judge, New Jersey Superior Court Vicinage Eight)* Appointed by Governor Thomas H. Kean to term beginning March 14, 1983. Reappointed by Governor Thomas H. Kean Feb 1988. Former Presiding Judge Family Division. Educated at Rutgers University J.D. 1969. Admitted to practice New Jersey 1969. In legal practice New Brunswick 1969-83.
Mailing address: P.O. Box 964, New Brunswick 08903.
Office: Middlesex County Courthouse, One John F. Kennedy Square, New Brunswick 08901.
Telephone: (732) 981-3168.

ESCALA, Gerald C. *(Judge, New Jersey Superior Court Vicinage Two)* Appointed by governor. Currently serves as Acting Assignment Judge.
Office: Bergen County Justice Center, 10 Main Street, Hackensack 07601.
Telephone: (201) 646-3148, 646-3151.

EYNON, David G. *(Retired Judge, New Jersey Superior Court)* Assumed office Dec 7, 1978. Former Presiding Judge Criminal Division. Served Vicinage Four. Retired, serves on recall. Former Judge, New Jersey County Court Camden County.
Office: 340 Camden County Hall of Justice, 101 South Fifth Street, Camden 08103-4001.
Telephone: (856) 379-2356.

FALCONE, Joseph A. *(Assignment Judge, New Jersey Superior Court Vicinage Five)* Appointed by governor. Served Vicinage Eleven. Former Presiding Judge Criminal Division.
Office: 618 Essex County Courts Building, 50 West Market Street, Newark 07102.
Telephone: (973) 693-6470, 693-6471.

FALK, Mark *(Magistrate Judge, United States District Court District of New Jersey)* Appointed by U.S. District Court judges to term beginning March 1, 2002.
Office: U.S. Courthouse, 50 Walnut Street, Newark 07102.
Telephone: (973) 645-3110.

FALL, Robert A. *(Judge, New Jersey Superior Court Appellate Division)* Appointed Judge Vicinage Fourteen by Governor Thomas H. Kean to term beginning June 6, 1986. Reappointed by Governor Jim Florio 1993. Former Presiding Judge Family Division. Assigned to Appellate Division by Chief Justice Deborah T. Poritz. Term expires at age seventy. Born Jersey City New Jersey Nov 11, 1945. Catholic. Educated at Monmouth College B.A. 1968 and University of Miami J.D. 1973. Admitted to practice New Jersey 1973 and Florida 1973. E-5 U.S. Army 1969-70.
Mailing address: P.O. Box 4617, Toms River 08754-4617.
Office: 100 East Water Street, Toms River 08754.
Telephone: (732) 736-7201, 736-7202.

FARBER, James A. *(Judge, New Jersey Superior Court Vicinage Ten)* Appointed by governor.
Office: Sussex County Judicial Center, 43-47 High Street, Newton 07860.
Telephone: (973) 579-0685.

FARRELL, Timothy G. *(Judge, New Jersey Superior Court Vicinage Fifteen)* Appointed by governor.
Office: Salem County Courthouse, 92 Market Street, Salem 08079.
Telephone: (856) 935-7510.

FARREN, Michael D. *(Judge, New Jersey Superior Court Vicinage Nine)* Appointed by governor. Currently serves as Presiding Judge Criminal Division and Acting Assignment Judge.
Mailing address: P.O. Box 1266, Freehold 07728-1266.
Office: Monmouth County Courthouse, Monument and Court Streets, Freehold 07728.
Telephone: (732) 677-4122.

FAST, Mahlon L. *(Judge, New Jersey Superior Court Vicinage Five)* Appointed by Governor Thomas H. Kean to term beginning April 11, 1986. Reappointed by Governor Jim Florio. Term expires at age seventy. Also serves as Designated Judge Special Civil Part. Born Newark New Jersey Feb 27, 1934. Educated at Rutgers University B.A. LL.B. Admitted to practice New Jersey 1960 and U.S. Court of Appeals Third Circuit 1960.

FAST, MAHLON L.—*Continued*

Author "A Guide to Landlord/Tenant Actions" New Jersey Institute for Continuing Legal Education 1992.

Office: 322 Hall of Records, 465 Dr. Martin Luther King Jr. Blvd., Newark 07102.

Telephone: (973) 693-6436, 693-6437.

FEINBERG, Linda R. *(Assignment Judge, New Jersey Superior Court Vicinage Seven)* Appointed by governor.

Mailing address: P.O. Box 8068, Trenton 08650.

Office: Mercer County Civil Courts, 175 South Broad Street, Trenton 08608.

Telephone: (609) 989-6200.

FERENCZ, Bradley J. *(Judge, New Jersey Superior Court Vicinage Eight)* Appointed by Governor Christine T. Whitman to term beginning June 2, 1997. Term expires June 2004.

Mailing address: P.O. Box 2691, New Brunswick 08903-2691.

Office: Middlesex County Family Court, 120 New Street, New Brunswick 08901.

Telephone: (732) 981-3021.

FERENTZ, Carol A. *(Judge, New Jersey Superior Court Vicinage Five)* Appointed by Governor Thomas H. Kean to term beginning Jan 13, 1984. Reappointed by Governor Jim Florio Jan 1991. Term expires at age seventy. Born New Jersey July 22, 1943. Catholic. Educated at Syracuse University B.A. 1965 and Seton Hall University J.D. 1972. Admitted to practice New Jersey 1972 and U.S. District Court District of New Jersey 1972. Began legal practice East Orange 1972.

Important Decision: In re Release of Juveniles' Identities to Albert Wise, Applicant (held: victim not entitled to obtain names and addresses of juveniles who had not been charged with any offense arising out of incident) 204 N.J. Super. 71 May 28, 1985. Master U.S. Justice Brennan Chapter since 1987 and New Jersey Chief Justice Vanderbilt Chapter 1989-91 Essex County Inns of Court. Member Essex County, New Jersey State and American Bar Associations. Faculty Lecturer "Proving a Personal Injury Case" Fall 1987 and "Premises Liability" since Fall 1988 New Jersey ICLE. Faculty Instructor "Recent Trends in Civil Law" New Jersey Judicial College Nov 1987-88 and Lecturer "Demonstrative Evidence in Products Liability Cases" Essex County Bar Association Legal Education March 1989. Republican. Former Secretary Republican Lawyers Association of New Jersey.

Office: 409 Hall of Records, 465 Dr. Martin Luther King Jr. Blvd., Newark 07102.

Telephone: (973) 693-5854, 693-5855.

FERGUSON, Kathryn C. *(Judge, United States Bankruptcy Court District of New Jersey)* Appointed by U.S. Court of Appeals Third Circuit judges.

Office: U.S. Courthouse, 402 East State Street, Trenton 08608.

Telephone: (609) 989-0494.

FISHER, Clarkson S., Jr. *(Judge, New Jersey Superior Court Vicinage Nine)* Appointed by governor. Currently serves as Presiding Judge General Equity Division. Served Vicinage Eight.

Mailing address: P.O. Box 1266, Freehold 07728-1266.

Office: Monmouth County Courthouse, Monument and Court Streets, Freehold 07728.

Telephone: (732) 431-7135.

FISHER, Michael Brooke *(Judge, New Jersey Superior Court Vicinage Fifteen)* Appointed by governor.

Office: Cumberland County Courthouse, West Broad and Fayette Streets, Bridgeton 08302.

Telephone: (856) 453-4397.

FITZPATRICK, Patrick F. X. *(Judge, New Jersey Superior Court Vicinage Two)* Appointed by governor.

Office: Bergen County Justice Center, 10 Main Street, Hackensack 07601.

Telephone: (201) 646-3224, 646-3265.

FLORIA, Sallyanne *(Judge, New Jersey Superior Court Vicinage Five)* Appointed by governor.

Office: Gibraltar Building, Twelfth Floor, 212 Washington Street, Newark 07102.

Telephone: (973) 693-5877, 693-5878.

FLYNN, Terence P. *(Judge, New Jersey Superior Court Vicinage Five)* Appointed by governor. Served Vicinage Six.

Office: 1106 Essex County Courts Building, 50 West Market Street, Newark 07102.

Telephone: (973) 693-6746, 693-6747.

FORD, Marlene Lynch *(Judge, New Jersey Superior Court Vicinage Fourteen)* Appointed by Governor Jim Florio to term beginning Oct 16, 1992. Reappointed by Governor Christine T. Whitman. Term expires at age seventy. Born Yuma Arizona Feb 23, 1954. Catholic. Educated at Georgian Court College B.A. magna cum laude 1976 and Seton Hall University J.D. 1979. Admitted to practice New Jersey 1979 and U.S. Court of Appeals Third Circuit 1979. In legal practice Jackson 1979-81 and Point Pleasant Beach 1981-86.

General Counsel H. Hovnanian Industries 1986-88 and 1990-92. General Counsel Democratic Delegation New Jersey General Assembly 1988-90. Member Ocean County and New Jersey State Bar Associations. Attended CLE sponsored by New Jersey Administrative Office of the Courts. Chair Assembly Judiciary Committee and Member New Jersey General Assembly 1984-86 and 1990-92.

Office: Ocean County Courthouse, 100 Hooper Avenue, Toms River 08753.

Telephone: (732) 506-5084.

FORESTER, William L. *(Judge, New Jersey Superior Court Vicinage Fifteen)* Appointed by governor. Former Designated Judge Special Civil Part.

Office: Salem County Courthouse, 92 Market Street, Salem 08079.

Telephone: (856) 935-7510.

FORRESTER, F. Lee *(Judge, New Jersey Superior Court Vicinage Seven)* Appointed by governor. Currently serves as Presiding Judge Family Division.

Mailing address: P.O. Box 8068, Trenton 08650.

Office: Mercer County Civil Courts, 175 South Broad Street, Trenton 08608.

Telephone: (609) 989-6647.

FOSTER, Joseph L. *(Judge, New Jersey Tax Court)* Appointed by governor. Currently serves New Jersey Superior Court Vicinage Fourteen.

Office: Ocean County Justice Complex, 120 Hooper Avenue, Toms River 08753.

Telephone: (732) 929-4706.

FRANCIS, Robert E. *(Judge, New Jersey Superior Court Vicinage Fifteen)* Appointed by governor. Former Acting Assignment Judge.

Mailing address: P.O. Box 429, Woodbury 08096.

Office: Gloucester County Courthouse, Woodbury 08096.

Telephone: (856) 853-3208.

FRANCIS, Travis L. *(Judge, New Jersey Superior Court Vicinage Eight)* Appointed by governor.

Mailing address: P.O. Box 964, New Brunswick 08903.

Office: Middlesex County Courthouse, One John F. Kennedy Square, New Brunswick 08901.

Telephone: (732) 981-3076.

FRANKLIN, Sheldon R. *(Judge, New Jersey Superior Court Vicinage Fourteen)* Appointed by Governor Christine T. Whitman to term beginning June 8, 1999. Term expires June 8, 2006. Served Vicinage Three. Born Lakewood New Jersey March 1, 1947. Educated at George Washington University B.A. 1969 and Rutgers University School of Law J.D. with high honors 1972. Admitted to practice New Jersey 1972, U.S. District Court District of New Jersey 1972 and U.S. Supreme Court 1979. In legal practice Lakewood and Brick Nov 1972 to June 1999.

Committeeman Jan 1, 1997 to June 8, 1999 and Mayor Jan 1, 1998 to Dec 31, 1998 Lakewood Township.

Office: 10 Ocean County Courthouse, 125 Washington Street, Toms River 08753.

Telephone: (732) 506-5024.

E-mail address: Sheldon_Franklin@Judiciary.state.nj.us

FRATTO, John A. *(Judge, New Jersey Superior Court Vicinage Four)* Appointed by Governor Thomas H. Kean to term beginning July 12, 1989. Reappointed by Governor Christine T. Whitman. Term expires at age seventy. Born Philadelphia Pennsylvania 1935. Educated at Temple University A.B. 1957 J.D. 1960. Staff member Temple Law Review 1958-59. Member Phi Delta Phi. Admitted to practice New Jersey 1962, U.S. Supreme Court 1969 and U.S. Court of Appeals Third Circuit 1976. Certified by Supreme Court of New Jersey Civil Trial Attorney.

Fellow American College of Trial Lawyers. Member Trial Attorneys of New Jersey, American Judicature Society, Camden County, New Jersey State and American Bar Associations. New Jersey National Guard 1961-68.

Office: 430 Camden County Hall of Justice, 101 South Fifth Street, Camden 08103-4001.

Telephone: (856) 379-2363.

FREEDMAN, Philip M. *(Retired Judge, New Jersey Superior Court)* Appointed by Governor Brendan T. Byrne to term beginning Sept 20, 1979. Reappointed by Governor Thomas H. Kean. Served Civil and Criminal Divisions Vicinage Five. Former Presiding Judge Family Division. Retired, serves on recall. Born Newark New Jersey Feb 1, 1940. Jewish. Educated at Tufts University B.A. 1961 and Cornell University J.D. 1964. Law Clerk to Hon. Sol Schulman, New Jersey County Court Hudson County 1964-65. Admitted to practice New Jersey 1965. Began legal practice East Orange 1965.

Member Essex County and New Jersey State Bar Associations.

Office: Wilentz Building, 212 Washington Street, Newark 07102.

Telephone: (973) 693-6803, 693-6804.

FREEMAN, Ronald J. *(Judge, New Jersey Superior Court Vicinage Four)* Appointed by governor.

Office: 260 Hall of Justice, 101 South Fifth Street, Camden 08103-4001.

Telephone: (856) 379-2364.

FUENTES, Jose L. *(Judge, New Jersey Superior Court Appellate Division)* Appointed Judge Vicinage Six by governor. Assigned to Appellate Division by Chief Justice Deborah T. Poritz. Born Cuba. Educated at Montclair State University 1978 and Rutgers University School of Law J.D. 1982. Former Judge, Union City Municipal Court.

Office: 1101 North Tower, 158 Headquarters Plaza, Morristown 07960-3965.

Telephone: (973) 631-6527.

FULLILOVE, Harold W. *(Judge, New Jersey Superior Court Vicinage Five)* Appointed by governor. Currently serves as Presiding Judge Criminal Division.

Office: 608 Essex County Courts Building, 50 West Market Street, Newark 07102.

Telephone: (973) 693-5862, 693-5863.

GAETA, Bruce A. *(Judge, New Jersey Superior Court Vicinage Two)* Appointed by Governor Thomas H. Kean.

Office: Bergen County Justice Center, 10 Main Street, Hackensack 07601.

Telephone: (201) 646-2333.

GAETA, Sebastian, Jr. *(Judge, New Jersey Superior Court Vicinage Two)* Appointed by governor.

Office: Bergen County Justice Center, 10 Main Street, Hackensack 07601.

Telephone: (201) 646-3462.

GALLIPOLI, Maurice J. *(Judge, New Jersey Superior Court Vicinage Six)* Appointed by governor. Currently serves as Presiding Judge Civil Division and Acting Assignment Judge. Born Jersey City New Jersey 1942. Educated at St. Peter's College B.S. 1963 and New York University LL.B. 1966. Admitted to practice New Jersey 1966, U.S. District Court District of New Jersey 1966, U.S. Court of Appeals Third Circuit 1982 and U.S. Supreme Court 1983. Certified by the Supreme Court of New Jersey as a Civil Trial Attorney 1985.

Fellow American College of Trial Lawyers and American Bar Foundation. Member Trial Attorney Certification Board Supreme Court of New Jersey 1986. Former Member National Panel of Arbitrators American Arbitration Association, National Association of Railroad Trial Counsel, Trial Attorneys of New Jersey, The Defense Research Institute, Inc. and The Association of Trial Lawyers of America (Associate member ATLA-NJ).

GALLIPOLI, MAURICE J.—*Continued*

Member Essex County, Hudson County (President 1985), New Jersey State and American Bar Associations.
Office: Courthouse, 583 Newark Avenue, Jersey City 07306.
Telephone: (201) 795-6736, 795-6737.

GAMBARDELLA, Rosemary *(Chief Judge, United States Bankruptcy Court District of New Jersey)* Chief Judge since Aug 12, 1998.
Office: U.S. Courthouse, Third Floor, 50 Walnut Street, Newark 07102-3550.
Telephone: (973) 645-2322.

GANNON, Edward V. *(Judge, New Jersey Superior Court Vicinage Eleven)* Appointed by governor. Served Vicinage Ten.
Office: Passaic County Courthouse, 77 Hamilton Street, Paterson 07505.
Telephone: (973) 247-8320.

GAROFOLO, Albert J. *(Judge, New Jersey Superior Court Vicinage One)* Appointed by governor. Currently serves as Presiding Judge Criminal Division.
Office: County Criminal Courthouse, 5909 Main Street, Mays Landing 08330.
Telephone: (609) 645-5837.

GARRUTO, Bryan D. *(Judge, New Jersey Superior Court Vicinage Eight)* Appointed by governor.
Mailing address: P.O. Box 964, New Brunswick 08903.
Office: Middlesex County Courthouse, One John F. Kennedy Square, New Brunswick 08901.
Telephone: (732) 981-3174.

GASIOROWSKI, Francis W. *(Judge, New Jersey Superior Court Vicinage Thirteen)* Appointed by governor.
Mailing address: P.O. Box 3000, Somerville 08876.
Office: Somerset County Historic Courthouse, Somerville 08876.
Telephone: (908) 231-7060.

GAYNOR, Robert E. *(Retired Judge, New Jersey Superior Court Appellate Division)* Appointed Judge Vicinage Seven by Governor Brendan T. Byrne to term beginning April 1, 1978. Assigned to Appellate Division by chief justice. Retired, serves on recall. Born Brooklyn New York Aug 10, 1918. Baptist. Educated at Rutgers University A.B. 1940, Fordham University and George Washington University LL.B. 1946. Admitted to practice New Jersey 1946. Began legal practice Newark 1946. In legal practice New Brunswick 1948-73. Magistrate, Municipal Court 1961-64. Judge, New Jersey County Court Somerset County May 1973 to April 1978.
Member Somerset County, New Jersey State and American Bar Associations. Captain USAS 1942-46. Republican. Enjoys golf and opera.
Mailing office: P.O. Box 977, Trenton 08625-0977.
Office: Hughes Justice Complex, Trenton 08625.
Telephone: (609) 633-9744.

GEIGER, Richard J. *(Judge, New Jersey Superior Court Vicinage Fifteen)* Appointed by Governor James E. McGreevey.
Office: Cumberland County Courthouse, West Broad and Fayette Streets, Bridgeton 08302.
Telephone: (856) 453-4690.

GELADE, Melvin L. *(Judge, New Jersey Superior Court Vicinage Eight)* Appointed by governor. Former Designated Judge Special Civil Part.
Mailing address: P.O. Box 964, New Brunswick 08903.
Office: Middlesex County Courthouse, One John F. Kennedy Square, New Brunswick 08901.
Telephone: (732) 981-3107.

GILES, F. Michael *(Judge, New Jersey Superior Court Vicinage Five)* Appointed by governor.
Office: 706 Essex County Courts Building, 50 West Market Street, Newark 07102.
Telephone: (973) 693-5864, 693-5865.

GILROY, William P. *(Judge, New Jersey Superior Court Vicinage Nine)* Appointed by governor. Currently serves as Presiding Judge Civil Division.
Mailing address: P.O. Box 1266, Freehold 07728-1266.
Office: Monmouth County Courthouse, Monument and Court Streets, Freehold 07728.
Telephone: (732) 677-4125.

GINDIN, William H. *(Recalled Judge, United States Bankruptcy Court District of New Jersey)* Appointed by U.S. Court of Appeals Third Circuit judges to term beginning Jan 18, 1985. Reappointed Jan 1999. Former Chief Judge. Retired. Appointed Recalled Judge by the Judicial Council of the Third Circuit. Born Perth Amboy New Jersey Sept 1, 1931. Jewish. Educated at Brown University A.B. with high honors 1953 and Yale University J.D. 1956. Member Phi Beta Kappa. Admitted to practice New Jersey 1956, U.S. Supreme Court 1965 and U.S. Court of Appeals Third Circuit 1979. In legal practice Plainfield 1956-72 and Bridgewater 1972-82. Administrative Law Judge, State of New Jersey 1982-85.
Board of Editors New Jersey State Bar Association Journal 1960-70. Adjunct Professor Rutgers University Law School at Camden. Fellow American Bar Foundation. Member National Conference of Bankruptcy Judges (Board of Governors 1989-92), Plainfield, Union County, Somerset County, Middlesex County, Mercer County, New Jersey State and American Bar Associations. Lecturer Professional Education Systems and ICLE. Member 1965-72 and Chairman 1967-72 Plainfield Human Relations Commission. President Plainfield Business Association 1969, Plainfield Rotary Club 1975-76 and Temple Sholom 1979-81. Board of Trustees 1981-84 and Vice President 1984-86 New Jersey West Hudson Valley Region Union of American Hebrew Congregations. Board of Trustees New Jersey Opera Festival. Board of Trustees Princeton Jewish Center 1996-98.
Office: U.S. Courthouse, Second Floor, 402 East State Street, Trenton 08608.
Telephone: (609) 989-2018.

GIOVINE, Peter J. *(Judge, New Jersey Superior Court Vicinage Fourteen)* Appointed by Governor Thomas H. Kean July 23, 1984 to term beginning Aug 29, 1984. Reappointed by Governor Jim Florio 1991. Term expires at age seventy. Currently serves as Presiding Judge Criminal Division. Born Orange New Jersey May 23, 1939. Catholic. Educated at Columbia University B.A. 1961 J.D. 1964. Admitted to practice New Jersey 1965. In legal practice Toms River 1965-84. Judge, Stafford Township Municipal Court 1973-83. Judge, Lacey Township Municipal Court 1974-83. Judge, Borough of Island Heights Municipal Court 1977-84. Judge,

GIOVINE, PETER J.—*Continued*

Borough of Lavallette Municipal Court 1979-84. Judge, Borough of Surf City Municipal Court 1980-84. Judge, Borough of South Toms River Municipal Court 1983-84.

Assistant Prosecutor Ocean County 1967-72. Attorney Board of Adjustment Dover Township 1974-77. Attorney Dover Township Parking Authority 1974-77. Former Prosecutor Brick Township. President Ocean County Municipal Court Judges Association 1975-77. Member Ocean County (President 1977-78), New Jersey State and American Bar Associations.

Office: Ocean County Justice Complex, 120 Hooper Street, Toms River 08753.

Telephone: (732) 929-2172.

GOLDMAN, Donald S. *(Judge, New Jersey Superior Court Vicinage Five)* Appointed by governor.

Office: 806 Essex County Courts Building, 50 West Market Street, Newark 07102.

Telephone: (973) 693-5866, 693-5867.

GRALL, Jane *(Judge, New Jersey Superior Court Vicinage Seven)* Appointed by governor.

Mailing address: P.O. Box 8068, Trenton 08650.

Office: Mercer County Civil Courts, 175 South Broad Street, Trenton 08608.

Telephone: (609) 989-6182.

GRANT, Glenn A. *(Judge, New Jersey Superior Court Vicinage Five)* Appointed by governor.

Office: Gibraltar Building, Tenth Floor, 212 Washington Street, Newark 07102.

Telephone: (973) 693-6814, 693-6815.

GRASSO, Vincent J. *(Judge, New Jersey Superior Court Vicinage Fourteen)* Appointed by governor. Currently serves as Presiding Judge Family Division.

Office: Ocean County Justice Complex, 120 Hooper Avenue, Toms River 08753.

Telephone: (732) 929-4792.

GRAVES, Ronald B. *(Judge, New Jersey Superior Court Vicinage Ten)* Appointed by governor.

Office: Sussex County Judicial Center, 43-47 High Street, Newton 07860.

Telephone: (973) 579-0680.

GRAZIANO, Anthony J. *(Judge, New Jersey Superior Court Vicinage Eleven)* Appointed by governor.

Office: Passaic County Admin. Bldg., 401 Grand Street, Paterson 07505.

Telephone: (973) 247-8446.

GREENAWAY, Joseph A., Jr. *(Judge, United States District Court District of New Jersey)* Appointed for life by President Bill Clinton July 25 1996 to term beginning Sept 20, 1996. Born London England 1957. Episcopalian. Educated at Columbia College B.A. 1978 and Harvard University J.D. 1981. Law Clerk to Hon. Vincent L. Broderick, U.S. District Court Southern District of New York 1982-83. Admitted to practice New York 1983 and U.S. District Court District of New Jersey 1985. In legal practice 1981-85.

With U.S. Attorney's Office Newark 1985-90. Attorney Legal Department Johnson & Johnson, New Brunswick 1990-96. Adjunct Professor Rutgers University School of Law. Member Federal Judges Association, New Jersey State, National and American Bar Associations. Weintraub Lecturer Rutgers University School of Law. Recipient Award of Excellence from Columbia University. Coach Westfield Athletic Association. Enjoys golfing.

Mailing address: P.O. Box 999, Newark 07101-0999.

Office: U.S. Courthouse, 50 Walnut Street, Newark 07102.

Telephone: (973) 622-4828.

Fax: (973) 622-4806

GREENBERG, Martin L. *(Retired Judge, New Jersey Superior Court)* Appointed by governor. Served Vicinages Five and Six. Former Presiding Judge General Equity Division. Retired, serves on recall.

Office: Brennan Courthouse, 583 Newark Avenue, Jersey City 07306.

Telephone: (201) 795-6675.

GREENE, Joseph F., Jr. *(Retired Judge, New Jersey Superior Court)* Appointed by governor. Served Vicinage Four. Retired, serves on recall.

Mailing address: ISP, P.O. Box 987, Trenton 08625.

Telephone: (609) 984-0076.

GUZMAN, Nestor F. *(Judge, New Jersey Superior Court Vicinage Eleven)* Appointed by governor. Currently serves as Presiding Judge Family Division.

Office: Passaic County Admin. Bldg., 401 Grand Street, Paterson 07505.

Telephone: (973) 247-8441.

HAGUE, Douglas T. *(Judge, New Jersey Superior Court Vicinage Eight)* Appointed by governor. Served Vicinage Five.

Mailing address: P.O. Box 964, New Brunswick 08903.

Office: Middlesex County Courthouse, One John F. Kennedy Square, New Brunswick 08901.

Telephone: (732) 981-3170.

HANEKE, G. Donald *(Magistrate Judge, United States District Court District of New Jersey)* Appointed by U.S. District Court judges.

Office: U.S. Courthouse, 50 Walnut Street, Newark 07102.

Telephone: (973) 645-6664.

HANSBURY, Stephan C. *(Judge, New Jersey Superior Court Vicinage Ten)* Appointed by governor.

Mailing address: P.O. Box 910, Morristown 07963-0910.

Office: Morris County Courthouse, Morristown 07960.

Telephone: (973) 656-4039.

HAPPAS, Jamie D. *(Judge, New Jersey Superior Court Vicinage Eight)* Appointed by governor.

Mailing address: P.O. Box 964, New Brunswick 08903-0964.

Office: Middlesex County Courthouse, One John F. Kennedy Square, New Brunswick 08901.

Telephone: (732) 981-3054.

HARPER, John J. *(Judge, New Jersey Superior Court Vicinage Ten)* Appointed by governor.

Mailing address: P.O. Box 910, Morristown 07963-0910.

Office: Morris County Courthouse, Morristown 07960.

Telephone: (973) 656-4024.

HARRINGTON, John E. *(Judge, New Jersey Superior Court Vicinage Three)* Appointed by Governor James E. McGreevey.

Office: Burlington County Court Facility, 49 Rancocas Road, Mount Holly 08060.

Telephone: (609) 518-2595.

HARRIS, Craig Randall *(Judge, New Jersey Superior Court Vicinage Five)* Appointed by governor.

Office: Gibraltar Building, Tenth Floor, 212 Washington Street, Newark 07102.

Telephone: (973) 693-6656, 693-6657.

HARRIS, Jonathan N. *(Judge, New Jersey Superior Court Vicinage Two)* Appointed by governor.

Office: Bergen County Justice Center, 10 Main Street, Hackensack 07601.

Telephone: (201) 646-2448.

HAVEY, James M. *(Judge, New Jersey Superior Court Appellate Division)* Appointed Judge by Governor Brendan T. Byrne to term beginning Aug 26, 1978. Reappointed 1978. Assigned to Appellate Division by chief justice. Term expires at age seventy. Currently serves as Presiding Judge Part G. Born Connecticut May 26, 1939. Catholic. Educated at University of Connecticut B.A. 1961 and Rutgers University J.D. 1964. Member Alpha Sigma Phi. Admitted to practice New Jersey 1964 and U.S. District Court District of New Jersey 1964. In legal practice Toms River 1965 and 1968-76. Judge, Brick Township Municipal Court 1969-72. Judge, New Jersey County Court Ocean County Aug 1976 to Dec 1978.

Assistant Public Defender State of New Jersey 1971-74. Author "Insurance Coverage in Groundwater Pollution Litigation" New Jersey Lawyer Summer 1983. Important Opinions: Lionel's Appliance Center, Inc. v. Citta 156 N.J. Super. Ct. 257 Law. Div. 1978; Jackson Tp. Etc. v. Hartford Acc. & Indemn. Co. 186 N.J. Super. Ct. 156 Law Div. 1982; Dreier Co., Inc. v. Unitronix Corp. 218 N.J. Super. Ct. 260 App. Div. 1986; Baltica Const. v. Planning Bd. 222 N.J. Super. Ct. 428 App. Div. 1988; and Wawa Food Market v. Planning Bd. 227 N.J. Super. Ct. 29 App. Div. 1988. Member New Jersey State and Ocean County (Ethics Committee) Bar Associations. Instructor ICLE 1986 and 1988. Republican. Parliamentarian New Jersey Assembly 1971-72. Member Toms River Board of Education 1967-69. Enjoys tennis, racquetball and skiing.

Mailing address: P.O. Box 4617, Toms River 08754-4617.

Office: 100 East Water Street, Toms River 08753.

Telephone: (732) 286-6411.

HAWKINS, Rudolph N., Jr. *(Judge, New Jersey Superior Court Vicinage Twelve)* Appointed by Governor Thomas H. Kean to term beginning July 19, 1985. Reappointed by Governor Jim Florio. Term expires at age seventy. Former Presiding Judge Family Division. Born Trenton New Jersey Dec 30, 1933.

Office: Union County Courthouse, Two Broad Street, Elizabeth 07207.

Telephone: (908) 659-3415.

HAYDEN, Katharine S. *(Judge, United States District Court District of New Jersey)* Appointed for life by President Bill Clinton to term beginning 1997. Born New York New York May 30, 1942. Educated at Marymount-Manhattan College B.A. 1963 and Seton Hall University M.A. 1971 J.D. 1975. Law Clerk to Hon. Robert L. Clifford, New Jersey Supreme Court 1975-76. In legal practice 1975-91. Judge, New Jersey Superior Court Vicinage Five 1991-97.

Assistant U.S. Attorney District of New Jersey 1976-78.

Mailing address: P.O. Box 999, Newark 07101-0999.

Office: 311 U.S. Post Office & Courthouse, Newark 07102.

Telephone: (973) 645-4611.

HAYSER, Raymond A. *(Judge, New Jersey Tax Court)* Appointed by governor. Currently serves New Jersey Superior Court Vicinage Seven. Served Vicinage Nine Family Division.

Mailing address: P.O. Box 8068, Trenton 08650.

Office: Mercer County Civil Courts, 175 South Broad Street, Trenton 08608.

Telephone: (609) 989-6166.

HEDGES, Ronald J. *(Magistrate Judge, United States District Court District of New Jersey)* Appointed by U.S. District Court judges to term beginning Feb 18, 1986. Reappointed 1994 and Feb 2002. Current term expires 2010. Born Hackensack New Jersey March 16, 1952. Roman Catholic. Educated at University of Maryland B.A. 1974 and Georgetown University Law Center J.D. 1977. Editor Georgetown Law Journal 1976-77. Law Clerk to Chief Justice Richard J. Hughes, New Jersey Supreme Court 1977-78. Admitted to practice New Jersey 1978. In legal practice Newark 1978-86.

Member New Jersey State Bar Association.

Office: U.S. Courthouse, 50 Walnut Street, Newark 07102.

Telephone: (973) 645-3827.

HEIMLICH, James C. *(Judge, New Jersey Superior Court Vicinage Twelve)* Appointed by governor. Former Designated Judge Special Civil Part.

Office: Union County Courthouse, Two Broad Street, Elizabeth 07207.

Telephone: (908) 659-3697.

HERMAN, Martin A. *(Judge, New Jersey Superior Court Vicinage Fifteen)* Appointed by Governor Thomas H. Kean.

Mailing address: P.O. Box 316, Woodbury 08096.

Office: Gloucester County Justice Center, Woodbury 08096.

Telephone: (856) 853-3516.

HERR, Marilyn Rhyne *(Judge, New Jersey Superior Court Vicinage Thirteen)* Appointed by governor.

Office: Hunterdon County Justice Center, 65 Park Avenue, Flemington 08822.

Telephone: (908) 788-1472.

HIGBEE, Carol E. *(Judge, New Jersey Superior Court Vicinage One)* Appointed by governor.

Office: County Civil Court Building, 1201 Bacharach Boulevard, Atlantic City 08401-4510.

Telephone: (609) 343-2190.

HIMMELBERGER, John G., Jr. *(Judge, New Jersey Superior Court Vicinage One)* Appointed by governor. Former Presiding Judge Civil Division.

Office: County Civil Court Building, 1201 Bacharach Boulevard, Atlantic City 08401-4510.

Telephone: (609) 343-2384.

HOCHBERG, Faith S. *(Judge, United States District Court District of New Jersey)* Appointed for life by President Bill Clinton to term beginning Nov 16, 1999. Born New Jersey 1950. Educated at Tufts University B.A. 1972 and Harvard Law School J.D. 1975. Law Clerk to Hon. Spottswood W. Robinson, III, U.S. Court of Appeals District of Columbia Circuit 1975-76. In legal practice Newark 1977-83 and 1987-90.

Assistant U.S. Attorney 1983-87 and U.S. Attorney 1994-99 District of New Jersey. Senior Deputy Chief Counsel Office of Thrift Supervision 1990-93 and Deputy Assistant Secretary for Law Enforcement 1993-94 U.S. Department of Treasury. Special Assistant to Chairman U.S. Securities and Exchange Commission 1976.

Office: Federal Building & U.S. Courthouse, 50 Walnut Street, Newark 07102.

Telephone: (973) 297-4851.

HOENS, Helen E. *(Judge, New Jersey Superior Court Appellate Division)* Appointed Judge Vicinage Thirteen by Governor Christine T. Whitman to term beginning March 31, 1994. Reappointed 2001. Former Presiding Judge Civil Division. Assigned to Appellate Division by Chief Justice Deborah T. Poritz. Term expires at age seventy. Born Elizabeth New Jersey July 31, 1954. Presbyterian. Educated at College of William & Mary B.A. with high honors 1976 and Georgetown University Law Center J.D. cum laude 1979. Special Project Editor Georgetown Law Journal 1978-79. Law Clerk to Hon. John J. Gibbons, U.S. Court of Appeals Third Circuit 1979-80. Admitted to practice New Jersey 1979, District of Columbia 1979, New York 1981, U.S. District Courts District of New Jersey 1979, District of Columbia 1979 and Southern District of New York 1981 and U.S. Courts of Appeals Second 1983 and Third 1985 Circuits. In legal practice New York 1980-85, Morristown New Jersey 1985-89 and Roseland New Jersey 1989-94.

Co-editor and Co-author Section "Special Education" *Disability Law: A Legal Primer* 1990 ed. and 1992 ed. Important Decisions: In re Adoption of an Adult by C. K. 314 N.J. Super. 604, 1998; Mandell v. Bell Atlantic NYNEX 315 N.J. Super. 273, 1998; FileNet Corp. v. Chubb Corp. 324 N.J. Super 476, 1999; and Sprint Spectrum v. Township of Warren 325 N.J. Super 61 1999. Member Somerset County, New Jersey State and American Bar Associations. Republican.

Office: 1101 North Tower, 158 Headquarters Plaza, Morristown 07960-3965.

Telephone: (973) 631-6359.

HOFFMAN, Ronald E. *(Judge, New Jersey Superior Court Vicinage Fourteen)* Appointed by governor.

Office: 125 Washington Street, Toms River 08753.

Telephone: (732) 288-7820.

HOGAN, Michael J. *(Judge, New Jersey Superior Court Vicinage Three)* Appointed by governor.

Office: Burlington County Court Facility, 49 Rancocas Road, Mount Holly 08060.

Telephone: (609) 518-2707.

HOLLAR-GREGORY, Michelle *(Judge, New Jersey Superior Court Vicinage Five)* Appointed by governor.

Office: 420 Hall of Records, 465 Dr. Martin Luther King Jr. Blvd., Newark 07102.

Telephone: (973) 693-6703, 693-6704.

HOLLENBECK, Harold C. *(Judge, New Jersey Superior Court Vicinage Two)* Appointed by Governor Thomas H. Kean to term beginning 1987. Reappointed by Governor Christine T. Whitman 1994. Term expires at age seventy. Born Passaic New Jersey Dec 29, 1938. Roman Catholic. Educated at Fairleigh Dickinson University B.A. 1961 and University of Virginia J.D. 1964. Admitted to practice New Jersey 1965. In legal practice Bergen County 1964-76 and 1983-87.

Council Member East Rutherford Borough 1967-70. Member State Assembly 1968-72 and State Senate 1971-73 New Jersey and U.S. House of Representatives (New Jersey) 1977-83.

Office: Bergen County Justice Center, 10 Main Street, Hackensack 07601.

Telephone: (201) 646-2754, 646-2755.

HOLSTON, John S., Jr. *(Judge, New Jersey Superior Court Vicinage Fifteen)* Appointed by Governor Thomas H. Kean to term beginning Jan 12, 1984. Reappointed by Governor Jim Florio Jan 12, 1991. Term expires at age seventy. Born Camden New Jersey July 14, 1940. Methodist. Educated at Dickinson College B.A. 1962 and Rutgers University LL.B. 1967. Law Clerk to Hon. William Kramer and Hon. John J. Kitchen, Gloucester County Court 1967-68. Admitted to practice New Jersey 1967, U.S. District Court District of New Jersey 1967, U.S. Court of Appeals Third Circuit 1977 and U.S. Supreme Court 1977. In legal practice Woodbury 1967-84. Former Judge, City of Woodbury, Borough of Swedesboro and Township of Woolwich Municipal Courts.

Former Borough Solicitor Woodbury Heights. Former Solicitor Woodbury Heights Zoning Board. Former City Prosecutor Woodbury. Former member Gloucester County Municipal Court Judges Association (President 1982-83). Member Gloucester County and New Jersey State Bar Associations. Recipient Distinguished Service Award from Woodbury Jaycees 1981. Captain USAR 1962. Former Director Robins Nest, Inc., Vice President and Director Woodbury Jaycees, Director and Solicitor Peoples Building & Loan Association and Director YMCA of Gloucester County (Vice President 1983) and Visiting Homemaker Service of Gloucester County. Former District Supervisor Transfer Inheritance Tax Bureau Gloucester County. Past President Woodbury Old-City Restoration Committee. Former member Executive Committee Greater Woodbury Chamber of Commerce and Advisory Board Carteret Savings & Loan Association. Member Kemble Memorial United Methodist Church Woodbury (Trustee and Chairman 100th Anniversary Committee). Vice President Woodbury Soccer Club. Enjoys sports and coaching youth sports (soccer, basketball and baseball).

Office: Family Court Building, Two South Broad Street, Woodbury 08096.

Telephone: (856) 686-7540.

HONIGFELD, Jared D. *(Judge, New Jersey Superior Court Vicinage Five)* Appointed by governor.

Office: 818 Essex County Courts Building, 50 West Market Street, Newark 07102.

Telephone: (973) 693-5868, 693-5869.

HORNSTINE, Louis F. *(Judge, New Jersey Superior Court Vicinage Four)* Appointed by governor. Served Vicinage One.

Office: 260 Camden County Hall of Justice, 101 South Fifth Street, Camden 08103-4001.

Telephone: (856) 379-2365.

HUGHES, John J. *(Magistrate Judge, United States District Court District of New Jersey)* Appointed by U.S. District Court judges 1991. Reappointed 1999, current term expires 2007. Born Trenton New Jersey April 21, 1946. Educated at Villanova University B.S. 1968 J.D. 1971. In legal practice New Jersey 1972.

Assistant Public Defender New Jersey 1972-75. Federal Public Defender Assistant-in-Charge Trenton and Camden offices New Jersey 1976-91. Former Trustee/ Member Association of Criminal Defense Lawyers of New Jersey. Fellow American Bar Foundation. Master Seton Hall Law School Inn of Court. Member Brehon Law Society, Judicial Conference Committee on Defender Services, Federal Magistrate Judges Association, New Jersey State and American Bar Associations. Lecturer Widener University School of Law, Federal Judicial Center, National Defense Investigator Association, New Jersey Institute for Continuing Legal Education, New Jersey Federal Bar Association, New Jersey Association of Criminal Defense Lawyers, Association of Trial Lawyers, Burlington and Morris Prosecutor Offices, Mercer County Bar Association, New Jersey Department of Law and Public Safety and Legal Services of New Jersey. Recipient Chief Judge Lawrence A. Whipple Memorial Award for excellence and devotion to law from Association of Criminal Defense Lawyers of New Jersey. Director Mobile Meals of Trenton. Trustee Georgian Court College.

Office: 6000 U.S. Courthouse, 402 East State Street, Trenton 08608.

Telephone: (609) 989-2144.

HUMPHREYS, Burrell Ives *(Retired Judge, New Jersey Superior Court)* Appointed Judge Vicinage Eleven by Governor Brendan T. Byrne to term beginning 1980. Served Vicinage Eleven 1980-83. Assignment Judge Vicinage Six 1983-90 and Vicinage Five 1990-94. Appointed to Appellate Division by Chief Justice Robert N. Wilentz 1994. Retired, serves on recall. Born New Jersey May 18, 1927. Unitarian. Educated at Dickinson College B.A. 1950 and Temple University LL.B. 1953. Editor-in-Chief Temple Law Review 1950. Law Clerk to Hon. Richard Hartshorne, U.S. District Court District of New Jersey. Admitted to practice New Jersey 1954, U.S. District Court District of New Jersey 1955, U.S. Court of Appeals Third Circuit 1955 and U.S. Supreme Court 1955. In legal practice Jersey City and Wayne.

Deputy Attorney General 1959-62 and former Special Attorney (escheat cases) New Jersey. County Prosecutor Passaic County 1975-80. Appointed Special Prosecutor by New Jersey Supreme Court to investigate and prosecute obstruction of justice and contempt of court by magistrates, police and other public officials. Member Panel of Hearing Examiners Division of Civil Rights, New Jersey. Former member Editorial Board New Jersey Law Journal. Important Decisions: Friedland v. Podhoretz 174 N.J. Super. Ct. 73 Law Div. 1980; State v. Alexander 184 N.J. Super. Ct. 615 Law Div. 1982; and St. John's Evangelical Lutheran Church v. City of Hoboken 195 N.J. Super. Ct. 414 Law Div. 1983. Former Faculty Member Rutgers University. Former Adjunct Professor Seton Hall University School of Law. Former Chair ad hoc New Jersey Supreme Court Committee on Jury Selection in Criminal Cases. Former Chairperson New Jersey Organized Crime Policy Board. Former Co-chairperson Attorney General and County Prosecutor's Task Force on Organized Crime. Former Member New Jersey Supreme Court Committees on Criminal Practice, Juvenile Practice, Ethics and Character and Fitness, Governor Brendan Byrne's Advisory Committee on Standards and Goals for New Jersey Criminal Justice System, New Jersey Criminal Justice Advisory Committee on Security and Privacy and President John F. Kennedy's Lawyers' Committee for Civil Rights Under Law. Former Chair Conference of New Jersey Assignment Judges and Conference of Presiding Judges of the New Jersey Criminal Division. Fellow American Bar Foundation. Member World Association of Jurists, Essex County, Hudson County, Passaic County (Former Member Bicentennial Committee), New Jersey State (Former Member Board of Trustees, Former Chairperson Creditor-Debtor Rights Section), Federal and American Bar Associations. Former Member Board of Trustees and Lecturer on Reorganization and Creditor-Debtor law New Jersey Institute for Continuing Legal Education. U.S. Army Infantry 1945-46. Board of Trustees Passaic County Legal Aid Society. Active in civic, church and service organizations, especially in fields of civil rights and liberties.

Office: Passaic County Courthouse, 77 Hamilton Street, Paterson 07505.

Telephone: (973) 247-8166.

HURLEY, James P. *(Judge, New Jersey Superior Court Vicinage Eight)* Appointed by governor.

Mailing address: P.O. Box 964, New Brunswick 08903.

Office: Middlesex County Courthouse, One John F. Kennedy Square, New Brunswick 08901.

Telephone: (732) 981-3114.

IADANZA, Eugene A. *(Judge, New Jersey Superior Court Vicinage Nine)* Appointed by governor. Currently serves as Presiding Judge Family Division.

Mailing address: P.O. Box 1266, Freehold 07728-1266.

Office: Monmouth County Courthouse, Monument and Court Streets, Freehold 07728.

Telephone: (732) 294-5938, 294-5939.

INNES, Paul *(Judge, New Jersey Superior Court Vicinage Seven)* Appointed by governor.

Mailing address: P.O. Box 8068, Trenton 08650.

Office: Mercer County Courthouse, 209 South Broad and Market Streets, Trenton 08608.

Telephone: (609) 278-7904.

IRENAS, Joseph E. *(Senior Judge, United States District Court District of New Jersey)* Appointed for life by President George Bush April 13, 1992 to term beginning June 30, 1992. Assumed Senior status July 1, 2002, serves by assignment. Born Newark New Jersey July 13, 1940. Jewish. Educated at Princeton University A.B. 1962, Harvard Law School J.D. cum laude 1965 and New York University School of Law. Law Clerk to Hon. Haydn Proctor, New Jersey Supreme Court 1965-66. Admitted to practice New Jersey 1965, U.S. District Courts District of New Jersey 1965, Eastern 1983 and Southern 1983 Districts of New York, U.S. Court of Appeals Third Circuit 1969, U.S. Supreme Court 1970 and New York 1982. In legal practice Newark 1966-92.

Important Decisions: Clever v. Cherry Hill Board of Education 838 F. Supp. 929, 1993; Bishop v. Okidata 864 F. Supp. 416, 1994; Atlantic Coast v. Board of Chosen Freeholders 931 F. Supp. 341, 1996; and Atlantic Coast v. Board of Chosen Freeholders 1997 WL 780909 Civ.A.No. 93-2669 D.N.J. Dec 18, 1997. Lecturer on Professional Responsibility Article 9, First Amend-

IRENAS, JOSEPH E.—*Continued*

ment, High Technology and the First Amendment Rutgers University School of Law 1985-86 and 1988-97. Vice Chairman Essex County District V-A Ethics Committee Supreme Court of New Jersey 1985-86. Member New Jersey Board of Bar Examiners 1986-88. Fellow Royal Chartered Institute of Arbitrators and American Bar Foundation. Member The American Law Institute, Camden County, New Jersey State and American Bar Associations. Lecturer Institute of Continuing Legal Education, Practising Law Institute, ALI-ABA and New Jersey Bar Association. Recipient Award for Distinguished Service from New Jersey Department of Health 1983. Former Chairman Board of United Hospitals of Newark. Former Member Executive Committee United Hospitals Foundation. Former Member 1988-92 and Treasurer 1990-92 United Way Essex County.

Office: U.S. Courthouse, One John F. Gerry Plaza, 400 Cooper Street, Camden 08102.

Telephone: (856) 757-5223.

ISABELLA, Joseph V. *(Judge, New Jersey Superior Court Vicinage Five)* Appointed by governor.

Office: 1218 Essex County Courts Building, 50 West Market Street, Newark 07102.

Telephone: (973) 693-6753, 693-6754.

ISMAN, James E. *(Judge, New Jersey Tax Court)* Appointed by governor. Currently serves New Jersey Superior Court Vicinage One.

Office: County Criminal Courthouse, 5909 Main Street, Mays Landing 08330.

Telephone: (609) 343-5815.

ISSENMAN, David J. *(Judge, New Jersey Superior Court Vicinage Twelve)* Appointed by governor. Served Vicinage Six.

Office: Union County Courthouse, Two Broad Street, Elizabeth 07027.

Telephone: (908) 659-3433.

IULIANI, Anthony J. *(Retired Judge, New Jersey Superior Court)* Appointed by Governor Thomas H. Kean to term beginning Dec 8, 1983. Reappointed. Served Vicinage Five. Retired, serves on recall. Born Newark New Jersey Nov 24, 1925. Roman Catholic. Educated at Seton Hall University B.S. 1948 J.D. 1954. Admitted to practice New Jersey 1955. In legal practice Newark 1955 to Nov 1980. Judge, New Jersey County Court Essex County Nov 25, 1980 to Dec 7, 1983, appointed by Governor Brendan T. Byrne.

First Assistant Corporation Counsel, Acting Corporation Counsel and Corporation Counsel Newark July 1962 to July 1970. Member Essex County and New Jersey State Bar Associations. Attended The National Judicial College Reno Nevada and New Jersey Judicial College.

Office: 514 Essex County Courts Building, 50 West Market Street, Newark 07102.

Telephone: (973) 693-5704.

JACKSON, James L. *(Judge, New Jersey Superior Court Vicinage One)* Appointed by Governor Christine T. Whitman to term beginning Feb 13, 1998. Term expires Feb 2005.

Office: County Civil Court Building, 1201 Bacharach Boulevard, Atlantic City 08401-4510.

Telephone: (609) 343-2152.

JACOBSON, Mary C. *(Judge, New Jersey Superior Court Vicinage Five)* Appointed by governor.

Office: 416 Hall of Records, 465 Dr. Martin Luther King Jr. Blvd., Newark 07102.

Telephone: (973) 693-6439, 693-6440.

JOHNSON, Harold U., Jr. *(Judge, New Jersey Superior Court Vicinage Fifteen)* Appointed by Governor James E. McGreevey.

Office: Cumberland County Courthouse, West Broad and Fayette Streets, Bridgeton 08302.

Telephone: (856) 453-4664.

KAHN, Roger M. *(Judge, New Jersey Tax Court)* Appointed by governor.

Office: Gibraltar Building, Eighth Floor, 212 Washington Street, Newark 07102.

Telephone: (973) 648-2105.

KANE, Joseph E. *(Judge, New Jersey Superior Court Vicinage One)* Appointed by governor. Also serves as Designated Judge Special Civil Part.

Office: County Civil Court Building, 1201 Bacharach Boulevard, Atlantic City 08401-4510.

Telephone: (609) 343-2191.

KANNEN, Bernard A. *(Retired Judge, New Jersey Superior Court)* Appointed by governor. Served Vicinage Fourteen. Retired, serves on recall.

Office: Ocean County Complex, 100 Washington Street, Toms River 08753.

Telephone: (732) 929-2042.

KAPALKO, Paul A. *(Judge, New Jersey Superior Court Vicinage Nine)* Appointed by governor.

Mailing address: P.O. Box 1266, Freehold 07728-1266.

Office: Monmouth County Courthouse, Monument and Court Streets, Freehold 07728.

Telephone: (732) 677-4128.

KASSEL, Michael *(Judge, New Jersey Superior Court Vicinage Four)* Appointed by governor.

Office: 220 Camden County Hall of Justice, 101 South Fifth Street, Camden 08103-4001.

Telephone: (856) 379-2366.

KELLY, Thomas P. *(Judge, New Jersey Superior Court Vicinage Seven)* Appointed by governor.

Mailing address: P.O. Box 8068, Trenton 08650.

Office: Mercer County Civil Courts, 175 South Broad Street, Trenton 08608.

Telephone: (609) 989-6180.

KENNEDY, James A. *(Judge, New Jersey Superior Court Vicinage Nine)* Appointed by Governor Brendan T. Byrne to term beginning Dec 8, 1981. Reappointed by Governor Thomas H. Kean Dec 1988. Former Presiding Judge Criminal Division.

Mailing address: P.O. Box 1266, Freehold 07728-1266.

Office: Monmouth County Courthouse, Monument and Court Streets, Freehold 07728.

Telephone: (732) 677-4134.

KENNY, Camille M. *(Judge, New Jersey Superior Court Vicinage Six)* Appointed by governor.

Office: Administration Building, 595 Newark Avenue, Jersey City 07306.

Telephone: (201) 795-6640.

KESTIN, Howard H. *(Judge, New Jersey Superior Court Appellate Division)* Appointed Judge Vicinage Eleven by governor. Assigned to Appellate Division by Chief Justice Robert N. Wilentz.

Office: Court Plaza North, Fifth Floor, 25 Main Street, Hackensack 07601-7015.

Telephone: (201) 996-1228.

KIESER, Fred, Jr. *(Judge, New Jersey Superior Court Vicinage Eight)* Appointed by governor. Also serves as Designated Judge Special Civil Part.

Mailing address: P.O. Box 2691, New Brunswick 08903.

Office: Middlesex County Family Court, 120 New Street, New Brunswick 08901.

Telephone: (732) 981-3106.

KIMMELMAN, Irwin I. *(Retired Judge, New Jersey Superior Court)* Appointed Judge Vicinage Five by governor. Served Vicinage Six. Former Presiding Judge General Equity Division. Assigned to Appellate Division by chief justice. Retired, serves on recall.

Office: 710 Essex County Courts Building, 50 West Market Street, Newark 07102.

Telephone: (973) 693-5578.

KING, Michael Patrick *(Judge, New Jersey Superior Court Appellate Division)* Appointed Judge by Governor Brendan T. Byrne to term beginning 1975. Assigned to Appellate Division by Chief Justice Richard J. Hughes 1976. Reappointed by Governor Thomas H. Kean 1983. Term expires at age seventy. Currently serves as Presiding Judge Part B. Born Dec 16, 1934. Educated at Fordham University B.S. 1956, University of Pennsylvania LL.B. cum laude 1959 and University of Virginia LL.M. in Judicial Process 1988. Admitted to practice New Jersey 1960, U.S. District Court District of New Jersey 1960 and U.S. Court of Appeals 1966. Began legal practice Camden 1960. Judge, Camden County District Court 1972-73. Judge, New Jersey County Court Camden County 1973-75.

Office: 216 Haddon Avenue, Suite 700, Westmont 08108-2815.

Telephone: (856) 854-3493.

KLEIN, Harriet Farber *(Judge, New Jersey Superior Court Vicinage Five)* Appointed by Governor Christine T. Whitman to term beginning Aug 18, 1998. Term expires 2005. Born Elizabeth New Jersey April 30, 1948. Educated at Douglass College B.A. with honors 1970 and Rutgers University School of Law at Newark J.D. 1973. Law Clerk to Hon. Irwin I. Kimmelman, New Jersey Superior Court Chancery Division Vicinage Five 1973-74. National Moot Court Team. Member Pi Sigma Alpha and Order of Barristers. Admitted to practice New Jersey 1973 and U.S. District Court District of New Jersey 1973. In legal practice Newark 1974-78 and Woodbridge 1979-98.

Bar Exam Reader 1978-87 and Member 1987-90 New Jersey Board of Bar Examiners. Member Advisory Committee on Bar Admissions New Jersey Supreme Court 1987-90. Member Essex County (Vice Chair 1988-90 and Co-chair 1990-92 Special Committee on the Role of Women in Law Firms, Vice Chair Equity Jurisprudence Committee 1989-90) and New Jersey State Bar Association (Co-chair Committee on Civil and Personal Rights Labor and Employment Law Section 1995-98). Listed in *Who's Who of American Women* since 1984 and *Who's Who in American Law* since 1990. Member Juvenile Conference Committee Maplewood Township 1995-98. Vice President of Band Columbia High School Music Parents Association 1999-2002.

Office: 302A Hall of Records, 465 Dr. Martin Luther King Jr. Blvd., Newark 07102.

Telephone: (973) 693-5814.

E-mail address: Harriet.Klein@judiciary.state.nj.us

KNIGHT, Edward R. *(Magistrate Judge, United States District Court District of New Jersey)* Appointed by U.S. District Court judges to term beginning Dec 1, 1976. Reappointed Dec 1, 1980, Dec 1, 1984, Dec 1, 1988, Dec 1, 1992, Dec 1996 and Dec 2000. Current term expires Nov 30, 2004. Serves part time. Born Milwaukee Wisconsin Oct 5, 1917. Educated at University of Wisconsin B.A. 1940 J.D. 1941 and New York University M.A. 1942 Ph.D. 1943. Admitted to practice Wisconsin 1941, New Jersey 1976 and U.S. District Courts District of New Jersey 1976 and Eastern District of Wisconsin 1976. In legal practice Atlantic City New Jersey since 1976. Judge, Margate City Municipal Court 1977-81.

Member State Bar of Wisconsin and New Jersey State Bar Association. Served to Captain USAAC 1943-45. Headmaster The Oxford Academy 1945-73.

Office: 400 Midtown Building, 1301 Atlantic Avenue, Atlantic City 08401-7212.

Telephone: (609) 348-4515.

KOBLITZ, Ellen L. *(Judge, New Jersey Superior Court Vicinage Two)* Appointed by governor. Currently serves as Presiding Judge Family Division.

Office: Bergen County Justice Center, 10 Main Street, Hackensack 07601.

Telephone: (201) 646-3439, 646-3592.

KOENIG, Paul T., Jr. *(Judge, New Jersey Superior Court Vicinage Seven)* Appointed by governor.

Mailing address: P.O. Box 8068, Trenton 08650.

Office: Mercer County Courthouse, 209 South Broad and Market Streets, Trenton 08608.

Telephone: (609) 989-6204.

KRACOV, Melvin S. *(Judge, New Jersey Superior Court Vicinage Six)* Appointed by governor.

Office: Courthouse, 583 Newark Avenue, Jersey City 07306.

Telephone: (201) 795-6645.

KREIZMAN, Ira E. *(Judge, New Jersey Superior Court Vicinage Nine)* Appointed by governor.

Mailing address: P.O. Box 1266, Freehold 07728-1266.

Office: Monmouth County Courthouse, Monument and Court Streets, Freehold 07728.

Telephone: (732) 677-4137.

KUGLER, Robert B. *(Judge, United States District Court District of New Jersey)* Former Magistrate Judge. Appointed Judge for life by President George W. Bush to term beginning Dec 4, 2002.

Office: U.S. Courthouse, One John F. Gerry Plaza, 400 Cooper Street, Camden 08102.

Telephone: (856) 757-5019.

KUMPF, Fred H. *(Judge, New Jersey Superior Court Vicinage Thirteen)* Appointed by governor.

Mailing address: P.O. Box 3000, Somerville 08876.

KUMPF, FRED H.—*Continued*

Office: Somerset County Courthouse, Somerville 08876.
Telephone: (908) 203-6180.

KUSKIN, Harold A. *(Judge, New Jersey Tax Court)* Appointed by governor.
Office: North Tower, First Floor, 77 Headquarters Plaza, Morristown 07960-3964.
Telephone: (973) 631-6400.

LANDAU, David *(Retired Judge, New Jersey Superior Court Appellate Division)* Appointed Judge Vicinage Five by Governor Brendan T. Byrne to term beginning Sept 6, 1977. Reappointed by Governor Thomas H. Kean Sept 1984. Assigned to Appellate Division by Chief Justice Robert N. Wilentz Sept 1986. Retired, serves on recall. Born Jersey City New Jersey Jan 8, 1930. Educated at Rutgers University 1950 and Harvard University Law School 1953. Admitted to practice District of Columbia 1953 and New Jersey 1956. In legal practice Newark 1962-77.

Deputy Attorney General New Jersey 1957-62. Counsel to New Jersey Insurance Law Revision Commission 1964-70. Member American Inns of Court, The American Law Institute and Essex County Bar Association. Captain USAFR (retired).
Office: 155 Morris Avenue, Springfield 07081.
Telephone: (973) 376-6039, 376-4179.

LANGLOIS, Catherine M. *(Judge, New Jersey Superior Court Vicinage Ten)* Appointed by governor.
Mailing address: P.O. Box 910, Morristown 07963-0910.
Office: Morris County Courthouse, Morristown 07960.
Telephone: (973) 656-3938.

LARIO, Frank M., Jr. *(Judge, New Jersey Superior Court Vicinage Four)* Appointed by Governor Jim Florio to term beginning Feb 23, 1993. Reappointed by Governor Christine T. Whitman Jan 10, 2000. Term expires at age seventy. Served Civil Division 1993-94, Family Division 1994-97 and Criminal Division since 1997. Born Philadelphia Pennsylvania July 1, 1937. Roman Catholic. Educated at Georgetown University A.B. cum laude 1959 and Rutgers University J.D. cum laude 1962. Associate Editor Rutgers Law Review 1961-62. National Moot Court Team 1961-62. Law Clerk to Hon. Vincent Haneman, Supreme Court of New Jersey 1962-63. Admitted to practice New Jersey 1962, U.S. District Court District of New Jersey 1963, U.S. Supreme Court 1969 and U.S. Court of Appeals Third Circuit 1978. In legal practice New Jersey 1993-96. Judge, Borough of Magnolia Municipal Court 1969-93, Borough of Audubon Park Municipal Court 1970-93, Borough of Woodlynne Municipal Court 1971-76 and Borough of Bellmawr Municipal Court 1976-93.

Member Character and Fitness Committee 1964-72, Committee on Municipal Courts 1980-92 and Committee on Character District IV 1983-92 Supreme Court of New Jersey. Secretary 1975-76 and President 1976-77 Camden County Municipal Judges Conference. Member Camden County (Chairman Blue Cross-Blue Shield Committee 1965-76, Immigration and Naturalization Committee 1974-83, Long Range Planning Committee 1976-78 and Attorney Arbitration Committee 1991-92; Board of Managers 1973-76; Secretary 1980-81, Treasurer 1981-82, Vice President 1982-83, President Elect 1983-84, President 1984-85; Chairman 1985 and Member 1986-90 Nominating Committee; Member Committee on Professionalism 1989-92), New Jersey State (Delegate General Council 1973-92, Chairman Municipal Courts of New Jersey Committee 1978-81), Federal and American Bar Associations. Instructor in Estate Planning 1962-69 and Legal Ethics 1973-78 Institute for Continuing Legal Education. Recipient Peter J. Devine, Jr. Award from Camden County Bar Association 1981 and 1994. Listed in *Who's Who in American Law* 1983-88. Chancellor 1968-69 and Board of Managers since 1970 Rutgers University Law School Alumni Association of South Jersey. Associate Captain Men of Malvern since 1968. Third Degree Member Knights of Columbus. Member Alumni Senate Georgetown University, Vesper Club, Tavistock Country Club and Union League of Philadelphia.
Office: 570 Hall of Justice, 101 South Fifth Street, Camden 08103-4001.
Telephone: (856) 379-2367.

LASKIN, Lee B. *(Judge, New Jersey Superior Court Vicinage Four)* Appointed by Governor Christine T. Whitman to term beginning Sept 23, 1994. Reappointed by Acting Governor Donald T. DiFrancesco 2001. Term expires at age seventy. Born Atlantic City New Jersey June 30, 1936. Jewish. Educated at American University and Rutgers University School of Law LL.B. 1961. Admitted to practice New Jersey 1962, U.S. District Court District of New Jersey 1962, U.S. Court of Appeals Third Circuit 1964 and U.S. Supreme Court 1966. In legal practice Camden, Haddonfield and Cherry Hill.

Assistant City Attorney Camden 1962-64. Assistant U.S. Attorney District of New Jersey 1964-66. Former Attorney Camden County Welfare Board. Former Arbitrator American Arbitration Association. Former Member New Jersey Institute of Municipal Attorneys. Member Camden County, New Jersey State and American Bar Associations. USMCR June 1957 to 1962. Republican. Assemblyman New Jersey 1968-69. Camden County Freeholder 1969-72. Chairman Camden County Republican Organization 1976-77. Senator Sixth Legislative District 1977-91. Member Senate Judiciary Committee 1984-91 and Joint Legislative Committee to oversee the operations of the State Commission on Investigation 1990. Former Scoutmaster Troop 18 Boy Scouts of America. Board of Directors South Camden YMCA, East Camden Lions Club and League of Women Voters. Former Counsel to Garden State Lodge of Brith Sholom.
Office: 120 Camden County Hall of Justice, 101 South Fifth Street, Camden 08103.
Telephone: (856) 225-7007.

LA VECCHIA, Jaynee *(Associate Justice, Supreme Court of New Jersey)* Appointed by Governor Christine T. Whitman to term beginning Feb 1, 2000. Term expires 2007. Born Paterson New Jersey Oct 9, 1954. Educated at Douglass College 1976 and Rutgers University at Newark J.D. 1979.

Former Deputy Attorney General and Director Aug 1, 1984 to Aug. 23, 1998 Division of Law State Department of Law and Public Safety and Commissioner State Department of Banking and Insurance Aug 24, 1998 to Jan 31, 2000. Director and Chief Administrative Law Judge Office of Administrative Law 1989 to July 31, 1994. Fellow American Bar Association. Member New Jersey State Bar Association. Former Assistant Counsel and Former Deputy Chief Counsel to Governor Thomas

LA VECCHIA, JAYNEE—*Continued*

H. Kean. Member Douglass College Alumnae Association.

Office: 158 Headquarters Plaza, North Tower, Suite 1101, Morristown 07960-3965.

Telephone: (973) 631-6379.

LAWSON, Lawrence M. *(Assignment Judge, New Jersey Superior Court Vicinage Nine)* Appointed by governor.

Mailing address: P.O. Box 1266, Freehold 07728-1266.

Office: 301 Monmouth County Courthouse, Monument and Court Streets, Freehold 07728.

Telephone: (732) 667-4100.

LeBLON, Vincent *(Judge, New Jersey Superior Court Vicinage Eight)* Appointed by governor.

Mailing address: P.O. Box 2691, New Brunswick 08903-2691.

Office: Middlesex County Family Court, 120 New Street, New Brunswick 08901.

Telephone: (732) 981-3192.

LE BON, Patricia Richmond *(Judge, New Jersey Superior Court Vicinage Three)* Appointed by governor. Also serves as Designated Judge Special Civil Part.

Office: Burlington County Court Facility, 49 Rancocas Road, Mount Holly 08060.

Telephone: (609) 518-2590.

LEFELT, Steven L. *(Judge, New Jersey Superior Court Appellate Division)* Appointed Judge Vicinage Eight by Governor Jim Florio to term beginning Nov 1, 1991. Reappointed by Governor Christine T. Whitman Nov 1, 1998. Assigned to Appellate Division by Chief Justice Deborah T. Poritz Aug 1, 1999. Term expires at age seventy. Born Bronx New York Nov 6, 1940. Educated at Rutgers University A.B. 1962 J.D. 1965. Editor Rutgers Law Review 1964-65. Admitted to practice New Jersey 1965, U.S. District Court District of New Jersey 1965, U.S. Court of Appeals Third Circuit 1965 and U.S. Supreme Court 1975. Judge Office of Administrative Law 1980-90.

Chief Litigator Prisoners Rights Defense Organization 1973-74. Editor *Collection Practice in New Jersey* 1972, *Aspects of Representing a Petitioner in Workers' Compensation* 1975 and *Try It—A Trial Techniques Monograph* 1976 ICLE. Author "Pretrial Mental Examinations: Compelled Cooperation and the Fifth Amendment" 10 American Criminal L. Rev. 431, 1972; "Toward a New Method of Awarding Compensation Benefits: Solving the Permanent Partial Problem in New Jersey" 28 Rutgers L. Rev. 587, 1975; "Workers' Compensation in New Jersey: A Critique of S802" 104, 425, 1979, "A Search for Agency Expertise in New Jersey" 110, 525, Nov 11, 1982, "Unobjected to Hearsay and the Residuum Rule in Administrative Hearings" July 4, 1985 and "An APA 'Contested Case' May Be No Contest" 129, 347, 1991 New Jersey L. Jour.; and *N.J. Administrative Law and Practice* 37 New Jersey Practice Series. Coauthor "The New Jersey Workmen's Compensation Law Study Commission Report, The Proponent's View" No. 67 New Jersey State B. Jour. Spring Issue, May 1974; "Respondent's Practice Under the New Workers' Compensation Rules" 1 *ICLE News Letter* 11 June 1975; and with Arthur Finkle "Union Representation in State Civil Service Contested Hearings" New Jersey L. Jour. Sept 26, 1985. Important Decision: Abbott v. Burke 119, N.J. 287, 1990. Adjunct Professor 1973-75, Assistant Dean and Director of Admissions 1976-78 and Associate Dean and Director of Admissions 1978-79 Rutgers Law School. Executive Director New Jersey Chapter The Association of Trial Lawyers of America 1971-72. Cochairperson Income Maintenance Commission 1978-80. Former Member Central Panel of Chief Administrative Law Judges. Neutral Bencher Sidney Reitman Employment Law American Inn of Court. Member New Jersey Supreme Court Committee on Model Civil Jury Charges. Member New Brunswick, Middlesex County, New Jersey State (Former Trustee and Second Vice President Criminal Law Section, Former Chairperson Subcommittee to Study Public Defender System, Former Member Committee on Recruitment, Legal Education and Admission to the Bar) and American (Former Member Section of Tort and Insurance Practice, Former Chairperson Subcommittee on State Administrative Practice and Procedures and Committee on State Practice and Procedures National Conference of Administrative Law Judges Judicial Administration Division and Member Section of Administrative Law and Regulatory Practice and Judicial Administration Division) Bar Associations. First Director Skills Training Course 1970-74 and Associate Director 1970-76 New Jersey ICLE. Captain U.S. Army 1965-67. Recipient Bronze Star Medal. Enjoys reading, movies, hiking and photography.

Office: 155 Morris Avenue, Springfield 07081-1216.

Telephone: (973) 921-9181.

LEHRER, Alexander D. *(Judge, New Jersey Superior Court Vicinage Nine)* Appointed by Governor Thomas H. Kean to term beginning May 14, 1984. Reappointed by Governor Jim Florio. Term expires at age seventy. Born Toms River New Jersey Sept 6, 1944. Jewish. Educated at University of Connecticut B.S. 1966 and University of Notre Dame J.D. with honors 1969. Law Clerk to Hon. Merritt Lane, Jr., New Jersey Superior Court Chancery Division 1969-70. Member Phi Epsilon Pi. Admitted to practice U.S. District Court 1969, New Jersey 1970, U.S. Court of Appeals 1971 and U.S. Supreme Court 1979. In legal practice Asbury Park 1970-78.

County Prosecutor 1978-83 and Assistant County Counsel 1984 Monmouth County. Special Counsel and Special Prosecutor Monmouth County. Instructor Monmouth County Police Academy 1978-83 and Brookdale Community College 1982-83. Member Monmouth County Criminal Justice Coordinating Council, Provost Marshals Guild, Monmouth County Crime Prevention Officers Association, Monmouth County Juvenile Officers Association, Monmouth County Police Chiefs Association, New Jersey Narcotic Enforcement Officers Association, International Police Chiefs Association, International Society of Law Enforcement and Criminal Justice Instructors, New Jersey County Prosecutors Association (Former Chairman Legislative Committee, State Director to National District Attorneys Association), New Jersey Trial Lawyers Association, Monmouth County Court Clerks Association, American Judicature Society, Monmouth County Legal Aid Society (Trustee 1976-79), Monmouth Bar Foundation (Trustee), Monmouth (Trustee 1977-81), New Jersey State, Federal and American Bar Associations. Faculty National College of District Attorneys Houston Texas 1979-80. Listed in *Who's Who in American Law Enforcement* 1980. During tenure as Monmouth County Prosecutor 1978-83 received awards

LEHRER, ALEXANDER D.—*Continued*
from Jewish War Veterans of the United States of America, Fort Monmouth Chapter Association of the United States of America, Long Branch Aerie Fraternal Order of Eagles, Monmouth County Police Chiefs Association, Monmouth County Firemen's Association, Middletown Jaycees, Provost Marshal Guild Fort Monmouth, Monmouth County Board of Chosen Freeholders, National Association of Counties, City of Asbury Park, City of Long Branch, Monmouth County Board of Health, New Jersey State Department of Education, New Jersey State Parole Board, Monmouth County Crime Prevention Officers Association, Monmouth County Fire Marshal, County Traffic Safety Officers Association, Monmouth County Juvenile Officers Association, Allenhurst Police Department, Association of the United States Army, Monmouth County Drunk Driving Task Force, Monmouth County Police Academy, New Jersey Office of Highway Safety, Monmouth County Municipal Judges Association, Drug Enforcement Administration of the United States and New Jersey Narcotic Enforcement Officers Association. Captain New Jersey National Guard 1969-79. Democrat. Former Advisory Board member Chelsea School Long Branch and Women's Resource and Survival Center Keyport. Advisory Board member Brookdale Community College Lincroft. Member Monmouth County Board of Drug Abuse Services since 1976. Trustee Monmouth County Chapter Boy Scouts of America National Council on Alcoholism. Active participant March of Dimes Crusade in Monmouth County.

Mailing address: P.O. Box 1266, Freehold 07728-1266.

Office: Monmouth County Courthouse, Monument and Court Streets, Freehold 07728.

Telephone: (732) 677-4140.

LENOX, Samuel D., Jr. *(Retired Judge, New Jersey Superior Court)* Appointed by governor. Served Vicinage Seven. Former Assignment Judge. Retired, serves on recall.

Mailing address: ISP, P.O. Box 987, Trenton 08625.

Telephone: (609) 984-0076.

LESTER, Betty Joan *(Judge, New Jersey Superior Court Vicinage Five)* Appointed by Governor Thomas H. Kean to term beginning March 1985. Reappointed by Governor Jim Florio 1992. Term expires at age seventy. Presiding Judge Criminal Division Sept 1996 to July 1, 1999. Born Bristol Pennsylvania Oct 14, 1945. Baptist. Educated at Howard University B.A. 1968 and Rutgers University Law School J.D. 1971. Awarded honorary LL.D. Marymount Manhattan College 1983. Admitted to practice New Jersey 1972. Judge 1977-80, Acting Court Administrator 1979 and Presiding Judge 1980-85, Newark Municipal Court.

Former Trial Attorney State Public Defender's Office. Member Committee to Study New Jersey Bar Admissions, Committee on Municipal Courts, Task Force on Women in the Courts, Task Force on Municipal Court Improvement and Task Force on Minority Concerns (Chair Essex Vicinage Committee on Minority Concerns) Supreme Court of New Jersey. Commissioner Commission on Accreditation of Law Enforcement Agencies. Member Essex County Municipal Court Judges Association, National Association of Women Judges, Essex County and New Jersey State Bar Associations. Recipient Special Achievement Award from National Association of Negro Business and Professional Women's Club 1977, Outstanding Attorney Award from Association of Black Women Lawyers 1980 and Mary Philbrook Award from Rutgers University Law School 1986. Listed in *Who's Who in American Law* 1985, *Who's Who Among Black Americans* 1985 and *World Who's Who of Women* 1986. Named Woman of the Year by Zonta Club International 1986. Member Coalition of 100 Black Women.

Office: 1206 Essex County Courts Building, 50 West Market Street, Newark 07102.

Telephone: (973) 623-5872, 623-5873.

LEVY, Kenneth S. *(Judge, New Jersey Superior Court Vicinage Five)* Appointed by governor.

Office: Gibraltar Building, Eighth Floor, 212 Washington Street, Newark 07102.

Telephone: (973) 648-3585.

LEVY, Paul Gans *(Retired Judge, New Jersey Superior Court Appellate Division)* Appointed Judge Vicinage Seven by Governor Brendan T. Byrne to term beginning Oct 6, 1978. Former Presiding Judge General Equity Division. Reappointed by governor. Assigned to Appellate Division by Chief Justice Robert N. Wilentz. Retired, serves on recall. Born New York New York Oct 6, 1936. Jewish. Educated at Princeton University A.B. 1958 and University of Pennsylvania LL.B. 1961. Law Clerk to Hon. Nathan L. Jacobs, New Jersey Supreme Court 1961-62. Admitted to practice New Jersey 1962. Began legal practice Trenton 1962. Judge, Lawrence Township Municipal Court 1972-73.

Deputy Attorney General 1962-64. Assistant Attorney General 1975-76 and First Assistant Attorney General 1977-78 New Jersey. Member New Jersey State Bar Association. Enjoys computers and golf.

Mailing address: P.O. Box 977, Trenton 08625-0977.

Office: Hughes Justice Complex, Trenton 08625.

Telephone: (609) 292-7572.

LEWINN, Laura *(Judge, New Jersey Superior Court Vicinage Seven)* Appointed by governor.

Mailing address: P.O. Box 8068, Trengton 08650.

Office: Mercer County Civil Courts, 175 South Broad Street, Trenton 08608.

Telephone: (609) 989-6060.

LIFLAND, John C. *(Senior Judge, United States District Court District of New Jersey)* Appointed for life by President Ronald Reagan. Assumed Senior status June 15, 2001, serves by assignment. Born Jersey City New Jersey July 13, 1933. Educated at Yale University A.B. 1954 and Harvard Law School LL.B. 1957. Law Clerk to Hon. T. F. Meaney, U.S. District Court District of New Jersey 1959-61. Admitted to practice New Jersey 1957 and New York 1960. In legal practice Newark New Jersey 1961-88.

Office: U.S. Courthouse, 50 Walnut Street, Newark 07102.

Telephone: (973) 645-3167.

LIHOTZ, Marie E. *(Judge, New Jersey Tax Court)* Appointed by governor. Currently serves as Presiding Judge New Jersey Superior Court Vicinage Three Family Division.

Office: Burlington County Court Facility, 49 Rancocas Road, Mount Holly 08060.

Telephone: (609) 518-2884.

LINARES, Jose L. *(Judge, United States District Court District of New Jersey)* Appointed for life by President George W. Bush to term beginning 2002. Born Havan Cuba 1953. Educated at Jersey City State University B.A. 1975 and Temple University School of Law J.D. 1978. In legal practice New Jersey 1980-2000. Judge, New Jersey Superior Court Vicinage Five 2000-02, appointed by Governor Christine T. Whitman.

Office: U.S. Courthouse, 50 Walnut Street, Newark 07102.

Telephone: (973) 645-6042.

LINTNER, Jack L. *(Judge, New Jersey Superior Court Appellate Division)* Appointed Judge Vicinage Eight by governor. Former Presiding Judge General Equity Division. Assigned to Appellate Division by Chief Justice Deborah T. Poritz.

Office: North Tower Suite 1101, 158 Headquarters Plaza, Morristown 07960-3965.

Telephone: (973) 631-6297, 631-6298.

LIPTON, Lois *(Judge, New Jersey Superior Court Vicinage Two)* Appointed by governor.

Office: Bergen County Justice Center, 10 Main Street, Hackensack 07601.

Telephone: (201) 752-4182.

LISA, Joseph F. *(Judge, New Jersey Superior Court Appellate Division)* Appointed Judge Vicinage Fifteen by governor. Former Presiding Judge Criminal Division. Assigned to Appellate Division by Chief Justice Deborah T. Poritz.

Office: 216 Haddon Avenue, Suite 700, Westmont 08108-2815.

Telephone: (856) 854-8581, 854-8583.

LISBOA, Severiano, III *(Judge, New Jersey Superior Court Vicinage Six)* Appointed by governor.

Office: Administration Building, 595 Newark Avenue, Jersey City 07306.

Telephone: (201) 795-6627, 795-6628.

LITTLE, Charles A. *(Judge, New Jersey Superior Court Vicinage Four)* Appointed by governor. Born Medford New Jersey 1937. Educated at Guilford College B.A. 1961 and Wake Forest College School of Law LL.B. 1964. Member Phi Delta Phi. Admitted to practice New Jersey 1965, U.S. District Court District of New Jersey 1965 and U.S. Supreme Court 1969.

National Panel of Arbitrators American Arbitration Association since 1971. Member New Jersey Defense Association (Supreme Court Committee on Superior Court Special Civil Part Rules 1984-88), Compensation Association of New Jersey State, The Association of Trial Lawyers of America (Medical Malpractice Panel 1983), Camden County and New Jersey State Bar Associations.

Office: 430 Camden County Hall of Justice, 101 South Fifth Street, Camden 08103-4001.

Telephone: (856) 379-2369.

LOCASCIO, Louis F. *(Judge, New Jersey Superior Court Vicinage Nine)* Appointed by governor.

Mailing address: P.O. Box 1266, Freehold 07728-1266.

Office: Monmouth County Courthouse, Monument and Court Streets, Freehold 07728.

Telephone: (732) 677-4142.

LOMBARDI, Sebastian P. *(Judge, New Jersey Superior Court Vicinage Five)* Appointed by governor.

Office: 1116 Essex County Courts Building, 50 West Market Street, Newark 07102.

Telephone: (973) 693-5818, 693-5819.

LONG, Virginia A. *(Associate Justice, Supreme Court of New Jersey)* Appointed by governor. Educated at Dunbarton College of the Holy Cross and Rutgers University. Captain Appellate Moot Court Team. Judge, New Jersey Superior Court Vicinage Twelve 1978-84, appointed by Governor Brendan T. Byrne. Judge and Presiding Judge, New Jersey Superior Court Appellate Division 1984-99.

Deputy Attorney General. Commissioner State Department of Banking.

Mailing address: P.O. Box 979, Trenton 08625-0979.

Office: Hughes Justice Complex, Trenton 08625.

Telephone: (609) 292-8090.

LONGHI, Robert A. *(Assignment Judge, New Jersey Superior Court Vicinage Eight)* Assumed office as Judge Law Division Dec 7, 1978. Served Civil Division from Dec 1983. Assignment Judge since May 1, 1994. Educated at University of Vermont B.A. 1958 and Syracuse University College of Law LL.B. 1961. Admitted to practice New Jersey 1962. Began legal practice New Brunswick. In legal practice New Jersey 1964-73. Judge, Middlesex County District Court July 6, 1973 to 1975, appointed by Governor William Thomas Cahill. Judge, New Jersey County Court Middlesex County 1976-78.

Attorney South Brunswick Board of Adjustment 1965-67 and South Brunswick Planning Board 1968-73. Prosecutor Borough of South River 1966-68 and 1973. Fellow American Bar Foundation. Member Middlesex County (Secretary Ethics Committee 1970-73) and American Bar Associations. U.S. Army 3/40th Armor Division 1962-64. Member Election Board Middlesex County 1972-73. Enjoys traveling, reading and playing golf.

Mailing address: P.O. Box 964, New Brunswick 08903-0964.

Office: Middlesex County Courthouse, One John F. Kennedy Square, New Brunswick 08901.

Telephone: (732) 981-3081.

LYONS, Raymond T. *(Judge, United States Bankruptcy Court District of New Jersey)* Appointed by U.S. Court of Appeals Third Circuit judges to term beginning April 13, 1999. Term expires April 2013.

Office: U.S. Courthouse, Second Floor, 402 East State Street, Trenton 08608.

Telephone: (609) 656-2565.

LYONS, Thomas N. *(Judge, New Jersey Superior Court Vicinage Twelve)* Appointed by governor.

Office: Union County Courthouse, Two Broad Street, Elizabeth 07207.

Telephone: (908) 659-3865.

MacKENZIE, Kenneth C. *(Judge, New Jersey Superior Court Vicinage Ten)* Assumed office Dec 7, 1978. Currently serves as Presiding Judge General Equity Division. Former Judge, New Jersey County Court Morris County.

Mailing address: P.O. Box 910, Morristown 07963-0910.

Office: Morris County Courthouse, Morristown 07960.

Telephone: (973) 656-4061.

MAHON, Roger F. *(Judge, New Jersey Superior Court Vicinage Thirteen)* Appointed by governor. Currently serves as Presiding Judge General Equity Division and Acting Assignment Judge.
Office: Hunterdon County Justice Center, 65 Park Avenue, Flemington 08822.
Telephone: (908) 788-1236.

MALONE, John F. *(Judge, New Jersey Superior Court Vicinage Twelve)* Appointed by governor. Currently serves as Presiding Judge Criminal Division.
Office: Union County Courthouse, Two Broad Street, Elizabeth 07207.
Telephone: (908) 659-3452.

MANNION, Thomas B. *(Retired Judge, New Jersey Superior Court)* Appointed by Governor Thomas H. Kean to term beginning Jan 29, 1986. Reappointed by Governor Jim Florio 1993. Served Vicinage Eight. Retired, serves on recall. Born Ireland Dec 29, 1925. Roman Catholic. Educated at Rutgers University B.A. 1950 LL.B. 1952. Admitted to practice New Jersey 1952 and District of Columbia 1952. Began legal practice New Brunswick.
Member Middlesex County Trial Lawyers Association, New Jersey Trial Attorneys Association, New Jersey Defense Association, New Brunswick, Middlesex County, New Jersey State and American Bar Associations. Corporal U.S. Army Infantry 1943-46.
Mailing address: P.O. Box 964, New Brunswick 08903.
Office: Middlesex County Courthouse, One John F. Kennedy Square, New Brunswick 08901.
Telephone: (732) 981-3170.

MANTINEO, Maureen B. *(Judge, New Jersey Superior Court Vicinage Six)* Appointed by Governor James E. McGreevey.
Office: Administration Building, 595 Newark Avenue, Jersey City 07306.
Telephone: (201) 795-6622, 795-6623.

MARGULIES, Seymour *(Retired Judge, New Jersey Superior Court)* Appointed by governor. Served Vicinage Six. Retired, serves on recall.
Office: Courthouse, 583 Newark Avenue, Jersey City 07306.
Telephone: (201) 795-6650, 795-6651.

MARMO, Ronald G. *(Judge, New Jersey Superior Court Vicinage Eleven)* Appointed by governor.
Office: Passaic County Courthouse, 77 Hamilton Street, Paterson 07505.
Telephone: (973) 247-8323.

MARSHALL, Walter L., Jr. *(Judge, New Jersey Superior Court Vicinage Fifteen)* Appointed by governor.
Mailing address: P.O. Box 847, Woodbury 08096.
Office: Gloucester County Justice Center, Woodbury 08096.
Telephone: (856) 853-3206.

MARTINI, William J. *(Judge, United States District Court District of New Jersey)* Appointed for life by President George W. Bush to term beginning Nov 20, 2002.
Office: U.S. Courthouse, 50 Walnut Street, Newark 07102.
Telephone: (973) 645-6340.

MARTINOTTI, Brian R. *(Judge, New Jersey Superior Court Vicinage Two)* Appointed by governor.
Office: Bergen County Justice Center, 10 Main Street, Hackensack 07601.
Telephone: (201) 678-6566.

MATHESIUS, Bill H. *(Judge, New Jersey Superior Court Vicinage Seven)* Appointed by governor.
Mailing address: P.O. Box 8068, Trenton 08650.
Office: Mercer County Courthouse, 209 South Broad and Market Streets, Trenton 08608.
Telephone: (609) 989-6643.

MAUTONE, Anthony R. *(Magistrate Judge, United States District Court District of New Jersey)* Appointed by U.S. District Court judges to term beginning Oct 12, 2000. Serves part time.
Office: U.S. Courthouse, 50 Walnut Street, Newark 07102.
Telephone: (973) 736-7755.

MAVEN, Susan F. *(Judge, New Jersey Superior Court Vicinage One)* Appointed by governor.
Office: County Civil Court Building, 1201 Bacharach Boulevard, Atlantic City 08401-4510.
Telephone: (609) 345-6700.

MAYER, Jessica R. *(Judge, New Jersey Superior Court Vicinage Eight)* Appointed by Governor James E. McGreevey.
Mailing address: P.O. Box 964, New Brunswick 08903.
Office: Middlesex County Courthouse, One John F. Kennedy Square, New Brunswick 08901.
Telephone: (732) 981-3086.

McCORMACK, Thomas M. *(Judge, New Jersey Superior Court Vicinage Five)* Appointed by Acting Governor Donald DiFrancesco to term beginning Dec 27, 2001. Term expires 2008. Born Newark New Jersey May 9, 1947. Educated at Kean University B.A. 1969 and Seton Hall University School of Law J.D. 1974. Admitted to practice New Jersey 1974 and New York 1985.
Member The Association of Trial Lawyers of America, Essex County, New Jersey State and American Bar Associations.
Office: 50 West Market Street, Newark 07102.
Telephone: (973) 693-6711.
Fax: (973) 424-2480
E-mail address: Thomas.McCormack-@judiciary.state.nj.us

McCORMICK, Ann Graf *(Judge, New Jersey Superior Court Vicinage Eight)* Appointed by governor.
Mailing address: P.O. Box 964, New Brunswick 08903.
Office: Middlesex County Courthouse, One John F. Kennedy Square, New Brunswick 08901.
Telephone: (732) 981-3105.

McDANIEL, Frederic R. *(Judge, New Jersey Superior Court Vicinage Twelve)* Appointed by Governor James E. McGreevey.
Office: Union County Courthouse, Two Broad Street, Elizabeth 07207.
Telephone: (908) 659-4100.

McDONNELL, Anne *(Judge, New Jersey Superior Court Vicinage Fifteen)* Appointed by governor. Currently serves as Presiding Judge Criminal Division and Act-

MCDONNELL, ANNE—*Continued*

ing Assignment Judge. Former Presiding Judge Civil Division and Designated Judge Special Civil Part.
Mailing address: P.O. Box 797, Woodbury 08096.
Office: Gloucester County Courthouse, Woodbury 08096.
Telephone: (856) 853-3562.

McGANN, James *(Judge, New Jersey Superior Court Vicinage Nine)* Appointed by governor.
Mailing address: P.O. Box 1266, Freehold 07728-1266.
Office: Monmouth County Courthouse, Monument and Court Streets, Freehold 07728.
Telephone: (732) 677-4180.

McGANN, Patrick J., Jr. *(Retired Judge, New Jersey Superior Court)* Appointed by Governor William T. Cahill to term beginning July 17, 1972. Reappointed by Governor Brendan T. Byrne 1979. Former Presiding Judge General Equity Division Vicinage Nine. Retired, serves on recall. Born Teaneck New Jersey May 17, 1927. Roman Catholic. Educated at Fordham University A.B. cum laude 1949 LL.B. 1954 J.D. 1954. Admitted to practice New Jersey 1955. In legal practice Red Bank 1955-68. Judge, New Jersey County Court Monmouth County 1968-72.
Important Decisions: State v. Fisher 112 N.J. Super. 319, 1970; State v. Palandrano 120 N.J. Super. 336, 1972; State v. Shapiro 122 N.J. Super. 409, 1973; In re Lucas 136 N.J. Super. 24, 1975; State v. Sinacore 151 N.J. Super. 106, 1977; State v. Singletary 155 N.J. Super. 505, 1977; Hunter v. Hartford Accident 155 N.J. Super. 16 Law Div. 1978; State v. Singletary 170 N.J. Super. 454 Law Div. 1979; State v. Ott 181 N.J. Super. 559 Law Div. 1981; Oceanport v. Hughes 186 N.J. Super. 109 Law Div. 1982; In re Riker Trust 192 N.J. Super. 225 Law Div. 1983; State v. Tate 194 N.J. Super. 622 Law Div. 1984, aff'd 198 N.J. Super. 285 App. Div. 1984, rev'd 102 N.J. Super. 64, 1986; State v. Decher 196 N.J. Super. 157 Law Div. 1984; Fidelity Union Bank v. Trim 204 N.J. Super. 434 Ch. Div. 1985, rev'd 210 N.J. Super. 476 App. Div. 1986; In re Del Guercio Estate 206 N.J. Super. 159 Law Div. 1985; Whispering Woods at Bamm Hollow v. Twp. of Middletown 220 N.J. Super. 161 Law Div. 1987; East Jersey Savings & Loan Assn. v. Shatto 226 N.J. Super. 473 Ch. Div. 1988; and Spyco, Inc. v. Domenus 226 N.J. Super. 482 Ch. Div. 1988. Member American Judicature Society, Monmouth and New Jersey State Bar Associations. Delegate and Second Vice President New Jersey Constitutional Convention 1966. Teaching member New Jersey Supreme Court Committee on Judicial Seminars since 1972. Member New Jersey Supreme Court Committees on Criminal Practice 1972-86 and Civil Practice since 1986. Chairman Committee on New Jersey Judicial College 1976. Recipient Man of the Year Award from Monmouth-Ocean Chapter New Jersey Conference of Christians and Jews 1971. Petty Officer Third Class USN 1945-46 and First Lieutenant U.S. Army 1951-53. Democrat. State Assembly New Jersey 1964-65. Member Serra Club of Monmouth County.
Office: Monmouth County Hall of Records, One East Main Street Second Floor, Freehold 07728.
Telephone: (732) 431-7135, 431-7136.

McKENZIE, A. Donald *(Retired Judge, New Jersey Superior Court)* Appointed by Governor Brendan T. Byrne to term beginning April 1976. Reappointed by Governor Thomas H. Kean April 1983. Served Vicinage Twelve. Retired, serves on recall. Born Schenectady New York Feb 15, 1924. Educated at Rutgers University B.A. 1945 and Cornell University LL.B. 1948. Awarded honorary LL.D. Cornell University 1969. Listed in *Who's Who in American Colleges and Universities.* Member Phi Beta Kappa. In legal practice Union 1948-70. Presiding Judge, Union County District Court 1970-72. Judge, New Jersey County Court Union County 1972-76.
Assistant Union County Attorney 1964-65. Member Union County (Nominating Committee, Chairman Legislative Committee 1969-70) and New Jersey State (Former delegate from Union County to General Council) Bar Associations. Attended National College of the State Judiciary 1971. Member Union County Ethics and Grievance Committee 1952-55 and 1968-70. Former Trustee Union Historical Society. Member Connecticut Farms Presbyterian Church (Elder).
Office: Union County Courthouse, Two Broad Street, Elizabeth 07207.
Telephone: (908) 659-4154.

McLAUGHLIN, John A. *(Judge, New Jersey Superior Court Vicinage Six)* Appointed by Governor Brendan T. Byrne to term beginning March 20, 1981. Reappointed by Governor Thomas H. Kean 1986. Educated at Seton Hall University B.A. and Seton Hall University School of Law. Admitted to practice New Jersey 1965.
First Assistant Prosecutor Hudson County 1975-81. Trustee Hudson County Bar Foundation. Member Hudson County (President 1979) and New Jersey State Bar Associations. State Assemblyman New Jersey 1966-67.
Office: Administration Building, 595 Newark Avenue, Jersey City 07306.
Telephone: (201) 795-6880, 795-6881.

McMANIMON, F. Patrick *(Judge, New Jersey Superior Court Vicinage Seven)* Appointed by governor. Also serves as Designated Judge Special Civil Part.
Mailing address: P.O. Box 8068, Trenton 08650.
Office: Mercer County Civil Courts, 175 South Broad Street, Trenton 08608.
Telephone: (609) 989-6179.

McMASTER, Jean B. *(Judge, New Jersey Superior Court Vicinage Fifteen)* Appointed by governor.
Office: Gloucester County Courthouse, Two South Broad Street, Woodbury 08096.
Telephone: (856) 686-7580.

McNEILL, John T., III *(Judge, New Jersey Superior Court Vicinage Four)* Appointed by governor.
Office: 370 Camden County Hall of Justice, 101 South Fifth Street, Camden 08103-4001.
Telephone: (856) 379-2371.

McVEIGH, Margaret Mary *(Judge, New Jersey Superior Court Vicinage Eleven)* Appointed by governor.
Office: Passaic County Courthouse, 77 Hamilton Street, Paterson 07505.
Telephone: (973) 247-8168.

MECCA, Daniel P. *(Judge, New Jersey Superior Court Vicinage Two)* Appointed by governor.
Office: Bergen County Justice Center, 10 Main Street, Hackensack 07601.
Telephone: (201) 646-2470, 646-2471.

MEEHAN, William C. *(Judge, New Jersey Superior Court Vicinage Two)* Appointed by Governor Thomas H. Kean to term beginning Jan 21, 1983. Reappointed by Governor Thomas H. Kean 1987. Term expires at age seventy. Currently serves as Presiding Judge Criminal Division. Born Jersey City New Jersey Oct 13, 1937. Roman Catholic. Educated at Boston College 1955-56, St. Peter's College B.S. 1960 and Fordham University LL.B. 1966 replaced by J.D. Recipient American Jurisprudence Award for Excellence 1966. Law Clerk to Hon. Clarkson S. Fisher, New Jersey Superior Court 1966-67. Admitted to practice New Jersey 1966. Certified Civil Trial Attorney New Jersey 1982. In legal practice Asbury Park 1967-68, Bloomfield 1968-69 and Hackensack 1969-83.

Prosecutor Fairview 1971-76, Bergenfield 1980-82 and Closter 1981-82. Special Tax Counsel to Edgewater Board of Health 1970-73, Borough of Edgewater 1972-76 and Edgewater Housing Authority 1973-80. Attorney Oradell Zoning Board of Adjustors and Planning Board 1976-82. Borough Attorney River Edge 1977-83 and Northvale 1981-82. Member Monmouth, Bergen County, New Jersey State and American Bar Associations. Specialist Four U.S. Army 1961-62. Revenue Officer IRS New York City 1960-66. Republican. Former Trustee Pascack Valley Hospital and Riverdell Board of Education. Former Officer and Counsel River Edge Blood Bank. President River Edge Rotary Club and St. Peter the Apostle School Board. Trustee Deaf Advocates. Enjoys golfing and fishing.

Office: Bergen County Justice Center, 10 Main Street, Hackensack 07601.

Telephone: (201) 646-2434, 646-2435.

MELENDEZ, Octavia *(Judge, New Jersey Superior Court Vicinage Four)* Appointed by Governor James E. McGreevey.

Office: 260 Camden County Hall of Justice, 101 South Fifth Street, Camden 08103-4001.

Telephone: (856) 379-2372.

MELLACI, Anthony J., Jr. *(Judge, New Jersey Superior Court Vicinage Nine)* Appointed by governor.

Mailing address: P.O. Box 1266, Freehold 07728-1266.

Office: Monmouth County Courthouse, Monument and Court Streets, Freehold 07728.

Telephone: (732) 677-4148.

MELONI, Louis R. *(Judge, New Jersey Superior Court Vicinage Four)* Appointed by Governor James E. McGreevey.

Office: 440 Camden County Hall of Justice, 101 South Fifth Street, Camden 08103-4001.

Telephone: (856) 379-2373.

MENDEZ, Julio L. *(Judge, New Jersey Superior Court Vicinage Fifteen)* Appointed by Governor James E. McGreevey.

Office: Cumberland County Courthouse, West Broad and Fayette Streets, Bridgeton 08302.

Telephone: (856) 453-4502.

MENYUK, Gail L. *(Judge, New Jersey Tax Court)* Appointed by Governor James E. McGreevey.

Mailing address: P.O. Box 975, Trenton 08625.

Office: Justice Complex, Trenton 08625.

Telephone: (609) 633-7370.

MERKELBACH, Donald W. *(Judge, New Jersey Superior Court Vicinage Five)* Appointed by governor.

Office: 916 Essex County Courts Building, 50 West Market Street, Newark 07102.

Telephone: (973) 693-5875, 693-5876.

MESSANO, Carmen *(Judge, New Jersey Superior Court Vicinage Six)* Appointed by governor.

Office: Administration Building, 595 Newark Avenue, Jersey City 07306.

Telephone: (201) 795-6645, 795-6646.

MESSINA, Joseph C. *(Judge, New Jersey Superior Court Vicinage Eight)* Appointed by Governor Thomas H. Kean to term beginning Feb 1986. Reappointed by Governor Jim Florio 1993. Term expires at age seventy. Currently serves as Presiding Judge General Equity Division. Born New Brunswick New Jersey Feb 24, 1940. Catholic. Educated at Princeton University B.A. 1961 and Yale Law School LL.B. 1964. Admitted to practice New Jersey 1965. In legal practice New Brunswick 1965-86.

Member Middlesex County, New Brunswick (President 1977-78) and New Jersey State Bar Associations.

Mailing address: P.O. Box 964, New Brunswick 08903.

Office: Middlesex County Courthouse, One John F. Kennedy Square, New Brunswick 08901.

Telephone: (732) 981-3117.

MICHELETTI, E. Benn *(Judge, New Jersey Superior Court Vicinage Nine)* Appointed by governor.

Mailing address: P.O. Box 1266, Freehold 07728-1266.

Office: Monmouth County Courthouse, Monument and Court Streets, Freehold 07728.

Telephone: (732) 677-4150.

MIDDLESWORTH, Charles, Jr. *(Judge, New Jersey Superior Court Vicinage One)* Appointed by governor.

Office: County Civil Courthouse, 1201 Bacharach Boulevard, Atlantic City 08401-4510.

Telephone: (609) 343-2356.

MILLARD, E. David *(Judge, New Jersey Superior Court Vicinage Three)* Appointed by governor.

Office: Burlington County Court Facility, 49 Rancocas Road, Mount Holly 08060.

Telephone: (609) 518-2855.

MILLENKY, Robert G. *(Judge, New Jersey Superior Court Vicinage Four)* Appointed by governor.

Office: 120 Camden County Hall of Justice, 101 South Fifth Street, Camden 08103-4001.

Telephone: (856) 379-2374.

MILLER, Elijah L., Jr. *(Judge, New Jersey Superior Court Vicinage Two)* Appointed by governor.

Office: Bergen County Justice Center, 10 Main Street, Hackensack 07601.

Telephone: (201) 646-3581.

MINIMAN, Christine L. *(Judge, New Jersey Superior Court Vicinage Eleven)* Appointed by governor. Served Vicinage Ten. Also serves as Designated Judge Special Civil Part.

Office: Passaic County Courthouse, 77 Hamilton Street, Paterson 07505.

Telephone: (973) 247-8143.

MORGAN, David W. *(Judge, New Jersey Superior Court Vicinage Fifteen)* Appointed by governor.
Mailing address: P.O. Box 666, Woodbury 08096.
Office: Gloucester County Justice Center, Woodbury 08096.
Telephone: (856) 853-3378.

MOSES, Sybil R. *(Assignment Judge, New Jersey Superior Court Vicinage Two)* Appointed by governor. Former Presiding Judge Criminal Division.
Office: Bergen County Justice Center, 10 Main Street, Hackensack 07601.
Telephone: (201) 646-2360.

MOYNIHAN, Scott J. *(Judge, New Jersey Superior Court Vicinage Twelve)* Appointed by Governor Christine T. Whitman to term beginning June 13, 1997. Term expires June 2004.
Office: Union County Courthouse, Two Broad Street, Elizabeth 07207.
Telephone: (908) 659-3685.

MULVIHILL, James F. *(Judge, New Jersey Superior Court Vicinage Eight)* Appointed by governor. Served Vicinage Nine.
Mailing address: P.O. Box 964, New Brunswick 08903.
Office: Middlesex County Courthouse, One John F. Kennedy Square, New Brunswick 08901.
Telephone: (732) 981-3188.

NARDI, Joseph M., Jr. *(Retired Judge, New Jersey Superior Court)* Appointed by Governor Thomas H. Kean to term beginning July 1989. Reappointed by Governor Christine T. Whitman. Presiding Judge Family Part Sept 1997. Served Vicinage Four. Retired, serves on recall. Born Camden New Jersey Jan 18, 1932. Educated at St. Joseph's College B.S. 1953 and Rutgers University School of Law J.D. 1956. Admitted to practice New Jersey 1956. In legal practice Haddonfield 1956-60. Judge Camden Municipal Court 1968-69 and Voorhees Township Municipal Court June 1981 to Jan 1983 and Jan 1988 to July 1989.
Assistant City Attorney 1960-61, First Assistant City Attorney 1961-64 and City Attorney 1964-67 Camden. Assistant Prosecutor Camden County 1967-68. Attorney Site Plan Review Board 1976-77 and Housing Authority 1977-78 Voorhees Township. Vice President League of Municipalities of New Jersey 1973. Member Camden County Ethics Commission 1978-89, Pathfinders Subcommittee on Domestic Violence 1990, Family Violence Committee 1990-91 and Juvenile Drug Offender Subcommittee Pretrial Population Committee 1990-91. Chairman Oversight Committee. President New Jersey Council of Juvenile and Family Court Judges. Member Voluntary Placement Committee, Children in Court ad hoc Committee, Scan Committee, Domestic Violence Working Group Committee and Family Division Practice. Participant Children in Court Seminar May 22-25, 1994 and Financial Statements in the Courtroom Seminar Jun 2-3, 1994 The National Judicial College and National Conference on Juvenile Justice March 19-22, 1995. Recipient Man of the Year Award, Italian-American TV Press Radio Award from Public Relations Association of America, Criminal Justice Alumni Award from St. Joseph's University and Bishop's Medal from the Bishop of the Diocese of Camden 1994. Named Knight of St. Gregory by Pope John Paul II 1995. Mayor City of Camden 1969-73. Member and Vice Chairman Board of Trustees St. Joseph's Preparatory School 1984-90. Former Trustee St. John the Baptist Church. Former Member Volunteer Community Agency Relations Committee. Member Dante Aligheri Lodge #354, DARE Program, Foster Parents Association and Rutgers Mentor Program.
Office: Olde Courthouse, Second Floor, 120 High Street, Burlington 08060.
Telephone: (609) 518-2880.

NATAL, Samuel D. *(Judge, New Jersey Superior Court Vicinage Four)* Appointed by governor.
Office: 570 Camden County Hall of Justice, 101 South Fifth Street, Camden 08103-4001.
Telephone: (856) 379-2375.

NELSON, Mark J. *(Judge, New Jersey Superior Court Vicinage Six)* Appointed by governor.
Office: Administration Building, 595 Newark Avenue, Jersey City 07306.
Telephone: (201) 795-6172.

NELSON, Michael J. *(Judge, New Jersey Superior Court Vicinage Five)* Appointed by governor.
Office: 1218 Essex County Courts Building, 50 West Market Street, Newark 07102.
Telephone: (973) 693-6794, 693-6795.

NEUSTADTER, Robert *(Retired Judge, New Jersey Superior Court)* Assumed office Dec 7, 1978. Reappointed by Governor Brendan T. Byrne March 9, 1979. Served Vicinage One. Retired, serves on recall. Born Atlantic City New Jersey Dec 17, 1930. Jewish. Educated at University of Pennsylvania B.S. in Economics 1953 J.D. 1956. Admitted to practice New Jersey 1957 and U.S. Supreme Court 1966. Began legal practice Atlantic City 1957. Magistrate, U.S. District Court District of New Jersey 1967-76. Judge, New Jersey County Court Atlantic County Oct 12, 1976 to Dec 7, 1978.
Member Atlantic County (President 1975-76), New Jersey State, Federal and American Bar Associations. Democrat. Board of Governors Atlantic City Medical Center. Private pilot.
Office: Atlantic County Criminal Courthouse, 5909 Main Street, Mays Landing 08330.
Telephone: (609) 645-5815.

NEWMAN, Richard *(Judge, New Jersey Superior Court Appellate Division)* Appointed Judge Vicinage Five by Governor Brendan T. Byrne to term beginning Nov 24, 1980. Assigned to Appellate Division by Chief Justice Robert N. Wilentz 1994. Educated at Yale College B.A. 1957 and Columbia University School of Law J.D. 1961. Admitted to practice New Jersey 1962.
Office: 155 Morris Avenue, Springfield 07081-1216.
Telephone: (973) 564-9777.

NICOLA, George J. *(Retired Judge, New Jersey Superior Court)* Appointed by governor. Served Vicinage Eight. Former Acting Assignment Judge. Retired, serves on recall. Former Judge, Middlesex County Juvenile and Domestic Relations Court.
Mailing address: P.O. Box 964, New Brunswick 08903.
Office: Middlesex County Courthouse, One John F. Kennedy Square, New Brunswick 08901.
Telephone: (732) 981-3094.

NIEVES, Dennis V. *(Judge, New Jersey Superior Court Vicinage Eight)* Appointed by Governor James E. McGreevey.
Office: Middlesex County Family Courthouse, 120 New Street, New Brunswick 08903.
Telephone: (732) 981-3043.

NUGENT, William E. *(Judge, New Jersey Superior Court Vicinage One)* Appointed by Governor James E. McGreevey.
Office: County Civil Court Building, 1201 Bacharach Boulevard, Atlantic City 08401-4510.
Telephone: (609) 343-2394.

O'BRIEN, Thomas E. *(Judge, New Jersey Superior Court Vicinage Fourteen)* Appointed by governor.
Office: 118 Washington Street, Toms River 08753.
Telephone: (732) 506-5199.

O'BRIEN, Thomas S. *(Retired Judge, New Jersey Superior Court Appellate Division)* Appointed Judge Vicinage Six by Governor William Cahill to term beginning 1972. Served as Assignment Judge 1975-83. Assigned to Appellate Division by Chief Justice Robert N. Wilentz. Retired, serves on recall. Born Yorklyn Delaware April 4, 1923. Educated at University of Notre Dame and Villanova University LL.B. 1949. Admitted to practice New Jersey 1950. In legal practice Ridgewood 1951-65. Judge, Bergen County District Court 1965-67. Judge, New Jersey County Court Bergen County 1967-72.
Assistant Prosecutor Bergen County 1956-60. Borough Attorney 1961-64 and Sewer Attorney 1964-65 Paramus. Attorney Ramsey Planning Board 1963. Member Bergen County Bar Association. USAAC ETO 1943-45. Recipient Distinguished Flying Cross Air Medal with oak leaf clusters.
Office: Bergen County Courthouse, 10 Main Street, Hackensack 07601.
Telephone: (201) 646-3670.

O'CONNOR, Amy *(Judge, New Jersey Superior Court Vicinage Thirteen)* Appointed by governor.
Office: Warren County Courthouse, 413 Second Street, Belvidere 07823.
Telephone: (908) 475-6196.

O'CONNOR, Edward T., Jr. *(Judge, New Jersey Superior Court Vicinage Six)* Appointed by governor.
Office: Administration Building, 595 Newark Avenue, Jersey City 07306.
Telephone: (201) 795-6630.

O'HAGAN, Robert W. *(Judge, New Jersey Superior Court Vicinage Nine)* Appointed by governor.
Mailing address: P.O. Box 1266, Freehold 07728-1266.
Office: Monmouth County Courthouse, Monument and Court Streets, Freehold 07728.
Telephone: (732) 677-4153.

O'HALLORAN, Kevin M. *(Retired Judge, New Jersey Superior Court)* Appointed by governor. Served Vicinage Two. Retired, serves on recall. Former Judge, Bergen County District Court.
Office: Bergen County Justice Center, 10 Main Street, Hackensack 07601-7015.
Telephone: (201) 646-2800.

OLES, Edward M. *(Judge, New Jersey Superior Court Vicinage Fourteen)* Appointed by governor.
Office: Ocean County Courthouse, 100 Hooper Avenue, Toms River 08753.
Telephone: (732) 506-5015.

OLIVIERI, Thomas P. *(Judge, New Jersey Superior Court Vicinage Six)* Appointed by governor.
Office: Courthouse, 583 Newark Avenue, Jersey City 07306.
Telephone: (201) 795-6652.

ORLANDO, Francis J., Jr. *(Assignment Judge, New Jersey Superior Court Vicinage Four)* Appointed by governor.
Office: 670 Camden County Hall of Justice, 101 South Fifth Street, Camden 08103-4001.
Telephone: (856) 379-2355.

ORLOFSKY, Stephen M. *(Judge, United States District Court District of New Jersey)* Appointed for life by President Bill Clinton to term beginning 1995. Born Bronx New York June 24, 1944. Educated at City College of the City University of New York B.A. 1965 and Rutgers University J.D. 1974. Law Clerk to Hon. Mitchell H. Cohen, U.S. District Court District of New Jersey 1974-76. In legal practice Cherry Hill 1980-95. Magistrate, U.S. District Court District of New Jersey 1976-80.
Office: U.S. Courthouse, One John F. Gerry Plaza, 400 Cooper Street, Camden 08102.
Telephone: (856) 757-5020.

O'SHAUGHNESSY, John A. *(Judge, New Jersey Superior Court Vicinage Six)* Appointed by governor.
Office: Administration Building, 595 Newark Avenue, Jersey City 07306.
Telephone: (201) 795-6654.

PAGE, Robert W. *(Judge, New Jersey Superior Court Vicinage Four)* Assumed office Dec 31, 1983. Term expires at age seventy. Former Presiding Judge Family Division. Born Lewisburg Pennsylvania Sept 10, 1935. Educated at Dickinson College A.B. and Rutgers University J.D. Law Clerk to Assignment Judge W. Orvyl Schalick, Camden County 1960. Member Theta Chi. Admitted to practice New Jersey 1960 and U.S. District Court District of New Jersey. Began legal practice Camden 1960. Judge, Workman's Compensation Court Camden 1973. Judge, Camden County Juvenile and Domestic Relations Court Aug 31, 1973 to Dec 30, 1983, appointed by Governor William T. Cahill.
Assistant U.S. Attorney Camden County. Author "Juvenile Justice in New Jersey" *A Manual for Judges* published by Administrative Office of the Courts Feb 1982. Important Opinions: State in the Interest of D.F. (placement when in need of treatment in a psychiatric facility) 138 N.J. Super. 383, 1975; Division of Youth and Family Services v. Huggins (removal of children from foster parents detrimental to emotional well-being) 148 N.J. Super.; State in the Interest of Virginia Doe juvenile (directing state agency DYFS to place juvenile in residential treatment facility to meet her needs) 169 N.J. Super. 585, 1979; In the Matter of Guardianship of DN, CN, EN and AN juvenile (termination of parental rights) 169 N.J. Super. 230, 1979; New Jersey Youth and Family Services v. State in the Interest of M.S. (child abuse and neglect) 185 N.J. Super. 1980; Division of Youth and Family Services v. C.M., In the Case of M.E.D. minors

PAGE, ROBERT W.—*Continued*
(children's mental and emotional disabilities related to lack of nurturing and care provided by mother) 181 N.J. Super. 190, 1981; Loughridge v. Loughridge (guidelines and principles for cases involving hidden assets and undisclosed income) Oct 1984; and Glover v. Glover (criteria for determining expenses to be considered in reimbursement of alimony cases) Oct 1984. Chair Conference of Presiding Judges. Member New Jersey Council of Juvenile and Family Court Judges, National Council of Juvenile and Family Court Judges and Camden County Bar Association. Lecturer New Jersey Administrative Office of the Courts and National Council of Juvenile and Family Court Judges 1982-86. Instructor New Jersey Judicial College 1982-86 and National Council Family Law 1985. Democrat. Board of Trustees Trinity Methodist Church. Enjoys tennis and camping.

Office: 220 Camden County Hall of Justice, 101 South Fifth Street, Camden 08103-4001.

Telephone: (856) 379-2376.

PALEY, Phillip Lewis *(Judge, New Jersey Superior Court Vicinage Eight)* Appointed by governor. Served Vicinage Seven.

Mailing address: P.O. Box 964, New Brunswick 08903.

Office: Middlesex County Courthouse, One John F. Kennedy Square, New Brunswick 08901.

Telephone: (732) 981-3201.

PARKER, Lorraine C. *(Judge, New Jersey Superior Court Appellate Division)* Appointed Judge Vicinage Ten by governor. Assigned to Appellate Division by Chief Justice Deborah T. Poritz.

Office: North Tower Suite 1101, 158 Headquarters Plaza, Morristown 07960-3965.

Telephone: (973) 631-6373, 631-6374.

PARRILLO, Anthony J. *(Judge, New Jersey Superior Court Appellate Division)* Appointed Judge Vicinage Seven by governor. Also served Vicinage Four. Former Presiding Judge General Equity Division. Assigned to Appellate Division by Chief Justice Deborah T. Poritz.

Mailing address: P.O. Box 977, Trenton 08650-0977.

Office: Hughes Justice Complex, Trenton 08650.

Telephone: (609) 943-5184, 943-5185.

PARSONS, George W., Jr. *(Judge, New Jersey Superior Court Vicinage Two)* Appointed by governor.

Office: Bergen County Justice Center, 10 Main Street, Hackensack 07601.

Telephone: (201) 646-2321, 646-2444.

PASSERO, Robert J. *(Assignment Judge, New Jersey Superior Court Vicinage Eleven)* Appointed by governor.

Office: 602 Passaic County Courthouse, 77 Hamilton Street, Paterson 07505.

Telephone: (973) 247-8139.

PAYNE, Edith K. *(Judge, New Jersey Superior Court Appellate Division)* Appointed Judge Vicinage Five by Governor Christine T. Whitman to term beginning Jan 6, 1996. Assigned to Appellate Division by Chief Justice Deborah T. Poritz Aug 1, 2002. Reappointed by Governor James E. McGreevey Jan 6, 2003. Educated at Mount Holyoke College B.A. 1964 and Rutgers University J.D. 1976. Board of Editors Rutgers Law Review. Law Clerk to Hon. Herman D. Michels, New Jersey Superior Court Appellate Division 1976-77. Admitted to practice New Jersey, New York, U.S. District Courts District of New Jersey and Southern District of New York and U.S. Courts of Appeals Second and Third Circuits. In legal practice Newark New Jersey.

Author Note 28 Rutgers L. Rev. 1030, 1975, Note 29 Rutgers L. Rev. 637, 1976 and "The Call for Reform" 12 *Journal of Insurance Regulation* 140 Winter 1993. Assistant Editor *The Forum* American Bar Association 1980-82. Board of Editors New Jersey L. Jour. 1989-96. Contributing Author *Environmental Dispute Handbook* Wiley 1991. Contributing Editor *Journal of Insurance Regulation* 1996. Adjunct Lecturer on Law Rutgers University 1985-97. Vice Chair Committee on Publications Section of Tort and Insurance Practice American Bar Association 1981-82. Chair Environmental Law Committee 1988 and Member Committee on Women in Law Firms 1988-91 Essex County Bar Association. Vice Chair 1988-89 and Chair 1989-91 Committee on Bar-Law School Relationships New Jersey State Bar Association. Member District Ethics Committee for Essex County District V-A 1990-96, Committee on Character 1991-96, Civil Practice Committee 1997-98 and since 2002 and Ad Hoc Committee on Bar Admissions 2000-02 Supreme Court of New Jersey. Member Willard Heckel Inn of Court (Vice President 1999-2000). Participant speaking on the admissibility of expert testimony in toxic tort litigation Product Liability and Toxic Tort Committee Seminar New Jersey State Bar Association Annual Meeting 1990, speaking on the admissibility of novel scientific opinions in toxic tort litigation Products Liability Practice for the 1990s Seminars ICLE 1991, speaking on proof of causation in toxic tort litigation Boardwalk Seminar The Association of Trial Lawyers of America 1991, Seminar on proving causation of disease ICLE 1992, "Nationwide Settlements of Toxic Tort Insurance Coverage Litigation" National Conference of Insurance Guaranty Funds Workshop 1993, workshops on insurer insolvency and guaranty association law National Conference of Insurance Guaranty Funds and seminars concerning hazardous waste and insurance claims Northwest Center for Professional Education. Member 1986-96 and Chair 1989-91 Board of Trustees Integrity, Inc. Volunteer Attorney American Civil Liberties Union 1996. Board of Trustees Newark Museum since 1996.

Office: Suite 1101 North Tower, 158 Headquarters Plaza, Morristown 07960-3965.

Telephone: (973) 631-6365, 631-6366.

PEER, Norman J. *(Judge, New Jersey Superior Court Vicinage Nine)* Appointed by Governor Christine T. Whitman to term beginning July 31, 1997. Born Orange New Jersey Sept 9, 1936. Episcopalian. Educated at Villanova University B.A. 1958 and Fordham University School of Law J.D. 1963. Admitted to practice New York 1964, U.S. District Court Southern District of New York 1964 and New Jersey 1965. In legal practice New York New York 1963-88 and Woodbridge New Jersey 1988-97. Judge, Municipal Court Atlantic Highlands March 19, 1972 to Jan 4, 1988.

Author "Private Placements of Securities" New Jersey L. Jour. 1987. Trustee Monmouth Bar Association 1991-92. Member New Jersey Supreme Court Committee on Domestic Violence 1999-2002. Former Member and President 1983 Monmouth Judges Association. Member Advisory Committee Monmouth County Children in Court, New Jersey Council of Juvenile and Family Court Judges, National Council of Juvenile and Family Court Judges, Monmouth County, New Jersey State,

PEER, NORMAN J.—*Continued*
New York State and American (Section of Economics of the Profession) Bar Associations. Attended numerous Conferences and Judicial Conferences on Family Law PCI 1998 and 1999. Lecturer on Corporate Law for Continuing Education for Accountants. Recipient National Endowment for the Humanities Grant from Harvard Legal Studies 1980, CPC Helen Herrmann Community Service Award 1992 and Silver Gull Award Monmouth Ocean Development Council 1997. Lieutenant Commander USNR 1958-70 (active duty 1958-60). Member Villanova University Investment Committee 1977-80. Trustee and Chairman Board of Trustees CPC Behavioral Healthcare, Inc. 1988-97. Vestryman St. George's by-the-River Episcopal Church 1994-96. Advisory Council Summit Bank 1994-97. Member Monmouth Beach Bath and Tennis Club 1978-86, Monmouth County Foster Parent Program since 1981 and Monmouth County Drunk Driving & Death by Auto Task Force 1983-88. Former Member Princeton Club of New York and Monmouth County Domestic Violence Working Group. Member Navesink Men's Hockey Team, Navesink Country Club (Board of Governors 1979-82 and since 2000, Secretary 2002-03), North Shrewsbury Ice Boat and Yacht Club. Ice hockey goalie. Enjoys golf, hockey, tennis, platform tennis, reading and grandchildren.

Mailing address: P.O. Box 1266, Freehold 07728.
Office: 71 Monmouth Park, Freehold 07728.
Telephone: (732) 683-2114.
Fax: (732) 294-5402
E-mail address: judgenpeer@judiciary.state.nj.us

PEIM, Stuart L. *(Judge, New Jersey Superior Court Vicinage Twelve)* Appointed by governor.
Office: Union County Courthouse, Two Broad Street, Elizabeth 07207.
Telephone: (908) 659-3693.

PEREKSTA, Darlene J. *(Judge, New Jersey Superior Court Vicinage Fourteen)* Appointed by governor.
Office: 118 Washington Street, Toms River 08753.
Telephone: (732) 288-7822.

PERFILIO, Joseph P. *(Judge, New Jersey Superior Court Vicinage Twelve)* Appointed by governor. Also serves as Designated Judge Special Civil Part.
Office: Union County Courthouse, Two Broad Street, Elizabeth 07207.
Telephone: (908) 659-3672.

PERRETTI, Serena *(Retired Judge, New Jersey Superior Court)* Appointed by governor. Served Vicinage Five. Retired, serves on recall.
Office: Justice Complex, Ninth Floor, 212 Washington Street, Newark 07102.
Telephone: (973) 693-6803, 693-6804.

PERRI, Jamie S. *(Judge, New Jersey Superior Court Vicinage Nine)* Appointed by governor.
Mailing address: P.O. Box 1266, Freehold 07728-1266.
Office: Monmouth County Courthouse, Monument and Court Streets, Freehold 07728.
Telephone: (732) 677-4160.

PERSKIE, Steven P. *(Judge, New Jersey Superior Court Vicinage One)* Appointed by governor.
Office: County Civil Court Building, 1201 Bacharach Boulevard, Atlantic City 08401-4510.
Telephone: (609) 345-6700.

PESKOE, Florence R. *(Retired Judge, New Jersey Superior Court)* Appointed by governor. Served Vicinage Nine. Retired, serves on recall.
Mailing address: P.O. Box 1266, Freehold 07728-1266.
Office: Monmouth County Courthouse, Monument and Court Streets, Freehold 07728.
Telephone: (732) 431-7090.

PETERSON, John A., Jr. *(Judge, New Jersey Superior Court Vicinage Fourteen)* Appointed by governor.
Office: Ocean County Courthouse, 118 Washington Street, Toms River 08753.
Telephone: (732) 929-2192.

PETRELLA, James J. *(Judge, New Jersey Superior Court Appellate Division)* Appointed Judge Vicinage Two by Governor Brendan T. Byrne to term beginning Feb 25, 1976. Assigned to Appellate Division by chief justice. Term expires at age seventy. Currently serves as Presiding Judge Part C. Born Bayonne New Jersey July 10, 1935. Educated at St. Peter's College A.B. cum laude 1957 and New York University J.D. 1962. Associate Editor New York University Law Review 1962. Admitted to practice New Jersey 1962 and U.S. District Court District of New Jersey 1962. Law Secretary to Chief Justice Joseph Weintraub, New Jersey Supreme Court 1962. Judge, North Arlington Municipal Court 1968-70. Judge, New Jersey County Court Bergen County 1973-76, appointed by Governor William T. Cahill.
Member Bergen County, Essex County and New Jersey State Bar Associations. First Lieutenant USAS 1957-59. Associate Counsel to Governor William Thomas Cahill 1970-73.
Office: Court Plaza North Fifth Floor, 25 Main Street, Hackensack 07601-7015.
Telephone: (201) 996-8005, 996-8006.

PETROLLE, Michael A. *(Judge, New Jersey Superior Court Vicinage Five)* Appointed by governor.
Office: 1006 Essex County Courts Building, 50 West Market Street, Newark 07102.
Telephone: (973) 693-5881.

PISANO, Joel A. *(Judge, United States District Court District of New Jersey)* Magistrate Judge 1991-2000, appointed by U.S. District Court judges. Appointed Judge for life by President Bill Clinton to term beginning Feb 16, 2000. Born Orange New Jersey March 3, 1949. Educated at Lafayette College B.A. 1971 and Seton Hall University J.D. 1974. In legal practice 1978-91.
Assistant Deputy Public Defender New Jersey 1974-78.
Mailing address: P.O. Box 999, Newark 07101.
Office: U.S. Post Office & Courthouse, Federal Square, Newark 07102.
Telephone: (973) 645-3136.

PISANSKY, John *(Judge, New Jersey Superior Court Vicinage Twelve)* Appointed by governor.
Office: Union County Courthouse, Two Broad Street, Elizabeth 07207.
Telephone: (908) 659-4158.

PISCAL, Francis P. *(Judge, New Jersey Superior Court Vicinage Fourteen)* Appointed by Governor Thomas H. Kean to term beginning July 21, 1989. Reappointed by Governor Christine T. Whitman 1996. Term expires at age seventy. Born Jersey City New Jersey Aug 12, 1939. Roman Catholic. Educated at Boston College A.B. cum laude 1961 and St. John's University LL.B. 1964. Admitted to practice New Jersey 1965 and U.S. District Court District of New Jersey 1965. In legal practice Toms River 1967-89. Judge, Pine Beach, Beachwood and Berkeley Inter-Municipal Court 1971-75. Judge, Seaside Heights Municipal Court 1971-75.

Vice Chairman District Ethics Committee 1979-83. Member since 1990 and Chairman since 1998 Committee on Civil Jury Charges Supreme Court of New Jersey. Member New Jersey State and American Bar Associations. Captain U.S. Army 1965-67. Enjoys golfing and reading.

Office: 213 Washington Street, Third Floor, Toms River 08753.

Telephone: (732) 506-5097.

PIZZUTO, Peter D. *(Judge, New Jersey Tax Court)* Appointed by governor.

Office: 125 State Street, Hackensack 07601.

Telephone: (201) 996-8029.

POGARSKY, Alan J. *(Judge, New Jersey Superior Court Vicinage Fourteen)* Appointed by governor. Served Vicinage Seven.

Office: 125 Washington Street, Toms River 08753.

Telephone: (732) 288-7834.

PORITZ, Deborah T. *(Chief Justice, Supreme Court of New Jersey)* Appointed by Governor Christine T. Whitman. Educated at Brooklyn College 1958, Columbia University, Brandeis University and University of Pennsylvania Law School J.D. 1977. Woodrow Wilson Fellow. In legal practice Princeton 1990-94.

Deputy Attorney General 1977-81, Assistant Chief Environmental Protection Section 1981-82, Deputy Attorney General in Charge of Appeals 1982-86, Chief of Banking, Insurance and Public Securities Section Jan 1984 to Jan 1986, Assistant Attorney General and Director Division of Law 1986-89 and Attorney General Jan 1994 to July 1996 (first woman to serve) New Jersey. Chief Counsel to Governor Thomas H. Kean Feb 1989 to Jan 1990.

Mailing address: P.O. Box 023, Trenton 08625.

Office: Hughes Justice Complex, Trenton 08625.

Telephone: (609) 292-2448.

PRESSLER, Sylvia B. *(Presiding Judge for Administration, New Jersey Superior Court Appellate Division)* Appointed Judge by governor. Assigneded to Appellate Division by chief justice. Also serves as Presiding Judge Part E.

Office: Court Plaza North, Fifth Floor, 25 Main Street, Hackensack 07601-7015.

Telephone: (201) 996-8002, 996-8003.

PULLEN, Lorraine *(Judge, New Jersey Superior Court Vicinage Eight)* Appointed by governor. Former Designated Judge Special Civil Part.

Mailing address: P.O. Box 2691, New Brunswick 08903-2691.

Office: Middlesex County Family Court, 120 New Street, New Brunswick 08901.

Telephone: (732) 981-3031.

PURSEL, John H. *(Judge, New Jersey Superior Court Vicinage Thirteen)* Appointed by governor.

Office: Warren County Courthouse, 413 Second Street, Belvidere 07823.

Telephone: (908) 475-6191.

QUINN, Joseph P. *(Judge, New Jersey Superior Court Vicinage Nine)* Appointed by governor.

Mailing address: P.O. Box 1266, Freehold 07728-1266.

Office: Monmouth County Courthouse, Monument and Court Streets, Freehold 07728.

Telephone: (732) 677-4161.

RAFFERTY, James E. *(Judge, New Jersey Superior Court Vicinage Fifteen)* Appointed by governor. Currently serves as Presiding Judge General Equity Division.

Mailing address: P.O. Box 246, Woodbury 08096.

Office: Gloucester County Courthouse, Woodbury 08096.

Telephone: (856) 853-3479.

RAND, Charles M. *(Judge, New Jersey Superior Court Vicinage Four)* Appointed by governor. Currently serves as Presiding Judge Family Division.

Office: 270 Camden County Hall of Justice, 101 South Fifth Street, Camden 08103-4001.

Telephone: (856) 379-2377.

RAND, David B. *(Judge, New Jersey Superior Court Vicinage Ten)* Appointed by governor.

Mailing address: P.O. Box 910, Morristown 07963-0910.

Office: Morris County Courthouse, Morristown 07960.

Telephone: (973) 656-4045.

RAUH, John R. *(Judge, New Jersey Superior Court Vicinage One)* Appointed by Governor James E. McGreevey.

Office: Cape May County Courthouse, Main Street, Cape May Court House 08210.

Telephone: (609) 345-6700.

RAVIN, Michael L. *(Judge, New Jersey Superior Court Vicinage Five)* Appointed by governor.

Office: 816 Essex County Courts Bldg., 50 West Market Street, Newark 07102.

Telephone: (973) 693-6729.

REISNER, Ronald Lee *(Judge, New Jersey Superior Court Vicinage Thirteen)* Appointed by Governor James E. McGreevey to term beginning Dec 21, 2001. Term expires Dec 21, 2008. Born Long Branch New Jersey Oct 8, 1947. Episcopalian. Educated at Wesleyan University B.A. 1969 and Duke University J.D. 1972. Law Clerk to Hon. Clarkson S. Fisher, U.S. District Court District of New Jersey 1972-74. Admitted to practice New Jersey 1972, U.S. District Court District of New Jersey 1972 and U.S. Court of Appeals Third Circuit 1973. In legal practice 1978-2001.

Assistant U.S. Attorney 1974-78. Township Attorney West Windsor Township 1987 and Old Bridge Township 1989-92. Planning Board Attorney Atlantic Highlands 1988-2001 and Marlboro Township 1993-94. Special Counsel Borough of Keansburg July 2000 to Dec 2001. Member Monmouth County, New Jersey State and American Bar Associations. Municipal Republican Chairman Oceanport 1992-2001. Member Monmouth County Republican Finance Committee 1992-2001. Secretary Board of Trustees YMCA Conference Center Silver Bay

REISNER, RONALD LEE—*Continued*

New York 1992-97. Member Trustee Search Committee Brookdale Community College 1996-2001. Enjoys tennis, golf, skiing and working out.
Mailing address: P.O. Box 1266, Freehold 07728-1266.
Office: Monmouth County Courthouse, Monument and Court Streets, Freehold 07728.
Telephone: (732) 677-4164.

REISNER, Susan L. *(Judge, New Jersey Superior Court Vicinage Eleven)* Appointed by governor. Currently serves as Presiding Judge General Equity Division.
Office: Passaic County Courthouse Annex, 63-65 Hamilton Street, Paterson 07505.
Telephone: (973) 247-8155.

RIVA, Joseph J. *(Judge, New Jersey Superior Court Vicinage Eleven)* Appointed by governor.
Office: Passaic County Courthouse, 77 Hamilton Street, Paterson 07505.
Telephone: (973) 247-8151.

RODRÍGUEZ, Ariel A. *(Judge, New Jersey Superior Court Appellate Division)* Appointed Judge Vicinage Six by Governor Thomas H. Kean to term beginning Dec 5, 1985. Reappointed by Governor Jim Florio 1992. Assigned to Appellate Division by Chief Justice Robert N. Wilentz. Born Havana Cuba. Methodist. Educated at Rutgers University B.A. 1970 J.D. 1973. Admitted to practice New Jersey 1973, U.S. District Court District of New Jersey 1973 and U.S. Supreme Court 1977. Certified by the Supreme Court of New Jersey as a Civil Trial Attorney. In legal practice Union City 1976-84.
Assistant Prosecutor Hudson County 1973-76. Senior Trial Counsel Fireman's Fund Insurance Company 1984-85. Author "Equatorial Guinea Constitutional Study" Oceana 1973. Lecturer on Law Hudson County Community College 1976-79. Member North Hudson Lawyers Club, Hudson County, New Jersey State and Cuban-American Bar Associations. Recipient Justice Medallion from Hudson County Bar Association 1986. Enjoys alpine skiing.
Office: W. J. Brennan Courthouse, 583 Newark Avenue, Jersey City 07306.
Telephone: (201) 659-6869, 659-7465.
Fax: (201) 659-0480
E-mail: ariel.rodriguez@judiciary.state.nj.us

RODRIGUEZ, Joseph H. *(Senior Judge, United States District Court District of New Jersey)* Appointed for life by President Ronald Reagan. Assumed Senior status, serves by assignment. Educated at La Salle College A.B. 1955 and Rutgers University Law School LL.B. 1958 replaced by J.D. 1968. Awarded honorary LL.D. St. Peter's College 1972, Rutgers University 1974, Seton Hall University 1976, Montclair State College 1985 and Kean College 1985. Certified Trial Attorney State of New Jersey. In legal practice Camden 1959 to Feb 1982.
Public Advocate/Public Defender New Jersey Feb 1982 to May 1985. Former Associate Editor New Jersey Law Journal. Instructor Rutgers University Law School 1972-82 and since 1993. Chairman State Board of Higher Education 1971-73 and State Commission of Investigation 1974-79. Former member Disciplinary Review Board and Civil Practice Committee New Jersey Supreme Court. Fellow American College of Trial Lawyers and American Bar Association. Judicial Fellow American College of Trial Lawyers. Member Judicial Conference Committee on the Judicial Branch, The American Law Institute, International Society of Barristers, New Jersey State (President 1978-79) and American (House of Delegates 1984-86, Chair National Conference of Federal Trial Judges 1995-96) Bar Associations. Lecturer Professional Trial Lawyers Seminar since 1969. Participant Central and East European Law Initiative American Bar Association Oct 1994. Recipient Trial Bar Award for Distinguished Service in the Cause of Justice from Trial Attorneys of New Jersey 1981, Friend of Hospice Award from Karen Ann Quinlan Center of Hope 1985, Man of the Year Award from National Hispanic Bar Association 1992, Peter J. Devine Award from Camden County Bar Association 1996, Spirit of Edison Award from Thomas Edison State College 1997, Medal of Honor Award from New Jersey State Bar Foundation 1999 and William J. Brennan, Jr. Award from Association of the Federal Bar of the State of New Jersey 1999. Inducted into Rutgers University Hall of Distinguished Alumni 1996. Board of Trustees Temple University 1976-80.
Office: 6060 U.S. Courthouse, One John F. Gerry Plaza, 400 Cooper Street, Camden 08102.
Telephone: (856) 757-5002.

RODRIGUEZ, Mathias E. *(Judge, New Jersey Superior Court Vicinage Eight)* Appointed by governor.
Mailing address: P.O. Box 964, New Brunswick 08903.
Office: Middlesex County Courthouse, One John F. Kennedy Square, New Brunswick 08901.
Telephone: (732) 981-3111.

ROHDE, George F., Jr. *(Judge, New Jersey Superior Court Vicinage Eleven)* Appointed by governor. Also serves as Designated Judge Special Civil Part.
Office: Passaic County Courthouse, 77 Hamilton Street, Paterson 07505.
Telephone: (973) 247-8235.

ROMA, Patrick J. *(Judge, New Jersey Superior Court Vicinage Two)* Appointed by Governor Christine T. Whitman to term beginning Jan 10, 1997. Term expires Jan 2004. Born New York New York July 7, 1949. Educated at Seton Hall University B.A. 1971, Cumberland School of Law J.D. 1975 and New York University LL.M. 1982. Law Clerk to Hon. John J. Cariddi, New Jersey Superior Court Vicinage Two. Admitted to practice New Jersey 1975, Florida 1975, District of Columbia 1976 and New York 1981. In legal practice Hudson and Bergen counties 1976-97.
Prosecutor Palisades Park 1981-89. Borough Attorney Haworth 1990-97 and Leonia 1996-97. Member The Florida Bar, Bergen County and New Jersey State Bar Associations. Attended Juvenile Justice College, Reno Nevada and Judicial College, Teaneck New Jersey. Enjoys fishing, hunting and boating.
Office: Bergen County Justice Center, 10 Main Street, Hackensack 07601.
Telephone: (201) 646-2311, 646-2312.

ROSA, Joseph, Jr. *(Judge, New Jersey Superior Court Vicinage Two)* Appointed by Acting Governor Donald DiFransesco to term beginning Feb 6, 2002. Term expires Feb 6, 2009. Born Hackensack New Jersey July 2, 1947. Roman Catholic. Educated at St. Peter's College B.A. 1969, Montclair State University M.A.

ROSA, JOSEPH, JR.—*Continued*

1972 and Fordham University J.D. 1973. Deans List. Admitted to practice New Jersey 1973, New York 1982, U.S. District Court District of New Jersey 1973 and U.S. Supreme Court 1978. In legal practice Hackensack Jan 1974 to Dec 1974, Newark Nov 1984 to June 1985, Montclair July 1985 to June 1995 and Lyndhurst July 1995. Former Administrative Law Judge, Office of Administrative Law July 1979 to Oct 1984.

Borough Prosecutor Jan 1975 to Sept 1979 and Jan 1976 to Sept 1979. Borough Public Defender Jan 1979 to Sept 1979 and Jan 1986 to Dec 1993. Borough Attorney Borough of Wallington Jan 1987 to 1990 and since Jan 1993. Special Solid Waste Counsel 1996-2000. Author "Landfill Rate Making in New Jersey" II No. 5 *Local Government Law Section Newsletter* New Jersey State Bar Association Feb 1986 and "Executive Agencies: Playing by the Rules" No. 122 *New Jersey Lawyer* Winter Issue Feb 1988. Member Bergen County, New Jersey State and American Bar Associations. Panelist "How to Practice Before the Office of Administrative Law" Legal Education Seminar Bergen County Bar Association March 1, 1986 and March 12, 1994 and "Solid Waste: It's Not Garbage Anymore—It's the Law" April 5, 1988 and "Medical Waste: What Is It? What To Do with It?" April 4, 1989 Public Utility Law Conference New Jersey State Bar Association. High school teacher Sept 1969 to June 1971. Councilman Borough of Wallington 1973-79 and 1985-86. Chairman Wallington United Way Committee 1975-77. Member Wallington Bicentennial Committee 1975-77. Board of Directors Meadowlands YMCA 1976-77. Director Bergen County Mental Health Law Project Aug 1978 to Feb 1979. Member Deborah Heart and Lung Association and Wallington Hillside Social and Athletic Club.

Office: Bergen County Justice Center, 10 Main Street, Hackensack 07601.
Telephone: (201) 752-4041.
Fax: (201) 646-0895
E-mail address: josephrosa@judiciary.state.nj.us

ROSEN, Joel B. *(Magistrate Judge, United States District Court District of New Jersey)* Appointed by U.S. District Court judges.
Office: U.S. Courthouse, One John F. Gerry Plaza, 400 Cooper Street, Camden 08102.
Telephone: (856) 757-5446.

ROSENBERG, David A. *(Judge, New Jersey Superior Court Vicinage Eight)* Appointed by governor.
Mailing address: P.O. Box 964, New Brunswick 08903.
Office: Middlesex County Courthouse, One John F. Kennedy Square, New Brunswick 08901.
Telephone: (732) 981-3032.

ROSS, Graham T. *(Assignment Judge, New Jersey Superior Court Vicinage Thirteen)* Appointed by Governor Thomas H. Kean to term beginning Aug 25, 1986. Reappointed by Governor Jim Florio June 7, 1993. Term expires at age seventy. Former Presiding Judge Family Division. Born Biloxi Mississippi June 29, 1944. Episcopalian. Educated at Gettysburg College B.A. 1966 and Seton Hall University School of Law J.D. 1969. Admitted to practice New Jersey 1969, U.S. District Court District of New Jersey 1969 and U.S. Supreme Court 1978. In legal practice Somerville 1969-86.

Member Somerset County and New Jersey State Bar Associations.
Mailing address: P.O. Box 3000, Somerville 08876.
Office: Somerset County Courthouse, Somerville 08876.
Telephone: (908) 231-7069.

ROTHSCHILD, James S. *(Judge, New Jersey Superior Court Vicinage Five)* Appointed by governor.
Office: 228 Hall of Records, 465 Dr. Martin Luther King Jr. Blvd., Newark 07102.
Telephone: (973) 693-5578.

ROTHSTADT, Garry S. *(Judge, New Jersey Superior Court Vicinage Eleven)* Appointed by governor.
Office: Passaic County Courthouse, 77 Hamilton Street, Paterson 07505.
Telephone: (973) 247-8317.

RUBIN, Stephen B. *(Judge, New Jersey Superior Court Vicinage Thirteen)* Appointed by governor.
Mailing address: P.O. Box 3000, Somerville 08876.
Office: Somerset County Courthouse, Somerville 08876.
Telephone: (908) 203-6160.

RUSSELL, Karen D. *(Judge, New Jersey Superior Court Vicinage Ten)* Appointed by Governor Thomas H. Kean to term beginning Oct 26, 1984. Reappointed by Governor Jim Florio 1991. Term expires at age seventy. Former Presiding Judge Civil Division. Currently serves as Acting Assignment Judge. Born Elizabeth New Jersey Nov 17, 1943. Religious affiliation: Unitarian. Educated at Wellesley College B.A., Boston University School of Law and Rutgers University Law School J.D. 1972. Admitted to practice New Jersey 1972. In legal practice Hackettstown 1977-84.

Supervising Attorney Dover Office Morris County Legal Aid Society 1972-77. Member National Association of Women Judges and Morris County Bar Association. Enjoys gardening, raising cattle and skiing.
Office: Sussex County Judicial Center, 43-47 High Street, Newton 07860.
Telephone: (973) 579-0652.

RUSSELLO, Mark M. *(Judge, New Jersey Superior Court Vicinage Two)* Appointed by governor.
Office: Bergen County Justice Center, 10 Main Street, Hackensack 07601.
Telephone: (201) 646-2440, 646-2441.

RYAN, Edward J. *(Judge, New Jersey Superior Court Vicinage Eight)* Appointed by governor.
Mailing address: P.O. Box 2691, New Brunswick 08903-2691.
Office: Middlesex County Family Court, 120 New Street, New Brunswick 08901.
Telephone: (732) 981-3046.

RYAN, Peter V. *(Judge, New Jersey Superior Court Vicinage Five)* Appointed by governor.
Office: Gibraltar Building, Ninth Floor, 212 Washington Street, Newark 07102.
Telephone: (973) 693-5781, 693-5782.

SABATINO, Jack M. *(Judge, New Jersey Superior Court Vicinage Seven)* Appointed by Acting Governor Donald DiFrancesco to term beginning March 30, 2001. Born Feb 21, 1958. Educated at Yale College B.A.

SABATINO, JACK M.—*Continued*
summa cum laude 1979 and Harvard Law School J.D. cum laude 1982.
Office: 175 South Broad Street, Trenton 08608.
Telephone: (609) 989-6949.

SABBATH, George E. *(Judge, New Jersey Superior Court Vicinage Eleven)* Appointed by Governor Christine T. Whitman to term beginning June 13, 1997. Term expires June 2004.
Office: Passaic County Courthouse, 77 Hamilton Street, Paterson 07505.
Telephone: (973) 247-8159.

SAPP-PETERSON, Paulette *(Judge, New Jersey Superior Court Vicinage Seven)* Appointed by governor. Currently serves as Presiding Judge Civil Division.
Mailing address: P.O. Box 8068, Trenton 08650.
Office: Mercer County Civil Courts, 175 South Broad Street, Trenton 08608.
Telephone: (609) 989-6823.

SCANCARELLA, Joseph F. *(Judge, New Jersey Superior Court Vicinage Eleven)* Appointed by Governor Thomas H. Kean to term beginning Dec 10, 1982. Reappointed. Term expires at age seventy. Presiding Judge Civil Division since July 1996. Born Clifton New Jersey Sept 26, 1938. Roman Catholic. Educated at Villanova University B.A. 1959 and Fordham University J.D. with honors 1962. Admitted to practice New Jersey 1963. Began legal practice Newark 1963. In legal practice Boonton 1964 and Passaic 1964-82.
City Attorney Passaic 1971-77. Attorney Planning Board Little Falls 1976-82. Assistant Counsel Passaic County 1981-82. Member Passaic County, New Jersey State and American Bar Associations. Specialist Five U.S. Army 1962-63. USAR 1963-68. Republican (inactive). General Assembly New Jersey Legislature 1967-72. Delegate to Republican National Presidential Convention 1976. Enjoys spectator and participant sports.
Office: Passaic County Courthouse, 77 Hamilton Street, Paterson 07505.
Telephone: (973) 247-8131.

SCHLOSSER, Marvin E. *(Judge, New Jersey Superior Court Vicinage Three)* Appointed by governor. Currently serves as Presiding Judge Criminal Division.
Office: Burlington County Court Facility, 49 Rancocas Road, Mount Holly 08060.
Telephone: (609) 518-2716.

SCHOTT, Francine A. *(Judge, New Jersey Superior Court Vicinage Five)* Appointed by governor.
Office: 429 Hall of Records, 465 Dr. Martin Luther King Jr. Blvd., Newark 07102.
Telephone: (973) 693-5883, 693-5884.

SCHULTZ, Francis B. *(Judge, New Jersey Superior Court Vicinage Six)* Appointed by governor.
Office: Administration Building, 595 Newark Avenue, Jersey City 07306.
Telephone: (201) 795-6966.

SCHWARTZ, Edward R. *(Judge, New Jersey Superior Court Vicinage Five)* Appointed by Governor Jim Florio to term beginning Jan 24, 1992. Reappointed by Governor Christine T. Whitman Jan 24, 1999. Term expires at age seventy. Born Paterson New Jersey Dec 29, 1934. Jewish. Educated at Williams College A.B. cum laude 1956 and Harvard Law School LL.B. 1959. Admitted to practice District of Columbia 1959, U.S. Courts of Appeals District of Columbia 1960 and Third 1968 Circuits, New Jersey 1963, U.S. District Court District of New Jersey 1963 and U.S. Supreme Court 1976. In legal practice Newark New Jersey 1963-83, Livingston New Jersey 1983-90 and Springfield New Jersey 1990-92.
Important Decisions: R.A. Intile Realty Co. v. Raho 259 N.J. Super. 1992, Leadership Real Estate v. Bernard Harper and Donald Kolpan 271 N.J. Super. 152, 1993 and Christian v. Ormsby 267 N.J. Super. 1993. Member Trial Attorneys of New Jersey, American Judicature Society, Essex County, New Jersey State and American Bar Associations. Attended New Jersey Judicial College Nov 1993 and Nov 1994. USAR JAGC 1960-63. Republican. Chairman Livingston Citizens for Tom Kean for Governor 1977. Enjoys reading, golfing, walking, swimming, watching TV sports and news, theater, movies, visiting art museums and traveling.
Office: 1116 Essex County Courts Building, 50 West Market Street, Newark 07102.
Telephone: (973) 693-6825, 693-6826.

SCULLY, Thomas F. *(Judge, New Jersey Superior Court Vicinage Nine)* Appointed by governor.
Mailing address: P.O. Box 1266, Freehold 07728-1266.
Office: Monmouth County Courthouse, Monument and Court Streets, Freehold 07728.
Telephone: (732) 677-4168.

SEGAL, Vincent D. *(Judge, New Jersey Superior Court Vicinage One)* Appointed by governor. Served Vicinage Four. Currently serves as Presiding Judge Family Division.
Office: County Civil Court Building, 1201 Bacharach Boulevard, Atlantic City 08401-4510.
Telephone: (609) 343-2348.

SELSER, John E. *(Judge, New Jersey Superior Court Vicinage Eleven)* Appointed by governor.
Office: Passaic County Admin. Bldg., 401 Grand Street, Paterson 07505.
Telephone: (973) 247-8587.

SELTZER, George L. *(Judge, New Jersey Superior Court Vicinage One)* Appointed by governor. Former Presiding Judge Family Division. Currently serves as Presiding Judge General Equity Division.
Office: County Civil Court Building, 1201 Bacharach Boulevard, Atlantic City 08401-4510.
Telephone: (609) 343-2307.

SERPENTELLI, Eugene D. *(Assignment Judge, New Jersey Superior Court Vicinage Fourteen)* Appointed by governor.
Office: Ocean County Courthouse, 118 Washington Street, Toms River 08753.
Telephone: (732) 929-2176.

SEYBOLT, Harry K. *(Judge, New Jersey Superior Court Vicinage Thirteen)* Appointed by Governor Christine T. Whitman to term beginning June 27, 1996. Born Dover New Jersey Jan 18, 1934. Educated at Syracuse University A.B. 1956 LL.B. 1961 replaced by J.D. 1974. Law Clerk to Hon. Eldon Mills and Hon. Scott M. Long, Jr., New Jersey County Court Morris County May 1962 to June 1963. Admitted to practice New Jersey 1963, U.S. District Court District of New Jersey 1963 and U.S. Supreme Court 1973. In legal practice Verona

SEYBOLT, HARRY K.—*Continued*

June 1964 to June 1965, Washington June 1965 to April 1970 and June 1973 to June 27, 1996 and Hackettstown April 1970 to July 1974 and April 1, 1996 to June 27, 1996.

Assignment Clerk Morris County Courthouse June 1963 to June 1964. Attorney Washington Borough 1971, Independence Township 1984-87, Belvidere 1992-96 and Mansfield Township Jan 1, 1996 to June 27, 1996. Trustee New Jersey State Bar Foundation 1980-87. Member Unauthorized Practice of Law Committee 1985-96, Committee on Complementary Dispute Resolution since 1996 and Civil/Special Civil Subcommittee since 1996 Supreme Court of New Jersey. Former Member Morris County and American Bar Associations. Member Marie L. Garibaldi Inn of Court, Warren County (Vice President 1979-80, President 1980-81, Immediate Past President 1981-82, Chairman and Member Nominating Committee 1982-90, Board of Trustees 1986-87) and New Jersey State (Trustee 1974-80 and 1987-90, Vice Chairman Land Use Planning and Community Affairs Committee 1980-81, Board of Directors Land Use Law Section 1981-90 and 1993-96, Member Judicial and County Prosecutorial Appointments Committee 1981-87, Trustee Liaison Election Committee 1987-90, Immigration, Naturalization and Americanism Section 1988-90, Construction and Public Contract Law Committee 1988-90 and Prepaid Legal Services Committee 1988-90, Member 1989-94, Chairman of Part B 1989-91 and Vice Chairman 1991-92 By-Laws Committee, Travel and Meetings Arrangement Committee since 1993) Bar Associations. Program Chairman Land Use Committee Annual Meeting New Jersey State Bar Association May 1981 and Program on Legal Fee Financing General Council Meeting New Jersey State Bar Foundation 1981. U.S. Army Sept 1956 to Sept 1958. Member Washington Borough Board of Education 1968-71 and Warren County Economic Development Task Force Oct 1993 to Feb 1994. Member Washington Kiwanis Club (President 1975-76).

Mailing address: P.O. Box 3000, Somerville 08876.
Office: Somerset County Courthouse, Somerville 08876.
Telephone: (908) 231-7075.

SHUSTER, Neil H. *(Judge, New Jersey Superior Court Vicinage Seven)* Appointed by governor. Former Presiding Judge Civil Division. Currently serves as Presiding Judge General Equity Division and Acting Assignment Judge.

Mailing address: P.O. Box 8068, Trenton 08650.
Office: 210 South Broad Street, Trenton 08608.
Telephone: (609) 292-4696.

SHWARTZ, Patty *(Magistrate Judge, United States District Court District of New Jersey)* Appointed by U.S. District Court judges to term beginning March 10, 2003.

Office: U.S. Courthouse, 50 Walnut Street, Newark 07102.
Telephone: (973) 645-6596.

SIMANDLE, Jerome B. *(Judge, United States District Court District of New Jersey)* Magistrate Judge Aug 11, 1983 to May 25, 1992. Appointed Judge for life by President George Bush to term beginning May 26, 1992. Born Binghamton New York April 29, 1949. Educated at Princeton University B.S.E. with high honors 1971, University of Stockholm, Sweden diploma in Social Science 1975 and University of Pennsylvania J.D. 1976. Recipient Rotary International Graduate Fellowship Stockholm Sweden 1974-75 and Edwin R. Keedy Award University of Pennsylvania Law School 1976. Associate Editor 1973-74 and Editor 1975-76 University of Pennsylvania Law Review. Law Clerk to Hon. John F. Gerry, U.S. District Court District of New Jersey 1976-78. Admitted to practice Pennsylvania 1977 and New Jersey 1978.

Assistant U.S. Attorney District of New Jersey 1978-83. Attorney-in-Charge U.S. Attorney's Office Trenton 1982-83. Important Decisions: Ferraro v. General Motors Corp. (class action litigation) 105 F.R.D. 429 D.N.J. 1984; Robbins v. Camden City Board of Education (proportionality of discovery) 105 F.R.D. 49 D.N.J. 1985; Brock v. Gerace (Fifth Amendment privilege) 110 F.R.D. 58 D.N.J. 1986; In re Matter of Extradition of Bertrand (extradition procedures) 1986 Westlaw 8845 D.N.J. 1986; Leased Optical Departments—Montgomery Ward Inc. v. Opti-Center, Inc. (amended pleadings) 120 F.R.D. 476 D.N.J. 1988; Glickman v. Chirlin (lawyer conflict of interest) 1988 Westlaw 65585 D.N.J. 1988; In re First Peoples Bank Shareholders Litigation (attorneys' fee in class action settlement) 121 F.R.D. 219 D.N.J. 1988; Occulto v. Adamar of New Jersey, Inc. (attorney misconduct) 125 F.R.D. 611 D.N.J. 1989; Lukas v. Nasco International, Inc. (Rule 11 sanctions) 128 F.R.D. 619 D.N.J. 1989; Johnston Development Group, Inc. v. Carpenters Local Union No. 1578 (deposition of opposing attorney) 130 F.R.D. 348 D.N.J. 1990; G-69 v. Degnan (protecting governmental privilege) 130 F.R.D. 326 and 339 D.N.J. 1990; Public Service Electric & Gas Co. v. Philadelphia Electric Co. (discovery in complex litigation) 130 F.R.D. 543 D.N.J. 1990; Harrison Beverage Co. v. Dribeck Importers, Inc. (amending pleadings; delay) F.R.D. 1990 Westlaw 211662 D.N.J. 1990; In re Request from L. Kasper-Ansermet, Examining Magistrate for the Republic and Canton of Geneva, etc. (international judicial assistance) 132 F.R.D. 622 D.N.J. 1990; Curley v. Cumberland Farms, Inc. (attorney ethics) F. Supp. D.N.J. 1990, aff'd F. Supp. 1991 Westlaw 7854 D.N.J. 1991; Camden Iron and Metal, Inc. v. Marubeni America Corp. (discovery of foreign documents) 138 F.R.D. 438 D.N.J. 1991; U.S. v. King 781 F. Supp. 315 D.N.J. 1991; Kaselaan & D'Angelo Associates, Inc. v. D'Angelo (attorney disqualification) 144 F.R.D. 235 D.N.J. 1992; Hunter v. Greenwood Trust Co. (federal question jurisdiction, remand) 856 F. Supp. 207 D.N.J. 1992; Resolution Trust Corp. v. DiDomenico (FIRREA negligence claims) 837 F. Supp. 623 D.N.J. 1993; Bryan v. Associated Container Transp. (long-arm jurisdiction) 837 F. Supp. 633 D.N.J. 1993; U.S. v. LiButti (sentencing, departures) 1994 Westlaw 774647 D.N.J. 1994; Hakimoglu v. Trump Taj Mahal Associates (gambling, Dram-Shop) 876 F. Supp. 625 D.N.J. 1994; Andrews v. Holloway (preliminary injunction to protect assets) 1995 Westlaw 875883 D.N.J. 1995; Watson v. City of Salem (discrimination in police hiring) 934 F. Supp. 643 D.N.J. 1996; Andrews v. Holloway (civil contempt) 1996 Westlaw 495148 D.N.J. 1996; and Reich v. D.C. Wiring, Inc. (res judicata) 940 F. Supp. 105, 132 Lab. Cas. P 33,458, 3 Wage & Hour Cas.2d (BNA) 885 D.N.J. 1996.

Guest Lecturer Legal Intern Program Rutgers Law School since 1987. Master, Camden Inn of Court since 1987. Member Lawyers Advisory Committee District of

SIMANDLE, JEROME B.—*Continued*

New Jersey 1983-95, Federal Judges Association, Judicial Conference of the U.S. (Committee on Court Administration and Case Management since 1991), New Jersey State and American Bar Associations. Lecturer on "Judicial Management of Complex Litigation" American Corporate Counsel Association, Tampa Florida March 1986 and "Hazardous Wastes, Superfund and Toxic Substances" ALI/ABA National Seminar, Washington D.C. Dec 1988. Panelist on "Fundamentals of Federal Court Practice" Federal Bar Association Oct 1986; "Federal Pretrial Practice and Procedure" ICLE Jan 1987; "Judicial Management of Complex Environmental Litigation" Federal Bar Association April 1987; "Liability for Hazardous Waste Management" ALI/ABA National Seminar, Washington D.C. April 1987; "Federal Court Practice" ICLE March 1989; and "Prosecuting Civil Claims Against the Government" New Jersey State Bar Association May 1990. Instructor "Search Warrants" Continuing Professional Education Program Internal Revenue Service June 1987. Speaker on "Management of Hazardous Waste Litigation: The Public/Private Partnership" New Jersey Corporate Counsel Association Nov 1988; "Managing Complex Litigation" Conference for U.S. Magistrates Federal Judicial Center, Boston Massachusetts July 1989; "Evaluating the Court-Annexed Arbitration Program" District of New Jersey Bench/Bar Meeting Third Circuit Judicial Conference, Pittsburgh Pennsylvania Sept 1989; "Federal Trial Court Practice" Camden County Bar Association Oct 1989; Symposium "Alternative Methods for Resolving Environmental Disputes" Villanova Pennsylvania March 1990; and "Managing Pretrial Discovery in Complex Litigation" Conference for U.S. Magistrates Federal Judicial Center, Arlington Virginia Sept 1990. Faculty for "Managing Complex Environmental Cases—Litigation and Settlement Perspectives" New Jersey State Judicial College Nov 1990. Recipient Special Achievement Award from U.S. Department of Justice 1982.

Office: 6010 U.S. Courthouse, One John F. Gerry Plaza, 400 Cooper Street, Camden 08102.

Telephone: (856) 757-5167.

SIMON, Marguerite T. *(Judge, New Jersey Superior Court Vicinage Two)* Appointed by governor. Currently serves as Presiding Judge General Equity Division.

Office: Bergen County Justice Center, 10 Main Street, Hackensack 07601.

Telephone: (201) 646-3757.

SIMONELLI, Marie P. *(Judge, New Jersey Superior Court Vicinage Five)* Appointed by governor.

Office: 307 Hall of Records, 465 Dr. Martin Luther King Jr. Blvd., Newark 07102.

Telephone: (973) 693-6806, 693-6807.

SIVILLI, Nancy *(Judge, New Jersey Superior Court Vicinage Five)* Appointed by governor.

Office: Gibraltar Building, Twelfth Floor, 212 Washington Street, Newark 07102.

Telephone: (973) 693-5885, 693-5886.

SKILLMAN, Stephen *(Judge, New Jersey Superior Court Appellate Division)* Appointed Judge Vicinage Eight by Governor Brendan T. Byrne March 1, 1981. Reappointed by Governor Thomas H. Kean 1988. Assigned to Appellate Division by Chief Justice Robert N. Wilentz. Term expires at age seventy. Currently serves as Presiding Judge Part A. Born East Orange New Jersey Dec 4, 1940. Educated at Amherst College B.A. cum laude 1962 and Harvard Law School LL.B. 1965. Law Clerk to Justice Frederick W. Hall, New Jersey Supreme Court 1965-66. Admitted to practice New Jersey 1965, U.S. District Court District of New Jersey 1965, U.S. Court of Appeals Third Circuit 1968 and U.S. Supreme Court 1969.

Deputy Attorney General Department of Law and Public Safety 1966-69. Assistant Attorney General 1969-73. First Assistant Attorney General 1973-74. Director Division of Law and Assistant Attorney General in Charge of Appeals 1973-80.

Mailing address: P.O. Box 977, Trenton 08625-0977.

Office: Hughes Justice Complex, Trenton 08625.

Telephone: (609) 984-2446.

SMALL, Joseph C. *(Presiding Judge, New Jersey Tax Court)* Appointed by Governor Jim Florio to term beginning June 21, 1991. Reappointed by Governor Christine T. Whitman June 21, 1998. Term expires at age seventy. Born New York New York March 23, 1943. Educated at Williams College B.A. 1965 and Columbia University J.D. 1975. Harlan Fiske Stone Scholar. Edward John Noble Leadership Fellow and International Fellow. Admitted to practice New Jersey 1975, U.S. District Court District of New Jersey 1975, New York 1976 and U.S. Tax Court 1981. In legal practice New York and New Jersey 1975-77, 1981-83 and 1988-91.

Deputy Attorney General 1977-81 and Executive Assistant to the Attorney General 1980-81 New Jersey. Counsel to the Director and Coordinator Tax Evasion Task Force New Jersey Division of Taxation 1983-88. Contributing Author Journal of State Taxation, Interstate Tax Reports, New Jersey Tax Notes and New Jersey L. Jour. Member Committee on the Tax Court Supreme Court of New Jersey 1990-92, 1997-98 and since 2001. Chairman National Conference of State Tax Judges 1999-2000. Member Mercer County, New Jersey State (Tax Section), New York State and American (Committee on State and Local Taxes Section of Taxation) Bar Associations. Frequent Lecturer on Criminal Tax Enforcement, Interstate Tax Cooperation, Cigarette Tax Administration, Transfer Inheritance Tax, New Jersey Tax Law and Procedures, Legal Issues in Property Taxation and Resolving Tax Disputes for Section of Taxation American Bar Association, New York University Institute on Federal Taxation, Fairleigh Dickinson University Tax Institute, National Association of Tax Administrators, Rutgers University School of Law, Tax Executive Institute, New Jersey Institute for Continuing Legal Education and National Conference of State Tax Judges. Program Assistant Office of Economic Opportunity 1967. Associate Director Urban Opinions Surveys Division of Mathematica 1971-74. Previously employed as a Consultant by Abt Associates, The Calspan Corporation and Mathematica, Inc. 1974-75. Former Director Columbia Law School Association. Director Lincoln Institute of Land Policy. Moot Court Judge Columbia University Law School.

Mailing address: Hughes Justice Complex, P.O. Box 975, Trenton 08625.

Telephone: (609) 292-8108.

SMITH, Donald A., Jr. *(Judge, New Jersey Superior Court Vicinage Fifteen)* Appointed by governor. Also serves as Designated Judge Special Civil Part.

Mailing address: P.O. Box 798, Woodbury 08096.

Office: Gloucester County Justice Center, Woodbury 08096.

Telephone: (856) 853-3501.

SMITH, Lawrence D. *(Judge, New Jersey Superior Court Vicinage Two)* Appointed by governor.

Office: Bergen County Justice Center, 10 Main Street, Hackensack 07601.

Telephone: (201) 646-2296.

SMITH, Stephen F., Jr. *(Judge, New Jersey Superior Court Vicinage Ten)* Appointed by Governor Thomas H. Kean to term beginning May 18, 1988. Reappointed by Governor Christine T. Whitman May 18, 1995. Term expires at age seventy. Born East Orange New Jersey June 7, 1942. Roman Catholic. Educated at St. Peter's College B.A. 1963 and Seton Hall University J.D. 1966. Admitted to practice New Jersey 1966 and U.S. District Court District of New Jersey 1966. In legal practice Morristown 1966-75.

Assistant Prosecutor Morris County 1975-81. Deputy First Assistant Prosecutor Essex County 1981-88. Member Morris County Bar Association.

Mailing address: P.O. Box 910, Morristown 07963-0910.

Office: Morris County Courthouse, Morristown 07960.

Telephone: (973) 676-3998.

SMITH, Thomas S., Jr. *(Judge, New Jersey Superior Court Vicinage Three)* Appointed by governor. Former Presiding Judge Family Division.

Office: Burlington County Court Facility, 49 Rancocas Road, Mount Holly 08060.

Telephone: (609) 518-2700.

SMITHSON, Andrew J. *(Judge, New Jersey Superior Court Vicinage Seven)* Appointed by governor.

Mailing address: P.O. Box 8068, Trenton 08650.

Office: Mercer County Civil Courts, 175 South Broad Street, Trenton 08608.

Telephone: (609) 989-6191.

SNYDER, Irvin J. *(Judge, New Jersey Superior Court Vicinage Four)* Appointed by governor. Currently serves as Designated Judge Criminal Division.

Office: 470 Camden County Hall of Justice, 101 South Fifth Street, Camden 08103-4001.

Telephone: (856) 225-7267.

SOGLUIZZO, Maureen P. *(Judge, New Jersey Superior Court Vicinage Six)* Appointed by governor.

Office: Administration Building, 595 Newark Avenue, Jersey City 07306.

Telephone: (201) 795-6775.

SOKALSKI, Ronald B. *(Judge, New Jersey Superior Court Vicinage Eleven)* Appointed by governor.

Office: Passaic County Courthouse, 77 Hamilton Street, Paterson 07505.

Telephone: (973) 247-8335.

SPAN, Miriam N. *(Judge, New Jersey Superior Court Vicinage Twelve)* Appointed by Governor Thomas H. Kean to term beginning Nov 2, 1984. Reappointed by Governor Jim Florio 1991. Term expires at age seventy. Currently serves as Presiding Judge General Equity Division. Born Newark New Jersey May 12, 1942. Educated at Rutgers University at Newark B.A. with honors 1964 LL.B. 1966. Law Clerk to Hon. Robert M. Matthews 1966. Admitted to practice New Jersey 1966 and Florida 1979. Began legal practice Newark New Jersey 1967. In legal practice Elizabeth, Trenton and Westfield New Jersey.

Former First Assistant Public Defender Union County, Assistant U.S. Attorney New Jersey and Assistant Deputy Public Advocate. Member Union County (Former Trustee, Treasurer and Secretary) and New Jersey State Bar Associations.

Office: Union County Courthouse, Two Broad Street, Elizabeth 07207.

Telephone: (908) 659-4186.

SPATOLA, Jo-Anne B. *(Judge, New Jersey Superior Court Vicinage Twelve)* Appointed by Governor Jim Florio December 1990 to term beginning Feb 1, 1991. Reappointed by Governor Christine T. Whitman Dec 1998. Term expires at age seventy. Currently serves as Presiding Judge Family Division. Born Bronx New York June 1, 1945. Roman Catholic. Educated at University of Maryland B.A. 1967 and Seton Hall University School of Law J.D. 1977. Admitted to practice New Jersey 1977, U.S. District Court District of New Jersey 1977 and U.S. Supreme Court 1985. In legal practice Westfield 1978-91.

Attorney Board of Social Services Union City 1984-88. Important Decision: State v. Myrick & Green 282 N.J. Super 285, 659 A.2d 976 Feb. 14, 1995. Member Women Lawyers in Union County (Vice President 1986-88, President 1988-90, Member Judicial/Prosecutorial Screening Committee 1989-90, Nominating Committee 1989-92), Union County and New Jersey State Bar Associations. Councilman 1985-91 and Mayor 1990 Scotch Plains Township. Enjoys gardening and cooking.

Office: Union County Courthouse, Two Broad Street, Elizabeth 07207.

Telephone: (908) 659-3423.

STANGER, George H., Jr. *(Assignment Judge, New Jersey Superior Court Vicinage Fifteen)* Appointed Judge by Governor Thomas H. Kean to term beginning July 8, 1983. Reappointed by Governor Jim Florio 1990. Assignment Judge since April 1, 2000. Term expires at age seventy. Born Vineland New Jersey Sept 12, 1942. Presbyterian. Educated at Syracuse University B.S. and Dickinson School of Law J.D. Member Sigma Chi and Tau Theta Upsilon. Admitted to practice New Jersey 1970. Began legal practice Vineland 1970. In legal practice Bridgeton 1973. First Lieutenant U.S. Army 1964-66.

Office: Cumberland County Courthouse, West Broad and Fayette Streets, Bridgeton 08302.

Telephone: (856) 453-4391, 453-4393.

STARK, Isabel B. *(Judge, New Jersey Superior Court Vicinage Two)* Appointed by governor.

Office: Bergen County Justice Center, 10 Main Street, Hackensack 07601.

Telephone: (201) 646-3015.

STECKROTH, Donald H. *(Judge, United States Bankruptcy Court District of New Jersey)* Appointed by U.S. Court of Appeals Third Circuit judges to term beginning Feb 2, 2001.

Office: Federal Building and U.S. Courthouse, Third Floor, 50 Walnut Street, Newark 07102-3550.

Telephone: (973) 645-6022.

STEIN, Kenneth R. *(Retired Judge, New Jersey Superior Court)* Appointed by governor. Served Vicinage Five. Retired, serves on recall.

Mailing address: ISP, P.O. Box 987, Trenton 08625.

Telephone: (609) 984-0076.

STERN, Edwin H. *(Judge, New Jersey Superior Court Appellate Division)* Appointed Judge Vicinage Five by governor. Assigned to Appellate Division by Chief Justice Robert N. Wilentz. Currently serves as Presiding Judge Part H.

Office: North Tower Suite 1101, 158 Headquarters Plaza, Morristown 07960-3965.

Telephone: (973) 631-6381, 631-6382.

STERN, Morris *(Judge, United States Bankruptcy Court District of New Jersey)* Appointed by U.S. Court of Appeals Third Circuit judges Dec 27, 2001.

Office: Federal Building, 50 Walnut Street, Newark 07102.

Telephone: (973) 368-1244.

Fax: (973) 645-3696

STOLTE, Barbara Clarke *(Judge, New Jersey Superior Court Vicinage Eight)* Appointed by Governor James E. McGreevey.

Mailing address: P.O. Box 2691, New Brunswick 08903-2691.

Office: Middlesex County Family Court, 120 New Street, New Brunswick 08901.

Telephone: (732) 981-3219.

STRELECKI, June *(Retired Judge, New Jersey Superior Court)* Appointed by Governor Brendan T. Byrne to term beginning April 1, 1978. Reappointed by Governor Thomas H. Kean 1983. Served Vicinage Five. Retired, serves on recall. Born Newark New Jersey May 28, 1928. Educated at Drew University B.A. cum laude 1950, American University and Harvard University LL.B. 1955. Admitted to practice New Jersey 1956. Judge, New Jersey County Court Essex County April 1974 to March 1978.

Deputy Attorney General 1956-59. Counsel to Governor Robert Baumle Meyner 1960-61. Assistant Prosecutor Essex County 1961-64. Director Department of Motor Vehicles 1964-70.

Mailing address: P.O. Box 8068, Trenton 08650.

Office: Mercer County Civil Courts, 209 South Broad and Market Streets, Trenton 08650.

Telephone: (609) 278-7113.

STROUMTSOS, Nicholas J., Jr. *(Judge, New Jersey Superior Court Vicinage Eight)* Appointed by governor. Served Vicinage Five.

Mailing address: P.O. Box 964, New Brunswick 08903.

Office: Middlesex County Courthouse, One John F. Kennedy Square, New Brunswick 08901.

Telephone: (732) 981-3102.

SUBRYAN, Randolph M. *(Judge, New Jersey Superior Court Vicinage Eleven)* Appointed by governor.

Office: Passaic County Courthouse, 77 Hamilton Street, Paterson 07505.

Telephone: (973) 247-8420.

SULLIVAN, Cornelius P. *(Judge, New Jersey Superior Court Vicinage Three)* Appointed by Governor Brendan T. Byrne to term beginning Jan 18, 1982. Reappointed by Governor Thomas H. Kean Jan 12, 1989. Term expires at age seventy. Former Presiding Judge Criminal Division. Born Lowell Massachusetts Nov 24, 1940. Educated at Providence College A.B. with honors 1962 and Boston University J.D. 1965. Admitted to practice New Jersey 1965. In legal practice Mount Holly 1968-70.

Assistant Deputy Public Defender 1970-73. Assistant Prosecutor 1973-75 and Prosecutor 1975-82 Burlington County. Member Burlington County and New Jersey State Bar Associations. Captain USAR Military Police 1966-67.

Office: Burlington County Court Facility, 49 Rancocas Road, Mount Holly 08060.

Telephone: (609) 518-2712.

SULLIVAN, Mark A., Jr. *(Judge, New Jersey Superior Court Vicinage Nine)* Appointed by Governor Thomas H. Kean to term beginning Feb 3, 1989. Reappointed by Governor Christine T. Whitman 1996. Term expires at age seventy. Also serves as Designated Judge Special Civil Part. Born Jersey City New Jersey Dec 11, 1946. Catholic. Educated at Georgetown University A.B. 1968 and Rutgers University J.D. 1973. Law Clerk to Hon. John F. Lynch, New Jersey Superior Court Appellate Division Part A 1973-74. Admitted to practice New Jersey 1973. Certified by the Supreme Court of New Jersey as a Civil Trial Attorney. In legal practice Belmar 1979-88.

Deputy Attorney General New Jersey 1974-79. Author "Liability of New Jersey National Guard" 1987 and "Definition of Hearsay" 1991 *New Jersey Lawyer.* Important Decisions: Aykan v. Goldzweig 238 N.J. Super. 389 Law Div. 1989, State v. M.Z. 241 N.J. Super. 444 Law Div. 1990, Loigman v. Keim 250 N.J. Super. 434 Law Div. 1991, Frantz v. Frantz 256 N.J. Super. 90 Ch. Div. 1992 and Petrocco v. AT&T 273 N.J. Super. 613 Law Div. 1994. Instructor in New Jersey Criminal Law Monmouth College 1981-82. Member American Inns of Court, Monmouth County, New Jersey State and American Bar Associations. Specialist E-4 U.S. Army 1969-70.

Mailing address: P.O. Box 1266, Freehold 07728-1266.

Office: Monmouth County Courthouse, Monument and Court Streets, Freehold 07728.

Telephone: (732) 677-4170.

SULLIVAN, Timothy J. *(Retired Judge, New Jersey Superior Court)* Appointed by governor. Served Vicinage Two. Retired, serves on recall.

Office: Bergen County Courthouse, 10 Main Street, Hackensack 07601-7015.

Telephone: (201) 646-2146.

SUPNICK, Samuel L. *(Retired Judge, New Jersey Superior Court)* Appointed by governor. Served Vicinage Four. Retired, serves on recall. Also serves as Designated Judge Special Civil Part.

Office: 530 Camden County Hall of Justice, 101 South Fifth Street, Camden 08103-4001.

Telephone: (856) 379-2379.

SUTER, Karen L. *(Judge, New Jersey Superior Court Vicinage Three)* Appointed by governor.

Office: Burlington County Court Facility, 49 Rancocas Road, Mount Holly 08060.

Telephone: (609) 518-2587.

SWEEN, Birger M. *(Retired Judge, New Jersey Superior Court)* Appointed by Governor Brendan T. Byrne to term beginning Jan 18, 1982. Reappointed by Governor Thomas H. Kean Dec 1986. Former Presiding Judge Family Division Vicinage Two. Retired, serves on recall. Born Englewood New Jersey April 19, 1929. Presbyterian. Educated at Rutgers University B.A. 1951 J.D. 1954. Admitted to practice District of Columbia 1954 and New Jersey 1957. Began legal practice Englewood 1957. In legal practice Hackensack 1959.

Counsel and Adjuster 1967 and Attorney Welfare Board 1968 Bergen County. Attorney Norwood Planning Board 1970-81, Demarest Planning Board 1972-75, Woodcliff Lake Borough 1973-81, Leonia Planning Board 1974-81, Washington Township Planning Board 1977-81 and Westwood Planning Board 1980-81. Prosecutor Leonia 1972-75 and 1977-81, Norwood 1973-79 and Washington Township 1976-77. Important Decision: Plaza Road Cooperatives v. Mae Gambert Finn (cooperative tenancy issue) 1983. Member 1973-75, Chairman 1975 and Secretary 1976 Bergen County Ethics Committee. Member Bergen County Attorneys Society (President 1963-64) and Bergen County Bar Association. USMCR 1947-49 (inactive). Specialists U.S. Army 1954-56. Woodcliff Lake Democratic Councilman and Bergen County Democratic Committeeman. Ordained Deacon and Ordained Elder Westside Presbyterian Church. Enjoys woodworking, photography, horticulture and travel.

Office: Bergen County Justice Center, 10 Main Street, Hackensack 07601.

Telephone: (201) 646-2750.

SWEENEY, John A. *(Assignment Judge, New Jersey Superior Court Vicinage Three)* Appointed by governor. Former Presiding Judge Family Division and Civil Division.

Office: Burlington County Court Facility, 49 Rancocas Road, Mount Holly 08060.

Telephone: (609) 518-2850.

SYPEK, Maria Marinari *(Judge, New Jersey Superior Court Vicinage Seven)* Appointed by governor.

Mailing address: P.O. Box 8068, Trenton 08650.

Office: Mercer County Courthouse, 209 South Broad and Market Streets, Trenton 08608.

Telephone: (609) 989-6797.

TALBERT, Patricia Medina *(Judge, New Jersey Superior Court Vicinage Five)* Appointed by governor.

Office: 1018 Essex County Courts Building, 50 West Market Street, Newark 07102.

Telephone: (973) 693-5893, 693-5894.

TELSEY, Norman *(Retired Judge, New Jersey Superior Court)* Assumed office Dec 7, 1978. Served Vicinage Fifteen. Retired, serves on recall. Born Brooklyn New York Dec 23, 1925. Jewish. Educated at Albright College B.S. 1949 and Brooklyn Law School J.D. 1951. Admitted to practice New York 1952 and New Jersey 1956. Began legal practice Flushing New York 1952. In legal practice Bridgeton New Jersey 1956 and Salem New Jersey 1965-71. Judge, New Jersey County Court Salem County Oct 8, 1976 to Dec 6, 1978, appointed by Governor Brendan T. Byrne.

Solicitor Salem Housing Authority 1962-76, Elsinboro Township 1964-76, Salem County Welfare Board 1967-76, Quinton Township 1970-76 and Upper Penns Neck Township 1971-73. Instructor in Commercial Law and Negotiable Instruments American Institute of Banking 1959-61. Member Salem County (President 1967) and New Jersey State Bar Associations. Radioman Third Class USN 1944-46. Member Deerfield Township Committee 1959-61. Democrat. Enjoys travel, jogging, photography and sports.

Office: 340 Hall of Justice, 101 South Fifth Street, Camden 08103-4001.

Telephone: (856) 225-7107.

TESTA, Joseph P. *(Judge, New Jersey Superior Court Vicinage Fifteen)* Appointed by governor. Former Presiding Judge Family Division.

Office: Cumberland County Courthouse, West Broad and Fayette Streets, Bridgeton 08302.

Telephone: (856) 453-4383, 453-4385.

THEEMLING, Frederick J., Jr. *(Judge, New Jersey Superior Court Vicinage Six)* Appointed by Governor James E. McGreevey.

Office: Administration Building, 595 Newark Avenue, Jersey City 07306.

Telephone: (201) 795-6971.

THOMPSON, Anne E. *(Senior Judge, United States District Court District of New Jersey)* Appointed for life by President Jimmy Carter to term beginning 1979. Chief Judge 1994 to June 1, 2001. Assumed Senior status June 1, 2001, serves by assignment. Born Philadelphia Pennsylvania July 8, 1934. Educated at Howard University B.A. 1955 LL.B. 1964 and Temple University M.A. 1957. Judge, Trenton Municipal Court 1972-75.

Attorney Office of the Solicitor U.S. Department of Labor 1964-65. Assistant Deputy Public Defender Trenton 1967-70. Municipal Prosecutor Lawrence Township 1970-72. Prosecutor Mercer County 1975-79.

Office: 4000 U.S. Courthouse, 402 East State Street, Trenton 08608.

Telephone: (609) 989-2123.

THOMPSON, Stephen W. *(Judge, New Jersey Superior Court Vicinage Four)* Appointed by governor.

Office: 470 Camden County Hall of Justice, 101 South Fifth Street, Camden 08103-4001.

Telephone: (856) 379-2380.

TODD, Daryl F., Sr. *(Judge, New Jersey Superior Court Vicinage One)* Appointed by Governor Christine T. Whitman to term beginning Dec 20, 2000. Born Tampa Florida April 1, 1942. Roman Catholic. Educated at University of Pennsylvania B.S. 1964 and Duke University School of Law J.D. 1967. Admitted to practice New Jersey 1967, U.S. District Court District of New Jersey 1967 and Florida 1975. In legal practice Linwood New Jersey Oct 31, 1967 to Dec 20, 2000.

Solicitor Somers Point Planning Board and Corbin City Zoning Board of Adjustment. Instructor in Municipal Land Use 1978 and Pinelands Moratorium Cause and Effect 1979 Stockton College Center for Environmental Research. Member 1979-81 and Vice Chairman 1980-81 District Fee Arbitration Committee. Former Panelist Early Settlement Program and Former Arbitrator Automobile Arbitration Program New Jersey Superior Court. Member Atlantic County (Recording Secretary and Executive Secretary 1972-76, Treasurer 1978-79) and New Jersey State Bar Associations. Board of Directors Cape Atlantic Legal Services 1968-70. Director 1969-70, Vice President 1970-71, President 1971-72 and Chairman of the Board 1972-73 Atlantic City Jaycees.

TODD, DARYL F., SR.—*Continued*

Member Charter Study Commission 1973-74, Board of Chosen Freeholders 1975-77 and Ethics Committee 1978 Atlantic County. Sponsor 1975-96, Minor League Director 1978-79 and Coach 1980-81 and 1988-89 Linwood Little League. Member 1979-94 and President 1992-94 Board of Trustees Stockton College Foundation. Member Secondary School Committee University of Pennsylvania 1980-2003. Coach Linwood Girls Softball League 1982. Member 1983 to Dec 20, 2000 and President 1985-87 and 1993 to Dec 20, 2000 Linwood Board of Education. Member 1983-92 and President 1985-88 Advisory Council Holy Spirit High School. Co-chairman Scholastic Rowing Association of America Championship Nationals 1998. Chairman Capital Campaign Our Lady of Sorrows Church. Interested in U.S. history with emphasis on the War Between the States.

Office: Atlantic County Civil Court Building, 1201 Bacharach Boulevard, Atlantic City 08401.

Telephone: (609) 343-2215, 345-6700.

Fax: (609) 343-2301

TODD, William C., III *(Judge, New Jersey Superior Court Vicinage One)* Appointed by governor. Currently serves as Presiding Judge Civil Division and Acting Assignment Judge.

Office: County Civil Court Building, 1201 Bacharach Boulevard, Atlantic City 08401-4510.

Telephone: (609) 343-2281.

TOLENTINO, Shirley A. *(Judge, New Jersey Superior Court Vicinage Six)* Appointed by governor.

Office: Administration Building, 595 Newark Avenue, Jersey City 07306.

Telephone: (201) 795-6668, 795-6669.

TOMASELLO, John *(Judge, New Jersey Superior Court Vicinage Fifteen)* Appointed by governor.

Mailing address: P.O. Box 846, Woodbury 08096.

Office: Gloucester County Courthouse, Woodbury 08096.

Telephone: (856) 853-3519.

TORACK, Edward V. *(Judge, New Jersey Superior Court Vicinage Two)* Appointed by governor.

Office: Bergen County Justice Center, 10 Main Street, Hackensack 07601.

Telephone: (201) 646-2180.

TRIARSI, John S. *(Judge, New Jersey Superior Court Vicinage Twelve)* Appointed by governor. Former Presiding Judge Criminal Division.

Office: Union County Courthouse, Two Broad Street, Elizabeth 07207.

Telephone: (908) 659-3443.

TROIANO, James G. *(Judge, New Jersey Superior Court Vicinage Five)* Appointed by governor.

Office: Gibraltar Building, Ninth Floor, 212 Washington Street, Newark 07102.

Telephone: (973) 693-6756, 693-6757.

TURNBACH, Edward J. *(Judge, New Jersey Superior Court Vicinage Fourteen)* Appointed by governor.

Office: Ocean County Justice Complex, 120 Hooper Avenue, Toms River 08753.

Telephone: (732) 929-2177.

UHRMACHER, Bette E. *(Judge, New Jersey Superior Court Vicinage Nine)* Appointed by governor. Served Vicinage Eight.

Mailing address: P.O. Box 1266, Freehold 07728-1266.

Office: Monmouth County Courthouse, Monument and Court Streets, Freehold 07728.

Telephone: (732) 677-4174.

VAZQUEZ, Peter J. *(Judge, New Jersey Superior Court Vicinage Five)* Appointed by governor.

Office: 1208 Essex County Courts Building, 50 West Market Street, Newark 07102.

Telephone: (973) 693-6453, 693-6454.

VELAZQUEZ, Hector R. *(Judge, New Jersey Superior Court Vicinage Six)* Appointed by Governor Christine T. Whitman to term beginning March 15, 1996. Reappointed by Governor James E. McGreevey 2003. Term expires at age seventy. Born Mayaquez Puerto Rico Dec 8, 1951. Educated at Lehigh University B.A. 1972 and State University of New York at Buffalo J.D. 1975. Admitted to practice New Jersey 1976, New York 1976 and U.S. District Courts District of New Jersey 1976 and Western District of New York 1977. In legal practice Buffalo and Lackawanna New York 1976-79 and Jersey City New Jersey 1979-96.

Member Hudson County, New Jersey Hispanic (Past President), New Jersey State and National Hispanic Bar Associations. Mentor Jersey City Board of Education. Member Jersey City Lions Club. Enjoys scuba diving, skiing, biking and golfing.

Office: Administration Building, 595 Newark Avenue, Jersey City 07306.

Telephone: (201) 795-6202.

VENA, Thomas R. *(Judge, New Jersey Superior Court Vicinage Five)* Appointed by governor.

Office: 916 Essex County Courts Building, 50 West Market Street, Newark 07102.

Telephone: (973) 693-5852, 693-5853.

VENEZIA, Deborah J. *(Judge, New Jersey Superior Court Vicinage Eight)* Appointed by governor.

Mailing address: P.O. Box 964, New Brunswick 08903.

Office: Middlesex County Courthouse, One John F. Kennedy Square, New Brunswick 08901.

Telephone: (732) 981-3206.

VENEZIA, Donald R. *(Judge, New Jersey Superior Court Vicinage Two)* Appointed by Governor Christine T. Whitman to term beginning Aug 1999. Born Jersey City New Jersey April 16, 1949. Catholic. Educated at St. Peter's College B.A. 1971 and Seton Hall University School of Law J.D. 1974. Law Clerk to Hon. Robert I. X. McAlvey, New Jersey Superior Court Vicinage Six. Admitted to practice New Jersey 1976. In legal practice 1980 to Aug 1999.

Assistant Prosecutor Hudson County 1977-80. Member Bergen County and Hudson County Bar Associations. Member New York Seaport Association.

Office: Bergen County Justice Center, 10 Main Street, Hackensack 07601.

Telephone: (201) 646-6779.

VERNIERO, Peter G. *(Associate Justice, Supreme Court of New Jersey)* Appointed by Governor Christine T. Whitman to term beginning Sept 1, 1999. Born Montclair New Jersey April 30, 1959. Educated at Drew

VERNIERO, PETER G.—*Continued*

University summa cum laude 1981 and Duke University J.D. with honors 1984. Law Clerk to Hon. Robert L. Clifford, Supreme Court of New Jersey 1984-85. Member Phi Beta Kappa. Admitted to practice New Jersey 1984.

Attorney General July 10, 1996 to Sept 1, 1999. Chief Counsel Jan 1994 to Feb 1995 and Chief of Staff Feb 1995 to July 10, 1996 to Governor Christine T. Whitman.

Office: Hunterdon County Justice Center, 65 Park Avenue, Flemington 08822.

Telephone: (908) 237-9440.

VICHNESS, Paul J. *(Judge, New Jersey Superior Court Vicinage Five)* Appointed by Governor Christine T. Whitman to term beginning Dec 1995. Reappointed by Governor James E. McGreevey Dec 2002. Term expires at age seventy. Born Bronx New York March 9, 1944. Educated at Hobart College B.A. 1965 and Seton Hall University School of Law J.D. 1968. Editorial Board Seton Hall Law Review 1967. Law Clerk to Hon. William J. Camarata, New Jersey Superior Court Vicinage Five 1967-68. Admitted to practice New Jersey 1968, U.S. District Court District of New Jersey 1968, U.S. Court of Appeals Third Circuit 1968 and U.S. Supreme Court 1991. In legal practice Newark 1971-87 and Fairfield 1987-95. Judge, Mount Olive and Netcong Municipal Courts 1975-87.

Assistant Deputy Public Defender Sept 1969 to April 1971. Member Essex County, New Jersey State and American Bar Associations.

Office: 1108 New Courts Building, 50 West Market Street, Newark 07102.

Telephone: (973) 693-5887.

VILLANO, Barbara Ann *(Judge, New Jersey Superior Court Vicinage Fourteen)* Appointed by governor.

Office: Ocean County Justice Complex, 120 Hooper Avenue, Toms River 08753.

Telephone: (732) 929-2173.

VILLANUEVA, Charles E. *(Retired Judge, New Jersey Superior Court)* Appointed Judge Vicinage Five by Governor Brendan T. Byrne to term beginning March 15, 1979. Reappointed by Governor Thomas H. Kean March 15, 1986. Assigned to Appellate Division by Chief Justice Robert N. Wilentz. Retired March 30, 1996, serves on recall. Born Orange New Jersey March 30, 1926. Episcopalian. Educated at Duke University A.B. 1948 LL.B. 1951. Admitted to practice District of Columbia 1951 and New Jersey 1952. In legal practice Newark 1952-79.

Member Essex County, New Jersey State and American Bar Associations. USN 1944-46.

Mailing address: P.O. Box 910, Morristown 07963-0910.

Office: Morris County Courthouse, Morristown 07960.

Telephone: (973) 656-4006.

VISALLI, Joseph C. *(Judge, New Jersey Superior Court Vicinage One)* Appointed by Governor Thomas H. Kean to term beginning March 21, 1986. Reappointed by Governor Jim Florio 1993. Term expires at age seventy. Born Philadelphia Pennsylvania Oct 6, 1941. Catholic. Educated at La Salle College B.S. and Duquesne University J.D. Managing Editor Duquesne Law Review 1970-71. Admitted to practice Pennsylvania 1971 and New Jersey 1972. In legal practice Cape May County 1972-86. Judge, Wildwood 1980-86, West Wildwood 1980-86 and North Wildwood 1983-86 Municipal Courts.

Assistant County Prosecutor Cape May County 1976-79. Member Cape May County and New Jersey State Bar Associations. First Lieutenant U.S. Army 1965-68.

Office: Cape May County Courthouse, Main Street, Cape May Court House 08210.

Telephone: (609) 463-6530.

VOGELSON, M. Allan *(Judge, New Jersey Superior Court Vicinage Four)* Appointed by Governor Jim Florio 1991. Reappointed by Governor Christine T. Whitman 1998. Currently serves as Presiding Judge Civil Division. Educated at Temple University B.S. 1961 and Rutgers University School of Law at Camden LL.B. 1964. Law Clerk to New Jersey County Court Camden County 1964-65. Admitted to practice New Jersey 1965, U.S. District Court District of New Jersey 1965, U.S. Court of Appeals Third Circuit, U.S. Court of Claims and U.S. Supreme Court. In legal practice 1965-91.

Assistant Prosecutor Camden County. Assistant Municipal Attorney City of Camden. Former Member New Jersey State and American Bar Associations. Member Camden County Bar Association. Member Reappointment Committee New Jersey State Legislature 1970. Member 1972-75 and Former Director Camden County Board of Freeholders.

Office: 660 Camden County Hall of Justice, 101 South Fifth Street, Camden 08103-4001.

Telephone: (856) 379-2381.

VOLKERT, Donald J., Jr. *(Judge, New Jersey Superior Court Vicinage Five)* Appointed by governor. Currently serves as Presiding Judge Family Division and Acting Assignment Judge.

Office: Gibraltar Building, Tenth Floor, 212 Washington Street, Newark 07102.

Telephone: (973) 693-5889, 693-5890.

WAKS, David *(Judge, New Jersey Superior Court Vicinage Eleven)* Appointed by governor.

Office: Passaic County Courthouse, 77 Hamilton Street, Paterson 07505.

Telephone: (973) 247-8147.

WALDMAN, Daniel M. *(Judge, New Jersey Superior Court Vicinage Nine)* Appointed by Governor James E. McGreevey.

Mailing address: P.O. Box 1266, Freehold 07728-1266.

Office: Monmouth County Courthouse, Monument and Court Streets, Freehold 07728.

Telephone: (732) 677-4177.

WALLACE, John E., Jr. *(Associate Justice, Supreme Court of New Jersey)* Appointed by Governor James E. McGreevey to term beginning May 20, 2003. Term expires 2010. Former Judge, New Jersey Superior Court Vicinage Fifteen. Former Judge, New Jersey Superior Court Appellate Division.

Office: 216 Haddon Avenue, Suite 700, Westmont 08108.

Telephone: (856) 858-8636.

WALLS, William H. *(Judge, United States District Court District of New Jersey)* Appointed for life by President Bill Clinton to term beginning 1994. Born Atlantic City New Jersey Nov 18, 1932. Educated at Dart-

WALLS, WILLIAM H.—*Continued* mouth College A.B. 1954 and Yale Law School LL.B. 1957. Law Clerk 1957-59. In legal practice Newark 1959-62, 1968-70 and 1972-75. Judge, Newark Municipal Court 1968-70. Judge, New Jersey County Court Essex County 1977-78. Judge, New Jersey Superior Court Vicinage Five 1979-94.

Assistant Corporation Counsel 1962-68 and Corporation Counsel 1970-73 Newark. Business Administrator City of Newark 1974-77.

Office: U.S. Courthouse, 50 Walnut Street, Newark 07102.

Telephone: (973) 645-2564.

WALSH, Charles J. *(Judge, New Jersey Superior Court Vicinage Two)* Appointed by governor.

Office: Bergen County Justice Center, 10 Main Street, Hackensack 07601.

Telephone: (201) 646-6772.

WALSH, James J. *(Retired Judge, New Jersey Superior Court)* Appointed by Governor Thomas H. Kean April 26, 1984 to term beginning July 13, 1984. Reappointed by Governor Jim Florio 1991. Served Vicinage Twelve. Retired, serves on recall. Born New York New York Jan 15, 1926. Roman Catholic. Educated at Seton Hall University and Rutgers University B.L. 1952 J.D. 1968. Admitted to practice District of Columbia 1952, New Jersey 1953 and U.S. District Court District of New Jersey 1953. Began legal practice Scotch Plains 1955. Judge, Scotch Plains Municipal Court 1979-84.

Assistant Municipal Attorney, Prosecutor and Board of Adjustment Attorney Scotch Plains 1965-66. Municipal Attorney Scotch Plains 1967-74 and Berkeley Heights 1975-84. Instructor in Administrative Law Kean College 1979-80. Member Union County Municipal Judges Association (Secretary-Treasurer 1983-84), New Jersey Council of Juvenile and Family Court Judges (Vice President 1990-91), National Council of Juvenile and Family Court Judges, New Jersey Institute of Municipal Attorneys, Plainfield, Union County, New Jersey State and American Bar Associations. Sergeant USAAC 1944-46. Republican. Enjoys traveling, flying, sailing and reading. Interested in the arts.

Office: Union County Courthouse, Two Broad Street, Elizabeth 07207.

Telephone: (908) 659-3682.

WATERS, John M., Jr. *(Judge, New Jersey Superior Court Vicinage Fifteen)* Appointed by governor.

Office: Cumberland County Courthouse, West Broad and Fayette Streets, Bridgeton 08302.

Telephone: (856) 453-4379.

WAUGH, Alexander P., Jr. *(Judge, New Jersey Superior Court Vicinage Eight)* Appointed by Governor Christine T. Whitman Jan 23, 1998. Term expires Jan 23, 2005. Born Glen Ridge New Jersey Feb 19, 1950. Educated at Columbia College B.A. 1972 and Rutgers University School of Law J.D. with honors 1975. Law Clerk to Hon. Lawrence A. Whipple, U.S. District Court District of New Jersey Sept 1975 to Sept 1976. Admitted to practice New Jersey 1975, U.S. District Court District of New Jersey 1975, U.S. Court of Appeals Third Circuit 1976 and U.S. Supreme Court 1981. In legal practice Newark 1976-78 and Princeton 1980-89.

Assistant Attorney General 1989-98. Author "Litigation in the District of New Jersey" New Jersey Lawyer Nov 1988. Fellow American Bar Foundation. Member Mercer County, Middlesex County, New Jersey State and American Bar Associations. Democrat. Assistant Counsel to Governor Brendan T. Byrne 1978-80.

Mailing address: P.O. Box 964, New Brunswick 08903.

Office: Middlesex County Courthouse, One John F. Kennedy Square, New Brunswick 08901.

Telephone: (732) 981-3184.

WEBER, Frederic G. *(Retired Judge, New Jersey Superior Court)* Assumed office Dec 7, 1978. Served Vicinage Ten. Retired, serves on recall. Former Judge, New Jersey County Court Sussex County.

Mailing address: P.O. Box 910, Morristown 07601.

Office: Morris County Courthouse, Morristown 07601.

Telephone: (973) 656-3929.

WECKER, Barbara Byrd *(Judge, New Jersey Superior Court Appellate Division)* Appointed Judge Vicinage Twelve by Governor Thomas H. Kean to term beginning Dec 23, 1985. Reappointed by Governor Jim Florio. Served Chancery Division Family Part Dec 1985 to Sept 1986, Law Division Civil Part Sept 1986 to Feb 1989 and Oct 1992 to Aug 1996 and Law Division Criminal Part Feb 1989 to Oct 1992. Assigned to Appellate Division by chief justice Sept 1996. Educated at Cornell University B.A. 1962, University of Missouri M.A. 1964 and Rutgers University J.D. with honors 1974. Staff member Rutgers Law Review. Member Phi Beta Kappa and Mortarboard. Admitted to practice New Jersey 1974, U.S. District Court District of New Jersey 1974 and U.S. Supreme Court 1983. In private legal practice Newark 1974-78 and Westfield 1978-85.

New Jersey Board of Bar Examiners 1984-85. Lecturer on Appellate Moot Court Rutgers University School of Law 1978-81. Trustee Legal Services of New Jersey, Inc. 1982-85 and New Jersey State Bar Foundation 1983-85.

Office: 155 Morris Avenue, Springfield 07081-1216.

Telephone: (973) 376-0595.

WEEKS, Renee Jones *(Judge, New Jersey Superior Court Vicinage Five)* Appointed by governor. Reappointed. Term expires at age seventy. Served Vicinage Twelve. Born Washington D.C. Dec 28, 1948. Catholic. Educated at Ursuline College B.A. 1970 and Rutgers University at Newark School of Law J.D. 1973. Member Alpha Kappa Alpha. Admitted to practice New Jersey 1973, District of Columbia 1977 and U.S. Supreme Court 1981. Former Acting Judge, Newark Municipal Court.

Deputy Attorney General New Jersey 1973-75. Assistant General Counsel Prudential Insurance 1975-89. Member National Association of Women Judges, National (Judicial Council Division) and American (Judicial Division) Bar Associations. Former Board Member New Jersey State Opera. Enjoys travel, music and volunteer projects.

Office: Gibraltar Building, Thirteenth Floor, 212 Washington Street, Newark 07102.

Telephone: (973) 693-5891, 693-5892.

WEFING, Dorothea O'C. *(Judge, New Jersey Superior Court Appellate Division)* Appointed Judge Vicinage Six by governor. Also served Vicinage Five. As-

WEFING, DOROTHEA O'C.—*Continued*

signed to Appellate Division by Chief Justice Robert N. Wilentz.

Office: Courthouse, 583 Newark Avenue, Jersey City 07306.

Telephone: (201) 659-8710.

WEISSBARD, Harvey *(Judge, New Jersey Superior Court Appellate Division)* Appointed Judge Vicinage Five by governor. Assigned to Appellate Division by Chief Justice Deborah T. Poritz.

Office: 155 Morris Avenue, Springfield 07081-1216.

Telephone: (973) 376-5649, 376-0354.

WELLERSON, Craig L. *(Judge, New Jersey Superior Court Vicinage Three)* Appointed by governor.

Office: Burlington County Court Facility, 49 Rancocas Road, Mount Holly 08060.

Telephone: (609) 518-2845.

WELLS, Harold B., III *(Judge, New Jersey Superior Court Appellate Division)* Assumed office as Judge Vicinage Three Dec 7, 1978. Former Assignment Judge. Assigned to Appellate Division by Chief Justice Deborah T. Poritz. Former Judge, New Jersey County Court Burlington County.

Office: 216 Haddon Avenue, Suite 700, Westmont 08108-2815.

Telephone: (856) 854-8826, 854-8925.

WENZEL, Glenn R. *(Judge, New Jersey Superior Court Vicinage Eleven)* Appointed by governor.

Office: Passaic County Admin. Bldg., 401 Grand Street, Paterson 07505.

Telephone: (973) 247-8438.

WERTHEIMER, William L'E. *(Judge, New Jersey Superior Court Vicinage Twelve)* Appointed by Governor Thomas H. Kean to term beginning Nov 9, 1984. Reappointed by Governor Jim Florio 1991. Former Presiding Judge Criminal Division. Currently serves as Presiding Judge Civil Division. Educated at Lafayette College B.A. 1964 and George Washington University J.D. 1967. Admitted to practice New Jersey 1970, U.S. District Court District of New Jersey 1970, New York 1981 and U.S. Court of Appeals Third Circuit.

Author Chapter X "Defense of Legal Malpractice Cases" *Professional Negligence* New Jersey Institute for Continuing Legal Education 1984. Important Decision: State v. Alvarado (criminal defendant may not use peremptory challenges to strike jurors on the basis of group association) 221 N.J. Super. 324 Law Div. 1987. Fellow International Society of Barristers. Master Richard F. Hughes Inn of Court. Member Union County Bar Association. Captain U.S. Army 1967-69.

Office: Union County Courthouse, Two Broad Street, Elizabeth 07207.

Telephone: (908) 659-4162.

WHITKEN, Melvin S. *(Judge, New Jersey Superior Court Vicinage Twelve)* Appointed by Governor Thomas H. Kean to term beginning Feb 3, 1989. Reappointed. Term expires at age seventy. Former Presiding Judge Family Division. Born Elizabeth New Jersey June 12, 1937. Jewish. Educated at Rutgers University B.A. 1959 and Seton Hall School of Law LL.B. 1962. Admitted to practice New Jersey 1962, U.S. District Court District of New Jersey 1962 and U.S. Supreme Court 1969. In legal practice East Orange 1973-80 and Livingston 1980-89. Judge, Fanwood Municipal Court 1972-89.

Assistant City Attorney Elizabeth 1966-67. Deputy Public Defender 1967-68. Former Member New Jersey Defense Association and New Jersey Trial Lawyers Association. Member New Jersey Supreme Court Committee on Municipal Courts since 1990, Union County and New Jersey State Bar Associations. Attended General Jurisdiction course The National Judicial College 1989 and 1990 and New Jersey Judicial College 1989 and 1990. New Jersey Air National Guard 1962-68. Enjoys reading, golf and skiing.

Office: Union County Courthouse, Two Broad Street, Elizabeth 07207.

Telephone: (908) 659-3428.

WIGENTON, Susan D. *(Magistrate Judge, United States District Court District of New Jersey)* Appointed by U.S. District Court judges. Reappointed to term beginning April 7, 2000, current term expires April 2008.

Office: U.S. Courthouse, 50 Walnut Street, Newark 07102.

Telephone: (973) 645-5903.

WILLIAMS, Rosemarie Ruggiero *(Judge, New Jersey Superior Court Vicinage Thirteen)* Appointed by Governor Jim Florio Feb 19, 1993. Reappointed by Governor Christine T. Whitman. Term expires at age seventy. Served Vicinage Seven 1993-2000. Currently serves as Environmental Judge. Born Plainfield New Jersey Dec 21, 1951. Lutheran. Educated at College of New Jersey B.A. summa cum laude 1978 and Villanova University J.D. 1981. Admitted to practice New Jersey 1981.

Deputy Attorney General 1981-93 and Supervisor 1989-91 and Section Chief 1991-93 Tort Claim Section Attorney General's Office. Professor College of New Jersey 1998. Vice President Mercer County Inns of Court 1998-2000. Former Member Committee on Criminal Practices Supreme Court of New Jersey. Member Model Civil Jury Charges Committee, Joseph Halpern American Inn of Court, Mercer County, Somerset County and New Jersey State Bar Associations.

Mailing address: P.O. Box 3000, Somerville 08876.

Office: Somerset County Courthouse, Somerville 08876.

Telephone: (908) 231-7195.

WILSON, Deanne M. *(Judge, New Jersey Superior Court Vicinage Ten)* Appointed by governor.

Mailing address: P.O. Box 910, Morristown 07963-0910.

Office: Morris County Courthouse, Morristown 07960.

Telephone: (973) 656-4058.

WILSON, Robert C. *(Judge, New Jersey Superior Court Vicinage Two)* Appointed by governor.

Office: Bergen County Justice Center, 10 Main Street, Hackensack 07601.

Telephone: (201) 752-4403.

WINARD, Theodore A. *(Judge, New Jersey Superior Court Vicinage Five)* Appointed by governor.

Office: 310 Hall of Records, 465 Dr. Martin Luther King Jr. Blvd., Newark 07102.

Telephone: (973) 693-6524, 693-6525.

WINFIELD, Novalyn L. *(Judge, United States Bankruptcy Court District of New Jersey)* Appointed by U.S. Court of Appeals Third Circuit judges.
Office: U.S. Courthouse, Third Floor, 50 Walnut Street, Newark 07102-3550.
Telephone: (973) 645-2187.

WINKELSTEIN, Michael *(Judge, New Jersey Superior Court Appellate Division)* Appointed Judge Vicinage One by governor. Former Assignment Judge. Assigned to Appellate Division by Chief Justice Deborah T. Poritz.
Office: County Civil Court Building, 1201 Bacharach Boulevard, Atlantic City 08401-4510.
Telephone: (609) 441-3482.

WIZMUR, Judith H. *(Judge, United States Bankruptcy Court District of New Jersey)* Appointed by U.S. Court of Appeals Third Circuit judges to term beginning Sept 5, 1985. Reappointed 1999, current term expires Sept 2013.
Office: 15 North Seventh Street, Camden 08102-1104.
Telephone: (856) 757-5126.

WOLFSON, Freda L. *(Judge, United States District Court District of New Jersey)* Former Magistrate Judge. Appointed Judge for life by President George W. Bush to term beginning Dec 4, 2002.
Office: U.S. Courthouse, One John F. Gerry Plaza, 400 Cooper Street, Camden 08102.
Telephone: (856) 757-5057.

WOLIN, Alfred M. *(Senior Judge, United States District Court District of New Jersey)* Appointed for life by President Ronald Reagan to term beginning Jan 6, 1988. Assumed Senior status Sept 18, 2000, serves by assignment. Born Orange New Jersey Sept 17, 1932. Jewish. Educated at University of Michigan B.A. 1954 and Rutgers University J.D. 1959. Member Phi Delta Phi. Admitted to practice New Jersey 1960, U.S. District Court District of New Jersey 1960 and U.S. Supreme Court 1963. In legal practice 1960-80. Judge, Union County District Court 1980-83. Judge Civil Part 1982-83 and Presiding Judge Criminal Part 1983-87, Superior Court Vicinage Twelve. Sat by assignment, U.S. Court of Appeals Third Circuit 1989. Sat by assignment U.S. District Court District of the Virgin Islands 1989-90 and 1992-93.
Attorney Board of Adjustment Roselle 1965-74. Chief Staff Attorney Union County Legal Aid Society 1965-74. Special Assistant Prosecutor Union County 1970. Municipal Prosecutor Township of Westfield 1973-74. Important Opinions: 250 opinions published and over 1,500 unpublished opinions on Westlaw and Lexis. Instructor in Trial Advocacy 1995 and Adjunct Professor 1995-99 Seton Hall University School of Law. Former Member Executive Committee Statewide Speedy Trial Committee, Criminal Practice Committee Conference of Presiding Criminal Judges and Criminal Justice Act Appointments Subcommittee U.S. Judicial Conference New Jersey Supreme Court. Secretary Union County Ethics Committee 1970-78. Chairman ad hoc Committee on Juror Utilization. Fellow American Bar Foundation. Master American Inns of Court. Member District Judges Association (President 1991-92), U.S. Alien Terrorist Removal Court, Federal Judges Association, American Judicature Society, Union County (Secretary 1970-74, President Elect 1975, President Judicial Appointments Committee 1976), New Jersey State (Professional Responsibility Committee 1992 and 1994, Judicial Selection Committee, Discipline of the Bar Committee, Lawyer Referral Committee) and American (Committee on Standards for Admissibility of Technology-Sophisticated Evidence) Bar Associations.
Attended Judicial Workshops for First and Third Circuit Judges 1988, Seminar for Newly Appointed Judges 1988, Third Circuit Annual Judicial Conference 1988-91 and Media Coverage of Criminal Cases Bench-Bar Conference New Jersey Law Center 1989. Lecturer-Panelist Prentice Hall Insurance Litigation Institute Seminar 1989 and 1990. Panelist The Sentencing Reform Act and Sentencing Guidelines Seminar Institute for Continuing Legal Education 1990; Tenth Annual U.S. District Court Judicial Conference 1992; and Seminar on State-Federal Relationships 1992 and 21st Century Courtroom Technology—A Demonstration and Discussion of the Multimedia Trial Twentieth Annual U.S. District Court Judicial Conference 1996 Association of the Federal Bar. Speaker Fourteenth Annual U.S. District Court Judicial Conference Federal Bar Association 1990 and "The Trial Lawyers Approach to Winning Patent Cases" Seminar for Executives, General Counsel, Litigation Managers and Patent Counsel Los Angeles 1997. Panel Participant Certified Civil and Criminal Trial Attorneys Young Lawyers Section Program on Professionalism New Jersey State Bar Association Convention 1990. Keynote Speaker Conference sponsored by Labor and Employment Law Section New Jersey State Bar Association and National Labor Relations Board 1991. Participant Case Management Skills Development Seminar Federal Judicial Center 1992 and National Workshop for District Court Judges 1993. Moderator Debate of Continuing Legal Education Division New York Patent and Trademark Association 1992. Participant/Panelist "From War Room to Courtroom" American Bar Association 1993. Speaker and Participant in panel and trial demonstration Eighth Annual Insurance Litigation Institute Prentice Hall New York City 1994 and San Francisco California 1994 and Scientific Evidence Panel Association of the Federal Bar 1995. Keynote Speaker and Participant "Beyond the Barr Decision" University of Rhode Island Seminar Naples Florida 1998, Marco Island Florida 1999 and Lucerne Switzerland 1999. Specialist Second Class U.S. Army 1954-56. Legislative Aide to New Jersey State Senator Matthew J. Rinaldo 1970-72. Congressional Field Representative to Congressman Matthew J. Rinaldo 12th Congressional District 1972-79. Participant Third Annual Challenge Cup American Cancer Society. Member Gender Bias Task Force Philadelphia and National Maritime Association.
Office: U.S. Courthouse, 50 Walnut Street, Newark 07102.
Telephone: (973) 645-2580.

WOMACK, Stephen H. *(Judge, New Jersey Superior Court Vicinage Eleven)* Appointed by governor.
Office: Passaic County Admin. Bldg., 401 Grand Street, Paterson 07505.
Telephone: (973) 247-8452.

YANNOTTI, Joseph L. *(Judge, New Jersey Superior Court Vicinage Two)* Appointed by governor.
Office: Bergen County Justice Center, 10 Main Street, Hackensack 07601.
Telephone: (201) 646-6769.

ZAMPINO, Thomas P. *(Judge, New Jersey Superior Court Vicinage Five)* Appointed by governor.

Office: Gibraltar Building, Tenth Floor, 212 Washington Street, Newark 07102.

Telephone: (973) 693-6706, 693-6707.

ZAZZALI, James *(Associate Justice, Supreme Court of New Jersey)* Appointed by Governor Christine T. Whitman to term beginning June 20, 2000. Born Newark New Jersey June 17, 1937. Roman Catholic. Educated at Georgetown University B.S. 1958 J.D. 1962. Law Clerk to Hon. Lawrence A. Whipple, New Jersey Superior Court 1964-65. Admitted to practice District of Columbia 1962, New Jersey 1963, New York 1988, U.S. District Courts District of Columbia and District of New Jersey, U.S. Court of Appeals Third Circuit and U.S. Supreme Court. In legal practice Washington D.C. and Newark and Trenton New Jersey 1962-2000.

Assistant County Prosecutor Essex County 1965-68. Former General Counsel New Jersey Sports and Exposition Authority. Former Special Master County Jails Essex, Monmouth and Bergen counties. Former State Attorney General. Former Adjunct Professor Seton Hall Law School. Member Essex County, Monmouth County, New Jersey State, Federal and American Bar Associations. Democrat. Chairman New Jersey State Commission of Investigation. Vice Chairman Disciplinary Review Board. Receiver Bloomfield College.

Office: 151 Bodman Place, Redbank 07701.

Telephone: (732) 530-7854.

ZUCKER-ZARETT, Barbara *(Judge, New Jersey Superior Court Vicinage Ten)* Appointed by governor.

Mailing address: P.O. Box 910, Morristown 07963-0910.

Office: Morris County Courthouse, Morristown 07960.

Telephone: (973) 656-4010.

NEW MEXICO

Capital SANTA FE

UNITED STATES DISTRICT COURT DISTRICT OF NEW MEXICO

The court sits at Albuquerque, Las Cruces, Las Vegas, Roswell, Santa Fe and Silver City. For descriptive information refer to the United States Courts section.

Chief Judge
James A. Parker

Judges
C. LeRoy Hansen
Martha Vazquez
Bruce Douglas Black
M. Christina Armijo
William Paul Johnson

Senior Judge
John Edwards Conway

Clerk
Robert M. March
U.S. Courthouse
333 Lomas Boulevard N.W.
Albuquerque, New Mexico 87102
(505) 348-2000

UNITED STATES MAGISTRATE JUDGES OF NEW MEXICO

Robert W. Ionta
Leslie C. Smith
Karen B. Molzen
Robert H. Scott
Lorenzo F. Garcia
Richard L. Puglisi
Lourdes A. Martinez

Recalled Magistrate Judges
Don J. Svet
Joe H. Galvan

UNITED STATES BANKRUPTCY COURT OF NEW MEXICO

Chief Judge
James S. Starzynski

Judge
Mark B. McFeeley

Bankruptcy Clerk
Norman H. Meyer
P.O. Box 546
Albuquerque, New Mexico 87103-0546
(505) 348-2500

NEW MEXICO SUPREME COURT

The Supreme Court is New Mexico's court of last resort. The court consists of five justices initially elected in partisan elections for eight-year terms. Subsequent eight-year terms are by retention vote. Vacancies are filled by the governor and appointees serve for the remainder of the unexpired term. The chief justice is elected by peer vote for a two-year term. The senior justice is determined by length of continuous service to the court; in the absence of the chief justice, the senior justice exercises the powers of the chief justice. Retired judges serve pro tempore by assignment of the chief justice.

The court has appellate jurisdiction over all District Court decisions in criminal cases imposing a death penalty or life imprisonment and in all other cases where appellate jurisdiction is not vested in the Court of Appeals. The court has original jurisdiction to issue extraordinary writs necessary to the exercise of proper jurisdiction and has jurisdiction to review by writ of certiorari decisions of the Court of Appeals. At its discretion, the court may review questions certified to it by a federal court. The court has supervisory and administrative control over all lower courts and exercises disciplinary control over judges and attorneys in the state.

The court sits at Santa Fe, generally in panels of three, and holds session all year.

Chief Justice
Petra Jimenez Maes

Senior Justice
Petra Jimenez Maes

Justices
Pamela B. Minzner
Patricio M. Serna
Richard C. Bosson
Edward L. Chavez

Clerk
Kathleen Jo Gibson
P.O. Box 848
Santa Fe, New Mexico 87504-0848
(505) 827-4860

Administrative Director
Gina M. Maestas
Administrative Office of the Courts
237 Don Gasper, Room 25
Santa Fe, New Mexico 87501
(505) 827-4800

NEW MEXICO COURT OF APPEALS

The Court of Appeals is New Mexico's intermediate appellate court. The court consists of ten judges initially elected in partisan elections for eight-year terms. Subsequent eight-year terms are by retention vote. Vacancies are filled by the governor and appointees serve for the remainder of the unexpired term. A chief judge is elected by peer vote to serve a two-year term. The senior judge is determined by length of service to the court; in the absence of the chief judge, the senior judge exer-

NEW MEXICO COURT OF APPEALS—*Continued*

cises the power of the chief judge. Retired judges may serve by assignment of the chief justice.

The court has appellate jurisdiction over judicial cases except criminal cases involving sentences of death or life imprisonment, appeals from the State Public Regulation Commission, and cases involving writs of habeas corpus. The court has discretionary jurisdiction over administrative appeals and in interlocutory decision cases.

The court sits in panels of three at Santa Fe but may sit elsewhere in the state as needed.

Chief Judge

James J. Wechsler

Judges

A. Joseph Alarid
Michael D. Bustamante
Celia Foy Castillo
Ira S. Robinson
Michael E. Vigil
Lynn Pickard
Jonathan B. Sutin
Cynthia A. Fry
Roderick T. Kennedy

NEW MEXICO DISTRICT COURTS

The District Courts are New Mexico's courts of general jurisdiction. The state is divided into thirteen judicial districts. Judges are elected initially in partisan elections by the voters in their respective districts for six-year terms. Subsequent six-year terms are by retention vote. Vacancies are filled by the governor and appointees serve for the remainder of the unexpired term. In judicial districts having more than one judge, a chief judge is elected by peer vote; length of term varies by district. Retired judges may serve by assignment of the chief justice.

The courts have original jurisdiction in all matters not excepted in the constitution or otherwise provided by law. The courts have jurisdiction over misdemeanors and exclusive jurisdiction over triable felonies. The courts have concurrent jurisdiction with the Probate Courts over informal proceedings for probate of wills or appointment of personal representatives and exclusive original jurisdiction over formal probate proceedings, estates of missing and protected persons, protection of incapacitated persons or minors and cases involving trusts. In each county a Children's Court may be established as a division of the District Court to exercise exclusive juvenile jurisdiction. A District Court may establish a Family Court Division in lieu of the Children's Court Division. The Family Court Division exercises the same jurisdiction as the Children's Court Division and additionally exercises exclusive jurisdiction over domestic relations and mental health cases. The courts have appellate jurisdiction and supervisory control over the lower courts. The courts also have rule-making authority and may issue writs necessary to the exercise of proper jurisdiction.

The courts sit at each county seat in the district.

FIRST JUDICIAL DISTRICT includes Los Alamos, Rio Arriba and Santa Fe counties. The court sits at Los Alamos, Tierra Amarilla and Santa Fe.

Chief Judge

James A. Hall

Judges

Tim Garcia
Daniel A. Sanchez
Carol J. Vigil
Stephen Pfeffer
Barbara J. Vigil
Michael E. Vigil

SECOND JUDICIAL DISTRICT includes Bernalillo County. The court sits at Albuquerque.

Chief Judge

W. John Brennan

Judges

Frank H. Allen
Ted Baca
James F. Blackmer
Susan M. Conway
Angela Jewell
Richard J. Knowles
Mark A. Macaron
Nan Nash
Ernesto Romero
W. Daniel Schneider
Deborah D. Walker
Marie A. Baca
Theresa M. Baca
Neil C. Candelaria
Valerie Mackie Huling
Tommy E. Jewell
William F. Lang
Albert S. Murdoch
Geraldine E. Rivera
Ross C. Sanchez
Robert L. Thompson
Wendy York

THIRD JUDICIAL DISTRICT includes Doña Ana County. The court sits at Las Cruces.

Chief Judge

Robert E. Robles

Judges

Stephen Bridgforth
Sylvia Cano-Garcia
Grace B. Duran
Larry Ramirez
Jerald A. Valentine

FOURTH JUDICIAL DISTRICT includes Guadalupe, Mora and San Miguel counties. The court sits at Santa Rosa, Mora and Las Vegas.

Chief Judge

Jay G. Harris

Judge

Eugenio S. Mathis

FIFTH JUDICIAL DISTRICT includes Chaves, Eddy and Lea counties. The court sits at Roswell, Carlsbad and Lovington.

Chief Judge

Jay W. Forbes

Judges

Gary L. Clingman
Alvin F. Jones
Don Maddox
James L. Shuler
Charles C. Currier
William P. Lynch
William A. McBee

SIXTH JUDICIAL DISTRICT includes Grant, Hidalgo and Luna counties. The court sits at Silver City, Lordsburg and Deming.

Chief Judge

Gary Jeffreys

Judge

Henry R. Quintero, Sr.

SEVENTH JUDICIAL DISTRICT includes Catron, Sierra, Socorro and Torrance counties. The court sits at Reserve, Truth or Consequences, Socorro and Estancia.

NEW MEXICO DISTRICT COURTS—*Continued*

Chief Judge
Edmund H. Kase, III

Judges
Thomas G. Fitch
Kevin Sweazea

EIGHTH JUDICIAL DISTRICT includes Colfax, Taos and Union counties. The court sits at Raton, Taos and Clayton.

Chief Judge
Peggy J. Nelson

Judge
Sam Sanchez

NINTH JUDICIAL DISTRICT includes Curry and Roosevelt counties. The court sits at Clovis and Portales.

Chief Judge
Robert C. Brack

Judges
Ted L. Hartley
Stephen K. Quinn

TENTH JUDICIAL DISTRICT includes De Baca, Harding and Quay counties. The court sits at Fort Sumner, Mosquero and Tucumcari.

Chief Judge
Ricky D. Purcell

ELEVENTH JUDICIAL DISTRICT includes McKinley and San Juan counties. The court sits at Gallup, Aztec and Farmington.

Chief Judge
William C. Birdsall

Judges
John A. Dean, Jr.
Douglas A. Echols
Grant L. Foutz
Thomas J. Hynes
Joseph L. Rich

TWELFTH JUDICIAL DISTRICT includes Lincoln and Otero counties. The court sits at Carrizozo and Alamogordo.

Chief Judge
Jerry H. Ritter

Judges
James Waylon Counts
Karen L. Parsons
Frank K. Wilson

THIRTEENTH JUDICIAL DISTRICT includes Cibola, Sandoval and Valencia counties. The court sits at Grants, Bernalillo and Los Lunas.

Chief Judge
Louis P. McDonald

Judges
Kenneth G. Brown
Camille Martinez-Olguin
John William Pope
William A. Sanchez

NEW MEXICO PROBATE COURTS

Probate Courts are courts of limited jurisdiction located in each county in New Mexico. Judges are elected at general elections in their respective counties for two-year terms.

The courts have concurrent original jurisdiction with the District Courts over informal proceedings for probate of wills or appointment of personal representatives. The District Courts have exclusive jurisdiction over other probate matters. Appeals are to the District Courts.

The courts sit at each county seat.

NEW MEXICO MAGISTRATE COURTS

Magistrate Courts are courts of limited jurisdiction in New Mexico. The courts are established in counties with populations of less than 200,000. Magistrate judges are elected within their respective counties in partisan elections for four-year terms. Vacancies are filled by the governor. In magistrate districts where two or more divisions operate as a single court, the director of the Administrative Office of the Courts designates a presiding magistrate judge to perform administrative duties.

The courts have civil jurisdiction in matters not exceeding $10,000 and criminal jurisdiction to commit to jail and to discharge or recognize the defendant to appear before the District Courts. The courts also have jurisdiction over misdemeanors, DWI and other traffic violations and other actions as provided by law.

The courts sit at each county seat.

BERNALILLO COUNTY METROPOLITAN COURT

The Bernalillo County Metropolitan Court began operation July 1, 1980 as an independent branch of the state Magistrate Court. Separate Metropolitan Courts may be established in counties with populations exceeding 200,000. Judges are elected initially in partisan elections by the voters in their respective districts for four-year terms. Subsequent four-year terms are by retention vote. Vacancies are filled by the governor. Appointees serve until the next general election. A chief judge is selected by peer vote.

The court has concurrent jurisdiction with the Magistrate Courts and has jurisdiction over county and municipal ordinance violations as well as civil jurisdiction over matters when the amount in controversy does not exceed $10,000. Appeals are to the District Courts.

The court sits at Albuquerque.

NEW MEXICO MUNICIPAL COURTS

Municipal Courts are courts of limited jurisdiction in New Mexico which may be established in incorporated cities or towns with populations of 1,000 or more. Judges are usually elected for four-year terms, but may also be appointed. Length of term may vary as determined by each municipality.

The courts have jurisdiction over all violations of municipal ordinances and over traffic violations. The courts are also authorized to issue subpoenas and warrants and may punish for contempt of court. Appeals are to the District Courts.

New Mexico Counties and County Seats

Bernalillo
Albuquerque

Catron
Reserve

Chaves
Roswell

Cibola
Grants

Colfax
Raton

Curry
Clovis

De Baca
Fort Sumner

Doña Ana
Las Cruces

Eddy
Carlsbad

Grant
Silver City

Guadalupe
Santa Rosa

Harding
Mosquero

Hidalgo
Lordsburg

Lea
Lovington

Lincoln
Carrizozo

Los Alamos
Los Alamos

Luna
Deming

McKinley
Gallup

Mora
Mora

Otero
Alamogordo

Quay
Tucumcari

Rio Arriba
Tierra Amarilla

Roosevelt
Portales

Sandoval
Bernalillo

San Juan
Aztec

San Miguel
Las Vegas

Santa Fe
Santa Fe

Sierra
Truth or Consequences

Socorro
Socorro

Taos
Taos

Torrance
Estancia

Union
Clayton

Valencia
Los Lunas

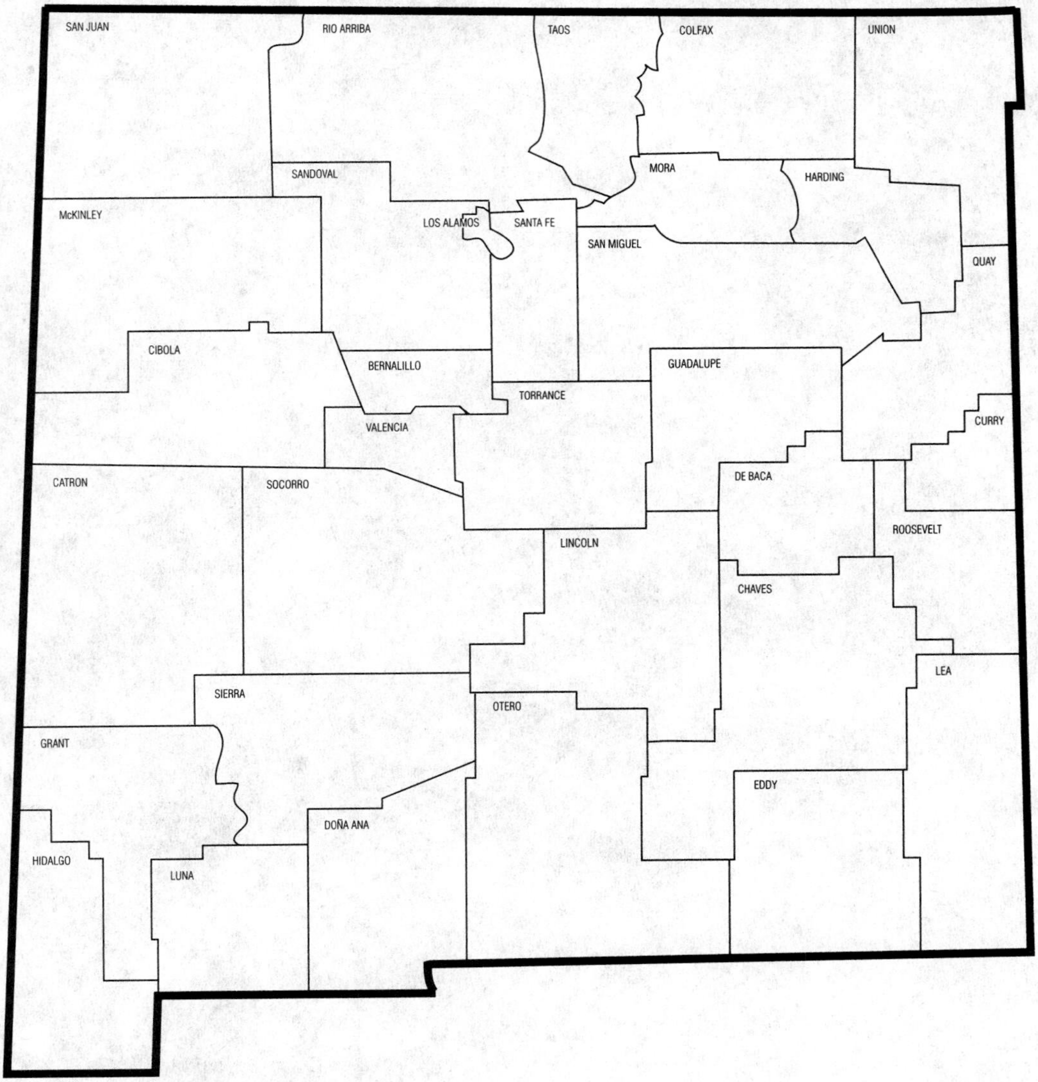
SAN JUAN
RIO ARRIBA
TAOS
COLFAX
UNION
SANDOVAL
MORA
HARDING
McKINLEY
LOS ALAMOS
SANTA FE
SAN MIGUEL
QUAY
CIBOLA
BERNALILLO
GUADALUPE
TORRANCE
CURRY
VALENCIA
CATRON
SOCORRO
DE BACA
ROOSEVELT
LINCOLN
CHAVES
LEA
SIERRA
OTERO
GRANT
EDDY
DOÑA ANA
HIDALGO
LUNA

UNITED STATES DISTRICT COURT DISTRICT OF NEW MEXICO

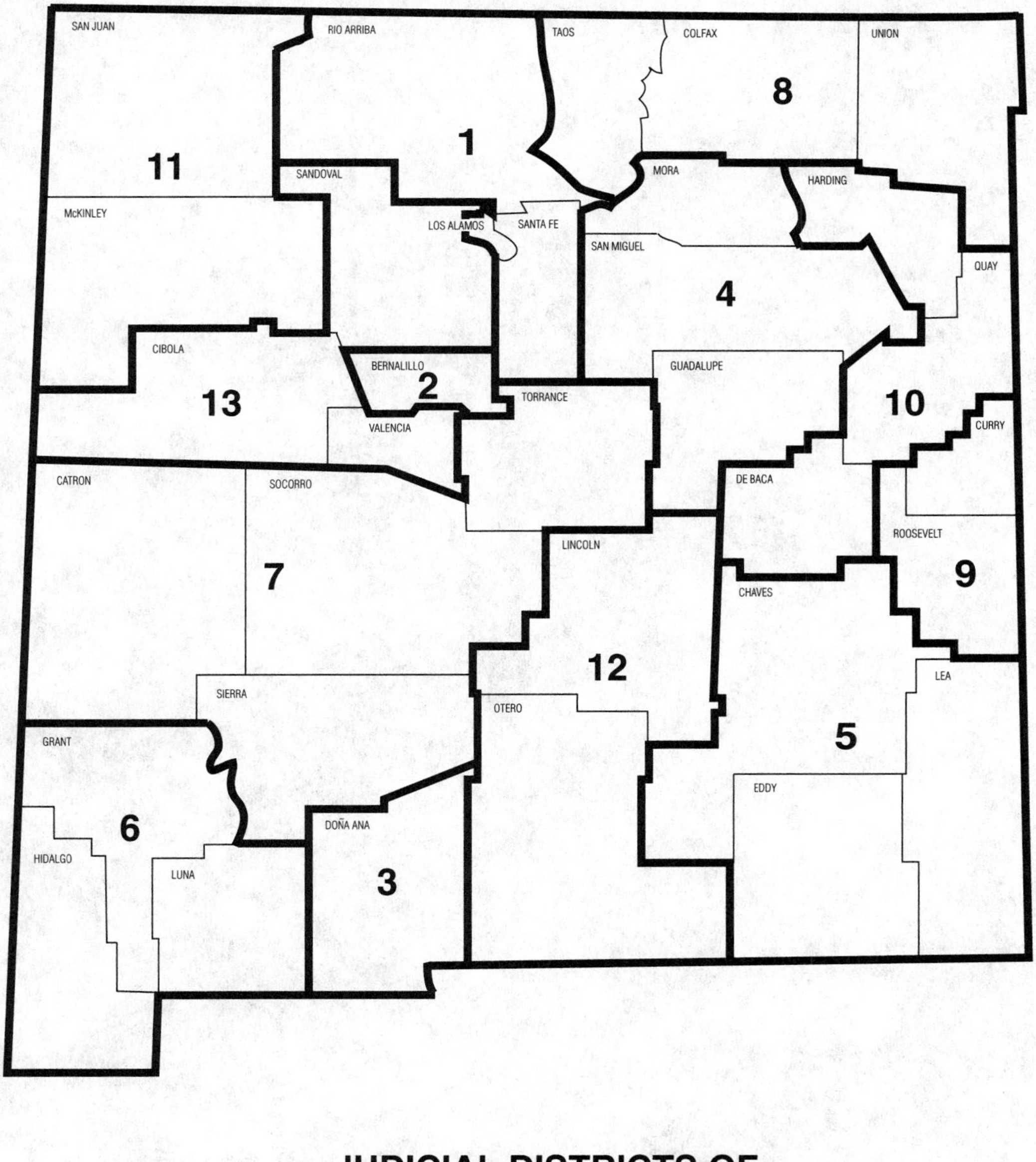
SAN JUAN
RIO ARRIBA
TAOS
COLFAX
UNION
8
1
11
SANDOVAL
MORA
HARDING
McKINLEY
LOS ALAMOS
SANTA FE
SAN MIGUEL
QUAY
4
CIBOLA
GUADALUPE
BERNALILLO
2
TORRANCE
10
13
VALENCIA
CURRY
CATRON
SOCORRO
DE BACA
ROOSEVELT
LINCOLN
9
7
CHAVES
12
LEA
SIERRA
OTERO
5
GRANT
EDDY
DOÑA ANA
6
HIDALGO
LUNA
3

JUDICIAL DISTRICTS OF NEW MEXICO DISTRICT COURTS

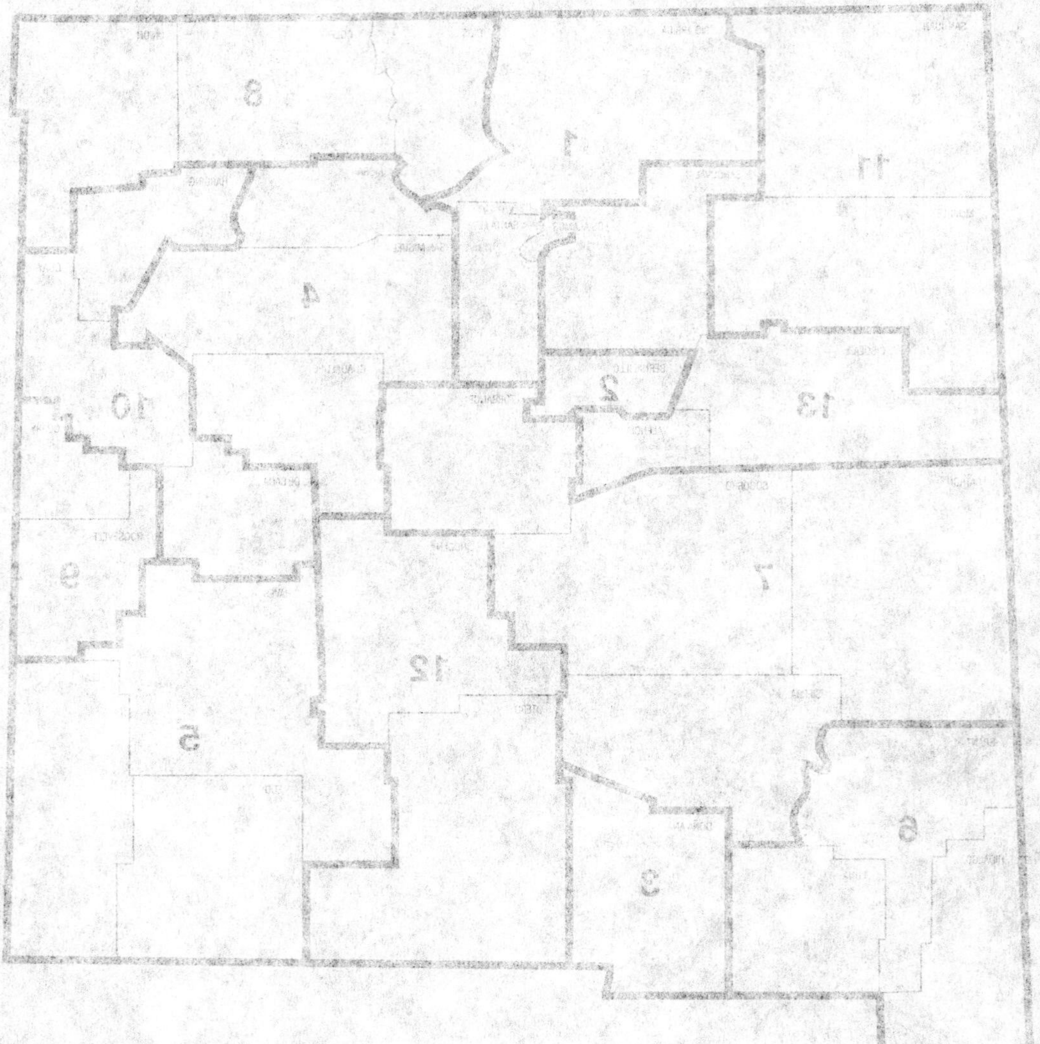
8
1
11
4
10
2
13
9
7
12
5
6
3

JUDICIAL DISTRICTS OF NEW MEXICO DISTRICT COURTS

NEW MEXICO

ALARID, A. Joseph *(Judge, New Mexico Court of Appeals)* Appointed by Governor Toney Anaya to term beginning Jan 1, 1984. Elected Nov 1984. Retained by election Nov 3, 1992 and 2000. Current term expires Dec 31, 2008. Former Chief Judge. Former Senior Judge. Born Albuquerque New Mexico Sept 4, 1948. Roman Catholic. Educated at University of New Mexico B.A. in Political Science 1970 and Georgetown University Law Center J.D. 1973. Member Delta Theta Phi. Admitted to practice New Mexico 1973, U.S. Supreme Court, U.S. Tax Court and U.S. Court of Military Appeals. Began legal practice Washington D.C. 1973. In legal practice Santa Fe New Mexico 1977-80. Judge, Bernalillo County Metropolitan Court 1980-81. Judge, New Mexico District Court Second Judicial District 1981-83.

Former Trial Attorney U.S. Department of Justice. Legislative Counsel to Senator Joseph M. Montoya 1974-77. Assistant Attorney General State of New Mexico 1977-79. General Counsel Energy and Mineral Department 1979-80. Adjunct Professor of Public Administration University of New Mexico 1980-81 and Summer 1992. Chairman New Mexico Judicial Conference 1983-85 and Supreme Court Judicial Performance Evaluation Subcommittee since 1990. Former Delegate National Conference of the Judiciary on Victims of Crime. Former Member Board of Bar Examiners. Member Supreme Court Committee on Judicial Performance Standards, State Bar of New Mexico, Albuquerque and American Bar Associations. Faculty Advisor "General Jurisdiction" The National Judicial College Fall 1985. Democrat. Board of Directors University of New Mexico Alumni Association 1981-84 (Executive Committee 1983-84), New Mexico Council on Crime and Delinquency 1982-84, La Companiá de Teatro de Albuquerque 1982-84 and Albuquerque Civic Light Opera Association. Advisory Board New Mexico Law-Related Education Project. Member Search Committee for Dean of the College of Arts and Sciences University of New Mexico 1987. Member Albuquerque Kiwanis Club. Enjoys New Mexico history, racquetball and skiing.

Office: 1117 Stanford N.E., Albuquerque 87131.
Telephone: (505) 841-4611.

ALLEN, Frank H. *(Judge, New Mexico District Court Second Judicial District)* Term expires Dec 31, 2008.

Mailing address: P.O. Box 488, Albuquerque 87103.
Office: 400 Lomas Boulevard N.W., Albuquerque 87102.
Telephone: (505) 841-7456.
Fax: (505) 841-5458

ARMIJO, M. Christina *(Judge, United States District Court District of New Mexico)* Appointed for life by President George W. Bush to term beginning Nov 15, 2001. Former Judge, New Mexico Court of Appeals.

Office: 760 U.S. Courthouse, 333 Lomas Boulevard N.W., Albuquerque 87102.
Telephone: (505) 348-2310.

BACA, Marie A. *(Judge, New Mexico District Court Second Judicial District)* Term expires 2008.

Mailing address: P.O. Box 488, Albuquerque 87103.
Office: 400 Lomas Boulevard N.W., Albuquerque 87102.
Telephone: (505) 841-7602.

BACA, Ted *(Judge, New Mexico District Court Second Judicial District)* Term expires Dec 31, 2008.

Mailing address: P.O. Box 488, Albuquerque 87103.
Office: 400 Lomas Boulevard N.W., Albuquerque 87102.
Telephone: (505) 841-7522.
Fax: (505) 841-5456

BACA, Theresa M. *(Judge, New Mexico District Court Second Judicial District)* Appointed by Governor Bruce King to term beginning May 1993. Elected Nov 1994. Retained by election Nov 1996 and 2002. Current term expires Dec 31, 2008. Born Albuquerque New Mexico July 14, 1950. Catholic. Educated at St. John's College A.B. 1972 and University of Pennsylvania J.D. 1975. Admitted to practice New Mexico 1978 and U.S. District Court District of New Mexico 1978. In legal practice Albuquerque 1978-85. Judge, Bernalillo County Metropolitan Court 1985-93.

Mailing address: P.O. Box 488, Albuquerque 87103.
Office: 400 Lomas Boulevard N.W., Albuquerque 87102.
Telephone: (505) 841-7512.
Fax: (505) 841-5455

BIRDSALL, William C. *(Chief Judge, New Mexico District Court Eleventh Judicial District)* Term expires Dec 31, 2008.

Office: 103 South Oliver, Aztec 87410.
Telephone: (505) 334-6151.
Fax: (505) 334-1940

BLACK, Bruce Douglas *(Judge, United States District Court District of New Mexico)* Appointed for life by President Bill Clinton. Born Detroit Michigan 1947. Educated at Albion College B.A. with honors 1969 and University of Michigan J.D. with honors 1971. Member Phi Beta Kappa. Admitted to practice New Mexico 1972, U.S. Courts of Appeals Tenth 1974 and Ninth 1982 Circuits and U.S. Supreme Court 1980. In legal practice Albuquerque 1972-75 and Santa Fe 1975-91. Former Judge, New Mexico Court of Appeals, appointed by Governor Bruce King to term beginning Aug 8, 1991.

Author "Optional Safety Devises: How Strict the Liability" 8 New Mexico L. Rev. 189, 1978, "What are the Lessee's Obligations When Settling Take-or-Pay Litigation" 6 New Mexico Natural Resources Law Reporter 15, 1991 and "The Use (or Abuse) of Expert Witnesses in Post-Daubert Employment Litigation" 17 Hofstra Labor and Employment L. Jour. 269, 2000. Important Decisions: City of Farmington v. Fawcett 114 N.M. 537, 843 P.2d 839, 1992; United States v. Dion L. 19 F. Supp.2d 1224 (D.N.M.) 1998; and Swanson v. Guthrie Independent School District 135 F.3d 694 (10th Cir)

BLACK, BRUCE DOUGLAS—*Continued*

1998. Chairman Rules of Civil Procedure Committee New Mexico Supreme Court 1983-89.

Office: 640 U.S. Courthouse, 333 Lomas Boulevard N.W., Albuquerque 87102.

Telephone: (505) 348-2260.

BLACKMER, James F. *(Judge, New Mexico District Court Second Judicial District)* Term expires Dec 31, 2008.

Mailing address: P.O. Box 488, Albuquerque 87103.

Office: 400 Lomas Boulevard N.W., Albuquerque 87102.

Telephone: (505) 841-7521.

Fax: (505) 841-5458

BOSSON, Richard C. *(Justice, New Mexico Supreme Court)* Term expires Dec 31, 2004. Former Judge and Chief Judge, New Mexico Court of Appeals.

Mailing address: P.O. Box 848, Santa Fe 87504-0848.

Telephone: (505) 827-4892.

BRACK, Robert C. *(Chief Judge, New Mexico District Court Ninth Judicial District)* Term expires Dec 31, 2008.

Office: 14 Curry County Courthouse, 700 North Main, Clovis 88101.

Telephone: (505) 762-4185.

Fax: (505) 763-5160

BRENNAN, W. John *(Chief Judge, New Mexico District Court Second Judicial District)* Appointed by Governor Bruce King to term beginning July 1, 1979. Elected 1984. Retained by election 1990, 1996 and 2002. Current term expires Dec 31, 2008. Born Albuquerque New Mexico Feb 25, 1947. Catholic. Educated at University of Notre Dame B.A. cum laude 1969 and University of New Mexico J.D. 1973. Staff member New Mexico Law Review 1971. Law Clerk to New Mexico Court of Appeals 1973. Admitted to practice New Mexico 1973. Began legal practice Albuquerque 1973.

Director Judicial Council. Member Juvenile Justice Advisory Committee, State Bar of New Mexico and Albuquerque Bar Association. Instructor New Mexico Magistrate Judicial College 1982. Recipient Crimestopper Award 1980. Democrat. Lecturer First Offenders Program. Director La Compania (bilingual theatre group). Member Kiwanis Club. Enjoys tennis.

Mailing address: P.O. Box 488, Albuquerque 87103.

Office: 400 Lomas Boulevard N.W., Albuquerque 87102.

Telephone: (505) 841-7499.

Fax: (505) 841-6785

BRIDGFORTH, Stephen *(Judge, New Mexico District Court Third Judicial District)* Appointed by Governor Gary E. Johnson 1997. Elected 2000. Retained by election 2002, current term expires Dec 31, 2008.

Office: 201 West Picacho Avenue, Suite A, Las Cruces 88005.

Telephone: (505) 523-8230.

Fax: (505) 523-8290

BROWN, Kenneth G. *(Judge, New Mexico District Court Thirteenth Judicial District)* Term expires Dec 31, 2008. Former Chief Judge.

Office: 100 Avenida de Justicia, Bernalillo 87004.

Telephone: (505) 867-2861.

BUSTAMANTE, Michael D. *(Judge, New Mexico Court of Appeals)* Elected to term beginning 1996. Retained by election 2002, current term expires Dec 31, 2010.

Office: 1117 Stanford N.E., Albuquerque 87131.

Telephone: (505) 841-4650.

CANDELARIA, Neil C. *(Judge, New Mexico District Court Second Judicial District)* Appointed by Governor Gary E. Johnson to term beginning Feb 8, 1999. Elected 2000, current term expires Dec 31, 2006. Born Norwich England Jan 19, 1956. Religious affiliation: United Church of Religious Science. Educated at University of Albuquerque B.S. 1983 and University of New Mexico J.D. 1986. Admitted to practice New Mexico 1986 and U.S. District Court District of New Mexico 1988. Judge, Bernalillo County Metropolitan Court 1994-99.

Deputy District Attorney Albuquerque 1986-94. U.S. Army 1974-77. Hobbies include collecting coins and old religious books.

Mailing address: P.O. Box 488, Albuquerque 87103.

Office: 400 Lomas Boulevard N.W., Albuquerque 87102.

Telephone: (505) 841-7484.

Fax: (505) 841-5457

E-mail address: albdnxc@jidmail.nmcourts.com

CANO-GARCIA, Sylvia *(Judge, New Mexico District Court Third Judicial District)* Elected to term beginning Jan 2003. Term expires Dec 31, 2008.

Office: 201 West Picacho Avenue, Suite A, Las Cruces 88005.

Telephone: (505) 523-8240.

Fax: (505) 523-8290

CASTILLO, Celia Foy *(Judge, New Mexico Court of Appeals)* Appointed by Governor Gary E. Johnson to term beginning 2001. Elected 2002, current term expires Dec 31, 2010.

Office: 201 West Picacho Avenue, Suite C, Las Cruces 88005.

Telephone: (505) 523-8261.

CHAVEZ, Edward L. *(Justice, New Mexico Supreme Court)* Term expires Dec 31, 2006.

Mailing address: P.O. Box 848, Santa Fe 87504-0848.

Telephone: (505) 827-4880.

CLINGMAN, Gary L. *(Judge, New Mexico District Court Fifth Judicial District)* Term expires Dec 31, 2008.

Office: 100 North Main, Lovington 88260.

Telephone: (505) 396-4768.

Fax: (505) 396-2428

CONWAY, John Edwards *(Senior Judge, United States District Court District of New Mexico)* Appointed for life by President Ronald Reagan to term beginning July 3, 1986. Former Chief Judge. Assumed Senior status Sept 1, 2000, serves by assignment. Born Joplin Missouri Sept 1, 1934. Protestant. Educated at U.S. Naval Academy B.S. 1956 and Washburn University School of Law LL.B. magna cum laude 1963. Editor-in-Chief Washburn Law Review 1962-63. Member Phi Alpha Delta. Admitted to practice New Mexico 1963, Kansas 1963, U.S. District Courts District of New Mexico 1963 and District of Kansas 1963, U.S. Court of Appeals Tenth Circuit 1964, U.S. Supreme Court 1971 and U.S. Claims Court 1984. In legal practice Santa Fe New

CONWAY, JOHN EDWARDS—*Continued*
Mexico 1963-64, Alamogordo New Mexico 1964-80 and Albuquerque New Mexico 1980-86.

City Attorney Alamogordo 1966-72. Member 1977-84 and Chairman 1980-84 New Mexico Disciplinary Board. Author Case Comment "Torts—Joint Enterprise—Imputed Contributory Negligence" Washburn Law Journal 1961 and "Extrajudicial Admissions of the Defendant in Malpractice Cases" The Trial Lawyers' Guide 1966. Vice Chairman 1972 and Chairman 1973-75 New Mexico Judicial Council. Vice Chairman 1984 and Chairman 1985-86 Governor's Organized Crime Prevention Commission. Member New Mexico State Bar Judicial Selection Committee 1974-86, National Commissioners on Uniform State Laws 1978-80, Federal Judges Association (Board of Directors), Albuquerque and American Bar Associations. Attended George Mason University School of Law LEC Economics Institute 1988. Recipient Outstanding Contribution Award for Chairman of Disciplinary Board State Bar of New Mexico 1983. Republican. Member New Mexico State Senate (Minority Leader 1973-80) 1970-80. Enjoys playing golf, reading and traveling.

Office: 740 U.S. Courthouse, 333 Lomas Boulevard N.W., Albuquerque 87102.

Telephone: (505) 348-2200.

CONWAY, Susan M. *(Judge, New Mexico District Court Second Judicial District)* Appointed by Governor Toney Anaya May 22, 1985 to term beginning July 1, 1985. Elected 1986. Retained by election 1990, 1996 and 2002. Current term expires Dec 31, 2008. Born Salem Massachusetts Sept 24, 1946. Educated at Barnard College, Columbia University B.A. 1968 and Northeastern University School of Law J.D. 1973. Admitted to practice New Mexico 1974, U.S. District Court District of New Mexico 1974 and U.S. Court of Appeals Tenth Circuit 1984. In legal practice Albuquerque 1977-85.

VISTA Attorney Albuquerque Legal Aid Society 1974-75. Attorney New Mexico Health and Social Services Department 1975-77. Co-author Final Report Task Force on Women and the Legal Profession 1991 and Guardian ad Litem Manual 1993 State Bar of New Mexico. Member Committee on Child Support Guidelines New Mexico Supreme Court 1986-88. Member New Mexico District Judges Association, National Association of Women Judges, State Bar of New Mexico (Member Committee on Interim Guidelines 1984-85 and Chairman Committee on Mediation and Arbitration 1985 Family Law Section, Member Committee on Alternative Methods of Dispute Resolution 1984-86, Task Force on Women and the Legal Profession 1989-91), New Mexico Women's and New Mexico Hispanic Bar Associations. Instructor Governor's Conference on Youth 1981, Governor's Conference on the New Mexico Equal Rights Amendment 1984, Child Support Guidelines New Mexico Judicial Conclave 1986 and various family law, civil law and procedure continuing legal education programs State Bar of New Mexico and New Mexico Trial Lawyers Association since 1986. Attended National Conference on Bioethics and the Law National Women Judges Association 1991 and National Conference of the State Judiciary on Bioethical Issues and General Jurisdiction course The National Judicial College.

Recipient Special Friend to Children Award from North American Council on Adoptable Children 1985, Outstanding Contribution Award from State Bar of New Mexico 1991, Governor's Award for Outstanding New Mexico Women 1994 and Outstanding Judge Award from Albuquerque Bar Association 1995. Playwright Ensemble Theatre Laboratory 1968-69. Secretary and Bookkeeper Citizens Housing Association, Inc. 1969-70. Previously employed as waitress, bartender, short-order cook and chambermaid. Democrat. Former member Board of Directors Albuquerque Rape Crisis Center. Volunteer Governor's Juvenile Code Task Force 1979-81. Board of Directors Shelter for Victims of Domestic Violence 1980-84 and Albuquerque Child Guidance Center 1986-89. Member 1983-85 and Vice Chair 1984 Albuquerque-Bernalillo County Child Abuse Council. Advisory Board of Directors Children's Psychiatric Hospital 1984. Executive Board since 1984, Director since 1984, Vice Chair 1984-85 and Chairwoman 1985-87 New Mexico Council on Crime and Delinquency. Member Domestic Violence Task Force Albuquerque Police Department 1987-88. Board of Directors since 1991 and Vice President 1992 Hogares, Inc. Member New Mexico Children's Lobby, New Mexico Women's Forum and Hispanic Women's Council of New Mexico. Enjoys cooking, reading, family and friends.

Mailing address: P.O. Box 488, Albuquerque 87103.

Office: 400 Lomas Boulevard N.W., Albuquerque 87102.

Telephone: (505) 841-7534.

Fax: (505) 841-5457

COUNTS, James Waylon *(Judge, New Mexico District Court Twelfth Judicial District)* Appointed by Governor Gary E. Johnson to term beginning Nov 5, 1999. Elected Nov 7, 2000. Retained by election 2002, current term expires Dec 31, 2008. Born Roswell New Mexico Aug 23, 1955. Catholic. Educated at University of New Mexico B.A. 1977 J.D. 1981. Admitted to practice New Mexico 1981 and U.S. District Court District of New Mexico 1982. In legal practice Albuquerque 1981-84 and Alamogordo 1989-1997.

Assistant City Attorney Alamagordo 1985-86. Assistant District Attorney Twelfth Judicial District 1997-99. Professor of Business Law I and II Park College 1990-96 and of Business Law Embry-Riddle Areo University since 1996. Member Otero County and Twelfth Judicial District Bar Associations. Republican. Member Rotary International.

Office: 1000 New York Avenue, Room 208, Alamogordo 88310-6937.

Telephone: (505) 434-0573.

Fax: (505) 434-8886

CURRIER, Charles C. *(Judge, New Mexico District Court Fifth Judicial District)* Elected to term beginning Jan 2003. Term expires Dec 31, 2008.

Mailing address: P.O. Box 1776, Roswell 88202-1776.

Office: 1600 Southeast Main, Roswell 88203.

Telephone: (505) 622-0536.

Fax: (505) 624-9610

DEAN, John A., Jr. *(Judge, New Mexico District Court Eleventh Judicial District)* Term expires Dec 31, 2004.

Office: 920 Municipal Drive, Farmington 87401.

Telephone: (505) 326-2256.

DURAN, Grace B. *(Judge, New Mexico District Court Third Judicial District)* Elected to term beginning Nov 1996. Retained by election Nov 2002, current term expires Dec 31, 2008. Educated at University of New

DURAN, GRACE B.—*Continued*
Mexico B.S. 1974 J.D. 1977. Admitted to practice New Mexico 1978. In legal practice Las Cruces 1979-91.
Office: 201 West Picacho, Suite A, Las Cruces 88005.
Telephone: (505) 523-8292.
Fax: (505) 523-8299
E-mail address: lcrdgbd@nmcourts.com

ECHOLS, Douglas A. *(Judge, New Mexico District Court Eleventh Judicial District)* Term expires Dec 31, 2004.
Office: 920 Municipal Drive, Farmington 87401.
Telephone: (505) 564-3017.

FITCH, Thomas G. *(Judge, New Mexico District Court Seventh Judicial District)* Appointed by Gary E. Johnson to term beginning May 20, 1995. Elected Jan 1, 1997. Retained by election 2002, current term expires Dec 31, 2008. Born Grand Rapids Michigan Nov 7, 1942. Educated at Rutgers Men's College B.A. 1964 and University of Kentucky College of Law J.D. with honors 1972. Notes Editor Kentucky Law Review 1971-72. Law Clerk to Hon. James S. Chenault, Kentucky Circuit Court Circuit Twenty-five 1971-72. Member Order of the Coif. Admitted to practice New Mexico 1972 and U.S. Court of Appeals Tenth Circuit 1975. In legal practice Socorro 1972-95.
Mailing address: P.O. Drawer 1129, Socorro 87801.
Office: 200 Church Street, Socorro 87801-4581.
Telephone: (505) 835-0050.
Fax: (505) 838-5217

FORBES, Jay W. *(Chief Judge, New Mexico District Court Fifth Judicial District)* Term expires Dec 31, 2008.
Office: 102 North Canal, Suite 345, Carlsbad 88220.
Telephone: (505) 885-4828.
Fax: (505) 885-2458

FOUTZ, Grant L. *(Judge, New Mexico District Court Eleventh Judicial District)* Term expires Dec 31, 2008.
Office: 201 West Hill Street, Room 4, Gallup 87301.
Telephone: (505) 726-2062.
Fax: (505) 722-9172

FRY, Cynthia A. *(Judge, New Mexico Court of Appeals)* Elected to term beginning Dec 1, 2000. Term expires Dec 31, 2006. Born Albuquerque New Mexico March 20, 1953. Educated at Colorado College B.A. 1975 and University of New Mexico School of Law J.D. 1981. Admitted to practice New Mexico 1981, U.S. District Court District of New Mexico 1982, U.S. Courts of Appeals Tenth 1983 and Ninth 1999 Circuits and U.S. Supreme Court 1995. In legal practice Albuquerque 1981-2000.
Member State Bar of New Mexico (Member 1993-2000 and Chair 1994 Appellate Practice Section, Member Appellate Rules Committee 1995-2000).
Mailing address: P.O. Box 2008, Santa Fe 87504-2008.
Telephone: (505) 827-4925.

GALVAN, Joe H. *(Recalled Magistrate Judge, United States District Court District of New Mexico)* Appointed Magistrate Judge by U.S. District Court judges. Appointed Recalled Magistrate Judge by the Judicial Council of the Tenth Circuit. Former Chief Judge, New Mexico District Court Third Judicial District.
Office: Federal Building, 200 East Griggs Avenue, Las Cruces 88001.
Telephone: (505) 528-1470.

GARCIA, Lorenzo F. *(Magistrate Judge, United States District Court District of New Mexico)* Appointed by U.S. District Court judges.
Office: 680 U.S. Courthouse, 333 Lomas Boulevard N.W., Albuquerque 87102.
Telephone: (505) 348-2320.

GARCIA, Tim *(Judge, New Mexico District Court First Judicial District)* Elected to term beginning Jan 2003. Term expires Dec 31, 2008.
Mailing address: P.O. Drawer 40, Tierra Amarilla 87575.
Office: #2 Main Street, Tierra Amarilla 87575.
Telephone: (505) 588-0267.
Fax: (505) 588-9898.

HALL, James A. *(Chief Judge, New Mexico District Court First Judicial District)* Appointed by Governor Gary E. Johnson to term beginning April 3, 1995. Elected Nov 5, 1996 and 2002. Current term expires Dec 31, 2008. Born Muncie Indiana. Presbyterian. Educated at DePauw University B.A. 1979 and University Michigan J.D. 1983. Admitted to practice New Mexico 1984.
Mailing address: P.O. Box 2268, Santa Fe 87504.
Office: 100 Catron, Santa Fe 87504.
Telephone: (505) 827-5044.
Fax: (505) 827-5055

HANSEN, C. LeRoy *(Judge, United States District Court District of New Mexico)* Appointed for life by President George Bush to term beginning Oct 5, 1992. Educated at University of Iowa B.S.M.E. 1956 and University of New Mexico School of Law J.D. 1961. Chairman Board of Editors Natural Resources Journal 1960-61. Law Clerk to Hon. Irwin S. Moise, New Mexico Supreme Court 1961-62. Member Tau Beta Pi, Pi Tau Sigma and Order of the Coif. In legal practice 1962-92.
Adjunct Professor of Trial Practice University of New Mexico School of Law 1989-90. Board of Bar Examiners New Mexico Supreme Court 1982-84. President 1993-94 and Member 1993-2000 The H. Vearl Payne Inn of Court The American Inns of Court. Member Twentieth Judicial Council of the Tenth Circuit 1999-2001. Former Chairman New Mexico Appellate Judicial Selection Commission. Fellow New Mexico Bar Foundation and American College of Trial Lawyers. Honorary Member State Bar of New Mexico (Board of Bar Commissioners 1983-85, Former Chairman Federal Bar Committee and Trial Practice Section). Member Judicial Conference of the U.S. (Committee on the Budget since 1999), American Board of Trial Advocates and Albuquerque Bar Association. Engineer Sandia Corporation 1956-60.
Office: 660 U.S. Courthouse, 333 Lomas Boulevard N.W., Albuquerque 87102.
Telephone: (505) 348-2240.
Fax: (505) 348-2246

HARRIS, Jay G. *(Chief Judge, New Mexico District Court Fourth Judicial District)* Elected to term beginning Jan 1, 1985. Retained by election 1990, 1996 and 2002. Current term expires Dec 31, 2008. Born Las Ve-

HARRIS, JAY G.—*Continued*

gas New Mexico June 25, 1944. Protestant. Educated at New Mexico Highlands University B.A. cum laude 1966 and University of Colorado J.D. 1969. Admitted to practice New Mexico 1969 and Colorado 1969. Began legal practice Las Vegas New Mexico 1969.

Member State Bar of New Mexico, Fourth Judicial District and American Bar Associations. Democrat. Member Kiwanis Club of Las Vegas (Past President and Lieutenant Governor Division I), Las Vegas Shrine Club and Masons (Past Master). Enjoys fishing and woodworking.

Mailing address: P.O. Box 1540, Las Vegas 87701-1540.
Office: 500 West National Street, Las Vegas 87701.
Telephone: (505) 425-3900.
Fax: (505) 425-6307

HARTLEY, Ted L. *(Judge, New Mexico District Court Ninth Judicial District)* Term expires Dec 31, 2008.
Office: 700 North Main Street, Suite 13, Clovis 88101.
Telephone: (505) 769-0963.

HULING, Valerie Mackie *(Judge, New Mexico District Court Second Judicial District)*
Mailing address: P.O. Box 488, Albuquerque 87103.
Telephone: (505) 841-7425.

HYNES, Thomas J. *(Judge, New Mexico District Court Eleventh Judicial District)* Term expires Dec 31, 2004.
Office: 103 South Oliver, Aztec 87410.
Telephone: (505) 334-4895.

IONTA, Robert W. *(Magistrate Judge, United States District Court District of New Mexico)* Appointed by U.S. District Court judges to term beginning Feb 1985. Reappointed Feb 1989, Feb 1993, Feb 1997 and Feb 2001. Current term expires Feb 2005. Serves part time.
Mailing address: P.O. Box 1059, Gallup 87305-1059.
Telephone: (505) 863-4438.

JEFFREYS, Gary *(Chief Judge, New Mexico District Court Sixth Judicial District)* Appointed by Governor Gary E. Johnson. Elected Nov 1998. Retained by election Nov 2002, current term expires Dec 31, 2008. Born Sayre Oklahoma Jan 18, 1947. Educated at University of Arkansas B.S.B.A. 1969 and University of New Mexico J.D. 1972. Admitted to practice New Mexico 1972. In legal practice Deming 1972-97.
Office: 700 South Silver Street, Room 56, Deming 88030.
Telephone: (505) 546-2344.
Fax: (505) 546-2994
E-mail address: demdgmj@nmcourts.com

JEWELL, Angela *(Judge, New Mexico District Court Second Judicial District)* Term expires Dec 31, 2008.
Mailing address: P.O. Box 488, Albuquerque 87103.
Office: 400 Lomas Boulevard N.W., Albuquerque 87102.
Telephone: (505) 841-6748.
Fax: (505) 841-5454

JEWELL, Tommy E. *(Judge, New Mexico District Court Second Judicial District)* Term expires Dec 31, 2008.
Mailing address: P.O. Box 488, Albuquerque 87103.
Office: 5100 Second Street N.W., Albuquerque 87102.
Telephone: (505) 841-7392.
Fax: (505) 841-5915

JOHNSON, William Paul *(Judge, United States District Court District of New Mexico)* Appointed for life by President George W. Bush to term beginning Dec 28, 2001. Former Judge, New Mexico District Court Fifth Judicial District.
Office: 770 U.S. Courthouse, 333 Lomas Boulevard N.W., Albuquerque 87102.
Telephone: (505) 348-2330.

JONES, Alvin F. *(Judge, New Mexico District Court Fifth Judicial District)* Term expires Dec 31, 2008. Former Chief Judge.
Mailing address: P.O. Box 1776, Roswell 88202-1776.
Office: 1600 Southeast Main, Roswell 88203.
Telephone: (505) 625-2411.
Fax: (505) 624-9510

KASE, Edmund H., III *(Chief Judge, New Mexico District Court Seventh Judicial District)* Term expires Dec 31, 2008.
Mailing address: P.O. Drawer 1129, Socorro 87801.
Office: 200 Church Street, Socorro 87801.
Telephone: (505) 835-0050.
Fax: (505) 838-5217

KENNEDY, Roderick T. *(Judge, New Mexico Court of Appeals)* Term expires Dec 31, 2004.
Mailing address: P.O. Box 2008, Santa Fe 87504-2008.
Telephone: (505) 827-4911.

KNOWLES, Richard J. *(Judge, New Mexico District Court Second Judicial District)* Assumed office 1995. Elected 1996. Retained by election 2002, current term expires Dec 31, 2008.
Mailing address: P.O. Box 488, Albuquerque 87103.
Office: 400 Lomas Boulevard N.W., Albuquerque 87102.
Telephone: (505) 841-7472.
Fax: (505) 841-5458

LANG, William F. *(Judge, New Mexico District Court Second Judicial District)* Assumed office Feb 25, 1994. Elected 1996. Retained by election 2002, current term expires Dec 31, 2008. Educated at University of New Mexico B.A. 1979 J.D. 1982. Law Clerk to Chief Judge Mary Walters, New Mexico Court of Appeals Sept 1982 to June 1983. In legal practice Oct 1983 to June 1988. Child Support Hearing Officer, New Mexico District Court Second Judicial District July 1, 1988 to Feb 1, 1991. Judge March 1, 1991 to May 31, 1992, Presiding Judge Criminal Division Sept 1, 1991 to May 1, 1992 and Chief Judge June 1, 1992 to Feb 25, 1994, Bernalillo County Metropolitan Court.

Attorney New Mexico State Corporation Commission Office of General Counsel June 1983 to Sept 1983. President New Mexico Magistrate—Metropolitan Judges Association 1992-93. Former Member New Mexico Judicial Information Systems Council, New Mexico Supreme Court Commission on Finance and the Courts and New

LANG, WILLIAM F.—*Continued*

Mexico Chief Judges Council. Member State Bar of New Mexico.
Mailing address: P.O. Box 488, Albuquerque 87103.
Office: 400 Lomas Boulevard N.W., Albuquerque 87102.
Telephone: (505) 841-7562.
Fax: (505) 841-5458

LYNCH, William P. *(Judge, New Mexico District Court Fifth Judicial District)* Term expires Dec 31, 2008.
Mailing address: P.O. Box 1776, Roswell 88202-1776.
Office: 401 North Main, Roswell 88201.
Telephone: (505) 624-0859.
Fax: (505) 624-9510

MACARON, Mark A. *(Judge, New Mexico District Court Second Judicial District)* Appointed by Governor Gary E. Johnson Feb 1997. Elected Jan 1, 1999. Retained by election 2002, current term expires Dec 31, 2008. Born Springer New Mexico Sept 9, 1952. Christian. Educated at New Mexico Military Institute A.A. with honors 1972, University of Arizona B.S. 1974 and George Mason University J.D. 1980. Law Clerk to New Mexico Court of Appeals 1981. Admitted to practice New Mexico 1981. In legal practice Albuquerque 1982-83. Judge, Bernalillo County Metropolitan Court Jan 1987 to Feb 1997.
Deputy District Attorney Second Judicial District Jan 1983 to Jan 1987. Member Code of Judicial Conduct Committee and Professionalism Committee New Mexico Supreme Court. Captain New Mexico National Guard JAG 1982-88. Republican. Member Kiwanis Club.
Mailing address: P.O. Box 488, Albuquerque 87103.
Office: 400 Lomas Boulevard N.W., Albuquerque 87102.
Telephone: (505) 841-7480.
Fax: (505) 841-5457

MADDOX, Don *(Judge, New Mexico District Court Fifth Judicial District)* Term expires Dec 31, 2008.
Office: 100 North Main, Lovington 88260.
Telephone: (505) 396-4430.
Fax: (505) 396-2428

MAES, Petra Jimenez *(Chief Justice, New Mexico Supreme Court and Senior Justice, New Mexico Supreme Court)* Assumed office. Elected Nov 5, 2002, current term expires Dec 31, 2010.
Mailing address: P.O. Box 848, Santa Fe 87504-0848.
Telephone: (505) 827-4883.

MARTINEZ, Lourdes A. *(Magistrate Judge, United States District Court District of New Mexico)* Appointed by U.S. District Court judges to term beginning April 1, 2003. Born Delta Colorado Oct 21, 1949. Educated at New Mexico State University B.S. 1971 and University of New Mexico law degree 1980. Law Clerk to Hon. Dan Sosa, Jr., New Mexico Supreme Court 1980-82. Member Order of the Coif. Admitted to practice New Mexico 1980 and U.S. District Court District of New Mexico 1982. In legal practice Las Cruces 1987-98. Judge, New Mexico District Court Third Judicial District Dec 28, 1998 to March 30, 2003.
Member Symphony Board, Hospital Foundation Board and Catholic Diocese Board.
Office: Federal Building, 200 East Griggs Street, Las Cruces 88001.
Telephone: (505) 528-1650.
Fax: (505) 528-1655

MARTINEZ-OLGUIN, Camille *(Judge, New Mexico District Court Thirteenth Judicial District)* Term expires Dec 31, 2008.
Mailing address: P.O. Box 758, Grants 87020.
Office: 515 West High Street, Grants 87020.
Telephone: (505) 287-2104.
Fax: (505) 771-8897

MATHIS, Eugenio S. *(Judge, New Mexico District Court Fourth Judicial District)* Elected June 2, 1992 to term beginning Nov 30, 1992. Retained by election Nov 5, 1996 and 2002. Current term expires Dec 31, 2008. Former Chief Judge. Born Las Vegas New Mexico Nov 4, 1954. Catholic. Educated at Stanford University B.A. 1976 and University of New Mexico School of Law J.D. 1979. Admitted to practice New Mexico 1979 and U.S. District Court District of New Mexico 1980. In legal practice Las Vegas 1979-82.
Mailing address: P.O. 1540, Las Vegas 87701-1540.
Office: 501 West National, Las Vegas 87701.
Telephone: (505) 425-7131.
Fax: (505) 425-6307

McBEE, William A. *(Judge, New Mexico District Court Fifth Judicial District)* Elected to term beginning Jan 2003. Term expires Dec 31, 2008.
Office: 100 North Main, Lovington 88260.
Telephone: (505) 396-8573.
Fax: (505) 396-2428

McDONALD, Louis P. *(Chief Judge, New Mexico District Court Thirteenth Judicial District)* Term expires Dec 31, 2008.
Office: 100 Avenida de Justicia, Bernalillo 87004.
Telephone: (505) 867-0563.
Fax: (505) 285-5755

McFEELEY, Mark B. *(Judge, United States Bankruptcy Court District of New Mexico)* Appointed by U.S. District Court judges Sept 28, 1981. Reappointed by U.S. Court of Appeals Tenth Circuit judges. Former Chief Judge Bankruptcy Court. Also Chief Judge, Bankruptcy Appellate Panel Tenth Circuit. Selected by the Judicial Council of the Tenth Circuit. Chief Judge Appellate Panel since June 3, 1999. Born Orlando Florida May 5, 1944. Presbyterian. Educated at U.S. Merchant Marine Academy B.S. 1966 and University of New Mexico J.D. cum laude 1972. Editor New Mexico Law Review 1971-72. Law Clerk to Hon. Oliver Seth, U.S. Court of Appeals Tenth Circuit 1972-73. Member Phi Kappa Phi. Admitted to practice New Mexico 1972, U.S. District Court District of New Mexico 1972 and U.S. Court of Appeals Tenth Circuit 1972. Began legal practice Santa Fe 1974.
Member American Bankruptcy Institute, National Conference of Bankruptcy Judges and State Bar of New Mexico. Democrat.
Mailing address: P.O. Box 546, Albuquerque 87103-0546.
Telephone: (505) 348-2525.

MINZNER, Pamela B. *(Justice, New Mexico Supreme Court)* Appointed by Governor Bruce King Dec

MINZNER, PAMELA B.—*Continued*

1994. Elected 2002, current term expires Dec 31, 2010. Former Chief Justice. Born Meridian Mississippi Nov 19, 1943. Congregationalist. Educated at Miami University B.A. cum laude 1965 and Harvard Law School LL.B. 1968. Member Gamma Phi Beta. Admitted to practice Massachusetts 1968 and New Mexico 1972. Began legal practice Boston Massachusetts 1968. In legal practice Albuquerque New Mexico 1971-73. Judge, New Mexico Court of Appeals, appointed by Governor Toney Anaya to term beginning January 1984.

Member Governor's Commission on Higher Education 1983-84. Co-author with Robert T. Lawrence *A Student's Guide to Estates in Land and Future Interests: Text, Examples, Problems & Answers* Matthew Bender 1981. Author "The Management and Control of Separate and Community Property" *American Community Property Law* Lawyers' Cooperative Publishing Co. 1982. Adjunct Professor of Law 1973-77, Associate Professor of Law 1977-80 and Professor of Law 1980-83 University of New Mexico School of Law. Faculty member Instituto Preparativo Legal University of New Mexico School of Law 1975 and 1979 (summers). Member State Bar of New Mexico and American Bar Association. Attended National Endowment for the Humanities Summer Humanities Seminar for Law Teachers Stanford Law School 1982 and University of Chicago Law School 1978. Recipient Faculty Award from University of New Mexico Class of 1981 and Class of 1977. Honorary Faculty member Delta Theta Phi 1978. Democrat. Chairman General Honors Council 1977-79 and Law School Curriculum Committee 1982-83 University of New Mexico. Enjoys reading, bridge and movies.

Mailing address: P.O. Box 848, Santa Fe 87504-0848.
Telephone: (505) 827-4889.

MOLZEN, Karen B. *(Magistrate Judge, United States District Court District of New Mexico)* Appointed by U.S. District Court judges to term beginning April 26, 1999. Term expires April 2007.

Office: Federal Building, 200 East Griggs Avenue, Las Cruces 88001.
Telephone: (505) 528-1480.

MURDOCH, Albert S. *(Judge, New Mexico District Court Second Judicial District)* Term expires Dec 31, 2008.

Mailing address: P.O. Box 488, Albuquerque 87103.
Office: 400 Lomas Boulevard N.W., Albuquerque 87102.
Telephone: (505) 841-7538.
Fax: (505) 841-5456

NASH, Nan *(Judge, New Mexico District Court Second Judicial District)* Term expires Dec 31, 2008.

Mailing address: P.O. Box 488, Albuquerque 87103.
Office: 400 Lomas Boulevard N.W., Albuquerque 87102.
Telephone: (505) 841-7531.
Fax: (505) 841-5454

NELSON, Peggy J. *(Chief Judge, New Mexico District Court Eighth Judicial District)* Appointed by Governor Garrey Carruthers to term beginning Feb 1, 1988. Elected Nov 1988. Retained by election Nov 1990, 1996 and 2002. Current term expires Dec 31, 2008. Born St. Paul Minnesota Sept 5, 1947. Educated at University of California at Los Angeles B.A. magna cum laude 1969 J.D. 1973. Member Phi Beta Kappa. Admitted to practice New Mexico 1973, California 1973 and U.S. Court of Appeals Tenth Circuit 1973. In legal practice Taos 1973-87.

Member National Women Judges Association, State Bar of California and State Bar of New Mexico (Task Force on Women in the Profession, Co-Chair Legal Services and Programs). Recipient Outstanding Community Service Award 1985, Outstanding Contribution Award from State Bar of New Mexico 1991, 1994 and 1996, Governor's Award for Outstanding New Mexico Women 1996 and Outstanding Judicial Service Award from State Bar of New Mexico 1997. Board Member Taos Municipal Schools 1985-88. Participant in local and state domestic violence projects since 1978.

Office: 105 Albright, Suite H, Taos 87571.
Telephone: (505) 758-3173.
Fax: (505) 751-1281

PARKER, James A. *(Chief Judge, United States District Court District of New Mexico)* Appointed for life by President Ronald Reagan to term beginning Nov 13, 1987. Chief Judge since Sept 2, 2000. Born Houston Texas Jan 8, 1937. Episcopalian. Educated at Rice University B.A. 1959 and University of Texas LL.B. with honors 1962. Articles Editor Texas Law Review 1961-62. Member Phi Delta Phi, Chancellors and Order of the Coif. Admitted to practice Texas 1962, New Mexico 1963, U.S. District Court District of New Mexico 1963 and U.S. Court of Appeals Tenth Circuit 1963. In legal practice Albuquerque New Mexico 1963-87.

Important Decisions: Jackson v. State of New Mexico (State of New Mexico must provide residential care for individuals with developmental disabilities where care providers have recommended community placement) 757 F. Supp. 1243 D. N.M. Dec 28, 1990; United States v. Miller (search and seizure issues involving train travelers) 811 F. Supp. 1485 D. N.M. 1993; United States v. Corrow (first criminal prosecution under Native American Graves Protection and Repatriation Act) 941 F. Supp. 1553 D. N.M. 1996; United States v. Gonzales (Native American defendant's rights under Religious Freedom Restoration Act) 957 F. Supp. 1225 D. N.M. 1997; United States v. Martinez CR 97-359 JP, 1997 WL 665678 D. N.M. Oct 22, 1997; Navajo Nation v. Intermountain Steel Buildings, Inc. (tribal exhaustion rule required parties to exhaust their remedies in Navajo tribal court before resorting to federal district court) 42 F. Supp.2d 1222 D. N.M. 1999; United States v. Gonzalez (mediated plea negotiations that resolved three death penalty cases) No. CR 95-538MV D. N.M. 1999; and United States v. Wen Ho Lee (improper handling of classified information) No. CR 99-1417 JP D. N.M. 1999. Member Judicial Conference Standing Committee on Rules of Practice and Procedure 1993-99. Member American Board of Trial Advocates, American Judicature Society, Federal Judges Association, State Bar of New Mexico (Board of Bar Commissioners 1983-84) and State Bar of Texas. Recipient Outstanding Judge Award from Albuquerque Bar Association 1993 and 2000 and State Bar of New Mexico 1994. Board of Visitors University of New Mexico School of Law.

Office: 770 U.S. Courthouse, 333 Lomas Boulevard N.W., Albuquerque 87102.
Telephone: (505) 348-2220.
Fax: (505) 348-2225

PARSONS, Karen L. *(Judge, New Mexico District Court Twelfth Judicial District)* Term expires Dec 31, 2008.

Mailing address: P.O. Box 427, Carrizozo 88301.
Office: 300 Central Street, Carrizozo 88301.
Telephone: (505) 648-2902.
Fax: (505) 648-2581

PFEFFER, Stephen *(Judge, New Mexico District Court First Judicial District)* Appointed by Governor Gary E. Johnson Jan 1996 to term beginning Feb 14, 1997. Elected Nov 1998. Retained by election 2002, current term expires Dec 31, 2008. Born New York New York Oct 13, 1947. Educated at University of Denver B.A. 1969 J.D. 1973. Law Clerk to Hon. John Brooks, Jr., Colorado District Court Second Judicial District 1972. Admitted to practice Colorado 1973 and New Mexico 1977. In legal practice Pueblo Colorado 1973-76, Los Alamos New Mexico 1973-78 and Santa Fe New Mexico 1978-97.

Assistant City Attorney Pueblo Colorado 1973-76. Member Oliver Seth American Inn of Court, State Bar of New Mexico and First Judicial District Bar Association. Democrat.

Mailing address: P.O. Box 2268, Santa Fe 87504.
Office: 100 Catron, Santa Fe 87504.
Telephone: (505) 827-5047.
Fax: (505) 827-5055

PICKARD, Lynn *(Judge, New Mexico Court of Appeals)* Term expires Dec 31, 2006. Former Chief Judge.

Mailing address: P.O. Box 2008, Santa Fe 87504-2008.
Telephone: (505) 827-4903.

POPE, John William *(Judge, New Mexico District Court Thirteenth Judicial District)* Appointed by Governor Bruce King to term beginning Dec 18, 1992. Retained by election. Current term expires Dec 31, 2008. Born San Francisco California March 12, 1947. Educated at University of New Mexico B.A. 1969 J.D. 1973. Law Clerk to Hon. Benigno C. Hernandez, New Mexico Court of Appeals 1973. Admitted to practice New Mexico 1973, U.S. District Court District of New Mexico 1973 and U.S. Court of Appeals Tenth Circuit 1976. In legal practice Belen 1974-85 and Albuquerque 1985-87. Judge, Workers' Compensation Administration 1987-92.

Author *Workers' Compensation in New Mexico* 1991 and *Advanced Workers' Compensation in New Mexico* 1992 National Business Institute. Instructor in Criminal Justice 1983-92 and Adjunct Professor of Law 1989-92 University of New Mexico. Member State Bar of New Mexico, Valencia County (Vice President 1975-81) and Albuquerque Bar Associations. Instructor Workers' Compensation Seminars New Mexico Continuing Legal Education twice yearly 1988-92 and National Business Institute twice yearly 1988-92. Democrat. Member New Mexico Central Democratic Committee 1972-85. State Chair Common Cause 1980-82. President Valencia County Historical Society 1981-83. Enjoys running, swimming, historical research and photography.

Mailing address: P.O. Box 1089, Los Lunas 87031.
Office: 444 Luna Avenue, Los Lunas 87031.
Telephone: (505) 865-9654.
Fax: (505) 866-6813

PUGLISI, Richard L. *(Magistrate Judge, United States District Court District of New Mexico)* Appointed by U.S. District Court judges.

Office: U.S. Courthouse, 333 Lomas Boulevard N.W., Albuquerque 87102.
Telephone: (505) 348-2360.

PURCELL, Ricky D. *(Chief Judge, New Mexico District Court Tenth Judicial District)* Term expires Dec 31, 2008.

Mailing address: P.O. Box 1067, Tucumcari 88401.
Office: 300 South Third Street, Tucumcari 88401.
Telephone: (505) 461-4422.
Fax: (505) 461-4498

QUINN, Stephen K. *(Judge, New Mexico District Court Ninth Judicial District)* Appointed by Governor Garrey Carruthers to term beginning May 8, 1989. Elected 1990. Retained by election 1996 and 2002. Current term expires Dec 31, 2008. Former Chief Judge. Born El Paso Texas Aug 26, 1943. Presbyterian. Educated at Eastern New Mexico University B.A. 1968 and University of New Mexico School of Law J.D. 1974. Comment Editor New Mexico Law Review 1972-74. Admitted to practice New Mexico 1974 and U.S. District Court District of New Mexico 1974. In legal practice Clovis 1974-89.

Board of Directors Southern New Mexico Legal Services. U.S. Army 1968-71. Enjoys music and running.

Office: 3 Curry County Courthouse, 700 North Main, Clovis 88101.
Telephone: (505) 762-9529.
Fax: (505) 763-5160

QUINTERO, Henry R., Sr. *(Judge, New Mexico District Court Sixth Judicial District)* Term expires Dec 31, 2008.

Mailing address: P.O. Box 2339, Silver City 88062.
Office: 201 North Cooper, Silver City 88061.
Telephone: (505) 538-2975.
Fax: (505) 388-5439

RAMIREZ, Larry *(Judge, New Mexico District Court Third Judicial District)* Appointed by Governor Bill Richardson 2003.

Office: 201 West Picacho, Suite A, Las Cruces 88005.
Telephone: (505) 523-8200.

RICH, Joseph L. *(Judge, New Mexico District Court Eleventh Judicial District)* Term expires Dec 31, 2008.

Office: 201 West Hill Street, Room 4, Gallup 87301.
Telephone: (505) 722-4341.
Fax: (505) 722-9172

RITTER, Jerry H. *(Chief Judge, New Mexico District Court Twelfth Judicial District)* Term expires Dec 31, 2008.

Office: 203 Otero County Courthouse, 1000 New York Avenue, Alamogordo 88310-6937.
Telephone: (505) 473-3030.
Fax: (505) 437-0752

RIVERA, Geraldine E. *(Judge, New Mexico District Court Second Judicial District)* Term expires Dec 31, 2008.

Mailing address: P.O. Box 488, Albuquerque 87103.
Office: 5100 Second Street N.W., Albuquerque 87102.
Telephone: (505) 841-7311.
Fax: (505) 841-7317

ROBINSON, Ira S. *(Judge, New Mexico Court of Appeals)* Term expires 2008.
Mailing address: P.O. Box 2008, Santa Fe 87504-2008.
Telephone: (505) 827-4909.

ROBLES, Robert E. *(Chief Judge, New Mexico District Court Third Judicial District)* Term expires Dec 31, 2008.
Office: 201 West Picacho Avenue, Suite A, Las Cruces 88005.
Telephone: (505) 523-8220.
Fax: (505) 523-8290

ROMERO, Ernesto *(Judge, New Mexico District Court Second Judicial District)* Elected to term beginning Jan 2003. Term expires Dec 31, 2008.
Mailing address: P.O. Box 488, Albuquerque 87103.
Office: 400 Lomas Boulevard N.W., Albuquerque 87102.
Telephone: (505) 841-7574.
Fax: (505) 841-5454

SANCHEZ, Daniel *(Judge, New Mexico District Court First Judicial District)* Elected Nov 1998 to term beginning Dec 1998 . Retained by election 2002, current term expires Dec 31, 2009. Born Dixon New Mexico Oct 13, 1948. Presbyterian. Educated at University of New Mexico B.S. 1970 and Antioch School of Law J.D. 1976. Admitted to practice New Mexico 1979, U.S. District Court District of New Mexico, U.S. Court of Appeals Tenth Circuit and U.S. Supreme Court. In legal practice Santa Fe 1984-98.
Special Assistant Attorney General New Mexico Land Office and Office of the State Engineer 1979-84. County Attorney Santa Fe County 1985-89. Democrat. Board of Directors SER Jobs for Progress Santa Fe. Enjoys hunting, fishing and golf.
Mailing address: P.O. Box 2268, Santa Fe 87504-2268.
Office: 100 Catron, Santa Fe 87504.
Telephone: (505) 827-5056.
E-mail address: sfeddas@nmcourts.com

SANCHEZ, Ross C. *(Judge, New Mexico District Court Second Judicial District)* Appointed by Governor Toney Anaya to term beginning Aug 1985. Elected 1986. Retained by election 1990, 1996 and 2002. Current term expires Dec 31, 2008. Born Albuquerque New Mexico Aug 2, 1940. Catholic. Educated at University of New Mexico B.A. 1963 M.A.T.S. 1968 and Oklahoma City University School of Law J.D. 1973. Admitted to practice Oklahoma 1973 and New Mexico 1975. Began legal practice Oklahoma City Oklahoma 1973. In legal practice New Mexico 1975-82. Judge, Bernalillo County Metropolitan Court Jan 1, 1983 to Aug 2, 1985.
Assistant Professor of Business Law, Labor Law, Real Estate Law and Insurance Eastern New Mexico University 1973-78. Member New Mexico Hispanic Bar Association, State Bar of New Mexico and Albuquerque Bar Association. New Mexico Air National Guard 1963-71. School teacher 1963-68. Democrat. Chairman of the Board Southern New Mexico Legal Services. Member Kiwanis. Enjoys walking, jogging and playing handball and racquetball.
Mailing address: P.O. Box 488, Albuquerque 87103.
Office: 400 Lomas Boulevard N.W., Albuquerque 87102.
Telephone: (505) 841-7476.
Fax: (505) 841-5456

SANCHEZ, Sam *(Judge, New Mexico District Court Eighth Judicial District)* Term expires Dec 31, 2008.
Mailing address: P.O. Box 160, Raton 87740.
Office: North Third Street, Raton 87740.
Telephone: (505) 455-5584.
Fax: (505) 445-2626

SANCHEZ, William A. *(Judge, New Mexico District Court Thirteenth Judicial District)* Elected to term beginning Dec 7, 1992. Retained by election 1996 and 2002. Current term expires Dec 31, 2008. Former Chief Judge. Born Albuquerque New Mexico Feb 11, 1954. Catholic. Educated at University of New Mexico B.B.A. 1976 J.D. 1980. Admitted to practice New Mexico 1980. In legal practice Albuquerque 1980-83 and Los Lunas 1983-93.
Member State Bar of New Mexico and Valencia County Bar Association (Executive Committee 1983-92). Previously employed as an accountant. Democrat. Enjoys basketball, volleyball and chess.
Mailing address: P.O. Box 1089, Los Lunas 87031.
Office: 444 Luna Avenue, Los Lunas 87031.
Telephone: (505) 865-4010.
Fax: (505) 866-5819

SCHNEIDER, W. Daniel *(Judge, New Mexico District Court Second Judicial District)* Assumed office Dec 1994. Elected 1996. Retained by election 2002, current term expires Dec 31, 2008. Educated at Northern Illinois University B.A. 1970, University of New Mexico J.D. 1973 and Boston University M.A. 1983. Admitted to practice New Mexico 1973, Colorado 1978, U.S. District Courts District of New Mexico, District of Colorado and District of Maryland and U.S. Court of Military Appeals. In legal practice Albuquerque Aug 1986 to Dec 1994.
Assistant District Attorney Bernalillo County June 1978 to March 1979. Deputy District Attorney Park County Colorado March 1979 to Aug 1980. Member New Mexico District Judges Association, State Bar of New Mexico and Colorado Bar Association. U.S. Army Oct 1974 to June 1978. U.S. Army JAG Aug 1980 to July 1986. Colonel New Mexico National Guard since 1986.
Mailing address: P.O. Box 488, Albuquerque 87103.
Office: 400 Lomas Boulevard N.W., Albuquerque 87102.
Telephone: (505) 841-7494.
Fax: (505) 841-5456

SCOTT, Robert H. *(Magistrate Judge, United States District Court District of New Mexico)* Appointed by U.S. District Court judges to term beginning April 1, 2003. Born Albuquerque New Mexico April 21, 1947. Educated at University of New Mexico B.A. 1969 J.D. 1972. Admitted to practice New Mexico 1972, U.S. District Court District of New Mexico 1972 and U.S. Supreme Court 1976. In legal practice Albuquerque 1972-84. Judge, Bernalillo County Probate Court 1985-89. Judge, New Mexico District Court Second Judicial District 1989 to March 30, 2003, appointed by Governor Garrey Carruthers.
President Elect New Mexico District Judges Association. Member New Mexico Trial Lawyers Association,

SCOTT, ROBERT H.—*Continued*

The Association of Trial Lawyers of America, State Bar of New Mexico and Albuquerque Bar Association.

Office: 620 U.S. Courthouse, 333 Lomas Boulevard N.W., Albuquerque 87102.
Telephone: (505) 348-2300.
Fax: (505) 348-2305

SERNA, Patricio M. *(Justice, New Mexico Supreme Court)* Elected to term beginning 1996. Retained by election, current term expires Dec 31, 2008. Chief Justice Jan 5, 2001 to 2002. Educated at University of Albuquerque B.S. 1962, University of Denver College of Law J.D. 1970 and Harvard Law School LL.M. Honorary LL.D. University of Denver College of Law 2002. Judge and Chief Judge, New Mexico District Court First Judicial District 1985-96.

Assistant Attorney General New Mexico 1975-79. Adjunct Professor of Law and Constitutional Law Georgetown University School of Law and Catholic University School of Law. President National Consortium on Racial and Ethnic Fairness in the Courts April 2002. Member Conference of Chief Justices, New Mexico Hispanic Bar Association, National Hispanic Bar Association, State Bar of New Mexico and American Bar Association. Named one of the top 100 Most Influential Hispanics in the United States by *Hispanic Business Magazine* Oct 2001. Recipient President's Award from Catholic University of America School of Law 2001, Outstanding Hispanic Attorney of the Year Award from New Mexico Hispanic Bar Association April 2002 and Judge of the Year Award from National Hispanic Bar Association Convention 2002. Special Assistant to Commissioner Federal Equal Employment Opportunity Commission for four years.

Mailing address: P.O. Box 848, Santa Fe 87504-0848.
Telephone: (505) 827-4887.

SHULER, James L. *(Judge, New Mexico District Court Fifth Judicial District)* Appointed by Governor Toney Anaya to term beginning Dec 28, 1986. Elected 1988. Retained by election 1990, 1996 and 2002. Current term expires Dec 31, 2008. Born Carlsbad New Mexico June 19, 1949. Episcopalian. Educated at University of Arizona B.A. 1973 and Pepperdine University School of Law J.D. 1976. Member Phi Alpha Delta. Admitted to practice New Mexico 1976, U.S. District Court District of New Mexico 1977 and U.S. Court of Appeals Tenth Circuit 1977. In legal practice Carlsbad 1976-86.

Member New Mexico Trial Lawyers Association, The Association of Trial Lawyers of America and National Association of Criminal Defense Lawyers. Democrat. Member New Mexico State School Board 1985-86. Enjoys hunting, golf and reading.

Office: 102 North Canal, Suite 315, Carlsbad 88220.
Telephone: (505) 887-7101.
Fax: (505) 885-2458

SMITH, Leslie C. *(Magistrate Judge, United States District Court District of New Mexico)* Appointed by U.S. District Court judges to term beginning 1995. Reappointed 2003, current term expires 2011. Born Baltimore Maryland July 15, 1941. Educated at Vanderbilt University B.A. 1962, University of Kentucky College of Law J.D. with high distinction 1971 and University of Western Australia, Perth LL.M. 1978. Articles Editor Kentucky Law Journal 1970-71. Member Order of the Coif. Admitted to practice New Mexico 1971, U.S. District Court District of New Mexico 1972, U.S. Court of Appeals Tenth Circuit 1981, U.S. Supreme Court 1975 and U.S. Tax Court. In legal practice Truth or Consequences 1971-89. Judge, New Mexico District Court Seventh Judicial District 1989-95, appointed by Governor Garrey Carruthers. Former Panel Member by Designation, New Mexico Supreme Court.

Public Defender Sierra County 1977-81. Village Attorney Williamsburg 1977-89. Board of Editors New Mexico Bar Journal and New Mexico Bar Bulletin since 1995. Important Decisions: Rivera v. Brazos Lodge Corp. (New Mexico Supreme Court Panel Member) 111 N.M. 670, 808 P.2d 955, 1991; State v. Swafford (New Mexico Supreme Court Panel Member) 112 N.M. 3, 810 P.2d 1223, 1991; Roux v. Lovelace Health System, Inc. (determination of group health insurer's subrogation rights) 947 F. Supp. 1534 D. N.M. 1997; City of Las Cruces v. El Paso Electric Co. (municipal condemnation of private utility) 904 F. Supp. 1238 D. N.M. 1995, WL 1090945 D. N.M. July 15, 1997, WL 1089567 D. N.M. 1997; Betsuie v. United States (discretionary function exception to the FTCA) 65 F. Supp.2d 1218 D. N.M. 1999; United States v. 36.06 Acres of Land (validity of attorney's charging lien against former client) 70 F. Supp.2d 1272 D. N.M. 1999; Jones v. Southwest Airlines (pretext with respect to racial discrimination action under Title VII) 99 F. Supp.2d 1322 D. N.M. 2000; Bogan v. Sandoval County (the highway signs cases); Bolton v. Valencia County (the bond cases); Volkman v. El Paso Natural Gas (catastrophic injury to child); FHP v. Hospital Corporation of America (complex business litigation); Otero County, et al. v. State of New Mexico (statewide collective bargaining case); The New Mexico Breast Implant Cases (pre-trial matters, discovery and management of over 60 court cases); Archdiocese of Santa Fe v. Underwriters Insurance Lloyds, and 13 other insurance carriers (coverage arising out of pedophilia cases); and Parker v. General Motors (products liability involving trunk release). Instructor in Evidence, Australian Constitutional Law and Torts University of Western Australia, Perth 1975. Adjunct Professor of Business Law Truth or Consequences Community College 1976-77. Member Advisory Opinions Committee 1971-77 and Judicial Selection Committee 1981-88 and Chair Bench-Bar Relations Committee 1990-92 State Bar of New Mexico. Board of Directors New Mexico Trial Lawyers Association 1982-89. Member Standing Committee on Rules of Civil Procedure 1988-95, Subcommittee on Judicial Evaluation 1990-92 and Standing Committee on Rules of Evidence 1993-95 New Mexico Supreme Court. Chair New Mexico Judicial Grievance Board 1989-92. President Judge Albert Fountain Inn of Court American Inns of Court 1997-99. Fellow New Mexico State Bar Foundation.

Graduate General Jurisdiction Course 1989, Advanced Evidence Course 1992, Mediation Course 1993 and Managing the Complex Case 1994 The National Judicial College. Attended Magistrate Judge Orientation 1995 and Mediation Course 1999 Federal Judicial Center and Program on Economics for Federal Judges 1998 and Program on Economics in Public Law 2001 George Mason University. CLE Instructor "Workshop for United States Magistrate Judges" Federal Judicial Center, "Resolving Disputes Without Litigation" and "The New Alimony Rules" State Bar of New Mexico, "What Lawyers Do Wrong in the Courtroom" State Bar of New Mexico Convention and "New Roles for Managing Family Con-

SMITH, LESLIE C.—*Continued*

flict." Recipient Outstanding Judicial Service Award from State Bar of New Mexico 1993, President's Award from Editorial Advisory Committee State Bar of New Mexico 1994 and Century of Achievement Award from State Bar of New Mexico 1999. Listed in *Who's Who in American Law* and *Who's Who in the World*. Captain USAF 1962-68. Recipient Distinguished Flying Cross and several Air Medals. Board of Directors First Sierra National Bank 1973-75 and 1981-83 and Sierra County Chamber of Commerce 1976-80. President Bertha Schwartz Fine Arts Society 1974-75 and Truth or Consequences Rotary Club 1982-83. Board of Directors 1974-75 and 1979-80, Vice Chair 1980-81 and Chair and Vice Chair 1981-82 and 1986-87 Ralph Edwards Fiesta. Coach Hot Springs High School Mock Trial Team 1990-95. Organizer Sierra County and Torrance County Teen Court 1991-95. Advisory Board Truth or Consequences Community College. Life Member VFW.

Office: Federal Building, 200 East Griggs Avenue, Las Cruces 88001.
Telephone: (505) 528-1460.

STARZYNSKI, James S. *(Chief Judge, United States Bankruptcy Court District of New Mexico)* Appointed by U.S. Court of Appeals Tenth Circuit judges Aug 14, 1998. Term expires 2012. Chief Judge since Jan 1, 2001.

Mailing address: P.O. Box 546, Albuquerque 87103-0546.
Telephone: (505) 348-2420.

SUTIN, Jonathan B. *(Judge, New Mexico Court of Appeals)* Appointed by Governor Gary E. Johnson to term beginning Feb 12, 1999. Elected 2000, current term expires Dec 31, 2009. Born Indiana May 7, 1938. Educated at University of Colorado B.A. 1960 and University of New Mexico School of Law J.D. 1963. Editor-in-Chief Natural Resources Journal 1963. Admitted to practice New Mexico 1963. In legal practice Albuquerque 1965-99.

USMCR. Enjoys running, reading and playing handball.

Office: 1117 Stanford N.E., Albuquerque 87131.
Telephone: (505) 841-4609.
E-mail address: coajbs@nmcourts.com

SVET, Don J. *(Recalled Magistrate Judge, United States District Court District of New Mexico)* Appointed Magistrate Judge by U.S. District Court judges. Appointed Recalled Magistrate Judge by the Judicial Council of the Tenth Circuit.

Office: 630 U.S. Courthouse, 333 Lomas Boulevard N.W., Albuquerque 87102.
Telephone: (505) 348-2340.

SWEAZEA, Kevin *(Judge, New Mexico District Court Seventh Judicial District)* Term expires Dec 31, 2008.

Mailing address: P.O. Drawer 1129, Socorro 87801.
Office: 200 Church Street, Socorro 87801.
Telephone: (505) 835-0050.
Fax: (505) 838-5217

THOMPSON, Robert L. *(Judge, New Mexico District Court Second Judicial District)* Elected to term beginning Jan 1985. Retained by election Nov 1990, 1996 and 2002. Current term expires Dec 31, 2008. Born Albuquerque New Mexico April 2, 1944. Baptist. Educated at University of New Mexico B.S. 1967 and University of Tulsa J.D. 1970. Member Phi Delta Phi. Admitted to practice New Mexico 1971. Began legal practice Albuquerque 1972. Substitute Judge, Albuquerque Municipal Court 1976-79. Judge, Bernalillo County Metropolitan Court 1983-85.

Member State Bar of New Mexico and Albuquerque Bar Association. Democrat.

Mailing address: P.O. Box 488, Albuquerque 87103.
Office: 400 Lomas Boulevard N.W., Albuquerque 87102.
Telephone: (505) 841-7515.
Fax: (505) 841-5457

VALENTINE, Jerald A. *(Judge, New Mexico District Court Third Judicial District)* Term expires Dec 31, 2008. Former Chief Judge.

Office: 201 West Picacho Avenue, Suite A, Las Cruces 88005.
Telephone: (505) 523-8235.
Fax: (505) 523-8290

VAZQUEZ, Martha *(Judge, United States District Court District of New Mexico)* Appointed for life by President Bill Clinton to term beginning 1993. Born Santa Barbara California Feb 21, 1953. Educated at University of Notre Dame B.A. 1975 J.D. 1978. In legal practice Santa Fe 1981-93.

Assistant Public Defender New Mexico 1979-81.

Mailing address: P.O. Box 2710, Santa Fe 87504-2710.
Telephone: (505) 988-6330.

VIGIL, Barbara J. *(Judge, New Mexico District Court First Judicial District)* Term expires Dec 31, 2008.

Mailing address: P.O. Box 2268, Santa Fe 87504.
Office: 100 Catron, Santa Fe 87504.
Telephone: (505) 827-4195.
Fax: (505) 827-5055

VIGIL, Carol J. *(Judge, New Mexico District Court First Judicial District)* Elected to term beginning Dec 10, 1998. Retained by election 2002, current term expires Dec 31, 2008. Child Support Hearing Officer Sept 1988 to June 1994. Special Commissioner Domestic Violence and Mental Competency since July 1994. First American Indian woman to serve a state court of general jurisdiction and first American Indian judge to serve in New Mexico. Born Santa Fe New Mexico Oct 24, 1947. Catholic. Educated at University of New Mexico Bachelor of University Studies 1974 J.D. 1978. Admitted to practice New Mexico 1979, U.S. District Court District of New Mexico 1980 and U.S. Court of Appeals Tenth Circuit 1980. In legal practice April 1984 to Aug 1988. Judge pro tem Jicarilla Tribal Court, San Juan Tribal Court and Cochiti Pueblo Tribal Court.

Staff Attorney Indian Pueblo Services, Inc. July 1978 to Aug 1980. Assistant Attorney General New Mexico Aug 1980 to March 1984. Director National American Indian Bar Association April 1981 to April 1984. Chairperson 1981-84 and Vice Chairperson 1984-86 Board of Trustees Northern New Mexico Legal Services Inc. Committee Member All Indian Pueblo Council Constitutional Revision Committee 1986-87. Member Governor's Commission on Rape Prevention and Prosecution 1987-89. Member Rules of Evidence Committee 1993 and Judicial Information System Council 1993 New Mexico Supreme Court. Former Member Espanola Bar Associa-

VIGIL, CAROL J.—*Continued*

tion. Member New Mexico Indian Bar Association, State Bar of New Mexico (Advisory Opinions Committee May 1984 to Jan 1985, Pro Bono Committee 1984-90, Chair-elect 1987-88 and Chair 1988-89 Indian Law Section, Member Minority Involvement in the State Bar Task Force since 1988, Women and the Legal Profession Standing Committee for Implementation of Task Force Report March 1991, Sex Bias in the Judiciary Committee 1993), Santa Fe and American (Judicial Administration Division Lawyers Conference on Affordable Justice Committee 1990-91) Bar Associations. Instructor Indian Child Welfare Act 1979, in Indian Law for members of Acoma and Laguna pueblo Indians August 1980 and National American Indian Court Judges Association June 1981. Speaker "The Changing Role of the Guardian Ad Litem" The Changing Area of Custody Litigation State Bar of New Mexico Conference 1985. Presenter Tax Consequences for Native American Businesses on and off the reservation Eight Northern Pueblos Council 1990, Domestic Violence Against the Elderly 1992, Bias in Domestic Violence State of New Mexico Court Clerks 1993 and Winning Your Case in a Culturally Diverse Court Room State Bar of New Mexico Aug 1994. Faculty Advisor The National Judicial College Nov 1992. Attended Panel on Cultural Diversity in the Bar Annual Bar Convention Oct 1994 and General Jurisdiction Course The National Judicial College Oct 1997. Faculty Due Process in the Administration Law Fair Hearing Process The National Judicial College July 1995. Recipient Governors Award for Outstanding New Mexico Women 1993 and Plaque for Excellence in the Fair Adjudication of Rights in Domestic Violence Cases from Northern New Mexico Women's Bar Association 1994. Conveyance Examiner Division of Resource Development and Protection Bureau of Indian Affairs July 1977 to August 1977. Board Member and Secretary Visitor Hospitality Center, Inc. 1981-82. Member Economic Development Committee for Pueblo of Tesuque June 1981 to 1988, Board of Education for Tesuque Pueblo 1984-86, New Mexico Indian Business Association 1984-88 and New Mexico Business Women's Association Aug 1985 to 1986. Board Member Nov 1983 to Oct 1984 and Member since Nov 1983 Southwestern Association on Indian Affairs. Board Santa Fe Mountain Center, Inc. Jan 1985. Board of Visitors University of New Mexico School of Law 1985-87. Board of Directors Pueblo North 1988-89.

Mailing address: P.O. Box 2268, Santa Fe 87504-2268.
Office: Judicial Complex, Santa Fe 87504.
Telephone: (505) 827-5083.
Fax: (505) 827-5055
E-mail address: sfedcjv@jidmailnmcourts.com

VIGIL, Michael E. *(Judge, New Mexico Court of Appeals)* Term expires Dec 31, 2004.
Mailing address: P.O. Box 2008, Santa Fe 87504-2008.
Telephone: (505) 827-4906.

VIGIL, Michael E. *(Judge, New Mexico District Court First Judicial District)* Term expires Dec 31, 2008. Former Chief Judge.
Mailing address: P.O. Box 2268, Santa Fe 87504.
Office: 100 Catron, Santa Fe 87504.
Telephone: (505) 827-5053.
Fax: (505) 827-5055

WALKER, Deborah D. *(Judge, New Mexico District Court Second Judicial District)* Term expires Dec 31, 2008.
Mailing address: P.O. Box 488, Albuquerque 87103.
Office: 400 Lomas Boulevard N.W., Albuquerque 87102.
Telephone: (505) 841-6778.
Fax: (505) 841-5454

WECHSLER, James J. *(Chief Judge, New Mexico Court of Appeals)* Assumed office 1994. Elected 1998, current term expires Dec 31, 2006.
Mailing address: P.O. Box 2008, Santa Fe 87504-2008.
Telephone: (505) 827-4908.

WILSON, Frank K. *(Judge, New Mexico District Court Twelfth Judicial District)* Term expires Dec 31, 2008. Former Chief Judge.
Office: 1000 New York Avenue, Room 261, Alamogordo 88310-6937.
Telephone: (505) 439-1333.
Fax: (505) 434-8886

YORK, Wendy *(Judge, New Mexico District Court Second Judicial District)* Term expires Dec 31, 2008.
Mailing address: P.O. Box 488, Albuquerque 87103.
Office: 400 Lomas Boulevard N.W., Albuquerque 87102.
Telephone: (505) 841-7434.
Fax: (505) 841-5457

NEW YORK

Capital ALBANY

UNITED STATES DISTRICT COURTS DISTRICTS OF NEW YORK

Within New York there are four United States District Courts. For descriptive information refer to the United States Courts section.

EASTERN DISTRICT includes Kings, Nassau, Queens, Richmond and Suffolk counties and concurrently with the Southern District the waters within the counties of Bronx and New York. The court sits at Brooklyn, Central Islip, Hauppauge and Hempstead (including the village of Uniondale).

Chief Judge

Edward R. Korman

Judges

Raymond J. Dearie
Carol Bagley Amon
Denis R. Hurley
David G. Trager
John Gleeson
Nina Gershon
Arthur D. Spatt
Sterling Johnson, Jr.
Joanna Seybert
Allyne Ross
Frederic Block
Nicholas G. Garaufis

Senior Judges

Jacob Mishler
Thomas C. Platt, Jr.
I. Leo Glasser
Jack B. Weinstein
Charles P. Sifton
Leonard D. Wexler

Clerk

Robert C. Heinemann
U.S. Courthouse
225 Cadman Plaza East
Brooklyn, New York 11201
(718) 260-2270

NORTHERN DISTRICT includes Albany, Broome, Cayuga, Chenango, Clinton, Columbia, Cortland, Delaware, Essex, Franklin, Fulton, Greene, Hamilton, Herkimer, Jefferson, Lewis, Madison, Montgomery, Oneida, Onondaga, Oswego, Otsego, Rensselaer, St. Lawrence, Saratoga, Schenectady, Schoharie, Tioga, Tompkins, Ulster, Warren and Washington counties. The court sits at Albany, Auburn, Binghamton, Malone, Syracuse, Utica and Watertown.

Chief Judge

Frederick J. Scullin, Jr.

Judges

Thomas J. McAvoy
Lawrence E. Kahn
Norman A. Mordue
David N. Hurd

Senior Judges

Howard G. Munson
Neal P. McCurn

Clerk

Lawrence K. Baerman
P.O. Box 7367
Syracuse, New York 13261-7367
(315) 234-8500

SOUTHERN DISTRICT includes Bronx, Dutchess, New York, Orange, Putnam, Rockland, Sullivan and Westchester counties and concurrently with the Eastern District the waters within the Eastern District. The court sits at New York City, White Plains and the Middletown Wallkill area of Orange County.

Chief Judge

Michael B. Mukasey

Judges

Charles L. Brieant
John S. Martin, Jr.
Allen G. Schwartz
Denise Cote
Denny Chin
John G. Koeltl
Sidney H. Stein
Jed S. Rakoff
Alvin K. Hellerstein
Colleen McMahon
Naomi Reice Buchwald
George B. Daniels
Laura Taylor Swain
Kimba M. Wood
Loretta A. Preska
Deborah A. Batts
Lewis A. Kaplan
Harold Baer, Jr.
Shira A. Scheindlin
Barbara S. Jones
Richard C. Casey
Richard M. Berman
William Pauley, III
Victor Marrero
Gerard E. Lynch

Senior Judges

Constance Baker Motley
Thomas P. Griesa
Robert L. Carter
Robert J. Ward
William C. Conner
Gerard L. Goettel
Leonard B. Sand
Shirley Wohl Kram
Peter K. Leisure
Miriam Goldman Cedarbaum
Milton Pollack
Morris E. Lasker
Whitman Knapp
Kevin Thomas Duffy
Richard Owen
Charles S. Haight, Jr.
Robert Workman Sweet
John E. Sprizzo
John F. Keenan
Louis L. Stanton
Robert Patterson, Jr.
Lawrence M. McKenna

Clerk

J. Michael McMahon
U.S. Courthouse
500 Pearl Street
New York, New York 10007-1312
(212) 805-0136

WESTERN DISTRICT includes Allegany, Cattaraugus, Chautauqua, Chemung, Erie, Genesee, Livingston, Monroe, Niagara, Ontario, Orleans, Schuyler, Seneca, Steuben, Wayne, Wyoming and Yates counties. The court sits at Buffalo, Canandaigua, Elmira, Jamestown and Rochester.

UNITED STATES DISTRICT COURTS DISTRICTS OF NEW YORK—*Continued*

Chief Judge
Richard J. Arcara

Judges
David G. Larimer
William M. Skretny
Charles J. Siragusa

Senior Judges
John T. Curtin
John T. Elfvin
Michael A. Telesca

Clerk
Rodney C. Early
304 U.S. Courthouse
68 Court Street
Buffalo, New York 14202-3498
(716) 551-4211

UNITED STATES MAGISTRATE JUDGES OF NEW YORK

EASTERN DISTRICT

Aaron Simon Chrein
Michael L. Orenstein
Marilyn D. Go
Roanne L. Mann
Robert M. Levy
Cheryl L. Pollak
Lois S. Bloom
Joan Marie Azrack
Steven M. Gold
Arlene Rosario Lindsay
Viktor V. Pohorelsky
E. Thomas Boyle
William D. Wall

NORTHERN DISTRICT

Gustave J. DiBianco
Gary L. Sharpe
Randolph F. Treece
David R. Homer
David E. Peebles
Larry A. Kudrle

SOUTHERN DISTRICT

Michael H. Dolinger
Theodore H. Katz
Martin R. Goldberg
Andrew J. Peck
Douglas F. Eaton
George A. Yanthis
Frank Maas
Gabriel W. Gorenstein
James C. Francis, IV
Mark D. Fox
Ronald L. Ellis
Lisa Margaret Smith
Henry B. Pitman
Kevin Nathaniel Fox
Debra Freeman

WESTERN DISTRICT

Leslie G. Foschio
Hugh B. Scott
Jonathan W. Feldman
H. Kenneth Schroeder, Jr.

Recalled Magistrate Judge
Victor E. Bianchini (Western)

UNITED STATES BANKRUPTCY COURTS OF NEW YORK

EASTERN DISTRICT

Chief Judge
Conrad B. Duberstein

Judges
Jerome Feller
Melanie L. Cyganowski
Carla E. Craig
Dorothy Eisenberg
Stan Bernstein
Dennis E. Milton

Bankruptcy Clerk
Joseph P. Hurley
75 Clinton Street
Brooklyn, New York 11201-4201
(718) 330-2188

NORTHERN DISTRICT

Chief Judge
Stephen D. Gerling

Judge
Robert E. Littlefield, Jr.

Bankruptcy Clerk
Richard G. Zeh, Sr.
327 U.S. Courthouse
445 Broadway
Albany, New York 12207-2965
(518) 257-1661

SOUTHERN DISTRICT

Chief Judge
Stuart M. Bernstein

Judges
Prudence Carter Beatty
Adlai S. Hardin, Jr.
Cecelia G. Morris
Allan L. Gropper
Cornelius Blackshear
Arthur J. Gonzalez
Robert E. Gerber
Robert D. Drain

Recalled Judge
Burton R. Lifland

Bankruptcy Clerk
Kathleen Farrell
Alexander Hamilton Custom House
Sixth Floor, One Bowling Green
New York, New York 10004-1408
(212) 668-2870

WESTERN DISTRICT

Chief Judge
John Charles Ninfo, II

Judges
Michael J. Kaplan
Carl L. Bucki

Bankruptcy Clerk
Paul R. Warren
250 Olympic Towers
300 Pearl Street
Buffalo, New York 14202-0250
(716) 551-4130

NEW YORK COURT OF APPEALS

The Court of Appeals is New York's court of last resort. The court consists of a chief judge and six associate judges appointed to fourteen-year terms. Judges are appointed by the governor with the advice and consent of the Senate from a list of candidates provided by the Commission on Judicial Nominations.

The chief judge appoints a chief administrator of the courts, who is called the chief administrative judge if the appointee is a judge. Two deputy chief administrative judges assist in the daily operations of the trial courts. One deputy chief administrative judge supervises the trial courts of New York City and the other super-

NEW YORK COURT OF APPEALS—*Continued*

vises the trial courts outside New York City. In addition, a deputy chief administrative judge for management support supervises the internal operations of the Office of Court Administration. Administrative judges are also assigned in each judicial district and in each of the major New York City courts.

The jurisdiction of the court is limited to the review of questions of law except in cases involving the death penalty or when the Appellate Division of the Supreme Court, in reversing or modifying a final or interlocutory judgment or order, finds new facts and a final judgment or order is entered pursuant to that finding. The court also hears appeals from determinations of the State Commission on Judicial Conduct. Appeals involving the death penalty or the constitutionality of a state or federal statute are taken directly to the court.

The court sits en banc at Albany and recesses during July and August.

Chief Judge
Judith S. Kaye

Associate Judges
George Bundy Smith
Richard C. Wesley
Albert M. Rosenblatt
Susan Phillips Read
Carmen Beauchamp Ciparick
Victoria A. Graffeo

Clerk
Stuart M. Cohen
Court of Appeals Hall
20 Eagle Street
Albany, New York 12207-1095
(518) 455-7700

New York State Unified Court System

Chief Administrative Judge
Jonathan Lippman
Office of Court Administration
25 Beaver Street
New York, New York 10004
(212) 428-2100

NEW YORK SUPREME COURT

SUPREME COURT APPELLATE DIVISION

The Supreme Court Appellate Division is New York's court of intermediate appellate jurisdiction and consists of four judicial departments. Justices are designated by the governor from among the Supreme Court justices. The presiding justice serves to the end of his or her term as a Supreme Court justice. Associate justices serve five-year terms or to the end of their Supreme Court terms, whichever is shorter. Retirement is mandatory at age seventy; however, retired justices may be certificated to serve for as many as three two-year terms.

The court hears appeals from the special and trial terms of the Supreme Court, from County Courts and from various other courts of original instance. The court has appellate jurisdiction over final and many intermediate orders rendered in these courts as well as original jurisdiction in certain matters. Where established by the Appellate Division, Appellate Terms exercise jurisdiction over civil and criminal appeals from various local courts and certain criminal appeals from County Courts in the Second Judicial Department. Appeals from the Appellate Division are to the Court of Appeals. Appeals from the Appellate Terms are to the Appellate Division in civil matters and to the Court of Appeals in criminal matters. The Appellate Division has authority to regulate admission to the bar and the conduct of its members.

The court sits in panels of four or five justices. Four justices constitute a quorum, and no more than five justices may hear any particular case.

---

*Certificated

FIRST JUDICIAL DEPARTMENT includes Bronx and New York counties. The court sits at Manhattan.

Presiding Justice
John T. Buckley

Associate Justices
Richard T. Andrias
David Friedman
Luis A. Gonzalez
George D. Marlow
Eugene L. Nardelli
David B. Saxe
Peter Tom
Milton L. Williams*
Betty Weinberg Ellerin*
Alfred D. Lerner*
Angela Mazzarelli
Ernst H. Rosenberger*
Joseph P. Sullivan*
Richard W. Wallach*

SECOND JUDICIAL DEPARTMENT includes Dutchess, Kings, Nassau, Orange, Putnam, Queens, Richmond, Rockland, Suffolk and Westchester counties. The court sits at Brooklyn.

Presiding Justice
A. Gail Prudenti

Associate Justices
Thomas A. Adams
Barry A. Cozier
Sandra J. Feuerstein
William D. Friedmann*
Gabriel M. Krausman*
William F. Mastro
Howard Miller
David S. Ritter
Fred T. Santucci
Nancy E. Smith
Myriam J. Altman
Stephen G. Crane
Anita R. Florio
Gloria Goldstein*
Daniel F. Luciano*
Leo F. McGinity*
Sondra Miller*
Reinaldo E. Rivera
Robert W. Schmidt
Sandra L. Townes

THIRD JUDICIAL DEPARTMENT includes Albany, Broome, Chemung, Chenango, Clinton, Columbia, Cortland, Delaware, Essex, Franklin, Fulton, Greene, Hamilton, Madison, Montgomery, Otsego, Rensselaer, St. Lawrence, Saratoga, Schenectady, Schoharie, Schuyler, Sullivan, Tioga, Tompkins, Ulster, Warren and Washington counties. The court sits at Albany.

Presiding Justice
Anthony V. Cardona

Associate Justices
Anthony J. Carpinello
Anthony T. Kane
Thomas E. Mercure
Karen K. Peters
Edward O. Spain
D. Bruce Crew, III
John A. Lahtinen
Carl J. Mugglin
Robert S. Rose

FOURTH JUDICIAL DEPARTMENT includes Allegany, Cattaraugus, Cayuga, Chautauqua, Erie, Genesee, Herkimer, Jefferson, Lewis, Livingston, Monroe, Niagara, Oneida, Onondaga, Ontario, Orleans, Oswego, Sene-

NEW YORK SUPREME COURT—*Continued*

ca, Steuben, Wayne, Wyoming and Yates counties. The court sits at Rochester.

Presiding Justice

Eugene F. Pigott, Jr.

Associate Justices

Christopher J. Burns	Jerome C. Gorski
Samuel L. Green	Leo F. X. Hayes*
Robert G. Hurlbutt	L. Paul Kehoe
John F. Lawton*	Elizabeth W. Pine
Henry J. Scudder	Donald J. Wisner

SUPREME COURT

The Supreme Court is New York's court of general trial jurisdiction. Justices are elected by judicial district to serve fourteen-year terms. Retirement is mandatory at age seventy; however, retired justices may be certificated to serve for as many as three two-year terms. The Chief Administrative Judge may designate judges of the Court of Claims, County-level Courts (including County Courts, Surrogate's Courts and Family Courts) and the Civil and Criminal Courts of the City of New York to serve as Acting Supreme Court Justices. These assignments are based upon need and the availability of judges and are temporary with no specified length of term. Acting Supreme Court Justices have the full authority of regular Supreme Court Justices.

The court has unlimited original jurisdiction, but it generally hears cases outside the jurisdiction of other courts, such as civil matters beyond the jurisdiction of lower courts; divorce, separation and annulment proceedings; equity suits such as mortgage foreclosures and injunctions; and criminal prosecution of felonies and indictable misdemeanors in New York City, where there is no County Court to handle these cases. The court may issue writs necessary to the exercise of proper jurisdiction.

The court sits at the county seats and other places as designated.

---

*Certificated

FIRST JUDICIAL DISTRICT consists of New York County. The court sits at Manhattan.

Justices

Sheila Abdus Salaam	Rolando T. Acosta
Eileen C. Bransten	Herman Cahn*
William J. Davis*	Leland G. DeGrasse
Carol Robinson Edmead	Nicholas Figueroa
Fern A. Fisher	Helen E. Freedman
Ira Gammerman*	Phyllis Gangel-Jacob*
Budd G. Goodman*	Emily Jane Goodman
Sherry Klein Heitler	Carol E. Huff
Marcy L. Kahn	Barbara R. Kapnick
Edward H. Lehner	Doris Ling-Cohan
Joan B. Lobis	Richard B. Lowe, III
Joan A. Madden	William P. McCooe*
Karla Moskowitz	Eduardo Padro
Richard Lee Price	Charles E. Ramos
Rosalyn H. Richter	Alice Schlesinger
Martin Schoenfeld	Jacqueline Silbermann
Stanley L. Sklar*	Milton A. Tingling Jr.
Harold Tompkins*	Laura Visitacion-Lewis
Troy K. Webber	Lottie E. Wilkins
James A. Yates	

SECOND JUDICIAL DISTRICT includes Kings and Richmond counties. The court sits at Brooklyn and at St. George, Staten Island.

Justices

Thomas P. Aliotta	Gloria Cohen Aronin*
Melvin S. Barasch*	Frank J. Barbaro*
Betsy Barros	Ariel E. Belen
Michael J. Brennan	Joseph F. Bruno
Bert A. Bunyan	Cheryl E. Chambers
Nicholas A. Clemente*	Anthony J. Cutrona
Gloria M. Dabiri	Carolyn E. Demarest
Patricia M. DiMango	Lewis L. Douglass*
Joseph J. Dowd*	Deborah A. Dowling
Anne G. Feldman*	William J. Garry*
Gerald P. Garson*	Michael J. Garson
Abraham G. Gerges	Robert J. Gigante
L. Priscilla Hall	Ira B. Harkavy*
Gerald S. Held*	Muriel Shaff Hubsher*
Allen Z. Hurkin-Torres	James W. Hutcherson*
Richard D. Huttner	M. Randolph Jackson
Laura Lee Jacobson	Diana A. Johnson
Theodore T. Jones, Jr.	Lawrence S. Knipel
Herbert Kramer	Robert S. Kreindler*
Alan L. Lebowitz	John M. Leventhal
Joseph S. Levine*	Yvonne Lewis
Plummer E. Lott	Louis John Marrero
Larry D. Martin	Reynold N. Mason
Christopher J. Mega*	Philip G. Minardo
Mark I. Partnow	Michelle Weston Patterson
Michael L. Pesce	Edward M. Rappaport
Frank V. Ponterio*	François A. Rivera
Gustin L. Reichbach	Howard A. Ruditzky
Gerard H. Rosenberg	Martin Schneier
Leon Ruchelsman	James G. Starkey
Jules L. Spodek*	James P. Sullivan
Marsha L. Steinhardt	David B. Vaughan
Albert Tomei	
Virginia E. Yancey	

THIRD JUDICIAL DISTRICT includes Albany, Columbia, Greene, Rensselaer, Schoharie, Sullivan and Ulster counties. The court sits at Albany, Hudson, Catskill, Troy, Schoharie, Monticello and Kingston.

Justices

Vincent G. Bradley	James B. Canfield
Joseph R. Cannizzaro	George Ceresia, Jr.
John G. Connor*	E. Michael Kavanagh
Thomas W. Keegan	Bernard Malone, Jr.
Thomas J. Spargo	Leslie E. Stein
Joseph C. Teresi	

FOURTH JUDICIAL DISTRICT includes Clinton, Essex, Franklin, Fulton, Hamilton, Montgomery, St. Lawrence, Saratoga, Schenectady, Warren and Washington counties. The court sits at Plattsburgh, Elizabethtown, Malone, Johnstown, Lake Pleasant, Fonda, Canton, Ballston Spa, Schenectady, Warren County Center, Hudson Falls and Salem.

Justices

Richard T. Aulisi	Robert P. Best*
Vito C. Caruso	James P. Dawson
David R. Demarest	Stephen A. Ferradino
G. Thomas Moynihan, Jr.	Thomas D. Nolan, Jr.

NEW YORK SUPREME COURT—*Continued*

Jan H. Plumadore
Joseph M. Sise
Vincent J. Reilly, Jr.
Frank B. Williams

FIFTH JUDICIAL DISTRICT includes Herkimer, Jefferson, Lewis, Oneida, Onondaga and Oswego counties. The court sits at Herkimer, Watertown, Lowville, Utica, Rome, Syracuse, Oswego and Pulaski.

Justices

Edward D. Carni
Michael E. Daley
Hugh A. Gilbert
Samuel D. Hester
Deborah H. Karalunas
Joseph D. McGuire
Robert J. Nicholson
William R. Roy*
John R. Tenney*
John V. Centra
Brian F. DeJoseph
John W. Grow*
Robert F. Julian
Charles T. Major
Thomas J. Murphy*
Anthony J. Paris
Anthony F. Shaheen
James C. Tormey, III

SIXTH JUDICIAL DISTRICT includes Broome, Chemung, Chenango, Cortland, Delaware, Madison, Otsego, Schuyler, Tioga and Tompkins counties. The court sits at Binghamton, Elmira, Norwich, Cortland, Delhi, Wampsville, Cooperstown, Watkins Glen, Owego and Ithaca.

Justices

Kevin M. Dowd
Patrick D. Monserrate
William O'Brien, III
Walter J. Relihan, Jr.*
Joseph P. Hester, Jr.
Robert C. Mulvey
Judith F. O'Shea
Phillip R. Rumsey

SEVENTH JUDICIAL DISTRICT includes Cayuga, Livingston, Monroe, Ontario, Seneca, Steuben, Wayne and Yates counties. The court sits at Auburn, Geneseo, Rochester, Canandaigua, Waterloo, Ovid, Bath, Hornell, Corning, Lyons and Penn Yan.

Justices

Francis A. Affronti
David Michael Barry
Raymond E. Cornelius
Kenneth R. Fisher
Harold L. Galloway
William P. Polito
Thomas A. Stander
Thomas Van Strydonck
John J. Ark
Eugene W. Bergin*
David Daniel Egan
Evelyn Frazee
Robert J. Lunn
Andrew V. Siracuse*
Joseph D. Valentino

EIGHTH JUDICIAL DISTRICT includes Allegany, Cattaraugus, Chautauqua, Erie, Genesee, Niagara, Orleans and Wyoming counties. The court sits at Belmont, Little Valley, Olean, Mayville, Buffalo, Batavia, Lockport, Albion and Warsaw.

Justices

Ralph A. Boniello III
Kevin M. Dillon
Eugene M. Fahey
Amy J. Fricano
Joseph R. Glownia
John P. Lane*
Joseph G. Makowksi
Salvatore R. Martoche
Joseph D. Mintz
Peter J. Notaro
Janice M. Rosa
Frank A. Sedita, Jr.
Robert E. Whelan
Nelson H. Cosgrove
Vincent Doyle, Jr.*
Joseph S. Forma
Joseph Gerace*
Barbara Howe
David J. Mahoney*
Frederick J. Marshall
John A. Michalek
Patrick H. NeMoyer
John F. O'Donnell
Rose H. Sconiers
Donna M. Siwek
Penny M. Wolfgang

NINTH JUDICIAL DISTRICT includes Dutchess, Orange, Putnam, Rockland and Westchester counties. The court sits at Newburgh, Goshen, Carmel, New City and White Plains.

Justices

Daniel D. Angiolillo
Orazio R. Bellantoni
James V. Brands
James R. Cowhey*
Thomas A. Dickerson
Mark C. Dillon
S. Barrett Hickman*
Linda S. Jamieson
Joan B. Lefkowitz
J. Emmett Murphy
Francis A. Nicolai
Joseph G. Owen
Peter P. Rosato*
William E. Sherwood
Robert A. Spolzino
Joseph K. West*
Louis A. Barone*
George M. Bergerman
Nicholas Colabella
John P. DiBlasi
Janet DiFiore
W. Denis Donovan*
Judith A. Hillery
John R. La Cava
John K. McGuirk
Aldo A. Nastasi*
Andrew P. O'Rourke
Peter C. Patsalos*
Kenneth W. Rudolph
Mary H. Smith
John W. Sweeny, Jr.

TENTH JUDICIAL DISTRICT includes Nassau and Suffolk counties. The court sits at Mineola and Riverhead.

Justices

Bruce D. Alpert
Paul J. Baisley, Jr.
John C. Bivona
Stephen A. Bucaria
James M. Catterson
John Copertino*
Joseph Covello
Kenneth A. Davis
Robert W. Doyle
John P. Dunne*
Anthony J. Falanga
Patrick Henry*
John J. J. Jones, Jr.
William J. Kent, III
William R. LaMarca
Robert A. Lifson
Roy S. Mahon
Edward G. McCabe
Denise F. Molia
Robert Webster Oliver*
Anthony L. Parga
Emily Pines
Ira J. Raab
Robert A. Ross
Sandra L. Sgroi
Elaine Jackson Stack*
William L. Underwood, Jr.*
Ira H. Wexner*
Allan L. Winick*
Michele M. Woodard
Leonard B. Austin
Howard Berler*
Donald R. Blydenburgh
John W. Burke*
Peter Fox Cohalan
Ralph F. Costello
R. Bruce Cozzens, Jr.
Joseph A. DeMaro
John J. Dunn*
Elizabeth H. Emerson
Ralph P. Franco*
Zelda Jonas*
Burton S. Joseph*
Ute Wolff Lally
H. Patrick Leis, III
Daniel J. Loughlin*
Anthony F. Marano
Edward W. McCarty, III
Geoffrey J. O'Connell
Alan D. Oshrin
Thomas P. Phelan
Arthur G. Pitts
Robert Roberto, Jr.*
Marvin E. Segal*
Peter B. Skelos
Melvyn Tanenbaum
Ira B. Warshawsky
Mary M. Werner
Thomas F. Whelan
F. Dana Winslow

ELEVENTH JUDICIAL DISTRICT includes Queens County. The court sits at Jamaica, Kew Gardens and Long Island City.

Justices

Laura D. Blackburne
Richard Lance Buchter
James P. Dollard
Roberta L. Dunlop
Evelyn L. Braun
Arthur J. Cooperman
Joseph P. Dorsa
Joan Marie Durante

NEW YORK SUPREME COURT—*Continued*

Luther V. Dye	Randall T. Eng
Steven W. Fisher	Timothy J. Flaherty
Phyllis Orlikoff Flug	William T. Glover*
Simeon Golar*	David Goldstein
Joseph G. Golia	Marguerite A. Grays
Duane A. Hart	Ronald D. Hollie
Stanley B. Katz*	Peter Joseph Kelly
Orin R. Kitzes	Robert C. Kohm
Alan Le Vine*	Daniel Lewis
Robert J. McDonald	Peter J. O'Donoghue
Thomas V. Polizzi*	Arnold N. Price*
Jaime A. Rios	Joseph J. Risi*
Martin E. Ritholtz	Sheri S. Roman
Roger N. Rosengarten	Joseph Rosenzweig*
Seymour Rotker	Frederick Sampson
Patricia Satterfield	Frederick D. Schmidt*
Martin J. Schulman	Mark H. Spires*
Sidney F. Strauss	Janice A. Taylor
Charles J. Thomas	Jeremy S. Weinstein
Allan B. Weiss	

TWELFTH JUDICIAL DISTRICT includes Bronx County. The court sits at Bronx.

Justices

John A. Barone	Louis C. Benza*
Lawrence H. Bernstein*	Janice L. Bowman
Jerry L. Crispino*	Edward M. Davidowitz*
Laura G. Douglas	Gerald V. Esposito
Yvonne Gonzalez	Alexander Hunter, Jr.
Bertram D. Katz*	Sallie Manzanet
LaTia W. Martin	Douglas E. McKeon
Donna Marie Mills	Dianne T. Renwick
Nelson S. Roman	Norma Ruiz
Alan J. Saks	George D. Salerno
Barry Salman	Howard R. Silver
Harold Silverman*	David Stadtmauer
Betty Owen Stinson	Lucindo Suarez
Anne E. Targum*	Kenneth Thompson, Jr.
Edwin Torres*	Paul A. Victor

NEW YORK COURT OF CLAIMS

The Court of Claims is a special trial court of statewide jurisdiction in New York. Judges are appointed by the governor with the advice and consent of the Senate for nine-year terms. A presiding judge is designated to serve for the remainder of his or her term.

The court has jurisdiction of claims against the state of New York. Trials are not heard by a jury; a judge presides and renders a decision.

The court sits at Albany, with branches throughout the state. Of the sixty-four judges currently sitting on the court, forty-five of them are designated acting Supreme Court justices and hear felony cases, mainly in New York City.

‡Acting Supreme Court Justice

Presiding Judge

James J. Lack

Judges

Michael R. Ambrecht‡	Phylis S. Bamberger‡
Antonio I. Brandveen‡	John J. Brunetti‡
Edward D. Burke‡	Russell P. Buscaglia‡
Joan B. Carey‡	Gregory Carro‡
Thomas J. Carroll‡	Caesar D. Cirigliano‡
Margaret L. Clancy‡	Robert J. Collini‡
Francis T. Collins	Donald J. Corbett, Jr.
Michael A. Corriero‡	Vincent M. Del Giudice‡
Matthew J. D'Emic‡	William C. Donnino‡
Albert J. Emanuelli‡	Joseph Fisch‡
Diane L. Fitzpatrick	Anthony I. Giacobbe‡
Robert J. Hanophy‡	Judith A. Hard
Alan L. Honorof‡	Richard M. Klein‡
Richard C. Kloch, Sr.‡	Dan Lamont‡
Ferris D. Lebous	Jonathan Lippman
Albert Lorenzo‡	Joseph J. Maltese‡
Guy J. Mangano, Jr.‡	Martin Marcus‡
Alan C. Marin	Daniel Martin‡
Dominic R. Massaro‡	Thomas J. McNamara
Nicholas V. Midey, Jr.	Stephen J. Mignano
Renee Forgensi Minarik	Richard A. Molea‡
Michael F. Mullen‡	S. Michael Nadel
Edgar Carroll NeMoyer	Victor M. Ort‡
Philip J. Patti	Stephen J. Rooney‡
Frank S. Rossetti‡	Mario J. Rossetti‡
Terry Jane Ruderman	Thomas H. Scuccimarra
Edward A. Sheridan‡	Norman I. Siegel‡
Richard E. Sise	Leslie Crocker Snyder‡
Lewis Bart Stone‡	Charles J. Tejada‡
Ronald H. Tills‡	Rena K. Uviller‡
Alton R. Waldon, Jr.	William A. Wetzel‡
Ronald A. Zweibel‡	

NEW YORK COUNTY COURT

The County Court is a court of superior jurisdiction established in every county in New York except the five counties of New York City (Bronx, Kings, New York, Queens and Richmond counties). Judges are elected in each county for ten-year terms. Retirement is mandatory at age seventy.

The court has jurisdiction of all criminal offenses committed within the county, although in practice most minor offenses are handled by lower courts. The court has limited jurisdiction of civil cases generally involving amounts up to $25,000. County Courts in the Third and Fourth Judicial Departments of the Supreme Court Appellate Division also exercise appellate jurisdiction over cases from the lower courts. Some County Courts also exercise the jurisdiction of the Surrogate's Court and Family Court.

†Also exercises Surrogate's Court jurisdiction
**Also exercises Family Court jurisdiction
#Also exercises Surrogate's Court and Family Court jurisdiction
‡Acting Supreme Court Justice

County	Judge
Albany	Thomas A. Breslin‡
	Stephen W. Herrick
Allegany	Thomas Paul Brown#
	James E. Euken#
Broome	Patrick H. Mathews**
	Martin E. Smith
Cattaraugus	Larry M. Himelein#
	Michael L. Nenno#
Cayuga	Peter E. Corning**
Chautauqua	John T. Ward

NEW YORK COUNTY COURT—*Continued*

Chemung	Peter C. Buckley#
	James T. Hayden#
Chenango	W. Howard Sullivan#
Clinton	Patrick R. McGill
	Kevin K. Ryan†
Columbia	Paul Czajka#
Cortland	William F. Ames#
	Emerson R. Avery, Jr.#
Delaware	Carl F. Becker#
Dutchess	Thomas J. Dolan‡
	Gerald V. Hayes
Erie	Michael L. D'Amico
	Sheila A. DiTullio
	Timothy J. Drury
	Michael F. Pietruszka
	Shirley Troutman
Essex	Andrew Halloran#
Franklin	Robert G. Main, Jr.#‡
Fulton	Richard C. Giardino†
	Polly A. Hoye†
Genesee	Robert C. Noonan†‡
Greene	Daniel Kevin Lalor#
	George J. Pulver, Jr.#
Hamilton	S. Peter Feldstein#
Herkimer	Patrick L. Kirk†
Jefferson	Kim H. Martusewicz
Lewis	Charles C. Merrell#
Livingston	Gerard J. Alonzo, Jr.#
	Ronald A. Cicoria#
Madison	Biagio J. DiStefano#
	Dennis K. McDermott#
Monroe	Elma A. Bellini
	John J. Connell
	Frank P. Geraci, Jr.
	Richard A. Keenan
	Patricia D. Marks‡
	Alex R. Renzi
Montgomery	Felix J. Catena
Nassau	Donald E. Belfi
	Meryl J. Berkowitz
	Jeffrey S. Brown
	Joseph C. Calabrese
	Jerald S. Carter‡
	Daniel J. Cotter
	Donald P. DeRiggi
	John Michael Galasso‡
	Frank A. Gulotta, Jr.
	Richard A. LaPera
	Daniel Palmieri
	George R. Peck
	David P. Sullivan
	Claire I. Weinberg
Niagara	Peter L. Broderick, Sr.†
	Sara Sheldon Sperrazza†
Oneida	Barry M. Donalty
	Michael L. Dwyer
Onondaga	Anthony F. Aloi
	Joseph E. Fahey
	William D. Walsh
Ontario	Craig J. Doran**
	James R. Harvey**
Orange	Jeffrey G. Berry‡
	Nicholas DeRosa‡
	Stewart A. Rosenwasser
Orleans	James P. Punch#

Oswego	Walter W. Hafner, Jr.
	James W. McCarthy
Otsego	Brian D. Burns#
	Michael V. Coccoma#
Putnam	Robert E. Miller#
	James T. Rooney#
Rensselaer	Patrick J. McGrath
Rockland	William A. Kelly
	William K. Nelson‡
	Kenneth H. Resnik
St. Lawrence	Eugene L. Nicandri
Saratoga	Jerry J. Scarano
Schenectady	Michael C. Eidens
Schoharie	George R. Bartlett, III#
Schuyler	J. C. Argetsinger#
Seneca	Dennis F. Bender#
Steuben	Peter C. Bradstreet**
	Joseph W. Latham**
Suffolk	Stephen L. Braslow
	James F. X. Doyle
	Joseph Farneti
	Ralph T. Gazzillo
	C. Randall Hinrichs
	James C. Hudson
	Martin J. Kerins
	Donald Kitson‡
	Louis J. Ohlig
	Jeffrey Arlen Spinner
	Gary J. Weber
Sullivan	Frank J. LaBuda†
	Burton Ledina†
Tioga	Vincent A. Sgueglia#
Tompkins	John C. Rowley#
	M. John Sherman#
Ulster	J. Michael Bruhn
Warren	John Austin†
Washington	Philip A. Berke#
	Gordon M. Hemmett, Jr.#
Wayne	Dennis M. Kehoe#
	John B. Nesbitt#
	Stephen R. Sirkin#
Westchester	Lester B. Adler
	Kenneth H. Lange
	Fred L. Shapiro‡
	Sam D. Walker
	Barbara Gunther Zambelli
Wyoming	Mark H. Dadd#
	Michael F. Griffith#
Yates	W. Patrick Falvey#‡

NEW YORK COURTS OF LIMITED OR SPECIAL JURISDICTION

The following courts sit at places designated locally. The courts in New York City sit at many branch locations.

NEW YORK SURROGATE'S COURT

The Surrogate's Court is a court of special jurisdiction established in every county in New York. Surrogates are elected for ten-year terms in each county outside New York City and for fourteen-year terms in each county of New York City. Retirement is mandatory at age seventy.

The court hears cases involving the affairs of decedents, including the probate of wills and the administration of estates. The court has concurrent jurisdiction

NEW YORK SURROGATE'S COURT—*Continued*

with the Family Court in adoption cases. In some counties jurisdiction is handled by the County Court.

*Surrogate's jurisdiction handled by County Court Judge
‡Acting Supreme Court Justice

County	Surrogate
Albany	Cathyrn M. Doyle
Allegany	*
Bronx	Lee L. Holzman
Broome	Eugene E. Peckham
Cattaraugus	*
Cayuga	Mark H. Fandrich
Chautauqua	Stephen W. Cass
Chemung	*
Chenango	*
Clinton	*
Columbia	*
Cortland	*
Delaware	*
Dutchess	James D. Pagones
Erie	Joseph S. Mattina‡
Essex	*
Franklin	*
Fulton	*
Genesee	*
Greene	*
Hamilton	*
Herkimer	*
Jefferson	Peter A. Schwerzmann
Kings	Michael H. Feinberg
Lewis	*
Livingston	*
Madison	*
Monroe	Edmund A. Calvaruso
Montgomery	Guy P. Tomlinson
Nassau	John B. Riordan
New York	Eve M. Preminger
	Renee R. Roth
Niagara	*
Oneida	John G. Ringrose
Onondaga	Peter N. Wells
Ontario	Frederick G. Reed
Orange	Elaine Slobod
Orleans	*
Oswego	John J. Elliott‡
Otsego	*
Putnam	*
Queens	Robert L. Nahman
Rensselaer	Christian F. Hummel
Richmond	John A. Fusco
Rockland	Alfred J. Weiner‡
St. Lawrence	Kathleen Martin Rogers
Saratoga	Harry W. Seibert, Jr.
Schenectady	Barry D. Kramer‡
Schoharie	*
Schuyler	*
Seneca	*
Steuben	Marianne Furfure
Suffolk	John M. Czygier, Jr.
Sullivan	*
Tioga	*
Tompkins	*
Ulster	Joseph J. Traficanti, Jr.
Warren	*
Washington	*
Wayne	*
Westchester	Anthony A. Scarpino, Jr.
Wyoming	*
Yates	*

NEW YORK FAMILY COURT

The Family Court is a court of special jurisdiction established in each county in New York and the city of New York. In counties outside New York City judges are elected for ten-year terms; in New York City judges are appointed by the mayor for ten-year terms. Retirement is mandatory at age seventy for elected judges.

The court hears matters involving children and families, including abuse and neglect, support of dependent relatives and children born out of wedlock, juvenile delinquency, child protection, persons in need of supervision, foster care placements, permanent termination of custody due to permanent neglect, family offenses and paternity determinations. The court has concurrent jurisdiction with the Surrogate's Court in adoption cases. In some counties jurisdiction is handled by the County Court.

*Family Court jurisdiction handled by County Court Judge
‡Acting Supreme Court Justice

NEW YORK CITY FAMILY COURT

Judges

Jody Adams	Michael A. Ambrosio‡
Mary E. Bednar	Stephen J. Bogacz
Robert F. Clark	Rhoda J. Cohen
Alma Cordova	Tandra L. Dawson
Guy P. De Phillips	Lee Hand Elkins
Mary Ellen Fitzmaurice	Nora L. Freeman
Rhea G. Friedman	Sidney H. Gribetz
Paul H. Grosvenor	Bryanne A. Hamill
Paula J. Hepner	John Hunt
George L. Jurow	Susan R. Larabee
Joseph M. Lauria	Arnold Lim
Fran L. Lubow	Harold J. Lynch
Terrence J. McElrath	Maureen A. McLeod
Martin P. Murphy	Jane Pearl
Myrna M. Martinez Perez	Ralph J. Porzio
	Sheldon M. Rand
Clark V. Richardson	Marybeth S. Richroath
Gayle P. Roberts	Barbara Salinitro
Sara P. Schechter	Marian R. Shelton
Gloria Sosa-Lintner	Betty E. Staton
Carol A. Stokinger	Helen C. Sturm
Jeffrey S. Sunshine‡	Daniel Turbow
Stewart H. Weinstein	

COUNTIES OUTSIDE NEW YORK CITY

County	Judge
Albany	W. Dennis Duggan
	Gerard E. Maney
	Beverly Cipollo Tobin
Allegany	*
Broome	Mary Rita Connerton
	Spero Pines
	Herbert B. Ray
Cattaraugus	*

NEW YORK FAMILY COURT—*Continued*

Cayuga	*
Chautauqua	Judith S. Claire
Chemung	David M. Brockway
Chenango	*
Clinton	Timothy J. Lawliss
Columbia	*
Cortland	*
Delaware	*
Dutchess	Damian J. Amodeo‡
	Peter M. Forman
Erie	Kevin M. Carter
	James H. Dillon
	Patricia Anne Maxwell
	Margaret O. Szczur
	Sharon S. Townsend‡
Essex	*
Franklin	*
Fulton	David F. Jung
Genesee	Eric R. Adams
Greene	*
Hamilton	*
Herkimer	Henry A. La Raia
Jefferson	Richard V. Hunt
Lewis	*
Livingston	*
Madison	*
Monroe	Gail A. Donofrio
	Joan S. Kohout
	Marilyn L. O'Connor
	John J. Rivoli
	Anthony J. Sciolino
	Ann Marie Taddeo
Montgomery	Philip V. Cortese
Nassau	Ruth C. Balkin
	Lawrence J. Brennan
	Kenneth S. Diamond
	Julianne S. Eisman
	Carnell T. Foskey
	Richard S. Lawrence
	John G. Marks
	John B. Pessala
Niagara	John F. Batt
Oneida	Frank S. Cook
	James R. Griffith‡
	Bernadette T. Romano
	David E. Seaman
Onondaga	Michael L. Hanuszczak
	Bryan R. Hedges
	Martha Walsh Hood
	David G. Klim
	Robert J. Rossi
Ontario	*
Orange	Andrew P. Bivona
	Debra J. Kiedaisch
	Carol S. Klein
Orleans	*
Oswego	David J. Roman
Otsego	*
Putnam	*
Rensselaer	Catherine Cholakis
	Linda C. Griffin
Rockland	Margaret Garvey
	William P. Warren
St. Lawrence	Barbara R. Potter
Saratoga	Gilbert L. Abramson
	Courtenay W. Hall
Schenectady	Jo Anne Assini
	Mark L. Powers
Schoharie	*
Schuyler	*
Seneca	*
Steuben	*
Suffolk	Gregory J. Blass
	Peter G. Dounias
	David Freundlich‡
	Joan M. Genchi
	Dudley L. Lehman
	Barbara Lynaugh
	Marion T. McNulty‡
	Ettore A. Simeone
	Patrick A. Sweeney
	Kerry R. Trainor
Sullivan	Mark M. Meddaugh
Tioga	*
Tompkins	*
Ulster	Marianne O. Mizel
	Mary MacMaster Work
Warren	J. Timothy Breen
Washington	*
Wayne	*
Westchester	Joan O. Cooney
	Sandra B. Edlitz
	Nilda Morales Horowitz
	David Klein
	Bruce E. Tolbert
Wyoming	*
Yates	*

CITY COURTS IN NEW YORK

City Courts are established in cities outside the city of New York. Part-time judges are elected for six-year terms and full-time judges are elected for ten-year terms. Retirement is mandatory at age seventy.

The courts have jurisdiction in civil cases up to $15,000. The courts have criminal jurisdiction over misdemeanors.

§Acting Judge **Administrative Judge
+Chief Judge #Supervising Judge
‡Acting Supreme Court Justice

City	Judge
Albany	William A. Carter
	Cheryl F. Coleman
	E. David Duncan
	John C. Egan, Jr.
	Thomas K. Keefe
Amsterdam	Howard M. Aison
	Paul L. Wollman
Auburn	Michael F. McKeon
	Thomas J. Shamon
Batavia	Robert J. Balbick
	Don B. Iwanicki
Beacon	Rebecca S. Mensch§
	Timothy G. Pagones‡
Binghamton	Deborah Jo L. Harter§
	John T. Hillis
	Mary Anne Lehmann
	Robert C. Murphy
Buffalo	Thomas P. Amodeo+**

CITY COURTS IN NEW YORK—*Continued*

Buffalo—Cont.	Patrick M. Carney
	Diane Y. Devlin
	Joseph A. Fiorella
	Thomas P. Franczyk
	Debra L. Givens
	Andrew C. Lo Tempio
	Sharon M. Lo Vallo
	David M. Manz
	James A. W. McLeod
	Henry J. Nowak, Jr.
	E. Jeanette Ogden
	Robert T. Russell, Jr.
Canandaigua	Stephen D. Aronson
	John A. Schuppenhauer§
Cohoes	Walter J. Forman
	Caroline Guresz
	Stephen J. Van Ullen
Corning	Robert H. Cole, Sr.§
	David B. Kahl
Cortland	Elizabeth Burns
	Thomas A. Meldrim
Dunkirk	Walter F. Drag
	John M. Kuzdale
Elmira	Steven W. Forrest
	Thomas E. Ramich
Fulton	Spencer J. Ludington
	Jerome A. Mirabito§
Geneva	Timothy J. Buckley
	Walter C. Gage
	Elisabeth A. Toole
Glen Cove	Richard J. McCord
	Joel B. Meirowitz
Glens Falls	David B. Krogmann
	Richard P. Tarantino
Gloversville	Vincent DeSantis
	Mario J. Papa
Hornell	Joseph Edward Damrath
	David A. Shults
Hudson	William F. Cranna
	Barry D. Sack
Ithaca	Marjorie Z. Olds
	Judith A. Rossiter
Jamestown	James Abdella
	John L. LaMancuso
Johnstown	Frederick R. Stortecky
	Thomas C. Walsh
Kingston	Edward T. Feeney
	James P. Gilpatric
Lackawanna	Joseph V. Deren§
	Frederic J. Marrano
Little Falls	Bart M. Carrig§
	Edward J. Rose
Lockport	William J. Watson
	David R. Wendt
Long Beach	Stanley A. Smolkin
	Roy Tepper
Mechanicville	James F. Hughes§
	Joseph W. Sheehan
Middletown	Richard J. Guertin
	Michael Schwartz
Mount Vernon	Brenda Dowery-Rodriquez
	Colleen Duffy
	William Edwards
	Adam Seiden
Newburgh	Anthony G. Austria, Jr.
	Jeanne M. Patsalos
New Rochelle	John P. Colangelo
	Gail B. Rice
	Preston S. Scher
Niagara Falls	Angelo J. Morinello
	Robert M. Restaino
	Mark Anthony Violante+
North Tonawanda	R. Thomas Burgasser
	William R. Lewis
Norwich	Maureen A. Byrne§
	James E. Downey
Ogdensburg	A. Michael Gebo
	George E. Silver
Olean	William H. Mountain III
	Daniel R. Palumbo§
Oneida	Anthony P. Eppolito
	Michael J. Misiaszek§
Oneonta	William K. Atchinson, Jr.
	Walter L. Terry, III
Oswego	James M. Metcalf
	Thomas A. Reynolds§
Peekskill	Barry Birbrower
	William L. Maher
Plattsburgh	Penelope D. Clute
	Mark J. Rogers§
Port Jervis	Victoria Brace Campbell
	Robert A. Onofry
Poughkeepsie	Lee David Klein
	Ronald J. McGaw
Rensselaer	Kathleen L. Robichaud
Rochester	Marjorie L. Byrnes
	Melchor E. Castro
	Teresa D. Johnson
	Roy Wheatley King
	Stephen K. Lindley
	Thomas Rainbow Morse
	Ann E. Pfeiffer
	John R. Schwartz+
	Ellen Yacknin
Rome	John C. Gannon
	Daniel C. Wilson
Rye	John L. Alfano
	Peter Lane
Salamanca	William J. Gabler§
	William H. Mountain III
Saratoga Springs	James E. D. Doern
	Douglas C. Mills
Schenectady	Karen A. Drago
	Guido A. Loyola
	Vincent W. Versaci
Sherrill	Neal P. Rose
Syracuse	James H. Cecile
	Stephen J. Dougherty
	David S. Gideon§
	Thomas W. Higgins, Jr.
	Langston C. McKinney
	Jeffrey R. Merrill#
	Kate Rosenthal
	Jack Schultz§
	Karen M. Uplinger
	Kevin G. Young
Tonawanda	Joseph J. Cassata, Jr.
	Salvatore M. Rua§
Troy	Henry R. Bauer
	Matthew J. Turner

CITY COURTS IN NEW YORK—*Continued*

Utica	John S. Balzano Gerald J. Popeo
Watertown	James Coulter Harberson, Jr. Eugene R. Renzi
Watervliet	Thomas E. Lamb Susan B. Reinfurt
White Plains	Andrew K. Brotmann Jo Ann Friia Barbara A. Leak Rosanna H. Washington
Yonkers	Robert C. Cerrato Thomas R. Daly Arthur J. Doran, Jr. Edmund G. Fitzgerald, Jr. Richard B. Liebowitz Michael A. Martinelli

THE CIVIL COURT OF THE CITY OF NEW YORK

The Civil Court of the City of New York is established for the counties of Bronx, Kings, New York, Queens and Richmond. Judges are elected for ten-year terms. Special Housing Part judges are appointed by the administrative judge for five-year terms; these judges are not constitutional judges. Retirement is mandatory for all judges at age seventy.

The court has jurisdiction over civil cases involving up to $25,000. The court also includes a Small Claims Part for informal disposition of matters not exceeding $3,000.

‡Acting Supreme Court Justice

Judges

Rachel Amy Adams
Augustus C. Agate
Richard N. Allman
Loren Baily-Schiffman
Jack M. Battaglia
Harold B. Beeler‡
Arthur Birnbaum
Dorothy Chin Brandt‡
Mary Ann Brigantti-Hughes
Matthew F. Cooper
Marylin G. Diamond‡
David Elliot
Laura Safer Espinoza‡
Paul G. Feinman
Louise Gruner Gàns‡
Darrell Lori Gavrin‡
Lenora Gerald
Ira R. Globerman‡
Ferne J. Goldstein
Stephen S. Gottlieb
Raymond Guzman
Sylvia O. Hinds-Radix
Debra A. James‡
Joan M. Kenney
Kevin J. Kerrigan
Stephen A. Knopf
Sarah L. Krauss
Donald Scott Kurtz
Harold A. Adler
Francis Alessandro
Michael B. Aloise
Bruce M. Balter
Bernadette Bayne
Lucy A. Billings
John A. K. Bradley‡
Richard Fredric Braun‡
Raymond L. Bruce
Denis J. Butler
Raul Cruz
Timothy J. Dufficy
Arthur F. Engoron
Saralee E. Evans‡
Marcy S. Friedman‡
Robin S. Garson
Anthony V. Gazzara
Judith J. Gische‡
Lila P. Gold
James J. Golia
Stanley B. Green‡
Wilma Guzman
Barbara Jaffe
Deborah A. Kaplan
Cynthia S. Kern
Susan K. Knipps
Shirley Werner Kornreich‡
Diane Alexis Lebedeff‡
Jeffrey D. Lebowitz‡
Robert D. Lippmann‡
Charles J. Markey
Esther M. Morgenstern‡
Valerie Brathwaite Nelson
Barbara I. Panepinto‡
Steven W. Paynter
Eric I. Prus
Irving Rosen
Alice Fisher Rubin
Wayne P. Saitta
Saliann Scarpulla
David I. Schmidt‡
Howard E. Sherman‡
Bernice Daun Siegal
Joseph S. Silverman‡
Karen S. Smith
Jane S. Solomon‡
Faviola Soto
John E. H. Stackhouse‡
Robert M. Stolz
Peter Paul Sweeney
Delores J. Thomas
Analisa Torres
Wavny Toussaint
George R. Villegas
Edgar G. Walker
Betty J. Williams
Louis B. York‡
Judith S. Lieb
Margarita López Torres
Judith N. McMahon
Eileen N. Nadelson
Paula J. Omansky‡
Jose Padilla, Jr.‡
Kibbie F. Payne‡
Diccia T. Pineda-Kirwan
Eileen A. Rakower
Karen B. Rothenberg‡
Robert A. Sackett
Debra Rose Samuels
Arthur M. Schack
Marilyn Shafer‡
Martin Shulman‡
Debra Silber
Anil C. Singh
Kathryn M. Smith‡
Martin M. Solomon
Ellen M. Spodek
Michael D. Stallman‡
Philip S. Straniere
Fernando Tapia
Walter B. Tolub‡
Robert E. Torres
Alison Y. Tuitt
Eric N. Vitaliano
Dolores L. Waltrous
Geoffrey D. Wright

THE CRIMINAL COURT OF THE CITY OF NEW YORK

The Criminal Court of the City of New York is established for the counties of Bronx, Kings, New York, Queens and Richmond. Judges are appointed by the mayor for ten-year terms.

The court has trial jurisdiction of misdemeanors and violations. The judges also act as arraigning magistrates for all criminal offenses.

‡Acting Supreme Court Justice

Judges

Bruce Allen‡
Herbert I. Altman‡
Jeffrey M. Atlas‡
A. Kirke Bartley, Jr.
Carol Berkman‡
Denis John Boyle‡
John N. Byrne‡
Fernando M. Camacho
John W. Carter
Danny K. Chun
Robert L. Cohen‡
John P. Collins‡
Laura E. Drager‡
Ralph A. Fabrizio
JoAnn Ferdinand‡
Daniel P. FitzGerald‡
William E. Garnett
James D. Gibbons
Joel M. Goldberg‡
James P. Griffin‡
Joseph A. Grosso‡
Allen G. Alpert‡
Efrain L. Alvarado‡
Steven L. Barrett‡
Peter J. Benitez‡
Joel L. Blumenfeld‡
James M. Burke
Alex M. Calabrese
Richard D. Carruthers‡
John Cataldo‡
Darcel D. Clark
Ellen M. Coin
Joseph J. Dawson
William M. Erlbaum‡
Thomas A. Farber
Neil Jon Firetog‡
Bernard J. Fried‡
Michael A. Gary‡
Arlene D. Goldberg‡
Ethan Greenberg
Michael A. Gross‡
Joseph E. Gubbay

THE CRIMINAL COURT OF THE CITY OF NEW YORK—*Continued*

William M. Harrington
Roger S. Hayes‡
Nicholas J. Iacovetta‡
Martin G. Karopkin
Judy Harris Kluger‡
Barry Kron‡
Leslie G. Leach‡
Gene R. Lopez
Seth L. Marvin
Joseph Kevin McKay‡
Suzanne J. Melendez
William Miller‡
Salvatore J. Modica
William I. Mogulescu‡
John S. Moore‡
Barbara F. Newman‡
Michael J. Obus‡
Sheryl L. Parker‡
Ruth Pickholz‡
Robert M. Raciti
Leonard P. Rienzi‡
Micki A. Scherer‡
Arlene R. Silverman‡
Charles H. Solomon‡
Larry R. C. Stephen
Joan C. Sudolnik‡
Megan Tallmer‡
Laura A. Ward‡
Renee Allyn White‡
Bonnie G. Wittner‡
Gerald Harris
Charles J. Heffernan, Jr.
Diane R. Kiesel
Eileen Koretz
John B. Latella, Jr.‡
Judith Anne Levitt
Alan D. Marrus‡
Robert C. McGann‡
Edward J. McLaughlin‡
Alan J. Meyer‡
Deborah Stevens Modica
Suzanne M. Mondo
Pauline A. Mullings
Patricia M. Nunez
Eugene Oliver, Jr.‡
Ann T. Pfau
Charles A. Posner
Donna G. Recant
Neil E. Ross
Robert G. Seewald‡
Brenda S. Soloff‡
Michael R. Sonberg
Robert H. Straus‡
Ruth Levine Sussman‡
John P. Walsh‡
Richard M. Weinberg
Patricia A. Williams‡
Douglas S. Wong‡

NEW YORK DISTRICT COURTS

District Courts are courts of lesser jurisdiction established in Nassau and Suffolk counties. Nassau District includes the entire county of Nassau; Suffolk District includes the five westernmost towns of Suffolk County. Judges are elected for six-year terms. Retirement is mandatory at age seventy.

The courts have civil jurisdiction in actions involving money or real property when the amount in controversy does not exceed $15,000 and in small claims actions up to $3,000. The courts have jurisdiction of misdemeanors and violations. The judges also act as arraigning magistrates for all criminal offenses.

NASSAU COUNTY DISTRICT

Judges

Joel K. Asarch
Alfred D. Cooper, Sr.
Thomas Feinman
Kenneth L. Gartner
Steven M. Jaeger
Norman Janowitz
Randy Sue Marber
Martin J. Massell
Adam H. Moser
Sondra K. Pardes
Christopher G. Quinn
Francis D. Ricigliano
Joseph P. Spinola
Valerie Bullard
Scott Fairgrieve
Michael A. Fiechter
David A. Gross
Dana Mitchell Jaffe
Susan T. Kluewer
Edward A. Maron
Howard S. Miller
William J. O'Brien
Erica L. Prager
Margaret C. Reilly
Lea Ruskin

SUFFOLK COUNTY DISTRICT

Judges

Salvatore A. Alamia
Stephen M. Behar, Sr.
William J. Burke, III
Lawrence J. Donohue
Madeleine A. Fitzgibbon
Paul M. Hensley
John Kelly
Gaetan B. Lozito
William B. Rebolini
Anthony A. Tafuri
Hertha C. Trotto
Sonia M. Veras
Patrick J. Barton
Howard M. Bergson
Kevin J. Crowley
Patricia M. Filiberto
Steven Hackeling
Barbara R. Kahn
Steven A. Lotto
Carol MacKenzie
Joseph A. Santorelli
John J. Toomey, Jr.
Georgia A. Tschiember

TOWN AND VILLAGE JUSTICE COURTS

Town and Village Justice Courts also exist in New York and are not courts of record. These courts handle minor civil and criminal matters. The method of selecting judges, their terms of office and the jurisdiction of the courts vary throughout the state.

New York Counties and County Seats

Albany
Albany
Allegany
Belmont
Bronx
Bronx
Broome
Binghamton
Cattaraugus
Little Valley
Cayuga
Auburn
Chautauqua
Mayville
Chemung
Elmira
Chenango
Norwich
Clinton
Plattsburgh
Columbia
Hudson
Cortland
Cortland
Delaware
Delhi
Dutchess
Poughkeepsie
Erie
Buffalo
Essex
Elizabethtown
Franklin
Malone
Fulton
Johnstown
Genesee
Batavia
Greene
Catskill
Hamilton
Lake Pleasant
Herkimer
Herkimer
Jefferson
Watertown
Kings
Brooklyn

COUNTIES AND COUNTY SEATS—*Continued*

Lewis
Lowville

Livingston
Geneseo

Madison
Wampsville

Monroe
Rochester

Montgomery
Fonda

Nassau
Mineola

New York
New York City

Niagara
Lockport

Oneida
Utica

Onondaga
Syracuse

Ontario
Canandaigua

Orange
Goshen

Orleans
Albion

Oswego
Oswego

Otsego
Cooperstown

Putnam
Carmel

Queens
Jamaica

Rensselaer
Troy

Richmond
St. George

Rockland
New City

St. Lawrence
Canton

Saratoga
Ballston Spa

Schenectady
Schenectady

Schoharie
Schoharie

Schuyler
Watkins Glen

Seneca
Waterloo

Steuben
Bath

Suffolk
Riverhead

Sullivan
Monticello

Tioga
Owego

Tompkins
Ithaca

Ulster
Kingston

Warren
Queensbury

Washington
Hudson Falls
Salem

Wayne
Lyons

Westchester
White Plains

Wyoming
Warsaw

Yates
Penn Yan

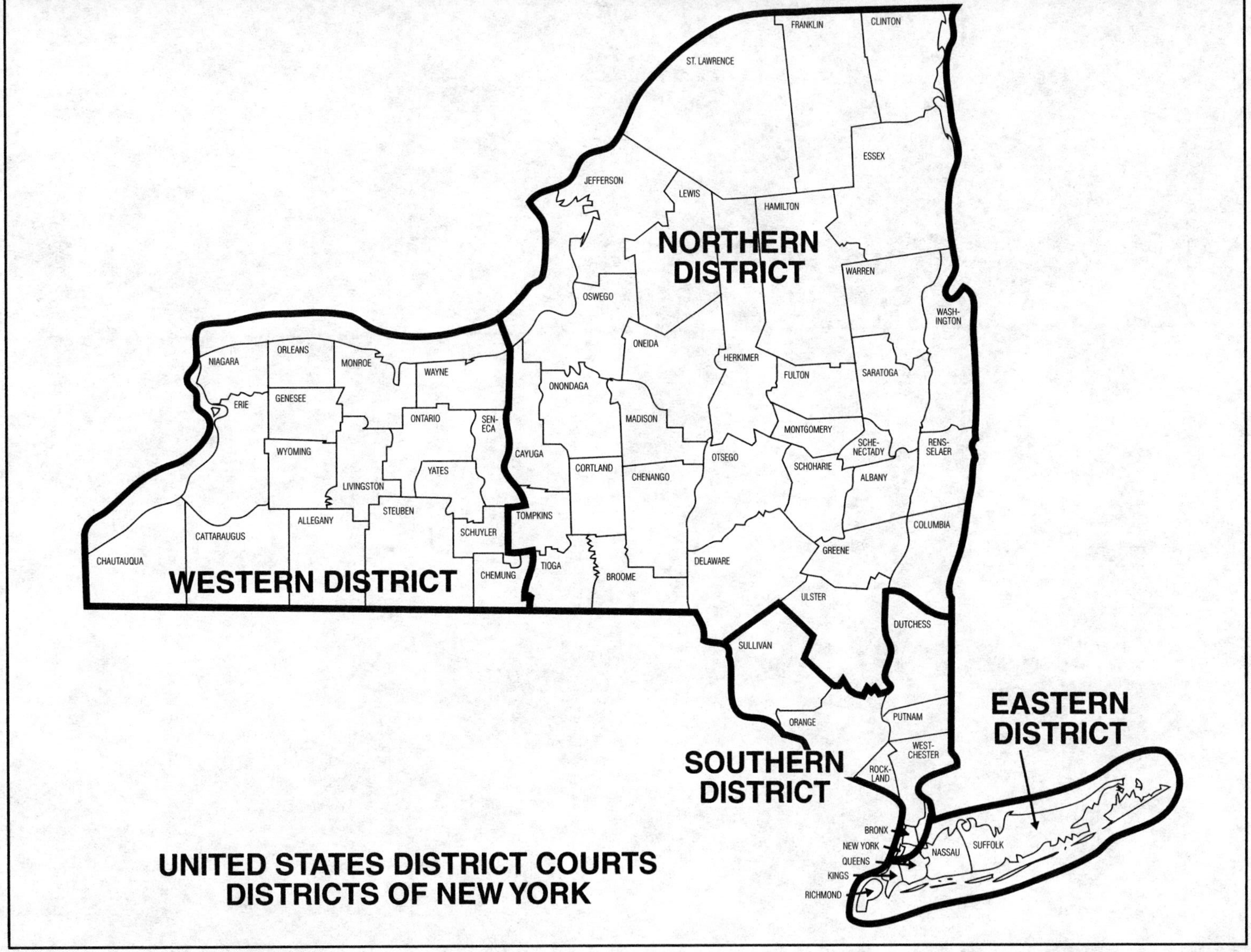
NORTHERN DISTRICT
WESTERN DISTRICT
SOUTHERN DISTRICT
EASTERN DISTRICT
UNITED STATES DISTRICT COURTS
DISTRICTS OF NEW YORK
FRANKLIN
CLINTON
ST. LAWRENCE
ESSEX
JEFFERSON
LEWIS
HAMILTON
WARREN
OSWEGO
WASH-INGTON
ONEIDA
HERKIMER
FULTON
SARATOGA
NIAGARA
ORLEANS
MONROE
WAYNE
ONONDAGA
ERIE
GENESEE
ONTARIO
SEN-ECA
MADISON
MONTGOMERY
SCHE-NECTADY
RENS-SELAER
WYOMING
CAYUGA
CORTLAND
CHENANGO
OTSEGO
SCHOHARIE
ALBANY
YATES
LIVINGSTON
STEUBEN
ALLEGANY
TOMPKINS
COLUMBIA
CATTARAUGUS
SCHUYLER
GREENE
CHAUTAUQUA
DELAWARE
CHEMUNG
TIOGA
BROOME
ULSTER
DUTCHESS
SULLIVAN
PUTNAM
ORANGE
WEST-CHESTER
ROCK-LAND
BRONX
NEW YORK
QUEENS
KINGS
RICHMOND
NASSAU
SUFFOLK

© Forster-Long, Inc. *THE AMERICAN BENCH: Judges of the Nation*

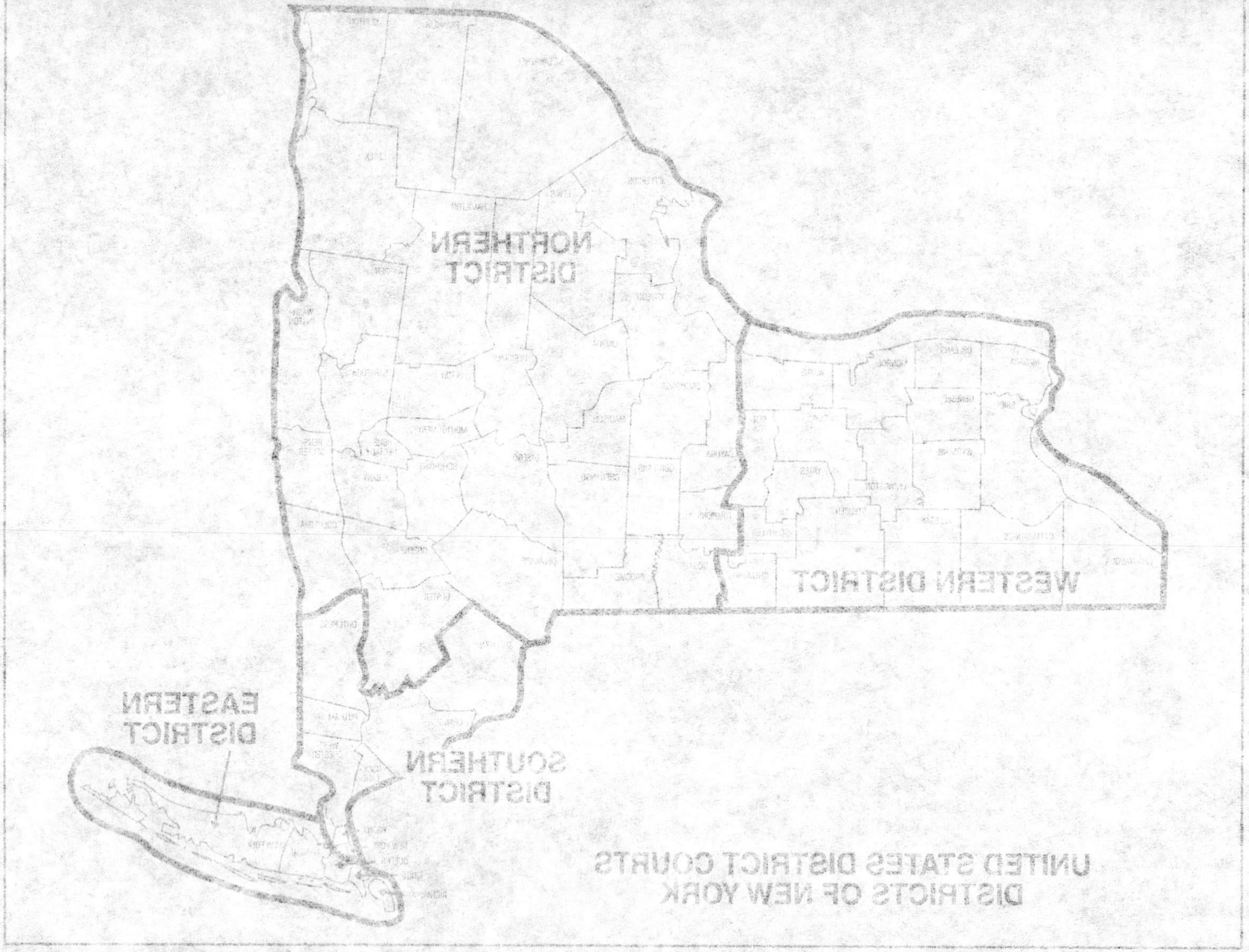
NORTHERN DISTRICT
WESTERN DISTRICT
SOUTHERN DISTRICT
EASTERN DISTRICT
UNITED STATES DISTRICT COURTS
DISTRICTS OF NEW YORK

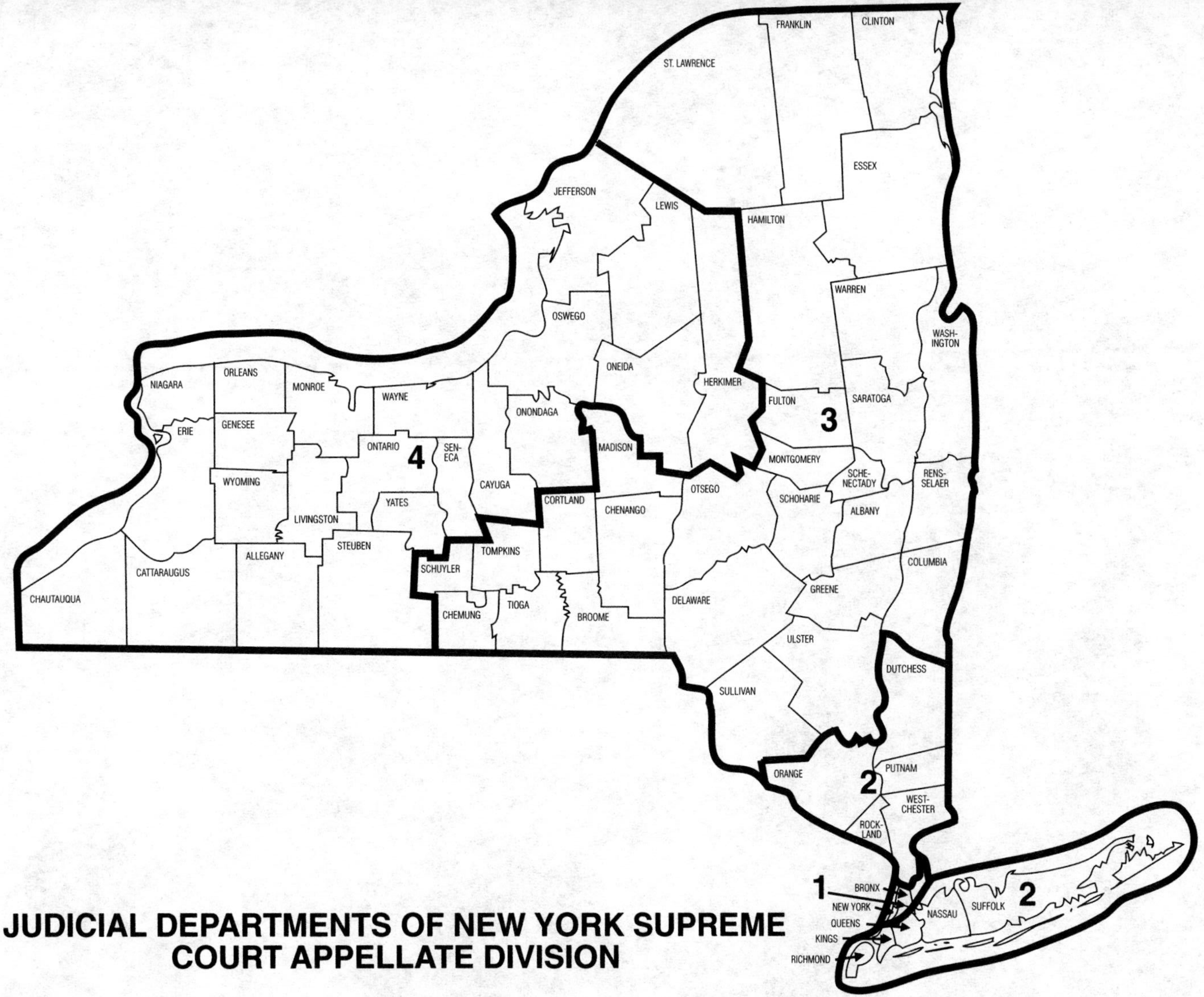
FRANKLIN
CLINTON
ST. LAWRENCE
ESSEX
JEFFERSON
LEWIS
HAMILTON
WARREN
OSWEGO
WASH-
INGTON
ONEIDA
HERKIMER
NIAGARA
ORLEANS
MONROE
WAYNE
FULTON
SARATOGA
3
ONONDAGA
ERIE
GENESEE
ONTARIO
4
SEN-
ECA
MADISON
MONTGOMERY
SCHE-
NECTADY
RENS-
SELAER
WYOMING
YATES
CAYUGA
CORTLAND
CHENANGO
OTSEGO
SCHOHARIE
ALBANY
LIVINGSTON
STEUBEN
ALLEGANY
TOMPKINS
SCHUYLER
COLUMBIA
CATTARAUGUS
CHAUTAUQUA
CHEMUNG
TIOGA
BROOME
DELAWARE
GREENE
ULSTER
DUTCHESS
SULLIVAN
ORANGE
PUTNAM
2
WEST-
CHESTER
ROCK-
LAND
1
BRONX
NEW YORK
QUEENS
KINGS
RICHMOND
NASSAU
SUFFOLK
2

JUDICIAL DEPARTMENTS OF NEW YORK SUPREME COURT APPELLATE DIVISION

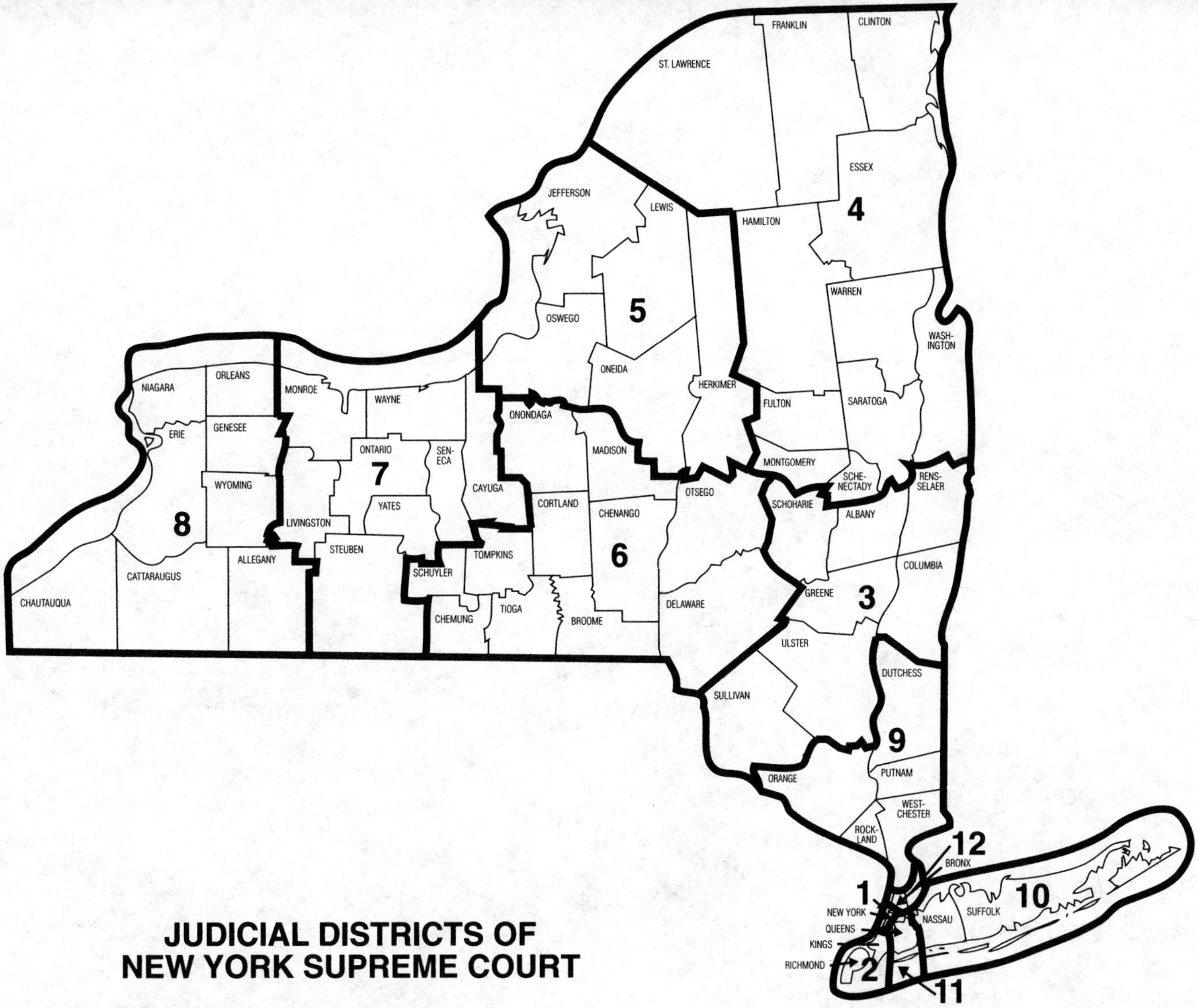
FRANKLIN
CLINTON
ST. LAWRENCE
ESSEX
4
JEFFERSON
LEWIS
HAMILTON
WARREN
5
OSWEGO
WASH-
INGTON
ONEIDA
HERKIMER
ORLEANS
NIAGARA
MONROE
WAYNE
FULTON
SARATOGA
ONONDAGA
GENESEE
ERIE
ONTARIO
SEN-
ECA
MADISON
MONTGOMERY
7
SCHE-
NECTADY
RENS-
SELAER
WYOMING
CAYUGA
OTSEGO
YATES
CORTLAND
SCHOHARIE
CHENANGO
ALBANY
8
LIVINGSTON
STEUBEN
ALLEGANY
TOMPKINS
6
COLUMBIA
SCHUYLER
CATTARAUGUS
GREENE
3
CHAUTAUQUA
DELAWARE
CHEMUNG
TIOGA
BROOME
ULSTER
DUTCHESS
SULLIVAN
9
PUTNAM
ORANGE
WEST-
CHESTER
ROCK-
LAND
12
BRONX
1
10
NEW YORK
NASSAU
SUFFOLK
QUEENS
KINGS
RICHMOND
2
11

JUDICIAL DISTRICTS OF NEW YORK SUPREME COURT

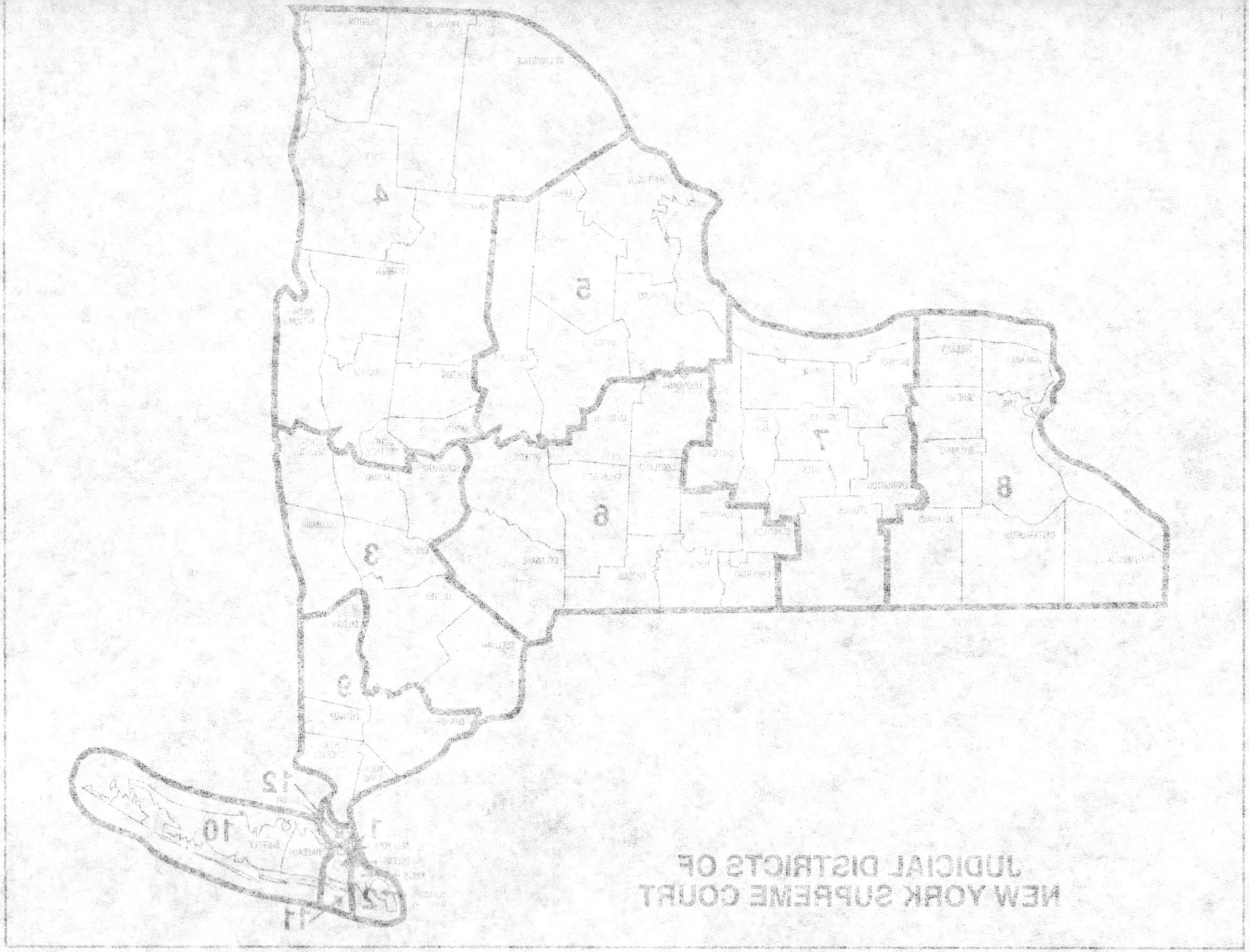
JUDICIAL DISTRICTS OF
NEW YORK SUPREME COURT
1
2
3
4
5
6
7
8
9
10
11
12

NEW YORK

ABDELLA, James *(Judge, Jamestown City Court)* Appointed by City Council to term beginning Jan 11, 1994. Currently serves as Acting Judge. Born Gloversville New York June 21, 1934. Methodist. Educated at College of William & Mary B.A. 1956 and University of Michigan J.D. 1959. Admitted to practice New York 1960 and U.S. Supreme Court 1964. Began legal practice Jamestown.

President Jamestown Estate Planning Council 1968-69. Member Jamestown (President 1978-79) and New York State Bar Associations. President Jamestown Optimist Club 1971-72, Jamestown Babe Ruth World Series Committee 1991-93 and Jamestown Rotary Club 1993-94. Author "Just Here 'N There" *Pennysaver* since 1991 and in *Weekly Sentinel* Mayville New York for sixteen years.

Office: City Hall, Jamestown 14701-5433.
Telephone: (716) 483-7561.
Fax: (716) 483-7519

ABDUS SALAAM, Sheila *(Justice, New York Supreme Court First Judicial District)* Former Judge, The Civil Court of the City of New York.

Office: 71 Thomas Street, New York 10013.
Telephone: (212) 815-0878.
Fax: (212) 815-0892
E-mail address: sabdussa@courts.state.ny.us

ABRAMSON, Gilbert L. *(Judge, Saratoga County Family Court)*

Office: Saratoga County Municipal Center, 35 West High Street, Ballston Spa 12020-0600.
Telephone: (518) 884-9207.

ACOSTA, Rolando T. *(Justice, New York Supreme Court First Judicial District)* Acting Justice May 1998 to Dec 2002. Elected Justice Nov 2002 to term beginning Jan 1, 2003. Term expires Dec 31, 2016. Born Santiago Dominican Republic Dec 24, 1955. Christian. Educated at Columbia College B.A. 1979 and Columbia University School of Law J.D. 1982. Admitted to practice New York 1983. In legal practice 1982-97. Judge, The Civil Court of the City of New York Jan 1, 1998 to Dec 31, 2002.

Staff Attorney 1982-88, Attorney-in-Charge Jan 1994 to Nov 1995 and Director of Government Nov 1995 to Dec 1997 Legal Aid Society. Deputy Commissioner 1988-92 and First Deputy Commissioner 1992-93 for Law Enforcement New York City Commission on Human Rights. Author "A Response to [Prof.] Burt Neuborne" 23 Fordham Urban L. Jour. 1996. Important Decisions: John v. Bastien (showing that a belated summary judgment motion is meritorious is insufficient to excuse untimely filing of the motion) 178 Misc. 2d 664 N.Y. Civ. Ct. 1988; Eina Realty v. Calixte (a written rent demand which violates provisions of the Fair Debt Collection Practices Act could not serve as adequate predicate for a nonpayment proceeding against a tenant) 178 Misc. 2d 80 N.Y. Civ. Ct. 1988; Roxborough Apt. Corp. v. Becker (nonprimary residence proceeding) 177 Misc. 2d 408 N.Y. Civ. Ct. 1998; Alsaedi v. Alsaedi (oral contract to temporarily transfer a lottery agent's license in violation of law is not enforceable on public policy grounds) 177 Misc. 2d 440 N.Y. Civ. Ct. 1998; Zhai v. Chemical Bank (Civil Court has authority to vacate a prior order issued by Supreme Court where the prior order was issued upon default) 180 Misc. 2d 442 N.Y. Civ. Ct. 1999; and Pierno v. Adames (procedural consequences of a plaintiff's failure to file proof of service in New York County Civil Court actions as opposed to those in Supreme and County Court) 179 Misc. 2d 381 N.Y. Civ. Ct. 1999. Member New York County Lawyers' Association, Association of the Bar of the City of New York, Dominican and Puerto Rican Bar Associations. Recipient Community Service Award from Audubon Partnership for Economic Development 1999, Life of Gold Award from American Association of Retired Persons 1999 and Columbia University Medal for Excellence 2000. Democrat. Officer and Chair of Policy Commission The Hispanic Federation 1990-97. President Community School Board Six 1997. Founding Board Member Upper-Manhattan Empowerment Zone. Presiding Justice Harlem Community Justice Center. Board Member Columbia Law School Alumni Association. Enjoys sports and reading.

Office: 170 East 121st Street, New York 10035.
Telephone: (212) 360-4123, 360-4124.
E-mail address: racosta@courts.state.ny.us

ADAMS, Eric R. *(Judge, Genesee County Family Court)*

Office: Genesee County Courts Facility, One West Main Street, Batavia 14020.
Telephone: (585) 344-2550.
Fax: (585) 344-8520

ADAMS, Jody *(Judge, New York City Family Court)* Appointed by mayor.

Office: 60 Lafayette Street, New York 10013.
Telephone: (212) 374-4177.
Fax: (212) 374-2623

ADAMS, Rachel Amy *(Judge, The Civil Court of the City of New York)* Currently assigned to Family Court.

Office: 283 Adams Street, Sixth Floor, Brooklyn 11201.
Telephone: (718) 643-3445.
Fax: (718) 643-3733

ADAMS, Thomas A. *(Associate Justice, New York Supreme Court Appellate Division Second Judicial Department)* Elected Justice Tenth Judicial District. Appointed Associate Justice Appellate Division by Governor George E. Pataki. Former Judge, Nassau County District Court.

Office: Supreme Court Building, 100 Supreme Court Drive, Mineola 11501.
Telephone: (516) 571-2961.

ADLER, Harold A. *(Judge, The Civil Court of the City of New York)* Currently assigned to The Criminal Court of the City of New York.

Office: 215 East 161st Street, Bronx 10451.
Telephone: (718) 590-2927.
Fax: (718) 590-7297

ADLER, Lester B. *(Judge, Westchester County Court)*
Office: 111 Dr. Martin Luther King Jr. Blvd., White Plains 10601.
Telephone: (914) 995-4518.
Fax: (914) 995-3427

AFFRONTI, Francis A. *(Justice, New York Supreme Court Seventh Judicial District)* Elected to term beginning Jan 1, 1990. Term expires Dec 31, 2003. Born Rochester New York Aug 14, 1941. Catholic. Educated at St. John Fisher College B.B.A. 1963 and University of San Francisco. Admitted to practice New York 1970 and U.S. District Court Western District of New York 1972. Began legal practice Rochester 1970. Judge, Monroe County Family Court Jan 1, 1984 to Dec 31, 1989.
Assistant District Attorney Monroe County 1970-76. Member Monroe County Bar Association. Republican.
Office: 436 Hall of Justice, Rochester 14614-2185.
Telephone: (585) 428-5397.
Fax: (585) 428-3557

AGATE, Augustus C. *(Judge, The Civil Court of the City of New York)*
Office: 89-17 Sutphin Boulevard, Jamaica 11435.
Telephone: (718) 262-7391.

AISON, Howard M. *(Judge, Amsterdam City Court)* Born Amsterdam New York Oct 12, 1945. Jewish. Educated at Syracuse University B.A. 1967 and Brooklyn Law School J.D. 1970. Member Phi Epsilon Pi. Admitted to practice New York 1972 and U.S. District Court Northern District of New York 1974. In legal practice Amsterdam 1973-85. Former Judge, Montgomery County Court, elected to term beginning Jan 1, 1986.
District Attorney Montgomery County 1979-85. Member County Judges Association of the State of New York and Montgomery County Bar Association. Captain U.S. Army 1970-72. Democrat.
Office: 208 Public Safety Building, One Guy Park Avenue Extension, Amsterdam 12010.
Telephone: (518) 842-9510.
Fax: (518) 843-8474

ALAMIA, Salvatore A. *(Judge, Suffolk County District Court)* Currently serves as Acting Judge, Suffolk County Court.
Mailing address: P.O. Box 9075, Central Islip 11722-9075.
Office: Cohalan Court Complex, 400 Carleton Avenue, Central Islip 11722.
Telephone: (631) 853-4919.

ALESSANDRO, Francis M. *(Judge, The Civil Court of the City of New York)* Born New York New York.
Office: 851 Grand Concourse, Bronx 10451.
Telephone: (718) 590-3607.

ALFANO, John L. *(Judge, Rye City Court)* Currently serves as Acting Judge.
Office: 21 McCullough Place, Rye 10580.
Telephone: (914) 967-1599.
Fax: (914) 967-3308

ALIOTTA, Thomas P. *(Justice, New York Supreme Court Second Judicial District)* Former Judge, The Civil Court of the City of New York.
Office: Homeport, 355 Front Street, Staten Island 10304.
Telephone: (718) 876-6425.

ALLEN, Bruce *(Judge, The Criminal Court of the City of New York)* Appointed by mayor. Currently serves as Acting Justice, New York Supreme Court First Judicial District.
Office: 111 Centre Street, New York 10013.
Telephone: (212) 374-8005.

ALLMAN, Richard N. *(Judge, The Civil Court of the City of New York)* Currently assigned to The Criminal Court of the City of New York.
Office: 120 Schermerhorn Street, Brooklyn 11201.
Telephone: (718) 643-4775.

ALOI, Anthony F. *(Judge, Onondaga County Court)*
Office: Courthouse, 401 Montgomery Street, Syracuse 13202.
Telephone: (315) 671-1054.
Fax: (315) 671-1176

ALOISE, Michael B. *(Judge, The Civil Court of the City of New York)* Currently assigned to The Criminal Court of the City of New York.
Office: 125-01 Queens Boulevard, Room 234D, Kew Gardens 11415.
Telephone: (718) 520-1799.
Fax: (718) 520-4712

ALONZO, Gerard J., Jr. *(Judge, Livingston County Court)* Also serves Livingston County Surrogate's Court and Livingston County Family Court. Former Acting Justice, New York Supreme Court Seventh Judicial District.
Office: Livingston County Courthouse, Two Court Street, Geneseo 14454-1030.
Telephone: (585) 243-7068.
Fax: (585) 243-7067

ALPERT, Allen G. *(Judge, The Criminal Court of the City of New York)* Appointed by mayor. Currently assigned to Family Court. Also serves as Acting Justice, New York Supreme Court Twelfth Judicial District.
Office: 900 Sheridan Avenue, Bronx 10451.
Telephone: (718) 590-3391.

ALPERT, Bruce D. *(Justice, New York Supreme Court Tenth Judicial District)* Former Judge, Nassau County District Court.
Office: Supreme Court Building, 100 Supreme Court Drive, Mineola 11501.
Telephone: (516) 571-2954.

ALTMAN, Herbert I. *(Judge, The Criminal Court of the City of New York)* Appointed by mayor. Currently serves as Acting Justice, New York Supreme Court First Judicial District.
Office: 100 Centre Street, New York 10013.
Telephone: (212) 374-8109.

ALTMAN, Myriam J. *(Associate Justice, New York Supreme Court Appellate Division Second Judicial Department)* Acting Justice First Judicial District Sept 1987 to Dec 1987. Elected Justice First Judicial District Nov 1987 to term beginning Dec 1988. Appointed Associate Justice Appellate Division by Governor Mario Cuomo to term beginning Jan 1, 1994. Reappointed to Appellate Division by Governor George E. Pataki to term beginning Jan 1, 1999. Judge, The Civil Court of the City of New York Jan 1978 to Dec 1987.
Office: 100 Centre Street, Room 1710, New York 10013.
Telephone: (212) 374-6298.

ALVARADO, Efrain L. *(Judge, The Criminal Court of the City of New York)* Appointed by Mayor Edward I. Koch to term beginning Aug 1988. Reappointed by Mayor David Dinkins to term beginning 1991 and by Mayor Rudolph Giuliani 2000. Current term expires Dec 31, 2010. Acting Justice, New York Supreme Court Twelfth Judicial District since 1994.
Office: 851 Grand Concourse, Bronx 10451.
Telephone: (718) 590-5263.
E-mail address: ealvarad@courts.state.ny.us

AMBRECHT, Michael R. *(Judge, New York Court of Claims)* Appointed by Governor George E. Pataki. Currently serves as Acting Justice, New York Supreme Court First Judicial District.
Office: 100 Centre Street, New York 10013.
Telephone: (212) 227-1610.

AMBROSIO, Michael A. *(Judge, New York City Family Court)* Appointed by Mayor Edward I. Koch to term beginning March 20, 1983. Reappointed by Mayor David Dinkins 1992 and by Mayor Michael Bloomberg 2002. Current term expires Sept 3, 2012. Former Supervising Judge. Currently serves as Acting Justice, New York Supreme Court Second Judicial District. Born Brooklyn New York April 23, 1945. Roman Catholic. Educated at Fordham University A.B. 1966 and Harvard University J.D. cum laude 1969. Member Phi Beta Kappa. Admitted to practice New York 1970. Began legal practice New York 1970.
Treasurer Bronx Legal Services Corporation 1979-83. Adjunct Instructor New York Law School 1981-83. Member Federal Bar Council and The Association of the Bar of the City of New York.
Office: 120 Schermerhorn Street, Brooklyn 11201.
Telephone: (718) 643-5953.
Fax: (718) 643-3290
E-mail address: mambrosio@courts.state.ny.us

AMES, William F. *(Judge, Cortland County Court)* Also serves Cortland County Surrogate's Court and Cortland County Family Court.
Office: 301 County Courthouse, 46 Greenbush Street, Cortland 13045-2725.
Telephone: (607) 758-5556.
Fax: (607) 753-1899

AMODEO, Damian J. *(Judge, Dutchess County Family Court)* Elected to term beginning Jan 1, 1989. Reelected Nov 1998, current term expires Dec 31, 2008. Currently serves as Acting Justice, New York Supreme Court Ninth Judicial District.
Office: 50 Market Street, Poughkeepsie 12601-3204.
Telephone: (845) 486-2521.
E-mail address: damodeo@courts.state.ny.us

AMODEO, Thomas P. *(Chief Judge, Buffalo City Court)* Elected to term beginning Jan 1, 1990. Reelected Nov 7, 1994, current term expires Dec 31, 2004. Currently serves as Administrative Judge. Born Buffalo New York Sept 12, 1951. Roman Catholic. Educated at Canisius College B.A. cum laude 1973 and Gonzaga University School of Law J.D. cum laude 1976. Admitted to practice New York 1977, U.S. District Court Southern District of New York 1981 and U.S. Court of Appeals Second Circuit 1985. In legal practice Buffalo 1977-90.
Assistant Corporation Counsel Buffalo 1985-90. Member New York State Association of City Court Judges and Bar Association of Erie County (Bench and Bar Committee). Recipient Leadership Award from North Buffalo Community Center Dec 1989, David Morrisey Civic Award from University District Civic Association March 1990, Founders Award from North Buffalo Youth Hockey May 1990 and Judiciary Citation of Honor Award from Columbus Day Committee April 1993. Zone Chairman Democratic Party Erie County 1985-90. Legal Counsel Buffalo Urban Renewal Agency 1984-85. Advisory Board Criminal Law Erie County College since 1993. Founder Greater Buffalo Italian Festival. Director and Coach North Buffalo Baseball Association. Director North Buffalo Community Center. Director and Founder North Buffalo Youth Hockey Association.
Office: 50 Delaware Avenue, Buffalo 14202.
Telephone: (716) 847-8207.
Fax: (716) 847-8273

AMON, Carol Bagley *(Judge, United States District Court Eastern District of New York)* Magistrate 1987-90. Appointed Judge for life by President George Bush Aug 7, 1990. Born Richmond Virginia April 23, 1946. Educated at College of William & Mary B.S. 1968 and University of Virginia School of Law J.D. 1971.
Staff Attorney Communications Satellite Corporation 1971-73. Trial Attorney Narcotics Task Force U.S. Department of Justice 1973-74. Assistant U.S. Attorney 1974-86, Chief of Frauds 1978-80, Chief of General Crimes 1981-82 and Senior Litigation Counsel 1984-86 Eastern District of New York.
Office: U.S. Courthouse, 225 Cadman Plaza East, Brooklyn 11201.
Telephone: (718) 260-2410.

ANDRIAS, Richard T. *(Associate Justice, New York Supreme Court Appellate Division First Judicial Department)* Assumed office as Justice First Judicial District Jan 1, 1988. Appointed Associate Justice Appellate Division by Governor George E. Pataki June 1996. Born Mount Vernon New York April 7, 1943. Educated at Bowdoin College B.A. cum laude with high honors in Economics 1965 and Columbia University School of Law LL.B. cum laude 1970. Visiting Scholar London School of Economics Graduate Law School 1974. Member Beta Theta Pi, Phi Beta Kappa and Phi Delta Phi. Admitted to practice New York 1971, U.S. District Courts Southern 1975 and Eastern 1975 Districts of New York and U.S. Court of Appeals Second Circuit 1975. In legal practice New York City since 1970. Judge, The Criminal Court of the City of New York Feb 3, 1983 to Dec 31, 1987, appointed by Mayor Edward Koch.
Author "Criminal Defendant in England" Oct 29, 1974, "Criminal Trials in England" Nov 29, 1974 and "Impeachment of a Defendant Witness—England and America" May 30, 1975 New York L. Jour., "The Impact of Defendants' Psychiatric Disorders on Case Flow in the Criminal Justice System" 5 *Critical Issue in American Psychiatry and the Law* 1987, "Shed Your Robes: Three Reasons for Aggressive Judicial Leadership in Coping with the HIV Epidemic" 29 No. 2 Judges Journal 4, 1990, "Rape Myths: A Persistent Problem in Defining and Prosecuting Rape" 7 No. 2 Criminal Justice Journal American Bar Association 2 Summer 1992, "Urban Criminal Justice: Has the Response to the HIV Epidemic Been 'Fair'" XX No. 3 Fordham Urban L. Jour. 497, 1993, "The Criminal Justice System and the Resurgent TB Epidemic" 9 No. 1 Criminal Justice Journal American Bar Association 2 Spring 1994, "Jury

ANDRIAS, RICHARD T.—*Continued*

Trials, Russian Style: An American Jurist Reports on a Country's First Steps Toward a New Method of Justice" 11 No. 2 Criminal Justice Journal American Bar Association 14 Summer 1996 and "Seeking Justice for the Victim" 21 No. 2 *Update on Law Related Education* 22 Spring 1997. Important Decisions: People of the State of New York v. Museum of Modern Art 2453 A.D.2d 211, 699 N.Y.S.2d 3, 1999 N.Y. App. Div. LEXIS 2969; City of New York v. Stringfellow's of N.Y., Ltd. 253 A.D.2d 110, 684 N.Y.S.2d 544, 1999 N.Y. App. Div. LEXIS 935; Community Service Society v. New York Community Trust A.D.2d 713 N.Y.S.2d 712, 2000 N.Y. App. Div. LEXIS 9291; and Khan v. New York Times Co. 269 A.D.2d 74, 710 N.Y.S.2d 41, 2000 N.Y. App. Div LEXIS 7134. Member New York County Lawyers' Association, The Association of the Bar of the City of New York, New York State and American Bar Associations. Honored for support of alternatives to incarceration of women by Citizen Advocates for Justice Feb 1984. U.S. Army Intelligence 1965-67 and 1st Cavalry Division Vietnam 1966-67. Recipient Bronze Star and Air Medal. Democrat. Member 1972-78, Secretary 1974-75 and Chairman 1976-77 Community Board 12 Manhattan. Board member Bronx Legal Services Corp. (Chairman 1980-83). Governor's Task Force on Rape and Sexual Violence 1989-90.

Office: 27 Madison Avenue & 25th Street, New York 10010.

Telephone: (212) 340-0436.

ANGIOLILLO, Daniel D. *(Justice, New York Supreme Court Ninth Judicial District)* Former Acting Justice. Elected Nov 2, 1999 to term beginning Jan 1, 2000. Term expires Dec 31, 2013. Born Jan 6, 1952. Educated at Boston College B.S. cum laude 1974, St. John's University School of Law J.D. 1977 and Cornell University Institute on Organized Crime 1979. In legal practice White Plains 1977-79. Judge, Westchester County Court Jan 1994 to Dec 1999.

Assistant District Attorney Westchester County March 1979 to Nov 1985. Principal Law Clerk to Hon. Kenneth H. Lange, Westchester County Court Nov 1985 to Dec 1993. Author "At What Age May a Child Testify Under Oath?" 2 No. 1 *The Navigator.* Adjunct Professor of Criminal Law and Procedure and The Rights of Crime Victims Manhattanville College and Business Law I Iona College. Past President White Plains Bar Association. Chairman Scholarship Committee and Board of Directors Columbian Lawyers Association. Member Westchester County and New York State Bar Associations. Instructor "Unified Court System" Orientation Seminar for Newly-Elected and Newly-Appointed Judges. Former Vice President and Board of Directors Lions International. Former Member Advisory Board Victims Assistance Services Westchester County. Board of Directors and Secretary N.Y.S. Prader-Willi Syndrome Alliance. Parishioner and Lector Our Lady of Sorrows Church White Plains. Volunteer Alumni Admission Boston College. Member Development Committee Children's Rehabilitation Center St. Agnes Hospital, Criminal Justice Advisory Board, Order Sons of Italy, Italian Civic Association and Enrico Fermi Scholarship Fund.

Office: County Courthouse, 111 Dr. Martin Luther King Jr. Blvd., White Plains 10601.

Telephone: (914) 995-4512.

Fax: (914) 995-4010

E-mail address: DANGIOLI@courts.state.ny.us

ARCARA, Richard J. *(Chief Judge, United States District Court Western District of New York)* Appointed for life by President Ronald Reagan to term beginning 1988. Chief Judge since Jan 1, 2003. Born Buffalo New York June 6, 1940. Educated at St. Bonaventure University B.A. 1962 and Villanova University School of Law J.D. 1965. In legal practice Buffalo 1968-69.

Assistant U.S. Attorney 1969-73, First Assistant U.S. Attorney 1973-74 and U.S. Attorney 1975-81 Western District of New York. District Attorney Erie County 1982-88.

Office: 609 U.S. Courthouse, 68 Court Street, Buffalo 14202.

Telephone: (716) 551-5626.

ARGETSINGER, J. C. *(Judge, Schuyler County Court)* Elected to term beginning Jan 1, 1998. Also serves Schuyler County Surrogate's Court and Schuyler County Family Court.

Office: 35 Courthouse, 105 Ninth Street, Watkins Glen 14891.

Telephone: (607) 535-7015.

Fax: (607) 535-4918

ARK, John J. *(Justice, New York Supreme Court Seventh Judicial District)*

Office: 545 Hall of Justice, 99 Exchange Boulevard, Rochester 14614-2185.

Telephone: (585) 428-3547.

Fax: (585) 428-3570

ARONIN, Gloria Cohen *(Justice, New York Supreme Court Second Judicial District)* Former Acting Justice. Certificated. Also serves as Justice, New York Supreme Court Appellate Term Second and Eleventh Judicial Districts. Former Judge, The Civil Court of the City of New York.

Office: 360 Adams Street, Brooklyn 11201.

Telephone: (718) 643-7080.

E-mail address: garonin@courts.state.ny.us

ARONSON, Stephen D. *(Judge, Canandaigua City Court)* Acting City Judge 1982-83. Elected Judge to term beginning Jan 1, 1984. Reelected 1986 and to subsequent terms. Born Seneca Falls New York Jan 22, 1948. Jewish. Educated at Syracuse University B.S. 1970 and Suffolk University Law School J.D. 1975. Admitted to practice New York 1976, Florida 1977 and U.S. Supreme Court 1980. Began legal practice Canandaigua New York 1976.

Instructor Unified Court System for Town and Village Magistrates. Member Ontario County Bar Association (President 1984). Republican. Coordinator Drug Treatment Court.

Office: City Hall, Two North Main Street, Canandaigua 14424-1448.

Telephone: (585) 396-5011.

Fax: (585) 396-5012

E-mail address: saronson@courts.state.ny.us

ASARCH, Joel K. *(Judge, Nassau County District Court)*

Office: 99 Main Street, Hempstead 11550.

Telephone: (516) 572-2137.

E-mail address: asarch@courts.state.ny.us

ASSINI, Jo Anne *(Judge, Schenectady County Family Court)*
Office: 620 State Street, Schenectady 12305-2114.
Telephone: (518) 388-4305.
Fax: (518) 388-4496

ATCHINSON, William K., Jr. *(Judge, Oneonta City Court)* Former Acting Judge.
Office: Public Safety Building, 81 Main Street, Oneonta 13820.
Telephone: (607) 432-4480.
Fax: (607) 432-2328
E-mail address: watchins@courts.state.ny.us

ATLAS, Jeffrey M. *(Judge, The Criminal Court of the City of New York)* Appointed by mayor to term beginning May 28, 1980. Reappointed by mayor 1989 and Mayor Rudolph Giuliani 1999. Current term expires Dec 31, 2009. Acting Justice, New York Supreme Court First Judicial District since 1982. Born New York New York Dec 7, 1939. Jewish. Educated at Syracuse University A.B. 1960 and Fordham University School of Law 1964. Law Clerk to Hon. Charles M. Metzner, U.S. District Court Southern District of New York 1960-64. Member Tau Epsilon Phi. Admitted to practice New York 1964, U.S. District Court District of New York 1967 and U.S. Court of Appeals 1967. In legal practice New York City 1964 and 1970-80.

Assistant 1964-70 and Superseding (Special) 1974-75 District Attorney New York County. Receiver in Bankruptcy 1970-71. Commissioner of Appraisal 1971-74. Important Decisions: People v. Colon (speedy trial) aff'd 59 N.Y.2d 521; People v. Adais (obscenity, constitutionality) 114 Misc. 2d 773; People v. Thompson (speedy trial) aff'd 120 Misc. 2d 444; People v. De Jesus (misdemeanor-felony enhancement) 122 Misc. 2d 190; People v. Brandt (statutory interpretation) 119 Misc. 2d 841; and People v. Hunter (obligations of prosecutor) Misc. 2d. Lecturer on Law Columbia University School of Law since 1997. Instructor in Trial Advocacy Benjamin N. Cardozo Law School, New York Law School, Columbia University, Brooklyn Law School and Hofstra University School of Law. Fellow Guggenheim Fellowship Program in Criminal Justice Yale University Law School 1984-85. Fellow New York Bar Foundation. Member Anti-Bias Committee and Former Chair Personnel Committee New York Supreme Court First Judicial District. Member New York County Lawyers' Association (Former Chairman Young Lawyers Committee), Criminal Court Judges Association (Former Chair Education Committee, Former Vice President, Member Legislative Committee), New York State (Judiciary and Criminal Justice Sections) and American (Former Second Circuit Delegate to Consumer Litigation Committee Section of Litigation) Bar Associations. Lecturer statewide judicial educational seminars. Republican. Past President Republican Club. Former County Committeeman (Member Law Committee). Former New York City Coordinator New York State Young Republican Club. Director Gateway Job Corps. Lecturer on law to civic groups. Enjoys playing tennis, building miniature ships, photography, sketching and reading history of law and Japanese fiction.
Office: 100 Centre Street, New York 10013.
Telephone: (212) 374-4762.

AULISI, Richard T. *(Justice, New York Supreme Court Fourth Judicial District)*
Office: Supreme Court Chambers, 15 West Fulton Street, Gloversville 12078.
Telephone: (518) 773-2333.
Fax: (518) 773-9875

AUSTIN, John *(Judge, Warren County Court)* Also serves Warren County Surrogate's Court. Born Cambridge New York May 31, 1935. Educated at Dartmouth College A.B. in Sociology 1957 and Albany Law School of Union University J.D. 1969. Admitted to practice New York 1970. Began legal practice Glens Falls 1970. Former Judge, Warren County Family Court, appointed by Governor Mario Cuomo to term beginning June 6, 1984.

Law Assistant Warren County Court 1975-79 and New York Supreme Court 1980-84. Author "Municipal Annexation in New York" Albany L. Rev. 1969. Member Warren County and New York State Bar Associations. E-4 U.S. Army 1958-60. Editorial Director The Glens Falls Times 1960-67. Councilman 1969-72 and Supervisor 1972-74 Town of Queensbury.
Office: Warren County Municipal Center, 1340 State Route 9, Lake George 12845-9803.
Telephone: (518) 761-7697.

AUSTIN, Leonard B. *(Justice, New York Supreme Court Tenth Judicial District)*
Office: Supreme Court Building, 100 Supreme Court Drive, Mineola 11501.
Telephone: (516) 571-2683.
Fax: (516) 571-0131
E-mail address: laustin@courts.state.ny.us

AUSTRIA, Anthony G., Jr. *(Judge, Newburgh City Court)*
Office: Public Safety Building, 57 Broadway, Newburgh 12550.
Telephone: (845) 565-1244.
Fax: (845) 565-1244

AVERY, Emerson R., Jr. *(Judge, Cortland County Court)* Also serves Cortland County Surrogate's Court and Cortland County Family Court.
Office: 301 Cortland County Courthouse, 46 Greenbush Street, Cortland 13045-2725.
Telephone: (607) 753-5001.
Fax: (607) 758-5531

AZRACK, Joan Marie *(Magistrate Judge, United States District Court Eastern District of New York)* Appointed by U.S. District Court judges to term beginning 1990. Educated at Rutgers University B.S. 1974 and New York Law School J.D. 1979.
Office: 333 U.S. Courthouse, 225 Cadman Plaza East, Brooklyn 11201.
Telephone: (718) 260-2530.

BAER, Harold, Jr. *(Judge, United States District Court Southern District of New York)* Appointed for life by President Bill Clinton to term beginning Aug 1994. Educated at Hobart College magna cum laude 1954 and Yale Law School 1957. Member Phi Beta Kappa. In legal practice 1967-70. Justice, New York Supreme Court First Judicial District Jan 1, 1983 to Oct 1992.

Assistant Counsel New York State Commission on the Governmental Operations of the City of New York 1959-60 and Special Unit New York State Investigations Commission 1960-61. Assistant U.S. Attorney May 1961

BAER, HAROLD, JR.—*Continued*

to July 1966 and First Deputy Assistant U.S. Attorney and Chief Criminal Division Feb 1970 to Aug 1971 Southern District of New York. Executive Director Civilian Complaint Review Board New York City Police Department 1966-67. Executive Judicial Officer Judicial Arbitration & Mediation Services, Inc. Oct 13, 1992 to 1994. Author "Marijuana/The Public Policy" *Marijuana, The Non-Narcotic Dangerous Drug* Community Service Society of New York 1970, Book Review *Desert Exile: The Uprooting of a Japanese American Family* by Uoshiko Uchida 4 No. 1 New York Law School Journal of International and Comparative Law 1982, "Watching the Watchman" New York L. Jour. Aug 28, 1991, "Why I Quit the New York Bench" *The New York Times* Op-Ed page Oct 1, 1992, "From Judge to Rent-a-Judge: Reflections on the State of Public and Private Adjudication" 3 No. 22 World Arbitration & Mediation Report Nov 1992, "Is There a Threat to Judicial Independence in the United States Today?" 26 No. 1 Fordham Urban L. Jour. Nov 1998 and Book Review *The Federal Impeachment Process—A Constitutional and Historical Analysis* by Michael J. Gerhardt Michigan L. Rev. May 1998. Co-editor with Whitney North Seymour, Jr., Richard N. Gottfried, Francis B. Looney, Robert B. McKay, Nicholas Scoppetta and Peter Tufo *Blow the Whistle on Crime: A Citizens' Guide to the Facts About Crime in NYC, What is Wrong with Our Criminal Justice System and What Can You Do About It* Nov 1979. Co-author with Suzanne H. Baer "Judge Who Hired Via Want Ad Offers a Guide for Job Seekers" 196 No. 67 New York L. Jour. Oct 3, 1986 and with Robert Meade, Esq. "How to Win Motions in Supreme Court" New York L. Jour. July 12, 1991.

Adjunct Professor of White Collar Crime and the Correctional System New York Law School. Lecturer on The Oresteia and Our Criminal Justice System Harvard University. Ex Officio Member Board of Directors New York County Lawyers' Association since 1981. Ex Officio Network of Bar Leaders since 1983. Chairman Equal Opportunity Commission U.S. District Court Southern District of New York since 1998. Former Vice President, Secretary and Treasurer Association of Supreme Court Justices of the City of New York. Former Trustee Federal Bar Council and National Council on Crime and Delinquency. Former Secretary Association of Justices of the Supreme Court of the State of New York. Former Member Board of Directors Committee for Modern Courts and Disciplinary Committee New York Supreme Court Appellate Division First Judicial Department. Fellow New York State Bar Association (Former House of Delegates) and American Bar Association. Member The Association of the Bar of the City of New York (Committee on Professional Discipline since 1995, Special Committee to Encourage Judicial Service since 1997). CLE Lecturer Practising Law Institute, The American Law Institute, Local and State Bar Associations and American Bar Association since 1991. Former Board of Directors Retarded Infants Services. Former Board of Trustees Community Service Society.

Office: 2230 U.S. Courthouse, 500 Pearl Street, New York 10007-1312.
Telephone: (212) 805-0184.

BAILY-SCHIFFMAN, Loren *(Judge, The Civil Court of the City of New York)*

Office: 141 Livingston Street, Room 705, Brooklyn 11201.
Telephone: (718) 643-3312.
Fax: (718) 643-3733

BAISLEY, Paul J., Jr. *(Justice, New York Supreme Court Tenth Judicial District)* Former Judge, Suffolk County District Court.

Office: 204A Supreme Court Annex, 215 Griffing Avenue, Riverhead 11901.
Telephone: (631) 852-3888.
Fax: (631) 852-3745

BALBICK, Robert J. *(Judge, Batavia City Court)*

Office: Genesee Courts Facility, One West Main Street, Batavia 14020.
Telephone: (585) 344-2550.
Fax: (585) 344-8556
E-mail address: rbalbick@courts.state.ny.us

BALKIN, Ruth C. *(Judge, Nassau County Family Court)* Elected to term beginning Jan 1, 1995. Educated at Adelphi University B.A. summa cum laude 1973 and St. John's University School of Law J.D. 1976. Member Phi Beta Kappa. Admitted to practice New York 1977, U.S. District Courts Eastern 1977 and Southern 1977 Districts of New York, U.S. Court of Appeals Second Circuit 1979 and U.S. Supreme Court 1981. In legal practice 1977-87.

Counsel to Town Board 1987-89 and Executive Assistant to Presiding Supervisor and Counsel 1989-94 Town of Hempstead. Member Nassau County Judicial Committee on Women in the Courts since 1996. Board of Directors Jewish Lawyers Association of Nassau County. Representative of OCA Anti-Discrimination Panel for Nassau Courts. Member Family Court Judges Association, National Women Judges Association, Nassau County Women's Bar Association, Bar Association of Nassau County (Chair Municipal Law Committee 1989-91, Director 1993-96, Board of Directors We Care Association since 1996, Board of Directors since 2001, Member Matrimonial and Family Law Committees) and New York State Bar Association. Keynote Speaker Nassau County Women's Bar Association June 7, 2000. Lecturer on Post Judgment Relief, Appellate Practice and Domestic Violence Nassau Academy of Law; Developments in Family Law, Custody, Child Abuse and Neglect and Grandparent Visitation Matrimonial and Family Law Committees Nassau County Bar Association; Domestic Violence Judicial Training Seminar for Nassau County Judges; and Child Abuse and Neglect and Family Offenses New York State Bar Association. Recipient Pathfinders Award from Town of Hempstead 1995. Honored by Tough Love Organization 1999 and Coalition of Child Abuse and Neglect April 2000. Lecturer Student Mentoring Program Alverta B. Gray Schultz Middle School, League of Women Voters, FOCUS (For Our Children and Us), F.A.C.T. (Family and Children Together), Grandparents Reaching Out (Grandparent Support Group) and Business and Professional Women's Club of New York State. Lifetime Member Hadassah. Member Hewlett East Rockaway Jewish Centre and St. John's University Law School Alumni Association.

Office: 1200 Old Country Road, Westbury 11590.
Telephone: (516) 571-9154.
Fax: (516) 571-9335

BALTER, Bruce M. *(Judge, The Civil Court of the City of New York)*
Office: 141 Livingston Street, Brooklyn 11201.
Telephone: (718) 643-3700.
Fax: (718) 643-8997

BALZANO, John S. *(Judge, Utica City Court)*
Office: 411 Oriskany Street West, Utica 13502.
Telephone: (315) 724-8043.
Fax: (315) 792-8038

BAMBERGER, Phylis S. *(Judge, New York Court of Claims)* Appointed by governor. Currently serves as Acting Justice, New York Supreme Court Twelfth Judicial District.
Office: 851 Grand Concourse, Bronx 10451.
Telephone: (718) 590-3670.
Fax: (718) 590-6338

BARASCH, Melvin S. *(Justice, New York Supreme Court Second Judicial District)* Certificated.
Office: 360 Adams Street, Brooklyn 11201.
Telephone: (718) 643-5250.
E-mail address: mbarasch@courts.state.ny.us

BARBARO, Frank J. *(Justice, New York Supreme Court Second Judicial District)* Certificated.
Office: 360 Adams Street, Brooklyn 11201.
Telephone: (718) 643-5891.
E-mail address: fbarbaro@courts.state.ny.us

BARONE, John A. *(Justice, New York Supreme Court Twelfth Judicial District)* Elected Nov 7, 2000 to term beginning Jan 1, 2001. Term expires Dec 31, 2014. Born New York New York July 31, 1948. Educated at Fordham University B.A. with honors 1970 and Harvard Law School J.D. 1973. Admitted to practice New York 1974, U.S. District Courts Southern 1974 and Eastern 1986 Districts of New York and U.S. Court of International Trade 1991. In legal practice New York City Jan 1976 to Nov 1982 and Dec 1988 to May 1992. Judge, The Criminal Court of the City of New York May 1992 to Dec 2000.

Assistant Counsel New York Department of City Planning 1973-76. Law Secretary to Hon. Harold Silverman, The Civil Court of the City of New York 1982-88. Author Introduction *The Advocate* U.S. Court of International Trade 1993 and "The Bellacosa Dissents" New York L. Jour. 1995. Member New York County Lawyers' Association, Columbian Lawyers Association of New York, Bronx County and New York State Bar Associations. Captain USAR 1974-80. Director St. Barnabas Hospital and Alcoholism Council of New York. Advisory Board Congress of Italian American Organization. Member Student Sponsor Partnership. Enjoys fishing, playing piano and singing. Interested in literature, history and philosophy.
Office: 851 Grand Concourse, Bronx 10451.
Telephone: (718) 590-3767.

BARONE, Louis A. *(Justice, New York Supreme Court Ninth Judicial District)* Certificated. Born New Rochelle New York April 11, 1929. Roman Catholic. Educated at Iona College B.A. 1951 and New York Law School J.D. 1954. Admitted to practice New York 1955 and U.S. Supreme Court 1967. Began legal practice New Rochelle 1961. Former Judge, Westchester County Family Court, elected to term beginning Jan 2, 1983.

USMCR 1948-50. Republican. Board of Supervisors Westchester County 1957-63. Chairman Republican City Committee of New Rochelle 1961-63 and 1980-82. Past President Boys Club Alumni New Rochelle. Enjoys music and playing golf.
Office: County Courthouse, 111 Dr. Martin Luther King Jr. Blvd., White Plains 10601.
Telephone: (914) 995-4739.
Fax: (914) 995-4010

BARRETT, Steven L. *(Judge, The Criminal Court of the City of New York)* Appointed by mayor. Currently serves as Acting Justice, New York Supreme Court Twelfth Judicial District.
Office: 851 Grand Concourse, Bronx 10451.
Telephone: (718) 590-3757.
Fax: (718) 590-8914

BARROS, Betsy *(Justice, New York Supreme Court Second Judicial District)* Former Judge, The Civil Court of the City of New York.
Office: 360 Adams Street, Brooklyn 11201.
Telephone: (718) 643-3780.
E-mail address: bbarros@courts.state.ny.us

BARRY, David Michael *(Justice, New York Supreme Court Seventh Judicial District)*
Office: 545 Hall of Justice, 99 Exchange Boulevard, Rochester 14614-2185.
Telephone: (585) 428-2929.
Fax: (585) 428-2513

BARTLETT, George R., III *(Judge, Schoharie County Court)* Also serves Schoharie County Surrogate's Court and Schoharie County Family Court.
Mailing address: P.O. Box 669, Schoharie 12157-0669.
Office: 290 Main Street, Schoharie 12157.
Telephone: (518) 295-8383.
Fax: (518) 295-8451

BARTLEY, A. Kirke, Jr. *(Judge, The Criminal Court of the City of New York)* Appointed by Mayor Rudolph Giuliani.
Office: 100 Centre Street, New York 10013.
Telephone: (212) 374-5729.
Fax: (212) 374-2579

BARTON, Patrick J. *(Judge, Suffolk County District Court)*
Office: 375 Commack Road, Deer Park 11729.
Telephone: (631) 854-1950.

BATT, John F. *(Judge, Niagara County Family Court)*
Office: Courthouse, 175 Hawley Street, Lockport 14094-2758.
Telephone: (716) 439-7185.
Fax: (716) 439-7170
E-mail address: jbatt@courts.state.ny.us

BATTAGLIA, Jack M. *(Judge, The Civil Court of the City of New York)*
Office: 141 Livingston Street, Brooklyn 11201.
Telephone: (718) 643-8830.
Fax: (718) 643-3733

BATTS, Deborah A. *(Judge, United States District Court Southern District of New York)* Appointed for life by President Bill Clinton to term beginning 1994. Born Philadelphia Pennsylvania April 13, 1947. Educated at Radcliffe College A.B. 1969 and Harvard Law School J.D. 1972. Law Clerk to Hon. Lawrence W. Pierce, U.S.

BATTS, DEBORAH A.—*Continued*
District Court Southern District of New York 1972-73. In legal practice New York City 1973-79.

Assistant U.S. Attorney Criminal Division Southern District of New York 1979-84. Special Associate Counsel Department of Investigation New York City 1990-91.

Office: 2510 U.S. Courthouse, 500 Pearl Street, New York 10007-1312.
Telephone: (212) 805-0186.

BAUER, Henry R. *(Judge, Troy City Court)*
Office: Criminal Court, Second Floor, 51 State Street, Troy 12180.
Telephone: (518) 271-1602.

BAYNE, Bernadette *(Judge, The Civil Court of the City of New York)*
Office: 141 Livingston Street, Brooklyn 11201.
Telephone: (718) 643-8474.
Fax: (718) 643-3733

BEATTY, Prudence Carter *(Judge, United States Bankruptcy Court Southern District of New York)*
Office: Hamilton Custom House, Sixth Floor, One Bowling Green, New York 10004-1408.
Telephone: (212) 668-5637.

BECKER, Carl F. *(Judge, Delaware County Court)* Elected to term beginning Jan 1, 2003. Term expires Dec 31, 2012. Also serves Delaware County Surrogate's Court and Delaware County Family Court. Born Endicott New York Jan 31, 1948. Presbyterian. Educated at Clarkson College 1970 and Albany Law School of Union University J.D. 1973. Admitted to practice New York 1974. In legal practice Stamford 1974-2002.

Social Services Attorney and Assistant County Attorney Delaware County July 1, 1974 to May 21, 2002. Member New York State and American Bar Associations. Republican. Member Rotary International.

Office: Delaware County Courthouse, Three Court Street, Delhi 13753.
Telephone: (607) 746-2423.
Fax: (607) 746-3253
E-mail address: cfbecker@courts.state.ny.us

BEDNAR, Mary E. *(Judge, New York City Family Court)* Appointed by mayor.
Office: 60 Lafayette Street, New York 10013.
Telephone: (212) 374-4177.
Fax: (212) 374-2623

BEELER, Harold B. *(Judge, The Civil Court of the City of New York)* Currently serves as Acting Justice, New York Supreme Court First Judicial District.
Office: 71 Thomas Street, New York 10013.
Telephone: (212) 815-0875.

BEHAR, Stephen M., Sr. *(Judge, Suffolk County District Court)*
Mailing address: P.O. Box 9075, Central Islip 11722-9075.
Office: Cohalan Court Complex, 400 Carleton Avenue, Central Islip 11722.
Telephone: (631) 853-4916.

BELEN, Ariel E. *(Justice, New York Supreme Court Second Judicial District)* Elected to term beginning Jan 1, 1995.
Office: 360 Adams Street, Brooklyn 11201.
Telephone: (718) 643-5485.
E-mail address: abelen@courts.state.ny.us

BELFI, Donald E. *(Judge, Nassau County Court)*
Office: Nassau County Courthouse, 262 Old Country Road, Mineola 11501.
Telephone: (516) 571-3563.
Fax: (516) 571-2160

BELLANTONI, Orazio R. *(Justice, New York Supreme Court Ninth Judicial District)* Born Port Chester New York May 12, 1941. Roman Catholic. Educated at Fordham University A.B. 1963 J.D. 1966. Admitted to practice New York 1967, U.S. Supreme Court 1970 and U.S. District Court Southern District of New York 1973. Began legal practice White Plains New York 1969. Former Judge, Westchester County Family Court, elected to term beginning Jan 1, 1984.

Assistant District Attorney Westchester County 1969-72. Law Clerk to Hon. James R. Caruso, Westchester County Court 1973-76 and Hon. Russell R. Leggett, New York Supreme Court 1977-83. Member Columbian Lawyers Bar of Westchester, Port Chester-Rye, Westchester County and U.S. Justinian Bar Associations. Captain USAR 1967-69. Republican.

Office: 111 Dr. Martin Luther King Jr. Blvd., White Plains 10601.
Telephone: (914) 995-4361.
Fax: (914) 995-4010

BELLINI, Elma A. *(Judge, Monroe County Court)*
Office: 545 Hall of Justice, 99 Exchange Boulevard, Rochester 14614-2186.
Telephone: (585) 428-2616.
Fax: (585) 428-4533

BENDER, Dennis F. *(Judge, Seneca County Court)* Also serves Seneca County Surrogate's Court and Seneca County Family Court.
Office: Courthouse, 48 West Williams Street, Waterloo 13165.
Telephone: (315) 539-6291.
Fax: (315) 539-7850

BENITEZ, Peter J. *(Judge, The Criminal Court of the City of New York)* Appointed by mayor. Currently serves as Acting Justice, New York Supreme Court Twelfth Judicial District.
Office: 851 Grand Concourse, Bronx 10451.
Telephone: (718) 590-6272.
Fax: (718) 590-8914

BENZA, Louis C. *(Justice, New York Supreme Court Twelfth Judicial District)* Certificated. Currently serves Third Judicial District. Born New York New York July 15, 1929. Catholic. Educated at Seton Hall University B.S. 1952 LL.B. 1957. Admitted to practice New York 1958, U.S. District Court Southern District of New York and U.S. Supreme Court 1965. In legal practice Bronx 1959-69 and 1973-78. Former Judge, New York Court of Claims, appointed by Governor Mario Cuomo to term beginning March 26, 1984.

Important Decisions: Grayford John Mesick, et al. v. State of New York (state liability in personal injury claim) 1984, aff'd 118 A.D.2d 214; Judith Cordts, Ind., etc. v. State of New York (death; negligent maintenance of state highway) 1985, aff'd A.D.2d Third Dept. Dec 4, 1986; Santangelo v. State of New York (injury to police officer) 129 Misc. 2d 898, aff'd A.D.2d 647, aff'd 71 N.Y.2d 393; and Charbonneau v. State of New York

BENZA, LOUIS C.—*Continued*

148 Misc. 2d 891, aff'd A.D.2d 815, aff'd 81 N.Y.2d dub nom Dreger. Former Member Bronx County and New York State Bar Associations. Member Albany County Bar Association. Participant Unified Court System judicial seminars. First Lieutenant USMCR 1952-54. Democrat. Deputy Borough President Bronx 1970-72. District Administrator and General Counsel to Congressman Herman Badillo 1973-75. Administrative Assistant and General Counsel to Congressman Robert A. Garcia 1978-80 and Congressman Mario Biaggi 1981-84. Former Member Community School Board No. 8 New York City. Former Chairman Advisory Committee Office of Telecommunications New York City, 47th Precinct Youth Council and Fund-Raising Committee Police Athletic League Bronx County. Former District Together Chairman Greater New York Council Boy Scouts of America. Former Director Community Boards Bronx County. Former Vice President and Board Member Small Business Development Corporation Bronx County. Former Board Member Bronx Frontier Corporation, University Heights Development Corporation and Columbian Lawyers. President Board of Trustees St. Barnabas' Hospital, Bronx. Interests include hunting, swimming and fishing.

Office: 201 Courthouse, 16 Eagle Street, Albany 12207.

Telephone: (518) 487-5860.

BERGERMAN, George M. *(Justice, New York Supreme Court Ninth Judicial District)* Born New York New York Aug 19, 1934. Jewish. Educated at Trinity College, Hartford Connecticut B.A. 1956 and New York University School of Law J.D. 1959. Admitted to practice New York 1961. In legal practice Spring Valley 1961-66 and Pearl River 1966-85. Justice, Town of Orangetown Justice Court 1975-85. Former Judge, Rockland County Family Court, elected to term beginning Jan 1985.

Deputy Town Attorney Orangetown 1970-74. Tribunal Administrator American Arbitration Association 1960-61. Member New York State Association of Magistrates, Association of Judges of the Family Court of the State of New York, The Association of the Bar of the City of New York, Rockland County and New York State Bar Associations. USAFR 1959-64. Former Republican Committeeman Rockland County. Former Director United Way Rockland County and Big Brothers and Big Sisters of Rockland County, Inc. Past President and Director Rotary Club Pearl River Rockland County. Past Master and Member Athelstane Masonic Lodge 839. Former Trustee Nyack Hospital. Former Associate Member Excelsior Fire Engine Company of Pearl River. Member B'nai B'rith, NAACP and Nyack Branch. Interests include golfing, reading and sports.

Office: Courthouse, New City 10956.

Telephone: (845) 638-5355.

Fax: (845) 638-5834

BERGIN, Eugene W. *(Justice, New York Supreme Court Seventh Judicial District)* Elected to term beginning Jan 1983. Reelected 1996. Certificated. Born Rochester New York Sept 5, 1931. Roman Catholic. Educated at University of Notre Dame 1953 and Georgetown University 1959. Admitted to practice New York 1960. Judge, Monroe County Court June 1973 to Jan 1983, appointed by Governor Nelson A. Rockefeller.

Office: 514 Hall of Justice, 99 Exchange Boulevard, Rochester 14614-2185.

Telephone: (585) 428-5541.

Fax: (585) 428-4122

E-mail address: ebergin@courts.state.ny.us

BERGSON, Howard M. *(Judge, Suffolk County District Court)*

Office: 3105 Veteran's Memorial Highway, Ronkonkoma 11779.

Telephone: (631) 854-9680

BERKE, Philip A. *(Judge, Washington County Court)* Elected to term beginning Jan 1, 1983. Reelected 1992 and 2002. Current term expires Dec 31, 2012. Also serves Washington County Surrogate's Court and Washington County Family Court. Born Granville New York Jan 25, 1936. Educated at Dartmouth College B.A. 1958 and Cornell University J.D. 1961. Recipient American Jurisprudence Award in Labor Law 1961. Member Tau Epsilon Phi and Phi Alpha Delta. Admitted to practice New York 1961. In legal practice Granville 1961-82. Justice, Granville Justice Court July 1, 1963 to Dec 31, 1970.

District Attorney Washington County Jan 1, 1971 to Dec 31, 1976. Member New York Surrogates Association, New York Family Court Association, New York County Judges Association, Washington County Magistrates Association, Washington County (Secretary-Treasurer 1982-83, President 1984-85) and New York State Bar Associations. Private U.S. Army 1961-67. Former Member Granville Hook and Ladder Company. Member Granville Rotary Club (Past President), Granville Lodge No. 55 Masons and Dartmouth Alumni Club of Glens Falls and Vicinity (Secretary-Treasurer 1966-78). Enjoys playing tennis and skiing.

Office: County Courthouse, Building C, 383 Broadway, Fort Edward 12828.

Telephone: (518) 746-2515.

Fax: (518) 746-2531

BERKMAN, Carol *(Judge, The Criminal Court of the City of New York)* Appointed by mayor. Currently serves as Acting Justice, New York Supreme Court First Judicial District.

Office: 100 Centre Street, New York 10013.

Telephone: (212) 374-5855.

BERKOWITZ, Meryl J. *(Judge, Nassau County Court)*

Office: County Courthouse, 262 Old Country Road, Mineola 11501.

Telephone: (516) 571-1488.

Fax: (516) 571-2160

BERLER, Howard *(Justice, New York Supreme Court Tenth Judicial District)* Elected to term beginning Jan 1, 1992. Certificated. Born Brooklyn New York Oct 6, 1930. Educated at Fairleigh Dickinson University B.S. magna cum laude 1952 and Brooklyn Law School LL.B. 1957. Editor Brooklyn Law Review. Admitted to practice New York 1957. In legal practice New York City 1957-61 and Suffolk County since 1961. Arbitrator, Small Claims Court New York City 1960-63. Judge, Suffolk County District Court Jan 1, 1972 to Dec 31, 1983. Judge, Suffolk County Family Court Jan 1, 1984 to Dec 31, 1991.

BERLER, HOWARD—*Continued*

Assistant District Attorney Suffolk County 1963-67. Assistant District Attorney, Chief Trial Assistant and Chief Administrative Assistant District Court Bureau 1967-71. Author preface to *The "How" of Criminal Law* by Francis M. Conlon, Looseleaf Law Publications, Inc. 1976. Member ISLIP Lawyers Association, Suffolk County and Suffolk County Criminal Bar Associations. Former Chairman Red Cross and United Fund for Central ISLIP. Former Director Suffolk County Heart Association and Columbus Park Civic Association. Former Trustee Leukemia Society, Inc. of Suffolk County. Former Council member Carleton Park Civic Association. Organizer and first President Suffolk County Police Memorial Fund. Member Elks and Jewish Centre of Bayshore (Trustee). Enjoys jogging, reading and auto mechanics.

Office: 430 U.S. Courthouse, 170 Federal Plaza, Central Islip 11722.

Telephone: (631) 853-6321.

Fax: (631) 853-6320

BERMAN, Richard M. *(Judge, United States District Court Southern District of New York)* Appointed for life by President Bill Clinton to term beginning Nov 23, 1998. Born New York New York Sept 11, 1943. Educated at Cornell University B.S. 1964, New York University School of Law J.D. 1967 and Fordham University M.S.W. 1996. In legal practice 1970-74 and New York City 1986-95. Judge, New York City Family Court 1995-98, appointed by Mayor Rudolph Giuliani.

General Counsel Warner Cable Corporation 1978-86. Executive Assistant to U.S. Senator Jacob Javits 1974-77.

Office: 201 U.S. Courthouse, 40 Centre Street, New York 10007-1581.

Telephone: (212) 805-6715.

BERNSTEIN, Lawrence H. *(Justice, New York Supreme Court Twelfth Judicial District)* Elected to term beginning Jan 2, 1979. Reelected 1992. Certificated. Born New York New York Dec 18, 1932. Jewish. Educated at City College of the City University of New York B.A. magna cum laude 1954 and Columbia University LL.B. Member Phi Beta Kappa. Stone Scholar 1957. Admitted to practice New York 1957 and U.S. District Court Southern District of New York 1960. Began legal practice New York County 1957. Judge, The Criminal Court of the City of New York 1970-78.

Assistant District Attorney New York County 1957-63. Member Bronx County Bar Association. Democrat. Councilman 1966-70. Enjoys playing golf and reading.

Office: 851 Grand Concourse, Bronx 10451.

Telephone: (718) 590-3765.

Fax: (718) 590-8914

BERNSTEIN, Stan *(Judge, United States Bankruptcy Court Eastern District of New York)* Appointed by U.S. Court of Appeals Second Circuit judges to term beginning Nov 1, 1996. Term expires Nov 1, 2010. Born Los Angeles California April 20, 1941. Educated at Brandeis University B.A. with honors 1962, Harvard University Ph.D. 1970 and Rutgers University School of Law J.D. 1973. Member Phi Beta Kappa. Admitted to practice Michigan 1974, Ohio 1974, California 1984, Arizona 1989 and Massachusetts 1991. In legal practice Detroit Michigan, Los Angeles California, Phoenix Arizona and Boston Massachusetts 1974-96. Judge, United States Bankruptcy Court Eastern District of Michigan 1982-84.

Author *Collier Bankruptcy Compensation Guide* rev. ed. 1997. Assistant Professor University of California at Davis 1967-70, Rutgers University and Livingston University 1970-73 and University of Toledo College of Law 1973-74. Enjoys reading and sailing.

Office: Long Island Federal Courthouse, 290 Federal Plaza, Central Islip 11722.

Telephone: (631) 712-6200.

E-mail address: judgestan@msn.com

BERNSTEIN, Stuart M. *(Chief Judge, United States Bankruptcy Court Southern District of New York)* Appointed by U.S. Court of Appeals Second Circuit judges. Chief Judge since Feb 1, 2000.

Office: Hamilton Custom House, Sixth Floor, One Bowling Green, New York 10004.

Telephone: (212) 668-2304.

BERRY, Jeffrey G. *(Judge, Orange County Court)* Elected to term beginning Jan 1, 1991. Reelected 2000, current term expires Dec 31, 2010. Currently serves as Acting Justice, New York Supreme Court Ninth Judicial District. Born Newburgh New York May 7, 1947. Roman Catholic. Educated at State University of New York at New Paltz B.S. 1969 and University of Tulsa College of Law J.D. 1974. Law Clerk to Hon. Paul F. Murphy, Orange County Family Court. Member Order of Barristers. Admitted to practice New York 1975, U.S. District Courts Eastern 1977 and Southern 1977 Districts of New York and U.S. Supreme Court 1978. In legal practice Newburgh 1977-90. Judge, Newburgh City Court 1984-90.

Board of Directors County Judges Association of the State of New York. Member and Vice President 2000-01 New York State Judges Education Committee on Criminal Law and Procedure. Member Newburgh, Orange County (Board of Directors 1985-89, Secretary 1990-91) and New York State Bar Associations. Lecturer at New York State Judges Education Seminars. Named Alumnus of the Year by State University of New York at New Paltz 1985. Board of Trustees Johnes Home for Aged Couples since 1981 and Hospice of Orange and Sullivan Counties since 1996. President Board of Directors College at New Paltz Foundation 1983-87. Enjoys playing tennis, fly fishing and collecting antiques, art glass and oriental carpets.

Office: Orange County Government Center, 255-275 Main Street, Goshen 10924.

Telephone: (845) 291-3120.

BEST, Robert P. *(Justice, New York Supreme Court Fourth Judicial District)* Elected to term beginning Jan 1, 1989. Certificated. Born DuBois Pennsylvania June 20, 1929. Educated at Hobart College B.A. 1951 and Albany Law School of Union University LL.B. cum laude 1954. Recent Decisions Editor Albany Law Review 1953-54. Admitted to practice New York 1954 and U.S. Supreme Court 1974. Began legal practice Gloversville 1958. Judge, Fulton County Court Jan 1, 1979 to Dec 31, 1988. Former Surrogate, Fulton County Surrogate's Court.

Confidential Law Clerk to Hon. Willard L. Best, New York Supreme Court 1958-70. District Attorney Fulton County 1977-78. Member Federated (Delegate Fourth Judicial District), Fulton County and New York State Bar Associations. Attended The National Judicial Col-

BEST, ROBERT P.—*Continued*

lege 1982. Lieutenant USN (Legal Officer) 1955-58. Mayor City of Gloversville 1969-73.

Office: Supreme Court Chambers, Courthouse, Johnstown 12095.

Telephone: (518) 736-5533.

Fax: (518) 762-1158

BIANCHINI, Victor E. *(Recalled Magistrate Judge, United States District Court Western District of New York)* Appointed Magistrate Judge U.S. District Court Southern District of California by U.S. District Court Judges to term beginning May 28, 1974. Served part time. Appointed Recalled Magistrate Judge U.S. District Court Western District of New York by the Judicial Council of the Second Circuit. Born San Pedro California Feb 21, 1938. Educated at San Diego State College (now California State University at San Diego) B.A. 1960, University of San Diego J.D. 1963 and Naval Justice School 1964. Law Clerk to Hon. James M. Carter, U.S. District Court 1963-64. Listed in *Who's Who in American Colleges and Universities* 1960. Admitted to practice California 1964. Judge, El Cajon Municipal Court San Diego County Aug 1982 to Nov 30, 1998, appointed by Governor Edmund G. Brown, Jr. Former Judge, Superior Court of California County of San Diego, assumed office Dec 1, 1998.

U.S. Commissioner 1968-69. Author "Vietnamese Law" *Dicta* San Diego County Bar Association 1967, Book Review "How Can You Defend Those People?" Western State University School of Law Criminal Justice Reporter Fall 1984, "Misinterpreting Habit and Custom Evidence: Are California Appellate Courts Kicking the Habit?" *California Evidence Law Reporter* 1985, "The Uniform Child Custody Jurisdiction Act: A Cursory Review" *San Diego Trial Lawyer's Magazine* 1986, "Hearsay Rule—Hospital Records" California Judges Association May 1988 and "Hearsay Rule—Official Records Exception, Mystery or Magic?" San Diego Trial Lawyers Association Trial Bar News Part I June 1988 Part II July 1988. Associate Professor of Business Law California State University at San Diego 1969-73 and of Labor Law Western State University School of Law 1975. Founding Dean until 1980 and Professor since 1978 National University School of Law. Member National Council of U.S. Magistrates (Chairman By-laws Committee), State Bar of California, San Diego County (Board of Directors 1978, Treasurer 1979-80, Chairman Legal Ethics and Unlawful Practices Committee) and American (Subcommittee on Courts and the Community National Conference on Special Court Judges Judicial Administration Division) Bar Associations. Faculty member California Continuing Judicial Studies Program 1986, California Center for Judicial Education and Research and The National Judicial College, Reno Nevada. Administrative Law Officer California Agricultural Labor Relations Board. Named Outstanding Professor by National University 1984. Colonel USMCR since 1960. Recipient Bronze Star with "V" and three air medals. General Court-Martial Judge USMCR. Chairperson Vietnam Veterans Post Traumatic Stress Disorder Committee. Chairman Board of Visitors University of San Diego School of Law. Certified AAU Boxing Referee/Judge. Volunteer worker with free legal clinic for runaway juveniles Ocean Beach 1970 and with disadvantaged youth South Bay San Diego Region since 1976. Enjoys flying.

Office: 510 U.S. Courthouse, 68 Court Street, Buffalo 14202-3498.

Telephone: (716) 332-1765.

BILLINGS, Lucy A. *(Judge, The Civil Court of the City of New York)* Elected Nov 4, 1997 to term beginning Jan 1, 1998. Term expires Dec 31, 2007. Served The Criminal Court of the City of New York 1998. Born Watertown New York May 4, 1948. Educated at Smith College B.A. magna cum laude 1970 and University of California Boalt Hall School of Law J.D. with high honors 1973. Member Phi Beta Kappa. Admitted to practice Vermont 1974, U.S. District Courts District of Vermont 1974, District of Utah 1976 and Eastern 1982 and Southern 1982 Districts of New York, U.S. Courts of Appeals Second 1974 and Tenth 1976 Circuits, Utah 1976 and New York 1982. Former Acting Justice, New York Supreme Court.

Staff Attorney Vermont Legal Aid 1973-75. Supervisor Public Benefits and Health Unit 1976-78, Senior Attorney 1978-82 and Chairperson Public Benefits and Health Task Forces 1980-82 Utah Legal Services. Staff Counsel Children's Rights Project ACLU National Headquarters 1986-89. Consultant Northern Manhattan Improvement Corporation 1996-97. Author "Developing Regulations for the Safe Abatement of Lead Paint" New York University Environmental L. Jour. 7, 1992; "Tenants of Federally Financed Housing Lose Rights to Lead Paint Abatement" 26 Clearinghouse Review 1583, 1993; "Local and Federal Statutory and Regulatory Bases for Preventing Lead Poisoning" 29 Clearinghouse Review 382, 1995 and 26 Trial Lawyers Quarterly 32, 1996; "The Future of Legal Services: Legal and Ethical Implications of the LSC Restrictions" 25 Fordham Urban L. Jour. 608, 1998; and "The Proposed 'Class Action Fairness Act'" 54 *Record* 637, 1999. Member Administrative Procedure Committee Utah State Bar Association 1976-82. Member Federal Task Force on Lead Hazard Reduction and Financing 1993-95. Member New York County Lawyers' Association (Chairperson Civil Rights Committee since 2002, Member Women's Rights Committee, Civil Practice Committee, Judicial Section), New York State Trial Lawyers Association, New York State Trial Lawyers Institute, The Association of Trial Lawyers of America, National Association of Women Judges (Foster Care Task Committee), The Association of the Bar of the City of New York (Council on Judicial Administration, Litigation Committee, Federal Courts Committee, Civil Court Committee), New York Women's (Litigation Committee, Criminal Law Committee), New York State (Civil Rights Committee) and Vermont Bar Associations.

Instructor "Actions Under 42 U.S.C. § 1983; Class Actions; Lead Poisoning Prevention; Federal Housing Quality Standards; and EPSDT" National Legal Aid and Defender Association 1993-95, The Association of Trial Lawyers of America 1994 and New York State Trial Lawyers Institute Spring and Fall 1994; 'Lead Poisoning Prevention" New York City Civil Court Judges 1994; "Selected Civil Issues" 2001 and "Landlord-Tenant Issues" 2002 Judicial Seminars; and "Civil Rights Implications of Security Measures Combatting Terrorism" New York County Lawyers Association 2002. Member Judicial Seminars Curriculum Committee 1999-2002. Recipient Legal Services Award from The Association of the Bar of the City of New York 1996. Chairperson and

BILLINGS, LUCY A.—*Continued*

Member Board of Directors Food Research Action Center National Support Center for Legal Services 1978-87. Co-founder and Member Board of Directors Mental Health Advocacy Group 1980-82. Director of Legal Support Community Action for Legal Services 1982. Director of Litigation 1982-86 and Director of Special Litigation and Training 1989-97 Bronx Legal Services. Co-founder, Member Board of Directors and Chairperson Litigation Committee New York City Coalition to End Lead Poisoning 1983-97. Board of Directors Legal Services Alumni Association 1986-88. Head Coach and Chief Girls' Division American Youth Soccer Organization 1990-97. Coach and Umpire Little League 1992-97. Advisory Board Sino-American Cross-Cultural Training Project Advisory Board New York University School of Social Work 1997-98. Participant Judicial Externship Program Rutgers School of Law Summer and Fall 1999, Moot Court Competition New York Law School 2000 and Orientation Program City University of New York School of Law 2001-02.

Office: 111 Centre Street, Room 650, New York 10013.

Telephone: (212) 374-8061.

Fax: (212) 374-0402

BIRBROWER, Barry *(Judge, Peekskill City Court)* Former Acting Judge.

Office: Two Nelson Avenue, Peekskill 10566.

Telephone: (914) 737-3405.

Fax: (914) 736-1889

BIRNBAUM, Arthur *(Judge, The Civil Court of the City of New York)* Currently assigned to The Criminal Court of the City of New York.

Office: 215 East 161st Street, Bronx 10451.

Telephone: (718) 590-2944.

BIVONA, Andrew P. *(Judge, Orange County Family Court)* Elected to term beginning Jan 1, 1989. Reelected 1998, current term expires Dec 31, 2008. Former Judge, Newburgh City Court. Former Acting Justice, New York Supreme Court Ninth Judicial District.

Office: Orange County Courthouse, 285 Main Street, Goshen 10924.

Telephone: (845) 291-3020.

Fax: (845) 291-3051

BIVONA, John C. *(Justice, New York Supreme Court Tenth Judicial District)*

Mailing address: P.O. Box 9070, Central Islip 11722.

Office: 531 Court Complex, 400 Carleton Avenue, Central Islip 11722.

Telephone: (631) 853-5155.

Fax: (631) 853-3288

BLACKBURNE, Laura D. *(Justice, New York Supreme Court Eleventh Judicial District)* Elected Nov 1999. Serves Criminal Term Queens County since Jan 1, 2000. Educated at The Ohio State University B.S. 1959, New York University 1960-61, Cornell University 1979-80 and St. John's University School of Law J.D. 1979. Honorary LL.D. St. John's University 1986 and Niagara University 1991. Member Alpha Kappa Alpha. Admitted to practice New York, U.S. District Courts Eastern and Southern Districts of New York and U.S. Supreme Court. In legal practice New York 1992-95. Judge, The Civil Court of the City of New York Nov 1995 to Dec 31, 1999.

Important Decisions: People v. Calero N.Y.L.J. March 18, 1998, People v. Jagdish Singh N.Y.L.J. March 26, 1998, People v. Leslie Seide N.Y.L.J. April 6, 1998, People v. All Island Truck Leasing Corp. N.Y.L.J. June 29, 1998 and People v. M'Allah El N.Y.L.J. Sept 11, 1998. Adjunct Professor of Law University of Massachusetts 1984-85. Visiting Professor of Law St. John's University School of Law 1985-90. Member Character and Fitness Committee for Admission to the Bar Second Judicial Department 1985-92. Member National Association of Women Judges and Macon B. Allen Black Bar Association. Life Member NAACP. Coordinator "Not Just for Blacks and Jews in Conversation" Queens County. Convener Judicial Friends Queens County.

Office: 125-01 Queens Boulevard, Room E-337, Kew Gardens 11415.

Telephone: (718) 520-4584.

BLACKSHEAR, Cornelius *(Judge, United States Bankruptcy Court Southern District of New York)*

Office: Hamilton Custom House, Sixth Floor, One Bowling Green, New York 10004-1408.

Telephone: (212) 668-5632.

BLASS, Gregory J. *(Judge, Suffolk County Family Court)*

Office: Millbrook Office Campus, 877 East Main Street, Riverhead 11901.

Telephone: (631) 852-3907.

Fax: (631) 852-2851

BLOCK, Frederic *(Judge, United States District Court Eastern District of New York)* Appointed for life by President Bill Clinton to term beginning 1994. Born Brooklyn New York June 6, 1934. Educated at Indiana University A.B. 1956 and Cornell Law School LL.B. 1959. Law Clerk to New York Supreme Court Appellate Division 1959-61. In legal practice Patchogue 1961-62, Port Jefferson 1962-68, 1974-77, 1979-81 and 1983-85, Centereach 1968-74 and Smithtown 1977-79, 1981-83 and 1985-94.

Office: U.S. Courthouse, 225 Cadman Plaza East, Brooklyn 11201.

Telephone: (718) 260-2420.

BLOOM, Lois S. *(Magistrate Judge, United States District Court Eastern District of New York)* Appointed by U.S. District Court judges to term beginning May 18, 2001. Educated at State University of New York at Stony Brook B.A. 1981 and State University of New York at Buffalo J.D. 1985.

Office: U.S. Courthouse, 225 Cadman Plaza East, Brooklyn 11201.

Telephone: (718) 260-4590.

BLUMENFELD, Joel L. *(Judge, The Criminal Court of the City of New York)* Appointed by Mayor Ed Koch. Currently serves as Acting Justice, New York Supreme Court Eleventh Judicial District.

Office: 25-10 Court Square, Long Island City 11101.

Telephone: (718) 520-3906.

Fax: (718) 520-2539

BLYDENBURGH, Donald R. *(Justice, New York Supreme Court Tenth Judicial District)*

Office: 522 Cohalan Court Complex, 400 Carleton Avenue, Central Islip 11722-9070.

Telephone: (631) 853-7703.

Fax: (631) 853-7542

BOGACZ, Stephen J. *(Judge, New York City Family Court)* Appointed by Mayor Rudolph Giuliani March 1, 1995. Reappointed Sept 13, 1995, current term expires Sept 13, 2005. Served Kings County 1995-97. Currently serves Queens County. Born Brooklyn New York. Educated at Fordham University B.A. 1970 M.A. 1971 J.D. 1974. Admitted to practice New York 1976, U.S. District Courts Eastern 1980 and Southern 1980 Districts of New York and U.S. Supreme Court 1980. In legal practice New York 1976-77.

Assistant Corporation Counsel 1977-83 and Deputy Borough Chief 1983-84 Bronx Family Court, Borough Chief Queens Family Court 1984-87 and Coordinator of Special Projects 1985-95, Deputy Chief 1987-93 and First Deputy Chief 1993-95 Family Court Division Office of the Corporation Counsel. Author "Juveniles in New York Under the *Miranda* Rule: Twenty-Five Years Later" Outside Counsel New York L. Jour. March 20, 1992, "Appellate Conflict Over the *Rosàrio/Ranghelle* Rule" Outside Counsel New York L. Jour. Aug 24, 1992, Essay "Robert F. Kennedy Remembered" New York L. Jour. June 4, 1993, "Bright Lines and Opaque Containers: Searching for Reasonable Rules in Automobile Cases" Outside Counsel New York L. Jour. Sept 22, 1993 and 10 No. 3 Touro L. Rev. Spring 1994, "Toward a More Balanced Method For Questioning Juveniles" Perspective New York L. Jour. Jan 14, 1994, "Destroyed *Rosario:* Completing the Picture" New York Criminal Law News Oct 1995, *New York Juvenile Delinquency Practice* LEXIS Law Publishing Co. 1998 2nd ed. 2002 and annual cumulative supplements 1999-2001 and "Re-Thinking Criminal Discovery and the *Rosario* Rule" 9 No. 2 Criminal Justice Journal Summer New York State Bar Association 2001. Important Decisions: Matter of C.V. (M.V.) 4 New York L. Jour. 30, June 10, 1996; Matter of Meleick H. 170 Misc. 2d 230, 647 N.Y.S.2d 669, 1996; Matter of Susan Marie A. (David M., Sr.) 6 New York L. Jour. 39 Oct 25, 1999; and Matter of Tiffany A. 183 Misc. 2d 391, 703 N.Y.S.2d 381, 2000. Member Queens County (Chair 1993-95 and Member since 1993 Juvenile Justice Committee), New York State and American Bar Associations. Faculty "Juvenile Delinquency Practice" New York State Division of Criminal Justice Services 1987 and Queens Bar Association 1995 and 1998-2001; 25th Anniversary of Family Court The Association of the Bar of the City of New York 1987; "Delinquency Issues" New York State Association of County Attorneys 1992 and 1994; Trial Advocacy Workshop New York City Office of the Corporation Counsel since 1996; "Evidence for the Criminal Practitioner" New York State Bar Association 1999; "Defending Juvenile Delinquency Cases" New York Appellate Division Second Department 2000; and "Juvenile Delinquency Motion Practice" New York State Court System CLE for Court Attorneys 2003. Panelist "Media Access to Juvenile Delinquency Proceedings" The Association of the Bar of the City of New York 1998. Moot Court Judge Fordham University School of Law and New York University School of Law 1989-94, 1995-98 and 2002. Participant New York City Leadership Institute 1993.

Office: 89-14 Parsons Boulevard, Jamaica 11432.
Telephone: (718) 520-3985.
Fax: (718) 520-5085

BONIELLO, Ralph A., III *(Justice, New York Supreme Court Eighth Judicial District)* Elected to term beginning Jan 2001. Term expires Dec 2014. Born Niagara Falls New York June 18, 1944. Roman Catholic. Educated at Ohio University B.A. 1966, State University of New York at Buffalo School of Law J.D. 1969 and McGill University Law School Certificate in Air and Space Law 1970. Moot Court. Admitted to practice New York 1970, U.S. District Court Western District of New York 1970, U.S. Court of Appeals Second Circuit 1971 and Florida 1983. In legal practice Niagara Falls New York May 1, 1970 to Dec 31, 2000.

General Counsel Niagara County Industrial Development Agency 1990-94 and 1998-99. County Attorney Niagara County Jan 2000 to Dec 31, 2000. Former General Counsel Niagara Falls Chamber of Commerce. Instructor in Real Estate Law and Development Niagara University 1972-78. Arbitrator American Arbitration Association. Member The Florida Bar, Niagara Falls (President 1988-89), Niagara County (Past President) and New York State Bar Associations. Recipient Chairman's Award from Niagara Falls Area Chamber of Commerce 1995. Past President and Former Member Board of Education Lewiston-Porter Central School District. Former Director Niagara Hospice, Inc. Former Board of Directors State University of New York at Buffalo School of Law Alumni Association. Former Member Niagara University Advisory Council. Board of Trustees and Former Director Niagara Falls Family YMCA. Enjoys family, hiking, snow skiing and traveling. Personal Statement or Quote: "A judge should never forget that he or she is elected to represent all of the people."

Office: Niagara Civic Building, 775 Third Street, Niagara Falls 14302-1710.
Telephone: (716) 278-1840.
Fax: (716) 278-1809
E-mail address: rboniello@courts.state.ny.us

BOWMAN, Janice L. *(Justice, New York Supreme Court Twelfth Judicial District)* Elected to term beginning Jan 1, 1997. Term expires Dec 31, 2010. Born New York. Educated at Howard University B.A., Pratt Institute M.S. and Brooklyn Law School J.D. Member Alpha Kappa Alpha. Judge, The Civil Court of the City of New York Jan 1, 1992 to Dec 31, 1996.

Assistant Corporation Counsel New York City Law Department. Member Bronx Women's Bar Association, Metropolitan Women's Bar Association, Bronx and National Bar Associations. Member Links, Inc.

Office: 851 Grand Concourse, Bronx 10451.
Telephone: (718) 590-3794.
Fax: (718) 590-8914

BOYLE, Denis John *(Judge, The Criminal Court of the City of New York)* Appointed by Mayor David Dinkins Aug 13, 1991. Reappointed 2001, current term expires Dec 31, 2011. Currently serves as Acting Justice, New York Supreme Court Twelfth Judicial District. Born Bronx New York May 15, 1953. Roman Catholic. Educated at Fordham University B.S. 1975 J.D. 1978. Admitted to practice New York 1978.

Law Clerk to Hon. Thomas B. Galligan, New York Court of Claims and New York City Criminal Court 1978-91. Instructor Mercy College 1989-90. Member The Association of the Bar of the City of New York and Bronx County Bar Association.

Office: 851 Grand Concourse, Bronx 10451.
Telephone: (718) 590-3781.
Fax: (718) 590-8914

BOYLE, E. Thomas *(Magistrate Judge, United States District Court Eastern District of New York)* Appointed

BOYLE, E. THOMAS—*Continued*
by U.S. District Court judges to term beginning July 31, 1995. Term expires July 31, 2003. Born Paterson New Jersey April 30, 1939. Educated at College of the Holy Cross B.S. 1961 and University of Virginia LL.B. 1964. Staff member 1962-63 and Editorial Board 1963-64 Virginia Journal of International Law. Admitted to practice New York 1965, U.S Courts of Appeals Second 1973 and Federal 1985 Circuits and U.S. District Courts Eastern 1974, Southern 1974 and Western 1992 Districts of New York. In legal practice New York City 1965-66, Smithtown 1976-88 and Hauppauge 1988-95.

Attorney Federal Defender Services Appeals Unit 1972-75. County Attorney Suffolk County 1988-92. Author "Omnibus Crime Bill S-5A-AS-43," 51 New York State Bar Journal and "The Independent (Non-Lawyer) Escrow Agent" May 1992 and "Bonded Escrow Agents-The Time Has Come" Dec 1992 *The Suffolk Lawyer.* Adjunct Faculty New York Law School 1982-83. Member Legal Aid Society of Suffolk County, Alexander Hamilton Inn of Court, Association of the Bar of the City of New York, Suffolk County (Trustee 1984-85, Director 1985-88, Member Judiciary Committee 1992-95), New York State (Committee on Judicial Selection 1992-95) and American Bar Associations. Recipient award for public service in civil rights from Brookhaven Branch NAACP 1980 and President's Award from Suffolk County Bar Association May 1980. Assistant Counsel to Speaker New York State Assembly 1977-78 and Senate Minority 1978-79. Calendar Counsel to Senate Minority New York State Legislature 1979-80. Legal Aid Society of Suffolk County 1966-71. Board of Directors 1982-86 and President 1985 Community Youth Services Stony Brook New York. Chairman Presidential Reception 1985 and Board of Directors 1985-88 Holy Cross College Club of Long Island. Board of Directors Nassau-Suffolk Legal Services, Inc. 1986-88. Chair Code Revision Advisory Committee 1992-93, Commissioner Fire and Public Safety 1993-95, Trustee 1993-95 and Chair Board of Assessment Review 1994-95 Village of Old Field.

Office: Long Island Federal Courthouse, 834 Federal Plaza, Central Islip 11722-4449.
Telephone: (631) 712-5710.

BRADLEY, John A. K. *(Judge, The Civil Court of the City of New York)* Appointed by Mayor Edward Koch to term beginning Aug 23, 1979. Elected 1980, 1990 and 2000. Current term expires Dec 31, 2010. Currently serves as Acting Justice, New York Supreme Court First Judicial District.
Office: 111 Centre Street, New York 10013.
Telephone: (212) 374-8481.

BRADLEY, Vincent G. *(Justice, New York Supreme Court Third Judicial District)* Appointed by Governor Hugh L. Carey to term beginning June 9, 1981. Elected 1981 and 1995. Current term expires Dec 31, 2009. Born Kingston New York Oct 3, 1939. Catholic. Educated at New York State Maritime College B.S. 1962 and Fordham University School of Law LL.B. 1967 replaced by J.D. Admitted to practice New York 1967. Began legal practice Kingston 1967.

Former New York State Estate Tax Attorney Ulster County. Member Ulster County and New York State Bar Associations. Former State and County Democratic Party Ulster Committeeman.
Office: Courthouse, 285 Wall Street, Kingston 12401-3817.
Telephone: (845) 340-3225.

BRADSTREET, Peter C. *(Judge, Steuben County Court)* Also serves Steuben County Family Court.
Office: Steuben County Office Building, Davidson Way, Bath 14810.
Telephone: (607) 776-9631.
Fax: (607) 776-7019
E-mail address: pbradstr@courts.state.ny.us

BRANDS, James V. *(Justice, New York Supreme Court Ninth Judicial District)* Former Acting Justice. Former Judge, Dutchess County Family Court.
Office: Courthouse, 10 Market Street, Poughkeepsie 12601.
Telephone: (845) 486-2531.
E-mail address: jbrands@courts.state.ny.us

BRANDT, Dorothy Chin *(Judge, The Civil Court of the City of New York)* Elected to term beginning Jan 1, 1988. Reelected 1998, current term expires Dec 31, 2008. Currently assigned to The Criminal Court of the City of New York. Also serves as Acting Justice, New York Supreme Court Eleventh Judicial District.

Important Decisions: People v. Durch 140 Misc. 2d 353, Spirer v. Adams 144 Misc. 2d 903 and People v. Leiberman 141 Misc. 2d 561. Assistant Dean Harvard Law School 1975-78. Adjunct Professor New York University 1985-87 and Brooklyn Law School since 1987.
Office: 125-01 Queens Boulevard, Kew Gardens 11415.
Telephone: (718) 520-3616.
Fax: (718) 520-4712

BRANDVEEN, Antonio I. *(Judge, New York Court of Claims)* Appointed by Governor Mario Cuomo to term beginning Jan 1, 1987. Reappointed by Governor George E. Pataki to subsequent term. Currently serves as Acting Justice, New York Supreme Court Tenth Judicial District. Born New York 1946. Roman Catholic. Educated at Fordham University School of Business Administration B.S. 1969 and New York University School of Law J.D. 1972. Admitted to practice New York 1974, U.S. District Courts Eastern 1974 and Southern 1974 Districts of New York and U.S. Supreme Court 1977. Judge Housing Part 1980-85 and Judge 1985-86, The Civil Court of the City of New York. Judge, The Criminal Court of the City of New York 1985-86.

Staff Attorney General Counsel's Office New York City Health and Hospitals Corporation 1972-74. With Harlem Legal Services, Inc. 1974. Court Attorney New York Supreme Court First Judicial District 1975-80. Important Decisions: People v. Arol Development Corp. 132 Misc. 2d 200, 1986; People v. Almando Garcia 132 Misc. 2d 350, 1986; and York 77 Assoc. v. Silberman New York L. Jour. Nov 21, 1985. Adjunct Professor of Legal Methods Touro College Jacob D. Fuchsberg Law Center since 1991. Member Harlem Lawyers Association (President 1978-80), Metropolitan Black (Vice President 1985-91, Board Member 1988-91) and New York State (House of Delegates 1979-81) Bar Associations. Attended National Institute of Trial Advocacy Boulder Colorado 1976. Participant judicial seminars New York State Office of Court Administration since 1981. First Lieutenant USAF 1967-72. Board of Directors Central

BRANDVEEN, ANTONIO I.—*Continued*

Harlem Senior Citizens Coalition, Inc. Interests include reading, writing, computers and sports.

Office: New York State Supreme Court, 100 Supreme Court Drive, Mineola 11501-4815.

Telephone: (516) 571-2883.

Fax: (516) 571-0828

E-mail address: tveen@aol.com

BRANSTEN, Eileen C. *(Justice, New York Supreme Court First Judicial District)* Former Acting Justice. Former Judge, The Civil Court of the City of New York.

Office: 60 Centre Street, Room 649, New York 10007.

Telephone: (212) 374-4692.

Fax: (212) 374-1268

E-mail address: ebranste@courts.state.ny.us

BRASLOW, Stephen L. *(Judge, Suffolk County Court)* Also serves as Acting Judge, Suffolk County Surrogate's Court. Former Judge, Suffolk County District Court.

Mailing address: P.O. Box 9007, Riverhead 11901.

Office: Court Complex, 210 Center Drive, Riverhead 11901.

Telephone: (631) 852-1731.

BRAUN, Evelyn L. *(Justice, New York Supreme Court Eleventh Judicial District)* Former Judge, The Civil Court of the City of New York.

Office: 125-01 Queens Boulevard, Kew Gardens 11415.

Telephone: (718) 520-2859.

BRAUN, Richard Fredric *(Judge, The Civil Court of the City of New York)* Elected Nov 7, 1989 to term beginning Jan 1, 1990. Reelected Nov 2, 1999, current term expires Dec 31, 2009. Acting Justice, New York Supreme Court First Judicial District since May 12, 1997. Born Bronx New York March 24, 1947. Jewish. Educated at Queens College B.A. 1969 and Brooklyn Law School J.D. 1975. Associate Editor Brooklyn Law Review 1973-75. Admitted to practice Pennsylvania 1975, New York 1976, U.S. District Courts Western District of Pennsylvania 1975 and Eastern 1977 and Western 1977 Districts of New York and U.S. Court of Appeals Second Circuit 1979. In legal practice New York City 1985-89.

Staff Attorney Legal Services Northwestern Pennsylvania 1975-76. Staff Attorney and Senior Attorney The Legal Aid Society of New York City 1977-80 and 1981-84. Author Book Reviews 1974 and "Waiver of Deportation Under Section 241(f) of the Immigration and Naturalization Act" 1975 Brooklyn L. Rev. Important Decisions: Simeonov v. Tiegs 159 Misc. 2d 54, 602 N.Y.S.2d 1014, 1993; O'Neill v. City of New York 160 Misc. 2d 1086, 612 N.Y.S.2d 303, 1994; United Car & Limousine Foundation, Inc. v. New York City Taxi and Limousine Company 178 Misc. 2d 734, 600 N.Y.S.2d 805 Sup. Ct. N.Y. County 1999; Mayor of City of New York v. Council of City of New York 182 Misc. 2d 330, 696 N.Y.S.2d 761 Sup. Ct. N.Y. County 1999; Brad H. v. City of New York 185 Misc. 2d 420, 712 N.Y.S.2d 336 Sup. Ct. N.Y. County 2000 and 188 Misc. 2d 470, 729 N.Y.S.2d 348 Sup. Ct. N.Y. County 2001; Kellogg v. Travis 188 Misc. 2d 164, 728 N.Y.S.2d 645 Sup. Ct. N.Y. County 2001; and Minieri v. Knittel 188 Misc. 2d 298, 727 N.Y.S.2d 872 Sup. Ct. N.Y. County 2001. Clinical Instructor in Law Hofstra University School of Law 1980-81. Lecturer on Introduction to Landlord-Tenant Law New York University Oct 12, 1995. Member Jewish Lawyers Guild (Board of Governors since 1996), New York County Lawyers' Association (Civil Court Committee and Practice Section 1984-96, Co-chair Judicial Liaison Committee Civil Court Practice Section 1993-95) and New York State Trial Lawyer Association.

Lecturer on Non-jury trials, Inquests, and Jury Trials to newly elected judges Civil Court of the City of New York 1994, 1996 and 1997; on Motion Practice The New York Lawyers Network 1996; on Premises Liability New York State Trial Lawyers Institute 1996; on Tips and Tactics for Successful Mediation and Arbitration 2001; and Guardian and Court Evaluator Training Certification Program Metropolitan Women's Bar Association 2002. Panelist "Slip, Trip and Fall Cases" July 13, 1999, July 11, 2000 and Aug 22, 2001, Judicial Faculty Member Trial Techniques Advanced Program Feb 22, 2000 and Judicial Faculty Presenter Trial Practice Workshop Program May 31, 2000 New York State Trial Lawyers Institute. Facilitator for Discussion Roundtable on Civil Law and Court Proceedings July 22, 1999 and July 19, 2000 and Member Civil Law Curriculum Development Committee 1999, 2000 and 2001 Annual Judicial Seminars Office of Court Administration. Organizer and Moderator "Use of Depositions at Trial" Seminar Jan 20, 2000, Co-organizer and Moderator "Use of X-rays, MRIs, CT-Scans and Radiological Reports at Trial" Educational Program May 24, 2000 and Education Chair Board of Judges of The Civil Court of the City of New York. Program Chair Association of the Bar of the City of New York Dec 11, 2001. Chair Education Committee New York State Association of Supreme Court Justices by Designation and Board of Judges of The Civil Court of the City of New York. Recipient Certificate of Appreciation from New York County Lawyers' Association 1994 and from Board of Directors New York State Trial Lawyers Institute various years 1996-2001. Democrat. Delegate Manhattan Democratic Party Judicial Nominating Convention 1982 and 1984. President Village Independent Democrats 1984-86. Manhattan Coordinator Blacks and Jews in Conversation. Member Middle College High School Career Fair and Brooklyn Law School Mentor Program. Enjoys cycling, tennis, theatre and movies.

Office: 111 Centre Street, New York 10013.

Telephone: (212) 374-8432.

E-mail address: rbraun@courts.state.ny.us

BREEN, J. Timothy *(Judge, Warren County Family Court)* Appointed by Governor George E. Pataki to term beginning June 4, 1999. Elected to term beginning Jan 1, 2000, current term expires Dec 31, 2009. Born Glens Falls New York July 12, 1948. Roman Catholic. Educated at LeMoyne College B.A. with honors 1970 and Albany Law School of Union University J.D. 1974. Admitted to practice New York 1975, U.S. District Court Northern District of New York 1975 and U.S. Supreme Court 1978. Hearing Examiner, New York Family Court 1985-99.

Member Association of Judges of the Family Court of the State of New York, Warren County and New York State Bar Associations. Instructor New York State Bar

BREEN, J. TIMOTHY—*Continued*
Association CLE Spring 1998. USAR 1970-76. Republican.
Office: Warren County Municipal Center, 1340 State Route 9, Lake George 12845.
Telephone: (518) 761-6500.
Fax: (518) 761-6230

BRENNAN, Lawrence J. *(Judge, Nassau County Family Court)*
Office: 1200 Old Country Road, Westbury 11590.
Telephone: (516) 571-9020.
Fax: (516) 571-9335

BRENNAN, Michael J. *(Justice, New York Supreme Court Second Judicial District)* Former Judge, The Civil Court of the City of New York, assigned to The Criminal Court of the City of New York.
Office: 120 Schermerhorn Street, Brooklyn 11201.
Telephone: (718) 643-7161.
E-mail address: mbrennan@courts.state.ny.us

BRESLIN, Thomas A. *(Judge, Albany County Court)* Currently serves as Acting Justice, New York Supreme Court Third Judicial District. Also serves as Supervising Judge, Criminal Courts Third Judicial District. Former Judge, Albany County Family Court.
Office: 342 Albany County Courthouse, 16 Eagle Street, Albany 12207-1019.
Telephone: (518) 487-5370.
Fax: (518) 487-5138

BRIEANT, Charles L. *(Judge, United States District Court Southern District of New York)* Appointed for life by President Richard M. Nixon to term beginning 1971. Former Chief Judge. Born Ossining New York March 13, 1923. Episcopalian. Educated at Columbia University B.A. 1947 LL.B. 1949. Admitted to practice New York 1949. In legal practice White Plains 1949-71. Justice, Ossining Town Justice Court 1952-58.
Special Assistant District Attorney Westchester County 1958-59. Former Village Attorney Briarcliff Manor. U.S. Army WWII. Water Commissioner 1948-51 and Town Supervisor 1960-63 Ossining. Assistant Counsel New York State Joint Legislative Committee on Fire Insurance 1968. Member Westchester County Legislature Second District. Vestryman Episcopal Church. Member Westchester County Republican Committee 1957-71 and Sons of the American Revolution.
Office: U.S. Courthouse, 300 Quarropas Street, White Plains 10601-4150.
Telephone: (914) 390-4077.

BRIGANTTI-HUGHES, Mary Ann *(Judge, The Civil Court of the City of New York)*
Office: 851 Grand Concourse, Bronx 10451.
Telephone: (718) 590-2935.

BROCKWAY, David M. *(Judge, Chemung County Family Court)* Appointed by Governor George E. Pataki to term beginning March 12, 2000. Elected to term beginning Jan 1, 2001. Current term expires Dec 31, 2010. Born Ithaca New York Sept 10, 1950. Episcopalian. Educated at Colgate University A.B. cum laude 1972 and Albany Law School of Union University J.D. 1975. Admitted to practice New York 1976 and U.S. District Courts Northern 1976 and Western 1981 Districts of New York. In legal practice Elmira 1980-2000. Justice, Horseheads Village Court 1980-2000.
Assistant Public Defender 1975-80 and Project Attorney Office for Aging 1980-2000 Chemung County. Editor *The Magistrate* New York State Magistrates Association 1989-2000 and *Brockway's Bench Book* 1999-2003. Instructor Elmira College 1981. Member New York State Magistrates Association (Vice President 1992-94 and 1998-2000), Chemung County, New York State and American Bar Associations. Instructor New York State Unified Court System Continuing Judicial Education since 1989. Named New York State Magistrate of the Year 1988.
Mailing address: P.O. Box 588, Elmira 14902-0588.
Office: 203-209 William Street, Elmira 14901.
Telephone: (607) 737-2901.
Fax: (607) 737-2961
E-mail address: dbrockwa@courts.state.ny.us

BRODERICK, Peter L., Sr. *(Judge, Niagara County Court)* Also serves Niagara County Surrogate's Court.
Office: Courthouse, 175 Hawley Street, Lockport 14094-2758.
Telephone: (716) 439-7150.
Fax: (716) 439-7157
E-mail address: pbroderi@courts.state.ny.us

BROTMANN, Andrew K. *(Judge, White Plains City Court)*
Office: 77 South Lexington Avenue, White Plains 10601.
Telephone: (914) 422-6050.
Fax: (914) 422-6058

BROWN, Jeffrey S. *(Judge, Nassau County Court)*
Office: County Courthouse, 262 Old Country Road, Mineola 11501.
Telephone: (516) 571-3378.
Fax: (516) 571-2160

BROWN, Thomas Paul *(Judge, Allegany County Court)* Also serves Allegany County Surrogate's Court and Allegany County Family Court.
Office: Courthouse, Seven Court Street, Belmont 14813.
Telephone: (585) 268-5800.
Fax: (585) 268-7090
E-mail address: tbrown@courts.state.ny.us

BRUCE, Raymond L. *(Judge, The Civil Court of the City of New York)*
Office: 111 Centre Street, New York 10013.
Telephone: (212) 791-6000.

BRUHN, J. Michael *(Judge, Ulster County Court)* Elected Nov 1993 to term beginning Jan 1, 1994. Term expires Dec 31, 2003. Born Kingston New York Jan 27, 1943. Catholic. Educated at Union College B.A. 1964 and Albany Law School of Union University LL.B. replaced by J.D. 1967. Admitted to practice New York 1967. In legal practice Kingston 1967-93. Judge, Kingston City Court 1982-93.
Member New York State Association of Magistrates, Ulster County Magistrates Association, County Judges Association of the State of New York, Ulster County and New York State Bar Associations. Enjoys golf.
Office: Courthouse, 285 Wall Street, Kingston 12401-0906.
Telephone: (845) 340-3730.

BRUNETTI, John J. *(Judge, New York Court of Claims)* Appointed by governor. Currently serves as Act-

BRUNETTI, JOHN J.—*Continued*

ing Justice, New York Supreme Court Fifth Judicial District.

Office: 408 Onondaga County Courthouse, 401 Montgomery Street, Syracuse 13202.
Telephone: (315) 671-1058.
Fax: (315) 671-1178

BRUNO, Joseph F. *(Justice, New York Supreme Court Second Judicial District)* Acting Justice Jan 1991 to Dec 2001. Former Judge, The Civil Court of the City of New York.

Office: 360 Adams Street, Brooklyn 11201.
Telephone: (718) 643-3123.
E-mail address: jbruno@courts.state.ny.us

BUCARIA, Stephen A. *(Justice, New York Supreme Court Tenth Judicial District)* Elected to term beginning Jan 1, 1996. Born Aug 29, 1948. Roman Catholic. Educated at Fairfield university B.A. 1970, State University of New York at Albany M.A. 1971 and Hofstra University School of Law J.D. 1976. Admitted to practice New York 1977. In legal practice 1979-87. Judge, Nassau County District Court 1994-95.

Assistant District Attorney Nassau County 1976-79. Law Secretary to Hon. Gabriel S. Kohn, New York Court of Claims 1987-89 and Hon. Angelo D. Roncallo, New York Supreme Court Tenth Judicial District 1990-93. Co-author "Prepaid Legal Services Have Arrived" Hofstra L. Rev. 1975. Author "Warning Signs on the Cyber Highway" New York L. Jour. May 22, 1995. Important Decisions: Super 7 Food Stores Inc. v. Mama Properties Feb 21, 1996, Island Rock Gym Corp. v. Skyline Holding Corp. Jan 29, 1997, Constance Fay Klein Ecker v. Zwaik & Bernstein, P.C. June 6, 1997, Harmon v. Harmon Oct 10, 1997, Gumo v. Inc. Village of Malverne Jan 13, 1998, "John Doe" v. Saint Francis Hospital Nov 27, 1998, Bordan v. North Shore University Hospital Feb 4, 1999, John C. DiCocco v. Center For Developmental Disabilities, Inc. Oct 4, 1999, Matter of Patricia Serio v. Board of Education of Valley Stream Union Free School District Feb 28, 2000, Roy H. Stevens v. Jeanne M. Stevens March 13, 2000, Foster v. Peninsula Counseling Center March 17, 2000, Doe v. Port Washington Union Free School District April 14, 2000, Koko Contracting Inc. v. Continental Environmental Asbestos Removal Corp. June 5, 2000, Luigi Cappellino v. Atco Mechanical June 19, 2000, The N.Y. and Presbyterian Hospital v. Allstate Ins. Co. Oct 16, 2000, Rox Riv 83 Partners v. Thomas Ettinger Nov 6, 2000, Kemelman v. Delta Air Lines, Inc. Nov 17, 2000, Edgar Beltran v. Town of Oyster Bay Jan 29, 2001, Nature's Trees, Inc. v. County of Nassau April 24, 2001 and Newsday, Inc. v. Office of the District Attorney of Nassau County July 10, 2001. Participant "Students Thinking Inspirationally & Responsibly" S.T.I.R. Program 1994 and Speaker Student Mentoring Program 1995 Bar Association of Nassau County. Presided at Mock Trial Tournament Nassau County Bar Association 1991-95.

Office: 100 Supreme Court Drive, Mineola 11501.
Telephone: (516) 571-2073.
Fax: (516) 571-1575

BUCHTER, Richard Lance *(Justice, New York Supreme Court Eleventh Judicial District)* Former Acting Justice. Former Judge, The Civil Court of the City of New York.

Office: 125-01 Queens Boulevard, Kew Gardens 11415.
Telephone: (718) 520-3524.

BUCHWALD, Naomi Reice *(Judge, United States District Court Southern District of New York)* Magistrate Judge April 3, 1980 to Sept 23, 1999 and Chief Magistrate Judge Jan 1994 to Jan 1996. Appointed Judge for life by President Bill Clinton to term beginning Sept 24, 1999. Born Feb 14, 1944. Educated at Brandeis University B.A. cum laude 1965 and Columbia University LL.B. cum laude 1968. Editor Columbia Journal of Law and Social Problems 1967-68. Member Phi Beta Kappa and Omicron Delta Epsilon. Admitted to practice New York 1968, U.S. Court of Appeals Second Circuit 1969, U.S. District Courts Eastern 1970 and Southern 1970 Districts of New York and U.S. Supreme Court 1978. In legal practice New York 1968-73.

Assistant U.S. Attorney Southern District of New York 1973-80. Deputy Chief 1976-79 and Chief 1979-80 U.S. Attorney's Office Civil Division Southern District of New York. Author "Abuse of Process: Sewer Service" 3 Columbia Jour. of Law and Social Problems 17, 1967. Member The Association of the Bar of the City of New York, Federal Bar Council (Trustee 1976-82 and 1998-2000, Vice President 1982-84) and New York State Bar Association. Recipient Commissioner's Special Citation from the Food and Drug Administration 1978, William B. Tendy Award for Outstanding Public Service from Robert B. Fiske Association and Class of 1968 Excellence in Public Service Award from Columbia Law School.

Office: 2270 U.S. Courthouse, 500 Pearl Street, New York 10007-1312.
Telephone: (212) 805-0194.

BUCKI, Carl L. *(Judge, United States Bankruptcy Court Western District of New York)* Appointed by U.S. Court of Appeals Second Circuit judges. Former Judge, Bankruptcy Appellate Panel Second Circuit, selected by the Judicial Council of the Second Circuit.

Office: 350 Olympic Towers, 300 Pearl Street, Buffalo 14202-0250.
Telephone: (716) 551-4207.

BUCKLEY, John T. *(Presiding Justice, New York Supreme Court Appellate Division First Judicial Department)* Elected Justice Fifth Judicial District to term beginning Jan 1, 1995. Appointed Associate Justice Appellate Division by Governor George E. Pataki. Term expires Dec 31, 2008. Born Utica New York Feb 8, 1936. Roman Catholic. Educated at Georgetown University B.S. with honors in History 1958 and Albany Law School of Union University LL.B. 1961. Admitted to practice New York 1961, U.S. District Court Northern District of New York 1965, U.S. Supreme Court 1968, Florida 1977 and District of Columbia 1979. In legal practice Utica 1962-79. Acting Judge, Nassau County Court March 1981. Acting Judge, Suffolk County Court April 1982 to May 1982. Judge, Oneida County Court 1980 to Dec 31, 1994.

Past President County Judges Association of the State of New York. First Vice President Association of Justices of the Supreme Court of the State of New York. Member New York State Bar Association (House of Delegates since 1999, Former Presiding Member Judiciary Section). Captain USAR JAGC 1961-69. Former

BUCKLEY, JOHN T.—*Continued*

Pistol Permit Officer Oneida County. Member Oneida County Jail Advisory Board. Member State Assembly New York 1967-72. Counsel on Court Reform 1973 and Assistant Counsel 1974 Judiciary Committee State Assembly New York. Member St. Mary's Parish, Clinton New York.
Office: 27 Madison Avenue at 25th Street, New York 10010.
Telephone: (212) 340-0400.

BUCKLEY, Peter C. *(Judge, Chemung County Court)* Also serves Chemung County Surrogate's Court and Chemung County Family Court. Former Judge, Elmira City Court.
Mailing address: P.O. Box 588, Elmira 14902-0588.
Office: Courthouse, 224 Lake Street, Elmira 14901.
Telephone: (607) 737-2940.
Fax: (607) 732-3343

BUCKLEY, Timothy J. *(Judge, Geneva City Court)*
Office: Public Safety Building, 255 Exchange Street, Geneva 14456.
Telephone: (315) 789-6560.
Fax: (315) 781-2802

BULLARD, Valerie *(Judge, Nassau County District Court)*
Office: 99 Main Street, Hempstead 11550.
Telephone: (516) 572-2103.
E-mail address: bullard@courts.state.ny.us

BUNYAN, Bert A. *(Justice, New York Supreme Court Second Judicial District)* Former Judge, The Civil Court of the City of New York, elected to term beginning Jan 1, 1995, assigned to The Criminal Court of the City of New York.
Office: 360 Adams Street, Brooklyn 11201.
Telephone: (718) 643-3985.

BURGASSER, R. Thomas *(Judge, North Tonawanda City Court)* Serves part time.
Office: North Tonawanda City Hall, 216 Payne Avenue, North Tonawanda 14120.
Telephone: (716) 693-1010.

BURKE, Edward D. *(Judge, New York Court of Claims)* Appointed by Governor George E. Pataki. Currently serves as Acting Justice, New York Supreme Court Tenth Judicial District.
Office: 106A Supreme Court Annex, 215 Griffing Avenue, Riverhead 11901.
Telephone: (631) 852-2881.
Fax: (631) 852-2884

BURKE, James M. *(Judge, The Criminal Court of the City of New York)* Appointed by mayor.
Office: 120 Schermerhorn Street, Brooklyn 11201.
Telephone: (718) 643-8400.
Fax: (718) 643-3538

BURKE, John W. *(Justice, New York Supreme Court Tenth Judicial District)* Certificated.
Office: Supreme Court Building, 100 Supreme Court Drive, Mineola 11501.
Telephone: (516) 571-3360.

BURKE, William J., III *(Judge, Suffolk County District Court)*
Office: Court Complex, 400 Carleton Avenue, Central Islip 11722.
Telephone: (631) 853-4918.
Fax: (631) 853-7611

BURNS, Brian D. *(Judge, Otsego County Court)* Also serves Otsego County Surrogate's Court and Otsego County Family Court.
Office: 197 Main Street, Cooperstown 13326.
Telephone: (607) 547-4358.

BURNS, Christopher J. *(Associate Justice, New York Supreme Court Appellate Division Fourth Judicial Department)* Elected Justice Eighth Judicial District. Appointed Associate Justice Appellate Division by Governor George E. Pataki.
Office: 50 Delaware Avenue, Buffalo 14202.
Telephone: (716) 851-3263.
Fax: (716) 852-6367
E-mail address: cjburns@courts.state.ny.us

BURNS, Elizabeth *(Judge, Cortland City Court)* Serves part time.
Office: 25 Court Street, Cortland 13045.
Telephone: (607) 753-1811.

BUSCAGLIA, Russell P. *(Judge, New York Court of Claims)* Appointed by Governor George E. Pataki to term beginning May 27, 1997. Term expires March 31, 2006. Currently serves as Acting Justice, New York Supreme Court Eighth Judicial District. Born Buffalo New York Sept 12, 1950. Educated at State University of New York at Buffalo B.A. with honors 1972 J.D. 1975. Admitted to practice New York 1976, U.S. District Court Western District of New York 1976, U.S. Court of Appeals Second Circuit 1990 and U.S. Supreme Court 1984. In legal practice Buffalo 1976-77.
Assistant District Attorney Erie County 1977-89. Assistant U.S. Attorney Department of Justice Western District of New York 1989-95. Deputy Attorney General New York 1995-97. Adjunct Professor of Law State University of New York at Buffalo School of Law. Member Bar Association of Erie County and New York State Bar Association.
Office: Erie County Hall, 92 Franklin Street, Buffalo 14202.
Telephone: (716) 851-3447.
Fax: (716) 851-3316

BUTLER, Denis J. *(Judge, The Civil Court of the City of New York)*
Office: 89-17 Sutphin Boulevard, Jamaica 11435.
Telephone: (718) 520-3685.

BYRNE, John N. *(Judge, The Criminal Court of the City of New York)* Appointed by mayor. Currently serves as Acting Justice, New York Supreme Court Twelfth Judicial District.
Office: 851 Grand Concourse, Bronx 10451.
Telephone: (718) 590-3870.
Fax: (718) 590-8914

BYRNE, Maureen A. *(Acting Judge, Norwich City Court)*
Office: One Court Plaza, Norwich 13815.
Telephone: (607) 334-1224.
Fax: (607) 334-8494

BYRNES, Marjorie L. *(Judge, Rochester City Court)* Office: 6 Hall of Justice, 99 Exchange Boulevard, Rochester 14614.
Telephone: (585) 428-2435.
Fax: (585) 428-2741

CAHN, Herman *(Justice, New York Supreme Court First Judicial District)* Former Acting Justice. Certificated. Born Germany Nov 4, 1932. Jewish. Educated at City College of the City University of New York B.A. 1953 and Harvard University J.D. 1956. Admitted to practice New York 1956 and U.S. Supreme Court 1964. Began legal practice New York City 1956. Former Judge, The Civil Court of the City of New York, elected to term beginning Jan 1, 1977.
Member New York County Lawyers' Association and New York State Bar Association.
Office: 60 Centre Street, New York 10007.
Telephone: (212) 374-8354.

CALABRESE, Alex M. *(Judge, The Criminal Court of the City of New York)* Appointed by Mayor Rudolph Giuliani.
Office: 120 Schermerhorn Street, Brooklyn 11201.
Telephone: (718) 923-8225.
Fax: (718) 923-8223

CALABRESE, Joseph C. *(Judge, Nassau County Court)* Born Brooklyn New York Nov 24, 1944. Catholic. Educated at St. John's University B.B.A. 1966 J.D. 1971. Member Alpha Phi Delta. Admitted to practice New York 1972 and U.S. District Court Eastern District of New York 1973. In legal practice New York City area since 1976. Former Judge, Nassau County District Court, appointed to term beginning Jan 3, 1985.
Assistant District Attorney Nassau County 1972-75. Assistant Town Attorney Hempstead 1975-77. General and Labor Counsel Sanitary District 6 Town of Hempstead 1977-85. Member New York State District Attorneys Association 1972-75, National District Attorneys Association 1972-74, Catholic Lawyers' Guild, Nassau County (Member Criminal Law and Procedure Committee 1972-74, Admissions/Membership Committee 1973-78 and 1986-89, Municipal Law Committee 1976-86, Public Relations Committee 1977-80, Professional Ethics Committee since 1981, Community Chairman Library Lecture Series 1977-78 and Courts Committee 1987-89) and New York State (Committee on Prosecution 1972-75 and member Municipal Law Section since 1975) Bar Associations. Republican. Teacher St. Aidan's Catholic Elementary School Sept 1967 to Feb 1972. Customs Inspector Treasury Department summers 1967, 1969 and 1970. Member Franklin Square Republican Club (First Vice President 1972, President 1973-74 and Committeeman 1974-85). Alternate Delegate 10th Judicial District Republican Judicial Convention 1979-84. Community Chairman Heart Fund 1974 and 1975. Usher St. Catherine of Sienna Roman Catholic Church. Member Sons of Italy America Lodge 2245, Police Boys' Club (Soccer coach 1976-81), Franklin Square Athletic Association and Kiwanis (President 1975-76, Board of Governors 1976-81, Long Island South Central Division Public Relations Chairman 1977). Enjoys swimming and playing tennis and golf.
Office: Nassau County Courthouse, 262 Old Country Road, Mineola 11501.
Telephone: (516) 571-3423.
Fax: (516) 571-2160

CALVARUSO, Edmund A. *(Surrogate, Monroe County Surrogate's Court)* Former Justice, New York Supreme Court Seventh Judicial District.
Office: 541 Hall of Justice, 99 Exchange Boulevard, Rochester 14614-2186.
Telephone: (585) 428-2482.
Fax: (585) 428-2650
E-mail address: ecalvaru@courts.state.ny.us

CAMACHO, Fernando M. *(Judge, The Criminal Court of the City of New York)* Appointed by Mayor Rudolph Giuliani.
Office: 120 Schermerhorn Street, Brooklyn 11201.
Telephone: (718) 520-3855.
Fax: (718) 520-4712

CAMPBELL, Victoria Brace *(Judge, Port Jervis City Court)* Former Acting Judge. Appointed Judge by Common Council Nov 1996 to term beginning Jan 1, 1997. Term expires Dec 31, 2003. Born Port Jervis New York June 19, 1961. Catholic. Educated at State University of New York at New Paltz B.A. 1984 and New York Law School J.D. 1987. Admitted to practice New Jersey 1987 and New York 1988. In legal practice Port Jervis New York 1988-98.
Member Womans Bar of Orange County, Womans Bar of Rockland County, Womans Bar of Sullivan County, Bankruptcy Bar of Hudson Valley, Port Jervis and Orange County Bar Associations.
Office: 14-18 Hammond Street, Port Jervis 12771-2495.
Telephone: (845) 858-4034.
Fax: (845) 856-2767

CANFIELD, James B. *(Justice, New York Supreme Court Third Judicial District)* Elected Nov 5, 1991 to term beginning Jan 1, 1992. Term expires Dec 31, 2005. Born Utica New York Aug 11, 1940. Roman Catholic. Educated at Siena College B.A. with honors 1962 and Albany Law School of Union University J.D. LL.B. 1965. Admitted to practice New York 1965, U.S. District Court Northern District of New York 1965 and U.S. Supreme Court 1975. In legal practice Troy 1965-85.
District Attorney Rensselaer County 1985-91. Member Association of Justices of the Supreme Court of the State of New York and Rensselaer County Bar Association. Attended annual New York State Judicial Conference Seminars.
Office: Courthouse, Congress and Second Streets, Troy 12180.
Telephone: (518) 270-3779.
Fax: (518) 270-9162

CANNIZZARO, Joseph R. *(Justice, New York Supreme Court Third Judicial District)*
Office: 269 Courthouse, 16 Eagle Street, Albany 12207.
Telephone: (518) 487-5160.

CARDONA, Anthony V. *(Presiding Justice, New York Supreme Court Appellate Division Third Judicial Department)* Elected Justice Third Judicial District 1990. Administrative Judge 1992 to Sept 7, 1993. Appointed Associate Justice Appellate Division by Governor Mario Cuomo Sept 8, 1993. Presiding Justice since Jan 1, 1994. Educated at Manhattan College and Albany Law School of Union City. In legal practice 1971-84. Judge, Albany County Family Court 1985-90.

CARDONA, ANTHONY V.—*Continued*

Former Assistant Public Defender Albany County. Former Town Attorney Coeymans. Co-chair Family Violence Task Force. Member Capital District Trial Lawyers Association, Association of Justices of the Supreme Court of the State of New York, National Italian-American Bar Association (Upstate New York Chapter), Albany County, New York State and American (Executive Committee Council of Chief Judges) Bar Associations. USN 1963-67. Board of Trustees Albany Law School.

Office: 357 Albany County Courthouse, Eagle Street, Albany 12207.
Telephone: (518) 487-5170.
Fax: (518) 487-5042

CAREY, Joan B. *(Judge, New York Court of Claims)* Appointed by governor. Currently serves as Acting Justice, New York Supreme Court First Judicial District. Also serves as Deputy Chief Administrative Judge New York City Courts. Former Judge, The Criminal Court of the City of New York.
Office: 100 Centre Street, New York 10013.
Telephone: (212) 374-8540.
Fax: (212) 374-3003

CARNEY, Patrick M. *(Judge, Buffalo City Court)*
Office: 50 Delaware Avenue, Buffalo 14202.
Telephone: (716) 847-8281.
Fax: (716) 847-8257

CARNI, Edward D. *(Justice, New York Supreme Court Fifth Judicial District)* Former Judge, Syracuse City Court.
Office: Onondaga County Courthouse, 401 Montgomery Street, Syracuse 13202.
Telephone: (315) 671-1108.
Fax: (315) 671-1177
E-mail address: ecarni@courts.state.ny.us

CARPINELLO, Anthony J. *(Associate Justice, New York Supreme Court Appellate Division Third Judicial Department)* Elected Justice Third Judicial District 1994 to term beginning Jan 1, 1995. Appointed Associate Justice Appellate Division by Governor George E. Pataki June 25, 1996. Educated at Union College 1970 and Albany Law School of Union University 1973. Law Clerk to New York Supreme Court Appellate Division Third Judicial Department 1973-74. In legal practice Albany 20 years.
Office: 279 River Street, Fourth Floor, Troy 12180.
Telephone: (518) 270-3795.

CARRIG, Bart M. *(Acting Judge, Little Falls City Court)*
Office: City Hall, 659 East Main Street, Little Falls 13365.
Telephone: (315) 823-1690.
Fax: (315) 823-1623

CARRO, Gregory *(Judge, New York Court of Claims)* Appointed by Governor George E. Pataki. Currently serves as Acting Justice, New York Supreme Court First Judicial District. Former Judge, The Civil Court of the City of New York. Former Judge, The Criminal Court of the City of New York.
Office: 111 Centre Street, Room 114, New York 10013.
Telephone: (212) 374-8068.

CARROLL, Thomas J. *(Judge, New York Court of Claims)* Appointed by governor. Currently serves as Acting Justice, New York Supreme Court Second Judicial District.
Office: 120 Schermerhorn Street, Brooklyn 11201.
Telephone: (718) 643-8003.
Fax: (718) 643-3813
E-mail address: tcarrol@courts.state.ny.us

CARRUTHERS, Richard D. *(Judge, The Criminal Court of the City of New York)* Appointed by mayor. Currently serves as Acting Justice, New York Supreme Court First Judicial District.
Office: 100 Centre Street, New York 10013.
Telephone: (212) 374-8162.

CARTER, Jerald S. *(Judge, Nassau County Court)* Elected to term beginning Jan 1, 1998. Term expires Dec 2007. Currently serves as Acting Justice, New York Supreme Court Tenth Judicial District. Educated at Fisk University B.A. cum laude 1974 and Howard University J.D. 1977. Admitted to practice New York 1978 and U.S. District Courts Eastern and Southern Districts of New York. In legal practice Hempstead 1980-96. Justice, Hempstead Village Justice Court 1989-96. Judge, Nassau County District Court 1996.

Assistant District Attorney Nassau County 1977-80. Negotiating Attorney Hempstead School District 1983-90. Important Decision: In re Connecticut (regarding the murder of Martha Moxley and whether investigator hired by the brother of Ethel Kennedy on behalf of his two sons, considered suspects by the police could be compelled to testify before a Connecticut grand jury) 1999. Adjunct Professor of Trial Practice Touro College Jacob D. Fuchsberg Law Center Jan 2000. Member Nassau County Bar Association. Republican. Enjoys scuba diving.
Office: Nassau County Courthouse, 262 Old Country Road, Mineola 11501.
Telephone: (516) 571-3560.

CARTER, John W. *(Judge, The Criminal Court of the City of New York)* Appointed by Mayor Rudolph Giuliani.
Office: 120 Schermerhorn Street, Brooklyn 11201.
Telephone: (718) 643-8400.
Fax: (718) 643-3538

CARTER, Kevin M. *(Judge, Erie County Family Court)*
Office: One Niagara Plaza, Buffalo 14202.
Telephone: (716) 858-8077.
Fax: (716) 858-8432

CARTER, Robert L. *(Senior Judge, United States District Court Southern District of New York)* Appointed for life by President Richard M. Nixon to term beginning Sept 1972. Assumed Senior status, serves by assignment. Born Caryville Florida March 11, 1917. Protestant. Educated at Lincoln University A.B. magna cum laude 1937, Howard University LL.B. magna cum laude 1940 and Columbia University LL.M. 1941. Honorary D.C.L. Lincoln University 1965. Honorary LL.D. Northeastern University 1988, College of the Holy Cross 1994 and Howard University May 1995. Honorary Doctor of Humane Letters New School for Social Research May 1998. Recipient Rosenwald Fellowship 1940. Admitted to practice New York 1945. In legal practice New York City Sept 1969 to Aug 1972.

CARTER, ROBERT L.—*Continued*

Counsel NAACP 1945-68. Special Assistant U.S. Attorney Southern District of New York 1962. Contributing Author "Equality" *The African Forum* Pantheon Press 1965. Author "The Warren Court and Desegregation" University of Michigan L. Rev. 1968, "The Federal Rules of Civil Procedure as a Vindicator of Civil Rights" 137 University of Pennsylvania L. Rev. 2179, 1989, "Thurgood Marshall While at the NAACP" Editorial Page *Washington Post* Jan 1993, "Thirty-Five Years Later: New Perspectives on *Brown,*" "*Race in America, The Struggle for Equality*" 83 University Wisconsin Press 1993 and "In Tribute: Charles Hamilton Houston" 111 Harvard L. Rev. 2149, 1998. Adjunct Professor of Law New York University 1965-70, Yale University 1976-77, University of Michigan 1976 and Haywood Burns Chair in Civil Rights City University of New York School of Law 1999-2000. Member Mayor's Judiciary Committee 1966-72, Temporary Commission on the State Court System 1970-72 and New York State Special Commission on Attica 1971-72. Founder and Co-chairman National Conference of Black Lawyers 1968-72. Chairman Subcommittee on Legal Representation for the Indigent 1968-72 and Member Departmental Committee on Court Administration of the First and Second Judicial Departments New York State Supreme Court. Former Member Council on Foreign Relations. Member The Association of the Bar of the City of New York (Executive Committee, Judiciary Committee, Admissions Committee, Grievances Committee, Bill of Rights Committee, Court Conduct Committee 1960-72) and American Bar Association. Recipient Alumni Award for Distinguished Postgraduate Achievement from Howard University 1980, Emory Buckner Medal for Outstanding Public Service from Federal Bar Council Nov 1995 and Medal of Freedom from Harvard Law School Sept 2000. Second Lieutenant USAAC 1941-44. Democrat. Director Veterans Affairs American Veterans Committee 1948-49. Member American Delegation to United Nations Conference on Crime and Treatment of Offenders, Stockholm Sweden 1965 and United Nations Conference of African Jurists on African Legal Process and Individual Rights, Addis Ababa Ethiopia 1971. Past President National Committee Against Discrimination in Housing. Council of Advisors and Former Chairman Board of Directors Northside Center for Child Development Inc. Former Board Member American Civil Liberties Union, United Housing Foundation, Alvin Ailey Dance Theatre and Phelps Stokes Fund. Board of Governors Columbia University School of Law. Enjoys jogging, opera, ballet and bridge.

Office: 2220 U.S. Courthouse, 500 Pearl Street, New York 10007-1312.

Telephone: (212) 805-0196.

CARTER, William A. *(Judge, Albany City Court)*

Office: Public Safety Building, Morton Avenue and Broad Street, Albany 12202.

Telephone: (518) 462-6714.

CARUSO, Vito C. *(Justice, New York Supreme Court Fourth Judicial District)* Elected Nov 1994 to term beginning Jan 1, 1995. Term expires Dec 31, 2008. Born Boston Massachusetts March 20, 1949. Roman Catholic. Educated at State University of New York at New Paltz B.A. 1971. Admitted to practice New York 1977 and U.S. District Court Northern District of New York 1977. In legal practice Schenectady 1977-95.

Counsel Town of Duanesburg 1978-80. Deputy Assistant County Attorney Schenectady County 1980-94. Important Decisions: Sgambellone v. Wheatley (CPUR 3103 [c] sanctions) 165 Misc. 2d 954, 1995; McCauley v. McCauley (child support standards act) 172 Misc. 2d 611, 1997; Polimeni v. Minolta Corporation (bulk supplier doctrine in products liability cases) aff'd 227 A.D.2d 64 Sept 26, 1995; and Myers v. City of Schenectady (SCEA retirees' entitlement to continue health insurance coverage) 1996 aff'd A.D.2d Nov 26, 1997. Member Schenectady County and New York State Bar Associations. Recipient Pro Bono Award from New York State Bar Association 1986. Republican. County Republican Chairman Schenectady 1984-94. Board of Directors Annie Schaffer Senior Center 1989-97. Board of Trustees Schenectady Community College 1989-92. Member Rotterdam Elks Lodge 2157, Knights of Columbus and Sons of Italy. Enjoys golf, computers and carpentry.

Office: Schenectady County Courthouse, 612 State Street, Schenectady 12305.

Telephone: (518) 388-4327.

Fax: (518) 347-1972

CASEY, Richard C. *(Judge, United States District Court Southern District of New York)* Appointed for life by President Bill Clinton to term beginning Nov 23, 1997. Born Ithaca New York Jan 19, 1933. Educated at College of the Holy Cross B.S. 1955 and Georgetown University Law Center LL.B. 1958. In legal practice New York City 1964-97.

Legal Investigator District Attorney's Office New York County 1958. Assistant U.S. Attorney Southern District of New York 1959-63. Counsel Special Commission State of New York 1963-64.

Office: 920 U.S. Courthouse, 500 Pearl Street, New York 10007-1312.

Telephone: (212) 805-0260.

CASS, Stephen W. *(Surrogate, Chautauqua County Surrogate's Court)*

Mailing address: P.O. Box C, Mayville 14757-0299.

Office: Gerace Office Building, Three North Erie Street, Mayville 14757.

Telephone: (716) 753-4337.

Fax: (716) 753-4600

E-mail address: scass@courts.state.ny.us

CASSATA, Joseph J., Jr. *(Judge, Tonawanda City Court)*

Office: City Hall, 200 Niagara Street, Tonawanda 14150.

Telephone: (716) 693-3484.

Fax: (716) 693-1612

CASTRO, Melchor E. *(Judge, Rochester City Court)*

Office: 6 Hall of Justice, 99 Exchange Boulevard, Rochester 14614.

Telephone: (585) 428-2437.

Fax: (585) 428-4134

E-mail address: mcastro@courts.state.ny.us

CATALDO, John *(Judge, The Criminal Court of the City of New York)* Appointed by mayor. Currently

CATALDO, JOHN—*Continued*

serves as Acting Justice, New York Supreme Court First Judicial District.

Office: 100 Centre Street, New York 10013.

Telephone: (212) 374-6370.

CATENA, Felix J. *(Judge, Montgomery County Court)* Appointed by Governor George E. Pataki to term beginning March 9, 1999. Elected Nov 1999, current term expires Dec 31, 2009. Born Amsterdam New York March 3, 1957. Roman Catholic. Educated at American University B.A. 1979 and California Western School of Law J.D. 1985. Admitted to practice New York 1986, California 1987, District of Columbia 1987 and U.S. District Courts Northern District of New York 1986 and Central 1987, Eastern 1988 and Southern 1988 Districts of California. In legal practice Amsterdam New York Jan 1990 to March 8, 1999. Judge, Amsterdam City Court Jan 1995 to March 8, 1999.

Prosecuting Attorney U.S. Department of Labor Jan 1987 to Dec 1989. Assistant District Attorney Montgomery County Jan 1990 to March 1992. Corporation Counsel City of Amsterdam Jan 1992 to Dec 1994. President Montgomery County Bar Association 1997 and 1998. Board of Directors Capital District Italian-American Bar Association. Member Montgomery County Magistrate's Association and Fulton County Bar Association. Lecturer Newly Elected Judges School Dec 2000 and Annual Judicial Training Seminar July 2001. Member Curriculum Committee New York State Judicial Education and Training. Member Local Elections Division Republican National Committee Jan 1979 to Aug 1981 and Montgomery County Republican Committee 1990-94. President St. Anthony's/Holy Name Society. Chairman Board of Directors Montgomery County Chamber of Commerce. Board of Directors Amsterdam Little Giants Football League, Inc., Greater Amsterdam Volunteer Ambulance Corps. and Community Health Center, Inc. Member Executive Committee Amsterdam Youth Court, Elks Club of Amsterdam, Kiwanis Club and Knights of Columbus.

Mailing address: P.O. Box 1500, Fonda 12068-1500.

Office: Courthouse, Route 30A, Extension Broadway, Fonda 12068.

Telephone: (518) 853-3834.

Fax: (518) 853-8396

E-mail address: fjcatena@courts.state.ny.us

CATTERSON, James M. *(Justice, New York Supreme Court Tenth Judicial District)*

Office: 205A Supreme Court Annex, 215 Griffing Avenue, Riverhead 11901.

Telephone: (631) 852-2833.

Fax: (631) 852-2714

CECILE, James H. *(Judge, Syracuse City Court)* Serves part time.

Office: Public Safety Building, Second Floor, 511 South State Street, Syracuse 13202-2179.

Telephone: (315) 477-2786.

Fax: (315) 474-2601

E-mail address: jcecile@courts.state.ny.us

CEDARBAUM, Miriam Goldman *(Senior Judge, United States District Court Southern District of New York)* Appointed for life by President Ronald Reagan to term beginning March 4, 1986. Assumed Senior status March 31, 1998. Born New York New York 1929. Jewish. Educated at Barnard College B.A. cum laude 1950 and Columbia University School of Law LL.B. 1953. James Kent Scholar and Harlan Fiske Stone Scholar. Recipient Jane Marx Murphy Prize. Board of Revising Editors Columbia Law Review 1951-53. Law Clerk to Hon. Edward Jordan Dimock, U.S. District Court Southern District of New York 1953-54. Admitted to practice New York 1954, U.S. District Courts Southern 1956 and Eastern 1980 Districts of New York, U.S. Court of Appeals Second 1956, Fifth 1980 and Eleventh 1980 Circuits and U.S. Supreme Court 1958. In legal practice New York 1959-62 and 1979-86. Acting Village Justice 1978-82 and Village Justice 1982-86.

Assistant U.S. Attorney Southern District of New York 1954-57. Attorney U.S. Department of Justice 1958-59. First Assistant Counsel Moreland Commission on the Alcoholic Beverage Control Law New York State 1963-64. Associate Counsel The Museum of Modern Art 1965-79. Author "Women on the Federal Bench" 73 Boston University L. Rev. 39, 1993 and "Women on the Federal Bench—A Progress Report" 10 Columbia Journal of Gender and Law 23, 2000. Important Decisions: Cahill v. Anderson 659 F. Supp. 1115, 1986; Walk-In v. Breuer Capital 651 F. Supp. 1009, 1986; Boxer v. Gottlieb 652 F. Supp. 1056, 1987; Bowlus v. Alexander & Alexander 659 F. Supp. 914, 1987; U.S. v. Chuang 696 F. Supp. 910, 1988; Murray v. NBC 718 F. Supp. 249, 1989; USA v. Willis 737 F. Supp. 269, 1990 and 778 F. Supp. 205, 1991; Doherty v. Thornburgh 750 F. Supp. 131, 1990; New York News Inc. v. Metropolitan Transportation Authority et. al. 753 F. Supp. 133 S.D.N.Y. 1990; Tuxxedo Network v. Hughes Communications 753 F. Supp. 514 S.D.N.Y. 1990; United States of America v. Disomma 769 F. Supp. 575 S.D.N.Y. 1991; United States of American v. Sprecher 783 F. Supp. 133, 1992; United Rope v. Kimberly Line 785 F. Supp. 446 S.D.N.Y. 1992; Landgray Associates v. 450 Lexington Venture 788 F. Supp. 776 S.D.N.Y. 1992; The Walt Disney Company, Walt Disney Pictures and Television, and Buena Vista Home Video v. Goodtimes Home Video Corp. 830 F. Supp. 762 S.D.N.Y. 1993; Sansevera v. E.I. DuPont de Nemours & Co. 859 F. Supp. 106 S.D.N.Y. 1994; Mitsui & Co., Ltd. v. Oceantrawl Corp. 906 F. Supp. 202 S.D.N.Y. 1995; John E. Grimmer, et al. V. Lord Day & Lord, Barrett Smith, et al. 937 F. Supp. 255 S.D.N.Y. 1996; Papa's-June Music, Inc. v. Ramsey McLean 921 F. Supp. 1154 S.D.N.Y. 1996; Lebbeus Woods V. Universal City Studios, Inc., et al., 920 F. Supp. 62 S.D.N.Y. 1996; SEG Sports Corp. and Miracle Promotions Incorporated v. The State Athletic Commission, et al. 952 F. Supp. 202 S.D.N.Y. 1997; Latino Officers Association, et al. v. The City of New York, et al. 966 F. Supp. 238 S.D.N.Y. 1997; Miramax Films Corp. v. Columbia Pictures Entertainment, Inc. and Mandalay Entertainment, Inc. 996 F. Supp. 294 S.D.N.Y. 1998; New York Stock Exchange, Inc. v. New York, New York Hotel, LLC, et al. 69 F. Supp.2d 479 S.D.N.Y. 1999; Pilates, Inc. v. Current Concepts and Kenneth Endelman 120 F. Supp. 2d 286 S.D.N.Y. 2000; Lennox Lewis v. Hasim Rahman, et al. 147 F. Supp.2d 225 S.D.N.Y. 2001; The Martha Graham School and Dance Foundation, Inc., et al. v. Martha Graham Center of Contemporary Dance, Inc., et al. 153 F. Supp.2d 512 S.D.N.Y. 2001; and The Martha Graham School and Dance Foundation, et al. v. Martha Graham Center of Contemporary Dance, Inc., et al. 224 F. Supp.2d 567 S.D.N.Y. 2002.

CEDARBAUM, MIRIAM GOLDMAN—*Continued*

Member Judicial Conference Committee on Defender Services 1993-99. Member Federal Bar Council, Copyright Society of the U.S.A. (Trustee, Member Executive Committee 1979-82), The American Law Institute, The Association of the Bar of the City of New York (Committee on Copyright and Literary Property 1982-84, Committee on the Bicentennial 1988-92), New York State (Chairman Committee on Federal Legislation 1978-80, Committee on District, City, Village and Town Courts 1983-84) and American (Chairman Committee on Pictorial, Graphic, Sculptural and Choreographic Works 1979-81, Member Committee on Federal Practice and Procedure 1983-84) Bar Associations. Recipient Barnard Medal of Distinction May 14, 1991. Co-Counsel Local Association to Promote Residential Diversity 1968-86. Member Advisory Committee on Labor Relations of Local School Board 1976-77 and Board of Architectural Review 1977-78. Trustee Barnard College. Board of Visitors Columbia Law School. Hobbies include history, languages and tennis.

Office: 1330 U.S. Courthouse, 500 Pearl Street, New York 10007-1312.

Telephone: (212) 805-0198.

CENTRA, John V. *(Justice, New York Supreme Court Fifth Judicial District)*

Office: Onondaga County Courthouse, 401 Montgomery Street, Syracuse 13202.

Telephone: (315) 671-1105.

CERESIA, George B., Jr. *(Justice, New York Supreme Court Third Judicial District)* Elected to term beginning Jan 1, 1994. Term expires Dec 31, 2007. Born Troy New York May 31, 1943. Educated at State University of New York at Albany B.A. 1965 and Albany Law School of Union University J.D. 1968. Admitted to practice New York 1969 and U.S. District Court Northern District of New York 1969. In legal practice Troy 1969 to June 1987. Justice, North Greenbush Town Justice Court Jan 1, 1972 to June 28, 1987. Clerk, Rensselaer County Surrogate's Court 1975 and 1978-86. Acting Judge, Troy Police Court July and Nov 1986. Surrogate, Rensselaer County Surrogate's Court June 28, 1987 to Dec 31, 1993.

Assistant Public Defender Rensselaer County 1970-71. Member and Former Chair Gender Fairness Committee and Member Anti-Bias Panel Third Judicial District. Member Rensselaer County Magistrates Association, New York State Association of Magistrates, The Surrogates' Association of the State of New York, Association of Justices of the Supreme Court of the State of New York and Rensselaer County Bar Association (Past President). Lecturer "Probate & Administration Practice Skills" 1981, "Estate Planning, Will Drafting, Probate & Administration Practice Skills" 1982, "Obtaining Letters in Contested & Uncontested Estate Proceedings" 1984 and "Deposition Practice and Practicalities in State and Federal Court" 1995 New York State Bar Association. Panelist Forum on Increasing Minorities on Juries The Fund for Modern Courts 1992, "Planning Today for Tomorrow" New York State Association for Retarded Children, Inc. 1993, "The Judges Speak" New York State Bar Association 1994 and "The Art of Trial Advocacy: Jury Selection" Albany Law School of Union University 1996. Coach CYO Boys' Basketball 1980-92. Manager Twin Town Little League 1981-85. Manager 1984-88 and President 1989 Twin Town Senior League Baseball. Judge Moot Court and Gabrielli Competitions Albany Law School of Union University. Advisor Explorer Scouting. Member Association of Retarded Children (Guardianship Committee Rensselaer County Chapter) and North Greenbush Youth Council.

Office: Courthouse, Congress and Second Streets, Troy 12180.

Telephone: (518) 270-3728.

CERRATO, Robert C. *(Judge, Yonkers City Court)* Elected to term beginning Jan 1, 2001. Term expires Dec 31, 2010. Born Yonkers New York March 25, 1947. Roman Catholic. Educated at Manhattan College B.S.B.A. 1970 and Pace University School of Law J.D. 1980. Admitted to practice New York 1982. In legal practice Yonkers 1982-2001.

Adjunct Professor of Business Law Mercy College. Member Columbian Lawyers Association of Brooklyn, Yonkers Lawyers Association, The Association of Trial Lawyers of America, Westchester County and New York State Bar Associations. Member Yonkers Republican Party. Member Operation Santa Claus. Interests include music, physical fitness and golf.

Office: Justice Center, 100 South Broadway, Yonkers 10701.

Telephone: (914) 377-6365.

CHAMBERS, Cheryl E. *(Justice, New York Supreme Court Second Judicial District)* Former Judge, The Civil Court of the City of New York, elected to term beginning Jan 1, 1995.

Office: 360 Adams Street, Room 527, Brooklyn 11201.

Telephone: (718) 643-2677.

E-mail address: cchambers@courts.state.ny.us

CHIN, Denny *(Judge, United States District Court Southern District of New York)* Appointed for life by President Bill Clinton to term beginning 1994. Born Kowloon Hong Kong April 13, 1954. Educated at Princeton University B.A. 1975 and Fordham University School of Law J.D. 1978. Law Clerk to Hon. Henry F. Werker, U.S. District Court Southern District of New York 1978-80. In legal practice New York City 1980-82 and 1986-94.

Assistant U.S. Attorney Southern District of New York 1982-86.

Office: 1020 U.S. Courthouse, 500 Pearl Street, New York 10007-1312.

Telephone: (212) 805-0200.

CHOLAKIS, Catherine *(Judge, Rensselaer County Family Court)*

Office: 1504 Fifth Avenue, Troy 12180-4107.

Telephone: (518) 270-3761.

Fax: (518) 272-6573

E-mail address: ccholaki@courts.state.ny.us

CHREIN, Aaron Simon *(Magistrate Judge, United States District Court Eastern District of New York)* Appointed by U.S. District Court judges to term beginning 1976. Chief Magistrate Judge 1988-2000. Educated at University of Pennsylvania Wharton School of Finance and Commerce 1955 and New York University School of Law 1962.

Office: U.S. Courthouse, 225 Cadman Plaza East, Brooklyn 11201.

Telephone: (718) 260-2500.

CHUN, Danny K. *(Judge, The Criminal Court of the City of New York)* Appointed by mayor.
Office: 120 Schermerhorn Street, Brooklyn 11201.
Telephone: (718) 643-8400.
Fax: (718) 643-3538

CICORIA, Ronald A. *(Judge, Livingston County Court)* Also serves Livingston County Surrogate's Court and Livingston County Family Court. Former Acting Justice, New York Supreme Court Seventh Judicial District.
Office: Livingston County Courthouse, Two Court Street, Geneseo 14454-1030.
Telephone: (585) 243-7088.
Fax: (585) 243-7067

CIPARICK, Carmen Beauchamp *(Associate Judge, New York Court of Appeals)* Appointed by Governor Mario Cuomo Dec 1, 1993 to term beginning Jan 4, 1994. First Hispanic to serve on the Court of Appeals. Judge, The Criminal Court of the City of New York 1978-82. Justice, New York Supreme Court First Judicial District 1982-93.
Office: 3700 Chanin Building, 122 East 42nd Street, New York 10168-0002.
Telephone: (212) 661-2144.

CIRIGLIANO, Caesar D. *(Judge, New York Court of Claims)* Appointed by governor. Currently serves as Acting Justice, New York Supreme Court Twelfth Judicial District.
Office: 851 Grand Concourse, Bronx 10451.
Telephone: (718) 590-3673.
Fax: (718) 590-7302

CLAIRE, Judith S. *(Judge, Chautauqua County Family Court)* Elected 1998. Term expires Dec 31, 2008. Born Dec 29, 1950. Educated at University of Massachusetts B.A. 1972 and State University of New York at Buffalo School of Law J.D. 1975. In legal practice 1978-91.
Staff Attorney Health Planning Commission 1976-77. Confidential Assistant and Matrimonial Referee to Hon. Joseph Gerace, New York Supreme Court Eighth Judicial District 1992-98. Member Bar Association of Erie County, Jamestown and New York State Bar Associations. Listed in *Who's Who in American Law* 4th Edition. Member Chautauqua County Commission on Families 1978-98, Soccer Boosters 1991-98, Breast Cancer Support Group 1993-98, Family Services Board 1994-98, Girl Scouts of America 1994-98 and Falconer High School Compact Team 1995-98. Board Member 1983-93 and Chairman 1992-93 Lenna Civic Center. Developed P.E.A.C.E. program (Parent Education and Custody Effectiveness) serving at risk children and their families 1993. Former Member Hospice, Visiting Nurse Association Board and Boys and Girls Club.
Mailing address: P.O. Box 149, Mayville 14757-0149.
Office: Gerace Office Building, Three North Erie Street, Mayville 14757.
Telephone: (716) 753-4351.
Fax: (716) 753-4350

CLANCY, Margaret L. *(Judge, New York Court of Claims)* Appointed by Governor George E. Pataki. Currently serves as Acting Justice, New York Supreme Court Twelfth Judicial District.
Office: 851 Grand Concourse, Bronx 10451.
Telephone: (718) 590-8917.
Fax: (718) 590-8914

CLARK, Darcel D. *(Judge, The Criminal Court of the City of New York)* Appointed by Mayor Rudolph Giuliani.
Office: 215 East 161st Street, Bronx 10451.
Telephone: (718) 590-2927.
Fax: (718) 590-7297

CLARK, Robert F. *(Judge, New York City Family Court)* Appointed by mayor.
Office: 151-20 Jamaica Avenue, Jamaica 11432.
Telephone: (718) 298-0197.

CLEMENTE, Nicholas A. *(Justice, New York Supreme Court Second Judicial District)* Certificated. Currently serves Third Judicial District.
Office: Sullivan County Courthouse, 414 Broadway, Monticello 12071.
Telephone: (845) 794-9776.
E-mail address: nclemente@courts.state.ny.us

CLUTE, Penelope D. *(Judge, Plattsburgh City Court)* Appointed by Plattsburgh City Council to term beginning Jan 3, 2002. Term expires Jan 3, 2012. Born Detroit Michigan Dec 3, 1945. Educated at Michigan State University B.A. cum laude 1967 and Wayne State University J.D. cum laude 1973. Editor Wayne State University Law Review 1972-73. Admitted to practice Michigan 1974, New York 1978 and U.S. District Court Northern District of New York 1978. In legal practice Plattsburgh New York Aug 1978 to Dec 1988.
Staff Attorney Center for the Administration of Justice Wayne State University 1973-76. Hearings Administrator Michigan Department of Corrections 1976-78. District Attorney Clinton County New York Jan 1, 1989 to Dec 31, 2001. Co-author with Paul Bishop "How State and Local Governments Can Economize by Implementing Criminal Justice Standards" American Bar Association 1976. Author *Legal Manual on Parole* 1977 and *Hearing Officer Handbook* 1977 Michigan Department of Corrections, *The Legal Aspects of Prisons and Jails* Chas. C. Thomas & Son 1980, Column "You and the Law" *Senior Sentinel* 1986, Column "What Are My Rights?" *Plattsburgh Press-Republican* March 1986 to Dec 1988, "How Prosecutors Can Make a Difference Pro-Actively Handling Domestic Violence Cases" New York State Bar Journal July/Aug 1994, "Taking the Terror Out of Testifying" New York State Trooper Newsletter Dec 1996 and *Child Sexual Abuse Prosecution Manual* 1992. Adjunct Professor of Administering Corrections Within the Law, Issues and Trends in Corrections, Sociology of Law and The Constitution in Prison State University of New York at Plattsburgh 1978-84. Member New York City Judges Association, Clinton County and American Bar Associations. Trainer/Educator Clinton County Child Abuse Prevention Council 1989-94, The SAFER Program 1992-2001 and Domestic Violence Task Force 1994-2001. Democrat. Paralegal Investigator Mandel Legal Aid Clinic University of Chicago Law School 1968-69. Former Moderator DWI Victim Impact Panels STOP-DWI Program. Enjoys photography, skiing and researching local crime in the nineteenth century.
Office: 41 City Hall Place, Plattsburgh 12901.
Telephone: (518) 563-7870.
Fax: (518) 563-3124
E-mail address: pclute@courts.state.ny.us

COCCOMA, Michael V. *(Judge, Otsego County Court)* Elected to term beginning Jan 1, 1995. Also serves Otsego County Surrogate's Court and Otsego County Family Court.

Office: County Office Building, 197 Main Street, Cooperstown 13326.
Telephone: (607) 547-4212.
Fax: (607) 547-6412

COHALAN, Peter Fox *(Justice, New York Supreme Court Tenth Judicial District)* Elected Nov 1986 to term beginning Jan 1, 1987. Reelected Nov 2000, current term expires Dec 31, 2008. Born Rockville Centre New York Jan 10, 1938. Educated at Manhattan College B.A. 1959 and Fordham University School of Law J.D. 1963. Awarded honorary LL.D. Dowling College 1977 and honorary L.H.D. New York Institute of Technology 1982. Law Clerk to Suffolk County Court 1964. Admitted to practice New York 1964 and U.S. District Court Eastern District of New York 1964. In legal practice Merrick 1964-66, Islip 1966-67 and Sayville 1967-72.

Deputy Town Attorney Islip 1966-67. Lecturer on Municipal Law at various Long Island universities, colleges and high schools over the last 30 years. Former member Nassau County Bar Association. Member Suffolk County (Chairman Municipal Law Committee 1970) and New York State Bar Associations. Recipient Frank C. Moore Award from New York State Government 1974, Tree of Life Award from Jewish National Fund 1985 and Judge of the Year Award from Columbian Lawyers Association of Suffolk County June 1990. Named Man of the Year in Public Administration by C. W. Post College/Long Island University 1976. Town Supervisor Islip 1972-79. County Executive Suffolk County 1980-86. Member Suffolk County Republican Committee 1969-86 and New York State Republican Committee 1973-86. Alternate Delegate 1972 and Delegate 1980 and 1984 Republican National Conventions. Interests include the study of American, British and French history; solving double crostics and *New York Times* crossword puzzles; Italian opera; tennis; and walking.

Office: 235 Griffing Avenue, Riverhead 11901.
Telephone: (631) 852-2395.
Fax: (631) 852-2719

COHEN, Rhoda J. *(Judge, New York City Family Court)* Appointed by mayor.

Office: 60 Lafayette Street, New York 10013.
Telephone: (212) 374-4177.
Fax: (212) 374-2623

COHEN, Robert L. *(Judge, The Criminal Court of the City of New York)* Appointed by mayor. Currently serves as Acting Justice, New York Supreme Court Twelfth Judicial District.

Office: 215 East 161st Street, Bronx 10451.
Telephone: (718) 590-2943.

COIN, Ellen M. *(Judge, The Criminal Court of the City of New York)* Appointed by mayor. Former Judge, The Civil Court of the City of New York.

Office: 100 Centre Street, New York 10013.
Telephone: (212) 374-7350.

COLABELLA, Nicholas *(Justice, New York Supreme Court Ninth Judicial District)* Former Acting Justice. Elected Justice to term beginning Jan 1, 1988. Reelected Nov 2001, current term expires Dec 31, 2015. Also serves as Justice, New York Supreme Court Appellate Term Ninth and Tenth Judicial Districts. Born Bronxville New York May 22, 1936. Roman Catholic. Educated at New York University B.S. 1959 and Albany Law School J.D. 1962. Admitted to practice New York 1962 and U.S. District Courts Eastern 1970 and Southern 1970 Districts of New York. In legal practice Eastchester 1964-82. Justice, Eastchester Town Justice Court 1981-82. Judge, Westchester County Court 1982-87.

Member New York State Association of Magistrates, Association of Justices of the Supreme Court of the State of New York, Buffalo and Westchester County Bar Associations. Attended New York State Judicial Seminars. Member Sons of Italy and Columbus Lawyers. Enjoys golf and reading.

Office: County Courthouse, 111 Dr. Martin Luther King Jr. Blvd., White Plains 10601.
Telephone: (914) 995-4752.

COLANGELO, John P. *(Judge, New Rochelle City Court)*

Office: 475 North Avenue, New Rochelle 10801-3405.
Telephone: (914) 654-2286.

COLE, Robert H., Sr. *(Acting Judge, Corning City Court)*

Office: City Hall, 12 Civic Center Plaza, Corning 14830-2884.
Telephone: (607) 936-4111.

COLEMAN, Cheryl F. *(Judge, Albany City Court)*

Office: 209 City Hall, Eagle and Corning Place, Albany 12207.
Telephone: (518) 434-5034.
Fax: (518) 434-5034

COLLINI, Robert J. *(Judge, New York Court of Claims)* Appointed by Governor George E. Pataki. Currently serves as Acting Justice, New York Supreme Court Second Judicial District.

Office: 120 Schermerhorn Street, Brooklyn 11201.
Telephone: (718) 643-8576.

COLLINS, Francis T. *(Judge, New York Court of Claims)* Appointed by Governor George E. Pataki.

Office: 65 South Broadway, Room 220, Saratoga Springs 12866.
Telephone: (518) 583-5340.
Fax: (518) 583-5345

COLLINS, John P. *(Judge, The Criminal Court of the City of New York)* Appointed by mayor. Currently serves as Acting Justice, New York Supreme Court Twelfth Judicial District. Also serves as Administrative Judge Criminal Term.

Office: 851 Grand Concourse, Bronx 10451.
Telephone: (718) 590-3672.
Fax: (718) 590-8914

CONNELL, John J. *(Judge, Monroe County Court)* Appointed by Governor Mario Cuomo to term beginning May 29, 1984. Elected Nov 1984 and Nov 1994. Current term expires Dec 31, 2004. Born Rochester New York June 25, 1947. Roman Catholic. Educated at Le Moyne College B.A. 1969 and Albany Law School of Union University J.D. 1973. Admitted to practice New York 1974, U.S. District Court 1974 and U.S. Supreme Court 1979. Began legal practice Schenectady 1974.

Chief Assistant District Attorney Schenectady County Feb 1974 to July 1976. Assistant District Attorney July 1976 to May 1984 and Second Assistant District Attor-

CONNELL, JOHN J.—*Continued*
ney Jan 1982 to May 1984 Monroe County. Important Decisions: People v. Lomack (confession) March 1985 and Matter of Grand Jury of Monroe County 130 Misc. 2d 505. Instructor Regional Police Training Academy 1976-86. Member New York State District Attorneys Association, National District Attorneys Association, American Judicature Society, Monroe County, New York State and American Bar Associations. Democrat. Member Rochester Museum and Science Center, Landmark Society and Ancient Order of Hibernians. Enjoys sports and scuba diving.
Office: 545 Hall of Justice, 99 Exchange Boulevard, Rochester 14614-2186.
Telephone: (585) 428-2422.
Fax: (585) 428-3538

CONNER, William C. *(Senior Judge, United States District Court Southern District of New York)* Appointed for life by President Richard M. Nixon to term beginning Jan 4, 1974. Assumed Senior status April 1, 1987, serves by assignment. Born Wichita Falls Texas March 27, 1920. Presbyterian. Educated at University of Texas B.B.A. 1941 LL.B. 1942. Editor Texas Law Review. Recipient McKie Scholarship. Admitted to practice Texas 1942 and New York 1950. In legal practice New York City 1946-73.
Board of Editors *Manual for Complex Litigation* since 1976. Member New York Patent Law Association (President 1972-73) and American Judicature Society. Recipient Jefferson Medal from New Jersey Patent Law Association 1975. Lieutenant USNR 1942-45. Republican. Member St. Andrews Golf Club. Enjoys golf and amateur radio.
Office: U.S. Courthouse, 300 Quarropas Street, White Plains 10601-4150.
Telephone: (914) 390-4166.

CONNERTON, Mary Rita *(Judge, Broome County Family Court)*
Mailing address: P.O. Box 1766, Binghamton 13902-1766.
Office: 65 Hawley Street, Binghamton 13901.
Telephone: (607) 778-6074.
Fax: (607) 778-2439

CONNOR, John G. *(Justice, New York Supreme Court Third Judicial District)* Elected Nov 1981 to term beginning Jan 1, 1982. Reelected 1996. Certificated. Born Albany New York June 24, 1931. Catholic. Educated at St. Michael's College and Albany Law School LL.B. 1957. Admitted to practice New York 1958 and U.S. District Courts Northern 1975 and Southern 1975 Districts of New York. In legal practice Hudson 1958-82.
District Attorney Columbia County 1965-68. Important Decisions: MTR Con Ed v. Public Service (freedom of expression first amendment—the right to refrain from speaking) 127 Misc. 2d 1085 April 1985 and Quirk v. Regan (lag payroll of government employee held as unconstitutional) 148 Misc. 2d 300 Jan 1991. U.S. Army 1952-54. Enjoys piano and organ jazz.
Office: 20 Columbia County Courthouse, 401 Union Street, Hudson 12534.
Telephone: (518) 828-3079.

COOK, Frank S. *(Judge, Oneida County Family Court)*
Office: Oneida County Courthouse, 200 Elizabeth Street, Utica 13501.
Telephone: (315) 798-5926.
Fax: (315) 798-6422

COONEY, Joan O. *(Judge, Westchester County Family Court)* Also serves as Supervising Judge Family Courts Ninth Judicial District.
Office: 111 Dr. Martin Luther King Jr. Blvd., White Plains 10601.
Telephone: (914) 995-6347.
Fax: (914) 995-4675

COOPER, Alfred D., Sr. *(Judge, Nassau County District Court)*
Office: 99 Main Street, Hempstead 11550.
Telephone: (516) 572-2122.
E-mail address: adcooper@courts.state.ny.us

COOPER, Matthew F. *(Judge, The Civil Court of the City of New York)* Currently assigned to The Criminal Court of the City of New York.
Office: 100 Centre Street, New York 10013.
Telephone: (212) 374-5834.

COOPERMAN, Arthur J. *(Justice, New York Supreme Court Eleventh Judicial District)* Elected Nov 1982 to term beginning Jan 1, 1983. Reelected Nov 1996, current term expires Dec 31, 2003. Born Bronx New York. Educated at New York University B.A. 1955 LL.B. 1960. Admitted to practice New York 1960. Judge, The Civil Court of the City of New York 1980-82.
Member Queens County Bar Association. First Lieutenant U.S. Army Signal Corps 1955-57. Member New York State Assembly 1969-79.
Office: 125-01 Queens Boulevard, Kew Gardens 11415.
Telephone: (718) 520-3497.
E-mail address: acooperm@courts.state.ny.us

COPERTINO, John *(Justice, New York Supreme Court Tenth Judicial District)* Elected to term beginning Jan 1, 1988. Certificated. Born New York New York Dec 10, 1928. Catholic. Educated at City College of the City University of New York B.S. 1950 and Fordham University LL.B. 1955. Admitted to practice New York 1955, U.S. District Courts for Eastern 1957 and Southern 1957 Districts of New York, U.S. Supreme Court 1959 and U.S. Court of Appeals Second Circuit 1962. Began legal practice New York City 1955. In legal practice Woodside 1956, Selden 1956-63 and Setauket 1964-67. Judge, Suffolk County District Court 1969-77. Judge, Suffolk County Court Jan 1, 1978 to Dec 31, 1987. Former Associate Justice, New York Supreme Court Appellate Division Second Judicial Department, appointed by Governor George E. Pataki.
Assistant District Attorney Feb 1962 to July 1964 and April 1967 to Dec 1968. Important Decisions: People v. Mancuso 59 Misc. 2d 941, 1969; People v. Cannistra 60 Misc. 2d 559, 1969; People v. Rosgaard 61 Misc. 2d 151, 1969; People v. O'Donnell 61 Misc. 2d 194, 1969; People v. Hariton 61 Misc. 2d 209, 1969; People v. Dionne 61 Misc. 2d 211, 1969; People v. Mackey 61 Misc. 2d 799, 1969; People v. East Island News Corporation 61 Misc. 2d 923, 1969; People v. Simonetti 62 Misc. 2d 285, 1969; People v. Creighton 71 Misc. 2d

COPERTINO, JOHN—*Continued*

370, 1972; Palagonia v. Pappas 79 Misc. 2d 830, 1974; Estates Roofing Co., Inc. v. Savo 85 Misc. 2d 1028, 1976; People v. Seymour 104 Misc. 2d 482, 1980; People v. Angelillo 105 Misc. 2d 338, 1980; People v. Trocchio 107 Misc. 2d 610, 1980; People v. Armioia 109 Misc. 2d 1038, 1981; People v. Lucarano 111 Misc. 2d 661, 1981; People v. Doe 110 Misc. 2d 595, 1981; Bay Pasture Co. v. Schwartz 116 Misc. 2d 48, 1982; People v. Pasciuto 122 Misc. 2d 158, 1983; People v. Troiano 127 Misc. 2d 738, 1985; People ex rel Kinkade v. Finnerty 128 Misc. 2d 515, 1985; Matter of Michalski v. Noah Home Improvement 128 Misc. 2d 901, 1985; People v. Russo and Stony Brook Systems, Inc. 128 Misc. 2d 876, N.Y.S.2d 276 1985; People v. Davis 130 Misc. 2d 681, 1985; People v. Abney 135 Misc. 2d. 797, 516 N.Y.S.2d 578; and People v. Greene 137 Misc. 2d 771, 522 N.Y.S.2d 752. Adjunct Instructor in Business Law Suffolk County Community College 1975-76. Member Suffolk County Columbian Lawyers Association, Suffolk County Magistrates Association, American Justinian Society of Jurists, National District Attorneys Association, Suffolk County, New York State and American Bar Associations. Special Agent U.S. Army Counterintelligence Corps 1951-53. Republican. Charter member Dr. Vincent Sellar's Lodge Sons of Italy. Member Selden-Coram Lions Club 1957-64, Selden Post 1633 American Legion 1957-68, Sacred Heart Council 4402 Knights of Columbus 1957-70 (Charter Advocate 1957), Port Jefferson Lodge 2138 Elks 1959-72 (Charter Justice Subordinate), Lions Club of the Setaukets since 1964 (President 1969-70), UNICO Brookhaven Chapter 1977 and Coalition of Italian-Americans Association 1966.

Office: 4 Court Complex, 210 Center Drive, Riverhead 11901.
Telephone: (631) 852-1969
Fax: (631) 852-1546

CORBETT, Donald J., Jr. *(Judge, New York Court of Claims)* Appointed by Governor Mario M. Cuomo to term beginning July 6, 1983. Reappointed Dec 30, 1985 and Dec 1994. Current term expires Dec 31, 2003. Former Presiding Judge. Born Rochester New York April 2, 1936. Roman Catholic. Educated at University of Notre Dame B.A. 1958 and Albany Law School of Union University LL.B. 1961 J.D. 1968. Admitted to practice New York 1961, U.S. District Court Western District of New York 1963, U.S. Supreme Court 1966 and U.S. Tax Court 1973. Began legal practice Rochester 1961. Judge Jan 1, 1975 to July 12, 1983 and Administrative Judge 1976-83, Monroe County Family Court.

Chairman Family Court Rules and Advisory Committee Administrative Board New York State. Member Monroe County, New York State (Member Technical Advisory Committee on Juvenile Justice) and American (Delegate to National Conference of Special Court Judges Judicial Administration Division 1980-82) Bar Associations. Member 1976 and Chairman 1977-83 Family Court Advisory and Rules Committee Administrative Board New York State. Member and Vice Chairman Temporary State Commission to Recodify the Family Court Act. Chairman Departmental Advisory Committee for Operation of Law Guardian Panels (Fourth Department). Former member Independent Review Board New York State Division for Youth. Member Mental Health Advisory Committee on Children and Youth New York State. Recipient Hannah G. Solomon Award for Humanitarian Service 1978. Democrat. Past President Monroe County Travelers Aid Society. Former Chairman Rochester Housing Authority. Former Vice President Boys Club of Rochester. Consultant to National Adoption Listing Service. Treasurer and member Board of Directors Action for Child Protection.

Office: 500 Court Exchange Building, 144 Exchange Boulevard, Rochester 14614-2108.
Telephone: (585) 262-4100.
Fax: (585) 325-3421
E-mail address: djcorb@frontiernet.net

CORDOVA, Alma *(Judge, New York City Family Court)* Appointed by mayor.

Office: 900 Sheridan Avenue, Bronx 10451.
Telephone: (718) 590-3376.
Fax: (718) 590-7305

CORNELIUS, Raymond E. *(Justice, New York Supreme Court Seventh Judicial District)* Elected to term beginning Jan 1, 1986. Reelected Nov 1999, current term expires Dec 31, 2013. Born Rochester New York Nov 20, 1936. Presbyterian. Educated at Harpur College State University of New York at Binghamton B.A. 1959 and University of Michigan Law School J.D. 1962. Admitted to practice New York 1963, U.S. District Court Western District of New York 1964, U.S. Supreme Court 1972 and Florida 1973. In legal practice Rochester New York 1962-65. Judge, Monroe County Family Court 1978-85.

Assistant District Attorney Monroe County 1965-77. Member Association of Justices of the Supreme Court of the State of New York (Co-chair Education Committee 1992-94 and 1995-96), Seventh Judicial District Supreme Court Justices Association (President 1991) and Monroe County Bar Association (Member and Dean-Elect Academy of Law Committee). Participant Judicial Seminars New York State Office of Court Administration 1982, 1989, 1993, 1994 and 2001. Lecturer Evidence Seminar 1996, Article 81 Mental Hygiene Law Seminar 1998 and Jury Selection Seminar 2002 Monroe County Bar Association. Member Rotary International (Past President Pittsford Club, Paul Harris Fellow).

Office: 509 Hall of Justice, Rochester 14614-2185.
Telephone: (585) 428-5487.
Fax: (585) 428-2987
E-mail address: recornel@courts.state.ny.us

CORNING, Peter E. *(Judge, Cayuga County Court)* Also serves Cayuga County Family Court.

Office: Courthouse, Third Floor, 154 Genesee Street, Auburn 13021-3435.
Telephone: (315) 255-4306.

CORRIERO, Michael A. *(Judge, New York Court of Claims)* Appointed by governor. Currently serves as Acting Justice, New York Supreme Court First Judicial District. Former Judge, The Criminal Court of the City of New York.

Office: 111 Centre Street, New York 10013.
Telephone: (212) 374-7155.
Fax: (212) 748-5080

CORTESE, Philip V. *(Judge, Montgomery County Family Court)*

Mailing address: P.O. Box 1500, Fonda 12068-1500.
Office: Montgomery County Courthouse, 58 Broadway, Fonda 12068.

CORTESE, PHILIP V.—*Continued*
Telephone: (518) 853-8135.
Fax: (518) 853-8148

COSGROVE, Nelson H. *(Justice, New York Supreme Court Eighth Judicial District)*
Office: Erie County Hall, 92 Franklin Street, Buffalo 14202-2721.
Telephone: (716) 851-3271.
Fax: (716) 851-4696
E-mail address: ncosgrove@courts.state.ny.us

COSTELLO, Ralph F. *(Justice, New York Supreme Court Tenth Judicial District)* Former Judge, Suffolk County District Court.
Office: 312 Supreme Court Building, 235 Griffing Avenue, Riverhead 11901.
Telephone: (631) 852-2422.
Fax: (631) 852-2779

COTE, Denise *(Judge, United States District Court Southern District of New York)* Appointed for life by President Bill Clinton to term beginning 1994. Born St. Cloud Minnesota Oct 13, 1946. Educated at St. Mary's College B.A. 1968 and Columbia University M.A. 1969 J.D. 1975. Law Clerk to Hon. Jack B. Weinstein, U.S. District Court Eastern District of New York 1975-76. In legal practice New York City 1976-77 and 1985-91.
Assistant U.S. Attorney 1977-85 and Chief Criminal Division 1991-94 Southern District of New York.
Office: 1040 U.S. Courthouse, 500 Pearl Street, New York 10007-1312.
Telephone: (212) 805-0202.

COTTER, Daniel J. *(Judge, Nassau County Court)* Elected to term beginning Jan 1, 1995.
Office: Nassau County Courthouse, 262 Old Country Road, Mineola 11501.
Telephone: (516) 571-2331.
Fax: (516) 571-2160

COVELLO, Joseph *(Justice, New York Supreme Court Tenth Judicial District)* Former Judge, Nassau County District Court, elected to term beginning Jan 1, 1995.
Office: Supreme Court Building, 100 Supreme Court Drive, Mineola 11501.
Telephone: (516) 571-3895.

COWHEY, James R. *(Justice, New York Supreme Court Ninth Judicial District)* Elected Nov 1987 to term beginning Jan 1, 1988. Certificated. Born Richmond County New York Jan 4, 1930. Educated at Wagner College 1947-49 and Brooklyn Law School LL.B. 1951. Admitted to practice New York, U.S. Supreme Court 1958 and U.S. District Courts Eastern and Southern Districts of New York. Began legal practice New York City 1951. In legal practice White Plains 1954-60. Judge, Westchester County Court Jan 1, 1981 to Dec 31, 1987.
Assistant District Attorney Westchester County 1960-75. Legal Secretary to Hon. George Beisheim, Jr., New York Supreme Court Ninth Judicial District 1976-80. Member New York State District Attorneys Association, Northern Westchester, White Plains, Westchester County and New York State Bar Associations. Attended College Law Enforcement Institute. U.S. Army Intelligence Corps and 101st Airborne Division 1951-53. With Home Title Guaranty Company (now Chicago Title Insurance Company) White Plains 1953-54. Former volunteer defense attorney for Westchester County Bar Association and Legal Aid Society 1956-60. Area Chairman for United Fund, Heart Fund, American Cancer Society (Westchester Division) and Cancer Fund. Member Battle Hill Association of White Plains, American Legion (Past Judge Advocate Post 135), Elks and Church of Saints John and Mary.
Office: County Courthouse, 111 Dr. Martin Luther King Jr. Blvd., White Plains 10601.
Telephone: (914) 995-4313.
Fax: (914) 995-4182

COZIER, Barry A. *(Associate Justice, New York Supreme Court Appellate Division Second Judicial Department)* Elected Justice Second Judicial District to term beginning Jan 1, 1993. Appointed Associate Justice Appellate Division by Governor George E. Pataki March 2001. Deputy Chief Administrative Judge New York City Courts Jan 1994 to Dec 1995 and New York State Courts Jan 1996 to Dec 1997. Born New York New York July 19, 1951. Educated at State University of New York at Stony Brook B.A. magna cum laude 1971 and New York University School of Law J.D. 1975. Admitted to practice New York 1976, U.S. District Courts Eastern 1976 and Southern 1976 Districts of New York and U.S. Supreme Court 1979. In legal practice Brooklyn 1976-80 and New York City 1982-86. Judge and Hearing Examiner, New York City Family Court Dec 1986 to Dec 1992.
Associate General Counsel Family Law Litigation Office of Legal Affairs Human Resources Administration City of New York Jan 1980 to Oct 1981. Author Chapter "Summary Judgment" *Commercial Litigation in New York State Court* West. Adjunct Professor of Juvenile Justice Survey Fordham University School of Law. Member Alternative Dispute Resolution Advisory Committee New York State Unified Court System. Member New York County Lawyers' Association, New York State Judicial Council, Federal Judicial Council, Metropolitan Black Bar Association, The Association of the Bar of the City of New York (Executive Committee 1998-2002), Brooklyn and National Bar Associations. Recipient Wayne E. Scarborough Award from New York City Association of Criminal Court Judges, Distinguished Alumni Award from New York University School of Law, Golda Meir Award from Jewish Lawyers Guild and Chairman's Award from Manhattan Advisory Board New York Urban League. Board of Directors Covenant House 1993-99 and Law Alumni Association, Inc. New York University School of Law since 1996. Enjoys jogging, jazz and African-American art.
Office: 140 Grand Street, Suite 503, White Plains 10601.
Telephone: (914) 328-5066.
Fax: (914) 328-5946
E-mail address: bcozier@courts.state.ny.us

COZZENS, R. Bruce, Jr. *(Justice, New York Supreme Court Tenth Judicial District)* Elected Nov 1997 to term beginning Jan 1, 1998. Term expires Dec 31, 2011. Born Buffalo New York Feb 12, 1949. Episcopalian. Educated at University of Virginia B.A. 1971 and Pace University J.D. 1980. Admitted to practice New York 1981, U.S. District Courts Eastern 1984 and Southern 1984 Districts of New York and U.S. Supreme Court 1997. In legal practice Mineola 1981-97.
Member Bar Association of Nassau County and American Bar Association (Judicial Division). Seminar

COZZENS, R. BRUCE, JR.—*Continued*

Instructor Bar Association of Nassau County and New York State Bar Association. Member Nassau County Industrial Development Agency 1991-97 and Town of Oyster Bay Zoning Board 1997.

Office: Supreme Court Building, 100 Supreme Court Drive, Mineola 11501.

Telephone: (516) 571-2484.

Fax: (516) 571-1575

E-mail address: bcozzens@courts.state.ny.us

CRAIG, Carla E. *(Judge, United States Bankruptcy Court Eastern District of New York)* Appointed by U.S. Court of Appeals Second Circuit judges to term beginning Feb 28, 2000. Term expires Feb 2014.

Office: 75 Clinton Street, Brooklyn 11201-4201.

Telephone: (718) 330-2188.

CRANE, Stephen G. *(Associate Justice, New York Supreme Court Appellate Division Second Judicial Department)* Acting Justice Jan 1984 to Feb 1989. Appointed Justice First Judicial District by Governor Mario Cuomo to term beginning March 21, 1989. Elected 1989. Appointed Associate Justice Appellate Division by Governor George E. Pataki March 23, 2001. Term expires Dec 31, 2003. Administrative Judge Civil Branch July 1996 to March 22, 2001. Born Mount Vernon New York Oct 5, 1938. Educated at Cornell University School of Industrial and Labor Relations B.S. 1960 LL.B. with distinction 1963 replaced by J.D. Recipient Williams Press Official Reports Award and Law Week Award. Member Kosmos, Moot Court, Pi Delta Epsilon and Phi Delta Phi. Admitted to practice New York 1963, U.S. District Courts Southern 1963 and Eastern 1964 Districts of New York, U.S. Court of Appeals Second Circuit 1972 and U.S. Supreme Court 1974. In legal practice New York City 1963-66 and 1980-81. Judge, The Criminal Court of the City of New York March 1981 to March 1989, appointed by Mayor Edward I. Koch.

Senior Law Assistant Sept 1966 to Dec 1976 and Chief Law Assistant Dec 1976 to May 1979 to New York Supreme Court Appellate Division First Judicial Department. Counsel to Office of Court Administration May 1979 to Nov 1980. Co-author with David Curtis *Dayan, a Pictorial Biography* Citadel Press 1967 and with James V. Sullivan "Legal Aspects of Common Real Estate Transactions" Baruch College 1972. Author "The Adequacy of Costs Allowable in Litigation" Sixteenth Annual Report of the Judicial Conference 246, 1971 reprinted New York L. Jour. Feb 22, 23 and 24, 1971; "Litigating Parallel Civil and Criminal Actions" *Bill of Particulars* New York State Trial Lawyers Association Sept 1985; "Constructive Knowledge Under *People v. Bartolomeo*" *The Panelist* Office of Projects Development, Appellate Division First Department Winter 1985-86; "City's Courthouses: Attention Must Be Paid" New York L. Jour. 2 May 6, 1992; "Deteriorating Court Facilities and Their Impact on Justice" Bill of Particulars New York State Trial Lawyers Association June 1993; book review "Commercial Litigation in New York State Courts"; and Perspective "Case Management: Changing the Culture" New York L. Jour. 2 c. 3-4 Dec 4, 1997. Editor-in-Chief Robert L. Haig *New York County Lawyer* Feb/March 1996. Adjunct Associate Professor of Real Property Transactions and Securities Markets and Regulation Bernard M. Baruch College of the City University of New York 1969-78. Instructor Seminars on Judicial Practice and Ethics Benjamin N. Cardozo School of Law 1985-91 and since 1993.

Important Decisions 1981-83: People v. Reid (filing of prosecutor's information changing theory of misdemeanor prosecution vitiates exclusions from statutory speedy trial time applicable to former pleading) 110 Misc. 2d 1083, 443 N.Y.S.2d 600, 1981; People v. Joseph W. F. (unsealing of transcript sealed after acquittal will not be granted to assist complainant in civil suit against defendant for same transaction) 111 Misc. 2d 752, 444 N.Y.S.2d 1007, 1981; People v. Brown (lookout for three card Monte game who never possessed the cards can nevertheless be charged with accessorial liability for promoting gambling and possessing gambling devices) 112 Misc. 2d 471, 447 N.Y.S.2d 129, 1982; People v. Parris (prosecutor's failure to plead essential elements of a crime is a nonwaivable jurisdictional defect that cannot be cured by amendment under CPL 200.70 and that can be raised beyond the deadline for an omnibus motion under CPL Article 255) 113 Misc. 2d 1066, 450 N.Y.S.2d 721, 1982; Matter of District Council No. 9 v. Metropolitan Transportation Authority (competitive bidding required for contracts to paint subway stations by a not-for-profit corporation rehabilitating the chronic unemployable) 115 Misc. 2d 810, 454 N.Y.S.2d 663, 1982 aff'd 92 A.D.2d 791 leave to appeal granted 93 A.D.2d 787 1983; Stylianides v. DeLorean Co. (no cause of action is stated for damage to an employee's reputation because of scandal surrounding financial collapse of employer; benefit granting motion by president of employer to dismiss the cause of action for insufficiency will be given to non-moving co-defendant, the employer) 115 Misc. 2d 861, 454 N.Y.S.2d 799, 1982; People v. Florentino (antifraud provisions of Martin act applied for the first time to trading by an insider-fiduciary on nonpublic information; this application not unconstitutional) 116 Misc. 2d 692, 456 N.Y.S.2d 638, 1982; Taylor v. Eli Haddad Corp. (upholding sufficiency of causes of action under Loft Law, discussing its constitutionality and resolving numerous procedural and substantive claims often arising thereunder including the rejection of claims for attorney's fees under Real Prop. Law §234) 118 Misc. 2d 253, 460 N.Y.S.2d 886, 1983; Fort Tryon Nursing Home v. Kavanaugh (finding law office failure in a default in not answering a motion until the return date in violation of CPLR 2214b) 118 Misc. 2d 320, 460 N.Y.S.2d 473, 1983; and People v. Twine (analyzing the nature of a new misdemeanor information filed after 90 days to correct the place of occurrence and rejecting a statutory speedy trial challenge to new pleading) 121 Misc. 2d 762, 468 N.Y.S.2d 559, 1983.

Important Decisions 1984-85: People v. Walden (rejecting the application of a title theory under the Uniform Commercial Code in a robbery prosecution involving larceny of the item whose title might have passed to the defendant) 124 Misc. 2d 615, 478 N.Y.S.2d 501, 1984; People v. Garcia (discussing the interaction in a gun possession case of a motion to dismiss in furtherance of justice) 126 Misc. 2d 579, 482 N.Y.S.2d 996, 1984; People v. Rakusz (holding that defendant can be found criminally responsible for a police officer's injury sustained while defendant, resisting arrest, tried to put his hand in his own pocket where the officer, who reached in first, cut his finger on a knife) 127 Misc. 2d 1, 484 N.Y.S.2d 784, 1985; People v. Cox (dismissing an indictment for a technical failure of corroboration in

CRANE, STEPHEN G.—*Continued*

the grand jury but upholding geographical jurisdiction of prosecution for bribing a witness in Florida to induce him to refrain from testifying in New York) 127 Misc. 2d 336, 486 N.Y.S.2d 143, 1985; People v. Jose C. (authorizing resubmission to the grand jury of charges it had previously dismissed because it had misperceived the law and thereby failed to give a fair and impartial investigation) 127 Misc. 2d 689, 487 N.Y.S.2d 499, 1985; People v. Nuzzi (disqualifying the D.A. and appointing a special prosecutor where defendant's first cousin was as assistant in the district attorney's office on the ground that if the district attorney were to prosecute it would project an image of impropriety even though defendant could demonstrate no prejudice) 128 Misc. 2d 502, 489 N.Y.S.2d 836 vacated sub. nom. Morgenthau v. Crane 113 AD 2d 20; People v. Matthew Scala (upholding the qualifications of a clinical certified social worker with psychotherapeutic training and forensic experience to examine a defendant in connection with a plea of not responsible by reason of mental disease or defect and to render an opinion and testify as to dangerousness following acceptance of the plea) 128 Misc. 2d 831, 491 N.Y.S.2d 555; 83rd Street Tenants, Inc. v. Brandywynne (invalidating service in Switzerland by mail as appropriate service under CPLR 313—even though such service was valid as personal service in Switzerland it did not constitute personal service in accordance with New York law) 130 Misc. 2d 590, 496 N.Y.S.2d 888, 1985; and Levess v. Celebrity Knitwear (discussing a gap in the CPLR that permitted a Sheriff to levy on a judgment debtor's bank accounts, thus incurring poundage and fees, which the judgment debtor was required to pay as a condition to releasing the judgment lien on these accounts when the debtor tardily posted an undertaking on appeal) 130 Misc. 2d 1055, 498 N.Y.S.2d 974.

Important Decisions 1986: Finkelstein v. Bishins (clarifying the purpose of CPLR Article 54 and transmuting a motion erroneously brought thereunder into one for partial summary judgment enforcing that part of a Florida divorce decree that awarded to the wife shares to a cooperative apartment in New York) 131 Misc. 2d 314, 499 N.Y.S.2d 319; Mandel v. Grunfeld (denying leave to amend a complaint to assert new causes of action in a law firm dissolution, that had already been asserted in a pending federal action) N.Y.L.J 1 and 12 Jan 7, 1986; Borgeest v. Canandaigua National Bank & Trust Co. (granting a preliminary injunction against a bank from adversely reporting on plaintiff's credit for refusing to begin payments on his guaranteed student loans because the bank had refused without excuse to certify the balance due when plaintiff attempted to refinance at terms more favorable to plaintiff that had been offered by the Federal Student Loan Marketing Association) 7 *New York Law Journal* Jan 9, 1986; Hirth v. 25-26 East Owners Corp. (granting preliminary injunctive relief in favor of a cooperative tenant enforcing house rules to require an upstairs neighbor to carpet the floors and curb her dog) 12 N.Y.L.J. Jan 22, 1986; Matter of Ares—Abrams (upholding a tenant group challenge to a "red herring" plan of cooperative conversion based on the failure of the Attorney General to consider the detailed tenant specifications before allowing the plan to become effective) N.Y.L.J. 1 and 12 c. 1 Jan 23, 1986; and People v. Bernhard Goetz (dismissed counts charging attempted murder and related crimes due to erroneous instructions to the grand jury concerning the defense of justification and due to post-indictment developments that undermined confidence in the basis for indictment) 131 Misc. 2d 1, N.Y.S.2d aff'd 116 AD 2d 316 reversed 68 N.Y. 2d 96, 1986.

Important Decisions 1987: People v. Bernhard Goetz (holding that a missing witness charge is appropriate when the witness becomes unavailable by invoking his Fifth Amendment privilege where the prosecutor procured this unavailability by withholding immunity solely for purposes of trial strategy) 135 Misc. 2d 888, 516 N.Y.S.2d 1007, 1987; People v. Eddie Hernandez (detailing the procedure at a hearing to controvert opinions of a defendant's fitness to stand trial and imposing on defendant a burden of going forward to attack the presumption of competence) N.Y.L.J. 13 c. 1 April 15, 1987 and N.Y.L.J. 1, 13 c. 4 April 24, 1987; People v. Kelvin Davis (denying the prosecutor's motion to strike notice of a defense of not responsible by reason of mental disease or defect but requiring defendant to turn over his mental health expert's notes and any report he may put in writing, calling on legislature to enact procedures for greater cooperation in the exchange of information when this defense is raised) 136 Misc. 2d 1076, 519 N.Y.S.2d 776, 1987; People v. Bernhard Goetz (denying the district attorney's motion to permit his presentence memorandum to be made public and calling on the Chief Judge to adopt standards guiding trial judges in regulating publicity by the attorneys and litigants during the pendency of the case) New York L. Jour. 17 c. 2 Oct 19, 1987; People v. Bernhard Goetz (outlining sentencing considerations under the 1980 gun law and explaining how a sentence of other than one year may be imposed if it is equally severe without the need for finding that a one year sentence would be unduly harsh) 137 Misc. 2d 380, 520 N.Y.S.2d 919, 1987, modified 141 A.D.2d 466, affirmed N.Y.2d 1988; and Matter of Saferstein v. Wendy (establishing guides in determining an application for a preliminary injunction in aid of arbitration authorized by a recent enactment CPLR 7502 c) 137 Misc. 2d 1032, 523 N.Y.S.2d 725, 1987.

Important Decisions 1988-90: People v. John Gaston (holding that due diligence to secure the presence of defendant is still required for the prosecution to exclude periods of a defendant's absence on a bench warrant for statutory speedy trial purposes) N.Y.L.J. 1 and 13 c. 3 March 22, 1988; Drexel Burnham Lambert, Inc. v. Ruebsamen (denying an attachment in aid of arbitration which is limited to the ground that this provisional remedy is necessary to prevent rendering the award ineffectual and is unavailable on the ground of the non-domicile of respondents) 138 Misc. 2d 884, 525 N.Y.S.2d 184, 1988, affirmed on other grounds 139 A.D.2d 323; People v. John Nelson and Guillermo Rafael Tejada (determining two motions by prosecutors to vacate their defaults, granting one and denying the other and establishing standards to relieve a district attorney from the consequences of failing to respond to a defendant's motion) 1988; People v. Stanley Evans (rejecting the application by the Police Department to vacate an order requiring it to furnish defendant an auto crime expert to examine motor vehicles, the subjects of his arson prosecution, on due process grounds because the Police Department has a monopoly of such expertise which is necessary to his defense) 141 Misc. 2d 781, 534 N.Y.S.2d 640 N.Y.L.J. 25 c. 1 Nov 25, 1988; People v.

CRANE, STEPHEN G.—*Continued*

David Woods and Jerry Mason (dismissing one indictment and upholding another from attack based on bifurcated presentation of charges or instructions under People v. Cade 140 A.D.2d 99 and People v. Wilkins 68 N.Y.2d 269) N.Y.L.J. 22 c. 5 Feb 22, 1989; Matter of Suson MABSTOA (permitting late notice of claim to be filed where respondent had received timely actual notice in an improper form) N.Y.L.J. 24 c. 3 May 5, 1989; Matter of Cotter v. Shearson Lehman Hutton (denying judicial enforcement of subpoenas served in arbitration proceeding on ground that petitioners had elected a remedy to rely on the arbitrators to enforce their subpoenas, and if the arbitrators possess enforcement power, CPLR 2308(b) requires the court to defer to the arbitration tribunal) 145 Misc. 2d 235, 546 N.Y.S.2d 319 Sept 29, 1989 N.Y.L.J. 22 c. 3 Nov 7, 1989; People v. Carrasquillo (holding that no notice pursuant to CPL 710.30 is required for the people to prove a prompt procedure whereby an undercover officer confirms that the back-up team has arrested the correct person) N.Y.L.J. 1 and 27 c. 4 Dec 11, 1989; People v. Jorge Martinez (suppressing cocaine because an anonymous radio communication of a man with a gun two and a half hours earlier ten blocks away failed to support the required justification which was not enriched because defendant wore the same color jacket and the officer saw a bulge in its pocket not perceived to be a gun) N.Y.L.J. 25 c. 3 Dec 26, 1989; Matter of Cowen & Co.—Lasry & Schaeffer (granting sanctions for a frivolous motion where the movant was unreasonable in ignoring the true state of facts thereby establishing a constructive intent to delay resolution of the underlying controversy) N.Y.L.J. 21 and 28 c. 8 May 14, 1990; People v. Herbert Rivera (suppressing a loaded firearm where the police lacked sufficient justification to ask defendant to stand and to touch the undefined bulge in the front of his pants) N.Y.L.J. 19 c. 2 Aug 15, 1990; and People v. Shimkon Batashure (denying 30.30 speedy trial dismissal for the People's appellate delay because defendant consented to it by failing to move to dismiss the appeal for lack of prosecution or to oppose their application to enlarge their time to perfect the appeal sought eight and one-half months after the filing deadline) N.Y.L.J. 23 c. 1 Nov 8, 1990.

Important Decisions 1991-92: People v. Edward Suarez (dismissing a drug prosecution in the interest of justice where the defendant, a homeless man with a positive HIV test, had sold a single codeine tablet and a single glutethmide pill to an undercover officer, but had not, unlike prior cases of dismissals in favor of defendants with AIDS, become terminally ill) N.Y.L.J. 22 c. 4 Feb 1, 1991; People v. Muneer Hussein and Bassam Ayoub (denying dismissal of an indictment for failure to voir dire the grand jurors regarding their bias in the Palestinian-Israeli conflict and their exposure to publicity over the demonstration at the Israeli mission during which the arrests occurred, because the defendants could not prove prejudice or special circumstances) 150 Misc. 2d 119, 568 N.Y.S.2d 296 March 14, 1991; People v. Gega (interpreting the new procedure to inspect grand jury minutes and reduce the charge; holding that the prosecutor may change a choice to appeal or re-present to a second grand jury within 30 days subject to extension for good cause) 151 Misc. 2d 70, 580 N.Y.S.2d 639 Jan 28, 1992; People v. Lucas Gonzalez (suppressing line up identifications because the homeless fillers were markedly different in grooming in comparison to defendant and a photographic procedure that preceded these line ups was unduly suggestive inasmuch as defendant's photo appeared twice in the mug books) N.Y.L.J. 26 c. 1 May 12, 1992; The Dormitory Authority of the State of New York v. The Gruzen Partnership (deciding, for the first time, that the Dormitory Authority is entitled to a trial preference pursuant to CPLR 3404 (a)(1) as a "board of officers of the State" and explaining the meaning of this phrase) Misc. 2d N.Y.S.2d N.Y.L.J. 30 c. 3 July 7, 1992; Agin v. Krest Associates (interpreting new provisions of CPLR 310 for service of process on partnerships as supplementing the earlier procedure for serving partners under CPLR 308) 157 Misc. 2d 994, 599 N.Y.S.2d 367, 1992; and Morgenthau v. Clifford and Altman (action to forfeit proceeds of a crime pursuant to CPLR Article 13-A, this decision clarified the concept of "proceeds" and interpreted the recent enactment authorizing release of attached proceeds to pay for retaining counsel in the forfeiture action and the related criminal prosecution) 157 Misc. 2d 331, 597 N.Y.S.2d 843, 1992.

Important Decisions Jan 1993 to May 1993: Waterside Tenants Association v. Waterside Redevelopment Co. (invalidating parking garage increases for Mitchell-Lama housing tenants in the absence of regulations governing applications by owners for such increases) N.Y.L.J. 22 c. 5 Jan 20, 1993; Sony Corporation of America v. Cabasso (excluding from the attorney-client privilege information as to the source of funds paid by a client into the attorney's escrow account) N.Y.L.J. 30 c. 6 Feb 19, 1993; Matter of Shearson Lehman Brothers, Inc. (Rinzler) (denying a stay of arbitration of a customer's loss claim, although barred by limitations, because petitioner had just succeeded in a related action in compelling the very arbitration it now sought to stay, thus relegating the time bar defense to the arbitrators) 156 Misc. 2d 773, 594 N.Y.S.2d. 593, 1993; Matter of Shapiro (New York City Police Department) (analyzing the administrative hearing in a gun license revocation proceeding to determine that it is not held pursuant to direction by law so that the question of substantial evidence is not presented which would otherwise require that pursuant to CPLR 7804 (g) such cases be transferred to the Appellate Division) 157 Misc. 2d 28, 595 N.Y.S.2d 864, 1993, aff'd 201 A.D.2d 333; People v. Baghai-Kermani (holding that a Rosario violation that infects two counts of a ten count indictment requires vacatur of convictions on all counts where the prosecutor had urged the fact-finder to consider all transactions in determining guilt or innocence on each count) N.Y.L.J. 22 c. 2 March 19, 1993, modified 199 A.D. 2d 36; Matter of Silver v. Dinkins (granting an Article 78 petition to review and enjoin the siting of a municipal garage fueling facility unless and until proper consideration was given to the 'fair share' criteria of the New York City Charter and its Uniform Land Use Review Procedure; this being the first case to interpret the 'fair share' standards and procedures) 158 Misc. 2d 550, 601 N.Y.S.2d 366, 1993, aff'd for the reasons stated by Crane, J. 196 A.D.2d 757, 602 N.Y.S.2d 540, leave to appeal denied 82 N.Y.2d 659; Samuels v. City of New York (upholding the denial of the release from in rem foreclosure of real property belonging to the estate of a decedent who had been incompetent at the time property taxes came due and the city foreclosed) N.Y.L.J. 26 c. 4 May 19, 1993; and Merchant Factors Corp. v. Wolfson, Kapit, Melzer,

CRANE, STEPHEN G.—*Continued*

Milowsky, Ettinger & Wieselthier, P.C. (upholding the sufficiency of a complaint by a lender against the accountants of the borrower for negligence because the defendant was aware of plaintiff's role, that its financial statements were being used to extend credit and that defendant intended plaintiff to rely on its financial statements) N.Y.L.J. 26 c. 2 May 21, 1993.

Important Decisions June 1993 to Dec 1993: Matter of Yancey v. Hernandez-Pinero (dismissing an Article 78 proceeding for a defect in following the new commencement-by-filing provisions of CPLR 304 and 306-a in that petitioner filed proof of service simultaneously with purchasing the index number and filing his pleading) 158 Misc. 2d 514, 601 N.Y.S.2d 206 June 4, 1993; Lothar's of California, Inc. v. Weintraub (holding illegal and unenforceable an accountant's contingent fee agreement and leaving both parties where they were at the time of suit) 158 Misc. 2d 460, 601 N.Y.S.2d 231, 1993, aff'd for the reasons stated by Crane, J. A.D.2d N.Y.L.J. 26 c. 3 Dec 27, 1994; Wexner v. Burlington Air Express, Inc. (upholding a claim for damage to a painting brought about when defendant delivered a crate to plaintiff's apartment; the limitations in the Airbill are inapplicable to a claim of damages for defendant's negligence after completion of the delivery of other property that was subject of the Airbill) N.Y.L.J. 22 c. 4 July 21, 1993; Warendorf v. M.R. Beal & Co. (holding that litigation activity for two and one half years did not waive defendants' right to arbitrate the controversy pursuant to procedures of the Federal Arbitration Act although this would be a waiver if New York law applied) N.Y.L.J. 22 c. 4 Sept 15, 1993; Radin v. Avis Rent-a-Car System (declaring the extent to which a car rental company may recover from the driver of its leased car for amounts paid to a party injured by the negligence of the driver over the minimum statutory amount for which it was a self insurer) 159 Misc. 2d 370, 604 N.Y.S.2d 662, 1993; Mansdorf v. New York Football Giants (denying an injunction that would have prevented defendant from refusing to renew plaintiff's season subscription to twenty seats that defendant had withheld due to plaintiff's prior resales at prices in excess of face value) N.Y.L.J. 29 c. 3 Oct 28, 1993; 27 Victoria Owners Corp. v. Colbert (granting mandatory injunctive relief to compel a cooperator to allow the cooperative corporation to replace windows and waterproof his terrace) N.Y.L.J. 22 c. 3 Nov 3, 1993; and Sansol Industries v. 345 E. 56th St. Owners (declaring the unavailability of the notice of pendency to an action to compel conveyance of stock and proprietary leases for fifty apartments in a cooperative) 159 Misc. 2d 822, 606 N.Y.S. 856, 1993.

Important Decisions Feb 1994 to May 1994: In re New York County Data Entry Worker Product Liability Litigation (Bost-Manuel v. Unisys Corp; Karolisyn-Morris v. International Business Machines Corp.) (granting a protective order against plaintiffs' demand to inspect the workers' compensation files and OSHA forms respecting injuries to defendants' own data entry workers) N.Y.L.J. 23 c. 1 Aug 23, 1994 overruled by Blanco v. American Telephone & Telegraph Co. 223 A.D.2d 156 modified 90 N.Y.2d 257, 1997; Vojtech Blau, Inc. v. Sara (granting a joint trial but denying consolidation where a defendant would lose statute of limitations defenses against some of the plaintiffs if the cases were consolidated) 160 Misc. 2d 431, 609 N.Y.S.2d 515, 1994; Kidder, Peabody & Co. v. Marvin and Matter of Smith Barney Sheason v. Rosenfield (explaining why New York courts have jurisdiction over proceedings relating to arbitration pursuant to provisions in brokerage agreements specifying the facilities of a New York based arbitral tribunal; and describing the nature of 'participation in arbitration' before the National Association of Securities Dealers) 161 Misc. 2d 12 N.Y.S.2d, N.Y.L.J. 25 c. 6 April 7, 1994; Liberty Cable Co. v. Roofcom Associates (enjoining a building owner, fearful of health risks, from removing microwave equipment installed by plaintiff, cable television supplier, on the roof of the building because removal would violate agreements between the parties and would interrupt service to subscribers in several buildings) N.Y.L.J. 28 c. 2 April 29, 1994; and Melsten v. Board of Managers 178-184 East Second St. Condominium (holding inapplicable to the resale by a foreclosing mortgagee, which had previously bought in the property at the foreclosure sale, a provision in the condominium by-laws giving the condominium association the right of first refusal on the sale of apartments) N.Y.L.J. 28 c. 2 May 2, 1994.

Important Decisions June 1994 to Dec 1994: King v. Eastman Kodak Co. (dismissing repetitive stress injury actions against Kodak as parent of manufacturer-supplier of allegedly defective products because plaintiffs failed to establish facts to support theories of piercing the corporate veil, apparent manufacturer, concerted action or agency) N.Y.L.J. 22 c. 4 June 21, 1994; Hulse v. A.B. Dick Co. (granting a protective order preventing non-settling defendants from discovering the terms of confidential settlement agreements between plaintiffs and co-defendants in repetitive stress injury actions) N.Y.L.J. 22 c. 3 Aug 10, 1994; Johansen v. Honeywell, Inc. (master decision on statute of limitations defenses to repetitive stress injury claims) 167 Misc. 2d 496, 642 N.Y.S.2d 459 Aug 17, 1994; In re New York County Data Entry Worker Product Liability Litigation (Brooks v. International Business Machines Corp.) (holding that the statute of limitations in repetitive stress injury cases is three years from the earlier of onset of symptoms or last use of the allegedly injurious product) N.Y.L.J. 23 c. 1 Aug 23, 1994; Gray Line New York Tours v. New York Double Decker Tours (denying a preliminary injunction to prohibit competitors from operating double decker tour buses until certified as safe, movant having failed to establish a likelihood of success on the merits) N.Y.L.J. 22 c. 3 Aug 26, 1994; Gillin v. Patterson, Belknap, Webb & Tyler (rejecting the defenses of equitable estoppel and res judicata in a lawyer malpractice action stemming from the decision of the matrimonial court in the underlying action that the client had failed to make out a case for rescission of the separation agreement the making of which was attributable to the alleged legal malpractice) N.Y.L.J. 22 c. 4 Sept 2, 1994; and People v. Alamo Rent A Car (holding that General Business Law §391-g forbids rental car companies from discriminating against persons under 25 years of age solely on the basis of their age and establishing that insurance coverage through the New York Automobile Insurance Plan (assigned risk plan) is available substantially to cover the renters' risks for such rentals) N.Y.L.J. 26 c. 1, Misc. 2d, N.Y.S.2d Dec 13, 1994.

Important Decisions 1995: Fone-A-Car v. Fischbein, Badillo, Wagner and Itzler (finding service on a law firm partnership invalid under CPLR 310(c) and 308 for

CRANE, STEPHEN G.—*Continued*

failure to mail a copy of process to a partner rather than, as was done in this case, to the partnership) N.Y.L.J. 26 c. 1 Jan 4, 1995; Sandusky v. McCummings (interpreting the revised "Son of Sam' law as inapplicable to funds generated from a verdict in favor of the perpetrator against the transit police who used excessive force in shooting him in the back as he was fleeing from mugging plaintiff in this action) 164 Misc. 2d 700, 625 N.Y.S.2d 457 March 16, 1995; Morrissey v. Ecclesiastical Communications Corp. (dismissing defamation action against Catholic news publication based on truth and opinion of report of plaintiff's organization's disruption of mass to protest its support of gay and lesbian Catholics) N.Y.L.J. 31 c. 1 May 25, 1995; Matter of Bramson v. Brown (upholding determination of Board of Trustees of police pension fund denying a line-of-duty accidental disability retirement to petitioner who claimed her post traumatic stress disorder stemmed from trauma suffered during investigation of a homicide years earlier) N.Y.L.J. 22 c. 4 July 28, 1995; 80-02 Leasehold Co. v. Rogers (granting summary judgment on guarantee of tenant's obligations under lease despite defenses the tenant itself might assert) N.Y.L.J. 21 c. 5 Aug 9, 1995; Senfeld v. I.S.T.A. Holding Co. (setting attorneys fees pursuant to RPL §234 in favor of plaintiffs) N.Y.L.J. 21 c. 5 Aug 16, 1995 aff'd 235 A.D.2d 345; Osorno v. AD 1619 Co. (exploring case law applicable to claims under Labor Law §240(1) made by window washers and discussing circumstances under which such claims may be unrelated to construction activity) N.Y.L.J. 29 c. 6 Nov 6, 1995; Matter of Samsung America v. Pro Elite (holding arbitration unavailable under agreement that was conditioned on approval of third party licensor which never signed agreement) N.Y.L.J. 26 c. 4 Nov 21, 1995; and Matter of Maxi Cohen—Four Way Features, Inc. (rejecting recommendation of special referee and fixing value of petitioner's shares pursuant to BCL 1118 and establishing that neither party bears burden of proving value) 168 Misc. 2d 91, 636 N.Y.S.2d 994 Dec 29, 1995.

Important Decisions 1996: Matter of Three Parkway Partners, L.P. v. Marsh & McLennan (compelling an appraisal to fix fair market rental of office premises to determine rent for renewal period and refusing to declare appropriate methodology be applied in appraisal) N.Y.L.J. 26 c. 2 Jan 3, 1996; Hospital Audiences, Inc. v. New York City Department of Health (withholding mandatory injunctive relief that would have compelled defendant to continue to pay under plaintiff's contract to provide Directly Observed Preventative Therapy to tuberculosis and AIDS patients where plaintiff failed to establish that defendant was unjustified in terminating contract) N.Y.L.J. 29 c. 1 Jan 18, 1996; Matter of Civil Service Employees Association, Inc. v. New York State Unified Court System (rejecting petition to mandamus the respondent to establish standard and policy that would conform personnel rules of the Unified Court System to recent amendment to Civil Service Law §75 permitting disciplined employee to be represented by the union; the court system is not required to adopt standards and policies identical to Civil Service Law) N.Y.L.J. 29 c. 4 Jan 22, 1996; Devine v. New York Convention Center Operating Corp. (interpreting Labor Law §201-d and denying injunctive relief relegating plaintiffs to preferred procedures of collective bargaining grievance provisions and remedies before PERB for alleged discrimination on basis of union membership) 167 Misc. 2d 372, 639 N.Y.S.2d 904 Feb 27, 1996; Rodbell v. New York State Legislative Ethics Committee (rejecting petitioner's constitutional attack on Ethics in Government Act requiring candidates for member of legislature to file a financial disclosure statement) N.Y.L.J. 26 c. 5 May 24, 1996; Grutman Katz Greene & Humphrey v. Goldman (dismissing law firm's action in quantum meruit for additional compensation above contemporaneously billed regular time charges and dismissing client's counterclaims for legal malpractice and ethical infractions) N.Y.L.J. 27 c. 2 June 11, 1996; Citibank v Intercontinental Bank (finding lack of personal jurisdiction over bank that merely placed a check into the usual banking channels for collection and ultimate payment by a New York bank, rejecting plaintiff's attempt to collaterally estop defendant on the basis of a prior case where defendant had acted through an agent) 169 Misc. 2d 342, 646 N.Y.S.2d 261 July 12, 1996; Mike Schechter Associates v. Major League Baseball Players Association (dismissing claims for conversion and punitive damages in action for breach of agency agreement to promote licensing of merchandise and memorabilia of major league baseball players) N.Y.L.J. 28 c. 5 Aug 19, 1996; and Reliance Insurance Company of New York v. Chemical Bank (holding that issuer of bond for guardian of incompetent person had no claim as subrogee against bank where defaulting fiduciary maintained account from which she made unauthorized withdrawals) N.Y.L.J. 22 c. 1 Sept 5, 1996.

Important Decisions since 1997: Elite Model Management Corp. v. Crawford (finding outside the statute of frauds a contract to manage fashion model and upholding model's counterclaim for conversion of funds diverted by plaintiff from related corporation that owed them to model-defendant) N.Y.L.J. 27 c. 2 Jan 7, 1997; Seinfeld v. Robinson (approving settlement of a stockholders' derivative action but denying any fees to plaintiffs' counsel because the action brought no substantial benefit, monetary or non-monetary, to the corporation whose directors were required to pass two resolution that would expire in four years) 172 Misc. 2d 159, 656 N.Y.S.2d 707 Feb 21, 1997 rev'd 246 A.D.2d 291 N.Y.L.J. 25 c. 4 Aug 31, 1998; People v. Alamo Rent A Car (holding that penalties for a violation of General Business Law §391-g were unavailable for the failure to prove that respondents knowingly violated the statute and analyzing the concept of knowingly as required knowledge that insurance was available) Misc. 2d N.Y.S.2d Oct 3, 1997; Republic of New York Securities Corporation v. Lloyd (denying vacatur of an arbitration award to delete attorneys fees where the Uniform Submission Agreement set forth respondents' claim for them, and rejecting attack on award as irrational for lack of evidence where the only reference to their amount in the arbitration hearing was in closing arguments) N.Y.L.J. 28 c. 6 Oct 27, 1997; Infante v. City of New York (denying motions to set aside a verdict in favor of a plaintiff who fell on a sidewalk adjacent to a service station) N.Y.L.J. 26 c. 6 Feb 24, 1998, modified 258 A.D.2d 333 N.Y.L.J. 31 c. 4 Feb 17, 1999; Hall v. King (corporate dissolution) 177 Misc. 2d 126, 675 N.Y.S.2d 810 May 21, 1998 aff'd 265 A.D.2d 244, 1999; Makastchian v. Oxford Health Plans (certifying a class complaining of termination of health care coverage) N.Y.L.J. 28 c. 1 Aug 3, 1998 modified N.Y.L.J. March

CRANE, STEPHEN G.—*Continued*
9, 2000 26 c. 1; Vacco v. Aramony (upholding the authority of the Attorney General to sue former officers and directors under the Not for Profit Corporations Law for breach of fiduciary duties and fraud) N.Y.L.J. 22 c. 6 Aug 7, 1998; State of New York v. Philip Morris (denying motion by tobacco product manufacturers to compel disclosure by the Attorney General of individual recipient data in Medicaid expense) N.Y.L.J. 22 c. 5 Sept 2, 1998; City of New York v. Show World (construing the amended zoning resolution applicable to adult establishments by applying a ration of 60:40 to stock and floor area accessible to customers) 178 Misc. 2d 812, 683 N.Y.S.2d 376 Aug 28, 1998; City of New York v. Stringfellow's of New York, Ltd. (applying language defining adult establishments) N.Y.L.J. 26 c. 1 Nov 10, 1998, rev'd 253 A.D.2d 110, 1999, 684 N.Y.S.2d 544; State of New York v. Philip Morris (granting a defense motion to compel answers by former Attorney General and former Assistant Attorney General concerning the state of their knowledge of facts on which to pursue fraud claims) N.Y.L.J. 29 c. 1 Dec 10, 1998; and State of New York v. Philip Morris (approving tobacco industry master settlement agreements as fair, reasonable and adequate and approving the Attorney General's allocation of the proceeds among the members of the class of Counties, the City of New York and the State of New York also as fair, reasonable and adequate) 179 Misc. 2d 435, 686 N.Y.S.2d 564 Dec 23, 1998.

Important Decisions since 1999: Miller v. Weyerhaeuser, Co. (dismissing action against a defaulting defendant against which personal jurisdiction was lacking) 179 Misc. 2d 471, 685 N.Y.S.2d 393 Jan 13, 1999; City of New York v. Dezer Properties (denying application of adult eating and drinking establishment under the 60/40 rule) N.Y.L.J. 28 c. 1 March 22, 1999 reversed 259 A.D.2d 116, 1999 reversed 2000; City of New York v. Stringfellow's of New York, Ltd. (granting plaintiffs' motion to vacate an order that allowed an adult eating and drinking establishment to reopen under the 60/40 rule with the condition that the occupancy be limited to one-half the number allowed by the public assembly permit) N.Y.L.J. 28 c. 2 March 22, 1999; Fourth Federal Savings Bank v. Nationwide Associates (setting forth various guiding principles in foreclosure actions where referees to compute are used) 183 Misc. 2d 165, 701 N.Y.S.2d 814 Oct 21, 1999; Banc of America Commercial Finance Corp. v. Issacharoff (difference between fraud that induces a contract and fraud that relates to and duplicates a claim of breach of contract) 188 Misc. 2d 790, 728 N.Y.S.2d 861 Sept 19, 2000; McCluskey v. Ferriter (denying motion to vacate dismissal of complaint for refusal of plaintiff's counsel to proceed to trial) N.Y.L.J. 30 c. 5 Jan 12, 2001; Baisi v. Gonzalez (dissent in dog bite case) 286 A.D.2d 313, 728 N.Y.S.2d 697 Aug 8, 2001 rev'd N.Y.2d 2002 W.L. 46897 Jan 15, 2002; People v. Anthony Sorbello (applying CPL 240.75 retroactively to case appealed before effective date of statute but decided thereafter) 285 A.D.2d 88, 729 N.Y.S.2d 747 Aug 27, 2001; O'Neal v. Archdioceses of New York (dissenting from grant of summary judgment dismissing the complaint of victim of another resident of Pius 12 facility) 286 A.D.2d 757 Sept 24, 2001; Bindit Corp. v. Inflight Advertising, Inc. (declaring that prior litigation over alleged antitrust violations during the life of a patent did not bar similar claims by the licensor after the patent expired) N.Y.L.J. 16, 3 Oct 16, 2001; and DeLuca v. Gallo (holding that upon renunciation of the proceeds of a wrongful death action by the distributee of the decendent, the next distributee in line can maintain the action and the measure of her recovery is not limited to the amount that the renouncing distributee would have been entitled to recover) N.Y.L.J. 17, 3 Jan 7, 2002.

Member Advisory Committee for A Manual for Managing Notorious Cases National Center for State Courts 1990-92. Member Executive Committee Board of Justices First Judicial District. Member Jewish Lawyers Guild, New York County Lawyers' Association (Former Co-Chair Continuing Legal Education Institute, Chair History Committee, Member Judicial Section, Board of Directors Executive Committee), New York State Trial Lawyers Association, Association of Supreme Court Justices of the City of New York, Association of Justices of the Supreme Court of the State of New York, Hispanic National and New York State (Member Commission on Legal Services for the Middle Income, Committee on Jury Selection Council of Judicial Associations) Bar Associations. Past President Cornell Law Association. President Advisory Council Cornell Law School. Chair Executive Committee Curia. Member Anti-Defamation League of B'nai B'rith (Member Regional Board, Executive Committee, National Legal Affairs Committee). Chair Board of Trustees New York County Public Access Law Library.

Office: 60 Centre Street, Room 669, New York 10007.

Telephone: (212) 374-4726.

CRANNA, William F. *(Judge, Hudson City Court)* Former Acting Judge.

Office: 427-429 Warren Street, Hudson 12534.

Telephone: (518) 828-3100.

Fax: (518) 828-3628

CREW, D. Bruce, III *(Associate Justice, New York Supreme Court Appellate Division Third Judicial Department)* Elected Justice Sixth Judicial District to term beginning Jan 1, 1983. Reelected 1996. Appointed Associate Justice Appellate Division by Governor Mario Cuomo to term beginning Jan 1, 1991. Reappointed by the governor. Administrative Judge Sixth Judicial District 1987-90. Born Elmira New York Sept 27, 1937. Catholic. Educated at Colgate University B.A. 1959 and Albany Law School of Union University LL.B. 1962. Staff member Albany Law Review 1962. Confidential Clerk to Hon. Harold E. Simpson, New York Supreme Court 1962-64. Admitted to practice New York.

Assistant District Attorney 1968-71 and District Attorney 1973-83 Chemung County. Author "Criminal Discovery in New York State—Selected Issues." Faculty Member Department of Criminal Justice Elmira College since 1974. Lecturer Student School of Nursing Arnot Ogden Memorial Hospital, Student School of Nursing St. Joseph's Hospital, Corning Community College, Bureau of Criminal Prosecution and Defense Services New York State Division of Criminal Justice Services, New York State District Attorneys Association and The Practising Law Institute. Member Governor's Task Force on Criminal Justice Standards and Goals 1977, Criminal Procedure Law Advisory Committee to New York State Office of Court Administration since 1980, New York State District Attorneys Association (President 1976-77, Executive Committee 1973-83), Chemung County (Com-

CREW, D. BRUCE, III—*Continued*

mittee on Criminal Discovery) and New York State (Committee on Criminal Discovery Criminal Justice Section since 1978) Bar Associations. Former member Executive Committee Chemung County Republican Party. Board member Elmira Neighborhood House 1964-67, Elmira Child and Family Services 1965-68, Elmira Little Theatre 1966-70 (Past President), Elmira Country Club 1968-70 (Former Vice President) and Chemung County Legal Services 1974. Member Community Advisory Board Elmira Junior League 1974-79. Chairman Lawyers Division St. Joseph's Hospital Capital Fund Drive 1975 and United Way Campaign 1981. Chairman Annual Fund Drive Mount Saviour Monastery 1981. Member Advisory Board Chemung County Stop DWI Program 1982. Communicant St. Patrick's Church.

Mailing address: P.O. Box 588, Elmira 14902-0588.

Office: Supreme Court Chambers, 203 Lake Street, Elmira 14901.

Telephone: (607) 737-2080.

Fax: (607) 737-2072

E-mail address: dbcrew@courts.state.ny.us

CRISPINO, Jerry L. *(Justice, New York Supreme Court Twelfth Judicial District)* Elected to term beginning 1992. Certificated. Term expires 2004. Born Manhattan New York April 17, 1930. Educated at Manhattan College B.A. 1952, New York University and Fordham University School of Law LL.B. 1955. Admitted to practice New York 1955 and U.S. Supreme Court 1959.

Member Columbian Lawyers Association of Brooklyn, Bronx County and New York State Bar Associations. New York National Guard 1955-58. Administrative Assistant to U.S. Congressman Alfred E. Santangelo 1962-63. Associate Counsel to Joint Legislative Committee on the Study of New York State Alcoholic Beverage Laws 1964. Member Community Planning Board No. 11, 1965-67. Past President and Former Chairman of the Board Columbus-Esca Alliance. Former Director Bronx Foundation for Senior Citizens and Victory Day Care Center, Inc. Former Member Board of Directors National Multiple Sclerosis Society. Member Chester Civic Association, Bronx County Catholic Interracial Council, Fordham University School of Law Alumni Association, Manhattan College Alumni Association, La Salle University Alumni Association and Order of the Sons of Italy.

Office: 851 Grand Concourse, Bronx 10451.

Telephone: (718) 590-3763.

Fax: (718) 590-8914

CROWLEY, Kevin J. *(Judge, Suffolk County District Court)*

Mailing address: P.O. Box 9075, Central Islip 11722-9075.

Office: Cohalan Court Complex, 400 Carleton Avenue, Central Islip 11722.

Telephone: (631) 853-5520.

CRUZ, Raul *(Judge, The Civil Court of the City of New York)*

Office: 851 Grand Concourse, Bronx 10451.

Telephone: (718) 590-3601.

CURTIN, John T. *(Senior Judge, United States District Court Western District of New York)* Appointed for life by President Lyndon B. Johnson to term beginning Dec 23, 1967. Assumed Senior status, serves by assignment. Born Buffalo New York Aug 24, 1921. Roman Catholic. Educated at Canisius College B.S. 1945 and University of Buffalo LL.B. 1949. Admitted to practice New York 1949, U.S. District Court Western District of New York 1950, U.S. Court of Appeals Second Circuit 1961, U.S. Court of Military Appeals 1953 and U.S. Supreme Court 1962. Began legal practice Buffalo 1949.

U.S. Attorney Western District of New York 1961-67. Member National Legal Aid and Defender Organization, Bar Association of Erie County (Nominating Committee 1965 and 1967), New York State, Federal and American Bar Associations. Lieutenant Colonel USMC 1942-45 USMCR 1952-54. Democrat.

Office: 624 U.S. Courthouse, 68 Court Street, Buffalo 14202.

Telephone: (716) 551-4221.

CUTRONA, Anthony J. *(Justice, New York Supreme Court Second Judicial District)*

Office: 360 Adams Street, Brooklyn 11201.

Telephone: (718) 643-5084.

E-mail address: acutrona@courts.state.ny.us

CYGANOWSKI, Melanie L. *(Judge, United States Bankruptcy Court Eastern District of New York)* Appointed by U.S. Court of Appeals Second Circuit judges to term beginning March 1, 1993. Term expires March 1, 2007. Born Chicago Illinois June 8, 1952. Educated at Grinnell College A.B. with honors 1974, Cornell University and State University of New York at Buffalo J.D. magna cum laude 1981. Senior Editor Buffalo Law Review 1979-81. Law Clerk to Hon. Charles L. Brieant, U.S. District Court Southern District of New York 1981-82. Admitted to practice New York 1982, U.S. District Courts Eastern 1982, Southern 1982 and Western 1982 Districts of New York, U.S. Supreme Court 1989 and U.S. Court of Appeals Second Circuit. In legal practice New York City 1982-93.

Author "Polish-Am. Legal Experience in Buffalo" Buffalo L. Rev. 1982 and "Summary Judgment in Second Circuit" St. John's L. Rev. 1989. Important Decisions: In re Slater (recognition of state court judgment) WL 9971a, 1996; In re Malandra (untimely complaint in Chapter 7) 206 B.R. 667, 1997; In re Taibbi (class actions in Chapter 7) 213 B.R. 261, 1997; and In re Gurney's Inn Corporate Liquidation Trust WL 757558, 1997. Adjunct Professor St. John's University School of Law. Member National Conference of Bankruptcy Judges and New York State (Executive Committee, Commercial and Federal Litigation Section) Bar Association. Participant Various CLE programs sponsored by the New York State Bar Association. Enjoys gardening and cycling.

Office: Long Island Federal Courthouse, 290 Federal Plaza, Central Islip 11722.

Telephone: (631) 712-6200.

CZAJKA, Paul *(Judge, Columbia County Court)* Also serves Columbia County Surrogate's Court and Columbia County Family Court.

Office: Courthouse, 401 Union Street, Hudson 12534.

Telephone: (518) 822-0453.

CZYGIER, John M., Jr. *(Surrogate, Suffolk County Surrogate's Court)*

Office: 320 Center Drive, Riverhead 11901.

Telephone: (631) 852-1745.

Fax: (631) 852-1777

DABIRI, Gloria M. *(Justice, New York Supreme Court Second Judicial District)* Elected to term beginning Jan 1, 1995. Former Judge, New York City Family Court.
Office: 360 Adams Street, Brooklyn 11201.
Telephone: (718) 643-6246.
E-mail address: gdabiri@courts.state.ny.us

DADD, Mark H. *(Judge, Wyoming County Court)* Also serves Wyoming County Surrogate's Court and Wyoming County Family Court.
Office: Courthouse, 147 North Main Street, Warsaw 14569-1193.
Telephone: (585) 786-2253.
Fax: (585) 786-2818

DALEY, Michael E. *(Justice, New York Supreme Court Fifth Judicial District)*
Office: 542 County Office and Court Facility, 301 North Washington Street, Herkimer 13350.
Telephone: (315) 867-1185.
Fax: (315) 867-1531

DALY, Thomas R. *(Judge, Yonkers City Court)* Appointed by Mayor Terence Zaleski Feb 14, 1995. Elected to term beginning Jan 1, 2001. Current term expires Dec 31, 2011. Born Bronx New York Dec 16, 1953. Roman Catholic. Educated at St. John's University B.A. cum laude 1975 J.D. 1978. Law Clerk to Hon. Benjamin F. Nolan, New York City Civil Court 1979-81. Admitted to practice New York 1979 and Florida 1992. In legal practice Yonkers New York 1981-95.
Court Attorney The Civil Court of the City of New York 1979-81. Senior Court Attorney Yonkers City Court April 1995 to Dec 2000. Member Yonkers Lawyers Association (President 1999-2000). Democratic Party District and Ward Leader 1989-94 and 1996-2000. Member Yonkers Historical Society, Yonkers Male Glee Club, Ancient Order of Hibernians and Knights of Columbus. Enjoys historical re-enactment, historical board and miniature wargaming.
Office: Justice Center, 100 South Broadway, Yonkers 10701.
Telephone: (914) 377-6367.

D'AMICO, Michael L. *(Judge, Erie County Court)* Elected to term beginning Jan 1, 1987. Reelected 1996, current term expires Dec 31, 2006.
Office: Erie County Hall, 92 Franklin Street, Buffalo 14202.
Telephone: (716) 858-8388.
Fax: (716) 851-3251

DAMRATH, Joseph Edward *(Judge, Hornell City Court)* Assumed office 1989. Serves part time. Born Hornell New York Oct 25, 1951. Educated at Le Moyne College B.A. 1973, Duquesne University M.A. 1975 and University of Toledo College of Law J.D. 1980. Admitted to practice New York 1981. In legal practice New York since 1981.
Important Decisions: People v. Rice 148 Misc.2d 204, 1990; Valentino v. Principio 174 Misc.2d 709, 1997; City of Hornell v. Harrison 192 Misc.2d 273, 2002; and City of Hornell v. Glover 2002 N.Y. Slip Op. 40345(U). Member Attorney Grievance Committee. Member City Court Judges Association and New York State Bar Association. Member 21st Regiment Georgia Volunteer Infantry. Enjoys family life, reading, Civil War re-enacting and living histories, yard work and baseball.
Mailing address: P.O. Box 627, Hornell 14843-0627.
Office: 82 Main Street, Hornell 14843.
Telephone: (607) 324-7531.
Fax: (607) 324-6325

DANIELS, George B. *(Judge, United States District Court Southern District of New York)* Appointed for life by President Bill Clinton to term beginning April 17, 2000. Born Allendale South Carolina May 13, 1953. Educated at Yale University B.A. 1975 and University of California Boalt Hall School of Law J.D. 1978. Law Clerk to Chief Justice Rose Elizabeth Bird, California Supreme Court 1980-81. In legal practice 1981-83. Judge, The Criminal Court of the City of New York 1989-90 and 1993-95. Justice, New York Supreme Court First Judicial District 1995-2000.
Trial Attorney Legal Aid Society of New York 1978-80. Assistant U.S. Attorney Eastern District of New York 1983-89. Counsel to mayor New York City 1990-93.
Office: 410 U.S. Courthouse, 40 Centre Street, New York 10007-1581.
Telephone: (212) 805-6735.

DAVIDOWITZ, Edward M. *(Justice, New York Supreme Court Twelfth Judicial District)* Former Acting Justice. Appointed Justice by Governor George E. Pataki to term beginning June 2002. Certificated. Born New York New York Oct 24, 1932. Educated at Allegheny College B.A. 1954 and Cornell Law School LL.B. 1959. Admitted to practice New York 1959 and U.S. District Courts Eastern 1968 and Southern 1968 Districts of New York. In legal practice New York 1965-76. Judge, New York Court of Claims March 25, 1986 to June 2002, appointed by Governor Mario Cuomo.
Assistant District Attorney New York County 1959-65. With Office of the Investigation of the New York City Criminal Justice System Office of the Special Prosecutor 1976-86. Author "The Practice of Criminal Law Under the CPLR and Related Civil Procedure Statutes" New York State Bar Association. Member The Association of the Bar of the City of New York (Council on Judicial Administration, Council on Criminal Justice, Criminal Courts Committee, Criminal Law Committee) and New York State Bar Association (Special Committee to report upon legislative proposals in the "Mayor's Survey of the Criminal Justice System" Criminal Justice Section 1981). Attended annual seminars for judges in the New York State Judicial system. First Lieutenant USAF 1957-59. Trustee Blythedale Children's Hospital.
Office: 851 Grand Concourse, Bronx 10451.
Telephone: (718) 590-3662.
Fax: (718) 590-8914
E-mail address: edavidow@courts.state.ny.us

DAVIS, Kenneth A. *(Justice, New York Supreme Court Tenth Judicial District)* Elected Nov 8, 1994 to term beginning Jan 3, 1995. Term expires Dec 31, 2008. Born New York New York Oct 5, 1946. Jewish. Educated at Hofstra University B.A. 1968 and University of Akron Law Center J.D. 1971. Admitted to practice New York 1974, U.S. District Courts Eastern 1975 and Southern 1975 District of New York, U.S. Supreme Court 1988 and U.S. Court of Appeals Second Circuit 1989. In legal practice Nassau County 1990-92. Judge, Nassau County District Court 1993-94.
Assistant District Attorney Nassau County 1974-75.

DAVIS, KENNETH A.—*Continued*
Deputy Town Attorney Oyster Bar 1981-90. Member Nassau-Suffolk Trial Lawyers Association and Nassau County Bar Association. Captain Field Artillery USAS 1977. Republican. Enjoys racquetball and rafting.
Office: Supreme Court Building, 100 Supreme Court Drive, Mineola 11501.
Telephone: (516) 571-2613.

DAVIS, William J. *(Justice, New York Supreme Court First Judicial District)* Former Acting Justice. Elected Justice to term beginning Jan 1, 1987. Reelected 2000. Certificated. Also serves as Justice, New York Supreme Court Appellate Term First Judicial Department. Born Concord North Carolina Oct 19, 1932. Judge, The Criminal Court of the City of New York March 8, 1981 to Dec 31, 1986.
Office: 60 Centre Street, New York 10007.
Telephone: (212) 374-4502.

DAWSON, James P. *(Justice, New York Supreme Court Fourth Judicial District)* Elected to term beginning Jan 1, 1995. Educated at St. Michael's College and Albany Law School of Union University 1971. Admitted to practice New York 1972. In legal practice Elizabethtown 1975-92. Judge, Essex County Court 1992-94.
Office: Essex County Courthouse, 100 Court Street, Box 217, Elizabethtown 12932.
Telephone: (518) 873-3612.
Fax: (518) 873-3529

DAWSON, Joseph J. *(Judge, The Criminal Court of the City of New York)* Appointed by Mayor Rudolph Giuliani.
Office: 215 East 161st Street, Bronx 10451.
Telephone: (718) 590-2927.
Fax: (718) 590-7297

DAWSON, Tandra L. *(Judge, New York City Family Court)* Appointed by Mayor Rudolph Giuliani.
Office: 900 Sheridan Avenue, Bronx 10451.
Telephone: (718) 590-3376.
Fax: (718) 590-7305

DEARIE, Raymond J. *(Judge, United States District Court Eastern District of New York)* Appointed for life by President Ronald Reagan to term beginning 1986. Born Rockville Center New York June 4, 1944. Educated at Fairfield University B.A. 1966 and St. John's University J.D. 1969. In legal practice New York City 1969-71 and 1977-80.
Chief Appeals Division 1971-74, General Crimes Section 1974-76 and Criminal Division 1976-77, Executive Assistant U.S. Attorney 1977, Chief Assistant U.S. Attorney 1980-82 and U.S. Attorney 1982-86 Eastern District of New York.
Office: U.S. Courthouse, 225 Cadman Plaza East, Brooklyn 11201.
Telephone: (718) 260-2430.

DeGRASSE, Leland G. *(Justice, New York Supreme Court First Judicial District)* Former Judge, The Civil Court of the City of New York.
Office: 60 Centre Street, New York 10007.
Telephone: (212) 374-4735.

DeJOSEPH, Brian F. *(Justice, New York Supreme Court Fifth Judicial District)*
Office: 333 East Washington Street, Eighth Floor, Syracuse 13202.
Telephone: (315) 428-3215.
Fax: (315) 428-3250

DEL GIUDICE, Vincent M. *(Judge, New York Court of Claims)* Appointed by Governor George E. Pataki. Currently serves as Acting Justice, New York Supreme Court Second Judicial District.
Office: 120 Schermerhorn Street, Room 309B, Brooklyn 11201.
Telephone: (718) 643-7496.

DEMAREST, Carolyn E. *(Justice, New York Supreme Court Second Judicial District)* Appointed by Governor Mario Cuomo June 1990. Elected to term beginning Jan 1, 1992, current term expires Dec 31, 2005. Born Hackensack New Jersey July 13, 1946. Educated at New York University B.A. 1967 and New York Law School J.D. 1972. Recipient American Jurisprudence Awards in Contracts and Ethics. Articles Editor New York Law Forum 1969-72. Law Clerk to Hon. Stanley P. Danzig, The Civil Court of the City of New York 1973-76. Admitted to practice New York 1973, U.S. District Courts Eastern 1973 and Southern 1973 Districts of New York, U.S. Court of Appeals Second Circuit 1973 and U.S. Supreme Court 1978. In legal practice New York City 1972-73 and 1984-85. Judge, The Civil Court of the City of New York March 1983 to Dec 31, 1983 and March 1985 to July 2, 1985. Judge, New York City Family Court July 3, 1985 to June 1990, appointed by Mayor Edward I. Koch.
Assistant Corporation Counsel Appeals Division New York City 1976-84. Instructor Bernard M. Baruch College of the City University of New York 1985. Chair Committee on Women in Prison New York State Women Judges Association. Member Association of Supreme Court Justices of the City of New York, Association of Justices of the Supreme Court of the State of New York, National Association of Women Judges, The Association of the Bar of the City of New York, Brooklyn and New York State (Committees on Judicial Administration and Attorney Professionalism) Bar Associations. Faculty CLE programs. Member Civil Law Curriculum Committee for Judicial Seminars.
Office: 360 Adams Street, Brooklyn 11201.
Telephone: (718) 643-5874.
E-mail address: cdemares@courts.state.ny.us

DEMAREST, David R. *(Justice, New York Supreme Court Fourth Judicial District)* Elected Nov 1993 to term beginning Jan 1, 1994. Term expires Dec 31, 2007. Born College Point New York Aug 30, 1948. Educated at St. Lawrence University B.A. 1970 and Albany Law School of Union University J.D. 1973. Admitted to practice New York 1974 and U.S. District Court Northern District of New York 1974. In legal practice 1974-83.
Principal Law Clerk to Hon. Edmund L. Shea, New York Supreme Court 1983-84. Principal Law Clerk and Confidential Law Advisor to New York State Unified Court System 1984-93. Lecturer on campus legal issues, risk management, social responsibility and alcohol awareness various college campuses. Chair Advisory Committee Court Reporting Curriculum Mater Dei College. Executive Council New York State Conference of Bar Leaders. Board of Directors North Country Legal

DEMAREST, DAVID R.—*Continued*

Services, Inc. and St. Lawrence County Legal Assistance Corporation. Delegate House of Delegates New York State Bar Association. Member Association of Justices of the Supreme Court of the State of New York and St. Lawrence County Bar Association (President and Director). Lecturer to bar groups on Uniform Rules for the Trial Courts of the State of New York. Commissioned Second Lieutenant USAR 1970 (active duty Oct 1973 to Jan 1974). Committeeman and Treasurer Potsdam Town Republican Committee. International President Phi Kappa Sigma. Chairman St. Lawrence County Industrial Development Agency. Vice Chair Seaway Valley Crime Stoppers, Inc. Volunteer Music Theater North. Member Elks.

Office: Courthouse, 48 Court Street, Canton 13617-1194.

Telephone: (315) 379-0326.

Fax: (315) 379-2311

E-mail address: ddemares@courts.state.ny.us

DeMARO, Joseph A. *(Justice, New York Supreme Court Tenth Judicial District)* Former Judge, Nassau County Family Court.

Office: Supreme Court Building, 100 Supreme Court Drive, Mineola 11501.

Telephone: (516) 571-2949.

D'EMIC, Matthew J. *(Judge, New York Court of Claims)* Appointed by Governor George E. Pataki to term beginning July 11, 1996. Term expires July 11, 2005. Currently serves as Acting Justice, New York Supreme Court Second Judicial District. Born Brooklyn New York Dec 16, 1952. Roman Catholic. Educated at Fordham College B.A. 1974 and Brooklyn Law School J.D. 1977. Law Clerk to Hon. Ronald J. Aiello, New York Supreme Court Second Judicial District 1993-96. Admitted to practice New York 1978 and U.S. District Courts Eastern 1978 and Southern 1978 Districts of New York. In legal practice 1978-93.

Member Catholic Lawyers Guild (Vice President 1990-95), Court of Claims Judges Association, Bay Ridge Lawyers Association, Brooklyn and New York State Bar Associations. Recipient Distinguished Alumni Award from Xaverian High School, Community Service Award from National Information Bureau for Jewish Life, Service Award from Guild for Exceptional Children, Grand Marshall's Award from Ragamuffin Parade and Deputy Marshall's Award from Bay Ridge St. Patrick's Parade Committee. Trustee Xaverian High School 1985-91. Director Guild for Exceptional Children since 1990, The Cathedral Club of Brooklyn since 1994 and Mercy Home for Children since 1996.

Office: 360 Adams Street, Brooklyn 11201.

Telephone: (718) 643-8762.

Fax: (718) 643-1144

E-mail address: mdemic@courts.state.ny.us

DE PHILLIPS, Guy P. *(Judge, New York City Family Court)* Appointed by Mayor Edward Koch to term beginning Feb 17, 1983. Reappointed by Mayor David Dinkins to term beginning Dec 1, 1992 and by Mayor Michael Bloomberg 2002. Term expires Nov 30, 2012. Born New York New York March 30, 1937. Educated at Manhattan College B.A. cum laude 1959, St. John's University LL.B. 1962 and New York University LL.M. 1965. Staff member St. John's Law Review 1960-61. Member Phi Alpha Theta, Epsilon Sigma Pi and Phi Delta Phi. Admitted to practice New York 1962 and U.S. District Courts Southern 1964 and Eastern 1964 Districts of New York. Began legal practice New York City 1962.

Law Assistant 1968-72, Law Secretary to Hon. Vincent Lupiano 1972-82 and Principal Appellate Law Assistant 1982-83, New York Supreme Court Appellate Division First Judicial Department. Member Queens County Bar Association (American Legal Principles Committee, Family Law Committee).

Office: 151-20 Jamaica Avenue, Jamaica 11432.

Telephone: (718) 298-0197.

DEREN, Joseph V. *(Acting Judge, Lackawanna City Court)*

Office: City Hall, 714 Ridge Road, Lackawanna 14218-1588.

Telephone: (716) 827-6486.

Fax: (716) 825-1874

DeRIGGI, Donald P. *(Judge, Nassau County Court)* Elected Nov 1993 to term beginning Jan 1, 1994. Term expires Dec 31, 2003. Educated at Villanova University B.A. 1958 and St. John's University School of Law LL.B. 1961. Admitted to practice New York 1962 and U.S. District Courts Eastern 1969 and Southern 1969 Districts of New York. In legal practice Jericho 1970-88.

Assistant District Attorney Nassau County 1963-70. E-3 U.S. Army 1961-62. Mayor City of Glen Cove 1988-93.

Office: Nassau County Courthouse, 262 Old Country Road, Mineola 11501.

Telephone: (516) 571-2241.

Fax: (516) 571-2160

DeROSA, Nicholas *(Judge, Orange County Court)* Currently serves as Acting Justice, New York Supreme Court Ninth Judicial District. Former Judge, Newburgh City Court.

Office: Orange County Courthouse, 285 Main Street, Goshen 10924.

Telephone: (845) 291-3115.

DeSANTIS, Vincent *(Judge, Gloversville City Court)* Elected Nov 1993 to term beginning Feb 1, 1994. Re-elected Nov 1999, current term expires Dec 31, 2005. Former Acting Judge. Born Gloversville New York May 14, 1948. Roman Catholic. Educated at C. W. Post College B.A. 1970 and St. John's University School of Law J.D. 1977. Admitted to practice New York 1978. In legal practice Gloversville since 1978.

Office: City Hall, Three Frontage Road, Gloversville 12078.

Telephone: (518) 773-4527.

Fax: (518) 773-4599

DEVLIN, Diane Y. *(Judge, Buffalo City Court)*

Office: 50 Delaware Avenue, Buffalo 14202.

Telephone: (716) 847-8265.

Fax: (716) 847-8257

DIAMOND, Kenneth S. *(Judge, Nassau County Family Court)* Currently serves as Supervising Judge. Former Judge, Nassau County District Court, elected to term beginning Jan 1, 1989.

Office: 1200 Old Country Road, Westbury 11590.

Telephone: (516) 571-9362.

Fax: (516) 571-9335

DIAMOND, Marylin G. *(Judge, The Civil Court of the City of New York)* Currently serves as Acting Justice, New York Supreme Court First Judicial District.
Office: 60 Centre Street, New York 10007.
Telephone: (212) 374-8374.

DiBIANCO, Gustave J. *(Magistrate Judge, United States District Court Northern District of New York)* Appointed by U.S. District Court judges to term beginning 1987. Educated at Brooklyn College B.A. 1966 J.D. 1969.
Mailing address: P.O. Box 7396, Syracuse 13261-7396.
Telephone: (315) 234-8600.

DiBLASI, John P. *(Justice, New York Supreme Court Ninth Judicial District)* Elected to term beginning Jan 1, 1995. Former Judge, Mount Vernon City Court.
Office: County Courthouse, 111 Dr. Martin Luther King Jr. Blvd., White Plains 10601.
Telephone: (914) 995-4725.

DICKERSON, Thomas A. *(Justice, New York Supreme Court Ninth Judicial District)* Former Judge, Westchester County Court.
Office: 111 Dr. Martin Luther King Jr. Blvd., White Plains 10601.
Telephone: (914) 995-3824.
Fax: (914) 289-4184
E-mail address: judgetad@aol.com

DiFIORE, Janet *(Justice, New York Supreme Court Ninth Judicial District)* Former Judge, Westchester County Court.
Office: 111 Dr. Martin Luther King Jr. Blvd., White Plains 10601.
Telephone: (914) 995-4736.
Fax: (914) 995-4010

DILLON, James H. *(Judge, Erie County Family Court)*
Office: One Niagara Plaza, Buffalo 14202.
Telephone: (716) 858-8181.
Fax: (716) 858-8432

DILLON, Kevin M. *(Justice, New York Supreme Court Eighth Judicial District)*
Office: 77 West Eagle Street, Buffalo 14202.
Telephone: (716) 851-3279.
Fax: (716) 851-3292
E-mail address: kdillon@courts.state.ny.us

DILLON, Mark C. *(Justice, New York Supreme Court Ninth Judicial District)*
Office: 111 Dr. Martin Luther King Jr. Blvd., White Plains 10601.
Telephone: (914) 995-4917.
E-mail address: mdillon@courts.state.ny.us

DiMANGO, Patricia M. *(Justice, New York Supreme Court Second Judicial District)* Acting Justice April 1995 to Dec 2001. Elected Justice to term beginning Jan 1, 2002. Term expires Dec 31, 2015. Born Washington D.C. June 19, 1953. Catholic. Educated at Brooklyn College B.S. cum laude 1973, Columbia University M.A. with honors 1974 and St. John's University School of Law J.D. 1980. Recipient American Jurisprudence Award in New York Practice and Moot Court Scholarship Award. Admitted to practice New York 1981 and U.S. District Courts Eastern and Southern Districts of New York. Judge, The Criminal Court of the City of New York April 1995 to Dec 31, 2001, appointed by Mayor Rudolph Giuliani.
Assistant District Attorney Kings County Aug 1980 to Jan 1986. Special Assistant U.S. Attorney Eastern District of New York 1984-85. Law Clerk to Hon. Steven W. Fisher 1986-90, Hon. Luigi R. Marano 1990-91 and Hon. Reinaldo E. Rivera 1991-95, New York Supreme Court Second Judicial District. Co-author with Hon. Steven W. Fisher "Confessions in New York: An Overview" 2 June 1986 and "Fighting the Inevitable—An Important Development in the Law of Inevitable Discovery" 3 June 1987 Kings County Criminal Bar Association Journal. Author "A Concise Summary of the Sentencing Statutes Under the Penal Law and Criminal Procedure Law" 6 Kings County Criminal Bar Association Journal Jan 1993. Important Decisions: People v. Reginald Cobb Docket No. 97K037720, 1997 and Pamela Chan Solomon v. Michael Solomon 2001 N.Y. Slip Op. 40051. Adjunct Associate Professor St. John's University since 1991. Member Pro Bono Panel on Uncontested Matrimonials. Assigned Counsel Panel Review Board. Member Columbian Lawyers Association (First and Second Departments), Brooklyn Women's Bar Association (Second Vice President, Board of Directors 1993-94, Chair By-laws Committee), Richmond County Women's Bar Association, Kings County Criminal Bar Association (Treasurer), Richmond County and Brooklyn Bar Associations (Chair Criminal Law Section 1993-94, Board of Trustees). Attended Judicial Seminar since 1995 and Criminal Court Judge's Seminar 1995-98. Recipient Distinguished Service Award from the Brooklyn Bar Association 1994. Member Congress of Italo-American Organizations and Coalition of Italo-American Association. Second Vice President Amicus Curiae.
Office: 120 Schermerhorn Street, Brooklyn 11201.
Telephone: (718) 643-8045.
Fax: (718) 643-3813
E-mail address: pdimango@courts.state.ny.us

DiSTEFANO, Biagio J. *(Judge, Madison County Court)* Also serves Madison County Surrogate's Court and Madison County Family Court.
Mailing address: P.O. Box 545, Wampsville 13163.
Office: Courthouse, Wampsville 13163.
Telephone: (315) 366-2381.
Fax: (315) 366-2739

DiTULLIO, Sheila A. *(Judge, Erie County Court)* Elected Nov 1995 to term beginning Jan 1, 1996. Term expires Dec 31, 2005. Born Lockport New York. Christian. Educated at Houghton College B.A. 1977 and Western New England College School of Law J.D. 1980. Admitted to practice New York 1982.
Lecturer on Trial Technique State University of New York at Buffalo 1995-98. Enjoys gardening, jogging and fly fishing.
Office: Erie County Hall, 92 Franklin Street, Buffalo 14202.
Telephone: (716) 858-2143.
Fax: (716) 851-3334
E-mail address: sditulli@courts.state.ny.us

DOERN, James E. D. *(Judge, Saratoga Springs City Court)*
Office: 3 City Hall, 474 Broadway, Saratoga Springs 12866-2295.
Telephone: (518) 581-1797.
Fax: (518) 584-3097

DOLAN, Thomas J. *(Judge, Dutchess County Court)* Elected Nov 3, 1992 to term beginning Jan 1, 1993. Reelected 2002, current term expires Dec 31, 2012. Acting Justice, New York Supreme Court Ninth Judicial District since Jan 1, 2000. Born Bronx New York Oct 24, 1943. Roman Catholic. Educated at Fordham University B.S. 1965 and St. John's University School of Law J.D. 1968. Admitted to practice New York 1968, U.S. Court of Appeals for the Armed Forces 1968, U.S. District Courts Eastern 1975 and Southern 1975 Districts of New York and U.S. Supreme Court 1980.

Assistant District Attorney Dutchess County April 23, 1973 to Jan 1, 1993. Member Dutchess County and New York State Bar Associations. Recipient Two Bronze Star Medals, Two Army Commendations Medals, Vietnam Campaign and Service Medals and Vietnam Cross of Gallantry. Captain JAGC U.S. Army 1968-73 (Vietnam 1970-71). Military Judge USAR 1975-78. President East Fishkill Republican Club 1977. Coach East Fishkill Girls Softball League. Member Exchange Club Southern Dutchess, VFW, NRA and American Legion. Enjoys coaching youth athletics, hunting, camping and fishing. Interested in conservation.

Office: Courthouse, 10 Market Street, Poughkeepsie 12601-3203.

Telephone: (845) 486-2210.

Fax: (845) 473-5403

DOLINGER, Michael H. *(Magistrate Judge, United States District Court Southern District of New York)* Appointed by U.S. District Court judges to term beginning March 12, 1984. Reappointed 1992 and 2000. Current term expires 2008. Born New York New York Sept 29, 1946. Jewish. Educated at Columbia University B.A. magna cum laude 1968 J.D. 1972. Harlan Fiske Stone Scholar. Editor-in-Chief Columbia Law Review 1971-72. Law Clerk to Hon. Wilfred Feinberg, U.S. Court of Appeals Second Circuit 1972-73. Admitted to practice New York 1973, U.S. District Courts Southern 1974 and Eastern 1974 Districts of New York and U.S. Court of Appeals Second Circuit 1974. In legal practice New York City 1973-76.

Assistant U.S. Attorney 1976-84, Deputy Chief Appellate Attorney 1979-82 and Deputy Chief 1982-84 Civil Division Southern District of New York.

Office: 1670 U.S. Courthouse, 500 Pearl Street, New York 10007-1312.

Telephone: (212) 805-0204.

DOLLARD, James P. *(Justice, New York Supreme Court Eleventh Judicial District)* Former Judge, The Civil Court of the City of New York.

Office: 88-11 Sutphin Boulevard, Jamaica 11435.

Telephone: (718) 262-3802.

DONALTY, Barry M. *(Judge, Oneida County Court)*

Office: Oneida County Courthouse, Elizabeth Street, Utica 13501.

Telephone: (315) 798-5289.

DONNINO, William C. *(Judge, New York Court of Claims)* Appointed by Governor Mario Cuomo to term beginning 1989. Reappointed by Governor George E. Pataki. Currently serves as Acting Justice, New York Supreme Court Twelfth Judicial District. Educated at Queens College of the City University of New York B.A. 1963 and Fordham University School of Law J.D. 1966. Admitted to practice New York 1966, U.S. District Courts Eastern 1968 and Southern 1968 Districts of New York, U.S. Court of Appeals Second Circuit 1968 and U.S. Supreme Court 1970. In legal practice 1988-89.

Assistant District Attorney New York County 1969-71. Deputy Commissioner and Counsel New York State Department of Correctional Services 1973-75. Chief Appeals Bureau District Attorney's Office Nassau County 1975-81. Chief Assistant District Attorney Kings County 1982-88. Co-author "The Agency Defense in Drug Cases" New York L. Jour. 1 April 27, 1978 and "Exigent Circumstances for a Warrantless Home Arrest" 45 Albany L. Rev. 90. Author "Practice Commentaries" *McKinney's New York Penal Law* 1984 and *New York Court of Appeals on Criminal Law 2d* West Group 1985 2nd ed. 1997. Member Advisory Committee on Criminal Law and Procedure 1977-92 and Committee to Revise the Criminal Jury Instructions since 1992, Chair Advisory Committee on Evaluation of Cameras in the Court 1990 and Co-chair Committee on Automation and Technology for Judges 1994-95 New York Office of Court Administration. Member Advisory Committee to the Law Revision Commission on the Defense of Insanity 1979-80 and New York State Advisory Commission on Criminal Sanctions 1982. Former Member New York State Association of Criminal Defense Lawyers. Member The American Law Institute, The Association of the Bar of the City of New York (Committee on Criminal Law 1979-82) and New York State Bar Association. Assistant Counsel to Governor Nelson Aldrich Rockefeller 1971-73. Counsel to Committee on Crime and Correction New York State Senate 1988-89. Member Fordham Law Alumni Association.

Office: 851 Grand Concourse, Bronx 10451.

Telephone: (718) 590-3775.

Fax: (718) 590-4505

E-mail address: wdonnino@courts.state.ny.us

Website address: http://ourworld.compuserve.com/homepages/w_c_d

DONOFRIO, Gail A. *(Judge, Monroe County Family Court)*

Office: Hall of Justice, 99 Exchange Boulevard, Rochester 14614-2187.

Telephone: (585) 428-5597.

DONOHUE, Lawrence J. *(Judge, Suffolk County District Court)*

Mailing address: P.O. Box 9075, Central Islip 11722-9075.

Office: Cohalan Court Complex, 400 Carleton Avenue, Central Islip 11722.

Telephone: (631) 853-4916.

DONOVAN, W. Denis *(Justice, New York Supreme Court Ninth Judicial District)* Certificated.

Office: County Courthouse, 111 Dr. Martin Luther King Jr. Blvd., White Plains 10601.

Telephone: (914) 995-4746.

Fax: (914) 995-4184

DORAN, Arthur J., Jr. *(Judge, Yonkers City Court)* Former Chief Judge.

Office: Justice Center, 100 South Broadway, Yonkers 10701.

Telephone: (914) 377-6350.

DORAN, Craig J. *(Judge, Ontario County Court)* Also serves Ontario County Family Court.
Office: Courthouse, 27 North Main Street, Canandaigua 14424-1447.
Telephone: (585) 396-4479.
Fax: (585) 396-4580
E-mail address: cdoran@courts.state.ny.us

DORSA, Joseph P. *(Justice, New York Supreme Court Eleventh Judicial District)* Former Judge, The Civil Court of the City of New York.
Office: 88-11 Sutphin Boulevard, Jamaica 11435.
Telephone: (718) 520-3899.

DOUGHERTY, Stephen J. *(Judge, Syracuse City Court)*
Office: Public Safety Building, 511 South State Street, Syracuse 13202.
Telephone: (315) 477-2787.
Fax: (315) 474-2601

DOUGLAS, Laura G. *(Justice, New York Supreme Court Twelfth Judicial District)* Former Judge, The Civil Court of the City of New York.
Office: 851 Grand Concourse, Bronx 10451.
Telephone: (718) 590-3584.
Fax: (718) 590-8914

DOUGLASS, Lewis L. *(Justice, New York Supreme Court Second Judicial District)* Former Acting Justice. Certificated. Born Brooklyn New York Dec 12, 1930. Protestant. Educated at Brooklyn College B.S. 1953 and St. John's University LL.B. 1956. Member Phi Beta Sigma. Admitted to practice New York 1956, U.S. Court of Appeals Second Circuit 1962, U.S. Supreme Court 1962 and U.S. District Court Eastern District of New York 1963. In legal practice Brooklyn 1956-61. Former Judge, The Criminal Court of the City of New York, appointed by Mayor Ed Koch to term beginning May 28, 1978. Former Judge, New York Court of Claims, appointed by governor.

Investigator and Hearing Officer New York State Rent Commission June 1956 to Nov 1958. Attorney Corporation Counsel's Office City of New York Nov 1958 to Dec 1961. Assistant U.S. Attorney Eastern District of New York Dec 1961 to March 1966. Trial Attorney Interstate Commerce Commission 1966-67. Deputy Director and General Counsel Non-Profit Housing Center Jan 1969 to June 1972. Executive Deputy Commissioner New York State Department of Correctional Services May 1975 to June 1978. Author "Bedford-Stuyvesant: A Community Corporation" in *Housing Patterns for Action* Joint Strategy and Action Committee 1969; "Investing in Real Estate" Black Enterprise Oct 1972; and *Minority Enterprise Opportunities* HUD 1971. Important Decisions: Mardikus v. Arger (grounds for corporate dissolution) 116 Misc. 2d 1028, 1982; McLean v. Michaelowsky (resolution of dispute over division of attorney's fee) 117 Misc. 2d 699, 1983, 458 N.Y.S.2d 1005; People v. Colon (use of grand jury testimony as evidence in-chief) 122 Misc. 2d 1084, 473 N.Y.S.2d 301, 1984; People v. Reid (first decision in state to permit testimony of expert witness on Rape Trauma Syndrome) Misc. 2d 1984; and People v. Lopez (first decision ordering drug dealer to make restitution of over two million dollars to drug programs) 139 Misc. 2d 448. Visiting Instructor in Political Science New York City Community College 1964-67. Adjunct Professor of Law and Evidence John Jay College of Criminal Justice of the City University of New York since 1980. Adjunct Professor of Business Law York College of the City University of New York since 1982 and St. John's University since 1983. Recipient Social Action Award from Phi Beta Sigma 1963 and Ford Foundation Grant to study European New Towns 1969. Librarian Brooklyn Public Library Feb 1953 to June 1953. Investigator Department of Welfare New York City June 1954 to Sept 1954 and June 1955 to Sept 1955. Deputy Executive Director Bedford-Stuyvesant Restoration Corporation April 1967 to Dec 1968. Executive Vice President Black Enterprise Magazine June 1972 to May 1975. Director Bedford-Stuyvesant Registration Drive 1962. Local organizer Civil Rights March to Washington D.C. 1963. Chairman Speakers Bureau Brooklyn Branch NAACP (Past Vice President and Treasurer). Member U.S. Census Bureau Advisory Committee on the Black Population for 1980 census.
Office: 360 Adams Street, Brooklyn 11201.
Telephone: (718) 643-5086.
E-mail address: ldouglass@courts.state.ny.us

DOUNIAS, Peter G. *(Judge, Suffolk County Family Court)* Former Judge and Supervising Judge, Suffolk County District Court.
Office: Cohalan Court Complex, 400 Carleton Avenue, Central Islip 11722.
Telephone: (631) 853-4268.
Fax: (631) 853-4359

DOWD, Joseph J. *(Justice, New York Supreme Court Second Judicial District)* Certificated. Former Judge, The Civil Court of the City of New York.
Office: 360 Adams Street, Brooklyn 11201.
Telephone: (718) 643-5888.
E-mail address: jdowd@courts.state.ny.us

DOWD, Kevin M. *(Justice, New York Supreme Court Sixth Judicial District)* Born Queens New York Aug 12, 1949. Roman Catholic. Educated at State University of New York at Cortland B.A. 1971 and College of William & Mary Marshall-Wythe School of Law J.D. 1974. Admitted to practice New York 1975 and U.S. District Court Northern District of New York 1975. Former Judge, Chenango County Court, elected to term beginning Jan 1, 1986.

Assistant District Attorney 1976-79 and District Attorney 1980-85 Chenango County. Member County Judges Association of the State of New York, American Judges Association, Chenango County and New York State Bar Associations. Republican. Enjoys jogging.
Office: Courthouse, West Park Place, Norwich 13815.
Telephone: (607) 337-1740.
Fax: (607) 336-3648

DOWERY-RODRIQUEZ, Brenda *(Judge, Mount Vernon City Court)* Associate Judge Jan 1986 to Dec 31, 1988. Appointed Judge by Mayor Ronald Blackwood to term beginning Jan 1, 1987. Elected 1989 and 1999. Current term expires Dec 31, 2009. Born Shelbyville Kentucky Feb 5, 1946. Catholic. Educated at St. Augustine's College B.A 1967 and University of Santa Clara J.D. 1975. Member Phi Alpha Delta. Admitted to practice New York 1977, U.S. District Court Southern District of New York 1978 and District of Columbia 1979. In legal practice Bronx New York 1978-80 and Mount Vernon New York since 1978.

Member Association of Black Lawyers of Westchester, Mount Vernon (Treasurer, Secretary), Westchester

DOWERY-RODRIQUEZ, BRENDA—*Continued*

County and New York State Bar Associations. Recipient award from Association of Black Lawyers of Westchester 1987. Previously worked as social worker, Department of Social Services Bronx New York. Hobbies include photography, travel, movies and reading fiction.
Office: Roosevelt Square, Mount Vernon 10550-2019.
Telephone: (914) 665-2400.
Fax: (914) 699-1230

DOWLING, Deborah A. *(Justice, New York Supreme Court Second Judicial District)* Former Judge, The Civil Court of the City of New York.
Office: 360 Adams Street, Brooklyn 11201.
Telephone: (718) 643-5340.
E-mail address: ddowling@courts.state.ny.us

DOWNEY, James E. *(Judge, Norwich City Court)*
Office: One Court Plaza, Norwich 13815.
Telephone: (607) 334-1224.
Fax: (607) 334-8494

DOYLE, Cathryn M. *(Surrogate, Albany County Surrogate's Court)*
Office: Albany County Courthouse, Albany 12207.
Telephone: (518) 487-5391.

DOYLE, James F. X. *(Judge, Suffolk County Court)*
Office: 8 Court Complex, 210 Center Drive, Riverhead 11901.
Telephone: (631) 852-1640.
Fax: (631) 852-3547

DOYLE, Robert W. *(Justice, New York Supreme Court Tenth Judicial District)* Elected to term beginning Jan 1, 1982. Reelected 1995, current term expires Dec 31, 2009. Also serves as Presiding Justice, New York Supreme Court Appellate Term Ninth and Tenth Judicial Districts. Born Brooklyn New York May 7, 1935. Catholic. Educated at Niagara University and St. John's University LL.B. 1959. Admitted to practice New York 1960. Began legal practice Mineola 1960. Judge, Suffolk County Court 1977-82.
Member Catholic Lawyers Guild, New York State Supreme Court Judges Association, Nassau-Suffolk Trial Lawyers Association and Suffolk County Bar Association. Conservative-Republican.
Office: 420 Federal Building, 170 Federal Way, Central Islip 11722.
Telephone: (631) 853-6317.

DOYLE, Vincent E., Jr. *(Justice, New York Supreme Court Eighth Judicial District)* Elected to term beginning Jan 1, 1979. Reelected 1992. Certificated. Former Administrative Judge. Born Buffalo New York Oct 17, 1932. Roman Catholic. Educated at Canisius College and University of Buffalo (now State University of New York at Buffalo) J.D. 1956. Admitted to practice New York 1956, U.S. District Court Western District of New York 1959 and U.S. Supreme Court 1964. In legal practice Buffalo 1956-78.
Public Defender City of Buffalo 1957-59. Instructor State University of New York at Buffalo Law School since 1974. Chairman Criminal Procedure Law Advisory Committee New York State Office of Court Administration 1984-95. President Association of Justices of the Supreme Court of the State of New York 1989-90. Member Eighth Judicial District Supreme Court Judges (President 1983), Erie County Trial Lawyers (Board of Governors 1974-76), Bar Association of Erie County (Board of Directors 1974-75, President 1976-77) and New York State Bar Association (House of Delegates 1975-77, Chairman 1981-83, Executive Committee Criminal Justice Section). Lecturer Office of Court Administration, Bar Association of Erie County and New York State Bar Association. Recipient Outstanding Jurist Award from Bar Association of Erie County 1988, Outstanding Jurist Award from Erie County Matrimonial and Family Law Committee 1993, Distinguished Alumni Award from State University of New York at Buffalo School of Law 1994 and Outstanding Jurist of the Year Award from Judges and Police Conference of Erie County 1997. Named One of 100 Most Influential People in Western New York by Business First 1998.
Office: Niagara Civic Building, 775 Third Street, Niagara Falls 14302.
Telephone: (716) 278-1815.
E-mail address: vdoyle@courts.state.ny.us

DRAG, Walter F. *(Judge, Dunkirk City Court)* Acting Judge Jan 1, 1985 to Dec 31, 1989. Elected Judge to term beginning Jan 1, 1990. Reelected 1995 and 2001. Current term expires Dec 31, 2007. Born Dunkirk New York Jan 28, 1950. Roman Catholic. Educated at Colgate University A.B. with honors 1972 and State University of New York at Buffalo J.D. 1977. Admitted to practice New York 1978 and U.S. District Court Western District of New York 1978. Began legal practice Dunkirk 1978.
City Attorney Dunkirk 1978-79. Deputy County Attorney Chautauqua County July 1, 1984 to Nov 30, 1988. Housing Authority Counsel Dunkirk since July 1979. Instructor Fredonia State University College (part of State University of New York) 1979-81 and 1984. Member Bar Association of Northern Chautauqua County (Secretary 1983-84, President 1984-85), Bar Association of Erie County, New York State and American Bar Associations. Board of Directors Dunkirk Chamber of Commerce 1989-96.
Office: City Hall, 342 Central Avenue, Dunkirk 14048-2122.
Telephone: (716) 366-2055.
Fax: (716) 366-3622

DRAGER, Laura E. *(Judge, The Criminal Court of the City of New York)* Appointed by Mayor Ed Koch. Currently serves as Acting Justice, New York Supreme Court First Judicial District.
Office: 111 Centre Street, New York 10013.
Telephone: (212) 374-8001.

DRAGO, Karen A. *(Judge, Schenectady City Court)* Former Judge, Schenectady Police Court.
Office: 531 Liberty Street, Schenectady 12305.
Telephone: (518) 382-5239.
Fax: (518) 382-5241

DRAIN, Robert D. *(Judge, United States Bankruptcy Court Southern District of New York)* Appointed by U.S. Court of Appeals Second Circuit judges to term beginning May 24, 2002. Term expires May 2016.
Office: Hamilton Custom House, Sixth Floor, One Bowling Green, New York 10004-1408.
Telephone: (212) 668-2301.

DRURY, Timothy J. *(Judge, Erie County Court)* Appointed by Governor Mario Cuomo to term beginning Feb 1987. Elected 1987 and 1997. Current term expires

DRURY, TIMOTHY J.—*Continued*

Dec 31, 2007. Born Buffalo New York Dec 17, 1940. Educated at Georgetown University A.B. 1963 and State University of New York School of Law LL.B. 1967. Admitted to practice New York 1968. Associate Judge, Buffalo City Court 1980-87.

Member Bar Association of Erie County.

Office: Erie County Hall, 92 Franklin Street, Buffalo 14202.

Telephone: (716) 858-8448.

Fax: (716) 851-3335

DUBERSTEIN, Conrad B. *(Chief Judge, United States Bankruptcy Court Eastern District of New York)* Appointed by U.S. District Court judges 1981. Appointed Recalled Judge by the Judicial Council of the Second Circuit. Chief Judge since 1984. Born New York Oct 22, 1915. Educated at Brooklyn College and St. John's University School of Law 1941. Honorary LL.D. St. John's University 1991. Staff member St. John's Law Review. Admitted to practice New York 1942.

Chairman Bankruptcy Committee Brooklyn Bar Association. Member Bankruptcy Committee New York State Bar Association. Fellow American College of Bankruptcy and American Bar Association (Committee on Bankruptcy). Member Commercial Law League of America, American Bankruptcy Institute and National Conference of Bankruptcy Judges. Lecturer on Bankruptcy at various law schools, bar associations, bankruptcy seminars and educational programs. Recipient Annual Award for Outstanding Achievement in the Science of Jurisprudence and Public Service from Brooklyn Bar Association 1992 and Medal of Honor from St. John's University. USAS 1943-46. Recipient Purple Heart, Bronze Star Medal and Combat Infantry Badge. President St. John's University Council. Director St. John's Law Alumni Association. Member Loughlin Society of St. John's University, Military Order of the Purple Heart for the State of New York, Disabled American Veterans, American Legion and Historical Society of the Supreme Court of the United States.

Office: 75 Clinton Street, Brooklyn 11201-4201.

Telephone: (718) 330-2188.

DUFFICY, Timothy J. *(Judge, The Civil Court of the City of New York)*

Office: 89-17 Sutphin Boulevard, Jamaica 11435.

Telephone: (718) 262-7100.

DUFFY, Colleen *(Judge, Mount Vernon City Court)*

Office: 30 Roosevelt Square, Mount Vernon 10550-2060.

Telephone: (914) 665-2400.

DUFFY, Kevin Thomas *(Senior Judge, United States District Court Southern District of New York)* Appointed for life by President Richard M. Nixon to term beginning Oct 17, 1972. Assumed Senior status, serves by assignment. Born New York New York Jan 10, 1933. Roman Catholic. Educated at Fordham University A.B. 1954 LL.B. 1958. Law Clerk to Hon. J. Edward Lumbard, U.S. Court of Appeals Second Circuit 1955-58. Admitted to practice New York 1958, U.S. District Court Southern District of New York 1959 and U.S. Court of Appeals Second Circuit 1959. In legal practice New York City 1961-69.

Assistant Chief, Criminal Division U.S. Attorney's Office Southern District of New York 1958-61. Regional Administrator Securities Exchange Commission New York Reg. Office 1969-72. Author "Reforming SIPC" 7 The Review of Securities Regulation 985, 1974, "Foreign Sovereign Immunity in the Second Circuit After Texas Trading and Verlinden" 48 Brooklyn L. Rev. 979, 1982 and "The Civil Rights Act: A Need For Re-Evaluation of the Non-Exhaustion Doctrine Applied to Prison Section 1983 Lawsuits" 4 Pace L. Rev. 61, 1983. Co-author with Aron and Rosner *Cross-Examination of Witnesses: The Litigator's Puzzle* 1989 and *Impeachment of Witnesses* 1990 Shepard's McGraw-Hill. Adjunct Professor of Securities Law Brooklyn Law School 1975-81 and Trial Advocacy New York University 1983-84, Pace University 1984-85 and Fordham University School of Law 1993-95. Member The American Law Institute, Federal Bar Council, The Association of the Bar of the City of New York, Westchester County and New York State Bar Associations. Lecturer Practising Law Institute, Attorney General's Advocacy Program and National Institute for Trial Advocacy. Recipient Distinguished Service Award from Securities and Exchange Commission 1972, Excellence in Law Award from Fordham University Alumni 1984, Gold Medal for Excellence in the Law from Fordham Law School Alumni 1984, Distinguished Public Service Award from County Lawyers Association 1994 and William O. Douglas Award from Association of Securities and Exchange Commission Alumni 1995. Member Fordham Law School Alumni Association (Trustee 1969-77, Vice President since 1977).

Office: 1205 U.S. Courthouse, 40 Centre Street, New York 10007-1581.

Telephone: (212) 805-6125.

DUGGAN, W. Dennis *(Judge, Albany County Family Court)* Assumed office 1994. Term expires Dec 31, 2003. Born Salamanca New York June 25, 1949. Roman Catholic. Educated at University of Notre Dame 1972 and Albany Law School of Union University J.D. 1976. Admitted to practice New York 1977, U.S. District Court Northern District of New York 1977, U.S. Supreme Court 1980 and U.S. Court of Appeals Second Circuit 1982. In legal practice 1978-94.

Assistant Corporation Counsel, Chief Labor Counsel and Chief Labor Negotiator 1978-86 and Executive Deputy Corporation Counsel 1986-88 Albany. Counsel Department of Economic Development Albany 1992-94. Author "Courting Trouble" March 2, 1997 and "Courting Hope" Oct 1999 *Albany Times Union*, "Electronic Recording in Family Court" March 6, 1997, "Handling Domestic Violence Cases in Family Court" May 1997, "Case Management in Family Court" July 1997, "Family Court Case Load Study" Oct 1997 and "So What's a Grandparent to Do?" Family L. Rev. New York State Bar Association Spring 2000. Regular Contributor Albany County Bar Association Newsletter. Important Opinions: Benoit v. Benoit N.Y.L.J. Dec 15, 1995, Kahler v. Terrell N.Y.L.J. July 31, 2000, Matter of "LL" N.Y.L.J. Dec 28, 2000, Webster v. Ryan N.Y.L.J. Jan 23, 2001 and N.Y.L.J. June 29, 2001, Matter of T./P. Children 165 Misc. 2d 333, Matter of Judy T 170 Misc. 2d 506, Matter of James T 172 Misc. 2d 427, Raymond v. Raymond 174 Misc. 2d 158 and Sweet v. Sweet 177 Misc. 2d 454. Lecturer "View from the Bench" Albany Law School of Union University 1995-99. Instructor in Business Law Schenectady County Community College. Judicial Representative National Minority Confinement Conference. Member Deputy Chief Judge's Committee on Standards and Goals, New

DUGGAN, W. DENNIS—*Continued*
York State Family Court Advisory and Rules Committee and Judicial Institute Committee. Member Notre Dame Law Association, Family Court Judges Association (Chair Legislative Committee), National Council of Juvenile and Family Court Judges, American Judges Association (Former Member House of Delegates), American Judicature Society (Director), Capital District Women's, Capital District Black, Albany County, New York State and American Bar Associations.

Lecturer "Getting Through the First Year" New Judges School 1997-2001 and Judicial Seminar on Child Abuse 1999 Office of Court Administration; "How We Protect the Ones We Love" Women's Law Caucus on Domestic Violence Oct 1999; "Improving Our Responses to Child Sexual Abuse" CASA Conference Syracuse, New York Oct 1999; "Youth Making a Difference" Youth Court Conference Albany, New York Nov 1999; "Case Management in Family Court" Tarrytown, New York 1999 and "Tropea, Five Years of Relocation Experience" July 2001 New York State Annual Judicial Seminar; "Custody Relocation Cases" Oneida County Bar Association Feb 2001; "Resolving Custody Disputes" New York State Dispute Resolution Association May 2001; and Forum on Family Court National Council of Juvenile and Family Court Judges, Cincinnati, Ohio Sept 2001. Moderator Sidebar Program American Judicature Society 1999. Graduate National Institute for Trial Advocacy. Previously employed as Journeyman Structural Ironworker Ironworkers Local 12. Former Member Albany-Colonie Chamber of Commerce and Sorin Society. Manager-Coach Westland Hills Little League. Parent Leader Boy Scouts of America. Assistant Den Leader Cub Scouts. Advisor Youth Court Albany County. Member Domestic Violence Committee Council of Community Services, Supreme Court Historical Society, Albany Police Neighborhood Watch Program, Big Brothers-Big Sisters, Adirondack Mountain Club and Notre Dame Club of North Eastern New York. FAA Licensed Pilot.

Office: One Van Tromp Street, Albany 12207.
Telephone: (518) 427-3531.
Fax: (518) 427-3562
E-mail address: wduggan@courts.state.ny.us

DUNCAN, E. David *(Judge, Albany City Court)*
Office: 209 City Hall, Eagle and Corning Place, Albany 12207.
Telephone: (518) 434-5034.
Fax: (518) 434-5034

DUNLOP, Roberta L. *(Justice, New York Supreme Court Eleventh Judicial District)* Elected Nov 1991 to term beginning Jan 1, 1992. Term expires Dec 31, 2005. Judge, The Civil Court of the City of New York 1987-91. Former Judge-in-Charge Queens County Branch.
Office: 125-01 Queens Boulevard, Kew Gardens 11415.
Telephone: (718) 520-3501.

DUNN, John J. *(Justice, New York Supreme Court Tenth Judicial District)* Certificated. Former Judge, Suffolk County Family Court.
Office: 203A Supreme Court Annex, 215 Griffing Avenue, Riverhead 11901.
Telephone: (631) 852-3742.
Fax: (631) 852-2574

DUNNE, John P. *(Justice, New York Supreme Court Tenth Judicial District)* Certificated. Former Judge, Nassau County Court.
Office: Supreme Court Building, 100 Supreme Court Drive, Mineola 11501.
Telephone: (516) 571-3310.

DURANTE, Joan Marie *(Justice, New York Supreme Court Eleventh Judicial District)*
Office: 88-11 Sutphin Boulevard, Jamaica 11435.
Telephone: (718) 520-3726.
Fax: (718) 520-6409

DWYER, Michael L. *(Judge, Oneida County Court)*
Office: Oneida County Courthouse, Elizabeth Street, Utica 13501.
Telephone: (315) 798-5299.

DYE, Luther V. *(Justice, New York Supreme Court Eleventh Judicial District)* Elected to term beginning Jan 1, 1994. Term expires Dec 31, 2007. Judge, The Civil Court of the City of New York Jan 1, 1989 to Dec 31, 1993.
Office: 88-11 Sutphin Boulevard, Jamaica 11435.
Telephone: (718) 520-3735.

EATON, Douglas F. *(Magistrate Judge, United States District Court Southern District of New York)* Appointed by U.S. District Court judges.
Office: 1360 U.S. Courthouse, 500 Pearl Street, New York 10007-1312.
Telephone: (212) 805-6175.

EDLITZ, Sandra B. *(Judge, Westchester County Family Court)*
Office: 111 Dr. Martin Luther King Jr. Blvd., White Plains 10601.
Telephone: (914) 995-3384.
Fax: (914) 995-4675
E-mail address: sedlit@wes_fam_nys_u

EDMEAD, Carol Robinson *(Justice, New York Supreme Court First Judicial District)* Former Judge, The Civil Court of the City of New York.
Office: 71 Thomas Street, Room 209, New York 10013.
Telephone: (212) 815-0865.
E-mail address: cedmead@courts.state.ny.us

EDWARDS, William *(Judge, Mount Vernon City Court)*
Office: 30 Roosevelt Square, Mount Vernon 10550-2060.
Telephone: (914) 665-2400.

EGAN, David Daniel *(Justice, New York Supreme Court Seventh Judicial District)* Appointed by Governor George E. Pataki to term beginning May 31, 2000. Elected to term beginning Jan 1, 2001, current term expires Dec 31, 2014. Born Rochester New York April 22, 1939. Roman Catholic. Educated at Rochester Institute of Technology B.S. 1962 and Albany Law School of Union University LL.B. cum laude 1967. Staff writer Albany Law Review 1966-1967. Admitted to practice New York 1967 and U.S. District Court Western District of New York 1968. Began legal practice Rochester 1967. Justice, Gates Town Justice Court 1980-83. For-

EGAN, DAVID DANIEL—*Continued*
mer Judge, Monroe County Court, elected to term beginning Jan 1, 1984.
Office: Hall of Justice, 99 Exchange Boulevard, Rochester 14614-2185.
Telephone: (585) 428-2008.

EGAN, John C., Jr. *(Judge, Albany City Court)*
Office: Public Safety Building, Morton Avenue and Broad Street, Albany 12202.
Telephone: (518) 462-6714.

EIDENS, Michael C. *(Judge, Schenectady County Court)* Elected to term beginning Jan 1, 1995.
Office: Courthouse, 612 State Street, Schenectady 12305.
Telephone: (518) 388-4215.

EISENBERG, Dorothy *(Judge, United States Bankruptcy Court Eastern District of New York)*
Office: Long Island Federal Courthouse, 290 Federal Plaza, Central Islip 11722.
Telephone: (631) 712-6200.

EISMAN, Julianne S. *(Judge, Nassau County Family Court)*
Office: 1200 Old Country Road, Westbury 11590.
Telephone: (516) 571-9015.
Fax: (516) 571-9335

ELFVIN, John T. *(Senior Judge, United States District Court Western District of New York)* Appointed for life by President Gerald R. Ford to term beginning Jan 10, 1975. Assumed Senior status 1987. Born Montour Falls New York June 30, 1917. Educated at Cornell University B.E.E. 1942, Harvard Law School and Georgetown University J.D. 1947. Board of Editors Georgetown Law Journal. Law Clerk to Hon. E. Barrett Prettyman, U.S. Court of Appeals District of Columbia Circuit 1947-48. Admitted to practice District of Columbia 1948 and New York 1949. In legal practice New York City 1948-51 and Buffalo Sept 1951 to Oct 1955, May 1958 to April 1969 and Jan 1970 to July 1972. Justice, New York Supreme Court April 22, 1969 to Dec 31, 1969.
Assistant U.S. Attorney Oct 1955 to May 1958 and U.S. Attorney July 1972 to Jan 1975 Western District of New York. Republican. Board of Supervisors Erie County 1962-65. Buffalo Common Council 1966-69. Chairman Erie County Board of Ethics 1970-72.
Office: 716 U.S. Courthouse, 68 Court Street, Buffalo 14202.
Telephone: (716) 551-4226.

ELKINS, Lee Hand *(Judge, New York City Family Court)* Appointed by Mayor Rudolph Giuliani.
Office: 283 Adams Street, Sixth Floor, Brooklyn 11201.
Telephone: (718) 643-4546.
Fax: (718) 643-5103

ELLERIN, Betty Weinberg *(Associate Justice, New York Supreme Court Appellate Division First Judicial Department)* Elected Justice First Judicial District 1976. Appointed Associate Justice Appellate Division by Governor Mario Cuomo March 1985. Certificated. First woman appointed to that bench. Former Presiding Justice Appellate Division. Born Bronx New York June 21, 1929. Jewish. Educated at Indiana University 1946-47 and New York University B.A. cum laude 1950 LL.B. 1952 replaced by J.D. Member Justinian Society. Admitted to practice New York 1953 and U.S. District Courts Eastern 1953 and Southern 1953 Districts of New York. Began legal practice New York City 1953. Former Judge, The Civil Court of the City of New York, elected Nov 1976 to term beginning Jan 1, 1977. Deputy Chief Administrative Judge, New York Unified Court System Jan 1982 to March 1985.
Law Secretary to Hon. Harry B. Frank, The Civil Court of the City of New York 1955-65 and New York Supreme Court 1965-75; and to Presiding Justice Jacob Markowitz, New York Supreme Court Appellate Term First Judicial Department Jan 1976 to Sept 1976. Chief Law Assistant New York Supreme Court Appellate Term Jan 1976 to Sept 1976. Former Member New York State Sentencing Guidelines Committee and Committee to Implement the recommendations of the New York Task Force on Women in the Courts. Director National Conference of Metropolitan Courts. Member New York Judicial Committee on Women in the Courts, Advisory Committee on Judicial Ethics, National Association of Women Lawyers (Former Business Manager), National Association of Women Judges (Vice President, Chair National Task Force on Gender Bias in the Courts), Women's Bar Association of the State of New York (Director), The Association of the Bar of the City of New York (Executive Committee, Past Vice President, Former Chair Committee on Women in the Courts) and New York Women's Bar Association (President 1969-70, Director). Recipient Founders Award from Women's Bar Association of the State of New York, Florence E. Allen Award from New York University School of Law and New York Women's Bar Association, Tom Clark Award from National Conference of Metropolitan Courts, Harlan Fiske Stone Award from Association of Trial Lawyers of the City of New York (first woman recipient) and Annual Law Day Award from New York State Trial Lawyers Association. Vice-President HIAS, Inc. (President Women's Division). Enjoys opera, ballet and reading.
Office: 27 Madison Avenue at 25th Street, New York 10010.
Telephone: (212) 340-0457.
Fax: (212) 340-0555

ELLIOT, David *(Judge, The Civil Court of the City of New York)*
Office: 89-17 Sutphin Boulevard, Jamaica 11435.
Telephone: (718) 262-7394.

ELLIOTT, John J. *(Surrogate, Oswego County Surrogate's Court)* Currently serves as Acting Justice, New York Supreme Court Fifth Judicial District.
Office: Courthouse, 25 East Oneida Street, Oswego 13126-2693.
Telephone: (315) 349-3295.
Fax: (315) 349-8514

ELLIS, Ronald L. *(Magistrate Judge, United States District Court Southern District of New York)* Appointed by U.S. District Court judges.
Office: 1970 U.S. Courthouse, 500 Pearl Street, New York 10007-1312.
Telephone: (212) 805-0242.

EMANUELLI, Albert J. *(Judge, New York Court of Claims)* Appointed by Governor George E. Pataki. Cur-

EMANUELLI, ALBERT J.—*Continued*
rently serves as Acting Justice, New York Supreme Court Twelfth Judicial District.
Office: 851 Grand Concourse, Bronx 10451.
Telephone: (718) 590-3784.
Fax: (718) 590-8914

EMERSON, Elizabeth H. *(Justice, New York Supreme Court Tenth Judicial District)*
Office: 7 Court Complex, 210 Center Drive, Riverhead 11901.
Telephone: (631) 852-2781.
Fax: (631) 852-3732

ENG, Randall T. *(Justice, New York Supreme Court Eleventh Judicial District)* Former Judge, The Criminal Court of the City of New York.
Office: 125-01 Queens Boulevard, Kew Gardens 11415.
Telephone: (718) 520-3481.
E-mail address: reng@courts.state.ny.us

ENGORON, Arthur F. *(Judge, The Civil Court of the City of New York)*
Office: 111 Centre Street, New York 10013.
Telephone: (212) 791-6000.

EPPOLITO, Anthony P. *(Judge, Oneida City Court)*
Office: 109 North Main Street, Oneida 13421.
Telephone: (315) 363-1310.
Fax: (315) 363-3230

ERLBAUM, William M. *(Judge, The Criminal Court of the City of New York)* Appointed by mayor. Currently serves as Acting Justice, New York Supreme Court Eleventh Judicial District.
Office: 125-01 Queens Boulevard, Kew Gardens 11415.
Telephone: (718) 520-2215.

ESPINOZA, Laura Safer *(Judge, The Civil Court of the City of New York)* Currently assigned to The Criminal Court of the City of New York. Also serves as Acting Justice, New York Supreme Court Twelfth Judicial District.
Office: 215 East 161st Street, Bronx 10451.
Telephone: (718) 590-6398.

ESPOSITO, Gerald V. *(Justice, New York Supreme Court Twelfth Judicial District)* Elected to term beginning Jan 1, 1995. Administrative Judge Civil Division since Oct 2002. Educated at Fordham University School of Business B.S. 1957 and Fordham University School of Law J.D. 1960. Admitted to practice New York 1960 and U.S. District Courts Eastern and Southern Districts of New York. In legal practice New York 1961-69 and 1974-94.

Law Secretary to Hon. William Kapelman, New York Supreme Court District One 1970-73. Important Opinions: Huggins v. Board of Education Jan 22, 1996; Gregorio v. City of New York NYLJ April 2, 1996; Matter of Liechtensein 171 Misc.2d 29, 1996; Barnes v. City of New York NYLJ Jan 5, 1999; Sabater v. Lead Indus. Assn. 183 Misc.2d 759, 2000; Lara v. Verde NYLJ April 16, 2001; M. Colon v. H&B Plumbing & Heating, et al. NYLJ March 29, 2002; and A. Hamilton v. New Branford, Inc., et al. NYLJ April 4, 2002. Board Member New York Judicial Conference since Jan 2002. Member Columbian Lawyers Association, New York City Supreme Court Justices Association, New York State Supreme Court Justices Association and Bronx County Bar Association (Civil Branch Committee). Lecturer on Trying Labor Law Cases Sections 200, 202, 220, 240, 241 and Industrial Code New York State Trial Lawyers Association and Defense Bar. Speaker Law Day public high schools since 1996. Advisory Board The Astor Home. Co-founder senior citizen center. Member Community Planning Board, 49th Police Precinct Council, Allerton Avenue Homeowners Association, Morris Park Civic Association and Beth Jacob Beth-Miriam School.
Office: 851 Grand Concourse, Bronx 10451.
Telephone: (718) 590-3942.
Fax: (718) 590-1206

EUKEN, James E. *(Judge, Allegany County Court)* Also serves Allegany County Surrogate's Court and Allegany County Family Court.
Office: Courthouse, Seven Court Street, Belmont 14813.
Telephone: (585) 268-5800.
Fax: (585) 268-7090
E-mail address: jeuken@courts.state.ny.us

EVANS, Saralee E. *(Judge, The Civil Court of the City of New York)* Currently serves as Acting Justice, New York Supreme Court First Judicial District.
Office: 111 Centre Street, New York 10013.
Telephone: (212) 374-8156.

FABRIZIO, Ralph A. *(Judge, The Criminal Court of the City of New York)* Appointed by mayor.
Office: 215 East 161st Street, Bronx 10451.
Telephone: (718) 590-2927.
Fax: (718) 590-7297

FAHEY, Eugene M. *(Justice, New York Supreme Court Eighth Judicial District)* Former Judge, Buffalo City Court.
Office: 50 Delaware Avenue, Buffalo 14202.
Telephone: (716) 851-3283.
Fax: (716) 851-3317
E-mail address: efahey@courts.state.ny.us

FAHEY, Joseph E. *(Judge, Onondaga County Court)* Elected to term beginning Jan 1, 1997. Term expires Dec 31, 2006. Born Syracuse New York June 30, 1949. Roman Catholic. Educated at University of Tennessee at Knoxville B.S. 1971 and Syracuse University College of Law J.D. 1975. Admitted to practice New York 1976, U.S. District Court Northern District of New York 1977, U.S. Court of Appeals Second Circuit 1980 and U.S. Supreme Court 1980. In legal practice Syracuse 1979-96.

Senior Staff Attorney Frank H. Hiscock Legal Aid Society 1976-80. Commissioner of Education Syracuse Jan 1, 1986 to Dec 31, 1993. Adjunct Professor of Basic Trial Practice Syracuse University College of Law since 1994. Member Central New York Women's Bar Association and Onondaga County Bar Association. Democrat. Interests include photography and writing. Personal Statement or Quote: "In the legal profession, the only currency an attorney has is truthfulness and integrity. Don't squander it."
Office: Courthouse, 401 Montgomery Street, Syracuse 13202.
Telephone: (315) 671-1050.
Fax: (315) 671-1176
E-mail address: JFAHEY@courts.state.ny.us

FAIRGRIEVE, Scott *(Judge, Nassau County District Court)*
Office: 99 Main Street, Hempstead 11550.
Telephone: (516) 571-2141.
E-mail address: fairgrieve@courts.state.ny.us

FALANGA, Anthony J. *(Justice, New York Supreme Court Tenth Judicial District)* Elected Nov 1999 to term beginning Jan 1, 2000. Term expires Dec 31, 2013. Born Brooklyn New York Dec 5, 1935. Catholic. Educated at Georgetown University B.S.S. 1957 LL.B. 1960. Admitted to practice District of Columbia 1960, New York 1962, U.S. Supreme Court 1971 and U.S. District Courts Eastern 1978 and Southern 1978 Districts of New York. In legal practice Carle Place and Mineola New York 1963-94. Judge, Nassau County District Court Jan 1, 1995 to Dec 31, 1999.

Adjunct Professor in Trial Techniques Hofstra University School of Law since 1983. President Columbian Lawyers Association of Nassau County. Chairman of the Board Nassau Lawyers Association of Long Island, Inc. Director Criminal Courts Bar Association of Nassau County. Member Justinian Society, Bar Association of Nassau County and New York State Bar Association. Member East Meadow Kiwanis and Chamber of Commerce.

Office: Matrimonial Center, 400 County Seat Drive, Mineola 11501.
Telephone: (516) 571-0017.
Fax: (516) 571-0029

FALVEY, W. Patrick *(Judge, Yates County Court)* Appointed by Governor Mario Cuomo to term beginning May 3, 1988. Elected Nov 1988 and Nov 1998. Current term expires Dec 31, 2008. Currently serves as Acting Justice, New York Supreme Court Seventh Judicial District. Also serves Yates County Surrogate's Court and Yates County Family Court. Born Penn Yan New York Aug 31, 1946. Educated at Hobart College B.A. 1968 and John Marshall Law School J.D. 1975. Law Clerk to Hon. Lyman H. Smith, Jr., New York Supreme Court Seventh Judicial District 1976-77. Admitted to practice New York 1976, U.S. District Court Western District of New York 1979 and U.S. Supreme Court 1984. In legal practice Penn Yan 1976-88.

Assistant Public Defender 1977-80 and District Attorney 1981-88 Yates County. Member The Surrogates' Association of the State of New York, Family Court Judges Association of the City of New York, County Judges Association of the State of New York (Executive Committee), American Judges Association, American Judicature Society, Yates County (Past President) and New York State Bar Associations. Recipient Distinguished Jurist Award from Center for Dispute Settlement 1996. First Lieutenant U.S. Army Jan 9, 1969 to Sept 30, 1974 (served in South Vietnam). Participant in many community activities.

Office: 415 Liberty Street, Penn Yan 14527.
Telephone: (315) 536-5128.
Fax: (315) 536-5197

FANDRICH, Mark H. *(Surrogate, Cayuga County Surrogate's Court)*
Office: Courthouse, 152 Genesee Street, Auburn 13021-3471.
Telephone: (315) 255-4316.
Fax: (315) 255-4322

FARBER, Thomas A. *(Judge, The Criminal Court of the City of New York)* Appointed by Mayor Rudolph Giuliani.
Office: 120 Schermerhorn Street, Brooklyn 11201.
Telephone: (718) 643-8400.
Fax: (718) 643-3538

FARNETI, Joseph *(Judge, Suffolk County Court)* Former Judge, Suffolk County District Court. Former Acting Justice, New York Supreme Court Tenth Judicial District.
Mailing address: P.O. Box 9007, Riverhead 11901-9007.
Office: Court Complex, 210 Center Drive, Riverhead 11901.
Telephone: (631) 852-2169.
Fax: (631) 852-2855

FEENEY, Edward T. *(Judge, Kingston City Court)*
Office: One Garraghan Drive, Kingston 12401.
Telephone: (845) 338-2974.
Fax: (845) 338-1443

FEINBERG, Michael H. *(Surrogate, Kings County Surrogate's Court)* Elected Nov 1996 to term beginning Jan 1, 1997. Former Judge, The Civil Court of the City of New York. Former Justice, New York Supreme Court Second Judicial District.
Office: Two Johnson Street, Brooklyn 11201.
Telephone: (718) 643-4336.

FEINMAN, Paul G. *(Judge, The Civil Court of the City of New York)*
Office: 111 Centre Street, New York 10013.
Telephone: (212) 374-8460.

FEINMAN, Thomas *(Judge, Nassau County District Court)*
Office: 99 Main Street, Hempstead 11550.
Telephone: (516) 572-2125.

FELDMAN, Anne G. *(Justice, New York Supreme Court Second Judicial District)* Former Acting Justice. Certificated. Born New York New York March 30, 1930. Jewish. Educated at Antioch College A.B. 1951 and Yale University LL.B. 1954. Board of Editors Yale Law Review. Admitted to practice New York 1955, U.S. District Court Southern District of New York and U.S. Supreme Court. Began legal practice New York City 1955. Hearing Officer, New York City Commission on Human Rights 1974-77. Judge, The Civil Court of the City of New York 1978-90. Former Judge, New York Court of Claims, appointed by Governor Mario Cuomo to term beginning July 1, 1990.
Office: 360 Adams Street, Brooklyn 11201.
Telephone: (718) 643-8092.
Fax: (718) 643-7984
E-mail address: afeldman@courts.state.ny.us

FELDMAN, Jonathan W. *(Magistrate Judge, United States District Court Western District of New York)* Appointed by U.S. District Court judges.
Office: 2330 Federal Building, 100 State Street, Rochester 14614-1322.
Telephone: (716) 263-5757.

FELDSTEIN, S. Peter *(Judge, Hamilton County Court)* Also serves Hamilton County Surrogate's Court and Hamilton County Family Court.
Mailing address: P.O. Box 780, Indian Lake 12842-0780.
Office: Family Court Chambers, White Birch Lane, Indian Lake 12842.
Telephone: (518) 648-5411.
Fax: (518) 648-6286

FELLER, Jerome *(Judge, United States Bankruptcy Court Eastern District of New York)* Appointed by U.S. Court of Appeals Second Circuit judges April 15, 1985 to term beginning Sept 23, 1985. Reappointed Sept 1999, current term expires Sept 2013. Born Brooklyn New York July 3, 1941. Educated at Yeshiva University B.A. with honors 1962 and New York Law School J.D. with honors 1966. Admitted to practice New York 1967 and U.S. Courts of Appeals First 1971 and Second 1978 Circuits.
Trial Attorney 1969-74, Branch Chief 1974-79 and Assistant Regional Administrator 1979-85 New York Regional Office U.S. Securities and Exchange Commission.
Office: 75 Clinton Street, Brooklyn 11201-4201.
Telephone: (718) 330-2188.

FERDINAND, JoAnn *(Judge, The Criminal Court of the City of New York)* Appointed by Mayor Ed Koch. Currently serves as Acting Justice, New York Supreme Court Second Judicial District.
Office: Brooklyn Treatment Court, 360 Adams Street, Brooklyn 11201.
Telephone: (718) 643-3185.
E-mail address: jferdina@courts.state.ny.us

FERRADINO, Stephen A. *(Justice, New York Supreme Court Fourth Judicial District)* Appointed by Governor Mario Cuomo 1994. Elected to term beginning Jan 1, 1995, current term expires Dec 31, 2008. Born Ballston Spa New York Aug 16, 1941. Roman Catholic. Educated at Siena College B.A. 1963 and Albany Law School of Union University J.D. 1966. Admitted to practice New York 1966 and U.S. District Court District of New York 1966. In legal practice Ballston Spa 1966-80. Acting Justice, Ballston Spa Village Justice Court 1967-68. Judge, Saratoga County Family Court 1981-94.
Town Attorney Charlton, Day, Greenfield, Hadley, Providence, Saratoga and Waterford 1968-90. Assistant District Attorney 1969-73 and First Assistant District Attorney 1974-80 Saratoga County. Important Decisions: Hogan v. Kivlin (father charged with abuse, lack of proof) 1985; Towne v. Towne (relocation case) 1988; Smith v. Strait (paternity) 1988; and In the Matter of Ricky AA (adoption) 1989. Former Member New York State District Attorneys Association and New York State Association of Magistrates. Member Saratoga County Magistrates Association, Association of Judges of the Family Court of the State of New York, National Council of Juvenile and Family Court Judges, American Justinian Society of Jurists, Saratoga County (Former Director) and New York State (Fourth Judicial District Representative Criminal Justice Section 1977-80) Bar Associations. Lecturer "Warrants, Search and Seizure" New York State Division of Local Police 1974. Panelist "Role of the Law Guardian" Albany Law School of Union University 1982. Speaker "Family Values" College of St. Rose 1993. Lecturer to Town Justices for training sponsored by Office of Court Administration. Frequent Speaker on Family Law to Parents Without Partners. Republican. Former Director and President Benedict Memorial Hospital. Former Member and Director Ballston Spa Rotary Club. Former Director Ballston Spa Junior Baseball League. Founder, Former Director and Chairman Saratoga County CYO Basketball League. Former Chairman March of Dimes and National Red Cross fund drives Ballston Spa. Original Incorporator for Meals on Wheels Ballston Spa. Former Member Ballston Spa Jaycees. Member Advisory Board Boy Scouts of America, Saratoga YMCA, Elks, Knights of Columbus, Saratoga Springs Historical Society, New York State Basketball Coaches Association and Siena College Alumni Association (Former Director National Executive Committee). Coach Saratoga Central Catholic High School Girls Varsity Basketball 1986-94. Enjoys sports, card collecting and swimming.
Mailing address: P.O. Box 2380, Malta 12020-2380.
Telephone: (518) 581-1006.

FEUERSTEIN, Sandra J. *(Associate Justice, New York Supreme Court Appellate Division Second Judicial Department)* Elected Justice Tenth Judicial District 1994. Appointed Associate Justice Appellate Division by Governor George E. Pataki 1999. Born Jan 21, 1946. Educated at University of Vermont, Hunter College of the City University of New York and Yeshiva University Benjamin N. Cardozo School of Law J.D. cum laude. Admitted to practice New York, U.S. District Courts Eastern and Southern Districts of New York, U.S. Tax Court and U.S. Supreme Court. Matrimonial Referee, New York State Supreme Court Nassau County 1985-86. Judge, Nassau County District Court 1987-93.
Co-author *Handling a Criminal Case in New York: Practice Guide* Lawyers Cooperative 1088. Adjunct Professor Hofstra University School of Law 1998. Master Franklin D. Roosevelt Inns of Court 1989. Member since 1994 and Chair 1995-96 Gender Bias Committee and Co-chair Task Force on Reducing Litigation Cost and Delay since 1996 Tenth Judicial District; Member Advisory Committee on Judicial Ethics for New York State since 1996; and Task Force on Family Violence for New York State since 1996 Office of Court Administration. Member Nassau County Judicial Advisory Council, Bar Association of Nassau County (Director 1988-91, Vice Chair 1993-96 and Chair since 1996 Judicial Section), Nassau-Suffolk Women's (Vice President 1986-88), Nassau County Women's (President 1988-89) and New York State Women's (Vice President 1990-91) Bar Associations. Lecturer "Federal and State Civil Motion Practice" New York State Bar Association 1991. Chair Domestic Violence Seminar Nassau County 1995. Co-chair Domestic Violence Seminar Tenth Judicial District 1997 and 1998. Recipient Humanitarian Award from Education Assistance Corporation 1992 and Pathfinder Award from Town of Hempstead 1992. Named Judge of the Year by Court Officers Benevolent Association of Nassau County 1992 and Long Beach Lawyers Association 1996 and Woman of the Year by Merrick Chamber of Commerce 1993. Board of Directors South Nassau Communities Hospital and Noreen T. Holland Breast Cancer Foundation. Member Kiwanis Club (Merrick Chapter) and Long Island Center for Business and Professional Women. Life Member American Cancer Society and Cancer Care, Long Beach Memorial Hospital

FEUERSTEIN, SANDRA J.—*Continued*
Auxiliary, Hadassah and National Council of Jewish Women.
Office: Supreme Court Building, 100 Supreme Court Drive, Mineola 11501.
Telephone: (516) 571-3337.

FIECHTER, Michael A. *(Judge, Nassau County District Court)*
Office: 99 Main Street, Hempstead 11550.
Telephone: (516) 572-2139.
E-mail address: fiechter@courts.state.ny.us

FIGUEROA, Nicholas *(Justice, New York Supreme Court First Judicial District)* Former Acting Justice Twelfth Judicial District. Currentlyo serves Civil Term First Judicial District. Born New York New York Oct 1, 1933. Educated at City College of the City University of New York School of Business B.B.A. 1956 and Brooklyn Law School LL.B. 1964. Admitted to practice New York 1964, U.S. District Courts Southern 1973 and Eastern 1975 Districts of New York and U.S. Court of Appeals Second Circuit 1973. Former Judge, The Criminal Court of the City of New York, appointed by Mayor Edward Koch to term beginning May 28, 1980.
Assistant District Attorney Bronx County 1966-69. Assistant U.S. Attorney Southern District of New York 1972-75. Associate Counsel Knapp Commission for Investigation of Police Corruption. Member Puerto Rican Bar Association (President 1980). First Lieutenant U.S. Army 1956-58. Deputy Public Administrator 1969-70.
Office: 100 Centre Street, New York 10013.
Telephone: (212) 374-5719.
Fax: (212) 748-5095

FILIBERTO, Patricia M. *(Judge, Suffolk County District Court)*
Mailing address: P.O. Box 9075, Central Islip 11722-9075.
Office: Cohalan Court Complex, 400 Carleton Avenue, Central Islip 11722.
Telephone: (631) 853-7601.

FIORELLA, Joseph A. *(Judge, Buffalo City Court)*
Office: 50 Delaware Avenue, Buffalo 14202.
Telephone: (716) 847-8271.
Fax: (716) 847-8257

FIRETOG, Neil Jon *(Judge, The Criminal Court of the City of New York)* Appointed by Mayor Edward I. Koch March 22, 1983. Reappointed by Mayor David Dinkins to term beginning Jan 1, 1991 and by Mayor Rudolph W. Giuliani 2000. Current term expires Dec 31, 2010. Currently serves as Acting Justice, New York Supreme Court Second Judicial District. Born New York New York March 14, 1947. Educated at University of Michigan B.A. 1969 J.D. 1972.
Office: 360 Adams Street, Brooklyn 11201.
Telephone: (718) 643-3184.
E-mail address: nfiretog@courts.state.ny.us

FISCH, Joseph *(Judge, New York Court of Claims)* Appointed by Governor Mario Cuomo to term beginning July 1, 1990. Reappointed by Governor George E. Pataki 2001, current term expires June 30, 2008. Currently serves as Acting Justice, New York Supreme Court Twelfth Judicial District. Born New York New York Jan 10, 1933. Jewish. Educated at New York University B.A. 1953 and Harvard Law School LL.B. 1956. Member Phi Beta Kappa and Pi Sigma Alpha. President Harvard Law School Forum. Admitted to practice New York 1958, U.S. District Court Southern District of New York 1975 and U.S. Supreme Court 1978.
Assistant Counsel and Chief Counsel New York State Commission of Investigation 1959-77. Chief Assistant District Attorney Queens County 1977-84. Executive Assistant District Attorney Queens County 1987-90. Deputy District Attorney Kings County 1990. Important Decisions: People v. Louis Berrios 150 Misc. 2d 229, 568 N.Y.S.2d 512, 1991; People v. Gregory Ezeonu Misc. 2d 588 N.Y.S.2d 116, 1992; People v. Anthony Marchese 160 Misc. 2d 212, 608, N.Y.S.2d 776, 1994; People v. Paul Malcolm 161 Misc. 2d N.Y.S.2d 746, 1994; People v. Juan Ortiz 283 A.D.2d 377; and People v. Sherain Bryant 278 A.D.2d 7. Lecturer John Jay College of Criminal Justice 1988. Instructor in Organized Crime Seminars New York State Police 1975-77. Member New York County Lawyers' Association, American Judges Association and The Association of the Bar of the City of New York. Named Man of the Year by Knights of Pythias 1965 and Man in the News by *New York Times* 1971. Recipient Public Service Award from National Committee for Furtherance of Jewish Education 1984 and Distinguished Law Enforcement Award from New York State Association of Chiefs of Police and International Association of Chiefs of Police 1985. SP-3 U.S. Army JAG 1956-58. Democrat. Deputy Inspector General Metropolitan Transportation Authority 1984-85. Executive Director Office of Professional Discipline 1985-87. National President National Committee for Furtherance of Jewish Education. Member Harvard-Radcliffe Club of Westchester. Enjoys pocket billiards, photography, art and collecting Judaica.
Office: 851 Grand Concourse, Bronx 10451.
Telephone: (718) 590-6368.
Fax: (718) 590-7296

FISHER, Fern A. *(Justice, New York Supreme Court First Judicial District)* Currently serves as Administrative Judge, The Civil Court of the City of New York. Former Judge, The Civil Court of the City of New York.
Office: 111 Centre Street, New York 10013.
Telephone: (212) 374-8082.
Fax: (212) 374-5709
E-mail address: ffisher@courts.state.ny.us

FISHER, Kenneth R. *(Justice, New York Supreme Court Seventh Judicial District)* Born Westport Connecticut March 22, 1952. Educated at Williams College B.A. 1974 and Vermont Law School J.D. 1977. Staff member Vermont Law Review. Admitted to practice New York 1978 and U.S. District Courts Eastern, Northern, Southern and Western Districts of New York. Former Magistrate Judge, U.S. District Court Western District of New York, appointed by U.S. District Court judges to term beginning April 20, 1988.
Assistant District Attorney 1977-84 (Special Assistant to Chief of Appeals in charge of Appeals Bureau Administration 1982-84) and Deputy County Attorney 1984-88 Monroe County. Special Assistant U.S. Attorney Organized Crime and Racketeering Division U.S. Department of Justice 1981-84. Special Counsel to District Attorney Steuben County 1981-86. Author Note "Abandonment of *Lex Loci Delicti?* Toward a Functional Approach to Choice-of-Law in Vermont" 2 Vermont

FISHER, KENNETH R.—*Continued*

L. Rev. 133, 1977. Member Greater Rochester Association for Women Attorneys.

Office: 545 Hall of Justice, 99 Exchange Boulevard, Rochester 14614-2185.
Telephone: (585) 428-2888.
Fax: (585) 428-2983

FISHER, Steven W. *(Justice, New York Supreme Court Eleventh Judicial District)* Former Acting Justice. Currently serves as Administrative Judge. Former Judge, The Criminal Court of the City of New York.

Office: 88-11 Sutphin Boulevard, Jamaica 11435.
Telephone: (718) 520-3798.
Fax: (718) 520-2499

FitzGERALD, Daniel P. *(Judge, The Criminal Court of the City of New York)* Appointed by mayor. Currently serves as Acting Justice, New York Supreme Court First Judicial District.

Office: 100 Centre Street, New York 10013.
Telephone: (212) 374-5862.

FITZGERALD, Edmund G., Jr. *(Judge, Yonkers City Court)* Elected Nov 1999 to term beginning Jan 1, 2000. Term expires Dec 31, 2009. Born New York New York. Roman Catholic. Educated at Fordham University B.A. 1966 J.D. 1972. Admitted to practice New York 1977 and U.S. District Courts Eastern 1981 and Southern 1981 Districts of New York. In legal practice Yonkers 1977-81 and 1987-99.

Senior Assistant Corporate Counsel Yonkers 1981-87. Republican.

Office: Justice Center, 100 South Broadway, Yonkers 10701.
Telephone: (914) 377-6392.
Fax: (914) 377-6395
E-mail address: egfitzge@courts.state.ny.us

FITZGIBBON, Madeleine A. *(Judge, Suffolk County District Court)* Currently serves as Supervising Judge.

Mailing address: P.O. Box 9075, Central Islip 11722-9075.

Office: Cohalan Court Complex, 400 Carleton Avenue, Central Islip 11722.
Telephone: (631) 853-4917.

FITZMAURICE, Mary Ellen *(Judge, New York City Family Court)* Appointed by mayor. Former Supervising Judge.

Office: 210 Joralemon Street, Brooklyn 11201.
Telephone: (718) 643-6476.

FITZPATRICK, Diane L. *(Judge, New York Court of Claims)* Appointed by Governor George E. Pataki. Educated at Albany Law School 1978. Admitted to practice New York 1979 and U.S. District Courts Northern 1979 and Western 1980 Districts of New York. In legal practice Syracuse 1979-98.

Law Clerk to Onondaga County Court 1987-91. Member Town Board Lafayette 1992-98.

Office: Salina Place, Second Floor, 205 South Salina Street, Syracuse 13202.
Telephone: (315) 466-7161.
Fax: (315) 466-7164

FLAHERTY, Timothy J. *(Justice, New York Supreme Court Eleventh Judicial District)* Former Judge, The Civil Court of the City of New York.

Office: 25-10 Court Square, Long Island City 11101.
Telephone: (718) 520-2615.

FLORIO, Anita R. *(Associate Justice, New York Supreme Court Appellate Division Second Judicial Department)* Acting Justice Jan 1981 to Dec 1983. Elected Justice Twelfth Judicial District to term beginning Jan 1, 1984. Appointed Associate Justice Appellate Division by Governor Mario Cuomo 1994. Term expires Dec 31, 2011. Born New York New York Nov 22, 1936. Roman Catholic. Educated at Manhattanville College B.A. 1958, Fordham University School of Law LL.B. 1963 and New York University School of Law LL.M. 1966. Law Clerk to Hon. Vincent A. Giaquinto 1963-64. Admitted to practice New York 1963 and U.S. Supreme Court 1968. In legal practice New York 1964-69. Judge, The Criminal Court of the City of New York 1977-84.

Assistant District Attorney Bronx County Feb 1969 to Oct 1970. Law Secretary to Justice Joseph P. Sullivan, New York Supreme Court Appellate Division First Judicial Department Jan 1973 to Dec 1974. Deputy Secretary of State and Counsel to New York State April 1975 to Dec 1977. Past President New York State Association of Women Judges. Former Director National Association of Women Judges. Treasurer Board of Justices of the Twelfth Judicial District. President Association of Supreme Court Justices of the City of New York. Co-chair New York State Unified Court System's Jury Selection Uniformity Committee. Member Columbian Lawyers Association-First Judicial Department, Metropolitan Women's (President 1969-71, Past Officer, Past Director) and Bronx County (Past President, Officer and Director) Bar Associations. Recipient Charles A. Rapall Award from Columbian Lawyers Association 1989. Founder and Director Judges and Lawyers Breast Cancer Alert (JALBCA).

Office: 851 Grand Concourse, Bronx 10451.
Telephone: (718) 590-3660.

FLUG, Phyllis Orlikoff *(Justice, New York Supreme Court Eleventh Judicial District)* Elected to term beginning Jan 1, 1990. Term expires Dec 31, 2003. Educated at Bernard M. Baruch College of the City University of New York B.B.A. 1960 and Syracuse University College of Law J.D. 1963. Admitted to practice New York 1964, U.S. District Courts Eastern 1965 and Southern 1965 Districts of New York, U.S. Tax Court 1965, U.S. Court of Appeals Second Circuit 1966 and U.S. Supreme Court 1989. In legal practice New York June 1964 to Jan 1974 and Jan 1981 to Dec 1983. Hearing Examiner Parking Violations Bureau April 1972 to Jan 1974. Per Diem Administrative Law Judge 1982-83. Judge, The Civil Court of the City of New York 1984-89.

Taxi and Limousine Commission Dec 1973 to Jan 1974 New York City. Assistant District Attorney Queens County Jan 1974 to Dec 1974. Law Secretary Civil Court Queens County Jan 1975 to Oct 1976. Principal Law Clerk to Supreme Court Justice Queens County Oct 1976 to Dec 1980. Author *Conspiracy: Historical Perspective* Arno Press 1972. Assistant Professor of Law Nassau Community College Sept 1969 to Jan 1974. Adjunct Lecturer on Continuing Legal Education Queens College of the City University of New York 1992. Adjunct Associate Professor Queensborough Community College since 1993. Member Appellate Division Griev-

FLUG, PHYLLIS ORLIKOFF—*Continued*
ance Committee Second and Eleventh Judicial Districts 1981-83 and Speaker's Bureau Office of Court Administration 1996. President 1982-83 and Chairperson Board of Directors 1991-92 Brandeis Association. Chair Program Committee 1980 and 1991-92 and Board of Managers 1981-83 Queens County Bar Association. Member Queens Assistant District Attorneys Association, New York City Board of Civil Court Judges (Vice President 1988-89), Association of Supreme Court Justices of the City of New York (Board of Directors), Association of Justices of the Supreme Court of the State of New York, National Association of Women Judges (Board of Directors since 1992, Treasurer 1997-2000 and Vice President since 2000 New York State Chapter, National Finance Chair 2002) and New York State Women's Bar Association (Queen's Chapter). Recipient Outstanding Achievement Award from Baruch College Alumni Association 1988. Troop Leader 1963-67, Career Day Speaker 1991, Gold Award Key Note Speaker 1991 and Scholar Program Instructor 1991 Girl Scouts of America. Board of Trustees Conservative Synagogue of Jamaica 1976-97. New York State Delegate to International Women's Year Convention, Houston Texas 1977. Paralegal Advisory Board 1984-88 and Black, Jewish People-to-People Project 1990 Queens College of the City University of New York. Judge Froessel Moot Court Competition New York Law School 1990-91, 1993 and 1995-96. Board of Directors Judges and Lawyers Breast Cancer Alert (JALBCA) 1995-99. Member Jamaica Estates Civic Association (Bulletin Committee 1980), State of Israel Bond (Queens Women's Professional Division Committee 1981-83) and Parents Association Board P.S. 178 and P.S. 131 Queens.

Office: 88-11 Sutphin Boulevard, Jamaica 11435.
Telephone: (718) 520-3743.
Fax: (718) 520-4682
E-mail address: poflug@courts.state.ny.gov

FORMA, Joseph S. *(Justice, New York Supreme Court Eighth Judicial District)* Elected to term beginning Jan 1, 1987. Reelected 2000, current term expires Dec 31, 2014. Born Buffalo New York March 23, 1942. Roman Catholic. Educated at University of Buffalo B.A. cum laude 1962 and State University of New York at Buffalo J.D. 1965. Staff member New York University Law Review. Admitted to practice New York 1965. Began legal practice Buffalo 1965. Judge, Buffalo City Court 1976-82. Judge, Erie County Court Jan 1, 1983 to Dec 31, 1986.

Instructor Buffalo Police Academy 1971-73. Member Bar Association of Erie County (Lecturer 1972-73). Democrat. Councilman-at-large 1974-75. Enjoys the outdoors and photography.

Office: Erie County Hall, 92 Franklin Street, Buffalo 14202-2721.
Telephone: (716) 851-3355.
Fax: (716) 851-3319
E-mail address: jforma@courts.state.ny.us

FORMAN, Peter M. *(Judge, Dutchess County Family Court)*
Office: 50 Market Street, Poughkeepsie 12601-3204.
Telephone: (845) 486-2526.
E-mail address: pforman@courts.state.ny.us

FORMAN, Walter J. *(Judge, Cohoes City Court)*
Mailing address: P.O. Box 678, Cohoes 12047-0678.
Office: 97 Mohawk Street, Cohoes 12047.
Telephone: (518) 233-2133.

FORREST, Steven W. *(Judge, Elmira City Court)* Appointed by mayor to term beginning July 1, 1996. Elected to term beginning Jan 1, 1998, current term expires Dec 31, 2003. Born Sedalia Missouri Oct 3, 1955. Methodist. Educated at Denison University B.A. 1977 and DePaul University J.D. 1980. Admitted to practice New York 1981. In legal practice Elmira since 1981.

Assistant Corporation Counsel 1984-87 and Assistant Public Defender 1985-96 Elmira. Instructor in Business Law II Corning Community College 1984-87. Member Chemung County and New York State Bar Associations. Attended Judicial Training sponsored by New York State since 1996. Named Kiwanian of the Year 1983. Recipient Judd Hoover Community Service Award 1996. Enjoys sports.

Office: Elmira City Hall, 317 East Church Street, Elmira 14901-2790.
Telephone: (607) 737-5681.
Fax: (607) 737-5820
E-mail address: sforrest@courts.state.ny.us

FOSCHIO, Leslie G. *(Magistrate Judge, United States District Court Western District of New York)* Appointed by U.S. District Court judges to term beginning Feb 1, 1991. Reappointed Jan 1999, current term expires Jan 2007. Born Buffalo New York Oct 29, 1940. Roman Catholic. Educated at University of Buffalo B.A. cum laude 1962 and State University of New York at Buffalo LL.B. cum laude 1965. Comment Editor Buffalo Law Review 1964-65. Law Clerk to Hon. William B. Lawless, Jr., New York Supreme Court Eighth Judicial District 1965. Honorary Member Alpha Phi Delta. Admitted to practice New York 1966, U.S. Courts of Appeals Seventh 1973, Second 1977 and District of Columbia 1977 Circuits, U.S. District Court Western District of New York 1975, U.S. Supreme Court 1975 and U.S. Tax Court 1980. In legal practice Buffalo 1978-81.

Attorney Office of Counsel State University of New York 1965-66. Assistant District Attorney 1966-68 and Senior Assistant District Attorney 1968-69 Western District of New York. Corporation Counsel City of Buffalo 1975-77. Commissioner of Motor Vehicles State of New York 1981-83. General Counsel (Vice President and Secretary) Barrister Information Systems Corporation 1983-91. Author Case Note "Zoning Ordinance—Constitutionality of Privately or Publicly Establishes Setback line" 13 Buffalo L. Rev. 285, 1963; Case Note "Unconstitutionality of New York City Minimum Wage Law—A Limitation on Municipal Rule Police Powers" 13 Buffalo L. Rev. 149, 1963; Comment "Condonation and the New York Separate Roofs Defense" 13 Buffalo L. Rev. 603, 1964; "Operations Research in Criminal Justice: A Legal View, in Studying Social Systems" Mickle and Hoelscher eds. University of Pittsburgh Press 1973; Chapter 3 "New York State Regulatory Reform" Report of Action Unit No. 5 New York State Bar Association 1981; "Access and Disclosures of Motor Vehicles Records—Your Privacy and Government's Need to Know" 6 No. 1 Journal of Law and Communications Feb 1984; "Legal System Defends Religious Freedom" Western New York Catholic May 1984; "Law Day, A Time to Consider the Mother of All of Our Liberties" Op. Ed. Buffalo News May 1, 1984; and "The United

FOSCHIO, LESLIE G.—*Continued*

States Commissioner and Magistrate Judge System—A Legal History" III Nos. 3, 4 & 5 Federal Bar News.

Important Decisions: Daniel v. American Board of Emergency Medicine 802 F. Supp. 912 W.D.N.Y. 1992; Fiske v. Church of St. Mary of the Angels 802 F. Supp. 872 W.D.N.Y. 1992; Vendetti v. Fiat Auto, S.p.A. 802 F. Supp. 886 W.D.N.Y. 1992; Hydroflow v. Enidine, Inc. 145 F.R.D. 626 W.D.N.Y. 1993; United States v. Clarke 822 F. Supp. 990 W.D.N.Y. 1993; Kinley Corp. v. Ancira 859 F. Supp. 652 W.D.N.Y. 1994; Burns v. Imagine Films 164 F.R.D. 594 W.D.N.Y. 1996; United States v. Johnson 886 F. Supp. 1057 W.D.N.Y. 1995; Idylwoods Associates v. Mader Capital, Inc. 915 F. Supp. 1290 W.D.N.Y. 1996; Westmoreland Capital Corp. v. Findlay 916 F. Supp. 242 W.D.N.Y. aff'd 100 F.3d 263, 2d Cir. 1996; United States v. Collins 921 F. Supp. 1028 W.D.N.Y. 1996; R. E. Turner, Inc. v. Connecticut Indemnity 925 F. Supp. 139 W.D.N.Y. 1996; Koseck v. United States of America 1996 WL328140 W.D.N.Y. 1996; Idylwoods v. Mader 1997 WL815398 W.D.N.Y. 1997; Daniel v. American Board of Emergency Medicine 988 F. Supp. 127 W.D.N.Y. 1997; In re Pfohl Brothers Landfill Litigation 26 F. Supp. 2d 512 W.D.N.Y. 1998; In re Pfohl Brothers Landfill Litigation 68 F. Supp. 2d 236 W.D.N.Y. 1999; Hyatt Corporation v. Women's International Bowling Congress, Inc. 1999 WL 1041520 W.D.N.Y. 1999; In re Pfohl Bros. Landfill Litigation 68 F. Supp. 2d 236 W.D.N.Y. 1999; United States v. Bidloff 82 F. Supp. 2d 86 W.D.N.Y. 2000; Roberts-Gordon, LLC v. Superior Radiant Products, Ltd. 85 F. Supp. 2d 202 W.D.N.Y. 2000; United States v. King 2000 W.L. 362026 W.D.N.Y. 2000; Nagele v. Electronic Data System Corp. 193 F.R.D. 94 W.D.N.Y. 2000; Booth Oil Site Administrative Group v. Safety-Kleen Corporation 194 F.R.D. 76 W.D.N.Y. 2000; Mainline Contracting Corp. v. Chopra-Lee, Inc. 109 F. Supp. 2d 110 W.D.N.Y. 2000; McKinley Associates, LLC v. McKesson HBOC, Inc. 110 F. Supp. 2d 169 W.D.N.Y. 2000 aff'd 8 Fed.Appx. 31 2d Cir. 2001; TIG Ins. Co. v. Town of Cheektowaga 142 F. Supp. 2d 343 W.D.N.Y. 2000; Burt Rigid Box Inc. v. Travelers Property Cas. Corp. 126 F. Supp. 2d 596 W.D.N.Y. 2001; Mercer v. Herbert 133 F. Supp. 2d 219 W.D.N.Y. 2001; United States v. Parker 165 F. Supp. 2d 431 W.D.N.Y. 2001.

Assistant Professor of Law 1965-73, Associate Professor of Law 1973-75 and Assistant Dean Notre Dame Law School. Lecturer State University of New York at Buffalo Law School 1966-67, 1978 and 1979. Member Region One Executive Committee American Association of Motor Vehicle Administrators 1981-83 and Committee on Unjust Criticism of Courts 1988-90. Former Commercial Arbitrator American Arbitration Association. Life Fellow New York Bar Foundation and American Bar Foundation. Member Federal Magistrate Judges Association, Bar Association of Erie County (Chair Administrative Law and Procedure Committee 1978-81 and Law Day Committee 1983-84, Director 1988-91) and New York State (Member 1979-97 and Chairman Subcommittee on Regulatory Process Action Unit No. 5, 1980-82, Chair Computer Law Committee 1986-90, Member Courts and Community Relations Committee 1987-89, Executive Committee Business Law Section 1987-93). Panelist "Counseling Governmental and Corporate Clients: How Can the Public Interest Be Served?" Model Public Interest Law Conference Sept 29, 1978. Presenter "Deregulation in New York—The Work of Action N.Y.B.A. Unit No. 5" Administrative Law Program Oct 24, 1980, "Standard Software Licensing Agreements" Oct 22, 1986, "Standard Software License Agreements, Computer Law: Practical Approaches to the Acquisition and Marketing of Computer Goods and Services" Business Law Section Oct 1987 and Nov 16, 1988, "Computer Software—Copyright, Trade Secret & Acquisition Issues—An Intellectual Property Forum for the General Practitioner" Special Committee on Patents and Copyright Law and Computer Law Committee Section on Business Law Jan 17, 1990, "Arrest and Pre-Trial Proceedings on Federal Criminal Practice, Basic Federal Criminal Practice" April 22, 1994, "Resolving Intellectual Property Disputes, Intellectual Property Law: How It Can Help Your Business" Intellectual Property Law Section Fall Meeting Bolton Landing Oct 1, 1994 and "Deposition Practice—A View from the Federal Bench" April 21, 1995 and Oct 17, 1997 New York State Bar Association; "Considerations in Negotiating a Computer Hardware and Software Agreement" Corporation, Banking and Business Law Section Cleveland Bar Association Oct 11, 1989; and "A Chronicle for the Nineties—Computer Systems and the Lawyer" Oct 20, 1990, "Sanctions and Summary Judgment" 1991 and "Objections to Report and Recommendations of Magistrate Judges" Federal Civil Practice Seminar Feb 25, 1995 Bar Association of Erie County.

Named one of Outstanding Young Men of America by U.S. Jaycees 1970 and 1977. Recipient Distinguished Public Service Award from New York State Jaycees 1976, Award for Outstanding Achievement in Highway Safety by a public official from New York State RID (Remove Intoxicated Drivers) 1982, Roy Thorp Award for Outstanding Service to Benefit Highway Safety from New York State Association of Traffic Safety Board 1982, Distinguished Alumnus Award from General Alumni Association State University of New York at Buffalo June 3, 1983, Distinguished Alumnus Award for Achievements in Public Service from Law Alumni Association State University of New York at Buffalo School of Law May 8, 1987 and Outstanding Alumnus Award from H. C. Technical High School Alumni Association June 23, 1997. Listed in *Who's Who in American Law* 4th ed., *Who's Who in United States Executives* 1990 and *Who's Who in America* Millennium Edition. Democratic candidate New York State Assembly General Election 1968. Endorsed candidate for mayor of Buffalo Democratic Primary 1977. Director 1976-79, Treasurer 1979-80, Vice President 1980-81 and President 1981-82 Member Law Alumni Association State University of New York at Buffalo. President 1978-87 and Trustee since 1978 Theodore Roosevelt Inaugural National Historic Site. Trustee Theodore Roosevelt Association 1981-99. Director 1996-98 and Vice President of Membership 1998-99 Alumni Association State University of New York at Buffalo. Enjoys reading.

Office: 424 U.S. Courthouse, 68 Court Street, Buffalo 14202.

Telephone: (716) 332-7850.

FOSKEY, Carnell T. *(Judge, Nassau County Family Court)*

Office: 1200 Old Country Road, Westbury 11590.
Telephone: (516) 571-9022.
Fax: (516) 571-9335

FOX, Kevin Nathaniel *(Magistrate Judge, United States District Court Southern District of New York)* Appointed by U.S. District Court judges.

Office: 540 U.S. Courthouse, 40 Centre Street, New York 10007.

Telephone: (212) 805-6705.

FOX, Mark D. *(Magistrate Judge, United States District Court Southern District of New York)* Appointed part-time Magistrate May 31, 1988. Appointed full-time Magistrate Judge Sept 3, 1991. Reappointed 1999, current term expires Sept 2007. Born Bronx New York Aug 4, 1943. Educated at State University of New York at Buffalo B.A. 1964 and Brooklyn Law School J.D. 1967. In legal practice Port Jervis 1977 to May 31, 1998.

Assistant District Attorney Bronx County Jan 1970 to Nov 1971 and Orange County Nov 1971 to Jan 1, 1973. Chief Trial Attorney, Chief Attorney and Public Defender Orange County Legal Aid Society 1973-77. Editorial Board Federal Bar Council Newsletter 1997-2000. Visiting Instructor in Trial Practice Harvard University Law School Jan 2000. Former Director New York State Defenders Association. Former Member Law Guardian Advisory Committee Appellate Division Second Department Ninth Judicial District. Member Committee on Security and Facilities Judicial Conference of the U.S. since Nov 4, 1996. Member Federal Bar Council, Federal Magistrate Judges Association, Orange County (Former Chair Criminal Law Committee), New York State (Former Member Executive Committee Criminal Justice Section) and American Bar Associations. Lecturer on Criminal Law and Federal Civil Practice New York State Bar Association and New York State Office of Court Administration. Investigator U.S. Army 1967 to Jan 1970.

Office: U.S. Courthouse, 300 Quarropas Street, White Plains 10601-4150.

Telephone: (914) 390-4124.

FRANCIS, James C., IV *(Magistrate Judge, United States District Court Southern District of New York)* Appointed by U.S. District Court judges to term beginning Oct 28, 1985. Reappointed Oct 1993 and 2001. Current term expires Oct 2009. Born Tulsa Oklahoma Oct 3, 1952. Presbyterian. Educated at Yale University B.A. summa cum laude 1974 J.D. 1978 and Harvard University M.P.P. 1978. Editorial Board Yale Law Journal 1977-78. Law Clerk to Hon. Robert L. Carter, U.S. District Court Southern District of New York 1978-79. Member Phi Beta Kappa. Admitted to practice New York 1979, U.S. District Courts Southern 1979 and Eastern 1980 Districts of New York and U.S. Court of Appeals Second Circuit 1980.

Staff Attorney The Legal Aid Society of New York 1979-85. Author "United Jewish Organizations and the Need to Recognize Aggregate Voting Rights" 87 Yale L. Jour. 571, 1978, "Current Discovery Disputes" *Civil Practice and Litigation Techniques in Federal Courts* ALI-ABA 1993, "Practicing Before United States Magistrate Judges" 5 Practical Litigator 15, 1994, "Pretrial Management" *Federal Civil Practice* Georgene Vairo ed. 1989, 1993 and 1997 Supplement and "Pretrial Management" *Moore's Federal Practice* Chapters 29, 31, 34 and 35 3rd ed. 1997. Co-author with J. Chaifitz and A. Cohen "Mandatory Law School Pro Bono Programs" 50 Record 170, 1995. Important Decisions: Polycast Technology Corp. v. Uniroyal, Inc. (legal ethics) 129 F.R.D. 621 S.D.N.Y. 1990; Lewis v. Velez (prison discipline; evidence) 149 F.R.D. 474 S.D.N.Y. 1993; Hogarth v. Thornburgh (disability discrimination) 833 F. Supp. 1077 S.D.N.Y. 1993; Bank Brussels Lambert v. Credit Lyonnais (Suisse) S.A. (attorney-client privilege) 160 F.R.D. 437 S.D.N.Y. 1995; MFS/Sun Life Trust—High Yield Series v. Van Dusen Airport Services Co. (leveraged buyout; fraudulent conveyance) 910 F. Supp. 913 S.D.N.Y. 1995; Shea v. Icelandair (age discrimination in employment; damages) 925 F. Supp. 1014 S.D.N.Y 1996; Phillips v. Kidder Peabody & Co. (securities fraud) 933 F. Supp. 303, 1996; Iannone v. Frederic R. Harris, Inc. (sex harassment and retaliation) 941 F. Supp. 403 S.D.N.Y. 1996; Bank of New York v. Meridien Biao Bank Tanzania Ltd. (custody or control of documents) 171 F.R.D. 135 S.D.N.Y. 1997; Chi Chao Yuan v. Rivera (abuse and neglect; liability of caseworker) 48 F. Supp. 2d 335 S.D.N.Y. 1999; Madanes v. Madanes (foreign privilege against self-incrimination) 186 F.R.D. 279 S.D.N.Y. 1999; and Mathias v. Jacobs (discovery sanctions) 197 F.R.D. 29 S.D.N.Y. 2000. Member Federal Magistrate Judges Association, Federal Bar Council, The Association of the Bar of the City of New York and New York State Bar Association. Democrat. Member Professional Advisory Board Epilepsy Institute. Interests include travel and soccer.

Office: 1960 U.S. Courthouse, 500 Pearl Street, New York 10007-1312.

Telephone: (212) 805-0206.

FRANCO, Ralph P. *(Justice, New York Supreme Court Tenth Judicial District)* Elected to term beginning Jan 1, 1995. Certificated. Born Brooklyn New York June 20, 1927. Catholic. Educated at Brooklyn College A.A. 1949 and Brooklyn Law School LL.B. 1952. Admitted to practice New York 1953, U.S. District Courts Eastern 1958 and Southern 1958 Districts of New York and U.S. Supreme Court 1960. In legal practice Brooklyn and Freeport 1953-88. Justice, Freeport Village Justice Court 1977-88. Judge, Nassau County District Court Feb 1988 to Dec 31, 1994.

Law Secretary to Justice, New York Supreme Court 1960-64. Member Catholic Lawyers Guild, Columbian Lawyers Association, Nassau County Lawyers Association, Nassau County Magistrates Association (President 1985-86), New York State Association of Magistrates and Nassau County Bar Association. Hospital Corpsman First Class USN 1945-47. Past President Freeport Rotary Club. Lifetime member Freeport Harbor Civic Association. Honorary member Freeport Fire Department. Member American Legion, Knights of Columbus and Order of Sons of Italy. Enjoys fishing and boating.

Office: Supreme Court Building, 100 Supreme Court Drive, Mineola 11501.

Telephone: (516) 571-2727.

FRANCZYK, Thomas P. *(Judge, Buffalo City Court)* Appointed by Mayor Anthony M. Masullo to term beginning Jan 1, 1997. Elected Nov 1997 to term beginning Jan 1, 1998, current term expires Dec 31, 2007. Born Buffalo New York Sept 10, 1957. Roman Catholic. Educated at State University of New York at Buffalo B.A. with honors 1979 and Syracuse University College of Law J.D. 1982. Member Order of the Coif. Admitted to practice New York 1983 and U.S. District Court Western District of New York 1983. In legal practice Buffalo 1985-86.

Assistant District Attorney Erie County 1982-85 and 1986-96. Instructor in Trial Technique, Plea Bargaining

FRANCZYK, THOMAS P.—*Continued*

and Jury Selection State University of New York at Buffalo School of Law since 1995. Member New York State Association of City Court Judges, Erie County, New York State and American Bar Associations. Attended Annual New York State Judges Conference Rye 1998. Named Prosecutor of the Year by Buffalo Police Department Detective's Association 1991. Recipient Christopher Ionnine Award from National Alliance for the Mentally Ill 1999. Democrat. Teacher and Instructor Youth Court since 1997. Enjoys guitar and cooking.

Office: 50 Delaware Avenue, Buffalo 14202.
Telephone: (716) 847-8283.
Fax: (716) 847-8257

FRAZEE, Evelyn *(Justice, New York Supreme Court Seventh Judicial District)* Elected to term beginning Jan 1, 1993. Term expires Dec 31, 2006. Educated at State University of New York College at Oneonta B.A. 1972 and Rutgers University School of Law at Camden J.D. 1978. Editor-in-Chief Rutgers Law Review 1977-78. Recipient Corpus Juris Secundum Award. Admitted to practice New York 1979 and U.S. District Court Western District of New York 1980. In legal practice Rochester 1978-80.

Law Clerk to Hon. Andrew V. Siracuse, New York Supreme Court Seventh Judicial District 1980-92. Member Monroe County and New York State Bar Associations.

Office: 545 Hall of Justice, 99 Exchange Boulevard, Rochester 14614-2185.
Telephone: (585) 428-2486.
Fax: (585) 428-2698
E-mail address: efrazee@courts.state.ny.us

FREEDMAN, Helen E. *(Justice, New York Supreme Court First Judicial District)* Former Acting Justice. Elected Justice to term beginning Jan 1, 1989. Reelected 2002, current term expires Dec 31, 2016. Former Justice, New York Supreme Court Appellate Term First Judicial Department. Born New York New York 1942. Educated at Smith College B.A. 1963 and New York University School of Law LL.B. 1967. Admitted to practice New York 1967, U.S. District Courts Eastern 1970 and Southern 1970 Districts of New York and U.S. Supreme Court 1979. Began legal practice New York. Judge, The Civil Court of the City of New York Jan 1, 1979 to Dec 31, 1988.

Author *New York Objections* James Publishing 1st ed.1998, revised 1999, 2000 and 2001. Adjunct Professor of Law and Mass Torts Spring 1999 and Spring 2000. Recipient Judicial Excellence Award from Conference of State Trial Judges American Bar Association 1998.

Office: 60 Centre Street, New York 10007.
Telephone: (212) 374-8387.

FREEMAN, Debra *(Magistrate Judge, United States District Court Southern District of New York)* Appointed by U.S. District Court judges.

Office: 631 U.S. Courthouse, 40 Centre Street, New York 10007-1581.
Telephone: (212) 805-4250.

FREEMAN, Nora L. *(Judge, New York City Family Court)* Appointed by mayor.

Office: 283 Adams Street, Sixth Floor, Brooklyn 11201.
Telephone: (718) 643-4546.
Fax: (718) 643-5103

FREUNDLICH, David *(Judge, Suffolk County Family Court)* Elected to term beginning Jan 1, 1989. Reelected Nov 1998, current term expires Dec 31, 2008. Also serves as Supervising Judge. Currently serves as Acting Justice, New York Supreme Court Tenth Judicial District.

Office: Cohalan Court Complex, 400 Carleton Avenue, Central Islip 11722.
Telephone: (631) 853-4318.
Fax: (631) 853-6218

FRICANO, Amy J. *(Justice, New York Supreme Court Eighth Judicial District)* Former Judge, Niagara County Court.

Office: Niagara County Civic Center, 775 Third Street, Niagara Falls 14302.
Telephone: (716) 278-1810.
Fax: (716) 278-1809
E-mail address: africano@courts.state.ny.us

FRIED, Bernard J. *(Judge, The Criminal Court of the City of New York)* Appointed by mayor. Currently serves as Acting Justice, New York Supreme Court First Judicial District.

Office: 111 Centre Street, New York 10013.
Telephone: (212) 374-8452.

FRIEDMAN, David *(Associate Justice, New York Supreme Court Appellate Division First Judicial Department)* Acting Justice Jan 1994 to Dec 1997. Elected Justice Second Judicial District to term beginning Jan 1998. Appointed Associate Justice Appellate Division by Governor George E. Pataki. Judge, The Civil Court of the City of New York Jan 1990 to Dec 1993.

Office: 27 Madison Avenue at 25th Street, New York 10010.
Telephone: (212) 340-0400.

FRIEDMAN, Marcy S. *(Judge, The Civil Court of the City of New York)* Currently serves as Acting Justice, New York Supreme Court First Judicial District.

Office: 80 Centre Street, New York 10013.
Telephone: (212) 374-4573.

FRIEDMAN, Rhea G. *(Judge, New York City Family Court)* Appointed by Mayor Ed Koch.

Office: 151-20 Jamaica Avenue, Jamaica 11432.
Telephone: (718) 298-0197.

FRIEDMANN, William D. *(Associate Justice, New York Supreme Court Appellate Division Second Judicial Department)* Elected Justice to term beginning Jan 1, 1980. Appointed Associate Justice Appellate Division by Governor Mario Cuomo to term beginning Jan 1994. Certificated. Born New York New York Aug 2, 1927. Unitarian. Educated at Hunter College of the City University of New York A.B. cum laude 1950 and New York University School of Law LL.B. 1953 LL.M. in Trade Regulation 1958. Admitted to practice New York, U.S. Supreme Court, U.S. Court of Appeals and U.S. District Court. In legal practice New York City 1952-76 and Flushing 1978-80. Acting Judge, The Criminal Court of the City of New York 1981-82. Judge, The

FRIEDMANN, WILLIAM D.—*Continued*

Civil Court of the City of New York Jan 1, 1981 to Dec 31, 1986.

Assistant District Attorney Queens County 1962-63. Assistant Administrator and General Counsel 1976-77 and Commissioner 1977-78 Environmental Protection Administration New York City. Emergency Energy Coordinator New York City 1976-78. Coordinator Mayor's Hazardous Matter Task Force New York City 1978. Professor Paralegal Program Queens College of the City University of New York 1984. Associate Professor of Law Long Island University since 1984. National Panel of Arbitrators American Arbitration Association. Member American Judicature Society, Federal Bar Council, Federal Bar Association of New Jersey, Federal Bar Association of Connecticut, The Association of the Bar of the City of New York, Bankruptcy Lawyers, Queens County, New York State and American Bar Associations. Instructor in Corporation Law Queens College Continuing Education Program 1984. Counsel Assembly Committee on Judiciary New York State 1979 and Senate Democratic Minority New York State 1980.

Office: 88-11 Sutphin Boulevard, Jamaica 11435.
Telephone: (718) 520-3753.
Fax: (718) 520-6405
E-mail address: wfriedma@courts.state.ny.us

FRIIA, Jo Ann *(Judge, White Plains City Court)*
Office: 77 South Lexington Avenue, White Plains 10601.
Telephone: (914) 422-6064.
Fax: (914) 422-6058

FURFURE, Marianne *(Surrogate, Steuben County Surrogate's Court)* Currently serves as Acting Judge, Steuben County Court.
Office: Courthouse, 13 East Pulteney Square, Bath 14810.
Telephone: (607) 776-8492.
Fax: (607) 776-4921

FUSCO, John A. *(Surrogate, Richmond County Surrogate's Court)*
Office: County Courthouse, St. George, Staten Island 10301.
Telephone: (718) 390-5400.

GABLER, William J. *(Acting Judge, Salamanca City Court)* Appointed by mayor to term beginning Dec 30, 1991. Reappointed to term beginning Jan 1, 1993. Reappointed to subsequent term. Also serves as Hearing Examiner Family Court since 1985. Born Olean New York June 2, 1952. Baptist. Educated at State University of New York at Buffalo B.S. magna cum laude 1974 and Albany Law School of Union University J.D. 1977. Member Beta Gamma Sigma. Admitted to practice New York 1978, U.S. District Court Western District of New York 1978 and U.S. Supreme Court 1982. In legal practice Allegany 1981-85.

Assistant Public Defender Monroe County 1978-81. Assistant Professor of Business Law St. Bonaventure University 1982-85. Adjunct Instructor in Business Law Jamestown Community College 1990-93. Member Allegany County and Cattaraugus County (President 1989) Bar Associations. Instructor in Basic Matrimonial Practice sponsored by New York State Bar Association Fall 1994. Listed in *Who's Who in American Law* 8th ed. Democrat. Enjoys golf, racquetball and long distance running.

Office: Municipal Center, Salamanca 14779.
Telephone: (716) 945-4153.
Fax: (716) 945-2362

GAGE, Walter C. *(Judge, Geneva City Court)*
Office: Public Safety Building, 255 Exchange Street, Geneva 14456.
Telephone: (315) 789-6560.
Fax: (315) 781-2802

GALASSO, John Michael *(Judge, Nassau County Court)* Elected Nov 4, 1997 to term beginning Jan 1, 1998. Term expires Dec 31, 2007. Currently serves as Acting Justice, New York Supreme Court Tenth Judicial District. Born Glen Cove New York Dec 26, 1944. Roman Catholic. Educated at C. W. Post College of Long Island University B.A. 1966 and St. John's University School of Law J.D. 1969. Admitted to practice New York 1969, U.S. Court of Appeals Second Circuit 1973, U.S. Supreme Court 1973, U.S. District Courts Eastern 1975 and Southern 1975 Districts of New York, U.S. Court of Appeals for the Armed Forces 1979, U.S. Court of Customs and Patent Appeals 1979, U.S. Court of Federal Claims 1979, U.S. Tax Court 1979 and U.S. Court of International Trade 1983. In legal practice 1978-91. Judge, Nassau County District Court Jan 28, 1991 to Dec 31, 1997.

Assistant District Attorney Nassau County 1969-78. Vice Chairman Board 113 Region 17 Selective Service System since 1984. Member Columbian Lawyers, Nassau County District Court Judges Association (Vice President since 1997), Nassau County Court Judges Association, District Court Judges Association of the State of New York (Vice President 1997), Bar Association of Nassau County, New York State and American Bar Associations. Recipient Bench and Bar Award from Uniformed Court Officers of Nassau County April 15, 1994, Judiciary Award from Catholic Lawyers Guild of the Diocese of Rockville Centre Oct 8, 1998 and Fidelis Juri Award from Court Officers Benevolent Association of Nassau County Oct 25, 2002. Private E-2 U.S. Army Nov 1970 to May 1971. Hearing Officer Environmental Quality Review Board Oyster Bay 1978-91. Member Republican Committee Town of Oyster Bay 1987-91. Alumni Board St. Dominic High School. Member Italian-American Citizens Club of Oyster Bay, St. Dominic Usher Society and Catholic Lawyers Guild.

Office: County Courthouse, 262 Old Country Road, Mineola 11501-4255.
Telephone: (516) 571-2408.
Fax: (516) 571-1491
E-mail address: jgalasso@courts.state.ny.us

GALLOWAY, Harold L. *(Justice, New York Supreme Court Seventh Judicial District)*
Office: 545 Hall of Justice, 99 Exchange Boulevard, Rochester 14614-2185.
Telephone: (585) 428-2011.
Fax: (585) 428-5887

GAMMERMAN, Ira *(Justice, New York Supreme Court First Judicial District)* Certificated. Former Judge, The Civil Court of the City of New York.
Office: 60 Centre Street, New York 10007.
Telephone: (212) 374-4715.
E-mail address: igammerm@courts.state.ny.us

GANGEL-JACOB, Phyllis B. *(Justice, New York Supreme Court First Judicial District)* Acting Justice 1989-93. Elected Justice to term beginning Jan 1, 1994. Certificated. Also serves as Justice, New York Supreme Court Appellate Term First Judicial Department since Oct 1999. Born New York New York April 21, 1930. Jewish. Educated at Brooklyn College of the City University of New York B.A. 1951 and New York University School of Law J.D. 1966. Contributor Intramural Law Review 1965. Admitted to practice New York 1966, U.S. District Courts Eastern 1973 and Southern 1973 Districts of New York and U.S. Supreme Court 1974. In legal practice New York 1966-84. Conference Master, New York City Family Court 1980-81. Small Claims Arbitrator 1975-85 and Judge, The Civil Court of the City of New York Jan 1, 1985 to 1994. Assigned to The Criminal Court of the City of New York 1987.

Consultant on Revision of Family Court Forms Office of Court Administration New York 1978. Author cassette tape on *Divorce in New York State* 1975, "Some Words of Caution About Divorce Mediation" 23 No. 4 Hofstra L. Rev. Summer 1995 and "Bring in the Lawyers" *Trial Magazine* Aug 1997. Contributor *Protocal for Alternative Dispute Resolution in Matrimonial Cases* New York State Courts. Published Decisions 1985-89: Great Universal Capital Corp. v. Singer (usury) Spec. Term Part I Aug 29, 1985 N.Y.L.J. Nov 26, 1985; Estate of Leo Rosenstock v. Brown (landlord-tenant, cure of lease violation) Part 18 Jan 29, 1986 N.Y.L.J. June 9, 1986; Zeller v. Krouk (personal jurisdiction) Spec. Term Part I June 6, 1986 rev. July 7, 1986 N.Y.L.J. Oct 28, 1986; Miller & Wrubel PC v. Marque Royale Motors, Inc. (modification of contracts) Spec. Term Part I July 30, 1986 N.Y.L.J. Oct 20, 1986; Hartford Insurance Group v. Posen 134 Misc. 2d 334, 511 N.Y.S.2d 1 No. 7081, 02148/86 N.Y. Civ. Ct. Oct 14, 1986; Galan Industries, Inc. v. Loizeaux 134 Misc. 2d 641, 512 N.Y.S.2d 625 No. 68351/86, 7149 N.Y. Civ. Ct. Dec 29, 1986; Art Board, Inc. v. Worldwide Business Exchange Corp. 134 Misc. 2d 350, 510 N.Y.S.2d 973 No. 7082, 14788/85 N.Y. Civ. Ct. Dec 29, 1986; 216-220 East 67th Street Associates v. Quinn 136 Misc. 2d 188, 518 N.Y.S.2d 302 No. 7500, 59447/87 N.Y. Civ. Ct. June 10, 1987; CL Realty v. Eliran 137 Misc. 2d 955, 522 N.Y.S.2d 763 No. 7834 L&T38247/86 N.Y. Civ. Ct. Oct 8, 1987; Koplik v. Arnott 137 Misc. 2d 944, 522 N.Y.S.2d 770 No. 7833, 132778/87 N.Y. Civ. Ct. Oct 26, 1987; Matter of Martin B. 138 Misc. 2d 685, 525 N.Y.S.2d 469 No. 928/80, 1181/80, 95021/87, 7970 N.Y. Sup. Ct. Dec 24, 1987; Carriage Court Inn, Inc. v. Rains 138 Misc. 2d 444, 524 N.Y.S.2d 647 No. 7935, 98670/87 N.Y. Civ. Ct. Jan 26, 1988; Olsen v. 432 East 57th Street Corp. 145 Misc. 2d 970, 548 N.Y.S.2d 864 No. 1233, 00012/89 N.Y. Sup. Ct. Nov 30, 1989.

Published Decisions since 1990: Morgan v. Morgan Manhattan Storage Co., Inc. N.Y. Sup. Ct. N.Y.L.J. April 9, 1990 and April 24 1992; Legasto v. Legasto N.Y. Sup. Ct. N.Y.L.J. April 13, 1990; Steel v. Steel 152 Misc. 2d 880, 579 N.Y.S.2d 531 No. 2557, 73378/89 N.Y. Sup. Ct. April 27, 1990 and N.Y.L.J. 26 Col. 1 May 17, 1990; Grenvil Realty Corp. v. Commissioner of New York State Division of Housing and Community Renewal N.Y. Sup. Ct. N.Y.L.J. May 23, 1990; Matter of Baby J. N.Y. Sup. Ct. N.Y.L.J. June 7, 1990; Morgenthau v. Garcia 148 Misc. 2d 900, 561 N.Y.S.2d 867 No. 1835, 46426/89 N.Y. Sup. Ct. June 11, 1990 and N.Y.L.J. 24 Col. 2 June 21, 1990; Audubon Avenue Associates v. State Division of Housing and Community Renewal, Office of Rent Administration 148 Misc. 2d 831, 563 N.Y.S.2d 590 No. 1884, 27894/89 N.Y. Sup. Ct. July 3, 1990 and N.Y.L.J. Aug 6, 1990; Gabai v. Grinker 148 Misc. 2d 359, 560 N.Y.S.2d 384 No. 1758, 46181/89 N.Y. Sup. Ct. Sept 11, 1990 and N.Y.L.J. 26 Col. 1 April 20, 1990; New York City Police Department v. Kirchgaessner N.Y. Sup. Ct. N.Y.L.J. Jan 15, 1991; G. D. v. Herkommer N.Y. Sup. Ct. N.Y.L.J. April 22, 1991; Aminu v. The Port Authority of New York and New Jersey N.Y. Sup. Ct. N.Y.L.J. April 29, 1991; Odom v. Woodstock Terrace Mutual Housing Corp. N.Y. Sup. Ct. N.Y.L.J. May 13, 1991; Counihan v. City of New York 152 Misc. 2d 443, 576 N.Y.S.2d 745 No. 2479, 10368/91 N.Y. Sup. Ct. May 23, 1991 and N.Y.L.J. June 17, 1991; Council of Trade Waste Associations, Inc. v. City of New York 152 Misc. 2d 43, 574 N.Y.S.2d 883 No. 2393, 9689/91 N.Y. Sup. Ct. July 12, 1991; Koch v. Plainview-Old Bethpage Road Runners Club N.Y. Sup. Ct. N.Y.L.J. 22 July 19, 1991; Gewirtz v. Wenig N.Y.L.J. Aug 8, 1991; Harmon v. Harmon N.Y. Sup. Ct. N.Y.L.J. Aug 19, 1991; Sanchez v. Sanchez N.Y. Sup. Ct. N.Y.L.J. Aug 26, 1991; Barclays Bank of New York, National Association v. Delgeo Fast Foods, Inc. N.Y. Sup. Ct. N.Y.L.J. Sept 5, 1991; Johnson v. City of New York 152 Misc. 2d 576, 578 N.Y.S.2d 977, No. 2454, 46956/90 N.Y. Sup. Ct. Sept 30, 1991 and Oct 9, 1991; Kirkpatrick v. 60 Sutton Corp. N.Y. Sup. Ct. N.Y.L.J. Oct 22, 1991; Mullady v. Bogard 583 N.Y.S.2d 744 No. 2776, 42314/91 N.Y. Sup. Ct. Feb 24, 1992; BNY Financial Corp. v. Moran 584 N.Y.S.2d 261 No. 2852, 22138/90 N.Y. Sup. Ct. April 10, 1992 N.Y.L.J. May 7, 1992; Lieberman v. Lieberman 587 N.Y.S.2d 107 No. 2901, 63642/89 N.Y. Sup. Ct. June 10, 1992; Dawson v. Higgins 588 N.Y.S.2d 93 No. 14558/91, 2910 N.Y. Sup. Ct. June 23, 1992 N.Y.L.J. 27 July 8, 1992; Johnson v. Johnson N.Y. Sup. Ct. N.Y.L.J. Aug 19, 1992; Moskowitz v. Lieberman 158 Misc. 2d 1031, 602 N.Y.S.2d 752 N.Y. Sup. April 13, 1993; Carter v. Bane 159 Misc. 2d 786, 606 N.Y.S.2d 548 N.Y. Sup. Oct 28, 1993; McNamara v. Coughlin 162 Misc. 2d 504, 616 N.Y.S.2d 886 N.Y. Sup. June 15, 1994, 165 Misc. 2d 397, 627 N.Y.S.2d 278 N.Y. Sup. April 20, 1995; Bryan v. Hammons 173 Misc. 2d 894, 662 N.Y.S.2d 691, 1997 N.Y. Slip Op. 97480 N.Y. Sup. July 23, 1997; Schrader v. Cuevas 179 Misc. 2d 11, 686 N.Y.S.2d 251, 1998 N.Y. Slip Op. 98677 N.Y. Sup. Oct 9, 1998; City of New York Com'n on Human Rights v. Salinas Realty Corp. 183 Misc. 2d 897, 705 N.Y.S.2d 885, 2000 N.Y. Slip Op. 20153 N.Y. Sup. March 15, 2000; and Medical Soc. of State of N.Y., Inc. v. Levin 185 Misc. 2d 536, 712 N.Y.S.2d 745 N.Y. Sup. June 9, 2000.

Adjunct Professor of Family Law Department of Law Bernard M. Baruch College of the City University of New York 1983-85. Lecturer on Judicial Process and Ethics Benjamin N. Cardozo School of Law 1992. Faculty Member in Comparative Family Law Hofstra University School of Law Study Abroad Program, Nice France July 1999 and July 2000. President New York State Association of Women Judges. Member Board of Justices of New York Supreme Court, New York County Lawyers' Association, The Women Judges Fund for Justice, National Association of Women Judges, American Judicature Society, The Association of the Bar of the City of New York, New York City Women's, Puerto Rican, New York Women's and New York State Bar

GANGEL-JACOB, PHYLLIS B.—*Continued*

Associations. Speaker Practicing Legal Education Program "Custody" 1976-77, "Matrimonial Law" 1987 and "Landlord and Tenant Law" 1987 New York County Lawyers' Association CLE; "Support Enforcement" Matrimonial Committee New York Women's Bar Association 1991; "Alternative Dispute Resolution" Annual Meeting New York State Bar Association 1992; and "The Child Support Guidelines: Realities and Myths" The Association of the Bar of the City of New York 1992. Attended Certificate Program The National Judicial College 1989. Panelist Public Forum on the Newly Enacted Child Support Standards Act New York State Commission on Child Support The Association of the Bar of the City of New York 1989; "Is There a Feminine Jurisprudence?" NYU Law Women's Panel Discussion New York University School of Law 1991; "Spousal Maintenance" Women's Bar Association of the State of New York 1992; "A Case Study of Valuing a Real Estate Business for Trial Purposes" 1992, "Role of a Law Guardian" 1993, "The Anatomy of a Matrimonial Action: Inception to Conclusion" Matrimonial Law Section 1993 and "Enforcement Proceedings" Matrimonial Law Section 1995 New York County Lawyers' Association; "Child Support—What Lies Ahead?" New York State Bar Association Annual Meeting 1993; "Divorce: Litigation or Mediation?" Benjamin N. Cardozo School of Law 1994; "Treatment of Women by the Judicial System" United Federation of Teachers Forum 1994; "Child Support Guidelines; After *Cassano*" American Matrimonial Lawyers 1995; "Bankruptcy Proceedings and Matrimonial Actions" Women's Bar Association 1995; "Legal Ethics: The Core Issues" Hofstra University School of Law 1996; "Conflicts of Interest and Disciplinary Issues Arising from Sexual Relationships with Clients" New York State Bar Association 1998; and "Bridge the Gap" 2000 Program Law Library Association of Greater New York 2000. Moderator "Bankruptcy Law and the 'Bankrupt' Marriage" Panel Discussion The Association of the Bar of the City of New York 1991. Co-chair "Memorial Tribute to Justice Thurgood Marshall" New York County Lawyers' Association and Metropolitan Black Bar 1993. Commentator "Current Developments in Matrimonial Law" The Association of the Bar of the City of New York 1994. Program Participant "Jewel of the Hudson—The New York Apartment Under Equitable Distribution" Committee on Matrimonial Law Forum Evening 1987 and "New Certification Rules in Matrimonial Actions" 1994 New York County Lawyers' Association. District Director District II Conference 2000 National Association of Women Judges 2000. Chair "Reception and Lecture in Honor of Women's History Month and in Memory of Ethel B. Danzig" Judicial Section New York County Lawyers' Association 2000. Worked for Bureau of Attendance New York City Board of Education 1959-63. Founder Coalition on Women's Legislative Issues. Former Board Member Community Research Initiative on AIDS and HIV-related Clinical Research and Institute for Community Living. Supporter The Nature Conservancy, Group for the North Fork and Metropolitan Museum of Art.
Office: 60 Centre Street, New York 10007.
Telephone: (212) 374-8572.

GANNON, John C. *(Judge, Rome City Court)*
Office: 100 West Court Street, Rome 13440.
Telephone: (315) 337-6440.
Fax: (315) 338-0343

GANS, Louise Gruner *(Judge, The Civil Court of the City of New York)* Currently serves as Acting Justice, New York Supreme Court First Judicial District.
Office: 60 Centre Street, New York 10007.
Telephone: (212) 374-8515.
Fax: (212) 374-3326

GARAUFIS, Nicholas G. *(Judge, United States District Court Eastern District of New York)* Appointed for life by President Bill Clinton to term beginning Aug 28, 2000. Born Paterson New Jersey Sept 28, 1948. Educated at Columbia College B.A. 1969 and Columbia University J.D. 1974.
Former Chief Counsel Federal Aviation Administration.
Office: 659 U.S. Courthouse, 225 Cadman Plaza East, Brooklyn 11201.
Telephone: (718) 260-2540.

GARNETT, William E. *(Judge, The Criminal Court of the City of New York)* Appointed by mayor.
Office: 120 Schermerhorn Street, Brooklyn 11201.
Telephone: (718) 643-2374.

GARRY, William J. *(Justice, New York Supreme Court Second Judicial District)* Certificated.
Office: 360 Adams Street, Brooklyn 11201.
Telephone: (718) 643-7090.
E-mail address: wgarry@courts.state.ny.us

GARSON, Gerald P. *(Justice, New York Supreme Court Second Judicial District)* Certificated.
Office: 360 Adams Street, Brooklyn 11201.
Telephone: (718) 643-5099.
E-mail address: ggarson@courts.state.ny.us

GARSON, Michael J. *(Justice, New York Supreme Court Second Judicial District)*
Office: 360 Adams Street, Brooklyn 11201.
Telephone: (718) 643-4860.
E-mail address: mgarson@courts.state.ny.us

GARSON, Robin S. *(Judge, The Civil Court of the City of New York)*
Office: 141 Livingston Street, Brooklyn 11201.
Telephone: (718) 643-5069.

GARTNER, Kenneth L. *(Judge, Nassau County District Court)*
Office: 99 Main Street, Hempstead 11550.
Telephone: (516) 572-2143.

GARVEY, Margaret *(Judge, Rockland County Family Court)*
Office: One South Main Street, Suite 300, New City 10956.
Telephone: (845) 638-5328.

GARY, Michael A. *(Judge, The Criminal Court of the City of New York)* Appointed by Mayor Ed Koch. Currently serves as Acting Justice, New York Supreme Court Second Judicial District.
Office: 360 Adams Street, Brooklyn 11201.
Telephone: (718) 643-3875.
E-mail address: mgary@courts.state.ny.us

GAVRIN, Darrell Lori *(Judge, The Civil Court of the City of New York)* Elected to term beginning Jan 1, 1993. Acting Justice, New York Supreme Court Eleventh Judicial District since June 1999. Formerly served The Criminal Court of the City of New York. Educated at State University of New York at Stony Brook B.A. cum laude 1973 and Hofstra University School of Law J.D. 1976. Admitted to practice New York, U.S. District Courts Eastern and Southern Districts of New York and U.S. Supreme Court. In legal practice Sept 1976 to Feb 1977. Small Claims Arbitrator, The Civil Court of the City of New York March 1988 to March 1991.

Counsel Board of Standards and Appeals of the City of New York June 1977 to Jan 1981. Principal Law Clerk to New York State Supreme Court Justices Jan 1981 to Dec 1992. Author "An Experiment Worth Keeping? Closed Circuit Television in Child Abuse Cases" LI No. 6 March-April 1988 and "Personal Reflections on the Retirement of Justice Joseph S. Calabretta" LV No. 3 March 1992 Queens Bar Bulletin. Coauthor with Nelson E. Timken "Outside Counsel: Enhanced Sanctions for Driving While Intoxicated" 215 No. 2 New York L. Jour. 1 Jan 3, 1996 and "Outside Counsel: Complying with C.P.L. §710.30 Notice Requirements" 215 No. 62 New York L. Jour. 1 April 1, 1996. Advisory Board Latino Lawyers Association of Queens County 1999. Former Member National Association of Women Judges. Member Association of Law Secretaries to Justices of the Supreme and Surrogate Courts (Board of Directors, Vice President), Board of Judges of The Civil Court of the City of New York, New York State Association of Women Judges, Designated Supreme Court Judges Association, Criminal Courts Bar Association of Queens County (Board of Directors), Women's Bar Association of the State of New York, The Association of the Bar of the City of New York (Civil Court Committee), Queens County (Board of Managers), Queens County Women's (Board of Trustees), New York County, New York State and American Bar Associations. Speaker Orientation for Incoming Assistant District Attorneys Queens County Sept 1996, Sept 1997 and Sept 1998, Queens Women's Political Caucus March 10, 1997, Not Just for Jews and Blacks in Conversation Queens County Criminal Court May 1998 and 1999 and P.E.A.C.E. Program June 2001. Faculty Member Lorman Educational Services Dec 1, 2000. Instructor Summer Judicial Seminar New York State Office of Court Administration July 2001. Named Outstanding Young Woman of America by U.S. Jaycees 1979 and 1988. Recipient Distinguished Service Award from St. John's University School of Law 1985 and Citation of Honor from President of the Borough of Queens Sept 30, 1987. Member Legislative Advisory Committee 24th Assembly District. Trial Judge Mock Trial City University of New York April 27, 1999. President Brandies Association. Advisory Board Paralegal Studies Continuing Education Program Queens College. Advisory Board Moot Court and Executive Board Alumni Association Hofstra University School of Law. Board of Directors Queens Women's Center. Member Queens Mediation Network, Hollis Hills Jewish Center Sisterhood, Hollis Hills Civic Association, Jewish Lawyers Guild and Judges and Lawyers Breast Cancer (Board of Directors).

Office: 88-11 Sutphin Boulevard, Jamaica 11435.
Telephone: (718) 520-2580.

GAZZARA, Anthony V. *(Judge, The Civil Court of the City of New York)*

Office: 89-17 Sutphin Boulevard, Jamaica 11435.
Telephone: (718) 262-7373.

GAZZILLO, Ralph T. *(Judge, Suffolk County Court)* Currently serves as Supervising Judge Superior Criminal Court. Former Judge, Suffolk County District Court. Former Acting Justice, New York Supreme Court Tenth Judicial District.

Mailing address: P.O. Box 9007, Riverhead 11901-9007.
Office: Court Complex, 210 Center Drive, Riverhead 11901.
Telephone: (631) 852-2583.
Fax: (631) 852-3854

GEBO, A. Michael *(Judge, Ogdensburg City Court)* Former Acting Judge. Educated at St. Lawrence University B.A. 1973 and Albany Law School of Union University J.D. 1976. Admitted to practice New York 1977.

Member St. Lawrence County and New York State Bar Associations.

Office: 330 Ford Street, Ogdensburg 13669.
Telephone: (315) 393-3941.
Fax: (315) 393-6839

GENCHI, Joan M. *(Judge, Suffolk County Family Court)* Former Judge, Suffolk County District Court.

Mailing address: P.O. Box 9075, Central Islip 11722-9075.
Office: Cohalan Court Complex, 400 Carleton Avenue, Central Islip 11722.
Telephone: (631) 853-4302.

GERACE, Joseph *(Justice, New York Supreme Court Eighth Judicial District)* Elected to term beginning Jan 1992. Certificated. Term expires Dec 31, 2003. Educated at Denison University A.B. 1949 and Albany Law School of Union University J.D. 1952. In legal practice Albany 1952-53, Lakewood 1953-60 and Jamestown 1961-74.

County Executive Chautauqua County 1975-83. Commissioner New York State Department of Agriculture and Markets May 11, 1983 to Dec 31, 1986. Director Office of Rural Affairs Jan 1, 1987 to Sept 9, 1990 and Office of Mandate Review Sept 10, 1990 to Dec 1991 New York State. Important Decisions: Packard Estates Homeowners Association v. Paige Development Corporation Slip Opinion 1996 06845 4th Dept.; Niagara Mohawk v. Dunkirk 221 A.D.2d 912, 87 NY2 1054, 88 NY2 803, 659 N.Y.S.2d 632 4th Dept. May 30, 1997; Matter of Chautauqua County Commissioner of Health v. John Doe Oct 16, 1997; OAG v. Desert Gas Exploration Company Slip Opinion 1997 05074 4th Dept; Webber v. Dunkirk Slip Opinion 1997 03679 4th Dept; Farnham, Cobb v. Kittinger 83 NY2 520, 192 A.D.2d 1062, 168 A.D.2d 923; Sauberan v. Ohl 1997 Slip Opinion 4th Dept 05061; AAC Contracting v. United Coastal 199 A.D.2d 1067; Cowan v. Sea Lion 195 A.D.2d 1002; Welch v. Westfield 222 A.D.2d 1053, 221 A.D.2d 912, 87 NY2 1054; Niagara Mohawk v. Ferranti 83 N.Y. 953, 201 A.D.2d 902, 157 M2 606; ITT v. Bailey 166 M2 24; Held v. S.U.N.Y. 165 M2 577; Integra v. Gordon 164 M2 691; Benson v. Syntex 161 M2 822, 1996 Slip Opinions 05730 4th Dept; Sanchez v. Eckstrom 160 M2 918; Kennedy v. Valley Forge 84 NY2 963; Key Bank v. Becker 88 NY2 899, 206 A.D.2d 953; JWO v. Jacobson, Weakely and Olson 229 A.D.2d 936; Gillson

GERACE, JOSEPH—*Continued*

v. Denis Slip Opinion 08477; and Brecht v. Copper Sands Slip Opinion 02355.
Office: Courthouse, One North Erie Street, Mayville 14757.
Telephone: (716) 753-4245.
Fax: (716) 753-4993
E-mail address: jgerace@courts.state.ny.us

GERACI, Frank P., Jr. *(Judge, Monroe County Court)* Former Judge, Rochester City Court.
Office: 545 Hall of Justice, 99 Exchange Boulevard, Rochester 14614-2186.
Telephone: (585) 428-4315.
Fax: (585) 428-4262

GERALD, Lenora *(Judge, The Civil Court of the City of New York)*
Office: 125-01 Queens Boulevard, Kew Gardens 11415.
Telephone: (718) 520-3855.
Fax: (718) 520-4712

GERBER, Robert E. *(Judge, United States Bankruptcy Court Southern District of New York)* Appointed by U.S. Court of Appeals Second Circuit judges to term beginning Sept 5, 2000. Term expires Sept 2014.
Office: Hamilton Custom House, Sixth Floor, One Bowling Green, New York 10004-1408.
Telephone: (212) 668-5627.

GERGES, Abraham G. *(Justice, New York Supreme Court Second Judicial District)* Elected to term beginning Jan 1, 1991. Term expires Dec 31, 2004. Born Brooklyn New York March 20, 1934. Educated at Brooklyn College and New York Law School LL.B. 1964. Admitted to practice New York 1965, U.S. District Courts Eastern 1966 and Southern 1966 Districts of New York and U.S. Supreme Court 1975. Arbitrator, The Civil Court of the City of New York 1972-86.
Editor *The Jurist* Newsletter of the Association of Justices of the Supreme Court of the State of New York. Guest Lecturer The New School, Baruch College, Long Island University and New York University. Former Chairperson Office of Court Administration Speakers Bureau. Former Member Eastern District Committee for the Defense of Indigent Defendants, New York State Democratic Screening Committee for Candidates to the Court of Appeals, Mayor's Committee of Administrative Justice, State of New York Legal Defense Panel for Indigent Defendants and Brooklyn Women's Bar Association. Chairperson Facilities Committee and Technicians Committee Kings County Supreme Court. Member New York County Lawyers' Association, Association of Justices of Supreme Court of the State of New York (President 2001, Chairperson Education Committee and Publicity Committee), The Supreme Court Justices Association of the City of New York (Secretary), American Judges Association, Brooklyn, New York State and American (New York State Delegate National Conference of State Trial Judges 1995-2002) Bar Associations. Guest Lecturer New York Police Department Police Academy and Judicial Seminar Office of Court Administration. Councilman New York City 1974-90. Chairperson Government Operations Committee, Economic Development Committee, Standards and Ethics Committee, Subcommittee on Criminal Court System and Select Committee for the Homeless. Past President Brooklyn Heights Chapter B'nai B'rith. Council of Advisors Christian Herald.
Office: 360 Adams Street, Brooklyn 11201.
Telephone: (718) 875-3060.
Fax: (718) 243-2542

GERLING, Stephen D. *(Chief Judge, United States Bankruptcy Court Northern District of New York)* Appointed by U.S. Court of Appeals Second Circuit judges to term beginning Oct 4, 1985. Reappointed 1999, current term expires Oct 3, 2013. Born Herkimer New York May 31, 1942. Catholic. Educated at Niagara University B.A. 1964 and St. John's University J.D. 1967. Admitted to practice New York 1968. In legal practice Utica 1969-85. Former Judge, Bankruptcy Appellate Panel Second Circuit, selected by the Judicial Council of the Second Circuit.
Former Assistant Attorney Oneida County. Former Assistant Counsel to Speaker New York Assembly. Former Special Counsel Town of Whitestown. Important Decisions: In re ICS Cybernetics 111 B.R. 32; In re Kleist 114 B.R. 366; In re Copy Crafters Quickprint, Inc. 92 B.R. 973; In re Fischel 103 B.R. 44; In re Santa Maria 128 B.R. 32; and In re SPI Communications & Marketing, Inc. 112 B.R. 507. Adjunct Professor of Law Syracuse University College of Law 1996-2000. Former Member Oneida County and New York State Bar Associations. Lecturer numerous Bankruptcy seminars Oneida County Bar Association CLE and New York State Bar Association CLE. Named Citizen of the Year by Whitestown Post American Legion 1984. Captain U.S. Army Military Police 1967-69 (Vietnam 1968-69). Recipient Bronze Star. Former Member Greater Whitestown Recreation Committee, Utica Rotary Club and Whitestown Kiwanis. Past Exalted Ruler Elks Utica Lodge 33. Former member Advisory Board Whitestown Community Center and Sadaquada Golf Club. Founder Whitestown Youth Hockey Association, Inc. Interests include boating, coaching youth sports and skiing.
Office: 220 Federal Building, 10 Broad Street, Utica 13501.
Telephone: (315) 793-8111.

GERSHON, Nina *(Judge, United States District Court Eastern District of New York)* Former Magistrate Judge Southern District of New York. Appointed Judge for life by President Bill Clinton. Educated at Cornell University B.A. 1962 and Yale Law School LL.B. 1965. Fulbright Scholar London School of Economics 1965-66.
Office: U.S. Courthouse, 225 Cadman Plaza East, Brooklyn 11201.
Telephone: (718) 260-2650.

GIACOBBE, Anthony I. *(Judge, New York Court of Claims)* Appointed by Governor George E. Pataki. Currently serves as Acting Justice, New York Supreme Court Second Judicial District.
Office: Homeport, 355 Front Street, Staten Island 10304.
Telephone: (718) 876-6433.
Fax: (718) 876-6416

GIARDINO, Richard C. *(Judge, Fulton County Court)* Appointed by Governor George E. Pataki to term beginning June 10, 1996. Elected Nov 1996, term expires Dec 2006. Also serves Fulton County Surrogate's Court. Born Gloversville New York Dec 9, 1958. Roman Catholic. Educated at Siena College B.A. cum

GIARDINO, RICHARD C.—*Continued*

laude 1981 and Albany Law School of Union University J.D. 1984. Admitted to practice New York 1985.

Assistant District Attorney Nassau County 1985-86. Assistant District Attorney 1986-91 and District Attorney 1992-96 Fulton County. Part-time Instructor in Criminal Law I & II Fulton Montgomery Community College since 1986. Member County Judges Association of the State of New York, The Surrogates' Association of the State of New York, Fulton County and New York State Bar Associations. Attended New York State Judges Training Dec 1996 and Annual State Seminars. Recipient Traffic Safety Board Award 1998 and Cooperative Extension Community Service Award 1998. Republican. Chairman Fulton County Domestic Violence Task Force 1998. Co-director VISTA Fulton County 1999-2000. Co-chair Mayor's Task Force on Teen Violence since 1999.

Office: Fulton County Building, 223 West Main Street, Johnstown 12095.
Telephone: (518) 736-5695.
Fax: (518) 762-5078
E-mail address: richg@superior.net

GIBBONS, James D. *(Judge, The Criminal Court of the City of New York)* Appointed by mayor.
Office: 120 Schermerhorn Street, Brooklyn 11201.
Telephone: (718) 643-8400.
Fax: (718) 643-3538

GIDEON, David S. *(Acting Judge, Syracuse City Court)*
Office: Public Safety Building, 511 South State Street, Syracuse 13202.
Telephone: (315) 477-2785.

GIGANTE, Robert J. *(Justice, New York Supreme Court Second Judicial District)*
Office: Homeport, 355 Front Street, Staten Island 10304.
Telephone: (718) 876-6444.
E-mail address: rgigante@courts.state.ny.us

GILBERT, Hugh A. *(Justice, New York Supreme Court Fifth Judicial District)* Elected Nov 3, 1989 to term beginning Jan 1, 1990. Term expires Dec 31, 2003. Currently serves as Supervising Judge Family Court. Educated at Fordham University B.A. with honors 1962 and Albany Law School of Union University J.D. with honors 1965. Notes Editor Albany Law Review 1963-65. Admitted to practice New York 1965. Judge, Jefferson County Family Court 1978-83. Surrogate, Jefferson County Surrogate's Court 1984-89.
Office: 317 Washington Street, Tenth Floor, Watertown 13601.
Telephone: (315) 785-7918.

GILPATRIC, James P. *(Judge, Kingston City Court)*
Office: One Garraghan Drive, Kingston 12401.
Telephone: (845) 338-2974.
Fax: (845) 338-1443

GISCHE, Judith J. *(Judge, The Civil Court of the City of New York)* Currently serves as Acting Justice, New York Supreme Court First Judicial District. Former Acting Justice, New York Supreme Court Twelfth Judicial District.
Office: 80 Centre Street, Room 122, New York 10013.
Telephone: (212) 374-1487.
Fax: (212) 374-3907
E-mail address: jgische@courts.state.ny.us

GIVENS, Debra L. *(Judge, Buffalo City Court)*
Office: 50 Delaware Avenue, Buffalo 14202.
Telephone: (716) 847-8207.

GLASSER, I. Leo *(Senior Judge, United States District Court Eastern District of New York)* Appointed for life by President Ronald Reagan to term beginning Jan 28, 1982. Assumed Senior status, serves by assignment. Born New York New York April 6, 1924. Jewish. Educated at City College of the City University of New York B.A. 1943 and Brooklyn Law School LL.B. 1948. Awarded honorary LL.D. Brooklyn Law School. Editor-in-Chief Brooklyn Law Review. Admitted to practice New York 1948. Judge, Family Court Oct 1969 to June 1977.

Professor of Law Feb 1948 to Oct 1969 and Dean Sept 1977 to Dec 1981 Brooklyn Law School. Member American Bar Association. Technician Fifth Class U.S. Army 1943-46. Recipient Bronze Star. Board of Directors Hebrew Free Loan Society.
Office: U.S. Courthouse, 225 Cadman Plaza East, Brooklyn 11201.
Telephone: (718) 260-2440.

GLEESON, John *(Judge, United States District Court Eastern District of New York)* Appointed for life by President Bill Clinton to term beginning Oct 1994. Educated at Georgetown University B.A. 1975 and University of Virginia School of Law J.D. 1980. Law Clerk to Hon. Boyce F. Martin, Jr., U.S. Court of Appeals Sixth Circuit Sept 1980 to Oct 1981. In legal practice New York Oct 1981 to Feb 1985.

Assistant U.S. Attorney Eastern District of New York Feb 1985 to Oct 1994 (Deputy Chief Appeals Oct 1986 to Aug 1987, Chief Appeals Sept 1987 to June 1989, Chief Special Prosecutions June 1989 to Jan 1990, Chief Organized Crime Jan 1990 to June 1993 and Chief Criminal Division June 1993 to Oct 1994). Co-author with John C. Jeffries, Jr. "The Federalization of Organized Crime: The Advantages of Federal Prosecution" 46 Hastings L. Jour. 1095, 1995 and with Gordon Mehler and David C. James *Federal Criminal Practice: A Second Circuit Handbook* Lexis Nexis 2002. Author "Sentence Bargaining Under The Guidelines" 8 Federal Sentencing Reporter 314, 1996 and "Supervising Criminal Investigations: The Proper Scope of the Supervisory Power of Federal Judges" 5 Journal of Law and Policy 423, 1997. Assistant Adjunct Professor of Law Brooklyn Law School 1990-97 and New York University School of Law since 1995. Distinguished Visiting Professor of Law University of Virginia School of Law 1994. Member Defender Services Committee Judicial Conference of the U.S., The American Law Institute and The Association of the Bar of the City of New York. Recipient Attorney General's Award for Distinguished Service for investigation and prosecution of *United States v. John Gotti, et al.* Dec 1992.
Office: U.S. Courthouse, 225 Cadman Plaza East, Brooklyn 11201.
Telephone: (718) 260-2450.

GLOBERMAN, Ira R. *(Judge, The Civil Court of the City of New York)* Currently serves as Acting Justice, New York Supreme Court Twelfth Judicial District.
Office: 851 Grand Concourse, Bronx 10451.
Telephone: (718) 590-3761.
Fax: (718) 590-8914

GLOVER, William T. *(Justice, New York Supreme Court Eleventh Judicial District)* Certificated.
Office: 88-11 Sutphin Boulevard, Jamaica 11435.
Telephone: (718) 520-3026.
Fax: (718) 520-3708

GLOWNIA, Joseph R. *(Justice, New York Supreme Court Eighth Judicial District)*
Office: Erie County Hall, 92 Franklin Street, Buffalo 14202.
Telephone: (716) 851-3442.
Fax: (716) 851-3320
E-mail address: jglownia@courts.state.ny.us

GO, Marilyn D. *(Magistrate Judge, United States District Court Eastern District of New York)* Appointed by U.S. District Court judges to term beginning 1993. Educated at Radcliffe College B.A. 1973 and Harvard Law School J.D. 1977. Law Clerk to Hon. William M. Marutani, Pennsylvania Court of Common Pleas District One Trial Division. In legal practice New York 1984-93.
Office: U.S. Courthouse, 225 Cadman Plaza East, Brooklyn 11201.
Telephone: (718) 260-2550.

GOETTEL, Gerard L. *(Senior Judge, United States District Court Southern District of New York)* Magistrate 1971-76. Appointed Judge for life by President Gerald R. Ford to term beginning April 7, 1976. Assumed Senior status, serves District of Connecticut by assignment. First serving U.S. Magistrate elevated to District Judge. Born New York New York Aug 5, 1928. Educated at The Citadel, Duke University B.A. 1950 and Columbia University J.D. 1955. Harlan Fiske Stone Scholar. Admitted to practice New York 1955.
Assistant U.S. Attorney 1955-58. Deputy Chief Attorney General's Special Group on Organized Crime 1958-59. Assistant Counsel New York Court on the Judiciary 1970-71. Author "Why the Crime Syndicate Can't Be Touched" Harpers 1960. Adjunct Professor of Law Fordham University Law School 1978-87 and Pace University Law School 1988-90. Chairman District Court Committees on the Criminal Justice Act and Discovery 1982-93. Member Committee on the Criminal Justice Act Judicial Conference of the U.S. 1981-87 and Committee on the Pre-Trial Phase of Litigation Second Circuit 1984-86. Lieutenant USCG 1951-53 and USCGR 1953-60. Enjoys playing tennis and golf.
Office: Federal Building, 14 Cottage Place, Waterbury, Connecticut 06702.
Telephone: (203) 575-7891.

GOLAR, Simeon *(Justice, New York Supreme Court Eleventh Judicial District)* Certificated.
Office: 88-11 Sutphin Boulevard, Jamaica 11435.
Telephone: (718) 520-2599.
Fax: (718) 520-6433

GOLD, Lila P. *(Judge, The Civil Court of the City of New York)* Currently assigned to The Criminal Court of the City of New York.
Office: 120 Schermerhorn Street, Brooklyn 11201.
Telephone: (718) 643-3320.

GOLD, Steven M. *(Magistrate Judge, United States District Court Eastern District of New York)* Appointed by U.S. District Court judges to term beginning Feb 23, 1993. Reappointed 2001, current term expires 2009. Born Brooklyn New York Aug 28, 1955. Educated at Wesleyan University B.A. 1977 and Yale Law School J.D. 1980. Law Clerk to Hon. Herbert E. Murray, U.S. District Court District of Maryland 1980-81. Admitted to practice New York 1981, U.S. District Courts District of Maryland 1981 and Eastern 1982 and Southern 1982 Districts of New York and U.S. Courts of Appeals Fourth 1981 and Second 1987 Circuits. In legal practice New York 1981-85.
Assistant U.S. Attorney Eastern District of New York 1985-90. General Counsel Department of Investigation New York City 1990-93.
Office: U.S. Courthouse, 225 Cadman Plaza East, Brooklyn 11201.
Telephone: (718) 260-2560.

GOLDBERG, Arlene D. *(Judge, The Criminal Court of the City of New York)* Appointed by mayor. Currently serves as Acting Justice, New York Supreme Court First Judicial District.
Office: 100 Centre Street, New York 10013.
Telephone: (212) 748-5100.

GOLDBERG, Joel M. *(Judge, The Criminal Court of the City of New York)* Appointed by Mayor Ed Koch. Currently serves as Acting Justice, New York Supreme Court Second Judicial District.
Office: 120 Schermerhorn Street, Brooklyn 11201.
Telephone: (718) 643-5425.
E-mail address: jgoldberg@courts.state.ny.us

GOLDBERG, Martin R. *(Magistrate Judge, United States District Court Southern District of New York)* Appointed by U.S. District Court judges to term beginning March 12, 1992. Reappointed March 12, 1996 and March 2000. Current term expires March 2004. Serves part time. Born Bronx New York April 20, 1945. Educated at Fairleigh Dickinson University B.A. with honors 1966 and New York Law School J.D. 1969. Admitted to practice New York 1970, Florida 1975 and U.S. District Court Southern District of New York 1981. In legal practice Orange County since 1981.
With Orange County District Attorney's Office 1972-81. Member New York State Criminal Attorneys Association, Federal Bar Council, Middletown, Orange County and New York State Bar Associations. U.S. Army National Guard. Enjoys all sports and reading.
Mailing address: P.O. Box 2083, Middletown 10940-0618.
Telephone: (845) 343-1130.

GOLDSTEIN, David *(Justice, New York Supreme Court Eleventh Judicial District)* Appointed by Governor Mario Cuomo to term beginning June 19, 1990. Elected Nov 1990 to term beginning Jan 1, 1991. Born New York New York Aug 9, 1943. Jewish. Educated at New York University B.A. 1965 J.D. 1968. Recipient American Jurisprudence Awards in Commercial Law, Insurance Law and Labor Law. Law Clerk to Hon. Matthew M. Levy, New York Supreme Court Aug 1968 to Sept 1969. Member Zeta Beta Tau. Admitted to practice New York 1968, U.S. Court of Appeals Second Circuit 1969, U.S. District Courts Eastern 1971 and Southern 1971 Districts of New York and U.S. Supreme Court 1972. In legal practice Jan 1970 to July 1974 and Oct 1980 to

GOLDSTEIN, DAVID—*Continued*

April 1982. Judge, The Civil Court of the City of New York Jan 1, 1988 to June 18, 1990.

Law Secretary to Hon. Arnold L. Fein July 1974 to Oct 1980 and Hon. Bentley Kassal Oct 7, 1982 to Dec 31, 1988, New York Supreme Court Appellate Division First Judicial Department and to Administrative Judge Shanley N. Egeth, The Civil Court of the City of New York April 1982 to Oct 1982. Author "Suicide and New York Law Under Policies of Insurance" 23 No. 3 New York University Intramural L. Rev. 163 March 1968. Important Opinions: Victoria Kitchen v. Leiner 138 Misc.2d 556, Paradiso v. Colonial Townhouses 138 Misc.2d 1002, Chrysler Credit Corp. v. Shaw 139 Misc.2d 154, Peritz v. Kaye 140 Misc. 2d 224, Modern Thermographic Testing v. MABSTOA 141 Misc.2d 617, Rubin v. Dondysh 146 Misc.2d 37, Bruckner v. Jaitor Apartments Co. 147 Misc.2d 796, Matter of Yvette S. 163 Misc.2d 902, Giannakoulopoulos v. Koukoumelis 164 Misc.2d 541, National Indemnity Co. v. Ryder Truck Rental 165 Misc.2d 848, Janello v. Parker 167 Misc.2d 239, Zwerling v. Zwerling 167 Misc.2d 782, Burton v. Ontra, Inc. 167 Misc.2d 977, Peralta v. La Placita Dominca Market Corp. 170 Misc.2d 340, Meachum v. Outdoor World Corp. 171 Misc.2d 354, People v. Stanley Joyner 171 Misc.2d 544, Fairman v. Santos 174 Misc.2d 85, Matter of Brussels Leasing v. Henne 174 Misc.2d 535, Pugach v. Borja 175 Misc.2d 683, Vasquez v. Vasquez 175 Misc.2d 847, Dobress v. North Shore University Hosp. 178 Misc.2d 205, City of New York v. "Scandals" 178 Misc.2d 267, Lightman v. Flaum 179 Misc.2d 1007, Strignano v. Jamaica Hosp. 181 Misc.2d 155 and Council of the City of New York v. Guiliani 183 Misc.2d 799.

Member Task Force on Reducing Litigation Cost and Delay Eleventh Judicial District since 1996, Alternative Dispute Resolution Advisory Committee Unified Court System since March 1999 and Judicial Conference of the State of New York since 1999. Former Member Executive Board Board of Judges The Civil Court of the City of New York. Member Association of Justices of the Supreme Court of the City of New York, Association of Justices of the Supreme Court of the State of New York, Brandeis Association, Inc. (Board of Directors), New York State Trial Lawyers Association, The Association of the Bar of the City of New York (Committee on State Courts of Superior Jurisdiction since Sept 1999, Queens County, Queens County Women's and New York State Bar Associations. Faculty Panel Member "The Give and Take of Negotiation" *A Primer on the Evaluation and Negotiation of a Tort Case* CLE Seminar New York State Bar Association June 11, 1999. Democrat. Democratic Delegate Queens County Judicial Convention 1972, 1973, 1981, 1985 and 1986. Member 28th Assembly District 1974-86 and Executive Committee 1984-86 New York State Democratic Committee and Queens County Democratic Committee. Charter Member 1957. Personal Statement or Quote: Be direct, concise and courteous with the court and your adversary."

Office: 88-11 Sutphin Boulevard, Jamaica 11435.
Telephone: (718) 520-3757.
Fax: (718) 520-5084

GOLDSTEIN, Ferne J. *(Judge, The Civil Court of the City of New York)* Currently assigned to The Criminal Court of the City of New York.

Office: 141 Livingston Street, Brooklyn 11201.
Telephone: (718) 643-2525.
Fax: (718) 643-3733

GOLDSTEIN, Gloria *(Associate Justice, New York Supreme Court Appellate Division Second Judicial Department)* Former Acting Justice. Elected Justice to term beginning Jan 1, 1993. Appointed Associate Justice Appellate Division by Governor Mario Cuomo to term beginning Jan 1994. Certificated. Born Brooklyn New York Dec 25, 1931. Jewish. Educated at Brooklyn College B.A. and Brooklyn Law School LL.B. magna cum laude 1956. Editor Brooklyn Law Review 1954-56. Admitted to practice New York 1956 and U.S. District Court District of New York 1957. Began legal practice Brooklyn 1956. Judge, The Civil Court of the City of New York Jan 1, 1979 to Dec 31, 1992.

Office: 45 Monroe Place, Brooklyn 11201.

GOLIA, James J. *(Judge, The Civil Court of the City of New York)*

Office: 100 Centre Street, New York 10013.
Telephone: (718) 262-7357.

GOLIA, Joseph G. *(Justice, New York Supreme Court Eleventh Judicial District)* Elected to term beginning Jan 1, 1987. Reelected to term beginning Jan 1, 2001, current term expires Dec 31, 2014. Also serves as Justice, New York Supreme Court Appellate Term Second and Eleventh Judicial Districts. Born New York New York May 17, 1938. Roman Catholic. Educated at New York University B.S. 1959 and New York Law School LL.B. 1965. Member Phi Delta Phi and Theta Chi. Admitted to practice New York 1966, U.S. District Courts Eastern 1975 and Southern 1975 Districts of New York, U.S. Supreme Court 1979 and District of Columbia 1981. Judge, The Civil Court of the City of New York 1982-86, appointed by Mayor Edward I. Koch.

Legal staff Hartford Insurance Group, New York June 1965 to Jan 1968. Assistant District Attorney Jan 1968 to Oct 1973 (Deputy Chief Youth Bureau Queens County). Principal Law Clerk to Hon. Bernard Dubin, New York Supreme Court Eleventh Judicial District Oct 1973 to Nov 1982. Important Decisions: Sherwood Village Co-op A, Inc. v. Slovik 134 Misc. 2d 952, 513 N.Y.S.2d 580; People of the State of New York v. Santana 159 Misc. 2d 301, 704 N.Y.S.2d 1016; People of the State of New York v. Modeste 159 Misc. 2d 250, 603 N.Y.S.2d 955; People of the State of New York v. Johnson 153 Misc. 2d 537, 590 N.Y.S.2d 682; Moriarity v. New York Racing Association, Inc. 134 Misc. 2d 952, 513 N.Y.S.2d 580; People of the State of New York v. Gallman 152 Misc. 2d 1033, 579 N.Y.S.2d 561; People of the State of New York v. Ruiz 151 Misc. 2d 757, 573 N.Y.S.2d 845; Yechazel Michaeli v. Greater New York Savings Bank 124 Misc. 2d 840, 469 N.Y.S.2d 279; People of the State of New York v. Martinez 151 Misc. 2d 1016, 574 N.Y.S.2d 434; People of the State of New York v. Edward Adorno 128 Misc. 2d 389, 489 N.Y.S.2d 441; and People of the State of New York v. Elvin Rodriguez 124 Misc. 2d 393, 477 N.Y.S.2d 441. U.S. Army 1961-66.

Office: 88-11 Sutphin Boulevard, Jamaica 11435.
Telephone: (718) 520-3741.

GONZALEZ, Arthur J. *(Judge, United States Bankruptcy Court Southern District of New York)* Appointed by U.S. Court of Appeals Second Circuit judges.
Office: Hamilton Custom House, Fifth Floor, One Bowling Green, New York 10004-1408.
Telephone: (212) 668-2894.

GONZALEZ, Luis A. *(Associate Justice, New York Supreme Court Appellate Division First Judicial Department)* Elected Justice First Judicial District and Twelfth Judicial District. Appointed Associate Justice Appellate Division by Governor George E. Pataki. Former Justice, New York Supreme Court Appellate Term First Judicial Department. Administrative Judge 1999 to March 2002. Former Judge, The Civil Court of the City of New York, elected to term beginning Jan 1, 1987.
Office: 27 Madison Avenue at 25th Street, New York 10010.
Telephone: (212) 340-0576.

GONZALEZ, Yvonne *(Justice, New York Supreme Court Twelfth Judicial District)* Former Judge, The Civil Court of the City of New York.
Office: 851 Grand Concourse, Bronx 10451.
Telephone: (718) 590-6358.
Fax: (718) 590-8914

GOODMAN, Budd G. *(Justice, New York Supreme Court First Judicial District)* Elected to term beginning Jan 1, 1984. Reelected to term beginning Jan 1, 1998. Certificated. Born New York Dec 23, 1929. Jewish. Educated at New York University A.B. 1950 LL.B. 1953. Member Rota Legal Society. Admitted to practice New York 1954 and U.S. District Courts Southern 1963 and Eastern 1963 Districts of New York. In legal practice New York City 1957-70. Judge, The Civil Court of the City of New York 1970-83.

Staff Trial Attorney Legal Aid Society Feb 1956 to Oct 1957. Co-author with Leventhal *Charges to the Jury & Requests to Charge in a Criminal Case* Volumes I and II Callaghan & Co. 1983 and with Waltuch "Declarations Against Penal Interest: The Majority Has Emerged" XXVIII No. 1 New York Law School L. Rev. 1983. Important Decisions: People v. Guzman Misc. 198, N.Y.L.J.; People v. Willie Sumlin 105 Misc. 2d 134, 1980; and People v. Eric Pollicott aka Norman Fontanelle N.Y.L.J. 1980. Adjunct Assistant Professor City University of New York Urban Legal Study Program 1977-78. Judge and Trial Advocacy Trainer Hofstra Law School 1978, Legal Aid Society 1980 and District Attorney's Office 1981. Former member New York County Lawyers' and American Bar Association. Member National Conference of State Trial Judges (Drug Abuse Committee), Hunter College Trial Institute for Judges, Association of the Supreme Court Judges for the State and City of New York, Civil Court Committee on Continuing Education and The Association of the Bar of the City of New York since 1972. Corporal U.S. Army JAG 1953-55. Assistant Chief Counsel Joint Legislative Committee on Higher Education 1966-67. Assistant Counsel Joint Legislative Committee to Study Revisions on Corporation Laws 1968. Democratic State Committeeman representing 65th A.D. for six years. President Park River Independent Democratic Club for two years. Member Executive Committee West Side Democratic Club and Park River Independent Democratic Club. Election District Captain for Reform Independent Democratic Club and West Side Democratic Club. Alternate Delegate New York State Democratic Gubernatorial Convention 1966. Member American Civil Liberties Union since 1958, B'nai B'rith since 1973 (President Manhattan West Lodge 1973-74), Psychoanalytic Seminar Interdisciplinary Study Group 1975-78 and Society of American Magicians. Enjoys tennis and travel.
Office: 60 Centre Street, New York 10007.
Telephone: (212) 374-8381.

GOODMAN, Emily Jane *(Justice, New York Supreme Court First Judicial District)* Former Acting Justice. Former Judge, The Civil Court of the City of New York.
Office: 60 Centre Street, Room 551, New York 10007.
Telephone: (212) 374-4742.
E-mail address: egoodman@courts.state.ny.us

GORENSTEIN, Gabriel W. *(Magistrate Judge, United States District Court Southern District of New York)* Appointed by U.S. District Court judges to term beginning March 2, 2001. Former Judge, The Criminal Court of the City of New York, appointed by Mayor Rudolph Giuliani.
Office: 431 U.S. Courthouse, 40 Centre Street, New York 10007-1581.
Telephone: (212) 805-4260.

GORSKI, Jerome C. *(Associate Justice, New York Supreme Court Appellate Division Fourth Judicial Department)* Elected Justice Eighth Judicial District to term beginning Jan 1989. Appointed Associate Justice Appellate Division by Governor George E. Pataki Aug 2001. Born Feb 16, 1937. Educated at Niagara University B.A. cum laude 1958 and Georgetown University Law Center J.D. 1962. Board of Editors Georgetown University Law Review. Law Clerk to Hon. John J. Sirica, U.S. District Court District of Columbia 1962-63. Admitted to practice New York 1962. In legal practice New York 1963-88.

Author "The Exclusionary Rule and the Question of Standing" 50 Georgetown L. Jour. 585. President Lawyers Club of Buffalo 1984. Member Jury Selection Uniformity Committee 1993-94, Advisory Committee on Judicial Ethics since 1995 and Pattern Jury Instruction Committee since 1997. Member Western New York Trial Lawyers Association, The Association of Trial Lawyers of America, Association of Justices of the Supreme Court of the State of New York, Erie County (Board of Directors 1977-80) and New York State Bar Associations. Attended "Financial Statements in the Courtroom" The National Judicial College Nov 1993. Lecturer Judicial Seminars July 1994 and New York State Bar Association Seminars. Board of Directors Buffalo Hearing and Speech Center 1972-84. Board of Trustees Studio Arena Theater 1974-84 and Erie County United Way 1979-88. Chairman Eight County Diocesan Catholic Charities Appeal 1980. Member Daemen College Scholarship Fund Committee 1985-88. Board of Advisors Niagara University since 1999.
Office: 50 Delaware Avenue, Buffalo 14202.
Telephone: (716) 851-3363.
Fax: (716) 852-6365
E-mail address: jcgorski@courts.state.ny.us

GOTTLIEB, Stephen S. *(Judge, The Civil Court of the City of New York)* Currently assigned to Family Court. Former Acting Justice, New York Supreme Court.
Office: 89-17 Sutphin Boulevard, Jamaica 11435.
Telephone: (718) 262-7378.

GRAFFEO, Victoria A. *(Associate Judge, New York Court of Appeals)* Appointed by Governor George E. Pataki to term beginning Dec 1, 2000. Term expires Dec 1, 2014. Born Rockville Centre New York April 13, 1952. Roman Catholic. Educated at State University of New York at Oneonta B.A. with honors 1974 and Albany Law School of Union University J.D. 1977. Admitted to practice New York 1978, U.S. District Court Northern District of New York 1978, U.S. Supreme Court 1993 and U.S. Court of Appeals Second Circuit 1995. In legal practice Colonie 1978-82. Justice, New York Supreme Court Third Judicial District Sept 1996 to March 1998, appointed by Governor George E. Pataki. Associate Justice, New York Supreme Court Appellate Division Third Judicial Department March 1998 to Nov 2000, appointed by Governor George E. Pataki.

Chief Counsel to Assembly Minority Leader New York Jan 1989 to Dec 1994. Solicitor General New York Jan 1995 to Sept 1996. Member Women's Bar Association of the State of New York, National Italian American (New York State Greater Capital Chapter), Albany County and New York State Bar Associations. Recipient Kate Stoneman Award from Albany Law School of Union University 1999 and Distinguished Member Award from Capital District Women's Bar Association 2000. Named one of 100 Women of Excellence by Albany Colonie Chamber of Commerce 2000. Member Zonta Club of Albany.

Office: 20 Eagle Street, Albany 12207.
Telephone: (518) 487-5330.

GRAYS, Marguerite A. *(Justice, New York Supreme Court Eleventh Judicial District)* Former Judge, The Civil Court of the City of New York.

Office: 88-11 Sutphin Boulevard, Jamaica 11435.
Telephone: (718) 520-2500.

GREEN, Samuel L. *(Associate Justice, New York Supreme Court Appellate Division Fourth Judicial Department)* Elected Justice Eighth Judicial District to term beginning Jan 1, 1979. Reelected 1992. Appointed Associate Justice Appellate Division by governor. Born Feb 10, 1935. Educated at State University of New York at Buffalo B.S.B.A. J.D. Awarded honorary D.H.L. Canisius College 1977. Began legal practice Buffalo. Judge, Buffalo City Court 1973-79.

Lecturer on Constitutional Law Buffalo Police Training Academy. Member American Judges Association, New York State City Court Judges Association, Bar Association of Erie County, New York State and National Bar Associations. Testified before New York State Assembly regarding runaways and teenage prostitution. Named one of Buffalo's Outstanding Citizens by Buffalo Courier Express 1974. Listed in *Who's Who in the East* 1975-76. Chairman Task Force Against Youthful Prostitution. Board of Directors Buffalo Urban League and Buffalo Council on World Affairs. Member NAACP, Buffalo 4-H Program and Advisory Council Daeman College School of Social Work.

Office: 50 Delaware Avenue, Buffalo 14202.
Telephone: (716) 851-3415.
Fax: (716) 852-6367

GREEN, Stanley B. *(Judge, The Civil Court of the City of New York)* Currently serves as Acting Justice, New York Supreme Court Twelfth Judicial District.

Office: 851 Grand Concourse, Bronx 10451.
Telephone: (718) 590-3591.
Fax: (718) 590-8914

GREENBERG, Ethan *(Judge, The Criminal Court of the City of New York)* Appointed by Mayor Rudolph Giuliani to term beginning Oct 1997. Reappointed 2000, current term expires Dec 31, 2010. Born New Rochelle New York Aug 7, 1957. Jewish. Educated at Yale College B.A. cum laude 1978 and Columbia University School of Law J.D. 1981. Harlan Fiske Stone Scholar. Admitted to practice New York 1982, U.S. District Courts Eastern 1985 and Southern 1985 Districts of New York and U.S. Court of Appeals Second Circuit 1989. In legal practice New York City 1985-97.

Assistant District Attorney New York County Aug 1981 to Feb 1985. Author "Penal Law's Unequal Treatment of Violent Acts Against Police" New York L. Jour. Nov 6, 1996. Important Opinions: People v. Robles 691 N.Y.S.2d 697, 1999; People v. Patterson 708 N.Y.S.2d 815, 2000; and People v. Brown 711 N.Y.S.2d 707, 2000. Adjunct Professor of New York Civil Practice Seton Hall University School of Law since 2002.

Office: 215 East 161st Street, Room 9-20, Bronx 10451.
Telephone: (718) 590-2942.
Fax: (718) 590-7297
E-mail address: egreenbe@courts.state.ny.us

GRIBETZ, Sidney H. *(Judge, New York City Family Court)* Appointed by Mayor Rudolph W. Giuliani to term beginning May 1999. Term expires May 2009.

Office: 900 Sheridan Avenue, Bronx 10451.
Telephone: (718) 590-3321.
Fax: (718) 590-7305
E-mail address: sgribetz@courts.state.ny.us

GRIESA, Thomas P. *(Senior Judge, United States District Court Southern District of New York)* Appointed for life by President Richard M. Nixon June 30, 1972 to term beginning Sept 22, 1972. Former Chief Judge. Assumed Senior status, serves by assignment. Born Kansas City Missouri Oct 11, 1930. Christian Scientist. Educated at Harvard University B.A. cum laude 1952 and Stanford University LL.B. 1958. Admitted to practice Washington 1958 and New York 1961. In legal practice New York City 1961-72.

With U.S. Department of Justice Washington D.C. 1958-60. Member The Association of the Bar of the City of New York, New York State and Washington State Bar Associations. Lieutenant j.g. USCG 1952-54.

Office: 1630 U.S. Courthouse, 500 Pearl Street, New York 10007-1312.
Telephone: (212) 805-0210.

GRIFFIN, James P. *(Judge, The Criminal Court of the City of New York)* Appointed by mayor. Currently serves as Acting Justice, New York Supreme Court Eleventh Judicial District.

Office: 125-01 Queens Boulevard, Kew Gardens 11415.
Telephone: (718) 520-5064.

GRIFFIN, Linda C. *(Judge, Rensselaer County Family Court)*

Office: 1504 Fifth Avenue, Troy 12180-4107.
Telephone: (518) 270-3761.
Fax: (518) 272-6573
E-mail address: lgriffin@courts.state.ny.us

GRIFFITH, James R. *(Judge, Oneida County Family Court)* Elected to term beginning Jan 4, 1999. Acting Justice, New York Supreme Court since 2001. Born Rome New York June 2, 1954. Presbyterian. Educated at Princeton University A.B. 1976 and Columbia University School of Law J.D. 1980. Editor-in-Chief Columbia Journal of Environmental Law. Admitted to practice New York. In legal practice 1981-88.

Director Oneida County Legal Aid Society. Member Oneida County and New York State (Chairman Committee on Citizenship Education) Bar Associations. Staff member Permanent Subcommittee on Investigations U.S. Senate 1976-77. Committeeman, Rome City Chairman and Oneida County Chairman Oneida County Republican Committee. State Republican Committeeman Delegate to Supreme Court Convention Fifth Judicial District. Trustee First Presbyterian Church, Rome New York. Coach and judge high school mock trial. Assistant Youth Soccer Coach YMCA. Member Rotary Club.

Office: 301 West Dominick Street, Rome 13440.
Telephone: (315) 356-1117.
Fax: (315) 337-0480

GRIFFITH, Michael F. *(Judge, Wyoming County Court)* Also serves Wyoming County Surrogate's Court and Wyoming County Family Court.

Office: Courthouse, 147 North Main Street, Warsaw 14569-1193.
Telephone: (585) 786-2253.
Fax: (585) 786-2818

GROPPER, Allan L. *(Judge, United States Bankruptcy Court Southern District of New York)* Appointed by U.S. Court of Appeals Second Circuit judges to term beginning Oct 4, 2000. Term expires Oct 2014.

Office: Hamilton Custom House, Sixth Floor, One Bowling Green, New York 10004-1408.
Telephone: (212) 668-5660.

GROSS, David A. *(Judge, Nassau County District Court)*

Office: 99 Main Street, Hempstead 11550.
Telephone: (516) 572-2149.
E-mail address: gross@courts.state.ny.us

GROSS, Michael A. *(Judge, The Criminal Court of the City of New York)* Appointed by mayor. Currently serves as Acting Justice, New York Supreme Court Twelfth Judicial District.

Office: 851 Grand Concourse, Bronx 10451.
Telephone: (718) 590-7181.
Fax: (718) 590-8914

GROSSO, Joseph A. *(Judge, The Criminal Court of the City of New York)* Appointed by mayor. Currently serves as Acting Justice, New York Supreme Court Eleventh Judicial District.

Office: 125-01 Queens Boulevard, Kew Gardens 11415.
Telephone: (718) 520-6652.

GROSVENOR, Paul H. *(Judge, New York City Family Court)* Appointed by mayor. Currently serves as Supervising Judge.

Office: 283 Adams Street, Sixth Floor, Brooklyn 11201.
Telephone: (718) 643-4546.
Fax: (718) 643-5103

GROW, John W. *(Justice, New York Supreme Court Fifth Judicial District)* Elected to term beginning Jan 1, 1983. Reelected 1996. Certificated. Born Rome New York March 4, 1932. Presbyterian. Educated at St. Lawrence University B.A. 1954 and Cornell Law School LL.B. 1959. Member Phi Delta Phi and Omicron Delta Kappa. Admitted to practice New York 1959. In legal practice Rome 1959-82.

Former Corporation Counsel City of Rome New York. Fellow New York Bar Foundation. Member Rome (Past President), Oneida County and New York State Bar Associations. Captain U.S. Army 1954-56 and USAR 1956-60. Republican. Enjoys golf, gardening, racquetball and cross-country skiing.

Office: Oneida County Courthouse, 300 North James Street, Rome 13440.
Telephone: (315) 336-0772.
Fax: (315) 337-0846

GUBBAY, Joseph E. *(Judge, The Criminal Court of the City of New York)* Appointed by Mayor Rudolph Giuliani.

Office: 120 Schermerhorn Street, Brooklyn 11201.
Telephone: (718) 643-8400.
Fax: (718) 643-3538

GUERTIN, Richard J. *(Judge, Middletown City Court)*

Office: Two James Street, Middletown 10940.
Telephone: (845) 346-4050.

GULOTTA, Frank A., Jr. *(Judge, Nassau County Court)* Appointed by Governor George E. Pataki June 29, 1995. Elected Nov 1995 to term beginning Jan 1, 1996, current term expires Dec 31, 2005. Born New York Nov 2, 1939. Catholic. Educated at Trinity College B.A. 1961 and Columbia University School of Law J.D. 1964. Admitted to practice New York 1965, U.S. Supreme Court 1970 and U.S. District Court Eastern District of New York 1972. In legal practice Minneola 1969-95.

Assistant District Attorney Nassau County Jan 1, 1965 to Sept 15, 1969. Chairman Grievance Committee Tenth Judicial District 1992-95. Member New York State District Attorneys Association, New York State Sheriff's Association, Columbian Lawyers Association (Director), National Association of Criminal Defense Lawyers, National District Attorneys Association, The Association of Trial Lawyers of America, American Academy of Professional Law Enforcement, Former Assistant District Attorneys Association (Past President, Director), County Judges Association of the State of New York (Vice President), American Judicature Society, American Judges Association, Criminal Courts, Nassau County (President 1996-97, Chairman 1982-84 and Former Vice Chairman Grievance Committee, Chair Pre-Paid Legal Service Committee and Lawyers Counseling Committee, Member Criminal Law and Procedure Committee, Matrimonial Law Committee), New York State and American Bar Associations. Recipient Frank A. Gulotta Criminal Justice Award from Former Assistant District Attorneys Association and Man of the Year Award from Middle Earth Crisis Center. Director Syosset South Little League 1981-83. Member Massapequa Elks Lodge 2162, Knights of Columbus Council 5091, South Woodbury Civic Association, Trinity College Alumni Association, Columbia University School of Law Alumni Association, American Diabetes Association, American Committee on

GULOTTA, FRANK A., JR.—*Continued*

Italian Migration (Director) and Italian-Americans in Government. Enjoys gardening and reading.

Office: Nassau County Courthouse, 262 Old Country Road, Mineola 11501.

Telephone: (516) 571-2631.

Fax: (516) 571-0811

GURESZ, Caroline *(Judge, Cohoes City Court)*

Mailing address: P.O. Box 678, Cohoes 12047-0678.

Office: 7 City Hall, First Floor, 97 Mohawk Street, Cohoes 12047.

Telephone: (518) 233-8202.

Fax: (518) 233-8202

GUZMAN, Raymond *(Judge, The Civil Court of the City of New York)* Currently assigned to The Criminal Court of the City of New York.

Office: 100 Centre Street, New York 10013.

Telephone: (212) 374-2067.

Fax: (212) 374-2579

GUZMAN, Wilma *(Judge, The Civil Court of the City of New York)* Elected to term beginning 1999. Term expires 2009. Born New York City. Catholic. Educated at John Jay College of Criminal Justice of the City University of New York B.S. 1978 and St. John's University School of Law J.D. 1986. Admitted to practice New York 1986, New Jersey 1987 and U.S. District Courts Eastern and Southern Districts of New York. In legal practice New York City 1986-98.

Member New York State Trial Lawyers Association, Bronx, Bronx Women's and Metropolitan Women's Bar Associations. Speaker on law related programs Board of Education. Mentor St. Catherine Academy and New York City Alternative School Program. Enjoys swimming, bowling and dancing. Personal Statement or Quote: "God grant me the courage to change the things I can change, the serenity to accept those I cannot, and the wisdom to know the difference."

Office: 851 Grand Concourse, Bronx 10451.

Telephone: (718) 590-2682.

E-mail address: wguzman@courts.state.ny.us

HACKELING, Steven *(Judge, Suffolk County District Court)*

Mailing address: P.O. Box 9075, Central Islip 11722-9075.

Office: Court Complex, 400 Carleton Avenue, Central Islip 11722.

Telephone: (631) 853-4915.

HAFNER, Walter W., Jr. *(Judge, Oswego County Court)*

Office: Public Safety Center, 39 Churchill Road, Oswego 13126.

Telephone: (315) 349-8666.

HAIGHT, Charles S., Jr. *(Senior Judge, United States District Court Southern District of New York)* Appointed for life by President Gerald Ford to term beginning 1976. Assumed Senior status Sept 23, 1995, serves by assignment. Born New York City Sept 23, 1930. Educated at Yale University B.A. 1952 LL.B. 1955. In legal practice New York City 1957-76.

Trial Attorney Civil Division U.S. Department of Justice 1955-57.

Office: 1940 U.S. Courthouse, 500 Pearl Street, New York 10007-1312.

Telephone: (212) 805-0214.

HALL, Courtenay W. *(Judge, Saratoga County Family Court)*

Office: Saratoga County Municipal Center, 35 West High Street, Ballston Spa 12020-0600.

Telephone: (518) 884-9207.

HALL, L. Priscilla *(Justice, New York Supreme Court Second Judicial District)* Acting Justice March 1990 to July 1990. Elected Justice Nov 2, 1993 to term beginning Jan 1, 1994. Term expires Dec 31, 2007. Born Cuero Texas Oct 2, 1946. Educated at Howard University B.A. magna cum laude 1968 and Columbia University M.S. with honors 1969 J.D. 1973. Member Phi Beta Kappa. Admitted to practice New York 1974, U.S. District Court Southern District of New York 1976 and U.S. Supreme Court 1978. Judge, The Criminal Court of the City of New York Feb 1986 to March 1990. Judge, New York Court of Claims July 1990 to Jan 1994, appointed by Governor Mario Cuomo.

Corporate Attorney General Electric Aug 1973 to Feb 1974. Assistant District Attorney New York County Feb 1974 to June 1979 (Criminal Court Assistant, Supreme Court Assistant, Deputy Chief of Grand Jury). Inspector General Department of Employment Oct 1979 to March 1982 and Human Resources Administration Nov 1982 to Feb 1986 New York City. Assistant Attorney General Department of Law New York State April 1982 to Nov 1982. Author "The History of Section Six of the Federal Trade Commission Act" The Record of the Association of the Bar of the City of New York 1972. Important Decisions: People v. Tufano 135 Misc. 2d 222, 1987; People v. Malone 140 Misc. 2d 602, 1988; People v. Wiggans 140 Misc. 2d 602, 1988; People v. Kelvin N.Y.L.J. 29 col. 1 Oct 20, 1988; People v. Prudent N.Y.L.J. 1 col. 3 March 29, 1989; and People v. Stewart & Baxter N.Y.L.J. 27 col. 6 Oct 8, 1992. Member Committee on the Profession and the Courts, Judicial Friends, Association of Black Women Attorneys (Past President, Former Board Member), New York State Association of Women Judges, Inc. (Board of Directors, Treasurer, President Elect), Federal Bar Council (Public Service Committee), The Association of the Bar of the City of New York (Chair Committee to Encourage Judicial Service, Committee on Lectures and Continuing Education), Brooklyn, Metropolitan Black (Chairman 1988-93 and Member Board of Directors), Kings County Criminal, New York State, National (Judicial Council) and American Bar Associations.

Panelist "Women and the Law" New York Law School. Presenter "An Update—Search and Seizure, Miranda" Judicial Council National Bar Association July 1987; "Arraignments" Orientation Seminar Dec 1988 and "Child Witness Verification" Annual Summer Judicial Seminar 1989 Office of Court Administration; "Motions to Dismiss Based upon a Defect in the Grand Jury" Annual Seminar on Criminal Law, Procedure and Evidence 1992; "Mapp Hearings" and "Discovery" 1993 Brooklyn Law School; "Capital Case Update: Focus on Selecting and Managing the Capital Case Injury" Judicial Seminar July 2000; "Presidential Showcase Programs: A Town Meeting on Diversity in the Legal Profession" American Bar Association July 9, 2000; "What

HALL, L. PRISCILLA—*Continued*

It Takes: Building and Reflecting on Qualification for the Judiciary" Presidential Showcase Seminar Past III Aug 9, 2000 and "Impact of Human Rights Violations and Racism on Economic Development: A Precursor to the World Conference on Racism" International Affiliate Meeting Johannesburg, South Africa June 19, 2001 National Bar Association; and "Managing High Profile Trials" Mid Atlantic Association for Court Management Oct 4, 2000. Recipient African-American Business and Professional Women Award from *Dollars and Sense Magazine* Aug 5, 1989, Distinguished Women of New York City Award from Human Resources Administration Women Advisors 1989, Professional Woman Award from The Bronx Club National Association of Negro Business and Professional Women's Clubs, Inc. April 1991, Outstanding Service Award from National Bar Association July 27, 1992, Public Service and Dedication to the African-American Community Award from National Black Prosecutors Association Feb 26, 1993, Community Service Award from Kappa Sigma Chapter Sigma Gamma Rho Nov 13, 1993, The Pinnacle Woman of the Year Award from *Being Single Magazine* and The Gillette Company June 1994, Tenth Year Anniversary Award from Metropolitan Black Bar Association Nov 1994, Positive Role Model Award from The Black American Roots Society June 17, 1995, Taking Charge of Our Future Award from Hofstra Black Law Students Association March 22, 1996, Judicial Sunshine Award from Tort Law Section New York County Lawyers Association Jan 23, 2001 and Leadership Award from New York State Association of Women Judges Jan 27, 2001. Board of Directors Protestant Board of Guardians. Member Revson Advisory Committee Urban Legal Studies Program Center for Legal Education and Urban Policy City College of the City University of New York 1989-90 and 1990-91. Life Subscribing Member NAACP. Board of Governors Daytop Village. Member Church Women United in Brooklyn, Inc.

Office: 360 Adams Street, Brooklyn 11201.
Telephone: (718) 643-7088.
Fax: (718) 643-6244

HALLORAN, Andrew *(Judge, Essex County Court)* Also serves Essex County Surrogate's Court and Essex County Family Court.

Mailing address: P.O. Box 505, Elizabethtown 12932.
Office: Essex County Courthouse, 100 Court Street, Elizabethtown 12932.
Telephone: (518) 873-3326.
Fax: (518) 873-3732

HAMILL, Bryanne A. *(Judge, New York City Family Court)* Appointed by mayor.

Office: 283 Adams Street, Sixth Floor, Brooklyn 11201.
Telephone: (718) 643-4546.
Fax: (718) 643-5103

HANOPHY, Robert J. *(Judge, New York Court of Claims)* Appointed by governor. Currently serves as Acting Justice, New York Supreme Court Eleventh Judicial District.

Office: 125-01 Queens Boulevard, Kew Gardens 11415.
Telephone: (718) 520-3238.
Fax: (718) 520-2494

HANUSZCZAK, Michael L. *(Judge, Onondaga County Family Court)*

Office: Onondaga County Courthouse, 401 Montgomery Street, Syracuse 13202.
Telephone: (315) 671-2010.
Fax: (315) 671-1166
E-mail address: mhanuszc@courts.state.ny.us

HARBERSON, James Coulter, Jr. *(Judge, Watertown City Court)* Appointed by City Council to term beginning April 1, 1986. Elected Nov 4, 1986 and 1996. Current term expires Dec 31, 2006. Born Boston Massachusetts Jan 28, 1941. Catholic. Educated at Colgate University B.A. 1964 and St. John's University School of Law J.D. 1971. Law Clerk to Hon. Henry Hudson, New York Supreme Court Fifth Judicial District June 1974 to Jan 1976. Admitted to practice New York 1972, U.S. District Court Northern District of New York 1972 and U.S. Supreme Court 1976. In legal practice Watertown Aug 1971 to Dec 1986.

Assistant District Attorney Jefferson County 1973-86. Assistant Corporation Counsel 1975-82 and Corporation Counsel 1982-86 Watertown. Important Decisions: Armstrong v. Boyce 135 Misc. 2d 148, 513 N.Y.S.2d 613, 1987; P. v. Tederson 150 Misc. 2d 813, 570 N.Y.S.2d 891, 1981; P. v. Blanchette (found P.L. Section 240.20 Subd. 3 unconstitutional based on P. v. Dietze 75 N.Y.2d 47) 147 Misc. 2d 50, 554 N.Y.S.2d 388; People v. Bauer (passive resistance by protestors found to be resisting arrest under N.Y. Penal Law 205.30) 161 Misc. 2d 588, 614 N.Y.S.2d 871 April 22, 1994; People v. Nancy C. 188 Misc. 2d 383, 727 N.Y.S.2d 867; and People v. Freeman N.Y.L.J. 21 Nov 30 , 2001. Member Jefferson County and New York State Bar Associations. Participant New York Judicial Conference Dec 1986. Speaker on Landlord-Tenant Law New York State Court Administration Judicial Seminars 1993. Faculty Member Continuing Education Program Freedom Village Justice's Programs. Recipient Alcohol and Substance Abuse Council Award 1996. Project Director Neighborhood Youth Corps U.S. Department of Labor, Watertown 1966-68. Member Jefferson County Committee on Domestic Abuse since 1994. Interests include golf, hockey and reading.

Office: Municipal Building, 245 Washington Street, Watertown 13601.
Telephone: (315) 785-7785.
Fax: (315) 785-7817

HARD, Judith A. *(Judge, New York Court of Claims)* Appointed by Governor George E. Pataki.

Mailing address: P.O. Box 7344, Albany 12224.
Office: Capital Station, Albany 12224.
Telephone: (518) 432-3907.
Fax: (518) 432-3908

HARDIN, Adlai S., Jr. *(Judge, United States Bankruptcy Court Southern District of New York)* Appointed by U.S. Court of Appeals Second Circuit judges. Former Judge, Bankruptcy Appellate Panel Second Circuit, selected by the Judicial Council of the Second Circuit.

Office: U.S. Courthouse, 300 Quarropas Street, White Plains 10601-4150.
Telephone: (914) 390-4155.

HARKAVY, Ira B. *(Justice, New York Supreme Court Second Judicial District)* Acting Justice Feb 5, 1992 to 2000. Elected Justice to term beginning Jan 1, 2001. Certificated. Born New York New York April 13,

HARKAVY, IRA B.—*Continued*

1931. Jewish. Educated at Brooklyn College of the City University of New York B.A. cum laude 1951 and Columbia University School of Law J.D. 1954. Member Phi Alpha Delta. Admitted to practice New York 1954, U.S. District Courts Eastern 1956 and Southern 1956 Districts of New York, U.S. Supreme Court 1960, U.S. Court of Appeals Second Circuit 1967 and U.S. Customs Court. In legal practice New York City 1954-82. Arbitrator 1964-81 and Judge Jan 1, 1982 to Dec 31, 2000, The Civil Court of the City of New York.

Important Decisions 1982-84: Baskerdeow Balram v. Sylvia Etheridge 113 Misc. 2d. 251, 449 N.Y.S.2d 389 N.Y.L.J. March 31, 1982; Brooklyn Machinery Warehouse Corp. v. Integrated Display Systems Inc. N.Y.L.J. May 10, 1982; Long Island Anesthesiology Service, P.C. v. Cristoral Solis 114 Misc. 2d 561, 452 N.Y.S.2d 139, June 3, 1982; Bank of Commerce v. Michael De Santis and James K. Noonan 114 Misc. 2d 491, 451 N.Y.S.2d 974 N.Y.L.J. June 22, 1982; Marvin H. Greene, Maurice T. Greene, Bernard Goldberg, Norman Greenberg, Irvin Forrest d/b/a Greenboro Realty v. Jaqueline Resch and Ethel Verducci 114 Misc. 2d 780, 452 N.Y.S.2d 314 N.Y.L.J. 1 July 21, 1982; Seymour Englard v. Martin Davis N.Y.L.J. July 28, 1982 and N.Y.L.J. Weekly Real Estate Law Digest Sept 8, 1982; Charles Beck d/b/a Beck Real Estate v. Natalie Richuiso and Elsa V. Ferdinand and Kathleen A. Ferdinand N.Y.L.J. Aug 11, 1982 and N.Y.L.J. Weekly Real Estate Law Digest Sept 15, 1982; Banner Casualty Company v. Nationwide Insurance Company 115 Misc. 2d 453, 454 N.Y.S.2d 264 Sept 3, 1982; Luch Urso v. Waldbaum, Inc., Frank Nappi, Paul Ramirez and The City of New York N.Y.L.J. Oct 8, 1982; Glen Oaks Village Owners, Inc., Proprietary Lessee v. Malti and Rajkumar L. Balwani, Lessor 115 Misc. 2d 948, 454 N.Y.S.2d 802 N.Y.L.J. Oct 13, 1982 and New York Post Oct 14, 1982; Leroy Wilson Jr. v. New York City Transit Authority 115 Misc. 2d 1017, 454 N.Y.S.2d 962 N.Y.L.J. Nov 9, 1982; Jeron Co., Inc. v. Mark Hwang N.Y.L.J. Nov 17, 1982 and Real Estate Weekly Jan 10, 1983; Rafolin Construction Corp. v. Juana Lippman and John Dee 116 Misc. 2d 920, 457 N.Y.S.2d 712 N.Y.L.J. Dec 22, 1982 and Real Estate Weekly March 21, 1983; Brooklyn Union Gas Company v. Hadley-White Management Corp. 118 Misc. 2d 699, 461 N.Y.S.2d 208 N.Y.L.J. April 27, 1983; Royal Insurance Company v. Swetlana Rzhevsky 119 Misc. 2d 38, 462 N.Y.S.2d 161 N.Y.L.J. July 28, 1983; Ocean Farragut Associates v. Henry and Barbara Sawyer 119 Misc. 2d 712, 464 N.Y.S.2d 346 Real Estate Weekly Dec 26, 1983; Mary C. Giamboi and Joseph J. Giamboi v. New York City Transit Authority 120 Misc. 2d 33, 465 N.Y.S.2d 160 N.Y.L.J. Aug 11, 1983; George Izraelewitz v. Manufacturers Hanover Trust Company 120 Misc. 2d 125, 465 N.Y.S.2d 486 N.Y.L.J. Sept 8, 1983; U.S. Nemrod, Inc. v. Wheel House Dive Shop, Inc. 120 Misc. 2d 156, 465 N.Y.S.2d 674 N.Y.L.J. Sept 30, 1983; The Park Management v. John F. Delucie and Charles H. Berg N.Y.L.J. Sept 19, 1983; Esther Marks v. City of New York 121 Misc. 2d 303, 467 N.Y.S.2d 137, Sept 12, 1983; Kimwal Realty Corp. v. John Marhoffer 121 Misc. 2d 499, 478 N.Y.S.2d 96, Oct 26, 1983; Martin Abramowitz v. The Workmen's Circle N.Y.L.J. Dec 12, 1983; Atlantic Leasing Co. Inc. v. Castro Convertible Corp. N.Y.L.J. Jan 12, 1984; Kenneth Kanarick v. Mannie & Al's Service Station 123 Misc. 2d 221, 473 N.Y.S.2d 327 N.Y.L.J. March 27, 1984; Kalmon Dolgin Affiliates, Inc. v. Berman N.Y.L.J. June 13, 1984; Sidney Kitrosser et al. v. Travelers Insurance Company N.Y.L.J. June 26, 1984; General Electric Credit Corp. v. Phillip Brody 124 Misc. 2d 805, 478 N.Y.S.2d 532 July 5, 1984; Lillian Gellerman v. Allstate Insurance Company 124 Misc. 2d 882, 478 N.Y.S.2d 247 July 9, 1984; Evins Exterminating Co. Inc. v. Progressive Management Corp. N.Y.L.J. Aug 20, 1984; Linton Realty Corp. v. Nannette Saffon and the Department of Social Service of the City of New York 125 Misc. 2d 166, 479 N.Y.S.2d 141, N.Y.L.J. Sept 10, 1984 and Real Estate Weekly Sept 26, 1984; Massachusetts Higher Education Assistance Corporation v. Lucia Bruno a/k/a Karen Mangan Misc. 2d, N.Y.S.2d N.Y.L.J. Oct 1, 1984; and HSU v. Emerson Collision, Inc. 126 Misc. 2d 385, 481 N.Y.S.2d 1001 Nov 28, 1984.

Important Decisions 1985-89: Joseph Cacucciolo v. The City of New York 127 Misc. 2d 315, 486 N.Y.S.2d 829 N.Y.L.J. April 3, 1985; Henry L. Mallardi v. District Council 37 Health and Security Plan Trust 128 Misc. 2d 696, 490 N.Y.S.2d 968 June 7, 1985; People of the State of New York v. Mickey Garcia 128 Misc. 2d 810, 491 N.Y.S.2d 552 June 14, 1985; The Home Indemnity Company v. Castel Construction, Inc. and Gemelli Realty Corp. 128 Misc. 2d 1026, 492 N.Y.S.2d 353 July 15, 1985; People v. Inkyoon Ahm and Tae Ho Chong N.Y.L.J. Sept 26, 1985 and New York Times 29 Sept 21, 1985; People v. Siegel St. Pharmacy, Inc. and Afzal F. Sheikh, et al. N.Y.L.J. Dec 16, 1985; Gropack v. Glen Oaks Village Owners Inc. N.Y.L.J. April 23, 1986; Accad v. DiMattina N.Y.L.J. Sept 10, 1986; GBT Warehouse, Inc. v. Interstate Brake Products N.Y.L.J. Sept 17, 1986; A/P Associates v. The Long Island College Hospital N.Y.L.J. Sept 17, 1986; Miller v. Koss N.Y.L.J. Sept 22, 1986; Brooklyn Law School v. Pelligrini N.Y.L.J. Sept 24, 1986 and N.Y.L.J. Weekly Real Estate Law Digest Nov 5, 1986; Satenspiels Markets, Inc. v. Hing Lung Chinese Restaurant, Inc. N.Y.L.J. Jan 8, 1987; Walcott v. Manufacturers Hanover Trust 133 Misc. 2d 725, 507 N.Y.S.2d 961 N.Y.L.J. Jan 6, 1987; People v. Carlos Rodriguez N.Y.L.J. Feb 27, 1987; People v. Derek Townsend N.Y.L.J. May 14, 1987; Edelman v. New York City Board of Education N.Y.L.J. July 13, 1987; Son Chai Yi v. Aiello N.Y.L.J. Nov 18, 1987; Department of Housing Preservation and Development of the City of New York v. Sterling Street Corp. and Morris Gross N.Y.L.J. Dec 17, 1987; Licari v. Mullig N.Y.L.J. Jan 26, 1987; J. J. Balan, Inc. v. Ace Dodge, Inc. N.Y.L.J. April 19, 1988; Merrill Lynch Pierce Fenner & Smith, Inc. v. Hristos Xanthoudakis and Laurie Xanthoudakis 140 Misc. 2d 595, 531 N.Y.S.2d 487 N.Y.L.J. Aug 16, 1988; Atlas Door Corp. v. Elite Associates, Inc. N.Y.L.J. Oct 21, 1988; Brodsky v. Gaulke N.Y.L.J. Jan 12, 1989 and N.Y.L.J. Realty Law Digest Feb 1, 1989; Lentini v. Tishman Speyer 52 Venture N.Y.L.J. Feb 2, 1989; Chan v. Rivera N.Y.L.J. May 17, 1989; Kings County District Attorneys Office v. Debra Underwood 143 Misc. 2d 965, 543 N.Y.S.2d 247 N.Y.L.J. June 15, 1989; Trimman Painting and Decorating Corp. v. Zilber N.Y.L.J. July 26, 1989; Taylor v. City of New York et al. 144 Misc. 2d 1029, 545 N.Y.S.2d 521 N.Y.L.J. Aug 30, 1989; and Judah Dick v. Citibank (Hannah Freund v. Citibank) 145 Misc. 2d 563, 548 N.Y.S.2d 133 N.Y.L.J. Sept 30, 1989.

Important Decisions 1990-92: Shabi v. State Farm Mutual Automobile Insurance Co. N.Y.L.J. Jan 18,

HARKAVY, IRA B.—*Continued*

1990; 19th Street Realty Co. v. New Broadway Toy Mfg. Co. N.Y.L.J. Feb 14, 1990; Saintune v. Leger N.Y.L.J. Feb 20, 1990; King v. Faustin N.Y.L.J. March 26, 1990; Cohen v. City of New York N.Y.L.J. May 7, 1990; Trinman Painting and Decorating Corp. v. Victor Zilber as 7-A Administrator N.Y.L.J. May 30, 1990; Shabi v. State Farm Mutual Automobile Insurance Co. N.Y.L.J. May 31, 1990; Fromantz v. Altman N.Y.L.J. June 22, 1990; Accad v. DiMattina N.Y.L.J. Aug 8, 1990; Aponte v. City of New York N.Y.L.J. Aug 22, 1990; Butts v. Marx 148 Misc. 2d 405, 560 N.Y.S.2d 268 N.Y.L.J. Sept 25, 1990; LaManna v. King Tut Restaurant, Inc. N.Y.L.J. Sept 26, 1990; Zakshevsky v. City of New York 149 Misc. 2d 52, 562 N.Y.S.2d 371 N.Y.L.J. Dec 10, 1990; Dent's Out Ltd. v. O'Shaughnessy N.Y.L.J. June 24, 1991; Travelers Indemnity Co. v. Agoli 151 Misc. 2d 947, 574 N.Y.S.2d 134 N.Y.L.J. Aug 29, 1991; Mojica v. MVAIC N.Y.L.J. Sept 12, 1991; Adler v. Halberstam N.Y.L.J. Sept 30, 1991; Continental Insurance Co. v. Skyview Fuel Oil Company N.Y.L.J. Nov 5, 1991; Grossbard v. Casella N.Y.L.J. Dec 3, 1991; Stec v. St. Paul Fire and Marine Insurance Co. N.Y.L.J. Dec 26, 1991; Cox v. Parkway Realty N.Y.L.J. Feb 25, 1992; Level Line, Inc. v. Balzano N.Y.L.J. March 27, 1992; People v. Benito Lopez N.Y.L.J. April 17, 1992; People v. Berris Asphill N.Y.L.J. April 29, 1992; Tucker v. City of New York Misc. 2d N.Y.S.2d N.Y.L.J. May 26, 1992; People v. Donald Peterkin N.Y.L.J. July 13, 1992; People v. Samuel Ramirez N.Y.L.J. Aug 10, 1992; People v. Donovan Castell N.Y.L.J. Aug 18, 1992; and People v. Jose M. Gonzalez N.Y.L.J. Dec 22, 1992.

Important Decisions since 1993: People v. Thomas McCord N.Y.L.J. Feb 3, 1994; People v. Colbert Wong N.Y.L.J. Feb 8, 1994; People v. John Cureton N.Y.L.J. March 4, 1994; People v. Michael Lipovsky N.Y.L.J. April 1, 1994; People v. Steve Miller N.Y.L.J. April 6, 1994; People v. Mustafa Omron N.Y.L.J. May 16, 1994; People v. Victor Rivera N.Y.L.J. June 3, 1994; People v. Steve Miller N.Y.L.J. June 21, 1994; People v. Tyrone Adams and Victor Adams Dec 20, 1994; People v. Marcus Graham and Gary Van Dorn N.Y.L.J. April 3, 1995; People v. Mark McEwen N.Y.L.J. April 7, 1995; People v. Bobby Trim N.Y.L.J. May 22, 1995; Pensabene v. Pensabene N.Y.L.J. Oct 27, 1995; Slater v. Slater N.Y.L.J. Dec 29, 1995; Guglielmo v. Guglielmo N.Y.L.J. Jan 2, 1996; Kedio v. Kedio N.Y.L.J. Jan 26, 1996; Brown v. Brown N.Y.L.J. March 18, 1996; Howard v. Howard N.Y.L.J. March 22, 1996; Jurdak v. Jurdak N.Y.L.J. April 9, 1996; People v. Shawn Sims N.Y.L.J. July 5, 1996; People v. Phillip Allen N.Y.L.J. Aug 16, 1996; People v. Michael Price N.Y.L.J. Oct 15, 1996; People v. John Vento N.Y.L.J. Dec 27, 1996; Lopez v. Lopez N.Y.L.J. 38 June 13, 1997; Chifari v. Chifari N.Y.L.J. 31 Sept 25, 1997; Melucci v. Melucci N.Y.L.J. 27 Oct 28, 1997; Allsopp v. Allsopp N.Y.L.J. 32 Dec 12, 1997; Lipovsky v. Lipovsky N.Y.L.J. 30 Feb 27, 1998; Termini v. Termini N.Y.L.J. 33 June 8, 1998; Salimeni v. Salimeni N.Y.L.J. 24 Aug 20, 1998; Orlando v. Orlando N.Y.L.J. 29 Oct 20, 1998; Lobdell v. Lobdell N.Y.L.J. 33 March 1, 1999; Saponaro v. Saponaro N.Y.L.J. 35 April 30, 1999; Sherman v. Sherman N.Y.L.J. 26 Aug 12, 1999; People v. Edward Madden N.Y.L.J. 32 Sept 29, 1999; Mazzone v. Mazzone N.Y.L.J. 34 Jan 25, 2000; People v. Zakity Abdul Malik N.Y.L.J. 32 March 2, 2000; Campbell v. Rockefeller University N.Y.L.J. 30 Sept 21, 2000; Barreto v. Pall Corp. N.Y.L.J. 28 Oct 31, 2000; Bankhead v. N.Y.C. Police Officer Erick Wolf N.Y.L.J. 28 Nov 21, 2000; Trepel v. Greenman-Pederson, Inc. N.Y.L.J. 30 Feb 8, 2001; Lieber v. Diamantstein N.Y.L.J. 20 July 19, 2001; Ades v. Microsoft Corporation N.Y.L.J. 27 Oct 9, 2001; and The Board of Education v. Hankins N.Y.L.J. 23 Dec 17, 2001.

Special Deputy Attorney General Election Fraud Bureau 1954-57. Adjunct Professor of Business Law Brooklyn College of the City University of New York Department of Economics 1988-93. Former Member Association of Arbitrators of The Civil Court of The City of New York, American Judges Association and The Association of the Bar of the City of New York. Arbitrator National Panel of Arbitrators American Arbitration Association 1975-81. Member Board of Judges of The Civil Court of the City of New York (Vice President 1989-94 and President 1994-96), New York State Trial Lawyers Association, Brooklyn (Committees: Civil Court, Court Facilities, Grievance, Continuing Education), New York State (Court Facilities Subcommittee Judicial Section) and American Bar Associations. Recipient Presidential Medal of Honor from Brooklyn College 1975, Citation of Merit from Brooklyn Borough President 1976, 1981, 1991 and 1996, Annual Award from Flatbush-Nostrand Chamber of Commerce 1979, Certificate of Merit from New York City 1981, Distinguished Service Award from Brooklyn Bar Association 1996 and Annual Recognition Award from Jewish Community Council of Kings Bay 1996. Listed in *Who's Who in the East* since 1975, *Who's Who in American Law* since 1977 and *Who's Who in America.* Named Trustee of the Year by American Library Association 1995. Member 1965-67 and Secretary 1966-67 Community Board 4 of Brooklyn. Chairman Community Board 14 of Brooklyn 1967-81. Member Coordinating Council of the Alumni Association of the Senior Colleges of the City University of New York 1965-83 (Chairman 1973-74), Borough of Manhattan Community College Advisory Council 1974-77, Committee for Public Higher Education Executive Board and Ad Hoc Committee for City University 1967-83, Flatbush Development Corporation Advisory Board 1975-76, Brooklyn Civic Council 1975-85 (Trustee 1977-81), Brooklyn College Foundation (Board of Directors 1958-82, Secretary 1958-64 and 1971-78, Vice President/Secretary 1966-70), Madison Jewish Center (Advisory Board 1960-72, member 1972-92 and Chairman 1981-83 Board of Trustees, Vice President 1975-77, Secretary 1977-78 and 1981-92, President 1978-81), Brooklyn/Staten Island Council of B'nai B'rith (Member since 1960, President Kings County Lodge 1965-67, Chairman Anti-Defamation League Borough of Brooklyn 1967-70 and Committee on Community Affairs 1978-79, member Executive Board Brooklyn Council 1967-70, member Regional Board Anti-Defamation League 1983-90, President Brooklyn Unity Lodge 1985-90), Boy Scouts of America (Institutional Representative 1967-69, Chairman Pack Committee Pack 353, 1969-72), Brooklyn Public Library (Trustee since 1975, Secretary 1977-79, Vice President 1979-82, President 1982-85), Jewish Community Council of Bay Park (Executive Board since 1987, President since 1991) and Council of Jewish Organizations of Flatbush (Executive Board since 1986). Member Search Committee for Selection of President 1969 and 1979 Brooklyn College. Board of Directors

HARKAVY, IRA B.—*Continued*

Brooklyn College B'nai B'rith JACY Hillel Foundation since 1975 (Vice President 1977-78, President 1978-81, Trustee 1981-83, Chairman of the Board 1983-90), American Library Trustee Association since 1985 (Region II Vice President 1989-93) and Brooklyn College Alumni Association since 1993 (Executive Board 1955-86, Secretary 1956-61, Vice President 1961-73, President 1973-83). Board of Trustees Kings Bay YMHA-YWHA since 1979 (Vice President 1986-89 and 1992, First Vice President 1989-97, President 1997-2001). Founder Midwood-Kings Highway Development Corporation (Chairman of the Board 1976-82, Chairman Emeritus 1982-87).

Office: 360 Adams Street, Room 735, Brooklyn 11201.
Telephone: (718) 643-7082.
Fax: (718) 643-3722

HARRINGTON, William M. *(Judge, The Criminal Court of the City of New York)* Appointed by mayor.
Office: 100 Centre Street, New York 10013.
Telephone: (212) 374-6216.
Fax: (212) 374-2579

HARRIS, Gerald *(Judge, The Criminal Court of the City of New York)* Appointed by Mayor Rudolph W. Giuliani.
Office: 100 Centre Street, New York 10013.
Telephone: (212) 374-6216.
Fax: (212) 374-2579

HART, Duane A. *(Justice, New York Supreme Court Eleventh Judicial District)* Former Judge, The Civil Court of the City of New York.
Office: 88-11 Sutphin Boulevard, Jamaica 11435.
Telephone: (718) 520-2501.

HARTER, Deborah Jo L. *(Acting Judge, Binghamton City Court)*
Office: 46 Hawley Street, Fifth Floor, Binghamton 13901.
Telephone: (607) 772-7006.

HARVEY, James R. *(Judge, Ontario County Court)* Also serves Ontario County Family Court.
Office: Courthouse, 27 North Main Street, Canandaigua 14424-1447.
Telephone: (585) 396-4260.
Fax: (585) 396-4087
E-mail address: jharvey@courts.state.ny.us

HAYDEN, James T. *(Judge, Chemung County Court)* Also serves Chemung County Surrogate's Court and Chemung County Family Court.
Mailing address: P.O. Box 588, Elmira 14902-0588.
Office: Justice Building, Second Floor, 203 William Street, Elmira 14901.
Telephone: (607) 737-2923.
Fax: (607) 737-2913

HAYES, Gerald V. *(Judge, Dutchess County Court)*
Office: Dutchess County Courthouse, 10 Market Street, Poughkeepsie 12601-3203.
Telephone: (845) 486-2225.

HAYES, Leo F. X. *(Associate Justice, New York Supreme Court Appellate Division Fourth Judicial Department)* Elected Justice Fifth Judicial District to term beginning Jan 1, 1974. Reelected 1987 and 2001. Appointed Associate Justice Appellate Division by Governor George E. Pataki. Certificated. Term expires Dec 31, 2004. Born Syracuse New York July 31, 1932. Roman Catholic. Educated at LeMoyne College B.B.A. 1956 and Albany Law School of Union University LL.B. 1959. Admitted to practice New York 1960. District Attorney Onondaga County 1971-74.
Office: Onondaga County Courthouse, 401 Montgomery Street, Syracuse 13202.
Telephone: (315) 671-1095.
Fax: (315) 671-1185

HAYES, Roger S. *(Judge, The Criminal Court of the City of New York)* Appointed by Mayor Rudolph Giuliani. Currently serves as Acting Justice, New York Supreme Court Twelfth Judicial District.
Office: 851 Grand Concourse, Bronx 10451.
Telephone: (718) 590-7344.
Fax: (718) 590-8914

HEDGES, Bryan R. *(Judge, Onondaga County Family Court)*
Office: 105 Onondaga County Courthouse, 401 Montgomery Street, Syracuse 13202.
Telephone: (315) 671-2040.
Fax: (315) 671-1169
E-mail address: bhedges@courts.state.ny.us

HEFFERNAN, Charles J., Jr. *(Judge, The Criminal Court of the City of New York)* Appointed by mayor. Currently assigned to Family Court.
Office: 89-14 Parsons Boulevard, Jamaica 11432.
Telephone: (718) 520-3985.

HEITLER, Sherry Klein *(Justice, New York Supreme Court First Judicial District)* Former Acting Justice. Former Judge, The Civil Court of the City of New York.
Office: 60 Centre Street, New York 10007.
Telephone: (212) 374-8379.

HELD, Gerald S. *(Justice, New York Supreme Court Second Judicial District)* Elected to term beginning April 1974. Reelected 1988. Certificated. Term expires Dec 31, 2005. Born New York Dec 9, 1932. Jewish. Educated at Brooklyn College of the City University of New York 1952 and Brooklyn Law School 1954. Admitted to practice New York 1955. Republican.
Office: 360 Adams Street, Brooklyn 11201.
Telephone: (718) 643-7024.
E-mail address: gheld@courts.state.ny.us

HELLERSTEIN, Alvin K. *(Judge, United States District Court Southern District of New York)* Appointed for life by President Bill Clinton to term beginning Nov 30, 1998. Born New York City Dec 28, 1933. Educated at Columbia College B.A. 1954 and Columbia University J.D. 1956. Law Clerk to Hon. Edmund L. Palmieri, U.S. District Court Southern District of New York 1956-57. In legal practice New York City 1960-98.
Office: 910 U.S. Courthouse, 500 Pearl Street, New York 10007-1312.
Telephone: (212) 805-0152.

HEMMETT, Gordon M., Jr. *(Judge, Washington County Court)* Elected Nov 1989 to term beginning Jan 1, 1990. Reelected 1999, current term expires Dec 31, 2009. Also serves Washington County Surrogate's Court and Washington County Family Court. Born Rochester New York Aug 5, 1940. Protestant. Educated at Alle-

HEMMETT, GORDON M., JR.—*Continued*

gheny College B.A. 1962 and Syracuse University College of Law J.D. 1965. Admitted to practice New York 1965. In legal practice Glens Falls 1965-71 and Hudson Falls 1971-85.

District Attorney Washington County 1982-89. Member Washington County and New York State Bar Associations. Member Hudson Falls Rotary Club, Adirondack Chapter American Red Cross and Hudson Falls-UBY Chamber of Commerce. Enjoys traveling, fishing, hunting and outdoor recreation.

Office: Washington County Courthouse, Building C, 383 Broadway, Fort Edward 12828.

Telephone: (518) 746-2506.

HENRY, Patrick *(Justice, New York Supreme Court Tenth Judicial District)* Elected to term beginning Jan 1, 1991. Certificated. Also serves as Supervising Judge, Suffolk County Criminal Courts. Born Islip New York Aug 8, 1929. Episcopalian. Educated at Massachusetts Maritime Academy B.S. 1951 and Washington and Lee University J.D. 1960. Admitted to practice New York 1964.

District Attorney Suffolk County 1978-90. Instructor in Business Law, Criminal Procedure and Criminal Law Suffolk Community College 1967-71. Member Suffolk County Bar Association. Lieutenant USN 1952-54.

Office: Supreme Court Building, 235 Griffing Avenue, Riverhead 11901-3090.

Telephone: (631) 852-2327.

Fax: (631) 852-2328

HENSLEY, Paul M. *(Judge, Suffolk County District Court)*

Office: C-158 North County Complex, Veteran's Memorial Highway, Hauppauge 11788.

Telephone: (631) 853-5419.

Fax: (631) 853-5951

HEPNER, Paula J. *(Judge, New York City Family Court)* Appointed by Mayor David Dinkins to term beginning Aug 21, 1990. Reappointed by Mayor Rudolph Giuliani Jan 2000, current term expires Dec 31, 2009. Born Philadelphia Pennsylvania Sept 29, 1948. Educated at Ohio Wesleyan University B.A. 1970 and Hofstra University School of Law J.D. 1977. Admitted to practice New York 1978, U.S. District Courts Eastern 1978 and Southern 1978 Districts of New York and U.S. Tax Court 1980. In private legal practice New York 1978-90.

Staff Attorney Protection and Advocacy System for Developmental Disabilities, Inc. 1975-79. Director Handicapped Children's Rights Project Advocates for Children of New York, Inc. 1979-83 and Education Rights Project Public Education Association 1983-85. Consulting Attorney Center for Independence of the Disabled in New York, Inc. 1984-86. Supervising Attorney Human Resources Administration New York City 1986-90. Member Professional Advisory Board and Co-chair Legal and Legislative Committee Coalition on Sexuality and Disability, Inc. 1980-90. Member Lesbian and Gay Law Association of Greater New York, LAMBDA Legal Defense and Education Fund, Association of Lesbian and Gay Judges (President), National Association of Women Judges, The Association of the Bar of the City of New York and New York Women's Bar Association. Citizens Advisory Council Task Force on the Disabled New York State Assembly 1981-85.

Office: 283 Adams Street, Sixth Floor, Brooklyn 11201.

Telephone: (718) 643-4546.

Fax: (718) 643-5103

HERRICK, Stephen W. *(Judge, Albany County Court)* Former Judge, Albany City Court.

Office: 256 Albany County Courthouse, Columbia and Eagle Streets, Albany 12207.

Telephone: (518) 487-5030.

Fax: (518) 487-5020

HESTER, Joseph P., Jr. *(Justice, New York Supreme Court Sixth Judicial District)* Born Binghamton New York Sept 13, 1939. Roman Catholic. Educated at Yale University B.A. 1961 and Syracuse University College of Law LL.B. 1964. Note Contributor Syracuse L. Rev. 1963. Law Clerk to Onondaga County Family Court 1965. Member Phi Delta Phi. Admitted to practice New York 1966, Pennsylvania 1973 and U.S. Supreme Court 1974. In legal practice Binghamton New York 1967-91 and Montrose Pennsylvania 1973-91. Former Judge, Broome County Family Court, elected to term beginning Jan 1, 1992.

Former Member Pennsylvania and American Bar Associations. Member Broome County and New York State Bar Associations. Chairman Broome County Republican Party 1982-83. Member 1972-75 and President 1974 Binghamton City Council. Member Choir and Lay Lector St. Patrick's Church, Binghamton New York. Enjoys tennis, squash and reading American history.

Mailing address: P.O. Box 1766, Binghamton 13902-1766.

Office: Broome County Courthouse, 92 Court Street, Binghamton 13901-3301.

Telephone: (607) 778-2428.

HESTER, Samuel D. *(Justice, New York Supreme Court Fifth Judicial District)*

Office: Oneida County Courthouse, 200 Elizabeth Street, Utica 13501.

Telephone: (315) 798-5889.

Fax: (315) 798-6436

HICKMAN, S. Barrett *(Justice, New York Supreme Court Ninth Judicial District)* Elected to term beginning Jan 1, 1986. Certificated 1999 and 2001. Born Danbury Connecticut Oct 3, 1929. Baptist. Educated at Hamilton College A.B. 1951 and Cornell University LL.B. 1959. Staff member Cornell University Law Review. Admitted to practice New York 1959. Began legal practice White Plains 1959. In legal practice Mahopac 1977-78. Justice, Carmel Town Justice Court 1965-76. Judge, Putnam County Court Jan 1, 1979 to Dec 31, 1985. Judge, Putnam County Family Court Jan 1, 1979 to Dec 31, 1985. Surrogate, Putnam County Surrogate's Court Jan 1, 1979 to Dec 31, 1985.

District Attorney Putnam County 1977-78. Member Putnam County, Westchester County, New York State and American Bar Associations. USAF 1952-56.

Office: 40 Gleneida Avenue, Carmel 10512.

Telephone: (845) 225-3224.

HIGGINS, Thomas W., Jr. *(Judge, Syracuse City Court)*
Office: Public Safety Building, Second Floor, 511 South State Street, Syracuse 13202-2179.
Telephone: (315) 477-2769.
Fax: (315) 474-2601
E-mail address: thiggins@courts.state.ny.us

HILLERY, Judith A. *(Justice, New York Supreme Court Ninth Judicial District)* Elected to term beginning Jan 1, 1992. Term expires Dec 31, 2005. Born Oneonta New York July 26, 1943. Educated at State University of New York at Buffalo B.A. 1966 J.D. 1967. Admitted to practice New York 1967, U.S. District Courts Southern 1969 and Eastern 1969 Districts of New York, U.S. Court of Appeals Second Circuit 1969 and U.S. Supreme Court 1976. Began legal practice Poughkeepsie 1967. Justice, Poughkeepsie Town Justice Court July 30, 1975 to Dec 31, 1978. Judge, Dutchess County Family Court Jan 2, 1979 to Dec 31, 1982. Judge, Dutchess County Court Jan 1, 1983 to Dec 31, 1991.
Member Dutchess County Magistrates Association, New York State Magistrates Association, Association of Justices of the Supreme Court of the State of New York, Dutchess County and New York State Bar Associations. Member Poughkeepsie South Rotary and Rotary International. Enjoys golfing, sailing, racquetball and swimming.
Office: Courthouse, 10 Market Street, Poughkeepsie 12601.
Telephone: (845) 486-2220.
Fax: (845) 473-5403

HILLIS, John T. *(Judge, Binghamton City Court)*
Office: Governmental Plaza, 38 Hawley Street, Binghamton 13901.
Telephone: (607) 772-7006.
Fax: (607) 772-7041

HIMELEIN, Larry M. *(Judge, Cattaraugus County Court)* Elected Nov 1992 to term beginning Jan 1, 1993. Reelected 2002, current term expires Dec 31, 2012. Also serves Cattaraugus County Surrogate's Court and Cattaraugus County Family Court. Born Buffalo New York June 27, 1949. Episcopalian. Educated at Ithaca College B.A. 1971 and Suffolk University Law School J.D. 1975. Admitted to practice New York 1976, U.S. District Court Western District of New York and U.S. Court of Appeals Second Circuit. In legal practice Gowanda 1976-81.
District Attorney Cattaraugus County 1982-92. Member County Judges Association of the State of New York, Association of Judges of the Family Court of the State of New York, The Surrogates' Association of the State of New York, Bar Association of Erie County, Cattaraugus County and New York State Bar Associations. Attended "Child Support Guidelines and Valuing Professional Licenses" Judicial Seminars 1993, 1994 and 1995. Member 1987-96 and President 1990-96 Board of Directors Tri-County Hospital. Member Arson Task Force and Traffic Safety Board 1982-92. Enjoys running, golf, weight lifting and travel. Has competed in five marathons and two triathlons.
Office: Courthouse, 303 Court Street, Little Valley 14755.
Telephone: (716) 938-9111.
Fax: (716) 938-6413

HINDS-RADIX, Sylvia O. *(Judge, The Civil Court of the City of New York)*
Office: 141 Livingston Street, Brooklyn 11201.
Telephone: (718) 643-5060.
Fax: (718) 643-3733

HINRICHS, C. Randall *(Judge, Suffolk County Court)*
Mailing address: P.O. Box 9007, Riverhead 11901-9007.
Office: Court Complex, 210 Center Drive, Riverhead 11901.
Telephone: (631) 853-7549.

HOLLIE, Ronald D. *(Justice, New York Supreme Court Eleventh Judicial District)* Former Judge, The Civil Court of the City of New York.
Office: 125-01 Queens Boulevard, Kew Gardens 11415.
Telephone: (718) 520-4737.
Fax: (718) 520-2494

HOLZMAN, Lee L. *(Surrogate, Bronx County Surrogate's Court)*
Office: 851 Grand Concourse, Bronx 10451.
Telephone: (718) 590-4515.
Fax: (718) 537-5158

HOMER, David R. *(Magistrate Judge, United States District Court Northern District of New York)* Appointed by U.S. District Court judges to term beginning 1995. Educated at Brown University B.A. 1969 and Syracuse University J.D. cum laude. Editor Syracuse Law Review 1975.
Office: 441 U.S. Courthouse, 445 Broadway, Albany 12207-2967.
Telephone: (518) 257-1850.

HONOROF, Alan L. *(Judge, New York Court of Claims)* Appointed by Governor George E. Pataki. Currently serves as Acting Justice, New York Supreme Court Tenth Judicial District. Also serves as Acting Judge, Nassau County Court.
Office: Nassau County Courthouse, West Wing, 262 Old Country Road, Mineola 11501.
Telephone: (516) 571-3833.
Fax: (516) 571-2137
E-mail address: sailjudge@yahoo.com

HOOD, Martha Walsh *(Judge, Onondaga County Family Court)*
Office: Onondaga County Courthouse, 401 Montgomery Street, Syracuse 13202.
Telephone: (315) 671-2020.
Fax: (315) 671-1167
E-mail address: mhood@courts.state.ny.us

HOROWITZ, Nilda Morales *(Judge, Westchester County Family Court)*
Office: 111 Dr. Martin Luther King Jr. Blvd., White Plains 10601.
Telephone: (914) 995-3623.
Fax: (914) 995-4675

HOWE, Barbara *(Justice, New York Supreme Court Eighth Judicial District)* Born Neptune New Jersey May 16, 1947. Educated at University of Connecticut B.A. with highest honors 1969, Cornell University M.A. 1974 Ph.D. 1976 and State University of New York at Buffalo J.D. 1980. Member Phi Beta Kappa. Admitted to practice New York 1981, Florida 1981, U.S. District

HOWE, BARBARA—*Continued*

Court Western District of New York 1981, U.S. Supreme Court 1984 and U.S. Tax Court 1986. Former Judge, Buffalo City Court, elected to term beginning Jan 1, 1988.

Assistant Professor of Sociology 1974-81, Associate Professor of Sociology 1981-87 and Adjunct Associate Professor of Sociology since 1988 State University of New York at Buffalo. Member The Florida Bar, Bar Association of Erie County and New York State Bar Association.

Office: One Niagara Plaza, Buffalo 14202.
Telephone: (716) 858-4798.
Fax: (716) 858-4873

HOYE, Polly A. *(Judge, Fulton County Court)* Elected Nov 2001 to term beginning Jan 2002. Term expires Dec 2011. Also serves Fulton County Surrogate's Court. Born Utica New York Nov 15, 1957. Episcopalian. Educated at William Smith College B.A. magna cum laude 1979 and Albany Law School of Union University J.D. 1982. Admitted to practice New York 1983 and U.S. District Court Northern District of New York 1983. In legal practice Gloversville 1983-96.

Assistant District Attorney Dec 1989 to June 1996 and District Attorney June 1996 to Dec 2001 Fulton County. Member Fulton-Hamilton Counties Magistrates' Association, County Judges Association of the State of New York, The Surrogates' Association of the State of New York, Fulton County and New York State (House of Delegates) Bar Associations. Parishioner St. John's Episcopal Church, Johnstown New York. Member Soroptimists International of Fulton County. Enjoys travel, winter sports and fishing.

Office: 216 Fulton County Office Building, 223 West Main Street, Johnstown 12095.
Telephone: (518) 736-5691.
Fax: (518) 762-6372

HUBSHER, Muriel Shaff *(Justice, New York Supreme Court Second Judicial District)* Certificated. Former Judge, The Criminal Court of the City of New York, appointed by Mayor Ed Koch.

Office: 360 Adams Street, Brooklyn 11201.
Telephone: (718) 643-5125.
E-mail address: mhubsher@courts.state.ny.us

HUDSON, James C. *(Judge, Suffolk County Court)*
Mailing address: P.O. Box 9007, Riverhead 11901-9007.
Office: Court Complex, 210 Center Drive, Riverhead 11901.
Telephone: (631) 852-3850.
E-mail address: jhudson@courts.state.ny.us

HUFF, Carol E. *(Justice, New York Supreme Court First Judicial District)* Elected to term beginning Jan 1, 1989. Reelected 2002, current term expires Dec 31, 2016. Born Kansas City Missouri. Episcopalian. Educated at Barnard College B.A. 1971 and New York University J.D. 1974. Admitted to practice New York 1975, District of Columbia and U.S. District Court Southern District of New York. Housing Part Judge 1985-87 and Judge 1987-88, The Civil Court of the City of New York.

Member American Bar Association.
Office: 60 Centre Street, New York 10007.
Telephone: (212) 374-8369.

HUGHES, James F. *(Acting Judge, Mechanicville City Court)*
Office: 36 North Main Street, Mechanicville 12118.
Telephone: (518) 664-9876.

HUMMEL, Christian F. *(Surrogate, Rensselaer County Surrogate's Court)* Former Judge, Rensselaer County Family Court.

Office: Courthouse, Congress and Second Streets, Troy 12180.
Telephone: (518) 270-3721.
Fax: (518) 272-5452
E-mail address: chummel@courts.state.ny.us

HUNT, John *(Judge, New York City Family Court)* Appointed by Mayor Rudolph Giuliani.
Office: 151-20 Jamaica Avenue, Jamaica 11432.
Telephone: (718) 298-0197.

HUNT, Richard V. *(Judge, Jefferson County Family Court)*
Office: 175 Arsenal Street, Watertown 13601-2560.
Telephone: (315) 785-3001.
Fax: (315) 785-3198

HUNTER, Alexander Wayman, Jr. *(Justice, New York Supreme Court Twelfth Judicial District)* Acting Justice 1993-94. Elected Justice to term beginning Jan 1, 1995. Term expires Dec 31, 2008. Born New York County New York July 2, 1949. Protestant. Educated at Temple University B.A. 1971 and State University of New York at Buffalo J.D. 1974. Member Phi Alpha Delta. Admitted to practice New York 1975, U.S. District Courts Eastern 1975 and Southern 1975 Districts of New York, U.S. Court of Appeals Second Circuit 1975, U.S. Supreme Court 1979 and Florida 1980. Arbitrator, The Civil Court of the City of New York Small Claims Division 1982-86. Judge, The Criminal Court of the City of New York May 15, 1986 to Dec 31, 1994.

Assistant District Attorney Bronx 1974-77. Law Clerk to Hon. Albert P. Williams, New York Supreme Court First Judicial District 1978 to May 1986. Adjunct Professor of Law Pace University School of Law since 1988. Assistant Adjunct Professor of Legal Research and Writing Bronx Community College since 1990. Member Judicial Friends since 1986. Vice President 1984-85 and Director 1986-92 Black Bar Association of Bronx County. Member The Association of the Bar of the City of New York (Council on Judicial Administration since 1996), The Florida Bar, Metropolitan Black and Bronx County Bar Associations. Faculty summer Judicial Seminars Office of Court Administration 1989, 1994, 1995 and 1996. Recipient Distinguished Service Award from District Attorney's Office Bronx 1978 and Achievement Award from Black Bar Association of Bronx County 1986. Democrat. Corresponding Secretary Committee of One Hundred Democrats Bronx County 1985-86. Board of Visitors Pace University School of Law. Board of Managers East Side House Settlement. Coach Pelham Parkway Little League 1984-86. Enjoys sports, fishing, diving and sailing.

Office: 851 Grand Concourse, Room 533, Bronx 10451.
Telephone: (718) 590-3777.
Fax: (718) 590-7302

HURD, David N. *(Judge, United States District Court Northern District of New York)* Magistrate Judge Jan 18, 1991 to Sept 23, 1999. Appointed Judge for life by

HURD, DAVID N.—*Continued*

President Bill Clinton to term beginning Sept 24, 1999. Born Hancock New York 1937. Educated at Cornell University B.S. 1959 and Syracuse University LL.B. 1963. Board of Editors Syracuse Law Review 1962-63. Member Order of the Coif. Admitted to practice New York 1963.

Assistant District Attorney Oneida County 1966-67. Fellow American College of Trial Lawyers. Member Rome, Albany County, Oneida County and New York State Bar Associations.

Office: Federal Building, 10 Broad Street, Utica 13501.

Telephone: (315) 793-9572.

HURKIN-TORRES, Allen Z. *(Justice, New York Supreme Court Second Judicial District)*

Office: 360 Adams Street, Brooklyn 11201.

Telephone: (718) 643-5343.

HURLBUTT, Robert G. *(Associate Justice, New York Supreme Court Appellate Division Fourth Judicial Department)* Elected Justice Fifth Judicial District to term beginning Jan 1, 1988. Appointed Associate Justice Appellate Division by Governor George E. Pataki. Term expires Dec 31, 2015. Born Canandaigua New York Nov 8, 1939. Protestant. Educated at Union College A.B. 1961 and Albany Law School of Union University LL.B. with honors 1964 replaced by J.D. Comments Editor Albany Law Review 1963-64. Admitted to practice New York 1964. Began legal practice Oswego 1964. Judge, Oswego County Court April 28, 1982 to Dec 31, 1987, appointed by Governor Hugh L. Carey.

District Attorney Oswego County Jan 1977 to April 1982. Adjunct Professor of Business Law 1970-72 and Criminal Law 1978-82 State University of New York at Oswego. Member Oswego County (President 1977-78) and New York State Bar Associations.

Office: Oswego County Courthouse, 25 East Oneida Street, Oswego 13126.

Telephone: (315) 349-3271.

Fax: (315) 343-9090

HURLEY, Denis R. *(Judge, United States District Court Eastern District of New York)* Appointed for life by President George Bush to term beginning 1991. Born Baldwin New York Oct 24, 1937. Educated at University of Pennsylvania B.S. 1959, Columbia University M.B.A. 1962 and Fordham University J.D. 1966. In legal practice Syracuse 1966-68 and Riverhead 1970-83. Judge, Suffolk County Family Court 1983-87. Acting Justice, New York Supreme Court 1987-88. Judge, Suffolk County Court 1988-91.

Principal Assistant District Attorney 1968-70, Special Prosecutor 1974-75 and Senior Assistant County Attorney 1980-81 Suffolk County. Member Suffolk County Legislature 1978-79.

Office: Long Island Federal Courthouse, 100 Federal Plaza, Central Islip 11722-4438.

Telephone: (631) 712-5650.

HUTCHERSON, James W. *(Justice, New York Supreme Court Second Judicial District)* Certificated.

Office: 360 Adams Street, Brooklyn 11201.

Telephone: (718) 643-8094.

E-mail address: jhutcherson@courts.state.ny.us

HUTTNER, Richard D. *(Justice, New York Supreme Court Second Judicial District)* Elected 1986 to term beginning Jan 1, 1987. Reelected 2000, current term expires Dec 31, 2014. Currently serves Eleventh Judicial District. Born Bronx New York Feb 3, 1935. Jewish. Educated at Brooklyn College of the City University of New York B.A. 1956 and Brooklyn Law School J.D. 1962. Admitted to practice New York 1962, U.S. District Court Southern District of New York 1963, U.S. Court of Appeals Second Circuit 1963 and U.S. Supreme Court 1970. Began legal practice New York City 1962. Judge and Administrative Judge, New York City Family Court 1983-85.

Member Brooklyn Bar Association. Chairman New York City Taxi and Limousine Commission 1977-79. Enjoys tennis, jogging and reading. Personal Statement or Quote: "Be a boy scout (or girl scout). Be prepared!"

Office: 88-17 Sutphin Boulevard, Jamaica 11435.

Telephone: (718) 262-7368.

E-mail address: rhuttner@courts.state.ny.us

IACOVETTA, Nicholas J. *(Judge, The Criminal Court of the City of New York)* Appointed by mayor. Currently serves as Acting Justice, New York Supreme Court Twelfth Judicial District.

Office: 851 Grand Concourse, Bronx 10451.

Telephone: (718) 590-3859.

Fax: (718) 590-8914

IWANICKI, Don B. *(Judge, Batavia City Court)* Former Acting Judge.

Office: Genesee County Courts Facility, One West Main Street, Batavia 14020.

Telephone: (585) 344-2550.

Fax: (585) 344-8556

E-mail address: diwanick@courts.state.ny.us

JACKSON, M. Randolph *(Justice, New York Supreme Court Second Judicial District)* Elected to term beginning Jan 1, 1989. Former Judge, The Civil Court of the City of New York.

Office: 360 Adams Street, Brooklyn 11201.

Telephone: (718) 643-2116.

E-mail address: rjackson@courts.state.ny.us

JACOBSON, Laura Lee *(Justice, New York Supreme Court Second Judicial District)* Former Judge, The Civil Court of the City of New York.

Office: Kings County Civic Center, 360 Adams Street, Brooklyn 11201.

Telephone: (718) 643-3804.

JAEGER, Steven M. *(Judge, Nassau County District Court)* Elected Nov 6, 2001 to term beginning Jan 1, 2002. Born Brooklyn New York Jan 24, 1951. Jewish. Educated at University of Pennsylvania B.A. 1973 and New York University J.D. 1976. Admitted to practice New York 1977, District of Columbia, U.S. District Courts Eastern 1977 and Southern 1977 District of New York and U.S. Court of Appeals Second Circuit. In legal practice March 1977 to Sept 1978 and Jan 1984 to Dec 1999. Former Hearing Officer Small Claims Assessment Review New York Supreme Court Tenth Judicial District.

Associate Appellate Counsel Criminal Appeals Bureau The Legal Aid Society of the City of New York Sept 1978 to April 1981. Principal Law Clerk to Hon. Alexander Vitale April 1981 to Dec 1983 and Hon. Meryl J. Berkowitz Jan 2000 to Dec 2001, Nassau County Court. Legal Counsel to Board of Directors Huntington's Disease Society of America, Inc. 1989-99. Former Arbitra-

JAEGER, STEVEN M.—*Continued*
tor Compulsory Arbitration Program American Arbitration Association. Member Jewish Lawyers Association of Nassau County (Board of Directors since 2000), Bar Association of Nassau County and New York State Bar Association. President and Board Member Greater New York-Long Island Chapter 1991-96 and Board Member and Secretary since 1997 Huntington's Disease Society of America, Inc. Member Small Business Council Long Island Association 1996-99 and Concerned Long Island Mountain Bikers since 1998. Associate Member Law & Order Lodge #142 Fraternal Order of Police. Member Manhasset Hills-Herricks Civic Association, Kiwanis Club of the Nassau County Courthouse and Men's Club Temple Judea of Manhasset.
Office: 99 Main Street, Hempstead 11550.
Telephone: (516) 572-2151.
Fax: (516) 572-2562
E-mail address: sjaeger@courts.state.ny.us

JAFFE, Barbara *(Judge, The Civil Court of the City of New York)* Currently assigned to The Criminal Court of the City of New York.
Office: 111 Centre Street, New York 10013.
Telephone: (212) 374-6216.

JAFFE, Dana Mitchell *(Judge, Nassau County District Court)*
Office: 99 Main Street, Hempstead 11550.
Telephone: (516) 572-2113.
E-mail address: jaffe@courts.state.ny.us

JAMES, Debra A. *(Judge, The Civil Court of the City of New York)* Elected to term beginning Jan 1, 1995. Currently serves as Acting Justice, New York Supreme Court First Judicial District.
Office: 111 Centre Street, New York 10013.
Telephone: (212) 374-8499.
Fax: (212) 374-0402
E-mail address: djames@courts.state.ny.us

JAMIESON, Linda S. *(Justice, New York Supreme Court Ninth Judicial District)* Former Judge, Westchester County Family Court.
Office: 111 Dr. Martin Luther King Jr. Blvd., White Plains 10601.
Telephone: (914) 995-3824.
E-mail address: ljamieso@courts.state.ny.us

JANOWITZ, Norman *(Judge, Nassau County District Court)*
Office: 99 Main Street, Hempstead 11550.
Telephone: (516) 572-2147.

JOHNSON, Diana A. *(Justice, New York Supreme Court Second Judicial District)* Former Judge, The Civil Court of the City of New York.
Office: 360 Adams Street, Brooklyn 11201.
Telephone: (718) 643-8750.
E-mail address: djohnson@courts.state.ny.us

JOHNSON, Sterling, Jr. *(Judge, United States District Court Eastern District of New York)* Appointed for life by President George Bush to term beginning 1991. Educated at Brooklyn College of the City University of New York B.A. 1963 and Brooklyn Law School LL.B. 1966.
Assistant U.S. Attorney Southern District of New York 1967-70. Executive Liaison Officer Drug Enforcement Administration 1974-75. Special Narcotics Prosecutor New York City 1975-91. Commissioner U.S. Sentencing Commission since 1999. Member New York State District Attorneys Association, National District Attorneys Association, National Organization of Black Law Enforcement Executives, National Black Prosecutors Association, New York State and American (Executive Committee National Conference of Federal Trial Judges Judicial Division) Bar Associations. USMC 1952-55. Police Officer New York City 1956-67. Member Police Athletic League.
Office: U.S. Courthouse, 225 Cadman Plaza East, Brooklyn 11201.
Telephone: (718) 260-2460.

JOHNSON, Teresa D. *(Judge, Rochester City Court)* Appointed by Mayor Thomas Ryan to term beginning July 1990. Elected Nov 1990 and 2000. Current term expires Dec 31, 2010. Born Akron Ohio 1953. Educated at Yale University B.A. with honors 1975 and Boalt Hall School of Law J.D. 1978. Admitted to practice California 1979, District of Columbia 1983 and New York 1983. In legal practice Rochester New York 1983-88.
Trial Attorney U.S. Department of Justice Washington D.C. 1979-83. First Assistant County Attorney Monroe County 1988-90. Member Greater Rochester Association of Women Attorneys and Monroe County Bar Association.
Office: 6 Hall of Justice, 99 Exchange Boulevard, Rochester 14614.
Telephone: (585) 428-2096.
Fax: (585) 428-4265

JONAS, Zelda *(Justice, New York Supreme Court Tenth Judicial District)* Certificated. Former Judge, Nassau County District Court. Former Judge, Nassau County Court.
Office: Supreme Court Building, 100 Supreme Court Drive, Mineola 11501.
Telephone: (516) 571-2883.
Fax: (516) 571-1427
E-mail address: zjonas@courts.state.ny.us

JONES, Barbara S. *(Judge, United States District Court Southern District of New York)* Appointed for life by President Bill Clinton. Born Inglewood California Dec 31, 1947. Educated at Mount St. Mary's College B.A. 1968 and Temple University J.D. 1973.
Special Attorney 1973 and Special Attorney Manhattan Strike Force 1973-77 Organized Crime and Racketeering Criminal Division U.S. Department of Justice. Assistant U.S. Attorney 1977-87, Chief General Crimes Unit 1983-84 and Chief Organized Crime Unit 1984-87 Southern District of New York. First Assistant District Attorney New York County 1987-95.
Office: U.S. Courthouse, 40 Centre Street, New York 10007-1581.
Telephone: (212) 805-6186.

JONES, John J. J., Jr. *(Justice, New York Supreme Court Tenth Judicial District)* Former Acting Justice. Born Brooklyn New York June 30, 1926. Roman Catholic. Educated at Trinity College, St. John's University LL.B. 1949 and New York University. Admitted to practice New York 1950. In legal practice Brooklyn 1950-55 and Stony Brook 1955-71. Judge, Suffolk District Court 1971-73. Judge, Suffolk County Family Court 1974. Judge, Suffolk County Court 1975-77. Former Justice, New York Supreme Court Tenth Judicial District,

JONES, JOHN J. J., JR.—*Continued*
elected to term beginning Jan 1, 1978. Former Judge, Suffolk County Court.

Deputy Receiver of Taxes Town of Brookhaven 1959-60. Special Town Attorney Brookhaven 1960-71. Lecturer Suffolk Academy of Law. Member Suffolk County Criminal, Suffolk County, New York State and American Bar Associations. Named Judge of the Year by Suffolk County Criminal Bar Association 1976. USNR 1944-45. Democrat. Assistant Counsel New York State Joint Legislative Committee 1965-67. Member Stony Brook Fire Department and Knights of Columbus. Enjoys golf, tennis and music.

Office: 18 Court Complex, 210 Center Drive, Riverhead 11901.
Telephone: (631) 852-1429.
Fax: (631) 852-2730

JONES, Theodore T., Jr. *(Justice, New York Supreme Court Second Judicial District)*
Office: 360 Adams Street, Brooklyn 11201.
Telephone: (718) 643-5880.
E-mail address: tjones@courts.state.ny.us

JOSEPH, Burton S. *(Justice, New York Supreme Court Tenth Judicial District)* Elected to term beginning March 1997. Certificated. Born Maspeth New York 1929. Educated at Long Island University B.A. 1949, Adelphi University 1949-50 and Brooklyn Law School LL.B./J.D. 1956. Admitted to practice New York 1957, U.S. District Courts Eastern and Southern Districts of New York and U.S. Supreme Court. In legal practice Brooklyn 1957-68 and Wantagh 1968-70. Judge, Nassau County District Court 1977-84. Judge Jan 1, 1985 to 1997 and Supervising Judge 1990-97, Nassau County Family Court.

Chief and Senior Deputy County Attorney Nassau County 1971-76. Important Decisions: Emanuel S. v. Joseph E. (grandparents visitation) 161 A.D.2d 83, 78 N.Y.2d 178, 1988; Ocean Rock Associates v. Cruz (warranty of habitability) 51 N.Y.2d 1001, aff'd 66 A.D.2d 878; and People v. Shore Realty Corp. (constitutionality of county fire prevention ordinance) 127 Misc. 2d 419. Adjunct Evening Professor of Law Nassau Community College since 1974. Member Bar Association of Nassau County (We Care Committee), New York State and American Bar Associations. Lectured at numerous seminars for Law Guardians and committees for Bar Association of Nassau County.

Office: Supreme Court Building, 100 Supreme Court Drive, Mineola 11501.
Telephone: (516) 571-2878.

JULIAN, Robert F. *(Justice, New York Supreme Court Fifth Judicial District)*
Office: Oneida County Courthouse, 200 Elizabeth Street, Utica 13501.
Telephone: (315) 798-5877.
Fax: (315) 798-6457

JUNG, David F. *(Judge, Fulton County Family Court)*
Office: 11 North William Street, Johnstown 12095.
Telephone: (518) 762-3840.
Fax: (518) 762-9540

JUROW, George L. *(Judge, New York City Family Court)* Appointed by Mayor Edward Koch to term beginning June 7, 1982. Reappointed by mayor 1989 and Mayor Rudolph Giuliani 1999. Current term expires Dec 31, 2009. Born New York New York Feb 3, 1943. Educated at University of Pennsylvania B.S. with honors 1963, Yale Law School J.D. with honors 1966 and Adelphi University Ph.D. 1971. Editor Yale Law Journal 1964-66. Admitted to practice New York 1967.

First Deputy Commissioner New York City Department of Mental Health 1973-79. Member The Association of the Bar of the City of New York.

Office: 60 Lafayette Street, New York 10013.
Telephone: (212) 374-4177.
Fax: (212) 374-2623

KAHL, David B. *(Judge, Corning City Court)*
Office: 12 Civic Center Plaza, Corning 14830-2884.
Telephone: (607) 936-4111.
Fax: (607) 936-0519

KAHN, Barbara R. *(Judge, Suffolk County District Court)*
Mailing address: P.O. Box 9075, Central Islip 11722-9075.
Office: Cohalan Court Complex, 400 Carleton Avenue, Central Islip 11722.
Telephone: (631) 853-4918.

KAHN, Lawrence E. *(Judge, United States District Court Northern District of New York)* Appointed for life by President Bill Clinton to term beginning Aug 1, 1996. Born Troy New York Dec 8, 1937. Educated at Union University A.B. with honors 1959, Harvard University J.D. with honors 1962 and Oxford University Post Graduate Certificate in International Law 1963. Admitted to practice New York 1963. Began legal practice Albany 1963. Justice, New York Supreme Court Third Judicial District Jan 1, 1974 to Aug 1, 1996.

Assistant Corporation Counsel Albany 1963-69. Author *Divorce Lawyer's Casebook* St. Martin's Press 1972 and *When Couples Part* Franklin Watts 1982. Adjunct Professor Sage College of Albany since 1976 and Albany Law School of Union University since 1990. Named Outstanding Young Man of New York State 1967. E6 New York National Guard 1955-65. Active in many civic and community organizations.

Office: 424 U.S. Courthouse, 445 Broadway, Albany 12207-2947.
Telephone: (518) 257-1830.

KAHN, Marcy L. *(Justice, New York Supreme Court First Judicial District)* Former Judge, The Criminal Court of the City of New York, appointed by Mayor Ed Koch.
Office: 100 Centre Street, New York 10013.
Telephone: (212) 374-5894.
Fax: (212) 374-5853

KANE, Anthony T. *(Associate Justice, New York Supreme Court Appellate Division Third Judicial Department)* Elected Justice Third Judicial District. Appointed Associate Justice Appellate Division by Governor George E. Pataki. Born New York New York Feb 10, 1945. Educated at Iona College B.A. 1966 and Cornell Law School J.D. 1969. Admitted to practice New York 1970, U.S. Tax Court 1971 and U.S. District Court Southern District of New York 1972. In legal practice Monticello 1969-84. Judge, Sullivan County Family Court Jan 1985 to Dec 31, 1991. Judge, Sullivan County Court Jan 1992 to Dec 31, 1995.

With Sullivan County Legal Services 1969-71 and

KANE, ANTHONY T.—*Continued*

Public Defender's Office Sullivan County 1974. Adjunct Associate Professor Sullivan County Community College 1982-84. Member Association of Justices of the Supreme Court of the State of New York, Sullivan County (Board of Directors 1983-84) and New York State Bar Associations.

Office: Courthouse, 414 Broadway, Monticello 12701.
Telephone: (845) 794-8811.

KAPLAN, Deborah A. *(Judge, The Civil Court of the City of New York)*

Office: 111 Centre Street, New York 10013.
Telephone: (212) 791-6000.

KAPLAN, Lewis A. *(Judge, United States District Court Southern District of New York)* Appointed for life by President Bill Clinton to term beginning Aug 22, 1994. Born Staten Island New York Dec 23, 1944. Educated at University of Rochester A.B. with high honors in Political Science 1966 and Harvard Law School J.D. cum laude 1969. Law Clerk to Hon. Edward M. McEntee, U.S. Court of Appeals First Circuit 1969-70. Admitted to practice New York 1970. In legal practice New York City 1970-94.

Member Committee on Automation and Technology Judicial Conference of the U.S. since 1997. Fellow American College of Trial Lawyers. Member The American Law Institute, Federal Bar Council, The Association of the Bar of the City of New York, New York State and American Bar Associations. Village Trustee 1988-91. Member Trustees' Council University of Rochester 1982-88.

Office: 1310 U.S. Courthouse, 500 Pearl Street, New York 10007-1312.
Telephone: (212) 805-0216.

KAPLAN, Michael J. *(Judge, United States Bankruptcy Court Western District of New York)* Appointed by U.S. Court of Appeals Second Circuit judges. Former Chief Judge. Former Judge, Bankruptcy Appellate Panel Second Circuit, selected by the Judicial Council of the Second Circuit.

Office: 350 Olympic Towers, 300 Pearl Street, Buffalo 14202-0250.
Telephone: (716) 551-4208.

KAPNICK, Barbara R. *(Justice, New York Supreme Court First Judicial District)* Acting Justice Jan 1992 to Dec 2001. Elected Justice to term beginning Jan 1, 2002. Term expires Dec 31, 2015. Former Judge, The Civil Court of the City of New York.

Office: 60 Centre Street, New York 10007.
Telephone: (212) 374-5699.
E-mail address: bkapnick@courts.state.ny.us

KARALUNAS, Deborah H. *(Justice, New York Supreme Court Fifth Judicial District)*

Office: Hughes State Office Building, Eighth Floor, 333 East Washington Street, Syracuse 13202.
Telephone: (315) 428-3256.
Fax: (315) 428-3250

KAROPKIN, Martin G. *(Judge, The Criminal Court of the City of New York)* Appointed by Mayor Edward Koch to term beginning May 14, 1986. Reappointed 1993, current term expires Dec 2003. Born Brooklyn New York Oct 27, 1946. Jewish. Educated at State University of New York at Stony Brook B.A. 1967 and Brooklyn Law School J.D. 1972. Admitted to practice New York 1972, U.S. District Courts Eastern 1977 and Southern 1977 Districts of New York and U.S. Supreme Court 1980.

Former member New York County Lawyers' Association. Member Brooklyn Bar Association. Former Inspector General New York City Fire Department.

Office: 120 Schermerhorn Street, Brooklyn 11201.
Telephone: (718) 643-8400.
Fax: (718) 643-3538

KATZ, Bertram D. *(Justice, New York Supreme Court Twelfth Judicial District)* Former Acting Justice. Certificated. Former Judge, The Civil Court of the City of New York.

Office: 851 Grand Concourse, Bronx 10451.
Telephone: (718) 590-6360.
Fax: (718) 590-8914

KATZ, Stanley B. *(Justice, New York Supreme Court Eleventh Judicial District)* Elected to term beginning Jan 1, 1988. Certificated. Judge, The Civil Court of the City of New York Jan 1, 1984 to Dec 31, 1987.

Office: 125-01 Queens Boulevard, Kew Gardens 11415.
Telephone: (718) 520-6844.
Fax: (718) 520-2236

KATZ, Theodore H. *(Magistrate Judge, United States District Court Southern District of New York)* Appointed by U.S. District Court judges.

Office: 1660 U.S. Courthouse, 500 Pearl Street, New York 10007-1312.
Telephone: (212) 805-0218.

KAVANAGH, E. Michael *(Justice, New York Supreme Court Third Judicial District)*

Office: Supreme Court Chambers, 255 Wall Street, Kingston 12401-0906.
Telephone: (845) 340-3888.
Fax: (845) 340-3893

KAYE, Judith S. *(Chief Judge, New York Court of Appeals)* Appointed by Governor Mario Cuomo to term beginning Sept 12, 1983. Reappointed by Governor George E. Pataki. Chief Judge since March 23, 1993. First woman to occupy the State Judiciary's highest office. Educated at Barnard College B.A. 1958 and New York University LL.B. cum laude 1962. Admitted to practice New York 1963. In legal practice New York City 1963-83.

Office: Court of Appeals Hall, 20 Eagle Street, Albany 12207.
Telephone: (518) 455-7700.
Office: 230 Park Avenue, Suite 826, New York 10169-0007.
Telephone: (212) 661-6787.

KEEFE, Thomas K. *(Judge, Albany City Court)*

Office: 209 City Hall, Eagle and Corning Place Albany 12207.
Telephone: (518) 434-5115.

KEEGAN, Thomas W. *(Justice, New York Supreme Court Third Judicial District)* Elected to term beginning Jan 1, 1992. Term expires Dec 31, 2005. Currently serves as Administrative Judge. Born Albany New York Oct 14, 1940. Roman Catholic. Educated at Siena College B.A. 1962 and Villanova University School of Law LL.D. 1965. Admitted to practice New York 1966, U.S.

KEEGAN, THOMAS W.—*Continued*
District Court Northern District of New York 1966, U.S. Court of Appeals Second Circuit 1969 and U.S. Supreme Court 1970. In legal practice Albany 1966-89. Judge, Albany Police Court 1973-89. Judge, Albany County Court 1989-91.

Assistant Corporation Counsel 1966-71 and Executive Deputy Corporation Counsel 1971-73 Albany. Important Decisions: Cable Television Association of New York v. New York State Commission on Cable Television (upheld Commission's interpretation of the Executive Law and Commission's authority to promulgate regulations) 588 N.Y.S.2d 81; Medical Society of the State of New York v. Sobol (amendment to Education Law §6524 declared unconstitutional, as applied to the triennial registration renewal fees of physicians) 583 N.Y.S.2d 145; Lawyer's Fund for Client Protection v. Manufacturers Hanover Trust Co. (drawee bank was liable for amount of forged check, attorney possessed neither apparent nor implied authority to endorse or collect proceeds of check) 153 Misc. 2d 360, 581 N.Y.S.2d 133; People v. Craver (held that value of murder defendant's admissions to newspaper reporter outweighed reporter's constitutionally based privilege against disclosure) 150 Misc. 2d 631, 569 N.Y.S.2d 859; and People v. Richard (surgical removal of bullet fragments from shoulder would constitute unreasonable search and seizure under the Fourth Amendment to the U.S. Constitution) 145 Misc. 2d 755, 548 N.Y.S.2d 369. Member Capital District Trial Lawyers Association, New York State Trial Lawyers Association, Albany County and New York State Bar Associations. Recipient numerous awards and recognition from legal and civic organizations. Member Albany County Democratic Committee. Active in various civic organizations. Enjoys fishing.

Office: 433-A Albany County Courthouse, 16 Eagle Street, Albany 12207.

Telephone: (518) 487-5150.

KEENAN, John F. *(Senior Judge, United States District Court Southern District of New York)* Appointed for life by President Ronald Reagan Sept 20, 1983 to term beginning Oct 21, 1983. Assumed Senior status, serves by assignment. Educated at Manhattan College B.B.A. 1951 and Fordham University Law School LL.B. 1954. Awarded honorary LL.D. from Manhattan College 1989 and Mount Saint Vincent College. Admitted to practice New York 1954 and U.S. District Court Southern District of New York 1970. In legal practice New York City Aug 1956 to Dec 1956.

Assistant District Attorney Dec 17, 1956 to June 30, 1976, Assistant District Attorney in Charge of Supreme Court Bureau April 1, 1968 to Dec 31, 1969, Assistant District Attorney in Charge of Homicide Bureau Jan 1, 1970 to June 30, 1973, Administrative Assistant District Attorney in Charge of Trials Jan 1, 1974 to April 15, 1974 and Chief Assistant District Attorney April 15, 1974 to June 30, 1976 New York County. Chief Assistant District Attorney Queens County July 1, 1973 to Dec 31, 1973. Deputy Attorney General Special Prosecutor of Corruption in New York City June 30, 1976 to April 9, 1979. Criminal Justice Coordinator City of New York June 9, 1982 to Oct 20, 1983. Lecturer on Criminal Law and Trial Techniques Short Course for Prosecuting and Defense Attorneys Northwestern University School of Law 1968-90 and on Trial Advocacy Harvard University Law School 1979-83, 1989, 1994 and 1998. Adjunct Professor of Criminal Justice John Jay College of Criminal Justice Graduate School 1979-83 and Trial Advocacy Fordham University School of Law 1992-93. Guest Lecturer Yale University Law School, University of Michigan Law School, Northwestern University School of Law, Columbia University School of Law, St. John's University School of Law, New York University School of Law and Fordham University School of Law.

Member Disciplinary Committee to Regulate Conduct of Attorneys First Judicial Department 1979-83 and Judicial Panel on Multidistrict Litigation since June 1998. Former Member Advisory Committee on Criminal Rules Judicial Conference of the U.S. and Criminal Justice Executive Committee New York State Bar Association. Member Criminal Procedure Law Advisory Committee Judicial Conference of the State of New York (Chairman 1980-83). Faculty Member National College of District Attorneys 1974-80. Former Lecturer on Trial Tactics New York State District Attorneys Association. Lecturer and Panel Member at American Bar Association, Practising Law Institute and New York State Bar Association Programs on Case Management, Fed. R. Civ. P. 11 and Sentencing Subjects. Recipient Outstanding Prosecution Services from New York State Bar Association 1978, New York Criminal Bar Association Annual Award 1979, Frank S. Hogan Award from New York State District Attorneys Association 1981, Medal of Honor as Distinguished Alumnus from Fordham University School of Law 1988, Medal of Achievement from New York County Lawyers' Association 1992, Emory R. Buckner Award for Outstanding Public Service from Federal Bar Council 1993, The Charles Carroll Award from Catholic Lawyers Guild 1994 and Ellis Island Medal of Honor from The National Ethnic Coalition of Organizations Foundation, Inc. 1998. U.S. Army July 1954 to July 1956. Chairman and President New York City Off-Track Betting Corporation April 9, 1979 to June 9, 1982. Board of Governors and Chairman Board of Trustees 1981-83 Daytop Village. Vice President Fordham University School of Law Alumni Association. Advisory Board Center for Research in Crime and Justice New York University School of Law.

Office: 1930 U.S. Courthouse, 500 Pearl Street, New York 10007-1312.

Telephone: (212) 805-0220.

KEENAN, Richard A. *(Judge, Monroe County Court)*

Office: 545 Hall of Justice, 99 Exchange Boulevard, Rochester 14614-2186.

Telephone: (585) 428-1912.

Fax: (585) 428-3551

KEHOE, Dennis M. *(Judge, Wayne County Court)* Also serves Wayne County Surrogate's Court and Wayne County Family Court.

Office: 323 Hall of Justice, 54 Broad Street, Lyons 14489-1199.

Telephone: (315) 946-5435.

Fax: (315) 946-5434

KEHOE, L. Paul *(Associate Justice, New York Supreme Court Appellate Division Fourth Judicial Department)* Elected Justice Seventh Judicial District to term beginning Jan 1, 1993. Appointed Associate Justice Appellate Division by Governor George E. Pataki. Term expires Dec 31, 2006. Administrative Judge Seventh Judicial District 1996-2000. Born Carthage New York May 21, 1938. Roman Catholic. Educated at Syracuse Univer-

KEHOE, L. PAUL—*Continued*

sity B.S. 1959 J.D. magna cum laude 1962. Admitted to practice New York 1962, U.S. District Court Northern District of New York 1963 and U.S. Supreme Court 1967. In legal practice Watertown 1962-66 and Wolcott and Lyons 1966-92.

District Attorney Wayne County 1967-71. Member Wayne County (Past President), New York State and American Bar Associations. U.S. Army 1962-63. Member State Assembly 1979-80 and State Senate 1981-92 New York.

Office: 50 East Avenue, Rochester 14604.

Telephone: (585) 530-3205.

KELLY, John *(Judge, Suffolk County District Court)* Mailing address: P.O. Box 9075, Central Islip 11722-9075.

Office: Cohalan Court Complex, 400 Carleton Avenue, Central Islip 11722.

Telephone: (631) 853-5520.

KELLY, Peter Joseph *(Justice, New York Supreme Court Eleventh Judicial District)* Elected Nov 2002 to term beginning Jan 1, 2003. Born Jamaica New York 1958. Educated at Iona College B.A. magna cum laude 1980 and St. John's University School of Law J.D. 1983. Admitted to practice New York 1984, U.S. District Court Southern District of New York 1997 and U.S. Supreme Court 1997. Judge, The Civil Court of the City of New York Jan 1999 to Dec 2002.

Office: 88-11 Sutphin Boulevard, Jamaica 11435.

Telephone: (718) 262-7376.

KELLY, William A. *(Judge, Rockland County Court)* Elected to term beginning Jan 1, 1988. Reelected 1997, current term expires Dec 31, 2007. Roman Catholic. Educated at Fordham University B.S. with honors 1966 and Brooklyn Law School J.D. with honors 1969. Admitted to practice New York 1966, U.S. District Courts Eastern 1970 and Southern 1970 Districts of New York, U.S. Supreme Court 1970 and U.S. Court of Appeals Second Circuit 1983. In legal practice New City 1982-87. Justice, Clarkstown Town Justice Court 1982-87.

Assistant Corporation Counsel New York City 1966-69. Assistant District Attorney Bronx County 1969-82 (Deputy Chief Supreme Court Trial Bureau and Deputy Chief Homicide Trial Bureau). Instructor Rockland Community College 1983-87. Former member Rockland County Bar Association. Member Federal Bar Council and New York State Bar Association. President Ancient Order of Hibernians New City Chapter since 1982. Board of Directors Clarkstown Drug Abuse Board since 1983 and Big Brothers/Big Sisters of Rockland County since 1984. Member New City Rotary since 1997.

Office: Courthouse, One South Main Street, New City 10956.

Telephone: (845) 638-5386.

Fax: (845) 638-5312

KENNEY, Joan M. *(Judge, The Civil Court of the City of New York)* Elected to term beginning Jan 1, 2001. Term expires Dec 31, 2010. Born Brooklyn New York April 15, 1959. Educated at State University of New York at Binghamton B.A. magna cum laude 1982 and State University of New York at Buffalo J.D. 1985. Admitted to practice New York 1986 and U.S. District Courts Eastern and Southern Districts of New York. In legal practice New York City 1985-97.

Court Attorney New York Supreme Court First Judicial District 1997-2000. President Harbor House Owner's Corp. Former Chair Jane Street Association. Interests include photography and film.

Office: 111 Centre Street, New York 10013.

Telephone: (212) 791-6000.

E-mail address: jkenney@courts.state.ny.us

KENT, William J., III *(Justice, New York Supreme Court Tenth Judicial District)* Elected to term beginning Jan 1, 2000. Term expires Dec 31, 2013. Born Brooklyn New York May 15, 1938. Catholic. Educated at University of Arizona B.A. with honors 1960 and Fordham University School of Law LL.B. 1963. Admitted to practice New York 1964, U.S. District Courts Eastern 1964 and Southern 1964 Districts of New York and U.S. Court of Appeals Second Circuit 1964. Began legal practice Brooklyn 1964. In legal practice New York City 1966. Judge, Suffolk County District Court Jan 1, 1984 to Dec 31, 1992. Judge, Suffolk County Family Court Jan 1, 1993 to Dec 31, 1999.

Senior Assistant District Attorney 1968-71 and Chief Deputy County Attorney 1980-84 Suffolk County. Deputy Town Attorney Islip 1972-80. Member Suffolk County Bar Association. Republican. Former Committeeman 53rd Election District Town of Islip. Board of Directors East End Republican Club. Member Sayville Yacht Club. Enjoys skiing and golf.

Mailing address: P.O. Box 9070, Central Islip 11722-9070.

Office: S-24 Cohalan Courthouse, 400 Carleton Avenue, Central Islip 11722.

Telephone: (631) 853-5471.

Fax: (631) 853-3281

KERINS, Martin J. *(Judge, Suffolk County Court)* Mailing address: P.O. Box 9007, Riverhead 11901-9007.

Office: Court Complex, 210 Center Drive, Riverhead 11901.

Telephone: (631) 852-2670.

KERN, Cynthia S. *(Judge, The Civil Court of the City of New York)*

Office: 111 Centre Street, New York 10013.

Telephone: (212) 374-8458.

KERRIGAN, Kevin J. *(Judge, The Civil Court of the City of New York)*

Office: 89-17 Sutphin Boulevard, Jamaica 11435.

Telephone: (718) 262-7382.

KIEDAISCH, Debra J. *(Judge, Orange County Family Court)* Former Acting Justice, New York Supreme Court Ninth Judicial District.

Office: Orange County Courthouse, 285 Main Street, Goshen 10924.

Telephone: (845) 291-3050.

Fax: (845) 291-4520

KIESEL, Diane R. *(Judge, The Criminal Court of the City of New York)* Appointed by Mayor Rudolph Giuliani.

Office: 215 East 161st Street, Bronx 10451.

Telephone: (718) 590-2927.

Fax: (718) 590-7297

E-mail address: dkiesel@courts.state.ny.us

KING, Roy Wheatley *(Judge, Rochester City Court)* Assumed office Jan 1997. Currently serves as Supervis-

KING, ROY WHEATLEY—*Continued*
ing Judge. Born Cat Island Bahamas July 16, 1936. Religious affiliation: Church of God in Christ. Educated at Drake University B.A. and Syracuse University College of Law J.D. In legal practice Rochester 1965-97.

Adjunct Professor Department of African and Afro-American Studies State University of New York at Brockport. Former member Board of Governors, Minority Attorney's Committee, Strategic Planning Committee, Judiciary Committee, Special Committee to Review Judicial Screening Process and Rodenbeck Award Committee Academy of Law. Member Seventh Judicial District Gender Fairness Committee, Rochester Black and Monroe County (Trustee 1973-74 and 1991-93, Secretary 1991-93) Bar Associations. Recipient West Indian and American Community Award 1984, Charles F. Crimi Award from Monroe County Bar Association 1995, Fossie and Steven McClary Award from Seneca District No. 293 Boy Scouts of America 1997 and service award from Full Gospel Tabernacle Church 1997. U.S. Army 1956-58. Chairman Board of Trustees Progressive Church of God in Christ. Board of Trustees Prison Outreach, Inc. Mentor Greater Rochester Minority Achiever's Program YMCA. Member Biracial Partnerships for Community Progress.

Office: 6 Hall of Justice, 99 Exchange Boulevard, Rochester 14614.
Telephone: (585) 428-2477.
Fax: (585) 428-2746
E-mail address: rwking@courts.state.ny.us

KIRK, Patrick L. *(Judge, Herkimer County Court)* Also serves Herkimer County Surrogate's Court.
Office: 5509 Court Facility, 301 North Washington Street, Herkimer 13350-0749.
Telephone: (315) 867-1171.
Fax: (315) 867-1344

KITSON, Donald *(Judge, Suffolk County Court)* Elected to term beginning Jan 1, 1989. Reelected 1998, current term expires Dec 31, 2008. Currently serves as Acting Justice, New York Supreme Court Tenth Judicial District. Born New York New York Dec 29, 1936. Catholic. Educated at Lafayette College B.S.B.A. 1958 and St. John's University LL.B. 1965. Member Phi Delta Theta. Admitted to practice New York 1966 and U.S. District Courts Eastern 1973 and Southern 1973 Districts of New York. Judge, Suffolk County District Court Dec 1, 1980 to Dec 31, 1988.

Trial Attorney Rackets and Anti-Corruption Bureau and Chief Economic Crime Unit Suffolk County District Attorney's Office 1973-80. Important Decision: Somma v. Wehrle Index No. 96-14896, 1996. Instructor State University of New York at Farmingdale 1973-80 and Southampton College 1974-75. Member Suffolk County Bar Association (Lecturer Academy of Law since 1984, Chairman Bench Bar Committee, Professional Ethics Committee, Committee on Professionalism). Previously employed as Negligence Claims Manager with Crawford & Co. Atlanta Georgia. Republican. Little League Coach. Member Boy Scouts of America and Knights of Columbus. Enjoys skiing, tennis, bicycling, running, hiking and touring. Personal Statement or Quote: "Timeliness is next to godliness."

Mailing address: P.O. Box 9070, Central Islip 11722.
Office: Court Complex, 400 Carleton Avenue, Central Islip 11722.
Telephone: (631) 853-4507.
Fax: (631) 853-7683

KITZES, Orin R. *(Justice, New York Supreme Court Eleventh Judicial District)* Elected to term beginning Jan 1, 1995. Former Judge, The Civil Court of the City of New York.
Office: 88-11 Sutphin Boulevard, Jamaica 11435.
Telephone: (718) 261-2198.
Fax: (718) 520-2363

KLEIN, Carol S. *(Judge, Orange County Family Court)*
Office: Orange County Courthouse, 285 Main Street, Goshen 10924.
Telephone: (845) 291-3040.
Fax: (845) 291-4520

KLEIN, David *(Judge, Westchester County Family Court)*
Office: 420 North Avenue, Third Floor, New Rochelle 10801.
Telephone: (914) 813-5650.
Fax: (914) 813-5580

KLEIN, Lee David *(Judge, Poughkeepsie City Court)*
Mailing address: P.O. Box 300, Poughkeepsie 12602.
Office: Civic Center Plaza, Poughkeepsie 12601.
Telephone: (845) 451-4091.
Fax: (845) 485-6795

KLEIN, Richard M. *(Judge, New York Court of Claims)* Appointed by Governor George E. Pataki. Currently serves as Acting Justice, New York Supreme Court Tenth Judicial District. Former Judge, Suffolk County District Court.
Office: 3B-45 New York State Office Building, Veterans Memorial Highway, Hauppauge 11788.
Telephone: (631) 952-4955.
Fax: (631) 952-2070

KLIM, David G. *(Judge, Onondaga County Family Court)*
Office: Onondaga County Courthouse, 401 Montgomery Street, Syracuse 13202.
Telephone: (315) 671-2050.
Fax: (315) 671-1170
E-mail address: dklim@courts.state.ny.us

KLOCH, Richard C., Sr. *(Judge, New York Court of Claims)* Appointed by Governor George E. Pataki. Currently serves as Acting Justice, New York Supreme Court Eighth Judicial District. Born North Tonawanda New York May 8, 1951. Roman Catholic. Educated at State University of New York at Buffalo B.A. with honors 1973 J.D. 1976. Admitted to practice New York 1977 and U.S. District Court Western District of New York 1977. In legal practice Tonawanda 1977-88. Former Judge, North Tonawanda City Court, appointed by Mayor Elizabeth C. Hoffman to term beginning Jan 1, 1986.

City Attorney North Tonawanda Jan 1978 to Dec 1985. Commissioner Selective Service System.
Office: 92 Franklin Street, Buffalo 14202.
Telephone: (716) 851-3245.

KLUEWER, Susan T. *(Judge, Nassau County District Court)*
Office: 99 Main Street, Hempstead 11550.
Telephone: (516) 572-2159.
E-mail address: kluewer@courts.state.ny.us

KLUGER, Judy Harris *(Judge, The Criminal Court of the City of New York)* Appointed by mayor. Currently serves as Administrative Judge. Also serves as Acting Justice, New York Supreme Court First Judicial District.
Office: 100 Centre Street, New York 10013.
Telephone: (212) 374-3207.
Fax: (212) 374-3004

KNAPP, Whitman *(Senior Judge, United States District Court Southern District of New York)* Appointed for life by President Richard M. Nixon to term beginning Sept 20, 1972. Assumed Senior status, serves by assignment. Born New York New York Feb 24, 1909. Episcopalian. Educated at Yale University B.A. 1931 and Harvard University LL.B. cum laude 1934. Awarded honorary LL.D. City College of the City University of New York 1992. Staff member Harvard Law Review. Admitted to practice New York 1935. In legal practice New York City 1935-38, 1941 and 1950-72.
Assistant District Attorney New York County 1938-41 and 1942-50. Special Counsel New York State Youth Commission 1950-53 and Waterfront Commission of New York Harbor 1953-54. Chairman Commission to Investigate Allegations of Police Corruption and Anti-Corruption Procedures City of New York 1970-72. Author "Why Argue an Appeal? If So, How?" The Association of the Bar of the City of New York 1959 and "Counsel on Appeal" McGraw-Hill 1968. Member The Association of the Bar of the City of New York (Secretary 1946-49, Chairman Executive Committee 1970-71). Republican.
Office: 1201 U.S. Courthouse, 40 Centre Street, New York 10007-1581.
Telephone: (212) 805-6165.

KNIPEL, Lawrence S. *(Justice, New York Supreme Court Second Judicial District)* Former Judge, The Civil Court of the City of New York.
Office: 360 Adams Street, Brooklyn 11201.
Telephone: (718) 643-7654.
E-mail address: lknipel@courts.state.ny.us

KNIPPS, Susan K. *(Judge, The Civil Court of the City of New York)* Currently assigned to New York City Family Court.
Office: 60 Lafayette Street, New York 10013.
Telephone: (212) 374-1844.
Fax: (212) 374-2623

KNOPF, Stephen A. *(Judge, The Civil Court of the City of New York)* Currently assigned to The Criminal Court of the City of New York.
Office: 89-17 Sutphin Boulevard, Jamaica 11435.
Telephone: (718) 520-3059.

KOELTL, John G. *(Judge, United States District Court Southern District of New York)* Appointed for life by President Bill Clinton to term beginning 1994. Born New York City Oct 25, 1945. Educated at Georgetown University A.B. 1967 and Harvard Law School J.D. 1971. Law Clerk to Hon. Edward Weinfeld, U.S. District Court Eastern District of New York 1971-72 and Hon. Potter Stewart, U.S. Supreme Court 1972-73. In legal practice New York City 1975-94.
Assistant Special Prosecutor Watergate Special Prosecution Force 1973-74.
Office: 1030 U.S. Courthouse, 500 Pearl Street, New York 10007-1312.
Telephone: (212) 805-0222.

KOHM, Robert C. *(Justice, New York Supreme Court Eleventh Judicial District)* Former Judge, The Civil Court of the City of New York.
Office: 125-01 Queens Boulevard, Kew Gardens 11415.
Telephone: (718) 520-2397.
Fax: (718) 520-8603

KOHOUT, Joan S. *(Judge, Monroe County Family Court)* Also serves as Acting Judge, Monroe County Court.
Office: 545 Hall of Justice, 99 Exchange Boulevard, Rochester 14614-2186.
Telephone: (585) 428-5486.
Fax: (585) 428-2597

KORETZ, Eileen *(Judge, The Criminal Court of the City of New York)* Appointed by Mayor Rudolph Giuliani.
Office: 100 Centre Street, New York 10013.
Telephone: (646) 264-1318.

KORMAN, Edward R. *(Chief Judge, United States District Court Eastern District of New York)* Appointed for life by President Ronald Reagan to term beginning Dec 16, 1985. Chief Judge since March 19, 2000. Born New York New York Oct 25, 1942. Educated at Brooklyn College B.A. 1963, Brooklyn Law School LL.B. 1966 and New York University LL.M. 1971. Law Clerk to Hon. Kenneth B. Keating, New York Court of Appeals 1966-68. In legal practice New York City 1968-70 and 1982-85.
Assistant U.S. Attorney 1970-72, Chief Assistant U.S. Attorney 1974-78 and U.S. Attorney 1978-82 Eastern District of New York. Assistant to Solicitor General of U.S. 1972-74. Professor of Law Brooklyn Law School 1984-85. Chairman Mayor's Committee on New York City Marshals 1983-85. Former Member Temporary Commission of Investigation New York.
Office: U.S. Courthouse, 225 Cadman Plaza East, Brooklyn 11201.
Telephone: (718) 260-2470.

KORNREICH, Shirley Werner *(Judge, The Civil Court of the City of New York)* Elected to term beginning Jan 1, 1995. Term expires Dec 31, 2004. Currently serves as Acting Justice, New York Supreme Court First Judicial District. Born Lakewood New Jersey May 31, 1950. Educated at New York University B.A. cum laude 1972 and New York University School of Law J.D. 1975. Member Phi Beta Kappa. Admitted to practice New York 1976 and U.S. District Courts District of New Jersey 1975 and Eastern 1979 and Southern 1979 Districts of New York.
Appellate Attorney Nassau County March 1977 to March 1979 and New York City March 1979 to Oct 1986. Trial Lawyer Criminal Defense Division Legal Aid Society Oct 1986 to Nov 1988. Law Assistant to Acting Justice Ira R. Goldman New York Supreme Court Twelfth Judicial District Nov 1988 to Dec 1995. Editor Matthew Bender and Co. Oct 1975 to March 1977. Small Claims Arbitrator 1992 and 1993. Member The Association of the Bar of the City of New York

KORNREICH, SHIRLEY WERNER—*Continued*

(Criminal Advocacy Committee 1990-93, Committee on Juvenile Justice 1993-96, Committee on Drugs and the Law since 1996). Participant Charles W. Froessel Moot Court Competition 1990, 1991 and 1998; Annual Jerome Prince Evidence Competition 1991, 1993 and 1994 and Externship Program 1998-2002 and Lawyering Program 1999, 2000, 2001 and 2002 New York University School of Law; and Externship Program Fordham University School of Law 2002 and 2003. Member School Committee Society for the Advancement of Judaism 1993-96. Co-chair Hotline since 1996, Board of Directors since 1997, Vice President 2000 and Assistant Secretary 2001 Judges and Lawyers Breast Cancer Alert. Member Building Committee 1998-99, Gabbai 1998-99 and Kiddush Committee 1999-2001 Minyan M'at (Ansche Chesed Synagogue). Secretary 50 West 96th Street Co-op Board 2001. Advisory Board Rebecca & Ivry Prozdor 2000-03.

Office: 111 Centre Street, New York 10013.
Telephone: (212) 374-8466.
E-mail address: skornrei@courts.state.ny.us

KRAM, Shirley Wohl *(Senior Judge, United States District Court Southern District of New York)* Appointed for life by President Ronald Reagan to term beginning May 23, 1983. Assumed Senior status, serves by assignment. Born New York New York. Educated at Hunter College of the City University of New York and Brooklyn Law School LL.B. 1950. Judge, New York City Family Court 1971-83.

Former Assistant Attorney in charge of Harlem Office Legal Aid Society (Chief Narcotics and Mental Health Division).

Office: 2101 U.S. Courthouse, 40 Centre Street, New York 10007-1581.
Telephone: (212) 805-6315.

KRAMER, Barry D. *(Surrogate, Schenectady County Surrogate's Court)* Currently serves as Acting Justice, New York Supreme Court Fourth Judicial District.

Office: Courthouse, 612 State Street, Schenectady 12305-2113.
Telephone: (518) 388-4211.
Fax: (518) 377-6378

KRAMER, Herbert *(Justice, New York Supreme Court Second Judicial District)* Former Acting Justice. Former Judge, The Civil Court of the City of New York.

Office: 360 Adams Street, Brooklyn 11201.
Telephone: (718) 643-7020.
E-mail address: hkramer@courts.state.ny.us

KRAUSMAN, Gabriel M. *(Associate Justice, New York Supreme Court Appellate Division Second Judicial Department)* Elected Justice to term beginning Jan 1, 1983. Appointed Associate Justice Appellate Division by governor. Certificated. Born Brooklyn New York. Jewish. Educated at Brooklyn College of the City University of New York B.S. with honors 1957 and New York Law School LL.B. with honors 1959. Staff Editor New York Law Forum 1958-59. Admitted to practice New York 1960. In legal practice New York 1960-69. Law Clerk to Hon. Irwin Brownstein, The Civil Court of the City of New York and Hon. Frank Vaccaro, New York Supreme Court Second Judicial District 1968-79. Judge, The Civil Court of the City of New York 1980-82.

Office: 45 Monroe Place, Brooklyn 11201.
Telephone: (718) 722-6435.

KRAUSS, Sarah L. *(Judge, The Civil Court of the City of New York)* Elected to term beginning Jan 1, 1995. Currently assigned to The Criminal Court of the City of New York.

Office: 141 Livingston Street, Brooklyn 11201.
Telephone: (718) 643-3174.
Fax: (718) 643-3733

KREINDLER, Robert S. *(Justice, New York Supreme Court Second Judicial District)* Acting Justice April 1973 to March 1997. Appointed Justice by Governor George E. Pataki March 3, 1997. Certificated. Born New York New York March 28, 1927. Educated at Brooklyn College of the City University of New York and Brooklyn Law School LL.B. 1950. Admitted to practice New York 1951, U.S. District Courts Southern 1951 and Eastern 1952 Districts of New York, U.S. Court of Appeals Second Circuit 1955 and U.S. Supreme Court 1955. In legal practice New York City 1951-57 and 1962-68. Judge, The Civil Court of the City of New York Sept 1966 to Dec 1966. Judge, The Criminal Court of the City of New York Dec 1968 to March 1997.

Assistant U.S. Attorney Eastern District of New York 1957-61 (Chief Organized Crime and Racketeering Section and Criminal Division). Former Trustee Federal Bar Council (Chairman Criminal Law Committee). Former member National Association of Defense Lawyers in Criminal Cases, New York State District Attorneys Association, National Panel of Arbitrators American Arbitration Association, Kings County Criminal, Brooklyn (Co-chairman Criminal Courts Committee, member Federal Courts Committee) and American (Criminal and Judicial Sections) Bar Associations. USAAC PTO 1945-47. Member Brooklyn College Alumni Association (Past President Lawyers Group). Master Mason. Past Chancellor Knights of Pythias. Former member and Director Ocean Parkway Jewish Center.

Office: 360 Adams Street, Brooklyn 11201.
Telephone: (718) 643-7072.
Fax: (718) 643-4994
E-mail address: rkreindl@courts.state.ny.us

KROGMANN, David B. *(Judge, Glens Falls City Court)* Appointed part-time Judge by Glens Falls Common Council to term beginning March 2, 1982. Elected to subsequent terms. Elected full-time Judge to term beginning Jan 1, 2001, current term expires Dec 31, 2010. Born Jamaica New York April 9, 1945. Lutheran. Educated at Wittenberg University B.A. with honors 1967 and Washington and Lee University J.D. 1974. Member Pi Kappa Alpha. Admitted to practice New York 1974. In legal practice Glens Falls.

Deputy County Attorney 1974-76. Town Attorney Lake Luzerne, Bolton Landing, Horicon and Stony Creek. School Board Attorney Glens Falls Common School District. Member New York State Association of City Court Judges, Warren County and New York State Bar Associations. First Lieutenant U.S. Army 1969-73 (Army Intelligence). Recipient Army Commendation Medal. Board of Directors Crandall Public Library (Pres-

KROGMANN, DAVID B.—*Continued*

ident) and Southern Adirondack Library System. Enjoys family activities and all sports.

Office: 42 Ridge Street, Glens Falls 12801.
Telephone: (518) 798-4714.
Fax: (518) 798-0137

KRON, Barry *(Judge, The Criminal Court of the City of New York)* Appointed by mayor. Currently serves as Acting Justice, New York Supreme Court Eleventh Judicial District. Former Judge, The Civil Court of the City of New York.

Office: 125-01 Queens Boulevard, Kew Gardens 11415.
Telephone: (718) 520-2259.

KUDRLE, Larry A. *(Magistrate Judge, United States District Court Northern District of New York)* Appointed by U.S. District Court judges to term beginning Jan 24, 2002.

Office: 53 Court Street, Plattsburgh 12901-2834.
Telephone: (518) 561-6274.

KURTZ, Donald Scott *(Judge, The Civil Court of the City of New York)*

Office: 141 Livingston Street, Brooklyn 11201.
Telephone: (718) 643-8931.
Fax: (718) 643-3733

KUZDALE, John M. *(Judge, Dunkirk City Court)* Currently serves as Acting Judge.

Office: City Hall, 342 Central Avenue, Dunkirk 14048-2122.
Telephone: (716) 366-2055.
Fax: (716) 366-3622

LaBUDA, Frank J. *(Judge, Sullivan County Court)* Elected Nov 5, 1996 to term beginning Jan 1, 1997. Term expires Dec 31, 2007. Also serves Sullivan County Surrogate's Court. Born Bronx New York Dec 15, 1949. Catholic. Educated at City University of New York B.A. with honors 1971 and Case Western Reserve University J.D. with honors 1974. Member Phi Beta Kappa. Admitted to practice New York 1975, U.S. Court of Appeals for the Armed Forces 1975 and U.S. District Court Southern District of New York 1990. In legal practice Goshen 1989-96. Justice, Mamakaing Town Justice Court 1992-96.

Chief Assistant District Attorney Sullivan County 1979-89. Assistant Instructor Case Western Reserve University School of Law 1974. Assistant Professor of Law Sullivan County Community College 1985-87. Member New York State Bar Association. Attended judicial conferences since 1985. Recipient Meritorious Service Award. Major JAGC 1975-78 and Operation Desert Storm 1989-90 U.S. Army. Political Affiliation: Democrat Conservative. Member Wurtsboro Fire Co. No. One American Legion, Veterans of Foreign Wars and Vietnam Veterans of America. Enjoys big game hunting, backpacking and maintaining a beef farm in Sullivan County.

Mailing address: P.O. Box 5012, Monticello 12701.
Office: Government Center, 100 North Street, Monticello 12701.
Telephone: (845) 794-1248.
Fax: (845) 794-0310
Office: Sullivan County Courthouse, 414 Broadway, Monticello 12701.
Fax: (845) 794-6208

LA CAVA, John R. *(Justice, New York Supreme Court Ninth Judicial District)* Born Yonkers New York Feb 4, 1947. Catholic. Educated at Fordham University B.A. 1969 J.D. 1973. Admitted to practice New York 1974. Began legal practice White Plains 1973. Judge, Yonkers City Court Feb 19, 1985 to Dec 31, 1988, appointed by Mayor Angelo Martinelli. Former Judge, Westchester County Court, elected to term beginning Jan 1, 1989.

Senior Assistant District Attorney Westchester County 1973-85. Member Yonkers Lawyers Association, Columbian Lawyers Association of Westchester County and Westchester County Bar Association. USAR 1970-75. Major New York Guard. Member Fordham Law Alumni Association, Westchester Citizens Committee on Crime and Delinquency, Enrico Fermi Scholarship Fund and John D. Calandra Lodge Sons of Italy.

Office: Courthouse, 111 Dr. Martin Luther King Jr. Blvd., White Plains 10601.
Telephone: (914) 995-4320.
Fax: (914) 995-4184

LACK, James J. *(Presiding Judge, New York Court of Claims)* Appointed by Governor George E. Pataki.

Office: State Office Building, Third Floor, Veterans Memorial Highway, Hauppauge 11787.
Telephone: (631) 952-6542.
Fax: (631) 952-6727

LAHTINEN, John A. *(Associate Justice, New York Supreme Court Appellate Division Third Judicial Department)* Elected Justice Fourth Judicial District to term beginning 1997. Appointed Associate Justice Appellate Division by Governor George E. Pataki March 6, 2000. Educated at Colgate University and Albany Law School of Union University. Admitted to practice New York 1971. In legal practice Plattsburgh 1971-97.

Mailing address: P.O. Box 38, Plattsburgh 12901.
Office: 36 Oak Street, Plattsburgh 12901.
Telephone: (518) 562-1446.
Fax: (518) 562-1792

LALLY, Ute Wolff *(Justice, New York Supreme Court Tenth Judicial District)* Former Judge, Nassau County District Court.

Office: Supreme Court Building, 100 Supreme Court Drive, Mineola 11501.
Telephone: (516) 571-2323.

LALOR, Daniel Kevin *(Judge, Greene County Court)* Elected to term beginning Jan 1, 1991. Reelected Nov 7, 2000, current term expires Dec 31, 2010. Also serves Greene County Surrogate's Court and Greene County Family Court. Born Catskill New York June 14, 1944. Roman Catholic. Educated at Georgetown University A.B. 1966 J.D. 1969. Admitted to practice New York 1969, District of Columbia, Florida, U.S. District Courts Northern and Southern Districts of New York and U.S. Supreme Court. In legal practice Catskill 1972-87.

Attorney Law Department Metropolitan Life 1969-72. Public Defender 1972-76, Assistant District Attorney 1978-86 and District Attorney 1987-90 Greene County. Important Decisions: People v. Diener 583 N.Y.S.2d 781; Matter of Guida N.Y.L.J. Nov 1, 1991; and People v. Ferrari N.Y.L.J. Nov 17, 1992. Guest Lecturer Greene Community College. Member New York State Defenders Association, New York State District Attorneys Association, National District Attorneys Association, The Asso-

LALOR, DANIEL KEVIN—*Continued*
ciation of the Bar of the City of New York, The District of Columbia Bar, The Florida Bar, New York State and American Bar Associations. Democrat. Member Elks.
Office: Courthouse, 320 Main Street, Catskill 12414.
Telephone: (518) 943-5609.
Fax: (518) 943-7763

LaMANCUSO, John L. *(Judge, Jamestown City Court)*
Office: City Hall, Jamestown 14701-5433.
Telephone: (716) 483-7561.
Fax: (716) 483-7519

LaMARCA, William R. *(Justice, New York Supreme Court Tenth Judicial District)*
Office: Matrimonial Center, 400 County Seat Drive, Mineola 11501.
Telephone: (516) 571-5908.

LAMB, Thomas E. *(Judge, Watervliet City Court)*
Office: City Hall, 15th Street and Broadway, Watervliet 12189.
Telephone: (518) 270-3803.
Fax: (518) 270-3812

LAMONT, Dan *(Judge, New York Court of Claims)* Appointed by Governor George E. Pataki June 1995. Reappointed June 1996, current term expires Dec 31, 2004. Currently serves as Acting Justice, New York Supreme Court Third Judicial District. Born Albany New York Feb 26, 1942. Educated at Hamilton College A.B. 1964 and Albany Law School of Union University J.D. with honors 1967. Began legal practice Albany 1967. In legal practice Cobleskill 1971-78. Judge, Schoharie County Court Jan 1, 1979 to July 25, 1995.
Assistant County Attorney Schoharie County 1972-73. Town Attorney Cobleskill 1977-78. Member Schoharie County and New York State Bar Associations. Lieutenant USNR JAG 1968-71. Member Exchange Club of Cobleskill.
Mailing address: P.O. Box 369, Schoharie 12157.
Office: County Courthouse, Schoharie 12157.
Telephone: (518) 295-8640.
Fax: (518) 295-8638

LANE, John P. *(Justice, New York Supreme Court Eighth Judicial District)* Certificated. Former Judge, New York Court of Claims, appointed by Governor George E. Pataki.
Office: 92 Franklin Street, Buffalo 14202.
Telephone: (716) 851-3435.
Fax: (716) 851-3264
E-mail address: jlane@courts.state.ny.us

LANE, Peter *(Judge, Rye City Court)*
Office: 21 McCullough Place, Rye 10580.
Telephone: (914) 967-1599.
Fax: (914) 967-3308

LANGE, Kenneth H. *(Judge, Westchester County Court)*
Office: 111 Dr. Martin Luther King Jr. Blvd., White Plains 10601.
Telephone: (914) 995-4301.
Fax: (914) 995-4182

LaPERA, Richard A. *(Judge, Nassau County Court)*
Office: County Courthouse, 252 Old Country Road, Mineola 11501.
Telephone: (516) 571-2768.
Fax: (516) 571-1093

LARABEE, Susan R. *(Judge, New York City Family Court)* Appointed by mayor.
Office: 60 Lafayette Street, New York 10013.
Telephone: (212) 374-4177.
Fax: (212) 374-2623

LA RAIA, Henry A. *(Judge, Herkimer County Family Court)* Elected to term beginning Jan 1, 1985. Reelected 1994, current term expires Dec 31, 2004. Born Warsaw New York Aug 5, 1940. Roman Catholic. Educated at Cornell University A.B. 1964 and St. John's University School of Law LL.B. 1967. Member Theta Chi. Admitted to practice New York 1968 and U.S. District Court Northern District of New York 1972. Began legal practice East Rochester 1967. In legal practice Ilion 1970.
Assistant District Attorney 1970-75 and District Attorney 1978-84 Herkimer County. Instructor in Business Law Herkimer County Community College 1974. Member Governor Carey's DWI Task Force, New York State Association of District Attorneys (Stop DWI Committee 1980-84), Herkimer County and New York State Bar Associations. Captain U.S. Army Military Intelligence 1968-70. President Herkimer County Chamber of Commerce 1974-75.
Mailing address: P.O. Box 749, Herkimer 13350-0749.
Office: County Office Building, 109 Mary Street, Herkimer 13350.
Telephone: (315) 867-1139.
Fax: (315) 867-1369
E-mail address: hlaraia@courts.state.ny.us

LARIMER, David G. *(Judge, United States District Court Western District of New York)* Former Magistrate. Appointed Judge for life by the President. Former Chief Judge.
Office: 250 Federal Building, 100 State Street, Rochester 14614-1324.
Telephone: (716) 263-5894.

LASKER, Morris E. *(Senior Judge, United States District Court Southern District of New York)* Appointed for life by President Lyndon B. Johnson to term beginning June 24, 1968. Assumed Senior status, serves U.S. District Court District of Massachusetts by assignment. Born New York July 17, 1917. Educated at Harvard University B.A. 1938 and Yale University LL.B. 1941.
Office: 4730 U.S. Courthouse, One Courthouse Way, Boston, Massachusetts 02210-3002.
Telephone: (617) 748-9132.

LATELLA, John B., Jr. *(Judge, The Criminal Court of the City of New York)* Appointed by Mayor Ed Koch. Currently serves as Acting Justice, New York Supreme Court Eleventh Judicial District.
Office: 125-01 Queens Boulevard, Kew Gardens 11415.
Telephone: (718) 520-3508.

LATHAM, Joseph W. *(Judge, Steuben County Court)* Elected Nov 1998 to term beginning Jan 1, 1999. Term expires Dec 31, 2008. Also serves Steuben County Family Court. Born North Hornell New York June 13, 1947. Christian. Educated at Cornell University B.A.

LATHAM, JOSEPH W.—*Continued*

1969, Syracuse University M.P.A. 1974 J.D. 1974. Member Phi Alpha Delta. Admitted to practice New York 1975 and U.S. District Court Western District of New York 1975. Surrogate, Steuben County Surrogate's Court 1997-98.

Past President and Former Trustee Steuben County Bar Association. Member Association of Judges of the Family Court of the State of New York, County Judges Association of the State of New York and The Surrogates' Association of the State of New York. Recipient Pro Bono Service Award from New York State Bar Association 1973. Specialist Six USAR 1970-76. President Bethesda Foundation. Chairman Board of Trustees Supreme Court Law Library Bath New York. Senior Active Member Bath Rotary Club. Member Elks Lodge 364. Judge Advocate Steuben County American Legion.

Office: Steuben County Courthouse, Three East Pulteney Square, Bath 14810.

Telephone: (607) 776-9631.

Fax: (607) 776-6940

LAURIA, Joseph M. *(Judge, New York City Family Court)* Appointed by mayor. Currently serves as Administrative Judge.

Office: 60 Lafayette Street, New York 10013.

Telephone: (212) 374-3711.

Fax: (212) 374-2127

LAWLISS, Timothy J. *(Judge, Clinton County Family Court)*

Office: 13 County Government Center, 137 Margaret Street, Plattsburgh 12901-2933.

Telephone: (518) 565-4404.

Fax: (518) 565-4688

LAWRENCE, Richard S. *(Judge, Nassau County Family Court)*

Office: 1200 Old Country Road, Westbury 11590.

Telephone: (516) 571-9104.

Fax: (516) 571-9335

LAWTON, John F. *(Associate Justice, New York Supreme Court Appellate Division Fourth Judicial Department)* Elected Justice to term beginning Jan 1, 1983. Reelected 1996. Appointed Associate Justice Appellate Division by Governor Mario Cuomo 1986. Reappointed to Appellate Division by Governor George E. Pataki. Certificated. Educated at Niagara University B.S. 1950 and St. John's University School of Law LL.B. with honors 1955. Admitted to practice New York 1955, U.S. District Courts Northern and Western Districts of New York, U.S. Court of Appeals Second Circuit and U.S. Supreme Court. In legal practice Syracuse 1955-82.

Captain USAR 1950-65 (active Korean War 1951-53). Member Onondaga County Legislature 1970-77 (Republican Floor Leader 1976, Chairman 1976-77).

Office: Onondaga County Courthouse, Syracuse 13202-2127.

Telephone: (315) 671-1090.

Fax: (315) 671-1180

LEACH, Leslie G. *(Judge, The Criminal Court of the City of New York)* Appointed by mayor. Currently serves as Acting Justice, New York Supreme Court Eleventh Judicial District.

Office: 125-01 Queens Boulevard, Kew Gardens 11415.

Telephone: (718) 520-2218.

Fax: (718) 520-4712

LEAK, Barbara A. *(Judge, White Plains City Court)*

Office: 77 South Lexington Avenue, White Plains 10601.

Telephone: (914) 422-6061.

Fax: (914) 422-6058

LEBEDEFF, Diane Alexis *(Judge, The Civil Court of the City of New York)* Housing Part Judge 1980-82. Elected Judge to term beginning Jan 1, 1983. Reelected 1992 and 2002. Current term expires Dec 31, 2012. Acting Justice, New York Supreme Court First Judicial District since 1988. Born Detroit Michigan June 25, 1943. Educated at University of Michigan B.A. 1965 J.D. 1968. Admitted to practice New York 1969 and Michigan 1969.

Associate Appellate Counsel Legal Aid Society New York City 1968-71. Attorney Division of Criminal Justice Services New York State 1971-73. General Counsel Department of Rent and Housing Maintenance New York City 1976-80 and New York City Rent Guidelines 1976-80. Member New York County Lawyers' Association (Chair Elder Law Committee since 1999), New York State Association of Women Judges (Board of Directors since 1984, Vice President 1990-92, President 1992-95), National Association of Women Judges (Board of Directors 1993-95), The Association of the Bar of the City of New York, New York State and American Bar Associations. Member New York City Community Board 2, 1979-80.

Office: 60 Centre Street, Room 626, New York 10007.

Telephone: (212) 374-8561.

E-mail address: dlebedef@courts.state.ny.us

LEBOUS, Ferris D. *(Judge, New York Court of Claims)* Appointed by Governor George E. Pataki.

Office: State Office Building, 44 Hawley Street, Binghamton 13901-4418.

Telephone: (607) 721-8623.

Fax: (607) 721-8590

LEBOWITZ, Alan L. *(Justice, New York Supreme Court Second Judicial District)* Born Brooklyn New York. Jewish. Educated at Long Island University B.A. 1957 and Brooklyn Law School J.D. 1960. Member Iota Theta. Admitted to practice New York 1961. In legal practice Brooklyn 1961-85. Former Judge, The Civil Court of the City of New York, elected to term beginning Jan 1, 1986.

Assistant Corporate Counsel 1961-65, Committee Counsel 1966-67 and City Counsel 1966-67 City of New York. Senate Minority Counsel 1967-70. Senate Minority Finance Counsel 1976-81. Adjunct Instructor in Business Law New York City Technical College 1978-80, Para Legal Studies Brooklyn College of the City University of New York 1981-83 and Para Legal Studies Kingsborough Community College 1983-93. Member Kings County Criminal Bar (Legislative Chairman 1972-77, Judiciary Committee), Brooklyn (Chair Continuing Legal Education Committee, Assigned Counsel Committee) and New York State Bar Associations. Named one of Outstanding Young Men of America by Junior Chamber of Commerce and East Flatbush Man of the Year. Recipient Scroll of Honor from Jewish War Veterans and Brooklyn Bar Service Award and The Louis Sangiorgio Award for Outstanding Service as a Jurist Jan 9,

LEBOWITZ, ALAN L.—*Continued*

2003. Personnelman Third Class USN 1951-55. Vice President Madison Democratic Club 1966-70. Executive Vice President Kings County Young Democrats 1967-70. Law Chairman Kings County Democratic Executive Committee 1980-85. Counsel East Flatbush Civic Association, Affiliated Block Associations of East Flatbush and Dynamite Youth Drug Program. County Commander Kings County Council Jewish War Veterans 1977-78. Post Commander Post 335 Jewish War Veterans of the United States. Member Zeradetha Lodge Masons, Knights of Pythias, B'nai B'rith and Jews and Blacks in Conversation. Enjoys reading history novels and mysteries, golf and all sports.

Office: Homeport, 355 Front Street, Staten Island 10304.

Telephone: (718) 876-6440.

Fax: (718) 876-6441

E-mail address: alebowitz@courts.state.ny.us

LEBOWITZ, Jeffrey D. *(Judge, The Civil Court of the City of New York)* Currently serves as Acting Justice, New York Supreme Court Eleventh Judicial District.

Office: 125-01 Queens Boulevard, Kew Gardens 11415.

Telephone: (718) 520-2846.

LEDINA, Burton *(Judge, Sullivan County Court)* Appointed by Governor George E. Pataki to term beginning June 27, 1996. Reappointed Jan 15, 1997. Elected Nov 4, 1997, current term expires Dec 31, 2007. Also serves Sullivan County Surrogate's Court. Born Elizabeth New Jersey Jan 5, 1940. Jewish. Educated at Syracuse University A.B. 1961 and New York University School of Law LL.B. 1964. Admitted to practice New York 1964, U.S. District Courts Northern 1964, Eastern 1967 and Southern 1967 Districts of New York, U.S. Court of Appeals Second Circuit 1966 and U.S. Supreme Court 1970. In legal practice Monticello 1964-96. Justice, Monticello Village Justice Court 1969-78. Justice, Thompson Town Justice Court 1977-96.

Chairman Unlawful Practice of Law Committee 1971-72 and Lawyer Referral and Pro Bono Committee 1983-86. Director Sullivan County Legal Services Corporation 1968-69. Member Panel of Arbitrators American Arbitration Association 1970-78. Member Sullivan County Magistrates' Association, New York State Association of Magistrates, Sullivan County (Director 1966-70 and 1983, Secretary-Treasurer 1966-68, Vice President 1983-84, President 1984-85), New York State (Legal Aid Committee 1968-70, House of Delegates 1984-85, Family Law Section) and American Bar Associations. Attended Annual Summer Judicial Seminar July 1997-2002, Orientation Seminar for New Judges Dec 8-12, 1997 and Capital Cases Training Program Dec 15-16, 1997 New York State Unified Court System. Recipient Harris Gordon Memorial Award from Holiday Mountain Ski Club March 13, 1994. Republican. Member Holiday Mountain Ski Club, Inc., Masons, Otsiningo Bodies A.A.S.R., Kalurah Temple, Shriners Organization, Fallsburg Lions Club, Elks Lodge 1544, Temple Sholom and Landfield Avenue Synagogue. Interests include genealogy, local history, golf and skiing.

Mailing address: P.O. Box 5012, Monticello 12701.

Office: County Government Center, 100 North Street, Monticello 12701.

Telephone: (845) 794-3000.

Fax: (845) 791-6252

LEFKOWITZ, Joan B. *(Justice, New York Supreme Court Ninth Judicial District)* Elected to term beginning Jan 1991. Term expires Dec 31, 2004. Born Manhattan New York June 28, 1949. Jewish. Educated at New York University B.A. with honors 1970 and Brooklyn Law School J.D. 1973. Law Assistant The Civil Court of the City of New York Aug 1974 to Oct 1975. Admitted to practice New York 1974, U.S. District Courts Eastern 1975 and Southern 1975 Districts of New York and U.S. Supreme Court 1982. In legal practice White Plains 1976-85. Part-time Hearing Examiner Oct 1984 to Oct 1985, Hearing Examiner Nov 1985 to May 1987 and Judge May 1987 to Dec 1990, Westchester County Family Court.

Important Decisions (published in New York Law Journal): Matter of S.K., M.K. & C.K. (child abuse finding is not prima facie evidence of other abuse) March 20, 1989, Matter of C. & D. (non-respondent parent's presence is permitted in abuse proceeding) April 17, 1989, Matter of Richard E. (reasonable adjournment for hearing is not a speedy trial violation) May 16, 1989, J.C. v. K.R. (emergency jurisdiction for custody is reserved for extraordinary cases) June 13, 1989, Matter of Ileana and Luis (duplicate abuse petition dismissed for agency's unclean hands) July 3, 1989, Matters of Ibn W. et al. (malnutrition is basis for neglect under Family Court Act) Aug 14, 1989, Matter of Maria B. (abuse petition dismissed for insufficient corroboration) Sept 1, 1989, Matter of Elizabeth O. (expert testimony alone is sufficient to corroborate child's statements) Sept 20, 1989, Paul T. v. Maria S. (best interests of child require that father be granted sole custody) Nov 13, 1989, Matter of Patricia F. (Child Support Standards Act does not apply in issue settled before effective date) Dec 14, 1989, Matter of Gerald S. (court calls for changes in law to protect children from abuse) Feb 9, 1990, Matter of C.C. (Child Support Standards Act guidelines may be applied to case filed before effective date) March 13, 1989, Matter of Richard H. (juvenile delinquency petition is dismissed in interest of justice) June 7, 1990, Matter of Daniel N. (willful leaving of parent's home is requisite for emancipation) June 14, 1990, Matter of Jose C. (designated felony petition requires two prior delinquency findings) Aug 21, 1990 and Foster v. Bohrmann (parties held not to be in default absent proper, fixed closing date). Adjunct Professor Pace University since 1990. Member White Plains, Westchester Women's (Former Member Board of Directors), Westchester County (Sections: Criminal Law, Family Law) and New York State (Courts and the Community Committee) Bar Associations. Democrat. Member Advisory Committee on the Abused Spouse Assistance Services Mental Health Association. Former Member Board of Directors Young Israel of Scarsdale. Member Yonkers Task Force and Board of Directors Anti-Defamation League.

Office: County Courthouse, 111 Dr. Martin Luther King Jr. Blvd., White Plains 10601.

Telephone: (914) 995-4906.

Fax: (914) 995-4184

LEHMAN, Dudley L. *(Judge, Suffolk County Family Court)* Former Judge, Suffolk County District Court.

Office: Cohalan Court Complex, 400 Carleton Avenue, Central Islip 11722.

Telephone: (631) 853-7752.

Fax: (631) 853-7569

LEHMANN, Mary Anne *(Judge, Binghamton City Court)* Elected Nov 3, 1996 to term beginning Jan 1, 1997. Term expires Dec 31, 2006. Born Orange County California Sept 8, 1957. Roman Catholic. Educated at Colgate University B.A. with honors 1979 and Albany Law School of Union University J.D. 1983. Admitted to practice New York 1984 and U.S. District Court Northern District of New York 1993.

Assistant District Attorney 1984-85, Second Assistant District Attorney 1985-86 and Senior Assistant District Attorney in charge of Local Courts 1986-88 and in charge of Drug Prosecutions 1988-96 Broome County. Adjunct Faculty in Special Prosecutions: Drug and Alcohol Broome Community College. Member Broome County and New York State Bar Associations. Lecturer Statewide Basic Prosecutors School Albany, Bureau of Municipal Police, Regional Police Trainings and Jury Selection New York State Bar Association. Recipient Certificate for Outstanding Contributions in the Field of Drug Enforcement from Drug Enforcement Agency U.S. Department of Justice 1995. Named 1997 Woman of Achievement by Broome County Status of Women's Council. Participant numerous church activities and civic boards.

Office: Governmental Plaza, 38 Hawley Street, Binghamton 13901.

Telephone: (607) 772-7006.

Fax: (607) 772-7041

LEHNER, Edward H. *(Justice, New York Supreme Court First Judicial District)* Former Acting Justice. Born Queens New York March 6, 1933. Jewish. Educated at City College of the City University of New York B.B.A. 1954 and New York University School of Law LL.B. cum laude 1957. Admitted to practice New York 1958 and U.S. District Courts Southern 1960 and Eastern 1960 Districts of New York. In legal practice New York City 1957-72. Former Judge, The Civil Court of the City of New York, elected to term beginning Jan 1, 1981.

Attorney Towers Mart International, Inc. 1962-64. Coauthor "Goodman-Dearie Expiration Leaves Co-op Conversions Radically Altered" Nov 16, 1977, "Co-op Conversion Law: Impact in Suburbia" Sept 20, 1978, "City Proposes Remedies for Illegal Conversions of Lofts to Residences" Nov 15, 1978, "Lehner-Flynn Law's Impact on Protecting Senior Citizens" Sept 14, 1979 and "Recent Statutory Changes & Case Law Developments, Conversions of Residential Cooperatives, Lofts" Dec 24 and 26, 1980 New York L. Jour. Important Decisions: Municipal Art Society v. City of New York (sale of Coliseum was invalid because it provided "cash sale" of a zoning bonus) 137 Misc. 2d 832; Mixon v. Phillips (preliminary injunction requiring the City to provide a homeless person, who had an HIV infection but did not have AIDS, with non-congregate housing so that he would not be in close proximity to persons with infectious diseases) N.Y.L.J. Jan 13, 1985; Love v. Koch (City of New York required to see that all mentally ill persons who are in need of care and treatment at a hospital are in fact admitted to hospital) N.Y.L.J. Nov 4, 1988; Grant v. Cuomo (city to investigate all reports of suspected child abuse within 24 hours of receipt of report) 134 Misc. 2d 83, modified 130 A.D. 2d 154, aff'd 73 N.Y. 2d 820; Tarman v. Rowe (purchaser of an occupied apartment under a non-eviction cooperative conversion plan could not evict a tenant based on a claimed need of personal use of the apartment) 112 Misc. 2d 708, aff'd 90 A.D. 452; Scotia Associates v. Bond (tenant's pro bono attorney may recover compensation from landlord if tenant wins lawsuit) 126 Misc. 2d 885; Mann v. 125 East 50th Street Corp. (hotel resident who had no other address could not be deemed a "transient") 124 Misc. 2d 115, aff'd 126 Misc. 2d 1016; Washington Post Company v. N.Y. State Insurance Department (under the Freedom of Information Law, a newspaper reporter was entitled to obtain a copy of insurance company minutes which had been filed with the Insurance Department) 114 Misc. 2d 601, aff'd 61 N.Y. 2d 557; Matter of Nyazi (mental hospital to release a non-English speaking patient unless it provided an interpreter to enable him to be treated) 111 Misc. 2d 414; Association of Messenger Services, Inc. v. City of New York (invalidated the order of the City Traffic Commissioner barring bicycles from certain midtown Manhattan streets during specified hours) 136 Misc. 2d 869; and Kaswan v. Aponte (city restrictions on areas where street peddling is authorized are inapplicable to one who holds disabled veterans peddlers license) 142 Misc. 2d 298, aff'd N.Y.L.J. April 12, 1990.

Member New York County Lawyers' Association and The Association of the Bar of the City of New York (Committee on State Legislation 1971-72). Lecturer Forum on Cooperative Conversion The Association of the Bar of the City of New York 1978 and Cooperative and Condominium Conversion New York Law Journal Forum 1979. Member State Assembly New York 1973-80 (Judiciary Committee 1975-80, Housing Committee 1977-80, Cities Committee, Corporations, Authorities and Commissions Committee, Government Employees Committee, Higher Education Committee, Real Property Taxation Committee). Member Citizens Union Committee on State Legislation 1970-72. Served as volunteer attorney to represent people arrested during anti-Vietnam War rally Washington D.C. 1972. Board of Trustees Fort Tryon Jewish Center, Mount Sinai Jewish Center and Inwood B'nai B'rith Lodge. Board of Directors YMHA of Washington Heights.

Office: 60 Centre Street, New York 10007.

Telephone: (212) 374-8563.

LEIS, H. Patrick, III *(Justice, New York Supreme Court Tenth Judicial District)* Former Judge, Suffolk County Court.

Mailing address: P.O. Box 9070, Central Islip 11722-9070.

Office: S-32 Cohalan Court Complex, 400 Carleton Avenue, Central Islip 11722.

Telephone: (631) 853-6092.

Fax: (631) 852-3289

LEISURE, Peter K. *(Senior Judge, United States District Court Southern District of New York)* Appointed for life by President Ronald Reagan to term beginning 1984. Assumed Senior status March 21, 1997, serves by assignment. Born New York New York March 21, 1929. Educated at Columbia University School of Law, Yale University B.A. 1952 and University of Virginia School

LEISURE, PETER K.—*Continued*
of Law LL.B. 1958. In legal practice New York City 1958-61 and 1966-84.
Assistant U.S. Attorney Southern District of New York 1962-66.
Office: 1910 U.S. Courthouse, 500 Pearl Street, New York 10007-1312.
Telephone: (212) 805-0226.

LERNER, Alfred D. *(Associate Justice, New York Supreme Court Appellate Division First Judicial Department)* Elected Justice Eleventh Judicial District to term beginning Jan 1973. Associate Justice Appellate Division Second Judicial Department Oct 1997 to Jan 1998. Appointed Associate Justice Appellate Division First Judicial Department by Governor George E. Pataki to term beginning Jan 1998. Certificated. Associate Justice Appellate Term Second and Eleventh Judicial Districts April 1985 to Sept 1987. Administrative Judge Eleventh Judicial District Oct 1986 to Oct 1997. Presiding Justice Appellate Division Jan 1998 to Jan 1999.
Office: 27 Madison Avenue at 25th Street, New York 10010.
Telephone: (212) 340-0440.

LEVENTHAL, John Michael *(Justice, New York Supreme Court Second Judicial District)* Elected Nov 1994 to term beginning Jan 1, 1995. Term expires Dec 2008. Born New York New York Nov 28, 1948. Educated at Case Western Reserve University B.A. 1970, Hunter College of the City University of New York M.S. 1974 and Brooklyn Law School J.D. 1979. Law Clerk to Hon. Louis R. Rosenthal, The Civil Court of the City of New York 1980-82. Admitted to practice New York 1980, U.S. District Courts Eastern 1980 and Southern 1980 Districts of New York and U.S. Court of Appeals Second Circuit 1988. In legal practice Brooklyn Sept 1982 to Dec 1994.
Editor-in-Chief *Veritas* Brooklyn Law School Alumni Association 1982-84 and *Barrister* Brooklyn Bar Association 1982-94. Author or Co-author "Verdict Sheets—Objection and Appeal" 6 No. 1 Kings County Criminal B. Jour. June 1990, "Public Trial: Keeping the Undercover 'Undercover'" New York L. Jour. 1 Nov 3, 1992, "Courtroom Show-Ups: Identification of the Worst Kind" New York L. Jour. 1 April 27, 1994, "Renunciation of Property Interests Under EPTL §2-1.11" New York L. Jour. 1 March 23, 1995, "Do Not Open Unless . . . Review of Civil Rights Law §50-1" New York L. Jour. 1 Sept 6, 1995 and *The Jurist* 5 Fall/Winter 1995 and "Judicial Selection System Under Attack: An Overview of *France v. Pataki*" *The Jurist* 11 Spring 1996. Important Decisions: People v. Qike (suppressing a tape illegally obtained by a defendant by eavesdropping on his wife) 182 Misc. 2d 737, 1999; People v. Miterko (defendant moved to dismiss an indictment on the ground that Criminal Procedure Laws were violated since the People failed to obtain permission to present case to a Grand Jury) 2000, Small v. MUAIC (wrongful death action referred to the court solely for the purpose of a jury trial on the issue of damages) 185 Misc. 2d 664, 2000; People v. Torres (incarcerated defendant moved ex parte for an order to allow a polygraphist to enter the prison to administer a lie detector test) 185 Misc. 2d 108, 2000; People v. Mallet (detaining subway train is not stop or seizure of defendant) 164 Misc. 2d 1009; People v. Ramos (newly obtained records warrant new trial on sexual abuse) 166 Misc. 2d 515; People v. Smoot 166 Misc. 2d 862; People v. Patterson/Smart (police officer's failure to report discharge of weapon is admissible) 169 Misc. 2d 787; People v. Sommerville (motion to suppress contents of personal diary is granted) 170 Misc. 2d 1024; People v. Owusu (defendant's unaltered teeth are not "dangerous instruments") 172 Misc. 2d 357; People v. Calderon 173 Misc. 2d 435; People v. Kheyfits (criminal mischief regarding jointly owned property) 174 Misc. 2d 516; People v. Arnold (double jeopardy) 174 Misc. 2d 585; People v. Truick 175 Misc. 2d 460; People v. Damsky 177 Misc. 2d 884; People v. Gellineau 178 Misc. 2d 790; People v. Arnold 178 Misc. 2d 285; People v. Seeley (propriety of devices used in seeking records filed with law enforcement authorities) 179 Misc. 2d 42; People v. Salazar 180 Misc. 2d 128; People v. Williams 180 Misc. 2d 203; People v. Emerhall 181 Misc. 2d 460; People v. Cubero 181 Misc. 2d 431; and People v. Lugo 181 Misc. 2d 811. Trustee 1987-94 and Member Grievance Committee 1991-94 Brooklyn Bar Association. Member Task Force on Reducing Litigation Cost and Delay 1996-97 and Chair Gender Fairness Committee since 1999 Second Judicial District. Member Oversight Committee for Criminal Defense Organizations since 1997 and Assigned Counsel Committee Second and Eleventh Judicial Districts since 1999 Appellate Division Second Department. Delegate National Conference of Special Court Judges American Bar Association since 1999.
Moderator High Profile Cases and the Press Seminar 1991 and "Aggressive Policing Under the Gun: Saving Lives v. Costing Lives and Implications for the Criminal Justice System" Panel Discussion June 6, 2000 Brooklyn Law School. Speaker "Recurring Issues in Domestic Violence Cases" Columbia Lawyers Association of Brooklyn April 1, 1997, "What Can Judges Do to Stop Domestic Violence?" Second Annual Domestic Violence Awareness Fair Battered Women's Justice Center Pace University Oct 8, 1997 and "The Future—Criminal Justice Through Collaboration" NYS Division of Criminal Justice Services Saratoga Springs Nov 28, 2000. Panelist Resolving Gaps in Domestic Violence Resources Symposium Brooklyn Hospital Center May 12, 1997, Judicial Seminar on Child Abuse/Sexual Assault New York City March 5, 1998, "The Trial of Domestic Violence Cases: Cutting Edge Issues for Law Enforcement and Advocates: Domestic Violence Court Innovations" Kings County District Attorney's Fourth Annual Domestic Violence Conference Oct 6, 1999 and "New York Domestic Violence Courts" Ninth Annual Domestic Violence Conference National District Attorneys Association Oct 23, 1999 to Oct 27, 1999. Keynote Speaker Conference on Domestic Violence and the Police International Association of Chiefs of Police Kingsboro College Sept 19, 1997. Named Educator of the Year by City Tabernacle Church S.D.A. Nov 1979. Recipient Distinguished Service Award from Brooklyn Bar Association 1985, 1990 and 1994 and In the Trenches Award from The Lawyers Committee Against Domestic Violence Fordham University School of Law March 30, 2000. Math teacher Intermediate School 151 Sept 1971 to June 1976. Chairperson Law Committee Kings County Democratic County Committee 1990-94. Part-time Counsel to New York State Assembly 1991-94. Director Brooklyn Law School Alumni Association since 1983. Master Cornerstone Lodge 194 F. & A.M. 1985. Attorney Crime Victim's Political Platform 1993-94. Co-chair Second Manhattan

LEVENTHAL, JOHN MICHAEL—*Continued*

Masonic District Blood Drive since 1996. Commissioner of Appeals Grand Lodge of the State of New York since 1997. Grand Representative Grand Lodge of South Carolina since 1997. Amateur boxer and Golden Gloves Quarter Finalist 1972. Past President New York Rugby Club. Youth Soccer Coach and Youth Basketball Coach. Gym enthusiast. Enjoys chess.

Office: 360 Adams Street, Brooklyn 11201.
Telephone: (718) 643-8490.
E-mail address: jleventh@courts.state.ny.us

LE VINE, Alan *(Justice, New York Supreme Court Eleventh Judicial District)* Certificated.

Office: 88-11 Sutphin Boulevard, Jamaica 11435.
Telephone: (718) 520-3761.

LEVINE, Joseph S. *(Justice, New York Supreme Court Second Judicial District)* Elected to term beginning Jan 1, 1984. Reelected 1997. Certificated. Born Brooklyn New York Aug 24, 1932. Educated at Cornell University B.A. 1954 and New York University School of Law J.D. 1959. Admitted to practice New York 1960, U.S. District Courts Eastern 1962 and Southern 1962 Districts of New York and U.S. Court of Appeals for the Armed Forces 1993. Began legal practice Brooklyn 1960. Judge, The Civil Court of the City of New York 1975-83. Judge-in-Charge, Kings County 1981-83.

Assistant District Attorney 1960-65. Law Secretary to Hon. Thomas R. Jones 1965-67 and to Hon. O. D. Williams 1969-74. Important Decision: Mertsaris v. Physicians Hospital (medical malpractice—$7,500,000 verdict) 1982. Instructor Richmond Memorial Hospital & Health Center Emergency Medical Services 1983-84. Vice President Civil Court Board of Judges 1980-81. Member Brooklyn and New York State (Committee on Courts and the Community) Bar Associations. Chairman Moot Court Finals American Bar Association Law School Division 1981. Board of Advisors New York Dispute Resolution Center since 1981. Vice President and Director Respect for Law Alliance, Inc. Recipient PACK Award from Kings County Panel on Automotive Complaints 1978-82. First Lieutenant U.S. Army 2nd Armored Division 1954-56 and Brigadier General New York Guard. Member State Assembly New York 1967-68. Enjoys photography and antique automobiles.

Office: 360 Adams Street, Brooklyn 11201.
Telephone: (718) 643-7022.
E-mail address: jlevine@courts.state.ny.us

LEVITT, Judith Anne *(Judge, The Criminal Court of the City of New York)* Appointed by mayor.

Office: 100 Centre Street, New York 10013.
Telephone: (212) 374-6216.
Fax: (212) 374-2579

LEVY, Robert M. *(Magistrate Judge, United States District Court Eastern District of New York)* Appointed by U.S. District Court judges to term beginning March 21, 1995.

Author *Rights of People with Mental Disabilities* Southern Illinois University Press 1996. Adjunct Professor of Law New York University School of Law, Columbia University School of Law and Brooklyn Law School since 1990. Member Federal Bar Council and The Association of the Bar of the City of New York.

Office: U.S. Courthouse, 225 Cadman Plaza East, Brooklyn 11201.
Telephone: (718) 260-2340.

LEWIS, Daniel *(Justice, New York Supreme Court Eleventh Judicial District)* Former Judge, The Criminal Court of the City of New York.

Office: 125-01 Queens Boulevard, Kew Gardens 11415.
Telephone: (718) 520-4662.

LEWIS, William R. *(Judge, North Tonawanda City Court)*

Office: City Hall, 216 Payne Avenue, North Tonawanda 14120-5446.
Telephone: (716) 693-1010.
Fax: (716) 743-1754

LEWIS, Yvonne *(Justice, New York Supreme Court Second Judicial District)* Elected to term beginning Jan 6, 1992. Term expires Dec 31, 2005. Born Detroit Michigan Jan 23, 1944. Catholic. Educated State University of New York at Geneseo B.A. 1967 and State University of New York at Buffalo J.D. 1973. Admitted to practice New York 1974, U.S. District Courts Eastern and Southern Districts of New York and U.S. Court of Appeals Second Circuit. Judge, The Civil Court of the City of New York 1987-91.

Assistant Clinic Professor Elderly Clinic Hofstra University School of Law 1984-86. Member Advisory Committee of Judicial Ethics. Member National Association of Women Judges, National Lawyers Guild, American Judges Association, The Association of the Bar of the City of New York, Brooklyn Women's Bar Association, Inc., Brooklyn and Metropolitan Black Bar Associations. Board of Education and Teacher Buffalo 1968-70. Member Judicial Friends and Women in Government Mentoring Program.

Office: 360 Adams Street, Brooklyn 11201.
Telephone: (718) 643-3191.
Fax: (718) 643-4995
E-mail address: ylewis@courts.state.ny.us

LIEB, Judith S. *(Judge, The Civil Court of the City of New York)* Currently assigned to The Criminal Court of the City of New York.

Office: 215 East 161st Street, Bronx 10451.
Telephone: (718) 590-2927.
Fax: (718) 590-7297

LIEBOWITZ, Richard B. *(Judge, Yonkers City Court)* Elected to term beginning Jan 1, 1992. Reelected 2001. Born Yonkers New York May 4, 1935. Educated at Manhattan College B.S. 1957 and Fordham University J.D. 1960. Admitted to practice New York 1960 and U.S. District Court Southern District of New York 1987. In legal practice New York City 1968-80 and White Plains 1980-91.

Member Yonkers Lawyers Association, Westchester County and New York State Bar Associations. Attended National Institute for Trial Advocacy. Trustee Westchester Community College since 1994.

Office: Justice Center, 100 South Broadway, Yonkers 10701.
Telephone: (914) 377-6363.

LIFLAND, Burton R. *(Recalled Judge, United States Bankruptcy Court Southern District of New York)* Ap-

LIFLAND, BURTON R.—*Continued*
pointed Recalled Judge by the Judicial Council of the Second Circuit. Former Chief Judge. Former Chief Judge, Bankruptcy Appellate Panel Second Circuit, selected by the Judicial Council of the Second Circuit.
Office: Hamilton Custom House, Sixth Floor, One Bowling Green, New York 10004-1408.
Telephone: (212) 668-5663.

LIFSON, Robert A. *(Justice, New York Supreme Court Tenth Judicial District)* Elected to term beginning Jan 1, 1995.
Mailing address: P.O. Box 9070, Central Islip 11722-9070.
Office: S-34 Cohalan Court Complex, 400 Carleton Avenue, Central Islip 11722.
Telephone: (631) 853-5138.
Fax: (631) 853-5798

LIM, Arnold *(Judge, New York City Family Court)* Appointed by Mayor Rudolph Giuliani.
Office: 283 Adams Street, Sixth Floor, Brooklyn 11201.
Telephone: (718) 643-4546.
Fax: (718) 643-5103

LINDLEY, Stephen K. *(Judge, Rochester City Court)*
Office: Hall of Justice, 99 Exchange Boulevard, Rochester 14614.
Telephone: (585) 428-1965.
Fax: (585) 428-4134

LINDSAY, Arlene Rosario *(Magistrate Judge, United States District Court Eastern District of New York)* Appointed by U.S. District Court judges to term beginning 1994. Educated at University of Dayton B.A. 1968 and New York University J.D. 1975.
Office: Long Island Federal Courthouse, 100 Federal Plaza, Central Islip 11722-4438.
Telephone: (631) 712-5730.

LING-COHAN, Doris *(Justice, New York Supreme Court First Judicial District)* Former Judge, The Civil Court of the City of New York.
Office: 60 Centre Street, New York 10007.
Telephone: (212) 374-4574.
E-mail address: dlingcoh@courts.state.ny.us

LIPPMAN, Jonathan *(Judge, New York Court of Claims)* Appointed by Governor George E. Pataki to term beginning June 28, 1995. Reappointed April 30, 1998, current term expires March 30, 2007. Chief Administrative Judge, Office of Court Administration New York State Unified Court System since Jan 1, 1996. Born New York New York May 19, 1945. Educated at New York University B.A. with honors 1965 J.D. 1968. Admitted to practice New York 1968 and U.S. District Courts Eastern and Southern Districts of New York.
Law Clerk to Hon. Samuel A. Spiegel, New York Supreme Court and New York County Surrogate's Court 1974-77. Principal Court Attorney New York Supreme Court First Judicial District Civil Term 1977-83. Chief Clerk and Executive Officer Civil Branch New York County Supreme Court 1983-89. Deputy Chief Administrator for Management Support New York Unified Court System 1989-95. Author "Divorce Reform Aids Families, Children" Jan 27, 1999, "CLE: Have It Your Way" April 5, 1999, "Interaction Between Legislative, Judicial Branches Essential" May 5, 1999 and "Differentiated Case Management" Dec 8, 1999 New York L. Jour. Member Conference of State Court Administrators, National Association for Court Management and New York State Bar Association. Lecturer to judges, non-judicial personnel, bar groups and law schools. Vice President New York University Law Alumni Association. Recipient Benjamin Cardozo Award from Jewish Lawyers Guild March 13, 1996, Chief Justice Harlan Fisk Stone Memorial Award from Association of Trial Lawyers of the City of New York Oct 1996 and Robert L. Haig Award from Committee for Commercial and Federal Litigation New York Bar Association May 1998.
Office: Office of Court Administration, 25 Beaver Street, New York 10004.
Telephone: (212) 428-2100.
Fax: (212) 428-2188
E-mail address: jlippman@courts.state.ny.us

LIPPMANN, Robert D. *(Judge, The Civil Court of the City of New York)* Elected Nov 1983 to term beginning Jan 1984. Reelected 1993, current term expires Dec 31, 2003. Currently serves as Acting Justice, New York Supreme Court First Judicial District. Born New York New York April 10, 1936. Educated at Oberlin College B.A. 1958, Syracuse University LL.B. 1961 and Columbia University LL.M. 1962. Admitted to practice New York 1962, U.S. District Courts Eastern 1964 and Southern 1964 Districts of New York, U.S. Court of Appeals Second Circuit 1964 and U.S. Supreme Court 1981.
Member The Association of the Bar of the City of New York, Puerto Rican Bar Association of New York, Metropolitan Women's, New York State and American Bar Associations.
Office: 111 Centre Street, New York 10013.
Telephone: (212) 374-8454.
Fax: (212) 374-5709

LITTLEFIELD, Robert E., Jr. *(Judge, United States Bankruptcy Court Northern District of New York)* Appointed by U.S. Court of Appeals Second Circuit judges to term beginning 1995. Educated at University of Denver B.A. and Albany Law School of Union University J.D. Former Judge, Bankruptcy Appellate Panel Second Circuit, selected by the Judicial Council of the Second Circuit.
Former Chapter 7 Trustee, Former Chapter 11 Trustee, Chapter 13 Standing Trustee 1979-95 and Chapter 12 Standing Trustee 1979-95 Northern District of New York. Former President National Association of Chapter 13 Trustees. Lecturer on Consumer Bankruptcy at numerous seminars and educational forums.
Office: 327 U.S. Courthouse, 445 Broadway, Albany 12207-2965.
Telephone: (518) 257-1661.

LOBIS, Joan B. *(Justice, New York Supreme Court First Judicial District)* Former Judge, The Civil Court of the City of New York.
Office: 60 Centre Street, New York 10007.
Telephone: (212) 374-8383.

LOPEZ, Gene R. *(Judge, The Criminal Court of the City of New York)* Appointed by mayor.
Office: 120 Schermerhorn Street, Brooklyn 11201.
Telephone: (718) 643-8400.
Fax: (718) 643-3538

LÓPEZ TORRES, Margarita *(Judge, The Civil Court of the City of New York)* Currently assigned to The Criminal Court of the City of New York.
Office: 120 Schermerhorn Street, Brooklyn 11201.
Telephone: (718) 643-8400.

LORENZO, Albert *(Judge, New York Court of Claims)* Appointed by Governor George E. Pataki. Currently serves as Acting Justice, New York Supreme Court Twelfth Judicial District.
Office: 851 Grand Concourse, Bronx 10451.
Telephone: (718) 590-3905.
Fax: (718) 590-8914

LO TEMPIO, Andrew C. *(Judge, Buffalo City Court)*
Office: 50 Delaware Avenue, Buffalo 14202.
Telephone: (716) 847-8285.
Fax: (716) 847-8257

LOTT, Plummer E. *(Justice, New York Supreme Court Second Judicial District)* Elected to term beginning Jan 1, 1995. Former Judge, The Criminal Court of the City of New York.
Office: 360 Adams Street, Brooklyn 11201.
Telephone: (718) 643-5349.
E-mail address: jamcmahon@juno.com

LOTTO, Steven A. *(Judge, Suffolk County District Court)*
Mailing address: P.O. Box 9075, Central Islip 11722-9075.
Office: Cohalan Court Complex, 400 Carleton Avenue, Central Islip 11722.
Telephone: (631) 853-4920.

LOUGHLIN, Daniel J. *(Justice, New York Supreme Court Tenth Judicial District)* Certificated. Former Judge, Suffolk County District Court.
Mailing address: P.O. Box 9070, Central Islip 11722-9070.
Office: S-33 Cohalan Court Complex, 400 Carleton Avenue, Central Islip 11722.
Telephone: (631) 853-7620.
Fax: (631) 853-7622

LO VALLO, Sharon M. *(Judge, Buffalo City Court)*
Office: 50 Delaware Avenue, Buffalo 14202.
Telephone: (716) 847-8200.

LOWE, Richard B., III *(Justice, New York Supreme Court First Judicial District)* Former Judge, The Criminal Court of the City of New York.
Office: 100 Centre Street, New York 10013.
Telephone: (212) 374-8151.
Fax: (212) 374-6923
E-mail address: rlowe@courts.state.ny.us

LOYOLA, Guido A. *(Judge, Schenectady City Court)*
Office: 215 Civil Court City Hall, Jay Street, Schenectady 12305.
Telephone: (518) 382-5077.
Fax: (518) 382-5080

LOZITO, Gaetan B. *(Judge, Suffolk County District Court)*
Mailing address: P.O. Box 9075, Central Islip 11722-9075.
Office: Cohalan Court Complex, 400 Carleton Avenue, Central Islip 11722.
Telephone: (631) 853-4920.

LUBOW, Fran L. *(Judge, New York City Family Court)* Appointed by mayor.
Office: 151-20 Jamaica Avenue, Jamaica 11432.
Telephone: (718) 298-0197.

LUCIANO, Daniel F. *(Associate Justice, New York Supreme Court Appellate Division Second Judicial Department)* Elected Justice Tenth Judicial District 1982. Appointed Associate Justice Appellate Division by Governor George E. Pataki May 30, 1996. Certificated. Formerly served Appellate Term Ninth and Tenth Judicial Districts.
Mailing address: P.O. Box 9070, Central Islip 11722-9070.
Office: Cohalan Court Complex, 400 Carleton Avenue, Central Islip 11722.
Telephone: (631) 853-7725.
Fax: (631) 853-7444

LUDINGTON, Spencer J. *(Judge, Fulton City Court)*
Office: Municipal Building, 141 South First Street, Fulton 13069.
Telephone: (315) 593-8400.
Fax: (315) 592-3415

LUNN, Robert J. *(Justice, New York Supreme Court Seventh Judicial District)* Elected to term beginning Jan 1, 1995.
Office: 545 Hall of Justice, 99 Exchange Boulevard, Rochester 14614-2185.
Telephone: (585) 428-2883.
Fax: (585) 428-4517
E-mail address: rlunn@courts.state.ny.us

LYNAUGH, Barbara *(Judge, Suffolk County Family Court)* Hearing Examiner June 1993 to Dec 2000. Elected Nov 2000 to term beginning Jan 2001. Term expires Dec 2010. Born Brooklyn New York Aug 13, 1952. Catholic. Educated at State University of New York at Old Westbury B.A. 1981 and Hofstra University School of Law J.D. with honors 1984. Admitted to practice New York 1986.

Staff Attorney Family Court Division Suffolk County Legal Aid Society May 1985 to May 1993. Member Suffolk County Women's Bar Association and Suffolk County Bar Association (Professional Ethics Committee, Bench Bar Committee, Family Court Committee, Matrimonial Bar Committee).
Office: Cohalan Court Complex, 400 Carleton Avenue, Central Islip 11722.
Telephone: (631) 853-4286.
Fax: (631) 853-4359
E-mail address: blynaugh@courts.state.ny.us

LYNCH, Gerard E. *(Judge, United States District Court Southern District of New York)* Appointed for life by President Bill Clinton to term beginning Aug 31, 2000. Born Brooklyn New York Sept 4, 1951. Educated at Columbia University B.A. 1972 J.D. 1975. Law Clerk to Hon. Wilfred Feinberg, U.S. Court of Appeals Second Circuit 1975-76 and Hon. William J. Brennan, Jr., U.S. Supreme Court 1976-77. In legal practice New York City 1992-2000.

Assistant U.S. Attorney 1980-83 and Chief Criminal Division 1990-92 Southern District of New York. Asso-

LYNCH, GERARD E.—*Continued*

ciate Counsel Office of Independent Counsel (Iran/Contra) 1988-90.

Office: 803 U.S. Courthouse, 40 Centre Street, New York 10007-1581.

Telephone: (212) 805-0427.

LYNCH, Harold J. *(Judge, New York City Family Court)* Appointed by Mayor Edward Koch to term beginning Aug 1, 1984. Reappointed 1994, current term expires 2004. Born New York New York Sept 23, 1941. Roman Catholic. Educated at Fordham University B.A. 1963 and New York University LL.B. 1966. Admitted to practice New York 1966 and U.S. District Courts Southern 1976 and Eastern 1976 Districts of New York. Began legal practice New York City 1967.

Assistant Corporation Counsel New York City 1967-70. Law Assistant to New York Supreme Court 1970-76. Law Secretary to Presiding Justice Francis T. Murphy, New York Supreme Court Appellate Division First Judicial Department 1977-84. Member New York State Family Court Judges Association and New York County Lawyers' Association. Recipient awards from New York Small Claims Arbitrators and New York City Law Secretaries and Law Assistants Association. Specialist Four New York State National Guard 1967-70. Republican. Member Ancient Order of Hibernians and Emerald Society. Enjoys chess and fine restaurants.

Office: 900 Sheridan Avenue, Bronx 10451.

Telephone: (718) 590-3376.

Fax: (718) 590-7305

MAAS, Frank *(Magistrate Judge, United States District Court Southern District of New York)* Appointed by U.S. District Court judges to term beginning June 1999. Term expires June 2007. Educated at State University of New York at Binghamton B.A. 1972 and New York University J.D. 1976. Staff member 1974-75 and Articles Editor 1975-76 New York University Journal of International Law and Politics. Law Clerk to Hon. Henry F. Werker, U.S. District Court Southern District of New York 1976-78. Admitted to practice New York 1977, U.S. District Courts Southern 1977, Eastern 1990 and Northern 1995 Districts of New York and U.S. Court of Appeals Second Circuit 1981. In legal practice Oct 1978 to Feb 1980 and since Oct 1986.

Assistant U.S. Attorney Criminal Division Southern District of New York Feb 1980 to Oct 1986. Deputy Commissioner June 1995 to Sept 1996 and First Deputy Commissioner 1996-99 New York City Department of Investigation. Former Member New York Council of Defense Lawyers. Member Federal Magistrate Judges Association, Federal Bar Council, The Association of the Bar of the City of New York (Member 1983-85 and Chair Pretrial Detention Subcommittee 1984-85 Committee on Juvenile Justice, Member 1985-88 and Chair Subcommittee on Front Running and Insider Trading 1988-89 Committee on Commodities Regulation, Member Council on Judicial Administration since 1997) and New York State Bar Association (Executive Committee Federal and Commercial Litigation Section since 1984).

Office: 740 U.S. Courthouse, 500 Pearl Street, New York 10007-1312.

Telephone: (212) 805-6727.

MacKENZIE, Carol *(Judge, Suffolk County District Court)* Currently serves as Acting Judge.

Mailing address: P.O. Box 9075, Central Islip 11722-9075.

Office: Cohalan Court Complex, 400 Carleton Avenue, Central Islip 11722.

Telephone: (631) 853-4919.

MADDEN, Joan A. *(Justice, New York Supreme Court First Judicial District)* Former Judge, The Civil Court of the City of New York.

Office: 60 Centre Street, New York 10007.

Telephone: (212) 374-5654.

MAHER, William L. *(Judge, Peekskill City Court)*

Office: Two Nelson Avenue, Peekskill 10566.

Telephone: (914) 737-3405.

Fax: (914) 736-1889

MAHON, Roy S. *(Justice, New York Supreme Court Tenth Judicial District)* Former Judge, Nassau County District Court.

Office: Supreme Court Building, 100 Supreme Court Drive, Mineola 11501.

Telephone: (516) 571-2837.

MAHONEY, David J. *(Justice, New York Supreme Court Eighth Judicial District)* Certificated.

Office: 50 Delaware Avenue, Buffalo 14202.

Telephone: (716) 851-3397.

Fax: (716) 851-3440

E-mail address: dmahoney@courts.state.ny.us

MAIN, Robert G., Jr. *(Judge, Franklin County Court)* Elected 1987 to term beginning Jan 1, 1988. Reelected Nov 1997, current term expires Dec 31, 2007. Currently serves as Acting Justice, New York Supreme Court Fourth Judicial District. Also serves Franklin County Surrogate's Court and Franklin County Family Court. Born Malone New York May 12, 1951. Roman Catholic. Educated at Middlebury College A.B. 1973 J.D. 1976. Admitted to practice New York 1977 and U.S. District Court Northern District of New York 1977. In legal practice Malone 1976-87.

Former Village Attorney Malone. Former Adjunct Professor of Business Law North Country Community College. Member Franklin County (Former Secretary) and New York State Bar Associations. Republican. Trustee and Former Chair Alice Hyde Hospital Medical Center. President Farrar Home. Board of Directors Morningside Cemetery.

Office: Courthouse, 355 West Main Street, Malone 12953.

Telephone: (518) 481-1732.

MAJOR, Charles T. *(Justice, New York Supreme Court Fifth Judicial District)* Elected to term beginning Jan 1, 1995.

Office: Onondaga County Courthouse, 401 Montgomery Street, Syracuse 13202.

Telephone: (315) 671-1106.

MAKOWSKI, Joseph G. *(Justice, New York Supreme Court Eighth Judicial District)*

Office: Erie County Hall, 92 Franklin Street, Buffalo 14202.

Telephone: (716) 851-3295.

Fax: (716) 851-3384

E-mail address: jmakowski@courts.state.ny.us

MALONE, Bernard J., Jr. *(Justice, New York Supreme Court Third Judicial District)*
Office: 271 Albany County Courthouse, 16 Eagle Street, Albany 12207.
Telephone: (518) 487-5130.
Fax: (518) 487-5137
E-mail address: bmalone@courts.state.ny.us

MALTESE, Joseph J. *(Judge, New York Court of Claims)* Appointed by Governor George E. Pataki July 3, 1996. Currently serves as Acting Justice, New York Supreme Court Second Judicial District. Former Judge, The Civil Court of the City of New York.
Office: Homeport, 355 Front Street, Staten Island 10304.
Telephone: (718) 876-6429.
Fax: (718) 876-6428
E-mail address: jmaltese@courts.state.ny.us

MANEY, Gerard E. *(Judge, Albany County Family Court)* Also serves as Supervising Judge Family Courts Third Judicial District.
Office: One Van Tromp Street, Albany 12207.
Telephone: (518) 427-3560.
Fax: (518) 427-3562
E-mail address: gmaney@courts.state.ny.us

MANGANO, Guy J., Jr. *(Judge, New York Court of Claims)* Currently serves as Acting Justice, New York Supreme Court Second Judicial District.
Office: 120 Schermerhorn Street, Brooklyn 11201.
Telephone: (718) 643-4191.
E-mail address: gmangano@courts.state.ny.us

MANN, Roanne L. *(Magistrate Judge, United States District Court Eastern District of New York)* Appointed by U.S. District Court judges to term beginning 1994. Educated at Yale College B.A. magna cum laude 1972 and Stanford Law School J.D. Managing Editor Stanford Law Review 1975. Law Clerk to U.S. Court of Appeals District of Columbia Circuit. In legal practice New York 1986-94.
Office: U.S. Courthouse, 225 Cadman Plaza East, Brooklyn 11201.
Telephone: (718) 260-2350.

MANZ, David M. *(Judge, Buffalo City Court)*
Office: 50 Delaware Avenue, Buffalo 14202.
Telephone: (716) 847-8269.
Fax: (716) 847-8257

MANZANET, Sallie *(Justice, New York Supreme Court Twelfth Judicial District)* Former Judge, The Civil Court of the City of New York.
Office: 851 Grand Concourse, Bronx 10451.
Telephone: (718) 590-3666.
Fax: (718) 590-8914

MARANO, Anthony F. *(Justice, New York Supreme Court Tenth Judicial District)* Former Judge, Nassau County District Court.
Office: Matrimonial Center, 400 County Seat Drive, Mineola 11501.
Telephone: (516) 571-0021.

MARBER, Randy Sue *(Judge, Nassau County District Court)*
Office: 99 Main Street, Hempstead 11550.
Telephone: (516) 571-2133.

MARCUS, Martin *(Judge, New York Court of Claims)* Appointed by governor. Currently serves as Acting Justice, New York Supreme Court Twelfth Judicial District.
Office: 851 Grand Concourse, Bronx 10451.
Telephone: (718) 590-6364.
Fax: (718) 590-7296

MARIN, Alan C. *(Judge, New York Court of Claims)* Appointed by Governor George E. Pataki.
Office: 71 Thomas Street, Suite 8399, New York 10013.
Telephone: (917) 538-8547.

MARKEY, Charles J. *(Judge, The Civil Court of the City of New York)*
Office: 89-17 Sutphin Boulevard, Jamaica 11435.
Telephone: (718) 262-7120.

MARKS, John G. *(Judge, Nassau County Family Court)* Former Judge, Nassau County District Court.
Office: 1200 Old Country Road, Westbury 11590.
Telephone: (516) 571-9010.

MARKS, Patricia D. *(Judge, Monroe County Court)* Elected to term beginning Jan 1, 1985. Reelected 1994, current term expires Dec 31, 2004. Currently serves as Acting Justice, New York Supreme Court Seventh Judicial District. Also serves as Supervising Judge Criminal Courts Seventh Judicial District. Born Flushing New York Oct 8, 1949. Catholic. Educated at Vassar College B.A. 1971 and Albany Law School of Union University J.D. 1974. Admitted to practice New York 1975 and U.S. District Court Western District of New York 1975. In legal practice Monroe County 1975-84. Former Acting Judge, Monroe County Family Court.
Legal Assistant Monroe County Department of Social Services 1975-76. Assistant District Attorney Monroe County 1976-84. Instructor Criminal Justice Training Center 1977-83. Chair New York State Committee on Criminal Jury Instructions since 1992 and Evidence Curriculum New York State Judicial Seminars. Former Member Greater Rochester Association for Women Attorneys, Monroe County (Board of Trustees 1983-85) and New York State Bar Associations. Member Judicial Capital Cases Resource Committee, New York State Association of Women Judges, County Judges Association of the State of New York (Program Chair 1989 and 1990, Second Vice President 1991, President 1992-93, Member Executive Committee) and National Association of Women Judges. Lecturer Police Academy seminars for law enforcement New York State Bar Association May 1998 and Nov 1999. Participant Judicial Leadership in Education University of Memphis and Judicial Leadership Training in Administration National Center State Courts. Recipient Distinguished Citizen Award from Rochester Police Department Rosewood Club 1994. Democrat. Board of Directors Adam Walsh Child Resources Center 1985-86, Rochester Society for the Prevention of Cruelty to Children 1985-99, Community Partners for Youth since 1988 and Rochester Women's Network 1990-92. Advisory Council Highland Hospital OB-GYN 1988-91. Member Adam Walsh Resource Center and Rape Crisis Service Advisory Committee. Enjoys bowling and baseball.
Office: 545 Hall of Justice, 99 Exchange Boulevard, Rochester 14614-2185.
Telephone: (585) 428-5276.
Fax: (585) 428-2990

MARLOW, George D. *(Associate Justice, New York Supreme Court Appellate Division First Judicial Department)* Former Acting Justice Ninth Judicial District. Acting Justice Second Judicial District 1987, 1988 and 1997. Elected Justice Ninth Judicial District to term beginning Jan 1, 1999. Term expires Dec 31, 2013. Appointed Associate Justice Appellate Division by Governor George E. Pataki to term beginning March 21, 2001. Term expires March 20, 2006. Born New York New York June 8, 1941. Jewish. Educated at St. Lawrence University B.A. 1963, St. John's University School of Law J.D. 1966 and University of Nevada at Reno Masters of Judicial Studies 1997. Law Clerk to Hon. Albert M. Rosenblatt, Dutchess County Court 1976-79. Admitted to practice New York 1967, U.S. District Courts Eastern 1968 and Southern 1968 Districts of New York, U.S. Court of Appeals Second Circuit 1968 and U.S. Supreme Court 1980. In legal practice Poughkeepsie and Hopewell 1976-83. Justice, Poughkeepsie Town Justice Court 1980-83. Judge, Dutchess County Family Court 1984-92. Judge, Dutchess County Court Jan 1, 1993 to 1999.

Assistant District Attorney Queens County 1967-71. Senior Assistant District Attorney Dutchess County 1971-75. Co-author with Adina C. Gilbert "Ex Parte Orders of Protection in Cases of Domestic Violence" New York L. Jour. 1 July 16, 1987, reprinted 20 No. 1 Family L. Rev. New York State Bar Association March 1988 and with Thomas P. Flaherty "Invidious Discrimination: New Rules of Judicial Conduct" New York L. Jour. 1 June 9, 1997. Author "Opinions of the New York State Advisory Committee on Judicial Ethics; Their Language and Rhetoric" 69 No. 7 New York State B. Jour. 32 Nov 1997, "From Black Robes to White Lab Coats: The Ethical Implications of a Judge's Sua Sponte, Ex Parte Acquisition of Social and Other Scientific Evidence During the Decision Making Process" 72 Book 32 St. John's L. Rev. June 1998 and "Perspective" New York L. Jour. 2 July 30, 1998. Important Decisions: Ritz v. Ritz 152 Misc. 2d 432; Dutchess County Department of Social Services o/b/o T.G. v. Mr. and Mrs. G. 141 Misc. 2d 641; Desmond v. Desmond 134 Misc. 2d 62; Matter of Janet C. 130 Misc. 2d 1043; Matter of T. G. 128 Misc. 2d 914; Department of Social Services v. Barbara M. 123 Misc. 2d 523; People v. Hall 117 Misc. 2d 1085; A.K.A.B. & D. Mobile Home Rentals, Inc. v. Marshall 114 Misc. 2d 622; Wheeler v. Wheeler N.Y.S.L.J. Aug 2, 1985; Department of Social Services o/b/o SDG v. Mr. and Mrs. G. N.Y.L.J. Oct 26, 1989 and Family L. Rev. New York State Bar Association Dec 1989; People v. Edmonds 157 Misc. 2d 966; People v. Curtis 160 Misc. 2d 508 N.Y.L.J. Feb 1, 1994; People v. Nesbitt N.Y.L.J. Aug 23, 1994; People v. Patterson 165 Misc. 2d 299 N.Y.L.J. May 8, 1995; People v. Gordon and King N.Y.L.J. Oct 20, 1995; People v. McMorris N.Y.L.J. Oct 30, 1995; People v. McIntosh 173 Misc. 2d 724 Jan 30, 1997, 173 Misc. 2d 727 July 8, 1997 and 178 Misc. 2d 433 Aug 25, 1998 N.Y.L.J.; People v. Dixon 172 Misc. 2d 292 N.Y.L.J. March 13, 1997; Maraziti v. Weber 185 Misc. 2d 624; and LaValle v. State of New York 185 Misc. 2d 699.

Member Family Law Curriculum Committee 1987-91, New York State Family Court Advisory and Rules Committee 1987-92, New York State Adoption Advisory Committee 1993, New York State Advisory Committee on Criminal Law and Procedure 1993-99, Criminal Law Curriculum Committee 1993-2001, Committee to Promote Gender Fairness in the Courts Ninth Judicial District since 1998 and New York State Commission on Fiduciary Appointments since 2000. Member since 1987 and Co-chair since 1996 New York State Advisory Committee on Judicial Ethics. Co-chair Capital Case Judicial Resource Committee since 1995. Member Dutchess County Magistrates Association, New York State Association of Magistrates, County Judges Association of the State of New York (Liaison to Bar Criminal Justice Section 1993-99), Association of Judges of the Family Court of the State of New York (Chair Domestic Violence Committee 1986-89, Chair Public Relations Committee 1990-92), Association of Justices of the Supreme Court of the State of New York, Mid-Hudson Women's, Dutchess County (President 1991-92, Chair Endowment Fund since 1995) and New York State (House of Delegates 1992-94) Bar Associations. Faculty Member and Coordinator Advanced Judicial Education Programs for Dutchess County's Town and Village Justices since 1985. Instructor Dutchess County Task Force on Child Protection 1986-90. Faculty Member Annual Judicial Training Seminar for all New York State Judges and Justices since 1987, Annual Seminars on Judicial Ethics, Judicial Writing and Capital Case Litigation since 1991 and Seminar on New York State's New Death Penalty Statutes and Judicial Ethics since 1995. Guest Lecturer seminars Law Guardian Advisory Committee Ninth Judicial District 1986-90, on American courts and domestic violence and child abuse for judges, lawyers, police and other professionals Dominica Jan 13-26, 1991 and Seminar on Basic Criminal Law Practice New York State Bar Association 1995 and 1998. State Alumni Liaison The National Judicial College 1991-98. President Dogwood Knolls Civic Association 1976-77. Board Member Dutchess County Alcoholism Information and Referral Center 1976-79 and Mid-Hudson Vietnam Veterans Outreach Center 1984-86. Board of Directors Dutchess County Jewish Community Center 1977-79. Advisory Board Dutchess County Mediation Center 1989-94. Board of Trustees Vassar Brothers Hospital 1991-99. Member Committee to Enhance Racial Harmony in Dutchess County 1992-94 and Southern Dutchess Exchange Club.

Office: 27 Madison Avenue, New York 10010.
Telephone: (212) 340-0593.

MARON, Edward A. *(Judge, Nassau County District Court)* Elected Nov 1999 to term beginning Jan 1, 2000. Term expires Dec 31, 2005. Born Brooklyn New York. Jewish. Educated at Yeshiva University B.A. 1961 and St. John's University School of Law J.D. 1964. Member Phi Delta Phi. Admitted to practice New York 1964 and U.S. Supreme Court 1968. In legal practice New York 1964-99. Administrative Law Judge, New York City 1995-99.

Member Nassau County District Court Judges Association, District Court Judges Association of the State of New York, Criminal Court Bar Association of Nassau County, Bar Association of Nassau County, Brooklyn and New York State Bar Associations.

Office: 99 Main Street, Hempstead 11550.
Telephone: (516) 572-2127.
Fax: (516) 572-2538
E-mail address: emaron@courts.state.ny.us

MARRANO, Frederic J. *(Judge, Lackawanna City Court)* Appointed Acting Judge by mayor to term beginning Aug 8, 1985. Reappointed to subsequent terms.

MARRANO, FREDERIC J.—*Continued*

Currently serves as Chief Judge. Born Lackawanna New York July 8, 1951. Roman Catholic. Educated at State University of New York at Fredonia B.A. 1973. Admitted to practice New York 1979. Began legal practice Lackawanna and Buffalo 1979.

Member New York State Trial Lawyers Association, New York State Defenders Association, Inc., American Judicature Society, Bar Association of Erie County, New York State and American Bar Associations. Participant seminar for New York State Judges New York State Office of Court Administration, Syracuse Aug 1986. Worked for Bethlehem Steel Corporation 1973-77. Democrat. Member Knights of Columbus, St. Anthony's Holy Name Society and Galanti Athletic Association. Interests include fishing and astronomy.

Office: City Hall, 714 Ridge Road, Lackawanna 14218-1588.
Telephone: (716) 827-6672.
Fax: (716) 825-1874

MARRERO, Louis John *(Justice, New York Supreme Court Second Judicial District)*
Office: 360 Adams Street, Brooklyn 11201.
Telephone: (718) 643-7026.
E-mail address: lmarrero@courts.state.ny.us

MARRERO, Victor *(Judge, United States District Court Southern District of New York)* Appointed for life by President Bill Clinton Oct 5, 1999 to term beginning Dec 1, 1999. Born Santurce Puerto Rico Sept 1, 1941. Educated at New York University B.A. cum laude 1964, University of Sheffield, England 1966-67 and Yale Law School J.D. 1968. Fulbright Scholar. Editor Yale Law Journal. In legal practice 1982-93.

Visiting Lecturer on Real Estate, Land Use and Environmental Law Yale Law School 1985-87 and Columbia University School of Law 1990-93. Chairman New York State Chief Judge's Committee to Improve the Availability of Legal Services. Co-chair Chief Judge's Pro Bono Review Committee. Member Governor's Task Force on Bias-Related Violence and The Association of the Bar of the City of New York (Vice President, Member Executive Committee, Judiciary Committee, Committee for Modern Courts, Delegate House of Delegates New York State Bar Association). Recipient Root/Stimson Public Service Award from New York State Bar Association 1992, Pro Bono Publico Award from American Bar Association 1993 and Ellis Island Medal of Honor 1999. Former Ambassador U.S. Representative on the Economic and Social Council of the United Nations and Permanent Representative of the U.S. to Organization of American States. Former Undersecretary U.S. Department of Housing and Urban Development. Former First Assistant Counsel to Governor Hugh L. Carey. Former Special Counsel to New York City Comptroller. Former Assistant Administrator Model Cities Administration. Former Executive Director Department of City Planning. Former Assistant to Mayor John V. Lindsay New York City. Founder, First Chairman of the Board and Director/Trustee Puerto Rican Legal Defense and Education Fund. Vice Chairman of the Board and Director/Trustee New York Public Library. Board of Directors/Trustees New York Telephone Company and Consolidated Edison Company. Director/Trustee State University of New York, The Cooper Union for the Advancement of Science and Art, Educational Broadcasting Corporation and New York City Partnership.

Office: 414 U.S. Courthouse, 40 Centre Street, New York 10007-1581.
Telephone: (212) 805-6374.

MARRUS, Alan D. *(Judge, The Criminal Court of the City of New York)* Appointed by Mayor Edward Koch to term beginning Feb 17, 1983. Reappointed by Mayor David Dinkins Nov 24, 1992. Acting Justice, New York Supreme Court Second Judicial District since Jan 1, 1986. Educated at Brooklyn College B.A. 1967 and George Washington University J.D. cum laude 1970. Associate George Washington Law Review 1968-70.
Office: 120 Schermerhorn Street, Brooklyn 11201.
Telephone: (718) 643-7156.
E-mail address: amarrus@courts.state.ny.us

MARSHALL, Frederick J. *(Justice, New York Supreme Court Eighth Judicial District)*
Office: Erie County Hall, 92 Franklin Street, Buffalo 14202.
Telephone: (716) 851-3407.
Fax: (716) 851-3315
E-mail address: fmarshall@courts.state.ny.us

MARTIN, Daniel *(Judge, New York Court of Claims)* Appointed by Governor George E. Pataki. Currently serves as Acting Justice, New York Supreme Court Tenth Judicial District.
Office: Supreme Court Building, 100 Supreme Court Drive, Mineola 11501.
Telephone: (516) 571-3891.
Fax: (516) 571-1095

MARTIN, John S., Jr. *(Judge, United States District Court Southern District of New York)* Appointed for life by President George Bush May 22, 1990. Educated at Manhattan College B.A. 1957 and Columbia University School of Law LL.B. 1961. James Kent Scholar. Admitted to practice New York 1961. Began legal practice New York.
Office: 1620 U.S. Courthouse, 500 Pearl Street, New York 10007-1312.
Telephone: (212) 805-0228.

MARTIN, Larry D. *(Justice, New York Supreme Court Second Judicial District)* Former Judge, The Civil Court of the City of New York.
Office: 360 Adams Street, Brooklyn 11201.
Telephone: (718) 643-7028.
E-mail address: ldmartin@courts.state.ny.us

MARTIN, LaTia W. *(Justice, New York Supreme Court Twelfth Judicial District)* Former Acting Justice. Former Judge, The Criminal Court of the City of New York, appointed by Mayor Rudolph Giuliani. Former Judge, The Civil Court of the City of New York.
Office: 851 Grand Concourse, Bronx 10451.
Telephone: (718) 590-3919.
Fax: (718) 590-8914

MARTINELLI, Michael A. *(Judge, Yonkers City Court)* Elected Nov 7, 1995 to term beginning Jan 1, 1996. Term expires Dec 31, 2005. Born Mt. Vernon New York Nov 30, 1950. Roman Catholic. Educated at University of Notre Dame B.A. 1972 and St. John's University J.D. 1975. Admitted to practice 1976, U.S. District Court Southern District of New York 1979 and

MARTINELLI, MICHAEL A.—*Continued*

U.S. Supreme Court 1991. In legal practice Yonkers 1976-95 and New York City 1983-88.

Member Yonkers Lawyers Association (President 1993-94), Columbian Lawyers Association of Westchester County (Founding Member Board of Directors, President 2003-04), Women's Bar Association of Westchester County and Westchester County Bar Association. Named Man of the Year by Yonkers Tenants Coalition 1979. Republican. Member Enrico Fermi Scholarship Committee. Little League Manager. Enjoys music, baseball, history and reading. Personal Statement or Quote: "A life is not important, except in the impact it has on other lives" (Jackie Robinson).

Office: Justice Center, 100 South Broadway, Yonkers 10701.

Telephone: (914) 377-6368.

Fax: (914) 377-6395

E-mail address: mamartin@courts.state.ny.us

MARTOCHE, Salvatore R. *(Justice, New York Supreme Court Eighth Judicial District)*

Office: One Niagara Plaza, Buffalo 14202.

Telephone: (716) 858-4782.

Fax: (716) 858-4783

MARTUSEWICZ, Kim H. *(Judge, Jefferson County Court)*

Office: Courthouse, 195 Arsenal Street, Watertown 13601-2577.

Telephone: (315) 785-3010.

Fax: (315) 786-6931

E-mail address: kmartuse@courts.state.ny.us

MARVIN, Seth L. *(Judge, The Criminal Court of the City of New York)* Appointed by Mayor Rudolph W. Giuliani.

Office: 215 East 161st Street, Bronx 10451.

Telephone: (718) 590-2927.

Fax: (718) 590-7297

E-mail address: smarvin@courts.state.ny.us

MASON, Reynold N. *(Justice, New York Supreme Court Second Judicial District)* Elected to term beginning Jan 5, 1998. Term expires Dec 31, 2011. Born Grenada West Indies Oct 31, 1949. Methodist. Educated at Brooklyn College of the City University of New York B.A. cum laude 1977 and New York Law School J.D. 1982. Admitted to practice New York 1983, U.S. District Courts Eastern 1983 and Southern 1983 Districts of New York and U.S. Supreme Court 1991. Judge, The Civil Court of the City of New York Jan 1, 1995 to 1997.

Assistant Corporate Counsel and Corporate Counsel New York City 1983-85. Instructor Monroe College 1983-84 and Brooklyn College of the City University of New York 1993-94. Member Brooklyn, New York State and Caribbean-American Bar Associations. Attended Annual Judicial Conference New York 1995-97. E-4 U.S. Army 1971-73. Enjoys reading, jogging and travel.

Office: 360 Adams Street, Brooklyn 11201.

Telephone: (718) 643-8038.

E-mail address: rmason@courts.state.ny.us

MASSARO, Dominic R. *(Judge, New York Court of Claims)* Appointed by Governor Mario Cuomo Dec 13, 1986. Reappointed by Governor George E. Pataki June 13, 1996. Acting Justice, New York Supreme Court Twelfth Judicial District since 1987. Educated at New York University B.S. M.P.A., Long Island University M.S. and New York Law School J.D. Honorary Diploma Academic Pontifical Tiberian Academy, Rome. Honorary degrees in law, letters and judicial administration.

Human Rights Commissioner New York City 1967-70 and New York State 1971-75. U.S. Regional Director of ACTION 1976-77. Author "Cesare Beccaria—The Father of Criminal Justice: His Impact on Anglo-American Jurisprudence" Universitas Internationalis Press Pescia Italy 1991, "Provisional Remedies" *Enforcing Judgments in New York* West Publishing Company 1996 and "Foreordained Failure: New York's Experiment with Political Review of Constitutionality" Sept 1998 and "Taking Title to New York: The Enduring Authority of Roman Law" Jan 2000 New York State B. Jour. President National Commission for Social Justice 1989-91. Principal Representative American Judges Association to the United Nations since 1992. Delegate Rome Conference on the Creation of the International Criminal Court 1998. Director American Justinian Society of Jurists. Member New York State Appeals Board Selective Service System 1972-76. Member New York State (Committee on Federal Constitution since 1987) and American Bar Associations. Named Outstanding Young Man of America by U.S. Jaycees 1965 and Outstanding Citizen of Bronx County 1986. Recipient Police Honor Legion of the City of New York 1964, International Dorso Prize 1991 and Lehman LaGuardia Award in Civil Rights from Anti-Defamation League of B'nai B'rith 1994. Knighted Grand Cross by Organization of Latin American States at the United Nations 1989, by The Vatican 1994, by Republic of Italy 1998 and by Sovereign Order of Malta 2002. Major New York Guard JAGC. Woodrow Wilson Visiting Fellow since 1992. President Gramacy Boys Club of New York 1973-74 and Bronx Chamber of Commerce 1985-87. Director Lavelle School for the Blind since 1976. President Emeritus The Conference of Presidents of Major Italian American Organizations. Diplomat Colombian Academy of International Law.

Office: 851 Grand Concourse, Bronx 10451.

Telephone: (718) 590-3771.

MASSELL, Martin J. *(Judge, Nassau County District Court)*

Office: 99 Main Street, Hempstead 11550.

Telephone: (516) 571-2200.

MASTRO, William F. *(Associate Justice, New York Supreme Court Appellate Division Second Judicial Department)* Elected Justice Second Judicial District. Appointed Associate Justice Appellate Division by Governor George E. Pataki.

Office: 130 Stuyvesant Place, Staten Island 10301.

Telephone: (718) 390-5357.

Fax: (718) 720-6403

E-mail address: wmastro@courts.state.ny.us

MATHEWS, Patrick H. *(Judge, Broome County Court)* Also serves Broome County Family Court.

Mailing address: P.O. Box 1766, Binghamton 13902-1766.

Office: 65 Hawley Street, Binghamton 13901.

Telephone: (607) 778-2431.

Fax: (607) 778-6133

MATTINA, Joseph S. *(Surrogate, Erie County Surrogate's Court)* Elected to term beginning Jan 1, 1982. Reelected 1991 and 2001, current term expires Dec 31, 2011. Currently serves as Acting Justice, New York Su-

MATTINA, JOSEPH S.—*Continued*
preme Court Eighth Judicial District. Born Buffalo New York March 19, 1933. Roman Catholic. Educated at University of Buffalo 1950-53 J.D. 1956. Member Alpha Sigma Phi. Admitted to practice New York 1956. In legal practice Buffalo 1957-65. Judge, Buffalo City Court 1965-69. Judge, Erie County Court 1969-74. Justice, New York Supreme Court Eighth Judicial District 1974-81.

Assistant District Attorney Erie County 1958-63. Coauthor with Hon. James M. Burns *Sentencing* The National Judicial College 1978. Adjunct Professor of Criminal Justice State University of New York at Buffalo 1969-90. Member Bar Association of Erie County, New York State and American Bar Associations. Instructor The National Judicial College 1970-92. Named Outstanding Citizen of the Year by *The Buffalo News* 1969 and one of the 200 Young Citizens of the United States by *Time* Magazine 1974. Recipient Certificate of Commendation from New York State Developmental Disabilities Council 1989, Award for Outstanding Contributions to Litigants and Attorneys from Matrimonial Bar of Erie County 1990, Distinguished Alumnus Award from State University of New York at Buffalo School of Law 1991, Treat Award for Excellence from National College of Probate Judges Sept 1998 and Edwin F. Jaeckle Award from State University of New York at Buffalo School of Law and Law Alumni Association Nov 1998. Inducted into The National Judicial College Hall of Fame 1988 (Charter Member). Past President and Chairman of the Board Buffalo Columbus Hospital. Chairman Research and Planning Council United Way. Interests include golf and writing.

Office: Erie County Hall, 92 Franklin Street, Buffalo 14202.
Telephone: (716) 854-7867.
Fax: (716) 853-3741
E-mail address: jmattina@courts.state.ny.us

MAXWELL, Patricia Anne *(Judge, Erie County Family Court)*
Office: One Niagara Plaza, Buffalo 14202.
Telephone: (716) 858-8188.
Fax: (716) 858-8432

MAZZARELLI, Angela *(Associate Justice, New York Supreme Court Appellate Division First Judicial Department)* Former Acting Justice. Elected Justice First Judicial District. Appointed Associate Justice Appellate Division by governor. Former Judge, The Civil Court of the City of New York.
Office: 27 Madison Avenue at 25th Street, New York 10010.
Telephone: (212) 340-0400.

McAVOY, Thomas J. *(Judge, United States District Court Northern District of New York)* Appointed for life by President Ronald Reagan. Former Chief Judge. Educated at Albany Law School of Union University J.D. cum laude 1964. Articles Editor Albany Law Review. Admitted to practice New York 1964 and U.S. District Court Northern District of New York 1964. In legal practice Binghamton 1964-86. Legislator Broome County 1972-86.
Office: 225 Federal Building, 15 Henry Street, Binghamton 13901.
Telephone: (607) 773-2892.

McCABE, Edward G. *(Justice, New York Supreme Court Tenth Judicial District)* Elected to term beginning Jan 1, 1986. Reelected 1999, current term expires Dec 31, 2013. Currently serves as Administrative Judge Nassau County.
Office: Supreme Court Building, 100 Supreme Court Drive, Mineola 11501.
Telephone: (516) 571-2684.

McCARTHY, James W. *(Judge, Oswego County Court)* Elected Nov 1992 to term beginning Jan 1, 1993. Reelected 2002, current term expires Dec 31, 2012. Born Syracuse New York. Catholic. Educated at State University of New York at Oswego B.A. with honors 1970 and Union University J.D. 1977. Admitted to practice New York 1978 and U.S. District Courts Northern 1978 and Western 1979 Districts of New York. In legal practice Oswego since 1978. Judge, Oswego City Court Oct 14, 1988 to Dec 31, 1992.

Assistant City Attorney 1978-83 and City Attorney 1983-88 Oswego. U.S. Army 1971-74.
Office: Public Safety Center, 39 Churchill Road, Oswego 13126.
Telephone: (315) 349-3286.
Fax: (315) 349-8525

McCARTY, Edward W., III *(Justice, New York Supreme Court Tenth Judicial District)* Elected Nov 5, 1991 to term beginning Jan 1, 1992. Term expires Dec 31, 2005. Born Brooklyn New York Oct 25, 1945. Roman Catholic. Educated at Siena College B.S. 1967, St. John's University School of Law J.D. 1970 and New York University 1983. Admitted to practice New York 1971, U.S. District Courts Eastern 1974 and Southern 1974 Districts of New York and U.S. Court of Appeals Second Circuit 1974. Judge, Nassau County District Court 1985-91.

Special Prosecutor—Professional Conduct 1971-72. Assistant District Attorney Nassau County 1972-85. Important Decisions: Fallarino v. Board of Education 160 Misc. 2d. 682, Matter of Fein v. Fein 160 Misc. 2d. 760, People v. King 137 Misc. 2d. 1070 and Heritage County v. Cutrone 137 Misc. 2d. 839. Instructor in Trial Techniques Hofstra University School of Law since 1978. Member Nassau County and New York State Bar Associations. Instructor in Trial Techniques National Institute of Trial Advocacy since 1979. Colonel USAR JAGC. Republican. Competes in triathlons.
Office: Supreme Court Building, 100 Supreme Court Drive, Mineola 11501.
Telephone: (516) 571-2154.

McCOOE, William P. *(Justice, New York Supreme Court First Judicial District)* Certificated. Also serves as Justice, New York Supreme Court Appellate Term First Judicial Department.
Office: 60 Centre Street, Room 401, New York 10007.
Telephone: (212) 374-8578.

McCORD, Richard J. *(Judge, Glen Cove City Court)*
Office: 13 Glen Street, Glen Cove 11542-2776.
Telephone: (516) 676-0109.
Fax: (516) 676-1570

McCURN, Neal P. *(Senior Judge, United States District Court Northern District of New York)* Appointed for life by President Jimmy Carter Nov 13, 1979. Former Chief Judge. Assumed Senior status, serves by as-

MCCURN, NEAL P.—*Continued*
signment. Born Syracuse New York April 6, 1926. Roman Catholic. Educated at Syracuse University A.B. 1950 LL.B. 1952 replaced by J.D. 1968. Notes and Comment Editor Syracuse University Law Review. Member Phi Delta Phi (Magistrate). Admitted to practice New York 1952, U.S. District Court Northern District of New York 1952 and U.S. Court of Appeals Second Circuit 1966. Began legal practice Syracuse 1952.

Fellow American College of Trial Lawyers. Member American Judicature Society (Board of Directors 1977-81), American Bar Foundation, Onondaga County (Past President), New York State (Chairman Committee on State Constitution and Conference of Local Bar Delegates, Regional Vice Chairman Committee on Judiciary, member Council of Judicial Associations, Committees on Judicial Discipline and Removal, Judicial Administration, Annual Meeting and Young Lawyers) and American (Division of Judicial Administration) Bar Associations. Recipient Distinguished Service Award from Syracuse University College of Law 1978. Cadet Midshipman USNR-USMS 1944-46. Lieutenant j.g. 1946-50. Democrat. Past President Hiscock Legal Aid Society, Syracuse Law College Alumni Association and Syracuse University Alumni Association. Former Chairman Onondaga County Chapter American Red Cross. Chairman Urban League of Central New York (Board of Directors) and Onondaga County Chapter National Foundation. Vice Chairman Human Rights Commission of Syracuse and Onondaga County and Board of Visitors Syracuse Law College. Board of Directors United Way of Central New York (Executive Committee). Member Steering Committee Coalition of Northeast Municipalities, Central New York Chapter March of Dimes (New York State Executive Committee) and Advisory Council Maria Regina College.

Mailing address: P.O. Box 7365, Syracuse 13261-7365.
Telephone: (315) 234-8590.

McDERMOTT, Dennis K. *(Judge, Madison County Court)* Also serves Madison County Surrogate's Court and Madison County Family Court.
Mailing address: P.O. Box 545, Wampsville 13163.
Office: Courthouse, Wampsville 13163.
Telephone: (315) 366-2360.
Fax: (315) 366-2722

McDONALD, Robert J. *(Justice, New York Supreme Court Eleventh Judicial District)* Former Acting Justice. Former Judge, The Civil Court of the City of New York.
Office: 25-10 Court Street, Long Island City 11101.
Telephone: (718) 520-3914.
Fax: (718) 520-8577

McELRATH, Terrence J. *(Judge, New York City Family Court)* Appointed by mayor.
Office: 100 Richmond Terrace, Staten Island 10301.
Telephone: (718) 390-5462.

McGANN, Robert C. *(Judge, The Criminal Court of the City of New York)* Appointed by Mayor Edward Koch to term beginning Feb 5, 1986. Reappointed Jan 1, 1988 and by Mayor Rudolph W. Giuliani Jan 1, 1998. Current term expires Jan 2008. Currently serves as Acting Justice, New York Supreme Court Eleventh Judicial District. Born Queens New York June 11, 1948. Roman Catholic. Educated at Fordham University B.A. 1969 and New York Law School J.D. 1972. Recipient Dean's Award 1972. Book Review Editor New York Law Forum 1971-72. Member Phi Delta Phi. Magister Dwight Inn. Admitted to practice New York 1973, U.S. District Courts Eastern 1975 and Southern 1975 Districts of New York and U.S. Court of Appeals Second Circuit 1975.

Assistant District Attorney Queens County 1972-76. Special Assistant Attorney General 1976-81. Inspector General Department of Personnel New York City 1981-86. Author Comment "Declarations Against Penal Interests" New York Law Forum 1971 and "Prosecution of Arson" Fire Engineering Magazine 1978. Adjunct Assistant Professor of Criminal Justice St. John's University since 1978. Member Blackstone Club, Association of Criminal Court Judges of the City of New York, The Association of the Bar of the City of New York, Queens Criminal Courts and Queens County Bar Associations. Participant National College of District Attorneys Houston 1974 and seminar on Organized Crime Cornell Institute 1977. Member St. Thomas the Apostle Parish Youth Council. Interests include golf, reading and travel.
Office: 25-10 Court Street, Long Island City 11101.
Telephone: (718) 520-3928.

McGAW, Ronald J. *(Judge, Poughkeepsie City Court)*
Mailing address: P.O. Box 300, Poughkeepsie 12602.
Office: Civic Center Plaza, Poughkeepsie 12601.
Telephone: (845) 451-4091.
Fax: (845) 485-6795

McGILL, Patrick R. *(Judge, Clinton County Court)*
Office: 317 County Government Center, 137 Margaret Street, Plattsburgh 12901-2933.
Telephone: (518) 565-4657.
Fax: (518) 565-4887

McGINITY, Leo F. *(Associate Justice, New York Supreme Court Appellate Division Second Judicial Department)* Elected Justice Tenth Judicial District to term beginning Jan 1, 1982. Appointed Associate Justice Appellate Division by Governor George E. Pataki. Certificated. Born Garden City New York Aug 9, 1927. Roman Catholic. Educated at Georgetown University B.A. 1950 and New York Law School LL.B. 1954. Admitted to practice New York 1954. Began legal practice Mineola 1954. Former Supervising Judge, Criminal Courts of Nassau County. Judge, Formerly served as Administrative Judge Nassau County. Judge Nassau County Court 1976-81.

Member Nassau County Criminal Coordinating Council, Catholic Lawyers Guild, Bar Association of Nassau County, Nassau Lawyers Association of Long Island Inc. and Criminal Courts Bar Association (President 1963). Recipient Norman F. Lent Memorial Award from Nassau County Criminal Courts Bar Association 1980. Private First Class USMC 1945-46. Member Town Council Hempstead 1969-76. Board of Sponsors Mercy Hospital. President Baldwin Interfaith Conference 1966 and The Society of the Friendly Sons of Saint Patrick 1984-85.
Office: Supreme Court Building, 100 Supreme Court Drive, Mineola 11501.
Telephone: (516) 571-3320.

McGRATH, Patrick J. *(Judge, Rensselaer County Court)* Born Troy New York Jan 14, 1953. Catholic. Educated at Manhattan College B.A. magna cum laude

MCGRATH, PATRICK J.—*Continued*

1975 and Albany Law School of Union University J.D. 1978. Chief Clerk to Albany County Surrogate's Court 1978-80. Member Phi Beta Kappa. Admitted to practice New York 1979. Former Judge, Troy City Court, assumed office May 16, 1985.

Author *New York Practice Guide: Probate and Estate Administration* Matthew Bender 1985. Member New York State Bar Association.

Office: Rensselaer County Courthouse, Congress & Second Streets, Troy 12180.

Telephone: (518) 270-3737.

McGUIRE, Joseph D. *(Justice, New York Supreme Court Fifth Judicial District)* Elected Nov 2001 to term beginning Jan 1, 2002. Term expires Dec 31, 2015. Born Rochester New York July 6, 1944. Catholic. Educated at St. John Fisher College B.A. 1966 and Albany Law School of Union University J.D. 1969. Law Clerk to Hon. Fred A. Young, New York Court of Claims 1970-73. Admitted to practice New York 1970 and U.S. District Court District of New York 1970. In legal practice Rochester 1969-70 and Lowville 1970-98. Judge, Lewis County Court Jan 1, 1999 to Dec 31, 2001.

Office: Courthouse, 7660 State Street, Lowville 13367-1396.

Telephone: (315) 376-5347.

E-mail address: JMCGUIRE@courts.state.ny.us

McGUIRK, John K. *(Justice, New York Supreme Court Ninth Judicial District)* Former Judge, Orange County Family Court.

Office: 255 Main Street, Goshen 10924.

Telephone: (845) 291-3140.

McKAY, Joseph Kevin *(Judge, The Criminal Court of the City of New York)* Appointed to term beginning Feb 17, 1984. Reappointed 1993, current term expires Dec 31, 2003. Currently serves as Acting Justice, New York Supreme Court Second Judicial District. Educated at Fordham University A.B. 1966 and New York University School of Law J.D. 1969. Admitted to practice New York 1969, U.S. District Courts Southern 1973 and Eastern 1973 Districts of New York, U.S. Court of Appeals Second Circuit 1974, U.S. Supreme Court 1974 and U.S. Tax Court 1978. In legal practice New York City 1974-81. Judge, The Civil Court of the City of New York July 14, 1983 to Feb 16, 1984.

Assistant District Attorney New York County Aug 1969 to Jan 1974. Inspector General New York City Department of Sanitation Aug 1981 to July 1983. Member New York County Lawyers' Association (Federal Courts Committee since 1978), The Association of the Bar of the City of New York, New York State (Federal Courts Committee 1978-82) and American Bar Associations.

Office: 120 Schermerhorn Street, Brooklyn 11201.

Telephone: (718) 643-7158.

E-mail address: jmckay@courts.state.ny.us

McKENNA, Lawrence M. *(Senior Judge, United States District Court Southern District of New York)* Appointed for life by President George Bush to term beginning 1990. Assumed Senior status May 24, 2002, serves by assignment. Born New York New York Nov 7, 1933. Educated at Fordham College A.B. 1956 and Columbia University School of Law LL.B. 1959. In legal practice New York City 1959-90.

Office: 1640 U.S. Courthouse, 500 Pearl Street, New York 10007-1312.

Telephone: (212) 805-0230.

McKEON, Douglas E. *(Justice, New York Supreme Court Twelfth Judicial District)* Former Judge, The Civil Court of the City of New York.

Office: 851 Grand Concourse, Bronx 10451.

Telephone: (718) 590-6366.

Fax: (718) 590-8914

McKEON, Michael F. *(Judge, Auburn City Court)* Elected Nov 1998 to term beginning Jan 1, 1999. Term expires Dec 31, 2008. Born Auburn New York May 1, 1953. Catholic. Educated at College of Wooster B.A. 1975 and Duquesne University J.D. 1978. Law Clerk to Hon. Robert E. White, New York Supreme Court Seventh Judicial District 1979-86. Admitted to practice New York 1979. In legal practice Auburn 1979-96.

Assistant Corporate Counsel 1986-92 and Corporate Counsel 1996-98 City of Auburn. Adjunct Professor of Criminal Justice Cayuga Community College since 1981. Member Cayuga County and New York State Bar Associations. Democrat. Enjoys golfing, reading and walking.

Office: 153 Genesee Street, Auburn 13021-3434.

Telephone: (315) 253-1570.

Fax: (315) 253-1085

E-mail address: mmckeon@courts.state.ny.us

McKINNEY, Langston C. *(Judge, Syracuse City Court)*

Office: Public Safety Building, Second Floor, 511 South State Street, Syracuse 13202-2179.

Telephone: (315) 477-2766.

Fax: (315) 474-2601

E-mail address: lmckinne@courts.state.ny.us

McLAUGHLIN, Edward Jude *(Judge, The Criminal Court of the City of New York)* Appointed by Mayor Edward Koch to term beginning March 22, 1983. Reappointed by Mayor David Dinkins Nov 22, 1992 and by Mayor Michael Bloomberg Nov 26, 2002. Current term expires Nov 30, 2012. Currently serves as Acting Justice, New York Supreme Court First Judicial District. Born Ithaca New York Aug 24, 1946. Roman Catholic. Educated at Fordham University B.A. 1969 and Georgetown University J.D. 1972. Editor American Criminal Law Review 1971-72. Admitted to practice New York 1973 and U.S. District Court Southern District of New York. Began legal practice New York City 1973.

Assistant District Attorney New York County 1972-77. Special Assistant Attorney General 1977-81. Deputy Executive Director Executive Advisory Commission on the Administration of Justice 1981-83. Member The Association of the Bar of the City of New York (Former member Criminal Courts Committee) and New York State Bar Association.

Office: 100 Centre Street, New York 10013.

Telephone: (212) 374-5861.

E-mail address: emclaugh@courts.state.ny.us

McLEOD, James A. W. *(Judge, Buffalo City Court)*

Office: 50 Delaware Avenue, Buffalo 14202.

Telephone: (716) 847-8267.

Fax: (716) 847-8257

McLEOD, Maureen A. *(Judge, New York City Family Court)* Appointed by mayor.
Office: 900 Sheridan Avenue, Bronx 10451.
Telephone: (718) 590-3376.
Fax: (718) 590-7305

McMAHON, Colleen *(Judge, United States District Court Southern District of New York)* Appointed for life by President Bill Clinton to term beginning Oct 26, 1998. Born Columbus Ohio July 18, 1951. Educated at The Ohio State University B.A. 1973 and Harvard Law School J.D. 1976. In legal practice New York 1976-95. Judge, New York Court of Claims 1995-98, appointed by Governor George E. Pataki. Former Acting Justice, New York Supreme Court First Judicial District.
Office: U.S. Courthouse, 300 Quarropas Street, White Plains 10601-4150.
Telephone: (914) 390-4146.

McMAHON, Judith N. *(Judge, The Civil Court of the City of New York)*
Office: 927 Castleton Avenue, West New Brighton 10310.
Telephone: (718) 390-5417.

McNAMARA, Thomas J. *(Judge, New York Court of Claims)* Appointed by Governor George E. Pataki.
Office: 65 South Broadway, Room 210, Saratoga Springs 12866.
Telephone: (518) 583-5330.
Fax: (518) 583-5335

McNULTY, Marion T. *(Judge, Suffolk County Family Court)* Elected to term beginning Jan 1, 1988. Currently serves as Acting Justice, New York Supreme Court Tenth Judicial District. Born Queens New York Jan 30, 1951. Roman Catholic. Educated at Thomas More College B.A. 1972 and Fordham University J.D. 1975. Admitted to practice New York 1976 and U.S. District Courts Eastern 1981 and Southern 1981 Districts of New York.
Assistant District Attorney 1975-83 and Assistant County Attorney 1983-87 Suffolk County. Member Association of Judges of the Family Court of the State of New York, National Association of Women Judges, American Judges Association, Suffolk County Criminal, Suffolk County Women's and Suffolk County Bar Associations.
Mailing address: P.O. Box 9070, Central Islip 11722-9070.
Office: F-36 Cohalan Court Complex, 400 Carleton Avenue, Central Islip 11722.
Telephone: (631) 853-4332.
Fax: (631) 853-7412
E-mail address: mmcnulty@courts.state.ny.us

MEDDAUGH, Mark M. *(Judge, Sullivan County Family Court)* Former Acting Justice, New York Supreme Court Third Judicial District.
Office: Government Center, 100 North Street, Monticello 12701.
Telephone: (845) 794-3000.
Fax: (845) 794-8300

MEGA, Christopher J. *(Justice, New York Supreme Court Second Judicial District)* Certificated. Former Presiding Judge, New York Court of Claims, appointed by governor.
Office: 18 Richmond Terrace, Staten Island 10301.
Telephone: (718) 390-5415.

MEIROWITZ, Joel B. *(Judge, Glen Cove City Court)*
Office: 13 Glen Street, Glen Cove 11542-2776.
Telephone: (516) 676-0109.
Fax: (516) 676-1570

MELDRIM, Thomas A. *(Judge, Cortland City Court)*
Office: 25 Court Street, Cortland 13045.
Telephone: (607) 753-1811.
Fax: (607) 753-9932
E-mail address: tmeldrim@courts.state.ny.us

MELENDEZ, Suzanne J. *(Judge, The Criminal Court of the City of New York)* Appointed by Mayor Rudolph Giuliani.
Office: 125-01 Queens Boulevard, Kew Gardens 11415.
Telephone: (718) 520-3855.
Fax: (718) 520-4712

MENSCH, Rebecca S. *(Acting Judge, Beacon City Court)* Appointed by Mayor Clara Lou Gould Dec 2000. Born Rome New York March 21, 1967. Educated at Vassar College B.A. 1988 and Albany Law School of Union University J.D. 1991. Admitted to practice Connecticut 1991 and New York 1992. In legal practice Poughkeepsie New York Jan 1992 to June 2001.
Member Mid-Hudson Women's Bar Association (Board Member 1992-99, President 1996-97). Member Ethics Committee City of Beacon.
Office: One Municipal Plaza, Suite 2, Beacon 12508.
Telephone: (845) 838-5030.

MERCURE, Thomas E. *(Associate Justice, New York Supreme Court Appellate Division Third Judicial Department)* Elected Justice to term beginning Jan 1, 1982. Appointed Associate Justice Appellate Division by Governor Mario Cuomo to term beginning Jan 1, 1988. Born Dover New Jersey Dec 5, 1943. Catholic. Educated at St. Michael's College B.A. 1965 and Georgetown University Law Center J.D. 1968. Admitted to practice New York 1969, U.S. District Court Northern District of New York 1969 and U.S. Supreme Court 1974. Began legal practice Fort Edward 1969. Judge, Washington County Court 1981-82.
Assistant District Attorney 1973-76 and District Attorney 1977-80 Washington County. Important Decision: Washington County CEASE, Inc. v. Richard A. Persico et al. 99 A.D.2d 321, 473 N.Y.S.2d 610. Member New York State Supreme Court Justices Association, Washington County and New York State Bar Associations. New York State National Guard 1968-74.
Mailing address: P.O. Box 346, Fort Edward 12828-0346.
Office: Washington County Courthouse, 383 Broadway, Fort Edward 12828.
Telephone: (518) 746-2540.

MERRELL, Charles C. *(Judge, Lewis County Court)* Also serves Lewis County Surrogate's Court and Lewis County Family Court.
Office: Courthouse, 7660 North State Street, Lowville 13367-1396.
Telephone: (315) 376-5366.

MERRILL, Jeffrey R. *(Supervising Judge, Syracuse City Court)* Elected to term beginning Jan 1, 1984. Reelected 1993, current term expires Dec 31, 2003. Born Geneva New York May 16, 1945. Presbyterian. Edu-

MERRILL, JEFFREY R.—*Continued*

cated at Colgate University B.A. 1967 and Syracuse University J.D. 1971. Member Sigma Nu. Admitted to practice New York 1972, U.S. District Court Northern District of New York 1974 and U.S. Supreme Court 1980. Began legal practice Syracuse 1972.

Assistant District Attorney 1972-74, Senior Assistant District Attorney 1977-84 and S.T.O.P.-D.W.I. Coordinator 1982-84 Onondaga County. Deputy Sheriff Seneca County 1968-69 and Onondaga County 1969-72. Republican. Executive Board Orange Pack and President Lacrosse Club Syracuse University.

Office: Public Safety Building, Second Floor, 511 South State Street, Syracuse 13202-2179.
Telephone: (315) 477-2767.
Fax: (315) 474-2601
E-mail address: jmerrill@courts.state.ny.us

METCALF, James M. *(Judge, Oswego City Court)*
Office: Conway Municipal Center, 20 West Oneida Street, Oswego 13126.
Telephone: (315) 343-0415.
Fax: (315) 343-0531

MEYER, Alan J. *(Judge, The Criminal Court of the City of New York)* Appointed by mayor. Currently serves as Acting Justice, New York Supreme Court Second Judicial District.
Office: 18 Richmond Terrace, Staten Island 10301.
Telephone: (718) 390-8408.
E-mail address: ameyer@courts.state.ny.us

MICHALEK, John A. *(Justice, New York Supreme Court Eighth Judicial District)* Elected Nov 1994 to term beginning Jan 1, 1995. Term expires Dec 31, 2008. Born Lackawanna New York June 12, 1951. Roman Catholic. Educated at Canisius College B.A. 1973 and Albany Law School of Union University J.D. 1976. Admitted to practice New York 1977, U.S. District Court Western District of New York 1978 and U.S. Supreme Court 1994. In legal practice Lackawanna, Hamburg and West Seneca 1977-95.

Assistant District Attorney Erie County 1977-85. Bureau Chief Justice Court Bureau Erie County District Attorneys Office 1981-85. Member Thomas More Guild, The Advocates, New York State Trial Lawyers Association, The Association of Trial Lawyers of America, Police and Judges Executive Conference, Association of Justices of the Supreme Court of the State of New York, Supreme Court Justices Association Eighth Judicial District (President), Bar Association of Erie County and New York State Bar Association. Speaker and Instructor PEACE Conference. Member Democratic Committee Town of Hamburg 1984-94 and Democratic Executive Committee Erie County 1987-94. Town Supervisor Town of Hamburg 1993. Former Member Board of Trustees ECC Community College. Sponsor St. Francis High School National Honor Society. Judge Moot Court Competition. Member Lions Club (Past President), Knights of Columbus and School Board St. Francis High School. Enjoys writing, jogging, traveling, skiing and coaching swimming, soccer and basketball.

Office: Erie County Hall, 92 Franklin Street, Buffalo 14202.
Telephone: (716) 851-3438.
Fax: (716) 851-3323
E-mail address: jmichalek@courts.state.ny.us

MIDEY, Nicholas V., Jr. *(Judge, New York Court of Claims)* Appointed by Governor George E. Pataki.
Office: Salina Place, Second Floor, 205 South Salina Street, Syracuse 13202.
Telephone: (315) 466-7151.
Fax: (315) 466-7154

MIGNANO, Stephen J. *(Judge, New York Court of Claims)* Appointed by Governor George E. Pataki.
Office: 140 Grand Street, Ninth Floor, White Plains 10601.
Telephone: (914) 289-2320.
Fax: (914) 289-2323

MILLER, Howard *(Associate Justice, New York Supreme Court Appellate Division Second Judicial Department)* Elected Justice Ninth Judicial District. Appointed Associate Justice Appellate Division by Governor George E. Pataki.
Office: Rockland County Courthouse, One South Main Street, New City 10956.
Telephone: (845) 638-5353.
Fax: (845) 708-2937

MILLER, Howard S. *(Judge, Nassau County District Court)*
Office: 99 Main Street, Hempstead 11550.
Telephone: (516) 572-2156.
E-mail address: miller@courts.state.ny.us

MILLER, Robert E. *(Judge, Putnam County Court)* Also serves Putnam County Surrogate's Court and Putnam County Family Court.
Office: County Office Building, 40 Gleneida Avenue, Carmel 10512.
Telephone: (845) 225-3641.
Fax: (845) 225-4395

MILLER, Sondra *(Associate Justice, New York Supreme Court Appellate Division Second Judicial Department)* Elected Justice to term beginning Jan 1, 1987. Appointed Associate Justice Appellate Division by Governor Mario Cuomo. Certificated. Former Judge, Westchester County Family Court.
Office: 140 Grand Street, White Plains 10601.
Telephone: (914) 285-4910.

MILLER, William *(Judge, The Criminal Court of the City of New York)* Appointed by mayor. Currently serves as Supervising Judge. Also serves as Acting Justice, New York Supreme Court Second Judicial District.
Office: 120 Schermerhorn Street, Brooklyn 11201.
Telephone: (718) 643-8400.
E-mail address: wmiller@courts.state.ny.us

MILLS, Donna Marie *(Justice, New York Supreme Court Twelfth Judicial District)* Currently serves First Judicial District. Former Judge, The Civil Court of the City of New York.
Office: 111 Centre Street, New York 10013.
Telephone: (212) 374-8462.

MILLS, Douglas C. *(Judge, Saratoga Springs City Court)*
Office: 3 City Hall, 474 Broadway, Saratoga Springs 12866-2295.
Telephone: (518) 581-1797.
Fax: (518) 584-3097

MILTON, Dennis E. *(Judge, United States Bankruptcy Court Eastern District of New York)* Appointed by

MILTON, DENNIS E.—*Continued*

U.S. Court of Appeals Second Circuit judges to term beginning April 30, 2001. Term expires April 2015.
Office: 75 Clinton Street, Brooklyn 11201-4201.
Telephone: (718) 330-2188.

MINARDO, Philip G. *(Justice, New York Supreme Court Second Judicial District)*
Office: 18 Richmond Terrace, Staten Island 10301.
Telephone: (718) 390-5356.
E-mail address: pminardo@courts.state.ny.us

MINARIK, Renee Forgensi *(Judge, New York Court of Claims)* Appointed by Governor George E. Pataki.
Office: 500 Court Exchange Building, 144 Exchange Boulevard, Rochester 14614.
Telephone: (585) 262-2320.
Fax: (585) 262-5715

MINTZ, Joseph D. *(Justice, New York Supreme Court Eighth Judicial District)* Elected to term beginning Jan 1, 1979. Reelected 1992, current term expires Dec 31, 2004. Born Buffalo New York May 9, 1933. Educated at Buffalo Law School J.D. 1956. Editorial Board Buffalo Law Review 1955-56. Admitted to practice New York 1956 and U.S. District Court Western District of New York 1956. Began legal practice Buffalo 1958.

Public Defender Legal Aid Bureau Buffalo 1957-58. Administrator Erie County Bar Association Aid to Indigent Prisoners Society, Inc. 1962-78. Member New York State Defender Association (President 1966-67), Trial Lawyers Association of Erie County (Treasurer 1977-79), National Association of Defense Lawyers in Criminal Cases, Bar Association of Erie County and New York State Bar Association. Counsel Variety Club of Buffalo, Inc. 1970-75.
Office: 50 Delaware Avenue, Buffalo 14202.
Telephone: (716) 851-3433.
Fax: (716) 851-3265
E-mail address: jmintz@courts.state.ny.us

MIRABITO, Jerome A. *(Acting Judge, Fulton City Court)* Appointed by mayor to term beginning Jan 1, 2000. Serves part time. Born Fulton New York Jan 30, 1954. Catholic. Educated at LeMoyne College 1976 and University of Louisville J.D. 1979. Member Brandies Society. Admitted to practice New York 1980. In legal practice Fulton since 1980.

City Attorney Fulton 1980-85, 1992, 1994 and 1995. Attorney Community Development Agency Fulton. Member New York State Association of City Court Judges, Oswego County, New York State and American Bar Associations. Past President Fore and Police Commission City of Fulton. Former member Board of Directors United Way of Oswego County. Trustee Fulton Savings Bank. Chairman Board of Directors Oswego County Catholic Charities. Vice Chairman Board of Directors St. Luke Health Services, Inc. Board of Directors Greater Fulton Chamber of Commerce (Chairman 2001-02), Fulton Community Revitalization Corporation and Ticor Title Guarantee Corporation. Board of Trustees A. L. Lee Memorial Hospital. Member Workforce Development Board Oswego County. Enjoys sports, landscaping and reading.
Office: Municipal Building, 141 South First Street, Fulton 13069.
Telephone: (315) 593-8400.
Fax: (315) 592-3415
E-mail address: jmirabit@courts.state.ny.us

MISHLER, Jacob *(Senior Judge, United States District Court Eastern District of New York)* Appointed for life by President Dwight D. Eisenhower to term beginning Sept 27, 1960. Former Chief Judge. Assumed Senior status, serves by assignment. Born New York New York April 20, 1911. Educated at New York University B.A. J.D. Admitted to practice New York 1934. Justice, New York Supreme Court Sept 1, 1959 to Dec 31, 1959.
Office: Long Island Federal Courthouse, 100 Federal Plaza, Central Islip 11722.
Telephone: (631) 712-5630.

MISIASZEK, Michael J. *(Acting Judge, Oneida City Court)*
Office: Oneida Municipal Building, 109 North Main Street, Oneida 13421.
Telephone: (315) 363-1310.
Fax: (315) 363-3230

MIZEL, Marianne O. *(Judge, Ulster County Family Court)* Elected to term beginning Jan 1, 1994. Term expires Dec 31, 2003. Born Athens New York March 7, 1954. Reformed Protestant. Educated at State University of New York at New Paltz B.A. 1976 and Widener University School of Law J.D. 1980. Admitted to practice New York 1981. In legal practice Catskill 1981-82 and Kingston 1981-93.

Assistant Corporation Counsel 1986-88 and Corporation Counsel Jan 1992 to Dec 1992 Kingston. Important Decisions: Matter of Ursula J. 169 Misc. 2d 148, Matter of Melanie J. 615 N.Y.S.2d 555 and Matter of Doe 161 Misc. 2d 935. Instructor in Marriage and Family Brandywine College 1977-78. Member Law Guardian Panel Greene County 1981-83 and Ulster County since 1982. Member Law Guardian Liaison Committee since Jan 1991, Appellate Division Law Guardian Advisory Committee since Jan 1991, National Association of Women Lawyers, New York State Women's Bar Association (Mid-Hudson Chapter), Ulster County (Board of Directors 1989-92), New York State (Family Law Section, Committee on Family Court since Feb 1990) and American Bar Associations. Republican. Board of Directors Children's Home of Kingston 1987, Kingston Area Library Jan 1991 to Dec 1991 and since Feb 1993 and Boys and Girls Club. Member Advisory Board Y.W.C.A. Day Care Center 1985-86, City of Kingston Planning Board Oct 1986 to May 1988 and Jan 1992 to Dec 1992, City of Kingston Historic Landmarks Commission 1988 to Dec 1991 (Chairperson 1988-90, Vice Chairperson 1990-91), Ulster County Child Abuse Task Force (Board of Directors 1987-88), League of Women Voters, Kingston Junior League and Mid-Hudson Chapter American Heart Association. Enjoys reading and scuba diving.
Office: 16 Lucas Avenue, Kingston 12401-0906.
Telephone: (845) 340-3614.
Fax: (845) 340-3626
E-mail address: mmizel@courts.state.ny.us

MODICA, Deborah Stevens *(Judge, The Criminal Court of the City of New York)* Appointed by Mayor Rudolph Giuliani.
Office: 125-01 Queens Boulevard, Kew Gardens 11415.
Telephone: (718) 520-3855.
Fax: (718) 520-4712

MODICA, Salvatore J. *(Judge, The Criminal Court of the City of New York)* Appointed by mayor.
Office: 120 Schermerhorn Street, Brooklyn 11201.
Telephone: (718) 643-8400.
Fax: (718) 643-3538

MOGULESCU, William I. *(Judge, The Criminal Court of the City of New York)* Appointed by mayor. Currently serves as Acting Justice, New York Supreme Court Twelfth Judicial District.
Office: 851 Grand Concourse, Bronx 10451.
Telephone: (718) 590-7342.
Fax: (718) 590-8914

MOLEA, Richard A. *(Judge, New York Court of Claims)* Appointed by Governor George E. Pataki. Currently serves as Acting Justice, New York Supreme Court Ninth Judicial District.
Office: 111 Dr. Martin Luther King Jr. Blvd., White Plains 10601.
Telephone: (914) 995-7519.
Fax: (914) 995-4182
E-mail address: rmolea@courts.state.ny.us

MOLIA, Denise F. *(Justice, New York Supreme Court Tenth Judicial District)* Elected Nov 1998 to term beginning Jan 1, 1999. Term expires Dec 31, 2012.
Office: 114A Supreme Court Annex, 215 Griffing Avenue, Riverhead 11901.
Telephone: (631) 852-3750.
Fax: (631) 852-2867

MONDO, Suzanne M. *(Judge, The Criminal Court of the City of New York)* Appointed by Mayor Rudolph Giuliani. Former Judge, The Civil Court of the City of New York.
Office: 100 Centre Street, New York 10013.
Telephone: (212) 374-6216.
Fax: (212) 374-2579

MONSERRATE, Patrick D. *(Justice, New York Supreme Court Sixth Judicial District)* Former Administrative Justice. Former Judge, Broome County Court.
Mailing address: P.O. Box 1766, Binghamton 13902-1766.
Office: Broome County Courthouse, Court Street, Binghamton 13901.
Telephone: (607) 778-2201.
Fax: (607) 778-2398

MOORE, John S. *(Judge, The Criminal Court of the City of New York)* Appointed by Mayor Ed Koch to term beginning Feb 24, 1987. Reappointed by Mayor David Dinkens Dec 21, 1990 and by Mayor Rudolph W. Giuliani 2000. Current term expires Dec 31, 2010. Currently serves as Acting Justice, New York Supreme Court Twelfth Judicial District. Born Englewood New Jersey Oct 11, 1947. Catholic. Educated at Fairfield University B.A. with honors 1969 and Fordham University School of Law J.D. 1972. Admitted to practice New York 1972 and U.S. District Courts Eastern 1973 and Southern 1973 Districts of New York.
Bureau Chief Bronx District Attorneys Office 1973-87. Member Association of Criminal Court Judges of the City of New York, Acting Supreme Court Judges Association, Bronx and New York State Bar Associations. Attended CLE Courses Supreme Court Conference and Criminal Court Conference. Board Member Bronx Alternative for Special Education. Enjoys boating, golf and travel.
Office: 851 Grand Concourse, Bronx 10451.
Telephone: (718) 590-3760.
Fax: (718) 590-8914

MORDUE, Norman A. *(Judge, United States District Court Northern District of New York)* Appointed for life by President Bill Clinton to term beginning Dec 4, 1998. Born Elmira New York June 26, 1942. Educated at Syracuse University B.A. 1966 and J.D. with honors 1971. Admitted to New York 1972. Judge, Onondaga County Court 1983-85. Justice, New York Supreme Court Fifth Judicial District Jan 1, 1986 to Dec 4, 1998.
Law Clerk and Chief Assistant District Attorney Onondaga County 1970-82. Adjunct Professor of Law "Trial Practice" Syracuse University College of Law. Member Association of Justices of the Supreme Court of the State of New York and Onondaga County Bar Association. Lecturer New York State Bar Association. Participant CLE for New York Supreme Court Justices. Recipient Letterwinner of Distinction from Syracuse University. Platoon Leader U.S. Army Infantry Vietnam. Recipient Purple Heart, Combat Infantryman's Badge, Distinguished Service Cross, Bronze Star and Air Medal.
Mailing address: P.O. Box 7336, Syracuse 13261-7336.
Telephone: (315) 234-8570.

MORGENSTERN, Esther M. *(Judge, The Civil Court of the City of New York)* Currently assigned to Family Court. Also serves as Acting Justice, New York Supreme Court Second Judicial District.
Office: 283 Adams Street, Sixth Floor, Brooklyn 11201.
Telephone: (718) 643-5624.
Fax: (718) 643-5103

MORINELLO, Angelo J. *(Judge, Niagara Falls City Court)*
Office: Public Safety Building, 520 Hyde Park Boulevard, Niagara Falls 14302-2725.
Telephone: (716) 278-9822.
Fax: (716) 278-9809

MORRIS, Cecelia G. *(Judge, United States Bankruptcy Court Southern District of New York)* Appointed by U.S. Court of Appeals Second Circuit judges to term beginning July 1, 2000. Term expires June 30, 2014. Born Quanah Texas May 26, 1946. Educated at West Texas State University A.B. 1968 and John Marshall Law School J.D. 1977.
Office: 176 Church Street, Poughkeepsie 12601.
Telephone: (845) 452-4200.

MORSE, Thomas Rainbow *(Judge, Rochester City Court)* Appointed by Mayor William A. Johnson, Jr. to term beginning Jan 4, 1999. Elected Nov 2, 1999, current term expires Dec 31, 2009. Born Rochester New York. Episcopalian. Educated at Wesleyan University B.A. 1971 and New England School of Law J.D. magna cum laude 1978. Managing Editor New England Law Review 1977-78. Admitted to practice New York 1978

MORSE, THOMAS RAINBOW—*Continued*
and U.S. District Court Western District of New York 1979.

Assistant District Attorney Monroe County 1980-98. Member Monroe County Bar Association. Recipient Charles F. Crimi Award from Monroe County Bar Association (the only prosecutor to receive award for "dedication to the fair representation of the poor and disadvantaged") 1997. Democrat. Board Member Alternatives for Battered Women (Past President). Interests include family, woodworking and juggling.

Office: 6 Hall of Justice, 99 Exchange Boulevard, Rochester 14614.
Telephone: (585) 428-5248.
Fax: (585) 428-2741
E-mail address: tmorse@courts.state.ny.us

MOSER, Adam H. *(Judge, Nassau County District Court)*
Office: 99 Main Street, Hempstead 11550.
Telephone: (516) 572-2145.
E-mail address: moser@courts.state.ny.us

MOSKOWITZ, Karla *(Justice, New York Supreme Court First Judicial District)* Born New York New York June 8, 1941. Former Judge, The Civil Court of the City of New York.
Office: 60 Centre Street, Room 532, New York 10007.
Telephone: (212) 374-8520.
Fax: (212) 374-3929
E-mail address: kmoskowi@courts.state.ny.us

MOTLEY, Constance Baker *(Senior Judge, United States District Court Southern District of New York)* Appointed for life by President Lyndon B. Johnson to term beginning Sept 9, 1966. Chief Judge June 1, 1982 to Sept 30, 1986. Assumed Senior status Oct 1, 1986. First Black woman appointed to U.S. District Court. Born New Haven Connecticut Sept 14, 1921. Episcopalian. Educated at New York University B.A. 1943 and Columbia University LL.B. 1946. Honorary LL.D. Howard University 1966, Fordham University 1970, New York University School of Law 1985, Yale University 1987, Georgetown University 1989, Tulane University 1990, Claremont University 1991, Middlebury College 1994, Syracuse University 1999 and Harvard University 2000. Honorary D.P.S. Russell Sage College 1997. Admitted to practice New York 1948.

Staff member and Chief Staff Attorney NAACP Legal Defense and Education Fund, Inc. 1945-65. Author "Massive Resistance: America's Second Civil War" 41 No. 1 Arkansas L. Rev. 123, 1988 and Bar Association Journal, Inc., "The Supreme Court, Civil Rights Litigation, and Deja Vu" 76 No. 3 Cornell L. Rev. 643 March 1991, "My Personal Debt to Thurgood Marshall" 101 No. 1 Yale L. Jour. 19 Oct 1991, "Civil Rights-Civil Liberties Litigation in the U.S. Supreme Court: Are the State Courts Our Only Hope?" 9 Harvard Blackletter Journal 101 Spring 1992, "The Historical Setting of *Brown* and Its Impact on the Supreme Court's Decisions" 61 No. 1 Fordham L. Rev. Oct 1992, "It's Time to Bar Peremptory Challenges" III No. 4 *Voir Dire* American Board of Trial Advocates Fall 1996 and *Equal Justice Under Law, an Autobiography* Farrar, Straus & Giroux June 1998. Member The Association of the Bar of the City of New York and American Bar Association (Section of Criminal Justice). Inducted into National Women's Hall of Fame 1993 and Connecticut Women's Hall of Fame 1998. Recipient 20th Anniversary Award from Association of Black Women Attorneys 1996, James Weldon Johnson Medal from The Johnson Memorial Foundation, Inc. 1996, Equal Justice Award from NAACP Legal Defense and Educational Fund, Inc. 1997, Kate Stoneman Award from Albany Law School 1997, Emmory Buckner Award from Federal Bar Council 2000 and Presidential Citizens Medal 2001. Democrat. New York State Advisory Council on Employment and Unemployment Insurance 1958-64. Member State Senate New York 1964-69 (First Black woman in State Senate). Borough President Manhattan 1965-66 (First woman to hold office).

Office: 2540 U.S. Courthouse, 500 Pearl Street, New York 10007-1312.
Telephone: (212) 805-0232.

MOUNTAIN, William H., III *(Judge, Olean City Court and Judge, Salamanca City Court)* Acting Judge Olean City Court 1979-84. Judge since 1984. Judge Salamanca City Court since 1991. Born Olean New York May 23, 1946. Roman Catholic. Educated at Gettysburg College B.A. and Albany Law School of Union University J.D. Member Phi Kappa Psi. Admitted to practice New York 1973, U.S. District Court District of New York 1973 and U.S. Supreme Court 1980. In legal practice Olean since 1973.

Member New York State Association of City Court Judges, Cattaraugus County, New York State and American Bar Associations. E-5 USAR 1968-75.
Mailing address: P.O. Box 631, Olean 14760-0631.
Office: Municipal Building, Olean 14760.
Telephone: (716) 376-5620.
Fax: (716) 376-5623

MOYNIHAN, G. Thomas, Jr. *(Justice, New York Supreme Court Fourth Judicial District)* Former Judge, Warren County Court.
Office: Warren County Municipal Center, 1340 State Route 9, Lake George 12845.
Telephone: (518) 761-6547.

MUGGLIN, Carl J. *(Associate Justice, New York Supreme Court Appellate Division Third Judicial Department)* Elected Justice Sixth Judicial District to term beginning Jan 1, 1986. Appointed Associate Justice Appellate Division by Governor George E. Pataki. Born Walton New York March 6, 1937. Presbyterian. Educated at Syracuse University B.S.B.A. 1958 J.D. 1961. Law Clerk to Hon. Walter L. Terry, New York Supreme Court Sixth Judicial District 1973-79. Admitted to practice New York 1962 and U.S. Supreme Court 1976. In legal practice Endicott 1961-62 and Walton 1962-85.

District Attorney Delaware County 1965-67. Member Delaware County, Otsego County and New York State Bar Associations. Republican (inactive). Member Kiwanis Club and Masons. Enjoys golfing, camping, canoeing and cross country skiing.
Office: One Gardiner Place, Walton 13856.
Telephone: (607) 865-8600.

MUKASEY, Michael B. *(Chief Judge, United States District Court Southern District of New York)* Appointed for life by President Ronald Reagan to term beginning 1987. Chief Judge since March 12, 2000. Born Bronx New York July 28, 1941. Educated at Columbia University A.B. 1963 and Yale Law School LL.B. 1967. In legal practice New York City 1967-72 and 1976-87.

MUKASEY, MICHAEL B.—*Continued*
Assistant U.S. Attorney 1972-76 and Chief Official Corruption Unit 1975-76 Southern District of New York.
Office: 2240 U.S. Courthouse, 500 Pearl Street, New York 10007-1312.
Telephone: (212) 805-0234.

MULLEN, Michael F. *(Judge, New York Court of Claims)* Appointed by Governor Mario M. Cuomo to term beginning Jan 1, 1987. Reappointed by Governor George E. Pataki 1995. Current term expires Dec 31, 2004. Currently serves as Acting Justice, New York Supreme Court Tenth Judicial District. Born Bronx New York. Roman Catholic. Educated at Fairfield University A.B. 1959 and St. John's University LL.B. 1962. Research Assistant St. John's Law Review 1960-62. Admitted to practice New York 1963, U.S. District Courts Eastern and Southern Districts of New York 1975 and U.S. Court of Appeals Second Circuit 1975. In legal practice New York City 1965-67 and Huntington 1976-86.
Law Clerk to Associate Justice Fred J. Munder, New York Supreme Court Appellate Division Second Judicial Department 1968-75. Counsel to Senator Bernard C. Smith New York 1977-78. Referee in Incompetency 1976-86. Assistant Counsel to Senate Majority New York State 1979-86. Important Decisions: Matter of Henry v. New York State Commission of Investigation 141 Misc. 2d 849, aff'd 143 A.D.2d 914; Matter of Gazza v. New York State Department of Environmental Conservation 159 Misc. 2d 591 aff'd 217A.D.2d 202 aff'd 89 N.Y.2d 603; and People v. Lavalle 181 Misc. 2d 916 (capital case). Lecturer Suffolk Academy of Law. Member Suffolk County Bar Association. Enjoys reading and Irish poetry.
Mailing address: P.O. Box 9007, Riverhead 11901-9007.
Office: Criminal Courts Building, 210 Center Drive South, Riverhead 11901.
Telephone: (631) 852-2166.
Fax: (631) 852-2729

MULLINGS, Pauline A. *(Judge, The Criminal Court of the City of New York)* Appointed by Mayor Rudolph Giuliani.
Office: 125-01 Queens Boulevard, Kew Gardens 11415.
Telephone: (718) 520-3855.
Fax: (718) 520-4712

MULVEY, Robert C. *(Justice, New York Supreme Court Sixth Judicial District)*
Mailing address: P.O. Box 70, Ithaca 14851-0070.
Office: Tompkins County Courthouse, 320 North Tioga Street, Ithaca 14850.
Telephone: (607) 272-0674.
Fax: (607) 272-0691

MUNSON, Howard G. *(Senior Judge, United States District Court Northern District of New York)* Appointed for life by President Gerald R. Ford to term beginning 1976. Former Chief Judge. Assumed Senior status Nov 5, 1990, serves by assignment. Born Claremont New Hampshire July 26, 1924. Educated at University of Pennsylvania B.S. in Economics 1948 and Syracuse University LL.B. 1952. Member Justinian Law Society, Alpha Tau Omega and Phi Delta Phi. Admitted to practice New York. In legal practice Syracuse 1952-76.
Member Advisory Council Onondaga County District Attorney. Fellow American College of Trial Lawyers. Member National Panel of Arbitrators American Arbitration. Member National Association of Railroad Trial Counsel, Onondaga County and New York State Bar Associations. U.S. Army ETO 1943-45. Recipient Bronze Star and Purple Heart. With Employers' Assurance Corp. Ltd. 1949-50. Chairman Ethics Committee Onondaga County Legislature. Member Syracuse Board of Education (President) and Board of Directors WCNY-TV. Member Kiwanis.
Mailing address: P.O. Box 7376, Syracuse 13261-7376.
Telephone: (315) 234-8580.

MURPHY, J. Emmett *(Justice, New York Supreme Court Ninth Judicial District)* Elected Nov 1996 to term beginning Jan 1, 1997. Term expires Dec 31, 2010. Born Yonkers New York March 12, 1941. Educated at Manhattan College B.A. 1963 and Fordham University School of Law J.D. 1966. Admitted to practice New York 1966 and U.S. District Courts Eastern 1975 and Southern 1975 Districts of New York. Judge 1980-86 and Chief Judge 1986-91, Yonkers City Court. Judge, Westchester County Court Jan 1, 1992 to Dec 31, 1996.
First Deputy Corporation Counsel Yonkers Law Department.
Office: Courthouse, Nineteenth Floor, 111 Dr. Martin Luther King Jr. Blvd., White Plains 10601.
Telephone: (914) 995-4521.
Fax: (914) 995-4323

MURPHY, Martin P. *(Judge, New York City Family Court)* Appointed by Mayor Rudolph Giuliani. Currently serves as Supervising Judge, The Criminal Court of the City of New York.
Office: 100 Centre Street, New York 10013.
Telephone: (212) 374-6216.

MURPHY, Robert C. *(Judge, Binghamton City Court)* Serves part time.
Office: Governmental Plaza, 38 Hawley Street, Binghamton 13901.
Telephone: (607) 772-7006.
Fax: (607) 772-7041

MURPHY, Thomas J. *(Justice, New York Supreme Court Fifth Judicial District)* Elected to term beginning Jan 1, 1977. Reelected 1990. Certificated. Born Syracuse New York May 25, 1930. Roman Catholic. Educated at LeMoyne College 1948-51 and Syracuse University LL.D. 1954. Admitted to practice New York 1955. Began legal practice Syracuse 1955.
Member Onondaga County Bar Association. Republican. Member Board of Supervisors 1965-69 and County Legislature 1969-70 Onondaga County. Member State Assembly New York 1971-76.
Office: Onondaga County Courthouse, 401 Montgomery Street, Syracuse 13202.
Telephone: (315) 671-1107.
Fax: (315) 671-1181
E-mail address: tjmurphy@courts.state.ny.us

NADEL, S. Michael *(Judge, New York Court of Claims)* Appointed by Governor George E. Pataki.
Mailing address: Justice Building, Seventh Floor, Empire State Plaza, Albany 12223.
Office: 26 Broadway, Tenth Floor, New York 10004.
Telephone: (212) 361-8110.

NADELSON, Eileen N. *(Judge, The Civil Court of the City of New York)*
Office: 111 Centre Street, New York 10013.
Telephone: (212) 374-8161.

NAHMAN, Robert L. *(Surrogate, Queens County Surrogate's Court)* Former Judge, The Civil Court of the City of New York. Former Justice, New York Supreme Court Eleventh Judicial District.
Office: 88-11 Sutphin Boulevard, Jamaica 11435.
Telephone: (718) 520-3132.

NARDELLI, Eugene L. *(Associate Justice, New York Supreme Court Appellate Division First Judicial Department)* Former Acting Justice. Elected Justice First Judicial District to term beginning Jan 1, 1986. Appointed Associate Justice Appellate Division by governor. Acting Presiding Justice Jan 2002 to March 2002. Born Italy June 11, 1934. Catholic. Educated at Fordham University B.S.S. 1956 J.D. 1960. Admitted to practice New York 1960. Began legal practice New York City 1960. Judge, The Civil Court of the City of New York Jan 1, 1975 to Dec 31, 1985.
Member American Justinian Society of Judges (Past President 1984-86), New York County Lawyers' Association and The Association of the Bar of the City of New York. Past President Columbus Citizens Foundation, Inc., New York. Former Counsel to Neighborhood Conservation Bureau of New York.
Office: 27 Madison Avenue, New York 10010.
Telephone: (212) 340-0408.

NASTASI, Aldo A. *(Justice, New York Supreme Court Ninth Judicial District)* Elected to term beginning Jan 1, 1984. Reelected 1997. Certificated. Born Manhattan New York Sept 18, 1932. Catholic. Educated at Fordham University B.S.S. 1954 J.D. 1959. Admitted to practice New York 1960, U.S. District Courts Eastern and Southern Districts of New York and U.S. Supreme Court. In legal practice New York City 1960-74. Judge, Yonkers City Court 1975-79. Judge, Westchester County Court 1980-83.
Member Columbia Lawyers Association of Westchester County (Board of Directors) and Westchester County Bar Association. First Lieutenant USMC 1954-56. Republican. Member City Council Yonkers 1972-75 (Majority Leader). Formerly active in various youth clubs and home owners organizations. Enjoys golf and studying history and governments of the world.
Office: County Courthouse, 111 Dr. Martin Luther King Jr. Blvd., White Plains 10601.
Telephone: (914) 995-4314.
Fax: (914) 995-4182

NELSON, Valerie Brathwaite *(Judge, The Civil Court of the City of New York)*
Office: 89-17 Sutphin Boulevard, Jamaica 11435.
Telephone: (718) 262-7100.

NELSON, William K. *(Judge, Rockland County Court)* Currently serves as Acting Justice, New York Supreme Court Ninth Judicial District.
Office: Courthouse, One South Main Street, New City 10956.
Telephone: (845) 638-5336.
Fax: (845) 638-5312

NeMOYER, Edgar Carroll *(Judge, New York Court of Claims)* Appointed by Governor Mario Cuomo to term beginning March 25, 1985. Reappointed 1994 and 2002. Born Buffalo New York June 5, 1932. Educated at Georgetown University 1950-52, University of Buffalo B.A. 1954, State University of New York at Buffalo J.D. 1961 and University of Wisconsin (Fellow) LL.M. 1962. Staff Member Buffalo Law Review 1959-61. Member Phi Delta Phi. Admitted to practice New York 1961, District of Columbia 1962, U.S. Court of Military Appeals 1963 and U.S. Supreme Court 1967. In legal practice Buffalo 1963-84. Justice, New York Supreme Court 1984.
Assistant U.S. Attorney, First Assistant U.S. Attorney and Acting U.S. Attorney Western District of New York 1967-69. Deputy Corporation Counsel Buffalo 1969. Law Clerk to Hon. James B. Kane, New York Supreme Court Eighth Judicial District 1976-77. Author "Jones Act" 9 Buffalo L. Rev. 390, 1960 and "Negotiated Justice" 47 Denver L. Jour. 367, 1970. Associate Professor State University of New York at Albany School of Criminal Justice 1969-71. Lecturer State University of New York at Buffalo School of Law 1979-83. Member Erie County Trial Lawyers Association (Treasurer 1980-82), Bar Association of Erie County, New York State, Federal and American Bar Associations. Named Man of the Year by Ancient Order of Hibernians 1984 and Citizen of the Year by Buffalo Police Detective Sergeants and Detective Association 1986. Captain USAF 1955-58. Longshoreman Buffalo 1946-55. Patrolman Buffalo Police Department 1954-55 and 1958-61. Undersheriff summer 1970 and District Committeeman 1982-84 Erie County. Member NAACP, American Legion, Men's Sustaining Society of Mercy Hospital and MENSA. Enjoys sailing.
Office: 125 Main Street, Buffalo 14203-3026.
Telephone: (716) 847-3438.
Fax: (716) 842-1982
E-mail address: cdnyc11@attglobal.net

NeMOYER, Patrick H. *(Justice, New York Supreme Court Eighth Judicial District)*
Office: 92 Franklin Street, Buffalo 14202.
Telephone: (716) 851-3353.
Fax: (716) 851-3345
E-mail address: pnemoyer@courts.state.ny.us

NENNO, Michael L. *(Judge, Cattaraugus County Court)* Also serves Cattaraugus County Surrogate's Court and Cattaraugus County Family Court. Former Judge, Salamanca City Court.
Office: County Office Building, 1701 Lincoln Avenue, Olean 14760.
Telephone: (716) 373-8035.
Fax: (716) 373-0449

NESBITT, John B. *(Judge, Wayne County Court)* Also serves Wayne County Surrogate's Court and Wayne County Family Court.
Office: Hall of Justice, 54 Broad Street, Lyons 14489-1199.
Telephone: (315) 946-5441.
Fax: (315) 946-5429

NEWMAN, Barbara F. *(Judge, The Criminal Court of the City of New York)* Appointed by mayor. Currently serves as Acting Justice, New York Supreme Court Twelfth Judicial District.
Office: 851 Grand Concourse, Bronx 10451.
Telephone: (718) 590-7834.
Fax: (718) 590-8914

NICANDRI, Eugene L. *(Judge, St. Lawrence County Court)* Appointed by Governor Mario Cuomo March 1985 to term beginning May 29, 1985. Elected Nov 1985 and Nov 1995. Current term expires Dec 31, 2005. Born Seneca Falls New York June 8, 1938. Roman Catholic. Educated at University of Rochester B.A. 1960 and Albany Law School of Union University J.D. 1965. Admitted to practice New York 1965 and U.S. District Court Northern District of New York 1967. In legal practice Massena 1965-85.

Village Attorney Village of Massena 1966-69 and 1971-83. Town Attorney Town of Massena 1971-85. Member St. Lawrence County, New York State and American Bar Associations.

Office: County Courthouse, 48 Court Street, Canton 13617-1197.
Telephone: (315) 379-2214.
Fax: (315) 379-9934

NICHOLSON, Robert J. *(Justice, New York Supreme Court Fifth Judicial District)*
Office: 25 East Oneida Street, Oswego 13126.
Telephone: (315) 349-3270.
Fax: (315) 349-3299

NICOLAI, Francis A. *(Justice, New York Supreme Court Ninth Judicial District)* Currently serves as Administrative Judge. Born White Plains New York Nov 2, 1939. Educated at U.S. Coast Guard Academy B.S. 1961 and New York Law School J.D. 1970. Admitted to practice New York 1971, U.S. District Courts Eastern and Southern Districts of New York, U.S. Court of Appeals Second Circuit and U.S. Court of Appeals for the Armed Forces. Judge, Westchester County Court March 1982 to 1983, appointed by Governor Hugh Carey.

Associate Professor Pace University 1984-85. Ninth District Delegate Association of Justices of the Supreme Court of the State of New York. Member Columbian Lawyers of Westchester County and Confederation of Columbian Lawyers Association. Recipient Distinguished Service Award from Columbian Lawyers of Westchester County 1995. Lieutenant Commander USCG 1957-73. Board of Visitors Pace University School of Law. Member Advisory Committee Paralegal Program Mercy College.

Office: 111 Dr. Martin Luther King Jr. Blvd., White Plains 10601.
Telephone: (914) 995-4100.
Fax: (914) 995-4111

NINFO, John Charles, II *(Chief Judge, United States Bankruptcy Court Western District of New York)* Appointed by U.S. Court of Appeals Second Circuit judges. Chief Judge since Jan 1, 2000. Former Judge, Bankruptcy Appellate Panel Second Circuit, selected by the Judicial Council of the Second Circuit.

Office: 1400 Federal Building, 100 State Street, Rochester 14614-1367.
Telephone: (716) 263-3148.

NOLAN, Thomas D., Jr. *(Justice, New York Supreme Court Fourth Judicial District)* Former Judge, Saratoga County Family Court.

Office: Saratoga County Municipal Center, 30 McMaster Street, Ballston Spa 12020.
Telephone: (518) 884-4703.

NOONAN, Robert C. *(Judge, Genesee County Court)* Elected Nov 1996 to term beginning Jan 1, 1997. Term expires Dec 31, 2006. Currently serves as Acting Justice, New York Supreme Court Eighth Judicial District. Also serves Genesee County Surrogate's Court. Born Batavia New York Aug 6, 1947. Educated at St. Lawrence University B.S. 1969 and Fordham University School of Law J.D. 1975. Admitted to practice U.S. District Court Western District of New York 1977, U.S. Supreme Court 1980 and New York. In legal practice Batavia 1976-96.

Assistant District Attorney 1976-80 and District Attorney 1988-96 Genesee County. Member Bar Association of Erie County, Genesee County and New York State Bar Associations.

Office: Genesee County Courts Facility, One West Main Street, Batavia 14020.
Telephone: (585) 344-2550.
Fax: (585) 344-8517
E-mail address: rnoonan@courts.state.ny.us

NOTARO, Peter J. *(Justice, New York Supreme Court Eighth Judicial District)* Former Judge, Erie County Family Court.
Office: 50 Delaware Avenue, Buffalo 14202.
Telephone: (716) 851-3259.
Fax: (716) 850-3325
E-mail address: pnotaro@courts.state.ny.us

NOWAK, Henry J., Jr. *(Judge, Buffalo City Court)*
Office: 50 Delaware Avenue, Buffalo 14202.
Telephone: (716) 847-8200.

NUNEZ, Patricia M. *(Judge, The Criminal Court of the City of New York)* Appointed by Mayor Rudolph Giuliani.
Office: 120 Schermerhorn Street, Brooklyn 11201.
Telephone: (212) 374-6216.
Fax: (212) 374-5292

O'BRIEN, William F., III *(Justice, New York Supreme Court Sixth Judicial District)* Elected Nov 5, 1996. Term expires Dec 31, 2010. Born Johnstown Pennsylvania Feb 2, 1942. Roman Catholic. Educated at LeMoyne College B.B.A. 1963 and Syracuse University College of Law J.D. 1966. Admitted to practice New York 1966. Judge, Madison County Court 1983-96.

District Attorney Madison County 1974-81. Sergeant USAF NYANG 174th TFG Syracuse New York Nov 1966 to Nov 1972.

Office: Madison County Courthouse, Wampsville 13163.
Telephone: (315) 366-2321.
Fax: (315) 366-2721

O'BRIEN, William J. *(Judge, Nassau County District Court)*
Office: 99 Main Street, Hempstead 11550.
Telephone: (516) 572-2101.
E-mail address: o'brien@courts.state.ny.us

OBUS, Michael J. *(Judge, The Criminal Court of the City of New York)* Appointed by Mayor Ed Koch to term beginning Aug 26, 1986. Reappointed 1995, current term expires Dec 31, 2005. Currently serves as Acting Justice, New York Supreme Court First Judicial District. Educated at Rutgers University B.A. 1970 and Columbia University School of Law J.D. 1973.

Office: 100 Centre Street, New York 10013.
Telephone: (212) 374-5854.
Fax: (212) 374-2579
E-mail address: mobus@courts.state.ny.us

O'CONNELL, Geoffrey J. *(Justice, New York Supreme Court Tenth Judicial District)* Former Judge, Nassau County District Court.
Office: Supreme Court Building, 100 Supreme Court Drive, Mineola 11501.
Telephone: (516) 571-2325.

O'CONNOR, Marilyn L. *(Judge, Monroe County Family Court)*
Office: Hall of Justice, Third Floor, 99 Exchange Boulevard, Rochester 14614-2187.
Telephone: (585) 428-1904.
Fax: (585) 428-2597
E-mail address: moconnor@courts.state.ny.us

O'DONNELL, John F. *(Justice, New York Supreme Court Eighth Judicial District)* Former Judge, Erie County Family Court.
Office: Erie County Hall, 92 Franklin Street, Buffalo 14202.
Telephone: (716) 851-3373.
Fax: (716) 851-3326
E-mail address: jodonnel@courts.state.ny.us

O'DONOGHUE, Peter J. *(Justice, New York Supreme Court Eleventh Judicial District)* Former Judge, The Civil Court of the City of New York.
Office: 88-11 Sutphin Boulevard, Jamaica 11435.
Telephone: (718) 520-3799.

OGDEN, E. Jeanette *(Judge, Buffalo City Court)*
Office: 50 Delaware Avenue, Suite 650, Buffalo 14202.
Telephone: (716) 847-8240.
Fax: (716) 847-6409
E-mail address: eogden@courts.state.ny.us

OHLIG, Louis J. *(Judge, Suffolk County Court)* Elected to term beginning Jan 1, 1997. Term expires Dec 31, 2006. Born Brooklyn New York June 21, 1934. Roman Catholic. Educated at Hofstra University, C. W. Post College B.A. 1961 and Brooklyn Law School LL.B. 1961. Admitted to practice New York 1962. Began legal practice Huntington 1962. In legal practice East Northport 1967. Judge, Suffolk County District Court Dec 7, 1976 to Dec 31, 1996.
Assistant District Attorney Suffolk County 1966-74. Member Suffolk County District Court Judges Association since 1976, Huntington Lawyers Club since 1965, New York State District Attorney's Association 1966-74, Suffolk County and New York State 1965-76 Bar Associations. Petty Officer Second Class USNR Korean War 1952-56. Republican Committeeman and Zone Vice Chairman twenty years. Member Huntington Elks Lodge 1565, Eagles Lodge 1815, Northport American Legion Post 694, Northport Kiwanis Club and Knights of Columbus Father Thomas A. Judge Council 6893 East Northport. Soccer coach. Enjoys boating and bowling.
Mailing address: P.O. Box 9007, Riverhead 11901-9007.
Office: Court Complex, 210 Center Drive, Riverhead 11901.
Telephone: (631) 852-2163.

OLDS, Marjorie Z. *(Judge, Ithaca City Court)* Elected to term beginning 1990. Reelected, current term expires 2007. Currently serves Drug Court. Born Washington D.C. June 16, 1950. Educated at Johns Hopkins University B.A. with honors 1972 and Cornell University Law School J.D. 1976. Admitted to practice New York 1977. Judge, Ithaca City Court Jan 1990 to Dec 1995, appointed by Mayor Ben Nichols.
Assistant District Attorney 1976-82. Co-founder Law Guardian Office Ithaca.
Office: 118 East Clinton Street, Ithaca 14850.
Telephone: (607) 273-2263.

OLIVER, Eugene, Jr. *(Judge, The Criminal Court of the City of New York)* Appointed by mayor. Currently serves as Supervising Judge. Also serves as Acting Justice, New York Supreme Court First Judicial District.
Office: 215 East 161st Street, Bronx 10451.
Telephone: (718) 590-2927.

OLIVER, Robert Webster *(Justice, New York Supreme Court Tenth Judicial District)* Certificated. Former Judge, Suffolk County District Court.
Mailing address: P.O. Box 9070, Central Islip 11722-9070.
Office: D64 Cohalan Court Complex, 400 Carleton Avenue, Central Islip 11722.
Telephone: (631) 853-7735.
Fax: (631) 853-6094

OMANSKY, Paula J. *(Judge, The Civil Court of the City of New York)* Currently serves as Acting Justice, New York Supreme Court First Judicial District.
Office: 71 Thomas Street, New York 10013.
Telephone: (212) 815-0862.
Fax: (212) 815-0892.

ONOFRY, Robert A. *(Judge, Port Jervis City Court)*
Office: 14-18 Hammond Street, Port Jervis 12771-2495.
Telephone: (845) 858-4034.
Fax: (845) 856-2767

ORENSTEIN, Michael L. *(Magistrate Judge, United States District Court Eastern District of New York)* Appointed by U.S. District Court judges to term beginning 1991. Educated at Cornell University B.A. 1961 and New York University School of Law J.D. 1965.
Office: Long Island Federal Courthouse, 100 Federal Plaza, Central Islip 11722-4438.
Telephone: (631) 712-5700.

O'ROURKE, Andrew P. *(Justice, New York Supreme Court Ninth Judicial District)* Former Judge, New York Court of Claims, appointed by Governor George E. Pataki.
Office: Courthouse, One South Main Street, New City 10956.
Telephone: (845) 638-5982.

ORT, Victor M. *(Judge, New York Court of Claims)* Appointed by Governor George E. Pataki. Currently serves as Acting Justice, New York Supreme Court Tenth Judicial District.
Office: Nassau County Courthouse, 252 Old Country Road, Mineola 11501.
Telephone: (516) 571-3259.
Fax: (516) 571-1349
E-mail address: vort@courts.state.ny.us

O'SHEA, Judith F. *(Justice, New York Supreme Court Sixth Judicial District)* Currently serves as Administrative Judge. Former Judge, Chemung County Family Court.
Mailing address: P.O. Box 588, Elmira 14902.
Office: 203 Lake Street, Elmira 14901.

O'SHEA, JUDITH F.—*Continued*

Telephone: (607) 737-3560.
Fax: (607) 737-3562

OSHRIN, Alan D. *(Justice, New York Supreme Court Tenth Judicial District)* Currently serves as Administrative Judge.

Mailing address: P.O. Box 9070, Central Islip 11722-9070.

Office: Court Complex, 400 Carleton Avenue, Central Islip 11722.

Telephone: (631) 853-5368.
Fax: (631) 853-7741

OWEN, Joseph G. *(Justice, New York Supreme Court Ninth Judicial District)* Acting Justice 1984-93. Elected Justice to term beginning Jan 1, 1994. Term expires Dec 31, 2007. Born Chester New York Nov 7, 1933. Catholic. Educated at City College of the City University of New York B.A. in Social Sciences 1955 and Fordham University School of Law LL.B. 1959. Admitted to practice New York 1959 and U.S. District Courts Southern 1959 and Eastern 1960 Districts of New York. In legal practice New York City 1959-63 and Goshen 1963-84. Justice, Wallkill Town Justice Court 1974-84. Surrogate, Orange County Surrogate's Court 1984-93.

Member The Surrogates' Association of the State of New York, New York State Association of Magistrates, Association of Justices of the Supreme Court of the State of New York, Orange County Magistrates Association (President 1978-79), Goshen (President 1979), Orange County, New York State and American Bar Associations. Major USAR and National Guard 1955-70. President Republican Club 1970-75 and Republican Committeeman 1972-74 Town of Wallkill. Member Knights of Columbus, American Legion, Kiwanis, Club of Middletown, Circleville Fire Company and Old Monroe Village. Enjoys walking and reading.

Office: 255 Main Street, Goshen 10924.

Telephone: (845) 291-3130.
Fax: (845) 291-3045

OWEN, Richard *(Senior Judge, United States District Court Southern District of New York)* Appointed for life by President Richard M. Nixon to term beginning 1974. Assumed Senior status Sept 9, 1989, serves by assignment. Born New York New York Dec 11, 1922. Religious affiliation: Society of Friends. Educated at Dartmouth College A.B. 1947 and Harvard University LL.B. 1950. Admitted to practice New York 1950. In legal practice New York City 1950-74.

Assistant U.S. Attorney Southern District of New York 1953-55. Special Assistant Attorney General 1954. Senior Trial Attorney Antitrust Division U.S. Department of Justice 1955-58. Associate Counsel New York State Moreland Committee on Alcoholic Beverage Control Laws 1963-64. Assistant Professor New York Law School 1951-53. First Lieutenant USAAC 1942-45. Recipient Distinguished Flying Cross with oak leaf cluster and Air Medal with three oak leaf clusters. Republican. Trustee Manhattan School of Music. Member American Society of Composers, Authors and Publishers, Century Association, Metropolitan Opera Club, Pine Pond Yacht Club (Commodore 1967-70) and Chelsea Yacht Club. Librettist and opera composer.

Office: 2903 U.S. Courthouse, 40 Centre Street, New York 10007-1581.

Telephone: (212) 805-6155.

PADILLA, Jose A., Jr. *(Judge, The Civil Court of the City of New York)* Elected to term beginning Jan 1, 1995. Term expires Dec 2004. Currently serves as Acting Justice, New York Supreme Court First Judicial District. Born New York New York Sept 21, 1959. Educated at Fordham University 1980 and New York University School of Law 1983. Root-Tilden Scholar. Admitted to practice New York and U.S. District Courts Eastern and Southern Districts of New York.

Office: 111 Centre Street, Room 453, New York 10013.

Telephone: (212) 374-8072.
Fax: (212) 374-6311

PADRO, Eduardo *(Justice, New York Supreme Court First Judicial District)* Former Judge, The Civil Court of the City of New York, elected to term beginning Jan 1, 1995.

Office: 100 Centre Street, New York 10013.

Telephone: (212) 374-4626.

PAGONES, James D. *(Surrogate, Dutchess County Surrogate's Court)* Former Judge, Dutchess County Family Court.

Office: Courthouse, 10 Market Street, Poughkeepsie 12601-3203.

Telephone: (845) 486-2242.
Fax: (845) 486-2234

PAGONES, Timothy G. *(Judge, Beacon City Court)* Currently serves as Acting Justice, New York Supreme Court Ninth Judicial District.

Office: One Municipal Plaza, Suite 2, Beacon 12508.

Telephone: (845) 838-5030.
Fax: (845) 838-5041

PALMIERI, Daniel *(Judge, Nassau County Court)* Elected to term beginning Jan 1, 1995. Judge, Nassau County District Court Jan 1, 1989 to Dec 31, 1994.

Office: Nassau County Courthouse, 262 Old Country Road, Mineola 11501.

Telephone: (516) 571-3765.
Fax: (516) 571-3256

PALUMBO, Daniel R. *(Acting Judge, Olean City Court)*

Mailing address: P.O. Box 631, Olean 14760-0631.

Office: Municipal Building, Olean 14760.

Telephone: (716) 376-5620.
Fax: (716) 376-5623

PANEPINTO, Barbara I. *(Judge, The Civil Court of the City of New York)* Currently serves as Supervising Judge. Also serves as Acting Justice, New York Supreme Court Second Judicial District.

Office: 927 Castleton Avenue, West New Brighton, Staten Island 10310.

Telephone: (718) 390-5425.
Fax: (718) 390-8108

PAPA, Mario J. *(Judge, Gloversville City Court)* Currently serves as Acting Judge.

Office: City Hall, Three Frontage Road, Gloversville 12078.

PAPA, MARIO J.—*Continued*

Telephone: (518) 773-4527.
Fax: (518) 773-4599

PARDES, Sondra K. *(Judge, Nassau County District Court)*
Office: 99 Main Street, Hempstead 11550.
Telephone: (516) 571-2200.

PARGA, Anthony L. *(Justice, New York Supreme Court Tenth Judicial District)* Former Judge, Nassau County District Court.
Office: Supreme Court Building, 100 Supreme Court Drive, Mineola 11501.
Telephone: (516) 571-2373.

PARIS, Anthony J. *(Justice, New York Supreme Court Fifth Judicial District)* Born Syracuse New York Aug 14, 1948. Roman Catholic. Educated at Syracuse University B.A. 1970 J.D. 1973. Law Clerk to Onondaga County Family Court 1972-73. Admitted to practice New York 1974, U.S. District Courts Northern District of New York 1976 and District of Columbia 1976 and U.S. Court of Appeals District of Columbia Circuit 1976. In legal practice Syracuse 1974-93. Former Judge, Onondaga County Family Court, elected Nov 1992 to term beginning Jan 1, 1993.
Assistant District Attorney Onondaga County 1977-89. Board of Directors Onondaga County Bar Foundation. Member Association of Judges of the Family Court of the State of New York, Association of Justices of the Supreme Court of the State of New York and Onondaga County Bar Association. Guest Lecturer on all aspects of domestic relations at various conferences and symposiums. Board of Directors Ronald McDonald House Charities of the City of New York and Columbus Foundation. Volunteer various community functions. Enjoys jogging, coaching, swimming and spending time with family.
Office: Onondaga County Courthouse, 401 Montgomery Street, Syracuse 13202.
Telephone: (315) 671-1104.

PARKER, Sheryl L. *(Judge, The Criminal Court of the City of New York)* Appointed by mayor. Currently serves as Acting Justice, New York Supreme Court Second Judicial District.
Office: 120 Schermerhorn Street, Brooklyn 11201.
Telephone: (718) 643-8400.
E-mail address: sparker@courts.state.ny.us

PARTNOW, Mark I. *(Justice, New York Supreme Court Second Judicial District)*
Office: 120 Schermerhorn Street, Brooklyn 11201.
Telephone: (718) 643-8576.

PATSALOS, Jeanne M. *(Judge, Newburgh City Court)* Former Acting Judge. Appointed by City Council to term beginning Jan 1998. Term expires Dec 31, 2003. Born Newburgh New York March 29, 1964. Educated at State University of New York at Binghamton and Syracuse University School of Law J.D. 1989. Admitted to practice New York 1991. In legal practice 1991-2002.
Member New York State Association of City Court Judges.
Office: Public Safety Building, 57 Broadway, Newburgh 12550.
Telephone: (845) 568-0647.
Fax: (845) 565-1244

PATSALOS, Peter C. *(Justice, New York Supreme Court Ninth Judicial District)* Certificated. Born Newburgh New York March 21, 1929. Greek Orthodox. Educated at Seton Hall University B.S. and New York Law School J.D. Admitted to practice New York 1963. Began legal practice Newburgh 1963. Judge, Newburgh City Court 1977-83. Former Judge, Orange County Court, elected to term beginning Jan 1, 1984.
New York P.E.R.B. Mediator and Fact Finder 1968-73. Important Decisions: People v. Hellman 476 (criminal) New York Misc. 2d 1984 and People v. L. Blank (criminal) New York Misc. 2d 1985. President New York State Association of City Court Judges 1982-83. Member New York State Bar Association (Judicial Delegate). Recipient Appreciation Award from Newburgh Bar Association 1976, Excellence Award from Newburgh P.B.A. 1980, Friend of Education Award from Newburgh Teachers Association 1981 and Award of Merit from New York State Trial Lawyers Association 1982. City Councilman and President pro tem Newburgh 1965-73. Attorney and Chief Labor Negotiator Newburgh School District 1973-77.
Office: 255 Main Street, Goshen 10924.
Telephone: (845) 291-3135.

PATTERSON, Michelle Weston *(Justice, New York Supreme Court Second Judicial District)* Currently serves as Justice, New York Supreme Court Appellate Term Second and Eleventh Judicial Districts.
Office: 360 Adams Street, Brooklyn 11201.
Telephone: (718) 643-5882.
E-mail address: mpatterson@courts.state.ny.us

PATTERSON, Robert P., Jr. *(Senior Judge, United States District Court Southern District of New York)* Appointed for life by President Ronald Reagan to term beginning 1988. Assumed Senior status Dec 31, 1998, serves by assignment. Born New York New York July 11, 1923. Educated at Harvard College B.A. 1947 and Columbia University School of Law LL.B. 1950. In legal practice New York City 1950-52 and 1956-88.
Assistant Counsel New York State Crime Commission 1952-53. Assistant U.S. Attorney Southern District of New York 1953-56. Special Hearing Officer for Conscientious Objectors U.S. Department of Justice 1961-68. Assistant Counsel Banking and Currency Committee U.S. Senate 1954.
Office: 2550 U.S. Courthouse, 500 Pearl Street, New York 10007-1312.
Telephone: (212) 805-0238.

PATTI, Philip J. *(Judge, New York Court of Claims)* Appointed by Governor George E. Pataki.
Office: 500 Court Exchange Building, 144 Exchange Boulevard, Rochester 14614-2108.
Telephone: (585) 325-4500.
Fax: (585) 262-5715

PAULEY, William H., III *(Judge, United States District Court Southern District of New York)* Appointed for life by President Bill Clinton to term beginning Oct 28, 1998. Born Glen Cove New York Aug 14, 1952. Educated at Duke University A.B. 1974 J.D. 1977. In legal practice New York City 1978-98.
Deputy County Attorney Nassau County 1978. Assis-

PAULEY, WILLIAM H., III—*Continued*

tant Counsel to Minority Leader New York State Assembly 1984-98.

Office: 2210 U.S. Courthouse, 500 Pearl Street, New York 10007-1581.

Telephone: (212) 805-6387.

PAYNE, Kibbie F. *(Judge, The Civil Court of the City of New York)* Currently serves as Acting Justice, New York Supreme Court First Judicial District.

Office: 111 Centre Street, New York 10013.

Telephone: (212) 374-8497.

PAYNTER, Steven W. *(Judge, The Civil Court of the City of New York)* Currently assigned to The Criminal Court of the City of New York.

Office: 125-01 Queens Boulevard, Kew Gardens 11415.

Telephone: (718) 520-3855.

Fax: (718) 520-4712

PEARL, Jane *(Judge, New York City Family Court)* Appointed by Mayor Rudolph Giuliani.

Office: 900 Sheridan Avenue, Bronx 10451.

Telephone: (718) 590-3376.

Fax: (718) 590-7305

PECK, Andrew J. *(Magistrate Judge, United States District Court Southern District of New York)* Appointed by U.S. District Court judges 1994 to term beginning Feb 27, 1995. Reappointed 2003, current term expires Feb 27, 2011. Born New York New York Jan 1, 1953. Jewish. Educated at Cornell University A.B. with honors 1974 and Duke University School of Law J.D. with honors 1977. Notes and Comments Editor Duke Law Journal 1975-77. Law Clerk to Hon. Paul Roney, U.S. Court of Appeals Fifth Circuit 1977-78. Member Order of the Coif. Admitted to practice New York 1978, U.S. District Courts Eastern 1979 and Southern 1979 Districts of New York, U.S. Courts of Appeals Fourth 1980, Ninth 1980, Second 1982, Eleventh 1982, Third 1983, Fifth 1984, Sixth 1990, Seventh 1990, Eighth 1990, Tenth 1990 and Federal 1990 Circuits and U.S. Supreme Court 1983. In legal practice New York City 1978-95.

Important Opinions: In re Towers Financial Corporation 1995-97. Member Federal Magistrate Judges Association and American Bar Association. Past President and Board of Directors Berkshire Hills-Emanuel Camps, Inc. (non-profit camp for children and senior adults). Member Baker Street Irregulars and other Sherlock Holmes societies. Member Mystery Writers of America (Board of Directors).

Office: 1370 U.S. Courthouse, 500 Pearl Street, New York 10007-1312.

Telephone: (212) 805-0036.

Fax: (212) 805-7933

PECK, George R. *(Judge, Nassau County Court)*

Office: County Courthouse, 262 Old Country Road, Mineola 11501.

Telephone: (516) 571-2800.

PECKHAM, Eugene E. *(Surrogate, Broome County Surrogate's Court)* Assumed office 2001. Born Stamford Connecticut Aug 11, 1940. Educated at Wesleyan University B.A. 1962 with honors and distinction and Harvard University J.D. 1965. Admitted to practice New York 1965, U.S. District Court Northern District of New York 1965, Florida 1981, U.S. Tax Court 1974 and U.S. Court of Appeals Second Circuit 1975. In legal practice Binghamton 1965-2000.

Author "New Estate Planning Techniques for Small & Medium Sized Estates" 54, 514 Dec 1982 reprinted in *The Monthly Digest of Tax Articles* 37 May 1983, "*White v. U.S.* Upholds Full Deductibility of Attorney's Fees on Estate Tax Returns" 59, 55 May 1987, "Employee Business Expenses and the 2% Limit for Miscellaneous Deductions" 62, 60 April 1990, "Sometimes Plain Vanilla Is Best: The Impact of Chapter 14 on Family Limited Partnerships and Limited Liability Companies" 67, 50 Nov 1995, "Post Mortem Tax Planning Will Continue as Vital Element in Handling Large Estates" 71, 39 Dec 1999, "New Era for Estate Administration in New York Has Reduced Estate Tax but Many Requirements Still Apply" 72 Sept 2000, "Phase-Ins, Phase-Outs, Refunds and Sunsets Mark New Tax Bill, a/k/a EGTRRA 2001" 73, 41 Oct 2001 and "Last Resort Estate Planning Finds Acceptance in Statutes & Cases Relying on Substituted Judgment" 74, 33 March-April 2002 New York State B. Jour.; "Forming the Not for Profit Organization and Obtaining Tax Exemption" Committee on CLE New York State Bar Association May 5, 1989; "Estate Planning in a Volatile Economy" CLE Satellite Network May 7, 1991; and "Investment of Guardianship Funds" 6 Warren's Heaton Legislative and Case Digest 5 April 2002. Co-author with Allen J. Hall "Buy Sell Agreements Frozen" 63 New York State B. Jour. 50 Oct 1991. Board of Editors New York State B. Jour. since 1998 and Warren's Heaton on Surrogates' Courts since 2001.

Adjunct Lecturer 1972-77, Adjunct Assistant Professor 1977-81, Adjunct Associate Professor 1981-87 and Adjunct Professor since 1987 State University of New York at Binghamton. Visiting Lecturer 1978 and Adjunct Professor 1984 Cornell University. Treasurer Joint Legislative Advisory Committee on the Estates Powers and Trust Law since 1990. Fellow American College of Trusts and Estates Counsel. Member Federation of Bar Associations of the Sixth Judicial District (Vice President 1983-84, President 1984-85), Broome County and New York State (House of Delegates 1990-94 and 1995-2002, Vice President 1999-2002) Bar Associations. Listed in *Who's Who in American Law* since 1977 and *Who's Who in America* since 2000. Recipient Alumni Recognition Award from State University of New York at Binghamton Alumni Association 1984. Chairman Finance Committee 1982-83 and Vice Chairman 1996-2000 Broome County Republican Committee.

Peace Corps Volunteer Peru 1966-67. Director 1970-77 and President 1974-76 Binghamton Girls Club. Member 1971-74, Deacon 1971-74, Moderator 1973-74 and Trustee 1980-83 and 1993-96 First Presbyterian Church Binghamton. Director 1975-82, Member Executive Committee 1976-82 and President 1977-79 Foundation of State University of New York at Binghamton. Director Roberson Museum and Science Center 1977-80 and 1987-95 and A. Lindsay and Olive B. O'Connor Foundation since 1982. Secretary 1984-2001 and Director 1984-2001 Dr. G. Clifford and Florence B. Decker Foundation. Member 1985-90 and Chair 1999-2001 Broome County Board of Ethics. President Estate Planning Council 1986 and President The Samaritan Counseling Center 1987 The Southern Tier, Inc. Member 1987-2000 and Chairman 1996-2000 Foundation Board Binghamton Boys and Girls Club. Director since 1996 and Co-founder Community Foundation for Southern

PECKHAM, EUGENE E.—*Continued*

Central New York, Inc. Member Broom County United Way.
Office: Broome County Courthouse, Court Street, Binghamton 13902.
Telephone: (607) 778-2111.

PEEBLES, David E. *(Magistrate Judge, United States District Court Northern District of New York)* Appointed by U.S. District Court judges to term beginning May 22, 2000.
Mailing address: P.O. Box 7345, Syracuse 13261-7345.
Telephone (315) 234-8620.

PEREZ, Myrna M. Martinez *(Judge, New York City Family Court)* Appointed by mayor.
Office: 900 Sheridan Avenue, Bronx 10451.
Telephone: (718) 590-3376.
Fax: (718) 590-7305

PESCE, Michael L. *(Justice, New York Supreme Court Second Judicial District)* Former Acting Justice. Elected Justice to term beginning Jan 1, 1990. Term expires Dec 31, 2003. Former Administrative Judge. Currently serves as Presiding Justice, New York Supreme Court Appellate Term Second and Eleventh Judicial Districts. Born Italy March 1, 1943. Educated at City College of the City University of New York B.A. 1964, New School for Social Research M.A. 1966 and Detroit College of Law J.D. 1969. Member Delta Theta Phi. Admitted to practice New York 1970. Began legal practice New York City 1970. In legal practice Brooklyn 1974-80. Judge, The Criminal Court of the City of New York 1981-83. Judge, The Civil Court of the City of New York 1981-89.
Member American Justinian Society, Columbian Lawyers Association, Brooklyn Women's and Brooklyn Bar Associations. Member State Assembly New York 1973-80. Member Selection Committee Revlon Harmony Awards. Board of Directors Visiting Nurse Association.
Office: 360 Adams Street, Brooklyn 11201.
Telephone: (718) 643-7078.
Fax: (718) 643-8753
E-mail address: mpesce@courts.state.ny.us

PESSALA, John B. *(Judge, Nassau County Family Court)* Former Judge, Nassau County District Court.
Office: 1200 Old Country Road, Westbury 11590.
Telephone: (516) 571-9005.
Fax: (516) 571-9335

PETERS, Karen K. *(Associate Justice, New York Supreme Court Appellate Division Third Judicial Department)* Elected Justice to term beginning Jan 1, 1993. Appointed Associate Justice Appellate Division by Governor Mario Cuomo Feb 1994. Born Rockville Centre New York July 29, 1947. Educated at George Washington University B.A. 1969 and New York University School of Law J.D. cum laude 1972. Admitted to practice New York 1973 and U.S. Supreme Court 1979. In legal practice New Paltz 1973-79. Judge, Ulster County Family Court 1984-92.
Visiting Assistant District Attorney Dutchess County 1979. Counsel New York State Division of Alcoholism and Alcohol Abuse 1979-83. Director New York State Assembly Government Operations Committee 1983. Assistant Professor State University of New York at New Paltz 1973-74, 1976-79 and 1984. Chairperson Gender Bias Committee Third Judicial District 1991-93. Member Association of Judges of the Family Court of the State of New York, Association of Justices of the Supreme Court of the State of New York, Women's Bar Association of the State of New York, Ulster County and New York State (Special Committee on Lawyer Alcoholism and Drug Abuse 1980-94) Bar Associations. Lecturer and Participant numerous seminars on Family Law, Women and the Law, Alcoholism and the Law and Case Management and Settlement Skills. Lecturer Guardian Training Programs New York Supreme Court Appellate Division Third Judicial Department and Albany Law School, Domestic Violence Education Programs New York Medical College, New York State Task Force on Permanency Planning for Foster Children and Annual Judicial Seminars New York State Office of Court Administration. Recipient Tribute to Women Award from YWCA 1987, Dean's Award from State University of New York at New Paltz 1989, Harold D. Koreman Award 1992, Martin Luther King, Jr. Award 1992 and Gabrielli Memorial Award 1999. Prepared and presented testimony on dispositional alternatives 1980 and on PINS jurisdiction and dispositional alternatives 1982 New York State Temporary Commission to Recodify the Family Court Act, on Labelling and Advertising of Alcoholic Beverages Bureau of Alcohol, Tobacco and Firearms U.S. Department of the Treasury 1981, on Criteria for Supplemental Grants Under Federal Drunk Driving Legislation National Highway Traffic Safety Administration U.S. Department of Transportation 1982 and on surrogate parenting legislation New York State Senate Child Care Committee 1987. Former Director New York State Coalition for Children of Alcoholic Families. Director Planned Parenthood of Ulster County. Member NAACP.
Office: Ulster County Courthouse, 281 Wall Street, Kingston 12401-3817.
Telephone: (845) 340-3757.

PFAU, Ann T. *(Judge, The Criminal Court of the City of New York)* Appointed by Mayor Rudolph Giuliani. Currently serves as Deputy Chief Administrative Judge Management Support. Also serves as Administrative Judge, New York Supreme Court Second Judicial District.
Office: 360 Adams Street, Brooklyn 11201.
Telephone: (718) 643-7086.
Office: 25 Beaver Street, New York 10004.
Telephone: (212) 428-2120.
Fax: (212) 428-2190

PFEIFFER, Ann E. *(Judge, Rochester City Court)* Elected to term beginning Jan 1, 1986. Reelected 1995, current term expires Dec 31, 2005. Born Dansville New York March 22, 1953. Educated at Rosary Hill (now Doemen College) B.A. magna cum laude 1975 and State University of New York at Buffalo J.D. 1979. Recipient Moot Court Award. Member Order of Barristers. Admitted to practice New York 1980 and U.S. District Court Western District of New York 1980. In legal practice Rochester 1982-85.
Assistant Public Defender Monroe County 1979-82. Member Greater Rochester Association of Women Attorneys and Women's Bar Association of the State of New York (Board of Directors 1986-87). Democrat.
Office: 6 Hall of Justice, 99 Exchange Boulevard, Rochester 14614.

PFEIFFER, ANN E.—*Continued*
Telephone: (585) 428-2470.
Fax: (585) 428-4265

PHELAN, Thomas P. *(Justice, New York Supreme Court Tenth Judicial District)* Former Judge, Nassau County District Court.
Office: Supreme Court Building, 100 Supreme Court Drive, Mineola 11501.
Telephone: (516) 571-2874.

PICKHOLZ, Ruth *(Judge, The Criminal Court of the City of New York)* Appointed by mayor. Currently serves as Acting Justice, New York Supreme Court First Judicial District.
Office: 100 Centre Street, New York 10013.
Telephone: (212) 374-6216.
Fax: (212) 374-2579

PIETRUSZKA, Michael F. *(Judge, Erie County Court)* Elected to term beginning 1999. Term expires Dec 31, 2008. Born Buffalo New York Oct 20, 1956. Roman Catholic. Educated at Canisius College B.A. magna cum laude 1978 and Syracuse University College of Law J.D. cum laude 1981. Recipient American Jurisprudence Award 1981 and International Legal Studies Award 1981. Named Phi Delta Phi Graduate of the Year by Comstock Inn 1981. Executive Editor Syracuse Journal of International Law & Commerce 1980-81. Member Phi Delta Phi. Admitted to practice New York 1982, U.S. District Court Western District of New York 1982, U.S. Court of International Trade 1985 and U.S. Supreme Court 1986. In legal practice Buffalo 1982-87. Judge, Buffalo City Court Jan 1, 1988 to 1998, appointed by Mayor James Griffin.

Assistant Corporation Counsel 1983-86 and Director Division of Parking Enforcement 1986-87 Buffalo. General Counsel Buffalo Municipal Housing Authority 1987. Author "Our Law and You" (weekly column) AMPOL Eagle 1982-83 and "Columns of Justice" (bi-weekly column) *Metro Community News* 1990-91. Contributor "Analysis of the Draft of Principles of Act Regarding Judges, Lay Judges, and Junior Judges for the Slovak Republic" CEELI Project American Bar Association 1997. Associate Editor Polish American Journal since 1993. New York State Bar Association Representative U.S. Secretary of State's Advisory Committee on Private International Law Annual Meeting 1990. Master of the Bench Charles S. Desmond Chapter American Inns of Court. Member Judges and Police Conference of Erie County, New York State Eighth Judicial District Judicial Advisory Council, County Judges Association of the State of New York, Advocates Club of Western New York (Past President), American Judges Association, The Association of Trial Lawyers of America, Bar Association of Erie County, New York State and American (Secretary, Member Executive Committee National Conference of Special Court Judges) Bar Associations. Investment Panel Moderator Conference on Trade and Investment in Central Europe 1990. Attended Second International Conference on Regional and Municipal Cooperation, Prague Czech Republic 1991. Workshop Presenter New York State Sister Cities Convention Rochester 1992. Judicial Seminar Faculty "Problems in Local Criminal Courts" 1993, "What Do Your Sentences Really Mean?" 1994, "Selected Topics in Vehicle and Traffic Law" 1995, "Jenna's Law: A New Sentencing Scheme for First Time Violent Offenders" 1999 and "Jenna's Law/Sentencing Issues—Legal Update Seminar for Court Attorneys" 2000; Chairman Local Criminal Court Sentencing Subcommittee 1996; and Panelist Local Criminal Court Workshop 1997 and Domestic Violence Program for the Criminal and Family Courts 1998 New York State Unified Court System. Faculty "Petit Larceny: A Jury Trial Demonstration" Erie Institute of Law 1997.

Recipient Jurist Citation of Honor from National Columbus Day Committee 1988, Martin Luther King, Jr. Human Relations Award from Western New York Chapter of Southern Christian Leadership Conference 1991, Northwest Buffalo Community Service Award 1991 and Certificate of Honor from New York State Bar Association 1992, 1993 and 1994. Named Man of the Year by Pulaski Police Association 1989 and Am-Pol Eagle Citizen of the Year 1991. Listed in *Who's Who in America 2000-Millennium Edition* 1999. Democrat. President Western New York Chapter Kosciuszko Foundation. Member Forest District Civic Association, Professional and Businessman's Association, Northwest Buffalo Community Center, Floss Avenue Men's Choir and Orchestra, St. Gabriel's Parish, Chopin Singing Society, NAACP, Polish Cadets, Buffalo Urban League, Buffalo-Rzeszow Sister City, Inc., Buffalo Canoe Club, Knights of Columbus, The Polish American Congress (Vice President Western New York Division), Polish American/Jewish American Council of Western New York, Polish Arts Club of Buffalo, St. Joseph's Guild and West Side Business and Taxpayers Association. Enjoys travel.
Office: Erie County Hall, 92 Franklin Street, Buffalo 14202.
Telephone: (716) 858-2896.
Fax: (716) 851-3332
E-mail address: pietruszka@aol.com *or* mpietrus-@courts.state.ny.us
Website address: http://members.aol.com/pietruszka/index.html

PIGOTT, Eugene F., Jr. *(Presiding Justice, New York Supreme Court Appellate Division Fourth Judicial Department)* Elected Justice Eighth Judicial District. Appointed Associate Justice Appellate Division by Governor George E. Pataki.
Office: 50 Delaware Avenue, Buffalo 14202.
Telephone: (716) 851-3412.
Fax: (716) 853-9235

PINE, Elizabeth W. *(Associate Justice, New York Supreme Court Appellate Division Fourth Judicial Department)*
Office: Courthouse, 50 East Avenue, Rochester 14604.
Telephone: (585) 530-3210.
Fax: (585) 530-3245

PINEDA-KIRWAN, Diccia T. *(Judge, The Civil Court of the City of New York)*
Office: 89-17 Sutphin Boulevard, Jamaica 11435.
Telephone: (718) 262-7100.

PINES, Emily *(Justice, New York Supreme Court Tenth Judicial District)* Elected to term beginning Jan 1, 2002. Term expires Dec 31, 2015. Born New York New York Nov 20, 1950. Educated at Hofstra University B.A. magna cum laude 1972 and Hofstra University School of Law J.D. with distinction 1976. Admitted to practice New York 1977. Judge, Suffolk County District Court Jan 1, 1999 to Dec 31, 2001.

Assistant Corporate Counsel New York City 1980-86.

PINES, EMILY—*Continued*
Deputy County Attorney Suffolk County 1988-92. Town Attorney Brookhaven 1993-98. Member Suffolk County Matrimonial, Suffolk County Women's (Officer, Director), Suffolk County and New York State (Ethics Committee) Bar Associations. Named Municipal Attorney of the Year by The Association of the Bar of the City of New York 1983.

Office: Court Complex, 400 Carleton Avenue, Central Islip 11722.
Telephone: (631) 853-5160.

PINES, Spero *(Judge, Broome County Family Court)*
Mailing address: P.O. Box 1766, Binghamton 13902.
Office: 65 Hawley Street, Binghamton 13901.
Telephone: (607) 778-2156.
Fax: (607) 778-2439

PITMAN, Henry B. *(Magistrate Judge, United States District Court Southern District of New York)* Appointed by U.S. District Court judges.

Office: 750 U.S. Courthouse, 500 Pearl Street, New York 10007-1312.
Telephone: (212) 805-6105.

PITTS, Arthur G. *(Justice, New York Supreme Court Tenth Judicial District)* Elected to term beginning Jan 1, 2000. Term expires Dec 31, 2013. Born Feb 8, 1952. Educated at Colgate University B.A. 1973 and St. John's Law University J.D. 1981. In legal practice Lindenhurst 1982-87 and Mineola Sept 1992 to Dec 1992. Judge, Suffolk County Court Jan 1993 to Dec 1999. Acting Surrogate, Suffolk County Surrogate's Court 1995-97.

Town Supervisor Babylon Jan 1988 to Sept 1992. Member New York State Association of Magistrates, Association of Justices of the Supreme Court of the State of New York, Suffolk County Women's Bar Association, Suffolk County and New York State Bar Associations. Former Member Executive Board Association of Towns of the State of New York. Board of Trustees Catholic Charities. Board Member Diocese of Rockville Centre. Member Sons of the American Legion, Ancient Order of Hibernians and Loyal Order of Moose.

Mailing address: P.O. Box 9007, Riverhead 11901.
Office: 5 Court Complex, 210 Center Drive, Riverhead 11901.
Telephone: (631) 852-2174.
Fax: (631) 852-2769
E-mail address: apitts@courts.state.ny.us

PLATT, Thomas Collier, Jr. *(Senior Judge, United States District Court Eastern District of New York)* Appointed for life by President Richard M. Nixon to term beginning May 17, 1974. Chief Judge 1988-95. Assumed Senior status Feb 1, 2001, serves by assignment. Born New York New York May 29, 1925. Episcopalian. Educated at Yale University B.A. 1947 LL.B. 1950. Admitted to practice New York 1950, U.S. District Courts Southern 1953, Eastern 1953 and Northern 1966 Districts of New York, U.S. Treasury Department 1953, U.S. Court of Appeals Second Circuit 1954 and U.S. Court of Claims 1972. In legal practice New York City 1950-53 and 1956-74. Acting Police Justice, Incorporated Village of Lloyd Harbor 1958-63.

Assistant U.S. Attorney Eastern District of New York 1953-56. Village Attorney Incorporated Village of Laurel Hollow 1957-74. Former member The Association of the Bar of the City of New York (Federal Courts Committee, Municipal Courts Committee), Bar Association of Nassau County, New York State and American Bar Associations. Ensign USNR 1943-46. Republican. Suffolk County Republican Committeeman 1957-74. Alternate Delegate Republican National Convention 1964, 1968 and 1972. Delegate Republican State Convention 1966. Enjoys sailboat cruising, racing and tennis.

Office: Long Island Federal Courthouse, 1044 Federal Plaza, Central Islip 11722-4438.
Telephone: (631) 712-5600.

PLUMADORE, Jan H. *(Justice, New York Supreme Court Fourth Judicial District)* Currently serves as Administrative Judge. Born Potsdam New York July 29, 1942. Roman Catholic. Educated at St. Lawrence University B.S. 1964 and Albany Law School of Union University J.D. 1968. Member Alpha Tau Omega and Alpha Omicron. Admitted to practice New York 1970. Began legal practice Saranac Lake 1970. Former Judge, Franklin County Court, elected to term beginning Jan 1, 1978. Former Surrogate, Franklin County Surrogate's Court. Former Judge, Franklin County Family Court.

Town Attorney Harrietstown 1971-77 and St. Armand 1973-77. Important Decisions: People v. Boots et al. (state's jurisdiction over Indians) 106 Misc. 2d 522, 434 N.Y.S.2d 850, 1980; People v. Thompson et al. (defendant appearance) 107 Misc. 2d 258, 433 N.Y.S.2d 961, 1980; People v. Lawrence (case dismissal) 106 Misc. 2d 482, 434 N.Y.S.2d 311, 1980; Matter of Jason ZZ (revocation of consent to adoption) 79 A.D.2d 737, 434 N.Y.S.2d 759, 1980; People v. Boots et al. (appellate affirmation of case dismissal) 83 A.D.2d 705, 442 N.Y.S.2d 286, 1981; People v. Herne (waiver of indictment and prosecution) 110 Misc. 2d 152, 441 N.Y.S.2d 936, 1981; People v. Slocum (leaving scene of accident) 126 Misc. 2d 364, 481 N.Y.S.2d 984 rev'd 112 A.D. 2d 641, 492 N.Y.S.2d 195, 1984; People v. Morse (types and issues re: blood tests in vehicular prosecutions) 127 Misc. 2d 468, 486 N.Y.S.2d 621, 1985; and Woodbeck v. Caputo and Associates (no Dram Shop contribution liability where Plaintiff was person served) 131 Misc. 2d 321, 500 N.Y.S.2d 481, 1986. Member New York State Trial Lawyers Association, New York State Family Court Judges Association, New York State Surrogate Court Judges Association, New York State County Court Judges Association, Franklin County and New York State Bar Associations. Captain U.S. Army 1968-70 (active duty in Vietnam 1969-70). Recipient Bronze Star and Vietnamese Medal of Honor. Republican. Franklin County Legislator 1974-77. Republican County Chairman 1976-77. Chairman Association of Adirondack County Governments 1976-77 and Tri-Lakes Council of Local Governments 1976-77. Member 1980 Winter Olympics Organizing Committee since 1974, Elks, Kiwanis, VFW and American Legion. Volunteer football coach Saranac Lake High School since 1964. Rugby player and referee. Enjoys skiing.

Office: Supreme Court Chambers, 30 Main Street, Saranac Lake 12983-1794.
Telephone: (518) 891-3816.

POHORELSKY, Viktor V. *(Magistrate Judge, United States District Court Eastern District of New York)* Appointed by U.S. District Court judges to term beginning Jan 31, 1995. Reappointed 2003, current term expires Jan 31, 2011. Born Ludwigsburg Germany March 15, 1949. Episcopalian. Educated at Tulane University

POHORELSKY, VIKTOR V.—*Continued*

B.S. 1971 J.D. summa cum laude 1980. Editor-in-Chief Tulane Law Review 1979-80. Law Clerk to Hon. John Minor Wisdom, U.S. Court of Appeals Fifth Circuit 1980-81. Member Order of the Coif. Admitted to practice New York 1982, U.S. District Courts Eastern 1982 and Southern 1982 Districts of New York and U.S. Court of Appeals Second Circuit 1985. In legal practice New York 1982-84 and 1991-95.

Assistant U.S. Attorney Southern District of New York 1984-91.

Office: U.S. Courthouse, 225 Cadman Plaza East, Brooklyn 11201.
Telephone: (718) 260-2400.

POLITO, William P. *(Justice, New York Supreme Court Seventh Judicial District)* Elected Nov 5, 1996 to term beginning Jan 2, 1997. Term expires Dec 31, 2010. Born Rochester New York Nov 5, 1938. Roman Catholic. Educated at University of Toronto B.A. 1960 and Syracuse University College of Law LL.B. 1963. Admitted to practice New York 1963. In legal practice Rochester 1963-96.

Town Attorney Webster 1981-83. Member Monroe County and New York State Bar Associations. Monroe County Legislator 1987-91. Legal Aid Attorney and First Assistant 1964-69.

Office: 545 Hall of Justice, 99 Exchange Boulevard, Rochester 14614-2185.
Telephone: (585) 428-5271.
Fax: (585) 428-3554

POLIZZI, Thomas V. *(Justice, New York Supreme Court Eleventh Judicial District)* Elected to term beginning Jan 1, 1995. Certificated.

Office: 88-11 Sutphin Boulevard, Jamaica 11435.
Telephone: (718) 520-3722.
Fax: (718) 520-3044
E-mail address: tpolizzi@courts.state.ny.us

POLLACK, Milton *(Senior Judge, United States District Court Southern District of New York)* Appointed for life by President Lyndon B. Johnson to term beginning 1967. Assumed Senior status Sept 29, 1983, serves by assignment. Born New York New York Sept 29, 1906. Educated at Columbia University B.A. 1927 J.D. 1929. In legal practice New York City 1929-67.

Office: 2102 U.S. Courthouse, 40 Centre Street, New York 10007-1581.
Telephone: (212) 805-6115.

POLLAK, Cheryl L. *(Magistrate Judge, United States District Court Eastern District of New York)* Appointed by U.S. District Court judges.

Office: U.S. Courthouse, 225 Cadman Plaza East, Brooklyn 11201.
Telephone: (718) 260-2360.

PONTERIO, Frank V. *(Justice, New York Supreme Court Second Judicial District)* Certificated. Former Judge, The Civil Court of the City of New York, elected to term beginning Jan 1, 1987.

Office: 18 Richmond Terrace, Staten Island 10301.
Telephone: (718) 390-5212.
E-mail address: fponterio@courts.state.ny.us

POPEO, Gerald J. *(Judge, Utica City Court)*

Office: 411 Oriskany Street West, Utica 13502.
Telephone: (315) 724-6213.
Fax: (315) 792-8038

PORZIO, Ralph J. *(Judge, New York City Family Court)* Appointed by Mayor Rudolph Giuliani.

Office: 100 Richmond Terrace, Staten Island 10301.
Telephone: (718) 390-5462.

POSNER, Charles A. *(Judge, The Criminal Court of the City of New York)* Appointed by Mayor Rudolph Giuliani.

Office: 120 Schermerhorn Street, Brooklyn 11201.
Telephone: (718) 643-8400.
Fax: (718) 643-3538

POTTER, Barbara R. *(Judge, St. Lawrence County Family Court)*

Office: Courthouse, 48 Court Street, Canton 13617-1199.
Telephone: (315) 379-2410.
Fax: (315) 386-3197

POWERS, Mark L. *(Judge, Schenectady County Family Court)*

Office: 620 State Street, Schenectady 12305-2114.
Telephone: (518) 388-4305.
Fax: (518) 388-4496

PRAGER, Erica L. *(Judge, Nassau County District Court)*

Office: 99 Main Street, Hempstead 11550.
Telephone: (516) 572-2129.
E-mail address: prager@courts.state.ny.us

PREMINGER, Eve M. *(Surrogate, New York County Surrogate's Court)* Born Vienna Austria Sept 20, 1935. Educated at Antioch College and Columbia University LL.B. 1960. Stone Scholar. Staff member Columbia Law Review. Recipient Jane Marks Murphy Prize. Admitted to practice New York 1961. Former Justice, New York Supreme Court First Judicial District.

Instructor Columbia Law School 1971-76. Member The Association of the Bar of the City of New York. President Correctional Association of New York.

Office: 31 Chambers Street, New York 10007.
Telephone: (212) 374-4500.

PRESKA, Loretta A. *(Judge, United States District Court Southern District of New York)* Appointed for life by President George Bush Aug 12, 1992 to term beginning Sept 18, 1992. Educated at College of St. Rose B.A. 1970, Fordham University J.D. 1973 and New York University LL.M. in Trade Regulation 1978. Admitted to practice New York 1974, U.S. District Courts Eastern 1974 and Southern 1974 Districts of New York, U.S. Court of Appeals Second Circuit 1974 and U.S. Supreme Court 1977. In legal practice Sept 1973 to Sept 1992.

Member New York County Lawyers' Association, Federal Bar Council and New York State Bar Association.

Office: 1320 U.S. Courthouse, 500 Pearl Street, New York 10007-1312.
Telephone: (212) 805-0240.

PRICE, Arnold N. *(Justice, New York Supreme Court Eleventh Judicial District)* Elected to term beginning Jan 1, 1992. Certificated. Former Judge, The Civil

PRICE, ARNOLD N.—*Continued*

Court of the City of New York, elected to term beginning Jan 1, 1989.

Office: 88-11 Sutphin Boulevard, Jamaica 11435.

Telephone: (718) 520-3056.

PRICE, Richard Lee *(Justice, New York Supreme Court First Judicial District)* Acting Justice First Judicial District Jan 1981 to June 1981 and Nov 1981 to Jan 22, 1982. Former Acting Justice Twelfth Judicial District. Born Sept 19, 1940. Educated at Roanoke College B.A. in Political Science 1961 and New York Law School J.D. 1964. Awarded honorary LL.D. Shaw University 1980. Staff member New York Law Forum. Recipient American Jurisprudence Awards in New York Practice, Torts and Common Law Pleadings. Recipient Trial Lawyers Library Award. Moot Court. Admitted to practice New York 1965, U.S. District Courts Eastern and Southern Districts of New York, U.S. Customs Court, U.S. Court of Appeals Second Circuit and U.S. Supreme Court. In legal practice New York City 1965-69. Former Judge, The Civil Court of the City of New York, elected to term beginning Jan 1, 1981.

With Consumer Frauds Bureau and Labor Bureau Attorney General's Office 1962-64. Law Secretary to Hon. Harry W. Davis June 1969 to May 1976, Counsel to Administrative Judges June 1976 to Dec 1980 and Chief Law Assistant 1976-80 The Civil Court of the City of New York. Author "Small Claims in New York City" New York L. Jour. 1 Jan 21, 1980; *A Guide to Small Claims Court* Office of Court Administration 1980; "The New Morality and Landlord-Tenant Law: Hudson View and Its Progeny" New York State B. Jour. 33 Oct 1983; "The Damages Dilemma in Warranty of Habitability Cases—Analysis and Solution" New York L. Jour. 1 Dec 7, 1983; "Issues in Marital Rape Exemption" New York L. Jour. Law Day Edition 38 Dec 7, 1983 and May 1, 1984; "Landlord Liability—Breach of Warranty of Habitability" 16 No. 1 Trial Lawyers Quar. 13, 1984; "Observations from the Bench on Non-Stranger Rape Trials" 22 No. 1 Court Review Winter 1985; "Voir Dire" *Bill of Particulars* New York State Trial Lawyers Association March 1985; "Pro Se—A Judicial Dilemma" New York L. Jour. 1 June 3, 1985; "Battered Woman Syndrome—A Defense Begins to Emerge" New York L. Jour. 1 Nov 29, 1985; "The Judge" New York State Bar Association/New York State Education Department Dec 1985; "I.A.S." (Criminal Term) *Bill of Particulars* New York State Trial Lawyers Association Feb/March 1986; "Criminal Law—Competing Interest" *Metropolitan Women's Bar Association Bulletin* 1988 and 12 No. 1 *Benchmark* American Judges Association 1989; "Separate But Equal" 12 No. 4 *Benchmark* American Judges Association Winter 1989; "Judicial Goals and Priorities" President's Message 28 No. 3 *Court Review* 1991; "Incest and the Legal System" New York L. Jour. 2 April 24, 1992; "Should Judges Be Elected" *State Government News* Aug 1992; "Listening to the Jurors" New York L. Jour. Dec 20, 1993; and "The Reluctant Witness" New York L. Jour. 2 July 8, 1994. Instructor in Small Claims Manhattan Community College and Law for the Layperson Murry Bergtraum Evening Adult School since 1983. Lecturer on Small Claims Pace University.

President Civil Court Law Secretaries Association 1973-75 and Arbitrators Association of the Small Claims Court 1979-80. Member Panel to Review New York Probation July 1987. Chair Gender Bias Committee Twelfth Judicial District since Dec 1987. Member Jewish Lawyers Guild (Board of Directors since 1969), The Council of New York Law Associates, New York State Trial Lawyers Association (Chair Committee on Judicial Administration and Procedure 1982), New York County Lawyers' Association (Co-chair Task Force on Domestic Violence 1996-98, Director 1998, Chair Law-Related Education Committee, Supreme Court Committee, Committee on Women's Rights), National Association of Women Judges (Projects Committee, National Task Force on Gender Bias in the Courts, International Community Outreach Committee, Bias in Judicial Selection and Evaluation Committee), American Judicature Society (Criminal Justice Reform Committee 1995-96), American Judges Association (Secretary, Vice President and President 1991-92, Chair Domestic Violence Committee), American Judges Foundation (Former Treasurer), Black Bar Association of Bronx County, The Association of the Bar of the City of New York (Former Member Committee on Women in the Courts, Member Committee on Women in the Profession, Council on Judicial Administration), Puerto Rican Bar Association of New York, Metropolitan Women's (Board of Directors, Chair Criminal Law Committee and Task Force on Discrimination of Women in the Courts), New York Criminal and Civil Courts (Vice President), Bronx Women's (Treasurer since 1998, Board of Directors, Chair Gender Bias Committee), New York Women's (Former Chair Committee on Gender Bias), New York State (Former Chair Committee on District, City, Village and Town Courts; Chair Committee on Citizenship Education, Committee on Justice and the Community; Member Ad Hoc Committee on Jury System) and American (Task Force on Law-Related Education, Committee on Courts and the Community and National Conference of State Trial Judges Judicial Administration Division) Bar Associations.

Member Curriculum Development Committee in the area of Evidence 1984-86. Board Member New York State Criminal Court Judges Training Committee. Faculty member 1985 and Facilitator Gender Bias Program 1986 judicial seminars Office of Court Administration. Lecturer Government Career Information Symposium New York University Feb 24, 1978; Orientation for New Arbitrators 1978-80; Orientation Program for New Law Assistants in the Family Court March 8, 1979; Orientation Program for Newly Elected Judges in Civil Court Jan 1979 and Jan 1980; "Criminal Justice System—An Inside View" Educational Alliance Gladys Herzman Lecture Forum Oct 7, 1983, 1984, 1986 and 1990; "Court Unification, Selection of Judges and Judicial Politics" Fordham University March 6 and 13, 1984; "The Small Claims Court" Baruch College April 2, 1984; "Marital Rape" New York Women's Bar Association Dec 11, 1984; "Battered Women and the System" Women's Ensemble Theatre and WBAI Feb 26, 1986; Advisory Council of the Abused Spouse Assistance Services Mental Health Association of Westchester March 31, 1986; "Judges Role in Law Related Education" American Judges Association, Toronto Oct 1988; and "Battered Women's Syndrome" Bar Association of Nassau County Oct 31, 1988. Panelist "Rape" Women in the Law Today Legal Association of Women New York Law School Oct 27, 1984; "Youth on Justice: A Public Forum" New York State Bar Association and New York Daily News May 15, 1985; "Youth and Our Justice System—Justice for All" Presidential Showcase

PRICE, RICHARD LEE—*Continued*

American Bar Association and The Association of the Bar of the City of New York Aug 8, 1993; and "Jury Reform and Its Challenges" New York State Conference of Bar Leaders and New York State Bar Association May 20, 1994.

Moderator "Orders of Protection: A Practical Approach" New York Women's Bar Association April 10, 1985; Criminal Jury Selection Bronx Court Monitoring Project Oct 23, 1988; and "Cameras in the Courtroom—Pass or Fail" Metropolitan Women's Bar Association Spring 1989. Moderator and Chair "Sex Discrimination in the Courts" Metropolitan Women's Bar Association May 22, 1985. Moderator New York Courts and Battered Women I and Coordinator New York Courts and Battered Women II Fourth Annual Conference on the Legal Rights of Battered Women 1984. Moderator and Coordinator Family Court Practice for Advocates, Moderator Family Court Practice for Attorneys and Welcome Speaker Fifth Annual Conference on the Legal Rights of Battered Women Nov 13, 1985, 1986 and 1987. Presenter "Happy Birthday Constitution" 1987, Twelfth Annual Conference Nov 1988, "Rights and Responsibilities" Oct 25-27, 1989, "Bill of Rights, Etc." Oct 1990, Oct 1991 and Oct 1992 and "Law, Youth and Citizenship" 1993, 1994, 1996, 1997, 1998 and 2000 Annual Statewide Conference on Law Related Education New York State Bar Association; "Youth at Risk" New York County Lawyers' Association March 1989; Court Officer Academy Office of Court Administration May 1989; and "Connecting Students to the Courts: Proven Programs and Strategies to Teach the Justice System" New York State Bar Association Annual Conference on Law Related Education Oct 28, 1999 and Oct 2000. Speaker "Implementation of Recommendations to Eliminate Gender Bias in the Courts" Brooklyn Bar Association May 3, 1990, "Public Education and the Law" New York State Bar Association Jan 1993, 1994, 1995 and 1996, "Power—Control" Domestic Violence Conference Oct 4, 1991, Symposium "Domestic Violence in the Courtroom" Nov 15, 1991, "Domestic Violence" New York State Criminal Court Judges Training Project April 30, 1992 and May 6, 1992, Forum on Domestic Violence Nov 4, 1992, "Needs of the Courts" Network of Bar Leaders Nov 18, 1992 and "Education for Arbitrators" June 1993, 1994 and 1995 New York County Lawyers' Association, "Gender Bias in the Courtroom" *Best Talk* WPIX-TV Nov 11, 1992, Orientation and Training of Arbitrators The Association of the Bar of the City of New York Dec 16, 1992, "Law Related Education" Court Attorneys Seminar Twelfth Judicial District Jan 28, 1993, "Judicial Fairness" Regional Conference American Judges Association Feb 20, 1993 and "Operation Cooperation" New York State Bar Association May 25, 1994.

Listed in *Who's Who in the East, Who's Who in American Law, Men of Achievement, Who's Who in World Jewry, Community Leaders and Noteworthy Americans, Personalities of America, International Book of Honor, Two Thousand Notable Americans, Community Leaders of the World, Who's Who of Contemporary Achievement, Who's Who in American Jewry, Personalities of the East, Community Leaders of America, Directory of Distinguished Americans, Dictionary of International Biography, Biography International, The International Directory of Distinguished Leadership, Biography of the Year* and *Men and Women of Distinction.* Recipient Lower East Side Jewish Festival Public Service Award June 9, 1985, Award of Achievement from New York State Bar Association May 15, 1986 and 1993, Achievement in Law Related Education Award from New York City Board of Education June 6, 1986, Gender Fairness Award from Bronx Women's Bar Association Sept 24, 1992 and Judicial Excellence Award from The Association of Arbitrators Nov 16, 1992.

Lecturer Public School Experimental Gates Program Seventh Grade Class Grand Street Academy Oct 20, 1982; "The Court System and the Law" Fourth Grade Class Jan 28, 1983 and Oct 16, 1983 and Informal Workshop for Teachers Oct 16, 1983 Public School 196; and Orientation for Five New York City Chapters of New York Public Interest Research Groups College of Staten Island. Former Chairman Cooperative Village Health Drive. Chairman Manhattan Borough President's Safety Commission 1972-77. Board of Directors East Side Torah Center. Member Community School Board District 1, 1973-80 (Vice Chairman 1973-74 and 1979-80). President Lawyers Lodge 2929 B'nai B'rith 1976-78 and 1986-90. Executive Officer Lieutenant Seventh Precinct Auxiliary Police 1980. Vice President Education Alliance Alumni Association. Board of Governors District I B'nai B'rith. Advisory Council on Violence and the Family American Psychological Association. Advisory Board Law, Government and Community Service Magnet High School 1994. Board of Trustees Educational Alliance. Member Coordinating Council of Cooperatives 1973-91. Member East River Housing Committee (Chairman 1969, 1974, 1975, and 1977-81), Manhattan Borough President's Planning Board 3, 1969-77, National Organization for Women, New York Regional Board Anti-Defamation League of B'nai B'rith (Law Committee), Governor's Commission on Child Support (Chair Committee on Setting the Support Amount 1984-90), Bialystoker Synagogue (Board of Trustees 1966-79), Citizens Committee for the Equal Rights Amendment, Lower East Side Businessmen's Association (Board of Directors 1977-80) and B'nai B'rith Career and Counseling Services (Advisory Board 1984-86).

Office: 851 Grand Concourse, Bronx 10451.
Telephone: (718) 590-3590.
E-mail address: rprice@courts.state.ny.us

PRUDENTI, A. Gail *(Presiding Justice, New York Supreme Court Appellate Division Second Judicial Department)* Acting Justice Tenth Judicial District 1996-2000. Elected Justice Tenth Judicial District to term beginning 2001. Appointed Associate Justice Appellate Division by Governor George E. Pataki to term beginning 2001. District Administrative Judge Suffolk County 1999-2001. Presiding Justice since Feb 2002. Educated at Marymount College B.A. 1974 and University of Aberdeen, Scotland LL.B. 1978. In legal practice 1982-91. Law Clerk to Suffolk County Surrogate's Court 1978-80. Justice, New York Supreme Court Tenth Judicial District 1992-94. Surrogate, Suffolk County Surrogate's Court 1995-2000.

Assistant District Attorney Suffolk County 1980-82. Author *Guidelines for Guardians ad Litem* 1995, 1997 and 2000, "Helpful Hints from the Surrogate" *Suffolk Lawyer* 1996, "Leadership Among Us" *The Jurist* 1998 and "Viewpoints" *Newsday* Oct 6, 1999. Member Gender Bias and Anti-Discrimination Panel since 1992 and Chairperson Mental Health Curriculum Committee for Trial Judges 2001 Office of Court Administration. Mem-

PRUDENTI, A. GAIL—*Continued*

ber Chief Judge's Committees on Matrimonial Rules 1993-94 and Public Access to Court Records since 2002 and Chief Administrative Judge's Judicial Legislative Group since 1997. Member Executive Committee The Surrogates' Association of the State of New York 1995-2000. Co-chair Chief Judge's Task Force on Delay in the Courts since 1997. Fellow New York Bar Foundation. Member Columbian Lawyers Association of Suffolk County (Board of Directors since 1994), New York State Trial Lawyers Association, American Justinian Society of Jurists, Association of Justices of the Supreme Court of the State of New York, Suffolk County Women's Bar Association, Suffolk County (Co-chair Surrogate's Court Committee 1990) and New York State (Treasurer 1996, Secretary 1997, Associate Presiding Member 1998 and Presiding Member 1999 Judicial Section) Bar Associations.

Lecturer Surrogate's Court Practice, Guardianship Practice Under Article 81, Continuing Legal Education Programs, Guidelines for Guardians ad Litem and Surrogate's Practice for Legal Secretaries and Paralegals Suffolk Academy of Law and Suffolk County Bar Association 1992-2000; Changes in Estate Tax Laws Diocese of Brooklyn and Queens 1996; Probate and Administration Proceedings (Contested and Uncontested) Trusts and Estates Section New York State Bar Association 1996-1998; and Judicial Training Seminars Office of Court Administration since 1996. Recipient Judicial Appreciation Award from Columbian Lawyers of Nassau County, Inc. 1995, District Attorney's Millennium 2000 Award for Outstanding Public Service Jan 2000, Directors Award from Suffolk County Bar Association May 2000 and Community Service Award from American Red Cross Nov 2000. Named Supreme Court Committee Honoree 2001 and Surrogate's Court Committee Honoree 2001 Suffolk County Bar Association. Board of Directors John T. Mather Memorial Hospital 1999-2002.

Office: 45 Monroe Place, Brooklyn 11201.
Telephone: (718) 722-6400.
Fax: (718) 855-2884

PRUS, Eric I. *(Judge, The Civil Court of the City of New York)*
Office: 141 Livingston Street, Brooklyn 11201.
Telephone: (718) 643-3172.
Fax: (718) 643-3733

PULVER, George J., Jr. *(Judge, Greene County Court)* Also serves Greene County Surrogate's Court and Greene County Family Court.
Office: Courthouse, 320 Main Street, Catskill 12414.
Telephone: (518) 943-5711.
Fax: (518) 943-1864

PUNCH, James P. *(Judge, Orleans County Court)* Also serves Orleans County Surrogate's Court and Orleans County Family Court.
Mailing address: Three North Main Street, Albion 1411.
Office: Courthouse, 243 South Main Street, Albion 14411-1497.
Telephone: (585) 589-5458.

QUINN, Christopher G. *(Judge, Nassau County District Court)*
Office: 99 Main Street, Hempstead 11550.
Telephone: (516) 572-2123.
E-mail address: quinn@courts.state.ny.us

RAAB, Ira J. *(Justice, New York Supreme Court Tenth Judicial District)* Born June 20, 1935. Educated at City College of the City University of New York B.B.A. 1955, Brooklyn Law School J.D. 1957, New York University M.P.A. 1959, Long Island University M.S. 1961, New York Law School 1961 and Adelphi University M.B.A. 1990. Admitted to practice New York 1958, U.S. District Courts Eastern 1960 and Southern 1960 Districts of New York, U.S. Supreme Court 1967, U.S. Tax Court 1976 and U.S. Court of Appeals Second Circuit 1977. Arbitrator, The Civil Court of the City of New York 1970-96, Nassau County District Court 1978-96 and U.S. District Court Eastern District of New York 1986-96. Law Guardian, Nassau County Family Court 1976-96. Special Master, New York Supreme Court First Judicial District 1977-96. Hearing Officer, New York Supreme Court Tenth Judicial District 1982-96. Administrative Law Judge, New York City Parking Violations Bureau 1991-93. Former Judge and Presiding Judge, Nassau County District Court, elected to term beginning Jan 1, 1997.

Agent Society for the Prevention of Cruelty to Children Westchester County 1958. Counsel 1959 and Trial Commissioner 1976 New York City Correction Department. Staff Counsel U.S. Small Business Administration 1961-63. Assistant Corporation Counsel Tort Division New York City 1963-70. Counsel Investigation Committee on Willowbrook State School 1970. General Counsel Society for the Prevention of Cruelty to Children Richmond County 1970-81. Counsel Parking Enforcement and Traffic Control Agents 1970-91. Editorial Board *Court Review* American Judges Association 1975-79 and 1982-83. Arbitrator American Arbitration Association 1975-95, Long Island Better Business Bureau 1976-89, Judicate National Private Court System 1987-89 and New York State Attorney General Lemon Law Program 1987-91. Former Member Jewish Lawyers Association of Nassau County, Nassau County Lawyers Association, Association of Arbitrators of the Small Claims Division of The Civil Court of the City of New York (President 1974), Association of Arbitrators of the Small Claims Division Nassau County District Court (President 1985-88), New York State Defenders Association, American Judicature Society, International Association of Jewish Lawyers and Jurists (Executive Committee 1978-93, International Council in Israel 1981-93, Bill of Rights of Privacy Committee 1982, Board of Directors American Section 1984-96), New York State (New York State Constitutional Committee 1985-89; Secretary District, City, Village and Town Courts Committee 1986-89) and American (Judicial Administration Division 1985-96, Executive Committee Lawyers Conference 1989-95, Chairperson Courts and Community Committee 1987-92) Bar Associations. Member American Judges Foundation (Treasurer 1974-75 and 1976-77, Trustee 1975-77 and since 1979, President 1977-79, Chair Board of Trustees 1979-83), American Judges Association (Chairperson Educational Film Committee 1974-77, Civil Court Operations Committee 1975-76, Speakers' Bureau Committee 1976-77, International Conference Committee 1983-85, Legislative Committee 1983-96 and Resolutions Committee since 1995; Governor New York District 1974-78, 1982-96 and since 1998, National Treasurer 1978-82; Member Executive Committee 1978-84 and 1986; Historian since 1986) and Nassau County Bar Association

RAAB, IRA J.—*Continued*

(Matrimonial and Family Law Committee 1978-96; Courts Committee since 1978; Criminal Law and Procedure Committee since 1979; Lawyer Referral Service 1980-96; Mock Trial Panel 1983, 1985 and 1986; Chair Supreme Court Justices Portrait Subcommittee 1983-84; Speakers Bureau since 1983; Assigned Counsel Subcommittee for State and Federal Courts 1984-89; Court Security Subcommittee 1985-86; Professional Ethics Committee 1985-91; District Court Committee 1985-2000; Conciliation Committee 1987-91).

Instructor in Landlord-Tenant Law Paralegal Course School District Fifteen 1982-85. Recipient William H. Burnett Award from American Judges Association 1983 and Presidential Recognition Award from President Ronald Reagan 1985. Named Man of the Year by Nassau Council Chambers of Commerce 1987 and Lawyer of the Month by Nassau County Bar Association April 1989. Democrat. President Professional Group Legal Services Association 1977-79. U.N. Delegate Foundation for the Establishment of an International Criminal Court 1977. U.S. Delegate to International Conference on Human Rights 1977. Board of Directors 1979-94, Vice President 1979-84 and Chairperson Board of Directors 1985-89 Woodmere Merchants Association. Secretary 1978-89 and Executive Vice President 1980-81 Community Mediation Center Suffolk County. Advisory Board Community Dispute Center Nassau County 1979-81 and Hewlett H.S. Business Alliance since 1994. Secretary Congregation Aish Kodesh 1993-2002. Chair Wall Street Synagogue Businessmen's Luncheon Club 1968-79. Member Knights of Pythias 1958-81 (Chancellor Commander 1962, Grand Lodge Rank 1980) and League of Women Voters of Five Towns 1979-89. Pro-Bono Counsel for Poor Consumers Federal Trade Commission 1974-85 and New York City Patrolmen's Benevolent Association 1974-81.

Office: Supreme Court Building, 100 Supreme Court Drive, Mineola 11501.
Telephone: (516) 571-2870.
Fax: (516) 571-2555
E-mail address: iraab@courts.state.ny.us

RACITI, Robert M. *(Judge, The Criminal Court of the City of New York)* Appointed by Mayor Rudolph Giuliani. Former Judge, The Civil Court of the City of New York.

Office: 125-01 Queens Boulevard, Kew Gardens 11415.
Telephone: (718) 520-3855.
Fax: (718) 520-4712

RAKOFF, Jed S. *(Judge, United States District Court Southern District of New York)* Appointed for life by President Bill Clinton Jan 4, 1996 to term beginning March 1, 1996. Born Philadelphia Pennsylvania Aug 1, 1943. Jewish. Educated at Swarthmore College B.A. 1964, Oxford University, England M.Phil. 1966 and Harvard Law School J.D. cum laude 1969. Law Clerk to Hon. Abraham L. Freedman, U.S. Court of Appeals Third Circuit 1969-70. Admitted to practice New York 1971, U.S. District Court Southern District of New York 1972, U.S. Court of Appeals Second Circuit 1973 and District of Columbia 1985. In legal practice New York 1970-72 and 1980-96.

Assistant U.S. Attorney 1973-80 and Chief Business and Securities Fraud Prosecutions 1978-80 Southern District of New York. Author five books and 103 articles. Lecturer on Civil and Criminal Litigation Columbia University School of Law since 1988. Director New York Council of Defense Lawyers 1990-94. Fellow American Board of Criminal Lawyers and American College of Trial Lawyers (Chair New York Chapter 1993-94). Member The Association of the Bar of the City of New York (Chair Criminal Law Committee 1986-89). Chair RICO Litigation Seminar New York Law Journal 1984-94. Democrat. Executive Board New York Chapter American Jewish Committee 1972-95. Enjoys skiing and songwriting.

Office: 1340 U.S. Courthouse, 500 Pearl Street, New York 10007-1312.
Telephone: (212) 805-0401.
Fax: (212) 805-7935

RAKOWER, Eileen A. *(Judge, The Civil Court of the City of New York)*

Office: 111 Centre Street, New York 10013.
Telephone: (212) 374-8102.

RAMICH, Thomas E. *(Judge, Elmira City Court)* Born June 23, 1950. Roman Catholic. Educated at St. John Fisher College B.A. cum laude 1972 and St. John's University School of Law J.D. 1975. Admitted to practice New York 1976 and U.S. District Court Western District of New York 1976. Began legal practice Elmira. Former Judge, Elmira Recorder's Court, elected to term beginning Jan 1, 1982. Enjoys wood working and golf.

Office: City Hall, 317 East Church Street, Elmira 14901-2790.
Telephone: (607) 737-5681.
Fax: (607) 737-5820
E-mail address: tramich@courts.state.ny.us

RAMOS, Charles E. *(Justice, New York Supreme Court First Judicial District)* Former Judge, The Civil Court of the City of New York.

Office: 60 Centre Street, New York 10007.
Telephone: (212) 374-8216.

RAND, Sheldon M. *(Judge, New York City Family Court)* Appointed by Mayor Abraham Beame to term beginning Dec 27, 1977. Reappointed by Mayor Edward Koch Oct 27, 1987 and Mayor Rudolph W. Giuliani 1997. Current term expires 2007. Born Woonsocket Rhode Island. Educated at New York University B.S. 1959 and Brooklyn Law School LL.B. 1961. Admitted to practice New York 1962. In legal practice New York 1962-73.

Member The Association of the Bar of the City of New York. USAR 1962-68. Enjoys art, music and movies.

Office: 60 Lafayette Street, New York 10013.
Telephone: (212) 374-4177.
Fax: (212) 374-2623

RAPPAPORT, Edward M. *(Justice, New York Supreme Court Second Judicial District)*

Office: 360 Adams Street, Brooklyn 11201.
Telephone: (718) 643-7084.
E-mail address: erappaport@courts.state.ny.us

RAY, Herbert B. *(Judge, Broome County Family Court)* Elected to term beginning Jan 1, 1986. Reelected Nov 1995, current term expires Dec 31, 2005. Born Binghamton New York Oct 1, 1934. Protestant. Educated at Duke University B.A. 1957 and Cornell Law

RAY, HERBERT B.—*Continued*

School J.D. 1961. Admitted to practice New York 1961 and U.S. District Court Northern District of New York. Justice, Chenango Town Justice Court 1975-82.

Former Member Broome County Magistrates Association (Past President), New York State Trial Lawyers Association, New York State Association of Magistrates and The Association of Trial Lawyers of America. Member Association of Judges of the Family Court of the State of New York and Broome County Bar Association. Instructor various judicial seminars Office of Court Administration. Sergeant U.S. Army 1961.

Mailing address: P.O. Box 1766, Binghamton 13902.
Office: 65 Hawley Street, Binghamton 13901.
Telephone: (607) 778-2156.
Fax: (607) 778-2439

READ, Susan Phillips *(Associate Judge, New York Court of Appeals)* Appointed by Governor George E. Pataki. Former Presiding Judge, New York Court of Claims, appointed by Governor George E. Pataki.

Mailing address: P.O. Box 7344, Albany 12224.
Office: Capitol Station, Albany 12224.
Telephone: (518) 432-3472.

REBOLINI, William B. *(Judge, Suffolk County District Court)*

Mailing address: P.O. Box 9075, Central Islip 11722-9075.
Office: Cohalan Court Complex, 400 Carleton Avenue, Central Islip 11722.
Telephone: (631) 853-4921.

RECANT, Donna G. *(Judge, The Criminal Court of the City of New York)* Appointed by Mayor Rudolph Giuliani.

Office: 100 Centre Street, New York 10013.
Telephone: (212) 374-8451.

REED, Frederick G. *(Surrogate, Ontario County Surrogate's Court)*

Office: Courthouse, 27 North Main Street, Canandaigua 14424-1447.
Telephone: (585) 396-4053.
Fax: (585) 396-4086

REICHBACH, Gustin L. *(Justice, New York Supreme Court Second Judicial District)* Educated at State University of New York at Buffalo B.A. magna cum laude 1967 and Columbia University School of Law J.D. 1970. Admitted to practice New York 1972, California 1975, U.S. District Courts Eastern and Northern Districts of California and Eastern and Southern Districts of New York and U.S. Supreme Court. In legal practice New York 1972-90 and California 1974-76. Former Judge, The Civil Court of the City of New York, elected to term beginning Jan 1, 1991.

Author "Raising and Litigating Electronic Surveillance Claims" 1975. Instructor in Law and Justice Brooklyn College 1972-74. Recipient David Michaels Award for Outstanding Efforts in Promoting Integrity in the Criminal Justice System from New York State Bar Association Jan 1992.

Office: 120 Schermerhorn Street, Brooklyn 11201.
Telephone: (718) 643-4680.
E-mail address: greichbach@courts.state.ny.us

REILLY, Margaret C. *(Judge, Nassau County District Court)*

Office: 99 Main Street, Hempstead 11550.
Telephone: (516) 572-2107.
E-mail address: reilly@courts.state.ny.us

REILLY, Vincent J., Jr. *(Justice, New York Supreme Court Fourth Judicial District)* Former Acting Justice. Born Brooklyn New York July 15, 1942. Roman Catholic. Educated at College of the Holy Cross B.A. 1964 and Albany Law School of Union University J.D. 1967. Admitted to practice New York 1967. In legal practice Schenectady 1968-84. Justice, Niskayuna Town Justice Court 1977-84. Former Judge, Schenectady County Family Court, elected to term beginning Jan 1, 1985.

Chairman Law Guardian Advisory Committee New York Supreme Court Appellate Division. Member Commission on Substance Abuse in the Profession 1999, Statewide Law Guardian Advisory Committee, Association of Judges of the Family Court of the State of New York, Schenectady County (President 1994-95) and New York State Bar Associations. Recipient Harold Korman Award of Excellence from New York State Trial Lawyers Association 1997. Former Coordinator High School Mock Trial Competition for Schenectady.

Office: Schenectady County Courthouse, 612 State Street, Schenectady 12305.
Telephone: (518) 388-4350.

REINFURT, Susan B. *(Judge, Watervliet City Court)* Currently serves as Acting Judge.

Office: City Hall, 15th Street and Broadway, Watervliet 12189.
Telephone: (518) 270-3803.
Fax: (518) 270-3812

RELIHAN, Walter J., Jr. *(Justice, New York Supreme Court Sixth Judicial District)* Elected Nov 1991 to term beginning Jan 1992. Certificated. Born Binghamton New York Oct 17, 1930. Educated at Cornell University B.A. 1952 J.D. 1959. Admitted to practice New York 1959, U.S. District Court Northern District of New York 1959 and U.S. Supreme Court 1964. In legal practice Binghamton 1960-67.

Chief Counsel New York State Office of General Services 1967-71. Counsel and Vice Chancellor for Legal Affairs State University of New York 1971-78. University Counsel and Secretary of Corporation Cornell University 1979-91. Important Decisions: 33 published opinions. Member Tompkins County and New York State Bar Associations. Recipient Board of Trustees Recognition Award from Cornell University 1991. Lieutenant j.g. USNR 1952-56. President Cornell Law Association 1996-98. Member Cornell University Council 1997-2001. Member Advisory Council Cornell University Law School.

Mailing address: P.O. Box 70, Ithaca 14851-0070.
Office: 320 North Tioga Street, Ithaca 14850.
Telephone: (607) 277-1441.
Fax: (607) 272-0690

RENWICK, Dianne T. *(Justice, New York Supreme Court Twelfth Judicial District)* Former Judge, The Civil Court of the City of New York.

Office: 851 Grand Concourse, Bronx 10451.
Telephone: (718) 590-3782.
Fax: (718) 590-8914

RENZI, Alex R. *(Judge, Monroe County Court)*
Office: 545 Hall of Justice, 99 Exchange Boulevard, Rochester 14614-2186.
Telephone: (585) 428-2331.

RENZI, Eugene R. *(Judge, Watertown City Court)* Serves part time.
Office: Municipal Building, 245 Washington Street, Watertown 13601.
Telephone: (315) 785-7785.
Fax: (315) 785-7917

RESNIK, Kenneth H. *(Judge, Rockland County Court)*
Office: 200 Courthouse, One South Main Street, New City 10956.
Telephone: (845) 638-5340.
Fax: (845) 638-5312

RESTAINO, Robert M. *(Judge, Niagara Falls City Court)*
Office: Public Safety Building, 520 Hyde Park Boulevard, Niagara Falls 14302-2725.
Telephone: (716) 278-9821.
Fax: (716) 278-9809

REYNOLDS, Thomas A. *(Acting Judge, Oswego City Court)*
Office: Conway Municipal Center, 20 West Oneida Street, Oswego 13126.
Telephone: (315) 343-0415.
Fax: (315) 343-0531

RICE, Gail B. *(Judge, New Rochelle City Court)* Currently serves as Acting Judge.
Office: 475 North Avenue, New Rochelle 10801-3405.
Telephone: (914) 654-2286.

RICHARDSON, Clark V. *(Judge, New York City Family Court)* Appointed by Mayor Rudolph Giuliani. Currently serves as Supervising Judge.
Office: 900 Sheridan Avenue, Bronx 10451.
Telephone: (718) 590-3376.
Fax: (718) 590-7305

RICHROATH, Marybeth S. *(Judge, New York City Family Court)* Appointed by mayor.
Office: 283 Adams Street, Sixth Floor, Brooklyn 11201.
Telephone: (718) 643-4546.
Fax: (718) 643-5103

RICHTER, Rosalyn H. *(Justice, New York Supreme Court First Judicial District)* Acting Justice Twelfth Judicial District Feb 1997 to Feb 2000. Former Acting Justice First Judicial District. Educated at Barnard College B.A. 1976 and Brooklyn Law School J.D. 1979. Admitted to practice New York 1980. Administrative Law Judge, New York City Office of Administrative Trials 1987-90. Former Judge, The Criminal Court of the City of New York, appointed by Mayor David Dinkins to term beginning Aug 1990. Supervising Judge Jan 1998 to Jan 2000.
Office: 60 Centre Street, New York 10007.
Telephone: (212) 374-8542.
E-mail address: rrichter@courts.state.ny.us

RICIGLIANO, Francis D. *(Judge, Nassau County District Court)*
Office: 99 Main Street, Hempstead 11550.
Telephone: (516) 571-2200.

RIENZI, Leonard P. *(Judge, The Criminal Court of the City of New York)* Appointed by mayor. Currently serves as Acting Justice, New York Supreme Court Second Judicial District.
Office: 18 Richmond Terrace, Staten Island 10301.
Telephone: (718) 390-5433.
E-mail address: lrienzi@courts.state.ny.us

RINGROSE, John G. *(Surrogate, Oneida County Surrogate's Court)* Elected to term beginning Jan 1, 1980. Reelected 1989 and 1999. Current term expires Dec 31, 2009. Born Rome New York Sept 11, 1935. Roman Catholic. Educated at Syracuse University B.A. 1957 J.D. 1960. Member Phi Delta Phi. Admitted to practice New York 1960. In legal practice Rome 1960-79.
Member The Surrogates' Association of the State of New York (Vice President, President, Member Advisory Committee Office of Court Administration), Rome, Oneida County (Director three years) and New York State (Sections: Judicial, Trusts and Estates) Bar Associations.
Office: Oneida County Office Building, Eighth Floor, 800 Park Avenue, Utica 13501.
Telephone: (315) 797-9230.
Fax: (315) 797-9237

RIORDAN, John B. *(Surrogate, Nassau County Surrogate's Court)* Former Judge, Nassau County District Court.
Office: 262 Old Country Road, Mineola 11501.
Telephone: (516) 571-2040.
Fax: (516) 571-3864
E-mail address: jriordan@courts.state.ny.us

RIOS, Jaime A. *(Justice, New York Supreme Court Eleventh Judicial District)* Elected to term beginning Jan 1, 1995. Also serves as Justice, New York Supreme Court Appellate Term Second and Eleventh Judicial Districts. Former Judge, The Civil Court of the City of New York.
Office: 125-01 Queens Boulevard, Kew Gardens 11415.
Telephone: (718) 520-7144.

RISI, Joseph J. *(Justice, New York Supreme Court Eleventh Judicial District)* Former Acting Justice. Certificated. Former Judge, The Civil Court of the City of New York.
Office: 25-10 Court Square, Long Island City 11101.
Telephone: (718) 520-3919.

RITHOLTZ, Martin E. *(Justice, New York Supreme Court Eleventh Judicial District)* Former Acting Justice. Born Salem New Jersey Aug 6, 1946. Educated at Columbia College B.A. 1968 and Hebrew University of Jerusalem LL.B. 1974. Admitted to practice Israel 1975, New York 1976, U.S. District Courts Eastern 1976 and Southern 1976 Districts of New York and U.S. Supreme Court 1980. In legal practice Brooklyn New York March 1975 to June 1978. Judge, The Civil Court of the City of New York, elected to term beginning Jan 1996.
Principal Law Clerk to Hon. Martin Rodell Jan 1981 to May 1982, Hon. Eugene P. Bambrick Jan 1983 to Dec 1989, Hon. Angelo Graci Jan 1990 to Dec 1993 and Hon. Luther V. Dye Jan 1994 to Dec 1995 New York Supreme Court Eleventh Judicial District. Important Decisions: City & Suburban Delivery Systems Inc. v. Green's Cards & Gifts Inc. 167 Misc. 2d 283 Feb 29,

RITHOLTZ, MARTIN E.—*Continued*

1996; Suffolk Chiropractic Center v. GEICO 171 Misc. 2d 855 Feb 7, 1997; Royal Insurance Company of America v. Martyn N.Y.L.J. 30 c. 4 March 13, 1997; Guzman v. Members America Credit Union 172 Misc. 2d 192 April 14, 1997; Malik v. Cukrowski 172 Misc. 2d 360 May 8, 1997; Santana v. Country-Wide Insurance Company 177 Misc. 2d 1 May 27, 1998; Rombom v. New York City Transit Authority 177 Misc. 2d 1043 Aug 3, 1998; Dollar Rent A Car Systems v. Fishbein N.Y.L.J. 32 c. 5 April 22, 1999; Klein v. Seenauth 180 Misc. 2d 213 March 25, 1999; and Elrac, Inc. v. Cruz 1999 WL 1059798, 182 Misc.2d 523 Nov 4, 1999. Adjunct Professor of Jewish Law Touro College Aug 1984 to Feb 1988. President Brandeis Bar Association 1986. Second Vice President Association of Law Secretaries to the Justices of the Supreme and Surrogate's Courts Jan 1993 to Dec 1995. Vice President Board of Judges Civil Court of the City of New York Queens County since Jan 1998. Member Queens County Bar Association (Chairman Continuing Legal Education Sept 1988 to Dec 1998, Member Nominating Committee 1993 to Dec 1995, Dean Academy of Law since Jan 1999). Lecturer "Interaction Between Jewish and American Law in American Courts: A Judge's Perspective" March 1997 and "The Enforcement of a Jewish Marriage Contract in Civil Court: Is Jewish Law a Religious Law" Nov 1998 Touro College. Recipient William Goodstein Memorial Award from Association of Law Secretaries of New York City April 1999. President Jamaica Regular Democratic Club 1980. Delegate to Democratic Judicial Convention for the Eleventh Judicial District 1982-87. Board of Directors Jewish Community Baseball League 1983-86 and Queens Jewish Community Council 1996-98. Coach Young Israels of Far Rockaway and Bayswater Little League Baseball 1993. Member Columbia College Alumni Secondary Schools Committee.

Office: 88-11 Sutphin Boulevard, Jamaica 11435.
Telephone: (718) 520-3159.

RITTER, David S. *(Associate Justice, New York Supreme Court Appellate Division Second Judicial Department)* Elected Justice to term beginning Jan 1, 1985. Appointed Associate Justice Appellate Division by Governor Mario Cuomo. Reappointed to Appellate Division by Governor George E. Pataki 1998, current term expires Dec 31, 2003. Born Middletown New York Nov 25, 1934. Protestant. Educated at Union College A.B. 1956 and Cornell University Law School LL.B. 1959. Member Delta Upsilon. Admitted to practice New York 1959. In legal practice Middletown 1962-65. Judge, Orange County Court Jan 1981 to Dec 31, 1984.

Special Assistant to Attorney General 1959-62. Confidential Law Secretary to Hon. Clare J. Hoyt, New York Supreme Court 1966-69. Assistant District Attorney, Executive Assistant District Attorney and Chief Assistant District Attorney 1970-76 and District Attorney 1976-80 Orange County. Member District Attorney's Association of New York State, Middletown, Orange County and New York State Bar Associations. Member Advisory Committee on Criminal Law and Procedure Judicial Conference of New York State. Instructor School for Newly Elected Judges 1987 and 1988 and annual judicial seminar.

Office: County Government Center, 255-285 Main Street, Goshen 10924.
Telephone: (845) 291-3145.
Fax: (845) 291-3043

RIVERA, François A. *(Justice, New York Supreme Court Second Judicial District)*

Office: 360 Adams Street, Brooklyn 11201.
Telephone: (718) 643-5195.

RIVERA, Reinaldo E. *(Associate Justice, New York Supreme Court Appellate Division Second Judicial Department)* Elected Justice Second Judicial District Nov 1991 to term beginning Jan 2, 1992. Appointed Associate Justice Appellate Division by Governor George E. Pataki June 11, 2002. Term expires Dec 31, 2005. First Hispanic judge appointed to Appellate Division Second Judicial Department in 106 years. Born Puerto Rico 1951. Catholic. Educated at St. Peter's College B.S. 1973, St. John's University School of Law J.D. 1976 and Columbia University School of Law LL.M. 1977. Admitted to practice New Jersey 1976, U.S. District Courts District of New Jersey 1977 and District of New York 1978, New York 1978 and U.S. Supreme Court 1982. In legal practice New York City 1977-91.

Member Character and Fitness Committee New York Supreme Court Appellate Division Second Judicial Department 1985-91. Adjunct Professor St. John's University School of Law. Member Brooklyn, Puerto Rican and Hispanic National Bar Associations. Attended Office of Court Administration Judicial Seminars since 1992. Lieutenant Colonel New York Guard since Nov 1992. Board of Directors Alumni Association St. John's University School of Law since 1992.

Office: 360 Adams Street, Brooklyn 11201.
Telephone: (718) 643-8183.

RIVOLI, John J. *(Judge, Monroe County Family Court)*

Office: Hall of Justice, Third Floor, 99 Exchange Boulevard, Rochester 14614-2187.
Telephone: (585) 428-2227.
Fax: (585) 428-2597

ROBERTO, Robert, Jr. *(Justice, New York Supreme Court Tenth Judicial District)* Elected to term beginning Jan 1, 1984. Reelected 1997. Certificated. Born New York New York June 28, 1930. Catholic. Educated at Adelphi University B.A. 1952 and Brooklyn Law School J.D. 1955. Member Delta Theta Phi (Dean 1977-78). Admitted to practice New York 1956, U.S. District Courts Eastern 1962 and Southern 1962 Districts of New York and U.S. Supreme Court 1965. Began legal practice Mineola 1956. Judge, Nassau County District Court 1978-83.

Assistant Attorney General New York 1956-62. Law Secretary to Hon. Albert A. Oppido, New York Supreme Court Tenth Judicial District 1962-71. Executive Assistant District Attorney Nassau County 1971-74. Adjunct Faculty Nassau Community College 1978-79 and New York Institute of Technology. Chief Counsel Joint Bar Association Grievance Committee Tenth Judicial District 1975-78. Member Nassau County Lawyers Association (Director 1977-78), Columbian Lawyers Association (Director), Former Assistant District Attorneys Association, New York State District Attorneys Association and Bar Association of Nassau County (Federal Courts Committee, Criminal Law Committee, Courts Committee, World Peace Through Law Committee). Past Exalted Ruler Elks. Past President Manhasset Youth Council and Roslyn Kiwanis Club. Former Chairman Inde-

ROBERTO, ROBERT, JR.—*Continued*

pendent Citizens Committee for the Selection of School Board Candidates. Chairman Nassau County Task Force on Vandalism and Committee to Develop an Anti-Vandalism Education Program. Appointed by Manhasset Board of Education to Citizens Advisory Committee on Education. Member Cellini Lodge, Sons of Italy and St. Mary's Roman Catholic Church Manhasset. Enjoys golf, tennis and skiing.

Office: Supreme Court Building, 100 Supreme Court Drive, Mineola 11501.
Telephone: (516) 571-2427.

ROBERTS, Gayle P. *(Judge, New York City Family Court)* Appointed by Mayor Rudolph Giuliani.
Office: 900 Sheridan Avenue, Bronx 10451.
Telephone: (718) 590-3376.
Fax: (718) 590-7305

ROBICHAUD, Kathleen Leahey *(Judge, Rensselaer City Court)*
Office: City Hall, 505 Broadway, Rensselaer 12144.
Telephone: (518) 462-6751.
Fax: (518) 462-3307

ROGERS, Kathleen Martin *(Surrogate, St. Lawrence County Surrogate's Court)* Elected to term beginning Jan 1, 1989. Reelected 1998, current term expires Dec 31, 2008.
Office: Courthouse, 48 Court Street, Canton 13617-1199.
Telephone: (315) 379-2217.
Fax: (315) 379-2372

ROGERS, Mark J. *(Acting Judge, Plattsburgh City Court)*
Office: 53 Court Street, Plattsburgh 12901.
Telephone: (518) 561-3700.
Fax: (518) 563-3124

ROMAN, David J. *(Judge, Oswego County Family Court)* Elected Nov 1988 to term beginning Jan 1, 1989. Reelected 1998, current term expires Dec 31, 2008. Born Rome New York Feb 15, 1951. Roman Catholic. Educated at Cornell University B.S. 1973 and Albany Law School of Union University J.D. 1976. Law Clerk to Hon. John O'C. Conway, New York Supreme Court 1976-77. Admitted to practice New York 1977 and U.S. District Court Northern District of New York 1977. In legal practice Oswego 1976-88.

Town Attorney Town of Minetto 1980-88. New York State District Tax Attorney and Appraiser Oswego County 1983-88. Law Clerk to Hon. Donald K. Comstock, Oswego County Family Court 1986-88. Important Decisions: Matter of DSS v. Moody (statutory minimum child support award of $25 per month per NYS CSSA may be pre-empted and a $0.00 order is permissible under certain specified circumstances) 188 A.D.2nd 1001 (4th Dept 1992) aff'd 83 N.Y.2d 65 1993 and Atty General NYS v. Moody U.S. 114 S. Ct. 1837, 1994. Member New York State Advisory Committee on Judicial Ethics, Law Guardian Advisory Committee for the New York Supreme Court Fourth Appellate Division Fourth Judicial Department, Association of Judges of the Family Court of the State of New York (President 1995-97), Oswego County (President 1985-87), New York State and American Bar Associations. President Board of Directors Fornham Youth Center, Inc. 1979-86 and Oswego YMCA 1989 and 1990. Enjoys golf, racquetball and swimming.

Office: Public Safety Center, 39 Churchill Road, Oswego 13126.
Telephone: (315) 349-3350.
Fax: (315) 349-3457
E-mail address: droman@courts.state.ny.us

ROMAN, Nelson S. *(Justice, New York Supreme Court Twelfth Judicial District)* Former Judge, The Civil Court of the City of New York.
Office: 851 Grand Concourse, Bronx 10451.
Telephone: (718) 590-8917.

ROMAN, Sheri S. *(Justice, New York Supreme Court Eleventh Judicial District)* Elected to term beginning Jan 1, 1995. Term expires Dec 31, 2008. Educated at State University of New York at Buffalo B.A. cum laude 1969, Georgetown University Law Center J.D. 1972 and New York University LL.M. in Criminal Justice 1976. Member Phi Beta Kappa. Staff member American Criminal Law Review. Admitted to practice New York 1973. Judge, The Criminal Court of the City of New York May 20, 1985 to Dec 31, 1994.

First Vice President New York Women's Bar Association 1987.

Office: 125-01 Queens Boulevard, Kew Gardens 11415.
Telephone: (718) 520-4416.
E-mail address: sroman@courts.state.ny.us

ROMANO, Bernadette T. *(Judge, Oneida County Family Court)* First woman elected judge in Oneida County. Educated at St. Mary's College B.S. cum laude 1974 and Syracuse University J.D. magna cum laude 1989. In legal practice Syracuse and Utica 1989-94.

First Assistant District Attorney Oneida County 1994-2000. Co-Chair Domestic Violence Coalition Oneida County since 1995. Member Oneida County Bar Association. Named Woman of the Year by Metro-Utica Business and Professional Woman's Group 2000. Recipient Governor's Justice Award to End Domestic Violence 2001. Board of Directors Boys and Girls Club of Greater Utica, Mohawk Valley Performing Arts and National Center for Missing and Exploited Children.

Office: Oneida County Courthouse, 200 Elizabeth Street, Utica 13501.
Telephone: (315) 731-3474.
Fax: (315) 731-3469

ROONEY, James T. *(Judge, Putnam County Court)* Also serves Putnam County Surrogate's Court and Putnam County Family Court.
Office: County Office Building, 40 Gleneida Avenue, Carmel 10512.
Telephone: (845) 225-3641.
Fax: (845) 225-4395

ROONEY, Stephen J. *(Judge, New York Court of Claims)* Appointed by Governor George E. Pataki. Currently serves as Acting Justice, New York Supreme Court Second Judicial District. Former Judge, The Criminal Court of the City of New York.
Office: 18 Richmond Terrace, Staten Island 10301.
Telephone: (718) 390-5157.
Fax: (718) 390-5230
E-mail address: srooney@courts.state.ny.us

ROSA, Janice M. *(Justice, New York Supreme Court Eighth Judicial District)* Former Judge, Erie County Family Court.
Office: Erie County Hall, 99 Franklin Street, Buffalo 14202.
Telephone: (716) 851-3236.

ROSATO, Peter P. *(Justice, New York Supreme Court Ninth Judicial District)* Elected to term beginning Jan 1, 1988. Reelected 2001. Certificated. Currently serves as Supervising Judge Criminal Courts Ninth Judicial District. Born Yonkers New York April 29, 1932. Roman Catholic. Educated at Iona College B.A. 1957 and The Ohio State University J.D. 1959. Contributor Ohio State Law Journal. Member Phi Delta Phi. Admitted to practice New York 1960, U.S. Supreme Court 1965 and U.S. District Court Southern District of New York 1973. Began legal practice Yonkers 1960. Judge, Yonkers City Court Jan 1, 1981 to Dec 31, 1982. Judge, Westchester County Court Jan 1, 1983 to Dec 31, 1987.
Instructor in Criminal Law Elizabeth Seton College 1982-83. President Yonkers Lawyers Association. Corporal U.S. Army 332nd Engineering Aviation Battalion 1951-53. Republican. President Enrico Fermi Scholarship Foundation 1978-79. Enjoys sports, home repairs and gardening.
Office: 140 Grand Street, White Plains 10601.
Telephone: (914) 995-4730.
Fax: (914) 995-4396

ROSE, Edward J. *(Judge, Little Falls City Court)*
Office: City Hall, 659 East Main Street, Little Falls 13365.
Telephone: (315) 823-1690.
Fax: (315) 823-1623

ROSE, Neal P. *(Judge, Sherrill City Court)*
Office: 373 Sherrill Road, Sherrill 13461.
Telephone: (315) 363-0996.
Fax: (315) 363-1176

ROSE, Robert S. *(Associate Justice, New York Supreme Court Appellate Division Third Judicial Department)* Elected Justice Sixth Judicial District to term beginning Jan 1, 1988. Reelected Nov 2001, current term expires 2015. Appointed Associate Justice Appellate Division by Governor George E. Pataki to term beginning March 2000. Reappointed 2001. Born Bronxville New York Sept 11, 1943. Educated at St. Lawrence University B.A. 1965 and Albany Law School of Union University J.D. 1968. Captain U.S. Army 1969-72.
Office: Courthouse, 92 Court Street, Binghamton 13902-1766.
Telephone: (607) 778-2473.
Fax: (607) 778-2405

ROSEN, Irving *(Judge, The Civil Court of the City of New York)* Elected Nov 4, 1991 to term beginning Jan 1, 1992. Reelected 2001, current term expires Dec 31, 2011. Born New York New York July 19, 1934. Religious affiliation: Hebrew. Educated at New York University B.S. in Economics and Labor Relations 1955 LL.M. in Labor Law 1964 and Brooklyn Law School LL.B. 1958. Admitted to practice New York 1958, U.S. District Courts Southern 1964 and Eastern 1965 Districts of New York, U.S. Tax Court 1965 and U.S. Supreme Court 1996. In legal practice New York City. Former Judge, The Criminal Court of the City of New York.
Associate Counsel and Deputy Counsel New York State Assembly 1975-88. Principal Law Clerk to Supreme Court Judge 1989-91. Bronx Vice President Board of Judges Association of Civil Court Judges of the City of New York. Member Jewish Lawyers Guild, Bronx Women's, Bronx County and New York State Bar Associations. U.S. Army Infantry and Reserve 1958-64. Past President Robert F. Kennedy Democratic Organization. Trustee and Treasurer Riverdale Temple. Area Coordinator Riverdale Branch of Habitat International. Member New York State Masonic Order, Brotherhood Lodge. Enjoys classical music, chess, swimming, physical fitness, economics and religious history.
Office: 851 Grand Concourse, Bronx 10451.
Telephone: (718) 590-3604.
Fax: (718) 590-7292

ROSENBERG, Gerard H. *(Justice, New York Supreme Court Second Judicial District)* Former Acting Justice. Former Judge, The Civil Court of the City of New York.
Office: 360 Adams Street, Brooklyn 11201.
Telephone: (718) 643-7074.
E-mail address: grosenbe@courts.state.ny.us

ROSENBERGER, Ernst H. *(Associate Justice, New York Supreme Court Appellate Division First Judicial Department)* Elected Justice First Judicial District to term beginning Jan 1, 1977. Reelected 1990. Appointed Associate Justice Appellate Division by Governor Mario Cuomo. Reappointed to Appellate Division by Governor George E. Pataki. Certificated. Born Hamburg Germany Aug 31, 1931. Jewish. Educated at City College of the City University of New York B.A. 1955, New York Law School J.D. 1958 and University of Virginia LL.M. 1996. Editor-in-Chief New York Law School Law Review. Recipient Moot Court Award. National Moot Court. Admitted to practice New York 1958, U.S. District Courts Southern 1959 and Eastern 1961 Districts of New York, U.S. Customs Court 1962, U.S. Court of Appeals Second Circuit 1962 and U.S. Supreme Court 1970. Judge, The Criminal Court of the City of New York 1972-76.
Technical Assistance and Evaluations Consultant to Director of Legal Services Office of Economic Opportunity Washington D.C. Adjunct Professor of Law New York Law School. Guest Lecturer Pratt Institute 1965-68, Brooklyn Law School, St. John's University, John Jay College of Criminal Justice of the City University of New York, New School and New York City Police Department Homicide Investigator's Course. Polsky Judicial Fellow The Aspen Institute 2000. Member National Conference of State Trial Judges, American Judges Association, American Judicature Society, American Society for Legal History, Association of Justices of the Supreme Court of the State of New York (Committee on Judicial Ethics, Chairman Committee on Reform of the Law), New York County Lawyers' Association (Cochairman Trial Practice Course, member Committee on Penal and Correctional Reform, Committee on Civil Rights and Committee on Practical Legal Education), The Association of the Bar of the City of New York (Committee on Criminal Courts, Law and Procedure, Committee on Art and Entertainment, Committee on Lectures and Continuing Education and Advisor Special Committee on Criminal Justice), New York State (Executive Committee Criminal Justice Section, Chairman Committee to Improve the Effectiveness of the Criminal Justice System) and American (Criminal Justice Section,

ROSENBERGER, ERNST H.—*Continued*

Judicial Administration Division) Bar Associations. One of two judges from the U.S. invited by West German Foreign Office to make an official visit to West Germany to study legal systems June 1975. Designated judicial representative from New York at meeting sponsored by U.S. Department of Justice on the Future and Standards of Defender Services in the U.S. Attended Northwestern University summer course in Criminal Law and Practice 1960 and National College of the State Judiciary at University of Nevada 1976. Guest Lecturer Appellate Division Special Projects Course in Criminal Law and New York County Lawyers' Association. Listed in *New York Magazine* and *Village Voice* compilations of outstanding judges in New York and Ralph Nader's "Verdicts on Lawyers." Corporal USAS 1949-51. Democrat. One of the founding directors of New York Offender Aid and Restoration, program for rehabilitation of offenders through individual volunteer contact. Director The Blue Card, a self-help charitable organization for refugees from Germany, now concerned mainly with problems of the aging.

Office: 27 Madison Avenue at 25th Street, New York 10010.

Telephone: (212) 340-0450.

Fax: (212) 889-4412

ROSENBLATT, Albert M. *(Associate Judge, New York Court of Appeals)* Appointed by Governor George E. Pataki. Born New York New York Jan 17, 1936. Jewish. Educated at University of Pennsylvania B.A. 1957 and Harvard University J.D. 1960. Admitted to practice New York 1961. Began legal practice New York City 1961. Judge, Dutchess County Court 1976-81. Former Justice, New York Supreme Court, elected to term beginning Jan 1, 1981. Former Associate Justice, New York Supreme Court Appellate Division Second Judicial Department, appointed by Governor Mario Cuomo. Chief Administrative Judge, New York State Unified Court System 1987-89.

District Attorney Dutchess County 1969-75. Author "Flag Desecration Statutes: History and Analysis" Washington University L. Quar. 1972 and "New York's New Drug Laws and Sentencing Statutes" New York L. Jour. 1973, "The Complete Search Warrant Annotated" O.P.S. 1974 and 1976, "A Legal House of Cards" *Harper's* July 1977, "The Sherlock Holmes Crossword" (monograph on the origins of the Baker Street Irregulars) 1985 and "Lawyers as Wordsmiths" New York State B. Jour. Nov/Dec 1997. Co-author with wife Dr. Julia Carlson Rosenblatt "Six Member Juries in Criminal Cases, Legal and Psychological Considerations" St. John's L. Rev. 1973. Instructor at Annual Judicial Training Seminar since 1973 and Dutchess Community College 1974. Visiting Faculty Member Trial Advocacy Workshop Harvard Law School 1998 and 1999. President New York State District Attorneys Association 1974. Member Dutchess County and New York State Bar Associations. Recipient Outstanding New York State Prosecutor Award 1974. USAR 1970. Republican. Moot Court Judge Harvard Law School 1992 and 1996. Certified professional ski instructor. Member Professional Ski Instructors of America and Baker Street Irregulars. Author several skiing articles in *Ski, Skiing Magazine* and Sports Monday *New York Times.*

Office: 10 Market Street, Second Floor, Poughkeepsie 12601-3228.

Telephone: (845) 486-6444.

ROSENGARTEN, Roger N. *(Justice, New York Supreme Court Eleventh Judicial District)* Former Acting Justice. Born London England Aug 1, 1937. Educated at City College of the City University of New York B.B.A. 1961 and Brooklyn Law School J.D. 1972. Admitted to practice New York 1973, U.S. District Courts Eastern 1975 and Southern 1975 Districts of New York and U.S. Supreme Court 1979. Former Judge, The Civil Court of the City of New York, elected Nov 6, 1990 to term beginning Jan 1, 1991.

Assistant District Attorney Queens County 1973-77. Principal Law Clerk to New York Supreme Court and New York Surrogate's Court 1977-91. Important Decisions: People v. Stokner (inadequacy of criminal pleading) 152 Misc. 2d 463, 1991; Farenga v. Maniatis (personal liability of attorney/executor of will never offered for probate) 164 Misc. 2d 231; Forest Hills Gardens v. Kemp (discovery in a civil action under CPLR) 165 Misc. 2d 915; People v. Harris (sex offender registration: finding not subject to stipulation) 178 Misc. 2d 858; and People v. Sheldon (criminal liability of passenger in stolen vehicle) 180 Misc. 2d 876. Adjunct Professor of Legal Medicine Queens College of the City University of New York since 1984. Member Brandeis Association (President 1986-87) and Queens County Bar Association. Lecturer on Scientific Aspects of Intoxicated Driving Cases Queens County Bar Association 1992. Recipient Certificate of Honor from New York State Bar Association. U.S. Army 1961. Member Board of Directors Jamaica Estates Association (Past Vice President).

Office: 125-01 Queens Boulevard, Kew Gardens 11415.

Telephone: (718) 520-4763.

ROSENTHAL, Kate *(Judge, Syracuse City Court)*

Office: Public Safety Building, Second Floor, 511 South State Street, Syracuse 13202-2179.

Telephone: (315) 477-2775.

Fax: (315) 474-2601

E-mail address: krosenth@courts.state.ny.us

ROSENWASSER, Stewart A. *(Judge, Orange County Court)*

Office: Orange County Courthouse, 285 Main Street, Goshen 10924.

Telephone: (845) 291-3110.

ROSENZWEIG, Joseph *(Justice, New York Supreme Court Eleventh Judicial District)* Elected Nov 1988 to term beginning Jan 1, 1989. Certificated. Born New York City April 21, 1929. Educated at City College of the City University of New York B.S.S. cum laude 1950 and Yale Law School LL.B. 1953. Admitted to practice New York 1953. Judge, The Civil Court of the City of New York 1977-88.

Office: 125-01 Queens Boulevard, Kew Gardens 11415.

Telephone: (718) 520-3556.

E-mail address: jrosenzw@courts.state.ny.us

ROSS, Allyne *(Judge, United States District Court Eastern District of New York)* Magistrate Judge 1986-94.

ROSS, ALLYNE—*Continued*

Appointed Judge for life by President Bill Clinton to term beginning 1994. Born New York New York April 5, 1946. Educated at Wellesley College B.A. 1967 and Harvard Law School J.D. 1970. In legal practice New York City 1971-76.

Staff Attorney Boston Legal Assistant Project 1970-71. Attorney U.S. Attorney's Office 1976-86 (Chief Appeals Division 1983-86) Eastern District of New York.

Office: U.S. Courthouse, 225 Cadman Plaza East, Brooklyn 11201.

Telephone: (718) 260-2380.

ROSS, Neil E. *(Judge, The Criminal Court of the City of New York)* Appointed by mayor. Former Judge, The Civil Court of the City of New York, appointed by Mayor Rudolph Giuliani to term beginning May 1998.

Office: 100 Centre Street, New York 10013.

Telephone: (212) 374-6216.

Fax: (212) 374-2579

ROSS, Robert A. *(Justice, New York Supreme Court Tenth Judicial District)*

Office: Matrimonial Center, 400 County Seat Drive, Mineola 11501.

Telephone: (516) 571-0760.

ROSSETTI, Frank S. *(Judge, New York Court of Claims)* Appointed by Governor Nelson A. Rockefeller to term beginning May 26, 1972. Reappointed by Governor Hugh Carey Dec 28, 1977, by Governor Mario Cuomo 1986 and by Governor George E. Pataki 1995. Current term expires Dec 2004. Currently serves as Acting Justice, New York Supreme Court Tenth Judicial District. Born New York New York March 30, 1935. Catholic. Educated at Manhattan College B.B.A. 1958 and New York Law School LL.B. 1961. Admitted to practice New York 1961. Began legal practice New York City 1961.

Assistant Counsel to State Commission on Revision of Penal Law 1964-68. Member Columbian Lawyers Association, New York County Lawyers' Association, Association of Lawyers of the Criminal Courts of the City of New York and The Association of the Bar of the City of New York. Democrat. Former member New York County Democratic Law Committee and Lawyers' Committee to Aid Indigent Citizens in East Harlem. Delegate to 1967 New York State Constitutional Convention representing 29th Senatorial District (appointed Chairman Subcommittee on State Finances and Subcommittee on Local Government and Home Rule). Assistant Counsel to Minority Leader of State Assembly 1971. Appointed member Local Draft Board Eight 1970. Member Columbus Citizens Committee and Manhattan College Alumni Association. Former member East Harlem Civic League.

Office: Supreme Court Building, 100 Supreme Court Drive, Mineola 11501.

Telephone: (516) 571-2873.

Fax: (516) 571-0745

ROSSETTI, Mario J. *(Judge, New York Court of Claims)* Appointed by governor. Currently serves as Acting Justice, New York Supreme Court Eighth Judicial District.

Office: Erie County Hall, 92 Franklin Street, Buffalo 14202.

Telephone: (716) 851-3381.

Fax: (716) 851-3327

E-mail address: mrossetti@courts.state.ny.us

ROSSI, Robert J. *(Judge, Onondaga County Family Court)*

Office: Onondaga County Courthouse, 401 Montgomery Street, Syracuse 13202.

Telephone: (315) 671-2030.

Fax: (315) 671-1168

ROSSITER, Judith A. *(Judge, Ithaca City Court)*

Office: 118 East Clinton Street, Ithaca 14850.

Telephone: (607) 273-2263.

Fax: (607) 277-3702

ROTH, Renee R. *(Surrogate, New York County Surrogate's Court)* Elected to term beginning Jan 1, 1983. Reelected 1996, current term expires Dec 31, 2010. Educated at City College of New York B.A. 1961 and Fordham University School of Law J.D. 1969. Admitted to practice New York 1969 and U.S. District Courts Southern 1977 and Eastern 1977 Districts of New York. Law Assistant and Referee Kings County Surrogate's Court 1969-82.

Author monthly column "Wills, Estates and Surrogate Practice" New York L. Jour. 1976-83. Adjunct Professor Fordham University School of Law since 1980. Lecturer United Jewish Appeal, Federation of Jewish Philanthropies, Yeshiva University, Hunter College, St. John's University, Hadassah, Archdiocese of Brooklyn, Surrogate's Association of New York, The Association of the Bar of the City of New York, New York County Lawyers' Association, New York State Trial Lawyers Association, New York Women's Bar Association, Brooklyn Bar Association, Park Avenue Synagogue, East Midwood Jewish Center, Consular Law Society and Westchester County Bar Association. Member New York County Lawyers' Association (Chairperson since 1974), Surrogates' Association of New York, The Association of the Bar of the City of New York and New York Women's Bar Association. Trustee Brooklyn Law Library and St. Francis College. President City College Alumni Association 1977-79. Member Metropolitan Council of American Jewish Congress.

Office: 31 Chambers Street, New York 10007.

Telephone: (212) 374-8280.

ROTHENBERG, Karen B. *(Judge, The Civil Court of the City of New York)* Elected to term beginning 1998. Deputy Supervising Judge 1999-2000. Supervising Judge since 2001. Currently serves as Acting Justice, New York Supreme Court Second Judicial District. Educated at Brooklyn Law School J.D. 1981. In legal practice Brooklyn 1982-97.

Adjunct Assistant Professor New York City Technical College 1988-90. Arbitrator New York State Arbitration Committee 1979-85. Appeals Board Member New York State Department of Motor Vehicles 1985-97. Member Grievance Committee Second and Eleventh Judicial Districts 1996-97. Member Lawyers' Torah Club, New York State Trial Lawyers Association, Brooklyn Women's Bar Association (Former Vice President and Cochair Judicial Screening Committee), Brooklyn (Former Member Judicial Screening Committee), New York State and American Bar Associations. Lecturer "Your Case Is Not Dead!", "Civility and Professionalism" and "Winning Civil Court Motions" Brooklyn Bar Association; and Advanced Trial Techniques and "Trying an Auto Crash Case" New York State Trial Lawyers Association.

ROTHENBERG, KAREN B.—*Continued*

Recipient Sybil Hart Kooper Award 2001 and Recognition Award for Leadership Achievement 2002 from Brooklyn Women's Bar Association and Judiciary Award of Merit from Kings County Housing Court Bar Association 2001.
Office: 141 Livingston Street, Brooklyn 11201.
Telephone: (718) 643-2860.
Fax: (718) 643-3537

ROTKER, Seymour *(Justice, New York Supreme Court Eleventh Judicial District)* Former Acting Justice. Born New York New York July 11, 1933. Educated at City College of the City University of New York B.A. 1955 and New York University LL.B. 1957. Admitted to practice New York 1957, U.S. District Courts Southern 1959 and Eastern 1959 Districts of New York and U.S. Supreme Court 1960. Began legal practice New York City 1957. Former Judge and Supervising Judge, The Criminal Court of the City of New York, appointed by Mayor Edward Koch May 31, 1978.
With District Attorney's Office Bronx 1960-78. Instructor Adelphi University Lawyers Assistant Program since 1976. Member The Association of the Bar of the City of New York.
Office: 125-01 Queens Boulevard, Kew Gardens 11415.
Telephone: (718) 520-4659.
E-mail address: srotker@courts.state.ny.us

ROWLEY, John C. *(Judge, Tompkins County Court)* Also serves Tompkins County Surrogate's Court and Tompkins County Family Court. Former Judge, Ithaca City Court.
Mailing address: P.O. Box 70, Ithaca 14851-0070.
Office: Courthouse, 320 North Tioga Street, Ithaca 14851.
Telephone: (607) 277-4957.
Fax: (607) 272-0559

ROY, William R. *(Justice, New York Supreme Court Fifth Judicial District)* Appointed by Governor Nelson A. Rockefeller to term beginning May 4, 1971. Elected to term beginning Jan 1, 1972. Reelected 1985. Certificated. Former Administrative Justice. Born Hartford Connecticut March 23, 1929. Roman Catholic. Educated at Syracuse University B.A. 1951 J.D. 1956. Member Phi Gamma Delta and Phi Delta Phi. Admitted to practice New York 1956 and U.S. District Court District of New York 1957.
Member Onondaga County (Chairman Trial Lawyers Section 1970-71 and Bench and Bar Committee 1975-77), New York State (Insurance Negligence and Compensation Section Trial Lawyers Section) and American Bar Associations. Lieutenant j.g. USCG 1951-53. Republican. Past President Alumni Association. Past Vice President Varsity Club. Former Chairman Alumni Ball. Former Member Board of Visitors College of Law and Orange Pack Syracuse University. Trustee Neurosurgical Research and Education Memorial Fund, Inc. Member National Foundation (City Campaign Director two years).
Office: Onondaga County Courthouse, 401 Montgomery Street, Syracuse 13202.
Telephone: (315) 671-1109.
Fax: (315) 671-1186

RUA, Salvatore M. *(Acting Judge, Tonawanda City Court)*
Office: City Hall, 200 Niagara Street, Tonawanda 14150.
Telephone: (716) 693-3484.
Fax: (716) 693-1612

RUBIN, Alice Fisher *(Judge, The Civil Court of the City of New York)*
Office: 141 Livingston Street, Room 606, Brooklyn 11201.
Telephone: (718) 643-5960.
Fax: (718) 643-3733

RUCHELSMAN, Leon *(Justice, New York Supreme Court Second Judicial District)* Former Acting Justice. Former Judge, The Civil Court of the City of New York. Former Judge, New York Court of Claims, appointed by Governor George E. Pataki.
Office: 360 Adams Street, Brooklyn 11201.
Telephone: (718) 643-5121.
E-mail address: lruchelsman@courts.state.ny.us

RUDERMAN, Terry Jane *(Judge, New York Court of Claims)* Appointed by Governor George E. Pataki.
Office: 140 Grand Street, Fifth Floor, White Plains 10601.
Telephone: (914) 289-2310.
Fax: (914) 289-2219

RUDITZKY, Howard A. *(Justice, New York Supreme Court Second Judicial District)* Former Judge, The Civil Court of the City of New York, assigned to The Criminal Court of the City of New York.
Office: 360 Adams Street, Brooklyn 11201.
Telephone: (718) 643-3656.

RUDOLPH, Kenneth W. *(Justice, New York Supreme Court Ninth Judicial District)* Elected to term beginning Jan 1, 1995. Term expires Dec 31, 2008. Currently serves as Justice Appellate Term Ninth and Tenth Judicial Districts. Born New York July 29, 1936. Catholic. Educated at Fordham University B.S. 1958 J.D. 1961. Admitted to practice New York 1961 and U.S. District Court Southern District of New York 1963. In legal practice Bronx 1962-70 and New Rochelle 1970-90. Acting Judge 1983-90 and Judge 1991-94, New Rochelle City Court.
Former Member New York State Association of City Court Judges. Member New York State Magistrates Association, Association of Justices of the Supreme Court of The State of New York, New Rochelle, Westchester County and New York State Bar Associations. Former Commissioner New Rochelle Human Rights Commission. Board of Trustees New Rochelle Boys' and Girls' Club. Board of Directors Frank M. Reed Foundation for the Handicapped. Member Society of Friendly Sons of St. Patrick and New Rochelle Kiwanis Club (Past President). Enjoys golf, skiing, reading, carpentry and professional and collegiate sports.
Office: 140 Grand Street, White Plains 10601.
Telephone: (914) 995-4364.
E-mail address: kwr@courts.state.ny.us

RUIZ, Norma *(Justice, New York Supreme Court Twelfth Judicial District)* Former Judge, The Civil Court of the City of New York.
Office: 851 Grand Concourse, Bronx 10451.
Telephone: (718) 590-3773.
Fax: (718) 590-8914

RUMSEY, Phillip R. *(Justice, New York Supreme Court Sixth Judicial District)*
Office: 46 Greenbush Street, Suite 301, Cortland 13045-2725.
Telephone: (607) 756-3480.
Fax: (607) 753-0854

RUSKIN, Lea *(Judge, Nassau County District Court)*
Office: 99 Main Street, Hempstead 11550.
Telephone: (516) 572-2117.
E-mail address: ruskin@courts.state.ny.us

RUSSELL, Robert T., Jr. *(Judge, Buffalo City Court)*
Office: 50 Delaware Avenue, Buffalo 14202.
Telephone: (716) 847-8231.
Fax: (716) 847-8257

RYAN, Kevin K. *(Judge, Clinton County Court)* Also serves Clinton County Surrogate's Court. Former Judge, Plattsburgh City Court.
Office: 315 County Government Center, 137 Margaret Street, Plattsburgh 12901-2933.
Telephone: (518) 565-4630.
Fax: (518) 565-4769

SACK, Barry D. *(Judge, Hudson City Court)*
Office: 427-429 Warren Street, Hudson 12534.
Telephone: (518) 828-3100.
Fax: (518) 828-3628

SACKETT, Robert A. *(Judge, The Civil Court of the City of New York)* Former Judge, The Criminal Court of the City of New York.
Office: 851 Grand Concourse, Bronx 10451.
Telephone: (718) 590-5231.

SAITTA, Wayne P. *(Judge, The Civil Court of the City of New York)* Currently assigned to the Criminal Court of the City of New York.
Office: 100 Centre Street, New York 10013.
Telephone: (718) 643-8400.
Fax: (718) 643-3538

SAKS, Alan J. *(Justice, New York Supreme Court Twelfth Judicial District)* Former Acting Justice. Elected to term beginning Jan 1, 1996. Term expires Dec 31, 2003. Born New York New York Jan 9, 1933. Jewish. Educated at Queens College B.A. cum laude 1953 and Cornell University LL.B. 1956. Recipient Federal Bar Association Prize 1956. Member Phi Alpha Delta and Phi Alpha Theta. Admitted to practice New York 1957, U.S. District Courts Southern 1959 and Eastern 1959 Districts of New York and U.S. Court of Appeals Second Circuit 1965. Began legal practice New York City 1957. Judge, The Civil Court of the City of New York, Jan 1, 1982 to Dec 31, 1995.
Office: 851 Grand Concourse, Bronx 10451.
Telephone: (718) 590-3779.
Fax: (718) 590-8914

SALERNO, George D. *(Justice, New York Supreme Court Twelfth Judicial District)* Former Judge, The Civil Court of the City of New York.
Office: 851 Grand Concourse, Bronx 10451.
Telephone: (718) 590-2678.

SALINITRO, Barbara *(Judge, New York City Family Court)* Appointed by Mayor Rudolph Giuliani.
Office: 151-20 Jamaica Avenue, Jamaica 11432.
Telephone: (718) 298-0197.

SALMAN, Barry *(Justice, New York Supreme Court Twelfth Judicial District)* Acting Justice 1981-90. Appointed Justice by Governor Mario Cuomo to term beginning May 1990. Elected 1990, current term expires Dec 31, 2004. Born Bronx New York May 20, 1940. Jewish. Educated at Hunter College of the City University of New York B.A. 1962 and St. John's University School of Law J.D. 1965. Member Delta Theta Phi. Admitted to practice New York 1965, U.S. District Courts Southern and Eastern Districts of New York and U.S. Supreme Court. Law Secretary to Hon. Alvin F. Klein, The Civil Court of the City of New York 1967-70. In legal practice New York City 1965-67 and 1970-78. Judge, The Civil Court of the City of New York 1977-90.

Author "The Grand Jury: Alibi and the Burden of Proof" 3 No. 1, 1985/1986 and "The '911' Dilemma—Emergency Response Telephone System" March 1989 Bronx County B. Jour.; and "The Nature of Assumption of Risk" 2 No. 1 *The Advocate* Journal of the Bronx County Bar Association Sept 1993. Adjunct Professor of Political Science College of New Rochelle 1979-80. Instructor Institute for Legal Assistant and Paralegal Training 1980-81. Adjunct Associate Professor of Political Science since 1980, Instructor in Paralegal Programs since 1985 and Chairman Paralegal Advisory Board Lehman College of the City University of New York. Adjunct Associate Professor of Torts and Criminal Law Bronx Community College of the City University of New York since 1988. President Supreme Court Justices Association Twelfth Judicial District. Former Director Bronx County Bar Association. Member Association of Supreme Court Justices of the City of New York (Board of Directors), Jewish Lawyers Guild, New York State Trial Lawyers Association, The Association of Trial Lawyers of America and New York State Bar Association (Judicial Committee, Ad Hoc Committee of the Jury System). Recipient Meritorious Service Award from New York City Division American Cancer Society and Lincoln Citation and Award from John F. Kennedy Library for the Minorities. Inducted into Hall of Fame Hunter College of the City University of New York. E-4 USAR 1962-68. Major Civil Affairs Regiment New York Guard. City Council New York City 1970-78. Founder and Chairman Advisory Board Lehman College Paralegal Program. Board of Directors New York City Division and Chairman Emeritus Bronx Unit American Cancer Society. Board of Directors St. John's University School of Law Alumni Association. Member University Council St. John's University. Interests include sports and animals.
Office: 851 Grand Concourse, Bronx 10451.
Telephone: (718) 590-3795.
Fax: (718) 590-1286

SAMPSON, Frederick D. R. *(Justice, New York Supreme Court Eleventh Judicial District)* Elected to term beginning Jan 1, 1995. Former Judge, The Civil Court of the City of New York.
Office: 25-10 Court Square, Long Island City 11101.
Telephone: (718) 520-3903.

SAMUELS, Debra Rose *(Judge, The Civil Court of the City of New York)*
Office: 111 Centre Street, Room 646, New York 10013.
Telephone: (212) 374-8493.

SAND, Leonard B. *(Senior Judge, United States District Court Southern District of New York)* Appointed for life by President Jimmy Carter to term beginning June 7, 1978. Assumed Senior status, serves by assignment. Born New York New York May 24, 1928. Jewish. Educated at New York University B.S. magna cum laude 1947 and Harvard University LL.B. cum laude 1951. Law Clerk to Hon. Irving R. Kaufman, U.S. District Court Southern District of New York 1952-53. Admitted to practice New York 1953, U.S. Court of Appeals Second Circuit 1954, U.S. District Courts Southern 1955 and Eastern 1969 Districts of New York and District of Columbia 1969 and U.S. Supreme Court 1956. Began legal practice New York City 1954.

Assistant U.S. Attorney Southern District of New York 1953-54. Assistant Solicitor General of the U.S. 1956-59. Co-author with Siffert, Reiss, Sexton and Thrope *Modern Federal Jury Instructions* Matthew Bender 1985. Adjunct Professor of Law New York University since 1985. Fellow American College of Trial Lawyers 1977. President Elect Federal Bar Council 1977. Member The Association of the Bar of the City of New York and American Bar Association. Ensign USNR 1951-52. Delegate New York State Constitutional Convention 1967.

Office: 1650 U.S. Courthouse, 500 Pearl Street, New York 10007-1312.

Telephone: (212) 805-0244.

SANTORELLI, Joseph A. *(Judge, Suffolk County District Court)* Currently serves as Acting Judge, Suffolk County Court.

Mailing address: P.O. Box 9007, Riverhead 11901-9007.

Office: Court Complex, 210 Center Drive, Riverhead 11902.

Telephone: (631) 853-7418.

SANTUCCI, Fred T. *(Associate Justice, New York Supreme Court Appellate Division Second Judicial Department)* Former Judge, The Civil Court of the City of New York.

Office: 88-11 Sutphin Boulevard, Jamaica 11435.

Telephone: (718) 520-3747.

SATTERFIELD, Patricia P. *(Justice, New York Supreme Court Eleventh Judicial District)* Former Acting Justice. Born Christchurch Virginia July 10, 1942. Protestant. Educated at Howard University B.M.E. 1964, Indiana University School of Music M.M. 1967 and St. John's University School of Law J.D. 1977. Member Pi Kappa Lambda. Admitted to practice New York 1978, U.S. District Courts Eastern 1979 and Southern 1979 Districts of New York and U.S. Court of Appeals Second Circuit 1980. Former Judge, The Civil Court of the City of New York, elected to term beginning Jan 1, 1991.

Assistant Deputy Counsel New York State Office of Court Administration 1977-90. Member Association of Women Judges, Association of Civil Court Judges of the City of New York, Macon B. Allen, Queens Women's, Metropolitan Black and Queens County Bar Associations. Named Outstanding Community Leader of the Year by Alpha Kappa Alpha Sorority Epsilon Omega Chapter 1991. Democrat. Member Queens Women's Network, Jack and Jill of America, Inc. and Cultural Diversity Committee St. John's School of Law. Board of Directors St. John's University Law Alumni Association and St. Albans Human Resources Center. Interested in developing and implementing programs for young people interested in studying law. Mentors teenage mothers. Enjoys bridge, singing and camping.

Office: 88-11 Sutphin Boulevard, Jamaica 11435.

Telephone: (718) 520-3731.

SAXE, David B. *(Associate Justice, New York Supreme Court Appellate Division First Judicial Department)* Elected Justice First Judicial District. Appointed Associate Justice Appellate Division by Governor George E. Pataki. Former Judge, The Civil Court of the City of New York.

Office: 27 Madison Avenue at 25th Street, New York 10010.

Telephone: (212) 340-0401.

SCARANO, Jerry J. *(Judge, Saratoga County Court)*

Office: 30 McMaster Street, Ballston Spa 12020-0600.

Telephone: (518) 885-2214.

SCARPINO, Anthony A., Jr. *(Surrogate, Westchester County Surrogate's Court)* Elected Nov 2000 to term beginning Jan 1, 2001. Born Mount Vernon New York July 18, 1951. Roman Catholic. Educated at University of Connecticut B.S.B.A. magna cum laude 1973 and Syracuse University College of Law J.D. 1976. Recipient Dean's Outstanding Student Award and Paul Shipman Andrews Memorial Award. President Law Student Senate. Listed in *Who's Who in American Colleges and Universities.* Member Sigma Chi, Phi Delta Phi and Beta Gamma Sigma. Judicial Intern to Hon. Irving Kendall, Mount Vernon City Court 1974-76. Admitted to practice New York 1977, U.S. District Court Southern District of New York and U.S. Supreme Court. Began legal practice Mount Vernon 1977. Judge, Mount Vernon City Court Jan 1, 1984 to Dec 31, 1988. Judge, Westchester County Court Jan 1, 1989 to Dec 31, 1993. Acting Justice July 1989 to 1993 and Justice Jan 1, 1994 to Dec 31, 2000, New York Supreme Court Ninth Judicial District.

Former Assistant Corporation Counsel City of Mount Vernon Law Department. Adjunct Professor graduate programs Long Island University and Iona College. Coordinator Simon Wiesenthal Center's Task Force Against Hate Ninth Judicial District. Member Task Force on Bias and Hate Crimes Westchester County. Member Columbian Lawyers Association, Women's Bar Association, Mount Vernon and Westchester County Bar Associations. Former Special Agent FBI. Former Assistant Vice President Bankers Trust Company. Democrat. Member Society of Former Special Agents FBI and Italian Civic Association. Enjoys tennis.

Office: 140 Grand Street, Eighth Floor, White Plains 10601.

Telephone: (914) 995-3722.

SCARPULLA, Saliann *(Judge, The Civil Court of the City of New York)*

Office: 111 Centre Street, New York 10013.

Telephone: (212) 791-6000.

SCHACK, Arthur M. *(Judge, The Civil Court of the City of New York)* Elected Nov 1998 to term beginning Jan 1, 1999. Term expires Dec 31, 2008. Assigned to The Criminal Court of the City of New York Jan 1, 1999 to Jan 28, 2002. Born Brooklyn New York June 29, 1945. Jewish. Educated at Brooklyn College B.A. 1966, Indiana University M.A. 1968 and New York Law School J.D. cum laude 1980. Admitted to practice New

SCHACK, ARTHUR M.—*Continued*
York 1981 and U.S. District Courts Eastern 1984 and Southern 1984 Districts of New York. In legal practice New York City 1981-98.

Counsel Major League Baseball Players Association Aug 1982 to Dec 31, 1998. Important Decisions: People v. Mahmodoo (resisting arrest charge stands even if underlying charge unconstitutional) 182 Misc. 2d 77, 698 N.Y.S.2d 445, 1999; People v. Santoriello (New York City Administrative code section banning commercial banner advertising from parasail unconstitutional) 183 Misc. 2d 54, 702 N.Y.S.2d 53, 27 Aviation Report 12447, 1999; and People v. McCullum (mace is a deadly or dangerous weapon) 184 Misc. 2d 70, 706 N.Y.S.2d 616, 2000. Member Brooklyn (Criminal Court Committee since 1999), New York State (Committee on Judicial Administration since 2000) and American Bar Associations (National Conference of State Trial Judges Judicial Division). Recipient Silver Beaver Award from Boy Scouts of America 1982, George Meany Award from Boy Scouts of America and AFL-CIO 1989 and Albert Smallheiser Award from UFT. Social Studies teacher Feb 1968 to June 1982. Democrat. Member 1983-98 and Chairman 1986-89 Community Board 10 Brooklyn. President Stars and Stripes Democratic Club of the 49th Assembly District 1990-98. Staff Ten Mile River Scout Camps 1962-70. Executive Board Brooklyn Council (Camping Chairman 1985-90, Commissioner 1990-91, President 1991-93) since 1985, Greater New York Councils since 1990 and National Council since 1996 Boy Scouts of America. Enjoys reading, camping and traveling.

Office: 100 Centre Street, New York 10013.
Telephone: (718) 643-4078.
Fax: (212) 374-3177
E-mail address: aschack@courts.state.ny.us

SCHECHTER, Sara P. *(Judge, New York City Family Court)* Appointed by Mayor Edward Koch to term beginning Feb 17, 1983. Reappointed 1988 and 1998. Current term expires 2008. Educated at Barnard College B.A. 1965 and New York University Law School J.D. 1968. Admitted to practice New York 1968. Began legal practice New York City 1968.

Assistant General Counsel New York City Human Resources Administration 1980-83. Member New York City Family Court Judges Association, New York State Family Court Judges Association and The Association of the Bar of the City of New York.

Office: 60 Lafayette Street, New York 10013.
Telephone: (212) 374-4177.
Fax: (212) 374-2623

SCHEINDLIN, Shira A. *(Judge, United States District Court Southern District of New York)* Appointed for life by President Bill Clinton to term beginning Nov 14, 1994. Born Washington D.C. Aug 16, 1946. Educated at University of Michigan B.A. cum laude 1967, Columbia University M.A. 1969 and Cornell University J.D. cum laude 1975. Woodrow Wilson Fellow 1967-68. Board of Editors Cornell Law Review 1972-74. Law Clerk to Hon. Charles L. Brieant, U.S. District Court Southern District of New York 1976-77. Admitted to practice New York, U.S. District Courts Eastern and Southern Districts of New York, U.S. Court of Appeals Second Circuit and U.S. Supreme Court. In legal practice New York 1986-94. Magistrate Judge, U.S. District Court Eastern District of New York 1982-86.

Assistant U.S. Attorney Eastern District of New York 1977-81. General Counsel Department of Investigation City of New York 1981-82. Author "Legal Services—Past and Present" 59 Cornell L. Rev. 960, 1974 and "Discovering the Discoverable: A Bird's Eye View of Discovery in a Complex Multi-District Class Action Litigation" 52 Brooklyn L. Rev. 397, 1986. Co-author with Hon. Charles L. Brieant, Jr. "Venue in the Second Circuit: A Topic Whose Time Has Come, A Review of Civil and Criminal Venue Cases 1970-76" Annual Second Circuit Review Brooklyn L. Rev. 1977, with Stacy Caplow "Portrait of a Lady: The Woman Lawyer in the 1980's" New York Law School L. Rev. 391, 1990, with John Elofson, Esq. "Judges, Juries, and Sexual Harassment" 17 Yale Law and Policy Review 813, 1999 and with Jeffrey Rabkin "Electronic Discovery in Federal Civil Litigation: Is Rule 34 Up to the Task?" Boston College L. Rev. May 2000. Important Decisions: Playboy Enterprises, Inc. v. Chuckleberry Publishing Inc. 939 F. Supp. 1032 S.D.N.Y. 1996; Ringling Bros.-Barnum & Bailey Combined Shows v. B.E. Windows Corp. 937 F. Supp. 204 S.D.N.Y. 1996; United States v. Santiago 950 F. Supp. 590 S.D.N.Y. 1996; Eve of Milady v. Impression Bridal, Inc. 957 F. Supp. 484 S.D.N.Y. 1997; New York Magazine v. Metropolitan Transit Authority 987 F. Supp. 254 S.D.N.Y. 1997; U.S. v. Livoti 22 F. Supp.2d 235, 1998; Nabisco, Inc. v. PF Brands 50 F. Supp.2d 188 S.D.N.Y. 1999; Polar International Brokerage v. Reeve 187 F.R.D. 108 S.D.N.Y. 1999; Allendale Mutual Ins. Co. v. Excess Ins. Co. 62 F. Supp.2d 1116 S.D.N.Y. 1999; United States v. Nachamie 98 Cr. 1238, 2000 WL 12139 S.D.N.Y. Jan 6, 2000; and United States v. Nachamie 98 Cr. 1238, 2000 WL 37993 S.D.N.Y. Jan 14, 2000. Adjunct Professor of Law Brooklyn Law School 1983-98. Member Bankruptcy Judge Selection Committee and Magistrate Judge Selection Committee Eastern District of New York, Bankruptcy Selection Committee Southern District of New York, Second Circuit Judicial Conference Planning Committee, Southern District Advisory Group Civil Justice Reform Act of 1990, Advisory Committee on Civil Rules Judicial Conference of the U.S., Justice Resource Center (Board of Directors), New York County Lawyers' Association (Chair Tort Law Section, Member Board of Directors, Executive Committee), New York State Association of Women Judges (Vice President, Board of Directors), Federal Bar Council (Vice President, Board of Directors, Member Planning Committee Winter Meeting), The Association of the Bar of the City of New York (Council on Judicial Administration, Committee on Women in the Profession, Committee on Criminal Advocacy) and New York State Bar Association (Chair Section on Commercial and Federal Litigation, Member Finance Committee House of Delegates, Board of Directors New York Bar Foundation). Recipient Special Achievement Award from U.S. Department of Justice April 1980. Enjoys jogging, hiking and cooking.

Office: 1050 U.S. Courthouse, 500 Pearl Street, New York 10007-1312.
Telephone: (212) 805-0246.

SCHER, Preston S. *(Judge, New Rochelle City Court)*
Office: 475 North Avenue, New Rochelle 10801-3405.
Telephone: (914) 654-2289.

SCHERER, Micki A. *(Judge, The Criminal Court of the City of New York)* Appointed by Mayor Ed Koch. Currently serves as Administrative Judge Criminal Term First Judicial District. Also serves as Acting Justice, New York Supreme Court First Judicial District.
Office: 100 Centre Street, New York 10013.
Telephone: (212) 374-8015.
Fax: (212) 748-5129

SCHLESINGER, Alice *(Justice, New York Supreme Court First Judicial District)* Former Acting Justice. Former Judge, The Civil Court of the City of New York.
Office: 60 Centre Street, Room 557, New York 10007.
Telephone: (212) 374-4744.

SCHMIDT, David I. *(Judge, The Civil Court of the City of New York)* Currently serves as Acting Justice, New York Supreme Court Second Judicial District.
Office: 120 Schermerhorn Street, Brooklyn 11201.
Telephone: (718) 643-3190.
E-mail address: dschmidt@courts.state.ny.us

SCHMIDT, Frederick D. *(Justice, New York Supreme Court Eleventh Judicial District)* Certificated. Former Judge, The Civil Court of the City of New York.
Office: 88-11 Sutphin Boulevard, Jamaica 11435.
Telephone: (718) 520-3143.

SCHMIDT, Robert W. *(Associate Justice, New York Supreme Court Appellate Division Second Judicial Department)* Elected Justice Tenth Judicial District. Appointed Associate Justice Appellate Division by Governor George E. Pataki.
Office: Supreme Court Building, 100 Supreme Court Drive, Mineola 11501.
Telephone: (516) 571-2061.

SCHNEIER, Martin *(Justice, New York Supreme Court Second Judicial District)* Former Acting Justice. Former Judge, The Civil Court of the City of New York.
Office: 360 Adams Street, Brooklyn 11201.
Telephone: (718) 243-2474.
E-mail address: mschneier@courts.state.ny.us

SCHOENFELD, Martin *(Justice, New York Supreme Court First Judicial District)* Elected to term beginning Jan 1, 1995. Term expires Dec 31, 2008. Currently serves as Justice, New York Supreme Court Appellate Term First Department. Born New York New York March 17, 1947. Jewish. Educated at Brooklyn College of the City University of New York B.A. 1968 and Syracuse University College of Law J.D. with honors 1971. Editorial Board Syracuse Law Review. Moot Court Board. Recipient Junior of the Year Award from Syracuse University Student Bar Association 1970 and American Jurisprudence Award 1971. Admitted to practice New York 1972, U.S. District Courts Southern 1973 and Eastern 1973 Districts of New York and U.S. Supreme Court 1976. Began legal practice New York City 1972. Assigned to The Criminal Court of The City of New York two years. Judge, The Civil Court of the City of New York Jan 1, 1985 to Dec 31, 1994.

Principal Law Clerk to Hon. Jerome W. Marks, New York Supreme Court First Judicial District Sept 1978 to Dec 1984. Author "Great Eastern Liquor Corp. v. S.L.A." 21 Syracuse L. Rev. 1034, 1970, "What's in a Name?" March 17, 1976 and "Artists and Exclusive Contracts" June 21, 1978 New York L. Jour. Author more than fifty published opinions. Former Small Claims and Commercial Arbitrator National Panel of Arbitrators American Arbitration Association. Member New York County Lawyers' Association, New York State Trial Lawyers Association, The Association of the Bar of the City of New York (Committees on State Legislation 1974-76, Courts of Superior Jurisdiction 1981-83 and Criminal Justice Operations and Budget 1988-91) and New York State Bar Association (Committee on Copyright Law 1979-81, Committee on Supreme Courts 1981-83, Committee on AIDS and the Law since 1993). Guest Judge Monrad G. Paulsen Moot Court Competition Benjamin N. Cardozo School of Law. Participant Trial Advocacy Program Brooklyn Law School and Moot Court Competition The Association of the Bar of the City of New York. Lecturer Alumnae Association of the Women's Law Class New York University and New York County Lawyers' Association. Counsel for Volunteer Lawyers for the Arts. Member B'nai B'rith Performing Arts Lodge, Young Israel Synagogue, Guardian/Friends of Juan Baez and American Tinnitus Association. Enjoys athletics, music and reading.
Office: 60 Centre Street, New York 10007.
Telephone: (212) 374-8202.

SCHROEDER, H. Kenneth, Jr. *(Magistrate Judge, United States District Court Western District of New York)* Appointed by U.S. District Court judges to term beginning June 1, 2000.
Office: 418 U.S. Courthouse, 68 Court Street, Buffalo 14202-3406.
Telephone: (716) 551-3301.

SCHULMAN, Martin J. *(Justice, New York Supreme Court Eleventh Judicial District)* Elected to term beginning Jan 1, 1995. Former Judge, The Civil Court of the City of New York.
Office: 88-11 Sutphin Boulevard, Jamaica 11435.
Telephone: (718) 261-2271.

SCHULTZ, Jack *(Acting Judge, Syracuse City Court)*
Office: Public Safety Building, 511 South State Street, Syracuse 13202.
Telephone: (315) 477-2785.

SCHUPPENHAUER, John A. *(Acting Judge, Canandaigua City Court)*
Office: City Hall, Two North Main Street, Canandaigua 14424-1448.
Telephone: (585) 396-5011.
Fax: (585) 396-5012

SCHWARTZ, Allen G. *(Judge, United States District Court Southern District of New York)* Appointed for life by President Bill Clinton Nov 22, 1993 to term beginning Jan 12, 1994. Born Brooklyn New York Aug 23, 1934. Jewish. Educated at City College of the City University of New York B.B.A. 1955 and University of Pennsylvania LL.B. 1958. Research Editor University of Pennsylvania Law Review 1956-58. Admitted to practice New York 1958, U.S. District Courts Eastern 1961 and Southern 1961 Districts of New York, U.S. Court of Appeals Second Circuit 1968 and U.S. Supreme Court 1970. In legal practice New York City 1959-93.

Assistant District Attorney 1959-62. Corporation Counsel New York City 1978-81. Member Criminal Justice Coordinating Committee New York City 1978-79.

SCHWARTZ, ALLEN G.—*Continued*
Member The Association of the Bar of the City of New York (Criminal Courts Law and Procedure Committee 1972-75, Municipal Affairs Committee 1980, Chair Committee on Public Law Offices 1982-83). Recipient Hogan-Morgenthau Award 1980, Achievement Award from the School of Business Alumni Society of the City College of the City University of New York 1981, Award for Distinguished Service from Corporation Counsel 1994, Award from Frank S. Hogan Associates, Inc. 1995 and President's Medal from Baruch College 2001. USAR 1958-65. Ex Officio Member Board of Ethics New York City 1978-81.

Office: 1350 U.S. Courthouse, 500 Pearl Street, New York 10007-1312.
Telephone: (212) 805-0248.
Fax: (212) 805-7921

SCHWARTZ, John R. *(Chief Judge, Rochester City Court)* Appointed by Mayor Thomas J. Ryan to term beginning June 28, 1983. Elected 1983 and 1993. Current term expires Dec 31, 2003. Born Rochester New York July 9, 1944. Roman Catholic. Educated at John Carroll University B.S.B.A. 1966 and Albany Law School of Union University J.D. 1969. Admitted to practice New York 1970 and U.S. District Court Western District of New York 1970. In legal practice Rochester 1970-83.

Town Attorney Ogden 1972-74. Member Monroe County, New York State and American Bar Associations. Counsel to State Senate New York 1970-73. Attorney School District Town of Livonia 1980-83. Board of Directors Center for Dispute Settlement Inc. and School of Holy Childhood Inc. (Chairman). Member Greater Rochester Fights Back (Chair Criminal Justice Task Force, Member Executive Committee).

Office: 108 Hall of Justice, 99 Exchange Boulevard, Rochester 14614.
Telephone: (585) 428-2450.
Fax: (585) 428-2737
E-mail address: jschwart@courts.state.ny.us

SCHWARTZ, Michael *(Judge, Middletown City Court)* Appointed to term beginning Jan 1999. Term expires 2005. Serves part time. Educated at Brandeis University B.A. 1960 and New York University J.D. 1963. Admitted to practice New York 1963, U.S. District Courts Eastern 1966 and Southern 1966 Districts of New York and U.S. Supreme Court 1967. In legal practice 1971-72 and 1984-89. Hearing Examiner, Orange County Family Court 1984-85.

Assistant District Attorney Appeals Bureau Kings County 1964-68. Associate Appellate Counsel Legal Aid Society, Inc. 1968-71. Executive Assistant District Attorney Orange County 1972-81. Principal Law Clerk to Family Court Judge 1981-83 and County Court part-time 1985-89 and full time 1989-2000 Orange County. Special Assignment as Principal Law Clerk to County Court Judge Brinks Trial 1982-84. Adjunct Professor Mercy College at Harriman College 1978-81, John Jay College 1984-85 and Orange County Community College 1985-87. Member City of Middletown, Orange County and New York State Bar Associations.

Office: Two James Street, Middletown 10940.
Telephone: (845) 346-4050.
Fax: (845) 343-5737

SCHWERZMANN, Peter A. *(Surrogate, Jefferson County Surrogate's Court)*
Office: 175 Arsenal Street, Seventh Floor, Watertown 13601-2562.
Telephone: (315) 785-3019.
Fax: (315) 785-5194

SCIOLINO, Anthony J. *(Judge, Monroe County Family Court)* Elected Nov 1986 to term beginning Jan 1, 1987. Reelected 1996, current term expires Dec 31, 2006. Born Rochester New York Feb 6, 1945. Roman Catholic. Educated at Columbia University B.A. 1967 and Cornell Law School J.D. 1970. Admitted to practice New York 1971. In legal practice Rochester 1971-86.

Assistant District Attorney Monroe County May 1973 to Oct 1976. Member Monroe County (former Trustee) and New York State Bar Associations. Republican. City Council member Rochester 1980-86. Member Rochester Rotary Club. Enjoys theater and travel.

Office: Hall of Justice, Third Floor, 99 Exchange Boulevard, Rochester 14614-2187.
Telephone: (585) 428-2049.
Fax: (585) 428-2597

SCONIERS, Rose H. *(Justice, New York Supreme Court Eighth Judicial District)* Elected to term beginning Jan 1, 1994. Term expires Dec 31, 2007. Born Waverly Virginia Sept 23, 1945. Episcopalian. Educated at Long Island University B.A. 1969 and State University of New York at Buffalo School of Law J.D. 1973. Admitted to practice New York 1974, U.S. District Court Western District of New York 1975, U.S. Court of Appeals Second Circuit 1978 and U.S. Supreme Court 1978. In legal practice Niagara Falls 1975. Judge, Buffalo City Court 1988-93.

Assistant Corporation Counsel Law Department Buffalo 1975-79. Executive Attorney Legal Aid Bureau of Buffalo 1980-87. Important Decisions: People v. Lyons (miscellaneous reports on the privilege of a news gatherer against disclosure of confidential sources or information) 151 Misc. 2d 718, 574 N.Y.S. 2d 126, 1991; People (Deyver) v. Travis 172 Misc. 2d 83, 657 N.Y.S. 2d 306; Taxation & Fin. v. Bramhall 172 Misc. 2d 934, 660 N.Y.S. 2d 329; Valvo v. Seneca Nation 170 Misc. 2d 512, 650 N.Y.S. 2d 937; Morris v. Freudenheim 168 Misc. 2d 417, 641 N.Y.S. 2d 788; Travelers Ins. Co. v. Heppner 166 Misc. 2d 682, 630 N.Y.S. 2d 666; Zylinski v. Marine Drive Apartments 178 Misc. 2d 769, 680 N.Y.S. 2d 830; and Duncan v. Mt. St. Mary's Hospital 176 Misc. 2d 201, 672 N.Y.S. 2d 657. Lecturer New York State Urban Center 1971-72 and State University of New York 1983-84. Past President Buffalo Chapter National Bar Association. Former Member New York State Judicial Records Disposition Committee and Board of Directors New York State Defenders Association. Vice President Association of Justices of the Supreme Court of the State of New York. Member Judicial Commission on Minorities and Criminal Procedure Law Committee Office of Court Administration. Member Bar Association of Erie County, New York State (Committee on Legal Aid, Secretary Judicial Council) and American (Delegate The National Conference of State Trial Judges Judicial Division) Bar Associations.

Attended "The Appearance of Justice: Juries, Judges and the Media" The Jury Project Princeton University Nov 11, 1994. Recipient Outstanding Achievement in Law Award from Bison Assembly 48, 1980, Community Award from Phyllis Weatley Club Nov 5, 1982, Excel-

SCONIERS, ROSE H.—*Continued*
lence in Leadership Award from Xi Epsilon Omega Chapter Alpha Kappa Alpha 1983, Outstanding Black Woman in Justice Award from North Region Black Political Caucus Nov 3, 1984, Lawyer of the Year Award from Buffalo Chapter National Bar Association Nov 10, 1984, Award of Merit for Professional Achievement from Rho Lambda Chapter Alpha Phi Alpha Dec 4, 1987, Frank F. Hughes Memorial Award from Afro-American Police Association 1988, Distinguished Service Award from St. John African Methodist Episcopalian Church June 29, 1990, Outstanding Church and Community Service Award from St. Luke African Methodist Episcopalian Zion Church Feb 24, 1991, Community Service Award from Afro-American Police Association 1992 and Sojourner Truth Award from National Association of Negro Business and Professional Women's Clubs, Inc. June 20, 1993. Past President University of Buffalo Law Alumni Association, Community Planning Assistance Center of Western New York, Inc. and New York State Association of Council Members and College Trustees. Former Chairperson 13th Street Multi-Purpose Center, Inc. and Friends of the School of Architecture and Environmental Design State University of New York at Buffalo. Former Member Board of Directors Longview Protestant Home for Children and Buffalo Chapter American Red Cross. Member Presidential Search Advisory Committee State University of New York at Buffalo 1981-82. President Erie County Chapter The LINKS, Inc. Board of Trustees Children's Hospital of Buffalo. Council Member State University of New York at Buffalo.

Office: Third and Cedar Streets, Niagara Falls 14302.
Telephone: (716) 278-1815.
E-mail address: rsconiers@courts.state.ny.us

SCOTT, Hugh B. *(Magistrate Judge, United States District Court Western District of New York)* Appointed by U.S. District Court judges. Former Judge, Buffalo City Court.

Office: 414 U.S. Courthouse, 68 Court Street, Buffalo 14202.
Telephone: (716) 551-4010.

SCUCCIMARRA, Thomas H. *(Judge, New York Court of Claims)* Appointed by Governor George E. Pataki April 24, 2001 to term beginning June 5, 2001. Term expires March 31, 2006. Born Peekskill New York May 27, 1948. Educated at Southampton College B.A. 1970 and Vermont Law School J.D. 1977. Admitted to practice New York 1978 and U.S. District Courts Eastern 1978 and Southern 1978 Districts of New York. In legal practice Peekskill 1978-2001. Acting Justice, Coldspring Village Court 1984-2000. Acting Justice, Nelsonville Village Court 1986-2000. Judge, Philipstown City Court 1985-2000. Judge, Putnam County Court June 2000 to Dec 31, 2000.

President City of Peekskill Bar Association 1984 and Putnam County Magistrates Association 1989-92. Board of Directors Columbian Lawyers Association of Westchester County. Member New York State Association of Magistrates, National Judges Association, White Plains, Westchester County, Westchester County Women's, New York State and American Bar Associations. Republican. Former Member Board of Directors Butterfield Memorial Hospital and Coldspring/Garrison Chamber of Commerce. Enjoys scuba diving (Assistant Instructor), skiing, hiking and antique autos.

Office: 140 Grand Street, Suite 910, White Plains 10601.
Telephone: (914) 289-2330.
Fax: (914) 289-2333

SCUDDER, Henry J. *(Associate Justice, New York Supreme Court Appellate Division Fourth Judicial Department)* Elected Justice Seventh Judicial District. Appointed Associate Justice Appellate Division by Governor George E. Pataki. Former Surrogate, Steuben County Surrogate's Court.

Office: 19 East Pulteney Square, Bath 14810-1575.
Telephone: (607) 776-9623.
Fax: (607) 776-7168

SCULLIN, Frederick J., Jr. *(Chief Judge, United States District Court Northern District of New York)* Appointed for life by President George Bush Feb 10, 1992. Chief Judge since April 2000. Born Syracuse New York Nov 5, 1939. Educated at Niagara University 1961 and Syracuse University College of Law J.D. 1964. Admitted to practice Florida and New York. In legal practice 1967-69 and 1980-82.

Assistant District Attorney Onondaga County 1969-71. Prosecutor and Assistant in Charge of Albany Regional Office Statewide Organized Task Force 1971-78. Chief Prosecutor Governor's Council for Prosecution of Organized Crime Florida 1978-80. U.S. Attorney Northern District of New York 1982-92. Member Federal Bar Council, The Florida Bar, Onondaga County (Board of Directors 1988-90), New York State, Federal and American Bar Associations. Infantry Commander 173rd Airborne Brigade U.S. Army Vietnam. Colonel USAR (retired 1991). Past Member and Chairman City of Syracuse and County of Onondaga Drug and Alcohol Abuse Commission. Member Law College Association Syracuse University.

Mailing address: P.O. Box 7255, Syracuse 13261-7255.
Telephone: (315) 234-8560.

SEAMAN, David E. *(Judge, Niagara County Family Court)*

Office: Courthouse, 175 Hawley Street, Lockport 14094-2758.
Telephone: (716) 439-7172.
Fax: (716) 439-7170
E-mail address: dseaman@courts.state.ny.us

SEDITA, Frank A., Jr. *(Justice, New York Supreme Court Eighth Judicial District)* Elected to term beginning Jan 1, 1994. Term expires Dec 31, 2007. Born Buffalo New York April 1, 1935. Roman Catholic. Educated at Canisius College B.S. summa cum laude 1957 and University of Buffalo (now State University of New York at Buffalo) LL.B. 1960. Admitted to practice New York 1961 and U.S. District Court Western District of New York 1961. Began legal practice Buffalo 1961. Judge, Erie County Family Court 1977-89. Associate Judge 1989 and Chief Judge 1990-93, Buffalo City Court.

Assistant Corporation Counsel 1968 and Senior Deputy Corporation Counsel 1970 City of Buffalo. Important Decision: Donovan and Klice v. Rapid Ray Printing and Copying Inc. and Paul M. Tarapacki 403 N.Y.S.2d 407, 1978, aff'd Erie County Court 1978. Lecturer in Criminal Law D'Youville College 1979. Member American

SEDITA, FRANK A., JR.—*Continued*

Judicature Society, Police and Justices Conference of Western New York and Bar Association of Erie County. Chairman Task Force on School Discipline Buffalo Public Schools 1979. Member Forest District Civic Association and Knights of Columbus. Enjoys reading.

Office: 50 Delaware Avenue, Buffalo 14202.
Telephone: (716) 851-3226.
Fax: (716) 851-3329
E-mail address: fsedita@courts.state.ny.us

SEEWALD, Robert G. *(Judge, The Criminal Court of the City of New York)* Appointed by Mayor Edward Koch to term beginning May 1981. Reappointed 1983 and 1993. Current term expires Dec 2003. Currently serves as Acting Justice, New York Supreme Court Twelfth Judicial District.

Office: 215 East 161st Street, Bronx 10451.
Telephone: (718) 590-2940.

SEGAL, Marvin E. *(Justice, New York Supreme Court Tenth Judicial District)* Elected 1989. Certificated. Educated at University of Miami J.D. 1952. Admitted to practice Florida 1952. In legal practice twenty-nine years. Master, The Civil Court of the City of New York 1968. Judge and Acting Supervising Judge, Nassau County District Court 1983-89. Former Acting Judge, Nassau County Court. Former Acting Judge, The Criminal Court of the City of New York.

Co-author "The Right of Marine Repairmen to a Seaworthy Vessel." Past President Nassau County District Court Judges' Association. Former member American Arbitration Association. Member Jewish Lawyers of Nassau County, The Maritime Law Association of the U.S., The Florida Bar and Nassau County Bar Association. Captain USAF JAG. Member Nassau County American Revolution Bicentennial Commission 1975-77 and Nassau County Human Rights Commission 1980-83. Board of Directors Nassau-Suffolk Division Cystic Fibrosis 1978-83. Former District Deputy Grand Master Eighth Masonic District of Manhattan. Board of Trustees B'nai B'rth North Hills Lodge. Member Shelter Rock Jewish Center.

Office: 100 Supreme Court Drive, Mineola 11501.
Telephone: (516) 571-2742.

SEIBERT, Harry W., Jr. *(Surrogate, Saratoga County Surrogate's Court)* Elected Nov 3, 1992 to term beginning Jan 1, 1993. Reelected Nov 5, 2002, current term expires Dec 31, 2012. Born Ballston Spa New York Oct 3, 1941. Roman Catholic. Educated at LeMoyne College B.S. 1963 and Albany Law School J.D. 1966. Admitted to practice New York 1966. In legal practice Ballston Spa 1966-92.

Village Attorney Ballston Spa 1969-91. First Assistant County Attorney Saratoga County 1984-92. Member Saratoga County Bar Association.

Office: 30 McMaster Street, Ballston Spa 12020-0600.
Telephone: (518) 884-4722.
Fax: (518) 884-4774

SEIDEN, Adam *(Judge, Mount Vernon City Court)* Currently serves as Associate Judge.

Office: Roosevelt Square, Mount Vernon 10550-2019.
Telephone: (914) 665-2400.

SEYBERT, Joanna *(Judge, United States District Court Eastern District of New York)* Appointed for life by President Bill Clinton Jan 12, 1994. Educated at St. John's University School of Law J.D. 1971. Judge, Nassau County District Court 1987-92. Judge, Nassau County Court 1992-94.

Trial Staff Attorney Legal Aid Society of New York City 1971-73. Senior Trial Attorney Federal Defender Service 1973-76. Senior Staff Attorney Legal Aid Society of Nassau County 1976-79. Deputy Bureau Chief Nassau County Attorney's Office 1980-87.

Office: Long Island Federal Courthouse, 100 Federal Plaza, Central Islip 11722-4438.
Telephone: (631) 712-5610.

SGROI, Sandra L. *(Justice, New York Supreme Court Tenth Judicial District)* Former Judge, Suffolk County District Court.

Mailing address: P.O. Box 9075, Central Islip 11722-9075.
Office: S-23 Court Complex, 400 Carleton Avenue, Central Islip 11722.
Telephone: (631) 853-4537.
Fax: (631) 853-5427

SGUEGLIA, Vincent A. *(Judge, Tioga County Court)* Also serves Tioga County Surrogate's Court and Tioga County Family Court.

Mailing address: P.O. Box 307, Owego 13827.
Office: Courthouse, 16 Court Street, Owego 13827.
Telephone: (607) 687-0544.
Fax: (607) 687-3240

SHAFER, Marilyn *(Judge, The Civil Court of the City of New York)* Currently serves as Acting Justice, New York Supreme Court First Judicial District.

Office: 80 Centre Street, New York 10013.
Telephone: (212) 374-3254.
Fax: (212) 374-2593

SHAHEEN, Anthony F. *(Justice, New York Supreme Court Fifth Judicial District)* Elected to term beginning Jan 1, 1984. Reelected Nov 4, 1997, current term expires Dec 31, 2011. Born Utica New York June 9, 1935. Catholic. Educated at Utica College of Syracuse University 1957 and Syracuse University College of Law LL.B. 1959. Admitted to practice New York 1960. In legal practice Utica 1960-83.

Corporation Counsel City of Utica 1971-72. Member Association of Justices of the Supreme Court of the State of New York, Oneida County and New York State Bar Associations. Attended New York Judicial Seminars 1984-99. New York Army National Guard 1961-66. Chairman Oneida County Republican Party 1977-83.

Office: Oneida County Courthouse, 200 Elizabeth Street, Utica 13501.
Telephone: (315) 798-5466.
Fax: (315) 798-6431

SHAMON, Thomas J. *(Judge, Auburn City Court)* Currently serves as Acting Judge.

Office: 153 Genesee Street, Auburn 13021-3434.
Telephone: (315) 253-1570.
Fax: (315) 253-1085

SHAPIRO, Fred L. *(Judge, Westchester County Court)* Elected to term beginning Jan 1, 1995. Currently serves as Acting Justice, New York Supreme Court Ninth Judicial District.

Office: 111 Dr. Martin Luther King Jr. Blvd., White Plains 10601.
Telephone: (914) 995-4510.
Fax: (914) 995-4323

SHARPE, Gary L. *(Magistrate Judge, United States District Court Northern District of New York)* Appointed by U.S. District Court judges to term beginning 1997. Educated at Buffalo University B.A. magna cum laude 1971 and Cornell Law School J.D. 1974. Member Phi Beta Kappa.
Mailing address: P.O. Box 7346, Syracuse 13261-7346.
Telephone: (315) 234-8610.

SHEEHAN, Joseph W. *(Judge, Mechanicville City Court)*
Office: City Hall, 36 North Main Street, Mechanicville 12118.
Telephone: (518) 664-9876.
Fax: (518) 664-8606

SHELTON, Marian R. *(Judge, New York City Family Court)* Appointed by Mayor Rudolph Giuliani.
Office: 900 Sheridan Avenue, Bronx 10451.
Telephone: (718) 590-3376.
Fax: (718) 590-7305

SHERIDAN, Edward A. *(Judge, New York Court of Claims)* Appointed by Governor George E. Pataki. Currently serves as Acting Justice, New York Supreme Court Third and Fourth Judicial Districts.
Office: 65 South Broadway, Room 240, Saratoga Springs 12866.
Telephone: (518) 583-5352.
Fax: (518) 583-5355

SHERMAN, Howard E. *(Judge, The Civil Court of the City of New York)* Currently serves as Supervising Judge. Also serves as Acting Justice, New York Supreme Court Twelfth Judicial District.
Office: 851 Grand Concourse, Bronx 10451.
Telephone: (718) 466-3117.

SHERMAN, M. John *(Judge, Tompkins County Court)* Elected to term beginning Jan 1, 1994. Also serves Tompkins County Surrogate's Court and Tompkins County Family Court. Born Syracuse New York Sept 9, 1949. Educated at Harvard University B.A. magna cum laude 1971 and Syracuse University College of Law J.D. 1975. Admitted to practice New York 1976 and U.S. District Court Northern District of New York 1980. Began legal practice Herkimer 1976. In legal practice Ithaca since 1978. Acting Judge Jan 1, 1984 to Dec 31, 1988 and Judge Jan 1, 1989 to Dec 31, 1993, Ithaca City Court.
Chief Assistant District Attorney Herkimer County 1976-78. Assistant District Attorney Tompkins County 1978-80. City Prosecutor Ithaca 1980-82. Member Tompkins County Bar Association. Board of Directors Alpha House. Chair Advisory Board Ithaca City Youth Bureau.
Mailing address: P.O. Box 70, Ithaca 14851-0070.
Office: Courthouse, 320 North Tioga Street, Ithaca 14851.
Telephone: (607) 277-2355.
Fax: (607) 272-0684

SHERWOOD, William E. *(Justice, New York Supreme Court Ninth Judicial District)* Elected Nov 1993 to term beginning Jan 1, 1994. Term expires Dec 31, 2007. Born Nyack New York July 26, 1940. Protestant. Educated at Syracuse University B.A. 1962 and New York Law School J.D. 1970. Admitted to practice New York 1971, U.S. District Court Southern District of New York 1981 and U.S. Supreme Court 1984. In legal practice Spring Valley 1971-78 and Pomona 1978-93. Town Judge, Stony Point Town Court 1988-93.
Assistant District Attorney Rockland County 1974-75. Town Attorney Stony Point 1978-84. Member Rockland County and New York State Bar Associations.
Office: County Courthouse, One South Main Street, New City 10956.
Telephone: (845) 638-5634.

SHULMAN, Martin *(Judge, The Civil Court of the City of New York)* Currently serves as Supervising Judge. Also serves as Acting Justice, New York Supreme Court First Judicial District.
Office: 111 Centre Street, New York 10013.
Telephone: (212) 374-8070.

SHULTS, David A. *(Judge, Hornell City Court)*
Mailing address: P.O. Box 627, Hornell 14843-0627.
Office: 82 Main Street, Hornell 14843.
Telephone: (518) 664-9876.
Fax: (518) 664-8606

SIEGAL, Bernice Daun *(Judge, The Civil Court of the City of New York)*
Office: 89-17 Sutphin Boulevard, Jamaica 11435.
Telephone: (718) 262-7354.

SIEGEL, Norman I. *(Judge, New York Court of Claims)* Appointed by Governor George E. Pataki. Currently serves as Acting Justice, New York Supreme Court Fifth Judicial District.
Office: Oneida County Courthouse, 200 Elizabeth Street, Utica 13501.
Telephone: (315) 793-6096.
Fax: (315) 798-6045

SIFTON, Charles P. *(Senior Judge, United States District Court Eastern District of New York)* Appointed for life by President Jimmy Carter to term beginning Oct 26, 1977. Former Chief Judge. Assumed Senior status, serves by assignment. Born New York New York March 18, 1935. Educated at Harvard University B.A. summa cum laude 1957 and Columbia University LL.B. 1961. Admitted to practice New York 1961, U.S. District Court Southern District of New York 1962, U.S. Courts of Appeals Second 1966 and District of Columbia 1977 Circuits and U.S. Supreme Court 1969. Began legal practice New York City 1961.
Assistant U.S. Attorney Southern District of New York 1966-69. Member The Association of the Bar of the City of New York. Staff member U.S. Senate Foreign Relations Committee 1962-64.
Office: U.S. Courthouse, 225 Cadman Plaza East, Brooklyn 11201.
Telephone: (718) 260-2300.

SILBER, Debra *(Judge, The Civil Court of the City of New York)*
Office: 141 Livingston Street, Brooklyn 11201.
Telephone: (718) 643-4386.
Fax: (718) 643-3733

SILBERMANN, Jacqueline W. *(Justice, New York Supreme Court First Judicial District)* Elected to term beginning Jan 1, 1991. Term expires Dec 31, 2004. Currently serves as Administrative Judge for Matrimonial Matters and New York Supreme Court First Judicial District Civil Term. Born Brooklyn New York. Educated at Bryn Mawr College B.A. cum laude 1959 and Ford-

SILBERMANN, JACQUELINE W.—*Continued*
ham University School of Law J.D. cum laude 1972. Admitted to practice New York 1973, U.S. District Courts Eastern 1973 and Southern 1973 Districts of New York and U.S. Supreme Court. Judge, The Civil Court of the City of New York 1984-90.
Office: 60 Centre Street, New York 10007.
Telephone: (212) 374-4733.
Fax: (212) 374-1803

SILVER, George E. *(Judge, Ogdensburg City Court)*
Office: 330 Ford Street, Ogdensburg 13669.
Telephone: (315) 393-3941.
Fax: (315) 393-6839

SILVER, Howard R. *(Justice, New York Supreme Court Twelfth Judicial District)* Former Acting Justice. Born Bronx New York Sept 23, 1934. Jewish. Educated at Bernard M. Baruch College of the City University of New York B.B.A. 1956 and Brooklyn Law School LL.B. 1961. Admitted to practice New York 1962. Former Judge, The Civil Court of the City of New York, appointed by Mayor Edward I. Koch to term beginning Dec 1, 1982.
Chief Legal Officer and Trial Commissioner New York City Fire Department 1975-81. Member The Association of the Bar of the City of New York and Bronx County Bar Association.
Office: 851 Grand Concourse, Bronx 10451.
Telephone: (718) 590-6356.
Fax: (718) 590-8914

SILVERMAN, Arlene R. *(Judge, The Criminal Court of the City of New York)* Appointed by mayor. Currently serves as Acting Justice, New York Supreme Court First Judicial District.
Office: 111 Centre Street, New York 10013.
Telephone: (212) 374-8075.

SILVERMAN, Harold *(Justice, New York Supreme Court Twelfth Judicial District)* Former Acting Justice. Certificated. Former Judge, The Civil Court of the City of New York.
Office: 851 Grand Concourse, Bronx 10451.
Telephone: (718) 590-3793.
Fax: (718) 590-8914

SILVERMAN, Joseph S. *(Judge, The Civil Court of the City of New York)* Currently serves as Acting Justice, New York Supreme Court Second Judicial District.
Office: 120 Schermerhorn Street, Brooklyn 11201.
Telephone: (718) 643-7410.
E-mail address: jsilverman@courts.state.ny.us

SIMEONE, Ettore A. *(Judge, Suffolk County Family Court)*
Office: Cohalan Court Complex, 400 Carleton Avenue, Central Islip 11722.
Telephone: (631) 853-4935.
Fax: (631) 853-7629

SINGH, Anil C. *(Judge, The Civil Court of the City of New York)*
Office: 111 Centre Street, New York 10013.
Telephone: (212) 791-6000.

SIRACUSE, Andrew V. *(Justice, New York Supreme Court Seventh Judicial District)* Elected to term beginning Jan 1, 1975. Reelected 1988. Certificated. First Democrat to serve Seventh Judicial District in 134 years. Born Brooklyn New York Dec 14, 1928. Educated at Syracuse University B.S. 1953 J.D. 1956. Member Alpha Phi Delta (President) and Phi Delta Phi. Admitted to practice New York 1959 and U.S. District Courts Eastern 1959, Western 1959 and Southern 1959 Districts of New York. In legal practice New York City 1961-63 and Rochester 1965-75.
Counsel New York Central Railroad 1956-61. Senior Assistant Corporation Counsel City of Rochester 1963-65. Town Attorney Town of Penfield 1971-74. Coauthor *Bench Book.* Editor Case Book on Labor Law Sections 240(1) July 1993 amended Sept 1995. Editorial Board *Bench Book for Trial Judges—New York* since 1989. Author article on motion for summary judgment *Trial Lawyers Quarterly* March 1992 revised July 1996, article on New York State Labor Law Sections 200, 241(6) and 240(1) and "Re: *Ross v. Curtis-Palmer Hydro-Electric Company* Decision New Rules—New Game" New York L. Jour. Former Member New York State Trial Lawyers Association. Chairman Committee to Review Mental Hygiene Commitment Hearing Procedures in Monroe County 1982. Member Fourth Judicial Department and Seventh Judicial District Rules Committee (Tax Certiorari Committee) 1978, Committee on Civil Practice and Procedure 1980-81, Association of Justices of the Supreme Court of the State of New York (Representative Seventh Judicial District 1989-90, First Vice President 1995, President 1996), Association of Supreme Court Justices of the Seventh Judicial District (President 1987 and Executive Board), Monroe County (Bench and Bar Committee since 1987, Board of Trustees 1991-93, Former Member Subcommittee to Assist in Formulation of Court Guidelines) and Wayne County Bar Associations. Representative to Judicial Conference Fourth Judicial Department 1988-89. Lecturer on Criminal Evidence and Anatomy of a Trial New York State Unified Court System Judicial Seminar 1982 and 1987, seminars on Evidence and Trial Procedure, Commercial Litigation and Community Affairs Forum on Cameras in the Courtroom New York State Bar Association 1987 and 1989, and on Labor Law Sections 240, 241 and 200 Defense Attorneys of New York. Chairman and Participant "Judges' Walk-Through Program" Monroe County Bar Association 1985. Moot Court Judge Cornell University. Member Executive Committee Association of Towns 1973-74. Lecturer Finger Lakes Building Officials Association School. Former Member Board of Directors Rochester General Hospital and Alumni Association of Utica College of Syracuse University. Former Member Board of Trustees McQuaid Jesuit High School, Rochester and Mary Cariola Children's Center, Inc. Board of Trustees Bryant and Stratton Business Institute. Member Penfield-Perinton Kiwanis Club (President 1968, Program Chairman children's activities, Trustee Kiwanis Kidney Fund), Vince Lombardi Chapter Order of the Sons of Italy, United Commercial Travelers and St. Joseph's Parish. Active in coordinating youth recreation activities. Guest speaker youth forums and service organizations.
Office: 545 Hall of Justice, 99 Exchange Boulevard, Rochester 14614-2185.
Telephone: (585) 428-5288.
Fax: (585) 428-2995

SIRAGUSA, Charles J. *(Judge, United States District Court Western District of New York)* Appointed for life by President Bill Clinton to term beginning Dec 15, 1997. Born Rochester New York Aug 10, 1947. Edu-

SIRAGUSA, CHARLES J.—*Continued*
cated at LeMoyne College B.A. 1969 and Albany Law School of Union University J.D. 1976. Justice, New York Supreme Court Seventh Judicial District 1993-97.
Assistant District Attorney Monroe County 1977-92.
Office: 1360 Federal Building, 100 State Street, Rochester 14614-1363.
Telephone: (716) 263-6237.

SIRKIN, Stephen R. *(Judge, Wayne County Court)* Also serves Wayne County Surrogate's Court and Wayne County Family Court.
Office: 213 Hall of Justice, 54 Broad Street, Lyons 14489-1199.
Telephone: (315) 946-5443.
Fax: (315) 946-5428

SISE, Joseph M. *(Justice, New York Supreme Court Fourth Judicial District)* Elected to term beginning Jan 24, 1999. Born Amsterdam New York Jan 26, 1963. Catholic. Educated at Siena College B.A. 1985 and Albany Law School of Union University J.D. 1988. Admitted to practice New York 1989 and U.S. District Court Southern District of New York 1989. Judge, Montgomery County Court Jan 1, 1996 to Jan 1999.
Assistant District Attorney Bronx County 1988-90, Montgomery County 1990-95 and Fulton County 1991-94. Attorney Montgomery County Department of Social Services 1995. Member County Judges Association of the State of New York, Association of Justices of the Supreme Court of the State of New York, Fulton County, Montgomery County and Schenectady County Bar Associations. Republican. Member Knights of Columbus.
Mailing address: P.O. Box 1500, Fonda 12068-1500.
Office: Montgomery County Courthouse, Fonda 12068.
Telephone: (518) 853-4432.
Fax: (518) 853-8378

SISE, Richard E. *(Judge, New York Court of Claims)* Appointed by Governor George E. Pataki.
Mailing address: P.O. Box 7344, Albany 12224.
Office: Capitol Station, Albany 12224.
Telephone: (518) 432-3435.
Fax: (518) 432-3428

SIWEK, Donna M. *(Justice, New York Supreme Court Eighth Judicial District)*
Office: 50 Delaware Avenue, Tenth Floor, Buffalo 14202.
Telephone: (716) 851-3394.
Fax: (716) 851-3318
E-mail address: dsiwek@courts.state.ny.us

SKELOS, Peter B. *(Justice, New York Supreme Court Tenth Judicial District)* Former Judge, Nassau County District Court, elected to term beginning Jan 1, 1995.
Office: Supreme Court Building, 100 Supreme Court Drive, Mineola 11501.
Telephone: (516) 571-2823.
E-mail address: pskelos@courts.state.ny.us

SKLAR, Stanley L. *(Justice, New York Supreme Court First Judicial District)* Former Acting Justice. Elected Justice to term beginning Jan 1, 1986. Reelected 1999. Certificated 2003. Born Manhattan New York 1932. Educated at Columbia College B.A. with honors in Government and Spanish 1953 and Columbia University LL.B. 1956. Harlan Fiske Stone Scholar. Student Faculty Assistant to Professor Jack B. Weinstein. Judge, The Civil Court of the City of New York Jan 1, 1977 to Dec 31, 1985.
Author "Shoplifting: What You Need to Know About the Law" Fairchild Publications New York 1982, "Affirmative Defenses in Criminal Cases in New York" New York L. Jour. March 20, 1985, "Declarations Against Penal Interest" *The Panelist* 1985 and "Suppression Law Outline" (revised annually). Contributing Author "Pre-Trial Criminal Practice" New York State Bar Association 1984. Chair Board of Justices New York County since 2001. Member Association of Supreme Court Justices of the City of New York (President 2000-01), American Judicature Society and The Association of the Bar of the City of New York. Instructor Annual New Judges Seminar and various judicial and bar seminars.
Office: 60 Centre Street, New York 10007.
Telephone: (212) 374-8597.

SKRETNY, William M. *(Judge, United States District Court Western District of New York)* Appointed for life by President George Bush to term beginning Oct 1, 1990. Born Buffalo New York March 8, 1945. Roman Catholic. Educated at Canisius College A.B. 1966, Howard University J.D. 1969 and Northwestern University LL.M. 1972. Admitted to practice Illinois 1969, U.S. District Courts Northern District of Illinois 1969 and Western District of New York 1973, U.S. Courts of Appeals Seventh 1969 and Second 1973 Circuits and New York 1972. In legal practice Buffalo New York 1981-83 and 1988-90.
Assistant U.S. Attorney Northern District of Illinois and Western District of New York 1971-75. First Assistant U.S. Attorney Western District of New York 1975-81. Special Counsel U.S. Attorney General's Advocacy Institute 1979. Staff Attorney Office of Special Prosecutor U.S. Department of Justice 1980. First Deputy District Attorney Erie County New York 1983-89. Member Judicial Conference of Security and Facilities 1994. Chair Subcommittee on Planning and Space Management. Liaison Committee for Long Range Planning. Member Advocates Society of Western New York, Western New York Trial Lawyers Association, Federal Judges Association, Bar Association of Erie County and American Bar Association (Judicial Committee on Security and Facilities Judicial Administration Division). Republican.
Office: 507 U.S. Courthouse, 68 Court Street, Buffalo 14202.
Telephone: (716) 551-3086.

SLOBOD, Elaine *(Surrogate, Orange County Surrogate's Court)* Former Judge, Orange County Family Court.
Office: Surrogate's Courthouse, 30 Park Place, Goshen 10924.
Telephone: (845) 291-2300.
Fax: (845) 291-2543

SMITH, George Bundy *(Associate Judge, New York Court of Appeals)* Appointed by Governor Mario Cuomo to term beginning Sept 1992. Born New Orleans Louisiana April 7, 1937. Educated at Yale University B.A. 1959 LL.B. 1962 and New York University M.A. 1967 Ph.D. 1974. Admitted to practice New York 1963. Judge, The Civil Court of the City of New York May 1975 to 1979. Justice, New York Supreme Court First

SMITH, GEORGE BUNDY—*Continued*

Judicial District 1979-87. Associate Justice, New York Supreme Court Appellate Division First Judicial Department Jan 1987 to Sept 1992.

Office: 61 Broadway, 29th Floor, New York 10006-2704.

Telephone: (212) 363-5990.

Office: Court of Appeals Hall, 20 Eagle Street, Albany 12207.

Telephone: (518) 455-7746.

SMITH, Karen S. *(Judge, The Civil Court of the City of New York)*

Office: 111 Centre Street, New York 10013.

Telephone: (212) 374-8057.

E-mail address: kssmith@courts.state.ny.us

SMITH, Kathryn M. *(Judge, The Civil Court of the City of New York)* Currently serves as Acting Justice, New York Supreme Court Second Judicial District.

Office: 120 Schermerhorn Street, Brooklyn 11201.

Telephone: (718) 643-8172.

E-mail address: ksmith@courts.state.ny.us

SMITH, Lisa Margaret *(Magistrate Judge, United States District Court Southern District of New York)* Appointed by U.S. District Court judges to term beginning May 20, 1995. Born Hamilton New York April 25, 1955. Educated at Earlham College B.A. 1977 and Duke University School of Law J.D. 1980. Admitted to practice New York 1981, U.S. District Courts Eastern 1983, Southern 1983 and Northern 1985 Districts of New York, U.S. Courts of Appeals Second 1984 and Eighth 1994 Circuits and U.S. Supreme Court 1985.

Assistant District Attorney Kings County 1980-85 and 1986-87. Assistant Attorney General New York State Department of Law 1985-86. Assistant U.S. Attorney Southern District of New York 1987-95. Board of Editors Federal Courts L. Rev and Federal Bar Council Newsletter. Important Decisions: Donato v. Fitzgibbons 172 F.R.D. 75 April 1, 1997; Sharkey v. Lasmo 992 F. Supp. 321 Jan 21, 1998; and Am-Haul v. Contractors Casualty 33 F. Supp. 2d 235, Nov 13, 1998. Member New York State Association of Women Judges, National Association of Women Judges, Federal Magistrate Judges Association, Westchester Women's and Westchester Bar Associations. Member Judges and Lawyers Breast Cancer Awareness.

Office: U.S. Courthouse, 300 Quarropas Street, White Plains 10601-4150.

Telephone: (914) 390-4130.

SMITH, Martin E. *(Judge, Broome County Court)* Elected Nov 8, 1990 to term beginning Jan 1, 1991. Reelected 2000, current term expires Dec 31, 2010. Born Binghamton New York May 3, 1945. Roman Catholic. Educated at Niagara University B.A. 1967 and Syracuse University College of Law J.D. 1970. Member Phi Alpha Delta. Admitted to practice New York 1971 and U.S. District Court Northern District of New York 1985. In legal practice Binghamton 1977-91.

Assistant District Attorney Westchester County 1970-75 (Deputy Chief Frauds Bureau 1972-75). Senior Assistant District Attorney Broome County 1975-77. Adjunct Faculty Criminal Justice Program State University of New York at Binghamton 1977-88. Former Member New York State Trial Lawyers Association and National District Attorneys Association. Member Broome County, Westchester County and New York State Bar Associations. Attended National District Attorneys College 1972. Enjoys family and sports.

Mailing address: P.O. Box 1766, Binghamton 13902-1766.

Office: Broome County Courts Building, 65 Hawley Street, Binghamton 13901.

Telephone: (607) 778-2418.

Fax: (607) 778-6135

SMITH, Mary H. *(Justice, New York Supreme Court Ninth Judicial District)* Elected Nov 5, 2002. Former Judge, Yonkers City Court. Former Judge, Westchester County Court, elected to term beginning Jan 1, 1995.

Office: 111 Dr. Martin Luther King Jr. Blvd., White Plains 10601.

Telephone: (914) 995-4367.

Fax: (914) 995-4323

E-mail address: masmith@courts.state.ny.us

SMITH, Nancy E. *(Associate Justice, New York Supreme Court Appellate Division Second Judicial Department)* Elected Justice Seventh Judicial District. Appointed Associate Justice Appellate Division by Governor George E. Pataki. Former Judge, Monroe County Court.

Office: Courthouse, 50 East Avenue, Rochester 14604.

Telephone: (585) 530-3280.

Fax: (585) 530-3287

SMOLKIN, Stanley A. *(Judge, Long Beach City Court)*

Office: One West Chester Street, Long Beach 11561.

Telephone: (516) 431-1000.

Fax: (516) 431-4372

SNYDER, Leslie Crocker *(Judge, New York Court of Claims)* Appointed by governor. Currently serves as Acting Justice, New York Supreme Court First Judicial District. Educated at Radcliffe College A.B. with honors 1962, Harvard Business School 1963 and Case Western Reserve Law School J.D. with honors 1966. Associate Editor Case Western Reserve Law Review. National Moot Court Team. Member Order of the Coif. Admitted to practice New York 1966. In legal practice New York City 1966-68 and 1979-82. Former Judge, The Criminal Court of the City of New York, appointed by Mayor Edward Koch to term beginning March 1983.

Assistant District Attorney New York County 1968-76 (Chief Supreme Court Trial Bureau and Consumer Frauds Bureau; Chief and Founder first Sex Crimes Prosecution Bureau in U.S.; first woman allowed to try felony cases; first and only woman in Homicide Bureau). Special Assistant Attorney General Chief of Trials New York State Office of the Special Prosecutor Sept 1976 to June 1979. Deputy Criminal Justice Coordinator for City of New York and Coordinator Arson Strike Force Sept 1982 to March 1983. Author proposed reform of Penal Law 130 Sex Crimes and articles about proposed reform New York L. Jour. Dec 13 and 14, 1978. Member Criminal Procedure Law Advisory Committee to Chief Judge, New York State District Attorneys Association, The Association of the Bar of the City of New York (Former member Criminal Courts Committee, Sex and Law Committee), New York Women's (Former First and Third Vice President, former Chair State Legislation Committee, President 1982-83, Chair Criminal Law Committee and Judiciary Committee) and New York State Bar Associations. Lecturer to legal,

SNYDER, LESLIE CROCKER—*Continued*
civic, community and medical groups on criminal trials, women in law, sex crimes and homicides. Speaker at numerous homicide and sex crimes seminars. Former member Mayor's Committee on City Marshals. Language: French.
Office: 100 Centre Street, New York 10013.
Telephone: (212) 374-3033.

SOLOFF, Brenda S. *(Judge, The Criminal Court of the City of New York)* Appointed by mayor. Currently serves as Acting Justice, New York Supreme Court First Judicial District.
Office: 100 Centre Street, New York 10013.
Telephone: (212) 374-7181.

SOLOMON, Charles H. *(Judge, The Criminal Court of the City of New York)* Appointed by mayor. Former Supervising Judge New York County Branch. Currently serves as Acting Justice, New York Supreme Court First Judicial District.
Office: 111 Centre Street, New York 10013.
Telephone: (212) 748-5157.

SOLOMON, Jane S. *(Judge, The Civil Court of the City of New York)* Elected to term beginning Jan 1, 1987. Reelected 1996, current term expires Dec 31, 2006. Acting Justice, New York Supreme Court First Judicial District since March 1993. Born Brooklyn New York Aug 27, 1945. Jewish. Educated at Vassar College A.B. 1967 and New York University School of Law J.D. 1970. Admitted to practice New York 1971, U.S. District Courts Southern 1972 and Eastern 1973 Districts of New York and Northern District of California 1983, U.S. Court of Appeals Second Circuit 1972 and U.S. Supreme Court 1974. In legal practice New York 1970-86.

Author "Real Estate Aspects of the 1984 Amendments to the Bankruptcy Code" 90 Commercial L. Jour. p. 288, June/July 1985 republished 58 New York State B. Jour. p. 28, July 1986. Member The Association of the Bar of the City of New York (Entertainment Committee 1972-76, Committee on the Civil Court 1974-77, Committee on Bankruptcy and Corporate Reorganization 1977-80, Chair 1984-86 Committee on Municipal Affairs, member Special Committee on Election Law 1985-86, Committee to Encourage Judicial Access). Democrat.
Office: 60 Centre Street, New York 10007.
Telephone: (212) 374-8596.

SOLOMON, Martin M. *(Judge, The Civil Court of the City of New York)*
Office: 141 Livingston Street, Brooklyn 11201.
Telephone: (718) 643-2868.
Fax: (718) 643-3733

SONBERG, Michael R. *(Judge, The Criminal Court of the City of New York)* Former Judge, The Civil Court of the City of New York.
Office: 215 East 161st Street, Bronx 10451.
Telephone: (718) 590-2927.
Fax: (718) 590-7297
E-mail address: mrsonberg@abanet.org

SOSA-LINTNER, Gloria *(Judge, New York City Family Court)* Appointed by Mayor Edward I. Koch to term beginning March 22, 1988. Reappointed 1992 and 2002. Born New York New York. Catholic. Educated at Barnard College B.A. 1970 and New York University School of Law J.D. 1975. Admitted to practice New York 1976 and U.S. District Courts Eastern 1983 and Southern 1983 Districts of New York.

Vice President Hispanic Judges Association 1991-92. Member New York State, Puerto Rican (President 1984-86) and American Bar Associations.
Office: 60 Lafayette Street, New York 10013.
Telephone: (212) 374-8996.
Fax: (212) 374-2623

SOTO, Faviola *(Judge, The Civil Court of the City of New York)* Currently serves as Acting Justice, New York Supreme Court First Judicial District.
Office: 111 Centre Street, New York 10013.
Telephone: (212) 374-8495.
Fax: (212) 401-9179

SPAIN, Edward O. *(Associate Justice, New York Supreme Court Appellate Division Third Judicial Department)* Elected Justice Third Judicial District Nov 1991. Appointed Associate Justice Appellate Division by Governor Mario Cuomo Dec 30, 1994. Administrative Judge Third Judicial District 1994-95. Born Troy New York Oct 19, 1941. Roman Catholic. Educated at Boston College A.B. 1963 and Albany Law School of Union University LL.B. cum laude 1966. Admitted to practice New York 1966 and U.S. District Court Northern District of New York 1966. Began legal practice Troy 1966. Deputy Chief Clerk Rensselaer County Surrogate's Court 1977. Judge, Troy Police Court Jan 1, 1978 to May 13, 1985. Judge, Rensselaer County Family Court 1985-1991.

Assistant District Attorney Rensselaer County 1967. Deputy Corporation Counsel Troy 1970-72. Member Association of Justices of the Supreme Court of the State of New York, Rensselaer County and New York State Bar Associations. USN JAGC 1967-70.
Office: Rensselaer County Courthouse, Congress and Second Streets, Troy 12180.
Telephone: (518) 270-3707.
Fax: (518) 270-0066
E-mail address: espain@courts.state.ny.us

SPARGO, Thomas J. *(Justice, New York Supreme Court Third Judicial District)*
Office: 40 Steuben Street, Sixth Floor, Suite 603, Albany 12207.
Telephone: (518) 487-5018.

SPATT, Arthur D. *(Judge, United States District Court Eastern District of New York)* Appointed for life by President George Bush to term beginning Dec 15, 1989. Born Brooklyn New York Dec 13, 1925. Jewish. Educated at The Ohio State University and Brooklyn Law School LL.B. cum laude 1949. Book Review Editor Brooklyn Law Review 1948-49. Admitted to practice New York 1950, U.S. District Courts Eastern and Southern Districts of New York and U.S. Court of Appeals Second Circuit. In legal practice New York City 1950-78. Justice, New York Supreme Court Tenth Judicial District 1979-82. Administrative Judge Nassau County 1982-86. Associate Justice, New York Supreme Court Appellate Division Second Judicial Department 1986-89.

Member Long Beach Lawyers Association, Association of Justices of the Supreme Court of the State of New York, Bar Association of Nassau County, Federal

SPATT, ARTHUR D.—*Continued*
and American Bar Associations. Navigation Petty Officer USN 1944-46.
Office: Long Island Federal Courthouse, 1024 Federal Plaza, Central Islip 11722.
Telephone: (631) 712-5620.

SPERRAZZA, Sara Sheldon *(Judge, Niagara County Court)* Also serves Niagara County Surrogate's Court.
Office: Courthouse, 175 Hawley Street, Lockport 14094-2758.
Telephone: (716) 439-7140.
Fax: (716) 439-7157
E-mail address: ssperraz@courts.state.ny.us

SPINNER, Jeffrey Arlen *(Judge, Suffolk County Court)* Elected to term beginning Jan 1, 1999. Term expires Dec 31, 2008. Also serves as Acting Judge, Suffolk County Family Court. Born New York New York. Educated at Ithaca College B.A. 1981 and Touro College Jacob D. Fuchsberg Law Center J.D. 1987. Admitted to practice Connecticut 1987, New York 1988, U.S. District Courts District of Connecticut 1988 and Eastern 1991, Northern 1991, Southern 1991 and Western 1991 Districts of New York, U.S. Court of Appeals for the Armed Forces 1991 and U.S. Supreme Court 1991. In legal practice East Hartford Connecticut and Hartford Connecticut 1988-91 and Syosset New York, Huntington New York and Babylon New York 1991-97. Small Claims Arbitrator Sept 1991 to Dec 1997 and Judge Jan 1998 to Dec 1998, Suffolk County District Court.
Important Decisions: Northwood Village Inc. v. Curet ("Curet I") N.Y.L.J. 34, 4 May 6, 1998; Albert v. Olympic Parking Service N.Y.L.J. 35, 2 July 28, 1998; Curran v. Ciaramelli N.Y.L.J. 34, 3 Nov 10, 1998; Northwood Village Inc. v. Curet ("Curet II") N.Y.L.J. 1, 5 Nov 27, 1998 and 35, 5 Nov 30, 1998; People v. Victor Casa No. I460-98; People v. Vivian Miranda No. I196A-98; People v. Serena Miranda-Martin No. I196B-98; People v. Roberto Rivera No. I2196A-98; People v. Mark Burns No. I2196B-98; People v. Christopher LaRusso No. I1889-98; and People v. Joseph Spreeman No. I1606-99. Instructor in Paralegal Studies New York Institute of Technology 1993-94. Member Alexander Hamilton Inn of Court, American Inns of Court, Suffolk County Criminal Bar Association and Suffolk County Bar Association (Committees on Criminal Law and Family Court). Member Conservative Party of New York State. Director and Advisor The Lumiere Ballet Company and The Long Island Youth Ballet. Member Babylon Masonic Lodge #793 and John Bosco Lodge #2384. Interests include automobiles, automobile mechanics, hiking, travel, rollerblading, bicycling, American and European history, reading and boating.
Office: Court Complex, 400 Carleton Avenue, Central Islip 11722.
Telephone: (631) 853-4263.
Fax: (631) 853-7629
E-mail address: jspinner@courts.state.ny.us

SPINOLA, Joseph P. *(Judge, Nassau County District Court)*
Office: 99 Main Street, Hempstead 11550.
Telephone: (516) 571-2200.

SPIRES, Mark H. *(Justice, New York Supreme Court Eleventh Judicial District)* Elected to term beginning Jan 1, 1995. Certificated. Former Housing Part Judge, The Civil Court of the City of New York.
Office: 125-01 Queens Boulevard, Kew Gardens 11415.
Telephone: (718) 520-6737.

SPODEK, Ellen M. *(Judge, The Civil Court of the City of New York)*
Office: 141 Livingston Street, Brooklyn 11201.
Telephone: (718) 643-5069.

SPODEK, Jules L. *(Justice, New York Supreme Court Second Judicial District)* Elected to term beginning Jan 1, 1981. Reelected 1994. Certificated. Born New York New York June 5, 1928. Jewish. Educated at Brooklyn College B.A. 1950 and New York University LL.B. 1952. Admitted to practice New York 1953, U.S. District Courts Eastern 1955 and Southern 1955 Districts of New York and U.S. Supreme Court 1972. In legal practice New York City 1953. Judge, The Civil Court of the City of New York Jan 1, 1975 to Dec 30, 1980.
Board of Directors Association of Supreme Court Justices of the City of New York. Member Brooklyn Bar Association. Lecturer Brooklyn Bar Association and New York County Lawyers' Association. USMC 1952. Board of Directors Kings Bay "Y" Brooklyn. Enjoys sailing.
Office: 360 Adams Street, Brooklyn 11201.
Telephone: (718) 643-3922.
E-mail address: jspodek@courts.state.ny.us

SPOLZINO, Robert A. *(Justice, New York Supreme Court Ninth Judicial District)* Appointed by Governor George E. Pataki May 31, 2001 to term beginning July 10, 2001. Elected Nov 6, 2001 to term beginning Jan 2002, current term expires Dec 31, 2015. Born Mount Vernon New York April 30, 1959. Catholic. Educated at Georgetown University A.B. cum laude 1980 and St. John's University School of Law J.D. 1983. Law Clerk to Hon. Kenneth H. Lange, Westchester County Court 1984-85 and Hon. Leon D. Lazer, New York Supreme Court Appellate Division Second Judicial Department 1985-86. Admitted to practice New York 1984, U.S. District Courts Eastern 1984, Southern 1984, Northern 1999 and Western 1999 Districts of New York, U.S. Court of Appeals Second Circuit 1987 and U.S. Supreme Court 1987. In legal practice Mount Kisco 1987-99 and White Plains 1999-2001.
Village Attorney Mount Kisco 1988-95. Member Columbian (Italian-American) Lawyers of Westchester County, Northern Westchester (President 1992-93), Westchester County, New York State and American Bar Associations. President Mount Kisco Lions Club 1991-92.
Office: 111 Dr. Martin Luther King Jr. Blvd., White Plains 10601.
Telephone: (914) 995-4300.
Fax: (212) 401-9112
E-mail address: rspolzin@courts.state.ny.us

SPRIZZO, John E. *(Senior Judge, United States District Court Southern District of New York)* Appointed for life by President Ronald Reagan to term beginning Nov 10, 1981. Assumed Senior status Jan 1, 2000, serves by assignment. Born Brooklyn New York Dec 23, 1934. Catholic. Educated at St. John's University B.A. summa cum laude 1956 LL.B. summa cum laude 1959. Editor St. John's Law Review 1958-59. Member Delta Theta Phi. Admitted to practice New York 1960,

SPRIZZO, JOHN E.—*Continued*

U.S. Supreme Court 1963, U.S. District Courts Southern District of New York 1964 and District of Columbia 1980 and U.S. Courts of Appeals Second 1964 and District of Columbia 1980 Circuits. Began legal practice New York City and Washington D.C. 1960. In legal practice New York 1960-81.

Assistant U.S. Attorney Southern District of New York 1963-68 (Chief Appellate Attorney 1965-66, Assistant Chief Criminal Division 1966-68). Co-author "Criminal Procedure" Brooklyn L. Rev. 1975 and "Sentencing and Parole Guidelines" National L. Rev. 1978. Associate Professor Fordham University School of Law 1968-72. Member The Association of the Bar of the City of New York and American Bar Association. Commissioner Knapp Commission 1971-72. Enjoys opera, football, music and the theatre.

Office: 2201 U.S. Courthouse, 40 Centre Street, New York 10007-1581.
Telephone: (212) 805-6135.

STACK, Elaine Jackson *(Justice, New York Supreme Court Tenth Judicial District)* Elected to term beginning Jan 2000. Certificated. Educated at Hunter College 1948-52, Long Island University B.A. 1971 M.S.L.S. 1973 and St. John's University School of Law J.D. 1979. In legal practice May 1986 to July 1991. Judge, Nassau County District Court Jan 1997 to Dec 1999.

Assistant District Attorney Nassau County Sept 1979 to May 1986. Special Assistant U.S. Attorney Southern District of New York Sept 1985 to May 1986. Board of Directors Women's Bar Association of State of New York 1985-86. Master Theodore Roosevelt Inn of Court 1987-89 and 1998-2001. Member Grievance Committee Tenth Judicial District Nov 1988 to Nov 1996 and Second Department Screening Panel 1995-97. Director New York State Defenders Association 1994-97. Fellow American Bar Foundation. Honorary Member Family Law Inns of Court. Member National Association of Women Judges (Nassau/Suffolk Delegate), Criminal Courts Bar Association (Director since 1994), Bar Association of Nassau County (Women in the Courts Committee since 1992, Board of Directors 1999-2001, Matrimonial Committee since 2000), New York State (House of Delegates 1990-91, Committee on Courts of Appellate Jurisdiction 1992-96, Executive Committee Criminal Justice Section 1994-2001) and American Bar Associations. Recipient Women's Roll of Honor from Town of North Hempstead 2000 and Norman Lent Award from Criminal Courts Bar Association 2001. Deputy Mayor Village of East Hills 1988-91 and 1994-95. Board of Managers The Greens Condominium since 1995. Board of Directors Coalition Against Domestic Violence 1996. Director St. John's University School of Law Alumni Association since 2000.

Office: Matrimonial Center, 400 County Seat Drive, Mineola 11501.
Telephone: (516) 571-5810.
Fax: (516) 571-1600
E-mail address: ejstack@courts.state.ny.us

STACKHOUSE, John E. H. *(Judge, The Civil Court of the City of New York)* Elected to term beginning Jan 1, 1984. Reelected 1993, current term expires Dec 31, 2003. Currently serves as Acting Justice, New York Supreme Court First Judicial District. Born New York New York April 3, 1939. Jewish. Educated at The Citadel B.A. 1960 and St. John's University LL.B. 1966. Moot Court. Listed in *Who's Who in American Colleges and Universities.* Admitted to practice New York 1970, U.S. District Courts Southern 1973 and Eastern 1973 Districts of New York and U.S. Court of Appeals Second Circuit 1974. Began legal practice New York City 1970.

Author "Denial of Justice: Criminal Process in the U.S." Brooklyn L. Rev. 1977. Member New York State Bar Association (Committee on CLE 1979-80). Trial Advocacy Faculty Benjamin N. Cardozo School of Law 2002. First Lieutenant (courier) U.S. Army Corps 1961-66. Democrat. Assistant Counsel Board of Ethics New York City 1970-71. Judicial Delegate 1975-82 and Democratic District Leader 1979-82 Sixty-fourth Assembly District. Founder and Chairperson Chelsea Anti-Crime Task Force. Member Community Advisory Board Bayview Correctional Facility for Women and Committee for an Integrated Chelsea. Enjoys poetry, painting, running and swimming.

Office: 111 Centre Street, New York 10013.
Telephone: (212) 374-8014.
E-mail address: jstackho@courts.state.ny.us

STADTMAUER, David *(Justice, New York Supreme Court Twelfth Judicial District)* Acting Justice Nov 1980 to Dec 1988. Elected Justice to term beginning Jan 1, 1989. Reelected to term beginning Jan 1, 2003, current term expires Dec 31, 2016. Born Brooklyn New York Dec 16, 1934. Jewish. Educated at Yeshiva University B.A. 1956, New York Law School LL.B. 1960 and New York University School of Law LL.M. 1977. Admitted to practice New York 1961. In legal practice New York City 1961-65. Judge, The Civil Court of the City of New York Jan 1, 1974 to Dec 31, 1988.

Law Secretary to New York State Supreme Court Justice 1966-72. Commissioner New York City Civil Service Commission 1972-73. Former Member Mayor's Cabinet. Author "Exhibit A: The Human Body" New York State B. Jour. Jan 1988 and "1914: An Arbitration in Galicia" New York L. Jour. 2 Dec 2, 1996. Adjunct Professor 1979-94 and Former Member Judicial Faculty of the Advanced Practice Institute Hofstra University. Member New York County Lawyers' Association, New York State Trial Lawyers Association, The Association of Trial Lawyers of America, The Association of the Bar of the City of New York, Bronx County and New York County Bar Associations. Recipient Bernard Revel Memorial Award in Arts and Sciences from Yeshiva University Alumni Association 1976. Vice President Executive Committee Yeshiva University Alumni Association since 1977. Board of Directors Palisades Gardens Foundation since 1975. Member National Jewish Commission on Law and Public Affairs 1970-75. Enjoys chess, reading and traveling.

Office: 851 Grand Concourse, Bronx 10451.
Telephone: (718) 590-7179.

STALLMAN, Michael D. *(Judge, The Civil Court of the City of New York)* Arbitrator 1980-86. Appointed Judge by Mayor Edward Koch to term beginning Aug 8, 1986. Elected Nov 1986 and 1996. Current term expires Dec 31, 2006. Currently serves as Acting Justice, New York Supreme Court First Judicial District. Born New York New York Oct 18, 1950. Jewish. Educated at City College of the City University of New York B.A. magna cum laude 1971, New York University Law School J.D. 1974, Columbia Law School 1982 and Harvard

STALLMAN, MICHAEL D.—*Continued*

Law School 1986. Staff member Moot Court Board 1972-74. Law Clerk to Hon. Martin Evans, New York Supreme Court First Judicial District 1978-86. Admitted to practice New York 1975, U.S. District Court Southern District of New York 1975, U.S. Supreme Court 1979 and U.S. Court of Appeals Second Circuit 1981.

Assistant District Attorney New York County 1974-78. Co-author with Hon. Martin Evans "Deferred Sentence: Common Law Alternative to Judge's Dilemma" New York L. Jour. 1982. Contributing Author Chapter 1 "Organization of the New York Courts," Chapter 3 "Subject Matter Jurisdiction," Chapter 17 "Undertakings," Chapter 18 "Property Paid into Court or Transferred During Litigation," Chapter 22 "Calendar Practice and Trial Preference," Chapter 25 "Former Adjudication: Res Judicata and Collateral Estoppel," Chapter 28 "Provisional Remedies," Chapter 30 "Recovery of Chattel," Chapter 34 "Records of Clerks of Court and Sealing," and Chapter 35 "Actions Against Villages" *Weinstein-Korn-Miller CPLR Handbook* 2nd ed. Matthew Bender and Co. revised 1992-98. Adjunct Assistant Professor Bernard M. Baruch College of the City University of New York 1984-85. Adjunct Professor of Law Touro Law School 1985-88, City University of New York 1985-87 and Yeshiva University Benjamin N. Cardozo School of Law 1988-96. Member New York County Lawyers' Association (Committee on Professional Ethics since 1982), The Association of the Bar of the City of New York (Former Chair Committee on Legislation and Election Law, Former Chair Task Force on New York State Constitutional Convention) and New York State Bar Association (Committee on Civil Practice Law and Rules). Advisory Board Andrew Glover Youth Program since 1977. Member Community Planning Board 1984-86 and Town & Village Conservative Synagogue. Interests include classical music, travel and historical preservation.

Office: 111 Centre Street, New York 10013.

Telephone: (212) 374-8446.

STANDER, Thomas A. *(Justice, New York Supreme Court Seventh Judicial District)* Elected Nov 1990 to term beginning Jan 1, 1991. Term expires Dec 31, 2004. Born Detroit Michigan March 14, 1945. Educated at Denison University B.A. with honors 1967 and Syracuse University J.D. 1970. Admitted to practice New York 1971, Connecticut 1971 and U.S. District Court Western District of New York 1973. In legal practice Rochester New York 1972-90. Justice, Fairport Village Justice Court 1975-90.

Member Monroe County and New York State Bar Associations.

Office: 545 Hall of Justice, 99 Exchange Boulevard, Rochester 14614-2185.

Telephone: (585) 428-2082.

Fax: (585) 428-2994

STANTON, Louis L. *(Senior Judge, United States District Court Southern District of New York)* Appointed for life by President Ronald Reagan to term beginning 1985. Assumed Senior status Oct 1, 1996. Born New York New York Oct 1, 1927. Educated at Yale University B.A. 1950 and University of Virginia School of Law J.D. 1955 LL.B. 1955. In legal practice New York City 1955-85.

Office: 2250 U.S. Courthouse, 500 Pearl Street, New York 10007-1312.

Telephone: (212) 805-0252.

STARKEY, James G. *(Justice, New York Supreme Court Second Judicial District)* Assigned as Justice Second Judicial District 1976-82 and 1987-2002. Term expires Dec 31, 2003. Born Brooklyn New York July 21, 1933. Catholic. Educated at St. Michael's College B.A. cum laude 1954, St. John's University School of Law J.D. cum laude 1957 and New York University School of Law LL.M. in Taxation 1985. St. Thomas More Scholar. Legislation Editor St. John's Law Review 1956-57. Member Delta Theta Phi (Dean John Jay Senate 1956-57) and Delta Epsilon Sigma. Admitted to practice New York, U.S. District Court Southern District of New York, U.S. Court of Appeals Second Circuit and U.S. Supreme Court. In legal practice New York City 1961-73. Judge, The Criminal Court of the City of New York 1973-82. Judge, New York Court of Claims Jan 1, 1987 to Dec 31, 2002, appointed by Governor Mario Cuomo.

Assistant U.S. Attorney Civil and Criminal Divisions Southern District of New York 1957-61. Author "Trial in Absentia" 53 St. John's L. Rev. 721, 1979 and New York State B. Jour. 30 Jan 1982, "Fact and Fiction Concerning 'Turnstile Justice'" New York L. Jour. 1 March 13, 1981 and "Reading Tea Leaves: The Fifth Amendment and Tax Records" 17 Loyola University of Chicago L. Jour. 67, 1985. Important Decisions: People v. Caban 90 Misc. 2d 43, 1977; People v. Powell 98 Misc. 2d 460, 1979; People v. McCray 104 Misc. 2d 782, 1980; People v. Beaudonvine 136 Misc. 2d 179, 1987; People v. Anglin 136 Misc. 2d 987, 1987; People v. Bacote 143 Misc. 2d 535, 1989; People v. Paris 150 Misc. 2d 266, 1991; People v. Sanchez 151 Misc. 2d 431, 1991; People v. Machado 159 Misc. 2d 94, 1993; People v. Tucker 171 Misc. 2d 1, 1996; and People v. Branch 175 Misc. 2d 933, 1998. Associate Professor of Law St. John's University School of Law 1982-87. President Catholic Lawyers Guild of Brooklyn 1968-69, Lawyers Club of Brooklyn 1971-72 and St. Patrick Society of Brooklyn 1976. Member Federal Bar Council, The Association of the Bar of the City of New York, Brooklyn and New York State (Member Action Unit No. 7 Study of Proper, Effective and Efficient Administration of Justice in the Criminal Justice System, Member Judicial Section) Bar Associations. Lecturer on Law of Trial in Absentia County Judges Association of the State of New York Jan 23, 1981 and on The Criminal Trial in New York English Magistrates Association Sept 29, 1981. Faculty Member New York State Trial Judges Association judicial seminar Aug 2-5, 1982.

Office: 360 Adams Street, Brooklyn 11201.

Telephone: (718) 643-8552.

Fax: (718) 643-2095

STATON, Betty E. *(Judge, New York City Family Court)* Appointed by mayor.

Office: 283 Adams Street, Sixth Floor, Brooklyn 11201.

Telephone: (718) 643-4546.

Fax: (718) 643-5103

STEIN, Leslie E. *(Justice, New York Supreme Court Third Judicial District)* Elected Nov 2001 to term beginning Jan 1, 2002. Term expires Dec 31, 2015. Born New York New York Dec 25, 1956. Jewish. Educated

STEIN, LESLIE E.—*Continued*

at Macalester College B.A. with honors 1978 and Albany Law School J.D. magna cum laude 1981. Law Clerk to Hon. Leonard J. Litz 1981-83 and Hon. G. Douglas Griset 1981-83, Schenectady County Family Court. Member Phi Beta Kappa and Justinian Society. Admitted to practice New York 1982 and U.S. Supreme Court 1989. In legal practice Albany 1983-96. Judge, Albany City Court Jan 1, 1997 to Dec 2001, appointed by Mayor Gerald D. Jennings.

Important Decisions: Dicostanzo v. Hughes (negligence/vehicle and traffic law) 172 Misc. 2d 368, 1997; Albank v. Foland (debtor/creditor law) 177 Misc. 2d 569, 1998; Brown v. Solomon and Solomon, PC (fair debt collection practices act sanctions) 181 Misc. 2d 461, 1999; Selby v. Albany Police 186 Misc. 2d 518, 2000; and Mater of Embee Corp. v. Ringler 2002 Slip Op 22734. Member since 1998 and Chair since 2001 Gender Fairness Committee New York State Unified Court System Third Judicial District. Co-chair Judicial Seminars Local Courts Curriculum Committee New York State Office of Court Administration 1999-2001. Former Member and Secretary-Treasurer 2000-01 New York State Association of City Court Judges. Fellow American Academy of Matrimonial Lawyers. Member New York State Judicial Institute on Professionalism in the Law, Association of Justices of the Supreme Court of the State of New York, New York State Association of Women Judges (Board of Directors since 1999), Women's Bar Association of the State of New York (Board of Directors 1986-2000, Secretary 1996-97, Vice President 1997-98), Capital District Women's Bar Association (Board of Directors 1985-2000, Vice President 1992-93, President 1993-94), Albany County and New York State (Executive Committee Family Law Section 1990-97, Committee on Women in the Law 1995-98, Task Force on Diversity in the Courts since 2001) Bar Associations. Lecturer CLE New York State Bar Association since 1985. Coordinator and Lecturer on Civil Actions, Small Claims and Commercial Claims July 1999, Coordinator Landlord/Tenant Issues July 1999 and Infant Compromises and Case Settlement Techniques July 2000 New York Unified Court Systems. Trainer/Lecturer Albany County Bar Association, Women's Bar Association of the State of New York, Third Judicial Department Law Guardian Program, Third Judicial District Hearing Examiners, Legal Aid Society, New York State Employees Assistance Program and New York State Office of Court Administration. Lecturer various seminars on debtor/creditor law and matrimonial and family law. Recipient Marilyn R. Menge Memorial Award from Women's Bar Association of the State of New York May 1997 and Distinguished Member Award from Capital District Women's Bar Association June 1999. Board of Directors Men's Coalition Against Battering 1983-88. Member 1993-2001, Vice President 1997-98 and President Aug 1998 to Dec 1999 Professional Women's Network. Member Hunger Action Network of New York State 1994, Albany County League of Women Voters 1995-97, Albany County Ethics Commission 1996 and The Sage Colleges Legal Studies Advisory Board since June 2000. Former Member Advisory Committee Fund for Modern Courts.

Office: 40 Steuben Street, Suite 601, Albany 12207.
Telephone: (518) 434-2145.
Fax: (518) 434-5980

STEIN, Sidney H. *(Judge, United States District Court Southern District of New York)* Appointed for life by President Bill Clinton to term beginning May 1, 1995. Educated at Princeton University A.B. 1967 and Yale Law School J.D. 1972. Editor Yale Law Journal. Law Clerk to Chief Judge Stanley H. Fuld, New York Court of Appeals. In legal practice 1981 to May 1995.

Columnist on New York Court of Appeals New York Law Journal. Former Board of Director New York Lawyers for the Public Interest. Former Member Governor's Judicial Screening Committee for the First Department. Fellow New York Bar Foundation and American Bar Foundation. Member New York County Lawyers' Association, American Judicature Society, Federal Bar Council, The Association of the Bar of the City of New York, New York State and American Bar Associations. Former Board of Directors and Chairman Yale Law School Fund. Former Board of Directors Prisoner's Legal Services of New York.

Office: U.S. Courthouse, 500 Pearl Street, New York 10007-1312.
Telephone: (212) 805-0192.

STEINHARDT, Marsha L. *(Justice, New York Supreme Court Second Judicial District)* Elected to term beginning Jan 1, 1995. Former Judge, The Civil Court of the City of New York.

Office: 360 Adams Street, Brooklyn 11201.
Telephone: (718) 643-5127.
E-mail address: msteinhardt@courts.state.ny.us

STEPHEN, Larry R. C. *(Judge, The Criminal Court of the City of New York)* Appointed by Mayor Rudolph Giuliani. Former Judge, The Civil Court of the City of New York.

Office: 851 Grand Concourse, Bronx 10451.
Telephone: (718) 590-2927.
Fax: (718) 590-7297

STINSON, Betty Owen *(Justice, New York Supreme Court Twelfth Judicial District)* Former Judge, The Civil Court of the City of New York.

Office: 851 Grand Concourse, Room 6M-21, Bronx 10451.
Telephone: (718) 590-3664.

STOKINGER, Carol A. *(Judge, New York City Family Court)* Appointed by Mayor Rudolph Giuliani.

Office: 900 Sheridan Avenue, Bronx 10451.
Telephone: (718) 590-3376.
Fax: (718) 590-7305

STOLZ, Robert M. *(Judge, The Civil Court of the City of New York)*

Office: 100 Centre Street, New York 10013.
Telephone: (212) 374-3319.

STONE, Lewis Bart *(Judge, New York Court of Claims)* Appointed by Governor George E. Pataki to term beginning June 2000. Acting Justice, New York Supreme Court First Judicial District since June 2000. Born Brooklyn New York March 5, 1938. Educated at Rensselaer Polytechnic Institute B.Ch.E. 1958 and Harvard Law School LL.B. cum laude 1962. Admitted to practice New York 1963. In legal practice New York Aug 1962 to June 1967 and Jan 1, 1972 to Dec 31, 1999.

Pro Bono Representative Lawyers Committee for Civil Rights Under Law Aug 1964 and Lawyers Constitutional Defense Committee Aug 1965. Member 1977-88 and

STONE, LEWIS BART—*Continued*

Chairman 1985-87 Committee on Housing and Urban Development New York County Lawyers' Association. Commissioner on Uniform Laws New York State June 1997 to June 2000. Senior Economic Legal Consultant Brcko Law Revision Commission May 2000 and June 2000. Former Member Cooperative Housing Lawyers Group (Secretary 1979-80). Member American College of Real Estate Lawyers, The Association of the Bar of the City of New York (Real Property Law Committee June 1984 to May 1988 and June 1989 to June 1994, Committee on Uniform Laws July 1999 to June 2001, Committee on Courts of Superior Jurisdiction since July 2002) and New York State Bar Association (Cooperatives and Condominium Committee since 1980, Executive Committee Business Law Section 1985-87). Lecturer New School of Social Research Oct 1981 to May 1982. Assistant Counsel June 15, 1967 to Dec 31, 1970 and Special Assistant Jan 1, 1971 to Dec 31, 1971 to Governor Nelson A. Rockefeller. Counsel Committee on Housing and Urban Development New York State Senate Jan 1972 to Dec 1973. President New York Chapter 1973-75 and Member National Governing Board 1974-76 Ripon Society. Member May 1983 to March 1999, Deputy Treasurer May 1983 to Dec 1983 and Treasurer Jan 1984 to March 1999 New York Republican State Committee. Delegate Republican National Convention 1988. Director 1972-88 and President 1978-85 Jewish Conciliation Board of America. Director 1975-85 and Vice President 1977-80 Optometric Center of New York. Director 1978-93 and Member Executive Committee 1986-89 Jewish Board of Family and Children's Services. Trustee National Dropout Prevention Center 1988-90. Director 1993 to June 2000, Counsel 1993-98, Secretary 1988 to June 2000 and Member Executive Committee 1997 to June 2000 Deafness Research Foundation. Member Battery Park City Authority April 1999 to June 2000.

Office: 100 Centre Street, New York 10013.
Telephone: (212) 374-5814.

STORTECKY, Frederick R. *(Judge, Johnstown City Court)* Currently serves as Acting Judge.

Office: 105 City Hall, 33-41 East Main Street, Johnstown 12095.
Telephone: (518) 762-0007.
Fax: (518) 762-2720

STRANIERE, Philip S. *(Judge, The Civil Court of the City of New York)*

Office: 927 Castleton Avenue, West New Brighton, Staten Island 10310.
Telephone: (718) 390-5130.
Fax: (718) 390-8108
E-mail address: pstraniere@courts.state.ny.us

STRAUS, Robert H. *(Judge, The Criminal Court of the City of New York)* Appointed by Mayor Ed Koch. Currently serves as Acting Justice, New York Supreme Court Twelfth Judicial District.

Office: 851 Grand Concourse, Bronx 10451.
Telephone: (718) 590-3791.
Fax: (718) 590-7837

STRAUSS, Sidney F. *(Justice, New York Supreme Court Eleventh Judicial District)*

Office: 25-10 Court Square, Long Island City 11101.
Telephone: (718) 520-2611.

STURM, Helen C. *(Judge, New York City Family Court)* Appointed by Mayor Rudolph Giuliani.

Office: 60 Lafayette Street, New York 10013.
Telephone: (212) 374-4177.
Fax: (212) 374-2623

SUAREZ, Lucindo *(Justice, New York Supreme Court Twelfth Judicial District)* Currently serves First Judicial District. Also serves as Presiding Justice, New York Supreme Court Appellate Term First Judicial Department. Former Judge, The Civil Court of the City of New York.

Office: 60 Centre Street, Room 401, New York 10007.
Telephone: (212) 374-8373.

SUDOLNIK, Joan C. *(Judge, The Criminal Court of the City of New York)* Appointed by mayor. Currently serves as Acting Justice, New York Supreme Court First Judicial District.

Office: 111 Centre Street, New York 10013.
Telephone: (212) 374-8485.

SULLIVAN, David P. *(Judge, Nassau County Court)*

Office: County Courthouse, 262 Old Country Road, Mineola 11501.
Telephone: (516) 571-2800.

SULLIVAN, James P. *(Justice, New York Supreme Court Second Judicial District)* Former Judge, The Civil Court of the City of New York.

Office: 360 Adams Street, Brooklyn 11201.
Telephone: (718) 643-6246.

SULLIVAN, Joseph P. *(Associate Justice, New York Supreme Court Appellate Division First Judicial Department)* Elected Justice to term beginning Jan 1, 1973. Re-elected to terms beginning Jan 1, 1987 and Jan 1, 2001. Appointed Associate Justice Appellate Division by Governor Hugh Carey Jan 1, 1978. Certificated. Presiding Justice 2000-01. Born Bronx New York March 17, 1931. Roman Catholic. Educated at St. John's University B.A. 1952 LL.B. 1957 and University of Virginia School of Law LL.M. 1984. Admitted to practice New York 1957 and U.S. District Courts Southern 1959 and Eastern 1959 Districts of New York. Began legal practice New York City 1957. Judge, The Civil Court of the City of New York Jan 1, 1969 to Dec 31, 1972.

Member The Association of the Bar of the City of New York, Bronx County, New York State and American Bar Associations. Corporal U.S. Army 1953-55. Enjoys reading, tennis, bicycle riding and golf.

Office: 27 Madison Avenue at 25th Street, New York 10010.
Telephone: (212) 340-0455.

SULLIVAN, W. Howard *(Judge, Chenango County Court)* Also serves Chenango County Surrogate's Court and Chenango County Family Court. Born Norwich New York June 18, 1942. Catholic. Educated at LeMoyne College B.B.A. 1964 and Temple University School of Law LL.B. 1970. Admitted to practice New York 1971, U.S. District Court District of New York and U.S. Supreme Court 1975. Began legal practice Norwich 1971. Former Judge, Norwich City Court, elected to term beginning Nov 1977.

Tax Attorney New York State 1974-76. District Attorney Chenango County 1976. Instructor in Real Estate State University of New York 1973-77. Member American Judicature Society, Chenango County (President

SULLIVAN, W. HOWARD—*Continued*

1981), New York State and American Bar Associations. Recipient American Legion Citizenship Award 1978 and Bronze Key Award from Chenango County Alcohol Council 1979. Worked for Traveler's Insurance Company 1964-71. Chairman Chenango County Democratic Party 1974-75. President Norwich YMCA, Chenango County Council of the Arts and Big Brothers/Big Sisters. Enjoys fishing, running and racquetball.

Office: County Office Building, Five Court Street, Norwich 13815-1676.

Telephone: (607) 337-1825.

Fax: (607) 337-1834

SUNSHINE, Jeffrey S. *(Judge, New York City Family Court)* Appointed by Mayor Rudolph Giuliani. Currently serves as Acting Justice, New York Supreme Court Second Judicial District.

Office: Homeport, 355 Front Street, Staten Island 10304.

Telephone: (718) 876-7311.

SUSSMAN, Ruth Levine *(Judge, The Criminal Court of the City of New York)* Appointed by Mayor Rudolph Giuliani. Currently serves as Acting Justice, New York Supreme Court Twelfth Judicial District. Former Judge, New York City Family Court, appointed by Mayor Rudolph Giuliani.

Office: 215 East 161st Street, Bronx 10451.

Telephone: (718) 590-2927.

Fax: (718) 590-7297

SWAIN, Laura Taylor *(Judge, United States District Court Southern District of New York)* Appointed for life by President Bill Clinton to term beginning Aug 31, 2000. Born Brooklyn New York Nov 21, 1958. Educated at Harvard-Radcliffe College A.B. 1979 and Harvard Law School J.D. 1982. Law Clerk to Hon. Constance Baker Motley, U.S. District Court Southern District of New York 1982-83. In legal practice 1982-96. Judge, U.S. Bankruptcy Court Eastern District of New York 1996-2000.

Member New York State Board of Law Examiners 1986-96.

Office: 426 U.S. Courthouse, 40 Centre Street, New York 10007.

Telephone: (212) 805-0417.

SWEENEY, Patrick A. *(Judge, Suffolk County Family Court)* Former Judge, Suffolk County District Court.

Office: Cohalan Court Complex, 400 Carleton Avenue, Central Islip 11722.

Telephone: (631) 853-4315.

Fax: (631) 853-3204

SWEENEY, Peter Paul *(Judge, The Civil Court of the City of New York)*

Office: 141 Livingston Street, Brooklyn 11201.

Telephone: (718) 643-8474.

Fax: (718) 643-3733

SWEENY, John W., Jr. *(Justice, New York Supreme Court Ninth Judicial District)* Former Acting Justice. Former Judge, Putnam County Court, elected to term beginning Jan 1, 1987.

Office: Courthouse, 40 Gleneida Avenue, Carmel 10512.

Telephone: (845) 225-3641.

SWEET, Robert Workman *(Senior Judge, United States District Court Southern District of New York)* Appointed for life by President Jimmy Carter to term beginning May 18, 1978. Assumed Senior status, serves by assignment. Born Yonkers New York Oct 15, 1922. Protestant. Educated at Yale University B.A. 1944 LL.B. 1948. Admitted to practice New York 1949 and U.S. Court of Appeals Second Circuit 1951. Began legal practice New York City 1948.

Assistant U.S. Attorney Southern District of New York 1953-55. Hearing Officer New York City Transit Authority 1975-77. Member New York Law Institute, New York County Lawyers' Association, The Association of the Bar of the City of New York, New York State and American Bar Associations. Lieutenant j.g. USNR 1943-46. Deputy Mayor City of New York 1966-69.

Office: 1920 U.S. Courthouse, 500 Pearl Street, New York 10007-1312.

Telephone: (212) 805-0254.

SZCZUR, Margaret O. *(Judge, Erie County Family Court)*

Office: One Niagara Plaza, Buffalo 14202.

Telephone: (716) 858-8150.

Fax: (716) 858-8432

TADDEO, Ann Marie *(Judge, Monroe County Family Court)* Currently serves as Supervising Judge.

Office: Hall of Justice, Third Floor, 99 Exchange Boulevard, Rochester 14614-2187.

Telephone: (585) 428-5488.

Fax: (585) 428-4068

TAFURI, Anthony A. *(Judge, Suffolk County District Court)*

Mailing address: P.O. Box 9075, Central Islip 11722-9075.

Office: Cohalan Court Complex, 400 Carleton Avenue, Central Islip 11722.

Telephone: (631) 853-4915.

TALLMER, Megan *(Judge, The Criminal Court of the City of New York)* Appointed by mayor. Currently serves as Acting Justice, New York Supreme Court Twelfth Judicial District. Former Judge, The Civil Court of the City of New York.

Office: 851 Grand Concourse, Bronx 10451.

Telephone: (718) 590-3632.

Fax: (718) 590-8914

TANENBAUM, Melvyn *(Justice, New York Supreme Court Tenth Judicial District)* Acting Justice 1979-82. Elected Justice to term beginning Jan 1, 1983. Reelected 1996, current term expires Dec 31, 2010. Born Brooklyn New York Jan 20, 1935. Educated at New York University B.S. 1955, New York Law School LL.B. 1957 replaced by J.D. and University of Virginia School of Law LL.M. 1992. Staff member New York Law Forum. Admitted to practice New York 1958, U.S. District Courts Eastern 1963 and Southern 1963 Districts of New York, U.S. Supreme Court 1963 and U.S. Court of Appeals Second Circuit 1966. In legal practice Huntington 1958-74. Judge, Suffolk County Court May 28, 1974 to Dec 31, 1982.

Assistant County Attorney Suffolk County 1971-73. Author "Have the Courts Kept Up?" 23 No. 4, 1984, "We Should Change the Judicial Compensation System" 24 No. 1, 1985, "Evaluating Judicial Performance" 24

TANENBAUM, MELVYN—*Continued*

No. 2, 1985, "Accountability with Independence" 24 No. 3, 1985, "Changes and Advances" 31 No. 4, 27, 1992, "The State Court Funding Crisis" 32 No. 1, 21, 1993, "An International Criminal Court" 32 No. 2, 17, 1993, and "You Are Special" 32 No. 2, 40, 1993 *Judges Journal.* Co-author with Hon. Stanley Mosk foreword *School Crime and Violence, Victim's Rights* Rapp, Carrington and Nicholson 1986. Co-author Bench Book and Manual of Pattern Jury Instructions "RSFSR Bench Book for the Jury Trial of Criminal Cases" (Bench Book and Manual of Pattern Jury Instructions) 1993. Fulbright Professor of Law Ministry of Justice Russian Academy of Jurisprudence International Law Institute Moscow and Fulbright Visiting Professor of Law Rostov State University Law Department, North Caucasian Social Law School, Academy of Civil Services Institute of Business Management Law College, Academy of Law in Tula, Ministry of the Interior Law School and St. Petersburg Higher School of Law 1996-97.

Former member New York Trial Lawyers Association (Former member Board of Governors and Judiciary Committee 1971-74), The Association of Trial Lawyers of America, New York State County Judges Association (First Vice President 1980-81, President Elect 1981-82, President 1982-83, former member Executive Committee and Legislative Committee) and Nassau County Bar Association (Trial Lawyers Section). Fellow American Bar Foundation. Associate Member National Center for State Courts. Member National Courts and Community Committee since 1993, American Judicature Society, Suffolk County Court Judges Association (Presiding Officer 1979-83, President 1980-83), Association of Justices of the Supreme Court of the State of New York (Co-chairperson Committee on Evaluation of Judicial Performance since 1985 and Task Force of Court Structure 1997, District Member Executive Committee since 1994, Chairperson Court Management Committee since 1995), Suffolk County (Co-chairperson Courthouse Facilities Committee 1991-94, Chairperson Strategic Planning Committee since 1996, Committee on Supreme Court, former member County Court Committee) and New York State (Council Member and Delegate 1982-83 and 1985-92, Member Committee on Unified Court System since 1983, Co-chairman Council of Judicial Association Committee on Evaluation of Judicial Performance since 1986, Member Special Committee for Improvement in the Law/Simplification of the Law since 1984, Committee on Continuing Education for the Judiciary since 1992, Committee on Judicial Administration and Committee on Community Relations Judicial Section, Member Committee to Improve the Effectiveness of the Criminal Justice System Criminal Justice Section, Former Member Municipal Law Section) Bar Associations. Member American Bar Association (Board Member representing Second Circuit 1978-84, Chairperson Elect, Vice Chairperson, Secretary, Member 1978-86 and 1988-90 Executive Committee, Chairperson of Conference 1984-85, Chairperson Committee on Evaluation of Judicial Performance 1985-90, Chairperson 1982 and Member 1983-86 and 1989-93 Committee on Plans and Development 1982, Chairperson Funding for Courts Committee since 1993, Co-chairperson Committee on State and Federal Relations since 1993 National Conference of Special Court Judges; Member Committee on Improving Judicial Performance 1982, Committee on Guidelines for Judicial Selection 1983-84, Executive Committee 1984-85 and 1987-96, Vice Chairperson 1990-91, Chairperson Elect 1991-92, Chairperson 1992-93, Liaison to Section of Tort and Insurance Practice 1993-94, Liaison to Section of International Law and Practice 1993-97, Liaison to National Bar Association 1993-97 Judicial Administration Division; Member Advisory Task Force on Haiti Projects since 1993 Section of International Law and Practice; Participant Meetings and Briefings at United Nations 1992-96 and at U.S. Mission 1993-96 Standing Committee on World Order Under Law).

Participant Faculty Training Session The National Judicial College Nov 1985, National Symposium on the Child Victim of Sexual Abuse 1985, National Conference on Judicial Education 1987, National Conference on Birth, Death and Law 1988, "Drugs and Crime in America; A Clear and Present Danger" 1988, National Conference of the Judiciary on the Court Related Needs of the Elderly and Persons With Disabilities 1991, National Conference on the Crisis in America's System of Justice 1993 and National Conference of Family Violence March 1994. Participant and Group Discussion Leader "Custody Decision Making—The Best Interest of the Child" 1985. Faculty Member and Moderator Seminar "Pre-natal Drug Abuse: Legal and Treatment Issues" Fourteenth National Conference on Juvenile Justice 1987. Faculty Member and Speaker on "Fetal Abuse and Neglect; Emerging New Issues" National Council of Juvenile and Family Court Judges Conference 1987. Member Planning Committee, Faculty and Lecturer Seminar on Life Support Decisions The National Conference of the State Judiciary on Bioethical Issues 1989. Speaker "Crisis in State Court Funding" Conference of Chief Justices Education Program 1993, "A Partnership for Safe Communities, Courts, Education and Literacy" Symposium 1993, Program in Honor of Women of Color in the Judiciary 1993, Dinner in Honor of Women in the Judiciary 1993 and Fund for Modern Courts Public Forum on Alternative Dispute Resolution and the Role of Courts May 1995. Conferee The New York Fair Trial Free Press Conference May 1996. Lecturer Case Management Seminar for Federal Administrative Law Judges Oct 1996 and Round Table Groups in Moscow and St. Petersburg McArthur Foundation and U.S. Information Service. Invitee Medina Seminar on Judicial Decision-Making and Competing Values in Contemporary America Princeton University 1991 and 1992 and Conference of Chief Justices Education Programs July 1992 and Jan 1993. Lecturer and Presenter Karelia Rule of Law Project Program on Civil Law, Contracts and Securities Petrozavodsk Republic of Karelia. Presenter Seminar on Domestic Violence NIS U.S. Women's Consortium and ABA-CEELI and "Human Rights and the Role of Advocacy in a Democratic Society" Russian Lawyers Guild, Council of Europe, Ministry of Justice of the Russian Federation, Ministry of Foreign Affairs of the Russian Federation and The Branch of Human Rights of International Informatization Academy (NGO). Assistant Counsel and Special Counsel Suffolk County Water Authority Oakdale 1959-63. Associate Counsel South Huntington Water District 1969-74. Former Counsel Suffolk County Board of Elections. Former Special Deputy Attorney General Election Frauds Bureau New York State.

Office: 440 U.S. Courthouse, 170 Federal Plaza, Central Islip 11722.

Telephone: (631) 853-6323.

TAPIA, Fernando *(Judge, The Civil Court of the City of New York)*
Office: 851 Grand Concourse, Bronx 10451.
Telephone: (718) 590-3601.

TARANTINO, Richard P. *(Judge, Glens Falls City Court)* Currently serves as Acting Judge.
Office: 42 Ridge Street, Glens Falls 12801.
Telephone: (518) 798-4714.
Fax: (518) 798-0137

TARGUM, Anne E. *(Justice, New York Supreme Court Twelfth Judicial District)* Former Acting Justice. Certificated. Former Judge, The Civil Court of the City of New York.
Office: 851 Grand Concourse, Bronx 10451.
Telephone: (718) 590-6362.
Fax: (718) 590-1011

TAYLOR, Janice A. *(Justice, New York Supreme Court Eleventh Judicial District)* Former Judge, The Civil Court of the City of New York, elected to term beginning Jan 1, 1995.
Office: 88-11 Sutphin Boulevard, Jamaica 11435.
Telephone: (718) 520-3728.

TEJADA, Charles J. *(Judge, New York Court of Claims)* Appointed by Governor Mario Cuomo to term beginning 1990. Currently serves as Acting Justice, New York Supreme Court First Judicial District. Educated at City College of the City University of New York and New York University School of Law 1973. Former Judge, The Civil Court of the City of New York. Former Judge, New York City Family Court.
Staff Attorney and Attorney-in-Charge Harlem Office Legal Aid Society 1975-79. Counsel QUERER, Inc. Former Instructor St. John's University School of Law and Seton Hall University School of Law. Adjunct Professor of Law Yeshiva University Benjamin N. Cardozo School of Law since 1997. Past President Association of Judges of Hispanic Heritage and Puerto Rican Bar Association. Former Member Board of Directors Legal Aid Society of the City of New York and New York County Lawyers' Association. Former Member Executive Committee Association of the Bar of the City of New York. Member Franklin H. Williams Judicial Commission on Minorities. Regional Director Office for Civil Rights U.S. Department of Education 1979-85. Former Trustee College of New Rochelle. Former Participant Mentor/Teaching Program Thurgood Marshall Academy George W. Wingate High School. Board of Directors Project Youth Reach. Member Committee to Promote Public Trust and Confidence in the Legal System.
Office: 100 Centre Street, New York 10013.
Telephone: (212) 374-4741.
Fax: (212) 748-5089

TELESCA, Michael A. *(Senior Judge, United States District Court Western District of New York)* Appointed for life by the President. Former Chief Judge. Assumed Senior status, serves by assignment. Born Rochester New York Nov 25, 1929. Catholic. Educated at University of Rochester A.B. 1952 and University of Buffalo LL.B. 1955. Admitted to practice New York 1957. Began legal practice Rochester 1957. Former Surrogate, Monroe County Surrogate's Court, elected to term beginning Jan 1, 1973.
Important Decisions: Matter of Wilkinson 75 Misc. 2d 1024, 1973; Matter of Cooper 76 Misc. 2d 166, 349 N.Y.S.2d 613, 1973; Matter of DeBelardino 77 Misc. 2d 253, aff'd 47 A.D.2d 589, 1974-75; Matter of Schnelle 353 N.Y.S.2d 902, 1974; Matter of Stone 80 Misc. 2d 762, 1974; Matter of Masline aff'd 52 A.D.2d 739; Matter of Flores 78 Misc. 2d 481, 1974; Matter of Peck 79 Misc. 2d 1053, 1974; Matter of Marafioti 80 Misc. 2d 206, 1974; Matter of Bihansky aff'd 81 Misc. 2d 979, 1975-76; Matter of Miller 80 Misc. 2d 916, 1975; Matter of Dow 81 Misc. 2d 506, 1975; Matter of Figliola 81 Misc. 2d 979, 1975; Matter of Frank 83 Misc. 2d 314, 1975; Matter of Kolodij 85 Misc. 2d 946, 1975; and Matter of Willey 85 Misc. 2d 380, 1976. Former member Departmental Committee New York Supreme Court Fourth Judicial Department. Member National College of Probate Judges, Monroe County and American Bar Associations. Staff Legal Officer USMC 1955-57. Republican. Board of Governors Genesee Hospital and Board of Directors Association for Retarded Children. Member St. Helen's Parish.
Office: 272 Federal Building, 100 State Street, Rochester 14614-1323.
Telephone: (716) 263-5785.

TENNEY, John R. *(Justice, New York Supreme Court Fifth Judicial District)* Elected Nov 1968 to term beginning Jan 1, 1969. Reelected Nov 1982 and Nov 1996. Certificated. Born North Arlington New Jersey March 4, 1930. Educated at Colgate University 1952 and Cornell University LL.B. 1955. Admitted to practice New York 1955. In legal practice Brooklyn 1955-57, Albany 1957-58 and Utica 1958-68.
Assistant Attorney General 1957-58. Author "Justice, Fair Play and Equity in Divorce Actions" New York State B. Jour. 1995. President 1993, Officer and Director Association of Supreme Court Justices of the State of New York. Presiding Member Council of Judicial Associations. Member Oneida County, New York State and American Bar Associations. Recipient Community Service Award from Faxton Hospital and Director's Award from Oneida County Bar Association. Chairman Oneida County Republican Committee 1962-68. Delegate Republican National Convention 1964 and 1968. Former Chairman and Past President Board of Managers Faxton Hospital. Past President Yahnundasis Golf Club. Enjoys golfing and sailing.
Office: Oneida County Courthouse, 200 Elizabeth Street, Utica 13501.
Telephone: (315) 798-5860.
Fax: (315) 797-0531

TEPPER, Roy *(Judge, Long Beach City Court)*
Office: One West Chester Street, Long Beach 11561.
Telephone: (516) 431-1000.
Fax: (516) 431-4372

TERESI, Joseph C. *(Justice, New York Supreme Court Third Judicial District)* Elected Nov 2, 1993 to term beginning Jan 1, 1994. Term expires Dec 31, 2007. Born Albany New York Dec 5, 1946. Roman Catholic. Educated at Boston College B.S. with honors 1968 and Albany Law School of Union University J.D. 1971. Admitted to practice New York 1972, U.S. District Court Northern District of New York 1972 and U.S. Court of Appeals Second Circuit 1983. In legal practice Albany 1972-93.
Public Defender Albany County 1972-93. Member Capital District Trial Lawyers Association, Association of Justices of the Supreme Court of the State of New York, Albany County and New York State Bar Associa-

TERESI, JOSEPH C.—*Continued*

tions. First Lieutenant U.S. Army Military Intelligence 1971-74.
Office: 451 Albany County Courthouse, Albany 12207.
Telephone: (518) 487-5140.

TERRY, Walter L., III *(Judge, Oneonta City Court)*
Office: Public Safety Building, 81 Main Street, Oneonta 13820.
Telephone: (607) 432-4480.
Fax: (607) 432-2328
E-mail address: wterry@courts.state.ny.us

THOMAS, Charles J. *(Justice, New York Supreme Court Eleventh Judicial District)* Elected to term beginning Jan 1, 1989. Reelected 2002, current term expires Dec 31, 2016. Born Bronx New York June 5, 1934. Judge, The Civil Court of the City of New York Jan 1, 1983 to Dec 31, 1988.
Office: 88-11 Sutphin Boulevard, Jamaica 11435.
Telephone: (718) 520-3733.

THOMAS, Delores J. *(Judge, The Civil Court of the City of New York)*
Office: 141 Livingston Street, Brooklyn 11201.
Telephone: (718) 643-5069.

THOMPSON, Kenneth L., Jr. *(Justice, New York Supreme Court Twelfth Judicial District)* Former Judge, The Civil Court of the City of New York.
Office: 851 Grand Concourse, Bronx 10451.
Telephone: (718) 590-3668.
Fax: (718) 590-8914

TILLS, Ronald H. *(Judge, New York Court of Claims)* Appointed by Governor George E. Pataki. Currently serves as Acting Justice, New York Supreme Court Eighth Judicial District.
Office: 25 Delaware Avenue, Buffalo 14202.
Telephone: (716) 858-4868.
Fax: (716) 858-4871
E-mail address: rtills@courts.state.ny.us

TINGLING, Milton A., Jr. *(Justice, New York Supreme Court First Judicial District)* Former Judge, The Civil Court of the City of New York.
Office: 60 Centre Street, New York 10007.
Telephone: (212) 374-3799.
Fax: (212) 374-3326

TOBIN, Beverly Cipollo *(Judge, Albany County Family Court)* Appointed by Governor Mario Cuomo to term beginning March 1988. Elected Nov 1988 and Nov 1998. Current term expires Dec 31, 2008. Educated at Albany Law School LL.B. 1962. Admitted to practice New York 1962, U.S. District Court Northern District of New York 1962 and U.S. Supreme Court 1967.
Office: One Van Tromp Street, Albany 12207.
Telephone: (518) 427-3530.
Fax: (518) 427-3562

TOLBERT, Bruce E. *(Judge, Westchester County Family Court)* Former Judge, Yonkers City Court.
Office: 111 Dr. Martin Luther King Jr. Blvd., White Plains 10601.
Telephone: (914) 995-3615.
Fax: (914) 995-4675

TOLUB, Walter B. *(Judge, The Civil Court of the City of New York)* Currently serves as Acting Justice, New York Supreme Court First Judicial District.
Office: 60 Centre Street, New York 10007.
Telephone: (212) 374-8550.
Fax: (212) 374-1788

TOM, Peter *(Associate Justice, New York Supreme Court Appellate Division First Judicial Department)* Former Judge, The Civil Court of the City of New York.
Office: 27 Madison Avenue at 25th Street, New York 10010.
Telephone: (212) 340-0403.
Fax: (212) 340-0571

TOMEI, Albert *(Justice, New York Supreme Court Second Judicial District)* Former Acting Justice. Former Judge, The Civil Court of the City of New York.
Office: 360 Adams Street, Brooklyn 11201.
Telephone: (718) 643-3804.
E-mail address: atomei@courts.state.ny.us

TOMLINSON, Guy P. *(Surrogate, Montgomery County Surrogate's Court)*
Mailing address: P.O. Box 1500, Fonda 12068-1500.
Office: 50 New Courthouse, 58 Broadway, Fonda 12068.
Telephone: (518) 853-8108.
Fax: (518) 853-8230

TOMPKINS, Harold *(Justice, New York Supreme Court First Judicial District)* Former Acting Justice. Certificated. Former Judge, The Civil Court of the City of New York, elected to term beginning Jan 1982.
Office: 60 Centre Street, New York 10007.
Telephone: (212) 374-8542.
Fax: (212) 227-2920
E-mail address: htompkin@courts.state.ny.us

TOOLE, Elisabeth A. *(Judge, Geneva City Court)* Currently serves as Acting Judge.
Office: Public Safety Building, 255 Exchange Street, Geneva 14456.
Telephone: (315) 789-6560.
Fax: (315) 781-2802

TOOMEY, John J., Jr. *(Judge, Suffolk County District Court)*
Office: 3105 Veteran's Memorial Highway, Ronkonkoma 11779.
Telephone: (631) 854-9680.
Fax: (631) 854-9683

TORMEY, James C., III *(Justice, New York Supreme Court Fifth Judicial District)* Currently serves as Administrative Judge. Former Judge, Syracuse City Court.
Office: Onondaga County Courthouse, 401 Montgomery Street, Syracuse 13202.
Telephone: (315) 671-1100.
Fax: (315) 671-1183

TORRES, Analisa *(Judge, The Civil Court of the City of New York)* Currently assigned to The Criminal Court of the City of New York.
Office: 111 Centre Street, New York 10013.
Telephone: (212) 374-8479.

TORRES, Edwin *(Justice, New York Supreme Court Twelfth Judicial District)* Certificated. Currently serves First Judicial District.
Office: 100 Centre Street, New York 10013.
Telephone: (212) 374-5817.
Fax: (212) 374-1953

TORRES, Robert E. *(Judge, The Civil Court of the City of New York)* Currently assigned to The Criminal Court of the City of New York.
Office: 215 East 161st Street, Bronx 10451.
Telephone: (718) 590-7502.

TOUSSAINT, Wavny *(Judge, The Civil Court of the City of New York)*
Office: 141 Livingston Street, Brooklyn 11201.
Telephone: (718) 643-5069.

TOWNES, Sandra L. *(Associate Justice, New York Supreme Court Appellate Division Second Judicial Department)* Elected Justice Fifth Judicial District. Appointed Associate Justice Appellate Division by Governor George E. Pataki. Former Judge, Syracuse City Court.
Office: 405 Onondaga County Courthouse, 401 Montgomery Street, Syracuse 13202.
Telephone: (315) 671-1187.

TOWNSEND, Sharon S. *(Judge, Erie County Family Court)* Elected 1991. Reelected 2001, current term expires Jan 31, 2011. Supervising Judge Jan 1, 1996 to Dec 31, 2002. Administrative Judge Eighth Judicial District since Jan 1, 2003. Also serves as Acting Justice, New York Supreme Court Eighth Judicial District. Educated at University of Connecticut School of Law 1979.
Office: 92 Franklin Street, Buffalo 14202.
Telephone: (716) 851-3273.
Fax: (716) 855-1611
E-mail address: stownsen@courts.state.ny.us

TRAFICANTI, Joseph J., Jr. *(Surrogate, Ulster County Surrogate's Court)* Also serves as Deputy Chief Administrative Judge Courts Outside New York City.
Mailing address: P.O. Box 1800, Kingston 12402-1800.
Office: 244 Fair Street, Kingston 12401.
Telephone: (845) 340-3350.
Fax: (845) 340-3352
Office: 2001 Agency Building Four, Four Empire State Plaza, Albany 12223-1450.
Telephone: (518) 474-3828.
Fax: (518) 473-5514
E-mail address: jtrafica@courts.state.ny.us

TRAGER, David G. *(Judge, United States District Court Eastern District of New York)* Appointed for life by President Bill Clinton to term beginning Jan 1994. Born Dec 23, 1937. Educated at Columbia College A.B. 1959 and Harvard Law School LL.B. 1962. Admitted to practice New York 1963. In legal practice 1963-67.

Assistant Corporation Counsel Appeals Division City of New York 1967. Law Clerk to Hon. Kenneth B. Keating, New York Court of Appeals 1968-69. Chief Appeals Division 1970-72 and U.S. Attorney 1974-78 Eastern District of New York U.S. Attorney's Office. Author "Contract Zoning" Maryland L. Rev. Spring 1963, Introduction to criminal procedure of Second Circuit Review "Harmless Error: A Doctrine for All Seasons" 39 Brooklyn L. Rev. 1043 Spring 1973 and "The Law of Standing Under the Fourth Amendment" 41 Brooklyn L. Rev. 423 Spring 1975. Associate Professor of Law 1972-74, Professor of Law 1978-94 and Dean 1983-93 Brooklyn Law School. Member Committee on State Legislation 1966-67, Committee on Federal Legislation 1973-74, Committee on Criminal Advocacy 1980-83 and Executive Committee 1983-87 The Association of the Bar of the City of New York. Chairman Brooklyn Citizens Independent Non-Partisan Judicial Screening Panel 1973, U.S. Magistrate Merit Panel Eastern District of New York 1981-82 and Temporary New York State Commission of Investigation 1983-90. Member Second Circuit Committee on Speedy Trial Guidelines 1978-79 and Criminal Justice Panel Committee for Modern Courts, Inc. 1977-79 and 1981-82. Vice President 1978-82, Trustee 1982-84, President Elect 1984-86, President 1986-88 and President Emeritus 1988-93 Federal Bar Council. Member 1978-83 and Vice Chairman 1981-83 Committee on Professional Ethics New York State Bar Association. Reporter Subcommittee on Court Management Advisory Committee on Planning for the District Courts Judicial Council of the Second Circuit 1979-81. Member 1981-89 and Chairman 1982-89 Mayor's Committee on the Judiciary. Trustee Fund for Modern Courts 1983-93. Board of Directors Legal Aid Society 1988-93. Member The American Law Institute and American Bar Association (Committee on Law School Accreditation Section of Legal Education and Admission to the Bar since 1989). Member New York City Charter Revision Committee 1986-89. Board of Directors Prospect Park Alliance 1987-88 and Daytop Village 1987-93. Member 1988-95 and Chairman 1989-95 Board of Trustees Eden II School for Autistic Children, Inc. Board of Trustees The Brooklyn Hospital Center since 1994.
Office: U.S. Courthouse, 225 Cadman Plaza East, Brooklyn 11201.
Telephone: (718) 260-2510.

TRAINOR, Kerry R. *(Judge, Suffolk County Family Court)*
Office: Cohalan Court Complex, 400 Carleton Avenue, Central Islip 11722.
Telephone: (631) 853-4330.
Fax: (631) 853-7569

TREECE, Randolph F. *(Magistrate Judge, United States District Court Northern District of New York)* Appointed by U.S. District Court judges to term beginning April 26, 2001. Term expires April 26, 2009. Born Troy New York Sept 25, 1948. Educated at Siena College B.B.A. 1970 and Albany Law School J.D. 1976. Admitted to practice New York 1977, U.S. District Court Northern District of New York 1977 and U.S. Supreme Court 1980. In legal practice Albany Aug 1976 to Sept 1987.

Assistant Public Defender Resselaer County Sept 1977 to May 1985. Assistant Attorney General New York Sept 1987 to Sept 1995. First Deputy Capital Defender New York Sept 1995 to Feb 1999. General Counsel Office of State Comptroller since Feb 1999. Author "How Far We Have Come Since Magna Carta" 1993 and "Jury of One's Peers, Jury Panels, Minority and Third Judicial Districts" Capital District Black Bar Association. Contributing Writer *Place for Jazz* since 1997 and *Urban Voices* 2000. Adjunct Instructor Hudson Valley Community College Sept 1977 to Dec 1978 and Junior College of Albany Sept 1980 to Dec 1984. Adjunct Professor of Trial Tactics Albany Law School since Jan 1989. Panel Member and Co-chair Subcommittee on In-

TREECE, RANDOLPH F.—*Continued*

clusion and Representation on Juries New York Jury Project 1995. Member Attorney Advisory Group U.S. Court of Appeals Second Circuit 2001. Member Franklin H. Williams Commission on Minorities in the Judiciary, Capital District Trial Lawyers Association, New York Bar Foundation (Committee on Public Understanding of the Law 1996-2000, Treasurer 2000, Board of Trustees), Federal Magistrate Judges Association, Capital District Women's (Advisory Board of Directors), Capital District Black (Founder, Past President, Vice President), Albany County (Board of Directors since 1994, Chair Admission Committee 2000, Secretary 2003), Rensselaer County, New York State (House of Delegates 2001, Committee of Bar Leaders, Committee on Minorities in the Profession, Judicial Selection Committee, Co-chair Minority Counsel Project) and National Bar Associations. Recipient Root/Stimson Award from New York State Bar Association 1993, Thurgood Marshall Justice Award from Albany Chapter NAACP Jan 1996, Roland J. Smith Award from New York Chapter American Civil Liberties Union Oct 1997, Alumni Distinguished Service Award from Albany Law School Oct 1999, President's Award from Albany County Bar Association Feb 2000, Frederick Douglas Award from Center for Law and Justice April 2002 and Millennium Award from Franklin H. Williams Commission on Minorities Oct 2002. Inducted into Troy Boys and Girls Club Hall of Fame April 2000 and Lansingburgh High School Hall of Fame Sept 2001. Named Man of the Year by Capital District Chapter The Links April 2000 and Citizen of the Year by Omega Phi Psi Nov 2001. USAR 1976. Accountant Peat Marwick and Mitchell June 1970 to Sept 1973. Member Blue Ribbon Commission Rensselaer County Democratic Party 1985. Treasurer Tri-County Afro-American Renaissance Council 1969-73. Board of Directors and Tutor Motivation of Black Youth (MOBY) 1970-73. Board of Trustees Hudson Valley Community College since 1985. Board of Directors Lansingburgh Boys Club 1986-92. Coach and Referee Youth Basketball League YMCA since 1989. Associate 1992-95 and Member July 2001 Board of Trustees Siena College. Member Minority Committee Alumni Association 1997-98, Student Affairs Task Force 1997-98, Advisory Committees NAACP Legal Assistance Program since 1999 and Government Law Center since 1999 and Board of Trustees July 2001 Albany Law School. Former Member, Board of Directors, Executive Vice Chair 1992-95 and Chair 1996 Urban League of Northeastern New York. Board of Trustees Albany Law School. Member 100 Black Men of the Capital Region and NAACP.

Office: U.S. Courthouse, 445 Broadway, Albany 12207-2925.
Telephone: (518) 474-3444.
Fax: (518) 473-9104
E-mail address: rtreece@osc.state.ny.us

TROTTO, Hertha C. *(Judge, Suffolk County District Court)* Currently serves as Acting Judge, Suffolk County Court.

Office: Cohalan Court Complex, 400 Carleton Avenue, Central Islip 11722.
Telephone: (631) 853-7418.

TROUTMAN, Shirley *(Judge, Erie County Court)* Former Judge, Buffalo City Court.

Office: Erie County Hall, 92 Franklin Street, Buffalo 14202.
Telephone: (716) 858-8452.

TSCHIEMBER, Georgia A. *(Judge, Suffolk County District Court)*

Office: Court Complex, 400 Carleton Avenue, Central Islip 11722.
Telephone: (631) 853-7418.
Fax: (631) 853-5402

TUITT, Alison Y. *(Judge, The Civil Court of the City of New York)*

Office: 851 Grand Concourse, Bronx 10451.
Telephone: (718) 590-3606.

TURBOW, Daniel *(Judge, New York City Family Court)* Appointed by Mayor Rudolph Giuliani.

Office: 283 Adams Street, Sixth Floor, Brooklyn 11201.
Telephone: (718) 643-4546.
Fax: (718) 643-5103

TURNER, Matthew J. *(Judge, Troy City Court)* Elected Nov 1998 to term beginning Jan 1, 1999. Born Mount Kisco New York Nov 23, 1964. Catholic. Educated at Catholic University of America B.A. 1986 and Albany Law School of Union University J.D. 1989. Admitted to practice New York 1991. In legal practice Albany Sept 1989 to Jan 1993 and Troy since Jan 1993.

Deputy Corporation Counsel City of Troy Jan 1993 to Jan 1995. Assistant Public Defender Rensselaer County Jan 1995 to Jan 1999.

Office: 51 State Street, Third Floor, Troy 12180.
Telephone: (518) 274-2816.
Fax: (518) 271-2360
E-mail address: mjturner@courts.state.ny.us

UNDERWOOD, William L., Jr. *(Justice, New York Supreme Court Tenth Judicial District)* Elected to term beginning Jan 1, 1973. Reelected 1986. Certificated. Born Patchogue New York Feb 27, 1928. Educated at Long Island University 1945-47, Brooklyn Law School LL.B. 1950 LL.M. 1951, New York University 1952 and Johns Hopkins University 1954. Admitted to practice New York 1951. In legal practice Patchogue 1952-63. Justice of the Peace, Town of Brookhaven Sept 1963 to Dec 1965. Judge, Suffolk District Court Jan 1966 to Dec 1972.

Member Suffolk County Bar Association. USN JAGD 1952-54. Fire Commissioner Davis Park Fire Department. Warden Village of Patchogue Fire Department. Member Patchogue Congregational Church, Patchogue Rotary Club and Farm Bureau.

Office: 101 Supreme Court Building, 235 Griffing Avenue, Riverhead 11901.
Telephone: (631) 852-2365.
Fax: (631) 852-1961

UPLINGER, Karen M. *(Judge, Syracuse City Court)*

Office: Public Safety Building, Second Floor, 511 South State Street, Syracuse 13202-2179.
Telephone: (315) 477-2765.
Fax: (315) 474-2601
E-mail address: kuplinge@courts.state.ny.us

UVILLER, Rena K. *(Judge, New York Court of Claims)* Appointed by governor. Currently serves as Act-

UVILLER, RENA K.—*Continued*
ing Justice, New York Supreme Court First Judicial District.
Office: 100 Centre Street, New York 10013.
Telephone: (212) 374-4968.
Fax: (212) 374-0607

VALENTINO, Joseph D. *(Justice, New York Supreme Court Seventh Judicial District)* Elected to term beginning Jan 1, 2002. Term expires Dec 31, 2015. Born New York New York Nov 1, 1946. Roman Catholic. Educated at Niagara University B.A. 1968 and St. John's University School of Law J.D. 1971. Admitted to practice New York 1973, U.S. District Court Western District of New York 1973 and U.S. Supreme Court 1976. Began legal practice Rochester 1973. Judge, Rochester City Court Jan 1, 1983 to Dec 31, 2001.
Assistant District Attorney 1974-82. Member Monroe County, New York State and American Bar Associations. Democrat.
Office: Hall of Justice, 99 Exchange Boulevard, Rochester 14614.
Telephone: (585) 428-2034.
Fax: (585) 428-1885
E-mail address: jvalenti@courts.state.ny.us

VAN STRYDONCK, Thomas M. *(Justice, New York Supreme Court Seventh Judicial District)* Currently serves as Administrative Judge.
Office: 545 Hall of Justice, 99 Exchange Boulevard, Rochester 14614-2185.
Telephone: (585) 428-2885.
Fax: (585) 428-2105

VAN ULLEN, Stephen J. *(Judge, Cohoes City Court)*
Mailing address: P.O. Box 678, Cohoes 12047-0678.
Office: 7 City Hall, First Floor, 97 Mohawk Street, Cohoes 12047.
Telephone: (518) 233-8202.
Fax: (518) 233-8202

VAUGHAN, David B. *(Justice, New York Supreme Court Second Judicial District)*
Office: 360 Adams Street, Brooklyn 11201.
Telephone: (718) 643-7076.
E-mail address: dvaughan@courts.state.ny.us

VERAS, Sonia M. *(Judge, Suffolk County District Court)*
Mailing address: P.O. Box 9075, Central Islip 11722-9075.
Office: Cohalan Court Complex, 400 Carleton Avenue, Central Islip 11722.
Telephone: (631) 853-7601.

VERSACI, Vincent W. *(Judge, Schenectady City Court)*
Office: 215 City Hall, Jay Street, Schenectady 12305.
Telephone: (518) 382-5077.
Fax: (518) 382-5080

VICTOR, Paul A. *(Justice, New York Supreme Court Twelfth Judicial District)* Elected Nov 2, 1999 to term beginning Jan 1, 2000. Born Bronx New York March 11, 1933. Catholic. Educated at Fordham University B.S. 1954 J.D. 1959. Staff member Fordham Law Review 1957-59. Law Clerk to Hon. Adrian Burke, New York Court of Appeals 1959-61. Admitted to practice New York 1959, U.S. District Courts Eastern 1962 and Southern 1962 Districts of New York, U.S. Supreme Court 1968 and U.S. Court of Appeals Second Circuit 1969. In legal practice New York 1964-98. Arbitrator, The Civil Court of the City of New York 1971-80. Judge, The Civil Court of the City of New York Jan 1, 1999 to Dec 31, 1999.
Assistant District Attorney Bronx County 1962-64. Important Decisions: Holman v. City of New York 181 Misc. 2d 15, 691 N.Y.S.2d 739, 1999 N.Y. slip op. 99247; Daniel v. Motor Vehicle Acc. Indemnification Corp. 181 Misc. 2d 941, 694 N.Y.S.2d 913, 1999 N.Y. slip op. 99414; Curia v. Brooks, Weinger, Robbins & Leeds, Inc. 182 Misc. 2d 36, 696 N.Y.S.2d 776, 1999 N.Y. slip op. 99473 Sept 21, 1999; Pacurib v. Villacruz N.Y.L.J. 32 c. 4 Dec 6, 1999; Mingman Acupuncture Services, P.C. v. American Transit Insurance Co. Misc. 2d N.Y.S.2d 1999; McClester v. New York City Health and Hospitals Corp. N.Y.L.J. 25 c. 6 Dec 30, 1999; Marte v. City of New York N.Y.L.J. 32 c. 4 Dec 6, 1999; and Cameron v. Greens N.Y.L.J. 30 c. 6 Jan 13, 2000. Arbitrator American Arbitration Association 1970-98. Panel Member Medical Malpractice Mediation Panel New York Supreme Court Twelfth Judicial District 1977-89. Commissioner Law Revision Commission 1984-86. Member Columbian Lawyers Association, Justinian Law Society and Bronx County Bar Association (Former Director). Attended Annual Judicial Seminars Office of Court Administration. Lieutenant USAF 1955-57. Counsel to Assemblyman Alexander Chananau 1969-70, Assemblyman George Friedman 1994-95, Senator Martin Connor 1995-96 and Assemblyman Roberto Ramirez 1997-98. Founder and Former Member Belmont-Arthur Avenue Local Development Corporation. Former Member Bronx County Community Planning Board No. 6 and Belmont Civic Association.
Office: 851 Grand Concourse, Bronx 10451.
Telephone: (718) 590-3837.
Fax: (718) 590-8914

VILLEGAS, George R. *(Judge, The Civil Court of the City of New York)*
Office: 851 Grand Concourse, Bronx 10451.
Telephone: (718) 590-3601.

VIOLANTE, Mark Anthony *(Chief Judge, Niagara Falls City Court)* Appointed by Mayor O'Laughlin to term beginning Dec 1986. Elected 1987, 1993 and 1995. Current term expires Dec 31, 2005. Chief Judge since Dec 13, 1995. Acting Judge, Niagara County Court since Feb 2000. Born Niagara Falls New York Jan 22, 1951. Roman Catholic. Educated at John Carroll University B.A. 1973 and South Texas College of Law J.D. 1977. Editor-in-Chief South Texas Law Journal 1976. Member Order of Lytae. Admitted to practice New York 1977. In legal practice Niagara Falls Aug 1977 to Dec 1995.
Assistant Corporation Counsel Aug 16, 1977 to June 9, 1983 and Former Corporation Counsel Niagara Falls. Special Assistant District Attorney for Appellate Practice 1980, Assistant Public Defender June 9, 1983 to Dec 1986 and Former Public Defender Niagara County. Adjunct Professor Niagara University Fall 1979 to 1981 and Fall 1988, Niagara County Community College Spring 1995 and "A Critical Look at Therapeutic Diversionary Courts: Drug Rehabilitation Courts and Domestic Violence Courts" State University of New York at Buffalo Spring 2001 and 2002. Chairman and Supervising Judge Planning Committee Niagara Falls Drug Court

VIOLANTE, MARK ANTHONY—*Continued*

1996. Organizational Member National Association of Drug Court Professionals 1996-97. Supervising Judge Coalition and Planning Committee Niagara Falls Domestic Violence Court 1997. Member Domestic Violence Fatality Review Commission Niagara County 1998. Former Member The Association of Trial Lawyers of America and Erie County Bar Association. Member New York State Association of City Court Judges, American Justinian Society of Jurists and Niagara Falls Bar Association (Board of Directors 1980, President 1985, Member 1985-87 and Chairman Grievance Committee).

Faculty Member "Attending a Revolution: Building Program Evaluation and Domestic Violence Intervention Strategies from the Ground Up by Utilizing Existing Community Resources" Family Violence Research: An International Conference University of New Hampshire July 1998, "Collaboration for Effective Case Management" Nov 1998 and "Developing Linkages for Vocational, Educational and Employment Opportunities for Drug Court Participants" Dec 1999 New York Association of Drug Treatment Court Professionals, "Drug Courts: Sharing Resources in Multi-jurisdictional Courts" National Association of Drug Court Professionals June 1999 and "The Changing Face of Criminal Justice: Domestic Violence Courts—Issues and Updates" New York Association for Alternative Sentencing Programs April 2000. Attended "Comprehensive Drug Court Judicial Training" The National Drug Court Institute Georgetown Law Center March 1999. Participant Domestic Violence Roundtable New York State Unified Court System and Center for Court Innovation Nov 2001. Board of Directors Niagara Chapter National Conference of Christians and Jews 1988, Family and Children's Service of Niagara 1988 and Horizon Health Services, Inc. 1997. Volunteer Catholic Worker 1996-97.

Office: Public Safety Building, 520 Hyde Park Boulevard, Niagara Falls 14302-2725.
Telephone: (716) 278-9820.
Fax: (716) 278-9809
E-mail address: maviolan@courts.state.ny.us

VISITACION-LEWIS, Laura *(Justice, New York Supreme Court First Judicial District)* Former Judge, The Criminal Court of the City of New York, appointed by mayor.

Office: 60 Centre Street, New York 10007.
Telephone: (212) 374-8364.
E-mail address: lvlewis@courts.state.ny.us

VITALIANO, Eric N. *(Judge, The Civil Court of the City of New York)*

Office: 927 Castleton Avenue, West New Brighton, Staten Island 10310.
Telephone: (718) 390-5428.
Fax: (718) 390-8108

WALDON, Alton R., Jr. *(Judge, New York Court of Claims)* Appointed by Governor George E. Pataki to term beginning Jan 10, 2000. Born Lakeland Florida Dec 21, 1936. Catholic. Educated at John Jay College of Criminal Justice B.S. 1968 and New York Law School J.D. 1973. Member Sigma Pi Phi. Admitted to practice New York 1974. In legal practice New York City 1975-2000.

Member American Judges Association, Macon B. Allen Bar Association, New York State and American Bar Associations. Former Member 33rd District New York State Assembly and 10th District New York State Senate. Former Member 6th District U.S. House of Representatives. Former Commissioner of Investigation New York State. Former Deputy Commissioner of Human Rights. 33° Mason. Enjoys sports and music. Personal Statement or Quote: "The only way to keep up is to stay ahead."

Office: 26 Broadway, New York 10004.
Telephone: (212) 361-8140.
Fax: (212) 361-8143

WALKER, Edgar G. *(Judge, The Civil Court of the City of New York)* Formerly assigned to The Criminal Court of the City of New York.

Office: 89-17 Sutphin Boulevard, Jamaica 11435.
Telephone: (718) 262-7385.

WALKER, Sam D. *(Judge, Westchester County Court)* Former Judge and Acting Judge, Mount Vernon City Court.

Office: 111 Dr. Martin Luther King Jr. Blvd., White Plains 10601.
Telephone: (914) 995-3824.

WALL, William D. *(Magistrate Judge, United States District Court Eastern District of New York)* Appointed by U.S. District Court judges to term beginning June 1, 2000. Educated at Rutgers University A.B. 1971 and Fordham University J.D. 1977. In legal practice New York 1979-2000.

Office: Long Island Federal Courthouse, 100 Federal Plaza, Central Islip 11722.
Telephone: (631) 712-5720.

WALLACH, Richard W. *(Associate Justice, New York Supreme Court Appellate Division First Judicial Department)* Elected Justice to term beginning Jan 1, 1977. Reelected 1990. Appointed Associate Justice Appellate Division by Governor Mario Cuomo to term beginning 1986. Reappointed by Governors Mario Cuomo and George E. Pataki. Certificated. Born New York New York Sept 16, 1927. Jewish. Educated at Harvard University A.B. magna cum laude 1949 LL.B. 1952. Member Phi Beta Kappa. Admitted to practice New York 1952, U.S. Tax Court 1959 and U.S. Supreme Court 1969. Began legal practice New York City 1952. Judge, The Civil Court of the City of New York 1970-76.

Author "Johnson and Boswell, Treasure House of the Law" New York State B. Jour. 1973, "The Living Corpse" (Evidence Law Critique) Trial Lawyers Quarterly 1974, "The Application of Judicial Discretion" New York L. Jour. 1978 and "Marshaling Evidence in a Criminal Case" New York L. Jour. 1978. Important Decision: Matter of Goldstick 177 A.D.2d 225, 1992. Adjunct Professor Fordham University School of Law 1975-84. Chairman National Conference of Special Court Judges American Bar Association 1976. Member The Association of the Bar of the City of New York (Ethics Committee 1972-75). Faculty National College of the State Judiciary 1973 and since 1976. Staff Sergeant USAR JAGC 1951-54. Political party affiliation: Democrat, Liberal. Interested in eighteenth century literature. Enjoys tennis.

Office: 27 Madison Avenue at 25th Street, New York 10010.
Telephone: (212) 340-0461.

WALSH, John P. *(Judge, The Criminal Court of the City of New York)* Appointed by mayor. Currently

WALSH, JOHN P.—*Continued*

serves as Supervising Judge Arraignment Parts. Also serves as Acting Justice, New York Supreme Court First Judicial District.

Office: 100 Centre Street, New York 10013.

Telephone: (212) 374-7171.

WALSH, Thomas C. *(Judge, Johnstown City Court)*

Office: 105 City Hall, 33-41 East Main Street, Johnstown 12095.

Telephone: (518) 762-0007.

Fax: (518) 762-2720

WALSH, William D. *(Judge, Onondaga County Court)*

Office: Onondaga County Courthouse, 401 Montgomery Street, Syracuse 13202.

Telephone: (315) 671-1056.

Fax: (315) 671-1176

WALTROUS, Dolores L. *(Judge, The Civil Court of the City of New York)*

Office: 141 Livingston Street, Brooklyn 11201.

Telephone: (718) 643-8826.

Fax: (718) 643-3733

WARD, John T. *(Judge, Chautauqua County Court)*

Mailing address: P.O. Box 292, Mayville 14757-0292.

Office: Courthouse, One North Erie Street, Mayville 14757.

Telephone: (716) 753-4347.

Fax: (716) 753-4993

WARD, Laura A. *(Judge, The Criminal Court of the City of New York)* Appointed by Mayor Rudolph Giuliani. Currently serves as Acting Justice, New York Supreme Court First Judicial District.

Office: 100 Centre Street, New York 10013.

Telephone: (212) 374-6216.

Fax: (212) 374-2579

WARD, Robert J. *(Senior Judge, United States District Court Southern District of New York)* Appointed for life by President Richard M. Nixon to term beginning 1972. Assumed Senior status Feb 1, 1991, serves by assignment. Born New York New York Jan 31, 1926. Educated at Harvard University S.B. 1945 LL.B. 1949. Admitted to practice New York 1949. In legal practice New York City 1949-51 and 1961-72.

Assistant District Attorney New York County 1951-55. Assistant U.S. Attorney Southern District of New York 1956-61. Member The Association of the Bar of the City of New York and New York State Bar Association. USNR 1944-46.

Office: U.S. Courthouse, 40 Centre Street, New York 10007-1581.

Telephone: (212) 805-6145.

WARREN, William P. *(Judge, Rockland County Family Court)*

Office: One South Main Street, Suite 300, New City 10956.

Telephone: (845) 638-5327.

WARSHAWSKY, Ira B. *(Justice, New York Supreme Court Tenth Judicial District)* Elected Nov 1997 to term beginning Jan 1, 1998. Term expires Dec 31, 2011. Born Newark New Jersey April 4, 1945. Jewish. Educated at Rutgers University B.A. 1966 and Brooklyn Law School J.D. 1969. Admitted to practice New York 1970, U.S. Court of Appeals for the Armed Forces, U.S. Court of Federal Claims, U.S. District Court Eastern District of New York, U.S. Court of Appeals Federal Circuit and U.S. Supreme Court. Judge, Nassau County District Court 1987-97.

Deputy Bureau Chief Legal Aid Society 1970-72. Assistant District Attorney Nassau County 1972-74. Past President Nassau County District Court Judges Association and Former Assistant District Attorneys' Association. Member Theodore Roosevelt American Inn of Court, Jewish Lawyers Association, Bar Association of Nassau County (Chair Community Relations Committee 1993-95, Dean Nassau Academy of Law 1995-97, Board of Directors 1995-98 and since 2001), New York State (Former Chair County Court Committee) and American (Judicial Division, Section of Criminal Justice) Bar Associations. Instructor National Institute for Trial Advocacy Hofstra University School of Law 1995-2002 and Widener University School of Law 1996-2001. Attended and Lectured New York State Judicial Seminars Office of Court Administration. Lecturer on Ethics and Criminal Law Nassau Academy of Law. Named Humanitarian of the Year by Educational and Assistance Corporation 1996. Recipient President's Award from Bar Association of Nassau County 1997. Republican. Past President Community Reform Temple of Westbury and East Meadow Jewish Community Relations Council. Past Regional President Long Island and National First Vice President North American Federation of Temple Brotherhoods. Merit Badge Counselor Nassau County Boy Scouts. Member Rutgers University Mentor Program. Enjoys reading and golfing.

Office: Supreme Court Building, 100 Supreme Court Drive, Mineola 11501.

Telephone: (516) 571-3351.

Fax: (516) 571-0163

E-mail address: iwarshaw@courts.state.ny.us

WASHINGTON, Rosanna H. *(Judge, White Plains City Court)* Former Acting Judge.

Office: 77 South Lexington Avenue, White Plains 10601.

Telephone: (914) 422-6048.

Fax: (914) 422-6058

WATSON, William J. *(Judge, Lockport City Court)*

Office: Municipal Building, One Locks Plaza, Lockport 14094.

Telephone: (716) 439-6684.

Fax: (716) 439-6684

WEBBER, Troy K. *(Justice, New York Supreme Court First Judicial District)* Former Acting Justice Twelfth Judicial District. Former Judge, The Civil Court of the City of New York.

Office: 851 Grand Concourse, Bronx 10451.

Telephone: (718) 590-8932.

WEBER, Gary J. *(Judge, Suffolk County Court)* Elected Nov 1992 to term beginning Jan 1, 1993. Reelected Nov 2002, current term expires Dec 31, 2012. Also serves as Acting Surrogate, Suffolk County Surrogate's Court. Born Huntington New York Aug 14, 1944. Roman Catholic. Educated at Syracuse University Bachelor degree cum laude 1966 J.D. 1968 and New York University School of Law LL.M. in Criminal Justice 1976. Admitted to practice New York 1968, Florida 1970 and U.S. District Courts Eastern 1980 and South-

WEBER, GARY J.—*Continued*
ern 1980 Districts of New York. In legal practice Quogue 1975-80 and Westhampton Beach 1980-93.

Assistant District Attorney Suffolk County 1970-75. Member Suffolk County Criminal Bar, Suffolk County, New York State and American Bar Associations. Republican.

Mailing address: P.O. Box 9007, Riverhead 11901-9007.

Office: Court Complex, 210 Center Drive, Riverhead 11901.

Telephone: (631) 852-2176.

Fax: (631) 852-3857

WEINBERG, Claire I. *(Judge, Nassau County Court)* Former Judge, Nassau County District Court.

Office: County Courthouse, 262 Old Country Road, Mineola 11501.

Telephone: (516) 571-2628.

Fax: (516) 571-2160

E-mail address: cweinber@courts.state.ny.us

WEINBERG, Richard M. *(Judge, The Criminal Court of the City of New York)* Appointed by mayor.

Office: 100 Centre Street, New York 10013.

Telephone: (212) 374-5893.

WEINER, Alfred J. *(Surrogate, Rockland County Surrogate's Court)* Currently serves as Acting Justice, New York Supreme Court Ninth Judicial District.

Office: One South Main Street, Suite 270, New City 10956.

Telephone: (845) 638-5365.

Fax: (845) 638-5944

WEINSTEIN, Jack B. *(Senior Judge, United States District Court Eastern District of New York)* Appointed for life by President Lyndon B. Johnson to term beginning April 15, 1967. Assumed Senior status, serves by assignment. Born Wichita Kansas Aug 10, 1921. Religious affiliation: Hebrew. Educated at Brooklyn College of the City University of New York B.A. 1943 and Columbia University LL.B. 1948. Law Clerk to Hon. Stanley H. Fuld, New York Court of Appeals 1949-50. Admitted to practice New York 1949.

County Attorney Nassau County 1963-65. Author "Morgan's Basic Problems of Evidence" 1975 and "Advisory Opinions and Rule-Making Power" The Ohio State University Lecture Spring 1976. Co-author "Cases and Materials on Evidence" 1957, "Cases and Materials on Civil Procedure" 1961, *New York Civil Practice* (ten volumes) 1963, *Manual of CPLR* 1967 and *Weinstein's Evidence* (six volumes) 1975. Author numerous articles for bar association and legal journals. Professor of Law 1952-67 and Adjunct Professor since 1967 Columbia University. Reporter and Consultant on Practice and Procedure New York State Temporary Commission on Courts 1955-58. Representative First Judicial Department Advisory Committee on Civil Procedure New York Judicial Conference 1962-66. Draftsman State Credit Crime Act 1966 and Interstate and International Procedure Act. Chairman Board of Directors Nassau County Law Services Committee 1966. Member Advisory Committee on Rules of Evidence for Committee of Practice and Procedure 1965-75 and Subcommittee on Federal Jurisdiction Committee on Court Administration 1969-75 Judicial Conference of the U.S., Special Committee on Individual Assignment System U.S. District Courts Eastern District of New York 1967, Panel Annual Judicial Conference 1971 (Chairman) and Committee on Pro Se Prisoner Proceedings 1971 Second Circuit, Special Advisory Committee to Chief Justice on Problems Relating to Civil Litigation 1971 and National Conference of the Judiciary Williamsburg Virginia 1971. Member International Association of Jewish Lawyers and Jurists, National Legal Aid and Defenders Association, Society of American Law Teachers, Society of Public Teachers of Law (England), Institute for Judicial Administration, American Judicature Society, The American Law Institute, The Association of the Bar of the City of New York, Bar Association of Nassau County, New York State and American Bar Associations.

Lieutenant USNR 1942-46. Special Counsel New York Joint Legislative Committee on Motor Vehicle Problems 1952-54. Research Assistant State Senate New York 1952-54. Board of Governors Law Affiliates of Brooklyn College Alumni Association 1975. Board of Directors CARE 1986-87 and United Jewish Appeal Federation 1986-94. Member New York City Advisory Narcotics Council 1960-62, New York State Commission on the Revision and Simplification of the Constitution and Commission to Prepare for a Constitutional Convention 1966 (Commissioner), Police Science Advisory Committee State University Technical and Agricultural College Farmingdale 1967, Jewish Communal Affairs Commission American Jewish Committee 1973, American Association of University Professors, Lay Board Riverside Hospital for Adolescent Drug Users (Chairman 1954-56), Temple Emanuel of Great Neck and American Academy of Arts and Sciences.

Office: U.S. Courthouse, 225 Cadman Plaza East, Brooklyn 11201.

Telephone: (718) 260-2520.

WEINSTEIN, Jeremy S. *(Justice, New York Supreme Court Eleventh Judicial District)* Former Acting Justice. Also serves as Supervising Judge, The Civil Court of the City of New York. Former Judge, The Civil Court of the City of New York. Former Judge-in-Charge Queens County.

Office: 89-17 Sutphin Boulevard, Jamaica 11435.

Telephone: (718) 262-7333.

WEINSTEIN, Stewart H. *(Judge, New York City Family Court)* Appointed by mayor.

Office: 283 Adams Street, Sixth Floor, Brooklyn 11201.

Telephone: (718) 643-4546.

Fax: (718) 643-5103

WEISS, Allan B. *(Justice, New York Supreme Court Eleventh Judicial District)* Former Judge, The Civil Court of the City of New York, elected to term beginning Jan 1, 1995.

Office: 88-11 Sutphin Boulevard, Jamaica 11435.

Telephone: (718) 520-3755.

WELLS, Peter N. *(Surrogate, Onondaga County Surrogate's Court)* Elected to term beginning Jan 1, 1989. Reelected 1998, current term expires Dec 31, 2008.

Office: Onondaga County Courthouse, 401 Montgomery Street, Syracuse 13202-2173.

Telephone: (315) 671-2098.

Fax: (315) 671-1162

WENDT, David R. *(Judge, Lockport City Court)* Former Acting Judge.

Office: Municipal Building, One Locks Plaza, Lockport 14094.

Telephone: (716) 439-6684.

Fax: (716) 439-6684

WERNER, Mary M. *(Justice, New York Supreme Court Tenth Judicial District)* Appointed by Governor Mario Cuomo June 9, 1991. Elected Nov 1991. Term expires Dec 31, 2005. Administrative Judge Suffolk County Feb 1994 to Jan 1999. Educated at St. John's University Teachers College 1951-54, Dowling College B.A. in Humanities 1974 and St. John's University School of Law J.D. 1977. Admitted to practice New York 1978, U.S. District Courts Eastern 1979 and Southern 1979 Districts of New York and U.S. Supreme Court 1981.

Assistant District Attorney Suffolk County Sept 1977 to June 1991 (Deputy Bureau Chief and Assistant District Attorney Rackets Bureau March 1979 to Aug 1987, Special Assignment to New York State Organized Crime Task Force Aug 1983 to Oct 1984, Bureau Chief Family Crime Bureau Aug 1987 to June 1991). Contributor *Treatise on Child Abuse for Physicians* by Dr. Milton Gordon and *Handbook on Domestic Violence* and *Practicum Handbook on Criminal Law* Suffolk County Bar Association. Past President Suffolk County Women's Bar Association. Former Director Suffolk County Criminal Bar Association. Former Officer Suffolk Academy of Law. Former Member New York State Advisory Committee on Criminal Procedure. Director Alexander Hamilton Inns of Court and New York State Association of Women Judges. Member Suffolk County (Former Director, Member Nominating Committee 1995-97) and New York State Bar Associations. Moderator, Panelist and Lecturer for numerous programs on child abuse, domestic violence, criminal law and trial advocacy Suffolk Academy of Law, Suffolk County Medical Society and Suffolk County Bar Association as well as various other professional and civic organizations. Recipient Humanitarian Award from Education and Assistance Corporation, Award from Long Island Women's Coalition, Award from Victim's Information Bureau of Suffolk County, Certificate of Merit from Governor Mario Cuomo, Citations from Suffolk County Bar Association, Certificates of Distinguished Merit from Suffolk Academy of Law, Award from Drug Enforcement Administration U.S. Department of Justice and Child Abuse and Family Violence Professional Award. Former Director St. John's University School of Law Alumni Association. Former Chairperson Child Abuse Task Force. Former Member Suffolk County Task Force on Family Violence. Director Cleary School for the Deaf. Member New York State Family Violence Task Force.

Office: Court Complex, 210 Center Drive, Riverhead 11901.

Telephone: (631) 852-2157.

Fax: (631) 852-2156

WESLEY, Richard C. *(Associate Judge, New York Court of Appeals)* Appointed by governor. Born Canandaigua New York Aug 1, 1949. Educated at State University of New York at Albany B.A. with honors 1971 and Cornell Law School J.D. 1974. Associate Editor Cornell Law Review 1973-74. Admitted to practice New York 1974. In legal practice Rochester 1974-76 and Geneseo 1976-86. Former Justice New York Supreme Court Seventh Judicial District, elected to term beginning Jan 1, 1987. Former Associate Justice, New York Supreme Court Appellate Division Fourth Judicial Department.

Author "Recent Developments in Welfare Law" 87 No. 5 Cornell L. Rev. Important Decisions: Application of Dohring 537 N.Y.S.2d 767, 142 Misc. 2d 429, 1989; Spose v. Ragu Foods, Inc. 537 N.Y.S.2d 739, 142 Misc. 2d 366, 1989; Matter of Subaru of America v. McKelvey 532 N.Y.S.2d 617, 141 Misc. 2d 41, 1988; Huebner v. Caldwell & Cook, Inc. 526 N.Y.S.2d 356, 139 Misc. 2d 288, 1988; Samper v. University of Rochester et al. 528 N.Y.S. 958, 139 Misc. 2d 580, aff'd and modified 144 A.D.2d 940-941, 1988, aff'd 144 A.D.2d 1046-1047, 1988; Blanco v. American Telephone & Telegraph Company (product liability rep.) 1997 WL 729116 CCH P 15, 116 NY Nov 25, 1997; Park Slope Jewish Center v. Congregation B'nai Jacob 90 N.Y.2d 517, 686 N.E.2d 1330; Rudolph Steiner Fellowship Foundation v. De Luccia 90 N.Y.2d 453, 685 N.E.2d 192; Matter of Liquidation of New York Agency and Other Assets of Bank of Credit and Commerce Intern., S.A. 90 N.Y.2d 410, 683 N.E.2d 756; Buckley v. National Freight, Inc. 90 N.Y.2d 210, 681, N.E.2d 1287; Itri Brick & Concrete Corp. v. Aetna Casualty & Surety Co., 89 N.Y.2d 786, 680 N.E.2d 1200; People v. Wilson 89 N.Y.2d 754, 680 N.E.2d 598; People v. Vasquez 89 N.Y.2d 521, 678 N.E.2d 482; People v. Burdo 1997 WL 677307 NY Oct 30, 1997; Anello v. Zoning Board of Appeals of the Village of Dobbs Ferry 89 N.Y.2d 535, 678 N.E.2d 870; Di Ponzio v. Riordan 224 A.D.2d 139; Nuzzo v. Griffin Technology, Inc. 222 A.D.2d 184, Doty v. Navistar Intern. Transp. Corp. 219 A.D.2d 32; Caruso v. Russell P. LeFrois Builders, Inc. 217 A.D.2d 256; People by Abrams v. Oliver Schools, Inc. 206 A.D.2d 143; People v. Buie 201 A.D.2d 156; People v. Herner 156 Misc. 2d 735; and Schwartz v. Hudacs 149 Misc. 2d 1024. Vice President Seventh Judicial District Supreme Court Justices Association. Member Monroe County Bench/Bar Committee, Association of Justices of the Supreme Court of the State of New York, Livingston County, Monroe County and Ontario County Bar Associations. Lecturer and Faculty Member judicial seminar July 1989. Member Curriculum Committee judicial seminar July 1990. Lecturer on "Deposition Practice and Practicalities in State and Federal Courts" New York State Bar Association Nov 1990. Named Legislator of the Year by Livingston-Wyoming ARC 1985. Recipient Distinguished Service Award from United University Professors 1985. Republican. Counsel to James Emery Minority Leader New York State Assembly 1979-82. New York State Assemblyman 1983-86. Board of Directors Myers' Memorial Foundation and Center for Dispute Settlement. Enjoys skiing, jogging, coaching boys and girls soccer and baseball, playing golf, traveling and reading.

Office: Livingston County Government Center, Six Court Street, Geneseo 14454-1030.

Telephone: (585) 243-7910.

Office: Court of Appeals Hall, 20 Eagle Street, Albany 12207.

Telephone: (518) 455-7736.

WEST, Joseph K. *(Justice, New York Supreme Court Ninth Judicial District)* Appointed by Governor George E. Pataki to term beginning May 1999. Certificated. Born Yonkers New York Sept 11, 1929. Methodist. Educated at Howard University B.S. 1952 and Brooklyn

WEST, JOSEPH K.—*Continued*
Law School J.D. 1961. Member Alpha Phi Alpha. Admitted to practice New York 1962, U.S. Supreme Court 1967 and U.S. District Court Southern District of New York 1973. Began legal practice Yonkers 1962. Judge, Yonkers City Court 1983-84. Judge, Westchester County Court Jan 1985 to May 1999. Supervising Judge, Criminal Courts Ninth Judicial District Jan 1991 to Dec 1995.

Former Deputy District Attorney and Chief of Superior Court Trial Bureau. Member Yonkers Lawyers Association and Westchester County Bar Association. First Lieutenant U.S. Army 1952-56. Graduate Artillery Officer's Candidate School March 1954. Republican. Board of Directors Saint Joseph's Hospital, Westchester Community Opportunity Program and Yonkers Big Brothers/ Big Sisters. Member Ludlow Park Homeowner's Association, NAACP and Institutional African Methodist Episcopal Zion Church. Enjoys travel and sports.

Office: Courthouse, 111 Dr. Martin Luther King Jr. Blvd., White Plains 10601.
Telephone: (914) 995-4305.
E-mail address: jwest@courts.state.ny.us

WETZEL, William A. *(Judge, New York Court of Claims)* Appointed by Governor George E. Pataki. Currently serves as Acting Justice, New York Supreme Court First Judicial District.

Office: 111 Centre Street, New York 10013.
Telephone: (212) 374-8007.
Fax: (212) 748-5922

WEXLER, Leonard D. *(Senior Judge, United States District Court Eastern District of New York)* Appointed for life by President Ronald Reagan to term beginning June 23, 1983. Assumed Senior status, serves by assignment. Born Brooklyn New York Nov 11, 1924. Educated at Indiana University B.S. 1947 and New York University J.D. 1950. Admitted to practice New York 1951, U.S. District Court District of New York 1956 and U.S. Supreme Court 1959. Began legal practice Suffolk County 1951.

Important Decisions: Baby Jane Doe 1983, Roache v. Bolar (patent) 1984, King & Brown v. County of Nassau (peremptory challenges) 1984 and Fonar v. General Electric and Hitachi (MRI patent) 1992. Chartered Suffolk County Criminal Bar Association 1964. Private U.S. Army Tank Destroyer 1943-45. Attorney Suffolk County Republican Party 1977-83. Judge-in-Charge planning and construction of Long Island Federal Courthouse. Enjoys sailing and touring foreign countries.

Office: Long Island Federal Courthouse, 100 Federal Plaza, Central Islip 11722-4438.
Telephone: (631) 712-5640.

WEXNER, Ira H. *(Justice, New York Supreme Court Tenth Judicial District)* Certificated. Currently serves as Acting Judge, Nassau County Court. Born Brooklyn New York March 15, 1929. Religious affiliation: Hebrew. Educated at University of Miami B.B.A. 1951 J.D. 1953. Member Tau Epsilon Rho and Phi Sigma Delta. Admitted to practice Florida 1953 and New York 1954. Began legal practice New York City 1954. Judge, Nassau County District Court 1984-87. Former Judge, Nassau County Court, elected to term beginning Jan 1, 1988.

Member Bar Association of Nassau County, The Florida Bar and Brooklyn Bar Association. Private First Class U.S. Army 1946-48. Legislative Counsel to State Assemblyman New York 1968-71. Member Nassau County Cerebral Palsy Association. Past Chancellor Commander Knights of Pythias. Member Jewish War Veterans and Disabled American Veterans. Enjoys tennis, travel, reading and sports.

Office: County Courthouse, 262 Old Country Road, Mineola 11501.
Telephone: (516) 571-2797.
Fax: (516) 571-1485

WHELAN, Robert E. *(Justice, New York Supreme Court Eighth Judicial District)*

Office: 50 Delaware Avenue, Ninth Floor, Buffalo 14202.
Telephone: (716) 851-3421.
Fax: (716) 851-3324
E-mail address: rwhelan@courts.state.ny.us

WHELAN, Thomas F. *(Justice, New York Supreme Court Tenth Judicial District)*

Office: 102 Supreme Court Building, 235 Griffing Avenue, Riverhead 11901.
Telephone: (631) 852-2375.
Fax: (631) 852-3550

WHITE, Renee Allyn *(Judge, The Criminal Court of the City of New York)* Appointed by Mayor Edward Koch to term beginning Jan 25, 1985. Reappointed to subsequent term. Supervising Judge New York County Branch 1987-89. Acting Justice, New York Supreme Court First Judicial District since Jan 1, 1988. Born Bronx New York Sept 22, 1945. Educated at Hofstra University B.A. 1966 and Brooklyn Law School J.D. 1969. Admitted to practice New York 1969, U.S. District Courts Southern 1977 and Eastern 1977 Districts of New York and U.S. Supreme Court 1978. Began legal practice New York City 1969. Administrative Law Judge, New York City 1978-84. Judge, The Civil Court of the City of New York June 1984 to Jan 1985.

Trial Attorney Family Court Division Aug 1969 to March 1970 and Criminal Defense Division March 1970 to May 1974 New York City Legal Aid Society. Attorney-in-Charge Criminal Justice Section Indigent Defendants Legal Panel New York Supreme Court Appellate Division First Judicial Department May 1974 to Oct 1978. Editor 1975-77, Co-Editor 1980 and Author *Criminal Trial Advocacy* New York Supreme Court Appellate Division First Judicial Department. Author "Trial Preparation and Voir Dire Techniques—A Defense View" *Basic Criminal Practice* New York State Bar Association 1978, 1979, 1980 and 1983. Co-author "Avoiding Malpractice in Criminal Law" *New York Practice Manual* New York State Bar Association 1980. Important Decisions: People v. Barnwell 143 Misc. 2d 922, 1989 and People v. Pantaleo 141 Misc. 2d 251, 1988. Adjunct Instructor in Appellate Advocacy Delaware Law School 1974. Member The Association of the Bar of the City of New York (Committee on Criminal Justice Operations and Budget 1984-87, Committee on Criminal Courts 1984-87, Council on Judicial Administration 1990-93), New York Women's and New York State (Secretary 1981-83, Vice Chair 1983-85, and Chair 1985-87 Criminal Justice Section, Member House of Delegates 1985-88 and 1991-94, Member 1988 and Chair 1992-96 Special Committee on AIDS and the Law, Nominating Committee 1989 and 1990, Task Force on Court Reorganization since 1997) Bar Associations. Teaching Assistant in Trial Advocacy Practising Law Institute 1976-78. Chairperson "Handling Offenses in Lo-

WHITE, RENEE ALLYN—*Continued*

cal Criminal Court" Oct 30, 1981 and "The Prosecution, Defense and Judicial View of the Trial of a Felony Case" June 1983 New York State Bar Association Continuing Legal Education Program. Listed in *Who's Who in American Law, Who's Who in the East, Who's Who of American Women, Who's Who in America* and *Who's Who in the World.* Enjoys travel, jazz and the theatre.

Office: 100 Centre Street, New York 10013.
Telephone: (212) 374-7148.

WILKINS, Lottie E. *(Justice, New York Supreme Court First Judicial District)* Former Judge, The Civil Court of the City of New York.

Office: 71 Thomas Street, New York 10013.
Telephone: (212) 815-0850.
Fax: (212) 815-0892

WILLIAMS, Betty J. *(Judge, The Civil Court of the City of New York)*

Office: 120 Schermerhorn Street, Brooklyn 11201.
Telephone: (718) 643-8400.
Fax: (718) 643-3538

WILLIAMS, Frank B. *(Justice, New York Supreme Court Fourth Judicial District)* Former Judge, Saratoga County Court.

Office: 201 Supreme Court Chambers, 433 Broadway, Saratoga Springs 12866.
Telephone: (518) 581-9454.

WILLIAMS, Milton L. *(Associate Justice, New York Supreme Court Appellate Division First Judicial Department)* Acting Justice 1978-84. Elected Justice First Judicial District to term beginning Jan 1, 1985. Appointed Associate Justice Appellate Division by governor. Certificated. Administrative Judge, New York Supreme Court First Judicial District Criminal Term 1983-85. Deputy Chief Administrative Judge New York City Courts since 1985. Presiding Justice March 2002 to Dec 2002. Born Augusta Georgia Nov 14, 1932. Roman Catholic. Educated at New York University B.S. 1960 and New York Law School LL.B. 1963. Awarded honorary LL.D. New York Law School, St. John's University and Long Island University. Recipient American Jurisprudence Award in Constitutional Law. Member Sigma Pi Phi. Admitted to practice New York 1965, U.S. District Courts Eastern 1965 and Southern 1965 Districts of New York, U.S. Supreme Court 1968 and U.S. Customs Court 1971 (now U.S. Court of International Trade). Began legal practice New York 1965. Judge 1977-84 and Supervising Judge New York County 1978-79, The Criminal Court of the City of New York.

Staff Attorney Allstate Insurance Company May 1963 to Feb 1966. Trial Attorney Manhattan and Bronx Surface Transit Authority Feb 1966 to Sept 1966. Regional Counsel Small Business Administration Sept 1966 to May 1968. General Counsel and Director Hunts Point Legal Services May 1968 to June 1970. Associate General Counsel for the Commission to investigate allegations of police corruption and the city's anti-corruption procedures June 1970 to Oct 1971. Special Prosecutor New York City Civil Service Commission Oct 1971 to March 1974. Executive Director New York State Special Commission on Attica Jan 1972 to Sept 1972. Commissioner New York City Division of Veterans' Affairs 1974-77. Author "Evicting Drug Dealers" RAM Digest, National Association of Home Builders Spring 1991. Important Decisions: Nickels v. New York City Housing Authority 208 A.D.2d 203 aff'd 85 N.Y.2d 917; PSNY v. Anthony Leslie 232 A.D.2d 94 lv denied 91 N.Y.2d 875 cert denied 531 U.S. 1199 (Leslie v. Artuz); Johnson v. New York City Health and Hospitals Corp. 246 A.D.2d 88 lv denied 92 N.Y.2d 816; Hertz v. GEICO 250 A.D.2d 181 appeal dismissed 93 N.Y.2d 1040; Hirschfeld v. City of New York 253 A.D.2d 53 lv denied 93 N.Y.2d 814; PSNY v. Richard Wigfall 253 A.D.2d 80 lv denied 93 N.Y.2d 981; Manuel Cruz v. NYNEX 263 A.D.2d 285; PSNY v. Paul Rivera 257 A.D.2d 172 aff'd 94 N.Y.2d 908; Walter Scott v. Bell Atlantic 280 A.D.2d 180; and Lowinger v. Lowinger 733 A.D.2d 33.

Instructor New York Community College 1967-69. Adjunct Associate Professor John Jay College 1973-77. Adjunct Professor Manhattan Community College 1980-85. Member State Committee on Sentencing Guidelines 1983-86, Catholic Lawyers Guild (Former Secretary, former member Board of Governors), Harlem Lawyers Association (Former Board Member, Secretary and Vice President, Past President), New York County Lawyers' Association (Former Board Member) and The Association of the Bar of the City of New York. Attended Conference of New York State Trial Judges Summer 1978, Institute of Court Management Conferences 1979 and 1980, "Calendar Control and Management" and "Innovative Trends in the Expeditious Trial of Criminal Matters" L.E.A.A. conferences 1981-82, Courses on Judicial General Law Nov 1983 and Leadership for Chief and Presiding Judges April 1992 The National Judicial College, Workshop on Operation "Weed and Seed" U.S. Department of Justice San Diego California Oct 1992 and "The Criminal Justice System and the Public: Are They Communicating?" The Association of the Bar of the City of New York Criminal Justice Retreat. Recipient Charles Carrol Award from Catholic Lawyers Guild, Harlan Fiske Stone Award from New York State Trial Lawyers Association, Humanitarian Award and Judge Capozolli Award from New York County Lawyers' Association, Outstanding Achievement Award from Bronx Black Bar Association, Golda Meir Award from Jewish Lawyers Guild and Metropolitan Black Bar Association Award. Petty Officer (Radioman Second Class) USN 1951-55. Colonel New York State Guard JAGC. Police Officer New York City 1957-63. Democrat. Former Sponsor Executive Internship Program. Former Lecturer Central Labor Rehabilitation Council of New York, Inc. Former member Board of Directors U.S.O. Former member 100 Black Men. Board of Trustees St. Patrick's Cathedral, Catholic Charities of New York, Inner-City Scholarship Fund and St. John's University. Member American Association of the Sovereign Military Order of Malta, Bequests and Planned Gifts Committee New York Archdiocese, De Witt Clinton Alumni Association, New York Law School Alumni Association, NAACP and Urban League.

Office: 27 Madison Avenue at 25th Street, New York 10010.
Telephone: (212) 340-0430.
Fax: (212) 340-0554

WILLIAMS, Patricia Anne *(Judge, The Criminal Court of the City of New York)* Appointed by mayor. Currently serves as Acting Justice, New York Supreme Court Twelfth Judicial District.

Office: 851 Grand Concourse, Bronx 10451.

WILLIAMS, PATRICIA ANNE—*Continued*
Telephone: (718) 590-3792.
Fax: (718) 590-7837

WILSON, Daniel C. *(Judge, Rome City Court)* Elected to term beginning Jan 1, 1978. Reelected 1985 and 1993. Current term expires Dec 31, 2003. Born Rome New York Nov 8, 1946. Roman Catholic. Educated at St. Bonaventure University B.A. with honors 1967 and Cornell University J.D. 1970. Admitted to practice New York 1971 and U.S. District Court Northern District of New York 1978. Began legal practice Utica 1971. In legal practice Rome since 1976.

Assistant District Attorney Oneida County March 1971 to Oct 1976. First Assistant Corporation Counsel Oct 1976 to Dec 1976 and Corporation Counsel Jan 1977 to Dec 1977 City of Rome. Instructor in Criminal Justice Mohawk Valley Community College 1972-85. Former member American Bar Association and New York State District Attorneys Association. Past President Oneida County Magistrates Association and New York State Association of City Court Judges. Member Cornell Law Association, Oneida County and Rome Bar Associations. Named Rome Optimist Respect for Law Honoree of Year 1984. Recipient Silver Beaver Award from Boy Scouts of America 1990. Republican. Alternate Delegate Fifth Judicial District Convention 1971-77. Former Member Rome Chamber of Commerce. Former Board Member Rome Chapter American Red Cross. Past President Rome Catholic School Board. Former Director Alumni Association and Past President Parents Association Rome Catholic High School. Lector St. Paul's Church. Member Boy Scouts of America (District Chairman 1981-83, President Revolutionary Trails Council 2002-03), Rome Kiwanis Club (Executive Board and Stop D.W.I. Program), Rome Club (President Board of Governors 1985-86) and Elks Lodge 96 (Judicial Committee). Enjoys gardening. Interested in economics and government affairs.

Office: 100 West Court Street, Rome 13440.
Telephone: (315) 337-6440.
Fax: (315) 338-0343
E-mail address: dcwilson@courts.state.ny.us

WINICK, Allan L. *(Justice, New York Supreme Court Tenth Judicial District)* Elected to term beginning Jan 1, 1993. Certificated. Also serves as Justice, New York Supreme Court Appellate Term Ninth and Tenth Judicial Districts. Born Brooklyn New York 1927. Educated at New York University B.A. 1947 J.D. 1950. Staff member New York University Law Review. Member Beta Gamma Sigma. Admitted to practice New York 1950. Former Arbitrator, Nassau County District Court and The Civil Court of the City of New York. Judge, Nassau County Court 1982-92.

Member Bar Association of Nassau County, New York State and American Bar Associations. Lecturer New York State Bar Association, Bar Association of Nassau County and Adelphi University. Advisory Council Continuing Legal Education Panel for 18B Attorneys Nassau Academy of Law. Recipient Norman F. Lent Memorial Medal from the Criminal Courts Bar Association of Nassau County. USAS WWII. Deputy Commissioner Nassau County Board of Elections 1977-82. Former Counsel Nassau Democratic County Committee. Vice President and Director Masonic Brotherhood Foundation. Board of Directors Kiwanis Club of Peninsula and American Committee on Italian Migration. Member Hancock-Dirigo-Adelphi Lodge No. 23 (Master 1958) and Guiding Light Olympia Lodge No. 808 Masons (District Deputy Grand Master First Masonic District 1961 and Commissioner of Appeals Grand Lodge State of New York).

Office: Supreme Court Building, 100 Supreme Court Drive, Mineola 11501.
Telephone: (516) 571-2736.

WINSLOW, F. Dana *(Justice, New York Supreme Court Tenth Judicial District)* Elected Nov 1996 to term beginning Jan 1, 1997. Educated at American University B.A. 1966 and Catholic University of America J.D. 1969. Admitted to practice New York, U.S. District Courts Eastern and Southern Districts of New York, U.S. Court of Appeals Second Circuit and U.S. Supreme Court. In legal practice New York City 1969-73, Mineola 1973-78 and 1980-89 and Garden City 1979-80 and 1989-96. Justice, Old Westbury Village Justice Court 1991-96.

Prosecuting Attorney Roslyn Harbor 1983-85. Village Attorney Centre Island 1988-96. Legal Counsel and Advisor Tae Kwon Do World Cup Championship 1993. Special County Attorney Hamilton County 1995-96. Town Attorney Lake Pleasant 1995-96. Adjunct Professor Department of Business Law St. John's University 1998-2000. Chair Advisory Committee New York State Judicial Institute since 2000. Member Nassau County Magistrates Association (Director 1996), Association of Justices of the Supreme Court of the State of New York and New York State Association of Magistrates. Listed in *Who's Who in the World, Who's Who in America, Biographies of Distinguished Americans* and *Who's Who Among Lawyers.* Special Agent Military Intelligence U.S. Army 1962-65. Founding President and Chairperson Winslow Therapeutic Riding Unlimited, Ltd. since 1974 and Long Island Riding for the Handicapped, Inc. 1979-97. Founder and Chairperson Board of Directors Helping Hand Horse Show 1979-86. Director 1983-87 and Chairperson National Equestrian Sports Day 1986 North American Riding for the Handicapped Association. Board of Directors 1985-88 and President 1988 Glen Players.

Office: 100 Supreme Court Drive, Mineola 11501.
Telephone: (516) 571-2480.
Fax: (516) 571-0213
E-mail address: dwinslo1@yahoo.com

WISNER, Donald J. *(Associate Justice, New York Supreme Court Appellate Division Fourth Judicial Department)* Elected Justice Seventh Judicial District. Appointed Associate Justice Appellate Division by Governor George E. Pataki. Former Judge, Monroe County Court.

Office: Courthouse, 50 East Avenue, Rochester 14604.
Telephone: (585) 530-3230.
Fax: (585) 530-3245

WITTNER, Bonnie G. *(Judge, The Criminal Court of the City of New York)* Appointed by Mayor Edward Koch to term beginning July 14, 1983. Reappointed 1991 and 2001. Current term expires Dec 31, 2010. Currently serves as Acting Justice, New York Supreme Court First Judicial District. Born New York New York April 19, 1948. Educated at Wheaton College B.A. cum laude 1969, George Washington University 1969-70 and Boston College Law School J.D. 1972. Admitted to

WITTNER, BONNIE G.—*Continued*

practice New York 1973. Began legal practice New York City 1973.

With Legal Aid Society New York City 1972-77 and State Attorney General's Office 1977-83 (Deputy Bureau Chief Antitrust Bureau 1980-83). Member The Association of the Bar of the City of New York (Trade Regulation Committee), New York Women's and New York State Bar Associations. Board of Directors Wheaton College Alumnae Association. Member Wheaton College Sesquicentennial Advisory Committee.

Office: 100 Centre Street, New York 10013.
Telephone: (212) 394-5841.
Fax: (212) 748-5069
E-mail address: bwittner@courts.state.ny.us

WOLFGANG, Penny M. *(Justice, New York Supreme Court Eighth Judicial District)* Term expires Dec 31, 2013. Educated at Fairleigh Dickinson University B.A. in Political Science magna cum laude 1961, University of Michigan School of Law 1962 and New York University law degree 1964. Admitted to practice New York 1964. Began legal practice Buffalo 1964. Former Judge, Erie County Court, elected to term beginning Jan 1, 1979.

Former Attorney-in-Charge Appeals Division Legal Aid Bureau of Buffalo, Inc. Part-time faculty member State University of New York at Buffalo School of Law. Instructor Erie County Law Enforcement Training Academy. Member Bar Association of Erie County and New York State Bar Association. Board of Directors The Police and Judges Conference, Respect for Law Alliance and Buffalo Council on World Affairs. WKBW TV Public Service Series "The Law and You," WGRZ TV Public Service Series segment "Legal Grounds," WKBW radio program "The Penny Wolfgang Show" and Adelphia Cable TV Show on legal matters. Enjoys tennis and theatre.

Office: Erie County Hall, 92 Franklin Street, Buffalo 14202.
Telephone: (716) 851-3269.
Fax: (716) 851-3331
E-mail address: pwolfgang@courts.state.ny.us

WOLLMAN, Paul L. *(Judge, Amsterdam City Court)*
Office: 208 Public Safety Building, One Guy Park Avenue Extension, Amsterdam 12010.
Telephone: (518) 842-9510.
Fax: (518) 843-8474

WONG, Douglas S. *(Judge, The Criminal Court of the City of New York)* Appointed by mayor. Currently serves as Acting Justice, New York Supreme Court Eleventh Judicial District.

Office: 125-01 Queens Boulevard, Kew Gardens 11415.
Telephone: (718) 520-2221.

WOOD, Kimba M. *(Judge, United States District Court Southern District of New York)* Appointed for life by President Ronald Reagan April 20, 1988 to term beginning July 28, 1988. Born Port Townsend Washington Jan 2, 1944. Educated at Connecticut College B.A. 1965, London School of Economics and Political Science, England M.Sc. 1966 and Harvard Law School J.D. 1969. Admitted to practice District of Columbia 1969, U.S. District Courts Eastern 1974, Southern 1974 and Western 1981 Districts of New York, U.S. Court of Appeals Second Circuit 1975 and U.S. Supreme Court 1980. In legal practice District of Columbia 1969-71 and New York City 1971-88.

Member The American Law Institute, New York State (Chairman Antitrust Law Section 1983-84, Member House of Delegates 1984) and American (Judicial Representative Section of Antitrust Law 1989-91) Bar Associations.

Office: 1610 U.S. Courthouse, 500 Pearl Street, New York 10007-1312.
Telephone: (212) 805-0258.

WOODARD, Michele M. *(Justice, New York Supreme Court Tenth Judicial District)*
Office: Matrimonial Center, 400 County Seat Drive, Mineola 11501.
Telephone: (516) 571-0766.

WORK, Mary MacMaster *(Judge, Ulster County Family Court)*
Office: 16 Lucas Avenue, Kingston 12401-0906.
Telephone: (845) 340-3601.
Fax: (845) 340-3626
E-mail address: mwork@courts.state.ny.us

WRIGHT, Geoffrey D. *(Judge, The Civil Court of the City of New York)* Currently assigned to Family Court.

Office: 283 Adams Street, Sixth Floor, Brooklyn 11201.
Telephone: (718) 643-6274.
E-mail address: gdwright@courts.state.ny.us

YACKNIN, Ellen *(Judge, Rochester City Court)*
Office: Hall of Justice, 99 Exchange Boulevard, Rochester 14614.
Telephone: (585) 428-2444.

YANCEY, Virginia E. *(Justice, New York Supreme Court Second Judicial District)* Former Acting Justice. Former Judge, New York City Family Court, appointed by mayor.

Office: 360 Adams Street, Brooklyn 11201.
Telephone: (718) 643-5266.
E-mail address: vyancey@courts.state.ny.us

YANTHIS, George A. *(Magistrate Judge, United States District Court Southern District of New York)* Appointed by U.S. District Court judges.

Office: U.S. Courthouse, 300 Quarropas Street, White Plains 10601-4150.
Telephone: (914) 390-4088.

YATES, James A. *(Justice, New York Supreme Court First Judicial District)* Former Acting Justice. Former Judge, New York Court of Claims, appointed by governor.

Office: 100 Centre Street, New York 10013.
Telephone: (212) 374-4526.
Fax: (212) 374-0607
E-mail address: jyates@courts.state.ny.us

YORK, Louis B. *(Judge, The Civil Court of the City of New York)* Elected to term beginning Jan 1, 1987. Reelected 1996, current term expires Dec 31, 2006. Currently serves as Acting Justice, New York Supreme Court First Judicial District.

Office: 111 Centre Street, New York 10013.
Telephone: (212) 374-5658.

YOUNG, Kevin G. *(Judge, Syracuse City Court)* Elected Nov 7, 1995 to term beginning Jan 1, 1996. Term expires Dec 31, 2005. Born Syracuse New York March 10, 1951. Catholic. Educated at Syracuse University B.S. 1975 J.D. 1978. Admitted to practice New York 1983. In legal practice Syracuse 1984-95.

Assistant District Attorney Onondaga County 1988-95. Member Onondaga County Bar Association. Attended several CLE seminars, two judicial seminars and one computer seminar. Counsel to Speaker of New York Assembly 1984-90. Committee Member Onondaga County Democratic Party. Enjoys basketball, golf, swimming, biking and listening to good rock and roll.

Office: Public Safety Building, Second Floor, 511 South State Street, Syracuse 13202-2179.

Telephone: (315) 477-2768.

Fax: (315) 474-2601

E-mail address: kyoung@courts.state.ny.us

ZAMBELLI, Barbara Gunther *(Judge, Westchester County Court)* Former Judge, Mount Vernon City Court.

Office: 111 Dr. Martin Luther King Jr. Blvd., White Plains 10601.

Telephone: (914) 995-4904.

Fax: (914) 995-4184

ZWEIBEL, Ronald A. *(Judge, New York Court of Claims)* Appointed by governor. Currently serves as Acting Justice, New York Supreme Court First Judicial District.

Office: 100 Centre Street, New York 10013.

Telephone: (212) 374-8625.

Fax: (212) 374-5920

NORTH CAROLINA

Capital RALEIGH

UNITED STATES DISTRICT COURTS DISTRICTS OF NORTH CAROLINA

Within North Carolina there are three United States District Courts. For descriptive information refer to the United States Courts section.

EASTERN DISTRICT includes Beaufort, Bertie, Bladen, Brunswick, Camden, Carteret, Chowan, Columbus, Craven, Cumberland, Currituck, Dare, Duplin, Edgecombe, Franklin, Gates, Granville, Greene, Halifax, Harnett, Hertford, Hyde, Johnston, Jones, Lenoir, Martin, Nash, New Hanover, Northampton, Onslow, Pamlico, Pasquotank, Pender, Perquimans, Pitt, Robeson, Sampson, Tyrrell, Vance, Wake, Warren, Washington, Wayne and Wilson counties and the portion of Durham County which includes the Federal Correctional Institution at Butner. The court sits at Elizabeth City, Fayetteville, Greenville, New Bern, Raleigh, Wilmington and Wilson.

Chief Judge
Terrence W. Boyle

Judge
Malcolm J. Howard

Senior Judges
W. Earl Britt
James C. Fox

Clerk
David W. Daniel
P.O. Box 25670
Raleigh, North Carolina 27611-5670
(919) 645-1777

MIDDLE DISTRICT includes Alamance, Cabarrus, Caswell, Chatham, Davidson, Davie, Durham (excluding the area included in the Eastern District), Forsythe, Guilford, Hoke, Lee, Montgomery, Moore, Orange, Person, Randolph, Richmond, Rockingham, Rowan, Scotland, Stanly, Stokes, Surry and Yadkin counties. The court sits at Durham, Greensboro and Winston-Salem.

Chief Judge
N. Carlton Tilley, Jr.

Judges
Frank W. Bullock, Jr.
William L. Osteen, Sr.
James Arthur Beaty, Jr.

Clerk
J. P. Creekmore
P.O. Box 2708
Greensboro, North Carolina 27402-2708
(336) 332-6000

WESTERN DISTRICT includes Alexander, Alleghany, Anson, Ashe, Avery, Buncombe, Burke, Caldwell, Catawba, Cherokee, Clay, Cleveland, Gaston, Graham, Haywood, Henderson, Iredell, Jackson, Lincoln, Macon, Madison, McDowell, Mecklenburg, Mitchell, Polk, Rutherford, Swain, Transylvania, Union, Watauga, Wilkes and Yancey counties. The court sits at Asheville, Bryson City, Charlotte, Shelby and Statesville.

Chief Judge
Graham C. Mullen

Judges
Richard L. Voorhees
Lacy H. Thornburg

Clerk
Frank G. Johns
210 Federal Building
401 West Trade Street
Charlotte, North Carolina 28202
(704) 350-7400

UNITED STATES MAGISTRATE JUDGES OF NORTH CAROLINA

EASTERN DISTRICT
Louise W. Flanagan
William Norton Mason
William A. Webb

MIDDLE DISTRICT
Russell A. Eliason
P. Trevor Sharp

WESTERN DISTRICT
Carl Horn III
H. Brent McKnight
Max O. Cogburn, Jr.

Recalled Magistrate Judge
Wallace W. Dixon (Middle)

UNITED STATES BANKRUPTCY COURTS OF NORTH CAROLINA

EASTERN DISTRICT

Chief Judge
J. Rich Leonard

Judge
A. Thomas Small

Bankruptcy Clerk
Peggy B. Deans
P.O. Box 2807
Wilson, North Carolina 27894-2807
(252) 237-0248

MIDDLE DISTRICT

Chief Judge
William L. Stocks

UNITED STATES DISTRICT COURTS DISTRICTS OF NORTH CAROLINA—*Continued*

Judge
Catharine R. Carruthers

Recalled Judge
James Boyd Wolfe, Jr.

Bankruptcy Clerk
William L. Schwenn
P.O. Box 26100
Greensboro, North Carolina 27402-6100
(336) 333-5647

WESTERN DISTRICT

Chief Judge
George R. Hodges

Judge
J. Craig Whitley

Recalled Judge
Marvin R. Wooten

Bankruptcy Clerk
Geraldine Treutelaar Crockett
P.O. Box 34189
Charlotte, North Carolina 28234-4189
(704) 350-7500

SUPREME COURT OF NORTH CAROLINA

The Supreme Court is North Carolina's court of last resort. The court consists of a chief justice and six associate justices elected in statewide elections for eight-year terms. Vacancies may be filled by the governor. Retirement is mandatory at age seventy-two. Justices who retire before the mandatory retirement age may be appointed by the governor to serve as emergency justices. After age seventy-two, emergency justices and retired justices may be recalled to serve as needed.

The court exercises exclusive appellate jurisdiction over first-degree murder cases in which the defendant is sentenced to death or life imprisonment and over final orders by the Utilities Commission for general rate cases. The court also has appellate jurisdiction over cases involving substantial constitutional issues, cases of dissent in the Court of Appeals and cases which have been granted a review at the court's discretion. The court exercises original jurisdiction over the censure and removal of judges and has supervisory control and rule-making authority over the lower courts. The court may issue writs necessary to the exercise of proper jurisdiction.

The court sits en banc at Raleigh.

Chief Justice
I. Beverly Lake, Jr.

Associate Justices
Sarah E. Parker
Mark D. Martin
Robert H. Edmunds, Jr.
Robert F. Orr
George Wainwright, Jr.
Edward T. Brady

Clerk
Christie Speir Cameron
Justice Building
P.O. Box 1841
Raleigh, North Carolina 27602
(919) 733-3723

Director
John M. Kennedy
Administrative Office of the Courts
Justice Building
P.O. Box 2448
Raleigh, North Carolina 27602
(919) 733-7107

NORTH CAROLINA COURT OF APPEALS

The Court of Appeals is North Carolina's intermediate appellate court. The court consists of a chief judge and fourteen associate judges elected in statewide elections for eight-year terms. Vacancies may be filled by the governor. A chief judge is chosen by and serves at the pleasure of the Supreme Court chief justice. Retirement is mandatory at age seventy-two. Judges who retire before the mandatory retirement age may be appointed by the governor to serve as emergency judges; those assigned to the Superior Court are designated emergency special judges. After age seventy-two, emergency judges and retired judges may be recalled to serve as needed.

The court has appellate jurisdiction over cases appealed from the trial courts except those cases heard directly by the Supreme Court. The court also hears appeals from the Industrial Commission, the Commissioner of Insurance, the State Board of Contract Appeals, the State Bar, the Property Tax Commission, the Department of Human Resources, the Commissioner of Banks, the Administrator of Savings and Loans, the Secretary of Environment, Health and Natural Resources and the Utilities Commission in cases other than those concerning general rates. Appeals from decisions of other administrative agencies are heard first in the Superior Courts.

Judges sit in panels of three. The court regularly sits at Raleigh but may sit in various localities throughout the state as authorized by the Supreme Court.

Chief Judge
Sidney S. Eagles, Jr.

Associate Judges
James A. Wynn, Jr.
Linda M. McGee
Robert C. Hunter
J. Douglas McCullough
John Marsh Tyson
Ann Marie Calabria
Sanford Steelman, Jr.
Eric L. Levinson
John C. Martin
Patricia Ann Timmons-Goodson
Robin E. Hudson
Wanda G. Bryant
Richard A. Elmore
Martha A. Geer

Retired Judges
Donald L. Smith
Joseph R. John, Sr.
John B. Lewis, Jr.
Ralph A. Walker

NORTH CAROLINA SUPERIOR COURTS

The Superior Courts are North Carolina's courts of general jurisdiction. The state is divided into forty-seven districts or sets of districts for administrative purposes (sixty-two districts for electoral purposes) and comprises eight judicial divisions. For electoral purposes the following districts have been divided into two or more electoral districts: District 10, District 12, District 14, District 18, District 21 and District 26. Resident, special, retired and emergency judges serve the courts as assigned by the chief justice.

Resident judges are elected in statewide elections to eight-year terms. Vacancies may be filled by the governor. Resident judges are required to rotate among the districts in their divisions, spending six months in each district. Each district has at least one resident judge who handles administrative tasks for the district. In districts with more than one resident judge, the judge senior in service exercises these supervisory powers. In addition, special judges are appointed by the governor and may hold court in any county. Retirement is mandatory at age seventy-two. Judges who retire before the mandatory retirement age may be appointed by the governor to serve as emergency judges. After age seventy-two, emergency judges and retired judges may be recalled to serve as needed.

The courts have original jurisdiction in all felony cases and certain misdemeanor cases, such as those which originate by grand jury indictment. The courts exercise concurrent jurisdiction with the District Courts in general civil cases, but the Superior Courts are the proper courts for cases involving $10,000 or more. The courts exercise appellate jurisdiction over misdemeanor convictions from the District Courts and over certain administrative agencies, except those cases which are heard directly by the Court of Appeals or Supreme Court. In criminal appeals from the District Courts, the defendant is granted a trial de novo. The courts may also hear appeals of decisions from Superior Court clerks in probate and estate matters.

The courts sit at each county seat on a rotating basis.

FIRST JUDICIAL DIVISION includes District 1, District 2, District 3A, District 6A, District 6B, District 7A, District 7B and District 7C.

SECOND JUDICIAL DIVISION includes District 3B, District 4A, District 4B, District 5, District 8A and District 8B.

THIRD JUDICIAL DIVISION includes District 9, District 9A, District 10, District 14, District 15A and District 15B.

FOURTH JUDICIAL DIVISION includes District 11A, District 11B, District 12, District 13, District 16A and District 16B.

FIFTH JUDICIAL DIVISION includes District 17A, District 17B, District 18, District 19B, District 21 and District 23.

SIXTH JUDICIAL DIVISION includes District 19A, District 19C, District 20A, District 20B and District 22.

SEVENTH JUDICIAL DIVISION includes District 25A, District 25B, District 26, District 27A and District 27B.

EIGHTH JUDICIAL DIVISION includes District 24, District 28, District 29, District 30A and District 30B.

---

*Senior Resident Judge

DISTRICT 1 includes Camden, Chowan, Currituck, Dare, Gates, Pasquotank and Perquimans counties and is part of the First Judicial Division. The court sits at Camden, Edenton, Currituck, Manteo, Gatesville, Elizabeth City and Hertford.

Resident Judges
J. Richard Parker*
Jerry R. Tillett

DISTRICT 2 includes Beaufort, Hyde, Martin, Tyrrell and Washington counties and is part of the First Judicial Division. The court sits at Washington, Swan Quarter, Williamston, Columbia and Plymouth.

Resident Judge
William C. Griffin, Jr.*

DISTRICT 3A includes Pitt County and is part of the First Judicial Division. The court sits at Greenville.

Resident Judges
W. Russell Duke, Jr.*
Clifton W. Everett, Jr.

DISTRICT 3B includes Carteret, Craven and Pamlico counties and is part of the Second Judicial Division. The court sits at Beaufort, New Bern and Bayboro.

Resident Judges
Benjamin G. Alford*
Kenneth F. Crow

DISTRICT 4A includes Duplin, Jones and Sampson counties and is part of the Second Judicial Division. The court sits at Kenansville, Trenton and Clinton.

Resident Judge
Russell J. Lanier, Jr.*

DISTRICT 4B includes Onslow County and is part of the Second Judicial Division. The court sits at Jacksonville.

Resident Judge
Charles H. Henry*

DISTRICT 5 includes New Hanover and Pender counties and is part of the Second Judicial Division. The court sits at Wilmington and Burgaw.

Resident Judges
Ernest Berlin Fullwood*
W. Allen Cobb, Jr.
Jay D. Hockenbury

DISTRICT 6A includes Halifax County and is part of the First Judicial Division. The court sits at Halifax.

Resident Judge
Dwight L. Cranford*

DISTRICT 6B includes Bertie, Hertford and Northampton counties and is part of the First Judicial Division. The court sits at Windsor, Winton and Jackson.

Resident Judge
Cy A. Grant*

DISTRICT 7A includes Nash County and is part of the First Judicial Division. The court sits at Nashville.

NORTH CAROLINA SUPERIOR COURTS—*Continued*

Resident Judge
Quentin T. Sumner*

DISTRICT 7B includes part of Edgecombe and Wilson counties and is part of the First Judicial Division. The court sits at Wilson.

Resident Judge
Milton F. Fitch, Jr.

DISTRICT 7C includes part of Edgecombe and Wilson counties and is part of the First Judicial Division. The court sits at Tarboro.

Resident Judge
Frank R. Brown*

DISTRICT 8A includes Greene and Lenoir counties and is part of the Second Judicial Division. The court sits at Snow Hill and Kinston.

Resident Judge
Paul L. Jones*

DISTRICT 8B includes Wayne County and is part of the Second Judicial Division. The court sits at Goldsboro.

Resident Judge
Jerry Braswell*

DISTRICT 9 includes Franklin, Granville, Vance and Warren counties and is part of the Third Judicial Division. The court sits at Louisburg, Oxford, Henderson and Warrenton.

Resident Judges
Robert H. Hobgood*
Henry W. Hight, Jr.

DISTRICT 9A includes Caswell and Person counties and is part of the Third Judicial Division. The court sits at Yanceyville and Roxboro.

Resident Judge
W. Osmond Smith, III*

DISTRICT 10 includes Wake County and is part of the Third Judicial Division. The court sits at Raleigh.

Resident Judges
Donald W. Stephens*
Stafford G. Bullock
Howard E. Manning, Jr.
Narley L. Cashwell
Abraham Penn Jones
Evelyn W. Hill

DISTRICT 11A includes Harnett and Lee counties and is part of the Fourth Judicial Division. The court sits at Lillington and Sanford.

Resident Judge
Wiley F. Bowen*

DISTRICT 11B includes Johnston County and is part of the Fourth Judicial Division. The court sits at Smithfield.

Resident Judge
Knox V. Jenkins, Jr.*

DISTRICT 12 includes Cumberland County and is part of the Fourth Judicial Division. The court sits at Fayetteville.

Resident Judges
E. Lynn Johnson*
Gregory A. Weeks
Jack Thompson
James Floyd Ammons, Jr.

DISTRICT 13 includes Bladen, Brunswick and Columbus counties and is part of the Fourth Judicial Division. The court sits at Elizabethtown, Bolivia and Whiteville.

Resident Judges
William C. Gore, Jr.*
Ola M. Lewis

DISTRICT 14 includes Durham County and is part of the Third Judicial Division. The court sits at Durham.

Resident Judges
Orlando F. Hudson, Jr.*
A. Leon Stanback, Jr.
Ronald L. Stephens
Kenneth C. Titus

DISTRICT 15A includes Alamance County and is part of the Third Judicial Division. The court sits at Graham.

Resident Judges
J. B. Allen, Jr.*
James C. Spencer, Jr.

DISTRICT 15B includes Chatham and Orange counties and is part of the Third Judicial Division. The court sits at Pittsboro and Hillsborough.

Resident Judge
Wade Barber, Jr.*

DISTRICT 16A includes Hoke and Scotland counties and is part of the Fourth Judicial Division. The court sits at Raeford and Laurinburg.

Resident Judge
B. Craig Ellis*

DISTRICT 16B includes Robeson County and is part of the Fourth Judicial Division. The court sits at Lumberton.

Resident Judges
Robert F. Floyd, Jr.*
Gary Lynn Locklear

DISTRICT 17A includes Rockingham County and is part of the Fifth Judicial Division. The court sits at Wentworth.

Resident Judges
Melzer A. "Pat" Morgan, Jr.*
vacancy

DISTRICT 17B includes Stokes and Surry counties and is part of the Fifth Judicial Division. The court sits at Danbury and Dobson.

Resident Judges
A. Moses Massey*
Andy Cromer

DISTRICT 18 includes Guilford County and is part of the Fifth Judicial Division. The court sits at Greensboro and High Point.

Resident Judges
W. Douglas Albright*
Catherine C. Eagles
Henry E. Frye, Jr.
Lindsay R. Davis, Jr.
John O. Craig, III

NORTH CAROLINA SUPERIOR COURTS—*Continued*

DISTRICT 19A includes Cabarrus County and is part of the Sixth Judicial Division. The court sits at Concord.

Resident Judge

William Erwin Spainhour*

DISTRICT 19B includes Montgomery, Moore and Randolph counties and is part of the Fifth Judicial Division. The court sits at Troy, Carthage and Asheboro.

Resident Judges

Russell G. Walker, Jr.*
James M. Webb

DISTRICT 19C includes Rowan County and is part of the Sixth Judicial Division. The court sits at Salisbury.

Resident Judge

Larry G. Ford*

DISTRICT 20A includes Anson and Richmond counties and is part of the Sixth Judicial Division. The court sits at Wadesboro and Rockingham.

Resident Judge

Michael Earle Beale*

DISTRICT 20B includes Stanly and Union counties and is part of the Sixth Judicial Division. The court sits at Albemarle and Monroe.

Resident Judges

Susan Chandler Taylor*
W. David Lee

DISTRICT 21 includes Forsyth County and is part of the Fifth Judicial Division. The court sits at Winston-Salem.

Resident Judges

Judson Davie DeRamus, Jr.*
William Z. Wood, Jr.
L. Todd Burke
Ronald E. Spivey

DISTRICT 22 includes Alexander, Davidson, Davie and Iredell counties and is part of the Sixth Judicial Division. The court sits at Taylorsville, Lexington, Mocksville and Statesville.

Resident Judges

Mark E. Klass*
Kimberly Susan Taylor
Christopher Collier

DISTRICT 23 includes Alleghany, Ashe, Wilkes and Yadkin counties and is part of the Fifth Judicial Division. The court sits at Sparta, Jefferson, Wilkesboro and Yadkinville.

Resident Judge

Michael Etna Helms*

DISTRICT 24 includes Avery, Madison, Mitchell, Watauga and Yancey counties and is part of the Eighth Judicial Division. The court sits at Newland, Marshall, Bakersville, Boone and Burnsville.

Resident Judges

James L. Baker, Jr.*
Charles Philip Ginn

DISTRICT 25A includes Burke and Caldwell counties and is part of the Seventh Judicial Division. The court sits at Morganton and Lenoir.

Resident Judges

Beverly Tate Beal*
Robert C. Ervin

DISTRICT 25B includes Catawba County and is part of the Seventh Judicial Division. The court sits at Newton.

Resident Judges

Timothy S. Kincaid*
Nathaniel J. Poovey

DISTRICT 26 includes Mecklenburg County and is part of the Seventh Judicial Division. The court sits at Charlotte.

Resident Judges

Robert P. Johnston*
W. Robert Bell
J. Gentry Caudill
Yvonne M. Evans
Marcus L. Johnson
Richard D. Boner
David S. Cayer

DISTRICT 27A includes Gaston County and is part of the Seventh Judicial Division. The court sits at Gastonia.

Resident Judges

Jesse B. Caldwell, III*
Timothy L. Patti

DISTRICT 27B includes Cleveland and Lincoln counties and is part of the Seventh Judicial Division. The court sits at Shelby and Lincolnton.

Resident Judges

Forrest Donald Bridges*
James W. Morgan

DISTRICT 28 includes Buncombe County and is part of the Eighth Judicial Division. The court sits at Asheville.

Resident Judges

Dennis Jay Winner*
Ronald K. Payne

DISTRICT 29 includes Henderson, McDowell, Polk, Rutherford and Transylvania counties and is part of the Eighth Judicial Division. The court sits at Hendersonville, Marion, Columbus, Rutherfordton and Brevard.

Resident Judges

Zoro J. Guice, Jr.*
E. Penn Dameron, Jr.

DISTRICT 30A includes Cherokee, Clay, Graham, Macon and Swain counties and is part of the Eighth Judicial Division. The court sits at Murphy, Hayesville, Robbinsville, Franklin and Bryson City.

Resident Judge

James U. Downs*

DISTRICT 30B includes Haywood and Jackson counties and is part of the Eighth Judicial Division. The court sits at Waynesville and Sylva.

Resident Judge

Janet Marlene Hyatt*

NORTH CAROLINA SUPERIOR COURTS—*Continued*

SPECIAL SUPERIOR COURT JUDGES

Steve A. Balog
Albert Diaz
Thomas D. Haigwood
Clarence E. Horton, Jr.
John R. Jolly, Jr.
Ripley E. Rand
Gary E. Trawick
G. K. Butterfield, Jr.
Richard L. Doughton
D. Jack Hooks, Jr.
Jack W. Jenkins
Charles C. Lamm, Jr.
Ben F. Tennille

EMERGENCY SUPERIOR COURT JUDGES

Napoleon B. Barefoot, Sr.
Anthony M. Brannon
Clarence W. Carter
Robert L. Farmer
Donald M. Jacobs
James E. Lanning
Peter M. McHugh
James E. Ragan, III
Claude S. Sitton
Henry V. Barnette, Jr.
David H. Beard
Robert Burroughs, Sr.
Preston Cornelius
Howard R. Greeson, Jr.
David Q. LaBarre
Jerry Cash Martin
F. Fetzer Mills
J. Milton Read, Jr.

RETIRED-RECALLED SUPERIOR COURT JUDGES

Cary Walter Allen
James C. Davis
Robert W. Kirby
Hollis M. Owens, Jr.
Julius A. Rousseau, Jr.
Thomas W. Seay, Jr.
Giles R. Clark
Marvin Kenneth Gray
Robert Dobbins Lewis
Herbert O. Phillips, III

NORTH CAROLINA DISTRICT COURTS

The District Courts are courts of limited jurisdiction in North Carolina. The state is divided into thirty-nine District Court districts for administrative purposes (forty districts for electoral purposes). For electoral purposes, District 9 is divided into two electoral districts. Judges are elected in their districts for four-year terms. Magistrates also serve each county and are appointed by the senior resident Superior Court judge upon nomination by the county's Superior Court clerk. A chief judge for each district is appointed by the chief justice for a four-year term. Retirement is mandatory at age seventy-two. Judges who retire before the mandatory retirement age may be appointed by the governor to serve as emergency judges. After age seventy-two, emergency judges and retired judges may be recalled to serve as needed.

The courts exercise original jurisdiction in nearly all misdemeanor cases, infractions, probable cause hearings in most felony cases, all juvenile proceedings, mental health hospital commitment and recommitment hearings and domestic relations cases. The courts exercise concurrent jurisdiction with the Superior Courts in general civil cases, but cases involving less than $10,000 and domestic relations cases, regardless of the amount in controversy, are heard in the District Courts. Civil cases in which the amount in controversy is $3,000 or less may be designated as small claims cases and assigned to a magistrate for hearing. In addition to small claims cases, magistrates exercise jurisdiction over certain worthless check cases in which the amount of the check does not exceed $2,000. They may also accept written appearances, waivers of trial or hearing and pleas of guilty or admissions of responsibility, and enter judgments in misdemeanor or infraction cases involving certain alcohol, traffic, hunting, fishing, boating and littering offenses and state park and recreation area rule offenses. Magistrates may also conduct initial appearances, grant bail before trial in noncapital cases and issue arrest and search warrants.

The courts sit at each county seat and may also sit in other cities and towns specifically authorized by the General Assembly.

DISTRICT 1 includes Camden, Chowan, Currituck, Dare, Gates, Pasquotank and Perquimans counties. The court sits at Camden, Edenton, Currituck, Manteo, Gatesville, Elizabeth City and Hertford.

Chief Judge
Grafton G. Beaman

Judges
C. Christopher Bean
J. Carlton Cole
Edgar L. Barnes
Amber D. Malarney

DISTRICT 2 includes Beaufort, Hyde, Martin, Tyrrell and Washington counties. The court sits at Washington, Swan Quarter, Williamston, Columbia and Plymouth.

Chief Judge
James W. Hardison

Judges
Samuel G. Grimes
Michael A. Paul
Regina Rogers Parker

DISTRICT 3A includes Pitt County. The court sits at Greenville, Farmville and Ayden.

Chief Judge
David A. Leech

Judges
Patricia G. Hilburn
Joseph A. Blick, Jr.
Galen Braddy
Charles M. Vincent

DISTRICT 3B includes Carteret, Craven and Pamlico counties. The court sits at Beaufort, New Bern, Bayboro and Havelock.

Chief Judge
Jerry F. Waddell

Judges
Cheryl Lynn Spencer
Paul M. Quinn
Karen A. Alexander
Peter Mack, Jr.

DISTRICT 4 includes Duplin, Jones, Onslow and Sampson counties. The court sits at Kenansville, Trenton, Jacksonville and Clinton.

Chief Judge
Leonard W. Thagard

Judges
Wayne G. Kimble, Jr.
William M. "Mac" Cameron, III
Carol A. Jones
Paul A. Hardison
Louis F. Foy, Jr.
Sarah Cowen Seaton
Henry L. Stevens IV

DISTRICT 5 includes New Hanover and Pender counties. The court sits at Wilmington and Burgaw.

Chief Judge
John J. Carroll, III

NORTH CAROLINA DISTRICT COURTS—*Continued*

Judges

John W. Smith	Elton G. Tucker
J. H. Corpening, II	Shelly Sveda Holt
Rebecca W. Blackmore	James H. Faison, III

DISTRICT 6A includes Halifax County. The court sits at Halifax, Roanoke Rapids and Scotland Neck.

Chief Judge
Harold Paul McCoy, Jr.

Judge
Alma L. Hinton

DISTRICT 6B includes Bertie, Hertford and Northampton counties. The court sits at Windsor, Winton and Jackson.

Chief Judge
Alfred W. Kwasikpui

Judges
Thomas R. J. Newbern
W. Rob Lewis, II

DISTRICT 7 includes Edgecombe, Nash and Wilson counties. The court sits at Tarboro, Nashville, Wilson, Rocky Mount (Edgecomb County) and Rocky Mount (Nash County).

Chief Judge
John L. Whitley

Judges

Joseph J. Harper, Jr.	John M. Britt
Pell C. Cooper	Robert A. Evans
William G. Stewart	William C. Farris

DISTRICT 8 includes Greene, Lenoir and Wayne counties. The court sits at Snow Hill, Kinston, Goldsboro, LaGrange and Mount Olive.

Chief Judge
Joseph E. Setzer

Judges
David B. Brantley
Lonnie W. Carraway
R. Leslie Turner
Rose Vaughn Williams
Elizabeth A. Heath

DISTRICT 9 includes Franklin, Granville, Vance and Warren counties. The court sits at Louisburg, Oxford, Warrenton and Henderson.

Chief Judge
Charles W. Wilkinson, Jr.

Judges
J. Larry Senter
H. Weldon Lloyd, Jr.
Daniel F. Finch
J. Henry Banks
Garey H. Ballance

DISTRICT 9A includes Caswell and Person counties. The court sits at Yanceyville and Roxboro.

Chief Judge
Mark E. Galloway

Judge
L. Michael Gentry

DISTRICT 10 includes Wake County. The court sits at Raleigh, Apex, Wendell, Wake Forest and Fuquay-Varina.

Chief Judge
Joyce Amelia Hamilton

Judges

James R. Fullwood	Anne B. Salisbury
William C. Lawton	Michael R. Morgan
Robert B. Rader	Paul G. Gessner
Alice C. Stubbs	Kristin H. Ruth
Craig Croom	Kris D. Bailey
Jennifer M. Green	Monica M. Bousman
Jane Powell Gray	Shelley H. Desvousges

DISTRICT 11 includes Harnett, Johnston and Lee counties. The court sits at Lillington, Smithfield, Sanford, Dunn, Benson, Clayton and Selma.

Chief Judge
Albert A. Corbett, Jr.

Judges

Edward H. McCormick	Franklin F. Lanier
Marcia Stewart	Jacquelyn L. Lee
Jimmy L. Love, Jr.	Addie M. Harris Rawls
George R. Murphy	

DISTRICT 12 includes Cumberland County. The court sits at Fayetteville.

Chief Judge
Anna Elizabeth Keever

Judges

John S. Hair, Jr.	Robert J. Stiehl, III
Edward A. Pone	C. Edward Donaldson
Kimbrell Kelly Tucker	John W. Dickson
Cheri L. Beasley	Dougald Clark, Jr.

DISTRICT 13 includes Bladen, Brunswick and Columbus counties. The court sits at Elizabethtown, Bolivia, Whiteville, Shallotte and Tabor City.

Chief Judge
Jerry Arnold Jolly

Judges
Napoleon B. Barefoot, Jr.
Thomas V. Aldridge, Jr.
Nancy C. Phillips
Douglas B. Sasser
Marion R. Warren

DISTRICT 14 includes Durham County. The court sits at Durham.

Chief Judge
Elaine M. O'Neal

Judges
Richard G. Chaney
Craig B. Brown
Ann E. McKown
Marcia H. Morey
James T. Hill

DISTRICT 15A includes Alamance County. The court sits at Graham and Burlington.

Chief Judge
James Kent Washburn

NORTH CAROLINA DISTRICT COURTS—*Continued*

Judges
Ernest J. Harviel
Bradley Reid Allen, Sr.
James K. Roberson

DISTRICT 15B includes Chatham and Orange counties. The court sits at Pittsboro, Hillsborough, Siler City and Chapel Hill.

Chief Judge
Joseph Moody Buckner

Judges
Alonzo Brown Coleman, Jr.
Charles T. L. Anderson
M. Patricia DeVine

DISTRICT 16A includes Hoke and Scotland counties. The court sits at Raeford and Laurinburg.

Chief Judge
Warren L. Pate

Judges
William C. McIlwain
Richard T. Brown

DISTRICT 16B includes Robeson County. The court sits at Fairmont, Lumberton, Maxton, Pembroke, Red Springs, Rowland and St. Pauls.

Chief Judge
J. Stanley Carmical

Judges
Herbert L. Richardson
John B. Carter, Jr.
William Jeffrey Moore
James Gregory Bell

DISTRICT 17A includes Rockingham County. The court sits at Eden, Madison, Reidsville and Wentworth.

Chief Judge
Richard W. Stone

Judge
Frederick B. Wilkins, Jr.

DISTRICT 17B includes Stokes and Surry counties. The court sits at Danbury, Dobson and Mount Airy.

Chief Judge
Otis M. "Bud" Oliver

Judges
Charles M. Neaves, Jr.
Spencer G. Key, Jr.

DISTRICT 18 includes Guilford County. The court sits at Greensboro and High Point.

Chief Judge
William L. Daisy

Judges

Lawrence McSwain	Thomas G. Foster, Jr.
Joseph E. Turner	Wendy Melton Enochs
Susan Elizabeth Bray	Patrice A. Hinnant
A. Robinson Hassell	H. Thomas Jarrell, Jr.
Susan R. Burch	Teresa H. Vincent
William K. Hunter	

DISTRICT 19A includes Cabarrus County. The court sits at Concord and Kannapolis.

Chief Judge
William G. Hamby, Jr.

Judges
Donna Hedgepeth Johnson
Martin B. McGee
Michael G. Knox

DISTRICT 19B includes Montgomery, Moore and Randolph counties. The court sits at Troy, Carthage, Asheboro and Liberty.

Chief Judge
William M. Neely

Judges
Vance B. Long
Michael A. Sabiston
Jayrene R. Maness
Lee W. Gavin
Scott C. Etheridge

DISTRICT 19C includes Rowan County. The court sits at Salisbury.

Chief Judge
Charlie Brown

Judges
Beth Spencer Dixon
William C. Kluttz, Jr.
Kevin G. Eddinger

DISTRICT 20 includes Anson, Richmond, Stanly and Union counties. The court sits at Wadesboro, Rockingham, Albemarle, Monroe, Hamlet and Southern Pines.

Chief Judge
Tanya T. Wallace

Judges

Joseph J. Williams	Christopher W. Bragg
Kevin M. Bridges	Lisa D. Thacker
Hunt Gwyn	Scott T. Brewer

DISTRICT 21 includes Forsyth County. The court sits at Kernersville and Winston-Salem.

Chief Judge
William B. Reingold

Judges

Chester C. Davis	William T. Graham, Jr.
Victoria L. Roemer	Laurie L. Hutchins
Lisa V. L. Menefee	Lawrence J. Fine
Denise S. Hartsfield	

DISTRICT 22 includes Alexander, Davidson, Davie and Iredell counties. The court sits at Taylorsville, Lexington, Mocksville, Statesville, Thomasville and Mooresville.

Chief Judge
Samuel Cathey

Judges

James M. Honeycutt	Jimmy Laird Myers
Wayne L. Michael	L. Dale Graham
Julia Shuping Gullett	Theodore S. Royster, Jr.
April C. Wood	Mary F. Covington

NORTH CAROLINA DISTRICT COURTS—*Continued*

DISTRICT 23 includes Alleghany, Ashe, Wilkes and Yadkin counties. The court sits at Sparta, Jefferson, Wilkesboro and Yadkinville.

Chief Judge
Edgar B. Gregory

Judges
David V. Byrd
Jeanie Reavis Houston
Mitchell L. McLean

DISTRICT 24 includes Avery, Madison, Mitchell, Watauga and Yancey counties. The court sits at Newland, Marshall, Bakersville, Boone and Burnsville.

Chief Judge
Alexander Lyerly

Judges
William A. Leavell, III
Kyle David Austin
Bruce B. Briggs

DISTRICT 25 includes Burke, Caldwell and Catawba counties. The court sits at Morganton, Lenoir, Newton and Hickory.

Chief Judge
Robert Monroe Brady

Judges
Gregory R. Hayes
C. Thomas Edwards
Sherri Wilson Elliott
Amy R. Sigmon
L. Suzanne Owsley
Burford A. Cherry
John R. Mull

DISTRICT 26 includes Mecklenburg County. The court sits at Charlotte.

Chief Judge
Fritz Y. Mercer, Jr.

Judges
H. William Constangy
Philip Howerton, Jr.
Rickye McKoy-Mitchell
Louis A. Trosch, Jr.
Nancy Black Norelli
Avril U. Sisk
Becky Thorne Tin
Thomas F. Moore
Jane V. Harper
Elizabeth D. Miller
Lisa C. Bell
Regan A. Miller
Hugh B. Lewis
Nathaniel P. Proctor
Elizabeth M. Currence
Ben S. Thalheimer

DISTRICT 27A includes Gaston County. The court sits at Gastonia.

Chief Judge
Dennis J. Redwing

Judges
Joyce Albright Brown
James A. Jackson
John K. Greenlee
Angela G. Hoyle
Ralph C. Gingles, Jr.

DISTRICT 27B includes Cleveland and Lincoln counties. The court sits at Shelby and Lincolnton.

Chief Judge
Larry James Wilson

Judges
Anna F. Foster
K. Dean Black
Charles A. Horn, Jr.

DISTRICT 28 includes Buncombe County. The court sits at Asheville.

Chief Judge
Gary S. Cash

Judges
Peter L. Roda
Shirley Hastings Brown
Rebecca B. Knight
Marvin P. Pope Jr.
Patricia K. Young

DISTRICT 29 includes Henderson, McDowell, Polk, Rutherford and Transylvania counties. The court sits at Hendersonville, Marion, Columbus, Rutherfordton and Brevard.

Chief Judge
Robert S. Cilley

Judges
Mark E. Powell
David Kennedy Fox
Laura J. Bridges
C. Randy Pool
C. Dawn Skerrett

DISTRICT 30 includes Cherokee, Clay, Graham, Haywood, Jackson, Macon and Swain counties. The court sits at Murphy, Hayesville, Robbinsville, Waynesville, Sylva, Franklin, Bryson City and Canton.

Chief Judge
John J. Snow, Jr.

Judges
Danny E. Davis
Steven J. Bryant
Richlyn D. Holt
Bradley B. Letts

EMERGENCY DISTRICT COURT JUDGES

Philip W. Allen
Sarah P. Bailey
Solomon G. Cherry
J. Patrick Exum
Rodney R. Goodman
James A. Harrill, Jr.
Robert W. Johnson
Lillian B. Jordan
C. Jerome Leonard, Jr.
Stanley Peele
Russell G. Sherrill, III
E. Burt Aycock, Jr.
Donald L. Boone
William A. Christian
J. Keaton Fonvielle
Lawrence Hammond, Jr.
Pattie S. Harrison
William G. Jones
R. Kason Keiger
Donald W. Overby
Margaret L. Sharpe
Catherine C. Stevens

RETIRED-RECALLED DISTRICT COURT JUDGES

Abner Alexander
Lowry M. Betts
William A. Creech
Spencer B. Ennis
Harley B. Gaston, Jr.
Walter P. Henderson
Edmund Lowe
Elton C. Pridgen
Claude W. Allen, Jr.
Daphene L. Cantrell
T. Yates Dobson, Jr.
Robert T. Gash
Roland Harris Hayes
Jack E. Klass
J. Bruce Morton
Samuel McDowell Tate

North Carolina Counties and County Seats

Alamance
Graham

Alexander
Taylorsville

Alleghany
Sparta

Anson
Wadesboro

Ashe
Jefferson

Avery
Newland

Beaufort
Washington

Bertie
Windsor

Bladen
Elizabethtown

Brunswick
Bolivia

Buncombe
Asheville

Burke
Morganton

Cabarrus
Concord

Caldwell
Lenoir

Camden
Camden

Carteret
Beaufort

Caswell
Yanceyville

Catawba
Newton

Chatham
Pittsboro

Cherokee
Murphy

Chowan
Edenton

Clay
Hayesville

Cleveland
Shelby

Columbus
Whiteville

Craven
New Bern

Cumberland
Fayetteville

Currituck
Currituck

Dare
Manteo

Davidson
Lexington

Davie
Mocksville

Duplin
Kenansville

Durham
Durham

Edgecombe
Tarboro

Forsyth
Winston-Salem

Franklin
Louisburg

Gaston
Gastonia

Gates
Gatesville

Graham
Robbinsville

Granville
Oxford

Greene
Snow Hill

Guilford
Greensboro

Halifax
Halifax

Harnett
Lillington

Haywood
Waynesville

Henderson
Hendersonville

Hertford
Winton

Hoke
Raeford

Hyde
Swan Quarter

Iredell
Statesville

Jackson
Sylva

Johnston
Smithfield

Jones
Trenton

Lee
Sanford

Lenoir
Kinston

Lincoln
Lincolnton

Macon
Franklin

Madison
Marshall

Martin
Williamston

McDowell
Marion

Mecklenburg
Charlotte

Mitchell
Bakersville

Montgomery
Troy

Moore
Carthage

Nash
Nashville

New Hanover
Wilmington

Northampton
Jackson

Onslow
Jacksonville

Orange
Hillsborough

Pamlico
Bayboro

Pasquotank
Elizabeth City

Pender
Burgaw

Perquimans
Hertford

Person
Roxboro

Pitt
Greenville

Polk
Columbus

Randolph
Asheboro

Richmond
Rockingham

Robeson
Lumberton

Rockingham
Wentworth

Rowan
Salisbury

Rutherford
Rutherfordton

Sampson
Clinton

Scotland
Laurinburg

Stanly
Albemarle

Stokes
Danbury

Surry
Dobson

Swain
Bryson City

Transylvania
Brevard

Tyrrell
Columbia

Union
Monroe

Vance
Henderson

Wake
Raleigh

Warren
Warrenton

Washington
Plymouth

Watauga
Boone

Wayne
Goldsboro

Wilkes
Wilkesboro

Wilson
Wilson

Yadkin
Yadkinville

Yancey
Burnsville

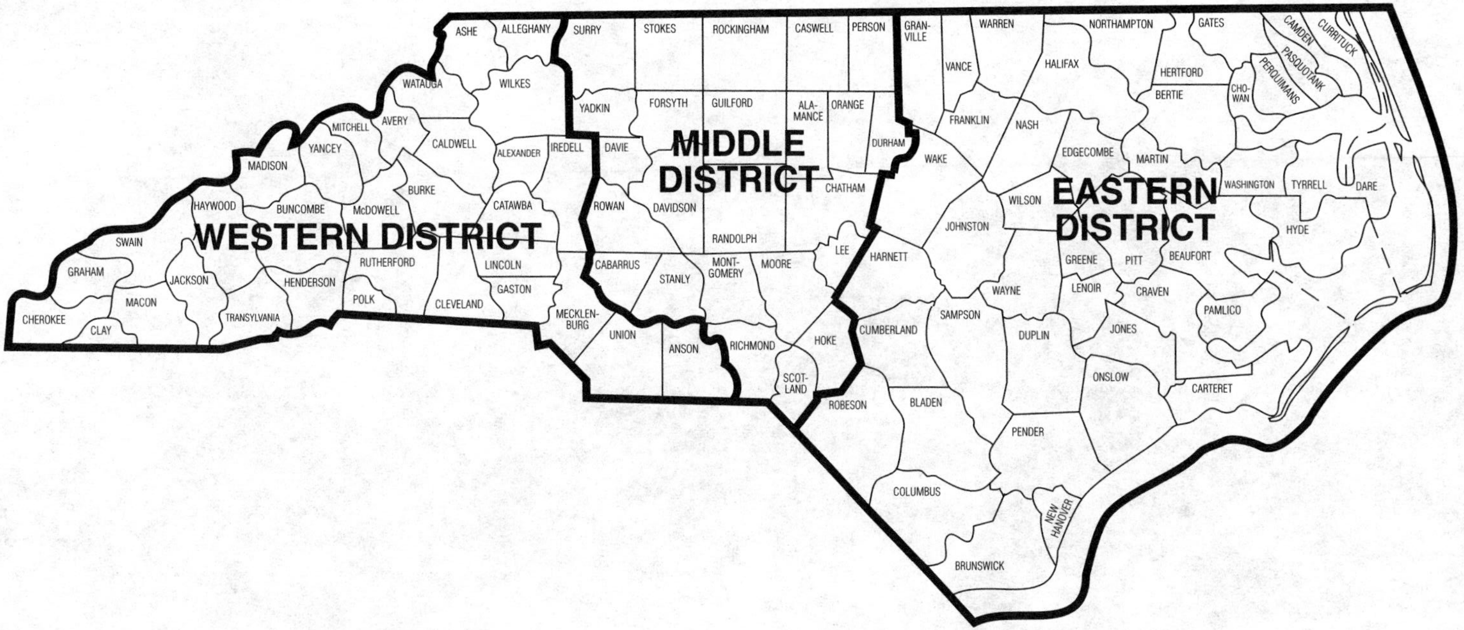

WESTERN DISTRICT
MIDDLE DISTRICT
EASTERN DISTRICT
ASHE
ALLEGHANY
SURRY
STOKES
ROCKINGHAM
CASWELL
PERSON
GRAN-VILLE
WARREN
NORTHAMPTON
GATES
CAMDEN
CURRITUCK
PASQUOTANK
PERQUIMANS
CHO-WAN
HERTFORD
BERTIE
HALIFAX
VANCE
WATAUGA
WILKES
YADKIN
FORSYTH
GUILFORD
ALA-MANCE
ORANGE
DURHAM
FRANKLIN
NASH
EDGECOMBE
MARTIN
WASHINGTON
TYRRELL
DARE
HYDE
MITCHELL
AVERY
CALDWELL
ALEXANDER
IREDELL
DAVIE
YANCEY
MADISON
BURKE
CATAWBA
ROWAN
DAVIDSON
CHATHAM
WAKE
WILSON
JOHNSTON
HAYWOOD
BUNCOMBE
McDOWELL
RANDOLPH
LEE
HARNETT
GREENE
PITT
BEAUFORT
SWAIN
RUTHERFORD
LINCOLN
CABARRUS
STANLY
MONT-GOMERY
MOORE
WAYNE
LENOIR
CRAVEN
PAMLICO
GRAHAM
JACKSON
HENDERSON
GASTON
MACON
POLK
CLEVELAND
CHEROKEE
CLAY
TRANSYLVANIA
MECKLEN-BURG
UNION
ANSON
RICHMOND
HOKE
CUMBERLAND
SAMPSON
DUPLIN
JONES
SCOT-LAND
ROBESON
BLADEN
ONSLOW
CARTERET
PENDER
COLUMBUS
NEW HANOVER
BRUNSWICK

UNITED STATES DISTRICT COURTS DISTRICTS OF NORTH CAROLINA

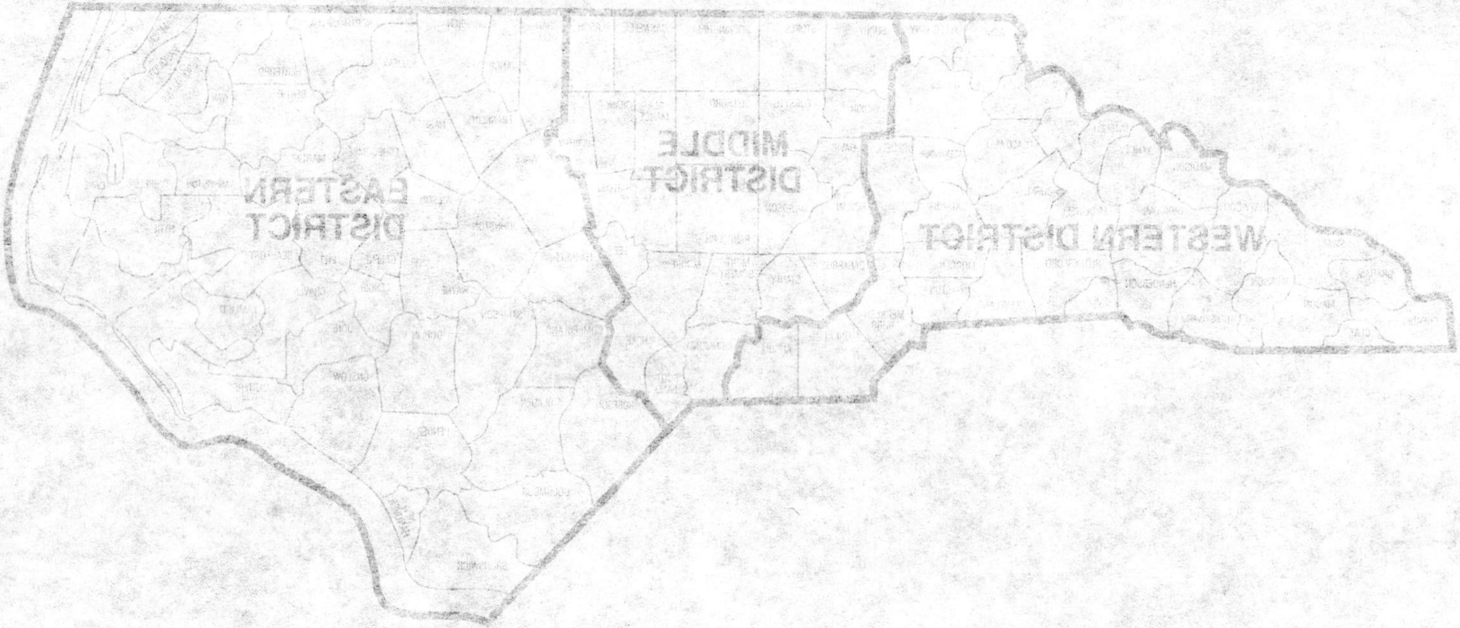
EASTERN DISTRICT
MIDDLE DISTRICT
WESTERN DISTRICT

UNITED STATES DISTRICT COURTS DISTRICTS OF NORTH CAROLINA

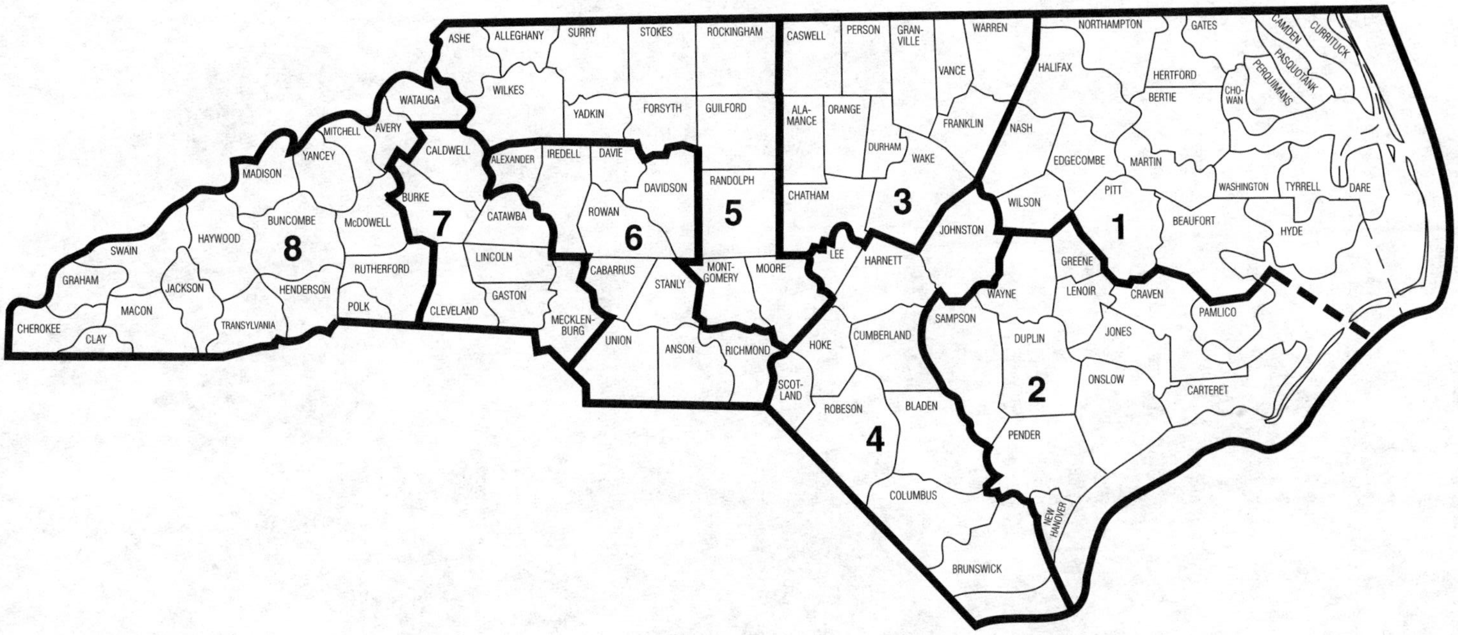
ASHE
ALLEGHANY
SURRY
STOKES
ROCKINGHAM
CASWELL
PERSON
GRAN-VILLE
WARREN
NORTHAMPTON
GATES
CAMDEN
CURRITUCK
PASQUOTANK
PERQUIMANS
HERTFORD
BERTIE
CHO-WAN
HALIFAX
VANCE
WILKES
WATAUGA
YADKIN
FORSYTH
GUILFORD
ALA-MANCE
ORANGE
DURHAM
FRANKLIN
NASH
EDGECOMBE
MARTIN
WASHINGTON
TYRRELL
DARE
MITCHELL
AVERY
YANCEY
MADISON
CALDWELL
ALEXANDER
IREDELL
DAVIE
DAVIDSON
RANDOLPH
CHATHAM
WAKE
WILSON
PITT
BEAUFORT
HYDE
BURKE
CATAWBA
ROWAN
BUNCOMBE
McDOWELL
HAYWOOD
SWAIN
GRAHAM
CHEROKEE
CLAY
MACON
JACKSON
TRANSYLVANIA
HENDERSON
POLK
RUTHERFORD
CLEVELAND
LINCOLN
GASTON
MECKLEN-BURG
CABARRUS
STANLY
UNION
ANSON
RICHMOND
MONT-GOMERY
MOORE
LEE
HARNETT
JOHNSTON
GREENE
LENOIR
CRAVEN
PAMLICO
WAYNE
SAMPSON
CUMBERLAND
HOKE
SCOT-LAND
ROBESON
BLADEN
DUPLIN
JONES
ONSLOW
CARTERET
PENDER
NEW HANOVER
COLUMBUS
BRUNSWICK
1
2
3
4
5
6
7
8

JUDICIAL DIVISIONS OF NORTH CAROLINA SUPERIOR COURTS

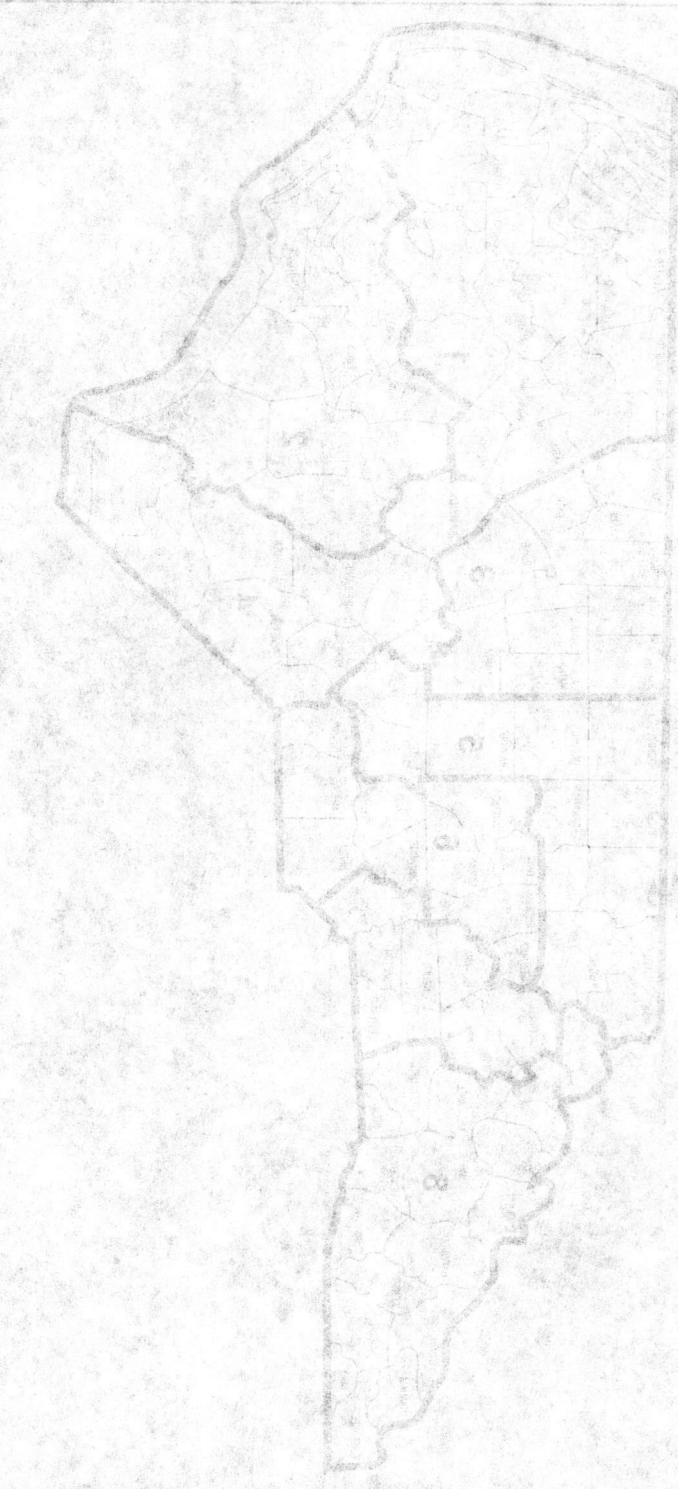

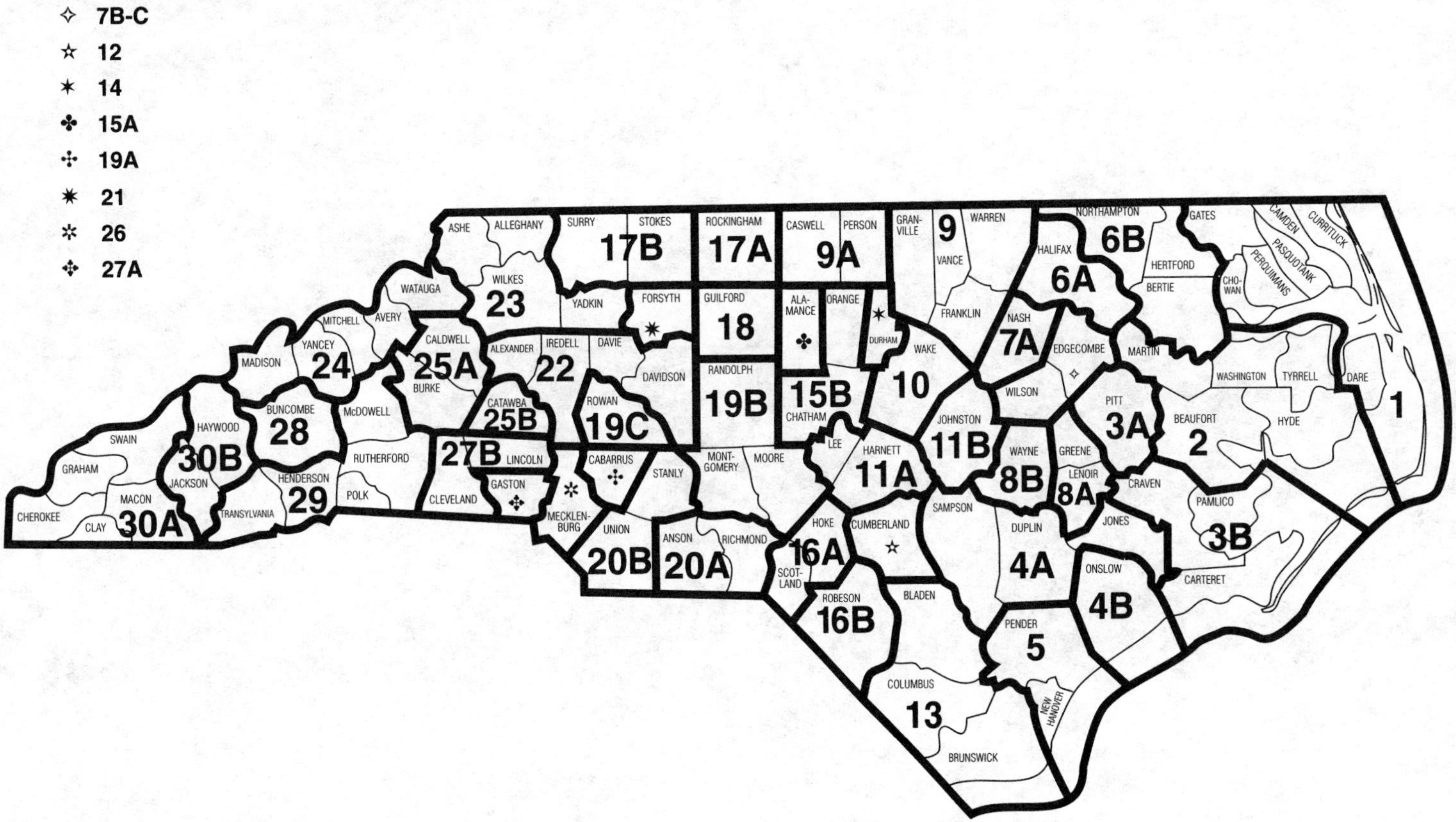

✧ 7B-C
☆ 12
✶ 14
✤ 15A
✣ 19A
✷ 21
✲ 26
✥ 27A
ASHE
ALLEGHANY
SURRY
STOKES
17B
ROCKINGHAM
17A
CASWELL
PERSON
9A
GRAN-VILLE
9
WARREN
VANCE
NORTHAMPTON
6B
GATES
CAMDEN
CURRITUCK
PASQUOTANK
PERQUIMANS
CHO-WAN
HERTFORD
BERTIE
HALIFAX
6A
WATAUGA
WILKES
23
YADKIN
FORSYTH
GUILFORD
18
ALA-MANCE
ORANGE
DURHAM
FRANKLIN
NASH
7A
EDGECOMBE
MARTIN
MITCHELL
AVERY
CALDWELL
25A
BURKE
ALEXANDER
IREDELL
DAVIE
22
DAVIDSON
MADISON
YANCEY
24
RANDOLPH
19B
15B
CHATHAM
WAKE
10
WILSON
WASHINGTON
TYRRELL
DARE
1
HYDE
BUNCOMBE
28
McDOWELL
CATAWBA
25B
ROWAN
19C
JOHNSTON
11B
PITT
3A
BEAUFORT
2
HAYWOOD
30B
SWAIN
GRAHAM
RUTHERFORD
27B
LINCOLN
CABARRUS
STANLY
MONT-GOMERY
MOORE
LEE
HARNETT
11A
WAYNE
8B
GREENE
LENOIR
8A
CRAVEN
JACKSON
HENDERSON
29
POLK
CLEVELAND
GASTON
MECKLEN-BURG
UNION
20B
ANSON
20A
RICHMOND
HOKE
16A
SCOT-LAND
CUMBERLAND
SAMPSON
DUPLIN
4A
JONES
PAMLICO
3B
CHEROKEE
CLAY
MACON
30A
TRANSYLVANIA
ROBESON
16B
BLADEN
ONSLOW
4B
CARTERET
PENDER
5
COLUMBUS
13
NEW HANOVER
BRUNSWICK

DISTRICTS OF NORTH CAROLINA SUPERIOR COURTS

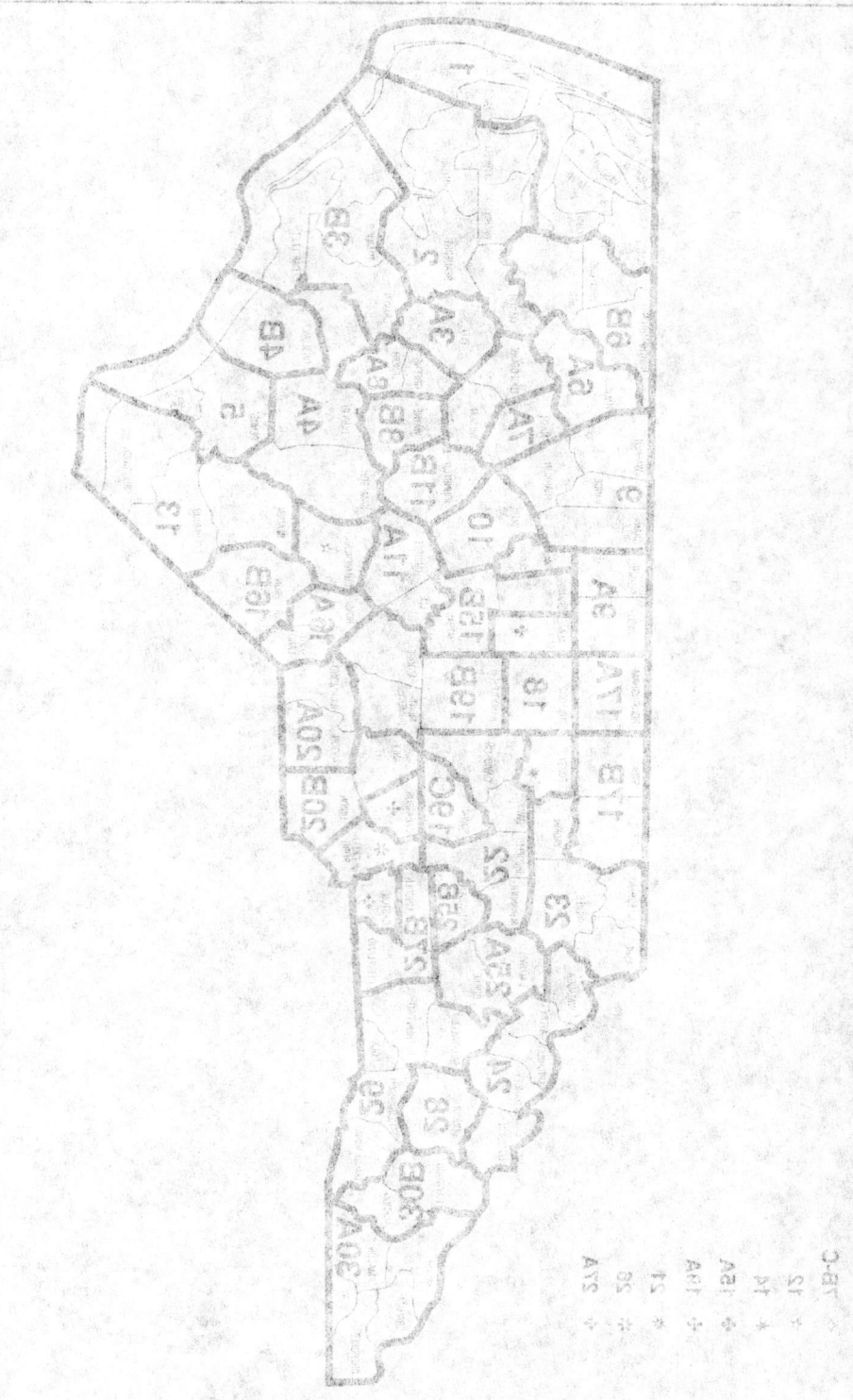

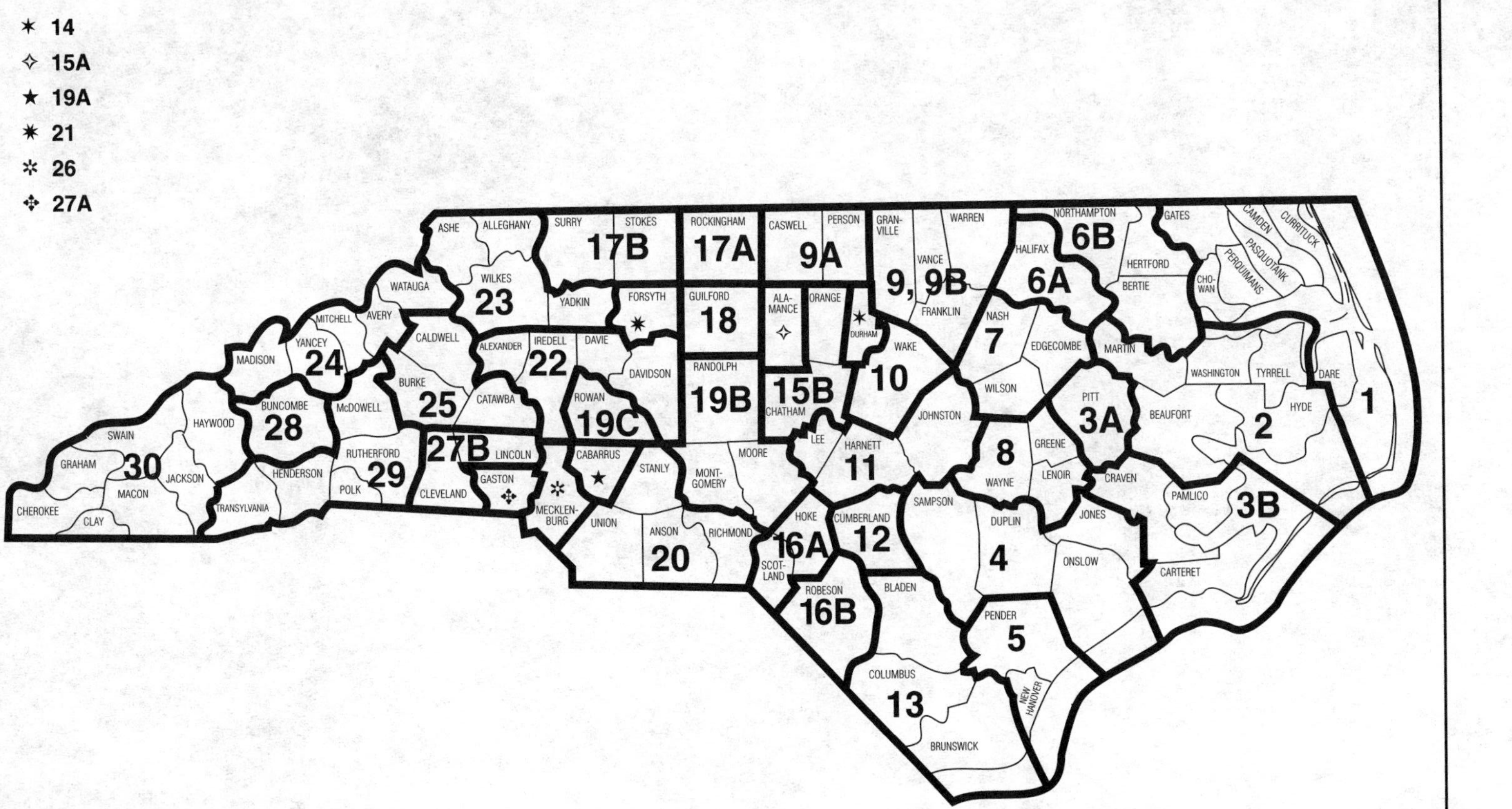

14
15A
19A
21
26
27A
1
2
3A
3B
4
5
6A
6B
7
8
9, 9B
9A
10
11
12
13
15B
16A
16B
17A
17B
18
19B
19C
20
22
23
24
25
27B
28
29
30
CURRITUCK
CAMDEN
PASQUOTANK
PERQUIMANS
CHO-WAN
GATES
HERTFORD
BERTIE
NORTHAMPTON
HALIFAX
WARREN
VANCE
FRANKLIN
GRAN-VILLE
PERSON
CASWELL
ROCKINGHAM
STOKES
SURRY
ALLEGHANY
ASHE
WATAUGA
WILKES
YADKIN
FORSYTH
GUILFORD
ALA-MANCE
ORANGE
DURHAM
WAKE
NASH
EDGECOMBE
MARTIN
WASHINGTON
TYRRELL
DARE
HYDE
BEAUFORT
PITT
WILSON
JOHNSTON
GREENE
LENOIR
WAYNE
CRAVEN
PAMLICO
CARTERET
JONES
ONSLOW
DUPLIN
SAMPSON
PENDER
NEW HANOVER
BRUNSWICK
COLUMBUS
BLADEN
CUMBERLAND
HARNETT
LEE
CHATHAM
RANDOLPH
MOORE
HOKE
SCOT-LAND
ROBESON
RICHMOND
MONT-GOMERY
ANSON
STANLY
UNION
CABARRUS
MECKLEN-BURG
ROWAN
DAVIDSON
DAVIE
IREDELL
ALEXANDER
CATAWBA
LINCOLN
GASTON
CLEVELAND
CALDWELL
BURKE
AVERY
MITCHELL
YANCEY
MADISON
McDOWELL
RUTHERFORD
POLK
BUNCOMBE
HENDERSON
TRANSYLVANIA
HAYWOOD
JACKSON
SWAIN
GRAHAM
MACON
CHEROKEE
CLAY

DISTRICTS OF NORTH CAROLINA DISTRICT COURTS

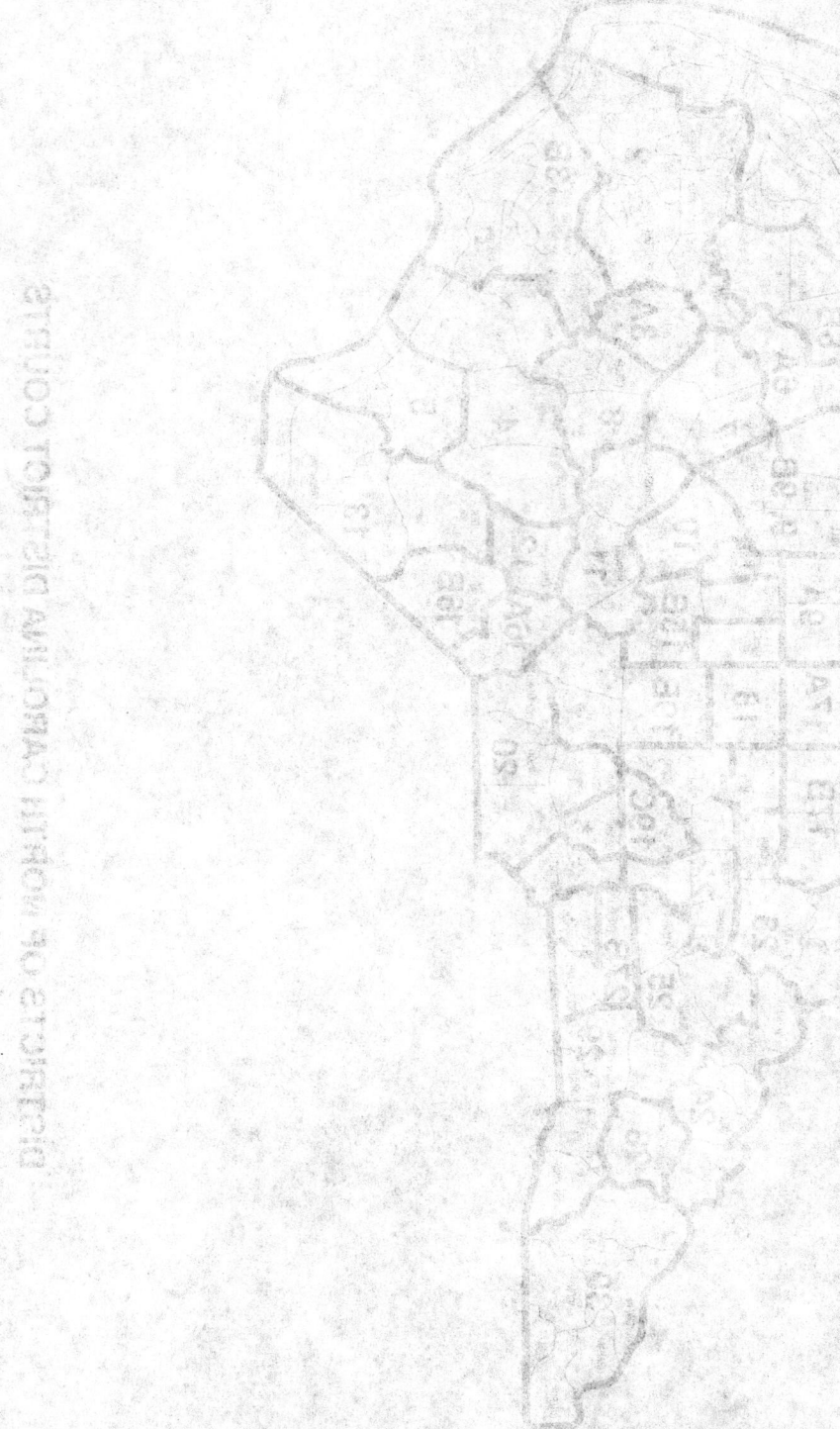

NORTH CAROLINA

ALBRIGHT, W. Douglas *(Resident Judge, North Carolina Superior Court Fifth Judicial Division District 18)* Assumed office 1975. Elected to subsequent terms. Current term expires 2006. Senior Resident Judge since 1984. Born West Lafayette Indiana Jan 19, 1939. Educated at Duke University A.B. 1961 and American University LL.B. 1964. Recipient American Jurisprudence Award in Constitutional Law. Member Phi Beta Kappa. Admitted to practice North Carolina 1964. In legal practice 1964-66.

Assistant Solicitor Guilford County Superior Court 1966-68. Chief District Prosecutor Eighteenth Judicial District 1968-69. District Attorney Superior Court Eighteenth Prosecutorial District 1969-75. President North Carolina District Attorneys Association 1973-74. President 1995-96 and Former Chairman North Carolina Conference of Superior Court Judges. Member Chief Justice's Commission on Professionalism 1999-2000. Former member North Carolina Judicial Council. Former Delegate National Conference of State Trial Judges. Former Chairman Continuing Legal Education Committee and News Media & Administration of Justice Committee. Former member Governor's Committee on Fair Sentencing Procedures. Member North Carolina Judicial Standards Commission and Governor's Study Commission on Length of Sentences. Member The North Carolina State Bar, Greensboro and North Carolina (Vice President 1985-86, Member Long Range Planning Committee 2000) Bar Associations. Attended The National Judicial College 1978. Member First Presbyterian Church (Ruling Elder, Teacher Young Men's Bible Class).

Mailing address: P.O. Box 3008, Greensboro 27402.

Telephone: (336) 574-4300.

ALDRIDGE, Thomas V., Jr. *(Judge, North Carolina District Court District 13)*

Office: 110-A Courthouse Square, Whiteville 28472.

Telephone: (910) 641-3070.

ALEXANDER, Abner *(Retired-Recalled Judge, North Carolina District Court)* Elected to term beginning 1968. Reelected 1972, 1976, 1980, 1984 and 1988. Former Chief Judge. Retired, serves by recall. Former Emergency Judge. Born Winston-Salem North Carolina May 20, 1929. United Methodist. Educated at Guilford College A.B. 1952 and Wake Forest University LL.B. 1957. Admitted to practice North Carolina 1957. Began legal practice Winston-Salem 1957.

Assistant U.S. Attorney 1960. Member North Carolina State Bar, Forsyth County and American Bar Associations. Sergeant U.S. Army 1952-54. Republican. Member Exchange Club, Masons and Shriners. Enjoys athletic activities.

Mailing address: P.O. Box 20099, Winston-Salem 27120.

Office: Forsyth County Hall of Justice, Winston-Salem 27120.

ALEXANDER, Karen A. *(Judge, North Carolina District Court District 3B)*

Office: 204 Craven County Courthouse Annex, 302 Broad Street, New Bern 28560-4903.

Telephone: (252) 514-4782.

ALFORD, Benjamin G. *(Resident Judge, North Carolina Superior Court Second Judicial Division District 3B)* Currently Senior Resident Judge.

Mailing address: P.O. Box 1187, New Bern 28563.

Office: c/o Clerk of Superior Court, Craven County Courthouse, New Bern 28562.

Telephone: (252) 672-1654.

ALLEN, Bradley Reid, Sr. *(Judge, North Carolina District Court District 15A)* Appointed by Governor James B. Hunt, Jr. to term beginning Feb 2000. Elected to term beginning Dec 2, 2002, current term expires Dec 2004. Born Burlington North Carolina July 21, 1962. Methodist. Educated at University of North Carolina at Chapel Hill B.S. 1985 and Campbell University School of Law J.D. 1988. Admitted to practice North Carolina 1988. In legal practice Burlington 1988-89.

Assistant District Attorney 1989-97 and Chief Assistant District Attorney 1997-2000 Alamance County.

Office: 120 Criminal Courts Building, 212 West Elm Street, Graham 27253.

Telephone: (336) 438-1018.

Fax: (336) 570-6984

ALLEN, Cary Walter *(Retired-Recalled Judge, North Carolina Superior Court)* Formerly served Eighth Judicial Division District 28. Retired, serves by recall. Former Emergency Judge. Former Chief Judge, North Carolina District Court Twenty-eighth Judicial District.

Mailing address: 557 Cronfields Lane, Asheville 28803.

ALLEN, Claude W., Jr. *(Retired-Recalled Judge, North Carolina District Court)* Former Chief Judge. Retired, serves by recall. Former Emergency Judge.

Mailing address: P.O. Box 631, Oxford 27565.

ALLEN, J. B., Jr. *(Resident Judge, North Carolina Superior Court Third Judicial Division District 15A)* Elected to term beginning Jan 1, 1987. Reelected 1994 and 2002. Current term expires Dec 31, 2010. Currently Senior Resident Judge. Born Burlington North Carolina July 9, 1938. Methodist. Educated at Elon College B.A. 1963 and University of North Carolina at Chapel Hill School of Law J.D. 1971. Admitted to practice North Carolina 1971. Began legal practice Burlington 1971. Chief Judge, North Carolina District Court Fifteenth Judicial District A Dec 28, 1972 to Dec 31, 1986.

Assistant District Attorney 1971-72. Member Alamance County, Fifteenth Judicial District A and North Carolina State Bar Associations. Attended numerous CLE conferences and seminars. Employed by Burlington Industries 1956-58, AT&T 1958-64 and North Carolina State Probation Office 1964-69. Democrat. Member Masons, Shriners, Moose Lodge, Salvation Army Boys'

ALLEN, J. B., JR.—*Continued*

Council and Emmanuel United Methodist Church. Enjoys golf.

Office: 245 Criminal Courts Building, 212 West Elm Street, Graham 27253.

Telephone: (336) 570-6870.

ALLEN, Philip W. *(Emergency Judge, North Carolina District Court)* Elected to term beginning Dec 1, 1986. Reelected 1990. Retired, serves by recall. Born Durham North Carolina Aug 13, 1946. Presbyterian. Educated at University of North Carolina at Chapel Hill A.B. 1969 J.D. 1972. Admitted to practice North Carolina 1972. In legal practice Yanceyville 1972-78. Assistant District Attorney 1978-81. District Attorney 1981-86.

Mailing address: c/o Rockingham County Clerk of Superior Court, P.O. Box 127, Wentworth 27375-0127.

AMMONS, James Floyd, Jr. *(Resident Judge, North Carolina Superior Court Fourth Judicial Division District 12)* Elected to term beginning Nov 25, 1998. Reelected Nov 5, 2002, current term expires Dec 31, 2010. Certified Juvenile Court Judge since Nov 1994. Born Portsmouth Virginia June 26, 1955. United Methodist. Educated at Louisburg Junior College A.A. with honors 1975 and University of North Carolina at Chapel Hill A.B. 1977 J.D. 1980. Member Phi Theta Kappa, Phi Delta Phi and Sigma Phi Epsilon. Admitted to practice North Carolina 1981. In legal practice Fayetteville 1981-82. Judge, North Carolina District Court District 12 Nov 7, 1988 to Nov 25, 1998, appointed by Governor James G. Martin.

Assistant District Attorney Twelfth District 1982-88. Adjunct Professor of Business Law I and II Fayetteville Technical Community College 1981-87 and Criminal Justice Fayetteville Police Academy 1982-88 and 1995-98. Member North Carolina Association of Superior Court Judges and The North Carolina State Bar. Graduate The National Judicial College 1989. Democrat. Member Fayetteville Kiwanis.

Mailing address: P.O. Box 363, Fayetteville 28302.

Office: Cumberland County Courthouse, Fayetteville 28302.

Telephone: (910) 678-2900.

ANDERSON, Charles T. L. *(Judge, North Carolina District Court District 15B)*

Mailing address: P.O. Box 1088, Hillsborough 27278.

Telephone: (919) 732-8181.

AUSTIN, Kyle David *(Judge, North Carolina District Court District 24)*

Mailing address: P.O. Box 219, Pineola 28662.

Telephone: (828) 733-0887.

AYCOCK, E. Burt, Jr. *(Emergency Judge, North Carolina District Court)* Elected to term beginning Dec 6, 1976. Reelected 1980, 1984, 1988, 1992 and 1996. Former Chief Judge. Retired, serves by recall. Born New Orleans Louisiana Sept 30, 1942. Presbyterian. Educated at University of North Carolina B.A. 1964 Law School 1968. Admitted to practice North Carolina 1968. Began legal practice Tarboro 1968. In legal practice Greenville 1971-73.

Assistant District Attorney 1973-76. Past President North Carolina Association of District Court Judges and North Carolina Conference of Chief District Court Judges. Chair Arbitration Subcommittee and Member North Carolina Supreme Court Committee on Alternative Dispute Resolution. Member The North Carolina State Bar and North Carolina Bar Association (Former Vice President, Council Member Section of Alternative Dispute Resolution). Democrat.

Mailing address: P.O. Box 8147, Greenville 27835.

BAILEY, Kris D. *(Judge, North Carolina District Court District 10)* Educated at Freed Hardeman University B.S. 1979, Winthrop University M.S. 1981 and University of Georgia School of Law J.D. 1995.

Church Deacon. Volunteer Special Olympics and HOPE for kids. Coach Youth Soccer.

Mailing address: P.O. Box 351, Raleigh 27602.

Office: Wake County Courthouse, Raleigh 27601.

Telephone: (919) 755-4101.

BAILEY, Sarah P. *(Emergency Judge, North Carolina District Court)* Retired, serves by recall.

Mailing address: c/o Edgecombe County Clerk of Superior Court, P.O. Drawer 9, Tarboro 27886.

Office: Edgecomb County Courthouse, Tarboro 27886.

BAKER, James L., Jr. *(Resident Judge, North Carolina Superior Court Eighth Judicial Division District 24)* Elected Nov 1994 to term beginning Jan 1, 1995. Reelected Nov 2002, current term expires Dec 31, 2010. Currently Senior Resident Judge. Born Asheville North Carolina Sept 15, 1954. Baptist. Educated at Mars Hill College B.A. 1977 and Mercer University J.D. 1980. Recipient American Jurisprudence Award in Real Property 1980. National Moot Court Team 1980. Member Phi Alpha Delta. Admitted to practice North Carolina, U.S. District Courts Middle and Western Districts of North Carolina, U.S. Courts of Appeals Fourth, Fifth and Eleventh Circuits and U.S. Supreme Court.

Assistant District Attorney District 24 1983-94. Member North Carolina Judicial Standards Commission 1997-2002. Attended The National Judicial College 1996. Chairman and Member County Board of Education 1986-90.

Mailing address: P.O. Box 940, Marshall 28753.

Telephone: (828) 649-2328.

Fax: (828) 649-2778

E-mail address: JudgeJBaker@aol.com

BALLANCE, Garey M. *(Judge, North Carolina District Court District 9)*

Mailing address: P.O. Box 616, Warrenton 27589.

Telephone: (919) 693-5193.

BALOG, Steve A. *(Special Judge, North Carolina Superior Court)* Appointed by governor.

Office: 245 Criminal Courts Building, 212 West Elm Street, Graham 27253.

Telephone: (336) 438-1019.

BANKS, J. Henry *(Judge, North Carolina District Court District 9)*

Mailing address: P.O. Box 1482, Henderson 27536.

Telephone: (919) 693-5193.

BARBER, Wade, Jr. *(Resident Judge, North Carolina Superior Court Third Judicial Division District 15B)* Assumed office Jan 2, 1998. Currently Senior Resident Judge.

Office: Old Courthouse, 104 East King Street, Hillsborough 27278.

Telephone: (919) 732-8181.

BAREFOOT, Napoleon B., Sr. *(Emergency Judge, North Carolina Superior Court)* Retired, serves by recall. Born Wilmington North Carolina Sept 11, 1930. Presbyterian. Educated at Wake Forest University B.S. 1955 LL.B. 1958. Admitted to practice North Carolina 1958. In legal practice 1958-70. Judge, North Carolina District Court Fifth Judicial District 1970-78.

Assistant District Attorney 1967-70. Member New Hanover County and North Carolina Bar Associations. Staff Sergeant USAF 1950-53. Democrat. Enjoys hunting and fishing.

Office: 519 New Hanover County Judicial Building, 316 Princess Street, Wilmington 28401.

BAREFOOT, Napoleon Bonaparte, Jr. *(Judge, North Carolina District Court District 13)* Appointed by Governor James G. Martin to term beginning Jan 1991. Elected Nov 1996 and 2000. Current term expires 2004. Born Wilmington North Carolina Jan 19, 1956. Methodist. Educated at Wake Forest University B.S. 1978 J.D. 1982. Admitted to practice North Carolina 1983. In legal practice Swan Quarter 1983-84.

Assistant District Attorney 1984-91. Former Member North Carolina District Attorneys Association (Secretary-Treasurer 1987). Member North Carolina Association of District Court Judges and North Carolina Bar Association. Chairman Family Assistance Agency Brunswick County 1997-98. Chairman Administrative Board Camp Methodist Church. Vice Chair Criminal Justice Partnership. Treasurer Brunswick Community College Foundation. Enjoys golfing, snow skiing and hunting.

Mailing address: P.O. Box 127, Bolivia 28422.
Office: Brunswick County Complex, Bolivia 28422.
Telephone: (910) 641-3070.

BARNES, Edgar L. *(Judge, North Carolina District Court District 1)* Appointed by Governor James B. Hunt, Jr. to term beginning June 23, 1995. Elected Nov 1996 and Nov 2000. Current term expires Dec 31, 2004. Born Bladen County North Carolina. Christian. Educated at University of North Carolina at Wilmington B.A. and North Carolina Central University School of Law J.D. Research Editor North Carolina Central Law Journal 1991-93. Admitted to practice North Carolina 1986. In legal practice Dare County 1988-95.

Mailing address: P.O. Drawer 406, Elizabeth City 27909.
Telephone: (252) 331-4750.
Fax: (252) 331-4814

BARNETTE, Henry V., Jr. *(Emergency Judge, North Carolina Superior Court)* Retired, serves by recall.

Mailing address: P.O. Box 351, Raleigh 27602.
Office: Wake County Courthouse, Raleigh 27602.

BEAL, Beverly Tate *(Resident Judge, North Carolina Superior Court Seventh Judicial Division District 25A)* Elected Nov 1990, 1994 and 2002. Current term expires Dec 31, 2010. Currently Senior Resident Judge. Born Lenoir North Carolina Feb 7, 1947. Presbyterian. Educated at Wake Forest University B.A. 1968 J.D. 1974. Member Phi Alpha Delta. Admitted to practice North Carolina 1974, U.S. District Courts Western 1977 and Middle 1978 Districts of North Carolina. In legal practice Lenoir 1974-91.

Important Decision: Batcheldor et al v. Boyd et al (exhumation of body for DNA comparison testing, affirms Beal, J. order allowing exhumation) N.C. App. Dec 15, 1992. Chair Judicial Education Committee and Member Pattern Jury Instruction Committee North Carolina Conference of Superior Court Judges. Member North Carolina Bar Association. E-5 U.S. Army 1968-71. Democrat. Member Optimist Club of Lenoir. Enjoys reading, book collecting and TV news.

Mailing address: P.O. Box 796, Morganton 28680.
Telephone: (828) 432-2827.

BEALE, Michael Earle *(Resident Judge, North Carolina Superior Court Sixth Judicial Division District 20A)* Currently Senior Resident Judge. Born Wilmington North Carolina Jan 3, 1950. Baptist. Educated at University of Rhode Island B.A. with honors 1972 and University of North Carolina J.D. 1976. Member Phi Kappa Phi. Admitted to practice North Carolina 1976 and U.S. District Court Middle District of North Carolina 1978. Former Judge and Chief Judge, North Carolina District Court District 20, appointed by Governor James B. Hunt, Jr. Sept 1, 1981.

Former Assistant District Attorney. Member Committee of Richmond County Criminal Justice Partnership, Richmond County, Twentieth Judicial District and North Carolina Bar Associations. Democrat. District Committee Boy Scouts of America 1981-82. Former District Director North Carolina Wildlife Federation. Life Member Trout Unlimited. Member Ducks Unlimited, National Wild Turkey Federation and Delta Waterfowl Association. Board of Deacons, Member and Former Teacher First Baptist Church of Southern Pines. Enjoys waterfowl hunting, trout fishing, saltwater fishing, photography, decoy collecting and running.

Mailing address: P.O. Box 1064, Wadesboro 28170-1064.
Telephone: (704) 694-4344.

BEAMAN, Grafton G. *(Chief Judge, North Carolina District Court District 1)* Elected to term beginning Dec 2, 1974. Reelected 1978, 1982, 1986, 1990, 1994, 1998 and Nov 5, 2002. Current term expires Dec 1, 2006. Chief Judge since Dec 3, 1990. Born Norfolk Virginia Sept 21, 1940. Educated at University of North Carolina at Chapel Hill B.S.B.A. 1963 LL.B. 1966 replaced by J.D. 1969. Law Clerk to U.S. District Court 1966-67. Member Phi Alpha Delta. Admitted to practice North Carolina 1966 and U.S. District Courts Western 1966 and Eastern 1967 Districts of North Carolina. In legal practice Elizabeth City 1967-74. Magistrate, U.S. District Court Eastern District of North Carolina 1971 to Jan 14, 1974, served part time.

Member District Court Judges Association (Executive Committee 1990-91), The North Carolina State Bar, First Judicial District (Executive Committee 1967-68 and 1990-91, Secretary-Treasurer 1969-70, Vice President 1970-71 and President 1971-72), North Carolina and American (Delegate to National Conference of Special Court Judges Judicial Administration Division Annual Meeting 1984, 1985, 1987, 1988 and 1991) Bar Associations. Voted Boss of the Year by Elizabeth City Legal Secretaries Association 1971. Recipient North Carolina Freedom Guard Second Place Award in Citizenship from North Carolina Jaycees 1974-75. Democrat. Life member General Alumni Association University of North Carolina at Chapel Hill. Former Chairman Pasquotank County Chapter American Red Cross. Former Board member and Treasurer Museum of the Albemarle 1972-77. Former member and State Director Elizabeth City Jaycees. Division Chairman United Fund Campaign 1969. Mem-

BEAMAN, GRAFTON G.—*Continued*

ber Elizabeth City Area Chamber of Commerce (Board of Directors 1970-73), Rotary (Board member 1986-87), University North Carolina Law Alumni Association (Board of Directors 1989-91) and Christ Episcopal Church (Former Layreader, former Vestryman, Vestry Secretary 1972, Chancellor 1973). Enjoys reading, boating and traveling.

Mailing address: P.O. Drawer 406, Elizabeth City 27907-0406.

Office: Pasquotank County Courthouse, Elizabeth City 27909.

Telephone: (252) 331-4750.

Fax: (252) 331-4814

BEAN, C. Christopher *(Judge, North Carolina District Court District 1)*

Mailing address: P.O. Box 588, Edenton 27932.

Telephone: (252) 331-4750.

BEARD, David H. *(Emergency Judge, North Carolina Superior Court)* Retired, serves by recall.

Mailing address: P.O. Box 489, Windsor 27983.

BEASLEY, Cheri L. *(Judge, North Carolina District Court District 12)*

Mailing address: P.O. Box 363, Fayetteville 28302.

Telephone: (910) 678-2901.

BEATY, James Arthur, Jr. *(Judge, United States District Court Middle District of North Carolina)* Appointed for life by President Bill Clinton to term beginning Nov 1, 1994. Born Whitmire South Carolina June 28, 1949. Baptist. Educated at Western Carolina University B.A. cum laude 1971 and University of North Carolina J.D. 1974. Admitted to practice North Carolina 1974. Began legal practice Winston-Salem 1974. Special Judge, North Carolina Superior Court Oct 29, 1981 to Dec 31, 1988, appointed by Governor James B. Hunt, Jr. Resident Judge, North Carolina Superior Court Judicial Division Three Twenty-first District D Jan 1, 1989 to Oct 31, 1994.

Member North Carolina Real Estate Commission 1979-81. Member North Carolina Association of Black Lawyers (Vice President and Secretary 1976-78), North Carolina Conference of Superior Court Judges (Secretary-Treasurer 1982), The North Carolina State Bar, Forsyth County and Winston-Salem Bar Associations. Named Outstanding Trial Judge of the Year by North Carolina Academy of Trial Lawyers 1990. President Forsyth County Young Democrat Club 1979. Enjoys golf, woodworking and reading.

Office: 248 Federal Building, 251 North Main Street, Winston-Salem 27101-3914.

Telephone: (336) 734-2540.

BELL, James Gregory *(Judge, North Carolina District Court District 16B)*

Office: Robeson County Courthouse, Box 18, Lumberton 28358.

Telephone: (910) 671-3355.

BELL, Lisa C. *(Judge, North Carolina District Court District 26)* Elected Nov 1998 to term beginning Jan 1999. Reelected 2002, current term expires Dec 31, 2006.

Office: 700 East Fourth Street, Suite 3304, Charlotte 28202.

Telephone: (704) 347-7801.

BELL, W. Robert *(Resident Judge, North Carolina Superior Court Seventh Judicial Division District 26)*

Office: 700 East Fourth Street, Charlotte 28202.

Telephone: (704) 347-7800.

BETTS, Lowry M. *(Retired-Recalled Judge, North Carolina District Court)* Former Chief Judge. Retired, serves by recall. Former Emergency Judge.

Office: c/o Chatham County Clerk of Superior Court, Chatham County Courthouse, Pittsboro 27312.

BLACK, K. Dean *(Judge, North Carolina District Court District 27B)* Appointed by Governor James B. Hunt, Jr. to term beginning Feb 25, 2000. Elected Nov 2000, current term expires Dec 2004. Born Mooresville North Carolina Dec 12, 1951. Presbyterian. Educated at University of North Carolina at Chapel Hill B.A. 1974 and Wake Forest University School of Law J.D. 1977. Admitted to practice North Carolina 1977. In legal practice Denver North Carolina 1977-99.

Member The North Carolina State Bar and North Carolina Bar Association. Member Rotary.

Office: Cleveland County Courthouse, 100 Justice Place, Shelby 28150.

Telephone: (704) 484-4801.

BLACKMORE, Rebecca W. *(Judge, North Carolina District Court District 5)* Appointed by Governor James B. Hunt, Jr. Nov 1993. Elected 1994, Nov 1998 and 2002. Current term expires Dec 3, 2006. Born Durham North Carolina Sept 4, 1953. Methodist. Educated at University of North Carolina at Wilmington B.A. cum laude and University of North Carolina at Chapel Hill J.D. 1983. Admitted to practice North Carolina 1983. In legal practice 1983-93.

Former Vice President North Carolina Bar Association. Member North Carolina Association of District Court Judges (Education Committee) and American Bar Association (Judicial Division). Faculty The National Judicial College. Named Distinguished Alumnus by University of North Carolina at Wilmington 1994. Board of Directors YWCA.

Office: 328 New Hanover County Judicial Bldg., 316 Princess Street, Wilmington 28401.

Telephone: (910) 341-1121.

Fax: (910) 341-4071

BLICK, Joseph A., Jr. *(Judge, North Carolina District Court District 3A)* Appointed by Governor James B. Hunt, Jr. to term beginning June 1999. Elected Nov 2002, current term expires Nov 2006. Born Jacksonville North Carolina Jan 4, 1954. Roman Catholic. Educated at University of North Carolina at Chapel Hill B.A. 1976 and Wake Forest University J.D. 1981. Admitted to practice North Carolina 1982. In legal practice Southern Pines Aug 1981 to March 1983.

Assistant District Attorney March 1983 to June 1999. Member North Carolina Association of District Court Judges and The North Carolina State Bar. Democrat. Member Athletic Boosters Club Rose High School. Interests include reading and coaching football and baseball.

Mailing address: P.O. Box 8147, Greenville 27835.

Telephone: (252) 695-7275.

E-mail address: joeb107@hotmail.com

BONER, Richard D. *(Judge, North Carolina Superior Court Seventh Judicial Division District 26)* Elected Nov 1998 to term beginning Jan 1, 1999. Term expires

BONER, RICHARD D.—*Continued*

Dec 31, 2006. Born Davidson County North Carolina April 7, 1949. Presbyterian. Educated at University of North Carolina A.B. in Journalism 1971 J.D. 1975. Admitted to practice North Carolina 1975. In legal practice Charlotte 1980-87. Special Judge, North Carolina Superior Court 1987-88. Judge, North Carolina District Court District 26 Jan 1, 1989 to Dec 31, 1998.

Assistant Public Defender Twenty-sixth District 1975-78. Assistant City Attorney Charlotte 1978-80. Member The North Carolina State Bar and North Carolina Bar Association. Republican. Chairman Precinct Organization Mecklenburg County GOP 1985-87. Member North Carolina State Republican Executive Committee 1985-87. Enjoys collecting Civil War artifacts, oil painting and reading.

Office: 700 East Fourth Street, Charlotte 28202.
Telephone: (704) 347-7800.

BOONE, Donald L. *(Emergency Judge, North Carolina District Court)* Retired, serves by recall.

Mailing address: P.O. Box 3008, Greensboro 27402-3008.

BOUSMAN, Monica M. *(Judge, North Carolina District Court District 10)*

Mailing address: P.O. Box 351, Raleigh 27602.
Telephone: (919) 755-4101.

BOWEN, Wiley F. *(Resident Judge, North Carolina Superior Court Fourth Judicial Division District 11A)* Appointed by Governor James B. Hunt, Jr. Jan 12, 1981. Elected 1982, 1990 and Nov 3, 1998. Current term expires 2006. Currently Senior Resident Judge. Born Hoffman North Carolina Aug 27, 1931. Baptist. Educated at Wake Forest University B.S. 1958 LL.B. 1961 replaced by J.D. and Campbell University M.B.A. 1986. Member Phi Delta Phi and Kappa Sigma. Admitted to practice North Carolina 1961. Began legal practice Dunn 1961.

Former Attorney Harnett County and City of Dunn. Member Eleventh Judicial District and North Carolina Bar Associations. Sergeant U.S. Army 1952-54. Democrat.

Mailing address: P.O. Box 1045, Lillington 27546.
Office: 301 West Cornelius Harnett Boulevard, Lillington 27546.
Telephone: (910) 814-4488.
Fax: (910) 814-1662

BOYLE, Terrence W. *(Chief Judge, United States District Court Eastern District of North Carolina)* Appointed for life by President Ronald Reagan to term beginning May 3, 1984. Chief Judge since 1997. Born Passaic New Jersey Dec 22, 1945. Educated at Brown University B.A. 1967 and Washington College of Law of American University J.D. 1970. In legal practice Elizabeth City 1974-84.

Minority Counsel Housing Subcommittee Committee on Banking and Currency U.S. House of Representatives 1970-73. Legislative Assistant to U.S. Senator Jesse Helms 1973.

Office: 306 East Main Street, Elizabeth City 27909.
Telephone: (919) 645-1777.

BRADDY, Galen *(Judge, North Carolina District Court District 3A)*

Mailing address: P.O. Box 8147, Greenville 27835.
Telephone: (252) 695-7270.

BRADY, Edward T. *(Associate Justice, Supreme Court of North Carolina)*

Mailing address: P.O. Box 1841, Raleigh 27602.
Telephone: (919) 733-3717.

BRADY, Robert Monroe *(Chief Judge, North Carolina District Court District 25)* Elected to term beginning Dec 3, 1990. Reelected Nov 1994, Nov 1998 and 2002. Current term expires 2006. Born Salisbury North Carolina April 2, 1949. Methodist. Educated at Wake Forest University B.A. 1971 J.D. 1974. Admitted to practice North Carolina 1974. In legal practice Lenoir 1974-90.

Attorney Caldwell County 1980-90. Member North Carolina Association of District Court Judges, The North Carolina State Bar, Caldwell County, Twenty-fifth Judicial District and North Carolina Bar Associations. Republican.

Office: District Court Building, 111 Main Avenue N.E., Hickory 28601.
Telephone: (828) 327-7500.
E-mail address: bobandsheila@earthlink.net

BRAGG, Christopher W. *(Judge, North Carolina District Court District 20)*

Mailing address: c/o Clerk of Superior Court, P.O. Box 5038, Monroe 28111.
Office: Union County Courthouse, Monroe 28111.
Telephone: (704) 982-3095.

BRANNON, Anthony M. *(Emergency Judge, North Carolina Superior Court)* Appointed by Governor James B. Hunt, Jr. to term beginning Nov 1977. Elected Nov 1978 and 1984. Term extended by statute to comply with Federal Voting Rights Statute. Retired, serves by recall. Former Senior Resident Judge. Born Durham North Carolina June 30, 1937. Educated at University of North Carolina A.B. 1960 LL.B. 1962. Admitted to practice North Carolina 1962, U.S. District Courts Eastern 1965 and Middle 1965 Districts of North Carolina and U.S. Court of Appeals Fourth Circuit 1965. In legal practice Ashboro 1963 and Durham 1964-77.

District Attorney Fourteenth Judicial District 1971-77. Adjunct Professor of Business Law University of North Carolina, Administration of the Criminal Justice System Duke University and Evidence and Criminal Trial Practice North Carolina Central University School of Law. Member Conference of Superior Court Judges, The North Carolina State Bar, Fourteenth Judicial District, North Carolina and American Bar Associations. Instructor in CLE for all North Carolina bar associations and law schools. Private USAR 1962-68. Democrat.

Office: 278 Durham County Judicial Building, Sixth Floor, 201 East Main Street, Durham 27701.

BRANTLEY, David B. *(Judge, North Carolina District Court District 8)*

Mailing address: P.O. Box 267, Goldsboro 27533-0267.
Telephone: (252) 527-7891.

BRASWELL, Jerry *(Resident Judge, North Carolina Superior Court Second Judicial Division District 8B)* Former Special Judge, appointed by Governor James B. Hunt, Jr. Currently Senior Resident Judge. Born Rosewood North Carolina June 23, 1952. Educated at More-

BRASWELL, JERRY—*Continued*

house College B.S. with high honors 1974 and University of North Carolina at Chapel Hill J.D. 1977.
Mailing address: P.O. Box 267, Goldsboro 27533-0267.
Office: Wayne County Courthouse, Goldsboro 27533.
Telephone: (919) 731-2038.
Fax: (919) 731-2037

BRAY, Susan Elizabeth *(Judge, North Carolina District Court District 18)* Elected to term beginning Dec 5, 1996. Reelected 2000, current term expires 2004. Certified Juvenile Court Judge since Spring 1997. Born Reidsville North Carolina Sept 18, 1961. United Methodist. Educated at Wake Forest University B.A. cum laude 1983 and Southern Methodist University School of Law J.D. 1987. Member Phi Delta Phi. Admitted to practice North Carolina 1987 and Virginia 1989.
Assistant District Attorney District 18 1989-96. Member North Carolina Association of District Court Judges, The North Carolina State Bar, Virginia State Bar and Greensboro Bar Association. Member Women's Professional Forum and United Methodist Women. Enjoys tennis, bicycling, theatre, aerobics and travel.
Mailing address: P.O. Box 3008, Greensboro 27402-3008.
Office: Guilford County Courthouse, Greensboro 27402.
Telephone: (336) 574-4301.

BREWER, Scott T. *(Judge, North Carolina District Court District 20)*
Mailing address: c/o Clerk of Superior Court, P.O. Box 5038, Monroe 28111.
Office: Union County Courthouse, Monroe 28111.
Telephone: (704) 982-3095.

BRIDGES, Forrest Donald *(Resident Judge, North Carolina Superior Court Seventh Judicial Division District 27B)* Elected Nov 1994 to term beginning Jan 3, 1995. Reelected 2002, current term expires Dec 31, 2010. Currently Senior Resident Judge. Born Toluca North Carolina March 23, 1953. Presbyterian. Educated at University of North Carolina at Charlotte B.A. with honors 1974 and Wake Forest University J.D. 1977. Staff member Wake Forest Law Review 1976-77. Admitted to practice North Carolina 1977. In legal practice Shelby 1977-94.
Office: Cleveland County Courthouse, 100 Justice Place, Shelby 28150.
Telephone: (704) 484-4876.

BRIDGES, Kevin M. *(Judge, North Carolina District Court District 20)*
Mailing address: c/o Clerk of Superior Court, P.O. Box 668, Albemarle 28002.
Office: Stanly County Courthouse, Albemarle 28002.
Telephone: (704) 982-3095.

BRIDGES, Laura J. *(Judge, North Carolina District Court District 29)* Elected Nov 3, 1998.
Mailing address: c/o Clerk of Superior Court, P.O. Box 630, Rutherford 28139.
Office: Rutherford County Courthouse, Rutherford 28139.
Telephone: (828) 287-2604.

BRIGGS, Bruce B. *(Judge, North Carolina District Court District 24)*
Mailing address: P.O. Box 81, Mars Hill 28754.
Telephone: (828) 733-0887.

BRITT, John M. *(Judge, North Carolina District Court District 7)*
Mailing address: P.O. Box 1238, Tarboro 27886.
Telephone: (252) 234-7676.

BRITT, W. Earl *(Senior Judge, United States District Court Eastern District of North Carolina)* Appointed for life by President Jimmy Carter 1980. Chief Judge 1983-90. Assumed Senior status Dec 7, 1997, serves by assignment. Born McDonald North Carolina Dec 7, 1932. Educated at Wake Forest University B.S. 1956 LL.B. 1958 replaced by J.D. 1970. Research Assistant to Hon. Emery B. Denny, North Carolina Supreme Court 1958-59. Member Pi Kappa Alpha and Phi Alpha Delta. In legal practice Fairmont and Lumberton 1959-80.
Chairman State-Federal Judicial Council of North Carolina 1985-86. Member Judicial Conference Committee on Automation and Technology 1990-95. Fourth Circuit Representative to the Judicial Conference of the U.S. 1991-97. Member Federal Judges Association (Vice President 1994, President 1995-97) and North Carolina Bar Association (Vice President 1992-93). Recipient Distinguished Alumnus Award from Campbell University 1984. U.S. Army Nov 1953 to Sept 1955. Former Member Alumni Council of Wake Forest University and Wake Forest Lawyer Alumni Association. Former Member and Vice President Fairmont Rotary Club. Board of Trustees 1965-69 and Vice Chairman 1967-69 Southeastern General Hospital. Trustee Southeastern Community College 1965-70. Trustee 1967-72, Vice Chairman 1969-71 and Chairman 1972 Pembroke State University. Board of Governors 1972-75 and Vice Chairman 1973-75 University of North Carolina. Board of Visitors Wake Forest University School of Law. Charter Member and Past President Fairmont Jaycees.
Mailing address: P.O. Box 27504, Raleigh 27611-7504.
Telephone: (919) 645-1745.

BROWN, Charlie *(Chief Judge, North Carolina District Court District 19C)* Elected to term beginning Dec 3, 1998. Reelected 2002, current term expires Dec 2006. Chief Judge since Nov 16, 2001. Born Newport News Virginia Dec 21, 1965. Educated at Appalachian State University B.S. 1988 and University of South Dakota J.D. 1992. Admitted to practice North Carolina 1993.
With Department of Social Services Rowan County 1993-95. Assistant District Attorney 1995-98.
Office: 232 North Main Street, Salisbury 28144.
Telephone: (704) 639-7509.
Fax: (704) 639-7726

BROWN, Craig B. *(Judge, North Carolina District Court District 14)*
Office: 565 Durham County Judicial Building, Sixth Floor, 201 East Main Street, Durham 27701.
Telephone: (919) 564-7240.

BROWN, Frank R. *(Resident Judge, North Carolina Superior Court First Judicial Division District 7C)* Currently Senior Resident Judge.
Mailing address: P.O. Box 156, Tarboro 27886.
Telephone: (252) 823-4761.

BROWN, Joyce Albright *(Judge, North Carolina District Court District 27A)* Elected Nov 1992 to term beginning Dec 6, 1992. Reelected Nov 7, 1996 and 2000. Current term expires 2004. Born North Carolina. Methodist. Educated at Indiana Wesleyan University A.B. 1953 and University of North Carolina School of Law J.D. 1956. Admitted to practice North Carolina 1956. In legal practice Belmont 1960-92.

Member North Carolina Association of District Court Judges, North Carolina Judicial Conference and The North Carolina State Bar. Republican.

Mailing address: P.O. Box 706, Belmont 28012.
Telephone: (704) 852-3117.

BROWN, Richard T. *(Judge, North Carolina District Court District 16A)*

Mailing address: P.O. Box 769, Laurinburg 28353.
Telephone: (910) 875-9535.

BROWN, Shirley Hastings *(Judge, North Carolina District Court District 28)* Elected to term beginning Dec 3, 1990. Reelected Nov 1994, Nov 3, 1998 and 2002. Current term expires Dec 2006. Born Shelby North Carolina Aug 26, 1950. Religious affiliation: United Methodist Church. Educated at University of North Carolina B.A. 1977 J.D. 1979. Member Phi Beta Kappa. Admitted to practice North Carolina 1979 and U.S. District Court Western District of North Carolina 1986. In legal practice Asheville 1986-90.

Chief Prosecutor 28th Prosecutorial District 1981-86. Member North Carolina Association of District Court Judges, North Carolina Judicial Conference, The North Carolina State Bar and 28th Judicial District Bar. Attends CLE and CJE programs sponsored by North Carolina Institute of Government and Administrative Office of the Courts. Democrat. Owns and operates an Arabian horse farm. Enjoys reading, yoga and family-oriented activities.

Office: Buncombe County Courthouse, 60 Court Plaza, Asheville 28801-3583.
Telephone: (828) 232-2760.

BRYANT, Steven J. *(Judge, North Carolina District Court District 30)*

Mailing address: c/o Clerk of Superior Court, P.O. Box 1397, Bryson City 28713.
Office: Swain County Courthouse, Bryson City 28713.
Telephone: (828) 456-3796.

BRYANT, Wanda G. *(Associate Judge, North Carolina Court of Appeals)* Appointed by Governor Michael F. Easley to term beginning March 1, 2001. Reappointed Dec 2002, current term expires Dec 31, 2004. Born Brunswick County North Carolina June 26, 1956. Baptist. Educated at Duke University B.A. 1977 and North Carolina Central University School of Law J.D. 1982. Admitted to practice North Carolina 1982, District of Columbia 1987 and U.S. Supreme Court 2002. In legal practice Southport North Carolina Aug 1982 to Dec 1982.

Senior Deputy Attorney General North Carolina Attorney General's Office 1993-2001. Assistant U.S. Attorney Office of U.S. Attorney District of Columbia 1989-93. Assistant District Attorney North Carolina for five years. Member North Carolina Association of Women Attorneys, North Carolina Association of Black Lawyers, Wake County (Board of Directors since 2002) and North Carolina (Administration of Justice Task Force 2001-03) Bar Associations. Director Citizen's Rights Division North Carolina Department of Justice 1993-2001. Board of Directors Martin Street Human Services, Inc. Member Parent Teacher Association Douglas Elementary School. Enjoys traveling, reading and yoga.

Mailing address: P.O. Box 888, Raleigh 27602.
Office: One West Morgan Street, Raleigh 27601.
Telephone: (919) 733-0473.
Fax: (919) 733-8003
E-mail address: wbryant@coa.state.nc.us

BUCKNER, Joseph Moody *(Chief Judge, North Carolina District Court District 15B)* Elected 1994. Reelected 1998 and 2002. Current term expires 2006. Born Chatham County North Carolina 1960. Baptist. Educated at University of North Carolina at Chapel Hill B.A. 1982 J.D. 1987. Member Phi Delta Phi. Admitted to practice North Carolina 1987 and U.S. District Court Middle District of North Carolina 1987. In legal practice Chapel Hill.

Instructor The National Judicial College. Presenter "Domestic Law" North Carolina Bar Association. Attended New Judge's School North Carolina Judges Association. Democrat.

Mailing address: P.O. Box 1088, Hillsborough 27278.
Telephone: (919) 732-8181.
E-mail address: joebuck@mindspring.com

BULLOCK, Frank W., Jr. *(Judge, United States District Court Middle District of North Carolina)* Appointed for life by President Ronald Reagan to term beginning Dec 29, 1982. Chief Judge 1992 to Sept 21, 1999. Born Oxford North Carolina Nov 3, 1938. Presbyterian. Educated at University of North Carolina at Chapel Hill B.S. 1961 LL.B. 1963. Board of Editors North Carolina Law Review 1962-63. Law Clerk to Hon. Algernon Butler, U.S. District Court Eastern District of North Carolina 1963-64. Member Delta Theta Phi. Admitted to practice North Carolina 1963. In legal practice Raleigh 1964-68 and Greensboro 1973-82.

Assistant Director Administrative Office of the Courts State Judicial Department 1968-73. Author "North Carolina Labor Relations Practice" North Carolina Bar Association Foundation, Inc. 1979, *North Carolina Business Practice Handbook* Wake Forest University 1981 and "Prior Consistent Statements and the Premotive Rule" 24 Florida State University L. Rev. 509, 1997. Liaison Member Advisory Committee on Rules of Evidence. Member Standing Committee on Rules of Practice and Procedure Judicial Conference of the U.S. since 1996, The North Carolina State Bar and North Carolina Bar Association.

Mailing address: P.O. Box 3223, Greensboro 27402-3223.
Telephone: (336) 332-6070.

BULLOCK, Stafford G. *(Resident Judge, North Carolina Superior Court Third Judicial Division District 10)* Appointed by Governor James Eubert Holshouser, Jr. to term beginning April 1974. Elected to subsequent terms. Current term expires Dec 2004. Born Granville County North Carolina March 21, 1942. Baptist. Educated at Shaw University B.A. 1963 and Howard University J.D. 1969. Admitted to practice North Carolina 1971.

Mailing address: P.O. Box 351, Raleigh 27602.
Telephone: (919) 755-4100.

BURCH, Susan R. *(Judge, North Carolina District Court District 18)*
Mailing address: P.O. Box 3008, Greensboro 27402-3008.
Telephone: (336) 574-4301.

BURKE, L. Todd *(Resident Judge, North Carolina Superior Court Fifth Judicial Division District 21)*
Mailing address: P.O. Box 20099, Winston-Salem 27120-0099.
Telephone: (336) 761-2420.

BURROUGHS, Robert M., Sr. *(Emergency Judge, North Carolina Superior Court)* Elected to term beginning Jan 1, 1979. Reelected Nov 1986. Retired, serves by recall. Born Charlotte North Carolina March 10, 1937. Methodist. Educated at University of North Carolina at Chapel Hill A.B. 1959 J.D. 1962. Member Phi Delta Phi. Admitted to practice North Carolina 1962, U.S. Court of Military Appeals 1963, U.S. District Court Western District of North Carolina 1965 and U.S. Tax Court 1969. In legal practice Charlotte 1965-78.
Member American Judges Association, North Carolina Conference of Superior Court Judges, The North Carolina State Bar, Twenty-sixth Judicial District and North Carolina Bar Associations. Attended The National Judicial College. Captain USMCR 1962-70. Democrat. Member Masons, Scottish Rite, Oasis Shrine and Shrine Jesters. Enjoys travel, boats and photography.
Office: 3304 Mecklenburg County Criminal Courts Building, 700 East Fourth Street, Charlotte 28202.

BUTTERFIELD, G. K., Jr. *(Special Judge, North Carolina Superior Court)* Former Resident Judge First Judicial Division District 7B, elected to term beginning Jan 1, 1989. Appointed Special Judge by Governor Michael F. Easley. Born Wilson North Carolina April 27, 1947. Baptist. Educated at North Carolina Central University B.A. 1971 J.D. 1974. Admitted to practice North Carolina 1975, U.S. District Court Eastern District of North Carolina 1979 and U.S. Supreme Court 1985. In legal practice Wilson 1975-88. Former Associate Justice, North Carolina Supreme Court.
Member North Carolina Association of Black Lawyers and The North Carolina State Bar. E-4 U.S. Army 1968-70.
Mailing address: P.O. Box 2445, Wilson 27894-2445.
Telephone: (919) 733-4840.

BYRD, David V. *(Judge, North Carolina District Court District 23)* Elected Nov 1994 to term beginning Dec 5, 1994. Reelected Nov 3, 1998 and 2002. Current term expires Dec 2006. Certified Juvenile Court Judge since 1995. Born Elkin North Carolina Dec 27, 1960. Baptist. Educated at Appalachian State University B.A. cum laude 1983 and University of North Carolina School of Law J.D. 1989. Admitted to practice North Carolina 1989. County Magistrate 1983-86.
Assistant District Attorney 1989-94. Member North Carolina Association of District Court Judges, North Carolina Judicial Conference, American Judges Association, The North Carolina State Bar, Wilkes County and 23rd District Bar Associations. Attended summer and fall conferences North Carolina Association of District Court Judges 1995, 1996 and 1997. Ordained Minister Southern Baptist Church. Republican. Chairman Wilkes County Young Republicans 1990-92. Secretary Wilkes County Republican Party 1993-94. Member Child Fatality Review Team Ashe and Yadkin counties. Member Wilkes One-on-One and Community Based Alternatives Board, Wilkes Prison Ministry Board and Wilkes Criminal Justice Partnership Board. Enjoys golf, football, colonial history, computers and religion.
Office: Wilkes County Courthouse, 500 Courthouse Drive, Wilkesboro 28697.
Telephone: (336) 838-4246.

CALABRIA, Ann Marie *(Associate Judge, North Carolina Court of Appeals)* Former Judge, North Carolina District Court District 10.
Mailing address: P.O. Box 888, Raleigh 27602.
Office: Court of Appeals Building, One West Morgan Street, Raleigh 27601.
Telephone: (919) 715-4961.

CALDWELL, Jesse B., III *(Resident Judge, North Carolina Superior Court Seventh Judicial Division District 27A)* Appointed by Governor James B. Hunt, Jr. Aug 1993. Elected Nov 1994 and Nov 3, 1998. Current term expires 2006. Currently Senior Resident Judge. Born Winston-Salem North Carolina May 18, 1949. Methodist. Educated at University of North Carolina B.A. 1971 J.D. 1973. Admitted to practice North Carolina 1973 and U.S. District Court Western District of North Carolina 1973. In legal practice Gastonia 1973-1993.
Assistant Public Defender 1977-79 and Public Defender 1992-93 District 27A. Member North Carolina Conference of Superior Court Judges, North Carolina Judicial Conference and The North Carolina State Bar. Democrat. Enjoys reading, acting and directing in Little Theater productions, teaching Sunday school and spending time with family.
Office: Gaston County Courthouse, 325 North Marietta Street, Gastonia 28052.
Telephone: (704) 852-3125.

CAMERON, William M. "Mac", III *(Judge, North Carolina District Court District 4)* Appointed by Governor James B. Hunt, Jr. to term beginning March 1994. Elected Nov 1996 and Nov 2000. Current term expires Dec 2004. Born Wilmington North Carolina June 14, 1954. Methodist. Educated at North Carolina State University B.A. 1976 and Campbell University School of Law J.D. 1980. Admitted to practice North Carolina 1980. In legal practice Jacksonville 1980-94.
Mailing address: P.O. Box 395, Richlands 28574.
Telephone: (910) 296-2308.

CANTRELL, Daphene L. *(Retired-Recalled Judge, North Carolina District Court)* Retired, serves by recall. Former Emergency Judge.
Mailing address: 3304 Criminal Courts Building, 700 East Fourth Street, Charlotte 28202.

CARMICAL, J. Stanley *(Chief Judge, North Carolina District Court District 16B)* Appointed by Governor James G. Martin to term beginning June 30, 1989. Elected Nov 1990, Nov 1994, Nov 3, 1998 and Nov 2002. Current term expires Dec 2006. Born Lumberton North Carolina Oct 31, 1954. Presbyterian. Educated at Wake Forest University B.A. with honors 1977 and University of North Carolina Law School J.D. 1980. Member Phi Beta Kappa and Phi Alpha Theta. Admitted to practice North Carolina 1980, U.S. District Courts Eastern 1981 and Middle 1981 Districts of North Carolina and U.S. Court of Appeals Fourth Circuit 1982. In legal practice Lumberton 1980-89.

CARMICAL, J. STANLEY—*Continued*

Member North Carolina Association of District Court Judges (Former Secretary-Treasurer, Vice President), The North Carolina State Bar and Robeson County Bar Association. Attended National Judicial College Reno Nevada 1993. Recipient Distinguished Service Award from Lumberton Jaycees 1990 and District Court Judge of the Year from Rural Justice Project Dec 14, 1992. Democrat. President Kiwanis Club of Robeson 1985-86. Chairman of the Board Robeson County Group Home, Inc. 1989-91. Member Lumberton Youth and Family Commission 1990-91. Advisory Board Member Robeson Community Penalties Program 1991-92.

Office: Robeson County Courthouse, Box 18, Lumberton 28358.

Telephone: (910) 671-3355.

CARRAWAY, Lonnie W. *(Judge, North Carolina District Court District 8)*

Mailing address: P.O. Box 68, Kinston 28502.

Office: Lenoir County Courthouse, Kinston 28502.

Telephone: (252) 527-7891.

CARROLL, John J., III *(Chief Judge, North Carolina District Court District 5)*

Office: 519 New Hanover County Judicial Bldg., 316 Princess Street, Wilmington 28401.

Telephone: (910) 341-1120.

CARRUTHERS, Catharine R. *(Judge, United States Bankruptcy Court Middle District of North Carolina)* Appointed by U.S. Court of Appeals Fourth Circuit judges. Born Sept 24, 1954. Educated at University of North Carolina at Chapel Hill B.A. 1975 and Wake Forest University School of Law J.D. 1980. Law Clerk to Hon. Rufus W. Reynolds, U.S. Bankruptcy Court Middle District of North Carolina 1980-81.

Mailing address: P.O. Box 4798, Winston-Salem 27115-4798.

Telephone: (336) 631-5351.

CARTER, Clarence W. *(Emergency Judge, North Carolina Superior Court)* Former Senior Resident Judge Fifth Judicial Division District 17B. Retired, serves by recall. Former Judge, North Carolina District Court Seventeenth Judicial District B.

Mailing address: P.O. Box 441, King 27021.

CARTER, John B., Jr. *(Judge, North Carolina District Court District 16B)*

Office: Robeson County Courthouse, Box 18, Lumberton 28358.

Telephone: (910) 671-3355.

CASH, Gary S. *(Chief Judge, North Carolina District Court District 28)* Appointed by Governor James G. Martin Jan 31, 1986. Elected Nov 1986, 1990, 1994, Nov 3, 1998 and 2002. Current term expires Dec 2006. Chief Judge since Dec 2, 2002. Born Oxford North Carolina Aug 27, 1949. Presbyterian. Educated at Davidson College A.B. 1971, Yale University Divinity School 1971-72 and University of North Carolina J.D. 1976. Admitted to practice North Carolina 1976. In legal practice Asheville 1976-86. Democrat.

Office: Buncombe County Courthouse, Asheville 28801-3583.

Telephone: (828) 232-2760.

CASHWELL, Narley L. *(Resident Judge, North Carolina Superior Court Third Judicial Division District 10)*

Mailing address: P.O. Box 351, Raleigh 27602.

Telephone: (919) 755-4100.

CATHEY, Samuel *(Chief Judge, North Carolina District Court District 22)*

Mailing address: P.O. Box 186, Statesville 28677.

Telephone: (704) 878-4209.

CAUDILL, J. Gentry *(Resident Judge, North Carolina Superior Court Seventh Judicial Division District 26)*

Office: 700 East Fourth Street, Charlotte 28202.

Telephone: (704) 347-7800.

CAYER, David S. *(Resident Judge, North Carolina Superior Court Seventh Judicial Division District 26)* Born Winston-Salem North Carolina May 21, 1954. Educated at Washington and Lee University B.A. magna cum laude with honors in History 1976 and American University J.D. 1979. Admitted to practice North Carolina, Virginia, U.S. Court of Appeals Fourth Circuit and U.S. Supreme Court. In legal practice Arlington Virginia 1979-80. Former Judge and Former Cerified Juvenile Court Judge, North Carolina District Court District 26, elected to term beginning Dec 7, 1992.

Assistant Commonwealth's Attorney Arlington Virginia 1980-83. Attorney U.S. Department of Agriculture 1983-85 and Criminal Division U.S. Department of Justice 1985-86. Assistant U.S. Attorney Eastern District of Virginia 1986-88. Assistant District Attorney Mecklenburg County 1988-92. Member The North Carolina State Bar, Virginia State Bar and Mecklenburg County Bar Association (Continuing Legal Education Committee, Public Information and Education Committee, Criminal Courts and Defendants Committee, Legal Hotline, Criminal Law Section, Family Law Section). Speaker Continuing Legal Education Program and Law Explorers and Judge Moot Court Competition Young Lawyers Division Mecklenburg County Bar Association. Attended The National Judicial College 1993. Earned special commendations from the Drug Enforcement Administration, Internal Revenue Service and Attorney General. Republican. Lincoln Forum. Member Charlotte/Mecklenburg Blue Ribbon Bond Committee 1991, Myers Park Presbyterian Church, Battered Women's Shelter Resource Committee and Speakers' Bureau. Panelist/Speaker at numerous civic forums on Criminal Justice in Mecklenburg County. Enjoys spectator sports, traveling and reading.

Office: 700 East Fourth Street, Charlotte 28202.

Telephone: (704) 347-7800.

CHANEY, Richard G. *(Judge, North Carolina District Court District 14)* Appointed by Governor James G. Martin to term beginning Feb 15, 1985. Elected Nov 1986, 1990, 1994, Nov 3, 1998 and 2002. Current term expires Dec 2006. Born Annapolis Maryland Jan 27, 1950. Methodist. Educated at Duke University B.A. 1972 and University of North Carolina J.D. with honors 1976. Admitted to practice North Carolina 1976 and U.S. District Court District of North Carolina 1976. In legal practice Raleigh 1976-78 and Durham 1978-85.

Member North Carolina Association of District Court Judges, Durham County and North Carolina Bar Associations. Volunteer Coach YMCA. Enjoys sports, jogging and coaching.

Office: 565 Durham County Judicial Building, Sixth Floor, 201 East Main Street, Durham 27701.

Telephone: (919) 564-7240.

CHERRY, Burford A. *(Judge, North Carolina District Court District 25)*
Mailing address: P.O. Box 1292, Hickory 28603.
Telephone: (828) 327-7500.

CHERRY, Solomon G. *(Emergency Judge, North Carolina District Court)* Appointed by Governor James B. Hunt, Jr. to term beginning Jan 6, 1978. Elected 1978, 1982, 1986 and 1990. Retired, serves by recall. Born Elizabeth City North Carolina Dec 26, 1932. Episcopalian. Educated at University of North Carolina A.B. 1953 LL.B. 1956. Staff member North Carolina Law Review 1953. Member Phi Delta Phi. Admitted to practice North Carolina 1956 and U.S. District Court Eastern District of North Carolina 1958. In legal practice Windsor 1958-60 and Fayetteville 1960.

Former Assistant District Attorney and Public Defender Twelfth Judicial District 1970-73. Member The North Carolina State Bar and North Carolina Bar Association (Vice President 1988-89). Captain USAFR JAG 1956-58 (active duty 1956). Democrat.
Mailing address: P.O. Box 1501, Boone 28607.

CHRISTIAN, William A. *(Emergency Judge, North Carolina District Court)* Former Chief Judge. Retired, serves by recall.
Mailing address: c/o Lee County Clerk of Superior Court, P.O. Box 4209, Sanford 27331.

CILLEY, Robert S. *(Chief Judge, North Carolina District Court District 29)* Elected to term beginning Dec 5, 1988. Reelected 1992, 1996 and 2000. Current term expires 2004. Born Hickory North Carolina Nov 19, 1948. Educated at University of North Carolina at Chapel Hill A.B. 1971 J.D. 1974. Admitted to practice North Carolina 1974. In legal practice Brevard 1974-88.
Mailing address: c/o Trial Court Administrator, P.O. Box 188, Rutherfordton 28139.
Telephone: (828) 287-2604.

CLARK, Dougald, Jr. *(Judge, North Carolina District Court District 12)*
Mailing address: P.O. Box 363, Fayetteville 28302.
Telephone: (910) 678-2901.

CLARK, Giles R. *(Retired-Recalled Judge, North Carolina Superior Court)* Appointed by Governor James Holshouser, Jr. to term beginning Feb 19, 1975. Elected 1976, 1978 and 1986. Retired 1992, serves by recall. Born Elizabethtown North Carolina Dec 5, 1929. Baptist. Educated at East Carolina University B.S. 1953 and University of North Carolina J.D. 1958. Admitted to practice North Carolina 1958. Began legal practice Raleigh 1958. In legal practice Elizabethtown 1962-68. Judge, Bladen County Recorder's Court 1966-68. Judge, North Carolina District Court Thirteenth Judicial District 1968-75.

Arbitrator and Certified Mediator. Member North Carolina Bar Association. U.S. Army 1953-56.
Mailing address: P.O. Box 997, Elizabethtown 28337.

COBB, W. Allen, Jr. *(Resident Judge, North Carolina Superior Court Second Judicial Division District 5)* Appointed by governor to term beginning 1993. Elected Nov 1994 and Nov 2002. Current term expires Dec 2010. Educated at University of North Carolina at Chapel Hill A.B. 1974 and North Carolina Central University School of Law J.D. 1978. In legal practice Wilmington 1978-90. Former Judge, North Carolina District Court Fifth Judicial District, elected 1990.

Member Chief Justice's Task Force on Reorganization of North Carolina Court System 1998-99. Former Member The North Carolina Academy of Trial Lawyers, The Association of Trial Lawyers of America, North Carolina Association of District Court Judges, North Carolina and American Bar Associations. Member North Carolina Association of Superior Court Judges, The North Carolina State Bar, New Hanover County and Fifth Judicial District Bar Associations. Lecturer "Perspectives from the Bench" CLE Seminar The North Carolina State Bar 1995. Panelist "You and the Law" public TV video project University of North Carolina at Wilmington and New Hanover County 1997 and "Sentencing in Superior Court" Seminar University of North Carolina School of Law 1999. Member Wilmington North Carolina Chapter The Educational Foundation, Inc. 1980-93. Board of Trustees Wilmington Railroad Museum 1990-93. Board of Directors Keys, Inc. 1993-96 and The Wilmington Children's Museum 1998-2002. President The North Carolina Azalea Festival at Wilmington 1998, Cape Fear Council Boy Scouts of America 1999 and 2000 and The Wilmington Executives Club 2000. Board of Directors Friends and Citizens of Wilmington 6, Inc. Board of Trustees Cape Fear Community College. Participant Joint Civilian Orientation Conference U.S. Department of Justice. Member First Presbyterian Church (Board of Deacons 1995-98), Wilmington South Rotary Club, Committee on Legislative Affairs Wilmington Chamber of Commerce and BPO Elks Lodge No. 532.
Mailing address: P.O. Box 188, Wrightsville Beach 28480.
Telephone: (910) 341-1146.
Fax: (910) 341-4403
E-mail address: cobbwaj@aol.com

COGBURN, Max O., Jr. *(Magistrate Judge, United States District Court Western District of North Carolina)* Appointed by U.S. District Court judges.
Office: 325 U.S. Courthouse, 100 Otis Street, Asheville 28801-2611.
Telephone: (828) 771-7240.

COLE, J. Carlton *(Judge, North Carolina District Court District 1)*
Mailing address: P.O. Box 400, Hertford 27944.
Telephone: (252) 331-4750.

COLEMAN, Alonzo Brown, Jr. *(Judge, North Carolina District Court District 15B)* Appointed by Governor James B. Hunt, Jr. to term beginning Dec 1, 1995. Elected Nov 1996 and 1999. Current term expires Dec 2003. Born Burlington North Carolina June 30, 1937. Christian. Educated at Evansville College B.S. 1961 and University of North Carolina School of Law LL.B. 1964. Member Delta Theta Phi. Admitted to practice North Carolina 1965, U.S. District Courts Eastern and Middle Districts of North Carolina and U.S. Supreme Court. In legal practice Hillsborough 1965-95.

Former Attorney Orange County. Member The North Carolina State Bar (Councilor). Former Board Member and Lecturer North Carolina Academy of Trial Lawyers. Former North Carolina State Senator.
Mailing address: P.O. Box 1088, Hillsborough 27278.
Telephone: (919) 732-8181.

COLLIER, Christopher *(Resident Judge, North Carolina Superior Court Sixth Judicial Division District 22)*
Mailing address: P.O. Box 186, Statesville 28687.

COLLIER, CHRISTOPHER—*Continued*
Office: Iredell County Courthouse, Statesville 28687.
Telephone: (704) 878-4213.

CONSTANGY, H. William *(Judge, North Carolina District Court District 26)*
Office: 700 East Fourth Street, Suite 3304, Charlotte 28202.
Telephone: (704) 347-7801.

COOPER, Pell C. *(Judge, North Carolina District Court District 7)*
Mailing address: P.O. Drawer 9, Tarboro 27886.
Telephone: (252) 234-7676.

CORBETT, Albert A., Jr. *(Chief Judge, North Carolina District Court District 11)*
Mailing address: P.O. Box 955, Smithfield 27577.
Telephone: (910) 814-4670.

CORNELIUS, Preston *(Emergency Judge, North Carolina Superior Court)* Assumed office 1979. Elected to subsequent terms. Former Senior Resident Judge. Retired, serves by recall. Educated at North Carolina State University B.S. 1964 and University of North Carolina at Chapel Hill J.D. 1967. Former Judge, North Carolina District Court Twenty-second Judicial District.
Mailing address: c/o Senior Resident Superior Court Judge, P.O. Box 1343, Lexington 27293.

CORPENING, J. H., II *(Judge, North Carolina District Court District 5)*
Office: 519 New Hanover County Judicial Bldg., 316 Princess Street, Wilmington 28401.
Telephone: (910) 341-1120.

COVINGTON, Mary F. *(Judge, North Carolina District Court District 22)*
Mailing address: P.O. Box 186, Statesville 28687.
Telephone: (704) 878-4209.

CRAIG, John O., III *(Resident Judge, North Carolina Superior Court Fifth Judicial Division District 18)* Assumed office Feb 26, 2002.
Mailing address: P.O. Box 3008, Greensboro 27402.
Telephone: (336) 574-4300.

CRANFORD, Dwight L. *(Resident Judge, North Carolina Superior Court First Judicial Division District 6A)* Appointed by Governor James B. Hunt, Jr. Oct 2000. Elected Nov 5, 2002, current term expires Dec 2010. Currently Senior Resident Judge. Born Albemarle North Carolina July 26, 1932. Presbyterian. Educated at University of North Carolina A.B. 1954 J.D. 1960. Member Phi Alpha Delta. Admitted to practice North Carolina 1960, U.S. District Court Eastern District of North Carolina 1961 and U.S. Supreme Court 1966. In legal practice Roanoke Rapids 1960-92. Judge, North Carolina District Court District 6A Dec 5, 1992 to Oct 2000. U.S. Army 1954-57. Democrat.
Mailing address: P.O. Box 66, Halifax 27839.
Office: Halifax County Courthouse, Halifax 27839.
Telephone: (252) 583-2910.
Fax: (252) 583-1005

CREECH, William A. *(Retired-Recalled Judge, North Carolina District Court)* Appointed by Governor James B. Hunt, Jr. to term beginning Dec 7, 1982. Elected 1984, 1988 and 1992. Retired, serves by recall. Emergency Judge 1996-2000. Born Smithfield North Carolina Aug 5, 1925. United Methodist. Educated at University of Oslo, Norway 1947, University of North Carolina at Chapel Hill A.B. 1948, George Washington University 1949 and 1952-53, City of London School of Law Certificate in English and Comparative Law 1954 and Georgetown University J.D. 1958. Member Phi Gamma Delta. Admitted to practice North Carolina 1958. In legal practice Smithfield 1959-61 and Raleigh 1965-82.
Author "Law and Contemporary Problems" Duke L. Jour. 1966. Member The North Carolina State Bar and North Carolina Bar Association (Chairman Committee on Health 1971). Attended Judicial Courses Northwestern University 1962, The Brookings Institute 1982, The National Judicial College 1983 and Braxton Craven Inn of Court Duke University School of Law since 1993. Recipient Special Award for Outstanding Contribution to the Education of the Gifted and Talented from North Carolina Association of the Gifted and Talented 1988 and Award from Exceptional Children Division North Carolina Department of Public Instruction July 24, 2000. USN South Pacific WWII. Economic Assistant American Embassy Baghdad, Iraq 1949-51. International Economist Near East and African Division Bureau of Foreign Commerce Department of Commerce 1952-54. Economic Officer American Embassy London, England 1954-55. Democrat. Chief Counsel U.S. Senate Subcommittee on Constitutional Rights Judiciary Committee 1961-66. Member North Carolina House of Representatives 1975-78. Member North Carolina Senate 1979-82. Board of Trustees and Advisory Committee North Carolina Symphony Society, Inc. 1968-74. President The Wake County Historical Society, Inc. 1971-72. President and President Elect Raleigh Little Theater 1973-75. Board of Directors Leonidas Lafayette Polk Home Foundation since 1994, Methodist Home for Children 1996-2000 and Triangle World Affairs Council since 1998. Board of Directors and Vice President United Nations Association since 1997. Member Edenton Street United Methodist Church (Administrative Board 1972-85, Chairman of the Board 1973-75, Board Member Sheets Adult Day Care Center 1992-99), Lion's Club (Vice President 1977), Masons and American Legion.
Mailing address: P.O. Box 351, Raleigh 27602.

CROMER, Andy *(Resident Judge, North Carolina Superior Court Fifth Judicial Division District 17B)*
Mailing address: P.O. Box 1749, King 27021.
Telephone: (336) 983-8989.

CROOM, Craig *(Judge, North Carolina District Court District 10)*
Mailing address: P.O. Box 351, Raleigh 27602.
Telephone: (919) 755-4101.

CROW, Kenneth F. *(Resident Judge, North Carolina Superior Court Second Judicial Division District 3B)* Elected Nov 6, 2002 to term beginning Jan 2, 2003. Term expires Dec 31, 2010. Born Raleigh North Carolina Nov 18, 1962. Religious affiliation: Christian. Educated at University of North Carolina at Chapel Hill B.A. 1986 and Campbell University School of Law J.D. 1990. Member Pi Alpha Delta. Admitted to practice North Carolina 1991 and U.S. District Courts Eastern 1993 and Western 1993 Districts of North Carolina. In legal practice Dunn 1991 and New Bern 1994. Judge, North Carolina District Court District 3B Jan 30, 1995 to Jan 2003, appointed by Governor James B. Hunt, Jr.
Assistant District Attorney Prosecutorial District 3B 1991-94. Member The North Carolina State Bar, North

CROW, KENNETH F.—*Continued*

Carolina and American Bar Associations. Attended The National Judicial College Oct 1996. Democrat. Member Rotary International. Enjoys hunting, fishing, hiking and skiing.

Office: 204 Craven County Courthouse Annex, 302 Broad Street, New Bern 28560-4903.

Telephone: (252) 514-4782.

E-mail: Kenneth.F.Crow@aoc.state.nc.us

CURRENCE, Elizabeth M. *(Judge, North Carolina District Court District 26)*

Office: 700 East Fourth Street, Suite 3304, Charlotte 28202.

Telephone: (704) 347-7801.

DAISY, William L. *(Chief Judge, North Carolina District Court District 18)* Elected to term beginning 1980. Reelected 1984, 1988, 1992, 1996 and 2000. Current term expires 2004. Born Winston-Salem North Carolina Feb 14, 1943. Educated at Davidson College B.A. 1965 and University of North Carolina School of Law J.D. 1968. Admitted to practice North Carolina 1968 and U.S. Supreme Court 1977. In legal practice Greensboro 1974-80.

Assistant County Attorney Guilford County 1974-77. Member North Carolina District Judges Association and Greensboro Bar Association. Member Nat Greene Kiwanis Club. Enjoys golfing, traveling and cooking.

Mailing address: P.O. Box 3008, Greensboro 27402.

Telephone: (336) 574-4301.

E-mail address: William.L.Daisy@aoc.state.nc.us

DAMERON, E. Penn, Jr. *(Resident Judge, North Carolina Superior Court Eighth Judicial Division District 29)*

Mailing address: P.O. Box 188, Rutherfordton 28139.

Telephone: (828) 286-4690.

DAVIS, Chester C. *(Judge, North Carolina District Court District 21)*

Mailing address: P.O. Box 20099, Winston-Salem 27120-0099.

Telephone: (336) 761-2478.

DAVIS, Danny E. *(Judge, North Carolina District Court District 30)* Appointed by Governor James B. Hunt, Jr. to term beginning April 16, 1984. Elected 1986, 1990, 1994, Nov 3, 1998 and 2002. Current term expires Dec 2, 2006. Born Waynesville North Carolina Feb 22, 1953. Educated at Western Carolina University B.S. 1975 and Campbell University J.D. 1979. Notes and Comments Editor Campbell Law Review 1979. Admitted to practice North Carolina 1979 and U.S. District Court Western District of North Carolina 1982. Began legal practice Waynesville 1979.

Member The North Carolina State Bar, North Carolina and American Bar Associations. Democrat. Enjoys golf and racquetball.

Mailing address: P.O. Box 196, Waynesville 28786.

Telephone: (828) 456-3796.

Fax: (828) 452-2510

DAVIS, James C. *(Retired-Recalled Judge, North Carolina Superior Court)* Appointed by Governor James B. Hunt, Jr. to term beginning Nov 28, 1977. Elected 1978, 1984 and 1992. Retired, serves by recall. Former Emergency Judge. Born China Grove North Carolina July 30, 1929. Baptist. Educated at Catawba College B.A. 1957 and Wake Forest University J.D. 1959. Admitted to practice North Carolina 1960. In legal practice Salisbury 1960-66 and Concord 1967-77. Judge, Rowan County Recorder's Court 1964-66.

North Carolina House of Representatives 1961-62. Prosecuting Attorney Rowan County Court 1962-64. Certified Mediator. Member North Carolina State Bar, Cabarrus County, Nineteenth A Judicial District and North Carolina Bar Associations. Democrat. Honored by North Carolina with Order of The Long Leaf Pine (highest civilian award). Member Historic Cabarrus, Masons and Shriners.

Mailing address: P.O. Box 303, Concord 28026-0303.

DAVIS, Lindsay R., Jr. *(Resident Judge, North Carolina Superior Court Fifth Judicial Division District 18)*

Mailing address: P.O. Box 3008, Greensboro 27402.

Telephone: (336) 574-4300.

DeRAMUS, Judson Davie, Jr. *(Resident Judge, North Carolina Superior Court Fifth Judicial Division District 21)* Special Judge 1979-80. Elected Resident Judge 1980. Reelected 1988 and 1996. Current term expires Dec 31, 2004. Senior Resident Judge since Feb 8, 1989. Born Charlotte North Carolina Jan 6, 1945. Methodist. Educated at Duke University B.A. 1965 and University of North Carolina J.D. 1968. Law Clerk to Chief Judge Algernon L. Butler, U.S. District Court Eastern District of North Carolina 1969-70. Admitted to practice North Carolina 1968. In legal practice Winston-Salem 1970-79.

North Carolina House of Representatives 1974-79. Chairman Forsyth County Legislative Delegation 1979 and House Constitutional Amendments Committee 1979. President Conference of Superior Court Judges of North Carolina 1999-2000. Democrat.

Mailing address: P.O. Box 20099, Winston-Salem 27120-0099.

Telephone: (336) 761-2420.

DESVOUSGES, Shelley H. *(Judge, North Carolina District Court District 10)*

Mailing address: P.O. Box 351, Raleigh 27602.

Telephone: (919) 755-4101.

DeVINE, M. Patricia *(Judge, North Carolina District Court District 15B)*

Mailing address: P.O. Box 1088, Hillsborough 27278.

Telephone: (919) 732-8181.

DIAZ, Albert *(Special Judge, North Carolina Superior Court)* Resident Judge Seventh Judicial Division District 26 Nov 15, 2002 to Dec 31, 2002. Appointed Special Judge by Governor Michael F. Easley to term beginning Jan 1, 2003. Born Brooklyn New York Nov 28, 1960. Catholic. Educated at University of Pennsylvania B.S. 1983, New York University J.D. 1988 and Boston University M.S.B.A. 1993. Admitted to practice New York 1989, District of Columbia 1993 and North Carolina 1995. In legal practice Raleigh and Charlotte North Carolina Aug 1995 to Nov 2002.

Member North Carolina and American Bar Associations. Jag USMC since Nov 1988. Lieutenant Colonel USMCR.

Office: 700 East Fourth Street, Suite 3304, Charlotte 28202.

Telephone: (704) 347-7800.

Fax: (704) 347-7867

E-mail address: adiaz2@carolina.rr.com

DICKSON, John W. *(Judge, North Carolina District Court District 12)*
Mailing address: P.O. Box 363, Fayetteville 28302.
Telephone: (910) 678-2901.

DIXON, Beth Spencer *(Judge, North Carolina District Court District 19C)* Appointed by Governor Michael F. Easley to term beginning Jan 28, 2002.
Mailing address: P.O. Box 4237, Salisbury 28145-4237.
Telephone: (704) 639-7509.

DIXON, Wallace W. *(Recalled Magistrate Judge, United States District Court Middle District of North Carolina)* Magistrate Judge Eastern District of North Carolina June 20, 1983 to Oct 1999. Appointed Recalled Magistrate Judge District of South Carolina Oct 1999 to 2001 by the Judicial Council of the Fourth Circuit. Appointed Recalled Magistrate Judge Middle District of North Carolina Oct 2001 by the Judicial Council of the Fourth Circuit. Born Dunn North Carolina April 8, 1943. Southern Baptist. Educated at University of North Carolina at Chapel Hill B.S.B.A. 1965 and Wake Forest University J.D. 1972. Admitted to practice North Carolina 1972, U.S. District Courts Eastern 1972 and Western 1973 Districts of North Carolina and U.S. Court of Appeals Fourth Circuit 1980. Began legal practice Elizabeth City 1972. In legal practice Statesville 1973-80.
Assistant U.S. Attorney Eastern District of North Carolina 1980-83. Important Decisions: Thacker v. Dixon (change of name for religious reasons and the constitutional requirements imposed on prison officials to reflect the name change on prison records) 784 F. Supp. 286; Swann v. City of Goldsboro (federal discovery rules and the fee-setting device for experts at depositions) 137 F.R.D. 230; Mathis v. Parks (pendent claim and pendent party jurisdiction) 741 F. Supp. 567; Brooks v. Pembroke City Jail (summary judgment standard applied in a fourth amendment excessive force claim) 722 F. Supp. 1294; Stocks v. Sullivan (attorney fee award in Social Security cases) 717 F. Supp. 397; and Pratt v. U.S. Parole Commission (exclusionary rule does not apply to parole revocation proceedings) 717 F. Supp. 382. USMC 1966-69. Officer candidate, Second Lieutenant, First Lieutenant and Captain. Vietnam service 1967. Member Masons (Master), Rotary, Kiwanis and United Fund.
Mailing address: P.O. Box 1091, Durham 27702.
Telephone: (919) 541-5275.

DOBSON, T. Yates, Jr. *(Retired-Recalled Judge, North Carolina District Court)* Retired, serves by recall.
Mailing address: c/o Johnston County Clerk of Superior Court, P.O. Box 297, Smithfield 27577.

DONALDSON, C. Edward *(Judge, North Carolina District Court District 12)*
Mailing address: P.O. Box 363, Fayetteville 28302.
Telephone: (910) 678-2901.

DOUGHTON, Richard L. *(Special Judge, North Carolina Superior Court)* Appointed by governor.
Mailing address: P.O. Box 458, Sparta 28675.
Telephone: (336) 372-8949.

DOWNS, James U. *(Resident Judge, North Carolina Superior Court Eighth Judicial Division District 30A)* Appointed by Governor James B. Hunt, Jr. to term beginning June 29, 1983. Elected Nov 1984, 1990 and Nov 3, 1998. Current term expires 2006. Currently Senior Resident Judge. Born Shreveport Louisiana Sept 26, 1941. Baptist. Educated at Virginia Military Institute B.A. 1963 and Loyola University of the South LL.B. 1966. Member Delta Theta Phi. Admitted to practice Louisiana 1966, North Carolina 1971, U.S. District Courts Eastern 1973, Middle 1973 and Western 1973 Districts of North Carolina and U.S. Court of Appeals Fourth Circuit 1975. In legal practice Shreveport Louisiana 1968-71 and Franklin North Carolina 1971-83.
Member The North Carolina State Bar. Captain U.S. Army 1966-68. Democrat. Enjoys handball, golf, hunting and fishing.
Mailing address: P.O. Box 879, Franklin 28744.
Telephone: (828) 524-6414.

DUKE, W. Russell, Jr. *(Resident Judge, North Carolina Superior Court First Judicial Division District 3A)* Elected Nov 1990 to term beginning Jan 1, 1991. Reelected Nov 1991 and Nov 2000. Current term expires Dec 31, 2008. Currently Senior Resident Judge. Born Franklin County North Carolina Aug 28, 1947. Baptist. Educated at Wake Forest University 1970 J.D. 1974. Law Clerk to Hon. John Davis Larkins, Jr., U.S. District Court Eastern District of North Carolina 1974-76. Admitted to practice North Carolina 1974. In legal practice Farmville 1976-83 and Greenville 1984-88. Judge, North Carolina District Court Third Judicial District 1988-91.
Member North Carolina Conference of Superior Court Judges, North Carolina Judicial Conference, The North Carolina State Bar and North Carolina Bar Association. Former Mayor Town of Farmville. Member Rotary Club.
Mailing address: P.O. Box 835, Greenville 27835.
Telephone: (252) 695-7260.
Fax: (252) 830-3376
E-mail address: Wilton.Duke@AOC.STATE.NC.US

EAGLES, Catherine C. *(Resident Judge, North Carolina Superior Court Fifth Judicial Division District 18)* Appointed by Governor James B. Hunt, Jr. April 1993. Elected 1994 and 1996. Current term expires 2004. Born Memphis Tennessee Aug 30, 1958. Educated at Southwestern at Memphis B.A. 1979 and George Washington University J.D. 1982. Law Clerk to Hon. J. Smith Henley, U.S. Court of Appeals Eighth Circuit 1982-84. Member Phi Beta Kappa. Admitted to practice Missouri 1982, Arkansas 1983 and North Carolina 1984. In legal practice North Carolina 1984-93.
Member National Association of Women Judges, Conference of Superior Court Judges, American Judicature Society, North Carolina and American Bar Associations. Alumnus The National Judicial College 1993. Board of Directors YWCA. Member New Garden Friends Meeting, American Association of University Women and Women's Professional Forum.
Mailing address: P.O. Box 3008, Greensboro 27402.
Telephone: (336) 574-4300.

EAGLES, Sidney S., Jr. *(Chief Judge, North Carolina Court of Appeals)* Elected to term beginning Jan 1, 1983. Reelected 1990 and Nov 3, 1998. Current term expires 2006. Chief Judge since May 1, 1998. Born Asheville North Carolina Aug 5, 1939. Religious affiliation: Christian Church (Disciples of Christ). Educated at Wake Forest University B.A. 1961 J.D. 1964. Member Phi Delta Phi. Admitted to practice North Carolina 1964, U.S. Court of Military Appeals and U.S. Supreme Court. In legal practice Raleigh 1976-82.
Assistant Attorney General 1967-76 (Deputy Attorney General 1972-76). Counsel to Speaker of the House

EAGLES, SIDNEY S., JR.—*Continued*
1977-81. Author *Criminal Procedure Forms* VanCamp, Eagles & Corbett 1975, 1983 and 1989. Instructor Campbell University School of Law since 1976. Former Member Wake County Academy of Criminal Defense Attorneys and North Carolina Academy of Trial Lawyers. Member The American Law Institute, The North Carolina State Bar, Wake County, North Carolina and American (Chair Appellate Judges Conference 1992-93, Section of Criminal Justice, Judicial Administration Division, House of Delegates since 1992) Bar Associations. Recipient Justice Foundation Fellowship 1972. Colonel USAFR 1964-67 (retired). Democrat. Member Kiwanis Club of Raleigh. Enjoys reading, family, travel and dogs.

Mailing address: P.O. Box 888, Raleigh 27602.
Telephone: (919) 733-4230.

EDDINGER, Kevin G. *(Judge, North Carolina District Court District 19C)*
Mailing address: P.O. Box 4237, Salisbury 28145-4237.
Telephone: (704) 639-7509.

EDMUNDS, Robert Holt, Jr. *(Associate Justice, Supreme Court of North Carolina)* Elected Nov 7, 2000. Educated at Williams College 1967-69, Vassar College B.A. with honors 1971 and University of North Carolina School of Law J.D. 1975. Associate Justice Holderness Moot Court Bench. Admitted to practice North Carolina 1975, Virginia 1977, U.S. District Courts Eastern, Middle and Western Districts of North Carolina and U.S. Court of Appeals Fourth Circuit. Certified Specialist in Federal and State Criminal Law and Appellate Criminal Law by The North Carolina State Bar Board of Legal Specialization. In legal practice North Carolina 1993-98. Associate Judge, North Carolina Court of Appeals Jan 1999 to Dec 2000.

Assistant District Attorney District 18 North Carolina 1978-82. Assistant U.S. Attorney 1982-86 and U.S. Attorney 1986-93 Middle District of North Carolina. Former Member North Carolina Academy of Trial Lawyers. Member Guilford Inn of Court, Greensboro, North Carolina and American Bar Associations.

Mailing address: P.O. Box 1841, Raleigh 27602.
Office: Justice Building, Two East Morgan Street, Raleigh 27601.
Telephone: (919) 733-3712.

EDWARDS, C. Thomas *(Judge, North Carolina District Court District 25)*
Mailing address: P.O. Box 1627, Morganton 28680.
Telephone: (828) 433-0728.

ELIASON, Russell A. *(Magistrate Judge, United States District Court Middle District of North Carolina)* Appointed by U.S. District Court judges to term beginning July 1, 1976. Reappointed 1984, 1992 and 2000. Current term expires 2008. Born Minneapolis Minnesota Jan 28, 1944. Religious affiliation: Moravian. Educated at Yale University B.S. 1967, Wake Forest University 1967-68 and University of Minnesota J.D. 1970. Law Clerk to Hon. Martin Van Oosterhout, U.S. Court of Appeals Eighth Circuit 1970-71 and to Hon. Hiram Hamilton Ward, U.S. District Court Middle District of North Carolina 1972-74. Member Phi Alpha Delta. Admitted to practice Minnesota 1970, Iowa 1971, North Carolina 1973 and Nebraska 1975. Began legal practice South Sioux City Nebraska 1974.

Assistant U.S. Attorney Sioux City Iowa 1971-72 and Greensboro North Carolina 1975-76. Member Federal Magistrate Judges Association, Forsyth County, Minnesota State, Iowa State, North Carolina, Nebraska State and American Bar Associations. Attended seminar on Federal Habeas Corpus Asheville North Carolina 1985. Member Sons of Norway, Salem Band and Home Moravian Church. Enjoys music, reading and fishing.

Office: 224 Federal Building, 251 North Main Street, Winston-Salem 27101-3914.
Telephone: (336) 734-2520.

ELLIOTT, Sherri Wilson *(Judge, North Carolina District Court District 25)*
Office: 111 Main Avenue N.E., Hickory 28601.
Telephone: (828) 327-7500.

ELLIS, B. Craig *(Resident Judge, North Carolina Superior Court Fourth Judicial Division District 16A)* Appointed by Governor James B. Hunt, Jr. Jan 28, 1984. Elected 1984, 1988, 1994 and 2002. Current term expires Dec 31, 2010. Currently Senior Resident Judge. Born Wilmington North Carolina Jan 13, 1941. Presbyterian. Educated at University of Virginia B.S.Ed. 1964 and University of North Carolina J.D. 1970. Admitted to practice North Carolina 1970. Began legal practice Laurinburg 1970. Magistrate, U.S. District Court Middle District of North Carolina 1974-76. Judge, North Carolina District Court Sixteenth Judicial District Dec 6, 1976 to Jan 28, 1984.

President North Carolina Conference of Superior Court Judges 2002-03. Member Scotland County, Sixteenth Judicial District (Secretary 1973 and Vice President 1974) and North Carolina Bar Associations. Lieutenant USN 1964-68. Chairman Scotland County Democratic Executive Committee. Enjoys sailing and working with Boy Scouts.

Mailing address: P.O. Box 769, Laurinburg 28353.
Office: Scotland County Courthouse, Laurinburg 28353.
Telephone: (910) 277-3270.
Fax: (910) 277-3184

ELMORE, Richard A. *(Associate Judge, North Carolina Court of Appeals)*
Mailing address: P.O. Box 888, Raleigh 27602.
Office: Court of Appeals Building, One West Morgan Street, Raleigh 27601.
Telephone: (919) 733-0355.

ENNIS, Spencer B. *(Retired-Recalled Judge, North Carolina District Court)* Appointed by Governor James G. Martin to term beginning Feb 11, 1987. Elected 1988, 1992 and 1996. Retired, serves by recall. Former Emergency Judge. Born Rowan County North Carolina Dec 17, 1929. Presbyterian. Educated at Wake Forest University B.S. 1951 LL.B. 1953. Member Phi Alpha Delta. Admitted to practice North Carolina 1954. In legal practice Burlington and Graham Dec 1955 to Feb 11, 1987.

Assistant District Attorney 1964-67. Instructor Alamance Community College 1967-87. Member North Carolina Academy of Trial Lawyers, The North Carolina State Bar, Fifteenth Judicial District A (Former Secretary, Trustee, President 1983) and North Carolina Bar Associations. Attended General Trial Judges Course The National Judicial College 1988. Corporal U.S. Army

ENNIS, SPENCER B.—*Continued*

1953-55. Democrat. Former Secretary and Vice President Young Democrats Club. Former member State Advisory Committee for Senator Robert Morgan. Former Delegate and Chairman County and State Conventions. Former member Planning and Zoning Board, Board of Adjustments City of Burlington and Advisory Board Salvation Army. Former County Chairman Governor's Highway Safety Programs. Former committee member Heart Fund, March of Dimes, United Fund, Diabetes Association and Burlington Coaches Association. Former member Rural Community Development Association and Fire District. Member and Legal Advisor Masons, Shriners, Elks, Moose (Governor) and Lions. State Legal Advisor on National Supreme Forum and Toastmasters International. Enjoys golfing, gardening and cooking.

Office: 120 Criminal Courts Building, 212 West Elm Street, Graham 27253.

ENOCHS, Wendy Melton *(Judge, North Carolina District Court District 18)* Elected Nov 1994 to term beginning Dec 1994. Reelected Nov 3, 1998 and 2002. Current term expires Nov 2006. Born Gainesville Georgia. Presbyterian. Educated at University of North Carolina at Greensboro B.S. with honors 1988 and Campbell University J.D. 1991. Member Phi Alpha Delta. Admitted to practice North Carolina 1991.

Assistant District Attorney Guilford County 1991-94.

Mailing address: P.O. Box 3008, Greensboro 27402-3008.

Telephone: (336) 574-4301.

ERVIN, Robert C. *(Resident Judge, North Carolina Superior Court Seventh Judicial Division District 25A)*

Mailing address: P.O. Box 796, Morganton 28680.

Telephone: (828) 432-2827.

ETHERIDGE, Scott C. *(Judge, North Carolina District Court District 19B)*

Mailing address: P.O. Box 4906, Asheboro 27204-4906.

Telephone: (336) 318-6887.

EVANS, Robert A. *(Judge, North Carolina District Court District 7)*

Mailing address: P.O. Box 2762, Rocky Mount 27802.

Telephone: (252) 234-7676.

EVANS, Yvonne M. *(Resident Judge, North Carolina Superior Court Seventh Judicial Division District 26)* Former Judge and Chief Judge, North Carolina District Court District 26.

Office: 700 East Fourth Street, Charlotte 28202.

Telephone: (704) 347-7800.

EVERETT, Clifton W., Jr. *(Resident Judge, North Carolina Superior Court First Judicial Division District 3A)*

Mailing address: P.O. Box 7045, Greenville 27835.

Telephone: (252) 695-7260.

Fax: (252) 830-3376

EXUM, J. Patrick *(Emergency Judge, North Carolina District Court)* Retired, serves by recall.

Mailing address: c/o Lenoir County Clerk of Superior Court, P.O. Box 68, Kinston 28502-0068.

FAISON, James H., III *(Judge, North Carolina District Court District 5)* Appointed by Governor James B. Hunt, Jr. to term beginning July 21, 2000. Elected Nov 2001, current term expires Jan 2006. First African American male to become a District Court Judge for the Fifth Judicial District in over one hundred years. Born Wilmington North Carolina July 21, 1962. Missionary Baptist. Educated at North Carolina Central University B.A. cum laude J.D. 1987. Admitted to practice North Carolina 1989 and U.S. District Court Eastern District of North Carolina 1989.

Assistant District Attorney Fifth Judicial District 1992 to July 21, 2000. Staff Attorney Legal Services of the Lower Cape Fear. Member North Carolina Association of Assistant District Attorneys, North Carolina Black Lawyers Association, North Carolina Association of District Court Judges, The North Carolina State Bar, New Hanover County and North Carolina Bar Associations. Recipient Community Service Award from Wilmington Chapter Winston-Salem State University Alumni 1991 and Distinguished Service Award from Wilmington Jaycees 1997-98. Democrat. Assistant Pastor Friendship Missionary Baptist Church 1992-97. Guest Speaker Alumni Breakfast North Carolina Agricultural and Technical State University 1996, Pender County Black Focus 1997 and Drug Abuse Resistance Education Program New Hanover Sheriff's Department 2001. Pastor Byrd's Chapel Missionary Baptist Church since Feb 1998. Board of Advisors Wilmington YMCA. Board of Directors Cape Fear United Way, Lower Cape Fear Hospice and Community Boys and Girls Club. Board of Trustees Legal Services of the Lower Cape Fear. Member Youth Council Committee Kenansville Eastern Missionary Baptist Association (Instructor), Pender County Juvenile Crime Prevention Council and Burgaw Rotary Club. Personal Statement or Quote: "Preparation plus opportunity equals success. Stay focused on your goals and your dreams while putting God first."

Office: 519 New Hanover County Judicial Bldg., 316 Princess Street, Wilmington 28401.

Telephone: (910) 341-1120.

E-mail address: James.H.Faison@aoc.state.nc.us

FARMER, Robert L. *(Emergency Judge, North Carolina Superior Court)* Appointed by Governor James B. Hunt, Jr. to term beginning Dec 15, 1977. Elected 1978, 1984 and 1992. Retired, serves by recall. Born Johnston County North Carolina July 23, 1933. Methodist. Educated at University of North Carolina B.S. 1955 LL.B. 1960. Admitted to practice North Carolina 1960. Began legal practice Raleigh 1960.

North Carolina State Representative 1971-77. Member North Carolina Judicial Council 1973-75, Wake County and North Carolina Bar Associations. Member North Carolina General Statutes Commission 1975-77 and North Carolina Advisory Budget Commission 1977. Specialist Third Class U.S. Army 1955-57. Democrat. President Raleigh Jaycees 1966-67. Enjoys golf.

Mailing address: P.O. Box 351, Raleigh 27602.

Office: Wake County Courthouse, Raleigh 27602.

FARRIS, William C. *(Judge, North Carolina District Court District 7)*

Mailing address: P.O. Box 999, Wilson 27894.

Telephone: (252) 234-7676.

FINCH, Daniel F. *(Judge, North Carolina District Court District 9)* Appointed by Governor James B. Hunt, Jr. to term beginning Jan 24, 1995. Elected Nov 1996 and 2000. Current term expires Dec 2004. Born Oxford North Carolina. Baptist. Educated at University of North Carolina at Chapel Hill B.A. 1970 and Mercer

FINCH, DANIEL F.—*Continued*

University J.D. 1973. Admitted to practice North Carolina 1973 and U.S. District Court Eastern District of North Carolina 1979. In legal practice Oxford 1973-95.

Attorney Granville County Board of Education 1974-95. City Attorney Oxford 1975-95. Member North Carolina Bar Association. Attended "General Jurisdiction" The National Judicial College University of Nevada, Reno Summer 1997.

Mailing address: P.O. Box 597, Oxford 27565.

Telephone: (919) 693-9215, 693-5193.

FINE, Lawrence J. *(Judge, North Carolina District Court District 21)*

Mailing address: P.O. Box 20099, Winston-Salem 27120-0099.

Telephone: (336) 761-2478.

FITCH, Milton F., Jr. *(Resident Judge, North Carolina Superior Court First Judicial Division District 7B)* Appointed by Governor Michael F. Easley Dec 29, 2001. Elected Nov 4, 2002, current term expires Dec 31, 2010. Born Wilson North Carolina Oct 20, 1946. Educated at North Carolina Central University B.A. 1969 and North Carolina Central University School of Law J.D. 1971. Admitted to practice North Carolina 1975 and District of Columbia 1975. In legal practice Wilson North Carolina Nov 1975 to Dec 2001.

Member North Carolina General Assembly Nov 1984 to Dec 29, 2001. Member Mount Hebron Masonic Lodge #42.

Mailing address: P.O. Box 2445, Wilson 27894-2445.

Office: 115 East Nash Street, Third Floor, Wilson 27893.

Telephone: (252) 399-0008.

Fax: (252) 291-8635

E-mail address: Milton.F.Fitch@nccourts.nc.org

FLANAGAN, Louise W. *(Magistrate Judge, United States District Court Eastern District of North Carolina)* Appointed by U.S. District Court judges May 16, 1995. Reappointed May 16, 1999 and 2003. Current term expires May 15, 2007. Serves part time. Born Richmond Virginia June 26, 1962. Educated at Wake Forest University B.A. magna cum laude 1984 and University of Virginia J.D. 1988. Law Clerk to Hon. Malcolm J. Howard, U.S. District Court Eastern District of North Carolina 1988. Admitted to practice North Carolina 1988 and District of Columbia 1988. In legal practice Washington D.C. 1989-90 and Greenville 1990-99.

Member Fourth Circuit Judicial Conference, The District of Columbia Bar and The North Carolina State Bar.

Office: 103 U.S. Courthouse Annex, 215 South Evans Street, Greenville 27858-1133.

Telephone: (252) 830-1334.

FLOYD, Robert F., Jr. *(Resident Judge, North Carolina Superior Court Fourth Judicial Division District 16B)* Elected to term beginning Jan 1, 1997. Term expires Dec 31, 2004. Senior Resident Judge since March 6, 2002. Born Lumberton North Carolina March 30, 1954. Baptist. Educated at Campbell University B.S. cum laude 1976 J.D. 1979. Admitted to practice North Carolina 1979 and U.S. District Court Eastern District of North Carolina 1980. In legal practice Fairmont 1979-88. Judge, North Carolina District Court District 16B 1988-97.

Member The North Carolina State Bar and Robeson County Bar Association. Attended General Jurisdiction course The National Judicial College. Democrat. Former Deacon and Trustee First Baptist Church of Fairmont. Coach and Umpire Little League Baseball. Member Child Fatalities Task Force, Juvenile Multi-Purpose Board of Advisors, Civitan (Past President), Masons and Shriners.

Office: 18 Robeson County Courthouse, Lumberton 28358.

Telephone: (910) 671-3325.

Fax: (910) 671-3113

FONVIELLE, J. Keaton *(Emergency Judge, North Carolina District Court)* Retired, serves by recall.

Mailing address: P.O. Box 1867, Shelby 28151-1867.

FORD, Larry G. *(Resident Judge, North Carolina Superior Court Sixth Judicial Division District 19C)* Currently Senior Resident Judge.

Mailing address: P.O. Box 4156, Salisbury 28145-4156.

Telephone: (704) 639-7503.

FOSTER, Anna F. *(Judge, North Carolina District Court District 27B)*

Office: Cleveland County Courthouse, 100 Justice Place, Shelby 28150.

Telephone: (704) 484-4801.

FOSTER, Thomas G., Jr. *(Judge, North Carolina District Court District 18)*

Mailing address: P.O. Box 3008, Greensboro 27402-3008.

Telephone: (336) 574-4301.

FOX, David Kennedy *(Judge, North Carolina District Court District 29)* Assumed office Dec 2, 1996.

Mailing address: c/o Clerk of Superior Court, P.O. Box 965, Hendersonville 28739-0965.

Office: Henderson County Courthouse, Hendersonville 28739.

Telephone: (828) 287-2604.

FOX, James C. *(Senior Judge, United States District Court Eastern District of North Carolina)* Appointed for life by President Ronald Reagan to term beginning Nov 10, 1982. Assumed Senior status Jan 31, 2001, serves by assignment. Former Chief Judge. Born Atchison Kansas Nov 6, 1928. Episcopalian. Educated at University of North Carolina at Chapel Hill B.S.B.A. 1950 J.D. cum laude 1957. Recipient Block Award and Clark Award 1957. Board of Editors North Carolina Law Review 1957. Law Clerk to Hon. Don Gilliam, U.S. District Court 1957-58. Member Order of the Coif. Admitted to practice North Carolina 1957. Began legal practice Wilmington 1958.

Attorney New Hanover County 1967-81. Author Note "Injunction to Prohibit Use in State Court of Evidence Illegally Obtained by Federal Agents" 35 North Carolina L. Rev. 483, 1957, Book Review "Admiralty Law of the Supreme Court" 41 North Carolina L. Rev. 654, 1963 and "Removal Jurisdiction and Procedure" 10 No. 2 The Practical Lawyer Feb 1964. Member New Hanover County (President 1967-68), Fifth Judicial District (Secretary 1960-62), North Carolina (Lecturer 1964) and American Bar Associations. Recipient Conservation Service Award from Ducks Unlimited 1975. Corporal USAR 1951-59. Republican. Board of Directors Family Service Society 1961-66, Opportunities, Inc. of New Hanover County 1968-69, New Hanover School for

FOX, JAMES C.—*Continued*

Mentally Retarded Children 1968-71 and St. John's Art Gallery 1974. Director Law Alumni Association University of North Carolina 1963-66. President Law Foundation of University of North Carolina 1977-79. Member United Fund (President 1970). Interested in hunting and waterfowl conservation. Enjoys sailing and fishing.

Mailing address: P.O. Box 2143, Wilmington 28402-2143.

Telephone: (910) 815-4738.

FOY, Louis F., Jr. *(Judge, North Carolina District Court District 4)*

Mailing address: P.O. Box 460, Pollocksville 28573.

Telephone: (910) 296-2308.

FRYE, Henry E., Jr. *(Resident Judge, North Carolina Superior Court Fifth Judicial Division District 18)*

Mailing address: P.O. Box 3008, Greensboro 27402.

Telephone: (336) 574-4300.

FULLWOOD, Ernest Berlin *(Resident Judge, North Carolina Superior Court Second Judicial Division District 5)* Assumed office 1988. Senior Resident Judge since 1988. Born Wilmington North Carolina Oct 24, 1944. Educated at Wilmington College B.A. in History 1966 and North Carolina Central University Law School J.D. summa cum laude 1972. Recipient Dean's Scholarship for Academic Excellence and U.S. Law Week Award. Board of Editors North Carolina Law Journal. Member Delta Theta Phi. In legal practice 1976-88.

Assistant Professor of Law and Professor of Law North Carolina Central University Law School 1972-76. Board of Directors Legal Services of the Lower Cape Fear. Member State Advisory Council to The Legal Services Corporation. Member North Carolina Association of Black Lawyers, North Carolina Academy of Trial Lawyers, The North Carolina State Bar (Trust Account Committee), New Hanover County, Fifth Judicial District (Secretary), North Carolina and National Bar Associations. Faculty Member Civil Criminal Trial Skills Workshop North Carolina Academy of Trial Lawyers and Civil Settlement Technique Program North Carolina Association of Black Lawyers. U.S. Army (two years active duty). Former Director Community Boy's Club. Former Member North Carolina Organized Crime Council, Wilmington-New Hanover Planning Commission and American Red Cross. Life Member NAACP and Veterans of Foreign Wars. Referral Attorney North Carolina Civil Liberties Union, North Carolina Land Loss Program and Legal Services Pro Bono Program. Member Board of Trustees Ebenezer Baptist Church.

Office: 519 New Hanover County Judicial Bldg., 316 Princess Street, Wilmington 28401.

Telephone: (910) 341-1140.

FULLWOOD, James R. *(Judge, North Carolina District Court District 10)*

Mailing address: P.O. Box 351, Raleigh 27602.

Telephone: (919) 755-4101.

GALLOWAY, Mark E. *(Chief Judge, North Carolina District Court District 9A)*

Office: Person County Courthouse, 105 South Main Street, Roxboro 27573.

Telephone: (336) 597-0567.

GASH, Robert T. *(Retired-Recalled Judge, North Carolina District Court)* Elected to term beginning Dec 2, 1968. Reelected 1972, 1976, 1980 and 1984. Former Chief Judge. Retired, serves by recall. Born Brevard North Carolina Oct 6, 1924. Episcopalian. Educated at Brevard Junior College 1943 and University of North Carolina A.B. 1948 J.D. 1950. Admitted to practice North Carolina 1950. Began legal practice Brevard 1950. Judge, General County Court of Transylvania 1961-65.

State Senator 1953-54. Member American Judicature Society, North Carolina Association of District Judges (President 1975), North Carolina Conference of Chief Judges (President 1974 and 1984), Transylvania County (President 1966), Twenty-ninth Judicial District (President 1967), North Carolina and American Bar Associations. Named Delegate to National Conference of Special Court Judges. Attended National College of the State Judiciary 1975. Lieutenant j.g. USNR (naval aviator) 1943-45. Democrat. President Episcopal Foundation of West North Carolina 1976 and 1995-96.

Mailing address: c/o Transylvania County Clerk of Superior Court, 12 East Main Street, Brevard 28712.

GASTON, Harley Black, Jr. *(Retired-Recalled Judge, North Carolina District Court)* Elected to term beginning Dec 1, 1986. Reelected 1990, 1994 and Nov 3, 1998. Chief Judge April 19, 1995 to April 30, 2001. Retired May 1, 2001, serves by recall. Born Gastonia North Carolina April 16, 1929. Methodist. Educated at Duke University A.B. 1952 J.D. 1956. Admitted to practice North Carolina 1956 and U.S. District Court Western District of North Carolina 1957. In legal practice Belmont 1956-86.

City Attorney Belmont 1967-86. Member North Carolina State Bar, Gaston County and North Carolina Bar Associations. Attended Traffic Court Seminar American Bar Association Chicago 1986 and The National Judicial College Reno Nevada March 1987 to April 1987. Lieutenant j.g. USNR Korea 1952-54. Democrat. Member Board of Commissioners Gaston County 1976-84 (Vice Chairman 1979-82, Chairman 1982-84). Past President Belmont Rotary Club, Belmont United Fund and Belmont Chamber of Commerce. Past Commander American Legion Post 144. Past Chairman Building Committee First United Methodist Church. Board of Advisors Belmont Abbey College. Interests include yard work, hiking, camping, jogging, history and municipal government.

Office: Gaston County Courthouse, 325 North Marietta Street, Gastonia 28052.

GAVIN, Lee W. *(Judge, North Carolina District Court District 19B)*

Mailing address: P.O. Box 4906, Asheboro 27204-4906.

Telephone: (336) 318-6887.

GEER, Martha A. *(Associate Judge, North Carolina Court of Appeals)*

Mailing address: P.O. Box 888, Raleigh 27602.

Office: Court of Appeals Building, One West Morgan Street, Raleigh 27601.

Telephone: (919) 733-0496.

GENTRY, L. Michael *(Judge, North Carolina District Court District 9A)*

Mailing address: P.O. Box 94, Pelham 27311.

Telephone: (336) 597-0567.

GESSNER, Paul G. *(Judge, North Carolina District Court District 10)*
Mailing address: P.O. Box 351, Raleigh 27602.
Telephone: (919) 786-4245.

GINGLES, Ralph C., Jr. *(Judge, North Carolina District Court District 27A)*
Office: Gaston County Courthouse, 325 North Marietta Street, Gastonia 28052.
Telephone: (704) 852-3117.

GINN, Charles Philip *(Resident Judge, North Carolina Superior Court Eighth Judicial Division District 24)*
Mailing address: P.O. Box 940, Marshall 28753.
Telephone: (828) 265-5369.

GOODMAN, Rodney R. *(Emergency Judge, North Carolina District Court)* Former Chief Judge. Retired, serves by recall.
Mailing address: P.O. Box 68, Kinston 28502-0068.

GORE, William C., Jr. *(Resident Judge, North Carolina Superior Court Fourth Judicial Division District 13)* Currently Senior Resident Judge. Born Whiteville North Carolina Oct 27, 1951. Baptist (Sunday School teacher, member Family Life Council). Educated at University of North Carolina at Chapel Hill B.A. 1974 and North Carolina Central University J.D. magna cum laude 1977. Staff member North Carolina Central University Law Review 1976-77. Member Phi Sigma Kappa. Admitted to practice North Carolina 1977. Began legal practice Whiteville 1977. Former Chief Judge, North Carolina District Court Thirteenth Judicial District.

Assistant District Attorney 1979-80. Member North Carolina Academy of Trial Lawyers, District Court Judges Association, American Judicature Society, The North Carolina State Bar and American Bar Association. Named one of Outstanding Young Men of America 1982. Recipient Distinguished Service Award from Jaycees 1983. Listed in *Who's Who in American Law* 1984. Democrat. Member Columbus County Cotillion Club, Columbus County Law Officers Association and Columbus County Fair Advisory Board. Enjoys bass fishing, woodworking, gardening and reading.
Office: 106 Courthouse Square, Whiteville 28472.
Telephone: (910) 641-3060.

GRAHAM, L. Dale *(Judge, North Carolina District Court District 22)*
Mailing address: c/o Clerk of Superior Court, P.O. Box 100, Taylorsville 28681.
Office: Alexander County Courthouse, Taylorsville 28681.
Telephone: (704) 878-4209.

GRAHAM, William T., Jr. *(Judge, North Carolina District Court District 21)* Elected to term beginning 1996. Reelected 2000, current term expires 2004. Certified Juvenile Court Judge. Born Illinois Jan 15, 1959. Methodist. Educated at Duke University A.B. 1981 and Thomas M. Cooley Law School J.D. 1989.

Attended The National Judicial College Reno Nevada. Personal Statement or Quote: "Be on time."
Mailing address: P.O. Box 20099, Winston-Salem 27120-0099.
Office: Forsyth County Hall of Justice, Winston-Salem 27120.
Telephone: (336) 761-2478.

GRANT, Cy A. *(Resident Judge, North Carolina Superior Court First Judicial Division District 6B)* Elected to term beginning Jan 1, 1989. Reelected 1996, current term expires Dec 31, 2004. Currently Senior Resident Judge.
Mailing address: P.O. Box 489, Windsor 27983.
Telephone: (252) 794-9406.

GRAY, Jane Powell *(Judge, North Carolina District Court District 10)* Appointed by Governor Michael F. Easley to term beginning Feb 1, 2002. Term expires Nov 30, 2004. Born Richmond Virginia Nov 21, 1949. United Methodist. Educated at University of Florida B.A. 1972 and Campbell University School of Law J.D. 1979. Member Delta Theta Phi. Admitted to practice North Carolina 1979.

Associate Attorney General, Assistant Attorney General and Deputy Attorney General Attorney General's Office North Carolina 1980-99. Member North Carolina Association of District Court Judges, Wake County (President Elect 2000, President 2001) and North Carolina Bar Associations. General Counsel Speaker of the House North Carolina 1999-2001.
Mailing address: P.O. Box 351, Raleigh 27602.
Telephone: (919) 755-4101.
Fax: (919) 835-3226
E-mail address: Jane.P.Gray@nccourts.org

GRAY, Marvin Kenneth *(Retired-Recalled Judge, North Carolina Superior Court)* Resident Judge Twenty-sixth Judicial District 1986-87. Appointed Special Judge by Governor James B. Martin to term beginning Jan 1, 1987. Reappointed to subsequent terms. Retired, serves by recall. Former Emergency Judge. Born Gates County North Carolina March 8, 1931. Presbyterian. Educated at Wake Forest University B.A. 1958 J.D. 1960. Member Sigma Chi and Phi Delta Phi. Admitted to practice North Carolina 1960, U.S. District Courts Eastern and Western Districts of North Carolina and U.S. Court of Appeals Fourth Circuit. In legal practice Charlotte 1960-85.

Author various papers regarding investigation and trial of civil arson cases since 1978. Chairman Superior Court Bench Book Revision Committee. Charter Member North Carolina Association of Defense Attorneys. Member Mecklenburg Satellite Jail Task Force, Judicial Standards Commission, Supreme Court Alternative Dispute Resolution Committee, Capital Indigent Committee, Civil Procedure Study Commission, North Carolina Conference of Superior Court Judges, The Defense Research Institute, Inc., The North Carolina State Bar, Twenty-sixth Judicial District (Former member Executive Committee and Medico-Legal Committee, Former Chairman Calendar Committee, Unauthorized Practice Committee and Grievance and Ethics Committee), North Carolina (Litigation Section) and American (Section of Tort and Insurance Practice) Bar Associations. Graduate General Jurisdiction course The National Judicial College 1988. Lecturer "Rules, Code of Professional Ethics" Oct 1988 and CLE Program "Rule 5, Conflicts of Interest" 1988 Mecklenburg County Bar Association. Lecturer North Carolina Association of Defense Attorneys, North Carolina Justice Academy, North Carolina Claim Association, Charlotte Claim Association, Charlotte Fire Academy, North Carolina Chapter International Association of Arson Investigators and North Carolina Law Enforcement

GRAY, MARVIN KENNETH—*Continued*

Officers. Listed in *Who's Who in the Southwest* 15th ed. 300, 1976. USAF 1951-54.

Office: 3304 Mecklenburg County Criminal Courts Building, 700 East Fourth Street, Charlotte 28202.

GREEN, Jennifer M. *(Judge, North Carolina District Court District 10)*

Mailing address: P.O. Box 351, Raleigh 27602.
Telephone: (919) 755-4101.

GREENLEE, John K. *(Judge, North Carolina District Court District 27A)*

Office: Gaston County Courthouse, 325 North Marietta Street, Gastonia 28052.
Telephone: (704) 852-3117.

GREESON, Howard R., Jr. *(Emergency Judge, North Carolina Superior Court)* Elected to term beginning Jan 1, 1989. Reelected 1996. Retired Jan 31, 2002, serves by recall.

Mailing address: P.O. Box 2434, High Point 27261.

GREGORY, Edgar B. *(Chief Judge, North Carolina District Court District 23)*

Mailing address: P.O. Box 833, Wilkesboro 28697.
Telephone: (336) 838-4246.

GRIFFIN, William C., Jr. *(Resident Judge, North Carolina Superior Court First Judicial Division District 2)* Term expires Dec 31, 2010. Currently Senior Resident Judge.

Mailing address: P.O. Box 1152, Williamston 27892.
Telephone: (252) 792-7341.

GRIMES, Samuel G. *(Judge, North Carolina District Court District 2)*

Mailing address: P.O. Box 1297, Washington 27889.
Telephone: (252) 946-2660.

GUICE, Zoro J., Jr. *(Resident Judge, North Carolina Superior Court Eighth Judicial Division District 29)* Elected Nov 1990 to term beginning Jan 1991. Reelected Nov 3, 1998, current term expires 2006. Currently Senior Resident Judge. Educated at Mars Hill College, University of North Carolina B.A. 1963 and Wake Forest University J.D. 1969. Law Clerk to Hon. Woodrow Wilson Jones, U.S. District Court Western District of North Carolina 1969-72. In legal practice Rockingham 1972-74. Judge, North Carolina District Court Twenty-ninth Judicial District 1976-91.

Member North Carolina Bar Association. Attended North Carolina Superior Court Judges Conference. Democrat. Enjoys bass fishing.

Mailing address: P.O. Box 188, Rutherfordton 28139.
Telephone: (828) 286-4690.
Fax: (828) 286-4322

GULLETT, Julia Shuping *(Judge, North Carolina District Court District 22)*

Mailing address: P.O. Box 186, Statesville 28687.
Telephone: (704) 878-4209.

GWYN, Hunt *(Judge, North Carolina District Court District 20)*

Mailing address: c/o Clerk of Superior Court, P.O. Box 5038, Monroe 28111.
Office: Union County Courthouse, Monroe 28111.
Telephone: (704) 982-3095.

HAIGWOOD, Thomas D. *(Special Judge, North Carolina Superior Court)* Appointed by Governor James B. Hunt, Jr. March 10, 1999 to term beginning April 16, 1999. Term expires April 16, 2004. Born Columbia South Carolina Nov, 9 1945. Methodist. Educated at University of North Carolina at Chapel Hill LL.B. 1970. Law Clerk to Hon. John Davis Larkins, Jr., U.S. District Court Eastern District of North Carolina 1970-71. Admitted to practice North Carolina 1970, U.S. District Court Eastern District of North Carolina 1970 and U.S. Supreme Court 1974. In legal practice Greenville 1973-75.

Assistant District Attorney Third Prosecutorial District 1976-82 and District Attorney 3A Prosecutorial District 1983-99. President North Carolina Conference of District Attorneys 1993-94. Recipient Outstanding Leadership Award from North Carolina Victim Assistance Network 1997. Member Order of the Long Leaf Pine 1999. Enjoys camping, fishing and cooking.

Mailing address: P.O. Box 1465, Greenville 27835.
Office: Pitt County Courthouse, Greenville 27835.
Telephone: (252) 830-6460.
Fax: (252) 830-3376

HAIR, John S., Jr. *(Judge, North Carolina District Court District 12)*

Mailing address: P.O. Box 363, Fayetteville 28302.
Telephone: (910) 678-2901.

HAMBY, William G., Jr. *(Chief Judge, North Carolina District Court District 19A)* Chief Judge since Jan 5, 1998.

Mailing address: P.O. Box 70, Concord 28026-0070.
Telephone: (704) 786-4137.

HAMILTON, Joyce Amelia *(Chief Judge, North Carolina District Court District 10)* Appointed by Governor James G. Martin to term beginning Oct 1986. Elected Nov 1986, 1990, 1994, 1998 and 2002. Current term expires Dec 2006. Chief Judge since Dec 1, 2000. Born Camp LeJeune North Carolina Nov 13, 1949. Educated at University of North Carolina at Greensboro B.S. magna cum laude and University of North Carolina at Chapel Hill School of Law J.D. 1975. Alumni Scholar University of North Carolina at Greensboro. Admitted to practice North Carolina 1975. In legal practice Raleigh 1983 to Oct 1986.

Assistant District Attorney Tenth Judicial District Sept 1975 to April 1978. Executive Director North Carolina Academy of Trial Lawyers May 1978 to June 1979. Staff Attorney North Carolina Court of Appeals July 1979 to May 1983. Board of Directors Badger-Iredell Foundation 1983-84 and Reentry of Wake County 1987-92. Guardian Ad Litem Advisory Council since 1999. Member Governor's Crime Commission Aug 1983 to Feb 1986, North Carolina Association of Women Attorneys, The North Carolina State Bar and Wake County Bar Association (Board of Directors 1977-78, 1981 and 1994-95, Committee on Indigent Appointments 1984-86). Attended The National Judicial College 1987. Named Outstanding Young Woman of America 1978 and 1983. Named Woman of the Year by Raleigh Business and Professional Women's Club 1986. Inducted into YMCA Academy of Women 1988. Member Partners of Wake County 1982-83 and Raleigh Business and Professional Women's Club since 1976. Member Master Plan Advisory Committee North Carolina Department of Correction 1992 and Statewide Substance Abuse Task Force 1994-95. Member Advisory Council Domestic Offenders

HAMILTON, JOYCE AMELIA—*Continued*

Sentenced to Education Program 1993-96, Domestic Violence Council since 1997 and Supervised Visitation/ Exchange Center since 2002. Board of Trustees Summit House 1994-00. Community Advisor Junior League of Raleigh 1991-93. Foster parent 1990-93. Enjoys boating and traveling.

Mailing address: P.O. Box 351, Raleigh 27602.
Office: Wake County Courthouse, Raleigh 27602.
Telephone: (919) 755-4101.

HAMMOND, Lawrence T., Jr. *(Emergency Judge, North Carolina District Court)* Retired, serves by recall.

Mailing address: P.O. Box 4906, Asheboro 27204-4906.

HARDISON, James W. *(Chief Judge, North Carolina District Court District 2)* Appointed by Governor James B. Hunt, Jr. Jan 13, 1981. Elected 1984, 1988, 1992, 1996 and 2000. Current term expires Dec 31, 2004. Chief Judge since 1992. Born Martin County North Carolina Jan 7, 1939. Religious affiliation: Disciples of Christ. Member First Christian Church. Educated at University of North Carolina at Chapel Hill A.B. 1961 LL.B. 1964. Member Sigma Nu and Delta Theta Phi. Admitted to practice North Carolina 1964. Began legal practice Williamston 1971.

Special Agent FBI 1964-70. Former Assistant District Attorney. Member North Carolina District Court Judges Association and The North Carolina State Bar.

Mailing address: P.O. Box 1403, Washington 27889.
Telephone: (252) 946-2660.

HARDISON, Paul A. *(Judge, North Carolina District Court District 4)*

Mailing address: P.O. Box 1101, Jacksonville 28541.
Telephone: (910) 296-2308.

HARPER, Jane V. *(Judge, North Carolina District Court District 26)*

Office: 700 East Fourth Street, Suite 3304, Charlotte 28202.
Telephone: (704) 347-7801.

HARPER, Joseph J., Jr. *(Judge, North Carolina District Court District 7)*

Mailing address: P.O. Box 1238, Tarboro 27886.
Telephone: (252) 234-7676.

HARRILL, James A., Jr. *(Emergency Judge, North Carolina District Court)* Elected to term beginning Dec 1976. Reelected 1984, 1988 and 1992. Former Chief Judge. Retired, serves by recall. Born Raleigh North Carolina April 15, 1937. Presbyterian. Educated at University of North Carolina at Chapel Hill A.B. 1961 and Wake Forest University LL.B. 1964. Admitted to practice North Carolina 1966. Began legal practice Rockingham 1966. In legal practice Winston-Salem 1968-76.

Former Chief Prosecutor Twenty-first Judicial District. Member Forsyth County and North Carolina Bar Associations. E-3 USN 1957-59. Member Winston-Salem Kiwanis Club.

Mailing address: P.O. Box 20099, Winston-Salem 27120.
Office: Forsyth County Hall of Justice, Winston-Salem 27120.

HARRISON, Pattie S. *(Emergency Judge, North Carolina District Court)* Retired, serves by recall.

Mailing address: P.O. Box 822, Roxboro 27573.

HARTSFIELD, Denise S. *(Judge, North Carolina District Court District 21)*

Mailing address: P.O. Box 20099, Winston-Salem 27120-0099.
Telephone: (336) 761-2478.

HARVIEL, Ernest J. *(Judge, North Carolina District Court District 15A)*

Office: 120 Criminal Courts Building, 212 West Elm Street, Graham 27253.
Telephone: (336) 570-6871.

HASSELL, A. Robinson *(Judge, North Carolina District Court District 18)*

Mailing address: P.O. Box 3008, Greensboro 27402-3008.
Telephone: (336) 574-4301.

HAYES, Gregory R. *(Judge, North Carolina District Court District 25)*

Mailing address: P.O. Box 4, Hickory 28603.
Telephone: (828) 322-5508.
Fax: (828) 327-7572
E-mail address: hayes@abts.net

HAYES, Roland Harris *(Retired-Recalled Judge, North Carolina District Court)* Appointed by Governor James B. Hunt, Jr. to term beginning Sept 27, 1984. Elected to subsequent terms. Former Chief Judge. Retired Nov 30, 2002, serves by recall. Born Winston-Salem North Carolina Feb 4, 1931. Educated at Winston-Salem State University B.S. in Education 1952, Wake Forest University 1961-63 and North Carolina Central University School of Law J.D. 1971. Member Phi Alpha Delta and Omega Psi Phi. Began legal practice 1971.

Staff Attorney Legal Aid Society of Forsyth County 1971-72. Reginald Heber Smith Community Law Fellow. Member North Carolina Association of District Court Judges, North Carolina Association of Black Lawyers, Winston-Salem, Forsyth County, North Carolina and American Bar Associations. Worked as assistant cashier for Wachovia Bank and Trust Company 1952-68. Golden Heritage Life Member NAACP. Elder and Official Board Member Greater Cleveland Avenue Christian Church. Member Bachelor Benedict Club, Mules, Winston-Salem University Alumni Association and North Carolina Central University School of Law Alumni Association.

Mailing address: P.O. Box 20099, Winston-Salem 27120.
Office: Forsyth County Hall of Justice, Winston-Salem 27120.

HEATH, Elizabeth A. *(Judge, North Carolina District Court District 8)*

Mailing address: P.O. Box 267, Goldsboro 27533-0267.
Telephone: (252) 527-7891.

HELMS, Michael Etna *(Resident Judge, North Carolina Superior Court Fifth Judicial Division District 23)* Elected Nov 3, 1998. Currently Senior Resident Judge. Born North Wilkesboro North Carolina June 10, 1947. Episcopalian. Educated at University of North Carolina at Chapel Hill B.A. with honors 1975 J.D. with honors 1978. Staff member North Carolina Law Review 1977-78. Admitted to practice North Carolina 1978. In legal practice North Wilkesboro 1978-80. Judge, North Caroli-

HELMS, MICHAEL ETNA—*Continued*

na District Court District 23 Sept 1986 to 1998, appointed by Governor James G. Martin.

Assistant District Attorney Twenty-third Judicial District 1980-86. Instructor North Carolina Criminal Justice Training and Standards Division since 1985. Recipient Bronze Star 1969. CW-2 U.S. Army 1967-71. Republican. Secretary Republican Party 1982-87.

Office: 2064 Wilkes County Courthouse, 500 Courthouse Drive, Wilkesboro 28697.

Telephone: (336) 667-4706.

HENDERSON, Walter P. *(Retired-Recalled Judge, North Carolina District Court)* Elected May 1968 to term beginning Dec 1968. Elected to subsequent terms. Retired 1986, serves by recall. Former Emergency Judge. Born Jones County North Carolina Oct 19, 1927. Methodist. Educated at University of North Carolina at Chapel Hill.

Mailing address: P.O. Box 580, Trenton 28585.

HENRY, Charles H. *(Resident Judge, North Carolina Superior Court Second Judicial Division District 4B)* Currently Senior Resident Judge.

Mailing address: P.O. Box 845, Jacksonville 28541.

Telephone: (910) 938-3552.

HIGHT, Henry W., Jr. *(Resident Judge, North Carolina Superior Court Third Judicial Division District 9)* Term expires Dec 31, 2010.

Mailing address: P.O. Box 1682, Henderson 27536.

Telephone: (252) 738-7126.

HILBURN, Patricia Gwynett *(Judge, North Carolina District Court District 3A)*

Mailing address: P.O. Box 8147, Greenville 27835.

Telephone: (252) 695-7270.

HILL, Evelyn W. *(Resident Judge, North Carolina Superior Court Third Judicial Division District 10)*

Mailing address: P.O. Box 351, Raleigh 27602.

Telephone: (919) 755-4100.

HILL, James T. *(Judge, North Carolina District Court District 14)*

Office: 565 Durham County Judicial Building, Sixth Floor, 201 East Main Street, Durham 27701.

Telephone: (919) 564-7240.

HINNANT, Patrice A. *(Judge, North Carolina District Court District 18)* Elected to term beginning 1996. Reelected 2000, current term expires 2004. Born Greensboro North Carolina Aug 16, 1953. Episcopalian. Educated at Spelman College B.A. 1974 and North Carolina Central University J.D. 1978. Admitted to practice North Carolina. In legal practice Greensboro 1987-96.

Assistant Public Defender Greensboro 1983-87. Member North Carolina Association of Black Lawyers, North Carolina Association of District Court Judges, Greensboro, National and American Bar Associations. Board Member Junior League of Greensboro, Inc., Delta Sigma Theta Sorority, Inc. and Links, Inc. Personal Statement or Quote: "Keep the faith!"

Mailing address: P.O. Box 3008, Greensboro 27402-3008.

Telephone: (336) 574-4301.

HINTON, Alma L. *(Judge, North Carolina District Court District 6A)*

Mailing address: P.O. Box 66, Halifax 27839.

Office: Halifax County Courthouse, Halifax 27839.

Telephone: (252) 583-2910.

HOBGOOD, Robert H. *(Resident Judge, North Carolina Superior Court Third Judicial Division District 9)* Term expires Dec 31, 2010. Currently Senior Resident Judge.

Mailing address: 102 South Main Street, Louisburg 27549.

Telephone: (919) 496-2445.

Fax: (919) 497-1638

HOCKENBURY, Jay D. *(Resident Judge, North Carolina Superior Court Second Judicial Division District 5)* Elected Nov 8, 1994 to term beginning Jan 1, 1995. Reelected 2002, current term expires Dec 31, 2010. Born Wilmington Delaware Dec 14, 1947. Pentecostal. Educated at The Citadel B.A. with honors 1969 and Wake Forest University School of Law J.D. 1972. Member Phi Alpha Delta. Admitted to practice North Carolina 1972, U.S. District Court Eastern District of North Carolina 1972 and U.S. Court of Appeals Fourth Circuit 1973. In legal practice Wilmington 1972-94.

Adjunct Faculty Member-Group Facilitator The National Judicial College 2000. President Elect Fifth Judicial District The North Carolina State Bar 1995. Board of Directors Sentencing Services Fifth Judicial District. Member North Carolina Bar Association. Attended General Jurisdiction course The National Judicial College 1996. Instructor Structured Sentencing Seminar University of North Carolina at Wilmington 1996. Panelist "11 Secrets to Success in the Courtroom: Fact and Expert Witness" Superior Court Judges Fall Conference Litigation Section North Carolina Bar Association 1999. Captain U.S. Army Infantry 1972. Republican. Past President Wilmington Railroad Museum Foundation. Presiding Judge North Carolina High School Mock Trial Competition Finals. Member Community Resource Council Wilmington Residential Facility for Women and North Carolina Community Justice Partnership Commission. Enjoys backpacking, gardening, civil war history and sailing.

Office: 341 New Hanover County Judicial Bldg., 316 Princess Street, Wilmington 28401.

Telephone: (910) 341-1140.

Fax: (910) 341-4071

E-mail address: hockbury@bellsouth.net

HODGES, George R. *(Chief Judge, United States Bankruptcy Court Western District of North Carolina)*

Mailing address: P.O. Box 34189, Charlotte 28234.

Telephone: (704) 350-7500.

HOLT, Richlyn D. *(Judge, North Carolina District Court District 30)*

Office: c/o Clerk of Superior Court, Haywood County Courthouse, 215 North Main Street, Waynesville 28786.

Telephone: (828) 456-3796.

HOLT, Shelly Sveda *(Judge, North Carolina District Court District 5)* Elected to term beginning June 22, 1992. Reelected 1996 and 2000. Current term expires Dec 5, 2004. Born Akron Ohio June 24, 1957. Educated at Kent State University B.A. cum laude 1978 and T. C. Williams School of Law University of Richmond J.D.

HOLT, SHELLY SVEDA—*Continued*

magna cum laude 1981. Admitted to practice North Carolina 1981.

Assistant District Attorney District 8, 1981-85 and District 5, 1986-92. Former Member Board of Directors North Carolina Association of Women Attorneys. Member North Carolina District Judges Association (Education Committee, Bench Book Committee) and New Hanover Bar Association (Secretary/Treasurer). Recipient Distinguished Service in Law Enforcement Award from Optimist Club of Cape Fear March 1992. Vice President Board of Directors YWCA. Member Board of Directors Community Penalties Program and Delphi, a Development Learning Assistance Center, Inc.

Office: 519 New Hanover County Judicial Bldg., 316 Princess Street, Wilmington 28401.

Telephone: (910) 341-1120.

HONEYCUTT, James M. *(Judge, North Carolina District Court District 22)*

Mailing address: P.O. Box 1064, Lexington 27293.

Telephone: (336) 249-4764, (704) 878-4209.

HOOKS, D. Jack, Jr. *(Special Judge, North Carolina Superior Court)* Former Resident Judge Fourth Judicial Division District 13. Appointed Special Judge by Governor Michael F. Easley. Former Judge and Chief Judge, North Carolina District Court Thirteenth Judicial District.

Office: 106 Courthouse Square, Whiteville 28472.

HORN, Carl, III *(Magistrate Judge, United States District Court Western District of North Carolina)* Appointed by U.S. District Court judges to term beginning April 3, 1993. Reappointed April 2001, current term expires April 2009. Currently serves as Chief Magistrate Judge. Born Charlotte North Carolina June 12, 1951. Roman Catholic. Educated at University of Virginia B.A. with honors 1973, University of South Carolina School of Law J.D. 1976 and Wheaton College M.A. 1981. Staff member South Carolina Law Review 1974-76. Admitted to practice North Carolina 1976, U.S. District Court Western District of North Carolina 1976 and U.S. Court of Appeals Fourth Circuit 1987. In legal practice Charlotte 1976-79 and 1984-93.

Chief Assistant U.S. Attorney Western District of North Carolina 1987-93. Author *Fourth Circuit Criminal Handbook* 1st ed. 1994, 2nd ed. 1995, 3rd ed. 1996, 4th ed. 1997, 5th ed. 1998, 6th ed. 1999, 7th ed. 2000, 8th ed. 2001, 9th ed. 2002 and 10th ed. 2003; *Fourth Circuit Model Jury Instructions* 1996; and *Federal Civil Practice in the Fourth Circuit* 1997. Editor *Fourth Circuit Criminal Reporter* Michie since 1994. Instructor in Constitutional Law and History Wheaton College 1981-82. Member Mecklenburg County and North Carolina Bar Associations. Speaker on federal criminal law and quality of life issues at numerous CLE seminars. Honored for distinguished service as a federal prosecutor by U.S. Department of Justice and several other federal agencies. Republican. Candidate for U.S. Congress 1984. Enjoys family, church, exercise and health, travel, reading and good conversation.

Office: 238 U.S. Courthouse, 401 West Trade Street, Charlotte 28202.

Telephone: (704) 350-7470.

Fax: (704) 350-7474

HORN, Charles A., Jr. *(Judge, North Carolina District Court District 27B)*

Office: Cleveland County Courthouse, 100 Justice Place, Shelby 28150.

Telephone: (704) 484-4801.

HORTON, Clarence E., Jr. *(Special Judge, North Carolina Superior Court)* Appointed by governor. Born Cabarrus County North Carolina May 4, 1940. Educated at University of North Carolina at Chapel Hill A.B. 1962 J.D. 1965. In legal practice Kannapolis 1965-66 and 1968-81. Judge, Domestic Relations and Juvenile Court Cabarrus County 1966 to Dec 31, 1967. Former Judge, North Carolina District Court District 19A, appointed by Governor James B. Hunt, Jr. to term beginning 1981. Former Associate Judge, North Carolina Court of Appeals, appointed by Governor James B. Hunt, Jr. to term beginning Jan 2, 1998.

Author "Coercive Governmental Intervention and the Family: A Comment on North Carolina's Proposed Standards" Campbell Law Review Fall 1984, "Principles of Valuation in North Carolina Equitable Distribution Actions" Institute of Government 1989 (revised 1993) and "Pension and Retirement Rights in North Carolina Equitable Distribution Cases." Lecturer on Income Tax Law Barber-Scotia College. Chair Custody Mediation Advisory Committee since 1988. Member Endangered Children Committee North Carolina Association of District Court Judges 1983-84. Member Administration of Justice Task Force, Criminal Courts Advisory Committee, Education and Bench Book Committees and Supreme Court ADR Committee. Faculty "Managing Equitable Distribution Trials Effectively" Special Topics Seminar April 1995. Lecturer on interstate custody disputes and on equitable distribution at the annual school for newly appointed or elected district court judges. Recipient Communication Achievement Award from Toastmasters International 1991. Named "Historian of the Year—West" by North Carolina Society of Historians 1998. Sunday School Teacher since 1981. Board of Directors Historic Cabarrus, Inc., Cabarrus Genealogy Society and Kannapolis History Associates. Faculty Leadership Kannapolis, Leadership Cabarrus and "Meet the Courts."

Mailing address: P.O. Box 70, Concord 28026-0070.

HOUSTON, Jeanie Reavis *(Judge, North Carolina District Court District 23)*

Office: Wilkes County Courthouse, 500 Courthouse Drive, Wilkesboro 28697.

Telephone: (336) 838-4246.

HOWARD, Malcolm J. *(Judge, United States District Court Eastern District of North Carolina)* Appointed for life by President Ronald Reagan to term beginning March 11, 1988. Born Kinston North Carolina June 24, 1939. Baptist. Educated at U.S. Military Academy B.S. 1962 and Wake Forest University J.D. 1970. Member Phi Alpha Delta. Admitted to practice North Carolina 1970. In legal practice Greenville 1974-88.

Assistant U.S. Attorney Raleigh 1972-73. Staff Assistant to the President 1974. Lieutenant Colonel U.S. Army (retired). Recipient Silver Star, Bronze Star (twice), Purple Heart and Combat Infantryman's Badge. Republican. Member Rotary Club. Enjoys hunting and fishing.

Mailing address: P.O. Box 5006, Greenville 27835-0078.

Telephone: (252) 830-4976.

HOWERTON, Philip F., Jr. *(Judge, North Carolina District Court District 26)*
Office: 700 East Fourth Street, Suite 3304, Charlotte 28202.
Telephone: (704) 347-7801.

HOYLE, Angela G. *(Judge, North Carolina District Court District 27A)*
Office: Gaston County Courthouse, 325 North Marietta Street, Gastonia 28052.
Telephone: (704) 852-3117.

HUDSON, Orlando F., Jr. *(Resident Judge, North Carolina Superior Court Third Judicial Division District 14)* Elected to term beginning Jan 1, 1989. Reelected 1996, current term expires Dec 31, 2004. Currently Senior Resident Judge. Former Judge, North Carolina District Court Fourteenth Judicial District.
Office: Durham County Judicial Building, Sixth Floor, Durham 27701.
Telephone: (919) 564-7230.

HUDSON, Robin E. *(Associate Judge, North Carolina Court of Appeals)* Elected Nov 2000 to term beginning Jan 2001. Term expires 2008. Educated at Yale University 1973 and University of North Carolina School of Law 1976. Admitted to practice North Carolina 1976. In legal practice Raleigh and Durham 1976 to Nov 2000.
Part-time Chair Review Board North Carolina Occupational Safety and Health Administration 1994-99. Member Advisory Council North Carolina Industrial Commission 1994-2000. Certified Mediator North Carolina Superior Court and Industrial Commission since 1994. Member North Carolina Association of Women Attorneys (Founder 1978), North Carolina Academy of Trial Lawyers (Board of Governors 1992-99) and Wake County Bar Association.
Mailing address: P.O. Box 888, Raleigh 27602.
Office: Court of Appeals Building, One West Morgan Street, Raleigh 27601.
Telephone: (919) 733-4225.

HUNTER, Robert "Bob" C. *(Associate Judge, North Carolina Court of Appeals)* Appointed by Governor James B. Hunt, Jr. July 1998. Elected Nov 3, 1998, current term expires 2006. Educated at University of North Carolina at Chapel Hill B.A. in Political Science 1966 J.D. 1969. Member Sigma Phi Epsilon, Alpha Phi Omega and Delta Theta Phi. In legal practice North Carolina 1969-98.
Assistant District Attorney 1969-70. Attorney McDowell County 1970-94. Former Chairman and Member North Carolina Courts Commission. Former Member North Carolina Academy of Trial Lawyers and North Carolina Sentencing Commission. Member McDowell County, Wake County, Twenty-ninth Judicial District, North Carolina and American Bar Associations. Former Member North Carolina Advisory Council on the Eastern Band of the Cherokee. North Carolina Representative 1980-98. Co-chair Legislative Highway Study Commission 1987-89. Chairman Southern Legislative Conference 1990. Former Chairman Council of State Governments. Former Member and Director North Carolina Victims' Assistance Network and McDowell Economic Development Association. Former Director McDowell United Fund. Former Member University of North Carolina Board of Visitors. Board of Directors Agency of Public Telecommunications 1981-82 and North Carolina Healthy Start. Rotarian. Member First Baptist Church.
Mailing address: P.O. Box 888, Raleigh 27602.
Telephone: (919) 733-4295.

HUNTER, William K. *(Judge, North Carolina District Court District 18)*
Mailing address: P.O. Box 3008, Greensboro 27402-3008.
Telephone: (336) 574-4301.

HUTCHINS, Laurie L. *(Judge, North Carolina District Court District 21)*
Mailing address: P.O. Box 20099, Winston-Salem 27120-0099.
Telephone: (336) 761-2478.

HYATT, Janet Marlene *(Resident Judge, North Carolina Superior Court Eighth Judicial Division District 30B)* Appointed Special Judge by Governor James B. Hunt, Jr. to term beginning Dec 21, 1984. Elected Resident Judge 1986, 1994 and 2002. Current term expires Dec 31, 2010. Currently Senior Resident Judge. Born Waynesville North Carolina Dec 14, 1953. Methodist. Educated at Wake Forest University B.A. with honors 1976 J.D. with honors 1980. Admitted to practice North Carolina 1980. In legal practice Waynesville 1980-84.
Member Longs Chapel United Methodist Church.
Mailing address: P.O. Box 665, Waynesville 28786.
Telephone: (828) 456-3134.
Fax: (828) 452-2510

JACKSON, James A. *(Judge, North Carolina District Court District 27A)*
Office: Gaston County Courthouse, 325 North Marietta Street, Gastonia 28052.
Telephone: (704) 852-3117.

JACOBS, Donald M. *(Emergency Judge, North Carolina Superior Court)* Retired, serves by recall.
Mailing address: P.O. Box 351, Raleigh 27602.
Office: Wake County Courthouse, Raleigh 27602.

JARRELL, H. Thomas, Jr. *(Judge, North Carolina District Court District 18)*
Mailing address: P.O. Box 3008, Greensboro 27402-3008.
Telephone: (336) 574-4301.

JENKINS, Jack W. *(Special Judge, North Carolina Superior Court)* Appointed by governor.
Mailing address: 2345 Airline Drive, Raleigh 27607.
E-mail address: jackwjenkins@yahoo.com

JENKINS, Knox V., Jr. *(Resident Judge, North Carolina Superior Court Fourth Judicial Division District 11B)* Currently Senior Resident Judge.
Mailing address: P.O. Box 2739, Smithfield 27577.
Telephone: (919) 934-0957.

JOHN, Joseph R., Sr. *(Retired Judge, North Carolina Court of Appeals)* Elected Nov 3, 1992 to term beginning Jan 10, 1993. Retired, serves by recall. Currently serves as Emergency Special Judge, North Carolina Superior Court. Born East Chicago Indiana Oct 13, 1939. Episcopalian. Educated at University of North Carolina at Chapel Hill A.B. 1960 M.A. 1967 J.D. 1971. Member Phi Delta Phi. Admitted to practice North Carolina 1971, U.S. District Court Middle District of North Carolina 1976, U.S. Supreme Court 1977 and U.S. Court of Appeals Fourth Circuit 1978. In legal

JOHN, JOSEPH R., SR.—*Continued*
practice Greensboro 1977-80. Judge, North Carolina District Court Eighteenth Judicial District 1980-84. Resident Judge, North Carolina Superior Court Judicial Division Three Eighteenth District E 1984-93.
Staff Attorney Greensboro Legal Aid Foundation 1971-72. Assistant District Attorney Office of District Attorney Eighteenth Judicial District 1972-77.
Mailing address: P.O. Box 351, Raleigh 27602.

JOHNSON, Donna Hedgepeth *(Judge, North Carolina District Court District 19A)*
Mailing address: P.O. Box 70, Concord 28026-0070.
Telephone: (704) 786-4137.

JOHNSON, E. Lynn *(Resident Judge, North Carolina Superior Court Fourth Judicial Division District 12)* Elected 1986, 1994 and 2002. Current term expires Dec 31, 2010. Currently Senior Resident Judge.
Mailing address: P.O. Box 363, Fayetteville 28302.
Telephone: (910) 678-2975.

JOHNSON, Marcus L. *(Resident Judge, North Carolina Superior Court Seventh Judicial Division District 26)*
Office: 700 East Fourth Street, Charlotte 28202.
Telephone: (704) 347-7800.

JOHNSON, Robert W. *(Emergency Judge, North Carolina District Court)* Retired, serves by recall.
Mailing address: c/o Iredell County Clerk of Superior Court, P.O. Box 186, Statesville 28687.

JOHNSTON, Robert P. *(Resident Judge, North Carolina Superior Court Seventh Judicial Division District 26)* Senior Resident Judge since Feb 1, 2003. Former Judge, North Carolina District Court Twenty-sixth Judicial District.
Office: 700 East Fourth Street, Charlotte 28202.
Telephone: (704) 347-7800.

JOLLY, Jerry Arnold *(Chief Judge, North Carolina District Court District 13)* Elected to term beginning Dec 3, 1984. Reelected 1988, 1992, 1996 and 2000. Current term expires 2004. Born Whiteville North Carolina Jan 20, 1949. Baptist. Educated at University of North Carolina at Chapel Hill A.B. 1971 and Wake Forest University J.D. 1979. Member Phi Delta Phi. Admitted to practice North Carolina 1979 and U.S. District Court Eastern District of North Carolina 1984. In legal practice Tabor City 1979-84.
Member North Carolina Association of District Court Judges, The North Carolina State Bar, Columbus County, Thirteenth Judicial District and North Carolina Bar Associations. Attended Summer and Fall Conferences of District Court Judges Administrative Office of Courts June 1992 and Sept-Oct 1992 and 12th Annual Review Sept 1992 and Torts Laws Oct 1992 Wake Forest University Law School. Democrat. Member Civitan Club of Tabor City. Past President, Secretary and associate member Tabor City Chamber of Commerce.
Mailing address: P.O. Box 36, Tabor City 28463.
Telephone: (910) 641-3070.

JOLLY, John R., Jr. *(Special Judge, North Carolina Superior Court)* Appointed by governor.
Mailing address: P.O. Box 351, Raleigh 27602.
Telephone: (919) 755-4100.

JONES, Abraham Penn *(Resident Judge, North Carolina Superior Court Third Judicial Division District 10)*
Mailing address: P.O. Box 351, Raleigh 27602.
Telephone: (919) 755-4100.

JONES, Carol A. *(Judge, North Carolina District Court District 4)*
Mailing address: P.O. Box 65, Kenansville 28349.
Telephone: (910) 296-2308.
Fax: (910) 296-2311

JONES, Paul L. *(Resident Judge, North Carolina Superior Court Second Judicial Division District 8A)* Currently Senior Resident Judge. Former Judge, North Carolina District Court District 8.
Mailing address: P.O. Box 68, Kinston 28502.
Telephone: (252) 527-2629.

JONES, William G. *(Emergency Judge, North Carolina District Court)* Elected to term beginning Dec 1976. Reelected 1980, 1984, 1988, 1992 and 1996. Former Chief Judge. Retired, serves by recall. Born Weston West Virginia Aug 7, 1945. Educated at Glenville State College 1963-64, Davidson College B.A. 1967 and University of North Carolina J.D. 1970. Law Clerk to Judge James B. McMillan, U.S. District Court Western District of North Carolina 1970-72. Admitted to practice North Carolina 1971. In legal practice 1973-75.
With Mecklenburg County Public Defender's Office 1975-76. Member North Carolina Bar Association. Democrat.
Office: 3304 Criminal Courts Building, 700 East Fourth Street, Charlotte 28202.

JORDAN, Lillian B. *(Emergency Judge, North Carolina District Court)* Retired, serves by recall.
Mailing address: P.O. Box 4906, Asheboro 27204-4906.

KEEVER, Anna Elizabeth *(Chief Judge, North Carolina District Court District 12)* Appointed by Governor James B. Hunt, Jr. to term beginning Feb 9, 1982. Elected Nov 1982, 1986, 1990, 1994, Nov 3, 1998 and 2002. Current term expires Dec 2006. Born Elkin North Carolina Oct 10, 1950. Methodist. Educated at University of North Carolina at Greensboro B.A. 1972 and University of North Carolina at Chapel Hill J.D. 1975. Member Phi Beta Kappa. Admitted to practice North Carolina 1975.
Assistant District Attorney Fayetteville 1975-82. Member North Carolina Association of District Court Judges (Chair Education Committee since 1987), North Carolina (Vice President 1990-91) and American (National Conference of Special Court Judges) Bar Associations. Member North Carolina Judicial Standards Commission. President Cumberland County Dispute Resolution Center 1987-90 and Board of Directors Women's Center of Fayetteville 1990-92. Board of Trustees University of North Carolina at Greensboro Alumni Association. Enjoys movies, plays and reading.
Mailing address: P.O. Box 363, Fayetteville 28302.
Telephone: (910) 678-2901.

KEIGER, R. Kason *(Emergency Judge, North Carolina District Court)* Elected to term beginning Dec 6, 1976. Reelected 1980, 1984, 1988 and 1992. Retired, serves by recall. Born Forsyth County North Carolina June 28, 1934. Presbyterian. Educated at University of North Carolina at Chapel Hill B.S. 1956 and Wake Forest University J.D. replaced LL.B. conferred 1960. Ad-

KEIGER, R. KASON—*Continued*

mitted to practice North Carolina 1960. Began legal practice Winston-Salem 1960. Judge, Kernersville Recorder's Court 1968.

Member North Carolina and American Bar Associations. Democrat. Private pilot. Enjoys scuba diving, jogging, photography, painting and music.

Mailing address: c/o Iredell County Clerk of Superior Court, P.O. Box 186, Statesville 28687.

KEY, Spencer G., Jr. *(Judge, North Carolina District Court District 17B)*

Mailing address: P.O. Box 456, Dobson 27017.

Telephone: (336) 386-3750.

KIMBLE, Wayne G., Jr. *(Judge, North Carolina District Court District 4)* Former Chief Judge.

Mailing address: P.O. Box 866, Kenansville 28540.

Telephone: (910) 296-2308.

KINCAID, Timothy S. *(Resident Judge, North Carolina Superior Court Seventh Judicial Division District 25B)* Elected Nov 3, 1998. Senior Resident Judge since Feb 1, 2002. Born Newton North Carolina Dec 9, 1952. Lutheran. Educated at Western Carolina University B.S. cum laude 1976, Campbell College School of Law J.D. 1979 and University of North Carolina at Chapel Hill 1982. Admitted to practice North Carolina 1979, U.S. District Court District of North Carolina 1979, U.S. Court of Appeals Fourth Circuit 1982 and U.S. Supreme Court 1982. Judge, North Carolina District Court District 25 1986-98, appointed by Governor James G. Martin.

Instructor in Business Law Catawba Valley Community College 1982-86. Member North Carolina Association of District Court Judges. USAR May 15, 1972 to May 15, 1979. Republican. Charter President Mountain View Lions Club. President North Carolina Child Support Council. Member Lion Lutheran Church. Enjoys travel, racquetball, skiing, collecting coins and music.

Mailing address: P.O. Box 9606, Hickory 28603.

Telephone: (828) 327-7500.

KIRBY, Robert W. *(Retired-Recalled Judge, North Carolina Superior Court)* Retired, serves by recall.

Office: Gaston County Courthouse, 325 North Marietta Street, Gastonia 28052.

KLASS, Jack E. *(Retired-Recalled Judge, North Carolina District Court)* Retired, serves by recall.

Mailing address: c/o Davidson County Clerk of Superior Court, P.O. Box 1064, Lexington 27293-1064.

KLASS, Mark E. *(Resident Judge, North Carolina Superior Court Sixth Judicial Division District 22)* Elected to term beginning Nov 3, 1998. Senior Resident Judge since Oct 1, 2001.

Mailing address: P.O. Box 1343, Lexington 27293.

Telephone: (704) 878-4213.

KLUTTZ, William C., Jr. *(Judge, North Carolina District Court District 19C)* Appointed by Governor James B. Hunt, Jr. to term beginning July 2, 1999.

Mailing address: P.O. Box 4237, Salisbury 28145-4237.

Telephone: (704) 639-7509.

KNIGHT, Rebecca B. *(Judge, North Carolina District Court District 28)* Elected May 1989 to term beginning Dec 3, 1990. Reelected 1994, Nov 3, 1998 and 2002. Current term expires Dec 2006. Born Lake Charles Louisiana Dec 14, 1955. Methodist. Educated at Appalachian State University B.S. with honors 1977 and Campbell University School of Law J.D. 1982. Admitted to practice North Carolina 1982 and U.S. District Court Western District of North Carolina. In legal practice Black Mountain 1982-84 and Asheville 1987-88.

Assistant County Attorney Buncombe County 1984-86 and 1988. Assistant District Attorney Twenty-eighth Judicial District Asheville 1989-90.

Office: Buncombe County Courthouse, 60 Court Plaza, Asheville 28801-3583.

Telephone: (828) 232-2760.

KNOX, Michael G. *(Judge, North Carolina District Court District 19A)*

Mailing address: P.O. Box 70, Concord 28026-0070.

Telephone: (704) 786-4137.

KWASIKPUI, Alfred W. *(Chief Judge, North Carolina District Court District 6B)*

Mailing address: P.O. Box 643, Jackson 27845.

Telephone: (252) 534-1785.

Fax: (252) 534-1308

LaBARRE, David Q. *(Emergency Judge, North Carolina Superior Court)* Retired, serves by recall. Former Judge and Chief Judge, North Carolina District Court Fourteenth Judicial District.

Office: 278 Durham County Judicial Building, Sixth Floor, 201 East Main Street, Durham 27701.

LAKE, I. Beverly, Jr. *(Chief Justice, Supreme Court of North Carolina)* Associate Justice 1995-2000. Elected Chief Justice 2000. Born Raleigh North Carolina. Educated at Wake Forest University B.S. 1955 J.D. 1960. In legal practice Raleigh 1960-69 and 1976-85. Special Judge, North Carolina Superior Court 1985-91. Associate Justice, North Carolina Supreme Court 1992-93.

Assistant Attorney General 1969-74 and Deputy Attorney General 1974-76 North Carolina Department of Justice. Member Association of Interstate Commerce Commission Practitioners, North Carolina Academy of Trial Lawyers, The North Carolina State Bar, Wake County and North Carolina Bar Associations. Member North Carolina Senate 1976-80. Eagle Scout 1948. Member Raleigh Chamber of Commerce 1977-83. Member Ridge Road Baptist Church of Raleigh since 1960.

Mailing address: P.O. Box 1841, Raleigh 27602.

Telephone: (919) 733-3711.

LAMM, Charles Cadmus, Jr. *(Special Judge, North Carolina Superior Court)* Appointed Special Judge by Governor James B. Hunt, Jr. to term beginning July 17, 1979. Reappointed May 2, 1984. Elected Resident Judge Nov 1984. Retired, served as Emergency Judge by recall. Reappointed Special Judge by Governor James B. Hunt, Jr. Sept 1, 1995. Reappointed to subsequent term. Born Wilson North Carolina Nov 10, 1944. Methodist. Educated at Wake Forest University B.A. 1966 J.D. 1969. Member Phi Delta Phi. Admitted to practice North Carolina 1969. In legal practice Boone 1969-79.

Important Decisions: State v. Johnson (first degree murder by poison) 317 N.C. 193, 1986 and Branks v. Kern (veterinary negligence) 320 N.C. 621, 1987. Member Pattern Jury Committee North Carolina Superior Court since 1988. Member North Carolina Conference of Superior Court Judges (Former Vice President), The North Carolina State Bar and North Carolina Bar Association. Attended General Jurisdiction Course The Na-

LAMM, CHARLES CADMUS, JR.—*Continued*

tional Judicial College 1981 and Rural Justice Conference American Bar Association 1990. Instructor in bar seminars North Carolina Bar Association. Democrat. Board of Directors Senator Sam J. Ervin, Jr. Library.

Mailing address: P.O. Box 229, Terrell 28682.

LANIER, Franklin F. *(Judge, North Carolina District Court District 11)*

Mailing address: P.O. Box 104, Buies Creek 27506.
Telephone: (910) 814-4670.

LANIER, Russell J., Jr. *(Resident Judge, North Carolina Superior Court Second Judicial Division District 4A)* Elected to term beginning Jan 1, 1995. Reelected 2002, current term expires Dec 31, 2010. Currently Senior Resident Judge. Born Chapel Hill North Carolina July 20, 1944. Presbyterian. Educated at Campbell University B.S. 1965 and University of North Carolina at Chapel Hill J.D. 1968. Admitted to practice North Carolina 1968. In legal practice Kenansville 1968-92. Judge, North Carolina District Court Fourth Judicial District 1992-94.

Member North Carolina Academy of Trial Lawyers, The North Carolina State Bar and North Carolina Bar Association. Attended North Carolina Conference of Superior Court Judges. Recipient Governor's Volunteer Award 1991. Member Beulaville Presbyterian Church. Assistant football coach East Duplin High School since 1975. Interests include golf and Carolina football.

Mailing address: P.O. Box 26, Kenansville 28349.
Telephone: (910) 296-2305.
Fax: (910) 296-1085
E-mail address: RussellL@duplinnet.com

LANNING, James E. *(Emergency Judge, North Carolina Superior Court)* Retired, serves by recall. Former Judge and Chief Judge, North Carolina District Court District 26.

Office: 700 East Fourth Street, Suite 3304, Charlotte 28202.

LAWTON, William C. *(Judge, North Carolina District Court District 10)* Appointed by Governor James Martin to term beginning Oct 7, 1991. Elected Nov 1992, 1996 and 2000. Current term expires Dec 2004. Born Richmond Virginia Feb 21, 1946. Christian. Educated at North Carolina State University B.S. with honors 1968 and Georgetown University Law Center J.D. 1972. Editor Law and Policy in International Business 1971-72. Law Clerk to Hon. F. T. Dupree, Jr., U.S. District Court Eastern District of North Carolina 1972-74. Member Delta Theta Phi and Golden Chain. Admitted to practice North Carolina 1972, U.S. District Courts Eastern and Middle Districts of North Carolina and U.S. Court of Appeals Fourth Circuit. In legal practice Raleigh 1972-91.

Co-author Case Note "Law & Policy in International Business" International L. Jour. 1971. Instructor in Business Law North Carolina State University 1990-95. Member The North Carolina State Bar, Wake County (Public Service Committee, Membership Committee, Board of Directors) and North Carolina (Patent, Trademark and Copyright Committee, General Practice Committee) Bar Associations. Democrat. Former Member Board of Directors Raleigh Rescue Mission. Former Member Rotary Club. Enjoys running, writing poetry and reading.

Mailing address: P.O. Box 351, Raleigh 27602.
Office: Wake County Courthouse, Raleigh 27601.
Telephone: (919) 755-4101.

LEAVELL, William A., III *(Judge, North Carolina District Court District 24)* Elected to term beginning Dec 5, 1994. Reelected Nov 3, 1998 and Nov 2002. Current term expires Dec 2006. Born Sarasota Florida May 4, 1953. Christian. Educated at Eckerd College B.A. 1975 and Florida State University J.D. with honors 1986. Admitted to practice Washington 1986 and North Carolina 1988. In legal practice Seattle Washington 1986-88, Asheville North Carolina 1988 and Spruce Pine North Carolina 1989-94.

Town Attorney Town of Bakersville 1994. Instructor in Business Law 1989 and in Real Estate Law 1994 Mayland Community College. Member North Carolina Association of District Court Judges (Board of Governors), North Carolina Judicial Conference, The North Carolina State Bar and 24th Judicial District Bar Association. Instructor in Boundary Law CLE Asheville 1993. Republican. Vice Chairman Mitchell County Republican Party 1993. Chairman Boy Scouts Toe River District. Member Fork Mountain Volunteer Fire Department and Mitchell County Canines. Interests include training dogs for search and rescue, playing the upright bass at church and playing Bluegrass and Old Time music.

Mailing address: P.O. Box 98, Bakersville 28705.
Telephone: (828) 733-2395.
E-mail address: Leavell03@aol.com

LEE, Jacquelyn L. *(Judge, North Carolina District Court District 11)*

Mailing address: P.O. Box 1965, Sanford 27331-1965.
Telephone: (910) 814-4670.

LEE, W. David *(Resident Judge, North Carolina Superior Court Sixth Judicial Division District 20B)*

Mailing address: P.O. Drawer 829, Monroe 28111-0829.
Telephone: (704) 289-6487.

LEECH, David A. *(Chief Judge, North Carolina District Court District 3A)*

Mailing address: P.O. Box 8147, Greenville 27835.
Telephone: (252) 695-7270.

LEONARD, C. Jerome, Jr. *(Emergency Judge, North Carolina District Court)* Retired, serves by recall.

Office: 3304 Criminal Courts Building, 700 East Fourth Street, Charlotte 28202.

LEONARD, J. Rich *(Chief Judge, United States Bankruptcy Court Eastern District of North Carolina)* Clerk of Court 1979-92 and Magistrate Judge 1981-92. Appointed by U.S. Court of Appeals Fourth Circuit judges to term beginning June 23, 1992. Chief Judge since Aug 6, 1999. Born Lexington North Carolina Oct 8, 1949. Protestant. Educated at University of North Carolina at Chapel Hill A.B. 1971 M.Ed. 1973 and Yale University J.D. 1976. Morehead Scholar. Recipient John J. Parker Medal, Frank Porter Graham Award and Howard W. Odom Award. Law Clerk to Hon. Franklin Taylor Dupree, Jr., U.S. District Court Eastern District of North Carolina 1976-78. Member Order of the Golden Fleece and Phi Beta Kappa. Admitted to practice North Carolina 1976 and U.S. Court of Appeals Fourth Circuit 1976. In legal practice Raleigh 1978-79.

LEONARD, J. RICH—*Continued*

Co-author with Patrice Solberg "Notary Public Guidebook" Institute of Government 1976. Author "Congressional Action Changes Federal Practice" Winter 1980 and "A Quick Look at Changes in the Federal Rules" Winter 1980 *Barnotes,* "Rule 11 in the Federal Courts of North Carolina" North Carolina State Bar Quarterly Summer 1987 and "After the Clerkship: Was It Worth It?" North Carolina Lawyer Feb 1991. Editorial Board Bankruptcy Clerks Manual 1988-90 and District Clerks Manual since 1990. Reporter Eastern District Advisory Group. Adjunct Professor of Civil Procedure North Carolina Central University School of Law 1985-86. Liaison Member Advisory Committee on Civil Rules 1989-92. Pilot Program for National Fine Center since 1990. Member Education and Training Committee Federal Judicial Center 1985-91, Clerks Advisory Committee to Director of Administrative Office since 1985, Judicial Conference Committee on Court Administration and Case Management (Subcommittee on Case Management and CHASER Subcommittee) 1989-92, Fourth Circuit Judicial Conference, North Carolina State-Federal Judicial Council (Secretary), North Carolina Federal Bar Advisory Council (Secretary), National Council of Magistrate Judges, National Conference of Bankruptcy Judges, Federal Court Clerks Association, Wake County (Board of Directors 1978-89), North Carolina (Trial Practice Curriculum Committee, Bench, Bar and Law School Committee, Technology and the Law Committee) and American Bar Associations.

Lecturer "Civil Trial Walk-Through" Young Lawyers Division April 1988, "Seizures Under the Supplemental Rules" Admiralty Law April 1988, "Federal Practice in North Carolina" Practical Skills Course Aug 1988-91, "Tricks and Traps of Federal Civil Practice" View from the Federal Bench Dec 1990 and Course Planner and Moderator Federal Appellate Practice May 1988 North Carolina Bar Association Seminars; "Developments in the Law" Conference of Clerks of District Courts New Orleans Louisiana June 1988; "Defending Indigent Clients in Federal Court" Campbell Law School Symposium Oct 1988; "The Changing Federal Rules" New Orleans Louisiana Jan 1989 and "Recent Legal Developments Affecting Clerks Offices" Chicago Illinois July 1990 Workshops for Chief Deputy Clerks of the U.S. District Courts; "Case Management in a Small Court" Workshop for Clerks of the Small U.S. District Courts Atlanta Georgia April 1989; "Pre-Judgment and Post-Judgment Remedies in Federal Court" Surviving and Prospering in Federal Court Nov 1989 and "Workings of the Justice System—A Primer for Reporters" Media and the Law Symposium May 1990 North Carolina Bar Association; "Understanding the Federal Rules of Civil Procedure" Workshop for Court Administrators Dallas Texas Aug 1990; "Handling Pro Se Litigants: Some Observations" Workshop for Pro Se Law Clerks in Federal Courts Washington D.C. Aug 1990; "Recent Legal Developments Affecting Clerks Offices" Workshop for Clerks of Medium-Sized Federal Courts Atlanta Georgia Feb 1991; "Federal Practice in North Carolina" North Carolina Paralegal Association Annual Conference March 1991; "Civil Case Management" Workshop for Judges of the Fourth Circuit March 1991; "Recent Legal Developments Affecting Court Operations" Conference of District Court Clerks Houston Texas April 1991; and "Implementing the Civil Justice Reform Act of 1990" and "Management of District Courts" Conference of Chief District Judges Naples Florida May 1991. Recipient of first Director's Award for Outstanding Leadership 1992. Board of Directors Ligon Middle School PTA 1989-91. President Ligon Sports Club 1989-91. Enjoys gardening and volleyball.

Mailing address: P.O. Drawer 2807, Wilson 27894-2807.

Telephone: (252) 291-6413.

LETTS, Bradley B. *(Judge, North Carolina District Court District 30)* Appointed by Governor James B. Hunt, Jr. to term beginning Aug 2000. Educated at University of North Carolina at Chapel Hill B.A. 1990 and University of Mississippi J.D. 1994. Admitted to practice North Carolina 1995.

Assistant District Attorney Thirtieth Judicial District Oct 1995 to March 1997. Attorney General Eastern Band of Cherokee Indians March 1997 to Oct 1999. Member North Carolina and American Bar Associations.

Mailing address: P.O. Box 23, Sylva 28779.

Telephone: (828) 456-3796.

LEVINSON, Eric L. *(Associate Judge, North Carolina Court of Appeals)* Born Charlotte North Carolina. Educated at Georgetown University, University of Georgia B.B.A. cum laude 1989, University of London, England 1989 and University of North Carolina at Chapel Hill J.D. 1992. Member James B. and Carolyn E. Davis Society 1992. Admitted to practice North Carolina 1992. Former Judge, North Carolina District Court District 26, appointed by Governor James B. Hunt, Jr. to term beginning Sept 3, 1996.

Assistant District Attorney District 19B 1992-96. Member The North Carolina State Bar and Mecklenburg County Bar Association. Member Charlotte Jaycees and Hands on Charlotte. Youth Group Advisor. At-Risk Student Mentor/Advisor Hawthorne Middle School.

Mailing address: P.O. Box 888, Raleigh 27602.

Office: Court of Appeals Building, One West Morgan Street, Raleigh 27601.

Telephone: (919) 715-5111.

LEWIS, Hugh B. *(Judge, North Carolina District Court District 26)*

Office: 700 East Fourth Street, Suite 3304, Charlotte 28202.

Telephone: (704) 347-7801.

LEWIS, John B., Jr. *(Retired Judge, North Carolina Court of Appeals)* Elected Associate Judge to term beginning Jan 1, 1989. Reelected to subsequent term. Retired, serves by recall. Currently serves as Emergency Special Judge, North Carolina Superior Court. Born Farmville North Carolina Sept 21, 1936. Presbyterian. Educated at University of North Carolina at Chapel Hill A.B. 1958 LL.B. 1961. Member Chi Phi and Phi Delta Phi. Admitted to practice North Carolina 1961. In legal practice Farmville 1961 and 1966-82. Special Judge, North Carolina Superior Court Aug 27, 1982 to Dec 31, 1988.

Chairman North Carolina Property Tax Commission 1980-82 and North Carolina Judicial Standards Commission since 1997. Member The North Carolina State Bar, Pitt County and North Carolina Bar Associations. Captain USNR 1980-91 (active duty 1961-66). Board of Visitors Wake Forest University School of Law 1994-2000.

Mailing address: P.O. Box 4, Farmville 27828.

LEWIS, Ola M. *(Resident Judge, North Carolina Superior Court Fourth Judicial Division District 13)* Former Special Judge, appointed by Governor James B. Hunt, Jr. to term beginning 2000. Educated at Fayetteville State University B.S. magna cum laude 1986 and North Carolina Central University School of Law J.D. 1990. Admitted to practice North Carolina 1990. In legal practice Raleigh 1990-91. Former Judge, North Carolina District Court District 13, appointed by Governor James B. Hunt, Jr.

Assistant District Attorney North Carolina 1991-93. Member North Carolina Association of Superior Court Judges and The North Carolina State Bar. Attended The National Judicial College. Volunteer Hope Harbor Homes Domestic Violence Shelter and Providence Home Shelter for Children. Member NAACP and March of Dimes.

Mailing address: 399 North Shore Drive, Southport 28461.

Telephone: (910) 253-8502.

LEWIS, Robert Dobbins *(Retired-Recalled Judge, North Carolina Superior Court)* Elected to term beginning Jan 1, 1975. Reelected 1982 and 1990. Retired, serves by recall. Born Asheville North Carolina April 19, 1929. Baptist. Educated at Duke University A.B. 1951 and University of North Carolina School of Law LL.B. 1956. Staff member North Carolina Law Review 1953-54. Admitted to practice North Carolina 1956. In legal practice Asheville 1956-71.

Prosecutor General County Court Buncombe County 1967-71. District Attorney Twenty-eighth District Buncombe County 1971-75. Member North Carolina Conference of Superior Court Judges, The North Carolina State Bar, Buncombe County, North Carolina and American Bar Associations. Lieutenant j.g. USN 1951-53. Democrat. Enjoys golf.

Office: Buncombe County Courthouse, 60 Court Plaza, Asheville 28801-3583.

LEWIS, W. Rob, II *(Judge, North Carolina District Court District 6B)* Elected to term beginning Dec 1, 1994. Reelected Nov 3, 1998 and 2002. Current term expires Dec 2006. Born New York New York March 6, 1955. Educated at State University of New York at Brockport B.S. 1977 M.S. 1978 and University of Cincinnati J.D. 1981. Admitted to practice North Carolina 1981 and U.S. District Court Eastern District of North Carolina 1982. In legal practice Ahoskie 1982-94.

Member North Carolina Association of Black Lawyers. Democrat. Chair Roanoke Chowan Community College Trustees. Life Member NAACP. Enjoys coaching little league baseball and recreational league basketball.

Mailing address: P.O. Box 86, Winton 27986.

Office: Hertford County Courthouse, Winton 27986.

Telephone: (252) 534-1785.

LLOYD, H. Weldon, Jr. *(Judge, North Carolina District Court District 9)*

Office: c/o Clerk of Superior Court, 101 Vance County Courthouse, 156 Church Street, Henderson 27536.

Telephone: (919) 693-5193.

LOCKLEAR, Gary Lynn *(Resident Judge, North Carolina Superior Court Fourth Judicial Division District 16B)* Born Robeson County North Carolina Feb 6, 1949. Baptist. Educated at University of North Carolina at Pembroke B.S. 1970, Appalachian State University M.A. 1972 and University of North Carolina School of Law J.D. 1979. Admitted to practice North Carolina 1979. In legal practice Lumberton 1982-88. Former Judge and Chief Judge, North Carolina District Court District 16B, elected to term beginning Dec 1988.

Assistant District Attorney 1979-82. Instructor University of North Carolina at Pembroke 1979-82. Member The North Carolina State Bar, Robeson County and Sixteenth Judicial District Bar Associations. Enjoys boating and fishing.

Office: Robeson County Courthouse, Box 18, Lumberton 28358.

Telephone: (910) 671-3325.

LONG, Vance B. *(Judge, North Carolina District Court District 19B)*

Mailing address: P.O. Box 4906, Asheboro 27204-4906.

Telephone: (336) 318-6887.

LOVE, Jimmy L., Jr. *(Judge, North Carolina District Court District 11)*

Mailing address: P.O. Box 1897, Sanford 27331-1897.

Telephone: (910) 814-4670.

LOWE, Edmund *(Retired-Recalled Judge, North Carolina District Court)* Retired, serves by recall. Former Emergency Judge.

Mailing address: P.O. Box 3008, Greensboro 27402.

LYERLY, Alexander *(Chief Judge, North Carolina District Court District 24)* Elected to term beginning Dec 1, 1980. Reelected 1984, 1988, 1992, 1996 and 2000. Current term expires 2004. Chief Judge since April 1995. Born Banner Elk North Carolina May 22, 1944. Catholic. Educated at Lees-McRae College A.A. 1965, Appalachian State University B.S. with honors 1971 and South Texas College of Law J.D. 1975. Member Delta Theta Phi. Admitted to practice Texas 1975 and North Carolina 1976. Began legal practice Houston Texas 1975. In legal practice Newland North Carolina 1976-80.

School teacher 1971-72. Member Banner Elk Town Council 1976-80. Author "Avoidance of Medical Malpractice" 1979. Adjunct Instructor Lees-McRae College 1976-83. Instructor in Criminal Justice Mayland College 1979-80 and Caldwell Community College 1981-82. Member State Bar of Texas, North Carolina Trial Lawyers Association, The Association of Trial Lawyers of America, North Carolina (Administration of Justice Committee), American and International (Family Law Committee) Bar Associations. Named an Outstanding Young American 1979. Republican. Member Avery County Republican Executive Committee. Former Treasurer North Carolina Young Republicans. Member Knights of Columbus, Kiwanis Club (President 1978) and Avery County Chamber of Commerce (President 1978-80). Vice Chairman Board of Trustees Crossnore School. Board of Advisors Sloop Memorial and Cannon Memorial Hospitals. Enjoys horseback riding, painting and collecting antiques.

Mailing address: P.O. Box 127, Banner Elk 28604.

Telephone: (828) 733-0887.

MACK, Peter, Jr. *(Judge, North Carolina District Court District 3B)*

Office: 204 Craven County Courthouse Annex, 302 Broad Street, New Bern 28560-4903.

Telephone: (252) 514-4782.

MALARNEY, Amber D. *(Judge, North Carolina District Court District 1)*
Mailing address: Drawer 406, Elizabeth City 27907-0406.
Telephone: (252) 331-4750.

MANESS, Jayrene R. *(Judge, North Carolina District Court District 19B)*
Mailing address: P.O. Box 1116, Carthage 28327.
Telephone: (336) 318-6887.

MANNING, Howard E., Jr. *(Resident Judge, North Carolina Superior Court Third Judicial Division District 10)* Former Special Judge.
Mailing address: P.O. Box 351, Raleigh 27602.
Telephone: (919) 755-4100.

MARTIN, Jerry Cash *(Emergency Judge, North Carolina Superior Court)* Retired, serves by recall. Born Surry County North Carolina Aug 1, 1948. Educated at Wake Forest University B.A. 1970 J.D. 1972. Member Phi Alpha Delta. Admitted to practice North Carolina 1972. Began legal practice Mount Airy 1972. Former Chief Judge, North Carolina District Court Seventeenth Judicial District B.

Assistant District Attorney Twenty-seventh Judicial District 1972-73 and Seventeenth Judicial District 1973-78. Member North Carolina Association of District Court Judges, Seventeen B Judicial District, Surry County and North Carolina Bar Associations. Democrat. Enjoys bicycling, running and reading.
Mailing address: P.O. Box 345, Dobson 27017.

MARTIN, John C. *(Associate Judge, North Carolina Court of Appeals)* Elected Nov 1992 and 2000. Term expires 2008. Born Durham North Carolina Nov 9, 1943. Methodist. Educated at Wake Forest University B.A. 1965 J.D. 1967. Member Phi Delta Phi. Admitted to practice North Carolina 1967, U.S. District Courts Middle 1967, Eastern 1972 and Western 1975 Districts of North Carolina and U.S. Court of Appeals Fourth Circuit 1976. In legal practice Durham 1969-77 and 1988-92. Resident Judge, North Carolina Superior Court Judicial Division Two Fourteenth District 1977-85. Judge, North Carolina Court of Appeals Jan 1, 1985 to Jan 1, 1988.

Arbitrator U.S. District Court Middle District of North Carolina 1988-92. Member North Carolina Conference of Superior Court Judges 1977-84 (Pattern Jury Instructions Drafting Committee 1978-84, Trial Judges' Bench Book Drafting Committee 1984-87), Legislative Research Commission Study Committee on the Rules of Evidence 1980, North Carolina News Media/Administration of Justice Council 1987 and Panel of Arbitrators American Arbitration Society 1988-92. Former Member North Carolina Association of Defense Attorneys and North Carolina Academy of Trial Lawyers. Chairman North Carolina Judicial Standards Commission since 2001. Member Education Study Committee North Carolina Judicial Branch since 2001. Member State—Federal Judicial Council of North Carolina (Chair 1987), North Carolina Judicial Conference (Vice President 1999-2002), Tenth Judicial District Bar, The North Carolina State Bar, Durham County (Board of Directors 1991-92), Wake County, North Carolina (Bench Bar and Law School Liaison Committee 1987-91, Judicial Campaign Oversight Committee 1990, Chair Administration of Justice Study Committee 1990-92, Litigation Section Council 1991-94, Administration of Justice Task Force 1995-96, Vice President 1997-98, Convention Planning Committee 1997-2001, Appellate Rules Study Committee 1999-2001) and American (Judicial Division) Bar Associations. Attended The National Judicial College Reno Nevada 1979 and Justice Executives' Program University of North Carolina at Chapel Hill 1982. Named Outstanding Young Man of the Year of Durham 1976. Listed in *Who's Who in America, Who's Who in American Law* and *Who's Who in the South and Southwest.* First Lieutenant U.S. Army 1967-69. Democrat. Chairman Leadership Development Course Durham Chamber of Commerce 1974. Member 1975-77 and Chair Public Works Committee 1976-77 Durham City Council. Member Panel of Arbitrators Duke University Private Adjudication Center 1988-92. Member Hayes-Barton United Methodist Church. Enjoys running, golfing, boating and fishing.
Mailing address: P.O. Box 888, Raleigh 27602.
Telephone: (919) 733-4293.

MARTIN, Mark D. *(Associate Justice, Supreme Court of North Carolina)* Elected Nov 3, 1998. Born April 29, 1963. Educated at Western Carolina University B.S.B.A. summa cum laude 1985, University of North Carolina School of Law J.D. with honors 1988 and University of Virginia School of Law LL.M. in Judicial Process 1998. Editor-in-Chief North Carolina Journal of International Law and Commercial Regulation 1987-88. Law Clerk to Hon. Clyde Henry Hamilton, U.S. District Court District of South Carolina 1988-90. Member Phi Alpha Delta, Phi Kappa Phi, Pi Gamma Mu and Omicron Delta Epsilon. Honorary Member Beta Gamma Sigma. Admitted to practice North Carolina 1988, South Carolina 1990, U.S. District Courts Eastern 1990 and Western 1990 Districts of North Carolina and District of South Carolina 1990, U.S. Court of Appeals Fourth Circuit 1991 and U.S. Supreme Court. In legal practice Raleigh North Carolina 1990-91. Resident Judge, North Carolina Superior Court Judicial Division One Third District A 1992-94. Associate Judge, North Carolina Court of Appeals Dec 16, 1994 to 1999.

Adjunct Professor of Law University of North Carolina at Chapel Hill School of Law. Adjunct Faculty North Carolina Central University School of Law. Member Legislation and Law Reform Committee North Carolina Conference of Superior Court Judges 1994. Member Appellate Courts Computer Committee since 1995. Co-chair Legislative Liaison Committee since 1995 and Secretary since 1997 North Carolina Judicial Conference. Member Wake County, North Carolina (Minorities in Profession Committee since 1995, Multidisciplinary Task Force 1999-2001, Council Litigation Section since 2000, Vice President 2000-01, Member Strategic Planning/Emergency Trends Committee since 2001) and American (Judicial Division, Committee on Coalition for Justice) Bar Associations. Attended General Jurisdiction course The National Judicial College 1993. Recipient Order of the Long Leaf Pine from State of North Carolina 1992 and Distinguished Alumnus Award from Western Carolina University 1995. Legal Counsel to Governor James G. Martin 1991-92. Member United Way Combined Campaign 1990-91, North Carolina Council for Women 1992, Master Plan Advisory Committee North Carolina Department of Correction 1992 and Greenville Noon Rotary 1993-94. Participant Council of State Governments Toll Fellowship Program 2001. Fellow North Car-

MARTIN, MARK D.—*Continued*
olina Institute of Political Leadership. Enjoys walking and reading.
Mailing address: P.O. Box 1841, Raleigh 27602.
Office: Justice Building, Two East Morgan Street, Raleigh 27601.
Telephone: (919) 733-3714.

MASON, William Norton *(Magistrate Judge, United States District Court Eastern District of North Carolina)* Appointed by U.S. District Court judges Aug 14, 1995. Served part time 1990-95. Born Winston-Salem North Carolina Aug 31, 1951. Educated at University of North Carolina Bachelors degree 1973 and Wake Forest University J.D. 1977. Admitted to practice North Carolina 1977 and U.S. District Court Eastern District of North Carolina 1985. In legal practice Wilmington 1984-95.
Assistant District Attorney 5th Judicial District 1977-81. Member U.S. Magistrate Judges Association and North Carolina Bar Association.
Mailing address: P.O. Box 2862, Wilmington 28402-2862.
Telephone: (910) 815-4814.

MASSEY, A. Moses *(Resident Judge, North Carolina Superior Court Fifth Judicial Division District 17B)* Currently Senior Resident Judge. Former Judge, North Carolina District Court District 17B.
Mailing address: P.O. Box 1749, King 27021.
Telephone: (336) 983-8989.

McCORMICK, Edward H. *(Judge, North Carolina District Court District 11)* Elected to term beginning Dec 3, 1984. Reelected 1988, 1992, 1996 and 2000. Current term expires Dec 2004. Former Chief Judge. Born Harnett County North Carolina July 2, 1935. Presbyterian. Educated at University of North Carolina at Chapel Hill A.B. in Economics 1961 LL.B. 1964. Admitted to practice North Carolina 1964, U.S. District Court Eastern District of North Carolina 1964 and U.S. Supreme Court 1976. In legal practice Lillington 1964-84.
Mayor Town of Lillington 1970-72. Attorney Harnett County 1971-82. Member Child Support Council 1988-89. Chairman Juvenile Procedures Manual Committee 1989-92 and Member Advisory Committee on Child Custody and Mediation 1989-91 and Insurance Committee since 1995 Administrative Office of the Court. Former Member North Carolina Academy of Trial Lawyers, The North Carolina State Bar, Eleventh Judicial District (President 1983-84), Harnett County (President 1967-68) and North Carolina (Pro Bono Committee 1991-92, Committee on Appeals 1992-97) Bar Associations. Board of Directors Lee—Harnett Criminal Justice Alliance since 1997. Member Harnett County Criminal Justice Council since 1998 and Indigent Fee Commission 1999-2000. Recipient Distinguished Service Award from Jaycees 1972. Named Lillington Man of the Year 1983. Specialist Five U.S. Army Airborne Division 1954-58. Treasurer 1969 and Chairman 1970-72 and 1979-80 Harnett County Democratic Executive Committee. Advancement Chairman 1967-81 and Chairman 1980 Golden Leaf District Boy Scouts of America. President Lillington Chamber of Commerce 1968, Harnett County Development Association 1968-69 and Lillington Middle School PTA 1981. Past President Shawtown PTA. Member Lillington Rotary Club 1967-72 and since 1984 (President 1970-71).
Mailing address: P.O. Box 1780, Lillington 27546-1780.
Telephone: (910) 814-4670.
E-mail address: mccormicked@worldnet.att.net

McCOY, Harold Paul, Jr. *(Chief Judge, North Carolina District Court District 6A)*
Mailing address: P.O. Box 66, Halifax 27839.
Office: Halifax County Courthouse, Halifax 27839.
Telephone: (252) 583-2910.

McCULLOUGH, J. Douglas *(Associate Judge, North Carolina Court of Appeals)* Elected to term beginning Feb 9, 2001. Term expires Jan 2, 2009. Born Tyler Texas May 28, 1945. Episcopalian. Educated at University of North Carolina A.B. 1967 and University of South Carolina J.D. with honors 1970. Managing Editor South Carolina Law Review 1969-70. Admitted to practice South Carolina 1970, District of Columbia 1976, North Carolina 1982 and U.S. District Court Eastern District of North Carolina 1982. In legal practice New Bern North Carolina 1996-2001.
Assistant U.S. Attorney Eastern District of North Carolina 1981-96. Member The District of Columbia Bar and The North Carolina State Bar. Republican. Enjoys boating, jogging and golfing.
Mailing address: P.O. Box 888, Raleigh 27602.
Telephone: (919) 733-4226.
Fax: (919) 733-8003

McGEE, Linda M. *(Associate Judge, North Carolina Court of Appeals)* Appointed by Governor James B. Hunt, Jr. Jan 1995. Elected 1996, current term expires 2004. Born Marion North Carolina Sept 20, 1949. Educated at University of North Carolina at Chapel Hill B.A. 1971 J.D. 1973. In legal practice Boone 1978-95.
First Executive Director North Carolina Academy of Trial Lawyers 1973-78. Board of Governors North Carolina Bar Association 1983-86. Board Member North Carolina Board of Law Examiners 1986-93. Member North Carolina Association of Women Attorneys, The Association of Trial Lawyers of America, Watauga County and American Bar Associations. Trustee Caldwell Community College and Technical Institute 1981-89. Co-founder Blue Ridge Dispute Settlement Center. Member American Association of University Women, Women's Forum of North Carolina and Northminster Presbyterian Church, Hickory.
Mailing address: P.O. Box 888, Raleigh 27602.
Office: Court of Appeals Building, One West Morgan Street, Raleigh 27601.
Telephone: (919) 733-4228.

McGEE, Martin B. *(Judge, North Carolina District Court District 19A)*
Mailing address: P.O. Box 70, Concord 28026-0070.
Telephone: (704) 786-4137.

McHUGH, Peter M. *(Emergency Judge, North Carolina Superior Court)* Retired, serves by recall. Born Buffalo New York Sept 19, 1947. Episcopalian. Educated at Cornell University B.A. 1969 and University of North Carolina J.D. 1974. Admitted to practice North Carolina 1974. Began legal practice Reidsville 1974. Former Judge and Chief Judge, North Carolina District Court Seventeenth Judicial District A, appointed by Governor James B. Hunt, Jr. to term beginning Dec 15, 1977.

MCHUGH, PETER M.—*Continued*

Member Rockingham County, 17A Judicial District, North Carolina and American Bar Associations. Specialist Five USAS 1970-72. Democrat.

Mailing address: P.O. Box 97, Wentworth 27375-0097.

McILWAIN, William C. *(Judge, North Carolina District Court District 16A)*

Mailing address: P.O. Box 769, Laurinburg 28353.

Telephone: (910) 875-9535.

McKNIGHT, H. Brent *(Magistrate Judge, United States District Court Western District of North Carolina)* Appointed by U.S. District Court judges. Former Judge, North Carolina District Court Twenty-sixth Judicial District.

Office: 168 Federal Building, 401 West Trade Street, Charlotte 28202.

Telephone: (704) 350-7480.

McKOWN, Ann E. *(Judge, North Carolina District Court District 14)* Assumed office Jan 30, 1998. Elected Nov 3, 1998 and 2002. Current term expires Dec 31, 2006.

Office: 565 Durham County Judicial Building, Sixth Floor, 201 East Main Street, Durham 27701.

Telephone: (919) 564-7240.

McKOY-MITCHELL, Rickye *(Judge, North Carolina District Court District 26)* Appointed by Governor James B. Hunt, Jr. to term beginning July 1998. Elected Nov 1998 and 2002. Current term expires Dec 2006. Born Dunn North Carolina May 20, 1959. Baptist. Educated at University of North Carolina at Chapel Hill B.A. 1981 J.D. 1984. Reginald Heber Smith Fellow 1984-86. Member Delta Sigma Theta, Order of Oldwell and Order of Valkyries. Admitted to practice North Carolina 1984 and U.S. District Court Western District of North Carolina 1986.

Attorney Advisor Office of Hearings and Appeals Social Security Administration 1986-88 and Senior Trial Attorney Equal Employment Opportunity Commission 1988-94 Western District of North Carolina. Assistant District Attorney Mecklenburg County 1994-98. Member North Carolina Association of Women Attorneys (Board of Directors 1990-94), North Carolina Association of Black Lawyers (Scholarship Chair Leary Charlotte Chapter), The North Carolina State Bar and Mecklenburg County Bar Association (Board of Directors). Attended District Court Judges Conferences Oct 1998, Oct 1999 and June 1999, Family Law Seminar Dec 1998 and Enhancing Judicial Skills in Domestic Violence Cases National Council of Juvenile and Family Court Judges Dec 1999. Member Mecklenburg Democratic Party, Black Political Caucus, Mecklenburg County Democratic Women and Charlotte Women's Political Caucus. Board of Directors Smart Start since 1999 and Children's Law Center (Program Committee 1996-98). Deacon, Youth Church Leader and Sunday School Teacher Mount Carmel Baptist Church. Member The Links, Jack and Jill of America and Junior League of Charlotte. Enjoys watching movies, nature walking, family picnics and arts/crafts.

Office: 700 East Fourth Street, Suite 3304, Charlotte 28202.

Telephone: (704) 347-7801.

McLEAN, Mitchell L. *(Judge, North Carolina District Court District 23)* Elected Nov 3, 1998.

Office: Wilkes County Courthouse, 500 Courthouse Drive, Wilkesboro 28697.

Telephone: (336) 838-4246.

McSWAIN, Lawrence *(Judge, North Carolina District Court District 18)* Former Chief Judge.

Mailing address: P.O. Box 3008, Greensboro 27402-3008.

Telephone: (336) 574-4301.

MENEFEE, Lisa V. L. *(Judge, North Carolina District Court District 21)*

Mailing address: P.O. Box 20099, Winston-Salem 27120-0099.

Telephone: (336) 761-2478.

MERCER, Fritz Y., Jr. *(Chief Judge, North Carolina District Court District 26)*

Office: 700 East Fourth Street, Suite 3304, Charlotte 28202.

Telephone: (704) 347-7801.

MICHAEL, Wayne L. *(Judge, North Carolina District Court District 22)* Elected Nov 3, 1998.

Mailing address: c/o Clerk of Superior Court, P.O. Box 1064, Lexington 27293-1064.

Office: Davidson County Courthouse, Lexington 27293.

Telephone: (704) 878-4209.

MILLER, Elizabeth D. *(Judge, North Carolina District Court District 26)*

Office: 700 East Fourth Street, Suite 3304, Charlotte 28202.

MILLER, Regan A. *(Judge, North Carolina District Court District 26)*

Office: 700 East Fourth Street, Suite 3304, Charlotte 28202.

Telephone: (704) 333-1700.

MILLS, F. Fetzer *(Emergency Judge, North Carolina Superior Court)* Retired, serves by recall.

Mailing address: c/o Anson County CSC, P.O. Box 1064, Wadesboro 28170.

MOORE, Thomas F. *(Judge, North Carolina District Court District 26)*

Office: 700 East Fourth Street, Suite 3304, Charlotte 28202.

Telephone: (704) 347-7801.

MOORE, William Jeffrey *(Judge, North Carolina District Court District 16B)*

Office: Robeson County Courthouse, Box 18, Lumberton 28358.

Telephone: (910) 671-3355.

MOREY, Marcia H. *(Judge, North Carolina District Court District 14)*

Office: 565 Durham County Judicial Building, Sixth Floor, 201 East Main Street, Durham 27701.

Telephone: (919) 564-7240.

MORGAN, James W. *(Resident Judge, North Carolina Superior Court Seventh Judicial Division District 27B)* Certified Juvenile Court Judge since April 1994. Born Shelby North Carolina Nov 21, 1954. United Methodist. Educated at University of North Carolina at Chapel Hill B.S. 1977 and Campbell University School

MORGAN, JAMES W.—*Continued*

of Law J.D. 1982. Member Phi Alpha Delta. Admitted to practice North Carolina 1982 and U.S. District Court Western District of North Carolina 1983. In legal practice Shelby 1982-90. Former Chief Judge, North Carolina District Court District 27B, elected to term beginning Dec 1990.

Member North Carolina Association of District Court Judges, The North Carolina State Bar, Twenty-seventh Judicial District and Cleveland County Bar Associations. Attended CLE courses sponsored by the North Carolina Association of District Court Judges 1990-97. Democrat. Member Shelby Rotary Club. Enjoys golf.

Mailing address: 100 Justice Place, Shelby 28150.
Telephone: (704) 484-4876.

MORGAN, Melzer A. "Pat", Jr. *(Resident Judge, North Carolina Superior Court Fifth Judicial Division District 17A)* Appointed July 1981 by Governor James B. Hunt, Jr. to term beginning Sept 1, 1981. Elected Nov 1982, Nov 1990 and Nov 3, 1998. Current term expires Dec 31, 2006. Currently Senior Resident Judge. Born Smithfield North Carolina March 17, 1940. Presbyterian. Educated at University of North Carolina A.B. 1962 J.D. 1967. Member Phi Alpha Delta. Admitted to practice North Carolina 1967, U.S. District Court Middle District of North Carolina 1969, U.S. Supreme Court 1971 and U.S. Court of Appeals Fourth Circuit 1976. In legal practice Reidsville 1967-81.

Member Commission on Race Relations in the Legal Profession in North Carolina since 1993. Member since 2000 and Vice Chair 2000-02 North Carolina Indigent Defense Services Commission. Member Foreign Language Advisory Committee Administrative Office of the Courts, Guilford Inn of Court, The North Carolina State Bar, North Carolina (Vice President 1984-85) and American Bar Associations. Attended Charter Session National College of Criminal Defense Lawyers and Public Defenders 1973, General Jurisdiction Course The National Judicial College 1982 and National Judicial Ethics Forum American Judicature Society 1989 and 1992. Lecturer on Evidence and Legal Ethics New Judges School North Carolina Bar Association, North Carolina Academy of Trial Lawyers, University of North Carolina School of Law and Wake Forest University School of Law. Recipient Community Unity Award from Reidsville Human Relations Council, NAACP and Chamber of Commerce 2000. Volunteer United States Peace Corps Dominican Republic 1962-64. Democrat. Past President Reidsville Rotary Club and Reidsville YMCA. President Greater Reidsville Habitat for Humanity, Inc. 1989-91. Stakeholder Adviser North Carolina Department of Corrections Futures Project 1997. Elder and Deacon Presbyterian Church. Enjoys family, hiking, traveling, cross-country skiing, sailing and gardening.

Mailing address: P.O. Box 97, Wentworth 27375-0097.
Office: Rockingham County Courthouse, Wentworth 27375.
Telephone: (336) 342-8750.

MORGAN, Michael R. *(Judge, North Carolina District Court District 10)*
Mailing address: P.O. Box 351, Raleigh 27602.
Telephone: (919) 755-4101.

MORTON, J. Bruce *(Retired-Recalled Judge, North Carolina District Court)* Former Chief Judge. Retired, serves by recall. Former Emergency Judge.
Mailing address: P.O. Box 3008, Greensboro 27402.

MULL, John R. *(Judge, North Carolina District Court District 25)*
Office: 111 Main Avenue N.E., Hickory 28601.
Telephone: (828) 327-7500.

MULLEN, Graham C. *(Chief Judge, United States District Court Western District of North Carolina)* Appointed for life by President George Bush to term beginning Sept 11, 1990. Chief Judge since Jan 28, 1998. Born Charlotte North Carolina April 20, 1940. Educated at Duke University B.A. 1962 J.D. 1969. In legal practice Gastonia 1969-90.
Office: 230 Federal Building, 401 West Trade Street, Charlotte 28202.
Telephone: (704) 350-7450.

MURPHY, George R. *(Judge, North Carolina District Court District 11)*
Mailing address: P.O. Box 1780, Lillington 27546-1780.
Telephone: (910) 814-4670.

MYERS, Jimmy Laird *(Judge, North Carolina District Court District 22)* Elected to term beginning Dec 5, 1994. Reelected Nov 3, 1998 and 2002. Current term expires Dec 2006. Certified Juvenile Court Judge. Born Winston-Salem North Carolina March 11, 1953. Religious affiliation: United Methodist. Educated at Wake Forest University B.A. cum laude 1975, Emory University M.Div. magna cum laude 1978 and University of North Carolina at Chapel Hill J.D. 1991. Member Theta Phi Theological Honor Society. Admitted to practice North Carolina 1991. In legal practice Lexington 1991-94 and Advance 1992-94.

Member Christian Legal Society, North Carolina Association of District Court Judges, North Carolina Judicial Conference, North Carolina and American (National Conference of Special Court Judges Judicial Division) Bar Associations. Attended Advanced Special Courts course The National Judicial College June 1995. Lieutenant Commander USNR since 1988 (active duty 1985-88). Republican. Member Lexington Civil War Roundtable, Mocksville Lions Club, Clemmons Rotary, Mocksville Post 174 American Legion, Farmington Masonic Lodge 265, Winston-Salem Scottish Rite, Lincoln Forum and Winston-Salem York Rite. Enjoys playing golf and hunting.

Office: c/o clerk of Superior Courts, Davie County Courthouse, 140 South Main Street, Mocksville 27028.
Telephone: (704) 878-4209.
E-mail address: JLMYERS@yadtel.net

NEAVES, Charles M., Jr. *(Judge, North Carolina District Court District 17B)*
Mailing address: P.O. Box 456, Dobson 27017.
Telephone: (336) 386-3750.

NEELY, William M. *(Chief Judge, North Carolina District Court District 19B)* Elected to term beginning Dec 1, 1980. Reelected 1984, 1988, 1992, 1996 and 2000. Current term expires Dec 6, 2004. Certified Juvenile Court Judge. Born Asheboro North Carolina Oct 23, 1949. Presbyterian. Educated at College of Charleston B.S. 1971 and University of South Carolina School of Law J.D. 1976. Admitted to practice North Carolina

NEELY, WILLIAM M.—*Continued*

1976. In legal practice Charlotte 1976-77 and Asheboro 1977-80.

Member 1987-93 and Chairman 1992-93 North Carolina Juvenile Law Study Commission. President North Carolina District Court Judges Association Fall 2000 to Fall 2001. Member Governor's Crime Commission 1986-92. Member The North Carolina State Bar, Randolph County, Judicial District 19B and North Carolina (Vice President June 23, 2001 to June 22, 2002) Bar Associations. Previously employed as Director Student Activities College of Charleston 1971-73. Republican. Enjoys beef cattle and sailing.

Mailing address: P.O. Box 4906, Asheboro 27204-4906.

Telephone: (336) 328-3270.

NEWBERN, Thomas R. J. *(Judge, North Carolina District Court District 6B)*

Mailing address: c/o Clerk of Superior Court, P.O. Box 370, Windsor 27983.

Office: Bertie County Courthouse, Windsor 27983.

Telephone: (252) 534-1785.

NORELLI, Nancy Black *(Judge, North Carolina District Court District 26)* Educated at Wellesley College B.A. with honors 1972 and Northeastern University J.D. 1976. Admitted to practice North Carolina 1977 and Massachusetts 1977.

President Mecklenburg County Bar Association 1999-2000.

Office: 3304 Criminal Courts Building, 700 East Fourth Street, Charlotte 28202.

Telephone: (704) 347-7801.

OLIVER, Otis M. "Bud" *(Chief Judge, North Carolina District Court District 17B)* Elected to term beginning Dec 3, 1990. Reelected 1994, Nov 3, 1998 and Nov 2002. Current term expires Dec 2006. Born Mount Airy North Carolina March 19, 1938. Baptist. Educated at University of North Carolina at Chapel Hill LL.B. Member Delta Theta Phi. Admitted to practice North Carolina 1963. In legal practice Mount Airy 1963-90.

Board of Governors North Carolina Association of District Court Judges since 1994. City Commissioner Mount Airy 1969-73 and 1979-90. Member North Carolina Academy Trial Lawyers, Surry County, North Carolina and American Bar Associations. Democrat. Enjoys sports.

Mailing address: P.O. Box 456, Dobson 27017.

Office: 201 East Kapp Street, Dobson 27017.

Telephone: (336) 386-3750.

O'NEAL, Elaine M. *(Chief Judge, North Carolina District Court District 14)* Elected to term beginning Dec 1994. Reelected Nov 3, 1998 and 2002. Current term expires Dec 2006. Certified Juvenile Court Judge since 1996. Born Durham North Carolina March 18, 1962. Baptist. Educated at North Carolina Central University B.S. in Mathematics cum laude 1984 J.D. 1991. Member Delta Sigma Theta. Admitted to practice North Carolina 1991. In legal practice Durham 1991-94.

Member Commission on Accreditation for Law Enforcement Agencies, Inc. Member North Carolina Association of Black Lawyers, North Carolina Association of District Court Judges, American Judges Association, Durham County and North Carolina Bar Associations. Attended Advanced Special Court Jurisdiction course The National Judicial College 1995. Recipient Clifton Johnson Community Service Award 1991 and Clifton Johnson Community Alumni Service Award 1996 from North Carolina Central University School of Law and Student Pro Bono Award from North Carolina Bar Association 1991. Named Woman of the Year by Women's Caucus North Carolina Central University School of Law 1991. Staff Specialist Duke University Medical Center 1984-91. Board of Directors Durham Companions 1994-95. Co-chair Durham County Juvenile Task Force since 1995. Member Advisory Board Durham County Youth Services since 1995. Member First Calvary Baptist Church.

Office: Durham County Judicial Building, Sixth Floor, 201 East Main Street, Durham 27701.

Telephone: (919) 560-6807.

ORR, Robert F. *(Associate Justice, Supreme Court of North Carolina)* Elected Nov 8, 1994. Reelected 2002, current Term expires Dec 2010. Born Norfolk Virginia Oct 11, 1946. Educated at University of North Carolina A.B. 1971 J.D. 1975. Admitted to practice North Carolina 1975. In legal practice Asheville 1975-86. Former Associate Judge, North Carolina Court of Appeals, appointed by Governor James G. Martin to term beginning Sept 2, 1986.

Adjunct Professor of Law North Carolina Central University School of Law since 1989. Member The North Carolina State Bar, Twenty-eighth Judicial District and North Carolina (Commission for the Delivery of Civil Legal Services) Bar Associations. U.S. Army 1968-71. Republican. Board of Trustees Historic Preservation Foundation of North Carolina 1982-85. Member North Carolina Beverage Control Commission 1985-86, Governor's Crime Commission, Asheville Revitalization Commission 1977-81 and Asheville-Buncombe Historic Resources Commission 1980-81. Member Secretary of the Interior's National Park System Advisory Board 1990-94. Member North Carolina 2000 (Chairman 1992), Committee for Excellence in Education, Goal 6: Safe and Drug Free Schools. Interests include historic preservation, fly fishing, sports and national parks conservation.

Mailing address: P.O. Box 1841, Raleigh 27602.

Telephone: (919) 733-3715.

OSTEEN, William L., Sr. *(Judge, United States District Court Middle District of North Carolina)* Appointed for life by President George Bush to term beginning June 18, 1991. Born Greensboro North Carolina July 15, 1930. Educated at Guilford College A.B. 1953 and University of North Carolina School of Law LL.B. 1956. In legal practice North Wilkesboro 1956-58 and Greensboro 1958-69 and 1974-91.

U.S. Attorney Middle District of North Carolina 1969-74.

Mailing address: P.O. Box 3485, Greensboro 27402-3485.

Telephone: (336) 332-6090.

OVERBY, Donald W. *(Emergency Judge, North Carolina District Court)* Retired, serves by recall.

Mailing address: P.O. Box 351, Raleigh 27602.

OWENS, Hollis M., Jr. *(Retired-Recalled Judge, North Carolina Superior Court)* Retired, serves by recall. Former Judge, North Carolina District Court Twenty-ninth Judicial District.

Mailing address: P.O. Box 64, Rutherfordton 28139.

OWSLEY, L. Suzanne *(Judge, North Carolina District Court District 25)* Elected Nov 3, 1998. Reelected 2002, current term expires Nov 2006. Educated at Wake Forest University 1982.
Office: 111 Main Avenue N.E., Hickory 28601.
Telephone: (828) 327-7500.

PARKER, J. Richard *(Resident Judge, North Carolina Superior Court First Judicial Division District 1)* Elected to term beginning Dec 1992. Reelected 1994 and 2002. Current term expires 2010. Currently Senior Resident Judge. Born Franklin Virginia Feb 26, 1948. Methodist. Educated at University of North Carolina at Chapel Hill A.B. 1970 and Wake Forest University J.D. 1974. Admitted to practice North Carolina 1974. Judge, North Carolina District Court First Judicial District 1979-92.
Mailing address: P.O. Box 1761, Manteo 27954.
Telephone: (252) 475-9138.
E-mail address: Judy.Stallings@AOC.State.NC.US

PARKER, Regina Rogers *(Judge, North Carolina District Court District 2)*
Mailing address: P.O. Box 1132, Williamston 27892.
Telephone: (252) 946-2660.

PARKER, Sarah E. *(Associate Justice, Supreme Court of North Carolina)* Elected Nov 3, 1992 to term beginning Jan 11, 1993. Reelected Nov 5, 1996, current term expires 2004. Born Charlotte North Carolina Aug 23, 1942. Educated at Meredith College 1960-62, University of North Carolina at Chapel Hill A.B. 1964 J.D. 1969. Received honorary D.H.L. Queens College 1998. Staff member North Carolina Law Review 1967-69. Admitted to practice North Carolina 1969. In legal practice Charlotte 1969-84. Associate Judge, North Carolina Court of Appeals 1985-92.
Former Member American Association of Railroad Trial Counsel. Member North Carolina Association of Women Attorneys, National Association of Women Judges, Institute for Judicial Administration, Mecklenburg County, Wake County, North Carolina and American Bar Associations. Past President Mecklenburg County Democratic Women's Club. Former Member State Democratic Party Executive Committee. Former Member Board of Directors Charlotte YMCA. Board of Visitors University of North Carolina at Chapel Hill. Board of Directors The Leadership Forum of North Carolina, Inc. Member Christ Episcopal Church, Charlotte.
Mailing address: P.O. Box 1841, Raleigh 27602.
Telephone: (919) 733-3716.

PATE, Warren L. *(Chief Judge, North Carolina District Court District 16A)*
Mailing address: P.O. Drawer 1569, Raeford 28376.
Telephone: (910) 875-9535.

PATTI, Timothy L. *(Resident Judge, North Carolina Superior Court Seventh Judicial Division District 27A)* Former Chief Judge, North Carolina District Court District 27A.
Office: Gaston County Courthouse, 325 North Marietta Street, Gastonia 28052.
Telephone: (704) 852-3125.

PAUL, Michael A. *(Judge, North Carolina District Court District 2)*
Mailing address: P.O. Box 278, Washington 27889-0278.
Telephone: (252) 946-2660.

PAYNE, Ronald K. *(Resident Judge, North Carolina Superior Court Eighth Judicial Division District 28)*
Office: Buncombe County Courthouse, 60 Court Plaza, Asheville 28801-3584.
Telephone: (828) 232-2777.

PEELE, Stanley *(Emergency Judge, North Carolina District Court)* Appointed to term beginning Nov 1969. Elected to subsequent terms. Former Chief Judge. Retired, serves by recall. Born Virginia July 1932. Educated at University of North Carolina J.D. 1959. Admitted to practice North Carolina 1959. Began legal practice Chapel Hill 1959. Assistant Judge, Recorder's Court 1965-69.
Carrboro Town Attorney 1968-69. Member North Carolina Bar Association. Sergeant First Class USAS 1950-53. Democrat. Member Orange County Youth Task Force and Botanical Garden Foundation. Founder, Board member and Big Brother Volunteers for Youth. Sponsor Child Care Networks. Helpline Crisis Volunteer. Active in Dispute Settlement Center of Chatham County and Teen Court. Columnist for local newspaper. Author *A Simple Guide to Spiritual Healing*. Involved with organizations that help children with juvenile court and custody matters.
Office: c/o Orange County Clerk of Superior Court, Orange County Courthouse, Hillsborough 27278.

PHILLIPS, Herbert O., III *(Retired-Recalled Judge, North Carolina Superior Court)* Appointed by Governor James B. Hunt, Jr. to term beginning June 1982. Elected Nov 1982 and 1986. Retired, serves by recall. Born Morehead City North Carolina Oct 7, 1928. Presbyterian. Educated at University of North Carolina at Chapel Hill B.S. 1949 LL.B. 1951. Admitted to practice North Carolina 1951. Began legal practice Morehead City 1951. Judge, North Carolina District Court Third Judicial District 1968-82.
County Attorney Carteret County 1963-68. Member North Carolina Conference of District Judges (Secretary 1975, Vice President 1976, President 1977-78) and North Carolina Bar Association. Member Masons, Scottish Rite and Shriners. Enjoys hunting, sailing, flying and fishing.
Mailing address: 1913 Evans Street, Morehead City 28557.

PHILLIPS, Nancy C. *(Judge, North Carolina District Court District 13)*
Mailing address: P.O. Box 86, Elizabethtown 28337.
Telephone: (910) 641-3070.

PONE, Edward A. *(Judge, North Carolina District Court District 12)*
Mailing address: P.O. Box 363, Fayetteville 28302.
Telephone: (910) 678-2901.

POOL, C. Randy *(Judge, North Carolina District Court District 29)*
Office: c/o clerk of Superior Court, McDowell County Courthouse, 21 South Main Street, Marion 28752.
Telephone: (828) 287-2604.

POOVEY, Nathaniel J. *(Resident Judge, North Carolina Superior Court Seventh Judicial Division District 25B)*
Mailing address: P.O. Box 9606, Hickory 28603.
Telephone: (828) 327-7500.

POPE, Marvin P., Jr. *(Judge, North Carolina District Court District 28)* Appointed by Governor James B. Hunt, Jr. to term beginning Jan 26, 2001. Term expires 2004. Born Asheville North Carolina Jan 26, 1949. Educated at Lenior-Rhyne College A.B. 1970 and Wake Forest University J.D. 1973. Staff member Wake Forest Law Review. Admitted to practice North Carolina 1973 and U.S. District Court District of North Carolina 1973. In legal practice Asheville 1973 to Jan 26, 2001.

Member North Carolina Academy of Trial Lawyers, The North Carolina State Bar, North Carolina and American Bar Associations. Democrat. Member Asheville Jaycees and Masons. Enjoys hunting, fishing, horses, crafts and stained glass.

Office: Buncombe County Courthouse, 60 Court Plaza, Asheville 28801-3583.

Telephone: (828) 232-2760.

POWELL, Mark E. *(Judge, North Carolina District Court District 29)*

Mailing address: P.O. Box 6182, Hendersonville 28793.

Telephone: (828) 287-2604.

PRIDGEN, Elton C. *(Retired-Recalled Judge, North Carolina District Court)* Retired, serves by recall.

Mailing address: P.O. Box 856, Smithfield 27577.

PROCTOR, Nathaniel P. *(Judge, North Carolina District Court District 26)*

Office: 700 East Fourth Street, Suite 3304, Charlotte 28202.

Telephone: (704) 347-7801.

QUINN, Paul M. *(Judge, North Carolina District Court District 3B)*

Mailing address: P.O. Box 3633, Morehead City 28557.

Telephone: (252) 514-4782.

RADER, Robert Blackwell *(Judge, North Carolina District Court District 10)* Appointed by Governor James B. Hunt, Jr. to term beginning Sept 1, 1994. Elected Dec 1, 1996 and Dec 1, 2000. Current term expires Dec 1, 2004. Born Morganton North Carolina Oct 1, 1956. Presbyterian. Educated at North Carolina State University B.A. 1978 and Campbell University School of Law J.D. 1985. Admitted to practice North Carolina 1986. In legal practice Raleigh 1986-94. Democrat.

Mailing address: P.O. Box 351, Raleigh 27602.

Telephone: (919) 755-4101.

RAGAN, James Edward, III *(Emergency Judge, North Carolina Superior Court)* Appointed by Governor James B. Hunt, Jr. to term beginning Feb 1994. Elected Nov 6, 1994. Former Senior Resident Judge Second Judicial Division District 3B. Retired, serves by recall. Born New Bern North Carolina July 21, 1941. Methodist. Educated at North Carolina State University B.S. 1963 and University of Baltimore LL.B. 1967. Admitted to practice Maryland 1969 and North Carolina 1975. Judge and Chief Judge, North Carolina District Court District 3B 1979-94.

Office: Superior Court Judges Office, 421 Craven Street, New Bern 28563.

RAND, Ripley E. *(Special Judge, North Carolina Superior Court)* Appointed by Governor Michael F. Easley.

Mailing address: P.O. Box 351, Raleigh 27602.

Telephone: (919) 755-4100.

RAWLS, Addie M. Harris *(Judge, North Carolina District Court District 11)*

Mailing address: c/o Clerk of Superior Court, P.O. Box 297, Smithfield 27577.

Telephone: (910) 814-4670.

READ, J. Milton, Jr. *(Emergency Judge, North Carolina Superior Court)* Retired, serves by recall. Former Chief Judge, North Carolina District Court Fourteenth Judicial District.

Office: 278 Durham County Judicial Building, Sixth Floor, 201 East Main Street, Durham 27701.

REDWING, Dennis J. *(Chief Judge, North Carolina District Court District 27A)*

Office: Gaston County Courthouse, 325 North Marietta Street, Gastonia 28052.

Telephone: (704) 852-3117.

REINGOLD, William B. *(Chief Judge, North Carolina District Court District 21)* Appointed by Governor James G. Martin April 3, 1986. Elected 1988, 1992, 1996 and 2000. Current term expires Dec 2004. Chief Judge since March 6, 1998.

Mailing address: P.O. Box 20099, Winston-Salem 27120-0099.

Telephone: (336) 761-2478.

RICHARDSON, Herbert L. *(Judge, North Carolina District Court District 16B)* Former Chief Judge.

Office: Robeson County Courthouse, Box 18, Lumberton 28358.

Telephone: (910) 671-3355.

ROBERSON, James K. *(Judge, North Carolina District Court District 15A)* Elected to term beginning Dec 4, 2001. Term expires Dec 2005. Educated at East Carolina University B.S. 1972 and Wake Forest University J.D. 1975. Admitted to practice North Carolina 1975, U.S. District Court Middle District of North Carolina, U.S. Court of Appeals Fourth Circuit and U.S. Supreme Court.

Office: 120 Criminal Courts Building, 212 West Elm Street, Graham 27253.

Telephone: (336) 438-1018.

RODA, Peter L. *(Judge, North Carolina District Court District 28)* Appointed by Governor James B. Hunt, Jr. April 6, 1979. Elected 1982, 1986, 1990, 1994, 1998 and 2002. Current term expires Dec 2006. Born Rochester New York Feb 8, 1935. Baptist. Educated at Amherst College B.A. cum laude 1956 and Duke University J.D. 1962. Member Theta Xi and Phi Delta Phi. Admitted to practice North Carolina 1962. Began legal practice Asheville 1965.

Asheville City Solicitor 1968-70. Public Defender Twenty-eighth Judicial District 1973-79. Named Asheville's Outstanding Young Man 1968. Democrat.

Office: Buncombe County Courthouse, Asheville 28801-3583.

Telephone: (828) 232-2760.

ROEMER, Victoria L. *(Judge, North Carolina District Court District 21)*
Mailing address: P.O. Box 20099, Winston-Salem 27120-0099.
Telephone: (336) 761-2478.

ROUSSEAU, Julius A., Jr. *(Retired-Recalled Judge, North Carolina Superior Court)* Appointed by Governor Robert Walter Scott to term beginning Dec 8, 1972. Elected to subsequent terms. Former Senior Resident Judge. Retired, serves by recall. Former Emergency Judge. Born Wilkes County North Carolina Dec 3, 1930. Educated at University of North Carolina A.B. LL.B. 1956. Admitted to practice North Carolina 1956.
Mailing address: P.O. Box 1291, North Wilkesboro 28659.

ROYSTER, Theodore S., Jr. *(Judge, North Carolina District Court District 22)*
Mailing address: P.O. Box 1064, Lexington 27293-1064.
Telephone: (704) 878-4209.

RUTH, Kristin Holmquist *(Judge, North Carolina District Court District 10)* Elected Nov 4, 1998 to term beginning Dec 7, 1998. Reelected 2002, current term expires Nov 2006. Born Salina Kansas Sept 28, 1956. Methodist. Educated at Kansas State University B.S. 1978 and Campbell University School of Law J.D. Admitted to practice North Carolina 1991 and Texas 1992. In legal practice Raleigh 1991-92 and Apex 1992-98 North Carolina.
Member Wake County (Board of Directors since 2000) and North Carolina (Board of Directors Tenth Judicial District since 2000) Bar Associations. Attended New Judges School Nov 1998 and Feb 1999 and Conference on North Carolina Child Support May 1999. Democrat. Member Kiwanis Club, Association of American Business Women, Business and Professional Women, Apex United Methodist Church and Apex Educational Foundation. Enjoys running in 5K events, horseback riding and softball.
Mailing address: P.O. Box 351, Raleigh 27602.
Telephone: (919) 755-4101.

SABISTON, Michael A. *(Judge, North Carolina District Court District 19B)* Appointed by Governor James G. Martin to term beginning March 23, 1992. Elected Nov 1994, Nov 3, 1998 and Nov 2002. Current term expires 2006. Born Mobile Alabama Oct 13, 1953. Baptist. Educated at University of North Carolina at Greensboro B.S. with honors 1977 and Wake Forest University J.D. 1982. Admitted to practice North Carolina 1982. In legal practice Troy 1983-88.
Assistant District Attorney Judicial District 19B 1988-92. Republican.
Mailing address: P.O. Box 666, Troy 27371.
Telephone: (336) 318-6887.

SALISBURY, Anne B. *(Judge, North Carolina District Court District 10)* Elected to term beginning Dec 3, 1990. Reelected 1994, 1998 and 2002. Current term expires Dec 2006. Certified Juvenile Court Judge since 1995. Born Charlotte North Carolina May 17, 1949. Presbyterian. Educated at Salem College A.B. 1971, North Carolina State University M.Ed. 1978 and Campbell University J.D. 1982. Member Phi Alpha Delta. Admitted to practice North Carolina 1982 and U.S. District Court Eastern District of North Carolina 1982. Certified Specialist in Family Law by The North Carolina State Bar Board of Legal Specialization since 1989. In legal practice Raleigh 1982-90.
Member The North Carolina State Bar, Wake County (Board of Directors 2000-02, Member Endowment Committee) and North Carolina Bar Associations. Instructor "Use of Constructive and Resulting Trusts in Equitable Distribution" Family Law CLE Wake Forest University School of Law 1994. Democrat. Junior League Community Advisor 1993-94. Member Cary Community Choir. Enjoys weightlifting and children.
Mailing address: P.O. Box 351, Raleigh 27602.
Office: Wake County Courthouse, Raleigh 27601.
Telephone: (919) 755-4101.

SASSER, Douglas B. *(Judge, North Carolina District Court District 13)*
Office: 110-A Courthouse Square, Whiteville 28472.
Telephone: (910) 641-3070.

SEATON, Sarah Cowen *(Judge, North Carolina District Court District 4)* Appointed by Governor James B. Hunt, Jr. to term beginning July 2, 1999. Elected 2002, current term expires Dec 2006. Born Williamston North Carolina June 21, 1960. Baptist. Educated at North Carolina State University B.A. 1981 and Campbell University School of Law J.D. 1985. Admitted to practice North Carolina 1986, U.S. District Court Eastern District of North Carolina and U.S. Supreme Court.
Assistant District Attorney Fourth Prosecutorial District of North Carolina 1986 to June 1999.
Mailing address: P.O. Box 1378, Jacksonville 28541.
Telephone: (910) 296-2308.

SEAY, Thomas W., Jr. *(Retired-Recalled Judge, North Carolina Superior Court)* Appointed by Governor Dan Killian Moore to term beginning July 1, 1967. Reelected to subsequent terms. Retired, serves by recall. Born Salisbury North Carolina April 14, 1926. Member Central United Methodist Church. Educated at Duke University A.B. 1949 J.D. 1952. Admitted to practice North Carolina 1952. Began legal practice Salisbury 1952. Judge, Rowan County Court 1958-60.
Prosecuting Attorney Rowan County 1956-58. Member North Carolina Senate 1963 and 1965. Member American Judicature Society, The North Carolina State Bar, Rowan County, North Carolina and American Bar Associations. Participant 1968 and 1972 and Faculty Advisor 1974 National College of the State Judiciary. U.S. Army 1944-46. Democrat. Member Masons, York Rite, Shriners, American Legion and Kiwanis Club of Salisbury.
Mailing address: P.O. Box 286, Spencer 28159.

SENTER, J. Larry *(Judge, North Carolina District Court District 9)*
Mailing address: P.O. Box 3, Franklinton 27525.
Telephone: (919) 693-5193.

SETZER, Joseph E. *(Chief Judge, North Carolina District Court District 8)*
Mailing address: P.O. Box 267, Goldsboro 27533-0267.
Telephone: (252) 527-7891.

SHARP, P. Trevor *(Magistrate Judge, United States District Court Middle District of North Carolina)* Appointed by U.S. District Court judges.
Mailing address: P.O. Box 3195, Greensboro 27402.
Telephone: (336) 332-6120.

SHARPE, Margaret L. *(Emergency Judge, North Carolina District Court)* Elected Nov 1988 to term beginning Dec 5, 1988. Reelected Nov 3, 1992. Retired, serves by recall. Born Washington D.C. May 22, 1934. Educated at Duke University Diploma in Nursing 1955, University of North Carolina at Greensboro B.A. magna cum laude 1976 and Wake Forest University J.D. 1978. Member Phi Beta Kappa and Phi Alpha Delta. Admitted to practice North Carolina 1978 and U.S. District Court Middle District of North Carolina 1978. In legal practice Winston-Salem 1978-88.

Member Forsyth County Women Attorneys, North Carolina Women Attorneys, North Carolina Sixteenth District and North Carolina Bar Associations. Democrat. President Forsyth County Democratic Women 1976-77. Board Member FIRST Drug Rx Program and Winston-Salem Arts Council. Member Leadership Winston-Salem. Enjoys gardening and travel. Interests include environmental and health issues.

Mailing address: 844 Glen Echo Trail, Winston-Salem 27106.

Telephone: (336) 724-6245.

Fax: (336) 724-6245

E-mail address: marglsharpe@yahoo.com

SHERRILL, Russell Graham, III *(Emergency Judge, North Carolina District Court)* Appointed by Governor James B. Hunt, Jr. to term beginning Jan 9, 1979. Elected 1980, 1984, 1988, 1992 and 1996. Former Chief Judge. Retired, serves by recall. Certified Juvenile Court Judge since 1992. Born Raleigh North Carolina June 9, 1944. Educated at North Carolina State University B.A. 1967 and University of North Carolina J.D. 1971. Law Clerk to Hon. Earl W. Vaughan, North Carolina Court of Appeals 1971-72. Member Phi Delta Phi. Admitted to practice North Carolina 1971. Began legal practice Raleigh 1971.

Associate Attorney General North Carolina Department of Justice 1972-73. Assistant District Attorney Tenth Judicial District 1973-79. Secretary 1994-95 and Co-chair Legislative Committee 1995-97 North Carolina Judicial Conference. Member North Carolina District Court Judges Association (Co-chairman Legislation Committee 1990-98) and Wake County Bar Association. E-6 North Carolina National Guard 1968-76. Democrat. Board member Wake County Child Abuse Prevention, Inc. and Artspace, Inc. (Former Vice President). Member City of Raleigh Arts Commission 1978-82 (Chairman 1982), Raleigh Arts Foundation (Admissions and Allocations Committee 1987-90), Terpsichorean Club and Raleigh Jaycees. Enjoys reading, art and book collecting, sailing, hiking and photography.

Mailing address: P.O. Box 351, Raleigh 27602.

SIGMON, Amy R. *(Judge, North Carolina District Court District 25)*

Office: 111 Main Avenue N.E., Hickory 28601.

Telephone: (828) 327-7500.

SISK, Avril U. *(Judge, North Carolina District Court District 26)* Appointed to term beginning Jan 5, 2001.

Office: 700 East Fourth Street, Suite 3304, Charlotte 28202.

Telephone: (704) 347-7801.

SITTON, Claude S. *(Emergency Judge, North Carolina Superior Court)* Appointed by Governor James B. Hunt, Jr. to term beginning Sept 3, 1980. Elected Nov 1980, 1986 and 1994. Former Senior Resident Judge Seventh Judicial Division District 25A. Retired, serves by recall. Born Arden North Carolina Dec 24, 1937. Baptist. Educated at Mars Hill Junior College A.A. 1958, University of North Carolina at Chapel Hill A.B. 1960 and Wake Forest University School at Law J.D. replaced LL.B. conferred 1963. Member Phi Alpha Delta. Admitted to practice North Carolina 1963 and U.S. Supreme Court 1973. In legal practice Morganton 1963-80.

Member Burke County, North Carolina and American Bar Associations. Attended The National Judicial College 1983, 1988, 1993 and 1996.

Mailing address: P.O. Box 796, Morganton 28680.

SKERRETT, C. Dawn *(Judge, North Carolina District Court District 29)*

Mailing address: P.O. Box 426, Cedar Mountain 28718.

Telephone: (828) 287-2604.

SMALL, A. Thomas *(Judge, United States Bankruptcy Court Eastern District of North Carolina)* Appointed by U.S. District Court judges to term beginning Dec 14, 1982. Reappointed by U.S. Court of Appeals Fourth Circuit judges 1986. Term expires Sept 2014. Former Chief Judge. Born Columbia South Carolina Oct 4, 1943. Educated at Duke University A.B. 1965 and Wake Forest University School of Law J.D. 1969. Member Kappa Sigma and Phi Alpha Delta. Admitted to practice North Carolina 1969. In legal practice Greensboro 1969-72 and Raleigh 1973-82.

Vice President and Associate General Counsel First Union Corporation 1969-82. Associate Director and General Counsel Community Enterprise Development Corporation Anchorage Alaska 1972-73. Instructor Campbell University School of Law 1979-81. Member North Carolina (Bankruptcy Council 1979-82) and American Bar Associations. Republican. Enjoys tennis.

Mailing address: P.O. Drawer 2747, Raleigh 27602-2747.

Telephone: (919) 856-4603.

SMITH, Donald L. *(Retired Judge, North Carolina Court of Appeals)* Associate Judge 1988-89. Retired, serves by recall. Currently serves as Emergency Special Judge, North Carolina Superior Court since Sept 1, 1995. Born Sampson County North Carolina March 23, 1939. Educated at University of North Carolina at Chapel Hill, Pembroke University and Wake Forest University School of Law 1964. In legal practice North Carolina 1989-94. Resident Judge, North Carolina Superior Court Second Judicial Division District Ten 1973-75 and 1985-86. Special Judge, North Carolina Superior Court 1975-85 and 1986-88.

Important Decisions: Revco v. Board of Pharmacy 1975, State v. Columbus Christian Academy 1978, State v. James Hutchins (McDowell Co.) and State v. Small (Robeson Co.). Member North Carolina Municipal Attorneys Association, The North Carolina State Bar, Tenth District and Wake County Bar Associations. Attended North Carolina Conference of Superior Court Judges 1973-88 and North Carolina Judicial Conference. Member Governor's Standards Policies and Goal Commission 1986-88. Member Raleigh Kiwanis Club and First Baptist Church of Lumberton.

Mailing address: P.O. Box 351, Raleigh 27602.

SMITH, John W. *(Judge, North Carolina District Court District 5)* Elected to term beginning Dec 1,

SMITH, JOHN W.—*Continued*
1988. Reelected 1992, 1996 and 2000. Current term expires Dec 2004. Former Chief Judge. Educated at Davidson College B.A. 1969 and Wake Forest University School of Law J.D. 1972. Admitted to practice North Carolina 1972, U.S. Tax Court 1973 and U.S. District Court Eastern District of North Carolina 1974. In legal practice Raleigh 1972-74.

Assistant District Attorney Fifth Judicial District 1974-88. Author *North Carolina Drunk Driving Law* Professional Education Seminars, Inc. 1984 and *The North Carolina Safe Roads Act* Institute of Government Publications 1984. Founding Board of Directors North Carolina Judicial Conference 1993-95. Member North Carolina Association of District Court Judges (Secretary/Treasurer 1991-92, President Elect 1992-93, President 1994), The North Carolina State Bar and New Hanover County Bar Association (Board of Directors 1986-88 and 2000-03). Graduate General Jurisdiction Course The National Judicial College 1989. First Lieutenant U.S. Army 1972 and Captain USAR 1979. Democrat.

Office: 332 New Hanover County Judicial Bldg., 316 Princess Street, Wilmington 28401.
Telephone: (910) 341-1120.

SMITH, W. Osmond, III *(Resident Judge, North Carolina Superior Court Third Judicial Division District 9A)* Currently Senior Resident Judge.

Mailing address: P.O. Box 1777, Yanceyville 27379.
Office: Caswell County Courthouse, Yanceyville 27379.
Telephone: (336) 694-7208.

SNOW, John J., Jr. *(Chief Judge, North Carolina District Court District 30)*

Office: c/o Clerk of Superior Court, 201 Cherokee County Courthouse, 75 Peachtree Street, Murphy 28906.
Telephone: (828) 456-3796.

SPAINHOUR, William Erwin *(Resident Judge, North Carolina Superior Court Sixth Judicial Division District 19A)* Appointed by Governor James B. Hunt, Jr. to term beginning Jan 1, 1998. Elected Nov 1998, current term expires Nov 2006. Currently Senior Resident Judge. Born Lenoir North Carolina Nov 23, 1942. Presbyterian. Educated at Davidson College A.B. 1964 and University of North Carolina J.D. 1970. Admitted to practice North Carolina 1970, U.S. District Court Middle District of North Carolina 1970, U.S. Court of Appeals Fourth Circuit 1977 and U.S. Supreme Court 2001. In legal practice Concord 1970 to Jan 1, 1998.

Author "Lawyer Depression: A Catch-22?" and "Of Elephants and Birehouses" The North Carolina State B. Jour. and "I Found Atticus Finch" The North Carolina State B. Jour. reprinted in Rhode Island B. Jour. President The North Carolina State Bar 1996-97. Chairman The North Carolina Sentencing and Policy Advisory Commission since 1999. Fellow American College of Trial Lawyers. Recipient Silver Beaver Award from Boy Scouts of America 1982. Second Lieutenant, First Lieutenant and Captain U.S. Army active duty 1965-68. President Concord Rotary Club 1989-90.

Mailing address: P.O. Box 303, Concord 28026-0303.
Telephone: (704) 786-4279.
Fax: (704) 788-2587

SPENCER, Cheryl Lynn *(Judge, North Carolina District Court District 3B)*

Office: 204 Craven County Courthouse Annex, 302 Broad Street, New Bern 28560-4903.
Telephone: (252) 514-4782.

SPENCER, James C., Jr. *(Resident Judge, North Carolina Superior Court Third Judicial Division District 15A)* Appointed by Governor James B. Hunt, Jr. to term beginning Feb 18, 1994. Elected Nov 1994 and Nov 2002. Current term expires Dec 31, 2010. Born Asheboro North Carolina Oct 24, 1940. Episcopalian. Educated at University of North Carolina at Chapel Hill A.B. 1963 J.D. 1967. Law Clerk to Hon. John Davis Larkins, Jr., U.S. District Court Eastern District of North Carolina 1967-69. Member Phi Delta Phi. Admitted to practice North Carolina 1967, U.S. District Courts Eastern and Middle Districts of North Carolina and U.S. Court of Appeals Fourth Circuit. In legal practice Burlington 1969-94.

Office: 245 Criminal Courts Building, 212 West Elm Street, Graham 27253.
Telephone: (336) 438-1019.

SPIVEY, Ronald E. *(Resident Judge, North Carolina Superior Court Fifth Judicial Division District 21)* Appointed by Governor James B. Hunt, Jr. to term beginning Feb 8, 2001. Born Sanford North Carolina Nov 20, 1959. Methodist. Educated at North Carolina State University B.A. 1982 and Wake Forest University J.D. 1985. Admitted to practice North Carolina 1985 and U.S. Court of Appeals for the Armed Forces 1988. In legal practice Winston-Salem 1985-86. Judge, North Carolina District Court District 21 Oct 1994 to 2001, appointed by Governor James B. Hunt, Jr.

Assistant District Attorney 1987-94. Member North Carolina Governor's Crime Commission, North Carolina Domestic Violence Commission and Forsyth County Bar Association. Democrat. Enjoys basketball and golf.

Mailing address: P.O. Box 20099, Winston-Salem 27120-0099.
Telephone: (336) 761-2420.
E-mail address: RSJUDGE@AOL.COM

STANBACK, A. Leon, Jr. *(Resident Judge, North Carolina Superior Court Third Judicial Division District 14)* Assumed office 1989. Elected to subsequent term. Educated at North Carolina Central University B.S. 1965 J.D. 1968. Staff member North Carolina Central Law Journal. In legal practice 1968-69 and 1971-89.

Assistant District Attorney Guilford County 1969-71. Commissioner North Carolina Parole Commission 1985-89. Author "Thoughts on Jury Trials" *The Litigator* North Carolina Bar Association 1999 and "Professionalism and Legal Ethics in the Practice of Criminal Law—A Judge's Perspective" Wake Forest Law School Continuing Legal Education Series. Member Judicial Council National Bar Association. Member North Carolina Conference of Superior Court Judges, Guilford County Association of Black Lawyers (Past President), North Carolina Academy of Trial Lawyers, North Carolina Association of Black Lawyers (Former Vice President), George White Bar Association, Durham County, North Carolina (Medico-Legal Liaison Committee) and American Bar Associations. Panel Member New Rules of Evidence North Carolina Academy of Trial Lawyers. Attended The Philosophy of Law and Judging Harvard University Law School 2000, Seminar on Professionalism in the Practice of Law North Carolina Central Uni-

STANBACK, A. LEON, JR.—*Continued*
versity School of Law 2001, "A View from the Bench" Seminar North Carolina Bar Association, Criminal Law Trial Practice Seminar Wake Forest University School of Law and National Institute for Trial Advocacy. Guest Faculty Trial Advocacy Course University of North Carolina School of Law 2001.

Recipient Outstanding Trial Judge of the Year Award from North Carolina Academy of Trial Lawyers 1998, Certificate of Appreciation from Hayes-Taylor YMCA and Award for Service to the North Carolina Judiciary from North Carolina Central University School of Law Alumni Association. Member Governor's Minority Advisory Council 1985-89. Member Minority Business Resource Center Advisory Committee U.S. Department of Transportation 1988-89. Trial Judge Fullwood Competition Finals North Carolina Central University School of Law 1998 and Wade Edwards High School Mock Trial Competition North Carolina Academy of Trial Lawyers. Board of Directors Durham County Friends of Guardian Ad Litem, North Carolina Central University School of Law Alumni Association, Greensboro Legal Aid Foundation and Durham Community Penalties Program. Member Steward Board Saint Joseph A.M.E. Church, North Carolina Black Child Development Institute, North Carolina Council on the Status of Women, Greensboro Minority Business League, Executive Committee NAACP Greensboro, Planning Division United Way of Greater Greensboro and Steering Committee Black Achiever's Program Durham YMCA.

Office: Durham County Judicial Building, Sixth Floor, Durham 27701.
Telephone: (919) 564-7072.

STEELMAN, Sanford L., Jr. *(Associate Judge, North Carolina Court of Appeals)* Elected to term beginning Jan 1, 2003. Born Elmhurst Illinois Sept 11, 1951. Baptist. Educated at Davidson College A.B. with honors 1973 and University of North Carolina at Chapel Hill J.D. 1976. Admitted to practice North Carolina 1976, U.S. District Courts Western 1978 and Middle 1984 Districts of North Carolina and U.S. Court of Appeals Fourth Circuit 1986. In legal practice Monroe 1976-94. Resident Judge Dec 19, 1994 to 2001 and Senior Resident Judge 2001-02, North Carolina Superior Court Sixth Judicial Division District 20B.

County Attorney Union County 1991-94. Attorney Village of Marvin 1994. Member Budget Advisory Committee Administrative Office of the Courts 1999-2002. Member 2000-02 and Chairman 2001-02 Superior Court Subcommittee Alternative Dispute Resolution Committee North Carolina Judicial Council. Member Union County, 20th Judicial District and North Carolina Bar Associations. Attended General Jurisdiction course The National Judicial College April-May 1996. Named Jaycee of the Year 1979. Councilman and Mayor pro tempore Town of Weddington 1985-94. President Monroe Jaycees 1980-81. Chairman Standby Selective Service Board Union and Anson Counties 1982-94. Sunday School Teacher and Member Communion Committee First Baptist Church Matthews since 1985. Board Member Criminal Justice Partnership Stanly County 1994-2002. Member Task Force Sun Valley High School 1998 and North Carolina Dispute Resolution Commission since 2003. Member Courthouse Security Advisory Committee 2000 and Chairman Criminal Justice Partnership Board 2001-02 Union County. Interests include local history and writing the history of the town of Weddington.

Mailing address: P.O. Box 888, Raleigh 27602.
Telephone: (919) 733-4227.
Fax: (919) 733-8003
E-mail address: snj@coa.state.nc.us

STEPHENS, Donald W. *(Resident Judge, North Carolina Superior Court Third Judicial Division District 10)* Appointed Special Judge by Governor James B. Hunt, Jr. to term beginning Jan 1, 1985. Elected Resident Judge 1986, 1988 and 1996. Current term expires Dec 31, 2004. Senior Resident Judge since Jan 1, 2001. Born Durham North Carolina Oct 9, 1945. Southern Baptist. Educated at University of North Carolina at Chapel Hill B.S. 1967 J.D. with honors 1970. Staff member North Carolina Law Review 1969-70. Member Order of the Coif. Admitted to practice North Carolina 1970, U.S. District Court Eastern District of North Carolina 1978, U.S. Supreme Court 1978 and U.S. Court of Appeals Fourth Circuit 1979.

Assistant District Attorney Durham 1975-78. Special Deputy Attorney General North Carolina 1978-84. USMC JAGC 1971-74. Member Democratic Party. Active in animal and environmental preservation. Enjoys golf.

Mailing address: P.O. Box 351, Raleigh 27602.
Telephone: (919) 755-4100.

STEPHENS, Ronald L. *(Resident Judge, North Carolina Superior Court Third Judicial Division District 14)* Former Special Judge.

Office: Durham County Judicial Building, Sixth Floor, Durham 27701.
Telephone: (919) 564-7230.

STEVENS, Catherine C. *(Emergency Judge, North Carolina District Court)* Retired, serves by recall.

Office: Gaston County Courthouse, 325 North Marietta Street, Gastonia 28052.

STEVENS, Henry L., IV *(Judge, North Carolina District Court District 4)*

Mailing address: P.O. Box 866, Kenansville 28349.
Telephone: (910) 296-2308.

STEWART, Marcia *(Judge, North Carolina District Court District 11)* Elected to term beginning Dec 2001. Term expires Dec 2005. Born Saginaw Michigan July 18, 1969. Protestant. Educated at Michigan State University B.A. 1991 and Campbell University J.D. Admitted to practice North Carolina 1995. In legal practice Smithfield 1995-2000.

Member American Bar Association.
Mailing address: P.O. Box 2066, Smithfield 27577.
Telephone: (910) 814-4670.
E-mail address: judgemks@bellsouth.net

STEWART, William G. *(Judge, North Carolina District Court District 7)*

Mailing address: P.O. Box 999, Wilson 27894.
Telephone: (252) 234-7676.

STIEHL, Robert J., III *(Judge, North Carolina District Court District 12)*

Mailing address: P.O. Box 363, Fayetteville 28302.
Telephone: (910) 678-2901.

STOCKS, William L. *(Chief Judge, United States Bankruptcy Court Middle District of North Carolina)* Appointed by U.S. Court of Appeals Fourth Circuit jud-

STOCKS, WILLIAM L.—*Continued*

ges to term beginning Nov 24, 1993. Term expires Nov 24, 2007. Born Greenville North Carolina Sept 24, 1942.

Mailing address: P.O. Box 3603, Greensboro 27402-3603.

Telephone: (336) 333-5080.

E-mail address: william_stocks@ncmb.uscourts.gov

STONE, Richard W. *(Chief Judge, North Carolina District Court District 17A)*

Mailing address: P.O. Box 97, Wentworth 27375.

Telephone: (336) 342-8740.

STUBBS, Alice C. *(Judge, North Carolina District Court District 10)* Appointed by Governor James B. Hunt, Jr. 1997. Elected Nov 3, 1998 and 2002. Current term expires Dec 2006.

Mailing address: P.O. Box 351, Raleigh 27602.

Telephone: (919) 755-4101.

SUMNER, Quentin T. *(Resident Judge, North Carolina Superior Court First Judicial Division District 7A)* Currently Senior Resident Judge. Born Rocky Mount North Carolina Oct 10, 1950. Baptist. Educated at North Carolina Central University B.A. 1972 J.D. 1975. Staff member North Carolina Law Review 1974. Member Omega Psi Phi and Phi Alpha Delta. Admitted to practice North Carolina 1975. Began legal practice Wilson 1975, in legal practice Rocky Mount 1976. Former Judge, North Carolina District Court Seventh Judicial District, appointed by Governor James B. Hunt, Jr. Aug 1983.

Member Redevelopment Commission City of Rocky Mount and Nash County Industrial Development Board. Part-time Instructor Edgecombe Technical College since 1978 and North Carolina Wesleyan College. Member Nash-Edgecombe and Seventh Judicial District Bar Associations. Named Omega Man of the Year 1983. Board of Directors Friends of Youth, Inc., Cities in Schools, Inc., Red Cross and Rocky Mount Meals on Wheels. Enjoys golf, horseback riding, tennis and skiing.

Mailing address: P.O. Box 1215, Rocky Mount 27802-1215.

Telephone: (252) 459-4707.

TATE, Samuel McDowell *(Retired-Recalled Judge, North Carolina District Court)* Elected to term beginning Dec 2, 1974. Reelected to subsequent terms. Retired, serves by recall. Born Morganton North Carolina June 10, 1923. Presbyterian. Educated at Davidson College A.B. 1948 and University of North Carolina J.D. 1953. Admitted to practice North Carolina 1953. Began legal practice Morganton 1953.

Lecturer on Juvenile Law at local technical institute 1977. President North Carolina Association of District Court Judges 1982-83. Private First Class U.S. Army ETO 1944-45. Democrat. Enjoys nature study, particularly ornithology.

Mailing address: c/o Burke County Clerk of Superior Court, P.O. Box 796, Morganton 28680.

TAYLOR, Kimberly Susan *(Resident Judge, North Carolina Superior Court Sixth Judicial Division District 22)* Born Durham North Carolina Feb 19, 1955. Presbyterian. Educated at Duke University A.B. with honors 1977 and University of North Carolina at Chapel Hill J.D. with honors 1981. Staff member North Carolina Law Review. Member Phi Delta Phi and Order of the Coif. Admitted to practice North Carolina 1981 and U.S. District Court Western District of North Carolina 1981. In legal practice Taylorsville 1981-86. Former Judge, North Carolina District Court District 22, elected to term beginning Dec 1, 1986.

Author "Attorney Mediation in Domestic Cases" North Carolina L. Rev. 1980. Member North Carolina Association of District Court Judges (Chair Education Committee), The North Carolina State Bar and North Carolina Bar Association. Democrat. Chairperson Alexander County Democratic Women. Member Alexander County Board of Elections. Enjoys scuba diving and horseback riding.

Mailing address: P.O. Box 186, Statesville 28687.

Office: Iredell County Courthouse, Statesville 28687.

Telephone: (704) 878-4213.

TAYLOR, Susan Chandler *(Resident Judge, North Carolina Superior Court Sixth Judicial Division District 20B)* Appointed by Governor Michael F. Easley to term beginning 2002. Currently Senior Resident Judge. Former Judge, North Carolina District Court District 20.

Mailing address: P.O. Drawer 829, Monroe 28111-0829.

Telephone: (704) 289-6487.

TENNILLE, Ben F. *(Special Judge, North Carolina Superior Court)* Appointed by governor.

Office: North Carolina Business Law Center, 200 South Elm Street, Greensboro 27401.

Telephone: (336) 334-5252.

THACKER, Lisa D. *(Judge, North Carolina District Court District 20)* Assumed office Jan 2, 1998.

Mailing address: c/o Clerk of Superior Court, P.O. Box 1064, Wadesboro 28170.

Office: Anson County Courthouse, Wadesboro 28170.

Telephone: (704) 982-3095.

THAGARD, Leonard W. *(Chief Judge, North Carolina District Court District 4)*

Mailing address: P.O. Box 866, Kenansville 28540.

Telephone: (910) 296-2308.

THALHEIMER, Ben S. *(Judge, North Carolina District Court District 26)*

Office: 700 East Fourth Street, Suite 3304, Charlotte 28202.

Telephone: (704) 347-7801.

THOMPSON, Jack *(Resident Judge, North Carolina Superior Court Fourth Judicial Division District 12)* Elected to term beginning Jan 1, 1991. Reelected Nov 3, 1998, current term expires Jan 1, 2007. Born Fayetteville North Carolina June 14, 1941. Presbyterian. Educated at Wake Forest University B.A. 1963 J.D. 1965. Member Phi Alpha Delta. Admitted to practice North Carolina 1965. In legal practice Fayetteville 1967-70 and 1974-90.

District Attorney Twelfth District 1970-75. Member North Carolina Academy of Trial Lawyers, The North Carolina State Bar and North Carolina Bar Association. Attended General Jurisdiction Course The National Judicial College 1993. Recipient Outstanding Trial Court Judge Award from North Carolina Academy of Trial Lawyers 1997. First Lieutenant Military Police Corps U.S. Army 1965-67. Democrat.

Mailing address: P.O. Box 363, Fayetteville 28302.

Office: Cumberland County Courthouse, Fayetteville 28302.

Telephone: (910) 678-2900.

THORNBURG, Lacy H. *(Judge, United States District Court Western District of North Carolina)* Appointed for life by President Bill Clinton.
Office: 241 U.S. Courthouse, 100 Otis Street, Asheville 28801-2611.
Telephone: (828) 771-7250.

TILLETT, Jerry R. *(Resident Judge, North Carolina Superior Court First Judicial Division District 1)*
Mailing address: P.O. Box 1761, Manteo 27954.
Telephone: (252) 475-9138.

TILLEY, N. Carlton, Jr. *(Chief Judge, United States District Court Middle District of North Carolina)* Appointed for life by President Ronald Reagan to term beginning Nov 4, 1988. Chief Judge since Sept 22, 1999. Born Rock Hill South Carolina Dec 16, 1943. Presbyterian. Educated at Wake Forest University B.S. J.D. Law Clerk to Hon. Eugene A. Gordon, U.S. District Court 1969-71. Admitted to practice North Carolina 1969. In legal practice Greensboro 1977-88.
Assistant U.S. Attorney 1971-73 and U.S. Attorney 1974-77 U.S. District Court Middle District of North Carolina.
Mailing address: P.O. Box 3443, Greensboro 27402.
Office: 324 West Market Street, Greensboro 27401.
Telephone: (336) 332-6080.

TIMMONS-GOODSON, Patricia Ann *(Associate Judge, North Carolina Court of Appeals)* Appointed by Governor James B. Hunt, Jr. to term beginning Feb 21, 1997. Elected Nov 3, 1998, current term expires Dec 31, 2006. Born Florence South Carolina Sept 18, 1954. Baptist. Member First Baptist Church Fayetteville. Educated at University of North Carolina at Chapel Hill B.A. in Speech/English 1976 J.D. 1979. Named to Holderness Moot Court Bench. Member Order of Valkyries and Order of the Old Well. Admitted to practice North Carolina 1981. Began legal practice Fayetteville 1981. Judge, North Carolina District Court District 12 Sept 17, 1984 to Feb 20, 1997, appointed by Governor James B. Hunt., Jr. (one of the youngest persons to serve on the District 12 bench).
Clerk Cumberland County Sheriff's Department Sept 1979 to Nov 1979. District Manager U.S. Census Bureau Nov 1979 to Aug 1980. Assistant District Attorney Cumberland County May 1, 1981 to July 15, 1983. Staff Attorney Lumbee River Legal Services, Inc. July 18, 1983 to Sept 14, 1984. Member North Carolina Association of Black Lawyers, North Carolina Association of Women Attorneys, North Carolina Association of District Court Judges, Cumberland County, North Carolina, and American Bar Associations. Named Distinguished Young Alumna by University of North Carolina at Chapel Hill 1992. Recipient Leadership Award from North Carolina Legislative Black Caucus 1995 and Service Award from Fayetteville Chapter NAACP 1996. Democrat. Member Fayetteville Chapter of Links, Inc. and First Baptist Church (Sunday School teacher). Enjoys travel, golf and reading.
Mailing address: P.O. Box 888, Raleigh 27602.
Office: Court of Appeals Building, One West Morgan Street, Raleigh 27601.
Telephone: (919) 733-4229.

TIN, Becky Thorne *(Judge, North Carolina District Court District 26)*
Office: 700 East Fourth Street, Suite 3304, Charlotte 28202.
Telephone: (704) 347-7801.

TITUS, Kenneth C. *(Resident Judge, North Carolina Superior Court Third Judicial Division District 14)* Former Judge and Chief Judge, North Carolina District Court District 14.
Office: Durham County Judicial Building, Sixth Floor, Durham 27701.
Telephone: (919) 564-7230.

TRAWICK, Gary E. *(Special Judge, North Carolina Superior Court)* Appointed by governor.
Mailing address: P.O. Box 956, Burgaw 28425.
Telephone: (910) 259-1229.

TROSCH, Louis A., Jr. *(Judge, North Carolina District Court District 26)*
Office: 700 East Fourth Street, Suite 3304, Charlotte 28202.
Telephone: (704) 347-7801.

TUCKER, Elton G. *(Judge, North Carolina District Court District 5)*
Office: 519 New Hanover County Judicial Bldg., 316 Princess Street, Wilmington 28401.
Telephone: (910) 341-1120.

TUCKER, Kimbrell Kelly *(Judge, North Carolina District Court District 12)*
Mailing address: P.O. Box 363, Fayetteville 28302.
Telephone: (910) 678-2901.

TURNER, Joseph E. *(Judge, North Carolina District Court District 18)* Elected to term beginning Dec 5, 1988. Reelected Nov 5, 1992, Nov 3, 1996 and Nov 7, 2000. Current term expires Dec 6, 2004. Certified Juvenile Court Judge since Aug 2, 1993. Born Greensboro North Carolina June 11, 1950. Presbyterian. Educated at Davidson College B.A. 1972 and University of North Carolina J.D. 1976. Associate Justice Holderness Moot Court Bench. Admitted to practice North Carolina 1976, U.S. District Court Middle District of North Carolina 1976 and U.S. Court of Appeals Fourth Circuit 1977. In legal practice Greensboro 1976-83.
Assistant Public Defender Eighteenth Judicial District 1983-88. Former member Greensboro Criminal Defense Lawyers Association (Treasurer 1986-88), Public Defenders Association of North Carolina (Vice President 1987), North Carolina College of Advocacy, North Carolina Academy of Trial Lawyers, The Association of Trial Lawyers of America, North Carolina and American Bar Associations. Member North Carolina Association of District Court Judges, North Carolina Judicial Conference, The North Carolina State Bar, Greensboro and North Carolina Bar Associations. Attended Special Court course The National Judicial College March 1989. Recipient Greensboro Criminal Defense Lawyers Association Award for Outstanding Achievement in Trial of Criminal Cases Jan 28, 1988. Democrat. Legal Counsel and Director Greensboro Jaycees. Elder First Presbyterian Church (former Deacon). Board of Directors Summit House (community-based alternative sentencing program for prison-bound mothers with young children). Chair Criminal Justice Partnership Advisory Board. Assistant

TURNER, JOSEPH E.—*Continued*

Scoutmaster Boy Scouts of America. Enjoys recreational sports, coaching soccer and reading.

Mailing address: P.O. Box 3008, Greensboro 27402-3008.

Telephone: (336) 574-4301.

TURNER, R. Leslie *(Judge, North Carolina District Court District 8)*

Mailing address: P.O. Box 68, Kinston 28502-0068.

Office: Lenoir County Courthouse, Kinston 28502.

Telephone: (252) 527-7891.

TYSON, John Marsh *(Associate Judge, North Carolina Court of Appeals)* Assumed office 2001. Born Cumberland County North Carolina July 14, 1953. Educated at University of North Carolina at Wilmington B.A. 1974, London School of Economic and Political Science, England 1977, Campbell University School of Law J.D. cum laude 1979 and Duke University M.B.A. 1988. In legal practice 1993-2000.

Real Estate Manager and Counsel Family Dollar Stores, Inc. 1980-82. Real Estate Director and Counsel Revco Drug Stores, Inc. 1982-93. Contributing Author "Mean Consolidated Forecasting: A Process to Improve the Accuracy and Sensitivity of Economic Forecasts" *MBA Forecasts* Duke University 107, 1989. Author "The Philosophy of Negotiation" *Retail Leasing Reporter* May 1990; "Drafting, Interpreting, and Enforcing Commercial and Shopping Center Leases" 14 Campbell L. Rev. 275, 1992; and "Presumed Guilty Until Proven Innocent: Using Results of Statistical or Econometric Studies as Evidence" 10 St. Thomas L. Rev. 387 Winter 1998. Adjunct Professor of Law Campbell University School of Law since 1987. Certified Mediator North Carolina Administrative Office of the Courts and Dispute Resolution Commission for Superior Court Mediations since 1992 and U.S. District Court Mediations 1993. Member Panel of Arbitrators American Arbitration Association, U.S. Supreme Court Bar, The North Carolina State Bar, Virginia State Bar, Cumberland County, Wake County and North Carolina (Development Committee 1994-96) Bar Associations. Instructor CLE North Carolina Bar Association 1992 and 1993. Panelist Land Use Symposium Campbell University School of Law 1993.

Listed in *Who's Who in American Law, Who's Who in the South & Southwest, Who's Who in Finance & Industry* and *Who's Who in Real Estate* 1987-2000. Recipient Distinguished Alumnus Award from Campbell University 1991. North Carolina National Guard 1989-96. Colonel Staff Judge Advocate U.S. Service Command Division III since 1999. Probation/Parole Officer North Carolina Department of Corrections 1975-76. Senior Vice President of Development Blockbuster Entertainment Group 1996. Previously worked as public school teacher junior and senior high schools and Special Deputy Sheriff Cumberland County. Member North Carolina Republican Party, Capital Area Republican Club, Cumberland County Republican Party. Board of Visitors Campbell University School of Law since 1992. Vice Chairman and Chairman Cumberland County Joint Planning and Zoning Board 1993-2001. Patron and Bronze Sponsor Ducks Unlimited. Member First Presbyterian Church (Former Chairman Board of Deacons), Campbell University National Alumni Association (President 1999-2001), Duke University Alumni Association, University of North Carolina at Wilmington Alumni Association, Association of MBA Executives, Inc., Fayetteville Kiwanis Club, Fayetteville Chamber of Commerce and National Rifle Association.

Mailing address: P.O. Box 888, Raleigh 27602.

Office: Court of Appeals Building, One West Morgan Street, Raleigh 27601.

Telephone: (919) 733-4294.

E-mail address: jtyson@coa.state.nc.us

VINCENT, Charles M. *(Judge, North Carolina District Court District 3A)* Elected to term beginning Dec 4, 2000. Term expires Nov 30, 2004. Born Charlotte North Carolina Sept 27, 1946. Episcopalian. Educated at University of North Carolina at Chapel Hill A.B. 1968 J.D. 1972. Law Clerk to Hon. John D. Larkins, Jr., U.S. District Court Eastern District of North Carolina 1973-74. Admitted to practice North Carolina 1974. In legal practice Greenville 1975-2000.

Former Member North Carolina Academy of Trial Lawyers and National Association of Criminal Defense Attorneys. Listed in *The Best Lawyers in America* 1995-2002. Republican. Mayor pro tem Greenville 1977-79. Distinguished Past President Kiwanis Club. Advisory Board Salvation Army. Interests include golf, Civil War history and reading. Personal Statement or Quote: "Pay attention to detail."

Mailing address: P.O. Box 8147, Greenville 27835.

Office: Pitt County Courthouse, Greenville 27834.

Telephone: (252) 695-7274.

Fax: (252) 830-3196

E-mail address: judgevincent@hotmail.com

VINCENT, Teresa H. *(Judge, North Carolina District Court District 18)*

Mailing address: P.O. Box 3008, Greensboro 27402-3008.

Telephone: (336) 574-4301.

VOORHEES, Richard L. *(Judge, United States District Court Western District of North Carolina)* Appointed for life by President Ronald Reagan to term beginning Oct 28, 1988. Chief Judge 1991-98. Born Syracuse New York June 5, 1941. Presbyterian. Educated at Davidson College B.A. 1963 and University of North Carolina at Chapel Hill J.D. 1968. Member Phi Delta Phi. Admitted to practice North Carolina 1968, U.S. Tax Court 1969 and U.S. Court of Appeals Fourth Circuit 1978. In legal practice Gastonia 1968-88.

Instructor in Medical Law and Ethics and Business Law Gaston College 1980-82. Former Member Fourth Circuit Judicial Council 1991-92. Member Court Administration and Case Management Committee U.S. Judicial Conference since 1992. Member Twenty-seven A Judicial District (President 1982-84) and North Carolina Bar Associations. Lieutenant 1963-68 and Captain 1969 USAR.

Office: 250 Federal Building, 401 West Trade Street, Charlotte 28202.

Telephone: (704) 350-7440.

WADDELL, Jerry F. *(Chief Judge, North Carolina District Court District 3B)*

Office: 204 Craven County Courthouse Annex, 302 Broad Street, New Bern 28560-4903.

Telephone: (252) 514-4782.

WAINWRIGHT, George L., Jr. *(Associate Justice, Supreme Court of North Carolina)* Elected Nov 3, 1998.

WAINWRIGHT, GEORGE L., JR.—*Continued*

Term expires 2006. Born Wilson North Carolina Dec 10, 1943. Educated at University of North Carolina at Chapel Hill A.B. 1966 and Wake Forest University School of Law J.D. 1984. Morehead Scholar. Admitted to practice North Carolina 1985 and U.S. District Court. In legal practice Beaufort 1986-90. Former Judge, North Carolina District Court Third Judicial District B, appointed by Governor James G. Martin to term beginning Jan 14, 1991. Former Resident Judge, North Carolina Superior Court Judicial Division One District 3B. U.S. Coast Guard 1966-72.

Member North Carolina Bar Association. Attended New Series Appellate Judges Seminar Summer 2000. Member Lookout Rotary Morehead City.

Mailing address: P.O. Box 1841, Raleigh 27602.

Telephone: (919) 733-3713.

WALKER, Ralph A. *(Retired Judge, North Carolina Court of Appeals)* Assumed office as Associate Judge Jan 1, 1995. Retired, serves by recall. Currently serves as Emergency Special Judge, North Carolina Superior Court. Born Morganton North Carolina Jan 23, 1936. Educated at Wake Forest University B.B.A. 1958 J.D. 1963. Former Resident Judge, North Carolina Superior Court Judicial Division Three District 18. Former Judge, Guilford County Domestic Relations Court. Associate Judge, North Carolina Court of Appeals 1992-93.

County Attorney Guilford County. Member American Arbitration Association, The North Carolina State Bar, Greensboro and Wake County Bar Associations. Participant The National Judicial College 1976. Member Guilford County Republican Executive Committee and Guilford County Board of Elections. Chairman North Carolina Property Tax Commission. Board of Directors Kiwanis International, Greensboro Urban Ministry and LINKS Substance Abuse Program. Board of Visitors Wake Forest Law School. Deacon and Elder 1974-93 and Member First Presbyterian Church.

Mailing address: P.O. Box 3008, Greensboro 27402.

WALKER, Russell G., Jr. *(Resident Judge, North Carolina Superior Court Fifth Judicial Division District 19B)* Appointed Special Judge by Governor James B. Hunt, Jr. to term beginning June 7, 1982. Elected Resident Judge Nov 1984, 1992 and 2000. Current term expires Dec 31, 2008. Currently Senior Resident Judge. Born Winston-Salem North Carolina Oct 10, 1943. Presbyterian. Educated at Wake Forest University B.B.A. 1966 J.D. 1969. Member Phi Alpha Delta. Admitted to practice North Carolina 1969 and U.S. District Court Eastern District of North Carolina 1969. In legal practice Asheboro 1978 and 1981-82.

Assistant Attorney General and Revisor of Statutes 1969-73. District Attorney Prosecutorial District 19B 1979-80. Member National Conference of Commissioners on Uniform State Laws, North Carolina Conference of Superior Court Judges, The North Carolina State Bar and North Carolina Bar Association. General Counsel and Assistant to President of Food Line Super Markets 1973-78. Democrat.

Office: Randolph County Courthouse, 145 Worth Street, Asheboro 27203.

Telephone: (336) 328-3186.

WALLACE, Tanya T. *(Chief Judge, North Carolina District Court District 20)*

Mailing address: P.O. Box 1607, Albemarle 28002-1607.

Telephone: (704) 982-3095.

WARREN, Marion R. *(Judge, North Carolina District Court District 13)*

Mailing address: P.O. Box 127, Bolivia 28422.

Office: Brunswick County Complex, Bolivia 28422.

Telephone: (910) 641-3070.

WASHBURN, James Kent *(Chief Judge, North Carolina District Court District 15A)* Appointed by Governor James B. Hunt, Jr. to term beginning Oct 1, 1980. Elected 1980, 1984, 1988, 1992, 1996 and 2000. Current term expires Dec 2004. Born Nashville Tennessee Nov 23, 1939. Educated at Belmont College B.A. in Psychology magna cum laude 1962, Vanderbilt University M.A. in English 1969 and University of North Carolina J.D. with honors 1973. Staff member North Carolina Law Review 1972-73. Member Order of the Coif. Admitted to practice North Carolina 1973. Began legal practice Burlington 1973.

Former Administrative Assistant and Assistant Director Urban Renewal Asheville and Greensboro. Member The North Carolina State Bar and American Bar Association. Attended Justice Executives Program University of North Carolina 1982. Former member Alamance Business Club. Former Director Domestic Violence and Child Abuse Services of Alamance County. Past President and Former Member Burlington Kiwanis. Former Board member Christian Counseling Center. Former member North Carolina Council on Alcoholism, Eagle Review Board Cherokee Council Boy Scouts of America and Alamance County Cancer Society. Member and Deacon First Baptist Church. Member Alamance County Law Enforcement Executive Association and Volunteers for People. Enjoys photography and making furniture.

Office: 120 Criminal Courts Building, 212 West Elm Street, Graham 27253.

Telephone: (336) 438-1132.

WEBB, James M. *(Resident Judge, North Carolina Superior Court Fifth Judicial Division District 19B)* Former Senior Resident Judge District 20A.

Mailing address: P.O. Drawer 1916, Southern Pines 28388-1916.

Telephone: (910) 347-3009.

WEBB, William A. *(Magistrate Judge, United States District Court Eastern District of North Carolina)* Appointed by U.S. District Court judges to term beginning Oct 18, 1999. Term expires Oct 18, 2007.

Office: U.S. Courthouse, 310 New Bern Avenue, Raleigh 27601.

Telephone: (919) 645-1700.

WEEKS, Gregory A. *(Resident Judge, North Carolina Superior Court Fourth Judicial Division District 12)* Elected to term beginning Jan 1, 1989. Reelected 1996, current term expires Dec 31, 2004.

Mailing address: P.O. Box 363, Fayetteville 28302.

Telephone: (910) 678-2975.

WHITLEY, J. Craig *(Judge, United States Bankruptcy Court Western District of North Carolina)* Appointed by U.S. Court of Appeals Fourth Circuit judges.

Mailing address: P.O. Box 34189, Charlotte 28234.

Telephone: (704) 350-7500.

WHITLEY, John L. *(Chief Judge, North Carolina District Court District 7)*
Mailing address: P.O. Box 999, Wilson 27894.
Telephone: (252) 234-7676.

WILKINS, Frederick B., Jr. *(Judge, North Carolina District Court District 17A)* Assumed office Feb 17, 1998. Elected Nov 3, 1998 and 2002. Current term expires Dec 31, 2006.
Mailing address: P.O. Box 97, Wentworth 27375.
Telephone: (336) 342-8740.

WILKINSON, Charles W., Jr. *(Chief Judge, North Carolina District Court District 9)* Elected to term beginning Dec 6, 1976. Reelected 1980, 1984, 1988, 1992, 1996 and 2000. Current term expires Dec 2004. Born Oxford North Carolina Aug 28, 1941. Baptist. Educated at Campbell College A.A. 1961, East Carolina University B.S. 1963 and University of North Carolina J.D. 1967. Admitted to practice North Carolina 1967. In legal practice Oxford 1968-76.
With Office of the North Carolina Attorney General Raleigh 1967. Member North Carolina Bar Association. Democrat. Enjoys fishing, hunting and boating.
Mailing address: 506 Country Club Drive, Oxford 27565.
Telephone: (919) 693-5193.

WILLIAMS, Joseph J. *(Judge, North Carolina District Court District 20)* Appointed by Governor James B. Hunt, Jr. March 1994. Elected Nov 1996 and 2000. Current term expires 2004. Born Waxham North Carolina Sept 12, 1964. Methodist. Educated at University of North Carolina at Chapel Hill B.A. in Political Science and History 1985 and North Carolina Central University J.D. 1988. Admitted to practice North Carolina 1988 and U.S. District Court Eastern District of North Carolina 1989. In legal practice Whiteville 1988-89.
Assistant District Attorney 1989-94. Active in Weddington United Methodist Church Orchestra. Enjoys water sports and outdoor activities including hiking and eco-tourism.
Mailing address: P.O. Box 1658, Monroe 28111.
Telephone: (704) 982-3095.

WILLIAMS, Rose Vaughn *(Judge, North Carolina District Court District 8)*
Mailing address: P.O. Box 267, Goldsboro 27533-0267.
Telephone: (252) 527-7891.

WILSON, Larry James *(Chief Judge, North Carolina District Court District 27B)*
Office: Cleveland County Courthouse, 100 Justice Place, Shelby 28150.
Telephone: (704) 484-4801.

WINNER, Dennis Jay *(Resident Judge, North Carolina Superior Court Eighth Judicial Division District 28)* Currently Senior Resident Judge.
Office: Buncombe County Courthouse, 60 Court Plaza, Asheville 28801-3584.
Telephone: (828) 232-2777.

WOLFE, James Boyd, Jr. *(Recalled Judge, United States Bankruptcy Court Middle District of North Carolina)* Appointed Judge by U.S. District Court judges Aug 1, 1977. Reappointed by U.S. Court of Appeals Fourth Circuit judges 1987. Former Chief Judge. Appointed Recalled Judge by the Judicial Council of the Fourth Circuit. Born Greensboro North Carolina Dec 24, 1921. Presbyterian. Educated at Duke University A.B. 1947 LL.B. 1950. Member Phi Delta Phi. Admitted to practice North Carolina 1951. Began legal practice Greensboro 1951. Senior Judge, Greensboro Municipal County Court 1953-56.
Member The North Carolina State Bar, Greensboro (President 1985-86, Immediate Past President 1986-87), Eighteenth Judicial District, North Carolina and American Bar Associations. Colonel USMCR 1943-46 (retired 1983). Past President Greensboro Civitan Club. Former Board member Children's Home Society, YMCA and Greensboro City Club. Board member Salvation Army. Member Greensboro Country Club. Enjoys tennis and golf.
Mailing address: P.O. Box 1708, Greensboro 27402-1708.
Telephone: (336) 333-5729.

WOOD, April C. *(Judge, North Carolina District Court District 22)*
Mailing address: P.O. Box 186, Statesville 28687.
Telephone: (704) 878-4209.

WOOD, William Z., Jr. *(Resident Judge, North Carolina Superior Court Fifth Judicial Division District 21)* Elected Nov 1990 to term beginning Jan 1, 1991. Reelected Nov 3, 1998, current term expires 2007. Born Raleigh North Carolina March 23, 1947. Religious affiliation: Moravian. Educated at University of North Carolina at Chapel Hill A.B. 1969 J.D. 1972. Admitted to practice North Carolina 1972 and U.S. District Court Middle District of North Carolina 1972. In legal practice Winston-Salem 1972-90.
Instructor in Trial Advocacy Course and Judge of Final Trial Competition Wake Forest University School of Law 1991-93. Instructor in Trial Advocacy Seminar Wake Forest University School of Law 1998 and Institute of Government Sentencing Seminar University of North Carolina School of Law 1998. Member Joseph Branch Chapter Inns of Court, American Judicature Society, North Carolina and Twenty-first Judicial District Bar Associations. Speaker "View from the Bench" Greensboro 1992 and High Point 1996. Judge High School Trial Competition North Carolina Academy of Trial Lawyers 1997-99. Member North Carolina Democratic Party. Member State Executive Committee 1972-73. President North Carolina Eye and Human Tissue Bank 1980-81.
Mailing address: P.O. Box 20099, Winston-Salem 27120-0099.
Office: Forsyth County Hall of Justice, Winston-Salem 27101.
Telephone: (336) 761-2420.
Fax: (336) 761-2089

WOOTEN, Marvin R. *(Recalled Judge, United States Bankruptcy Court Western District of North Carolina)* Appointed Judge by U.S. District Court judges to term beginning May 1, 1976. Reappointed to subsequent terms. Former Chief Judge. Appointed Recalled Judge by the Judicial Council of the Fourth Circuit. Born Clinton North Carolina May 5, 1928. Presbyterian. Educated at Presbyterian Junior College A.A. 1947 and Wake Forest University J.D. 1950. Admitted to practice North Carolina 1950. Began legal practice Hickory 1953. Judge, Hickory Municipal and Juvenile Courts 1959-62.
Chairman Parole Board 1965-68 and Chairman Utili-

WOOTEN, MARVIN R.—*Continued*

ties Commission 1968-76. Sergeant First Class U.S. Army 1950-53. Democrat.

Mailing address: P.O. Box 34189, Charlotte 28234.

Telephone: (704) 350-7500.

WYNN, James A., Jr. *(Associate Judge, North Carolina Court of Appeals)* Assumed office 1999. Born Robersonville North Carolina March 17, 1954. Educated at University of North Carolina at Chapel Hill B.A. 1975, Marquette University Law School J.D. 1979 and University of Virginia LL.M. 1995. In legal practice Wilson and Greenville 1984-90. Associate Judge, North Carolina Court of Appeals 1990-98. Associate Justice, North Carolina Supreme Court 1998.

Assistant Appellate Defender 1983-84. Former Member Board of Trustees Pitt Community College. Former Member Supreme Court Permanent Family Task Force. Board of Governors American Judicature Society. Member Appellate Judges Judicial Education Committee, North Carolina Courts Commission, North Carolina Judicial Council Liaison Committee, National Conference of Commissioners on Uniform State Laws, North Carolina Association of Black Lawyers (Judicial Council Secretary), North Carolina Judicial Conference (Treasurer), Naval Reserve Judge Advocate Association, The North Carolina State Bar, State Bar of Wisconsin, North Carolina (Former Member Commission on Public Trust and the Legal Profession and Public Information Committee, Vice President, Member Bench Bar Liaison Committee), National (Judicial Division) and American (Executive Committee, Membership Chairman and Secretary Appellate Judges Conference Judicial Administration Division, Member Task Force to Draft Guidelines for Selection of State Court Judges) Bar Associations. Presenter "Abuse of Discretion" Family Law Forum North Carolina Bar Association 1995 and "Use of DNA and Scientific Evidence" Professor Blakely Evidence Seminar Series University of North Carolina at Chapel Hill 1995. Participant Seminar on "Science and Statistics for Judges" Duke University, two year study on the Ethical, Legal and Social Implications of the "Human Genome Project" University of Virginia, and study group on "Enhancing Minority Participation in Research" Tuskegee University. Faculty "The Community of Courts: The Compleat Appellate Judge" and Military Appellate Judges Seminar. Recipient Appellate Judge of the Year Award from North Carolina Academy of Trial Lawyers 1995 and MLK Achievement Award from General Baptist Convention of North Carolina 1996. Former Member North Carolina Health Care Advisory Board.

Mailing address: P.O. Box 888, Raleigh 27602.

Office: Court of Appeals Building, One West Morgan Street, Raleigh 27601.

Telephone: (919) 733-6185.

YOUNG, Patricia K. *(Judge, North Carolina District Court District 28)*

Office: Buncombe County Courthouse, 60 Court Plaza, Asheville 28801-3583.

Telephone: (828) 232-2760.

NORTH DAKOTA

Capital BISMARCK

UNITED STATES DISTRICT COURT DISTRICT OF NORTH DAKOTA

United States District Court District of North Dakota is divided into four divisions. For descriptive information refer to the United States Courts section.

Northeastern Division includes Benson, Cavalier, Grand Forks, Nelson, Pembina, Ramsey, Rolette, Towner, Traill and Walsh counties. The court sits at Grand Forks.

Northwestern Division includes Bottineau, Burke, Divide, McHenry, McKenzie, Mountrail, Pierce, Renville, Sheridan, Ward, Wells and Williams counties. The court sits at Minot.

Southeastern Division includes Barnes, Cass, Dickey, Eddy, Foster, Griggs, LaMoure, Ransom, Richland, Sargent, Steele and Stutsman counties. The court sits at Fargo.

Southwestern Division includes Adams, Billings, Bowman, Burleigh, Dunn, Emmons, Golden Valley, Grant, Hettinger, Kidder, Logan, McIntosh, McLean, Mercer, Morton, Oliver, Sioux, Slope and Stark counties. The court sits at Bismarck.

Chief Judge
Daniel L. Hovland

Judge
Ralph R. Erickson

Senior Judges
Patrick A. Conmy
Rodney S. Webb

Clerk
Edward J. Klecker
P.O. Box 1193
Bismarck, North Dakota 58502-1193
(701) 530-2300

UNITED STATES MAGISTRATE JUDGES OF NORTH DAKOTA

Dwight C. H. Kautzmann
Karen K. Klein
Alice R. Senechal

UNITED STATES BANKRUPTCY COURT OF NORTH DAKOTA

Judge
William Alexander Hill

Bankruptcy Clerk
Ellen A. Johanson
210 U.S. Courthouse
655 First Avenue North
Fargo, North Dakota 58102-4932
(701) 297-7100

NORTH DAKOTA SUPREME COURT

The Supreme Court is North Dakota's court of last resort. The court consists of a chief justice and four justices elected in nonpartisan elections for staggered ten-year terms. Vacancies are filled by the governor from a list provided by the Judicial Nominating Committee or by special election called by the governor. Appointees serve for a minimum of two years and then until the next general election, at which time the office is filled by election for the remainder of the term. The chief justice is selected by Supreme Court justices and District Court judges from among the members of the Supreme Court for a five-year term or until the end of the elected term. Upon retirement, a justice may be appointed by the chief justice to serve as surrogate judge within the unified judicial system and may accept assignments as desired.

The court has final appellate jurisdiction over cases from the District Courts. The court has original jurisdiction in habeas corpus cases and cases of public concern that affect the sovereign rights of the state or its franchises or privileges and may issue original and remedial writs necessary to the exercise of proper jurisdiction. The court controls admission and licensing of attorneys and supervises the conduct of members of the bench and bar. The court also has rule-making authority and administrative control over the lower courts.

The court sits at Bismarck, with a quorum necessary to conduct judicial business.

Chief Justice
Gerald W. VandeWalle

Justices
Carol Ronning Kapsner
Mary Muehlen Maring
William A. Neumann
Dale V. Sandstrom

Clerk
Penny Miller
State Capitol, Dept. 180
600 East Boulevard Avenue
Bismarck, North Dakota 58505
(701) 328-2221

Court Administrator
Ted C. Gladden
State Capitol, Dept. 180
600 East Boulevard Avenue
Bismarck, North Dakota 58505-0530
(701) 328-4216

NORTH DAKOTA COURT OF APPEALS

The Court of Appeals is North Dakota's court of intermediate appellate jurisdiction. Established by the 1987

NORTH DAKOTA COURT OF APPEALS—*Continued*

State Legislature as an experimental appellate court, it began operation on July 1, 1987. Its lifespan was extended by the Legislature in 1993 as an unfunded temporary court and extended again in 1995 and 2000; it will be in operation until the year 2004. The court may be composed of active or retired District Court judges, retired Supreme Court justices or lawyers, all of whom serve on a rotating basis.

The court hears and decides cases as assigned by the Supreme Court, which may then review those decisions.

The court consists of two panels of three judges each. A majority vote of the three judges on a panel is necessary to pronounce a decision. The court sits at Bismarck but may sit at other locations as needed.

NORTH DAKOTA DISTRICT COURTS

The District Courts are North Dakota's trial courts of general and limited jurisdiction. In 1979, North Dakota was divided into seven judicial districts by the Supreme Court. There is a District Court in each of the state's fifty-three counties. On January 1, 1995, the County Courts were consolidated into the District Courts. Judges previously serving the County Courts were elected to the District Courts for initial staggered terms of two, four or six years. Subsequent terms are now six years. Judges already serving the District Courts are elected in nonpartisan elections in their districts for six-year terms. Vacancies are filled by the governor from a list provided by the Judicial Nominating Committee or by special election called by the governor. Appointees serve for a minimum of two years and then until the next general election, at which time the office is filled by election for the remainder of the term. A presiding judge is elected by the judges in each district as chief judicial administrator for the district. The presiding judge in each district may appoint referees to preside over certain matters in lieu of judges. Upon retirement, a judge may be appointed by the chief justice of the Supreme Court to serve as surrogate judge within the unified judicial system and may accept assignments as desired.

The courts have original limited and general jurisdiction in all cases as provided by law. The courts have jurisdiction in all criminal and civil cases. The courts also serve as juvenile courts and exercise original and exclusive jurisdiction over minors alleged to be unruly, delinquent or deprived. The courts also have appellate jurisdiction over decisions of many administrative agencies. The courts may issue original and remedial writs necessary to the exercise of proper jurisdiction.

EAST CENTRAL JUDICIAL DISTRICT includes Cass, Steele and Traill counties. The court sits at Fargo and Hillsboro.

Presiding Judge
Norman J. Backes

Judges

Georgia Dawson
Lawrence A. LeClerc
Frank L. Racek
John C. Irby
Michael O. McGuire
Cynthia Rothe-Seeger

NORTHEAST JUDICIAL DISTRICT includes Benson, Bottineau, Cavalier, McHenry, Pembina, Pierce, Ramsey, Renville, Rolette, Towner and Walsh counties. The court sits at Bottineau, Cavalier, Devils Lake, Grafton, Langdon and Rugby.

Presiding Judge
M. Richard Geiger

Judges
Lee A. Christofferson
Laurie A. Fontaine
Donovan J. Foughty
Lester S. Ketterling
John C. McClintock, Jr.

NORTHEAST CENTRAL JUDICIAL DISTRICT includes Grand Forks and Nelson counties. The court sits at Grand Forks.

Presiding Judge
Debbie Gordon Kleven

Judges
Bruce E. Bohlman
Karen Kosanda Braaten
Lawrence E. Jahnke
Joel Douglas Medd

NORTHWEST JUDICIAL DISTRICT includes Burke, Divide, McKenzie, Mountrail, Ward and Williams counties. The court sits at Minot, Stanley, Watford City and Williston.

Presiding Judge
Robert W. Holte

Judges
Gary A. Holum
Douglas L. Mattson
William McLees, Jr.
David W. Nelson
Gerald H. Rustad

SOUTH CENTRAL JUDICIAL DISTRICT includes Burleigh, Emmons, Grant, Kidder, Logan, McIntosh, McLean, Mercer, Morton, Oliver, Sheridan and Sioux counties. The court sits at Bismarck, Linton, Mandan and Washburn.

Presiding Judge
Benny A. Graff

Judges

Gail Hagerty
Donald L. Jorgensen
Bruce A. Romanick
Robert O. Wefald
Bruce B. Haskell
Burton L. Riskedahl
Thomas J. Schneider

SOUTHEAST JUDICIAL DISTRICT includes Barnes, Dickey, Eddy, Foster, Griggs, LaMoure, Ransom, Richland, Sargent, Stutsman and Wells counties. The court sits at Ellendale, Jamestown, New Rockford, Valley City and Wahpeton.

Presiding Judge
John T. Paulson

Judges
James M. Bekken
Ronald E. Goodman
John E. Greenwood
Richard W. Grosz
Mikal Simonson

SOUTHWEST JUDICIAL DISTRICT includes Adams, Billings, Bowman, Dunn, Golden Valley, Hettinger, Slope and Stark counties. The court sits at Bowman and Dickinson.

NORTH DAKOTA DISTRICT COURTS—*Continued*

Presiding Judge
Allan L. Schmalenberger

Judges
Zane C. Anderson
Ronald L. Hilden

SURROGATE DISTRICT COURT JUDGES
Gordon O. Hoberg
William F. Hodny
Jon R. Kerian
Everett Nels Olson
Kirk Smith

NORTH DAKOTA MUNICIPAL COURTS

Municipal Courts are courts of limited jurisdiction in North Dakota. Since 1981, each municipality has the option of deciding whether or not to have a municipal judge. In cities with a population of 3,000 or more, judges are required to be licensed attorneys unless an attorney is unavailable or not interested in serving. Judges are elected by their respective municipalities for four-year terms. Vacancies are filled by the executive officer of the municipality.

The courts have exclusive jurisdiction of all violations of municipal ordinances except certain juvenile violations. They also exercise jurisdiction over traffic cases.

North Dakota Counties and County Seats

Adams
Hettinger

Barnes
Valley City

Benson
Minnewaukan

Billings
Medora

Bottineau
Bottineau

Bowman
Bowman

Burke
Bowbells

Burleigh
Bismarck

Cass
Fargo

Cavalier
Langdon

Dickey
Ellendale

Divide
Crosby

Dunn
Manning

Eddy
New Rockford

Emmons
Linton

Foster
Carrington

Golden Valley
Beach

Grand Forks
Grand Forks

Grant
Carson

Griggs
Cooperstown

Hettinger
Mott

Kidder
Steele

LaMoure
LaMoure

Logan
Napoleon

McHenry
Towner

McIntosh
Ashley

McKenzie
Watford City

McLean
Washburn

Mercer
Stanton

Morton
Mandan

Mountrail
Stanley

Nelson
Lakota

Oliver
Center

Pembina
Cavalier

Pierce
Rugby

Ramsey
Devils Lake

Ransom
Lisbon

Renville
Mohall

Richland
Wahpeton

Rolette
Rolla

Sargent
Forman

Sheridan
McClusky

Sioux
Fort Yates

Slope
Amidon

Stark
Dickinson

Steele
Finley

Stutsman
Jamestown

Towner
Cando

Traill
Hillsboro

Walsh
Grafton

Ward
Minot

Wells
Fessenden

Williams
Williston

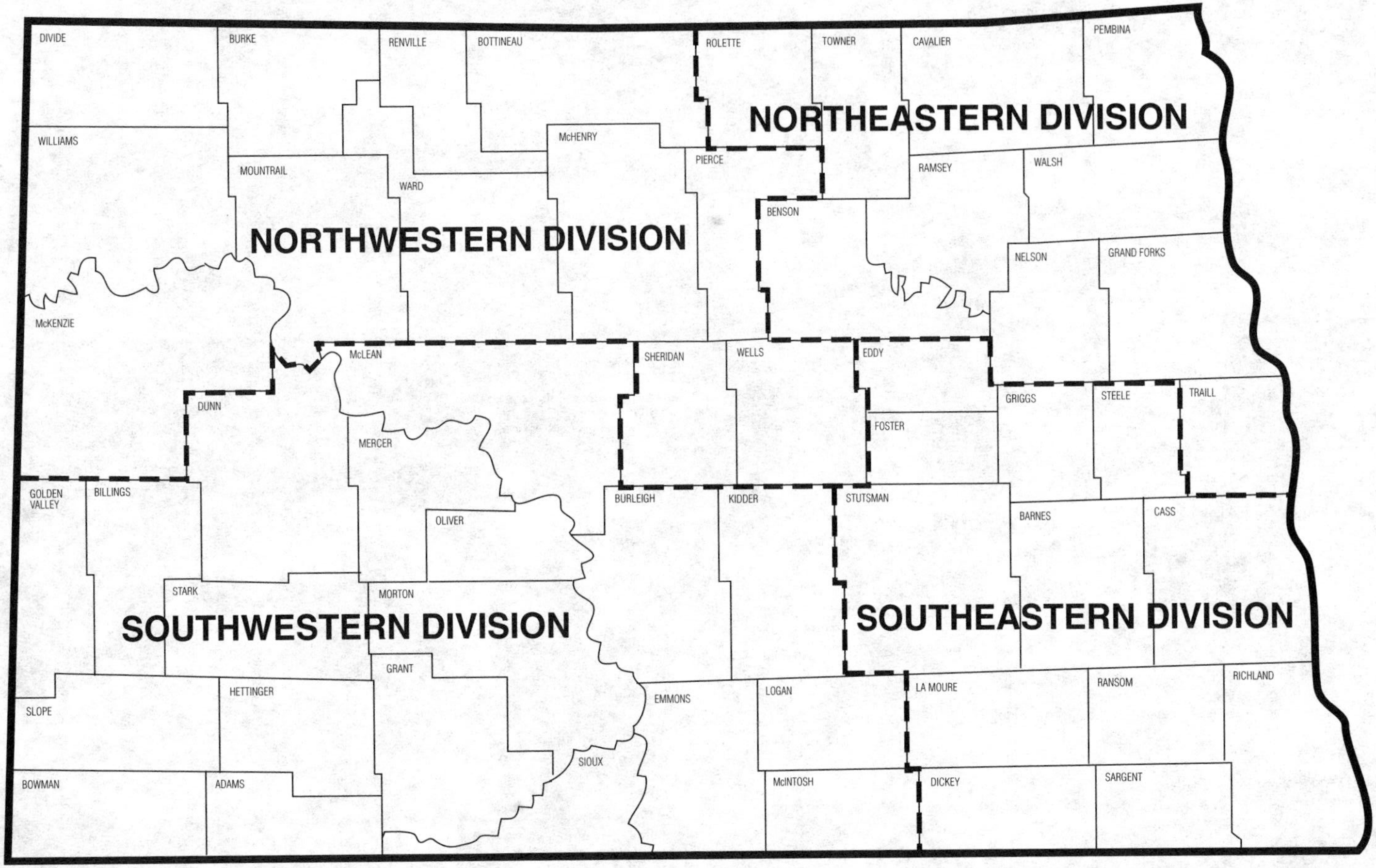

NORTHEASTERN DIVISION
NORTHWESTERN DIVISION
SOUTHWESTERN DIVISION
SOUTHEASTERN DIVISION
DIVIDE
BURKE
RENVILLE
BOTTINEAU
ROLETTE
TOWNER
CAVALIER
PEMBINA
WILLIAMS
MOUNTRAIL
WARD
McHENRY
PIERCE
RAMSEY
WALSH
BENSON
NELSON
GRAND FORKS
McKENZIE
McLEAN
SHERIDAN
WELLS
EDDY
GRIGGS
STEELE
TRAILL
FOSTER
DUNN
MERCER
GOLDEN VALLEY
BILLINGS
OLIVER
BURLEIGH
KIDDER
STUTSMAN
BARNES
CASS
STARK
MORTON
GRANT
HETTINGER
SLOPE
EMMONS
LOGAN
LA MOURE
RANSOM
RICHLAND
SIOUX
BOWMAN
ADAMS
McINTOSH
DICKEY
SARGENT

DIVISIONS OF UNITED STATES DISTRICT COURT DISTRICT OF NORTH DAKOTA

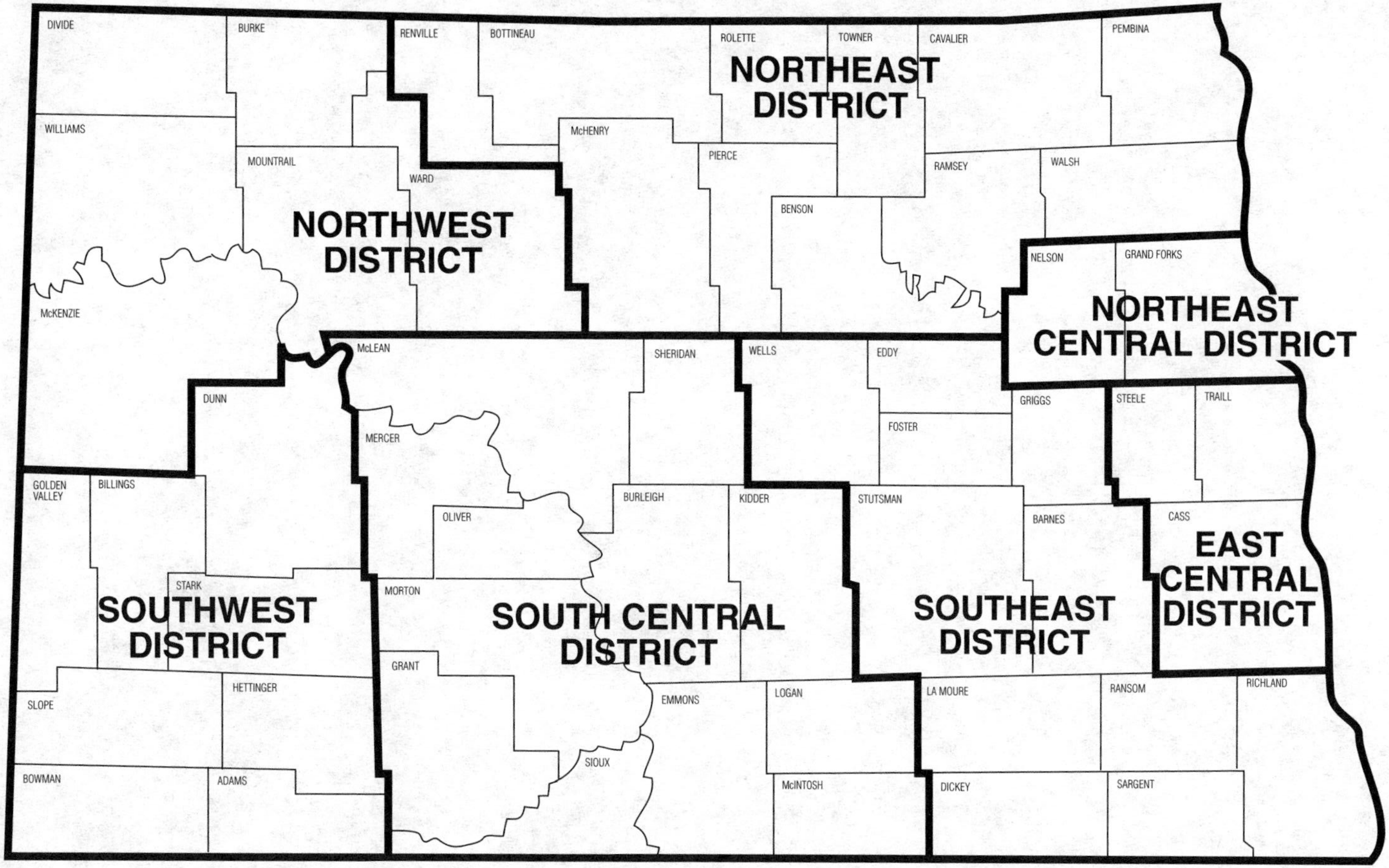
NORTHWEST DISTRICT
NORTHEAST DISTRICT
NORTHEAST CENTRAL DISTRICT
EAST CENTRAL DISTRICT
SOUTHEAST DISTRICT
SOUTH CENTRAL DISTRICT
SOUTHWEST DISTRICT
DIVIDE
BURKE
RENVILLE
BOTTINEAU
ROLETTE
TOWNER
CAVALIER
PEMBINA
WILLIAMS
MOUNTRAIL
WARD
McHENRY
PIERCE
BENSON
RAMSEY
WALSH
NELSON
GRAND FORKS
McKENZIE
McLEAN
SHERIDAN
WELLS
EDDY
FOSTER
GRIGGS
STEELE
TRAILL
DUNN
MERCER
OLIVER
BURLEIGH
KIDDER
STUTSMAN
BARNES
CASS
GOLDEN VALLEY
BILLINGS
STARK
MORTON
GRANT
HETTINGER
SLOPE
EMMONS
LOGAN
LA MOURE
RANSOM
RICHLAND
SIOUX
BOWMAN
ADAMS
McINTOSH
DICKEY
SARGENT

JUDICIAL DISTRICTS OF NORTH DAKOTA DISTRICT COURTS

NORTH DAKOTA

ANDERSON, Zane C. *(Judge, North Dakota District Court Southwest Judicial District)* Elected Nov 1994 to term beginning Jan 1, 1995. Reelected Nov 2000, current term expires Dec 31, 2006. Born Hettinger North Dakota July 13, 1951. Lutheran. Educated at University of North Dakota B.A. with honors 1973 J.D. with honors 1978. Member Phi Delta Phi. Admitted to practice North Dakota 1978, U.S. District Courts District of North Dakota 1980 and District of Minnesota 1983 and Minnesota 1983. In legal practice Bowman 1978-90. Judge, Adams, Bowman, Hettinger and Slope County Courts 1991 to Dec 31, 1994.

State's Attorney Bowman County 1978-83. Attended General Jurisdiction Course The National Judicial College April 1991. Enjoys running, basketball and golf.

Mailing address: P.O. Box 1507, Dickinson 58602-1507.

Office: Third and Sims, Dickinson 58601.

Telephone: (701) 264-7658.

Fax: (701) 227-7428

BACKES, Norman J. *(Presiding Judge, North Dakota District Court East Central Judicial District).*

Mailing address: P.O. Box 2806, Fargo 58108-2806.

Office: Cass County Courthouse, 211 South Ninth Street, Fargo 58103.

Telephone: (701) 241-5680.

Fax: (701) 241-5709

BEKKEN, James M. *(Judge, North Dakota District Court Southeast Judicial District)* Elected to term beginning Jan 1, 1995. Reelected 1998, current term expires Dec 31, 2004. Born Grand Forks North Dakota July 15, 1948. Lutheran. Educated at University of North Dakota B.S. in Education cum laude 1970 J.D. with distinction 1977. Special Projects Editor North Dakota Law Review 1976-77. Member Kappa Sigma. Admitted to practice North Dakota 1977. In legal practice New Rockford 1977-82. Assistant County Justice 1977-82. Former Judge, New Rockford Municipal Court. Judge, Benson, Eddy, Foster and Wells County Courts Jan 1, 1983 to Dec 31, 1994.

Former Member North Dakota Judicial Conduct Commission and North Dakota Association of County Judges (Past President). Member North Dakota Association of District Judges (President 1999-2000, Former Secretary-Treasurer), North Dakota Judicial Conference (Chair 2001-03)and State Bar Association of North Dakota. Instructor North Dakota Supreme Court Municipal Judges Institute 1987 and 1988. Discussion Leader Evidence Course and Faculty Advisor The National Judicial College May 1987. Previously employed as public school teacher in Minnesota and North Dakota. Past President New Rockford Commercial Club. Past President and Board member Fourth Corporation. Past Secretary New Rockford Community Development Corporation. Member New Rockford Kiwanis (Past President and Secretary) and Minnesota-Dakotas Kiwanis (Past Lieutenant Governor, Governor and Member District Board). Enjoys reading and sports.

Mailing address: P.O. Box 32, New Rockford 58356-0032.

Office: Eddy County Courthouse, 524 Central Avenue, New Rockford 58356.

Telephone: (701) 947-5777.

Fax: (701) 947-2067

E-mail address: jbekken@ndcourts.com

BOHLMAN, Bruce E. *(Judge, North Dakota District Court Northeast Central Judicial District)* Assumed office Nov 1, 1987. Former Presiding Judge. Educated at University of North Dakota J.D. Admitted to practice North Dakota.

Former Law Professor and Former Director Clinical Legal Education Program University of North Dakota.

Mailing address: P.O. Box 6347, Grand Forks 58206-6347.

Office: Grand Forks County Courthouse, 124 South Fourth Street, Grand Forks 58201.

Telephone: (701) 795-3824.

Fax: (701) 795-3886

BRAATEN, Karen Kosanda *(Judge, North Dakota District Court Northeast Central Judicial District)*

Mailing address: P.O. Box 6347, Grand Forks 58206-6347.

Office: Grand Forks County Courthouse, 124 South Fourth Street, Grand Forks 58201.

Telephone: (701) 795-3824.

Fax: (701) 795-3886

CHRISTOFFERSON, Lee A. *(Judge, North Dakota District Court Northeast Judicial District)* Former Presiding Judge.

Mailing address: P.O. Box 70, Devils Lake 58301-0070.

Office: Ramsey County Courthouse, 524 Fourth Avenue, Devils Lake 58301.

Telephone: (701) 662-1300.

Fax: (701) 662-8539

CONMY, Patrick A. *(Senior Judge, United States District Court District of North Dakota)* Appointed for life by President Ronald Reagan to term beginning Dec 17, 1985. Chief Judge Jan 1, 1986 to Dec 31, 1992. Assumed Senior status Jan 5, 2000, serves by assignment. Born Fargo North Dakota Jan 5, 1934. Catholic. Educated at Harvard College 1955 and Georgetown University Law Center 1959. Admitted to practice North Dakota 1959 and Virginia 1959. In legal practice Bismarck 1959-85.

Bismarck City Commissioner (Police and Fire portfolios) 1968-76. Member House of Representatives (Chairman House Judiciary) 1976-85. Former Honorary Consular Agent Republic of France. Former member State Bar Association of North Dakota (President 1971-72). Member Burleigh County Bar Association. Member Bismarck Civic Chorus and local theatre. Emcee for regional pag-

CONMY, PATRICK A.—*Continued*

eants. Enjoys sailing, singing, automobiles and performing arts.

Mailing address: P.O. Box 1578, Bismarck 58502-1578.

Telephone: (701) 530-2315.

DAWSON, Georgia *(Judge, North Dakota District Court East Central Judicial District)* Elected to term beginning Jan 1, 1995. Former Judge, Cass County Court.

Mailing address: P.O. Box 2806, Fargo 58108-2806.

Office: Cass County Courthouse, 211 South Ninth Street, Fargo 58103.

Telephone: (701) 241-5680.

Fax: (701) 241-5709

ERICKSON, Ralph R. *(Judge, United States District Court District of North Dakota)* Appointed for life by President George W. Bush. Former Judge, North Dakota District Court East Central Judicial District.

Office: 655 First Avenue North, Suite 410, Fargo 58102.

Telephone: (701) 297-7080.

Fax: (701) 297-7085

FONTAINE, Laurie A. *(Judge, North Dakota District Court Northeast Judicial District)*

Office: Pembina County Courthouse, 301 Dakota Street West #3, Cavalier 58220-4100.

Telephone: (701) 265-8783.

Fax: (701) 265-4514

FOUGHTY, Donovan J. *(Judge, North Dakota District Court Northeast Judicial District)* Elected to term beginning Jan 1, 1995. Former Judge, Ramsey and Towner County Courts.

Mailing address: P.O. Box 70, Devils Lake 58301-0070.

Office: Ramsey County Courthouse, 524 Fourth Avenue, Devils Lake 58301.

Telephone: (701) 662-1308.

Fax: (701) 662-8539

GEIGER, M. Richard *(Presiding Judge, North Dakota District Court Northeast Judicial District)* Elected to term beginning Jan 1, 1995. Former Judge, Walsh County Court.

Office: Walsh County Courthouse, 600 Cooper Avenue, Grafton 58237-1509.

Telephone: (701) 352-1311.

Fax: (701) 352-4542

GOODMAN, Ronald E. *(Judge, North Dakota District Court Southeast Judicial District)* Elected Nov 1994 to term beginning Jan 1, 1995. Reelected 1998, current term expires Dec 31, 2004. Born Grand Forks North Dakota Sept 17, 1947. Catholic. Educated at St. John's University B.A. 1969 and University of North Dakota M.A. cum laude 1974 J.D. 1981. Research Editor North Dakota Law Review 1980-81. Admitted to practice North Dakota 1981, U.S. District Court District of North Dakota 1982 and U.S. Tax Court 1986. In legal practice Oakes 1981-90. Judge, Dickey and LaMoure County Courts Jan 5, 1991 to Dec 31, 1994.

Instructor in Business Law Valley City State College 1982. Board of Governors State Bar Association of North Dakota 1988-90. President North Dakota District Judges Association 1998-99. USAF 1969-73. Member American Legion, Veterans of Foreign Wars, Lions Club and Knights of Columbus.

Mailing address: P.O. Box 336, Ellendale 58436-0036.

Office: Dickey County Courthouse, 309 North Second Street, Ellendale 58436.

Telephone: (701) 349-3249.

Fax: (701) 349-3560

GRAFF, Benny A. *(Presiding Judge, North Dakota District Court South Central Judicial District)* Appointed by governor to term beginning Feb 1, 1974. Elected 1975, 1980, 1986, 1992 and 1998. Current term expires Dec 31, 2004. Born Hibbing Minnesota Oct 14, 1938. Methodist. Educated at Hibbing Junior College A.S. 1958 and University of North Dakota B.S. in Chemical Engineering 1961 J.D. 1964. Member Order of the Coif. Editor North Dakota Law Review. Admitted to practice North Dakota 1964 and Wisconsin 1970. Began legal practice Mandan North Dakota 1964. In legal practice Racine Wisconsin 1970-71 and Carrington North Dakota 1971-74.

Important Decision: Square Butte Electric Cooperative v. Hilken 1975. Member Legal Staff Senate Subcommittee on Judicial Improvement 1971, North Dakota Council of Presiding Judges (Chairman since 1987) and State Bar Association of North Dakota. Sergeant USAF 1963-69. Democrat.

Mailing address: P.O. Box 1013, Bismarck 58502-1013.

Office: Burleigh County Courthouse, 514 East Thayer Avenue, Bismarck 58501.

Telephone: (701) 222-6682.

Fax: (701) 222-6689

GREENWOOD, John E. *(Judge, North Dakota District Court Southeast Judicial District)* Appointed by Governor Edward T. Schafer July 14, 1999 to term beginning Sept 1, 1999. Elected 2002, current term expires December 31, 2008. Born Harvey North Dakota. Catholic. Educated at University of North Dakota B.S. 1971 J.D. 1975. Admitted to practice North Dakota 1975. In legal practice Jamestown 1975-93.

State's Attorney Stutsman County 1993-99. Member State Bar Association of North Dakota. Enjoys golfing, biking and reading.

Office: 511 Second Avenue S.E., Jamestown 58401.

Telephone: (701) 252-9044.

Fax: (701) 251-1006

E-mail address: Johng@SEJD.COURT.STATE.ND.US

GROSZ, Richard W. *(Judge, North Dakota District Court Southeast Judicial District)*

Office: Richland County Courthouse, 418 Second Avenue North, Wahpeton 58075.

Telephone: (701) 671-1510.

Fax: (701) 671-1512

HAGERTY, Gail *(Judge, North Dakota District Court South Central Judicial District)* Elected to term beginning Jan 1, 1995. Born Bismarck North Dakota March 17, 1953. Lutheran. Educated at University of North Dakota B.A. cum laude 1975 J.D. 1978. Admitted to practice North Dakota 1978 and Minnesota 1978. Judge, Burleigh County Court Jan 1987 to Dec 31, 1994.

Assistant Attorney General 1978-80. Assistant State's Attorney 1980-82. State's Attorney 1982-87. Member National Association of Women Judges and State Bar Association of North Dakota. Chair North Dakota Legal

HAGERTY, GAIL—*Continued*
Counsel for Indigent Commission 1985-89. Board of Trustees Trinity Lutheran Church. Member Rotary Club.

Mailing address: P.O. Box 1013, Bismarck 58502-1013.

Office: Burleigh County Courthouse, 514 East Thayer Avenue, Bismarck 58501.

Telephone: (701) 222-6682.

Fax: (701) 222-6689

HASKELL, Bruce B. *(Judge, North Dakota District Court South Central Judicial District)* Elected Nov 1994 to term beginning Jan 1, 1995. Reelected 2000, current term expires Dec 31, 2006. Born Breckenridge Minnesota Aug 18, 1957. Catholic. Educated at University of North Dakota B.A. 1980 J.D. 1983. Note Author North Dakota Law Review 1982-83. Admitted to practice North Dakota 1983 and U.S. District Court District of North Dakota 1984.

Assistant Attorney General North Dakota 1983-85. Assistant State's Attorney Morton County 1985-87 and Burleigh County 1987-94. Member Inns of Court, American Judicature Society, Big Muddy and North Dakota Bar Associations. Member Elks Club. Enjoys hunting, fishing, golf, scuba diving and riding Harley-Davidsons.

Mailing address: P.O. Box 1013, Bismarck 58502-1013.

Office: Burleigh County Courthouse, 514 East Thayer Avenue, Bismarck 58501.

Telephone: (701) 222-6682.

Fax: (701) 222-6689

HILDEN, Ronald L. *(Judge, North Dakota District Court Southwest Judicial District)* Elected to term beginning Jan 1, 1995. Former Judge, Stark County Court.

Mailing address: P.O. Box 1507, Dickinson 58602-1507.

Office: Stark County Courthouse, Third and Sims, Dickinson 58601.

Telephone: (701) 264-7658.

Fax: (701) 227-7428

HILL, William Alexander *(Judge, United States Bankruptcy Court District of North Dakota)* Appointed by U.S. District Court judges to term beginning March 21, 1984. Reappointed by U.S. Court of Appeals Eighth Circuit judges May 24, 1988. Also Judge, Bankruptcy Appellate Panel Eighth Circuit. Selected by the Judicial Council of the Eighth Circuit to term beginning Sept 1996. Born Carmel California Aug 21, 1946. Episcopalian. Educated at University of North Dakota B.S.B.A. 1968 J.D. 1971. Editorial staff member North Dakota Law Review 1969-71. Law Clerk to Chief Judge Paul Benson, U.S. District Court District of North Dakota 1972-74. Member Sigma Nu and Phi Alpha Delta. Admitted to practice North Dakota 1971, Minnesota 1974, U.S. District Court 1974, U.S. Court of Appeals Eighth Circuit 1974 and U.S. Tax Court 1978. In legal practice Fargo North Dakota 1974-83. Part-time Magistrate, U.S. District Court District of North Dakota 1975-83.

Deputy Secretary of State 1971-72. Member National Conference of Bankruptcy Judges, State Bar Association of North Dakota, Cass County and Minnesota State Bar Associations. Republican. Member Fargo Chamber of Commerce, Historical Society, Masons and Boy Scouts.

Office: 350 U.S. Courthouse, 655 First Avenue North, Fargo 58102-4952.

Telephone: (701) 297-7140.

HOBERG, Gordon O. *(Surrogate Judge, North Dakota District Court)* Appointed by Governor Allen Olson to term beginning July 1, 1983. Elected to term beginning Jan 1, 1985. Reelected 1990. Retired, serves by assignment. Born Burnstad North Dakota Sept 13, 1929. Lutheran. Educated at Jamestown College B.S. 1956 and University of North Dakota J.D. 1959. Admitted to practice North Dakota 1959. In legal practice Wishek 1959 and Napoleon 1962.

State's Attorney Logan County 1962-82. President Third Judicial District Bar Association 1962. Member State Bar Board 1962, Stutsman County, Southeast Judicial District and American Bar Associations. Sergeant U.S. Army 1950-52. Board member 28th Legislative District. President Napoleon Airport Authority. Member American Legion, VFW, Lions and Alumni Board of Jamestown College. Enjoys horseback riding, racquetball, swimming, skiing and camping.

Mailing address: RR 1, P.O. Box 232, Wishek 58495-0232.

HODNY, William F. *(Surrogate Judge, North Dakota District Court)* Elected to term beginning Jan 1, 1975. Reelected 1980, 1986 and 1992. Retired, serves by assignment. Born Walsh County North Dakota Dec 3, 1932. Educated at University of North Dakota Ph.B. 1957 and J.D. with honors 1960. Editor-in-Chief North Dakota Law Review 1959-60. Member Phi Delta Phi and Order of the Coif. Admitted to practice North Dakota 1960. Began legal practice Mandan 1960. Judge, Morton County Court 1967-74.

Member State Bar Association of North Dakota. USAF 1950-53. Enjoys horse breeding, hunting, fishing, dog training, field trials, farming and ranching.

Mailing address: 1725 County Road 81, Mandan 58554-8726.

HOLTE, Robert W. *(Presiding Judge, North Dakota District Court Northwest Judicial District)* Elected to term beginning Jan 1, 1995. Former Judge, Burke, Divide and Mountrail County Courts.

Mailing address: P.O. Box 940, Stanley 58784-0940.

Office: Mountrail County Courthouse, North Main Street, Stanley 58784.

Telephone: (701) 628-2515.

Fax: (701) 628-1515

HOLUM, Gary A. *(Judge, North Dakota District Court Northwest Judicial District)* Elected to term beginning Jan 1, 1993. Reelected 1998, current term expires Dec 31, 2004. Born Minot North Dakota March 19, 1937. Lutheran. Educated at Harvard University 1955-56, University of North Dakota B.S.B.A. 1960 J.D. 1971. Member Phi Delta Theta and Phi Alpha Delta. Admitted to practice North Dakota 1971 and U.S. District Court District of North Dakota 1971. Began legal practice Minot 1971. Judge, Ward County Court July 1, 1981 to Dec 31, 1992.

Former Member North Dakota Judicial Qualifications Commission and Executive Committee National Conference of Special Court Judges. Member North Dakota Association of County Judges (Past President), North Dakota District Judges Association (Past President), State Bar Association of North Dakota and American Bar Association. U.S. Army 1961-62. Staff Sergeant North Dakota National Guard 1960-66. First Lutheran Church Centennial Commission 1983-84. Former Member Board of Directors YMCA, Second Story and Trinity Medical Center. Board of Directors Minot State Uni-

HOLUM, GARY A.—*Continued*
versity Foundation (Past President). Enjoys gardening, hunting and fishing.
Mailing address: P.O. Box 5005, Minot 58702-5005.
Office: Ward County Courthouse, 315 Third Street S.E., Minot 58701.
Telephone: (701) 857-7605.
Fax: (701) 857-7606
E-mail address: GHolum@ndcourts.com

HOVLAND, Daniel L. *(Chief Judge, United States District Court District of North Dakota)* Appointed for life by President George W. Bush to term beginning Nov 26, 2002.
Mailing address: P.O. Box 670, Bismarck 58502-0670.
Office: 220 East Rosser Avenue, Bismarck 58501-3869.
Telephone: (701) 530-2320.
Fax: (701) 530-2325

IRBY, John C. *(Judge, North Dakota District Court East Central Judicial District)*
Mailing address: P.O. Box 2806, Fargo 58108-2806.
Office: Cass County Courthouse, 211 South Ninth Street, Fargo 58103.
Telephone: (701) 241-5680.
Fax: (701) 241-5709

JAHNKE, Lawrence E. *(Judge, North Dakota District Court Northeast Central Judicial District)* Former Presiding Judge.
Mailing address: P.O. Box 6347, Grand Forks 58206-6347.
Office: Grand Forks County Courthouse, 124 South Fourth, Grand Forks 58205.
Telephone: (701) 795-3824.
Fax: (701) 795-3886

JORGENSEN, Donald L. *(Judge, North Dakota District Court South Central Judicial District)* Elected Nov 1984 to term beginning Jan 1, 1985. Reelected 1990, 1996 and 2002. Current term expires Dec 31, 2008. Served Southwest Judicial District 1985-95. Born Kenmare North Dakota Sept 23, 1944. Roman Catholic. Educated at University of North Dakota Ph.B. 1967 J.D. 1970. Member Phi Alpha Delta. Admitted to practice North Dakota 1970 and U.S. District Court District of North Dakota 1973. In legal practice Mayville 1970-71 and Dickinson 1973-82. Judge, Stark County Court 1983-84.
Instructor Dickinson State College 1974-85. Chairman Rural Courts Committee National Council of Juvenile and Family Court Judges since 1993. Member American Judicature Society, State Bar Association of North Dakota and American Bar Association. Attended The National Judicial College Nov 1983, July 1985 and Aug 1985. Earned Diploma of Judicial Skills American Academy of Judicial Education 1992. Captain U.S. Army (Chief, Legal Section USAISC) 1971-73.
Mailing address: P.O. Box 219, Mandan 58554-0219.
Office: Morton County Courthouse, 210 Second Avenue N.W., Mandan 58554.
Telephone: (701) 667-3357.
Fax: (701) 667-3385

KAPSNER, Carol Ronning *(Justice, North Dakota Supreme Court)* Appointed by Governor Edward T. Schafer 1998. Elected 2000. Born Bismarck North Dakota. Educated at College of St. Catherine B.A., Oxford University, England, Indiana University M.A. and University of Colorado School of Law J.D. 1977. In legal practice Bismarck 1977-98.
Former Member Board of Governors North Dakota Trial Lawyers Association and North Dakota Bar Association. Past President Burleigh County Bar Association.
Office: 600 East Boulevard Avenue, Department 180, Bismarck 58505-0530.
Telephone: (701) 328-4494.
Fax: (701) 328-4480

KAUTZMANN, Dwight C. H. *(Magistrate Judge, United States District Court District of North Dakota)* Appointed part-time Magistrate by U.S. District Court judges to term beginning June 1978. Reappointed 1982, 1986, 1990 and 1994. Appointed full-time Magistrate Judge 1996. Current term expires 2004. Born Bismarck North Dakota Dec 30, 1945. Roman Catholic. Educated at North Dakota State University B.A. 1968 and University of North Dakota J.D. 1971. Member Phi Alpha Delta. Recipient Pi Omega Award 1967, Distinguished Service Award North Dakota State University 1967 and Thormsgard Moot Court Award 1969. Admitted to practice North Dakota 1971, U.S. District Court District of North Dakota 1971, U.S. Court of Appeals Eighth Circuit 1974, U.S. Supreme Court 1977 and U.S. Court of Military Appeals 1992. In legal practice Mandan since 1971. Judge, Mandan Municipal Court 1973-76.
Chairman Legal Services Committee of North Dakota 1976-79. Member Governor's Committees on Privacy and Security and Juvenile Justice 1976, North Dakota Trial Lawyers Association (President 1990-91), National Association of Criminal Defense Lawyers, Inc., State Bar Association of North Dakota (Secretary-Treasurer 1974-75, President 1987-88) and American Bar Association (Executive Council Young Lawyers Section 1974-76). President Mandan Public School District #1, 1978-83. Member United Fund Drive 1971. Reader Christ the King Church 1972-74. Elks Exalted Ruler 1978-79. Interests include reading, horseback riding and historical research of courts and judges.
Mailing address: P.O. Box 1578, Bismarck 58502-1578.
Telephone: (701) 530-2340.

KERIAN, Jon R. *(Surrogate Judge, North Dakota District Court)* Appointed by Governor Arthur Link to term beginning April 15, 1980. Elected 1980 and 1986. Retired 1992. Appointed Surrogate Judge by North Dakota Supreme Court Chief Justice Dec 28, 1992. Serves by assignment. Born Grafton North Dakota Oct 23, 1927. Roman Catholic. Educated at University of North Dakota Ph.B. 1955 LL.B. 1957 J.D. 1971. Member Phi Delta Phi. Admitted to practice North Dakota 1957. Began legal practice Grand Forks 1958. In legal practice Bismarck 1961-67 and Minot 1967-80.
Assistant Attorney General 1961-67. Assistant City Attorney Minot 1968-76. Author *Valuation of Advertising Rights* National Academy of Sciences 1965. Editor Trial Judges Newsletter 1986-92. Board of Editors The Judges Journal. Adjunct Professor of Constitutional History and Business Law Bismarck State College 1965-67. Member State Bar Association of North Dakota (Board of Governors 1975-81, President 1979-80), Western States Bar Conference (President 1982-83) and American Bar Association (Executive Committee National Conference of State Trial Judges 1983-89). Master Sergeant U.S. Army Infantry in Korea 1951-52. Previously

KERIAN, JON R.—*Continued*
worked as apprentice car man, section laborer and night janitor for Great Northern Railway. Enjoys studying and collecting serious music and central and northern European-style cooking.
Mailing address: P.O. Box 340, Minot 58702-0340.

KETTERLING, Lester S. *(Judge, North Dakota District Court Northeast Judicial District)* Elected to term beginning Jan 1, 1995. Reelected 1996 and 2002. Current term expires Dec 31, 2008. Born Wishek North Dakota Oct 5, 1940. Lutheran. Educated at University of North Dakota B.Ph. 1962 LL.B. 1964. Admitted to practice North Dakota 1964 and U.S. District Court District of North Dakota 1974. In legal practice Westhope 1966-86. Justice, Bottineau County Justice Court 1967-83. Judge, Bottineau, Renville and Rolette County Courts Jan 5, 1987 to Dec 31, 1994.
Member American Blind Lawyers Association, State Bar Association of North Dakota, Northeast Judicial District and American Bar Associations.
Office: Bottineau County Courthouse, 314 West Fifth Street, Bottineau 58318-1200.
Telephone: (701) 228-3618.
Fax: (701) 228-2336

KLEIN, Karen K. *(Magistrate Judge, United States District Court District of North Dakota)* Appointed by U.S. District Court judges.
Office: 440 U.S. Courthouse, 655 First Avenue North, Fargo 58102-4952.
Telephone: (701) 297-7070.

KLEVEN, Debbie Gordon *(Presiding Judge, North Dakota District Court Northeast Central Judicial District)* Elected Nov 1994 to term beginning Jan 1, 1995. Reelected Nov 1996 and 2002. Current term expires Dec 31, 2008. Born Valley City North Dakota June 14, 1958. Lutheran. Educated at University of North Dakota B.S. magna cum laude 1980 J.D. with distinction 1983. Former staff member North Dakota Law Review. Admitted to practice North Dakota 1983. Judge, Grand Forks County Court Jan 1, 1991 to Dec 31, 1994.
Mailing address: P.O. Box 6347, Grand Forks 58206-6347.
Office: Grand Forks County Courthouse, 124 South Fourth Street, Grand Forks 58205.
Telephone: (701) 795-3824.
Fax: (701) 795-3886

LeCLERC, Lawrence A. *(Judge, North Dakota District Court East Central Judicial District)* Former Presiding Judge.
Mailing address: P.O. Box 2806, Fargo 58108-2806.
Office: Cass County Courthouse, 211 South Ninth Street, Fargo 58103.
Telephone: (701) 241-5680.
Fax: (701) 241-5709

MARING, Mary Muehlen *(Justice, North Dakota Supreme Court)* Appointed by Governor Edward T. Schafer to term beginning 1996. Elected 1996 and 1998. Current term expires Dec 31, 2008. Born Devils Lake North Dakota. Educated at University of North Dakota School of Law J.D. 1975. Law Clerk to Hon. Bruce C. Stone, Minnesota District Court Fourth Judicial District 1975-76. In legal practice 1976-96.
Past President North Dakota Trial Lawyers Association and East Central District Bar Association.
Office: 600 East Boulevard Avenue, Department 180, Bismarck 58505-0530.
Telephone: (701) 328-2221.
Fax: (701) 328-4480

MATTSON, Douglas L. *(Judge, North Dakota District Court Northwest Judicial District)*
Mailing address: P.O. Box 5005, Minot 58702-5005.
Office: Ward County Courthouse, 315 S.E. Third, Minot 58701.
Telephone: (701) 857-7604.
Fax: (701) 857-7606

McCLINTOCK, John C., Jr. *(Judge, North Dakota District Court Northeast Judicial District)* Elected to term beginning Jan 1, 1995. Born Rugby North Dakota Feb 11, 1961. Lutheran. Educated at University of North Dakota B.S.B.A. 1983 J.D. 1986. Member Phi Alpha Delta. Admitted to practice North Dakota 1991 and U.S. District Court District of North Dakota 1991. In legal practice 1991-95.
Former Assistant State's Attorney Pierce County. Member North Dakota Jury Standards Committee, North Dakota Judicial Conference (Executive Committee), State Bar Association of North Dakota and American Bar Association. Employed by Price Waterhouse, Minneapolis Minnesota 1986-89 and Merchants Bank of Rugby 1989-91. Former Chairman Good Samaritan Health Services Foundation. Former President Bethany Lutheran Church of Rugby. Former Treasurer Rugby Job Authority. Member Rugby Lions Club. Enjoys basketball, softball, hunting and fishing.
Mailing address: P.O. Box 387, Rugby 58368-0387.
Office: Pierce County Courthouse, 240 Second Street S.E., Rugby 58368.
Telephone: (701) 776-5375.
Fax: (701) 776-6893

McGUIRE, Michael O. *(Judge, North Dakota District Court East Central Judicial District)* Appointed by Governor Arthur Albert Link Nov 1979. Elected 1980, 1986, 1992 and 1998. Current term expires Dec 31, 2004. Former Presiding Judge. Born Bismarck North Dakota March 20, 1941. Educated at Moorhead State University B.A. 1967 and University of North Dakota J.D. 1971. Admitted to practice North Dakota 1972. Began legal practice Fargo 1972. Judge, Cass County Court with Increased Jurisdiction 1978-82.
Author "Winning Strategies for Defense of Marijuana Cases" The National Journal of Criminal Defense Vol. 1 No. 2 Fall 1975. Member American Judges Association, State Bar Association of North Dakota, Cass County and American (Criminal Specialization Committee 1976-79) Bar Associations. Faculty Advisor The National Judicial College April and May 1986. Attended National College of Criminal Defense Lawyers, Public Defenders Houston Texas 1975 and The National Judicial College 1979 and 1984. Recipient Outstanding Contribution and Leadership Award from National Association of Criminal Defense Lawyers 1977-78 and Distinguished Alumni Award Moorhead State University Sept 27, 1980. Specialist Fourth Class U.S. Army 1960-62 and Airman First Class USAF 1965-66. Member Veterans Administration Research and Development Committee on Human Studies 1977-84. President and Board member Centre Inc. Half-

MCGUIRE, MICHAEL O.—*Continued*

way House. Board of Directors Fargo Youth Commission 1986-87.

Mailing address: P.O. Box 2806, Fargo 58108-2806.

Office: Cass County Courthouse, 211 South Ninth Street, Fargo 58103.

Telephone: (701) 241-5680.

Fax: (701) 241-5709

McLEES, William W., Jr. *(Judge, North Dakota District Court Northwest Judicial District)* Elected to term beginning Jan 1, 1995. Reelected 2000, current term expires Dec 31, 2006. Born Valley City North Dakota April 14, 1951. Catholic. Educated at University of North Dakota B.A. 1973 J.D. 1976. Admitted to practice North Dakota 1976. In legal practice Williston 1976 and Watford City 1977-82. Judge, Billings, Dunn, Golden Valley and McKenzie County Courts March 1, 1978 to Dec 31, 1994.

Member North Dakota Judicial Conference, North Dakota Judges Association, State Bar Association of North Dakota, Upper Missouri (Past President) and American Bar Associations. Attended The National Judicial College Spring 1986 and Advanced Course in Special Courts Jurisdiction The National Judicial College June 1993. Past President Watford City Rotary Club. Public Address Announcer Watford City High School basketball and football games. Member Epiphany Parish, Knights of Columbus (Past Grand Knight) and Watford City Golf Club. Enjoys golf, basketball, snow skiing, water skiing, fishing and ice hockey.

Mailing address: P.O. Box 5005, Minot 58702-5005.

Office: Courthouse, Minot 58701.

Telephone: (701) 857-7602.

Fax: (701) 857-7606

E-mail address: bmclees@ndcourts.com

MEDD, Joel Douglas *(Judge, North Dakota District Court Northeast Central Judicial District)* Appointed by Governor Arthur Link Oct 1979. Elected 1980, 1986, 1992 and 1998. Current term expires Dec 31, 2004. Former Presiding Judge. Born Langdon North Dakota April 30, 1947. Educated at University of North Dakota B.A. 1969 J.D. 1975. Board of Editors North Dakota Law Review. Admitted to practice North Dakota 1975. Judge, Benson County Court 1975-79. Judge, Williams County Court 1979. Former Municipal Judge and Tribal Appeals Judge.

Author "Legal Problems of Migrants" North Dakota L. Rev. 1974 and book review "By What Right" North Dakota L. Rev. 1975. Author newspaper column "Points of Law" 1975-79. Chairman Criminal Justice Advisory Board Devils Lake 1975-79 and Civil Legal Services Committee. Member Legislative Court System Committee 1977, State District Court Personnel Advisory Committee 1992-98 and Court Technology Committee since 1992. Former member Association of County Judges with Increased Jurisdiction (Secretary-Treasurer). Chair Jury Management Committee North Dakota Judicial Conference. Fellow American Bar Foundation. Member American Judicature Society (North Dakota Director 1986-89), State Bar Association of North Dakota, Grand Forks Area and American (Member Committee on Jury Management and Delegate and Chair National Conference of State Trial Judges Judicial Division) Bar Associations. Recipient Outstanding Alumni Award from Phi Alpha Delta 1977, Silver Beaver Award for service to scouting from Boy Scouts of America 1986, Outstanding Member Award from Disabled American Veterans 1986, Lifetime Achievement Award in Teaching Trial Advocacy from University of North Dakota School of Law 1997 and Pro Bono Publico Award from State Bar Association of North Dakota. Named one of five Outstanding Young North Dakotans by Jaycees 1982. Captain USAS 1969-72. Board Member Grand Forks Symphony. Member Lions Club (President 1987), VFW, DAV (Commander 1986) and American Legion. Boy Scouts of America leader. Enjoys photography, sports, tennis, table tennis and boating.

Mailing address: P.O. Box 6347, Grand Forks 58206-6347.

Office: Grand Forks County Courthouse, 124 South Fourth Street, Grand Forks 58205.

Telephone: (701) 795-3824.

Fax: (701) 795-3886

E-mail address: jmedd@ndcourts.com

NELSON, David W. *(Judge, North Dakota District Court Northwest Judicial District)*

Mailing address: P.O. Box 2047, Williston 58802-2047.

Office: Williams County Courthouse, 205 East Broadway, Williston 58801.

Telephone: (701) 572-1705.

Fax: (701) 572-1758

NEUMANN, William A. *(Justice, North Dakota Supreme Court)* Elected to term beginning Jan 1, 1993. Reelected 2002, current term expires Dec 31, 2012. Born Minot North Dakota Feb 11, 1944. Lutheran (ELCA). Educated at University of North Dakota B.S.B.A. 1965 and Stanford Law School J.D. 1968. Admitted to practice North Dakota 1969 and U.S. District Court District of North Dakota 1969. In legal practice Williston 1969-70 and Bottineau 1970-79. Judge, North Dakota District Court Northeast Judicial District, appointed by Governor Arthur E. Link to term beginning Oct 1, 1979.

Chair Elect 1985-87 and Chair 1987-89 North Dakota Judicial Conference. Member American Judicature Society (Board of Directors since 1998), State Bar Association of North Dakota and American Bar Association.

Office: 600 East Boulevard, First Floor Judicial Wing, Department 180, Bismarck 58505-0530.

Telephone: (701) 328-2221.

Fax: (701) 328-4480

OLSON, Everett Nels *(Surrogate Judge, North Dakota District Court)* Assumed office Jan 1, 1979. Elected to term beginning Jan 1, 1985. Reelected 1990 and 1996. Retired, serves by assignment. Former Presiding Judge. Born Hettinger North Dakota July 12, 1939. Congregationalist. Educated at Dickinson State College B.A. 1962 and University of North Dakota LL.B. 1965. Admitted to practice North Dakota 1965. Began legal practice New Town 1965. In legal practice Minot 1968-79. Tribal Judge, Fort Benthold Reservation 1965-68.

Instructor in Criminal Procedure and Evidence Minot State College 1974-76. Member National Council of Juvenile and Family Court Judges, State Bar Association of North Dakota, Ward County and American Bar Associations.

Mailing address: 1801 Parkside Drive, Minot 58701-6839.

PAULSON, John T. *(Presiding Judge, North Dakota District Court Southeast Judicial District)* Elected to

PAULSON, JOHN T.—*Continued*
term beginning Jan 1, 1981. Reelected 1986, 1992 and 1998. Current term expires Dec 31, 2004. Presiding Judge since 1995. Born Valley City North Dakota Jan 6, 1943. Episcopalian. Educated at University of North Dakota School of Law J.D. 1967. Member Phi Delta Phi. Admitted to practice North Dakota 1967, U.S. District Court District of North Dakota 1968 and U.S. Supreme Court 1978. Began legal practice Valley City 1967. Municipal Judge 1968-70.

State's Attorney Barnes County 1970-80. Instructor on Business Law and Legal Environment of Business Valley City State University 1970-87. President North Dakota Judges Association 1995. Member State Bar Association of North Dakota and Southeast Judicial District Bar Association. Attended The National Judicial College 1981. Past President Valley City Kiwanis Club, Valley City Aerie 2192 Fraternal Order of Eagles and Advisory Board Children's Hospital Fargo.

Mailing address: P.O. Box 993, Valley City 58072-0993.

Office: Barnes County Courthouse, 230 Fourth Street N.W., Valley City 58072.

Telephone: (701) 845-8525.

Fax: (701) 845-8537

RACEK, Frank L. *(Judge, North Dakota District Court East Central Judicial District)* Elected to term beginning Jan 1, 1995. Former Judge, Cass County Court.

Mailing address: P.O. Box 2806, Fargo 58108-2806.

Office: Cass County Courthouse, 211 South Ninth Street, Fargo 58103.

Telephone: (701) 241-5680.

Fax: (701) 241-5709

RISKEDAHL, Burton L. *(Judge, North Dakota District Court South Central Judicial District)* Elected to term beginning Jan 1, 1995. Born Bismarck North Dakota Sept 8, 1940. Educated at Jamestown College B.A. 1962, University of Denver M.S.W. 1964 and William Mitchell College of Law J.D. 1973. Admitted to practice North Dakota 1973. Began legal practice Bismarck 1974. Former Justice, Sioux County Justice Court. Judge, Burleigh County Court Oct 15, 1979 to Dec 31, 1994.

Mailing address: P.O. Box 1013, Bismarck 58502-1013.

Office: Burleigh County Courthouse, 514 East Thayer Avenue, Bismarck 58501.

Telephone: (701) 222-6682.

Fax: (701) 222-6689

ROMANICK, Bruce A. *(Judge, North Dakota District Court South Central Judicial District)*

Mailing address: P.O. Box 1013, Bismarck 58502-1013.

Office: Burleigh County Courthouse, 514 East Thayer Avenue, Bismarck 58501.

Telephone: (701) 222-6682.

Fax: (701) 222-6689

ROTHE-SEEGER, Cynthia A. *(Judge, North Dakota District Court East Central Judicial District)* Appointed by Governor George A. Sinner to term beginning March 27, 1988. Elected 1988, 1990, 1996 and 2002. Current term expires Dec 31, 2008. Born Rolette North Dakota Nov 15, 1948. Lutheran. Educated at University of North Dakota B.A. 1970 M.A. 1972 J.D. 1975. Admitted to practice North Dakota 1975. Began legal practice Fargo 1975. Juvenile Supervisor, Cass County Juvenile Court 1975. Magistrate 1981-82 and Judge 1983-88, Cass County Court.

Legal Advisor Fargo Police Department 1976. Assistant State's Attorney 1976-78 and State's Attorney 1978-81 Cass County. Former Member North Dakota Association of County Judges (Secretary-Treasurer 1984). Member North Dakota District Judges Association, North Dakota Judicial Conference, State Bar Association of North Dakota, Cass County and American Bar Associations. Attended courses on Special Court Jurisdiction 1982 and General Court Jurisdiction 1988 The National Judicial College. Attended course on "Domestic Violence/Child Abuse" The National Judicial College and North Dakota Judicial System 1988. Recipient Recognition Award from Law Women's Caucus 1982 and 1987-88 and "Healing the Hurt" Award from Rape and Abuse Crisis Center 1983. Former Board member Rape and Abuse Crisis Center and United Way. Member Advisory Council Centre, Inc. and Advisory Board Alliance for Sexual Abuse Prevention and Treatment. Enjoys reading, playing the piano, walking, movies and spectator sports (hockey, basketball).

Mailing address: P.O. Box 2806, Fargo 58108-2806.

Office: Cass County Courthouse, 211 South Ninth Street, Fargo 58103.

Telephone: (701) 241-5680.

Fax: (701) 241-5709

RUSTAD, Gerald H. *(Judge, North Dakota District Court Northwest Judicial District)*

Mailing address: P.O. Box 2047, Williston 58802-2047.

Office: Williams County Courthouse, 205 East Broadway, Williston 58801.

Telephone: (701) 572-1705.

Fax: (701) 572-1758

SANDSTROM, Dale V. *(Justice, North Dakota Supreme Court)* Elected to term beginning Dec 31, 1992. Reelected 1996, current term expires Dec 31, 2006. Born North Dakota. Educated at North Dakota State University B.S. in Political Science, University of North Dakota School of Law J.D. and Harvard Law School.

Former Staff Attorney North Dakota Criminal Justice Commission. Former Assistant Attorney General and Chief Consumer Fraud and Antitrust Division North Dakota. State Securities Commissioner 1981-83. Member North Dakota Public Service Commission 1983-92.

Office: State Capitol, 600 East Boulevard Avenue, Bismarck 58505-0530.

Telephone: (701) 328-2221.

Fax: (701) 328-4480

SCHMALENBERGER, Allan L. *(Presiding Judge, North Dakota District Court Southwest Judicial District)*

Mailing address: P.O. Box 1507, Dickinson 58602-1507.

Office: Stark County Courthouse, Third and Sims, Dickinson 58601.

Telephone: (701) 264-7658.

Fax: (701) 227-7428

SCHNEIDER, Thomas J. *(Judge, North Dakota District Court South Central Judicial District)* Elected to term beginning Jan 1, 1995. Former Judge, Mandan Mu-

SCHNEIDER, THOMAS J.—*Continued*

nicipal Court. Former Judge, Grant, Morton and Sioux County Courts.

Mailing address: P.O. Box 219, Mandan 58554-0219.

Office: Morton County Courthouse, 210 Second Avenue N.W., Mandan 58554.

Telephone: (701) 667-3386.

Fax: (701) 667-3385

SENECHAL, Alice R. *(Magistrate Judge, United States District Court District of North Dakota)* Appointed by U.S. District Court judges. Serves part time.

Mailing address: P.O. Box 5576, Grand Forks 58206-5576.

Telephone: (701) 775-3117.

SIMONSON, Mikal *(Judge, North Dakota District Court Southeast Judicial District)* Elected Nov 8, 1994 to term beginning Jan 1, 1995. Reelected Nov 3, 1998 to term beginning Jan 1, 1999. Born Portland Oregon Nov 18, 1947. Episcopalian. Educated at Valley City State College B.S. 1969 and University of North Dakota J.D. 1976. Member Phi Delta Phi. Admitted to practice North Dakota 1976 and U.S. District Court District of North Dakota 1976. In legal practice Valley City 1976-85. Judge, Barnes County Court Jan 1, 1986 to Dec 31, 1994.

Assistant State's Attorney 1976-80 and State's Attorney 1981-85 Barnes County. President North Dakota County Judges Association 1993. Member State Bar Association of North Dakota, Barnes County (Past President), Southeast North Dakota and American Bar Associations. Attended General Jurisdiction Course Oct 1987 and Criminal Evidence Course Oct 1992 The National Judicial College. Secondary school teacher Ashley 1969-70 and Fort Yates 1970-73. Member Country Club and Eagles. Enjoys golf, spectator sports, baseball cards and fishing.

Mailing address: P.O. Box 993, Valley City 58072-0993.

Office: Barnes County Courthouse, 230 Fourth Street N.W., Valley City 58072.

Telephone: (701) 845-8592.

Fax: (701) 845-8537

SMITH, Kirk *(Surrogate Judge, North Dakota District Court)* Elected to term beginning Jan 3, 1977. Reelected to subsequent terms. Retired Jan 1, 2001. Appointed Surrogate Judge by North Dakota Supreme Court. Serves by assignment. Former Presiding Judge. Born Cogswell North Dakota Feb 5, 1930. Catholic. Educated at North Dakota State University 1947-50 and University of North Dakota Ph.B. 1956 J.D. 1957. Associate Editor North Dakota Law Review 1956-57. Law Clerk to Judge Charles J. Vogel, U.S. Court of Appeals Eighth Circuit 1957. Admitted to practice North Dakota 1957. In legal practice Enderlin 1958-59 and Grand Forks 1959-63. Justice of the Peace, Grand Forks April 1960 to June 1961. Justice, Grand Forks County Justice Court June 1961 to Jan 1963. Judge, Grand Forks County Court with Increased Jurisdiction Jan 1963 to Jan 1977.

Chair North Dakota Judicial Conference 1997-99. Member American Judicature Society (North Dakota Director 1982-86), State Bar Association of North Dakota and American Bar Association. U.S. Speaker on Court Organization and Due Process of Law U.S. Information Agency, Kathmandu Nepal 1993. Participant People to People Judicial Study Group to Czech Republic, Poland and Hungary Sept 21 to Oct 3, 2001. Chairman Courts Task Force North Dakota Criminal Justice Commission 1974. Quartermaster Second Class USN 1951-54. Member American Legion (Past Commander), DAV, VFW and Kiwanis Club (Past President).

Mailing address: 2610 Belmont Road, Grand Forks 58201-7510.

E-mail address: kirksmith1@aol.com

VandeWALLE, Gerald W. *(Chief Justice, North Dakota Supreme Court)* Appointed by Governor Arthur L. Link to term beginning Aug 15, 1978. Elected 1978, 1984 and Nov 1994. Current term expires Dec 31, 2004. Chief Justice since Jan 1, 1993. Born Noonan North Dakota Aug 15, 1933. Roman Catholic. Educated at University of North Dakota B.Sc. with honors 1955 J.D. magna cum laude 1958. Editor-in-Chief North Dakota Law Review 1957-58. Member Phi Alpha Delta, Phi Eta Sigma, Beta Alpha Psi, Beta Gamma Sigma and Order of the Coif. Admitted to practice North Dakota 1958, U.S. District Court District of North Dakota 1958 and U.S. Court of Appeals Eighth Circuit 1958.

Assistant Attorney General 1958-74 and First Assistant Attorney General 1975-78 North Dakota. Important Decisions: Bergstrom v. Bergstrom 271 NW 2d, 546, 1978, Morgan v. Hatch 274 NW 2d 563, 1979 and Heitkamp v. Quill Corporation 470 NW 2d 203, 1991. Instructor in Business Law Bismarck State College 1972-76. Member Federal-State Jurisdiction Committee Judicial Conference of the U.S. since 1997. Chair Research Advisory Council since 1997 and Chairperson National Center for State Courts. Board of Directors and Past President Conference of Chief Justices. Member American Judicature Society and American Bar Association (Co-chair Committee on Bar Admissions 1991-99 and Vice Chairperson Council Section of Legal Education and Admissions to the Bar). First chair of North Dakota Judicial Conference 1985-87. Recipient Education and Law Award from North Dakota Council of School Attorneys 1987, Sioux Award from University of North Dakota 1992, "Love Without Fear" Award from Abused Adult Resource Center Feb 1995, Outstanding Alumnus Award from Beta Alpha Psi April 1995 and Distinguished Service Award from State Bar Association of North Dakota June 1998. Political affiliation: Independent. Former Secretary Bismarck/Mandan Symphony. Former President Church Counsel. Former Chair Board of Capital Credit Union. Board of Directors Bismarck Meals on Wheels. Former President North Dakota Unit of American Contract Bridge League. Member Elks and Knights of Columbus. Enjoys playing duplicate bridge (Life Master Rank).

Office: State Capitol, Judicial Wing, 600 East Boulevard Avenue, Bismarck 58505-0530.

Telephone: (701) 328-2221.

Fax: (701) 328-4480

WEBB, Rodney S. *(Senior Judge, United States District Court District of North Dakota)* Appointed for life by President Ronald Reagan to term beginning 1988. Former Chief Judge. Assumed Senior status Jan 1, 2002, serves by assignment. Born Cavalier North Dakota June 21, 1935. Educated at University of North Dakota B.S. 1957 J.D. 1959. In legal practice Grafton 1959-81. Judge, Grafton Municipal Court 1975-81.

State's Attorney Walsh County 1967-74. Special As-

WEBB, RODNEY S.—*Continued*

sistant Attorney General North Dakota 1970-81. U.S. Attorney District of North Dakota 1981-87.

Office: 410 U.S. Courthouse, 655 First Avenue North, Fargo 58102-4952.

Telephone: (701) 297-7040.

WEFALD, Robert O. *(Judge, North Dakota District Court South Central Judicial District)* Elected to term beginning Jan 1, 1999. Term expires Dec 31, 2004. Educated at University of North Dakota B.A. 1964 and University of Michigan Law School J.D. 1970. Admitted to practice North Dakota 1970.

Attorney General North Dakota Jan 1, 1981 to Dec 31, 2004.

Mailing address: P.O. Box 1013, Bismarck 58502-1013.

Office: Burleigh County Courthouse, 514 East Thayer Avenue, Bismarck 58501.

Telephone: (701) 222-6682.

Fax: (701) 222-6689

E-mail address: rwefald@ndcourts.com

OHIO

Capital COLUMBUS

UNITED STATES DISTRICT COURTS DISTRICTS OF OHIO

Within Ohio there are two United States District Courts. For descriptive information refer to the United States Courts section.

NORTHERN DISTRICT consists of two divisions.

Eastern Division includes Ashland, Ashtabula, Carroll, Columbiana, Crawford, Cuyahoga, Geauga, Holmes, Lake, Lorain, Mahoning, Medina, Portage, Richland, Stark, Summit, Trumbull, Tuscarawas and Wayne counties. The court sits at Akron, Cleveland and Youngstown.

Western Division includes Allen, Auglaize, Defiance, Erie, Fulton, Hancock, Hardin, Henry, Huron, Lucas, Marion, Mercer, Ottawa, Paulding, Putnam, Sandusky, Seneca, Van Wert, Williams, Wood and Wyandot counties. The court sits at Lima and Toledo.

Chief Judge

Paul R. Matia

Judges

Lesley Wells
Solomon Oliver, Jr.
Kathleen M. O'Malley
Donald Clark Nugent
James S. Gwin
John R. Adams
James G. Carr
David A. Katz
Peter C. Economus
Patricia Anne Gaughan
Dan Aaron Polster

Senior Judges

John M. Manos
Ann Aldrich
John W. Potter
David D. Dowd, Jr.
Samuel H. Bell

Clerk

Geri M. Smith
U.S. Courthouse
801 West Superior Avenue
Cleveland, Ohio 44113
(216) 357-7000

SOUTHERN DISTRICT consists of two divisions.

Eastern Division includes Athens, Belmont, Coshocton, Delaware, Fairfield, Fayette, Franklin, Gallia, Guernsey, Harrison, Hocking, Jackson, Jefferson, Knox, Licking, Logan, Madison, Meigs, Monroe, Morgan, Morrow, Muskingum, Noble, Perry, Pickaway, Pike, Ross, Union, Vinton and Washington counties. The court sits at Columbus.

Western Division includes Adams, Brown, Butler, Champaign, Clark, Clermont, Clinton, Darke, Greene, Hamilton, Highland, Lawrence, Miami, Montgomery, Preble, Scioto, Shelby and Warren counties. The court sits at Cincinnati and Dayton.

Chief Judge

Walter Herbert Rice

Judges

James L. Graham
Susan J. Dlott
Algenon L. Marbley
Gregory Lynn Frost
Sandra S. Beckwith
Edmund A. Sargus, Jr.
Thomas M. Rose

Senior Judges

S. Arthur Spiegel
John D. Holschuh
Herman J. Weber, Jr.
George C. Smith

Clerk

Kenneth J. Murphy
260 U.S. Courthouse
85 Marconi Boulevard
Columbus, Ohio 43215
(614) 719-3000

UNITED STATES MAGISTRATE JUDGES OF OHIO

NORTHERN DISTRICT

Jack B. Streepy
Patricia A. Hemann
Nancy A. Vecchiarelli
William H. Baughman, Jr.
James S. Gallas
Vernelis K. Armstrong
George J. Limbert

SOUTHERN DISTRICT

Mark R. Abel
Michael R. Merz
Timothy S. Hogan
Norah McCann King
Terence P. Kemp
Sharon L. Ovington

Recalled Magistrate Judge

David S. Perelman (Northern)

UNITED STATES BANKRUPTCY COURTS OF OHIO

NORTHERN DISTRICT

Chief Judge

William T. Bodoh

Judges

Richard Lyle Speer
Marilyn Shea-Stonum
Russ Kendig
Arthur I. Harris
Randolph Baxter
Pat Morgenstern-Clarren
Mary Ann Whipple

Bankruptcy Clerk

Kenneth J. Hirz
3001 Key Tower
127 Public Square
Cleveland, Ohio 44114-1309
(216) 522-4373

UNITED STATES DISTRICT COURTS DISTRICTS OF OHIO—*Continued*

SOUTHERN DISTRICT

Chief Judge

Thomas F. Waldron

Judges

Barbara Jackson Sellers
J. Vincent Aug, Jr.
Charles M. Caldwell
Jeffery P. Hopkins
John E. Hoffman, Jr.

Recalled Judges

Burton Perlman
William A. Clark
Donald E. Calhoun, Jr.

Bankruptcy Clerk

Michael D. Webb
120 West Third Street
Dayton, Ohio 45402
(937) 225-2516

SUPREME COURT OF OHIO

The Supreme Court is Ohio's court of last resort. The court consists of a chief justice and six justices. Justices are nominated in partisan primaries but run on nonpartisan ballots at general elections for six-year terms. Vacancies occurring between elections are filled by the governor. Retirement is mandatory at the end of the term in which a justice turns seventy; however, retired justices may serve by assignment of the chief justice.

The court has appellate jurisdiction over cases which originate in the Courts of Appeals, involve the death penalty, involve state or federal constitutional law and cases which are significant or of public interest from any lower court. The court has exclusive appellate jurisdiction over appeals from the Public Utilities Commission and concurrent appellate jurisdiction with the Courts of Appeals over appeals from the Board of Tax Appeals. The court has original jurisdiction over matters relating to the practice of law and admission to the bar in Ohio. The court may issue writs necessary to the exercise of proper jurisdiction and exercises rule-making authority and general superintending control over all courts in the state.

The court sits en banc at Columbus.

Chief Justice

Thomas J. Moyer

Justices

Alice Robie Resnick	Francis E. Sweeney
Paul E. Pfeifer	Deborah L. Cook
Evelyn Lundberg Stratton	Maureen O'Connor

Clerk

Marcia J. Mengel
30 East Broad Street, Second Floor
Columbus, Ohio 43215-3431
(614) 466-3931

Administrative Director

Steven C. Hollon
30 East Broad Street, Third Floor
Columbus, Ohio 43215-3414
(614) 466-2653

OHIO COURTS OF APPEALS

The Courts of Appeals are Ohio's courts of intermediate appellate jurisdiction. The state is divided into twelve appellate districts, with at least three judges serving each district. Judges are nominated in partisan primaries but run on nonpartisan ballots at general elections for six-year terms. Vacancies occurring between elections are filled by the governor. Retirement is mandatory at the end of the term in which a judge turns seventy; however, retired judges may serve by assignment of the chief justice.

The courts have appellate jurisdiction over matters of law and in some cases hear appeals on questions of both law and fact. The courts have jurisdiction over cases appealed from the Courts of Common Pleas, County Courts, Municipal Courts and the Court of Claims and over actions of administrative officers and agencies. The courts have concurrent appellate jurisdiction with the Supreme Court over appeals from the Board of Tax Appeals. The courts may issue writs necessary to the exercise of proper jurisdiction.

Judges sit in panels of three. The courts sit at the county seats within each appellate district on prescribed days or as the need arises.

FIRST DISTRICT includes Hamilton County. The court sits at Cincinnati.

Judges

Rupert A. Doan	Robert H. Gorman
Lee H. Hildebrandt, Jr.	Mark P. Painter
Ralph Winkler	J. Howard Sundermann, Jr.

SECOND DISTRICT includes Champaign, Clark, Darke, Greene, Miami and Montgomery counties. The court sits at Urbana, Springfield, Greenville, Xenia, Troy and Dayton.

Judges

James A. Brogan
Mike Fain
Thomas J. Grady
William H. Wolff, Jr.
Frederick N. Young

THIRD DISTRICT includes Allen, Auglaize, Crawford, Defiance, Hancock, Hardin, Henry, Logan, Marion, Mercer, Paulding, Putnam, Seneca, Shelby, Union, Van Wert and Wyandot counties. The court sits at Lima, Wapakoneta, Bucyrus, Defiance, Findlay, Kenton, Napoleon, Bellefontaine, Marion, Celina, Paulding, Ottawa, Tiffin, Sidney, Marysville, Van Wert and Upper Sandusky.

Judges

Thomas F. Bryant
Robert Richard Cupp
Stephen R. Shaw
Sumner E. Walters

FOURTH DISTRICT includes Adams, Athens, Gallia, Highland, Hocking, Jackson, Lawrence, Meigs, Pickaway, Pike, Ross, Scioto, Vinton and Washington counties. The court sits at West Union, Athens, Gallipolis, Hillsboro, Logan, Jackson, Ironton, Pomeroy, Circleville, Waverly, Chillicothe, Portsmouth, McArthur and Marietta.

OHIO COURTS OF APPEALS—*Continued*

Judges

Peter B. Abele
David T. Evans
William H. Harsha
Roger L. Kline

FIFTH DISTRICT includes Ashland, Coshocton, Delaware, Fairfield, Guernsey, Holmes, Knox, Licking, Morgan, Morrow, Muskingum, Perry, Richland, Stark and Tuscarawas counties. The court sits at Ashland, Coshocton, Delaware, Lancaster, Cambridge, Millersburg, Mount Vernon, Newark, McConnelsville, Mount Gilead, Zanesville, New Lexington, Mansfield, Canton and New Philadelphia.

Judges

John F. Boggins
Julie A. Edwards
Sheila G. Farmer
W. Scott Gwin
William B. Hoffman
John W. Wise

SIXTH DISTRICT includes Erie, Fulton, Huron, Lucas, Ottawa, Sandusky, Williams and Wood counties. The court sits at Sandusky, Wauseon, Norwalk, Toledo, Port Clinton, Fremont, Bryan and Bowling Green.

Judges

Peter M. Handwork
Richard W. Knepper
Judith Ann Lanzinger
Mark L. Pietrykowski
Arlene Singer

SEVENTH DISTRICT includes Belmont, Carroll, Columbiana, Harrison, Jefferson, Mahoning, Monroe and Noble counties. The court sits at St. Clairsville, Carrollton, Lisbon, Cadiz, Steubenville, Youngstown, Woodsfield and Caldwell.

Judges

Mary DeGenaro
Gene Donofrio
Joseph J. Vukovich
Cheryl L. Waite

EIGHTH DISTRICT includes Cuyahoga County. The court sits at Cleveland.

Judges

Patricia Ann Blackmon
Anthony Calabrese, Jr.
Frank D. Celebrezze, Jr.
Colleen Conway Cooney
Michael J. Corrigan
Ann Dyke
Sean C. Gallagher
Diane J. Karpinski
Anne L. Kilbane
Timothy E. McMonagle
Kenneth A. Rocco
James J. Sweeney

NINTH DISTRICT includes Lorain, Medina, Summit and Wayne counties. The court sits at Elyria, Medina, Akron and Wooster.

Judges

William R. Baird
William G. Batchelder
Donna J. Carr
Lynn C. Slaby
Beth Whitmore

TENTH DISTRICT includes Franklin County. The court sits at Columbus.

Judges

Donna Bowman
Susan Brown
Peggy L. Bryant
Dana Deshler
William A. Klatt
Cynthia C. Lazarus
Charles R. Petree
Lisa L. Sadler

ELEVENTH DISTRICT includes Ashtabula, Geauga, Lake, Portage and Trumbull counties. The court sits at Jefferson, Chardon, Painesville, Ravenna and Warren.

Judges

Judith A. Christley
Donald R. Ford
Diane V. Grendell
William M. O'Neill
Cynthia Westcott Rice

TWELFTH DISTRICT includes Brown, Butler, Clermont, Clinton, Fayette, Madison, Preble and Warren counties. The court sits at Georgetown, Hamilton, Batavia, Wilmington, Washington Court House, London, Eaton and Lebanon.

Judges

Stephen W. Powell
Anthony Valen
James E. Walsh
William W. Young

OHIO COURTS OF COMMON PLEAS

The Courts of Common Pleas are Ohio's courts of general jurisdiction, with one court established in each county. The judges of each court are nominated in partisan primaries but run on nonpartisan ballots at general elections for six-year terms. Vacancies occurring between elections are filled by the governor. Retirement is mandatory at the end of the term in which a judge turns seventy; however, retired judges may serve by assignment of the chief justice.

The courts have original jurisdiction over civil cases in which the amount in controversy exceeds $500 and over all criminal felony cases. The courts also exercise jurisdiction over juvenile, domestic relations and probate matters. In some counties, separate divisions have been created within the courts to handle these cases. Juvenile Divisions of the courts have exclusive original jurisdiction over children under age eighteen, including juvenile delinquency and dependency and neglect cases, as well as adult cases involving paternity, child abuse, nonsupport, contributing to the delinquency of minors and failure to send children to school. Domestic Relations Divisions handle all proceedings involving divorce or dissolution of marriage, annulment, separation, alimony, child custody and support and visitation rights. Family Divisions handle both juvenile and domestic relations matters. Probate Divisions have jurisdiction over probate of wills, supervision of estates and guardianships, adoption proceedings, determination of insanity or mental competence, issuance of marriage licenses and certain eminent domain matters. In those counties which do not have a separate Juvenile, Domestic Relations or Family Division, the Probate Division also handles juvenile matters. The courts have appellate jurisdiction over cases involving orders from most administrative agencies, including the Liquor Control Commission. These appeals are filed with the Court of Common Pleas of Franklin County. Appeals involving licensing, other than liquor and admission to examinations, are filed in the court of the

OHIO COURTS OF COMMON PLEAS—*Continued*

county in which the business or applicant resides. Appeals from the Courts of Common Pleas are heard on the record in the Courts of Appeals.

The courts sit at each county seat.

County	Judge
Adams	David D. Wilson
Allen	David R. Kinworthy
	Jeffrey L. Reed
	Matt C. Staley
	Richard K. Warren
Ashland	Jeffrey L. Runyan
	Damian J. Vercillo
Ashtabula	Charles G. Hague
	Alfred W. Mackey
	Ronald W. Vettel
	Gary L. Yost
Athens	L. Alan Goldsberry
	Robert William Stewart
	Michael W. Ward
Auglaize	Frederick D. Pepple
	Mark E. Spees
Belmont	J. Mark Costine
	Jennifer L. Sargus
	John M. Solovan, II
Brown	Margaret A. Clark
	Robert Alan Corbin
Butler	H. J. Bressler
	Ronald Richard Craft
	Matthew J. Crehan
	Sharon L. Kennedy
	David J. Niehaus
	Patricia Shanes Oney
	Charles Lloyd Pater
	Randy T. Rogers
	Michael J. Sage
	Keith Spaeth
	Leslie C. Spillane
Carroll	William J. Martin
	John H. Weyand
Champaign	John C. Newlin
	Roger B. Wilson
Clark	Thomas J. Capper
	Richard P. Carey
	Gerald F. Lorig
	Joseph N. Monnin
	Richard O'Neill
Clermont	Jerry R. McBride
	Robert P. Ringland
	Michael J. Voris
	William Walker
	Stephanie Wyler
Clinton	G. Allen Gano
	John William Rudduck
Columbiana	Thomas M. Baronzzi
	C. Ashley Pike
	David Tobin
Coshocton	Richard I. Evans
	C. Fenning Pierce
Crawford	Steven Douglas Eckstein
	Russell Benson Wiseman
Cuyahoga	Chris Boyko
	Mary J. Boyle
	Janet E. Burney
	Janet R. Burnside
	Kenneth R. Callahan
Cuyahoga—Cont.	James P. Celebrezze
	Brian J. Corrigan
	John E. Corrigan
	Patrick F. Corrigan
	William J. Coyne
	John J. Donnelly
	Timothy M. Flanagan
	Alison L. "Nelson" Floyd
	Carolyn B. Friedland
	Stuart A. Friedman
	Nancy A. Fuerst
	Eileen Gallagher
	John W. Gallagher
	Daniel Gaul
	Lillian J. Greene
	Burt W. Griffin
	Peggy Foley Jones
	Cheryl S. Karner
	Judith Kilbane Koch
	Ann T. Mannen
	David T. Matia
	Bridget M. McCafferty
	Timothy P. McCormick
	Nancy R. McDonnell
	Timothy J. McGinty
	Christine T. McMonagle
	Richard J. McMonagle
	John Peter O'Donnell
	Kathleen O'Malley
	Thomas J. Pokorny
	Anthony J. Russo
	Joseph D. Russo
	Joseph F. Russo
	Michael Joseph Russo
	Nancy Margaret Russo
	Shirley Strickland Saffold
	Peter M. Sikora
	Ronald Suster
	John D. Sutula
	Kathleen Ann Sutula
	Jose A. Villanueva
	vacancy
Darke	Jonathan P. Hein
	Michael Douglas McClurg
Defiance	Stephen W. Ruyle
	Joseph N. Schmenk
Delaware	Everett H. Krueger
	Kenneth Jerome Spicer
	William Duncan Whitney
Erie	Robert C. DeLamatre
	Ann B. Maschari
	Beverly K. McGookey
Fairfield	Joseph T. Clark
	S. Farrell Jackson
	Chris Allen Martin
	Steven O. Williams
Fayette	Nancy D. Hammond
	Victor D. Pontious, Jr.
Franklin	Lawrence A. Belskis
	John P. Bessey
	Kim Alana Browne
	Jennifer L. Brunner
	David E. Cain
	John A. Connor
	Dale A. Crawford
	David W. Fais
	Daniel T. Hogan

OHIO COURTS OF COMMON PLEAS—*Continued*

Franklin—Cont.	David L. Johnson
	Katherine S. Lias
	James W. Mason
	Patrick M. McGrath
	Nodine Miller
	Deborah (Piperni) O'Neill
	Beverly Y. Pfeiffer
	Dana S. Preisse
	Richard S. Sheward
	Carole R. Squire
	Alan C. Travis
	Michael H. Watson
	vacancy
Fulton	James E. Barber
	Michael J. Bumb
Gallia	D. Dean Evans
	William S. Medley
Geauga	Forrest W. Burt
	Charles E. Henry
	H. F. Inderlied, Jr.
Greene	Joseph Timothy Campbell
	Robert A. Hagler
	Steven Leroy Hurley
	Robert W. Hutcheson
	Stephen Arthur Wolaver
Guernsey	David A. Ellwood
	Robert S. Moorehead, Jr.
Hamilton	Kim Wilson Burke
	James Charles Cissell
	Thomas H. Crush
	Penelope R. Cunningham
	David P. Davis
	Patrick T. Dinkelacker
	Dennis S. Helmick
	Sylvia Sieve Hendon
	Charles J. Kubicki, Jr.
	Thomas R. Lipps
	Melba D. Marsh
	Steven E. Martin
	Norbert A. Nadel
	Frederick Dickson Nelson
	Richard A. Niehaus
	Ronald A. Panioto
	Robert P. Ruehlman
	Mark R. Schweikert
	Robert Edward Taylor
	Susan Laker Tolbert
	Ann Marie Tracey
	John Andrew West
Hancock	Allan H. Davis
	Joseph H. Niemeyer
	Reginald J. Routson
Hardin	David C. Faulkner
	James S. Rapp
Harrison	Michael K. Nunner
	Matthew Paul Puskarich
Henry	Keith P. Muehlfeld
Highland	Kevin L. Greer
	Jeffrey J. Hoskins
Hocking	Thomas H. Gerken
	Frederick E. Mong
Holmes	Thomas C. Lee
	Thomas D. White
Huron	Timothy Lee Cardwell
	Earl R. McGimpsey
Jackson	Leonard F. Holzapfel
	Stephen D. Michael
Jefferson	Joseph J. Bruzzese, Jr.
	David Earl Henderson
	Samuel W. Kerr
Knox	Otho S. Eyster
	James M. Ronk
Lake	Richard L. Collins, Jr.
	Colleen Ann Falkowski
	Theodore R. Klammer
	Eugene A. Lucci
	Paul H. Mitrovich
	Martin O. Parks
	William W. Weaver
Lawrence	Frank J. McCown
	C. David Payne
	W. Richard Walton
Licking	Robert H. Hoover
	Jon R. Spahr
	Russell A. Steiner
Logan	Michael L. Brady
	Mark S. O'Connor
Lorain	David A. Basinski
	Mark A. Betleski
	Debra L. Boros
	Kosma J. Glavas
	Frank J. Horvath
	Thomas W. Janas
	Paulette J. Lilly
	Lynett McGough
	Edward M. Zaleski
Lucas	James D. Bates
	J. Ronald Bowman
	Robert G. Christiansen
	Charles J. Doneghy
	Joseph A. Flores
	Ruth Ann Franks
	James D. Jensen
	David Lewandowski
	Frederick H. McDonald
	Jack R. Puffenberger
	James Ray
	William J. Skow
	Charles S. Wittenberg
	Norman G. Zemmelman
	vacancy
Madison	Glenn S. Hamilton
	Robert D. Nichols
Mahoning	Maureen A. Cronin
	F. Theresa Dellick
	John M. Durkin
	James C. Evans
	R. Scott Krichbaum
	Robert G. Lisotto
	Timothy P. Maloney
	Beth A. Smith
Marion	Deborah A. Alspach
	Robert S. Davidson
	Thomas K. Jenkins
	Richard M. Rogers
Medina	Christopher Collier
	James L. Kimbler
	Mary R. Kovack
	John Joseph Lohn
Meigs	Fred W. Crow, III
	Larry Scott Powell

OHIO COURTS OF COMMON PLEAS—*Continued*

Mercer	Jeffrey R. Ingraham
	Mary Patricia Zitter
Miami	Robert J. Lindeman
	Lynnita K. C. Wagner
	Jeffrey M. Welbaum
Monroe	William D. Harris
	Walter R. Starr
Montgomery	Denise Martin Cross
	Giles Jackson Davis, Jr.
	Mary E. Donovan
	Jeffrey E. Froelich
	Barbara P. Gorman
	David A. Gowdown
	Michael T. Hall
	Mary Katherine Huffman
	John W. Kessler
	Judy King
	Nick Kuntz
	Dennis J. Langer
	Alice O. McCollum
	Michael B. Murphy
	Michael Tucker
	A. J. Wagner
Morgan	Dan W. Favreau
Morrow	Howard E. Hall
Muskingum	Mark C. Fleegle
	Joseph A. Gormley
	Jeffrey A. Hooper
	Howard S. Zwelling
Noble	John W. Nau
Ottawa	Kathleen Luebke Giesler
	Paul Clinton Moon
Paulding	Russell J. McMaster
	J. David Webb
Perry	Luann Cooperrider
	Linton D. Lewis, Jr.
Pickaway	P. Randall Knece
	Jan Michael Long
Pike	William Wray Bevens
	Cassandra S. Bolt-Meredith
Portage	Thomas J. Carnes
	John A. Enlow
	Jerry L. Hayes
	Joseph R. Kainrad
Preble	David N. Abruzzo
	Wilfrid Gavin Dues
Putnam	Randall L. Basinger
	Daniel R. Gerschutz
Richland	James DeWeese
	James D. Henson
	Philip Alan Mayer
	Ronald Spon
Ross	William J. Corzine
	Nicholas H. Holmes, Jr.
	Richard G. Ward
Sandusky	Brad Culbert
	Harry A. Sargeant, Jr.
	James Robert Sherck
Scioto	Howard H. Harcha, III
	James Wilson Kirsch
	William T. Marshall
	David E. Spears
Seneca	Michael Paul Kelbley
Seneca—Cont.	Paul F. Kutscher, Jr.
	Steve C. Shuff
Shelby	John D. Schmitt
	Norman P. Smith
Stark	Charles E. Brown, Jr.
	John G. Haas
	John R. Hoffman
	Robert Davis Horowitz
	Jim D. James
	Sara E. Lioi
	Richard D. Reinbold Jr.
	Lee Sinclair
	David E. Stucki
Summit	Jane Bond
	Patricia A. Cosgrove
	Carol J. Dezso
	James E. Murphy
	John Patrick Quinn, Jr.
	Marvin A. Shapiro
	Mary F. Spicer
	W. F. "Bill" Spicer
	Linda Tucci Teodosio
	Brenda Burnham Unruh
	James R. Williams
Trumbull	Richard L. James
	Peter J. Kontos
	Andrew D. Logan
	Walter W. McKay
	Pamela A. Rintala
	John M. Stuard
	Thomas A. Swift
Tuscarawas	Linda A. Kate
	Edward Emmett O'Farrell
	Elizabeth Lehigh Thomakos
Union	Charlotte M. Eufinger
	Richard E. Parrott
Van Wert	Rex D. Fortney
	Charles D. Steele
Vinton	N. Robert Grillo
	Jeffrey L. Simmons
Warren	Neal B. Bronson
	James Larry Flannery
	Michael E. Powell
	vacancy
Washington	Susan E. Boyer
	N. Edward Lane, Jr.
	Timothy A. Williams
Wayne	Robert J. Brown
	Raymond E. Leisy
	Mark K. Wiest
Williams	Steven R. Bird
	Anthony L. Gretick
Wood	Reeve Kelsey
	Alan Reed Mayberry
	Robert C. Pollex
	David E. Woessner
Wyandot	Kathleen A. Aubry

OHIO COURT OF CLAIMS

The Court of Claims consists of retired and active judges of the Supreme Court, Courts of Appeals and Courts of Common Pleas as assigned by the chief justice of the Supreme Court.

The court has exclusive original statewide jurisdiction over civil cases for claims against the state of Ohio, ex-

OHIO COURT OF CLAIMS—*Continued*

clusive original and appellate jurisdiction to determine compensation for victims of violent crime and exclusive jurisdiction over all civil cases that are initiated in other courts and removed to the Court of Claims. In victim compensation proceedings, appeals are to a single judge of the court. A panel of three judges may hear some cases involving complex issues of law or fact.

The court sits at Columbus but may sit in any county at the discretion of the chief justice of the Supreme Court.

OHIO MUNICIPAL COURTS

The Municipal Courts are courts of limited jurisdiction in Ohio. Judges are nominated by partisan primary or nominating petition and run on nonpartisan ballots at general elections, unless provisions of the city charter indicate otherwise. All judges are elected for six-year terms and may serve full or part time as provided by statute. Vacancies occurring between elections are filled by the governor. Retirement is mandatory at the end of the term in which a judge turns seventy; however, retired judges may serve by assignment of the chief justice.

The courts have jurisdiction in civil cases in which the amount in controversy does not exceed $15,000 and in criminal cases in which the sentence does not exceed one year. The courts may also conduct felony preliminary hearings. Appeals are heard on the record in the Courts of Appeals.

Municipal Court	Judge
Akron	Lynne S. Callahan John E. Holcomb Alison McCarty Carla D. Moore Elinore Marsh Stormer vacancy
Alliance	Robert G. Lavery
Ashland	Jacob M. Fridline
Ashtabula	Albert S. Camplese
Athens County Court sits at Athens	Douglas J. Bennett
Auglaize County Court sits at Wapakoneta	Gary W. Herman
Avon Lake	John F. Mackin
Barberton	Michael J. McNulty Michael L. Weigand
Batavia	See Clermont County
Bedford	Peter J. Junkin Brian J. Melling
Bellefontaine	John L. Ross
Bellevue	Kenneth P. Fox
Berea	Mark A. Comstock
Bowling Green	Mark B. Reddin
Brown County Court sits at Georgetown	Thomas F. Zachman vacancy
Bryan	Kent L. North
Bucyrus	See Crawford County
Cambridge	John M. Nicholson
Campbell	John P. Almasy
Canton	Stephen F. Belden Mary A. Falvey
Canton—Cont.	Richard J. Kubilus John A. Poulos James J. Scheer Susan Fornof-Lippencott
Celina	Craig Steven Albert
Champaign County Court sits at Urbana	
Chardon	
Chesapeake	See Lawrence County
Chillicothe	Thomas E. Bunch John B. Street
Cincinnati	See Hamilton County
Circleville	John R. Adkins
Clark County Court sits at Springfield	Susan H. Anderson Denise L. Moody Eugene S. Nevius
Clermont County Court sits at Batavia	Victor M. Haddad Thomas R. Herman James A. Shriver
Cleveland	Ronald Bruce Adrine C. Ellen Connally Emanuella D. Groves Mabel M. Jasper Larry A. Jones Kathleen A. Keough Mary Eileen Kilbane Ralph J. Perk, Jr. Raymond L. Pianka Angela R. Stokes Robert J. Triozzi Joseph Zone vacancy
Cleveland Heights	A. Deane Buchanan
Clinton County Court sits at Wilmington	Chad L. Carey
Columbiana County Court sits at Lisbon	Mark A. Frost Robert C. Roberts
Columbus	See Franklin County
Conneaut	Thomas E. Harris
Coshocton	David L. Hostetler
Crawford County Court sits at Bucyrus	James L. Hoover
Cuyahoga Falls	Kim R. Hoover vacancy
Dayton	James F. Cannon Daniel G. Gehres Bill C. Littlejohn John S. Pickrel vacancy
Defiance	John T. Rohrs, III
Delaware	David Sunderman
East Cleveland	Una H. R. Keenon
East Liverpool	Melissa Byers-Emmerling
Eaton	Paul D. Henry
Elyria	George H. Ferguson John R. Musson
Euclid	Deborah A. LeBarron
Fairborn	Catherine M. Barber
Fairfield	Joyce A. Campbell
Fairfield County Court sits at Lancaster	vacancy vacancy
Findlay	Vernon L. Preston Kevin C. Smith
Fostoria	John D. Hadacek

OHIO MUNICIPAL COURTS—*Continued*

Franklin	James D. Ruppert
Franklin County Court sits at Columbus	Michael T. Brandt
	James J. Fais
	Mark S. Froehlich
	James E. Green
	Janet A. Grubb
	Harland Hanna Hale
	Steven B. Hayes
	Bruce Jenkins
	Teresa L. Liston
	W. Dwayne Maynard
	H. William Pollitt, Jr.
	Marvin S. Romanoff
	Charles A. Schneider
	Anne Taylor
	Scott D. VanDerKarr
Fremont	Michael L. Burkett
Gallipolis	vacancy
Garfield Heights	Deborah J. Nicastro
	Jennifer P. Weiler
Girard	Michael A. Bernard
Hamilton	John G. Rosmarin
Hamilton County Court sits at Cincinnati	Lisa Conway Allen
	Nadine L. Allen
	Timothy S. Black
	John H. Burlew
	Ethna M. Cooper
	Karla J. Grady
	Cheryl D. Grant
	Guy C. Guckenberger
	William L. Mallory, Jr.
	Elizabeth B. Mattingly
	Heather S. Russell
	David C. Stockdale
	Ralph E. Winkler
	Robert C. Winkler
Hardin County Court sits at Kenton	William D. Hart
Hillsboro	David H. McKenna
Hocking County Court sits at Logan	Richard M. Wallar
Huron	Ralph C. Pisano, Jr.
Ironton	Oakley C. Collins, Jr.
Jackson County Court sits at Jackson	Lorene G. Johnston
Kent	See Portage County
Kenton	See Hardin County
Kettering	Thomas M. Hanna
	Robert L. Moore
Lakewood	Patrick Carroll
Lancaster	See Fairfield County
Lawrence County Court sits at Chesapeake	Donald R. Capper
Lebanon	Mark R. Bogen
Licking County Court sits at Newark	Michael F. Higgins
	Thomas M. Marcelain
Lima	William G. Lauber
	RicKard A. Workman
Logan	See Hocking County
London	See Madison County
Lorain	Mark Mihok
	Gus Nunez
Lyndhurst	Mary Kaye Bozza
Madison County Court sits at London	R. David Picken
Mansfield	Jerry E. Ault
	Jeff Payton
Marietta	Milt Nuzum
Marion	William R. Finnegan
Marysville	Michael Grigsby
Mason	George Parker
Massillon	Edward J. Elum
	Richard T. Kettler
Maumee	Gary L. Byers
Medina	Dale H. Chase
Mentor	John Frank Trebets
Miami County Court sits at Troy	Elizabeth Simms Gutmann
	Michael W. Hemm
Miamisburg	Robert E. Messham, Jr.
Middletown	Mark W. Wall
Morrow County Court sits at Mount Gilead	Lee W. McClelland
Mount Vernon	Paul E. Spurgeon
Napoleon	John S. Collier
Newark	See Licking County
New Philadelphia	Mary Wade Space
Newton Falls	Thomas L. Old
Niles	Thomas W. Townley
Norwalk	John S. Ridge
Oakwood	Robert L. Deddens
Oberlin	Thomas A. Januzzi
Oregon	Donald Z. Petroff
Ottawa County Court sits at Port Clinton	Frederick C. Hany, II
Painesville	Michael A. Cicconetti
Parma	Mary L. Dunning
	Timothy P. Gilligan
	Kenneth R. Spanagel
Perrysburg	S. Dwight Osterud
Portage County Court sits at Ravenna and Kent	Donald H. Martell
	Laurie J. Pittman
	Barbara Roush Watson
Port Clinton	See Ottawa County
Portsmouth	Russell Dee Kegley
	Richard T. Schisler
Ravenna	See Portage County
Rocky River	Donna C. Fitzsimmons
	Maureen A. Gravens
Sandusky	Erich J. O'Brien
Shaker Heights	K. J. Montgomery
Shelby	Jon Patrick Schaefer
Sidney	Donald G. Luce
South Euclid	Patricia Ann Kleri
Springfield	See Clark County
Steubenville	G. Daniel Spahn
Struthers	James R. Lanzo
Sylvania	Scott Ramey
Tiffin	Mark E. Repp
Toledo	Amy Berling
	Denise Ann Dartt
	Francis X. Gorman
	C. Allen McConnell

OHIO MUNICIPAL COURTS—*Continued*

Toledo—Cont.	Thomas J. Osowik Mary Grace Trimboli vacancy
Troy	See Miami County
Upper Sandusky	Thomas E. Osborn
Urbana	See Champaign County
Vandalia	Richard J. Bannister
Van Wert	Phil W. Campbell
Vermilion	Elizabeth Wakefield
Wadsworth	Stephen B. McIlvaine
Wapakoneta	See Auglaize County
Warren	Thomas P. Gysegem Terry Ivanchak
Washington Court House	Gary Creamer Stout
Wayne County Court sits at Wooster	D. William Evans, Jr. Stuart K. Miller
Willoughby	Larry Allen
Wilmington	See Clinton County
Wooster	See Wayne County
Xenia	Susan L. Goldie
Youngstown	Robert A. Douglas, Jr. Elizabeth A. Kobly Robert P. Milich
Zanesville	William D. Joseph

OHIO COUNTY COURTS

The County Courts have limited, countywide jurisdiction in those counties in Ohio which are not under the territorial jurisdiction of Municipal Courts. Judges are nominated by nominating petition and elected on nonpartisan ballots at general elections for six-year terms. All judges serve on a part-time basis. Retirement is mandatory at the end of the term in which a judge turns seventy; however, retired judges may serve by assignment of the chief justice.

The courts have exclusive original jurisdiction in civil cases in which the amount in controversy does not exceed $500 and original jurisdiction in civil cases in which the amount in controversy does not exceed $15,000. The courts exercise jurisdiction in forcible entry and detainer, traffic and nontraffic misdemeanor cases and small claims cases. The courts may also conduct felony preliminary hearings. Appeals are to the Courts of Appeals.

The courts sit at each county seat unless otherwise indicated.

County	Judge
Adams	Alan W. Foster
Ashtabula Court also sits at Geneva	Richard L. Stevens Robert S. Wynn
Belmont Court also sits at Bellaire and Martins Ferry	D. William Davis, Jr. Frank A. Fregiato Harry W. White
Butler Court also sits at Oxford and West Chester	J. B. Connaughton Robert A. Hendrickson Robert Hagen Lyons
Carroll	Charles A. Johnston
Darke	Gene R. Hoellrich Roger L. Hurley
Erie Court sits at Milan	Paul G. Lux
Fulton Court also sits at Swanton	James E. Hensal Colin J. McQuade
Harrison	vacancy
Highland Court sits at Greenfield	Robert J. Judkins
Holmes	Jane Ellen Irving
Jefferson Court sits at Dillonvale, Toronto and Wintersville	Michael C. Bednar Joseph M. Corabi David J. Scarpone
Mahoning Court also sits at Canfield and Sebring	David D'Apolito Joseph M. Houser Scott D. Hunter Diane S. Vettori
Meigs	Steven L. Story
Monroe	James W. Peters
Montgomery Court sits at Huber Heights and Trotwood	James A. Hensley, Jr. James A. Hensley, Sr. James L. Manning James D. Piergies Connie S. Price-Testerman
Morgan	Michael D. Lowe
Muskingum	Kelly J. Cottrill vacancy
Noble	Lucien Young, III
Paulding	Patrick H. Young
Perry	Dean L. Wilson
Pike	Randy D. Deering
Putnam	Ann R. Cunningham Michael E. O'Malley
Sandusky Court sits at Clyde and Woodville	Herbert E. Adams John P. Dewey
Trumbull Court sits at Brookfield and Cortland	Thomas A. Campbell Ronald J. Rice
Tuscarawas	Brad L. Hillyer
Vinton	vacancy
Warren	James J. Heath Dallas P. Powers

OHIO MAYOR'S COURTS

Mayor's Courts may be created by any municipality that does not have a Municipal Court. The courts have original jurisdiction over minor criminal cases, mainly traffic violations. The elected or appointed mayor presides over the Mayor's Court. The courts are not authorized to hold jury trials. Appeals are de novo to the Municipal or County Court having jurisdiction.

Ohio Counties and County Seats

Adams
West Union

Allen
Lima

Ashland
Ashland

Ashtabula
Jefferson

Athens
Athens

Auglaize
Wapakoneta

Belmont
St. Clairsville

Brown
Georgetown

Butler
Hamilton

Carroll
Carrollton

Champaign
Urbana

Clark
Springfield

Clermont
Batavia

Clinton
Wilmington

Columbiana
Lisbon

Coshocton
Coshocton

Crawford
Bucyrus

Cuyahoga
Cleveland

Darke
Greenville

Defiance
Defiance

Delaware
Delaware

Erie
Sandusky

Fairfield
Lancaster

Fayette
Washington Court House

Franklin
Columbus

Fulton
Wauseon

Gallia
Gallipolis

Geauga
Chardon

Greene
Xenia

Guernsey
Cambridge

Hamilton
Cincinnati

Hancock
Findlay

Hardin
Kenton

Harrison
Cadiz

Henry
Napoleon

Highland
Hillsboro

Hocking
Logan

Holmes
Millersburg

Huron
Norwalk

Jackson
Jackson

Jefferson
Steubenville

Knox
Mount Vernon

Lake
Painesville

Lawrence
Ironton

Licking
Newark

Logan
Bellefontaine

Lorain
Elyria

Lucas
Toledo

Madison
London

Mahoning
Youngstown

Marion
Marion

Medina
Medina

Meigs
Pomeroy

Mercer
Celina

Miami
Troy

Monroe
Woodsfield

Montgomery
Dayton

Morgan
McConnelsville

Morrow
Mount Gilead

Muskingum
Zanesville

Noble
Caldwell

Ottawa
Port Clinton

Paulding
Paulding

Perry
New Lexington

Pickaway
Circleville

Pike
Waverly

Portage
Ravenna

Preble
Eaton

Putnam
Ottawa

Richland
Mansfield

Ross
Chillicothe

Sandusky
Fremont

Scioto
Portsmouth

Seneca
Tiffin

Shelby
Sidney

Stark
Canton

Summit
Akron

Trumbull
Warren

COUNTIES AND COUNTY SEATS—*Continued*

Tuscarawas
New Philadelphia

Union
Marysville

Van Wert
Van Wert

Vinton
McArthur

Warren
Lebanon

Washington
Marietta

Wayne
Wooster

Williams
Bryan

Wood
Bowling Green

Wyandot
Upper Sandusky

NORTHERN DISTRICT
WESTERN DIVISION
EASTERN DIVISION
SOUTHERN DISTRICT
WESTERN DIVISION
EASTERN DIVISION
WILLIAMS
FULTON
LUCAS
OTTAWA
WOOD
HENRY
DEFIANCE
SANDUSKY
ERIE
LORAIN
CUYAHOGA
LAKE
GEAUGA
ASHTABULA
TRUMBULL
PORTAGE
SUMMIT
MEDINA
HURON
SENECA
PAULDING
PUTNAM
HANCOCK
ASHLAND
MAHONING
WAYNE
STARK
COLUMBIANA
WYANDOT
CRAWFORD
RICHLAND
VAN WERT
ALLEN
HARDIN
MARION
MORROW
HOLMES
TUSCARAWAS
CARROLL
JEFFERSON
MERCER
AUGLAIZE
LOGAN
UNION
KNOX
COSHOCTON
HARRISON
SHELBY
DELAWARE
LICKING
GUERNSEY
BELMONT
DARKE
MIAMI
CHAMPAIGN
MUSKINGUM
MADISON
FRANKLIN
CLARK
NOBLE
MONROE
PREBLE
MONTGOMERY
FAIRFIELD
PERRY
GREENE
PICKAWAY
MORGAN
FAYETTE
WASHINGTON
BUTLER
WARREN
CLINTON
HOCKING
ATHENS
VINTON
HAMILTON
CLERMONT
HIGHLAND
ROSS
PIKE
JACKSON
MEIGS
GALLIA
BROWN
ADAMS
SCIOTO
LAWRENCE

UNITED STATES DISTRICT COURTS DISTRICTS OF OHIO

WILLIAMS
FULTON
LUCAS
OTTAWA
WOOD
6
HENRY
DEFIANCE
SANDUSKY
ERIE
LORAIN
CUYAHOGA
8
LAKE
ASHTABULA
11
GEAUGA
TRUMBULL
PORTAGE
SENECA
HURON
PAULDING
PUTNAM
HANCOCK
MEDINA
SUMMIT
9
ASHLAND
MAHONING
VAN WERT
WYANDOT
CRAWFORD
RICHLAND
WAYNE
STARK
COLUMBIANA
3
ALLEN
HARDIN
MERCER
AUGLAIZE
MARION
MORROW
HOLMES
CARROLL
TUSCARAWAS
KNOX
JEFFERSON
LOGAN
SHELBY
UNION
COSHOCTON
HARRISON
7
DELAWARE
DARKE
5
LICKING
CHAMPAIGN
MIAMI
GUERNSEY
BELMONT
MADISON
FRANKLIN
MUSKINGUM
2
CLARK
10
PREBLE
MONTGOMERY
FAIRFIELD
PERRY
NOBLE
MONROE
GREENE
MORGAN
PICKAWAY
FAYETTE
WASHINGTON
HOCKING
BUTLER
WARREN
CLINTON
ROSS
ATHENS
12
VINTON
HAMILTON
CLERMONT
HIGHLAND
1
MEIGS
PIKE
JACKSON
4
GALLIA
BROWN
ADAMS
SCIOTO
LAWRENCE

DISTRICTS OF OHIO COURTS OF APPEALS

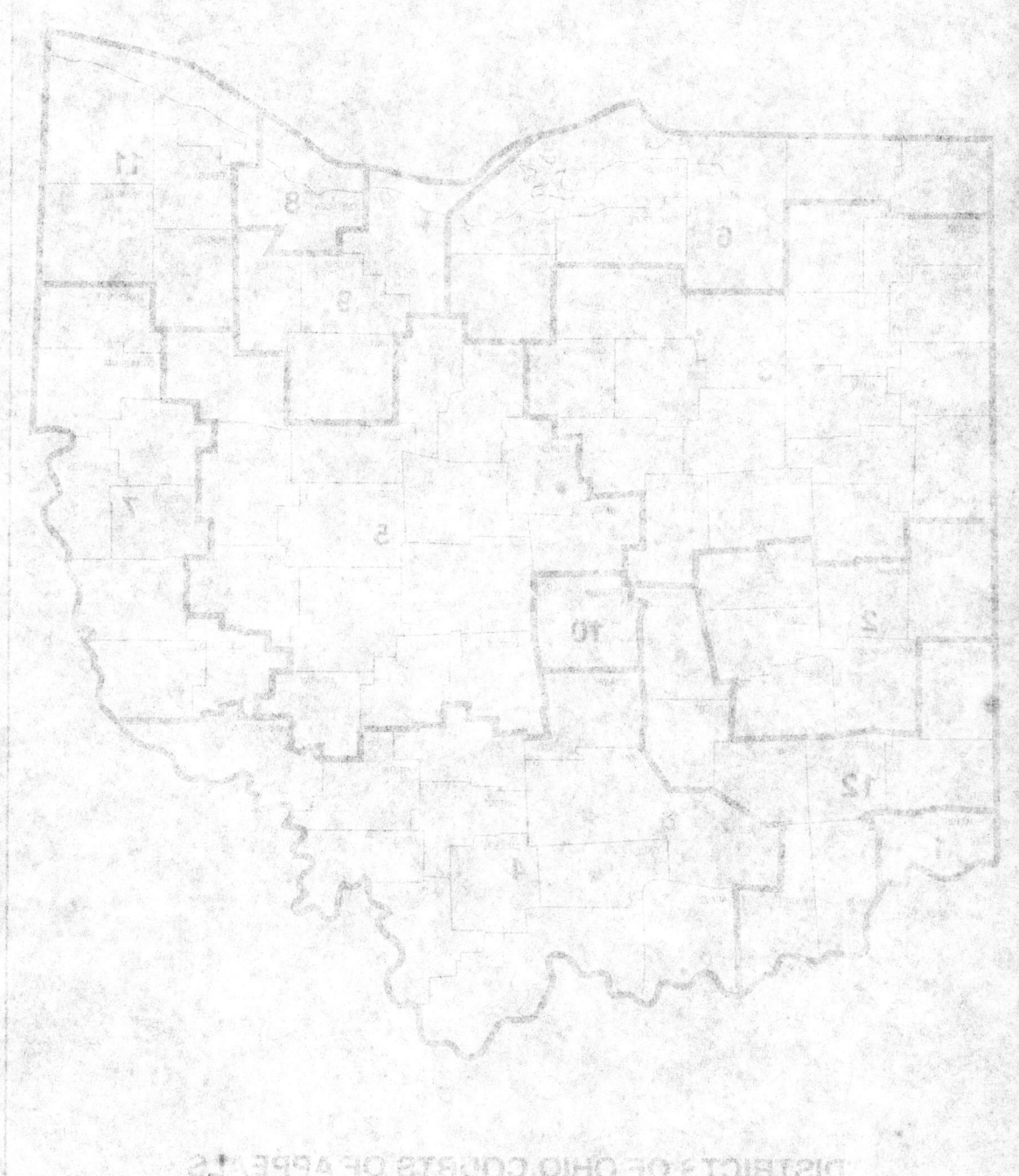

OHIO

ABEL, Mark R. *(Magistrate Judge, United States District Court Southern District of Ohio)* Appointed by U.S. District Court judges to term beginning 1971. Born Columbus Ohio July 28, 1944. Educated at Ohio University B.A. 1966 and The Ohio State University College of Law J.D. 1969. Law Clerk to Hon. Joseph P. Kinneary, U.S. District Court Southern District of Ohio 1969-71.

Member American Inns of Court, Columbus and Federal Bar Associations.

Office: 208 U.S. Courthouse, 85 Marconi Boulevard, Columbus 43215.

Telephone: (614) 719-3370.

ABELE, Peter B. *(Judge, Ohio Court of Appeals Fourth District)*

Office: Courthouse, Athens 45701.

Telephone: (740) 592-3247.

Fax: (740) 594-3303

E-mail address: pbabele@eurekanet.com

ABRUZZO, David N. *(Judge, Ohio Court of Common Pleas Preble County)* Elected to term beginning Jan 1, 1983. Reelected 1988, 1994 and 2000. Current term expires Dec 31, 2006. Born Detroit Michigan March 30, 1948. Catholic. Educated at Michigan State University B.A. with honors 1970 and The Ohio State University J.D. cum laude 1973. Admitted to practice Ohio 1973. Began legal practice Eaton.

Member Ohio Common Pleas Court Judges Association, Preble County, Ohio State and American (Judicial Administration Division) Bar Associations. Participant Ohio Judicial College. Republican. Enjoys sports and reading.

Office: 101 East Main Street, Eaton 45320-1791.

Telephone: (937) 456-8165.

Fax: (937) 456-9548

E-mail address: alice@preblecountyohio.net

ADAMS, Herbert E. *(Judge, Sandusky County Court)* Appointed by Governor Bob Taft to term beginning May 1, 2001. Born June 11, 1941. Educated at University of Illinois B.S. 1963 and Salmon P. Chase College of Law J.D. 1972. Admitted to practice Ohio 1972. In legal practice Gibsonburg and Fremont since 1973.

Office: 714 Court Street, Fremont 43420.

Telephone: (419) 355-1372.

Fax: (419) 332-1566

E-mail address: cooper-adams@core.com

ADAMS, John R. *(Judge, United States District Court Northern District of Ohio)* Appointed for life by President George W. Bush 2003. Born Orrville Ohio 1955. Educated at Bowling Green State University B.S. 1978 and University of Akron Law Center J.D. 1983. Law Clerk to Hon. W. F. "Bill" Spicer, Ohio Court of Common Pleas Summit County 1983-84. In legal practice Ohio 1984-99. Judge, Ohio Court of Common Pleas Summit County 1999-2003.

Office: 526 U.S. Courthouse, Two South Main Street, Akron 44308-1813.

Telephone: (330) 375-5900.

Fax: (330) 375-5875

ADKINS, John R. *(Judge, Circleville Municipal Court)*

Office: 151 East Franklin Street, Circleville 43113-0190.

Telephone: (740) 474-3175.

Fax: (740) 477-8291

E-mail address: cirmuncrt@earthlink.net

ADRINE, Ronald Bruce *(Judge, Cleveland Municipal Court)* Elected to term beginning Jan 1982. Reelected 1987, 1993 and 1999. Current term expires Jan 2006. Born April 21, 1947. Educated at Fisk University B.A. 1969 and Cleveland-Marshall College of Law Cleveland State University J.D. 1973. Admitted to practice Ohio, U.S. Supreme Court, U.S. Courts of Appeals Sixth and District of Columbia Circuits and U.S. District Court Northern District of Ohio. In legal practice Cleveland 1977-78 and 1979-82.

Assistant Prosecuting Attorney Cuyahoga County June 1974 to Jan 1977. Staff Counsel U.S. House of Representatives Select Committee on Assassinations June 1978 to April 1979. Attended The National Judicial College Limited Jurisdiction Course.

Mailing address: P.O. Box 94894, Cleveland 44101-4894.

Office: 1200 Ontario Street, Cleveland 44113-1645.

Telephone: (216) 664-4974.

Fax: (216) 664-6737

ALBERT, Craig Steven *(Judge, Chardon Municipal Court)* Elected to term beginning Jan 1, 1988. Reelected 1993 and 1999. Current term expires Dec 31, 2005. Born Cincinnati Ohio April 30, 1945. Jewish. Educated at University of Cincinnati B.B.A. 1967 and University of Texas J.D. 1970. Admitted to practice Ohio 1972 and U.S. District Court Northern District of Ohio 1974.

Office: 111 Water Street, Chardon 44024.

Telephone: (440) 286-2639.

Fax: (440) 286-2679

ALDRICH, Ann *(Senior Judge, United States District Court Northern District of Ohio)* Appointed for life by President Jimmy Carter to term beginning May 24, 1980. Assumed Senior status May 12, 1995, serves by assignment. Born Providence Rhode Island June 28, 1927. Educated at Columbia University B.A. 1948 and New York University LL.B. 1950 LL.M. 1964 J.S.D. 1967. In legal practice Washington D.C. 1952-53 and Darien Connecticut 1961-68.

Attorney General Counsel's Staff International Bank for Reconstruction and Development 1951-52 and Federal Communications Commission 1953-60. Civilian Attorney Subic Bay Naval Station 1954-56.

Office: 17B U.S. Courthouse, 801 West Superior Avenue, Cleveland 44113-1839.

Telephone: (216) 357-7200.

Fax: (216) 357-7205

ALLEN, Larry *(Judge, Willoughby Municipal Court)* Elected to term beginning Jan 1, 1994. Reelected Nov 1999, current term expires Dec 31, 2005. Born Emporium Pennsylvania Aug 18, 1938. Roman Catholic. Educated at Kent State University B.A. 1966 and Cleveland-

ALLEN, LARRY—*Continued*

Marshall College of Law J.D. 1971. Admitted to practice Ohio 1972, U.S. District Court Northern District of Ohio 1973, New York 1983, U.S. Supreme Court 1983 and U.S. Court of Appeals Sixth Circuit 1989. In legal practice Willoughby Ohio 1977-94.

Law Director and Prosecutor Willoughby 1979-92. State Certified Instructor Lakeland Community College Police Academy. Instructor in Criminal Law Lakeland Community College. Former Member Supreme Court Criminal Law and Procedures Committee, Local Government and Law Committee, Local Corrections Planning Committee, Advisory Committee on Substance Abuse and Court Procedures and New York State Bar Association. Member Association of Municipal and County Judges of Ohio (Ohio Supreme Court Alcohol and Drug Abuse Committee), Northern Ohio Municipal Judges Association (Past President), American Judges Association (Board of Governors), Lake County and Ohio State Bar Associations. Attended numerous legal and judicial conferences Ohio Judicial College, Ohio Supreme Court CLE and Harvard Law School CLE. USN. Administrative Vice President North Eastern Council Boy Scouts of America. President Willoughby Rotary. Honorary Member Lake County Association of Chiefs of Police. Member Knights of Columbus, AOPA and AARP. Enjoys flying airplanes and fishing.

Office: One Public Square, Willoughby 44094-7888.
Telephone: (440) 953-4183.
Fax: (440) 953-4149
E-mail address: judge@willoughbycourt.com

ALLEN, Lisa Conway *(Judge, Hamilton County Municipal Court)*

Office: Courthouse, 1000 Main Street, Cincinnati 45202.

ALLEN, Nadine L. *(Judge, Hamilton County Municipal Court)*

Office: 1000 Main Street, Cincinnati 45202.
Telephone: (513) 946-5154.
Fax: (513) 946-5157
E-mail address: nallen@cms.hamilton-co.org

ALMASY, John P. *(Judge, Campbell Municipal Court)*

Office: 351 Tenney Avenue, Campbell 44405-1603.
Telephone: (330) 755-2165.
Fax: (330) 750-3058

ALSPACH, Deborah A. *(Judge, Ohio Court of Common Pleas Marion County)* Serves Domestic Relations and Juvenile Divisions.

Office: Marion County Courthouse, Marion 43302-3089.
Telephone: (740) 387-8935.
Fax: (740) 382-3798
E-mail address: domrelations@acc-net.com

ANDERSON, Susan H. *(Judge, Clark County Municipal Court)* Appointed by Governor Richard F. Celeste to term beginning Jan 4, 1991. Elected Nov 1991 and Nov 1997. Current term expires Dec 31, 2003. Born Warren Ohio June 12, 1943. Lutheran. Educated at The Ohio State University B.A. 1963 and University of Dayton J.D. 1982. Law Clerk to Hon. Joseph D. Kerns, Ohio Court of Appeals Second District 1983-84. Admitted to practice U.S. District Court Southern District of Ohio 1982. In legal practice Springfield Ohio 1984-85.

Assistant Prosecutor Clark County 1985-90.

Office: 50 East Columbia Street, Springfield 45502.
Telephone: (937) 328-3768.
Fax: (937) 328-3755
E-mail address: sanderson@ci.springfield.oh.us

ARMSTRONG, Vernelis K. *(Magistrate Judge, United States District Court Northern District of Ohio)* Appointed by U.S. District Court judges.

Office: 318 U.S. Courthouse, 1716 Spielbusch Avenue, Toledo 43624.
Telephone: (419) 259-6217.

AUBRY, Kathleen A. *(Judge, Ohio Court of Common Pleas Wyandot County)*

Office: 109 South Sandusky Avenue, Room 34, Upper Sandusky 43351-1435.
Telephone: (419) 294-1727.
Fax: (419) 209-0251

AUG, J. Vincent, Jr. *(Judge, United States Bankruptcy Court Southern District of Ohio)* Also Judge, Bankruptcy Appellate Panel Sixth Circuit. Selected by the Judicial Council of the Sixth Circuit. Term expires 2004. Former Magistrate, U.S. District Court Southern District of Ohio.

Office: 800 Atrium II, 221 East Fourth Street, Cincinnati 45202.
Telephone: (513) 684-2572.

AULT, Jerry E. *(Judge, Mansfield Municipal Court)*

Office: 30 North Diamond Street, Mansfield 44902-1702.
Telephone: (419) 755-9622.
Fax: (419) 755-9650

BAIRD, William R. *(Judge, Ohio Court of Appeals Ninth District)* Assumed office Jan 3, 1983. Elected to subsequent terms. Born Akron Ohio Dec 29, 1934. Episcopalian. Educated at Amherst College A.B. 1956 and Case Western Reserve University J.S.D. 1959. Admitted to practice Ohio 1959. Judge, Ohio Court of Common Pleas Summit County Jan 1, 1977 to Jan 2, 1983.

Director of Law City of Akron 1966-76. Member Akron and American Bar Associations. Past President Ohio Municipal Attorneys Association. Sergeant USAR 1959-69. Councilman Fairlawn Ohio 1960-66.

Office: 161 South High Street, Fifth Floor, Akron 44308-1671.
Telephone: (330) 643-2250.
Fax: (330) 643-2091

BANNISTER, Richard J. *(Judge, Vandalia Municipal Court)*

Mailing address: P.O. Box 429, Vandalia 45377.
Office: 245 James E. Bohanan Memorial Drive, Vandalia 45377-2393.
Telephone: (937) 898-3996.
Fax: (937) 415-2222

BARBER, Catherine M. *(Judge, Fairborn Municipal Court)*

Office: 44 West Hebble Avenue, Fairborn 45324.
Telephone: (937) 754-3040.
Fax: (937) 879-4422

BARBER, James E. *(Judge, Ohio Court of Common Pleas Fulton County)* Appointed by Governor Richard F. Celeste to term beginning Dec 29, 1986. Elected 1986,

BARBER, JAMES E.—*Continued*

1992 and 1998. Current term expires Dec 31, 2004. Born Wauseon Ohio May 16, 1946. United Methodist. Educated at Northwestern University B.A. 1968 and University of Toledo J.D. 1973. Admitted to practice Ohio 1973 and U.S. District Court Northern District of Ohio 1975. In legal practice Wauseon 1973-86.

Law Director City of Wauseon 1982-86. Associate Editor *Courts, Health Science & Law*. Instructor Owens Technical College 1975-76. Fellow Ohio State Bar Foundation. Former Member The Association of Trial Lawyers of America. Member Ohio Judicial Conference, Ohio Common Pleas Judges Association, American Judges Association, Fulton County, Northwest Ohio, Ohio State and American Bar Associations. First Lieutenant U.S. Army 1969-72. Republican. Past Executive Secretary and Vice Chairman Corrections Commission Northwest Ohio. Past President and Board of Trustees Wauseon Public Library. District Representative Boy Scouts of America. Member 33° Scottish Rite and Masons.

Office: Courthouse, 210 South Fulton Street, Wauseon 43567.
Telephone: (419) 337-9260.
Fax: (419) 337-9293
E-mail address: jbarber@fultoncounty.oh.com

BARONZZI, Thomas M. *(Judge, Ohio Court of Common Pleas Columbiana County)* Serves Probate and Juvenile Divisions.

Office: 260 West Lincoln Way, Lisbon 44432.
Telephone: (330) 424-4071.
Fax: (330) 424-6670
E-mail address: judgepike@prodigy.net

BASINGER, Randall L. *(Judge, Ohio Court of Common Pleas Putnam County)*

Office: 245 East Main, Suite 302, Ottawa 45875-1968.
Telephone: (419) 523-6200.
Fax: (419) 523-5284
E-mail address: basinger@nwbright.net

BASINSKI, David A. *(Judge, Ohio Court of Common Pleas Lorain County)* Serves Domestic Relations Division.

Office: 226 Middle Avenue, Elyria 44035-5629.
Telephone: (440) 329-5365.
Fax: (440) 329-5438

BATCHELDER, William G. *(Judge, Ohio Court of Appeals Ninth District)* Appointed by Governor Bob Taft to term beginning March 15, 1999. Elected 2000, current term expires Feb 15, 2007. Born Medina Ohio Dec 19, 1942. Anglican. Educated at Ohio Wesleyan University B.A. 1964 and The Ohio State University College of Law J.D. 1967. Honorary Graduate University of Akron Law Center. National Moot Court Team. Member Tau Epsilon Rho. Admitted to practice Ohio 1967, U.S. District Court Northern District of Ohio and U.S. Court of Appeals Sixth Circuit. In legal practice Medina 1967-98. Judge, Ohio Court of Common Pleas Medina County Jan 2, 1999 to March 1999.

Adjunct Professor University of Akron Law Center 2000. Member Medina County, Summit County and Ohio State Bar Associations. Lecturer Continuing Legal Education at numerous judicial and bar associations. U.S. Army JAG 1968. Member Ohio House of Representatives 1968-99 (speaker pro tem two terms). Member American Legion, Vietnam Vets of America and Farm Bureau. Enjoys reading and jogging.

Office: 161 South High Street, Fifth Floor, Akron 44308-1671.
Telephone: (330) 643-2250.
Fax: (330) 643-2091
E-mail address: william@ninth.courts.state.oh.us

BATES, James D. *(Judge, Ohio Court of Common Pleas Lucas County)* Appointed by Governor Richard F. Celeste March 22, 1990. Elected Nov 1990, Nov 1994 and 2000. Current term expires Jan 3, 2007. Born Rome New York Sept 5, 1947. Lutheran. Educated at Ithaca College B.A. with honors 1969 and University of Toledo J.D. 1972. Admitted to practice Ohio 1972, U.S. Supreme Court 1980 and U.S. Court of Appeals Sixth Circuit 1984. In legal practice Toledo 1972-90.

Office: Lucas County Courthouse, 700 Adams Street, Toledo 43624-1678.
Telephone: (419) 213-4578.
Fax: (419) 213-4181

BAUGHMAN, William H., Jr. *(Magistrate Judge, United States District Court Northern District of Ohio)* Appointed by U.S. District Court judges to term beginning Feb 16, 2000. Term expires Feb 15, 2008. Born Greensburg Pennsylvania June 23, 1949. Roman Catholic. Educated at St. Vincent College B.A. 1971 and University of Notre Dame Law School J.D. 1974. Executive Editor Notre Dame Lawyer 1973-74. Law Clerk to Hon. Roger J. Kiley and Hon. John Paul Stevens, U.S. Court of Appeals Seventh Circuit Sept 1974 to Sept 1975. Admitted to practice Ohio 1974, U.S. Courts of Appeals Seventh 1975, Sixth 1978 and Third 1987 Circuits, U.S. District Courts Northern District of Ohio 1976 and Western District of Michigan 1996, U.S. Tax Court 1993 and U.S. Supreme Court 1994. In legal practice Cleveland 1976-2000.

Author Survey "Euthanasia: Criminal, Tort, Constitutional and Legislative Considerations" 48 No. 1202 Notre Dame Law 1227-1252, 1973; "Taking a Civil Appeal from the Trial Court to the Court of Appeals" *Ohio Appellate Practice* Ohio Legal Center Institute 1981; "Federal Cross Appeals—A Guide and a Proposal" 42 Ohio State L. Jour. 505, 1981; "The Appendix—Sixth Circuit Practice" 15 University of Toledo L. Rev. 949, 1984; "Effective Appellate Motions Practice" *The Appellate Process in Civil Cases* The Defense Research Institute, Inc. 1984; "Taking a Civil Appeal from a District Court to the Sixth Circuit" *Sixth Circuit Appellate Practice Institute Sourcebook* American Bar Association 1990; "Error in the Trial Court—Making a Record for Appeal" 64 Cleveland B. Jour. 302, 1993; "New Rules for the Supreme Court" 65 Cleveland B. Jour. 26 Aug 1994; "Statutory Privileges and Appellate Review—*Polikoff* Revisited" 68 Cleveland B. Jour. 12 Oct 1997; "The General Assembly Redefines 'Final Orders'" 69 Cleveland B. Jour. 28 June 1998; and "The Joint Appendix, Sixth Circuit Practice" *Sixth Circuit Federal Practice Manual 97* 2nd ed. 1999. Adjunct Professor of Ohio Appellate Practice Fall 1992 and Advanced Brief Writing and Oral Argument since 1994 Cleveland-Marshall College of Law. Life Member Judicial Conference of the Sixth Circuit. Chair Section of Litigation Cleveland Bar Association 1993-94. Master Bencher William K. Thomas Inn of Court since 2000. Attended National Session National Institute for Trial Advocacy

BAUGHMAN, WILLIAM H., JR.—*Continued*

Boulder Colorado 1977. USAR. Member University Heights Board of Zoning Appeals 1993-2000.

Office: U.S. Courthouse 10A, 801 West Superior Avenue, Cleveland 44113-1846.

Telephone: (216) 357-7220.

Fax: (216) 357-7224

E-mail address: Gudrun_Swoboda_Gazzo-@ohnd.uscourts.gov

BAXTER, Randolph *(Judge, United States Bankruptcy Court Northern District of Ohio)* Also Judge, Bankruptcy Appellate Panel Sixth Circuit. Selected by the Judicial Council of the Sixth Circuit.

Office: 3205 Key Tower, 127 Public Square, Cleveland 44114-1309.

Telephone: (216) 522-4373.

BECKWITH, Sandra S. *(Judge, United States District Court Southern District of Ohio)* Appointed for life by President George Bush to term beginning Feb 21, 1992. Born Norfolk Virginia Dec 4, 1943. Methodist. Educated at University of Cincinnati B.A. 1965 J.D. 1968. Admitted to practice Ohio 1969, Indiana 1976, U.S. District Courts Southern District of Ohio 1971 and Southern District of Indiana 1976, U.S. Supreme Court 1977 and Florida 1979. In legal practice Harrison Ohio 1969-77 and Cincinnati Ohio 1979-82 and 1986-92. Judge, Hamilton County Municipal Court 1977-79 and 1982-86. Judge, Ohio Court of Common Pleas Hamilton County 1986-89.

Commissioner 1989-92 and President 1991 Board of Commissioners Hamilton County. Author "Ohio Domestic Relations Law: Recent Developments" 74 No. 3. Women Lawyers Journal Spring 1988, "Domestic Relations Law Changing" Client Memorandum Graydon, Head & Ritchey Spring 1989, "Domestic Relations Hot Tips, Personal Residence: Tax Consequences" Domestic Relations Seminar Cincinnati Bar Association Jan 1990 and "Divorce Changes in the Works" Client Memorandum Graydon, Head & Ritchey Winter 1991. Important Decisions: G & C Langenbrunner, Inc. v. Davis Construction Co. et al. 21 Ohio Misc. 2d 11, 488 N.E.2d 506, 1984; Cincinnati Bell, Inc. v. Cooper d.b.a. Cooper Construction Co. 23 Ohio Misc. 2d 9, 491 N.E.2d 411, 1985; State Department of Mental Retardation and Developmental Disabilities Office of Support v. Moore 21 Ohio Misc. 2d 9, 21 O.B.R. 354, 487 N.E.2d 9, 1985; United States, ex rel. Pedicone v. Mazak Corp. 807 F. Supp. 1350, 1992; In re Suburban Motor Freight, Inc. 156 B.R. 790, 1992, aff'd 998 F.2d 338, 6th Cir. 1993; Morgan v. Rinehart 834 F. Supp. 233, 1992, aff'd without op. sub nom. Morgan v. Columbus 7 F.3d 234, 6th Cir. 1993; Wexell v. Komar Industries, Inc. 1993 WL 650863 Jan 12, 1993, aff'd 18 F.3d 916 Fed. Cir. 1993; United States v. Stith 824 F. Supp. 128, 1993, aff'd 1994 U.S. App. LEXIS 30157, 6th Cir. Oct 18, 1994; United States v. Moored 997 F.2d 139, 6th Cir. 1993; Petropoulos v. Columbia Gas of Ohio, Inc. 840 F. Supp. 511, 1993; James v. Runyan 868 F. Supp. 911, 1994; In re Cincinnati Radiation Litigation Case No. C-1-94-126, 1995 U.S. Dist. LEXIS 401, Jan 11, 1995; Buck v. Fries & Fries, Inc. 953 F. Supp. 896, 1996; In re Purdue 187 B.R. 188, 1995; and Kutschbach v. Davies 885 F. Supp. 1079, 1995.

Adjunct Professor of Appellate Advocacy University of Cincinnati College of Law. Member Code of Professional Responsibility Commission (established by Chief Justice Frank D. Celebrezze) 1984. Former Member Greater Cincinnati Women Lawyers' Association, The Lawyers Club, Ohio Academy of Trial Lawyers, The Association of Trial Lawyers of America, Ohio Municipal and County Judges Association (Chair Summer Conference 1983), National Association of Women Judges, The Florida Bar, Cincinnati (Chair Long Range Planning Task Force for CLE, Member CLE Committee and Attorney Assistance Committee), Dearborn-Ohio County, Indiana State and Ohio State Bar Associations. Attended Annual Seminar/Conferences National Association of Women Judges 1982-86, Annual Ohio Judges' Conferences 1982-89, Federal Judges School 1992, Sixth Circuit Conferences 1992 and 1994, Sixth and Eighth Circuit Seminar 1993 and Federal Judges Annual Seminar 1993. Recipient Betty Kuhn Memorial Prize for Top Woman Law Graduate 1965, awards for Superior Judicial Service from Ohio Supreme Court 1977, 1978, 1982, 1983 and 1984, Outstanding Achievement Award from Cincinnati Women's Political Caucus 1988, Women Helping Women Award from Soroptomists 1989 and A.C.E.S. for service to the children of Hamilton County 1989. Named Career Woman of Achievement by YWCA 1984. Republican. Chair Hamilton County Solid Waste Management Policy Committee and Ad Hoc Committee for the State Office Building. Advisory Board College of Business Administration Xavier University. Member ex officio Tender Mercies, Inc. Class Representative College of Law Alumni, Board Member Friends of Women's Studies and Board of Visitors University of Cincinnati. Board Member United Way of Cincinnati, Great Rivers Girl Scout Council and Red Cross. Member Governor's Committee on Prison Crowding 1984-90, Greater Cincinnati Sports & Special Events Commission, Ad Hoc Committee for Performing Arts Center, Coalition to Prevent Domestic Violence, The Cincinnatus Association, Hamilton County Republican Party Early Birds, Leadership Cincinnati Chamber of Commerce, Ohio Federation of Republican Women, Cincinnati Women's Political Caucus, League of Women Voters, Ohio Job Training Partnership, Inc. and Greater Cincinnati Film Commission. Interests include travel, history and antique collecting.

Office: 810 U.S. Courthouse, 100 East Fifth Street, Cincinnati 45202-3976.

Telephone: (513) 564-7610.

BEDNAR, Michael C. *(Judge, Jefferson County Court)* Elected Nov 3, 1998 to term beginning Jan 1, 1999. Term expires Dec 31, 2004. Born Martins Ferry Ohio Dec 23, 1958. Catholic. Educated at Kent State University B.G.S. with honors 1981 and University of Akron J.D. Admitted to practice Ohio 1984, West Virginia 1996, U.S. District Courts Southern District of Ohio 1986 and Northern 1996 and Southern 1996 Districts of West Virginia and U.S. Supreme Court 1999. In legal practice Steubenville Ohio since 1995.

Police Prosecutor Steubenville 1990-99. Village Solicitor Adena, Tiltonsville, Mt. Pleasant, Rayland and New Athens. Member Jefferson County (Former Treasurer, Secretary and Member Executive Board) and Ohio State Bar Associations. Member Jefferson County Township Trustee Association, Southern Jefferson County Party

BEDNAR, MICHAEL C.—*Continued*
Political Club, Jefferson County Farm Bureau, Pine Valley Sportsman Club and Indian Club.
Mailing address: P.O. Box 2207, Wintersville 43953-4136.
Telephone: (740) 264-7644.
Fax: (740) 264-6720
E-mail address: mbednar@blakehersheybednar.com

BELDEN, Stephen F. *(Judge, Canton Municipal Court)* Appointed by Governor George V. Voinovich to term beginning Jan 3, 1997. Elected Nov 2, 1999, current term expires Jan 1, 2006. Born Canton Ohio July 19, 1954. Roman Catholic. Educated at Marquette University B.A. summa cum laude 1976 and Case Western Reserve University J.D. 1979. Member Phi Beta Kappa and Alpha Sigma Nu. Admitted to practice Ohio 1979, South Carolina 1981, U.S. District Courts Northern District of Ohio 1987 and District of South Carolina and U.S. Courts of Appeals Sixth 1987 and Fourth Circuits. In legal practice Charleston South Carolina 1983-87 and Canton Ohio 1987-97.
Author "Hospitals, Nurses and 'Hired Guns': The Proposed Amendments to Evid. R. 601(D)" 26 No. 2 OACTA 1991. Member Stark County Bar Association (Grievance Committee 1990-93, Courts Arbitration Committee 1990-97, Criminal Law Committee since 1997). Commander USNR JAGC (retired). Board of Trustees Stark County Bluecoats. Member Canton Rotary Club and St. Michael Church. Enjoys golfing, running, sailing and reading.
Office: 218 Cleveland Avenue S.W., Canton 44702-1912.
Telephone: (330) 489-3214.
Fax: (330) 471-8860
E-mail address: sfbelden@ci.canton.oh.us

BELL, Samuel H. *(Senior Judge, United States District Court Northern District of Ohio)* Appointed for life by President Ronald Reagan to term beginning Dec 31, 1982. Assumed Senior status, serves by assignment. Born Rochester New York Dec 31, 1925. Presbyterian. Educated at College of Wooster B.A. 1947, American University and Akron University Law School J.D. 1952. Member Phi Alpha Theta. Admitted to practice Ohio 1952. Began legal practice Cuyahoga Falls 1956. Judge, Cuyahoga Falls Municipal Court 1968-73. Judge, Ohio Court of Common Pleas Summit County 1973-77. Judge, Ohio Court of Appeals Ninth District 1977-82.
Former Assistant Solicitor and Trial Counsel City of Tallmadge, Assistant Prosecuting Attorney Summit County and Special Counsel Attorney General Ohio. Former Member Ohio Municipal Judges Association, Ohio Common Pleas Judges Association and Ohio Appellate Judges Association. Fellow Akron Bar Foundation. Member Charles F. Scanlon American Inn of Court (President 1981-92), Federal Judges Association (Board of Directors), Akron and Ohio State Bar Associations. Recipient Distinguished Alumni Award from University of Akron Law Center 1983, St. Thomas More Award 1987 and Distinguished Alumni Award from University of Akron 1988. Trustee Deans Club. Member Advisory Board University of Akron School of Law.
Office: 433 U.S. Courthouse, Two South Main Street, Akron 44308-5836.
Telephone: (330) 375-5764.

BELSKIS, Lawrence A. *(Judge, Ohio Court of Common Pleas Franklin County)* Elected Nov 1990 to term beginning Feb 9, 1991. Reelected Nov 1996 and 2002. Current term expires Feb 2009. Serves Probate Division. Born Chicago Illinois Aug 10, 1946. Roman Catholic. Educated at DePauw University, Marquette University B.S. 1969 and Capital University J.D. 1975. Law Clerk to Probate Division Ohio Court of Common Pleas Franklin County 1972-75. Admitted to practice Ohio 1975, Florida 1976, U.S. District Court Southern District of Ohio 1976 and District of Columbia 1979. In legal practice Columbus Ohio 1975-91.
Author and National Speaker on probate and estate planning. Former Chairman Probate Court Committee and InterProfessional Committee Columbus Bar Association. Former Member Rules of Superintendence Committee Supreme Court of Ohio. Co-chairman Legislative Committee, Member Probate Law and Procedure Committee and Board Member Ohio Judicial Conference. Fellow American College of Trust and Estate Counsel. Member Ohio Association of Probate Judges (President 1999-2001, Member Forms and Rules Committee, Board Member), National College of Probate Judges (President Elect 2001-02, Board Member) and Ohio State Bar Association (Board of Governors Estate Planning, Trust and Probate Section). Recipient Flaschner Award from Judicial Division American Bar Association 2001. Former Chairman Westerville Music and Arts Festival. Former Board Member Capital University Law School Alumni Association, Ronald McDonald House Charities of Central Ohio, Inc. and Westerville Area Chamber of Commerce (President 1989). Director Western Golf Association. Board Member Recreation Unlimited and Capital University. Advisory Board Dave Thomas Center for Adoption Law. Member Charity Newsies, The Agonis Club and Knights of Columbus.
Office: 373 South High Street, 22nd Floor, Columbus 43215-6311.
Telephone: (614) 462-3830.
Fax: (614) 462-7422
E-mail address: lawrence_belskis@fccourts.org

BENNETT, Douglas J. *(Judge, Athens County Municipal Court)* Appointed by Governor Richard F. Celeste to term beginning Jan 1, 1985. Elected 1985, 1991 and 1997. Current term expires Dec 31, 2003. Born Ann Arbor Michigan Aug 6, 1949. Educated at Ohio University B.A. 1971 and Ohio Northern University J.D. 1975. Admitted to practice Ohio 1975 and U.S. District Court Southern District of Ohio 1976. In legal practice Columbus 1975-80.
Public Defender Athens County 1980-84. Member American Judges Association, American Judicature Society, Athens, Ohio State and American Bar Associations.
Office: Eight East Washington Street, Athens 45701.
Telephone: (740) 592-3328.
Fax: (740) 592-3331
E-mail address: dbennett@eurekanet.com

BERLING, Amy *(Judge, Toledo Municipal Court)*
Office: 555 North Erie Street, Toledo 43624-1391.
Telephone: (419) 245-1941.
Fax: (419) 245-1802
E-mail address: amy.berling@noris.org

BERNARD, Michael A. *(Judge, Girard Municipal Court)*
Office: 100 North Market, Girard 44420-2522.
Telephone: (330) 545-3177.
Fax: (330) 545-7045

BESSEY, John P. *(Judge, Ohio Court of Common Pleas Franklin County)*
Office: 369 South High Street, #6A, Columbus 43215-4554.
Telephone: (614) 462-3550.
Fax: (614) 462-3868
E-mail address: john_bessey@fccourts.org

BETLESKI, Mark A. *(Judge, Ohio Court of Common Pleas Lorain County)* Elected Nov 3, 1998 to term beginning Jan 3, 1999. Term expires Jan 2, 2005. Born Lorain Ohio Jan 17, 1958. Roman Catholic. Educated at The Ohio State University B.A. 1982 and University of Toledo College of Law J.D. cum laude 1986. Member Order of the Coif. Admitted to practice Ohio 1986 and U.S. District Court Northern District of Ohio 1986. In legal practice Akron 1986-87 and Elyria 1987-99.
Member Lorain County and Ohio State Bar Associations. Democrat.
Office: 308 Second Street, Elyria 44035.
Telephone: (440) 329-5722.
Fax: (440) 329-5729
E-mail address: judgebetleski@hotmail.com

BEVENS, William Wray *(Judge, Ohio Court of Common Pleas Pike County)* Serves Probate and Juvenile Divisions.
Office: 230 Waverly Plaza, Suite 600, Waverly 45690.

BIRD, Steven R. *(Judge, Ohio Court of Common Pleas Williams County)* Serves Probate and Juvenile Divisions.
Office: One Courthouse Square, Second Floor, Bryan 43506-1789.
Telephone: (419) 636-1548.
Fax: (419) 636-5405
E-mail address: juvcourt@powersupply.net

BLACK, Timothy S. *(Judge, Hamilton County Municipal Court)*
Office: 1000 Main Street, Cincinnati 45202.
Telephone: (513) 946-5138.
Fax: (513) 946-5140

BLACKMON, Patricia Ann *(Judge, Ohio Court of Appeals Eighth District)* Elected Nov 1990. Reelected Nov 1996 and 2002. Current term expires 2009. First black woman elected to Ohio Court of Appeals. Educated at Tougaloo College B.A. magna cum laude 1972 and Cleveland State University Cleveland-Marshall College of Law J.D. 1975. Member Delta Sigma Theta. Admitted to practice Ohio 1976 and U.S. Supreme Court 1985. Began legal practice Ohio 1980.
Research Assistant and Counselor 1974-77 and Assistant Director 1977 Victims/Witness Program. Assistant Prosecutor 1977-86 and Chief Prosecutor 1986-90 Cleveland. Former Staff Attorney UAW Legal Services Plan and Ohio Turnpike Commission. District Director for Ohio, Michigan and West Virginia National Association of Women Judges. Member Providence Baptist Church.
Office: One Lakeside Avenue, Cleveland 44113.
Telephone: (216) 443-6358.
Fax: (216) 443-2044
E-mail address: PB1702@aol.com

BODOH, William T. *(Chief Judge, United States Bankruptcy Court Northern District of Ohio)* Appointed by U.S. Court of Appeals Sixth Circuit judges Feb 12, 1985 to term beginning June 10, 1985. Reappointed June 9, 1999, current term expires June 2013. Chief Judge since July 1, 2001. Also Judge, Bankruptcy Appellate Panel Sixth Circuit. Selected by the Judicial Council of the Sixth Circuit to term beginning 2003. Born Newark Ohio Sept 5, 1938. Episcopalian. Educated at Ohio University B.S.C. 1961 and The Ohio State University College of Law J.D. 1964. Member Pi Kappa Alpha and Phi Delta Phi. Admitted to practice Ohio 1964, U.S. Supreme Court 1970, U.S. District Court Northern District of Ohio 1972 and U.S. Court of Appeals Sixth Circuit 1980. Began legal practice Columbus 1964. In legal practice Cleveland 1967-72 and Youngstown 1972-85.
Author *A Local Rules Guide for Ohio Northern District Bankruptcy Court* Professional Education Systems, Inc. 1988; "A Few Useful Provisions—The Adoption of the Bill of Rights" Ohio State Alumni Magazine Jan 1991; "The Parameters of the Non-Plan Liquidating Chapter 11: Refining the *Lionel* Standard" 9 Bankruptcy Development Journal 1, 1992; "On Judging Judges" 55 No. 4 Ohio State L. Jour. 889, 1994; "Protective Orders in the Bankruptcy Court: The Congressional Mandate of Bankruptcy Code Section 107 and Its Constitutional Implications" 24 Hastings Constitutional Law Quarterly 67 Fall 1996; "Inequality Among Creditors: The Unconstitutional Use of Successor Liability to Create a New Class of Priority Creditors" 4 American Bankruptcy Institute L. Rev. 325 Winter 1996; and "Bankruptcy Reform: An Orderly Development of Public Policy?" 49 Cleveland State L. Rev. 191, 2001. Member ex officio Judicial Council of the Sixth Circuit 1990-93. Fellow American College of Bankruptcy. Member National Conference of Bankruptcy Judges (Board of Governors 1988-93) and American Bankruptcy Institute (Board of Directors since 1994). Former Member Advisory Board Salvation Army. Former Member Board of Trustees Easter Seal Society of Eastern Ohio. President Youngstown Symphony Society 1973-75. Member National Council College of Law since 1972, Former Member and Chair 1990-92 Alumni Advisory Council and President Law Alumni Association 1994-95 The Ohio State University. Interests include sailing, fly fishing, Civil War history and antique automobile restoration.
Mailing address: P.O. Box 147, Youngstown 44501-0147.
Office: 301 U.S. Courthouse, 10 East Commerce Street, Youngstown 44503.
Telephone: (330) 746-6829.
Fax: (330) 746-0480
E-mail address: william_bodoh@ohnb.uscourts.gov

BOGEN, Mark R. *(Judge, Lebanon Municipal Court)*
Office: City Building, 50 South Broadway, Lebanon 45036-1777.
Telephone: (513) 932-3060.
Fax: (513) 933-7212

BOGGINS, John F. *(Judge, Ohio Court of Appeals Fifth District)* Elected to term beginning Feb 11, 2001. Term expires Feb 2007. Born Mineral City Ohio July 1, 1932. Catholic. Educated at Kent State University B.A. 1955 and The Ohio State University J.D. 1958. Admitted to practice Ohio 1958, U.S. District Court Northern District of Ohio 1959, U.S. Court of Appeals Sixth Cir-

BOGGINS, JOHN F.—*Continued*

cuit and U.S. Supreme Court 1970. In legal practice Canton 1958-93. Judge, Ohio Court of Common Pleas Stark County Feb 9, 1993 to Feb 10, 2001.

Legal Drafter and Researcher Ohio Legislature 1956-58. Member Stark County and Ohio State Bar Associations. Republican. Member Board of Trustees Canton Ex-Newsies Charitable Association.

Office: 110 Central Plaza South, Suite 320, Canton 44702.
Telephone: (330) 451-7245.
Fax: (330) 451-7249

BOLT-MEREDITH, Cassandra S. *(Judge, Ohio Court of Common Pleas Pike County)* Appointed by Governor George V. Voinovich to term beginning Oct 7, 1996. Elected Nov 3, 1996 and Nov 1997. Current term expires Jan 2004. Born Chillicothe Ohio May 22, 1949. Methodist. Educated at University of Cincinnati College Conservatory of Music B.M. 1971, Cleveland Institute of Music M.M., Case Western Reserve University and Capital University J.D. Member Phi Alpha Delta. Admitted to practice Ohio 1986.

Assistant Prosecutor Pike County 1986-87. Counsel The Parry Company 1992-96. Member Ohio State Bar Association (Board of Governors Intellectual Property Committee). Republican. Member Pike County Chamber of Commerce.

Office: 100 East Second Street, Waverly 45690-1302.
Telephone: (740) 947-2212.
Fax: (740) 947-1729
E-mail address: judge@zoomnet.net

BOND, Jane *(Judge, Ohio Court of Common Pleas Summit County)* Former Judge, Akron Municipal Court.

Office: 209 South High Street, Akron 44308-1610.
Telephone: (330) 643-2238.
Fax: (330) 643-2405
E-mail address: jbond@cpcourt.summitoh.net

BOROS, Debra L. *(Judge, Ohio Court of Common Pleas Lorain County)* Elected to term beginning Jan 3, 1999. Term expires Dec 31, 2004. Serves Domestic Relations Division. Born Elyria Ohio Sept 27, 1959. Catholic. Educated at The Ohio State University B.A., University of Toledo and Cleveland-Marshall College of Law J.D. 1987. Admitted to practice Ohio 1988, U.S. District Court Northern District of Ohio 1990 and Pennsylvania 1995.

Assistant Prosecuting Attorney Lorain County 1988-92 and 1995-98 and Jefferson County 1992-94. Member Juvenile Rule and Procedures Committee, Ohio Association of Juvenile and Family Court Judges, Lorain County and Ohio State Bar Associations. Member American Cancer Society.

Office: 348 Second Street, Elyria 44035.
Telephone: (440) 328-2201.
Fax: (440) 328-2211
E-mail address: jdboros@hotmail.com

BOWMAN, Donna *(Judge, Ohio Court of Appeals Tenth District)* Assumed office Jan 2, 1987.

Office: 373 South High Street, 24th Floor, Columbus 43215-4578.
Telephone: (614) 462-4032.
Fax: (614) 462-7249

BOWMAN, J. Ronald *(Judge, Ohio Court of Common Pleas Lucas County)* Former Judge, Toledo Municipal Court.

Office: 700 Adams Street, Toledo 43624-1678.
Telephone: (419) 213-4565.
Fax: (419) 213-4181
E-mail address: rbowman@co.lucas.oh.us

BOYER, Susan E. *(Judge, Ohio Court of Common Pleas Washington County)* Appointed by Governor Richard F. Celeste to term beginning Jan 20, 1986. Elected Nov 1986, Nov 1988, 1994 and 2000. Current term expires Dec 31, 2006. Born Deep River Ontario Dec 7, 1948. Educated at Kent State University B.A. 1970 and University of Akron Law Center J.D. 1973. Admitted to practice Ohio 1973 and U.S. District Courts Northern 1974 and Southern 1978 Districts of Ohio. In legal practice Akron 1973-78 and Marietta 1978-86.

Assistant Prosecutor Summit County 1974-77 and Washington County 1982-85. Assistant City Law Director Marietta 1985-86.

Office: 205 Putnam Street, Marietta 45750-2922.
Telephone: (740) 373-6623.
Fax: (740) 373-5713

BOYKO, Chris *(Judge, Ohio Court of Common Pleas Cuyahoga County)* Assumed office Jan 29, 1996. Educated at Mount Union College B.A. with honors 1976 and Cleveland Marshall College of Law Cleveland State University J.D. 1979. Admitted to practice Ohio 1979, Florida 1985, U.S. Tax Court 1986, U.S. Supreme Court 1988 and U.S. Court of Appeals Sixth Circuit 1990. In legal practice 1979-93 and 1994-96. Judge, Parma Municipal Court Sept 7, 1993 to Dec 1993.

Assistant Prosecutor 1981-87, Prosecutor 1987 to Sept 6, 1993 and Director of Law 1987 to Sept 6, 1993 City of Parma. Chief Legal Counsel Southwest Enforcement Bureau 1991-93. General Counsel and Executive Vice President Copy America, Inc. 1994-95. Legal Advisor to S.W.A.T. Team Parma Police Department. Former Member Cuyahoga County Prosecutors Club. Co-administrator Judicial Corrections Board. Chair Veteran's Service Committee Ohio Court of Common Pleas. Board of Trustees Cleveland Bar Association. Member The Florida Bar, Parma (Former Trustee, Past President), Cuyahoga County, Ukrainian and American Bar Associations. Faculty Member Ohio Judicial College and The National Judicial College. Speaker FBI Lecture Series. Member Parma Community Drug Task Force 1988-93. Host "Sidebar" Cox Cable Legal Show. Member Citizens League of Greater Cleveland, Parma Lodge No. 1938 Brotherhood of Elks, Advisory Council and Ambassador's Club Parmadale Children's Services, Mount Union College Alumni Association, Cleveland Marshall College of Law Alumni Association, Amvets, Sons of American Legion and St. Anthony of Padua Church. Enjoys martial arts, running, weightlifting and reading.

Office: 1200 Ontario Street, Room 19-C, Cleveland 44113-1678.
Telephone: (216) 443-8726.
Fax: (216) 348-4035

BOYLE, Mary J. *(Judge, Ohio Court of Common Pleas Cuyahoga County)*

Office: 1200 Ontario Street, Room 21D, Cleveland 44113-1678.
Telephone: (216) 443-8738.
Fax: (216) 348-4033

BOZZA, Mary Kaye *(Judge, Lyndhurst Municipal Court)*
Office: 5301 Mayfield Road, Lyndhurst 44124-2484.
Telephone: (440) 461-6500.
Fax: (440) 442-1910
E-mail address: mkb@core.com

BRADY, Michael L. *(Judge, Ohio Court of Common Pleas Logan County)* Serves Probate and Juvenile Divisions.
Office: 101 South Main Street, Room 6, Bellefontaine 43311.
Telephone: (937) 599-7249.
Fax: (937) 599-7297
E-mail address: mbrady@co.logan.oh.us

BRANDT, Michael T. *(Judge, Franklin County Municipal Court)*
Office: 375 South High Street, Columbus 43215-4593.
Telephone: (614) 645-8296.
Fax: (614) 645-7803
E-mail address: michael_brandt@fccourts.org

BRESSLER, H. J. *(Judge, Ohio Court of Common Pleas Butler County)* Born Baltimore Maryland Dec 31, 1939. Methodist. Educated at Miami University B.A. cum laude 1964 and Salmon P. Chase College of Law, Northern Kentucky University J.D. 1968. Member Order of Curia. Admitted to practice Ohio 1968. Began legal practice Hamilton 1969. Former Judge, Butler County Court, elected to term beginning Jan 1, 1981.
Past President Greater Hamilton Trial Lawyers Association. Member Ohio Academy of Trial Lawyers, American Academy of Trial Lawyers, Municipal and County Judges Association of Ohio (President 1991), Butler County (Past President) and Ohio State Bar Associations. E-5 U.S. Army 1958-61. Previously worked as Credit Manager for Procter & Gamble and for U.S. Shoe Corporation. Republican. Interests include running and horse shows.
Office: Government Services Center, Third Floor, 315 High Street, Hamilton 45011.
Telephone: (513) 887-3290.
Fax: (513) 887-3285

BROGAN, James A. *(Judge, Ohio Court of Appeals Second District)* Elected to term beginning Feb 11, 1981. Reelected 1986, 1992 and 1998. Current term expires 2005. Presiding Judge 1982-86 and 1995-96. Born Chicago Illinois Oct 23, 1939. Catholic. Educated at University of Notre Dame A.B. 1961 and Georgetown University J.D. 1964. Admitted to practice Ohio 1964, U.S. District Courts Southern 1967 and Northern 1975 Districts of Ohio and U.S. Supreme Court 1971.
First Assistant Prosecuting Attorney Montgomery County Dec 1969 to Feb 1981. Instructor Sinclair Community College since 1970 and University of Dayton since 1986. Member Board of Grievances and Discipline Ohio Supreme Court 1983-95. Chief Justice Ohio Courts of Appeals Association 1996. Fellow American College of Trial Lawyers, Ohio State Bar Foundation and American Bar Foundation. Member Dayton, Ohio State and American Bar Associations. Chairman Board of Trustees 1998 and Instructor Ohio Judicial College. Named Outstanding Ohio Assistant Prosecuting Attorney by Ohio Prosecuting Attorneys Association 1980. Colonel USAR JAGC (retired). Democrat. President Catholic Social Services Board 1983-84 and Man to Man Associates 1984-85. Enjoys tennis and golf.
Mailing address: P.O. Box 972, Dayton 45401.
Office: 41 North Perry Street, Dayton 45422.
Telephone: (937) 225-4464.
Fax: (937) 496-7724
E-mail address: jbrogan@mcohio.org

BRONSON, Neal B. *(Judge, Ohio Court of Common Pleas Warren County)* Appointed by Governor Richard F. Celeste to term beginning Feb 10, 1987. Elected 1988, 1994 and 2000. Current term expires Dec 31, 2006. Born Bronx New York April 14, 1948. Educated at Boston University B.S. 1969 and University of Cincinnati J.D. 1972. Admitted to practice Ohio 1972 and U.S. District Court Southern District of Ohio 1973. In legal practice Franklin 1972-77 and Lebanon 1977-87.
Assistant Prosecuting Attorney Warren County 1972. Assistant Attorney General Ohio 1981-87. Member Ohio Common Pleas Judges Association, Warren County (President 1985) and Ohio State Bar Associations. Member 1976-85 and President 1978-80 Board of Directors and Campaign Chairman 1980 Warren County United Way. Board Member and President 1978-79 and Campaign Chairman 1979 Warren County Unit American Cancer Society. Enjoys family activities, basketball, racquetball and reading.
Office: 500 Justice Drive, Lebanon 45036-2398.
Telephone: (513) 695-1231.
Fax: (513) 695-2920
E-mail address: bronnb@co.warren.oh.us

BROWN, Charles E., Jr. *(Judge, Ohio Court of Common Pleas Stark County)*
Office: 115 Central Plaza North, Canton 44702-1490.
Telephone: (330) 451-7720.
Fax: (330) 451-7740

BROWN, Robert J. *(Judge, Ohio Court of Common Pleas Wayne County)* Elected to term beginning Jan 1, 1987. Reelected 1992 and 1998. Current term expires Dec 31, 2004. Born Cleveland Ohio May 3, 1949. Catholic. Educated at The Ohio State University B.A. and University of Toledo J.D. Admitted to practice Ohio 1980.
Member Ohio Common Pleas Judges Association, Wayne County and Ohio State Bar Associations. Member Wooster Noon Lions Club (Lions International).
Office: 107 West Liberty Street, Wooster 44691-4862.
Telephone: (330) 287-5540.
Fax: (330) 264-2560

BROWN, Susan *(Judge, Ohio Court of Appeals Tenth District)* Born Zanesville Ohio Aug 9, 1952. Catholic. Educated at Kent State University B.S. 1974, The Ohio State University M.A. 1979 and Capital Law School J.D. 1983. Staff member Capital University Law Review. Member Kappa Delta Phi. Admitted to practice Ohio 1983. In legal practice Columbus 1985-94. Commissioner, Ohio Court of Claims 1987-94. Former Judge, Ohio Court of Common Pleas Franklin County, elected to term beginning Jan 2, 1995.
Assistant Attorney General Claims Section Ohio 1984. Member Commission of Professionalism Supreme Court of Ohio and Columbus Bar Association. Formerly employed as sixth grade teacher Madison Local School District 1975-76 and flight attendant 1976. Operations Board Buckeye Ranch, Inc. Board of Directors Capital University Law School Alumni Association. Interests in-

BROWN, SUSAN—*Continued*

clude plants and hiking. Personal Statement or Quote: "The road to success is always under construction."

Office: 373 South High Street, 24th Floor, Columbus 43215-6313.
Telephone: (614) 462-4050.
Fax: (614) 462-7249
E-mail address: sbrown@co.franklin.oh.us

BROWNE, Kim Alana *(Judge, Ohio Court of Common Pleas Franklin County)* Serves Domestic Relations and Juvenile Divisions.

Office: 373 South High Street, Sixth Floor, Columbus 43215-4520.
Telephone: (614) 462-4444.
Fax: (614) 462-7440
E-mail address: kim_browne@fccourts.org

BRUNNER, Jennifer L. *(Judge, Ohio Court of Common Pleas Franklin County)*

Office: 369 South High Street, Columbus 43215-3550.
Telephone: (614) 462-6281.
Fax: (614) 462-7643
E-mail address: jennifer_brunner@fccourts.org

BRUZZESE, Joseph J., Jr. *(Judge, Ohio Court of Common Pleas Jefferson County)* Born Steubenville Ohio Sept 21, 1951. Roman Catholic. Educated at Ohio Northern University B.S. 1973 and Claude W. Pettit College of Law Ohio Northern University J.D. 1976. Recipient American Jurisprudence Awards in Contracts. Member Sigma Pi. Admitted to practice Ohio 1976. Began legal practice Steubenville 1976. Former Judge, Jefferson County Court, elected to term beginning Jan 1, 1981.

Instructor in Real Estate The Ohio State University at Lima 1975-76. Member Ohio Academy of Trial Lawyers, The Association of Trial Lawyers of America, Jefferson County, Ohio State and American Bar Associations. Previously worked as pipe fitter helper Weirton Steel. Democrat. Member Toronto Rod and Gun Club, Jefferson County Sportsmen's Association, League of Ohio Sportsmen, Ohio Farm Bureau and Amsterdam Moose. Enjoys hunting and fishing.

Office: 301 Market Street, Steubenville 43952-2149.
Telephone: (740) 283-8543.
Fax: (740) 283-8686
E-mail address: jbreeze@clover.net

BRYANT, Peggy L. *(Judge, Ohio Court of Appeals Tenth District)* Assumed office Jan 26, 1987. Elected 1994. Former Judge, Franklin County Municipal Court.

Office: 373 South High Street, 24th Floor, Columbus 43215-4578.
Telephone: (614) 462-3612.
Fax: (614) 462-7249
E-mail address: plbryant@co.franklin.oh.us

BRYANT, Thomas F. *(Judge, Ohio Court of Appeals Third District)* Elected 1988 to term beginning Feb 9, 1989. Reelected 1994 and 2000. Current term expires 2006.

Office: 204 North Main Street, Lima 45801.
Telephone: (419) 223-1861.
Fax: (419) 224-3828
E-mail address: bryant@third.courts.state.oh.us

BUCHANAN, A. Deane *(Judge, Cleveland Heights Municipal Court)*

Office: 40 Severance Circle, Cleveland Heights 44118.
Telephone: (216) 291-3184.
Fax: (216) 291-2459

BUMB, Michael J. *(Judge, Ohio Court of Common Pleas Fulton County)* Elected to term beginning Feb 9, 1985. Reelected 1990, 1996 and 2002. Current term expires 2009. Serves Probate and Juvenile Divisions. Born Bellevue Ohio Jan 8, 1953. Catholic. Educated at The Ohio State University B.A. with honors 1975 and University of Toledo J.D. with honors 1978. Member Phi Alpha Delta. Admitted to practice Ohio 1978. Began legal practice Wauseon 1978.

Former Assistant Prosecuting Attorney. Member District I Juvenile Court Association (Secretary-Treasurer), Ohio State Probate Judges Association, Ohio State Juvenile Judges Association, National Probate Judges Association, National Juvenile Judges Association, Fulton County and Ohio State Bar Associations. Director Law Enforcement Seminars Fulton County 1979-84. Recipient Superior Judicial Service Award from Ohio Supreme Court 1985 and Outstanding Leadership Award from Ohio Educational Service Association. Former Assistant Manager in Agri-Business. Republican. Former Trustee Big Brothers Big Sisters of Northwestern Ohio and Northwest Ohio Community Action Commission. Former Chairman Fulton County Local Advisory Board Ohio Children's Trust Fund. Member Ducks Unlimited, Fulton County Child Protective Services Team, Fulton County Farm Bureau and Elks Lodge 1734. Enjoys golf, travel, gardening and woodworking.

Office: 210 South Fulton Street, Wauseon 43567-1211.
Telephone: (419) 337-9242.
Fax: (419) 337-9284

BUNCH, Thomas E. *(Judge, Chillicothe Municipal Court)* Elected Nov 2, 1993 to term beginning Jan 1, 1994. Reelected Nov 2, 1999, current term expires Dec 31, 2005. Born Chillicothe Ohio Oct 8, 1949. Roman Catholic. Educated at University of Dayton B.S. 1971, University of Florida M.B.A. 1972 and University of Toledo J.D. magna cum laude 1980. Notes and Comment Editor University of Toledo Law Review 1978-80. Member Gamma Beta Sigma. Admitted to practice Ohio 1980. In legal practice Chillicothe 1980-93.

Assistant City Law Director Chillicothe 1988-93. Captain U.S. Army 1972-77. Chairman Civil Service Commission Chillicothe 1983-87. Enjoys running, golf and gardening.

Office: 26 South Paint Street, Chillicothe 45601.
Telephone: (740) 774-4710.
Fax: (740) 774-1101
E-mail address: tbunch@bright.net

BURKE, Kim Wilson *(Judge, Ohio Court of Common Pleas Hamilton County)*

Office: 1000 Main Street, Room 500, Cincinnati 45202.
Telephone: (513) 946-5770.
Fax: (513) 946-5779

BURKETT, Michael L. *(Judge, Fremont Municipal Court)*

Office: 323 South Front Street, Fremont 43420-0071.
Telephone: (419) 332-1572.
Fax: (419) 332-1570

BURLEW, John H. *(Judge, Hamilton County Municipal Court)*
Office: 1000 Main Street, Cincinnati 45202.
Telephone: (513) 946-5122.
Fax: (513) 946-5124

BURNEY, Janet E. *(Judge, Ohio Court of Common Pleas Cuyahoga County)* Serves Juvenile Division.
Office: 2163 East 22nd Street, Cleveland 44115-2998.
Telephone: (216) 443-8411.
Fax: (216) 443-3386

BURNSIDE, Janet R. *(Judge, Ohio Court of Common Pleas Cuyahoga County)* Appointed by Governor Richard F. Celeste to term beginning Jan 13, 1991. Elected Nov 1992, Nov 1994 and Nov 2000. Current term expires Jan 10, 2007. Born Columbus Ohio Nov 18, 1946. Protestant. Educated at The Ohio State University B.S. cum laude 1967 M.S. 1970 J.D. cum laude 1977. Senior Staff Editor Ohio State Law Journal 1975-77. Law Clerk to Hon. Alvin I. Krenzler, Ohio Court of Appeals Eighth District 1977-78. Admitted to practice Ohio 1977, U.S. District Court Northern District of Ohio 1979, U.S. Court of Appeals Sixth Circuit 1982 and U.S. Supreme Court 1983. In legal practice Cleveland 1978-91. Acting Judge, Cleveland Heights Municipal Court 1985-91.

Author Case Note "Private Plaintiff Versus Member News Media—An Application of *Gertz v. Welch*" 36 Ohio State L. Jour. 929, 1975; Note "Involuntary Interprison Transfers of State Prisoners After *Meachum v. Fano* and *Montanye v. Haymes*" 37 Ohio State L. Jour. 845, 1976; and "When Can the Prosecution Appeal?" 6 No. 1 Cuyahoga Criminal Defense Lawyers Association Newsletter Spring 1983. Co-author "Alternate Delivery Systems: Liability for Patient Diagnosis and Treatment Decisions" 1 No. 5 Oct 1987 and 1 No. 6 Nov 1987 *Ohio Health Law Insider* and *Ohio Rules of Evidence Trial Book* Lexis Law Publishing 1999. Assistant Editor Cuyahoga Criminal Defense Lawyers Association Newsletter 1980-86. Important Decision: May v. Tandy Corp. (held Ohio's tort reform statute requiring reduction of verdict for collateral financial benefits received by plaintiff unconstitutional as violation of right to jury trial under Ohio constitution) Case no. 165883 Sept 25, 1991. Lecturer on Law Cleveland-Marshall College of Law 1980. Life Member since 1985 Eighth District Judicial Conference (Chair Corporate and Business Law Section 1997). Chair Criminal Court Committee Ohio Court of Common Pleas Cuyahoga County. Co-chair Canon 7 Subcommittee Ohio Common Pleas Judges Association 1996. Member Ohio Judicial Conference (Civil Law and Procedure Committee 1993, Strategic Planning Committee 1997, Chair Publications Committee 1997-2001), Cleveland (Member 1988-91 and Vice Chair 1988 Alternate Dispute Resolution Committee), Cuyahoga County (Board of Trustees since 1995, Chair Common Pleas Court Committee 1995-97, Member Golf Outing Committee since 1996), Ohio Women's (Co-chair Mentoring Project 1995-98), Ohio State and American Bar Associations. Judicial Panelist "Anatomy of Employment Rights Case" Employment Rights Section The Association of Trial Lawyers of America National Convention Chicago Illinois July 1994. Faculty Member Ohio Judicial College. Recipient Judicial Excellence Award from Lodge 14 Fraternal Order of Police 1992. Technical Staff Bell Telephone Laboratories 1968-74. President Ohio State Chapter National Organization for Women 1973. Member Executive Committee 1979-91 and Ward Leader Cleveland Heights Ward Four 1980-91 Cuyahoga County Democratic Party. Chairman Cleveland Heights Charter Review Committee 1982. Trustee Legal Aid Society of Cleveland 1983-92. Enjoys golf.
Office: 1200 Ontario Street, Cleveland 44113-1678.
Telephone: (216) 443-8671.
Fax: (216) 348-4035
E-mail address: cpjrb@www.cuyahoga.oh.us

BURT, Forrest W. *(Judge, Ohio Court of Common Pleas Geauga County)* Elected 1994. Reelected to subsequent term.
Office: 100 Short Court Street, Chardon 44024-1238.
Telephone: (440) 285-2222.
Fax: (440) 286-2127

BYERS, Gary L. *(Judge, Maumee Municipal Court)*
Office: 400 Conant Street, Maumee 43537-3397.
Telephone: (419) 897-7140.
Fax: (419) 897-7128
E-mail address: court@maumee.org

BYERS-EMMERLING, Melissa *(Judge, East Liverpool Municipal Court)*
Office: 126 West Sixth Street, East Liverpool 43920-5025.
Telephone: (330) 385-5151.
Fax: (330) 385-1566

CAIN, David E. *(Judge, Ohio Court of Common Pleas Franklin County)* Elected to term beginning Jan 7, 1987. Appointed by Governor George V. Voinovich 1992. Elected 1994 and 2000. Current term expires Jan 4, 2007. Born Akron Ohio June 11, 1943. Educated at Spring Arbor College A.A. 1963, Ohio University B.S.J. 1965 and Capital University Law School J.D. 1973. Comments Editor Capital University Law Review 1972. Admitted to practice Ohio 1973 and U.S. District Court Southern District of Ohio 1974. In legal practice Columbus 1974-86.

Past President Ohio Common Pleas Judges Association. Member Columbus and Ohio State Bar Associations. Recipient Private Sector Initiative Commendation from President Ronald Reagan Oct 26, 1983. Reporter Columbus Dispatch 1967-77. Republican. Member Columbus City Council 1980-83. President Press Club of Ohio 1975-76. Board of Trustees Community Resource Center 1984-90. Board Member House of Hope and Maryhaven, Inc.
Office: 369 South High Street, #7D, Columbus 43215-4554.
Telephone: (614) 462-3777.
Fax: (614) 462-2462
E-mail address: david_cain@fccourts.org

CALABRESE, Anthony O., Jr. *(Judge, Ohio Court of Appeals Eighth District)* Former Judge, Ohio Court of Common Pleas Cuyahoga County.
Office: One Lakeside Avenue, Cleveland 44113.

CALDWELL, Charles M. *(Judge, United States Bankruptcy Court Southern District of Ohio)* Appointed by U.S. Court of Appeals Sixth Circuit judges.
Office: 170 North High Street, Columbus 43215-2403.
Telephone: (614) 469-6638.

CALHOUN, Donald E., Jr. *(Recalled Judge, United States Bankruptcy Court Southern District of Ohio)* Appointed Judge by U.S. Court of Appeals Sixth Circuit

CALHOUN, DONALD E., JR.—*Continued*
judges to term beginning May 2, 1985. Appointed Recalled Judge by the Judicial Council of the Sixth Circuit 1999. Born Columbus Ohio May 15, 1926. United Church of Christ. Educated at The Ohio State University B.A. 1949 J.D. 1951. Senior Class President The Ohio State University College of Law. Member Delta Theta Phi (President). Admitted to practice Ohio 1951. In legal practice Columbus 1951-85.

Member Columbus Bar Association (President 1967-68). Speaker Family Farmer Bankruptcy Seminar 1987 and Bankruptcy Litigation Seminar 1988 Professional Education Systems, Inc. Recipient Leadership Award from Columbus Bar Association 1972. Seaman USNR 1944-46. Republican Committeeman Ward 21 Columbus 1958-85. Member Columbus Board of Education 1963-72. Past President University Club of Columbus. Enjoys gardening, tennis and hiking.

Office: 170 North High Street, Columbus 43215-2403.
Telephone: (614) 469-6638.

CALLAHAN, Kenneth R. *(Judge, Ohio Court of Common Pleas Cuyahoga County)*
Office: 1200 Ontario Street, Cleveland 44113-1678.
Telephone: (216) 443-8748.
Fax: (216) 348-4032

CALLAHAN, Lynne S. *(Judge, Akron Municipal Court)*
Office: 217 South High Street, Akron 44308-1611.
Telephone: (330) 375-2009.
Fax: (330) 375-2123
E-mail address: judgelsc@aol.com

CAMPBELL, Joseph Timothy *(Judge, Ohio Court of Common Pleas Greene County)*
Office: 45 North Detroit Street, Xenia 45385.

CAMPBELL, Joyce A. *(Judge, Fairfield Municipal Court)*
Office: 4951 Dixie Highway, Fairfield 45014.
Telephone: (513) 867-6002.
Fax: (513) 867-6001
E-mail address: jcampbell@fairfield-city.org

CAMPBELL, Phil W. *(Judge, Van Wert Municipal Court)* Appointed by Governor Richard F. Celeste to term beginning March 1, 1987. Elected Nov 1987, Nov 1993 and Nov 1999. Current term expires Dec 31, 2005. Born Van Wert Ohio May 17, 1947. Educated at Bowling Green State University B.S.Ed. 1973 and The Ohio State University J.D. 1976. Admitted to practice Ohio 1976 and U.S. Tax Court 1985. In legal practice Defiance 1976-78 and Van Wert 1980-87.

Managing Attorney Legal Aid Society 1978-80. Member Supreme Court Rules Advisory Committee since 1991. Member Ohio Defense Attorneys Association, Ohio Academy of Trial Lawyers, Van Wert, Northwest Ohio and Ohio State (Unauthorized Practice of Law Committee) Bar Associations. Life Member Van Wert Jaycees (President 1982). Member Mental Health Board 1985-87 (President 1986-87), Van Wert Lions (President 1991), Area Agency on Aging 1981-85 and Counter Attack Program 1980-82. Board of Trustees Wassenberg Art Center 1980-83. Member St. Paul's United Church of Christ, Trinity Friends. Enjoys farming and photography.

Office: 124 South Market Street, Van Wert 45891-1729.
Telephone: (419) 238-5767.
Fax: (419) 238-5865
E-mail address: jcampbell@fairfield-city.org

CAMPBELL, Thomas A. *(Judge, Trumbull County Court)* Appointed by Governor George V. Voinovich to term beginning Jan 1, 1995. Reelected 1996 and 1998. Current term expires Dec 31, 2004. Born Greenville Pennsylvania Jan 24, 1959. Educated at Kent State University B.A. 1983 and University of Akron J.D. 1989. Admitted to practice Ohio 1989 and U.S. Court of Appeals Sixth Circuit 1990. In legal practice Akron 1989-91 and Warren 1991. Judge, Trumbull County Court 1992.

Member Municipal-County Judges of Ohio, Inc., Akron, Trumbull County and Ohio State Bar Associations. Member Ohio Judicial Conference. Republican. Councilman 1978-79 and Mayor 1979-83 Orangeville Ohio. Member Rotary and Faithful Club. Enjoys baseball.

Office: 180 North Mecca Street, Cortland 44410.
Telephone: (330) 637-5023.
Fax: (330) 637-5021

CAMPLESE, Albert S. *(Judge, Ashtabula Municipal Court)* Elected to term beginning Dec 10, 1993. Reelected Nov 1995 and 2001. Current term expires Dec 31, 2007. Born Ashtabula Ohio. Catholic. Educated at Ohio Northern University B.A. cum laude 1980 and Cleveland-Marshall College of Law J.D. 1985. Law Clerk to Hon. Joseph Mahoney, Hon. Ronald Verrel, Hon. Ronald Varkettte, Hon. John Cardinal and Hon. Joseph Mallone, Ohio Court of Common Pleas Ashtabula County 1983-85. Admitted to practice Ohio 1985 and U.S. District Court Northern District of Ohio 1985. In legal practice Ashtabula 1985-93.

Municipal Prosecutor Ashtabula Ohio 1985-93. Member Association of Municipal and County Court Judges, Northeastern Ohio Judges Association, American Judges Association, Ashtabula and American Bar Associations. Developed model prosecution plan for prosecution of welfare fraud cases for Ohio Task Force on Welfare Fraud. Speaker on welfare fraud Ohio Task Force annual conference. Facilitator of several seminars on welfare fraud. Recipient "Integrity Award" from U.S. Inspector General 1991, Certificate of Recognition June 14, 1991 and Recognition Award June 15, 1993 from Ohio State Auditor's Office. Parish Council Mount Carmel Church 1993-96. Former Board Member Ashtabula County YMCA. Enjoys woodworking/carving, golf and skiing.

Office: 110 West 44th Street, Ashtabula 44004.
Telephone: (440) 992-7108.
Fax: (440) 998-5786

CANNON, James F. *(Judge, Dayton Municipal Court)* Appointed by Governor Richard F. Celeste to term beginning Feb 23, 1987. Elected 1987, 1993 and 1999. Current term expires Jan 2006. Born Greenfield Ohio March 31, 1931. Protestant. Educated at Wright State University B.A. with honors 1973 M.S. 1974 and University of Dayton J.D. 1978. Member Phi Alpha Delta. Admitted to practice Ohio 1978 and U.S. District Court Southern District of Ohio 1978. In legal practice Dayton 1978-86.

Assistant Prosecutor Montgomery County 1978-80. Member Dayton, Ohio State and American Bar Associa-

CANNON, JAMES F.—*Continued*

tions. Attended Ohio Judicial College and The National Judicial College 1988. Master Sergeant USAF 1950-70.
Office: 301 West Third Street, Dayton 45402-1424.
Telephone: (937) 333-4367.
Fax: (937) 333-5085
E-mail address: james.cannon@ci.dayton.oh.us

CAPPER, Donald R. *(Judge, Lawrence County Municipal Court)*
Mailing address: P.O. Box 126, Chesapeake 45619-0126.
Office: 10916 County Road One, Chesapeake 45619-7020.
Telephone: (740) 886-8590.
Fax: (740) 867-3547
E-mail address: dcapper@zoomnet.net

CAPPER, Thomas J. *(Judge, Ohio Court of Common Pleas Clark County)*
Office: Courthouse, 101 North Limestone, Springfield 45502-1120.
Telephone: (937) 328-2464.
Fax: (937) 328-2463

CARDWELL, Timothy Lee *(Judge, Ohio Court of Common Pleas Huron County)* Serves Probate and Juvenile Divisions.
Office: Two East Main Street, Norwalk 44857.

CAREY, Chad L. *(Judge, Clinton County Municipal Court)*
Office: 69 North South Street, Box 71, Wilmington 45177-2276.
Telephone: (937) 382-0266.
Fax: (937) 383-0130
E-mail address: ccmc@erinet.com

CAREY, Richard P. *(Judge, Ohio Court of Common Pleas Clark County)* Serves Probate and Juvenile Divisions. Born Springfield Ohio April 29, 1958. Roman Catholic. Educated at University of Notre Dame B.A. 1980 and Ohio Northern University Pettit College of Law J.D. 1982. Executive Editor Ohio Northern University Law Review 1981-82. Admitted to practice Ohio 1983 and U.S. District Court Southern District of Ohio 1988. In legal practice Springfield 1983-84. Former Judge, Clark County Municipal Court, appointed by Governor George V. Voinovich to term beginning Jan 22, 1993.
Assistant Prosecuting Attorney Clark County 1984-92. Member Municipal-County Judges of Ohio, Inc., American Judges Association, Springfield Bar & Law Library Association and Ohio State Bar Association.
Office: 50 East Columbia Street, Springfield 45502.

CARNES, Thomas J. *(Judge, Ohio Court of Common Pleas Portage County)* Appointed by Governor Richard F. Celeste to term beginning Jan 19, 1989. Elected 1990, 1996 and 2002. Current term expires Feb 8, 2009. Serves Probate and Juvenile Divisions. Born Magnolia Ohio July 24, 1946. Lutheran. Educated at Ohio Wesleyan University B.A. 1968 and Case Western Reserve University J.D. 1971. Admitted to practice Ohio 1973, U.S. District Court Northern District of Ohio 1979 and U.S. Supreme Court 1979. In legal practice Ravenna and Kent. Judge, Portage County Municipal Court Jan 2, 1980 to Jan 18, 1989.
Assistant Prosecutor 1973-74 and Public Defender 1974-80 Portage County. Instructor Ohio Judicial College 1986-87. Member Ohio Municipal Judges Association, Portage County and Ohio State Bar Associations. Attended The National Judicial College 1980. Democrat. Trustee United Way Portage County and Reed Memorial Library. Enjoys sports and coaching youth athletics.
Probate Court office: 203 West Main Street, Third Floor, Ravenna 44266.
Telephone: (330) 297-3870.
Fax: (330) 297-3894
Juvenile Court office: 8000 Infirmary Road, Ravenna 44266.
Telephone: (330) 297-0881.
Fax: (330) 297-2227

CARR, Donna J. *(Judge, Ohio Court of Appeals Ninth District)* Former Judge, Akron Municipal Court.
Office: 161 South High Street, Fifth Floor, Akron 44308-1671.
Telephone: (330) 643-2250.
Fax: (330) 643-2091
E-mail address: donna@ninth.courts.state.oh.us

CARR, James G. *(Judge, United States District Court Northern District of Ohio)* Magistrate Judge Sept 29, 1979 to May 8, 1994. Appointed Judge for life by President Bill Clinton May 9, 1994. Born Boston Massachusetts Nov 14, 1940. Roman Catholic. Educated at Kenyon College A.B. 1962, Freiburg West Germany (German Academic Exchange Commission and Fulbright Commission Grant) 1962-63 and Harvard University Law School LL.B. 1966. Member Phi Beta Kappa. Admitted to practice Illinois 1966 and Ohio 1972. Began legal practice Chicago Illinois 1966. In legal practice Evanston Illinois 1968-70.
Author "Final Report: National Wiretapping Commission" Government Printing Office 1976, *The Law of Electronic Surveillance* Clark Boardman 1977 and 2nd ed. 1986, *Criminal Law Review* (anthology) Clark Boardman since 1979 and *Criminal Law Handbook* Clark Boardman since 1984. Co-author *Anderson's Ohio Family Law* Anderson 1975 and 2nd ed. 1989 and *Juvenile Law: Cases & Materials* Michie/Bobbs Merrill 1980 and 2nd ed. 1989. Professor of Law University of Toledo 1970-79. Member Toledo and American Bar Associations. Recipient Fulbright Research Fellowship (Bonn West Germany) 1977-78. Member Child Abuse Prevention Center Board 1973-77 and 1979-81, Lucas County Mental Health Board 1981-86 and Lucas County Children Services Board 1987-92.
Office: 203 U.S. Courthouse, 1716 Spielbusch Avenue, Toledo 43624.
Telephone: (419) 259-6420.

CARROLL, Patrick *(Judge, Lakewood Municipal Court)*
Office: 12650 Detroit Avenue, Lakewood 44107.
Telephone: (216) 529-6700.
Fax: (216) 529-7687

CELEBREZZE, Frank Daniel, Jr. *(Judge, Ohio Court of Appeals Eighth District)* Born Cleveland Ohio Feb 22, 1952. Roman Catholic. Educated at Cleveland State University B.S. and Cleveland-Marshall College of Law. Extern to Hon. Alvin I. Krenzler, U.S. District Court Northern District of Ohio. Admitted to practice Ohio 1983. In legal practice Columbus 1983-87 and Cleveland 1987-93. Former Judge, Ohio Court of Com-

CELEBREZZE, FRANK DANIEL, JR.—*Continued*

mon Pleas Cuyahoga County, elected to term beginning Jan 11, 1993. Seaman USN Nov 1974 to Nov 1980.

Office: One Lakeside Avenue, Cleveland 44113-1085.
Telephone: (216) 443-6350.
Fax: (216) 443-2044

CELEBREZZE, James P. *(Judge, Ohio Court of Common Pleas Cuyahoga County)* Serves Domestic Relations Division.

Office: One Lakeside Avenue, Courtroom #4, Cleveland 44113-1082.
Telephone: (216) 443-8806.
Fax: (216) 443-2063

CHASE, Dale H. *(Judge, Medina Municipal Court)* Elected to term beginning Jan 1, 1988. Reelected 1993 and 1999. Current term expires Dec 31, 2005. Born Medina Ohio July 25, 1950. Roman Catholic. Educated at American University B.A. 1972 and Catholic University of America Columbus School of Law J.D. 1975. Admitted to practice Ohio 1975 and U.S. Supreme Court 1980. In legal practice Medina 1975-87.

Office: 135 North Elmwood Avenue, Medina 44256-0491.
Telephone: (330) 723-3287.
Fax: (330) 225-1108
E-mail address: dhchase@medinamunicipalcourt.org

CHRISTIANSEN, Robert G. *(Judge, Ohio Court of Common Pleas Lucas County)* Assumed office Jan 3, 1983. Elected to term beginning Dec 31, 1984. Reelected 1986, 1992 and 1998. Current term expires Dec 31, 2004. Born Buffalo New York April 19, 1948. Educated at Bowling Green State University B.A. 1970 and University of Toledo J.D. 1972. Member Phi Alpha Delta. Admitted to practice Ohio 1973. Began legal practice Toledo 1975. Judge, Toledo Municipal Court 1981.

Member United Methodist Church and Arthritis Foundation.

Office: Courthouse, 700 Adams Street, Toledo 43624-1678.
Telephone: (419) 213-4575.
Fax: (419) 213-4181

CHRISTLEY, Judith A. *(Judge, Ohio Court of Appeals Eleventh District)* Elected to term beginning Feb 9, 1987. Reelected 1992 and 1998. Current term expires Feb 2004. Born Pittsburgh Pennsylvania Dec 26, 1943. Methodist. Educated at The Ohio State University B.A. 1966 and Cleveland-Marshall College of Law J.D. 1978. Admitted to practice Ohio 1979. In legal practice Ravenna 1979-84. Referee, Portage County Municipal Court 1980-84. Chief Referee, Cleveland Municipal Courts 1984-87.

Assistant Prosecutor Portage County 1979-80. Adjunct Instructor in Business Law and other law related topics Hiram Weekend College since 1984. Secretary-Treasurer Ohio Courts of Appeals Judges Association. Member Ashtabula County and Ohio State Bar Associations. Attended The National Judicial College 1986, Ohio Judicial College and Institute of Judicial Administration for Intermediate Appellate Judges New York University 1988. Named Woman of the Year by Western Reserve Chapter American Association of University Women 1984. Teacher secondary education 1966-69. Market support representative IBM 1969-71. Republican. Past President Portage Alcohol and Drug Abuse Services Board and Portage County Executive Women's Network. Member Rotary International (Past President Mantua Chapter, President Andover Chapter).

Office: 111 High Street N.E., Warren 44481-1098.
Telephone: (330) 675-2661.
Fax: (330) 675-2655
E-mail address: jachristley-@11thappeal.co.trumbull.oh.us

CICCONETTI, Michael A. *(Judge, Painesville Municipal Court)* Elected Nov 2, 1993 to term beginning Jan 1, 1994. Reelected 1999, current term expires Dec 31, 2005. Born Painesville Ohio April 24, 1951. Roman Catholic. Educated at St. Leo College B.A. summa cum laude 1975 and Cleveland-Marshall College of Law J.D. 1980. Admitted to practice Ohio 1980, Florida 1981, U.S. District Court 1981 and U.S. Court of Appeals Sixth Circuit 1982. In legal practice Painesville Ohio 1980-93. Clerk Painesville Municipal Court 1975-80.

Trustee Painesville Township 1980-93. Member The Florida Bar, Lake County and Ohio State Bar Associations. Recipient nationwide recognition for creative sentencing from Connie Chung Tonight, John Walsh Show, Lou Dobbs Moneyline and MSNBC's Abrams Report. Democrat. Former Precinct Committeeman. Member Painesville Exchange Club, Knights of Columbus, Elks and VFW. Enjoys bowling, hunting, gardening, cooking and playing golf.

Mailing address: P.O. Box 601, Painesville 44077.
Office: Seven Richmond Street, Painesville 44077.
Telephone: (440) 639-4852.
Fax: (440) 352-0028
E-mail address: judgemike@pmcourt.org

CISSELL, James Charles *(Judge, Ohio Court of Common Pleas Hamilton County)* Serves Probate Division.

Office: 230 East Ninth Street, Room 10150, Cincinnati 45202.

CLARK, Joseph T. *(Judge, Ohio Court of Common Pleas Fairfield County)* Elected to term beginning Jan 1, 1983. Reelected 1988, 1994 and Nov 2000. Current term expires Dec 31, 2006. Presiding Judge 1986, 1989, 1990, 1995 and 2000. Born Lancaster Ohio Jan 29, 1941. Methodist. Educated at Ohio Northern University B.A. 1963 J.D. 1966 and University of Nevada-Reno M.J.S. 1993. Member Adelphian Senior Honor Society and Phi Alpha Delta. Admitted to practice Ohio 1966, U.S. Supreme Court, U.S. District Court Southern District of Ohio and U.S. Court of Military Appeals 1985. Began legal practice Lancaster 1966. Referee, Small Claims Court 1967-68. Judge 1979-82 and Presiding Judge 1982-83, Fairfield County Municipal Court. Certified Military Judge 1985.

City Prosecutor Lancaster 1967-73. Special Counsel to Ohio Attorney General 1970. Past Village Solicitor Bremen, Carroll, Lithopolis, Rushville and West Rushville. Editorial Review Committee *Resource Manual for Judges* State of Ohio 1985. Author chapter in *Ohio Judges Resource Manual* Ohio Judicial College/Ohio Judicial Conference 1988. Instructor in Real Estate Law Ohio University Branch 1969-71 and Search and Seizure Course Fairfield County Sheriff's Academy and Lancaster Police Academy. Chair Administration and General Court Reform Committee 1982-2000 and Member Board of Trustees Ohio Judicial Conference. Member Task Force for Jury Service 2002 and Rules Advisory Committee Supreme Court of Ohio. Fellow Ohio State Bar

CLARK, JOSEPH T.—*Continued*
Foundation. Member Ohio Jury Management Association (Board of Trustees), Ohio Common Pleas Judges Association (Board of Trustees), American Judges Association, Fairfield County (President 1976) and Ohio State Bar Associations. Recipient Diploma of Judicial Skills from American Academy of Judicial Education 1982. Inducted into Lancaster High School Hall of Fame Sept 2002. Faculty Member Ohio Judicial College since 1979 and The National Judicial College since 1999. Attended U.S. Constitution Course National Center for Constitutional Studies 1986, The National Judicial College University of Nevada-Reno and American Academy of Judicial Education University of Virginia School of Law, Washington and Lee University School of Law and University of Miami School of Law. Recipient Distinguished Service Award from Lancaster Jaycees 1972, Supreme Court of Ohio Award for Superior Judicial Service 1979, 1980, 1981 and 1982, Distinguished President's Award from Kiwanis International 1980, Certificate of Recognition from Peace Officer Training Council Ohio Attorney General's Office 1982, Certificate of Award from Ohio Department of Rehabilitation and Correction 1982, Supreme Court of Ohio Award for Excellent Judicial Service 1984 and Ben Franklin Award from Sertoma 1991. Named one of Outstanding Young Men of America 1972. Listed in *Who's Who in America* 1970 and 1991, *Who's Who in Ohio* 1974 and *Who's Who in American Law* 1985-86. Captain USN JAGC (retired). General Court-Martial Military Judge USN-USMC Trial Judiciary (retired). Member 1967-77 and President 1969 Fairfield County Young Republican Club. Vice Chairman and General Counsel Ohio League of Young Republican Clubs 1970. Chairman National Republican Party Voter Registration Drive Fairfield County 1971. Chairman 1972-73 and Member ten years Fairfield County Republican Executive Committee. Fairfield County Campaign Chairman for John W. Brown for Lieutenant Governor 1974 and Sam Speck for State Senate 1976. Member Central Committee twelve years and Century Club Fairfield Republican Party. Past President Sanderson Elementary School Parent-Teacher Organization. Past Vice President and Former Member Downtown Area Rehabilitation Effort. Former Member Lancaster Jaycees, Lancaster Athletic Booster Club and Board of Directors YMCA-YWCA. Past Solicitor United Appeal Campaign. Member Lancaster Kiwanis Club (President 1979-80), Salvation Army (Chairman 1985-86 and Member Advisory Board), Fairfield County Heart Board (Past President) and First United Methodist Church (Lay Leader 1990). Enjoys fishing, golf and woodcarving.

Office: Hall of Justice, 224 East Main Street, Lancaster 43130-3879.
Telephone: (740) 687-7044.
Fax: (740) 687-6701
E-mail address: jclark@co.fairfield.oh.us

CLARK, Margaret A. *(Judge, Ohio Court of Common Pleas Brown County)* Serves Probate and Juvenile Divisions. Born Cincinnati Ohio Sept 15, 1949. Roman Catholic. Educated at Edgecliff College B.A. 1971, Athenaeum of Ohio M.A. 1973 and University of Cincinnati J.D. 1977. Admitted to practice Ohio 1977 and U.S. District Court Southern District of Ohio 1978. Began legal practice Cincinnati 1978. In legal practice Georgetown since 1981. Referee, Ohio Courts of Common Pleas Brown County 1981-82 and Highland County 1982. Judge, Brown County Court Jan 1, 1983 to 2003.

Former Instructor Wilmington College, University of Cincinnati and Xavier University. President Municipal-County Judges of Ohio, Inc 1993. Member Cincinnati and Ohio State Bar Associations. Democrat. Board of Directors Cincinnati Area Chapter American Red Cross.

Mailing address: P.O. Box 379, Georgetown 45121.

CLARK, William A. *(Recalled Judge, United States Bankruptcy Court Southern District of Ohio)* Appointed by U.S. Court of Appeals Sixth Circuit judges. Appointed Recalled Judge by the Judicial Council of the Sixth Circuit.

Office: 120 West Third Street, Room 213, Dayton 45402.
Telephone: (937) 225-2955.

COLLIER, Christopher *(Judge, Ohio Court of Common Pleas Medina County)*
Office: 93 Public Square, Medina 44256-2205.
Telephone: (330) 725-9729.
Fax: (330) 764-8445

COLLIER, John S. *(Judge, Napoleon Municipal Court)*
Mailing address: P.O. Box 502, Napoleon 43545-0502.
Telephone: (419) 592-0766.
Fax: (419) 592-1805
E-mail address: lcollier@wcnet.org

COLLINS, Oakley C., Jr. *(Judge, Ironton Municipal Court)* Elected to term beginning Jan 1, 1982. Reelected 1987, 1993 and 1999. Current term expires Dec 31, 2005. Born Ironton Ohio June 29, 1947. Protestant. Educated at Ohio University B.A. 1969 and The Ohio State University J.D. 1973. Admitted to practice Ohio 1973. Began legal practice Ironton 1973.

City Prosecutor Ironton 1975-81. Assistant Prosecutor Lawrence County 1978-81. Member Ohio State and American Bar Associations. Recipient Superior Judicial Service Awards from Ohio Supreme Court 1982-84. Second Lieutenant Ohio National Guard 1973-78. Republican. Licensed Athletic Official. Enjoys golf.

Mailing address: P.O. Box 237, Ironton 45638-0237.
Telephone: (740) 532-3062.
Fax: (740) 533-6088

COLLINS, Richard L., Jr. *(Judge, Ohio Court of Common Pleas Lake County)*
Mailing address: P.O. Box 490, Painesville 44077.
Office: 47 North Park Place, Painesville 44077.
Telephone: (440) 350-2720.
Fax: (440) 350-2692

COMSTOCK, Mark A. *(Judge, Berea Municipal Court)* Elected Nov 2, 1999 to term beginning Jan 2, 2000. Term expires Jan 1, 2006. Born Rochester Pennsylvania July 20, 1954. Methodist. Educated at Wittenberg University B.A. 1976 and Gonzaga University School of Law J.D. 1979. Admitted to practice Ohio 1979 and U.S. District Court Northern District of Ohio 1988. In legal practice Berea 1979-94 and Middleburg Heights 1995-99.

Office: 11 Berea Commons, Berea 44017.
Telephone: (440) 826-5856.
Fax: (440) 891-3387

CONNALLY, C. Ellen *(Judge, Cleveland Municipal Court)* Elected to term beginning Jan 2, 1980. Reelected 1985, 1991 and 1997. Current term expires Jan 2, 2004. Born Cleveland Ohio Jan 26, 1945. Catholic. Educated at Bowling Green State University B.S. 1967 and Cleveland State University J.D. 1970 M.A. with honors 1997. Law Clerk to Hon. Alvin I. Krenzler, Ohio Court of Appeals Eighth District 1971-72. Member Alpha Kappa Alpha. Admitted to practice Ohio 1971, U.S. District Court Northern District of Ohio 1972 and U.S. Supreme Court 1975. Began legal practice Cleveland 1971. Referee, Cuyahoga County Probate Court 1972-80.

Formerly with Cleveland Board of Education and Law Department. Member Ohio Supreme Court Traffic Rules Commission 1981, Special Committee of Ohio Supreme Court to Evaluate Judicial Endorsements, National Conference of Black Lawyers, John M. Harlan Law Club (Secretary since 1976, Executive Committee, Board of Trustees), Black Women Lawyers Association of Cleveland (Treasurer 1975-76, Vice President 1976-77, President 1977-79, Historian since 1979), Cleveland Women Lawyers, Cleveland Lawyers Association, Greater Cleveland Municipal Judges Association, Ohio Municipal Judges Association, American Judges Association, Joint Cleveland-Cuyahoga County (Former Secretary Juvenile Court Committee, former member Bar Poll Committee, former Chairman Legal Aid Committee, member Finance Committee), Cuyahoga County (Board of Trustees 1976-79, Treasurer 1979-80) and National (Member Judicial Conference) Bar Associations. Awarded Certificate of Achievement from American Academy of Judicial Education, Guest Lecturer The National Judicial College Reno Nevada 1980, 1981 and 1982. Attended Ohio Judicial College 1980, 1981, 1982 and 1984 (Member Board of Trustees). Cited for Excellent Judicial Service 1980 and 1982 and for Outstanding Judicial Service 1981 by the Supreme Court. Former Assistant to Director HOPE (Housing Our People Economically). Democrat. Member Legal Aid Society of Cleveland (Board of Trustees 1974-77, Treasurer 1976-77), Northern Ohio Lung Association (Board of Trustees 1974-76, Executive Committee 1976-77), Ohio Lung Association (Executive Committee 1976-77), Bowling Green State University Alumni Association (Board of Trustees 1975-78, Treasurer 1976-77, Vice President 1977-78), Children Services of Cleveland (Board of Trustees 1978-80), Women's Space (Board of Trustees 1979-80), Camp Fire Girls of Cleveland (Board of Trustees 1980-82), Cleveland Society for the Blind (Board of Trustees since 1983), Community Action Against Drug Addiction (Board of Trustees since 1983), Cleveland Board of Education Law and Public Service Magnet School (Advisory Committee since 1981) and Adult Continuing Education (Advisory Committee since 1981) and People United to Save Humanity (PUSH).

Mailing address: P.O. Box 94894, Cleveland 44101-4894.
Office: 1200 Ontario Street, Cleveland 44113-1645.
Telephone: (216) 664-4972.
Fax: (216) 664-6737
E-mail address: cellenc@aol.com

CONNAUGHTON, J. B. *(Judge, Butler County Court)* Appointed by Governor George V. Voinovich March 1990. Elected Nov 8, 1994 and 2000. Current term expires Dec 31, 2006. Born Hamilton Ohio Sept 12, 1938. Roman Catholic. Educated at Xavier University B.S.B.A. 1960 and University of Cincinnati J.D. 1963. Admitted to practice Ohio 1964 and U.S. District Court Southern District of Ohio 1965. In legal practice Hamilton since 1964.

Trustee Hanover Township. Member Butler County, Ohio State and American Bar Associations. Republican. Former Legal Counsel Ohio Ducks Unlimited. State Chairman Quail Unlimited, Inc. Enjoys hunting and fishing.

Office: 101 High Street, First Floor, Hamilton 45011.
Telephone: (513) 887-3459.
Fax: (513) 887-3568

CONNOR, John A. *(Judge, Ohio Court of Common Pleas Franklin County)* Elected to term beginning Jan 6, 1993. Reelected 1998, current term expires Jan 2005. Born Akron Ohio July 28, 1940. Catholic. Educated at Mount St. Mary's College B.S. 1962 and The Ohio State University J.D. 1966. Member Phi Delta Phi. Admitted to practice Ohio 1966, U.S. District Court Southern District of Ohio and U.S. Supreme Court. In legal practice Franklin County and Columbus 1973-93.

Assistant Attorney General 1966-73. Member Ohio Common Pleas Judges Association, American Judges Association, Columbus (Common Pleas Court Committee and Dispute Resolution Committee), Ohio State (Civil Law Committee) and American (Executive Committee, Committees on Alternative Dispute Resolution, Court Management and Judicial Evaluation) Bar Associations. Democrat. President Mount St. Mary's College Ohio Alumni Association. Member St. Francis of Assisi Roman Catholic Church, 4° Knights of Columbus, Columbus Maennerchor, Columbus Country Club, Press Club of Ohio, Ancient Order of Hibernians, Loyal Order of Moose, Charity Newsies, Capital Club, Agonis Club, Shamrock Club and NAACP. Enjoys skiing, playing golf and jogging.

Office: 369 South High Street, #6D, Columbus 43215.
Telephone: (614) 462-3660.
Fax: (614) 462-3868
E-mail address: john_connor@fccourts.org

COOK, Deborah L. *(Justice, Supreme Court of Ohio)* Elected 1994 to term beginning 1995. Reelected Nov 2000, current term expires 2007. Educated at University of Akron B.A. 1974 J.D. 1978. Awarded honorary LL.D. University of Akron 1996. In legal practice Akron 1976-91. Judge, Ohio Court of Appeals Ninth District 1991-94.

Past President Akron Bar Foundation. Chair Commission on Public Legal Education. Fellow American Bar Foundation. Member Ohio Commission on Dispute Resolution and Conflict Management and Akron Bar Association. Board of Trustees Akron University School of Law, Stan Hywet Hall and Gardens, Summit County United Way and Volunteer Center. Volunteer Safe Landing Shelter and Mobile Meals.

Office: 30 East Broad Street, Third Floor, Columbus 43266-0419.
Telephone: (614) 466-3828.
Fax: (614) 752-5801
E-mail address: cookd@sconet.state.oh.us

COONEY, Colleen Conway *(Judge, Ohio Court of Appeals Eighth District)* Born Cleveland Ohio Oct 26, 1955. Roman Catholic. Educated at Case Western Reserve University B.S. cum laude 1978 J.D. 1981. Law Clerk to Hon. John V. Corrigan, Ohio Court of Appeals Eighth District 1981-84. Moot Court Board. Admitted to practice Ohio 1981, U.S. District Court Northern District

COONEY, COLLEEN CONWAY—*Continued*

of Ohio 1983 and U.S. Court of Appeals Sixth Circuit 1985. Former Judge, Cleveland Municipal Court, elected to term beginning Jan 4, 1992.

Assistant Prosecuting Attorney Cuyahoga County 1984-92. Member Municipal-County Judges of Ohio, Inc. (President 1998), American Judges Association and Ohio State Bar Association. Host Judge Municipal-County Judges of Ohio Summer Meeting July 1997. Board of Trustees Christian Legal Services, Regina High School and Case Western Reserve University School of Law Alumni Association.

Office: One Lakeside Avenue, Cleveland 44113.
Telephone: (216) 443-6367.
Fax: (216) 443-2044
E-mail address: ccc@8thappeals.com

COOPER, Ethna M. *(Judge, Hamilton County Municipal Court)*

Office: 1000 Main Street, Cincinnati 45202.
Telephone: (513) 946-5149.
Fax: (513) 946-5151

COOPERRIDER, Luann *(Judge, Ohio Court of Common Pleas Perry County)* Elected to term beginning Feb 9, 1991. Reelected 1996 and 2002. Current term expires 2009. Serves Probate and Juvenile Divisions. Born Thornville Ohio Dec 30, 1955. Lutheran. Educated at The Ohio State University B.S. 1978, Loyola University, Rome Italy 1980 and Capital University Law School J.D. 1983. Admitted to practice Ohio 1983. In legal practice Thornville 1983 to Feb 1991.

Night Prosecutor 1982-90. Assistant Prosecutor 1986-90. Instructor in Business Law The Ohio State University 1987-88 and Juvenile Law Hocking College since 1991. Trustee since 1996 and President 2003 Ohio Association of Juvenile and Family Court Judges. Member Women Judges Association, Perry County and Ohio State Bar Associations. Participant Ohio Common Pleas Judges Association annual meetings and Probate Juvenile Judges Association seminars. Named Perry County Person of the Year by Perry County Professional Business Women's Association 1986. Recipient Nettie Cronise Lutes Women in Law Award from Ohio State Bar Association 2001. Named project coordinator of two juvenile facilities built in Perry County. Member Executive Committee Democratic Party 1980-90. President Democratic Women 1988-90. Member American Cancer Society. Enjoys horses, boating and bicycling. Personal Statement or Quote: "Be as honest as you can be with everyone."

Mailing address: P.O. Box 167, New Lexington 43764-0167.
Telephone: (740) 342-1118.
Fax: (740) 342-5524
E-mail address: coop's@ascenture.net

CORABI, Joseph M. *(Judge, Jefferson County Court)*

Office: 1007 Franklin Avenue, Toronto 43964.
Telephone: (740) 537-2020.
Fax: (740) 537-1866

CORBIN, Robert Alan *(Judge, Ohio Court of Common Pleas Brown County)*

Office: 101 South Main Street, Georgetown 45121.
Telephone: (937) 378-4101.
Fax: (937) 378-4212

CORRIGAN, Brian J. *(Judge, Ohio Court of Common Pleas Cuyahoga County)*

Office: 1200 Ontario Street, Cleveland 44113.
Telephone: (216) 443-8747.
Fax: (216) 348-4032

CORRIGAN, John E. *(Judge, Ohio Court of Common Pleas Cuyahoga County)* Serves Probate Division.

Office: One Lakeside Avenue, Cleveland 44113.
Telephone: (216) 443-7557.
Fax: (216) 443-5445

CORRIGAN, Michael J. *(Judge, Ohio Court of Appeals Eighth District)* Appointed by Governor George V. Voinovich Dec 30, 1997. Born Cleveland Ohio Jan 31, 1949. Roman Catholic. Educated at Boston College B.A. cum laude 1971 and Cleveland-Marshall College of Law J.D. 1974. Admitted to practice Ohio 1974 and Florida 1974. Began legal practice Cleveland 1974. Judge, Ohio Court of Common Pleas Cuyahoga County Jan 12, 1983 to Dec 29, 1997.

Trial Attorney County Prosecutor's Office Cuyahoga County 1974-83. Lecturer Cleveland Police Academy. Member Ohio Common Pleas Judges Association, Ohio Judicial Conference, Cleveland and Ohio State Bar Associations. Seminar Lecturer Ohio Judicial College since 1983 and Ohio Legal Center Institute since 1983. Named One of Cleveland's Top Ten Trial Attorneys 1982. Recipient numerous awards for docket currency from Ohio Supreme Court. Laborer with Local 310, 1966-74. Former member Executive Committee Cuyahoga City Democratic Party. Former member Board of Directors Elks Club. Member St. Richard's Parents Club, St. Ignatius and Boston College Alumni Association. Enjoys gardening, racquetball and fishing.

Office: One Lakeside Avenue, Cleveland 44113.
Telephone: (216) 443-6360.
Fax: (216) 443-2044
E-mail address: mccorrig@aol.com

CORRIGAN, Patrick F. *(Judge, Ohio Court of Common Pleas Cuyahoga County)* Serves Juvenile Division.

Office: 2163 East 22nd Street, Cleveland 44115-2998.
Telephone: (216) 443-8415.
Fax: (216) 443-5794
E-mail address: kcorr1013@stratos.net

CORZINE, William J. *(Judge, Ohio Court of Common Pleas Ross County)*

Office: Two North Paint Street, Suite C, Chillicothe 45601-3109.
Telephone: (740) 702-3032.
Fax: (740) 702-3036

COSGROVE, Patricia A. *(Judge, Ohio Court of Common Pleas Summit County)*

Office: 209 South High Street, Akron 44308.
Telephone: (330) 643-2228.
Fax: (330) 643-8731

COSTINE, J. Mark *(Judge, Ohio Court of Common Pleas Belmont County)* Serves Probate and Juvenile Divisions.

Office: 101 West Main Street, St. Clairsville 43950-1154.
Telephone: (740) 699-2141.
Fax: (740) 699-2143
E-mail address: markcjmc@aol.com

COTTRILL, Kelly J. *(Judge, Muskingum County Court)*
Office: 27 North Fifth Street, Zanesville 43701.
Telephone: (740) 455-7138.
Fax: (740) 455-7157

COYNE, William J. *(Judge, Ohio Court of Common Pleas Cuyahoga County)* Elected 1994. Reelected to subsequent term.
Office: 1200 Ontario Street, Cleveland 44113.
Telephone: (216) 443-8755.
Fax: (216) 348-4092

CRAFT, Ronald Richard *(Judge, Ohio Court of Common Pleas Butler County)* Serves Juvenile Division.
Office: 280 North Fair Avenue, Hamilton 45011.

CRAWFORD, Dale A. *(Judge, Ohio Court of Common Pleas Franklin County)* Elected to term beginning Jan 8, 1983. Reelected 1988, 1994 and 2000. Current term expires Dec 31, 2006. Born East Orange New Jersey May 5, 1943. Educated at The Ohio State University B.S. 1965 J.D. 1968. Member Phi Delta Theta and Delta Theta Phi. Admitted to practice Ohio 1968 and Virginia 1969. In legal practice Columbus Ohio 1968 and 1970-79. Judge, Franklin County Municipal Court 1979-83.
Professor Virginia Polytechnic Institute and State University 1968-70, Capital University 1979-82 and 1986, and The Ohio State University 1981. Member Virginia State Bar, Columbus (Member Board of Governors), Ohio State (Delegate), Federal and American (Judicial Delegate) Bar Associations. Republican.
Office: 369 South High Street, Suite 8D, Columbus 43215-4554.
Telephone: (614) 462-3811.
Fax: (614) 462-2464
E-mail address: dale_crawford@fccourts.org

CREHAN, Matthew J. *(Judge, Ohio Court of Common Pleas Butler County)*
Office: Government Services Center, Third Floor, 315 High Street, Hamilton 45011.
Telephone: (513) 887-3591.
Fax: (513) 887-5667
E-mail address: crehanm@butlercountyohio.org

CRONIN, Maureen A. *(Judge, Ohio Court of Common Pleas Mahoning County)* Elected 1994. Reelected to subsequent term.
Office: 120 Market Street, Youngstown 44503.
Telephone: (330) 740-2154.
Fax: (330) 742-2529
E-mail address: vmalaska@earthlink.net

CROSS, Denise Martin *(Judge, Ohio Court of Common Pleas Montgomery County)* Elected to term beginning Jan 2001. Term expires Jan 2007. Serves Domestic Relations Division. Currently serves as Administrative Judge. Born Cincinnati Ohio May 16, 1953. African Methodist Episcopalian. Educated at Wilberforce University B.A. 1975 and University of Akron J.D. 1978. Law Clerk to Hon. Evan J. Reed, Ohio Court of Common Pleas Summit County 1976-78. Admitted to practice Pennsylvania 1978, Ohio 1987 and U.S. District Courts Western District of Pennsylvania 1981 and Southern District of Ohio 1987. Chief Magistrate, Juvenile Court 1991-2001.
Assistant Prosecutor Montgomery County 1988-90. Member Thurgood Marshall Law Society, Ohio State and National Bar Associations. Girl Scout Leader. Sunday School Teacher. Enjoys reading, dancing and tennis. Personal Statement or Quote: "To whom much is given much is expected."
Office: 301 West Third Street, Dayton 45422-4248.
Telephone: (937) 496-7538.
Fax: (937) 496-7443
E-mail address: brignerm@montcnty.org

CROW, Fred W., III *(Judge, Ohio Court of Common Pleas Meigs County)* Elected to term beginning Jan 1, 1989. Reelected 1994 and 2000. Current term expires Dec 31, 2006. Born Clarksburg West Virginia Feb 15, 1945. Episcopalian. Educated at Ohio University B.A. and The Ohio State University J.D. Admitted to practice Ohio 1970. In legal practice Pomeroy.
Prosecuting Attorney Meigs County 1977-88.
Office: 100 East Second Street, Pomeroy 45769-1030.
Telephone: (740) 992-6439.
Fax: (740) 992-3828

CRUSH, Thomas H. *(Judge, Ohio Court of Common Pleas Hamilton County)* Appointed by Governor James A. Rhodes June 1978. Elected to subsequent terms. Former Judge, Hamilton County Municipal Court.
Office: 1000 Main Street, Room 360, Cincinnati 45202-1217.
Telephone: (513) 946-5750.
Fax: (513) 946-5751

CULBERT, Brad *(Judge, Ohio Court of Common Pleas Sandusky County)* Elected to term beginning Feb 9, 1991. Reelected 1996 and 2002. Current term expires 2009. Serves Probate and Juvenile Divisions. Born Fremont Ohio Oct 1, 1957. Catholic. Educated at College of Wooster B.A. 1980 and University of Toledo J.D. 1983. Admitted to practice Ohio 1983. In legal practice Fremont 1983-90.
Assistant Prosecuting Attorney Sandusky County 1985-90. Member Ohio Association of Probate Judges, Ohio Association of Juvenile and Family Court Judges (Secretary), National Council of Juvenile and Family Court Judges, National College of Probate Judges, Sandusky County (President 1992) and Ohio State Bar Associations. President Fremont Kiwanis Club 1993-94. Enjoys family and advocating for children.
Office: 100 North Park Avenue, Fremont 43420-2476.
Telephone: (419) 334-6417.
Fax: (419) 334-6210
E-mail address: judgebc@co.sandusky.oh.us

CUNNINGHAM, Ann R. *(Judge, Putnam County Court)* Appointed by Governor Richard F. Celeste to term beginning March 25, 1985. Elected 1988, Nov 1994 and Nov 2000. Current term expires Dec 31, 2006. Born Ottawa Ohio Jan 15, 1938. Educated at The Ohio State University A.B. 1960 and Ohio Northern University J.D. 1967. Member Kappa Beta Phi. Admitted to practice Ohio 1968. Began legal practice Ottawa 1968.
Assistant Prosecuting Attorney Putnam County 1968-72. Member Putnam County (President 1974-75), Northwestern Ohio (Former Treasurer, Secretary, Vice President and President) and Ohio State Bar Associations. Worked for Ohio Department of Industrial and Economic Development Feb 1961 to Sept 1961, Columbus Better Business Bureau Oct 1961 to Nov 1962 and International Business Machines Nov 1962 to Nov 1964. Member 1968-76 and Treasurer 1971 Business and Profes-

CUNNINGHAM, ANN R.—*Continued*
sional Women's Association. Member Putnam County Mental Health and Mental Retardation Board 1970-77.
Office: 303 Courthouse, 245 East Main Street, Ottawa 45875-1968.
Telephone: (419) 523-3110.
Fax: (419) 523-5284

CUNNINGHAM, Penelope R. *(Judge, Ohio Court of Common Pleas Hamilton County)* Serves Domestic Relations Division.
Office: 800 Broadway, Cincinnati 45202-1267.
Telephone: (513) 946-9030.
Fax: (513) 946-9033
E-mail address: pcunningham@cms.hamilton-co.org

CUPP, Robert Richard *(Judge, Ohio Court of Appeals Third District)*
Office: 204 North Main Street, Lima 45801.

D'APOLITO, David *(Judge, Mahoning County Court)*
Office: 6000 Mahoning Avenue, Youngstown 44515.
Telephone: (330) 740-2001.
Fax: (330) 740-2036

DARTT, Denise Ann *(Judge, Toledo Municipal Court)* Appointed by Governor Richard F. Celeste. Elected to subsequent terms. Educated at Toledo College of Law J.D. 1978.
Former Assistant Public Defender Toledo Public Defender's Office. Former Staff Attorney Toledo College of Law. Former Special Counsel for Attorney General Anthony Celebrezze.
Office: 555 North Erie Street, Toledo 43624-1391.
Telephone: (419) 245-1950.
Fax: (419) 245-1802
E-mail address: denise.dartt@noris.org

DAVIDSON, Robert S. *(Judge, Ohio Court of Common Pleas Marion County)*
Office: Courthouse Square, 100 North Main Street, Marion 43302-3089.
Telephone: (740) 223-4210.
Fax: (740) 387-1321

DAVIS, Allan H. *(Judge, Ohio Court of Common Pleas Hancock County)* Elected to term beginning Nov 29, 1974. Reelected to subsequent terms. Current term expires Feb 2009. Serves Probate and Juvenile Divisions. Born Findlay Ohio Sept 17, 1943. United Methodist. Educated at Bowling Green State University B.S. in Business 1965 and Ohio Northern University J.D. 1968. President and Vice President Ohio Northern University Student Bar Association 1966-68. Admitted to practice Ohio 1968. Began legal practice Findlay 1968.
With Findlay Civil Service Commission 1972-74. Solicitor Village of Rawson 1972-74. Treasurer 1985-86, Secretary 1986-87 and President 1988-89 Ohio Association of Juvenile and Family Court Judges. Member Findlay-Hancock County (Secretary 1970 and President 1981), Ohio State and American Bar Associations. Named Outstanding Young Man of the Year 1976. Republican. Board of Trustees Big Brothers/Big Sisters of Hancock County since 1982. Member Findlay Hancock County Community Foundation (Chair since 1996), Hancock County Children's Services Board (President), Hancock County Alcoholism Council (Vice President), Findlay Rotary and Elks Club.
Office: 308 Dorney Plaza, Findlay 45840-3302.
Telephone: (419) 424-7079 (probate), 424-7066 (juvenile).
Fax: (419) 424-7081
E-mail address: ahdavis@co.hancock.oh.us

DAVIS, D. William, Jr. *(Judge, Belmont County Court)* Appointed by Governor James A. Rhodes to term beginning Feb 9, 1979. Elected 1980, 1986, 1992 and 1998. Current term expires Dec 31, 2004. Born Wheeling West Virginia Sept 5, 1948. Presbyterian. Educated at The Ohio State University B.A. 1970 J.D. 1973. Admitted to practice Ohio 1973 and U.S. District Court Southern District of Ohio 1974. In legal practice Columbus 1973-74, Bridgeport 1974-85 and Bellaire since 1985.
Member Belmont County (President 1988-89) and Ohio State Bar Associations. Captain USAR 1972-80. Democrat. Village Clerk Bridgeport 1978-79. Member Bridgeport Rotary Club (President 1977-78).
Office: 400 West 26th Street, Suite 100, Bellaire 43906.
Telephone: (740) 676-4490.
Fax: (740) 671-6100

DAVIS, David P. *(Judge, Ohio Court of Common Pleas Hamilton County)* Elected to term beginning Jan 4, 1997. Born Knott County Kentucky May 9, 1940. Methodist. Educated at Morehead State University 1965 and Salmon P. Chase College of Law 1972. Law Clerk to Hon. Gilbert Bettman, Ohio Court of Common Pleas. Member Phi Alpha Delta. Admitted to practice Ohio 1972. Began legal practice Cincinnati 1972. Referee 1980 and former Judge, Hamilton County Municipal Court, appointed by Governor James A. Rhodes Jan 5, 1981.
Assistant Prosecutor 1972-76. Member Municipal Court Judges Association, American Judges Association and Ohio State Bar Association. Republican.
Office: 1000 Main Street, Room 530, Cincinnati 45202.
Telephone: (513) 946-5890.
Fax: (513) 946-5894

DAVIS, Giles Jackson, Jr. *(Judge, Ohio Court of Common Pleas Montgomery County)*
Mailing address: P.O. Box 972, Dayton 45401.

DEDDENS, Robert L. *(Judge, Oakwood Municipal Court)* Elected Nov 4, 1989 to term beginning Jan 1, 1990. Reelected 1995 and 2001. Current term expires Dec 31, 2007. Born Cincinnati Ohio Sept 5, 1940. Roman Catholic. Educated at University of Cincinnati B.S.Ch.E. 1963 J.D. 1967. Staff member University of Cincinnati Law Review 1967. Admitted to practice Ohio 1967 and U.S. District Court Southern District of Ohio 1967. In legal practice Dayton since 1967.
Member Municipal-County Judges of Ohio, Inc., Dayton and Ohio State Bar Associations.
Office: 30 Park Avenue, Dayton 45419.
Telephone: (937) 293-3058.
Fax: (937) 297-2939

DEERING, Randy D. *(Judge, Pike County Court)*
Office: 106 North Market Street, Waverly 45690.
Telephone: (740) 947-4003.
Fax: (740) 947-7644

DeGENARO, Mary *(Judge, Ohio Court of Appeals Seventh District)*
Office: 120 Market Street, Fourth Floor, Youngstown 44503.
Telephone: (330) 740-2180.
Fax: (330) 740-2182
E-mail address: mdegenaro@aol.com

DeLAMATRE, Robert C. *(Judge, Ohio Court of Common Pleas Erie County)* Serves Domestic Relations and Juvenile Divisions.
Office: 323 Columbus Avenue, Fourth Floor, Sandusky 44870-2697.
Telephone: (419) 627-7782.
Fax: (419) 627-6600
E-mail address: rdelamatre@erie-county-ohio.net

DELLICK, F. Theresa *(Judge, Ohio Court of Common Pleas Mahoning County)* Serves Juvenile Division. Former Judge, Mahoning County Court.
Office: 300 East Scott Street, Youngstown 44505-2998.
Telephone: (330) 740-2244.
Fax: (330) 740-2286

DESHLER, Dana *(Judge, Ohio Court of Appeals Tenth District)* Appointed by governor 1991. Elected Nov 1992 and 1998. Current term expires 2004. Born Columbus Ohio April 8, 1937. Protestant. Educated at The Ohio State University B.A. 1960 and Franklin University LL.B. 1966 replaced by J.D. Admitted to practice Ohio 1966, U.S. District Court Southern District of Ohio 1967 and U.S. Court of Appeals Sixth Circuit 1974. In legal practice Columbus 1966-86. Judge 1987-91 and Administrative Judge 1990, Ohio Court of Common Pleas Franklin County.
Member House of Representatives Ohio 1980-86. Former Member Franklin County Legal Defender Commission. Treasurer Ohio Common Pleas Judges Association. Co-chairman Judicial Welfare Committee Ohio Judicial Conference. Member American Judicature Society and Ohio State Bar Association. Attended The National Judicial College, Reno Nevada 1988 and 1990. Ohio Army National Guard 1960-66. Member Charity Newsies (Past President) and Torch Club. Enjoys golf, art and travel.
Office: 373 South High Street, 24th Floor, Columbus 43215-4578.
Telephone: (614) 462-4054.
Fax: (614) 462-7249

DeWEESE, James *(Judge, Ohio Court of Common Pleas Richland County)* Elected Nov 1990 to term beginning Feb 5, 1991. Reelected 1996 and 2002. Current term expires 2009. Born Ohio Nov 16, 1946. Educated at Miami University, Ohio B.S. in Business summa cum laude 1968 and University of Dayton J.D. summa cum laude 1979. Editor-in-Chief University of Dayton Law Review 1978-79. Law Clerk to Hon. Leland R. Rutherford, Ohio Court of Appeals Fifth District 1977 and Magistrate Robert A. Steinberg, U.S. District Court Southern District of Ohio 1978. Admitted to practice Ohio 1979.
Member Richland County (President 1989) and Ohio State Bar Associations.
Office: 50 Park Avenue East, Mansfield 44902-1888.
Telephone: (419) 774-5567.
Fax: (419) 774-5516
E-mail address: judgedeweese@kosinet.com

DEWEY, John P. *(Judge, Sandusky County Court)* Appointed by Governor James A. Rhodes Oct 1975. Elected 1976, 1982, 1988, 1994 and 2000. Current term expires Dec 30, 2006. Born Fremont Ohio Feb 20, 1947. Presbyterian. Educated at Muskingum College B.A. 1969 and The Ohio State University J.D. 1972. Admitted to practice Ohio 1972. In legal practice Clyde 1972.
Member Civil Service Commission. City Solicitor Clyde 1975. Member Sandusky County and Ohio State Bar Associations. Republican. Enjoys golf.
Office: 123 West Buckeye Street, Clyde 43410-1998.
Telephone: (419) 547-9471.
Fax: (419) 547-0139
E-mail address: deweylaw@opman.com

DEZSO, Carol J. *(Judge, Ohio Court of Common Pleas Summit County)* Serves Domestic Relations Division.
Office: 209 South High, Akron 44308.
Telephone: (330) 643-2357.
Fax: (330) 643-2126

DINKELACKER, Patrick T. *(Judge, Ohio Court of Common Pleas Hamilton County)*
Office: 1000 Main Street, Room 370, Cincinnati 45202.
Telephone: (513) 946-5755.
Fax: (513) 946-5752

DLOTT, Susan J. *(Judge, United States District Court Southern District of Ohio)* Appointed for life by President Bill Clinton to term beginning Dec 26, 1995. Born Dayton Ohio Sept 11, 1949. Educated at University of Pennsylvania B.A. 1970 and Boston University School of Law J.D. 1973. Law Clerk to Hon. Alvin I. Krenzler and Hon. Jack G. Day, Ohio Court of Appeals Eighth District Aug 1973 to July 1974. Admitted to practice Ohio 1973, U.S. District Courts Southern 1975 and Northern 1989 Districts of Ohio and Eastern District of Kentucky 1984, U.S. Court of Appeals Sixth Circuit 1976, U.S. Supreme Court 1980 and Kentucky 1990. In legal practice Cincinnati Ohio April 1979 to Dec 1995.
Assistant U.S. Attorney Southern District of Ohio Feb 1975 to April 1979. Master of the Bench 1984-98 and President 1997-98 and since 2002 Potter Stewart Inn of Court. Trustee Cincinnati Bar Foundation 1993-95. Former Member Carl D. Kessler Inn of Court, Franklin Chapter American Inns of Court and Greater Cincinnati Women Lawyers Association. Life Member Sixth Circuit Judicial Conference. Member Cincinnati, Dayton, Kentucky, Ohio State (Gender in the Courts Subcommittee since 1994), Federal (Assistant Treasurer 1981-82, Treasurer 1982-83, Secretary 1983-84 and Vice President 1984-86 Cincinnati Chapter) and American Bar Associations. Instructor National Institute for Trial Advocacy. Honored by Cincinnati Leading Women 1998. Recipient Career Woman of Achievement Award from Y.W.C.A. 1996, Community Service Gift of Appreciation Award from Downtown Residents' Council 2000 and U.S. Postal Service Commendation and Service Award from Dayton Bar Association. Founding Member Women's Council of Democratic Senatorial Campaign Committee 1992-95. Alexis de Tocqueville Team Leader United Way Campaign 1994. Member Jan 20, 1988 to Dec 31, 1993 and Vice Chairman 1990-93 Ohio Building Authority. Member Design Team Selection Committee 1991 and Building Committee 1992-95 Aronoff Center for the Arts. National Co-chairman International Leadership Reunion United Jewish Appeal 1995. Co-chair Women's

DLOTT, SUSAN J.—*Continued*

Division Jewish Federation of Cincinnati 1995-96. Chairman Interreligious Relationships and Church-State Separation Committee 1984-88 and Board Member 1980-90 Jewish Community Relations Council of Cincinnati. Board of Trustees Cincinnati Fine Arts Fund since 2002. Former Volunteer Hamilton County Park District. Life Member NAACP and Hadassah. Member Leadership Cincinnati Alumni Association and Queen City Dog Training Club, Inc.

Office: 829 U.S. Courthouse, 100 East Fifth Street, Cincinnati 45202-3927.

Telephone: (513) 564-7630.

DOAN, Rupert A. *(Judge, Ohio Court of Appeals First District)* Assumed office Jan 5, 1981. Elected 1982, 1988, 1994 and 2000. Currently serves as Presiding Judge. Born Sept 13, 1933. Educated at Ohio Wesleyan University B.A. in Political Science 1955 and University of Cincinnati J.D. 1958. Admitted to practice Ohio 1958. Judge, Hamilton County Court 1966-67. Judge and Presiding Judge, Hamilton County Municipal Court 1967-75, appointed by Governor James A. Rhodes. Judge and Presiding Judge, Ohio Court of Common Pleas Hamilton County 1976-80.

Lecturer on Constitutional Law Ohio Wesleyan University. Chairman by Presidential appointment, Adjudication Committee National Highway Transportation Safety Advisory Commission until March 19, 1978. Member Ohio Courts of Appeals Judges Association (Chief Justice), American Judges Association (Past President), American Judicature Society and Ohio State Bar Association. Lecturer Judicial Seminars American Bar Association, Ohio Judicial Seminars and Cincinnati Bar Association Seminars. Recipient Nicholas Longworth Award from University of Cincinnati College of Law. Captain USAF three years active duty. Board of Trustees Wesley Foundation University of Cincinnati, St. Joseph Orphanage (Past President) and Methodist Union. Trustee Emeritus Twin Towers Methodist Home. Member Shiloh Community Methodist Church (Trustee), American Cancer Society Board (Past President) and Preservation Committee Old St. Mary's Church.

Office: 230 East Ninth Street, Twelfth Floor, Cincinnati 45202.

Telephone: (513) 946-3441.

Fax: (513) 946-3411

DONEGHY, Charles J. *(Judge, Ohio Court of Common Pleas Lucas County)* Term expires Dec 31, 2006. Born Toledo Ohio July 4, 1938. Educated at University of Toledo B.B.A. 1960 J.D. 1965. Member Alpha Phi Alpha. Admitted to practice Ohio 1965. Began legal practice Toledo 1968. Former Judge, Toledo Municipal Court, elected to term beginning Jan 2, 1978.

Assistant Prosecutor 1969-77 and Chief Assistant Prosecutor Jan 1977 to Dec 1977 Lucas County. Member Ohio Municipal Court Judges Association, American Judicature Society, American Judges, Toledo, Lucas County, Ohio State and American Bar Associations. Board Member Criminal Justice Regional Planning Unit. Captain U.S. Army 1966-68. Democrat. Board Member Court Diagnostic and Treatment Center, Boys Club, Central YMCA, Executive Committee Toledo University Law Alumni Association, United Central Services and Minority Law Scholarship Foundation. Former Board Member and Past President Economic Opportunity Planning Association of Greater Toledo, Inc., Toledo Old Town Community Organization, Old West End District Association and Jobs Training Center, Inc. Member All Saints Episcopal Church and Old Newsboys Goodfellow Association. Enjoys fishing, racquetball, tennis, music, bowling and jogging.

Office: Courthouse, 700 Adams Street, Toledo 43624-1678.

Telephone: (419) 213-4570.

Fax: (419) 213-4181

DONNELLY, John J. *(Judge, Ohio Court of Common Pleas Cuyahoga County)* Deputy Clerk 1965-69, Trial Referee 1969-73, Court Administrator and Chief Trial Referee 1973-80 Probate Division. Elected Judge to term beginning Dec 19, 1980. Reelected 1983, 1990, 1996 and 2002. Current term expires Dec 31, 2008. Serves Probate Division. Born Cleveland Ohio Feb 25, 1943. Roman Catholic. Educated at LaSalle College B.S. in Accounting 1965 and Cleveland-Marshall College of Law J.D. 1969. Admitted to practice Ohio 1969.

Co-author "Duties of the Probate Court Judge" Ohio Judicial College 1978. Lecturer in Probate Law and Procedure Cleveland-Marshall College of Law, Cleveland State University, Case Western Reserve School of Law and Ohio Department of Mental Health and Mental Retardation Division of Forensic Psychiatry. Member Ohio-Ukraine Rule of Law Committee, Ohio Legislative Service Commission (Select Committee on Standard Probate Forms), American Judicature Society, Ohio Probate Judges Association (President 1986-87), National College of Probate Judges, Cleveland, Cuyahoga County and Ohio State Bar Associations. Chairman Ohio Judicial Conference 1992-93. Chairman Judicial Conference of the Eighth Judicial District 1996-98. Member Ohio Supreme Court Continuing Legal Education Commission. Visiting Judges Committee Ohio Supreme Court 1987. Lecturer on Probate Law and Procedure Ohio Probate Judges Association, Ohio Legal Center Institute, Cleveland and Cuyahoga County Bar Associations. Recipient Superior Judicial Service Awards 1981-85, Presidential Award from Cleveland Bar Association 1984 and Outstanding Alumnus Award from Cleveland-Marshall College of Law 1986. Trustee Association for Retarded Citizens 1979-86, St. Augustine Manor 1982-88 (President 1987-88), Catholic Social Services Advisory Board 1983-88, St. Edward High School and Cleveland State University Law School Alumni Association. Member St. Ignatius High School Fathers Club 1980-84 and Magnificat High School Fathers Club 1981-85. Member Visiting Committee Cleveland State University 1992-2002. Enjoys golf.

Office: One Lakeside Avenue, Cleveland 44113.

Telephone: (216) 443-8975.

Fax: (216) 443-5446

DONOFRIO, Gene *(Judge, Ohio Court of Appeals Seventh District)* Elected Nov 1992 to term beginning Feb 9, 1993. Reelected Nov 1998, current term expires Feb 8, 2005. Born Youngstown Ohio Sept 2, 1953. Catholic. Educated at Youngstown State University B.A. 1975 and University of Akron J.D. 1978. Admitted to practice Ohio 1978 and Florida 1980. In legal practice Youngstown Ohio 1978-93.

Former Assistant Prosecutor Youngstown City and Mahoning County. Former Assistant Attorney General Ohio. Instructor Youngstown State University since 1990. Member The Florida Bar, Mahoning County, Ohio State and American Bar Associations. Democrat. Advi-

DONOFRIO, GENE—*Continued*

sory Board Canfield Career Education. Member Addiction Programs of Mahoning County. Enjoys skiing, boating and family.

Office: 120 Market Street, Fourth Floor, Youngstown 44503-1710.
Telephone: (330) 740-2180.
Fax: (330) 740-2182

DONOVAN, Mary E. *(Judge, Ohio Court of Common Pleas Montgomery County)*

Office: 41 South Perry Street, Room 103, Dayton 45422-2150.
Telephone: (937) 225-4376.
Fax: (937) 225-5406
E-mail address: donovanm@montcourt.org

DOUGLAS, Robert A., Jr. *(Judge, Youngstown Municipal Court)*

Office: 26 South Phelps Street, Youngstown 44503-1370.
Telephone: (330) 742-8857.
Fax: (330) 742-8845
E-mail address: rdoug31204@aol.com

DOWD, David D., Jr. *(Senior Judge, United States District Court Northern District of Ohio)* Appointed for life by President Ronald Reagan to term beginning Oct 8, 1982. Assumed Senior status, serves by assignment. Born Cleveland Ohio Jan 31, 1929. Educated at College of Wooster 1951 and University of Michigan Law School J.D. 1954. In legal practice Canton 1981. Judge, Ohio Court of Appeals Fifth District 1975-80, appointed by Governor James A. Rhodes. Justice, Ohio Supreme Court 1980.

Assistant Prosecuting Attorney 1961-67 and Prosecuting Attorney 1967-76 Stark County. Co-author "Anderson's Ohio Criminal Practice and Procedure." Former Lecturer University of Akron Law School. Member 1969 and Chairman 1975 Ohio Organized Crime Prevention Council, appointed by Governor James A. Rhodes. Member Technical Committee to the Ohio General Assembly (prepared first draft of Ohio's new Criminal Code effective 1974) 1970 and Advisory Committee to Ohio Supreme Court for formulation of Ohio Rules of Criminal Procedure 1971. Served on Commission for the Review of the National Policy Toward Gambling 1972-75, appointed by President Richard Nixon. President Ohio Prosecuting Attorneys Association 1973. Legal Officer U.S. Army in Western Germany 1955-57. Councilman-at-Large City of Massillon 1960. Member Central Presbyterian Church.

Office: U.S. Courthouse & Federal Bldg., Two South Main Street, Akron 44308.
Telephone: (330) 375-5834.

DUES, Wilfrid Gavin *(Judge, Ohio Court of Common Pleas Preble County)* Elected Nov 6, 1990 to term beginning Feb 9, 1991. Reelected 1996 and 2002. Current term expires 2009. Serves Probate and Juvenile Divisions. Born Coshocton Ohio Jan 5, 1950. Roman Catholic. Educated at University of Notre Dame B.A. 1972 and Ohio Northern University J.D. 1975. Member Delta Theta Phi. Admitted to practice Ohio 1975 and U.S. Court of Appeals Sixth Circuit 1987. In legal practice Eaton 1980-91.

Prosecuting Attorney Preble County 1981-91. Member Ohio Association of Probate Judges, Ohio Association of Juvenile and Family Court Judges, National College of Probate Judges, National Council of Juvenile and Family Court Judges, Preble County, Ohio State and American Bar Associations. Instructor Ohio Probate Clerks Association 1993 and 1994. Named Law Enforcement Officer of the Year by Optimists 1991 and Citizen of the Year by Chamber of Commerce 1992. Republican. Past President Eaton Athletic Boosters, Chamber of Commerce and United Way. Founder Preble County Youth Foundation. Enjoys running, skiing and golf.

Office: Courthouse, 101 East Main Street, Eaton 45320-1791.
Telephone: (937) 456-8136.
Fax: (937) 456-5803

DUNNING, Mary L. *(Judge, Parma Municipal Court)* Elected to term beginning Jan 1, 1996. Reelected 2001, current term expires Dec 31, 2007. Born Cleveland Ohio Oct 8, 1937. Educated at Baldwin-Wallace College B.A. 1982, John Marshall Law School J.D. 1986. and St. Luke's School of Nursing R.N. Admitted to practice Ohio 1986.

Assistant Prosecutor City of Parma 1993-94. Member Association of Municipal/County Judges of Ohio, Inc., Cleveland, Cuyahoga County and Ohio State Bar Associations. Councilwoman Parma 1968-72 and 1988-90. President Parma City Council 1990-92.

Office: Parma Municipal Court, 5555 Powers Boulevard, Parma 44129.
Telephone: (440) 887-7457.
Fax: (440) 887-7490

DURKIN, John M. *(Judge, Ohio Court of Common Pleas Mahoning County)* Appointed by Governor George V. Voinovich to term beginning Feb 18, 1997. Elected July 1, 1997 and 2003. Current term expires June 30, 2009. Born Youngstown Ohio July 23, 1958. Educated at University of Dayton B.A. 1980 J.D. 1983. Admitted to practice Ohio 1983 and Pennsylvania 1987.

Assistant Prosecuting Attorney City of Youngstown 1983-86. President Ohio Association of Drug Court Professionals since 1999. Member Mahoning County (President 1998-99, Chairperson Certified Grievance Committee) and Ohio State Bar Associations. Lecturer Mahoning County Bar Association and Ohio Judicial College. Named Lawyer of the Year by Mahoning County Bar Association 1997-98. Recipient Public Service Award from Community Corrections Association 1999.

Office: 120 Market Street, Youngstown 44503.
Telephone: (330) 740-2168.
Fax: (330) 742-5898
E-mail address: jdurkin@mahoningcounty.org

DYKE, Ann *(Judge, Ohio Court of Appeals Eighth District)* Assumed office Feb 9, 1987. Educated at John Carroll University and Cleveland State University Cleveland-Marshall College of Law. Admitted to practice 1969. Former Judge, Ohio Court of Common Pleas Cuyahoga County.

Office: One Lakeside Avenue, Cleveland 44113.
Telephone: (216) 443-6356.
Fax: (216) 443-2044

ECKSTEIN, Steven Douglas *(Judge, Ohio Court of Common Pleas Crawford County)* Elected to term beginning Feb 9, 1985. Reelected 1990, 1996 and 2002. Current term expires 2009. Serves Probate and Juvenile Divisions. Born Galion Ohio Oct 19, 1946. Religious affiliation: United Church of Christ (Evangelical and Re-

ECKSTEIN, STEVEN DOUGLAS—*Continued*

formed). Educated at Ohio Northern University B.A. 1969 J.D. 1972. Member Phi Alpha Delta. Admitted to practice Ohio 1972. Began legal practice Galion 1972. Acting Judge, County and Municipal Court 1977-84. Referee, Ohio Court of Common Pleas Domestic Relations Division 1979-85. Referee, Municipal Court Traffic and Small Claims 1981-84.

Member Ohio Probate and Juvenile Judges Association, Crawford County, Ohio State and American Bar Associations. Former Director of the Board Big Brothers Crawford County.

Office: 112 East Mansfield Street, Bucyrus 44820-2386.

Telephone: (419) 562-1896.

Fax: (419) 562-6538

ECONOMUS, Peter C. *(Judge, United States District Court Northern District of Ohio)* Appointed for life by President Bill Clinton. Born Youngstown Ohio June 10, 1943. Greek Orthodox. Educated at Youngstown State University A.B. 1967 and University of Akron J.D. 1970. Member Theta Xi. Admitted to practice Ohio 1971. Began legal practice Youngstown 1971. Judge, Ohio Court of Common Pleas Mahoning County 1982-97.

Trustee and Member Legislative Committee Ohio Common Pleas Judges Association. Member Civil Law Committee Ohio Judicial College. Recipient Outstanding Citizen Award from Buckeye Elks Lodge #73 1988, Public Service Award from Community Corrections Association 1989, "The Great Communicator Award" for Community Service from Youngstown Hearing and Speech Center 1995, Golden Gavel Award from Ohio Common Pleas Judges Association 1995, Outstanding Alumni Award from University of Akron Law Center Alumni Association 1996 and Ellis Island Medal of Honor 1999. Named Office Holder of the Year by Truman Johnson Women's Democratic Club 1990. Member State Victims Assistance Advisory Board 1986-95. Chairman Mahoning County Community Corrections Planning Board 1987-91. Board of Trustees University of Akron Law Center Alumni Association 1989-95. Member Committee to Celebrate Bicentennial of the U.S. Constitution Youngstown State University.

Office: 313 U.S. Courthouse, 125 Market Street, Youngstown 44503.

Telephone: (330) 746-7830.

EDWARDS, Julie A. *(Judge, Ohio Court of Appeals Fifth District)* Elected to term beginning Feb 10, 1999. Term expires Feb 2005. Educated at The Ohio State University B.A. summa cum laude J.D. 1978. Member Phi Beta Kappa, Phi Kappa Phi and Alpha Lambda Delta. Former Chief Referee and Judge Jan 1989 to Feb 1999, Ohio Court of Common Pleas Stark County.

Former Chief Juvenile Division Prosecutor's Office Stark County. Former Counsel Bureau of Support Stark County. Past President Ohio Association of Juvenile and Family Court Judges.

Office: 110 Central Plaza South, Suite 320, Canton 44702-1941.

Telephone: (330) 451-7766.

Fax: (330) 451-7249

E-mail address: info@fifthdist.org

ELLWOOD, David A. *(Judge, Ohio Court of Common Pleas Guernsey County)*

Office: 801 East Wheeling Avenue, Room E, Cambridge 43725-2358.

Telephone: (740) 432-9252.

Fax: (740) 432-7807

E-mail address: jdae33@yahoo.com

ELUM, Edward J. *(Judge, Massillon Municipal Court)* Elected Nov 7, 1995 to term beginning Jan 1, 1996. Reelected 2001, current term expires Jan 2008. Born Massillon Ohio Sept 14, 1952. Catholic. Educated at University of Notre Dame B.B.A. with honors 1974, The Ohio State University and Ohio Northern University J.D. with honors 1977. Admitted to practice Ohio 1977. In legal practice Massillon.

City Prosecutor Massillon 1978-81. Assistant Attorney General Ohio 1983-85. General Counsel for Higher Education Ohio 1985-90. Instructor in Federal Estate Taxation Stark State College of Technology 1998-99. Recipient Civil Liberties Award from Civil Liberties League of Massillon 1996 and Servant of the People Award from Grace Community Church of Massillon 1998. Lieutenant USNR. Democrat. Former Member Board of Trustees The Massillon Museum, Stark State College of Technology, Stark Development Board, Massillon Community Hospital, Massillon Main Street and Massillon Youth Center. Co-founder The Family Living Center. Advisory Board of Doctors Hospital. Member St. Joseph Catholic Church.

Office: Two James Duncan Plaza S.E., Massillon 44646-6690.

Telephone: (330) 830-1727.

Fax: (330) 830-1756

E-mail address: ejejudge@aol.com

ENLOW, John A. *(Judge, Ohio Court of Common Pleas Portage County)* Born Seguin Texas April 7, 1945. Educated at Ohio University A.B. 1967 and Akron University J.D. 1972. Admitted to practice Ohio 1972. Began legal practice Ravenna 1972. Former Judge, Portage County Municipal Court, appointed by Governor James A. Rhodes Jan 1, 1979.

Member Portage County and Ohio State Bar Associations. Republican.

Office: 203 West Main Street, Ravenna 44266-2778.

Telephone: (330) 297-3866.

Fax: (330) 297-5370

EUFINGER, Charlotte M. *(Judge, Ohio Court of Common Pleas Union County)* Serves Probate and Juvenile Divisions.

Office: Courthouse, 215 West Fifth Street, Marysville 43040.

EVANS, D. Dean *(Judge, Ohio Court of Common Pleas Gallia County)*

Office: 18 Locust Street, Room 1200, Gallipolis 45631-1244.

Telephone: (740) 446-4702.

Fax: (740) 441-2051

EVANS, D. William, Jr. *(Judge, Wayne County Municipal Court)*

Office: 538 North Market Street, Wooster 44691-3499.

Telephone: (330) 287-5663.

Fax: (330) 263-4043

EVANS, David T. *(Judge, Ohio Court of Appeals Fourth District)*
Mailing address: P.O. Box 708, Gallipolis 45631.
Office: 456 Second Avenue, Gallipolis 45631.
Telephone: (740) 446-2129.
Fax: (740) 446-8763

EVANS, James C. *(Judge, Ohio Court of Common Pleas Mahoning County)* Former Judge, Mahoning County Court, elected 1994.
Office: 120 Market Street, Youngstown 44503-1710.
Telephone: (330) 740-2152.
Fax: (330) 742-5890
E-mail address: jevans@mahoningcounty.org

EVANS, Richard I. *(Judge, Ohio Court of Common Pleas Coshocton County)* Appointed by Governor James A. Rhodes 1978. Elected 1980, 1986, 1992 and 1998. Current term expires Dec 2004. Served Probate and Juvenile Divisions 1978-80. Born Coshocton Ohio Oct 17, 1946. Methodist. Educated at The Ohio State University B.A. 1968 J.D. 1971. Admitted to practice Ohio 1971. Began legal practice Coshocton 1971. In legal practice Columbus 1973-77.

Assistant Prosecuting Attorney Coshocton County 1971-73. City Attorney Coshocton 1973. Title Attorney Lawyer's Title Insurance Corporation 1973-74. Assistant Elections Counsel Ohio Secretary of State 1974-77. Staff Attorney Ohio Elections Commission 1977. Important Decision: State of Ohio v. Miskimens, et al. (Ohio's "religious exemption" from prosecution for child endangerment or manslaughter for parents who use "faith healing" is unconstitutional), 490 N.E.2d 931, 22 Ohio Misc. 2d 43, 1984. Member Ohio Judicial Conference, Ohio Common Pleas Judges Association (1st Vice President), Coshocton County and Ohio State Bar Associations. Attends Ohio Common Pleas Judges Association annual meeting and Ohio Judicial College CLE courses. Captain USAR AGC 1971-78. Republican. Page Ohio Senate 1967-70. Researcher and Legislative Draftsman Legislative Reference Bureau Ohio General Assembly 1971. Enjoys carpentry and farming.
Office: 318 Main Street, Coshocton 43845.
Telephone: (740) 622-1595.
Fax: (740) 295-0021

EYSTER, Otho S. *(Judge, Ohio Court of Common Pleas Knox County)* Former Judge, Mount Vernon Municipal Court.
Office: 111 East High Street, Mount Vernon 43050.
Telephone: (740) 393-6779.
Fax: (740) 393-5096
E-mail address: kcacs@ecr.net

FAIN, Mike *(Judge, Ohio Court of Appeals Second District)* Elected to term beginning Feb 11, 1987. Reelected 1992 and 1998. Current term expires Feb 2005. Presiding and Administrative Judge since 2003. Born Miami Florida July 15, 1946. Methodist. Educated at Yale University B.A. 1968 and University of Pennsylvania J.D. 1972. Recipient American Jurisprudence Awards in Constitutional Law 1969 and International Public Law 1969. Admitted to practice Ohio 1973, U.S. District Court Southern District of Ohio 1973 and U.S. Court of Appeals Sixth Circuit 1980. In legal practice Dayton 1973-87.

Author *Code of Ethics* Montgomery County Democratic Party adopted March 1978 and monthly legal column in *Something Extra* magazine (newspaper supplement) 1981-82. Important Decisions: AAAA Enterprises, Inc. v. Riverplace Community Urban Redevelopment Corp. (abuse of discretion is proper standard of judicial review of municipality's "blighted area" finding for eminent domain purposes) 50 Ohio St. 3d 157, 553 N.E.2d 597, 1990; Lonigro v. Lonigro (test for appealability of an interlocutory order is whether appellant can wait to appeal, not whether it would be less convenient to do so) 55 Ohio App. 3d 30, 561 N.E.2d 573, 1989; Aviation Sales, Inc. v. Select Mobile Homes (circumstances under which seller's unilateral mistake entitles him to rescind the contract) 48 Ohio App. 3d 90, 548 N.E.2d 307, 1988; Howard v. Delco (employer not liable to estate of employee who is killed in car accident on way home from work when employer sends employee home knowing he is drunk) 41 Ohio App. 3d 145, 534 N.E.2d 936, 1987; and Wisecup v. Gulf Development (statute of limitations does not begin to run until actual injury occurs, even though plaintiff earlier discovers defendant's tortious conduct) 56 Ohio App. 3d 162, 1989. Adjunct Professor of Conflict of Laws University of Dayton School of Law 1988-91. Member Commission on Character and Fitness 1979-85 and Member 1991-98 and Chair 1998 Rules Advisory Committee Ohio Supreme Court. Chairman Criminal Law and Procedure Committee Ohio Judicial Conference 1991-94. Member Ohio Courts of Appeals Judges Association (Secretary-Treasurer 2003), Dayton, Ohio State and American Bar Associations. Attended Basic Review for Judges Ohio Judicial College 1987 and New York Appellate Judges Seminar Summer 1987. E-5 USNR 1969-75 (retired). Democrat. Counsel Board of Inquiry 1978-79 and General Counsel 1982-86 Montgomery County Democratic Party. President Yale Club of Dayton 1974-79. Representative Yale Alumni Association 1975-78. Trustee 1978-82 and President 1979 Western Ohio Epilepsy Association. Leadership Dayton Class of 1979. Chairman Leadership Dayton Alumni Association 1982-83. Trainer Legal Aspects of Boardsmanship. Voluntary Action Center United Way 1981-87. Member United Way of the Dayton Area (Chairman Committee on Agency Relationships 1983-85 and since 1987, Select Committee on Agency Affiliation Agreements 1983-84, Videotaped Boardsmanship Committee 1984-85). Enjoys programming computer simulations. Personal Statement or Quote: "Frame the issue artfully, and the rest is easy."
Office: 41 North Perry Street, Room 515, Dayton 45422.
Telephone: (937) 225-4464.
Fax: (937) 496-7724
E-mail address: fainm@mcohio.org

FAIS, David W. *(Judge, Ohio Court of Common Pleas Franklin County)* Special Probate Referee 1973-88. Assumed office as Judge 1988. Presiding Judge 1995-97 and since 2002. Born Columbus Ohio March 8, 1943. Educated at Otterbein College B.S. and Ohio Northern University College of Law J.D. Admitted to practice Ohio 1970. In legal practice Ohio 1972-88.

Assistant City Attorney Columbus 1970. Assistant Prosecutor Franklin County 1970-72. Assistant Law Director 1974-77 and Law Director 1977-88 Grandview Heights. Member Ohio Common Pleas Judges Association, American Judges Association, Columbus, Ohio State and American (Chairperson Judicial Corrections Board) Bar Associations. Attended The National Judicial College 1991. Recipient Judicial Excellence Award from Franklin County Trial Lawyers Association 1990-91.

FAIS, DAVID W.—*Continued*

Member Trinity Methodist Church, Otterbein College Alumni Association, Ohio Northern University Alumni Association, Agonis Club and Charity Newsies. Enjoys reading, playing tennis and golfing.

Office: 369 South High Street, Sixth Floor, Columbus 43215-4554.

Telephone: (614) 462-3660.

Fax: (614) 462-3868

E-mail address: david_fais@fccourts.org

FAIS, James J. *(Judge, Franklin County Municipal Court)*

Office: 375 South High Street, Columbus 43215.

Telephone: (614) 645-7655.

Fax: (614) 645-7802

E-mail address: james_fais@fccourts.org

FALKOWSKI, Colleen Ann *(Judge, Ohio Court of Common Pleas Lake County)* Serves Domestic Relations Division.

Mailing address: P.O. Box 490, Painesville 44077.

FALVEY, Mary A. *(Judge, Canton Municipal Court)*

Mailing address: P.O. Box 24218, Canton 44701-4218.

Office: 218 Cleveland Avenue S.W., Canton 44702-1912.

Telephone: (330) 489-3216.

Fax: (330) 471-8860

E-mail address: mafalvey@ci.canton.oh.us

FARMER, Sheila G. *(Judge, Ohio Court of Appeals Fifth District)* Elected to term beginning Feb 9, 1993. Reelected 1998, current term expires Feb 2005. Born Ohio Dec 5, 1945. Roman Catholic. Educated at Marymount College B.A. 1967, London School of Economics 1965-66 and Case Western Reserve University J.D. 1970. Admitted to practice Ohio 1970. Began legal practice Cleveland 1970. In legal practice Canton 1971-77. Presiding Judge, Massillon Municipal Court 1978-82. Judge, Ohio Court of Common Pleas Stark County Jan 1, 1985 to Feb 8, 1993.

Assistant Police Prosecutor Cleveland 1970-71. Assistant City Solicitor Canton 1971. Assistant Prosecuting Attorney Stark County 1972-75. Secretary Civil Service Commission 1976-77. Member National Association of Women Judges, American Judges Association, Stark County, Ohio State and American Bar Associations. Recipient U.S. Jaycettes Outstanding Woman in Government Award 1982 and Woman of the Year Award from Network, Inc. 1985. Republican. Board of Trustees Western Stark County United Way, Timken Mercy Medical Center, Palace Theater Association and Stark County Law Library. Board of Reference Right to Life Education Foundation, Domestic Violence Project and Next Step Group Home. Community Board Stark County Blue Cross. Member Sts. Phillip and James Church.

Office: 110 Central Plaza South, Suite 320, Canton 44702-1411.

Telephone: (330) 451-7447.

Fax: (330) 451-7249

FAULKNER, David C. *(Judge, Ohio Court of Common Pleas Hardin County)* Elected to term beginning Jan 1, 1987. Reelected 1992 and 1998. Current term expires Dec 31, 2004. Born Kenton Ohio Dec 7, 1939. Educated at Hiram College A.B. 1961 and The Ohio State University J.D. 1964. Associate Editor The Ohio State Law Journal 1963-64. Law Clerk to Hon. C. William O'Neill, Ohio Supreme Court 1964-65. Admitted to practice Ohio 1964. In legal practice Kenton 1966-86. Judge, Kenton Municipal Court 1979-86.

Law Director City of Kenton 1968-79. Adjunct Professor of Law Ohio Northern University since 1987. Member Hardin County and Ohio State Bar Associations.

Office: One Courthouse Square, Suite 370, Kenton 43326-2301.

Telephone: (419) 674-2256.

Fax: (419) 674-2264

FAVREAU, Dan W. *(Judge, Ohio Court of Common Pleas Morgan County)*

Office: 19 East Main Street, McConnelsville 43756-1197.

Telephone: (740) 962-3371.

Fax: (740) 962-4589

FERGUSON, George H. *(Judge, Elyria Municipal Court)* Elected to term beginning Jan 2, 1986. Reelected Nov 1991 and Nov 1997. Current term expires Jan 1, 2004. Born Lorain Ohio Dec 2, 1930. Roman Catholic. Educated at University of Notre Dame A.B. cum laude 1953 and The Ohio State University J.D. 1956. Admitted to practice Ohio 1956, U.S. District Court Northern District of Ohio 1962 and U.S. Supreme Court 1971. In legal practice Elyria 1961-85.

Solicitor City of Elyria 1976-85. Member Municipal-County Judges of Ohio, Inc., Lorain County and Ohio State Bar Associations. Attended The National Judicial College March 1987 to April 1987. Lieutenant Colonel USAF 1957-83. Assistant Trust Examiner Federal Reserve Bank of Cleveland 1960-61. Democrat.

Office: 328 East Broad Street, Elyria 44035-5577.

Telephone: (440) 323-6545.

Fax: (440) 322-2206

E-mail address: kmolnar@elyriamunicourt.org

FINNEGAN, William R. *(Judge, Marion Municipal Court)* Appointed by Governor Richard F. Celeste to term beginning Jan 9, 1989. Elected Nov 6, 1989, Nov 2, 1993 and Nov 1999. Current term expires Dec 31, 2005. Born Lancaster Ohio May 31, 1954. Roman Catholic. Educated at University of Dayton B.A. magna cum laude 1975 and The Ohio State University J.D. 1979. Admitted to practice Ohio 1979 and U.S. District Court Northern District of Ohio 1980.

Member Municipal-County Judges of Ohio, Inc., Marion County and Ohio State (Banking, Commercial and Bankruptcy Law Subcommittee since 1986) Bar Associations. Hobbies include amateur radio.

Office: 233 West Center Street, Marion 43302-3643.

Telephone: (740) 383-6049.

Fax: (740) 382-5274

E-mail address: nr8i@gte.net

FITZSIMMONS, Donna Congeni *(Judge, Rocky River Municipal Court)* Elected to term beginning Jan 1, 1994. Reelected Nov 1999, current term expires Jan 1, 2006. Born Cleveland Ohio March 10, 1951. Catholic. Educated at Boston College A.B. summa cum laude 1973 and George Washington University National Law Center J.D. cum laude 1976. Law Clerk to National Transportation Safety Board 1975-76. Member Phi Beta Kappa. Admitted to practice Maryland 1976, Ohio 1977, District of Columbia 1977, U.S. Courts of Appeals Fourth 1977 and Sixth 1980 Circuits and U.S. District

FITZSIMMONS, DONNA CONGENI—*Continued*

Courts Northern 1980 and Southern 1980 Districts of Ohio. In legal practice Washington D.C. 1976-77 and Cleveland Ohio 1985-94.

Assistant County Prosecutor Cuyahoga County 1977-80. Special Attorney Organized Crime and Racketeering Section U.S. Department of Justice 1980-84. Adjunct Professor of Trial Advocacy since 1987 and Instructor in Defending Medical Malpractice Cases 1991 Cleveland-Marshall College of Law. Life Member Eighth Judicial District Judicial Conference. Barrister Celebrezze Inn of Court. Member Cleveland Association of Civil Trial Attorneys, Ohio Academy of Civil Trial Attorneys, American Inns of Court, The Defense Research Institute, Inc., Northern Ohio Municipal Judges Association, Ohio Judicial Conference, National Association of Women Judges, American Judges Association, Cleveland (Judicial Selection Committee 1979-84, Trustee 1988-91, Member Investigation of Lawyer Jailings Committee 1992), Ohio State and American (Section of Litigation) Bar Associations. Instructor "Labor Racketeering" Inspector General Department of Labor In-Service 1985, "Money Laundering: New Investigative Tool" 1985 and "The Sound and the Fury: Organized Crime Violence" 1992 Federal Criminal Investigators' Conference, "Opening Statement Demonstration" Celebrezze Inn of Court 1989, "Medical Record Charting" University Hospitals of Cleveland 1992, "Ethical Questions in Neonatal Medicine" 1992 and "Obstetric/Neonatal Medical Malpractice" Medical Grand Rounds 1992 Fairview General Hospital, "Mock Medical Malpractice Trial" St. Luke's Hospital 1992 and "Trial Superstars" Cleveland Bar Association 1992. Instructor/Judge National Institute for Trial Advocacy 1990. Deputy Counsel President's Commission on Organized Crime 1984-85. Moot Court Judge Cleveland State University, Case Western Reserve University and Cleveland Bar Regional Competition 1984-88. Trustee Templum Domestic Violence Shelter & Child Advocacy Programs since 1994. Member Playhouse Square Foundation, Rocky River Preschool PTA, Rocky River Junior Women's League and National Italian American Foundation.

Office: 21012 Hilliard, Rocky River 44116.
Telephone: (440) 895-0060.
Fax: (440) 895-0061

FLANAGAN, Timothy M. *(Judge, Ohio Court of Common Pleas Cuyahoga County)* Serves Domestic Relations Division.

Office: One Lakeside Avenue, Cleveland 44113-1082.
Telephone: (216) 443-8812.
Fax: (216) 443-8888

FLANNERY, James Larry *(Judge, Ohio Court of Common Pleas Warren County)* Elected to term beginning Jan 1, 1987. Reelected 1992 and 1998. Current term expires Dec 31, 2004. Serves Domestic Relations Division. Born Dayton Ohio Aug 5, 1949. United Methodist. Educated at Bowling Green State University B.S. 1971 and University of Cincinnati J.D. 1974. Admitted to practice Ohio 1974 and U.S. Supreme Court 1975. In legal practice Lebanon 1974-86.

Chief Assistant Prosecutor 1974-80 and Prosecuting Attorney 1980-86 Warren County. Member Ohio Common Pleas Judges Association, National Council of Juvenile and Family Court Judges, Warren County and Ohio State Bar Associations. Judge Basic Review Seminar Ohio Judicial College March 2-4, 1987 and Family Law and Crucial Issues Seminar National College of Juvenile and Family Law Oct 23-28, 1988. First Lieutenant U.S. Army 1974-75. Republican. Member Lebanon Kiwanis Club. Enjoys sports.

Office: 500 Justice Drive, Lebanon 45036-2398.
Telephone: (513) 695-1340.
Fax: (513) 695-2929
E-mail address: flanjl@co.warren.oh.us

FLEEGLE, Mark C. *(Judge, Ohio Court of Common Pleas Muskingum County)*

Office: 401 Main Street, Zanesville 43701-3519.
Telephone: (740) 455-7142.
Fax: (740) 455-7177

FLORES, Joseph A. *(Judge, Ohio Court of Common Pleas Lucas County)* Elected to term beginning Jan 1, 1991. Reelected 1996 and 2002. Current term expires 2008. Serves Juvenile Division. Born Toledo Ohio Aug 2, 1934. Roman Catholic. Educated at University of Notre Dame B.A. 1956 and Ohio Northern University J.D. 1964. Awarded honorary LL.D. Adrian College 1991. Member Delta Theta Phi. Admitted to practice Ohio 1964, U.S. District Court Northern District of Ohio 1966 and U.S. Supreme Court 1970. In legal practice Findlay 1964-65 and Toledo 1966-81. Judge, Toledo Municipal Court 1981-90.

Member American Judicature Society, Toledo, Lucas County and Ohio State Bar Associations. Lieutenant Commander USNR 1957-79 (retired). Previously worked as teacher Lima Central Catholic High School 1962-64. Enjoys travel, reading and sports.

Office: 1801 Spielbusch Avenue, Toledo 43624.
Telephone: (419) 213-6778.
Fax: (419) 213-6898

FLOYD, Alison L. "Nelson" *(Judge, Ohio Court of Common Pleas Cuyahoga County)* Magistrate Domestic Relations Division March 1991 to Dec 2000. Elected Judge to term beginning Jan 2, 2001. Term expires Jan 1, 2007. Serves Juvenile Division. Born Brooklyn New York Feb 8, 1961. Educated at University of Virginia B.A. 1985 and Case Western Reserve University J.D. 1988. Law Clerk to Ohio Court of Common Pleas Cuyahoga County May 1989 to March 1991. Admitted to practice Ohio 1988 and U.S. District Court Northern District of Ohio 1989. In legal practice Cleveland 1988-89.

Life Member Eighth District Judicial Conference. Democrat. Board of Trustees The Phillis Wheatley Association. Enjoys reading, traveling and golfing.

Office: 2163 East 22nd Street, Cleveland 44115-2998.
Telephone: (216) 443-8404.
Fax: (216) 348-4448
E-mail address: CJALF@www.cuyahoga.oh.us

FORD, Donald R. *(Judge, Ohio Court of Appeals Eleventh District)* Elected to term beginning Feb 9, 1983. Reelected 1988, 1994 and 2000. Current term expires Feb 2007. Born Warren Ohio Nov 8, 1931. Roman Catholic. Educated at Bethany College B.A. cum laude 1953 and University of Michigan Law School J.D. 1956. Quarter Finalist Campbell Moot Court Competition. Member Bethany College Kalon Academic Society, Gamma Sigma Kappa, Sigma Nu (Commander Epsilon Chapter) and Phi Alpha Delta. Admitted to practice Ohio 1957. In legal practice Warren 1957-72. Judge, Warren Municipal Court Jan 1, 1972 to Dec 10, 1976.

FORD, DONALD R.—*Continued*

Judge, Ohio Court of Common Pleas Trumbull County 1976-82. Served Ohio Supreme Court by assignment.

Assistant Prosecutor Trumbull County 1962-68. Special Counsel Trumbull County Commissioners and Trumbull County Engineer 1969-71. Part-time Instructor in Criminal Law and Criminal Evidence Kent State University Trumbull Branch since 1972. Chair Rules Advisory Committee Ohio Supreme Court Jan 1, 1993 to Jan 1997. Member Trumbull County (Former Member Executive Committee), Ashtabula County, Ohio State and American Bar Associations. Named Trumbull County Democrat of the Year 1972. Recipient Distinguished Citizen Award from Warren Urban League 1975 and Spirit of '87 Award from Liberty Through Law Award 1987. Inducted into Ohio Elks Hall of Fame 1982. Past President Howland Athletic Club and Howland PTA. Former Chairman Cub Scouts, Trumbull County Red Cross Blood Drive, Muscular Dystrophy Drive and Fund Drive Fairhaven School for Retarded. Former Board member Trumbull County March of Dimes, Crippled Children's Society, Mental Health Center, County Agricultural Society, Council on Alcoholism, Warren Area Jaycees and Trumbull County Chapter American Red Cross. Board Member Warren Sports Hall of Fame. Hi-Y Advisor. Member Elks and United Appeal. Enjoys gardening and fishing.

Office: 111 High Street N.E., Warren 44481-1098.
Telephone: (330) 675-2663.
Fax: (330) 675-2655
E-mail address: drford@11thappeal.co.trumbull.oh.us

FORNOF-LIPPENCOTT, Susan J. *(Judge, Champaign County Municipal Court)* Assumed office. Elected 2001. Current term expires 2007.

Mailing address: P.O. Box 85, Urbana 43078.
Office: 205 South Main Street, Urbana 43078.
Telephone: (937) 653-7376.
Fax: (937) 652-4333

FORTNEY, Rex D. *(Judge, Ohio Court of Common Pleas Van Wert County)* Elected to term beginning Feb 8, 1985. Reelected 1990, 1996 and 2002. Current term expires Feb 8, 2009. Serves Probate and Juvenile Divisions. Born Van Wert Ohio Aug 21, 1950. Religious affiliation: United Church of Christ. Educated at Bluffton College B.A. with honors 1972 and Ohio Northern University J.D. 1975. Admitted to practice Ohio 1975, U.S. District Court Northern District of Ohio 1976 and U.S. Court of Appeals Sixth Circuit 1982. Began legal practice Van Wert 1976.

Director of Law Van Wert 1980-83. Member Van Wert County (Secretary-Treasurer 1980-82, Vice President 1983-84, President 1985-86), Northwest Ohio and Ohio State Bar Associations. Faculty Ohio Judicial College. Republican. Member Kiwanis Club (President 1985-86), YMCA (Board of Directors since 1987) and Civic Theater. Enjoys jogging and woodworking.

Office: 121 East Main, Room 104, Van Wert 45891-1786.
Telephone: (419) 238-0027.
Fax: (419) 238-7315
E-mail address: vwprobatecourt@bright.net

FOSTER, Alan W. *(Judge, Adams County Court)*

Office: 25 Courthouse, 110 West Main Street, West Union 45693-1347.
Telephone: (937) 544-2011.
Fax: (937) 544-8911

FOX, Kenneth P. *(Judge, Bellevue Municipal Court)* Elected to term beginning Jan 1, 1988. Reelected 1993 and 1999. Current term expires 2006. Born Bellevue Ohio June 14, 1936. Lutheran. Educated at The Ohio State University B.S. 1958 and Cleveland-Marshall College of Law J.D. 1967. Admitted to practice Ohio 1967. In legal practice Bellevue since 1967.

Member Huron County, Sandusky County and Ohio State Bar Associations. U.S. Army 1958-60. Republican. Member Elks, VFW, Eagles, Moose and American Legion. Enjoys boating, fishing, hunting and travel.

Office: 3000 Seneca Industrial Parkway, Bellevue 44811.
Telephone: (419) 483-5880.
Fax: (419) 484-8060

FRANKS, Ruth Ann *(Judge, Ohio Court of Common Pleas Lucas County)*

Office: Courthouse, 700 Adams Street, Toledo 43624.
Telephone: (419) 213-4572.
Fax: (419) 213-4181

FREGIATO, Frank A. *(Judge, Belmont County Court)*

Mailing address: P.O. Box 40, Martins Ferry 43935.
Telephone: (740) 633-3147.
Fax: (740) 633-6631
E-mail address: fregiato@aol.com

FRIDLINE, Jacob M. *(Judge, Ashland Municipal Court)*

Mailing address: P.O. Box 385, Ashland 44805-0385.
Telephone: (419) 289-8342.
Fax: (419) 289-8545

FRIEDLAND, Carolyn B. *(Judge, Ohio Court of Common Pleas Cuyahoga County)*

Office: 1200 Ontario Street, Cleveland 44113.
Telephone: (216) 443-8705.
Fax: (216) 348-4034

FRIEDMAN, Stuart A. *(Judge, Ohio Court of Common Pleas Cuyahoga County)* Appointed by Governor Richard F. Celeste to term beginning Feb 6, 1987. Elected 1988, 1994 and 2000. Current term expires Jan 1, 2007. Born Cleveland Ohio May 6, 1944. Jewish. Educated at University of Pennsylvania B.A. 1966, University of Michigan J.D. 1969 and University of London M.Sc. 1970. Law Clerk to Chief Judge Frank J. Battisti, U.S. District Court Northern District of Ohio 1970-72. Admitted to practice Ohio 1970, U.S. District Court Northern District of Ohio 1970, U.S. Court of Appeals Sixth Circuit 1972 and U.S. Supreme Court 1981. In legal practice Cleveland 1972-87.

Assistant Director of Law City of Cleveland 1977-87. Member Cleveland Bar Association. Board of Trustees Cleveland Music School Settlement 1981-86 and Cleveland Chapter American Jewish Committee since 1990. Member City Club of Cleveland. Enjoys music, travel and history.

Office: 1200 Ontario Street, Cleveland 44113.
Telephone: (216) 443-8708.
Fax: (216) 348-4035
E-mail address: cpsaf@www.cuyahoga.oh.us

FROEHLICH, Mark S. *(Judge, Franklin County Municipal Court)*
Office: 375 South High Street, Columbus 43215-4593.
Telephone: (614) 645-8849.
Fax: (614) 645-7185
E-mail address: mark_froehlich@fccourts.org

FROELICH, Jeffrey E. *(Judge, Ohio Court of Common Pleas Montgomery County)* Elected 1994. Reelected to subsequent term. Educated at Miami University B.A. with honors 1968 and University of Michigan J.D. 1972. Admitted to practice Ohio 1972. In legal practice Dayton since 1972. Former Judge, Montgomery County Court, elected to term beginning Jan 1, 1979.
Assistant Prosecuting Attorney 1972-76. Professor University of Dayton Law School 1976-80.
Mailing address: P.O. Box 972, Dayton 45401.
Office: 41 North Perry, Dayton 45422-2150.
Telephone: (937) 225-4440.
Fax: (937) 225-5406
E-mail address: froelicj@montcourt.org

FROST, Gregory Lynn *(Judge, United States District Court Southern District of Ohio)* Appointed for life by President George W. Bush to term beginning March 19, 2003. Born Newark Ohio April 17, 1949. Protestant. Educated at Wittenberg University B.A. 1971 and Ohio Northern University School of Law J.D. 1974. Editor Ohio Northern University Law Review 1973-74. Member Phi Mu Delta. Admitted to practice Ohio 1974. Began legal practice Newark 1974. Judge, Licking County Municipal Court Jan 1, 1983 to Feb 8, 1991, appointed by Governor James A. Rhodes. Judge, Ohio Court of Common Pleas Licking County Feb 9, 1991 to 2003.
Assistant Prosecutor Licking County 1974-78. Author "Branzburg v. Hayes-Newmen's Privilege" Ohio Northern L. Rev. 1973. Member Licking County, Ohio State, Federal and American Bar Associations. Recipient Superior Judicial Service Award from Ohio Supreme Court 1983. Republican. Member Masonic Lodge, Teheran Grotto, Shrine Club, Elks Club, Newark Area Chamber of Commerce, Moose Lodge, Newark Maennechor, Ancient Accepted Scottish Rites, Ducks Unlimited, Rotary Club and Honorable Order of Kentucky Colonels. Enjoys golf and swimming.
Office: 349 U.S. Courthouse, 85 Marconi Boulevard, Columbus 43215.
Telephone: (614) 719-3300.

FROST, Mark A. *(Judge, Columbiana County Municipal Court)* Elected 2001 to term beginning Jan 2002. Term expires 2007. Former Judge, Columbiana County Court.
Office: 41 North Park Avenue, Lisbon 44432.

FUERST, Nancy A. *(Judge, Ohio Court of Common Pleas Cuyahoga County)*
Office: 1200 Ontario Street, Cleveland 44113-1678.
Telephone: (216) 443-8687.
Fax: (216) 348-4092
E-mail address: cp1nf@www.cuyahoga.oh.us

GALLAGHER, Eileen *(Judge, Ohio Court of Common Pleas Cuyahoga County)* Elected Nov 1996 to term beginning Jan 6, 1997. Reelected 2001, current term expires Jan 2008. Born Cleveland Ohio Oct 23, 1956. Educated at Ohio Dominican College B.A. 1977 and Cleveland-Marshall College of Law J.D. 1987. Admitted to practice Ohio 1987, U.S. District Court Northern District of Ohio 1987 and U.S. Supreme Court 1992. In legal practice Cleveland 1987-96.
Member Cleveland and Ohio State Bar Associations. Attended "General Jurisdiction" Reno Nevada 1997 and "Advanced Evidence" Washington D.C. 1999 The National Judicial College.
Office: 1200 Ontario Street, Cleveland 44113-1678.
Telephone: (216) 443-8686.
Fax: (216) 348-4031

GALLAGHER, John W. *(Judge, Ohio Court of Common Pleas Cuyahoga County)* Elected 1994. Reelected to subsequent term. Serves Juvenile Division.
Office: 2163 East 22nd Street, Cleveland 44115.
Telephone: (216) 443-8418.
Fax: (216) 348-4447

GALLAGHER, Sean C. *(Judge, Ohio Court of Appeals Eighth District)* Former Judge, Cleveland Municipal Court.
Office: One Lakeside Avenue, Cleveland 44113.

GALLAS, James S. *(Magistrate Judge, United States District Court Northern District of Ohio)* Appointed by U.S. District Court judges to term beginning 1991. Reappointed 1999, current term expires 2007. Educated at Bethany College B.A. and Cleveland Marshall College of Law Cleveland State University LL.B. In legal practice Cleveland.
Assistant Attorney General. Member Supreme Court Historical Society, Anthony J. Celebrezze Inn of Court, American Judicature Society, Ohio State and Federal Bar Associations.
Office: 480 U.S. Courthouse & Federal Bldg., Two South Main Street, Akron 44308.
Telephone: (330) 375-5465.

GANO, G. Allen *(Judge, Ohio Court of Common Pleas Clinton County)* Serves Probate and Juvenile Divisions.
Office: 46 South South, Second Floor, Wilmington 45177-2297.
Telephone: (937) 382-2280.
Fax: (937) 383-1158

GAUGHAN, Patricia Anne *(Judge, United States District Court Northern District of Ohio)* Appointed for life by President Bill Clinton. Born Cleveland Ohio Oct 21, 1953. Roman Catholic. Educated at St. Mary's College B.A. magna cum laude 1975 and University of Notre Dame Law School J.D. 1978. Admitted to practice Ohio 1978 and Indiana 1978. In legal practice Cleveland 1984-87. Judge, Ohio Court of Common Pleas Cuyahoga County, elected to term beginning Jan 7, 1987.
Assistant Prosecutor Cuyahoga County 1978-83. Assistant U.S. Attorney 1983-84. Adjunct Professor of Law Cleveland-Marshall Law School 1983-87. Master of the Bench Harold H. Burton Inn of Court since 1991. Board of Directors National Conference of Metropolitan Courts. Treasurer Judicial Conference of the Eighth Judicial District. Member Ohio Common Pleas Judges Association, Federal Judges Association, Cleveland and Cuyahoga County Bar Associations. Recipient Edward F. Barrett Award for Trial Advocacy 1978. Named Prosecutor of the Year by Northern Ohio Patrolmen's Benevolent Association 1985. Democrat. Former Member Advisory Board Paralegal Studies Notre Dame College. Former Member Cuyahoga Women's Political Caucus, Chil-

GAUGHAN, PATRICIA ANNE—*Continued*

dren's Trust Board and Citizens League. Vice President Leukemia and Lymphoma Society. Member Paralegal Studies Board Ursuline College.

Office: U.S. Courthouse, 801 West Superior Avenue, Cleveland 44113.
Telephone: (216) 357-7210.

GAUL, Daniel *(Judge, Ohio Court of Common Pleas Cuyahoga County)*
Office: 1200 Ontario Street, Room 19D, Cleveland 44113-1678.
Telephone: (216) 443-8706.
Fax: (216) 348-4035
E-mail address: cpdxg@www.cuyahoga.oh.us

GEHRES, Daniel G. *(Judge, Dayton Municipal Court)* Elected to term beginning Jan 1, 1988. Reelected 1993 and 1999. Current term expires Dec 31, 2005. Born Van Wert Ohio March 6, 1953. Methodist. Educated at Manchester College B.S. 1975 and University of Dayton J.D. 1978. Member Phi Alpha Delta. Admitted to practice Ohio 1978 and U.S. District Court Southern District of Ohio 1979. In legal practice Dayton 1981-88.

Assistant Attorney General Ohio 1978-83. Member Dayton and Ohio State Bar Associations. Recipient Distinguished Service Award University of Dayton School of Law Alumni Association 1987. Treasurer Downtown Dayton Democratic Club 1982-85. President Montgomery County Young Democrats 1986. Member United Way 1983-85. Member Dayton Clean Community Advisory Board and University Row Neighborhood Association. Enjoys collecting political and Olympic memorabilia.

Office: 301 West Third Street, Dayton 45402-1424.
Telephone: (937) 333-4365.
Fax: (937) 333-5114
E-mail address: daniel.gehres@ci.dayton.oh.us

GERKEN, Thomas H. *(Judge, Ohio Court of Common Pleas Hocking County)* Elected Nov 4, 1988 to term beginning Jan 1, 1989. Reelected Nov 8, 1994 and 2000. Current term expires Jan 2007. Born Logan Ohio. Methodist. Educated at The Ohio State University B.A. 1975 and Northwestern School of Law J.D. 1978. Admitted to practice Ohio 1978. In legal practice Logan 1978-88. Judge, Ohio Court of Common Pleas Vinton County 1986.

Member Ohio Common Pleas Judges Association, American Judges Association, American Judicature Society and Hocking County Bar Association.

Office: One East Main Street, Third Floor, Logan 43138-1207.
Telephone: (740) 385-4027.
Fax: (740) 385-2614
E-mail address: cpcourt@ohiohills.com

GERSCHUTZ, Daniel Richard *(Judge, Ohio Court of Common Pleas Putnam County)* Serves Probate and Juvenile Divisions.
Office: 245 East Main Street, Ottawa 45875.

GIESLER, Kathleen Luebke *(Judge, Ohio Court of Common Pleas Ottawa County)* Serves Probate and Juvenile Divisions.
Office: 315 Madison, Port Clinton 43452.

GILLIGAN, Timothy P. *(Judge, Parma Municipal Court)*
Office: 5555 Powers Boulevard, Parma 44129-5462.
Telephone: (440) 887-7458.
Fax: (440) 887-7490

GLAVAS, Kosma J. *(Judge, Ohio Court of Common Pleas Lorain County)*
Office: Courthouse, 308 Second Street, Elyria 44035.
Telephone: (440) 329-5570.
Fax: (440) 284-3680
E-mail address: judgekjg@hotmail.com

GOLDIE, Susan L. *(Judge, Xenia Municipal Court)*
Office: 101 North Detroit Street, Xenia 45385-2926.
Telephone: (937) 376-7290.
Fax: (937) 376-7288

GOLDSBERRY, L. Alan *(Judge, Ohio Court of Common Pleas Athens County)* Appointed by Governor Richard F. Celeste to term beginning Jan 1, 1987. Elected Nov 1988, Nov 1990, Nov 1996 and 2002. Current term expires Feb 2009. Born Athens Ohio May 20, 1944. Protestant. Educated at Ohio University B.A. with high honors 1966 and Duke University School of Law J.D. 1969. Member Phi Beta Kappa and Phi Kappa Phi. Admitted to practice Ohio 1969, U.S. District Court Southern District of Ohio 1971 and U.S. Tax Court 1980. In legal practice Athens 1969-87.

Member Athens City School Board 1976-80. Solicitor Village of Glouster 1984-86. Member Athens County and Ohio State Bar Associations. Fulfilled CLE requirements for judges since 1987. Recipient Distinguished Service Award from Athens Jaycees 1979, Silver Beaver Award from Kootaga Council Boy Scouts of America 1985 and Alumni Merit Awards from Delta Upsilon fraternity 1985, 1987 and 1990. Democrat. Executive Board Member Southeastern Ohio Probation Alternative (SEPTA Center) since 1987. Board Member Athens County Chapter The Red Cross. Member Downtown Athens Kiwanis Club (Distinguished President 1976-77 and 1989-90), Athens Symposiarch Club, Athens Reading Club and Athens Historical Society and Museum (President).

Office: Courthouse, Third Floor, Athens 45701-2895.
Telephone: (740) 592-3236.
Fax: (740) 592-3020
E-mail address: agoldsberry@eurekanet.com

GORMAN, Barbara P. *(Judge, Ohio Court of Common Pleas Montgomery County)*
Mailing address: P.O. Box 972, Dayton 45401-0972.
Office: 41 North Perry Street, Dayton 45422-2150.
Telephone: (937) 225-4392.
Fax: (937) 225-5406
E-mail address: gormanb@montcourt.org

GORMAN, Francis X. *(Judge, Toledo Municipal Court)*
Office: 555 North Erie Street, Toledo 43624.
Telephone: (419) 245-1944.
Fax: (419) 245-1802
E-mail address: francis.gorman@noris.org

GORMAN, Robert H. *(Judge, Ohio Court of Appeals First District)* Elected to term beginning Feb 12, 1989. Reelected 1994 and 2000. Current term expires Feb 11, 2007. Presiding Judge 1991, 1995 and 2001. Born Cincinnati Ohio Aug 2, 1935. Episcopalian. Educated at Brown University A.B. 1957 and University of

GORMAN, ROBERT H.—*Continued*

Cincinnati LL.B. 1960. Member Sigma Nu and Phi Alpha Delta. Admitted to practice Ohio 1960, U.S. Court of Appeals Sixth Circuit 1961 and U.S. District Court Southern District of Ohio 1961. Began legal practice Cincinnati 1960. Judge, Hamilton County Municipal Court 1972-76. Judge, Ohio Court of Common Pleas Hamilton County 1976-89.

Member Committee on Revision of the Code of Judicial Conduct 1982, Committee on Revision of the Rules on Reporting Opinions 1983, Board of Commissioners on Grievances and Discipline for the Judiciary 1983-85 and 1996-98 and Committee on Review of Canon 7, 1990 Supreme Court of Ohio. Author *Anderson's Ohio Criminal Practice and Procedure* 8th ed. Anderson Publishing Co. 1989-2002. Adjunct Lecturer on Appellate Practice and Procedure University of Cincinnati College of Law. Chair Civil Rights Subcommittee Ohio Jury Instructions. Member Potter Stewart Cincinnati Inn of Court (President 1990-92), Ohio Common Pleas Judges Association (Vice President 1984-88), American Judges Association, Cincinnati (Executive Committee 1984-86, Co-chair Bench and Bar Conference 1992), and Ohio State Bar Associations. Lecturer and Trustee Ohio Judicial College 1986-91. Lecturer Ohio CLE Institute 1990 and Cincinnati Bar Association. Recorder Ohio State Bench and Bar Conference 1990. Co-author and Course Developer "Motions—Civ. R. 12(B), Summary, Judgment, and Discovery" Ohio Judicial College 1994 and 1998. Recipient Ohio Supreme Court Awards for Superior Judicial Service 1975 and 1976, Outstanding Jurist Award from Ohio Academy of Trial Lawyers 1979, Merit Award from Cincinnati Bar Association and the Academy of Medicine 1985, Adjunct Faculty Teaching Excellence Award from University of Cincinnati College of Law Alumni Association 1997 and Trustees' Award from Cincinnati Bar Association 2002. Captain USAF 1961-64. State Representative Ohio General Assembly 1965-66. Alumni Board of Trustees 1987-88, Advisory Board Civic Forum since 1998 and Board of Visitors since 1999 University of Cincinnati College of Law. Member "Let's Make Things Happen" Committee Legal Aid Society of Greater Cincinnati since 1999.

Office: 230 East Ninth Street, Twelfth Floor, Cincinnati 45202-1287.
Telephone: (513) 946-3421.
Fax: (513) 946-3411
E-mail address: Rgorman@cms.hamilton-co.org

GORMLEY, Joseph A. *(Judge, Ohio Court of Common Pleas Muskingum County)* Elected Nov 6, 1990 to term beginning Feb 9, 1991. Reelected 1996 and 2002. Current term expires 2009. Serves Juvenile and Probate Divisions. Born Zanesville Ohio July 7, 1940. Methodist. Educated at The Ohio State University B.A. 1962 J.D. 1965. Admitted to practice Ohio 1965. In legal practice Zanesville 1965-91.

Probate Court office: 401 Main Street, Zanesville 43701.
Telephone: (740) 455-7113.
Fax: (740) 455-7173
Juvenile Court office: 1860 East Pike, Zanesville 43701.
Telephone: (740) 453-0351.
Fax: (740) 453-1066

GOWDOWN, David A. *(Judge, Ohio Court of Common Pleas Montgomery County)*
Mailing address: P.O. Box 972, Dayton 45401-0972.
Office: 41 North Perry Street, Dayton 45422-2150.
Telephone: (937) 225-4416.
Fax: (937) 225-5406
E-mail address: gowdownd@montcourt.org

GRADY, Karla J. *(Judge, Hamilton County Municipal Court)*
Office: 1000 Main Street, Cincinnati 45202.
Telephone: (513) 946-5127.
Fax: (513) 946-5129

GRADY, Thomas J. *(Judge, Ohio Court of Appeals Second District)* Assumed office Feb 10, 1989. Elected 1994.
Office: Clark County Courthouse, 101 North Limestone Street, Springfield 45502.
Telephone: (937) 328-2653.
Fax: (937) 328-2652
E-mail address: tjgrady@erinet.com

GRAHAM, James L. *(Judge, United States District Court Southern District of Ohio)* Appointed for life by President Ronald Reagan Aug 15, 1986 to term beginning Nov 17, 1986. Born Columbus Ohio April 20, 1939. Educated at The Ohio State University B.A. 1962 J.D. summa cum laude 1962. Admitted to practice Ohio 1962 and Florida 1974. In legal practice Columbus Ohio 1969-86.

Author on various articles on tort law and civil procedure. Important Decision: Pinette v. Capitol Square. Fellow American College of Trial Lawyers. Member Columbus Bar Association. Lecturer Ohio Legal Center Institute, Capital University Trial Advocacy Institute and Ohio Judicial College. Advisory Board Salvation Army 1967-79. Member 1972-76 and Chairman 1975-76 Development Commission of the City of Columbus. Board of Trustees University Club of Columbus 1987-89. Member Dean's Council Capital University Law School since 1986. Interests include mentoring/tutoring inner city youth, collecting artifacts and documents of the American Civil War and restoring/maintaining vintage sports cars.
Office: 301 U.S. Courthouse, 85 Marconi Boulevard, Columbus 43215.
Telephone: (614) 719-3200.
E-mail address: James_L._Graham@ohsd.uscourts.gov

GRANT, Cheryl D. *(Judge, Hamilton County Municipal Court)*
Office: 1000 Main Street, Cincinnati 45202.
Telephone: (513) 946-5165.
Fax: (513) 946-5167
E-mail address: cgrant@cms.hamilton-co.org

GRAVENS, Maureen A. *(Judge, Rocky River Municipal Court)*
Office: 21012 Hilliard Boulevard, Rocky River 44116.
Telephone: (440) 895-0062.
Fax: (440) 895-0063

GREEN, James E. *(Judge, Franklin County Municipal Court)*
Office: 375 South High Street, Columbus 43215.
Telephone: (614) 645-8295.
Fax: (614) 645-7802
E-mail address: james_green@fccourts.org

GREENE, Lillian J. *(Judge, Ohio Court of Common Pleas Cuyahoga County)*
Office: 1200 Ontario Street, Cleveland 44113.
Telephone: (216) 443-8681.
Fax: (216) 348-4038
E-mail address: cpljg@www.cuyahoga.oh.us

GREER, Kevin L. *(Judge, Ohio Court of Common Pleas Highland County)* Serves Probate and Juvenile Divisions.
Office: 105 North High Street, Hillsboro 45133-1182.
Telephone: (937) 393-9981.
Fax: (937) 393-0926

GRENDELL, Diane V. *(Judge, Ohio Court of Appeals Eleventh District)*
Office: 111 High Street N.E., Warren 44481.
Telephone: (330) 675-2650.
Fax: (330) 675-2655

GRETICK, Anthony L. *(Judge, Ohio Court of Common Pleas Williams County)* Elected Nov 1994 to term beginning Jan 1, 1995. Reelected 2000, current term expires Dec 31, 2006. Born Chicago Illinois June 26, 1936. Unitarian. Educated at Northwestern University A.B. 1958 J.D. 1964. Admitted to practice Illinois 1964, Ohio 1965, U.S. District Court Northern District of Ohio 1966 and U.S. Supreme Court 1972. In legal practice Bryan 1964-95.

Prosecuting Attorney Williams County 1976-94. Member Williams County and Ohio State Bar Associations. Named Ohio Prosecutor of the Year 1993. Lieutenant Commander USNR 1958-61 (retired). Democrat.
Office: One Courthouse Square, Bryan 43506.
Telephone: (419) 636-2644.
Fax: (419) 636-9886
E-mail address: gretick@email.msn.com

GRIFFIN, Burt W. *(Judge, Ohio Court of Common Pleas Cuyahoga County)* Elected to term beginning Jan 3, 1975. Reelected 1980, 1986, 1992 and 1998. Current term expires Jan 2005. Born Cleveland Ohio Aug 19, 1932. Unitarian. Educated at Amherst College B.A. cum laude 1954 and Yale Law School J.D. 1959. Note and Comment Editor Yale Law Journal 1958-59. Law Clerk to Hon. George T. Washington, U.S. Court of Appeals District of Columbia Circuit 1959-60. Admitted to practice Ohio 1959 and U.S. District Court Northern District of Ohio 1960. In legal practice Cleveland 1962-66.

Assistant U.S. Attorney Northern District of Ohio 1960-62. Counsel President's Commission on the Assassination of President Kennedy 1964. Director Cleveland Legal Aid Society 1966-68 and Legal Services Program U.S. Office of Economic Opportunity 1968-69. Author *Mentally Retarded Offenders: A Handbook for Criminal Justice Personnel* 1980. Member Ohio Criminal Sentencing Commission 1991-95. Member Cleveland (Trustee 1970-72) and Cuyahoga County Bar Associations. Instructor in Sentencing Ohio Judicial College 1986 and Capital and Felony Sentencing The National Judicial College 1986-87. Recipient Award of Merit from Cleveland Bar Association 1986 and Law and Justice Service Award from Cleveland Urban League 1986. U.S. Army 1954-56. Democrat. Co-chairman Task Force on Violent Crime.
Office: 1200 Ontario Street, Cleveland 44113-1678.
Telephone: (216) 443-8736.
Fax: (216) 348-4033
E-mail address: cpbwg@www.cuyahoga.oh.us

GRIGSBY, Michael *(Judge, Marysville Municipal Court)*
Mailing address: P.O. Box 322, Marysville 43040.
Office: 125 East Sixth, Marysville 43040.
Telephone: (937) 644-9102.
Fax: (937) 644-1228

GRILLO, N. Robert *(Judge, Ohio Court of Common Pleas Vinton County)* Serves Probate and Juvenile Divisions. Born Akron Ohio Nov 7, 1956. Catholic. Educated at The Ohio State University B.S.B.A. cum laude 1979 and University of Toledo College of Law J.D. 1982. Member Delta Theta Phi, Beta Gamma Sigma and Phi Alpha Kappa. Admitted to practice Ohio 1983, West Virginia 1983, U.S. District Courts Southern District of Ohio 1983 and Southern District of West Virginia 1983, U.S. Tax Court 1983, Kentucky 1984 and U.S. Court of Appeals Fourth Circuit 1986. In legal practice Beckley West Virginia 1984-87 and McArthur Ohio since 1987. Former Judge, Vinton County Court, appointed by Governor George V. Voinovich to term beginning Oct 21, 1998.

Village Solicitor McArthur 1989-92, Wilkesville 1996-98 and Zaleski 1997-98. Member Kentucky, Ohio State and West Virginia Bar Associations. Recipient Award for Service to the Community from Ohio High School Athletic Association. Named Public Servant of the Year by Knights of Columbus. Republican. Radio Broadcaster of local high school sports. Coach basketball, soccer, cross-country and baseball. Enjoys running, weight lifting and working with children.
Office: 100 East Main Street, McArthur 45651-1267.

GROVES, Emanuella D. *(Judge, Cleveland Municipal Court)*
Office: 1200 Ontario Street, Cleveland 44113.
Telephone: (216) 664-4984.
Fax: (216) 644-4283

GRUBB, Janet A. *(Judge, Franklin County Municipal Court)*
Office: 375 South High Street, Columbus 43215-4593.
Telephone: (614) 645-8207.
Fax: (614) 645-7803
E-mail address: janet_grubb@fccourts.org

GUCKENBERGER, Guy C. *(Judge, Hamilton County Municipal Court)*
Office: 1000 Main Street, Cincinnati 45202.
Telephone: (513) 946-5169.
Fax: (513) 946-5171
E-mail address: gguck@cms.hamilton-co.org

GUTMANN, Elizabeth Simms *(Judge, Miami County Municipal Court)* Elected Nov 1999 to term beginning Jan 3, 2000. Term expires Dec 31, 2006. Born Munich Germany Oct 19, 1957. Episcopalian. Educated at Wright State University B.A. 1981 and University of Cincinnati J.D. 1984. Admitted to practice Ohio 1984. In legal practice Piqua 1984-86.

Assistant Public Defender Shelby County 1986-92. Municipal Prosecutor Piqua 1992-99. Member Ohio Judicial Conference (Criminal Law Committee), Ohio Municipal Judges Association, Miami County and Ohio State Bar Associations. Republican. Member Miami County YMCA and YWCA, Miami County CISV, Day-

GUTMANN, ELIZABETH SIMMS—*Continued*

ton Cycling Club and Bruckner Nature Center. Enjoys biking, traveling, reading and movies.

Office: 201 West Main Street, Troy 45373.
Telephone: (937) 332-6971.
Fax: (937) 440-3508
E-mail address: esg@woh.rr.com

GWIN, James S. *(Judge, United States District Court Northern District of Ohio)* Appointed for life by President Bill Clinton to term beginning Nov 10, 1997. Born Canton Ohio. Catholic. Educated at Kenyon College A.B. cum laude 1976 and University of Akron J.D. 1979. Staff member Akron Law Review. Admitted to practice Ohio 1979, U.S. Supreme Court 1988, U.S. District Court Northern District of Ohio and U.S. Court of Appeals Sixth Circuit. In legal practice Canton 1979-89. Former Judge, Ohio Court of Common Pleas Stark County, appointed by Governor Richard F. Celeste to term beginning April 1, 1989. Democrat.

Office: 510 U.S. Courthouse, Two South Main Street, Akron 44308.
Telephone: (330) 375-5934.

GWIN, W. Scott *(Judge, Ohio Court of Appeals Fifth District)* Elected to term beginning Feb 9, 1989. Reelected 1994 and 2000. Current term expires Feb 2007. Born Canton Ohio Nov 26, 1951. Catholic. Educated at John Carroll University B.A. cum laude 1973 and University of Akron J.D. 1976. Admitted to practice Ohio 1976. In legal practice Canton 1976-91.

Assistant Attorney General Ohio Department of Transportation 1976-84. Law Director Canton 1984-89. Contributing Editor *Stark Magazine.* Monthly Contributing Editor *Senior Forum.* Member Board of Commissioners on Grievances and Discipline Supreme Court of Ohio Jan 1, 1996 to Dec 31, 1998. Member Stark County Academy of Trial Lawyers, Stark County and Ohio State Bar Associations. Committee Person for CLE 1992-93 and 1996. Instructor in Appellate Practice. Precinct Committeeman City of Alliance. Member Roscoe Pound Foundation 1996. Board of Directors Imports Corp House of Laredo. Board Member Stark Technical College Court. Member Arthritis Foundation, Big Brothers/Big Sisters, Canton Chamber of Commerce, Canton Jaycees, Canton Preservation Society, Catholic Community League, Ducks Unlimited, Leadership Canton, Leadership Stark County Selection Committee, National Rifle Association, Rotary, St. John's Catholic Church, Stark County Certified Development and YMCA. Enjoys handball, racquetball, golf, tennis and antiques.

Office: 110 Central Plaza South, Suite 320, Canton 44702-1411.
Telephone: (330) 451-7750.
Fax: (330) 451-7249

GYSEGEM, Thomas P. *(Judge, Warren Municipal Court)*

Mailing address: P.O. Box 1550, Warren 44483-1550.
Office: 141 South Street, Warren 44483.
Telephone: (330) 841-2515.
Fax: (330) 841-2930
E-mail address: tgysegem@cisnet.com

HAAS, John G. *(Judge, Ohio Court of Common Pleas Stark County)*

Office: 115 Central Plaza North, Canton 44702-1490.
Telephone: (330) 451-7847.
Fax: (330) 451-7740

HADACEK, John D. *(Judge, Fostoria Municipal Court)*

Mailing address: P.O. Box 985, Fostoria 44830.
Office: 213 South Main Street, Fostoria 44830.
Telephone: (419) 435-8139.
Fax: (419) 435-1150
E-mail address: fosmunct@bright.net

HADDAD, Victor M. *(Judge, Clermont County Municipal Court)*

Office: 289 Main Street, Batavia 45103-2906.
Telephone: (513) 732-7967.
Fax: (513) 732-7051

HAGLER, Robert A. *(Judge, Ohio Court of Common Pleas Greene County)* Elected to term beginning Feb 3, 1973. Reelected to subsequent terms. Serves Probate Division. Born Xenia Ohio Jan 23, 1940. Protestant. Educated at Denison University B.A. 1962 and The Ohio State University J.D. 1965. Admitted to practice Ohio 1965.

Office: 45 North Detroit Street, Xenia 45385.
Telephone: (937) 562-5280.
Fax: (937) 562-5316
E-mail address: rhagler@co.greene.oh.us

HAGUE, Charles G. *(Judge, Ohio Court of Common Pleas Ashtabula County)* Serves Probate and Juvenile Divisions. Former Judge, Ashtabula Municipal Court.

Office: 25 West Jefferson Street, Ashtabula 44047.
Telephone: (440) 576-3451.
Fax: (440) 576-3633
E-mail address: ashprocourt1@suite224.net

HALE, Harland Hanna *(Judge, Franklin County Municipal Court)* Serves Environmental Division.

Office: 375 South High Street, 15C, Columbus 43215.

HALL, Howard E. *(Judge, Ohio Court of Common Pleas Morrow County)* Elected Nov 1998 to term beginning Jan 1, 1999. Term expires Dec 31, 2004. Born Cleveland Ohio Oct 4, 1945. Protestant. Educated at Bowling Green State University B.A. 1967 and University of Toledo J.D. 1970. Admitted to practice Ohio 1970, U.S. District Courts Northern and Southern Districts of Ohio, U.S. Court of Appeals Sixth Circuit and U.S. Supreme Court. In legal practice Parma 1970-72, Cardington 1972-99 and Mt. Gilead 1986-99.

Prosecuting Attorney Morrow County 1985-99. Member Ohio Common Pleas Judges Association, Ohio Association of Juvenile and Family Court Judges and Ohio Association of Probate Judges. Republican.

Office: 48 East High Street, Mount Gilead 43338-1458.
Telephone: (419) 947-4515.
Fax: (419) 947-6341

HALL, Michael T. *(Judge, Ohio Court of Common Pleas Montgomery County)* Appointed by Governor Bob Taft to term beginning Aug 23, 1999. Elected July 1, 2001 and 2002. Current term expires June 30, 2009. Educated at University of Dayton B.S. 1975 J.D. summa cum laude 1979. Associate Editor University of Dayton Law Review 1977-79. Law Clerk to Hon. John Michael Meagher, Ohio Court of Common Pleas Montgomery County 1978-79. Member Phi Delta Phi. Admitted to practice Ohio 1979 and Florida 1983. In legal practice

HALL, MICHAEL T.—*Continued*

Dayton Ohio 1979-99. Part-time Judge, Montgomery County Court, appointed by Governor George V. Voinovich.

Member 1986-99 and President 1994-96 Miami Valley Trial Lawyers Association. Member Ohio Common Pleas Judges Association, Dayton (Treasurer 1988-89) and American Bar Associations.

Mailing address: P.O. Box 972, Dayton 45401.
Office: 41 North Perry Street, Dayton 45422-2150.
Telephone: (937) 496-7951.
Fax: (937) 225-5406
E-mail address: hallm@montcourt.org

HAMILTON, Glenn S. *(Judge, Ohio Court of Common Pleas Madison County)* Elected Nov 1984 to term beginning 1985. Reelected Nov 1990, Nov 1996 and 2002. Current term expires Feb 2009. Serves Probate and Juvenile Divisions. Born Lexington Kentucky Jan 24, 1947. Methodist. Educated at Ohio Northern University B.A. 1970, Ball State University M.A. 1974 and University of Dayton J.D. 1977. Admitted to practice Ohio 1977.

Office: 205 Courthouse, One North Main Street, London 43140-1096.
Telephone: (740) 852-0756.
Fax: (740) 852-7134

HAMMOND, Nancy D. *(Judge, Ohio Court of Common Pleas Fayette County)* Serves Probate and Juvenile Divisions.

Office: 110 East Court Street, Washington Court House 43160.
Telephone: (740) 335-0640.
Fax: (740) 333-3598

HANDWORK, Peter M. *(Judge, Ohio Court of Appeals Sixth District)* Assumed office Jan 2, 1983. Elected 2000, current term expires Feb 7, 2007. Born Toledo Ohio Dec 2, 1941. Protestant. Educated at Lake Forest College B.A. 1963 and University of Toledo J.D. 1966. Admitted to practice Ohio 1966. Began legal practice Toledo 1966. Judge, Ohio Court of Common Pleas Lucas County Jan 1, 1977 to Jan 1, 1983, appointed by Governor James A. Rhodes.

Instructor College of Law 1971-75 and Adjunct Associate Professor of Paralegal Studies Community and Technical College since 1983 University of Toledo. Member Toledo (President), Toledo Junior, Ohio State, Federal (President Toledo Chapter 1971-73) and American Bar Associations. Named one of Ten Outstanding Young Men of Toledo 1972. Republican. Member Sylvania City School Board 1968-72. Enjoys golf, tennis and yard work.

Office: 800 Jackson Street, Toledo 43624.
Telephone: (419) 213-4755.
Fax: (419) 213-4844
E-mail address: handwork@co.lucas.oh.us

HANNA, Thomas M. *(Judge, Kettering Municipal Court)*

Office: 3600 Shroyer Road, Kettering 45429-2734.
Telephone: (937) 296-2543.
Fax: (937) 296-3284
E-mail address: thomas.hanna@ketteringoh.org

HANY, Frederick C., II *(Judge, Ottawa County Municipal Court)*

Office: 1860 East Perry Street, Port Clinton 43452-0777.
Telephone: (419) 734-4143.
Fax: (419) 732-2862

HARCHA, Howard H., III *(Judge, Ohio Court of Common Pleas Scioto County)* Elected Nov 5, 1996. Reelected 2002, current term expires Feb 2009. Born Portsmouth Ohio March 23, 1957. United Methodist. Educated at The Ohio State University B.S. 1979 and Ohio Northern University J.D. 1982. Member Phi Alpha Delta. Admitted to practice Ohio 1982 and U.S. District Courts Northern 1983 and Southern 1983 Districts of Ohio. Former Judge, Portsmouth Municipal Court, appointed by Governor George V. Voinovich to term beginning Feb 16, 1991.

Office: 602 Seventh Street, Room 307, Portsmouth 45662-3996.
Telephone: (740) 355-8207.
Fax: (740) 355-8230
E-mail address: hharcha@zoomnet.net

HARRIS, Arthur I. *(Judge, United States Bankruptcy Court Northern District of Ohio)* Appointed by U.S. Court of Appeals Sixth Circuit judges to term beginning Oct 7, 2002.

Office: 3101 Key Tower, 127 Public Square, Cleveland 44114-1309.
Telephone: (216) 552-4373.

HARRIS, Thomas E. *(Judge, Conneaut Municipal Court)* Appointed by Governor Richard F. Celeste to term beginning Jan 13, 1989. Elected Nov 1989, 1995 and 2001. Current term expires Dec 31, 2007. Born Troy Ohio June 4, 1957. Educated at University of Akron B.S.B.A. 1979 J.D. 1982. Admitted to practice Ohio 1982. In legal practice Jefferson 1982-85 and 1987-89 and Ashtabula 1985-87.

Assistant Prosecutor 1982-84 and Chief Assistant Prosecutor 1985-89 Ashtabula County. Member Ashtabula County, Ohio State and American Bar Associations. Past President Conneaut Exchange Club and Conneaut Rotary Club. Member Ducks Unlimited, United Way Fundraising and Chamber of Commerce. Enjoys golf, tennis and auto racing.

Office: 290 Main Street, Conneaut 44030.
Telephone: (440) 593-7410.
Fax: (440) 593-6402

HARRIS, William D. *(Judge, Ohio Court of Common Pleas Monroe County)*

Mailing address: P.O. Box 563, Woodsfield 43793-1099.
Telephone: (740) 472-0841.
Fax: (740) 472-2518
E-mail address: wmharris@1st.net

HARSHA, William H. *(Judge, Ohio Court of Appeals Fourth District)* Assumed office Feb 9, 1989. Elected 1994 and 2000.

Office: 14 South Paint Street, Suite 18, Chillicothe 45601.
Telephone: (740) 779-6662.
Fax: (740) 779-6665
E-mail address: bharsha@horizonview.net

HART, William D. *(Judge, Hardin County Municipal Court)*
Mailing address: P.O. Box 250, Kenton 43326.
Office: 111 West Franklin Street, Kenton 43326.
Telephone: (419) 674-4362.
Fax: (419) 674-4096
E-mail address: hcmc@bright.net

HAYES, Jerry L. *(Judge, Ohio Court of Common Pleas Portage County)* Elected to term beginning Jan 2, 1987. Reelected 1992 and 1998. Current term expires 2004. Serves Domestic Relations Division. Born Milwaukee Wisconsin May 5, 1934. Roman Catholic. Educated at Kent State University B.A. 1956 M.A. 1964 and University of Akron J.D. 1970. Member Phi Alpha Delta. Admitted to practice Ohio 1971 and District of Columbia 1979. Began legal practice Ravenna 1971. Judge, Portage County Municipal Court 1979-85.

Congressional Staff 1962. Associate Vice President Kent State University 1969-71. Contributing Editor *Ohio Judges Resource Manual* Ohio Judicial College 1985. Editor "The Chronicle" Journal of Ohio Municipal Judges Association. Instructor Kent State University 1980-2003, University of Akron 1983-85 and Hiram College 2003. USAR 1959-65. Republican. Public Affairs Officer Republican County Committee. Member Republican Finance Committee. President Akron University Law Alumni. Member Red Cross, Heart Fund and United Way. Host and writer "The Benchbook" (nationally syndicated N.P.R. Legal Affairs weekly radio program).
Office: 203 West Main Street, Ravenna 44266-2788.
Telephone: (330) 297-3880.
Fax: (330) 296-0190

HAYES, Steven B. *(Judge, Franklin County Municipal Court)*
Office: 375 South High Street, Columbus 43215.
Telephone: (614) 645-8204.
Fax: (614) 645-7185
E-mail address: steven_hayes@fccourts.org

HEATH, James J. *(Judge, Warren County Court)*
Office: 550 Justice Drive, Lebanon 45036-2397.
Telephone: (513) 695-1370.
Fax: (513) 695-2990
E-mail address: heatjj@co.warren.oh.us

HEIN, Jonathan P. *(Judge, Ohio Court of Common Pleas Darke County)* Elected Nov 1998 to term beginning Jan 1, 1999. Term expires Dec 31, 2004. Born Coldwater Ohio Jan 4, 1956. Christian. Educated at Miami University A.B. 1978 and University of Toledo J.D. 1981. Admitted to practice Ohio 1981 and U.S. District Courts Northern and Southern Districts of Ohio. In legal practice Greenville and Fort Recovery 1981-98.

Assistant Prosecuting Attorney 1985-93 and Prosecuting Attorney 1993-98 Darke County. Member Ohio Common Pleas Judges Association and Ohio State Bar Association. Republican.
Office: 504 South Broadway, Greenville 45331-1986.
Telephone: (937) 547-7325.
Fax: (937) 547-7323
E-mail address: darkecommonpleas@skyenet.com

HELMICK, Dennis S. *(Judge, Ohio Court of Common Pleas Hamilton County)* Elected Nov 2000 to term beginning April 1, 2001. Term expires April 2007. Born Cincinnati Ohio Nov 23, 1947. Roman Catholic. Educated at Xavier University B.S. 1969 and University of Cincinnati College of Law J.D. 1972. Admitted to practice Ohio 1972, U.S. District Courts Southern District of Ohio 1972 and Eastern District of Kentucky 1985, U.S. Courts of Appeals Sixth 1973 and District of Columbia 1980 Circuits, U.S. Tax Court 1974, U.S. Supreme Court 1978, District of Columbia 1982 and Texas 1993. In legal practice Cincinnati Ohio and Norwood Ohio 1972-90. Judge, Hamilton County Municipal Court Jan 4, 1990 to March 31, 2001.

Assistant Prosecutor Solicitor's Office City of Cincinnati 1974-84. Special Counsel Ohio Attorney General's Office 1983-90. Instructor in Law Enforcement for Police University of Cincinnati 1975-76. Member American Judges Association, American Judicature Society, Cincinnati (Former Member Board of Trustees) and Ohio State Bar Associations. Graduate of Leadership Cincinnati June 1996. Former Board Member and Director East End Learning Center and Norwood Federal Credit Union. Past President and Member Board of Trustees University of Cincinnati College of Law Alumni Association. Former Member Parish Council St. Mary's Church of Hyde Park.
Office: 1000 Main Street, Room 485, Cincinnati 45202-1217.
Telephone: (513) 946-5830.
Fax: (513) 946-5833

HEMANN, Patricia A. *(Magistrate Judge, United States District Court Northern District of Ohio)* Appointed by U.S. District Court judges to term beginning April 13, 1993. Reappointed October 2000, current term expires April 2009. Born Effingham Illinois June 28, 1942. Educated at University of Illinois B.A. cum laude 1964 and Cleveland State University Cleveland-Marshall College of Law J.D. summa cum laude 1980. Editor-in-Chief Cleveland State Law Review. Law Clerk to Hon. William K. Thomas, U.S. District Court Northern District of Ohio 1980-82. Admitted to practice Ohio 1980. In legal practice Cleveland 1982-93.

Author Note "Land Banking Tax Delinquent Properties" *Reform and Revitalization.* Former District Director National Association of Women Judges. Member Ohio Women's, Cleveland (Former Trustee, Member Justice for All Committee), Federal and American Bar Associations.
Office: 11B U.S. Courthouse, 801 West Superior Avenue, Cleveland 44113-1845.
Telephone: (216) 357-7135.

HEMM, Michael W. *(Judge, Miami County Municipal Court)*
Office: 201 West Main Street, Troy 45373-3240.
Telephone: (937) 332-6965.
Fax: (937) 332-6932
E-mail address: mwhemm@wesnet.com

HENDERSON, David Earl *(Judge, Ohio Court of Common Pleas Jefferson County)* Serves Domestic Relations Division.
Office: Courthouse, Steubenville 43952.

HENDON, Sylvia Sieve *(Judge, Ohio Court of Common Pleas Hamilton County)* Former Chief Referee. Serves Juvenile Division. Born Cincinnati Ohio March 23, 1944. Educated at Edgecliff College B.A. with honors 1965 and Chase Law School of Northern Kentucky University J.D. with honors 1975. Articles Editor Chase Law Review 1974-75. Member Phi Alpha Delta. Admitted to practice Ohio 1975 and U.S. Court of Appeals

HENDON, SYLVIA SIEVE—*Continued*
Sixth Circuit 1975. In legal practice Cincinnati 1975-83. Judge, Hamilton County Municipal Court 1983-91.

Important Decision: State v. Meadows (constitutionality of obscenity law) 1986. Guest Professor Chase Law School of Northern Kentucky University. Member National Association of Women Judges, American Judicature Society, Cincinnati and Ohio State Bar Associations. Recipient Superior Judicial Service Awards 1986-88. Republican.

Office: 800 Broadway, Cincinnati 45202-1225.
Telephone: (513) 946-9202.
Fax: (513) 946-9207
E-mail address: sylvia.sieve.hendon-@juvcourt.hamilton-co.org

HENDRICKSON, Robert A. *(Judge, Butler County Court)*
Office: 9113 Cincinnati Dayton Road, West Chester 45069.
Telephone: (513) 867-5070.
Fax: (513) 777-0558

HENRY, Charles E. *(Judge, Ohio Court of Common Pleas Geauga County)* Assumed office 1993. Presiding Judge 1996, 1999 and 2002. Serves Probate and Juvenile Divisions. Educated at Miami University, Ohio B.A. 1980 and Cleveland-Marshall College of Law J.D. 1985. In legal practice Geauga County 1985-93.

Assistant Prosecutor 1987-88 and Assistant Public Defender 1993 Geauga County. Established first CASA program in Northeast Ohio, an Indigent Guardian Program and a therapeutic youth center. Implemented use of creative disposition alternatives in unruly and delinquent juvenile cases. Eliminated probate case backlog and significantly reduced time needed for disposition. Member Ohio Association of Probate Judges, Ohio Association of Juvenile and Family Court Judges, Geauga County and Ohio State Bar Associations. Member State Senate Ohio 1988-92. Volunteer Peace Corps Lesotho Southern Africa 1980-82. Member Human Services Advisory Board and Geauga County Family First Council. Coach Kenston Athletic Association.

Office: 100 Short Court Street, Suite 3A, Chardon 44024.
Telephone: (440) 285-2222.
Fax: (440) 285-5025

HENRY, Paul D. *(Judge, Eaton Municipal Court)* Elected Nov 1991 to term beginning Jan 1, 1992. Reelected Nov 1997, current term expires Dec 31, 2004. Born Dayton Ohio May 2, 1948. Lutheran. Educated at Miami University B.S. 1970 M.S. 1976 and University of Dayton J.D. 1981. Admitted to practice Ohio 1981 and U.S. District Court District of Ohio 1981. In legal practice Eaton 1981-91.

Assistant County Attorney 1985-91. Member Association of Municipal/County Judges of Ohio, Inc., Preble County and Ohio State Bar Associations.

Mailing address: P.O. Box 65, Eaton 45320.
Telephone: (937) 456-4941, 456-6204.
Fax: (937) 456-4685

HENSAL, James E. *(Judge, Fulton County Court)*
Office: 224 South Fulton Street, Wauseon 43567-1352.
Telephone: (419) 337-9212.
Fax: (419) 337-9286

HENSLEY, James A., Jr. *(Judge, Montgomery County Court)* Elected 1994. Reelected to subsequent term.
Office: 6111 Taylorsville Road, Huber Heights 45424.
Telephone: (937) 496-7231.
Fax: (937) 496-7236
E-mail address: hensljrj@montcnty.org

HENSLEY, James A., Sr. *(Judge, Montgomery County Court)*
Office: 195 South Clayton Road, New Lebanon 45345-9601.
Telephone: (937) 687-9099.
Fax: (937) 687-7119
E-mail address: hensleyjsr@montcnty.org

HENSON, James D. *(Judge, Ohio Court of Common Pleas Richland County)* Elected to term beginning Jan 1, 1981. Reelected 1986, 1992 and 1998. Current term expires Dec 2004. Born Crestline Ohio Feb 19, 1942. Religious affiliation: Congregationalist. Educated at The Ohio State University B.A. 1966 J.D. 1969. Member Phi Alpha Delta. Admitted to practice Ohio 1969 and U.S. Supreme Court 1979. Began legal practice Cleveland 1969. In legal practice Mansfield 1973.

Assistant Prosecuting Attorney Richland County 1973-80. Important Decision: No Constitutional Right to be a Cheerleader in School (civil rights case). Member Richland County, Cuyahoga County and Ohio State Bar Associations. E-4 U.S. Army 1960-63. With FBI 1970-73. Army Security Agency Service in Japan. Republican. Fundraiser United Community Appeal (Multiple Sclerosis). 32° Mason. Member American Heart Fund, Kiwanis Club (President 1984-85), Optimist Club, American Legion and Elks. Enjoys writing, reading and active sports.

Office: 50 Park Avenue, Mansfield 44902-1888.
Telephone: (419) 774-5570.
Fax: (419) 774-5516
E-mail address: judgehenson@kosinet.com

HERMAN, Gary W. *(Judge, Auglaize County Municipal Court)* Elected to term beginning Jan 1, 1982. Reelected 1987, 1993 and 1999. Current term expires Dec 31, 2005. Born Lima Ohio June 11, 1949. United Church of Christ. Educated at Tarkio College B.A. 1971 and Ohio Northern University J.D. 1974. Admitted to practice Ohio 1974 and U.S. District Court Northern District of Ohio. Began legal practice Wapakoneta and St. Marys 1975.

Member Ohio Judges Association, Municipal-County Judges of Ohio, Inc., Auglaize County (President 1982) and Ohio State (Judicial Reform Committee) Bar Associations. Republican. Past President Sertoma Club. Former Board Member Family-Y. Participant Columbus Marathon 1982. Enjoys sailing, downhill skiing, long distance running, stained glass and wine making.

Mailing address: P.O. Box 11, Wapakoneta 45895.
Telephone: (419) 738-7870.
Fax: (419) 738-0543
E-mail address: gwherman@bright.net

HERMAN, Thomas R. *(Judge, Clermont County Municipal Court)* Elected Nov 5, 1991 to term beginning Jan 1, 1992. Reelected 1997, current term expires Dec 31, 2003. Born Cincinnati Ohio March 21, 1949. Roman Catholic. Educated at University of Cincinnati B.B.A. 1972 and Salmon P. Chase College of Law J.D. 1977. Law Clerk to Hon. Paul George, Ohio Court of Com-

HERMAN, THOMAS R.—*Continued*

mon Pleas Hamilton County 1972-73. Admitted to practice Ohio 1978 and U.S. District Court Southern District of Ohio 1978. In legal practice Amelia 1978-80 and Batavia 1980-91.

Assistant Prosecutor 1981-85 and Assistant Public Defender 1985-89. Solicitor Union Township Clermont County 1985-91. Board of Trustees Clermont County Law Library 1991. Member Ohio Association of Municipal and County Court Judges, American Judges Association, Clermont County, Cincinnati and American Bar Associations. Recipient Meritorious Service Award from Boy Scouts of America. Precinct Committeeperson Clermont County Republican Party 1986-91. Speaker DARE program commencement ceremonies. Member GLADD (Government Leaders Against Drunk Driving) and Kiwanis. Interests include family, church, golf and skiing.

Office: 289 Main Street, Batavia 45103-2906.
Telephone: (513) 732-7914.
Fax: (513) 732-7051

HIGGINS, Michael F. *(Judge, Licking County Municipal Court)* Appointed by governor to term beginning Jan 8, 1991. Elected 1996 and 2001. Current term expires Dec 2007. Born Sharon Pennsylvania. Presbyterian. Educated at Edinboro University of Pennsylvania B.S. 1970 and Capital University J.D. 1977. Law Clerk to Ohio Court of Common Pleas Licking County 1976-77. Admitted to practice Ohio 1977, U.S. District Court Southern District of Ohio 1980 and U.S. Supreme Court 1986. In legal practice Newark 1977-91.

Assistant Law Director City of Newark 1978-91. Law Director Buckeye Lake Village 1985-91. Member Licking County and Ohio State Bar Associations. USAR. Hobbies include fishing and shooting.

Office: 40 West Main Street, Newark 43055.
Telephone: (740) 349-6652.
Fax: (740) 345-4250
E-mail address: higginsmf@hotmail.com

HILDEBRANDT, Lee H., Jr. *(Judge, Ohio Court of Appeals First District)* Elected Nov 1984 to term beginning Feb 9, 1985. Reelected Nov 1990, Nov 1996 and 2002. Current term expires Feb 2009. Educated at University of Cincinnati B.A. 1969 and University of Toledo J.D. 1972. Member Phi Alpha Delta. Admitted to practice Ohio 1972, U.S. District Court Southern District of Ohio 1973, U.S. Court of Appeals Sixth Circuit 1973 and U.S. Supreme Court 1979. In legal practice Cincinnati 1972-79. Magistrate, Ohio Court of Common Pleas Hamilton County Division of Domestic Relations 1982-85.

Assistant Prosecuting Attorney Hamilton County 1978-82. Important Decisions: South Euclid Fraternal Order of Police v. D'Amico 29 Ohio St. 3d 50, 505 N.E.2d 268, 1987; Gahanna v. Eastgate Properties, Inc. 36 Ohio St. 3d 65, 521 N.E.2d 814, 1988; Cincinnati Bengals, Inc. v. Cincinnati 57 Ohio App. 3d 122, 567 N.E.2d 284, 1989; Ubelacker v. Cincom Sys. Inc. 80 Ohio App. 3d 97, 608 N.E.2d 858, 1992; Cincinnati v. Langan 94 Ohio App. 3d 22, 640 N.E.2d 200, 1994; and Morton International, Inc. v. Aetna Casualty and Surety Co. 106 Ohio App. 3d 653, 666 N.E.2d 1163, 1995. Lecturer on White Collar Crime University of Cincinnati Evening College 1978-80. Member Ohio Courts of Appeal Association (Chief Justice Elect) and Ohio State Bar Association. Instructor Capital Punishment seminars Ohio Association of Criminal Defense Lawyers and Cincinnati Bar Association Bench-Bar Conference. Board of Directors Pro Kids of Cincinnati and Lawyers' Club of Cincinnati.

Office: 230 East Ninth Street, Twelfth Floor, Cincinnati 45202-1287.
Telephone: (513) 946-3450.
Fax: (513) 946-3411
E-mail address: lhildebrandt@cms.hamilton-co.org

HILLYER, Brad L. *(Judge, Tuscarawas County Court)*

Office: 220 East Third Street, Uhrichsville 44683-1821.
Telephone: (740) 922-4795.
Fax: (740) 922-7020

HOELLRICH, Gene R. *(Judge, Darke County Court)* Elected to term beginning Jan 1, 1980. Reelected 1986, 1992 and 1998. Current term expires Dec 31, 2004. Born Defiance Ohio Sept 26, 1946. Lutheran. Educated at The Ohio State University B.A. 1968 J.D. summa cum laude 1971. Staff writer 1970 and Editor 1971 The Ohio State University Law Journal. Member Order of the Coif and Alpha Tau Omega. Admitted to practice Ohio 1971. Began legal practice Dayton 1971. In legal practice Greenville 1972.

With Greenville Civil Service Commission 1977-79. Author Case Note 1970, Case Note "Stanley v. Georgia" 1971 and article on Natural Resources 1971 The Ohio State University L. Jour. Member Darke County (Treasurer 1977, President 1978) and Ohio State Bar Associations. Captain USAS 1970-78 (active 1972). Previously worked as carpenter. Republican. Member Greenville Lions Club 1972-84. Enjoys bow hunting, woodworking, snowmobiling and reading.

Office: Courthouse, Greenville 45331-1990.
Telephone: (937) 547-7340.
Fax: (937) 547-7378
E-mail address: phoellrich@erinet.com

HOFFMAN, John E., Jr. *(Judge, United States Bankruptcy Court Southern District of Ohio)* Appointed by U.S. Court of Appeals Sixth Circuit judges to term beginning Feb 25, 2000. Term expires Feb 24, 2014.

Office: 120 West Third Street, Dayton 45402.
Telephone: (937) 225-2516.

HOFFMAN, John R. *(Judge, Ohio Court of Common Pleas Stark County)* Formerly served Domestic Relations Division. Serves Family Division.

Office: 110 Central Plaza South, Suite 602, Canton 44702-1414.
Telephone: (330) 451-7923.
Fax: (330) 451-7837

HOFFMAN, William B. *(Judge, Ohio Court of Appeals Fifth District)* Elected to term beginning Feb 9, 1991. Reelected 1996 and 2002. Current term expires Feb 2009. Born Canton Ohio July 1, 1951. Baptist. Educated at College of Wooster B.A. with honors 1973 and University of Akron J.D. 1976. Member Delta Theta Phi. Admitted to practice Ohio 1976, U.S. Court of Appeals Sixth Circuit 1984 and U.S. District Court Northern District of Ohio. In legal practice Canton 1976-87. Judge, Canton Municipal Court 1988-91.

City Prosecutor Canton 1977-87. Member Ohio State and American Bar Associations. Attended The National Judicial College 1989. Named one of Outstanding Young Men of America 1986. Recipient Certificate of

HOFFMAN, WILLIAM B.—*Continued*

Appreciation from Stark County Victim/Witness Program 1986 and 1990. Democrat. Advisory Board Stark County Epilepsy Association. Enjoys golf.
Office: 110 Central Plaza South, Suite 320, Canton 44721.
Telephone: (330) 451-7448.
Fax: (330) 451-7249

HOGAN, Daniel T. *(Judge, Ohio Court of Common Pleas Franklin County)* Elected Nov 5, 1996 to term beginning Jan 1, 1997. Reelected 2002, current term expires Dec 31, 2008. Born Niles Ohio May 17, 1952. Roman Catholic. Educated at Villanova University B.A. 1974 and Capital University Law School J.D. 1978. Admitted to practice Ohio 1978. In legal practice 1978-96.
Assistant City Prosecutor Columbus 1978-80. Assistant Prosecutor Franklin County 1980-96. Member Columbus and Ohio State Bar Associations. Attended Career Prosecutors School National College of District Attorneys Houston Texas 1988. Republican. Member American Heart Association. Enjoys golf.
Office: 369 South High Street, #9D, Columbus 43215.
Telephone: (614) 462-3770.
Fax: (614) 462-3676
E-mail address: daniel_hogan@fccourts.org

HOGAN, Timothy S. *(Magistrate Judge, United States District Court Southern District of Ohio)* Appointed by U.S. District Court judges to term beginning Oct 4, 1996. Born Columbus Ohio April 30, 1941. Catholic. Educated at University of Dayton B.A. 1964, Xavier University M.Ed. 1968 and Salmon P. Chase College of Law J.D. 1972. Admitted to practice Ohio 1973, U.S. District Court Southern District of Ohio 1973, U.S. Supreme Court 1976 and U.S. Court of Appeals Sixth Circuit 1979. In legal practice Cincinnati 1973-81. Former Judge Ohio Court of Common Pleas Hamilton County 1994-96 and Hamilton County Municipal Court, appointed by Governor James A. Rhodes to term beginning Jan 16, 1981.
Senior Assistant Prosecutor Cincinnati 1973-81. Solicitor Madeira 1978-81. Important Decisions: McDowell v. McCullion 11 Ohio Misc. 2d 23, 1983; State v. Howard 7 Ohio Misc. 2d 45, 1983; Marchioni v. Wilson 20 Ohio Misc. 2d 10, 1984; Fifth-Third Bank v. Gilbert 17 Ohio Misc. 2d 14, 1984; State v. Wymbs 10 Ohio Misc. 2d 26, 1984; Central Trust v. Cohen 14 Ohio Misc. 2d 23, 1984; State v. Scott 27 Ohio Misc. 2d 38, 1986; and C. G. & E. Company v. Goebel 28 Ohio Misc. 2d 4, 1986. Instructor in graduate and undergraduate courses University of Cincinnati and Cincinnati Police Academy. Former Member Ohio Municipal Judges Association, Ohio Common Pleas Judges Association, American Judges Association, Cincinnati, Ohio State and Federal Bar Associations. Attended The National Judicial College, American Academy of Judicial Education, Ohio Judicial College and Ohio Academy of Trial Lawyers. Rated Highly Recommended by Cincinnati Bar Association prior to 1981, 1985 and 1992 elections. Previously worked as teacher St. Gertrude School and Summit Country Day School. Republican. Former Board member Talbert House Inc. Board of Trustees Central Clinic and Bankers Club. Member Advisory Committee Citizens Concerned for Community Values. Member Fraternal Order of Police Associates and Cincinnati Athletic Club. Enjoys sports and reading.
Office: 706 U.S. Courthouse, 100 East Fifth Street, Cincinnati 45202-3976.
Telephone: (513) 564-7650.

HOLCOMB, John E. *(Judge, Akron Municipal Court)*
Office: 217 South High Street, Courtroom 907, Akron 44308.
Telephone: (330) 375-2052.
Fax: (330) 375-2474

HOLMES, Nicholas H., Jr. *(Judge, Ohio Court of Common Pleas Ross County)* Elected to term beginning Dec 11, 1978. Reelected to subsequent terms. Current term expires Dec 31, 2006. Born Madison Wisconsin Oct 20, 1942. Educated at Williams College B.A. 1965 and University of Cincinnati J.D. 1968. Admitted to practice Ohio 1969, U.S. District Court Southern District of Ohio 1970 and U.S. Supreme Court 1982. In legal practice Chillicothe 1969-78 and McArthur 1969-72.
Solicitor Village of McArthur 1969-72. Member Ross County, Ohio State and American Bar Associations. Member First Presbyterian Church. Enjoys reading, bridge, golf, tennis, fishing, trap shooting and darts.
Office: Two North Paint Street, Suite D, Chillicothe 45601.
Telephone: (740) 702-3038.
Fax: (740) 775-1065
E-mail address: niblick@bright.net

HOLSCHUH, John D. *(Senior Judge, United States District Court Southern District of Ohio)* Appointed for life by President Jimmy Carter to term beginning May 23, 1980. Former Chief Judge. Assumed Senior status, serves by assignment. Born Ironton Ohio Oct 12, 1926. Educated at Miami University B.A. cum laude 1948 and University of Cincinnati J.D. 1951. Editor-in-Chief Cincinnati Law Review. Law Clerk to Hon. Mell G. Underwood, U.S. District Court Southern District of Ohio 1952-54. Member Order of the Coif, Delta Upsilon, Phi Alpha Delta, Omicron Delta Kappa and Phi Beta Kappa. Admitted to practice Ohio 1951, U.S. District Court 1952, U.S. Court of Appeals Sixth Circuit 1953 and U.S. Supreme Court 1956. In legal practice Columbus 1951-52 and 1954-80.
Adjunct Professor The Ohio State University College of Law 1970-77. Fellow American College of Trial Lawyers. Member Columbus, Ohio State and American Bar Associations. Member St. Marks Episcopal Church.
Office: 109 U.S. Courthouse, 85 Marconi Boulevard, Columbus 43215.
Telephone: (614) 719-3310.

HOLZAPFEL, Leonard F. *(Judge, Ohio Court of Common Pleas Jackson County)*
Office: 226 East Main Street, Suite 6, Jackson 45640-1791.
Telephone: (740) 286-3601.
Fax: (740) 286-5203
E-mail address: cmnpleas@zoomnet.net

HOOPER, Jeffrey A. *(Judge, Ohio Court of Common Pleas Muskingum County)* Serves Domestic Relations Division. Former Judge, Muskingum County Court.
Office: 401 Main Street, Zanesville 43701.

HOOVER, James L. *(Judge, Crawford County Municipal Court)*
Office: 130 North Walnut, Bucyrus 44820-0550.
Telephone: (419) 562-2731.
Fax: (419) 562-7064
E-mail address: crawmuni@crawford-co.org

HOOVER, Kim R. *(Judge, Cuyahoga Falls Municipal Court)*
Office: 2310 Second Street, Cuyahoga Falls 44221.
Telephone: (330) 971-8209.
Fax: (330) 928-7722

HOOVER, Robert H. *(Judge, Ohio Court of Common Pleas Licking County)* Appointed by Governor George V. Voinovich Jan 5, 1996. Elected Nov 1996 and Nov 2002. Current term expires Feb 7, 2009. Serves Probate and Juvenile Divisions. Born Columbus Ohio 1948. Roman Catholic. Educated at Muskingum College B.A. 1970 and The Ohio State University College of Law J.D. 1975. Law Clerk to Licking County Courts 1976-77. Admitted to practice Ohio 1975 and U.S. Supreme Court 1979. Court Referee 1984-91. In legal practice Newark Ohio 1991-95.
Assistant County Prosecutor 1977-84. U.S. Army Military Police Corps 1971-73.
Office: Courthouse, Public Square, Newark 43055-5553.
Telephone: (740) 349-6125.
Fax: (740) 349-6168
E-mail address: jhoover@lcounty.com

HOPKINS, Jeffery P. *(Judge, United States Bankruptcy Court Southern District of Ohio)* Appointed by U.S. Court of Appeals Sixth Circuit judges.
Office: 800 Atrium Two, 221 East Fourth Street, Cincinnati 45202.
Telephone: (513) 684-2572.

HOROWITZ, Robert Davis *(Judge, Ohio Court of Common Pleas Stark County)* Serves Probate Division.
Office: 110 Central Plaza South, Suite 501, Canton 44702.

HORVATH, Frank J. *(Judge, Ohio Court of Common Pleas Lorain County)* Serves Probate Division.
Office: 226 Middle Avenue, Fourth Floor, Elyria 44035-5645.
Telephone: (440) 329-5179.
Fax: (440) 323-3595

HOSKINS, Jeffrey J. *(Judge, Ohio Court of Common Pleas Highland County)* Elected Nov 5, 2002 to term beginning Feb 9, 2003. Term expires Feb 8, 2009. Serves Domestic Relations Division. Born Hillsboro Ohio Feb 20, 1948. Methodist. Educated at University of Cincinnati, Ohio University B.S. summa cum laude 1972 and University of Notre Dame J.D. 1975. Admitted to practice Ohio 1975. In legal practice Hillsboro 1975-2003.
Member Lions Club and Elks Club. Enjoys farming.
Office: 105 North High Street, Hillsboro 45133.
Telephone: (937) 393-2422.

HOSTETLER, David L. *(Judge, Coshocton Municipal Court)*
Office: 760 Chestnut Street, Coshocton 43812.
Telephone: (740) 622-2871.
Fax: (740) 623-5928
E-mail address: judge@coshoctonmunicipalcourt.com

HOUSER, Joseph M. *(Judge, Mahoning County Court)*
Office: 127 Boardman-Canfield Road, Youngstown 44512.
Telephone: (330) 726-5546.
Fax: (330) 740-2035
E-mail address: jhouser@mbpu.com

HUFFMAN, Mary Katherine *(Judge, Ohio Court of Common Pleas Montgomery County)*
Mailing address: P.O. Box 972, Dayton 45401.
Telephone: (937) 496-7955.
Fax: (937) 225-5406.

HUNTER, Scott D. *(Judge, Mahoning County Court)*
Office: 72 North Broad Street, Canfield 44406.
Telephone: (330) 533-3643.
Fax: (330) 740-2034

HURLEY, Roger L. *(Judge, Darke County Court)* Assumed office Jan 1, 1979. Elected to term beginning Jan 1, 1983. Reelected 1988, 1994 and 2000. Current term expires Dec 31, 2006. Born Tucson Arizona Jan 7, 1948. Protestant. Educated at University of Akron B.S.E.E. 1971 J.D. 1974. Member Phi Kappa Tau and Phi Alpha Delta. Admitted to practice Ohio 1974. Began legal practice Greenville 1974.
Assistant County Prosecutor Darke County 1974-75. Village Solicitor New Madison 1975-78 and New Weston 1977-78. Instructor in Constitutional Law Greenville Police Department 1983. Member The Association of Trial Lawyers of America, Ohio Academy of Trial Lawyers, Darke County (President 1979) and Ohio State (General Practice Section) Bar Associations. Recipient Superior Judicial Award from the Supreme Court of Ohio. Certified Tennis Instructor USPTA. Head Coach girls varsity tennis, Assistant Coach boys tennis and Coach 7th grade boys basketball Greenville High School. Member Elks, Masonic Lodge, Antioch Temple and Shriners. Enjoys basketball and tennis.
Office: Courthouse, Third Floor, Greenville 45331-1990.
Telephone: (937) 547-7340.
Fax: (937) 547-7378

HURLEY, Steven Leroy *(Judge, Ohio Court of Common Pleas Greene County)* Serves Domestic Relations Division.
Office: 45 North Detroit Street, Xenia 45385.

HUTCHESON, Robert W. *(Judge, Ohio Court of Common Pleas Greene County)* Elected 1994. Reelected to subsequent term. Serves Juvenile Division.
Office: 2100 Greene Way Boulevard, Xenia 45385.
Telephone: (937) 562-4000.
Fax: (937) 562-4010

INDERLIED, H. F., Jr. *(Judge, Ohio Court of Common Pleas Geauga County)* Elected to term beginning Jan 1, 1981. Reelected Nov 1986, Nov 1992 and Nov 1998. Current term expires Dec 31, 2004. Born Portland Oregon Oct 23, 1940. Protestant. Educated at University of Arizona B.S. 1962 and Case Western Reserve University J.D. 1965. Member Phi Delta Phi. Admitted to practice Ohio 1965. In legal practice Cleveland 1965-72 and Chardon 1972-76. Judge, Chardon Municipal Court 1976-81.
Editorial Board *Ohio Jury Instructions* since 1990. Member Ohio Supreme Court Committee to study the impact of substance abuse on the courts 1990 and Trial

INDERLIED, H. F., JR.—*Continued*

Judges Panel Ohio-Ukraine Judiciary Program 1992. Fellow Ohio State Bar Foundation and Geauga County Bar Foundation. Former Member The Association of Trial Lawyers of America, Ohio Academy of Trial Lawyers (Governing Board of Trustees 1973-76) and Ohio Municipal Judges Association. Member Ohio Judicial Conference, Ohio Common Pleas Judges Association, Geauga County (Past President) and Ohio State Bar Associations. Faculty member Ohio Judicial College since 1978. Judicial Panelist Ohio Mock Trial Competition since 1994. Facilitator Ohio Bench-Bar Conference 1994. Vice Chair Ohio Judicial Conference Mentor Program for new judges and Judicial Corrections Board NEOCAP (a community based corrections facility). Attends CLE conferences regularly. Recipient Superior Judicial Service Awards from Ohio Supreme Court 1976-86, Humanitarian Award from Geauga County Exchange Club 1982 and Boss of the Year Award from Maple Leaf Chapter American Business Women's Association 1982. Republican. Enjoys reading, boating, hunting, fishing, water skiing, racquetball, basketball, softball, volleyball and watching other sports.

Office: 100 Short Court Street, Suite 1A, Chardon 44024-1238.
Telephone: (440) 285-2222.
Fax: (440) 286-2127
E-mail address: fubar1023@aol.com

INGRAHAM, Jeffrey R. *(Judge, Ohio Court of Common Pleas Mercer County)*
Office: 101 North Main, Room 301, Celina 45822.
Telephone: (419) 586-2122.
Fax: (419) 586-4000
E-mail address: judge.ingraham@mercercountyohio.org

IRVING, Jane Ellen *(Judge, Holmes County Court)* Appointed by Governor Richard F. Celeste to term beginning July 1, 1987. Elected Nov 1988, 1994 and 2000. Current term expires Dec 31, 2006. Born Millersburg Ohio Oct 8, 1947. Presbyterian. Educated at Bowling Green State University B.S. 1969 and The Ohio State University College of Law J.D. 1972. Admitted to practice Ohio 1972 and U.S. District Court Northern District of Ohio 1975. In legal practice Millersburg 1973-91.

Assistant Prosecutor Wayne County 1975-80 and Holmes County 1986-88. Associate Professor Ohio University 1972-73.

Office: One East Jackson Street, Suite 101, Millersburg 44654.
Telephone: (330) 674-4901.
Fax: (330) 674-5514

IVANCHAK, Terry *(Judge, Warren Municipal Court)*
Mailing address: P.O. Box 1550, Warren 44483.
Office: 141 South Street, Warren 44483.
Telephone: (330) 841-2518.
Fax: (330) 841-2760
E-mail address: tyivan@onecom.com

JACKSON, S. Farrell *(Judge, Ohio Court of Common Pleas Fairfield County)* Serves Domestic Relations Division.
Office: 224 East Main Street, Fourth Floor, Lancaster 43130.
Telephone: (740) 687-7087.
Fax: (740) 687-7169

JAMES, Jim D. *(Judge, Ohio Court of Common Pleas Stark County)* Serves Family Division.
Office: 110 Central Plaza South, Suite 604, Canton 44702-1414.
Telephone: (330) 451-7307.
Fax: (330) 451-7837
E-mail address: JudgeJames@co.stark.oh.us

JAMES, Richard L. *(Judge, Ohio Court of Common Pleas Trumbull County)* Appointed by Governor George V. Voinovich to term beginning Nov 1993. Elected Nov 1994 to term beginning Jan 1, 1995. Reelected 2000. Current term expires Dec 31, 2006. Serves Family Division. Born Warren Ohio Dec 20, 1950. Methodist. Educated at Hiram College B.A. 1973 and University of Akron J.D. 1981. Admitted to practice Ohio 1981. In legal practice Warren 1981-92.

Assistant City Law Director Warren 1987-92. Member Ohio Association of Juvenile and Family Court Judges (Trustee, Executive Committee), Ohio Association of Domestic Court Judges, Trumbull County and Ohio State Bar Associations. Community Medicine Clerkship Northeastern Ohio University College of Medicine 1995-96. Republican. Board of Directors American Heart Association and American Cancer Society. Officer Warren/Trumbull Urban League. Enjoys all outdoor sports.

Office: 220 South Main Avenue, Warren 44482.
Telephone: (330) 675-2605.
Fax: (330) 675-2322
E-mail address: drjames@co.trumbull.oh.us

JANAS, Thomas W. *(Judge, Ohio Court of Common Pleas Lorain County)*
Office: Courthouse, 308 Second Street, Elyria 44035.
Telephone: (440) 329-5518.
Fax: (440) 284-3794

JANUZZI, Thomas A. *(Judge, Oberlin Municipal Court)*
Mailing address: P.O. Box 179, Oberlin 44074-0179.
Telephone: (440) 775-1751.
Fax: (440) 775-0619

JASPER, Mabel M. *(Judge, Cleveland Municipal Court)* Elected Nov 1987 to term beginning Jan 5, 1988. Reelected 1993 and 1999. Current term expires Jan 2006. Born Alabama Oct 18, 1932. Educated at Kent State University B.S. and Cleveland-Marshall College of Law J.D. Member Delta Sigma Theta. Admitted to practice Ohio 1977. Began legal practice Cleveland 1977. Referee, Ohio Court of Common Pleas Cuyahoga County 1983-87.

Assistant Attorney General 1980-83. Member Cleveland and Cuyahoga County Bar Associations. Previously employed as school teacher.

Mailing address: P.O. Box 94894, Cleveland 44101-4894.
Office: 1200 Ontario Street, Cleveland 44113.
Telephone: (216) 664-4978.
Fax: (216) 664-4283

JENKINS, Bruce *(Judge, Franklin County Municipal Court)*
Office: 375 South High Street, Columbus 43215.
Telephone: (614) 645-8205.
Fax: (614) 645-7802
E-mail address: bruce_jenkins@fccourts.org

JENKINS, Thomas K. *(Judge, Ohio Court of Common Pleas Marion County)* Elected to term beginning

JENKINS, THOMAS K.—*Continued*

Jan 1, 1985. Reelected Nov 1990, 1996 and 2002. Current term expires 2009. Serves Probate, Juvenile and Family Divisions. Born Marion Ohio Sept 23, 1937. Presbyterian. Educated at Ohio Wesleyan University B.A. 1959, Ohio Northern University J.D. 1962 and Southern Methodist University LL.M. 1965. Admitted to practice Ohio 1962. In legal practice Marion 1963-84.

Board of Editors *Ohio Lawyer Magazine* 1987-92. Trustee 1988-96 and President 1995 Ohio State Bar Foundation. Trustee Ohio Judicial College 1990-96. Member Ohio State Bar Association (Executive Committee 1984-87). Enjoys sports and golf.

Office: 100 North Main Street, Marion 43302-3089.
Telephone: (740) 387-7614.
Fax: (740) 387-6638
E-mail address: tkj@marion.net

JENSEN, James D. *(Judge, Ohio Court of Common Pleas Lucas County)*
Office: 700 Adams Street, Toledo 43624-1678.
Telephone: (419) 213-4538.
Fax: (419) 213-4181

JOHNSON, David L. *(Judge, Ohio Court of Common Pleas Franklin County)* Elected to term beginning Jan 9, 1989. Reelected 1994 and 2000. Current term expires Jan 7, 2007. Born Springfield Ohio May 7, 1933. Educated at University of Omaha B.G.E. 1960, George Washington University M.B.A. 1972 and The Ohio State University J.D. 1976. Admitted to practice Ohio 1976.

Former Assistant Prosecuting Attorney Franklin County. Colonel U.S. Army 1953-76.

Office: 369 South High Street, Columbus 43215-4554.
Telephone: (614) 462-3664.
Fax: (614) 462-3476
E-mail address: david_johnson@fccourts.org

JOHNSTON, Charles A. *(Judge, Carroll County Court)* Appointed by Governor Richard F. Celeste to term beginning Feb 9, 1985. Elected Nov 1986, Nov 1988, 1994 and 2000. Current term expires Dec 31, 2006. Born Canton Ohio Oct 11, 1950. Presbyterian. Educated at Westminster College B.A. 1973 and Ohio Northern University J.D. 1976. Admitted to practice Ohio 1977, U.S. Court of Appeals Sixth Circuit 1984 and U.S. District Court Northern District of Ohio 1984. Began legal practice Carrollton Ohio 1977.

Member Carroll County, Stark County, Ohio State and American Bar Associations. Recipient Superior Judicial Service Award from Ohio Supreme Court 1985. Licensed Title Insurance Agent in Ohio for Chicago Title Insurance Company since 1983. Democrat. Precinct member Carroll County Central and Executive Democrat Party 1982-84. Member Lee Township Ruritans 1977-79, Carroll County Chamber of Commerce, Carroll County Co-operative Extension Advisory Committee, Buckeye Walking Horse Association and Carroll County Veterans Club (Social member). Enjoys golf and showing Tennessee Walking Horses.

Office: 119 South Lisbon Street, Suite 301, Carrollton 44615.
Telephone: (330) 627-5049.
Fax: (330) 627-3662

JOHNSTON, Lorene G. *(Judge, Jackson County Municipal Court)* Appointed by Governor Bob Taft Aug 2002. Elected 2002, current term expires Dec 31, 2007. Born Wellston Ohio Jan 15, 1952. Catholic. Educated at Miami University, Ohio B.S. 1974, Ohio University M.A. 1978 and University of Dayton J.D. 1982. Law Clerk to Ohio Court of Common Pleas Greene County 1981-82. Admitted to practice Ohio 1982, U.S. District Court Southern District of Ohio 1983, U.S. Supreme Court 1988 and U.S. Court of Appeals Sixth Circuit 1990. In legal practice Wellston 1982-2000.

Law Director Village of Hamden 1982-99 and City of Wellston 2000. Member Jackson County, Ohio State and American Bar Associations. Member City Council Wellston 1977. State Committeewoman 10th District Ohio 1978-82. Member Rotary. Enjoys golf.

Office: 350 Portsmouth Street, Suite 101, Jackson 45640-1791.
Telephone: (740) 286-4347.
Fax: (740) 286-0679
E-mail address: lorilaw@zoomnet.net

JONES, Larry A. *(Judge, Cleveland Municipal Court)*
Mailing address: P.O. Box 94894, Cleveland 44101-4894.
Office: 1200 Ontario Street, Cleveland 44113.
Telephone: (216) 664-4996.
Fax: (216) 664-4283

JONES, Peggy Foley *(Judge, Ohio Court of Common Pleas Cuyahoga County)*
Office: 1200 Ontario Street, Cleveland 44113-1678.
Telephone: (216) 443-8725.
Fax: (216) 348-4038
E-mail address: pmylott_2000@yahoo.com

JOSEPH, William D. *(Judge, Zanesville Municipal Court)* Elected to term beginning Nov 24, 1999. Reelected 2001, current term expires Dec 31, 2007. Born Athens Ohio March 3, 1944. Roman Catholic. Educated at University of Notre Dame B.A. 1966 and University of Cincinnati J.D. 1969. Admitted to practice Ohio 1969 and U.S. District Court Southern District of Ohio 1970. In legal practice Zanesville 1969-99.

Member Association of Municipal/County Judges of Ohio, Inc. and Muskingum County Bar Association.

Mailing address: P.O. Box 566, Zanesville 43702.
Office: 332 South Street, Zanesville 43702.
Telephone: (740) 454-3269.
Fax: (740) 455-0739
E-mail address: wdjoseph@prodigy.net

JUDKINS, Robert J. *(Judge, Highland County Court)* Elected to term beginning Jan 1, 1983. Reelected 1988, 1994 and 2000. Current term expires Dec 31, 2006. Born Hillsboro Ohio March 22, 1950. Methodist. Educated at Ohio Wesleyan University B.A. summa cum laude 1972 and University of Cincinnati J.D. 1975. Recipient Paxton Seasongood Award for Excellence in Appellate Advocacy from University of Cincinnati 1974. Member Phi Beta Kappa, Omicron Delta Kappa and Phi Kappa Psi. Admitted to practice Ohio 1975 and U.S. District Court Southern District of Ohio 1980. Began legal practice Greenfield 1980.

Instructor in Criminal Justice Rollins College. Former Trustee Southern Ohio Juvenile Detention Center. Member Highland County (President 1984-85), Ohio State and American Bar Associations. Captain USAF 1976-80. Recipient Commendation Medal for Meritorious Service 1980. Former Finance Chairman Highland County Re-

JUDKINS, ROBERT J.—*Continued*
publican Party. Member Greenfield Elks and Rotary Club. Enjoys tennis, swimming and family activities.
Mailing address: P.O. Box 378, Greenfield 45123-0378.
Office: 445 South Fourth Street, Greenfield 45123.
Telephone: (937) 981-2139.
Fax: (937) 981-2130

JUNKIN, Peter J. *(Judge, Bedford Municipal Court)* Appointed by Governor George V. Voinovich to term beginning May 1992. Elected 1996, current term expires Dec 31, 2003. Currently serves as Presiding Judge. Born Bedford Ohio 1947. Educated at Kalamazoo College B.A. 1969 and Case Western Reserve University J.D. 1972. Admitted to practice Ohio 1972, U.S. District Court District of Ohio 1974 and U.S. Supreme Court 1977. In legal practice Bedford 1972-92.
Member Cleveland, Cuyahoga County, Ohio State and American Bar Associations. Member Solon Civil Service Committee 1990-92. Chairman of Board Bedford Medical Center. Member University Hospital Health System Truste.
Office: 65 Columbus Road, Bedford 44146-2818.
Telephone: (440) 232-3420.
Fax: (440) 232-2510

KAINRAD, Joseph R. *(Judge, Ohio Court of Common Pleas Portage County)* Assumed office 1974. Elected 1979, 1985, 1991 and 1997. Current term expires Dec 31, 2003. Born Wayland Ohio May 29, 1933. Catholic. Educated at Kent State University B.A. and The Ohio State University J.D. Admitted to practice Ohio 1958. Began legal practice Ravenna 1958. Judge, Portage Municipal Court 1970-73.
Member Portage County and Ohio State Bar Associations. State Legislator 1963-69.
Office: 203 West Main Street, Ravenna 44266-2778.
Telephone: (330) 297-3858.
Fax: (330) 297-5370

KARNER, Cheryl S. *(Judge, Ohio Court of Common Pleas Cuyahoga County)* Referee Domestic Relations Division 1984-86. Appointed Judge by Governor Richard F. Celeste to term beginning Feb 6, 1989. Elected Nov 1990. Reelected to subsequent term. Serves Domestic Relations Division. Born Youngstown Ohio Aug 19, 1945. Educated at Case Western Reserve University B.A. with honors 1967 and Northwestern University School of Law J.D. with honors 1970. Admitted to practice Illinois 1970, U.S. District Courts Northern District of Illinois 1970 and Northern District of Ohio 1973, U.S. Courts of Appeals First, Third, Fourth, Sixth and Seventh Circuits 1972-73 and Ohio 1973. In legal practice Cleveland Ohio 1973-89.
Attorney Antitrust Division U.S. Department of Justice 1970-72. Author and Publisher "Family Law Facts Newsletter" 1987-89. Author "Relocation of Children" Cuyahoga County B. Jour. Jan 1990. Trustee Divorce Equity. Chair Guardian-Ad-Litem Project 1988-89. Member Ohio Judicial Conference, Cleveland (Program Chair Family Law Section 1988), Cuyahoga County (Chair Family Law Committee 1979-80 and Family Law Section 1988-89) and Ohio State Bar Associations. Lecturer Ohio Family Law Institute 1988, 1989 and 1990. Chairman Sex Abuse Seminar 1989 and Lecturer GAL Seminar 1990 Cuyahoga County Bar Association. Luncheon Speaker Ohio Academy of Trial Lawyers 1990. Democrat. Precinct Committeeman 1980-82. Officer 1978-80 and Member Executive Committee 1980-84 Cuyahoga Women's Political Caucus. Member Women Space 1978-80. Enjoys reading, boating and family activities.
Office: One Lakeside Avenue, Cleveland 44113-1082.
Telephone: (216) 443-8809.
Fax: (216) 443-8951
E-mail address: empress51@aol.com

KARPINSKI, Diane J. *(Judge, Ohio Court of Appeals Eighth District)* Elected Nov 5, 1994 to term beginning Feb 9, 1995. Reelected Nov 7, 2000, current term expires Feb 8, 2007. Born Cleveland Ohio June 3, 1935. Roman Catholic. Educated at The Ohio State University B.A. 1957 M.A. 1962 and Cleveland State University J.D. 1980. Admitted to practice Ohio 1981, U.S. Court of Appeals Sixth Circuit 1987 and U.S. District Court Northern District of Ohio 1985.
Assistant Attorney General 1982-95. Faculty Member The Ohio State University 1962-66 and Cleveland State University 1966-73 and 1975-81. Member Ohio Court of Appeals Judges Association, Cleveland (Appellate Court Committee since 1997), Cuyahoga County (Trustee since 1998, Member Certified Grievance Committee 1993-95 and since 1997, Law Day Panelist 1995-97, Appellate Court Committee since 1997) and Ohio State (Chair Independent Judiciary and Unjust Criticism of Judges Committee 2001-02) and American Bar Associations. Member Cuyahoga Democratic Women's League since 1980. President Women's Cosmopolitan Democratic League 1982-84. Second Vice President Federated Democratic Women of Ohio 1993. Founding Trustee East Side Catholic Shelter 1984-89. Past President Cleveland State University Chapter American Association of University Professors. Member Organizing Committee Parliamentarian Ohio Polish Congress 1995-2001, Butler A. Jones Endowed Lecture Series on "The American Dilemma Revisited" Cleveland State University since 1995, The City Club of Cleveland, Women's City Club and League of Women Voters. Choir Member Our Lady of Peace Parish 1990-2001.
Office: One Lakeside Avenue, Cleveland 44113-1085.
Telephone: (216) 443-6354.
Fax: (216) 443-2044

KATE, Linda A. *(Judge, Ohio Court of Common Pleas Tuscarawas County)* Serves Probate and Juvenile Divisions.
Office: 101 East High Avenue, New Philadelphia 44663-2636.
Telephone: (330) 365-3266.
Fax: (330) 364-3190

KATZ, David A. *(Judge, United States District Court Northern District of Ohio)* Appointed for life by President Bill Clinton to term beginning Oct 1994. Born Nov 1, 1933. Educated at The Ohio State University B.Sc. 1955 J.D. summa cum laude 1957. Associate Editor The Ohio State Law Journal. Member Order of the Coif. In legal practice Toledo 1957-93.
Trustee Toledo Bar Association Foundation (President 1986-93). Fellow Ohio State Bar Foundation. Member Toledo (Former Secretary and Board of Trustees), Ohio State and American Bar Associations. Recipient Harry Levinson Memorial Young Leadership Award from Jewish Welfare Federation of Toledo 1967, Outstanding Citizen Award from State of Israel 1979, Order of the Heel from Toledo Junior Bar Association 1993, William K. Douglas Distinguished Jurist Award from Ohio State

KATZ, DAVID A.—*Continued*

University College of Law 2001 and Community Service Award from Toledo Bar Association 2001. Past President Jewish Welfare Federation of Toledo and Temple B'nai Israel. Former Vice President and Trustee Jewish Educational Services of North America, Inc. Former Member Advisory Board Family Business Center University of Toledo College of Business Administration. Former Member Board of Trustees Toledo Jewish Community Foundation. Former Chairman Board of Trustees St. Vincent Medical Center. Former Solicitor United Way. Former Chairman Board of Directors Northwest Ohio Heart Center. Board of Trustees Advocates for Victims and Justice, Inc. Life Trustee St. Vincent Medical Center Foundation (Former Chairman). Trustee Toledo Symphony Orchestra and Mercy Health Partners (Executive Committee). Board of Directors and Secretary Seaway Food Town, Inc. Board Member Toledo Zoo Foundation.

Office: 210 U.S. Courthouse, 1716 Spielbusch Avenue, Toledo 43624.

Telephone: (419) 259-7488.

KEENON, Una H. R. *(Judge, East Cleveland Municipal Court)* Appointed by Governor Richard F. Celeste to term beginning Aug 25, 1986. Elected 1987, 1993 and 1999. Current term expires Dec 31, 2005. Born Nashville Tennessee Dec 30, 1933. Baptist. Educated at Tennessee State University B.A. 1953 and Cleveland-Marshall College of Law Cleveland State University J.D. cum laude 1975. Law Clerk to Hon. Ann Aldrich, U.S. District Court 1950-53. Member Alpha Kappa Alpha. Admitted to practice Ohio 1975 and U.S. District Court Northern District of Ohio 1977. In legal practice Cleveland 1980-83.

Attorney-in-Charge Juvenile Division Cuyahoga County Public Defender Office 1978-80. Managing Attorney U.A.W. Legal Services Plan 1983-86. Member Northern Ohio Municipal Judges Association (Vice President), Municipal-County Judges of Ohio, Inc. (Trustee), National Association of Women Judges, Norman S. Minor, Cleveland, Cuyahoga County, Ohio State, National and American Bar Associations. Attended Ohio Judicial College sessions. Recipient Most Deserving Graduate Award 1974-75, Leodis Harris Award 1981, Outstanding Pacesetter Award 1985, Minority Judges Award from Norman S. Minor Bar Association 1987, Official Recognition from Governor Richard F. Celeste 1989, Public Service Award from East Cleveland School District 1990, Tribute from Congressman L. Stokes 1990 and Certificate of Appreciation from Top Ladies of Distinction. Listed in *Who's Who of Women Executives* 1989-90 and *Who's Who of Women Lawyers* 1989-90. Social Worker Cuyahoga County Department of Human Services 1954-60. Teacher Cleveland Board of Education 1960-75. Member Democratic Executive Committee since 1975 and East Cleveland Democratic Club since 1986. Board of Trustees Cuyahoga County Library Board, YWCA, Arts, Inc., NAACP and Cleveland Treatment Center. Member Twenty-first District Congressional Caucus, Black Professional Association, Black Women Political Action Committee and Kiwanis Club of East Cleveland. Enjoys golfing, biking, reading, sewing and writing.

Office: 14340 Euclid Avenue East, East Cleveland 44112.

Telephone: (216) 681-2154.

Fax: (216) 681-2829

KEGLEY, Russell Dee *(Judge, Portsmouth Municipal Court)* Appointed by Governor Bob Taft.

Office: 728 Second Street, Portsmouth 45662.

KELBLEY, Michael Paul *(Judge, Ohio Court of Common Pleas Seneca County)* Appointed by Governor Richard F. Celeste to term beginning May 2, 1988. Elected to subsequent terms. Born Tiffin Ohio May 22, 1951. Catholic. Educated at John Carroll University A.B. magna cum laude 1973 and Case Western Reserve University Law School J.D. 1976. Member Phi Alpha Delta. Admitted to practice Ohio 1976, U.S. District Court Northern District of Ohio 1978 and U.S. Supreme Court 1980. In legal practice Tiffin 1976-88.

Instructor Tiffin University 1980. Member Seneca County and Ohio State Bar Associations.

Mailing address: P.O. Box 667, Tiffin 44883-0667.

Office: 103 South Washington, Third Floor, Tiffin 44883-2352.

Telephone: (419) 447-2982.

Fax: (419) 448-7103

E-mail address: cpc1@bright.net

KELSEY, Reeve *(Judge, Ohio Court of Common Pleas Wood County)* Appointed by Governor George V. Voinovich to term beginning Dec 1, 1998. Elected Nov 2000, current term expires Dec 31, 2006. Born Toledo Ohio Jan 18, 1948. Educated at Washington and Lee University B.A. cum laude 1970 and Duke University School of Law J.D. cum laude 1976. Member Omicron Delta Kappa and Omicron Delta Epsilon. Admitted to practice Ohio 1976. In legal practice 1976-94.

Assistant Attorney General Ohio 1995-98. Member Toledo (Member 1980-95 and Chairman 1983-86 Securities and Corporation Law Committee, Member Workers' Compensation Committee 1995-98, Roundtable Committee 1995-98, Common Pleas Court Committee 1995-98), Wood County, Ohio State (Member 1981-98 and Member Subcommittee on Close Corporations 1989-95 Corporation Law Committee) and American (Sections: Business Law, State and Local Government Law) Bar Associations. E-5 U.S. Army 1970-73. Mayor City of Perrysburg 1994-98. Member Perrysburg City Council 1988-93. Precinct Committeeman City of Toledo 1978-79. Member Republican Central and Executive Committee Wood County 1986-98. Republican District Chairman City of Perrysburg 1986-98. Board of Trustees Toledo Area Governmental Research Association 1978-84, ToledoScape (leadership training program) 1981-87, Sunset House (nonprofit nursing and rest home) 1985-91 and Wood County Mental Health Clinic 1986-92. Member of Vestry 1987-89 and Chancellor 1996-98 St. Timothy's Church. Board of Trustees since 1987, Assistant Secretary 1991-92, Member Executive Committee 1991-98, Secretary 1993-96 and Vice President 1996-98 Boys and Girls Club of Toledo. Member Perrysburg Chamber of Commerce, Bowling Green Chamber of Commerce, Rotary Club of Perrysburg, Historic Perrysburg, Wood County Historic Society and United States Masters Swimming Association.

Office: One Courthouse Square, Bowling Green 43402-2427.

Telephone: (419) 354-9220.

Fax: (419) 354-9223

E-mail address: rkelsey@co.wood.oh.us

KEMP, Terence P. *(Magistrate Judge, United States District Court Southern District of Ohio)* Appointed by U.S. District Court judges to term beginning 1987. Reappointed 1995 and 2003. Current term expires 2011. Born Huntingdon Pennsylvania. Educated at Brown University A.B. 1974 and University of Virginia School of Law J.D. 1977. Staff member Virginia Law Review. Law Clerk to Hon. Malcolm Muir, U.S. District Court Middle District of Pennsylvania 1977-79. Moot Court Board. Member Order of the Coif. In legal practice Huntingdon Pennsylvania 1979 and Columbus Ohio 1980-87.

Office: 172 U.S. Courthouse, 85 Marconi Boulevard, Columbus 43215.

Telephone: (614) 719-3410.

KENDIG, Russ *(Judge, United States Bankruptcy Court Northern District of Ohio)* Appointed by U.S. Court of Appeals Sixth Circuit judges.

Office: Federal Building, 201 Cleveland Avenue S.W., Canton 44702.

Telephone: (330) 489-4430.

KENNEDY, Sharon L. *(Judge, Ohio Court of Common Pleas Butler County)* Elected Nov 3, 1998 to term beginning Jan 4, 1999. Term expires Jan 4, 2005. Serves Domestic Relations Division. Born Cincinnati Ohio March 15, 1962. Catholic. Educated at University of Cincinnati B.S.W. 1980 J.D. 1991. Law Clerk to Hon. Matthew J. Crehan, Ohio Court of Common Pleas Butler County 1989-91. Admitted to practice Ohio 1991 and U.S. District Court Southern District of Ohio 1992. In legal practice Hamilton 1991-99. Magistrate, Butler County area courts 1995-98.

Member Ohio Domestic Relations Judges Association, Butler County and Ohio State Bar Associations. Past President Alcohol and Drug Addiction Services Board. Former Board Member YWCA. Vice President Senior Citizens Board. Mock Trial Advisor Lakota East.

Office: Government Services Center, 315 High Street, Hamilton 45011.

Telephone: (513) 887-3788.

Fax: (513) 785-5337

E-mail address: kennedysl@butlercountyohio.org

KEOUGH, Kathleen A. *(Judge, Cleveland Municipal Court)*

Office: 1200 Ontario Avenue, Cleveland 44113.

Telephone: (216) 664-4990.

Fax: (216) 664-4283

KERR, Samuel W. *(Judge, Ohio Court of Common Pleas Jefferson County)* Serves Probate and Juvenile Divisions. Former Judge, Jefferson County Court.

Mailing address: P.O. Box 549, Steubenville 43952-2184.

Telephone: (740) 283-8692.

Fax: (740) 283-8653 (probate), 283-8694 (juvenile)

KESSLER, John W. *(Judge, Ohio Court of Common Pleas Montgomery County)* Elected to term beginning Jan 3, 1981. Reelected 1986, 1992 and 1998. Current term expires Jan 2005. Currently serves as Presiding Judge. Born Dayton Ohio Oct 27, 1942. Educated at Miami University B.A. 1965 and University of Toledo J.D. 1968. Member Phi Kappa Tau and Delta Theta Phi. Admitted to practice Ohio 1968, U.S. District Court Southern District of Ohio 1969, U.S. Court of Appeals Sixth Circuit 1975 and U.S. Supreme Court 1977. Began legal practice Dayton 1968.

Assistant County Prosecutor 1968-71 and County Public Defender 1971-78 Montgomery County. Member Dayton, Ohio State and American Bar Associations.

Mailing address: P.O. Box 972, Dayton 45401-0972.

Office: 41 North Perry Street, Dayton 45422-2150.

Telephone: (937) 225-4384.

Fax: (937) 225-5406

E-mail address: kesslerj@montcourt.org

KETTLER, Richard T. *(Judge, Massillon Municipal Court)*

Office: Two James Duncan Plaza S.E., Massillon 44646-6690.

Telephone: (330) 830-1725.

Fax: (330) 830-1756

KILBANE, Anne L. *(Judge, Ohio Court of Appeals Eighth District)* Elected Nov 3, 1998 to term beginning Jan 2, 1999. Term expires Jan 1, 2005. Born Cleveland Ohio Sept 22, 1941. Roman Catholic. Educated at Seton Hill College B.A. 1963 and Cleveland-Marshall College of Law J.D. 1976. Member Delta Theta Phi. Admitted to practice Ohio 1977, U.S. District Courts Southern 1977 and Northern 1978 Districts of Ohio, U.S. Court of Appeals Sixth Circuit 1978 and U.S. Supreme Court 1985. In legal practice Columbus 1977-78 and Cleveland 1978-99.

Member Ohio Judicial Conference, Ohio Courts of Appeals Judges Association, National Lawyers Association, Ohio Women's (Founding Member), Cleveland (Appellate Committee since 1999), Cuyahoga County (Appellate Committee since 1999) and Ohio State (Negligence Committee since 1980, Insurance Committee since 1999) Bar Associations. Attended "Reflections on School Desegregation" Sept 16, 1998 and 1999; "1999 Bench-Bar Conference" March 19, 1999; "Conflict Resolution Services" March 24, 1999, April 28, 2000 and April 27, 2001; "1999 Medical Negligence Seminar" April 29, 1999; and "Joint Bar Ethics Symposium" March 22, 2001 Continuing Legal Education; "Ethics Cinema for Judges" Feb 12, 1999, "Felony DUI" April 30, 1999, "Domestic Violence Symposium" May 21, 1999, "Civil Issues Involving Children" Oct 22, 1999, "Permanent Custody Hearings" March 31, 2000, "Paternity Custody & Child Support" Aug 25, 2000 and "Insurance and Civil Liability" Oct 12, 2001 Judicial College Commission on Continuing Legal Education Supreme Court of Ohio; and "Advanced Evidence" The National Judicial College 1999. Team Instructor Trial Advocacy Course Cleveland-Marshall College of Law since 1990. Member Cleveland Artists Foundation, Lawyers Guild of the Diocese of Cleveland, West Side Irish-American Club, Irish Heritage Society, Alliance of Poles, Karlin Club and German Central Foundation.

Office: One Lakeside Avenue, Cleveland 44113.

Telephone: (216) 443-6324.

Fax: (216) 443-2044

KILBANE, Mary Eileen *(Judge, Cleveland Municipal Court)*

Mailing address: P.O. Box 94894, Cleveland 44101-4894.

Telephone: (216) 664-4998.

Fax: (216) 664-4283

KIMBLER, James L. *(Judge, Ohio Court of Common Pleas Medina County)* Former Judge, Wadsworth Municipal Court.
Office: 93 Public Square, Medina 44256.
Telephone: (330) 725-9736.
Fax: (330) 764-8791
E-mail address: kimbler@apk.net

KING, Judy *(Judge, Ohio Court of Common Pleas Montgomery County)* Serves Domestic Relations Division.
Office: 301 West Third Street, Dayton 45402.
Telephone: (937) 225-4091.
Fax: (937) 496-7835
E-mail address: lowman@cpcdir.co.montgomery.oh.us

KING, Norah McCann *(Magistrate Judge, United States District Court Southern District of Ohio)* Appointed by U.S. District Court judges to term beginning June 17, 1982. Reappointed 1990 and 1998. Current term expires June 16, 2006. Born Steubenville Ohio Aug 13, 1949. Roman Catholic. Educated at Rosary College B.A. cum laude 1971 and The Ohio State University J.D. summa cum laude 1975. Note and Comment Editor The Ohio State Law Journal 1974-75. Law Clerk to Hon. Joseph P. Kinneary, U.S. District Court Southern District of Ohio 1975-79. Member Order of the Coif. Admitted to practice Ohio 1975 and U.S. District Court Southern District of Ohio 1980. Began legal practice Columbus 1979.

Author Note "Parochial School Aid: A Public Perspective" 35 The Ohio State L. Jour. 104, 1974. Contributing Author *Real Estate Law Instructor's Manual* Center for Real Estate Education and Research The Ohio State University 1983. Assistant Professor The Ohio State University College of Administrative Science 1980-82. Member Federal Magistrate Judges Association, Columbus and Federal (Columbus Chapter) Bar Associations.
Office: 235 U.S. Courthouse, 85 Marconi Boulevard, Columbus 43215.
Telephone: (614) 719-3390.

KINWORTHY, David R. *(Judge, Ohio Court of Common Pleas Allen County)* Appointed by Governor John J. Gilligan to term beginning June 1974. Elected Nov 1974. Reelected to subsequent terms. Current term expires Feb 8, 2009. Serves Probate and Juvenile Divisions. Born Covington Kentucky Dec 11, 1935. Educated at Ohio Northern University B.A. 1960 J.D. 1965. Recipient Money and Banking Award as undergraduate and Wall Street Journal Award as law student. Admitted to practice Ohio 1965. Began legal practice Lima 1965. Assistant Prosecuting Attorney Allen County 1965-68 and 1972-74. Past President Ohio Association of Juvenile and Family Court Judges. Member Allen County and Ohio State Bar Associations. Corporal USMC 1954-57.
Mailing address: P.O. Box 1243, Lima 45802-1243.
Telephone: (419) 223-8501.
Fax: (419) 221-3432

KIRSCH, James Wilson *(Judge, Ohio Court of Common Pleas Scioto County)* Elected to term beginning Feb 9, 1979. Reelected 1984, 1990, 1996 and 2002. Current term expires 2009. Serves Probate and Juvenile Divisions. Born Portsmouth Ohio June 18, 1945. Methodist. Educated at The Ohio State University B.A. 1968 J.D. 1971. Member Phi Alpha Delta. Admitted to practice Ohio 1971 and U.S. District Court Southern District of Ohio 1972.

Assistant Prosecuting Attorney Scioto County 1975-76. Member National Council of Juvenile and Family Court Judges, Portsmouth Law Library Association, Ohio Association of Juvenile Court Judges, National Council of Juvenile and Family Court Judges, Ohio Association of Probate Judges, National Association of Probate Judges and Portsmouth Bar Association. Recipient Distinguished Service Award from Portsmouth Area Jaycees, Inc. 1977, Distinguished Golden Gavel Service Award from Ohio Association of Juvenile Court Judges Oct 12, 1983 and Certificate of Distinction from The Ohio State University College of Law Alumni Association 1983. Named one of Outstanding Young Men of America 1980. Member Men's Republican Club of Scioto County. Former member and former Chairman Advisory Board Retired Senior Volunteer Program. Board of Trustees and Past President Scioto County Tuberculosis & Respiratory Disease Association. Member of the Board The West Virginia-Ohio YMCA 1983. Chairman and Show Manager Portsmouth Charity Horse Show 1983 and 1984. Member Franklin Avenue United Methodist Church (Choir member, Sunday School teacher), Adams, Lawrence and Scioto Counties Mental Health Board (Former Chairman), Advisory Council Central Ohio Adolescent Center, Scioto County Children's Services Board, Scioto Memorial Hospital Auxiliary, Inc., The Ohio State Alumni Association, Kiwanis Club, Scioto Area Council Boy Scouts of America (Past President) and Portsmouth Area Jaycees, Inc. (Past President).
Office: 602 Seventh Street, Portsmouth 45662-3998.
Telephone: (740) 355-8290.
Fax: (740) 353-1095

KLAMMER, Theodore Rudolph *(Judge, Ohio Court of Common Pleas Lake County)* Serves Probate Division.
Mailing address: P.O. Box 490, Painesville 44077.

KLATT, William A. *(Judge, Ohio Court of Appeals Tenth District)*
Office: 373 South High Street, 24th Floor, Columbus 43215-4578.
Telephone: (614) 462-3610.
Fax: (614) 462-7249

KLERI, Patricia Ann *(Judge, South Euclid Municipal Court)*
Office: 1349 South Green Road, South Euclid 44121-3985.
Telephone: (216) 381-2880.
Fax: (216) 381-1195

KLINE, Roger L. *(Judge, Ohio Court of Appeals Fourth District)* Elected Nov 8, 1994 to term beginning Feb 9, 1995. Reelected 2000, current term expires Feb 9, 2007. Born Lima Ohio Jan 20, 1947. Educated at Ohio University B.B.A. 1974 and Capital University J.D. 1978. Admitted to practice Ohio 1978 and U.S. District Court Southern District of Ohio 1978. In legal practice Ashville 1978-84 and Circleville 1980-85. Judge, Ohio Court of Common Pleas Pickaway County 1985-95.

Prosecutor Pickaway County 1981-85. Member Teays Valley School Board 1978-81. Interests include sports.
Office: 121-A West Franklin Street, Circleville 43113.
Telephone: (740) 474-8977.
Fax: (740) 474-6870

KNECE, P. Randall *(Judge, Ohio Court of Common Pleas Pickaway County)* Elected 1994.

Office: 207 South Court Street, Second Floor, Circleville 43113.
Telephone: (740) 474-6026.
Fax: (740) 477-6334

KNEPPER, Richard W. *(Judge, Ohio Court of Appeals Sixth District)* Former Judge, Ohio Court of Common Pleas Lucas County.

Office: 800 Jackson Street, Toledo 43624.
Telephone: (419) 213-4755.
Fax: (419) 213-4844
E-mail address: knepper@co.lucas.oh.us

KOBLY, Elizabeth A. *(Judge, Youngstown Municipal Court)* Appointed by Governor Bob Taft to term beginning Sept 2000. Elected, current term expires Jan 1, 2008. Born Youngstown Ohio Oct 22, 1957. Educated at Youngstown State University B.S. 1980 and University of Akron Law Center J.D. 1988. Admitted to practice Ohio 1988 and Florida 1988. In legal practice Youngstown Ohio 1988-2000.

Office: 26 South Phelps Street, Youngstown 44503-1370.
Telephone: (330) 742-8853.
Fax: (330) 742-8845

KOCH, Judith Kilbane *(Judge, Ohio Court of Common Pleas Cuyahoga County)*

Office: 1200 Ontario Street, Cleveland 44113.
Telephone: (216) 443-8685.
Fax: (216) 348-4032

KONTOS, Peter J. *(Judge, Ohio Court of Common Pleas Trumbull County)*

Office: 161 High Street N.W., Warren 44481-1006.
Telephone: (330) 675-2569.
Fax: (330) 675-2580

KOVACK, Mary R. *(Judge, Ohio Court of Common Pleas Medina County)* Elected Nov 7, 2000 to term beginning Jan 1, 2001. Term expires Dec 31, 2006. Serves Domestic Relations Division. Born Cleveland Ohio May 22, 1963. Educated at College of Wooster B.A. with honors 1985 and Case Western Reserve University School of Law J.D. with honors 1989. Business Manager Case Western Reserve Law Review 1988-89. Law Clerk to Hon. Ann A. McManamon, Ohio Court of Appeals Eighth District 1989-91. Admitted to practice Ohio 1989, U.S. Court of Appeals Sixth Circuit 1991 and U.S. District Court Northern District of Ohio 1995. In legal practice Medina 1996-2000.

Law Clerk to Senior Judge Anthony J. Celebrezze, U.S. Court of Appeals Sixth Circuit 1991-95. Member Medina County and Ohio State Bar Associations. Named Woman of Distinction by YWCA 1999. Past President Federated Democratic Women of Medina County. Former Member Cleveland Orchestra Chorus. Member Leadership Medina County Class of 1998. Enjoys bike riding, choral singing and cooking.

Office: 99 Public Square, Medina 44256.
Telephone: (330) 725-9740.
Fax: (330) 764-8794
E-mail address: mrkovack@medinaco.org

KRICHBAUM, R. Scott *(Judge, Ohio Court of Common Pleas Mahoning County)* Elected Nov 7, 1990. Reelected 1996 and 2002. Current term expires 2009. Born Youngstown Ohio Jan 27, 1952. Catholic. Educated at Youngstown State University B.S.B.A. 1975 and University of Akron Law Center J.D. 1979. Law Clerk to Hon. Clyde W. Osborne, Ohio Court of Common Pleas Mahoning County 1975-80. Admitted to practice Ohio 1979, U.S. District Court Northern District of Ohio 1979 and U.S. Supreme Court 1985. In legal practice Youngstown 1980-91.

Special Assistant Prosecutor (Appropriations) 1982-85. Instructor Youngstown State University since 1992. Former Member Ohio Association of Trial Lawyers, Ohio Association of Criminal Defense Lawyers, National Association of Criminal Defense Lawyers, The Association of Trial Lawyers of America and American Bar Association. Bar Examiner Ohio State Board of Bar Examiners. Advisory Member Ohio Courts Futures Commission. Member Ohio Common Pleas Judges Association, American Judicature Society, Mahoning County (President) and Ohio State Bar Associations. Lecturer seminars Municipal-County Judges of Ohio, Inc. 1990 and 1991. Attended Ohio Judicial College 1991 and 1992. Listed in *The Best Lawyers in America* (criminal defense) 1989. Member Knights of Columbus, YMCA, Saxon Club and Crime Clinic. Enjoys golf.

Office: 120 Market Street, Youngstown 44503-1710.
Telephone: (330) 740-2156.
Fax: (330) 742-5893

KRUEGER, Everett H. *(Judge, Ohio Court of Common Pleas Delaware County)* Elected to term beginning Jan 1, 1995. Reelected to term beginning Jan 1, 2001, current term expires Dec 31, 2006. Born Muncie Indiana March 3, 1950. Educated at Hanover College B.A. 1972 and Capital University J.D. 1975. Admitted to practice Ohio 1975 and Indiana 1976. Began legal practice Delaware Ohio 1976. Judge, Delaware Municipal Court Jan 1, 1984 to Dec 31, 1994.

Member Commission on Professionalism 1993-94. Chair Elect Ohio Judicial Conference. Member American Judicature Society, Ohio Common Pleas Judges Association (Trustee), Columbus, Delaware County (President 1985-86) and Ohio State Bar Associations. Member Rotary. Enjoys snow skiing and reading.

Office: 91 North Sandusky Street, Third Floor, Delaware 43015.
Telephone: (740) 833-2550.
Fax: (740) 833-2549
E-mail address: ekrueger@co.delaware.oh.us

KUBICKI, Charles Joseph, Jr. *(Judge, Ohio Court of Common Pleas Hamilton County)*

Office: Courthouse, 1000 Main Street, Cincinnati 45202.

KUBILUS, Richard J. *(Judge, Canton Municipal Court)*

Office: City Hall, 218 Cleveland Avenue South, Canton 44702-1912.
Telephone: (330) 489-3210.
Fax: (330) 471-8860
E-mail address: rjkubilu@ci.canton.oh.us

KUNTZ, Nick *(Judge, Ohio Court of Common Pleas Montgomery County)* Elected 1994. Reelected to subsequent term. Serves Juvenile Division. Educated at University of Dayton B.S. 1965 and University of Toledo J.D. 1973. Admitted to practice Ohio 1974.

KUNTZ, NICK—*Continued*

Personal Statement or Quote: "Do your best and leave the rest to the Lord."
Office: 303 West Second Street, Dayton 45422-1413.
Telephone: (937) 225-4124.
Fax: (937) 224-8603
E-mail address: kuntzn@montcnty.org

KUTSCHER, Paul F., Jr. *(Judge, Ohio Court of Common Pleas Seneca County)* Serves Probate and Juvenile Divisions.
Office: 108 Jefferson Street, Tiffin 44883-2898.
Telephone: (419) 447-3121 (probate), 447-4912 (juvenile).
Fax: (419) 448-5060

LANE, N. Edward, Jr. *(Judge, Ohio Court of Common Pleas Washington County)* Elected to term beginning Jan 1, 1993. Reelected to subsequent term. Born Marietta Ohio July 23, 1950. Lutheran. Educated at Capital University B.A. 1972 J.D. 1977. Member Kappa Iota Lambda. Admitted to practice Ohio 1977, U.S. District Court Southern District of Ohio 1978 and U.S. Supreme Court 1987. In legal practice Marietta 1977-86. Judge, Marietta Municipal Court Jan 16, 1987 and Dec 31, 1992.

Former Member and Trustee Municipal-County Judges of Ohio, Inc. Member Ohio Judicial Conference, Ohio Common Pleas Judges Association, Washington County and Ohio State Bar Associations. Previously worked as public school teacher Columbus City Schools. Democrat. Former Board of Directors Marietta YMCA and Washington County Chapter American Cancer Society. Vice President Council St. Luke's Lutheran Church. Member Marietta Advertising Club and Marietta Morning Rotary Club. Enjoys skiing, golf and reading.
Office: 205 Putnam Street, Marietta 45750-2922.
Telephone: (740) 373-6623.
Fax: (740) 373-5713
E-mail address: edlane10@frognet.net

LANGER, Dennis J. *(Judge, Ohio Court of Common Pleas Montgomery County)* Elected 1994. Reelected to subsequent term.
Mailing address: P.O. Box 972, Dayton 45401-0972.
Office: 41 North Perry Street, Dayton 45402.
Telephone: (937) 225-4055.
Fax: (937) 225-5406
E-mail address: langerd@montcourt.org

LANZINGER, Judith Ann *(Judge, Ohio Court of Appeals Sixth District)* Elected Nov 2002. Term expires Feb 8, 2009. Born Toledo Ohio April 2, 1946. Roman Catholic. Educated at University of Toledo B.Ed. with honors 1968 J.D. with honors 1977 and University of Nevada Reno M.J.S. 1992. Member Kappa Delta Phi and Phi Kappa Psi. Admitted to practice Ohio 1978, U.S. District Courts Northern District of Ohio 1980 and Eastern District of Michigan 1985, U.S. Court of Appeals Sixth Circuit 1982 and U.S. Supreme Court 1985. In legal practice Toledo 1978-85. Judge, Toledo Municipal Court 1985-88. Judge, Ohio Court of Common Pleas Lucas County 1989-2003.

Author "Judges Teaching in Law School: Who, What, Where and Why Not?" Journal of Legal Education March 1993. Important Decision: State v. McDermott (counsel forced to testify against former client, state law privilege waived, attorney held in contempt) 1992. Adjunct Professor University of Toledo College of Law since 1988. President Toledo Civil Service Commission 1984-85, Toledo Junior Bar Association 1986 and Morrison Waite American Inns of Court 2000-02. Member Commission on Grievances and Discipline Ohio Supreme Court 1988-91 and Ohio State Criminal Sentencing Commission 1990-97. Co-chair Public Education and Awareness Task Force Ohio Courts Futures Commission since 1997. Member American Judicature Society, Ohio Common Pleas Judges Association, National Association of Women Judges, American Judges Association, Toledo (Board of Trustees 1982-85, Secretary 1983-85) and Ohio State Bar Associations. Faculty Member The National Judicial College since 1989. Faculty Member since 1989 and Vice Chair since 1997 Ohio Judicial College. Recorder and Facilitator various Bench-Bar conferences 1991 and 1992. Recipient Hall of Excellence Award from Ohio Foundation of Independent Colleges 1988-89. Employed as teacher 1966-69. Republican. Legal Advisor for high school mock trial programs. Church musician. Enjoys music, swimming, bicycling and reading.
Office: 800 Jackson Street, Toledo 43624.
Telephone: (419) 213-4755.
Fax: (419) 213-4844

LANZO, James R. *(Judge, Struthers Municipal Court)* Elected to term beginning Jan 1, 1994. Reelected 1999, current term expires Dec 31, 2005. Born Youngstown Ohio Dec 23, 1944. Roman Catholic. Educated at Youngstown State University B.S.Ed. 1966 and University of Akron J.D. 1971. Admitted to practice Ohio 1973 and U.S. District Court 1973. In legal practice Struthers since 1973. Small Claims Referee 1975-93.

Director of Law Struthers 1975-93. Member Mahoning County, Ohio State and American Bar Associations. Democrat. President SBA. Member Lions, Rotary (President), Knights of Columbus and St. Anthony Society. Enjoys sports.
Office: Six Elm Street, Struthers 44471-1904.
Telephone: (330) 755-1800.
Fax: (330) 755-2790

LAUBER, William G. *(Judge, Lima Municipal Court)*
Mailing address: P.O. Box 1529, Lima 45802-1529.
Office: 109 North Union Street, Lima 45801-4929.
Telephone: (419) 224-8966.
Fax: (419) 998-5526
E-mail address: munijudg@bright.net

LAVERY, Robert G. *(Judge, Alliance Municipal Court)* Elected Nov 1995 to term beginning Jan 1, 1996. Reelected Nov 2001, current term expires Dec 31, 2007. Born Dover Ohio May 1, 1951. Lutheran. Educated at Bowling Green State University B.S. 1973 and University of Toledo J.D. 1976. Member Delta Theta Phi. Admitted to practice Ohio 1976, U.S. District Court Northern District of Ohio 1976 and U.S. Court of Appeals Sixth Circuit 1982. In legal practice Alliance 1976-95.

Law Director Alliance 1991-95. Instructor Mount Union College 1981-86. Member Alliance (President 1984), Stark County and Ohio State Bar Associations. Enjoys golf.
Office: 470 East Market Street, Alliance 44601-2596.
Telephone: (330) 823-6181.
Fax: (330) 829-2231

LAZARUS, Cynthia C. *(Judge, Ohio Court of Appeals Tenth District)* Elected 1994 to term beginning 1995. Reelected to subsequent term.

Office: 373 South High Street, 24th Floor, Columbus 43215-4578.
Telephone: (614) 462-3613.
Fax: (614) 462-7249
E-mail address: cclazarus@co.franklin.oh.us

LeBARRON, Deborah A. *(Judge, Euclid Municipal Court)*

Office: 555 East 222nd Street, Euclid 44123-2029.
Telephone: (216) 289-8247.
Fax: (216) 289-8254

LEE, Thomas C. *(Judge, Ohio Court of Common Pleas Holmes County)* Serves Probate and Juvenile Divisions.

Office: One East Jackson Street, Suite 201, Millersburg 44654.
Telephone: (330) 674-5881.
Fax: (330) 674-5820
E-mail address: hcpjc@valkyrie.net

LEISY, Raymond E. *(Judge, Ohio Court of Common Pleas Wayne County)* Serves Probate and Juvenile Divisions.

Office: 107 West Liberty, Wooster 44691-4865.
Telephone: (330) 287-5575.
Fax: (330) 287-5427

LEWANDOWSKI, David *(Judge, Ohio Court of Common Pleas Lucas County)* Serves Domestic Relations Division.

Office: 429 North Michigan Street, Toledo 43624.
Telephone: (419) 213-6824.
Fax: (419) 213-6838
E-mail address: dlewan@co.lucas.oh.us

LEWIS, Linton D., Jr. *(Judge, Ohio Court of Common Pleas Perry County)* Appointed by Governor Richard F. Celeste to term beginning Sept 24, 1990. Elected Nov 6, 1990 to full term commencing July 6, 1992. Reelected 1998, current term expires 2004. Born Zanesville Ohio Dec 25, 1952. Catholic. Educated at The Ohio State University B.S. summa cum laude 1976 and University of Dayton J.D. 1979. Member Phi Alpha Delta, Phi Kappa Phi and Alpha Tau Omega. Admitted to practice Ohio 1979 and U.S. Supreme Court 1980. In legal practice Zanesville 1979-82 and New Lexington 1979-90. Judge, Perry County Court Jan 1, 1983 to Sept 23, 1990.

Assistant Prosecutor Muskingum County 1979-82. Instructor in Real Estate Hocking Technical College 1988 and Criminal Law and Forensics Central Ohio Technical College 2000-02. Former member Muskingum County Bar Association. Member Perry County (Past President), Ohio State (Judicial Reform Committee) and American (Judicial Reform Task Force Section of Administrative Law and Regulatory Practice) Bar Associations. Recipient Superior Judicial Service Awards from Ohio Supreme Court 1983, 1984, 1985 and 1986 and Division of Wildlife Award 1990. Honored by Perry County Alcohol & Drug Association 1990. Previously worked as substitute teacher Marysville and Crooksville Schools. Republican. Member Elks, Lions, Chamber of Commerce and Knights of Columbus. Enjoys sports, reading and travel.

Mailing address: P.O. Box 7, New Lexington 43764.
Telephone: (740) 342-1204.
Fax: (740) 342-5500

LIAS, Katherine S. *(Judge, Ohio Court of Common Pleas Franklin County)* Referee Domestic Relations Division March 1981 to Dec 1988. Elected Judge Nov 8, 1988 to term beginning Jan 1, 1989. Reelected Nov 8, 1994 and Nov 7, 2000. Current term expires Dec 31, 2006. Administrative Judge 1992, 1993, 1996, 1997, 1998, 1999, 2000, 2001 and 2002. Serves Domestic Relations and Juvenile Divisions. Born Trenton New Jersey Dec 21, 1941. Greek Orthodox. Educated at University of Delaware B.A. 1963 and Capital University Law School J.D. cum laude 1977. Recipient American Jurisprudence Award in Criminal Law. Hamilton Township P.T.A. Scholar. H. Rodney Sharp Scholar. Case Western Reserve University Fellow. Finalist Freshman Moot Court Competition 1975. Chief Justice Moot Court Board 1976-77. Member Kappa Delta Pi, Order of the Curia and Order of Barristers. Admitted to practice Ohio 1977, U.S. District Court Southern District of Ohio 1979 and U.S. Court of Appeals Sixth Circuit 1980. In legal practice Columbus 1977-81.

Narrator video project Divorce Equities, Inc. 1986 and videotape "Children in the Middle" Ohio University Telecommunications Center 1990. Member Creeds of Professionalism Committee 1990-91 and Teleconferencing Advisory Panel with Ohio Judicial College Ohio Supreme Court. Member Child Support Guidelines Advisory Commission Ohio Department of Human Services 1991. Member Task Force on Gender Fairness Ohio Supreme Court and Ohio State Bar Association 1991-92. Member Task Force on Domestic Violence Ohio Supreme Court 1995-96. Member Women Lawyers of Franklin County, Columbus (Family Law Committee since 1978, Municipal Court Committee 1980, Criminal Law Committee 1980-81) and Ohio State Bar Associations. Faculty Member Ohio Judicial College and Ohio CLE Institute. Chair Family Law Seminar Columbus Bar Association 1981. Instructor Legal Representation of the Homeless Legal Aid Society June 22, 1990. Member Public Education Videotape Program 1990-92, Chairman Domestic Violence Tape 1990-92, Vice Chair Family Law and Procedure Committee 1995 and Participant Mentor Program 1995-96 Ohio Judicial Conference. Participant Family Law Videotape Project Ohio Judicial College, Child/Elder Abuse videotape and panel discussion Center for the Advancement and Study of Ethics Capital University 1995, videotape project to aid pro se litigants in uncontested divorce proceedings Ohio Legal Assistance Foundation 1997 and "People's Law School" Columbus Bar Association 2000. Panel Member Franklin County Juvenile Court Truancy Summit 1999 and Franklin County Prostitution Project 1999. Originator Companionship Mediation Program 1999. Previously worked as professional actress 1963-73 and English teacher 1965-68. Republican. Member, Assistant Vice Chairman and President Elect Alumni Board of Advisors Capital University Law School 1985-88. Member Franklin County Children's Cabinet 1995-2001. Board Member Center for Psychology and Family Law Alternatives Athens. Member Columbus Housing Partnership Task Force 1989-90 and Franklin County Juvenile Delinquency Task Force 1991-92. Originator and Member Legal

LIAS, KATHERINE S.—*Continued*

Intern/Extern Court Program since 1990. Board of Trustees CHOICES Domestic Violence Shelter 1995-2000.

Office: 373 South High Street, Columbus 43215-4520.
Telephone: (614) 462-4445.
Fax: (614) 462-7440
E-mail address: kay_lias@fccourts.org

LILLY, Paulette J. *(Judge, Ohio Court of Common Pleas Lorain County)* Elected 1994. Reelected to subsequent term. Serves Domestic Relations Division.

Office: Administration Building, Fifth Floor, 226 Middle Avenue, Elyria 44035-5629.
Telephone: (440) 329-5357.
Fax: (440) 329-5438
E-mail address: judgelilly@centurytel.net

LIMBERT, George J. *(Magistrate Judge, United States District Court Northern District of Ohio)* Appointed by U.S. District Court judges to term beginning Nov 8, 1999. Term expires Nov 7, 2007. Born Youngstown Ohio Sept 11, 1940. Educated at Johns Hopkins University B.A. 1962 and Case Western Reserve University J.D. 1965 LL.M. 1971. Member Phi Delta Phi. Admitted to practice Ohio 1965, U.S. Supreme Court 1970 and U.S. Court of Appeals Sixth Circuit 1999. In legal practice Youngstown 1965 to July 10, 1995 and Jan 2, 1997 to Nov 8, 1999. Judge, Ohio Court of Common Pleas Mahoning County July 10, 1995 to Jan 1, 1997.

Member Mahoning County (Trustee 1976-86, President 1986-87) and Ohio State (Council of Delegates 1988-95) Bar Associations. Member Republican Executive Committee and Republican Central Committee Mahoning County 1984 to July 10, 1995. Member Zoning Commission Jan 1993 to July 10, 1995 and Township Trustee Jan 1998 to Nov 8, 1999 Boardman. Chairman June 1994 to July 10, 1995 and Assistant Treasurer June 1998 to Nov 8, 1999 Mahoning County Republican Organization. Trustee 1967-77 and President 1976-77 Children & Family Service Agency of Youngstown. Board of Trustees YMCA since Jan 1991, Youngstown State University April 13, 1993 to July 10, 1995 and Youngstown Central Area Community Improvement Corporation Feb 3, 1995 to Dec 2000. Member Pan-Arcadian Federation of America since 1967, American Hellenic Educational Progressive Association since 1984, Tod Homestead Cemetery Association since Dec 1992, Bremer Foundation since 1995 and St. John Greek Orthodox Church.

Office: Federal Bldg. & U.S. Courthouse, 125 Market Street, Youngstown 44503.
Telephone: (330) 743-2987.

LINDEMAN, Robert J. *(Judge, Ohio Court of Common Pleas Miami County)*

Office: 201 West Main Street, Troy 45373.
Telephone: (937) 332-6865.
Fax: (937) 332-7069
E-mail address: jlindeman@coax.net

LIOI, Sara E. *(Judge, Ohio Court of Common Pleas Stark County)*

Office: 115 Central Plaza North, Canton 44702.
Telephone: (330) 451-7708.
Fax: (330) 451-7740
E-mail address: judgelioi@co.stark.oh.us

LIPPS, Thomas R. *(Judge, Ohio Court of Common Pleas Hamilton County)* Serves Juvenile Division.

Office: 800 Broadway, Cincinnati 45202-1225.
Telephone: (513) 946-9211.
Fax: (513) 946-9216
E-mail address: thomas.lipps@juvcourt.hamilton-co.org

LISOTTO, Robert G. *(Judge, Ohio Court of Common Pleas Mahoning County)*

Office: 120 Market Street, Youngstown 44503.
Telephone: (330) 740-2150.
Fax: (330) 742-5882

LISTON, Teresa L. *(Judge, Franklin County Municipal Court)*

Office: 375 South High Street, Room 15A, Columbus 43215-4593.
Telephone: (614) 645-8280.
Fax: (614) 645-8255
E-mail address: listont@fcmclerk.com

LITTLEJOHN, Bill C. *(Judge, Dayton Municipal Court)*

Office: 301 West Third Street, Room 313, Dayton 45402-1424.
Telephone: (937) 333-4369.
Fax: (937) 333-4496
E-mail address: bill.littlejohn@ci.dayton.oh.us

LOGAN, Andrew D. *(Judge, Ohio Court of Common Pleas Trumbull County)* Elected 1994. Reelected to subsequent term. Former Judge, Trumbull County Court.

Office: 161 High Street N.W., Warren 44481-1006.
Telephone: (330) 675-2564.
Fax: (330) 675-2580

LOHN, John Joseph *(Judge, Ohio Court of Common Pleas Medina County)* Serves Probate and Juvenile Divisions.

Office: 93 Public Square, Medina 44256.

LONG, Jan Michael *(Judge, Ohio Court of Common Pleas Pickaway County)* Serves Probate and Juvenile Divisions.

Office: 207 South Court Street, Circleville 43113-1691.
Telephone: (740) 474-3117.
Fax: (740) 474-8451
E-mail address: jlong@pickaway.org

LORIG, Gerald F. *(Judge, Ohio Court of Common Pleas Clark County)* Former Judge, Springfield Municipal Court.

Office: 214 Courthouse, 101 N. Limestone Street, Springfield 45502-1120.
Telephone: (937) 328-2480.
Fax: (937) 328-2674

LOWE, Michael D. *(Judge, Morgan County Court)*

Office: 37 East Main Street, McConnelsville 43756.
Telephone: (740) 962-4031.
Fax: (740) 962-2895

LUCCI, Eugene A. *(Judge, Ohio Court of Common Pleas Lake County)* Elected to term beginning Jan 6, 2001. Term expires Jan 5, 2007. Born Youngstown Ohio Nov 29, 1954. Christian. Educated at Case Western Reserve University B.A. 1976 and Cleveland-Marshall College of Law J.D. 1980. Admitted to practice Ohio 1980, Florida 1982 and U.S. Supreme Court 1986. In legal practice Mentor Ohio 1980-2000.

LUCCI, EUGENE A.—*Continued*

Instructor Police Academy Lakeland Community College. Past President Lake County Bar Association. Associate Member Lake County Association of Police Chiefs. Member Ohio Judicial Conference, Ohio Common Pleas Judges Association (Legislative Committee), American Judges Association and American Judicature Society. Police Officer Cleveland 1975-77 and City of Painesville 1977-82. Special Sheriff's Detective Lake County 1995-2000. Republican. Past President Rotary Club of Painesville. Former Campaign Cabinet Captain Lake County United Way. Former Chairman AIDS Advisory Board of Lake County. Former Coordinator Law Explorers Post 2001. Former Board Member Forbes House (battered women's shelter). Former Legal Advisor ADAMHS Board (Alcohol, Drugs, Mental Health funding agency) and Parents Anonymous of Lake County. First Vice Chair Leadership Lake County, Inc. Chairman Paralegal Advisory Committee Lake Erie College. Judge and Competition Coordinator Regional Mock Trial Competition. Member Lake County Blue Coats.

Mailing address: P.O. Box 490, Painesville 44077-0490.

Office: Lake County Courthouse, 47 North Park Place, Painesville 44077.

Telephone: (440) 350-2100.

Fax: (440) 350-2210

E-mail address: judgelucci@lakecountyohio.org

LUCE, Donald G. *(Judge, Sidney Municipal Court)* Elected to term beginning Jan 1, 1984. Reelected 1989, 1996 and 2002. Current term expires Dec 31, 2007. Born Dedham Massachusetts Nov 12, 1948. Episcopalian. Educated at Bowling Green State University B.S. 1970 M.S. 1972 and Suffolk University Law School J.D. cum laude 1976. Admitted to practice Ohio 1976 and U.S. District Court Southern District of Ohio 1977. Began legal practice Sidney 1976.

Special Assistant City Solicitor 1979-80. Assistant Public Defender 1984. Member American Judges Association, Shelby County and Ohio State Bar Associations. First Lieutenant USAS 1970-78. Republican. Member Sidney City Board of Education 1980-84 (President 1984) and Upper Valley Joint Vocation School Board of Education 1980-84. Member Kiwanis and American Legion. Enjoys jogging, chess and reading.

Office: 110 West Court Street, Sidney 45365.

Telephone: (937) 498-0011.

Fax: (937) 498-8163

E-mail address: dluce@sidneyoh.com

LUX, Paul G. *(Judge, Erie County Court)* Elected 1994. Reelected to subsequent term.

Office: 150 West Mason Road, Milan 44846.

Telephone: (419) 499-4689.

Fax: (419) 499-3300

E-mail address: plux@cros.net

LYONS, Robert Hagen *(Judge, Butler County Court)*

Office: 118 West High Street, Oxford 45056.

Telephone: (513) 523-4748.

Fax: (513) 523-4737

MACKEY, Alfred W. *(Judge, Ohio Court of Common Pleas Ashtabula County)* Appointed by Governor Richard F. Celeste to term beginning March 29, 1989. Elected Nov 1990, Nov 1996 and 2002. Current term expires Feb 2009. Born Dorset Ohio Oct 2, 1941. Protestant. Educated at Hiram College B.A. 1963 and Case Western Reserve University J.D. 1967. Admitted to practice Ohio 1967 and U.S. Supreme Court 1973. In legal practice Ashtabula 1972-89.

Member Ashtabula County and Ohio State Bar Associations. Captain USMCR.

Office: 25 West Jefferson Street, Jefferson 44047-1092.

Telephone: (440) 576-3683.

Fax: (440) 576-2819

E-mail address: ashtacpcourt@suite224.net

MACKIN, John F. *(Judge, Avon Lake Municipal Court)*

Office: 32855 Walker Road, Avon Lake 44012.

Telephone: (440) 930-4103.

Fax: (440) 930-4128

MALLORY, William L., Jr. *(Judge, Hamilton County Municipal Court)*

Office: 1000 Main Street, Cincinnati 45202.

Telephone: (513) 946-5112.

Fax: (513) 946-5114

MALONEY, Timothy P. *(Judge, Ohio Court of Common Pleas Mahoning County)* Serves Probate Division.

Office: 120 Market Street, Youngstown 44503.

Telephone: (330) 740-2311.

Fax: (330) 740-2325

MANNEN, Ann T. *(Judge, Ohio Court of Common Pleas Cuyahoga County)*

Office: 1200 Ontario Street, Cleveland 44113-1678.

Telephone: (216) 443-8698.

Fax: (216) 348-4036

MANNING, James L. *(Judge, Montgomery County Court)* Elected 1994. Reelected to subsequent term.

Office: 195 South Clayton Road, New Lebanon 45345.

Telephone: (937) 687-9099.

Fax: (937) 687-9200

E-mail address: manning@montcnty.oh.org

MANOS, John M. *(Senior Judge, United States District Court Northern District of Ohio)* Appointed for life by President Gerald R. Ford to term beginning March 29, 1976. Assumed Senior status April 1, 1991, serves by assignment. Born Cleveland Ohio Dec 8, 1922. Educated at Case Institute of Technology B.S. 1944 and Cleveland-Marshall College of Law J.D. 1950. In legal practice Cleveland 1950-63. Judge, Ohio Court of Common Pleas Cuyahoga County 1963-69. Judge, Ohio Court of Appeals Eighth District 1969-76.

Law Director City of Bay Village 1954-56. Industries Representative Cleveland Regional Board of Review 1956-59.

Office: U.S. Courthouse, 801 West Superior Avenue, Cleveland 44113-1841.

Telephone: (216) 357-7265.

MARBLEY, Algenon L. *(Judge, United States District Court Southern District of Ohio)* Appointed for life by President Bill Clinton July 31, 1997 to term beginning Nov 7, 1997. Born Morehead City North Carolina Sept 19, 1954. Educated at University of North Carolina at Chapel Hill B.A. 1976 and Northwestern University School of Law J.D. 1979. In legal practice Chicago Illinois 1979-80 and Columbus Ohio 1986-97.

MARBLEY, ALGENON L.—*Continued*

Assistant Regional Attorney U.S. Department of Health and Human Services 1980-86.
Office: 349 U.S. Courthouse, 85 Marconi Boulevard, Columbus 43215.
Telephone: (614) 719-3260.

MARCELAIN, Thomas M. *(Judge, Licking County Municipal Court)* Appointed by Governor George V. Voinovich to term beginning Feb 9, 1991. Elected Nov 1993 and 1999. Current term expires Dec 31, 2005. Born Whiteman AFB Missouri Nov 24, 1957. Roman Catholic. Educated at Ashland University B.A. 1980 and Temple University J.D. 1983. Admitted to practice Ohio 1983 and U.S. District Court Southern District of Ohio 1985. In legal practice Newark 1983-89.
Attorney Nationwide Mutual Insurance Co. 1989-91. Member Licking County and Ohio State Bar Associations. City Councilman Newark 1987-91.
Office: 40 West Main Street, Newark 43055.
Telephone: (740) 349-6640.
Fax: (740) 345-4250
E-mail address: tmarcelain@mmsmisp.com

MARSH, Melba D. *(Judge, Ohio Court of Common Pleas Hamilton County)* Former Judge, Hamilton County Municipal Court.
Office: 1000 Main Street, Room 330, Cincinnati 45202.
Telephone: (513) 946-5866.
Fax: (513) 946-5868

MARSHALL, William T. *(Judge, Ohio Court of Common Pleas Scioto County)* Former Judge, Portsmouth Municipal Court.
Office: Courthouse, 602 Seventh Street, Portsmouth 45662.

MARTELL, Donald H. *(Judge, Portage County Municipal Court)*
Office: 203 West Main Street, Ravenna 44266.
Telephone: (330) 297-3632.
Fax: (330) 298-3033

MARTIN, Chris Allen *(Judge, Ohio Court of Common Pleas Fairfield County)* Former Judge, Fairfield County Municipal Court.
Office: 224 East Main Street, Lancaster 43130.

MARTIN, Steven E. *(Judge, Ohio Court of Common Pleas Hamilton County)*
Office: 1000 Main Street, Room 380, Cincinnati 45202-1217.
Telephone: (513) 946-5790.
Fax: (513) 946-5792

MARTIN, William J. *(Judge, Ohio Court of Common Pleas Carroll County)* Elected to term beginning Jan 1, 1983. Reelected 1988, 1994 and 2000. Current term expires Dec 31, 2006. Born Canton Ohio Feb 19, 1947. Presbyterian. Educated at The Ohio State University B.A. 1969 and Case Western Reserve University School of Law J.D. 1972. Admitted to practice Ohio 1972. Began legal practice Carrollton 1972.
Assistant Prosecuting Attorney 1973-81. Instructor Ohio Peace Officer Training Council 1974-75 and Minerva Police Academy 1984. Adjunct Professor of Law University of Akron 1985-93. Member Ohio Judicial Conference, Ohio Common Pleas Judges Association, Carroll County and Ohio State Bar Associations. Republican.
Mailing address: P.O. Box 367, Carrollton 44615.
Telephone: (330) 627-2450.
Fax: (330) 627-6389

MASCHARI, Ann B. *(Judge, Ohio Court of Common Pleas Erie County)*
Office: 323 Columbus Avenue, Sandusky 44870.
Telephone: (419) 627-7731.
Fax: (419) 627-6602

MASON, James W. *(Judge, Ohio Court of Common Pleas Franklin County)* Serves Domestic Relations and Juvenile Divisions.
Office: 373 South High Street, Sixth Floor, Columbus 43215-4598.
Telephone: (614) 462-4453.
Fax: (614) 462-7440
E-mail address: jim_mason@fccourts.org

MATIA, David T. *(Judge, Ohio Court of Common Pleas Cuyahoga County)* Elected Nov 3, 1998 to term beginning Jan 6, 1999. Term expires Jan 5, 2005. Born Lackawanna New York 1964. Educated at Miami University B.S.B.A. 1987 and Case Western Reserve University J.D. 1990. Admitted to practice Ohio 1990 and Kentucky 1991. In legal practice Louisville Kentucky 1991-92 and Cleveland Ohio 1992-98.
Member Cuyahoga County (Chair Common Pleas Court Committee, Member Certified Grievance Committee) and Ohio State Bar Associations. Personal Statement or Quote: "Be punctual and know your case well enough to explore resolution/settlement at every court appearance."
Office: 1200 Ontario Street, Cleveland 44113-1678.
Telephone: (216) 443-8695.
Fax: (216) 348-4037
E-mail address: judgematia@yahoo.com

MATIA, Paul R. *(Chief Judge, United States District Court Northern District of Ohio)* Appointed for life by President George Bush to term beginning Dec 20, 1991. Chief Judge since Feb 27, 1999. Born Cleveland Ohio Oct 2, 1937. Protestant. Educated at Case Western Reserve University B.A. cum laude 1959 and Harvard University J.D. 1962. Law Clerk to Ohio Court of Common Pleas Cuyahoga County 1963-66. Admitted to practice Ohio 1962 and U.S. District Court Northern District of Ohio. In legal practice Cleveland 1972-84. Judge, Ohio Court of Common Pleas Cuyahoga County Jan 5, 1985 to Dec 19, 1991.
Assistant Ohio Attorney General 1966-69. Administrative Assistant to Ohio Attorney General 1969-70. Member Cleveland and Cuyahoga County Bar Associations. Republican. Ohio State Senator 1971-75 and 1979-83.
Office: 19A U.S. Courthouse, 801 West Superior Avenue, Cleveland 44113-1834.
Telephone: (216) 357-7100.

MATTINGLY, Elizabeth B. *(Judge, Hamilton County Municipal Court)*
Office: 1000 Main Street, Room 230, Cincinnati 45202.
Telephone: (513) 946-5108.
Fax: (513) 946-5110
E-mail address: ematting@hamilton-co.org

MAYBERRY, Alan Reed *(Judge, Ohio Court of Common Pleas Wood County)* Serves Domestic Relations Division.
Office: One Courthouse Square, Bowling Green 43402.

MAYER, Philip Alan *(Judge, Ohio Court of Common Pleas Richland County)* Serves Probate Division.
Office: 50 Park Avenue East, Mansfield 44902.

MAYNARD, W. Dwayne *(Judge, Franklin County Municipal Court)*
Office: 375 South High Street, Columbus 43215-4593.
Telephone: (614) 645-8286.
Fax: (614) 645-7802
E-mail address: dwayne_maynard@fccourts.org

McBRIDE, Jerry R. *(Judge, Ohio Court of Common Pleas Clermont County)* Elected 1994. Reelected to subsequent term. Former Judge, Clermont County Municipal Court.
Office: 270 Main Street, Batavia 45103-3071.
Telephone: (513) 732-7104.
Fax: (513) 732-7987

McCAFFERTY, Bridget M. *(Judge, Ohio Court of Common Pleas Cuyahoga County)*
Office: 1200 Ontario Street, Cleveland 44113.
Telephone: (216) 443-8707.
Fax: (216) 348-4033

McCARTY, Alison *(Judge, Akron Municipal Court)* Appointed by Governor Bob Taft to term beginning May 10, 1999. Elected Nov 2, 1999, current term expires Jan 3, 2006. Born Akron Ohio April 5, 1962. Religious affiliation: non-denominational Christian. Educated at Wheaton College B.A. with honors 1984 and Wake Forest University School of Law J.D. 1987. Admitted to practice Ohio 1987.

Staff Attorney Ohio Court of Appeals Ninth District 1987-89. Assistant Prosecutor Summit County 1989-99. Member Ohio Municipal Court Association, Ohio Judicial Conference, Akron and Ohio State Bar Associations. Republican. Member Junior League of Akron, Covenant Community Church, Summit County Morbidity and Mortality Committee and Ohio Coalition on Sexual Assault. Enjoys aerobics, reading, child advocacy and spending time with family.
Office: 217 South High Street, #801, Akron 44308-1611.
Telephone: (330) 375-2611.
Fax: (330) 375-2642
E-mail address: mccaral@ci.akron.oh.us

McCLELLAND, Lee W. *(Judge, Morrow County Municipal Court)* Assumed office Jan 1, 2003. Term expires Dec 31, 2005. Born Galion Ohio May 7, 1947. Educated at Bowling Green State University B.A. 1969 and Case Western Reserve University J.D. 1974. Managing Editor Case Western Reserve Law Review 1973-74. Member Beta Theta Pi and Omicron Delta Kappa. Admitted to practice Ohio 1974. In legal practice Mansfield 1974-79 and Mount Gilead since 1979. Judge, Morrow County Court March 8, 1986 to Dec 31, 2002, appointed by Governor Richard F. Celeste.

Former Solicitor Village of Mount Gilead. Instructor in Real Estate Law Marion Technical Institute 1981-82. Trustee Ohio Municipal and County Judges Association. Member Morrow County and Ohio State Bar Associations. Faculty Member New Judges Orientation Ohio Judicial College 1998-2000. E-4 U.S. Army 1970-76. Battalion Legal Clerk U.S. Army Military Police School Fort Gordon Georgia. Democrat. Hobbies include antique cars, genealogy and computers.
Office: 48 East High Street, Mount Gilead 43338-1494.
Telephone: (419) 947-5045.
Fax: (419) 947-9161
E-mail address: mccelaw@bright.net

McCLURG, Michael Douglas *(Judge, Ohio Court of Common Pleas Darke County)* Serves Probate and Juvenile Divisions.
Office: 300 Garst Avenue, Greenville 45331.

McCOLLUM, Alice O. *(Judge, Ohio Court of Common Pleas Montgomery County)* Elected Nov 5, 2002 to term beginning Feb 9, 2003. Term expires Feb 8, 2009. Serves Probate Division. Born Oklahoma City Oklahoma Feb 1947. Educated at University of North Carolina at Greensboro B.A. in Mathematics 1969, University of Cincinnati College of Law J.D. 1972, Wright State University 1974-75 and University of Dayton 1975-77. Admitted to practice Ohio 1972, Michigan 1974 and U.S. District Courts Northern 1974 and Southern 1974 Districts of Ohio and Eastern 1974 and Western 1974 Districts of Michigan. In part-time legal practice Dayton 1975-79. Hearing Examiner, Ohio Civil Rights Commission April 1978 to Feb 1979. Judge Feb 9, 1979 to Feb 8, 2003, Administrative Judge 1983-84 and Presiding Judge 1985-86, Dayton Municipal Court, appointed by Governor James A. Rhodes (first woman to serve this court).

Co-director Legal Aid Society Dayton July 15, 1974 to Aug 31, 1975. Contributing Author *The Neurologic, Neurogenic and Neuropsychiatric Disorders Handbook* A. J. Giannini and R. L. Gilliland eds. 1982. Assistant Professor of Political Science and Director of Pre-Law Program Wilberforce University Sept 1974 to May 1976. Assistant Professor of Law and Assistant Director of Clinical Legal Studies July 1, 1976 to Feb 9, 1979 and Adjunct Professor since Feb 9, 1979 University of Dayton College of Law. Reginald Heber Smith Fellow Legal Aid Society Dayton 1972-74. Member Thurgood Marshall Law Society, Ohio Association of Probate Judges, National College of Probate Judges, Dayton (Professional Ethics Committee since July 1978), Ohio State, National and American Bar Associations. Recipient Marks of Excellence Award from Dayton Chapter National Forum for Black Public Administrators 2000, Foundation Award from Thurgood Marshall Law Society 2000, Joseph Cinque Award from BALSA University of Dayton School of Law 2001 and Women of Influence Award from YWCA 2002. Board Member Children's Medical Center, Central State University, Ohio Criminal Sentencing Commission, Dayton Foundation Self-Sufficiency Board, United Theological Seminary, Wright State University Foundation, Victoria Theatre Association, Wegerzyn Garden Center, Dayton Contemporary Dance Company and Senior Citizens Center of Greater Dayton. Advisory Board Sinclair Community College. Life Member NAACP. Interests include high school sports. Personal Statement or Quote: "Success is not measured by the position one reaches in life but by the obstacles she must overcome to become successful."
Office: 41 North Perry Street, Dayton 45402.
Telephone: (937) 225-4400.

MCCOLLUM, ALICE O.—*Continued*

Fax: (937) 496-3181
E-mail address: mccollua@montcourt.org

McCONNELL, C. Allen *(Judge, Toledo Municipal Court)*
Office: 555 North Erie Street, Toledo 43624.
Telephone: (419) 245-1946.
Fax: (419) 245-1802
E-mail address: callenmcc@noris.org

McCORMICK, Timothy P. *(Judge, Ohio Court of Common Pleas Cuyahoga County)* Elected 1994. Reelected to subsequent term.
Office: 1200 Ontario Street, #20C, Cleveland 44113.
Telephone: (216) 443-8745.
Fax: (216) 348-4034

McCOWN, Frank J. *(Judge, Ohio Court of Common Pleas Lawrence County)* Elected 1996 and 2002. Current term expires Feb 8, 2009. Born Ironton Ohio Feb 6, 1940. Methodist. Educated at Miami University, Ohio B.S.B.A. 1962 and The Ohio State University J.D. 1964. Associate Editor Ohio State Law Journal 1963-64. Member Phi Alpha Delta. Admitted to practice Ohio 1965. In legal practice Ironton 1965-97.

City Attorney Ironton 1965-80 and 1990-96. Assistant Attorney General Ohio 1980-90. Author weekly legal column *Ironton Tribunal* 1985-96. Instructor in Law Ohio University since 1974. Member Ohio State Bar Association. Democrat. Enjoys boating and traveling. Personal Statement or Quote: "Law is a profession. Treat it gently."
Office: Lawrence County Courthouse, One Veterans Square, Ironton 45638.
Telephone: (740) 533-4332.
Fax: (740) 533-4377
E-mail address: judgemac@hotmail.com

McDONALD, Frederick H. *(Judge, Ohio Court of Common Pleas Lucas County)*
Office: Courthouse, 700 Adams Street, Toledo 43624.
Telephone: (419) 213-4560.
Fax: (419) 213-4181

McDONNELL, Nancy R. *(Judge, Ohio Court of Common Pleas Cuyahoga County)* Elected Nov 1996 to term beginning Jan 3, 1997. Reelected 2002, current term expires Jan 2009. Born Cleveland Ohio Nov 30, 1959. Catholic. Educated at Catholic University of America B.A. magna cum laude 1982 and Cleveland-Marshall College of Law J.D. 1985. Admitted to practice Ohio 1985. In legal practice Cleveland 1985-96. Magistrate, Lakewood Municipal Court 1991-96.

Assistant County Prosecutor Cuyahoga County 1986-91. Member Lakewood Democratic Club. Member Junior Women's Club of Lakewood, St. Luke Parent Teacher Organization Board and Irish Civil Association. Enjoys family activities.
Office: 1200 Ontario Street, Cleveland 44113-1678.
Telephone: (216) 443-8756.
Fax: (216) 348-4037

McGIMPSEY, Earl R. *(Judge, Ohio Court of Common Pleas Huron County)* Elected Nov 1994 to term beginning May 15, 1995. Reelected Nov 2000, current term expires May 14, 2007. Born Cleveland Ohio Sept 6, 1941. Episcopalian. Educated at Wabash College B.A. 1963 and University of Washington J.D. 1971. Articles Editor Washington Law Review 1970-71. Law Clerk to Hon. Charles Stafford, Washington Supreme Court 1971-72. Member Order of the Coif. Admitted to practice Washington 1971, U.S. Supreme Court 1975, Ohio 1982, U.S. District Courts Eastern and Western Districts of Washington and Northern District of Ohio and U.S. Court of Appeals Ninth Circuit. In legal practice Norwalk Ohio 1982-95.

Assistant Attorney General Washington 1972-81. Former Member Washington State Bar Association. Member Ohio State Bar Association. Attended Criminal Evidence course The National Judicial College. Recipient Award of Merit from Boy Scouts of America 1992 and Commendation (for library board work) from Ohio State Senate 1995. Lieutenant j.g. USNR 1963-67. Republican. Former Member Norwalk Public Library Board. Volunteer Boy Scouts of America. Enjoys sailing, fly fishing, skiing, backpacking and woodworking.
Office: Two East Main Street, Norwalk 44857-1594.
Telephone: (419) 668-6162.
Fax: (419) 663-9334
E-mail address: judge@huroncountyclerk.com

McGINTY, Timothy J. *(Judge, Ohio Court of Common Pleas Cuyahoga County)* Elected to term beginning Jan 2, 1993. Reelected to subsequent term, current term expires Jan 1, 2005. Born Cleveland Ohio June 5, 1951. Catholic. Educated at Heidelberg College B.A. 1973, Cleveland-Marshall College of Law J.D. 1981 and University of Nevada Reno M.A. in Judicial Studies 2000. Admitted to practice Ohio 1981, U.S. District Court Northern District of Ohio 1984, U.S. Court of Appeals Sixth Circuit 1989 and U.S. Supreme Court 1989.

Probation Office/Investigator Ohio Court of Common Pleas 1973-81. Assistant Prosecutor Major Trial Division Cuyahoga County 1982-92. Member Criminal Rules Committee Ohio Court of Common Pleas, Cleveland (Criminal Law Committee) and Ohio State (Administration and Court Reform Committee, Criminal Law Committee) Bar Associations. Trustee St. Edward High School. Interests include history, photography, marathoning, backpacking and golfing.
Office: 1200 Ontario Street, Cleveland 44113.
Telephone: (216) 443-8758.
Fax: (216) 348-4033
E-mail address: tjmcginty@aol.com

McGOOKEY, Beverly K. *(Judge, Ohio Court of Common Pleas Erie County)* Elected Nov 1996 to term beginning Feb 9, 1997. Reelected Nov 2002, current term expires Feb 2009. Serves Probate Division. Born Sandusky Ohio. Educated at Bowling Green State University B.S. magna cum laude 1974 and University of Toledo College of Law J.D. 1980. Admitted to practice Ohio 1980 and U.S. District Court Northern District of Ohio 1981. In legal practice Sandusky Ohio 1980-85.

Assistant Prosecutor Erie County 1980-96. Member Ohio Association of Probate Judges, National College of Probate Judges, Erie County, Ohio State and American Bar Associations.
Office: 323 Columbus Avenue, Sandusky 44870-2691.
Telephone: (419) 627-7750.
Fax: (419) 626-9120

McGOUGH, Lynett *(Judge, Ohio Court of Common Pleas Lorain County)* Elected Nov 1988 to term beginning Jan 5, 1989. Reelected 1994 and 2000. Current term expires Jan 4, 2007. Catholic. Educated at Baldwin-Wallace College B.A. with honors 1978 and Cleve-

MCGOUGH, LYNETT—*Continued*

land-Marshall College of Law J.D. 1981. Admitted to practice Ohio 1981 and U.S. District Court Northern District of Ohio 1984. Began legal practice Lorain County.

Law Director City of North Ridgeville 1986-88. Author "CCA Boards Necessary to Coordinate Criminal Justice Efforts" Ohio Community Corrections Organization 1994. Member Lorain County and Ohio State Bar Associations. Named Woman of Achievement 1994. Chairman CCA Board. Member 317 Board. Enjoys gardening and scuba diving.

Office: 308 Second Street, Elyria 44035.
Telephone: (440) 329-5416.
Fax: (440) 284-3681
E-mail address: mcgough@mediaone.net

McGRATH, Patrick M. *(Judge, Ohio Court of Common Pleas Franklin County)*

Office: 369 South High Street, #7C, Columbus 43215-4554.
Telephone: (614) 462-3777.
Fax: (614) 462-2462
E-mail address: patrick_mcgrath@fccourts.org

McILVAINE, Stephen B. *(Judge, Wadsworth Municipal Court)*

Office: 120 Maple Street, Wadsworth 44281-1857.
Telephone: (330) 335-1596.
Fax: (330) 335-2723

McKAY, Walter W. *(Judge, Ohio Court of Common Pleas Trumbull County)* Assumed office Jan 1, 1987.

Office: 161 High Street N.W., Warren 44481.
Telephone: (330) 675-2577.
Fax: (330) 675-2580

McKENNA, David H. *(Judge, Hillsboro Municipal Court)* Elected Nov 1999 to term beginning Jan 1, 2000. Born Louisville Kentucky July 13, 1952. Presbyterian. Educated at University of North Carolina at Chapel Hill B.A. with honors 1974, University of Kentucky 1977 and University of Louisville J.D. 1985. Admitted to practice Kentucky 1985 and Ohio 1991. In legal practice Louisville Kentucky 1985-86 and Hillsboro Ohio since 1991.

Assistant Commonwealth Attorney Louisville 1986-91. Assistant County Prosecutor 1997-2000. Member Louisville, Highland County, Kentucky and Ohio State Bar Associations.

Office: 130 Homestead Avenue, Hillsboro 45133.
Telephone: (937) 393-3022.
Fax: (937) 393-3273

McMASTER, Russell J. *(Judge, Ohio Court of Common Pleas Paulding County)* Elected Nov 1992 to term beginning Feb 9, 1993. Reelected 1998, current term expires Feb 2005. Serves Probate and Juvenile Divisions. Born Toledo Ohio July 7, 1935. Presbyterian. Educated at Defiance College B.A. 1963 and University of Michigan Law School J.D. 1966. Admitted to practice Ohio 1966.

Prosecuting Attorney Paulding County 1969-77. Member Kiwanis.

Office: 115 North Williams Street, Second Floor, #202, Paulding 45879-1204.
Telephone: (419) 399-8255.
Fax: (419) 399-8261

McMONAGLE, Christine T. *(Judge, Ohio Court of Common Pleas Cuyahoga County)*

Office: 1200 Ontario Street, Cleveland 44113.
Telephone: (216) 443-8696.
Fax: (216) 348-4031

McMONAGLE, Richard J. *(Judge, Ohio Court of Common Pleas Cuyahoga County)*

Office: 1200 Ontario Street, Cleveland 44113-1678.
Telephone: (216) 443-8675.
Fax: (216) 348-4038

McMONAGLE, Timothy E. *(Judge, Ohio Court of Appeals Eighth District)* Assumed office 1995. Educated at University of Dayton and Cleveland State University Cleveland-Marshall College of Law. Admitted to practice Ohio 1974. Former Judge, Ohio Court of Common Pleas Cuyahoga County.

Office: One Lakeside Avenue, Cleveland 44113-1085.
Telephone: (216) 443-6359.
Fax: (216) 443-2044

McNULTY, Michael J. *(Judge, Barberton Municipal Court)*

Office: Municipal Building, 576 West Park Avenue, Barberton 44203.
Telephone: (330) 861-7212.
Fax: (330) 848-6779

McQUADE, Colin J. *(Judge, Fulton County Court)* Appointed by Governor Bob Taft to term beginning July 7, 1999. Elected 2000, current term expires Dec 31, 2006. Born Toledo Ohio June 13, 1955. Catholic. Educated at Adrian College B.A. magna cum laude 1977 and University of Toledo School of Law J.D. 1980. Admitted to practice Ohio 1980 and U.S. District Court District of Ohio 1980. In legal practice Swanton since 1980.

Village Solicitor Swanton and Metamura 1980-99. Member Toledo, Fulton County and Ohio State Bar Associations. Republican. Trustee Swanton Rotary Club.

Office: 128 North Main Street, Swanton 43558-1091.
Telephone: (419) 826-5636.
Fax: (419) 825-3324

MEDLEY, William S. *(Judge, Ohio Court of Common Pleas Gallia County)* Serves Probate and Juvenile Divisions. Born Akron Ohio. Methodist. Educated at University of Akron B.S.B.A. cum laude 1977 J.D. 1980. Member Phi Delta Gamma. Admitted to practice Ohio 1980 and U.S. District Court Northern District of Ohio 1981. In legal practice Akron 1981-84. Court Referee and Magistrate, Ohio Court of Common Pleas Gallia County 1988-92. Former Judge, Gallipolis Municipal Court, appointed by Governor George V. Voinovich to term beginning Jan 7, 1993.

Professor of Finance and Law University of Rio Grande 1986-93. Member Ohio Association of Court Referees and Magistrates (Board of Trustees 1990-91), Ohio Judges Association, Gallia County and Ohio State Bar Associations. Participant Contempt, Hearsay, Report Writing, General Update 92, Child Support, Court Security, Jury Standards, Faculty Development, Basic Review for Judges 93, Integrated Computer Justice, Strategic Planning for Courts, Protesting the Record and New DWI/DUS courses Ohio Judicial College; Driving While Intoxicated Law Update Course Ohio Police Officers Training Council; and mini-course on Judging The Ohio State University. E-3 U.S. Army Military Police 1972-

MEDLEY, WILLIAM S.—*Continued*

75. Republican. Advisor College Republicans. Member Lions, VFW, American Legion and American Veterans. Enjoys Sax Rohmer novels.

Office: 18 Locust Street, Room 1293, Gallipolis 45631.

MELLING, Brian J. *(Judge, Bedford Municipal Court)*

Office: 65 Columbus Road, Bedford 44146.
Telephone: (440) 232-3420.
Fax: (440) 232-2510

MERZ, Michael R. *(Magistrate Judge, United States District Court Southern District of Ohio)* Appointed by U.S. District Court judges to term beginning Nov 20, 1984. Reappointed Nov 20, 1992 and 2000. Current term expires Nov 20, 2008. Born Dayton Ohio March 29, 1945. Roman Catholic. Educated at Harvard University A.B. cum laude 1967 J.D. 1970. Irene Muir Jacobs Scholar 1963-64. Admitted to practice Ohio 1970, U.S. District Court Southern District of Ohio 1971, U.S. Supreme Court 1974 and U.S. Court of Appeals Sixth Circuit 1975. In legal practice Dayton 1970-77. Judge, Dayton Municipal Court 1977-84.

Author "The Meaninglessness of the Plain Meaning Rule" 4 University of Dayton L. Rev. 1, 1979. Author and Editor *Contempt Manual for Ohio Judges.* Published Decisions: State v. Foreman 54 Ohio Misc. 31, 376 N.E.2d 987, 1978; City of Dayton v. Peterson 56 Ohio Misc. 12, 381 N.E.2d 1154, 1978; City of Dayton v. Schenck 63 Ohio Misc. 14, 409 N.E.2d 284, 1980; City of Dayton v. Rutledge 7 Ohio Misc. 2d 14, 454 N.E.2d 611, 1983; City of Dayton v. Strausbaugh 10 Ohio Misc. 2d 29, 462 N.E.2d 462, 1984; State v. McGhee 12 Ohio Misc. 2d 18, 468 N.E.2d 400, 1984; Payne v. A. O. Smith Corp. 627 F. Supp. 226 S.D. Ohio 1985; United States v. Minisee 113 F.R.D. 121 S.D. Ohio 1986; Ullman v. Olwine 123 F.R.D. 237, 253 and 559 S.D. Ohio 1987 aff'd 857 F.2d 1475 6th Cir. 1988 cert. denied 489 U.S. 1080, 1989; Brown v. Springfield City Schools 689 F. Supp. 783 S.D. Ohio 1988; Miami Valley Carpenters District Council Pension Scheckelhoff 123 F.R.D. 263 S.D. Ohio 1988; Hopkins V. Elano Corp. 30 E.R.C. BNA 1782 S.D. Ohio 1989; Babcock Swine, Inc. v. Shelbco, Inc. 126 F.R.D. 43 S.D. Ohio 1989; Prather v. Dayton Power and Light Co. 54 F.E.P. 639 S.D. Ohio 1989, aff'd. 918 F.2d 1255, 6th Cir. 1990; Gall v. St. Elizabeth Medical Center 130 F.R.D. 85 S.D. Ohio 1990; Dolly, Inc. v. Spalding and Evenflo Companies, Inc. 16 U.S.P.Q.2d 1737, 1991; Insituform of North America, Inc. v. Midwest Pipeliners, Inc. 139 F.R.D. 622 S.D. Ohio 1991; Insituform of North America, Inc. v. Midwest Pipeliners, Inc. 780 F. Supp. 479 S.D. Ohio 1991; Dayco Products, Inc. v. Walker 142 F.R.D. 450 S.D. Ohio 1992; Hutchinson v. Cox 784 F. Supp. 1339 S.D. Ohio 1992; and Gearhardt v. Cadillac Plastics Group, Inc. 140 F.R.D. 349 S.D. Ohio 1992.

Adjunct Professor of Antitrust, Professional Responsibility, Federal Jurisdiction, Evidence and General Jurisprudence University of Dayton School of Law since 1979. Chair Civil Rules Subcommittee Ohio Supreme Court Rules Advisory Committee 1991-96. President Carl D. Kessler Inn of Court 1993-95. Fellow American Bar Foundation. Member Federal Magistrate Judges Association (Trustee Sixth Circuit 1997-2000), American Judicature Society, Dayton, Ohio State (Vice Chair Federal Courts Committee 1988-89, Chair Judicial Administration and Legal Reform Committee 1989-90), Federal and American (National Conference of Federal Trial Judges Judicial Administration Division) Bar Associations. Instructor in Contempt of Court and other topics Ohio Judicial College since 1979. Attended General Jurisdiction course The National Judicial College 1979. Recipient City of Dayton Outstanding Service Award 1982 and Ohio Superior Judicial Service Awards every year served from Dayton Municipal Court. Republican. Member 1981-95 and Chairman 1989-91 Board of Directors Dayton United Way. President Harvard Law School Association of Ohio 1989-90. Trustee since 1991 and President of the Board 1992-94 and 2000 Dayton and Montgomery County Public Library. Director Dayton Chapter National Conference of Christians and Jews 1988-92. Trustee Ohio Library Council 1997-2000.

Office: 902 Federal Building, 200 West Second Street, Dayton 45402.
Telephone: (937) 512-1550.
E-mail address: michael_merz@ohsd.uscourts.gov

MESSHAM, Robert E., Jr. *(Judge, Miamisburg Municipal Court)*

Office: 10 North First Street, Miamisburg 45342.
Telephone: (937) 866-2203.
Fax: (937) 866-0135

MICHAEL, Stephen D. *(Judge, Ohio Court of Common Pleas Jackson County)* Serves Probate and Juvenile Divisions.

Office: Courthouse, 226 East Main Street, Jackson 45640-1798.
Telephone: (740) 286-6405.
Fax: (740) 286-6537

MIHOK, Mark *(Judge, Lorain Municipal Court)*

Office: 100 West Erie Avenue, Lorain 44052-1646.
Telephone: (440) 244-2166.
Fax: (440) 244-3458

MILICH, Robert P. *(Judge, Youngstown Municipal Court)*

Office: 26 South Phelps Street, Youngstown 44503-1370.
Telephone: (330) 742-8855.
Fax: (330) 742-8845
E-mail address: bobmilich@aol.com

MILLER, Nodine *(Judge, Ohio Court of Common Pleas Franklin County)* Appointed by Governor George V. Voinovich to term beginning Jan 5, 1995. Elected Nov 1996 and Nov 1998. Current term expires Jan 2005. Former Presiding Judge. Lutheran. Educated at Miami University B.A. 1960 and Capital University Law School J.D. 1976. Admitted to practice Ohio 1976. In legal practice Columbus 1981-92. Judge, Franklin County Municipal Court 1992-95.

Attorney assigned to the Commissioner 1976-79, Attorney Inspector of Securities 1977-79 and Deputy Commissioner of Securities 1978-81 Division of Securities Ohio Department of Commerce. Chairman Rules Committee Ohio Court of Common Pleas Franklin County. Member Response Team to Ohio Futures Commission representing Ohio Common Pleas Judges Association. Member Franklin Inn 99 American Inns of Court, Columbus (Co-Chairman Bench/Bar Retreat 1999), Ohio State and American Bar Associations. Member Executive Committee, Chairman Civil Law and Procedure Commit-

MILLER, NODINE—*Continued*

tee and Mentor for newly elected Common Pleas Judges Ohio Judicial Conference. Board of Trustees Ohio Judicial College. Recipient Golden Nike Award from Ohio Federation of Business and Professional Women's Club, Inc. May 1971. Named Franklin County's 1970 Outstanding Career Woman by Columbus Citizen-Journal May 1971. Listed in *Who's Who in Government* 1974. Previously employed as Communications Specialist U.S. Department of State Oct 1962 to Dec 1963. State Telephone Chairman Ohio Committee to Reelect the President June 1972 to Nov 1972. City Ombudsman Columbus 1972-74. Member Sierra Club, Adirondack Mountain Club, Ascension Lutheran Church and Columbus Metropolitan Quilters. Enjoys quilting, hiking and fly fishing.

Office: 369 South High Street, Courtroom 6B, Columbus 43215-4554.
Telephone: (614) 462-3550.
Fax: (614) 462-3868
E-mail address: nodine_miller@fccourts.org

MILLER, Stuart K. *(Judge, Wayne County Municipal Court)*
Office: 538 North Market Street, Wooster 44691-3499.
Telephone: (330) 287-5663.
Fax: (330) 263-4043

MITROVICH, Paul H. *(Judge, Ohio Court of Common Pleas Lake County)* Elected Nov 1978 to term beginning Jan 5, 1979. Reelected Nov 1984, Nov 1990, Nov 1996 and 2002. Current term expires Jan 2009. Born Detroit Michigan July 25, 1934. Methodist. Educated at The Ohio State University B.S. 1960, University of Toledo College of Law J.D. 1965 and University of Nevada Reno M.J.S. 1992. Admitted to practice Ohio 1966 and U.S. District Court Northern District of Ohio 1972. In legal practice Willowick 1966-79.

Assistant Law Director Eastlake, Willoughby and Willowick 1970-73 and 1977-79. Prosecuting Attorney Lake County 1973-76. Author "Workmen's Compensation for Suicide After Traumatic Injury" 15 Cleveland Marshall L. Rev. 116, 1966; monthly column on Ethics for Cuyahoga County B. Jour. 1974-75; Chapter "Pre-Indictment Proceedings" *Ohio Prosecuting Attorney Manual* 1975; numerous articles for *Lake Legal Views* Lake County Bar Association Publication since 1979; and Analysis "Ohio Living Will Statute and Beyond" XVIII No. IV Ohio Northern University 1992. Coordinator Judicial Articles *Lake Legal Views* 1982-91. Important Decisions: Plumbing Connections, Inc. v. Kostelnik 60 Ohio Misc. 11, 430 N.E.2d 1340, 23 O.O. 3d 77, 1980; State v. Simpson 64 Ohio Misc. 42, 412 N.E.2d 956, 18 O.O. 3d 199, 1980; Jones v. Veit 6 Ohio Misc. 2d 4, 453 N.E.2d 1299, 6 O.B.R. 543, 1982; Hutter v. City of Wickliffe 7 Ohio Misc. 2d 21, 454 N.E.2d 601, 7 O.B.R. 121, 1983; Mramor v. Chapman 22 Ohio Misc. 2d 8, 488 N.E.2d 1257, 22 O.B.R. 182, 1984; Harris v. Prudential Ins. Co. of America 27 Ohio App. 3d 291, 501 N.E.2d 77, 27 O.B.R. 336, 1986; State v. Lambros 44 Ohio App. 3d 102, 541 N.E.2d 632, 1988; State v. Jurek 55 Ohio App. 3d 70, 562 N.E.2d 941, 1989; and State v. Jones 65 Ohio App. 3d 282, 583 N.E.2d 1023, 1989. Instructor in Law, Business Law, Constitutional Law and Constitutional History and Law for Paralegal program Lakeland Community College since 1986. Instructor in Law, Criminal Procedures and Constitutional Law including Arrest and Search and Seizure for Police Academy Lakeland Community College since 1986.

Former Member Ohio Prosecuting Attorney Association (Trustee 1974-75). Member Ohio Common Pleas Judges Association (Member 1979-92 and Chairman 1989 Ohio Government Committee), National District Attorneys Association, Lake County (Chairman Admissions to Bar Committee since 1977, Trustee since 1992) and Ohio State (District 18 Representative 1978-80, Practice of Law Committee 1980-83) Bar Associations. Attended Contempt Seminar March 13, 1981, Product Liability Seminar April 3, 1981, Administrative Appeals Seminar April 23, 1982, Determinate/Interdeterminate Sentencing Seminar April 22, 1983, Jury Instructions Seminar Sept 30, 1983, Evidence In Civil Cases Seminar Sept 28, 1984, Torts Today Seminar Feb 22, 1985, Computer Primer Seminar May 20, 1985, Judicial Immunity Seminar Feb 12, 1986, Child Sex Abuse Cases Seminar Oct 23, 1987, Tort Reform Seminar Jan 22, 1988, Ethics for Judges Seminar March 17, 1989, Fourth Amendment Update Feb 23, 1990, Felony Sentencing Seminar Nov 28, 1990, Judicial Ethics Sept 17, 1991 and Personnel Management for Judges Nov 5, 1992 Ohio Judicial College; Summer Conferences June 24-27, 1981, June 23-25, 1982, June 21-24, 1983, June 27-29, 1984, June 24-27, 1986, June 26-28, 1992 and June 24-26, 1992, Case and Legislative Law Update Sept 8, 1983 and Winter Conference Dec 1-12, 1992 Ohio Common Pleas Judges Association; Fact Finding, Decision Making, Communication Seminar July 27-31, 1981, Law of Evidence Seminar Aug 23-27, 1982, Constitutional Criminal Procedure Seminar June 10-16, 1984, Scholar's Seminar July 6-12, 1985, The Law of Evidence Seminar July 6-11, 1986 and Philosophical Ethics and Judicial Decision Making Seminar Aug 8-14, 1992 American Academy of Judicial Education; Justice, Law and Literature course University of Nevada Reno Jan 9-19, 1989; and Individual and Society Seminar The National Judicial College Oct 26-28, 1990. Recipient Excellent Judicial Service Award 1979 and Superior Judicial Service Awards 1980-86 from Ohio Supreme Court. USNR 1952-54. U.S. Army 1954-56. Lieutenant Colonel Ohio Military Reserve since 1987. Democrat. Lake County Charter Commission 1970. Member Lawyers Against Drugs since 1991. Enjoys antique cars, wood and metal working and collecting guns.

Mailing address: P.O. Box 490, Painesville 44077-0490.
Office: 47 North Park Place, Painesville 44077.
Telephone: (440) 350-2705.
Fax: (440) 350-2780

MONG, Frederick E. *(Judge, Ohio Court of Common Pleas Hocking County)* Serves Probate and Juvenile Divisions.
Office: One East Main Street, Logan 43138.
Telephone: (740) 385-3615.
Fax: (740) 385-6892
E-mail address: fmong@ohiohills.com

MONNIN, Joseph N. *(Judge, Ohio Court of Common Pleas Clark County)* Elected 1994 to term beginning 1995. Reelected 2000, current term expires Jan 1, 2007. Serves Domestic Relations and Juvenile Divisions.
Office: 101 East Columbia Street, Springfield 45502.
Telephone: (937) 328-2630.

MONNIN, JOSEPH N.—*Continued*

Fax: (937) 328-2639
E-mail address: ccjuvcourt@cs.com

MONTGOMERY, K. J. *(Judge, Shaker Heights Municipal Court)*
Office: 3355 Lee Road, Shaker Heights 44120-3499.
Telephone: (216) 491-1324.
Fax: (216) 491-1314

MOODY, Denise L. *(Judge, Clark County Municipal Court)*
Office: 50 East Columbia, Springfield 45502.

MOON, Paul Clinton *(Judge, Ohio Court of Common Pleas Ottawa County)* Elected to term beginning 1991. Born Port Clinton Ohio Dec 19, 1937. Educated at John Carroll University B.S.S. cum laude 1959, Catholic University of America 1960, Georgetown University J.D. 1962 and University of Kansas Law and Organizational Economics 2000. Admitted to practice Ohio 1962, U.S. Supreme Court 1971, U.S. District Court District of Ohio and U.S. Court of Appeals Sixth Circuit. In legal practice Port Clinton 1965-79. Judge, Port Clinton Municipal Court 1979-91.

Assistant City Solicitor and Police Prosecutor Port Clinton 1965-66. Former Special Counsel Ohio Attorney General. Former Editor *Chronicle* Newsletter for Judges and Legislators. Member Committee on Bi-Lingual Courts and Municipal Courts National Conference of Special Court Judges. Association of Municipal/County Judges of Ohio, Inc. (Trustee 1987-91), Ohio Common Pleas Judges Association, Ottawa County (President 1965 and 1968), Ohio State and American Bar Associations. Faculty Ohio Judicial College 1987-89. Second Lieutenant USAR June 6, 1959 to Dec 21, 1964. Member 1966-70 and President 1971-73 Port Clinton City Council. Board of Trustees Firelands College Bowling Green State University 1971-84. Legal Advisor Ohio Mock Trial Program 1987-88. Interested in music and historical restoration.

Office: 315 Madison Street, Port Clinton 43452-1936.
Telephone: (419) 734-6791.
Fax: (419) 734-6852
E-mail address: amadeus43452@yahoo.com

MOORE, Carla D. *(Judge, Akron Municipal Court)* Appointed by Governor Richard F. Celeste to term beginning June 1989. Elected Nov 1989, 1995 and 2001. Current term expires Dec 31, 2007. Born Akron Ohio Jan 29, 1952. Christian. Educated at University of Akron B.A. with honors 1974 and The Ohio State University College of Law J.D. 1977. Admitted to practice Ohio 1977, U.S. District Court Northern District of Ohio 1980 and U.S. Court of Appeals Sixth Circuit 1980. In legal practice Akron 1988-89.

Assistant Attorney General Ohio 1977-80. Assistant U.S. Attorney 1980-88. Adjunct Professor of Appellate Law Cleveland State University 1986-87. Member Akron Barristers Club, Akron, Ohio State and American Bar Associations. Instructor on Federal Tort Claims Act National Conference The Association of Trial Lawyers of America 1990 and 1992. Instructor Basic Review course 1993 and 1994 and Ethics for Judges course 1993, 1994, 1995, 1996 and 1997 Ohio Judicial College.

Office: 217 South High Street, #917, Akron 44308.
Telephone: (330) 375-2053.
Fax: (330) 375-2229
E-mail address: mooreca@ci.akron.oh.us

MOORE, Robert L. *(Judge, Kettering Municipal Court)*
Office: 3600 Shroyer Road, Kettering 45429-2734.
Telephone: (937) 296-2542.
Fax: (937) 296-3284
E-mail address: moore136@yahoo.com

MOOREHEAD, Robert S., Jr. *(Judge, Ohio Court of Common Pleas Guernsey County)* Serves Probate and Juvenile Divisions.
Office: 801 East Wheeling Avenue, Cambridge 43725.

MORGENSTERN-CLARREN, Pat E. *(Judge, United States Bankruptcy Court Northern District of Ohio)* Appointed by U.S. Court of Appeals Sixth Circuit judges to term beginning Dec 1, 1995. Term expires Dec 1, 2009. Educated at University of Michigan A.B. 1974, Case Western Reserve University J.D. 1977 and London School of Economics and Political Science, England LL.M. Mark of Distinction 1979. Member Order of the Coif. Judge, Bankruptcy Appellate Panel Sixth Circuit 1999-2002.

Office: 3201 Key Tower, 127 Public Square, Cleveland 44114-1309.
Telephone: (216) 522-4373.

MOYER, Thomas J. *(Chief Justice, Supreme Court of Ohio)* Elected to term beginning Jan 1, 1987. Reelected 1992 and 1998. Current term expires Dec 31, 2004. Born Sandusky Ohio April 18, 1939. Protestant. Educated at The Ohio State University B.A. 1961 J.D. 1964. Admitted to practice Ohio 1964. In legal practice Columbus 1966-69 and 1972-75. Referee for Commitments to Columbus State Hospitals 1968. Judge, Ohio Court of Appeals Tenth District 1979-86.

Assistant Attorney General 1964-66. Deputy Assistant 1969-71 and Executive Assistant 1975-79 to Governor James A. Rhodes. Member Columbus (President 1980-81) and Ohio State (Executive Committee, Council of Delegates) Bar Associations. Named Outstanding Young Man of Columbus by Columbus Jaycees 1969 and Outstanding Alumni of The Ohio State University June 1987. Inducted into Buckeye Boys State Hall of Fame June 1988. Recipient Award of Merit from Ohio State Legal Institute. Secretary Board of Trustees Franklin University. Member Crichton Club and Columbus Maennerchor. Enjoys sailing and tennis.

Office: 30 East Broad Street, Third Floor, Columbus 43266-0419.
Telephone: (614) 466-3627.
Fax: (614) 728-8064
E-mail address: moyert@sconet.state.oh.us

MUEHLFELD, Keith P. *(Judge, Ohio Court of Common Pleas Henry County)* Elected to term beginning May 9, 1999. Born Bryan Ohio Sept 10, 1951. Catholic. Educated at The Ohio State University B.S. cum laude 1973 and University of Toledo College of Law J.D. 1976. Admitted to practice Ohio 1976 and U.S. District Court Northern District of Ohio 1977. In legal practice Napoleon 1976-93. Former Judge, Napoleon Municipal Court, elected to term beginning Jan 1, 1988.

Law Director Napoleon City 1977-87. Former Member Municipal-County Judges of Ohio, Inc. Member Ohio Common Pleas Judges Association, Ohio Association of Juvenile and Family Court Judges, Henry Coun-

MUEHLFELD, KEITH P.—*Continued*

ty, Northwest Ohio and Ohio State Bar Associations. Panel Member Domestic Violence Seminar Defiance College 1992. Republican. Member Rotary Club. Enjoys tennis.
Mailing address: P.O. Box 70, Napoleon 43545-1747.
Office: Courthouse, Napoleon 43545.
Telephone: (419) 592-5926.
Fax: (419) 599-0803

MURPHY, James E. *(Judge, Ohio Court of Common Pleas Summit County)* Term expires Dec 31, 2006.
Office: 209 South High Street, Akron 44308-1413.
Telephone: (330) 643-2239.
Fax: (330) 643-2406

MURPHY, Michael B. *(Judge, Ohio Court of Common Pleas Montgomery County)* Serves Juvenile Division.
Office: 303 West Second Street, Dayton 45422.
Telephone: (937) 225-4780.
Fax: (937) 496-7843
E-mail address: murphym@montcnty.org

MUSSON, John R. *(Judge, Elyria Municipal Court)*
Office: 328 Broad Street, Elyria 44035-6434.
Telephone: (440) 323-4903.
Fax: (440) 323-4012

NADEL, Norbert A. *(Judge, Ohio Court of Common Pleas Hamilton County)* Assumed office 1980. Elected to subsequent terms. Presiding Judge 1982. Served Domestic Relations Division 1980-82. Serves General Division since 1982. Born Cincinnati Ohio Jan 3, 1939. Educated at University of Cincinnati A.B. 1961 and Samuel P. Chase College of Law (now Chase Law School of Northern Kentucky University) J.D. 1965. Court Constable, Ohio Court of Common Pleas Hamilton County 1963-65. Law Clerk to Justice Louis J. Schneider, Jr., Ohio Supreme Court 1965-66. Member Phi Alpha Delta. Admitted to practice Ohio 1965, U.S. District Court Southern District of Ohio 1968, U.S. Supreme Court 1968 and U.S. Court of Appeals Sixth Circuit 1971. In legal practice Cincinnati 1966-69. Administrator-Referee, Hamilton County Municipal Court 1968-69. Judge 1974-80 and Presiding Judge 1979, Hamilton County Municipal Court.
Assistant U.S. Attorney 1969-70 and First Assistant U.S. Attorney 1971-74 Southern District of Ohio Western Division. Assistant City Prosecutor Criminal Division Cincinnati 1966-68. Attorney-in-Charge Cincinnati Office of Drug Abuse Law Enforcement 1972-73. Member Ohio Common Pleas Judges Association. Honored by Mothers Against Drunk Drivers 1984. President Chase College of Law Alumni Association 1976 and 1983. Former Trustee Multiple Sclerosis Society of Cincinnati. Member Advisory Board Citizens Against Substance Abuse.
Office: 1000 Main Street, Room 560, Cincinnati 45202.
Telephone: (513) 632-8338.
Fax: (513) 632-7348

NAU, John W. *(Judge, Ohio Court of Common Pleas Noble County)*
Office: 300 Courthouse Square, Caldwell 43724-1243.
Telephone: (740) 732-4045.
Fax: (740) 732-0100

NELSON, Frederick Dickson *(Judge, Ohio Court of Common Pleas Hamilton County)*
Office: Courthouse, 1000 Main Street, Cincinnati 45202.

NEVIUS, Eugene S. *(Judge, Clark County Municipal Court)*
Office: 50 East Columbia Street, Springfield 45502.
Telephone: (937) 328-3763.
Fax: (937) 328-3755

NEWLIN, John C. *(Judge, Ohio Court of Common Pleas Champaign County)* Serves Probate and Juvenile Divisions.
Office: 200 North Main Street, Urbana 43078.
Telephone: (937) 652-2108.
Fax: (937) 652-2106

NICASTRO, Deborah J. *(Judge, Garfield Heights Municipal Court)*
Office: 5555 Turney Road, Garfield Heights 44125-3778.
Telephone: (216) 475-5045.
Fax: (216) 475-3087
E-mail address: dnicastro@garfieldhts.org

NICHOLS, Robert D. *(Judge, Ohio Court of Common Pleas Madison County)* Elected to term beginning Jan 1, 1975. Reelected 1980, 1986, 1992 and 1998. Current term expires Dec 31, 2004. Born Martins Ferry Ohio Oct 4, 1942. Episcopalian. Educated at Mount Union College B.A. 1964 and The Ohio State University College of Law J.D. 1967. Admitted to practice Ohio 1967. In legal practice London 1967-74. Judge, Madison County Court 1970-74.
Member Ohio Judicial Conference, Ohio Common Pleas Judges Association, Columbus, Madison County and Ohio State Bar Associations.
Office: One North Main Street, London 43140-0527.
Telephone: (740) 845-1781.
Fax: (740) 852-7144

NICHOLSON, John M. *(Judge, Cambridge Municipal Court)* Elected Nov 1989 to term beginning Jan 1990. Reelected Nov 1993 and Nov 1999. Current term expires Dec 2005. Born Cambridge Ohio June 6, 1953. Catholic. Educated at Yale University B.A. 1980 and Ohio Northern University J.D. 1983. Admitted to practice Ohio 1983. In legal practice Kenton 1983-85 and Cambridge 1985-89.
Assistant Prosecutor Guernsey County 1985-89. Member Guernsey County, Ohio State and American Bar Associations. Implemented (along with three other Ohio Municipal Courts) the first court mediation programs in Ohio for courts of smaller jurisdiction. Republican. Member American Red Cross, Kiwanis and Southeastern Ohio Celtic Society. Enjoys British and military history, travel, golf and skiing.
Office: 134 Southgate Parkway, Cambridge 43725.
Telephone: (740) 439-5585.
Fax: (740) 439-5666
E-mail address: jmn@cambridgeoh.com

NIEHAUS, David J. *(Judge, Ohio Court of Common Pleas Butler County)* Appointed by Governor James A. Rhodes to term beginning May 1, 1981. Elected 1982, 1984, 1986, 1992 and 1998. Current term expires Jan 2005. Formerly served Probate Division. Serves Juvenile Division. Born Hamilton Ohio March 29, 1944. Educated at The Ohio State University B.S.B.A. 1966 and

NIEHAUS, DAVID J.—*Continued*

Chase Law School of Northern Kentucky University J.D. 1971. Admitted to practice Ohio 1971. In legal practice Hamilton 1971-76 and Fairfield 1976-81. Referee, Butler County Juvenile Court 1971-81. Referee, Fairfield Municipal Court Small Claims Division 1980-81.

Member Butler County, Ohio State and American Bar Associations. With Budgets-Accounting Department Champion International Paper Company 1967-68. Probation Officer Juvenile Court 1968-71. Butler County Republican Party Executive Committee 1975-81. Member and President Board of Trustees Hamilton's German Village 1975-80 and Butler County Youth Service Bureau 1976-78. Board of Trustees The Children's Home, Hamilton 1978-80 and Catholic Social Services of Hamilton 1978-91. Board of Directors Family Services of Butler County 1982-87, Bunker Hill Haven since 1987 and Greater Hamilton Safety Council since 1992. Member St. Stephen's Parish Council 1981-84, Hamilton Community Foundation since 1987 and Mayor's Task Force on Racism 1991-95. Enjoys family activities and working on home and farm (including building and remodeling).

Office: 280 North Fair Avenue, Hamilton 45011.
Telephone: (513) 887-3313.
Fax: (513) 887-5592

NIEHAUS, Richard A. *(Judge, Ohio Court of Common Pleas Hamilton County)* Elected to term beginning April 1, 1983. Reelected 1988, 1994 and 2000. Current term expires April 1, 2007. Born Ironton Ohio Aug 23, 1944. Roman Catholic. Educated at Georgetown University A.B. in Government 1966, Chase Law School of Northern Kentucky University J.D. 1970 and University of Nevada-Reno Master's Degree 1998. Law Clerk to Hon. John Keefe, Ohio Court of Common Pleas Hamilton County 1969-70. Member Phi Alpha Delta. Admitted to practice Ohio 1970. Began legal practice Cincinnati 1970. Constable, Ohio Court of Common Pleas 1968-69. Judge, Hamilton County Municipal Court 1979-82.

Assistant City Solicitor Cincinnati 1970-77. Assistant Attorney General Ohio 1978-79. Important Decisions: State v. Taylor (probable cause to arrest) 1981; State v. Ray (ticket scalping ordinance of Cincinnati is unconstitutional); and State v. Sutorius (other acts evidence excited utterance, present condition exceptions to hearsay rule) 1997. Member American Judicature Society (Criminal Law Committee, Probation Committee Joint Session), Ohio Judges Association, American Association of Trial Judges, National Judges Association, Ohio State and American Bar Associations. Graduate The National Judicial College S.J. 1982. Instructor in Search and Seizure 1983 and Discussion Leader 1983 The National Judicial College. Member USCG Auxiliary. Recipient Superior Judicial Service Awards from Ohio Supreme Court 1980-82. Democrat. Board of Governors Salmon P. Chase College of Law Alumni 1980-82. President Georgetown University Alumni Association of Greater Cincinnati. Booth Chairman General Protestant Orphan's Home. Member Kolping Society and Don Simpson Scholarship Fund Committee. Enjoys photography and boating.

Office: 1000 Main Street, Room 520, Cincinnati 45202.
Telephone: (513) 946-5835.
Fax: (513) 946-5838

NIEMEYER, Joseph H. *(Judge, Ohio Court of Common Pleas Hancock County)*
Office: 300 South Main, Findlay 45840-3345.
Telephone: (419) 424-7008.
Fax: (419) 424-7437

NORTH, Kent L. *(Judge, Bryan Municipal Court)*
Mailing address: P.O. Box 546, Bryan 43506-1816.
Telephone: (419) 636-6939.
Fax: (419) 636-3417

NUGENT, Donald Clark *(Judge, United States District Court Northern District of Ohio)* Appointed for life by President Bill Clinton to term beginning July 5, 1995. Born Minneapolis Minnesota. Roman Catholic. Educated at Xavier University and Loyola University of Rome, Italy A.B. with honors 1970, Cleveland State University J.D. 1974 and University of Nevada M.J.S. with honors 1994. Member Delta Theta Phi. Admitted to practice Ohio 1974. In legal practice Cleveland 1974-84. Judge, Ohio Court of Common Pleas Cuyahoga County 1985-93. Judge, Ohio Court of Appeals Eighth District 1993-95.

Assistant Prosecuting Attorney Cuyahoga County 1975-84. Author "Judicial Bias" Cleveland State L. Rev. 1995. Instructor Cleveland State University 1985-99. Member Cleveland, Ohio State and Federal Bar Associations. USMC 1970-71. Democrat. Enjoys marathon running, golf and coaching.

Office: 15A U.S. Courthouse, 801 West Superior Avenue, Cleveland 44113-1842.
Telephone: (216) 357-7160.

NUNEZ, Gus *(Judge, Lorain Municipal Court)*
Office: 100 West Erie Avenue, Lorain 44052-1646.
Telephone: (440) 204-2150.
Fax: (440) 244-3458
E-mail address: Judge_Nunez@ci.lorain.oh.us

NUNNER, Michael K. *(Judge, Ohio Court of Common Pleas Harrison County)* Elected to term beginning April 18, 2003. Term expires 2009. Former Judge, Harrison County Court.
Office: 100 West Market Street, Cadiz 43907-1132.
Telephone: (740) 942-8500.

NUZUM, Milt *(Judge, Marietta Municipal Court)*
Mailing address: P.O. Box 615, Marietta 45750-1615.
Office: 301 Putnam Street, Marietta 45750.
Telephone: (740) 373-4474.
Fax: (740) 373-2547
E-mail address: judge@mariettacourt.com

O'BRIEN, Erich J. *(Judge, Sandusky Municipal Court)*
Office: 222 Meigs Street, Sandusky 44870-2889.
Telephone: (419) 627-5920.
Fax: (419) 627-5950

O'CONNOR, Mark S. *(Judge, Ohio Court of Common Pleas Logan County)* Appointed by Governor Richard F. Celeste to term beginning Aug 1, 1990. Elected Nov 1990, Nov 1992 and Nov 1998. Current term expires Dec 2004. Born Bellefontaine Ohio June 27, 1944. Roman Catholic. Educated at John Carroll University A.B. 1966 and The Ohio State University College of Law J.D. 1969. Member Alpha Sigma Nu. Admitted to practice Ohio 1969 and U.S. District Court Southern District of Ohio 1970. In legal practice Bellefontaine 1969-90.

O'CONNOR, MARK S.—*Continued*

City Prosecutor Bellefontaine 1971-73. Assistant County Prosecutor Logan County 1973-79. Important Decision: Williams v. Logan County Coop Power & Light (affidavit by plaintiff which contradicted an earlier deposition was held to be a sham; summary judgment granted to defendant) 62 Ohio Misc. 2d 196, 1991. Subcommittee Chair and Member Racial Fairness Implementation Task Force Supreme Court of Ohio. Member Ohio Common Pleas Judges Association, Logan County, Ohio State and American Bar Associations. Interests include golf, bridge and history.

Office: 101 South Main Street, Room 18, Bellefontaine 43311-3101.

Telephone: (937) 599-7260.

Fax: (937) 593-3379

E-mail address: mo'connor@co.logan.oh.us

O'CONNOR, Maureen *(Justice, Supreme Court of Ohio)*

Office: 30 East Broad Street, Third Floor, Columbus 43215.

O'DONNELL, John Peter *(Judge, Ohio Court of Common Pleas Cuyahoga County)*

Office: 1200 Ontario Street, Cleveland 44113.

O'FARRELL, Edward Emmett *(Judge, Ohio Court of Common Pleas Tuscarawas County)* Born Prairie du Chien Wisconsin June 21, 1946. Educated at Spring Hill College B.S. in Sociology 1970 and University of Notre Dame Law School J.D. 1973. Admitted to practice Ohio, U.S. District Courts Northern and Southern Districts of Ohio and U.S. Supreme Court. Former Judge, New Philadelphia Municipal Court, elected to term beginning Jan 1, 1982.

With Environmental Section Ohio Attorney General's Office 1974-75. Managing Attorney Southeastern Ohio Legal Services 1976-81. Member Executive Committee National Safety Council. Speaker Ohio Governor's Traffic Safety Conference 1982 and 1983, Wisconsin Governor's Traffic Safety Conference 1984, National Symposium St. Paul Minnesota 1984 and World Congress Chicago Illinois 1984 National Safety Council, National Highway Traffic Administration Convention Orlando Florida 1984 and Arkansas Highway Safety Conference 1984. Recipient Award for Outstanding Contribution in area of DWI from Stark County MADD 1982, Superior Judicial Service Awards from Ohio Supreme Court 1982-83 and Award for Outstanding Judicial Contribution to elimination of drunk drivers from Cuyahoga County MADD 1984. Recipient nationwide recognition for handling and sentencing those convicted for alcohol-related offenses from Cable Newsnetwork, Paul Harvey News Commentary, Washington Post, Los Angeles Times, Detroit Free Press, ABC-Radio Network, RKO-Radio Network, Cleveland Plain Dealer, Columbus Dispatch, Akron Beacon Journal, Canton Repository, Ohio Magazine, Wall Street Journal, Ladies Home Journal and Phil Donahue Show.

Office: 101 East High Avenue #202, New Philadelphia 44663-2599.

Telephone: (330) 365-3213.

Fax: (330) 602-8811

E-mail address: ofarrell@co.tuscarawas.oh.us

OLD, Thomas L. *(Judge, Newton Falls Municipal Court)* Elected to term beginning Jan 1, 1988. Reelected 1993 and 1999. Current term expires Dec 31, 2005. Born Youngstown Ohio Aug 24, 1946. Congregationalist. Educated at Mount Union College B.A. 1968 and University of Cincinnati J.D. 1973. Admitted to practice Ohio 1973 and U.S. District Court Northern District of Ohio 1976. In legal practice Warren 1973-87. Referee, Warren Municipal Court 1977-87.

Law Director Newton Falls 1978-87. Member Trumbull County and Ohio State Bar Associations. Sergeant U.S. Army 1968-70. Democrat. Board of Trustees First Congregational Church. Coach high school soccer. Former Board member Trumbull County Family Service Association and Children's Rehabilitation Center. Past President Kiwanis. Enjoys golf and skiing.

Office: 19 North Canal Street, Newton Falls 44444-1302.

Telephone: (330) 872-0302.

Fax: (330) 872-3899

E-mail address: judgetlo@aol.com

OLIVER, Solomon, Jr. *(Judge, United States District Court Northern District of Ohio)* Appointed for life by President Bill Clinton March 9, 1994 to term beginning May 9, 1994. Born Bessemer Alabama July 20, 1947. Educated at College of Wooster B.A. 1969, New York University School of Law J.D. 1972 and Case Western Reserve University M.A. 1974. Law Clerk to Hon. William Hastie, U.S. Court of Appeals Third Circuit 1975-76. In legal practice Wooster 1982-94.

Assistant U.S. Attorney 1976-82 and Special Assistant U.S. Attorney 1982-85 Northern District of Ohio.

Office: 17A U.S. Courthouse, 801 West Superior Avenue, Cleveland 44113-1838.

Telephone: (216) 357-7171.

O'MALLEY, Kathleen *(Judge, Ohio Court of Common Pleas Cuyahoga County)* Serves Domestic Relations Division.

Office: One Lakeside Avenue, Cleveland 44113-1082.

Telephone: (216) 443-8815.

Fax: (216) 698-2207

O'MALLEY, Kathleen McDonald *(Judge, United States District Court Northern District of Ohio)* Appointed for life by President Bill Clinton to term beginning 1994. Educated at Kenyon College magna cum laude 1979 and Case Western Reserve University School of Law J.D. 1982. Staff member Case Western Reserve Law Review. Law Clerk to Hon. Nathaniel R. Jones, U.S. Court of Appeals Sixth Circuit. Member Phi Beta Kappa and Order of the Coif. In legal practice 1983-91.

Chief Counsel to Attorney General 1991-92. First Assistant Attorney General and Chief of Staff to Attorney General 1992-94.

Office: 16A U.S. Courthouse, 801 West Superior Avenue, Cleveland 44113-1840.

Telephone: (216) 357-7240.

O'MALLEY, Michael E. *(Judge, Putnam County Court)*

Office: 245 East Main Street, Suite 303, Ottawa 45875-1968.

Telephone: (419) 523-3110.

Fax: (419) 523-5284

E-mail address: omal@bright.net

O'NEILL, Deborah (Piperni) *(Judge, Ohio Court of Common Pleas Franklin County)* Elected Nov 3, 1992 to term beginning Jan 7, 1993. Reelected 1998, current

O'NEILL, DEBORAH (PIPERNI) *—Continued*
term expires Jan 2005. Born Rochester New York. Catholic. Educated at St. John Fisher College B.S. with honors 1977 and University of Dayton School of Law J.D. 1980. Member Phi Alpha Delta. Admitted to practice Ohio 1980, U.S. District Court 1981, U.S. Court of Appeals Sixth Circuit 1981, U.S. Supreme Court 1983 and New York 1986. In legal practice Columbus Ohio 1980-92.

Member American Judges Association, Columbus and Ohio State Bar Associations. Attended Ohio Judicial College CLE. Board of Directors Ohio Hunger Task Force and March of Dimes. Hobbies include snow skiing, ice skating, physical fitness, reading and activities with children.

Office: 369 South High Street #9A, Columbus 43215-4554.
Telephone: (614) 462-3664.
Fax: (614) 462-3476

O'NEILL, Richard *(Judge, Ohio Court of Common Pleas Clark County)*
Office: Courthouse, Third Floor, 101 North Limestone, Springfield 45502-1120.
Telephone: (937) 328-2467.
Fax: (937) 328-2463

O'NEILL, William M. *(Judge, Ohio Court of Appeals Eleventh District)*
Office: 111 High Street N.E., Warren 44481.
Telephone: (330) 675-7006.
Fax: (330) 675-2655
E-mail address: wmoneill-@11thappeal.co.trumbull.oh.us

ONEY, Patricia Shanes *(Judge, Ohio Court of Common Pleas Butler County)* Born Welsh West Virginia May 30, 1942. Baptist. Educated at University of Cincinnati B.S. 1965 J.D. 1975 and University of Kentucky M.S. 1970. Member Phi Alpha Delta. Admitted to practice Ohio 1975 and U.S. District Court Western District of Ohio 1975. In legal practice Hamilton 1981-99. Former Judge, Butler County Court, appointed by Governor George V. Voinovich to term beginning Jan 14, 1993.

With Prosecutor's Office Green County 1975. With Public Defender's Office Montgomery County 1976-79. Former Member Municipal-County Judges of Ohio, Inc. and Ohio Trial Lawyers Association. Member Ohio Judicial Conference, Ohio Common Pleas Judges Association, Cincinnati (Communication Committee 1990), Middletown, Butler County and Ohio State Bar Associations. Volunteer for victim questions Oxford Crisis Center 1982-89 and YWCA Battered Persons 1982-90. Advisory Board Safe Program 1989 and CAP (Butler County Child Abuse Prevention Project). Member Reily Boosters (Secretary 1989-91), Oxford Business and Professional Women's Association 1990-91, Hamilton Chamber of Commerce 1990-2002, Middletown Chamber of Commerce, Oxford Chamber of Commerce, Fairfield Chamber of Commerce, Southeast Butler County Chamber of Commerce, Butler County Farm Bureau, Butler County Historical Society, Altrusa (service group promoting education, patriotism and business), Ohio Business and Professional Women's Association and Butler County Advisory Board on Domestic Violence. Enjoys scuba diving and gardening.

Office: Government Services Center, 315 High Street, Third Floor, Hamilton 45011.
Telephone: (513) 887-3286.
Fax: (513) 887-5646
E-mail address: oneyps@butlercountyohio.org

OSBORN, Thomas E. *(Judge, Upper Sandusky Municipal Court)*
Office: 119 North Seventh Street, Upper Sandusky 43351-1336.
Telephone: (419) 294-3809.
Fax: (419) 209-0474

OSOWIK, Thomas J. *(Judge, Toledo Municipal Court)*
Office: 555 North Erie Street, Toledo 43624.
Telephone: (419) 245-1954.
Fax: (419) 245-1802
E-mail address: thomas.osowik@noris.org

OSTERUD, S. Dwight *(Judge, Perrysburg Municipal Court)* Acting Judge 1982-89. Elected Judge Nov 7, 1989 to term beginning Jan 1, 1990. Reelected 1995 and 2001. Current term expires Dec 31, 2007. Born Toledo Ohio Aug 29, 1944. Lutheran. Educated at Washburn University 1962-64, University of Toledo B.Ed. 1970 J.D. 1974. Admitted to practice Ohio 1974 and U.S. District Court Northern District of Ohio 1976. In legal practice Toledo 1974-89.

Co-author "Planning New or Redesigning Court Facilities" *The Court Manager.* Mediator Toledo Municipal Court 1978-89. Fellow Ohio State Bar Foundation. Member Association of Municipal-County Judges of Ohio, Inc., Toledo, Lucas County, Wood County and Ohio State Bar Associations. Attended Intermediate Jurisdiction course The National Judicial College 1990. Instructor "This is the People's Court" seminar for magistrates Ohio Judicial College. Recipient Governor's Award for Community Service 1990 and Community Appreciation Award from Wood County Council of Alcoholism and Drug Abuse 1992. Inducted into Toledo-Libbey High School Hall of Fame. Member Executive Committee Wood County Democratic Party 1984-89. President Wood County Democratic Club 1985-87 and Perrysburg Democratic Club 1988. Former Board Member Perrysburg Alternative to Substance Abuse. Advisor and Institution Representative for Law and Government Explorer Post 2306. Judge Mock Trial Competition Ohio Center for Law-Related Education. Member Perrysburg Exchange Club (President 1990) and Perrysburg Rotary Club.

Office: 300 Walnut, Perrysburg 43551.
Telephone: (419) 872-7915.
Fax: (419) 872-7947
E-mail address: sdosterud@ci.perrysburg.oh.us

OVINGTON, Sharon L. *(Magistrate Judge, United States District Court Southern District of Ohio)* Appointed by U.S. District Court judges to term beginning Oct 28, 2002.
Office: 810 Federal Building, 200 West Second Street, Dayton 45402.
Telephone: (937) 512-1570.

PAINTER, Mark P. *(Judge, Ohio Court of Appeals First District)* Elected 1994 to term beginning 1995. Reelected 2000, current term expires Feb 8, 2007. Born

PAINTER, MARK P.—*Continued*

Cincinnati Ohio April 6, 1947. Educated at University of Cincinnati B.A. 1970 J.D. 1973. Admitted to practice Ohio 1973, U.S. District Court Southern District of Ohio 1973 and U.S. Supreme Court 1980. Began legal practice Cincinnati 1973. Judge, Hamilton County Municipal Court March 15, 1982 to 1995.

Author more than two-hundred and sixty opinions on criminal, tort, contract and other areas of law Ohio Official Reports and N.E. 2d 1982-2002; *Ohio Driving Under the Influence Law* Westgroup 11th ed. 2002 12th ed. 2003; and *The Legal Writer: 30 Rules for the Art of Legal Writing* 2002. Co-author *Ohio Driving Under the Influence Law* Westgroup 1988, 2nd ed. 1990, 3rd ed. 1994, 4th ed. 1995, 5th ed. 1996, 6th ed. 1997, 7th ed. 1998, 9th ed. 2000 and 10th ed. 2001. Lecturer on Business Law 1979-80 and Adjunct Professor of Law since 1990 University of Cincinnati. Member Ohio Supreme Court Board of Commissioners on Grievances and Discipline 1993-96. Master of the Bench Potter Stewart Inn of Court since 1986. Member American Judges Association, Cincinnati (Executive Committee 1988-90), Ohio State and American Bar Associations. Lecturer at ninety-five seminars. Recipient Superior Judicial Service Awards from Ohio Supreme Court 1982-85. Member Republican Central Committee 1972-82. President Eleventh Ward Republican Club 1975-82. Director Citizens School Committee 1974-76. Vice President M. J. Brueggeman Memorial Fund 1982-93. Trustee Cincinnati Free Store/Food Bank 1985-90 and Friends of the William Howard Taft Birthplace since 2001. Member Cincinnati Historical Society and Bankers Club. Interested in history.

Office: 230 East Ninth Street, Twelfth Floor, Cincinnati 45202-1287.
Telephone: (513) 946-3444.
Fax: (513) 946-3411
E-mail: mpainter@cms.hamilton-co.org

PANIOTO, Ronald A. *(Judge, Ohio Court of Common Pleas Hamilton County)* Elected to term beginning Jan 5, 1983. Reelected 1986, 1992 and 1998. Current term expires Dec 2004. Serves Domestic Relations Division. Born Cincinnati Ohio Dec 18, 1935. Catholic. Educated at University of Cincinnati B.A. 1963 and Salmon P. Chase College of Law (now Chase Law School of Northern Kentucky University) J.D. 1967. Law Clerk to Hon. Ferd Bader, Ohio Court of Common Pleas Hamilton County 1958-63. Admitted to practice Ohio 1967. Began legal practice Cincinnati 1967. Judge, Hamilton County Municipal Court 1975-82, appointed by Governor James A. Rhodes.

Assistant County Prosecutor Hamilton County 1968-75. Member Lawyer's Club of Cincinnati, American Judges Association, Cincinnati, Ohio State and American Bar Associations. Republican. Administrative Assistant to Congressman Donald Clancy 1967-68. Member Wyoming Golf Club, Queen City Club, DaVinci University Club, United Italian Societies of Greater Cincinnati (President) and Southern Ohio Dog and Game Protective Association. Enjoys woodworking and all sports.

Office: 800 Broadway, Room 225, Cincinnati 45202.
Telephone: (513) 946-9020.
Fax: (513) 946-8030

PARKER, George *(Judge, Mason Municipal Court)*
Office: 202 West Main Street, Mason 45040-1620.
Telephone: (513) 398-8901.
Fax: (513) 398-0190

PARKS, Martin O. *(Judge, Ohio Court of Common Pleas Lake County)* Elected Nov 1986 to term beginning Dec 24, 1986. Reelected Nov 1988, 1994 and 2000. Current term expires Jan 2007. Born Cleveland Ohio Jan 13, 1942. Catholic. Educated at John Carroll University B.S. 1964 and Case Western Reserve University J.D. 1968. Member Phi Delta Phi. Admitted to practice Ohio 1968, U.S. District Northern District of Ohio 1969 and U.S. Supreme Court 1977. In legal practice Painesville 1968-86.

Important Decision: State of Ohio v. Jeffrey Don Lundgren (leader of cult that killed a family of five) 90 CR 015 Lake County 1990. Instructor in Business Law Lakeland Community College 1975. Member Ohio Common Pleas Judges Association, American Judges Association and Lake County Bar Association. Member Lake County School Board 1976-77 and Painesville Township Local Board of Education 1982-86.

Mailing address: P.O. Box 490, Painesville 44077.
Office: 47 North Park Place, Painesville 44077.
Telephone: (440) 350-2736.
Fax: (440) 350-2780

PARROTT, Richard E. *(Judge, Ohio Court of Common Pleas Union County)* Assumed office 1991. Born Delaware Ohio May 26, 1934. Methodist. Educated at Ohio Northern University B.A. 1959 J.D. 1960. Member Phi Alpha Delta. Admitted to practice Ohio 1960, U.S. District Court Southern District of Ohio 1961 and U.S. Supreme Court 1996. Began legal practice Marysville 1960. Judge, Marysville Municipal Court Jan 1, 1982 to Feb 8, 1991.

Prosecuting Attorney Union County 1965-72. Member William Howard Taft American Inns of Court, American Judges Association, Union County, Ohio State and American Bar Associations. USAF 1955-57.

Mailing address: P.O. Box 723, Marysville 43040.
Office: Courthouse, Marysville 43040.
Telephone: (937) 645-3015.
Fax: (937) 645-3149
E-mail address: parrott@urec.net

PATER, Charles Lloyd *(Judge, Ohio Court of Common Pleas Butler County)*
Office: 315 High Street, Third Floor, Hamilton 45011.

PAYNE, C. David *(Judge, Ohio Court of Common Pleas Lawrence County)* Appointed by Governor George V. Voinovich Oct 7, 1993. Elected 1994, 1996 and 2002. Current term expires 2009. Serves Probate and Juvenile Divisions. Born Ironton Ohio June 2, 1957. Educated at University of Kentucky B.S. 1978 and Capital University J.D. 1986. Admitted to practice Ohio 1986. Began legal practice Ironton 1986.

Assistant Prosecuting Attorney 1986-88 and 1993. City Attorney Ironton 1991-93.

Office: Courthouse, One Veterans Square, Ironton 45638-1585.
Telephone: (740) 533-4372.
Fax: (740) 533-4412

PAYTON, Jeff *(Judge, Mansfield Municipal Court)*
Office: 30 North Diamond, Mansfield 44902-4702.
Telephone: (419) 755-9615.
Fax: (419) 755-9650

PEPPLE, Frederick D. *(Judge, Ohio Court of Common Pleas Auglaize County)* Elected to term beginning Jan 9, 1987. Reelected 1992 and 1998. Current term expires Jan 2005. Born Bluffton Ohio March 18, 1954. Educated at Bowling Green State University B.S.B.A. 1975 and Ohio Northern University J.D. 1978. Admitted to practice Ohio 1978 and U.S. District Court Northern District of Ohio 1978.

Member Auglaize County (Vice President 1988, President 1989) and Ohio State Bar Associations. Faculty Member National Conference on Court-Related Needs of the Elderly and Persons with Disabilities American Bar Association 1991. Named Distinguished Alumnus by College of Business Administration Bowling Green State University 1996.

Office: 201 Willipie Street, Suite 217, Wapakoneta 45895-1994.
Telephone: (419) 738-3118.
Fax: (419) 738-7953

PERELMAN, David S. *(Recalled Magistrate Judge, United States District Court Northern District of Ohio)* Appointed Magistrate Judge by U.S. District Court judges to term beginning Sept 14, 1979. Appointed Recalled Magistrate Judge July 13, 1999 by the Judicial Council of the Sixth Circuit. Educated at Case Western Reserve University 1958.

Office: 11A U.S. Courthouse, 801 West Superior Avenue, Cleveland 44113-1844.
Telephone: (216) 357-7140.

PERK, Ralph J., Jr. *(Judge, Cleveland Municipal Court)* Appointed by Governor George V. Voinovich to term beginning Feb 28, 1991. Elected Nov 3, 1991 and Nov 1997. Current term expires Dec 31, 2003. Educated at The Ohio State University B.S.B.A. 1968 and Cleveland State University J.D. 1983. Member Delta Theta Phi. Admitted to practice Ohio 1983, U.S. District Court Northern District of Ohio 1984 and U.S. Court of Appeals Sixth Circuit 1988. In legal practice Cleveland 1983-91.

Councilman City of Cleveland 1968-78. Member Justinian Forum, Northern Ohio Municipal Judges Association, American Judges Association, Cleveland, Cuyahoga County and Ohio State Bar Associations. First Lieutenant U.S. Army ROTC 1968-76. Member and President Cleveland Board of Education 1984-91.

Mailing address: P.O. Box 94894, Cleveland 44101-4894.
Office: 1200 Ontario Street, Cleveland 44113.
Telephone: (216) 664-4982.
Fax: (216) 664-4977

PERLMAN, Burton *(Recalled Judge, United States Bankruptcy Court Southern District of Ohio)* Appointed Judge by U.S. District Court judges to term beginning July 22, 1976. Reappointed to subsequent terms. Chief Judge 1986-93. Appointed Recalled Judge by the Judicial Council of the Sixth Circuit 1993. Reappointed 1997. Born Dec 17, 1924. Educated at Yale University B.E. in Metallurgical Engineering 1944 M.E. in Metallurgy 1947 and University of Michigan LL.B. 1952. Admitted to practice Connecticut 1952, New York 1953, U.S. Courts of Appeals Second 1953 and Sixth 1959 Circuits, U.S. Patent and Trademark Office 1954, Ohio 1959, U.S. District Courts Southern 1954 and Eastern 1954 Districts of New York and Southern District of Ohio 1959. In legal practice New York City 1952-58 and Cincinnati Ohio 1958-71. Magistrate, U.S. District Court Southern District of Ohio 1971-76.

Adjunct Professor University of Cincinnati Law School since 1976. Member Cincinnati, Federal and American Bar Associations. T-4 U.S. Army 1944-46. Metallurgical Engineer 1947-49.

Office: Atrium Two, Suite 800, 221 East Fourth Street, Cincinnati 45202.
Telephone: (513) 684-2572.

PETERS, James W. *(Judge, Monroe County Court)* Elected to term beginning Jan 1, 1989. Reelected 1994 and 2000. Current term expires Dec 31, 2006. Born Zanesville Ohio Sept 7, 1954. Educated at The Ohio State University B.A. 1976 and Capital University J.D. 1980. Admitted to practice Ohio 1980, West Virginia 1983, U.S. District Courts Northern and Southern Districts of Ohio and Northern and Southern Districts of West Virginia and U.S. Courts of Appeal Fourth and Sixth Circuits. In legal practice Woodsfield Ohio since 1980.

Assistant Prosecuting Attorney Wetzel County West Virginia 1983-88. Member Association of Municipal/County Judges of Ohio, Inc.

Office: 107 West Court Street, Woodsfield 43793.
Telephone: (740) 472-1681.
Fax: (740) 472-1718
E-mail address: judgejp1@1st.net
Website address: www.jjplaw.com

PETREE, Charles R. *(Judge, Ohio Court of Appeals Tenth District)* Elected to term beginning Feb 9, 1991. Reelected 1996 and 2002. Current term expires Feb 8, 2009. Born Columbus Ohio Aug 19, 1933. Protestant. Educated at The Ohio State University B.A. 1955 LL.B. 1960 replaced by J.D. Member Phi Delta Phi. Admitted to practice Ohio 1960, U.S. District Court Southern District of Ohio 1962 and U.S. Supreme Court 1992. In legal practice Columbus 1960-83. Judge, Franklin County Municipal Court 1983-84. Judge, Ohio Court of Common Pleas Franklin County 1984-91.

Office: 373 South High Street, 24th Floor, Columbus 43215-6313.
Telephone: (614) 462-4049.
Fax: (614) 462-7249
E-mail address: crpetree@co.franklin.oh.us

PETROFF, Donald Z. *(Judge, Oregon Municipal Court)* Elected to term beginning Jan 1, 1982. Reelected 1987, 1993 and 1999. Current term expires Dec 31, 2005. Born Toledo Ohio June 5, 1938. Christian. Educated at University of Toledo B.B.A. 1961 J.D. 1967. Member Phi Alpha Delta and Sigma Phi Epsilon. Admitted to practice Ohio 1967. Began legal practice Toledo 1967.

Member Ohio Judicial Conference, American Judges Association, Toledo and Ohio State Bar Associations. First Lieutenant U.S. Army Artillery 1961-64. Mayor City of Oregon 1971-73.

Office: 5330 Seaman Road, Oregon 43616.
Telephone: (419) 698-7009.
Fax: (419) 698-7013
E-mail address: court@ci.oregon.oh.us

PFEIFER, Paul E. *(Justice, Supreme Court of Ohio)* Elected Nov 1992 to term beginning Jan 3, 1993. Reelected 1998, current term expires Jan 2005. Born Bucyrus Ohio Oct 15, 1942. Protestant. Educated at The Ohio State University B.A. 1963 J.D. 1966. Admitted to practice Ohio 1967. In legal practice 1976-92.

Assistant Attorney General Ohio 1967-70. Assistant Prosecuting Attorney Crawford County 1973-76. Member House of Representatives 1971-72 and State Senate 1976-92 (Minority Floor Leader 1983-84, Assistant President pro tem 1985-86, Chairman Senate Judiciary Committee) Ohio. Member Grace United Methodist Church and Bucyrus Rotary Club.

Office: 30 East Broad Street, Third Floor, Columbus 43226-0419.
Telephone: (614) 466-2523.
Fax: (614) 466-6139
E-mail address: pfeiferp@sconet.state.oh.us

PFEIFFER, Beverly Y. *(Judge, Ohio Court of Common Pleas Franklin County)*
Office: 369 South High Street, #8C, Columbus 43215-4554.
Telephone: (614) 462-3811.
Fax: (614) 462-2464
E-mail address: beverly_pfeiffer@fccourts.org

PIANKA, Raymond L. *(Judge, Cleveland Municipal Court)*
Mailing address: P.O. Box 94894, Cleveland 44101-4894.
Office: 1200 Ontario Street, Cleveland 44113.
Telephone: (216) 664-4989.
Fax: (216) 664-4283

PICKEN, R. David *(Judge, Madison County Municipal Court)* Elected to term beginning Jan 1, 1994. Reelected 1999, current term expires Dec 31, 2005. Born Lorain Ohio Nov 2, 1945. Educated at Allegheny College B.A. 1967 and Case Western Reserve University School of Law J.D. 1974. Admitted to practice Ohio 1974 and U.S. District Court Southern District of Ohio 1975. In legal practice West Jefferson 1974-93.

Prosecutor Madison County Dec 1975. Member 1975-92 and President 1989 Ohio Prosecutor's Association. Member Madison County Bar Association. Chairman Madison County Republican Party 1986-92.

Mailing address: P.O. Box 646, London 43140-0646.
Telephone: (740) 852-1669.
Fax: (740) 852-0812

PICKREL, John S. *(Judge, Dayton Municipal Court)* Appointed by Governor Richard F. Celeste to term beginning Nov 21, 1984. Elected 1985, 1991 and 1997. Current term expires Jan 2004. Born Dayton Ohio April 7, 1945. Catholic. Educated at University of Dayton B.A. 1967 and The Ohio State University College of Law J.D. 1970. Admitted to practice Ohio 1970 and U.S. District Court Southern District of Ohio 1971. In legal practice Dayton 1970-84.

Member Municipal-County Judges of Ohio, Inc., American Judicature Society, American Judges Association, Dayton and Ohio State Bar Associations. Democrat. Member Montgomery County Democratic Club. Board member Dayton Mental Health Center. Member Downtown Dayton Kiwanis.

Office: 301 West Third Street, Dayton 45402-1424.
Telephone: (937) 333-4364.
Fax: (937) 333-5079
E-mail address: john.pickrel@ci.dayton.oh.us

PIERCE, C. Fenning *(Judge, Ohio Court of Common Pleas Coshocton County)* Appointed by Governor James A. Rhodes to term beginning Jan 2, 1981. Elected 1985, 1990, 1996 and 2002. Current term expires Feb 8, 2009. Serves Probate and Juvenile Divisions. Born Coshocton Ohio April 12, 1947. United Methodist. Educated at Ohio Wesleyan University B.A. in Economics 1969 and Vanderbilt University School of Law J.D. 1973. Admitted to practice Ohio 1973 and U.S. District Court Southern District of Ohio 1975. Began legal practice Columbus 1973. In legal practice Coshocton.

Former Member Ohio Criminal Sentencing Commission, Coshocton County and Ohio State Bar Associations. Past President Roscoe Village Foundation. Secretary Schooler Family Foundation. Board Member Echoing Hills Village Inc. for the Disabled and Salvation Army. Enjoys physical fitness and gourmet cooking.

Office: 426 Main Street, Coshocton 43812.
Telephone: (740) 622-1837.
Fax: (740) 623-6514

PIERGIES, James D. *(Judge, Montgomery County Court)* Elected 1994. Reelected to subsequent term.
Office: 6111 Taylorsville Road, Huber Heights 45424.
Telephone: (937) 225-5891.
Fax: (937) 496-7236
E-mail address: piergiesj@montcnty.org

PIETRYKOWSKI, Mark L. *(Judge, Ohio Court of Appeals Sixth District)*
Office: 800 Jackson Street, Toledo 43624.
Telephone: (419) 213-4755.
Fax: (419) 213-4844
E-mail address: pietry@co.lucas.oh.us

PIKE, C. Ashley *(Judge, Ohio Court of Common Pleas Columbiana County)* Elected Nov 6, 1990 to term beginning Feb 9, 1991. Reelected 1996 and Nov 2000. Current term expires Dec 31, 2006. Served Probate Division 1991-2000. Born Salem Ohio Jan 13, 1950. Educated at College of Wooster B.A. with honors 1972 and University of Akron J.D. 1975. Admitted to practice Ohio 1975, U.S. Supreme Court 1990 and U.S. District Court Northern District of Ohio. Judge, Columbiana County Court 1983-88.

Assistant Prosecuting Attorney 1976 and Assistant Public Defender 1977-79 Columbiana County. Member Columbiana County and Ohio State Bar Associations. Member First United Methodist Churck, Elks and Big Brothers/Big Sisters.

Office: Courthouse, Second Floor, 105 South Market Street, Lisbon 44432-1298.
Telephone: (330) 424-7777.
Fax: (330) 424-1379
E-mail address: judgepike@yahoo.com

PISANO, Ralph C., Jr. *(Judge, Huron Municipal Court)*
Office: 417 Main Street, Huron 44839.
Telephone: (419) 433-5430.
Fax: (419) 433-5120

PITTMAN, Laurie J. *(Judge, Portage County Municipal Court)*
Office: 203 West Main Street, Ravenna 44266.
Telephone: (330) 297-4278.
Fax: (330) 297-4283

POKORNY, Thomas J. *(Judge, Ohio Court of Common Pleas Cuyahoga County)*
Office: 1200 Ontario Street, Cleveland 44113.
Telephone: (216) 443-8728.
Fax: (216) 348-4038

POLLEX, Robert C. *(Judge, Ohio Court of Common Pleas Wood County)* Elected Nov 1984 to term beginning Feb 9, 1985. Reelected Nov 1990, Nov 1996 and 2002. Current term expires Feb 2009. Born Toledo Ohio Sept 12, 1947. Lutheran. Educated at University of Toledo B.S. in Physics 1969 J.D. 1973. Admitted to practice Ohio 1974. In legal practice Bowling Green 1974-80 and Perrysburg 1981-84.

Public Defender 1978-79 and Assistant Prosecuting Attorney 1980-84 Wood County. Municipal Attorney Village of Walbridge 1978-85, Elmore 1980-85, Bradner 1983-85 and Genoa 1984. Important Decision: In re Ruiz 27 Ohio Misc. 2d 31, 1986. Member The Association of Trial Lawyers of America and Wood County Bar Association.
Office: One Courthouse Square, Bowling Green 43402-2427.
Telephone: (419) 354-9210.
Fax: (419) 354-7626
E-mail address: rpollex@co.wood.oh.us

POLLITT, H. William, Jr. *(Judge, Franklin County Municipal Court)*
Office: 375 South High Street, #12A, Columbus 43215.
Telephone: (614) 645-7745.
Fax: (614) 645-7185
E-mail address: william_pollitt@fccourts.org

POLSTER, Dan Aaron *(Judge, United States District Court Northern District of Ohio)* Appointed for life by President Bill Clinton to term beginning Aug 10, 1998. Born Shaker Heights Ohio Dec 6, 1951. Jewish. Educated at Harvard University A.B. 1972 J.D. 1976.

Trial Attorney Antitrust Division U.S. Department of Justice 1976-82. Assistant U.S. Attorney Economic Crimes Division Northern District of Ohio 1982-98. Member Cleveland and Federal Bar Associations.
Office: 18B U.S. Courthouse, 801 West Superior Avenue, Cleveland 44113-1837.
Telephone: (216) 357-7190.

PONTIOUS, Victor D., Jr. *(Judge, Ohio Court of Common Pleas Fayette County)*
Office: 110 East Court Street, Washington Court House 43160.
Telephone: (740) 335-4750.
Fax: (740) 333-3522.

POTTER, John W. *(Senior Judge, United States District Court Northern District of Ohio)* Appointed for life by President Ronald Reagan to term beginning July 9, 1982. Assumed Senior status, serves by assignment. Born Toledo Ohio Oct 25, 1918. Protestant. Educated at University of Toledo Ph.B. with honors 1940 and University of Michigan J.D. 1946. Senior Editor University of Michigan Law Review. Member Phi Kappa Phi. Admitted to practice Ohio 1947, U.S. District Court Northern District of Ohio 1950 and U.S. Court of Appeals Sixth Circuit 1962. In legal practice Toledo 1947-69. Judge 1969-82 and Presiding Judge 1971-75 and 1977-81, Ohio Court of Appeals Sixth District.

Assistant Attorney General 1968-69. Fellow American Bar Foundation. Member American Judicature Society, Sixth Circuit District Judges Association, Federal Judges Association, Toledo (Executive Committee 1962-64), Lucas County, Ohio State and American Bar Associations. Attended New York University Law School Appellate Judges Seminar and numerous state and federal conferences and workshops. Recipient Leadership Award from Toledo Building Congress 1965 and Toledo Board of Realtors 1967 and Resolution of Recognition Award from Ohio House of Representatives. Named Outstanding Alumnus of University of Toledo 1966. Cited by Ohio Supreme Court for Outstanding Judicial Service 1973, by Kiwanis Club of Toledo for Distinguished Service as Mayor and by Toledo Bar Association for Recognition of Ten Years of Distinguished Service 1992. Recipient Award for Outstanding Research or Service in Law or Government from Ohio State Bar Foundation 1995. Captain U.S. Army Field Artillery ETO 1942-46. Recipient four Battle Stars and Bronze Star. Republican. Mayor Toledo 1961-67. Past President Ohio Municipal League. Former Board Member Cummings School and Conlon School. Past President and Member Kiwanis Club of West Toledo, University of Toledo Alumni Association and Committee on Relations with Toledo Spain. Former Associate Public Member Toledo Labor Management Committee. Former Board Member Toledo Zoological Society. Former Member Toledo Area Chamber of Commerce (Vice President 1973-74). Honorary Chairman Toledo Festival of Arts 1980. Member and Honorary Board Member Toledo Opera Association. Member Epworth United Methodist Church (Former Trustee), Old Newsboys Goodfellows Association, National Trust for Historic Preservation, Toledo Symphony Orchestra Association, Toledo Museum of Art and Maumee Valley Historical Society. Enjoys traveling and reading.
Office: 210 U.S. Courthouse, 1716 Spielbusch Avenue, Toledo 43624.
Telephone: (419) 259-6475.

POULOS, John A. *(Judge, Canton Municipal Court)*
Office: 218 Cleveland Avenue S.W., Canton 44702.
Telephone: (330) 489-3288.
Fax: (330) 471-8860

POWELL, Larry Scott *(Judge, Ohio Court of Common Pleas Meigs County)* Serves Probate and Juvenile Divisions.
Office: 100 East Second Street, Pomeroy 45769.

POWELL, Michael E. *(Judge, Ohio Court of Common Pleas Warren County)* Appointed by Governor Bob Taft to term beginning April 27, 2000. Elected Nov 8, 2000 and Nov 5, 2002. Current term expires Feb 2009. Serves Probate and Juvenile Divisions. Born Hamilton Ohio Nov 20, 1953. Educated at Ohio Northern University B.A. 1976 J.D. 1979. Admitted to practice Ohio 1979, U.S. District Court Southern District of Ohio 1986, U.S. Court of Appeals Sixth Circuit 1986 and U.S. Supreme Court 1987.

Assistant Prosecutor Warren County 1979-2000. Solicitor Village of Morrow 1987-2000. Member Warren County and Ohio State Bar Associations. Past President Lebanon Kiwanis. Advisory Board and Former Vice Chairman Warren County Salvation Army.
Office: 570 Justice Drive, Lebanon 45036.
Telephone: (513) 695-1245.

POWELL, MICHAEL E.—*Continued*
Fax: (513) 695-2345
E-mail address: poweme@co.warren.oh.us

POWELL, Stephen W. *(Judge, Ohio Court of Appeals Twelfth District)* Elected Nov 8, 1994 to term beginning 1995. Reelected Nov 7, 2000, current term expires 2007. Born Hamilton Ohio Jan 25, 1955. Presbyterian. Educated at Heidelberg College B.A. 1977 and University of Dayton School of Law J.D. 1981. Admitted to practice Ohio 1981 and U.S. District Court Southern District of Ohio 1982. In legal practice West Chester 1981-83 and Hamilton 1983-91. Referee, Probate, Juvenile and Domestic Relations Divisions Ohio Court of Common Pleas Butler County 1984-88. Judge, Butler County Court 1988-90. Judge, Probate Division Ohio Court of Common Pleas Butler County 1990-94.

Member Board of Township Trustees Union Township 1979-88. Member Judicial Conference Legislative Committee, Association of Municipal-County Judges of Ohio, Inc., Ohio Association of Probate Judges, Ohio Common Pleas Judges Association, National College of Probate Judges, American Judicature Society, Cincinnati, Butler County (Member Probate/Estate Planning Committee), Ohio State (Estate Planning Section) and American (Committee on Court Technology Judicial Administration Division, Young Lawyers Division, Section of Family Law) Bar Associations. Faculty Member Ohio Judicial College since 1997. Listed in *Who's Who Among Young American Professionals* 92nd edition, *Who's Who in American Law* since 1990, *Who's Who in America* since 1990 and *Who's Who in the World* 2000. Republican. Secretary Butler County Republican Central Committee 1980-88. Board Member United Way 1985-91. Kentucky Colonel 1989. Century Member Boy Scouts of America since 1990. Member Library Committee and Parks Committee Union Township and Elder-West Chester Presbyterian Church. Enjoys woodwork.

Mailing address: P.O. Box 1009, Middletown 45042-1901.
Telephone: (513) 425-6609.
Fax: (513) 425-8751
E-mail address: stephen@twelfth.courts.state.oh.us

POWERS, Dallas P. *(Judge, Warren County Court)* Elected Nov 8, 1988 to term beginning Jan 1, 1989. Reelected Nov 8, 1994 and 2000. Current term expires Dec 31, 2006. Currently serves as Administrative Judge. Born Mariba Kentucky Sept 11, 1934. Educated at University of Dayton B.S. 1957 and Chase Law School of Northern Kentucky University J.D. 1968. Admitted to practice Ohio 1968, U.S. District Court Southern District of Ohio 1971 and U.S. Tax Court 1978. Began legal practice Franklin 1970.

Member Warren County, Ohio State, Federal and American Bar Associations. First Lieutenant U.S. Army and Ohio National Guard 1958-68.

Office: 550 Justice Drive, Lebanon 45036-2397.
Telephone: (513) 695-1370.
Fax: (513) 695-2990
E-mail address: poweda@co.warren.oh.us

PREISSE, Dana S. *(Judge, Ohio Court of Common Pleas Franklin County)* Serves Domestic Relations and Juvenile Divisions.

Office: 373 South High Street, Sixth Floor, Columbus 43215-4520.
Telephone: (614) 462-5775.
Fax: (614) 462-7440
E-mail address: dana_preisse@fccourts.org

PRESTON, Vernon L. *(Judge, Findlay Municipal Court)*
Office: 206 Municipal Building, Findlay 45840.
Telephone: (419) 424-7144.
Fax: (419) 424-7803
E-mail address: vpreston@ci.findlay.oh.us

PRICE-TESTERMAN, Connie S. *(Judge, Montgomery County Court)*
Office: 195 South Clayton Road, New Lebanon 45345-9601.
Telephone: (937) 687-9099.
Fax: (937) 687-7119
E-mail address: pricejd@aol.com

PUFFENBERGER, Jack R. *(Judge, Ohio Court of Common Pleas Lucas County)* Elected to term beginning Jan 11, 1991. Reelected 1996 and 2002. Current term expires Jan 2009. Serves Probate Division. Judge, Toledo Municipal Court 1987-91.
Office: 700 Adams Street, Toledo 43624.
Telephone: (419) 213-4775.
Fax: (419) 213-4764
E-mail address: judgepuff@prodigy.net

PUSKARICH, Matthew Paul *(Judge, Ohio Court of Common Pleas Harrison County)* Serves Probate and Juvenile Divisions.
Office: 100 West Market Street, Cadiz 43907-1132.

QUINN, John Patrick, Jr. *(Judge, Ohio Court of Common Pleas Summit County)* Serves Domestic Relations Division.
Office: 209 South High, Akron 44308.

RAMEY, Scott *(Judge, Sylvania Municipal Court)*
Office: 6700 Monroe Street, Sylvania 43560-1995.
Telephone: (419) 885-8975.
Fax: (419) 885-8987
E-mail address: sylvania.court@sylvania.sev.org

RAPP, James S. *(Judge, Ohio Court of Common Pleas Hardin County)* Elected to term beginning Feb 9, 1991. Reelected 1996 and 2002. Current term expires 2009. Serves Probate and Juvenile Divisions. Born Hardin County Ohio Aug 31, 1951. Educated at Bowling Green State University B.A. 1972 and Ohio Northern University J.D. 1976. Recipient American Jurisprudence Award in Estates 1976. Admitted to practice Ohio 1976. In legal practice Kenton 1976-91. Judge, Kenton Municipal Court 1987-91.

Prosecuting Attorney Hardin County 1981-86. Member Committee to Review Rules of Superintendence 1993-97 Supreme Court of Ohio and Ohio Courts Futures Commission 1997-2000. Member Ohio Judicial Conference (Executive Committee 1998-2000, Member and Chair 1998-2000 Juvenile Law and Procedure Committee) and Ohio Association of Juvenile and Family Court Judges (Officer 1994-2002, President 2000-01). Member Elks, Moose and Knights of Columbus.

Office: One Courthouse Square, Suite 200/210, Kenton 43326-2301.
Telephone: (419) 674-2230.
Fax: (419) 674-2274
E-mail address: probjuv@bright.net

RAY, James *(Judge, Ohio Court of Common Pleas Lucas County)* Elected Nov 1988 to term beginning Jan 5, 1989. Reelected Nov 1994 and 2000. Current term expires Jan 4, 2007. Serves Juvenile Division. Born Richland Center Wisconsin April 25, 1940. Lutheran. Educated at St. Olaf College B.A. 1962, Luther Theological Seminary B.Th. 1966 and University of Toledo College of Law J.D. 1975. Admitted to practice Ohio 1976 and U.S. District Court Northern District of Ohio 1977. In legal practice Perrysburg 1976-81 and Toledo 1981-86.

Former President Ohio Association of Juvenile and Family Court Judges. President Elect/President National Council of Juvenile and Family Court Judges. Member Toledo, Lucas County and Ohio State Bar Associations. Previously worked as pastor, Our Saviour's Lutheran Church, Edmore Michigan 1966-70 and Faith Lutheran Church, Toledo Ohio 1970-76.

Office: 1801 Spielbusch Avenue, Toledo 43624.
Telephone: (419) 213-6717.
Fax: (419) 213-6898
E-mail address: jray@co.lucas.oh.us

REDDIN, Mark B. *(Judge, Bowling Green Municipal Court)* Elected to term beginning Jan 1, 1996. Reelected 2001, current term expires Dec 31, 2007. Born Bowling Green Ohio May 8, 1959. Presbyterian. Educated at Bowling Green State University B.S. 1981 and University of Dayton School of Law J.D. 1985. Admitted to practice Ohio 1985 and U.S. District Court Northern District of Ohio 1987. In legal practice Bowling Green 1985-95.

Member Association of Municipal/County Judges of Ohio, Inc., American Judicature Society, Toledo Women's, Wood County and Ohio State Bar Associations.

Mailing address: P.O. Box 326, Bowling Green 43402-0326.
Office: 711 South Dunbridge, Bowling Green 43402-8720.
Telephone: (419) 352-5263.
Fax: (419) 352-9407
E-mail address: bgmunict@wcnet.org

REED, Jeffrey L. *(Judge, Ohio Court of Common Pleas Allen County)* Elected to term beginning Feb 1999. Term expires Feb 2005. Born Lima Ohio March 10, 1958. Educated at The Ohio State University B.A. 1980 and Ohio Northern University J.D. 1983. Law Clerk to Ohio Court of Appeals Third District 1983-85. Admitted to practice Ohio 1983.

Assistant Prosecuting Attorney Allen County 1989-99. Member Allen County, Ohio State and American Bar Associations.

Mailing address: P.O. Box 1243, Lima 45802.
Telephone: (419) 223-8525.
Fax: (419) 224-9269
E-mail address: allenct@alpoha.wcoil.com

REINBOLD, Richard D., Jr. *(Judge, Ohio Court of Common Pleas Stark County)* Former Judge, Canton Municipal Court.

Office: 115 Central Plaza North, Canton 44702.
Telephone: (330) 451-7715.
Fax: (330) 451-7740
E-mail address: reinbold@co.stark.oh.us

REPP, Mark E. *(Judge, Tiffin Municipal Court)*
Office: 51 East Market Street, Tiffin 44883-2831.
Telephone: (419) 448-5412.
Fax: (419) 448-5419

RESNICK, Alice Robie *(Justice, Supreme Court of Ohio)* Elected 1988 to term beginning 1989. Reelected 1994 and 2000. Current term expires Jan 1, 2007. Born Erie Pennsylvania Aug 21, 1939. Catholic. Educated at Siena Heights College Ph.B. 1961 and University of Detroit J.D. 1964. Admitted to practice Ohio 1964 and Michigan 1965. In legal practice Ohio 1964-75 and Michigan 1965-75. Judge, Toledo Municipal Court 1976-83. Judge, Ohio Court of Appeals Sixth District Jan 14, 1983 to 1988.

Assistant County Prosecutor Lucas County 1964-75. Member National Association of Women Judges, Toledo, Lucas County and Ohio State Bar Associations. Recipient Woman of Achievement Award from Women in Communications Inc. 1983, Woman of the Year Award from Columbus Chapter American Association of University Women 1990, Women of Achievement Award from Franklin County YWCA 1994 and Making a Difference Award from District Seven National Association of Women Judges 1996. Listed in *Who's Who in America* 1984-98. Inducted into Ohio Hall of Fame 1995. Cochair Gender Fairness Task Force. Member Board of Trustees Guest House. Board of Directors Crime Stopper. Member Lucas County Democratic Business and Professional Women and Toledo Art Museum. Enjoys swimming, reading, gardening and painting.

Office: 30 East Broad Street, Columbus 43215-3431.
Telephone: (614) 466-3578.
Fax: (614) 752-6825
E-mail address: resnicka@sconet.state.oh.us

RICE, Cynthia Westcott *(Judge, Ohio Court of Appeals Eleventh District)*
Office: 111 High Street N.E., Warren 44481.

RICE, Ronald J. *(Judge, Trumbull County Court)*
Office: 7130 Brookwood Drive, Brookfield 44403.
Telephone: (330) 448-1726.
Fax: (330) 448-6310
E-mail address: rjrcolpa@msn.com

RICE, Walter Herbert *(Chief Judge, United States District Court Southern District of Ohio)* Appointed for life by President Jimmy Carter to term beginning June 4, 1980. Chief Judge since October 13, 1996. Born Pittsburgh Pennsylvania May 27, 1937. Educated at Northwestern University B.A. in History 1958, Columbia University M.B.A. 1962 J.D. replaced LL.B. conferred 1962 and Wright State University 1968. Awarded honorary LL.D. University of Dayton 1991. In legal practice 1966-69. Judge, Dayton Municipal Court 1970-71. Judge, Ohio Court of Common Pleas Montgomery County July 10, 1971 to June 4, 1980, appointed by Governor John J. Gilligan.

Assistant County Prosecutor 1964-66 and First Assistant County Prosecutor 1969 Montgomery County. Adjunct Professor Wright State University 1973-75. Adjunct Professor of Law University of Dayton 1976-92 and 1994-96. Founding Board Member and First President Carl D. Kessler Inn of Court. Chairman Montgomery County Trial Judges Conference. Convener Dayton Bar Association—Thurgood Marshall/Barbara Jordan Roundtable. Member Executive Committee Judicial Council of the Sixth Circuit. Former Member Ohio Judi-

RICE, WALTER HERBERT—*Continued*
cial Conference (Chairman Jury Instructions Committee and Standing Committee on Pattern Jury Instructions) and Ohio Common Pleas Judges Association (Executive Committee). Member Federal Judges Association and Dayton Bar Association (Former Chairman Common Pleas Court and Appellate Practice Committee and Civil Rights Committee). Recipient Award for Outstanding Judicial Service 1973, 1974 and 1976 and for Excellent Judicial Service 1976 and 1977 Ohio Supreme Court; Outstanding Jurist in Ohio from Ohio Academy of Trial Lawyers 1986; Public Official of the Year Award from National Association of Social Workers Ohio Region 1992; Humanitarian Award from National Conference of Christians and Jews 1993, Distinguished Service Award from Thurgood Marshall Law Society 1995, Paul Laurence Dunbar Humanitarian Award 1996 and NAACP President's Award 1996. Former Member Ohio Bureau of Adult Detention Facilities and Services Committee on the Development of Minimum Jail Standards in City and County Jails 1977. Chairman Task Force on Services for the Elderly 1977-79. Member Board of Visitors University of Dayton Law School since 1978. Chairman 2003 Committee 1989-96. Past President Dayton Area Counsel on Alcoholism and Drug Abuse. Past Chairman Montgomery County Supervisory Council on Crime and Delinquency. Past Vice Chairman and Board of Directors Pretrial Release. Past Chairman and Former Member Board of Trustees Stillwater Hospital. Former Member and Board of Directors Building Bridges. Former Member Board of Directors Montgomery County Community Action Agency, Dayton Area Chapter American Red Cross and Project Cure. Former Board Member and President Dayton Family Service Association. Chairman Dr. Martin Luther King, Jr. Memorial Committee and Dayton Aviation Heritage National Historical Park Commission. Board of Trustees Miami Valley Cultural Alliance and Montgomery County Volunteer Lawyers Project. Honorary Co-chair and Member Steering Committee of Race and Reconciliation Committee City of Dayton. Convener Barbara Jordan Committee.

Office: 909 Federal Building, 200 West Second Street, Dayton 45402.

Telephone: (937) 512-1500.

RIDGE, John S. *(Judge, Norwalk Municipal Court)*
Office: 45 North Linwood Avenue, Norwalk 44857.
Telephone: (419) 663-6771.
Fax: (419) 663-6749
E-mail address: jjsr@accnorwalk.com

RINGLAND, Robert P. *(Judge, Ohio Court of Common Pleas Clermont County)* Elected to term beginning Jan 2, 1983. Reelected 1988, 1994 and 2000. Current term expires Jan 1, 2007. Also serves Ohio Court of Claims. Born Cincinnati Ohio Oct 6, 1945. Methodist. Educated at The Ohio State University B.A. 1967 and University of Cincinnati College of Law J.D. 1970. Member Sphinx, Sigma Phi Epsilon (Chapter Vice President) and Phi Alpha Theta. Admitted to practice Ohio 1971, U.S. District Court Southern District of Ohio and U.S. Supreme Court. In legal practice Cincinnati and Batavia 1971-83. Judge, Clermont County Court 1977-83. Visiting Judge pro tem, Ohio Court of Appeals Twelfth District 1983-84 and 1986, Eighth District 1987, Tenth District 1990 and Second District 1992-93.

Assistant Prosecuting Attorney Clermont County 1974-77. Assistant Village Solicitor New Richmond 1976. Peer Review Consultant National Institute of Justice U.S. Department of Justice 1992. Contributor *Role of Libyan Intelligence and Security Services in International Terrorism* U.S. Army Counter Intelligence 1977. Author "Child Sex Abuse Evidence Problems" 12 No. 1 University of Dayton L. Rev. Fall 1986 and Winter 1987; "Child Abuse Evidence Outline" Ohio Judicial College 1987, 1988 and 1989; "They Must Not Speak a Useless Word—The Case For Hearsay Exception in Ohio" 14 No. 2 Ohio Northern University L. Rev. Winter 1988; "Child Sex Abuse Evidence Problems—Update 88" University of Dayton L. Rev. Fall 1988 and 14 No. 1, 1990; and "Further Guidance Needed in Ohio: *State v. Boston*—Its Rationale and Aftermath" II No. 1 Kentucky Children's Rights Journal Northern Kentucky University Winter 1992. Consultant *Local Prosecution of Environmental Crime* National Institute of Justice 1992.

Important Decisions: Males v. W. E. Gates & Associates 504 N.E.2d 494, Ohio Misc. 2d 13, 29 Ohio B. 229, 1985; Newmeyer v. Globe American Cas. Co. 504 N.E.2d 733, 29 Ohio Misc. 2d 4, 29 Ohio B. 168, 1985; Brinson v. Bethesda Hospital, Inc. 504 N.E.2d 496, 29 Ohio Misc. 2d 8, 29 Ohio B. 224, 1985; Margolis v. Pagano 528 N.E.2d 1331, 39 Ohio Misc. 2d 1, 1986; Bedinghaus v. Village of Moscow 536 N.E.2d 58, 41 Ohio Misc. 2d 1, 1987; Laxton v. Cincinnati Bell, Inc. 532 N.E.2d 787, 40 Ohio Misc. 2d 22, 1987; Seiger v. Yeager 542 N.E.2d 1119, 44 Ohio Misc. 2d 40, 1988; Mullen v. Al Castrucci Ford, Inc. 537 N.E.2d 1307, 42 Ohio Misc. 2d 35, 1989; Harris v. Elofskey 65 Ohio App. 3d 342, 583 N.E.2d 1344 Ohio App. 2d CA-11396, 8626 Nov 22, 1989; Hunt v. Mayfield 65 Ohio App. 3d 349, 583 N.E.2d 1349 Ohio App. 2d CA 11364, 8656 Nov 22, 1989; Blanchester Lumber and Supply, Inc. v. White 61 Ohio Misc. 2d 466, 580 N.E.2d 81 Ohio Com. Pl. 88-CV-0311, 1041 Dec 13, 1989; Felicity-Franklin Local School District Board of Education v. Nationwide Mutual Insurance Co. 56 Ohio Misc. 2d 19, 565 N.E.2d 618, 65 Ed. Law Rep. 166 Ohio Com.Pl. Dec 22, 1989; Pamer v. Pritchard Bros. 61 Ohio Misc. 2d 150, 575 N.E.2d 900 Ohio Com.Pl. 1067, 89-CV-0668 Sept 6, 1990; In re Fraternal Order of Police, Ohio Valley Lodge 112, 61 Ohio Misc. 2d 135, 575 N.E.2d 535, 30 Wage and Hour Cas. BNA 927, 119 Lab.Cas. P 35, 536 Ohio Com.Pl. 90-CV-0712 Dec 3, 1990; In re Kaman 62 Ohio Misc. 2d 288, 598 N.E.2d 236 Ohio Ct.Cl. V88-43657 July 26, 1991; Runge v. Norfolk Southern Corp. 62 Ohio Misc. 2d 74, 591 N.E.2d 1381 Ohio Com.Pl. 1261, 90-CV-0176 Aug 23, 1991; Pidgeon v. Ramar Land Corp. 62 Ohio Misc. 2d 223, 597 N.E.2d 562 Ohio Com.Pl. 1290, 91-CV-0151 Oct 23, 1991; Hanes v. Davis 62 Ohio Misc. 2d 468, 601 N.E.2d 685 Ohio Com.Pl. 91-C-114, 1295 April 14, 1992; Koob v. Rue 73 Ohio App.3d 418, 597 N.E.2d 550 Ohio App. 2 Dist. Greene County, 90-CA 131 9898 May 5, 1992; Natl. Am. Ins. Co. v. Clermont Cty. Bd. of Commrs. 65 Ohio Misc.2d 5, 640 N.E.2d 616 Ohio Com.Pl., 920CV-00709 Jan 22, 1993; Reed v. Miamisburg 96 Ohio App.3d 268, 644 N.E.2d 1094 Ohio App.2 Dist. Montgomery County 13446, 3493 July 29, 1993; Conley v. VanCamp 75 Ohio Misc.2d 29, 622 N.E. 2d 1, 662 N.E.2d 900 Ohio Com.Pl., 93-CV-0370 March 31, 1994; Estate of Waugh v. Shepherd 75 Ohio Misc. 2d 1, 662 N.E.2d 97 Ohio Com.Pl., 944-CV-0459 May 25, 1994; Doe v. Kahrs 75 Ohio Misc. 2d 7, 662 N.E.2d 101 Ohio Com.Pl., 94-CV000289 July 20, 1995;

RINGLAND, ROBERT P.—*Continued*

Clermont Cent. Soccer Association v. Cincinnati Insurance Company 82 Ohio Misc. 2d 31 Dec 8, 1995; Adamson v. Tate Twp. Board of Zoning Appeals 83 Ohio Misc. 2d 17 March 27, 1996; State v. Smith 83 Ohio Misc. 2d 21 May 13, 1996; Boyd v. Watson 83 Ohio Misc. 2d 88 July 15, 1996; Werden v. City of Milford 91 Ohio Misc. 2d 215, 698 N.E.2d 526, March 6, 1998; State v. Voland 99 Ohio Misc. 2d 61, 716 N.E.2d 299 March 10, 1999; Sannes v. Jeff Wyler Chevrolet, Inc. 107 Ohio Misc. 2d 11, 736 N.E.2d 116 Ohio Com.Pl., 97-CV-0916 July 1, 1999; Spradlin v. Williams 107 Ohio Misc. 2d 16, 736 N.E.2d 119 Ohio Com.Pl., 98-CV-0790 July 13, 1999; Tucker v. McQuery 107 Ohio Misc. 2d 31, 736 N.E.2d 569 Ohio Com.Pl., 95-CV-0777 Nov 10, 1999; Tucker v. McQuery 107 Ohio Misc. 2d 38, 736 N.E.2d 574 Ohio Com.Pl., 95-CV-0777 Nov 12, 1999; Mongold v. Estate of Gilbert 114 Ohio Misc. 2d 32, 2000; Winston S. & L. Co. v. Eastfork Trace, Inc. 119 Ohio Misc. 2d 83, 774 N.E.2d 355, 2001-Ohio-4386 Ohio Com.Pl. Aug 17, 2001; and State v. Sears 119 Ohio Misc. 2d 86, 774 N.E.2d 357, 168 Ed. Law Rep. 900, 2002-Ohio-4225 Ohio Com.Pl. Jan 17, 2002.

Guest Lecturer on Business Law University of Cincinnati 1982. Instructor in Criminal Procedures 1995-97, Criminal Law 1996, 1997, 1999, 2000 and 2001 and Criminal Evidence 1997, 1998, 1999 and 2000 University of Cincinnati Batavia Branch. Member Committee to establish guidelines in implementing Revised Code Section 2701.10 (Private Judge Bill) Ohio Supreme Court 1988-89. Member Felony and Misdemeanor Jury Instruction preparation Committee on Ohio Jury Instructions. Member Ohio Judicial College, Ohio Judicial Conference (Chairman Criminal Law and Procedure Committee 1995-2002), Ohio Common Pleas Judges Association (President 2002-03), American Judges Association, Cincinnati (Black Lawyers Association Roundtable since 1987), Clermont County, Ohio State, Federal and American Bar Associations. Lecturer on Child Sex Abuse Evidence Problems Spring Training Seminar Ohio Prosecuting Attorneys Association 1987 and Ohio Association of Criminal Defense Lawyers 1988, Child Sex Abuse Evidence Issues New Judges School March 1989 and Fourth Amendment Update Ohio Judicial College 1990. Speaker "Use of Expert Witness in Child Abuse Trial" Child Abuse Seminar Northern Kentucky Law School 1986. Faculty Member Child Abuse Seminar for Appellate Judges 1987 and 1988, Criminal Trial Objections Oct 1991 and Child Abuse Evidence for Appellate Judges May 1992 Ohio Judicial College. Attended CLE courses Ohio Judicial College, Managing the Complex Case and Evidence courses The National Judicial College and Constitutional Criminal Procedure American Academy of Judicial Education University of Virginia School of Law. Charter Member CLE Ohio Bar College.

Recipient Superior Judicial Service Awards from Ohio Supreme Court 1977-82, Bicentennial Spirit of '87 Liberty Through Law Award from Clermont Chamber of Commerce 1987, Silver Beaver Award 1988 and District Award of Merit from Dan Beard Council Boy Scouts of America, Excellence in Community Service Award from Clermont County Citizens for Community Values 1988 and Daniel S. Guy Award for Literary Excellence from Ohio Northern University 1988. Named Kentucky Colonel 1981. Listed in *Who's Who in the Mid-West* 20th ed. 1986-87, *Two Thousand Notable Americans* 3rd ed. 1987, *Who's Who in American Law* 5th ed. 1987-88 and 9th ed. 1996-97, *Men of Achievement* 12th ed. Cambridge, England, *Directory of Distinguished Americans* 4th ed. and *Who's Who in Society.* Lieutenant Colonel USAR (retired). Recipient Mershon Military Honor 1987 and Army Achievement Medal with oak leaf cluster 1989. Previously employed as laborer for Heekin Can Company. President Clermont County American Cancer Society 1973-83. Chairman Clermont County Mental Health and Retardation Board 1975. Founding Member Council on Alcoholism of Clermont County 1975-76. Member Advisory Board Family Service of Clermont County 1976-77. Trustee Clermont County Mental Health Council 1978. Board of Advisors St. Joseph's Orphanage 1980-1990. Member Advisory Board Clermont County Special Olympics 1983-86. Board of Directors Clermont County YMCA 1985-88. President The Ohio State University Alumni Club Clermont County 1987-88. Member 1988-97 and Chairman 1989-91 Public Awareness Advisory Council Ohio Victims of Crime. Member Clermont County Conference on Children and Family 1989. Former Member Board of Directors Batavia Chapter Rotary Club. Chairman Tescumseh District Brown and Clermont Counties Boy Scouts of America 1981-85. Member 1983-85 and Chairman Planning Committee Clermont County Jail Committee. Member Development Steering Committee Greater Cincinnati Region The Ohio State University 1988-90. Member Ohio Jail Advisory Board since 1997. Member Butler/Warren/Clermont Judicial Corrections Board for Planning Multi County Community Based Facility. Member Governor's Task Force on the Investigation and Prosecution of Child Abuse and Child Sexual Abuse Cases. Member American Legion, Eagles, Shriners of Cincinnati (Ambassador 1988), Scottish Rite of Cincinnati, Masons and Knights Templar. Enjoys fishing, racquetball, snorkeling, archeology and philately.

Office: Courthouse, 270 Main Street, Batavia 45103-3071.
Telephone: (513) 732-7378.
Fax: (513) 732-7987

RINTALA, Pamela A. *(Judge, Ohio Court of Common Pleas Trumbull County)* Elected 1994. Reelected to subsequent term. Serves Family Division.

Mailing address: P.O. Box 1209, Warren 44482.
Office: 220 South Main Street, Warren 44482.
Telephone: (330) 675-2341.
Fax: (330) 675-2322
E-mail address: drrintal@co.trumbull.oh.us

ROBERTS, Robert C. *(Judge, Columbiana County Municipal Court)* Assumed office Jan 2002. Former Judge, Columbiana County Court.

Office: 41 North Park Avenue, Lisbon 44432.
Telephone: (330) 424-5326.
Fax: (330) 424-6658

ROCCO, Kenneth A. *(Judge, Ohio Court of Appeals Eighth District)* Former Judge, Ohio Court of Common Pleas Cuyahoga County.

Office: One Lakeside Avenue, Cleveland 44113-1085.
Telephone: (216) 443-6350.
Fax: (216) 443-2044

ROGERS, Randy T. *(Judge, Ohio Court of Common Pleas Butler County)* Serves Probate Division.

Office: Courthouse, 101 High Street, Hamilton 45011.
Telephone: (513) 887-3303.
Fax: (513) 887-3629
E-mail address: rogersr@butlercountyohio.org

ROGERS, Richard M. *(Judge, Ohio Court of Common Pleas Marion County)* Elected to term beginning Jan 2, 1989. Reelected 1994 and 2000. Current term expires Jan 1, 2006. Born Lorain Ohio Dec 8, 1944. Methodist. Educated at Ohio Northern University B.A. 1966 J.D. 1972. Member Sigma Pi and Delta Theta Phi. Admitted to practice Ohio 1972 and U.S. District Court Northern District of Ohio 1973. In legal practice Marion 1972-81. Judge, Marion Municipal Court 1982-88.

Assistant Law Director and Police Prosecutor 1973-74 and Public Defender 1975 City of Marion. Assistant County Prosecutor Marion County 1976-81. Village Solicitor Village of LaRue 1976-81. Important Decisions: Augenstein v. Augenstein (deeds sufficient to convey reserve life estate) 107 Ohio Misc. 2d 44, 737 N.E.2d 613; In re Scioto Conservancy District (establishment of conservancy district) 108 Ohio Misc. 2d 1, 738 N.E.2d 109; Gary J. Brown, et al. v. Robert DuBois, et al. (landlord-tenant, installations by tenant become fixtures on termination of lease) 40 Ohio Misc. 2d 18, 1988; Marion Green Apartments v. Ronald Walter, et al. (forcible entry and detainer, objections to referee's report, Civ. R. 53(E)(2) and (7) inapplicable to eviction proceedings) 40 Ohio Misc. 2d 1, 1988; Lawrence Hines, et al. v. Thermal-Gard of Ohio, Inc. (applicability of Home Sales Solicitation Act to home improvement contracts) 46 Ohio Misc. 2d 11, 1988; and State v. Joseph Conroy (forfeiture of property in criminal actions) 50 Ohio Misc. 2d 15, 1988. Member Ohio Association of Municipal/County Judges, Inc. 1982-89 (Jury Instruction Committee 1982-85, Legislative Committee 1985-88, Board of Directors 1986-88, Chairman Judicial Administration Committee 1988), Ohio Supreme Court Traffic Rules Review Commission since 1989, Ohio Bar College, Ohio Judicial Conference (General Administration Committee 1984-85, Civil Law and Procedure Committee 1991-95, Vice Chairman Family Matters Video Committee since 1991, Ohio Jury Instruction Committee Editorial Board since 1994), Ohio State Bar Foundation (Board of Trustees 1997-99), Ohio Common Pleas Judges Association, Marion County (President 1985-86) and Ohio State (Modern Courts Committee 1982-85, Judicial Administration and Legal Reform Committee 1982-93 and Legislative Subcommittee 1989-93, Council of Delegates 1991-93, Civil Law and Procedure Committee 1993-95 and Board of Governors 1996-99, Vice Chair Criminal Justice Committee 2001-02, Chair Jury Instructions Committee since 2002) Bar Associations. Faculty Member "Journal Entries and Judgments" Ohio Judicial College. Judicial Panelist Ohio Mock Trial Program. Judge Burke E. Smith Intraschool Mock Trial Competition. Recipient Superior Judicial Service Awards from Ohio Supreme Court, Award of Appreciation from Big Brothers/Big Sisters Marion County, Ritter Award (for P.E.A.C.E. Program) from Ohio State Bar Foundation and Letter of Appreciation from Former U.S. Supreme Court Chief Justice Warren Burger. Listed in *International Who's Who of Contemporary Achievement, Who's Who in American Law, Who's Who in Law Enforcement, Who's Who in Society, Who's Who in the Midwest, Who's Who in the United States, Who's Who in the World* and *Who's Who of Emerging Leaders in America.* Sergeant E-5 U.S. Army 1968-69. Republican. Judge National Bicentennial Competition on the Constitution and Bill of Rights district competition, state competition and national competition 1989, 1993 and 1995. Member 1973-84, Treasurer 1976-80, Board of Directors 1976-84 and President 1980-81 Marion Active 20-40 Service Club. Member 1974-81, Chairman of the Board 1974-81 and President Marion Area Driver Re-education Project 1974-81. Member North Central Regional Council on Alcohol 1984-85. Board of Directors 1984-88, Member Internal Affairs Committee 1987-1990 and President 1986-87 Big Brothers/Big Sisters of Marion County. Board Member 1985-88 and Vice President 1986 St. Mary Elementary School Board. Board of Directors Marion Catholic High School Endowment Fund since 1988 (Vice President since 1991). Ex-officio Member 1986-87, Member 1988-94 and President 1990-91 Marion Catholic High School Board. Paralegal Advisory Committee Marion Technical College 1994-96. Member since 1982, President 1991-93 and Vice President since 1993 Marion County Law Library Association. Member Fellows of Criminal Justice Steering Committee The Ohio State University 1996-2000. Enjoys golf, tennis and scuba diving.

Office: Courthouse Square, 100 North Main Street, Marion 43302-3089.
Telephone: (740) 223-4220.
Fax: (740) 387-7131
E-mail address: judgermr@marion.net

ROHRS, John T., III *(Judge, Defiance Municipal Court)* Elected Nov 1993 to term beginning Jan 1, 1994. Reelected Nov 1999, current term expires Dec 2005. Born Defiance Ohio Dec 3, 1955. United Methodist. Educated at The Ohio State University B.A. 1978 and Ohio Northern University J.D. 1981. Admitted to practice Ohio 1982 and U.S. District Court Northern District of Ohio 1982. In legal practice Defiance 1982-94.

City Law Director Defiance 1984-94. Member Ohio Judicial Conference, Association of Municipal/County Judges of Ohio, Inc., American Judges Association, Defiance County (Secretary 2000, Treasurer 2001), Ohio State and American Bar Associations. Named Outstanding Public Official Serving Victims of Crime by Victim Services of Defiance County 1994. Member Rotary International and Society for the Preservation and Encouragement of Barbershop Quartet Singing in America.

Office: 324 Perry Street, Defiance 43512-2194.
Telephone: (419) 782-5756.
Fax: (419) 782-2018

ROMANOFF, Marvin S. *(Judge, Franklin County Municipal Court)* Appointed by Governor James A. Rhodes to term beginning March 8, 1979. Elected 1979, 1985, 1991 and 1997. Current term expires Jan 2004. Presiding and Administrative Judge 2001-02. Born Schenectady New York March 21, 1940. Educated at Yale University A.B. 1962 LL.B. 1965 replaced by J.D. Admitted to practice District of Columbia 1965, Ohio 1967, U.S. District Court Southern District of Ohio, U.S. Court of Appeals Sixth Circuit and U.S. Supreme Court. Began legal practice District of Columbia.

Former Staff Attorney Federal Power Commission. Former Assistant Prosecuting Attorney Franklin County. Trustee and Treasurer Ohio Municipal and County Judges Association (President 1996). Former Member Ohio Judicial Conference (Executive Committee), Columbus

ROMANOFF, MARVIN S.—*Continued*

and Ohio State Bar Associations. Recipient Superior Judicial Service Awards from Ohio Supreme Court 1979-85 and Award for Law Enforcement Initiative and Implementation from National Commission Against Drunk Driving 1988. Lieutenant Colonel Ohio Military Reserve. Former Member Governor's Special Task Force Against Drunk Driving and Governor's Highway Traffic Safety Committee. Member Lions Club, Masons and Shriners.

Office: 375 South High Street, Columbus 43215-4520.
Telephone: (614) 645-8287.
Fax: (614) 645-7803
E-mail address: marvin_romanoff@fccourts.org

RONK, James M. *(Judge, Ohio Court of Common Pleas Knox County)* Serves Probate and Juvenile Divisions.

Office: Courthouse, 111 East High Street, Mount Vernon 43050.
Telephone: (740) 393-6797.
Fax: (740) 393-6832

ROSE, Thomas M. *(Judge, United States District Court Southern District of Ohio)* Appointed for life by President George W. Bush to term beginning June 21, 2002. Born Circleville Ohio Oct 20, 1948. Methodist. Educated at Ohio University B.S.Ed. 1970 and University of Cincinnati J.D. 1973. Admitted to practice Ohio 1973 and U.S. District Court Southern District of Ohio. Judge, Ohio Court of Common Pleas Greene County, appointed by Governor George V. Voinovich to term beginning Feb 9, 1991 to June 20, 2002.

Member Greene County, Ohio State and American Bar Associations. With USAR. Member Rotary Club.

Office: 910 Federal Building, 200 West Second Street, Dayton 45402.
Telephone: (937) 512-1600.

ROSMARIN, John G. *(Judge, Hamilton Municipal Court)* Elected Nov 1995 to term beginning Jan 1, 1996. Reelected, current term expires Dec 31, 2007. Born Hamilton Ohio Sept 3, 1937. Catholic. Educated at University of Dayton B.S.Ch.E. and Chase Law School of Northern Kentucky University J.D. Admitted to practice Ohio 1964 and U.S. District Court Southern District of Ohio 1965. In legal practice Butler County 1964-96.

City Prosecutor Hamilton 1967-69. Former Member American Bar Association. Member Butler County and Ohio State Bar Associations. Named Man of the Year by Knights of Columbus 1996. Member Butler County Republican Party. Enjoys football, basketball, baseball and especially golf.

Office: 345 High Street, Second Floor, Hamilton 45011.
Telephone: (513) 785-7300.
Fax: (513) 867-7351

ROSS, John L. *(Judge, Bellefontaine Municipal Court)* Appointed by Governor Richard F. Celeste 1986. Elected 1987, 1993 and 2000. Current term expires Dec 30, 2005. Born Marietta Ohio Feb 3, 1947. Roman Catholic. Educated at Ohio University B.A. 1969 and The Ohio State University J.D. 1973. Admitted to practice Ohio 1974 and U.S. District Court Southern District of Ohio 1979. In legal practice Bellefontaine 1974-86.

Adjunct Professor of Business Law Urbana College 1981-86. Member Logan County (President 1983) and Ohio State (Traffic Law Committee 1975-80, Modern Courts Committee 1979-81) Bar Associations. U.S. Army 1969-71.

Office: 226 West Columbus Avenue, Bellefontaine 43311.
Telephone: (937) 599-6127.
Fax: (937) 599-2488

ROUTSON, Reginald J. *(Judge, Ohio Court of Common Pleas Hancock County)* Born Findlay Ohio Sept 25, 1953. Educated at Bowling Green State University B.A. 1975 M.A. with honors 1976 and University of Toledo J.D. 1980. Admitted to practice Ohio 1981 and U.S. District Court Northern District of Ohio 1981. In legal practice Findlay 1981-88. Acting Judge Dec 17, 1988 to Dec 31, 1988 and Former Judge, Findlay Municipal Court, appointed by Governor Richard F. Celeste to term beginning Jan 1, 1989.

Assistant Prosecutor Hancock County 1985-88. Solicitor Village of Arlington 1986-88. Instructor in Criminal Law Ohio Northern University College of Law since 1986 and University of Findlay 1990-91. Co-chairman Ohio Jury Management Study Committee. Member Municipal-County Judges of Ohio, Inc., American Judges Association, Findlay-Hancock County, Ohio State and American Bar Associations. Co-chairman Bench-Bar Conference 1993. Recipient awards from Hancock County Schools 1988, Findlay City Schools 1988, Hancock County Litter Prevention Board 1988 and 1989 and Ohio Department of Highway Safety 1989 and 1990. Board Member Findlay Arts Council, Lincoln Center for Abuse Prevention, Crime Prevention Association and Big Brothers/Big Sisters.

Office: 300 South Main Street, Findlay 45840-3345.
Telephone: (419) 424-7009.
Fax: (419) 424-7436

RUDDUCK, John William "Tim" *(Judge, Ohio Court of Common Pleas Clinton County)* Born Hillsboro Ohio Feb 14, 1949. Church of Christ. Educated at Miami University B.A. with honors in Political Science 1971 and The Ohio State University J.D. 1976. Member Alpha Delta Phi. Admitted to practice Ohio 1973 and U.S. District Court Southern District of Ohio. In legal practice Wilmington 1979-85. Former Judge, Clinton County Municipal Court, appointed by Governor Richard F. Celeste to term beginning Sept 13, 1985.

Assistant Attorney General 1976-79. Instructor in Business Law Southern State University 1979-80. Member Christian Legal Society. E-4 U.S. Army (Military Police 1971-73). Republican. President Wilmington Park Board 1981-85. Legal Officer American Legion. Secretary Elks 797 Golf Club. Deacon Wilmington Church of Christ. Enjoys golf, softball, basketball and collecting baseball cards.

Office: 46 South South Street, Wilmington 45177-2297.
Telephone: (937) 382-3640.
Fax: (937) 383-3455
E-mail address: cpjg@erinet.com

RUEHLMAN, Robert P. *(Judge, Ohio Court of Common Pleas Hamilton County)* Elected to term beginning Jan 3, 1987. Reelected 1992 and 1998. Current term expires Jan 2005. Presiding Judge 1996. Born Cincinnati Ohio April 5, 1952. Catholic. Educated at University of Cincinnati B.S. summa cum laude 1974 J.D. 1977. Member Delta Tau Delta. Admitted to practice

RUEHLMAN, ROBERT P.—*Continued*

Ohio 1977 and U.S. District Court Southern District of Ohio 1977.

Assistant Prosecuting Attorney 1977-83 and Chief Assistant Prosecuting Attorney (Head of County Arson Unit) 1983-87 Hamilton County. Member Ohio Judicial Conference, Ohio Common Pleas Judges Association, American Judges Association and Ohio State Bar Association. Named Judge of the Year 1996. Republican. Vice President 1983-84 and President 1985-86 Delhi Township Republican Club. Director 1980-82, Vice President 1983-84, Treasurer 1984-86 and President 1986 Hamilton County Republican Club. Enjoys swimming, scuba diving, running and the study of snakes.

Office: 1000 Main Street, Room 300, Cincinnati 45202-1217.
Telephone: (513) 946-5850.
Fax: (513) 946-5854

RUNYAN, Jeffrey L. *(Judge, Ohio Court of Common Pleas Ashland County)*
Office: 142 West Second Street, Ashland 44805-2101.
Telephone: (419) 282-4292.
Fax: (419) 281-8315
E-mail address: jeffreyr@voyager.net

RUPPERT, James D. *(Judge, Franklin Municipal Court)* Appointed by Governor Richard F. Celeste to term beginning Feb 20, 1985. Elected to subsequent terms. Current term expires Dec 31, 2005. Born Franklin Ohio Jan 16, 1936. Methodist. Educated at U.S. Military Academy B.S. 1960 and University of Cincinnati J.D. 1966. Associate Editor University of Cincinnati Law Review. Admitted to practice Ohio 1966, U.S. District Court Southern District of Ohio 1966, U.S. Courts of Appeals Sixth 1971 and Fifth 1981 Circuits and U.S. Supreme Court 1981. In legal practice Franklin since 1966.

Prosecuting Attorney Warren County 1968-72. Member Ohio Trial Lawyers Association, Association of Municipal/County Judges of Ohio, Inc., The Association of Trial Lawyers of America, Dayton, Warren County, Ohio State and American Bar Associations. Democrat. Member Franklin Historical Society, Carlisle Historical Society, Franklin High School Hall of Fame Committee and Warren County Area Progress Council. Enjoys golfing, skiing, swimming and art.

Mailing address: P.O. Box 369, Franklin 45005.
Office: Franklin Municipal Court, 35 East Fourth Street, Franklin 45005.
Telephone: (937) 746-2858.
Fax: (937) 743-7751
E-mail address: jdruppert@ruppertlaw.com

RUSSELL, Heather S. *(Judge, Hamilton County Municipal Court)*
Office: 1000 Main Street, #142, Cincinnati 45202.
Telephone: (513) 946-5133.
Fax: (513) 946-5136

RUSSO, Anthony J. *(Judge, Ohio Court of Common Pleas Cuyahoga County)* Serves Domestic Relations Division.
Office: One Lakeside Avenue, Cleveland 44113-1082.
Telephone: (216) 443-8866.
Fax: (216) 443-8956

RUSSO, Joseph D. *(Judge, Ohio Court of Common Pleas Cuyahoga County)*
Office: 1200 Ontario Street, Cleveland 44113-1678.
Telephone: (216) 443-8746.
Fax: (216) 348-4032
E-mail address: judgclear@aol.com

RUSSO, Joseph F. *(Judge, Ohio Court of Common Pleas Cuyahoga County)* Elected to term beginning Dec 3, 1998. Reelected Nov 2000. Serves Juvenile Division. Born Cleveland Ohio Nov 1957. Roman Catholic. Educated at Cleveland State University B.B.A. 1981 and Cleveland-Marshall College of Law J.D. 1986. Admitted to practice Ohio 1987 and U.S. District Court Northern District of Ohio 1987. In legal practice Cleveland 1987-98.

Assistant County Prosecutor Cuyahoga County 1987-98. Important Decision: In re Hunter (juvenile's motion to compel discovery was untimely where filed prior to probable cause hearing) 99 Ohio Misc. 2d 1999. Member Justinian Forum, Ohio Association of Juvenile and Family Court Judges, National Association of Juvenile Court Judges, Cleveland, Cuyahoga County and Ohio State Bar Associations.

Office: 2163 East 22nd Street, Cleveland 44115.
Telephone: (216) 443-8407.
Fax: (216) 443-3140

RUSSO, Michael Joseph *(Judge, Ohio Court of Common Pleas Cuyahoga County)*
Office: 1200 Ontario Street, Cleveland 44113.

RUSSO, Nancy Margaret *(Judge, Ohio Court of Common Pleas Cuyahoga County)* Elected Nov 1996 to term beginning Jan 7, 1997. Reelected 2002, current term expires Jan 2009. Born Cleveland Ohio 1956. Roman Catholic. Educated at West Liberty State College B.A., Cleveland-Marshall College of Law J.D. 1981 and Levin College of Urban Affairs M.P.A. 2000. Admitted to practice Ohio 1982 and U.S. District Court Northern District of Ohio 1982. In legal practice Cleveland May 1982 to Nov 1996.

Attorney Financial Investigations Unit Blue Cross/Blue Shield of Ohio May 1984 to Aug 1994. Attorney and SIU Special Investigator Nationwide Insurance March 1995 to Dec 1996. Adjunct Faculty Member CSU Levin College of Urban Affairs. Member Grievance Committee, Medical/Legal Committee, Insurance Law Committee and Criminal Justice Committee Cuyahoga County Bar Association. Member Committees on Criminal Rules, Civil Rules, Probation and Security Cuyahoga County Court of Common Pleas. Member Ohio Common Pleas Judges Association, Justinian Forum, American Judicature Society, Cleveland (Ethics Committee, Speakers Bureau, Bench/Bar Professionalism Initiative, CASE Legal Aid Program) and Ohio State Bar Associations. Attended Trial Lawyers College 1998 and "Children in Adult Courts" The National Judicial College. Recipient Outstanding Alumnus Award from Mentor Ridge Junior High School 1994. Inducted into Mentor High School Hall of Fame 1997. Named Judge of the Year by Mothers Against Drunk Driving 1999 and Parents of Murdered Children of Northeast Ohio 1999 and 2001. Graduate Leadership Cleveland 2000. Honorary Trustee Cleveland-Marshall College of Law. Judicial Volunteer Moot Court. Member Citizens League of Greater Cleveland, Cleveland City Club, Mothers Against Drunk Driving Educational Program, AIDS Task Force of Greater Cleveland, Providence House Shelter

RUSSO, NANCY MARGARET—*Continued*

for Children, St. George's Hunger Program, St. Augustine AIDS Hospice, CAMEO, Westside Irish-American Club, Italian Sons and Daughters of America, Mentor High School Alumni Association, West Liberty State College Alumni Association and Cleveland-Marshall Law Alumni Association.

Office: 1200 Ontario Street, Cleveland 44113-1678.
Telephone: (216) 443-8688.
Fax: (216) 348-4036

RUYLE, Stephen W. *(Judge, Ohio Court of Common Pleas Defiance County)* Elected to term beginning Feb 8, 1985. Reelected 1990, 1996 and 2002. Current term expires 2009. Serves Probate and Juvenile Divisions. Born Huntington Indiana April 13, 1947. Educated at Ohio Northern University B.S.Ed. 1969 and University of Toledo J.D. 1977. Member Phi Alpha Delta. Admitted to practice Ohio 1977. Began legal practice Van Wert 1978. In legal practice Defiance since 1978. Hearing Officer, State Personnel Board of Review 1977.

Instructor in Criminal Law, Evidence and Procedure, Constitutional Law and State and Local Government Defiance College 1980-2001. Member Northwest Ohio Probate and Juvenile Court Association, Ohio Association of Probate Judges, Ohio Association of Juvenile and Family Court Judges, Ohio Judicial Conference, Defiance County, Northwest Ohio and Ohio State Bar Associations. E-5 U.S. Army 1970-73. Junior high school teacher 1973-74. Republican. Active in Boy Scouts of America for twenty years (Advisory Board Black Swamp Council). Member Rotary and Evangelical Lutheran Church. Enjoys golf, fishing, history and youth work through Scouting.

Office: 221 Clinton Street, Defiance 43512.
Telephone: (419) 782-4181.
Fax: (419) 782-2437

SADLER, Lisa L. *(Judge, Ohio Court of Appeals Tenth District)* Elected Nov 2002 to term beginning July 1, 2003. Term expires 2009. Educated at Miami University, Ohio, The Ohio State University B.S. cum laude 1980 and Columbus University Law School J.D. 1984. Member Phi Kappa Phi. Admitted to practice Ohio 1984, U.S. District Court Southern District of Ohio 1985, U.S. Court of Appeals Sixth Circuit 1986, Florida 1987 and U. S. Supreme Court 1992. In legal practice Ohio 1984-92. Judge, Franklin County Municipal Court May 1992 to March 1996. Judge, Ohio Court of Common Pleas Franklin County March 6, 1996 to June 2003, appointed by Governor George V. Voinovich.

Assistant City Attorney Columbus July 1884 to Jan 1991. Deputy Chief Legal Counsel Office of the Governor Ohio Jan 1991 to May 1992. Member Franklin County Women Lawyers, The Florida Bar, Columbus and Ohio State Bar Associations. Recipient Summa Award from The Ohio State University 1978. Member Ohio State Alumni Association since 1980.

Office: 375 South High Street, Columbus 43215-4578.
Telephone: (614) 462-7244.
Fax: (614) 462-7249

SAFFOLD, Shirley Strickland *(Judge, Ohio Court of Common Pleas Cuyahoga County)* Elected 1994. Reelected to subsequent term. Born New Jersey Sept 12, 1951. Educated at Central State University B.A. 1983 and Cleveland-Marshall College of Law J.D. 1986. Admitted to practice Ohio 1987 and U.S. District Court Northern District of Ohio 1987. Former Judge, Cleveland Municipal Court, elected to term beginning Jan 1988.

Member American Judges Association, Cleveland, Cuyahoga County, Ohio State and National Bar Associations. Attended Tort Reform Seminar 1986 and Sentencing Guidelines Seminar 1986 Ohio Judicial College and full course at The National Judicial College 1986. Democrat. Enjoys tennis, racquetball, jogging, reading and gardening.

Office: 1200 Ontario Street, Cleveland 44113-1678.
Telephone: (216) 443-8735.
Fax: (216) 348-4036
E-mail address: o1492@aol.com

SAGE, Michael J. *(Judge, Ohio Court of Common Pleas Butler County)* Elected to term beginning Feb 9, 1991. Reelected 1996 and 2002. Current term expires Feb 2009. Born Cincinnati Ohio June 30, 1949. Educated at Miami University B.A. 1971 and University of Dayton J.D. 1979. Member Phi Alpha Delta. Admitted to practice Ohio 1979 and U.S. District Court Southern District of Ohio 1979. In legal practice Hamilton 1979-91.

Assistant Prosecuting Attorney State of Ohio 1980-86. Assistant Professor Department of Naval Science Miami University 1975-76. Member Cincinnati, Butler County, Ohio State and American Bar Associations. Captain USNR. Past President Butler County Chapter American Heart Association. President Butler County Family Service. Enjoys scuba diving.

Office: Government Services Center, 315 High Street, Third Floor, Hamilton 45011.
Telephone: (513) 887-3283.
Fax: (513) 887-3285
E-mail address: sagem@butlercountyohio.org

SARGEANT, Harry A., Jr. *(Judge, Ohio Court of Common Pleas Sandusky County)* Elected to term beginning Jan 1, 1979. Reelected 1984, 1990, 1996 and 2002. Current term expires Dec 31, 2008. Born Cleveland Ohio Feb 20, 1933. Educated at College of Wooster B.A. with honors in Political Science 1955 and The Ohio State University College of Law J.D. 1958. Admitted to practice Ohio 1958, U.S. District Court Northern District of Ohio 1961 and U.S. Supreme Court 1966. Judge, Fremont Municipal Court 1976-78.

Prosecuting Attorney Sandusky County 1965-75. Instructor in Local Government Law Terra Technical College 1977-78. Member Ohio Common Pleas Judges Association, American Judges Association, American Judicature Society, Sandusky County, Ohio State and American Bar Associations. USAFR 1958-64. Republican.

Office: 100 North Park Avenue, Fremont 43420.
Telephone: (419) 334-6169.
Fax: (419) 334-6122
E-mail address: cpcjudge2@nwonline.net

SARGUS, Edmund A., Jr. *(Judge, United States District Court Southern District of Ohio)* Appointed for life by President Bill Clinton Dec 22, 1995 to term beginning Aug 1, 1996. Born Wheeling West Virginia July 2, 1953. Educated at Brown University A.B. 1975 and Case Western Reserve University School of Law J.D. 1978. In legal practice Bellaire and St. Clairsville 1978-93.

Special Counsel Ohio Attorney General 1979-93. U.S.

SARGUS, EDMUND A., JR.—*Continued*
Attorney Southern District of Ohio 1993-96. Member City Council St. Clairsville 1988-91.
Office: 302 U.S. Courthouse, 85 Marconi Boulevard, Columbus 43215.
Telephone: (614) 719-3240.

SARGUS, Jennifer L. *(Judge, Ohio Court of Common Pleas Belmont County)*
Office: 101 West Main Street, St. Clairsville 43950-1154.
Telephone: (740) 699-2134.
Fax: (740) 695-4968

SCARPONE, David J. *(Judge, Jefferson County Court)*
Mailing address: P.O. Box 495, Dillonvale 43917.
Telephone: (740) 769-2903.
Fax: (740) 769-7640

SCHAEFER, Jon Patrick *(Judge, Shelby Municipal Court)* Appointed by Governor Richard F. Celeste to term beginning July 14, 1986. Elected 1987, 1993 and 1999. Current term expires Dec 31, 2005. Born Fremont Ohio Nov 20, 1948. Roman Catholic. Educated at Bethel College B.S. 1971 and Memphis State University J.D. 1974. Co-chairman Law Day Memphis State University 1973. Admitted to practice Ohio 1974 and U.S. District Courts Northern 1977 and Southern 1977 Districts of Ohio. In legal practice Shelby since 1974.
Law Director City of Shelby 1976-80. Member Ohio Trial Lawyers Association, Huron County, Richland County, Ohio State and American Bar Associations. Recipient Knights of Columbus Man of the Year Award 1984, Community Service Award for rescue work in flood July 2, 1987 and Sertoma International Distinguished Governor Award. Previously employed by Miller Boat Line, Crano Construction, Holiday Construction and J. B. Hunter. Member Knights of Columbus since 1974 (Grand Knight 1982-83), Shelby Sertoma Club since 1975 (President 1981-82, District Governor 1985-86), Heart Board 1975-76, St. Mary's Parish Council 1981-87 and Board of Directors Red Cross since 1987. Enjoys boating, fishing and reading.
Office: 18 West Main Street, Shelby 44875.
Telephone: (419) 342-2896.
Fax: (419) 342-6404

SCHEER, James J. *(Judge, Celina Municipal Court)* Appointed by Governor Richard F. Celeste to term beginning Dec 19, 1985. Elected 1987, 1993 and 1999. Current term expires Dec 31, 2005. Born Celina Ohio May 20, 1948. Roman Catholic. Educated at Ohio Northern University, Wright State University B.S. 1970 and The Ohio State University J.D. 1975. Admitted to practice Ohio 1975. In legal practice 1975-85.
Member Mercer County Bar Association (Past President). Named One of Ten Outstanding Young Lions in Ohio for 1986. Sergeant First Armored Division and First Cavalry Division U.S. Army 1971-72. Recipient Army Commendation Medal. Former member Mercer County Council on Drug and Alcohol. Member Lions Club (Past President), American Legion, Mercer County Sportsman, Mercer County Foundation, Knights of Columbus and Immaculate Conception Catholic Parish Council (Past President, President School Board and Cemetery Board).
Mailing address: P.O. Box 362, Celina 45822.
Telephone: (419) 586-6491.
Fax: (419) 586-4735

SCHISLER, Richard T. *(Judge, Portsmouth Municipal Court)* Appointed by Governor George V. Voinovich to term beginning Feb 10, 1997. Elected Nov 4, 1997, current term expires Dec 31, 2003. Born Portsmouth Ohio May 11, 1959. Episcopalian. Educated at Miami University A.B. 1961 and University of Cincinnati College of Law J.D. 1966. Board of Editors University of Cincinnati Law Review 1964-66. Admitted to practice Ohio 1967 and U.S. District Court Southern District of Ohio 1968. In legal practice Cincinnati 1967-70 and Portsmouth 1972-97.
City Solicitor Portsmouth 1979-97. Board of Governors Ohio State Bar Association 1995-97.
Office: 728 Second Street, Portsmouth 45662-4036.
Telephone: (740) 354-3283.
Fax: (740) 353-6645

SCHMENK, Joseph N. *(Judge, Ohio Court of Common Pleas Defiance County)* Former Judge, Defiance Municipal Court.
Mailing address: P.O. Box 386, Defiance 43512.
Office: 221 Clinton Street, Defiance 43512.
Telephone: (419) 782-5931.
Fax: (419) 782-2437

SCHMITT, John D. *(Judge, Ohio Court of Common Pleas Shelby County)*
Mailing address: P.O. Box 947, Sidney 45365-0947.
Telephone: (937) 498-7230.
Fax: (937) 498-7824
E-mail address: hizoner@bright.net

SCHNEIDER, Charles A. *(Judge, Franklin County Municipal Court)*
Office: 375 South High Street, Columbus 43215-4593.
Telephone: (614) 645-8206.
Fax: (614) 645-7803
E-mail address: charles_schneider@fccourts.org

SCHWEIKERT, Mark R. *(Judge, Ohio Court of Common Pleas Hamilton County)* Appointed by Governor Bob Taft to term beginning March 9, 1999. Elected 2000 and 2002. Born Cincinnati Ohio Sept 9, 1952. Presbyterian. Educated at The Ohio State University B.A. 1974 and Salmon P. Chase College of Law J.D. 1980. Admitted to practice Ohio 1980 and U.S. District Court Southern District of Ohio 1980. In legal practice Cincinnati 1980-95. Judge, Hamilton County Municipal Court Feb 6, 1995 to March 8, 1999, appointed by Governor George V. Voinovich.
Court Administrator Hamilton County 1981-95. Visiting Faculty Member Ukraine-Ohio Rule of Law Program Kiev, Ukraine 1995 and 1998. Chair Administration and Court Reform Committee Ohio Judicial Conference 2001-03. Member Ohio Common Pleas Judges Association, American Judges Association, Cincinnati, Ohio and American Bar Associations. Keynote Speaker and Faculty Member "Toward an Independent Judiciary in a Democratic Mongolia" (strategic planning for court reform) 1999.
Office: 1000 Main Street, Room 485, Cincinnati 45202.

SCHWEIKERT, MARK R.—*Continued*
Telephone: (513) 946-5117.
Fax: (513) 946-5119
E-mail address: mschweik@cms.hamilton-co.org

SELLERS, Barbara Jackson *(Judge, United States Bankruptcy Court Southern District of Ohio)* Appointed by U.S. Court of Appeals Sixth Circuit judges to term beginning July 1, 1986. Reappointed July 1, 2000, current term expires June 30, 2014. Born Richmond Virginia Oct 3, 1940. Presbyterian. Educated at Baldwin-Wallace College 1958-60, The Ohio State University B.A. cum laude 1962 and Capital University J.D. magna cum laude 1979. Staff member Capital University Law Review 1977-79. Law Clerk to Hon. Robert J. Sidman 1979-81 and to Hon. Thomas M. Herbert 1982-84, U.S. Bankruptcy Court Southern District of Ohio. Member Phi Beta Kappa, Alpha Gamma Delta and Order of the Curia. Admitted to practice Ohio 1979, U.S. District Court Southern District of Ohio 1981 and U.S. Court of Appeals Sixth Circuit 1986. In legal practice Columbus 1981-82 and 1984-86.

Member National Conference of Bankruptcy Judges, Commercial Law League of America, Columbus (Bankruptcy Committee) and American (Section of Litigation) Bar Associations. Speaker "The Jurisdictional Grant of the New Bankruptcy Courts and Its Impact Upon Domestic Relations Law" Joint Seminar on Bankruptcy and Domestic Relations Law Columbus Bar Association Spring 1981; "The Issue of Dischargeability in Bankruptcy and Its Impact Upon Domestic Relations" seminar on Domestic Relations Law Ohio Legal Center Institute, Columbus May 1982 and May 1983; "Disclosure Statements, The Plan of Reorganization, Confirmation and Modification of Plans" Advanced Reorganization Seminar Key Facts Legal Institute, Columbus June 15, 1984; "The 1984 Amendments to the Bankruptcy Code in Practice" Consumer Bankruptcy Law Seminar North Central Bankruptcy Institute, Capital University Dec 4, 1985; "Agriculture and Bankruptcy Law" North Central Bankruptcy Institute; "Views from the Bench" Consumer Association of Central Ohio 1988; "Current Issues in Chapter 13 of the Bankruptcy Code" Ad Hoc Creditors Association 1989; "Current Developments in Bankruptcy Law" Bankruptcy Law Seminar Columbus Bar Association 1989; "Partnership and Chapter 11" Commercial Law League Midwest Meeting March 1990; "Emerging Issues in Bankruptcy" Cleveland Bar Association Dec 1990; Creditor Education Coalition Bankruptcy Seminar Oct 1991; "Article 9 of the Uniform Commercial Code" CLE Institute Ohio State Bar Association Nov 1992; and "Filed-Rate Doctrine" Richmond Traffic Club Jan 1993. Panelist Mega Case Workshop, Breckenridge Colorado Aug 1990, "Creditors' Rights/Debtors' Rights" Bankruptcy Law Institute Columbus Bar Association May 1992 and "Lawyer/Judges Interchange Panel" Judicial Conference of the Sixth Circuit May 1992. Coordinator and Speaker "Chapter 13 of the Bankruptcy Code" Belmont County Bar Association May 1991. Democrat. Enjoys reading, music (piano, guitar and voice), travel, gardening, golf and bridge.

Office: 170 North High Street, Columbus 43215-2403.
Telephone: (614) 469-6638.

SHAPIRO, Marvin A. *(Judge, Ohio Court of Common Pleas Summit County)* Former Judge, Akron Municipal Court.
Office: 209 South High Street, Akron 44308.
Telephone: (330) 943-2628.

SHAW, Stephen R. *(Judge, Ohio Court of Appeals Third District)* Assumed office Feb 11, 1987. Elected to subsequent terms.
Office: 204 North Main Street, Lima 45801.
Telephone: (419) 223-1861.
Fax: (419) 224-3828
E-mail address: cpctshaw@midohio.net

SHEA-STONUM, Marilyn *(Judge, United States Bankruptcy Court Northern District of Ohio)* Appointed by U.S. Court of Appeals Sixth Circuit judges to term beginning Sept 19, 1994. Term expires 2008. Born Anaconda Montana June 6, 1947. Educated at Riverside City College A.A. with honors 1967, University of California at Santa Cruz A.B. with honors 1969 and Case Western Reserve University J.D. with honors 1975. Law Clerk to Hon. Frank J. Battisti, U.S. District Court Northern District of Ohio 1975-76. Member Order of Coif. Admitted to practice Ohio 1975, U.S. District Courts Northern District of Ohio 1975, Eastern District of Michigan 1982 and Eastern District of Wisconsin 1988, U.S. Courts of Appeals Sixth 1976 and Fourth 1978 Circuits, California 1976 and U.S. Supreme Court 1992. In legal practice Cleveland Ohio 1976-94.
Office: 240 U.S. Courthouse and Federal Bldg., Two South Main Street, Akron 44308.
Telephone: (330) 375-5780.

SHERCK, James Robert *(Judge, Ohio Court of Common Pleas Sandusky County)* Serves Domestic Relations Division. Former Judge, Fremont Municipal Court. Former Judge, Ohio Court of Appeals Sixth District.
Office: 100 North Park Avenue, Fremont 43420.

SHEWARD, Richard S. *(Judge, Ohio Court of Common Pleas Franklin County)* Elected to term beginning July 1, 1991. Reelected Nov 1996 and 2002. Current term expires July 1, 2009. Born Jackson Ohio May 21, 1944. Methodist. Educated at University of Miami, Ohio University B.B.A. 1967 and Capital University Law School J.D. 1974. Member Sigma Alpha Epsilon. Admitted to practice Ohio 1974, U.S. District Court Southern District of Ohio 1975 and U.S. Supreme Court 1978. In legal practice 1976-87. Mediator, State Board of Personnel Review 1977, State Department of Mental Health and Retardation 1977 and O.C.S.E.A. and A.F.S.C.M.E. 1977. Referee, Ohio Court of Common Pleas Franklin County Probate Division 1984-86. Judge, Franklin County Municipal Court July 13, 1987 to June 30, 1991, appointed by Governor Richard F. Celeste.

Assistant Prosecutor 1974-76 and Special Prosecutor 1978 Franklin County. Special Prosecutor Allen County 1978 and City Attorney's Office 1978. Editorial Advisor Gorsuch Publications 1979. Instructor Columbus Technical Institute 1977-80. Mediator Communication Workers of America 1977. Arbitrator Labor Panel American Arbitration Association since 1982. Member Franklin County Trial Lawyers Association (President 1984-85), Columbus (Chairman Criminal Law Committee 1985-87), Ohio State and American Bar Associations. Listed in *Who's Who in American Law* 2nd ed. 1979. Captain U.S. Army 1968-71. Elected to County Republican Central Committee 1980, 1982, 1984 and 1986 (Co-

SHEWARD, RICHARD S.—*Continued*
chairman Political Action Committee 1980-83, Chairman Republican Neighborhood Rallies 1980-84 and Republican Judicial Salute 1983-84, Member Administrative Screening Committee 1983-85, Delegate Republican State Convention 1984). President Buckeye Republican Club 1981. Volunteer Charity Newsies since 1981. Member Agonis Club since 1975, Jackson County Club of Franklin County since 1975 (President 1981-82), Upper Arlington Civic Association since 1976 (life member), Fraternal Order of Police Associates of Ohio, Inc. since 1977, 32° Masons Lodge No. 684 since 1979, Prosecuting Attorney's Alumni Club (Chairman 1979-85), Touchdown Club of Columbus since 1981, American Legion since 1984, VFW since 1984, Amvets since 1984 and Vietnam Veterans of America since 1984.
Office: 369 South High Street, #9C, Columbus 43215.
Telephone: (614) 462-3770, 462-3476.
Fax: (614) 462-3476
E-mail address: richard_sheward@fccourts.org

SHRIVER, James A. *(Judge, Clermont County Municipal Court)* Appointed by Governor George V. Voinovich to term beginning Jan 9, 1995. Elected Nov 7, 1995 and Nov 4, 1997. Current term expires Dec 31, 2003. Born Cincinnati Ohio Nov 1, 1956. United Methodist. Educated at University of Cincinnati B.S. with high honors 1979 J.D. 1982. Member Phi Beta Kappa. Admitted to practice Ohio 1982 and U.S. District Court Southern District of Ohio 1982. In legal practice Cincinnati 1982-95.

Assistant Prosecutor Clermont County 1984-95. Member Criminal Law and Procedure Committee Ohio Judicial Conference since 1998. Member Association of Municipal/County Judges of Ohio, Inc., Clermont County (Leader Scouts Explorer Post 1987-89), Ohio State and American Bar Associations. Speaker Criminal Law and Procedures Class 1995, "2001 Leadership Training" 1996 and 1998 and DARE Graduations since 1995. Recipient Exemplary Performance Award from Clermont County Law Enforcement Association 1987 and Certificate of Exemplary Services from Supreme Court of Ohio Chief Justice Thomas J. Moyer 1989. Republican. Member 1986-95 and Chairman 1990-95 Clermont County Republican Central Committee. Campaign Manager Voinovich/DeWine Election Campaign 1990. Regional Chairperson George Bush Reelection Campaign 1992. Regional Chairperson and Clermont County Chairperson Voinovich/Hollister Election Campaign 1994. Volunteer Task Force on Child Sexual Abuse Clermont County 1984-89. Member 1986-95 and Chairman 1989-95 Child Abuse and Neglect Advisory Board Clermont County. Director Clermont County Mediation Program 1987-95 and ADVOCATE Project 1987-95. Board Member Association for Retarded Citizens Clermont/Brown, Inc. 1989-95. Member Committee for Selection of Director Ohio Department of Youth Services 1990-91 and Community Corrections Board since 1995. Chairman Foster Parent Advisory Committee Clermont County 1992. Member Clermont Chamber of Commerce, Cherry Grove United Methodist Church (Building Committee 1980-81 and Chairman Administrative Council since 1983), Cincinnati District Mission Society of the United Methodist Church (Chairman since 1992), Clermont County Special Olympics Committee (Treasurer/Finance Chairperson 1987-95) and Centurions of Mercy of Clermont Mercy Hospital Development Council 1986-2000.
Office: 289 Main Street, Batavia 45103-2906.
Telephone: (513) 732-7967.
Fax: (513) 732-7051

SHUFF, Steve C. *(Judge, Ohio Court of Common Pleas Seneca County)*
Office: 103 South Washington Street, Tiffin 44883.
Telephone: (419) 448-1302.
Fax: (419) 443-7927
E-mail address: scs-court@bright.net

SIKORA, Peter M. *(Judge, Ohio Court of Common Pleas Cuyahoga County)* Serves Juvenile Division.
Office: 2163 East 22nd Street, Cleveland 44115.
Telephone: (216) 443-5818.
Fax: (216) 443-3127

SIMMONS, Jeffrey L. *(Judge, Ohio Court of Common Pleas Vinton County)* Former Judge, Vinton County Court.
Office: 100 East Main Street, McArthur 45651-1267.
Telephone: (740) 596-4319.
Fax: (740) 596-9611

SINCLAIR, Lee *(Judge, Ohio Court of Common Pleas Stark County)* Born Canton Ohio 1951. Educated at Kent State University B.A. 1973 and University of Akron J.D. 1976. Member Delta Theta Phi. Admitted to practice Ohio 1976.
Office: 115 Central Plaza North, Canton 44702.
Telephone: (330) 451-7789.
Fax: (330) 451-7740

SINGER, Arlene *(Judge, Ohio Court of Appeals Sixth District)* Born Toledo Ohio Oct 10, 1948. Jewish. Educated at University of Toledo B.A. 1972 J.D. 1976. Admitted to practice Ohio 1976, U.S. District Court Northern District of Ohio 1977 and U.S. Tax Court 1981. In legal practice Toledo 1976-91. Former Judge, Toledo Municipal Court, appointed by Governor Richard F. Celeste to term beginning Jan 1, 1991.

Assistant Prosecutor Lucas County 1989-91. Member Ohio Judicial Conference, Toledo Women's, Toledo, Lucas County and Ohio State Bar Associations. Democrat. State Representative Ohio 1987-88. Associate Member Vietnam Veterans of America.
Office: 800 Jackson, Toledo 43624.

SKOW, William J. *(Judge, Ohio Court of Common Pleas Lucas County)* Appointed by Governor Richard F. Celeste to term beginning Feb 28, 1986. Elected Nov 1986, Nov 1988, 1994 and 2000. Current term expires Jan 2, 2007. Born Toledo Ohio May 20, 1941. Educated at Harvard College A.B. 1963 and University of Michigan Law School J.D. 1966. Admitted to practice Ohio 1967 and U.S. District Court Northern District of Ohio 1969. In legal practice Toledo 1969-83. Judge, Toledo Municipal Court 1983-86.

Chief Legislative Assistant/Counsel to U.S. Congressman Thomas Ludlow Ashley 1977-81. Member Ohio Common Pleas Judges Association, American Judicature Society, Toledo, Lucas County, Ohio State and American Bar Associations. Graduate General Jurisdiction Course The National Judicial College 1984. Instructor and participant in miscellaneous Judicial seminars Ohio Judicial College. Recipient Order of the Heel Award for largest and most significant contributions to younger lawyers from Toledo Junior Bar Association 1988. Spe-

SKOW, WILLIAM J.—*Continued*
cialist Fifth Class U.S. Army 1967-69. Recipient Bronze Star April 21, 1969. Executive Committee Lucas County Democratic Party. Member Toledo Museum of Art, Toledo Zoological Society, Toledo Legal Aid Society and numerous other groups. Enjoys reading, golf and being a husband and father.
Office: Courthouse, 700 Adams Street, Toledo 43624.
Telephone: (419) 213-4566.
Fax: (419) 213-4181

SLABY, Lynn C. *(Judge, Ohio Court of Appeals Ninth District)* Appointed by Governor George V. Voinovich to term beginning Jan 9, 1995. Born Cleveland Ohio. Educated at University of Akron B.S. in Business Administration 1967 and University of Akron School of Law J.D. 1972. Admitted to practice Ohio, U.S District Court, U.S. Court of Appeals and U.S. Supreme Court. In legal practice Cuyahoga 1973, Akron 1974-81 and Summit County 1981-95.
Assistant Law Director Cuyahoga Falls 1973. Assistant Law Director, Assistant Prosecutor and Police Legal Advisor Akron 1974-81. Prosecuting Attorney Summit County 1981-95. Instructor University of Akron School of Law. Past President National District Attorneys Association and Ohio Prosecuting Attorneys Association. Past Chairman statewide committee to study Ohio's "not guilty by reason of insanity" plea. Board Member Ohio Family Support Association. Member Ohio Appellate Judges Association, Ohio Judges Association and American Bar Association (Council Member Criminal Justice Section, Member Victims Committee). Attended The National Judicial College and Ohio Judicial College. Lecturer various state seminars. Instructor National College of District Attorneys, The Akron Police Academy, The Sheriffs Academy and American Institute for Paralegal Studies, Inc. Recipient Outstanding Prosecutor of the Year 1988, Resolution of Honor Award 1991 and Leadership Award 1992 from Ohio Prosecuting Attorney Association; Leadership Award 1990 and Presidents Award 1995 from National District Attorneys Association; The Optimist Outstanding Law Enforcement Officer Award and Masonic Outstanding Community Service Award. Previously employed as Branch Manager for National City Bank and Trust Department Goodyear Bank. Former Board member Summit County Child Morbidity Review Board, Summit Forum and Child Abuse Prosecution Grant Project. Board of Directors Cleveland Christian Home for Children, High Street Christian Church, The Victim Witness Program, Big Brothers/Big Sisters and The All American Soap Box Derby.
Office: 161 South High Street, Suite 504, Akron 44308-1671.
Telephone: (330) 643-2250.
Fax: (330) 643-2091
E-mail address: lynn@ninth.courts.state.oh.us

SMITH, Beth A. *(Judge, Ohio Court of Common Pleas Mahoning County)* Serves Domestic Relations Division. Former Judge, Mahoning County Court.
Office: 120 Market Street, Youngstown 44503.
Telephone: (330) 740-2208.
Fax: (330) 740-2503

SMITH, George C. *(Senior Judge, United States District Court Southern District of Ohio)* Appointed for life by President Ronald Reagan to term beginning Dec 1, 1987. Assumed Senior status Jan 1, 2002, serves by continuous assignment. Born Columbus Ohio Aug 8, 1935. Presbyterian. Educated at The Ohio State University B.A. 1957 LL.B. 1959. Member Phi Eta Sigma, Sphinx, Bucket and Dipper and Romophos (President). Admitted to practice Ohio 1959, U.S. District Court Southern District of Ohio 1969 and U.S. Supreme Court 1971. In legal practice Columbus 1959-80. Judge, Franklin County Municipal Court 1980-85. Judge, Ohio Court of Common Pleas Franklin County 1985-87.
Assistant City Attorney and Assistant Attorney General Ohio 1959-65. Prosecuting Attorney 1971-80. Author numerous articles for teaching legal seminars. Important Decisions: Ent. Energy Co. v. Columbia Gas C2-85-1209 S.D. Ohio 1991, Martin v. Taft (Gov.) 840 F. Supp. 1175 S.D. Ohio 1993, U.S. v. General Electric 869 F. Supp. 1285 S.D. Ohio 1994 and U.S. v. Russell (41 Short North Posse defendants) CR2-95-44 (1-41) 1996. Lecturer on Business Law Columbus State University 1980-87. Visiting Lecturer and Judge in Residence University of Cincinnati College of Law 1993. Past President Lawyers Club of Columbus, The Association of Trial Lawyers of America and Ohio Prosecutors Association. Legislative Chair Ohio Municipal Court Association and Ohio Common Pleas Judges Association. Member Columbus Bar Foundation, Columbus, Ohio State and American Bar Associations. Chair Bench/Bar Conference Southern District of Ohio 1994. Lecturer Anti-Trust Section American Bar Association, Price-Waterhouse programs on complex cases Cleveland and Columbus, Lorman Educational seminars and Ohio Judicial College. Recipient Superior Judicial Service Award from Ohio Supreme Court and Ohio Prosecutor of the Year Award. Member Ohio Bicentennial Commission 2003. Past President Capital City, Buckeye Republican Club and 33° Association. President Athletic Club of Columbus. Trustee Leukemia Society. Elder Presbyterian Church. Member Scottish Rite, Masons (Honorary 33°), American Lung Association, Crime Stoppers, The Perry Group (President) and Ohio and Lake Erie Islands historical societies. Interests include history, swimming and fishing.
Office: 101 U.S. Courthouse, 85 Marconi Boulevard, Columbus 43215.
Telephone: (614) 719-3220.
Fax: (614) 469-5418

SMITH, Kevin C. *(Judge, Findlay Municipal Court)* Appointed by Governor George V. Voinovich to term beginning Dec 14, 1998. Elected Nov 2, 1999. Born Lima Ohio July 24, 1954. Catholic. Educated at U.S. Coast Guard Academy B.S. with honors 1976 and Cleveland State University J.D. cum laude 1982. Admitted to practice Ohio 1983 and U.S. District Court Northern District of Ohio 1983. In legal practice Findlay 1983-91. Magistrate Ohio Court of Common Pleas 1991-98.
Assistant Prosecuting Attorney 1983-91. Instructor University of Findlay since 1994. Member Findlay/Hancock County, Ohio State and American Bar Associations. USCG 1976-81. Board Member YMCA. Member Kiwanis.
Office: 208 Municipal Building, Findlay 45840-3306.
Telephone: (419) 424-7144.
Fax: (419) 424-7803
E-mail address: ksmith@ci.findlay.oh.us

SMITH, Norman P. *(Judge, Ohio Court of Common Pleas Shelby County)* Elected to term beginning Feb 9,

SMITH, NORMAN P.—*Continued*

1991. Reelected 1996 and 2002. Current term expires Feb 8, 2009. Serves Probate and Juvenile Divisions. Born Tiffin Ohio Sept 27, 1943. Educated at University of Dayton B.S. 1965 and University of Notre Dame J.D. 1968. Admitted to practice Ohio 1968 and U.S. District Court Southern District of Ohio 1968. In legal practice Sidney 1968-91 and Jackson Center 1977-91.

Prosecuting Attorney Shelby County 1973-76.

Mailing address: P.O. Box 4187, Sidney 45365-4187.
Telephone: (937) 498-7265.
Fax: (937) 498-7260
E-mail address: sheljuv@bright.net

SOLOVAN, John M., II *(Judge, Ohio Court of Common Pleas Belmont County)* Elected to term beginning 1997. Reelected 2002, current term expires 2009. Born Wheeling West Virginia. Educated at Xavier University B.S. magna cum laude 1968 and Boston College Law School J.D. 1971. Admitted to practice Massachusetts 1971, Ohio 1973, U.S. District Court Southern District of Ohio 1980 and U.S. Supreme Court 1982. Judge, Belmont County Court 1978-96.

Instructor Wheeling Jesuit University 1977-79. Member Belmont County and Ohio State Bar Associations. Captain U.S. Army JAGC 1972-75. Member Martins Ferry Elks and Rotary Club.

Office: 101 West Main Street, St. Clairsville 43950-1154.
Telephone: (740) 699-2138.
Fax: (740) 695-4968

SPACE, Mary Wade *(Judge, New Philadelphia Municipal Court)*

Office: 166 East High Avenue, New Philadelphia 44663-2540.
Telephone: (330) 364-4491.
Fax: (330) 364-6885

SPAETH, Keith *(Judge, Ohio Court of Common Pleas Butler County)* Former Judge, Fairfield Municipal Court.

Office: Government Services Center, 315 High Street, Third Floor, Hamilton 45011.
Telephone: (513) 887-3586.
Fax: (513) 785-5757
E-mail address: spaethkm@butlercountyohio.org

SPAHN, G. Daniel *(Judge, Steubenville Municipal Court)*

Office: 123 South Third Street, Steubenville 43952-2895.
Telephone: (740) 283-6028.
Fax: (740) 283-6167

SPAHR, Jon R. *(Judge, Ohio Court of Common Pleas Licking County)* Elected to term beginning Jan 1, 1983. Reelected 1988, 1994 and 2000. Current term expires Dec 31, 2006. Born New Castle Indiana Sept 20, 1939. Presbyterian. Educated at Miami University B.S. 1961 and The Ohio State University J.D. 1964. Member Phi Kappa Tau. Admitted to practice Ohio 1964 and U.S. District Court Southern District of Ohio 1965. Began legal practice Newark 1964. Judge, Licking County Municipal Court 1979-82.

Former Solicitor Village of Hebron. Instructor Central Ohio Technical College since 1983. Member Licking County, Ohio State and American Bar Associations. Instructor Ohio Judicial College since 1980. Recipient Superior Judicial Service Awards from Ohio Supreme Court 1979-81. Board member United Way and Rotary Club. Member Big Brothers/Big Sisters Association. Enjoys running, golf, tennis and gardening.

Office: Courthouse, Newark 43055.
Telephone: (740) 349-6181.
Fax: (740) 349-1414
E-mail address: jspahr@lcounty.com

SPANAGEL, Kenneth R. *(Judge, Parma Municipal Court)* Elected Nov 8, 1987 to term beginning Jan 1, 1988. Reelected Nov 5, 1993 and Nov 3, 1999. Current term expires Dec 31, 2005. Born Cleveland Ohio Oct 5, 1950. Lutheran. Educated at Northwestern University B.S. 1972 and Case Western Reserve University Law School J.D. 1975. Admitted to practice Ohio 1975 and U.S. Supreme Court 1981. In legal practice Parma and Cleveland 1975-87.

Member Northern Ohio Municipal Judges Association, Municipal-County Judges of Ohio, Inc. (Trustee), American Judges Association, Cleveland, Parma (Past President, Trustee, Co-chairman CLE Committee), Cuyahoga County (Co-chair Traffic Law Committee) and Ohio State (Council of Delegates since 1980, Chairman 1993-95 and Member Traffic Law Committee, Member Judicial Administration and Legal Reform Committees) Bar Associations. Lecturer on DWI, Traffic Law, Ethics and other topics CLE programs Parma Bar Association, Ohio State Bar Association, Case Western Reserve University Law School, Academy of Continuing Legal Education, Cleveland DWI Task Force Ohio CLE Institute and Ohio Judicial College. Member Parma Republican Club, Parma Heights Republican Club, Brooklyn Republican Club, North Royalton Republican Club and Seven Hills Republican Club. Former Board Member and Past President Samaritan Counseling Center. Board of Managers Ridgewood YMCA. Member Parma Exchange Club, Parma Chamber of Commerce, North Royalton Chamber of Commerce, Elks, Masons and Cleveland American Middle East Organization. Enjoys music, reading, Tai Chi, fishing and sports.

Office: 5555 Powers Boulevard, Parma 44129.
Telephone: (440) 887-7473.
Fax: (440) 887-7490
E-mail address: jdork1005@yahoo.com

SPEARS, David E. *(Judge, Ohio Court of Common Pleas Scioto County)* Elected 1994. Reelected to subsequent term. Serves Domestic Relations Division. Former Judge, Portsmouth Municipal Court.

Office: Courthouse, 602 Seventh Street, Portsmouth 45662.
Telephone: (740) 355-8316.
Fax: (740) 355-8205

SPEER, Richard Lyle *(Judge, United States Bankruptcy Court Northern District of Ohio)* Appointed by U.S. District Court judges to term beginning Sept 2, 1975. Reappointed by U.S. Court of Appeals Sixth Circuit judges Oct 1, 1986 and 2000. Term expires Oct 2014. Chief Judge July 1, 1997 to July 1, 2001. Born Norwalk Ohio Aug 14, 1941. Educated at Ohio Northern University B.S.Ed. 1963 J.D. 1966. Member Phi Mu Delta and Phi Alpha Delta. Admitted to practice Ohio 1966, U.S. District Courts Southern 1967 and Northern 1969 Districts of Ohio, U.S. Courts of Appeals Sixth 1968, Ninth 1981, District of Columbia 1981, Third 1982, Fourth 1982, Fifth 1982, Seventh 1982, Tenth 1983 and Eleventh 1983 Circuits, U.S. Supreme Court

SPEER, RICHARD LYLE—*Continued*

1970, U.S. Court of Military Appeals 1970 and U.S. Tax Court 1970. In legal practice Columbus 1968, Port Clinton 1969-70 and Oak Harbor 1970-75.

Instructor in Real Estate Law Terra Technical College since 1972. Member Toledo, Lucas County, Ottawa County (President 1970), Ohio State and American Bar Associations. Named Outstanding Real Estate Instructor for District Four by Ohio Association of Realtors 1978. Interested in Civil War history and genealogy.

Office: 113 U.S. Courthouse, 1716 Spielbusch Avenue, Toledo 43624.

Telephone: (419) 259-7559.

SPEES, Mark E. *(Judge, Ohio Court of Common Pleas Auglaize County)* Serves Probate and Family Divisions.

Office: 201 Willipie Street, #103, Wapakoneta 45895-1972.

Telephone: (419) 738-7710 (probate), 738-3930 (family).

Fax: (419) 739-7563

SPICER, Kenneth Jerome *(Judge, Ohio Court of Common Pleas Delaware County)* Serves Probate and Juvenile Divisions.

Office: 88 North Sandusky, Delaware 43015.

SPICER, Mary F. *(Judge, Ohio Court of Common Pleas Summit County)* Referee Probate Division July 1975 to Jan 1985. Elected Judge to term beginning Jan 3, 1985. Reelected Nov 1990, Nov 1996 and 2002. Current term expires Jan 2009. Born Akron Ohio Jan 20, 1937. Protestant. Educated at Heidelberg College B.A. 1958, University of Chicago M.A. 1960 and University of Akron J.D. 1965. Admitted to practice Ohio 1965. In legal practice Akron 1965-75.

Member Akron, Ohio State and American Bar Associations. Attends Ohio Judicial Seminars annually. Previously employed as psychiatric social worker Summit County Receiving Hospital Cuyahoga Falls. Republican. Member National Association of Social Workers, Zonta International, Crime Clinic, American Association of University Women, Summit County Historical Society, Greater Akron Humane Society, American Humane and U.S. Humane Society. Interests include animals, humane activities and civic service.

Office: 209 South High Street, Akron 44308-1610.

Telephone: (330) 643-2247.

Fax: (330) 643-2410

SPICER, W. F. "Bill" *(Judge, Ohio Court of Common Pleas Summit County)* Assumed office Aug 1980. Elected to subsequent terms. Current term expires 2009. Serves Probate Division. Born Akron Ohio Jan 12, 1942. Educated at University of Akron B.A. 1965 J.D. 1972 and The Ohio State University post graduate work 1969. Member Phi Kappa Tau. Admitted to practice Ohio 1972. Judge, Akron Municipal Court 1979-80.

Assistant City Prosecutor Akron 1973-75. Assistant U.S. Attorney 1975-78. Chief Trial Attorney Akron Law Department 1978-79. Member National College of Probate Judges, Ohio Probate Judges Association, American Judicature Society, Akron, Ohio State and American Bar Associations. Attended U.S. Attorney General Advocacy Institute May 1976 and The National Judicial College July 1979. Recipient Superior Judicial Service Award and Excellent Judicial Service Award from Ohio Supreme Court. Captain U.S. Army Vietnam 1965-67 and USAR 1967-72. Recipient Commendation Medal 1966. Instructor Hower Vocational School 1967-69. Member Church of the Good Shepherd United Methodist, VFW and Boy Scouts of America.

Office: 209 South High Street, Akron 44308-1668.

Telephone: (330) 643-2330.

Fax: (330) 643-2393

E-mail address: jbspicer@probate.summitoh.net

SPIEGEL, S. Arthur *(Senior Judge, United States District Court Southern District of Ohio)* Appointed for life by President Jimmy Carter to term beginning June 5, 1980. Assumed Senior status June 5, 1995, serves by assignment. Born Cincinnati Ohio Oct 24, 1920. Jewish. Educated at University of Cincinnati B.A. 1942 and Harvard Law School LL.B. 1948. Admitted to practice Ohio 1948, U.S. Court of Appeals Sixth Circuit 1949, U.S. District Court Southern District of Ohio 1949 and U.S. Supreme Court 1973. In legal practice Cincinnati 1948-80.

Instructor University of Cincinnati College of Law 1970-75. Member Cincinnati Lawyers Club, Cincinnati, Ohio State, Federal and American Bar Associations. Served to Captain USMC 1942-46.

Office: 838 U.S. Courthouse, 100 East Fifth Street, Cincinnati 45202-3976.

Telephone: (513) 564-7620.

SPILLANE, Leslie C. *(Judge, Ohio Court of Common Pleas Butler County)* Elected to term beginning Jan 2, 1987. Reelected 1992 and 1998. Current term expires 2004. Serves Domestic Relations Division. Born Hamilton Ohio May 28, 1943. Educated at Miami University B.A. 1965, Salmon P. Chase College of Law J.D. 1974 and University of Nevada Reno M.J.S. 1997. Member Order of Curia. Admitted to practice Ohio 1974. In legal practice Hamilton 1974-86. Referee, Domestic Relations Court 1979-81. Judge, Butler County Court 1982-86.

Assistant County Prosecutor 1976-79. Author "Spousal Support: The Other Ohio Lottery" Ohio Northern University L. Rev. 1998. Member Ohio Domestic Relations Judges Association, Ohio Academy of Trial Lawyers, National Association of Women Judges, National Association for Court Management, The Association of Trial Lawyers of America and Ohio State Bar Association. Republican.

Office: Government Services Center, Second Floor, 315 High Street, Hamilton 45011.

Telephone: (513) 887-3345.

Fax: (513) 785-5337

E-mail address: lspillane@butlercountyohio.org

SPON, Ronald *(Judge, Ohio Court of Common Pleas Richland County)* Serves Domestic Relations and Juvenile Divisions.

Office: 411 South Diamond Street, Mansfield 44902.

Telephone: (419) 774-5647.

Fax: (419) 774-5574

SPURGEON, Paul E. *(Judge, Mount Vernon Municipal Court)* Elected Nov 2, 1999 to term beginning Jan 1, 2000. Term expires Dec 31, 2005. Born Mount Vernon Ohio Feb 24, 1948. Educated at The Ohio State University B.S. 1970 and Capital University J.D. 1976. Admitted to practice Ohio 1976, U.S. District Courts

SPURGEON, PAUL E.—*Continued*

Northern and Southern Districts of Ohio and U.S. Supreme Court. In legal practice Mount Vernon 1978-99.

Member Ohio State Bar Association.

Office: Five North Gay Street, Mount Vernon 43050.
Telephone: (740) 393-9510.
Fax: (740) 393-5349

SQUIRE, Carole R. *(Judge, Ohio Court of Common Pleas Franklin County)* Elected to term beginning Jan 8, 2001. Term expires Jan 1, 2007. Serves Domestic Relations and Juvenile Divisions. Born Springfield Ohio July 21, 1953. Baptist. Educated at The Ohio State University B.A. 1974 J.D. 1977. Admitted to practice Ohio 1977 and U.S. Court of Appeals Sixth Circuit 1993. In legal practice Columbus 1982-83, 1987-89, 1995 and 1997. Juvenile Referee/Magistrate, Ohio Court of Common Pleas Franklin County 1991-94.

Assistant Prosecutor Diversion Unit Franklin County 1977. Staff Attorney The Ohio Legal Rights Services 1977-78. Attorney Advisor and General Counsel U.S. Department of the Navy 1979-82. Assistant Attorney General Ohio 1986-87. Instructor University of Maryland and Temple University, Germany 1980-82. Professorial Lecturer American University 1983-84. Member Ohio Association of Juvenile and Family Court Judges, Ohio Judicial Conference, National Council of Juvenile and Family Court Judges, Ohio State and National Bar Associations. Attended Ohio Bench Bar Conference March 7, 2002, Family Law Seminar March 8, 2002 and Juvenile Justice Seminar Dec 5, 2002 Ohio Judicial Conference, Jury Trial Seminar March 14, 2002 and Juvenile Justice Coalition Sept 19, 2002. Board Member Art for a Child Safe America. Founder and Director Project R.E.A.D. (Reading for Enlightenment and Delinquency Prevention). Sunday School Youth Department Superintendent Shiloh Baptist Church.

Office: 373 South High Street, Sixth Floor, Columbus 43215.
Telephone: (614) 462-5223.
Fax: (614) 462-7440
E-mail address: carole_squire@fccourts.org

STALEY, Matt C. *(Judge, Ohio Court of Common Pleas Allen County)* Serves Domestic Relations Division.

Mailing address: P.O. Box 1243, Lima 45802.
Telephone: (419) 223-8511.
Fax: (419) 227-3162

STARR, Walter R. *(Judge, Ohio Court of Common Pleas Monroe County)* Serves Probate and Juvenile Divisions.

Office: 101 North Main Street, Room 39, Woodsfield 43793-1099.
Telephone: (740) 472-1654.
Fax: (740) 472-2520

STEELE, Charles D. *(Judge, Ohio Court of Common Pleas Van Wert County)* Appointed by Governor Bob Taft to term beginning Feb 9, 1999. Elected 2000, current term expires Dec 31, 2006. Born Van Wert Ohio Nov 2, 1947. Methodist. Educated at Bowling Green State University B.S. 1972, St. Francis College M.S. 1977 and Ohio Northern University J.D. 1980. Admitted to practice Ohio 1981. In legal practice Van Wert 1981-99.

Assistant Prosecuting Attorney 1988-99. Member Van Wert County, Northwest Ohio and Ohio State Bar Associations. USMC 1966-69. USAR since 1982. Republican. Former Member County Central Committee. Former Member and Past President Van Wert City Council. Member Kiwanis, Elks, American Legion and VFW. Enjoys travel, reading and military history.

Office: 305 Courthouse, 121 East Main Street, Van Wert 45891-1729.
Telephone: (419) 238-6935.
Fax: (419) 238-2874
E-mail address: steelecharles@yahoo.com

STEINER, Russell A. *(Judge, Ohio Court of Common Pleas Licking County)* Elected to term beginning 1991. Reelected 1996 and 2002. Current term expires Dec 2008. Serves Domestic Relations Division. Born Lewisburg Ohio Nov 27, 1935. Catholic. Educated at University of Dayton B.Ch.E. 1965, The Ohio State University and Capital University J.D. 1972. Articles Editor Capital University Law Review 1972. Admitted to practice Ohio 1972. In legal practice Columbus 1972 and Newark 1974. Judge, Licking County Municipal Court Sept 23, 1983 to Dec 31, 1990, appointed by Governor Richard F. Celeste.

Arbitrator Columbus Mini-Arbitration Panel 1974-83. Contributor articles on Domestic Relations law Ohio Domestic Relations Law Journal. President Ohio Domestic Relations Judges Association 2000-01. Member American Family Court and Conciliators Conference, Licking County, Ohio State and American Bar Associations. Faculty Member Ohio Judicial Conference. E-4 U.S. Army 1958-60. Former Development Engineer Western Electric. Former Production Engineer and Environmental Control Coordinator Abbott Laboratories. Charter President Newark Evening Lions Club 1978. Life Member Disabled American Veterans.

Office: 75 East Main Street, Newark 43055.
Telephone: (740) 349-6215.
Fax: (740) 349-1485
E-mail address: steiner@alltel.net

STEVENS, Richard L. *(Judge, Ashtabula County Court)* Appointed by Governor James A. Rhodes to term beginning Dec 30, 1982. Elected 1984, 1986, 1992 and 1998. Current term expires Dec 31, 2004. Born Ashtabula Ohio April 6, 1947. Protestant. Educated at Kenyon College 1965-68 and Ohio Northern University B.A. with honors 1969 J.D. with honors 1976. Member Willis Society and Phi Kappa Phi. Admitted to practice Ohio 1977. Began legal practice Geneva 1977. In legal practice Jefferson 1981-82.

Member Ashtabula County, Ohio State and American Bar Associations. Previously worked as high school teacher and coach and construction worker. Former Chairman Geneva Downtown Revitalization Committee. Charter member Geneva Jaycees and Geneva-on-the-Lake Kiwanis Club. Member Geneva Rotary and Italian Sons and Daughters of America. Enjoys camping, traveling, golfing and music.

Office: 117 West Main Street, Geneva 44041.
Telephone: (440) 466-1184.
Fax: (440) 466-7171

STEWART, Robert William *(Judge, Ohio Court of Common Pleas Athens County)* Serves Probate and Juvenile Divisions.

Office: One South Court Street, Athens 45701.

STOCKDALE, David C. *(Judge, Hamilton County Municipal Court)*
Office: 1000 Main Street, Cincinnati 45202.
Telephone: (513) 946-5160.
Fax: (513) 946-5162
E-mail address: dstockda@cms.hamilton-co.org

STOKES, Angela R. *(Judge, Cleveland Municipal Court)*
Mailing address: P.O. Box 94894, Cleveland 44101-4894.
Office: 1200 Ontario Street, Cleveland 44113.
Telephone: (216) 664-4986.
Fax: (216) 664-4283

STORMER, Elinore Marsh *(Judge, Akron Municipal Court)* Elected Nov 1991. Reelected 1993 and 1999. Current term expires Jan 2, 2006. Born Bridgeport Connecticut Oct 9, 1956. Catholic. Educated at Davidson College 1978 and University of Akron J.D. 1982. Case and Comment Editor Akron Law Review 1981. Admitted to practice Ohio 1982. In legal practice Akron 1982-89.

General Counsel Summit County Executive 1989-91. Member Association of Municipal/County Judges of Ohio, Inc. (Trustee), Akron, Ohio State and American Bar Associations. Democrat. Trustee Ohio Community Corrections Organization. Board Member Weathervane Playhouse and Akron Urban League.

Office: 217 South High Street, Room 943, Akron 44308-1611.
Telephone: (330) 375-2054.
Fax: (330) 375-2238
E-mail address: stormel@ci.akron.oh.us

STORY, Steven L. *(Judge, Meigs County Court)*
Office: Courthouse, Pomeroy 45769.
Telephone: (740) 992-2279.
Fax: (740) 992-4570

STOUT, Gary Creamer *(Judge, Washington Court House Municipal Court)* Elected to term beginning Nov 17, 1977. Elected to subsequent terms. Current term expires Dec 31, 2005. Born Harlingen Texas March 2, 1945. Episcopalian. Educated at Ohio Northern University B.S. in Education 1967 J.D. 1970. Member Phi Alpha Delta and Phi Mu Delta. Admitted to practice Ohio 1971. In legal practice Xenia 1971-77 and Jeffersonville 1975-92. Referee, Ohio Court of Common Pleas Greene County Probate Division 1972-73.

Member Ohio Municipal Judges Association (Trustee), Ohio Judicial Conference, Fayette County (President 1986-87) and Ohio State Bar Associations. Attended Ohio State Bar College and Ohio Judicial College. Recipient All-Star Citizen of the Year Team Award from the Police Athletic League 1984. Specialist Fourth Class Ohio National Guard 1968-74. Republican. Member St. Andrews Episcopal Church, Washington Court House Rotary Club, Scottish Rite Masons, Shriners, Chamber of Commerce, Symposiarchs, Jeffersonville Masonic Lodge 648, Eastern Star and Elks. Enjoys hunting, fishing, camping and golfing.

Office: 119 North Main Street, Washington Court House 43160-1330.
Telephone: (740) 636-2350.
Fax: (740) 636-2359

STRATTON, Evelyn Lundberg *(Justice, Supreme Court of Ohio)* Appointed by Governor George V. Voinovich to term beginning March 4, 1996. Elected 1996 and 2002. Current term expires 2009. Youngest member to serve Supreme Court of Ohio. Born Bangkok Thailand Feb 25, 1953. Protestant. Educated at LeTourneau College 1971-74, University of Florida 1973, University of Akron B.A. 1976 and The Ohio State University J.D. 1978. Member Phi Delta Phi. Admitted to practice Ohio 1979, U.S. District Court Southern District of Ohio 1979 and U.S. Court of Appeals Sixth Circuit 1979. In legal practice 1979-88. Judge, Ohio Court of Common Pleas Franklin County Jan 3, 1989 to March 4, 1996 (youngest person and first woman to serve Ohio Court of Common Pleas Franklin County).

Former Member Columbus Defense Association, Ohio Association of Civil Trial Attorneys, The Association of Trial Lawyers of America, American Arbitration Association, American Inns of Court (President 1991-92), American Judges Association, Ohio Common Pleas Judges Association (Legislative Committee) and Ohio Judicial Conference (Chair Civil Law and Procedure Committee and Executive Committee 1993-96). Co-chair Security in Ohio Courts Committee Supreme Court of Ohio since 1992. Member Women Lawyers of Franklin County, Columbus Bar Foundation (Board of Trustees 1986-91, Vice President 1987-88), Columbus (Chair Common Pleas Court 1983-84, Member Board of Governors 1984-88 and 1990-92), Ohio State (Council of Delegates 1992-96, Judicial Administrative and Reform Committee) and American Bar Associations. Active in teaching both lawyers and judges in several seminars each year. Named one of Outstanding Young Women of America 1983 and 1985 and Woman of the Year by American Biographical Institute 1992. Recipient Commendation for Service from Ohio House of Representatives 1984. Listed in *Who's Who Among American Women* 14th, 15th, 16th, 18th and 21st editions and *Who's Who in American Law* 5th, 6th, 7th, 10th and 11th editions. Board of Trustees Franklin County Community Corrections Planning Board 1992-96, Ohio Community Corrections Organization since 1995, Dave Thomas Adoption Foundation since 1996 and ArChSafe (Art for a Child's Safe America) since 1997. Board of Directors Executive Club 1986-89. Member United Way 1982 and 1987, Ohio Affiliate National Society to Prevent Blindness 1989-99 (Secretary 1994-95, Member since 1989 and Chair since 1999 Board of Trustees), Women's Board Central Ohio Lung Association since 1989 (Zephyrus League since 1989), Alliance for Women in Community Corrections since 1993, Columbus Council of World Affairs (Board of Trustees 1990-99) and League Against Child Abuse (Women's Board 1989-94). Hobbies include piano, art, writing and cross-country skiing.

Office: 30 East Broad Street, Third Floor, Columbus 43266-0419.
Telephone: (614) 466-2926.
Fax: (614) 728-2021
E-mail address: strattonoe@sconet.state.oh.us

STREEPY, Jack B. *(Magistrate Judge, United States District Court Northern District of Ohio)* Appointed by U.S. District Court judges.
Office: 9B U.S. Courthouse, 801 West Superior Avenue, Cleveland 44113-1849.
Telephone: (216) 357-7230.

STREET, John B. *(Judge, Chillicothe Municipal Court)* Elected to term beginning Jan 1, 1996. Reelected 2001, current term expires Dec 31, 2007. Born Bad

STREET, JOHN B.—*Continued*

Cannstadt Germany May 11, 1956. Episcopalian. Educated at Wake Forest University B.A. cum laude 1978 and Washington and Lee University J.D. 1981. Admitted to practice Ohio 1981, U.S. District Court Southern District of Ohio, U.S. Court of Appeals Sixth Circuit and U.S. Supreme Court. In legal practice Chillicothe 1981-95.

Assistant Prosecuting Attorney Ross County 1993-95. Member Association of Municipal/County Judges of Ohio, Inc., Ohio Judicial Conference, American Judges Association, Ross County and Ohio State Bar Associations. President Chillicothe City Council 1989-95. Advisory Board Salvation Army. Member Rotary Club.

Mailing address: 626 Seminole Road, Chillicothe 45601.
Office: 26 South Paint Street, Chillicothe 45601.
Telephone: (740) 773-4202.
Fax: (740) 774-1101
E-mail address: jbstreet@bright.net

STUARD, John M. *(Judge, Ohio Court of Common Pleas Trumbull County)* Appointed by Governor Richard F. Celeste to term beginning Feb 14, 1991. Elected 1992, 1994 and 2000. Current term expires Dec 31, 2006. Born Sharon Pennsylvania March 26, 1939. Baptist. Educated at Thiel College A.B. 1961 and University of Kentucky J.D. 1965. Member Lambda Chi Alpha. Admitted to practice Ohio 1965. In legal practice Warren 1965-88. Judge, Trumbull County Court Jan 1, 1983 to Jan 1991.

City Prosecutor Warren 1968-70. City Solicitor Newton Falls 1971-72 and Orangeville 1977-82. Member Trumbull County and Ohio State Bar Associations. Antique weapon collector. Interests include hunting, conservation of wildlife and Civil War.

Office: 161 High Street N.W., Warren 44481-1006.
Telephone: (330) 675-2534.
Fax: (330) 675-2580
E-mail address: glipnir@aol.com

STUCKI, David E. *(Judge, Ohio Court of Common Pleas Stark County)* Appointed by Governor George V. Voinovich to term beginning Feb 10, 1993. Elected Nov 1994 and Nov 2000. Current term expires Jan 1, 2007. Serves Domestic Relations Division. Born Massillon Ohio May 8, 1959. American Baptist. Educated at University of Akron B.A. cum laude 1981 J.D. 1985. Law Clerk to Hon. Ira G. Turpin, Ohio Court of Common Pleas Stark County and Ohio Court of Appeals Fifth District 1980-85. Law Clerk and Bailiff Hon. Richard T. Kettler, Massillon Municipal Court 1983. Admitted to practice Ohio 1985, U.S. District Court Northern District of Ohio 1985 and U.S. Court of Appeals Sixth Circuit 1986. In legal practice as a sole practitioner Brewster 1985-93.

Prosecutor Massillon Municipal Court 1985-91. Member Governor's Council on Juvenile Justice since 1994. Member Ohio Supreme Court Commission for Certification of Attorneys as Specialists since 1998. Member Ohio Association of Domestic Relations Judges, Ohio Juvenile Judges Association, National Council of Juvenile and Family Court Judges, Stark County and Ohio State Bar Associations. Republican. Member Republican Central and Executive Committees 1978-93. Member Fairless Local Board of Education 1991-92. Board of Review Ohio Industrial Commissions 1991-93.

Office: 601 Citizens Savings Building, 110 Central Plaza South, Canton 44702-1414.
Telephone: (330) 451-7308.
Fax: (330) 451-7837
E-mail address: JudgeStucki@co.stark.oh.us

SUNDERMAN, David *(Judge, Delaware Municipal Court)*

Office: Justice Center, 70 North Union Street, Delaware 43015.
Telephone: (740) 368-1575.
Fax: (740) 368-1583
E-mail address: judgesunderman@municipalcourt.org

SUNDERMANN, J. Howard, Jr. *(Judge, Ohio Court of Appeals First District)* Elected 1995. Reelected to subsequent term. Presiding Judge 1998. Educated at University of Notre Dame B.A. 1963 and Georgetown University J.D. 1966. In legal practice Cincinnati 1969-79. Judge, Hamilton County Municipal Court 1980-88. Judge, Ohio Court of Common Pleas Hamilton County 1988-95.

Member Cincinnati and Ohio State Bar Associations. Former Member Cincinnatus Society, Leadership Cincinnati, Cincinnati Board of Education and Cincinnati Recreation Commission.

Office: 230 East Ninth Street, 12th Floor, Cincinnati 45202-1287.
Telephone: (513) 946-3424.
Fax: (513) 946-3411

SUSTER, Ronald *(Judge, Ohio Court of Common Pleas Cuyahoga County)* Assumed office Oct 5, 1995. Elected Nov 1996 and 2000. Current term expires Jan 2, 2007. Born Cleveland Ohio Oct 31, 1942. Catholic. Educated at Case Western Reserve University B.A. 1964 J.D. 1967. Admitted to practice Ohio 1967 and Florida 1975.

Former Assistant Prosecutor Cuyahoga County. Former Assistant Law Director Cleveland. Former Assistant Attorney General Ohio. Former State Representative Ohio.

Office: 1200 Ontario Street, Room 20B, Cleveland 44113-1678.
Telephone: (216) 443-8727.
Fax: (216) 348-4034

SUTULA, John D. *(Judge, Ohio Court of Common Pleas Cuyahoga County)*

Office: 1200 Ontario Street, Cleveland 44113-1678.
Telephone: (216) 443-8680.
Fax: (216) 348-4037

SUTULA, Kathleen Ann *(Judge, Ohio Court of Common Pleas Cuyahoga County)*

Office: 1200 Ontario Street, Suite 18-C, Cleveland 44113.
Telephone: (216) 443-8697.
Fax: (216) 348-4036
E-mail address: cpkas@www.cuyahoga.oh.us

SWEENEY, Francis E. *(Justice, Supreme Court of Ohio)* Assumed office 1992. Born Cuyahoga County Ohio Jan 24, 1934. Educated at Xavier University B.S.B.A. 1956 and Cleveland State University Cleveland-Marshall College of Law J.D. 1963. Judge, Ohio Court of Common Pleas Cuyahoga County 1970-88. Judge, Ohio Court of Appeals Eighth District 1988-92.

SWEENEY, FRANCIS E.—*Continued*

With Legal Department Allstate Insurance Company 1958-63. Assistant Prosecuting Attorney Cuyahoga County 1963-70. Professional football player Ottawa Roughriders 1956-58.

Office: 30 East Broad Street, Third Floor, Columbus 43266-0419.
Telephone: (614) 466-4425.
Fax: (614) 466-6138

SWEENEY, James J. *(Judge, Ohio Court of Appeals Eighth District)*
Office: One Lakeside Avenue, Cleveland 44113-1085.
Telephone: (216) 443-6357.
Fax: (216) 443-2044

SWIFT, Thomas A. *(Judge, Ohio Court of Common Pleas Trumbull County)* Appointed by Governor James A. Rhodes to term beginning Nov 5, 1979. Elected 1980, 1984, 1990, 1996 and 2002. Current term expires Feb 2009. Serves Probate Division. Born Youngstown Ohio March 25, 1942. Episcopalian. Educated at Kent State University B.A. 1965 and University of Akron J.D. 1969. Admitted to practice Ohio 1969 and Florida 1980. In legal practice Warren Ohio 1969-79.

Former Chair Mentor Program, Former Member Rules Advisory Committee and Chair Committee on Court Technology Supreme Court of Ohio. Member Ohio Association of Probate Judges (Past President, Chair Probate Code Revision Committee, Volunteer Guardian Standards Committee and Education Committee), Ohio Judicial Conference (Former Chair Judges Resource Manual, Chair Probate Law and Procedure Committee, Liaison Probate and Trust Law Section Ohio State Bar Association), National College of Probate Judges (Delegate, Chair Volunteer Guardian Standards Committee), American Judicature Society, American Judges Association, The Florida Bar, Trumbull County (Chair Probate Practice Committee and Media Relations Committee, Member Judicial and Legal Reform Committee), Ohio State (Elderly Law Committee) and American Bar Associations. Speaker Conference of National College of Probate Judges Spring 1999, Trumbull County Bar Association and Ohio State Bar Association. Attended seminars Ohio Judicial Conference. Board of Trustees, Faculty of Presenters, Faculty New Judges School and Member Strategic Planning Committee Ohio Judicial College. Faculty Member Probate Seminars Ohio Association of Probate Judges.

Recipient Good Citizenship Award from Daughters of the American Revolution 1980, Awards for Superior Judicial Service from Supreme Court of Ohio 1980-85 (award discontinued 1986), Outstanding Achievement in Mental Health Award from Trumbull County Board of Alcohol, Drug and Mental Health 1992, Public Service Award from Ohio Coalition for adult Protective Services 1996 and Silver Beaver Award from Boy Scouts of America. Named Public Official of the Year by National Association of Social Workers 1997. Former Member Board of Trustees Warren Rotary Club, Warren Area Jaycees, Trumbull County Mental Health Board, Northeast Ohio Council on Drug Abuse, Project Outreach, Children's Rehabilitation Center and YMCA. Board of Trustees Ohio United Way, Trumbull County Chapter American Red Cross, Leadership Ohio (Chair Constitution and By-Laws Committee) and Warren Trumbull Urban League. Member United Way of Trumbull County (Past President), Leadership Mahoning Valley (Board of Directors, Nominating Committee, Youth Leadership Selection Committee, National Issues Forum Committee), Ohio Department of Aging (Grandparents Raising Grandchildren Task Force), Ohio Adult Protective Services (Task Force on Elder Abuse), Western Reserve Council Boy Scouts (Former Member Board of Trustees, Past President, Member Advisory Board), Elks Lodge 296, Christ Episcopal Church (Former Vestryman) and Trumbull County Joint Committee on Suicide Prevention. Enjoys jogging, cycling and traveling.

Office: 161 High Street N.W., Warren 44481-1230.
Telephone: (330) 675-2520.
Fax: (330) 675-2524
E-mail address: trumbullprobate@aol.com

TAYLOR, Anne *(Judge, Franklin County Municipal Court)*
Office: 375 South High Street, #15D, Columbus 43215-4593.
Telephone: (614) 645-7643.
Fax: (614) 645-8255
E-mail address: anne_taylor@fccourts.org

TAYLOR, Robert Edward *(Judge, Ohio Court of Common Pleas Hamilton County)* Former Judge, Hamilton County Municipal Court.
Office: Courthouse, 1000 Main Street, Cincinnati 45202.
E-mail address: rtaylor@cms.hamilton-co.org

TEODOSIO, Linda Tucci *(Judge, Ohio Court of Common Pleas Summit County)* Elected Nov 2002 to term beginning Jan 1, 2003. Serves Juvenile Division. Born Canton Ohio Dec 8, 1956. Catholic. Educated at College of Wooster 1975-76 and University of Akron B.S. summa cum laude 1980 J.D. 1982. Staff Member Akron Law Review 1980-82. Member Alpha Gamma Delta, Kappa Delta Pi and Pi Lambda Theta. Admitted to practice Ohio 1982, U.S. District Court Northern District of Ohio 1983 and U.S. Court of Appeals Sixth Circuit 1985. In legal practice Akron Nov 1982 to Dec 1997. Magistrate and Referee, Akron Municipal Court Dec 1990-Nov 1997. Judge Jan 1, 1998 to Dec 31, 2002 and Administrative and Presiding Judge 2000 and 2002, Cuyahoga Falls Municipal Court.

Adjunct Faculty Member Dyke College Paralegal Program Dec 1988 to May 1990 and University of Akron Paralegal Program Sept 1994 to Dec 1994. Board of Trustees Akron Bar Association Foundation since 1998. Member Domestic Violence Task force since 1998, Summit County Criminal Justice Coordinating Council since 1998, Summit County Criminal Justice Advisory Board since 2001 and Summit County Judicial Corrections Board since 2003. Former Member Akron Metropolitan Municipal Judges Association (Secretary 1998-99), Ohio Association of Magistrates, Charles Scanlon American Inns of Court, National Institute of Municipal Law Officers, Federal and American Bar Associations. Member Ohio Judicial Conference, American Judges Association, Akron (Board of Trustees 1995-98, Chair Bench Bar Committee 1998-2001, Chair Law Week Committee since 2001) and Ohio State Bar Associations. Instructor "Report Writing for Referees" May 24, 1993, "Domestic Violence and Other Criminal Cases for Acting Judges" Sept 18, 1998, "Judicial Practice for Municipal Court Judges" June 1999 and New Judges Orientation Dec 3-4, 2001 Ohio Supreme Court Judicial College; "Advanced DUI Seminar" Ohio Association of

TEODOSIO, LINDA TUCCI—*Continued*

Criminal Defense Lawyers March 12, 1999; "Motions to Suppress in Municipal Court" May 18, 1999 and "Expectations of the Court Seminar" Oct 10, 2001 Akron Bar Association/University of Akron School of Law; and "The Role of Probation and Parole in Domestic Violence Cases" The Ohio Urban University Program Kent State University March 24, 2000.

Recipient Outstanding Service Award from Akron Bar Association 1999. Named Business Person of the Year by Stow Munroe Falls Chamber of Commerce 2001 andone of Most Influential Woman in Northeast Ohio by *Northern Ohio Live* Magazine June 2002. Member Federated Democratic Women of Ohio, Federated Democratic Women of Summit County, Cuyahoga Falls Democratic Club and Stow Democrats. Troop Leader Girl Scouts of America 1993-94. Volunteer Youth Motivational Task Force Akron Public Schools 1994-97. Member Women's Network since 1994, Junior Leadership Program Stow Munroe Falls since 1999, Ohio Community Corrections Organization since 2000 and Sons of Italy since 2000. Member since 1996 and Vice President since 2002 Board of Trustees University of Akron Law Alumni Association. Member since 1998 and Chair since 2002 Board of Trustees CYO and Community Services. Board of Trustees Western Reserve Outreach Center since 1998 and First Friday Club of Greater Akron since 2000. Friend of Stow Munroe Falls Library since 1999. Member Stow Munroe Falls Chamber of Commerce, Cuyahoga Falls Chamber of Commerce, Stow Rotary, League of Women Voters and Holy Family Parish (Eucharistic Minister since 1995, Minister of Hospitality since 1995, Member Athletic Commission since 1999).

Office: 650 Dan Street, Akron 44310.
Telephone: (330) 643-2995.
Fax: (330) 643-2894
E-mail address: teodosio@cpcourt.summitoh

THOMAKOS, Elizabeth Lehigh *(Judge, Ohio Court of Common Pleas Tuscarawas County)* Elected Nov 5, 1998 to term beginning Jan 1, 1999. Term expires Dec 31, 2004. Born Columbus Ohio Feb 27, 1963. United Methodist. Educated at Stephens College B.A. 1984 and University of Akron School of Law J.D. 1987. Admitted to practice Ohio 1987, U.S. District Court Northern District of Ohio 1988 and U.S. Court of Appeals Sixth Circuit 1988. In legal practice New Philadelphia 1987-98.

Member Federal Judicial Selection Committee Northern District of Ohio 1995-98. Member Ohio Common Pleas Judges Association, Ohio Judicial Conference, Tuscarawas County (President 1996, Former Secretary, Former Treasurer, Former Vice President) and Ohio State Bar Associations. Member Republican Executive Committee 1994-97. Board Member and Past President Big Brothers/Big Sisters of Tuscarawas, Carroll and Harrison Counties, Inc. Enjoys family and gourmet cooking.

Office: 101 East High Avenue, Suite 201, New Philadelphia 44663-2599.
Telephone: (330) 365-3289.
Fax: (330) 602-8811
E-mail address: thomakos@co.tuscarawas.oh.us

TOBIN, David *(Judge, Ohio Court of Common Pleas Columbiana County)* Elected to term beginning Jan 1, 1987. Reelected 1992 and 1998. Current term expires Dec 2004. Born East Liverpool Ohio June 3, 1949. Catholic. Educated at The Ohio State University B.A. 1971 and Ohio Northern University J.D. 1975. National Moot Court Team 1972-75. Admitted to practice Ohio 1975, U.S. District Court Northern District of Ohio 1976 and U.S. Supreme Court 1978. In legal practice East Liverpool 1975-87.

Prosecuting Attorney Columbiana County 1977-87. Instructor in Criminal Justice Kent State University 1985. Member Columbiana County and Ohio State Bar Associations. Attended Basic Review for Judges Ohio Judicial Conference 1987. Captain USAR 1971-81. Democrat. Member Red Cross, Rotary, Elks, American Legion and Church Boards. Enjoys photography, tennis, reading, running and home computing.

Office: 105 South Market Street, Lisbon 44432-1255.
Telephone: (330) 424-7777.
Fax: (330) 424-1739
E-mail address: dtobin@epohi.com

TOLBERT, Susan Laker *(Judge, Ohio Court of Common Pleas Hamilton County)* Serves Domestic Relations Division.

Office: 800 Broadway, Room 02-10, Cincinnati 45202.
Telephone: (513) 946-9016.
Fax: (513) 946-8040
E-mail: Susan.L.Tolbert@cmsts12.hamilton-co.org

TOWNLEY, Thomas W. *(Judge, Niles Municipal Court)*

Office: 15 East State Street, Niles 44446-5051.
Telephone: (330) 652-5863.
Fax: (330) 544-9025

TRACEY, Ann Marie *(Judge, Ohio Court of Common Pleas Hamilton County)* Appointed by Governor Richard F. Celeste to term beginning March 29, 1989. Elected Nov 6, 1990, 1996 and 2002. Current term expires 2009. Born Washington D.C. June 27, 1950. Educated at St. Mary's College B.A. with honors 1972 and University of Cincinnati J.D. with honors 1975. Editorial Board University of Cincinnati Law Review 1973-75. Admitted to practice Ohio 1975, U.S. Supreme Court 1980 and U.S. Court of Appeals Sixth Circuit 1983.

Assistant City Solicitor Cincinnati 1975-79. Assistant U.S. Attorney Southern District of Ohio 1979-89. Author "Minority Ownership Likely to Increase Diversity of Content Must Be Accorded Merit in FCC Licensing Hearings" 43 University of Cincinnati L. Rev. 669, 1974; "Caseload Ceilings on Indigent Defense Systems to Ensure Effective Assistance of Counsel" 43 University of Cincinnati L. Rev. 185, 1974; "Consumer Protection: An Expanded Role for the Local Prosecutor" 44 University of Cincinnati L. Rev. 81, 1975; and "The Child Witness: Competency and Confrontation" *Ohio Trial* Spring 1993. Adjunct Professor Xavier University. Member Ohio Supreme Court Futures Commission, Ohio Common Pleas Judges Association, National Association of Women Judges, American Judicature Society, Cincinnati, Ohio Women's, Ohio State and Federal Bar Associations. Attends numerous CLE programs. Lecturer for numerous CLE programs at Inns of Court, Ohio Academy of Trial Lawyers, Ohio Criminal Defense Lawyers Association, Ohio Judicial College and Ohio Common Pleas Judges Association. Adjunct Professor The National Judicial College.

Office: 1000 Main Street, Room 510, Cincinnati 45202-1217.

TRACEY, ANN MARIE—*Continued*
Telephone: (513) 946-5860.
Fax: (513) 946-5864
E-mail address: atracey@cms.hamilton-co.org

TRAVIS, Alan C. *(Judge, Ohio Court of Common Pleas Franklin County)*
Office: 369 South High Street, Columbus 43215-4554.
Telephone: (614) 462-6281.
Fax: (614) 462-2464
E-mail address: alan_travis@fccourts.org

TREBETS, John Frank *(Judge, Mentor Municipal Court)*
Office: 8500 Civic Center Boulevard, Mentor 44060-2418.
Telephone: (440) 974-5750.
Fax: (440) 974-5742

TRIMBOLI, Mary Grace *(Judge, Toledo Municipal Court)*
Office: 555 North Erie Street, Toledo 43624-1391.
Telephone: (419) 245-1940.
Fax: (419) 245-1802
E-mail address: mary.trimboli@noris.org

TRIOZZI, Robert J. *(Judge, Cleveland Municipal Court)*
Mailing address: P.O. Box 94894, Cleveland 44101-4894.
Telephone: (216) 664-4992.
Fax: (216) 664-4283

TUCKER, Michael *(Judge, Ohio Court of Common Pleas Montgomery County)*
Mailing address: P.O. Box 972, Dayton 45401.
Office: 41 North Perry Street, Dayton 45402.
Telephone: (937) 225-4448.
Fax: (937) 225-5406
E-mail address: tuckerm@montcourt.org

UNRUH, Brenda Burnham *(Judge, Ohio Court of Common Pleas Summit County)* Former Judge, Akron Municipal Court.
Office: 209 South High, Akron 44308-1610.
Telephone: (330) 643-2233.
Fax: (330) 643-2412

VALEN, Anthony *(Judge, Ohio Court of Appeals Twelfth District)* Elected to term beginning Feb 9, 1999. Term expires 2005. Born Middletown Ohio Jan 22, 1932. Religious affiliation: Greek Orthodox. Educated at Washington and Lee University B.A. 1955 and University of Cincinnati J.D. 1960. Admitted to practice Ohio 1960 and U.S. Supreme Court 1966. Former Judge, Ohio Court of Common Pleas Butler County, elected to term beginning Jan 1, 1989.
Mailing address: P.O. Box 1009, Middletown 45042.
Telephone: (513) 425-6609.
Fax: (513) 425-8751
E-mail address: anthony@twelfth.courts.state.oh.us

VanDerKARR, Scott D. *(Judge, Franklin County Municipal Court)*
Office: 375 South High Street, Columbus 43215-4593.
Telephone: (614) 645-8288.
Fax: (614) 645-7185
E-mail address: scott_vanderkarr@fccourts.org

VECCHIARELLI, Nancy A. *(Magistrate Judge, United States District Court Northern District of Ohio)* Appointed by U.S. District Court judges to term beginning 1998. Educated at Miami University, Ohio A.B. 1972 and University of Cincinnati J.D. 1977. Staff member University of Cincinnati Law Review. Law Clerk to Thomas J. Parrino, Ohio Court of Appeals District Eight 1977-79. Member Phi Beta Kappa and Order of the Coif. In legal practice 1979-85.
Assistant U.S. Attorney Civil Division 1986-87 and Criminal Division 1987-98 Northern District of Ohio. Member Anthony J. Celebrezze Inn of Court.
Office: 801 West Superior Avenue, Courtroom 10B, Cleveland 44113-1847.
Telephone: (216) 357-7130.

VERCILLO, Damian J. *(Judge, Ohio Court of Common Pleas Ashland County)* Serves Probate and Juvenile Divisions.
Office: 122 West Second Street, Ashland 44805-2190.
Telephone: (419) 282-4284.
Fax: (419) 281-5699

VETTEL, Ronald W. *(Judge, Ohio Court of Common Pleas Ashtabula County)* Elected to term beginning Jan 1, 1979. Reelected 1984, 1990, 1996 and 2002. Current term expires Dec 31, 2008. Born Ashtabula Ohio July 29, 1941. Catholic. Educated at University of Notre Dame A.B. 1963 LL.B. 1966. Admitted to practice Ohio 1966, U.S. District Court Northern District of Ohio 1968 and U.S. Supreme Court 1973. In legal practice Ashtabula 1966-79 and Conneaut 1968-72.
City Solicitor Conneaut 1968-72. Prosecuting Attorney Ashtabula County 1973-78. Instructor local Police Academy 1973-78. Judicial Board of Directors NEOCAP (community correctional facility). Member Ohio Judicial Conference, Ohio Common Pleas Judges Association, Ashtabula County and Ohio State Bar Associations. Former member Ohio Prosecuting Attorneys Association and National Prosecuting Attorneys Association. Graduate The National Judicial College 1979. Recipient Excellent Judicial Service Award 1981 and Superior Judicial Service Awards 1982-85 from Ohio Supreme Court. E-5 Ohio National Guard 1966-72. Democrat. Former Trustee Ashtabula County Airport Authority. Former Member Ashtabula County Budget Commission, Township Trustees and Clerks Association and Ashtabula North End Club. Member Elks Lodge 208. Enjoys fishing and other athletic and outdoor activities.
Office: 25 West Jefferson Street, Jefferson 44047-1092.
Telephone: (440) 576-3677.
Fax: (440) 576-2819
E-mail address: vettelctrptr@mail.com

VETTORI, Diane S. *(Judge, Mahoning County Court)*
Office: 605 East Ohio Avenue, Sebring 44672.

VILLANUEVA, Jose A. *(Judge, Ohio Court of Common Pleas Cuyahoga County)*
Office: 1200 Ontario Street, Cleveland 44113-1678.
Telephone: (216) 443-8737.
Fax: (216) 348-4034
E-mail address: cpjav@www.cuyahoga.oh.us

VORIS, Michael J. *(Judge, Ohio Court of Common Pleas Clermont County)* Elected Nov 1986 to term beginning Jan 2, 1987. Reelected 1992 and 1998. Current term expires Jan 2005. Serves Domestic Relations Division. Born Lancaster Ohio Dec 11, 1937. Educated at

VORIS, MICHAEL J.—*Continued*

Ohio University A.B. 1962, Salmon P. Chase College of Law J.D. 1967 and University of Cincinnati M.A.T. 1971. Member Phi Delta Theta and Phi Alpha Delta. Admitted to practice Ohio 1968 and U.S. District Court 1971. In legal practice Cincinnati 1968-84 and Batavia 1984-86. Domestic Relations Referee, Ohio Court of Common Pleas Clermont County 1978-79 and 1982. Judge, Clermont County Court 1983-86.

Author "The Domestic Violence Civil Protection Order and the Role of the Court" Akron L. Rev. Fall 1990-91 and article Ohio Northern L. Rev. Important Decisions: Bechtol v. Bechtol (permanent award of custody is supported by a substantial amount of credible and competent evidence) 49 Ohio St. 3d 21, 1990 and Felton v. Felton (Supreme Court of Ohio used his definition of domestic violence) 79 Ohio St. 3d 34, 1997. Adjunct Assistant Professor of Business Law and Social Sciences University of Cincinnati 1967-86. Co-chairperson Ohio Supreme Court and Ohio Judicial Conference Committee on Court Security 1993-98. Member Technology Committee Ohio Judicial Conference since 1999. Founder and Former Trustee Member Ohio Association of Family Court Judges. Former Member Ohio Municipal and County Judges Association. Member Ohio Common Pleas Judges Association, Ohio Association of Probate, Family and Juvenile Court Judges, Clermont County, Ohio State and American (Executive Committee National Conference of Special Court Judges, Former Member Local Task Force on Domestic Violence), Bar Associations. Charter member CLE 1983. Faculty Member Court Security Seminar Ohio Supreme Court 1989-90, Domestic Abuse The National Judicial College 1990 and Domestic Relations Update Ohio Judicial College April 2, 1991. Recipient Superior Judicial Service Award from Ohio Supreme Court 1983 and Continuing Legal Education Awards from Ohio State Bar 1984 and 1986. Named Public Official of the Year by Southwestern Ohio District National Association of Social Workers of Ohio 1993. Public school teacher 1964-67. Past President West Clermont Local Board of Education. Past President S.E.M. Manor, a Senior Citizen Housing Board sponsored by Southern Ohio Ecumenical Ministry. Member Clermont Senior Services Board. Public speaker on legal topics. Interests include grandchildren, computers, amateur radio (FCC licensed) and swimming.

Office: 2340 Clermont Center Drive, Suite 200, Batavia 45103-3043.
Telephone: (513) 732-7327.
Fax: (513) 732-7333

VUKOVICH, Joseph J. *(Judge, Ohio Court of Appeals Seventh District)*

Office: 120 Market Street, Fourth Floor, Youngstown 44503-1710.
Telephone: (330) 740-2180.
Fax: (330) 740-2182

WAGNER, A. J. *(Judge, Ohio Court of Common Pleas Montgomery County)*

Mailing address: P.O. Box 972, Dayton 45401.
Office: 41 South Perry Street, Dayton 45402.
Telephone: (937) 225-4409.
Fax: (937) 225-5406
E-mail address: wagnera@montcourt.org

WAGNER, Lynnita K. C. *(Judge, Ohio Court of Common Pleas Miami County)* Serves Probate and Juvenile Divisions.

Office: 201 West Main Street, Troy 45373-3239.
Telephone: (937) 332-6836.
Fax: (937) 440-3529

WAITE, Cheryl L. *(Judge, Ohio Court of Appeals Seventh District)* Elected Nov 1996 and 2002. Presiding Judge since Feb 2003. Educated at Youngstown State University 1982 and Cleveland-Marshall College of Law Cleveland State University J.D. 1985. Admitted to practice Ohio 1985, U.S. Court of Appeals Sixth Circuit 1986 and U.S. Supreme Court 1993.

Former Assistant Law Director City of Youngstown. Court of Appeals Representative to Ohio Criminal Sentencing Commission since Dec 2000. Member Ohio Court of Appeals Judges Association, Mahoning County, Ohio State (Committee on the Independent Judiciary and the Unjust Criticism of Judges) and American Bar Associations. Board of Trustees YWCA. Board of Directors Gateways to Better Living, Inc. Member Youngstown State University Alumni Association.

Office: 120 Market Street, Fourth Floor, Youngstown 44503-1710.
Telephone: (330) 740-2180.
Fax: (330) 740-2182

WAKEFIELD, Elizabeth *(Judge, Vermilion Municipal Court)*

Office: 687 Decatur Street, Vermilion 44089-1152.
Telephone: (440) 967-6543.
Fax: (440) 967-1467

WALDRON, Thomas F. *(Chief Judge, United States Bankruptcy Court Southern District of Ohio)* Chief Judge Bankruptcy Court since April 30, 1999. Also Judge, Bankruptcy Appellate Panel Sixth Circuit. Selected by the Judicial Council of the Sixth Circuit. Former Chief Judge Appellate Panel.

Office: 120 West Third Street, Room 121, Dayton 45402.
Telephone: (937) 225-2863.

WALKER, William *(Judge, Ohio Court of Common Pleas Clermont County)*

Office: 270 Main Street, Batavia 45103-3071.
Telephone: (513) 732-7102.
Fax: (513) 732-7987
E-mail address: wwalker@co.clermont.oh.us

WALL, Mark W. *(Judge, Middletown Municipal Court)* Appointed by Governor George V. Voinovich to term beginning Sept 6, 1994. Elected Nov 7, 1995 and 2001. Current term expires Dec 31, 2007. Born Middletown Ohio Dec 27, 1946. Roman Catholic. Educated at Miami University, Ohio B.A. 1968 and University of Cincinnati J.D. 1973. Admitted to practice Ohio 1973 and U.S. District Court Southern District of Ohio 1994. In legal practice Middletown 1973-94.

Member American Judicature Society, Ohio Judicial College, Middletown, Butler County, Ohio State and American Bar Associations. Sergeant U.S. Army Infantry 1968-70. Republican. Board of Trustees Safety Council of Southwest Ohio. Member VFW, American Legion, Disabled American Veterans and Knights of Columbus. Enjoys fishing, hiking, photography and reading.

Office: One City Centre Plaza, Middletown 45042.

WALL, MARK W.—*Continued*

Telephone: (513) 425-7822.
Fax: (513) 425-7846
E-mail address: markw@ci.middletown.oh.us

WALLAR, Richard M. *(Judge, Hocking County Municipal Court)*
Mailing address: P.O. Box 950, Logan 43138-1278.
Telephone: (740) 385-2250.
Fax: (740) 385-3826
E-mail address: rmw@hockinghills.net

WALSH, James E. *(Judge, Ohio Court of Appeals Twelfth District)* Elected Nov 6, 1990. Reelected 1996 and 2002. Current term expires 2009. Educated at Chase College B.S.B.A. 1962 J.D. 1966. Law Clerk to Hon. Fred B. Cramer, Ohio Court of Common Pleas Butler County 1965-66. In legal practice 1966-79. Judge, Fairfield Municipal Court 1979-91.

Former Assistant Prosecutor Butler County. Former Legal Counsel Fairfield and Hamilton City Boards of Education. Coach Fairfield High School Mock Trial teams. Life Member VFW Campbell Guard Post 1069. Member Fairfield Lions Club (Past President), Fairfield Hospital Association, Fairfield Safety Council and Elks Lodge No. 93.

Mailing address: P.O. Box 1009, Middletown 45042-1901.
Telephone: (513) 425-6609.
Fax: (513) 425-8751
E-mail address: james@twelfth.courts.state.oh.us

WALTERS, Sumner E. *(Judge, Ohio Court of Appeals Third District)* Born Van Wert Ohio July 5, 1949. Methodist. Educated at Stanford University 1967-68, Ohio Northern University A.B. with honors 1971 J.D. 1974. Admitted to practice Ohio 1974. Began legal practice Van Wert 1974. Acting Judge, Van Wert Municipal Court 1980-82. Former Judge, Ohio Court of Common Pleas Van Wert County, elected to term beginning Jan 1, 1983.

Member Ohio Judicial Conference, Ohio Common Pleas Judges Association, American Judges Association, Van Wert County, Northwest Ohio, Ohio State and American Bar Associations. Recipient Outstanding Young Man in America Award 1974. Republican.

Office: 204 North Main Street, Lima 45801.
Telephone: (419) 223-1861.
Fax: (419) 224-3828
E-mail address: walters@third.courts.state.oh.us

WALTON, W. Richard *(Judge, Ohio Court of Common Pleas Lawrence County)*
Office: One Veterans Square, Ironton 45638-1522.
Telephone: (740) 533-4329.
Fax: (740) 533-4377
E-mail address: walton@zoomnet.net

WARD, Michael W. *(Judge, Ohio Court of Common Pleas Athens County)*
Office: Court and Washington Streets, Athens 45701.
Telephone: (740) 593-3591.
Fax: (740) 592-3020
E-mail address: mward@athenscountygovernment.com

WARD, Richard G. *(Judge, Ohio Court of Common Pleas Ross County)* Appointed by Governor George V. Voinovich to term beginning Sept 1998. Elected Dec 1998 and 2002. Current term expires Feb 2009. Serves Probate and Juvenile Divisions. Born New Kensington Pennsylvania April 28, 1942. Educated at Duquesne University B.A. 1964 and Villanova University J.D. 1967. Admitted to practice Ohio 1968, U.S. District Court Southern District of Ohio 1971, U.S. Court of Appeals Sixth Circuit 1989 and U.S. Supreme Court 1989. In legal practice Chillicothe 1968-95.

Assistant Prosecuting Attorney 1968-76 and Prosecuting Attorney 1976-95 Ross County. Member Ross County and Ohio State Bar Associations.

Office: Two North Paint Street, Chillicothe 45601.
Telephone: (740) 774-1179.
Fax: (740) 774-3711
E-mail address: ctward@bright.net

WARREN, Richard K. *(Judge, Ohio Court of Common Pleas Allen County)* Elected to term beginning Jan 1, 1989. Reelected 1994 and 2000. Current term expires Dec 31, 2006. Born Bluffton Ohio Aug 18, 1941. Methodist. Educated at Heidelberg College B.A. 1963 and Ohio Northern University J.D. 1966. Member Delta Theta Phi. Admitted to practice Ohio 1966 and U.S. District Court Northern District of Ohio 1967. In legal practice Lima 1966-69 and Bluffton 1989.

Member Allen County, Ohio State and American Bar Associations. Attended The National Judicial College. Finalist Distinguished Service Award from Allen County for five years. Named Boss of the Year by Lima Sertoma and Assistant Prosecutor of the Year by State of Ohio 1981. Youth Leader and Sunday School Teacher St. Marks United Methodist Church. Enjoys basketball and playing the piano.

Mailing address: P.O. Box 1243, Lima 45802.
Telephone: (419) 223-8525.
Fax: (419) 224-9269

WATSON, Barbara Roush *(Judge, Portage County Municipal Court)* Appointed by Governor Richard F. Celeste to term beginning Feb 17, 1989. Elected Nov 7, 1989, Nov 5, 1991, and Nov 4, 1997. Current term expires Jan 1, 2004. Born Gallipolis Ohio Nov 13, 1936. Congregationalist. Educated at Ohio University B.A. with honors 1958, Stephen F. Austin State University M.A. with honors 1963 and University of Akron J.D. 1980. Admitted to practice Ohio 1980.

Assistant Prosecuting Attorney Portage County 1980-86. Member Akron Metropolitan Judges Association, Ohio Judicial College, Municipal-County Judges of Ohio, Inc., Portage County and Ohio State Bar Associations. Democrat. Member Ravenna Rotary Club and Kent State University Women. Interests include book discussion, gardening, hiking, camping and chamber music.

Office: 203 West Main Street, Ravenna 44266.
Telephone: (330) 297-4277.
Fax: (330) 297-4283

WATSON, Michael H. *(Judge, Ohio Court of Common Pleas Franklin County)*
Office: 369 South High Street, Room 7B, Columbus 43215-4554.
Telephone: (614) 462-3666.
Fax: (614) 462-2462
E-mail address: michael_watson@fccourts.org

WEAVER, William W. *(Judge, Ohio Court of Common Pleas Lake County)* Serves Juvenile Division.
Office: Juvenile Justice Center, 53 East Erie Street, Painesville 44077-3907.
Telephone: (440) 350-3126.
Fax: (440) 350-2724

WEBB, J. David *(Judge, Ohio Court of Common Pleas Paulding County)* Elected to term beginning Jan 1, 1987. Reelected 1992 and 1998. Current term expires Dec 31, 2004. Formerly served Domestic Relations Division. Born Effingham Illinois Jan 5, 1946. Catholic. Educated at University of Detroit B.A. 1968 and Ohio Northern University J.D. 1971. Admitted to practice Ohio 1971. In legal practice Paulding 1971-86.
Prosecuting Attorney Paulding County 1977-86. Member Paulding County and Ohio State Bar Associations. Republican. Member Paulding Kiwanis Club and Knights of Columbus.
Office: 115 North Williams Street, Suite 201, Paulding 45879-1298.
Telephone: (419) 399-8220.
Fax: (419) 399-8224

WEBER, Herman Jacob, Jr. *(Senior Judge, United States District Court Southern District of Ohio)* Appointed for life by President Ronald Reagan. Assumed Senior status Jan 1, 2002, serves by assignment. Born Lima Ohio May 20, 1927. United Methodist. Educated at Otterbein College B.A. 1949 and The Ohio State University J.D. summa cum laude 1951. Member Order of the Coif. Admitted to practice Ohio 1952. Began legal practice Fairborn 1952. Judge, Fairborn Mayor's Court 1956-58. Acting Judge, Fairborn Municipal Court 1958-60. Former Judge, Ohio Court of Common Pleas Greene County, elected to term beginning Jan 1, 1961. Former Judge, Ohio Court of Appeals Second District.
Member Ohio Criminal Justice Supervisory Commission 1977, American Judicature Society, Ohio Judicial Conference (Chairman 1981-82), Ohio Common Pleas Judges Association (President 1975), Cincinnati, Greene County (President 1962), Ohio State (Judicial Administration and Legal Reform Committee) and American Bar Associations. Attended National College of the State Judiciary 1975. Trustee Ohio Judicial College 1976. Recipient Excellent Achievement in Judicial Administration Award 1972. Named Senior Counselor by Cincinnati Bar Association 2002. ETM Third Class USNR 1945-46. City Council 1955-59 and Vice Mayor 1955-57 Fairborn. Chairman Greene County Mental Health Planning Project 1964. Enjoys golf and water sports.
Office: 801 U.S. Courthouse, 100 East Fifth Street, Cincinnati 45202-3976.
Telephone: (513) 564-7603.

WEIGAND, Michael L. *(Judge, Barberton Municipal Court)*
Office: 576 West Park Avenue, Barberton 44203-2584.
Telephone: (330) 753-2261.
Fax: (330) 848-6779
E-mail address: barboh@worldnet.att.net

WEILER, Jennifer P. *(Judge, Garfield Heights Municipal Court)* Elected to term beginning Jan 1, 2000. Term expires Dec 1, 2005. Born Cleveland Ohio. Educated at Ohio University A.B. summa cum laude 1974 and Cleveland State University J.D. cum laude 1979. Member Phi Beta Kappa. Admitted to practice Ohio 1979. In legal practice Brecksville 1984-99.
Law Clerk to Hon. Frank D. Celebrezze, Ohio Supreme Court 1982-83. Member Christian Legal Society, Cleveland, Cuyahoga County and Ohio State Bar Associations. Staff Member Ohio Judicial College. Member Domestic Violence Task Force St. Ignatius Loyola Society and Brecksville-Broadview Heights PSO.
Office: 5555 Turney Road, Garfield Heights 44125.
Telephone: (216) 475-4927.
Fax: (216) 475-3807
E-mail address: jweiler@ghmc.org

WELBAUM, Jeffrey M. *(Judge, Ohio Court of Common Pleas Miami County)* Elected 1994. Reelected to subsequent term.
Office: 201 West Main Street, Troy 45373-3239.
Telephone: (937) 332-6872.
Fax: (937) 332-7069
E-mail address: miamico@coax.net

WELLS, Lesley *(Judge, United States District Court Northern District of Ohio)* Appointed for life by President Bill Clinton to term beginning Feb 11, 1994. Born Muskegon Michigan Oct 6, 1937. Educated at Chatham College B.A. 1959 and Cleveland-Marshall College of Law J.D. cum laude 1974. Admitted to practice Ohio 1975, U.S. District Court Northern District of Ohio 1975 and U.S. Supreme Court 1989. Began legal practice Cleveland 1975. Judge, Ohio Court of Common Pleas Cuyahoga County March 31, 1983 to Feb 10, 1994.
Editor *ABAR III Federal Litigation Manual* 1980-81. Adjunct Assistant Professor of Law and Urban Policy 1980-82 and since 1990 and Adjunct Professor 1980-81 Cleveland State University College of Law. Chair Governor's Task Force on Family Violence 1984-86. Member Northwest Ordinance U.S. Constitution Commission 1986-88, National Women Judges Association, The American Law Institute, Cleveland, Cuyahoga County, Ohio State and American Bar Associations. Recipient Superior Judicial Service Award 1983, Merit Service Award 1983, Josephine Irwin Award for Outstanding Service 1984, Women's City Club Award 1985, Chatham College Outstanding Alumna Award 1988, Alumni Award for Civil Achievement from Cleveland State University 1992, Golden Gavel Award from Ohio Common Pleas Judges Association 1994 and Outstanding Alumni Award from Cleveland-Marshall Law Alumni Association 1994. President Legal Aid Society of Cleveland 1979-81. Member Visiting Committees College of Law and College of Urban Affairs Cleveland State University 1980-83 and 1990-94 and Bio-Medical Ethics Committee Case Western Reserve University School of Medicine 1986-94. Trustee Rose-Mary Center since 1986, Miami University 1988 and Urban League of Cleveland 1988-89. Fellow Institute for Humanities and Medicine 1991-92. Active in numerous boards and commissions. Interests include outdoors, philosophy, ethics, music, dance, art and science.
Office: 18A U.S. Courthouse, 801 West Superior Avenue, Cleveland 44113-1836.
Telephone: (216) 357-7120.

WEST, John Andrew *(Judge, Ohio Court of Common Pleas Hamilton County)* Former Judge, Hamilton County Municipal Court.
Office: 1000 Main Street, Cincinnati 45202-1217.

WEST, JOHN ANDREW—*Continued*

Telephone: (513) 946-5785.
Fax: (513) 946-5784

WEYAND, John H. *(Judge, Ohio Court of Common Pleas Carroll County)* Serves Probate and Juvenile Divisions.
Office: Courthouse, Carrollton 44615-1497.
Telephone: (330) 627-2323.
Fax: (330) 627-6004

WHIPPLE, Mary Ann *(Judge, United States Bankruptcy Court Northern District of Ohio)* Appointed by U.S. Court of Appeals Sixth Circuit judges to term beginning May 1, 2001.
Office: 111 U.S. Courthouse, 1716 Spielbusch Avenue, Toledo 43624.
Telephone: (419) 259-6327.

WHITE, Harry W. *(Judge, Belmont County Court)* Term expires Dec 31, 2006.
Office: 147 West Main Street, St. Clairsville 43950-1526.
Telephone: (740) 695-2875.
Fax: (740) 695-7285
E-mail address: western1@1st.net

WHITE, Thomas D. *(Judge, Ohio Court of Common Pleas Holmes County)*
Office: One East Jackson Street, Suite 301, Millersburg 44654-1249.
Telephone: (330) 674-5086.
Fax: (330) 674-0289
E-mail address: hccp@valkyrie.net

WHITMORE, Beth *(Judge, Ohio Court of Appeals Ninth District)* Former Judge, Ohio Court of Common Pleas Summit County.
Office: 161 South High Street, Fifth Floor, Akron 44308-1671.
Telephone: (330) 643-2250.
Fax: (330) 643-2091
E-mail address: beth@ninth.courts.state.oh.us

WHITNEY, William Duncan *(Judge, Ohio Court of Common Pleas Delaware County)* Serves Domestic Relations Division.
Office: 91 North Sandusky, Third Floor, Delaware 43015.

WIEST, Mark K. *(Judge, Ohio Court of Common Pleas Wayne County)*
Office: 107 West Liberty, Wooster 44691-4862.
Telephone: (330) 287-5530.
Fax: (330) 287-5416
E-mail address: mwiest@waynecountycourthouse.com

WILLIAMS, James R. *(Judge, Ohio Court of Common Pleas Summit County)* Former Judge, Akron Municipal Court.
Office: 209 South High, Akron 44308-2922.
Telephone: (330) 643-2241.
Fax: (330) 643-2413

WILLIAMS, Steven O. *(Judge, Ohio Court of Common Pleas Fairfield County)* Serves Probate and Juvenile Divisions.
Office: 224 East Main Street, Lancaster 43130-3863.
Telephone: (740) 687-7135.
Fax: (740) 687-0942

WILLIAMS, Timothy A. *(Judge, Ohio Court of Common Pleas Washington County)* Elected to term beginning Feb 9, 1997. Reelected 2002, current term expires Feb 8, 2009. Serves Probate and Juvenile Divisions. Born Marion Ohio March 17, 1958. Catholic. Educated at Ohio Northern University B.A. 1980 J.D. 1984. Associate Editor Ohio Northern University Law Review 1983-84. Admitted to practice Ohio 1984 and West Virginia 1984. In legal practice Marietta Ohio 1984-97.
Office: Courthouse, 205 Putnam Street, Marietta 45750-2922.
Telephone: (740) 373-6623.
Fax: (740) 376-7425
E-mail address: TimW@Frognet.net

WILSON, David D. *(Judge, Ohio Court of Common Pleas Adams County)*
Office: 110 West Main Street, West Union 45693-1347.
Telephone: (937) 544-2921.
Fax: (937) 544-8911

WILSON, Dean L. *(Judge, Perry County Court)*
Mailing address: P.O. Box 207, New Lexington 43764-1262.
Telephone: (740) 342-3156.
Fax: (740) 342-2188

WILSON, Roger B. *(Judge, Ohio Court of Common Pleas Champaign County)* Elected to term beginning Jan 1, 1971. Reelected 1976, 1982, 1988, 1994 and 2000. Current term expires Dec 31, 2006. Born Alton Illinois Jan 3, 1937. Educated at Denison University A.B. 1958 and The Ohio State University J.D. 1961. Admitted to practice Ohio 1961.
Office: 200 North Main Street, Urbana 43078.
Telephone: (937) 652-2221.
Fax: (937) 652-0196

WINKLER, Ralph *(Judge, Ohio Court of Appeals First District)* Elected 1998. Educated at University of Cincinnati B.A. 1959 and Salmon P. Chase College of Law J.D. with honors 1970. Admitted to practice Ohio 1970. Judge, Hamilton County Municipal Court 1977-81. Judge and Presiding Judge, Ohio Court of Common Pleas Hamilton County 1981-99.
First Assistant U.S. Attorney Southern District of Ohio.
Office: 230 East Ninth Street, Twelfth Floor, Cincinnati 45202-1287.
Telephone: (513) 946-3491.
Fax: (513) 946-3411
E-mail address: Rwinkler@cms.hamilton-co.org

WINKLER, Ralph E. *(Judge, Hamilton County Municipal Court)*
Office: 1000 Main Street, Room 178, Cincinnati 45202.
Telephone: (513) 946-5175.
Fax: (513) 946-5178
E-mail address: twinkler@cms.hamilton-co.org

WINKLER, Robert C. *(Judge, Hamilton County Municipal Court)*
Office: 1000 Main Street, #154, Cincinnati 45202.
Telephone: (513) 946-5143.
Fax: (513) 946-5145

WISE, John W. *(Judge, Ohio Court of Appeals Fifth District)* Elected 1995. Reelected to subsequent term. Educated at Ohio Northern University J.D. 1979. In legal practice for ten years. Former Judge, Canton Municipal Court, elected to term beginning 1990. Former Judge, Ohio Court of Common Pleas Stark County.

Office: 110 Central Plaza South, Suite 320, Canton 44702-1411.
Telephone: (330) 451-7701.
Fax: (330) 451-7249
E-mail address: infor@fifthdist.org

WISEMAN, Russell Benson *(Judge, Ohio Court of Common Pleas Crawford County)*
Mailing address: P.O. Box 588, Bucyrus 44820.
Office: 112 East Mansfield Street, Bucyrus 44820-2396.
Telephone: (419) 562-5771.
Fax: (419) 562-8011

WITTENBERG, Charles S. *(Judge, Ohio Court of Common Pleas Lucas County)*
Office: 700 Adams Street, Toledo 43624.
Telephone: (419) 213-4580.
Fax: (419) 213-4181
E-mail address: cwitten@co.lucas.oh.us

WOESSNER, David E. *(Judge, Ohio Court of Common Pleas Wood County)* Serves Probate and Juvenile Divisions.
Office: One Courthouse Square, Bowling Green 43402-2427.
Telephone: (419) 354-9231.
Fax: (419) 354-9357.

WOLAVER, Stephen Arthur *(Judge, Ohio Court of Common Pleas Greene County)*
Office: 45 North Detroit Street, Xenia 45385.

WOLFF, William H., Jr. *(Judge, Ohio Court of Appeals Second District)* Assumed office June 14, 1985. Born Dayton Ohio May 19, 1942. Catholic. Educated at Georgetown University A.B. 1964 J.D. 1967. Law Clerk to U.S. District Court District of Massachusetts 1967-68. Admitted to practice Ohio 1968 and Massachusetts 1968. Began legal practice Boston Massachusetts 1968. In legal practice Dayton Ohio 1969-75. Referee 1975 and Judge 1976-77, Dayton Municipal Court. Judge, Ohio Court of Common Pleas Montgomery County 1977-85.

Assistant Prosecutor Montgomery County 1970-75. Co-author with James A. Brogan and Shauna K. McSherry *Appellate Practice and Procedure in Ohio* Anderson 2nd ed. 2000. Instructor University of Dayton School of Law 1981-85 and 1987-2001. Chief Justice Ohio Courts of Appeals Judges Association 2003. Member Ohio Supreme Court Commission on Racial Fairness, Ohio Courts Futures Commission, Ohio Judicial Conference (Chair 1998-2000), Dayton (Executive Committee 1984 and 1986-90, President 1988-89), Ohio State (Bench-Bar Committee 1989-93, Legal Needs Assessment Implementation Committee) and American Bar Associations. Instructor Ohio Judicial College 1980-83, 1986, 1988, 1990, 1991, 1993, 1994 and 1995; The National Judicial College 1982-85; and Ohio CLE Institute 1990, 1991, 1992, 1993, 1994, 1995 and 1996. Democrat. Member since 1987 and Chairman 1987-89 Board of Visitors University of Dayton School of Law. Trustee Legal Aid Society of Dayton and Ohio Legal Assistance Foundation. Enjoys outdoor activities.

Mailing address: P.O. Box 972, Dayton 45401.
Office: 41 North Perry Street, Dayton 45422.
Telephone: (937) 225-4464.
Fax: (937) 496-7724
E-mail address: WolffW@Montcnty.org

WORKMAN, RicKard A. *(Judge, Lima Municipal Court)*
Mailing address: P.O. Box 1529, Lima 45802-1529.
Telephone: (419) 222-7861.
Fax: (419) 998-5526

WYLER, Stephanie *(Judge, Ohio Court of Common Pleas Clermont County)* Elected to term beginning Feb 9, 1991. Reelected 1996 and 2002. Current term expires 2009. Serves Probate and Juvenile Divisions. Born Cincinnati Ohio Aug 10, 1954. Protestant. Educated at Miami University 1971-73 and University of Cincinnati B.S. magna cum laude 1973-75 J.D. 1978. Admitted to practice Ohio 1978 and U.S. District Court Southern District of Ohio 1979. In legal practice Batavia since 1979. Judge pro tem 1981-86 and Judge, Clermont County Court Jan 1, 1987 to Feb 8, 1991.

Assistant Prosecuting Attorney 1979-81. Trustee Ohio Association of Juvenile and Family Court Judges. Member Clermont County Bar Association. Attended Twelfth Appellate District of Ohio Judicial Conference. Vice Chair Juvenile Law and Procedure Committee Ohio Judicial College. Recipient Chamber Athena Award for Outstanding Contribution to Community 1986. Republican. Secretary Clermont County Republican Club 1984-86. Chairman Eastern Area Community Chest. Director Greater Cincinnati Community Chest. Board Member Clermont College University of Cincinnati. Member LEAD Clermont and Committee of Management Clermont YMCA. Enjoys travel and sports.

Office: 2340 Clermont Center Drive, Suite 100, Batavia 45103.
Telephone: (513) 732-7243 (probate), 732-7696 (juvenile).
Fax: (513) 732-7695

WYNN, Robert S. *(Judge, Ashtabula County Court)*
Office: 25 West Jefferson Street, Jefferson 44047-1028.
Telephone: (440) 576-3617.
Fax: (440) 576-3441

YOST, Gary L. *(Judge, Ohio Court of Common Pleas Ashtabula County)* Born Covington Kentucky Sept 3, 1950. Roman Catholic. Educated at Findlay College B.A. cum laude 1972 and Case Western Reserve University J.D. 1975. Member Phi Mu Alpha and Phi Alpha Theta. Admitted to practice Ohio 1975, U.S. District Court Northern District of Ohio 1977 and U.S. Court of Appeals Sixth Circuit 1982. Began legal practice Ashtabula 1975. In legal practice Jefferson since 1977. Former Judge, Ashtabula County Court, elected to term beginning Jan 1, 1983.

Public Defender 1975-77 and Assistant Prosecutor 1979-82 Ashtabula County. Assistant Solicitor City of Ashtabula 1977-79. Important Decisions: State v. Jenkins (DWI-warrantless arrest) 10 Ohio Misc. 2d 7, 1983 and State v. Szalai (DWI-implied consent) 13 Ohio Misc. 2d 6, 1983. Instructor Ohio Institute for Paralegal Studies, American Paralegal Institute 1982-84 and Ashtabula County Peace Officer Training Academy since 1983.

YOST, GARY L.—*Continued*

Member Ohio Judicial Conference, Ohio Academy of Trial Lawyers, Ashtabula County and Ohio State Bar Associations. Democrat. Former Precinct Committeeman. Former Board member and Past President Ashtabula County Big Brothers/Big Sisters. Former member Ashtabula Kiwanis Club. Board member Civic Development Corporation. Enjoys music, photography, electronics and reading.

Office: 25 West Jefferson, Jefferson 44047-1092.
Telephone: (440) 576-3681.
Fax: (440) 576-2819
E-mail address: glyost@co.ashtabula.oh.us

YOUNG, Frederick N. *(Judge, Ohio Court of Appeals Second District)* Elected Nov 1992 to term beginning Feb 9, 1993. Reelected 1998, current term expires Feb 2005. Former Presiding Judge. Born Dayton Ohio Jan 1, 1932. Episcopalian. Educated at Wesleyan University B.A. with honors 1954 and Harvard Law School J.D. magna cum laude 1957. Member Phi Beta Kappa. Admitted to practice Ohio 1957 and U.S. District Court Southern District of Ohio 1959. In legal practice Dayton 1957-93.

Author "Corporate Separations: Some Revenue Rulings Under Section 355" 71 No. 5 Harvard L. Rev. 843, 1958. Important Decisions: State v. Rogan 94 Ohio App. 3d 140, 1994 and over 75 published opinions. Member Dayton and Ohio State Bar Associations. Legal Counsel The Children's Medical Center 1963-93 (Member 1963-93 and Chairman 1985-87 Board of Trustees). Chairman Montgomery County Republican Executive Committee 1977-82. Delegate Republican National Conventions 1976 and 1984. Member Ohio General Assembly 1968-76 (House Finance Committee 1968-76 and Ranking Member House Finance Appropriations Committee 1972-76, House Local Government and Urban Affairs Committee 1968-76, Member 1968-72 and Chairman 1968-72 Standing Subcommittee on Elections). Member Republican State Central and Executive Committee 1978-82. Member Kiwanis Club and The Lawyers Club (Secretary 1988-92). Interests include theatre, acting, reading and travel.

Mailing address: P.O. Box 972, Dayton 45401.
Office: 41 North Perry Street, Dayton 45422.
Telephone: (937) 225-4464.
Fax: (937) 496-7724
E-mail address: fnyoung@erinet.com

YOUNG, Lucien, III *(Judge, Noble County Court)*
Office: 100 Courthouse Square, Caldwell 43724.
Telephone: (740) 732-5795.
Fax: (740) 732-5702

YOUNG, Patrick H. *(Judge, Paulding County Court)*
Office: 201 East Caroline Street, #2, Paulding 45879-1204.
Telephone: (419) 399-5370.
Fax: (419) 399-3421

YOUNG, William W. *(Judge, Ohio Court of Appeals Twelfth District)* Elected to term beginning Feb 10, 1987. Reelected 1992 and 1998. Current term expires Feb 2005. Currently serves as Presiding Judge. Born Franklin Ohio Oct 6, 1937. Methodist. Educated at Miami University 1958 and Chase Law School of Northern Kentucky State College LL.B. 1961. Recipient Rebecca Bloom Bettman Scholarship. Admitted to practice Ohio 1961. Judge, Ohio Court of Common Pleas Warren County Jan 1, 1971 to Feb 9, 1987.

Prosecuting Attorney City of Lebanon 1963-70. Solicitor Village of Waynesville 1965-70. Assistant Attorney General 1965. Member Dayton, Warren County (President 1969), Ohio State and American Bar Associations. Republican. Member Elks. Enjoys sports car activities.

Mailing address: P.O. Box 1009, Middletown 45042-1901.
Telephone: (513) 425-6609.
Fax: (513) 425-8751
E-mail address: william@twelfth.courts.state.oh.us

ZACHMAN, Thomas F. *(Judge, Brown County Municipal Court)* Assumed office Feb 9, 2003. Term expires Dec 31, 2006. Judge, Brown County Court 1998-2002.

Office: 770 Mount Orab Pike, Georgetown 45121-1281.
Telephone: (937) 378-3638.
Fax: (937) 378-2462
E-mail address: tzachman@browncountycourt.org

ZALESKI, Edward M. *(Judge, Ohio Court of Common Pleas Lorain County)*
Office: 308 Second Street, Elyria 44035.
Telephone: (440) 329-5560.
Fax: (440) 329-5562

ZEMMELMAN, Norman G. *(Judge, Ohio Court of Common Pleas Lucas County)* Serves Domestic Relations Division.
Office: 429 North Michigan Street, Toledo 43624.
Telephone: (419) 213-6827.
Fax: (419) 213-6838

ZITTER, Mary Patricia *(Judge, Ohio Court of Common Pleas Mercer County)* Serves Probate and Juvenile Divisions.
Office: 101 North Main Street, Celina 45822.

ZONE, Joseph *(Judge, Cleveland Municipal Court)*
Mailing address: P.O. Box 94894, Cleveland 44101-4894.
Telephone: (216) 664-4980.
Fax: (216) 664-4283

ZWELLING, Howard S. *(Judge, Ohio Court of Common Pleas Muskingum County)* Born Zanesville Ohio Dec 11, 1936. Jewish. Educated at Muskingum College B.A. 1959 and Ohio Northern University J.D. 1962. Admitted to practice Ohio 1962, U.S. District Court 1963, U.S. Tax Court 1972 and U.S. Supreme Court 1972. Began legal practice Zanesville 1962. Former Judge, Zanesville Municipal Court, elected to term beginning Jan 1, 1984.

Author "Municipal Court Rules of Practice and Procedure" City of Zanesville June 1984. Member Committee on Dispute Resolution Supreme Court of Ohio since 1991. Member Municipal-County Judges of Ohio, Inc. (President 1997 and 1998, Board of Trustees), Muskingum County (President 1977), Ohio State and American Bar Associations. Democrat. City Council Zanesville 1965-69. President Zanesville Sertoma 1985. Enjoys sports, golf and handball.

Office: 401 Main Street, Zanesville 43701-3519.
Telephone: (740) 455-7142.
Fax: (740) 455-7177

OKLAHOMA

Capital OKLAHOMA CITY

UNITED STATES DISTRICT COURTS DISTRICTS OF OKLAHOMA

Within Oklahoma there are three United States District Courts. For descriptive information refer to the United States Courts section.

EASTERN DISTRICT includes Adair, Atoka, Bryan, Carter, Cherokee, Choctaw, Coal, Haskell, Hughes, Johnston, Latimer, LeFlore, Love, Marshall, McCurtain, McIntosh, Murray, Muskogee, Okfuskee, Okmulgee, Pittsburg, Pontotoc, Pushmataha, Seminole, Sequoyah and Wagoner counties. The court sits at Ada, Ardmore, Durant, Hugo, Muskogee, Okmulgee, Poteau and South McAlester.

Chief Judge
James Hardy Payne

Judge
Frank Howell Seay

Clerk
William B. Guthrie
P.O. Box 607
Muskogee, Oklahoma 74402-0607
(918) 687-2471

NORTHERN DISTRICT includes Craig, Creek, Delaware, Mayes, Nowata, Osage, Ottawa, Pawnee, Rogers, Tulsa and Washington counties. The court sits at Bartlesville, Miami, Pawhuska, Tulsa and Vinita.

Chief Judge
Terry C. Kern

Judges
Sven Erik Holmes
Claire V. Eagan

Senior Judges
H. Dale Cook
James O. Ellison

Clerk
Philip B. Lombardi
411 U.S. Courthouse
333 West Fourth Street
Tulsa, Oklahoma 74103-3819
(918) 699-4700

WESTERN DISTRICT includes Alfalfa, Beaver, Beckham, Blaine, Caddo, Canadian, Cimarron, Cleveland, Comanche, Cotton, Custer, Dewey, Ellis, Garfield, Garvin, Grady, Grant, Greer, Harmon, Harper, Jackson, Jefferson, Kay, Kingfisher, Kiowa, Lincoln, Logan, Major, McClain, Noble, Oklahoma, Payne, Pottawatomie, Roger Mills, Stephens, Texas, Tillman, Washita, Woods and Woodward counties. The court sits at Chickasha, Enid, Guthrie, Lawton, Mangum, Oklahoma City, Pauls Valley, Ponca City, Shawnee and Woodward.

Chief Judge
Robin J. Cauthron

Judges
David L. Russell
Timothy Dwight Leonard
Vicki Miles-LaGrange
Stephen P. Friot
Joe L. Heaton

Senior Judges
Ralph G. Thompson
Lee R. West
Wayne E. Alley

Clerk
Robert D. Dennis
1210 U.S. Courthouse
200 N.W. Fourth Street
Oklahoma City, Oklahoma 73102-3092
(405) 609-5000

UNITED STATES MAGISTRATE JUDGES OF OKLAHOMA

EASTERN DISTRICT

Kimberly E. West
Steven P. Shreder

NORTHERN DISTRICT

Frank H. McCarthy
Sam A. Joyner
Paul J. Cleary

WESTERN DISTRICT

Doyle W. Argo
Gary M. Purcell
Valerie K. Couch
Bana Burkett Roberts
Shon T. Erwin
Robert Bacharach

Recalled Magistrate Judge
Ronald L. Howland (Western)

UNITED STATES BANKRUPTCY COURTS OF OKLAHOMA

EASTERN DISTRICT

Judge
Tom R. Cornish

Bankruptcy Clerk
Therese Buthod
P.O. Box 1347
Okmulgee, Oklahoma 74447-1347
(918) 758-0126

NORTHERN DISTRICT

Chief Judge
Dana L. Rasure

UNITED STATES DISTRICT COURTS DISTRICTS OF OKLAHOMA—*Continued*

Judge
Terrence L. Michael

Bankruptcy Clerk
Michael L. Williams
105 Federal Building
224 South Boulder Avenue
Tulsa, Oklahoma 74103-3015
(918) 699-4000

WESTERN DISTRICT

Chief Judge
T. M. "Mike" Weaver

Judges
Richard L. Bohanon
Niles L. Jackson

Bankruptcy Clerk
Grant E. Price
Old Post Office Building
215 Dean A. McGee Avenue
Oklahoma City, Oklahoma 73102
(405) 609-5700

SUPREME COURT OF OKLAHOMA

The Supreme Court is Oklahoma's highest court of appellate jurisdiction. The court consists of nine justices initially appointed by the governor from a list submitted by the Judicial Nominating Commission. If the governor does not make the appointment within sixty days, the chief justice makes the appointment. Thereafter justices stand for retention in statewide nonpartisan elections to six-year terms. Each justice must be from a different electoral district. The chief justice and vice chief justice are elected by peer vote to two-year terms.

The court has appellate jurisdiction over all civil cases at law and in equity; additionally, in the event of a conflict over jurisdiction between the Supreme Court and the Court of Criminal Appeals, the Supreme Court makes the final determination. The court has superintending control of all inferior courts, agencies, commissions and boards created by law as well as administrative authority over all courts in the state except the Court on the Judiciary and a Senate Court of Impeachment. The court has jurisdiction in extraordinary writs and other writs necessary to the exercise of proper jurisdiction and exclusive jurisdiction over admission to the bar and the conduct of its members.

The court sits at Oklahoma City.

FIRST ELECTORAL DISTRICT includes Craig, Grant, Kay, Nowata, Osage, Ottawa, Pawnee, Rogers and Washington counties.

SECOND ELECTORAL DISTRICT includes Atoka, Bryan, Choctaw, Haskell, Johnston, Latimer, LeFlore, Marshall, McCurtain, McIntosh, Pittsburg, Pushmataha and Sequoyah counties.

THIRD ELECTORAL DISTRICT includes Oklahoma County.

FOURTH ELECTORAL DISTRICT includes Alfalfa, Beaver, Beckham, Blaine, Cimarron, Custer, Dewey, Ellis, Garfield, Harper, Kingfisher, Major, Roger Mills, Texas, Washita, Woods and Woodward counties.

FIFTH ELECTORAL DISTRICT includes Carter, Cleveland, Garvin, Grady, Jefferson, Love, McClain, Murray and Stephens counties.

SIXTH ELECTORAL DISTRICT includes Tulsa County.

SEVENTH ELECTORAL DISTRICT includes Adair, Cherokee, Creek, Delaware, Mayes, Muskogee, Okmulgee and Wagoner counties.

EIGHTH ELECTORAL DISTRICT includes Coal, Hughes, Lincoln, Logan, Noble, Okfuskee, Payne, Pontotoc, Pottawatomie and Seminole counties.

NINTH ELECTORAL DISTRICT includes Caddo, Canadian, Comanche, Cotton, Greer, Harmon, Jackson, Kiowa and Tillman counties.

Chief Justice
Joseph M. Watt (Ninth District)

Vice Chief Justice
Marian P. Opala (Third District)

Justices
Daniel J. Boudreau (Sixth District)
Rudolph Hargrave (Eighth District)
Ralph B. Hodges (Second District)
Yvonne Kauger (Fourth District)
Robert E. Lavender (First District)
Hardy Summers (Seventh District)
James R. Winchester (Fifth District)

Clerk
Michael Richie
State Capitol Building, Room B2
2300 North Lincoln Boulevard
Oklahoma City, Oklahoma 73105
(405) 521-2163

Director
Howard W. Conyers
Administrative Office of the Courts
1915 North Stiles, Suite 305
Oklahoma City, Oklahoma 73105
(405) 521-2450

OKLAHOMA COURT OF CRIMINAL APPEALS

The Court of Criminal Appeals is the highest court of criminal appeals in Oklahoma. The court consists of five judges initially appointed by the governor from a list submitted by the Judicial Nominating Commission. If the governor does not make the appointment within sixty days, the chief justice makes the appointment. Thereafter judges stand for retention in statewide nonpartisan elections to six-year terms. Each judge must be from a different electoral district. The positions of presiding judge and vice presiding judge rotate among the judges every two years.

The court has exclusive appellate jurisdiction in criminal cases appealed from the District Courts and the Municipal Criminal Courts of Record. Conflicts as to jurisdiction are determined by the Supreme Court. The court may issue writs necessary to the exercise of proper jurisdiction.

Three judges constitute a quorum, with the concurrence of three judges necessary for a decision. The court sits at Oklahoma City.

OKLAHOMA COURT OF CRIMINAL APPEALS—*Continued*

FIRST ELECTORAL DISTRICT includes Craig, Delaware, Mayes, Nowata, Ottawa, Rogers, Tulsa and Wagoner counties.

SECOND ELECTORAL DISTRICT includes Adair, Cherokee, Cleveland, Creek, Kay, Lincoln, Logan, Muskogee, Noble, Okfuskee, Okmulgee, Osage, Pawnee, Payne, Pottawatomie and Washington counties.

THIRD ELECTORAL DISTRICT includes Atoka, Bryan, Carter, Coal, Choctaw, Garvin, Grady, Haskell, Hughes, Jefferson, Johnston, Latimer, LeFlore, Love, Marshall, McClain, McCurtain, McIntosh, Murray, Pittsburg, Pontotoc, Pushmataha, Seminole, Sequoyah and Stephens counties.

FOURTH ELECTORAL DISTRICT includes Canadian and Oklahoma counties.

FIFTH ELECTORAL DISTRICT includes Alfalfa, Beaver, Beckham, Blaine, Caddo, Cimarron, Comanche, Cotton, Custer, Dewey, Ellis, Garfield, Grant, Greer, Harmon, Harper, Jackson, Kingfisher, Kiowa, Major, Roger Mills, Texas, Tillman, Washita, Woods and Woodward counties.

Presiding Judge

Charles A. Johnson (Second District)

Vice Presiding Judge

Stephen E. Lile (Fifth District)

Judges

Charles S. Chapel (First District)
Gary L. Lumpkin (Third District)
Reta M. Strubhar (Fourth District)

OKLAHOMA COURT OF CIVIL APPEALS

The Court of Civil Appeals is Oklahoma's intermediate appellate court. The court consists of twelve judges initially appointed by the governor from a list submitted by the Judicial Nominating Commission. If the governor does not make the appointment within sixty days, the chief justice makes the appointment. Thereafter judges stand for retention in statewide nonpartisan elections to six-year terms. Two judges are elected from each district. A chief judge and a vice chief judge are elected by peer vote to one-year terms. Retired judges may serve any state court at the pleasure of the Supreme Court.

The Court of Civil Appeals has jurisdiction over all civil cases as assigned to it by the Supreme Court. The court's decisions may be reviewed by the Supreme Court only if a majority of the justices certify the review. The court may dismiss any civil case assigned to it by the Supreme Court. The court may issue writs necessary to the exercise of proper jurisdiction.

The court sits in four divisions consisting of three-judge panels at Oklahoma City and Tulsa.

Chief Judge

Larry E. Joplin

Vice Chief Judge

Tom Colbert

Judges

Glenn D. Adams	Kenneth L. Buettner
Jerry L. Goodman	Carol M. Hansen
Carl B. Jones	Keith Rapp
John F. Reif	Ronald Stubblefield
Joe C. Taylor	E. Bay Mitchell III

OKLAHOMA DISTRICT COURTS

The District Courts are Oklahoma's courts of general jurisdiction. Oklahoma has twenty-six judicial districts served by district judges, associate district judges and special judges. For administration purposes judicial districts are combined into nine judicial administrative districts, each with a presiding judge. District and associate district judges are elected from their respective judicial districts in nonpartisan elections for four-year terms. Vacancies are filled by the governor from a list submitted by the Judicial Nominating Commission. If the governor does not fill the vacancy within sixty days, the chief justice makes the appointment. At least one associate district judge serves each county. Special judges are appointed by and serve at the pleasure of the district judges. Retired judges may serve any state court at the pleasure of the Supreme Court.

The courts have unlimited original jurisdiction of all justiciable matters as provided by law. The courts may review administrative action provided by statute and may issue writs necessary to implement orders, judgments or decrees. Appeals from the Municipal Courts Not of Record are by trial de novo.

The courts normally sit at the county seats within the judicial district, although they are empowered to sit anywhere in the state as authorized by rule of the Supreme Court.

FIRST JUDICIAL DISTRICT includes Beaver, Cimarron, Harper and Texas counties. The court sits at Beaver, Boise City, Buffalo and Guymon.

District Judge

Greg A. Zigler

County	Associate District Judge
Beaver	Gerald H. Riffe
Cimarron	Ronald L. Kincannon
Harper	Wayne Olmstead
Texas	Ryan D. Reddick

SECOND JUDICIAL DISTRICT includes Beckham, Custer, Ellis, Roger Mills and Washita counties. The court sits at Sayre, Arapaho, Arnett, Cheyenne and Cordell.

District Judge

Charles L. Goodwin

County	Associate District Judge
Beckham	Floyd "Doug" Haught
Custer	Jacqueline P. Duncan
Ellis	Joe L. Jackson
Roger Mills	Gale Smith
Washita	Joe Burch

County	Special Judge
Custer	Jill Carpenter Weedon

OKLAHOMA DISTRICT COURTS—*Continued*

THIRD JUDICIAL DISTRICT includes Greer, Harmon, Jackson, Kiowa and Tillman counties. The court sits at Mangum, Hollis, Altus, Hobart and Frederick.

District Judge
Richard B. Darby

County	Associate District Judge
Greer	Danny R. Deaver
Harmon	Winford Mike Warren
Jackson	Clark E. Huey
Kiowa	Norman L. Russell
Tillman	David A. Barnett

County	Special Judge
Jackson	C. Suzanne Mollison

FOURTH JUDICIAL DISTRICT includes Alfalfa, Blaine, Dewey, Garfield, Grant, Kingfisher, Major, Woods and Woodward counties. The court sits at Cherokee, Watonga, Taloga, Enid, Medford, Kingfisher, Fairview, Alva and Woodward.

District Judges
Ronald G. Franklin
Ray Dean Linder
John W. Michael

County	Associate District Judge
Alfalfa	Loren E. Angle
Blaine	Mark A. Moore
Dewey	Robert W. Collier
Garfield	Richard McBee Perry
Grant	Jack Hammontree
Kingfisher	Susie Pritchett
Major	N. Vince Barefoot
Woods	Mickey J. Hadwiger
Woodward	Joseph P. Marak, Jr.

County	Special Judge
Garfield	J. Bruce Harvey
	Gary L. Maxey

FIFTH JUDICIAL DISTRICT includes Comanche, Cotton, Jefferson and Stephens counties. The court sits at Lawton, Walters, Waurika and Duncan.

District Judges
David B. Lewis
George Womack Lindley
Charles Allen McCall
Mark R. Smith
Keith Byron Aycock

County	Associate District Judge
Comanche	C. William Stratton
Cotton	Leo A. Watson, Jr.
Jefferson	Jon Tom Staton
Stephens	Joe H. Enos

County	Special Judge
Comanche	Kenny D. Harris
	Taylor C. Stein
Stephens	William B. Buxton

SIXTH JUDICIAL DISTRICT includes Caddo and Grady counties. The court sits at Anadarko and Chickasha.

District Judge
Richard G. Van Dyck

County	Associate District Judge
Caddo	David E. Powell
Grady	Oteka Laverne Alford

County	Special Judge
Caddo	John E. Herndon
Grady	Timothy A. Brauer

SEVENTH JUDICIAL DISTRICT includes Oklahoma County. The court sits at Oklahoma City.

District Judges

Jerry D. Bass	Tammy Bass-Jones
Virgil C. Black	Susan W. Bragg
Susan P. Caswell	Nancy L. Coats
Bryan C. Dixon	Ray C. Elliott
Twyla Mason Gray	Noma Diane Gurich
David Harbour	Daniel L. Owens
Carolyn R. Ricks	Vicki Robertson
Barbara G. Swinton	

Associate District Judge
Nan J. Patton

Special Judges

James B. Croy	Donald Deason
D. Fred Doak	Daniel Durocher
Russell D. Hall	Lisa K. Hammond
Charles G. Hill	Carol Ann Hubbard
Charles G. Humble	Glenn M. Jones
Larry A. Jones	Roma M. McElwee
James H. Paddleford	Patricia G. Parrish
Gregory J. Ryan	Roger H. Stuart
Brian H. Upp	Geary L. Walke

EIGHTH JUDICIAL DISTRICT includes Kay and Noble counties. The court sits at Newkirk and Perry.

District Judge
D. W. Boyd

County	Associate District Judge
Kay	Leslie D. Page
Noble	Dan G. Allen

County	Special Judge
Kay	Robert H. Galbraith
	Douglas C. Revard

NINTH JUDICIAL DISTRICT includes Logan and Payne counties. The court sits at Guthrie and Stillwater.

District Judge
Donald L. Worthington

County	Associate District Judge
Logan	Larry R. Brooks
Payne	Robert M. Murphy, Jr.

County	Special Judge
Logan	William W. Wheeler
Payne	Phillip C. Corley
	Charles A. Meyers

TENTH JUDICIAL DISTRICT includes Osage County. The court sits at Pawhuska.

OKLAHOMA DISTRICT COURTS—*Continued*

District Judge
James Richard Pearman

Associate District Judge
Bruce David Gambill

Special Judge
John S. Boggs

ELEVENTH JUDICIAL DISTRICT includes Nowata and Washington counties. The court sits at Nowata and Bartlesville.

District Judge
Janice P. Dreiling

County	Associate District Judge
Nowata	Carl G. Gibson
Washington	Curtis L. DeLapp

County	Special Judge
Washington	Myrna L. Lansdown

TWELFTH JUDICIAL DISTRICT includes Craig, Mayes and Rogers counties. The court sits at Vinita, Pryor and Claremore.

District Judges
James D. Goodpaster
Dynda Rose Parks Post

County	Associate District Judge
Craig	Harry M. Wyatt, III
Mayes	Terry H. McBride
Rogers	J. Dwayne Steidley

County	Special Judge
Mayes	Gary J. Dean
Rogers	Sheila A. Condren
	L. Joe Smith

THIRTEENTH JUDICIAL DISTRICT includes Delaware and Ottawa counties. The court sits at Jay and Miami.

District Judge
Robert G. Haney

County	Associate District Judge
Delaware	Barry V. Denney
Ottawa	Robert E. Reavis, II

County	Special Judge
Delaware	Alicia Littlefield
Ottawa	William E. Culver

FOURTEENTH JUDICIAL DISTRICT includes Pawnee and Tulsa counties. The court sits at Pawnee and Tulsa.

District Judges

Sharron M. Bubenik	Doris L. Fransein
Gregory K. Frizzell	J. Michael Gassett
Tom C. Gillert	Jesse S. Harris
Linda G. Morrissey	Rebecca Nightingale
David L. Peterson	Jefferson D. Sellers
Ronald L. Shaffer	Deborah C. Shallcross
P. Thomas Thornbrugh	Jane P. Wiseman

County	Associate District Judge
Pawnee	Matthew D. Henry
Tulsa	Caroline E. Wall

County	Special Judge
Tulsa	Mark Barcus
	Terry H. Bitting
	Damon H. Cantrell
	Carlos J. Chappelle
	B. Darlene Crutchfield
	Kyle B. Haskins
	Russell Perry Hass
	Edward J. Hicks, III
	Charles R. Hogshead
	Allen Klein
	Gordon D. McAllister, Jr.
	Millie N. Otey
	Robert Perugino
	Clancy C. Smith
	Clifford J. Smith
	Sarah D. Smith
	C. Michael Zacharias

FIFTEENTH JUDICIAL DISTRICT includes Adair, Cherokee, Muskogee, Sequoyah and Wagoner counties. The court sits at Stilwell, Tahlequah, Muskogee, Sallisaw and Wagoner.

District Judges
James E. Edmondson
John C. Garrett
Mike Norman
G. Bruce Sewell

County	Associate District Judge
Adair	L. Elizabeth Brown
Cherokee	Mark L. Dobbins
Muskogee	Thomas H. Alford
Sequoyah	A. J. Henshaw, Jr.
Wagoner	Darrell G. Shepherd

County	Special Judge
Cherokee	Sandy Crosslin
Muskogee	Robin W. Adair
	A. Carl Robinson
Sequoyah	Dennis M. Sprouse
Wagoner	Forrest D. Nelson
	J. Jeffrey Payton

SIXTEENTH JUDICIAL DISTRICT includes Haskell, Latimer and LeFlore counties. The court sits at Stigler, Wilburton and Poteau.

District Judge
Danita E. Williams

County	Associate District Judge
Haskell	John N. Henderson
Latimer	Bill D. Welch
LeFlore	Ted A. Knight

County	Special Judge
LeFlore	Farley W. Ward

SEVENTEENTH JUDICIAL DISTRICT includes Choctaw, McCurtain and Pushmataha counties. The court sits at Hugo, Idabel and Antlers.

OKLAHOMA DISTRICT COURTS—*Continued*

District Judge
Willard Driesel

County	Associate District Judge
Choctaw	Don Ed Payne
McCurtain	Michael D. DeBerry
Pushmataha	Lowell Burgess, Jr.

County	Special Judge
McCurtain	Gary L. Brock
	John W. DeWitt

EIGHTEENTH JUDICIAL DISTRICT includes McIntosh and Pittsburg counties. The court sits at Eufaula and McAlester.

District Judge
Steven W. Taylor

County	Associate District Judge
McIntosh	Gene F. Mowery
Pittsburg	Thomas M. Bartheld

County	Special Judge
Pittsburg	Jim D. Bland

NINETEENTH JUDICIAL DISTRICT includes Bryan County. The court sits at Durant.

District Judge
Farrell M. Hatch

Associate District Judge
Rocky L. Powers

Special Judge
Trace C. Sherrill

TWENTIETH JUDICIAL DISTRICT includes Carter, Johnston, Love, Marshall and Murray counties. The court sits at Ardmore, Tishomingo, Marietta, Madill and Sulphur.

District Judges
John H. Scaggs
Thomas S. Walker

County	Associate District Judge
Carter	Lee Card
Johnston	Robert M. Highsmith
Love	Charles E. Roberts
Marshall	Richard A. Miller
Murray	Timothy K. Colbert

County	Special Judge
Carter	Charles G. Tate

TWENTY-FIRST JUDICIAL DISTRICT includes Cleveland, Garvin and McClain counties. The court sits at Norman, Pauls Valley and Purcell.

District Judges
Candace L. Blalock
William Hetherington, Jr.
Tom A. Lucas

County	Associate District Judge
Cleveland	vacancy
Garvin	Richard B. McClain
McClain	Noah H. Ewing, Jr.

County	Special Judge
Cleveland	Janet A. Foss
	Reginald D. Gaston
	H. Jequita Napoli
	Rodney David Ring
Garvin	Virgil R. Tipton
McClain	Gary D. Barger

TWENTY-SECOND JUDICIAL DISTRICT includes Hughes, Pontotoc and Seminole counties. The court sits at Holdenville, Ada and Wewoka.

District Judges
George W. Butner
Tom S. Landrith
Gary P. Snow

County	Associate District Judge
Hughes	Greggory M. Smith
Pontotoc	Martha K. Kilgore
Seminole	Lee G. Stilwell

County	Special Judge
Pontotoc	John David Miller
Seminole	Joseph Wrigley

TWENTY-THIRD JUDICIAL DISTRICT includes Lincoln and Pottawatomie counties. The court sits at Chandler and Shawnee.

District Judges
Douglas L. Combs
Paul Vassar

County	Associate District Judge
Lincoln	Craig Key
Pottawatomie	John D. Gardner

County	Special Judge
Pottawatomie	Mary A. Black

TWENTY-FOURTH JUDICIAL DISTRICT includes Creek, Okfuskee and Okmulgee counties. The court sits at Sapulpa, Okemah and Okmulgee.

District Judges
Charles M. Humphrey, III
John David Maley
Franklin D. Rahhal
Donald D. Thompson
Joe Sam Vassar

County	Associate District Judge
Creek	April Sellers White
Okfuskee	David N. Martin
Okmulgee	H. Michael Claver

County	Special Judge
Creek	Russell C. Miller
	Richard A. Woolery
Okmulgee	Duane A. Woodliff

TWENTY-FIFTH JUDICIAL DISTRICT includes Atoka and Coal counties. The court sits at Atoka and Coalgate.

District Judge
Doug Gabbard, II

OKLAHOMA DISTRICT COURTS—*Continued*

County	Associate District Judge
Atoka	Danny L. Scroggins
Coal	Richard E. Branam

TWENTY-SIXTH JUDICIAL DISTRICT includes Canadian County. The court sits at El Reno.

District Judge
Edward C. Cunningham

Associate District Judge
Gary E. Miller

Special Judges
Robert E. Davis
Gary D. McCurdy
John L. Wolking

OKLAHOMA WORKERS' COMPENSATION COURT

The Workers' Compensation Court is a court of special jurisdiction in Oklahoma that, effective July 1, 1978, replaced the State Industrial Court. The court consists of a presiding judge and nine judges appointed to six-year terms by the governor from a list supplied by the Judicial Nominating Commission. The presiding judge is appointed by the governor to a two-year term and may be reappointed for a second, consecutive two-year term. A vice presiding judge may be elected by peer vote to an unspecified term which runs concurrent with that of the presiding judge.

The court processes claims and administers laws coming under the workers' compensation statutes. Appeals are to the Supreme Court.

The court sits at Oklahoma City and Tulsa.

Presiding Judge
Richard L. Blanchard

Vice Presiding Judge
Susan Witt Conyers

Judges

Jerry L. Salyer
Ellen C. Edwards
Jimmy D. Filosa
Kenton W. Fulton
D. Craig Johnston
Richard G. Mason
Gene Prigmore
Cherri Farrar

OKLAHOMA COURT OF TAX REVIEW

The Court of Tax Review is a court of limited jurisdiction in Oklahoma. The chief justice assigns three district court judges on an as-needed basis from outside the congressional district in which a case occurs. The most senior judge amongst the three is designated as the presiding judge for each individual case.

The court has jurisdiction over cases involving alleged illegal tax levies by any political subdivision in the state. Appeals are to the Supreme Court.

The court sits at Oklahoma City.

OKLAHOMA MUNICIPAL CRIMINAL COURTS OF RECORD

The Municipal Criminal Courts of Record are courts of limited jurisdiction in Oklahoma established in cities with populations of more than 200,000. There are two courts, one in Oklahoma City and the other in Tulsa. Judges are appointed by their respective mayors to two-year terms.

The courts have jurisdiction over city ordinance violations when the penalty is less than $500 and/or a ninety-day jail sentence. The courts may hold jury trials when the case in question carries a penalty of more than $100 or a jail sentence of any length. Appeals are to the Court of Criminal Appeals.

The courts sit at Oklahoma City and Tulsa.

OKLAHOMA MUNICIPAL COURTS NOT OF RECORD

The Municipal Courts Not of Record are courts of limited jurisdiction in Oklahoma which may be established in any city or town having a population of 200,000 or less. Judges are appointed to two-year terms by the mayors of the cities and towns where the courts are established.

The courts have original jurisdiction of all city ordinance violations and may be required to supervise juveniles placed on parole, probation or suspended sentence. Appeals are by trial de novo in the District Courts.

Oklahoma Counties and County Seats

Adair
Stilwell

Alfalfa
Cherokee

Atoka
Atoka

Beaver
Beaver

Beckham
Sayre

Blaine
Watonga

Bryan
Durant

Caddo
Anadarko

Canadian
El Reno

Carter
Ardmore

Cherokee
Tahlequah

Choctaw
Hugo

Cimarron
Boise City

Cleveland
Norman

Coal
Coalgate

Comanche
Lawton

Cotton
Walters

Craig
Vinita

Creek
Sapulpa

Custer
Arapaho

Delaware
Jay

Dewey
Taloga

Ellis
Arnett

Garfield
Enid

COUNTIES AND COUNTY SEATS—*Continued*

Garvin
Pauls Valley

Grady
Chickasha

Grant
Medford

Greer
Mangum

Harmon
Hollis

Harper
Buffalo

Haskell
Stigler

Hughes
Holdenville

Jackson
Altus

Jefferson
Waurika

Johnston
Tishomingo

Kay
Newkirk

Kingfisher
Kingfisher

Kiowa
Hobart

Latimer
Wilburton

LeFlore
Poteau

Lincoln
Chandler

Logan
Guthrie

Love
Marietta

Major
Fairview

Marshall
Madill

Mayes
Pryor

McClain
Purcell

McCurtain
Idabel

McIntosh
Eufaula

Murray
Sulphur

Muskogee
Muskogee

Noble
Perry

Nowata
Nowata

Okfuskee
Okemah

Oklahoma
Oklahoma City

Okmulgee
Okmulgee

Osage
Pawhuska

Ottawa
Miami

Pawnee
Pawnee

Payne
Stillwater

Pittsburg
McAlester

Pontotoc
Ada

Pottawatomie
Shawnee

Pushmataha
Antlers

Roger Mills
Cheyenne

Rogers
Claremore

Seminole
Wewoka

Sequoyah
Sallisaw

Stephens
Duncan

Texas
Guymon

Tillman
Frederick

Tulsa
Tulsa

Wagoner
Wagoner

Washington
Bartlesville

Washita
Cordell

Woods
Alva

Woodward
Woodward

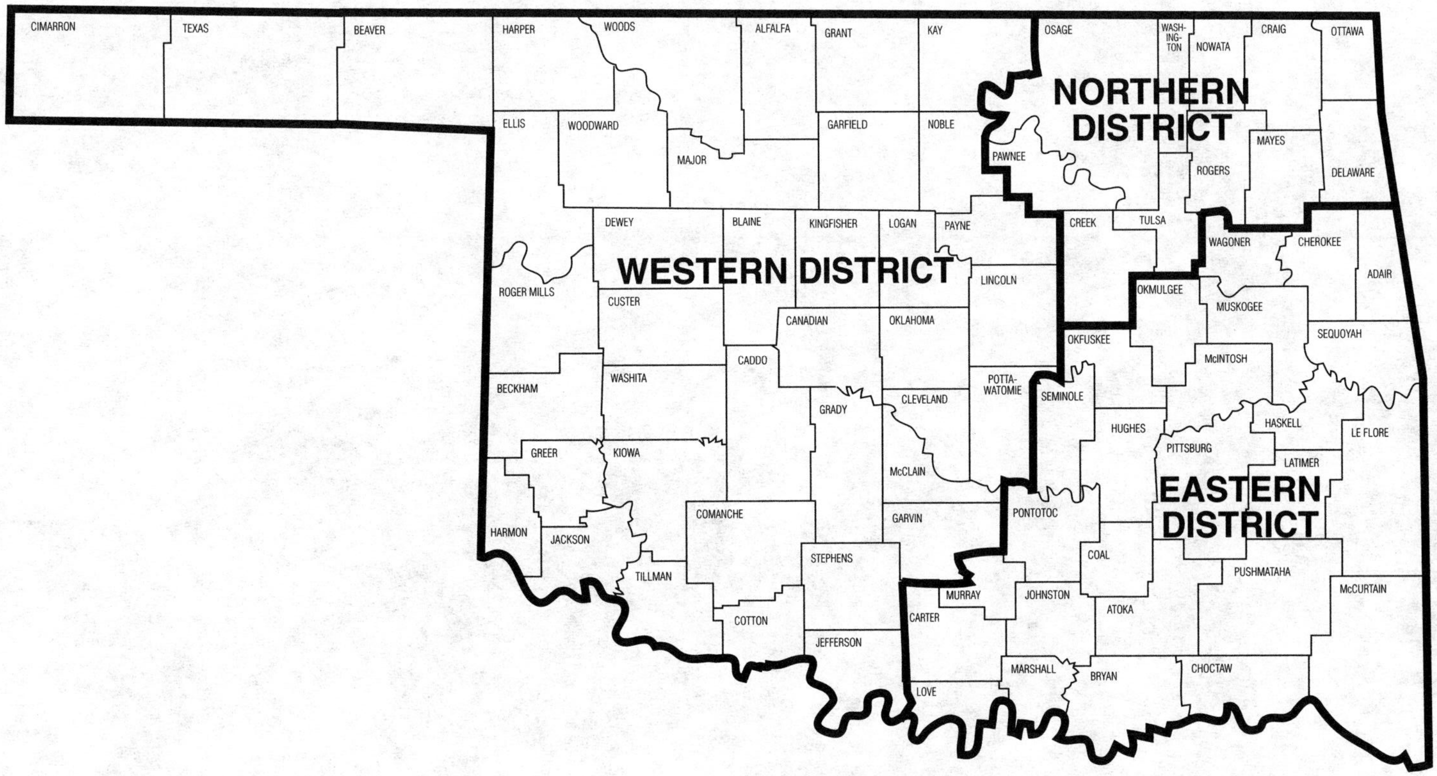
NORTHERN DISTRICT
WESTERN DISTRICT
EASTERN DISTRICT
CIMARRON
TEXAS
BEAVER
HARPER
WOODS
ALFALFA
GRANT
KAY
OSAGE
WASH-ING-TON
NOWATA
CRAIG
OTTAWA
ELLIS
WOODWARD
MAJOR
GARFIELD
NOBLE
PAWNEE
ROGERS
MAYES
DELAWARE
DEWEY
BLAINE
KINGFISHER
LOGAN
PAYNE
CREEK
TULSA
WAGONER
CHEROKEE
ADAIR
ROGER MILLS
CUSTER
LINCOLN
OKMULGEE
MUSKOGEE
SEQUOYAH
CANADIAN
OKLAHOMA
OKFUSKEE
McINTOSH
CADDO
BECKHAM
WASHITA
POTTA-WATOMIE
SEMINOLE
CLEVELAND
GRADY
HUGHES
HASKELL
LE FLORE
PITTSBURG
LATIMER
GREER
KIOWA
McCLAIN
GARVIN
PONTOTOC
COMANCHE
HARMON
JACKSON
COAL
STEPHENS
TILLMAN
PUSHMATAHA
McCURTAIN
MURRAY
JOHNSTON
ATOKA
CARTER
COTTON
JEFFERSON
MARSHALL
CHOCTAW
BRYAN
LOVE

UNITED STATES DISTRICT COURTS DISTRICTS OF OKLAHOMA

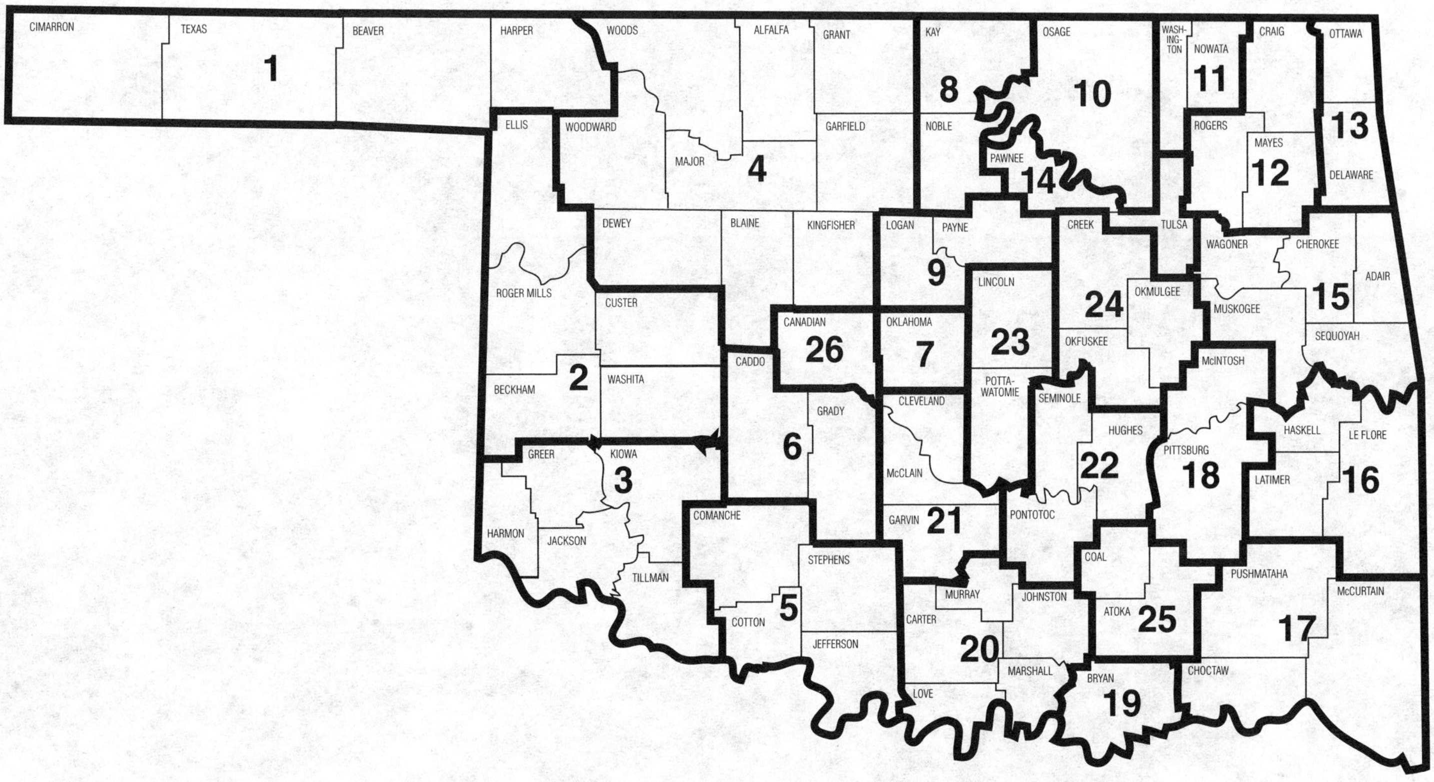
CIMARRON
TEXAS
BEAVER
HARPER
WOODS
ALFALFA
GRANT
KAY
OSAGE
WASH-ING-TON
NOWATA
CRAIG
OTTAWA
1
8
10
11
13
ELLIS
WOODWARD
MAJOR
4
GARFIELD
NOBLE
PAWNEE
14
ROGERS
MAYES
12
DELAWARE
DEWEY
BLAINE
KINGFISHER
LOGAN
PAYNE
9
CREEK
TULSA
WAGONER
CHEROKEE
ADAIR
15
ROGER MILLS
CUSTER
LINCOLN
23
24
OKMULGEE
MUSKOGEE
SEQUOYAH
CANADIAN
26
OKLAHOMA
7
OKFUSKEE
CADDO
POTTA-WATOMIE
McINTOSH
BECKHAM
2
WASHITA
GRADY
CLEVELAND
SEMINOLE
HUGHES
HASKELL
LE FLORE
GREER
KIOWA
6
PITTSBURG
18
22
3
McCLAIN
LATIMER
16
COMANCHE
GARVIN
21
PONTOTOC
HARMON
JACKSON
TILLMAN
STEPHENS
COAL
PUSHMATAHA
McCURTAIN
MURRAY
JOHNSTON
5
COTTON
CARTER
ATOKA
25
17
JEFFERSON
20
MARSHALL
CHOCTAW
BRYAN
LOVE
19

JUDICIAL DISTRICTS OF OKLAHOMA DISTRICT COURTS

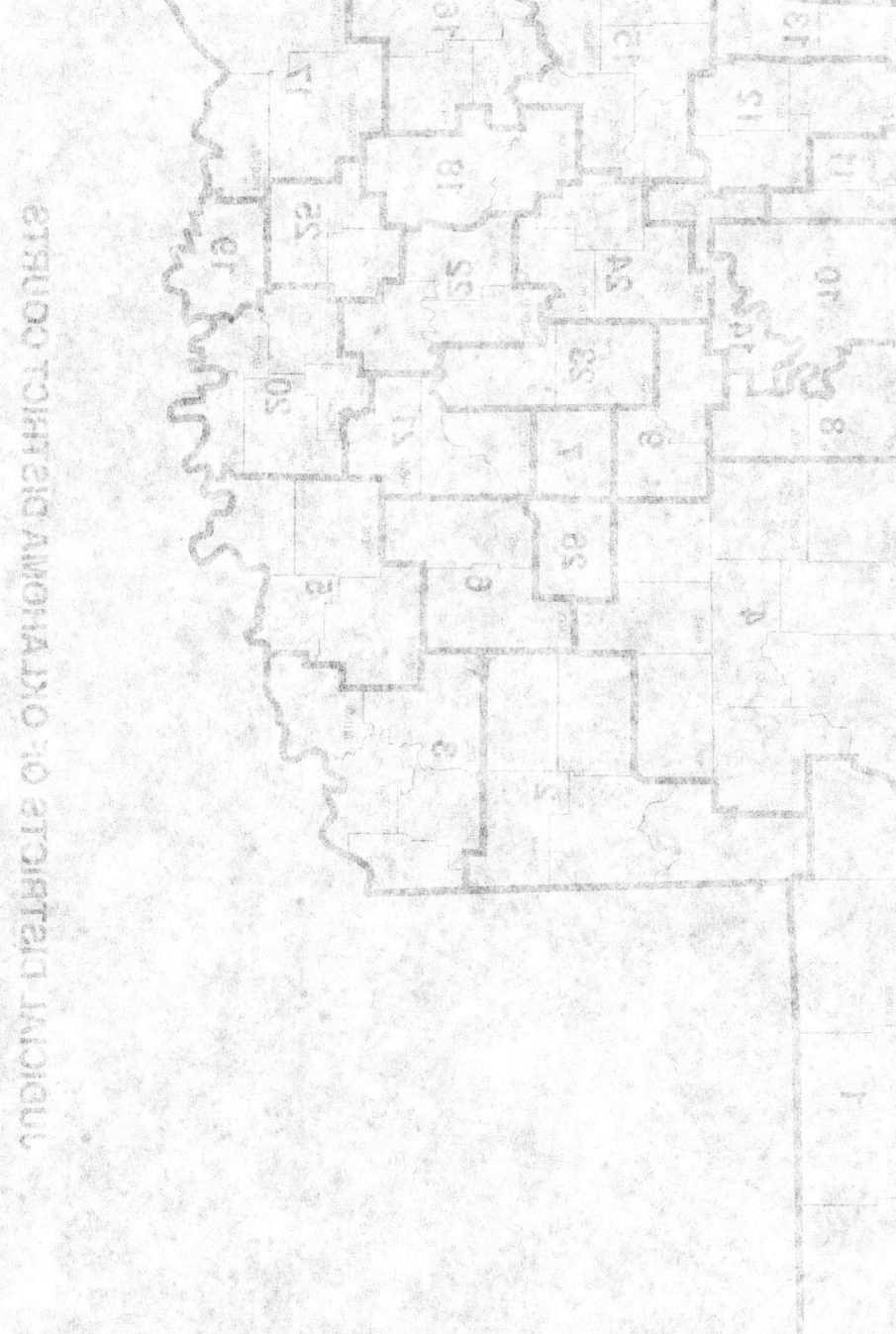

OKLAHOMA

ADAIR, Robin W. *(Special Judge, Oklahoma District Court Fifteenth Judicial District)* Serves Muskogee County.

Office: Muskogee County Courthouse, 220 State Street, Muskogee 74401.

Telephone: (918) 683-2997.

ADAMS, Glenn D. *(Judge, Oklahoma Court of Civil Appeals)* Former Chief Judge. Born Tulsa Oklahoma July 28, 1950. Baptist. Educated at John Brown University B.S.E. with honors 1973 and University of Oklahoma J.D. 1977. Editorial Board Oklahoma Law Review 1975-77. Law Clerk to Hon. Lester Reynolds, Oklahoma Court of Appeals 1978 and Vice-Chief Justice Pat Irwin, 1979-80 and Hon. Ralph Hodges, 1984 Oklahoma Supreme Court. Member Phi Delta Phi and Order of the Coif. Admitted to practice Oklahoma 1977, U.S. District Court Western District of Oklahoma 1977 and U.S. Court of Appeals Tenth Circuit 1982. In legal practice Oklahoma City 1977-78 and 1980 and Enid 1982-84. Former Associate District Judge, Oklahoma District Court Fourth Judicial District, appointed by Governor George P. Nigh to term beginning Oct 12, 1984.

General Counsel GEC Production Company 1980-81. Adjunct Professor University of Oklahoma College of Law. Member Garfield County, Cleveland County and Oklahoma Bar Associations. Attended General Jurisdiction and Judicial Writing courses The National Judicial College and Appellate Judges Institute New York University School of Law. Member First Baptist Church.

Office: 1915 North Stiles, Room 357, Oklahoma City 73105.

Telephone: (405) 521-3751.

ALFORD, Oteka Laverne *(Associate District Judge, Oklahoma District Court Sixth Judicial District)* Special Judge Jan 1979 to June 1979. Appointed Associate District Judge by Governor George P. Nigh to term beginning June 21, 1979. Elected Nov 1982, Nov 1986, Nov 1990, Nov 1994, Nov 1998 and Nov 2002. Current term expires Jan 2007. Serves Grady County. Born Lindsay Oklahoma June 2, 1948. Baptist. Educated at University of Oklahoma B.M. (piano) with honors 1970 J.D. 1973. Named Outstanding Sophomore. Editor Oklahoma Law Review 1971-73. Member Phi Delta Phi and Order of the Coif. Admitted to practice Oklahoma 1973. Began legal practice Oklahoma City 1973. In legal practice Lindsay 1977-79.

With Law Department Kerr-McGee Corporation 1973-74. Member Oklahoma Juvenile Justice Oversight Committee, Grady County and Oklahoma Bar Associations. Attended The National Judicial College 1980 and American Academy of Judicial Education 1987. Former member Board of Directors Youth Services of Grady County, Women's Service & Resource Center of Chickasha, Chisholm Trail Mental Health Clinics, Grady County Emergency Management Agency and Sooner Council Girl Scouts. Former Chairman Juvenile Foster Care Review Board. Former Member American Business Women's Association. Board of Directors Grady County Salvation Army. Enjoys playing piano and reading.

Mailing address: P.O. Box 605, Chickasha 73023.

Office: Grady County Courthouse, Chickasha 73023.

Telephone: (405) 224-5314.

Fax: (405) 224-8297

ALFORD, Thomas H. *(Associate District Judge, Oklahoma District Court Fifteenth Judicial District)* Former Special Judge. Serves Muskogee County.

Office: Muskogee County Courthouse, 220 State Street, Muskogee 74401.

Telephone: (918) 687-6388.

ALLEN, Dan G. *(Associate District Judge, Oklahoma District Court Eighth Judicial District)* Serves Noble County.

Office: 14 Noble County Courthouse, 300 Courthouse Drive, Perry 73077.

Telephone: (580) 336-2433.

ALLEY, Wayne E. *(Senior Judge, United States District Court Western District of Oklahoma)* Appointed for life by President Ronald Reagan to term beginning Aug 20, 1985. Assumed Senior status May 16, 1999, serves by assignment. Born Portland Oregon May 16, 1932. Educated at Stanford University A.B. with great distinction 1952 J.D. with honors 1957. Law Clerk to Hon. George Rossman, Oregon Supreme Court 1957. Member Phi Beta Kappa, Phi Delta Phi, Sigma Chi and Order of the Coif. Admitted to practice California 1957, Oregon 1957, U.S. District Court District of Oregon 1957, U.S. Court of Military Appeals 1959 and Oklahoma 1985. In legal practice Portland Oregon 1957-59.

Author "The Litigious Aftermath of Martial Law" 15 Oklahoma L. Rev. 17, 1962, "The Overseas Commander's Power to Regulate the Private Life" 37 Military L. Rev. 57, 1967, "Determinants of Military Judicial Decisions" 65 Military L. Rev. 85, 1974 and "Advocacy on Behalf of a Major Field Command" 94 Military L. Rev. 5, 1981. Important Decision: United States v. Calley 46 C.M.R. 1131, 1973. Dean and Professor of Law University of Oklahoma 1981-85. Former Member State Bar of California and American Bar Association. Fellow American Bar Foundation. Member Oregon State Bar, Oklahoma and Federal Bar Associations. Instructor Trial Advocacy Workshop Harvard Law School 1983, 1985 and 1987. Brigadier General U.S. Army JAGC 1959-81 (Military Judge 1968-75).

Office: 4001 U.S. Courthouse, 200 N.W. Fourth Street, Oklahoma City 73102.

Telephone: (405) 609-5160.

Fax: (405) 609-5171

ANGLE, Loren E. *(Associate District Judge, Oklahoma District Court Fourth Judicial District)* Serves Alfalfa County.

Office: Alfalfa County Courthouse, 300 South Grand, Cherokee 73728.

Telephone: (580) 596-2224.

ARGO, Doyle W. *(Magistrate Judge, United States District Court Western District of Oklahoma)* Appointed

ARGO, DOYLE W.—*Continued*

by U.S. District Court judges to term beginning April 17, 1987. Reappointed 1995 and 2003. Current term expires April 2011. Born Norman Oklahoma March 24, 1947. Educated at University of Oklahoma B.A. 1969 J.D. with honors 1976. Associate Editor Oklahoma Law Review 1974-76. Member Phi Delta Phi and Order of the Coif. Admitted to practice Oklahoma 1976, U.S. District Courts Northern 1979 and Western 1979 Districts of Oklahoma and U.S. Court of Appeals Tenth Circuit 1980. In legal practice Oklahoma City 1981-83 and Norman 1983-87. Judge, Norman Municipal Court 1984-87.

Assistant District Attorney 1976-79. General Counsel Oklahoma Bar Association 1979-81. Author "Scope of Attorney Work Product" Oklahoma Bar Association CLE 1986. Member Federal Magistrate Judges Association, Cleveland County, Oklahoma County, Oklahoma, Federal and American Bar Associations. Recipient Golden Gavel Award from Oklahoma Bar Association. Captain USAF 1969-73. Colonel USAFR (retired).

Office: 1301 U.S. Courthouse, 200 N.W. Fourth Street, Oklahoma City 73102.

Telephone: (405) 609-5220.

AYCOCK, Keith Byron *(District Judge, Oklahoma District Court Fifth Judicial District)* Former Special Judge.

Office: Comanche County Courthouse, 315 S.W. Fifth, Lawton 73501.

Telephone: (580) 581-4585.

BACHARACH, Robert *(Magistrate Judge, United States District Court Western District of Oklahoma)* Appointed by U.S. District Court judges March 29, 1999. Term expires March 29, 2007. Born Clarksdale Mississippi. Educated at University of Oklahoma B.A. with honors 1981 and Washington University J.D. 1985. Recipient Mary Collier Hitchcock Prize, Honor Scholar Award, American Jurisprudence Awards and Breckenridge Scholarship. Developments Editor Washington University Law Quarterly 1984-85. Law Clerk to Hon. William J. Holloway, Jr., U.S. Court of Appeals Tenth Circuit 1985-87. Member Order of Barristers and Order of the Coif. Admitted to practice Oklahoma 1985, U.S. District Courts Eastern, Northern and Western Districts of Oklahoma, U.S. Court of Appeals Tenth Circuit and U.S. Supreme Court. In legal practice Oklahoma City 1987-99.

Author Note "*Dirks v. SEC's Footnote Fourteen:* Horizontal and Vertical Reach" 62, 477, 1984 and Comment "Post-Trial Juror Interviews by the Press: The Fifth Circuit's Approach" 62, 783, 1985 Washington University Law Quarterly, "Section 1983 and the Availability of a Federal Forum: A Reappraisal of the Police Brutality Cases" 16 Memphis State University L. Rev. 353, 1986, "Section 1983 and an Administrative Exhaustion Requirement" 40 Oklahoma L. Rev. 407, 1987 and "Motions in Limine in Oklahoma State and Federal Courts" 24, Oklahoma City University L. Rev. 113, 1999. Adjunct Professor of Civil Pretrial Procedure 1997-99.

Office: 1305 U.S. Courthouse, 200 N.W. Fourth Street, Oklahoma City 73102.

Telephone: (405) 609-5320.

E-mail address: Judge_Robert_Bacharach-@okwd.uscourts.gov

BARCUS, Marc *(Special Judge, Oklahoma District Court Fourteenth Judicial District)* Appointed. Serves Tulsa County.

Office: 124 Tulsa County Courthouse, 500 South Denver Avenue, Tulsa 74103.

Telephone: (918) 596-5345.

BAREFOOT, N. Vince *(Associate District Judge, Oklahoma District Court Fourth Judicial District)* Serves Major County.

Office: Major County Courthouse, 500 East Broadway, Fairview 73737.

Telephone: (580) 227-4609.

BARGER, Gary D. *(Special Judge, Oklahoma District Court Twenty-first Judicial District)* Serves McClain County.

Office: 231 McClain County Courthouse, 121 North Second Street, Lawton 73080.

Telephone: (405) 527-6651.

BARNETT, David A. *(Associate District Judge, Oklahoma District Court Third Judicial District)* Appointed by Governor Henry Bellmon to term beginning May 4, 1988. Elected 1990, 1994, 1998 and 2002. Current term expires Jan 13, 2007. Serves Tillman County. Born Frederick Oklahoma Nov 27, 1945. Southern Baptist. Educated at Oklahoma State University B.S. 1969, Hardin-Simmons University M.B.A. 1973 and University of Oklahoma Law Center J.D. 1976. Admitted to practice Oklahoma 1976 and U.S. District Court Western District of Oklahoma 1984. In legal practice Weatherford 1976-88. Judge, Weatherford Municipal Court 1980-88.

Assistant Professor of Business Administration Southwest Oklahoma State University 1976-82. Former member American Bar Association. Member Oklahoma Bar Association. Staff Sergeant USAF 1969-73.

Mailing address: P.O. Box 97, Frederick 73542.

Office: Tillman County Courthouse, Frederick 73542.

Telephone: (580) 335-3710.

BARTHELD, Thomas M. *(Associate District Judge, Oklahoma District Court Eighteenth Judicial District)* Elected Nov 1994 to term beginning Jan 1995. Reelected 1998, current term expires Jan 2007. Serves Pittsburg County. Born Kansas City Missouri Nov 15, 1957. Educated at Oklahoma State University B.S. 1981 and University of Oklahoma J.D. 1984. Admitted to practice Oklahoma 1984, U.S. District Courts Eastern and Northern Districts of Oklahoma and U.S. Court of Appeals Tenth Circuit. In legal practice McAlester 1984-94.

City Prosecutor McAlester July 1986 to Jan 1994. Member Pittsburg County and Oklahoma Bar Associations.

Office: 115 East Carl Albert Parkway, McAlester 74501.

Telephone: (918) 423-6479.

BASS, Jerry D. *(District Judge, Oklahoma District Court Seventh Judicial District)* Former Special Judge and Associate District Judge.

Office: 800 Oklahoma County Courthouse, 321 Park Avenue, Oklahoma City 73102.

Telephone: (405) 713-7101.

BASS-JONES, Tammy *(District Judge, Oklahoma District Court Seventh Judicial District)*
Office: 722 Oklahoma County Courthouse, 321 Park Avenue, Oklahoma City 73102.
Telephone: (405) 713-1436.

BITTING, Terry H. *(Special Judge, Oklahoma District Court Fourteenth Judicial District)* Serves Tulsa County.
Office: 344 Tulsa County Courthouse, 500 South Denver Avenue, Tulsa 74103.
Telephone: (918) 596-5394.

BLACK, Mary A. *(Special Judge, Oklahoma District Court Twenty-third Judicial District)* Appointed. Serves Pottawatomie County.
Office: Pottawatomie County Courthouse, 325 North Broadway, Shawnee 74801.
Telephone: (405) 257-1296.

BLACK, Virgil C. *(District Judge, Oklahoma District Court Seventh Judicial District)* Appointed by Governor David Walters to term beginning Sept 23, 1991. Elected 1994, 1998 and 2002. Current term expires Jan 2007. Born San Antonio Texas Nov 2, 1945. Methodist. Educated at Oklahoma City University B.S. with honors 1975 J.D. 1978. Admitted to practice Oklahoma 1977, U.S. District Court Western District of Oklahoma 1978 and U.S. Court of Appeals Tenth Circuit 1986. In legal practice Oklahoma City 1983-91.
Assistant District Attorney 1977-83. Important Decision: Cox v. Oklahoma F90, 486, 1993. Member Oklahoma Trial Judges Association, Oklahoma Judicial Conference, American Inns of Court (Master), Oklahoma County and Oklahoma Bar Associations. Attended "Forensic Science and Evidence" 1993 and "Capital Litigation" 1997 The National Judicial College. Frequent Presenter on Criminal Law, Evidence and Trial Tactics Oklahoma Bar Association. Lieutenant Colonel U.S. Army 1965-92. Enjoys skeet shooting.
Office: 809 Oklahoma County Courthouse, 321 Park Avenue, Oklahoma City 73102.
Telephone: (405) 713-1451.

BLALOCK, Candace Landers *(District Judge, Oklahoma District Court Twenty-first Judicial District)* Elected to term beginning 1995. Reelected 1998 and 2002. Current term expires Jan 2007. Educated at University of Oklahoma B.A. 1965 M.A. 1971 and Oklahoma City University School of Law J.D. 1976. In legal practice 1977-81.
Legal Counsel Oklahoma Human Rights Commission 1976-80. Assistant District Attorney Garvin County 1981-94. Important Decision: In re Roger Dale Stafford (denied post conviction relief on the infamous Oklahoma City Steakhouse murder case). Board of Directors Oklahoma Trial Lawyers Association 1977-80. Chairman Serious Juvenile Offender Task Force 1994. Chair 1995 and State Judicial Representative 1996 Child Abuse Training and Coordination Council. Member Ruth Bader Ginsburg Inn of Court. Recipient Distinguished Service Award from Women's Resources Center 1979, Governor's Award from Women of the 80's 1981, Volunteer Award from Oklahoma Department of Human Services Southeast Region 1987, Governor's Volunteer Award 1988, Outstanding Jurist Award from Mental Health Services of Southern Oklahoma 1990 and Humanitarian Award from Department of Human Services Supervisors 1991. Named Outstanding Lawyer of the Month Oklahoma Bar Association 1994. Civilian Supervisor Special Services Department of the Army, Germany 1965-68. Personnel and Education Specialist Electric 1968-75. Assistant Municipal Counselor Oklahoma City 1975-80. Vice President United Nations Association 1977-80. Board of Directors McClain and Garvin Counties Youth and Family Services 1990-94. Member Valley United Methodist Church (Administration Board since 1982), Rotary and Optimist Club.
Mailing address: P.O. Box 356, Pauls Valley 73075.
Office: Garvin County Courthouse, Pauls Valley 73075.
Telephone: (405) 238-3486.

BLANCHARD, Richard L. *(Presiding Judge, Oklahoma Workers' Compensation Court)* Appointed by Governor Frank Keating to term beginning July 1, 1996. Reappointed 2002, current term expires June 2008. Born Waukeshaw Wisconsin Jan 17, 1949. Methodist. Educated at University of Tulsa B.A. 1972 J.D. 1976. Admitted to practice Oklahoma 1976 and U.S. District Court Northern District of Oklahoma 1976. In legal practice Tulsa 1976-83 and 1991-96.
Former Member Oklahoma Bar Association. Enjoys youth sports (baseball, basketball, football, swimming and soccer).
Office: 440 South Houston, Suite 210, Tulsa 74127.
Telephone: (918) 581-2714.

BLAND, Jim D. *(Special Judge, Oklahoma District Court Eighteenth Judicial District)* Serves Pittsburg County.
Office: Pittsburg County Courthouse, 115 East Carl Albert Parkway, McAlester 74501.
Telephone: (918) 423-6479.

BOGGS, John S. *(Special Judge, Oklahoma District Court Tenth Judicial District)* Appointed. Serves Osage County.
Office: Osage County Courthouse, 600 Grandview, Pawhuska 74056.
Telephone: (918) 287-4108.

BOHANON, Richard L. *(Judge, United States Bankruptcy Court Western District of Oklahoma)* Appointed by U.S. District Court judges to term beginning Dec 6, 1982. Reappointed by U.S. Court of Appeals Tenth Circuit judges May 12, 1986 and May 2000. Current term expires May 2014. Former Chief Judge Bankruptcy Court. Also Judge, Bankruptcy Appellate Panel Tenth Circuit. Selected by the Judicial Council of the Tenth Circuit. Born Oklahoma City Oklahoma Feb 9, 1935. Educated at Dartmouth College A.B. 1957, University of Oklahoma LL.B. 1960 and New York University LL.M. 1963. Law Clerk to Chief Judge A. P. Murrah, U.S. Court of Appeals Tenth Circuit 1960-61. Admitted to practice Oklahoma 1960. In legal practice Oklahoma City 1963-82.
Board of Governors National Conference of Bankruptcy Judges since 1982. President American Inn of Court XXIII.
Office: Old Post Office Building, 215 Dean A. McGee Avenue, Oklahoma City 73102.
Telephone: (405) 609-5660, 231-5140.

BOUDREAU, Daniel J. *(Justice, Supreme Court of Oklahoma)* Appointed by Governor Frank Keating to term beginning Oct 1999. Born Natick Massachusetts May 10, 1947. Educated at Boston College B.A. 1969,

BOUDREAU, DANIEL J.—*Continued*

Rutgers University M.A. in Social Work with honors 1972 and University of Tulsa J.D. with honors 1976. Staff member Tulsa Law Journal 1975-76. Admitted to practice Oklahoma 1976. Began legal practice Broken Arrow 1976. Special Judge 1980-83 and District Judge Sept 9, 1983 to 1992, Oklahoma District Court Fourteenth Judicial District, appointed by Governor George P. Nigh. Judge and Vice Chief Judge, Oklahoma Court of Civil Appeals 1992 to Oct 1999.

Adjunct Faculty in Domestic Relations University of Tulsa 1978-84. Member Oklahoma State Judges Organization, Tulsa County and Oklahoma Bar Associations. Graduate The National Judicial College and American Academy of Judicial Education. Former Board of Directors Legal Services of Eastern Oklahoma Corporation. Enjoys soccer and reading.

Office: 204 State Capitol, 2300 North Lincoln, Oklahoma City 73105.

Telephone: (405) 521-3843.

Fax: (405) 528-1607

BOYD, D. W. *(District Judge, Oklahoma District Court Eighth Judicial District)* Appointed by Governor Frank Keating 1996. Elected to term beginning 1999. Reelected 2002, current term expires Jan 2007.

Mailing address: P.O. Box 251, Newkirk 74647.

Office: Kay County Courthouse, Newkirk 74647.

Telephone: (580) 362-2445.

BRAGG, Susan W. *(District Judge, Oklahoma District Court Seventh Judicial District)*

Office: 223 Oklahoma County Courthouse, 321 Park Avenue, Oklahoma City 73102.

Telephone: (405) 713-1456.

BRANAM, Richard E. *(Associate District Judge, Oklahoma District Court Twenty-fifth Judicial District)* Serves Coal County.

Office: 12 Coal County Courthouse, 4 North Main, Coalgate 74538.

Telephone: (580) 927-2573.

BRAUER, Timothy A. *(Special Judge, Oklahoma District Court Sixth Judicial District)* Serves Grady County.

Office: Grady County Courthouse, Fourth Street and Choctaw Avenue, Chickasha 73023.

Telephone: (405) 224-3737.

BROCK, Gary L. *(Special Judge, Oklahoma District Court Seventeenth Judicial District)* Serves McCurtain County.

Office: McCurtain County Courthouse, 108 North Central, Idabel 74745.

Telephone: (580) 286-2221.

BROOKS, Larry R. *(Associate District Judge, Oklahoma District Court Ninth Judicial District)* Elected Aug 1994 to term beginning Jan 1995. Reelected 1998 and 2002. Current term expires Jan 2007. Serves Logan County. Born Oklahoma City Oklahoma March 8, 1949. Religious affiliation: Nazarene. Educated at Oklahoma State University B.S. 1971 M.S. 1973 and University of Oklahoma J.D. 1976. Admitted to practice Oklahoma 1976. In legal practice Idabel 1976-1977.

Assistant District Attorney Craig County Jan 1978 to Dec 1978 and Logan County Jan 1979 to July 1994. Member Oklahoma Judicial Conference and Oklahoma Bar Association. Attended Annual Short Course for Prosecuting Attorneys Northwestern University School of Law Chicago, Illinois 1985. Listed in *Who's Who in the South and Southwest* 1995-96, *Who's Who in American Law* 1996-97 and *Who's Who in America* 1997. Member Lions Club, National Railway Historical Society and Train Collectors Association.

Office: Logan County Courthouse, 301 East Harrison, Guthrie 73044.

Telephone: (405) 282-6114.

BROWN, L. Elizabeth *(Associate District Judge, Oklahoma District Court Fifteenth Judicial District)* Serves Adair County.

Office: Adair County Courthouse, 220 West Division, Stilwell 74960.

Telephone: (918) 696-2356.

Fax: (918) 696-5365

BUBENIK, Sharron M. *(District Judge, Oklahoma District Court Fourteenth Judicial District)* Special Judge Tulsa County Nov 1983 to Feb 1988. Elected District Judge to term beginning Feb 1988. Born San Antonio Texas Jan 23, 1943. Roman Catholic. Educated at Texas Tech University and University of Tulsa B.A. with honors 1975 J.D. 1978. Admitted to practice Oklahoma 1979. In legal practice Aug 1982 to Nov 1983.

Assistant City Prosecutor April 1979 to Nov 1980. Assistant City Attorney Nov 1980 to Aug 1982. Adjunct Professor of Law University of Tulsa 1981. Member Tulsa County Bar Association (Executive Committee 1984, Board of Directors 1985). Enjoys sailing and quilting.

Office: 708 Tulsa County Courthouse, 500 South Denver, Tulsa 74103.

Telephone: (918) 596-5350.

BUETTNER, Kenneth L. *(Judge, Oklahoma Court of Civil Appeals)* Appointed by Governor Frank Keating to term beginning Feb 26, 1996. Retained by election, current term expires 2006. Born Oklahoma City Oklahoma. Roman Catholic. Educated at Texas Christian University B.A. 1972 and Southern Methodist University J.D. 1975. Admitted to practice Oklahoma 1975, Texas 1975, U.S. District Courts Northern District of Texas 1975 and Western 1981 and Eastern 1982 Districts of Oklahoma, U.S. Court of Military Appeals 1976, Colorado 1980, U.S. Tax Court 1981, U.S. Supreme Court 1982 and U.S. Courts of Appeals Tenth 1980, Ninth 1985 and Eleventh 1995 Circuits. In legal practice Oklahoma City 1980-96.

Adjunct Professor of Pretrial Litigation and Texas Civil Procedure Oklahoma City University 1992-96. Member Luther Bohanon American Inn of Court, Oklahoma Bar Foundation, State Bar of Texas, Oklahoma County, Colorado, Oklahoma and American Bar Associations. Attended University of Kansas Law and Economic Center Institute for State Judges 1996 and "How to Write a Well-Written and Reasoned Opinion" American Academy of Judicial Education June 1997. Captain USAF JAG 1976-80. Member Leadership Edmond 1993-94. President Edmond Public Schools Foundation 1997. Trustee St. John's Endowment Fund and Oklahoma Foundation for Excellence.

Office: 1915 North Stiles, Room 357, Oklahoma City 73105.

Telephone: (405) 521-3751.

BURCH, Joe *(Associate District Judge, Oklahoma District Court Second Judicial District)* Serves Washita County.

Office: Washita County Courthouse, 111 East Main Street, Cordell 73632.

Telephone: (580) 832-3226.

BURGESS, Lowell, Jr. *(Associate District Judge, Oklahoma District Court Seventeenth Judicial District)* Serves Pushmataha County.

Office: Pushmataha County Courthouse, 203 S.W. Third Street, Antlers 74523.

Telephone: (580) 298-2553

BUTNER, George W. *(District Judge, Oklahoma District Court Twenty-second Judicial District)*

Mailing address: P.O. Box 656, Wewoka 74884.

Office: Seminole County Courthouse, Wewoka 74884.

Telephone: (405) 257-2545.

BUXTON, William B. *(Special Judge, Oklahoma District Court Fifth Judicial District)* Serves Stephens County.

Office: Stephens County Courthouse, 101 South Eleventh Street, Duncan 73533.

Telephone: (405) 255-3675.

CANTRELL, Damon H. *(Special Judge, Oklahoma District Court Fourteenth Judicial District)* Serves Tulsa County.

Office: Tulsa Juvenile Center, 315 South Gilcrease Museum Road, Tulsa 74127.

Telephone: (918) 596-5318.

CARD, Lee *(Associate District Judge, Oklahoma District Court Twentieth Judicial District)* Serves Carter County.

Office: 304 Carter County Courthouse, 20 B Street S.W., Ardmore 73401.

Telephone: (580) 223-3803.

CASWELL, Susan P. *(District Judge, Oklahoma District Court Seventh Judicial District)*

Office: 811 Oklahoma County Courthouse, 321 Park Avenue, Oklahoma City 73102.

Telephone: (405) 713-1466.

CAUTHRON, Robin J. *(Chief Judge, United States District Court Western District of Oklahoma)* Magistrate Judge Oct 15, 1986 to April 1991. Appointed Judge for life by President George Bush to term beginning April 1991. Chief Judge since Nov 26, 2001. Born Edmond Oklahoma July 14, 1950. Educated at University of Oklahoma B.A. 1970 J.D. 1977 and Central State University M.Ed. 1974. Editor Oklahoma Law Review. Law Clerk to Hon. Ralph G. Thompson, U.S. District Court Western District of Oklahoma Aug 1977 to Feb 1981. Member Order of the Coif. Admitted to practice Oklahoma 1977. In legal practice Idabel Aug 1982 to Feb 1983. Special Judge, Oklahoma District Court Seventeenth Judicial District Feb 1983 to Oct 1986.

Staff Attorney Legal Services of Eastern Oklahoma, Inc. Feb 1981 to Aug 1982. Author "Proving Attorney's Fees in Federal Court" 61 Oklahoma B. Jour. 2813, Oct 27, 1990. Instructor in "Practice in the Federal Court" Oklahoma University College of Law Legal Assistant Program 1982, 1987 and 1988. Former Member Oklahoma Judicial Conference (Vice President 1985 and Member Support Personnel Advisory Committee 1985), McCurtain County Bar Association (President 1986) and Tenth Circuit Judicial Conference Planning Committee 1992. Delegate National Conference on State-Federal Judicial Relationships 1992 and Second National Conference on Gender Bias in the Courts 1993. Oklahoma Fellow American Bar Foundation 1992. Co-chair Tenth Circuit Gender Bias Task Force. Master of the Bench since 1988 Luther Bohanon American Inn of Court XXIII (President 1991-92, Member Executive Committee since 1989). Member American Judicature Society, National Association of Women Judges (Resolutions Committee 1994), National Council of U.S. Magistrates (Tenth Circuit Representative to Board of Directors 1989-91), Oklahoma County (Bench and Bar Committee 1987-90, Board of Directors 1990-93), Oklahoma (Administration of Justice Committee since 1985, Vice Chair 1990 and 1994) and American (Judicial Administration Division) Bar Associations.

Graduate General Jurisdiction Course 1983 and Judge and Trial Course 1984 and Delegate National Conference on Jail and Prison Overcrowding 1985 The National Judicial College. Faculty Member "Discovery Disputes in the Western District" July 1987, "Practice in the Western District" Nov 1987 and June 1988 and "Special Appeals" Dec 1993 Oklahoma Bar Association CLE; "Role of the U.S. Magistrate" July 1988, Bench and Bar Conference Seminars May 1989 and April 1991, "Proving Attorney's Fees" Feb 1991 and "Discovery Disputes" May 1991 Oklahoma County Bar Association CLE; "Women in the Law" Oklahoma City University CLE Nov 1988; Trial Advocacy Program 1989 and 1993, "Federal Discovery Rules" Sept 1991 and "Mediation in Federal Court" Sept 1993 Oklahoma University CLE; "New Discovery Rules" Oklahoma Association Defense Counsel June 1993; Advocacy Institute Department of Justice Aug 1992; "Summary Jury Trials" Tenth Circuit Judges' Workshop Feb 1991; "Oklahoma Women '90's" Women's Education and Leadership Forum Sept 1991; and "What Judges Don't Like About Lawyers and Vice Versa" American Board of Trial Advocates Nov 1992. Panelist "Civil Justice Reform Act" Litigation Section American Bar Association Oct 1991. Named one of Outstanding Young Women of America 1984. Recipient Maurice Merrill Golden Quill Award from Oklahoma Bar Association 1991. Teacher Harding Middle School Oct 1971 to May 1974. Board of Directors Juvenile Diabetes Foundation 1989-92. Member First United Methodist Church (Secretary Board of Trustees 1987-90), Explorer Scouts Section Last Frontier Council Boy Scouts of America (Nominating Committee 1987), Oklahoma University College of Law Alumni Association and Edmond Educational Endowment.

Office: 3108 U.S. Courthouse, 200 N.W. Fourth Street, Oklahoma City 73102.

Telephone: (405) 609-5200.

CHAPEL, Charles S. *(Judge, Oklahoma Court of Criminal Appeals)* Appointed Jan 12, 1993. Educated at San Diego State University B.S., University of Tulsa College of Law J.D. and University of Virginia LL.M. Named outstanding law student by Oklahoma Bar Association 1968.

Trustee Oklahoma Bar Foundation. Trustee Jenks Public Schools Foundation.

Office: 230 State Capitol Building, Oklahoma City 73105.

Telephone: (405) 521-2158.

CHAPPELLE, Carlos J. *(Special Judge, Oklahoma District Court Fourteenth Judicial District)* Assumed office Oct 1995. Serves Tulsa County. Born July 28, 1951. Educated at University of Oklahoma B.B.A. 1973, Tulsa Junior College A.A.S. 1974 and University of Tulsa J.D. 1980. In legal practice Tulsa May 1981 to Oct 1995.

Adjunct Instructor Tulsa Junior College May 1982 to Dec 1995. Former Member Federal Judicial Advisory Committee. Member Council Oak Chapter American Inns of Court (President 1998-99), Oklahoma Trial Judges' Association, Oklahoma Judicial Conference, Tulsa County and Oklahoma Bar Associations. Instructor in Juvenile Law 1995 and 1998 Tulsa County Bar Association, in Adoptions Oklahoma Bar Association 1996, in Ryan Luke Bill Oklahoma Judicial Conference 1998 and in New Directions in Child Abuse University of Tulsa College of Law 1999. Computer Operator IBM/Atlantic Richfield June 1969 to Aug 1969. Sales Associate Chappelle Real Estate Co. June 1972 to June 1973. Real Estate Broker since June 1973. Former Commissioner Oklahoma Human Rights Commission. Former Member Board of Commissioners Tulsa Development Authority. Former Chairman and Member Tulsa City Board of Adjustment. Former Member Board of Directors University of Tulsa College of Law, Domestic Violence Intervention Services, Salvation Army Advisory Board, Camp Fire Girls, Tulsa Urban League, University of Tulsa Alumni Association and Street School. Executive Committee Tulsa 2000 Steering Committee. Board of Trustees Tulsa Junior College Foundation.

Office: 378 Tulsa County Courthouse, 500 South Denver Avenue, Tulsa 74103.
Telephone: (918) 596-5314.

CLAVER, H. Michael *(Associate District Judge, Oklahoma District Court Twenty-fourth Judicial District)* Former Special Judge. Serves Okmulgee County.

Office: Okmulgee County Courthouse, 315 West Seventh Street, Okmulgee 74447.
Telephone: (918) 756-1835.

CLEARY, Paul J. *(Magistrate Judge, United States District Court Northern District of Oklahoma)* Appointed by U.S. District Court judges to term beginning July 22, 2002.

Office: 411 U.S. Courthouse, 333 West Fourth Street, Tulsa 74103.
Telephone: (918) 699-4890.

COATS, Nancy L. *(District Judge, Oklahoma District Court Seventh Judicial District)*

Office: 712 Oklahoma County Courthouse, 321 Park Avenue, Oklahoma City 73102.
Telephone: (405) 713-1442.

COLBERT, Timothy K. *(Associate District Judge, Oklahoma District Court Twentieth Judicial District)* Serves Murray County.

Mailing address: P.O. Box 684, Sulphur 73086.
Office: Murray County Courthouse, Sulphur 73086.
Telephone: (580) 622-3440.

COLBERT, Tom *(Vice Chief Judge, Oklahoma Court of Civil Appeals)*

Office: 440 South Houston, Room 601, Tulsa 74127.
Telephone: (918) 581-2711.

COLLIER, Robert W. *(Associate District Judge, Oklahoma District Court Fourth Judicial District)* Elected to term beginning Jan 13, 1969. Reelected to subsequent terms. Serves Dewey County. Born Taloga Oklahoma May 28, 1938. Member Christian Church. Educated at Oklahoma State University B.S. 1960 and University of Oklahoma LL.B. 1963. Admitted to practice Oklahoma 1963. Began legal practice Taloga 1963.

County Attorney 1963-68. Member Oklahoma and American Bar Associations. Democrat. Enjoys farming, ranching and crop and livestock production.

Mailing address: P.O. Box 278, Taloga 73667.
Office: Dewey County Courthouse, Taloga 73667.
Telephone: (580) 328-5521.

COMBS, Douglas L. *(District Judge, Oklahoma District Court Twenty-third Judicial District)* Former Special Judge.

Office: 301 Pottawatomie County Courthouse, 325 North Broadway, Shawnee 74801.
Telephone: (405) 275-1296.

CONDREN, Sheila A. *(Special Judge, Oklahoma District Court Twelfth Judicial District)* Appointed July 1, 2000. Serves Craig, Mayes and Rogers counties. Born Wichita Kansas May 29, 1962. Educated at Kansas State University B.A. 1984 and University of Tulsa College of Law J.D. 1987. Staff member University of Tulsa Energy Law Journal 1986-87. Admitted to practice Oklahoma 1987, Kansas 1988, U.S. District Courts District of Kansas 1988 and Northern District of Oklahoma 1988. In legal practice Tulsa Oklahoma 1988-89.

Staff Attorney Department of Human Services Child Support Enforcement 1989-2000. Member American Inns of Court, Rogers County, Tulsa County and Oklahoma Bar Associations.

Office: 219 South Missouri, Claremore 74017.
Telephone: (918) 342-1366.
Fax: (918) 341-0874
E-mail address: Sheila.Condren@oscn.net

CONYERS, Susan Witt *(Vice Presiding Judge, Oklahoma Workers' Compensation Court)* Appointed by governor. Former Presiding Judge.

Office: 1915 North Stiles, Oklahoma City 73105.
Telephone: (405) 522-8600.

COOK, H. Dale *(Senior Judge, United States District Court Northern District of Oklahoma)* Appointed for life by President Gerald R. Ford to term beginning 1974. Also served Eastern and Western Districts. Former Chief Judge. Assumed Senior status Dec 31, 1991, serves by assignment. Born Guthrie Oklahoma April 14, 1924. Educated at University of Oklahoma B.S. in Business 1949 LL.B. 1950. Admitted to practice Oklahoma 1950. In legal practice Guthrie 1950 and Oklahoma City 1958-63 and 1965-71.

Logan County Attorney 1951-54. First Assistant U.S. Attorney 1954-58. Legal Counsel and Adviser to Governor of Oklahoma 1963-65. Director Bureau of Hearings and Appeals Social Security Administration HEW 1971-75. Member Bar Association of the District of Columbia, Tulsa County, Oklahoma (delegate to state conventions), Federal and American Bar Associations. Recipient Secretary's Special Citation from HEW 1973. USAAC 1943-45. Republican. Member Economic Opportunity Committee 1963-65 and Legal Advisory Council Oklahoma Highway Patrol 1969-70. President and Chairman of the Board Shepherd Mall State Bank 1969-71. Industrial Advisory Council Bureau for Business and Eco-

COOK, H. DALE—*Continued*
nomic Research University of Oklahoma 1970-71. Mason and Shriner.
Office: Federal Building, Second Floor, 224 South Boulder Avenue, Tulsa 74103.
Telephone: (918) 699-4130.

CORLEY, Phillip C. *(Special Judge, Oklahoma District Court Ninth Judicial District)* Serves Payne County.
Office: Payne County Courthouse, 606 South Husband Street, Stillwater 74074.
Telephone: (405) 372-4380.

CORNISH, Tom R. *(Judge, United States Bankruptcy Court Eastern District of Oklahoma)* Also Judge, Bankruptcy Appellate Panel Tenth Circuit. Selected by the Judicial Council of the Tenth Circuit to term beginning Feb 7, 1996.
Mailing address: P.O. Box 1347, Okmulgee 74447-1347.
Telephone: (918) 758-0366.

COUCH, Valerie K. *(Magistrate Judge, United States District Court Western District of Oklahoma)* Appointed by U.S. District Court judges to term beginning March 8, 1999. Term expires March 8, 2007. Educated at University of California B.A. 1974 and University of Oklahoma M.A. 1978 J.D. 1983. Cecil L. Hunt Memorial Scholarship. Staff member and Articles Editor Oklahoma Law Review. Judicial Intern to Oklahoma Court of Criminal Appeals 1981 and Oklahoma Supreme Court 1982. Member Order of the Coif. In legal practice May 1983 to March 1999.
Barrister Luther Bohanon American Inn of Court 1988-91. Master William J. Holloway, Jr. American Inn of Court since 1997. Fomer Member Federal Magistrate Judges Association and Oklahoma Health Lawyers Association. Fellow American Bar Foundation. Member Oklahoma County (Member Law-Related Education Panel since 1995, Vice President 2000-01, President 2002-03), Oklahoma (Chair Labor and Employment Law Section 1996-97, Member Diversity Committee since 2000, Member Bench and Bar Committee since 2000, Member Health Law Section) and American Bar Associations. Recipient Meritorious Award 1995 and 1998 and President's Award 2000.
Office: 1108 U.S. Courthouse, 200 N.W. Fourth Street, Oklahoma City 73102.
Telephone: (405) 609-5280.
Fax: (405) 609-5287
E-mail address: judge_valerie_couch-@okwd.uscourts.gov

CROSSLIN, Sandy *(Special Judge, Oklahoma District Court Fifteenth Judicial District)* Serves Cherokee County.
Office: Cherokee County Courthouse, 213 West Delaware, Tahlequah 74464.
Telephone: (918) 456-6179.

CROY, James B. *(Special Judge, Oklahoma District Court Seventh Judicial District)* Serves Oklahoma County.
Office: 602 Oklahoma County Courthouse, 321 Park Avenue, Oklahoma City 73102.
Telephone: (405) 713-1413.

CRUTCHFIELD, B. Darlene *(Special Judge, Oklahoma District Court Fourteenth Judicial District)* Serves Tulsa County.
Office: 357 Tulsa County Courthouse, 500 South Denver Avenue, Tulsa 73103.
Telephone: (918) 596-8756.

CULVER, William E. *(Special Judge, Oklahoma District Court Thirteenth Judicial District)* Appointed to term beginning Jan 11, 1999. Reappointed 2003, current term expires Jan 13, 2007. Serves Ottawa County. Born Travis AFB California July 11, 1956. Educated at East Central Oklahoma State University B.A. 1987 and University of Oklahoma College of Law J.D. 1995. Admitted to practice Oklahoma 1995, U.S. District Courts Eastern 1995, Western 1995 and Northern 1998 Districts of Oklahoma. In legal practice Seminole 1995-96.
Assistant District Attorney District 13 1996-99. President Ottawa County Bar Association 1997-98. Member Oklahoma Bar Association.
Office: Ottawa County Courthouse, 102 East Central, Miami 74354.
Telephone: (918) 542-2788.

CUNNINGHAM, Edward C. *(District Judge, Oklahoma District Court Twenty-sixth Judicial District)* Special Judge 1981-82 and Associate District Judge 1982-84. Appointed District Judge by Governor George P. Nigh to term beginning May 24, 1984. Elected 1986, 1990, 1994, 1998 and 2002. Current term expires Jan 2007. Born Suffern New York May 22, 1949. Catholic. Educated at University of Oklahoma B.B.A. 1974 J.D. 1978. Staff member American Indian Law Review 1977. Member Phi Delta Phi and Delta Sigma Pi. Admitted to practice Oklahoma 1979 and U.S. District Court Western District of Oklahoma 1980. Began legal practice El Reno 1978. In legal practice Yukon 1979. Former Judge, Oklahoma Court of Tax Review.
Member Canadian County (Chairman Law Day, Secretary/Treasurer, Vice President and President), Oklahoma and Federal Bar Associations. Named Outstanding Young Lawyer by Oklahoma Bar Association 1982. Recipient The Freedom Award 1983. USMC 1968-70. Member Lions, Elks, VFW, Canadian County Guidance Center (Board of Directors) and United Way (Board of Directors). Enjoys bridge.
Mailing address: P.O. Box 730, El Reno 73036.
Office: Canadian County Courthouse, El Reno 73036.
Telephone: (405) 262-1070.

DARBY, Richard B. *(District Judge, Oklahoma District Court Third Judicial District)* Special Judge 1987-90. Elected Associate District Judge to term beginning Jan 1991. Assumed office as District Judge. Former Judge, Oklahoma Court of Tax Review.
Office: Jackson County Courthouse, 101 North Main Street, Altus 73521.
Telephone: (580) 482-1665.

DAVIS, Robert E. *(Special Judge, Oklahoma District Court Twenty-sixth Judicial District)* Appointed. Serves Canadian County.
Mailing address: P.O. Box 730, El Reno 73036.
Office: Canadian County Courthouse, El Reno 73036.
Telephone: (405) 262-1070.

DEAN, Gary J. *(Special Judge, Oklahoma District Court Twelfth Judicial District)* Assumed office Jan 1,

DEAN, GARY J.—*Continued*
1999. Serves Mayes County. Born Oklahoma City Oklahoma Oct 6, 1940. Methodist. Educated at University of Oklahoma B.B.A. 1963 J.D. 1966. Member Phi Alpha Delta. Admitted to practice Oklahoma 1966, U.S. Supreme Court 1974 and U.S. Court of Appeals Tenth Circuit. In legal practice Pryor 1966-98.

Chair Family Law Section Oklahoma Bar Association 1997. Member American Bar Association. Recipient Presidential Citation for Outstanding Service from Oklahoma Bar Association 1997. Member Lions Club International.

Mailing address: P.O. Box 1047, Pryor 74362-1047.

Office: Mayes County Courthouse, Pryor 74361.

Telephone: (918) 825-6386.

Fax: (918) 825-7460

E-mail address: GARY.DEAN@OSCN.NET

DEASON, Donald *(Special Judge, Oklahoma District Court Seventh Judicial District)* Serves Oklahoma County.

Office: 527 Oklahoma County Courthouse, 321 Park Avenue, Oklahoma City 73102.

Telephone: (405) 713-2352.

DEAVER, Danny R. *(Associate District Judge, Oklahoma District Court Third Judicial District)* Serves Greer County.

Mailing address: P.O. Box 216, Mangum 73554.

Office: Greer County Courthouse, Mangum 73554.

Telephone: (580) 782-3509.

DeBERRY, Michael D. *(Associate District Judge, Oklahoma District Court Seventeenth Judicial District)* Serves McCurtain County.

Office: McCurtain County Courthouse, 106 North Central, Idabel 74745.

Telephone: (580) 286-2270.

DeLAPP, Curtis L. *(Associate District Judge, Oklahoma District Court Eleventh Judicial District)* Serves Washington County.

Office: Washington County Courthouse, 420 South Johnstone Street, Bartlesville 74003.

Telephone: (918) 337-2885.

DENNEY, Barry V. *(Associate District Judge, Oklahoma District Court Thirteenth Judicial District)* Elected to term beginning Jan 1999. Reelected 2002, current term expires Jan 2007. Serves Delaware County. Born Stillwater Oklahoma Jan 1, 1951. Methodist. Educated at Oklahoma State University B.S. 1973 M.S. 1974 and University of Tulsa J.D. 1985. Admitted to practice Oklahoma 1985. In legal practice Tulsa 1985-88 and Miami Oklahoma 1988-91.

Assistant District Attorney Thirteenth Judicial District Jan 1991 to Jan 1999. Member Oklahoma Bar Association. Board Member Encouragers. Community Services Chair Kiwanis Club. Enjoys running. Personal Statement or Quote: "There is no limit to what can be accomplished if you don't care who gets the credit."

Mailing address: P.O. Box 489, Jay 74346.

Office: Delaware County Courthouse, Jay 74346.

Telephone: (918) 253-4329.

DeWITT, John W. *(Special Judge, Oklahoma District Court Seventeenth Judicial District)* Serves McCurtain County.

Office: McCurtain County Courthouse, 106 North Central Avenue, Idabel 74745.

Telephone: (580) 286-2221.

DIXON, Bryan C. *(District Judge, Oklahoma District Court Seventh Judicial District)* Special Judge Jan 10, 1983 to Dec 29, 1985. Appointed District Judge by Governor George P. Nigh to term beginning Dec 30, 1985. Elected Nov 4, 1986, Nov 1990, Nov 1994, 1998 and 2002. Current term expires Jan 2007. Born Oklahoma City Oklahoma April 30, 1952. Methodist. Educated at University of Oklahoma B.A. with honors 1974 J.D. 1977. Member Phi Alpha Delta. Admitted to practice Oklahoma 1977 and U.S. District Court Western District of Oklahoma 1978. In legal practice Midwest City and Del City 1977-83. Judge, Del City Municipal Court 1981-83.

Member Oklahoma County and Oklahoma Bar Associations. Member Kiwanis.

Office: 821 Oklahoma County Courthouse, 321 Park Avenue, Oklahoma City 73102.

Telephone: (405) 713-1460.

DOAK, D. Fred *(Special Judge, Oklahoma District Court Seventh Judicial District)* Serves Oklahoma County.

Office: 202 Oklahoma County Courthouse, 321 Park Avenue, Oklahoma City 73102.

Telephone: (405) 713-7103.

DOBBINS, Mark L. *(Associate District Judge, Oklahoma District Court Fifteenth Judicial District)* Serves Cherokee County.

Office: Cherokee County Courthouse, 213 West Delaware, Tahlequah 74464.

Telephone: (918) 456-6179.

DREILING, Janice P. *(District Judge, Oklahoma District Court Eleventh Judicial District)* Elected Associate District Judge to term beginning Jan 10, 1983. Reelected 1986, 1990, 1994 and 1998. Assumed office as District Judge. Term expires Jan 2007. Served Oklahoma Court of Criminal Appeals Emergency Panel 1994-96. Born Kansas City Missouri Dec 7, 1944. Episcopalian. Educated at Kansas State University B.A. 1966 M.A. 1969 and University of Tulsa College of Law J.D. 1980. Member Phi Alpha Theta, Phi Delta Phi and Phi Kappa Phi. Admitted to practice Oklahoma 1980. In legal practice Bartlesville 1980-83.

Author "Women and Oklahoma Law: How It Has Changed, Who Changed It, and What Is Left" Oklahoma L. Rev. Fall 1987 and "Frozen Embryos, 'Gestational Hostesses' and Other Additions to the Family—The Future Revolution in Family Law" *Family Law Update* Oklahoma Bar Association Sept 1990. Vice President 1988 and 1996-97 Chair Subcommittee for Juvenile Legislation 1988-90 and President 1999 Oklahoma Judicial Conference. Member Oklahoma Judicial Education Board 1997-98 and Community Sentencing Council Eleventh Judicial District. Member Committee for Uniform Jury Instructions Oklahoma Court of Criminal Appeals. Member Washington County, Oklahoma and American Bar Associations. Recipient Diploma of Judicial Skills from the American Academy of Judicial Education University of Virginia 1986. Attended Judicial Education Training Seminar National Council of Juve-

DREILING, JANICE P.—*Continued*
nile and Family Court Judges University of Nevada 1997 and Criminal Sentencing Seminar University of Minnesota 1997. Named Woman of the Year by Women's Law Caucus 1980, American Association of University Women 1985 and Beta Sigma Phi 1988 and History Maker of the Year by Women's Network Women's History Week 1990. Recipient Women of Achievement Award in Politics from Oklahoma Division American Association of University Women 1991, Professional of the Year Award for Service to Children from Washington County Mental Health Association 1994 and Outstanding Service Award from Adult Protective Services 1994 and 1999. Member Oklahoma Juvenile Justice Oversight Committee 1986-92 and 2000. Co-Founder and Co-chair Steering Committee 1989 and Former Chair Washington County Youth Court. Chair Social and Minority Issues Subcommittee Project 2000, 1990. President Bluestem Girl Scout Council 1990-91. Board Member Green Country Village Inc. Member Rotary Club.
Office: Washington County Courthouse, 420 South Johnstone Street, Bartlesville 74003.
Telephone: (918) 337-2880.

DRIESEL, Willard *(District Judge, Oklahoma District Court Seventeenth Judicial District)* Former Judge, Oklahoma Court of Tax Review.
Office: McCurtain County Courthouse, 106 North Central Avenue, Idabel 74745.
Telephone: (580) 286-2171.

DUNCAN, Jacqueline P. *(Associate District Judge, Oklahoma District Court Second Judicial District)* Appointed Special Judge Oct 15, 1985. Elected Associate District Judge 1998. Reelected 2002, current term expires Jan 2007. Serves Custer County.
Mailing address: P.O. Box 180, Arapaho 73620.
Office: Custer County Courthouse, Arapaho 73620.
Telephone: (580) 323-3456.
Fax: (580) 331-1107

DUROCHER, Daniel *(Special Judge, Oklahoma District Court Seventh Judicial District)* Appointed. Serves Oklahoma County.
Office: 113 Oklahoma County Courthouse, 321 Park Avenue, Oklahoma City 73102.
Telephone: (405) 713-1157.

EAGAN, Claire V. *(Judge, United States District Court Northern District of Oklahoma)* Magistrate Judge Jan 27, 1998 to Oct 24, 2001. Appointed Judge for life by President George W. Bush to term beginning Oct 24, 2001. Born Bronx New York Oct 9, 1950. Roman Catholic. Educated at University of Fribourg, Switzerland, Trinity College B.A. cum laude 1972, University of Paris Institute of Comparative Law and Fordham University School of Law J.D. cum laude 1976. Staff member 1974-75 and Editor 1975-76 Fordham Law Review. Law Clerk to Chief Judge Allen E. Barrow, U.S. District Court Northern District of Oklahoma Sept 1976 to April 1978. Admitted to practice Oklahoma, New York, U.S. District Courts Eastern, Northern and Western Districts of Oklahoma, U.S. Courts of Appeals Fifth, Eighth, Tenth and Federal Circuits and U.S. Supreme Court. In legal practice Tulsa Oklahoma 1978-98. Former Adjunct Settlement Judge, Oklahoma District Court Fourteenth Judicial District. Instructor in Legal Research and Writing Legal Assistants' Program Tulsa Junior College Jan 1979 to May 1985. Professor of Appellate Advocacy Winter 1989, Introduction to Alternative Dispute Resolution Fall 1999 and Constitutional Law II Winter 2001 and Winter 2002 University of Tulsa College of Law. Former Chairman Admissions and Grievance Committee and Former Member Special Death Penalty Habeas Corpus Panel Northern District of Oklahoma. Fellow American Bar Foundation. Master Council Oak Chapter American Inns of Court (Member and Past President Executive Committee). Member Tulsa County (Former Chairman Young Lawyers Committee and Entertainment Committee, Former Member Executive Committee and Judicial Candidates Committee, Former Head of Publicity Law Day Committee, Member Professional Responsibility Committee), Oklahoma (Former Member Board of Governors and Member Young Lawyers Division) and American Bar Associations. Recipient Golden Rule Award from Tulsa County Bar Association and Mona Lambird Spotlight Award from Oklahoma Bar Association. Chair Manufacturing Division 1996 and Legal Division 1997 Tulsa Area United Way Campaign. Former Member Board of Directors Sooner Chapter Cystic Fibrosis Foundation. Former Member Board of Directors and Former Chairman Oklahoma Sinfonia. Former Member Board of Directors and Former Pro Bono Counsel in Adoption Matters Catholic Charities of the Diocese of Tulsa, Inc. Former Board of Trustees Gannon University. Sustaining Member Junior League of Tulsa, Inc.
Office: 333 West Fourth Street, Room 411, Tulsa 74103.
Telephone: (918) 699-4795.
Fax: (918) 699-4787

EDMONDSON, James E. *(District Judge, Oklahoma District Court Fifteenth Judicial District)*
Office: Muskogee County Courthouse, 220 State Street, Muskogee 74401.
Telephone: (918) 683-7786.

EDWARDS, Ellen C. *(Judge, Oklahoma Workers' Compensation Court)* Appointed by Governor Frank Keating.
Office: 440 South Houston, Suite 210, Tulsa 74127.
Telephone: (918) 581-2714.

ELLIOTT, Ray C. *(District Judge, Oklahoma District Court Seventh Judicial District)*
Office: 700 Oklahoma County Courthouse, 321 Park Avenue, Oklahoma City 73102.
Telephone: (405) 713-1428.

ELLISON, James O. *(Senior Judge, United States District Court Northern District of Oklahoma)* Appointed for life by President Jimmy Carter to term beginning 1979. Chief Judge 1992-94. Assumed Senior status Nov 7, 1994, serves by assignment. Born St. Louis Missouri Jan 11, 1929. Educated at University of Oklahoma B.A. 1951 LL.B. 1951. In legal practice Red Fork 1953-55 and Tulsa 1955-79.
Office: 310 Federal Building, 224 South Boulder Avenue, Tulsa 74103.
Telephone: (918) 699-4142.

ENOS, Joe H. *(Associate District Judge, Oklahoma District Court Fifth Judicial District)* Serves Stephens County.
Office: Stephens County Courthouse, 101 South Eleventh Street, Duncan 73533.
Telephone: (580) 255-0338.

ERWIN, Shon T. *(Magistrate Judge, United States District Court Western District of Oklahoma)* Appointed by U.S. District Court judges. Serves part time.
Office: 207 U.S. Courthouse, 410 S.W. Fifth Street, Lawton 73501.
Telephone: (580) 355-6340.

EWING, Noah Howard, Jr. *(Associate District Judge, Oklahoma District Court Twenty-first Judicial District)* Serves McClain County.
Office: 231 McClain County Courthouse, 121 N. Second Street, Purcell 73080.
Telephone: (405) 527-6651.

FARRAR, Cherri *(Judge, Oklahoma Workers' Compensation Court)* Appointed by governor.
Office: 1915 North Stiles, Oklahoma City 73105.
Telephone: (405) 522-8600.

FILOSA, Jimmy D. *(Judge, Oklahoma Workers' Compensation Court)* Appointed by Governor Frank Keating.
Office: 440 South Houston, Suite 210, Tulsa 74127.
Telephone: (918) 581-2714.

FOSS, Janet A. *(Special Judge, Oklahoma District Court Twenty-first Judicial District)* Serves Cleveland County.
Office: Cleveland County Courthouse, 200 South Peters, Norman 73069.
Telephone: (405) 360-9393.

FRANKLIN, Ronald G. *(District Judge, Oklahoma District Court Fourth Judicial District)*
Office: Garfield County Courthouse, 114 West Broadway, Enid 73701.
Telephone: (580) 237-0236.

FRANSEIN, Doris L. *(District Judge, Oklahoma District Court Fourteenth Judicial District)* Former Special Judge.
Office: 607 Tulsa County Courthouse, 500 South Denver Avenue, Tulsa 74103.
Telephone: (918) 596-5337.

FRIOT, Stephen P. *(Judge, United States District Court Western District of Oklahoma)* Appointed for life by President George W. Bush to term beginning Nov 19, 2001. Born Troy New York Aug 14, 1947. Protestant. Educated at University of Oklahoma B.A. 1969 J.D. 1972. Admitted to practice Oklahoma 1972, U.S. District Court Western District of Oklahoma 1972 and U.S. Supreme Court 1976.
Member Ruth Bader Ginsburg American Inn of Court and Oklahoma County Bar Association.
Office: 200 N.W. Fourth Street, Room 2006, Oklahoma City 73102.
Telephone: (405) 609-5500.
Fax: (405) 609-5513
E-mail address: Judge_Stephen_Friot-@okwd.uscourts.gov

FRIZZELL, Gregory Kent *(District Judge, Oklahoma District Court Fourteenth Judicial District)* Appointed by Governor Frank Keating April 1997 to term beginning May 7, 1997. Elected Nov 1998 and 2002. Current term expires Jan 2007. Educated at University of Tulsa B.A. with honors 1981 and University of Michigan J.D. 1984. Law Clerk to Hon. Thomas R. Brett, U.S. District Court Northern District of Oklahoma 1984-86. Admitted to practice Oklahoma 1985, U.S. District Courts Eastern 1985, Northern 1985 and Western 1985 Districts of Oklahoma, U.S. Court of Appeals Tenth Circuit 1986 and U.S. Supreme Court 1991. In legal practice Tulsa 1986-95.
General Counsel Oklahoma Tax Commission 1995-97. President Hudson-Hall-Wheaton Chapter American Inns of Court 1999-2000. Member Oklahoma Judicial Conference and Oklahoma Bar Association (Delegate 2001-02). Listed in *Who's Who in American Law* since 1996. Trustee Tulsa County Law Library. Member Rotary Club of Tulsa and Federalist Society.
Office: 706 Tulsa County Courthouse, 500 South Denver Avenue, Tulsa 74103.
Telephone: (918) 596-5415.

FULTON, Kenton W. *(Judge, Oklahoma Workers' Compensation Court)* Appointed by Governor Frank Keating to term beginning July 2, 1996. Reappointed July 2, 2002, current term expires July 1, 2008. Vice Presiding Judge July 1996 to Dec 1998. Presiding Judge Jan 1999 to Dec 2002. Born Arlington Virginia April 28, 1960. United Methodist. Educated at University of Maryland at College Park B.A. 1982 and University of South Carolina School of Law J.D. 1985. Member Phi Alpha Delta and Order of Wig and Robe. Admitted to practice Oklahoma 1985 and District of Columbia 1989. In legal practice Tulsa Oct 1985 to March 1989 and April 1991 to June 1992.
Trial Attorney Environment and Natural Resources Division U.S. Department of Justice March 1989 to March 1991. Staff Attorney Law Department Transok, Inc. June 1992 to June 1996. Member Council Oak Chapter American Inns of Court since 1997. Member Tulsa County Bar Association. Republican.
Office: 1915 North Stiles, Oklahoma City 73105.
Telephone: (405) 581-2714.
Fax: (918) 581-2678
E-mail address: kwfulton@owcc.state.ok.us

GABBARD, Doug, II *(District Judge, Oklahoma District Court Twenty-fifth Judicial District)* Appointed by Governor George P. Nigh to term beginning Aug 1, 1985. Elected Nov 4, 1986, Nov 6, 1990, Nov 8, 1994, Nov 1998 and 2002. Current term expires Jan 2007. Presiding Judge Southeastern Judicial Administrative District since 1991. Serves Oklahoma Court on the Judiciary since 1997. Born Lindsay Oklahoma March 27, 1952. Methodist. Educated at University of Oklahoma B.S. 1974 J.D. 1977. Admitted to practice Oklahoma 1978. In legal practice Atoka 1978-79. Judge, Atoka Municipal Court 1978-79. Presiding Judge, Oklahoma Court of Criminal Appeals Emergency Panel 1995-96. Former Judge, Oklahoma Court of Tax Review.
City Attorney Wapanucka 1979. Assistant District Attorney Atoka County 1979-82 and First Assistant District Attorney 1982-85 Nineteenth District. Director and Newsletter Editor Oklahoma Trial Judges Association since 1995. Member Oklahoma District Attorneys Association, National District Attorneys Association and Oklahoma Bar Association (Legal Education Committee, Legal Ethics Committee, Judicial Administration Com-

mittee). Attended The National Judicial College 1987. Recipient Outstanding Service Award from Oklahoma Disabled American Veterans 1979. Nominee Outstanding Young Oklahoman by Oklahoma Jaycees 1985. Listed in *Who's Who in American Law.* Enjoys jogging, building, painting and reading.

Office: Atoka County Courthouse, 201 East Court Street, Atoka 74525.

Telephone: (580) 889-2423.

GALBRAITH, Robert H. *(Special Judge, Oklahoma District Court Eighth Judicial District)* Serves Kay County.

Mailing address: P.O. Box 428, Newkirk 74647.

Office: Kay County Courthouse, Newkirk 74647.

Telephone: (580) 362-3350.

GAMBILL, Bruce David *(Associate District Judge, Oklahoma District Court Tenth Judicial District)* Former Special Judge. Serves Osage County.

Office: 203 Osage County Courthouse, 600 Grandview, Pawhuska 74056.

Telephone: (918) 287-4108.

GARDNER, John D. *(Associate District Judge, Oklahoma District Court Twenty-third Judicial District)* Elected Nov 6, 1990 to term beginning Jan 14, 1991. Reelected 1994, 1998 and 2002. Current term expires Jan 2007. Serves Pottawatomie County. Born Oklahoma City Oklahoma June 19, 1956. Episcopalian. Educated at University of Oklahoma B.A. with honors 1978 J.D. 1981. Admitted to practice Oklahoma 1981 and U.S. District Court Western District of Oklahoma 1981. In legal practice Shawnee 1983-91.

Office: Pottawatomie County Courthouse, 325 North Broadway, Shawnee 74801.

Telephone: (405) 275-4308.

GARRETT, John C. *(District Judge, Oklahoma District Court Fifteenth Judicial District)*

Office: Adair County Courthouse, 220 West Division Street, Stilwell 74960.

Telephone: (918) 696-6269.

GASSETT, J. Michael *(District Judge, Oklahoma District Court Fourteenth Judicial District)* Former Special Judge Tulsa County.

Office: Tulsa County Courthouse, 500 South Denver Avenue, Tulsa 74103.

Telephone: (918) 596-5310.

GASTON, Reginald D. *(Special Judge, Oklahoma District Court Twenty-first Judicial District)* Serves Cleveland County.

Office: Cleveland County Courthouse, 200 South Peters Avenue, Norman 73069.

Telephone: (405) 321-5638.

GIBSON, Carl G. *(Associate District Judge, Oklahoma District Court Eleventh Judicial District)* Serves Nowata County.

Office: Nowata County Courthouse, 229 North Maple Street, Nowata 74048.

Telephone: (918) 273-0808.

GILLERT, Tom C. *(District Judge, Oklahoma District Court Fourteenth Judicial District)*

Office: 501 Tulsa County Courthouse, 500 South Denver, Tulsa 74103.

Telephone: (918) 596-5324.

GOODMAN, Jerry L. *(Judge, Oklahoma Court of Civil Appeals)* Appointed by Governor David Walters to term beginning Aug 1, 1994. Retained by election Nov 7, 1996 and 2002. Current term expires Jan 2009. Former Chief Judge. Born Mangum Oklahoma April 17, 1939. Presbyterian. Educated at University of Tulsa B.A. 1961 and Georgetown University J.D. 1964. Member Phi Delta Phi. Admitted to practice Oklahoma 1964, U.S. District Court Northern District of Oklahoma 1965, U.S. Court of Appeals Tenth Circuit 1967 and U.S. Supreme Court 1983. In legal practice Tulsa 1964-92 and Oklahoma City 1992-94.

Member Tulsa County, Oklahoma and American Bar Associations. USNR 1965-71.

Office: 440 South Houston, Room 601, Tulsa 74127.

Telephone: (918) 581-2711.

GOODPASTER, James D. *(District Judge, Oklahoma District Court Twelfth Judicial District)* Former Judge, Oklahoma Court of Tax Review.

Mailing address: P.O. Box 1087, Pryor 74362.

Office: Mayes County Courthouse, Pryor 74361.

Telephone: (918) 825-0960.

GOODWIN, Charles L. *(District Judge, Oklahoma District Court Second Judicial District)* Serves Oklahoma Court of Tax Review.

Mailing address: P.O. Box 39, Clinton 73601.

Office: Custer County Courthouse, Arapaho 73620.

Telephone: (580) 323-2230.

GRAY, Twyla Mason *(District Judge, Oklahoma District Court Seventh Judicial District)* Elected to term beginning Dec 31, 1998. Reelected 2002, current term expires Jan 2007. Born Tulsa Oklahoma Oct 26, 1954. Christian. Educated at University of Central Oklahoma B.S. 1984 and University of Tulsa College of Law J.D. 1988. Staff member Mineral Law Review 1987-88. Law Intern to Hon. James O. Ellison, U.S. District Court Northern District of Oklahoma. Member Iota Tau Tau. Admitted to practice Oklahoma 1989. Judge, Oklahoma City Municipal Court 1994-98.

Member Oklahoma County and Oklahoma Bar Associations. Member Oklahoma House of Representatives 1980-84.

Office: 201 Oklahoma County Courthouse, 321 Park Avenue, Oklahoma City 73102.

Telephone: (405) 713-1133.

E-mail address: TWYLA.GRAY@OSCN.NET

GURICH, Noma Diane *(District Judge, Oklahoma District Court Seventh Judicial District)* Appointed by Governor Frank Keating July 1, 1998. Elected Nov 1998 to term beginning Jan 1999. Reelected 2002, current term expires Jan 2007. Presiding Judge Oklahoma-Canadian Judicial Administrative District since Jan 1, 2003. Born South Bend Indiana Sept 26, 1952. United Methodist. Educated at Indiana State University B.A. with honors 1975 and University of Oklahoma J.D. 1978. Research Editor American Indian Law Review 1977-78. Law Clerk to Oklahoma Court of Criminal Appeals 1976-78. Member Phi Alpha Delta. Admitted to practice Oklahoma 1978, U.S. District Courts Western

GURICH, NOMA DIANE—*Continued*

1978 and Northern 1986 Districts of Oklahoma, U.S. Court of Appeals Tenth Circuit 1978 and U.S. Supreme Court 1983. In legal practice Oklahoma City 1978-88. Judge and Presiding Judge, Oklahoma Workers' Compensation Court July 27, 1988 to June 30, 1998, appointed by Governor Henry Bellmon.

Member Faculty University of Oklahoma College of Law Graduate School of Successful Trial Advocacy. Guest Speaker in Trial Practice Oklahoma City University School of Law and Introduction to Law University of Central Oklahoma. Member Supreme Court Committee on Revision of the Rules for Perfecting Civil Appeals 1992, Oklahoma Judicial Education and Training Board 1997-98 and Oklahoma Supreme Court Standing Uniform Civil Jury Instructions Committee. Master William J. Holloway, Jr. American Inn of Court. Member Oklahoma Judicial Conference, Tenth Circuit Judicial Conference, Oklahoma Trial Judges Association, Oklahoma County, Oklahoma and American Bar Associations. Frequent Speaker and Author of numerous written materials for CLE, civic, professional and business organizations. Judge First Year Law Student Moot Court Competition University of Oklahoma College of Law. Member 1989-96 and President 1992-94 Board of Directors University of Oklahoma College of Law Association. Member Application Screening Committee Oklahoma School of Science and Mathematics since 1996. Presiding Judge Oklahoma High School Mock Trial Competition 1998 and 1999. Volunteer Course Monitor Oklahoma City Memorial Marathon 2001 and 2002. Annual Volunteer Rebuilding Together with Christmas in April Project. Volunteer Driver Mobile Meals and Habitat for Humanity. Member Community Advisory Board Junior League of Oklahoma City, Inc. Member Oklahoma City Kiwanis (Board of Directors) and St. Luke's United Methodist Church (Chair Administrative Board, Management Council and Arts at St. Luke's Council). Missionary to Russia 1993, 1997, 2000 and 2002. Enjoys music, sports and travel.

Office: 359 Oklahoma County Courthouse, 321 Park Avenue, Oklahoma City 73102.

Telephone: (405) 713-1107.

E-mail address: noma.gurich@oscn.net

HADWIGER, Mickey J. *(Associate District Judge, Oklahoma District Court Fourth Judicial District)* Serves Woods County.

Mailing address: P.O. Box 924, Alva 73717.

Office: Woods County Courthouse, Alva 73717.

Telephone: (580) 327-1596.

HALL, Russell D. *(Special Judge, Oklahoma District Court Seventh Judicial District)* Serves Oklahoma County.

Office: 502 Oklahoma County Courthouse, 321 Park Avenue, Oklahoma City 73102.

Telephone: (405) 713-1181.

HAMMOND, Lisa K. *(Special Judge, Oklahoma District Court Seventh Judicial District)* Serves Oklahoma County.

Office: Oklahoma Juvenile Justice Center, 5905 Classen Court, Oklahoma City 73118.

Telephone: (405) 713-6796.

HAMMONTREE, Jack *(Associate District Judge, Oklahoma District Court Fourth Judicial District)* Serves Grant County.

Office: Grant County Courthouse, 100 East Guthrie, Medford 73759.

Telephone: (580) 395-2258.

HANEY, Robert G. *(District Judge, Oklahoma District Court Thirteenth Judicial District)*

Office: 302 Ottawa County Courthouse, 102 East Central, Miami 74354.

Telephone: (918) 542-5574.

HANSEN, Carol M. *(Judge, Oklahoma Court of Civil Appeals)* Appointed by Governor George P. Nigh to term beginning July 1985. Retained by election 1986, 1988, 1994 and 2000. Current term expires Jan 2007. Former Vice Chief Judge and Chief Judge. Born Oklahoma City Oklahoma July 3, 1929. Presbyterian. Educated at Oklahoma City University B.A. magna cum laude 1950 J.D. 1974. Law Clerk to Hon. John B. Doolin, Oklahoma Supreme Court 1975-80. Member Phi Delta Phi, Gamma Phi Beta and Sigma Alpha Iota. Admitted to practice Oklahoma 1975 and U.S. District Court Western District of Oklahoma 1977. In legal practice Stillwater 1980-83. Municipal Judge, City of Stillwater 1983-84. Marshal, Oklahoma Supreme Court 1984-85.

Former member Payne County Bar Association. Member Oklahoma County, Oklahoma and American Bar Associations. Employed as school teacher 1950 and 1953. Reservation Agent Braniff Airways 1951-53.

Office: 1915 North Stiles, Room 357, Oklahoma City 73105.

Telephone: (405) 521-3751.

HARBOUR, David *(District Judge, Oklahoma District Court Seventh Judicial District)* Former Special Judge.

Office: 325 Oklahoma County Courthouse, 321 Park Avenue, Oklahoma City 73102.

Telephone: (405) 713-1166.

HARGRAVE, Rudolph *(Justice, Supreme Court of Oklahoma)* Assumed office 1979. Retained by election. Former Vice Chief Justice and Chief Justice. Born Shawnee Oklahoma Feb 15, 1925. Methodist. Educated at University of Oklahoma LL.B. 1949. Admitted to practice Oklahoma 1949. Began legal practice Wewoka 1949. Judge, Seminole County Court 1964-67. Seminole County Superior Judge 1967-69. District Judge, Oklahoma District Court Twenty-second Judicial District 1969-79.

Assistant Seminole County Attorney 1951-55. Member Seminole County, Oklahoma and American Bar Associations. Democrat. News Director Radio KWSH. Member Lions Club, Masonic Lodge and Boy Scouts of America Advisory Committee.

Office: State Capitol, Oklahoma City 73105.

Telephone: (405) 521-3847.

HARRIS, Jesse S. *(District Judge, Oklahoma District Court Fourteenth Judicial District)* Former Special Judge. Former Judge, Tulsa Municipal Criminal Court of Record.

Office: 508 Tulsa County Courthouse, 500 South Denver, Tulsa 74103.

Telephone: (918) 596-5320.

HARRIS, Kenny D. *(Special Judge, Oklahoma District Court Fifth Judicial District)* Assumed office May 1999. Serves Comanche County.

Office: Comanche County Courthouse, 315 South Fifth Street, Lawton 73501.

Telephone: (580) 581-4592.

HARVEY, J. Bruce *(Special Judge, Oklahoma District Court Fourth Judicial District)* Serves Garfield County.

Office: Garfield County Courthouse, 114 West Broadway, Enid 73701.

Telephone: (580) 237-5031.

HASKINS, Kyle B. *(Special Judge, Oklahoma District Court Fourteenth Judicial District)* Serves Tulsa County.

Office: 348 Tulsa County Courthouse, 500 South Denver, Tulsa 74103.

Telephone: (918) 596-5336.

HASS, Russell Perry *(Special Judge, Oklahoma District Court Fourteenth Judicial District)* Referee 1983-85. Appointed Special Judge July 31, 1985. Serves Tulsa County. Born Poteau Oklahoma Oct 23, 1950. Religious affiliation: Born Again Christian. Educated at Kansas State University B.S. 1972, Arizona State University 1974-76 and Tulsa University College of Law J.D. 1980. Law Clerk to Hon. Joe Jennings, Oklahoma District Court Fourteenth Judicial District 1979-80. Admitted to practice Oklahoma 1980 and U.S. District Court Northern District of Oklahoma 1982.

Assistant Public Defender 1980-83. Instructor in Business Law Tulsa Junior College 1984-86. Member American Judges Association and Oklahoma Bar Association. Attended The National Judicial College, National Council of Juvenile and Family Court Judges, Association of Family and Conciliation Courts Conference and Institute for State Court Judges Law and Organizational Economics Center University of Kansas 1997. Probation Officer Superior Court of Arizona Maricopa County Juvenile Division 1972-77. Enjoys running, reading, tennis, little league baseball and basketball.

Office: 379 Tulsa County Courthouse, 500 South Denver Avenue, Tulsa 74103.

Telephone: (918) 596-5397.

HATCH, Farrell M. *(District Judge, Oklahoma District Court Nineteenth Judicial District)* Appointed by Governor David Walters to term beginning April 20, 1993. Elected Nov 3, 1994. Born Dardanelle Arkansas July 4, 1935. Methodist. Educated at Hendrix College B.A. 1960, Duke University B.D. 1963 and University of Oklahoma J.D. 1968. Law Clerk to Hon. Elvin Brown, Oklahoma District Court. Member Delta Theta Phi. Admitted to practice Oklahoma 1968 and U.S. District Court Eastern District of Oklahoma 1970. In legal practice Durant 1968-93. Former Judge, Oklahoma Court of Tax Review.

Member Oklahoma and American Bar Associations. USN.

Office: Bryan County Courthouse, 402 West Evergreen, Durant 74701.

Telephone: (580) 924-3450.

HAUGHT, Floyd "Doug" *(Associate District Judge, Oklahoma District Court Second Judicial District)* Appointed by Governor George P. Nigh to term beginning May 2, 1983. Elected 1986, 1990, 1994, 1998 and 2002. Current term expires Jan 2007. Serves Beckham County. Born Harmon County Oklahoma Feb 7, 1950. United Methodist. Educated at Southwestern Oklahoma State College B.A. 1972 and Oklahoma City University J.D. 1980. Admitted to practice Oklahoma 1980. Began legal practice Oklahoma City 1980.

Member Oklahoma Bar Association. Lieutenant Colonel U.S. Army Field Artillery 1973-75 and Oklahoma Army National Guard since 1975.

Office: Beckham County Courthouse, 302 East Main Street, Sayre 73662.

Telephone: (580) 928-9332.

HEATON, Joe L. *(Judge, United States District Court Western District of Oklahoma)* Appointed for life by President George W. Bush to term beginning Dec 13, 2001. Educated at Northwestern Oklahoma State University B.A. 1973 and University of Oklahoma College of Law J.D. 1976. Board of Editors Oklahoma Law Review. Member Order of the Coif. Admitted to practice Oklahoma 1976, U.S. District Court Western District of Oklahoma 1977 and U.S. Court of Appeals Tenth Circuit. In legal practice Oklahoma City 1977-96.

Special Assistant U.S. Attorney 1992-93 and First Assistant U.S. Attorney 1996-2001 Western District of Oklahoma. Member Oklahoma County, Oklahoma and American Bar Associations. Member Oklahoma House of Representatives 1984-92.

Office: 5406 U.S. Courthouse, 200 N.W. Fourth Street, Oklahoma City 73102.

Telephone: (405) 609-5601.

HENDERSON, John N. *(Associate District Judge, Oklahoma District Court Sixteenth Judicial District)* Serves Haskell County.

Office: Haskell County Courthouse, 202 East Main Street, Stigler 74462.

Telephone: (918) 967-2500.

HENRY, Matthew D. *(Associate District Judge, Oklahoma District Court Fourteenth Judicial District)* Serves Pawnee County.

Office: Pawnee County Courthouse, 500 Harrison, Pawnee 74058.

Telephone: (918) 762-2105.

HENSHAW, A. J., Jr. *(Associate District Judge, Oklahoma District Court Fifteenth Judicial District)* Special Judge 1981-86. Appointed Associate District Judge by Governor George P. Nigh to term beginning April 16, 1986. Elected to term beginning Jan 1987. Re-elected 1990, 1994, 1998 and 2002. Current term expires Jan 2007. Serves Sequoyah County. Born Fort Smith Arkansas Nov 26, 1946. Methodist. Educated at Oklahoma State University 1965-66, Northeastern Oklahoma State University B.A. 1970 and Oklahoma City University J.D. 1980. Admitted to practice Oklahoma 1981. In legal practice Sallisaw 1981.

Member American Judges Association, Oklahoma and American Bar Associations. Attended Trial Judges Academy University of Virginia July 1982 and "Conduct of a Trial" Jackson Lake, Moran Wyoming July 1985. Secretary Sequoyah County Election Board 1974-81. Board of Directors Chamber of Commerce. Member 297 Mental Health Board and 32° Masons. Enjoys hunting and fishing.

Office: Sequoyah County Courthouse, 120 East Chickasaw, Sallisaw 74955.

Telephone: (918) 775-4613.

HERNDON, John E. *(Special Judge, Oklahoma District Court Sixth Judicial District)* Serves Caddo County.
Office: Caddo County Courthouse, 201 West Oklahoma, Anadarko 73005.
Telephone: (405) 247-3205.

HETHERINGTON, William, Jr. *(District Judge, Oklahoma District Court Twenty-first Judicial District)* Former Judge, Oklahoma Court of Tax Review.
Office: Cleveland County Courthouse, 200 South Peters Avenue, Norman 73069.
Telephone: (405) 447-3737.

HICKS, Edward J., III *(Special Judge, Oklahoma District Court Fourteenth Judicial District)* Serves Tulsa County.
Office: Tulsa Juvenile Center, 315 South Gilcrease Museum Road, Tulsa 74127.
Telephone: (918) 596-5909.

HIGHSMITH, Robert M. *(Associate District Judge, Oklahoma District Court Twentieth Judicial District)* Appointed by Governor Henry Bellmon to term beginning Oct 7, 1987. Elected Nov 1990, Nov 1994, 1998 and 2002. Current term expires Jan 2007. Serves Johnston County. Born Pensacola Florida Aug 3, 1950. Presbyterian. Educated at Central State University B.A.Ed. 1972 and Oklahoma City University School of Law J.D. 1976. Member Phi Delta Phi. Admitted to practice Oklahoma 1976, U.S. District Courts Eastern 1977 and Western 1977 Districts of Oklahoma and U.S. Court of Appeals Tenth Circuit 1979. In legal practice Oklahoma City 1978 and Ardmore 1985-86. Served Oklahoma Court of Criminal Appeals Emergency Panel 1994.
Assistant District Attorney and First Assistant District Attorney Twentieth Judicial District 1977-85. Member The Association of Trial Lawyers of America, Johnston County (President 1990), Love County and Oklahoma Bar Associations. Named Outstanding Assistant District Attorney by Oklahoma District Attorneys Association 1982. Previously employed as Oklahoma State Probation and Parole Officer and secondary school teacher. Enjoys reading, canoeing and fishing.
Office: Johnston County Courthouse, 403 West Main Street, Tishomingo 73460.
Telephone: (580) 371-2387.
E-mail address: Robert.Highsmith@OSCN.NET

HILL, Charles G. *(Special Judge, Oklahoma District Court Seventh Judicial District)* Serves Oklahoma County.
Office: 512 Oklahoma County Courthouse, 321 Park Avenue, Oklahoma City 73102.
Telephone: (405) 713-1185.

HODGES, Ralph B. *(Justice, Supreme Court of Oklahoma)* Appointed by Governor Henry Bellmon to term beginning April 19, 1965. Retained by election. Former Vice Chief Justice and Chief Justice. Born Anadarko Oklahoma Aug 4, 1930. Baptist. Educated at Oklahoma Baptist University B.A. and University of Oklahoma LL.B. Admitted to practice Oklahoma 1954. Began legal practice Durant 1954. Bryan County Attorney 1956-58. Judge, Oklahoma District Court District Nineteen Jan 1959 to April 1965.
Office: 200 State Capitol, Oklahoma City 73105.
Telephone: (405) 521-3844.

HOGSHEAD, Charles R. *(Special Judge, Oklahoma District Court Fourteenth Judicial District)* Serves Tulsa County.
Office: Tulsa County Courthouse. 500 South Denver Avenue, Tulsa 74103-3832.
Telephone: (918) 596-5354.

HOLMES, Sven Erik *(Judge, United States District Court Northern District of Oklahoma)* Appointed for life by President Bill Clinton Nov 21, 1994 to term beginning March 8, 1995. Born Grand Junction Colorado Feb 13, 1951. Lutheran. Educated at Harvard University A.B. 1973, University of Virginia School of Law J.D. 1980 and Georgetown University Law Center LL.M. 1987. Law Clerk to Hon. Thomas R. Brett, U.S. District Court Northern District of Oklahoma 1980-81. Admitted to practice Oklahoma 1980, District of Columbia 1985, U.S. Supreme Court 1994, U.S. District Courts Eastern, Northern and Western Districts of Oklahoma and District of Columbia, U.S. Tax Court and U.S. Claims Court. In legal practice Tulsa 1981-83 and Washington D.C. 1985-87 and 1989-95.
Adjunct Professor of Constitutional Law University of Tulsa College of Law since 1999. Member Bar Association of the District of Columbia and Oklahoma Bar Association. Campaign Coordinator Boren for Governor 1973-75. Administrative Assistant to Governor David L. Boren 1975-77. Executive Director Democrats for the 80's 1983-85. Designated Staff Member Senate Select Committee on Secret Military Assistance to Iran and the Nicaraguan Opposition 1987. General Counsel and Staff Director Senate Select Committee on Intelligence 1987-89.
Office: 4-508 U.S. Courthouse, 333 West Fourth Street, Tulsa 74103.
Telephone: (918) 699-4780.

HOWLAND, Ronald L. *(Recalled Magistrate Judge, United States District Court Western District of Oklahoma)* Appointed Magistrate Judge by U.S. District Court judges. Retired March 27, 1999. Appointed Recalled Magistrate Judge by the Judicial Council of the Tenth Circuit.
Office: 2017 U.S. Courthouse, 200 N.W. Fourth Street, Oklahoma City 73102.
Telephone: (405) 609-5340.

HUBBARD, Carol Ann *(Special Judge, Oklahoma District Court Seventh Judicial District)* Serves Oklahoma County.
Office: 543 Oklahoma County Courthouse, 321 Park Avenue, Oklahoma City 73102.
Telephone: (405) 713-1116.

HUEY, Clark E. *(Associate District Judge, Oklahoma District Court Third Judicial District)* Serves Jackson County.
Office: 301 Jackson County Courthouse, 101 North Main, Altus 73521.
Telephone: (580) 482-3155.

HUMBLE, Charles G. *(Special Judge, Oklahoma District Court Seventh Judicial District)* Serves Oklahoma County.
Office: 600 Oklahoma County Courthouse, 321 Park Avenue, Oklahoma City 73102.
Telephone: (405) 713-1167.

HUMPHREY, Charles M., III *(District Judge, Oklahoma District Court Twenty-fourth Judicial District)*

HUMPHREY, CHARLES M., III—*Continued*

Former Special Judge. Currently serves as Presiding Judge East Central Judicial Administrative District.

Office: Okmulgee County Courthouse, 315 West Seventh Street, Okmulgee 74447.

Telephone: (918) 756-0672.

JACKSON, Joe L. *(Associate District Judge, Oklahoma District Court Second Judicial District)* Serves Ellis County.

Mailing address: P.O. Box 151, Arnett 73832.

Office: Ellis County Courthouse, Arnett 73832.

Telephone: (580) 885-7601.

JACKSON, Niles L. *(Judge, United States Bankruptcy Court Western District of Oklahoma)* Appointed by U.S. Court of Appeals Tenth Circuit judges.

Office: Old Post Office Building, 215 Dean A. McGee Avenue, Oklahoma City 73102.

Telephone: (405) 609-5678.

JOHNSON, Charles A. *(Presiding Judge, Oklahoma Court of Criminal Appeals)* Appointed Oct 31, 1989. Former Vice Presiding Judge. Educated at University of Oklahoma B.A. LL.B. 1955. In legal practice Pawhuska and Ponca City.

Past President Kay County Bar Association.

Office: 230 State Capitol, Oklahoma City 73105.

Telephone: (405) 521-2159.

JOHNSTON, D. Craig *(Judge, Oklahoma Workers' Compensation Court)* Appointed by Governor Frank Keating to term beginning July 1, 1998. Term expires July 1, 2004. Former Vice Presiding Judge. Born Oklahoma City Oklahoma Nov 26, 1958. Educated at University of Central Oklahoma B.A. 1981 and Oklahoma City University J.D. 1984. Admitted to practice Oklahoma 1985, U.S. District Courts Eastern, Northern and Western Districts of Oklahoma and U.S. Court of Appeals Tenth Circuit. In legal practice Oklahoma City 1985-98.

Associate Editor TIPS Aviation Law Newsletter American Bar Association 1995-98. Member The Association of Trial Lawyers of America, Oklahoma and American Bar Associations. Enjoys family, golf and soccer.

Office: 1915 North Stiles, Oklahoma City 73105.

Telephone: (405) 522-8600.

E-mail address: cjohnston@owcc.state.ok.us

JONES, Carl B. *(Judge, Oklahoma Court of Civil Appeals)* Assumed office May 28, 1991. Former Chief Judge.

Office: 1915 North Stiles, Suite 357, Oklahoma City 73105.

Telephone: (405) 521-3751.

JONES, Glenn M. *(Special Judge, Oklahoma District Court Seventh Judicial District)* Serves Oklahoma County.

Office: 626 Oklahoma County Courthouse, 321 Park Avenue, Oklahoma City 73102.

Telephone: (405) 713-1420.

JONES, Larry A. *(Special Judge, Oklahoma District Court Seventh Judicial District)* Appointed to term beginning March 15, 1994. Serves Oklahoma County. Born Kansas City Missouri August 6, 1950. Christian (Independent). Educated at East Texas State University B.A. 1971 M.S. 1978 and Oklahoma City University J.D. 1981. Staff member Oklahoma City University Law Review 1980-81. Member Phi Delta Phi. Admitted to practice Oklahoma 1981 and U.S. District Court Western District of Oklahoma 1986. In legal practice Oklahoma City 1993-94.

Assistant District Attorney Oklahoma County 1981-93. Author "*Church v. State and the Supreme Court:* The Current Meaning of the Establishment Clause" 5 Oklahoma City University L. Rev. 683, 1981. Member American Inn of Court, Council of Juvenile and Family Court Judges, American Judges Association, Oklahoma Trial Judges Association and Oklahoma Bar Association. Attended Advanced Family Law course National College of Juvenile and Family Law Oct 1997. Participant "Summer College: Role of the Judge" National Council of Juvenile and Family Court Judges June 2000. Volunteer Boy Scouts of America. Enjoys researching and reading American history, religion, and law-related material.

Office: Juvenile Justice Center, Room C, 5905 North Classen Boulevard, Oklahoma City 73118.

Telephone: (405) 713-6763.

JOPLIN, Larry E. *(Chief Judge, Oklahoma Court of Civil Appeals)* Former Vice Chief Judge.

Office: 1915 North Stiles, Room 357, Oklahoma City 73105.

Telephone: (405) 521-3751.

JOYNER, Sam A. *(Magistrate Judge, United States District Court Northern District of Oklahoma)* Part-time Magistrate Judge Western District Jan 1976 to May 31, 1995. Appointed by U.S. District Court judges to term beginning June 1, 1995. Born Lawton Oklahoma Nov 3, 1941. Educated at George Washington University B.S. 1963 and University of Oklahoma 1959-61 J.D. with honors 1966 Masters of Liberal Studies 1987. Note Editor Oklahoma Law Review. Member Order of the Coif, Phi Delta Phi and Oklahoma and National Moot Court Teams. Admitted to practice Oklahoma 1966 and U.S. District Court Western District of Oklahoma. In legal practice Lawton since 1966. Former Assistant Judge, Lawton Municipal Court.

Author "Possession of Land as Notice to Subsequent Purchaser" 18 Oklahoma L. Rev. 179, 1965, "Abatement of Second Action When Parties Reversed" 19 Oklahoma L. Rev. 197, "Sonic Boom—A Legal Nightmare" 19 Oklahoma L. Rev. 3, 1966, "Law School and Legal Ethics—A Part of the Illness or the Cure?" 60 Oklahoma B. Jour. 743, 1989, "Humanities in Professional Education for Moral Development" Academic Conference Cameron University April 1992 and "A Planetary Survey of Feminist Jurisprudence: If Men Are from Mars and Women Are from Venus, Where Do Lawyers Come From?" 33 Tulsa L. Jour. 1019, 1998. Editor-in-Chief Federal Courts L. Rev. since 1998. Adjunct Professor of Professional Responsibility University of Oklahoma College of Law. Former Director Federal Magistrate Judges Association. Fellow American College of Trial Lawyers. Member Advisory Committee on U.S. Magistrates, Hudson-Hall-Wheaton Chapter American Inns of Court (Judicial Master 1995-96, President 1996), Comanche County, Oklahoma and American Bar Associations. Instructor CLE course Tulsa County Bar Association May 1997. Recipient Outstanding Young Man of Lawton Award from Lawton Jaycees 1970. Lieutenant Commander USNR 1970-75. Member Lawton Chamber of Commerce (Past member Board of Directors and Vice

JOYNER, SAM A.—*Continued*

President), Lawton YMCA (Past President and Treasurer), Lawton Industrial Foundation (Board of Directors), Wesley Foundation of Cameron College (Board of Directors) and First United Methodist Church (Sunday school teacher and youth sponsor). Member Oklahoma Visual Arts Coalition, Oklahoma Arts Institute, Tulsa Photo Collective and Philbrook Museum. Past member Lawton Noon Lions Club. Enjoys fine art photography.

Office: U.S. Courthouse, 333 West Fourth Street, Tulsa 74103.

Telephone: (918) 699-4760.

KAUGER, Yvonne *(Justice, Supreme Court of Oklahoma)* Appointed by Governor George P. Nigh to term beginning March 22, 1984. Retained by election 1986, 1988, 1994 and 2000. Current term expires Jan 2007. Former Vice Chief Justice. Former Chief Justice. Born Cordell Oklahoma Aug 3, 1937. Episcopalian. Educated at Southwestern State University B.S. magna cum laude 1958 and Oklahoma City University J.D. with honors 1969. Awarded honorary Doctor of Laws Oklahoma City University 1992. Recipient Dean's Award for First in Class 1969 and First Place International Scholarship Award from Iota Tau Tau 1969. Listed in *Who's Who Among Students in American Colleges and Universities* 1958. Member Iota Tau Tau and Delta Zeta. Admitted to practice Oklahoma 1969. Former Presiding Judge, Oklahoma Court on the Judiciary.

Staff Lawyer to Hon. Ralph B. Hodges, Supreme Court of Oklahoma 1972-84. Author "Reflections on Federalism: State Constitutions' Role as Nurturers of Individual Rights" Gonzaga L. Rev. Spring 1991. Important Decisions: Williams v. Lee Way Motor Freight 688 P.2d 1294 (Okla. 1984); Ellison v. Honorable Karl Gray 702 P.2d 360 (Okla. 1985); Oklahoma Water Resources Board v. Texas County Irrigation and Water Resources Association 711 P.2d 56 (Concurring opinion Okla. 1985); Cate v. Archon Oil Co. Inc. 695 P.2d 1352 (Okla. 1985); Fransen v. Echhardt 711 P.2d 926 (Okla. 1985); Seymour v. Swart 695 P.2d 509 (Okla. 1985); Maule v. Independent School District No. 9, 714 P.2d 198 (Okla. 1985); Westinghouse Electric Corp. v. Grand River Dam Authority 720 P.2d 713 (Okla. 1986); Centric Corp. v. Morrison-Knudsen Co. 731 P.2d 411 (Okla. 1986); Turner v. City of Lawton 733 P.2d 375 (Okla. 1987); Buckner v. General Motors Corp. 760 P.2d 803 (Okla. 1988); Haworth v. Central National Bank 769 P.2d 740 (Okla. 1989); Fling Resource Co. v. State ex rel. Okla. Tax Commission 780 P.2d 665 (Okla. 1989); City Service v. Okla. Tax Commission 774 P.2d 468 (Okla. 1989); Clifton v. Clifton 801 P.2d 693 (Okla. 1990); State v. Lynch 796 P.2d 1150 (Okla. 1990); and Williams v. Hook 62 OBJ 53 (Jan. 1991). Former Member William Holloway American Inn of Court. Member Washita County, Oklahoma (Law Schools and Bench and Bar Committees) and American (Law School Accreditation Committee) Bar Associations. Speaker Twentieth Annual William O. Douglas lecture series Nov 1990. Coordinator Sovereignty Symposiums (Indian law conference) since 1988.

Named one of Outstanding Young Women of America 1967, Woman of the Year by Oklahoma City Chapter of the Business and Professional Women's Club 1984 and by High Noon 1985, Distinguished Alumnus by Southwestern Oklahoma State University 1986 and Oklahoma City University 1986, Appellate Judge of the Year by Oklahoma Trial Lawyers Association 1987, State Delta Zeta of the Year 1987, Panhellenic Woman of the Year Dec 1990 and Woman of the Year by Red Lands Council of Girl Scouts 1990. Recipient National Delta Zeta Woman of the Year Award 1988 and Oklahoma City Pioneer Award 1988. Honored by Oklahoma Hospitality Club, Ladies in the News 1985 and Guthrie Pow Wow Professional Category 1985. Selected as 1984 Byliner Honoree by Women in Communications. Adopted by Cheyenne-Arapaho tribes 1984. Listed in *Who's Who of American Women* 1979, *Who's Who in American Law* 1979 and 1984 and *Who's Who in the Southwest* 1986. Inducted into Washita County Hall of Fame 1992. Previously employed as medical technologist Medical Arts Laboratory 1959-68. Former Member Board of Directors Civic Music Society, Oklahoma Theatre Center and Canterbury Choral Society. Founder Gallery of the Plains Indian. Co-Founder Red Earth (Largest Native American festival on North American continent). Member State Capitol Preservation Commission 1983-84. Participant and organizer Judicial Day Girl's State 1976-80. Keynote speaker Girl's State 1984. Board of Directors Lyric Theatre, Inc. (President 1981, Director Emeritus since 1984). Member Dean's Advisory Committee Oklahoma City University, First Lady of Oklahoma's Artisans' Alliance Committee and Washita County Historical Society (Lifetime). Interests include Native American art, historical preservation, musical theater, basketball and quilting.

Office: 242 State Capitol, Oklahoma City 73105.

Telephone: (405) 521-3841.

KERN, Terry C. *(Chief Judge, United States District Court Northern District of Oklahoma)* Appointed for life by President Bill Clinton to term beginning 1994. Born Clinton Oklahoma Sept 25, 1944. Educated at Oklahoma State University B.S. 1966 and University of Oklahoma J.D. 1969. Member Phi Eta Sigma, Phi Delta Phi and Beta Theta Pi. Admitted to practice Oklahoma 1969, U.S. District Courts Eastern 1974, Western 1979 and Northern 1993 Districts of Oklahoma and U.S. Court of Appeals Tenth Circuit 1979. In legal practice Ardmore 1970-94.

Board of Directors Tulsa County Bar Association. Master of the Bench American Inns of Court. Fellow Tulsa County Bar Foundation and American Bar Foundation. Member Committee on Security and Facilities Judicial Conference of the U.S. Member Oklahoma Bar Foundation, American Board of Trial Advocates, Tenth Circuit Judicial Council, Federal Judges Association and Oklahoma Bar Associations. Recipient Distinguished Service Award from Oklahoma Bar Foundation 1992 and Leadership Legacy Award 2001 and Distinguished Alumni Award 2001 from Oklahoma State University. Inducted into Gamma Lambda Chapter Beta Theta Pi Hall of Fame 2000. Member College of Law Alumni Association University of Oklahoma and Trinity Episcopal Church.

Office: 4-411 U.S. Courthouse, 333 West Fourth Street, Tulsa 74103.

Telephone: (918) 699-4770.

Fax: (918) 699-4771

KEY, Craig *(Associate District Judge, Oklahoma District Court Twenty-third Judicial District)* Serves Lincoln County.
Office: Lincoln County Courthouse, 811 Manvel Avenue, Chandler 74834.
Telephone: (405) 258-1254.

KILGORE, Martha K. *(Associate District Judge, Oklahoma District Court Twenty-second Judicial District)* Serves Pontotoc County.
Office: Pontotoc County Courthouse, 120 West 13th Street, Ada 74821.
Telephone: (580) 332-8940.

KINCANNON, Ronald L. *(Associate District Judge, Oklahoma District Court First Judicial District)* Serves Cimarron County.
Mailing address: P.O. Box 788, Boise City 73933.
Office: Cimarron County Courthouse, Boise City 73933.
Telephone: (580) 544-2471.

KLEIN, Allen *(Special Judge, Oklahoma District Court Fourteenth Judicial District)* Serves Tulsa County.
Office: 329 Tulsa County Courthouse, 500 South Denver Avenue, Tulsa 74103.
Telephone: (918) 596-5380.

KNIGHT, Ted A. *(Associate District Judge, Oklahoma District Court Sixteenth Judicial District)* Special Judge 1983-84. Appointed by Governor George P. Nigh March 13, 1984. Elected 1986, 1990, 1994, 1998 and 2002. Current term expires Jan 2007. Serves LeFlore County. Born Huntington Indiana Jan 22, 1950. Religious affiliation: Church of Christ. Educated at Northeastern State University B.S. 1972 and Oklahoma City University J.D. 1975. Member Phi Delta Phi. Admitted to practice Oklahoma 1975, U.S. District Court Eastern District of Oklahoma 1980 and U.S. Court of Appeals Tenth Circuit 1980. In legal practice Poteau 1976-78 and 1981-83.
Assistant District Attorney LeFlore and Latimer counties 1979-81. Important Decision: Wallace v. State 893 P.2d 504 (fining parents of truant child). Member Oklahoma Judicial Conference, National Council of Juvenile and Family Court Judges, LeFlore County and Oklahoma Bar Associations. Attended The National Judicial College, American Academy of Judges and Oklahoma Judges Conferences. Enjoys family, jogging and fishing.
Mailing address: P.O. Box 822, Poteau 74953.
Office: LeFlore County Courthouse, Poteau 74953.
Telephone: (918) 647-3196.

LANDRITH, Tom S. *(District Judge, Oklahoma District Court Twenty-second Judicial District)* Elected Nov 8, 1994 to term beginning Jan 5, 1995. Reelected 1998 and 2002. Current term expires Jan 2007. Born Ada Oklahoma April 10, 1947. Methodist. Educated at University of Oklahoma B.A. 1969 J.D. 1976. Admitted to practice Oklahoma 1976, U.S. District Court Eastern District of Oklahoma 1976 and U.S. Court of Appeals Tenth Circuit 1979. In legal practice Ada 1976-95. Special Judge, Oklahoma District Court Twenty-second Judicial District 1977-78.
Attended General Jurisdiction Course 1978 and Advanced Evidence Course 1995 The National Judicial College. First Lieutenant USAF 1969-72.
Mailing address: P.O. Box 99, Ada 74821.
Office: Pontotoc County Courthouse, Ada 74821.
Telephone: (580) 332-8940.

LANSDOWN, Myrna L. *(Special Judge, Oklahoma District Court Eleventh Judicial District)* Serves Washington County.
Office: Washington County Courthouse, 420 South Johnstone Street, Bartlesville 74003.
Telephone: (918) 337-2880.

LAVENDER, Robert E. *(Justice, Supreme Court of Oklahoma)* Appointed by Governor Henry Bellmon to term beginning June 24, 1965. Retained by election 1966, 1972, 1978, 1984, 1990, 1996 and 2002. Current term expires Jan 2009. Chief Justice 1979-81. Former Vice Chief Justice. Born Muskogee Oklahoma July 19, 1926. Member Village United Methodist Church. Educated at University of Tulsa LL.B. 1953. Honorary member Phi Alpha Delta. Admitted to practice Oklahoma 1953. In legal practice Tulsa and Claremore 1953-65. Former Assistant Court Clerk, Oklahoma District Court District Fourteen and Tulsa County Court of Common Pleas.
Former Assistant Tulsa City Attorney. Member Oklahoma Judicial Conference, American Judicature Society, Rogers County, Oklahoma and American (Appellate Judges Conference) Bar Associations. Attended Appellate Judges Seminar New York University and National College of the State Judiciary. Recipient First Annual Faculty and Alumni Award from University of Tulsa College of Law 1975. Seaman USNR 1944-46. Republican. 32° Mason Tulsa Consistory. Member American Legion Claremore Post. Former member Catoosa School Board. Enjoys reading and golf.
Office: 208 State Capitol, Oklahoma City 73105.
Telephone: (405) 521-3846.

LEONARD, Timothy Dwight *(Judge, United States District Court Western District of Oklahoma)* Appointed for life by President George Bush to term beginning Aug 21, 1992. Born Beaver Oklahoma Jan 22, 1940. Presbyterian. Educated at University of Oklahoma B.A. 1962 J.D. 1965. Member Phi Alpha Delta and Beta Theta Pi. Admitted to practice Oklahoma 1965, U.S. Court of Military Appeals 1966, U.S. District Courts Northern 1969 and Western 1969 Districts of Oklahoma and District of Columbia 1969, U.S. Court of Appeals Tenth Circuit 1969 and U.S. Supreme Court 1970. In legal practice Oklahoma City 1970-71 and 1988-89 and Beaver 1971-88.
Assistant Attorney General Oklahoma 1968-70. U.S. Attorney Western District of Oklahoma 1989-92. Coauthor *4 Days, 40 Hours* edited by Riva Poor 1970. Author *Tort Reform and Oklahoma Law* Continuing Education Seminar 1987. Guest Lecturer and Adjunct Professor Oklahoma City University 1988-89. Adjunct Professor University of Oklahoma School of Law Fall 2000 and Spring 2003. Chairman Office Management and Budget Subcommittee 1990-92. Member U.S. Attorney General's Advisory Committee 1990-92, Judicial Conference Committee on Financial Disclosure since 1998, Judicial Council of the Tenth Circuit 1999-2001 and Tenth Circuit Advisory Council since 2002. Fellow American Bar Foundation. Member Oklahoma County, Oklahoma, Federal and American Bar Associations. Instructor Civil Trial Advocacy Course U.S. Department of Justice Jan 1996 and May 2001. Annual Participant Judicial Conference of the Tenth Circuit and Oklahoma Bar Association Annual Meeting. Named Outstanding Legislator by

LEONARD, TIMOTHY DWIGHT—*Continued*

Oklahoma School Board Association 1988. Lieutenant USN JAGC 1965-68. USNR 1968-72. Military Aide White House 1967-68. Republican. Member 1979-88 and Minority Leader 1985-86 Oklahoma State Senate. Former Candidate Lieutenant Governor Oklahoma. Ex officio Member Oklahoma State Fair Board 1987-90. Member Governor's Council on Sports and Physical Education 1987-89. Former Member Donna Nigh Foundation. Enjoys basketball, running and reading.

Office: 5012 U.S. Courthouse, 200 N.W. Fourth Street, Oklahoma City 73102.

Telephone: (405) 609-5300.

Fax: (405) 609-5313

LEWIS, David B. *(District Judge, Oklahoma District Court Fifth Judicial District)* Appointed Special Judge to term beginning Jan 14, 1991. Assumed office as District Judge. Born Ardmore Oklahoma April 30, 1958. Baptist. Educated at University of Oklahoma B.B.A. with honors 1980 J.D. 1983. Member Phi Alpha Delta and Beta Gamma Sigma. Admitted to practice Oklahoma 1984 and U.S. District Court Western District of Oklahoma 1984.

Member Comanche County and Oklahoma (Board of Directors Young Lawyers Division since 1993) Bar Associations. Member Northwest Kiwanis Club and Roadbac, Inc. Enjoys reading, jogging and biking.

Office: Comanche County Courthouse, 300 S.W. Fifth Street, Lawton 73501.

Telephone: (580) 581-4585.

LILE, Stephen E. *(Vice Presiding Judge, Oklahoma Court of Criminal Appeals)* Assumed office Jan 4, 1999. Born Tulsa Oklahoma. Educated at University of Oklahoma B.A. 1970 J.D. 1973. Admitted to practice Oklahoma and U.S. Supreme Court 1987. In legal practice Oklahoma 1977-94. District Judge, Oklahoma District Court Fifth Judicial District 1994-99.

Former Assistant District Attorney Comanche County and Cotton County. Past President Comanche County Bar Association.

Office: 230 State Capitol Building, Oklahoma City 73105.

Telephone: (405) 521-4955.

LINDER, Ray Dean *(District Judge, Oklahoma District Court Fourth Judicial District)* Former Judge, Oklahoma Court of Tax Review.

Mailing address: P.O. Box 185, Alva 73717.

Office: Woods County Courthouse, Alva 73717.

Telephone: (580) 327-3226.

LINDLEY, George Womack *(District Judge, Oklahoma District Court Fifth Judicial District)* Special Judge 1974-76. Appointed Associate District Judge by Governor David Boren to term beginning April 27, 1976. Elected District Judge 1978. Reelected 1982, 1986, 1990, 1994, 1998 and 2002. Current term expires Jan 2007. Born Duncan Oklahoma July 12, 1945. Educated at Colorado College, University of Oklahoma B.A. 1967 and University of Texas J.D. 1970. Recipient Ford Foundation Fellowship and award for Best Brief in Geary, Brice and Lewis Moot Court Competition. Executive Board Criminal Law Association. Law Clerk to U.S. Court of Appeals Tenth Circuit 1970. Admitted to practice Texas 1970, Oklahoma 1971, U.S. District Court Western District of Oklahoma 1972 and U.S. Court of Appeals Tenth Circuit 1972.

Member State Bar of Texas, Stephens County, Oklahoma and American Bar Associations.

Office: Stephens County Courthouse, 101 South Eleventh Street, Duncan 73533.

Telephone: (580) 255-7954.

LITTLEFIELD, Alicia *(Special Judge, Oklahoma District Court Thirteenth Judicial District)* Serves Delaware County.

Mailing address: P.O. Box 489, Jay 74346.

Office: Delaware County Courthouse, Jay 74346.

Telephone: (918) 253-4329.

LUCAS, Tom A. *(District Judge, Oklahoma District Court Twenty-first Judicial District)*

Office: Cleveland County Courthouse, 200 South Peters Avenue, Norman 73069.

Telephone: (405) 329-2400.

LUMPKIN, Gary L. *(Judge, Oklahoma Court of Criminal Appeals)* Appointed by Governor Henry Bellmon Nov 15, 1988 to term beginning Jan 9, 1989. Retained by election Nov 6, 1990, Nov 5, 1996 and Nov 5, 2002. Current term expires Jan 11, 2009. Former Vice Presiding Judge. Presiding Judge 1993-94 and 2001-02. Born Wichita Falls Texas July 2, 1946. Baptist. Educated at Southwestern State College B.S. 1968 and University of Oklahoma J.D. 1974. Admitted to practice Oklahoma 1974 and U.S. District Courts Western 1974 and Eastern 1978 Districts of Oklahoma. Associate District Judge 1982-85 and District Judge 1985-89, Oklahoma District Court Twentieth Judicial District.

Staff Attorney Oklahoma Department of Consumer Affairs. First Assistant District Attorney Twentieth Judicial District 1976-82. Member Sentencing and Release Policy Committee 1990-92 and Truth in Sentencing Policy Advisory Commission 1992-97. Board of Directors National Center for State Courts. Fellow Oklahoma Bar Foundation. Member Court Liaison Uniform Criminal Jury Instruction Committee Oklahoma Court of Criminal Appeals. Member Committee on Uniform Civil Jury Instructions Oklahoma Supreme Court. Member Oklahoma Judicial Conference (Secretary-Treasurer 1987, President Elect 1988, President 1989), William J. Holloway, Jr. American Inns of Court CV (President 1993 and Chair Program Committee 1992), Marshall County and Oklahoma (Past Chairperson Criminal Law Committee, Member Law Related Education Committee) Bar Associations. Named one of the Outstanding Young Men of America U.S. Jaycees 1979 and Outstanding Assistant District Attorney Third Congressional District by Oklahoma District Attorneys Association 1981. Recipient Professionalism Award from William J. Holloway, Jr. American Inn of Court 1999. USMC 1968-71. Served to Colonel USMCR 1971-98 (retired). Member Veterans of Foreign Wars and Marine Corps Reserve Officers Association.

Office: 231 State Capitol Building, Oklahoma City 73105.

Telephone: (405) 521-4956.

MALEY, John David *(District Judge, Oklahoma District Court Twenty-fourth Judicial District)* Elected to term beginning Jan 1967. Reelected 1970, 1974, 1978, 1982, 1986, 1990, 1994, 1998 and 2002. Current term expires Jan 2007. Presiding Judge Appellate Division Oklahoma Court on the Judiciary since 1989. Born Ok-

MALEY, JOHN DAVID—*Continued*
mulgee Oklahoma Oct 15, 1930. Presbyterian. Educated at Washington and Lee University 1948-51 and University of Oklahoma B.A. 1952 LL.B. 1959 replaced by J.D. 1970. Admitted to practice Oklahoma 1959. Began legal practice Okmulgee 1959. Judge, Okmulgee County Court 1962-66.

Member Oklahoma Judicial Conference (President 1977), Okmulgee County, Oklahoma and American Bar Associations. Recipient Silver Beaver Award from Boy Scouts of America. Lieutenant Colonel USAF (retired). Democrat. Life Member Advisory Board Salvation Army. Board of Directors Tulsa Philharmonic Society. Member Lions Club and Executive Board Boy Scouts of America. Enjoys golf and classical music.

Mailing address: P.O. Box 1135, Okmulgee 74447.
Office: Okmulgee County Courthouse, Okmulgee 74447.
Telephone: (918) 756-0674.

MARAK, Joseph P., Jr. *(Associate District Judge, Oklahoma District Court Fourth Judicial District)* Appointed by Governor George P. Nigh to term beginning Sept 7, 1984. Elected 1986, 1990, 1994, 1998 and 2002. Current term expires Jan 2007. Serves Woodward County. Born El Paso Texas Aug 12, 1947. Roman Catholic. Educated at St. Mary of the Plains B.A. magna cum laude 1968, Central State University M.Ed. 1972 and Oklahoma City University J.D. 1977. Law Clerk to Hon. Charles F. Bliss, Jr., Oklahoma Court of Criminal Appeals 1977-78. Admitted to practice Oklahoma 1977. Began legal practice Oklahoma City 1977. In legal practice Guthrie 1977-78. Special Judge, Oklahoma District Court Seventh Judicial District 1978-82.

Assistant District Attorney District Twenty-six Oklahoma 1982-84. Former Member State Advisory Committee on Juvenile Justice. Chair Advisory Committee on Juvenile Justice Oklahoma Supreme Court. Member Oklahoma Bar Association. Presented and Attended Oklahoma Judicial Conference. Former member Lawton Evening Optimists and Rotary Club. Enjoys tennis, golf, hunting, fishing and history.

Office: Woodward County Courthouse, 1600 Main, Woodward 73801.
Telephone: (580) 256-3566.

MARTIN, David N. *(Associate District Judge, Oklahoma District Court Twenty-fourth Judicial District)* Serves Okfuskee County.
Mailing address: P.O. Box 106, Okemah 74859.
Office: Okfuskee County Courthouse, Okemah 74859.
Telephone: (918) 623-0900.

MASON, Richard G. *(Judge, Oklahoma Workers' Compensation Court)* Appointed by Governor Frank Keating. Former Presiding Judge.
Office: 1915 North Stiles, Oklahoma City 73105.
Telephone: (405) 522-8600.

MAXEY, Gary L. *(Special Judge, Oklahoma District Court Fourth Judicial District)* Serves Garfield County.
Office: Garfield County Courthouse, 114 West Broadway Avenue, Enid 73701.
Telephone: (580) 249-5953.

McALLISTER, Gordon D., Jr. *(Special Judge, Oklahoma District Court Fourteenth Judicial District)* Serves Tulsa County.
Office: 507 Tulsa County Courthouse, 500 South Denver Avenue, Tulsa 74103.
Telephone: (918) 596-8750.

McBRIDE, Terry H. *(Associate District Judge, Oklahoma District Court Twelfth Judicial District)* Special Judge 1994-98. Elected Associate District Judge 1998 to term beginning Jan 1999. Reelected 2002, current term expires Jan 2007. Serves Mayes County. Born Tulsa Oklahoma Oct 5, 1950. Baptist. Educated at Oklahoma State University B.S. 1975 and University of Tulsa J.D. 1979. Law Clerk to Hon. Milford M. McDougal, Oklahoma District Court District Fourteen 1975-76. Admitted to practice Oklahoma 1979, U.S. District Court Northern District of Oklahoma and U.S. Court of Appeals Tenth Circuit 1998. In legal practice Tulsa 1979-80 and Pryor 1985-90.

Assistant District Attorney 1980-85 and First Assistant District Attorney and Chief Prosecutor 1990-94 Twelfth Judicial District. Member Oklahoma Judicial Conference and Oklahoma Bar Association. Named Outstanding Young Man of America 1983. Board Member Boys & Girls Club. Advisor CASA. Enjoys flying, fishing and traveling.

Mailing address: P.O. Box 989, Pryor 74362.
Office: Mayes County Courthouse, Pryor 74362.
Telephone: (918) 825-3404.
E-mail address: Terry.McBride@oscn.net

McCALL, Charles Allen *(District Judge, Oklahoma District Court Fifth Judicial District)* Former Special Judge.
Office: 402 Comanche County Courthouse, 300 S.W. Fifth Street, Lawton 73501.
Telephone: (580) 581-4595.

McCARTHY, Frank H. *(Magistrate Judge, United States District Court Northern District of Oklahoma)* Appointed by U.S. District Court judges.
Office: U.S. Courthouse, 333 West Fourth Street, Tulsa 74103.
Telephone: (918) 699-4765.

McCLAIN, Richard B. *(Associate District Judge, Oklahoma District Court Twenty-first Judicial District)* Serves Garvin County.
Office: Garvin County Courthouse, 210 West Grant Street, Pauls Valley 73075.
Telephone: (405) 238-2542.

McCURDY, Gary D. *(Special Judge, Oklahoma District Court Twenty-sixth Judicial District)* Serves Canadian County.
Office: Canadian County Courthouse, 301 North Choctaw, El Reno 73036.
Telephone: (405) 262-1070.

McELWEE, Roma M. *(Special Judge, Oklahoma District Court Seventh Judicial District)* Serves Oklahoma County.
Office: 631 Oklahoma County Courthouse, 321 Park Avenue, Oklahoma City 73102.
Telephone: (405) 713-1121.

MEYERS, Charles A. *(Special Judge, Oklahoma District Court Ninth Judicial District)* Serves Payne County.

Office: Payne County Courthouse, 606 South Husband Street, Stillwater 74074.
Telephone: (405) 747-8383.

MICHAEL, John W. *(District Judge, Oklahoma District Court Fourth Judicial District)* Former Associate District Judge. Elected District Judge to term beginning Jan 1987. Born Ada Oklahoma Jan 4, 1946. Christian. Educated at Oklahoma State University B.A. 1968 and University of Oklahoma J.D. 1971. Admitted to practice Oklahoma 1972. Began legal practice Medford 1972. Captain USAR (inactive) since 1968.

Office: Garfield County Courthouse, 114 West Broadway, Enid 73701.
Telephone: (580) 237-0245.

MICHAEL, Terrence L. *(Judge, United States Bankruptcy Court Northern District of Oklahoma)* Appointed by U.S. Court of Appeals Tenth Circuit judges to term beginning June 9, 1997. Term expires June 8, 2011. Chief Judge Bankruptcy Court June 2, 1999 to June 1, 2001. Also Judge, Bankruptcy Appellate Panel Tenth Circuit. Selected by the Judicial Council of the Tenth Circuit to term beginning June 7, 2000. Educated at Doane College B.A. magna cum laude 1980 and University of Southern California J.D. 1983. Admitted to practice Nebraska 1983. In legal practice Omaha Nebraska 1983-97.

Member American Inns of Court (President Johnson/Sontag Chapter), National Conference of Bankruptcy Judges and Nebraska State Bar Association.

Office: 123 Federal Building, 224 South Boulder Avenue, Tulsa 74103-3015.
Telephone: (918) 699-4065.
Fax: (918) 699-4061

MILES-LaGRANGE, Vicki *(Judge, United States District Court Western District of Oklahoma)* Appointed for life by President Bill Clinton to term beginning 1994. Born Oklahoma City Oklahoma Sept 30, 1953. Educated at University of Ghana 1973, Vassar College B.A. 1974 and Howard University School of Law J.D. 1977. Law Clerk to Hon. Woodrow B. Seals, U.S. District Court Southern District of Texas 1977-79. In legal practice Oklahoma City 1986-93.

Trial Attorney Office of Enforcement Operations U.S. Department of Justice 1982-83. Assistant District Attorney Oklahoma County 1983-86. U.S. Attorney Western District of Oklahoma 1993-94. State Senator Oklahoma 1987-93.

Office: 5011 U.S. Courthouse, 200 N.W. Fourth Street, Oklahoma City 73102.
Telephone: (405) 609-5400.

MILLER, Gary E. *(Associate District Judge, Oklahoma District Court Twenty-sixth Judicial District)* Serves Canadian County.

Mailing address: P.O. Box 730, El Reno 73036.
Office: Canadian County Courthouse, El Reno 73036.
Telephone: (405) 262-1070.

MILLER, John David *(Special Judge, Oklahoma District Court Twenty-second Judicial District)* Serves Pontotoc County.

Mailing address: P.O. Box 99, Ada 74821.
Office: Pontotoc County Courthouse, Ada 74820.
Telephone: (580) 332-8940.

MILLER, Richard A. *(Associate District Judge, Oklahoma District Court Twentieth Judicial District)* Appointed by Governor George P. Nigh Feb 6, 1986. Elected Nov 7, 1986, Nov 6, 1990, Nov 1994, Nov 1998 and 2002. Current term expires Jan 2007. Serves Marshall County. Born July 3, 1953. Baptist. Educated at Northwest Missouri State University B.S. with honors 1975 and Oklahoma City University School of Law J.D. 1978. Staff member Oklahoma City University Law Review 1976-78. Member Phi Alpha Delta. Admitted to practice Oklahoma 1978, U.S. District Court Eastern District of Oklahoma 1980 and U.S. Court of Appeals Tenth Circuit 1980.

Assistant District Attorney Twentieth Judicial District 1978-86. Author "Survey of Oklahoma Law—Civil Procedure" Oklahoma City University L. Rev. 1978. Member Oklahoma Criminal Justice Task Force since 1988. Attended General Jurisdiction course The National Judicial College April-May 1988. Member Lions Club, Gideons and Masons. Board of Directors Baptist Retirement Village. Enjoys community theatre and long distance running.

Mailing address: P.O. Box 58, Madill 73446.
Office: Marshall County Courthouse, Madill 73446.
Telephone: (580) 795-3392.

MILLER, Russell C. *(Special Judge, Oklahoma District Court Twenty-fourth Judicial District)* Serves Creek County.

Mailing address: P.O. Box 1410, Sapulpa 74067.
Office: Creek County Courthouse, Sapulpa 74066.
Telephone: (918) 224-3702.

MITCHELL, E. Bay, III *(Judge, Oklahoma Court of Civil Appeals)* Appointed by Governor Frank Keating Feb 18, 2002.

Office: 1915 North Stiles, Suite 357, Oklahoma City 73105.
Telephone: (405) 521-3751.

MOLLISON, C. Suzanne *(Special Judge, Oklahoma District Court Third Judicial District)* Serves Jackson County.

Office: 303 Jackson County Courthouse, 101 North Main, Altus 73521.
Telephone: (580) 482-1980.

MOORE, Mark A. *(Associate District Judge, Oklahoma District Court Fourth Judicial District)* Appointed by the governor to term beginning April 1, 1993. Elected 1994, 1998 and 2002. Current term expires Jan 2007. Serves Blaine County. Born Alva Oklahoma Oct 2, 1958. Educated at Oklahoma State University B.S. with honors 1980 and University of Oklahoma J.D. with honors 1985. Managing Editor Oklahoma Law Review 1984-85. Member Order of the Coif. Admitted to practice Oklahoma 1985, U.S. District Court Western District of Oklahoma 1985 and U.S. Court of Appeals Tenth Circuit 1987. In legal practice Oklahoma City 1985-93.

Author "Production Revenue Standards Act—Where's Waldo Now" Oklahoma B. Jour. 1992. Adjunct Professor of Business Law University of Central Oklahoma 1992-93. Alternate Delegate Oklahoma Bar Association Oklahoma Judicial Conference 1998. Member Oklahoma and American Bar Associations. Named Watonga Citizen

MOORE, MARK A.—*Continued*

of the Year 1995. Recipient Judge of the Year Award from Oklahoma Child Support Association 2000. Chairman Oklahoma Children's Advisory Review Board 1998-99. President Watonga Kiwanis Club 1996-97. Lay Leader Watonga United Methodist Church 1996-2000.

Office: Blaine County Courthouse, 212 North Weigle Avenue, Watonga 73772.

Telephone: (580) 623-5025.

Fax: (580) 623-5971

MORRISSEY, Linda G. *(District Judge, Oklahoma District Court Fourteenth Judicial District)* Former Special Judge.

Office: 111 Tulsa County Courthouse, 500 South Denver Avenue, Tulsa 74103.

Telephone: (918) 596-5370.

MOWERY, Gene F. *(Associate District Judge, Oklahoma District Court Eighteenth Judicial District)* Serves McIntosh County.

Office: McIntosh County Courthouse, 110 North First Street, Eufaula 74432.

Telephone: (918) 689-2232.

MURPHY, Robert M., Jr. *(Associate District Judge, Oklahoma District Court Ninth Judicial District)* Appointed by Governor David Walters to term beginning May 1994. Elected Nov 1994, Nov 1998 and 2002. Current term expires Jan 2007. Serves Payne County. Born Stillwater Oklahoma Dec 31, 1949. Presbyterian. Educated at Oklahoma State University B.A. 1972 and University of Oklahoma J.D. 1975. Admitted to practice Oklahoma 1975, U.S. District Courts Western 1978 and Northern 1988 Districts of Oklahoma and U.S. Court of Appeals Tenth Circuit 1989. In legal practice Stillwater 1977-94.

Member Legal Aid of Western Oklahoma (President 1984), Oklahoma Judicial Conference (Civil Procedure Committee since 1992, Chairman Legislative Committee since 1996) and Oklahoma Bar Association (Chair Legal Services Committee 1988). Attended The National Judicial College Summer 1995. Member Rotary Club. Enjoys tennis, skiing and exercising.

Office: 606 South Husband, #301, Stillwater 74074.

Telephone: (405) 372-3999.

NAPOLI, H. Jequita *(Special Judge, Oklahoma District Court Twenty-first Judicial District)* Serves Cleveland County.

Office: Cleveland County Courthouse, 200 South Peters, Norman 73069.

Telephone: (405) 329-5733.

NELSON, Forrest D. *(Special Judge, Oklahoma District Court Fifteenth Judicial District)* Serves Wagoner County.

Office: Wagoner County Courthouse, 307 East Cherokee Street, Wagoner 74467.

Telephone: (918) 485-4508.

NIGHTINGALE, Rebecca *(District Judge, Oklahoma District Court Fourteenth Judicial District)*

Office: 631 Tulsa County Courthouse, 500 South Denver Avenue, Tulsa 74103.

Telephone: (918) 596-5390.

NORMAN, Mike *(District Judge, Oklahoma District Court Fifteenth Judicial District)*

Mailing address: P.O. Box 1350, Muskogee 74402.

Office: Muskogee County Courthouse, Muskogee 74401.

Telephone: (918) 687-1950.

OLMSTEAD, Wayne *(Associate District Judge, Oklahoma District Court First Judicial District)* Serves Harper County.

Office: Harper County Courthouse, 311 S.E. First, Buffalo 73834.

Telephone: (580) 735-2222.

OPALA, Marian P. *(Vice Chief Justice, Supreme Court of Oklahoma)* Appointed by Governor David L. Boren Nov 21, 1978. Retained by election 1980, 1982, 1988, 1994 and 2000. Current term expires Jan 2007. Chief Justice Jan 1, 1991 to Dec 31, 1992. Born Łodź Poland 1921. Educated at Oklahoma City University B.A. 1953 B.S.B. 1957 and New York University School of Law LL.M. 1968. Member Order of the Coif. Referee, Supreme Court of Oklahoma 1960-65. Judge, Oklahoma Workers' Compensation Court 1977-78.

Former Assistant County Attorney Oklahoma County. Former Staff Lawyer for Hon. Rooney McInerney. Administrative Director Oklahoma State Courts 1969-77. Frequent Lecturer at various national judicial and legal education programs. Commissioner National Conference of Commissioners on Uniform State Laws since 1982. Member The American Law Institute. Became U.S. Citizen 1953. Member Administrative Conference of the U.S. since Dec 1993.

Office: 238 State Capitol Building, Oklahoma City 73105.

Telephone: (405) 521-3839.

OTEY, Millie N. *(Special Judge, Oklahoma District Court Fourteenth Judicial District)* Serves Tulsa County.

Office: 173 Tulsa County Courthouse, 500 South Denver Avenue, Tulsa 74103.

Telephone: (918) 596-5364.

OWENS, Daniel L. *(District Judge, Oklahoma District Court Seventh Judicial District)* Currently serves as Presiding Judge Oklahoma-Canadian Judicial Administrative District.

Office: 304 Oklahoma County Courthouse, 321 Park Avenue, Oklahoma City 73102.

Telephone: (405) 713-1147.

PADDLEFORD, James H. *(Special Judge, Oklahoma District Court Seventh Judicial District)* Serves Oklahoma County.

Office: 217 Oklahoma County Courthouse, 321 Park Avenue, Oklahoma City 73102.

Telephone: (405) 713-1113.

PAGE, Leslie D. *(Associate District Judge, Oklahoma District Court Eighth Judicial District)* Appointed Special Judge to term beginning Dec 20, 1972. Assumed office as Associate District Judge. Serves Kay County. Born Ponca City Oklahoma June 8, 1942. Protestant. Educated at University of Oklahoma B.B.A. 1964 J.D. 1967. Admitted to practice Oklahoma 1967.

Member Oklahoma and American Bar Associations. Specialist Five USAS 1967-69. Republican.

Mailing address: P.O. Box 251, Newkirk 74647.

Office: Kay County Courthouse, Newkirk 74647.

Telephone: (580) 362-2326.

PARRISH, Patricia G. *(Special Judge, Oklahoma District Court Seventh Judicial District)* Appointed. Serves Oklahoma County.

Office: 113 Oklahoma County Courthouse, 321 Park Avenue, Oklahoma City 73102.

Telephone: (405) 713-1156.

PATTON, Nan J. *(Associate District Judge, Oklahoma District Court Seventh Judicial District)* Serves Oklahoma County.

Office: Oklahoma Juvenile Justice Center, 5905 North Classen Court, Room A, Oklahoma City 73118.

Telephone: (405) 713-6759.

PAYNE, Don Ed *(Associate District Judge, Oklahoma District Court Seventeenth Judicial District)* Serves Choctaw County.

Office: Choctaw County Courthouse, 300 East Jefferson, Hugo 74743.

Telephone: (580) 326-3384.

PAYNE, James Hardy *(Chief Judge, United States District Court Eastern District of Oklahoma)* Magistrate Judge Oct 1, 1988 to Oct 25, 2001. Appointed Judge for life by President George W. Bush to term beginning Oct 26, 2001. Chief Judge since Oct 27, 2002. Also serves Northern and Western Districts. Born Lubbock Texas March 5, 1941. United Methodist. Educated at University of Oklahoma B.S. 1963 J.D. 1966. Member Phi Alpha Delta. Admitted to practice Oklahoma 1966, U.S. District Courts Eastern and Northern Districts of Oklahoma, U.S. Court of Appeals Tenth Circuit and U.S. Supreme Court. In legal practice Muskogee 1973-88.

Member Muskogee County, Oklahoma and American Bar Associations. Captain USAF JAGC 1966-70. Lieutenant Colonel USAR JAGC since 1976. Enjoys playing golf and jogging.

Mailing address: P.O. Box 2459, Muskogee 74402-2459.

Telephone: (918) 687-2434.

PAYTON, J. Jeffrey *(Special Judge, Oklahoma District Court Fifteenth Judicial District)* Serves Wagoner County.

Office: Wagoner County Courthouse, 307 East Cherokee, Wagoner 74467.

Telephone: (918) 485-2144.

PEARMAN, James Richard *(District Judge, Oklahoma District Court Tenth Judicial District)* Appointed Special Judge to term beginning Jan 1, 1985. Elected District Judge 1986. Reelected 1990, 1994, 1998 and 2002. Current term expires Jan 2007. Currently serves as Presiding Judge Northeastern Judicial Administrative District. Currently serves Oklahoma Court of Criminal Appeals Emergency Panel and Oklahoma Court of Tax Review. Born Los Angeles California March 10, 1940. Southern Baptist. Educated at Oklahoma Baptist University B.A. 1963 and Oklahoma City University J.D. 1967. Admitted to practice Oklahoma 1968. In legal practice Oklahoma City 1968-70 and Tonkawa 1971-81.

Member Oklahoma Bar Association. Attended The National Judicial College 1985 and 1988. Enjoys fishing and hunting.

Office: 302 Osage County Courthouse, Pawhuska 74056.

Telephone: (918) 287-4767.

PERRY, Richard McBee *(Associate District Judge, Oklahoma District Court Fourth Judicial District)* Serves Garfield County.

Office: Garfield County Courthouse, 114 West Broadway, Enid 73701.

Telephone: (580) 237-0239.

PERUGINO, Robert *(Special Judge, Oklahoma District Court Fourteenth Judicial District)* Appointed to term beginning April 20, 1990. Serves Tulsa County.

Office: Tulsa Juvenile Center, 315 South Gilcrease Museum Road, Tulsa 74127.

Telephone: (918) 596-8740.

PETERSON, David L. *(District Judge, Oklahoma District Court Fourteenth Judicial District)* Appointed by Governor George Nigh 1985. Elected 1986, 1990, 1994, 1998 and 2002. Current term expires Jan 2007. Currently serves as Presiding Judge. Educated at Brigham Young University B.A. 1968 and University of Oklahoma J.D. 1972. Member Phi Alpha Delta. Admitted to practice Oklahoma 1973, U.S. District Court Northern District of Oklahoma 1973 and U.S. Supreme Court 1980. In legal practice Tulsa 1973-81.

Attended The National Judicial College 1982. U.S. Army 1968-70. Member Rotary Club of Tulsa.

Office: 701 Tulsa County Courthouse, 500 South Denver, Tulsa 74103.

Telephone: (918) 596-5300.

POST, Dynda Rose Parks *(District Judge, Oklahoma District Court Twelfth Judicial District)* Appointed Special Judge to term beginning Aug 1989. Assumed office as District Judge. Born Bartlesville Oklahoma Sept 6, 1952. Baptist. Educated at Oklahoma Baptist University B.A. magna cum laude 1974 and University of Oklahoma J.D. Admitted to practice Oklahoma 1980.

Member Mayes County and Oklahoma Bar Associations.

Office: Rogers County Courthouse, 219 South Missouri, Claremore 74017.

Telephone: (918) 341-3434.

POWELL, David E. *(Associate District Judge, Oklahoma District Court Sixth Judicial District)* Serves Caddo County.

Office: Caddo County Courthouse, 201 West Oklahoma, Anadarko 73005.

Telephone: (405) 247-5585.

POWERS, Rocky L. *(Associate District Judge, Oklahoma District Court Nineteenth Judicial District)* Appointed Special Judge to term beginning Oct 24, 1977. Elected Associate District Judge Nov 4, 1986. Reelected Nov 1990, Nov 1994, Nov 1998 and 2002. Current term expires Jan 2007. Serves Bryan County. Born Lawton Oklahoma July 3, 1951. Member First Baptist Church (choir). Educated at Southeastern State College B.A. 1973 and University of Tulsa J.D. 1976. Member Phi Delta Phi. Admitted to practice Oklahoma 1976 and U.S. District Court Northern District of Oklahoma 1977. Began legal practice Durant 1976. Alternate Municipal Court Judge 1977.

Member Oklahoma Judicial Conference, Bryan County and Oklahoma Bar Associations. Board of Directors

POWERS, ROCKY L.—*Continued*

Bryan County Youth Services, Inc. Enjoys music, writing and photography.

Office: Bryan County Courthouse, 402 West Evergreen Street, Durant 74701.

Telephone: (580) 924-3450.

PRIGMORE, Gene *(Judge, Oklahoma Workers' Compensation Court)* Appointed by Governor Frank Keating to term beginning Nov 16, 1998. Reappointed 2000, current term expires July 1, 2006. Born Freedom Oklahoma Jan 17, 1944. Educated at Northwestern Oklahoma State University B.A. 1966, Central State University M.A. with honors 1973 and University of Oklahoma J.D. 1980. Admitted to practice Oklahoma 1980. In legal practice Oklahoma City, Tulsa and Ada 1980-98.

Adjunct Professor Paralegal Courses Rose State College 1988-90. Member Oklahoma Bar Association. Instructor several seminars Oklahoma Bar Association. Specialist 4 U.S. Army 1966-68. Teacher and Coach 1968-78. Member Oklahoma City School Board 1986-89. Enjoys collecting baseball cards, reading, watching soccer games and playing golf.

Office: 1915 North Stiles Avenue, Oklahoma City 73105.

Telephone: (405) 522-8600.

E-mail address: gprigmore@owcc.state.ok.us

PRITCHETT, Susie *(Associate District Judge, Oklahoma District Court Fourth Judicial District)* Elected Nov 1994 to term beginning Jan 9, 1995. Reelected 1998 and 2002. Current term expires Jan 2007. Serves Kingfisher County. Born Houston Texas Oct 6, 1941. Evangelical Episcopalian. Educated at University of Oklahoma B.A. 1963 J.D. 1971 and University of Central Oklahoma M.T. 1965. Member Phi Alpha Delta and Iota Tau Tau. Admitted to practice Oklahoma 1971, U.S. District Courts Western 1973, Northern 1985 and Eastern 1987 Districts of Oklahoma and U.S. Court of Appeals Tenth Circuit 1973. In legal practice Oklahoma City 1984-91. Chief Administrative Law Judge, Office of Administrative Hearings State of Oklahoma 1991-95.

Assistant Public Defender Oklahoma County 1971-73. Assistant U.S. Attorney Western District of Oklahoma 1973-84. Author "Rules and Regulations of the Office of Administrative Hearings: Child Support" adopted by Oklahoma State Legislature as part of its code of administrative law 1994 and extensive revisions of Titles 56 and 43 of the Oklahoma statutes 1994. Member Ruth Bader Ginsburg Inn of Court, Kingfisher County (President Elect) and Oklahoma Bar Associations. Instructor Federal Law Enforcement Center. Recipient Commendation for Outstanding Service from Governor Frank Keating 1995. Member Rotary Club. Writer of newspaper column appearing in three rural papers. Enjoys reading, grandchildren and various crafts.

Office: 18 Kingfisher County Courthouse, 101 South Main, Kingfisher 73750.

Telephone: (405) 375-3869.

PURCELL, Gary M. *(Magistrate Judge, United States District Court Western District of Oklahoma)* Appointed by U.S. District Court judges. Former Special Judge, Oklahoma District Court Twenty-first Judicial District.

Office: 1423 U.S. Courthouse, 200 N.W. Fourth Street, Oklahoma City 73102.

Telephone: (405) 609-5260.

RAHHAL, Franklin D. *(District Judge, Oklahoma District Court Twenty-fourth Judicial District)* Former Associate District Judge. Former Judge, Oklahoma Court of Tax Review.

Mailing address: P.O. Box 222, Okemah 74859.

Office: Okfuskee County Courthouse, Okemah 74859.

Telephone: (918) 623-0725.

RAPP, Keith *(Judge, Oklahoma Court of Civil Appeals)* Appointed to term beginning Dec 13, 1984. Retained by election Nov 1990, Nov 1996 and Nov 2002. Current term expires Jan 2009. Former Vice Chief Judge. Former Chief Judge. Educated at Southwest Missouri State University B.S. in Mathematics and Chemistry 1958, University of Missouri graduate studies in Mathematics and Statistics, University of Arizona, University of Minnesota, University of Tulsa J.D. 1968 and University of Virginia M.L. in Judicial Process 1990. Associate Editor Tulsa Law Journal. Recipient Scholarship Key. Admitted to practice Oklahoma 1968, U.S. District Courts Northern, Eastern and Western Districts of Oklahoma, U.S. Court of Appeals Tenth Circuit and U.S. Supreme Court. Began legal practice Tulsa 1969. Judge, Bixby Municipal Court 1976-77. Alternate Judge, Tulsa Municipal Court 1977-78. District Judge, Oklahoma District Court Fourteenth Judicial District 1981-83.

Prosecutor Broken Arrow 1969-71. Public Defender Tulsa 1970-71. Author "Reliability of Identical Elements in Series" Electrotechnology, "A Rapid Reliability Estimator for Redundant Standby Configurations" 10th National Symposium Institute of Electrical & Electronic Engineers, article in *Handbook for Calculating the Reliability of Redundant Configurations* Honeywell Press, "Failure Mode, Effect & Criticality Analysis Procedure Guidelines" Evaluation Engineering, "Propaganda, a Klauswitzian Tool" and "Note on Universal Navy" submitted to United States Naval Institute and "The Unknowing Appellate Gideon: An Examination of the 'Burger Problem' Within State Appellate Structures" Oklahoma City L. Rev. 17 No. 2 Summer 1992. Contributing Author Tailhook Magazine. Instructor in Business Law Tulsa Junior College 1976-77 and in International Law 1976-77, Sino Soviet Relations 1977-78 and Chemical Bacteriological Nuclear Warfare 1979-80 Naval Reserve Officers School. Commander USNR (retired). Director Town and Country Bank 1976-81, Old General Insurance Co. 1977-81, Gumut Indemnity Co. 1977-81 and Canopus Oil and Gas Drilling 1980-81. Former aerospace engineer Avco Electronics, Douglas Aircraft, Aerospace Division Honeywell, Space Electronics Division Motorola and Air Arm Division Westinghouse. Former Regent Tulsa Junior College.

Office: 440 South Houston, Suite 601, Tulsa 74127.

Telephone: (918) 581-2711.

Fax: (918) 581-2403

RASURE, Dana L. *(Chief Judge, United States Bankruptcy Court Northern District of Oklahoma)* Appointed by U.S. Court of Appeals Tenth Circuit judges. Chief Judge since June 2, 2002.

Office: Federal Building, First Floor, 224 South Boulder Avenue, Tulsa 74103-3015.

Telephone: (918) 699-4085.

REAVIS, Robert E., II *(Associate District Judge, Oklahoma District Court Thirteenth Judicial District)* Serves Ottawa County.
Office: Ottawa County Courthouse, 102 East Central Avenue, Miami 74354.
Telephone: (918) 542-2862.

REDDICK, Ryan D. *(Associate District Judge, Oklahoma District Court First Judicial District)* Serves Texas County.
Office: Texas County Courthouse, 319 North Main Street, Guymon 73942.
Telephone: (580) 338-3412.

REIF, John F. *(Judge, Oklahoma Court of Civil Appeals)* Appointed by Governor George P. Nigh to term beginning June 8, 1984. Retained by election 1984, 1990, 1996 and 2002. Current term expires Jan 2009. Former Vice Chief Judge and Chief Judge. Born Tulsa Oklahoma June 19, 1951. Educated at University of Tulsa B.S. 1973 J.D. 1977. Law Clerk to Tulsa County District Attorney's Office. Admitted to practice Oklahoma 1978. Began legal practice Tulsa. Special Judge, Oklahoma District Court 1981-84.
Assistant District Attorney. Author "The Legal Status of Off-Duty Police Officers" Oral Roberts University L. Rev. May-June 1985. Adjunct Professor John Rogers School of Law University of Tulsa 1983, O. W. Coburn School of Law 1984-86 and School of Business since 1986 Oral Roberts University. Member Oklahoma Bar Association. Enjoys ice hockey, baseball and wildlife conservation.
Office: 440 South Houston, Suite 601, Tulsa 74127.
Telephone: (918) 581-2711.

REVARD, Douglas C. *(Special Judge, Oklahoma District Court Eighth Judicial District)* Serves Kay County.
Mailing address: P.O. Box 251, Newkirk 74647.
Office: Kay County Courthouse, Newkirk 74647.
Telephone: (580) 362-3740.

RICKS, Carolyn R. *(District Judge, Oklahoma District Court Seventh Judicial District)* Former Special Judge.
Office: 709 Oklahoma County Courthouse, 321 Park Avenue, Oklahoma City 73102.
Telephone: (405) 713-1433.

RIFFE, Gerald H. *(Associate District Judge, Oklahoma District Court First Judicial District)* Serves Beaver County.
Mailing address: P.O. Box 100, Beaver 73932.
Office: Beaver County Courthouse, Beaver 73932.
Telephone: (580) 625-3231.

RING, Rodney David *(Special Judge, Oklahoma District Court Twenty-first Judicial District)* Serves Cleveland County.
Office: Cleveland County Courthouse, 200 South Peters, Norman 73069.
Telephone: (405) 321-5638.

ROBERTS, Bana Burkett *(Magistrate Judge, United States District Court Western District of Oklahoma)* Appointed by U.S. District Court judges to term beginning June 1991. Reappointed June 1999, current term expires June 2007. Born Norman Oklahoma March 29, 1948. Educated at University of Oklahoma B.A. 1969 J.D. 1977. Member Phi Beta Kappa. Admitted to practice Oklahoma 1977. District Judge, Oklahoma District Court Seventh Judicial District 1988-91.
President William J. Holloway American Inn of Court and Oklahoma County Bar Association.
Office: 200 N.W. Fourth Street, Room 1021, Oklahoma City 73102.
Telephone: (405) 609-5240.

ROBERTS, Charles E. *(Associate District Judge, Oklahoma District Court Twentieth Judicial District)* Serves Love County.
Office: Love County Courthouse, 405 West Main Street, Marietta 73448.
Telephone: (580) 276-3373.

ROBERTSON, Vicki *(District Judge, Oklahoma District Court Seventh Judicial District)* Special Judge April 1, 1996 to April 15, 1999. Appointed District Judge by Governor Frank Keating to term beginning April 16, 1999. Born Ponca City Oklahoma Oct 5, 1949. Educated at University of Oklahoma B.S. with distinction 1970 and Oklahoma City University J.D. 1978. Member Phi Beta Kappa and Phi Delta Phi. Admitted to practice Oklahoma 1979. In legal practice Oklahoma City 1980-96.
Staff Attorney Hartford Insurance Group 1979-80. Member Oklahoma Judicial Conference (Special Vice President 1998), Oklahoma Trial Judges' Association, Oklahoma County (Board of Directors 1996-98, Vice President 1999), Oklahoma (Chairperson Credentials Committee to House of Delegates 1997) and American Bar Associations. Graduate General Jurisdiction Course The National Judicial College. Speaker CLE seminars Oklahoma County Bar Association and Oklahoma Bar Association. Former high school mathematics teacher. Member Downtown Exchange Club and Selection Committee Oklahoma Foundation for Excellence. Former high school coach girls tennis team. Enjoys golf, tennis, snow skiing and scuba diving.
Office: 315 Oklahoma County Courthouse, 321 Park Avenue, Oklahoma City 73102.
Telephone: (405) 713-1408.
E-mail address: RobertsonV@OSCN.NET

ROBINSON, A. Carl *(Special Judge, Oklahoma District Court Fifteenth Judicial District)* Serves Muskogee County.
Mailing address: P.O. Box 1350, Muskogee 74401.
Office: Muskogee County Courthouse, Muskogee 74401.
Telephone: (918) 684-1611.

RUSSELL, David L. *(Judge, United States District Court Western District of Oklahoma)* Appointed for life by President Ronald Reagan to term beginning Jan 12, 1982. Former Chief Judge. Also served Eastern and Northern Districts. Born Sapulpa Oklahoma July 7, 1942. Methodist. Educated at Oklahoma Baptist University B.S. 1963 and University of Oklahoma J.D. 1965. Member Order of the Coif. Admitted to practice Oklahoma 1965. Began legal practice 1965. In legal practice Oklahoma City since 1968.
Assistant Attorney General Oklahoma 1968-69. Legal advisor to Oklahoma Governor Dewey F. Bartlett 1969-70 and U.S. Senator 1973-75. U.S. Attorney 1975-77

RUSSELL, DAVID L.—*Continued*

and 1981-82. Member Oklahoma Bar Association. Lieutenant Commander USNR 1965-71. Republican.

Office: 3309 U.S. Courthouse, 200 N.W. Fourth Street, Oklahoma City 73102.

Telephone: (405) 609-5100.

RUSSELL, Norman L. *(Associate District Judge, Oklahoma District Court Third Judicial District)* Serves Kiowa County.

Office: Kiowa County Courthouse, 316 South Main Street, Hobart 73651.

Telephone: (580) 726-3594.

RYAN, Gregory J. *(Special Judge, Oklahoma District Court Seventh Judicial District)* Serves Oklahoma County.

Office: 109 Oklahoma County Courthouse, 321 Park Avenue, Oklahoma City 73105.

Telephone: (405) 713-1405.

SALYER, Jerry L. *(Judge, Oklahoma Workers' Compensation Court)* Appointed by Governor Henry Bellmon to term beginning July 1, 1988. Reappointed 1994 and 2000, current term expires July 1, 2006. Former Presiding Judge. Born Binger Oklahoma Sept 20, 1936. Protestant. Educated at University of Oklahoma B.A. 1959 J.D. with honors 1961. Second Place National Moot Court Competition 1961. Board of Editors Oklahoma L. Rev. 1958-61. Law Clerk to Hon. Ralph B. Hodges, Supreme Court of Oklahoma 1965-67. Member Phi Delta Phi and Order of the Coif. Admitted to practice Oklahoma 1961, U.S. Court of Military Appeals 1962, U.S. District Court Western District of Oklahoma 1968 and U.S. Court of Appeals Tenth Circuit 1971. In legal practice Oklahoma City 1967-88.

Member Oklahoma County, Oklahoma and American Bar Associations. Graduate College of Advocacy University of California Hastings College of the Law 1974. Attended Advanced Evidence course 1989, Advanced Workers' Compensation Law 1991 and Ethics for Judges course 1999 The National Judicial College and Common Law seminar Oxford, England 1998. Instructor Workers' Compensation seminar National Business Institute, Inc. 1990 and Oklahoma Bar Association 2001. Awarded Diploma of Humanities and Judging from American Academy of Judicial Education 1994. Colonel USAR since 1959 (active duty 1961-65). Honor Graduate 35 Basic Course JAGC 1962. Authority Counsel Oklahoma City Urban Renewal Authority 1979-88 and Oklahoma City Redevelopment Authority 1985-88. Republican. Member Muscular Dystrophy Association Western District of Oklahoma (Vice President 1974, President 1975). Enjoys running, snow skiing and reading.

Office: 1915 North Stiles, Oklahoma City 73105-4918.

Telephone: (405) 522-8600.

SCAGGS, John H. *(District Judge, Oklahoma District Court Twentieth Judicial District)* Appointed by Governor Henry Bellmon to term beginning Feb 14, 1989. Elected 1991, 1995, 1998 and 2002. Current term expires Jan 2007. Presiding Judge South Central Judicial Administrative District 1998-2001. Born Portland Oregon Jan 10, 1946. Methodist. Educated at Oklahoma City University B.A. 1967 and University of Oklahoma J.D. 1974. Note Editor Oklahoma Law Review 1973-74. Member Phi Alpha Delta and Order of the Coif. Admitted to practice Oklahoma 1974, U.S. District Courts Northern 1975 and Western 1975 Districts of Oklahoma and U.S. Supreme Court 1976. In legal practice Walters 1974-89.

Assistant District Attorney Cotton County 1976-78. President Oklahoma Judicial Conference 1997-98. Member Oklahoma Bar Association. Instructor for newly appointed/elected judges Oklahoma Judicial Conference. U.S. Army 1967-71. Oklahoma National Guard 1971-78. Little League Coach. Member Sulphur United Methodist Church, Murray County Players, Ardmore Oklahoma Holiday Chorale and Ardmore Oklahoma Little Theatre. Enjoys theater, choral music and running.

Mailing address: P.O. Box 58, Madill 73446.

Office: Marshall County Courthouse, Madill 73446.

Telephone: (580) 795-3392.

SCROGGINS, Danny L. *(Associate District Judge, Oklahoma District Court Twenty-fifth Judicial District)* Serves Atoka County.

Office: Atoka County Courthouse, 201 East Court Street, Atoka 74525.

Telephone: (580) 889-3400.

SEAY, Frank Howell *(Judge, United States District Court Eastern District of Oklahoma)* Appointed for life by the President. Chief Judge March 2, 2001 to Oct 26, 2002. Born Shawnee Oklahoma Sept 5, 1938. Methodist. Educated at Southern Methodist University 1956-57 and University of Oklahoma B.A. 1960 LL.B. 1963. Admitted to practice Oklahoma 1963 and U.S. District Court Eastern District of Oklahoma 1965. Began legal practice Seminole 1963. Former Associate District Judge and District Judge, Oklahoma District Court Twenty-second Judicial District. Former Judge and Presiding Judge 1975-78, Oklahoma Court of Bank Review.

Seminole County Attorney 1963-66. Assistant District Attorney 1967-68. Member Seminole County, Oklahoma and American Bar Associations. Democrat. Member Masonic Lodge, Elks Lodge and Lions Club.

Mailing address: P.O. Box 828, Muskogee 74402-0828.

Telephone: (918) 687-2437.

SELLERS, Jefferson D. *(District Judge, Oklahoma District Court Fourteenth Judicial District)*

Office: 713 Tulsa County Courthouse, 500 South Denver, Tulsa 74103.

Telephone: (918) 596-5375.

SEWELL, G. Bruce *(District Judge, Oklahoma District Court Fifteenth Judicial District)* Associate District Judge July 29, 1985 to Jan 7, 1995. Elected District Judge to term beginning Jan 9, 1995. Reelected 1998 and 2002. Current term expires Jan 2007. Chief Judge Cherokee County and Wagoner County. Born McAlester Oklahoma Feb 3, 1953. Baptist. Educated at Oklahoma State University B.S. 1976 and University of Tulsa J.D. 1979. Member Beta Gamma Sigma. Admitted to practice Oklahoma 1980. In legal practice Tulsa 1980-85.

Chairperson Legislative Committee Oklahoma Judicial Conference 1990. Chairperson Tulsa County Oklahoma Democratic Party 1980-82. Northeastern Oklahoma Coordinator Committee to Reelect President Jimmy Carter 1979-80. Enjoys thoroughbred racehorses.

Office: Wagoner County Courthouse, 307 East Cherokee Street, Wagoner 74467.

Telephone: (918) 485-2144.

SHAFFER, Ronald L. *(District Judge, Oklahoma District Court Fourteenth Judicial District)* Special Judge 1981-82. Elected District Judge to term beginning Jan 10, 1983. Reelected 1986, 1990, 1994, 1998 and 2002. Current term expires Jan 2007. Born Henryetta Oklahoma July 16, 1936. Christian. Educated at Oklahoma State University 1954-56 and University of Tulsa LL.B. 1964. Member Phi Alpha Delta. Admitted to practice Oklahoma 1964. In legal practice Tulsa 1965-66. Deputy Court Clerk 1957-64.

Assistant County Attorney 1964-65 and Assistant District Attorney 1966-81 Tulsa County. Instructor in Evidence and Criminal Procedure Tulsa Junior College 1970-81. Member Oklahoma Trial Lawyers Association, Tulsa County and Oklahoma Bar Associations. Attended Current Issues in Civil Litigation seminar The National Judicial College March 24-31, 1990. Named Outstanding District Court Trial Judge of 1986 by Oklahoma Trial Lawyers Association. Democrat. Enjoys hunting, golfing and fishing.

Office: 605 Tulsa County Courthouse, 500 South Denver, Tulsa 74103.

Telephone: (918) 596-5330.

SHALLCROSS, Deborah C. *(District Judge, Oklahoma District Court Fourteenth Judicial District)* Former Special Judge.

Office: 513 Tulsa County Courthouse, 500 South Denver, Tulsa 74103.

Telephone: (918) 596-5310.

SHEPHERD, Darrell G. *(Associate District Judge, Oklahoma District Court Fifteenth Judicial District)* Serves Wagoner County.

Office: Wagoner County Courthouse, 307 East Cherokee Street, Wagoner 74467.

Telephone: (918) 485-9599.

SHERRILL, Trace C. *(Special Judge, Oklahoma District Court Nineteenth Judicial District)* Serves Bryan County.

Office: Bryan County Courthouse, 402 West Evergreen Street, Durant 74701.

Telephone: (580) 924-3450.

SHREDER, Steven P. *(Magistrate Judge, United States District Court Eastern District of Oklahoma)* Appointed by U.S. District Court judges.

Mailing address: P.O. Box 7002, Muskogee 74402-7002.

Telephone: (918) 684-7960.

SMITH, Clancy C. *(Special Judge, Oklahoma District Court Fourteenth Judicial District)* Serves Tulsa County.

Office: 347 Tulsa County Courthouse, 500 South Denver, Tulsa 74103.

Telephone: (918) 596-5233.

SMITH, Clifford J. *(Special Judge, Oklahoma District Court Fourteenth Judicial District)* Serves Tulsa County.

Office: 124 Tulsa County Courthouse, 500 South Denver Avenue, Tulsa 74103.

Telephone: (918) 596-5345.

SMITH, Gale *(Associate District Judge, Oklahoma District Court Second Judicial District)* Serves Roger Mills County.

Mailing address: P.O. Box 737, Cheyenne 73628.

Office: Roger Mills County Courthouse, Cheyenne 73628.

Telephone: (580) 497-3359.

SMITH, Greggory M. *(Associate District Judge, Oklahoma District Court Twenty-second Judicial District)* Serves Hughes County.

Mailing address: P.O. Box 875, Holdenville 74848.

Office: Hughes County Courthouse, Holdenville 74848.

Telephone: (580) 379-3211.

SMITH, L. Joe *(Special Judge, Oklahoma District Court Twelfth Judicial District)* Serves Rogers County.

Office: Rogers County Courthouse, 219 South Missouri, Claremore 74017.

Telephone: (918) 341-4025.

SMITH, Mark R. *(District Judge, Oklahoma District Court Fifth Judicial District)* Appointed by Governor David Walters to term beginning May 18, 1992. Elected 1994, 1998 and 2002. Current term expires Jan 2007. Born Muskogee Oklahoma May 28, 1951. Baptist. Educated at Oklahoma State University B.S. 1973 and Oklahoma City University 1975. Admitted to practice Oklahoma 1975 and U.S. District Court Western District of Oklahoma 1980. In legal practice Lawton 1975-87. Judge, Lawton Municipal Court 1987-92.

Member Comanche County, Oklahoma and American Bar Associations. Democrat. Enjoys fishing and golfing.

Office: Comanche County Courthouse, 300 S.W. Fifth Street, Lawton 73501.

Telephone: (580) 581-4598.

SMITH, Sarah D. *(Special Judge, Oklahoma District Court Fourteenth Judicial District)* Serves Tulsa County.

Office: 345 Tulsa County Courthouse, 500 South Denver Avenue, Tulsa 74103.

Telephone: (918) 596-5384.

SNOW, Gary P. *(District Judge, Oklahoma District Court Twenty-second Judicial District)*

Mailing address: P.O. Box 1681, Seminole 74818.

Office: Seminole County Courthouse, Seminole 74818.

Telephone: (405) 382-0488.

SPROUSE, Dennis M. *(Special Judge, Oklahoma District Court Fifteenth Judicial District)* Serves Sequoyah County.

Office: Sequoyah County Courthouse, 120 East Chickasaw Street, Sallisaw 74955.

Telephone: (918) 775-4262.

STATON, Jon Tom *(Associate District Judge, Oklahoma District Court Fifth Judicial District)* Serves Jefferson County.

Office: Jefferson County Courthouse, 220 North Main Street, Waurika 73573.

Telephone: (580) 228-2180.

STEIDLEY, J. Dwayne *(Associate District Judge, Oklahoma District Court Twelfth Judicial District)* Former Special Judge. Serves Rogers County. Born Claremore Oklahoma March 8, 1959. Methodist. Educated at Oklahoma State University B.A. 1981 and Tulsa University J.D. 1984. Admitted to practice Oklahoma 1985 and

STEIDLEY, J. DWAYNE—*Continued*

U.S. District Court Northern District of Oklahoma. In legal practice Claremore 1985-98.

Member Rogers County and Oklahoma Bar Associations. Member State House of Representatives Oklahoma 1986-98.

Office: Rogers County Courthouse, 219 South Missouri Avenue, Claremore 74017.

Telephone: (918) 341-0950.

E-mail address: jdSteidley@OSCN.NET

STEIN, Taylor C. *(Special Judge, Oklahoma District Court Fifth Judicial District)* Appointed. Serves Comanche County.

Office: Comanche County Courthouse, 315 S.W. Fifth, Lawton 73501.

Telephone: (580) 581-4585.

STILWELL, Lee G. *(Associate District Judge, Oklahoma District Court Twenty-second Judicial District)* Special Judge 1983-87. Elected Associate District Judge to term beginning Jan 1987. Reelected 1990, 1994, 1998 and 2002. Current term expires Jan 2007. Serves Seminole County. Born Seminole Oklahoma July 30, 1952. Religious affiliation: Church of Christ. Educated at University of Oklahoma B.B.A. 1974 J.D. 1977. Admitted to practice Oklahoma 1977. In legal practice Wetumka 1977-81.

Part-time Assistant District Attorney Hughes County 1979-81. Assistant District Attorney Seminole, Hughes and Pontotoc counties 1981-83. Past President Seminole County Bar Association. Attended General Jurisdiction course The National Judicial College, Reno Nevada and "Conduct of a Jury Trial" American Judges Association. Enjoys church and family activities.

Mailing address: P.O. Box 678, Wewoka 74884.

Office: Seminole County Courthouse, Wewoka 74884.

Telephone: (405) 257-3386.

E-mail address: (405) 257-2631

E-mail address: Lee.Stillwell@oscn.net

STRATTON, C. William *(Associate District Judge, Oklahoma District Court Fifth Judicial District)* Former Special Judge. Serves Comanche County.

Office: Comanche County Courthouse, 300 S.W. Fifth Street, Lawton 73501.

Telephone: (580) 581-4570.

STRUBHAR, Reta M. *(Judge, Oklahoma Court of Criminal Appeals)* Appointed July 6, 1993. Former Vice Presiding Judge. Former Presiding Judge. First woman to sit on Oklahoma Court of Criminal Appeals. Educated at Phillips University B.S., University of Central Oklahoma M.A. and Oklahoma City University School of Law J.D. Associate District Judge, Oklahoma District Court Twenty-sixth Judicial District 1984-93.

Former Assistant District Attorney. Former Assistant Attorney General. Began Senior Life Skills seminar. Active in children's issues.

Office: 230 State Capitol Building, Oklahoma City 73105.

Telephone: (405) 521-2157.

E-mail address: rstrubhar@mail.occa.state.ok.us

STUART, Roger H. *(Special Judge, Oklahoma District Court Seventh Judicial District)* Serves Oklahoma County.

Office: Oklahoma Juvenile Justice Center, 5905 North Classen Court, Room B, Oklahoma City 73118.

Telephone: (405) 713-6754.

STUBBLEFIELD, Ronald J. *(Judge, Oklahoma Court of Civil Appeals)* Elected July 1982 to term beginning Jan 10, 1983. Retained by election 1986, 1992 and 1998. Current term expires Jan 2005. Former Presiding Judge. Born Bristow Oklahoma Dec 6, 1946. Unitarian. Educated at University of Oklahoma B.A. with honors 1968 J.D. 1975. Admitted to practice Oklahoma 1975. In legal practice Atoka 1975-78.

District Attorney Oklahoma District Nineteen 1979-82. Member Oklahoma Bar Association. E-4 U.S. Army 1968-70.

Office: 440 South Houston, Suite 601, Tulsa 74127.

Telephone: (918) 581-2711.

SUMMERS, Hardy *(Justice, Supreme Court of Oklahoma)* Appointed 1985. Retained by election 1986, 1988, 1994 and 2000. Current term expires Jan 2007. Former Vice Chief Justice. Former Chief Justice. Born Muskogee Oklahoma July 15, 1933. Educated at University of Oklahoma B.A. 1955 LL.B. 1957. Member Law Review and Order of the Coif. Admitted to practice Oklahoma 1957. In legal practice Muskogee 1962. Former District Judge, Oklahoma District Court Fifteenth Judicial District, appointed by Governor David Boren to term beginning Aug 18, 1976.

Assistant County Attorney 1960-62. Secretary County Election Board 1965-72. Chair Criminal Recodification Committee. Member Committee on Uniform Civil Jury Instructions Appellate Division Court of the Judiciary, Muskogee County (President 1976), Oklahoma and American Bar Associations. Named Distinguished Alumnus by University of Oklahoma College of Law 2000. Captain USAF JAGC 1957-60 USAFR 1960-63. Enjoys music, fishing, hunting, golf and other sports.

Office: 245 State Capitol, Oklahoma City 73105.

Telephone: (405) 521-3845.

SWINTON, Barbara G. *(District Judge, Oklahoma District Court Seventh Judicial District)* Former Special Judge.

Office: 105 Oklahoma County Courthouse, 321 Park Avenue, Oklahoma City 73102.

Telephone: (405) 713-7109.

TATE, Charles G. *(Special Judge, Oklahoma District Court Twentieth Judicial District)* Serves Carter County.

Office: 304 Carter County Courthouse, 20 B Street S.W., Ardmore 73401.

Telephone: (580) 223-3803.

TAYLOR, Joe C. *(Judge, Oklahoma Court of Civil Appeals)* Appointed by Governor David Walters to term beginning Jan 11, 1993. Retained by election Nov 1994 and 1998. Current term expires 2005. Former Vice Chief Judge. Former Chief Judge. Born Durant Oklahoma March 28, 1942. Church of Christ. Educated at Southeastern Oklahoma State University 1960-62, Oklahoma State University B.A. 1965 and University of Oklahoma J.D. 1968. Member Blue Key, Delta Theta Phi and Phi Sigma Epsilon. Admitted to practice Oklahoma 1968. In legal practice Norman 1968-69. Special Judge 1969-72, Associate District Judge 1972-76, District Judge 1976-93

TAYLOR, JOE C.—*Continued*
and Former Chief Judge, Oklahoma District Court Nineteenth Judicial District. Presiding Judge, Tribal Court of the Choctaw Nation of Oklahoma 1979-83. Administrative Judge, Southeastern Judicial Administrative District 1983-92. Presiding Judge, Trial Division Oklahoma Court on the Judiciary 1991-92.

Principal Author *Code of Procedure* Choctaw Nation of Oklahoma Tribal Court 1979. Author "Procedural Aspects of the Indian Child Welfare Act" *Sovereignty Symposium Handbook* 1989. Chairman Assembly of Presiding Judges 1990-92. Member Oklahoma Judicial Conference (President 1987, Past Vice President) and Oklahoma Bar Association (Vice Chairperson Administration of Justice Committee 1993). Attended General Jurisdiction 1972 and Writing 1988 The National Judicial College and American Academy of Judicial Education 1979 and 1983 (Diploma of Judicial Skills 1984). Listed in *Outstanding Young Men in America, Who's Who in Oklahoma, Who's Who in America* 1971 and *Who's Who in American Law.* Named Sorority Man of the Year by Delta Zeta 1962, Outstanding Young Man of Durant by Jaycees 1975 and Gourd Dance Honoree by Choctaw National Festival and Pow Wow 2002. Recipient Youth Advocate Award from Oklahoma Association of Youth Services 1986 and Leadership Legacy Award from Oklahoma State University Fall 2000. Lieutenant Colonel USAR since 1965. Chairman Board of Directors Youth Services of Bryan County 1974-93. Grand Marshal Veterans Day Parade Bryan County 2001. Past President Lions International. Former External Vice President Durant Jaycees. Former Member United Way. Director Noon Lions Club. Member Chamber of Commerce, Reserve Officers Association and Oklahoma Cattlemen's Association. Enjoys swimming, boating, hunting, ranching and football.

Office: 440 South Houston, Suite 601, Tulsa 74127.
Telephone: (918) 581-2711.

TAYLOR, Steven W. *(District Judge, Oklahoma District Court Eighteenth Judicial District)* Associate District Judge March 14, 1984 to Jan 8, 1995. Elected District Judge to term beginning Jan 9, 1995. Reelected 1998 and 2002. Current term expires Jan 2007. Former Presiding Judge East Central Judicial Administrative District. Born Henryetta Oklahoma June 7, 1949. Methodist. Educated at Oklahoma State University B.A. 1971 and University of Oklahoma J.D. 1974. Recipient American Jurisprudence Award 1973. Member Kappa Sigma. Admitted to practice Oklahoma 1974, U.S. Supreme Court 1977 and U.S. District Courts Northern 1980, Eastern 1980 and Western 1980 Districts of Oklahoma. Began legal practice McAlester 1978. Former Judge, Oklahoma Court of Tax Review.

City Councilman 1980-82 and Mayor 1982-84 McAlester. President Oklahoma Judicial Conference 1991. Major USMC 1974-78 (Special Court Martial Judge 1977-78). Member Rotary Club. Enjoys golf and running.

Office: Pittsburg County Courthouse, 115 East Carl Albert Parkway, McAlester 74501.
Telephone: (918) 423-6866.

THOMPSON, Donald D. *(District Judge, Oklahoma District Court Twenty-fourth Judicial District)* Appointed by Governor George Nigh to term beginning Feb 1982. Elected Nov 1982, 1986, 1990, 1994, 1998 and 2002. Current term expires Jan 2007. Born Sapulpa Oklahoma Sept 26, 1946. Protestant. Educated at University of Oklahoma B.A. 1968 J.D. 1971. Admitted to practice Oklahoma 1971 and U.S. District Court Northern District of Oklahoma 1972. Began legal practice Sapulpa 1971.

State Representative Oklahoma House of Representatives 1974-80. Member Oklahoma Bar Association. Recipient Certificate of Meritorious Service from Oklahoma Trial Lawyers Association 1975. Democrat. Member Rotary International. Enjoys golf, hunting and fishing.

Office: Creek County Courthouse, 222 East Dewey, Sapulpa 74066.
Telephone: (918) 224-3445.

THOMPSON, Ralph G. *(Senior Judge, United States District Court Western District of Oklahoma)* Appointed for life by President Gerald R. Ford to term beginning Oct 20, 1975. Chief Judge 1986-93. Assumed Senior status Dec 16, 1999, serves by assignment. Born Oklahoma City Oklahoma Dec 15, 1934. Member All Souls' Episcopal Church. Educated at University of Oklahoma B.B.A. 1956 LL.B. 1961. Member Phi Beta Kappa and Order of the Coif (alumnus). Admitted to practice Oklahoma 1961 and U.S. Supreme Court 1967. In legal practice Oklahoma City 1961-75. Special Justice, Oklahoma Supreme Court 1970.

Co-author Oklahoma Constitutional Amendment on Judicial Reform and with Bob Burke and Ralph G. Thompson *Bryce Harlow, Mr. Integrity* Oklahoma Heritage Association 2000. Member Teaching Team Trial Advocacy Workshop Harvard Law School since 1980. President U.S. District Judges Association of the Tenth Circuit 1992-94. Member Committees on Court Administration and Federal-State Jurisdiction, Elected U.S. District Judge Member 1997-2000 and Coordinator of Long Range Planning for Federal Courts 1999-2000 Judicial Conference of the U.S. Fellow American Bar Foundation. Appointed to Executive Committee by Chief Justice William Hubbs Rehnquist, Judicial Conference of the U.S. Member American Judicature Society, Oklahoma Bar Foundation (Trustee 1966-69), Oklahoma Young Lawyers Conference (President 1965), Oklahoma City Lawyers Club (President 1969), Association of Federal Trial Judges, Oklahoma County (Board of Directors 1974-77), Oklahoma (Member House of Delegates 1964, 1970 and 1971, Chairman International and Comparative Law Section 1973-75 and Organizing Chairman 1973 and Chairman 1974 General Practice Section) and American Bar Associations. Designed and served on the first Oklahoma Narcotics and Drug Abuse Council. Recipient Oklahoma City's Outstanding Young Man Award 1967, Judicial Service Award from Oklahoma County Bar Association Sept 24, 1988, Regents' Alumni Award from University of Oklahoma 1990, Distinguished Service Citation from University of Oklahoma 1993 and Journal Record Award 2001. Named one of Three Outstanding Young Oklahomans for 1968 by Oklahoma State Junior Chamber of Commerce, Outstanding Federal Trial Judge in Oklahoma by Oklahoma Trial Lawyers Association 1980 and Phi Beta Kappa of the Year from Phi Beta Kappa Association of Oklahoma City 1991. Inducted into Oklahoma Hall of Fame 1995. Nominee Pulitzer Prize 2000. Special Agent Office of Special Investigations USAF 1957-60. Colonel USAFR (retired). Recipient Legion of Merit from U.S. Air Force March 6, 1987. Republican. Member Oklahoma House of Representatives 1966-70 (Assistant Minority Floor Leader).

THOMPSON, RALPH G.—*Continued*

President Phi Beta Kappa Association of Oklahoma City 1985 and University of Oklahoma Dads Association 1986. Member Edward T. Devitt Distinguished Service to Justice Award Selection Committee 1997-99. Member American Red Cross of Oklahoma County (Chairman Board of Directors 1971-73), American National Red Cross (Chairman Thirteen-State Midwestern Area Advisory Council 1973) and University of Oklahoma Board of Visitors 1975-78. Honorary member Rotary International.

Office: 3301 U.S. Courthouse, 200 N.W. Fourth Street, Oklahoma City 73102.

Telephone: (405) 609-5120.

THORNBRUGH, P. Thomas *(District Judge, Oklahoma District Court Fourteenth Judicial District)*

Office: 601 Tulsa County Courthouse, 500 South Denver, Tulsa 74103.

Telephone: (918) 596-5340.

TIPTON, Virgil R. *(Special Judge, Oklahoma District Court Twenty-first Judicial District)* Appointed to term beginning May 1991. Serves Garvin County. Born Ada Oklahoma Nov 30, 1940. Presbyterian. Educated at East Central State College B.A. 1963 and University of Oklahoma J.D. 1973. Admitted to practice Oklahoma 1973 and U.S. District Court Western District of Oklahoma 1985. In legal practice Pauls Valley 1973-91.

City Attorney Pauls Valley 1975-91. Member Garvin County and Oklahoma Bar Associations. With Investigative Service Command Office of Naval Intelligence 1966-70. Member Kiwanis International (President 1983). Enjoys golf, tennis and amateur radio.

Office: Garvin County Courthouse, Box 356, 201 West Grant, Pauls Valley 73075.

Telephone: (405) 238-6561.

UPP, Brian H. *(Special Judge, Oklahoma District Court Seventh Judicial District)* Serves Oklahoma County.

Office: 115 Oklahoma County Courthouse, 321 Park Avenue, Oklahoma City 73102.

Telephone: (405) 713-7104.

VAN DYCK, Richard G. *(District Judge, Oklahoma District Court Sixth Judicial District)* Special Judge Oct 2, 1995 to Dec 18, 1997. Appointed District Judge by Governor Frank Keating Dec 19, 1997. Elected Nov 1998 and 2002. Current term expires Jan 2007. Born Chickasha Oklahoma July 11, 1957. Educated at University of Science and Arts of Oklahoma B.S. 1982 and Oklahoma City University J.D. 1988. Staff member Oklahoma City University Law Review 1986-88. Member Phi Delta Phi. Admitted to practice Oklahoma 1988 and U.S. District Court Western District of Oklahoma 1988. In legal practice Chickasha 1988-91.

Assistant District Attorney Sixth Judicial District 1987-95. Member Grady County, Caddo County and Oklahoma Bar Associations.

Mailing address: P.O. Box 605, Chickasha 73023.

Office: Grady County Courthouse, Chickasha 73018.

Telephone: (405) 224-3737.

VASSAR, Joe Sam *(District Judge, Oklahoma District Court Twenty-fourth Judicial District)*

Office: Creek County Courthouse, 110 West Seventh, Bristow 74010.

Telephone: (918) 367-5539.

VASSAR, Paul *(District Judge, Oklahoma District Court Twenty-third Judicial District)*

Office: Lincoln County Courthouse, 811 Manvel Avenue, Chandler 74834.

Telephone: (405) 258-1399.

WALKE, Geary L. *(Special Judge, Oklahoma District Court Seventh Judicial District)* Serves Oklahoma County.

Office: 123 Oklahoma County Courthouse, 321 Park Avenue, Oklahoma City 73102.

Telephone: (405) 713-7105.

WALKER, Thomas S. *(District Judge, Oklahoma District Court Twentieth Judicial District)* Special Judge July 11, 1975 to July 10, 1978. Associate District Judge Jan 8, 1979 to Jan 7, 1987. Elected District Judge to term beginning Jan 8, 1987. Reelected 1990, 1994, 1998 and 2002. Current term expires Jan 2007. Born Longview Texas Sept 18, 1945. Religious affiliation: Disciples of Christ. Educated at Phillips University B.A. with honors 1968 and University of Oklahoma J.D. 1974. Oklahoma Bar Foundation Scholar 1974. Recipient Moot Court Prize. Member Blue Key. Admitted to practice Oklahoma 1974. Began legal practice Norman 1974. Former Judge, Oklahoma Court of Tax Review.

Instructor University of Oklahoma 1974-75. Member American Judicature Society, American Judges Association, Judicial Conference of Oklahoma (Vice President 1978, President Elect 1992, President 1993), Carter County and Oklahoma Bar Associations. Attended American Academy of Judicial Education Trial Judges Academy. Listed in *Outstanding Young Men in America* 1971, 1972 and 1975. Recipient Outstanding Young Alum Award from Phillips University 1975. Staff Sergeant U.S. Army 1968-70. Currently Colonel Oklahoma Army National Guard. Recipient Outstanding Soldier Award from Fourth U.S. Army 1969.

Office: 304 Carter County Courthouse, 20 B Street S.W., Ardmore 73401.

Telephone: (580) 223-3803.

WALL, Caroline E. *(Associate District Judge, Oklahoma District Court Fourteenth Judicial District)* Serves Tulsa County.

Office: 404 Tulsa County Courthouse, 500 South Denver Avenue, Tulsa 74103.

Telephone: (918) 596-5305.

WARD, Farley W. *(Special Judge, Oklahoma District Court Sixteenth Judicial District)* Appointed. Serves LeFlore County.

Mailing address: P.O. Box 1056, Poteau 74953.

Office: LeFlore County Courthouse, Poteau 74953.

Telephone: (918) 647-8227.

WARREN, Winford Mike *(Associate District Judge, Oklahoma District Court Third Judicial District)* Elected Nov 6, 1990 to term beginning Jan 14, 1991. Reelected Nov 7, 1994, Nov 1998 and 2002. Current term expires Jan 2007. Serves Harmon County. Born Edmond Oklahoma Oct 13, 1954. Methodist. Educated at Southern Methodist University B.B.A. 1977 and University of Tulsa J.D. 1981. Admitted to practice Oklahoma 1981. In legal practice Hollis 1981-91. Judge, Hollis Municipal Court 1981-87.

Municipal Attorney Hollis 1987-91. President Harmon County Bar 2001-02. Member Harmon-Jackson County, Oklahoma and American Bar Associations. Group Facili-

WARREN, WINFORD MIKE—*Continued*

tator The National Judicial College 1996 and 1997 and Oklahoma Judicial Conference since 1999. Democrat. Member Lions Club and India Shriner Temple. Private pilot. Enjoys woodworking, snow skiing, piano playing and fishing.

Office: Harmon County Courthouse, 114 West Hollis Street, Hollis 73550.

Telephone: (580) 688-2553.

WATSON, Leo A., Jr. *(Associate District Judge, Oklahoma District Court Fifth Judicial District)* Appointed by Governor Henry Bellmon to term beginning May 1, 1989. Elected 1990, 1994, 1998 and 2002. Current term expires Jan 2007. Serves Cotton County. Born Sanford Florida May 4, 1945. Southern Baptist. Educated at University of Florida B.S.B.A. 1968 J.D. 1972. Member Phi Alpha Delta. Admitted to practice Oklahoma 1973, Florida 1973 and U.S. District Court Western District of Oklahoma 1973. In legal practice Duncan Oklahoma 1973-89. Judge, Comanche Municipal Court 1978-89.

Member The Florida Bar and Oklahoma Bar Association. Attended General Jurisdiction Course The National Judicial College 1989. First Lieutenant U.S. Army 1968-70.

Office: Cotton County Courthouse, 301 North Broadway, Walters 73573.

Telephone: (580) 875-3137.

WATT, Joseph M. *(Chief Justice, Supreme Court of Oklahoma)* Appointed by Governor David Walters to term beginning June 1, 1992. Retained by election 1994, 1996 and 2002. Current term expires Jan 2009. Former Vice Chief Justice. Chief Justice since Jan 2003. Born Austin Texas March 8, 1947. Educated at Texas Tech University B.A. 1969 and University of Texas J.D. 1972. Named Outstanding Law Student in the Nation by Delta Theta Phi 1972. Member Omicron Delta Kappa and Delta Theta Phi. Admitted to practice Texas 1972, Oklahoma 1974, U.S. District Court Western District of Oklahoma 1974 and U.S. Court of Appeals Tenth Circuit 1974. In legal practice Altus Oklahoma 1973-85. Special Judge 1985-86 and Associate District Judge 1986-91, Oklahoma District Court Third Judicial District. Judge, Appellate Division Oklahoma Court on the Judiciary 1997-2000.

City Prosecutor 1973-85 and City Attorney 1980-85 Altus Oklahoma. Important Decisions: Taylor v. Chubb Group of Insurance Companies (defines paralegal duties recoverable as attorney fees) OK 47, 874 P.2d 806, 1994 and Tuller v. Shallcross (directs that auto liability insurance existence and contents are discoverable) OK 133, 886 P.2d 481, 1994. Vice President 1990 and 1994, President Elect 1995 and President 1996 Oklahoma Judicial Conference. Supreme Court Liaison to Oklahoma Bar Association 1997-2002. Member Truth in Sentencing Commission, Supreme Court Long Range Planning Commission, Oklahoma Bench and Bar and Oklahoma Bar Association. Past President, Former Secretary and Paul Harris Fellow Altus Rotary Club. Interests include church, family and golf.

Office: 245 State Capitol Building, 2300 North Lincoln Boulevard, Oklahoma City 73105.

Telephone: (405) 521-3848.

Fax: (405) 521-6982

WEAVER, T. M. "Mike" *(Chief Judge, United States Bankruptcy Court Western District of Oklahoma)* Appointed by U.S Court of Appeals Tenth Circuit judges to term beginning June 30, 1998. Term expires June 30, 2012. Chief Judge since April 5, 2002. Born Seminole Oklahoma June 13, 1942. Presbyterian. Educated at University of Oklahoma B.B.A. 1965 and University of Oklahoma College of Law J.D. 1968. Article and Book Review Editor University of Oklahoma Law Review 1967-68. Member Phi Delta Phi and Order of the Coif. Admitted to practice Oklahoma 1968 and U.S. District Courts Western District of Oklahoma and Northern District of Texas. In legal practice Duncan Oklahoma 1968-98.

Office: Old Post Office Building, 215 Dean A. McGee Avenue, Oklahoma City 73102.

Telephone: (405) 609-5610.

E-mail address: t_mweaver@okwb.uscourts.gov

WEEDON, Jill Carpenter *(Special Judge, Oklahoma District Court Second Judicial District)* Serves Custer County.

Mailing address: P.O. Box 180, Arapaho 73620.

Office: Custer County Courthouse, Arapaho 73620.

Telephone: (580) 323-3456.

WELCH, Bill D. *(Associate District Judge, Oklahoma District Court Sixteenth Judicial District)* Serves Latimer County.

Office: Latimer County Courthouse, 109 North Central Avenue, Wilburton 74578.

Telephone: (918) 465-2071.

WEST, Kimberly E. *(Magistrate Judge, United States District Court Eastern District of Oklahoma)* Appointed by U.S. District Court judges to term beginning March 15, 2002.

Mailing address: P.O. Box 2999, Muskogee 74402-2999.

Telephone: (918) 684-7930.

WEST, Lee R. *(Senior Judge, United States District Court Western District of Oklahoma)* Appointed for life by President Jimmy Carter to term beginning Nov 5, 1979. Former Chief Judge. Assumed Senior status, serves by assignment. Born Clayton Oklahoma Nov 26, 1929. Protestant. Educated at University of Oklahoma B.A. with honors 1952 J.D. with honors 1956 and Harvard University LL.M. 1963. Recipient Outstanding Graduate Award University of Oklahoma 1956. Member winning team Moot Court Competition. Editor Oklahoma Law Review 1955-56. Member Phi Delta Phi (President Holmes Inn) and Order of the Coif. Admitted to practice Oklahoma 1956, U.S. District Courts Eastern 1956, Northern 1956 and Western 1956 Districts of Oklahoma and U.S. Court of Appeals Tenth Circuit 1956. In legal practice Ada 1961-65 and Tulsa 1978-79. District Judge, Oklahoma District Court Twenty-second Judicial District 1965-73. Special Justice, Supreme Court of Oklahoma 1967-73. Special Judge, Oklahoma Court of Criminal Appeals 1973-78.

Author "Collateral Source Rule sans Subrogation" 16 Oklahoma L. Rev. 395, "Federal Practice: Removal of Causes" 9 *Ibid* 333 and "Federal Practice: Jurisdictional Amount of Declaratory Judgment Suits" 8 *Ibid* 357. Member 1973-78 and Acting Chairman 1977 Civil Aeronautics Board Washington D.C. Instructor University of Oklahoma 1961-62. Ford Foundation Fellow in Law Harvard University 1962-63. Labor Arbitrator National

WEST, LEE R.—*Continued*

Mediation Board 1963-65. Member Pontotoc County (President 1959), Oklahoma and American Bar Associations. Recipient Outstanding Achievement Award from Aero Club of Washington D.C. 1978. Captain USMC 1952-56 (active duty 1952-54). Democrat. Interests include field trials and raising and breeding pointer dogs.

Office: 3001 U.S. Courthouse, 200 N.W. Fourth Street, Oklahoma City 73102.

Telephone: (405) 609-5140.

WHEELER, William W. *(Special Judge, Oklahoma District Court Ninth Judicial District)* Serves Logan County.

Office: 202 Logan County Courthouse, 301 East Harrison Street, Guthrie 73044.

Telephone: (405) 282-6941.

WHITE, April Sellers *(Associate District Judge, Oklahoma District Court Twenty-fourth Judicial District)* Former Special Judge. Serves Creek County.

Office: Creek County Courthouse, 222 East Dewey, Sapulpa 74066.

Telephone: (918) 224-0911.

WILLIAMS, Danita E. *(District Judge, Oklahoma District Court Sixteenth Judicial District)*

Mailing address: P.O. Box 1056, Poteau 74953.

Office: LeFlore County Courthouse, Poteau 74953.

Telephone: (918) 647-3351.

WINCHESTER, James R. *(Justice, Supreme Court of Oklahoma)* Appointed by Governor Frank Keating to term beginning Jan 4, 2000. Educated at University of Oklahoma B.A. and Oklahoma City University J.D. In legal practice Hinton April 1979 to Jan 1983. Associate District Judge Jan 1983 to Dec 1983. District Judge, Sixth Judicial District Dec 1983 to Aug 1997. U.S. Administrative Law Judge Aug 1997 to Jan 2000.

Executive Board Member 1992-96 and President 1995 Oklahoma Judicial Conference. Named Outstanding State Trial Court Judge by Oklahoma Trial Lawyers Association 1986. Member Leadership Oklahoma.

Office: 244 State Capitol, Oklahoma City 73105.

Telephone: (405) 521-3842.

E-mail address: james.winchester@oscn.net

WISEMAN, Jane P. *(District Judge, Oklahoma District Court Fourteenth Judicial District)* Appointed to term beginning Jan 3, 1977. Elected to subsequent terms. Current term expires Jan 2007. Born New Haven Connecticut June 18, 1947. Presbyterian. Educated at Cornell University B.A. 1969, University of North Carolina at Chapel Hill M.A. 1971 and University of Tulsa J.D. 1973. Staff member University of Tulsa Law Journal. Member Moot Court Team and Order of Barristers. Recipient Alumni Award from University of Tulsa Law School and American Jurisprudence Awards in Torts and Property. Admitted to practice Oklahoma 1974. In legal practice Tulsa 1974-77.

Adjunct Professor of Professional Responsibility University of Tulsa 1976-77 and 1986-87. Member Tulsa County, Oklahoma and American Bar Associations.

Office: 506 Tulsa County Courthouse, 500 South Denver Avenue, Tulsa 74103.

Telephone: (918) 596-5360.

WOLKING, John L. *(Special Judge, Oklahoma District Court Twenty-sixth Judicial District)* Serves Canadian County.

Office: Canadian County Courthouse, 201 North Choctaw Avenue, El Reno 73036.

Telephone: (405) 262-1070.

WOODLIFF, Duane A. *(Special Judge, Oklahoma District Court Twenty-fourth Judicial District)* Appointed Jan 16, 2001. Serves Okmulgee County. Born Norman Oklahoma Nov 7, 1941. Educated at University of Oklahoma B.A. 1963 J.D. 1966. Recipient American Jurisprudence Awards in Contracts 1964 and Bills and Notes 1965. Editor Oklahoma Law Review 1964-66 and The Advocate 1965-66. Member Phi Delta Phi. Admitted to practice Oklahoma 1966, U.S. Court of Appeals for the Armed Forces 1966 and U.S. District Court Eastern District of Oklahoma 1971. In legal practice Henryetta 1970 to Jan 16, 2001.

Associate Bar Examiner Seventh Judicial District 1973. Instructor in Business Law University of Maryland 1967-68. Trustee Oklahoma Bar Association Foundation 1989-91. Member Okmulgee County (President 1979) and Oklahoma (Board of Governors 1985-87, Professional Responsibility Tribunal 1987-93) Bar Associations. Named Henryettan of the Year 1976. Recipient Clarence Darrow Award from Oklahoma Criminal Defense Lawyers Association 1985. U.S. Army 1963-70 (Captain JAGC 1966-68). President Henryetta Chamber of Commerce 1975-76. President Henryetta Lions Club 1977. Director Oklahoma State and Education Employees Group Insurance Board 1994-2001.

Mailing address: P.O. Box 995, Okmulgee 74447.

Office: Okmulgee County Courthouse, 314 West Seventh, Okmulgee 74447.

Telephone: (918) 756-1835.

Fax: (918) 756-1839

WOOLERY, Richard A. *(Special Judge, Oklahoma District Court Twenty-fourth Judicial District)* Serves Creek County.

Office: Creek County Courthouse, 222 East Dewey, Sapulpa 74066.

Telephone: (918) 227-4080.

WORTHINGTON, Donald L. *(District Judge, Oklahoma District Court Ninth Judicial District)* Former Judge, Oklahoma Court of Tax Review.

Office: Payne County Courthouse, 606 South Husband, Stillwater 74074.

Telephone: (405) 372-3624.

WRIGLEY, Joseph *(Special Judge, Oklahoma District Court Twenty-second Judicial District)* Serves Seminole County.

Mailing address: P.O. Box 678, Wewoka 74884.

Office: Seminole County Courthouse, Wewoka 74884.

Telephone: (405) 257-2223.

WYATT, Harry M., III *(Associate District Judge, Oklahoma District Court Twelfth Judicial District)* Serves Craig County.

Office: Craig County Courthouse, 301 West Canadian Street, Vinita 74301.

Telephone: (918) 256-2577.

ZACHARIAS, C. Michael *(Special Judge, Oklahoma District Court Fourteenth Judicial District)* Appointed to term beginning Oct 1, 2001. Serves Tulsa County. Born Athol Springs New York May 22, 1939. Catholic. Edu-

ZACHARIAS, C. MICHAEL—*Continued*

cated at University of Tulsa B.S. 1968 J.D. 1970. Managing Editor Tulsa Law Journal 1969-70. Admitted to practice Oklahoma 1971 and U.S. Supreme Court 1986. In legal practice Claremore and Tulsa Feb 1972 to Sept 2001. Referee, Oklahoma Court of Criminal Appeals 1971-72.

Vice President and Member Board of Governors Oklahoma Bar Association 1982-86. Vice Chair Oklahoma Pardon and Parole Board 1994-96.

Office: 118 Tulsa County Courthouse, 500 South Denver, Tulsa 74103.

Telephone: (918) 596-5347.

Fax: (918) 596-4509

E-mail address: Michael.Zacharias@OSCN.NET

ZIGLER, Greg A. *(District Judge, Oklahoma District Court First Judicial District)* Former Associate District Judge.

Office: Texas County Courthouse, 319 North Main Street, Guymon 73942.

Telephone: (580) 338-3412.

OREGON

Capital SALEM

UNITED STATES DISTRICT COURT DISTRICT OF OREGON

The court sits at Coquille, Eugene or Springfield, Klamath Falls, Medford, Pendleton and Portland. For descriptive information refer to the United States Courts section.

Chief Judge
Ancer L. Haggerty

Judges
Michael R. Hogan
Ann L. Aiken
Garr M. King
Anna J. Brown

Senior Judges
Owen M. Panner
James A. Redden
Helen J. Frye
Malcolm F. Marsh
Robert E. Jones

Clerk
Donald M. Cinnamond
740 U.S. Courthouse
1000 Southwest Third Avenue
Portland, Oregon 97204-2902
(503) 326-8000

UNITED STATES MAGISTRATE JUDGES OF OREGON

Stephen M. Bloom	John P. Cooney
John A. Jelderks	Thomas M. Coffin
Donald C. Ashmanskas	Janice M. Stewart
Dennis J. Hubel	

Recalled Magistrate Judge
George E. Juba

UNITED STATES BANKRUPTCY COURT OF OREGON

Chief Judge
Albert E. Radcliffe

Judges
Elizabeth L. Perris
Frank R. Alley, III
Randall Lawson Dunn
Trish M. Brown

Recalled Judge
Donal D. Sullivan

Bankruptcy Clerk
Terence H. Dunn
1001 S.W. Fifth Avenue, Room 700
Portland, Oregon 97204
(503) 326-2231

OREGON SUPREME COURT

The Supreme Court is Oregon's court of last resort. The court consists of a chief justice and six justices elected in statewide nonpartisan elections for six-year terms. Vacancies are filled by the governor until a successor can be elected at the next general election. A chief justice is elected by peer vote for a six-year term. Retired justices may serve as senior judges upon assignment pro tem of the chief justice.

The court may, at its discretion, review any decision of the Court of Appeals and hears all appeals from the Oregon Tax Court. The court has original jurisdiction in mandamus, quo warranto and habeas corpus proceedings and may issue all writs necessary to the exercise of proper jurisdiction. The court has general administrative and supervisory authority over the courts of the state and admission to the bar.

The court may sit en banc or in panels of three to five justices. The court sits at Salem and holds session all year.

Chief Justice
Wallace P. Carson, Jr.

Justices

W. Michael Gillette	Robert D. Durham
R. William Riggs	Paul J. De Muniz
Thomas A. Balmer	vacancy

Case Records Administrator
Scott Crampton
Supreme Court Building
1163 State Street
Salem, Oregon 97301-2563
(503) 986-5550

State Court Administrator
Kingsley W. Click
Supreme Court Building
1163 State Street
Salem, Oregon 97301-2563
(503) 986-5500

OREGON COURT OF APPEALS

The Court of Appeals is Oregon's intermediate appellate court. The court consists of a chief judge and nine judges elected in statewide nonpartisan elections for six-year terms. Vacancies are filled by the governor until a successor can be elected at the next general election. A chief judge is appointed by the chief justice for a two-year term. Retired judges may serve as senior judges upon assignment pro tem of the chief justice.

The court has appellate jurisdiction over all matters from the Circuit Courts, except death penalty cases. The court may issue all writs necessary to the exercise of proper jurisdiction.

OREGON COURT OF APPEALS—*Continued*

The court may sit en banc or in panels of three judges. The court sits at Salem.

Chief Judge
Mary J. Deits

Judges

Walter Edmonds, Jr.	Jack L. Landau
Rick T. Haselton	Rex Armstrong
Virginia L. Linder	Robert Wollheim
Rives Kistler	David Brewer
David Schuman	

OREGON TAX COURT

The Tax Court is a court of special statewide jurisdiction in Oregon. As of September 1, 1997, the Tax Court consists of two divisions: the Regular Division and the Magistrate Division. The Regular Division consists of a single judge elected on a statewide nonpartisan ballot for a six-year term. A vacancy is filled by the governor until a successor can be elected at the next general election. The Magistrate Division consists of one presiding magistrate and one or more magistrates appointed by the Tax Court judge. Retired judges may serve as senior judges upon assignment pro tem of the chief justice.

The court has original jurisdiction over cases involving state tax laws including personal income taxes, corporate excise and income taxes, timber taxes, real and personal property taxes, inheritance taxes and gift taxes. The court hears cases involving certain tax refunds not exceeding $5,000, additional taxes or taxes assessed when no return was filed, refunds in homestead and rental assistance cases, and proceedings filed by taxpayers when cash values do not exceed $250,000 for real or personal property. Magistrate Division trials are informal proceedings and are not reported. Statutory rules of evidence do not apply. Magistrate decisions in small claims procedures are final while all other decisions may be appealed to the Regular Division. Appeals from the Regular Division go directly to the Supreme Court.

The court sits primarily at Salem, but may conduct trials at any county seat.

Judge
Henry C. Breithaupt

OREGON CIRCUIT COURTS

The Circuit Courts are Oregon's courts of general trial jurisdiction. The state is divided into twenty-seven judicial districts. On January 15, 1998, the district courts were abolished and all jurisdiction, authority, power, function and duties were transferred to the circuit courts. Judges are elected from their respective districts in nonpartisan elections for six-year terms. Vacancies are filled by the governor until a successor can be elected at the next general election. Presiding judges are appointed by the chief justice for two-year terms. Retired judges may serve as senior judges upon assignment pro tem of the chief justice.

The courts have general jurisdiction over all civil and criminal matters not exclusively reserved for some other court. The courts exercise juvenile and probate jurisdiction except in those counties where special courts or County Courts have jurisdiction. In Marion and Multnomah counties, separate court-established departments hear domestic relations and juvenile cases. Multnomah County also has a separate probate department. The courts exercise appellate jurisdiction over Justice Courts, Municipal Courts and County Courts. Appeals are to the Court of Appeals.

The courts sit at each county seat.

FIRST JUDICIAL DISTRICT includes Jackson County. The court sits at Medford.

Presiding Judge
Mark Schiveley

Judges

Philip Arnold	Patricia Crain
Daniel L. Harris	Lorenzo A. Mejia
Rebecca G. Orf	William G. Purdy
Raymond B. White	

SECOND JUDICIAL DISTRICT includes Lane County. The court sits at Eugene.

Presiding Judge
Mary Ann Bearden

Judges

Jack A. Billings	Charles D. Carlson
Cynthia Carlson	Ted Carp
Gregory G. Foote	Eveleen Henry
Bryan T. Hodges	Lauren S. Holland
Darryl Larson	Kip W. Leonard
Maurice K. Merten	Douglas S. Mitchell
Karsten H. Rasmussen	Lyle C. Velure

THIRD JUDICIAL DISTRICT includes Marion County. The court sits at Salem.

Presiding Judge
Paul J. Lipscomb

Judges

Pamela L. Abernethy	Richard D. Barber
Don A. Dickey	Dennis Graves
Joseph C. Guimond	Thomas M. Hart
Terry Ann Leggert	Albin W. Norblad
Joseph V. Ochoa	Jamese L. Rhoades
Susan M. Tripp	C. Gregory West
John B. Wilson	

FOURTH JUDICIAL DISTRICT includes Multnomah County. The court sits at Portland.

Presiding Judge
Dale R. Koch

Judges

Marshall L. Amiton	Dorothy Baker
Richard C. Baldwin	Frank L. Bearden
Douglas Beckman	Linda L. Bergman
Eric J. Bloch	Ronald E. Cinniger
Kimberly C. Frankel	Julie Frantz
Clifford L. Freeman	Alicia A. Fuchs
Sid A. Galton	David Gernant
Nely L. Johnson	Edward Jones
Henry Kantor	Paula Kurshner
Jerome E. LaBarre	Kristena A. LaMar
Marilyn Litzenberger	Michael S. Loy
Michael H. Marcus	Christopher J. Marshall
Jean Kerr Maurer	Maureen H. McKnight
Michael McShane	Keith E. Meisenheimer
Ellen F. Rosenblum	Susan M. Svetkey
Katherine Tennyson	Nan G. Waller

OREGON CIRCUIT COURTS—*Continued*

Elizabeth Welch
John Wittmayer
Jan G. Wyers
Janice R. Wilson
Merri S. Wyatt

FIFTH JUDICIAL DISTRICT includes Clackamas County. The court sits at Oregon City.

Presiding Judge
Robert R. Selander

Judges
Deanne L. Darling
Robert D. Herndon
Steven L. Maurer
Ronald D. Thom
vacancy
Patrick D. Gilroy
John K. Lowe
Eve L. Miller
Douglas Van Dyk

SIXTH JUDICIAL DISTRICT includes Morrow and Umatilla counties. The court sits at Heppner and Pendleton.

Presiding Judge
Jeff M. Wallace

Judges
Rudy Murgo
Ronald J. Pahl
Garry L. Reynolds

SEVENTH JUDICIAL DISTRICT includes Gilliam, Hood River, Sherman, Wasco and Wheeler counties. The court sits at Condon, Hood River, Moro, The Dalles and Fossil.

Presiding Judge
Paul G. Crowley

Judges
Donald W. Hull
John V. Kelly
Bernard Smith

EIGHTH JUDICIAL DISTRICT includes Baker County. The court sits at Baker City.

Presiding Judge
Gregory L. Baxter

NINTH JUDICIAL DISTRICT includes Malheur County. The court sits at Vale.

Presiding Judge
J. Burdette Pratt

Judge
Patricia Sullivan

TENTH JUDICIAL DISTRICT includes Union and Wallowa counties. The court sits at La Grande and Enterprise.

Presiding Judge
Phillip A. Mendiguren

Judge
Russell B. West

ELEVENTH JUDICIAL DISTRICT includes Deschutes County. The court sits at Bend.

Presiding Judge
Stephen Tiktin

Judges
Michael Adler
Alta J. Brady
Barbara Haslinger
Edward L. Perkins
Michael Cornelius Sullivan

TWELFTH JUDICIAL DISTRICT includes Polk County. The court sits at Dallas.

Presiding Judge
Charles Luukinen

Judges
Fred E. Avera
William M. Horner

THIRTEENTH JUDICIAL DISTRICT includes Klamath County. The court sits at Klamath Falls.

Presiding Judge
Cameron F. Wogan

Judges
Rodger J. Isaacson
Karla J. Knieps
Roxanne B. Osborne
Richard B. Rambo

FOURTEENTH JUDICIAL DISTRICT includes Josephine County. The court sits at Grants Pass.

Presiding Judge
Gerald C. Neufeld

Judges
Allan H. Coon
William J. Mackay
Loyd O'Neal

FIFTEENTH JUDICIAL DISTRICT includes Coos and Curry counties. The court sits at Coquille and Gold Beach.

Presiding Judge
Richard L. Barron

Judges
Paula Bechtold
Hugh C. Downer, Jr.
Michael J. Gillespie
Richard K. Mickelson
Martin E. Stone

SIXTEENTH JUDICIAL DISTRICT includes Douglas County. The court sits at Roseburg.

Presiding Judge
Joan G. Seitz

Judges
Thomas W. Kolberg
William L. Lasswell
Robert C. Millikan
Ronald Poole

SEVENTEENTH JUDICIAL DISTRICT includes Lincoln County. The court sits at Newport.

Presiding Judge
Robert James Huckleberry

Judges
Thomas O. Branford
Charles P. Littlehales

OREGON CIRCUIT COURTS—*Continued*

EIGHTEENTH JUDICIAL DISTRICT includes Clatsop County. The court sits at Astoria.

Presiding Judge
Paula J. Brownhill

Judge
Philip L. Nelson

NINETEENTH JUDICIAL DISTRICT includes Columbia County. The court sits at St. Helens.

Presiding Judge
Berkeley A. Smith

Judges
Ted E. Grove
Steven B. Reed

TWENTIETH JUDICIAL DISTRICT includes Washington County. The court sits at Hillsboro.

Presiding Judge
Marco Hernandez

Judges
Timothy P. Alexander
Mark Gardner
Donald R. Letourneau
Michael J. McElligott
Steven L. Price
Kirsten E. Thompson
Nancy W. Campbell
Thomas W. Kohl
John B. Lewis
Gayle Nachtigal
Keith R. Raines
Suzanne M. Upton

TWENTY-FIRST JUDICIAL DISTRICT includes Benton County. The court sits at Corvallis.

Presiding Judge
Janet S. Holcomb

Judges
Henry R. Dickerson, Jr.
Locke A. Williams

TWENTY-SECOND JUDICIAL DISTRICT includes Crook and Jefferson counties. The court sits at Prineville and Madras.

Presiding Judge
George W. Neilson

Judges
Daniel J. Ahern
Gary S. Thompson

TWENTY-THIRD JUDICIAL DISTRICT includes Linn County. The court sits at Albany.

Presiding Judge
Rick J. McCormick

Judges
Glen D. Baisinger
Carol R. Bispham
John A. McCormick
Daniel R. Murphy

TWENTY-FOURTH JUDICIAL DISTRICT includes Grant and Harney counties. The court sits at Canyon City and Burns.

Presiding Judge
William D. Cramer, Jr.

TWENTY-FIFTH JUDICIAL DISTRICT includes Yamhill County. The court sits at McMinnville.

Presiding Judge
John L. Collins

Judges
John W. Hitchcock
Ronald W. Stone
Carroll J. Tichenor

TWENTY-SIXTH JUDICIAL DISTRICT includes Lake County. The court sits at Lakeview.

Presiding Judge
Lane W. Simpson

TWENTY-SEVENTH JUDICIAL DISTRICT includes Tillamook County. The court sits at Tillamook.

Presiding Judge
David W. Hantke

Judge
Richard Roll

OREGON JUSTICE COURTS

The Justice Courts are courts of limited jurisdiction in Oregon. Justices are elected from their respective counties in nonpartisan elections for terms of varying lengths. Justices are not required to be attorneys.

The courts have jurisdiction over civil matters, including small claims jurisdiction, when the amount in controversy does not exceed $2,500, except in actions involving title to real property, false imprisonment, libel, slander or malicious prosecution. The courts have concurrent statutory jurisdiction over all criminal and civil and traffic offenses with the Circuit Court, except for presentation of felony trials. The courts can act as municipal courts as well. Appeals are to the Circuit Courts.

The courts sit in various places throughout the county.

County	Justice of the Peace
Baker	Larry D. Cole
	Yvonne Riggs
	Beverly C. Robertson
Columbia	Rod B. McLean
Deschutes	Stephen P. Forte
Douglas	Candace Hissong
	Carol Roberts
	Russell G. Trump
Gilliam	Cris Patnode
Grant	Terry Farrell
Harney	Dewey A. Newton
Hood River	Roberta K. Lee
Jackson	Robert H. King, Jr.
Klamath	Alfred L. Edgar
Lane	Cindy L. Cable
	Sheila M. Nelson
	Cynthia Sinclair
Linn	Jad Lemhouse
	Richard E. Triska
Malheur	Terry Thompson
Marion	Steven R. Summers
	Janice D. Zyryanoff
Morrow	Charlotte S. Gray
Sherman	Ronald McDermid

OREGON JUSTICE COURTS—*Continued*

Tillamook	Neal C. Lemery
Washington	James R. Shartel
Wheeler	Linda Keys
	Theressa W. Ward

OREGON COUNTY COURTS

County Courts are courts of limited jurisdiction established in seven counties of Oregon. The judges are county commissioners elected for six-year terms by the voters of their respective districts.

The courts have original jurisdiction over all probate matters in Gilliam, Grant, Harney, Malheur, Sherman and Wheeler counties. The courts have juvenile jurisdiction in Gilliam, Morrow, Sherman and Wheeler counties. The courts may grant preliminary injunctions or orders for any suit commenced in a Circuit Court for the county. Appeals are to the Circuit Courts.

The courts sit at the county seats.

OREGON MUNICIPAL COURTS

The Municipal Courts are courts of limited jurisdiction in Oregon. Judges may be either appointed by the city council or elected by the voters of the respective city. Terms of office vary among municipalities. Judges need not be lawyers.

The courts have jurisdiction over violations of municipal ordinances within their respective cities. The courts have concurrent jurisdiction with the District Courts over state liquor law violations and with the Justice Courts over misdemeanor state traffic offenses within municipal boundaries. Appeals are to the Circuit Courts.

Oregon Counties and County Seats

Baker
Baker City

Benton
Corvallis

Clackamas
Oregon City

Clatsop
Astoria

Columbia
St. Helens

Coos
Coquille

Crook
Prineville

Curry
Gold Beach

Deschutes
Bend

Douglas
Roseburg

Gilliam
Condon

Grant
Canyon City

Harney
Burns

Hood River
Hood River

Jackson
Medford

Jefferson
Madras

Josephine
Grants Pass

Klamath
Klamath Falls

Lake
Lakeview

Lane
Eugene

Lincoln
Newport

Linn
Albany

Malheur
Vale

Marion
Salem

Morrow
Heppner

Multnomah
Portland

Polk
Dallas

Sherman
Moro

Tillamook
Tillamook

Umatilla
Pendleton

Union
La Grande

Wallowa
Enterprise

Wasco
The Dalles

Washington
Hillsboro

Wheeler
Fossil

Yamhill
McMinnville

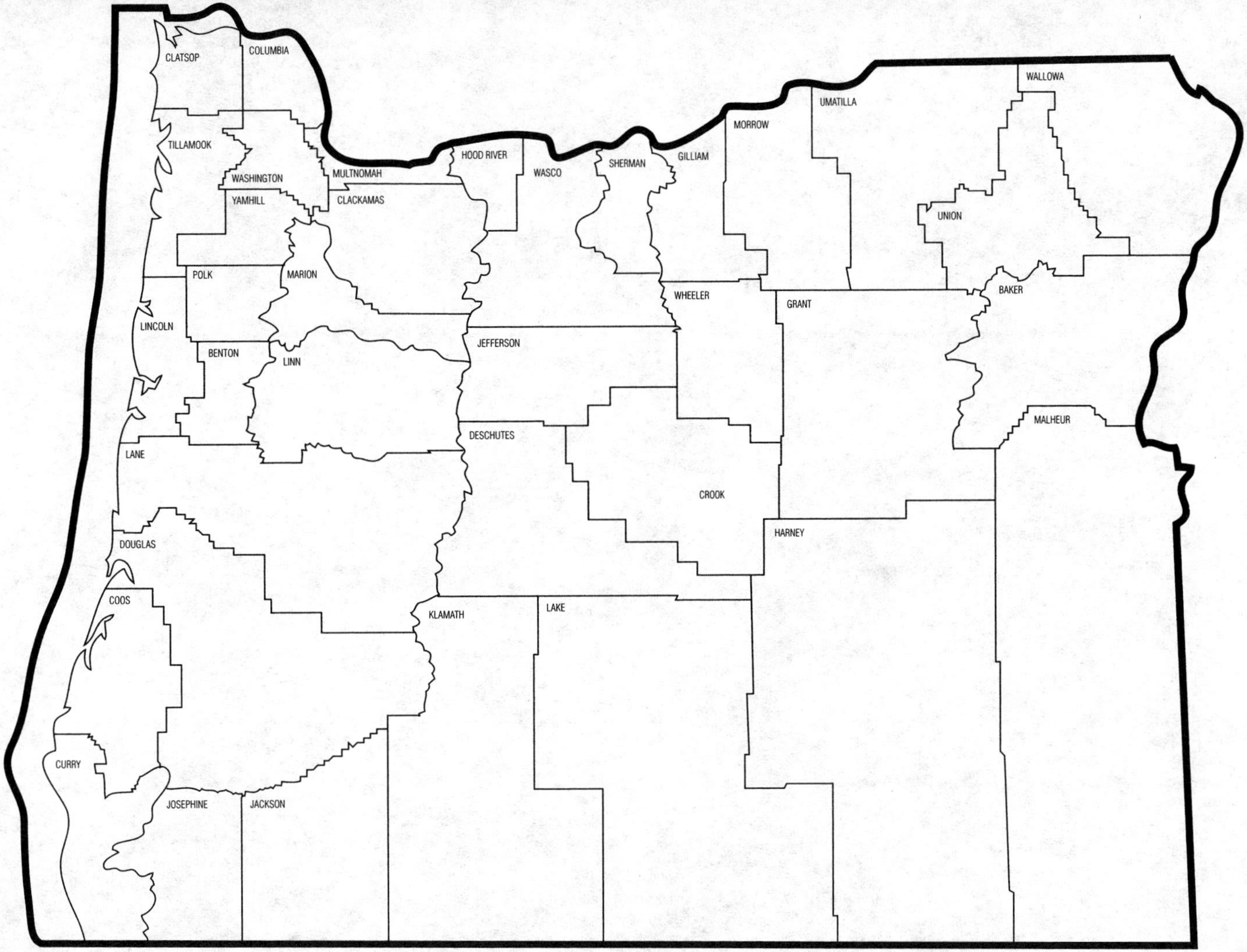
CLATSOP
COLUMBIA
TILLAMOOK
WASHINGTON
MULTNOMAH
YAMHILL
CLACKAMAS
HOOD RIVER
WASCO
SHERMAN
GILLIAM
MORROW
UMATILLA
WALLOWA
UNION
POLK
MARION
LINCOLN
BENTON
LINN
WHEELER
GRANT
BAKER
JEFFERSON
LANE
DESCHUTES
CROOK
MALHEUR
HARNEY
DOUGLAS
COOS
KLAMATH
LAKE
CURRY
JOSEPHINE
JACKSON

UNITED STATES DISTRICT COURT DISTRICT OF OREGON

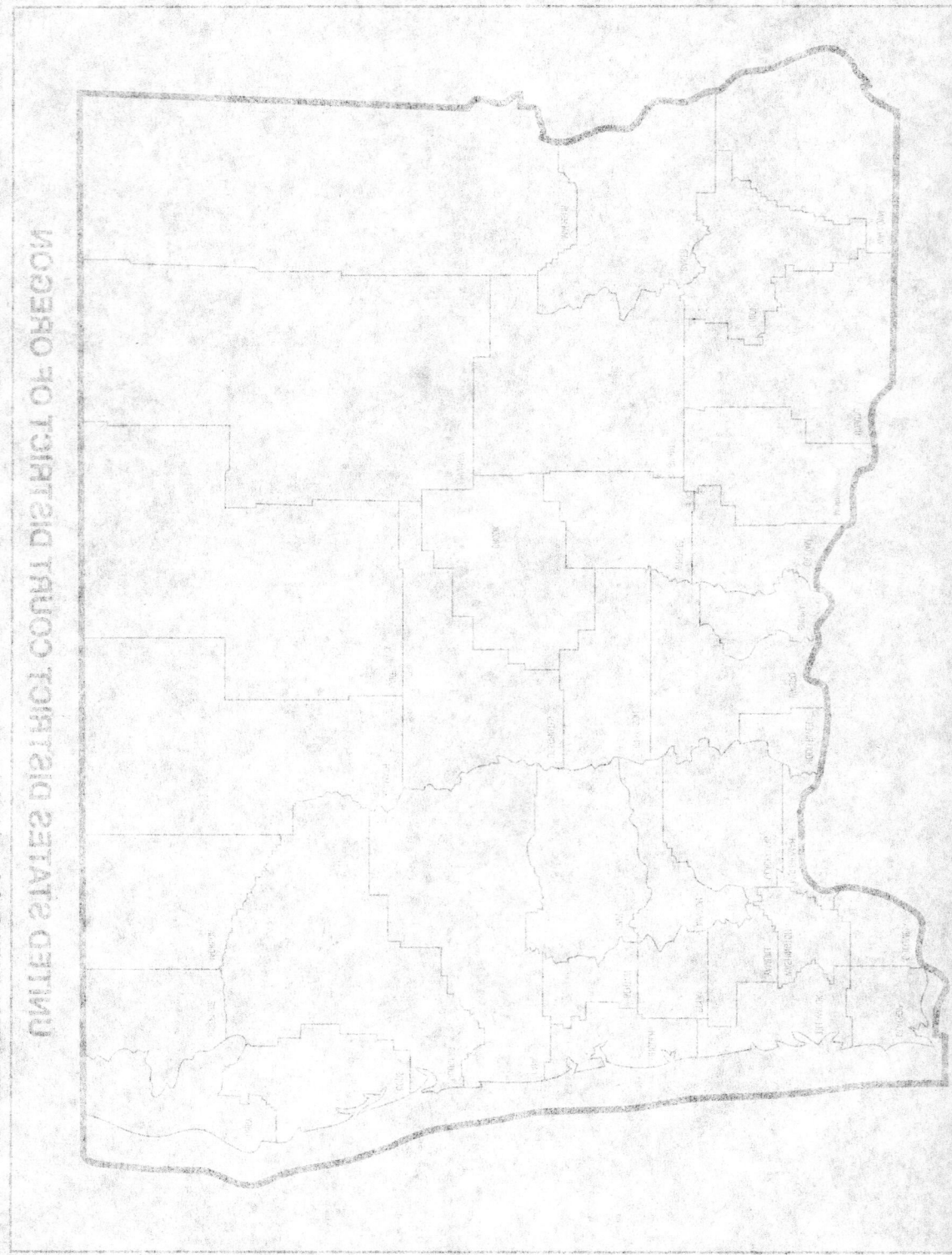

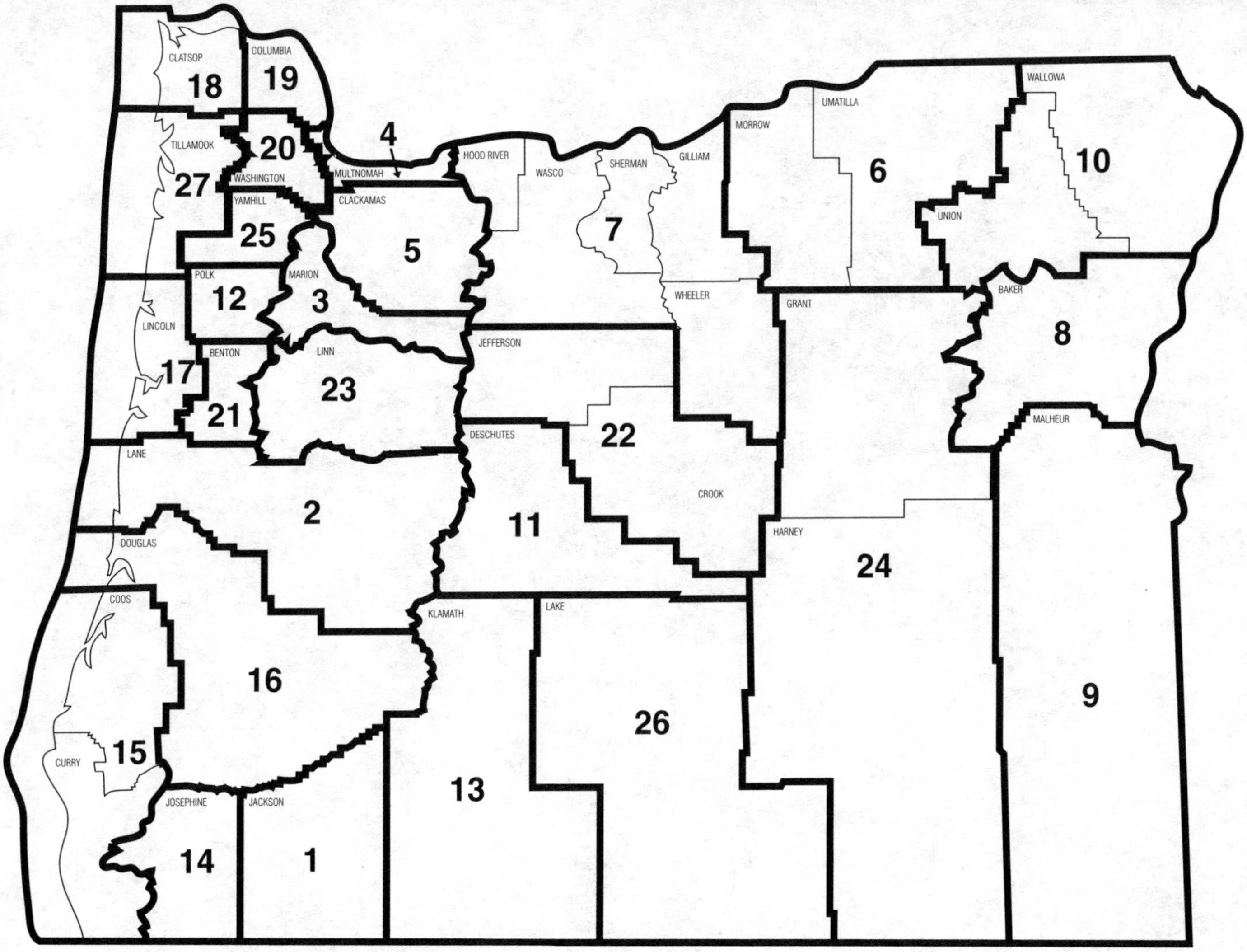
CLATSOP
18
COLUMBIA
19
TILLAMOOK
20
27
WASHINGTON
4
MULTNOMAH
YAMHILL
CLACKAMAS
25
5
POLK
12
MARION
3
LINCOLN
BENTON
LINN
17
23
21
LANE
2
DOUGLAS
COOS
16
15
CURRY
JOSEPHINE
JACKSON
14
1
HOOD RIVER
WASCO
SHERMAN
GILLIAM
7
WHEELER
JEFFERSON
DESCHUTES
22
CROOK
11
KLAMATH
13
LAKE
26
MORROW
UMATILLA
6
WALLOWA
10
UNION
BAKER
8
GRANT
MALHEUR
HARNEY
24
9

JUDICIAL DISTRICTS OF OREGON CIRCUIT COURTS

OREGON

ABERNETHY, Pamela L. *(Judge, Oregon Circuit Court Third Judicial District)* Appointed by governor Jan 1, 1995. Elected Nov 1996 and 2002. Current term expires Jan 5, 2009. Educated at University of California at Santa Cruz B.A. with honors 1973 and Willamette University College of Law J.D. cum laude 1980. Comments Editor Willamette Law Review. Admitted to practice Oregon and U.S. District Court District of Oregon. Judge, Marion County District Court Jan 4, 1993 to Dec 31, 1994, appointed by Governor Barbara Roberts.

Assistant Attorney General Trial Division 1981-84, Attorney-in-Charge Education and Human Services Section General Counsel Division 1984-86 and Special Litigation Unit Trial Division 1986-89 and Special Counsel to the Attorney General 1989-91 Oregon Department of Justice. Editor and Contributor *Oregon Attorney General's Public Records and Meetings Manual* 1989. Contributing Author Chapter on Institutional Litigation *The Office of Attorney General: Powers and Duties* Bureau of National Affairs 1990. Adjunct Professor of Trial Practice Willamette University since 1990. Former Member National Association of College and University Attorneys and Federal Bar Association. Chair Oregon Future of the Courts Committee. Toll Fellow Class of 2000 Council of State Governments. Member Oregon Women Lawyers Association, American Judges Association, Oregon State Bar (Former Chair Federal Practice and Procedure Committee) and Marion County Bar Association. Speaker "Trial Advocacy for Women: Complex Litigation" Oregon Law Institute 1985, "The School as a Community: Trends in National and Oregon Education Law" Oregon Department of Education Personnel Management Advisory Counsel 1986, "Conflicts in the Office of Attorney General" Annual Meeting Conference of the Western Attorneys General 1990, "Developments in Oregon Public Records Law" Government Law Section Oregon State Bar 1992, "Understanding the Indian Gaming Regulatory Act" Oregon Conference on Organized Crime 1992, "Indian Gaming Regulatory Act" Governor's Commission on Organized Crime 1992, "Future of the Oregon Courts—Preferred Scenario" Annual Meeting Oregon State Bar 1993 and "The Judicial Response to Non-Stranger Rape" Oregon District Judges Association 1994. Organizer, Moderator and Contributor "Ethics for Government Lawyers" Oregon Department of Justice 1989. Panelist "Americans with Disabilities Act" Civil Rights Section Oregon State Bar 1993. Recipient Meritorious Service Awards from Oregon Department of Justice 1983, 1984 and 1985. Field Volunteer 1965-66 and Mentor 1991-94 Amigos de Las Americas (immunization clinic in rural Guatemala). Counselor and Staff Trainer Trailblazer Camps (outdoor education program for inner city children) 1971-76 and 1978. Actress and Director Pentacle Theatre since 1982 (President and Board of Directors 1985-86 and 1992).

Mailing address: P.O. Box 12869, Salem 97309-0869.

Office: Marion County Courthouse, 100 High Street N.E., Salem 97301-3665.

Telephone: (503) 588-5051.

ADLER, Michael *(Judge, Oregon Circuit Court Eleventh Judicial District)* Term expires Jan 3, 2005.

Office: Deschutes County Courthouse, 1164 N.W. Bond, Bend 97701.

Telephone: (541) 388-5300.

AHERN, Daniel J. *(Judge, Oregon Circuit Court Twenty-second Judicial District)* Term expires Jan 5, 2009.

Office: Jefferson County Courthouse, 75 S.E. C Street, Madras 97741-1794.

Telephone: (541) 475-3317.

AIKEN, Ann L. *(Judge, United States District Court District of Oregon)* Appointed for life by President Bill Clinton to term beginning 1998. Born Salem Oregon Dec 29, 1951. Educated at University of Oregon B.S. 1974 J.D. 1979 and Rutgers University M.A. 1976. Law Clerk to Hon. Edwin E. Allen, Oregon Circuit Court Second Judicial District 1979-80. In legal practice 1980-82 and 1983-88. Judge, Lane County District Court 1988-92. Judge, Oregon Circuit Court Second Judicial District 1992-97.

Fundraiser/Field Staff Kulongoski for Governor 1982. Chief Clerk Oregon House of Representatives 1982-83.

Office: 286 Federal Building, 211 East Seventh Avenue, Eugene 97401.

Telephone: (541) 465-6409.

ALEXANDER, Timothy P. *(Judge, Oregon Circuit Court Twentieth Judicial District)* Term expires Jan 5, 2009. Former Presiding Judge.

Office: Washington County Courthouse, 150 North First, Hillsboro 97124.

Telephone: (503) 846-8772.

ALLEY, Frank R., III *(Judge, United States Bankruptcy Court District of Oregon)* Appointed by U.S. Court of Appeals Ninth Circuit judges.

Office: 151 West Seventh Avenue, Suite 300, Eugene 97401-2649.

Telephone: (541) 465-6767.

AMITON, Marshall L. *(Judge, Oregon Circuit Court Fourth Judicial District)* Term expires Jan 1, 2007. Born Portland Oregon April 9, 1945. Educated at Portland State University B.S. 1967 and Willamette University J.D. 1970. Admitted to practice Oregon 1970. In legal practice Portland 1970-85. Former Judge, Multnomah County District Court, appointed by Governor Victor Atiyeh to term beginning Jan 1985.

Member Oregon State Bar and Multnomah County Bar Association.

Office: Multnomah County Courthouse, 1021 S.W. Fourth, Portland 97204.

Telephone: (503) 988-3068.

ARMSTRONG, Rex *(Judge, Oregon Court of Appeals)* Elected Nov 1994 to term beginning Jan 3, 1995. Reelected May 2000, current term expires Jan 2007. Born Salem Oregon Feb 25, 1950. Educated at University of Pennsylvania B.A. cum laude 1974 and University of Oregon School of Law J.D. 1977. Managing Editor Oregon Law Review 1976-77. Law Clerk to Hon. Hans

ARMSTRONG, REX—*Continued*

A. Linde, Oregon Supreme Court 1977-78. Admitted to practice Oregon 1977, U.S. District Court District of Oregon 1978, U.S. Court of Appeals Ninth Circuit 1978 and U.S. Supreme Court 1980. In legal practice Portland 1978-94.

Author "Probing the Limits of Legislative Power" 56 Oregon L. Rev. 386, 1977; "Free Speech Fundamentalism" 70 Oregon L. Rev. 855; and "State Court Federalism" 30 Valparaiso University L. Rev. 493, 1996. Adjunct Professor of Legal Research Willamette University College of Law 1978 and Constitutional Theory Northwestern School of Law 1987. Member Oregon State Bar, Multnomah and American Bar Associations. Recipient Hugh M. Hefner First Amendment Award from Playboy Foundation 1988. Member Families with Children from China. Enjoys skiing, hiking and mountain climbing.

Office: Justice Building, Third Floor, 1162 Court Street N.E., Salem 97301-4095.

Telephone: (503) 986-5664.

ARNOLD, Philip *(Judge, Oregon Circuit Court First Judicial District)* Term expires Jan 3, 2005.

Office: Justice Building, 100 South Oakdale, Medford 97501.

Telephone: (541) 776-7171.

ASHMANSKAS, Donald C. *(Magistrate Judge, United States District Court District of Oregon)* Appointed by U.S. District Court judges to term beginning Sept 24, 1992. Reappointed Sept 24, 2000, current term expires Sept 23, 2008. Born Boston Massachusetts Aug 26, 1935. Educated at Boston College, University of Maine, Rutgers University B.A. 1960 and New York University J.D. 1966. Judge, Washington County District Court 1975-77. Judge, Oregon Circuit Court Twentieth Judicial District 1977-92.

Office: 1127 U.S. Courthouse, 1000 S.W. Third Avenue, Portland 97204-2902.

Telephone: (503) 326-8280.

AVERA, Fred E. *(Judge, Oregon Circuit Court Twelfth Judicial District)* Term expires Jan 3, 2005.

Office: Polk County Courthouse, 850 Main Street, Dallas 97338.

Telephone: (503) 623-5235.

BAISINGER, Glen D. *(Judge, Oregon Circuit Court Twenty-third Judicial District)* Assumed office Jan 15, 1998. Elected May 2000, current term expires Jan 1, 2007. Former Judge, Linn County District Court.

Mailing address: P.O. Box 1749, Albany 97321.

Telephone: (541) 967-3844.

BAKER, Dorothy *(Judge, Oregon Circuit Court Fourth Judicial District)* Assumed office Jan 15, 1998. Elected May 2000, current term expires Jan 1, 2007. Former Judge, Multnomah County District Court.

Office: Multnomah County Courthouse, 1021 S.W. Fourth, Portland 97204.

Telephone: (503) 988-3062.

BALDWIN, Richard C. *(Judge, Oregon Circuit Court Fourth Judicial District)* Term expires Jan 5, 2009.

Office: Multnomah County Courthouse, 1021 S.W. Fourth, Portland 97204.

Telephone: (503) 988-3052.

BALMER, Thomas A. *(Justice, Oregon Supreme Court)* Assumed office Sept 2001. Educated at Oberlin College B.A. 1974 and University of Chicago Law School J.D. 1977. In legal practice Boston Massachusetts 1977-79, Washington D.C. 1980-82 and Portland Oregon 1982-93 and 1997-2001.

Trial Attorney Antitrust Division U.S. Department of Justice 1979-80. Deputy Attorney General Oregon 1993-97. Adjunct Professor of Law Northwestern University School of Law. Member Advisory Committee Campaign for Equal Justice since 1992. Board Member 1989-93 and Chair 1992-93 Multnomah County Legal Aide Service, Inc. Board Member Chamber Music Northwest since 1998 and Classroom Law Project since 2000.

Office: Supreme Court Building, 1163 State Street, Salem 97301-2562.

Telephone: (503) 986-5717.

BARBER, Richard D. *(Judge, Oregon Circuit Court Third Judicial District)* Elected to term beginning Sept 2, 1974. Reelected 1980, 1986, 1992 and 1998. Current term expires Jan 3, 2005. Born Corvallis Oregon July 4, 1928. Educated at University of Oregon B.S. 1952 and Willamette University J.D. 1955. Admitted to practice Oregon 1955. Began legal practice Salem 1955. Judge pro tem, Municipal Court 1967-74. Judge pro tem, Oregon District Court 1967-74. Judge pro tem, Oregon Circuit Court 1972.

Important Decision: State v. John J. Rideout (first rape case brought by wife against husband while cohabiting) 1979. Instructor Willamette University Law School 1957 and 1960. Member Oregon Circuit Judges Association (President 1985), Oregon State Bar, Marion County (President 1970) and American Bar Associations. Petty Officer Third Class USN 1946-48. Republican. Enjoys music and golf.

Mailing address: P.O. Box 12869, Salem 97309-0869.

Office: Marion County Courthouse, 100 High Street N.E., Salem 97301.

Telephone: (503) 588-5033.

BARRON, Richard L. *(Presiding Judge, Oregon Circuit Court Fifteenth Judicial District)* Term expires Jan 3, 2005.

Office: Coos County Courthouse, 250 North Baxter, Coquille 97423.

Telephone: (541) 396-3121.

BAXTER, Gregory L. *(Presiding Judge, Oregon Circuit Court Eighth Judicial District)* Elected May 2000. Term expires Jan 1, 2007.

Office: Baker County Courthouse, Baker City 97814.

Telephone: (541) 523-6303.

BEARDEN, Frank L. *(Judge, Oregon Circuit Court Fourth Judicial District)* Term expires Jan 1, 2007. Born Pasadena California Dec 4, 1941. Educated at University of the Pacific B.A. 1963 and University of Denver J.D. 1966. Admitted to practice Oregon 1971, U.S. District Court District of Oregon 1974, U.S. Court of Appeals Ninth Circuit 1974 and U.S. Supreme Court 1977. Began legal practice Portland 1971. Former Judge, Multnomah County District Court.

Assistant Chief Deputy District Attorney Portland 1971-77. President District Judges Association 1987. Member Oregon District Judges Association (Past President), American Judges Association, Oregon State Bar and Multnomah County Bar Association. Political affiliation: Independent. Member Citizens for Docks Commit-

BEARDEN, FRANK L.—*Continued*
tee and Committee on Detention and Corrections. Enjoys skiing, running and playing golf.
Office: Multnomah County Courthouse, 1021 S.W. Fourth, Portland 97204.
Telephone: (503) 988-3803.

BEARDEN, Mary Ann *(Presiding Judge, Oregon Circuit Court Second Judicial District)* Term expires Jan 3, 2005.
Office: Lane County Courthouse, 125 East Eighth, Eugene 97401.
Telephone: (541) 682-4240.

BECHTOLD, Paula *(Judge, Oregon Circuit Court Fifteenth Judicial District)* Assumed office Jan 15, 1998. Elected May 2000, current term expires Jan 1, 2007. Judge, Coos County District Court Jan 1, 1995 to Jan 14, 1998.
Office: Coos County Courthouse, 250 North Baxter, Coquille 97423.
Telephone: (541) 756-2020.

BECKMAN, Douglas *(Judge, Oregon Circuit Court Fourth Judicial District)* Assumed office Jan 15, 1998. Elected May 2000, current term expires Jan 1, 2007. Former Judge, Multnomah County District Court.
Office: Multnomah County Courthouse, 1021 S.W. Fourth, Portland 97204.
Telephone: (503) 988-3201.

BERGMAN, Linda L. *(Judge, Oregon Circuit Court Fourth Judicial District)* Appointed by Governor Neil Goldschmidt Dec 1988. Elected 1990, 1996 and 2002. Current term expires Jan 5, 2009. Also serves as Chief Judge, Juvenile Court since May 1988. Born Elyria Ohio Jan 4, 1947. Protestant. Educated at University of Oklahoma B.A. 1970 and Lewis & Clark College Northwestern School of Law J.D. 1974. Admitted to practice Oregon 1974. Began legal practice Portland 1974. Former Judge, Multnomah County District Court, appointed by Governor Victor Atiyeh Jan 1980.
Instructor Lewis & Clark College Northwestern School of Law since 1980. Master American Inns of Court. Board member Oregon Law Related Education, Children & Youth Services Commission and Oregon Council on Alcoholism and Drug Addiction. Member Children's Justice Task Force 1990-91, Judicial Fitness Commission, Oregon Judicial Conference (Chair Judicial Conduct Committee 1985-88), National Association of Women Judges, Oregon Law Foundation (Secretary-Treasurer 1983-84, Second Vice President 1984-85, Chair 1986-87) and Oregon State Bar. Member Oregon Women's Political Caucus and National Women's Political Caucus. Board of Directors Our New Beginnings since 1983. Member Multnomah County Chemical Dependency Committee 1984-87.
Office: Multnomah County Courthouse, 1021 S.W. Fourth, Portland 97204.
Telephone: (503) 988-3041.

BILLINGS, Jack A. *(Judge, Oregon Circuit Court Second Judicial District)* Term expires Jan 5, 2009. Former Judge, Lane County District Court.
Office: Lane County Courthouse, 125 East Eighth, Eugene 97401.
Telephone: (541) 682-4250.

BISPHAM, Carol R. *(Judge, Oregon Circuit Court Twenty-third Judicial District)* Term expires Jan 3, 2005.
Mailing address: P.O. Box 1749, Albany 97321.
Telephone: (541) 967-3848.

BLOCH, Eric J. *(Judge, Oregon Circuit Court Fourth Judicial District)* Term expires Jan 3, 2005.
Office: Multnomah County Courthouse, 1021 S.W. Fourth, Portland 97204.
Telephone: (503) 988-3954.

BLOOM, Stephen M. *(Magistrate Judge, United States District Court District of Oregon)* Appointed by U.S. District Court judges to term beginning Oct 1, 1988. Reappointed 1992, 1996 and 2000. Current term expires 2004. Serves part time. Born San Francisco California June 10, 1948. Educated at Dartmouth College B.A. 1970, Stanford University and Willamette University 1977. Staff member Willamette Law Review. Admitted to practice Oregon 1977. USNR.
Mailing address: P.O. Box 490, Pendleton 97801-0490.
Telephone: (541) 276-2141.

BRADY, Alta J. *(Judge, Oregon Circuit Court Eleventh Judicial District)* Term expires Jan 1, 2007.
Office: Deschutes County Courthouse, 1164 N.W. Bond, Bend 97701.
Telephone: (541) 388-5300.

BRANFORD, Thomas O. *(Judge, Oregon Circuit Court Seventeenth Judicial District)* Assumed office Jan 15, 1998. Elected May 2000, current term expires Jan 1, 2007. Former Judge, Lincoln County District Court.
Mailing address: P.O. Box 100, Newport 97365.
Office: Lincoln County Courthouse, 225 West Olive, Newport 97365.
Telephone: (541) 265-4236.

BREITHAUPT, Henry C. *(Judge, Oregon Tax Court)*
Office: Robertson Building, Fourth Floor, 1241 State Street, Salem 97301.
Telephone: (503) 986-5645.

BREWER, David *(Judge, Oregon Court of Appeals)* Assumed office 1999. Elected Nov 2000, current term expires Jan 2007. Former Judge, Oregon Circuit Court Second Judicial District.
Office: Justice Building, Third Floor, 1162 Court Street N.E., Salem 97301-4095.
Telephone: (503) 986-5662.

BROWN, Anna J. *(Judge, United States District Court District of Oregon)* Appointed for life by President Bill Clinton to term beginning Oct 27, 1999. Born Portland Oregon 1952. Educated at Portland State University B.S. 1975 and Northwestern School of Law of Lewis & Clark College J.D. 1980. Recipient American Jurisprudence Award in Wills and Trusts. Admitted to practice Oregon 1980. Former Arbitrator, Oregon Circuit Court Fourth Judicial District. Former Judge, Multnomah County District Court. Former Judge, Oregon Circuit Court Fourth Judicial District.
Author "Homeowners Insurance" 2 *Insurance* 1986 and "Evidence in Summary Judgment Actions" 1986 CLE Oregon State Bar. Member Oregon State Bar (Member 1982-86, Secretary 1984-85 and Chairman 1985-86 Function and Organization Committee, Secretary 1987-88 and Chair 1988-89 Uniform Civil Jury In-

BROWN, ANNA J.—*Continued*

struction Committee), Multnomah County (Treasurer Young Lawyers Section 1984-85, Chairman Circuit Court Liaison Committee 1987-88) and American (State Membership Chairman 1984-86, Vice Chairman 1986-89 and Chair Elect 1989-90 Committee on Governmental Liability) Bar Associations. Officer and Member Alumni Board Northwestern School of Law of Lewis & Clark College 1983-86. Board of Regents St. Mary's Academy 1985-87.

Office: U.S. Courthouse, 1000 S.W. Third Avenue, Portland 97204.

Telephone: (503) 326-8350.

BROWN, Trish M. *(Judge, United States Bankruptcy Court District of Oregon)* Appointed by U.S. Court of Appeals Ninth Circuit judges to term beginning Dec 3, 1999. Term expires Dec 2, 2013. Born Billings Montana Sept 11, 1956. Unitarian. Educated at University of Pennsylvania B.S. 1978 and Washington and Lee University School of Law J.D. cum laude 1981. Law Clerk to Hon. Glen M. Williams, U.S. District Court Western District of Virginia 1981-82. Admitted to practice Virginia 1981, Oregon 1982, Washington 1986 and U.S. Supreme Court 1999. In legal practice Portland Oregon 1982-99.

Member Planning Committee Northwest Bankruptcy Institute 1993-96. Former Member Commercial Law League of America. Member American Bankruptcy Institute and Oregon State Bar (Chair Executive Committee Alternative Dispute Resolution Committee 1996-97, Member and Chair 1997-98 Debtor-Creditor Section). Interests include horses and bloodhounds.

Office: 1001 S.W. Fifth Avenue, Room 700, Portland 97204.

Telephone: (503) 326-4961.

E-mail address: Trish_Brown@orb.uscourts.gov

BROWNHILL, Paula J. *(Presiding Judge, Oregon Circuit Court Eighteenth Judicial District)* Term expires Jan 5, 2009. Former Judge Nineteenth Judicial District.

Mailing address: P.O. Box 835, Astoria 97103.

Office: Clatsop County Courthouse, Astoria 97103.

Telephone: (503) 325-8555.

CABLE, Cindy L. *(Justice of the Peace, Lane County Justice Court)* Elected to term beginning Jan 7, 1991. Reelected 1996 and 2002. Current term expires Dec 31, 2008. Born Florence Oregon Dec 31, 1958. Episcopalian. Educated at University of Oregon B.S. 1981.

Mailing address: P.O. Box N, Florence 97439.

Telephone: (541) 997-2535.

Fax: (541) 902-0639

CAMPBELL, Nancy W. *(Judge, Oregon Circuit Court Twentieth Judicial District)* Assumed office Jan 15, 1998. Elected May 2000, current term expires Jan 1, 2007. Former Judge, Washington County District Court.

Office: Washington County Courthouse, 150 North First, Hillsboro 97124.

Telephone: (503) 846-3443.

CARLSON, Charles D. *(Judge, Oregon Circuit Court Second Judicial District)* Term expires Jan 5, 2009.

Office: Lane County Courthouse, 125 East Eighth, Eugene 97401.

Telephone: (541) 682-4257.

CARLSON, Cynthia *(Judge, Oregon Circuit Court Second Judicial District)* Assumed office Jan 15, 1998. Elected May 2000, current term expires Jan 1, 2007. Former Judge, Lane County District Court.

Office: Lane County Courthouse, 125 East Eighth, Eugene 97401.

Telephone: (541) 682-4218.

CARP, Ted *(Judge, Oregon Circuit Court Second Judicial District)* Assumed office Jan 15, 1998. Elected 2002, current term expires Jan 5, 2009. Former Judge, Lane County District Court.

Office: Lane County Courthouse, 125 East Eighth, Eugene 97401.

Telephone: (541) 682-4497.

CARSON, Wallace P., Jr. *(Chief Justice, Oregon Supreme Court)* Appointed by Governor Victor Atiyeh to term beginning July 13, 1982. Elected Nov 1982, Nov 1988, Nov 1994 and 2000. Current term expires Jan 1, 2007. Born Salem Oregon June 10, 1934. Episcopalian. Educated at Stanford University B.A. 1956 and Willamette University College of Law J.D. 1962. Recipient University Honors Scholarship Stanford University 1952. Member Phi Delta Theta and Delta Theta Phi. Admitted to practice Oregon 1962, U.S. District Court District of Oregon 1963, U.S. Court of Appeals Ninth Circuit 1968, U.S. Supreme Court 1971 and U.S. Court of Military Appeals 1977. In legal practice Salem 1962-77. Judge, Oregon Circuit Court Third Judicial District 1977-82, appointed by Governor Robert W. Straub.

Oregon State Representative Marion County 1967-71 (House Majority Leader 1969-71). Oregon State Senator Marion and Linn Counties 1971-77 (Senate Minority Floor Leader). Author "Writ of Mandamus" Pleading and Practice Manual Oregon State Bar 1964 and "Last Things Last" Willamette L. Rev. 1983. Member Oregon State Bar, Marion County (Secretary-Treasurer 1965-67, Board member 1968-70) and American Bar Associations. Writer and lecturer CLE Program Oregon State Bar 1963-64, 1970-71 and 1973. Recipient Distinguished Service Award from Salem Jaycees 1968. Named one of Five Outstanding Young Men of Oregon 1968. Jet pilot USAF 1956-59. Colonel Oregon Air National Guard since 1970 (Staff Judge Advocate, Military Judge, Deputy Commander). Recipient Commander Trophy from Air Force Flight School 1956. Republican.

Office: Supreme Court Building, 1163 State Street, Salem 97301-2562.

Telephone: (503) 986-5700.

CINNIGER, Ronald E. *(Judge, Oregon Circuit Court Fourth Judicial District)* Elected Nov 7, 2000. Term expires Jan 1, 2007.

Office: Multnomah County Courthouse, 1021 S.W. Fourth, Portland 97204.

Telephone: (503) 988-3546.

COFFIN, Thomas M. *(Magistrate Judge, United States District Court District of Oregon)* Appointed by U.S. District Court judges.

Office: 102 U.S. Courthouse, 211 East Seventh Avenue, Eugene 97401.

Telephone: (541) 465-6476.

COLE, Larry D. *(Justice of the Peace, Baker County Justice Court)* Appointed by Governor Neil Goldschmidt to term beginning June 1, 1988. Elected Nov 1988, 1994 and 2000. Current term expires Dec 31, 2006. Al-

COLE, LARRY D.—*Continued*
so serves as Judge, Baker City, Haines and Sumpter Municipal Courts. Juvenile Court Referee since 1988. Born Baker City Oregon Sept 27, 1936. Protestant. Judge, Union Municipal Court 1974-89.

Chairman Oregon Special Courts Advisory Committee Oregon Supreme Court 1993-96 and Baker County Courthouse Security Committee 1994-2000. Member Criminal Justice Advisory Council, Oregon Municipal Judges Association (Executive Board 1975-83, President 1983-85), Oregon Justice of the Peace Association and National Judges Association (Chairman 1996 and Co-chairman 2000 Judicial Education Conference). Attended Oregon Judicial College sponsored by Oregon Supreme Court and Willamette University Salem Oregon 1976-79, American Judicial Academy Boulder Colorado 1978, courses on Small Claims 1984, Traffic Court 1984 and Legal Institute 1991-92 The National Judicial College, "Basic Civil Mediation" Mediation Center Eugene 1997, "Mental Health, Alcohol and Drug Use Issues in Mediation" 1998 and "Domestic Violence and Child Abuse Issues in Mediation" 1998. Recipient Meritorious Service Award from Oregon Municipal Judges Association Oct 1985 and Kenneth L. MacEachern Memorial Award (Outstanding Non-Attorney Judge in the United States) from National Judges Association 1995. Engineer Second Class USN 1954-57. Vice President Cole Brothers American Service 1978-90. Member Oregon Subordinate Grange Elkhorn No. 908 for 50 years, Teen Court and volunteer fire department. Enjoys flying, hunting, fishing and writing newspaper and magazine articles.

Office: 170 Baker County Courthouse, 1995 Third Street, Baker City 97814.
Telephone: (541) 523-8213.
Fax: (541) 523-8360
E-mail address: lcole@bakercounty.org
Website address: www.bakercounty.org

COLLINS, John L. *(Presiding Judge, Oregon Circuit Court Twenty-fifth Judicial District)* Appointed by Governor Barbara Roberts to term beginning Sept 11, 1992. Elected 1992 and 1998. Current term expires Jan 3, 2005. Presiding Judge since Jan 15, 1998. Former Judge Twelfth Judicial District. Born Salem Oregon. Educated at Oregon State University B.S. 1969, Willamette University J.D. 1972 and New York University LL.M. 1974. Comments Editor Willamette Law Review 1971-72. Member Order of Barristers. Admitted to practice Oregon 1972 and U.S. District Court District of Oregon 1973. In legal practice Dayton 1974.

Director of Corrections Yamhill, Polk and Marion counties 1974-75. Deputy Public Defender Portland 1975. District Attorney Yamhill County 1976-92. Instructor in Criminal Procedure and Civil Procedure Chemeketa Community College 1974-75. President Oregon District Attorneys Association 1983. Chair State Judicial Education Committee. Member Oregon Circuit Judges Association (President 2000, Member Executive Committee) and National District Attorneys Association (Board 1988-92). Attended general course The National Judicial College 1992. Recipient National Crime Victims Service Award from Attorney General Ashcroft 2001.

Office: Yamhill County Courthouse, McMinnville 97128.
Telephone: (503) 472-9371, 434-7497.
Fax: (503) 472-5802

COON, Allan H. *(Judge, Oregon Circuit Court Fourteenth Judicial District)* Term expires Jan 5, 2009. Former Judge, Josephine County District Court.

Office: 252 Josephine County Courthouse, 500 N.E. Sixth, Grants Pass 97526.
Telephone: (541) 476-2309.

COONEY, John P. *(Magistrate Judge, United States District Court District of Oregon)* Appointed by U.S. District Court judges.

Office: 302 U.S. Courthouse, 310 West Sixth Street, Medford 97501.
Telephone: (541) 776-4169.

CRAIN, Patricia *(Judge, Oregon Circuit Court First Judicial District)* Appointed by Governor John A. Kitzhaber to term beginning July 18, 1997. Elected Jan 1, 1999, current term expires Jan 3, 2005. Born Red Bluff California March 9, 1947. Educated at University of Oregon B.A. 1969 J.D. 1977. Admitted to practice Oregon 1977 and U.S. District Court District of Oregon 1977. In legal practice Ashland 1977-82 and Medford 1982-97.

Office: Justice Building, 100 South Oakdale, Medford 97501.
Telephone: (541) 776-7171.

CRAMER, William D., Jr. *(Presiding Judge, Oregon Circuit Court Twenty-fourth Judicial District)* Term expires Jan 5, 2009. Serves Grant and Harney counties.

Mailing address: P.O. Box 159, Canyon City 97820.
Office: Grant County Courthouse, 205 South Humbolt Street, Canyon City 97820.
Telephone: (541) 575-1438.
Office: Harney County Courthouse, 450 North Buena Vista, Burns 97720.
Telephone: (541) 573-5207.

CROWLEY, Paul G. *(Presiding Judge, Oregon Circuit Court Seventh Judicial District)* Assumed office Jan 15, 1998. Term expires Jan 3, 2005. Former Judge, Hood River County District Court.

Office: Hood River County Courthouse, 309 State Street, Hood River 97031.
Telephone: (541) 386-1862.

DARLING, Deanne L. *(Judge, Oregon Circuit Court Fifth Judicial District)* Assumed office Jan 15, 1998. Elected 2002, current term expires Jan 5, 2009. Serves Juvenile Court. Former Judge, Clackamas County District Court.

Office: 2123 Kaen Road, Oregon City 97045.
Telephone: (503) 557-2841.

DEITS, Mary J. *(Chief Judge, Oregon Court of Appeals)* Assumed office 1986. Elected to subsequent terms. Current term expires Jan 2005.

Office: Justice Building, Third Floor, 1162 Court Street N.E., Salem 97301-4095.
Telephone: (503) 986-5666.

De MUNIZ, Paul J. *(Justice, Oregon Supreme Court)* Elected Nov 7, 2000 to term beginning Jan 2001. Term expires Jan 2007. Judge 1990 to Jan 2001 and Presiding Judge Department One 1997-2000, Oregon Court of Appeals.

Office: Supreme Court Building, 1163 State Street, Salem 97301-2562.
Telephone: (503) 986-5709.

DICKERSON, Henry R., Jr. *(Judge, Oregon Circuit Court Twenty-first Judicial District)* Assumed office Jan 15, 1998. Elected May 2000, current term expires Jan 1, 2007. Former Judge, Benton County District Court.
Mailing address: P.O. Box 1870, Corvallis 97339.
Office: Benton County Courthouse, 120 N.W. Fourth, Corvallis 97330-4734.
Telephone: (541) 766-6830.

DICKEY, Don A. *(Judge, Oregon Circuit Court Third Judicial District)* Assumed office Jan 15, 1998. Elected 2002, current term expires Jan 5, 2009. Former Judge, Marion County District Court.
Mailing address: P.O. Box 12869, Salem 97309-0869.
Office: Marion County Courthouse, 100 High Street N.E., Salem 97301-3665.
Telephone: (503) 373-4445.

DOWNER, Hugh C., Jr. *(Judge, Oregon Circuit Court Fifteenth Judicial District)* Appointed by Governor Victor Atiyeh July 1, 1985. Elected May 1986, 1992 and 1998. Current term expires Jan 3, 2005. Born Cleveland Ohio April 27, 1946. Protestant. Educated at University of Michigan B.S.Eng. 1968 and Stanford University J.D. 1971. Admitted to practice California 1971 and Oregon 1972. In legal practice Portland Oregon 1975-78 and Gold Beach Oregon 1978-81. Judge, Curry County District Court 1981-85.
Assistant District Attorney Coos County Oregon 1972-75. U.S. Army Corps of Engineers 1971-72.
Mailing address: P.O. Box 810, Gold Beach 97444.
Office: Curry County Courthouse, Gold Beach 97444.
Telephone: (541) 247-2742.

DUNN, Randall Lawson *(Judge, United States Bankruptcy Court District of Oregon)* Appointed by U.S. Court of Appeals Ninth Circuit judges to term beginning Feb 1, 1998. Term expires Jan 31, 2012. Born Gary Indiana May 28, 1950. Educated at Northwestern University B.A. with honors 1972 and Stanford University J.D. 1975. Articles Editor Stanford Law Review 1974-75. Admitted to practice Utah 1975, Oregon 1977 and Washington 1986. In legal practice Salt Lake City Utah 1975-76 and Portland Oregon 1977-97.
Editor-in-Chief Oregon Debtor-Creditor Newsletter. Member Ninth Circuit Bankruptcy Education Committee (Chair), National Conference of Bankruptcy Judges (Editor-in-Chief Newsletter Committee, Board of Governors), Oregon State Bar (Executive Committee, Treasurer), Federal (Member Executive Committee and President Bankruptcy Section, Editor-in-Chief *Bankruptcy Briefs* Newsletter) and American Bar Associations. Past President, Former Treasurer and Former Board Member Beaverton Arts Commission. Board of Directors Portland Festival Symphony. Member Portland Opera Orchestra (2nd and E-flat clarinet). Enjoys playing the clarinet, reading, gardening and weight lifting.
Office: 1001 S.W. Fifth Avenue, Room 700, Portland 97204.
Telephone: (503) 326-4175.
Fax: (503) 326-5693
E-mail address: randall_dunn@orb.uscourts.gov

DURHAM, Robert D. *(Justice, Oregon Supreme Court)* Appointed by Governor Barbara Roberts to term beginning Jan 4, 1994. Elected 1994 and May 16, 2000. Current term expires 2007. Born Lynwood California May 10, 1947. Roman Catholic. Educated at Whittier College B.A. 1969 and University of Santa Clara J.D. 1972. Comments Editor Santa Clara Law Journal 1971-72. Law Clerk to Hon. Dean Bryson, Oregon Supreme Court 1972-74. Admitted to practice Oregon 1972, California 1973, U.S. District Court District of Oregon 1974, U.S. Court of Appeals Ninth Circuit 1980 and U.S. Supreme Court 1987. In legal practice Eugene Oregon 1974-83 and Portland Oregon 1983-91. Judge, Oregon Court of Appeals 1991-93.
Author Comment "Repairing the Duty to Repair—Implied Warranty of Habitability" 11 Santa Clara Lawyers 298, 1972 and "Litigation Under Section 1983" and "Torts Chapter on Wrongful Discharge" Continuing Legal Education Oregon State Bar. Member Lawyer's Committee Eugene and Portland American Civil Liberties Union 1978-91. Member Advisory Committee Joint Interim Judiciary Committee 1985. Chair Oregon Commission on Administrative Hearings 1988-89. Member Case Disposition Benchmarks Committee Oregon Supreme Court 1992-93. Member Council on Court Procedures 1992-93. Member Appellate Court Rules Committee 1994. Member Willamette Valley American Inns of Court (Team Leader Master of the Bench since 1992), Oregon Appellate Judges Association (President 1996-97), American Academy of Appellate Lawyers (Member Ninth Circuit Screening Committee since 1991, Co-chair Appellate Courts Liaison Committee 1994), Oregon State Bar (Chair Labor Law Section 1983-84, Member Administrative Law Committee Government Law Section 1986), Marion County and Multnomah County Bar Associations. Instructor Fair Hearing and Administrative Law Courses The National Judicial College 1992. Moderator Practical Skills Program New Lawyers Section Oregon Trial Lawyers Association 1993 and 1994. Co-chair and Instructor Oregon Appellate and Judicial Education Committee Continuing Legal Education Oct 1994. Speaker Employment Law for Trial Lawyers. Recipient Civil Rights Litigation Award from American Civil Liberties Union of Oregon 1988 and Ed Elliott Human Rights Award from Oregon Education Association 1990.
Office: Supreme Court Building, 1163 State Street, Salem 97301-2562.
Telephone: (503) 986-5725.

EDGAR, Alfred L. *(Justice of the Peace, Klamath County Justice Court)* Elected to term beginning Jan 2001. Term expires Jan 2007.
Mailing address: P.O. Box 516, Chiloquin 97624.
Telephone: (541) 783-2240.
E-mail address: wrjc@cvc.net

EDMONDS, Walter I., Jr. *(Judge, Oregon Court of Appeals)* Appointed by Governor Neil Goldschmidt to term beginning Jan 2, 1989. Elected 1990, 1996 and 2002. Current term expires Dec 31, 2008. Born Eugene Oregon Aug 30, 1943. Protestant. Educated at Linfield College B.A. 1965 and Willamette University College of Law J.D. 1967. Contributor Willamette Law Journal 1967. Admitted to practice Oregon 1967 and U.S. District Court District of Oregon 1967. In legal practice Madras 1967-68 and Redmond 1969-75. Judge Oct 1, 1975 to Jan 1, 1989 and Presiding Judge 1988, Oregon Circuit Court Eleventh Judicial District, appointed by Governor Robert W. Straub.
District Attorney Jefferson County 1968-69. Member Central Oregon Bar Association (President 1974), Oregon Circuit Court Judges Association (President 1985), Oregon Appellate Judges Association (President 1995), Oregon State Bar and American Bar Association. Named

EDMONDS, WALTER I., JR.—*Continued*

Boss of the Year by Central Oregon Legal Secretaries Association 1975. Listed in *Who's Who in Society* 1986. Member Advisory Commission on Prison Terms and Parole Standards 1985. Board of Director Building Blocks and Christian Television Station. Board of Visitors Willamette University College of Law. Interests include horses and cattle, mountain horsepacking and running.

Office: Justice Building, Third Floor, 1162 Court Street N.E., Salem 97301-4095.

Telephone: (503) 986-5670.

Fax: (503) 986-5865

E-mail address: walter.i.edmonds@state.or.us

FARRELL, Terry *(Justice of the Peace, Grant County Justice Court)* Term expires 2005.

Office: Courthouse, 201 South Humbolt, Canyon City 97820.

Telephone: (541) 575-1076.

FOOTE, Gregory G. *(Judge, Oregon Circuit Court Second Judicial District)* Term expires Jan 1, 2007. Born Santa Monica California Dec 5, 1947. Member Central Lutheran Church. Educated at University of Oregon B.S. 1969 J.D. 1972. Admitted to practice Oregon 1972 and U.S. District Court District of Oregon 1973. Began legal practice Eugene 1972. Judge, Lane County District Court 1977-81.

Author "Unconstitutionality of Oregon's Loitering Statute" Oregon L. Rev. 1972. Board of Directors Oregon Law Institute. Member Oregon Circuit Judges Association, Oregon Judicial Conference (Chairman Judicial Education Committee 1981-84), Oregon Trial Lawyers Association, The Association of Trial Lawyers of America, Oregon State Bar and Lane County Bar Association. Graduate 1978 and 1982 and Faculty member 1980 The National Judicial College. Enjoys backpacking, coaching, skiing, music and athletics.

Office: Lane County Courthouse, 125 East Eighth, Eugene 97401.

Telephone: (541) 682-4427.

FORTE, Stephen P. *(Justice of the Peace, Deschutes County Justice Court)* Elected to term beginning Jan 2, 2001. Term expires Jan 1, 2007. Born Dec 21, 1953. Educated at Northern Illinois University B.S. magna cum laude 1979 and University of Idaho J.D. 1982. Admitted to practice Oregon 1983. In legal practice Bend 1983-2000. Former Judge, Sisters Municipal Court.

Member Deschutes County and American Bar Associations.

Office: Administration Building, 1130 N.W. Harriman, Bend 97701-1947.

Telephone: (541) 388-6549.

E-mail address: stephenf@deschutes.org

FRANKEL, Kimberly C. *(Judge, Oregon Circuit Court Fourth Judicial District)* Term expires Jan 1, 2007. Former Judge, Multnomah County District Court.

Office: Multnomah County Courthouse, 1021 S.W. Fourth, Portland 97204.

Telephone: (503) 988-5101.

FRANTZ, Julie *(Judge, Oregon Circuit Court Fourth Judicial District)* Term expires Jan 5, 2009. Former Judge, Multnomah County District Court.

Office: Multnomah County Courthouse, 1021 S.W. Fourth, Portland 97204.

Telephone: (503) 988-3045.

FREEMAN, Clifford L. *(Judge, Oregon Circuit Court Fourth Judicial District)* Assumed office Jan 15, 1998. Elected 2002, current term expires Jan 5, 2009. Former Judge, Multnomah County District Court.

Office: Multnomah County Courthouse, 1021 S.W. Fourth, Portland 97204.

Telephone: (503) 988-3227.

FRYE, Helen J. *(Senior Judge, United States District Court District of Oregon)* Appointed for life by the President. Assumed Senior status, serves by assignment. Born Klamath Falls Oregon Dec 10, 1930. Educated at University of Oregon B.A. with honors 1953 M.A. 1961 J.D. 1966. Admitted to practice Oregon 1966. Began legal practice Eugene 1966. Former Judge, Oregon Circuit Court Second Judicial District, appointed by Governor Tom McCall to term beginning July 1971.

Contributor *Juvenile Law Handbook* Oregon State Bar 1970, *Oregon Lawyer's Trial Book—Evidence* Oregon State Bar 1972 and *Bench Book* Judicial Conference State of Oregon 1977. Important Circuit Court Decisions: Lane County Escrow and TransAmerican Insurance Company v. Smith and Coe 1974, State of Oregon v. Belinda Lederer 1975 and Green et al. v. Hayward 1976. Important Federal Decisions: Penk v. OSBHE 1985, Harrington v. City of Portland 1990, U.S. v. Wolfe 1986, D.B. v. Tewksbury 1982, Park n Fly v. Dollar Park n Fly 1981, Oregon v. City of Rajneeshpuram 1985 and Portland Audubon Society v. Lujan 1992. Instructor in Business Law University of Oregon 1970-71. Political affiliation: Independent.

Office: 1107 U.S. Courthouse, 1000 S.W. Third Avenue, Portland 97204-2902.

Telephone: (503) 326-8270.

FUCHS, Alicia A. *(Judge, Oregon Circuit Court Fourth Judicial District)* Term expires Jan 3, 2005.

Office: Multnomah County Courthouse, 1021 S.W. Fourth, Portland 97204.

Telephone: (503) 988-3731.

GALTON, Sid A. *(Judge, Oregon Circuit Court Fourth Judicial District)* Term expires Jan 3, 2005.

Office: Multnomah County Courthouse, 1021 S.W. Fourth, Portland 97204.

Telephone: (503) 988-5047.

GARDNER, Mark *(Judge, Oregon Circuit Court Twentieth Judicial District)* Term expires Jan 1, 2007.

Office: Washington County Courthouse, 150 North First, Hillsboro 97124.

Telephone: (503) 846-3503.

GERNANT, David *(Judge, Oregon Circuit Court Fourth Judicial District)* Assumed office Jan 15, 1998. Elected May 2000, current term expires Jan 1, 2007. Born Kalamazoo Michigan 1943. Jewish. Educated at Western Michigan University B.A. magna cum laude 1965 and Harvard Law School J.D. 1968. Admitted to practice District of Columbia 1969, Massachusetts 1969, Oregon 1973, U.S. Court of Appeals Ninth Circuit 1984, U.S. District Court District of Oregon 1985 and U.S. Supreme Court 1992. In legal practice Portland Oregon 1983-92. Former Judge, Multnomah County District Court Jan 4, 1993 to Jan 14, 1998, appointed by Governor Barbara Roberts.

Former Member Oregon Criminal Defense Lawyers Association, Oregon Gay and Lesbian Law Association (Board Member 1991-92), Oregon Trial Lawyers Associ-

GERNANT, DAVID—*Continued*
ation (Amicus Committee 1984-92) and National Lesbian and Gay Law Association. Attended Advanced Evidence and Problems in Criminal Evidence 1993 and Children in Court 1994 The National Judicial College. Enjoys grandchildren, photography, movies, plays, ballet and travel.
Office: Multnomah County Courthouse, 1021 S.W. Fourth, Portland 97204.
Telephone: (503) 988-3835.

GILLESPIE, Michael J. *(Judge, Oregon Circuit Court Fifteenth Judicial District)* Assumed office Jan 15, 1998. Term expires Jan 3, 2005. Former Judge, Coos County District Court and Curry County District Court.
Office: Coos County Courthouse, 250 North Baxter, Coquille 97423.
Telephone: (541) 396-3121.

GILLETTE, W. Michael *(Justice, Oregon Supreme Court)* Assumed office 1986. Elected to subsequent terms. Current term expires Jan 2005. Born Seattle Washington Dec 29, 1941. Educated at Whitman College A.B. cum laude 1963 and Harvard University LL.B. 1966. Member Phi Delta Theta. Admitted to practice Oregon 1966, American Samoa 1969 and U.S. Supreme Court 1973. Began legal practice Portland Oregon 1966. In legal practice Pago Pago American Samoa 1969-71 and Salem Oregon since 1971. Former Judge, Oregon Court of Appeals, appointed by Governor Robert Straub to term beginning Sept 5, 1977.
Instructor in Consumer Law Northwestern School of Law of Lewis & Clark College 1973-74 and Administrative Law Willamette University since 1984.
Office: Supreme Court Building, 1163 State Street, Salem 97301-2562.
Telephone: (503) 986-5705.

GILROY, Patrick D. *(Judge, Oregon Circuit Court Fifth Judicial District)* Appointed by Governor Thomas L. McCall Dec 11, 1974. Elected 1976, 1982, 1988, 1994 and May 2000. Current term expires Jan 1, 2007. Born Portland Oregon Aug 31, 1932. Catholic. Educated at University of Portland B.A. cum laude 1954 and University of San Francisco J.D. 1960. Admitted to practice Oregon 1960. Began legal practice Oregon City 1960.
Instructor University of Portland 1975-80. Member Oregon State Bar, Clackamas County (President 1970) and American Bar Associations. Captain USAF 1955-57.
Office: 104 Clackamas County Courthouse, 807 Main Street, Oregon City 97045.
Telephone: (503) 655-8687.

GRAVES, Dennis *(Judge, Oregon Circuit Court Third Judicial District)* Term expires Jan 1, 2007.
Mailing address: P.O. Box 12869, Salem 97309-0869.
Office: Marion County Courthouse, 100 High Street N.E., Salem 97301-3665.
Telephone: (503) 585-4939.

GRAY, Charlotte S. *(Justice of the Peace, Morrow County Justice Court)* Appointed by Governor Robert W. Straub to term beginning Dec 15, 1978. Elected 1980, 1986, 1992 and 1998. Current term expires Dec 31, 2004. Born Casper Wyoming July 30, 1940. Seventh Day Adventist.
Office: Courthouse, 100 Court Street, Heppner 97836.
Telephone: (541) 676-5264.
E-mail address: charlotte@co.morrow.or.us

GROVE, Ted E. *(Judge, Oregon Circuit Court Nineteenth Judicial District)* Term expires Jan 5, 2009.
Office: Columbia County Courthouse, 244 Strand Street, St. Helens 97051-2041.
Telephone: (503) 397-2327.

GUIMOND, Joseph C. *(Judge, Oregon Circuit Court Third Judicial District)* Assumed office Jan 15, 1998. Elected 2002, current term expires Jan 5, 2009. Former Judge, Marion County District Court.
Mailing address: P.O. Box 12869, Salem 97309-0869.
Office: Marion County Courthouse, 100 High Street N.E., Salem 97301-3665.
Telephone: (503) 588-5160.

HAGGERTY, Ancer L. *(Chief Judge, United States District Court District of Oregon)* Appointed for life by President Bill Clinton to term beginning 1994. Chief Judge since March 13, 2002. Born Vanport Oregon Aug 26, 1944. Educated at University of Oregon B.S. 1967 and University of California Hastings College of the Law J.D. 1973. In legal practice Portland 1977-88. Judge, Multnomah County District Court 1989-90. Judge, Oregon Circuit Court Fourth Judicial District 1990-93.
Law Clerk 1973 and Staff Attorney 1973-77 Metropolitan Public Defender Portland. USMC 1967-70.
Office: 1307 U.S. Courthouse, 1000 S.W. Third Avenue, Portland 97204-2902.
Telephone: (503) 326-8320.

HANTKE, David W. *(Presiding Judge, Oregon Circuit Court Twenty-seventh Judicial District)* Term expires Jan 3, 2005. Former Presiding Judge Nineteenth Judicial District. Formerly served Eighteenth Judicial District. Former Judge, Tillamook County District Court.
Office: Tillamook County Courthouse, 201 Laurel Avenue, Tillamook 97141.
Telephone: (503) 842-7914.

HARRIS, Daniel L. *(Judge, Oregon Circuit Court First Judicial District)* Appointed by Governor John A. Kitzhaber Aug 11, 1997 to term beginning Sept 19, 1997. Elected May 12, 1998, current term expires Jan 3, 2005. Educated at Brigham Young University B.S. 1977 and University of Oregon J.D. 1982. Associate Editor Oregon Law Review 1980-82. Admitted to practice Oregon 1983.
Office: Justice Building, 100 South Oakdale, Medford 97501.
Telephone: (541) 776-7171.
E-mail address: Daniel.Harris@state.or.us

HART, Thomas M. *(Judge, Oregon Circuit Court Third Judicial District)* Term expires Jan 3, 2005.
Mailing address: P.O. Box 12869, Salem 97309-0869.
Office: Marion County Courthouse, 100 High Street N.E., Salem 97301-3665.
Telephone: (503) 588-5627.

HASELTON, Rick T. *(Judge, Oregon Court of Appeals)* Appointed by Governor Barbara Roberts March 23, 1994. Elected 1994 and 2000. Current term expires Dec 31, 2006. Currently serves as Presiding Judge. Born Albany Oregon Nov 5, 1953. Educated at Stanford University B.A. with honors 1976 and Yale Law School J.D. 1979. Law Clerk to Hon. A. T. Goodwin, U.S. Court of Appeals Ninth Circuit 1979-80. Member Phi Beta Kappa. Admitted to practice Oregon 1979. In legal practice Portland 1980-94.

HASELTON, RICK T.—*Continued*

Author "Hobnobbing with the Wizards: An Operations Manual to the Ninth Circuit" *Appeal and Review* Oregon State Bar 1987. Important Decisions: Lakin v. Senco Products, Inc. 144 Or. App. 52, 925 P.2d 107 1996 aff'd 329 Or. 62, 987 P.2d 476, 1999; McCathern v. Toyota Motor Corp. 160 Or. App. 201, 985 P.2d 804, 1999 aff'd 332 Or. 59 P.3d 2001; and State v. Thorp 166 Or. App. 564, 2 P.2d 903, 2000 (dissenting). Member 1982-87 and 1993-94 and Chair 1986-87 Multnomah County Legal Aid Service Board. Member 1986-89 and Chair 1988-89 Oregon State Board of Bar Examiners. Member Ninth Circuit Advisory Committee on Rules 1991-93. Member Oregon State Bar (Chair 1993-94 and Member since 1993 Appellate Practice Section). Enjoys history, baseball trivia and good food.

Office: Justice Building, Third Floor, Salem 97310.

Telephone: (503) 986-5678.

HASLINGER, Barbara *(Judge, Oregon Circuit Court Eleventh Judicial District)* Assumed office Jan 15, 1998. Elected 2002, current term expires Jan 5, 2009. Former Judge, Deschutes County District Court.

Office: Deschutes County Courthouse, 1164 N.W. Bond, Bend 97701.

Telephone: (541) 388-5300.

HENRY, Eveleen *(Judge, Oregon Circuit Court Second Judicial District)* Assumed office Jan 15, 1998. Elected 2002, current term expires Jan 5, 2009. Former Judge, Lane County District Court.

Office: Lane County Courthouse, 125 East Eighth, Eugene 97401.

Telephone: (541) 682-4300.

HERNANDEZ, Marco *(Presiding Judge, Oregon Circuit Court Twentieth Judicial District)* Assumed office Jan 15, 1998. Elected 2002, current term expires Jan 5, 2009. Former Judge, Washington County District Court.

Office: Washington County Courthouse, 150 North First, Hillsboro 97124.

Telephone: (503) 846-3851.

HERNDON, Robert D. *(Judge, Oregon Circuit Court Fifth Judicial District)* Term expires Jan 3, 2005.

Office: 104 Clackamas County Courthouse, 807 Main Street, Oregon City 97045.

Telephone: (503) 655-8644.

HISSONG, Candace *(Justice of the Peace, Douglas County Justice Court)* Elected to term beginning Jan 1, 2001. Term expires Dec 31, 2006. Former Justice of the Peace, Gilliam County Justice Court.

Office: Courthouse, 1036 S.E. Douglas, Roseburg 97470.

Telephone: (541) 957-2409.

E-mail address: hissong@echoweb.net

HITCHCOCK, John W. *(Judge, Oregon Circuit Court Twenty-fifth Judicial District)* Term expires Jan 5, 2009. Formerly served Twelfth Judicial District.

Office: Yamhill County Courthouse, 535 N.E. Fifth Street, McMinnville 97128.

Telephone: (503) 434-7530.

HODGES, Bryan T. *(Judge, Oregon Circuit Court Second Judicial District)* Assumed office Jan 15, 1998. Elected May 2000, current term expires Jan 1, 2007. Born Eugene Oregon July 9, 1940. Educated at University of Oregon B.A. 1962 LL.B. 1965. Admitted to practice Oregon 1965. In legal practice Eugene 1965-74. Judge pro tem, Lane County District Court 1974-75. Judge, Lane County District Court Oct 1, 1975 to Jan 14, 1998, appointed by Governor Robert W. Straub.

Member Oregon State Bar and Lane County Bar Association. Member Central Lutheran Church. Enjoys chess, karate, reading, cooking and gardening.

Office: Lane County Courthouse, 125 East Eighth, Eugene 97401.

Telephone: (541) 682-4027.

HOGAN, Michael R. *(Judge, United States District Court District of Oregon)* Magistrate Judge Aug 13, 1973 to Sept 1991. Appointed Judge for life by President George Bush to term beginning Sept 1991. Former Chief Judge. Born Oregon City Oregon Sept 24, 1946. Baptist. Educated at University of Oregon B.A. with honors 1968 and Georgetown University J.D. 1971. Law Clerk to Hon. Robert C. Belloni, U.S. District Court District of Oregon 1971-72. Admitted to practice Oregon 1971, U.S. District Court District of Oregon 1971 and U.S. Court of Appeals Ninth Circuit 1971. In legal practice Portland 1972-73. Part-time Bankruptcy Judge, U.S. District Court District of Oregon 1973-80.

Author "Civil Rights Attorney Fees: The Curtain Call or the Main Act?" American Bar Association 1987, "Drawing the Line on Civil Rights Fees" The Brief American Bar Association 1988 and "Judicial Settlement Conferences: Empowering the Parties to Decide Through Negotiations" Willamette L. Rev. Summer 1991. Lecturer University of Oregon 1975-77 and Dispute Resolution Center Willamette University College of Law 1987-88. Member National Council of U.S. Magistrates, Oregon State Bar, Lane County and American Bar Associations. Lecturer National Institute for Trial Advocacy 1976-79, The National Judicial College 1979, Federal Judicial Center 1979-81 and various federal, state and local bar association seminars since 1973. Recipient Individual Award in Dispute Resolution Fifth Annual Conference on Dispute Resolution Willamette University College of Law 1988. Participant Lane County Crusade for Christ 1983. Member American Leadership Forum, Rotary Club, Myrtle Lodge 78, Masons, Alvord-Taylor Houses, Western Seminary and Campus Life. Enjoys skin diving.

Office: 260 U.S. Courthouse, 211 East Seventh Avenue, Eugene 97401.

Telephone: (541) 465-6773.

HOLCOMB, Janet S. *(Presiding Judge, Oregon Circuit Court Twenty-first Judicial District)* Term expires Jan 3, 2005.

Mailing address: P.O. Box 1870, Corvallis 97339.

Office: Benton County Courthouse, 120 N.W. Fourth, Corvallis 97330-4734.

Telephone: (541) 766-6843.

HOLLAND, Lauren S. *(Judge, Oregon Circuit Court Second Judicial District)* Assumed office Jan 15, 1998. Term expires Jan 3, 2005. Former Judge, Lane County District Court.

Office: Lane County Courthouse, 125 East Eighth, Eugene 97401.

Telephone: (541) 682-4415.

HORNER, William M. *(Judge, Oregon Circuit Court Twelfth Judicial District)* Assumed office Jan 15, 1998. Elected May 2000, current term expires Jan 1, 2007. Born San Francisco California June 11, 1943. Educated

HORNER, WILLIAM M.—*Continued*

at University of California at Davis A.B. 1965 and Willamette University College of Law J.D. 1968. Admitted to practice Oregon 1969. In legal practice Monmouth 1970-84. Former Judge, Polk County District Court April 1, 1987 to May 17, 1994, appointed by Governor Neil Goldschmidt.

District Attorney 1984-87. Captain U.S. Army. Interested in genealogy.

Office: Polk County Courthouse, 850 Main Street, Dallas 97338.

Telephone: (503) 623-9266.

HUBEL, Dennis J. *(Magistrate Judge, United States District Court District of Oregon)* Part-time Magistrate Judge 1995-97. Appointed by U.S. District Court judges to term beginning Jan 1, 1998. Term expires Dec 31, 2005. Born Nov 3, 1947. Educated at Cornell University B.S. 1969, University of Washington 1972-73 and Lewis and Clark College Northwestern School of Law J.D. cum laude 1976. Associate Editor Environmental Law 1974-76. Admitted to practice Oregon 1976, U.S. District Courts District of Oregon 1976, Eastern 1985 and Western 1985 Districts of Washington, U.S. Court of Appeals Ninth Circuit 1977, U.S. Supreme Court 1982 and Washington 1985. In legal practice Portland Oregon 1976-87 and Bend Oregon 1987-97.

Co-author "Clearcutting: Can You See The Forest For The Trees?" 5 Environmental Law 753, 1974. Author "Prelicensing Antitrust Review of Nuclear Electric Generating Plants" 6 Environmental Law 753, 1976; Chapter 48 "Insurance Supplement" *General Liability Coverage* 1992, Chapter 19 "Damages" *Injury to Chattels* 1990, Supplement 1992 and Supplement 1995 and Chapter 27 "Insurance" *Standard Provisions—Conditions* 1996 and Supplement 1999 Oregon State Bar; and "Voir Dire by the Struck Jury Method" *Litigation Journal* April 1993. Adjunct Professor of Wills and Trusts and of Professional Responsibility Lewis and Clark College Northwestern School of Law 1980-82. Chair Judicial Administration Work Group Gender Fairness Task Force 1996-97 and Professionalism Commission Oregon Supreme Court/Oregon State Bar since 2000. Co-founder J. R. Campbell American Inn of Court (President 1995-96). Member Gus Solomon American Inn of Court, Ninth Circuit Magistrate Judges Education Committee (Chair since 2001), American Board of Trial Advocates, Oregon State Bar (Member 1988-91, Secretary 1989-90 and Chairman 1990-91 Uniform Civil Jury Instruction Committee; Member 1991-94, Secretary 1992-93 and Chairman 1993-94 Civil Procedure and Practice Committee), Multnomah County, Washington State and Federal (Oregon Local Federal Rules Committee) Bar Associations. USN.

Office: 927 U.S. Courthouse, 1000 S.W. Third Avenue, Portland 97204-2902.

Telephone: (503) 326-8240.

Fax: (503) 326-8249

HUCKLEBERRY, Robert James *(Presiding Judge, Oregon Circuit Court Seventeenth Judicial District)* Term expires Jan 1, 2007. Born Portland Oregon April 29, 1948. Baptist. Educated at University of Utah B.S. 1971 and Lewis & Clark College J.D. 1974. Issue Editor and Staff member Environmental Law Review 1973-74. Law Clerk to Chief Judge Robert C. Belloni, U.S. District Court District of Oregon 1971. Member Phi Alpha Delta. Admitted to practice Oregon 1974. Began legal practice Newport 1975. Former Judge, Lincoln County District Court, appointed by Governor Victor Atiyeh to term beginning July 1, 1982.

Deputy District Attorney 1975-76 and District Attorney 1977-80 Lincoln County. Member Lincoln County Bar Association (President 1985). Sergeant USAFR 1966-72. Interested in calligraphy, art, piano, writing, football and racquetball.

Mailing address: P.O. Box 100, Newport 97365.

Office: Lincoln County Courthouse, 225 West Olive, Newport 97365.

Telephone: (541) 265-4236.

HULL, Donald W. *(Judge, Oregon Circuit Court Seventh Judicial District)* Appointed by Governor Barbara Roberts to term beginning Aug 7, 1991. Elected 1992 and 1998. Current term expires Jan 3, 2005. Born Portland Oregon April 1, 1944. Protestant. Educated at University of Oregon B.B.A. 1966 J.D. 1970. Admitted to practice Oregon 1970. Former Judge, Hood River County District Court.

District Attorney 1970-75 and County Counsel 1975-76 Hood River County. Colonel USAR JAGC.

Office: Hood River County Courthouse, 309 State Street, Hood River 97031.

Telephone: (541) 386-2676.

ISAACSON, Rodger J. *(Judge, Oregon Circuit Court Thirteenth Judicial District)* Term expires Jan 5, 2009. Former Presiding Judge. Former Judge, Klamath County District Court.

Office: 316 Main Street, Klamath Falls 97601.

Telephone: (541) 883-5503.

JELDERKS, John A. *(Magistrate Judge, United States District Court District of Oregon)* Appointed by U.S. District Court judges to term beginning July 1991. Reappointed 1999, current term expires July 2007. Former Judge, Oregon Circuit Court Seventh Judicial District.

Office: 1227 U.S. Courthouse, 1000 S.W. Third Avenue, Portland 97204-2902.

Telephone: (503) 326-8310.

JOHNSON, Nely L. *(Judge, Oregon Circuit Court Fourth Judicial District)* Term expires Jan 5, 2009. Born Botosani Romania Jan 5, 1947. Jewish. Educated at University of Wisconsin B.A. with honors 1969 J.D. 1972. Member Phi Kappa Phi. Admitted to practice Wisconsin 1972 and Oregon 1974. Began legal practice Milwaukee Wisconsin. Former Judge, Multnomah County District Court, elected to term beginning Jan 4, 1983.

Former Member Executive Committee Judicial Conference Education Committee and Public Safety Policy Commission. Former Chairperson Sentencing Task Force Subcommittee. Instructor Northwestern School of Law Lewis & Clark College 1980-85. Past President Oregon District Judges Association. Member Task Force on International Judicial Development and Chairperson International Relations Committee National Conference of State Trial Judges Judicial Administration Division American Bar Association. Member Oregon Circuit Judges Association, Oregon State Bar and Multnomah County Bar Association. Former Secretary Board of Directors The Musical Company. Former Board member

JOHNSON, NELY L.—*Continued*

YMCA. Gymnastics Judge. Enjoys painting, tennis and antiques.

Office: Multnomah County Courthouse, 1021 S.W. Fourth, Portland 97204.

Telephone: (503) 988-3404.

JONES, Edward *(Judge, Oregon Circuit Court Fourth Judicial District)* Term expires Jan 1, 2007.

Office: Multnomah County Courthouse, 1021 S.W. Fourth, Portland 97204.

Telephone: (503) 988-3540.

JONES, Robert E. *(Senior Judge, United States District Court District of Oregon)* Appointed for life by President George Bush to term beginning April 30, 1990. Assumed Senior status May 1, 2000, serves by assignment. Born Portland Oregon July 5, 1927. Presbyterian. Educated at University of Hawaii B.A. 1949 and Northwestern School of Law of Lewis & Clark College J.D. 1953. Awarded honorary LL.D. City University of Seattle 1984 and honorary L.H.D 1995 and honorary LL.D. 1995 Northwestern School of Law of Lewis & Clark College. Admitted to practice Oregon 1953. In legal practice Portland 1953-63. Judge, Oregon Circuit Court Fourth Judicial District 1963-83. Justice, Oregon Supreme Court 1983-90.

Former Member Oregon House of Representatives. Adjunct Professor of Evidence and Advocacy Northwestern School of Law of Lewis & Clark College since 1964. Chair Education Committee Ninth Circuit 1996-97. Former Chairman Oregon Commission on Prison Terms and Parole Studies. Former Member Oregon Evidence Revision Commission and Oregon Circuit Judges Association (President 1967). Member Oregon Trial Lawyers Association (President 1959), Oregon State Bar (Former Chairman Continuing Legal Education) and American Bar Association. Faculty Member The National Judicial College, American Academy of Judicial Education and Appellate Judges Seminars American Bar Association. Recipient Merit Award from Multnomah Bar Association 1979, Citizen Award from NCCJ 1988, Service to Mankind Award from Sertoma Club Oregon and James Madison Award from Sigma Delta Chi. Named Legal Citizen of the Year by Law Related Education Project 1988 and Distinguished Graduate by Northwestern School of Law of Lewis & Clark College. Captain USNR JAGC 1945-87. Board of Overseers Lewis & Clark College.

Office: 1407 U.S. Courthouse, 1000 S.W. Third Avenue, Portland 97204-2902.

Telephone: (503) 326-8340.

JUBA, George E. *(Recalled Magistrate Judge, United States District Court District of Oregon)* Appointed Magistrate Judge by U.S. District Court judges to term beginning Jan 14, 1971. Reappointed to subsequent terms. Appointed Recalled Magistrate Judge by the Judicial Council of the Ninth Circuit. Born Washougal Washington Jan 11, 1928. Protestant. Educated at Willamette University B.A. 1952 J.D. cum laude 1956. Admitted to practice Oregon 1956. Began legal practice Portland 1956. Judge, Oregon District Court Oct 1965 to Oct 1969.

Member Multnomah County Bar Association and Oregon State Bar. Seaman First Class USN 1946-48. Special Agent Federal Bureau of Investigation 1959-63. Republican. Enjoys golf, camping, fishing and swimming.

Office: U.S. Courthouse, 1000 S.W. Third Avenue, Portland 97204-2902.

Telephone: (503) 326-2917.

KANTOR, Henry *(Judge, Oregon Circuit Court Fourth Judicial District)* Assumed office Jan 1998. Elected 2002, current term expires Jan 2009. Born Newark New Jersey Feb 13, 1954. Educated at University of Pennsylvania B.A. cum laude 1976 and Lewis and Clark College Northwestern School of Law J.D. 1979. Extern to Hon. Alfred T. Goodwin, U.S. Court of Appeals Ninth Circuit 1978-79. Admitted to practice Oregon 1979, U.S. District Courts District of Oregon 1979 and District of Arizona 1990, U.S. Courts of Appeals Ninth 1979 and Sixth 1988 Circuits, U.S. Supreme Court 1988 and U.S. Court of Federal Claims 1994. In legal practice Portland 1979-95. Judge, Multnomah County District Court Jan 1995 to Jan 14, 1998, appointed by Governor Barbara Roberts.

Co-author "Class Actions and Shareholder Derivative Actions" *Federal Civil Litigation in Oregon* Oregon State Bar CLE 1994. Member 1987-93 and Chair 1991-93 Council on Court Procedures. Former Arbitrator American Stock Exchange, New York Stock Exchange, Pacific Stock Exchange, American Arbitration Association, National Association of Securities Dealers and Multnomah County Courts. Member Oregon Commission on Judicial Fitness and Disability, Oregon Circuit Judges Association, Oregon Judicial Conference, American Inns of Court (Master Owen M. Panner Inn), Oregon State Bar (Committee on Civility 1990-93, Lawyers Coordinating Committee 1990-93, Executive Committee Consumer Law Section 1995-98, Federal Practice and Procedure Committee), Multnomah County (Judicial Selection Committee 1988-91, Court Liaison Committee 1995-97), Federal and American (Committee on Class Actions Section of Litigation) Bar Associations. Speaker on Lender Liability 1980-90, Securities Arbitrations 1980-90 and Pleading Punitive Damages 1996 Oregon Trial Lawyers Association; Business Torts 1992, Federal Civil Litigation 1994, Litigation Institute 1996 and Consumer Law 1997 Oregon State Bar; Federal Rules Federal Bar Association 1993; and New Federal Rules 1994 and Class Action Securities Litigation 1995 NWSL. Attended The National Judicial College 1995 and 2002. Recipient Certificates of Appreciation from Oregon State Bar 1996-2002.

Office: Multnomah County Courthouse, 1021 S.W. Fourth, Portland 97204.

Telephone: (503) 988-3972.

E-mail address: henry.kantor@ojd.state.or.us

KELLY, John V. *(Judge, Oregon Circuit Court Seventh Judicial District)* Term expires Jan 3, 2005. Former Presiding Judge.

Mailing address: P.O. Box 1400, The Dalles 97058.

Office: Wasco County Courthouse, Fifth and Washington, The Dalles 97058.

Telephone: (541) 296-3196.

KEYS, Linda *(Justice of the Peace, Wheeler County Justice Court)* Elected to term beginning Jan 1, 1999. Term expires Dec 31, 2004.

Mailing address: P.O. Box 327, Fossil 97830.

Telephone: (541) 763-3460.

KING, Garr M. *(Judge, United States District Court District of Oregon)* Appointed for life by President Bill Clinton May 1, 1998. Born Pocatello Idaho Jan 28, 1936. Educated at University of Utah and Lewis & Clark College Northwestern School of Law LL.B. 1963. In legal practice Portland 1966-98.

Deputy District Attorney Multnomah County 1963-66.

Office: 907 U.S. Courthouse, 1000 S.W. Third Avenue, Portland 97204-2902.

Telephone: (503) 326-8230.

KING, Robert Henry, Jr. *(Justice of the Peace, Jackson County Justice Court)* Elected to term beginning Jan 1, 1979. Reelected 1984, 1990, 1996 and 2002. Current term expires Dec 2009. Born Los Angeles California Feb 24, 1945.

Publisher Gold Hill Nugget Newspaper 1976-77. Democrat. Involved with Little League and other youth-oriented activities.

Gold Hill office: 420 Sixth Avenue, Gold Hill 97525.

Telephone: (541) 855-1106.

KISTLER, Rives *(Judge, Oregon Court of Appeals)* Assumed office 1999. Elected 2000, current term expires Jan 2007. Educated at Williams College B.A. cum laude 1971, University of North Carolina M.A. 1978 and Georgetown University J.D. summa cum laude 1981. Law Clerk to Chief Judge Charles Clark, U.S. Court of Appeals Fifth Circuit 1981-82 and Hon. Lewis F. Powell, Jr., U.S. Supreme Court 1982-83. Admitted to practice Oregon 1984. In legal practice Portland 1983-87.

Assistant Attorney General Department of Justice Oregon 1987-99. Adjunct Professor of State Constitutional Law Lewis and Clark College Northwestern School of Law 1997 and 1999.

Office: Justice Building, Third Floor, 1162 Court Street N.E., Salem 97301-4095.

Telephone: (503) 986-5721.

KNIEPS, Karla J. *(Judge, Oregon Circuit Court Thirteenth Judicial District)* Term expires Jan 3, 2005.

Office: 316 Main Street, Klamath Falls 97601.

Telephone: (541) 883-5503.

KOCH, Dale R. *(Presiding Judge, Oregon Circuit Court Fourth Judicial District)* Assumed office Jan 15, 1998. Elected May 2000, current term expires Jan 1, 2007. Former Judge, Multnomah County District Court.

Office: Multnomah County Courthouse, 1021 S.W. Fourth, Portland 97204.

Telephone: (503) 988-5008.

KOHL, Thomas W. *(Judge, Oregon Circuit Court Twentieth Judicial District)* Term expires Jan 3, 2005.

Office: Washington County Courthouse, 150 North First, Hillsboro 97124.

Telephone: (503) 846-3589.

KOLBERG, Thomas W. *(Judge, Oregon Circuit Court Sixteenth Judicial District)* Term expires Jan 3, 2005. Former Presiding Judge.

Office: 201 Justice Building, 1036 S.E. Douglas, Roseburg 97470.

Telephone: (541) 957-2433.

KURSHNER, Paula *(Judge, Oregon Circuit Court Fourth Judicial District)* Assumed office Jan 15, 1998. Elected May 2000, current term expires Jan 1, 2007. Former Judge, Multnomah County District Court.

Office: Multnomah County Courthouse, 1021 S.W. Fourth, Portland 97204.

Telephone: (503) 988-5010.

LaBARRE, Jerome E. *(Judge, Oregon Circuit Court Fourth Judicial District)* Term expires Jan 1, 2007.

Office: Multnomah County Courthouse, 1021 S.W. Fourth, Portland 97204.

Telephone: (503) 988-3348.

LaMAR, Kristena A. *(Judge, Oregon Circuit Court Fourth Judicial District)* Appointed by Governor Victor Atiyeh to term beginning Nov 2, 1984. Elected to term beginning Jan 1985. Reelected May 8, 1990, 1996 and 2002. Current term expires Jan 5, 2009. Born Muskegon Michigan April 7, 1948. Educated at Purdue University B.A. with honors in Social Science 1970 and University of Michigan Law School J.D. 1973. Admitted to practice Oregon 1973, U.S. District Court District of Oregon 1974, U.S. Court of Appeals Ninth Circuit 1977, U.S. Supreme Court 1977 and U.S. Tax Court 1980. In legal practice Portland 1973-80. Referee, Multnomah County Juvenile Court 1981-84.

Legal Counsel to Senate Judiciary Committee Oregon Legislature 1981. Author *Divorce Guide for Oregon* Self-Counsel Press, Ltd. 1977; "Pre-Trial Settlement Conferences in Multnomah County" 27 Willamette L. Rev. 549, 1991; and "Judicially Hosted Settlement Conferences in Domestic Relations Cases" 34 *Family and Conciliation Courts Review* 219, 1996. Adjunct Professor of Law Lewis & Clark Law School 1981-85. Former Member Gus J. Solomon Chapter American Inns of Court (Treasurer 1988-89, President 1989-90, Secretary 1990-91). Member Society for Professionals in Dispute Resolution, Oregon Judicial Conference (Courtroom Professionalism Committee 1990-91, Chair Dispute Resolution Committee), Oregon State Bar (Chair Multnomah County Professional Responsibility Committee 1978-80, Secretary and Chair Uniform Civil Jury Instructions Committee 1987-90 and State Lawyers Assistance Committee 1993-96) and Multnomah County Bar Association (Treasurer 1983-85, Chair Alternative Dispute Resolution Section 2001, Member Executive Committee). Instructor in Family Law 1977, Practical Skills 1979, 1988 and 1991-93, Dissolution of Marriage 1987, Trial Advocacy 1987, Division of Marital Property 1989, Soft Tissue 1990, Civil Litigation 1990 and Insurance Law 1992 Oregon State Bar. Faculty Member in Dispute Resolution and Settlement Techniques The National Judicial College since 1989. Recipient Multnomah County Certificate of Merit 1983, Multnomah County Commendation for Superior Work, Productivity and Cooperation 1983, Individual Award of Merit from Center for Dispute Resolution Willamette University College of Law 1991 and Lezak Award of Merit from Alternative Dispute Resolution Section 2000. Named Legal Citizen of the Year (Classroom Law Project Award) 1994.

Office: Multnomah County Courthouse, 1021 S.W. Fourth, Portland 97204.

Telephone: (503) 988-3204.

LANDAU, Jack L. *(Judge, Oregon Court of Appeals)* Assumed office 1993. Elected May 2000, current term expires Jan 2007.
Office: Justice Building, Third Floor, 1162 Court Street N.E., Salem 97301-4095.
Telephone: (503) 986-5674.

LARSON, Darryl *(Judge, Oregon Circuit Court Second Judicial District)* Term expires Jan 5, 2009. Former Judge, Lane County District Court.
Office: Lane County Courthouse, 125 East Eighth, Eugene 97401.
Telephone: (541) 682-4259.

LASSWELL, William L. *(Judge, Oregon Circuit Court Sixteenth Judicial District)* Assumed office Jan 15, 1998. Elected May 2000, current term expires Jan 1, 2007. Former Judge, Douglas County District Court.
Office: 201 Justice Building, 1036 S.E. Douglas, Roseburg 97470.
Telephone: (541) 957-2420.

LEE, Roberta K. *(Justice of the Peace, Hood River County Justice Court)* Elected to term beginning Jan 2001. Term expires Dec 2006.
Office: 440 WaNaPa, Cascade Locks 97014.
Telephone: (541) 374-8558.

LEGGERT, Terry Ann *(Judge, Oregon Circuit Court Third Judicial District)* Assumed office Jan 15, 1998. Elected May 2000, current term expires Jan 1, 2007. Born Highland Park Michigan Dec 31, 1950. Methodist. Educated at University of Michigan B.A. 1973 and University of Oregon J.D. 1977. Admitted to practice Oregon 1977, U.S. District Court District of Oregon and U.S. Court of Appeals Ninth Circuit. Judge, Marion County District Court March 1994 to Jan 14, 1998, appointed by Governor Barbara Roberts.
Deputy District Attorney 1977-85. Assistant Attorney General 1985-94. Author Chapter on Venue *Juvenile Law Handbook* Oregon State Bar CLE. Adjunct Professor of Juvenile Law Willamette University since 1999. Member Marion County Bar Association. Board Member Local Relief Nursery. Enjoys skiing, climbing, rafting, mountain biking and golf.
Mailing address: P.O. Box 12869, Salem 97309-0869.
Office: Marion County Courthouse, 100 High Street N.E., Salem 97301-3665.
Telephone: (503) 588-5492.

LEMERY, Neal C. *(Justice of the Peace, Tillamook County Justice Court)* Elected Nov 7, 2000 to term beginning Jan 2, 2001. Term expires Jan 2007. Also Judge Pro Tem, Oregon Circuit Court since 2001. Born Tillamook Oregon July 28, 1953. Educated at Lewis & Clark College B.S. 1975 and Willamette University J.D. 1979. Admitted to practice Oregon 1980 and U.S. District Court District of Oregon 1980. In legal practice Tillamook 1980-86 and Rockaway Beach 1991-2000. Former Judge, Astoria, Cannon Beach, Garibaldi, Rockaway Beach and Tillamook Municipal Courts.
District Attorney Tillamook County 1986-90. Instructor Tillamook Bay Community College 1998. President Oregon Justices of the Peace Association 2002.
Office: Tillamook County Courthouse, 201 Laurel, Tillamook 97141.
Telephone: (503) 842-3416.
Website address: www.co.tillamook.or.us

LEMHOUSE, Jad *(Justice of the Peace, Linn County Justice Court)* Assumed office Jan 1997. Elected 2002, current term expires Jan 2009.
Office: 430 Smith Street, Harrisburg 97446.
Telephone: (541) 995-8311, 791-1638.

LEONARD, Kip Wethered *(Judge, Oregon Circuit Court Second Judicial District)* Appointed by Governor Neil Goldschmidt to term beginning Sept 1989. Elected Nov 1990, 1996 and 2002. Current term expires Jan 5, 2009. Former Presiding Judge. Born Eugene Oregon May 24, 1948. Educated at University of Oregon B.S. 1970 and Willamette University J.D. 1975. Admitted to practice Oregon 1975 and U.S. Court of Appeals Ninth Circuit 1978. In legal practice Eugene 1978-86. Judge pro tem, Lane County District Court 1978-80. Judge, Veneta Municipal Court 1981-86. Judge pro tem, Eugene Municipal Court 1984-86. Judge, Lane County District Court March 6, 1986 to Sept 1989, appointed by Governor Victor Atiyeh.
Deputy District Attorney Lane County 1975-78. Member Oregon State Bar.
Office: Lane County Courthouse, 125 East Eighth, Eugene 97401.
Telephone: (541) 682-4753.

LETOURNEAU, Donald R. *(Judge, Oregon Circuit Court Twentieth Judicial District)* Term expires Jan 1, 2007. Former Judge, Washington County District Court.
Office: Washington County Courthouse, 150 North First, Hillsboro 97124.
Telephone: (503) 846-3418.

LEWIS, John B. *(Judge, Oregon Circuit Court Twentieth Judicial District)* Assumed office Jan 15, 1998. Elected May 2000, current term expires Jan 1, 2007. Born Forest Grove Oregon June 16, 1946. Educated at Portland State University B.S. 1968 M.A. 1970 and Lewis & Clark College Northwestern School of Law J.D. 1975. Admitted to practice Oregon 1975 and U.S. District Court District of Oregon 1975. In legal practice Forest Grove and Hillsboro 1975-93. Municipal Judge, Hillsboro Municipal Court 1980-83. Judge, Washington County District Court Aug 13, 1993 to Jan 14, 1998, appointed by Governor Barbara Roberts.
Office: Washington County Courthouse, 150 North First, Hillsboro 97124.
Telephone: (503) 846-4403.

LINDER, Virginia L. *(Judge, Oregon Court of Appeals)* Assumed office 1997. Term expires Jan 2005.
Office: Justice Building, Third Floor, 1162 Court Street N.E., Salem 97301-4095.
Telephone: (503) 986-5659.

LIPSCOMB, Paul J. *(Presiding Judge, Oregon Circuit Court Third Judicial District)* Term expires Jan 1, 2007. Born Milwaukee Wisconsin May 11, 1948. Educated at Dartmouth College B.A. cum laude 1970 and Boston University School of Law J.D. cum laude 1975. Assistant Editor Boston University Law Review 1968-70. Law Clerk to Hon. Edward H. Howell, Oregon Supreme Court 1975-77. Admitted to practice Oregon 1975. In legal practice Salem 1977-86. Former Judge, Marion County District Court, appointed by Governor Victor Atiyeh to term beginning Oct 1, 1986.
Adjunct Professor Willamette University Law School since 1985. Member Oregon State Bar and Marion

LIPSCOMB, PAUL J.—*Continued*
County Bar Association. Enjoys hunting, fishing and mountain climbing.
Mailing address: P.O. Box 12869, Salem 97309-0869.
Office: Marion County Courthouse, 148 High Street N.E., Salem 97301.
Telephone: (503) 588-5024.

LITTLEHALES, Charles P. *(Judge, Oregon Circuit Court Seventeenth Judicial District)* Term expires Jan 1, 2007. Former Presiding Judge. Former Judge, Lincoln County District Court.
Mailing address: P.O. Box 100, Newport 97365.
Office: Lincoln County Courthouse, 225 West Olive, Newport 97365.
Telephone: (541) 265-4236.

LITZENBERGER, Marilyn *(Judge, Oregon Circuit Court Fourth Judicial District)* Term expires June 30, 2009.
Office: Multnomah County Courthouse, 1021 S.W. Fourth, Portland 97204.
Telephone: (503) 988-3957.

LOWE, John K. *(Judge, Oregon Circuit Court Fifth Judicial District)* Term expires Jan 1, 2007.
Office: 104 Clackamas County Courthouse, 807 Main Street, Oregon City 97045.
Telephone: (503) 655-8678.

LOY, Michael S. *(Judge, Oregon Circuit Court Fourth Judicial District)* Assumed office Jan 15, 1998. Elected 2002, current term expires Jan 5, 2009. Former Judge, Multnomah County District Court.
Office: Multnomah County Courthouse, 1021 S.W. Fourth, Portland 97204.
Telephone: (503) 988-3813.

LUUKINEN, Charles *(Presiding Judge, Oregon Circuit Court Twelfth Judicial District)* Appointed by Governor Victor Atiyeh to term beginning Jan 1, 1987. Elected 1988, 1994 and May 2000. Current term expires Jan 1, 2007. Born Astoria Oregon Dec 20, 1947. Catholic. Educated at Oregon State University B.S. 1970 and Willamette University J.D. 1975. Admitted to practice Oregon 1975 and U.S. District Court District of Oregon. In legal practice Dallas 1975-83 and Salem 1983-85. Judge, Polk County District Court 1985-86.
Member Oregon Circuit Judges Association (Secretary), Oregon District Court Judges Association, Oregon State Bar and Twelfth Judicial District Bar Association (President 1977). U.S. Army 1970-72. Previously worked as commercial fisherman.
Office: Polk County Courthouse, 850 Main Street, Dallas 97338.
Telephone: (503) 623-9245.

MACKAY, William J. *(Judge, Oregon Circuit Court Fourteenth Judicial District)* Assumed office Jan 1, 1998. Elected 2002, current term expires Jan 5, 2009. Former Judge, Josephine County District Court.
Office: 252 Josephine County Courthouse, 500 N.E. Sixth, Grants Pass 97526.
Telephone: (541) 476-2309.

MARCUS, Michael H. *(Judge, Oregon Circuit Court Fourth Judicial District)* Judge pro tem 1983-98. Reference Judge 1984-90. Assumed office Jan 15, 1998. Elected 2002, current term expires Jan 5, 2009. Born New Rochelle New York April 11, 1943. Educated at University of California at Berkeley A.B. 1966 and University of California Boalt Hall School of Law J.D. 1969. Note and Comment Editor California Law Review 1967-69. Law Clerk to Hon. Raymond Peters, California Supreme Court 1969-70. Member Pi Sigma Alpha and Order of the Coif. Admitted to practice California 1970, U.S. Court of Appeals Ninth Circuit 1970, U.S. Temporary Emergency Court of Appeals 1972, U.S. District Courts Northern District of California 1970 and District of Oregon 1975 and U.S. Supreme Court 1977. Judge pro tem 1980-90 and Judge March 5, 1990 to Jan 14, 1998 Multnomah County District Court.
Attorney San Francisco Neighborhood Legal Assistance Foundation 1970-74. Director of Litigation Multnomah County Legal Aid Service 1974-90. Author "Summary of Forcible Entry and Detainer Law" Oregon Judicial College 1977; chapter "Forcible Entry Detainer" *Pleading & Practice* 1978, 1980 and 1985 and "Forcible Entry Detainer" *Real Estate Disputes* Fall 1993 Oregon Bar Continuing Legal Education; "Landlord/Tenant Relations for Oregon" 1978 and "Landlord/Tenant Rights in Oregon" 1980, 1988, 1992 and 1994 Self Counsel Press; "Doctors, Lawyers and Nursing Home Transfers" The Portland Physician Nov 1981; *District Court Judges FED Casebook* since 1981; "Rent Increase Under HB 2915" Mobilehome Park Owners' Association Observer Nov/Dec 1985; chapter "Mediation in the Criminal Justice System" *Alternative Dispute Resolution Deskbook* Committee on Alternative Dispute Resolution Oregon Judicial Conference 1993 and 1996; and chapter "Mediation in the Criminal Justice System" *Arbitration and Mediation* Oregon Bar Continuing Legal Education 1994 and 1996. Contributing Editor *Oregon Real Estate and Land Use Digest* since 1979. Co-author "Landlord/Tenant" Continuing Legal Education 1981, 1983, 1985 and 1989. Contributing Author *SRO Housing Management Handbook* Burnside Consortium 1983. Important Decisions: Lockhart v. Louisiana-Pacific Corporation (dismissed wrongful discharge claim of male employee discharged for wearing facial jewelry) 102 Or. App. 593, 795 P.2d 602, 1990; State of Oregon v. Galligan (unauthorized departure conviction upheld) 213 Or. 35, 816 P.2d 602, 1991; In re Bors (method of determining corporation value was proper) 115 Or. App. 572, 839 P.2d 272, 1992; Juvenile Department of Multnomah County v. Cornett (child sexual abuse) 121 Or. App. 264, 855 P.2d 171, 1993; Koon v. City of Gresham (water district sought declarations that city had not effectively withdrawn territories from district) 123 Or. App. 513, 860 P.2d 848, 1993; In re Kelley (imposing remedial action for failure to pay child support) 128 Or. App. 123, 874 P.2d 1364, 1994; Juvenile Department of Multnomah County v. Cornett 318 Or. 323, 865 P.2d 1295, 1994; and Morris v. Nance (debtor's transfer of property to defendant) 1994 WL 718567 (Or. App.) 1994. Instructor Legal Writing Northwestern School of Law 1976-77 and Multnomah County Sheriff's Regional Law Enforcement Explorer Academy 1982-83.
Former Member Multnomah County Circuit Court Arbitration Panel and American Arbitration Association Commercial Panel. Former Senior Arbitrator National Panel of Consumer Arbitrators Better Business Bureau. Member District Court Liaison Committee 1981-83 and Alternative Dispute Resolution Committee 1992-94 Multnomah County Bar Association, Indigent Defense Committee 1992, Alternative Dispute Resolution 1992-93 and Sentencing Policy Committee 1996-97 Oregon Judicial

MARCUS, MICHAEL H.—*Continued*

Conference. Member Multnomah County Arbitration Commission, Oregon Council on Court Procedures, Oregon State Bar and State Bar of California. Faculty "Real Property" Oregon Bar Continuing Legal Education 1975, District Court Judges Continuing Legal Education 1984, Evergreen Legal Services Appellate Advocacy Training Conference 1985 and "Landlord/Tenant Law" Professional Education Systems Seminar 1986. Panelist Oregon Judicial College 1977, "Summary Judgments" Young Lawyers' U.S. District Court Federal Practice Continuing Legal Education Multnomah County Bar Association 1982, Issues in Mediation of Criminal Cases Conference on Mediation Policy and Practice Willamette University Center for Dispute Resolution 1990, Oregon Mediation Policy Dialogue 1991 and Multnomah County Landlord/Tenant Mediation Training 1994. Trainer Volunteer Lawyers Project Multnomah County Bar Association 1981, Sunriver Pro Bono Attorneys Training Seminar Oregon Legal Services 1985 and Multnomah County Circuit Court Alternative Dispute Resolution Program FED Mediation 1989. Speaker "Administrative Law: How to Squeeze Error Out of an Order" Continuing Legal Education Multnomah County Bar Association 1985, Landlord/Tenant Law Continuing Legal Education Marion County Bar Association 1988 and Continuing Legal Education Washington County Bar Association 1988, Landlord/Tenant Law and Ethics in Landlord/Tenant Litigation Oregon Pro Bono Attorneys Seminar 1988, Columbia County Legal Aid Continuing Legal Education Seminar 1992, Oregon State Bar Low Income Legal Services Committee Pro Bono Seminar 1993 and Oregon District Attorneys Association Winter Conference 1994. Lecturer Ethical Issues Representing Incompetent Clients Marion-Polk Legal Aid Service 1986.

Member Mayor's Low Income Multi-Family Housing Committee 1980, Health Division Committee on Nursing Home Transfers 1980 and 1983, Governors State Housing Energy Rating System Working Group 1985-86, State Long Term Solution Subcommittee Washington County Mobile Home Task Force 1985-86, Special Needs Advisory Committee PDC Downtown Low Income Housing Preservation Program 1988-89, Portland Community Housing Resource Board since 1989, Steering Committee Oregon HOUSING NOW! 1989-90, Metropolitan Human Relations Commission Task Force 1991-92, Fair Housing Advisory Task Force 1992, Advisory Committee DUI Case Disposition Evaluation Project MADD 1992, Housing Discrimination in Oregon History Project 1992-93, Oregon Campaign for Effective Crime Policy since 1994, Ballot Measure 11 Task Force Joint Judiciary Interim Committee 1996 and Data Standards Working Group 1996 and Evaluation Committee since 1996 Local Public Safety Coordinating Council. Interviewer Code Hearings Officer Hiring Portland Civil Service Board 1983. Board of Directors 1986-93 and Advisory Board since 1993 Resolutions Northwest (formerly known as Victim Offender Reconciliation Program of Multnomah County). Board of Directors Central City Concern since 1994.

Office: Multnomah County Courthouse, 1021 S.W. Fourth, Portland 97204.

Telephone: (503) 988-3250.

MARSH, Malcolm F. *(Senior Judge, United States District Court District of Oregon)* Appointed for life by President Ronald Reagan to term beginning March 24, 1987. Assumed Senior status April 16, 1998, serves by assignment. Born Portland Oregon Sept 24, 1928. Educated at University of Oregon School of Law LL.B. 1954 replaced by J.D. 1971. Admitted to practice Oregon 1954, U.S. District Court District of Oregon 1955 and U.S. Court of Appeals Ninth Circuit 1968. In legal practice Salem Sept 1954 to April 1987.

Fellow American College of Trial Lawyers. Member Oregon State Bar and American Bar Association. U.S. Army 1946-47.

Office: 1507 U.S. Courthouse, 1000 S.W. Third Avenue, Portland 97204-2902.

Telephone: (503) 326-8360.

MARSHALL, Christopher J. *(Judge, Oregon Circuit Court Fourth Judicial District)* Term expires Jan 5, 2009.

Office: Multnomah County Courthouse, 1021 S.W. Fourth, Portland 97204.

Telephone: (503) 988-3274.

MAURER, Jean Kerr *(Judge, Oregon Circuit Court Fourth Judicial District)* Assumed office Jan 15, 1998. Elected 2002, current term expires Jan 5, 2009. Former Judge, Multnomah County District Court.

Office: Multnomah County Courthouse, 1021 S.W. Fourth, Portland 97204.

Telephone: (503) 988-3804.

MAURER, Steven L. *(Judge, Oregon Circuit Court Fifth Judicial District)* Assumed office Jan 15, 1998. Elected May 2000, current term expires Jan 1, 2007. Former Judge, Clackamas County District Court.

Office: 104 Clackamas County Courthouse, 807 Main Street, Oregon City 97045.

Telephone: (503) 655-8643.

McCORMICK, John A. *(Judge, Oregon Circuit Court Twenty-third Judicial District)* Assumed office Jan 15, 1998. Elected May 2000, current term expires Jan 1, 2007. Born Salem Oregon Dec 15, 1946. Educated at University of Oregon B.S. 1969 J.D. 1976 and Midwestern University M.B.A. 1972. Admitted to practice Oregon 1976, U.S. District Court District of Oregon 1977 and U.S. Court of Appeals Ninth Circuit 1982. In legal practice Portland 1976-78 and Albany 1978-95. Judge, Albany Municipal Court 1990-95. Judge, Linn County District Court Jan 1, 1995 to Jan 14, 1998.

Member Oregon State Bar and Linn County Bar Association. USAF 1969-73. Enjoys hunting, fishing and traveling.

Mailing address: P.O. Box 1749, Albany 97321.

Telephone: (541) 967-3844.

McCORMICK, Rick J. *(Presiding Judge, Oregon Circuit Court Twenty-third Judicial District)* Term expires Jan 1, 2007. Born Goldendale Washington Aug 27, 1948. Educated at Oregon State University B.S. 1971 and Northwestern School of Law of Lewis & Clark College J.D. 1974. Staff member Environmental Law 1973-74. Admitted to practice Oregon 1974. Former Judge, Linn County District Court, appointed by Governor Victor Atiyeh Dec 21, 1981.

Mailing address: P.O. Box 1749, Albany 97321.

Telephone: (541) 967-3848.

McDERMID, Ronald *(Justice of the Peace, Sherman County Justice Court)* Appointed by Governor John A.

MCDERMID, RONALD—*Continued*

Kitzhaber to term beginning Sept 5, 2001. Elected Nov 2002, current term expires 2005.
Office: Courthouse, 500 Court Street, Moro 97039.
Telephone: (541) 565-3650.

McELLIGOTT, Michael J. *(Judge, Oregon Circuit Court Twentieth Judicial District)* Term expires Jan 1, 2007. Former Presiding Judge. Former Judge, Washington County District Court.
Office: Washington County Courthouse, 150 North First, Hillsboro 97124.
Telephone: (503) 846-8675.

McKNIGHT, Maureen H. *(Judge, Oregon Circuit Court Fourth Judicial District)* Term expires Jan 5, 2009.
Office: Multnomah County Courthouse, 1021 S.W. Fourth, Portland 97204.
Telephone: (503) 988-3986.

McLEAN, Rod B. *(Justice of the Peace, Columbia County Justice Court)* Appointed by Governor Barbara Roberts to term beginning May 1994. Elected 1994 and 2000. Current term expires Dec 31, 2006. Born Aloha Oregon Feb 28, 1935. Presbyterian.
Member Oregon Mediation Association, Oregon Justice of the Peace Association (Vice President) and National Judges Association. Attended The National Judicial College. Enjoys outdoors activities. Personal Statement or Quote: "There needs to be more humor in the world and in the legal system."
Mailing address: P.O. Box 189, Vernonia 97064.
Telephone: (503) 429-2441.
Fax: (503) 429-0151

McSHANE, Michael *(Judge, Oregon Circuit Court Fourth Judicial District)* Term expires Jan 5, 2009.
Office: Multnomah County Courthouse, 1021 S.W. Fourth, Portland 97204.
Telephone: (503) 988-3214.

MEISENHEIMER, Keith E. *(Judge, Oregon Circuit Court Fourth Judicial District)* Appointed by Governor John A. Kitzhaber to term beginning Nov 15, 1999. Elected May 2000, current term expires Jan 1, 2007. Born Berkeley California. Educated at University of California at Los Angeles B.A. 1970 and Lewis & Clark College Northwestern School of Law J.D. 1976. Admitted to practice Oregon 1976.
Member American Inns of Court.
Office: Multnomah County Courthouse, 1021 S.W. Fourth, Portland 97204.
Telephone: (503) 988-3985.
E-mail address: Keith.Meisenheimer@ojd.state.or.us

MEJIA, Lorenzo A. *(Judge, Oregon Circuit Court First Judicial District)* Term expires Jan 5, 2009.
Office: Justice Building, 100 South Oakdale, Medford 97501.
Telephone: (541) 776-7171.

MENDIGUREN, Phillip A. *(Presiding Judge, Oregon Circuit Court Tenth Judicial District)* Elected Nov 1996 to term beginning Jan 6, 1997. Reelected 2002, current term expires Jan 5, 2009. Born Ontario Oregon Jan 25, 1950. Catholic. Educated at University of Oregon B.S. in Political Science 1972 and Gonzaga University J.D. cum laude 1978. Admitted to practice Idaho 1978 and Oregon 1979. In legal practice La Grande Oregon 1978-96.
President Union County Bar Association. Specialist E-4 U.S. Army 1972-74. Interests include family, golf, fishing, hunting and University of Oregon sports.
Office: Union County Courthouse, 1008 K Avenue, La Grande 97850.
Telephone: (541) 962-9500.

MERTEN, Maurice K. *(Judge, Oregon Circuit Court Second Judicial District)* Term expires Jan 3, 2005. Born Portland Oregon May 30, 1945. Educated at University of Oregon B.S. 1966 J.D. 1969. Admitted to practice Oregon 1969, U.S. Supreme Court 1972, U.S. Courts of Appeals Second, Sixth and Ninth Circuits and U.S. District Court Eastern District of Kentucky. Judge pro tem Nov 1975 to July 1, 1976 and Former Judge, Lane County District Court, appointed by Governor Robert Straub to term beginning July 1, 1976.
With U.S. Department of Justice 1969-73 (Criminal Division Organized Crime and Racketeering Section 1969). Assistant District Attorney Lane County 1973-75. Member Oregon State Bar.
Office: Lane County Courthouse, 125 East Eighth, Eugene 97401.
Telephone: (541) 682-4258.

MICKELSON, Richard K. *(Judge, Oregon Circuit Court Fifteenth Judicial District)* Assumed office Jan 15, 1998. Term expires Jan 3, 2005. Born Seattle Washington March 13, 1947. Catholic. Educated at Seattle University B.A. 1969 and University of Oregon J.D. 1974. Admitted to practice Oregon 1974. In legal practice Brookings 1983-85. Judge, Curry County District Court July 15, 1985 to Jan 14, 1998, appointed by Governor Victor Atiyeh.
With District Attorney's Office Curry County 1978-83. Lieutenant Colonel USAR JAGC 1974-78.
Mailing address: P.O. Box 810, Gold Beach 97444.
Office: Curry County Courthouse, Gold Beach 97444.
Telephone: (541) 247-4511.

MILLER, Eve L. *(Judge, Oregon Circuit Court Fifth Judicial District)* Term expires Jan 3, 2005.
Office: 104 Clackamas County Courthouse, 807 Main Street, Oregon City 97045.
Telephone: (503) 655-8686.

MILLIKAN, Robert C. *(Judge, Oregon Circuit Court Sixteenth Judicial District)* Assumed office Jan 15, 1998. Elected 2002, current term expires Jan 5, 2009. Former Presiding Judge. Born San Francisco California July 10, 1946. Methodist. Educated at Willamette University B.A. 1968 J.D. 1971. Admitted to practice Oregon 1971, U.S. District Court District of Oregon and U.S. Court of Appeals Ninth Circuit. In legal practice Roseburg 1976-77. Judge, Douglas County District Court Aug 1, 1984 to Jan 14, 1998, appointed by Governor Victor Atiyeh.
With District Attorney's Office McMinnville 1972-73. Public Defender 1973-76 and District Attorney 1977-84 Roseburg. Instructor in Criminal Law Umpqua Community College 1979-81. Member Oregon State Bar, Douglas County and American Bar Associations. Attended The National Judicial College. Second Lieutenant USAF 1971-72. Enjoys golf, family and sports.
Office: 201 Justice Building, 1036 S.E. Douglas, Roseburg 97470.
Telephone: (541) 957-2422.

MITCHELL, Douglas S. *(Judge, Oregon Circuit Court Second Judicial District)* Term expires Jan 1, 2007.
Office: Lane County Courthouse, 125 East Eighth, Eugene 97401.
Telephone: (541) 682-4753.

MURGO, Rudy *(Judge, Oregon Circuit Court Sixth Judicial District)* Assumed office Jan 15, 1998. Term expires Jan 3, 2005. Former Presiding Judge. Former Judge, Umatilla County District Court.
Mailing address: P.O. Box 1307, Pendleton 97801.
Office: Umatilla County Courthouse, Pendleton 97801.
Telephone: (541) 278-0341.

MURPHY, Daniel R. *(Judge, Oregon Circuit Court Twenty-third Judicial District)* Elected May 17, 1994 to term beginning Oct 3, 1994. Reelected May 2000, current term expires Jan 1, 2007. Born Lebanon Oregon April 16, 1954. Educated at Oregon State University B.S. 1976 and Willamette University College of Law J.D. 1980. Admitted to practice Oregon 1981, U.S. District Court District of Oregon 1981 and New York 1992. In legal practice Lebanon Oregon 1981-88.
Deputy District Attorney Linn County 1988-94. Instructor in Trial Practice Willamette University College of Law 1992-97. Member National Council of Juvenile and Family Court Judges, American Judges Association, American Judicature Society, Oregon State Bar and New York State Bar Association.
Mailing address: P.O. Box 1749, Albany 97321.
Telephone: (541) 967-3848.

NACHTIGAL, Gayle *(Judge, Oregon Circuit Court Twentieth Judicial District)* Term expires Jan 3, 2005. Former Presiding Judge.
Office: Washington County Courthouse, 150 North First, Hillsboro 97124.
Telephone: (503) 846-4562.

NEILSON, George W. *(Presiding Judge, Oregon Circuit Court Twenty-second Judicial District)* Term expires Jan 5, 2009. Former Judge, Crook-Jefferson County District Court.
Office: Jefferson County Courthouse, 75 S.E. C Street, Madras 97741-1794.
Telephone: (541) 475-3317.

NELSON, Philip L. *(Judge, Oregon Circuit Court Eighteenth Judicial District)* Assumed office Jan 15, 1998. Term expires Jan 3, 2005. Former Judge, Clatsop County District Court.
Mailing address: P.O. Box 835, Astoria 97103.
Office: Clatsop County Courthouse, Astoria 97103.
Telephone: (503) 325-8536.

NELSON, Sheila M. *(Justice of the Peace, Lane County Justice Court)* Appointed to term beginning April 4, 2001. Elected 2002, current term expires Dec 31, 2008.
Office: 47674 School Street, Oakridge 97463.
Telephone: (541) 782-2175.

NEUFELD, Gerald C. *(Presiding Judge, Oregon Circuit Court Fourteenth Judicial District)* Term expires Jan 1, 2007.
Office: 252 Josephine County Courthouse, 500 N.E. Sixth, Grants Pass 97526.
Telephone: (541) 476-2309.

NEWTON, Dewey A. *(Justice of the Peace, Harney County Justice Court)* Elected to term beginning Jan 2001. Term expires Jan 2007.
Office: 450 North Buena Vista Avenue, Burns 97720.
Telephone: (541) 573-2346.

NORBLAD, Albin W. *(Judge, Oregon Circuit Court Third Judicial District)* Term expires Jan 1, 2007.
Mailing address: P.O. Box 12869, Salem 97309-0869.
Office: Marion County Courthouse, 100 High Street N.E., Salem 97301-3665.
Telephone: (503) 588-5028.

OCHOA, Joseph V. *(Judge, Oregon Circuit Court Third Judicial District)* Assumed office Jan 15, 1998. Elected May 2000, current term expires Jan 1, 2007. Former Judge, Marion County District Court.
Mailing address: P.O. Box 12869, Salem 97309-0869.
Office: Marion County Courthouse, 100 High Street N.E., Salem 97301-3665.
Telephone: (503) 373-4361.

O'NEAL, Loyd *(Judge, Oregon Circuit Court Fourteenth Judicial District)* Assumed office Jan 15, 1998. Elected May 2000, current term expires Jan 1, 2007. Born Stilwell Oklahoma June 20, 1944. Educated at California State University at Long Beach B.A. 1967 and Northwestern School of Law of Lewis & Clark College J.D. 1974. Admitted to practice Oregon 1974 and U.S. District Court District of Oregon 1974. Began legal practice Hillsboro. Judge, Josephine County District Court Jan 2, 1983 to Jan 14, 1998.
Instructor Portland Community College 1975-76 and Rogue Community College 1982-83.
Office: 252 Josephine County Courthouse, 500 N.E. Sixth, Grants Pass 97526.
Telephone: (541) 476-2309.

ORF, Rebecca G. *(Judge, Oregon Circuit Court First Judicial District)* Assumed office Jan 15, 1998. Elected 2002, current term expires Jan 5, 2009. Former Judge, Jackson County District Court.
Office: Justice Building, 100 South Oakdale, Medford 97501.
Telephone: (541) 776-7171.

OSBORNE, Roxanne B. *(Judge, Oregon Circuit Court Thirteenth Judicial District)* Term expires Jan 3, 2005. Former Presiding Judge. Former Judge, Klamath-Lake County District Court.
Office: 316 Main Street, Klamath Falls 97601.
Telephone: (541) 883-5503.

PAHL, Ronald J. *(Judge, Oregon Circuit Court Sixth Judicial District)* Term expires Jan 3, 2005.
Mailing address: P.O. Box 1307, Pendleton 97801.
Office: Umatilla County Courthouse, Pendleton 97801.
Telephone: (541) 278-0341.

PANNER, Owen M. *(Senior Judge, United States District Court District of Oregon)* Appointed for life by President Jimmy Carter to term beginning Feb 12, 1980. Former Chief Judge. Assumed Senior status 1992, serves by assignment. Born Chicago Illinois July 28, 1924. Presbyterian. Educated at University of Oklahoma LL.B. 1949. Editor Oklahoma Law Review 1948-49. Member Order of the Coif. Admitted to practice Oklahoma 1949 and Oregon 1950. In legal practice Bend Oregon 1950-80.

PANNER, OWEN M.—*Continued*

Fellow American College of Trial Lawyers. First Lieutenant U.S. Army 1943-46.

Office: 1207 U.S. Courthouse, 1000 S.W. Third Avenue, Portland 97204-2902.

Telephone: (503) 326-8290.

PATNODE, Cris *(Justice of the Peace, Gilliam County Justice Court)* Term expires 2009.

Mailing address: P.O. Box 427, Condon 97823-0427.

Office: Courthouse, 221 South Oregon Street, Condon 97823.

Telephone: (541) 384-3572.

PERKINS, Edward L. *(Judge, Oregon Circuit Court Eleventh Judicial District)* Assumed office Jan 15, 1998. Term expires Jan 3, 2005. Former Judge, Deschutes County District Court.

Office: Deschutes County Courthouse, 1164 N.W. Bond, Bend 97701.

Telephone: (541) 388-5300.

PERRIS, Elizabeth L. *(Judge, United States Bankruptcy Court District of Oregon)* Also Judge, Bankruptcy Appellate Panel Ninth Circuit. Selected by the Judicial Council of the Ninth Circuit.

Office: 1001 S.W. Fifth Avenue, Room 700, Portland 97204.

Telephone: (503) 326-4173.

POOLE, Ronald *(Judge, Oregon Circuit Court Sixteenth Judicial District)* Appointed by Governor Victor Atiyeh Aug 1, 1984. Elected Nov 1984, 1990, 1996 and 2002. Current term expires Jan 5, 2009. Born Winnsboro Texas Jan 2, 1946. Catholic. Educated at University of Texas at Austin B.A. 1968 J.D. 1972. Admitted to practice Oregon 1972 and Texas 1972. Began legal practice Roseburg Oregon 1972. Judge, Douglas County District Court 1979-84.

Member Oregon Circuit Judges Association (Former Secretary), Oregon State Bar and Douglas County Bar Association. E-4 USAR 1968-74. Member Roseburg Planning Commission 1977-78.

Office: 201 Justice Building, 1036 S.E. Douglas, Roseburg 97470.

Telephone: (541) 957-2430.

PRATT, J. Burdette *(Presiding Judge, Oregon Circuit Court Ninth Judicial District)* Assumed office Jan 15, 1998. Elected 2002, current term expires Jan 5, 2009. Born Nyssa Oregon Nov 16, 1950. Church of Jesus Christ of Latter-Day Saints. Educated at Boise State University B.B.A. 1973 and University of Idaho J.D. 1976. Editorial Board Idaho Law Review 1975-76. Admitted to practice Oregon 1976, Idaho 1985 and U.S. District Courts District of Oregon 1980 and District of Idaho 1985. In legal practice Nyssa Oregon 1976-90. Judge, Malheur County District Court May 7, 1990 to Jan 14, 1998, appointed by Governor Neil Goldschmidt.

Member Oregon Circuit Judges Association, Oregon State Bar and Malheur County Bar Association. Attended General Jurisdiction Course and Introduction to Personal Computers The National Judicial College. Board Member Nyssa School Board 1980-85. Scout Master and Explorer Advisor Boy Scouts of America. Enjoys fishing, gardening and white water rafting.

Office: Malheur County Courthouse, Box 3, 251 B Street West, Vale 97918.

Telephone: (541) 473-5194.

PRICE, Steven L. *(Judge, Oregon Circuit Court Twentieth Judicial District)* Assumed office Jan 15, 1998. Elected 2002, current term expires Jan 5, 2009. Former Judge, Washington County District Court.

Office: Washington County Courthouse, 150 North First, Hillsboro 97124.

Telephone: (503) 846-4999.

PURDY, William G. *(Judge, Oregon Circuit Court First Judicial District)* Term expires Jan 5, 2009.

Office: Justice Building, 100 South Oakdale, Medford 97501.

Telephone: (541) 776-7171.

RADCLIFFE, Albert E. *(Chief Judge, United States Bankruptcy Court District of Oregon)* Appointed by U.S. District Court judges to term beginning Dec 23, 1983. Reappointed by U.S. Court of Appeals Ninth Circuit judges Feb 17, 1988 and 2002. Term expires Feb 2016. Chief Judge since Sept 1, 1999. Born Portland Oregon April 23, 1947. Educated at University of Oregon B.A. 1969 J.D. 1972. Member Tau Kappa Epsilon and Phi Alpha Delta. Admitted to practice Oregon 1972, U.S. District Court District of Oregon 1973 and U.S. Court of Appeals Ninth Circuit 1983. In legal practice Eugene 1973-86.

Important Decisions: Tri City Service District v. Pacific Marine Dredging and Construction, et al. 79 B.R. 924, 16 Bankr. Ct. Dec. 915, 5 UCC Rep. Serv. 2d 1110 Bankr. D. Or. 1987; In re Luby 89 B.R. 120, 19 Collier Bankr. Cas. 2d 426 Bankr. D. Or. 1988; In re Williams Land Co., Inc. 91 B.R. 923, 19 Collier Bankr. Cas. 2d 1289 Bankr. D. Or. 1988; In re Derickson 104 B.R. 346, 64 A.F.T.R. 2d 89-5323, 89-2 USTC P 9480 Unempl. Ins. Rep. (CCH) P 14856A.56 Bankr. D. Or. 1989; In re Woodward 113 B.R. 680, 90-1 USTC P 50,244, 20 Bankr. Ct. Dec. 741 Bankr. L. Rep. P 1990; In re E Z Feed Cube Co., Ltd. 115 B.R. 684, 20 Bankr. Ct. Dec. 1049 Bankr. L. Rep. P 73, 427 Bankr. D. Or. 1990; In re McAllister 125 B.R. 393, 21 Bankr. Ct. Dec. 405 Bankr. D. Or. 1991; Roost v. Tyee Timbers, Inc. (In re Tyee Timbers, Inc.) 139 B.R. 520, 22 Bankr. Ct. Dec. 1437 Bankr. D. Or. 1992; In re Pad Enterprises, Inc. 139 B.R. 516, 22 Bankr. Ct. Dec. 1415 Bankr. D. Or. 1992; In re Garelli 162 B.R. 552, 88 Ed. L. Rep. 721 Bankr. L. Rep. P 75,690 Bankr. D. Or. 1994; In re Berry 166 B.R. 932, 31 Collier Bankr. Cas. 2d 290 Bankr. L. Rep. P 75,954 Bankr. D. Or. 1994; In re Heritage Mall Associates 184 B.R. 128, 27 Bankr. Ct. Dec. 614 Bankr. D. Or. 1995; In re Roost v. Reynolds (In re Reynolds) 189 B.R. 199 Bankr. L. Rep. P 76,825 Bankr. D. Or. 1995; In re Moore 200 B.R. 687 Bankr. D. Or. 1986; In re Ritacco 210 B.R. 595, 38 Collier Bankr. Cas. 2d 310 Bankr. D. Or. 1997.

Member National Conference of Bankruptcy Judges, U.S. District Court District of Oregon Historical Society, Oregon State Bar and Lane County Bar Association (Committees: Joint Medical-Legal Liaison 1980-81, Public Service and Information 1981-82, Joint Attorney-Realtor 1983-84, Bankruptcy Liaison since 1985). Named Jaycee of the Year by Eugene Junior Chamber of Commerce 1978. Paul Harris Fellow Eugene Southtowne Rotary Club 1985. Captain U.S. Army field artillery 1967-77. Member Southtowne Rotary Club (Rotary Foundation Committee, Handicapped Committee, Paul Harris Sustaining Members Committee, Aid to Homeless Committee 1991) and Eugene Junior Chamber of Commerce (Chapter legal counsel 1974-84). Board of Direc-

RADCLIFFE, ALBERT E.—*Continued*

tors Lane County Chapter American Red Cross 1979-82. Enjoys skiing, racquetball, tennis, camping, fishing and family activities.

Office: 151 West Seventh Avenue, Suite 300, Eugene 97401-2649.

Telephone: (541) 465-6802.

RAINES, Keith R. *(Judge, Oregon Circuit Court Twentieth Judicial District)* Term expires Jan 5, 2009.

Office: Washington County Courthouse, 150 North First, Hillsboro 97124.

Telephone: (503) 846-3457.

RAMBO, Richard B. *(Judge, Oregon Circuit Court Thirteenth Judicial District)* Assumed office Jan 15, 1998. Elected May 2000, current term expires Jan 1, 2007. Born Oregon Nov 23, 1948. Educated at University of Oregon B.S. 1974 J.D. 1977. Member Phi Beta Kappa. Admitted to practice Oregon 1977 and U.S. District Court District of Oregon 1982. In legal practice Klamath Falls. Judge pro tem Klamath Falls Municipal Court 1985-86. Judge, Klamath-Lake County District Court Jan 1, 1993 to Jan 14, 1998, appointed by Governor Barbara Roberts.

Public Defender Baker County 1977-78. Deputy District Attorney Baker County 1978-79 and Josephine County 1980-81. Member Oregon State Bar. Attended National Judicial College Reno.

Office: 316 Main Street, Klamath Falls 97601.

Telephone: (541) 883-5503.

RASMUSSEN, Karsten H. *(Judge, Oregon Circuit Court Second Judicial District)* Term expires Jan 1, 2007.

Office: Lane County Courthouse, 125 East Eighth, Eugene 97401.

Telephone: (541) 682-4253.

REDDEN, James A. *(Senior Judge, United States District Court District of Oregon)* Appointed for life by President Jimmy Carter to term beginning March 24, 1980. Former Chief Judge. Assumed Senior status March 13, 1995, serves by assignment. Born Springfield Massachusetts March 13, 1929. Catholic. Educated at Boston University 1949-51 and Boston College Law School LL.B. 1954. Senior Class President 1953-54. Admitted to practice Massachusetts 1954 and Oregon 1955. Began legal practice Springfield Massachusetts 1954. In legal practice Medford Oregon 1956-72.

Representative Oregon State Legislature 1963-69 (Minority Leader 1967 regular and special sessions). Oregon State Treasurer 1972-76. Oregon Attorney General 1977-80. Member American Board of Trial Advocates, Oregon Association of Defense Counsel, Oregon State Bar and Jackson County Bar Association. Private First Class U.S. Army 1946-48. Social worker Department of Public Welfare Springfield Massachusetts June 1954 to June 1955. Title Examiner Title and Trust Insurance Company Hillsboro Oregon 1955. Formerly employed as claims adjuster Allstate Insurance Company Portland Oregon. Democrat. Enjoys running.

Office: 1527 U.S. Courthouse, 1000 S.W. Third Avenue, Portland 97204-2902.

Telephone: (503) 326-8370.

REED, Steven B. *(Judge, Oregon Circuit Court Nineteenth Judicial District)* Term expires Jan 5, 2009.

Office: Columbia County Courthouse, 244 Strand Street, St. Helens 97051-2041.

Telephone: (503) 397-2327.

REYNOLDS, Garry L. *(Judge, Oregon Circuit Court Sixth Judicial District)* Term expires Jan 5, 2009.

Mailing address: P.O. Box 1307, Pendleton 97801.

Office: Umatilla County Courthouse, Pendleton 97801.

Telephone: (541) 278-0341.

RHOADES, Jamese L. *(Judge, Oregon Circuit Court Third Judicial District)* Term expires Jan 1, 2007. Former Judge, Marion County District Court.

Mailing address: P.O. Box 12869, Salem 97309-0869.

Office: Marion County Courthouse, 100 High Street N.E., Salem 97301-3665.

Telephone: (503) 588-7950.

RIGGS, R. William *(Justice, Oregon Supreme Court)* Assumed office 1998. Term expires Jan 2005. Born Hinsdale Illinois Nov 21, 1938. Educated at University of Oregon J.D. 1968. Articles Editor and member Managing Board Oregon Law Review 1967-68. Admitted to practice Oregon, U.S. Court of Appeals Ninth Circuit, U.S. District Court District of Oregon and U.S. Supreme Court. In legal practice 1968-78. Judge, Oregon Circuit Court Fourth Judicial District 1978-88, appointed by Governor Robert W. Straub. Judge, Oregon Court of Appeals May 1988 to 1998. Presiding Judge, Oregon Court of Appeals Panel Two 1995-98.

Visiting Lecturer on Trial Law University of Oregon and Lewis & Clark College since 1973. Secretary-Treasurer 1971-72, President 1973-74 and Former Member Board of Governors Oregon Trial Lawyers Association. Former member Board of Governors Western Trial Lawyers Association. Member The Association of Trial Lawyers of America (Judicial Member), Oregon State Bar (Member 1973-75 and Chairperson 1975 Unauthorized Practice of Law Committee, Member and Chairperson 1978-79 Committee on Function and Organization of the Bar), Multnomah County and American Bar Associations. Lecturer and author CLE programs Oregon State Bar since 1970. Captain USNR (active duty 1961-65).

Office: Supreme Court Building, 1163 State Street, Salem 97301-2562.

Telephone: (503) 986-5668.

RIGGS, Yvonne *(Justice of the Peace, Baker County Justice Court)* Elected to term beginning Jan 1, 2001. Term expires Dec 31, 2006.

Office: 235 Gover Lane, Halfway 97834.

Telephone: (541) 742-7171.

ROBERTS, Carol *(Justice of the Peace, Douglas County Justice Court)* Elected to term beginning Jan 1, 2001. Term expires Dec 31, 2006.

Office: 249 N.E. Main Street, Canyonville 97417.

Telephone: (541) 839-4389.

E-mail address: cvjc@pioneer-net.com

ROBERTSON, Beverly C. *(Justice of the Peace, Baker County Justice Court)* Elected to term beginning May 19, 1998. Term expires Nov 1, 2005. Currently serves as Presiding Justice of the Peace.

Office: 50 East Adams, Huntington 97907.

Telephone: (541) 869-2202.

ROLL, Richard *(Judge, Oregon Circuit Court Twenty-seventh Judicial District)* Assumed office Jan 15, 1998. Term expires Jan 3, 2005. Formerly served Eighteenth Judicial District. Former Judge, Tillamook County District Court.

Office: Tillamook County Courthouse, 201 Laurel Avenue, Tillamook 97141.

Telephone: (503) 842-2598.

ROSENBLUM, Ellen F. *(Judge, Oregon Circuit Court Fourth Judicial District)* Term expires Jan 1, 2007. Former Judge, Multnomah County District Court.

Office: Multnomah County Courthouse, 1021 S.W. Fourth, Portland 97204.

Telephone: (503) 988-5029.

SCHIVELEY, Mark *(Presiding Judge, Oregon Circuit Court First Judicial District)* Assumed office Jan 15, 1998. Elected 2002, current term expires Jan 5, 2009. Former Judge, Jackson County District Court.

Office: Justice Building, 100 South Oakdale, Medford 97501.

Telephone: (541) 776-7171.

SCHUMAN, David *(Judge, Oregon Court of Appeals)* Appointed by Governor John A. Kitzhaber to term beginning March 2001. Elected May 21, 2002, current term expires Dec 31, 2008. Born Chicago Illinois May 8, 1944. Educated at Stanford University B.A. 1966, San Francisco State University M.A. 1969, University of Chicago Ph.D. 1974 and University of Oregon School of Law J.D. 1984. Judicial Clerk to Hon. Hans A. Linde, Oregon Supreme Court 1984-85. Member Order of the Coif. Admitted to practice Oregon 1984, U.S. Court of Appeals Ninth Circuit 1985 and U.S. District Court District of Oregon 1997.

Assistant Attorney General Appellate Division 1985-87 and Deputy Attorney General Jan 1997 to Dec 2000 Oregon Department of Justice. Author "The Political Community, the Individual, and Control of Public School Curriculum" 63, 309-333, 1984, "Oregon's Remedy Guarantee: Article I, Section 10 of the Oregon Constitution" 65, 35-72, 1986 and "The Creation of the Oregon Constitution" 74, 611-641, 1995 Oregon L. Rev.; "The Right to 'Equal Privileges and Immunities': A State's Version of 'Equal Protection'" 13 Vermont L. Rev. 221-245, 1988; "Advocacy of State Constitutional Law Cases" 2 *Emerging Issues in State Constitutional Law* 275-297, 1989; "Beyond the Waste Land: Law Practice in the 1990s" 42 Hastings L. Jour. 1-13, 1990; "Taking Law Seriously: Communitarian Search and Seizure" 27 American Criminal L. Rev. 583-617, 1990 and revised version 3 The Responsive Community 32, 1993; "The Right to a Remedy" 65, 1197-1227, 1992 and "The Origins of State Constitutional Direct Democracy: William Simon U'Ren and the 'Oregon System'" 67, 947, 1994 Temple L. Rev.; "A Failed Critique of State Constitutionalism" 91 Michigan L. Rev. 274-280, 1992; and "State Constitutionalism Comes of Age in Oregon" 59 Albany L. Rev. 1741-1742, 1996. Assistant Professor 1987-92, Associate Professor 1992-97, Associate Dean for Academic Affairs 1994-96 and Professor Jan 2001 to March 2001 University of Oregon School of Law. Former Member American Bar Foundation and State Bar of Oregon. Recipient Ersted Award for Distinguished Teaching 1989 and Orlando Hollis Award for Excellence in Teaching 1993 from University of Oregon School of Law. Professor of English Deep Springs College 1974-81.

Office: 1162 Court Street N.E., Salem 97301.

Telephone: (503) 986-5672.

Fax: (503) 986-5865

E-mail address: david.schuman@state.or.us

SEITZ, Joan G. *(Presiding Judge, Oregon Circuit Court Sixteenth Judicial District)* Appointed by Governor Victor Atiyeh to term beginning Dec 20, 1985. Elected May 1986, 1992 and 1998. Current term expires Jan 3, 2005. Presiding Judge 1987-93, 1998-2001 and since 2003. Born Chicago Illinois July 14, 1949. Catholic. Educated at Southern Oregon College B.S. cum laude 1971 and Willamette University College of Law J.D. 1974. Admitted to practice Oregon 1974. In legal practice Roseburg 1982-85.

Deputy District Attorney Klamath County 1974-76. Assistant Public Defender 1976-79 and Assistant County Counsel 1979-82 Douglas County. Member Oregon State Bar and Douglas County Bar Association (President 1985).

Office: 201 Justice Building, 1036 S.E. Douglas, Roseburg 97470.

Telephone: (541) 957-2436.

SELANDER, Robert R. *(Presiding Judge, Oregon Circuit Court Fifth Judicial District)* Term expires Jan 5, 2009. Former Judge, Clackamas County District Court.

Office: 104 Clackamas County Courthouse, 807 Main Street, Oregon City 97045.

Telephone: (503) 655-8233.

SHARTEL, James R. *(Justice of the Peace, Washington County Justice Court)* Elected to term beginning Jan 1998. Term expires Jan 2004.

Office: 3700 S.W. Murray Boulevard, Beaverton 97005.

Telephone: (503) 681-6600.

E-mail address: James-Shartel@co.washington.or.us

SIMPSON, Lane W. *(Presiding Judge, Oregon Circuit Court Twenty-sixth Judicial District)* Assumed office Jan 15, 1998. Elected 2002, current term expires Jan 5, 2009. Former Judge, Klamath-Lake County District Court.

Office: Lake County Courthouse, 513 Center Street, Lakeview 97630.

Telephone: (541) 947-6051.

SINCLAIR, Cynthia *(Justice of the Peace, Lane County Justice Court)* Elected to term beginning Jan 1, 1997. Reelected 2002, current term expires Jan 1, 2009. Born St. Paul Minnesota. Catholic. Educated at California State University at Los Angeles B.A. 1972.

Former Court Clerk/Judicial Assistant Superior Court of California County of Los Angeles. Former Court Operations Specialist III Oregon Circuit Court Second Judicial District. Member Oregon Justices of the Peace Association (Treasurer) and National Judges Association. Attended Institute for Municipal and Justice Court Judges and The National Judicial College. Recipient Golden Rule Award for charity work. President Willamette Wildlife Rehabilitation. Board of Directors St. Vincent DePaul. Advisory Board Lane County Parks. Member Budget Committee Springfield School District. Literacy

SINCLAIR, CYNTHIA—*Continued*

tutor. Member Relief Nursery, Juvenile Justice Task Force and Animal Regulation Task Force.
Office: 220 Fifth Street, Springfield 97477.
Telephone: (541) 682-3621.
Fax: (541) 744-1190

SMITH, Berkeley A. *(Presiding Judge, Oregon Circuit Court Nineteenth Judicial District)* Assumed office Jan 15, 1998. Term expires Jan 3, 2005. Former Judge, Columbia County District Court.
Office: Columbia County Courthouse, 244 Strand Street, St. Helens 97051-2041.
Telephone: (503) 397-2327.

SMITH, Bernard *(Judge, Oregon Circuit Court Seventh Judicial District)* Term expires Jan 3, 2005.
Mailing address: P.O. Box 1400, The Dalles 97058.
Office: Wasco County Courthouse, Fifth and Washington, The Dalles 97058.
Telephone: (541) 296-2209.

STEWART, Janice M. *(Magistrate Judge, United States District Court District of Oregon)* Appointed by U.S. District Court judges Oct 13, 1993. Reappointed 2001, current term expires Oct 2009. Born Medford Oregon Feb 13, 1951. Educated at Stanford University A.B. with honors and distinction 1972 and University of Chicago J.D. 1975. Member Phi Beta Kappa. Moot Court Board. Admitted to practice Illinois 1975, Oregon 1977, U.S. District Court District of Oregon 1978 and U.S. Court of Appeals Ninth Circuit 1978. In legal practice Chicago 1975-76 and Portland 1976-93.
Important Decisions: Cleese v. Hewlett-Packard Co. 911 F. Supp. 1312, 7 NDLR P 306 D. Or., Dec 21, 1995; Nemo v. City of Portland 910 F. Supp. 491 D. Or., Dec 12, 1995; United States v. Lindstedt 1995 WL 774520, 76 A.F.T.R. 2d 95-7389, 77 A.F.T.R. 2d 96-558 D. Or., Dec 4, 1995; Plumeau v. Yamhill County School Dist. No. 40, 907 F. Supp. 1423, 105 Ed. Law Rep. 1006 D. Or., Nov 14, 1995; United States v. Brooks 1995 WL 555271, 76 A.F.T.R. 2d 95-5382 D. Or., June 8, 1995; United States v. Brooks 164 F.R.D. 501 D. Or., Apr 28, 1995; Adams v. J.C. Penney Co., Inc. 865 F. Supp. 1454 D. Or., Oct 6, 1994; Kanematsu Corp. v. M/V GRETCHEN W. 1994 WL 774554, 1995 A.M.C. 195 D. Or., Sept 27, 1994; Delyria v. Shalala 856 F. Supp. 1432, 45 Soc. Sec. Rep. Ser. 255, Unempl. Ins. Rep. (CCH) P 14242B D. Or., June 2, 1994; and Hells Canyon Preservation Council v. Richmond 841 F. Supp. 1039, 24 Envtl. L. Rep. 20,919 D. Or., Dec 9, 1993. Master Gus J. Solomon Chapter American Inns of Court 1988-92 and 1994-96. Lawyer Representative Ninth Circuit Judicial Conference 1990-93. Former Arbitrator Multnomah County American Arbitration Association and American Arbitration Service of Portland. Former Member Council on Court Procedures and Professional Liability Fund Defense Panel. Member Oregon State Bar (Member State Professional Responsibility Board 1982-85, Chair Procedure and Practice Committee 1985-88, Member Professionalism Committee 1989-92, Member Federal Practice and Procedure Committee since 1993) and Multnomah County Bar Association (Member Professional Responsibility Committee 1979-82, Member Judicial Selection Committee 1985-88, Director 1990-93, Member Professionalism Committee 1995-2000). Frequent speaker for continuing legal education seminars.
Office: 1027 U.S. Courthouse, 1000 S.W. Third Avenue, Portland 97204-2902.
Telephone: (503) 326-8260.

STONE, Martin E. *(Judge, Oregon Circuit Court Fifteenth Judicial District)* Term expires Jan 3, 2005.
Office: Coos County Courthouse, 250 North Baxter, Coquille 97423.
Telephone: (541) 396-3121.

STONE, Ronald W. *(Judge, Oregon Circuit Court Twenty-fifth Judicial District)* Elected Nov 7, 2000. Term expires Jan 1, 2007.
Office: Yamhill County Courthouse, 535 N.E. Fifth Street, McMinnville 97128.
Telephone: (503) 434-7530.

SULLIVAN, Donal D. *(Recalled Judge, United States Bankruptcy Court District of Oregon)* Clerk 1965-69. Appointed Judge by U.S. District Court judges to term beginning Sept 30, 1969. Reappointed to subsequent terms. Appointed Recalled Judge by the Judicial Council of the Ninth Circuit. Born St. Louis Missouri May 21, 1931. Educated at Loyola University, Illinois Institute of Technology and DePaul University 1957. Law Clerk to Justice Hall Lusk, Oregon Supreme Court 1958. Editor DePaul Law Review 1956. Admitted to practice Oregon 1957 and Illinois 1958. Began legal practice Salem Oregon 1959.
Deputy District Attorney Multnomah County 1960. Assistant Attorney General 1960-62 and First Assistant U.S. Attorney 1962-65 Oregon. Adjunct Professor of Creditors' Rights and Bankruptcy Northwestern School of Law of Lewis & Clark College 1981-83. Member National Conference of Bankruptcy Judges, Oregon State Bar, Multnomah County and American Bar Associations. Lecturer on Federal Practice CLE series Oregon State Bar 1968 and Federal Court Seminar Lewis & Clark College 1978. USMC 1950-52.
Office: 1001 S.W. Fifth Avenue, Room 700, Portland 97204.
Telephone: (503) 326-4186.

SULLIVAN, Michael Cornelius *(Judge, Oregon Circuit Court Eleventh Judicial District)* Appointed by Governor Neil Goldschmidt to term beginning Feb 19, 1988. Elected 1988, 1994 and May 2000. Current term expires Jan 1, 2007. Born Portland Oregon May 21, 1948. Catholic. Educated at Washington University B.S.B.A. 1970 and University of Oregon School of Law J.D. 1973. Admitted to practice Oregon 1973.
Deputy District Attorney Lane County 1974-77. District Attorney and County Counsel Jefferson County 1977-88. Former member Legislative Committee and Past President Oregon District Attorney's Association. Former Chairman and Former Hearings Officer Board on Police Standards and Training. Former Chairman Hispanic Relations Committee. Chairman Central Oregon Bar Association. President Circuit Court Judges Association. Colonel Oregon National Guard (retired). Former Chairman Task Force on Drug Abuse. Former Board Member Jefferson County Council on Alcoholism. Past President Kiwanis Club.
Office: Deschutes County Courthouse, 1100 N.W. Bond, Bend 97701.
Telephone: (541) 388-5300.

SULLIVAN, Patricia *(Judge, Oregon Circuit Court Ninth Judicial District)* Elected May 2000. Term expires Jan 1, 2007.

Office: Malheur County Courthouse, Box 3, 251 B Street West, Vale 97918.

Telephone: (541) 473-5178.

SUMMERS, Steven R. *(Justice of the Peace, Marion County Justice Court)* Elected to term beginning Jan 1997. Reelected 2002, current term expires Jan 2009.

Office: 111 West Locust, Suite 3, Stayton 97383.

Telephone: (503) 769-7656.

SVETKEY, Susan M. *(Judge, Oregon Circuit Court Fourth Judicial District)* Term expires Jan 1, 2007.

Office: Multnomah County Courthouse, 1021 S.W. Fourth, Portland 97204.

Telephone: (503) 988-3060.

TENNYSON, Katherine *(Judge, Oregon Circuit Court Fourth Judicial District)* Term expires Jan 5, 2009.

Office: Multnomah County Courthouse, 1021 S.W. Fourth, Portland 97204.

Telephone: (503) 988-3078.

THOM, Ronald D. *(Judge, Oregon Circuit Court Fifth Judicial District)* Elected Nov 7, 2000. Term expires Jan 1, 2007.

Office: 104 Clackamas County Courthouse, 807 Main Street, Oregon City 97045.

Telephone: (503) 655-8685.

THOMPSON, Gary S. *(Judge, Oregon Circuit Court Twenty-second Judicial District)* Assumed office Jan 15, 1998. Elected 2002, current term expires Jan 5, 2009. Born Lakeview Oregon Oct 23, 1945. Catholic. Educated at Oregon State University B.S. and Willamette University College of Law J.D. Admitted to practice Oregon 1972 and U.S. District Court District of Oregon 1979. In legal practice Prineville 1972-75. Former Judge, Crook-Jefferson County District Court July 1, 1990 to Jan 14, 1998, appointed by Governor Neil Goldschmidt.

District Attorney Crook County 1972-90. President Oregon District Attorneys Association 1981-82. Member Oregon State Bar and Central Oregon Bar Association.

Office: Crook County Courthouse, 300 East Third Street, Prineville 97754.

Telephone: (541) 447-6541.

THOMPSON, Kirsten E. *(Judge, Oregon Circuit Court Twentieth Judicial District)* Term expires Jan 5, 2009.

Office: Washington County Courthouse, 150 North First, Hillsboro 97124.

Telephone: (503) 846-8872.

THOMPSON, Terry *(Justice of the Peace, Malheur County Justice Court)* Term expires 2005.

Office: 251 B Street West, Vale 97918.

Telephone: (541) 473-5124.

E-mail address: tthompson@malheur.org

TICHENOR, Carroll J. *(Judge, Oregon Circuit Court Twenty-fifth Judicial District)* Term expires Jan 5, 2009.

Office: Yamhill County Courthouse, 535 N.E. Fifth Street, McMinnville 97128.

Telephone: (503) 434-7530.

TIKTIN, Stephen *(Presiding Judge, Oregon Circuit Court Eleventh Judicial District)* Term expires Jan 5, 2009.

Office: Deschutes County Courthouse, 1100 N.W. Bond, Bend 97701.

Telephone: (541) 388-5300.

TRIPP, Susan M. *(Judge, Oregon Circuit Court Third Judicial District)* Term expires Jan 5, 2009.

Mailing address: P.O. Box 12869, Salem 97309-0869.

Office: Marion County Courthouse, 100 High Street N.E., Salem 97301-3665.

Telephone: (503) 588-8485.

TRISKA, Richard E. *(Justice of the Peace, Linn County Justice Court)* Appointed by Governor Robert W. Straub to term beginning March 8, 1978. Elected 1978, 1984, 1990, 1996 and 2002. Current term expires 2009. Born Chicago Illinois Nov 24, 1932. Roman Catholic. Educated at Loyola University at Chicago B.S. 1959 M.S.W. 1963, DePaul University School of Law J.D. 1968 and Mount Angel Seminary M.A. with honors 1988. Admitted to practice Illinois 1968, Oregon 1971 and U.S. District Court District of Oregon 1972. In legal practice Albany Oregon 1972-78 and Lebanon Oregon 1978-87.

Author "The Legalities of Mushroom Experimentation" Linn-Benton Community College 1977. Member Oregon State Bar. Member Minor Court Rules Committee Oregon Supreme Court 1979-87. Previously employed as U.S. Probation and Parole Officer 1965-71. Member Linn County Planning Commission 1976-80. Chairman Linn County Mental Health Advisory Board 1978-87. Enjoys computer technology and basset hounds.

Mailing address: P.O. Box 283, Lebanon 97355.

Telephone: (541) 258-5777 (Lebanon), 367-5902 (Sweet Home).

E-mail address: rtriska@centurytel.net

TRUMP, Russell G. *(Justice of the Peace, Douglas County Justice Court)* Elected to term beginning Jan 1, 1987. Reelected 1992 and 1998. Current term expires Dec 31, 2004. Educated at Oregon State University B.S. 1981 and University of Oregon J.D. 1984. Admitted to practice Oregon 1984.

Member Oregon State Bar and Douglas County Bar Association.

Mailing address: P.O. Box 513, Drain 97435.

Telephone: (541) 836-2814.

UPTON, Suzanne M. *(Judge, Oregon Circuit Court Twentieth Judicial District)* Elected Nov 8, 1998 to term beginning Jan 4, 1999. Term expires Jan 3, 2005. Born Spokane Washington May 10, 1957. Educated at Western State College of Colorado B.A. 1979 and University of Oregon J.D. 1989. Admitted to practice Oregon 1990.

Deputy District Attorney Washington County May 1990 to Sept 1998. Director 1992-98 and President 1997-98 Washington County Bar Association. Director Washington County Women Lawyers 1993-98. Chair Washington County Judicial Screening Committee 1997. Named "most qualified" judicial candidate two Bar polls 1998.

Office: Washington County Courthouse, 150 North First, Hillsboro 97124.

Telephone: (503) 846-3590.

E-mail address: suzanne.upton@ojd.state.or.us

VAN DYK, Douglas *(Judge, Oregon Circuit Court Fifth Judicial District)* Term expires Jan 3, 2005.
Office: 104 Clackamas County Courthouse, 807 Main Street, Oregon City 97045.
Telephone: (503) 655-8688.

VELURE, Lyle C. *(Judge, Oregon Circuit Court Second Judicial District)* Term expires Jan 1, 2007.
Office: Lane County Courthouse, 125 East Eighth, Eugene 97401.
Telephone: (541) 682-4256.

WALLACE, Jeff M. *(Presiding Judge, Oregon Circuit Court Sixth Judicial District)* Assumed office Jan 15, 1998. Term expires Jan 3, 2005. Born Walla Walla Washington Oct 5, 1949. Episcopalian. Educated at University of Oregon B.S. with honors 1972 and Willamette University College of Law J.D. 1976. Admitted to practice Oregon 1976 and U.S. District Court District of Oregon 1977. In legal practice Pendleton 1976-77 and Milton-Freewater 1978-81. Former Judge, Morrow-Umatilla County District Court Jan 4, 1993 to Jan 14, 1998.
Deputy District Attorney Umatilla County 1984-87. District Attorney Morrow County 1987-93. Former Member Malheur County Bar Association. Member Sixth Judicial District Bar Association. Lieutenant Colonel USAR JAGC. Senior Military Judge USAR. City Administrator Weston 1981-83. Member Hermiston Kiwanis, Hermiston Masons and Heppner Lions Club. Enjoys running and music.
Mailing address: P.O. Box 1307, Pendleton 97801.
Office: Umatilla County Courthouse, Pendleton 97801.
Telephone: (541) 567-5225.

WALLER, Nan G. *(Judge, Oregon Circuit Court Fourth Judicial District)* Term expires Jan 5, 2009.
Office: Multnomah County Courthouse, 1021 S.W. Fourth, Portland 97204.
Telephone: (503) 988-3038.

WARD, Theressa W. *(Justice of the Peace, Wheeler County Justice Court)* Appointed by Governor Neil Goldschmidt to term beginning April 2, 1990. Elected Nov 6, 1990, 1996 and 2002. Current term expires Dec 31, 2008.
Office: 701 Adams Street, Fossil 97830.
Telephone: (541) 763-2047.
E-mail address: twward50@hotmail.com

WELCH, Elizabeth *(Judge, Oregon Circuit Court Fourth Judicial District)* Appointed by Governor Barbara Roberts to term beginning Jan 4, 1993. Elected 1994 and May 2000. Current term expires Jan 1, 2007. Chief Judge Family Court since 1994. Born Urbana Illinois. Jewish. Educated at University of Chicago B.A. 1963 J.D. 1965. Admitted to practice Illinois 1966, Oregon 1968, U.S. District Court District of Oregon 1969 and U.S. Court of Appeals Ninth Circuit 1970. In legal practice Portland Oregon 1979-89. Judge, Oregon Circuit Court Fourth Judicial District 1978-79. Judge, Multnomah County District Court 1989-92.
Senior Deputy District Attorney Multnomah County 1969-71 and 1973-75. Director Office of Justice Programs Portland 1971-73 and 1975-78. Author and Speaker on Juvenile Law, Family Law and Probate Law. Instructor Lewis & Clark College Northwestern School of Law 1970-78. Member 1971-73 and 1979-82 and Chair 1981-82 Committee on Future of Legal Profession. Member Council on Court Procedures 1989-92, Governor's Task Force on Drug Abuse and Pregnancy 1990-91, Juvenile Code Revision Committee 1991-92 and Select Committee on Support Guidelines. Member 1991-93 and Chair 1992-93 Access to Justice Committee Oregon State Bar. Chair Board of Directors Oregon Law Institute 1995-97. Chair Family Law Advisory Committee since 1989 and Juvenile Justice Council since 1996 Multnomah County.
Office: Multnomah County Courthouse, 1021 S.W. Fourth, Portland 97204.
Telephone (503) 988-3008.

WEST, C. Gregory *(Judge, Oregon Circuit Court Third Judicial District)* Appointed by Governor Victor Atiyeh to term beginning Aug 1, 1986. Elected May 1986, 1992 and 1998. Current term expires Jan 3, 2005. Former Presiding Judge. Born Littleton New Hampshire Jan 21, 1941. Catholic. Educated at University of New Hampshire B.A. 1969, University of Alaska 1968-69 and Willamette University College of Law J.D. 1972. Member Sigma Alpha Epsilon and Phi Delta Theta. Admitted to practice Oregon 1972. Began legal practice Salem 1972. Judge, Marion County District Court 1981-86.
Former Assistant City Attorney. Recipient highest overall rating of District Court Judges in poll by Oregon State Bar 1982. E-4 USAR 1964-70. Smokejumper Bureau of Land Management U.S. Department of the Interior Fairbanks Alaska 1964-69. Democrat. Enjoys duplicate bridge (Lifemaster since 1978, won twelve regional championships).
Mailing address: P.O. Box 12869, Salem 97309-0869.
Office: Marion County Courthouse, 100 High Street N.E., Salem 97301-3665.
Telephone: (503) 588-5135.

WEST, Russell B. *(Judge, Oregon Circuit Court Tenth Judicial District)* Term expires Jan 5, 2009.
Office: Union County Courthouse, 1008 K Avenue, La Grande 97850.
Telephone: (541) 962-9500.

WHITE, Raymond B. *(Judge, Oregon Circuit Court First Judicial District)* Assumed office Jan 15, 1998. Elected May 2000, current term expires Jan 1, 2007. Born Medford Oregon Sept 25, 1946. Educated at Pacific University 1964-65, Southern Oregon State College B.S.B.A. 1969 and University of Oregon J.D. 1972. Judge, Jackson County District Court March 11, 1981 to Jan 14, 1998, appointed by Governor Victor Atiyeh.
Office: Justice Building, 100 South Oakdale, Medford 97501.
Telephone: (541) 776-7171.

WILLIAMS, Locke A. *(Judge, Oregon Circuit Court Twenty-first Judicial District)* Term expires Jan 5, 2009.
Mailing address: P.O. Box 1870, Corvallis 97339.
Office: Benton County Courthouse, 120 N.W. Fourth, Corvallis 97330-4734.
Telephone: (541) 766-6827.

WILSON, Janice R. *(Judge, Oregon Circuit Court Fourth Judicial District)* Appointed by Governor Barbara Roberts to term beginning Jan 3, 1994. Elected Nov 1994 and May 2000. Current term expires Jan 1, 2007. Educated at Willamette University B.A. cum laude 1976 J.D. summa cum laude 1979. Law Clerk to U.S. District Court District of Oregon 1979 and Hon. Otto R. Skopil, Jr., U.S. Court of Appeals Ninth Circuit 1979-81. Admitted to practice Oregon 1979, U.S. District Court Dis-

WILSON, JANICE R.—*Continued*

trict of Oregon 1979 and U.S. Court of Appeals Ninth Circuit 1980. In legal practice Portland Oct 1981 to March 1991. Judge, Multnomah County District Court March 29, 1991 to Jan 2, 1994.

Special Prosecutor District Attorney's Office Multnomah County Spring 1990. Co-author "1989 Legislation (Labor and Employment)" Oregon State Bar Continuing Legal Education. Volunteer Attorney Senior Law Project 1982-90. Board of Directors May 1982 to Nov 1990 Volunteer Lawyers Project (Treasurer May 1984 to April 1985, Secretary April 1985 to Feb 1986, Vice President Feb 1986 to June 1988 and President June 1988 to June 1989). Member Judicial Conference Judicial Education Committee since 1991 (Member since 1993 and Vice Chair April 1994 Executive Committee). Member Policy Group for Intermediate Sanctions for Women Offenders Oregon Department of Corrections and Oregon Criminal Justice Council since 1994. Member Gus J. Solomon American Inn of Court and Multnomah County Bar Association (Member Jan 1987 to Feb 1990 and Chair Jan 1988 to Feb 1990 Judicial Selection Committee, Court Liaison Committee since July 1990). Attended General Jurisdiction Course The National Judicial College 1991. Panelist "Complex Litigation" Oct 1991, "Zealous Advocacy—The Good, the Bad, and the Ugly" April 1994 and "Ask the Lawyer" Aug 1994 Oregon Women Lawyers; and "Direct and Cross Examination of an HIV+ Client in an Employment Discrimination Case" Continuing Legal Education Sept 1994. Presenter "Evidence" Nov 1991, "Trial Dynamics" Jan 1993 and "Tips for the Litigator" April 1994 Continuing Legal Education Oregon Law Institute; "HIV in the Workplace" Continuing Legal Education Volunteer Lawyers Project March 1994; "Scientific Evidence" Continuing Legal Education Oregon Judicial Conference April 1994; "Novel and Scientific Evidence" Continuing Legal Education Oregon State Bar May 1994; and "Effective Techniques for Taking and Defending Depositions" Continuing Legal Education Multnomah County Bar Association June 1994. Moderator DUI Victims' Panel since 1992. Cooperating Attorney 1981-91, Chair Commission on Lesbian and Gay Rights 1987-90, Member Lawyers' Committee 1987-91, Board of Directors 1987-91 and Vice President for Litigation 1990-91 American Civil Liberties Union of Oregon. Volunteer Lawyer 1982-91, Board of Directors 1982-85 and Advisory Board 1989-91 Our New Beginnings, Inc. Chair 1985-86 and Vice Chair 1993-94 Multnomah County Community Corrections Advisory Committee. Volunteer Arbitrator Consumer Disputes Better Business Bureau 1987-91. Board of Visitors Willamette University College of Law since 1988. Board of Directors Phoenix Rising Foundation Jan 1993 to Feb 1996.

Office: Multnomah County Courthouse, 1021 S.W. Fourth, Portland 97204.

Telephone: (503) 988-3069.

WILSON, John B. *(Judge, Oregon Circuit Court Third Judicial District)* Assumed office Jan 15, 1998. Term expires Jan 3, 2005. Former Judge, Marion County District Court.

Mailing address: P.O. Box 12869, Salem 97309-0869.

Office: Marion County Courthouse, 100 High Street N.E., Salem 97301-3665.

Telephone: (503) 588-5030.

WITTMAYER, John *(Judge, Oregon Circuit Court Fourth Judicial District)* Assumed office Jan 15, 1998. Elected 2002, current term expires Jan 5, 2009. Former Judge, Multnomah County District Court.

Office: Multnomah County Courthouse, 1021 S.W. Fourth, Portland 97204.

Telephone: (503) 988-3165.

WOGAN, Cameron F. *(Presiding Judge, Oregon Circuit Court Thirteenth Judicial District)* Assumed office Jan 15, 1998. Term expires Jan 3, 2005. Born Montevideo Minnesota Nov 1, 1955. Protestant. Educated at Oregon State University B.A. with honors 1979 and University of Oregon J.D. 1984. Admitted to practice Oregon 1984 and U.S. District Court District of Oregon 1985. In legal practice Klamath Falls 1984-92. Judge, Klamath County District Court Aug 28, 1992 to Jan 14, 1998.

Member Oregon State Bar. Enjoys family activities and outdoor sports.

Office: 316 Main Street, Klamath Falls 97601.

Telephone: (541) 883-5503.

WOLLHEIM, Robert *(Judge, Oregon Court of Appeals)* Assumed office 1998. Term expires Jan 2005.

Office: Justice Building, Third Floor, 1162 Court Street N.E., Salem 97301-4095.

Telephone: (503) 986-5676.

WYATT, Merri S. *(Judge, Oregon Circuit Court Fourth Judicial District)* Assumed office Jan 15, 1998. Elected May 2000, current term expires Jan 1, 2007. Former Judge, Multnomah County District Court.

Office: Multnomah County Courthouse, 1021 S.W. Fourth, Portland 97204.

Telephone: (503) 988-3029.

WYERS, Jan G. *(Judge, Oregon Circuit Court Fourth Judicial District)* Term expires Jan 3, 2005.

Office: Multnomah County Courthouse, 1021 S.W. Fourth, Portland 97204.

Telephone: (503) 988-6760.

ZYRYANOFF, Janice D. *(Justice of the Peace, Marion County Justice Court)* Elected to term beginning Jan 2001. Term expires Jan 2007.

Office: 986 North Pacific Highway, Woodburn 97071.

Telephone: (503) 981-8101.

E-mail address: janicez@canby.com

PENNSYLVANIA

Capital HARRISBURG

UNITED STATES DISTRICT COURTS DISTRICTS OF PENNSYLVANIA

Within Pennsylvania there are three United States District Courts. For descriptive information refer to the United States Courts section.

EASTERN DISTRICT includes Berks, Bucks, Chester, Delaware, Lancaster, Lehigh, Montgomery, Northampton and Philadelphia counties. The court sits at Allentown, Easton, Lancaster, Philadelphia and Reading.

Chief Judge

James T. Giles

Judges

Franklin S. Van Antwerpen	Herbert J. Hutton
Ronald L. Buckwalter	Jay C. Waldman
William H. Yohn, Jr.	Harvey Bartle III
John R. Padova	Stewart Dalzell
Eduardo C. Robreno	J. Curtis Joyner
Bruce W. Kauffman	Anita B. Brody
Petrese Brown Tucker	Mary A. McLaughlin
R. Barclay Surrick	Berle M. Schiller
Cynthia M. Rufe	Legrome D. Davis
Timothy J. Savage	Michael M. Baylson
	James Knoll Gardner

Senior Judges

John P. Fullam	Charles R. Weiner
J. William Ditter, Jr.	Donald W. Van Artsdalen
Clarence C. Newcomer	Louis H. Pollak
Clifford Scott Green	James McGirr Kelly
Norma L. Shapiro	Marvin Katz
Thomas N. O'Neill, Jr.	Robert F. Kelly
Edmund V. Ludwig	Jan E. DuBois
Lowell A. Reed, Jr.	

Clerk

Michael E. Kunz
2609 U.S. Courthouse
601 Market Street
Philadelphia, Pennsylvania 19106-1796
(215) 597-7704

MIDDLE DISTRICT includes Adams, Bradford, Cameron, Carbon, Centre, Clinton, Columbia, Cumberland, Dauphin, Franklin, Fulton, Huntingdon, Juniata, Lackawanna, Lebanon, Luzerne, Lycoming, Mifflin, Monroe, Montour, Northumberland, Perry, Pike, Potter, Schuylkill, Snyder, Sullivan, Susquehanna, Tioga, Union, Wayne, Wyoming and York counties. The court sits at Harrisburg, Lewisburg, Scranton, Wilkes-Barre and Williamsport.

Chief Judge

Thomas I. Vanaskie

Judges

A. Richard Caputo
James M. Munley
Yvette Kane
Christopher C. Conner
John E. Jones III

Senior Judges

William J. Nealon, Jr.	Malcolm Muir
Sylvia H. Rambo	Richard P. Conaboy
William W. Caldwell	Edwin M. Kosik
James F. McClure, Jr.	

Clerk

Mary E. D'Andrea
P.O. Box 1148
Scranton, Pennsylvania 18501-1148
(570) 207-5600

WESTERN DISTRICT includes Allegheny, Armstrong, Beaver, Bedford, Blair, Butler, Cambria, Clarion, Clearfield, Crawford, Elk, Erie, Fayette, Forest, Greene, Indiana, Jefferson, Lawrence, McKean, Mercer, Somerset, Venango, Warren, Washington and Westmoreland counties. The court sits at Erie, Johnstown and Pittsburgh.

Chief Judge

Donetta W. Ambrose

Judges

Gary L. Lancaster	Robert J. Cindrich
Sean J. McLaughlin	Joy Flowers Conti
David S. Cercone	Terrence F. McVerry
Arthur J. Schwab	

Senior Judges

Maurice B. Cohill, Jr.	Donald E. Ziegler
Gustave Diamond	Alan N. Bloch
William L. Standish	Donald J. Lee

Clerk

Robert V. Barth, Jr.
P.O. Box 1805
Pittsburgh, Pennsylvania 15230-1805
(412) 208-7520

UNITED STATES MAGISTRATE JUDGES OF PENNSYLVANIA

EASTERN DISTRICT

James R. Melinson	M. Faith Angell
Arnold C. Rapoport	Charles B. Smith
Diane M. Welsh	Thomas J. Rueter
Carol Sandra Wells	Jacob P. Hart
Linda K. Caracappa	

MIDDLE DISTRICT

William Hartman Askey
J. Andrew Smyser
Thomas M. Blewitt
Malachy E. Mannion

UNITED STATES DISTRICT COURTS DISTRICTS OF PENNSYLVANIA—*Continued*

WESTERN DISTRICT

Ila Jeanne Sensenich	Robert C. Mitchell
Keith A. Pesto	Francis X. Caiazza
Susan Paradise Baxter	Amy Reynolds Hay

Recalled Magistrate Judges
Tullio Gene Leomporra (Eastern)
Peter B. Scuderi (Eastern)

UNITED STATES BANKRUPTCY COURTS OF PENNSYLVANIA

EASTERN DISTRICT

Chief Judge
Bruce I. Fox

Judges
Thomas M. Twardowski
Stephen Raslavich
Diane W. Sigmund
Kevin J. Carey

Bankruptcy Clerk
Joseph Simmons
400 Federal Building
900 Market Street
Philadelphia, Pennsylvania 19107-4299
(215) 408-4411

MIDDLE DISTRICT

Chief Judge
John J. Thomas

Judge
Mary D. France

Bankruptcy Clerk
Arlene Byers
274 U.S. Courthouse
197 South Main Street
Wilkes-Barre, Pennsylvania 18701-1598
(570) 826-6450

WESTERN DISTRICT

Chief Judge
Judith K. Fitzgerald

Judges
Bernard Markovitz
M. Bruce McCullough

Recalled Judges
Joseph L. Cosetti
Warren W. Bentz

Bankruptcy Clerk
Theodore S. Hopkins
5414 USX Tower
600 Grant Street
Pittsburgh, Pennsylvania 15219
(412) 644-2700

THE SUPREME COURT OF PENNSYLVANIA

The Supreme Court is Pennsylvania's court of last resort. The court consists of a chief justice and six justices initially elected at statewide partisan elections for ten-year terms. Subsequent ten-year terms are by retention vote. Vacancies may be filled by the governor with consent of the Senate. Appointees serve until the next general election, at which time they may run for election to office. The justice with the longest continuous service to the court is designated chief justice. Retirement is mandatory at age seventy; however, retired justices may serve as senior justices by assignment of the chief justice.

The court has appellate jurisdiction over cases originating in the Commonwealth Court and appeals of certain final orders issued by either the Common Pleas Court or specific constitutional and judicial agencies. The court has exclusive jurisdiction of appeals from the Court of Common Pleas in cases involving the death penalty, and over appeals originating from the Legislative Reapportionment Commission, the Court of Judicial Discipline (under limited conditions), the Minor Judiciary Education Board, the Pennsylvania Board of Law Examiners or the Disciplinary Board of the Supreme Court. The court has extraordinary jurisdiction to assume jurisdiction of any case pending before a lower court involving an issue of immediate public importance (this it can do on its own or upon petition from any party). The court has original jurisdiction to issue writs of habeas corpus, mandamus or quo warranto. The court exercises general supervisory control and rule-making authority over the court system.

The court sits en banc and exercises statewide jurisdiction, but three districts are established for the purpose of holding court.

EASTERN DISTRICT includes Philadelphia County. The court sits at Philadelphia.

MIDDLE DISTRICT includes Adams, Berks, Bradford, Bucks, Carbon, Centre, Chester, Clinton, Columbia, Cumberland, Dauphin, Delaware, Franklin, Fulton, Huntingdon, Juniata, Lackawanna, Lancaster, Lebanon, Lehigh, Luzerne, Lycoming, Mifflin, Monroe, Montgomery, Montour, Northampton, Northumberland, Perry, Pike, Schuylkill, Snyder, Sullivan, Susquehanna, Tioga, Union, Wayne, Wyoming and York counties. The court sits at Harrisburg.

WESTERN DISTRICT includes Allegheny, Armstrong, Beaver, Bedford, Blair, Butler, Cambria, Cameron, Clarion, Clearfield, Crawford, Elk, Erie, Fayette, Forest, Greene, Indiana, Jefferson, Lawrence, McKean, Mercer, Potter, Somerset, Venango, Warren, Washington and Westmoreland counties. The court sits at Pittsburgh.

Chief Justice
Ralph J. Cappy

Justices

Ronald D. Castille	Russell M. Nigro
Sandra Schultz Newman	Thomas G. Saylor
J. Michael Eakin	vacancy

Prothonotary
Charles W. Johns, Esq.
468 City Hall
Philadelphia, Pennsylvania 19107
(215) 560-6370

THE SUPREME COURT OF PENNSYLVANIA—*Continued*

Court Administrator

Zygmont A. Pines, Esq.
1515 Market Street, Suite 1414
Philadelphia, Pennsylvania 19102
(215) 560-6300

THE SUPERIOR COURT OF PENNSYLVANIA

The Superior Court is Pennsylvania's intermediate appellate court. For administrative purposes only, the state is divided into three districts. The court consists of a president judge and fourteen judges initially elected to ten-year terms at statewide partisan elections. Subsequent ten-year terms are by retention vote. Vacancies may be filled by the governor with consent of the Senate. Appointees serve until the next general election, at which time they may run for election to office. The president judge is elected to a five-year term by peer vote. Retirement is mandatory at age seventy; however, retired judges may serve as senior judges by assignment of the chief justice.

The court has exclusive appellate jurisdiction of all cases at law and equity from Courts of Common Pleas except those cases which are under the exclusive jurisdiction of the Supreme Court or the Commonwealth Court. The court hears a wide variety of appeals from the Courts of Common Pleas, including matters of contract, tort, domestic relations, nongovernment equity except for eminent domain and nonprofit corporation matters and most criminal cases. The court has original jurisdiction in applications made by the attorney general and district attorneys under the Wiretapping and Electronic Surveillance Control Act.

Judges sit in panels of three, but panel decisions may be reviewed by the court en banc at the discretion of the court.

EASTERN DISTRICT includes Bucks, Carbon, Chester, Delaware, Lehigh, Monroe, Montgomery, Northampton, Philadelphia, Pike and Wayne counties. The court sits at Philadelphia.

MIDDLE DISTRICT includes Adams, Berks, Bradford, Centre, Clinton, Columbia, Cumberland, Dauphin, Franklin, Fulton, Huntingdon, Juniata, Lackawanna, Lancaster, Lebanon, Luzerne, Lycoming, Mifflin, Montour, Northumberland, Perry, Schuylkill, Snyder, Sullivan, Susquehanna, Tioga, Union, Wyoming and York counties. The court sits at Harrisburg.

WESTERN DISTRICT includes Allegheny, Armstrong, Beaver, Bedford, Blair, Butler, Cambria, Cameron, Clarion, Clearfield, Crawford, Elk, Erie, Fayette, Forest, Greene, Indiana, Jefferson, Lawrence, McKean, Mercer, Potter, Somerset, Venango, Warren, Washington and Westmoreland counties. The court sits at Pittsburgh.

President Judge

Joseph A. Del Sole

Judges

Justin M. Johnson	Joseph A. Hudock
Kate Ford Elliott	Michael T. Joyce
Correale F. Stevens	John L. Musmanno
Joan Orie Melvin	Maureen E. Lally-Green
Debra McCloskey Todd	John T. Bender
Mary Jane Bowes	Richard B. Klein
Robert A. Graci	vacancy

THE COMMONWEALTH COURT OF PENNSYLVANIA

The Commonwealth Court is a court of special and appellate jurisdiction in Pennsylvania. For administrative purposes only, the state is divided into three districts. The court consists of a president judge and eight judges initially elected at statewide partisan elections for ten-year terms. Subsequent ten-year terms are by retention vote. Vacancies may be filled by the governor with consent of the Senate. Appointees serve until the next general election, at which time they may run for election to office. The president judge is elected to a five-year term by peer vote. Retirement is mandatory at age seventy; however, retired judges may serve as senior judges by assignment of the chief justice.

The court has exclusive jurisdiction in civil actions brought against the commonwealth government or an officer of the government (usually seeking equitable relief or declaratory judgment and not damages) and matters under the Election Code involving statewide offices, and concurrent jurisdiction with the Courts of Common Pleas in civil actions brought by the commonwealth government other than eminent domain matters. The court has appellate jurisdiction over cases from the Court of Common Pleas involving actions against the commonwealth that could not be initiated in the Commonwealth Court, actions by the commonwealth that could have been commenced in the Commonwealth Court, some appeals from decisions of the Liquor Board and the Department of Transportation, most local government matters other than contract matters (including actions for damages), eminent domain proceedings and matters involving the internal affairs of non-profit corporations.

Judges may sit en banc or in panels at the discretion of the court.

EASTERN DISTRICT includes Berks, Bucks, Carbon, Chester, Columbia, Delaware, Lackawanna, Lancaster, Lehigh, Luzerne, Monroe, Montgomery, Montour, Northampton, Northumberland, Philadelphia, Pike, Schuylkill, Sullivan, Susquehanna, Wayne and Wyoming counties. The court sits at Philadelphia.

MIDDLE DISTRICT includes Adams, Bradford, Centre, Clinton, Cumberland, Dauphin, Franklin, Fulton, Huntingdon, Juniata, Lebanon, Lycoming, Mifflin, Perry, Snyder, Tioga, Union and York counties. The court sits at Harrisburg.

WESTERN DISTRICT includes Allegheny, Armstrong, Beaver, Bedford, Blair, Butler, Cambria, Cameron, Clarion, Clearfield, Crawford, Elk, Erie, Fayette, Forest, Greene, Indiana, Jefferson, Lawrence, McKean, Mercer, Potter, Somerset, Venango, Warren, Washington and Westmoreland counties. The court sits at Pittsburgh.

President Judge

James Gardner Colins

Judges

Bernard L. McGinley	Doris A. Smith-Ribner
Dante R. Pellegrini	Rochelle S. Friedman
Bonnie B. Leadbetter	Renée L. Cohn
M. Hannah Leavitt	Robert E. Simpson, Jr.

PENNSYLVANIA COURTS OF COMMON PLEAS

The Courts of Common Pleas are courts of general jurisdiction in Pennsylvania. The state is divided into sixty judicial districts, each comprised of one or two counties. Judges are initially elected in partisan elections to ten-year terms by the voters of each district. Subsequent ten-year terms are by retention vote. Vacancies may be filled by the governor with consent of the Senate. Appointees serve until the next general election, at which time they may run for election to office. President judges are elected to five-year terms by peer vote, except in courts of seven or fewer judges where the judge with the longest continuous service to the court is designated the president judge. Retirement is mandatory at age seventy; however, retired judges may serve as senior judges by assignment of the chief justice.

The courts have original jurisdiction of all civil and criminal matters except those which are the exclusive jurisdiction of a lower court or the Commonwealth Court. The courts may establish specialized divisions as needed. In the First Judicial District the court consists of Trial, Family and Orphans' Divisions. In the Fifth Judicial District Civil, Criminal, Orphans' and Family Divisions have been established. Other districts have established Orphans' Divisions which handle probate matters. All courts hear appeals from certain state and most local government agencies as provided by statute. All but the First Judicial District hear appeals from district justice courts. The First Judicial District hears appeals from Philadelphia Municipal Court and the Traffic Court of Philadelphia. In addition, the Fifth Judicial District hears appeals from Pittsburgh Magistrates Court. The court may also issue writs of certiorari.

The courts sit at the county seats and elsewhere as prescribed by general rules or rule of court.

---

*Administrative Judge

FIRST JUDICIAL DISTRICT includes Philadelphia County. The court sits at Philadelphia.

President Judge
Frederica A. Massiah-Jackson

Judges

Howland W. Abramson
Norman Ackerman
Jacqueline F. Allen
Mark Israel Bernstein
Willis W. Berry, Jr.
Gwendolyn N. Bright
Genece E. Brinkley
Joan A. Brown
Sandy L. V. Byrd
Matthew D. Carrafiello
Ida K. Chen
Tama Myers Clark
Denis P. Cohen
Gene D. Cohen
Mary D. Colins
Amanda Cooperman
Nicholas M. D'Alessandro
Rose M. DeFino-Nastasi
Pamela Pryor Dembe
Thomas E. Dempsey
Alfred J. DiBona, Jr.
Victor J. DiNubile, Jr.
Gary F. Di Vito
Kevin M. Dougherty
Joseph A. Dych
Myrna P. Field*
James Fitzgerald, III*
Leslie Fleisher
Idee C. Fox
Steven R. Geroff
Gary S. Glazer
Richard J. Gordon, Jr.
Jane Cutler Greenspan
John W. Herron
Glynnis D. Hill
Renée Cardwell Hughes
Elizabeth Jackson
C. Darnell Jones, II
Barbara A. Joseph
Harold M. Kane
Joyce S. Kean
D. Webster Keogh
Marlene Lachman
Anne E. Lazarus
Benjamin Lerner
Kathryn Streeter Lewis
James Murray Lynn
Eugene E. J. Maier
William J. Manfredi
Robert J. Matthews
William J. Mazzola
Patricia A. McInerney
Margaret T. Murphy McKeown
Rayford A. Means
Sandra Mazer Moss
Arnold L. New
John J. O'Grady, Jr.
Joseph D. O'Keefe*
George W. Overton
Paul P. Panepinto
Joseph I. Papalini
Nitza I. Quiñones Alejandro
Lillian Harris Ransom
Lisa M. Rau
Robert J. Rebstock
Abram Frank Reynolds
Annette M. Rizzo
Shelley Robins New
Rosalyn K. Robinson
Peter F. Rogers
M. Teresa Sarmina
Albert Sheppard, Jr.
Karen Shreeves-Johns
Gregory E. Smith
Albert J. Snite, Jr.
Edward R. Summers
Esther R. Sylvester
Carolyn Engel Temin
Allan L. Tereshko
Earl W. Trent, Jr.
Thomas D. Watkins
Chris R. Wogan
Flora Barth Wolf
Sheila A. Woods-Skipper
John Milton Younge
Jerome A. Zaleski

SECOND JUDICIAL DISTRICT includes Lancaster County. The court sits at Lancaster.

President Judge
Michael A. Georgelis

Judges

Paul K. Allison
David L. Ashworth
James P. Cullen
Louis J. Farina
Leslie Gorbey
Jay J. Hoberg
Wayne G. Hummer, Jr.
Henry Kenderdine, Jr.
Joseph C. Madenspacher
Michael J. Perezous
Lawrence F. Stengel

THIRD JUDICIAL DISTRICT includes Northampton County. The court sits at Easton.

President Judge
Robert A. Freedberg

Judges
Stephen G. Baratta
F. P. Kimberly McFadden
William F. Moran
Jack Anthony Panella
Edward G. Smith

FOURTH JUDICIAL DISTRICT includes Tioga County. The court sits at Wellsboro.

President Judge
Robert E. Dalton, Jr.

FIFTH JUDICIAL DISTRICT includes Allegheny County. The court sits at Pittsburgh.

President Judge
Robert A. Kelly

Judges

Cheryl Lynn Allen
Max Baer
Cynthia A. Baldwin
Gerard M. Bigley*
David R. Cashman
Kim Berkeley Clark
Robert E. Colville
Robert J. Colville

PENNSYLVANIA COURTS OF COMMON PLEAS—*Continued*

Guido A. De Angelis
Kathleen A. Durkin
Kim D. Eaton
Judith L. A. Friedman
Robert P. Horgos
Walter R. Little
Paul F. Lutty, Jr.
Jeffrey A. Manning
Donna Jo McDaniel
Lester G. Nauhaus
Timothy P. O'Reilly
Alan S. Penkower
Eugene F. Scanlon, Jr.*
Randal B. Todd
R. Stanton Wettick, Jr.
Michael A. Della Vecchia
Ronald W. Folino
Robert C. Gallo
Joseph M. James*
Frank J. Lucchino
Donald E. Machen
Lee J. Mazur
Kathleen R. Mulligan
W. Terrence O'Brien
Lawrence J. O'Toole
Kevin G. Sasinoski
Eugene B. Strassburger, III
John A. Zottola
vacancy

SIXTH JUDICIAL DISTRICT includes Erie County. The court sits at Erie.

President Judge
William R. Cunningham

Judges
Fred P. Anthony
Shad F. Connelly
Stephanie Domitrovich
Elizabeth K. Kelly
John A. Bozza
Ernest DiSantis, Jr.
Michael E. Dunlavey
John J. Trucilla

SEVENTH JUDICIAL DISTRICT includes Bucks County. The court sits at Doylestown.

President Judge
R. Barry McAndrews

Judges
Kenneth G. Biehn
Michael J. Kane
Robert J. Mellon
John J. Rufe
Rea Boylan Thomas
David W. Heckler
Daniel J. Lawler
Alan M. Rubenstein
Susan Devlin Scott

EIGHTH JUDICIAL DISTRICT includes Northumberland County. The court sits at Sunbury.

President Judge
Robert B. Sacavage

Judges
Charles Horace Saylor
Wm. Harvey Wiest

NINTH JUDICIAL DISTRICT includes Cumberland County. The court sits at Carlisle.

President Judge
George E. Hoffer

Judges
Edgar B. Bayley
Edward E. Guido
Kevin A. Hess
J. Wesley Oler, Jr.

TENTH JUDICIAL DISTRICT includes Westmoreland County. The court sits at Greensburg.

President Judge
Daniel J. Ackerman

Judges
Alfred B. Bell
Gary P. Caruso
Rita Donovan Hathaway
Richard E. McCormick, Jr.
John E. Blahovec
John J. Driscoll
Anthony G. Marsili
William J. Ober
Debra Ann Pezze

ELEVENTH JUDICIAL DISTRICT includes Luzerne County. The court sits at Wilkes-Barre.

President Judge
Michael T. Conahan

Judges
Joseph M. Augello
Mark A. Ciavarella, Jr.
Chester B. Muroski
Patrick J. Toole, Jr.
Thomas F. Burke, Jr.
Ann H. Lokuta
Hugh F. Mundy
Peter P. Olszewski, Jr.

TWELFTH JUDICIAL DISTRICT includes Dauphin County. The court sits at Harrisburg.

President Judge
Joseph H. Kleinfelter

Judges
Bruce F. Bratton
Lawrence F. Clark, Jr.
Todd A. Hoover
Jeannine Turgeon
John F. Cherry
Scott A. Evans
Richard A. Lewis

THIRTEENTH JUDICIAL DISTRICT includes Greene County. The court sits at Waynesburg.

President Judge
H. Terry Grimes

Judge
William R. Nalitz

FOURTEENTH JUDICIAL DISTRICT includes Fayette County. The court sits at Uniontown.

President Judge
Conrad B. Capuzzi

Judges
Steve P. Leskinen
Gerald R. Solomon
John F. Wagner, Jr.
Ralph C. Warman

FIFTEENTH JUDICIAL DISTRICT includes Chester County. The court sits at West Chester.

President Judge
Howard F. Riley, Jr.

Judges
Jacqueline C. Cody
James P. MacElree, II
Paula Francisco Ott
Juan R. Sánchez
Robert J. Shenkin
Thomas G. Gavin
William P. Mahon
Katherine B. L. Platt
Anthony A. Sarcione
Phyllis R. Streitel

SIXTEENTH JUDICIAL DISTRICT includes Somerset County. The court sits at Somerset.

President Judge
Eugene E. Fike, II

Judges
John M. Cascio
Kim R. Gibson

PENNSYLVANIA COURTS OF COMMON PLEAS—*Continued*

SEVENTEENTH JUDICIAL DISTRICT includes Snyder and Union counties. The court sits at Middleburg and Lewisburg.

President Judge
Harold F. Woelfel, Jr.

Judge
Louise O. Knight

EIGHTEENTH JUDICIAL DISTRICT includes Clarion County. The court sits at Clarion.

President Judge
James G. Arner

NINETEENTH JUDICIAL DISTRICT includes York County. The court sits at York.

President Judge
John H. Chronister

Judges
Penny L. Blackwell
Michael J. Brillhart
Sheryl A. Dorney
John S. Kennedy
Stephen P. Linebaugh
Richard K. Renn
Gregory M. Snyder
John W. Thompson, Jr.
John C. Uhler

TWENTIETH JUDICIAL DISTRICT includes Huntingdon County. The court sits at Huntingdon.

President Judge
Stewart L. Kurtz

TWENTY-FIRST JUDICIAL DISTRICT includes Schuylkill County. The court sits at Pottsville.

President Judge
William E. Baldwin

Judges
Cyrus Palmer Dolbin
John E. Domalakes
Charles M. Miller
Jacqueline L. Russell
D. Michael Stine

TWENTY-SECOND JUDICIAL DISTRICT includes Wayne County. The court sits at Honesdale.

President Judge
Robert J. Conway

TWENTY-THIRD JUDICIAL DISTRICT includes Berks County. The court sits at Reading.

President Judge
Albert A. Stallone

Judges
Mary Ann Campbell
Thomas J. Eshelman
Arthur E. Grim
Scott D. Keller
Scott E. Lash
Stephen B. Lieberman
Linda K. Mowson Ludgate
Thomas G. Parisi
Jeffrey L. Schmehl
Peter W. Schmehl
Jeffrey K. Sprecher

TWENTY-FOURTH JUDICIAL DISTRICT includes Blair County. The court sits at Hollidaysburg.

President Judge
Thomas G. Peoples, Jr.

Judges
Hiram A. Carpenter, III
Jolene Grubb Kopriva
Daniel J. Milliron

TWENTY-FIFTH JUDICIAL DISTRICT includes Clinton County. The court sits at Lock Haven.

President Judge
Richard N. Saxton, Jr.

Judge
J. Michael Williamson

TWENTY-SIXTH JUDICIAL DISTRICT includes Columbia and Montour counties. The court sits at Bloomsburg and Danville.

President Judge
Scott W. Naus

Judge
Thomas A. James, Jr.

TWENTY-SEVENTH JUDICIAL DISTRICT includes Washington County. The court sits at Washington.

President Judge
David L. Gilmore

Judges
Katherine B. Emery
Debbie O'Dell-Seneca
Paul M. Pozonsky

TWENTY-EIGHTH JUDICIAL DISTRICT includes Venango County. The court sits at Franklin.

President Judge
H. William White

Judge
Oliver J. Lobaugh

TWENTY-NINTH JUDICIAL DISTRICT includes Lycoming County. The court sits at Williamsport.

President Judge
Clinton W. Smith

Judges
Dudley N. Anderson
Kenneth D. Brown
Nancy L. Butts
William S. Kieser

THIRTIETH JUDICIAL DISTRICT includes Crawford County. The court sits at Meadville.

President Judge
Gordon R. Miller

Judges
John F. Spataro
Anthony J. Vardaro

THIRTY-FIRST JUDICIAL DISTRICT includes Lehigh County. The court sits at Allentown.

President Judge
William H. Platt

Judges
Alan M. Black
Lawrence J. Brenner
William E. Ford
Carol K. McGinley

PENNSYLVANIA COURTS OF COMMON PLEAS—*Continued*

Edward D. Reibman
Robert L. Steinberg
Thomas A. Wallitsch

THIRTY-SECOND JUDICIAL DISTRICT includes Delaware County. The court sits at Media.

President Judge
Kenneth A. Clouse

Judges
Harry J. Bradley
Charles B. Burr, II
Joseph P. Cronin, Jr.
Barry C. Dozor
Kathrynann W. Durham
Maureen F. Fitzpatrick
Frank T. Hazel
Patricia H. Jenkins
Charles C. Keeler
Kevin F. Kelly
George Koudelis
Ann A. Osborne
George A. Pagano
James F. Proud
Robert C. Wright
Edward J. Zetusky, Jr.

THIRTY-THIRD JUDICIAL DISTRICT includes Armstrong County. The court sits at Kittanning.

President Judge
Joseph A. Nickleach

Judge
Kenneth G. Valasek

THIRTY-FOURTH JUDICIAL DISTRICT includes Susquehanna County. The court sits at Montrose.

President Judge
Kenneth W. Seamans

THIRTY-FIFTH JUDICIAL DISTRICT includes Mercer County. The court sits at Mercer.

President Judge
Francis J. Fornelli

Judges
Thomas R. Dobson
Michael J. Wherry

THIRTY-SIXTH JUDICIAL DISTRICT includes Beaver County. The court sits at Beaver.

President Judge
Robert E. Kunselman

Judges
George E. James
C. Gus Kwidis
John D. McBride
Peter O. Steege

THIRTY-SEVENTH JUDICIAL DISTRICT includes Forest and Warren counties. The court sits at Tionesta and Warren.

President Judge
Paul H. Millin

Judge
William F. Morgan

THIRTY-EIGHTH JUDICIAL DISTRICT includes Montgomery County. The court sits at Norristown.

President Judge
S. Gerald Corso

Judges
Kent H. Albright
R. Stephen Barrett
Emanuel A. Bertin
Thomas C. Branca
William R. Carpenter
Rhonda Lee Daniele
Thomas M. DelRicci
Toby L. Dickman
Calvin S. Drayer, Jr.
William J. Furber, Jr.
Richard J. Hodgson
Bernard A. Moore
William T. Nicholas
Steven T. O'Neill
Stanley R. Ott
Maurino J. Rossanese, Jr.
Joseph A. Smyth, Jr.
Paul W. Tressler
Arthur R. Tilson

THIRTY-NINTH JUDICIAL DISTRICT includes Franklin and Fulton counties. The court sits at Chambersburg and McConnellsburg.

President Judge
John R. Walker

Judges
Douglas W. Herman
Carol L. Van Horn
Richard J. Walsh

FORTIETH JUDICIAL DISTRICT includes Indiana County. The court sits at Indiana.

President Judge
William J. Martin

Judge
Gregory A. Olson

FORTY-FIRST JUDICIAL DISTRICT includes Juniata and Perry counties. The court sits at Mifflintown and New Bloomfield.

President Judge
Keith B. Quigley

Judge
C. Joseph Rehkamp

FORTY-SECOND JUDICIAL DISTRICT includes Bradford County. The court sits at Towanda.

President Judge
Jeffrey A. Smith

Judge
John C. Mott

FORTY-THIRD JUDICIAL DISTRICT includes Monroe County. The court sits at Stroudsburg.

President Judge
Ronald E. Vican

Judges
Jerome P. Cheslock
Linda Wallach Miller
Peter J. O'Brien
Margherita Patti Worthington

FORTY-FOURTH JUDICIAL DISTRICT includes Sullivan and Wyoming counties. The court sits at Laporte and Tunkhannock.

President Judge
Brendan J. Vanston

FORTY-FIFTH JUDICIAL DISTRICT includes Lackawanna County. The court sits at Scranton.

PENNSYLVANIA COURTS OF COMMON PLEAS—*Continued*

President Judge
Chester T. Harhut

Judges
Michael J. Barrasse
Patricia Corbett
Vito P. Geroulo
Robert A. Mazzoni
Carmen D. Minora
Terrence R. Nealon

FORTY-SIXTH JUDICIAL DISTRICT includes Clearfield County. The court sits at Clearfield.

President Judge
John K. Reilly, Jr.

Judge
Fredric J. Ammerman

FORTY-SEVENTH JUDICIAL DISTRICT includes Cambria County. The court sits at Ebensburg.

President Judge
Gerard Long

Judges
Timothy P. Creany
Norman A. Krumenacker, III
F. Joseph Leahey
Thomas A. Swope, Jr.

FORTY-EIGHTH JUDICIAL DISTRICT includes McKean County. The court sits at Smethport.

President Judge
John M. Cleland

FORTY-NINTH JUDICIAL DISTRICT includes Centre County. The court sits at Bellefonte.

President Judge
Charles C. Brown, Jr.

Judges
David E. Grine
Thomas King Kistler

FIFTIETH JUDICIAL DISTRICT includes Butler County. The court sits at Butler.

President Judge
Thomas J. Doerr

Judges
George H. Hancher
Marilyn J. Horan
William R. Shaffer
S. Michael Yeager

FIFTY-FIRST JUDICIAL DISTRICT includes Adams County. The court sits at Gettysburg.

President Judge
John D. Kuhn

Judges
Robert G. Bigham
Michael A. George

FIFTY-SECOND JUDICIAL DISTRICT includes Lebanon County. The court sits at Lebanon.

President Judge
Robert J. Eby

Judges
Bradford H. Charles
Samuel A. Kline
John C. Tylwalk

FIFTY-THIRD JUDICIAL DISTRICT includes Lawrence County. The court sits at New Castle.

President Judge
Ralph D. Pratt

Judges
J. Craig Cox
Dominick Motto
Thomas A. Piccione

FIFTY-FOURTH JUDICIAL DISTRICT includes Jefferson County. The court sits at Brookville.

President Judge
John H. Foradora

FIFTY-FIFTH JUDICIAL DISTRICT includes Potter County. The court sits at Coudersport.

President Judge
John B. Leete

FIFTY-SIXTH JUDICIAL DISTRICT includes Carbon County. The court sits at Jim Thorpe.

President Judge
Richard W. Webb

Judge
Roger N. Nanovic

FIFTY-SEVENTH JUDICIAL DISTRICT includes Bedford County. The court sits at Bedford.

President Judge
Daniel L. Howsare

Judge
Thomas S. Ling

FIFTY-EIGHTH JUDICIAL DISTRICT includes Mifflin County. The court sits at Lewistown.

President Judge
Timothy S. Searer

FIFTY-NINTH JUDICIAL DISTRICT includes Cameron and Elk counties. The court sits at Emporium and Ridgway.

President Judge
vacancy

SIXTIETH JUDICIAL DISTRICT includes Pike County. The court sits at Milford.

President Judge
vacancy

PHILADELPHIA MUNICIPAL COURT

The Municipal Court is a court of limited jurisdiction established in Philadelphia. Prior to 1969 municipal judges were appointed by the governor; since 1969 they have been elected initially at partisan elections for six-year terms. Subsequent six-year terms are by retention vote. Vacancies may be filled by the governor with consent of the Senate. Appointees serve until the next general election, at which time they may run for election to office. A president judge is elected by peer vote to a

PHILADELPHIA MUNICIPAL COURT—*Continued*

five-year term and may be reelected after a one-term interlude. Retirement is mandatory at age seventy; however, retired judges may serve as senior judges.

The court has jurisdiction over all criminal matters except summary traffic offenses in which the prison sentence does not exceed five years. The court also has jurisdiction over civil cases when the amount in controversy does not exceed $10,000. The court may hold arraignments, fix and accept bail and issue warrants. Appeals are to the Court of Common Pleas First Judicial District.

TRAFFIC COURT OF PHILADELPHIA

The Traffic Court is a court of limited jurisdiction established in Philadelphia. Judges are initially elected in partisan elections for six-year terms. Subsequent six-year terms are by retention vote. A president judge is appointed by the governor. Retirement is mandatory at age seventy; however, retired judges may serve as senior judges.

The court has exclusive jurisdiction over all summary offenses arising under the Motor Vehicle Code and over violations of city ordinances enacted pursuant to that code. Appeals are to the Court of Common Pleas First Judicial District.

PITTSBURGH MAGISTRATES COURT

The Magistrates Court is a court of limited jurisdiction established in Pittsburgh. Magistrates are appointed to four-year terms by the mayor with the approval of the city council. A chief magistrate is appointed by the mayor for a four-year term. Retirement is mandatory at age seventy.

The court exercises jurisdiction in criminal cases involving city ordinance violations and other specified offenses. The court also sits as a traffic court and exercises jurisdiction over summary offenses arising under the Motor Vehicle Code and related city ordinances. The court may issue arrest warrants, hold arraignments and preliminary hearings and commit to jail, bind over for trial or discharge defendants. Appeals are to the Court of Common Pleas Fifth Judicial District.

PENNSYLVANIA DISTRICT JUSTICE COURTS

District Justice Courts are courts of limited jurisdiction that exist in magisterial districts throughout the state except in Philadelphia County. Magisterial districts are established by the Supreme Court. District justices are elected in partisan elections by the voters in their respective districts for six-year terms. Retirement is mandatory at age seventy; however, retired justices may serve as senior district justices.

The courts have jurisdiction to conduct nonjury trials concerning criminal summary matters not involving delinquent acts as defined in 42 Pa.C.S. § 6301 *et seq.;* civil claims (other than claims against a commonwealth party as defined in 42 Pa.C.S. § 8501) where the amount in controversy does not exceed $8,000 exclusive of interests and costs in the following classes of actions: landlord-tenant actions, assumpsit actions (unless they involve a contract where the title to real estate may be in question), trespass actions, and fines and penalties imposed by any government agency; and all offenses under Title 34 (Game and Wildlife Code). The court may preside over preliminary arraignments and preliminary hearings, issue arrest warrants, fix and accept bail except in cases involving murder or voluntary manslaughter, and, in certain circumstances, accept guilty pleas to misdemeanors of the third degree. Appeals are to the Courts of Common Pleas.

Pennsylvania Counties and County Seats

Adams
Gettysburg

Allegheny
Pittsburgh

Armstrong
Kittanning

Beaver
Beaver

Bedford
Bedford

Berks
Reading

Blair
Hollidaysburg

Bradford
Towanda

Bucks
Doylestown

Butler
Butler

Cambria
Ebensburg

Cameron
Emporium

Carbon
Jim Thorpe

Centre
Bellefonte

Chester
West Chester

Clarion
Clarion

Clearfield
Clearfield

Clinton
Lock Haven

Columbia
Bloomsburg

Crawford
Meadville

Cumberland
Carlisle

Dauphin
Harrisburg

Delaware
Media

Elk
Ridgway

Erie
Erie

Fayette
Uniontown

Forest
Tionesta

Franklin
Chambersburg

Fulton
McConnellsburg

Greene
Waynesburg

Huntingdon
Huntingdon

Indiana
Indiana

Jefferson
Brookville

Juniata
Mifflintown

Lackawanna
Scranton

Lancaster
Lancaster

Lawrence
New Castle

Lebanon
Lebanon

Lehigh
Allentown

Luzerne
Wilkes-Barre

COUNTIES AND COUNTY SEATS—*Continued*

Lycoming
Williamsport

McKean
Smethport

Mercer
Mercer

Mifflin
Lewistown

Monroe
Stroudsburg

Montgomery
Norristown

Montour
Danville

Northampton
Easton

Northumberland
Sunbury

Perry
New Bloomfield

Philadelphia
Philadelphia

Pike
Milford

Potter
Coudersport

Schuylkill
Pottsville

Snyder
Middleburg

Somerset
Somerset

Sullivan
Laporte

Susquehanna
Montrose

Tioga
Wellsboro

Union
Lewisburg

Venango
Franklin

Warren
Warren

Washington
Washington

Wayne
Honesdale

Westmoreland
Greensburg

Wyoming
Tunkhannock

York
York

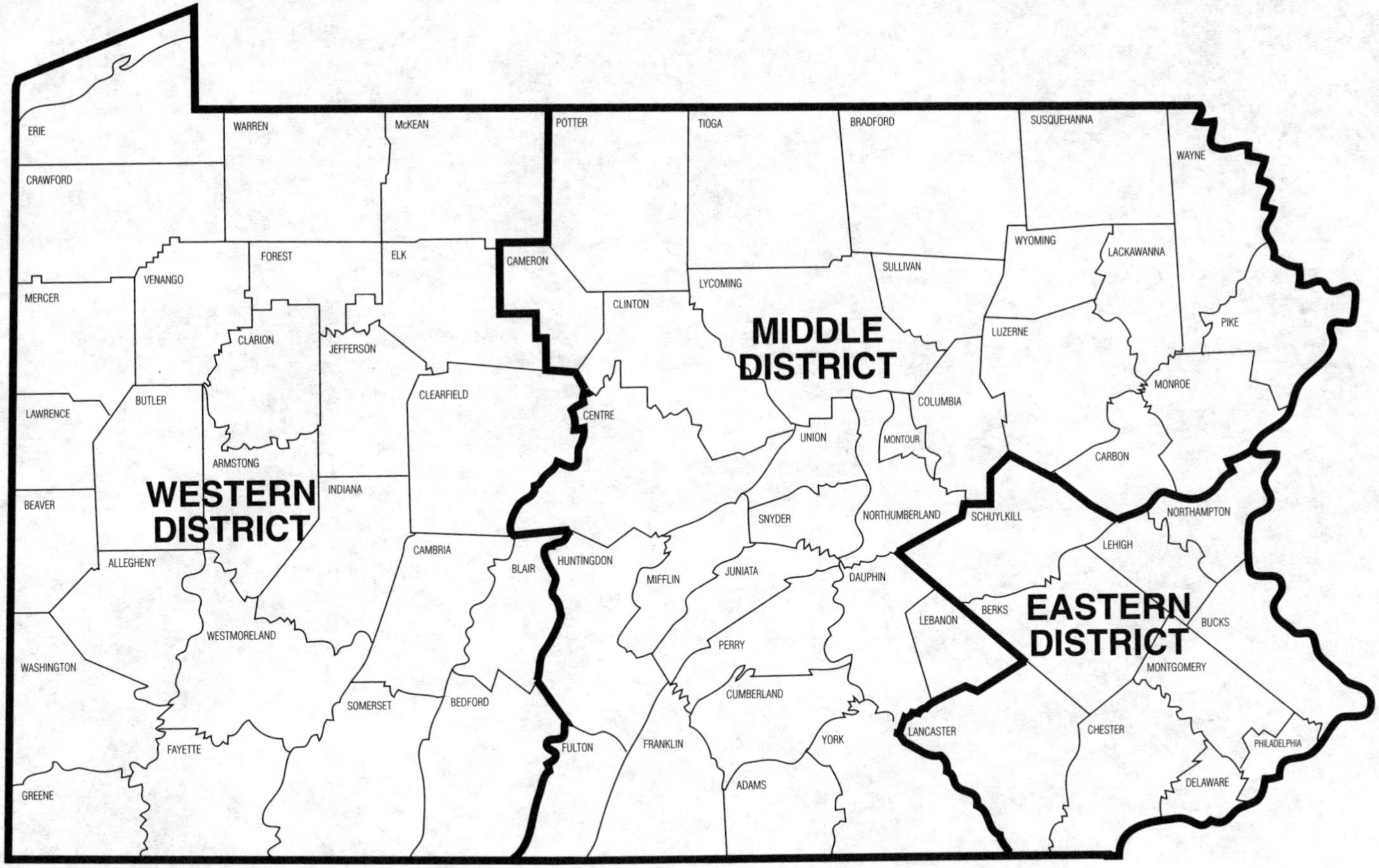
ERIE
CRAWFORD
WARREN
McKEAN
POTTER
TIOGA
BRADFORD
SUSQUEHANNA
WAYNE
WYOMING
LACKAWANNA
SULLIVAN
LYCOMING
CAMERON
ELK
FOREST
VENANGO
MERCER
CLARION
JEFFERSON
CLINTON
MIDDLE DISTRICT
LUZERNE
PIKE
MONROE
CLEARFIELD
LAWRENCE
BUTLER
CENTRE
COLUMBIA
UNION
MONTOUR
CARBON
ARMSTONG
WESTERN DISTRICT
INDIANA
BEAVER
SNYDER
NORTHUMBERLAND
SCHUYLKILL
NORTHAMPTON
ALLEGHENY
CAMBRIA
HUNTINGDON
BLAIR
LEHIGH
MIFFLIN
JUNIATA
DAUPHIN
BERKS
EASTERN DISTRICT
BUCKS
LEBANON
WESTMORELAND
PERRY
WASHINGTON
MONTGOMERY
SOMERSET
BEDFORD
CUMBERLAND
LANCASTER
CHESTER
FAYETTE
FULTON
FRANKLIN
YORK
PHILADELPHIA
DELAWARE
ADAMS
GREENE

UNITED STATES DISTRICT COURTS DISTRICTS OF PENNSYLVANIA

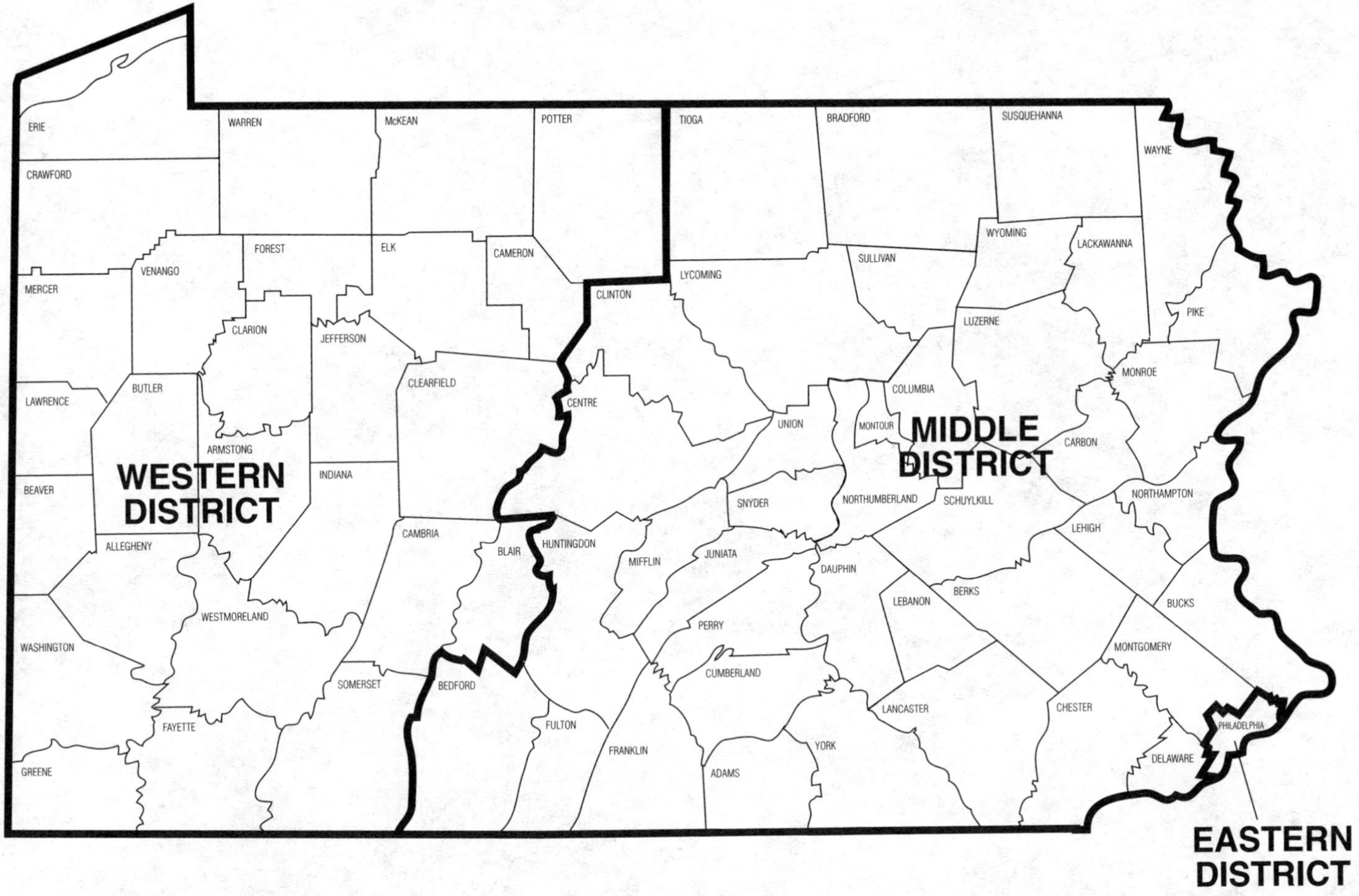
ERIE
CRAWFORD
MERCER
LAWRENCE
BEAVER
WASHINGTON
GREENE
WARREN
VENANGO
BUTLER
ALLEGHENY
FOREST
CLARION
ARMSTONG
WESTMORELAND
FAYETTE
McKEAN
ELK
JEFFERSON
INDIANA
CAMBRIA
SOMERSET
POTTER
CAMERON
CLEARFIELD
CENTRE
CLINTON
BLAIR
BEDFORD
HUNTINGDON
FULTON
FRANKLIN
MIFFLIN
JUNIATA
PERRY
CUMBERLAND
ADAMS
YORK
TIOGA
LYCOMING
UNION
SNYDER
BRADFORD
SULLIVAN
MONTOUR
COLUMBIA
NORTHUMBERLAND
DAUPHIN
LEBANON
LANCASTER
SUSQUEHANNA
WYOMING
LUZERNE
SCHUYLKILL
BERKS
CHESTER
LACKAWANNA
CARBON
LEHIGH
MONTGOMERY
DELAWARE
PHILADELPHIA
WAYNE
PIKE
MONROE
NORTHAMPTON
BUCKS
WESTERN DISTRICT
MIDDLE DISTRICT
EASTERN DISTRICT

DISTRICTS OF THE SUPREME COURT OF PENNSYLVANIA

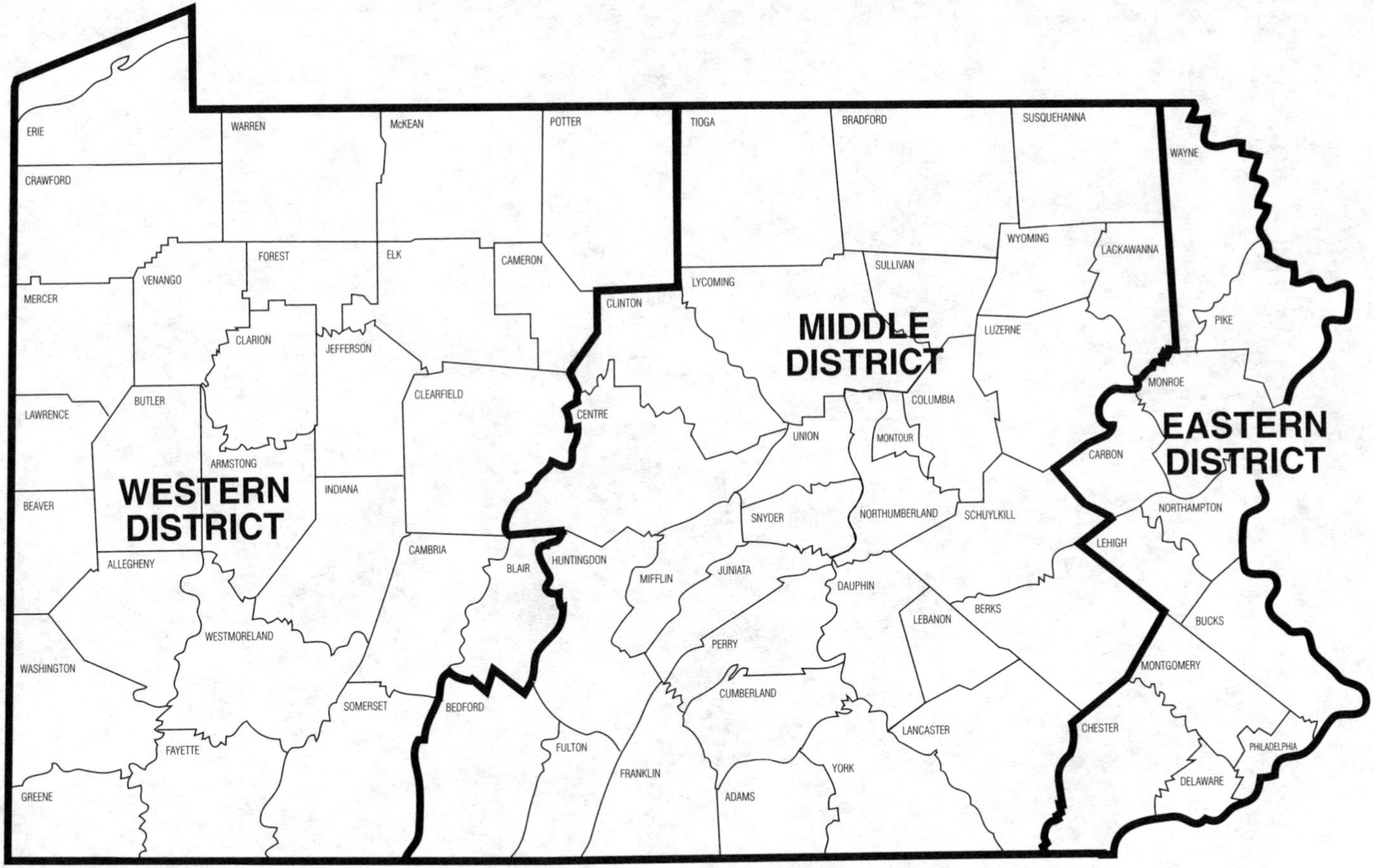

WESTERN DISTRICT
MIDDLE DISTRICT
EASTERN DISTRICT
ERIE
CRAWFORD
WARREN
McKEAN
POTTER
TIOGA
BRADFORD
SUSQUEHANNA
WAYNE
PIKE
FOREST
ELK
CAMERON
VENANGO
MERCER
CLINTON
LYCOMING
SULLIVAN
WYOMING
LACKAWANNA
CLARION
JEFFERSON
LUZERNE
MONROE
LAWRENCE
BUTLER
CLEARFIELD
CENTRE
UNION
COLUMBIA
MONTOUR
CARBON
ARMSTONG
INDIANA
BEAVER
NORTHAMPTON
SNYDER
NORTHUMBERLAND
SCHUYLKILL
LEHIGH
CAMBRIA
ALLEGHENY
BLAIR
HUNTINGDON
MIFFLIN
JUNIATA
DAUPHIN
BERKS
LEBANON
BUCKS
WESTMORELAND
PERRY
MONTGOMERY
WASHINGTON
SOMERSET
BEDFORD
CUMBERLAND
CHESTER
LANCASTER
FULTON
FAYETTE
PHILADELPHIA
FRANKLIN
YORK
DELAWARE
GREENE
ADAMS

DISTRICTS OF THE SUPERIOR COURT OF PENNSYLVANIA

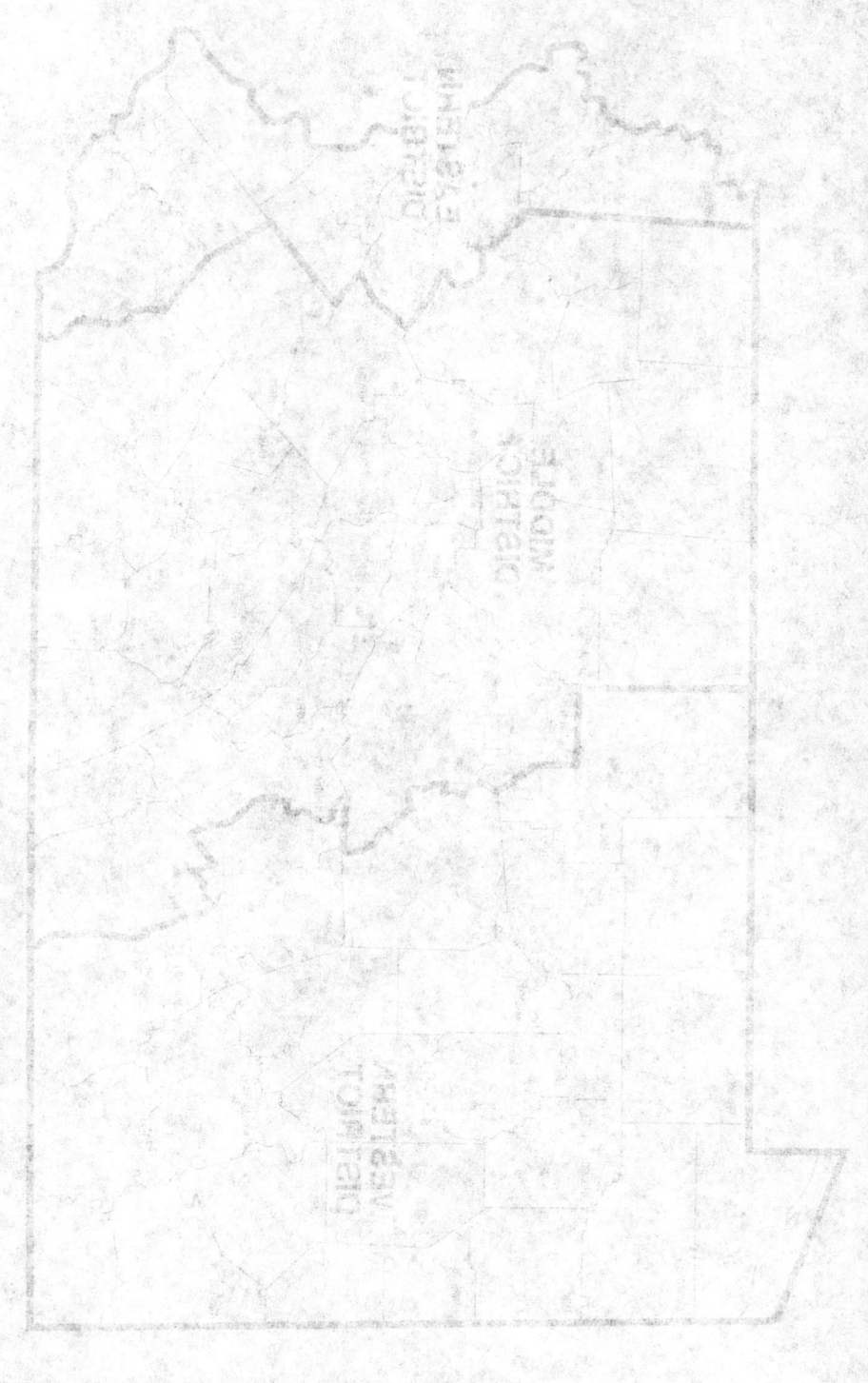

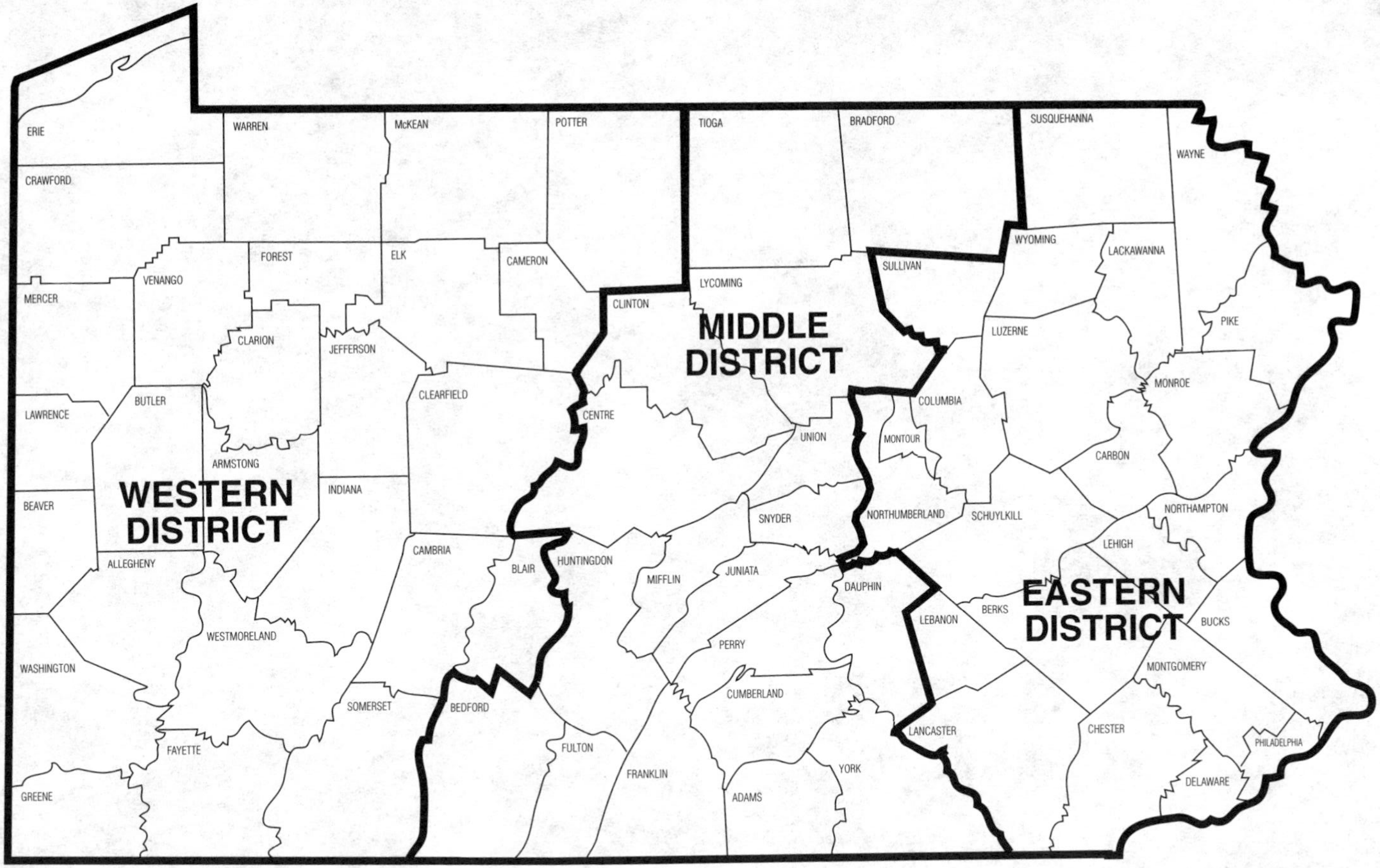
WESTERN DISTRICT
MIDDLE DISTRICT
EASTERN DISTRICT
ERIE
CRAWFORD
MERCER
LAWRENCE
BEAVER
WARREN
FOREST
VENANGO
CLARION
BUTLER
ARMSTONG
ALLEGHENY
WASHINGTON
GREENE
FAYETTE
WESTMORELAND
INDIANA
JEFFERSON
ELK
McKEAN
POTTER
CAMERON
CLEARFIELD
CAMBRIA
SOMERSET
BEDFORD
BLAIR
HUNTINGDON
CENTRE
CLINTON
FULTON
FRANKLIN
MIFFLIN
JUNIATA
PERRY
CUMBERLAND
ADAMS
YORK
TIOGA
LYCOMING
BRADFORD
SULLIVAN
UNION
SNYDER
MONTOUR
COLUMBIA
NORTHUMBERLAND
DAUPHIN
LEBANON
LANCASTER
SUSQUEHANNA
WYOMING
LUZERNE
LACKAWANNA
WAYNE
PIKE
MONROE
CARBON
SCHUYLKILL
NORTHAMPTON
LEHIGH
BERKS
BUCKS
MONTGOMERY
CHESTER
DELAWARE
PHILADELPHIA

DISTRICTS OF THE COMMONWEALTH COURT OF PENNSYLVANIA

DISTRICTS OF THE COMMONWEALTH COURT OF PENNSYLVANIA

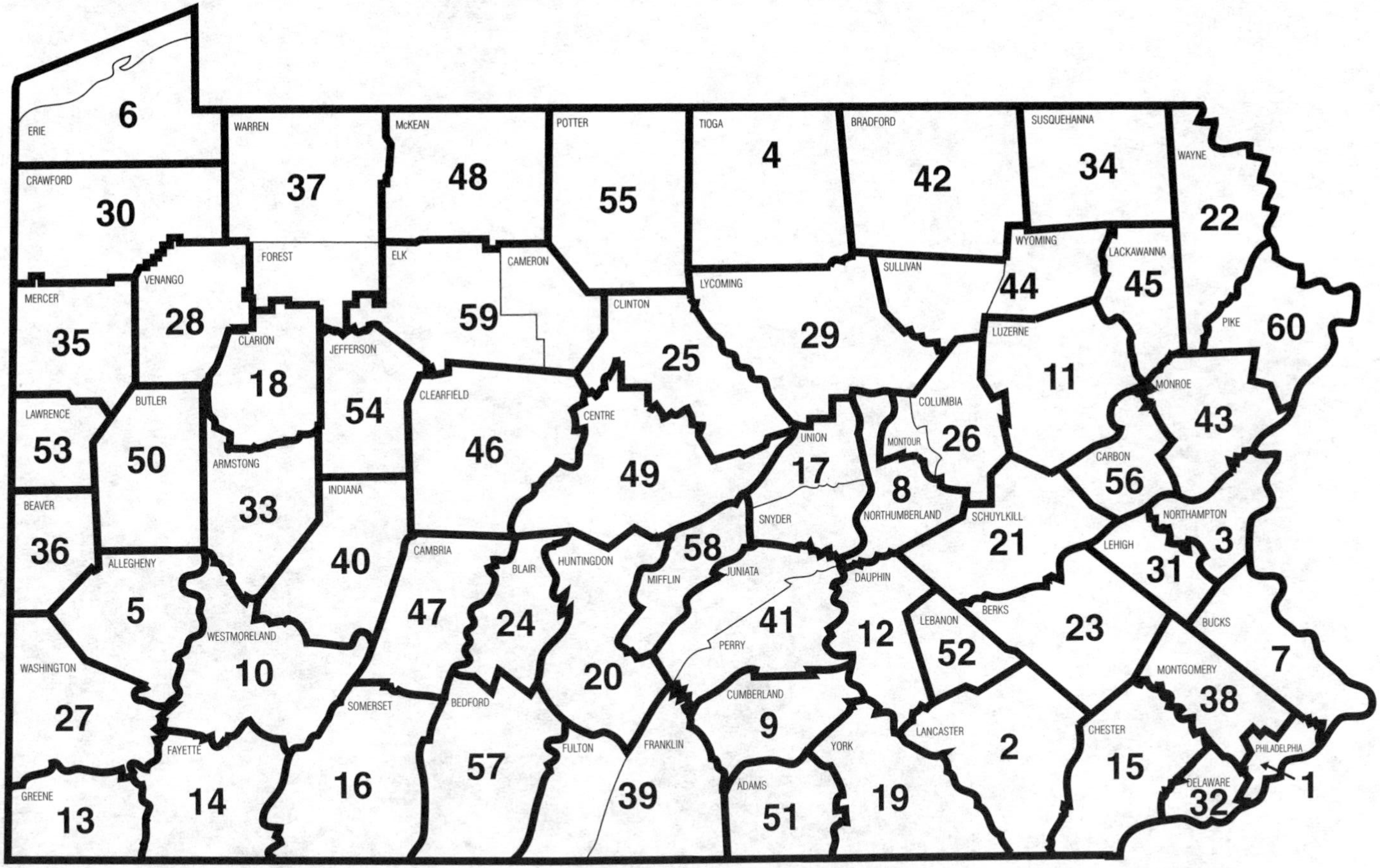
ERIE
6
CRAWFORD
30
WARREN
37
McKEAN
48
POTTER
55
TIOGA
4
BRADFORD
42
SUSQUEHANNA
34
WAYNE
22
FOREST
ELK
CAMERON
59
MERCER
35
VENANGO
28
CLARION
18
JEFFERSON
54
CLINTON
25
LYCOMING
29
SULLIVAN
WYOMING
44
LACKAWANNA
45
PIKE
60
LUZERNE
11
MONROE
43
LAWRENCE
53
BUTLER
50
ARMSTONG
33
CLEARFIELD
46
CENTRE
49
UNION
17
COLUMBIA
26
MONTOUR
8
CARBON
56
BEAVER
36
INDIANA
40
SNYDER
NORTHUMBERLAND
SCHUYLKILL
21
NORTHAMPTON
3
ALLEGHENY
5
CAMBRIA
47
BLAIR
24
HUNTINGDON
20
MIFFLIN
58
JUNIATA
41
DAUPHIN
12
LEHIGH
31
WESTMORELAND
10
PERRY
LEBANON
52
BERKS
23
BUCKS
7
WASHINGTON
27
SOMERSET
16
BEDFORD
57
CUMBERLAND
9
MONTGOMERY
38
FAYETTE
14
FULTON
FRANKLIN
39
YORK
19
LANCASTER
2
CHESTER
15
PHILADELPHIA
1
GREENE
13
ADAMS
51
DELAWARE
32

JUDICIAL DISTRICTS OF PENNSYLVANIA COURTS OF COMMON PLEAS

PENNSYLVANIA

ABRAMSON, Howland W. *(Judge, Pennsylvania Court of Common Pleas First Judicial District)*
Office: 1211 Criminal Justice Center, 1301 Filbert Street, Philadelphia 19107.
Telephone: (215) 683-7050.

ACKERMAN, Daniel J. *(President Judge, Pennsylvania Court of Common Pleas Tenth Judicial District)* Appointed by Governor Richard Thornburgh to term beginning May 7, 1980. Elected 1981. Retained by election 1991 and 2001. Current term expires Jan 2012. Born Pittsburgh Pennsylvania April 18, 1939. Educated at Thiel College B.A. with honors 1961 and University of Pittsburgh J.D. 1964. Admitted to practice Pennsylvania 1964. Began legal practice Latrobe 1964. In legal practice Greensburg 1966-80.
Office: Westmoreland County Courthouse, Two North Main Street, Greensburg 15601.
Telephone: (724) 830-3365.

ACKERMAN, Norman *(Judge, Pennsylvania Court of Common Pleas First Judicial District)*
Office: 290 City Hall, Philadelphia 19107.
Telephone: (215) 686-9540.

ALBRIGHT, Kent H. *(Judge, Pennsylvania Court of Common Pleas Thirty-eighth Judicial District)*
Mailing address: P.O. Box 311, Norristown 19404.
Office: Montgomery County Courthouse, Norristown 19401.
Telephone: (610) 278-3200.

ALLEN, Cheryl Lynn *(Judge, Pennsylvania Court of Common Pleas Fifth Judicial District)*
Office: 440 Ross Street, Room 5052, Pittsburgh 15219.
Telephone: (412) 350-0277.

ALLEN, Jacqueline F. *(Judge, Pennsylvania Court of Common Pleas First Judicial District)*
Office: 1222 Criminal Justice Center, 1301 Filbert Street, Philadelphia 19107.
Telephone: (215) 683-7083.

ALLISON, Paul K. *(Judge, Pennsylvania Court of Common Pleas Second Judicial District)*
Mailing address: P.O. Box 83480, Lancaster 17608-3480.
Office: Lancaster County Courthouse, 50 North Duke Street, Lancaster 17602.
Telephone: (717) 293-7292.

AMBROSE, Donetta W. *(Chief Judge, United States District Court Western District of Pennsylvania)* Appointed for life by President Bill Clinton. Born New Kensington Pennsylvania Nov 5, 1945. Educated at Duquesne University B.A. 1967 J.D. 1970. Law Clerk to Hon. Louis L. Manderino, The Commonwealth Court of Pennsylvania 1970-71. In legal practice New Kensington 1974-81. Judge, Pennsylvania Court of Common Pleas Tenth Judicial District 1982-93.
Assistant Attorney General Pennsylvania Department of Justice 1972-74. Assistant District Attorney Westmoreland County 1977-81.
Office: 620 U.S. Post Office & Courthouse, 700 Grant Street, Pittsburgh 15219.
Telephone: (412) 208-7350.

AMMERMAN, Fredric J. *(Judge, Pennsylvania Court of Common Pleas Forty-sixth Judicial District)*
Office: Clearfield County Courthouse, 230 East Market Street, Clearfield 16830.
Telephone: (814) 765-2641.

ANDERSON, Dudley N. *(Judge, Pennsylvania Court of Common Pleas Twenty-ninth Judicial District)*
Office: Lycoming County Courthouse, 48 West Third Street, Williamsport 17701.
Telephone: (570) 327-2318.

ANGELL, M. Faith *(Magistrate Judge, United States District Court Eastern District of Pennsylvania)* Appointed by U.S. District Court judges May 14, 1990. Reappointed May 1998, current term expires 2006. Born Buffalo New York 1938. Educated at Mount Holyoke College A.B. 1959, Bryn Mawr College M.S.S. 1965 and Temple University School of Law J.D. 1971. Admitted to practice Pennsylvania 1971, U.S. District Court Eastern District of Pennsylvania 1971, U.S. Court of Appeals Third Circuit 1974 and U.S. Supreme Court 1979. Administrative Law Judge, Office of Hearings and Appeals Social Security Administration 1988-90.
Assistant District Attorney City of Philadelphia 1971-72. Assistant Attorney General 1972-74, Deputy Attorney General and Chief Division of Civil Litigation 1974-78 Eastern Regional office Pennsylvania Department of Justice. Regional Counsel 1978-80 and Regional Director 1980-88 Interstate Commerce Commission. Adjunct Professor Clinical Program Temple University School of Law 1973-94. Member Committee on Racial and Gender Bias in the Justice System The Supreme Court of Pennsylvania 2000. Past President Philadelphia Chapter Federal Bar Association. Former Member United States Senior Executive Service. Co-Chair Commission on Gender Third Circuit Task Force on Equal Treatment in the Courts. Advisory Board Federal Courts 2000, Inc. Master Temple American Inns of Court. Member National Association of Women Judges, Federal Magistrate Judges Association and Philadelphia Bar Association. Named Women's Law Caucus Honoree 1996. Previously worked as social worker in child welfare, medical and community organizations. Former Director Social Service Department Wills Eye Hospital. Former Chief Social Worker Family Court Division Defender Association of Philadelphia. Member Executive Board Temple Law Alumni 1994-99. Former Member Child Welfare Advisory Board City of Philadelphia. Member Academy of Certified Social Workers.
Office: 3030 U.S. Courthouse, 601 Market Street, Philadelphia 19106.
Telephone: (215) 597-6079.
Fax: (215) 580-2165

ANTHONY, Fred P. *(Judge, Pennsylvania Court of Common Pleas Sixth Judicial District)* Elected to term

ANTHONY, FRED P.—*Continued*

beginning Jan 1, 1972. Retained by election 1981, 1991 and 2001. Current term expires Jan 2012. Former Administrative Judge Erie County Juvenile Court. Born Erie Pennsylvania Aug 26, 1935. Educated at University of Louisville A.B. 1956 J.D. 1958. Recipient Ford Foundation four-year scholarship. Admitted to practice 1958.

Member National Council of Juvenile and Family Court Judges, Pennsylvania Conference of State Trial Judges, Juvenile Court Judges Commission (Chairman 1975), Task Force for Delinquent and Deprived Youth Programs, Erie County Legal Services Board of Directors (Co-founder), Camp Hill Review Panel 1975, Pennsylvania, Kentucky and American Bar Associations. Delegate Standards and Goals Convention on Criminal Justice 1975 (Chairman Juvenile Delinquency Section). President Pennsylvania College of the Judiciary 1976. Recipient Citizen of the Year Award from Pennsylvania Northwest Division of the National Association of Social Workers 1976. USAF JAGC. Member Villa Maria Academy Board of Trustees, Youth Service Bureau Board of Directors (Co-founder), Catholic Social Services Board of Directors, Erie Guidance Center Board of Directors, St. Vincent's Hospital Nursing Association Board of Directors, Cystic Fibrosis Association Board of Directors (Past President), Youth Services Coordinating Council Board of Directors (Co-founder), Erie County Prison Rehabilitation Program Board of Directors, Christian Family Movement and Erie Serra Club (Board of Trustees, Past President). Volunteer Counsel Housing and Neighborhood Development Services and Community County Day School (Incorporator).

Office: Erie County Courthouse, 140 West Sixth Street, Erie 16501.

Telephone: (814) 451-6297.

ARNER, James G. *(President Judge, Pennsylvania Court of Common Pleas Eighteenth Judicial District)*

Office: Clarion County Courthouse, Main Street, Clarion 16214.

Telephone: (814) 226-9351.

ASHWORTH, David L. *(Judge, Pennsylvania Court of Common Pleas Second Judicial District)*

Mailing address: P.O. Box 83480, Lancaster 17608-3480.

Office: Lancaster County Courthouse, 50 North Duke Street, Lancaster 17602.

Telephone: (717) 299-8055.

ASKEY, William Hartman *(Magistrate Judge, United States District Court Middle District of Pennsylvania)* U.S. Commissioner 1964-71. Appointed Magistrate by U.S. District Court judges to term beginning June 21, 1971. Reappointed to subsequent terms. Serves part time. Born Williamsport Pennsylvania June 21, 1919. Educated at Bucknell University B.A. 1941 and University of Pittsburgh J.D. 1951. Member Phi Alpha Delta and Sigma Alpha Epsilon. Admitted to practice Pennsylvania 1952, U.S. District Court Middle District of Pennsylvania 1952 and U.S. Supreme Court 1960.

Member Charles F. Greevy Jr. American Inn of Court, Lycoming Law Association (Secretary 1959-61, Vice President 1961-68, President 1968-69, Chairman Nominating Committee), Pennsylvania (Real Property, Probate and Trust Law Section) and American (Sections: Judicial Administration Division, Senior Lawyers Division, Taxation) Bar Associations. Recipient Young Man of the Year Award from Williamsport Junior Chamber of Commerce 1954, Benjamin Rush Award from Lycoming County Medical Society 1956, Award for Dedicated Volunteer Service from Lycoming County Chapter American Red Cross 1973 and Volunteer Services Award from American Cancer Society 1992. Major USAF 1941-46. Former Member Board of Directors Lycoming County Chapter American Red Cross (Chairman Lycoming County Blood Program 1953-54, President Northeast Regional Blood Program 1962-68), Lycoming County Unit American Cancer Society 1955-94 (President 1957-58), Appalachia Educational Laboratory 1967-85 and Susquehanna Legal Services. Former Member and Secretary Board of Trustees YWCA. President Williamsport Community Concert Association 1962-68. Former member Wheel Club and Board of Directors Williamsport Junior Chamber of Commerce. Commissioner to General Assembly of United Presbyterian Church 1956. Board of Directors and Past President AAA North Central Pennsylvania. Member Masons Lodge 106, Williamsport Consistory AASR (Choir member since 1952, Past Presiding officer Chapter Rose Croix) and Ross Club. Member Episcopal Church of Our Savior (Vestry).

Office: 602 Penn Tower, 25 West Third Street, Williamsport 17701.

Telephone: (570) 323-9881.

AUGELLO, Joseph M. *(Judge, Pennsylvania Court of Common Pleas Eleventh Judicial District)* Former President Judge.

Office: Luzerne County Courthouse, 200 North River Street, Wilkes-Barre 18711.

Telephone: (570) 825-1547.

BAER, Max *(Judge, Pennsylvania Court of Common Pleas Fifth Judicial District)* Elected to term beginning Jan 1990. Retained by election Nov 1999, current term expires Jan 2010. Former Administrative Judge Family Division. Born Pittsburgh Pennsylvania Dec 24, 1947. Educated at University of Pittsburgh B.A. with honors 1971, Duquesne University J.D. with honors 1975 and Robert Morris College Masters of Tax Program course work 1987. Admitted to practice Pennsylvania 1975, U.S. District Courts Eastern 1975, Middle 1975 and Western 1975 Districts of Pennsylvania and U.S. Court of Appeals Third Circuit 1976. In legal practice Pennsylvania 1975-89.

Deputy Attorney General Pennsylvania 1975-79. Author two chapters *The Judge's Book* 1992 and "Custody Wars: The Creation of a New Weapon of Mass Destruction" 21 No. 4 Dec 1999 and "Family Law and Civility—Can They Co-Exist?" No. 1, 2002 Pennsylvania Family Lawyer. Lecturer on Family Law and Social Policy Carnegie Mellon University since 1991. Former Chair Domestic Relations Procedural Rules Committee The Supreme Court of Pennsylvania. Former Ex-officio Member Juvenile Court Judges' Commission. Member Task Force on Adoption Law and Task Force on the Law of Children and Youth Joint State Government Commission. Member Pennsylvania Conference of State Trial Judges (Former Chair Family Law Section, Member Education Committee), Allegheny County and Pennsylvania Bar Associations. Named Pennsylvania's Adoption Advocate of the Year 1997. Recipient Adoption

BAER, MAX—*Continued*

2002 Excellence Award for Judicial Innovation from U.S. Department of Health and Human Services.

Office: 817 City-County Building, 414 Grant Street, Pittsburgh 15219.

Telephone: (412) 350-3829.

Fax: (412) 350-3127

E-mail address: max.baer@court.allegheny.pa.us

BALDWIN, Cynthia A. *(Judge, Pennsylvania Court of Common Pleas Fifth Judicial District)* Elected Nov 1989 to term beginning Jan 1990. Retained by election Nov 1999, current term expires Jan 2010. Currently serves Civil Division (full-time) since Jan 2000. Served Family Division (full-time) Jan 1990 to Jan 2000 and Civil Division (part-time) Jan 1992 to Jan 2000. Born McKeesport Pennsylvania Feb 8, 1945. Educated at Pennsylvania State University B.A. 1966 M.A. in English 1974 and Duquesne University School of Law J.D. 1980. Honorary Doctor of Laws Point Park College 1999. Staff member Duquesne Law Review 1978-80. Member Delta Sigma Theta. Admitted to practice Pennsylvania 1980, U.S. District Court Western District of Pennsylvania 1980 and U.S. Supreme Court 1985. In legal practice McKeesport Aug 1987 to Dec 27, 1989.

Staff Attorney Neighborhood Legal Services Sept 1980 to Oct 1981. Deputy Attorney General Oct 1981 to Oct 1983 and Attorney-in-Charge Oct 1983 to July 1986 Western Regional Office Consumer Protection Commonwealth of Pennsylvania. Author "Silhouettes" Pittsburgh Legal Journal 3, 1989; "Professionalism" 139 No. 2 Pittsburgh Legal Journal 43, 1991 and "Avoiding Abuse" Pittsburgh Legal Journal 1, Dec 1994. Important Decisions: Marshall v. Marshall FD89-7879, July 2, 1990, aff'd Marshall v. Marshall Pa. Super. Ct. 591 A.2d 1960, 1991; Hock v. Hock FD84-7870, April 11, 1991, aff'd Hock v. Hock Pa. Super. Ct. Nos. 857 and 858 Pittsburgh 1991; Goldblum v. Goldblum FD88-3461, Jan 27, 1992, aff'd Goldblum v. Goldblum Pa. Super. Ct. 611 A.2d 296, 1992; Cobaugh v. Cobaugh v. Commonwealth of Pennsylvania State Employees' Retirement System 140 PLJ 430, 1992; and Gaydos v. Gaydos 693 A.2d 1368 Pa. Super. Ct. 1997 (aff'd in part, rev'd in part, case remanded). Adjunct Professor of Legal Research and Writing Sept 1984 to June 1986, Visiting Professor of Consumer Law, Criminal Law, Legal Research and Writing and Agency Aug 1986 to Aug 1987 and Adjunct Professor since Aug 1989 Duquesne University School of Law. Instructor Institute of Trial Advocacy Widener University School of Law since July 1991. Fulbright Scholarship Lecturer on Jurisprudence and Constitutional Law University of Zimbabwe May 1994 to Sept 1994. Executive Committee 1980-89, Vice President 1986-88, Executive Board 1993-94 and Board of Governors since 1994 Homer S. Brown Law Association. Member 1984-90 and Vice President 1986-88 Board of Directors Neighborhood Legal Services Association. Master Pittsburgh Chapter American Inns of Court 1992-99. Member Pennsylvania Commission on Crime and Delinquency since 1990. Chair Family Court Division Statewide Computerization Project since 1991 (nonfunctional at this time). Member Pennsylvania Conference of State Court Judges (Task Force of Gender Fairness in the Courts since 1992), Allegheny County and Pennsylvania (House of Delegates 1991-99, Board of Governors 1997-2000) Bar Associations.

Speaker on "Legal Bureaucracy: The Demise of Professionalism?" The David Glick Memorial Committee and Allegheny County Bar Association Oct 10, 1990. Panelist "Law Enforcement and the Judiciary" Feb 8, 1991 and "Law and the Judiciary" Feb 1993 Leadership Pittsburgh. Attended seminar on "A Judge's Philosophy of Law and Judging" American Academy of Judicial Education July 1992, seminar on "Gender Fairness Faculty Development" The National Judicial College Aug 1993 and "The Judge as Fact-Finder and Decision Maker" American Academy of Judicial Education Whitefish Montana Aug 12-18, 2000. Named one of Outstanding Young Women of America 1980, Distinguished Alum by Pennsylvania State University 1995 and Distinguished Daughter of the Commonwealth 1996. Recipient Achievement Award from NAACP 1980, Humanitarian Service Award from Penn State Forum on Black Affairs 1989, Community Achievement Award from N'AMAT USA, Pittsburgh Council NCJW, Hadassah, Whitney M. Young, Jr. Service Award from Boy Scouts of America 1991, Award in Recognition of Past, Present and Future Contributions from Forum of Black Affairs Penn State University 1991, Service Award in Recognition of Achievements and Contributions to the Community from Blue Cross and WPTT-22 1991, The Consortium of Doctors Award 1993, Outstanding Achievement Award by Duquesne University School of Law 1996, Susan B. Anthony Award from Women's Bar Association of Western Pennsylvania 1998, Pittsburgh Woman of the Year in Law and Government Award form Vectors/Pittsburgh 1999, Woman of the Year Award from Women's Law Association Duquesne University School of Law 1999, Appreciation Award from Federal Energy Technology Center National Women's History Month 1999, Barbara Stone Hollander Leadership Award from Chatham College 1999, Mon Valley Newsmaker of the Century Award from *McKeesport Daily News* 1999 and Alumni Fellow Award from Pennsylvania State University Alumni Association 2000. Listed in *Who's Who of American Women* 1983-88, *Who's Who in Emerging Leaders* 1987-88, *Who's Who in American Law* 1990-93 and *Who's Who Among African-Americans* 1990-95. Named one of 40 African-American Leaders and a Pittsburgher of the Century-African American by *Pittsburgh Magazine* 1999. English Teacher 1966-71 and Human Relations Counselor 1971-72 McKeesport Area School District. Instructor in Study Skills 1974-76 and in English Fall 1976 and Assistant Dean of Student Affairs in charge of Educational Opportunity Program 1976-77 Pennsylvania State University. Co-founder and Executive Director 1971-77 and Board of Directors 1977-82 McKeesport Counseling and Tutoring Service. Member 1971-78 and Chairperson 1973-79 Board of Directors Pittsburgh Urban League. Board of Directors McKeesport YWCA 1980-81, Greater Pittsburgh YWCA 1987-90, Pittsburgh Founders Council 1993 to Sept 1994, Magee-Women's Hospital 1994, United Way since 1993 and Duquesne University since 1997. Member 1981-93 and Executive Committee 1982-93 Alumni Council Pennsylvania State University. Advisory Board Pennsylvania State University since 1982 and Mon Valley Education Consortium since 1985. Vice President/President Elect 1987-89, President 1989-91 and Immediate Past President 1991-93 Penn State Alumni Association. Board of Trustees Pennsylvania State University. Published in *National Anthology of Poetry* late 1970's. Enjoys reading, writing poetry, fishing and gourmet cooking.

BALDWIN, CYNTHIA A.—*Continued*

Office: 820 City-County Building, 414 Grant Street, Pittsburgh 15219.

Telephone: (412) 350-3833.

BALDWIN, William E. *(President Judge, Pennsylvania Court of Common Pleas Twenty-first Judicial District)*

Office: Schuylkill County Courthouse, 401 North Second Street, Pottsville 17901.

Telephone: (570) 628-1301.

BARATTA, Stephen G. *(Judge, Pennsylvania Court of Common Pleas Third Judicial District)*

Office: 202 L and D Plaza, 101 Larry Holmes Drive, Easton 18042.

Telephone: (610) 559-2640.

BARRASSE, Michael J. *(Judge, Pennsylvania Court of Common Pleas Forty-fifth Judicial District)*

Office: Lackawanna County Courthouse, 200 North Washington Avenue, Scranton 18503.

Telephone: (570) 963-6452.

BARRETT, R. Stephen *(Judge, Pennsylvania Court of Common Pleas Thirty-eighth Judicial District)*

Mailing address: P.O. Box 311, Norristown 19404.

Office: Montgomery County Courthouse, Norristown 19401.

Telephone: (610) 278-3995.

BARTLE, Harvey, III *(Judge, United States District Court Eastern District of Pennsylvania)* Appointed for life by President George Bush to term beginning Sept 23, 1991. Born Bryn Mawr Pennsylvania June 6, 1941. Episcopalian. Educated at Princeton University A.B. with honors 1962 and University of Pennsylvania Law School LL.B. with honors 1965. Editor University of Pennsylvania Law Review 1963-65. Law Clerk to Hon. John Morgan Davis, U.S. District Court Eastern District of Pennsylvania 1965-67. Admitted to practice Pennsylvania 1965, U.S. District Court Eastern District of Pennsylvania 1965, U.S. Court of Appeals Third Circuit 1969 and U.S. Supreme Court 1978. In legal practice Philadelphia 1967-79 and 1981-91.

Commissioner National Conference of Commissioners on Uniform State Laws 1980-87. Member Philadelphia and American Bar Associations. Captain USAR 1966-72. Insurance Commissioner 1979-80 and Attorney General 1980-81 Pennsylvania.

Office: 16614 U.S. Courthouse, 601 Market Street, Philadelphia 19106-1714.

Telephone: (215) 597-2693.

BAXTER, Susan Paradise *(Magistrate Judge, United States District Court Western District of Pennsylvania)* Appointed by U.S. District Court judges to term beginning Aug 27, 2001. Term expires 2009.

Office: 227 U.S. Post Office & Courthouse, 617 State Street, Erie 16501.

Telephone: (814) 453-3457.

BAYLEY, Edgar B. *(Judge, Pennsylvania Court of Common Pleas Ninth Judicial District)* Elected to term beginning Jan 1, 1984. Retained by election 1993, current term expires Jan 2004. Born Bay Shore New York May 18, 1939. Protestant. Educated at St. Lawrence University B.A. 1961 and Dickinson School of Law LL.B. 1964. Admitted to practice Pennsylvania 1964. Began legal practice Carlisle 1964. In legal practice Camp Hill 1969-83.

Chief Public Defender 1968, First Assistant District Attorney 1969-75 and District Attorney 1976-83 Cumberland County. Adjunct Assistant Professor of Pennsylvania Criminal Law Practice Dickinson School of Law 1974-80. Member Pennsylvania Bar Association. Captain U.S. Army Infantry 1965-66.

Office: Cumberland County Courthouse, One Courthouse Square, Carlisle 17013.

Telephone: (717) 240-6294.

BAYLSON, Michael M. *(Judge, United States District Court Eastern District of Pennsylvania)* Appointed for life by President George W. Bush to term beginning July 12, 2002.

Office: 4001 U.S. Courthouse, 601 Market Street, Philadelphia 19106.

Telephone: (215) 597-7704.

BELL, Alfred B. *(Judge, Pennsylvania Court of Common Pleas Tenth Judicial District)* Elected Nov 3, 1999 to term beginning Jan 3, 2000. Term expires Jan 3, 2010. Born Greensburg Pennsylvania Nov 21, 1947. Catholic. Educated at California University of Pennsylvania B.A. and Duquesne University J.D. Admitted to practice Pennsylvania 1973, U.S. District Court Western District of Pennsylvania 1973, U.S. Supreme Court 1977 and U.S. Court of Appeals Third Circuit 1989. In legal practice Greensburg 1973-85.

First Assistant District Attorney 1985-2000. Member Pennsylvania Conference of State Trial Judges, Pennsylvania Association of Trial Judges and Westmoreland County Bar Association. Specialist Five U.S. Army 1969-75.

Office: Two North Main Street, Greensburg 15601.

Telephone: (724) 830-3805.

Fax: (724) 850-3975

BENDER, John T. *(Judge, The Superior Court of Pennsylvania)*

Office: 1201 Grant Building, 330 Grant Street, Pittsburgh 15219.

Telephone: (412) 565-2350.

BENTZ, Warren W. *(Recalled Judge, United States Bankruptcy Court Western District of Pennsylvania)* Appointed Judge by U.S. Court of Appeals Third Circuit judges to term beginning March 22, 1985. Appointed Recalled Judge by the Judicial Council of the Third Circuit March 1999. Former Chief Judge. Born Fairfield Nebraska Jan 8, 1926. Educated at University of Virginia, University of Michigan B.S. 1946, George Washington University, University of Toledo and Harvard Law School LL.B. 1954. Member and President Triangles Honor Society and Vulcans Honor Society. Member Sigma Chi. Admitted to practice Ohio 1954, Pennsylvania 1955, U.S. District Court Western District of Pennsylvania 1956, U.S. Court of Appeals Third Circuit 1960, U.S. Supreme Court 1972 and U.S. Tax Court 1983. In legal practice Erie Pennsylvania 1954-85.

Borough Solicitor Lake City 1966-85. Assistant Solicitor Erie County 1967-77. Member American Judicature Society, Erie County (Secretary 1959, Executive Committee 1966-72 and 1977-79, President 1978), Pennsylvania and American Bar Associations. Retired Lieutenant j.g. USNR (active duty 1943-46). Employed as Professional Engineer 1946-60. Registered Professional Engineer since 1956. Director MS Society and Clinic. Mem-

BENTZ, WARREN W.—*Continued*

ber Erie Yacht Club, Preservation Project of Erie, Erie Philharmonic (Former Vice President), Kiwanis (Past President), Shrine (Zem Zem Zailors), 33° Mason and YMCA (Board of Managers and Past President, Past President Handball Club). Enjoys handball and boating.

Office: 717 State Street, Suite 700, Erie 16501-1355.
Telephone: (814) 453-4408.

BERNSTEIN, Mark Israel *(Judge, Pennsylvania Court of Common Pleas First Judicial District)* Appointed by Governor Robert P. Casey to term beginning April 7, 1987. Elected Nov 1987. Retained by election Nov 1997, current term expires Jan 2008. Born New York New York Aug 18, 1947. Jewish. Educated at St. John's College B.A. 1969 and University of Pennsylvania Law School J.D. 1973. Admitted to practice Pennsylvania 1973, U.S. District Court Eastern District of Pennsylvania 1976 and U.S. Court of Appeals Third Circuit 1981. In legal practice Philadelphia 1973-87.

Assistant Public Defender 1974-76. Contributing Essayist "Jury Prerogatives: An American Political Inheritance" and Chairman Board of Editors "The Bill of Rights: A Bicentennial View" Bill of Rights Centennial Committee Pennsylvania Bar Association. Editor Pennsylvania Court of Common Pleas Trial Division Statistical Report 1989, 1990 and 1991. Author Chapters "Judicial Decision-Making" and "A Meditation on Judicial Morality" *The Judge's Book* 2nd ed. American Bar Association and The National Judicial College 1994, "Expert Testimony in Pennsylvania" Temple L. Rev. Summer 1995, "The Most Proactive Court" *Court Review* American Judges Association Fall 1996 and "Program Helps Reduce Backlog in Philadelphia" 80 No. 4 *Judicature* Jan and Feb 1997. Board of Governors American Judges Association 1999-2002. Member Civil Instruction Subcommittee Committee for Suggested Standard Civil Jury Instruction The Supreme Court of Pennsylvania since 2000. Secretary Board of Judges Pennsylvania Court of Common Pleas First Judicial District since 2000. Member The Delaware Valley Environmental American Inn of Court, The Temple American Inn of Court, American Judicature Society, Philadelphia, Pennsylvania and American (Judicial Division) Bar Associations.

Member Education Committee Pennsylvania Conference of State Trial Judges 1992-94. Organizer and Presenter Day Forward Case Management New Judge's Conference Feb 13 to Feb 16, 1996. Presenter "Prospering in a Day Forward Case Management System" Annual Meeting June 1996 and "Daubert—Frye: Will the Court Allow Your Expert to Testify" May 1999 Philadelphia Trial Lawyers Association; "Solving Problems Before They Arise Using ADR to Achieve Your Client's Objective" Alternative Dispute Committee Philadelphia Bar Association Nov 1997; "Civil Practice in the Philadelphia Court of Common Pleas" Feb 1998, "Myths & Realities About Jurors: An Inside Look at What Jurors Think" Oct 2001 and "New Pennsylvania Rule of Civil Procedure 207.1" Nov 2001 Pennsylvania Bar Institute; and "Medical Malpractice Kaleidoscope" July 2000, "Discovery Tips for Med Mal Cases: Laying the Foundation for Victory" Dec 2000 and "Products Liability Law & Strategy" Dec 2001 Pennsylvania Trial Lawyers Association. Faculty Member The National Judicial College June 1999 and 2001, Philadelphia New Judges School Nov 2001 and New Judges Conference State Conference of Trial Judges Jan 2002. Recipient Annual Foundation for Improvement of Justice, Inc. Award April 2000. Board of Directors West Mount Airy Neighbors (Vice Chairman 1980). Advisory Council Sudden Infant Death Resource Center. Member Executive Committee Philadelphia Lawyers Against Apartheid and Philadelphians for Recycling.

Office: 530 City Hall, Philadelphia 19107.
Telephone: (215) 686-7335.

BERRY, Willis W., Jr. *(Judge, Pennsylvania Court of Common Pleas First Judicial District)*

Office: 1409 Criminal Justice Center, 1301 Filbert Street, Philadelphia 19107.
Telephone: (215) 683-7124.

BERTIN, Emanuel A. *(Judge, Pennsylvania Court of Common Pleas Thirty-eighth Judicial District)*

Mailing address: P.O. Box 311, Norristown 19404.
Office: Montgomery County Courthouse, Norristown 19401.
Telephone: (610) 278-3163.

BIEHN, Kenneth G. *(Judge, Pennsylvania Court of Common Pleas Seventh Judicial District)* Appointed by Governor Richard Thornburgh to term beginning Dec 10, 1979. Elected 1981. Retained by election 1991 and 2001. Current term expires Jan 4, 2011. Former President Judge. Born Quakertown Pennsylvania July 10, 1939. Educated at Lafayette College A.B. cum laude 1961 and Duke University LL.B. with distinction 1964. Case Note Editor Duke Law Review. Member Phi Beta Kappa. Admitted to practice Pennsylvania 1964 and U.S. District Court Eastern District of Pennsylvania. In legal practice Quakerstown 1964-72.

District Attorney Bucks County 1972-79. Member Pennsylvania Commission on Crime and Delinquency (Chairman Victim Service Advisory Committee 1983-96 and Technology Committee since 1997). Recipient Allied Professional Award from National Organization of Victim Assistance 1989.

Office: Bucks County Courthouse, 55 East Court Street, Doylestown 18901.
Telephone: (215) 348-6066.

BIGHAM, Robert G. *(Judge, Pennsylvania Court of Common Pleas Fifty-first Judicial District)*

Office: Adams County Courthouse, 111-117 Baltimore Street, Gettysburg 17325.
Telephone: (717) 337-9857.

BIGLEY, Gerard M. *(Judge, Pennsylvania Court of Common Pleas Fifth Judicial District)* Elected to term beginning Jan 1, 1978. Retained by election 1987 and 1997. Current term expires Jan 2008. Currently serves as Administrative Judge Criminal Division. Born Pittsburgh Pennsylvania Aug 24, 1939. Roman Catholic. Educated at University of Pittsburgh B.B.A. 1961 and Duquesne University J.D. cum laude 1970. Staff member Duquesne Law Review. Member Phi Alpha Delta. Admitted to practice Pennsylvania 1970 and U.S. District Court Western District of Pennsylvania 1970. Began legal practice Pittsburgh 1970.

Police Legal Advisor Pittsburgh 1970-75. Assistant District Attorney Allegheny County 1976-77. Member Pennsylvania Conference of State Trial Judges, Allegheny County (Civil Division), Pennsylvania and American Bar Associations. Recipient Distinguished Alumnus Award from Duquesne University School of Law 1984.

BIGLEY, GERARD M.—*Continued*

Democrat. Member Muscular Dystrophy Association (Past Vice President Western Pennsylvania Chapter). Enjoys sports, hunting and fishing.

Office: 305 Allegheny County Courthouse, 436 Grant Street, Pittsburgh 15219.

Telephone: (412) 350-4434.

BLACK, Alan M. *(Judge, Pennsylvania Court of Common Pleas Thirty-first Judicial District)* Elected Nov 1997. Term expires Jan 2008. Born Bethlehem Pennsylvania Nov 20, 1938. Jewish. Educated at University of Pennsylvania B.S. in Economics with distinction 1960 and Harvard University J.D. 1963. Admitted to practice Pennsylvania 1964, U.S. District Court Eastern District of Pennsylvania 1965, U.S. Court of Appeals Third Circuit 1986 and U.S. Supreme Court 1986. In legal practice Allentown 1964-97.

Solicitor City of Allentown 1974-77. President Donald E. Wieand, Sr. American Inn of Court. Member Lehigh County, Pennsylvania and American Bar Associations. Attended Pennsylvania New Judges Conference Jan 1998, Pennsylvania State Trial Judges Conferences Feb and July 1998, 1999 and 2000 and General Jurisdiction Course The National Judicial College Oct 1998. Recipient Service Award from Confront, Inc. (drug rehabilitation organization) 1985. Democrat. Former Secretary and Board Member Lehigh County Mental Health/Mental Retardation Board. Former Board Member The Program for Women & Families, Inc. Former Wrestling Coach Salisbury Youth Association. President Adult Literacy Center of Lehigh Valley. Board of Governors Civic Theatre of Allentown. Founding Member Confront, Inc. Member Allentown Rotary. Interests include family and sports.

Office: Lehigh County Courthouse, 455 West Hamilton Street, Allentown 18101.

Telephone: (610) 782-3207.

E-mail address: alanblack@lehighcounty.org

BLACKWELL, Penny L. *(Judge, Pennsylvania Court of Common Pleas Nineteenth Judicial District)*

Office: York County Courthouse, 28 East Market Street, York 17401.

Telephone: (717) 771-9938.

BLAHOVEC, John E. *(Judge, Pennsylvania Court of Common Pleas Tenth Judicial District)*

Office: Westmoreland County Courthouse, Two North Main Street, Greensburg 15601.

Telephone: (724) 830-3835.

BLEWITT, Thomas M. *(Magistrate Judge, United States District Court Middle District of Pennsylvania)* Appointed by U.S. District Court judges to term beginning Feb 21, 1992. Reappointed Feb 21, 2000, current term expires Feb 20, 2008. Born Pittston Pennsylvania Nov 20, 1949. Roman Catholic. Educated at University of Scranton B.A. 1972, Marywood College M.P.A. 1979 and Temple University School of Law J.D. 1983. Admitted to practice Pennsylvania 1983, U.S. District Court Middle District of Pennsylvania 1986, U.S. Court of Appeals Third Circuit 1986 and U.S. Supreme Court 1987.

Assistant District Attorney Lackawanna County 1984-86. Assistant Federal Public Defender 1986-88 and 1989-92 U.S. District Court Middle District of Pennsylvania. Member Federal Magistrate Judges Association, Lackawanna County and Pennsylvania Bar Associations. Attended Mid-Atlantic Prosecution Course National College of District Attorneys 1984; Criminal Law Symposium 1984, 1985 and 1986, Grand Jury Practice Seminar 1986 and New Rules of Professional Conduct 1988 Pennsylvania Bar Institute; Trial Institute National Criminal Defense College 1986; Seminar for First Year Assistant Federal Public Defenders 1986, Advanced Defender Training Seminar 1990 and 1991; Workshop for Magistrate Judges of the First, Second, Third, Sixth and Seventh Circuits 1992 and Seminar for New United States Magistrate Judges 1992 Federal Judicial Center; Criminal Law Developments, Defense and Prosecution Dickinson School of Law 1987; Middle District of Pennsylvania Sentencing Guidelines Training Conference 1987; Death Penalty Resource Planning Conference American Bar Association 1988; and Video Program Americans with Disabilities Act ALI-ABA 1992. Instructor Sentencing Guidelines Seminar Middle District of Pennsylvania 1988 and Federal Public Defender 1989. Special Investigator Bureau of Consumer Protection U.S. Department of Justice 1972-80. Chairman Board of Directors Friendship House Children's Center. Member University of Scranton Alumni Society, University of Scranton Royals Club, Temple Law Alumni, University of Scranton Purple Club and Northeastern Pennsylvania Philharmonic. Patron Scranton Community Concerts.

Mailing address: P.O. Box 443, Scranton 18501-0443.

Telephone: (570) 207-5740.

BLOCH, Alan N. *(Senior Judge, United States District Court Western District of Pennsylvania)* Appointed for life by President Jimmy Carter. Assumed Senior status April 12, 1997, serves by assignment. Born Pittsburgh Pennsylvania April 12, 1932. Educated at University of Pennsylvania B.S. 1953 and University of Pittsburgh School of Law J.D. 1958. In legal practice Pittsburgh 1958-79.

Office: 837 U.S. Post Office & Courthouse, 700 Grant Street, Pittsburgh 15219.

Telephone: (412) 208-7360.

BOWES, Mary Jane *(Judge, The Superior Court of Pennsylvania)* Elected Nov 2001 to term beginning Jan 2002. Term expires Jan 2012. Born Pittsburgh Pennsylvania July 18, 1954. Educated at Georgetown University B.A. 1976 and University of Pittsburgh School of Law J.D. 1979. Judicial Law Clerk to Hon. Harry M. Montgomery and Hon. John P. Hester, The Superior Court of Pennsylvania and Chief Justice Henry X. O'Brien, The Supreme Court of Pennsylvania. In legal practice 1986-98.

Member Academy of Trial Lawyers of Allegheny County, Allegheny County and Pennsylvania Bar Associations. Recipient Pennsylvania's Best 50 Women in Business Award 1997. Past President Board Parental Stress Center and Georgetown University Alumni Club of Pittsburgh. Former Member Board of Trustees St. Clair Memorial Hospital and DePaul Institute. Past President and Member Board of Trustees St. Thomas More Society. Board of Trustees Duquesne University, St. Anthony School Programs and Pittsburgh Civic Light Opera. Member Pastoral Council St. Louise de Marillac.

Office: 2600 Grant Building, 330 Grant Street, Pittsburgh 15219.

Telephone: (412) 565-2342.

Fax: (412) 565-2317

BOZZA, John A. *(Judge, Pennsylvania Court of Common Pleas Sixth Judicial District)* Former President Judge.

Office: Erie County Courthouse, 140 West Sixth Street, Erie 16501.

Telephone: (814) 451-6294.

BRADLEY, Harry J. *(Judge, Pennsylvania Court of Common Pleas Thirty-second Judicial District)* Appointed by Governor Robert P. Casey to term beginning Aug 1, 1989. Elected Nov 3, 1990 and 2000. Current term expires Jan 2011. Born Philadelphia Pennsylvania Dec 15, 1936. Catholic. Educated at La Salle University B.A. with honors 1958 and Temple University School of Law J.D. with honors 1961. Associate Editor Temple Law Quarterly 1960-61. Law Clerk to Hon. John Lord, U.S. District Court Eastern District of Pennsylvania 1961-63. Member Phi Alpha Delta. Admitted to practice Pennsylvania 1962, U.S. Court of Appeals Third Circuit and U.S. Supreme Court. In legal practice Philadelphia 1963-64 and Media 1964-89.

Solicitor Springfield Township 1977-79. Author "Stock Options—Tax Practice" Journal of the American Bar Association 1964, and *Tax Magazine* 1964. Instructor in Property Widener University 1977-85. Member Pennsylvania Conference of State Trial Judges, Pennsylvania and American Bar Associations. Attended The National Judicial College and Oxford University. Republican. Member Knights of Columbus and various local charities. Enjoys cabinet making, cooking, reading and sports.

Office: Delaware County Courthouse, 201 West Front Street, Media 19063.

Telephone: (610) 891-4498.

BRANCA, Thomas C. *(Judge, Pennsylvania Court of Common Pleas Thirty-eighth Judicial District)*

Mailing address: P.O. Box 311, Norristown 19404.

Office: Montgomery County Courthouse, Norristown 19401.

Telephone: (610) 278-1067.

BRATTON, Bruce F. *(Judge, Pennsylvania Court of Common Pleas Twelfth Judicial District)* Appointed by Governor Tom Ridge to term beginning May 22, 2001. Elected Nov 2001 to term beginning Jan 2002, current term expires Jan 2012. Born Lewistown Pennsylvania June 25, 1949. Educated at Pennsylvania State University B.A. with honors 1973 and University of Pennsylvania J.D. 1976. Admitted to practice Pennsylvania 1976. In legal practice Harrisburg 1976-2001.

Solicitor Dauphin County Controller's Office 1981-2001. Former Member Pennsylvania Trial Lawyers Association. Member Dauphin County and Pennsylvania Bar Associations. Township Commissioner Susquehanna Township 1987-88.

Office: Dauphin County Courthouse, Front and Market Streets, Harrisburg 17101.

Telephone: (717) 780-6685.

Fax: (717) 780-6457

E-mail address: bbratton@dauphinc.org

BRENNER, Lawrence J. *(Judge, Pennsylvania Court of Common Pleas Thirty-first Judicial District)*

Office: Lehigh County Courthouse, 455 West Hamilton Street, Allentown 18101.

Telephone: (610) 782-3026.

BRIGHT, Gwendolyn N. *(Judge, Pennsylvania Court of Common Pleas First Judicial District)*

Office: 1208 Criminal Justice Center, 1301 Filbert Street, Philadelphia 19107.

Telephone: (215) 683-7041.

BRILLHART, Michael J. *(Judge, Pennsylvania Court of Common Pleas Nineteenth Judicial District)*

Office: York County Courthouse, 28 East Market Street, York 17401.

Telephone: (717) 771-9936.

BRINKLEY, Genece E. *(Judge, Pennsylvania Court of Common Pleas First Judicial District)*

Office: 1801 Vine Street, Suite 345, Philadelphia 19103.

Telephone: (215) 686-2660.

Fax: (215) 686-4224

BRODY, Anita B. *(Judge, United States District Court Eastern District of Pennsylvania)* Appointed for life by the President. Born New York New York May 25, 1935. Jewish. Educated at Wellesley College B.A. 1955 and Columbia University School of Law J.D. 1958. Member Moot Court Board. Admitted to practice New York 1958, Florida 1960 and Pennsylvania 1972. In legal practice Ardmore Pennsylvania 1972-81.

Assistant Attorney General New York 1958-60. Author "Deciding Who Gets Custody" *Philadelphia Inquirer* Sept 26, 1983 and "Professional Responsibility in Family Law" 1979. Important Decisions: The Philadelphia Center for Developmental Services, Inc. v. The Zoning Hearing Board of Plymouth Township 1984, O'Hara Sanitation Co. v. County of Montgomery, et al. 1986, Flax v. Reconstructionist Rabbinical College 1987 and Goldman v. Goldman 1987. Lecturer on Law University of Pennsylvania Law School 1978-79. Former Member Domestic Relations Committee Pennsylvania Supreme Court. Member Montgomery County, Pennsylvania and American Bar Associations. Visiting Lecturer "Issues in Family Law" Montgomery County Bar Association 1987 and "Custody of Children" University of Pennsylvania 1987. Speaker "The State ERA" We the Women 200 Philadelphia 1987. Panelist Family Law Symposium Pennsylvania Conference of State Trial Judges 1988. Republican. Board Member Deputy Sheriffs Education and Training and National Museum of Jewish American History.

Office: 4000 U.S. Courthouse, 601 Market Street, Philadelphia 19106-1744.

Telephone: (215) 597-3978.

BROWN, Charles C., Jr. *(President Judge, Pennsylvania Court of Common Pleas Forty-ninth Judicial District)* Elected Nov 1979 to term beginning Jan 1980. Retained by election Nov 1989 and Nov 1999. Current term expires Jan 2010. Born Bellefonte Pennsylvania June 22, 1937. Educated at Juniata College B.A. 1959 and New York University School of Law J.D. 1962. Admitted to practice Pennsylvania 1963. In legal practice Bellefonte 1963-80.

District Attorney Centre County 1966-78. Member Pennsylvania Conference of State Trial Judges, Centre County and Pennsylvania Bar Associations. Board of Trustees Juniata College. Enjoys collecting sports memorabilia.

Office: Centre County Courthouse, Bellefonte 16823.

Telephone: (814) 355-6732.

E-mail address: ccbrownj@co.centre.pa.us

BROWN, Joan A. *(Judge, Pennsylvania Court of Common Pleas First Judicial District)*
Office: 1215 Criminal Justice Center, 1301 Filbert Street, Philadelphia 19107.
Telephone: (215) 683-7062.

BROWN, Kenneth D. *(Judge, Pennsylvania Court of Common Pleas Twenty-ninth Judicial District)*
Office: Lycoming County Courthouse, 48 West Third Street, Williamsport 17701.
Telephone: (570) 327-2336.

BUCKWALTER, Ronald L. *(Judge, United States District Court Eastern District of Pennsylvania)* Appointed for life by President George Bush. Born Lancaster Pennsylvania Dec 11, 1936. Educated at Franklin and Marshall College A.B. 1958 and College of William & Mary J.D. 1962. Staff member William & Mary Law Review 1961-62. Member Phi Alpha Delta. Admitted to practice Pennsylvania 1963 and U.S. Supreme Court 1973. In legal practice Lancaster 1963-80. Former Judge, Pennsylvania Court of Common Pleas Second Judicial District, elected to term beginning Jan 1980.
District Attorney 1977-80. Member Pennsylvania Conference of State Trial Judges (Chairman Corrections Committee 1989), Federal Judges Association, Lancaster (President 1988) and Pennsylvania Bar Associations. Recipient Public Life and Letters Award from Phi Sigma Alpha. First Lieutenant U.S. Army 1968. President Lancaster County Prison Board. Advisory Board Boy Scouts of America and Lancaster REACT. Board of Directors YMCA and Lancaster Chapter American Cancer Society. Past President Franklin and Marshall Alumni Club, American Business Club and Buchanan PTO. Enjoys squash, racquetball, biking, swimming, reading and traveling.
Office: 14614 U.S. Courthouse, 601 Market Street, Philadelphia 19106-1714.
Telephone: (215) 597-3084.

BURKE, Thomas F., Jr. *(Judge, Pennsylvania Court of Common Pleas Eleventh Judicial District)*
Office: Luzerne County Courthouse, 200 North River Street, Wilkes-Barre 18711.
Telephone: (570) 830-5121.

BURR, Charles B., II *(Judge, Pennsylvania Court of Common Pleas Thirty-second Judicial District)* Elected Nov 4, 1999 to term beginning Jan 3, 2000. Term expires Jan 3, 2010. Born Pittsburgh Pennsylvania March 21, 1940. Episcopalian. Educated at Yale University B.S. 1962 and University of Pennsylvania Law School LL.B. 1966. Admitted to practice Pennsylvania 1968, U.S. District Court Eastern District of Pennsylvania 1968, U.S. Court of Appeals Third Circuit 1969 and U.S. Supreme Court 1975. In legal practice Philadelphia 1968-99.
Assistant U.S. Attorney Eastern District of Pennsylvania 1969-72. Author "Appellate Review as a Means of Controlling Criminal Sentencing Discretion—A Workable Alternative?" 33 University of Pittsburgh L. Rev. 1, 1971 and "Contribution, Indemnity, Settlements and Releases: What the Pennsylvania Comparative Negligence Statute Did Not Say" 24 Villanova L. Rev. 494, 1979. Adjunct Professor of Civil Pretrial Practice Villanova University School of Law 1992-97. Member Delaware County, Pennsylvania and American Bar Associations. Instructor "Effective Negotiating Techniques for Settling Difficult Cases" Pennsylvania Defense Institute Oct 2000 and "The Judicial Perspective on Expert Testimony" Pennsylvania Trial Lawyers Association Nov 2000. Republican. Solicitor Zoning Hearing Board Radnor Township 1975-99. Enjoys reading, traveling, recreational sports, crossword puzzles and grandparenting.
Office: Delaware County Courthouse, 201 West Front Street, Media 19063.
Telephone: (610) 891-5699.
Fax: (610) 891-5480
E-mail address: BurrC@co.delaware.pa.us

BUTTS, Nancy L. *(Judge, Pennsylvania Court of Common Pleas Twenty-ninth Judicial District)*
Office: Lycoming County Courthouse, 48 West Third Street, Williamsport 17701.
Telephone: (570) 327-2338.

BYRD, Sandy L. V. *(Judge, Pennsylvania Court of Common Pleas First Judicial District)*
Office: 1420 Criminal Justice Center, 1301 Filbert Street, Philadelphia 19107.
Telephone: (215) 683-7157.

CAIAZZA, Francis X. *(Magistrate Judge, United States District Court Western District of Pennsylvania)* Appointed by U.S. District Court judges. Born New Castle Pennsylvania Oct 17, 1935. Catholic. Educated at Duquesne University B.A. 1958 and University of Pittsburgh LL.B. 1961. Admitted to practice Pennsylvania 1961, U.S. District Court District of Pennsylvania 1964 and U.S. Supreme Court 1980. Began legal practice New Castle 1963. Former Judge, Pennsylvania Court of Common Pleas Fifty-third Judicial District, elected to term beginning Jan 4, 1982.
Important Decision: In re sheriff sales in Lawrence County No. 78, 1983. Member Pennsylvania Trial Lawyers Association, The Association of Trial Lawyers of America, Lawrence County and Pennsylvania Bar Associations. Private First Class Office of Judge Advocate USAS 1961-63. Former Board member Lark Workshop, YMCA, West Side Community Action Center (Legal Counsel for Kids, Inc.) and Eastside Community Center (Chairman Cerebral Palsy Fund Raising Drive). Enjoys jogging, baseball, football, piano and singing.
Office: 501 U.S. Post Office & Courthouse, 700 Grant Street, Pittsburgh 15219.
Telephone: (412) 208-7460.

CALDWELL, William W. *(Senior Judge, United States District Court Middle District of Pennsylvania)* Appointed for life by the President. Assumed Senior status, serves by assignment. Born Harrisburg Pennsylvania Nov 10, 1925. Educated at Dickinson College A.B. and Dickinson School of Law LL.B. Former Judge, Pennsylvania Court of Common Pleas Twelfth Judicial District, elected to term beginning Jan 1970.
Chairman Pennsylvania Board of Arbitration of Claims 1968-70. Member Dauphin County and Pennsylvania Bar Associations. USAAC 1943-45.
Mailing address: P.O. Box 11877, Harrisburg 17108-1877.
Telephone: (717) 221-3970.

CAMPBELL, Mary Ann *(Judge, Pennsylvania Court of Common Pleas Twenty-third Judicial District)*
Office: Berks County Services Center, Fourth Floor, 633 Court Street, Reading 19601.
Telephone: (610) 478-6421.

CAPPY, Ralph J. *(Chief Justice, The Supreme Court of Pennsylvania)* Born Pittsburgh Pennsylvania Aug 25,

CAPPY, RALPH J.—*Continued*

1943. Roman Catholic. Educated at University of Pittsburgh B.S. with honors 1965 J.D. 1968. Admitted to practice Pennsylvania 1968 and U.S. District Court Western District of Pennsylvania 1968. Began legal practice Pittsburgh 1968. Former Judge and Administrative Judge Civil Division, Pennsylvania Court of Common Pleas Fifth Judicial District, appointed by Governor Milton J. Sharp to term beginning June 23, 1978.

With Allegheny County Public Defender's Office 1970-78 (Director 1975-78). Lecturer on Constitutional Issues and Trial Tactics University of Pittsburgh 1971-73. Instructor City of Pittsburgh Training School and Allegheny County Police Academy 1970-73. Chairman Education Committee Pennsylvania Conference of State Trial Judges since 1985. Member Chief Justice's Committee on Continuing Judicial and Legal Education 1986. Democrat. Board of Directors Neighborhood Legal Services.

Office: 3130 One Oxford Center, Grant Street, Pittsburgh 15219.

Telephone: (412) 565-2700.

CAPUTO, A. Richard *(Judge, United States District Court Middle District of Pennsylvania)* Appointed for life by President Bill Clinton to term beginning Dec 15, 1997. Educated at Brown University A.B. 1960 and University of Pennsylvania Law School LL.B. 1963. In legal practice 1968-97.

Public Defender Luzerne County 1968. Member Luzerne County Law and Library Association, Federal Judges' Association (Board of Directors), Pennsylvania, Federal and American Bar Associations. USAF JAG 1964-67. Secretary and Director Stegmaier Brewing Company 1973-92. Director Unifax 1988-92. Director and Vice President Maplemoor, Inc. 1991-97. Director and Secretary/Treasurer The Luzerne Foundation 1994-97.

Mailing address: P.O. Box 1246, Scranton 18501-1246.

Telephone: (570) 207-5750.

CAPUZZI, Conrad B. *(President Judge, Pennsylvania Court of Common Pleas Fourteenth Judicial District)*

Office: Fayette County Courthouse, 61 East Main Street, Uniontown 15401.

Telephone: (724) 430-1233.

CARACAPPA, Linda K. *(Magistrate Judge, United States District Court Eastern District of Pennsylvania)* Appointed by U.S. District Court Judges to term beginning Nov 17, 2000.

Office: 3042 U.S. Courthouse, 601 Market Street, Philadelphia 19106-1789.

Telephone: (215) 597-7704.

CAREY, Kevin J. *(Judge, United States Bankruptcy Court Eastern District of Pennsylvania)* Appointed by U.S. Court of Appeals Third Circuit judges.

Office: 201 Federal Building, 900 Market Street, Philadelphia 19107-4297.

Telephone: (215) 408-2970.

CARPENTER, Hiram A., III *(Judge, Pennsylvania Court of Common Pleas Twenty-fourth Judicial District)*

Office: 360 Blair County Courthouse, 423 Allegheny Street, Hollidaysburg 16648.

Telephone: (814) 693-3070.

CARPENTER, William R. *(Judge, Pennsylvania Court of Common Pleas Thirty-eighth Judicial District)*

Mailing address: P.O. Box 311, Norristown 19404.

Office: Montgomery County Courthouse, Norristown 19401.

Telephone: (610) 278-5902.

CARRAFIELLO, Matthew D. *(Judge, Pennsylvania Court of Common Pleas First Judicial District)*

Office: 673 City Hall, Philadelphia 19107.

Telephone: (215) 686-2961.

CARUSO, Gary P. *(Judge, Pennsylvania Court of Common Pleas Tenth Judicial District)* Elected to term beginning Jan 6, 1986. Retained by election 1995, current term expires Jan 2006. Born Monessen Pennsylvania Oct 22, 1948. Roman Catholic. Educated at Waynesburg College B.A. cum laude 1970 and Duquesne University J.D. 1973. Admitted to practice Pennsylvania 1973. In legal practice Monessen 1973-79 and Rostraver 1979-85.

Member Pennsylvania Conference of State Trial Judges and Pennsylvania Bar Association.

Office: Westmoreland County Courthouse, Two North Main Street, Greensburg 15601.

Telephone: (724) 830-3815.

CASCIO, John M. *(Judge, Pennsylvania Court of Common Pleas Sixteenth Judicial District)*

Office: 212 Somerset County Courthouse, 111 East Union Street, Somerset 15501.

Telephone: (814) 445-1486.

CASHMAN, David R. *(Judge, Pennsylvania Court of Common Pleas Fifth Judicial District)*

Office: 533 Allegheny County Courthouse, 436 Grant Street, Pittsburgh 15219.

Telephone: (412) 350-3905.

CASTILLE, Ronald D. *(Justice, The Supreme Court of Pennsylvania)* Elected to term beginning Jan 1993. Term expires Dec 31, 2003. Born Miami Florida March 16, 1944. Educated at Auburn University B.S. 1966 and University of Virginia School of Law J.D. 1971. In legal practice Philadelphia 1991-93.

Deputy District Attorney 1971-85 and District Attorney 1986-91 Philadelphia. Vice President and Legislative Chairman National District Attorneys Association 1986-91. Commissioner President's Commission on Model State Drug Laws 1992. Member Pennsylvania Supreme Court Judicial Counsel. First Lieutenant USMC Vietnam 1966-68 (retired). Recipient Bronze Btar and two Purple Hearts. Executive Committee Cradle of Liberty Council Boy Scouts of America 1986-2000. Vice President and Secretary Philadelphia Vietnam Veterans Memorial Fund. Board of Directors Pennsylvania Center for Adapted Sports. Board Member Police Athletic League.

Office: 1818 Market Street, Suite 3730, Philadelphia 19103-3637.

Telephone: (215) 560-5663.

CERCONE, David S. *(Judge, United States District Court Western District of Pennsylvania)* Appointed for life by President George W. Bush to term beginning 2002. Born Pittsburgh Pennsylvania Nov 23, 1952. Roman Catholic. Educated at Westminster College B.A. magna cum laude 1974 and Duquesne University School of Law J.D. 1977. Law Clerk to Pennsylvania Court of Common Pleas 1978. Admitted to practice Pennsylvania 1977. In legal practice Pittsburgh, Stowe Township,

CERCONE, DAVID S.—*Continued*
McKees Rocks Borough and Allegheny County. Justice, Pennsylvania District Justice Court 1982-85. Judge Jan 6, 1986 to 2002 and Former Administrative Judge Criminal Division, Pennsylvania Court of Common Pleas Fifth Judicial District.

Assistant District Attorney Allegheny County 1979-81. Instructor University of Pittsburgh since 1984. Member Pennsylvania State Trial Judges Association and Allegheny County Bar Association. Board of Directors Boys Club of Western Pennsylvania. Enjoys playing classical piano.

Office: 1036 U.S. Courthouse, Tenth Floor, Seventh Avenue and Grant Street, Pittsburgh 15219.

Telephone: (412) 208-7363.

CHARLES, Bradford H. *(Judge, Pennsylvania Court of Common Pleas Fifty-second Judicial District)* Elected 1999 to term beginning Jan 2000. Term expires Jan 2010. Educated at Grove City College B.A. magna cum laude 1978 and Dickinson School of Law J.D. 1981. Trial and Appellate Moot Court Team. Member Order of Barristers. Admitted to practice Pennsylvania, U.S. District Courts Eastern and Middle Districts of Pennsylvania and U.S. Supreme Court. In legal practice 1985-94.

Assistant District Attorney 1986-90, First Assistant District Attorney 1990-94 and District Attorney 1994 Lebanon County. Instructor in Intensive Trial Advocacy Widener University School of Law since 1994. Chairman Lebanon County Criminal Rules Committee 1994-99. Member Executive Committee Pennsylvania District Attorneys Institute 1998-99. Board Certified in Civil Trial Advocacy. Member Pennsylvania Trial Lawyers Association. Instructor in How to Conduct a Preliminary Hearing for local police and Pennsylvania State Police and Crimes Code Orientation Pennsylvania Basic Prosecutors School. Recipient Paul Harris Fellowship Award from Lebanon Rotary Club 2000. Head Coach Neversink Knights Little League Baseball 1996-98. Former Chairman Lebanon City Zoning Hearing Board. Youth Sunday School Teacher Church of the Good Shepherd. Board of Directors Kiwanis Club. Volunteer Lebanon YMCA Swim Team. Master Swimmer (3rd in nation 1989). Swimming Official PIAA and NCAA.

Office: Lebanon County Courthouse, 400 South Eighth Street, Lebanon 17042.

Telephone: (717) 274-2801.

CHEN, Ida K. *(Judge, Pennsylvania Court of Common Pleas First Judicial District)*

Office: 27 South Twelfth Street, Suite 403, Philadelphia 19107.

Telephone: (215) 686-2545.

CHERRY, John F. *(Judge, Pennsylvania Court of Common Pleas Twelfth Judicial District)*

Office: Dauphin County Courthouse, Front and Market Streets, Harrisburg 17101.

Telephone: (717) 780-6680.

CHESLOCK, Jerome P. *(Judge, Pennsylvania Court of Common Pleas Forty-third Judicial District)* Elected Nov 1993 to term beginning Jan 1, 1994. Term expires Dec 31, 2003. Born West Hazleton Pennsylvania Dec 8, 1939. Roman Catholic. Educated at St. Francis College B.A. 1961 and Dickinson School of Law J.D. 1964. Admitted to practice Pennsylvania 1967. In legal practice East Stroudsburg 1967-81 and Stroudsburg 1981-93.

Public Defender 1969-71. Member Monroe County (President 1982) and Pennsylvania Bar Associations. Specialist 5 U.S. Army Feb 1965 to Feb 1967. President Stroudsburg Area School Board 1992-94.

Office: Monroe County Courthouse, Stroudsburg 18360.

Telephone: (570) 420-3630.

CHRONISTER, John H. *(President Judge, Pennsylvania Court of Common Pleas Nineteenth Judicial District)* Appointed by Governor Robert Casey to term beginning March 29, 1987. Elected 1987. Retained by election 1997, current term expires Jan 2008. Born York Pennsylvania July 21, 1944. United Church of Christ. Educated at Dickinson College B.A. 1965 and Dickinson School of Law J.D. 1968. Admitted to practice Pennsylvania 1968. In legal practice York 1968-87.

Member York County and Pennsylvania Bar Associations.

Office: York County Courthouse, 28 East Market Street, York 17401.

Telephone: (717) 771-9723.

CIAVARELLA, Mark A., Jr. *(Judge, Pennsylvania Court of Common Pleas Eleventh Judicial District)*

Office: Luzerne County Courthouse, 200 North River Street, Wilkes-Barre 18711.

Telephone: (570) 825-1544.

CINDRICH, Robert J. *(Judge, United States District Court Western District of Pennsylvania)* Appointed for life by President Bill Clinton to term beginning 1994. Born Washington Pennsylvania Sept 22, 1943. Educated at Wittenberg University A.B. 1965 and University of Pittsburgh School of Law J.D. 1968. Law Clerk to Hon. Ruggero Aldisert, U.S. Court of Appeals Third Circuit 1968-69. In legal practice Pittsburgh 1970-78 and 1981-94.

Assistant Public Defender 1969-70 and Assistant District Attorney 1970-72 Allegheny County. U.S. Attorney Western District of Pennsylvania 1978-81.

Office: 1014 U.S. Post Office & Courthouse, 700 Grant Street, Pittsburgh 15219.

Telephone: (412) 208-7370.

CLARK, Kim Berkeley *(Judge, Pennsylvania Court of Common Pleas Fifth Judicial District)*

Office: 440 Ross Street, Room 5065, Pittsburgh 15219.

Telephone: (412) 350-0269.

CLARK, Lawrence F., Jr. *(Judge, Pennsylvania Court of Common Pleas Twelfth Judicial District)*

Office: Dauphin County Courthouse, Front and Market Streets, Harrisburg 17101.

Telephone: (717) 780-6675.

CLARK, Tama Myers *(Judge, Pennsylvania Court of Common Pleas First Judicial District)* Assumed office Jan 1984. Retained by election 1993, current term expires Jan 2004. Born Boston Massachusetts. Educated at Morgan State University B.S. summa cum laude 1968 and University of Pennsylvania Master of City Planning 1972 J.D. 1972. Recipient Parekh Memorial Student Leadership Award 1968, Achievement and Merit Award from Student Government 1968 and Distinguished Honor Scholar Award 1968 from Morgan State University. Listed in *Who's Who in American Colleges and Univer-*

CLARK, TAMA MYERS—*Continued*

sities 1967. Law Clerk to Hon. Doris M. Harris, Pennsylvania Court of Common Pleas First Judicial District 1972-73. Member Alpha Kappa Alpha. Admitted to practice Pennsylvania 1972, U.S. District Court Eastern District of Pennsylvania 1973, U.S. Court of Appeals District of Columbia Circuit 1973 and U.S. Supreme Court 1981.

Assistant District Attorney 1973-80 and Deputy City Solicitor 1980-83 Philadelphia. Member Civil Procedural Rules Committee Domestic Relations Section and Criminal Procedural Rules Committee Pennsylvania Supreme Court. Member Barristers Association of Philadelphia, Pennsylvania Conference of State Trial Judges, The District of Columbia Bar, Philadelphia and National Bar Associations. Named one of Outstanding Young Women of America 1976. Recipient Legion of Honor Award from Chapel of Four Chaplains 1977, Distinguished Alumnus Award from Philadelphia Chapter Morgan State University Alumni Association 1984, Outstanding Woman of the Community Award from Bright Hope Baptist Church Women's Committee 1984, Morgan State University Distinguished Alumni of the Year Award from National Association for Equal Opportunity in Higher Education 1984 and Woman of the Year Award from National Sports Foundation 1985. Alternating-Current Speed Tester Molecular Electronics Division Westinghouse Corporation Summer 1966. Computer Programmer Western Electric Corporation Summer 1967. Instructor in Mathematics Bowie State College Summer 1969 and Summer 1970. Legal Intern New Communities Division Office of the General Counsel U.S. Department of Housing and Urban Development Summer 1971. Member Coalition of 100 Black Women (Philadelphia Chapter), Big Brothers/Big Sisters (Women's Committee), Penn Towne Chapter Links, Incorporated (National Trends and Services Committee), Women in Government Network, Corrections Task Force Criminal Justice Coordinating Commission, Project Review Committee on the Protection of Human Subjects Philadelphia Department of Health and Women & Girl Offenders Task Force Mayor's Commission for Women. American College Representative at International Workcamp Seminar in Japan and Korea National YMCA/YWCA 1965. Leader of American Exchange Students in Rio de Janeiro for Maryland Partners of the Alliance 1968. Student Legal Counselor Philadelphia Tenants' Union 1971-72. Volunteer Legal Advisor Girls' Club of Philadelphia 1972-73. Preceptor Legal Division "New Access Routes to Legal Careers" Program American Foundation for Negro Affairs 1978-80. Board of Directors Community Services Planning Council of Southeastern Pennsylvania, Prisoners' Family Welfare Association and New Directions for Women. Counsel Philadelphia Prisons' Board of Trustees.

Office: 313 City Hall, Philadelphia 19107.
Telephone: (215) 686-7320.

CLELAND, John M. *(President Judge, Pennsylvania Court of Common Pleas Forty-eighth Judicial District)* Appointed by Governor Richard Thornburgh to term beginning Oct 5, 1984. Elected 1985. Retained by election 1995, current term expires Jan 2006. Administrative Judge Regional Judicial Unit III 1992-98. Born Kane Pennsylvania Dec 24, 1947. Educated at Denison University B.A. 1969 and George Washington University National Law Center J.D. with honors 1972. Law Clerk to Hon. Barron P. McCune, U.S. District Court Western District of Pennsylvania 1972-74. Member Pi Delta Epsilon and Omicron Delta Kappa. Admitted to practice Pennsylvania 1972 and U.S. District Court Western District of Pennsylvania 1974. In legal practice Kane 1974-84.

Member Orphans' Court Rules Committee 1993-99 and Chief Justice's Advisory Committee on Continuing Judicial Education since 1994 Pennsylvania Supreme Court. Member Pennsylvania Conference of State Trial Judges (Executive Committee 1991-94, Co-Chairman Education Committee 1993-2000, Chair Juvenile Law Section 1999-2001), American Judicature Society, McKean County (Secretary 1980-82, Vice President 1984) and Pennsylvania Bar Associations. Attended General Jurisdiction Course The National Judicial College 1986 and American Academy of Judicial Education. Listed in *Who's Who in the East.* Fund Drive Chairman Kane Area United Way 1975. Chairman Economic Development Committee and Director Kane Chamber of Commerce 1976-79. Chairman Kane Area Recreational and Cultural Commission 1976-80. Elder and Trustee First United Church of Kane 1976-82 and 1990-93. Director 1976-84, Vice President and Secretary 1980-84 and President 1984 Kane Area Industrial Development Corporation. Treasurer Executive Committee McKean County Republican Committee 1978-84. President Kane Rotary Club 1980-81. Member Republican State Committee 1984. Member since 1984 and Chair since 1995 Advisory Board and Trustee 2001-03 University of Pittsburgh. President 1986-88 and Director 1986-91 and since 1999 Kane Area Historical Society. Director Northwestern Pennsylvania Camp Association since 1988. Chairperson FCI McKean Community Advisory Board 1989-92.

Office: McKean County Courthouse, 500 Main Street, Smethport 16749.
Telephone: (814) 887-3323.

CLOUSE, Kenneth A. *(President Judge, Pennsylvania Court of Common Pleas Thirty-second Judicial District)* Elected Nov 1991. Retained by election 2001, current term expires 2012. Former Acting President Judge. Educated at Haverford College and New York University Law School.

Office: Delaware County Courthouse, 201 West Front Street, Media 19063.
Telephone: (610) 891-5410.

CODY, Jacqueline C. *(Judge, Pennsylvania Court of Common Pleas Fifteenth Judicial District)*
Mailing address: P.O. Box 2748, West Chester 19380.
Office: 424 Chester County Courthouse, 2 North High Street, West Chester 19380.
Telephone: (610) 344-6604.

COHEN, Denis P. *(Judge, Pennsylvania Court of Common Pleas First Judicial District)*
Office: 27 South Twelfth Street, Suite 406, Philadelphia 19107.
Telephone: (215) 686-2650.

COHEN, Gene D. *(Judge, Pennsylvania Court of Common Pleas First Judicial District)*
Office: 364 City Hall, Philadelphia 19107.
Telephone: (215) 686-2620.

COHILL, Maurice B., Jr. *(Senior Judge, United States District Court Western District of Pennsylvania)* Appointed for life by President Gerald R. Ford to term

COHILL, MAURICE B., JR.—*Continued*

beginning June 1, 1976. Chief Judge July 2, 1985 to July 1, 1992. Assumed Senior status Nov 28, 1994, serves by assignment. Born Pittsburgh Pennsylvania Nov 26, 1929. United Presbyterian. Educated at Princeton University A.B. 1951 and University of Pittsburgh LL.B. 1956. Staff member University of Pittsburgh Law Review. Admitted to practice Pennsylvania 1956. Began legal practice Pittsburgh 1956. Judge, Allegheny County Juvenile Court July 1965 to Jan 1969. Judge, Allegheny County Court of Common Pleas Family Division Jan 1969 to June 1976.

Author section on Practice in Juvenile Court *Courts and Administrative Offices Handbook* Young Lawyers Section Allegheny County Bar Association 1967, "Revolution in the Juvenile Courts?" 1 No. 1 Pittsburgh Law Record 1967, "An Eye for an Eye" 1 No. 1 Pennsylvania Attorney General's Bulletin 1967, "Kent—A Warning on the Handling of Juveniles" 26 No. 1 Pennsylvania Chiefs of Police Association Bulletin 1967, "Drop-Outs, Squeeze-Outs, Push-Outs" 2 No. 3 Women's American ORT Pittsburgh Region 1969, "Delinquency" a two-part article in Family Magazine section The Pittsburgh Press 1969, "The United States Supreme Court and Juvenile Courts—An Overview" 9 Duquesne L. Rev. 573, 1971, "What Do I Do with Nancy?" The National Observer June 1975, "The Critics Don't Look in Their Eyes" The Pittsburgh Press Nov 1975, and "Janice's Only Problem Is Her Behavior" The National Observer Jan 1976. Member National Council of Juvenile and Family Court Judges, Allegheny County, Pennsylvania and American Bar Associations. Chairman Board of Fellows National Center for Juvenile Justice. Past President Pennsylvania Council of Juvenile Court Judges. Former member Pennsylvania Juvenile Court Judges Commission. Recipient Man of the Year in Law Award from Pittsburgh Jaycees 1968, Man of the Year in Good Government Award from Allegheny County League of Women Voters 1976 and Juvenile Law Award from Allegheny County Bar Association 1984. Captain USMC 1951-53. Republican. Board of Visitors University of Pittsburgh Graduate School of Social Work. Former member Allegheny Regional Planning Council.

Office: 803 U.S. Post Office & Courthouse, 700 Grant Street, Pittsburgh 15219.

Telephone: (412) 208-7380.

Office: U.S. Courthouse, 617 State Street, Erie 16501.

Telephone: (814) 452-3456.

COHN, Renée L. *(Judge, The Commonwealth Court of Pennsylvania)*

Office: 202 Paragon Centre, 1611 Pond Road, Allentown 18104.

Telephone: (610) 530-8225.

COLINS, James Gardner *(President Judge, The Commonwealth Court of Pennsylvania)*

Office: 900 The Widener Building, One South Penn Square, Philadelphia 19107.

Telephone: (215) 560-3010.

COLINS, Mary D. *(Judge, Pennsylvania Court of Common Pleas First Judicial District)*

Office: 229 City Hall, Philadelphia 19107.

Telephone: (215) 686-7926.

COLVILLE, Robert E. *(Judge, Pennsylvania Court of Common Pleas Fifth Judicial District)*

Office: 315 Allegheny County Courthouse, 436 Grant Street, Pittsburgh 15219.

Telephone: (412) 350-5547.

COLVILLE, Robert J. *(Judge, Pennsylvania Court of Common Pleas Fifth Judicial District)*

Office: 440 Ross Street, Room 5049, Pittsburgh 15219.

Telephone: (412) 350-0273.

CONABOY, Richard P. *(Senior Judge, United States District Court Middle District of Pennsylvania)* Appointed for life by President Jimmy Carter to term beginning Aug 6, 1979. Former Chief Judge. Assumed Senior status, serves by assignment. Chairman, U.S. Sentencing Commission Oct 7, 1994 to Oct 31, 1998. Born Minooka Pennsylvania June 12, 1925. Roman Catholic. Educated at University of Scranton B.A. 1946 and Catholic University of America LL.B. 1951. Awarded honorary LL.D. University of Scranton 1983. Admitted to practice Pennsylvania 1951. In legal practice Scranton 1951-62. Judge, Pennsylvania Court of Common Pleas Forty-fifth Judicial District 1962-78, appointed by Governor David L. Lawrence. President Judge 1978-79.

Pennsylvania Deputy Attorney General 1953-59. Examiner Pennsylvania Liquor Control Board 1959-62. Contributor Catholic University Law Review, Duquesne Law Review, Dickinson Law Paper, American Judges Journal, Philadelphia Bar Association (The Shingle) and Lackawanna County Bar Journal (Jurist). Important Decisions: Frank Augenti, Jr. v. Gifford R. Cappellini, et al. (cult-oriented child hostage-type lawsuit) M.D. Pa. Civil No. 79-222, 1979; Jewelcor Inc. v. St. Paul Fire & Marine Ins. Co. (fire loss) M.D. Pa. Civil No. 78-761, 1980; Michael J. Cefalo, et al. v. Frank P. Crossin, et al. (political firing) M.D. Pa. Civil No. 80-0104, 1980; Sovereign Order of St. John of Jerusalem, Inc. et al. v. Charles L. T. Pichel (church-related international systems) M.D. Pa. Civil No. 80-0501, 1981; USA v. Peter E. Galonis, et al. (illegal entry of foreign students to U.S. schools) M.D. Pa. Criminal 81-00112-01/05, 1982; Lucy McDonald v. USA (swine flu case) M.D. Pa. Civil No. 80-1070, 1983; In re Rope Antitrust Litigation (rope cases) MDL 652, 1989; Dombrowski, et al. v. Gould, Inc., et al. (environmental case) 85 F. Supp. 2d 456 M.D. Pa. 2000; and Gould, Inc., et al. v. A & M Battery & Tire, et al. (environmental-contribution) 232 F.3d 162 M.D. Pa. 2001. Lecturer University of Scranton, Marywood College, Harvard University, Pennsylvania Judicial College, Pennsylvania Bar Institute, The National Judicial College, The Association of Trial Judges of America, National Conference on Corrections, National Conference on Juvenile Justice and Pennsylvania Trial Lawyers Association. Member American Judicature Society, Pennsylvania Conference of State Trial Judges (President 1976-77), Federal District Judges Association, Pennsylvania Joint Council on the Criminal Justice System (President 1971-80), National Council on Crime and Delinquency, The Association of Trial Lawyers of America, Lackawanna County (Director), Pennsylvania and American Bar Associations.

Chairman Pennsylvania Governor's Conference on Criminal Justice Standards and Goals 1975 and Pennsylvania Commission on Sentencing Guidelines 1979-81. Former member Pennsylvania Supreme Court Criminal Rules Committee, Pennsylvania Camp Hill Review Panel

CONABOY, RICHARD P.—*Continued*

and Pennsylvania Governor's Justice Commission. Faculty member Pennsylvania College of Judiciary, National Conference on Juvenile Justice and National Conference on Corrections. Recipient Lion's Club Distinguished Service Award 1963 and 1964, National Foundation Service Award for Distinguished Voluntary Leadership 1970, United Fund Community Service Award 1975, Lackawanna Bar Association Recognition Awards 1976 and 1978, Honorary membership Alpha Sigma Lambda Society and Pi Sigma Alpha Honor Society 1982, Pennsylvania Trial Lawyers Association Achievement Award 1984 and Americanism Award from B'nai B'rith 1989. USAAC 1945-47. Sergeant U.S. Army 1947-49. Member Lackawanna County Democratic Committee (Chairman 1960-62) and Young Democrats of Lackawanna County (Past President). National Committeeman Young Democrats of Pennsylvania 1959-60. Former Chairman Board of Trustees Marywood College and University of Scranton. Former member Board of Directors Catholic University of America Law School National Alumni (Director), St. Mary's Hospital, Mercy Hospital, Everhart Museum (Chairman), Lackawanna United Fund, Holy Name Society, American Cancer Society, Scranton-Lackawanna Human Development Agency and Boy Scouts of America. Former member Scranton School Board (President 1953-62). Member Camp Hill Review Panel (juvenile placements), St. Francis of Assisi Roman Catholic Church, Lions, Elks and Knights of Columbus.

Mailing address: P.O. Box 189, Scranton 18501-0182.

Telephone: (570) 207-5710.

CONAHAN, Michael T. *(President Judge, Pennsylvania Court of Common Pleas Eleventh Judicial District)*

Office: Luzerne County Courthouse, 200 North River Street, Wilkes-Barre 18711.

Telephone: (570) 825-1573.

CONNELLY, Shad F. *(Judge, Pennsylvania Court of Common Pleas Sixth Judicial District)* Elected to term beginning Jan 6, 1986. Retained by election 1995, current term expires Jan 2006. Born Erie Pennsylvania Feb 16, 1945. Roman Catholic. Educated at University of Virginia B.A. 1969, Edinboro State University M.A. cum laude 1971 and Duquesne University J.D. 1974. Member Phi Alpha Delta. Admitted to practice Pennsylvania 1974 and U.S. District Court Western District of Pennsylvania 1974. In legal practice Erie 1974-76.

Assistant Public Defender 1975-76. Assistant District Attorney 1976-85. Instructor Mercyhurst College 1982-85. Member Erie County, Pennsylvania and American Bar Associations. Seaman First Class USN 1965-69. Democrat. Member Pennsylvania Commission on Crime and Delinquency since 2002. PIAA Basketball and Football Official. Enjoys weightlifting, softball, poetry and football.

Office: Erie County Courthouse, 140 West Sixth Street, Erie 16501.

Telephone: (814) 451-6315.

CONNER, Christopher C. *(Judge, United States District Court Middle District of Pennsylvania)* Appointed for life by President George W. Bush to term beginning Aug 2, 2002.

Mailing address: P.O. Box 983, Harrisburg 17108-0983.

Office: U.S. Courthouse, 228 Walnut Street, Harrisburg 17101.

Telephone: (717) 221-3945.

CONTI, Joy Flowers *(Judge, United States District Court Western District of Pennsylvania)* Appointed for life by President George W. Bush to term beginning August 30, 2002.

Office: 936 U.S. Courthouse, Ninth Floor, Seventh Avenue and Grant Street, Pittsburgh 15219.

Telephone: (412) 208-7330.

CONWAY, Robert J. *(President Judge, Pennsylvania Court of Common Pleas Twenty-second Judicial District)*

Office: Wayne County Courthouse, 925 Court Street, Honesdale 18431.

Telephone: (570) 253-0101.

COOPERMAN, Amanda *(Judge, Pennsylvania Court of Common Pleas First Judicial District)*

Office: 1221 Criminal Justice Center, 1301 Filbert Street, Philadelphia 19107.

Telephone: (215) 683-7080.

CORBETT, Patricia *(Judge, Pennsylvania Court of Common Pleas Forty-fifth Judicial District)*

Office: Lackawanna County Courthouse, 200 North Washington Avenue, Scranton 18503.

Telephone: (570) 963-6531.

CORSO, S. Gerald *(President Judge, Pennsylvania Court of Common Pleas Thirty-eighth Judicial District)* Appointed by Governor Richard Thornburgh to term beginning Feb 22, 1985. Born Washington D.C. March 2, 1939. Educated at University of Virginia B.A. 1962 and Villanova University School of Law J.D. 1965. Law Clerk to Hon. E. Arnold Forrest and Hon. William W. Vogel, Pennsylvania Court of Common Pleas Thirty-eighth Judicial District 1966-67. Admitted to practice Pennsylvania 1965, U.S. District Court Eastern District of Pennsylvania 1974 and U.S. Court of Appeals Third Circuit 1981. Began legal practice Ambler 1967.

Assistant District Attorney Montgomery County 1970-71. Municipal Solicitor Upper Moreland Township since 1974, Towamencin Township since 1982 and Upper Gwynedd-Towamencin Municipal Authority since 1984. Lecturer on Law Montgomery County Community College 1974-84. Member Montgomery County Trial Lawyers Association (President 1982), Montgomery (Chairman Law Day Public Relations Committee, member since 1974 and Chairman American Citizenship Committee, member Municipal Law Committee), Pennsylvania and American Bar Associations. Past President Ambler Jaycees and Inglewood Home and School Association. Former Director Ambler Kiwanis. Former Vice President and Secretary Germantown Cricket Club. Former Judge of Election. Committeeman since 1981. Solicitor Lodge Ruggero Bonghi. Member Towamencin Youth Association, Whitpain Recreation Association and Manufacturers Golf and Country Club.

Mailing address: P.O. Box 311, Norristown 19404.

Office: Montgomery County Courthouse, Norristown 19401.

Telephone: (610) 278-5917.

COSETTI, Joseph L. *(Recalled Judge, United States Bankruptcy Court Western District of Pennsylvania)* Former Chief Judge. Appointed Recalled Judge by the Judicial Council of the Third Circuit.
Office: 5436 USX Tower, 600 Grant Street, Pittsburgh 15219.
Telephone: (412) 644-4710.

COX, J. Craig *(Judge, Pennsylvania Court of Common Pleas Fifty-third Judicial District)*
Office: Lawrence County Government Center, 430 Court Street, New Castle 16101.
Telephone: (724) 656-1927.

CREANY, Timothy P. *(Judge, Pennsylvania Court of Common Pleas Forty-seventh Judicial District)*
Office: Cambria County Courthouse, 200 South Center Street, Ebensburg 15931.
Telephone: (814) 472-1404.

CRONIN, Joseph P., Jr. *(Judge, Pennsylvania Court of Common Pleas Thirty-second Judicial District)*
Office: Delaware County Courthouse, 201 West Front Street, Media 19063.
Telephone: (610) 891-5320.

CULLEN, James P. *(Judge, Pennsylvania Court of Common Pleas Second Judicial District)*
Mailing address: P.O. Box 83480, Lancaster 17608-3480.
Office: Lancaster County Courthouse, 50 North Duke Street, Lancaster 17602.
Telephone: (717) 209-3290.

CUNNINGHAM, William R. *(President Judge, Pennsylvania Court of Common Pleas Sixth Judicial District)*
Office: 215 Erie County Courthouse, 140 West Sixth Street, Erie 16501.
Telephone: (814) 451-6287.

D'ALESSANDRO, Nicholas M. *(Judge, Pennsylvania Court of Common Pleas First Judicial District)*
Office: 1801 Vine Street, Room 354, Philadelphia 19103.
Telephone: (215) 686-7912.

DALTON, Robert E., Jr. *(President Judge, Pennsylvania Court of Common Pleas Fourth Judicial District)*
Office: Tioga County Courthouse, 118 Main Street, Wellsboro 16901.
Telephone: (570) 724-1828.

DALZELL, Stewart *(Judge, United States District Court Eastern District of Pennsylvania)* Appointed for life by President George Bush Sept 16, 1991. Born Hackensack New Jersey Sept 18, 1943. Episcopalian. Educated at University of Pennsylvania B.S. with honors 1965 J.D with honors 1969. Member Beta Gamma Sigma. Admitted to practice Pennsylvania 1970 and U.S. Supreme Court 1970. In legal practice Philadelphia 1970-91.
Co-author "Is The Twenty-Seventh Amendment 200 Years Too Late?" 62 George Washington L. Rev. 501, 1994. Author "One Cheer for the Guidelines" 40 Villanova L. Rev. 317, 1995; Foreword "Judging Technology: An Eighteenth Century Institution Meets Twenty-first Century Cases" Law and Technology Issue 30 Creighton L. Rev. 1107, 1997; "Faces in the Courtroom" 146 University of Pennsylvania L. Rev. 961, 1998; and "A Voice for Liberty" 148 University of Pennsylvania L. Rev. 15, 1999. Important Decisions: American Civil Liberties Union v. Reno (first decision regarding Congressional attempt to limit content on the Internet) 929 F. Supp. 824, 865 E.D. Pa. 1996, aff'd 117 S. Ct. 2329, 1997; Lambert v. Blackwell (granted writ of habeas corpus and barred retrial) 962 F. Supp. 1521 E.D. Pa. 1997; consolidated civil rights actions brought by victims of the Philadelphia 39th Police District including one filed by the NAACP, ACLU and Police-Barrio Project; and civil actions and bankruptcy appeals of Foundation for New Era Philanthropy matter including the consolidated multi-district litigation involving Prudential Securities, Inc. Instructor Wharton School of Finance and Commerce University of Pennsylvania 1969-70. Member American Judicature Society, The American Law Institute, University of Pennsylvania American Inn of Court (President) and Junior Legal Club. Recipient Speiser Award 1969. Previously employed by National Broadcasting Company. Enjoys family, movies and music.
Office: 5614 U.S. Courthouse, 601 Market Street, Philadelphia 19106-1714.
Telephone: (215) 597-9773.

DANIELE, Rhonda Lee *(Judge, Pennsylvania Court of Common Pleas Thirty-eighth Judicial District)*
Mailing address: P.O. Box 311, Norristown 19404.
Office: Montgomery County Courthouse, Norristown 19401.
Telephone: (610) 278-3166.

DAVIS, Legrome D. *(Judge, United States District Court Eastern District of Pennsylvania)* Appointed for life by President George W. Bush to term beginning May 3, 2002. Former Judge, Pennsylvania Court of Common Pleas First Judicial District.
Office: 5918 U.S. Courthouse, 601 Market Street, Philadelphia 19106.
Telephone: (215) 597-7704.

DE ANGELIS, Guido A. *(Judge, Pennsylvania Court of Common Pleas Fifth Judicial District)*
Office: 440 Ross Street, Room 5069, Pittsburgh 15219.
Telephone: (412) 350-0390.

DeFINO-NASTASI, Rose Marie *(Judge, Pennsylvania Court of Common Pleas First Judicial District)*
Office: 544 City Hall, Philadelphia 19107.
Telephone: (215) 686-7510.

DELLA VECCHIA, Michael A. *(Judge, Pennsylvania Court of Common Pleas Fifth Judicial District)*
Office: 440 Ross Street, Room 5028, Pittsburgh 15219.
Telephone: (412) 350-0281.

DelRICCI, Thomas M. *(Judge, Pennsylvania Court of Common Pleas Thirty-eighth Judicial District)*
Mailing address: P.O. Box 311, Norristown 19404.
Office: Montgomery County Courthouse, Norristown 19401.
Telephone: (610) 278-3771.

DEL SOLE, Joseph A. *(President Judge, The Superior Court of Pennsylvania)* Elected to term beginning Jan 1984. Retained by election Nov 1993, current term expires Jan 2004. Born Pittsburgh Pennsylvania Nov 16, 1940. Roman Catholic. Educated at Carnegie Mellon University B.A. 1962, Duquesne University LL.B. 1965

DEL SOLE, JOSEPH A.—*Continued*
and University of Virginia LL.M. 1992. Associate member Duquesne Law Review 1963-65. Admitted to practice Pennsylvania 1965, U.S. District Court Western District of Pennsylvania 1965 and U.S. Court of Appeals Third Circuit 1966. In legal practice Pittsburgh 1965-78. Judge, Pennsylvania Court of Common Pleas Fifth Judicial District Civil Division 1978-84.

Co-author "Demise of Fair Trade in Pennsylvania." Former member Academy of Trial Lawyers of Allegheny County and Pennsylvania Bar Association. Member Allegheny County Bar Association. Attended Institute of Judicial Administration New York University 1988 and Master of Laws in the Judicial Process University of Virginia 1990 and 1991. Instructor New Judges School 1991 and 1993. Recipient President's Award from Pennsylvania Trial Lawyers Association 1988. Member Parish Council. Enjoys clay target shooting, reading and traveling.

Office: 2000 Oxford Drive, Suite 470, Bethel Park 15102.

Telephone: (412) 565-2542.

DEMBE, Pamela Pryor *(Judge, Pennsylvania Court of Common Pleas First Judicial District)* Elected to term beginning Jan 1990. Retained by election 1999, current term expires Jan 2010. Coordinating Judge Homicide and Major Felony Programs. Born Ohio May 4, 1947. Educated at Temple University 1970 J.D. 1977. Admitted to practice Pennsylvania 1977, U.S. Court of Appeals Third Circuit 1977 and U.S. Supreme Court 1977. In legal practice Philadelphia 1977-79.

Past President Pennsylvania Conference of State Trial Judges. President Brehon Law Society. Member National Association of Women Judges, American Judges Association, Philadelphia, Pennsylvania and American Bar Associations. President, Friends of the Free Library of Philadelphia.

Office: 1417 Criminal Justice Center, 1301 Filbert Street, Philadelphia 19107.

Telephone: (215) 683-7148.

DEMPSEY, Thomas E. *(Judge, Pennsylvania Court of Common Pleas First Judicial District)*

Office: 327 City Hall, Philadelphia 19107.

Telephone: (215) 686-4221.

DIAMOND, Gustave *(Senior Judge, United States District Court Western District of Pennsylvania)* Appointed for life by President Jimmy Carter to term beginning May 24, 1978. Former Chief Judge. Assumed Senior status, serves by assignment. Born Burgettstown Pennsylvania Jan 29, 1928. Greek Orthodox. Educated at Duke University A.B. 1951 and Duquesne University J.D. 1956. Named one of top 100 graduates of Duquesne University during its first 100 years. Law Clerk to Hon. Rabe F. Marsh, U.S. District Court Western District of Pennsylvania 1956-61. Admitted to practice Pennsylvania 1958, U.S. District Court Western District of Pennsylvania 1958, U.S. Supreme Court 1958 and U.S. Court of Appeals Third Circuit 1962. In legal practice Pittsburgh 1969-75 and Washington 1975-78.

Assistant U.S. Attorney 1961-63 and U.S. Attorney 1963-69 Western District of Pennsylvania. Important Decisions: Three Rivers Cablevision et al. v. City of Pittsburgh et al. 502 F. Supp. 1118 W.D. Pa. 1980; Ryden v. Johns-Manville et al. 518 F. Supp. 311 W.D. Pa. 1981; and U.S. v. Renfroe 634 F. Supp. 1536 W.D. Pa. 1986. Chairman Committee on Defender Services U.S. Judicial Conference 1990-95. Member National Lawyers Club, Federal Judges Association, Inc., Washington County, Allegheny County, Pennsylvania, Federal and American Bar Associations. Seaman First Class (radioman) USN 1946-48. Member Holy Cross Greek Orthodox Church. Enjoys gardening, golf and bridge.

Office: 821 U.S. Post Office & Courthouse, 700 Grant Street, Pittsburgh 15219.

Telephone: (412) 208-7390.

DiBONA, Alfred J., Jr. *(Judge, Pennsylvania Court of Common Pleas First Judicial District)* Elected to term beginning Jan 5, 1976. Retained by election 1985 and 1995. Current term expires Jan 2006. Born Philadelphia Pennsylvania Dec 7, 1934. Educated at Temple University B.S. 1957 LL.B. 1960. Moot Court. Member Phi Delta Phi. Admitted to practice Pennsylvania 1963, U.S. Court of Appeals Third Circuit and U.S. District Court Eastern District of Pennsylvania. Hearing Examiner, Pennsylvania Liquor Control Board.

Assistant District Attorney 1964-66. Adjunct Lecturer Department of Legal & Real Estate Studies Temple University since 1977. Member St. Thomas More Society, Justinian Society Board of Governors, National Conference of State Trial Judges (Judicial Education Committee), Philadelphia (Criminal Justice Committee, Bench Bar Conference and Municipal Court Committees), Pennsylvania and American Bar Associations. Past member Philadelphia County Board of Law Examiners. Participant 1976, 1978 and 1980 and Faculty Advisor 1981 The National Judicial College. Teacher Philadelphia public schools 1960-63. Member Temple Varsity Club, Prisoners' Family Welfare Association and Camp General Douglas MacArthur of the Order of Brotherly Love (Master 1966-68, reelected 1974). Board of Directors Horizon House and Greater Philadelphia Chapter of Unico National.

Office: 481 City Hall, Philadelphia 19107.

Telephone: (215) 686-8338.

DICKMAN, Toby L. *(Judge, Pennsylvania Court of Common Pleas Thirty-eighth Judicial District)*

Mailing address: P.O. Box 311, Norristown 19404.

Office: Montgomery County Courthouse, Norristown 19401.

Telephone: (610) 278-1694.

DiNUBILE, Victor J., Jr. *(Judge, Pennsylvania Court of Common Pleas First Judicial District)* Appointed by Governor Richard Thornburgh to term beginning June 19, 1981. Elected Nov 1981. Retained by election 1991 and 2001. Current term expires Jan 2012. Born Philadelphia Pennsylvania April 16, 1938. Roman Catholic. Educated at University of Pennsylvania A.B. with honors 1960 and Temple University LL.B. with honors 1963. Associate Editor Temple Law Quarterly. Member Theta Xi and Phi Alpha Delta. Admitted to practice Pennsylvania 1964. Began legal practice Philadelphia 1964.

Assistant District Attorney Philadelphia 1966-73. Member Defender Association, Citizens Crime Commission of Philadelphia, Lawyers Club of Philadelphia, American Judicature Society, Philadelphia, Pennsylvania and American Bar Associations.

Office: 684 City Hall, Philadelphia 19107.

Telephone: (215) 686-4214.

DiSANTIS, Ernest J., Jr. *(Judge, Pennsylvania Court of Common Pleas Sixth Judicial District)*
Office: Erie County Courthouse, 140 West Sixth Street, Erie 16501.
Telephone: (814) 451-6269.

DITTER, J. William, Jr. *(Senior Judge, United States District Court Eastern District of Pennsylvania)* Appointed for life by President Richard M. Nixon to term beginning Dec 2, 1970. Assumed Senior status, serves by assignment. Born Philadelphia Pennsylvania Oct 19, 1921. Methodist. Educated at Ursinus College B.A. 1943 and University of Pennsylvania LL.B. 1948. Awarded honorary LL.D. Ursinus College 1970. Associate Editor University of Pennsylvania Law Review 1947-48. Law Clerk to Pennsylvania Court of Common Pleas Thirty-eighth Judicial District 1948-51. Admitted to practice Pennsylvania 1948. Judge, Pennsylvania Court of Common Pleas Thirty-eighth Judicial District 1964-70.
Assistant District Attorney Montgomery County 1951 and 1953-60. Important Decisions: Bankruptcy proceedings and reorganization of the Reading Company (railroad reorganization case) and United States of America v. City of Philadelphia (police abuse) 482 F. Supp. 1248, 1979. Lecturer Villanova University Graduate School. Member Montgomery County, Pennsylvania, Federal and American Bar Associations. Captain USNR active duty 1943-46 and 1951-53. Republican. Charter President Ambler Jaycees. Regional Director Pennsylvania Jaycees. President Ambler Chamber of Commerce. Past President Board of Trustees Calvary Methodist Church. Member Junior Chamber International Senate, Ambler Rotary Club, American Legion and Masons. Board of Consultors Villanova University. Board of Directors Riverview Osteopathic Hospital 1964-71. Enjoys skiing, photography, bicycling, gardening and beekeeping.
Office: 3040 U.S. Courthouse, 601 Market Street, Philadelphia 19106-1769.
Telephone: (215) 597-9640.

DI VITO, Gary F. *(Judge, Pennsylvania Court of Common Pleas First Judicial District)*
Office: 229A City Hall, Philadelphia 19107.
Telephone: (215) 686-2636.

DOBSON, Thomas R. *(Judge, Pennsylvania Court of Common Pleas Thirty-fifth Judicial District)* Elected Nov 7, 1995 to term beginning Jan 1, 1996. Term expires Dec 31, 2005. Born Altoona Pennsylvania Aug 15, 1954. Educated at Bucknell University B.A. 1976 and University of Pittsburgh J.D. 1980. Law Clerk to Hon. John Q. Stranahan, Pennsylvania Court of Common Pleas Thirty-fifth Judicial District 1980-81. Admitted to practice Pennsylvania 1980. In legal practice Mercer 1981-91. Hearing Master Domestic Relations 1990-95.
Supervisory Assistant District Attorney 1991-95. Member Mercer County and Pennsylvania Bar Associations. Democrat. Enjoys golf, reading, computers and sky diving.
Office: Mercer County Courthouse, North Diamond Street, Mercer 16137.
Telephone: (724) 662-3800.

DOERR, Thomas J. *(President Judge, Pennsylvania Court of Common Pleas Fiftieth Judicial District)*
Mailing address: P.O. Box 1208, Butler 16003.
Office: Butler County Government Center, Butler 16001.
Telephone: (724) 284-5444.

DOLBIN, Cyrus Palmer *(Judge, Pennsylvania Court of Common Pleas Twenty-first Judicial District)*
Office: Schuylkill County Courthouse, 401 North Second Street, Pottsville 17901.
Telephone: (570) 628-1314.

DOMALAKES, John E. *(Judge, Pennsylvania Court of Common Pleas Twenty-first Judicial District)*
Office: Schuylkill County Courthouse, 401 North Second Street, Pottsville 17901.
Telephone: (570) 628-1300.

DOMITROVICH, Stephanie *(Judge, Pennsylvania Court of Common Pleas Sixth Judicial District)* Elected to term beginning Jan 1990. Retained by election 1999, current term expires Jan 2010. Born Rochester Pennsylvania March 20, 1954. Roman Catholic. Educated at Carlow College B.A. summa cum laude 1976, Duquesne University J.D. 1979 and University of Nevada at Reno M.J.S. in Trial Judges 1993 M.J.S. in Juvenile and Family Court Judges 1998. Member Phi Alpha Delta. Admitted to practice Pennsylvania 1981, U.S. District Courts Western 1982 and Middle 1989 Districts of Pennsylvania, U.S. Court of Appeals Third Circuit 1983 and U.S. Supreme Court 1985. In legal practice Erie 1981-89.
Assistant Solicitor Erie County 1983-89. Author "Jury Source Lists and the Community's Need to Achieve Racial Balance on the Jury" 33 No. 1 Duquesne L. Rev. Fall 1994 and "Utilizing an Effective Economic Approach to Family Court: A Proposal for a Statutory Unified Family Court in Pennsylvania" 37 No. 1 Duquesne L. Rev. Fall 1998. Important Decisions: Carnes v. Carnes (indigent has right to counsel in civil contempt proceedings) 7 Pa. D. & C. 4th 4, 1990, Bland v. Bland (court-ordered waiver of federal income tax dependency exemption) 8 Pa. D. & C. 4th 55, 1990 and Wozniak v. Wozniak (common law marriage invalidated by existing impediment) 74 Erie 124, 1990. Faculty Member Penn State Erie The Behrend College. Instructor in paralegal courses Pennsylvania State University since 1982. Immediate Past President Northwest Pennsylvania American Inn of Court. Treasurer Pennsylvania Conference of State Trial Judges. Member American Judges Association, Erie County, Pennsylvania, American and International Bar Associations. Faculty Member The National Judicial College and National Council for Juvenile and Family Court Judges. Named Woman of the Year by Women's Roundtable 1991 and Person of the Year by AHEPA 1992. Trustee Gannon University.
Office: Erie County Courthouse, 140 West Sixth Street, Erie 16501.
Telephone: (814) 451-6230.

DORNEY, Sheryl A. *(Judge, Pennsylvania Court of Common Pleas Nineteenth Judicial District)* Elected to term beginning Jan 4, 1988. Retained by election 1997, current term expires Jan 2008. Born Quakertown Pennsylvania Aug 21, 1949. Educated at Mansfield University B.A. with high honors 1971 and Valparaiso University School of Law J.D. 1974. Member Phi Alpha Delta. Admitted to practice Pennsylvania 1974, U.S. District

DORNEY, SHERYL A.—*Continued*

Court Middle District of Pennsylvania 1985 and U.S. Supreme Court 1999. In legal practice York 1985-87.

With District Attorney's Office York County 1975-84 (First Assistant District Attorney 1982-84). Solicitor York County Children and Youth Services 1986-87. Member Pennsylvania Conference of State Trial Judges, York County and Pennsylvania Bar Associations. Named to Pennsylvania Honor Roll of Women 1994. Named National Ecotrin Heart Patient of the Year 1996. Recipient Alumni Citation from Mansfield University 1997. Board of Directors York Division American Heart Association. Associate member White Rose Lodge Fraternal Order of Police. Honorary member Business and Professional Women. Member Unitarian Universalist Congregation of York Enjoys dogs.

Office: York County Courthouse, 28 East Market Street, York 17401.

Telephone: (717) 771-9725.

DOUGHERTY, Kevin M. *(Judge, Pennsylvania Court of Common Pleas First Judicial District)*

Office: 1801 Vine Street, Room 154, Philadelphia 19103.

Telephone: (215) 686-7277.

DOZOR, Barry C. *(Judge, Pennsylvania Court of Common Pleas Thirty-second Judicial District)*

Office: Delaware County Courthouse, 201 West Front Street, Media 19063.

Telephone: (610) 891-4523.

DRAYER, Calvin S., Jr. *(Judge, Pennsylvania Court of Common Pleas Thirty-eighth Judicial District)* Elected to term beginning Jan 1998. Term expires Jan 2008. Born Philadelphia Pennsylvania Sept 12, 1939. Protestant. Educated at Wesleyan University B.A. 1961, University of Pennsylvania LL.B. 1964 and Temple University LL.M. 1982. Law Clerk to Hon. Charles Klein, Pennsylvania Court of Common Pleas First Judicial District. Admitted to practice Pennsylvania 1965 and U.S. Court of Appeals Third Circuit. In legal practice Philadelphia 1965-72 and Norristown 1972-97.

Mailing address: P.O. Box 311, Norristown 19404.

Office: Montgomery County Courthouse, Norristown 19401.

Telephone: (610) 278-3759.

Fax: (610) 278-3162

E-mail address: Cdrayer@mail.montcopa.org

DRISCOLL, John J. *(Judge, Pennsylvania Court of Common Pleas Tenth Judicial District)* Appointed by Governor Robert P. Casey to term beginning Dec 16, 1994. Elected Nov 1995, current term expires Dec 31, 2005. Born Pittsburgh Pennsylvania Feb 13, 1942. Catholic. Educated at Villanova University B.S. in Economics 1963 and University of Pittsburgh J.D. 1966. Admitted to practice Pennsylvania 1966, U.S. District Court District of Pennsylvania 1972 and U.S. Court of Appeals Third Circuit 1986. In legal practice Greensburg 1970-81.

Law Clerk to Hon. Joseph A. Hudock, Pennsylvania Court of Common Pleas Tenth Judicial District 1978-81. District Attorney Westmoreland County 1982-94. Vice Chairman Supreme Court Committee on Criminal Procedural Rules. Member Westmoreland County and Pennsylvania Bar Associations. Lieutenant USNR. Board of Trustees Westmoreland Regional Hospital. Advisory Board University of Pittsburgh at Greensburg. Member Overly Foundation.

Office: Westmoreland County Courthouse, Two North Main Street, Greensburg 15601.

Telephone: (724) 830-3483.

DuBOIS, Jan E. *(Senior Judge, United States District Court Eastern District of Pennsylvania)* Appointed for life by President Ronald Reagan to term beginning July 27, 1988. Assumed Senior status April 15, 2002, serves by assignment. Born Philadelphia Pennsylvania Jan 17, 1931. Educated at University of Pennsylvania B.S. 1952 and Yale University Law School LL.B. 1957. Law Clerk to Hon. Harry E. Kalodner 1957-58. Recipient John Currier Gallagher Prize for Trial Advocacy from Yale University Law School. Member Beta Gamma Sigma and Beta Alpha Psi. Admitted to practice Pennsylvania 1958, U.S. District Court Eastern District of Pennsylvania 1958, U.S. Court of Appeals Third Circuit 1958 and U.S. Supreme Court 1982. In legal practice Philadelphia 1958-88.

Important Decisions: George Hertzke, et al. v. John Riley, et al. (restraints imposed by Federal Witness Protection Program did not encroach on liberty interests secured by Constitution) 715 F. Supp. 117 E.D. Pa. 1989; Norma Klein, et al. v. Drexel Burnham Lambert, Inc. (Federal Arbitration Act did not confer Federal jurisdiction notwithstanding fact that plaintiffs' underlying arbitration claims involved alleged violations of Federal law) 737 F. Supp. 319 E.D. Pa. 1990; EEOC v. READS, Inc. (prospective employer discriminated against plaintiff for a position as third grade counselor at two Catholic schools because she covered her head pursuant to her religious beliefs as a Muslim) 759 F. Supp. 1150 E.D. Pa. 1991; United States v. Ivy (Classified Information Procedures Act held constitutional in case involving charges of importing and exporting military articles and technology in violation of the Arms Export Control Act and the Comprehensive Anti-Apartheid Act) No. 91-CR-6002-04, 1993 WL 316215 E.D. Pa. Aug 12, 1993; Austin v. Pennsylvania Department of Corrections 876 F. Supp. 1437 E.D. Pa. 1995; and United States v. Stelmokas (Lithuanian born architect denaturalized for illegally entering the U.S.) No. 92-CV-3440, 1995 WL 464264 E.D. Pa. 1995 aff'd 100 F.3d 302 3d Cir. 1996. Faculty Academy of Advocacy Temple University Law School since 1991. Trustee 1981-89 and President 1987-88 Philadelphia Bar Foundation. Member Philadelphia, Pennsylvania and American Bar Associations. Faculty National Institute for Trial Advocacy 1981 and Pennsylvania Bar Institute 1991 and 1994. First Lieutenant U.S. Army 1952-54. Served to Captain USAR. Past President, Yale Law School Association of Philadelphia. President 1985-87 and Trustee Reform Congregation Keneseth Israel. Enjoys tennis and swimming.

Office: 12613 U.S. Courthouse, 601 Market Street, Philadelphia 19106-1766.

Telephone: (215) 597-5579.

DUNLAVEY, Michael E. *(Judge, Pennsylvania Court of Common Pleas Sixth Judicial District)*

Office: Erie County Courthouse, 140 West Sixth Street, Erie 16501.

Telephone: (814) 451-6374.

DURHAM, Kathrynann W. *(Judge, Pennsylvania Court of Common Pleas Thirty-second Judicial District)*
Office: Delaware County Courthouse, 201 West Front Street, Media 19063.
Telephone: (610) 891-8609.

DURKIN, Kathleen A. *(Judge, Pennsylvania Court of Common Pleas Fifth Judicial District)*
Office: 526 Allegheny County Courthouse, 436 Grant Street, Pittsburgh 15219.
Telephone: (412) 350-5652.

DYCH, Joseph A. *(Judge, Pennsylvania Court of Common Pleas First Judicial District)*
Office: 1219 Criminal Justice Center, 1301 Filbert Street, Philadelphia 19107.
Telephone: (215) 683-7074.

EAKIN, J. Michael *(Justice, The Supreme Court of Pennsylvania)* Elected to term beginning 2001. Born Mechanicsburg Pennsylvania Nov 18, 1948. Educated at Franklin & Marshall College B.A. 1970 and Dickinson School of Law J.D. 1975. In legal practice Pennsylvania 1980-89. Former Judge, The Superior Court of Pennsylvania, elected to term beginning Nov 1995.
Office: 4720 Old Gettysburg Road, Suite 405, Mechanicsburg 17055.
Telephone: (717) 731-0461.

EATON, Kim D. *(Judge, Pennsylvania Court of Common Pleas Fifth Judicial District)* Elected Nov 3, 1999 to term beginning Jan 3, 2000. Term expires Jan 1, 2010. Born Pittsburgh Pennsylvania April 27, 1956. Presbyterian. Educated at Pennsylvania State University B.A. 1978 and University of Pittsburgh J.D. 1981. Member Phi Alpha Delta. Admitted to practice Pennsylvania 1981 and U.S. District Court Western District of Pennsylvania 1982. In legal practice Pittsburgh 1982-99.
Member Allegheny County, Pennsylvania and American Bar Associations. Recipient Pro-Bono Award from Pennsylvania Bar Association and Olbum Award. Democrat. Enjoys golfing and skiing.
Office: 440 Ross Street, Room 5032, Pittsburgh 15219.
Telephone: (412) 350-5442.

EBY, Robert J. *(President Judge, Pennsylvania Court of Common Pleas Fifty-second Judicial District)* Appointed by Governor Richard Thornburgh to term beginning July 24, 1981. Elected Nov 1981. Retained by election 1991 and 2001. Current term expires Jan 2012. Born Lebanon Pennsylvania Aug 18, 1944. United Church of Christ. Educated at Dickinson College A.B. 1966 and Villanova University J.D. 1969.
Office: 400 South Eighth Street, Lebanon 17042.
Telephone: (717) 274-2801.

ELLIOTT, Kate Ford *(Judge, The Superior Court of Pennsylvania)* Elected Nov 1989 to term beginning Jan 1990. Retained by election Nov 1999, current term expires Jan 2010. Born Pittsburgh Pennsylvania June 8, 1949. Roman Catholic. Educated at University of Pittsburgh B.A. 1971 and Duquesne University M.S. 1973 J.D. 1978. Law Clerk to Hon. Harry M. Montgomery, The Superior Court of Pennsylvania 1978-80. Admitted to practice Pennsylvania 1978, U.S. District Court Western District of Pennsylvania 1978 and U.S. Supreme Court 1982.
Fellow American Bar Foundation. Member National Association of Women Judges, American Judicature Society, Women's Bar Association of Western Pennsylvania, Allegheny County, Pennsylvania and American Bar Associations.
Office: Two Chatham Center, Suite 1560, Pittsburgh 15219.
Telephone: (412) 565-7670.

EMERY, Katherine B. *(Judge, Pennsylvania Court of Common Pleas Twenty-seventh Judicial District)* Elected Nov 1995 to term beginning Jan 2, 1996. Term expires Dec 31, 2005. Born Canonsburg Pennsylvania Nov 23, 1955. Presbyterian. Educated at Pennsylvania State University B.A. in Economics 1978 and University of Dayton M.B.A. 1981 J.D. 1981. Admitted to practice Pennsylvania 1981.
Member Pennsylvania Judicial Dispute Committee, Pennsylvania Conference of State Trial Judges and Washington County Bar Association. Instructor of Family Law Topics Washington County Bar Association and Young Lawyers Division Pennsylvania Bar Association. Named Outstanding Woman of Achievement 1993 and Woman of the Year by Business and Professional Women 1995. Former School Director Canon-McMillan School District. Board Member United Cerebral Pralsy of Southwestern Pennsylvania. Member Canonsburg Business and Professional Women (Past President).
Office: 3005 Washington County Courthouse, One South Main Street, Washington 15301.
Telephone: (724) 228-6823.

ESHELMAN, Thomas J. *(Judge, Pennsylvania Court of Common Pleas Twenty-third Judicial District)* Elected to term beginning Jan 2, 1978. Retained by election 1987 and 1997. Current term expires Jan 2008. Born Jan 7, 1935. Protestant. Educated at Dickinson College A.B. 1956 LL.B. 1959. Admitted to practice Pennsylvania 1960 and U.S. Supreme Court 1968. Began legal practice Reading 1960. Register of Wills 1968-77. Democrat.
Office: Berks County Courthouse, Ninth Floor, 633 Court Street, Reading 19601.
Telephone: (610) 478-6684.

EVANS, Scott A. *(Judge, Pennsylvania Court of Common Pleas Twelfth Judicial District)*
Office: Dauphin County Courthouse, Front and Market Streets, Harrisburg 17101.
Telephone: (717) 780-6665.

FARINA, Louis J. *(Judge, Pennsylvania Court of Common Pleas Second Judicial District)*
Mailing address: P.O. Box 83480, Lancaster 17608-3480.
Office: Lancaster County Courthouse, 50 North Duke Street, Lancaster 17602.
Telephone: (717) 295-3525.

FIELD, Myrna P. *(Judge, Pennsylvania Court of Common Pleas First Judicial District)* Administrative Judge Family Division since Feb 12, 2002.
Office: 1801 Vine Street, Room 314, Philadelphia 19103.
Telephone: (215) 686-7970.

FIKE, Eugene E., II *(President Judge, Pennsylvania Court of Common Pleas Sixteenth Judicial District)* Elected to term beginning Jan 1986. Retained by election 1995, current term expires Jan 2006. Born Dec 8, 1939. Lutheran. Educated at Princeton University B.A. 1961 and University of Pennsylvania LL.B. 1964. Admitted to practice Pennsylvania 1967, U.S. District Court

FIKE, EUGENE E., II—*Continued*

Western District of Pennsylvania and U.S. Claims Court. In legal practice Somerset 1967-86.

Member Somerset County (President) and Pennsylvania Bar Associations. Captain U.S. Army Artillery 1965-66.

Office: 212 Somerset County Courthouse, 111 East Union Street, Somerset 15501.

Telephone: (814) 445-1506.

FITZGERALD, James J., III *(Judge, Pennsylvania Court of Common Pleas First Judicial District)* Administrative Judge Trial Division since Feb 12, 2002.

Office: 516 City Hall , Philadelphia 19107.

Telephone: (215) 686-2602.

FITZGERALD, Judith K. *(Chief Judge, United States Bankruptcy Court Western District of Pennsylvania)* Chief Judge since Jan 8, 2000.

Office: 5490 USX Tower, 600 Grant Street, Pittsburgh 15219.

Telephone: (412) 644-3541.

FITZPATRICK, Maureen F. *(Judge, Pennsylvania Court of Common Pleas Thirty-second Judicial District)*

Office: Delaware County Courthouse, 201 West Front Street, Media 19063.

Telephone: (610) 891-4341.

FLEISHER, Leslie *(Judge, Pennsylvania Court of Common Pleas First Judicial District)*

Office: 1419 Criminal Justice Center, 1301 Filbert Street, Philadelphia 19107.

Telephone: (215) 683-7154.

FOLINO, Ronald W. *(Judge, Pennsylvania Court of Common Pleas Fifth Judicial District)*

Office: 704 City-County Building, 414 Grant Street, Pittsburgh 15219.

Telephone: (412) 350-4535.

FORADORA, John H. *(President Judge, Pennsylvania Court of Common Pleas Fifty-fourth Judicial District)*

Office: Jefferson County Courthouse, 200 Main Street, Brookville 15825.

Telephone: (814) 849-1618.

FORD, William E. *(Judge, Pennsylvania Court of Common Pleas Thirty-first Judicial District)* Elected Nov 1991 to term beginning Jan 1, 1992. Retained by election Nov 2001, current term expires Dec 31, 2011. Born Allentown Pennsylvania Dec 9, 1950. Roman Catholic. Educated at De Sales University B.A. with honors 1972 and Dickinson School of Law J.D. 1975. Admitted to practice Pennsylvania 1975, U.S. District Courts Eastern 1982 and Middle 1982 Districts of Pennsylvania and U.S. Supreme Court 1986. In legal practice Allentown 1979-91.

Instructor De Sales University since 1990 and Chestnut Hill College since 1996. Member Lehigh County and Pennsylvania Bar Associations. Served to Captain USMC JAGC 1975-79. Enjoys running and reading biographies and history. Has finished six marathons.

Office: Lehigh County Courthouse, 455 West Hamilton Street, Allentown 18101.

Telephone: (610) 782-3022.

FORNELLI, Francis J. *(President Judge, Pennsylvania Court of Common Pleas Thirty-fifth Judicial District)*

Office: Mercer County Courthouse, North Diamond Street, Mercer 16137.

Telephone: (724) 662-3800.

FOX, Bruce I. *(Chief Judge, United States Bankruptcy Court Eastern District of Pennsylvania)* Chief Judge since April 15, 1999.

Office: Federal Building & Courthouse, Second Floor, 900 Market Street, Philadelphia 19107-4297.

Telephone: (215) 408-2974.

FOX, Idee C. *(Judge, Pennsylvania Court of Common Pleas First Judicial District)* Elected Nov 7, 1995 to term beginning Jan 1, 1996. Term expires Dec 31, 2005. Born New York New York May 27, 1953. Roman Catholic. Educated at State University of New York at Stony Brook B.A. 1974 and Washington University at St. Louis J.D. 1977. Admitted to practice Pennsylvania 1977. In legal practice 1977-95.

Office: 34 South Eleventh Street, Room 225, Philadelphia 19107.

Telephone: (215) 686-7924.

FRANCE, Mary D. *(Judge, United States Bankruptcy Court Middle District of Pennsylvania)* Appointed by U.S. Court of Appeals Third Circuit judges.

Mailing address: P.O. Box 908, Harrisburg 17108-0908.

Office: 320 Federal Building, 228 Walnut Street, Harrisburg 17101.

Telephone: (717) 901-2840.

Fax: (717) 901-2844.

FREEDBERG, Robert A. *(President Judge, Pennsylvania Court of Common Pleas Third Judicial District)* Elected to term beginning Jan 8, 1980. Retained by election 1989 and 1999. Current term expires Jan 2010. Born Easton Pennsylvania Feb 19, 1944. Jewish. Educated at Lafayette College B.A. with honors 1966 and Columbia University J.D. 1969. Law Clerk to Hon. Clinton B. Palmer, Pennsylvania Court of Common Pleas 1969-70. Admitted to practice Pennsylvania 1969 and U.S. District Court Eastern District of Pennsylvania 1971. Began legal practice Bethlehem 1970. In legal practice Easton 1971.

Assistant District Attorney 1973-79. Assistant City Solicitor Easton 1976-80. Instructor Lafayette College 1981. Member Judicial Council of Pennsylvania, Pennsylvania Conference of State Trial Judges, Northampton County, Pennsylvania and American Bar Associations. Recipient Lafayette College Award for Distinguished Judicial Service 1984.

Office: 252 Spring Garden Street, Easton 18042.

Telephone: (610) 253-6000.

FRIEDMAN, Judith L. A. *(Judge, Pennsylvania Court of Common Pleas Fifth Judicial District)*

Office: 712 City-County Building, 414 Grant Street, Pittsburgh 15219.

Telephone: (412) 350-5147.

FRIEDMAN, Rochelle S. *(Judge, The Commonwealth Court of Pennsylvania)* Elected Nov 1991 to term beginning Jan 1992. Retained by election Nov 2001, current term expires Jan 2012. Born Pittsburgh Pennsylvania April 30, 1938. Educated at University of Pittsburgh B.A. 1959 J.D. 1972. Law Clerk to Hon. James R. Mc-

FRIEDMAN, ROCHELLE S.—*Continued*

Gregor, Pennsylvania Court of Common Pleas Fifth Judicial District for 12 years. Admitted to practice Pennsylvania, U.S. District Court Western District of Pennsylvania, U.S. Court of Appeals Third Circuit and U.S. Supreme Court.

Solicitor Allegheny County 1972-74. Important Opinions: Georgia-Pacific v. Unemployment Compensation Board of Review 630 A.2d 948 Pa. Cmwlth. 1993; Empire Sanitary Landfill, Inc. v. Department of Environmental Resources Pa. Cmwlth. No. 216 M.D. 1994 filed Aug 17, 1994; Odette's, Inc. v. Department of Conservation and Natural Resources, Bureau of State Parks Pa. Cmwlth. No. 196 M.D. 1997 filed March 24, 1997, July 1, 1997 and Feb 12, 1998; Rothermel v. Department of Transportation 672 A.2d 837 Pa. Cmwlth. 1996 overruled by Dean v. Department of Transportation 718 A.2d 374 Pa. Cmwlth. 1998 rev'd 561 Pa. 503, 751 A.2d 1130, 2000; York Co. Transportation Authority v. Teamsters Local Union #430, 746 A.2d 1208 Pa. Cmwlth. 2000; West Chester Area Sch. Dist. v. Collegium Charter Sch. 760 A.2d 452 Pa. Cmwlth. 2000; Pa. State Building and Construction Trades Council, AFL-CIO v. Prevailing Wage Appeals Board 767 A.2d 605 Pa. Cmwlth. 2001; AFSCME v. Commonwealth of Pennsylvania Pa. Cmwlth. No. 149 M.D. 2001 filed April 6, 2001; Milici v. Workers' Compensation Appeal Board City of Philadelphia A.2d 2001 Pa. LEXIS 526 Pa. Cmwlth. July 18, 2001; and City of Philadelphia v. OLS Hotel Partners, L.P. A.2d 2001 Pa. LEXIS 542 Pa. Cmwlth. July 26, 2001. Member National Association of Women Judges, Bucks County, Pennsylvania and American Bar Associations. Personal Statement or Quote: "Be the best of whatever you are."

Office: 313 Hyde Park, Doylestown 18901.
Telephone: (215) 956-3712.
Fax: (215) 956-3715

FULLAM, John P. *(Senior Judge, United States District Court Eastern District of Pennsylvania)* Appointed for life by President Lyndon B. Johnson to term beginning 1966. Former Chief Judge. Assumed Senior status April 1, 1990, serves by assignment. Born Gardenville Pennsylvania Dec 10, 1921. Educated at Villanova University B.S. in Education 1942 and Harvard University LL.B. 1948. Admitted to practice Pennsylvania 1949. In legal practice Bristol 1948-60. Judge, Pennsylvania Court of Common Pleas Seventh Judicial District 1960-66.

Democratic candidate for Congress 1954-56. Member Delaware River Joint Toll Bridge Commission 1955-60 (Chairman 1958). Board of Directors New School of Music 1975-80. Trustee Bucks County Community College 1964-76 (First Chairman 1964-67).

Office: 15614 U.S. Courthouse, 601 Market Street, Philadelphia 19106-1780.
Telephone: (215) 597-0436.

FURBER, William J., Jr. *(Judge, Pennsylvania Court of Common Pleas Thirty-eighth Judicial District)*

Mailing address: P.O. Box 311, Norristown 19404.
Office: Montgomery County Courthouse, Norristown 19401.
Telephone: (610) 278-5900.

GALLO, Robert C. *(Judge, Pennsylvania Court of Common Pleas Fifth Judicial District)*

Office: 708 City-County Building, 414 Grant Street, Pittsburgh 15219.
Telephone: (412) 350-3831.

GARDNER, James Knoll *(Judge, United States District Court Eastern District of Pennsylvania)* Appointed for life by President George W. Bush to term beginning Nov 26, 2002. Former Judge and President Judge, Pennsylvania Court of Common Pleas Thirty-first Judicial District.

Office: 504 Hamilton Street, Room 4701, Allentown 18101-1500.
Telephone: (215) 597-7704.

GAVIN, Thomas G. *(Judge, Pennsylvania Court of Common Pleas Fifteenth Judicial District)* Elected to term beginning 1986. Retained by election 1995, current term expires Jan 2006. Former President Judge. Born Newark New Jersey Dec 22, 1943. Roman Catholic. Educated at Villanova University B.A. 1965 J.D. 1971. Admitted to practice Pennsylvania 1971. In legal practice West Chester 1971-85.

Assistant District Attorney Chester County 1972-75. Master Juvenile Court Chester County 1980-85. Officer Pennsylvania Conference of State Trial Judges. Member Chester County and American Bar Associations. Attended "Trial Techniques" The National Judicial College 1987. Captain USMC 1965-68. Member Knights of Columbus, Veterans of Foreign Wars and American Legion.

Mailing address: P.O. Box 2748, West Chester 19380.
Office: 2 North High Street, West Chester 19380.
Telephone: (610) 344-6181.

GEORGE, Michael A. *(Judge, Pennsylvania Court of Common Pleas Fifty-first Judicial District)*

Office: Adams County Courthouse, 111-117 Baltimore Street, Gettysburg 17325.
Telephone: (717) 334-9848.

GEORGELIS, Michael A. *(President Judge, Pennsylvania Court of Common Pleas Second Judicial District)* Elected to term beginning Jan 6, 1986. Retained by election 1995, current term expires Jan 1, 2006. Born Martins Ferry Ohio July 27, 1939. Greek Orthodox. Educated at Carnegie Mellon University B.S. 1961 and Cleveland-Marshall College of Law Cleveland State University J.D. cum laude 1974. Admitted to practice Pennsylvania 1974 and U.S. District Court Eastern District of Pennsylvania 1974. In legal practice Lancaster 1974-85.

Member Pennsylvania Conference of State Trial Judges, Lancaster, Pennsylvania and American Bar Associations. First Lieutenant U.S. Army Corps of Engineers 1961-62. Previously employed as sales engineer Carrier Corporation, production supervisor 3M Company and production superintendent Clecon Inc. Enjoys jogging, sports and medieval history.

Mailing address: P.O. Box 83480, Lancaster 17608-3480.
Office: Lancaster County Courthouse, 50 North Duke Street, Lancaster 17602.
Telephone: (717) 299-8075.

GEROFF, Steven R. *(Judge, Pennsylvania Court of Common Pleas First Judicial District)*
Office: 1414 Criminal Justice Center, 1301 Filbert Street, Philadelphia 19107.
Telephone: (215) 683-7139.

GEROULO, Vito P. *(Judge, Pennsylvania Court of Common Pleas Forty-fifth Judicial District)*
Office: Lackawanna County Courthouse, 200 North Washington Avenue, Scranton 18503.
Telephone: (570) 963-6597.

GIBSON, Kim R. *(Judge, Pennsylvania Court of Common Pleas Sixteenth Judicial District)* Elected to term beginning Jan 1998. Term expires Jan 2008. Born Trenton New Jersey May 29, 1948. Protestant. Educated at U.S. Military Academy B.S. 1970 and Dickinson School of Law J.D. summa cum laude 1975. Projects Editor Dickinson Law Review 1973-75. Admitted to practice Pennsylvania 1975 and U.S. District Court Western District of Pennsylvania. In legal practice Somerset 1978-97.
County Solicitor Somerset County 1988-97. Member Somerset County, Pennsylvania and American Bar Associations. U.S. Army and USAR 30 years (retired as Colonel 1996). Member Rotary Club. Enjoys baseball, golf, tae kwon do and reading.
Mailing address: P.O. Box 263, Somerset 15501.
Office: 212 Somerset County Courthouse, 111 East Union Street, Somerset 15501.
Telephone: (814) 445-1450.
Fax: (814) 445-1455
E-mail address: gibsonk@co.somerset.pa.us

GILES, James T. *(Chief Judge, United States District Court Eastern District of Pennsylvania)* Appointed for life by President Jimmy Carter. Chief Judge since Jan 1, 1999. Born Charlottesville Virginia Jan 31, 1943. Educated at Amherst College B.A. 1964 and Yale Law School LL.B. 1967. In legal practice Philadelphia 1968-79.
Field Attorney National Labor Relations Board Philadelphia Pennsylvania 1967-68. Clerk U.S. Equal Employment Opportunity Commission 1967.
Office: 17614 U.S. Courthouse, 601 Market Street, Philadelphia 19106-1771.
Telephone: (215) 597-0692.

GILMORE, David L. *(President Judge, Pennsylvania Court of Common Pleas Twenty-seventh Judicial District)* Elected to term beginning Jan 3, 1984. Retained by election Nov 1993, current term expires Jan 2004. Born Washington Pennsylvania Oct 28, 1944. Presbyterian. Educated at California State College B.S. 1966 and Duquesne University J.D. 1970. Managing Editor Duquesne Law Review 1969-70. Admitted to practice Pennsylvania 1970. Began legal practice Washington.
Assistant District Attorney 1971-72, County Solicitor 1974-76 and County Commissioner 1976-84 Washington County. Member Pennsylvania Bar Association. USMCR 1966-72. Democrat.
Office: 2001 Washington County Courthouse, One South Main Street, Washington 15301.
Telephone: (724) 228-6908.

GLAZER, Gary S. *(Judge, Pennsylvania Court of Common Pleas First Judicial District)*
Office: 1205 Criminal Justice Center, 1301 Filbert Street, Philadelphia 19107.
Telephone: (215) 683-7032.

GORBEY, Leslie *(Judge, Pennsylvania Court of Common Pleas Second Judicial District)*
Mailing address: P.O. Box 83480, Lancaster 17608-3480.
Office: Lancaster County Courthouse, 50 North Duke Street, Lancaster 17602.
Telephone: (717) 299-8070.

GORDON, Richard J., Jr. *(Judge, Pennsylvania Court of Common Pleas First Judicial District)* Currently serves Family Court.
Office: 1801 Vine Street, Room 116, Philadelphia 19103.
Telephone: (215) 686-7514.

GRACI, Robert A. *(Judge, The Superior Court of Pennsylvania)*
Office: 1017 Mumma Road, Suite 103, Wormleysburg 17043.
Telephone: (717) 731-1525.

GREEN, Clifford Scott *(Senior Judge, United States District Court Eastern District of Pennsylvania)* Appointed for life by President Richard M. Nixon Dec 9, 1971. Born Philadelphia Pennsylvania April 2, 1923. Presbyterian. Educated at Temple University B.S. in Economics with honors 1948 J.D. 1951. Awarded honorary LL.D. Temple University 1977. Recipient Robert E. Lamberton Award and A. Lincoln Meyers Award. Member Moot Court. Associate Editor Temple Law Quarterly. Judge, Pennsylvania Court of Common Pleas First Judicial District 1964-71.
Lecturer on Law Temple University School of Law. Member Philadelphia, Federal and American Bar Associations. Attended National College of the State Judiciary. Member Crime Prevention Association of Philadelphia, (Board of Directors), President's Commission on White House Fellows Philadelphia Regional Panel. First Recipient Judge William Hastie Award for service to the Community and Country from NAACP Legal Defense Fund Dec 4, 1985. USAAC 1943-46. Trustee Temple University.
Office: 15613 U.S. Courthouse, 601 Market Street, Philadelphia 19106-1781.
Telephone: (215) 597-9149.

GREENSPAN, Jane Cutler *(Judge, Pennsylvania Court of Common Pleas First Judicial District)* Appointed by Governor Robert P. Casey to term beginning April 27, 1987. Elected Nov 1989. Retained by election Nov 1999, current term expires Jan 2010. Born Newark New Jersey April 27, 1948. Jewish. Educated at Smith College A.B. 1970 and Rutgers University School of Law J.D. with high honors 1973. Notes and Comments Editor Rutgers Law Journal 1972-73. Law Clerk to Hon. Robert N. C. Nix Jr., The Supreme Court of Pennsylvania 1973-75. Admitted to practice New Jersey 1973, Pennsylvania 1974, U.S. District Courts District of New Jersey 1973 and Eastern District of Pennsylvania 1975, U.S. Court of Appeals Third Circuit 1977 and U.S. Supreme Court 1978.
Assistant District Attorney Philadelphia 1976-87. Author Case Note "Criminal Law—Sentencing—Appli-

GREENSPAN, JANE CUTLER—*Continued*

cation of the Rehabilitative Ideal in Sentencing First Time Marijuana Offenders" 3 Rutgers L. Jour. 370, 1972. Member three-judge panel Jackson, et al. v. Hendricks, et al. (Philadelphia County prison litigation) 1993. Adjunct Professor of Appellate Advocacy University of Pennsylvania Law School 1989-94. Member Attorney General's Family Violence Task Force 1985-87, Philadelphia Court Judicial Study Committee since 1990 and Criminal Procedural Rules Committee Supreme Court of Pennsylvania 1990-96. Member 1998-2000 and Chair 1999-2000 Orphans' Court Procedural Rules Committee Supreme Court of Pennsylvania. Founding Member Select Committee on Law Enforcement and Child Abuse Pilot Project 1979-81. Member 1981-87 and Chairman Legal Subcommittee 1983-86 Domestic Violence Task Force Mayor's Commission for Women. Former Member Pennsylvania District Attorney's Association and Philadelphia Elder Abuse Task Force. Master of the Bench University of Pennsylvania American Inn of Court since 1994. Member Pennsylvania Conference of State Trial Judges, National Association of Women Judges, Philadelphia (Executive Committee 1982-89, Nominating Committee 1984 and 1986, Chair Elect 1985 and Chair 1986 Criminal Justice Section, Board of Governors 1986, Long Range Planning Committee 1988-89) and American (Task Force on Merit Selection Section of Litigation since 1998) Bar Associations. Lecturer on Private Criminal Complaints and Economic Crime Pennsylvania District Attorney's Association Seminar 1979. Organizer Bench Bar Dialogue 1986. Faculty Member Criminal Law Symposium Pennsylvania Bar Institute 1988. Panelist Philadelphia Bench Bar Conference 1988 and 1989 and Seminar on Law and the Courts National Press Foundation and Philadelphia Bar Association 1990. Member 1982-88, Executive Board Member 1983-85 and Vice President 1985-88 Board of Trustees Child Psychiatry Center St. Christopher's Hospital for Children. Board Member Germantown Jewish Center, Anti-Defamation League and Support Center for Child Advocates. Member Rutgers University School of Law Alumni Association and Smith College Club of Philadelphia.

Office: 1206 Criminal Justice Center, 1301 Filbert Street, Philadelphia 19107.

Telephone: (215) 683-7035.

GRIM, Arthur E. *(Judge, Pennsylvania Court of Common Pleas Twenty-third Judicial District)* Elected to term beginning Jan 1988. Retained by election 1997, current term expires Jan 2008. Born Reading Pennsylvania Jan 27, 1943. United Church of Christ. Educated at Moravian College and Theological Seminary B.A. 1964 and Duquesne University J.D. 1972. Recipient American Jurisprudence Award 1972. Admitted to practice Pennsylvania 1972. In legal practice Reading 1972-87.

Solicitor City of Reading 1982-87. Adjunct Professor St. Joseph University and Alvernia College. Vice President Juvenile Justice Section Pennsylvania State Trial Judges Association. Vice Chair Pennsylvania Juvenile Court Judges Commission. Member Berks County and Pennsylvania Bar Associations. Named one of Outstanding Young Men of America 1974. Recipient Alvernia College Merit Award 1988, Award of Distinction from Pennsylvania Coalition Against Domestic Violence, Berks Women in Crisis Award, Partner of Education Award from Chamber of Commerce, Service to Youth Award from ProKids, Junior Achievement Education Award and Olivet Youth Club Award. Inducted into Southern Middle School Hall of Fame. Lieutenant USN 1965-69. Democrat. Chairman of the Board United Way. Board Member Civic Center. Advisory Board John Paul II School and Reading Hospital Mental Health. Member Berks Community Foundation Education Committee and Exeter Community Partnership. Enjoys mountain biking, sailing and skiing.

Office: Berks County Courthouse, Ninth Floor, 633 Court Street, Reading 19601.

Telephone: (610) 478-6688.

GRIMES, H. Terry *(President Judge, Pennsylvania Court of Common Pleas Thirteenth Judicial District)* Elected to term beginning Jan 6, 1986. Retained by election 1995, current term expires Dec 31, 2005. Born Baltimore Maryland Sept 2, 1942. United Methodist. Educated at California State University B.S. with honors 1972 and Ohio Northern University J.D. 1974. Member Phi Alpha Delta. Admitted to practice Pennsylvania 1975 and U.S. District Court Western District of Pennsylvania 1975. In legal practice Washington 1975-77 and Waynesburg 1977-86.

Instructor in Real Estate Law Pennsylvania State University 1975-78. Former member Washington County, Greene County and Pennsylvania Bar Associations. Member Pennsylvania Conference of State Trial Judges. Attended Conduct of the Criminal Trial Program Supreme Court of Pennsylvania 1985. Regularly attends seminars of Pennsylvania Conference of State Trial Judges. Major U.S. Army Artillery 1966-75. Republican. Member Sons of the American Revolution, Gideons International, Knights of Pythias and Reserve Officers Association (Life member). Enjoys farming.

Office: Greene County Courthouse, Waynesburg 15370.

Telephone: (724) 852-5212.

GRINE, David E. *(Judge, Pennsylvania Court of Common Pleas Forty-ninth Judicial District)* Appointed by Governor Richard Thornburgh to term beginning July 17, 1981. Elected Nov 1981. Retained by election 1991 and 2001. Current term expires Jan 2012. Born Washington D.C. March 7, 1945. Protestant. Educated at Pennsylvania State University B.S. 1969 and Dickinson School of Law J.D. 1973. Admitted to practice Pennsylvania 1973. In legal practice Bellefonte and State College 1973-81.

Legal Counsel to Pennsylvania Special Olympics 1977-81. District Attorney Centre County 1978-81. Member Centre County, Pennsylvania and American Bar Associations. Attended Pennsylvania Trial Lawyers College Boston Massachusetts 1974, Career Prosecutor's College Houston Texas 1980 and The National Judicial College 1982. E-4 U.S. Army 1964-66. Previously worked in construction and as police officer. Democrat. Enjoys hunting, fishing and skiing. Interested in automobiles.

Office: Centre County Courthouse, Bellefonte 16823.

Telephone: (814) 355-6733.

GUIDO, Edward E. *(Judge, Pennsylvania Court of Common Pleas Ninth Judicial District)*

Office: Cumberland County Courthouse, One Courthouse Square, Carlisle 17013.

Telephone: (717) 240-6290.

HANCHER, George H. *(Judge, Pennsylvania Court of Common Pleas Fiftieth Judicial District)*
Mailing address: P.O. Box 1208, Butler 16003.
Office: Butler County Government Center, Butler 16001.
Telephone: (724) 284-1447.

HARHUT, Chester T. *(President Judge, Pennsylvania Court of Common Pleas Forty-fifth Judicial District)* Appointed by Governor Robert P. Casey to term beginning April 30, 1987. Elected Nov 1987. Retained by election 1997, current term expires Jan 2008. Serves Family Division. Educated at Bethel College B.S. and University of Pittsburgh School of Law J.D. 1972.

Secretary Pennsylvania Conference of State Trial Judges. Graduate The National Judicial College May 1995. Former Co-chair Pennsylvania State Legislative Liaison Committee. Former member Pennsylvania Department of Public Welfare Dependency and Delinquency Health Care Services Work Group.

Office: Lackawanna County Courthouse, 200 North Washington Avenue, Scranton 18503.
Telephone: (570) 963-6306.

HART, Jacob P. *(Magistrate Judge, United States District Court Eastern District of Pennsylvania)* Appointed by U.S. District Court judges to term beginning Nov 17, 1997. Term expires Nov 16, 2005.
Office: 3041 U.S. Courthouse, 601 Market Street, Philadelphia 19106-1714.
Telephone: (215) 597-2733.

HATHAWAY, Rita Donovan *(Judge, Pennsylvania Court of Common Pleas Tenth Judicial District)*
Office: Westmoreland County Courthouse, Two North Main Street, Greensburg 15601.
Telephone: (724) 853-2140.

HAY, Amy Reynolds *(Magistrate Judge, United States District Court Western District of Pennsylvania)* Appointed by U.S. District Court judges to term beginning March 26, 2003.
Office: 501 U.S. Courthouse, Fifth Floor, Seventh Avenue and Grant Street, Pittsburgh 15219.
Telephone: (412) 208-7450.

HAZEL, Frank T. *(Judge, Pennsylvania Court of Common Pleas Thirty-second Judicial District)* Elected to term beginning 1981. Retained by election Nov 1991 and 2001. Current term expires Jan 2012. Born Delaware County Pennsylvania Dec 17, 1941. Educated at St. Joseph's College (now St. Joseph's University) A.B. in Political Science 1964 and Villanova University School of Law J.D. 1967. Recipient Scott Paper Company Scholarship for Leadership and Scholarship, St. Joseph's University Alumni Association Award for Excellence, Henry Trainer Award for Excellence in Political Science and Richard McCloskey Gold Medal for Loyalty and Service. Ford Foundation Fellow. Listed in *Who's Who in American Colleges and Universities.* Reimel Moot Court Club Champion and Semi-Finalist. Member Alpha Sigma Nu.

District Justice of the Peace 1970-75 and District Attorney 1976-81 Delaware County. Lecturer Pennsylvania State University. Member Minor Court Civil Procedural Rules Committee and Judicial Coordinating Committee Pennsylvania Supreme Court, Career Criminal Task Force Pennsylvania Commission on Crime and Delinquency, Pennsylvania Joint Council on Criminal Justice Committee to Study Pennsylvania's Unified Judicial System and Pennsylvania Commission on Sentencing. Member Pennsylvania District Attorneys Association (Chairman Task Force on Wiretapping and Electronic Surveillance, Vice President 1979, President 1980-81), Domestic Relations Association of Pennsylvania, Pennsylvania Trial Lawyers Association, National District Attorneys Association (Pennsylvania State Director, Commission on Victim-Witness Assistance), Delaware County (Grievance Committee 1971-73, Treasurer 1975, Board of Directors 1977-78, Criminal Rules Committee 1979-80), Pennsylvania and American Bar Associations. Lecturer on Pennsylvania Rules of Criminal Procedure for Pennsylvania Supreme Court Administrator's Office. Lecturer Pennsylvania District Attorneys Association, Criminal Justice Institute of St. Joseph's University, County Detectives Association of Pennsylvania, Pennsylvania State Constables Association and Juvenile Officers Association of Pennsylvania.

Office: Delaware County Courthouse, 201 West Front Street, Media 19063.
Telephone: (610) 891-5087.

HECKLER, David W. *(Judge, Pennsylvania Court of Common Pleas Seventh Judicial District)*
Office: Bucks County Courthouse, 55 East Court Street, Doylestown 18901.
Telephone: (215) 340-8058.

HERMAN, Douglas W. *(Judge, Pennsylvania Court of Common Pleas Thirty-ninth Judicial District)*
Office: Franklin County Courthouse, 157 Lincoln Way East, Chambersburg 17201.
Telephone: (717) 261-3840.

HERRON, John W. *(Judge, Pennsylvania Court of Common Pleas First Judicial District)* Appointed by Governor Robert Casey 1987. Elected Nov 1987. Retained by election 1997, current term expires Jan 2008. Former Administrative Judge Trial Division. Born Bryn Mawr Pennsylvania Jan 27, 1944. Methodist. Educated at Duke University B.A. 1966 and Dickinson School of Law J.D. 1969. Admitted to practice Pennsylvania 1969, U.S. District Court Eastern District of Pennsylvania 1969 and U.S. Supreme Court 1979. In legal practice Philadelphia 1969-71 and 1987.

Assistant District Attorney Philadelphia 1971-72. Acting Chief Disciplinary Counsel, Deputy Chief Disciplinary Counsel and Counsel-in-Charge The Disciplinary Board 1972-86, Member Judicial Study Committee and Chair Accountability Committee The Supreme Court of Pennsylvania. Deputy of Investigations District Attorney's Office Philadelphia 1986-87. Lecturer on Ethics and Trial Advocacy Beasley School of Law 1990-95. Member Pennsylvania Judicial Conduct Board 1993-96. Chair Judicial Ethics Education Committee Pennsylvania Conference of State Trial Judges. Member Committee on Racial and Gender Bias in the Justice System The Supreme Court of Pennsylvania. Member University of Pennsylvania Inn of Court, Philadelphia and Pennsylvania Bar Associations. Board of Directors Jenkins Memorial Law Library. Member Junior Legal Club.

Office: 300 City Hall, Philadelphia 19107.
Telephone: (215) 686-7344.

HESS, Kevin A. *(Judge, Pennsylvania Court of Common Pleas Ninth Judicial District)*
Office: Cumberland County Courthouse, One Courthouse Square, Carlisle 17013.
Telephone: (717) 240-6296.

HILL, Glynnis D. *(Judge, Pennsylvania Court of Common Pleas First Judicial District)*
Office: 1801 Vine Street, Room 329, Philadelphia 19103.
Telephone: (215) 686-4210.

HOBERG, Jay J. *(Judge, Pennsylvania Court of Common Pleas Second Judicial District)*
Mailing address: P.O. Box 83480, Lancaster 17608-3480.
Office: Lancaster County Courthouse, 50 North Duke Street, Lancaster 17602.
Telephone: (717) 299-8080.

HODGSON, Richard J. *(Judge, Pennsylvania Court of Common Pleas Thirty-eighth Judicial District)* Appointed by Governor Robert P. Casey to term beginning Oct 21, 1994. Elected to term beginning Jan 1, 1996, current term expires Dec 31, 2005. Born Philadelphia Pennsylvania Feb 21, 1948. Catholic. Educated at College of the Holy Cross B.A. in English 1970 and Villanova University School of Law J.D. 1973. Admitted to practice Pennsylvania 1973 and U.S. Supreme Court 1981. In legal practice Norristown 1979-94.
Assistant District Attorney 1973-76. Assistant Public Defender 1976-78. Member Doris Jonas Freed Inn of Court, Montgomery County and Pennsylvania Bar Associations. Enjoys squash, record collecting and travel.
Mailing address: P.O. Box 311, Norristown 19404.
Office: Montgomery County Courthouse, Norristown 19401.
Telephone: (610) 292-4922.
E-mail address: rhodgson@mail.montcopa.org

HOFFER, George E. *(President Judge, Pennsylvania Court of Common Pleas Ninth Judicial District)*
Office: Cumberland County Courthouse, One Courthouse Square, Carlisle 17013.
Telephone: (717) 240-6292.

HOOVER, Todd A. *(Judge, Pennsylvania Court of Common Pleas Twelfth Judicial District)*
Office: Dauphin County Courthouse, Front and Market Streets, Harrisburg 17101.
Telephone: (717) 780-6670.

HORAN, Marilyn J. *(Judge, Pennsylvania Court of Common Pleas Fiftieth Judicial District)*
Mailing address: P.O. Box 1208, Butler 16003.
Office: Butler County Courthouse, Butler 16001.
Telephone: (724) 284-5290.

HORGOS, Robert P. *(Judge, Pennsylvania Court of Common Pleas Fifth Judicial District)*
Office: 816 City-County Building, 414 Grant Street, Pittsburgh 15219.
Telephone: (412) 350-4398.

HOWSARE, Daniel Lee *(President Judge, Pennsylvania Court of Common Pleas Fifty-seventh Judicial District)* Elected Nov 1985 to term beginning Jan 6, 1986. Retained by election 1995, current term expires Jan 2006. Born Colerain Township Bedford County Pennsylvania Dec 16, 1948. Protestant. Educated at Pennsylvania State University B.S. 1971 and Duquesne University School of Law J.D. 1976. Admitted to practice Pennsylvania 1976 and U.S. District Court Western District of Pennsylvania 1985. In legal practice Bedford 1976-85.
District Attorney Bedford County 1980-85. Member Pennsylvania Conference of State Trial Judges, Bedford County and Pennsylvania Bar Associations. Attended General Jurisdiction Course The National Judicial College July 12, 1987 to Aug 7, 1987. Served U.S. Army. Previously employed as Juvenile Court Probation Officer Allegheny County. Member Rotary Club of Bedford County, National Historical Preservations Society and Ducks Unlimited. Enjoys raising Tennessee Walker horses and antiquing.
Office: Bedford County Courthouse, Annex One, 204 South Juliana Street, Bedford 15522.
Telephone: (814) 623-4810.

HUDOCK, Joseph A. *(Judge, The Superior Court of Pennsylvania)* Elected to term beginning Jan 3, 1990. Retained by election Nov 1999, current term expires Jan 2010. Born Greensburg Pennsylvania Nov 21, 1937. Roman Catholic. Educated at St. Vincent College B.A. 1959 and Duquesne University J.D. 1962. Recipient American Jurisprudence Awards. Listed in *Who's Who in American Colleges and Universities.* Admitted to practice Pennsylvania 1963. Judge, Pennsylvania Court of Common Pleas Tenth Judicial District Jan 3, 1978 to Jan 2, 1990.
Editorial Board *The Practical Litigator.* Past President Westmoreland American Inn of Court. Former Member Advisory Council Governors Justice Commission. Chairman Supreme Court Appellate Rules Committee. Member Westmoreland Academy of Trial Lawyers (Secretary), Pennsylvania Conference of State Trial Judges, Westmoreland County and Pennsylvania Bar Associations. Recipient Alumnus of Distinction Award from St. Vincent College 1987. Lieutenant Commander USN JAGC 1963-67. Democrat. President United Way of Central Westmoreland County and Mountain View Rotary Club. Vice Chairman Salvation Army Advisory Board.
Office: One Northgate Square, Garden Center Drive, Greensburg 15601.
Telephone: (724) 832-6540.

HUGHES, Renée Cardwell *(Judge, Pennsylvania Court of Common Pleas First Judicial District)* Elected to term beginning Dec 1, 1995. Term expires Dec 31, 2005. Born Lynchburg Virginia Dec 18, 1955. Baptist. Educated at University of Virginia B.A. 1978 and Georgetown University Law Center J.D. 1985. Admitted to practice Pennsylvania 1985 and U.S. Court of Appeals Third Circuit 1985.
Office: 1406 Criminal Justice Center, 1301 Filbert Street, Philadelphia 19107.
Telephone: (215) 683-7115.
Fax: (215) 683-7117
E-mail address: renee.hughes@courts.phila.gov

HUMMER, Wayne G., Jr. *(Judge, Pennsylvania Court of Common Pleas Second Judicial District)* Elected to term beginning Jan 1980. Retained by election Nov 1989 and Nov 1999. Current term expires Aug 2007. Born Harrisburg Pennsylvania Aug 18, 1937. Methodist. Educated at Hershey Junior College A.A. 1957, Lebanon Valley College A.B. 1959 and Dickinson School of Law J.D. 1962. Business Manager Dickinson Law Review 1961-62. Admitted to practice Pennsylvania

HUMMER, WAYNE G., JR.—*Continued*

1962, U.S. Court of Military Appeals 1964, U.S. District Court 1968 and U.S. Court of Appeals Third Circuit 1968. In legal practice Lititz 1966-79 and Lancaster 1966-79.

Assistant Public Defender Lancaster County 1968-70. Solicitor Lancaster County Recorder of Deeds office 1970-79. Counsel Lancaster County Courts Administration office 1977-79. Member Pennsylvania Conference of State Trial Judges, National Council of Juvenile and Family Court Judges, Lancaster County and Pennsylvania Bar Associations. Lieutenant USN 1963-66. Member American Business Club, Masons Brownstone Lodge No. 666 and Lititz United Methodist Church.

Mailing address: P.O. Box 83480, Lancaster 17608-3480.

Office: Lancaster County Courthouse, 50 North Duke Street, Lancaster 17602.

Telephone: (717) 299-8065.

HUTTON, Herbert J. *(Judge, United States District Court Eastern District of Pennsylvania)* Appointed for life by President Ronald Reagan to term beginning 1988. Born Philadelphia Pennsylvania Nov 26, 1937. Educated at Lincoln University A.B. 1959 and Temple University School of Law J.D. 1962. In legal practice Philadelphia 1964-88.

Attorney Pennsylvania Housing and Home Finance Agency 1962-64. Hearing Officer Board of Revision of Taxes 1982-88.

Office: 9614 U.S. Courthouse, 601 Market Street, Philadelphia 19106-1764.

Telephone: (215) 597-5646.

JACKSON, Elizabeth *(Judge, Pennsylvania Court of Common Pleas First Judicial District)*

Office: 27 South Twelfth Street, Suite 407, Philadelphia 19107.

Telephone: (215) 686-7518.

JAMES, George E. *(Judge, Pennsylvania Court of Common Pleas Thirty-sixth Judicial District)*

Office: Beaver County Courthouse, Third Street, Beaver 15009.

Telephone: (724) 728-5700.

JAMES, Joseph M. *(Judge, Pennsylvania Court of Common Pleas Fifth Judicial District)* Appointed by Governor Robert P. Casey to term beginning May 8, 1987. Elected Nov 1987. Retained by election Nov 1997, current term expires Jan 2008. Currently serves as Administrative Judge Civil Division. Born New Castle Pennsylvania May 5, 1948. Roman Catholic. Educated at University of Pittsburgh B.S. 1970 J.D. 1973. Law Clerk to Hon. Eunice L. Ross, Pennsylvania Court of Common Pleas Fifth Judicial District 1974-76. Admitted to practice Pennsylvania 1973 and U.S. District Court Western District of Pennsylvania 1973. In legal practice Pittsburgh 1973-83. Chief Magistrate, Pittsburgh Magistrates Court 1983-87.

Assistant District Attorney Allegheny County 1976-79. Adjunct Professor of Law Duquesne University School of Law 1990. Member Allegheny County Bar Association. Named Volunteer of the Year Western Pennsylvania Boys and Girls Club 1989. Member Allegheny County Democratic Committee 1976-79.

Office: 819 City-County Building, 414 Grant Street, Pittsburgh 15219.

Telephone: (412) 350-5598.

JAMES, Thomas A., Jr. *(Judge, Pennsylvania Court of Common Pleas Twenty-sixth Judicial District)* Assumed office 2000. Educated at Dickinson College B.A. 1970 J.D. 1974. Staff member Dickinson Law Review. Member Phi Beta Kappa. In legal practice Bloomsburg 1974-99.

Solicitor Columbia County 1991-99. Author "Landlord-Tenant: Contractual Basis for an Implied Warranty of Habitability in Leased Premises" 77 No. 1 Fall 1972, "Theft and Related Offenses in the New Pennsylvania Crimes Code: A New Concept in Property Offenses" 78 No. 1 Fall 1972 and "Custody Relocation Law in Pennsylvania: Time to Revisit *Gruber v. Gruber*" 107 No. 1 Summer 2002 Dickinson L. Rev. Lecturer Introduction to Paralegalism 1992 and "The People's Law School" 2000 Bloomsburg University. Past President Columbia-Montour Bar Association. Member Pennsylvania Trial Lawyers Association, The Association of Trial Lawyers of America, Pennsylvania Conference of State Trial Judges (Education Committee since 2002), Pennsylvania and American Bar Associations. Lecturer "Damages in Personal Injury Cases" Pennsylvania Bar Institute 1993. Attended The National Judicial College. Recipient Silver Beaver Award from Boy Scouts 1999. President and Co-owner Susquehanna Valley Land Abstract Company 1980-99. Member Leadership Program Bloomsburg Chamber of Commerce 1991. Executive Board Member 1991-98, Council President 1996-98, Member James E. West Fellowship and Member Scouting Heritage Society Boy Scouts. Chairman American Heart Association Columbia County for two years. Past President Bloomsburg School Board. Board of Directors Bloomsburg Theatre Ensemble. Board Member Columbia/Montour Mental Health Association and Bloomsburg United Way. Teacher and Member Wesley United Methodist Church. Member Bloomsburg Planning Commission, Elks Lodge 436 and Bloomsburg Kiwanis.

Mailing address: P.O. Box 380, Bloomsburg 17815.

Office: Columbia County Courthouse, Bloomsburg 17815.

Telephone: (570) 389-5662.

JENKINS, Patricia H. *(Judge, Pennsylvania Court of Common Pleas Thirty-second Judicial District)*

Office: Delaware County Courthouse, 201 West Front Street, Media 19063.

Telephone: (610) 891-4520.

JOHNSON, Justin M. *(Judge, The Superior Court of Pennsylvania)* Appointed by Governor Richard Thornburgh to term beginning Dec 16, 1980. Elected Nov 5, 1985. Retained by election Nov 1995, current term expires Dec 31, 2003. Born Wilkinsburg Pennsylvania Aug 19, 1933. Presbyterian. Educated at University of Chicago B.A. 1954 J.D. 1962 and University of Virginia. Member Alpha Delta Phi. Admitted to practice Pennsylvania 1962 and U.S. Supreme Court 1969. Began legal practice Pittsburgh 1962.

Assistant Solicitor 1964-70 and Solicitor and Assistant Secretary 1970-77 Board of Public Education School District of Pittsburgh. Adjunct Professor Duquesne University School of Law 1986-91. Fellow American Bar Foundation. Member 1969-89 and Chairman 1983-89

JOHNSON, JUSTIN M.—*Continued*

Pennsylvania Board of Law Examiners. Member National Conference of Bar Examiners, Allegheny County (Committees on Professional Ethics, Public Service, Nominating, Relations Between Bench and Bar, Civil Rights and Responsibilities), Pennsylvania (Member Committee on Legal Education and Admission to the Bar since 1969, former member Committees on Judicial Retention Election and Crime and Juvenile Delinquency), National and American Bar Associations. Recipient Dr. Martin Luther King Citizen's Award from Music and Arts Club of Pittsburgh 1971, Humanitarian and Community Service Award from COMPA 1978, Top Hat Award for Distinguished Judicial Service from *New Pittsburgh Courier* 1981, Homer S. Brown Service Award from Homer S. Brown Law Association and B.A.L.S.A. 1982, Man of the Year Award from Bethesda Presbyterian Church 1983, President's Award from Pennsylvania Trial Lawyers Association 1983, Award of Merit from Pittsburgh Young Adult Club of N.A.N.B.P.W.C. 1983, St. Thomas More Award from Pittsburgh Diocese 1985 and Public Service Award from Pittsburgh Chapter A.S.P.A. 1986. USAF active duty 1954-59 and USAFR 1963-73. Board of Trustees Princeton Theological Seminary and Carnegie-Mellon University. Board of Directors Homer S. Brown Law Association and Urban League of Pittsburgh. Former Commissioner Program to Aid Citizen Enterprise (PACE) and Pittsburgh Trust for Cultural Resources.

Office: 2702 Grant Building, 330 Grant Street, Pittsburgh 15219.

Telephone: (412) 565-3604.

JONES, C. Darnell, II *(Judge, Pennsylvania Court of Common Pleas First Judicial District)*

Office: 1207 Criminal Justice Center, 1301 Filbert Street, Philadelphia 19107.

Telephone: (215) 683-7038.

JONES, John E., III *(Judge, United States District Court Middle District of Pennsylvania)* Appointed for life by President George W. Bush to term beginning Aug 2, 2002. Born Pottsville Pennsylvania 1955. Educated at Dickinson College B.A. 1977 J.D. 1980. Law Clerk to President Judge Guy A. Bowe, Jr., Pennsylvania Court of Common Pleas Twenty-first Judicial District 1980-83. In legal practice Pennsylvania 1980-2002.

Office: 218 U.S. Courthouse, 240 West Third Street, Williamsport 17701.

Telephone: (570) 601-1497.

JOSEPH, Barbara A. *(Judge, Pennsylvania Court of Common Pleas First Judicial District)*

Office: 1410 Criminal Justice Center, 1301 Filbert Street, Philadelphia 19107.

Telephone: (215) 683-7127.

JOYCE, Michael T. *(Judge, The Superior Court of Pennsylvania)* Former Judge, Pennsylvania Court of Common Pleas Sixth Judicial District.

Office: 3250 West Lake Road, Erie 16505.

Telephone: (814) 878-5800.

JOYNER, J. Curtis *(Judge, United States District Court Eastern District of Pennsylvania)* Appointed for life by President George Bush to term beginning April 13, 1992. Born Newberry South Carolina April 18, 1948. Catholic. Educated at Central State University B.S. 1971 and Howard University School of Law J.D. 1974. Admitted to practice Pennsylvania 1975 and U.S. District Court Eastern District of Pennsylvania 1981. Judge, Pennsylvania Court of Common Pleas Fifteenth Judicial District 1987-92.

With District Attorney's Office Chester County 1975-87. Member Chester County Bar Foundation, Pennsylvania Trial Judges Association and Chester County Bar Association. Recipient "Trail-blazers in Law Enforcement" Award from Governor Richard Thornburgh 1986. Republican. Enjoys golf, jazz music and sailing.

Office: 8613 U.S. Courthouse, 601 Market Street, Philadelphia 19106-1714.

Telephone: (215) 597-1537.

KANE, Harold M. *(Judge, Pennsylvania Court of Common Pleas First Judicial District)*

Office: 591 City Hall, Philadelphia 19107.

Telephone: (215) 686-3753.

KANE, Michael J. *(Judge, Pennsylvania Court of Common Pleas Seventh Judicial District)* Elected to term beginning Jan 6, 1986. Retained by election 1995, current term expires Jan 2006. Born New York Oct 26, 1943. Educated at Dartmouth College A.B. with distinction 1965 and Duke University School of Law J.D. 1969. Managing Editor Duke Law Journal. Law Clerk to Hon. Francis L. Van Dusen, U.S. Court of Appeals Third Circuit 1969-70. Member Order of the Coif. Admitted to practice Pennsylvania 1969 and U.S. Court of Appeals Third Circuit 1969.

Assistant District Attorney 1970-72, Deputy District Attorney 1972-74, Chief of Prosecution 1974-79 and District Attorney 1979-86 Bucks County.

Office: Bucks County Courthouse, 55 East Court Street, Doylestown 18901.

Telephone: (215) 348-6063.

KANE, Yvette *(Judge, United States District Court Middle District of Pennsylvania)* Appointed for life by President Bill Clinton June 4, 1998 to term beginning Oct 27, 1998. Born Donaldsonville Louisiana Oct 11, 1953. Educated at Nicholls State University B.A. 1973 and Tulane University School of Law J.D. 1976. In legal practice Pennsylvania 1993-95.

Trial Attorney U.S. Equal Employment Opportunity Commission 1977-78. Assistant State Attorney General Colorado 1978-80. Deputy District Attorney Denver 1980-86. Deputy Commonwealth Attorney General Pennsylvania 1986-91. Commonwealth Secretary Pennsylvania 1995-98.

Mailing address: P.O. Box 11817, Harrisburg 17108-1817.

Telephone: (717) 221-3990.

KATZ, Marvin *(Senior Judge, United States District Court Eastern District of Pennsylvania)* Appointed for life by President Ronald Reagan to term beginning 1983. Assumed Senior status Aug 26, 1997, serves by assignment. Born Philadelphia Pennsylvania Nov 22, 1930. Educated at University of Pennsylvania B.A. 1951 and Yale Law School LL.B. 1954. Law Clerk to Hon. Francis X. McClanaghan, Pennsylvania Court of Common Pleas 1959-60. In legal practice Philadelphia 1954-77 and 1981-83.

Assistant to the Commissioner U.S. Internal Revenue Service 1977-81.

Office: 13613 U.S. Courthouse, 601 Market Street, Philadelphia 19106-1750.

Telephone: (215) 597-4405.

KAUFFMAN, Bruce W. *(Judge, United States District Court Eastern District of Pennsylvania)* Appointed for life by President Bill Clinton to term beginning Jan 20, 1998. Born Atlantic City New Jersey Dec 1, 1934. Educated at University of Pennsylvania B.A. 1956 and Yale Law School LL.B. 1959. Law Clerk to Hon. Vincent S. Haneman, Superior Court of New Jersey 1959-60. In legal practice Philadelphia 1960-80 and 1982-97. Justice, The Supreme Court of Pennsylvania 1980-82.

Office: 5613 U.S. Courthouse, 601 Market Street, Philadelphia 19106-1776.

Telephone: (215) 597-0888.

KEAN, Joyce S. *(Judge, Pennsylvania Court of Common Pleas First Judicial District)*

Office: 540 City Hall, Philadelphia 19107.

Telephone: (215) 686-7338.

KEELER, Charles C. *(Judge, Pennsylvania Court of Common Pleas Thirty-second Judicial District)*

Office: Delaware County Courthouse, 201 West Front Street, Media 19063.

Telephone: (610) 891-4043.

KELLER, Scott D. *(Judge, Pennsylvania Court of Common Pleas Twenty-third Judicial District)* Appointed by Governor Robert P. Casey to term beginning May 8, 1989. Elected Nov 1989. Retained by election Nov 1999, current term expires Jan 2010. Former President Judge. Born Chambersburg Pennsylvania July 23, 1950. Episcopalian. Educated at Albright College A.B. 1972 and American University J.D. 1975. Admitted to practice Pennsylvania 1975 and U.S. District Court Eastern District of Pennsylvania 1976. In legal practice Reading 1976-89.

Assistant District Attorney Berks County 1976-80. Solicitor Berks County 1988-89. Member Endlich Law Club, Pennsylvania Conference of State Trial Judges, Berks County and Pennsylvania Bar Associations. Attended General Orientation The National Judicial College 1990 and 1991. Chairman Berks County Republican Party 1986.

Office: Berks County Courthouse, Ninth Floor, 633 Court Street, Reading 19601.

Telephone: (610) 478-6431.

KELLY, Elizabeth K. *(Judge, Pennsylvania Court of Common Pleas Sixth Judicial District)*

Office: Erie County Courthouse, 140 West Sixth Street, Erie 16501.

Telephone: (814) 451-6363.

KELLY, James McGirr *(Senior Judge, United States District Court Eastern District of Pennsylvania)* Appointed for life by President Ronald Reagan to term beginning 1983. Assumed Senior status March 31, 1996, serves by assignment. Born Philadelphia Pennsylvania March 24, 1928. Educated at University of Pennsylvania B.S. 1951 and Temple University School of Law J.D. 1957. Law Clerk to Hon. Edward J. Griffiths, Pennsylvania Court of Common Pleas 1957-58. In legal practice Philadelphia 1962-83.

Assistant District Attorney Philadelphia 1958-60. Assistant U.S. Attorney Eastern District of Pennsylvania 1960-62. Special Assistant Commonwealth Attorney General Pennsylvania 1964-65.

Office: 8614 U.S. Courthouse, 601 Market Street, Philadelphia 19106-1762.

Telephone: (215) 597-5863.

KELLY, Kevin F. *(Judge, Pennsylvania Court of Common Pleas Thirty-second Judicial District)*

Office: Delaware County Courthouse, 201 West Front Street, Media 19063.

Telephone: (610) 891-4318.

KELLY, Robert A. *(President Judge, Pennsylvania Court of Common Pleas Fifth Judicial District)* Former Administrative Judge Orphans' Court Division.

Office: 330 Frick Building, 437 Grant Street, Pittsburgh 15219.

Telephone: (412) 350-5404.

KELLY, Robert F. *(Senior Judge, United States District Court Eastern District of Pennsylvania)* Appointed for life by President Ronald Reagan. Assumed Senior status July 17, 2001, serves by assignment. Born Rosemont Pennsylvania June 17, 1935. Educated at Villanova University B.S. in Economics 1957 and Temple University Law School 1957-60. Admitted to practice Pennsylvania 1961. Former Judge and Administrative Judge, Pennsylvania Court of Common Pleas Thirty-second Judicial District, elected to term beginning Jan 5, 1976.

Member Delaware County, Pennsylvania and American Bar Associations. Republican. Chairman Delaware County Republican Executive Committee 1971-75. Member St. Thomas Catholic Church.

Office: 11613 U.S. Courthouse, 601 Market Street, Philadelphia 19106-1765.

Telephone: (215) 597-0736.

KENDERDINE, Henry S., Jr. *(Judge, Pennsylvania Court of Common Pleas Second Judicial District)*

Mailing address: P.O. Box 83480, Lancaster 17608-3480.

Office: Lancaster County Courthouse, 50 North Duke Street, Lancaster 17602.

Telephone: (717) 293-7288.

KENNEDY, John S. *(Judge, Pennsylvania Court of Common Pleas Nineteenth Judicial District)*

Office: York County Courthouse, 28 East Market Street, York 17401.

Telephone: (717) 771-9830.

KEOGH, D. Webster *(Judge, Pennsylvania Court of Common Pleas First Judicial District)*

Office: 1201 Criminal Justice Center, 1301 Filbert Street, Philadelphia 19107.

Telephone: (215) 683-7020.

KIESER, William S. *(Judge, Pennsylvania Court of Common Pleas Twenty-ninth Judicial District)*

Office: Lycoming County Courthouse, 48 West Third Street, Williamsport 17701.

Telephone: (570) 327-2340.

KISTLER, Thomas King *(Judge, Pennsylvania Court of Common Pleas Forty-ninth Judicial District)* Elected Nov 1997 to term beginning Jan 2, 1998. Term expires Dec 31, 2007. Born Bellefonte Pennsylvania May 24, 1957. Presbyterian. Educated at Pennsylvania State University B.S. with distinction 1979 and Dickinson School of Law J.D. 1982. Admitted to practice Pennsylvania 1982 and U.S. Supreme Court 1985. In legal practice Bellefonte and State College 1982-97.

Member Centre County (Former Secretary) and Pennsylvania (Former Zone Governor House of Delegates)

KISTLER, THOMAS KING—*Continued*

Bar Associations. Member Kiwanis and YMCA. Enjoys skiing, hunting and shooting.
Office: Centre County Courthouse, Bellefonte 16823.
Telephone: (814) 355-8670.
E-mail address: tkkistler@co.centre.pa.us

KLEIN, Richard B. *(Judge, The Superior Court of Pennsylvania)* Elected Nov 2001 to term beginning Jan 2002. Term expires Jan 2012. Born Philadelphia Pennsylvania Dec 24, 1939. Jewish. Educated at Amherst College B.A. with honors 1961 and Harvard Law School J.D. with honors 1964. Member Phi Beta Kappa. Admitted to practice Pennsylvania 1964, U.S. District Court Eastern District of Pennsylvania 1965 and U.S. Court of Appeals Third Circuit 1965. In legal practice Philadelphia 1974-75. Judge, Pennsylvania Court of Common Pleas First Judicial District Jan 1972 to Jan 2002, appointed by Governor Milton J. Shapp.

Special Assistant Attorney General (assigned to prosecuting fraudulent insurance companies) 1967-71. Co-author *Trial Communication Skills* 1986 and revised edition March 1996 Shepard's McGraw-Hill. Important Opinions: Commonwealth v. Sherman 9 Phila. 261 1981, Blue v. Johns-Manville Corp. 10 Phila. 23 1983, Haines v. Raven Arms 24 Phila. 9 1992, In re Thorotrast Cases 26 Phila. 479 1994 and Frazier v. State Farm Mutual Auto Ins. 29 Phila. 443, 1995. Adjunct Lecturer in Law Temple University 1979-94. Member Philadelphia, Pennsylvania (House of Delegates) and American (Chair Futures Committee National Conference of State Trial Judges) Bar Associations. Presenter National Court Technology Conferences, American Bar Association meetings and Trial Communication, Ethics, Alternative Dispute Resolution, Legal Writing, Technology and Future Studies CLE courses. Named Outstanding Alumni by Friends' Central School. Recipient Humanitarian Award from Prisoners' Family Welfare Association. Chair Philadelphia Republican Policy Committee 1968-71. Past President Concerto Soloists and Prisoners' Family Welfare Association. Board Member Reading Terminal Preservation Fund. Member Musicians Union #77. Actively plays jazz drums and leads jazz group. Enjoys tennis and travel (educational leader for multiple trips abroad).
Office: 1700 Market Street, Suite 1650, Philadelphia 19103.
Telephone: (215) 560-4303.
Fax: (215) 560-4303

KLEINFELTER, Joseph H. *(President Judge, Pennsylvania Court of Common Pleas Twelfth Judicial District)*
Office: Dauphin County Courthouse, Front and Market Streets, Harrisburg 17101.
Telephone: (717) 780-6650.

KLINE, Samuel A. *(Judge, Pennsylvania Court of Common Pleas Fifty-second Judicial District)*
Office: 400 South Eighth Street, Lebanon 17042.
Telephone: (717) 274-2801.

KNIGHT, Louise O. *(Judge, Pennsylvania Court of Common Pleas Seventeenth Judicial District)*
Office: Union County Courthouse, 103 South Second Street, Lewisburg 17837.
Telephone: (570) 524-8641.

KOPRIVA, Jolene Grubb *(Judge, Pennsylvania Court of Common Pleas Twenty-fourth Judicial District)* Elected to term beginning Jan 4, 1988. Retained by election Nov 1997, current term expires Jan 2008. Born St. Clair Michigan Sept 5, 1953. Lutheran. Educated at Pennsylvania State University B.S. 1975 and Duquesne University J.D. 1978. Recent Decisions Editor Duquesne Law Review 1976-78. Member Phi Alpha Delta. Admitted to practice Pennsylvania 1978 and U.S. District Court Western District of Pennsylvania 1978. In legal practice Hollidaysburg 1978-87.

Member Pennsylvania Conference of Trial Court Judges 1988. Attended New Judges School A.O.P.C. 1988. Member Zion Lutheran Church and Soroptimist International of Blair County. Enjoys family, swimming and biking.
Office: 245 Blair County Courthouse, 423 Allegheny Street, Hollidaysburg 16648.
Telephone: (814) 693-3075.

KOSIK, Edwin M. *(Senior Judge, United States District Court Middle District of Pennsylvania)* Appointed for life by President Ronald Reagan. Assumed Senior status, serves by assignment. Born Dupont Pennsylvania May 5, 1925. Educated at Wilkes College A.B. 1949 and Dickinson School of Law LL.B. 1951. Former President Judge, Pennsylvania Court of Common Pleas Forty-fifth Judicial District.

Assistant U.S. Attorney 1953-58. Member Lackawanna County (Past President), Pennsylvania and American Bar Associations. U.S. Army ETO WWII. Chairman State Workmen's Compensation Board 1963-69. Member Polish National Catholic Church, Wilkes College Board of Trustees, Weston Field Handball Association and VFW.
Mailing address: P.O. Box 856, Scranton 18501-0856.
Telephone: (570) 207-5730.

KOUDELIS, George *(Judge, Pennsylvania Court of Common Pleas Thirty-second Judicial District)*
Office: Delaware County Courthouse, 201 West Front Street, Media 19063.
Telephone: (610) 891-4349.

KRUMENACKER, Norman A., III *(Judge, Pennsylvania Court of Common Pleas Forty-seventh Judicial District)*
Office: Cambria County Courthouse, 200 South Center Street, Ebensburg 15931.
Telephone: (814) 472-1415.

KUHN, John D. *(President Judge, Pennsylvania Court of Common Pleas Fifty-first Judicial District)* Elected to term beginning Jan 6, 1986. Retained by election 1995, current term expires Dec 31, 2005. Born Gettysburg Pennsylvania Aug 7, 1950. Presbyterian. Educated at Albright College B.A. 1972 and Dickinson School of Law J.D. 1975. Admitted to practice Pennsylvania 1975 and U.S. District Court Middle District of Pennsylvania 1976. In legal practice Harrisburg 1975-79 and Gettysburg 1979-85.

Member Adams County and Pennsylvania Bar Associations. Republican. Coaches youth soccer and baseball. Interested in history.
Office: Adams County Courthouse, 111-117 Baltimore Street, Gettysburg 17325.
Telephone: (717) 337-9848.

KUNSELMAN, Robert E. *(President Judge, Pennsylvania Court of Common Pleas Thirty-sixth Judicial District)* Appointed by Governor Richard Thornburgh April

KUNSELMAN, ROBERT E.—*Continued*
26, 1982. Elected Nov 1983. Retained by election 1993, current term expires Jan 3, 2004. Born Summerville Pennsylvania June 21, 1937. Roman Catholic. Educated at Geneva College B.A. 1959 and Duquesne University School of Law LL.B. 1963. Admitted to practice Pennsylvania 1963. In legal practice Beaver 1963-82.

Member Beaver County and Pennsylvania Bar Associations. USAR 1963-70.

Office: Beaver County Courthouse, Third Street, Beaver 15009.

Telephone: (724) 728-5700.

KURTZ, Stewart L. *(President Judge, Pennsylvania Court of Common Pleas Twentieth Judicial District)*

Office: Huntingdon County Courthouse, 223 Penn Street, Huntingdon 16652.

Telephone: (814) 643-4510.

KWIDIS, C. Gus *(Judge, Pennsylvania Court of Common Pleas Thirty-sixth Judicial District)*

Office: Beaver County Courthouse, Third Street, Beaver 15009.

Telephone: (724) 728-5700.

LACHMAN, Marlene *(Judge, Pennsylvania Court of Common Pleas First Judicial District)*

Office: 1413 Criminal Justice Center, 1301 Filbert Street, Philadelphia 19107.

Telephone: (215) 683-7136.

LALLY-GREEN, Maureen E. *(Judge, The Superior Court of Pennsylvania)* Appointed by Governor Thomas J. Ridge to term beginning May 1998. Elected Nov 1999, current term expires 2010. Born Sharpsville Pennsylvania. Educated at Duquesne University B.S. 1971 J.D. 1974. Admitted to practice Pennsylvania 1974, U.S. District Courts Western District of Pennsylvania 1975 and District of Columbia 1978 and U.S. Supreme Court 1980. In legal practice Pittsburgh 1974-75. Arbitrator, U.S. District Court Western District of Pennsylvania 1993 to June 1998.

Counsel Commodity Futures Trading Commission 1975-78 and Westinghouse Electric Corporation 1978-83. Appeals Research Associate to Hon. Nicholas P. Papadakos 1985-88 and Hon. John P. Flaherty, Jr. 1989-93, The Supreme Court of Pennsylvania. Consultant to Chief Justice John P. Flaherty, Jr., The Supreme Court of Pennsylvania 1993-98. Professor of Law Sept 1983 to June 1998 and Adjunct Faculty since 1999 Duquesne University School of Law. Member Criminal Procedural Rules Committee 1993-97 and Hearing Committee Disciplinary Board Summer 1995 to June 1998 The Supreme Court of Pennsylvania. Member Allegheny County (Secretary 1992-95 and Governor 1995-2001 Board of Directors and Pennsylvania (Commission on Women in the Profession since July 1994, Co-chair Quality of Work Life Committee since 2001, Member Executive Committee since 2001) Bar Associations. Recipient W.K. Kellogg Fellowship in International Development 1990-92, Outstanding Alumnus of Kennedy Christian High School Pellerite Award Dec 26, 1992, Most Responsive Professor Award 1996 and Distinguished Alumna Award 2001 from Duquesne University School of Law and President's Award from Chatham College. Named Woman of the Year by Women Law Students Duquesne University School of Law March 1997. Member 1984 to June 1998 and Chair 1986 to June 1998 Zoning Hearing Board Cranberry Township. Member since 1987 and President 1994-95 Western Pennsylvania Partners of the Americas (Board Member since 1996). Volunteer Counsel Volunteer Ambulance Corporation Cranberry Township 1990 to June 1998. Board Member Pennsylvanians for Modern Courts 1993 to June 1998. Former Member Alumni Board Duquesne Law Alumni Association and Duquesne University.

Office: 2420 Grant Building, 330 Grant Street, Pittsburgh 15219.

Telephone: (412) 565-2264.

LANCASTER, Gary L. *(Judge, United States District Court Western District of Pennsylvania)* Magistrate Judge 1987-93. Appointed Judge for life by President Bill Clinton. Born Brownsville Pennsylvania Aug 14, 1949. Educated at Slippery Rock State College B.S. 1971 and University of Pittsburgh School of Law J.D. 1974. In legal practice Pittsburgh 1978-87.

Regional Counsel Pennsylvania Human Relations Commission 1974-76. Assistant District Attorney Allegheny County 1976-78.

Office: 911 U.S. Post Office & Courthouse, 700 Grant Street, Pittsburgh 15219.

Telephone: (412) 208-7400.

LASH, Scott E. *(Judge, Pennsylvania Court of Common Pleas Twenty-third Judicial District)* Elected Nov 2, 1999 to term beginning Jan 3, 2000. Term expires Dec 31, 2009. Born Reading Pennsylvania Aug 14, 1956. Christian. Educated at Pennsylvania State University B.A. 1978 and University of Pittsburgh School of Law J.D. 1981. Admitted to practice Pennsylvania 1981, U.S. District Court Eastern District of Pennsylvania 1981 and U.S. Supreme Court 1998. In legal practice Reading 1981-99.

Office: Berks County Services Center, Fourth Floor, 633 Court Street, Reading 19601.

Telephone: (610) 478-4920.

E-mail address: slash@mail.countyofberks.com

LAWLER, Daniel J. *(Judge, Pennsylvania Court of Common Pleas Seventh Judicial District)*

Office: Bucks County Courthouse, 55 East Court Street, Doylestown 18901.

Telephone: (215) 348-8200.

LAZARUS, Anne E. *(Judge, Pennsylvania Court of Common Pleas First Judicial District)*

Office: 306 City Hall, Philadelphia 19107.

Telephone: (215) 686-7328.

LEADBETTER, Bonnie Brigance *(Judge, The Commonwealth Court of Pennsylvania)*

Office: 610 Sentry Park, Suite 210, Blue Bell 19422.

Telephone: (610) 832-1715.

Fax: (610) 832-1719

LEAHEY, F. Joseph *(Judge, Pennsylvania Court of Common Pleas Forty-seventh Judicial District)* Appointed by Governor Robert P. Casey to term beginning March 25, 1987. Elected Nov 7, 1989. Retained by election Nov 1999, current term expires Jan 1, 2010. Born Johnstown Pennsylvania Jan 31, 1938. Roman Catholic. Educated at University of Pittsburgh B.A. 1959 and Dickinson School of Law LL.B. with honors 1962. Admitted to practice Pennsylvania 1962. In legal practice Ebensburg 1966-87.

Examiner Pennsylvania Board of Law Examiners 1966-87. President Pennsylvania Bar Institute 1985-86.

LEAHEY, F. JOSEPH—*Continued*
Member Pennsylvania Bar Association. Lieutenant USN 1963-66.
Office: Cambria County Courthouse, 200 South Center Street, Ebensburg 15931.
Telephone: (814) 472-1525.

LEAVITT, M. Hannah *(Judge, The Commonwealth Court of Pennsylvania)*
Office: One Keystone Plaza, Suite 301, North Front & Market Streets, Harrisburg 17101.
Telephone: (717) 772-0763.

LEE, Donald J. *(Senior Judge, United States District Court Western District of Pennsylvania)* Appointed for life by President George Bush Nov 1989 to term beginning April 6, 1990. Assumed Senior status April 6, 2000, serves by assignment. Born Pittsburgh Pennsylvania July 24, 1927. Roman Catholic. Educated at University of Pittsburgh A.B. 1950 and Duquesne University School of Law LL.B. with honors 1954. Law Clerk to Hon. Rabe F. Marsh, Jr., U.S. District Court Western District of Pennsylvania 1957-58. Member St. Thomas More Society. Admitted to practice Pennsylvania 1954, U.S. Court of Appeals Third Circuit 1957 and U.S. Supreme Court 1984. In legal practice Pittsburgh 1954-84 and 1986-88. Judge, Pennsylvania Court of Common Pleas Fifth Judicial District 1984-86 and 1988-90.
Special Attorney General Pennsylvania 1963-74. Solicitor Borough of Green Tree 1963-84. Important Decisions: In re Janet Williams (upholding privilege of news media re: source in connection with Grand Jury subpoena) 963 F.2d 567, 3d Cir. 1992 and In re Chambers Development Securities Litigation (multidistrict litigation settlement; $95 million) 912 F. Supp. 882 W.D. Pa. 1995, 912 F. Supp. 852 W.D. Pa. 1995. Member Allegheny County and American Bar Associations. Recipient Bethel Park Good Neighbor Award 1985 and 1988, Distinguished Alumnus Award from Duquesne University Law Alumni Association 1993 and St. Thomas More Legal Society Award 1996. Seaman First Class USN 1945-47. Republican. Member Ad Hoc Committee Salvation Army. Enjoys fishing, cross-country skiing and bird watching.
Office: 916 U.S. Post Office & Courthouse, 700 Grant Street, Pittsburgh 15219.
Telephone: (412) 208-7410.

LEETE, John B. *(President Judge, Pennsylvania Court of Common Pleas Fifty-fifth Judicial District)* Appointed by Governor Robert P. Casey to term beginning Feb 19, 1988. Elected Nov 1989. Retained by election Nov 1999, current term expires Jan 1, 2010. Born Olean New York Oct 11, 1945. Episcopalian. Educated at University of Pittsburgh B.A. 1967 J.D. 1970. Admitted to practice Pennsylvania 1970 and U.S. District Court Western District 1970. In legal practice Pittsburgh July 1972 to June 1974 and Coudersport July 1976 to Feb 1988.
Staff Attorney and Chief Attorney Police Affairs Division Oct 1970 to July 1972 and Supervising Attorney and Deputy Program Director for Beaver, Butler and Lawrence Counties June 1974 to July 1976 Neighborhood Legal Services. Author "Treatment and Rehabilitation or Hard Time: Is the Focus of Juvenile Justice Changing" 29 Akron L. Rev. Spring 1996. Faculty Member Criminal Justice Administration Department Mansfield State University. Member Pennsylvania Juvenile Court Judges Commission, National Council of Juvenile and Family Court Judges, Pennsylvania Conference of State Trial Judges (Juvenile Court Section, Family Law Section), American Judges Association, Pennsylvania and American (Judicial Administration Division) Bar Associations. Recipient Distinguished Service Awards from Neighborhood Legal Services 1976 and Good Turn Award from Boy Scouts of America. Named One of Outstanding Young Men of America and Citizen of the Year by American Legion 1994. Listed in *Who's Who in the United States.* Past President Coudersport Rotary Club. Board of Directors American Cancer Society (Potter County Division). Member Potter County Historical Society.
Office: Potter County Courthouse, Room 30, Coudersport 16915.
Telephone: (814) 274-9720.
Fax: (814) 274-3363

LEOMPORRA, Tullio Gene *(Recalled Magistrate Judge, United States District Court Eastern District of Pennsylvania)* U.S. Commissioner 1966-71. Appointed Magistrate by U.S. District Court judges to term beginning March 12, 1971. Reappointed 1979 and 1987. Former Chief Magistrate Judge. Appointed Recalled Magistrate Judge by the Judicial Council of the Third Circuit. Roman Catholic. Educated at Wharton School of Finance and Commerce University of Pennsylvania B.S., University of Illinois and Georgetown University LL.B. J.D. Admitted to practice Pennsylvania 1951. Began legal practice Philadelphia 1951.
Professor La Salle College 1976-87. Member Philadelphia, Pennsylvania, Federal and American Bar Associations. Sergeant U.S. Army. Collects antique cars and clocks.
Office: 561 Madison Building, 400 Washington Street, Reading 19601.
Telephone: (610) 320-5097.

LERNER, Benjamin *(Judge, Pennsylvania Court of Common Pleas First Judicial District)* Assumed office June 1998. Born Philadelphia Pennsylvania Feb 2, 1941. Educated at Brandeis University B.A. cum laude 1962 and University of Pennsylvania Law School LL.B. magna cum laude 1965. Staff member University of Pennsylvania Law Review. Law Clerk to Hon. Stanley A. Weigel, U.S. District Court Northern District of California 1965-66. Member Order of the Coif. In legal practice Philadelphia Sept 1968 to June 1973, 1975 to Jan 1994, March 1994 to June 1996 and Jan 1998 to June 1998. Judge, Pennsylvania Court of Common Pleas First Judicial District June 1996 to Jan 1998.
Deputy Attorney General Pennsylvania Department of Justice June 1973 to Feb 1975. Chief Defender Defender Association of Pennsylvania 1975-90. Editorial Board *The Legal Intelligencer* 1992-96. Adjunct Professor of Trial Advocacy University of Pennsylvania Law School 1978-88. Member Pennsylvania Criminal Procedure Rules Committee 1977-86 and Hearing Committee 1.02 Disciplinary Board The Supreme Court of Pennsylvania 1980-86. Member Commission on Judicial Selection, Retention and Evaluation 1977-90 and Board of Governors 1992-95 Philadelphia Bar Association. Defender Board Member 1979-87, President 1983-85, Public Board Member 1991-96 and Board of Directors National Legal Aid and Defender Association. Member House of Delegates American Bar Association 1983-85. Fellow American College of Trial Lawyers. Teaching Team Member

LERNER, BENJAMIN—*Continued*

National Institute of Trial Advocacy 1975, 1977, 1978, 1980, 1985 and 1996. Recipient "Honorable Gerald F. Flood Memorial Award" from Philadelphia Bar Foundation 1978, Clara Shortridge Foltz Award from American Bar Association and National Legal Aid and Defender Association Dec 1987, Nochem S. Winnet Award Citizens Crime Commission of Delaware Valley Jan 1989, John Minor Wisdom Public Service and Professionalism Award from Section of Litigation American Bar Association Oct 1990 and Annual Award from Criminal Justice Section Philadelphia Bar Association Nov 1990. Member Philadelphia Regional Planning Council Pennsylvania Governor's Justice Commission 1977-78.

Office: 1220 Criminal Justice Center, 1301 Filbert Street, Philadelphia 19107.

Telephone: (215) 683-7077.

LESKINEN, Steve P. *(Judge, Pennsylvania Court of Common Pleas Fourteenth Judicial District)* Elected Nov 2001 to term beginning Jan 7, 2002. Term expires Jan 2012. Born Gardner Massachusetts Aug 6, 1953. Protestant. Educated at Bucknell University B.A. 1975 and University of Pennsylvania School of Law J.D. 1978. Admitted to practice Pennsylvania 1978. In legal practice Uniontown May 1978 to Jan 2002.

Assistant District Attorney Fayette County 1991-2001. Member Fayette County (President 1991) and Pennsylvania Bar Associations. Democrat. Interests include sports, boating, and skiing.

Office: Fayette County Courthouse, 61 East Main Street, Uniontown 15401.

Telephone: (724) 430-2060.

Fax: (724) 430-1001

E-mail address: leskinen439@yahoo.com

LEWIS, Kathryn Streeter *(Judge, Pennsylvania Court of Common Pleas First Judicial District)* Former Administrative Judge Orphans' Court Division.

Office: 342 City Hall, Philadelphia 19107.

Telephone: (215) 686-9532.

LEWIS, Richard A. *(Judge, Pennsylvania Court of Common Pleas Twelfth Judicial District)*

Office: Dauphin County Courthouse, Front and Market Streets, Harrisburg 17101.

Telephone: (717) 780-6660.

LIEBERMAN, Stephen B. *(Judge, Pennsylvania Court of Common Pleas Twenty-third Judicial District)*

Office: Berks County Courthouse, Ninth Floor, 633 Court Street, Reading 19601.

Telephone: (610) 478-6436.

LINEBAUGH, Stephen P. *(Judge, Pennsylvania Court of Common Pleas Nineteenth Judicial District)* Elected Nov 1997 to term beginning Jan 5, 1998. Term expires Jan 2008. Born York Pennsylvania Aug 25, 1947. Episcopalian. Educated at University of Pittsburgh B.A. 1969 J.D. 1972. Law Clerk to Pennsylvania Court of Common Pleas Nineteenth Judicial District 1972. Admitted to practice Pennsylvania 1972. In legal practice York 1973-97.

Assistant District Attorney York County 1973-74. Member Herbert B. Cohen American Inn of Court, York County, Pennsylvania and American Bar Associations. Personal Statement or Quote: "Common sense often makes good law" (Justice William O. Douglas).

Office: York County Government Center, 100 West Market Street, York 17401.

Telephone: (717) 771-9596.

Fax: (717) 771-2453

E-mail address: splinebaugh@york-county.org

LING, Thomas S. *(Judge, Pennsylvania Court of Common Pleas Fifty-seventh Judicial District)*

Office: 120 West John Street, Bedford 15522.

Telephone: (814) 623-4837.

LITTLE, Walter R. *(Judge, Pennsylvania Court of Common Pleas Fifth Judicial District)*

Office: 1700 Frick Building, 437 Grant Street, Pittsburgh 15219.

Telephone: (412) 350-5796.

LOBAUGH, Oliver J. *(Judge, Pennsylvania Court of Common Pleas Twenty-eighth Judicial District)*

Office: Venango County Courthouse, 1168 Liberty Street, Franklin 16323.

Telephone: (814) 432-9610.

LOKUTA, Ann H. *(Judge, Pennsylvania Court of Common Pleas Eleventh Judicial District)* Elected Nov 5, 1991 to term beginning Jan 2, 1992. Retained by election 2001, current term expires Jan 2012. First female judge in Luzerne County. Educated at King's College maxima cum laude 1975 and Hofstra University School of Law J.D. 1979. Pro Se Law Clerk to U.S. District Court Middle District of Pennsylvania 1980-82. Former Law Clerk to Hon. Arthur D. Dalessandro, Pennsylvania Court of Common Pleas Eleventh Judicial District. Member Delta Epsilon Sigma. Admitted to practice Pennsylvania 1979. Began legal practice Dupont 1983. Mental Health Hearing Officer Luzerne County 1983.

Solicitor Luzerne County Register of Wills 1985-87. Former Assistant District Attorney and Senior Trial Assistant Luzerne County. Former Assistant District Attorney Lackawanna County. Important Decisions: Fosko v. Board of Assessors Appeals of Luzerne County (constitutionality of taxing procedures in Pennsylvania) 646 A.2d 1275 and Lehigh Falls Fishing Club v. Andrejewski (Lehigh River navigable and therefore owned by the Commonwealth of Pennsylvania and held in trust for public use) 735 A.2d 718 aff'd. Lecturer on Constitutional Law King's College 1982. Instructor in Family Law and Criminal Law Luzerne County Community College 1993. Member Lackawanna County and Luzerne County (Former Member Executive Committee Young Lawyers' Division) Bar Associations. Former Board of Directors Penn's Wood Girl Scout Council and Women's Political Action Committee of Northeastern Pennsylvania. Former Board Member Taylor Long Term Nursing Center. Former Member Wilkes-Barre Quota Club, Slovak Cultural Society of Hazelton, General Pulaski Foundation and Wilkes-Barre Chapter American Business Women's Organization. Affiliate Polish Women's Alliance.

Office: Penn Place Building, 20 North Pennsylvania Avenue, Wilkes-Barre 18701.

Telephone: (570) 825-1613.

LONG, Gerard *(President Judge, Pennsylvania Court of Common Pleas Forty-seventh Judicial District)*
Office: Cambria County Courthouse, 200 South Center Street, Ebensburg 15931.
Telephone: (814) 472-1401.

LUCCHINO, Frank J. *(Judge, Pennsylvania Court of Common Pleas Fifth Judicial District)*
Office: 1700 Frick Building, 437 Grant Street, Pittsburgh 15219.
Telephone: (412) 350-4742.

LUDGATE, Linda K. Mowson *(Judge, Pennsylvania Court of Common Pleas Twenty-third Judicial District)* Elected to term beginning Jan 1, 1990. Retained by election Nov 1999, current term expires Jan 1, 2010. Born Rochester New York Aug 30, 1942. Protestant. Educated at Alvernia College B.A. magna cum laude 1977 and Temple University School of Law J.D. 1980. Member Phi Alpha Delta. Admitted to practice Pennsylvania 1980, U.S. District Court Eastern District of Pennsylvania 1980, U.S. Court of Appeals Third Circuit 1982 and U.S. Supreme Court 1984.

Conflict Counsel Central Pennsylvania Legal Services 1980-81. President and Founder Justice William Strong American Inn of Court. Member Pennsylvania Conference of State Trial Judges, National Association of Women Judges (National Board 1995), Berks County, Pennsylvania and American Bar Associations. Attended 1990-91 and Faculty Member 1993 and 1994 The National Judicial College. Chair "Meet Your Judges" forums National Conference of State Trial Judges. Recipient Ellen Frei Gruber Alumni Service Award from Alvernia College 1987, Berks County Trendsetter Award from YWCA 1990, The W. Richard Eshleman Award 1992, Beacon Award from Berks Women's Network 1992, Forrest Schaeffer Award from Berks County Prison Society 1997 and Altrusa Award 1999. Democrat. Former Member Board of Trustees Alvernia College. Founder Berks Women in Crisis, Berks Women's Network and Rape Crisis Center.
Office: Berks County Courthouse, Eighth Floor, 633 Court Street, Reading 19601.
Telephone: (610) 478-6448.

LUDWIG, Edmund V. *(Senior Judge, United States District Court Eastern District of Pennsylvania)* Appointed for life by President Ronald Reagan. Assumed Senior status May 20, 1997, serves by assignment. Born Philadelphia Pennsylvania May 20, 1928. Educated at Harvard University A.B. 1949 LL.B. 1952. Admitted to practice Pennsylvania 1953. In legal practice Philadelphia 1956-59 and Doylestown 1959-68. Former Judge, Pennsylvania Court of Common Pleas Seventh Judicial District, assumed office 1968.

Visiting Lecturer on Mental Health Law Villanova University School of Law 1984-97. Former Member Pennsylvania Conference of State Trial Judges (President 1981-82, Chairman Pennsylvania Chief Justice's Committee on Comprehensive Education 1984-85). Member Federal Judges Association (Executive Committee since 1998, Chair National Membership since 1998), Bucks County, Pennsylvania and American Bar Associations. Captain U.S. Army JAGC 1953-56. Republican. A principal drafter Pennsylvania Mental Health Procedures Act 143 of 1976. Member Juvenile Justice Alliance of Philadelphia (Co-chair since 1994) and Doylestown Historical Society (President since 1995).
Office: 12614 U.S. Courthouse, 601 Market Street, Philadelphia 19106-1775.
Telephone: (215) 580-2030.
E-mail address: chambers_of_judge_edmund_v._-udwig@paed.uscourts.gov

LUTTY, Paul F., Jr. *(Judge, Pennsylvania Court of Common Pleas Fifth Judicial District)*
Office: 814 City-County Building, 414 Grant Street, Pittsburgh 15219.
Telephone: (412) 350-5468.

LYNN, James Murray *(Judge, Pennsylvania Court of Common Pleas First Judicial District)*
Office: 27 South Twelfth Street, Suite 401, Philadelphia 19107.
Telephone: (215) 686-7330.

MacELREE, James Paul, II *(Judge, Pennsylvania Court of Common Pleas Fifteenth Judicial District)* Appointed by Governor Robert P. Casey Nov 1992. Elected Nov 1993, current term expires Jan 2004. Born Pennsylvania June 25, 1947. Episcopalian. Educated at West Chester University B.A 1970 and University of Maryland J.D. 1973. Admitted to practice Pennsylvania 1973 and U.S. Supreme Court 1983. In legal practice 1972-84.

First Assistant 1981-84 and District Attorney 1984-92 Chester County. Special Prosecutor Political Corruption 1975-76. Important Decisions: Curtis v. Klein 42 Chester Co. Rep. 147, 1994, Sunnegren v. Sunnegren 43 Chester Co. Rep. 189, 1995 and Reil v. Reil 43 Chester Co. Rep. 206, 1995. Instructor West Chester University and Delaware and Montgomery County Community College. Former Chairman Statewide Computer Committee and President 1989-90 Pennsylvania District Attorneys Association. Former Member Committees on Fee Dispute, Bench Bar and Lawyer Referral, Pennsylvania Commission on Crime and Delinquency, 1990 Prison Overcrowding Report Committee, National District Attorneys Association and Pennsylvania Trial Lawyers Association. Fellow American College of Prosecuting Attorneys. Appointed Member Judicial Conduct Board of Pennsylvania 1996-2000. Member Stively Inns of Court, Doris Jonas Freed Inns of Court (Family Court), Pennsylvania Association of Criminal Defense Lawyers, Pennsylvania Trial Judges Association, Chester County and Pennsylvania Bar Associations. Co-author Chester County Intermediate Punishment Organizational and Implementation Plan and Intermediate Punishment Plan. Instructor Pennsylvania Trial Lawyers Association, District Attorney Institute, Newly Elected Prosecutors Course and Basic Prosecutors Course Pennsylvania District Attorneys Association, Pennsylvania State Police Academy, Pennsylvania D.U.I. Association, Pennsylvania Chiefs of Police and Pennsylvania State Investigators Association. Recipient Governor's Certificate of Commendation from Municipal Police Officers Education and Training Commission, Award for Outstanding Assistance from Borough of West Chester, awards in Grand Jury, Crime Prevention and Senior Citizens from National Association of Counties and awards from Chamber of Commerce of West Chester, District Attorneys Police Education Council, Delaware County Community College, MADD Applauds Dynamic Deeds and County and State Detectives Association. Former Area Vice Chairman Committeeman. Region 3 Representative to Governor

MACELREE, JAMES PAUL, II—*Continued*

William Warren Scranton. Council Member Lenni Lenape District Chester County and Former Leader and District Vice Chairman Boy Scouts. Former Chester County Chairman March of Dimes. Former Vestry, Teacher and Committee Chairman Episcopal Church. Superintendent of Church School, Pastor Search Committee and May Fair Chairman Episcopal Church of the Advent. Enjoys fishing, hunting, boating, gardening and woodworking.

Mailing address: P.O. Box 2748, West Chester 19380.

Office: 203 Chester County Courthouse, 2 North High Street, West Chester 19380.

Telephone: (610) 344-6970.

MACHEN, Donald E. *(Judge, Pennsylvania Court of Common Pleas Fifth Judicial District)*

Office: 509 Allegheny County Courthouse, 436 Grant Street, Pittsburgh 15219.

Telephone: (412) 350-3250.

MADENSPACHER, Joseph C. *(Judge, Pennsylvania Court of Common Pleas Second Judicial District)*

Mailing address: P.O. Box 83480, Lancaster 17608-3480.

Office: Lancaster County Courthouse, 50 North Duke Street, Lancaster 17602.

Telephone: (717) 209-3131.

MAHON, William P. *(Judge, Pennsylvania Court of Common Pleas Fifteenth Judicial District)*

Mailing address: P.O. Box 2748, West Chester 19380.

Office: 302 Chester County Courthouse, 2 North High Street, West Chester 19380.

Telephone: (610) 344-4490.

MAIER, Eugene Edward J. *(Judge, Pennsylvania Court of Common Pleas First Judicial District)* Elected to term beginning Jan 4, 1982. Retained by election 1991 and 2001. Current term expires Jan 2012. Born Philadelphia Pennsylvania July 22, 1937. Roman Catholic. Educated at Temple University B.S. 1968 J.D. 1971. Recipient Constitutional Law Award 1969 and Constitutional History Award 1970 from Temple University. Admitted to practice Pennsylvania 1971, U.S. District Court District of Pennsylvania 1974 and U.S. Court of Appeals Third Circuit 1974. In legal practice Philadelphia 1971-81.

City Commissioner 1973-81 (Chairman 1980-81) Philadelphia. Author "The Presidential Franchise" 44 Temple Law Quarterly 595, 1971. Important Decisions: Trent v. Graduate Hospital, et al. CP#8208-6009 21 PHL 227, 1990 and Commonwealth v. Dennis Goeke CP#8512-3232-33. Lecturer on "Judicial Administration" Master in Public Administration Program Temple University Summer 1988 and 1989. Member Brehon Law Society (Board Member since 1980, President 1986-87), John Peter Zenger Law Society (Board Member since 1988, President since 1990), Philadelphia College of State Trial Judges (Corrections Committee 1983-91, Executive Board 1987-91, Zone Representative, Member Economics and Finance Committee), Philadelphia and Pennsylvania Bar Associations. Attended State Trial Judges Conferences annually since 1982 and Bench Bar Conferences annually since 1982. Recipient Judicial Excellence Award from Irish Society 1986 and various awards from fraternal groups. Previously employed as a sales representative, labor representative and in accounting. Member Temple Law Alumni Association (Board Member since 1990), Spring Garden Civic Association, West Frankford Civic Association, Knights of Columbus, Ancient Order of Hibernians, Men of Malvern and Alhambra.

Office: 390 City Hall, Philadelphia 19107.

Telephone: (215) 686-7551.

MANFREDI, William J. *(Judge, Pennsylvania Court of Common Pleas First Judicial District)* Assumed office 1983. Educated at University of Pennsylvania A.B. 1965 J.D. 1968.

Master American Inn of Court.

Office: 510 City Hall, Philadelphia 19107.

Telephone: (215) 686-4216.

MANNING, Jeffrey A. *(Judge, Pennsylvania Court of Common Pleas Fifth Judicial District)*

Office: 325 Allegheny County Courthouse, 436 Grant Street, Pittsburgh 15219.

Telephone: (412) 350-7387.

MANNION, Malachy E. *(Magistrate Judge, United States District Court Middle District of Pennsylvania)* Appointed by U.S. District Court judges to term beginning Jan 4, 2001. Educated at University of Scranton B.S. 1976 and Pace University School of Law J.D. 1979.

Office: 161 U.S. Courthouse, 197 South Main Street, Wilkes-Barre 18701.

Telephone: (570) 826-6229.

MARKOVITZ, Bernard *(Judge, United States Bankruptcy Court Western District of Pennsylvania)* Former Chief Judge.

Office: 5454 USX Tower, 600 Grant Street, Pittsburgh 15219.

Telephone: (412) 644-4533.

MARSILI, Anthony G. *(Judge, Pennsylvania Court of Common Pleas Tenth Judicial District)* Elected Nov 2, 1999 to term beginning Jan 3, 2000. Term expires Jan 3, 2010. Serves Family Court Division. Born Greensburg Pennsylvania Feb 12, 1951. Educated at Indiana University of Pennsylvania B.A. with honors 1973 and Duquesne University School of Law J.D. 1978. Admitted to practice Pennsylvania 1978 and U.S. Supreme Court 1988. In legal practice Greensburg 1978-99.

Assistant District Attorney Westmoreland County 1982-90. Part-time Instructor in Business Law Westmoreland Community College 1981-86. Member Westmoreland County Trial Academy, Westmoreland County and Pennsylvania Bar Associations. Attended Judicial Conference Summer Session July 2000. Panelist "Shared Physical Custody" Pennsylvania Bar Association Jan 2001. Past President Jeannette Rotary Club. Member Westmoreland County Chamber of Commerce and Recreation Commission of New Kensington. Enjoys golfing, jogging and coaching various little league teams.

Office: Westmoreland County Courthouse, Two North Main Street, Greensburg 15601.

Telephone: (724) 830-3489.

MARTIN, William J. *(President Judge, Pennsylvania Court of Common Pleas Fortieth Judicial District)*

Office: Indiana County Courthouse, Fourth Floor, 825 Philadelphia Street, Indiana 15701.

Telephone: (724) 465-3961.

MASSIAH-JACKSON, Frederica A. *(President Judge, Pennsylvania Court of Common Pleas First Judi-*

MASSIAH-JACKSON, FREDERICA A.—*Continued*
cial District) Elected to term beginning Jan 1984. Retained by election 1993, current term expires Jan 2004. Born Nov 10, 1950. Educated at Chestnut Hill College A.B. in Political Science 1971 and University of Pennsylvania Law School J.D. May 1974. Law Clerk to Hon. Robert N. C. Nix, Jr., Supreme Court of Pennsylvania 1974-76. Member Alpha Kappa Alpha. In legal practice Philadelphia 1976-83.
Office: 386 City Hall, Philadelphia 19107.
Telephone: (215) 686-2523.

MATTHEWS, Robert J. *(Judge, Pennsylvania Court of Common Pleas First Judicial District)* Appointed by Governor Tom Ridge to term beginning Dec 1, 1998. Elected Nov 4, 1999, current term expires Jan 3, 2010. Born Philadelphia Pennsylvania May 20, 1937. Roman Catholic. Educated at La Salle University B.S. and Temple University Law School J.D. 1971. Member Phi Alpha Delta. Admitted to practice Pennsylvania 1971, U.S. District Court Eastern District of Pennsylvania 1981, U.S. Courts of Appeals Third 1971 and Federal 1986 Circuits and U.S. Supreme Court 1995. In legal practice Philadelphia and Southampton 1971-98.
Law Clerk to Pennsylvania Court of Common Pleas First Judicial District 1974-98. Member Pennsylvania State Conference of Trial Judges, National Conference of Juvenile and Family Court Judges, Philadelphia, Bucks County, Pennsylvania and American Bar Associations. Attended numerous CLE courses Pennsylvania State Conference of Trial Judges and General Jurisdiction Course The National Judicial College April 2000. First Lieutenant U.S. Army. Assistant to Vice President of Administration McNeil Laboratories Inc. 1972-74. Interests include golf, swimming, reading and grandchildren.
Office: 34 South Eleventh Street, Room 203, Philadelphia 19107.
Telephone: (215) 686-7346.
E-mail address: rym@ccpjuvenile@1_jud_dist_pa

MAZUR, Lee J. *(Judge, Pennsylvania Court of Common Pleas Fifth Judicial District)* Appointed by Governor Robert P. Casey to term beginning May 1987. Elected Nov 1989. Retained by election Nov 1999, current term expires Jan 2010. Born Pittsburgh Pennsylvania Nov 21, 1939. Educated at St. Vincent College 1961 and West Virginia University College of Law J.D. 1964. Law Clerk to Judge Zavarella and Judge Rosenberg 1963-64. Admitted to practice Pennsylvania 1964.
Member Allegheny County and Pennsylvania Bar Associations. USAR 1964-70.
Office: 1700 Frick Building, 437 Grant Street, Pittsburgh 15219.
Telephone: (412) 350-5646.

MAZZOLA, William J. *(Judge, Pennsylvania Court of Common Pleas First Judicial District)* Elected Nov 3, 1981 to term beginning Jan 2, 1982. Retained by election Nov 1991 and Nov 2001. Current term expires Dec 2011. Born Philadelphia Pennsylvania Jan 8, 1945. Roman Catholic. Educated at St. Joseph's University B.S. 1966, Villanova University M.A. 1967 and University of Baltimore J.D. 1970. Admitted to practice Maryland 1970 and Pennsylvania 1973. In legal practice Baltimore Maryland 1970-73 and Philadelphia Pennsylvania 1973-82.
Assistant District Attorney Philadelphia County 1973-74. Important Decisions: Commonwealth v. Ball (arson insurance investigation) 1984, Commonwealth v. Santiago (prosecutorial misconduct) 1992, Commonwealth v. Foster (freedom of religion) 1998 and Commonwealth v. Ira Einhorn (trial in absentia, other crimes evidence) 2002. Instructor in Criminal Law Holy Family University 2002. Member Justinian Law Society, Pennsylvania Conference of State Trial Judges, American Judges Association, Philadelphia and Pennsylvania Bar Associations. Recipient Chapel of Four Chaplins from Legion of Honor 1981, Philadelphia Trial Judges Recognition Award 1982, Justinian Law Society Recognition Award 1982, Southeast Pennsylvania Heart Association Award 1983, UNICO National Appreciation Award and Italian Press Award. USAR 1969-75. New Jersey National Guard. Governor's Advisory Board Woodhaven Center for Mental Health 1977-84. Board of Managers NE YMCA. Member Parents Advisory Board Nazareth Academy, St. Joseph's Law Alumni, Commission on Social Justice Order Sons of Italy, UNICO (Past President Greater Philadelphia Chapter). Enjoys electronics, golf, music and gardening.
Office: 1301 Filbert Street, Suite 1412, Philadelphia 19107.
Telephone: (215) 683-7133.
Fax: (215) 683-7135
E-mail address: william.mazzola@courts.phila.gov

MAZZONI, Robert A. *(Judge, Pennsylvania Court of Common Pleas Forty-fifth Judicial District)*
Office: Lackawanna County Courthouse, 200 North Washington Avenue, Scranton 18503.
Telephone: (570) 963-6512.

McANDREWS, R. Barry *(President Judge, Pennsylvania Court of Common Pleas Seventh Judicial District)*
Office: Bucks County Courthouse, 55 East Court Street, Doylestown 18901.
Telephone: (215) 348-6872.

McBRIDE, John D. *(Judge, Pennsylvania Court of Common Pleas Thirty-sixth Judicial District)*
Office: Beaver County Courthouse, Third Street, Beaver 15009.
Telephone: (724) 728-5700.

McCLURE, James F., Jr. *(Senior Judge, United States District Court Middle District of Pennsylvania)* Appointed for life by President George Bush to term beginning May 7, 1990. Assumed Senior status April 7, 2001, serves by assignment. Born Danville Pennsylvania April 6, 1931. Presbyterian. Educated at Amherst College A.B. magna cum laude 1952 and University of Pennsylvania Law School J.D. cum laude 1957. Editorial Board University of Pennsylvania Law Review 1956-57. Member Phi Beta Kappa and Order of the Coif. Admitted to practice District of Columbia 1957 and Pennsylvania 1958. Began legal practice Washington D.C. 1957. In legal practice Philadelphia, New York City and Lewisburg 1958-84. President Judge, Pennsylvania Court of Common Pleas Seventeenth Judicial District May 14, 1984 to May 7, 1990, appointed by Governor Richard Thornburgh.
District Attorney Union County Jan 1974 to Sept 1975. Member 1967-74 and President 1968-74 Lewisburg Area School Board. Former member Pennsylvania Appellate Court Nominating Commission and Pennsylvania Supreme Court Advisory Committee on Appellate Court Rules. Member Union County and Pennsylvania

MCCLURE, JAMES F., JR.—*Continued*

(Former member House of Delegates, Board of Governors, Long Range Planning Committee and Committee to Study the Disciplinary Board of Supreme Court of Pennsylvania) Bar Associations. Former Lecturer Pennsylvania Bar Institute. Corporal U.S. Army 1952-54. Former Chairman Lewisburg Planning Commission. Member First Presbyterian Church of Lewisburg and Susquehanna Valley Chorale.

Office: 240 West Third Street, Williamsport 17701-6466.

Telephone: (570) 323-9772.

McCORMICK, Richard E., Jr. *(Judge, Pennsylvania Court of Common Pleas Tenth Judicial District)* Appointed by Governor Robert P. Casey to term beginning June 21, 1990. Elected 1991. Retained by election 2001, current term expires Jan 2012. Born Greensburg Pennsylvania Aug 10, 1950. Roman Catholic. Educated at Duquesne University B.S. 1972 J.D. cum laude 1980. Admitted to practice Pennsylvania 1980 and U.S. District Court Western District of Pennsylvania 1980. In legal practice Greensburg 1980-90.

Chief Trial Counsel and Public Defender Westmoreland County 1985-90. City Solicitor Greensburg 1987-90. Important Decisions: CRY, Inc. v. Mill Service, Inc. 1991 and Commonwealth v. CSX Transportation, Inc. 1992. Member Pennsylvania Conference of State Trial Judges (Zone Representative Executive Committee since 1992), Westmoreland and Pennsylvania Bar Associations. Attended annual and mid-annual seminars Pennsylvania Conference of State Trial Judges 1990-92. Legislative Assistant to U.S. Representative John H. Dent 1974-75. Democrat. Chairman Greensburg Democratic Committee 1986-90.

Office: Westmoreland County Courthouse, Two North Main Street, Greensburg 15601.

Telephone: (724) 830-3492.

McCULLOUGH, M. Bruce *(Judge, United States Bankruptcy Court Western District of Pennsylvania)* Appointed by U.S. Court of Appeals Third Circuit judges.

Office: 5464 USX Tower, 600 Grant Street, Pittsburgh 15219.

Telephone: (412) 644-4329.

McDANIEL, Donna Jo *(Judge, Pennsylvania Court of Common Pleas Fifth Judicial District)*

Office: 323 Allegheny County Courthouse, 436 Grant Street, Pittsburgh 15219.

Telephone: (412) 350-5434.

McFADDEN, F. P. Kimberly *(Judge, Pennsylvania Court of Common Pleas Third Judicial District)*

Office: 100 North Third Street, Suite 400, Easton 18042.

Telephone: (610) 253-8863.

McGINLEY, Bernard L. *(Judge, The Commonwealth Court of Pennsylvania)* Elected to term beginning Jan 1988. Retained by election 1997, current term expires Jan 2008. Born Pittsburgh Pennsylvania Jan 7, 1946. Educated at John Carroll University B.S. 1967, Loyola University of Rome 1965-66 and University of Pittsburgh J.D. 1970. Law Clerk to Hon. Robert A. Doyle, Pennsylvania Court of Common Pleas Fifth Judicial District 1974-77. Admitted to practice Pennsylvania 1970. Began legal practice Pittsburgh. Judge, Pennsylvania Court of Common Pleas Fifth Judicial District 1982-87. Assistant District Attorney 1971-74. Chairman Board of Viewers Pennsylvania Court of Common Pleas Fifth Judicial District 1977-81. Professor of Criminal Law Allegheny County Community College 1974-75. Member Allegheny County Bar Association. Captain USAR Medical Service Corps 1970-77.

Office: 104 Ellsworth Center, 5840 Ellsworth Avenue, Pittsburgh 15232.

Telephone: (412) 665-5503.

McGINLEY, Carol K. *(Judge, Pennsylvania Court of Common Pleas Thirty-first Judicial District)*

Office: Lehigh County Courthouse, 455 West Hamilton Street, Allentown 18101.

Telephone: (610) 782-3120.

McINERNEY, Patricia A. *(Judge, Pennsylvania Court of Common Pleas First Judicial District)*

Office: 1214 Criminal Justice Center, 1301 Filbert Street, Philadelphia 19107.

Telephone: (215) 683-7059.

McKEOWN, Margaret T. Murphy *(Judge, Pennsylvania Court of Common Pleas First Judicial District)*

Office: 27 South Twelfth Street, Suite 402, Philadelphia 19107.

Telephone: (215) 686-7918.

McLAUGHLIN, Mary A. *(Judge, United States District Court Eastern District of Pennsylvania)* Appointed for life by President Bill Clinton to term beginning June 23, 2000. Born Philadelphia Pennsylvania Nov 18, 1946. Educated at Gwynedd-Mercy College B.A. 1968, Bryn Mawr College M.A. 1969 and University of Pennsylvania Law School J.D. 1976. Law Clerk to Hon. Stanley S. Brotman, U.S. District Court District of New Jersey 1976-77. In legal practice 1977-80 and Philadelphia 1986-2000.

Assistant U.S. Attorney District of Columbia 1980-84. Chief Counsel Subcommittee on Terrorism, Technology and Government Committee on the Judiciary U.S. Senate 1995.

Office: 3809 U.S. Courthouse, 601 Market Street, Philadelphia 19106-1748.

Telephone: (215) 299-7704.

McLAUGHLIN, Sean J. *(Judge, United States District Court Western District of Pennsylvania)* Appointed for life by President Bill Clinton to term beginning 1994. Born Erie Pennsylvania Jan 4, 1955. Educated at Georgetown University A.B. 1977 J.D. 1980. Law Clerk to Hon. William Knox 1980, Hon. Gerald J. Weber 1980-81 and Hon. Maurice B. Cohill, Jr. 1981, U.S. District Court Western District of Pennsylvania. In legal practice Erie 1981-94.

Office: 240 U.S. Post Office & Courthouse, 617 State Street, Erie 16501.

Telephone: (814) 453-5759.

McVERRY, Terrence F. *(Judge, United States District Court Western District of Pennsylvania)* Appointed for life by President George W. Bush.

Office: 1008 U.S. Courthouse, Tenth Floor, Seventh Avenue and Grant Street, Pittsburgh 15219.

Telephone: (412) 208-7495.

MEANS, Rayford A. *(Judge, Pennsylvania Court of Common Pleas First Judicial District)*
Office: 1204 Criminal Justice Center, 1301 Filbert Street, Philadelphia 19107.
Telephone: (215) 683-7029.

MELINSON, James R. *(Magistrate Judge, United States District Court Eastern District of Pennsylvania)* Appointed by U.S. District Court judges 1990. Chief Magistrate Judge since 1997. Born Philadelphia Pennsylvania Sept 6, 1939. Roman Catholic. Educated at La Salle University B.A. with honors 1961 and Temple University J.D. 1968 M.Ed. 1973. Recipient Temple University School of Law Full Academic Scholarship. Chief Justice Moot Court. Admitted to practice Pennsylvania 1968 and U.S. Supreme Court 1975. In legal practice Philadelphia 1968-88. Former Judge, The Superior Court of Pennsylvania, appointed by Governor Robert P. Casey to term beginning Feb 1988.
Chief Negotiator School District of Philadelphia 1976-85. General Counsel International Association of Machinist and Aerospace Workers Local Lodge No. 159, 1980-88 and Whiting-Patterson Co., Inc. 1981-88. Consultant and Special Advisor for Labor Relations U.S. Department of Defense 1982-85. Important Decisions: Commonwealth of Pennsylvania v. Anderson (rights of retarded witness) 1988, Commonwealth of Pennsylvania v. Hill (drunk driving penalty) 1988 and Stenger v. The Morning Call (protecting litigant's privacy) 1989. Member Advisory Group since 1990 and Sub-chairman Committee of Judges since 1992 Civil Justice Reform Act U.S. District Court Eastern District of Pennsylvania. Member since 1997 and Member Statistics Subcommittee since 1999 Judicial Resources Committee Judicial Conference of the U.S. Former Member Society of Professionals in Dispute Resolution, Large City Negotiators Conference, Pennsylvania Conference of State Trial Judges, Appellate Judges Conference, American Judges Association, National Association of Educational Negotiators and American Arbitration Association. Charter Member Brehon Law Society (Past President). Member St. Thomas More Society, Judicial Council of the Third Circuit, Justinian Society, Federal Magistrate Judges Association, Philadelphia, Pennsylvania (Civil Litigation, Family Law, Real Property and Probate Sections), Federal and American (Chair Committee on Magistrate Judges 1995-96, Co-chair Committee on Membership 1995-96 Judicial Administration Division) Bar Associations. Attended "The Trial" course The National Judicial College April 1988.
Recipient Public Service Award from Pennsylvania School Boards Association 1979, Outstanding Service Award from School District of Philadelphia 1982, Distinguished Public Service Award from Emerald Education Committee 1984, President's Award from Philadelphia Association of School Administrators 1985, La Salle University Law Alumni Award 1988, Law Alumni/ae Certificate of Honor from Temple University 1988, Southeastern Pennsylvania Police Chief's Association Award 1994, Philadelphia Regional Veterans Award 1995 and Distinguished Jurist Award from John Peter Zenger Society 1999. Named Man of the Year by Emerald Society 1989. First Lieutenant U.S. Army artillery small unit commander 1961-63. Previously worked as Vice Principal and English instructor Olney High School and general worker Pennsylvania Fruit Company. Former Member Counseling or Referral Assistance, Inc. (CORA), Fellowship Commission, Order of the Sons of Italy of America and Police Athletic League. Board of Directors Catholic Social Services. Member Irish Society of Philadelphia, Emerald Education Committee, St. La Salle Club, La Salle University Alumni Association, La Salle University Education Alumni Association, La Salle University Law Alumni Association (President's Club 1980-88), Temple University Law Alumni Association, Knights of Columbus, Historical Society of the U.S. District Court Eastern District of Pennsylvania, Friendly Sons of St. Patrick, American Legion and National Osteoporosis Foundation.
Office: 3000 U.S. Courthouse, 601 Market Street, Philadelphia 19106-1714.
Telephone: (215) 597-5316.

MELLON, Robert J. *(Judge, Pennsylvania Court of Common Pleas Seventh Judicial District)*
Office: Bucks County Courthouse, 55 East Court Street, Doylestown 18901.
Telephone: (215) 348-6074.

MILLER, Charles M. *(Judge, Pennsylvania Court of Common Pleas Twenty-first Judicial District)*
Office: Schuylkill County Courthouse, 401 North Second Street, Pottsville 17901.
Telephone: (570) 628-1390.

MILLER, Gordon R. *(President Judge, Pennsylvania Court of Common Pleas Thirtieth Judicial District)* Elected Nov 1989 to term beginning Jan 1, 1990. Retained by election 1999, current term expires Jan 2010. Born Meadville Pennsylvania Jan 4, 1941. Episcopalian. Educated at Allegheny College B.A. 1962 and Case Western Reserve University J.D. 1966. Admitted to practice Pennsylvania 1966, Ohio 1966 and U.S. District Court Western District of Pennsylvania 1979. In legal practice Meadville Pennsylvania 1966-89.
Member American Judicature Society, Crawford County (Secretary 1969-72, Vice President 1981-82, President 1983-84), Pennsylvania and American Bar Associations. Attended General Jurisdiction Course The National Judicial College 1990. Member 1980-92 and President 1988-89 Board of Directors Meadville Public Library. Member since 1980 and President 1991-93 Board of Directors Meadville Medical Center. Trustee Allegheny College 1987-91.
Office: Crawford County Courthouse, 903 Diamond Park, Meadville 16335.
Telephone: (814) 333-7497.

MILLER, Linda Wallach *(Judge, Pennsylvania Court of Common Pleas Forty-third Judicial District)*
Office: Monroe County Courthouse, Stroudsburg 18360.
Telephone: (570) 420-3600.

MILLIN, Paul H. *(President Judge, Pennsylvania Court of Common Pleas Thirty-seventh Judicial District)* Appointed by Governor Robert P. Casey Nov 1994. Elected 1995, current term expires Dec 31, 2005. Born Warren Pennsylvania 1944. Methodist. Educated at Maryville College B.A. 1966 and University of Tennessee J.D. 1969. Admitted to practice Pennsylvania 1969. In legal practice Tionesta 1971-94.
District Attorney 1970-90. Member Pennsylvania Juvenile and Family Court Judges Association, National Council of Juvenile and Family Court Judges, American Judicature Society and American Judges Association. Attended Pennsylvania State Trial Judges Conferences

MILLIN, PAUL H.—*Continued*

1995, 1996 and 1997 and General Jurisdiction Course The National Judicial College 1997. Recipient Governor's Highway Traffic Safety Award 1997. U.S. Army 1969-71.

Office: Warren County Courthouse, 204 Fourth Avenue, Warren 16365.

Telephone: (814) 728-3530.

MILLIRON, Daniel J. *(Judge, Pennsylvania Court of Common Pleas Twenty-fourth Judicial District)*

Office: Blair County Courthouse, 423 Allegheny Street, Hollidaysburg 16648.

Telephone: (814) 693-3065.

MINORA, Carmen D. *(Judge, Pennsylvania Court of Common Pleas Forty-fifth Judicial District)*

Office: Lackawanna County Courthouse, 200 North Washington Avenue, Scranton 18503.

Telephone: (570) 963-6345.

MITCHELL, Robert C. *(Magistrate Judge, United States District Court Western District of Pennsylvania)* Appointed by U.S. District Court judges to term beginning Feb 17, 1972. Reappointed 1980, 1988 and 1996. Current term expires 2004. Born New York New York Aug 4, 1940. Educated at Dartmouth College A.B. 1962 and University of Pittsburgh M.B.A. 1964 J.D. 1967. Law Clerk to Hon. Louis Rosenberg, U.S. District Court Western District of Pennsylvania 1968-72. Admitted to practice Pennsylvania 1968, U.S. District Court Western District of Pennsylvania 1968, U.S. Supreme Court 1971 and U.S. Court of Appeals Third Circuit 1975.

Member American Judicature Society, National Council of United States Magistrates, Allegheny County and American Bar Associations.

Office: 524 U.S. Post Office & Courthouse, 700 Grant Street, Pittsburgh 15219.

Telephone: (412) 208-7470.

MOORE, Bernard A. *(Judge, Pennsylvania Court of Common Pleas Thirty-eighth Judicial District)* Appointed by Governor Robert P. Casey to term beginning July 17, 1989. Elected Nov 7, 1989 and Nov 2, 1999. Current term expires Jan 2010. Born Bryn Mawr Pennsylvania Nov 22, 1945. Educated at Temple University B.S. 1967 J.D. 1970. Admitted to practice Pennsylvania 1970.

Mailing address: P.O. Box 311, Norristown 19404.

Office: Montgomery County Courthouse, Norristown 19404.

Telephone: (610) 278-3188.

MORAN, William F. *(Judge, Pennsylvania Court of Common Pleas Third Judicial District)*

Office: 252 Spring Garden Street, Suite 2, Easton 18042.

Telephone: (610) 253-0700.

MORGAN, William F. *(Judge, Pennsylvania Court of Common Pleas Thirty-seventh Judicial District)*

Office: Warren County Courthouse, 204 Fourth Avenue, Warren 16365.

Telephone: (814) 728-3530.

MOSS, Sandra Mazer *(Judge, Pennsylvania Court of Common Pleas First Judicial District)* Elected to term beginning Jan 2, 1984. Retained by election 1993, current term expires Jan 2004. Born Vineland New Jersey Oct 10, 1942. Jewish. Educated at Temple University B.S. with honors 1964 J.D. 1975. Law Clerk to Hon. Eugene Gelfand, Pennsylvania Court of Common Pleas First Judicial District 1975-78. Admitted to practice Pennsylvania 1975. Began legal practice Philadelphia 1975.

Senior Deputy Administrator Arbitration Panels for Health Care 1978-80. Deputy City Solicitor Philadelphia 1980-83. Guest Lecturer Temple University School of Law since 1982. Member Philadelphia Bar Association (Civil/Judicial Procedures Committee 1978-84, Medico-Legal Committee 1978-84, Chair Women's Rights Committee 1981-83, Vice Chair Bylaws Committee 1982-83, Board of Governors 1983, Criminal Justice Section since 1984). Listed in *Philadelphia Magazine* as one of Outstanding Women Lawyers. Named one of Outstanding Professional Women by WIP (radio station). Assistant Director of Public Relations Alexander's Department Stores 1964-66 and Loehmann's Department Stores 1964-66 and copywriter for N. W. Ayer 1966-68. Member Democratic Women of Philadelphia. President Philadelphia Women's Political Caucus 1978-80. Legal Counsel Fifth Ward Democratic Executive Committee 1978-80. Board Member and Secretary Temple Law Alumni 1978-84. Cub Scout Leader 1980-82. Chair District Attorney's Domestic Violence Advisory Board. Enjoys bridge, theatre, art collecting, going to galleries and reading.

Office: 392 City Hall, Philadelphia 19107.

Telephone: (215) 686-7910.

MOTT, John C. *(Judge, Pennsylvania Court of Common Pleas Forty-second Judicial District)* Elected to term beginning Jan 4, 1988. Reelected 1997, current term expires Jan 2008. Born Canton (LeRoy Township) Pennsylvania May 23, 1955. Religious affiliation: Christian Church (Disciples). Educated at Mansfield University B.A. with high honors 1977 and Dickinson School of Law J.D. 1980. Law Clerk to Hon. Robert M. Kemp, Pennsylvania Court of Common Pleas Fourth Judicial District 1976 and Hon. Harold E. Sheely, Pennsylvania Court of Common Pleas Ninth Judicial District 1978-80. Admitted to practice Pennsylvania 1980, U.S. District Court Middle District of Pennsylvania 1983 and New York 1987. In legal practice Troy and Canton 1980-87.

Adjunct Professor of Criminal Justice Administration Mansfield University. Former member Pennsylvania Trial Lawyers Association and The Association of Trial Lawyers of America. Member Pennsylvania Conference of State Trial Judges, Bradford County (Former Secretary-Treasurer) and Pennsylvania Bar Associations. Attended General Jurisdiction Course The National Judicial College 1988. Attended mid-annual meeting and/or annual meeting Pennsylvania Conference of State Trial Judges since 1988. Listed in *Who's Who in American Law* and *Who's Who in Society*. Republican. Member 1982-87 and Chairman 1984-85 Bradford County Republican Committee. Former member Board of Directors Troy Community Hospital, Inc. and NyPenn Health Systems Agency, Inc. Deacon 1983-89 and Elder 1989-97 and since 1999 Canton Church of Christ (Disciples). Board of Directors Mansfield Foundation, Inc. Member Canton Lions Club (Past President), Loyal Order of Moose, Elks, Masons, Wheel Inn, Inc. and Hamilton Club. Enjoys athletics, current affairs and outdoor activities. Personal Statement or Quote: "Blessed are the

MOTT, JOHN C.—*Continued*
peacemakers: For they shall be called the children of God" (Matthew 5:9).
Office: Bradford County Courthouse, 301 Main Street, Towanda 18848.
Telephone: (570) 265-1709.

MOTTO, Dominick *(Judge, Pennsylvania Court of Common Pleas Fifty-third Judicial District)*
Office: Lawrence County Government Center, 430 Court Street, New Castle 16101.
Telephone: (724) 656-1925.

MUIR, Malcolm *(Senior Judge, United States District Court Middle District of Pennsylvania)* Appointed for life by President Richard M. Nixon to term beginning Nov 6, 1970. Assumed Senior status Aug 31, 1984. Born Englewood New Jersey Oct 20, 1914. Educated at Lehigh University A.B. magna cum laude 1935 and Harvard University LL.B. 1938. Admitted to practice Pennsylvania 1938. Began legal practice Williamsport 1938.
Member Pennsylvania (Treasurer 1965-69, President Elect 1970) and American Bar Associations. Lieutenant USNR 1942-45.
Office: 240 West Third Street, Suite 401, Williamsport 17701-6461.
Telephone: (570) 322-0287.

MULLIGAN, Kathleen R. *(Judge, Pennsylvania Court of Common Pleas Fifth Judicial District)* Currently serves Family Division.
Office: 440 Ross Street, Room 5045, Pittsburgh 15219.
Telephone: (412) 350-4146.

MUNDY, Hugh F. *(Judge, Pennsylvania Court of Common Pleas Eleventh Judicial District)*
Office: Luzerne County Courthouse, 200 North River Street, Wilkes-Barre 18711.
Telephone: (570) 825-1541.

MUNLEY, James M. *(Judge, United States District Court Middle District of Pennsylvania)* Appointed for life by President Bill Clinton to term beginning Oct 26, 1998. Born Scranton Pennsylvania June 28, 1936. Roman Catholic. Educated at University of Scranton B.S. 1958 and Temple University LL.B. 1963. Law Clerk to Chief Justice Michael J. Eagen, The Supreme Court of Pennsylvania 1963-64. Admitted to practice Pennsylvania 1964. In legal practice Scranton 1964-78. Hearing Examiner, Pennsylvania Department of Revenue 1973. Judge, Pennsylvania Court of Common Pleas Forty-fifth Judicial District Jan 2, 1978 to Oct 25, 1998.
Solicitor Carbondale Township. Former Solicitor Mayfield School District and Boroughs of Mayfield, Jermyn and Archbald. Author "A Right to Die: A Judicial Perspective" and "The Anthracite Coal Strike Commission of 1902" *The Barrister* and "Determining When Recusal Is Necessary" Pennsylvania L. Jour. Member since July 1986 and Chairman of the Board since Jan 1989 Judicial Inquiry and Review Board. Member Pennsylvania Board of Law Examiners, Pennsylvania Trial Lawyers Association, Lackawanna County, Pennsylvania and American Bar Associations. Recipient Frank J. O'Hara Award for Distinguished Achievement in the Law from University of Scranton, Community Leadership Award from Women's Resource Center of Scranton, Silver Beaver Award from Boy Scouts of America, Distinguished Service Award from The American Legion, Award in Recognition of Distinguished Service from Judicial Inquiry and Review Board and award in recognition of devoted and invaluable services from Bethel A.M.E. Church. U.S. Army 1958-60. Delegate to 1976 Democratic National Convention. Former Director First National Bank of Peckville. Former President Friendly Sons of St. Patrick. Member University of Scranton President's Club, Temple Alumni Association, VFW Post 7963, Knights of Columbus Council 2644 (4°) and Forest Lakes Council Boy Scouts of America. Former Mid-Valley Coordinator Lackawanna United Fund. Former Member Board of Directors St. Joseph's Hospital School of Nursing and Country Club of Scranton. Enjoys golfing, skiing and swimming.
Mailing address: P.O. Box 1247, Scranton 18501-1247.
Telephone: (570) 207-5780.

MUROSKI, Chester B. *(Judge, Pennsylvania Court of Common Pleas Eleventh Judicial District)*
Office: Luzerne County Courthouse, Annex II, 113 West North River Street, Wilkes-Barre 18711.
Telephone: (570) 822-0764.

MUSMANNO, John L. *(Judge, The Superior Court of Pennsylvania)* Born McKees Rocks Pennsylvania March 31, 1942. Educated at Washington & Jefferson College B.A. magna cum laude 1963 and Vanderbilt University J.D. 1966. Assistant Editor Vanderbilt Law Review 1965-66. Member Phi Beta Kappa. Admitted to practice Pennsylvania 1966 and U.S. Court of Appeals Third Circuit. Former Judge and Administrative Judge Civil Division, Pennsylvania Court of Common Pleas Fifth Judicial District, elected to term beginning Jan 1, 1982.
Member Pennsylvania Conference of State Trial Judges and Allegheny County Bar Association.
Office: 3150 One Oxford Centre, 301 Grant Street, Pittsburgh 15219.
Telephone: (412) 880-5800.

NALITZ, William R. *(Judge, Pennsylvania Court of Common Pleas Thirteenth Judicial District)* Elected to term beginning Jan 1998. Term expires Jan 2008. Born Pittsburgh Pennsylvania 1944. Roman Catholic. Educated at Georgetown University B.A. 1966 and Duquesne University J.D. 1973. Admitted to practice Pennsylvania 1973. In legal practice Waynesburg 1973-97.
County Solicitor Greene County 1992-96. Member Pennsylvania Conference of State Trial Judges, Greene County, Pennsylvania and American Bar Associations. First Lieutenant U.S. Army 1966-68 (Vietnam 1967-68).
Office: Greene County Courthouse, Waynesburg 15370.
Telephone: (724) 852-5312.
Fax: (724) 627-4716

NANOVIC, Roger N. *(Judge, Pennsylvania Court of Common Pleas Fifty-sixth Judicial District)*
Mailing address: P.O. Box 131, Jim Thorpe 18229.
Office: Carbon County Courthouse, Jim Thorpe 18229.
Telephone: (570) 325-3661.

NAUHAUS, Lester G. *(Judge, Pennsylvania Court of Common Pleas Fifth Judicial District)* Appointed by Governor Robert P. Casey to term beginning Nov 1994. Elected Nov 1997, current term expires Jan 5, 2008. Serves Criminal Division. Born Pittsburgh Pennsylvania

NAUHAUS, LESTER G.—*Continued*
July 16, 1943. Educated at University of Colorado B.A. 1965 and Duquesne University J.D. 1968. Admitted to practice Pennsylvania 1968, U.S. District Court Western District of Pennsylvania 1968, U.S. Court of Appeals Third Circuit and U.S. Supreme Court. In legal practice Pittsburgh 1968-94.

Public Defender Allegheny County 1978-94. Case Note Editor *Plain View* Pennsylvania Criminal Defense Lawyers. Associate Professor of Criminal Law Duquesne University since 1990. Visiting Lecturer University of Pittsburgh. Counselor Pittsburgh Chapter American Inns of Court. Member Allegheny County (Criminal Litigation Section) and American (Task Force Committee on Criminal Justice Standards) Bar Associations. Lecturer Criminal Law Symposium Pennsylvania Bar Institute and Search and Seizure Conference Pennsylvania Criminal Defense Lawyers. Recipient Liberty Award from Pennsylvania Criminal Defense Lawyers and Gideon Award from Public Defenders Association of Pennsylvania. Interested in computer science and woodworking.

Office: 326 Allegheny County Courthouse, 436 Grant Street, Pittsburgh 15219.

Telephone: (412) 350-5446.

Fax: (412) 350-5733

E-mail address: Nauhaus@Court.Allegheny.PA.US

NAUS, Scott W. *(President Judge, Pennsylvania Court of Common Pleas Twenty-sixth Judicial District)*

Mailing address: P.O. Box 380, Bloomsburg 17815.

Office: Columbia County Courthouse, Bloomsburg 17815.

Telephone: (570) 389-5663.

NEALON, Terrence R. *(Judge, Pennsylvania Court of Common Pleas Forty-fifth Judicial District)* Appointed by Governor Tom Ridge to term beginning June 29, 1998. Elected Nov 1999, current term expires Jan 2010. Born Scranton Pennsylvania April 15, 1959. Roman Catholic. Educated at University of Scranton B.S. 1981 and Dickinson School of Law J.D. 1984. National Champion Student Trial Advocacy Competition The Association of Trial Lawyers of America 1984. Member Order of Barristers. Admitted to practice Pennsylvania 1984, U.S. District Courts Middle 1984 and Eastern 1985 District of Pennsylvania, U.S. Court of Appeals Third Circuit 1985 and U.S. Supreme Court 1988.

Author "Bad Faith Liability and Delay Damages" Feb 1990 and "Discovery Issues in Products Liability Litigation" April 1991 Trial Advocacy Foundation of Pennsylvania; "Direct Examination of a Treating Physician" *My First Trial* Dec 1992 and "Peer Review Under the Motor Vehicle Financial Responsibility Law" *Fundamentals of Pennsylvania Automobile Insurance Law* Dec 1993 Pennsylvania Trial Lawyers Association; "Pa. R.C.P. 4003.6: The Death Knell to All Ex-Parte Contact Between the Defense and Treating Health Care Providers?" XXV Nos. 2-3 *The Barrister* Fall 1994; and "Juror Note-Taking in Civil Trials: An Idea Whose Time Has Come" 5 No. 2 *Civil Litigation Newsletter* Pennsylvania Bar Association Spring 2002. Contributing Author *Handbook for Pennsylvania Trial Judges: Management of Civil Jury Trials* Pennsylvania Conference of State Trial Judges 1st ed. 2000. Certified Specialist in Civil Trial Practice by National Board of Trial Advocacy since 1997. Former Member Pennsylvania Trial Lawyers Association (Board of Governors 1987-98, Assistant Treasurer 1992-93, Assistant Secretary 1993-94, Parliamentarian 1994-95, Treasurer 1995-96, Secretary 1996-97, Vice President 1997-98, President Elect 1998) and The Association of Trial Lawyers of America. Member Northeastern Pennsylvania Trial Lawyers Association (Board of Governors 1990-98, President 1992-93), Pennsylvania Conference of State Trial Judges (Education Committee since 1999), Lackawanna (Co-chair Bench-Bar Conference since 1988), Pennsylvania (Civil Litigation Council since 1996), Federal and American Bar Associations. Recipient President's Award from Lackawanna Bar Association 1995 and Pennsylvania Trial Lawyers Association 1999. Member 1994-98 and President 1995-96 Board of Directors Scranton Tomorrow. Member since 1998, Secretary 2000-02, Vice Chair since 2002 Board of Directors Northeast Regional Cancer Institute. Board of Trustees Mercy Health Partners since 2002.

Office: Lackawanna County Courthouse, 200 North Washington Avenue, Scranton 18503.

Telephone: (570) 963-6889.

Fax: (570) 496-7796

E-mail address: TRNealon@AOL.com

NEALON, William J., Jr. *(Senior Judge, United States District Court Middle District of Pennsylvania)* Appointed for life by President John F. Kennedy to term beginning Dec 15, 1962. Former Chief Judge. Assumed Senior status Jan 1, 1989, serves by assignment. Born Scranton Pennsylvania July 31, 1923. Roman Catholic. Educated at Miami University 1942, Villanova University B.S. 1947 and Catholic University of America LL.B. 1950. Awarded honorary LL.D. University of Scranton 1975. Admitted to practice Pennsylvania 1951. Began legal practice Scranton 1951. Hearing Examiner, Pennsylvania Liquor Control Board 1955-59. Judge, Pennsylvania Court of Common Pleas Forty-fifth Judicial District Jan 1960 to Dec 1962.

Lecturer University of Scranton 1951-59. Member Lackawanna and Pennsylvania Bar Associations. Recipient Americanism Award from Amos Lodge B'nai B'rith, Cyrano Award from University of Scranton Graduate School 1977, Distinguished Service Award from Pennsylvania Trial Lawyers Association 1979, Alumni Achievement Award from Catholic University 1981 and Judicial Achievement Award as Outstanding Federal Trial Judge from The Association of Trial Lawyers of America 1983. Named Distinguished Pennsylvanian by Philadelphia Chamber of Commerce 1980. First Lieutenant USMC 1942-45. Democrat. Commissioner Scranton Registration Commission 1953-55. Past Trustee Everhart Museum. Board of Trustees St. Michael's School for Boys. Trustee Lackawanna Junior College. Board member Scranton-Lackawanna Health and Welfare Authority. Board of Directors St. Mary's Hospital Lackawanna. Member Hospital Service Association of Northeast Pennsylvania, Lackawanna County Prison Board, Scranton Diocesan Liturgical Commission, Lackawanna County United Fund, March of Dimes, American Cancer Society, Heart Association, Association for Retarded Children and Scranton Country Club. Board of Directors Mercy Hospital Scranton and Catholic Youth Center.

Mailing address: P.O. Box 1146, Scranton 18501-1146.

Telephone: (570) 207-5700.

NEW, Arnold L. *(Judge, Pennsylvania Court of Common Pleas First Judicial District)*
Office: 606 City Hall, Philadelphia 19107.
Telephone: (215) 686-7260.

NEWCOMER, Clarence C. *(Senior Judge, United States District Court Eastern District of Pennsylvania)* Appointed for life by President Richard M. Nixon to term beginning Jan 4, 1972. Assumed Senior status, serves by assignment. Born Mount Joy Pennsylvania Jan 18, 1923. Episcopalian. Educated at Franklin & Marshall College A.B. 1944 and Dickinson School of Law LL.B. 1948. Admitted to practice Pennsylvania 1950. Began legal practice Lancaster 1950.
Special Deputy Attorney General Pennsylvania 1953-54. Assistant District Attorney 1960-64, First Assistant District Attorney 1964-68 and District Attorney 1968-72 Lancaster County. Important Decisions: Dickerson v. U.S. Steel Corp. (Title VII) 472 F. Supp. 1304 E.D. Pa. 1978; Fleer Corp. v. Topps Chewing Gum, Inc. (antitrust) 501 F. Supp. 485 E.D. Pa. 1980; United States v. Wade (hazardous waste) 577 F. Supp. 1326 E.D. Pa. 1983; and Apple Computer, Inc. v. Franklin Computer Corp. (copyright infringement) 545 F. Supp. 812 E.D. Pa. 1981. Member Pennsylvania Trial Lawyers Association, The Association of Trial Lawyers of America, Philadelphia, Lancaster County, Pennsylvania and Federal Bar Associations. Lieutenant j.g. USNR 1943-46. Member St. James Protestant Episcopal Church.
Office: 13614 U.S. Courthouse, 601 Market Street, Philadelphia 19106-1778.
Telephone: (215) 597-7847.

NEWMAN, Sandra Schultz *(Justice, The Supreme Court of Pennsylvania)* Elected to term beginning Jan 1996. Term expires Jan 2006. First woman elected to The Supreme Court of Pennsylvania. Educated at Drexel University, Temple University and Villanova University School of Law J.D. Awarded honorary J.D. by Gannon University 1996 and Widener University School of Law 1996. Admitted to practice Pennsylvania 1972. Judge, The Commonwealth Court of Pennsylvania 1993-95.
Assistant District Attorney Montgomery County 1972. Fellow Pennsylvania Bar Association and American Bar Foundation. Past President Pennsylvania Chapter American Academy of Matrimonial Lawyers. Chairperson Board of Consultors Villanova University School of Law. Advisory Board Biddle Law Library University of Pennsylvania and College of Business and Administration Drexel University.
Office: 100 Four Falls Corporate Center, Suite 400, West Conshohocken 19428.
Telephone: (610) 832-1700.

NICHOLAS, William T. *(Judge, Pennsylvania Court of Common Pleas Thirty-eighth Judicial District)* Elected to term beginning Jan 7, 1980. Retained by election 1989 and 1999. Current term expires Jan 2010. President Judge Jan 6, 1992 to Jan 6, 1997. Born New York New York Sept 3, 1938. Greek Orthodox. Educated at City College of the City University of New York B.A. 1961 and Temple University LL.B. 1964. Associate Editor Temple Law Quarterly 1963-64. Admitted to practice Pennsylvania 1965, U.S. District Court Eastern District of Pennsylvania 1965, U.S. Court of Appeals Third Circuit 1965 and U.S. Supreme Court 1970. Began legal practice Norristown 1965.
Assistant District Attorney 1968-71, First Assistant District Attorney 1971-76 and District Attorney 1976-80 Montgomery County. Member Pennsylvania District Attorneys Association (Vice President 1979), Montgomery County, Pennsylvania and American Bar Associations. Recipient Distinguished Public Service Award from Pennsylvania County Detectives Association 1978, Fraternal Order of Police Lodge 14, 1980 and Rape Crisis Center of Montgomery County 1984. Republican. Trustee Montgomery County Historical Society. Board member Montgomery County Emergency Service. Member Order of Ahepa Chapter 432.
Mailing address: P.O. Box 311, Norristown 19404.
Office: Montgomery County Courthouse, Norristown 19401.
Telephone: (610) 278-3160.

NICKLEACH, Joseph A. *(President Judge, Pennsylvania Court of Common Pleas Thirty-third Judicial District)* Elected to term beginning Jan 4, 1988. Retained by election 1997, current term expires Jan 2008. Born Kittanning Pennsylvania May 19, 1940. Catholic. Educated at St. Vincent College B.S. 1962 and Duquesne University School of Law J.D. 1966. Staff member Duquesne Law Review 1965-66. Law Clerk to Hon. Rabe F. Marsh, U.S. District Court Western District of Pennsylvania 1963-66. Admitted to practice Pennsylvania 1966 and U.S. District Court Western District of Pennsylvania 1966. In legal practice Kittanning 1966-88.
Hearing Examiner Pennsylvania Liquor Control Board 1970-72. District Attorney Armstrong County 1972-76. Member American Judicature Society, Armstrong County (Past President, Former Treasurer, Former Chairman CLE) and Pennsylvania Bar Associations. Attended General Jurisdiction course The National Judicial College 1988. Enjoys reading and coaching youth basketball.
Office: Armstrong County Courthouse, Kittanning 16201.
Telephone: (724) 548-3203.

NIGRO, Russell M. *(Justice, The Supreme Court of Pennsylvania)* Former Judge, Pennsylvania Court of Common Pleas First Judicial District.
Office: 1818 Market Street, Suite 3205, Philadelphia 19103.
Telephone: (215) 560-3082.

OBER, William J. *(Judge, Pennsylvania Court of Common Pleas Tenth Judicial District)*
Office: Westmoreland County Courthouse, Two North Main Street, Greensburg 15601.
Telephone: (724) 853-2202.

O'BRIEN, Peter J. *(Judge, Pennsylvania Court of Common Pleas Forty-third Judicial District)* Elected to term beginning Jan 6, 1986. Retained by election 1995, current term expires Jan 2006. Born Philadelphia Pennsylvania Aug 13, 1938. Roman Catholic. Educated at Villanova University B.S. in Economics 1959 J.D. 1962. Admitted to practice Pennsylvania 1962. In legal practice Mount Pocono 1967-85. Captain U.S. Army JAGC 1963-66.
Office: Monroe County Courthouse, Stroudsburg 18360.
Telephone: (570) 517-3012.

O'BRIEN, W. Terrence *(Judge, Pennsylvania Court of Common Pleas Fifth Judicial District)*
Office: 705 City-County Building, 414 Grant Street, Pittsburgh 15219.
Telephone: (412) 350-5898.

O'DELL-SENECA, Debbie *(Judge, Pennsylvania Court of Common Pleas Twenty-seventh Judicial District)* Elected Nov 1991 to term beginning Jan 6, 1992. Retained by election Nov 2001, current term expires Jan 2012. Born New Eagle Pennsylvania July 13, 1953. Presbyterian. Educated at West Virginia University B.S. with honors 1974 and Duquesne University J.D. 1977. Law Clerk to Hon. John F. Bell, Pennsylvania Court of Common Pleas Twenty-seventh Judicial District 1978-79. Member Pi Sigma Alpha. Admitted to practice Pennsylvania 1977 and U.S. District Court Western District of Pennsylvania 1978. In legal practice Washington 1977-91.

Assistant Public Defender 1978. Assistant District Attorney and Chief of Litigation 1980-84. Important Decision: In re Ringgold School District (expanding school law under Act 88) 53 W.D. 95 S.Ct. 94-2924, 1996. Member Pennsylvania Court of Judicial Discipline, Pennsylvania Conference of State Trial Judges, National Association of Women Judges, National Council of Juvenile and Family Court Judges, Washington County and Pennsylvania Bar Associations. Attended The National Judicial College, Pennsylvania Conference of State Trial Judges and Washington County Bench/Bars. Recipient BPW Pathfinders Award 1992 and Award from VFW 1997. Member Washington Community Theater, Mount Pleasant Township Community Singers and Church Choir. Enjoys reading, traveling, music and drama.

Office: 2002 Washington County Courthouse, One South Main Street, Washington 15301.

Telephone: (724) 228-6830.

O'GRADY, John J., Jr. *(Judge, Pennsylvania Court of Common Pleas First Judicial District)*

Office: 505 City Hall, Philadelphia 19107.

Telephone: (215) 686-2892.

O'KEEFE, Joseph D. *(Judge, Pennsylvania Court of Common Pleas First Judicial District)* Elected to term beginning Jan 3, 1984. Retained by election 1993, current term expires Jan 2004. Currently serves as Administrative Judge Orphans' Court Division. Born Philadelphia Pennsylvania Jan 13, 1944. Educated at St. Joseph's University B.S. 1966 and Duquesne University J.D. 1973. Law Clerk to Hon. Levy Anderson, Pennsylvania Court of Common Pleas 1973-74. Admitted to practice Pennsylvania 1973.

Assistant District Attorney Philadelphia 1974-83. General Counsel Philadelphia Housing Authority 1983. Member Procedural Rules Committee Orphans' Court, Lawyers Club of Philadelphia, Brehon Law Society, Pennsylvania Conference of State Trial Judges and Philadelphia Bar Association. First Lieutenant U.S. Army 1966-69. Former Vice President and General Manager Frederiksted Hotel Corporation St. Croix U.S. Virgin Islands. Board of Directors Law Alumni Association of St. Joseph's University. Member Center City Residents Association of Philadelphia. Interested in historic preservation.

Office: 519 City Hall, Philadelphia 19107.

Telephone: (215) 686-7902.

OLER, J. Wesley, Jr. *(Judge, Pennsylvania Court of Common Pleas Ninth Judicial District)* Elected Nov 1991 to term beginning Jan 1, 1992. Retained by election Nov 2001, current term expires Jan 1, 2012. Born Rochester New York Oct 12, 1941. Educated at Hamilton College B.A. 1963 and Georgetown University Law Center J.D. 1972. Staff member Georgetown Law Journal 1972. Law Clerk to Hon. Robert Lee Jacobs, The Superior Court of Pennsylvania 1972-74. Member Phi Beta Kappa. Admitted to practice Pennsylvania 1972, District of Columbia 1973, U.S. Supreme Court 1976 and U.S. District Court Middle District of Pennsylvania 1978. In legal practice Carlisle 1974-91.

Attorney Public Defenders Office Cumberland County 1978-87. Solicitor Borough of Carlisle 1986-91. Author *Pennsylvania Criminal Law: Defendant's Mental State* Michie Co. 1986. Member Cumberland County and Pennsylvania Bar Associations. Republican. Interested in aviation.

Office: Cumberland County Courthouse, One Courthouse Square, Carlisle 17013.

Telephone: (717) 240-6530.

OLSON, Gregory A. *(Judge, Pennsylvania Court of Common Pleas Fortieth Judicial District)*

Office: Indiana County Courthouse, Fourth Floor, 825 Philadelphia Street, Indiana 15701.

Telephone: (724) 465-3958.

OLSZEWSKI, Peter Paul, Jr. *(Judge, Pennsylvania Court of Common Pleas Eleventh Judicial District)*

Office: Luzerne County Courthouse, 200 North River Street, Wilkes-Barre 18711.

Telephone: (570) 823-4072.

O'NEILL, Steven T. *(Judge, Pennsylvania Court of Common Pleas Thirty-eighth Judicial District)*

Mailing address: P.O. Box 311, Norristown 19404.

Office: Montgomery County Courthouse, Norristown 19401.

Telephone: (610) 277-1304.

O'NEILL, Thomas N., Jr. *(Senior Judge, United States District Court Eastern District of Pennsylvania)* Appointed for life by President Ronald Reagan to term beginning Aug 30, 1983. Assumed Senior status July 6, 1996, serves by assignment. Born Hanover Pennsylvania July 6, 1928. Roman Catholic. Educated at Catholic University of America A.B. magna cum laude 1950 and University of Pennsylvania Law School LL.B. magna cum laude 1953. Fulbright Scholar University of London School of Economics, England 1955-56. Articles Editor University of Pennsylvania Law Review 1952-53. Law Clerk to Hon. H. F. Goodrich, U.S. Court of Appeals and Hon. Harold F. Burton, U.S. Supreme Court. Member Phi Beta Kappa, Phi Eta Sigma and Order of the Coif (Past President University of Pennsylvania chapter). In legal practice Philadelphia 1956-83.

Instructor in Appellate Advocacy University of Pennsylvania Law School 1973. Member Governor's Trial Court Nominating Commission for Philadelphia County 1978-82. Fellow American College of Trial Lawyers. President Pennsylvania Conference of County Bar Officers 1981-82. Life member The American Law Institute. Member Philadelphia (Chancellor 1976), Pennsylvania (Board of Governors 1978-81, House of Delegates) and Federal Bar Associations. Former member American Bar Association (House of Delegates 1976). Airman USNR 1948-53. Past President Law Alumni Society University of Pennsylvania. Former member Board of Overseers University of Pennsylvania Museum of Archeology and Anthropology.

Office: 4007 U.S. Courthouse, 601 Market Street, Philadelphia 19106-1714.

Telephone: (215) 597-2750.

O'REILLY, Timothy Patrick *(Judge, Pennsylvania Court of Common Pleas Fifth Judicial District)*
Office: 711 City-County Building, 414 Grant Street, Pittsburgh 15219.
Telephone: (412) 350-4847.

ORIE MELVIN, Joan *(Judge, The Superior Court of Pennsylvania)* Elected Nov 1997 to term beginning Jan 1998. Term expires Jan 2008. Born Pittsburgh Pennsylvania. Educated at University of Notre Dame B.A. 1978 and Duquesne University School of Law J.D. 1981. Magistrate 1985-87 and Chief Magistrate 1987-90, Pittsburgh Municipal Court. Judge, Pennsylvania Court of Common Pleas Fifth Judicial District 1990-98.
Corporate Counsel 1981-85. Member Allegheny County Women's Bar Association and Allegheny County Bar Association. Past President Allegheny County Prison Board. Board of Directors Vincentian Home. Member Community Problem Solving Troubled Youth Committee United Way, American Heart Association, St. Lucy's Guild for the Blind and Make-A-Wish Foundation.
Office: 3500 Grant Building, 330 Grant Street, Pittsburgh 15219.
Telephone: (412) 880-5888.

OSBORNE, Ann A. *(Judge, Pennsylvania Court of Common Pleas Thirty-second Judicial District)*
Office: Delaware County Courthouse, 201 West Front Street, Media 19063.
Telephone: (610) 891-4642.

O'TOOLE, Lawrence Joseph *(Judge, Pennsylvania Court of Common Pleas Fifth Judicial District)* Appointed by Governor Robert P. Casey Jan 1993 to term beginning March 5, 1993. Elected Nov 1993, current term expires Jan 2004. Born Pittsburgh Pennsylvania Aug 25, 1950. Catholic. Educated at La Salle University B.S. 1972 and Duquesne University J.D. 1975. Admitted to practice Pennsylvania 1975. In legal practice Pittsburgh.
Office: 513 Allegheny County Courthouse, 436 Grant Street, Pittsburgh 15219.
Telephone: (412) 350-7124.

OTT, Paula Francisco *(Judge, Pennsylvania Court of Common Pleas Fifteenth Judicial District)*
Mailing address: P.O. Box 2748, West Chester 19380.
Office: 230 Chester County Courthouse, 2 North High Street, West Chester 19380.
Telephone: (610) 344-6185.

OTT, Stanley R. *(Judge, Pennsylvania Court of Common Pleas Thirty-eighth Judicial District)* Elected to term beginning Jan 4, 1988. Retained by election Nov 1997, current term expires Jan 2008. Administrative Judge Montgomery County Orphans' Court since Sept 1994. Born Sellersville Pennsylvania April 15, 1949. United Church of Christ. Educated at Lafayette College A.B. 1971 and Cornell University J.D. 1974. Law Clerk to Hon. Richard S. Lowe, Pennsylvania Court of Common Pleas Thirty-eighth Judicial Circuit May 1974 to Aug 1975. Admitted to practice Pennsylvania 1974, U.S. District Court Eastern District of Pennsylvania 1974 and U.S. Supreme Court 1982. In legal practice Lansdale 1977-79 and Souderton 1980-87.
Assistant District Attorney Montgomery County Oct 1975 to Dec 1976. Adjunct Instructor in Business Law Eastern College 1991-93. Adjunct Instructor Temple University School of Law since 1994 and Villanova University School of Law since 2000. Member Pennsylvania Conference of State Trial Judges, Montgomery County, Pennsylvania and American Bar Associations. Frequent Lecturer Pennsylvania Bar Institute. Attended General Jurisdiction Course The National Judicial College Sept 1988. Member Souderton Area School Board 1976-77. Enjoys fly fishing.
Mailing address: P.O. Box 311, Norristown 19404.
Office: Montgomery County Courthouse, Airy and Swede Streets, Norristown 19401.
Telephone: (610) 278-3178.

OVERTON, George W. *(Judge, Pennsylvania Court of Common Pleas First Judicial District)* Elected Nov 6, 2001 to term beginning Jan 7, 2002. Term expires Jan 2012. Born Philadelphia Pennsylvania July 7, 1954. Baptist. Educated at Clark University B.A. 1976 and Widener University School of Law J.D. 1986. Admitted to practice Pennsylvania 1986 and New Jersey 1986.
Office: 1402 Criminal Justice Center, 1301 Filbert Street, Philadelphia 19107.
Telephone: (215) 683-7103.
Fax: (215) 683-7105
E-mail address: George.Overton@courts.phila.gov

PADOVA, John R. *(Judge, United States District Court Eastern District of Pennsylvania)* Appointed for life by President George Bush to term beginning 1992. Born Philadelphia Pennsylvania May 7, 1935. Educated at Villanova University A.B. 1956 and Temple University School of Law J.D. 1959. In legal practice Philadelphia 1960-92.
Office: 6614 U.S. Courthouse, 601 Market Street, Philadelphia 19106-1759.
Telephone: (215) 597-1178.

PAGANO, George A. *(Judge, Pennsylvania Court of Common Pleas Thirty-second Judicial District)*
Office: Delaware County Courthouse, 201 West Front Street, Media 19063.
Telephone: (610) 891-4261.

PANELLA, Jack Anthony *(Judge, Pennsylvania Court of Common Pleas Third Judicial District)* Appointed by Governor Robert P. Casey to term beginning Oct 24, 1991. Elected Nov 21, 1993, current term expires Dec 31, 2003. Born Brooklyn New York May 4, 1955. Catholic. Educated at St. John's University B.S. cum laude 1977 and Catholic University of America Columbus School of Law J.D. 1980. Law Clerk to Hon. Michael V. Franciosa, Pennsylvania Court of Common Pleas Third Judicial District 1980-82. Admitted to practice Pennsylvania 1980 and U.S. District Court Eastern District of Pennsylvania 1981. In legal practice Easton 1982-91.
Assistant County Solicitor 1982-87 and Solicitor 1987-91 Northampton County. Instructor of Criminal Justice Northampton Community College since 1998. Member Pennsylvania Conference of State Trial Judges, Juvenile Court Judges Association and Pennsylvania Bar Association.
Office: 2226 Northwood Avenue, Suite 7, Easton 18045-2290.
Telephone: (610) 515-0830.

PANEPINTO, Paul P. *(Judge, Pennsylvania Court of Common Pleas First Judicial District)* Appointed by Governor Robert P. Casey to term beginning June 25, 1990. Elected Nov 5, 1991. Retained by election 2001,

PANEPINTO, PAUL P.—*Continued*
current term expires Jan 2012. Former Administrative Judge Family Division. Born Philadelphia Pennsylvania June 25, 1949. Roman Catholic. Educated at Villanova University B.A. 1971 M.A. 1979 and Widener University School of Law J.D. 1976. Member Justinian Society. Admitted to practice Pennsylvania 1977, New Jersey 1977 and U.S. District Courts District of New Jersey 1977 and District of Pennsylvania 1978. In legal practice Philadelphia Pennsylvania 1977-90. Juvenile Master, Family Court Feb 1987 to June 1990.

Probation Officer Nov 1971 to June 1977 and Intake Unit Attorney June 1977 to Feb 1987 Family Court. Member Domestic Relations Rules Committee since 1996, Juvenile Court Judges Commission of Pennsylvania since 1996 and Pennsylvania Futures Commission on Justice in the 21st Century since Jan 1997. Member Lawyers Club of Philadelphia, National Council of Juvenile and Family Court Judges (National Trustee since July 2001), National Italian American Bar Association, Philadelphia (Sections: Family Law, Criminal Law) and Pennsylvania Bar Associations. Attended Pennsylvania Conference of State Trial Judges seminars twice annually since 1991 and Juvenile Court Judges Commission seminars annually since Oct 1991. Recipient Legion of Honor Award from Chapel of Four Chaplains 1982; Police Partnership Probation Award from Citizens Crime Commission South/Southwest Chapter 1988; Outstanding Alumnus of the Year Award from Widener University School of Law 1994; Justinian Society Award June 20, 1996; Columbus Civic Association of PA, Inc. Oct 13, 1997; award for outstanding service to the administration of justice Oct 8, 1998 and Family Law Section Award Dec 16, 1998 from Philadelphia Bar Association; Marvin E. Wolfgang Award for dedication to justice and the well-being of children in Philadelphia from Philadelphia CASA of the Juvenile Justice Center of Pennsylvania Aug 17, 1999; We the People Ethics Award from Philadelphia Exclusive Oct 22, 1999; and Man of the Year Award from Sons of Italy Roxborough Lodge #2217 Nov 14, 1999. Former Member Board of Directors Shalom, Inc. (Past President). Board of Directors Crime Prevention Association since 1996, Organized Anti-Crime Community Network since 1999 and Jenkins Memorial Law Library. National Advisory Board Member Point Breeze Performing Art Center since Jan 2000. Executive Council Widener University. Member Philadelphia Youth Council, Mayor's Cabinet for Children and Families, Men of Malvern Laymen's Retreat and Order of Sons of Italy of Roxborough Lodge #2217 (Vice President). Enjoys reading, swimming and playing golf.

Office: 1403 Criminal Justice Center, 1301 Filbert Street, Philadelphia 19107.
Telephone: (215) 683-7106.
E-mail address: paul.panepinto@courts.phila.gov

PAPALINI, Joseph I. *(Judge, Pennsylvania Court of Common Pleas First Judicial District)*
Office: 688 City Hall, Philadelphia 19107.
Telephone: (215) 686-7512.

PARISI, Thomas G. *(Judge, Pennsylvania Court of Common Pleas Twenty-third Judicial District)*
Office: Berks County Courthouse, 633 Court Street, Reading 19601.
Telephone: (610) 478-6354.

PELLEGRINI, Dante R. *(Judge, The Commonwealth Court of Pennsylvania)*
Office: 609 Frick Building, 437 Grant Street, Pittsburgh 15219.
Telephone: (412) 565-7919.

PENKOWER, Alan S. *(Judge, Pennsylvania Court of Common Pleas Fifth Judicial District)*
Office: 703 City-County Building, 414 Grant Street, Pittsburgh 15219.
Telephone: (412) 350-5444.

PEOPLES, Thomas G., Jr. *(President Judge, Pennsylvania Court of Common Pleas Twenty-fourth Judicial District)*
Office: 212 Blair County Courthouse, 423 Allegheny Street, Hollidaysburg 16648.
Telephone: (814) 693-3225.

PEREZOUS, Michael J. *(Judge, Pennsylvania Court of Common Pleas Second Judicial District)*
Mailing address: P.O. Box 83480, Lancaster 17608-3480.
Office: Lancaster County Courthouse, 50 North Duke Street, Lancaster 17602.
Telephone: (717) 299-8060.

PESTO, Keith A. *(Magistrate Judge, United States District Court Western District of Pennsylvania)* Appointed by U.S. District Court judges to term beginning March 1, 1994. Reappointed 1998 and 2002. Current term expires Feb 2006. Serves part time. Born Baltimore Maryland Sept 20, 1960. Roman Catholic. Educated at Johns Hopkins University B.A. 1980 and University of Pennsylvania J.D. 1983. Law Clerk to Hon. D. Brooks Smith, Pennsylvania Court of Common Pleas Twenty-fourth Judicial District 1985-86. Admitted to practice Pennsylvania 1984. In legal practice Altoona 1988-94.

Assistant District Attorney 1986-88. Instructor Pennsylvania State University 1985-87 and St. Francis College 1993-95. Republican. Member Habitat for Humanity.

Office: 206 Penn Traffic Building, 319 Washington Street, Johnstown 15901.
Telephone: (814) 536-4342.
Fax: (814) 533-4519

PEZZE, Debra Ann *(Judge, Pennsylvania Court of Common Pleas Tenth Judicial District)* Elected Nov 5, 1991 to term beginning Jan 1992. Retained by election 2001, current term expires Jan 2012. Born Pittsburgh Pennsylvania Dec 29, 1953. Educated Pennsylvania State University B.A. 1975 and Duquesne University School of Law J.D. 1979. Law Clerk to Hon. Austin L. Staley, U.S. Court of Appeals Third Circuit.

Assistant Public Defender Westmoreland County 1980-92. Member Pennsylvania Conference of State Trial Judges, Westmoreland County, Pennsylvania and American Bar Associations. Member Blessed Sacrament Cathedral.

Office: Westmoreland County Courthouse, Two North Main Street, Greensburg 15601.
Telephone: (724) 830-3782.

PICCIONE, Thomas A. *(Judge, Pennsylvania Court of Common Pleas Fifty-third Judicial District)*
Office: Lawrence County Government Center, 430 Court Street, New Castle 16101.
Telephone: (724) 656-2158.

PLATT, Katherine B. L. *(Judge, Pennsylvania Court of Common Pleas Fifteenth Judicial District)*
Mailing address: P.O. Box 2748, West Chester 19380.
Office: 424 Chester County Courthouse, 2 North High Street, West Chester 19380.
Telephone: (610) 344-4730.

PLATT, William H. *(President Judge, Pennsylvania Court of Common Pleas Thirty-first Judicial District)*
Office: Old Courthouse, 501 West Hamilton Street, Allentown 18101.
Telephone: (610) 782-3393.

POLLAK, Louis H. *(Senior Judge, United States District Court Eastern District of Pennsylvania)* Appointed for life by President Jimmy Carter to term beginning Sept 8, 1978. Assumed Senior status. Born New York New York Dec 7, 1922. Educated at Harvard University B.A. 1943 and Yale University LL.B. 1948. Law Clerk to Judge Wiley B. Rutledge 1948-49. Admitted to practice New York 1949, Connecticut 1956 and Pennsylvania 1976.
With Department of State as Assistant to Ambassador-at-large Philip C. Jessup 1951-53. Faculty Yale University Law School 1955-74 (Dean 1965-70) and University of Pennsylvania Law School 1974-78 (Dean 1975-78). Author *The Constitution and The Supreme Court: A Documentary History* World Books 1965.
Office: 16613 U.S. Courthouse, 601 Market Street, Philadelphia 19106-1777.
Telephone: (215) 597-9590.

POZONSKY, Paul M. *(Judge, Pennsylvania Court of Common Pleas Twenty-seventh Judicial District)*
Office: 1004 Washington County Courthouse, One South Main Street, Washington 15301.
Telephone: (724) 228-6826.

PRATT, Ralph D. *(President Judge, Pennsylvania Court of Common Pleas Fifty-third Judicial District)* Elected Nov 1985. Retained by election Nov 1995, current term expires Jan 2006. Born New Castle Pennsylvania 1940. Educated at Baldwin Wallace College B.S. and University of Pittsburgh M.S. J.D.
Member Pennsylvania Conference of State Trial Judges, American Judges Association, National Council of Juvenile and Family Court Judges, State Bar of California, Lawrence County, Ohio State, Pennsylvania and American Bar Associations. Attended The National Judicial College. Member House of Representatives Pennsylvania 1975-86.
Office: Lawrence County Government Center, 430 Court Street, New Castle 16101.
Telephone: (724) 656-2187.

PROUD, James F. *(Judge, Pennsylvania Court of Common Pleas Thirty-second Judicial District)*
Office: Delaware County Courthouse, 201 West Front Street, Media 19063.
Telephone: (610) 891-4527.

QUIGLEY, Keith B. *(President Judge, Pennsylvania Court of Common Pleas Forty-first Judicial District)* Appointed by Governor Milton J. Shapp to term beginning May 17, 1976. Elected 1977. Retained by election Nov 1987 and Nov 1997. Current term expires Jan 2008. Born Harrisburg Pennsylvania April 3, 1939. Lutheran. Educated at Gettysburg College B.S. 1961 and Dickinson School of Law LL.B. 1964. Admitted to practice Pennsylvania 1964. Began legal practice Lemoyne 1964. In legal practice New Bloomfield 1971.
District Attorney 1971-76. Important Decision: Constitutionality of D.U.I. legislation March 1983. E-4 USMCR 1957-60. Democrat. Health Service Organization Director. Interested in youth baseball, outdoors and history.
Mailing address: P.O. Box 668, New Bloomfield 17068.
Office: Perry County Courthouse, New Bloomfield 17068.
Telephone: (717) 582-2131.

QUIÑONES ALEJANDRO, Nitza I. *(Judge, Pennsylvania Court of Common Pleas First Judicial District)* Appointed by Governor Robert P. Casey to term beginning Dec 10, 1991. Retained by election, current term expires Jan 2011. Born Puerto Rico Jan 1951. Catholic. Educated at University of Puerto Rico B.B.A. cum laude 1972 J.D. 1975. Admitted to practice Puerto Rico 1975, Pennsylvania 1977, U.S. District Courts Eastern District of Pennsylvania 1977 and District of Puerto Rico 1977, U.S. Court of Appeals Third Circuit 1981 and U.S. Supreme Court 1983.
Member Hispanic Bar Association of Pennsylvania (Legal Education Fund), Philadelphia and Pennsylvania Bar Associations.
Office: 1418 Criminal Justice Center, 1301 Filbert Street, Philadelphia 19107.
Telephone: (215) 683-7151.

RAMBO, Sylvia H. *(Senior Judge, United States District Court Middle District of Pennsylvania)* Appointed for life by President Jimmy Carter to term beginning Aug 5, 1979. Chief Judge Sept 1, 1992 to Aug 31, 1999. Assumed Senior status April 18, 2001, serves by assignment. Born Royersford Pennsylvania April 17, 1936. Presbyterian. Educated at Dickinson College A.B. with honors 1958 and Dickinson School of Law J.D. 1962. Awarded honorary LL.D. Wilson College, Dickinson School of Law, Dickinson College, Shippensburg University of Pennsylvania and Widener University School of Law. Member Pi Beta Phi and Phi Alpha Delta. Admitted to practice Pennsylvania 1963. Began legal practice Carlisle 1963. Judge, Pennsylvania Court of Common Pleas Ninth Judicial District 1976-78.
Assistant Public Defender 1974-76. Chief Public Defender 1976. Important Decision: Three Mile Island 87 FRD 433. Assistant Adjunct Professor Dickinson School of Law 1973-76. Member Committee on the Administration of the Magistrate Judges System Pennsylvania Judicial Conference Sept 1996 to Sept 2002. Member Women Trial Judges Association, Federal Judges Association, Cumberland County and Pennsylvania Bar Associations. Democrat. Former member Chamber of Commerce, United Way and Governor's Commission on Crime and Delinquency. Board of Trustees Second Presbyterian Church. Board of Governors Dickinson School of Law.
Mailing address: P.O. Box 868, Harrisburg 17108-0868.
Telephone: (717) 221-3960.

RANSOM, Lillian Harris *(Judge, Pennsylvania Court of Common Pleas First Judicial District)*
Office: 1218 Criminal Justice Center, 1301 Filbert Street, Philadelphia 19107.
Telephone: (215) 683-7071.

RAPOPORT, Arnold C. *(Magistrate Judge, United States District Court Eastern District of Pennsylvania)* Appointed by U.S. District Court judges.
Office: 3401 U.S. Courthouse, 504 West Hamilton Street, Allentown 18101-1500.
Telephone: (610) 776-0369.

RASLAVICH, Stephen *(Judge, United States Bankruptcy Court Eastern District of Pennsylvania)* Appointed by U.S. Court of Appeals Third Circuit judges.
Office: 204 Federal Building, 900 Market Street, Philadelphia 19107-4295.
Telephone: (215) 408-2982.

RAU, Lisa M. *(Judge, Pennsylvania Court of Common Pleas First Judicial District)*
Office: 593 City Hall, Philadelphia 19107.
Telephone: (215) 686-3768.

REBSTOCK, Robert J. *(Judge, Pennsylvania Court of Common Pleas First Judicial District)*
Office: 1801 Vine Street, Room 343B, Philadelphia 19103.
Telephone: (215) 686-8845.

REED, Lowell A., Jr. *(Senior Judge, United States District Court Eastern District of Pennsylvania)* Appointed for life by President Ronald Reagan to term beginning May 6, 1988. Assumed Senior status June 21, 1999, serves by assignment. Born West Chester Pennsylvania 1930. Presbyterian. Educated at University of Wisconsin-Madison B.B.A. 1952 and Temple University School of Law J.D. 1958. Recipient Law Academy of Philadelphia Prize 1958. Law Clerk to Hon. Ethan Allen Doty, Pennsylvania Court of Common Pleas 1958-59. Member Phi Alpha Delta. Admitted to practice Pennsylvania 1959, U.S. District Court Eastern District of Pennsylvania 1961, U.S. Court of Appeals Third Circuit 1962 and U.S. Supreme Court 1970. In legal practice Philadelphia 1959-88.
Judge of Elections 1972-77. Author "Digest of Pennsylvania Workmen's Compensation and Occupational Disease Law" *United States Review* 1971-74 and "Pneumonconiosis and the Pennsylvania Law" *Joint Symposium on Coal Worker's Pneumonconiosis* Pennsylvania Lung Association, Pennsylvania Thoracic Society and Hahnemann Medical College and Hospital March 30, 1978. Author 1972 and Co-author revised manual 1975, 1980, 1982, 1985 and 1987 *Pennsylvania Workmen's Compensation Manual* Pennsylvania Bar Institute. Important Decisions: North East Women's Center v. McMonagle 745 F. Supp. 1082, 1990 and 749 F. Supp. 695, 1990 and over 800 opinions on LEXIS and WestLaw. Adjunct Professor of Litigation Practice Temple University School of Law and Graduate School 1966-82. Former Member Philadelphia Association of Defense Counsel (Secretary-Treasurer 1980-81, Vice President 1982, President 1983-84), Pennsylvania Defense Institute and National Association of Railroad Trial Counsel. Master Temple Inn of Court American Inns of Court (President 1990-93). Member National Panel of Arbitrators American Arbitration Association 1972-80, Eastern District Judicial Committees on Court Automation and Criminal Business, Philadelphia (Chairman Medico-Legal Committee 1976, Member Workers' Compensation Committee, Commission on Judicial Selection and Retention 1983-87, Committee to Celebrate Bicentennial of U.S. Constitution 1985-87) and American (Member Judicial Administration Division and Section of Litigation) Bar Associations. Author and Course Planner Pennsylvania Bar Institute since 1972. Attended Third Circuit Judicial Conferences since 1988. Listed in *Who's Who* and *Who's Who in American Law*. Lieutenant Commander Intelligence USNR 1952-57. Recipient U.S. Navy American Spirit Honor Medal 1952. Republican. Member Historical Society of the U.S. Supreme Court and Temple University Law Alumni Association (Executive Committee since 1995). Past President Rydal-Meadowbrook Civic Association. Director Abington School Board 1970-71. Trustee World Affairs Council of Philadelphia 1983-88 and Abington Memorial Hospital Health Care Corporation 1983-88 and 1990-93. Elder Abington Presbyterian Church.
Office: 11614 U.S. Courthouse, 601 Market Street, Philadelphia 19106-1705.
Telephone: (215) 597-0022.

REHKAMP, C. Joseph *(Judge, Pennsylvania Court of Common Pleas Forty-first Judicial District)*
Mailing address: P.O. Box 668, New Bloomfield 17068.
Office: Perry County Courthouse, New Bloomfield 17068.
Telephone: (717) 582-2131.

REIBMAN, Edward D. *(Judge, Pennsylvania Court of Common Pleas Thirty-first Judicial District)* Elected Nov 1991 to term beginning Jan 6, 1992. Retained by election 2001, current term expires Jan 2012. Born Easton Pennsylvania Aug 5, 1947. Jewish. Educated at Lafayette College A.B. 1969 and Duke University School of Law J.D. 1972. Law Clerk to Hon. Bryan Simpson, U.S. Court of Appeals Fifth Circuit 1972-73. Admitted to practice Florida 1972, U.S. Courts of Appeals Fifth 1972 and Fourth 1987 Circuits, Pennsylvania 1974, U.S. District Court Eastern District of Pennsylvania 1977 and U.S. Supreme Court 1977. In legal practice Easton Pennsylvania 1975-77 and Allentown Pennsylvania 1977-91.
Trial Attorney Civil Rights Division U.S. Department of Justice 1973-75. Important Decisions: Tyminski v. Commonwealth of Pennsylvania, Department of Transportation (jurisdiction to hear appeals of motor vehicle license suspension) 45 Lehigh L. Jour. 183, 1992; Quire v. Quire (contempt of court) 45 Lehigh L. Jour. 178, 1992; Shellenberger v. Shellenberger (child support, college tuition, medical expenses, age of majority) 45 Lehigh L. Jour. 174, 1992; Merchants Bank, N.A. v. J. L. Foster, Inc. (confession of judgment held unconstitutional as applied) 45 Lehigh L. Jour. 154, 1992; Kutz v. Kutz (motion to vacate or strike divorce decree) 44 Lehigh L. Jour. 820, 1992; Bennett v. Commonwealth of Pennsylvania, Department of Transportation (refusal to submit to chemical testing) 44 Lehigh L. Jour. 800, 1992; Gadek v. Allentown College of St. Francis de Sales (contract of employment for tenured member of academic faculty) 44 Lehigh L. Jour. 794, 1992; Kelly v. Kelly (contempt of court) 44 Lehigh L. Jour. 721, 1992; Darcy and Salem United Church of Christ v. Reverend Donald Overlock et al. (rights of a church, whether on local or broader level, to choose its minister without judicial intervention or oversight) 45 Lehigh L. Jour. 303, 1993; David Karl Schuster v. Commonwealth of Pennsylvania, Department of Transportation Bureau of Traffic Safety Operations (motorist's duty to assent to blood test cannot lawfully be burdened by adding requirement that motorist also sign form devised by hospi-

REIBMAN, EDWARD D.—*Continued*
tal) 45 Lehigh L. Jour. 309, 1993; Panebianco-Yip Heart Surgeons v. Joseph H. Boyer, Jr., M.D. (restrictive covenants which are restraint on free exercise of trade are disfavored by courts) 45 Lehigh L. Jour. 312, 1993; Barbara A. Weed v. L. Steven Weed (child support includes certain fixed expenses and these expenses do not increase proportionately with each additional child) 45 Lehigh L. Jour. 465, 1993; Mary D. Piechota v. Gregory J. Piechota and Stanley F. Piechota and Mary M. Piechota, h/w (exceptions to Master's Report) 45 Lehigh L. Jour. 484, 1993; Joseph J. DiMento v. Lynn J. DiMento and Ralph Bradley 45 Lehigh L. Jour. 695, 1993; Lillian Boger v. Abraham Boger 45 Lehigh L. Jour. 751, 1994; Aracelia Pabon v. Mercedes Pabon (proceeds from winning lottery ticket purchased prior to spouses' final separation constituted marital property and were therefore subject to equitable distribution) 45 Lehigh L. Jour. 6, 1994; Anne T. Wilkert v. Bruce E. Wilkert 46 Lehigh L. Jour. 70, 1994; School District of the City of Allentown v. Hotel and Restaurant Employees International Union, Local No. 391, AFL-CIO 46 Lehigh L. Jour. 85, 1994; Insulation Corporation of America v. Gary L. Brobston 46 Lehigh L. Jour. 4, 1994; and 318 Hamilton, Inc. t/a B & G Station v. Pennsylvania State Police, Bureau of Liquor Code Enforcement (the proper standard of review by Courts of Common Pleas of decisions of the LCB is de novo rather than abuse of discretion) 46 Lehigh L. Jour. 165, 1994.

Member Pennsylvania Conference of State Trial Judges (Judicial Ethics Committee since 1994), The Florida Bar, Lehigh County, Northampton County and Pennsylvania Bar Associations. Attended General Jurisdiction Course The National Judicial College Oct 1993. Facilitator seminar on "Child Abuse Victims in Court" Pennsylvania Conference of State Trial Judges July 1994. Sergeant USAR 1969-75. Democrat. Candidate for U.S. Congress Fifteenth District Pennsylvania 1988. Vice Chairman 1979-82, Member 1982-86 and Chairman 1983-86 Allentown Historic and Architectural Review Board. Board of Directors Lehigh Valley Legal Services 1981-87 (President 1982-85, Chief Labor Negotiator 1985-86), Allentown Literacy Council 1987-89 and Cities in Schools since 1994. Board of Associates Muhlenberg College since 1992. Member Congregation Keneseth Israel. Interests include tennis and child care.

Office: Old Courthouse, 501 West Hamilton Street, Allentown 18101.

Telephone: (610) 782-3930.

REILLY, John K., Jr. *(President Judge, Pennsylvania Court of Common Pleas Forty-sixth Judicial District)* Elected to term beginning Jan 1974. Retained by election 1983 and 1993. Current term expires Jan 2004. President Judge since Jan 1974. Born Winber Pennsylvania Oct 4, 1935. Presbyterian. Educated at Pennsylvania State University B.A. 1957 and Dickinson School of Law J.D. 1960.

Former District Attorney Clearfield County. Member Clearfield County and Pennsylvania Bar Associations. Attended Pennsylvania Conference of State Trial Judges. Past President Pennsylvania District Attorney's Association. U.S. Army 1960-61 and USAR 1962-68.

Office: Clearfield County Courthouse, 230 East Market Street, Clearfield 16830.

Telephone: (814) 765-2641.

RENN, Richard K. *(Judge, Pennsylvania Court of Common Pleas Nineteenth Judicial District)*

Office: York County Courthouse, 28 East Market Street, York 17401.

Telephone: (717) 771-4377.

REYNOLDS, Abram Frank *(Judge, Pennsylvania Court of Common Pleas First Judicial District)* Elected to term beginning Jan 1986. Retained by election 1995, current term expires Jan 2006. Former Supervising Judge Juvenile Division. Former Deputy Administrative Judge. Born Binghamton New York March 15, 1938. Educated at Park College B.A. cum laude 1969, University of Missouri M.A. 1970 and Rutgers University Law School J.D. 1973. Admitted to practice Pennsylvania 1973.

Certified Instructor U.S. Professional Tennis Association. Member Professional Tennis Registry.

Office: 1801 Vine Street, Room 159, Philadelphia 19103.

Telephone: (215) 686-8387.

RILEY, Howard F., Jr. *(President Judge, Pennsylvania Court of Common Pleas Fifteenth Judicial District)* Appointed by Governor Robert P. Casey to term beginning Dec 23, 1992. Elected Nov 1993 to term beginning Jan 3, 1994, current term expires Jan 2004. President Judge since Jan 4, 2000. Born Chester County Pennsylvania May 24, 1942. Educated at Villanova University B.S. 1964 J.D. 1967. Admitted to practice Pennsylvania, U.S. District Court Eastern District of Pennsylvania and U.S. Court of Appeals Third Circuit. In legal practice Devon May 1, 1971 to April 30, 1972 and Chester County May 1, 1972 to Dec 22, 1992.

Attorney House Counsel Office Allstate Insurance Company Nov 1969 to April 1971. Life Fellow Chester County Bar Foundation (Director since 1993) and Pennsylvania Bar Foundation. Charter Member John E. Stively, Jr. American Inn of Court (Member Executive Committee 1994-96). Member Pennsylvania Conference of State Trial Judges, Chester County (Chair Law Day Committee 1988-90 and 1992, Director 1989-91) and Pennsylvania Bar Associations. Graduate General Jurisdiction Course The National Judicial College July 11, 1993 to Aug 6, 1993. Recipient Public Service Award 1993 and President's Award 1988 from Chester County Bar Association. Specialist E-5 U.S. Army Sept 1967 to Aug 1969. Annual Volunteer 1952-92, Co-chairman 1965-67 and Chairman 1972-77 Goshen Country Fair. Life Member Goshen Fire Company (Director 1976-92, President 1982). Charter Member Westtown-Goshen Rotary Club. Member Chester County Fire-Fighters' Association, Chester County Historical Society, VFW and American Legion.

Mailing address: P.O. Box 2748, West Chester 19380.

Office: 230 Chester County Courthouse, 2 North High Street, West Chester 19380-0991.

Telephone: (610) 344-5706.

RIZZO, Annette M. *(Judge, Pennsylvania Court of Common Pleas First Judicial District)* Appointed by Governor Tom Ridge to term beginning Jan 4, 1999. Elected Nov 1999 to term beginning Jan 3, 2000. Term expires Jan 2010. Currently serves Criminal Division. Educated at University of Pennsylvania B.A. and Temple University School of Law J.D. 1983. Recipient Lena L. Hale Award 1983. Listed in *Who's Who in American Colleges and Universities*. Executive Board Moot Court

RIZZO, ANNETTE M.—*Continued*

Honor Society 1982-83. Member Pi Sigma Alpha. In legal practice Philadelphia 1985-91.

Assistant City Solicitor Philadelphia 1983-85. Senior Counsel Legal and Public Affairs CIGNA Companies 1992-98. Board Member Justinian Law Society 1990-97. Co-chair Membership Committee 1997 and Fee Dispute Committee 1998 Philadelphia Bar Association. Member Temple American Inn of Court. Board Member AMICI Center for Italian Studies University of Pennsylvania 1983-86 and Philadelphia Volunteers for the Indigent Program 1994-2000. Chair Law Subcommittee Philadelphia/Florence Sister Cities Committee since 1989. Advisory Board City of Philadelphia Airport Sept 1997 to Jan 2000. Board Member Casa Enrique Fermi since 2000 and Eastern State Penitentiary National Historic Landmark since 2000.

Office: 1415 Criminal Justice Center, 1301 Filbert Street, Philadelphia 19107.

Telephone: (215) 683-7142.

Fax: (215) 683-7144

ROBINS NEW, Shelley *(Judge, Pennsylvania Court of Common Pleas First Judicial District)*

Office: 1213 Criminal Justice Center, 1301 Filbert Street, Philadelphia 19107.

Telephone: (215) 683-7056.

ROBINSON, Rosalyn K. *(Judge, Pennsylvania Court of Common Pleas First Judicial District)*

Office: 27 South Twelfth Street, Suite 404, Philadelphia 19107.

Telephone: (215) 686-4030.

ROBRENO, Eduardo C. *(Judge, United States District Court Eastern District of Pennsylvania)* Appointed for life by President George Bush to term beginning July 27, 1992. Born Havana Cuba July 28, 1945. Educated at Westfield State College B.A. 1967, University of Massachusetts M.S. 1969 and Rutgers University School of Law J.D. 1975. Articles Editor Rutgers Law Journal 1977-78. Admitted to practice Pennsylvania 1978. In legal practice Philadelphia 1981-92.

Adjunct Faculty Member Rutgers University School of Law 1992-95. Fellow American Bar Foundation. Member Judicial Conference Committee on Bankruptcy Rules, The American Law Institute and Hispanic Bar Association of Pennsylvania.

Office: 7614 U.S. Courthouse, 601 Market Street, Philadelphia 19106-1745.

Telephone: (215) 597-4073.

ROGERS, Peter F. *(Judge, Pennsylvania Court of Common Pleas First Judicial District)*

Office: 1408 Criminal Justice Center, 1301 Filbert Street, Philadelphia 19107.

Telephone: (215) 683-7121.

ROSSANESE, Maurino J., Jr. *(Judge, Pennsylvania Court of Common Pleas Thirty-eighth Judicial District)* Assumed office 1989. Born Philadelphia Pennsylvania April 7, 1945. Educated at LaSalle College B.A. 1968, Temple University 1969-70 and Delaware Law School of Widener University J.D. 1975. Staff member Delaware Law Review. In legal practice Norristown 1978-84 and 1986-89 and Conshohocken 1984-85.

Assistant Public Defender 1977-80 and Chief Trial Division 1980-89 Public Defender's Office Montgomery County. Solicitor West Marshall Street Parking Authority 1985-89. Instructor in Criminal Law and Evidence Montgomery County Community College 1984-89. Member Montgomery County Trial Lawyers Association, Pennsylvania Public Defenders Association, Desmond J. McTighe American Inn of Court (Past President), Montgomery County and Pennsylvania Bar Associations. Teacher Overbrook High School Philadelphia School System 1968-77. Former Treasurer, Committeeman 1982-89 and Vice Chairman Hatfield Township Republican Committee. Former Assistant Coach North Penn Squires Football League. Former Pack Leader Cub Scouts. Board of Directors LaSalle High School Alumni. Treasurer LaSalle High School Crew Alumni Association. Solicitor Montgomery Soccer Association. Hunter Safety Instructor certified by Pennsylvania Game Commission. Member Industrial Development Authority Hatfield Township.

Mailing address: P.O. Box 311, Norristown 19404.

Office: Montgomery County Courthouse, Norristown 19401.

Telephone: (610) 278-3175.

RUBENSTEIN, Alan M. *(Judge, Pennsylvania Court of Common Pleas Seventh Judicial District)* Elected 1999 to term beginning Jan 2000. Term expires Jan 2010. Educated at Temple University B.A. 1967 and University of Toledo College of Law J.D. 1970. Articles and Comment Editor University of Toledo Law Review 1969-70. Admitted to practice Pennsylvania, U.S. District Court Eastern District of Pennsylvania, U.S. Court of Appeals Third Circuit and U.S. Supreme Court. In legal practice Philadelphia 1971-72.

Assistant District Attorney 1973-75. Deputy District Attorney 1975-79. Chief Deputy District Attorney and Chief of Trials 1979-82. Chief of Homicide 1983. First Assistant District Attorney 1983-86. District Attorney 1986-2000. Board of Directors 1986-97 and President 1993-94 and 1996-97 Pennsylvania District Attorneys Institute. Vice President 1990-91 and President 1991-92 Pennsylvania District Attorneys Association. Fellow American College of Prosecuting Attorneys. Member The Association of Trial Lawyers of America and American Judicature Society. Instructor Pennsylvania District Attorneys Institute 1986-99, Pennsylvania District Attorneys Association 1986-99 and Police/Prosecutors Training Institute 1989. Panelist and Speaker National Conference of Child Sex Abuse Investigations Criminal Justice Institute Harvard Law School Nov 2000. Named "Best District Attorney" in Philadelphia Area by *Philadelphia Magazine* 1988-89. Recipient Law Enforcement Commendation Medal from The National Society of the Sons of the American Revolution Nov 1992, Outstanding Services to Law Enforcement Award from Bucks County Fraternal Order of Police April 1993, Northeast Community Service Award May 1996, Diamond Achievement Award from Temple University College of Arts and Sciences May 1997, Excellence in Law Enforcement Award from Law Enforcement Square Club Feb 1998 and Justice Benjamin Cardozo Humanitarian Award from Cardozo Lodge May 2000. Listed in *Who's Who in American Law* and *Who's Who in America*. Member Drug Task Force Advisory Committee Office of Attorney General 1986-2000 and Attorney General's Task Force for Protection of Older Pennsylvanians 1998-2000. Advisor Board of Directors Joe Frazier's Golden Gloves 1992-93. Professional Boxing Judge.

RUBENSTEIN, ALAN M.—*Continued*

Member Boxing Scholarship Foundation and Honorable Order of Kentucky Colonels.

Office: Bucks County Courthouse, 55 East Court Street, Doylestown 18901.

Telephone: (215) 340-8222.

RUETER, Thomas J. *(Magistrate Judge, United States District Court Eastern District of Pennsylvania)* Appointed by U.S. District Court judges to term beginning Feb 22, 1994. Reappointed Feb 2002, current term expires Feb 2010. Born Philadelphia Pennsylvania July 12, 1955. Roman Catholic. Educated at University of Scranton B.A. summa cum laude 1977 and Dickinson School of Law J.D. 1980. Notes Editor Dickinson Law Review 1979-80. Law Clerk to Hon. Joseph L. McGlynn, Jr., U.S. District Court Eastern District of Pennsylvania 1980-82. Admitted to practice Pennsylvania 1980, New Jersey 1980, U.S. District Courts Eastern District of Pennsylvania 1980 and District of New Jersey 1980, U.S. Court of Appeals Third Circuit 1980 and U.S. Supreme Court 1984. In legal practice Philadelphia Pennsylvania 1982-85.

Assistant U.S. Attorney Criminal Division 1985-94 and Chief of Narcotics Section 1990-94 Eastern District of Pennsylvania U.S. Attorney's Office. Author Case Note "Criminal Procedure" 83 Dickinson L. Rev. 377, 1979, "Punitive Damage Liability of Municipal Corporations in Pennsylvania" 84 Dickinson L. Rev. 267, 1980, "Jonathan Roberts and the 'War Hawk' Congress of 1811-1812" *Pennsylvania Magazine of History and Biography* Oct 1980, "Mortgage Foreclosure in Pennsylvania" 85 Dickinson L. Rev. 275, 1981, "William Lewis, First United States Attorney" *The Shingle* Spring 1989, "Pennsylvania's Reasonable Expectations Doctrine: The Third Circuit's Perspective" Villanova L. Rev. Feb 2000 and "A Tribute to Judge Joseph L. McGlynn, Jr." *The Philadelphia Lawyer* Spring 2000. Important Decisions: Jackson v. Philadelphia Housing Authority 858 F. Supp. 464, 1994, Scott Paper Co. v. U.S. 943 F. Supp. 489, 1996 and Johnston v. Love 940 F. Supp. 489, 1996. Recipient citation for prosecuting *United States v. Houghton, et al.* from Insurance Crime Prevention Institute 1987, award for efforts in prosecuting *United States v. Jose Ortiz, et al.* from Fraternal Order of Police 1987, Award for Outstanding Service as Assistant U.S. Attorney from U.S. Department of Justice 1988, Certificate of Appreciation for outstanding contributions to drug enforcement from Drug Enforcement Administration 1988, Official Commendation for prosecution of cases arising from Operation Flying Kite *(United States v. LBS Bank—New York, Inc. et al.)* from U.S. Customs Service 1990 and Special Commendation for service as Assistant Director of Executive Office for Weed and Seed from U.S. Deputy Attorney General George T. Terwilliger, III 1992.

Office: 3038 U.S. Courthouse, 601 Market Street, Philadelphia 19106.

Telephone: (215) 597-0048.

RUFE, Cynthia M. *(Judge, United States District Court Eastern District of Pennsylvania)* Appointed for life by President George W. Bush to term beginning June 10, 2002. Born Philadelphia Pennsylvania Oct 30, 1948. Educated at Adelphi University B.A. 1970, Bloomsburg University Secondary Teaching Certification 1972 and State University of New York at Buffalo J.D. 1977. Judge, Pennsylvania Court of Common Pleas Seventh Judicial District Jan 1994 to June 9, 2002.

Assistant and Coordinator Juvenile Division 1977-82 and Deputy Public Defender 1980-81 Bucks County Public Defender's Office. Solicitor Bucks County Children and Youth Social Services Agency 1984-88. Guest Speaker on Child Abuse and Criminal Justice Temple University 1989-92 and Criminal Justice Bucks County Community College Career Day 1985-97. Member Appellate Court Procedural Rules Committee The Supreme Court of Pennsylvania since 1999. Former Member Pennsylvania College of Criminal Defense Lawyers, Pennsylvania Trial Lawyers Association, National College of Criminal Defense Lawyers, The Association of Trial Lawyers of America, Pennsylvania and American Bar Associations. Member Justinian Society, Pennsylvania Conference of State Trial Judges, National Council of Juvenile and Family Court Judges and Bucks County Bar Association (Board of Directors 1983-85, Chair Membership Committee 1983-85, Criminal Law Section 1987-88 and Bench-Bar Committee 1988-89). Speaker "Custody, Conciliation and Mediation" Annual Conference July 1997, "Criminal and Civil Statutory and Procedural Rules Update" Annual Conference July 2000, "Driving Under the Influence and License Suspensions" Mid-winter Conference Feb 2001 and "Families in Crisis" Seminar May 2001 Pennsylvania Conference of State Trial Judges; Criminal Justice Bucks County Police Training 1997-98; and Current Issues in Child Welfare Law Pennsylvania Bar Institute March 2000. Listed in *Who's Who in American Law* 1987-2003 and *Who's Who in America* 2002. Recipient Woman of Distinction Award from Soroptimist International of Indian Rock, Inc. 1994, M. J. Kirkpatrick Award for Leadership 1999 and Law and Justice Award from Pennsylvania Commission for Social Justice 2000. Secondary Education Teacher 1970-72. Founding Member and Board of Directors Organization to Prevent Teenage Suicide (OPTS) Inc. 1984-93. Member Advisory Council Big Brothers Big Sisters of Bucks County since 2000. Member Soroptimist International of Indian Rock, Inc. (Past President).

Office: 4000 U.S. Courthouse, 601 Market Street, Philadelphia 19106.

Telephone: (215) 597-7704.

RUFE, John J. *(Judge, Pennsylvania Court of Common Pleas Seventh Judicial District)* Appointed by Governor Robert P. Casey to term beginning Dec 4, 1989. Elected Nov 1991. Retained by election 2001, current term expires Jan 2012. Born Sellersville Pennsylvania Dec 12, 1939. Educated at Lafayette College A.B. 1962 and Duke University J.D. 1965. Law Clerk to Judge Edward G. Biester 1966-68. Admitted to practice Pennsylvania 1965, U.S. District Court Eastern District of Pennsylvania 1965 and U.S. Supreme Court 1979. In legal practice Sellersville 1965-89.

Member Bucks County and Pennsylvania Bar Associations.

Office: Bucks County Courthouse, 55 East Court Street, Doylestown 18901.

Telephone: (215) 348-6068.

Fax: (215) 340-8820

RUSSELL, Jacqueline L. *(Judge, Pennsylvania Court of Common Pleas Twenty-first Judicial District)*
Office: Schuylkill County Courthouse, 401 North Second Street, Pottsville 17901.
Telephone: (570) 628-1311.

SACAVAGE, Robert B. *(President Judge, Pennsylvania Court of Common Pleas Eighth Judicial District)*
Office: Northumberland County Courthouse, 201 Market Street, Sunbury 17801.
Telephone: (570) 988-4163.

SÁNCHEZ, Juan R. *(Judge, Pennsylvania Court of Common Pleas Fifteenth Judicial District)* Elected Nov 1997 to term beginning Jan 2, 1998. Term expires 2008. Born Vega Baja Puerto Rico Dec 22, 1955. Roman Catholic. Educated at City College of the City University of New York B.A. cum laude 1978 and University of Pennsylvania Law School J.D. 1981. Admitted to practice Pennsylvania 1982 and U.S. District Court Eastern District of Pennsylvania 1986. In legal practice West Chester 1983 to Dec 31, 1997.
Staff Attorney Legal Aid of Chester County, Inc. Sept 1981 to Aug 1983. Senior Trial Attorney Chester County Public Defender's Office Aug 15, 1983 to April 10, 1997. Important Opinions: Vanderlaag v. Fox & Lazlo, Inc., et al. 46 Ches. Co. Rep. 114, 1998; Board of Supervisors of Sadsbury Township v. Sadsbury Township Municipal Authority 46 Ches. Co. Rep. 130, 1998; Anthony Fragale and Donna Fragale, h/w v. Mark P. Brigham, M.D. Civil Action No. 95-10852, 331, 1999 Pa. Super. 1999; In re Richard Greist 47 Ches. Co. Rep. 140, 1999; and Commonwealth v. Friedman 47 Ches. Co. Rep. 174, 1999. Adjunct Professor Immaculata University and of Litigation Skills West Chester University. Member Chester County ad hoc Committee Pennsylvania District Justice Project since 1987. Member, Executive Committee and Master John E. Stively, Jr. American Inn of Court since 1996. Member Ethics Committee and Criminal Law Section since Dec 1999 Pennsylvania Conference of State Trial Judges. Master J. Willard O'Brien American Inn of Court. Former Member Pennsylvania Association of Criminal Defense Lawyers and Hispanic Bar Association. Member JNET Subcommittee, Regional Central Booking Committee, Criminal Justice Advisory Board, American Judges Association, Chester County and Pennsylvania Bar Associations. Attended State Trial Judges School for Newly Elected Judges Jan 1998; General Jurisdiction Course The National Judicial College July 1998 to Aug 1998; Rules of Evidence Workshop Sept 1998; Mid-Annual Conference Feb 1999-2002 and Annual Conference July 1999-2001 Pennsylvania Conference of State Trial Judges; Habeas Corpus Workshop Federal Judicial Center March 1999; "No Reversals—Correct Rulings: Evidence in Action" Workshop Aug 2000 and "Judge as Fact Finder and Decision Maker" Workshop Dec 2001 American Academy of Judicial Education; and Pennsylvania Conference of State Trial Judges. Assistant General Counsel to Republican Party 1990-94. Vice Chairman Area 12 Republican Committee 1990-94. Member 155th District Advisory Board 1990-94 and Republican Campaign Committee 1990-96 (Chairman Candidate Profile Subcommittee 1995-96). Republican Committeeman East Downington West Precinct 1990-97. Recipient V.A. Hospital Award for leadership in developing affordable housing and efforts in providing legal services to those with limited financial resources from Department of Veterans Affairs and Distinguished Community Service Award from La-Comunidad Hispana 1999 and Pride Award from Governor's Advisory Commission on Latino Affairs March 2001. Chairman Board of Directors Centro Guayacan 1981-85. Board of Directors and Coach Downingtown Little League 1988-93 and Downington Babe Ruth Baseball League 1993-97. Commissioner Housing Authority Chester County July 1992 to 1997. Advisory Board Member Riverside Care of Chester County 1992-97. Vice President and Board of Directors Legal Aid of Chester County, Inc. 1994-97. Board of Directors 1996-97 and Advisor Strategic Planning Committee 1999 United Way of Chester County. Former Member Downington Benefit Group, Inc., Downington Fire Department ad hoc Committee, Downington Home Rule Charter Commission, Chester County Hospital, Chester County Planning Commission Policy Plan Committee and National Association of Housing and Redevelopment Officials. Board Member Volunteer English Program Chester County since 1998. Corporate Board of Directors and Chairman Public Policy Committee YMCA of Central Chester County since 1994. Volunteer Attorney Legal Education Youth and Pro Bono Programs. Member Community Volunteers in Medicine. Interests include baseball and coaching.
Mailing address: P.O. Box 2748, West Chester 19380-0991.
Office: 230 Chester County Courthouse, Two North High Street, West Chester 19380.
Telephone: (610) 344-6184.

SARCIONE, Anthony A. *(Judge, Pennsylvania Court of Common Pleas Fifteenth Judicial District)*
Mailing address: P.O. Box 2748, West Chester 19380.
Office: 302 Chester County Courthouse, Two North High Street, West Chester 19380.
Telephone: (610) 344-5900.

SARMINA, M. Teresa *(Judge, Pennsylvania Court of Common Pleas First Judicial District)* Elected Nov 4, 1997 to term beginning Jan 6, 1998. Term expires Jan 2008. Currently serves Criminal Trial Division. Born Rochester Minnesota. Educated at St. Mary's College B.A. 1974, University of Chicago A.M. 1976 and Georgetown University Law Center J.D. 1982. Law Clerk to Hon. Nelson A. Diaz, Pennsylvania Court of Common Pleas First Judicial District 1982-84. Admitted to practice Pennsylvania 1982.
Assistant District Attorney Philadelphia 1984-89. Senior Deputy Attorney General 1989-97. Member Hispanic Bar Association and Philadelphia Bar Association. Attended General Jurisdiction, Advanced Evidence, Handling Capital Cases and Search, Seizure and Criminal Procedure courses The National Judicial College. Board Member Congreso de Latinos Unidos and Free Library of Philadelphia.
Office: 258 City Hall, Philadelphia 19107.
Telephone: (215) 686-7920.
E-mail address: M.Sarmina@Courts.Phila.Gov

SASINOSKI, Kevin G. *(Judge, Pennsylvania Court of Common Pleas Fifth Judicial District)*
Office: 507 Allegheny County Courthouse, 436 Grant Street, Pittsburgh 15219.
Telephone: (412) 350-2910.

SAVAGE, Timothy J. *(Judge, United States District Court Eastern District of Pennsylvania)* Appointed for

SAVAGE, TIMOTHY J.—*Continued*
life by President George W. Bush to term beginning Aug 19, 2002.
Office: 4006 U.S. Courthouse, 601 Market Street, Philadelphia 19106.
Telephone: (215) 597-7704.

SAXTON, Richard N., Jr. *(President Judge, Pennsylvania Court of Common Pleas Twenty-fifth Judicial District)*
Office: Clinton County Courthouse, 230 East Water Street, Lock Haven 17745.
Telephone: (570) 893-4013.

SAYLOR, Charles Horace *(Judge, Pennsylvania Court of Common Pleas Eighth Judicial District)* Assumed office 2002. Born Bethlehem Pennsylvania Jan 6, 1950. Roman Catholic. Educated at Pennsylvania State University B.A. 1971 and Dickinson School of Law J.D. 1974. Admitted to practice Pennsylvania 1974 and U.S. District Court Middle District of Pennsylvania 1979. Assistant Editor Dickinson Law Review 1973. Law Clerk to Pennsylvania Court of Common Pleas Eighth Judicial District 1974-76. In legal practice Sunbury 1976-2001.
Solicitor Rush Township 1979-2001, Point Township 1983-2001 and Northumberland County 1993-95. Assistant Editor Northumberland Legal Journal 1987-2001. Instructor Pennsylvania State University 1986. Member Pennsylvania Trial Lawyers Association, Northumberland County (Secretary-Treasurer 1985-2000, President 2001) and Pennsylvania Bar Associations. Republican. Trustee Northumberland County Law Library 1986-2001. Trustee 1988-93 and Vice President 1990-93 Priestley-Forsyth Memorial Library. Coach American Youth Soccer Association 1988-90. Assistant Coach Girls Track and Field Shikellamy High School 1992-93. Professionals Co-chair United Way 2000-01. Member YMCA (Member since 1991 and President 1997-98 Board of Directors, Chairman Sustaining Campaign 1992). Enjoys running and golf.
Office: Northumberland County Courthouse, 201 Market Street, Sunbury 17801.
Telephone: (570) 988-5445.

SAYLOR, Thomas G. *(Justice, The Supreme Court of Pennsylvania)* Elected 1997 to term beginning Jan 1998. Term expires Jan 2008. Born Meyersdale Pennsylvania Dec 14, 1946. Educated at University of Virginia B.A. 1969 and Columbia University School of Law J.D. 1972. In legal practice Pennsylvania 1972-82. Judge, The Superior Court of Pennsylvania 1993-97.
First Assistant District Attorney Somerset County 1973-76. First Deputy Attorney General Pennsylvania 1983-87. Member Appellate Judges Conference, American Law Institute, Cumberland County, Dauphin County, Pennsylvania and American Bar Associations. Director Pennsylvania Bureau of Consumer Protection 1982-83. Board of Overseers Widener University School of Law.
Office: Fulton Building, 16th Floor, 200 North Third Street, Harrisburg 17101.
Telephone: (717) 772-1599.

SCANLON, Eugene F., Jr. *(Judge, Pennsylvania Court of Common Pleas Fifth Judicial District)* Appointed by Governor Tom Ridge to term beginning May 14, 1998. Elected Nov 2, 1999, current term expires Jan 2010. Administrative Judge Family Division since April 2002. Born Pittsburgh Pennsylvania Oct 15, 1947. Roman Catholic. Educated at University of Pittsburgh B.A. 1969 and Duquesne University J.D. 1972. Admitted to practice Pennsylvania 1972, U.S. District Court Western District of Pennsylvania 1972, U.S. Court of Appeals Third Circuit 1976 and U.S. Supreme Court 1984. In legal practice Pittsburgh 1972-98.
Member Academy of Trial Lawyers of Allegheny County, Pennsylvania Defense Institute (Board of Directors 1980-85, President 1984-85) and International Association of Defense Counsel. Board of Directors 1985-98 and President 1990-98 Cystic Fibrosis Foundation. Former Member Board of Directors American Cancer Society. Board of Directors Pittsburgh Civic Light Opera since 1996 and Pittsburgh International Childrens Theater 1998-2000.
Office: 440 Ross Street, Room 5024, Pittsburgh 15219.
Telephone: (412) 350-6052.

SCHILLER, Berle M. *(Judge, United States District Court Eastern District of Pennsylvania)* Appointed for life by President Bill Clinton to term beginning June 6, 2000. Born Brooklyn New York June 17, 1944. Educated at Bowdoin College B.A. 1965 and New York University School of Law J.D. 1968. In legal practice Pennsylvania 1968-69 and 1972-93. Judge, The Superior Court of Pennsylvania 1996-2000.
Deputy Attorney General Pennsylvania Department of Justice 1971. Chief Counsel Federal Transit Administration 1994-96.
Office: 5614 U.S. Courthouse, 601 Market Street, Philadelphia 19106-1756.
Telephone: (215) 597-7704.

SCHMEHL, Jeffrey L. *(Judge, Pennsylvania Court of Common Pleas Twenty-third Judicial District)*
Office: Berks County Services Center, Fourth Floor, 633 Court Street, Reading 19601.
Telephone: (610) 478-6952.

SCHMEHL, Peter W. *(Judge, Pennsylvania Court of Common Pleas Twenty-third Judicial District)*
Office: Berks County Services Center, Fifth Floor, 633 Court Street, Reading 19601.
Telephone: (610) 478-6426.

SCHWAB, Arthur J. *(Judge, United States District Court Western District of Pennsylvania)* Appointed for life by President George W. Bush to term beginning Jan 1, 2003.
Office: 916 U.S. Courthouse, Ninth Floor, Seventh Avenue and Grant Street, Pittsburgh 15219.
Telephone: (412) 208-7423.

SCOTT, Susan Devlin *(Judge, Pennsylvania Court of Common Pleas Seventh Judicial District)*
Office: Bucks County Courthouse, 55 East Court Street, Doylestown 18901.
Telephone: (215) 348-6877.

SCUDERI, Peter B. *(Recalled Magistrate Judge, United States District Court Eastern District of Pennsylvania)* Appointed Magistrate Judge by U.S. District Court judges to term beginning Dec 11, 1974. Reappointed 1982 and 1990. Appointed Recalled Magistrate Judge by the Judicial Council of the Third Circuit. Born Philadelphia Pennsylvania April 12, 1928. Catholic. Educated at Temple University B.S. 1949 and Duke University LL.B. 1952. Admitted to practice Pennsylvania

SCUDERI, PETER B.—*Continued*

1952. Hearing Examiner, Pennsylvania Liquor Control Board 1963-71.

Member Philadelphia Bar Association. Republican. Enjoys golf and tennis.

Office: 3015 U.S. Courthouse, 601 Market Street, Philadelphia 19106-1714.

Telephone: (215) 597-2093.

SEAMANS, Kenneth W. *(President Judge, Pennsylvania Court of Common Pleas Thirty-fourth Judicial District)* Elected Nov 1987 to term beginning Jan 1988. Retained by election 1997, current term expires Jan 2008. Born Binghamton New York May 23, 1948. Educated at Pennsylvania State University B.A. with high distinction 1974 and Temple University J.D. 1977. District Justice 1980-88.

Member Pennsylvania Bar Association. USCG 1967-71.

Mailing address: P.O. Box 218, Montrose 18801.

Office: Susquehanna County Courthouse, Montrose 18801.

Telephone: (570) 278-4600.

SEARER, Timothy S. *(President Judge, Pennsylvania Court of Common Pleas Fifty-eighth Judicial District)* Elected Nov 1993 to term beginning Jan 3, 1994. Term expires Jan 2004. Born Lewistown Pennsylvania July 24, 1955. United Church of Christ. Educated at Pennsylvania State University B.S. 1977 and Duquesne University School of Law J.D. 1980. Admitted to practice Pennsylvania 1980, U.S. District Court Middle District of Pennsylvania 1985 and U.S. Court of Appeals Third Circuit 1991. In legal practice Lewistown 1980-94.

Solicitor 1984-88 and District Attorney 1988-94 Mifflin County. Member Pennsylvania Conference of State Trial Judges, Mifflin County and Pennsylvania Bar Associations. Attended General Jurisdiction Course The National Judicial College Sept 1994 to Oct 1994. Past President Lewistown Kiwanis Club. Former Board Member United Way of Mifflin-Juniata Counties. Enjoys golf and coaching youth basketball and baseball.

Office: Mifflin County Courthouse, 20 North Wayne Street, Lewistown 17044.

Telephone: (717) 248-4613.

SENSENICH, Ila Jeanne *(Magistrate Judge, United States District Court Western District of Pennsylvania)* Appointed by U.S. District Court judges to term beginning March 15, 1971. Reappointed March 15, 1979, March 15, 1987, March 1995 and March 2003. Current term expires March 2011. Born Pittsburgh Pennsylvania March 6, 1939. Presbyterian. Educated at Westminster College B.A. 1961 and Dickinson School of Law J.D. 1964. Awarded honorary J.D. from Dickinson School of Law 1994. Assistant Articles Editor Dickinson Law Review 1963-64. Admitted to practice Pennsylvania 1964. Began legal practice Greensburg 1964.

First Assistant Public Defender Westmoreland County 1970. Author "*Commonwealth v. Williams:* Voluntariness of a Confession as Affecting Admissibility into Evidence" 67 Dickinson L. Rev. 327, 1963, "United States Magistrates Act and Its Implementation in the Western District of Pennsylvania" Pittsburgh Legal Jour. July 1972 and "Compendium on the Law of Prisoner's Rights" Federal Judicial Center May 1979. Adjunct Professor of Law Duquesne University School of Law 1982-87. Visiting Fellow in the Daniel and Florence Guggenheim Program in Criminal Justice Yale Law School 1976-77. Member American Judicature Society, Federal Magistrate Judges Association (Past President), National Association of Women Judges, Women's Bar Association of Western Pennsylvania, Westmoreland County, Allegheny County, Pennsylvania and American (Committee on U.S. Magistrates National Conference of Special Court Judges Judicial Administration Division) Bar Associations. Faculty member Federal Judicial Center Washington, D.C. Selected as one of three magistrates in nation to study English judicial system and make recommendations on how U.S. federal system might benefit by English experience. Recipient Outstanding Alumni Award from Westminster College 1976. Democrat. Board of Trustees Emeritus Dickinson School of Law. Member Western Pennsylvania Blind Outdoor Leisure Development (B.O.L.D.). Enjoys skiing, sailing, bicycling, classical music and cooking.

Office: 518B U.S. Post Office & Courthouse, 700 Grant Street, Pittsburgh 15219-1952.

Telephone: (412) 208-7480.

SHAFFER, William R. *(Judge, Pennsylvania Court of Common Pleas Fiftieth Judicial District)* Elected to term beginning Jan 2000. Term expires Jan 2010. Born Butler Pennsylvania April 11, 1953. Educated at Allegheny College B.A. 1975 and University of Pittsburgh. Alden Scholar. Admitted to practice Pennsylvania 1975 and U.S. District Court Western District of Pennsylvania. In legal practice Butler 1979-83 and 1990-2000.

Assistant District Attorney Feb 1984 to July 1990. Member Butler County (Former Secretary) and Pennsylvania (Delegate Young Lawyers Division) Bar Associations.

Mailing address: P.O. Box 1208, Butler 16003-1208.

Office: Butler County Government Center, Butler 16001.

Telephone: (724) 284-5508.

E-mail address: wshaffer@co.butler.pa.js

SHAPIRO, Norma L. *(Senior Judge, United States District Court Eastern District of Pennsylvania)* Appointed for life by President Jimmy Carter to term beginning Sept 29, 1978. Assumed Senior status Dec 31, 1998, serves by assignment. Born Philadelphia Pennsylvania July 27, 1928. Jewish. Educated at University of Michigan B.A. with honors 1948 and University of Pennsylvania J.D. with honors 1951. Law Clerk to Hon. Horace Stern, The Supreme Court of Pennsylvania 1951-52. Member Order of the Coif (Chapter President 1973-75) and Tau Epsilon Rho. Admitted to practice Pennsylvania 1952. Began legal practice Philadelphia 1952.

Guest Editor "Women in the Law" *The Shingle* June 1972. Instructor 1951-52 and 1955-56 and Lecturer 1971 University of Pennsylvania Law School. Fellow American Bar Foundation. Member The American Law Institute, National Association of Women Lawyers, Philadelphia Trial Lawyers Association, American Judicature Society, Philadelphia (Former member Federal Civil Judicial Procedures Committee; Chairperson 1962 and 1974-75 and former member Women's Rights Committee; Secretary Medico-Legal Committee; Chairman Board of Governors 1977 and Public Relations Committee 1978), Pennsylvania (Former member House of Delegates, Special Committee on E.R.A., Committee on Civil Rights and Responsibilities and Professional Rights and Responsibilities Advisory Committee) Federal and American (Judicial Administration Division, Committee on

SHAPIRO, NORMA L.—*Continued*

Law and Mental Health; Sections: Family Law, Litigation, Business Law) Bar Associations. Former Reviewing Member Disciplinary Board Supreme Court of Pennsylvania Hearing Committee. Recipient Gowen Fellowship and Graduate Fellowship in Criminal Law for Study of Juvenile Court Law. Named Woman of the Year for Outstanding Achievement in the Community by Oxford Circle Jewish Community Center, Woman of Distinction by Golden Slipper Club. Recipient Bill of Rights Award from Federal Bar Association 1991 and Hannah G. Soloman Award from National Council of Jewish Women 1992. Vice President 1976 and President 1968-77 Lower Merion Board of School Directors. Vice President 1974-77 and Chairperson Legal Affairs Committee 1978 Jewish Community Relations Council of Greater Philadelphia. Former Trustee Women's Law Project. Past President Belmont Hills Home and School Association. Former Legislative Chairman Lower Merion School District Interschool Council. Former Legal Advisor Regional Council of Child Psychiatry. Former member Task Force on Mental Health of Children and Youth Commonwealth of Pennsylvania and Lawyers Advisory Panel Pennsylvania Governor's Commission on the Status of Women. Former Treasurer and Chairman Education Committee Human Relations Council of Philadelphia. Former Vice President and Parliamentarian Nes Ami Penn Valley Congregation. Member University of Pennsylvania Law Alumni Society, University of Pennsylvania Law School Board of Overseers (Associate Trustee) and National Council of Jewish Women.

Office: 10614 U.S. Courthouse, 601 Market Street, Philadelphia 19106-1774.

Telephone: (215) 597-9141.

SHENKIN, Robert J. *(Judge, Pennsylvania Court of Common Pleas Fifteenth Judicial District)* Elected Nov 1989 to term beginning Jan 1, 1990. Retained by election Nov 1999, current term expires Jan 3, 2010. Born Philadelphia Pennsylvania July 3, 1944. Educated at University of Michigan B.B.A. 1965 and Duke University J.D. with honors 1970. Law Clerk to Hon. Herbert S. Levin, Pennsylvania Court of Common Pleas First Judicial District 1970-71. Admitted to practice Pennsylvania 1970, U.S. District Court Eastern District of Pennsylvania and U.S. Supreme Court. In legal practice Chester County 1971-89.

Mailing address: P.O. Box 2748, West Chester 19380.

Office: 202 Chester County Courthouse, 2 North High Street, West Chester 19380.

Telephone: (610) 344-6180.

SHEPPARD, Albert W., Jr. *(Judge, Pennsylvania Court of Common Pleas First Judicial District)* Elected to term beginning Jan 1984. Retained by election Nov 1993, current term expires Jan 2004.

Office: 529 City Hall, Philadelphia 19107.

Telephone: (215) 686-7934.

SHREEVES-JOHNS, Karen *(Judge, Pennsylvania Court of Common Pleas First Judicial District)* Elected Nov 1999 to term beginning Jan 1, 2000. Term expires Jan 1, 2010. Born Philadelphia Pennsylvania July 8, 1956. Baptist. Educated at Fisk University B.A. 1978 and Howard University J.D. 1981. Admitted to practice Pennsylvania 1982 and U.S. District Court Eastern District of Pennsylvania 1983. In legal practice Philadelphia 1983-85.

Public Defender with Defender Association of Pennsylvania Sept 1985 to March 1999. Member Philadelphia Board of Judges, National Judicial Council and Philadelphia Bar Association. Deaconess Board Sharon Baptist Church. Member Philadelphia Chapter Howard University School of Law Alumni Association and Vine Memorial Baptist Church. Personal Statement or Quote: "To whom much is given, much shall be required. This statement acknowledges the great responsibility imposed upon the Judiciary as elected officials governing the lives of the people that appear before the court."

Office: 1217 Criminal Justice Center, 1301 Filbert Street, Philadelphia 19107.

Telephone: (215) 683-7068.

Fax: (215) 683-7070

SIGMUND, Diane W. *(Judge, United States Bankruptcy Court Eastern District of Pennsylvania)* Appointed by U.S. Court of Appeals Third Circuit judges.

Office: 203 Federal Building, 900 Market Street, Philadelphia 19107-4296.

Telephone: (215) 408-2978.

SIMPSON, Robert E., Jr. *(Judge, The Commonwealth Court of Pennsylvania)* Former Judge, Pennsylvania Court of Common Pleas Third Judicial District.

Office: Justice Building, 115 South Broad Street, Nazareth 18064.

Telephone: (610) 746-2807.

SMITH, Charles B. *(Magistrate Judge, United States District Court Eastern District of Pennsylvania)* Appointed by U.S. District Court judges. Former Judge, Pennsylvania Court of Common Pleas Fifteenth Judicial District.

Office: 3006 U.S. Courthouse, 601 Market Street, Philadelphia 19106-1714.

Telephone: (215) 597-0421.

SMITH, Clinton W. *(President Judge, Pennsylvania Court of Common Pleas Twenty-ninth Judicial District)*

Office: Lycoming County Courthouse, 48 West Third Street, Williamsport 17701.

Telephone: (570) 327-2370.

SMITH, Edward G. *(Judge, Pennsylvania Court of Common Pleas Third Judicial District)*

Office: 502 L and D Plaza, 101 Larry Holmes Drive, Easton 18042.

Telephone: (610) 559-1022.

SMITH, Gregory E. *(Judge, Pennsylvania Court of Common Pleas First Judicial District)* Appointed by Governor Robert P. Casey Nov 1991 to term beginning Jan 1992. Elected to term beginning 2002, current term expires Jan 2012. Born Lynchburg Virginia. Baptist. Educated at Lincoln University B.A. 1976 and Howard University J.D. 1979. Law Clerk to Hon. Darnell Jones, Pennsylvania Court of Common Pleas. In legal practice Philadelphia 1979-91.

Financial Secretary National Bar Association of the Judicial Council 1999-2001. Board Member and Chairman Compliance Committee Northwestern Human Services since 1999. Board Member Philadelphia Education Fund since 2002. Past President Board of Directors Warren E. Smith Center. Enjoys tennis and health club.

Office: 1301 Filbert Street, Suite 1407, Philadelphia 19107.

Telephone: (215) 683-7118.

SMITH, GREGORY E.—*Continued*

Fax: (215) 683-7120
E-mail address: Gregory.Smith@courts.phila.gov

SMITH, Jeffrey A. *(President Judge, Pennsylvania Court of Common Pleas Forty-second Judicial District)* Appointed by Governor Richard Thornburgh to term beginning Dec 27, 1983. Elected 1985. Retained by election 1995, current term expires Jan 2006. Born Sayre Pennsylvania Jan 31, 1953. Protestant. Educated at University of Pittsburgh B.A. in Economics cum laude 1974 and Dickinson School of Law J.D. 1979. Member Corpus Juris Society. Admitted to practice Pennsylvania 1979. Began legal practice Towanda 1979.

Special Prosecutor 1979-81. Assistant District Attorney 1981-82. Instructor American Institute of Banking 1980-82. Member Pennsylvania Conference of State Trial Judges, Bradford County and Pennsylvania Bar Associations. Member Advisory Committee on Jail Overcrowding Pennsylvania Commission on Crime and Delinquency. Attended General Jurisdiction course The National Judicial College April 1986. Republican. Treasurer Bradford County Young Republicans. Sustaining member Republican National Committee. Member Elks, Lions International, The Nature Conservancy and South Mountain Hunting Club. Board of Trustees Towanda Memorial Hospital. General Sullivan Council Executive Committee Boy Scouts of America. Enjoys basketball, cross-country skiing, reading, hunting, running and fishing.

Office: Bradford County Courthouse, 301 Main Street, Towanda 18848.
Telephone: (570) 265-1708.

SMITH-RIBNER, Doris A. *(Judge, The Commonwealth Court of Pennsylvania)*

Office: 920 The Widener Building, One South Penn Square, Philadelphia 19107.
Telephone: (215) 560-3694.

SMYSER, J. Andrew *(Magistrate Judge, United States District Court Middle District of Pennsylvania)* Appointed by U.S. District Court judges to term beginning June 15, 1982. Reappointed 1990 and 1998. Current term expires June 15, 2006. Born York Pennsylvania Oct 19, 1946. Presbyterian. Educated at Lehigh University B.A. with honors 1969 and Georgetown University J.D. 1972. Member Phi Delta Theta. Admitted to practice Pennsylvania 1972, U.S. District Court Middle District of Pennsylvania 1972 and U.S. Court of Appeals Third Circuit 1977. In legal practice York 1972.

Deputy Attorney General Pennsylvania Department of Justice 1972-79 (Director Office of Criminal Law 1975-79). Deputy District Attorney Dauphin County 1979-80. Assistant U.S. Attorney 1980-82. Member Dauphin County and Pennsylvania Bar Associations.

Office: 1160 Federal Building, 228 Walnut Street, Harrisburg 17101.
Telephone: (717) 221-3980.

SMYTH, Joseph A., Jr. *(Judge, Pennsylvania Court of Common Pleas Thirty-eighth Judicial District)* Former President Judge.

Mailing address: P.O. Box 311, Norristown 19404.
Office: Montgomery County Courthouse, Norristown 19401.
Telephone: (610) 278-3920.

SNITE, Albert John, Jr. *(Judge, Pennsylvania Court of Common Pleas First Judicial District)* Appointed by Governor Robert P. Casey to term beginning Dec 1991. Elected to term beginning Jan 6, 1992. Retained by election 2001, current term expires Jan 2012. Born Philadelphia Pennsylvania March 3, 1948. Educated at University of Pennsylvania B.S. 1969 and Dickinson School of Law J.D. 1973. Admitted to practice Pennsylvania 1973, U.S. District Court Eastern District of Pennsylvania 1977, U.S. Court of Appeals Third Circuit 1977 and U.S. Supreme Court 1981.

Office: 1401 Criminal Justice Center, 1301 Filbert Street, Philadelphia 19107.
Telephone: (215) 683-7100.
Fax: (215) 683-7102

SNYDER, Gregory M. *(Judge, Pennsylvania Court of Common Pleas Nineteenth Judicial District)* Elected Nov 1997 to term beginning Jan 1998. Term expires Jan 2008.

Office: York County Courthouse, 28 East Market Street, York 17401.
Telephone: (717) 771-9673.

SOLOMON, Gerald R. *(Judge, Pennsylvania Court of Common Pleas Fourteenth Judicial District)* Elected to term beginning Jan 1988. Retained by election 1997, current term expires Jan 2008. Born Republic Pennsylvania Feb 26, 1942. Orthodox. Educated at University of Pittsburgh B.A. 1965 and Temple University School of Law J.D. 1968. Member Phi Alpha Delta. Admitted to practice Pennsylvania 1968, U.S. District Court Western District of Pennsylvania 1969, U.S. Supreme Court 1980 and U.S. Court of Appeals Third Circuit 1982. In legal practice Uniontown 1968-88.

District Attorney Fayette County 1977-88. Former member Board of Examiners of Public Accountants Pennsylvania. Member Pennsylvania Conference of State Trial Judges, National Council of Juvenile and Family Court Judges, Fayette County (President 1982) and Pennsylvania Bar Associations. Recipient ALSA Man of the Year Award 1984 and Temple First Award. Enjoys running, reading and golf.

Office: Fayette County Courthouse, 61 East Main Street, Uniontown 15401.
Telephone: (724) 430-1234.

SPATARO, John F. *(Judge, Pennsylvania Court of Common Pleas Thirtieth Judicial District)* Elected to term beginning Jan 6, 2002. Term expires Dec 2011. Born Clearfield Pennsylvania Sept 30, 1953. Roman Catholic. Educated at Edinboro State College B.A. 1975 M.A. 1977 and Ohio Northern University J.D. with distinction 1980. Recipient Annual Daniel S. Guy Award for Excellence in Legal Journalism and American Jurisprudence Awards in Contracts III, Constitutional Law I, Sales, Federal Estate and Gift Tax and Labor Law. Listed in *Who's Who Among Students at American Universities and Colleges* 1976 and *The National Dean's List* 1978-79. Associate Editor Ohio Northern University Law Review 1978-79. Member Phi Kappa Phi and Willis Society. Admitted to practice Pennsylvania 1980 and U.S. District Court Western District of Pennsylvania 1981. In legal practice May 15, 1980 to March 1983.

Assistant District Attorney Feb 1983 to Dec 1991 and County Solicitor Jan 1992 to Dec 2001 Crawford County. Author "*Motorists Mutual Insurance Co. v. Bill:* A Narrow Scope of Liability for the Parents of Children Tortfeasors and the Application of Subrogation to Sec. 3109.09 of the Ohio Revised Code" 6 No. 3 and "The Impact of *United Steel-workers of America v. Weber* on

SPATARO, JOHN F.—*Continued*

Affirmative Action Planning" 7 No. 4 Ohio Northern University L. Rev. Former Member Pennsylvania Trial Lawyers Association. Member Inn of Court, Pennsylvania Conference of State Trial Judges, Crawford County and Pennsylvania Bar Associations. School Board Crawford Central School District 1987-91. Patron Meadville Public Library. Member Domestic Violence and Sexual Assault Advisory Committee, Crawford County Youth Soccer Association and Meadville Area Soccer Club. Coach Meadville Area Youth Baseball and Softball Association.

Office: Crawford County Courthouse, 903 Diamond Park, Meadville 16335.

Telephone: (814) 373-2711.

Fax: (814) 337-8198

E-mail address: jspataro@co.crawford.pa.us

SPRECHER, Jeffrey K. *(Judge, Pennsylvania Court of Common Pleas Twenty-third Judicial District)*

Office: Berks County Services Center, Fourth Floor, 633 Court Street, Reading 19601.

Telephone: (610) 478-6441.

STALLONE, Albert A. *(President Judge, Pennsylvania Court of Common Pleas Twenty-third Judicial District)* Appointed by Governor Robert Casey to term beginning July 13, 1987. Elected Nov 1987 and 1997. Current term expires Jan 2008. Born West Reading Pennsylvania April 5, 1933. United Methodist. Educated at Wesley College A.A. 1953, American University B.A. 1955 and Washington College of Law of American University LL.B. 1958. Co-editor American University Law Review 1958. Member Phi Sigma Kappa and Omicron Delta Kappa. Admitted to practice Pennsylvania 1959. In legal practice Reading 1959-87.

Assistant District Attorney 1960-64. Solicitor to Register of Wills 1973-80. President Pennsylvania Conference of State Trial Judges 2001-02. Member American Judicature Society, Berks County, Pennsylvania and American Bar Associations. Attended General Jurisdiction course The National Judicial College 1988. Recipient Award for Historic Restoration of Office Buildings in City of Reading 1984, Italian-American Citizen Award 1987, Wesley College Outstanding Alumni Award 1988 and Martin Luther King Image Award 1993. Democrat. Promoter Columbus '92 Commission for Berks County. President Board of Directors The Children's Home of Reading for 18 years. Fundraising Chairman Northwest Neighborhood Ministries. Enjoys antiques, motor home trips, golf, photography and restoring historic buildings.

Office: Berks County Courthouse, Eighth Floor, 633 Court Street, Reading 19601.

Telephone: (610) 478-6446.

STANDISH, William L. *(Senior Judge, United States District Court Western District of Pennsylvania)* Appointed for life by President Ronald Reagan to term beginning Nov 30, 1987. Assumed Senior status March 1, 2002, serves by assignment. Born Pittsburgh Pennsylvania Feb 16, 1930. Educated at Yale University B.A. and University of Virginia LL.B. Admitted to practice Pennsylvania 1957, U.S. District Court Western District of Pennsylvania 1957, U.S. Court of Appeals Third Circuit 1960 and U.S. Supreme Court 1967. In legal practice Pittsburgh 1957-80. Judge, Pennsylvania Court of Common Pleas Fifth Judicial District 1980-87.

Member Academy of Trial Lawyers of Allegheny County, Pittsburgh Chapter American Inns of Court, American Judicature Society, Allegheny County, Pennsylvania and American Bar Associations.

Office: 605 U.S. Post Office & Courthouse, 700 Grant Street, Pittsburgh 15219.

Telephone: (412) 208-7430.

STEEGE, Peter O. *(Judge, Pennsylvania Court of Common Pleas Thirty-sixth Judicial District)* Elected Nov 5, 1985 to term beginning Jan 6, 1986. Retained by election Nov 7, 1995, current term expires Jan 2006. Born Hartford Connecticut Nov 9, 1933. Presbyterian. Educated at Wesleyan University A.B. 1955 and University of Chicago J.D. 1958.

Office: Beaver County Courthouse, Third Street, Beaver 15009.

Telephone: (724) 728-5700.

STEINBERG, Robert L. *(Judge, Pennsylvania Court of Common Pleas Thirty-first Judicial District)* Elected to term beginning Jan 1998. Term expires Jan 2008. Born Nov 26, 1951. Educated at American University B.S. 1973 and Western New England College School of Law J.D. 1976.

Public Defender 1976-78. Assistant District Attorney 1978-83, Deputy District Attorney 1985-88, First Assistant District Attorney 1988-91 and District Attorney 1991-97. Author "Juvenile Court: Practice and Procedure" *Manual for Pennsylvania Prosecutors* and "Mental Infirmity Defenses" Pennsylvania Bar Institute. Member Lehigh County, Pennsylvania and American Bar Associations. Instructor Pennsylvania District Attorneys Association and Pennsylvania Bar Institute. Recipient Colonel John K. Schafer Award for excellence in law enforcement. Member Victim Services Advisory Board April 1996 to Dec 1997.

Office: Lehigh County Courthouse, 455 West Hamilton Street, Allentown 18101.

Telephone: (610) 782-3960.

STENGEL, Lawrence F. *(Judge, Pennsylvania Court of Common Pleas Second Judicial District)*

Mailing address: P.O. Box 83480, Lancaster 17608-3480.

Office: Lancaster County Courthouse, 50 North Duke Street, Lancaster 17602.

Telephone: (717) 293-7296.

STEVENS, Correale F. *(Judge, The Superior Court of Pennsylvania)* Elected Nov 1997 to term beginning Jan 1998. Term expires Jan 2008. Born Hazleton Pennsylvania. Educated at Pennsylvania State University B.A. 1964 and Dickinson School of Law J.D. 1972. Associate Editor Dickinson Law Review. Judge, Pennsylvania Court of Common Pleas Eleventh Judicial District 1991-98.

City Solicitor 1976-79 and City Authority Solicitor 1979-84 Hazleton. District Attorney Luzerne County 1987-91. Member Pennsylvania House of Representatives 1980-87. Executive Board Wilkes-Barre Law and Library Association.

Office: 300 Laurel Professional Center, 121 Airport Road, Hazleton 18202.

Telephone: (570) 459-3990.

STINE, D. Michael *(Judge, Pennsylvania Court of Common Pleas Twenty-first Judicial District)*
Office: Schuylkill County Courthouse, 401 North Second Street, Pottsville 17901.
Telephone: (570) 628-1312.

STRASSBURGER, Eugene B., III *(Judge, Pennsylvania Court of Common Pleas Fifth Judicial District)* Appointed by Governor Milton J. Shapp to term beginning June 29, 1978. Elected Nov 1979. Retained by election Nov 1989 and Nov 1999. Current term expires Jan 2010. Former Administrative Judge Family Division. Born Columbus Ohio Nov 28, 1943. Jewish. Educated at Yale University B.A. summa cum laude 1964 and Harvard University J.D. cum laude 1967. Law Clerk to Hon. Henry X. O'Brien, The Supreme Court of Pennsylvania 1967-70. Member Phi Beta Kappa. Admitted to practice Pennsylvania 1967, U.S. Court of Appeals Third Circuit 1970 and U.S. Supreme Court 1971. In legal practice Pittsburgh 1968-78.
Assistant City Solicitor 1970, Executive Assistant City Solicitor 1971-74 and Deputy City Solicitor 1974-78 City of Pittsburgh Law Department. Adjunct Professor of Federal and Pennsylvania Procedure Duquesne University Law School 1971-72 and of Local Government Law University of Pittsburgh Law School 1975-77. Former Member and Chair Pennsylvania Supreme Court Domestic Relations Committee. Former Member Juvenile Court Judges' Commission. Member Joint Task Force to Ensure Gender Fairness in Courts, Pennsylvania Conference of State Trial Judges and Pennsylvania Bar Association. Member Pennsylvania Joint Family Law Council, The American Law Institute (Project on Law and Family Dissolution), Pennsylvania Conference of State Trial Judges, Allegheny County (Committees on Opportunities for Minorities in the Legal Profession, Court Rules and Juvenile Law, Executive Committee and Gender Bias Subcommittee Women in the Law, Sections: Civil Litigation, Family, Juvenile Law) and Pennsylvania (Family Law Section) Bar Associations. Democrat. Former member and officer Board of Directors Neighborhood Legal Services Association. Former Member Board of Directors Pittsburgh-Allegheny County Chapter American Red Cross. Board of Directors Pennsylvania CASA, PERSAD and Women's Center and Shelter. Member Fertile Octogenarians, Allegheny County Bar Association Softball League and B'nai B'rith. Enjoys softball, golf and playing bridge.
Office: 709 City-County Building, 414 Grant Street, Pittsburgh 15219.
Telephone: (412) 350-7138.

STREITEL, Phyllis R. *(Judge, Pennsylvania Court of Common Pleas Fifteenth Judicial District)*
Mailing address: P.O. Box 2748, West Chester 19380.
Office: 102 Chester County Courthouse, Two North High Street, West Chester 19380.
Telephone: (610) 344-4494.

SUMMERS, Edward R. *(Judge, Pennsylvania Court of Common Pleas First Judicial District)*
Office: 34 South Eleventh Street, Room 220, Philadelphia 19107.
Telephone: (215) 686-8318.

SURRICK, R. Barclay *(Judge, United States District Court Eastern District of Pennsylvania)* Appointed for life by President Bill Clinton to term beginning July 14, 2000. Born Media Pennsylvania Dec 18, 1937. Episcopalian. Educated at Dickinson College A.B. 1960 and Dickinson School of Law LL.B. 1965. Admitted to practice Pennsylvania 1965. Began legal practice Media 1965. Judge, Pennsylvania Court of Common Pleas Thirty-second Judicial District Jan 3, 1978 to July 13, 2000.
Member Delaware County Bar Association. First Lieutenant USAS 1961-67. Republican. Board of Commissioners Nether Providence Township Delaware County 1974-78. Enjoys sailing.
Office: 5118 U.S. Courthouse, 601 Market Street, Philadelphia 19106-1754.
Telephone: (215) 597-7704.

SWOPE, Thomas A., Jr. *(Judge, Pennsylvania Court of Common Pleas Forty-seventh Judicial District)* Elected to term beginning Jan 4, 1988. Retained by election 1997, current term expires Jan 2008. Born Johnstown Pennsylvania April 21, 1934. Catholic. Educated at University of Notre Dame B.A. with honors 1956 and University of Pennsylvania J.D. 1959. Admitted to practice Pennsylvania 1960. In legal practice Ebensburg 1960-88.
Deputy Attorney General 1960-61. Assistant District Attorney 1965-70. Adjunct Professor of Business Law St. Francis College 1967-2000. Attended The National Judicial College July 1988. U.S. Army and Pennsylvania National Guard 1959-65.
Office: Cambria County Courthouse, 200 South Center Street, Ebensburg 15931.
Telephone: (814) 472-1492.

SYLVESTER, Esther R. *(Judge, Pennsylvania Court of Common Pleas First Judicial District)* Former Administrative Judge Family Division.
Office: 692 City Hall, Philadelphia 19107.
Telephone: (215) 686-7946.

TEMIN, Carolyn Engel *(Judge, Pennsylvania Court of Common Pleas First Judicial District)* Assumed office Jan 1, 1984.
Office: 1404 Criminal Justice Center, 1301 Filbert Street, Philadelphia 19107.
Telephone: (215) 683-7109.

TERESHKO, Allan L. *(Judge, Pennsylvania Court of Common Pleas First Judicial District)* Former Supervising Judge Domestic Relations Division. Currently serves as Supervising Judge Civil Trial Division.
Team Leader Day Forward Program Major Civil Jury Trials.
Office: 234 City Hall, Philadelphia 19107.
Telephone: (215) 686-7324.

THOMAS, John J. *(Chief Judge, United States Bankruptcy Court Middle District of Pennsylvania)* Appointed by U.S. Court of Appeals Third Circuit judges.
Office: U.S. Courthouse, 197 South Main Street, Wilkes-Barre 18701-1598.
Telephone: (570) 826-6336.

THOMAS, Rea Boylan *(Judge, Pennsylvania Court of Common Pleas Seventh Judicial District)*
Office: Bucks County Courthouse, 55 East Court Street, Doylestown 18901.
Telephone: (215) 348-6709.

THOMPSON, John W., Jr. *(Judge, Pennsylvania Court of Common Pleas Nineteenth Judicial District)*
Office: York County Courthouse, 28 East Market Street, York 17401.
Telephone: (717) 771-9329.

TILSON, Arthur R. *(Judge, Pennsylvania Court of Common Pleas Thirty-eighth Judicial District)*
Mailing address: P.O. Box 311, Norristown 19404.
Office: Montgomery County Courthouse, Norristown 19401.
Telephone: (610) 278-3910.

TODD, Debra McCloskey *(Judge, The Superior Court of Pennsylvania)* Elected Nov 1999 to term beginning Jan 2000. Term expires Jan 2010. Born Ellwood City Pennsylvania Oct 15, 1957. Educated at Chatham College with honors 1979 and University of Pittsburgh School of Law J.D. 1982. In legal practice Pittsburgh 1987-99. Special Master, Pennsylvania Court of Common Pleas Fifth Judicial District 1989-99.
In-house Litigation Attorney USX Corporation 1982-87. Member Academy of Trial Lawyers of Allegheny County, Allegheny County, Pennsylvania and American Bar Associations.
Office: Two Chatham Center, Suite 220, Pittsburgh 15219.
Telephone: (412) 565-2680.

TODD, Randal B. *(Judge, Pennsylvania Court of Common Pleas Fifth Judicial District)*
Office: 440 Ross Street, Room 5069, Pittsburgh 15219.
Telephone: (412) 350-0341.

TOOLE, Patrick J., Jr. *(Judge, Pennsylvania Court of Common Pleas Eleventh Judicial District)* Appointed by Governor Milton J. Shapp to term beginning Feb 28, 1978. Former President Judge. Born Wilkes-Barre Pennsylvania Sept 16, 1933. Catholic. Educated at King's College B.A. 1957 and Temple University LL.B. 1960. Admitted to practice Pennsylvania 1961. Began legal practice Wilkes-Barre 1960.
District Attorney Luzerne County 1971-78. President Pennsylvania District Attorneys Association 1977. Recipient Distinguished Public Service Award from County Detectives Association of Pennsylvania 1976. Corporal U.S. Army 1953-55.
Office: Luzerne County Courthouse, 200 North River Street, Wilkes-Barre 18711.
Telephone: (570) 825-1667.

TRENT, Earl W., Jr. *(Judge, Pennsylvania Court of Common Pleas First Judicial District)* Assumed office Jan 2002. Currently serves Juvenile Court Division. Educated at University of Pittsburgh B.A. 1967 and Howard University School of Law J.D. 1970.
Former General Counsel American Baptist Churches nationwide. Member Barristers Association of Philadelphia, Pennsylvania Trial Lawyers Association, Philadelphia and National Bar Associations. Recipient North Philadelphia Action Branch Award of Appreciation 1984, William Ming Award 1995 and Cecil B. Moore Award Oct 1999 NAACP. Executive Board and Chair Legal Redress Committee Philadelphia Branch NAACP for 25 years. Member Governor's Commission on African American Affairs for four years. Board of Directors John F. Kennedy Community Mental Health/Mental Retardation Center, Baptist Joint Committee on Public Affairs in Washington, D.C., ACLU of Pennsylvania and Homemaker's Inc. of Philadelphia.
Office: 1801 Vine Street, Room 347, Philadelphia 19103.
Telephone: (215) 686-4057.
Fax: (215) 686-4220
E-mail address: earl.trent@courts.phila.gov

TRESSLER, Paul W. *(Judge, Pennsylvania Court of Common Pleas Thirty-eighth Judicial District)* Appointed by Governor Richard Thornburgh to term beginning April 6, 1983. Elected Nov 1983. Retained by election Nov 1993, current term expires Jan 2004. Administrative Judge Juvenile Division 1985-90. Administrative Judge Criminal Division 1997-2000. Born Lancaster Pennsylvania March 29, 1940. Protestant. Educated at Susquehanna University B.A. cum laude 1962 and University of Pennsylvania J.D. 1966. Law Clerk to Hon. J. William Ditter, Jr., Pennsylvania Court of Common Pleas Thirty-eighth Judicial District 1966-68. Admitted to practice Pennsylvania 1966. In legal practice 1974-80.
Assistant District Attorney 1968-73 and First Assistant District Attorney 1980-83 Montgomery County. Special Assistant to Pennsylvania Attorney General's Office 1982-83. Instructor Fox Valley Technical College since 1990. Past President Juvenile Section Pennsylvania Association of State Trial Judges. Member Montgomery County Bar Association (Chairman Criminal Rules Committee). Instructor Office of Juvenile Justice and Delinquency Prevention since 1985. Member National Center for Missing and Exploited Children since 2001. Enjoys studying Civil War and is a numismatic.
Mailing address: P.O. Box 311, Norristown 19404-0311.
Office: Montgomery County Courthouse, Norristown 19401.
Telephone: (610) 278-3993.

TRUCILLA, John J. *(Judge, Pennsylvania Court of Common Pleas Sixth Judicial District)* Elected Nov 6, 2001 to term beginning Jan 2002. Term expires Jan 2012. Born Erie Pennsylvania Oct 3, 1960. Educated at University of Dayton B.A. 1982 J.D. 1985. Law Clerk to Hon. Shad F. Connelly, Pennsylvania Court of Common Pleas Sixth Judicial District Jan 1986 to Jan 1988. Admitted to practice Pennsylvania, U.S. District Court Western District of Pennsylvania, U.S. Court of Appeals Third Circuit and U.S. Supreme Court. In legal practice Jan 2001 to June 2001.
Assistant District Attorney Erie County Jan 1988 to April 1990 and June 2001 to Dec 2001. Assistant U.S. Attorney April 1990 to Jan 2001 and Chief Erie Division 1994-2001 Western District of Pennsylvania. Adjunct Professor of Criminal Law and Procedure and Constitutional Law Pennsylvania State University 1989-96 and Criminal Law and Procedure Gannon University since Jan 2002. Member Northwest Pennsylvania American Inns of Court. Instructor Northwest Training Center Pennsylvania State Police Academy 1997-2001.
Office: Erie County Courthouse, 140 West Sixth Street, Erie 16501.
Telephone: (814) 451-6481.

TUCKER, Petrese Brown *(Judge, United States District Court Eastern District of Pennsylvania)* Appointed for life by President Bill Clinton to term beginning July 14, 2000. Born Philadelphia Pennsylvania May 27, 1951. Educated at Temple University B.A. with honors 1973 J.D. 1976. Law Clerk to Hon. Lawrence Prattis, Penn-

TUCKER, PETRESE BROWN—*Continued*

sylvania Court of Common Pleas July 1976 to July 1978. Admitted to practice Pennsylvania 1976 and U.S. District Court Eastern District of Pennsylvania 1976. In legal practice 1977-78 and Jan 1986 to April 5, 1987. Judge April 6, 1987 to July 13, 2000 and Administrative Judge Orphans' Division April 1, 1996 to July 13, 2000, Pennsylvania Court of Common Pleas First Judicial District.

Assistant Chief Rape Unit July 1978 to March 1985 and Assistant Chief Child Abuse Unit March 1985 to Jan 1986 District Attorney's Office Philadelphia. Senior Trial Attorney Southeastern Pennsylvania Transportation Authority Nov 1986 to April 5, 1987. Adjunct Professor Great Lakes College Association Sept 1984 to Dec 1985 and Trial Advocacy Course Temple University School of Law Spring 1991, Spring 1992 and Spring 1993. Member Barristers Association of Philadelphia, Pennsylvania Conference of State Trial Judges, National Council of Juvenile and Family Court Judges (Juvenile Court Section), Philadelphia (Chairperson Domestic Abuse Committee Family Law Section Jan 1990), Pennsylvania, National (Advisory Board Philadelphia Chapter Women Lawyers Division, Chairperson Advisory Committee for the Probation Department, Member Education Committee and Judicial Accountability Committee Trial Division) and American Bar Associations. Recipient Award of Merit from Italian-American Press Knights of Legion Sept 30, 1988, Distinguished Service Award from Family Law Section 1990, University Mentor and Appreciation Award from Temple University Feb 1990, Certificate of Appreciation from Women Against Abuse and Victims of Domestic Violence Philadelphia Municipal Court 1992 and Certificate of Appreciation from Special Project Connect Greater Philadelphia Urban Affairs Coalition May 3, 1996. Board of Directors Girls Inc. of Greater Philadelphia and Southern New Jersey since Jan 1990 (Chair Personnel Committee, Member Marketing Committee). Board Member Germantown YWCA. Member The Forum of Executive Women.

Office: 3810 U.S. Courthouse, 601 Market Street, Philadelphia 19106-1796.

Telephone: (267) 299-7610.

TURGEON, Jeannine *(Judge, Pennsylvania Court of Common Pleas Twelfth Judicial District)* Elected to term beginning Jan 6, 1992. Retained by election 2001, current term expires Jan 2012. Served Juvenile Division 1996-97. First woman elected to Twelfth Judicial District. Born Ephrata Pennsylvania March 19, 1953. Educated at Chatham College B.A. 1974 and University of Pittsburgh School of Law J.D. 1977. Law Clerk to Hon. Genevieve Blatt, The Commonwealth Court of Pennsylvania 1977-79. In legal practice Pennsylvania 1979-91.

Author "A Custody System that Works" *Jurispondence* Pennsylvania Conference of State Trial Judges Dec 1995 republished *The Pennsylvania Lawyer* Nov-Dec 1996, "How to [Create] 'A Custody System That Works'" *The County Line* Pennsylvania Bar Association July 1996, "Judges: Should Pharmacological Treatment Be a Condition of Certain Sex Offenders' Probation or Parole?" *Jurispondence* Pennsylvania Conference of State Trial Judges May 1997 and "PFA Court—A Problem Solving Court" *Pennsylvania Family Lawyer* Dec 2001. Chair Joint Task Force on Gender Fairness in Courts Pennsylvania Bar Association and Pennsylvania Conference of State Trial Judges 1996 to August 1997. Member since March 1997 and Chair Domestic Relations Rules Committee and Member Suggested Standard Jury (Civil) Instructions Committee The Supreme Court of Pennsylvania. Member Attorney General's Family Violence Task Force since 1998. Co-chair Central Pennsylvania Judges and Lawyers Concerned for Lawyers and Judges. Member Computer Project Committee Pennsylvania Court of Common Pleas. Member Pennsylvania Conference of State Trial Judges (Executive Committee July 1996 to July 1997, Economics and Benefits Committee July 1996 to July 1997, Nominating Committee Juvenile Section 1997-98, Advisory Board Committee since 1996, Chair Family Law Section since 1996), Dauphin County (Board of Directors 1984-86 and 1990-91, Founding Member Community Task Force on Seminars for Separating Parents since 1993, Chairperson Public Relations Committee 1994, Chair Meet the Judges Forum since 1994, Domestic Relations Section) and Pennsylvania (Delegate House of Delegates Young Lawyers Division 1985-87, Council Member Section of Civil Litigation 1995-96, Civil Rules Committee since 1995) Bar Associations.

Speaker "Domestic Violence Program" 1995 and "Juvenile Justice in Pennsylvania: Balanced Approach" Feb 1997 Pennsylvania Conference of State Trial Judges. Course Planner "Alternate & Dispute Resolution" Mid Year Meeting Pennsylvania Bar Association Feb 1995. Presenter "Professionalism Program" May 1995 and "Protection from Abuse—Recent Rule Changes and Litigation Techniques" Family Law Section Summer Meeting Bermuda July 9-11, 1998 Pennsylvania Bar Association. Member Conference Steering Committee "Fractured Families & Fragmented Courts" Commission on Women in the Profession Pennsylvania Bar Association 1996 and 1997. Attended "Separating Families Presentation" Feb 1996 and "Equitable Distribution and Pensions" Feb 1997 Pennsylvania Conference of State Trial Judges. Participant "Victim-Judge Focus Group" Restorative Justice Policy Forum April 4, 1997, "Understanding Sexual Violence" State Justice Institute May 8-10, 1997, and "Domestic Violence Knows No Bounds: Interstate Enforcement and Technology Conference" CLE Seminar Pennsylvania Coalition Against Domestic Violence Nov 13-14, 1997. Lecturer PBI and Daubert/Frye Seminar Philadelphia Lawyers Association. Recipient Mae Carvell Award from North Atlantic Region Venture Club of America 1993, Distinguished Service to Legal Education Award from Widener School of Law 1994, Eagleville Hospital Award June 1995 and Distinguished Award Outside Field of Detention from Juvenile Detention Center Association of Pennsylvania 1996. Harrisburg Delegate "President's Summit for America's Future" April 27-29, 1997. Board of Directors 1988-90, Member Nominating Committee 1989 and Chair Diversification Committee 1988-90 Capitol Region Economic Development Corporation. Board of Directors Capitol Region Health Futures 1997. Member Junior League of Harrisburg 1978-94 (Chairperson Grantsmanship Committee 1980, Member 1986-87 and Chairperson 1988 Civic Pride Committee). Founding Member 1984 and Vice Chairperson 1985-86 Dauphin County Victim/Witness Program. Advisory Committee Communities in Schools since 1996. Sunday School Teacher St. Stephen's Cathedral since 1996. Chair Youth at Risk Work Group Harrisburg Community Alliance since 1997. Vice Chair Tri-County Alliance for Youth since 1998. Member Pennsylvania Coalition Against Domestic Violence, Protection From

TURGEON, JEANNINE—*Continued*

Abuse Database Project Advisory Committee and The Harrisburg Center for Healthy Child Development.
Office: Dauphin County Courthouse, Front and Market Streets, Harrisburg 17101.
Telephone: (717) 780-6655.

TWARDOWSKI, Thomas M. *(Judge, United States Bankruptcy Court Eastern District of Pennsylvania)* Appointed by U.S. District Court judges to term beginning April 28, 1975. Reappointed 1981. Appointed by U.S. Court of Appeals Third Circuit judges 1987. Reappointed 1999. Former Chief Judge. Born Reading Pennsylvania Feb 4, 1941. Roman Catholic. Educated at University of Notre Dame B.A. 1962 and Villanova University School of Law J.D. 1965. Member Order of the Coif. Associate Editor Villanova Law Review. Law Clerk to Hon. Ralph C. Body, U.S. District Court Eastern District of Pennsylvania 01965-67. Admitted to practice Pennsylvania 1965. Began legal practice Paoli 1967. In legal practice Westchester 1971-74.
Member Berks County, Pennsylvania and American Bar Associations. Enjoys all sports, painting and poetry.
Office: 301 Madison Building, 400 Washington Street, Reading 19601.
Telephone: (610) 320-5093.

TYLWALK, John C. *(Judge, Pennsylvania Court of Common Pleas Fifty-second Judicial District)*
Office: 400 South Eighth Street, Lebanon 17042.
Telephone: (717) 274-2801.

UHLER, John C. *(Judge, Pennsylvania Court of Common Pleas Nineteenth Judicial District)* Elected Nov 2, 1989 to term beginning Jan 1, 1990. Retained by election Nov 4, 1999, current term expires Jan 1, 2010. Acting President Judge Sept 1995 to Jan 1996. President Judge Jan 1996 to Jan 2001. Born Harrisburg Pennsylvania June 24, 1944. Lutheran. Educated at Bucknell University B.S. 1966 and Dickinson School of Law J.D. with honors 1969. Senior Law Clerk to Hon. R. Dixon Herman, U.S. District Court Middle District of Pennsylvania 1970-71. Admitted to practice Pennsylvania 1969, U.S. District Court Middle District of Pennsylvania 1971, U.S. Court of Appeals Third Circuit 1972 and U.S. Supreme Court 1978. In legal practice York.
Assistant U.S. Attorney Middle District of Pennsylvania 1971-73. District Attorney York County 1978-81. Lawyer Delegate Third Circuit Court of Appeals Judicial Conference of the U.S. 1987. President Juvenile Judges Section since 2001, Former Chairman President Judges Committee and Member Ethics Committee Pennsylvania Conference of State Trial Judges. Member York County, Pennsylvania and Federal Bar Associations. Panelist and Presenter seminars on Judicial Ethics, Professionalism, Discovery, Immigration, Criminal Law, Judicial Administration and Juvenile Law. Enjoys tennis, biking, bridge, photography and hiking.
Office: York County Courthouse, 28 East Market Street, York 17401.
Telephone: (717) 771-9806.
Fax: (717) 852-4931
E-mail address: jcuhler@york-county.org

VALASEK, Kenneth G. *(Judge, Pennsylvania Court of Common Pleas Thirty-third Judicial District)*
Office: Armstrong County Courthouse, Kittanning 16201.
Telephone: (724) 548-3457.

VAN ANTWERPEN, Franklin S. *(Judge, United States District Court Eastern District of Pennsylvania)* Appointed for life by President Ronald Reagan to term beginning Dec 21, 1987. Born Passaic New Jersey Oct 23, 1941. Protestant. Educated at University of Maine B.S. in Engineering Physics 1964 and Temple University School of Law J.D. 1967. Moot Court Justice. Admitted to practice Pennsylvania 1969, U.S. District Court Eastern District of Pennsylvania 1971, U.S. Court of Appeals Third Circuit 1971 and U.S. Supreme Court 1972. In legal practice New York New York 1967-70 and Easton Pennsylvania 1970-79. Judge, Pennsylvania Court of Common Pleas Third Judicial District 1979-87.
Solicitor Palmer Township 1971-79. Important Decision: United States v. Scarfo (major 18-defendant organized crime trial) 711 F. Supp. 1315, 1988. Adjunct Professor of Business Law Northampton Community College 1976-81. Member Judicial Working Group U.S. Sentencing Commission 1992-93. Member Committee on Defender Services Judicial Conference of the U.S. 1997. Member National Lawyers Club, American Judicature Society, Northampton County, Pennsylvania, Federal and American (Committee on Judicial Education) Bar Associations. Instructor Continuing Legal Education Seminar on Evidence Pennsylvania Bar Institute June 1991. Recipient George Palmer Award from Palmer Township, Law Enforcement Award from National Society of Sons of the American Revolution and Alumni Achievement Award from Newark Academy. Named Man of the Year by Palmer Township and Alumnus Who Has Made a Difference in the World by University of Maine. Member Pomfret Club and Union League of Philadelphia.
Office: Holmes Building, Fourth Floor, 101 Larry Holmes Drive, Easton 18042-7722.
Telephone: (610) 252-6522.

VAN ARTSDALEN, Donald W. *(Senior Judge, United States District Court Eastern District of Pennsylvania)* Appointed for life by President Richard M. Nixon to term beginning 1970. Assumed Senior status, serves by assignment. Born Doylestown Pennsylvania Oct 21, 1919. Educated at Williams College 1937-40 and University of Pennsylvania LL.B. 1948. Admitted to practice Pennsylvania 1948 and U.S. Supreme Court 1956. In legal practice Doylestown 1948-70.
District Attorney Bucks County 1954-58. Canadian Army 1940-42 and U.S. Army 1942-45.
Office: 3040 U.S. Courthouse, 601 Market Street, Philadelphia 19106-1779.
Telephone: (215) 597-7704.

VANASKIE, Thomas I. *(Chief Judge, United States District Court Middle District of Pennsylvania)* Appointed for life by President Bill Clinton to term beginning March 1, 1994. Chief Judge since Sept 1, 1999. Educated at Lycoming College B.A. magna cum laude 1975 and Dickinson School of Law J.D. cum laude 1978. Editorial Staff Dickinson Law Review. Law Clerk to Chief Judge William J. Nealon, U.S. District Court Middle District of Pennsylvania. Recipient Chieftain Award from Lycoming College and M. Vashti Burr Award from Dickinson School of Law. Appellate Moot Court Board and International Law Moot Court Team.

VANASKIE, THOMAS I.—*Continued*

Member Woolsack Society and Phi Kappa Phi. Began legal practice Scranton 1980.

Former Member Board of Directors Northeastern Pennsylvania Trial Lawyers Association. Former Member Board of Directors and Chair Continuing Legal Education Committee Lackawanna Bar Association. Former Member Lawyers' Advisory Committee and Civil Justice Reform Act Group U.S District Court Middle District of Pennsylvania. Liaison Judge Task Force on Equal Treatment in the Courts, Member Automation Committee and Co-Chair Library Resource Task Force U.S. Court of Appeals Third Circuit. President 1990-92 and Board of Governors Our Lady of Lourdes Regional High School Alumni Association. Board Member Scranton Preparatory School.

Mailing address: P.O. Box 913, Scranton 18501-0913.

Telephone: (570) 207-5720.

VAN HORN, Carol L. *(Judge, Pennsylvania Court of Common Pleas Thirty-ninth Judicial District)*

Office: Franklin County Courthouse, 157 Lincoln Way East, Chambersburg 17201.

Telephone: (717) 261-3836.

VANSTON, Brendan J. *(President Judge, Pennsylvania Court of Common Pleas Forty-fourth Judicial District)*

Office: Wyoming County Courthouse, One Courthouse Square, Tunkhannock 18657.

Telephone: (570) 836-3151.

VARDARO, Anthony J. *(Judge, Pennsylvania Court of Common Pleas Thirtieth Judicial District)* Elected Nov 1991 to term beginning Jan 6, 1992. Retained by election 2001, current term expires Jan 2012. Born Meadville Pennsylvania April 9, 1954. Roman Catholic. Educated at Allegheny College B.A. 1976 and University of Pittsburgh J.D. 1979. Admitted to practice Pennsylvania 1979 and U.S. District Court Western District of Pennsylvania 1982. In legal practice Meadville 1979-91.

Solicitor Crawford County 1988-91. Member American Inns of Court, Crawford County and Pennsylvania Bar Associations. Democrat. Chairman Crawford County Democratic Party 1982-86. Enjoys golf, antiques and carpentry.

Office: Crawford County Courthouse, 903 Diamond Park, Meadville 16335.

Telephone: (814) 333-7493.

VICAN, Ronald E. *(President Judge, Pennsylvania Court of Common Pleas Forty-third Judicial District)* Elected to term beginning Jan 1982. Retained by election 1991 and 2001. Current term expires Jan 2012. Born Baltimore Maryland Sept 12, 1946. Methodist. Educated at Dickinson College B.A. 1968 and Dickinson School of Law J.D. with honors in Roman and Civil law 1971. Member Sigma Chi. Admitted to practice Pennsylvania 1971. In legal practice Stroudsburg 1971-81.

Public Defender Monroe County 1973-80. Important Decision: Commonwealth v. Ludwig (closed circuit testimony in sexual child abuse cases). Member Monroe County and Pennsylvania Bar Associations. Former Solicitor Pleasant Valley Manor, Inc. Former Member Pocono Mountains Municipal Airport Authority. Member Cherrylane Methodist Church, Salvation Army (Honorary Board member), F & AM Barger Lodge No. 325 and BPOE Lodge No. 319. Enjoys sailing, physical fitness, reading and classical music.

Office: Monroe County Courthouse, Monroe Street, Stroudsburg 18360.

Telephone: (570) 420-3610.

WAGNER, John F., Jr. *(Judge, Pennsylvania Court of Common Pleas Fourteenth Judicial District)* Appointed by Governor Robert P. Casey to term beginning Nov 1987. Elected Nov 1989. Retained by election Nov 1999, current term expires Dec 31, 2009. Born Pittsburgh Pennsylvania Aug 26, 1947. Presbyterian. Educated at Indiana University of Pennsylvania B.S. 1969 and University of Pittsburgh J.D. 1972. Admitted to practice Pennsylvania 1972. In legal practice Connellsville 1972-87.

Assistant District Attorney Fayette County 1976-87. Instructor Pennsylvania State University since 1990. Member Fayette County and Pennsylvania Bar Association. Captain Pennsylvania Army National Guard 1972-84. Enjoys jogging.

Office: Fayette County Courthouse, 61 East Main Street, Uniontown 15401.

Telephone: (724) 430-1236.

WALDMAN, Jay C. *(Judge, United States District Court Eastern District of Pennsylvania)* Appointed for life by President Ronald Reagan to term beginning 1988. Born Pittsburgh Pennsylvania Nov 16, 1944. Educated at University of Wisconsin B.S. 1966 and University of Pennsylvania Law School LL.B. 1969. Law Clerk to Hon. Gwilym A. Price, Jr., Pennsylvania Court of Common Pleas 1969-70. In legal practice Pittsburgh 1970-71 and Philadelphia 1986-88.

Assistant U.S. Attorney Western District of Pennsylvania 1971-75. Deputy Assistant U.S. Attorney General Criminal Division Washington D.C. 1975-77. General Counsel Commonwealth of Pennsylvania 1981-86. Commissioner Pennsylvania Convention Center Authority 1986-88. Director Thornburgh for Governor Commission Philadelphia 1978. Counsel to Governor Richard Thornburgh 1979-81.

Office: 9613 U.S. Courthouse, 601 Market Street, Philadelphia 19106-1763.

Telephone: (215) 597-9644.

WALKER, John R. *(President Judge, Pennsylvania Court of Common Pleas Thirty-ninth Judicial District)*

Office: Franklin County Courthouse, 157 Lincoln Way East, Chambersburg 17201.

Telephone: (717) 261-3844.

WALLITSCH, Thomas A. *(Judge, Pennsylvania Court of Common Pleas Thirty-first Judicial District)* Appointed by Governor Robert P. Casey to term beginning April 23, 1991. Elected Nov 1991. Retained by election 2001, current term expires Jan 2012. Born Allentown Pennsylvania June 25, 1948. Lutheran. Educated at Dickinson College A.B. 1970, Duquesne University School of Law J.D. 1973 and University of Pennsylvania M.G.A. 1993. Staff member Duquesne Law Review 1972-73. Admitted to practice Pennsylvania 1973, U.S. District Court Eastern District of Pennsylvania, U.S. Court of Appeals Third Circuit and U.S. Supreme Court. In legal practice Allentown 1973-91.

Assistant County Solicitor 1976, Chief Public Defender 1976 and Solicitor to County Controller 1984-87 Lehigh County. Adjunct Professor of Political Science

WALLITSCH, THOMAS A.—*Continued*

Muhlenberg College since 1994. Vice Chair Appellate Rules Committee The Supreme Court of Pennsylvania. Member Pennsylvania Conference of State Trial Judges (Co-chair Education Committee), Lehigh County, Pennsylvania and American Bar Associations. Instructor numerous PBI programs. Captain USAR 1970-78. Member Democratic State Committee 1980. Member STOP Violence Against Women Planning Committee Pennsylvania Commission on Crime and Delinquency, Rotary, United Way and Pennsylvania Society.

Office: Lehigh County Courthouse, 455 West Hamilton Street, Allentown 18101-1614.
Telephone: (610) 782-3024.
Fax: (610) 820-3658

WALSH, Richard J. *(Judge, Pennsylvania Court of Common Pleas Thirty-ninth Judicial District)*

Office: Franklin County Courthouse, 157 Lincoln Way East, Chambersburg 17201.
Telephone: (717) 261-3161.

WARMAN, Ralph C. *(Judge, Pennsylvania Court of Common Pleas Fourteenth Judicial District)* Appointed by Governor Tom Ridge to term beginning June 6, 1996. Elected May 1997, current term expires Jan 2008. Born Ellwood City Pennsylvania Oct 22, 1943. Protestant. Educated at California University of Pennsylvania B.S. 1965 and West Virginia University J.D. 1970. Admitted to practice West Virginia 1970, Pennsylvania 1971 and U.S. District Courts Southern District of West Virginia 1970 and Western District of Pennsylvania 1974.

Assistant District Attorney 1977-87 and District Attorney 1991-96 Fayette County.

Office: Fayette County Courthouse, 61 East Main Street, Uniontown 15401.
Telephone: (724) 430-4021.

WATKINS, Thomas D. *(Judge, Pennsylvania Court of Common Pleas First Judicial District)*

Office: 469 City Hall, Philadelphia 19107.
Telephone: (215) 686-7916.

WEBB, Richard W. *(President Judge, Pennsylvania Court of Common Pleas Fifty-sixth Judicial District)* Elected to term beginning Jan 6, 1992. Retained by election 2001, current term expires Jan 2012. Born Palmerton Pennsylvania April 29, 1944. Lutheran. Educated at Pennsylvania State University B.A. 1966 and University of Pittsburgh J.D. 1969. Admitted to practice Pennsylvania 1970, U.S. Supreme Court 1976 and U.S. Court of Appeals Third Circuit 1985. In legal practice Palmerton 1970-92.

Public Defender 1973-75 and District Attorney 1976-92 Carbon County. Member Pennsylvania Conference of State Trial Judges, American Judicature Society, Carbon County (Chancellor 1991), Pennsylvania and American Bar Associations. Democrat. Enjoys golfing, shooting and skiing.

Mailing address: P.O. Box 131, Jim Thorpe 18229.
Office: Carbon County Courthouse, Jim Thorpe 18229.
Telephone: (570) 325-9419.

WEINER, Charles R. *(Senior Judge, United States District Court Eastern District of Pennsylvania)* Appointed for life by President Lyndon B. Johnson to term beginning 1967. Assumed Senior status, serves by assignment. Born Philadelphia Pennsylvania June 21, 1922. Educated at Temple University LL.B. 1950 and University of Pennsylvania M.A. in Political Science 1967 Ph.D. in Political Science 1976. Admitted to practice Pennsylvania 1951. Judge, Special Court on Regional Rail Reorganization 1982-96.

Assistant District Attorney Philadelphia County 1952-53. Former Lecturer on Political Science University of Pennsylvania and Temple University. Former Adjunct Professor of Political Science University of Pennsylvania. Adjunct Professor of Political Science Temple University. Appointed to President Lyndon B. Johnson's Advisory Commission on Inter-Governmental Relations, U.S. National Commission for UNESCO 1974 and Judicial Panel on Multidistrict Litigation 1978. County Board of Law Examiners since 1959. Member Practising Law Institute (Board of Directors), The American Law Institute, American Trial Lawyers Foundation, Philadelphia, Pennsylvania and American Bar Associations. Lecturer Practising Law Institute and The American Law Institute. Faculty member and Planning Committee Conference and Seminars for District Court Judges. Recipient Philadelphia Fellowship Award, Temple University Founder's Day Award, University of Pennsylvania Alumni Award and Berean Institute Founder's Award. USNR WWII. Pennsylvania Senate 1952-67 (Minority Floor Leader 1959-60 and 1963-64, Majority Floor Leader 1961-62). Fellow Harry S. Truman Library Institute. Chairman National Council of Overseers and Executive Committee Dropsie University and Fellowship Commissioners' Committee on Opportunities for Higher Education. Director Berean Institute, Philadelphia Psychiatric Center and World Affairs Council (Chairman Program Committee). Board of Trustees Federation of Jewish Charities (Executive Committee), Allied Jewish Appeal (Executive Committee), Baldwin School and B'rith Sholom Foundation. Board of Directors Mental Health Association of Southeastern Pennsylvania. Honorary Trustee John Marshall House. Board of Governors Institute of Human Resources Development Hahnemann Medical College. Board Member Athenaeum of Philadelphia. Former member Friends of the Philadelphia Orchestra Association, Lyric Opera (Board of Directors), Academy of Natural Sciences of Philadelphia, Pennsylvania Historical Society and University of Pennsylvania Museum. Member Philadelphia Public Policy Committee, VISTA (U.N.U.S.A.), State Board of Arts and Sciences, Franklin Inn Club, Philadelphia Tribune Charities, Philadelphia Wharton Center, Parkside YMCA, Big Brothers Association, Crime Prevention Association, Thouron Scholarship Committee University of Pennsylvania and Smithsonian Institute. Graduate of the Barnes Institute and other art museum courses.

Office: 6613 U.S. Courthouse, 601 Market Street, Philadelphia 19106-1770.
Telephone: (215) 923-4450.

WELLS, Carol Sandra *(Magistrate Judge, United States District Court Eastern District of Pennsylvania)* Appointed by U.S. District Court judges.

Office: 3016 U.S. Courthouse, 601 Market Street, Philadelphia 19106-1714.
Telephone: (215) 597-7833.

WELSH, Diane M. *(Magistrate Judge, United States District Court Eastern District of Pennsylvania)* Appointed by U.S. District Court judges.
Office: 3029 U.S. Courthouse, 601 Market Street, Philadelphia 19106-1714.
Telephone: (215) 597-1207.

WETTICK, R. Stanton, Jr. *(Judge, Pennsylvania Court of Common Pleas Fifth Judicial District)* Appointed by Governor Milton J. Shapp July 1976. Elected 1977. Retained by election 1987 and 1997. Current term expires Jan 2008. Educated at Amherst College B.A. cum laude 1960 and Yale University LL.B. 1963. Admitted to practice Pennsylvania 1963. Began legal practice Pittsburgh 1963.
Executive Director Neighborhood Legal Services Association 1969-76. Instructor University of Pittsburgh School of Law since 1966. Member Allegheny County, Pennsylvania and American Bar Associations.
Office: 818 City-County Building, 414 Grant Street, Pittsburgh 15219.
Telephone: (412) 350-5953.

WHERRY, Michael J. *(Judge, Pennsylvania Court of Common Pleas Thirty-fifth Judicial District)*
Office: Mercer County Courthouse, North Diamond Street, Mercer 16137.
Telephone: (724) 662-3800.

WHITE, H. William *(President Judge, Pennsylvania Court of Common Pleas Twenty-eighth Judicial District)* Elected to term beginning Jan 4, 1988. Retained by election Nov 1997, current term expires Jan 2008. Born Brookville Pennsylvania Aug 29, 1942. Protestant. Educated at Dickinson College A.B. and University of Pittsburgh School of Law J.D. 1967. Book Review Editor University of Pittsburgh Law Review 1966-67. Admitted to practice Pennsylvania 1967, U.S. District Court Western District of Pennsylvania 1972, U.S. Court of Appeals Third Circuit 1978 and U.S. Supreme Court 1978. In legal practice Franklin 1972-87.
Former member Pennsylvania Trial Lawyers Association and The Association of Trial Lawyers of America. Member Venango County (President 1984-85) and Pennsylvania Bar Associations. Attended General Jurisdiction course The National Judicial College 1988. Captain U.S. Army JAGC 1967-72.
Office: Venango County Courthouse, 1168 Liberty Street, Franklin 16323.
Telephone: (814) 432-9610.
E-mail address: wwhite@co.venango.pa.us

WIEST, Wm. Harvey *(Judge, Pennsylvania Court of Common Pleas Eighth Judicial District)* Elected Nov 4, 1997 to term beginning Jan 2, 1998. Term expires Jan 1, 2008. Born Dalmatia Pennsylvania July 8, 1945. United Church of Christ. Educated at Susquehanna University B.S.B.A. 1967 and Cleveland Marshall College of Law J.D. with honors 1971. Editorial Staff Cleveland Marshall Law Review 1970-71. Admitted to practice Pennsylvania 1971 and U.S. District Court Middle District of Pennsylvania 1972. In legal practice Dalmatia and Sunbury 1971-97.
Member Northumberland County and Pennsylvania Bar Associations. Attended Juvenile Court Judges Commission of the Commonwealth of Pennsylvania, Pennsylvania Conference of State Trial Judges and National Council of Juvenile and Family Court Judges. Member F&AM, Scottish Rite, Palatines to America (Past State President), Northumberland County Historical Society, Gratz Historical Society, The Pennsylvania German Society, Sons of the American Revolution (Past President William McClay Chapter, Former Aide to State President), Johannes Schwalm Historical Association, Inc., Cleveland Marshall Law Alumni Association, Northumberland County Council for the Arts and Mahanoy & Mahantongo Historical and Preservation Society (Founder and President). Organist Trinity UCC for 44 years. Interests include genealogy, Odyssey of the Mind, family activities and music.
Office: Northumberland County Courthouse, 201 Market Street, Sunbury 17801.
Telephone: (570) 988-4166.
E-mail address: ncjudge2@ptdprolog.net

WILLIAMSON, J. Michael *(Judge, Pennsylvania Court of Common Pleas Twenty-fifth Judicial District)*
Office: Clinton County Courthouse, 230 East Water Street, Lock Haven 17745.
Telephone: (570) 893-4014.

WOELFEL, Harold F., Jr. *(President Judge, Pennsylvania Court of Common Pleas Seventeenth Judicial District)* Appointed by Governor Robert P. Casey to term beginning Oct 12, 1990. Elected 1991. Retained by election 2001, current term expires Jan 2012. Born Darby Pennsylvania Jan 22, 1951. Educated at Pennsylvania State University B.S. 1972 and Temple University School of Law J.D. 1976. Admitted to practice Pennsylvania 1976 and U.S. District Court Middle District of Pennsylvania 1976. In legal practice Selinsgrove 1976-90.
Member Snyder County (Past President) and Pennsylvania Bar Associations. Attended General Jurisdiction Course The National Judicial College.
Mailing address: P.O. Box 217, Middleburg 17842.
Office: Snyder County Courthouse, Middleburg 17842.
Telephone: (570) 837-4238.

WOGAN, Chris R. *(Judge, Pennsylvania Court of Common Pleas First Judicial District)*
Office: 1212 Criminal Justice Center, 1301 Filbert Street, Philadelphia 19103.
Telephone: (215) 683-7053.

WOLF, Flora Barth *(Judge, Pennsylvania Court of Common Pleas First Judicial District)* Elected to term beginning Jan 6, 1992. Retained by election 2001, current term expires Dec 31, 2011. Educated at Connecticut College B.A. 1964, Johns Hopkins University M.A.T. 1965 and University of Pennsylvania Law School J.D. 1980. Recipient Edwin R. Keedy Moot Court Award 1979. Admitted to practice Pennsylvania and U.S. Court of Appeals Third Circuit.
Assistant City Solicitor Commercial Litigation Unit 1980-83 and Water Department 1983-85 and Divisional Deputy City Solicitor Code Enforcement Unit 1985-91 Philadelphia. Board of Managers and Bar Association Representative 1990-92 and Chair Advisory Board since 1994 Philadelphia Foundation. Member University of Pennsylvania American Inn of Court, Juvenile Justice Alliance and National Association of Women Judges. Public school teacher elementary and junior high schools 1964-67. Assistant to the Dean Institute for Paralegal Training 1976-77. Board Member Citizen's Committee for Public Education in Philadelphia 1968-77 and 1980-83 and Fredora Wolf Foundation since 1982. Member 1974-79 and 1989-96 and President 1974-76 Board of

WOLF, FLORA BARTH—*Continued*
Trustees and Member Long Range Planning Committee 1988 Miquon School. Participant Community Leadership Seminars 1983-84. Board of Directors since 1994 and President 2001-02 New Directions for Women. Board of Directors National Child Labor Committee 1995-99, Pennsylvania Citizen Service Project 1995-2000 and Jewish Family and Children's Services since 1997. Advisory Board Cancer Patient Legal Advocacy Network 1997.
Office: 1801 Vine Street, Room 353, Philadelphia 19103.
Telephone: (215) 686-2614, 686-2615.

WOODS-SKIPPER, Sheila A. *(Judge, Pennsylvania Court of Common Pleas First Judicial District)*
Office: 1216 Criminal Justice Center, 1301 Filbert Street, Philadelphia 19107.
Telephone: (215) 683-7065.

WORTHINGTON, Margherita Patti *(Judge, Pennsylvania Court of Common Pleas Forty-third Judicial District)*
Office: Monroe County Courthouse, Stroudsburg 18360.
Telephone: (570) 420-3607.

WRIGHT, Robert C. *(Judge, Pennsylvania Court of Common Pleas Thirty-second Judicial District)* Elected Nov 1991 to term beginning Jan 6, 1992. Retained by election 2001, current term expires Jan 2012. Former Juvenile Court Liaison Judge. Formerly served Motion Hearing Division. Currently serves Trial Division. Born Chester Pennsylvania Nov 5, 1944. Episcopalian. Educated at George Washington University B.A. 1966 and Villanova University J.D. 1969. Member Tau Epsilon Phi. Admitted to practice Pennsylvania 1970 and U.S. District Court Eastern District of Pennsylvania 1974. In legal practice Chester 1970-91.
Former Solicitor Delaware County Manpower Commission, Chester Housing Authority and Darby Township Zoning Hearing Board. Member Judicial Ethics Committee Pennsylvania Conference of State Trial Judges, Delaware County, Pennsylvania and American Bar Associations. Attended General Jurisdiction Course The National Judicial College. Recipient Chester Black Expo-Humanitarian Award 1982, Man of the Year Award from Chester Scholarship Fund 1982, 1984 and 1988, Victim-Witness Rights Award from Domestic Abuse Project of Delaware County 1988, Community Leadership Award from Concord Day Care Center Parents Association 1988 and Man of the Year Award from Republican Council of Delaware County 1991. Listed in *Who's Who Among Black Americans* 1986-91. Previously worked as social studies teacher Franklin Elementary School. Republican. State Legislator 159th District 1981-91 (Judiciary Committee, Urban Affairs Committee, Joint State Government Commission Task Force on the Decedent's Estate Laws, Former Special Investigative Committee on Pennsylvania State Police). Past President Republican Council of Delaware County. Former Member Board of Directors Southeast Delco Family YMCA and Citizens for Action Now. Board of Directors Chester Education Foundation and Boys and Girls Club of Chester. Former Member Executive Board Chester Branch NAACP. Vestry Saint Mary's Episcopal Church (Former Member).
Office: Delaware County Courthouse, 201 West Front Street, Media 19063.
Telephone: (610) 891-4511.

YEAGER, S. Michael *(Judge, Pennsylvania Court of Common Pleas Fiftieth Judicial District)*
Mailing address: P.O. Box 1208, Butler 16003.
Office: Butler County Government Center, Butler 16001.
Telephone: (724) 284-1391.

YOHN, William H., Jr. *(Judge, United States District Court Eastern District of Pennsylvania)* Appointed for life by the President. Born Pottstown Pennsylvania Nov 20, 1935. United Church of Christ. Educated at Princeton University A.B. magna cum laude 1957 and Yale Law School J.D. 1960. Admitted to practice Pennsylvania 1961 and District of Columbia 1961. Began legal practice Pottstown 1961. Former Judge, Pennsylvania Court of Common Pleas Thirty-eighth Judicial District, appointed by Governor Richard Thornburgh to term beginning May 13, 1981.
Assistant District Attorney 1962-65. Instructor American Institute of Banking 1963-66. Board of Directors Federal Judicial Center since 1999. Member Joint State Government Task Force on Decedents' Estates Laws 1972-80, Pennsylvania Conference of State Trial Judges, Montgomery County (Director 1967-70) and Pennsylvania Bar Associations. Corporal USMCR 1960-66. Pennsylvania House of Representatives 1968-80 (Chairman Finance Committee 1979-80, Chairman 1973-74 and 1979-80 and Vice Chairman 1975-78 Ethics Committee). Chairman Board of Directors The Greater Pottstown Drug Abuse Prevention Program, Inc. 1970-78 and Pottstown Memorial Medical Center 1974-95. Board of Directors Progress Pottstown 1979-81.
Office: 14613 U.S. Courthouse, 601 Market Street, Philadelphia 19106-1753.
Telephone: (215) 597-4361.

YOUNGE, John Milton *(Judge, Pennsylvania Court of Common Pleas First Judicial District)*
Office: 1405 Criminal Justice Center, 1301 Filbert Street, Philadelphia 19107.
Telephone: (215) 683-7112.

ZALESKI, Jerome A. *(Judge, Pennsylvania Court of Common Pleas First Judicial District)* Appointed by Governor Milton J. Shapp Jan 4, 1972. Born Philadelphia Pennsylvania June 21, 1933. Educated at La Salle College B.S. 1959 and Temple University J.D. 1963.
Office: 34 South Eleventh Street, Room 209, Philadelphia 19107.
Telephone: (215) 686-7326.

ZETUSKY, Edward J., Jr. *(Judge, Pennsylvania Court of Common Pleas Thirty-second Judicial District)*
Office: Delaware County Courthouse, 201 West Front Street, Media 19063.
Telephone: (610) 891-4221.

ZIEGLER, Donald E. *(Senior Judge, United States District Court Western District of Pennsylvania)* Appointed for life by President Jimmy Carter to term beginning May 22, 1978. Chief Judge 1994 to Jan 2001. Assumed Senior status Oct 1, 2001, serves by assignment. Born Pittsburgh Pennsylvania Oct 1, 1936. Catholic. Educated at Duquesne University B.A. 1958 and

ZIEGLER, DONALD E.—*Continued*

Georgetown University LL.B. 1961. Staff member Georgetown Law Journal 1960-61. Admitted to practice Pennsylvania 1962, U.S. Court of Appeals Third Circuit 1964 and U.S. Supreme Court 1967. In legal practice Pittsburgh 1962-78. Judge, Pennsylvania Court of Common Pleas Fifth Judicial District Civil Division 1974-78.

Author "Constitutional Rights of the Accused—Developing Dichotomy Between Federal and State Law" 48 Pennsylvania Bar Association Quarterly 421, 1977, "Collegiality and the Courts" *Judicature Magazine* 1991 and "The Unwritten Rules of Professional Conduct" Pittsburgh Legal Journal. Important Decisions: Perks v. Firestone Tire and Rubber Co. 611 F.2d 1363, 3d Cir. 1979, EEOC v. Allegheny County 519 F. Supp. 1328 W.D.Pa. 1981, Patton v. Yount 537 F. Supp. 873 W.D.Pa. 1982 and Keystone Bituminous Coal Association v. DeBenedictis 581 F. Supp. 511 W.D.Pa. 1984. Adjunct Professor Duquesne University School of Law since 1994. Former Member Judicial Council of the Third Circuit. Member Academy of Trial Lawyers of Allegheny County, Federal Judges Association, Judicial Conference of the U.S., Allegheny County (Bench-Bar Committee, Rules Committee, Committee on Professionalism), Pennsylvania and American Bar Associations. Recipient First Century Graduate Award from Duquesne University Century Club 1978, Liberty Watch Award from Pennsylvania Association of Criminal Defense Lawyers 1999, Recognition Award from Academy of Trial Lawyers of Allegheny County 1999 and Joseph F. Weis, Jr. Distinguished Service Award 2001. Airman First Class USAF and Pennsylvania Air National Guard 1961-67. Democrat. Treasurer Big Brothers of Allegheny County 1971-74. Duquesne University Century Club. Enjoys golf and bass fishing.

Office: 649 U.S. Post Office & Courthouse, 700 Grant Street, Pittsburgh 15219.

Telephone: (412) 208-7440.

ZOTTOLA, John A. *(Judge, Pennsylvania Court of Common Pleas Fifth Judicial District)*

Office: 529 Allegheny County Courthouse, 436 Grant Street, Pittsburgh 15219.

Telephone: (412) 350-3676.

RHODE ISLAND

Capital PROVIDENCE

UNITED STATES DISTRICT COURT DISTRICT OF RHODE ISLAND

The court sits at Providence. For descriptive information refer to the United States Courts section.

Chief Judge
Ernest C. Torres

Judges
Mary M. Lisi
William E. Smith

Senior Judge
Ronald R. Lagueux

Clerk
David A. DiMarzio
356 Federal Building
Two Exchange Terrace
Providence, Rhode Island 02903-1779
(401) 752-7220

UNITED STATES MAGISTRATE JUDGES OF RHODE ISLAND

Robert W. Lovegreen
David L. Martin

Recalled Magistrate Judge
Jacob Hagopian

UNITED STATES BANKRUPTCY COURT OF RHODE ISLAND

Judge
Arthur N. Votolato

Bankruptcy Clerk
Susan M. Thurston
The Federal Center
380 Westminster Street
Providence, Rhode Island 02903-3256
(401) 528-4477

RHODE ISLAND SUPREME COURT

The Supreme Court is Rhode Island's court of last resort. The court consists of a chief justice and four associate justices appointed by the governor and confirmed by the Legislature to serve for life during good behavior. Prior to 1994, justices were elected by the Legislature. The chief justice may appoint a general magistrate to enforce orders of restitution. Retired justices may serve by assignment of the chief justice.

The court exercises final appellate jurisdiction over all courts, determines the constitutionality of legislation and issues writs necessary to the exercise of proper jurisdiction. The court has general supervision of all lower courts and regulates admission to the bar and discipline of its members.

The court sits en banc for hearing appeals, but may also sit in panels of three justices for show causes. The court sits at Providence and recesses during July, August and September.

Chief Justice
Frank J. Williams

Associate Justices
Robert G. Flanders, Jr.
Maureen McKenna Goldberg
Francis X. Flaherty
Paul A. Suttell

Clerk
Brian Burns
Frank Licht Judicial Complex
250 Benefit Street
Providence, Rhode Island 02903
(401) 222-3272

State Court Administrator
John H. Barrette
Frank Licht Judicial Complex
250 Benefit Street
Providence, Rhode Island 02903
(401) 222-3266

RHODE ISLAND SUPERIOR COURT

The Superior Court is Rhode Island's court of general jurisdiction. Justices are appointed by the governor with the consent of the Senate to serve for life during good behavior. The presiding justice may appoint magistrates to handle victim restitution cases. General magistrates are appointed by the chief justice of the Supreme Court. Retired justices may serve at the direction of the chief justice and by assignment of the presiding justice.

The court has original jurisdiction in all equity cases and real estate title disputes, except actions for possessions of tenements let or held at will or by passive consent; and exclusive original jurisdiction of all other civil actions in which the amount in controversy exceeds $10,000. The court has concurrent jurisdiction with the District Court in cases involving $5,000 to $10,000. The court's criminal jurisdiction extends to all felonies and matters brought by indictment of the grand jury. The court hears civil and criminal appeals de novo from the District Court and appeals from Probate and Municipal Courts. The court may issue writs necessary to the exercise of proper jurisdiction. Appeals are to the Supreme Court.

The court sits in Kent, Newport, Providence and Washington counties.

Presiding Justice
Joseph F. Rodgers, Jr.

RHODE ISLAND SUPERIOR COURT—*Continued*

Associate Justices

Alice Bridget Gibney	Robert D. Krause
Melanie W. Thunberg	Vincent A. Ragosta
Mark A. Pfeiffer	Patricia A. Hurst
Francis J. Darigan, Jr.	Judith C. Savage
Michael A. Silverstein	Stephen Fortunato, Jr.
Edward C. Clifton	Netti C. Vogel
William A. Dimitri, Jr.	O. Rogeriee Thompson
Gilbert V. Indeglia	Stephen P. Nugent
Edwin J. Gale	Susan E. McGuirl
Daniel A. Procaccini	Jeffrey A. Lanphear
vacancy	

General Magistrate
Patricia L. Harwood

Special Magistrate
Joseph A. Keough

Magistrates
William J. McAtee
Susan L. Revens

RHODE ISLAND WORKERS' COMPENSATION COURT

The Workers' Compensation Court is a court of limited statewide jurisdiction in Rhode Island. The court was established by the General Assembly in 1991 to replace the Rhode Island Workman's Compensation Commission which had existed since 1954. Judges are appointed by the governor with the consent of the Senate to serve for life during good behavior.

The court has original jurisdiction in all issues of controversy relating to workers' compensation cases. Appeals are to the Supreme Court.

The court sits in Providence.

Chief Judge
Robert F. Arrigan

Associate Judges

John Rotondi, Jr.	George E. Healy
Debra L. Olsson	Bruce Q. Morin
Janette A. Bertness	Edward P. Sowa, Jr.
Dianne M. Connor	George T. Salem, Jr.
Hugo L. Ricci, Jr.	

RHODE ISLAND FAMILY COURT

The Family Court is a court of limited jurisdiction in Rhode Island. Justices are appointed by the governor with the consent of the Senate to serve for life during good behavior. The chief judge may appoint magistrates to hear reciprocal support cases and to assist the justices in Providence, Kent, Newport and Washington counties. Retired justices may serve at the direction of the chief justice and by assignment of the chief judge.

The court has exclusive jurisdiction over juvenile and domestic relations cases involving matters of divorce including distribution of property, alimony, support, custody and support of children and petitions for separate maintenance; delinquent, wayward, dependent, abused, mentally defective or mentally disordered children; adoptions; child marriages; and paternity proceedings. The court also has exclusive original jurisdiction over appeals from any administrative agency or board which affect or concern children under the age of eighteen. Serious felony cases may be waived after a hearing to Superior Court for persons between the ages of sixteen and eighteen. Appeals are to the Supreme Court.

The court sits in Kent, Newport, Providence and Washington counties.

Chief Judge
Jeremiah S. Jeremiah, Jr.

Associate Justices

Haiganush R. Bedrosian	Pamela M. Macktaz
Raymond E. Shawcross	Michael B. Forte
Kathleen A. Voccola	Howard I. Lipsey
John A. Mutter	Gilbert T. Rocha
Francis J. Murray, Jr.	Stephen J. Capineri
vacancy	

General Magistrate
John J. O'Brien, Jr.

Magistrates

Debra E. DiSegna	Everett C. Sammartino, Sr.
George N. DiMuro	Angela M. Bucci Paulhus
Jeanne L. Shepard	Edward H. Newman
Patricia K. Asquith	

RHODE ISLAND DISTRICT COURT

The District Court is a court of limited statewide jurisdiction. Judges are appointed by the governor with consent of the Senate to serve for life during good behavior. The chief judge may appoint a magistrate to hear and determine such matters as assigned by the chief judge. Retired judges may serve at the direction of the chief justice and by assignment of the chief judge.

The court has original jurisdiction of all civil cases in which the amount in controversy is less than $5,000 except equity cases, of all actions for possession of tenements or estates let or held by will or by passive consent and replevin actions involving $5,000 or less; and concurrent jurisdiction with the Superior Court in cases involving $5,000 to $10,000. Criminal jurisdiction extends to cases in which the punishment does not exceed $500 or imprisonment for more than one year and to felony preliminary arraignments. The court exercises exclusive original jurisdiction over violations of minimum housing standards. A Small Claims Division handles cases involving $1,500 or less. The court hears appeals from the Traffic Tribunal. The Sixth Division also handles involuntary civil commitments and reviews decisions of various regulatory boards and agencies. All trials are held without a jury. Appeals are heard de novo in the Superior Court.

There are four divisions consisting of the Second, Third, Fourth and Sixth; the First, Fifth and Seventh Divisions consolidated with the Sixth in 1993. The court sits at places designated by the chief judge.

SECOND DIVISION includes Newport County.

THIRD DIVISION includes Kent County.

FOURTH DIVISION includes Washington County.

SIXTH DIVISION includes Bristol and Providence counties.

Chief Judge
Albert E. DeRobbio

RHODE ISLAND DISTRICT COURT—*Continued*

Associate Judges

Michael A. Higgins	Robert K. Pirraglia
Patricia D. Moore	Stephen P. Erickson
Robert J. Rahill	Walter Gorman
John Michael McLoughlin	Frank J. Cenerini
Elaine T. Bucci	Madeline Quirk
Richard A. Gonnella	Jeanne E. LaFazia

Magistrates

Joseph P. Ippolito, Jr.
Christine S. Jabour

RHODE ISLAND TRAFFIC TRIBUNAL

The Traffic Tribunal is a court of limited statewide jurisdiction in Rhode Island. It was established in 1999 to succeed the Administrative Adjudication Court which had previously replaced the Administrative Adjudication Division of the Department of Transportation in 1992. The tribunal currently consists of four judges and three magistrates under the supervision of the Chief Judge of the District Court. Judges are appointed by the governor with consent of the Senate to serve for life during good behavior. As the judges resign or retire they will be replaced by additional magistrates who are appointed by the Chief Judge of the District Court with consent of the Senate to serve for eight-year terms.

The tribunal exercises jurisdiction over most traffic cases and is responsible for distributing and controlling traffic summonses and maintaining driver violation records. The tribunal also exercises appellate jurisdiction over traffic cases heard in Municipal Courts. Appeals are to the District Court.

The court sits full time at Providence and certain times at Woonsocket and Wakefield.

Judges

Marjorie R. Yashar
Lillian M. Almeida
Albert R. Ciullo
Edward C. Parker

Magistrates

Aurendina G. Veiga
Domenic A. DiSandro, III
William T. Noonan

RHODE ISLAND PROBATE COURTS

The Probate Courts are courts of limited jurisdiction in Rhode Island. Judges are appointed by the mayor or town council for two-year terms. In New Shoreham, the town council acts as judge of probate.

The courts have jurisdiction over all matters related to the settlement of estates and the appointment of guardians.

RHODE ISLAND MUNICIPAL COURTS

The Rhode Island Municipal Courts are courts of limited jurisdiction in Rhode Island. Judges are appointed by the city council for two-year terms.

The courts have jurisdiction over minor traffic violations and municipal ordinances. The courts also enforce the minimum housing standards ordinance. Appeals for traffic violations are to the Traffic Tribunal.

Rhode Island Counties

Bristol

Kent

Newport

Providence

Washington

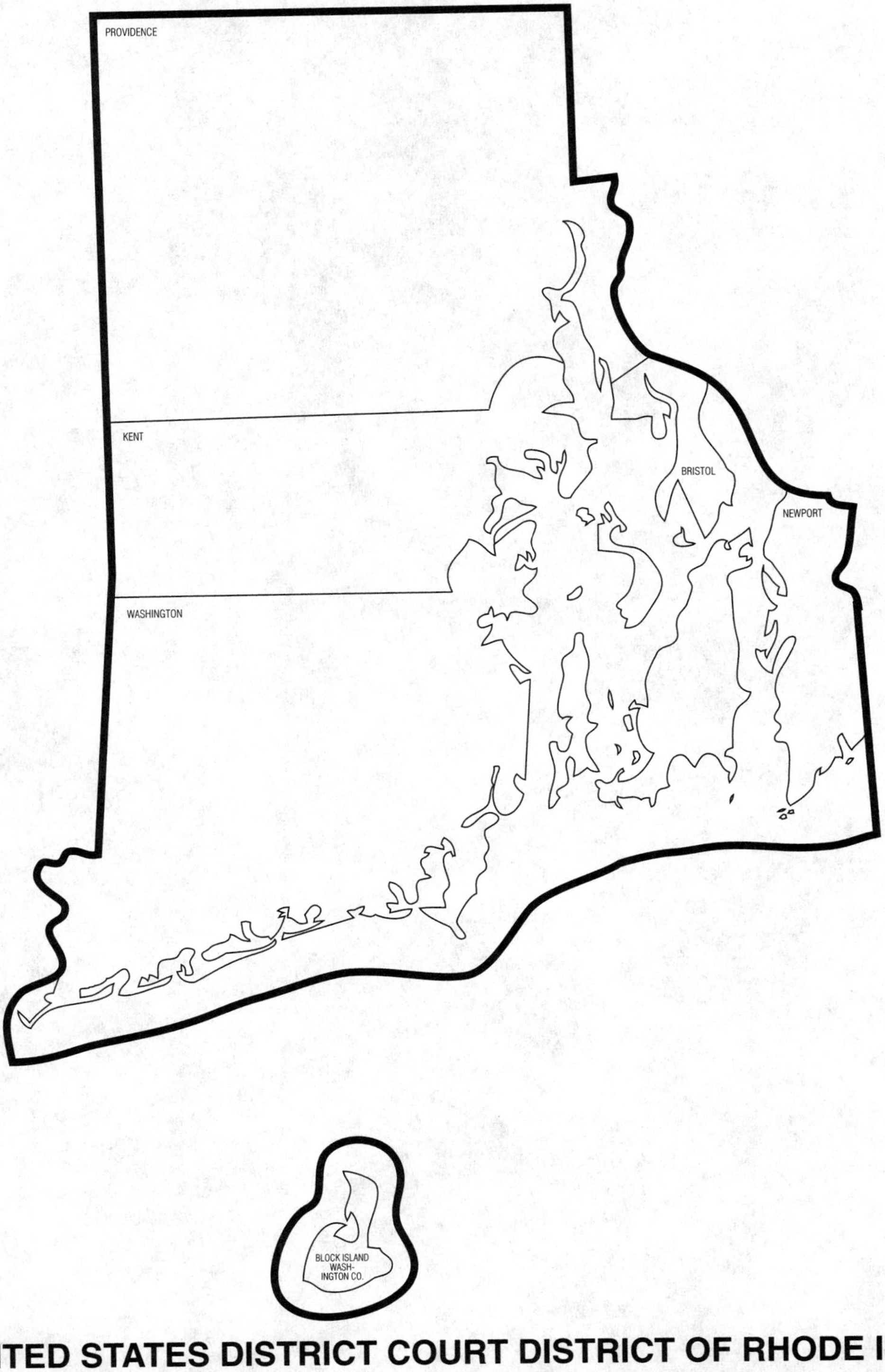
PROVIDENCE
KENT
WASHINGTON
BRISTOL
NEWPORT
BLOCK ISLAND WASH-INGTON CO.

UNITED STATES DISTRICT COURT DISTRICT OF RHODE ISLAND

RHODE ISLAND

ALMEIDA, Lillian M. *(Judge, Rhode Island Traffic Tribunal)* Appointed for life by Governor Edward DiPrete to term beginning July 1986. Educated at Salve Regina B.A. and Suffolk University J.D.

Member Rhode Island Trial Judges Association and Rhode Island Bar Association (Centennial Committee). Member Mercymount Country Day School (Advisory Board) and Rhode Island Legal Educational Partnership.

Office: 345 Harris Avenue, Providence 02909-1082.

Telephone: (401) 222-1184.

ARRIGAN, Robert F. *(Chief Judge, Rhode Island Workers' Compensation Court)* Appointed for life by Governor J. Joseph Garrahy to Workman's Compensation Commission to term beginning May 12, 1978. Appointed Chief Judge by Governor Bruce Sundlun Dec 19, 1991. Born Providence Rhode Island. Roman Catholic. Educated at Providence College A.B. 1957 and Georgetown University Law Center J.D. 1961. Admitted to practice Rhode Island 1961 and U.S. District Court District of Rhode Island 1969. In legal practice Providence 1961-78. Judge, Providence Municipal Court 1975-78.

Vice Chair Workers' Compensation Commission 1978-84. Workers' Compensation Commissioner 1984-91. Adjunct Professor of Workers' Compensation Law Roger Williams College 1980-91. Member American Judicature Society, American Judges Association and Rhode Island Bar Association (Committee for Workers' Compensation). Past President Eastern Association of Workers' Compensation Boards and Commissions. Board of Regents Workers' Compensation College and Member International Association of Industrial Accident Boards and Commissions. Lieutenant USAR. Member Georgetown University Alumni Association and University Club.

Office: J. Joseph Garrahy Judicial Complex, One Dorrance Plaza, Providence 02903.

Telephone: (401) 458-5000.

ASQUITH, Patricia K. *(Magistrate, Rhode Island Family Court)* Appointed by Chief Judge.

Office: J. Joseph Garrahy Judicial Complex, One Dorrance Plaza, Providence 02903.

Telephone: (401) 458-5310.

BEDROSIAN, Haiganush R. *(Associate Justice, Rhode Island Family Court)* Appointed for life by Governor J. Joseph Garrahy to term beginning June 5, 1980. First woman appointed to Family Court. Born Providence Rhode Island. Religious affiliation: Armenian Apostolic. Educated at Brown University A.B. 1965 and Suffolk University Law School J.D. 1971. Law Clerk and Legal Research Assistant to Hon. Thomas J. Paolino, Rhode Island Supreme Court 1971-72. Admitted to practice Rhode Island 1971 and U.S. District Court District of Rhode Island 1971. In legal practice 1973-80.

Elementary school teacher Brockton School System 1965-66 and Attleboro School System 1966-71. Assistant General Counsel Providence & Worcester Railroad Company 1972-73. Special Assistant Attorney General Rhode Island 1973-74. Important Decisions: In re Nicholas (adoption proceedings) June 22, 1982 and In re Gerald (competency of minor to testify in delinquency proceeding) Nov 30, 1982. Instructor in Law 1972 and since 1980 and Paralegal Certificate Course Roger Williams College, Rhode Island College 1975 and University of Rhode Island 1976. Member Rhode Island District Court Committee on Adoption of Rules of Criminal Procedure 1971, Governor's Advisory Commission on Women since 1972 (Subcommittee to Study and Analyze the Interstate Compact as it Applied to Women Offenders 1972-74, Chairwoman Legal Subcommittee on Incarceration of Women Offenders 1976-77, member Advisory Committee on Incarcerated Women 1981-84), Special Commission to Study the Operation of Cranston City Government 1972 (Secretary Recreational Subcommittee) and Rhode Island Task Force on Juvenile Probation New England Resource Center Judge Baker Child Guidance Center 1984. Member Rhode Island Women Lawyers Association (Secretary 1972-73, President 1973-74), Rhode Island Coalition of Women Lawyers, Rhode Island Trial Judges Association, National Association of Women Judges, American Correctional Association (National Public Policy Standards Committee since 1983), National Council of Juvenile and Family Court Judges, The Association of Trial Lawyers of America (Recording Secretary 1975-76, Vice President 1977-78 and President 1978-80 Rhode Island Chapter), National District Attorneys Association 1973-74, American Judicature Society 1973-80 and 1982-84, Rhode Island (Secretary Nominating Committee 1979, Home of Delegates since 1979, Chairwoman Standing Committee on Discrimination Because of Sex 1979-81) and American 1971-82 (Sections: Family Law, Tort and Insurance Practice, Young Lawyers Division) Bar Associations.

Named Armenian of the Year by Armenian Masonic Degree Team of Rhode Island 1981. Volunteer Campaign Worker for Richard Israel (Republican candidate for attorney general) 1974. Republican Candidate for Office of Rhode Island Secretary of State 1976. Member Rhode Island Women's Political Caucus 1974-79. Board of Directors and Chairwoman Youth Vision, Inc. 1982-83. Board of Directors and President The Honorable Angelo C. Rossi Scholarship Fund 1982-83. Corporation member since 1978, Advisory Committee since 1980, Executive Committee 1981-82 and Chairperson Bench/Bar Relations Subcommittee since 1981 and Annual Law Day Subcommittee 1983-84 Roger Williams College. Member Pembroke College Alumnae Association since 1965, Armenian Students Association since 1965, Suffolk University Law School Alumnae since 1971, National Organization for Women since 1971 (Chairperson Legal Subcommittee 1971-73, Member Subcommittee to Study Rhode Island Women Offenders 1972-73), Committee to Select Recipient The Loggia Luce Moderna Scholarship Fund and YMCA since 1981 and Rhode Island Task Force on Learning Disabilities, Inc. Enjoys reading and music.

Office: J. Joseph Garrahy Judicial Complex, One Dorrance Plaza, Providence 02903.

Telephone: (401) 458-5310.

BERTNESS, Janette A. *(Associate Judge, Rhode Island Workers' Compensation Court)* Appointed for life by Governor Bruce Sundlun to term beginning July 15, 1993. Born New York New York Dec 22, 1957. Educated at Clark University B.A. 1979, Brown University M.S. 1982 and Suffolk University Law School J.D. with honors 1986. Staff Writer 1984-85 and Technical Editor 1985-86 Suffolk University Law Review. Law Clerk to Hon. Florence K. Murray, Rhode Island Supreme Court 1986-87. Admitted to practice Rhode Island 1986 and U.S. District Court District of Rhode Island 1987. In legal practice Providence 1987-93.

Author Survey 19 473, Survey 19 415 and Comment 19 1023 Suffolk University L. Rev. 1985. Regent International Association of Industrial Accident Boards and Commissions. Member Eastern Association of Workers' Compensation Boards and Commissions. Member National Association of Women Judges, American Judicature Society, Rhode Island Bar Foundation and American Bar Association. Faculty Twenty-third International Workers' Compensation College International Association of Industrial Accident Boards and Commissions 1996. Past President and Board of Directors Rhode Island Legal/Educational Partnership.

Office: J. Joseph Garrahy Judicial Complex, One Dorrance Plaza, Providence 02903.

Telephone: (401) 458-5000.

BUCCI, Elaine T. *(Associate Judge, Rhode Island District Court)* Appointed for life by Governor Bruce Sundlun to term beginning Sept 30, 1994. Born Providence Rhode Island Sept 6, 1957. Educated at Boston College B.A. 1979 and Suffolk University Law School J.D. 1982.

Clerk Providence Probate Court 1988-94. Former Member Children's Code Commission. Member Rhode Island Trial Judges Association. Recipient Outstanding Young Women in America Award 1985 and 1986. Listed in *Who's Who in American Politics* 1985 and *Who's Who Among American Women* 1995. State Representative 1984-92. Deputy Majority Leader 1991-92. Member House Committees on Labor 1985, Corporations 1986-87, Health Education and Welfare 1988 and Judiciary 1989-92.

Office: Judicial Complex, One Dorrance Plaza, Providence 02903.

Telephone: (401) 458-5201.

CAPINERI, Stephen J. *(Associate Justice, Rhode Island Family Court)* Appointed Magistrate by Chief Judge to term beginning Oct 10, 1996. Appointed Associate Justice for life by Governor Lincoln Almond Jan 3, 2001. Born East Providence Rhode Island July 6, 1954. Educated at Providence College and Suffolk University Law School. Judge, East Providence Probate Court 1985-96.

Member Rhode Island Trial Judges Association and Rhode Island Bar Association.

Office: J. Joseph Garrahy Judicial Complex, One Dorrance Plaza, Providence 02903.

Telephone: (401) 458-5310.

CENERINI, Frank J. *(Associate Judge, Rhode Island District Court)* Appointed for life by Governor Bruce Sundlun to term beginning 1994. Born Providence Rhode Island Dec 31, 1944. Educated at Providence College A.B. 1966, Columbia University M.S. 1968 and Suffolk University Law School J.D. 1975.

Casework Supervisor Rhode Island Child Welfare Services. Deputy City Solicitor Warwick. Member Children's Code Commission. Member Justinian Law Society of Rhode Island, Rhode Island and American Bar Associations. Major USAR.

Office: Judicial Complex, One Dorrance Plaza, Providence 02903.

Telephone: (401) 458-5201.

CIULLO, Albert R. *(Judge, Rhode Island Traffic Tribunal)* Appointed for life by Governor Bruce Sundlun to term beginning Aug 1993. Born Oct 5, 1942. Educated at Providence College B.A. 1966 and Boston University J.D. 1969.

Assistant City Solicitor Providence 1970-76. Member Rhode Island Trial Judges Association and American Bar Association.

Office: 345 Harris Avenue, Providence 02909-1082.

Telephone: (401) 222-1184.

CLIFTON, Edward C. *(Associate Justice, Rhode Island Superior Court)* Appointed for life by Governor Bruce Sundlun to term beginning Sept 1994. Born March 6, 1945. Educated at University of California at Berkeley and University of California at Los Angeles. Judge, Providence Municipal Court 1979-84. Former Associate Judge, Rhode Island District Court, appointed by Governor Bruce Sundlun Feb 1993.

Providence City Solicitor 1985-91. Member Rhode Island Black Lawyers Association and Rhode Island Bar Association. U.S. Army 1966-68.

Office: Frank Licht Judicial Complex, 250 Benefit Street, Providence 02903.

Telephone: (401) 222-3250.

CONNOR, Dianne M. *(Associate Judge, Rhode Island Workers' Compensation Court)* Appointed for life by Governor Lincoln Almond to term beginning July 2000. Born Pawtucket Rhode Island Aug 18, 1957. Educated at University of Rhode Island B.A. 1979 and New England School of Law J.D. 1982. Admitted to practice Rhode Island 1982 and U.S. District Court District of Rhode Island 1982. In legal practice Rhode Island Jan 1992 to July 2000.

Author *Workers' Compensation Practice in Rhode Island* 1993, 1994 and 1995 and *Sports and Torts—An Analysis of the Law Surrounding Injuries in Golf and Ski Accidents* 1997 CLE Rhode Island Bar Association. Member Rhode Island Trial Judges Association and Rhode Island Bar Association. Lecturer "Arbitration of Personal Injury Cases in Rhode Island" Rhode Island Trial Lawyers Association 1996. Attended Ultimate Trial Advocacy Program Harvard Law School March 1998. Member Junior League of Rhode Island. Enjoys golf.

Office: One Dorrance Plaza, Providence 02903.

Telephone: (401) 458-5000.

Fax: (401) 734-9334

E-mail address: d.connor@courts.state.ris.us

DARIGAN, Francis J., Jr. *(Associate Justice, Rhode Island Superior Court)* Appointed for life by Governor Bruce Sundlun to term beginning June 28, 1991. Born Providence Rhode Island Sept 21, 1942. Roman Catholic. Educated at Providence College A.B. 1964, Suffolk University J.D. 1971 and University of Rhode Island M.A. 1974. Admitted to practice Rhode Island 1971, U.S. District Court District of Rhode Island 1972 and U.S. Supreme Court 1979. In legal practice Providence 1971-84. Associate Judge, Rhode Island District Court Jan 26, 1984 to June 27, 1991.

DARIGAN, FRANCIS J., JR.—*Continued*

City Council Member Providence 1970-74. Author "Recent Developments in the Law 1992" Rhode Island Bar Association 1992. Instructor in Court Management Roger Williams University and in Criminal Law Providence College. Chairperson Rhode Island Commission on Women in the Courts since 1990. Chair Sentence Bench Mark Review Commission Rhode Island Superior Court. Past President Rhode Island Trial Judges Association. Member Rhode Island and American (National Conference of State Trial Judges Judicial Division) Bar Associations. Attended General Jurisdiction course The National Judicial College 1984. Recipient Neil J. Houston, Jr. Award for dedicated service to the criminal justice system from Justice Assistance 1989 and Hon. Anthony Giannini Award for outstanding contributions to law related education in Rhode Island from Rhode Island Legal Education Partnership. Captain U.S. Army Military Intelligence 1965-67. Member Providence Charter Commission 1978-80. Chair Committee on Women and Minorities since 1999. Trustee St. Michael the Archangel Parish South Providence. Former Grand Knight. Member Rhode Island Historical Society, Elks Lodge 14, Knights of Columbus and Audubon Society. Enjoys reading, gardening and physical fitness.

Office: Frank Licht Judicial Complex, 250 Benefit Street, Providence 02903.

Telephone: (401) 222-3250.

DeROBBIO, Albert E. *(Chief Judge, Rhode Island District Court)* Appointed for life by Governor Edward DiPrete to term beginning Jan 6, 1987. Born Providence Rhode Island July 13, 1929. Educated at Boston College B.S. 1951 and Boston University School of Law LL.B. 1956. Admitted to practice Rhode Island 1956. Associate Judge, Rhode Island District Court Dec 1976 to Jan 1979. Associate Justice, Rhode Island Superior Court 1979-87, appointed by Governor J. Joseph Garrahy.

Legal Counsel Department of Social Services 1960-66. With Rhode Island Attorney General's Department 1967-76. Instructor in Criminal Law Roger Williams University since 1982. Vice Chair Commission on Criminal Justice. Member Roger Williams American Inn of Court. Member Providence Plantations Lion's Club (Board), State Law Day Chairmen, United Commercial Travelers, Luggia Luce Moderna, Grand Lodge of Rhode Island (First Vice President) and Order of Sons of Italy in America.

Office: J. Joseph Garrahy Judicial Complex, One Dorrance Plaza, Providence 02903.

Telephone: (401) 458-5201.

DIMITRI, William A., Jr. *(Associate Justice, Rhode Island Superior Court)* Appointed for life by Governor Lincoln Almond to term beginning July 24, 1996. Born Cranston Rhode Island April 24, 1930. Educated at Providence College 1957, Boston University School of Law, New England School of Law and Bates College of Law. Admitted to practice U.S. District Courts District of Rhode Island and District of Massachusetts and U.S. Courts of Appeals First and Second Circuits.

With Rhode Island Attorney General's Office 1967-73. Assistant U.S. Attorney District of Rhode Island 1974-78. Member Rhode Island Superior Court Advisory Committee 1974-75. Member Bar of the Commonwealth of Massachusetts, National Association of Criminal Defense Lawyers, National District Attorneys Association, The Association of the Trial Lawyers of America, Rhode Island (Public Relations Committee 1973-74, Nominating Committee 1974, Criminal Law Committee 1980-88) and Federal Bar Associations. Listed in *Best Lawyers in America* since 1989. Member since 1985 and Chairman of the Board since 1988 Southern New England School of Law.

Office: Frank Licht Judicial Complex, 250 Benefit Street, Providence 02903.

Telephone: (401) 222-3250.

DiMURO, George N. *(Magistrate, Rhode Island Family Court)* Appointed by Chief Judge.

Office: J. Joseph Garrahy Judicial Complex, One Dorrance Plaza, Providence 02903.

Telephone: (401) 458-5310.

DiSANDRO, Domenic A., III *(Magistrate, Rhode Island Traffic Tribunal)* Appointed by Chief Judge.

Office: 345 Harris Avenue, Providence 02909-1082.

Telephone: (401) 222-1184.

DiSEGNA, Debra E. *(Magistrate, Rhode Island Family Court)* Appointed by Chief Judge. Born Providence Rhode Island June 20, 1955. Educated at Rhode Island College B.A. 1977 and Suffolk University J.D. 1982.

Former State Prosecutor. Member Family Law American Inn of Court, National Council of Juvenile and Family Court Judges and Rhode Island Bar Association.

Office: J. Joseph Garrahy Judicial Complex, One Dorrance Plaza, Providence 02903.

Telephone: (401) 458-5310.

ERICKSON, Stephen P. *(Associate Judge, Rhode Island District Court)* Appointed for life by Governor Edward DiPrete to term beginning June 1990. Born Newport Rhode Island May 1, 1951. Educated at University of Rhode Island 1973 and Boston University School of Law J.D. 1976. Member Phi Kappa Phi and Delta Sigma Rho. Admitted to practice Rhode Island 1976.

Adjunct Professor of Law, Roger Williams College since 1979. State Representative 1978-86. Director of Legal Affairs Office of the Governor 1986-90.

Office: Judicial Complex, One Dorrance Plaza, Providence 02903.

Telephone: (401) 458-5201.

FLAHERTY, Francis X. *(Associate Justice, Rhode Island Supreme Court)* Appointed for life by governor to term beginning 2003.

Office: Frank Licht Judicial Complex, 250 Benefit Street, Providence 02903.

Telephone: (401) 222-3274.

FLANDERS, Robert G., Jr. *(Associate Justice, Rhode Island Supreme Court)* Appointed for life by Governor Lincoln Almond to term beginning April 1, 1996. Born July 9, 1949. Educated at Brown University and Harvard Law School.

Glocester Town Solicitor. Member Rhode Island and American Bar Associations. Assistant Executive Counsel to Governor Edward DiPrete.

Office: Frank Licht Judicial Complex, 250 Benefit Street, Providence 02903.

Telephone: (401) 222-3274.

FORTE, Michael B. *(Associate Justice, Rhode Island Family Court)* Appointed for life by Governor Edward DiPrete to term beginning March 25, 1987. Born Central Falls Rhode Island June 5, 1952. Educated at University

FORTE, MICHAEL B.—*Continued*
of Rhode Island B.A. 1974 and Franklin Pierce Law Center J.D. 1977. Admitted to practice Rhode Island 1977 and U.S. District Court District of Rhode Island 1977.

Tax Assessor 1977-78. Bail Commissioner Newport County 1979-87. Member Rhode Island Senate 1983-87 (Deputy Majority Leader 1984-87, Chairman Medical Malpractice Commission, Vice Chairman Judiciary Committee, Member Special Legislation Committee and Joint Committee on the Environment). Town Solicitor Little Compton 1984-86. Member Commission on Judicial Tenure & Discipline 1985-87 and Governmental Relations Committee. Member Family Court Bench/Bar Committee, District Court Bench/Bar Committee, National Council of Juvenile and Family Court Judges, Rhode Island Trial Judges Association (Board of Directors), Newport County, Rhode Island and American Bar Associations. Board of Directors Newport County Red Cross 1979, Tiverton-Little Compton Rotary Club and Friends of Sakonnet Lighthouse. Fund Drive Chairman Little Compton Heart Association. Treasurer Tiverton Boys & Girls Club. Advisory Board National Head Injury Foundation. President Little Compton Little League. Member Little Compton Historical Society, Preservation Society of Newport County and Sakonnet Preservation Association (President).

Office: J. Joseph Garrahy Judicial Complex, One Dorrance Plaza, Providence 02903.

Telephone: (401) 458-5310.

FORTUNATO, Stephen J., Jr. *(Associate Justice, Rhode Island Superior Court)* Appointed for life by Governor Bruce Sundlun to term beginning Sept 23, 1994. Born Providence Rhode Island Jan 31, 1942. Educated at Providence College A.B. with honors 1965 and George Washington University J.D. with honors 1970. Admitted to practice Rhode Island 1971, U.S. District Court District of Rhode Island 1971 and U.S. Supreme Court 1975.

Author "Instructing on Reasonable Doubt After *Victor v. Nebraska*" 41 Villanova L. Rev. 365, 1996 and Summary "Judgment in Rhode Island: Is It Time to Wrap the Mantra in Celotex" 2 Roger Williams University L. Rev. 153, 1997. Adjunct Professor of Remedies Roger Williams University School of Law since 1997. Member American Inns of Court, American Judges Association, American Judicature Association and Rhode Island Bar Association. State Senate (Vice Chairman Judiciary Committee) 1976-80.

Office: Frank Licht Judicial Complex, 250 Benefit Street, Providence 02903.

Telephone: (401) 222-3250.

GALE, Edwin J. *(Associate Justice, Rhode Island Superior Court)* Appointed for life by Governor Lincoln Almond to term beginning Feb 8, 2001. Born Brattleboro Vermont April 8, 1943. Religious affiliation: United Church of Christ. Educated at U.S. Naval Academy B.S. 1965 and University of Santa Clara J.D. 1972. Comments and Notes Editor Santa Clara Lawyer 1971-72. Member St. Thomas More Society. Admitted to practice California 1972, Rhode Island 1980, U.S. District Courts Northern District of Ohio 1973, District of Rhode Island 1977 and District of Massachusetts 1978 and U.S. Court of Appeals First Circuit 1978.

Attorney Oct 2, 1972 to Feb 7, 2001 and U.S. Attorney 1993-94 U.S. Department of Justice. Member Inns of Court and Rhode Island Bar Association. USN 1961-70. Captain USNR 1970-94 (retired). Enjoys hiking, sailing and canoeing.

Office: Frank Licht Judicial Complex, 250 Benefit Street, Providence 02903.

Telephone: (401) 222-3250.

GIBNEY, Alice Bridget *(Associate Justice, Rhode Island Superior Court)* Appointed for life by Governor J. Joseph Garrahy to term beginning Jan 20, 1984. Born West Warwick Rhode Island July 1, 1947. Educated at Rhode Island College B.A. 1969 and Catholic University J.D. 1972. Awarded honorary LL.D. Rhode Island College 1986. Admitted to practice Rhode Island 1972.

Assistant U.S. Attorney 1978-79. Commissioner Workers' Compensation Committee 1982-84. Adjunct Professor Roger Williams University School of Law. Chairperson Commission on Judicial Tenure and Discipline. Member Roger Williams Inn of Courts, Rhode Island and American Bar Associations. Director Buttonwoods Beach Association.

Office: Frank Licht Judicial Complex, 250 Benefit Street, Providence 02903.

Telephone: (401) 222-3250.

GOLDBERG, Maureen McKenna *(Associate Justice, Rhode Island Supreme Court)* Appointed for life by Governor Lincoln Almond to term beginning May 30, 1997. Born Pawtucket Rhode Island Feb 11, 1951. Educated at Providence College A.B. 1973 and Suffolk University Law School J.D. 1978. Admitted to practice Rhode Island 1978, Massachusetts 1978 and U.S. Court of Appeals First Circuit 1979. Former Associate Justice, Rhode Island Superior Court, appointed by Governor Edward DiPrete 1990.

Assistant Attorney General Criminal Division 1978-84. Town Solicitor South Kingstown 1985-87 and Westerly 1987-90. Acting Town Manager Westerly 1990. Special Legal Counsel Rhode Island State Police. Member Rhode Island Trial Judges Association, National Association of Women Judges, Pawtucket, Rhode Island and American Bar Associations.

Office: Frank Licht Judicial Complex, 250 Benefit Street, Providence 02903.

Telephone: (401) 222-3280.

GONNELLA, Richard A. *(Associate Judge, Rhode Island District Court)* Appointed for life by Governor Lincoln Almond.

Office: Judicial Complex, One Dorrance Plaza, Providence 02903.

Telephone: (401) 458-5201.

GORMAN, Walter *(Associate Judge, Rhode Island District Court)* Appointed for life by Governor Bruce Sundlun to term beginning Feb 1993. Born Providence Rhode Island April 21, 1937. Educated at Providence College A.B. 1961 and Boston University School of Law LL.B. 1964.

Trial Attorney U.S. Department of Justice 1964-87. Deputy Attorney General Rhode Island 1987-93. Fellow Public Affairs Stanford University 1973-74.

Office: J. Joseph Garrahy Judicial Complex, One Dorrance Plaza, Providence 02903.

Telephone: (401) 458-5201.

HAGOPIAN, Jacob *(Recalled Magistrate Judge, United States District Court District of Rhode Island)*

HAGOPIAN, JACOB—*Continued*

Appointed Magistrate Judge by U.S. District Court judges. Appointed Recalled Magistrate Judge by the Judicial Council of the First Circuit 1995. Born Providence Rhode Island July 3, 1927. Religious affiliation: Armenian Apostolic. Educated at George Washington University A.B. 1957, Georgetown University Law Center and Washington College of Law J.D. 1960. Admitted to practice Virginia 1961, Rhode Island 1964, U.S. Supreme Court 1964, U.S. District Courts District of Rhode Island and Eastern District of Virginia, U.S. Court of Appeals District of Columbia Circuit, U.S. Court of Customs and Patent Appeals, U.S. Court of Federal Claims and U.S. Tax Court. Appellate Judge, U.S. Court of Military Review 1967-70.

Former Consultant Rhode Island Commission to Reform Criminal Procedures. Former Director Roger Williams College Law Center. Author "Free Speech in the Military" Congressional Record, 90th Congress Vol. 113 No. 180 at A5434, Nov 1967; "Due Process of Law and Military Justice Today" Rhode Island B. Jour. Jan 1969; "Police Intrusions and the Fourth Amendment" Criminal Law Reporter, Bureau of National Affairs Feb 1969; "Administrative Due Process" Congressional Hearings, Armed Services HR 523, June 8, 1971; "Forcing Open the State Courthouse Doors: Federal Court Deference and Its Challenge to the States" 16 No. 2 Suffolk University L. Rev. Rhode Island Survey 1982; and "U.S. Magistrate Judges—A Look at the Growth and Development" 39 No. 7 Federal Bar News and Journal Aug 1992. Co-author *Courts of Military Review Rules of Practice and Procedure* AFM 111-4, AR 27-13, NAVSO P-2319 CG 241A Aug 1, 1969; *Federal Practice Manual* West Publishing Company 1970; and "State Courts as Guardians of Constitutional Liberties" Boston B. Jour. April 1979 reprinted in Rhode Island B. Jour. Dec 1979. Faculty Member Federal Jurisdiction Providence College and Constitutional Law Roger Williams College (Director 1970-71 and Chairman Advisor Committee on Law Center). Lecturer Federal Judicial Center Washington D.C. Adjunct Professor of Constitutional Rights and Liberties American University Center for the Administration of Justice since 1971. Visiting Professor U.S. Naval War College 1993. Appointed Honors Faculty Fellow Honors Program University of Rhode Island 1997-98. Adjunct Professor Suffolk University Law School. Member Code Committee Uniform Code of Military Justice since 2000. Member Institute of Judicial Administration, American Judges Association, U.S. Army and USAF Clemency and Parole Board, Federal (Past President Rhode Island Chapter, National Council, National Chairman Committee on Criminal Law, Chair U.S. Magistrate Judges Committee) and American (Former Consultant Section of Criminal Justice, Vice Chairman Committee on Adequate Defense and Incentives in the Military, Former Secretary-Reporter Committee on Military Law) Bar Associations. Awarded U.S. Legion of Merit by direction of President for judicial and legal service to government and U.S. Legion of Merit First Oak Leaf Cluster for duties as Appellate Judge. Colonel U.S. Army JAGC (retired) 1944-70. Chief, Criminal Law Division OTJAG U.S. Department of the Army 1965-67, Group Supervisor Defense Appellate Division U.S. Army Judiciary 1969 and Deputy Staff Judge Advocate, U.S. Commander in Berlin 1960-61. Recipient Graduate Certificates Graduate Thesis Program in International Law 1964 The Judge Advocate General School and Industrial College of the Armed Forces 1967 and 1969. Recipient Army Commendation Medal with oak leaf cluster. Former Member Advisory Committee to the President and Board of Trustees on the Administration of Justice American University.

Office: 279 Federal Building, Two Exchange Terrace, Providence 02903-1779.

Telephone: (401) 752-7010.

HARWOOD, Patricia L. *(General Magistrate, Rhode Island Superior Court)* Appointed by Chief Justice.

Office: Frank Licht Judicial Complex, 250 Benefit Street, Providence 02903.

Telephone: (401) 222-3250.

HEALY, George E. *(Associate Judge, Rhode Island Workers' Compensation Court)* Appointed for life by Governor Bruce Sundlun to term beginning July 3, 1991. Born Providence Rhode Island July 5, 1950. Educated at Northeastern University B.A. 1973 and Suffolk University Law School J.D. 1976. Admitted to practice Rhode Island 1976.

Member Commission on Judicial Tenure and Discipline. Member Eastern and International IABCs.

Office: J. Joseph Garrahy Judicial Complex, One Dorrance Plaza, Providence 02903.

Telephone: (401) 458-5000.

HIGGINS, Michael A. *(Associate Judge, Rhode Island District Court)* Appointed for life by Governor J. Joseph Garrahy to term beginning May 23, 1980. Also serves as Administrative Judge. Born Ballinamore Ireland March 31, 1944. Educated at Providence College A.B. 1967 and Catholic University of America School of Law J.D. 1971.

Member Commission on Judicial Tenure and Discipline, Rhode Island Port Authority, Rhode Island Economic Development Council, American Trial Lawyers Association, Rhode Island and American Bar Associations. State Representative 1972-80 and Majority Leader 1977-80. Board of Trustees South County Hospital. Member Washington Park Citizens Association.

Office: Judicial Complex, One Dorrance Plaza, Providence 02903.

Telephone: (401) 458-5201.

HURST, Patricia A. *(Associate Justice, Rhode Island Superior Court)* Appointed for life by Governor Edward DiPrete to term beginning July 18, 1990. Born Canadaigua New York Feb 19, 1951. Educated at Coe College B.A. 1972 and Suffolk University Law School J.D. 1978. Admitted to practice Rhode Island 1978, Massachusetts 1978, U.S. Supreme Court 1988, U.S. Court of Appeals Third Circuit and U.S. Tax Court.

Member Rhode Island Women's Bar Association, Rhode Island Trial Lawyers Association, American Trial Lawyers Association and American Bar Association (Judicial Administration Division). Chair Providence Zoning Board of Review. Legal Counsel Providence Civic Center Authority and Providence School Committee. Member College Corporation, Roger Williams University, Hospital Corporation, Butler Hospital, Rhode Island Legal Education Partnership, Women's Mentoring Program and Rhode Island Department of Corrections.

Office: Frank Licht Judicial Complex, 250 Benefit Street, Providence 02903.

Telephone: (401) 222-3250.

INDEGLIA, Gilbert V. *(Associate Justice, Rhode Island Superior Court)* Appointed for life by Governor Lincoln Almond. Born Providence Rhode Island Aug 31, 1941. Educated at Boston College A.B. 1963 and University of Michigan Law School J.D. 1966. Judge, South Kingstown Probate Court 1971-73. Former Associate Judge, Rhode Island District Court, appointed by Governor Edward DiPrete to term beginning June 16, 1989.

Assistant Town Solicitor South Kingstown 1971-73. Member Advisory Committee on the Code of Judicial Ethics and District Court Bench-Bar Committee. Member Rhode Island Trial Judges Association and Rhode Island Bar Association. Attended National Judicial College. Rhode Island Air National Guard 1972. Member 1977-84 and President 1981-84 South Kingstown Town Council. State Representative 1984-89 and Deputy Minority Leader 1988-89. Board of Trustees South Kingstown Public Library 1975-77. Board of Directors Sargent Rehabilitation Center and Kingston Improvement Association. Member Tavern Hall Club and Pettaquamscutt Historical Society.

Office: Frank Licht Judicial Complex, 250 Benefit Street, Providence 02903.

Telephone: (401) 222-3250.

IPPOLITO, Joseph P., Jr. *(Magistrate, Rhode Island District Court)* Appointed by Chief Judge to term beginning 1991. Born Medford Massachusetts Jan 14, 1954. Educated at Tufts University and Suffolk University Law School.

Assistant Attorney General. Member Rhode Island Bar Association.

Office: Judicial Complex, One Dorrance Plaza, Providence 02903.

Telephone: (401) 458-5201.

JABOUR, Christine S. *(Magistrate, Rhode Island District Court)* Appointed for life by governor to term beginning 2003.

Office: Judicial Complex, One Dorrance Plaza, Providence 02903.

Telephone: (401) 458-5201.

JEREMIAH, Jeremiah S., Jr. *(Chief Judge, Rhode Island Family Court)* Appointed for life by Governor Edward DiPrete to term beginning March 7, 1986. Chief Judge since March 13, 1987. Born Providence Rhode Island June 17, 1935. Religious affiliation: Congregational. Educated at Boston University B.A. 1957 J.D. 1961. Law Clerk to Hon. Thomas J. Paolino, Rhode Island Supreme Court 1962. Admitted to practice Rhode Island 1961, U.S. Supreme Court 1965, U.S. District Court District of Rhode Island 1966 and U.S. Court of Appeals First Circuit. In legal practice Cranston for twenty-three years.

Assistant Solicitor 1963-78 and Solicitor 1978-84 Cranston. Former Consultant Charter Review Commission. Executive Legal Counsel to Governor Edward D. DiPrete 1984-85. Co-chair Governor's Juvenile Justice Reform Task Force. Member Judicial Performance Evaluation Committee and Advisory Council to the Chief Justice Rhode Island Supreme Court. Member Governor's Juvenile Justice Advisory Council, Governor's Justice Commission, Attorney General's Task Force on Sexual and Violent Physical Abuse of Children, New England Chief Judges Association, National Council of Juvenile and Family Court Judges (Former Co-chair Metropolitan Court Judges, Member Board of Trustees, Committees on Diversity and Juvenile Law), Rhode Island (Family Court Bench/Bar Committee) and American (National Conference of Special Court Judges Judicial Administration Division, Commission on Homelessness and Poverty, Committees on Courts and the Community, Domestic Law Issues and Judicial Ethics) Bar Associations. Creator Rhode Island Family and Juvenile Drug Court. Launched New England's first Family Truancy Court. Attended The National Judicial College 1987 and 1995. Presenter "Family Courts: The Nature and Trends" Annual Conference 1997 and "Effective Coordination of Jurisdiction and Services in Family Court" Annual Conference 1999 National Council of Juvenile and Family Court Judges and "Family Court Caseflow Management and Mediation in Child Protection Cases" Annual Meeting American Bar Association 1998. Inducted into Cranston Hall of Fame 1988. Recipient Certificate of Appreciation for Outstanding Service and Dedication to the Young People and Their Families of Rhode Island from U.S. Department of Justice, Giannini Award from Rhode Island Legal/Educational Partnership and Jack and Ruth Eckerd Achievement for Youth Award. Artillery Officer USAR 1957-67. Executive Counsel to Governor Edward DiPrete 1984-86. Former Senior Deacon, Moderator and Chairman Board of Trustees Edgewood Congregational Church. Former Director Legal Aid Society of Rhode Island. Advisory Board and Corporate Member Bradley Hospital. Advisory Panel YMCA Teen Court. Honorary Member and Former Director Cranston Rotary Club. Member Families First, Gang Violence Commission, Cranston Chamber of Commerce (Past President, Former Director), Volunteers in Cranston Schools (Former Director), Father and Family Network of Rhode Island, Batterer's Intervention Program Standards Oversight Committee Rhode Island Commission on Criminal Justice, Big Brothers of Rhode Island (Advisory Board), Advisory Committee to Combat Underage Drinking Department of Mental Health, Retardation and Hospitals, Governor's Commission to Study the Placement of Children in Foster/Adoptive Care and Governor's Advisory Council Department of Children, Youth and Families.

Office: J. Joseph Garrahy Judicial Complex, One Dorrance Plaza, Providence 02903.

Telephone: (401) 458-5310.

KEOUGH, Joseph A. *(Special Magistrate, Rhode Island Superior Court)* Appointed by Presiding Justice.

Office: Frank Licht Judicial Complex, 250 Benefit Street, Providence 02903.

Telephone: (401) 222-3250.

KRAUSE, Robert D. *(Associate Justice, Rhode Island Superior Court)* Appointed for life by Governor Edward DiPrete to term beginning Nov 20, 1986. Born Cleveland Ohio June 10, 1945. Educated at Amherst College B.A. 1967 and Georgetown University J.D. 1970. Law Clerk to Hon. Alexander Harvey II, U.S. District Court District of Maryland 1970-71. Admitted to practice District of Columbia 1970, California 1976 and Rhode Island 1980.

Assistant U.S. Attorney 1974-78 and Chief of Appel-

KRAUSE, ROBERT D.—*Continued*
late Section 1977-78 Southern District of California. Assistant U.S. Attorney District of Rhode Island 1982-86.
Office: Frank Licht Judicial Complex, 250 Benefit Street, Providence 02903.
Telephone: (401) 222-3250.

LaFAZIA, Jeanne E. *(Associate Judge, Rhode Island District Court)* Appointed for life by governor.
Office: Judicial Complex, One Dorrance Plaza, Providence 02903.
Telephone: (401) 458-5201.

LAGUEUX, Ronald R. *(Senior Judge, United States District Court District of Rhode Island)* Appointed for life by President Ronald Reagan to term beginning Sept 5, 1986. Former Chief Judge. Assumed Senior status Nov 30, 2001, serves by assignment. Born Lewiston Maine June 30, 1931. Educated at Bowdoin College A.B. cum laude 1953 and Harvard University LL.B. 1956. Admitted to practice Rhode Island 1957, U.S. District Court District of Rhode Island 1958, U.S. Court of Appeals First Circuit 1960, Interstate Commerce Commission 1963 and U.S. Supreme Court 1967. In legal practice Providence 1956-68. Associate Justice, Rhode Island Superior Court June 24, 1968 to Sept 4, 1986.
Executive Counsel to Governor John Hubbard Chaffee 1963-65.
Office: 208 Federal Building, Two Exchange Terrace, Providence 02903-1779.
Telephone: (401) 752-7060.

LANPHEAR, Jeffrey A. *(Associate Justice, Rhode Island Superior Court)* Appointed for life by Governor Don Carcieri to term beginning 2003.
Office: Frank Licht Judicial Complex, 250 Benefit Street, Providence 02903.
Telephone: (401) 222-3250.

LIPSEY, Howard I. *(Associate Justice, Rhode Island Family Court)* Appointed for life by Governor Bruce Sundlun to term beginning Aug 20, 1993. Born Providence Rhode Island Jan 24, 1936. Educated at Providence College B.A. 1957 and Georgetown University Law Center J.D. 1960.
Past Chair Rhode Island Trial Lawyers Association. Former Member Board of Governors The Association of Trial Lawyers of America. Fellow American Academy of Matrimonial Lawyers and American College of Trial Lawyers. Member Rhode Island and American (Member Family Law Council) Bar Associations. Captain USAR JAGC. Member B'Nai B'rith, Temple Emanuel, Rhode Island Jewish Historical Society and Touro Fraternal Association.
Office: J. Joseph Garrahy Judicial Complex, One Dorrance Plaza, Providence 02903.
Telephone: (401) 458-5310.

LISI, Mary M. *(Judge, United Stated District Court District of Rhode Island)* Appointed for life by President Bill Clinton to term beginning May 1994. Born Providence Rhode Island Sept 4, 1950. Educated at University of Rhode Island B.A. 1972 and Temple University School of Law J.D. 1977. In legal practice Providence 1981-82.
Office: 310 Federal Building, Two Exchange Terrace, Providence 02903-1779.
Telephone: (401) 752-7040.

LOVEGREEN, Robert W. *(Magistrate Judge, United States District Court District of Rhode Island)* Appointed by U.S. District Court judges Oct 30, 1992 to term beginning March 1, 1993. Reappointed 2001. Educated at Brown University A.B. 1960 and University of Virginia School of Law J.D. 1963. Law Clerk to Hon. William E. Powers, Rhode Island Supreme Court Jan 1964 to Dec 1964. Admitted to practice Rhode Island 1963 and Massachusetts 1985. In legal practice 1965-93.
Office: 282 Federal Building, Two Exchange Terrace, Providence 02903-1779.
Telephone: (401) 752-7110.

MACKTAZ, Pamela M. *(Associate Justice, Rhode Island Family Court)* Appointed for life by Governor J. Joseph Garrahy to term beginning Jan 1984. Born Boston Massachusetts May 3, 1942. Jewish. Educated at Suffolk University B.A. 1963 LL.B. 1966. Admitted to practice Massachusetts 1967 and Rhode Island 1970. In legal practice Boston Massachusetts 1967-69 and Woonsocket Rhode Island 1970-84.
Member 1973-79 and Chairman 1979-83 Rhode Island Parole Board. Director State Legal Aid Society. Co-chair General's Domestic Violence Task Force, School Violence Task Force and Supreme Court Task Force on Domestic Violence. Member Rhode Island and American (National Conference of Special Court Judges Judicial Administration Division since 1987) Bar Associations. Board member Easter Seals Society of Rhode Island.
Office: J. Joseph Garrahy Judicial Complex, One Dorrance Plaza, Providence 02903.
Telephone: (401) 458-5310.

MARTIN, David L. *(Magistrate Judge, United States District Court District of Rhode Island)* Appointed by U.S. District Court judges to term beginning Sept 29, 1998. Educated at University of Rhode Island B.A. with distinction 1968 and University of Virginia School of Law J.D. 1973. Admitted to practice Rhode Island 1973. In legal practice Rhode Island 1981-98.
Office: 372 Federal Building, Two Exchange Terrace, Providence 02903-1779.
Telephone: (401) 752-7080.

McATEE, William J. *(Magistrate, Rhode Island Superior Court)* Appointed by Presiding Justice.
Office: Frank Licht Judicial Complex, 250 Benefit Street, Providence 02903.
Telephone: (401) 222-3250.

McGUIRL, Susan E. *(Associate Justice, Rhode Island Superior Court)* Appointed for life by Governor Lincoln Almond.
Office: Frank Licht Judicial Complex, 250 Benefit Street, Providence 02903.
Telephone: (401) 222-3250.

McLOUGHLIN, John Michael *(Associate Judge, Rhode Island District Court)* Appointed for life by Governor Bruce Sundlun to term beginning Sept 30, 1994. Born Bridgeport Connecticut May 15, 1940. Roman Catholic. Educated at Boston College B.S. 1962 and University of Baltimore J.D. 1966. Admitted to practice Maryland 1967, Rhode Island 1975, U.S. District Courts District of Maryland 1968 and District of Rhode Island 1975, U.S. Court of Appeals District of Columbia Circuit 1974 and U.S. Supreme Court 2000. In legal practice Hyattsville Maryland and Washington, D.C. 1967-74 and Rhode Island 1974-94.

MCLOUGHLIN, JOHN MICHAEL—*Continued*

Counsel to Liquor Control Board Prince George County 1969-75. Assistant Attorney General Rhode Island 1975-80 and 1986-94. Bail Commissioner 1980-85. Instructor Bryant College 1975-80. Former Member The District of Columbia Bar, Maryland State Bar Association, Inc. and Prince George's County Bar Association. Member National District Attorneys Association, Washington County, Rhode Island and American Bar Associations. Attended General Jurisdiction course The National Judicial College 1996. President Young Democrats Prince George County 1971. Chairman South Kingtown Democratic Town Committee 1980-84. Member Boston College Alumni Club of Rhode Island, Lions, Elks and Friendly Sons of St. Patrick. Enjoys reading, sailing and travel.

Office: J. Joseph Garrahy Judicial Complex, One Dorrance Plaza, Providence 02903.

Telephone: (401) 458-5201.

MOORE, Patricia D. *(Associate Judge, Rhode Island District Court)* Appointed for life by Governor Edward DiPrete to term beginning Jan 6, 1987. Born Brooklyn New York July 11, 1939. Educated at Wellesley College B.A. 1961 and University of Connecticut School of Law J.D. 1979. Admitted to practice Rhode Island 1979.

Office: Judicial Complex, One Dorrance Plaza, Providence 02903.

Telephone: (401) 458-5201.

MORIN, Bruce Q. *(Associate Judge, Rhode Island Workers' Compensation Court)* Appointed for life by Governor Bruce Sundlun to term beginning Oct 31, 1991. Educated at University of Rhode Island B.A. 1967 and Catholic University Law School.

Lieutenant USNR JAGC 1970-74. State Senator 1974-76 and 1980-83.

Office: J. Joseph Garrahy Judicial Complex, One Dorrance Plaza, Providence 02903.

Telephone: (401) 458-5000.

MURRAY, Francis J., Jr. *(Associate Justice, Rhode Island Family Court)* Appointed for life by Governor Bruce Sundlun to term beginning 1994. Born Brockton Massachusetts. Educated at Marquette University M.A. 1973 and Franklin Pierce Law Center J.D. 1976.

Office: J. Joseph Garrahy Judicial Complex, One Dorrance Plaza, Providence 02903.

Telephone: (401) 458-5320.

MUTTER, John A. *(Associate Justice, Rhode Island Family Court)* Appointed for life by Governor Bruce Sundlun to term beginning Oct 1994. Born Pawtucket Rhode Island March 27, 1927. Educated at Providence College B.A. 1949 and Boston University School of Law J.D. 1956. Admitted to practice Rhode Island 1957, U.S. District Court District of Rhode Island and U.S. Court of Appeals First Circuit. First Judge, Pawtucket Municipal Court June 1973.

With Department of Social Welfare Pawtucket 1950-53. Chief Counsel 1980 and Attorney Legal Aide Society of Rhode Island. Counselor Edward P. Gallogly Inn of Court. Member Rhode Island Trial Lawyers Association, American Judges Association (President), American Judicature Society, Rhode Island and American Bar Associations. Attended National College of the State Judiciary 1974. USN. Past President Children's Friend and Service. President Providence County Kennel Club. Co-writer and Co-director "That Summer in Philadelphia." Communicant St. Joseph's Church. Member Pawtucket Community Players, Providence College and Boston College Alumni Association.

Office: J. Joseph Garrahy Judicial Complex, One Dorrance Plaza, Providence 02903.

Telephone: (401) 458-5310.

NEWMAN, Edward H. *(Magistrate, Rhode Island Family Court)* Appointed by Chief Judge.

Office: J. Joseph Garrahy Judicial Complex, One Dorrance Plaza, Providence 02903.

Telephone: (401) 458-5310.

NOONAN, William T. *(Magistrate, Rhode Island Traffic Tribunal)* Appointed by Chief Judge.

Office: 345 Harris Avenue, Providence 02909-1082.

Telephone: (401) 222-1184.

NUGENT, Stephen P. *(Associate Justice, Rhode Island Superior Court)* Appointed for life by Governor Lincoln Almond to term beginning March 28, 2000. Born Providence Rhode Island Jan 23, 1948. Educated at Brown University B.A. 1969 and Boston University School of Law J.D. 1973 LL.M. 1975. Law Clerk to Rhode Island Superior Court 1973-74. Admitted to practice Rhode Island 1973, Massachusetts 1973, U.S. District Courts District of Rhode Island 1973 and District of Massachusetts 1973, U.S. Court of Appeals First Circuit 1973 and U.S. Supreme Court 1981. In legal practice Providence Rhode Island 1980-97.

Assistant Attorney General Rhode Island 1974-79. Chief Public Defender Rhode Island 1997-2000. Member Rhode Island Bar Association.

Office: 250 Benefit Street, Providence 02903.

Telephone: (401) 222-3250.

O'BRIEN, John J., Jr. *(General Magistrate, Rhode Island Family Court)* Appointed by Chief Judge to term beginning 1987. Born Providence Rhode Island April 19, 1931. Educated at Brown University A.B. and Boston University School of Law J.D. 1956.

Assistant U.S. Attorney and Civil Chief and Supervisory Assistant 1969-96. Interim U.S. Attorney 1997. Member Rhode Island Bar Association. Member Federal Employees Retirement Association.

Office: J. Joseph Garrahy Judicial Complex, One Dorrance Plaza, Providence 02903.

Telephone: (401) 458-5310.

OLSSON, Debra L. *(Associate Judge, Rhode Island Workers' Compensation Court)* Appointed for life by Governor Bruce Sundlun to term beginning July 15, 1991. Educated at Wellesley College B.A. 1979 and Suffolk University Law School J.D. 1982. Admitted to practice Massachusetts 1982 and Rhode Island 1983.

Chief Legal Counsel Workers' Compensation Department 1985-91. Member Rhode Island Trial Judges Association.

Office: J. Joseph Garrahy Judicial Complex, One Dorrance Plaza, Providence 02903.

Telephone: (401) 458-5000.

PARKER, Edward C. *(Judge, Rhode Island Traffic Tribunal)* Appointed for life by Governor Bruce Sundlun to term beginning 1993. Born Pawtucket Rhode Island

PARKER, EDWARD C.—*Continued*

March 27, 1939. Educated at Boston College A.B. 1961 and New England School of Law J.D. 1966.

Former Deputy Attorney General. Vice Chair Pawtucket Housing Authority. Member Witness Protection Review Board, Supreme Court Character and Fitness Commission, Governor's Justice Commission and State Crime Lab Commission. USAR six years. Executive Director Fire Safety Board of Appeal and Review. Member Sons of Irish Kings and Boston College Alumni.

Office: 345 Harris Avenue, Providence 02909-1082.

Telephone: (401) 222-1184.

PAULHUS, Angela M. Bucci *(Magistrate, Rhode Island Family Court)* Appointed by Chief Judge.

Office: J. Joseph Garrahy Judicial Complex, One Dorrance Plaza, Providence 02903.

Telephone: (401) 458-5310.

PFEIFFER, Mark A. *(Associate Justice, Rhode Island Superior Court)* Appointed for life by Governor Edward DiPrete to term beginning Oct 27, 1988. Born Bristol Rhode Island May 11, 1948. Educated at Dartmouth College A.B. 1970 and Cornell University Law School J.D. 1975.

Vice President and General Counsel Old Colony Bank. Senate Minority Legal Counsel 1975-80. Director Business Regulation 1986-88. Member Bristol School Committee.

Office: Frank Licht Judicial Complex, 250 Benefit Street, Providence 02903.

Telephone: (401) 222-3250.

PIRRAGLIA, Robert K. *(Associate Judge, Rhode Island District Court)* Appointed for life by Governor J. Joseph Garrahy to term beginning Jan 3, 1984. Educated at Providence College and George Washington University National Law Center.

Special Assistant 1977 and Legal Counsel 1979-82 to J. Joseph Garrahy.

Office: Judicial Complex, One Dorrance Plaza, Providence 02903.

Telephone: (401) 458-5201.

PROCACCINI, Daniel A. *(Associate Justice, Rhode Island Superior Court)* Appointed for life by Governor Lincoln Almond.

Office: Frank Licht Judicial Complex, 250 Benefit Street, Providence 02903.

Telephone: (401) 222-3250.

QUIRK, Madeline *(Associate Judge, Rhode Island District Court)* Appointed for life by governor.

Office: Judicial Complex, One Dorrance Plaza, Providence 02903.

Telephone: (401) 458-5201.

RAGOSTA, Vincent A. *(Associate Justice, Rhode Island Superior Court)* Appointed for life by Governor Edward DiPrete Feb 12, 1988. Born Providence Rhode Island Feb 12, 1924. Roman Catholic. Educated at University of Rhode Island B.S. in Accounting with highest honors 1949 and Boston College LL.B. 1951 replaced by J.D. Member Phi Kappa Phi, Theta Delta Chi and Beta Gamma Sigma. Admitted to practice Rhode Island 1951, U.S. District Court District of Rhode Island 1952 and U.S. Court of Appeals First Circuit 1965. Began legal practice Providence 1951. Former Associate Judge, Rhode Island District Court May 18, 1978 to Feb 11, 1988, appointed by Governor J. Joseph Garrahy.

Providence City Prosecutor 1953-60. Providence Assistant City Solicitor 1953-66. Commissioner Providence Bureau of Licenses 1977-78. Member Governor's Advisory Council on Social Welfare, The Association of Trial Lawyers of America, American Arbitration Association, American Judicature Society, Rhode Island and American Bar Associations. Awarded Star of Italian Solidarity with rank of Cavaliere by Republic of Italy 1975. Recipient Verrazzano Day Award 1995 and Distinguished Public Service Award from Justinian Law Society of Rhode Island 2000. Staff Sergeant U.S. Army 1943-46 Pacific Theater of Operations WWII. Past President and member House of Delegates Rhode Island Arthritis Foundation. Supreme Trustee Order of Sons of Italy in America. Incorporator of Rhode Island Hospital. Board of Directors Federal Hill House Association. Director Verrazzano Day Observance Committee. Member VFW, American Legion, Knights of Columbus, Elks and YMCA. Enjoys travel, handball and jogging.

Office: Frank Licht Judicial Complex, 250 Benefit Street, Providence 02903.

Telephone: (401) 222-3250.

RAHILL, Robert J. *(Associate Judge, Rhode Island District Court)* Appointed for life by Governor Bruce Sundlun to term beginning Feb 3, 1993. Born Nov 16, 1932. Educated at Rhode Island College B.Ed. 1954 M.Ed. 1963 and Suffolk University Law School J.D. 1977.

Registrar of Motor Vehicles 1969-73. Director Rhode Island Department of Transportation 1973-77. Executive Assistant for Policy to Governor J. Joseph Garrahy 1977-78. Lieutenant Colonel (retired) twenty-two years Active and National Guard. Incorporator Memorial Hospital of Rhode Island.

Office: Judicial Complex, One Dorrance Plaza, Providence 02903.

Telephone: (401) 458-5201.

REVENS, Susan L. *(Magistrate, Rhode Island Superior Court)* Appointed by Presiding Justice to term beginning 2001. Born Providence Rhode Island Feb 8, 1952. Educated at University of Rhode Island B.A. 1974 and Suffolk University Law School J.D. 1977. In legal practice 1978-94.

Attorney 1977-78 and Volunteer Attorney 1992-93 Rhode Island Legal Services, Inc. Assistant Administrator for Planning and Caseflow Management 1995-97, Executive Assistant 1997-99, Deputy Administrator 1999-2001 and Administrator since 2001 Rhode Island Superior Court. Instructor in Law Community College of Rhode Island 1978-79. Former Member American Bar Association. Member Rhode Island Bar Association (Committee on Availability of Legal Services 1979-81 and 1985-87). Member Rhode Island Board of Regents for Education 1973-75, Corporation of Women and Infants Hospital of Rhode Island since 1984, Kent County YMCA Board of Management 1986-89, Warwick School Department Advisory Committee on Gifted and Talented Education 1988-92 and University of Rhode Island Foundation 1986-89. Troop Leader 1986-87 and Member Nominating Committee 1986-88 Girl Scouts of Rhode

REVENS, SUSAN L.—*Continued*
Island. Program Instructor St. Catherine's Religious Education 1986-92.
Office: Frank Licht Judicial Complex, 250 Benefit Street, Providence 02903.
Telephone: (401) 222-3250.

RICCI, Hugh L., Jr. *(Associate Judge, Rhode Island Workers' Compensation Court)* Appointed for life by Governor Don Carcieri to term beginning 2003.
Office: One Dorrance Plaza, Providence 02903.
Telephone: (401) 458-5000.

ROCHA, Gilbert T. *(Associate Justice, Rhode Island Family Court)* Appointed for life by governor. Born East Providence Rhode Island Oct 17, 1931. Educated at Boston College B.S. 1954. Awarded honorary LL.D. Boston College Law School 1957. Associate Judge, Rhode Island District Court 1993-94.
Legal Counsel to East Providence Housing Authority. Secretary Commission to Revise Rhode Island Constitution. Member Rhode Island Trial Judges Association. State Senator 1959-67. Secretary Rhode Island Democratic State Central Committee. Member Boston College Varsity Club, Boston College Club of Rhode Island, Rhode Island Chapter Boston College Law School Alumni Association and Memorial Hospital of Rhode Island.
Office: J. Joseph Garrahy Judicial Complex, One Dorrance Plaza, Providence 02903.
Telephone: (401) 458-5310.

RODGERS, Joseph F., Jr. *(Presiding Justice, Rhode Island Superior Court)* Appointed for life by Governor Philip W. Noel to term beginning Nov 30, 1976. Presiding Justice since June 19, 1991. Born Providence Rhode Island Nov 18, 1941. Roman Catholic. Educated at Providence College A.M. 1962 and Boston University LL.B. 1966. Admitted to practice Rhode Island 1967. Began legal practice Providence 1967. Judge, Rhode Island District Court May 7, 1974 to Nov 30, 1976.
Instructor Rhode Island Junior College 1975-77 and Roger Williams University. Delegate National Conference of the Judiciary on the Rights of Victims of Crime 1983. Chair Commission to Study Election Laws and Commission on Judicial Tenure and Discipline. Member Rhode Island Bar Association. Democrat. Rhode Island State Senator 1968-74 (Chairman Senate Judiciary 1972-74). President Young Democrats of Rhode Island. Member Democratic Study Group on Vice Presidential Selection. Member National Democratic Committee to Reform Selection of Vice Presidential Candidates.
Office: Frank Licht Judicial Complex, 250 Benefit Street, Providence 02903.
Telephone: (401) 222-3250.

ROTONDI, John, Jr. *(Associate Judge, Rhode Island Workers' Compensation Court)* Appointed for life by Governor J. Joseph Garrahy to term beginning Aug 19, 1982. Born Providence Rhode Island Sept 28, 1942. Educated at University of Rhode Island B.A. 1964 and Suffolk University Law School J.D. Admitted to practice Rhode Island 1968.
Deputy City Solicitor 1976-81 and City Solicitor 1981-82 Providence. Former Member Commission on Judicial Tenure and Discipline 1986-89.
Office: J. Joseph Garrahy Judicial Complex, One Dorrance Plaza, Providence 02903.
Telephone: (401) 458-5000.

SALEM, George T., Jr. *(Associate Judge, Rhode Island Workers' Compensation Court)* Appointed for life by Governor Lincoln Almond.
Office: J. Joseph Garrahy Judicial Complex, One Dorrance Plaza, Providence 02903.
Telephone: (401) 458-5000.

SAMMARTINO, Everett C., Sr. *(Magistrate, Rhode Island Family Court)* Appointed by Chief Judge to term beginning Feb 12, 1996. Serves part-time. Born Providence Rhode Island April 19, 1931. Educated at Brown University A.B. and Boston University School of Law J.D. 1956.
Assistant U.S. Attorney 1969-96 and Interim U.S. Attorney 1997. Former Civil Chief and Supervisory Assistant U.S. Attorney's Office. Instructor in Litigation Roger Williams University School of Law. Member Rhode Island Bar Association. Member Federal Employees Retirement Association.
Office: J. Joseph Garrahy Judicial Complex, One Dorrance Plaza, Providence 02903.
Telephone: (401) 458-5310.

SAVAGE, Judith Colenback *(Associate Justice, Rhode Island Superior Court)* Appointed for life by Governor Bruce Sundlun to term beginning Feb 3, 1993. Born Pontiac Michigan Oct 9, 1957. Educated at Wellesley College B.A. 1979 and Case Western Reserve University School of Law J.D. 1982. Admitted to practice Pennsylvania 1982, Rhode Island 1984, U.S. Courts of Appeals Third 1984 and First 1985 Circuits and U.S. District Court District of Rhode Island 1985. Editor-in-Chief Case Western Reserve Law Review 1981-82. Law Clerk to U.S. Court of Appeals Third Circuit.
Member Rhode Island Women's Bar Association, Rhode Island and American Bar Associations. Executive Counsel to Governor Bruce Sundlun 1991-93.
Office: Frank Licht Judicial Complex, 250 Benefit Street, Providence 02903.
Telephone: (401) 222-3250.

SHAWCROSS, Raymond E. *(Associate Justice, Rhode Island Family Court)* Appointed for life by Governor Edward DiPrete Dec 23, 1986 to term beginning Feb 6, 1987. Born Providence Rhode Island Oct 2, 1945. Roman Catholic. Educated at Providence College B.A. 1968 and Suffolk University J.D. 1973. Admitted to practice Rhode Island 1974, U.S. District Court District of Rhode Island 1974 and U.S. Supreme Court 1979. In legal practice Cranston.
Faculty National College of Juvenile and Family Law. Board of Trustees National Council of Juvenile and Family Court Judges. Chair Model Code on Family and Domestic Violence Committee. Member Family Court Bench-Bar Committee and Rhode Island Bar Association. Rhode Island National Guard 1968-74. Counsel to Majority Leader House of Representatives 1981-87. Counsel Rhode Island Child Welfare Services 1974-78. Chief Counsel Department of Social and Rehabilitation Services 1978-81. Member Children's Code Commission

SHAWCROSS, RAYMOND E.—*Continued*
since 1978, Commission on Child Kidnapping and Commission on Adoption Law.
Office: J. Joseph Garrahy Judicial Complex, One Dorrance Plaza, Providence 02903.
Telephone: (401) 458-5310.

SHEPARD, Jeanne L. *(Magistrate, Rhode Island Family Court)* Appointed by Chief Judge.
Office: J. Joseph Garrahy Judicial Complex, One Dorrance Plaza, Providence 02903.
Telephone: (401) 458-5310.

SILVERSTEIN, Michael A. *(Associate Justice, Rhode Island Superior Court)* Appointed for life by Governor Bruce Sundlun to term beginning 1994. Born Providence Rhode Island Sept 28, 1933. Educated at Brown University A.B. 1956 and Boston University J.D. 1959.
Fellow American Bar Foundation. Member Association of Commercial Finance Attorneys, American Bankruptcy Institute, Rhode Island and American Bar Associations. Board of Trustees Roger Williams University. Member Woonsocket Industrial Development Corporation.
Office: Frank Licht Judicial Complex, 250 Benefit Street, Providence 02903.
Telephone: (401) 222-3250.

SMITH, William E. *(Judge, United Stated District Court District of Rhode Island)* Appointed for life by President George W. Bush to term beginning Dec 2, 2002. Educated at Georgetown University B.A. 1982 J.D. cum laude 1987. George F. Baker Scholar. Staff member American Criminal Law Review. In legal practice Providence 1987-2002. Judge, West Warwick Municipal Court 1993-98.
Office: Federal Building, Two Exchange Terrace, Providence 02903.
Telephone: (401) 752-7220.

SOWA, Edward P., Jr. *(Associate Judge, Rhode Island Workers' Compensation Court)* Appointed for life by Governor Lincoln Almond to term beginning March 28, 2000.
Office: J. Joseph Garrahy Judicial Complex, One Dorrance Plaza, Providence 02903.
Telephone: (401) 458-5000.

SUTTELL, Paul A. *(Associate Justice, Rhode Island Supreme Court)* Appointed for life by Governor Don Carcieri to term beginning 2003. Born Providence Rhode Island Jan 10, 1949. Educated at Northwestern University B.A. 1971 and Suffolk University Law School J.D. 1976. Admitted to practice Rhode Island 1976, U.S. District Court District of Rhode Island 1976 and Massachusetts 1977. In legal practice Providence Rhode Island 1976-90 and Little Compton Rhode Island 1983-90. Former Associate Justice, Rhode Island Family Court, appointed by Governor Edward DiPrete to term beginning July 9, 1990.
Counsel to Minority Leader 1979-82, Member 1983-90 and Deputy Minority Leader 1985-90 House of Representatives Rhode Island. Member National Council of Juvenile and Family Court Judges, Rhode Island and American Bar Associations. Delegate to Rhode Island Republican State Central Committee 1981-90 and Republican National Convention 1988. Member Little Compton Republican Town Committee 1987-90. Deacon 1995-99 and Chair 1997-99 United Congregational Church of Little Compton. Member Sakonnet Preservation Association, Rhode Island Agricultural Lands Preservation Commission, Newport County Convention and Visitors Bureau, Stopover Shelters of Newport County, Rhode Island Lung Association, Newport County Division American Heart Association, Friends of Sakonnet Lighthouse and Society of Colonial Wars.
Office: Frank Licht Judicial Complex, 250 Benefit Street, Providence 02903.
Telephone: (401) 222-3274.

THOMPSON, O. Rogeriee *(Associate Justice, Rhode Island Superior Court)* Appointed for life by Governor Lincoln Almond. Born Anderson South Carolina Aug 8, 1951. Educated at Brown University B.A. 1973 and Boston University School of Law J.D. 1976. Former Associate Judge, Rhode Island District Court, appointed by Governor Edward DiPrete to term beginning 1988.
Assistant City Solicitor Providence 1980-82. Member Supreme Court Committee to Study Future of the Courts and on Women and the Courts. Member Rhode Island Women's Bar Association, Rhode Island Black Lawyers Association, National Conference of Black Lawyers and Rhode Island Bar Association.
Office: Frank Licht Judicial Complex, 250 Benefit Street, Providence 02903.
Telephone: (401) 222-3250.

THUNBERG, Melanie Wilk *(Associate Justice, Rhode Island Superior Court)* Appointed for life by Governor Edward DiPrete to term beginning Feb 20, 1987. Born Providence Rhode Island Sept 15, 1951. Educated at Trinity College B.A. 1973 and Suffolk University Law School J.D. 1978. Member Phi Beta Kappa. Admitted to practice Rhode Island 1978, U.S. District Court District of Rhode Island 1978 and U.S. Court of Appeals First Circuit 1981.
Assistant Attorney General Rhode Island Criminal Division. Member State Commission on Judicial Tenure and Discipline. Member Rhode Island Trial Judges Association (Judicial Education Committee).
Office: Frank Licht Judicial Complex, 250 Benefit Street, Providence 02903.
Telephone: (401) 222-3250.

TORRES, Ernest C. *(Chief Judge, United States District Court District of Rhode Island)* Appointed for life by President Ronald Reagan to term beginning 1988. Chief Judge since Dec 1, 1999. Born New Bedford Massachusetts Oct 6, 1941. Educated at Dartmouth College A.B. 1963 and Duke University School of Law J.D. 1968. In legal practice Providence 1968-80 and 1986-88. Associate Justice, Rhode Island Superior Court 1980-85.
Member 1975-80 and Deputy Minority Leader 1977-80 State House of Representatives Rhode Island.
Office: U.S. Courthouse, One Exchange Terrace, Providence 02903-1779.
Telephone: (401) 752-7020.

VEIGA, Aurendina G. *(Magistrate, Rhode Island Traffic Tribunal)* Appointed by Chief Judge to term beginning 1999. Born Newport Rhode Island. Roman Catholic. Educated at Salve Regina College B.A.S. cum laude 1980 and Temple University School of Law J.D. 1983. Admitted to practice Rhode Island 1983. In legal practice Providence 1989-99. Bail Commissioner, Rhode Island District Court 1989-99.
Assistant Public Defender 1983-89. Member American

VEIGA, AURENDINA G.—*Continued*

Judges Association, Rhode Island and American Bar Associations.

Office: 345 Harris Avenue, Providence 02909-1082.
Telephone: (401) 222-1184.
E-mail address: AVEIGA@courts.state.ri.us

VOCCOLA, Kathleen A. *(Associate Justice, Rhode Island Family Court)* Appointed for life by Governor Edward DiPrete to term beginning June 5, 1989. Born Providence June 22, 1950. Educated at University of Rhode Island B.A. 1972 and Suffolk University Law School J.D. 1977. In legal practice 1978-89.

Assistant City Solicitor Cranston 1979-85. Administrator State Liquor Control 1985-89. Member Rhode Island Trial Lawyers Association, Rhode Island, New York State and American Bar Associations.

Office: J. Joseph Garrahy Judicial Complex, One Dorrance Plaza, Providence 02903.
Telephone: (401) 458-5310.

VOGEL, Netti C. *(Associate Justice, Rhode Island Superior Court)* Appointed for life by Governor Bruce Sundlun to term beginning Sept 1994. Born Chicago Illinois March 2, 1947. Educated at Roosevelt University B.A. 1971 and New England School of Law J.D. 1975.

Former Member Commission on Judicial Tenure and Discipline and Supreme Court Committee on Unauthorized Practice of Law. Member American Inn of Courts, Rhode Island Bar Foundation, Rhode Island (Member Executive Committee and House of Delegates 1985-84, Officer 1992-94) and American Bar Associations.

Office: Frank Licht Judicial Complex, 250 Benefit Street, Providence 02903.
Telephone: (401) 222-3250.

VOTOLATO, Arthur N. *(Judge, United States Bankruptcy Court District of Rhode Island)* Appointed by U.S. District Court judge to term beginning June 25, 1968. Reappointed by U.S. Court of Appeals judges. Also Chief Judge, Bankruptcy Appellate Panel First Circuit. Selected by the Judicial Council of the First Circuit. Born Providence Rhode Island Aug 20, 1930. Educated at University of Rhode Island B.A. 1953 and Boston University School of Law LL.B. 1956. Admitted to practice Rhode Island 1956 and U.S. District Court District of Rhode Island 1957. In legal practice Providence 1956-62. Judge, First Circuit Bankruptcy Appellate Panel (Maine) and Chief Judge, First Circuit Bankruptcy Appellate Panel (Massachusetts) 1981-84.

Chief Special Counsel Rhode Island Department of Public Works 1962-68. Author "Injunctions and Restraining Orders Under the Bankruptcy Act" Rhode Island Bar Annual 1970-71 and "A Review of Recent Equal Protection Challenges to the Dischargeability of Alimony Provisions of Section 17a(7) of the Bankruptcy Act" 13 Suffolk L. Rev. Rhode Island Survey 1979. Editorial Advisory Board 1975-90 and Digest Editor 1975-84 American Bankruptcy L. Jour. Editor National Conference of Bankruptcy Judges Newsletter 1970-75. Important Decisions: In re Wasserman 3 B.C.D. 467 Bankr. D.R.I. 1977; In re Hagan 41 B.R. 122 Bankr. D.R.I. 1984; In re Cournoyer 43 B.R. 354 Bankr. D.R.I. 1984; In re Gibbons 52 B.R. 861 Bankr. D.R.I. 1985; Monzack v. A.D.B. Investors (In re EMB Assocs., Inc.) 92 B.R. 9 Bankr. D.R.I. 1988, later proceeding In re Max Sugarman Funeral Home, Inc. 94 B.R. 16 Bankr. D.R.I. 1988, later proceeding In re EMB Assocs., Inc. 100 B.R. 629 Bankr. D.R.I. 1989, aff'd in part and rev'd in part, Max Sugarman Funeral Home, Inc. v. A.D.B. Investors 127 B.R. 408 D.R.I. 1989, vacated, in part, remanded Max Sugarman Funeral Home, Inc. v. A.D.B. Investors 926 F.2d 1248 1st Cir. 1991, later proceeding In re Max Sugarman Funeral Home, Inc. 130 B.R. 119 Bankr. D.R.I. 1991, on remand Monzack v. A.D.B. Investors 1992 Bankr. LEXIS 2074 Bankr. D.R.I. 1992; In re Newport Offshore, Ltd. 75 B.R. 919, aff'd 871 F.2d 223 1st Cir. Mass. March 31, 1989, judgment aff'd by U.S. v. Energy Resources Co., Inc. 110 S. Ct. 2139, 1990; In re Cardinale 142 B.R. 42 Bankr. D.R.I. 1992; and In re Flynn 143 B.R. 798 Bankr. D.R.I. 1992.

Adjunct Professor of Bankruptcy Law Roger Williams College 1977-82. Chairman Committee on Consolidation of Clerk's Office. Former Member Rhode Island Trial Lawyers Association and The Association of Trial Lawyers of America. Fellow American College of Bankruptcy. Member Bankruptcy Judges Advisory Committee Administrative Office of the U.S. Courts 1988-91. Member Northeast Bankruptcy Law Institute (Board of Advisors 1991), National Conference of Bankruptcy Judges (Liaison Committee on Special Court Judges 1973, Member Committee on Conference Newsletter 1973, First Circuit Board of Governors 1973-76, Liaison Committee to the Federal Courts Study Committee 1988-90), Rhode Island (Form Book Project 1960-62, Committee on Property Law 1964-66, Committee on Continuing Legal Education Programming 1976-77, Federal Court Bench/Bar Committee 1980-81, Committee on Creditor-Debtor Rights 1986), Federal (Secretary Rhode Island Chapter 1988-90) and American (Committee on Standards of Judicial Conduct 1970-71 and Member 1969-75 National Conference of Special Court Judges) Bar Associations. Speaker/Panelist Continuing Legal Education Speaker's Program Rhode Island Bar Association 1969-80, Eastern Regional Conference of Referees in Bankruptcy 1970, Advanced Seminar on Bankruptcy Practising Law Institute 1985, First Circuit Judicial Conference 1985 and Seminar on Bankruptcy Litigation and New England Cambridge Massachusetts 1989. Judge for mock trials Rhode Island Legal/Education Partnership 1988-90. Airman First Class USAF 1950-51. Republican Candidate for Rhode Island Attorney General 1962. Board of Management Greater Providence YMCA 1973-75. Board of Directors Ocean State Marathon Committee 1979-83. Trustee University of Rhode Island Foundation since 1988. Former Member Urban League of Rhode Island (Board of Directors 1980-81, Member Education Committee 1980-81, Scholarship Committee 1980-81). Member Boston University Alumni Association since 1956, Narragansett Bay Yachting Association 1960-81, Aircraft Owners and Pilots Association since 1981 and Mooney Aircraft Pilots Association since 1988. Enjoys running, sailing, skiing and flying.

Office: The Federal Center, 380 Westminster Street, Providence 02903-3256.
Telephone: (401) 528-4487.

WILLIAMS, Frank J. *(Chief Justice, Rhode Island Supreme Court)* Appointed for life by Governor Lincoln Almond to term beginning Jan 4, 2001. Born Cranston Rhode Island Aug 24, 1940. Educated at Boston University, College of Liberal Arts B.A., Boston University School of Law J.D. and Bryant College LL.M. in Taxation. Former Probate Judge, Towns of Hopkinton and West Greenwich. Associate Justice, Rhode Island Superi-

WILLIAMS, FRANK J.—*Continued*

or Court Dec 15, 1995 to Jan 4, 2001, appointed by Governor Lincoln Almond.

Town Moderator Richmond. Solicitor Towns of Coventry, West Greenwich, Hopkinton, Barrington and Bristol. Captain U.S. Army 1962-67. Recipient Bronze Star, three Air Medals, Combat Infantryman's Badge, Army Commendation Medal, two Vietnam Campaign Medals, Aerial Observer Wings and Republic of Vietnam Gallantry Cross with Silver Star for Valor. President The Ulysses Grant Association. Chair The Lincoln Forum and Rhode Island Housing and Mortgage Finance Corporation. Trustee The John F. Fogarty Foundation for the Mentally Retarded. Board of Trustees South County Hospital.

Office: Frank Licht Judicial Complex, 250 Benefit Street, Providence 02903.

Telephone: (401) 222-3274.

YASHAR, Marjorie R. *(Judge, Rhode Island Traffic Tribunal)* Appointed for life by governor to term beginning 1985. Born Newton Massachusetts. Educated at Wellesley College A.B. 1962 and Boston University School of Law J.D. 1967.

Member Providence Home Rule Charter Commission.

Office: 345 Harris Avenue, Providence 02909-1082.

Telephone: (401) 222-1184.

SOUTH CAROLINA

Capital COLUMBIA

UNITED STATES DISTRICT COURT DISTRICT OF SOUTH CAROLINA

United States District Court District of South Carolina consists of eleven divisions. For descriptive information refer to the United States Courts section.

Aiken Division includes Aiken, Allendale and Barnwell counties. The court sits at Aiken.

Anderson Division includes Anderson, Oconee and Pickens counties. The court sits at Anderson.

Beaufort Division includes Beaufort, Hampton and Jasper counties. The court sits at Beaufort.

Charleston Division includes Berkeley, Charleston, Clarendon, Colleton, Dorchester and Georgetown counties. The court sits at Charleston.

Columbia Division includes Kershaw, Lee, Lexington, Richland and Sumter counties. The court sits at Columbia.

Florence Division includes Chesterfield, Darlington, Dillon, Florence, Horry, Marion, Marlboro and Williamsburg counties. The court sits at Florence.

Greenville Division includes Greenville and Laurens counties. The court sits at Greenville.

Greenwood Division includes Abbeville, Edgefield, Greenwood, McCormick, Newberry and Saluda counties. The court sits at Greenwood.

Orangeburg Division includes Bamberg, Calhoun and Orangeburg counties. The court sits at Orangeburg.

Rock Hill Division includes Chester, Fairfield, Lancaster and York counties. The court sits at Rock Hill.

Spartanburg Division includes Cherokee, Spartanburg and Union counties. The court sits at Spartanburg.

Chief Judge
Joseph F. Anderson, Jr.

Judges

C. Weston Houck
David C. Norton
Cameron McGowan Currie
Terry L. Wooten
G. Ross Anderson, Jr.
Henry M. Herlong, Jr.
Patrick Michael Duffy
Margaret B. Seymour

Senior Judges
Sol Blatt, Jr.
Matthew J. Perry, Jr.

Clerk
Larry W. Propes
Federal Courthouse
1845 Assembly Street
Columbia, South Carolina 29201-2431
(803) 765-5816

UNITED STATES MAGISTRATE JUDGES OF SOUTH CAROLINA

Robert Stuart Carr
Robert L. Buchanan, Jr.
Bristow Marchant
Bruce H. Hendricks
William M. Catoe, Jr.
Joseph R. McCrorey
George C. Kosko
Thomas E. Rogers, III

UNITED STATES BANKRUPTCY COURT OF SOUTH CAROLINA

Chief Judge
Wm. Thurmond Bishop

Judge
John E. Waites

Bankruptcy Clerk
Brenda K. Argoe
P.O. Box 1448
Columbia, South Carolina 29202-1448
(803) 765-5436

SOUTH CAROLINA SUPREME COURT

The Supreme Court is South Carolina's court of last resort. The court consists of a chief justice and four associate justices elected by the General Assembly for staggered ten-year terms. If an unexpired term does not exceed one year, the governor may fill the vacancy for the remainder of that term. Retired justices may serve as needed.

The court has appellate jurisdiction in cases involving the death penalty, public utility rates, significant constitutional issues, public bond issues and the election laws. The court may, at its discretion, review decisions of the Court of Appeals. The court has original jurisdiction to issue original and remedial writs. Administrative control of all courts in the state is vested in the Chief Justice. The court may answer questions certified to it by the federal courts or appellate courts of other states. The court regulates the admission to the bar and the practice of law in the state.

The court sits en banc at Columbia and holds session all year.

Chief Justice
Jean Hoefer Toal

Associate Justices
James E. Moore
John H. Waller, Jr.
E. C. Burnett, III
Costa M. Pleicones

Clerk
Daniel E. Shearouse
P.O. Box 11330
Columbia, South Carolina 29211
(803) 734-1080
Fax: (803) 734-1499

SOUTH CAROLINA SUPREME COURT—*Continued*

Director
Rosalyn Woodson Frierson
South Carolina Court Administration
1015 Sumter Street, Suite 200
Columbia, South Carolina 29201
(803) 734-1800

SOUTH CAROLINA COURT OF APPEALS

The Court of Appeals is South Carolina's court of intermediate appellate jurisdiction. The court began temporary operation September 1, 1983 and was established by the voters as a permanent court November 1984. The court consists of a chief judge and eight associate judges elected by the General Assembly. Permanent terms began July 1, 1985 with length of initial terms staggered by two-year increments. Subsequent terms are six years. If an unexpired term does not exceed one year, the governor may fill the vacancy for the remainder of that term.

The court exercises appellate jurisdiction over cases from the Circuit Court and Family Court except cases over which the Supreme Court has exclusive jurisdiction. The Supreme Court, at its discretion, may review any decision of the court.

The court may sit in three panels of three judges or en banc. The court may sit in any county as needed.

Chief Judge
Kaye G. Hearn

Associate Judges

Ralph K. Anderson, Jr.	Donald W. Beatty
Carol Connor	C. Tolbert Goolsby, Jr.
William L. Howard, Sr.	Thomas E. Huff
John W. Kittredge	H. Samuel Stilwell

SOUTH CAROLINA CIRCUIT COURT

The Circuit Court is South Carolina's court of general jurisdiction. In civil matters the court is known as the Court of Common Pleas, and in criminal matters the court is known as the Court of General Sessions. The state is divided into sixteen judicial circuits. Judges are elected by the General Assembly for six-year terms. If an unexpired term does not exceed one year, the governor may fill the vacancy for the remainder of that term. Judges rotate among the circuits as assigned by the chief justice. However, each circuit has at least one resident circuit judge who maintains an office in the judge's home county within the circuit. Judges-at-Large may serve the entire state. Retired judges may serve as needed.

The court has original jurisdiction of civil and criminal cases except those cases which are under the exclusive jurisdiction of another court. The court has limited appellate jurisdiction of cases from Magistrate Courts, Municipal Courts, Probate Courts and some administrative agencies. Equity matters are heard by Masters-in-Equity.

The court sits at each county seat.

FIRST JUDICIAL CIRCUIT includes Calhoun, Dorchester and Orangeburg counties. The court sits at St. Matthews, St. George and Orangeburg.

Judges
Diane Schafer Goodstein
James C. Williams, Jr.

SECOND JUDICIAL CIRCUIT includes Aiken, Bamberg and Barnwell counties. The court sits at Aiken, Bamberg and Barnwell.

Judge
Rodney A. Peeples

THIRD JUDICIAL CIRCUIT includes Clarendon, Lee, Sumter and Williamsburg counties. The court sits at Manning, Bishopville, Sumter and Kingstree.

Judges
Thomas W. Cooper, Jr.
Howard P. King

FOURTH JUDICIAL CIRCUIT includes Chesterfield, Darlington, Dillon and Marlboro counties. The court sits at Chesterfield, Darlington, Dillon and Bennettsville.

Judges
John Michael Baxley
Paul M. Burch

FIFTH JUDICIAL CIRCUIT includes Kershaw and Richland counties. The court sits at Camden and Columbia.

Judges
G. Thomas Cooper, Jr.
J. Ernest Kinard, Jr.
L. Casey Manning

SIXTH JUDICIAL CIRCUIT includes Chester, Fairfield and Lancaster counties. The court sits at Chester, Winnsboro and Lancaster.

Judge
Paul E. Short, Jr.

SEVENTH JUDICIAL CIRCUIT includes Cherokee and Spartanburg counties. The court sits at Gaffney and Spartanburg.

Judge
J. Derham Cole

EIGHTH JUDICIAL CIRCUIT includes Abbeville, Greenwood, Laurens and Newberry counties. The court sits at Abbeville, Greenwood, Laurens and Newberry.

Judges
James W. Johnson, Jr.
Wyatt T. Saunders, Jr.

NINTH JUDICIAL CIRCUIT includes Berkeley and Charleston counties. The court sits at Moncks Corner and Charleston.

Judges
Deadra L. Jefferson
Daniel F. Pieper
Roger M. Young

TENTH JUDICIAL CIRCUIT includes Anderson and Oconee counties. The court sits at Anderson and Walhalla.

Judges
Alexander S. Macaulay
J. Cordell Maddox, Jr.
J. C. Nicholson, Jr.

SOUTH CAROLINA CIRCUIT COURT—*Continued*

ELEVENTH JUDICIAL CIRCUIT includes Edgefield, Lexington, McCormick and Saluda counties. The court sits at Edgefield, Lexington, McCormick and Saluda.

Judges

William P. Keesley
Marc H. Westbrook

TWELFTH JUDICIAL CIRCUIT includes Florence and Marion counties. The court sits at Florence and Marion.

Judge

Baxter Hicks Harwell, Jr.

THIRTEENTH JUDICIAL CIRCUIT includes Greenville and Pickens counties. The court sits at Greenville and Pickens.

Judges

John C. Few
Henry F. Floyd
Edward W. Miller
Larry R. Patterson

FOURTEENTH JUDICIAL CIRCUIT includes Allendale, Beaufort, Colleton, Hampton and Jasper counties. The court sits at Allendale, Beaufort, Walterboro, Hampton and Ridgeland.

Judges

Perry M. Buckner
Jackson V. Gregory

FIFTEENTH JUDICIAL CIRCUIT includes Georgetown and Horry counties. The court sits at Georgetown and Conway.

Judges

John L. Breeden, Jr.
Steven H. John
Paula H. Thomas

SIXTEENTH JUDICIAL CIRCUIT includes Union and York counties. The court sits at Union and York.

Judges

Lee S. Alford
John C. Hayes, III

CIRCUIT COURT JUDGES-AT-LARGE

James R. Barber, III	James E. Brogdon, Jr.
R. Markley Dennis, Jr.	Kenneth G. Goode
J. Mark Hayes, II	Alison Renee Lee
Reginald I. Lloyd	James E. Lockemy
John M. Milling	Clifton Newman

SOUTH CAROLINA FAMILY COURT

The Family Court is a statewide court of limited jurisdiction in South Carolina. It was established July 1, 1977, to replace the family court system which was in effect in only some counties. Judges are elected by the General Assembly for six-year terms. If an unexpired term does not exceed one year, the governor may fill the vacancy for the remainder of that term. Family court judges rotate among all counties in the circuit they serve. Judges may be rotated to other circuits at the discretion of the chief justice. Retired judges may serve as needed.

The court has exclusive jurisdiction over marriage, divorce, legal separation, custody, visitation rights, termination of parental rights, adoption, support, alimony, division of marital property and change of name. The court also has exclusive jurisdiction over minors under the age of seventeen alleged to have violated state or municipal ordinances; however, most traffic and fish and game violations may be tried in Magistrate or Municipal Courts. In cases where a child is charged with murder or rape, the case may be transferred to the Circuit Court, where the accused is tried as an adult. The court may issue writs of habeas corpus and such processes necessary to the exercise of proper jurisdiction. Appeals are to the Court of Appeals.

The boundaries of the Family Court circuits are the same as those of the Circuit Court.

FIRST JUDICIAL CIRCUIT includes Calhoun, Dorchester and Orangeburg counties. The court sits at St. Matthews, Summerville and Orangeburg.

Judges

Anne Gue Jones
Nancy Chapman McLin
William J. Wylie, Jr.

SECOND JUDICIAL CIRCUIT includes Aiken, Bamberg and Barnwell counties. The court sits at Aiken, Bamberg and Barnwell.

Judges

Dale Moore Gable
Peter R. Nuessle

THIRD JUDICIAL CIRCUIT includes Clarendon, Lee, Sumter and Williamsburg counties. The court sits at Manning, Bishopville, Sumter and Kingstree.

Judges

George M. McFaddin, Jr.
Marion D. Myers
R. Wright Turbeville

FOURTH JUDICIAL CIRCUIT includes Chesterfield, Darlington, Dillon and Marlboro counties. The court sits at Chesterfield, Darlington, Dillon and Bennettsville.

Judges

Roger E. Henderson
Jamie Lee Murdock, Jr.
James H. Spruill, III

FIFTH JUDICIAL CIRCUIT includes Kershaw and Richland counties. The court sits at Camden and Columbia.

Judges

Rolly W. Jacobs
Leslie K. Riddle
Donna S. Strom
H. Bruce Williams

SIXTH JUDICIAL CIRCUIT includes Chester, Fairfield and Lancaster counties. The court sits at Chester, Winnsboro and Lancaster.

Judges

Walter B. Brown, Jr.
Brooks P. Goldsmith

SOUTH CAROLINA FAMILY COURT—*Continued*

SEVENTH JUDICIAL CIRCUIT includes Cherokee and Spartanburg counties. The court sits at Gaffney and Spartanburg.

Judges
Georgia V. Anderson
Wesley L. Brown
James F. Fraley, Jr.

EIGHTH JUDICIAL CIRCUIT includes Abbeville, Greenwood, Laurens and Newberry counties. The court sits at Abbeville, Greenwood, Laurens and Newberry.

Judges
Joseph W. McGowan, III
John M. Rucker
Billy A. Tunstall, Jr.

NINTH JUDICIAL CIRCUIT includes Berkeley and Charleston counties. The court sits at Moncks Corner and Charleston.

Judges
Judy C. Bridges
Jocelyn B. Cate
Wayne M. Creech
Paul W. Garfinkel
Jack Alan Landis
Frances Segars-Andrews

TENTH JUDICIAL CIRCUIT includes Anderson and Oconee counties. The court sits at Anderson and Walhalla.

Judges
Timothy M. Cain
Tommy B. Edwards
Barry W. Knobel

ELEVENTH JUDICIAL CIRCUIT includes Edgefield, Lexington, McCormick and Saluda counties. The court sits at Edgefield, Lexington, McCormick and Saluda.

Judges
Kellum W. Allen
Richard W. Chewning, III
C. David Sawyer, Jr.

TWELFTH JUDICIAL CIRCUIT includes Florence and Marion counties. The court sits at Florence and Marion.

Judges
Mary E. Buchan
Wylie H. Caldwell, Jr.
A. E. Morehead, III

THIRTEENTH JUDICIAL CIRCUIT includes Greenville and Pickens counties. The court sits at Greenville and Pickens.

Judges
Stephen S. Bartlett
Timothy L. Brown
Robert N. Jenkins, Sr.
Alvin D. Johnson
R. Kinard Johnson, Jr.
Aphrodite K. Konduros

FOURTEENTH JUDICIAL CIRCUIT includes Allendale, Beaufort, Colleton, Hampton and Jasper counties. The court sits at Allendale, Beaufort, Walterboro, Hampton and Ridgeland.

Judges
Robert S. Armstrong
Jane D. Fender
Gerald C. Smoak, Jr.

FIFTEENTH JUDICIAL CIRCUIT includes Georgetown and Horry counties. The court sits at Georgetown and Conway.

Judges
H. T. Abbott, III
H. E. Bonnoitt, Jr.
Lisa A. Kinon

SIXTEENTH JUDICIAL CIRCUIT includes Union and York counties. The court sits at Union and Rock Hill.

Judges
Robert E. Guess
Henry T. Woods

SOUTH CAROLINA PROBATE COURT

The Probate Court is a court of special jurisdiction in South Carolina. Judges are elected in countywide elections for four-year terms. Associate judges may be appointed by and serve at the pleasure of probate judges.

The court has jurisdiction over marriage licenses, administration of estates of deceased persons, guardianship or conservatorship of minors and incompetents, minor settlements under $25,000 and involuntary commitments to mental institutions of mentally ill or chemically dependent persons. The court also has exclusive jurisdiction over trusts and concurrent jurisdiction with the Circuit Court over powers of attorney. The court may issue writs necessary to the exercise of proper jurisdiction.

The court sits at each county seat.

County	Judge
Abbeville	Carol F. Speer
Aiken	Sue H. Roe
Allendale	Brenda P. Bennett
Anderson	Martha D. Newton
Bamberg	Nancy Hand Green
Barnwell	Branna Woodward Williams
Beaufort	Francis M. Simon
Berkeley	Keith Kornahrens, Sr.
Calhoun	Frederick W. Robinson
Charleston	Irvin G. Condon
Cherokee	William R. Douglas
Chester	Lois Roddey
Chesterfield	Edwin Malloy Davis
Clarendon	Barney L. Morris
Colleton	I. A. Smoak, III
Darlington	Marvin I. Lawson
Dillon	Jasper G. Rogers
Dorchester	Tiffany Provence
Edgefield	Robert E. Peeler
Fairfield	Pamela W. Renwick
Florence	William Kenneth Eaton
Georgetown	Waldo A. Maring
Greenville	Debora Faulkner
Greenwood	Frank R. Addy, Jr.
Hampton	Sheila Odom
Horry	Deirdre Edmonds
Jasper	Joseph N. Malphrus, Jr.
Kershaw	Harriett P. Pierce
Lancaster	Sandra S. Estridge

SOUTH CAROLINA PROBATE COURT—*Continued*

Laurens	Kaye W. Fridy
Lee	Catherine F. Harris
Lexington	Daniel R. Eckstrom
Marion	T. Carroll Atkinson
Marlboro	Mark Heath
McCormick	Ronnie D. Kidd
Newberry	Kelly Baker Nobles
Oconee	Sandra Burgess Orr
Orangeburg	Vivian E. Ross-Bennett
Pickens	Kathy P. Zorn
Richland	Amy W. McCulloch
Saluda	Margaret N. Upchurch
Spartanburg	Raymond C. Eubanks, Jr.
Sumter	Dale Atkinson
Union	Donna P. Cudd
Williamsburg	Rudell M. Gamble
York	John P. Gettys

SOUTH CAROLINA MAGISTRATE COURTS

The Magistrate Courts are courts of limited jurisdiction in South Carolina. There are over two hundred eighty courts. The magistrates are appointed by the governor with the advice and consent of the Senate. Terms are four years.

The courts have civil jurisdiction over matters in which the amount in controversy does not exceed $7,500 and criminal jurisdiction over cases in which the penalty does not exceed a $500 fine or thirty days imprisonment, generally. The magistrates may conduct preliminary hearings, set bail and issue arrest and search warrants. Appeals are to the Circuit Court.

SOUTH CAROLINA MUNICIPAL COURTS

Municipal Courts are courts of limited jurisdiction in South Carolina. In 1980, Act 480 incorporated the municipal courts into the unified judicial system and created uniformity in the courts' jurisdiction. There are over two hundred municipal courts. Judges serve terms not exceeding four years as determined by the council of the municipality.

The courts have criminal jurisdiction to try all offenses against city and state ordinances or laws in which the penalty does not exceed a $500 fine or thirty days imprisonment, generally. The courts may set bail and issue arrest and search warrants. Appeals are to the Circuit Court.

South Carolina Counties and County Seats

Abbeville
Abbeville

Aiken
Aiken

Allendale
Allendale

Anderson
Anderson

Bamberg
Bamberg

Barnwell
Barnwell

Beaufort
Beaufort

Berkeley
Moncks Corner

Calhoun
St. Matthews

Charleston
Charleston

Cherokee
Gaffney

Chester
Chester

Chesterfield
Chesterfield

Clarendon
Manning

Colleton
Walterboro

Darlington
Darlington

Dillon
Dillon

Dorchester
St. George

Edgefield
Edgefield

Fairfield
Winnsboro

Florence
Florence

Georgetown
Georgetown

Greenville
Greenville

Greenwood
Greenwood

Hampton
Hampton

Horry
Conway

Jasper
Ridgeland

Kershaw
Camden

Lancaster
Lancaster

Laurens
Laurens

Lee
Bishopville

Lexington
Lexington

Marion
Marion

Marlboro
Bennettsville

McCormick
McCormick

Newberry
Newberry

Oconee
Walhalla

Orangeburg
Orangeburg

Pickens
Pickens

Richland
Columbia

Saluda
Saluda

Spartanburg
Spartanburg

Sumter
Sumter

Union
Union

Williamsburg
Kingstree

York
York

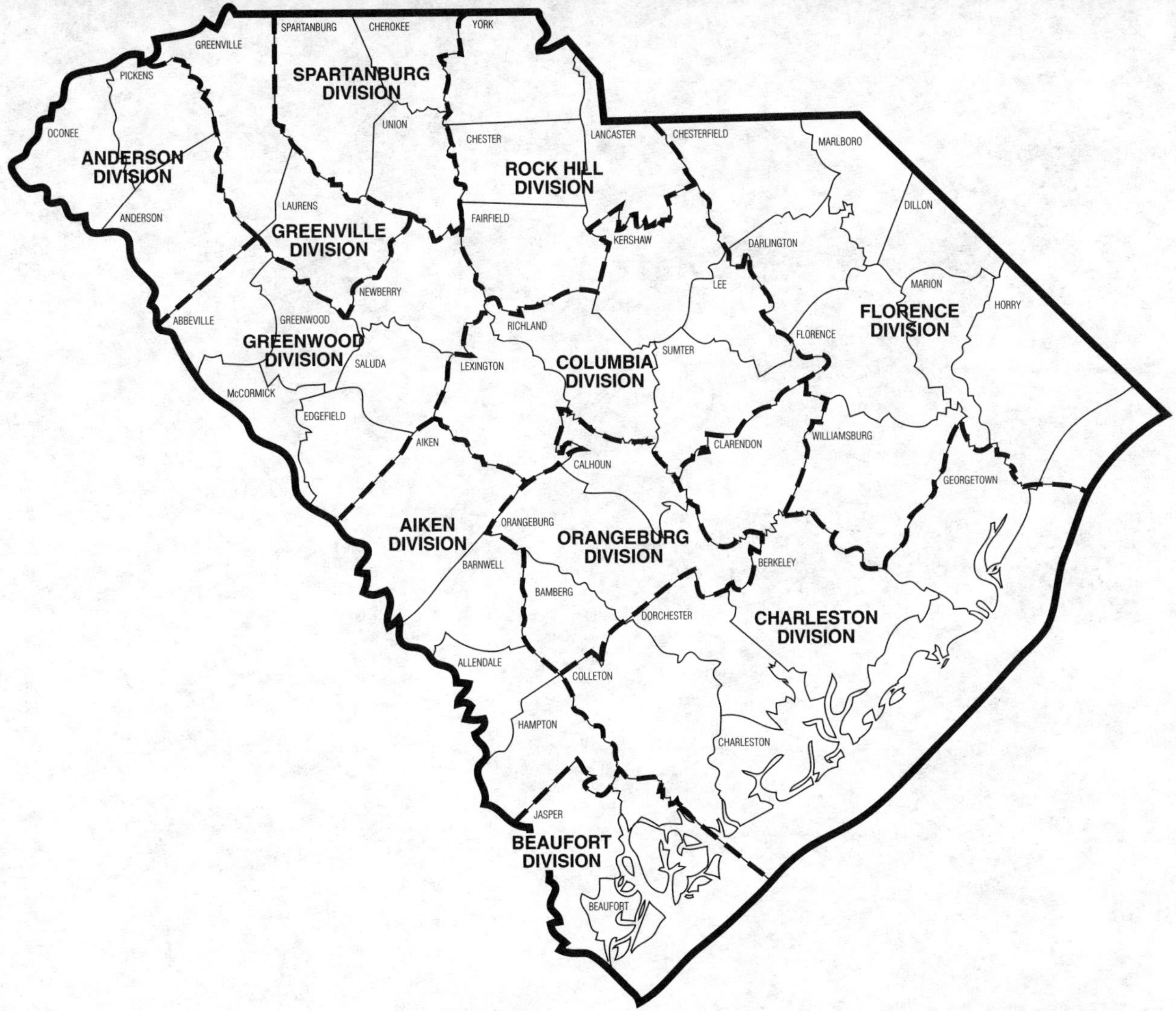
SPARTANBURG
CHEROKEE
YORK
GREENVILLE
PICKENS
SPARTANBURG DIVISION
UNION
OCONEE
ANDERSON DIVISION
CHESTER
LANCASTER
CHESTERFIELD
MARLBORO
ROCK HILL DIVISION
DILLON
LAURENS
ANDERSON
FAIRFIELD
GREENVILLE DIVISION
KERSHAW
DARLINGTON
MARION
NEWBERRY
LEE
HORRY
FLORENCE DIVISION
ABBEVILLE
GREENWOOD
RICHLAND
FLORENCE
GREENWOOD DIVISION
SUMTER
SALUDA
LEXINGTON
COLUMBIA DIVISION
McCORMICK
EDGEFIELD
WILLIAMSBURG
AIKEN
CLARENDON
CALHOUN
GEORGETOWN
AIKEN DIVISION
ORANGEBURG
ORANGEBURG DIVISION
BARNWELL
BERKELEY
BAMBERG
DORCHESTER
CHARLESTON DIVISION
ALLENDALE
COLLETON
HAMPTON
CHARLESTON
JASPER
BEAUFORT DIVISION
BEAUFORT

DIVISIONS OF UNITED STATES DISTRICT COURT DISTRICT OF SOUTH CAROLINA

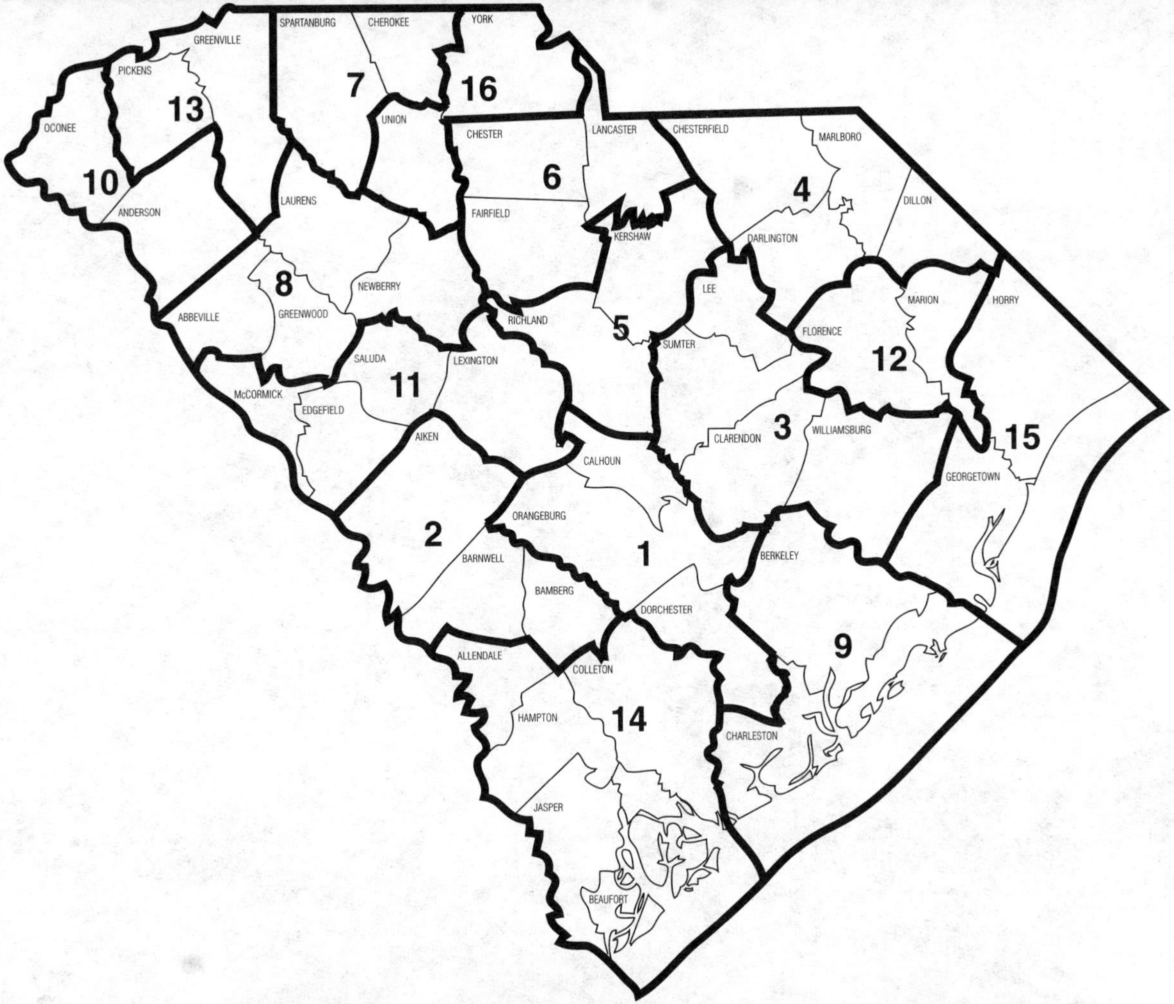
OCONEE
PICKENS
GREENVILLE
13
10
ANDERSON
SPARTANBURG
CHEROKEE
7
UNION
YORK
16
CHESTER
6
FAIRFIELD
LANCASTER
KERSHAW
CHESTERFIELD
MARLBORO
4
DILLON
DARLINGTON
LAURENS
8
NEWBERRY
GREENWOOD
ABBEVILLE
RICHLAND
5
LEE
SUMTER
FLORENCE
MARION
12
HORRY
SALUDA
11
LEXINGTON
McCORMICK
EDGEFIELD
AIKEN
CALHOUN
CLARENDON
3
WILLIAMSBURG
15
GEORGETOWN
2
ORANGEBURG
1
BARNWELL
BAMBERG
BERKELEY
DORCHESTER
9
ALLENDALE
COLLETON
14
HAMPTON
CHARLESTON
JASPER
BEAUFORT

JUDICIAL CIRCUITS OF SOUTH CAROLINA CIRCUIT COURT AND SOUTH CAROLINA FAMILY COURT

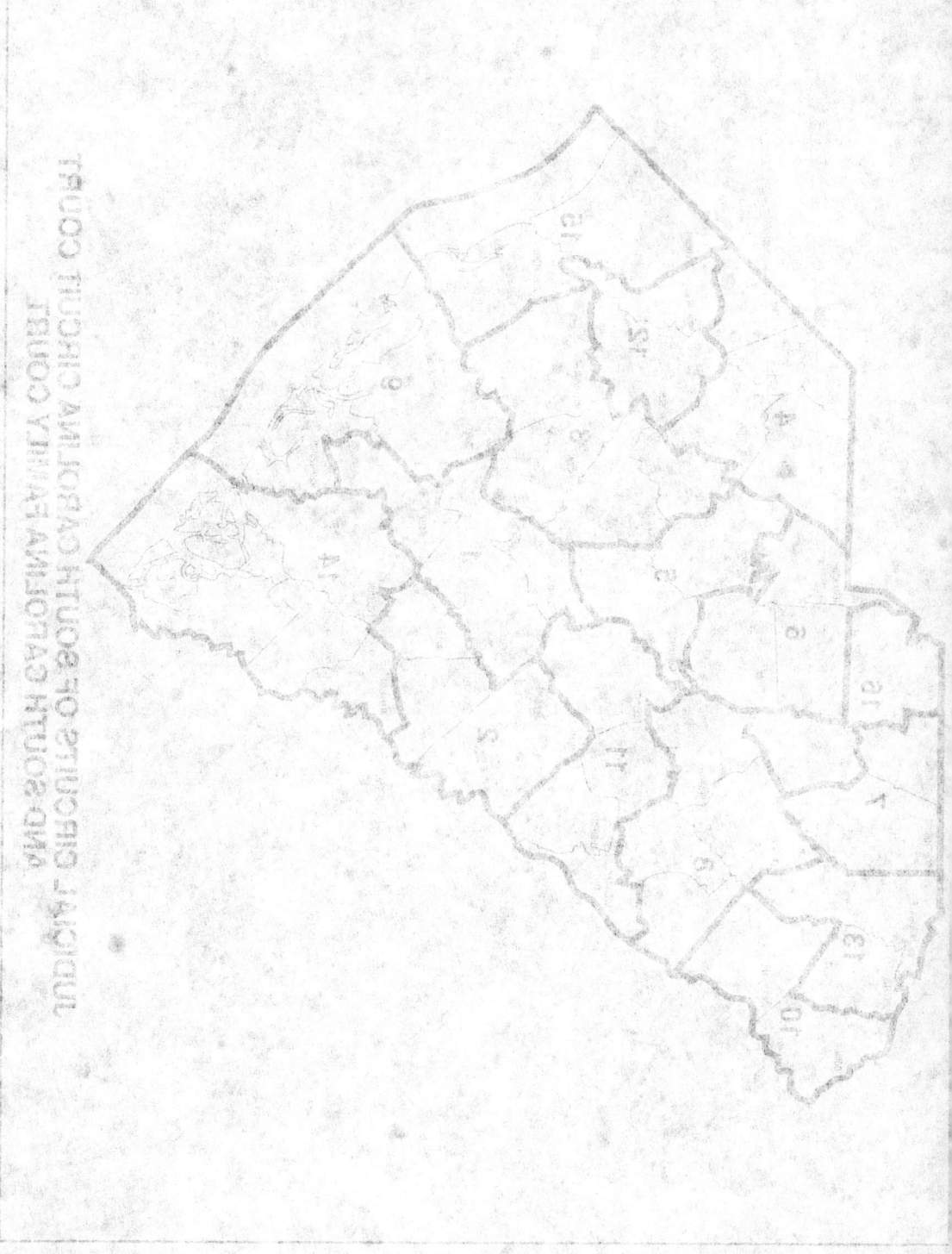

SOUTH CAROLINA

ABBOTT, H. T., III *(Judge, South Carolina Family Court Fifteenth Judicial Circuit)* Term expires 2008.

Mailing address: P.O. Box 377, Conway 29528-0377.

Telephone: (843) 915-8997.

Fax: (843) 915-8971

ADDY, Frank R., Jr. *(Judge, Greenwood County Probate Court)* Appointed by Governor Jim Hodges to term beginning June 29, 1999. Elected 2000 and 2002. Current term expires Dec 31, 2006. Born Greenwood South Carolina Nov 5, 1967. Methodist. Educated at University of South Carolina B.A. cum laude 1990 J.D. 1993. Articles Editor ABA Real Property Probate and Trust Journal 1992-93. Member International Law Society. Admitted to practice South Carolina 1993 and U.S. District Court District of South Carolina 1997. In legal practice Greenwood 1993-2000.

Deputy Solicitor Eighth Judicial Circuit 1993-97.

Mailing address: P.O. Box 1210, Greenwood 29648-1210.

Telephone: (864) 942-8625.

Fax: (864) 942-8620

ALFORD, Lee S. *(Judge, South Carolina Circuit Court Sixteenth Judicial Circuit)* Elected by General Assembly to term beginning May 13, 1998. Term expires 2004. Born Rock Hill South Carolina May 16, 1942. Methodist. Educated at University of South Carolina A.B. 1968 J.D. 1971. Member Phi Alpha Delta. Admitted to practice South Carolina 1971, U.S. Court of Appeals Fourth Circuit 1971, U.S. District Court District of South Carolina 1972 and U.S. Supreme Court 1974. In legal practice York 1971-79. Judge, York County Probate Court Jan 4, 1979 to June 30, 1992. Judge, South Carolina Family Court Sixteenth Judicial Circuit July 1, 1992 to 1998.

Hearing Officer York School District One 1975-79. Member National College of Probate Judges 1979, American Judicature Society 1979, York County Young Lawyers Association (President 1976-77), South Carolina Probate Judges Association (Past President), South Carolina Bar and York County Bar Association. Recipient York Distinguished Service Award 1977 and one of the Three Outstanding Young Men in South Carolina Award 1977. Named Shriner of the Year 1989. Airman Second Class USAF 1960-64. Judge Advocate American Legion Post 34. 32° Mason. Member Western York County United Way (Past President), York Red Cross Chapter (Chairman), Shriners (Trustee, Member Board of Directors), York County Mental Health Association (Past President), South Carolina Mental Health Association, York County Association for Retarded Citizens, South Carolina Association for Retarded Citizens, York School District One E.S.A.A. Advisory Committee (Chairman), Elks and Moose. Past President York Jaycees, Camp ARC Council, York Rotary Club and South Carolina United Way. Past State Vice President and Legal Counsel 1973-74 to South Carolina Jaycees. Past Commander Catawba Power Squadron. Enjoys jogging, tennis, golf and basketball.

Office: Moss Justice Center, 1675-1J York Highway, York 29745-7434.

Telephone: (803) 628-3048.

Fax: (803) 628-3139

ALLEN, Kellum W. *(Judge, South Carolina Family Court Eleventh Judicial Circuit)* Term expires 2004.

Office: Lexington County Courthouse, 139 East Main Street, Lexington 29072-3456.

Telephone: (803) 359-8452.

Fax: (803) 359-8505

ANDERSON, G. Ross, Jr. *(Judge, United States District Court District of South Carolina)* Appointed for life by President Jimmy Carter to term beginning May 23, 1980. Born Anderson South Carolina Jan 29, 1929. Educated at University of South Carolina J.D. 1954. Honorary LL.D. University of South Carolina 1984 and Anderson College 1998. Assistant Editor University of South Carolina Law Review 1953-54. Member Omicron Delta Kappa and Order of Wig and Robe. Admitted to practice South Carolina 1954. In legal practice Anderson 1954-80.

Founding Member 1958, Board of Directors 1958-78, Vice President 1979-71 and President 1971-72 South Carolina Trial Lawyers Association. President Anderson County Bar Association 1960. Board of Governors The Association of Trial Lawyers of America 1969-71. Board of Governors 1977-80 and Former Circuit Vice President South Carolina Bar. Board of Directors Federal Judges Association 1993-97. Fellow American Bar Foundation, International Academy of Trial Lawyers and International Society of Barristers. Member Fourth Circuit Judicial Conference. Participating Attorney Chief Justice's Conference 1972. Named Outstanding Trial Judge of the Year by South Carolina Trial Lawyers Association 1984. Recipient War Horse Award from Southern Trial Lawyers Association 1990 and Distinguished Judicial Service Award from The Civil Justice Foundation The Association of Trial Lawyers of America Convention 1997. Member House of Representatives South Carolina 1955-56.

Mailing address: P.O. Box 2147, Anderson 29622-2147.

Telephone: (864) 226-9799.

ANDERSON, Georgia V. *(Judge, South Carolina Family Court Seventh Judicial Circuit)* Elected by General Assembly May 1995 to term beginning July 1, 1995. Reelected 2001, current term expires June 30, 2007. Born Loris South Carolina. Methodist. Educated at University of South Carolina B.S. 1974 J.D. 1978. Admitted to practice South Carolina 1978.

Office: Spartanburg County Judicial Center, Second Floor, 180 Magnolia Street, Spartanburg 29306-2392.

Telephone: (864) 562-4395.

Fax: (864) 585-0904

E-mail address: gvandersonj@scjd.state.sc.us

ANDERSON, Joseph F., Jr. *(Chief Judge, United States District Court District of South Carolina)* Ap-

ANDERSON, JOSEPH F., JR.—*Continued*

pointed for life by President Ronald Reagan to term beginning Dec 11, 1986. Chief Judge since Oct 1, 2000. Born Edgefield South Carolina Nov 16, 1949. Methodist. Educated at Clemson University B.A. with honors 1972 and University of South Carolina J.D. with honors 1975. Executive Editor University of South Carolina Law Review 1973-75. Law Clerk to Chief Judge Clement F. Haynsworth, U.S. Court of Appeals Fourth Circuit 1975-76. Member Phi Alpha Delta. Admitted to practice South Carolina 1976, U.S. District Court District of South Carolina 1976, U.S. Court of Appeals Fourth Circuit 1976 and U.S. Supreme Court 1986. In legal practice Edgefield 1976-86.

Author two articles in South Carolina Law Review. Member Judicial Conference of the Fourth Circuit and South Carolina Bar. Named one of three Outstanding Young Men in South Carolina by South Carolina Jaycees 1980. USAR 1976-80. Democrat. South Carolina House of Representatives 1980-86. Hobbies include restoring antique and classic automobiles.

Mailing address: P.O. Box 447, Columbia 29202-0447.

Telephone: (803) 765-5136.

ANDERSON, Ralph King, Jr. *(Associate Judge, South Carolina Court of Appeals)* Elected by General Assembly Feb 14, 1996 to term beginning March 15, 1996. Born Timmonsville South Carolina Nov 13, 1936. Educated at Clemson University 1954-56 and University of South Carolina School of Law LL.B. 1959 replaced by J.D. 1970. Judge-at-Large, South Carolina Circuit Court Sept 14, 1979 to March 15, 1996.

Member House of Representatives 1973 to Sept 13, 1979. Chairman County Board of Registration 1961-62 and County Democratic Party 1966-70. President Howe Springs Volunteer Fire Company, Inc. 1971-72. Chairman Board of Deacons Greenwood Baptist Church Florence 1968-75 and Unity Baptist Church 1988-91. Board of Trustees Bethea Baptist Home 1976-81.

Mailing address: P.O. Box 1562, Florence 29503-1562.

Telephone: (843) 665-3039.

Fax: (843) 665-8211

ARMSTRONG, Robert S. *(Judge, South Carolina Family Court Fourteenth Judicial Circuit)* Term expires June 30, 2007.

Mailing address: P.O. Box 1693, Ridgeland 29936-1693.

Office: 602 Second Avenue, Ridgeland 29936.

Telephone: (843) 726-5571.

Fax: (843) 726-8032

ATKINSON, Dale *(Judge, Sumter County Probate Court)*

Office: 141 North Main Street, Sumter 29150.

Telephone: (803) 436-2166.

Fax: (803) 436-2407

ATKINSON, T. Carroll *(Judge, Marion County Probate Court)*

Mailing address: P.O. Box 583, Marion 29571-0583.

Telephone: (843) 423-8244.

Fax: (843) 431-5026

BARBER, James R., III *(Judge-at-Large, South Carolina Circuit Court)* Elected by General Assembly April 9, 1997 to term beginning Aug 19, 1997. Reelected 2003, current term expires 2009. Born Birmingham Alabama Dec 20, 1943. Educated at University of South Carolina B.A. 1966 J.D. 1969.

Member Central Midlands Planning Board 1977-83, Richland County Council 1977-86 (Chairman 1978) and Richland Memorial Hospital Foundation 1991-94. Board of Directors 1978-86, Vice President 1982-86 and Honorary President 1986 South Carolina Association of Counties. Board of Trustees Richland Memorial Hospital 1990-94. Board Richland County Cancer Society.

Mailing address: P.O. Box 2766, Columbia 29202-2766.

Office: 1701 Main Street, Room 224, Columbia 29201.

Telephone: (803) 576-1779.

Fax: (803) 576-1782

BARTLETT, Stephen S. *(Judge, South Carolina Family Court Thirteenth Judicial Circuit)* Term expires June 30, 2007.

Mailing address: P.O. Box 757, Greenville 29602-0757.

Office: 301 University Ridge, Suite 600, Greenville 29601.

Telephone: (864) 467-5841.

Fax: (864) 467-5615

BAXLEY, John Michael *(Judge, South Carolina Circuit Court Fourth Judicial Circuit)* Elected Feb 9, 2000 by General Assembly to term beginning June 25, 2000. Term expires 2006. Educated at Clemson University B.A. 1978 and University of South Carolina J.D. 1982.

Chairman Darlington County Bar Association. Recipient South Carolina Family of the Year Award 1985. Named Legislator of the Year by South Carolina American Ex-POW's 1988, South Carolina Association of the Deaf 1989, Youth Division South Carolina NAACP 1989, South Carolina Rural Water Association 1991 and South Carolina Mental Health Association 1997. Member House of Representatives South Carolina (Chairman Freshman Legislative Caucus 1987-88, Member House Judiciary Committee 1987-98, Joint Legislative Committee on AIDS, Joint Legislative Solid Waste Disposal Committee, Joint Legislative Committee on the Problems of the Disabled) 1987-98. Former Member Board of Directors Hartsville Red Cross and Crimestoppers. Board of Directors Hartsville Christmas in April and Butler Heritage Foundation. Three-gallon blood donor American Red Cross. Interpreter for the deaf. Member First Baptist Church.

Office: 531 East Carolina Avenue, Hartsville 29550-4311.

Telephone: (843) 383-4114.

Fax: (843) 383-4116

BEATTY, Donald W. *(Associate Judge, South Carolina Court of Appeals)* Elected by General Assembly April 9, 2003 to term beginning June 2003. Former Judge, South Carolina Circuit Court, assumed office 1995.

Mailing address: P.O. Box 11629, Columbia 29211.

Telephone: (803) 734-1890.

BENNETT, Brenda P. *(Judge, Allendale County Probate Court)* Elected to term beginning Jan 1, 1986. Reelected 1989, 1993, 1997 and 2002. Current term ex-

BENNETT, BRENDA P.—*Continued*

pires Dec 31, 2006. Born Beaufort South Carolina Nov 7, 1947. Baptist.
Mailing address: P.O. Box 603, Allendale 29810-0603.
Office: Courthouse Complex, Allendale 29810.
Telephone: (803) 584-3157.
Fax: (803) 584-7053

BISHOP, Wm. Thurmond *(Chief Judge, United States Bankruptcy Court District of South Carolina)* Appointed by U.S. Court of Appeals Fourth Circuit judges. Chief Judge since Oct 1, 2000.
Mailing address: P.O. Box 1448, Columbia 29202-1448.
Telephone: (803) 765-5850.

BLATT, Sol, Jr. *(Senior Judge, United States District Court District of South Carolina)* Appointed for life by President Richard M. Nixon to term beginning May 28, 1971. Former Chief Judge. Assumed Senior status, serves by assignment. Born Sumter South Carolina Aug 20, 1921. Episcopalian. Educated at University of South Carolina LL.B. 1946. Admitted to practice South Carolina 1946. Began legal practice Barnwell 1946.
Member South Carolina Bar and American Bar Association. Lieutenant USNR 1942-46. Board of Trustees University of South Carolina 1946-71. Enjoys golf.
Mailing address: P.O. Box 835, Charleston 29402-0835.
Telephone: (843) 579-1470.

BONNOITT, H. E., Jr. *(Judge, South Carolina Family Court Fifteenth Judicial Circuit)* Elected by General Assembly to term beginning July 1, 1991. Reelected 1995 and 2001. Current term expires June 30, 2007. Born Charleston South Carolina. Protestant. Educated at University of South Carolina A.B. 1965 J.D. 1973. Admitted to practice South Carolina 1973, U.S. Court of Appeals Fourth Circuit 1974 and U.S. District Court District of South Carolina 1983. In legal practice Georgetown 1973-91.
Public Defender Georgetown County 1978-85. Member South Carolina Bar, Georgetown County (President 1989-90) and American Bar Associations. Lieutenant USN 1965-69. Lieutenant Commander USNR 1969-79. Mayor City of Georgetown 1986-91. Enjoys fishing, tennis and reading.
Mailing address: P.O. Drawer 421270, Georgetown 29442-1270.
Office: 715 Prince Street, Room 300, Georgetown 29440.
Telephone: (843) 546-2214.
Fax: (843) 546-4927

BREEDEN, John L., Jr. *(Judge, South Carolina Circuit Court Fifteenth Judicial Circuit)* Elected Judge-at-Large to term beginning Feb 14, 1996. Elected Judge by General Assembly. Born Columbia South Carolina Dec 27, 1942. Educated at University of South Carolina B.A. 1966 J.D. 1973. In legal practice 1973-78.
Deputy Assistant Solicitor Fifteenth Judicial Circuit 1978-81. County Attorney 1981-88 and Master-in-Equity 1981-96 Horry County.
Office: 1301 Second Avenue, #3B71, Conway 29526-5005.
Telephone: (843) 915-8982.
Fax: (843) 915-6074

BRIDGES, Judy C. *(Judge, South Carolina Family Court Ninth Judicial Circuit)* Term expires 2004.
Office: 100 Broad Street, Suite 368, Charleston 29401.
Telephone: (843) 958-4439.
Fax: (843) 958-4435

BROGDON, James E., Jr. *(Judge-at-Large, South Carolina Circuit Court)* Elected by General Assembly Feb 14, 1996 to term beginning May 9, 1996. Reelected 2002, current term expires 2008. Born Laurinburg North Carolina May 29, 1952. Educated at Wofford College B.A. cum laude 1974 and University of South Carolina J.D. 1977.
Attorney Marion County 1989-96. Member City Council 1983-92 and Mayor Pro Tem 1985-92 Marion. Elder Marion Presbyterian Church.
Mailing address: P.O. Box 1041, Marion 29571-1041.
Office: 200 South Main, Marion 29571.
Telephone: (843) 423-5122.
Fax: (843) 423-6961

BROWN, Timothy L. *(Judge, South Carolina Family Court Thirteenth Judicial Circuit)* Term expires 2004.
Mailing address: P.O. Box 757, Greenville 29602-0757.
Office: 301 University Ridge, Greenville 29601.
Telephone: (864) 467-5851.
Fax: (864) 467-5929

BROWN, Walter B., Jr. *(Judge, South Carolina Family Court Sixth Judicial Circuit)* Term expires 2008.
Mailing address: P.O. Drawer 180, Winnsboro 29180-0180.
Office: 115 A South Congress Street, Second Floor, Winnsboro 29180.
Telephone: (803) 712-6734.
Fax: (803) 635-6529

BROWN, Wesley L. *(Judge, South Carolina Family Court Seventh Judicial Circuit)* Term expires 2004.
Mailing address: P.O. Box 1002, Gaffney 29342-1002.
Telephone: (864) 487-2568.
Fax: (864) 487-2776

BUCHAN, Mary E. *(Judge, South Carolina Family Court Twelfth Judicial Circuit)* Term expires June 30, 2007.
Mailing address: P.O. Box 63, Marion 29571-0063.
Office: 101 West Court Street, Marion 29571.
Telephone: (843) 423-5141.
Fax: (843) 423-9498

BUCHANAN, Robert L., Jr. *(Magistrate Judge, United States District Court District of South Carolina)* Appointed by U.S. District Court judges to term beginning April 1, 1979. Reappointed April 1, 1983, April 1987, April 1991, April 1995, April 1999 and April 2003. Current term expires April 2007. Serves part time. Born Aiken South Carolina May 22, 1951. Presbyterian. Educated at Erskine College A.B. 1973 and University of South Carolina School of Law J.D. 1976. Member Omicron Delta Kappa and Philomathean Literary Society. Admitted to practice South Carolina 1976 and U.S. District Court District of South Carolina 1976. Began legal practice Aiken 1976.
Member South Carolina Trial Lawyers Association, The Association of Trial Lawyers of America, American Judicature Society, South Carolina Bar, Aiken County (Secretary 1977-78 and Treasurer 1984-86) and Ameri-

BUCHANAN, ROBERT L., JR.—*Continued*

can Bar Associations. Political affiliation: Independent. Former member Board of Directors Aiken County Unit American Cancer Society. Football coach Aiken Elementary School 1976-82. Member First Presbyterian Church Aiken (Ruling Elder, former Deacon). Enjoys family activities and athletics.

Mailing address: P.O. Box 463, Aiken 29802-0463.
Telephone: (803) 649-2586.

BUCKNER, Perry M. *(Judge, South Carolina Circuit Court Fourteenth Judicial Circuit)*

Mailing address: P.O. Drawer 470, Walterboro 29488-0470.
Office: 101 Hampton Street, Walterboro 29488.
Telephone: (843) 549-7878.
Fax: (843) 549-9876

BURCH, Paul M. *(Judge, South Carolina Circuit Court Fourth Judicial Circuit)* Elected by General Assembly May 29, 1991 to term beginning July 1, 1991. Reelected 1992 and 1998. Current term expires 2004. Born Charlotte North Carolina Feb 10, 1954. United Methodist. Educated at University of South Carolina B.G.S. 1976 M.C.J. 1978 J.D. 1980. Admitted to practice South Carolina 1980 and U.S. District Court District of South Carolina 1984. In legal practice Pageland 1980-91.

Instructor in Criminal Justice University of South Carolina 1978-91. Attended General Jurisdiction Course 1992 and Advanced Evidence Course 1994 The National Judicial College. Member House of Representatives South Carolina 1988-91. Councilman Chesterfield County 1983-88. Member Jamil Shrine Temple. Past Master Mt. Moriah Masonic Lodge 58.

Mailing address: P.O. Box 276, Pageland 29728-0276.
Office: 601 West McGregor Street, Pageland 29728.
Telephone: (843) 672-3270.
Fax: (843) 672-5960

BURNETT, E. C., III *(Associate Justice, South Carolina Supreme Court)* Elected by General Assembly to term beginning April 10, 1995. Reelected 2000, current term expires July 31, 2010. Born Spartanburg South Carolina Jan 26, 1942. Educated at Wofford College A.B. 1964 and University of South Carolina J.D. 1969. Judge, Spartanburg County Probate Court Jan 1976 to May 1980. Former Judge, South Carolina Family Court, elected by General Assembly May 1980. Judge, South Carolina Circuit Court Seventh Judicial Circuit Sept 17, 1981 to March 21, 1995.

Member South Carolina Bar and American Bar Association. Member House of Representatives South Carolina 1973-74. Elder Mt. Calvary Presbyterian Church.

Mailing address: P.O. Box 804, Roebuck 29376-0804.
Telephone: (864) 596-2595.
Fax: (864) 596-2964

CAIN, Timothy M. *(Judge, South Carolina Family Court Tenth Judicial Circuit)* Elected by General Assembly Feb 2000 to term beginning April 14, 2000. Term expires June 30, 2004. Born Seneca South Carolina Jan 19, 1961. Methodist. Educated at University of South Carolina School of Law J.D. 1986. Admitted to practice South Carolina 1986 and U.S. District Court District of South Carolina 1987. In legal practice Walhalla.

Assistant Public Defender Oconee County 1987. Assistant Solicitor Tenth Judicial District 1988-90. County Attorney Oconee County 1992-2000. Member South Carolina Bar and Oconee County Bar Association.

Mailing address: P.O. Box 678, Walhalla 29691-0678.
Office: 211 West Main Street, Walhalla 29691.
Telephone: (864) 638-4290.
Fax: (864) 638-4293

CALDWELL, Wylie H., Jr. *(Judge, South Carolina Family Court Twelfth Judicial Circuit)* Assumed office March 1, 1980. Elected by General Assembly. Reelected to subsequent terms. Current term expires 2004. Born Florence South Carolina Aug 29, 1942. Lutheran. Educated at University of South Carolina B.A. 1964 J.D. 1967. Member Kappa Alpha. Admitted to practice South Carolina 1967. Began legal practice Florence 1967.

Former City Prosecutor and City Attorney Florence. Former Assistant Solicitor 12th Judicial Circuit. Former Councilman Florence County. Member National Council of Juvenile and Family Court Judges, Family Court Judges Council, South Carolina Bar and Florence County Bar Association.

Office: City-County Complex Box V, 180 North Irby Street, Florence 29501-3456.
Telephone: (843) 665-3079.
Fax: (843) 662-9240

CARR, Robert Stuart *(Magistrate Judge, United States District Court District of South Carolina)* Appointed by U.S. District Court judges to term beginning Sept 1, 1975. Reappointed Sept 1, 1983, Sept 1991 and Sept 1999. Current term expires Sept 2007. Born Atlanta Georgia Jan 25, 1946. Baptist. Educated at Furman University B.S. 1967 and University of South Carolina J.D. 1971. Law Clerk to Hon. Robert F. Chapman, U.S. District Court District of South Carolina 1971-72. Admitted to practice South Carolina 1971, U.S. District Court District of South Carolina 1972 and U.S. Court of Appeals Fourth Circuit 1974. In legal practice Columbia 1972-75.

Adjunct Professor College of Charleston since 1982. Past President National Council of United States Magistrates. Member South Carolina Bar, Federal and American (Former Chairman National Conference of Special Court Judges Judicial Administration Division 1986-87) Bar Associations. Colonel USAR (retired). Legal Assistant to U.S. Senator Strom Thurmond 1971.

Mailing address: P.O. Box 835, Charleston 29402-0835.
Telephone: (843) 579-1440.

CATE, Jocelyn B. *(Judge, South Carolina Family Court Ninth Judicial Circuit)*

Office: 100 Broad Street, Suite 256, Charleston 29401.
Telephone: (843) 958-4406.
Fax: (843) 958-4437

CATOE, William M., Jr. *(Magistrate Judge, United States District Court District of South Carolina)* Appointed by U.S. District Court judges.

Mailing address: P.O. Box 10262, Greenville 29603-0262.
Telephone: (864) 241-2740.

CHEWNING, Richard W., III *(Judge, South Carolina Family Court Eleventh Judicial Circuit)* Reelected 2001, current term expires June 30, 2007.
Office: Lexington County Courthouse, 139 East Main Street, Lexington 29072-3456.
Telephone: (803) 359-8451.
Fax: (803) 356-8620

COLE, J. Derham *(Judge, South Carolina Circuit Court Seventh Judicial Circuit)*
Mailing address: P.O. Box 1744, Spartanburg 29304-1744.
Office: 180 Magnolia Street, Second Floor, Spartanburg 29306.
Telephone: (864) 596-2685.
Fax: (864) 596-3592

CONDON, Irvin G. *(Judge, Charleston County Probate Court)*
Office: Estate Division, 84 Broad Street, Charleston 29401.
Telephone: (843) 958-5183.
Fax: (843) 958-5044

CONNOR, Carol *(Associate Judge, South Carolina Court of Appeals)* Elected by General Assembly June 2, 1993 to term beginning July 20, 1993. Born Kingstree South Carolina Jan 23, 1950. Methodist. Educated at Converse College B.A. with honors 1972 and University of South Carolina J.D. 1976. Admitted to practice Texas 1976, South Carolina 1977, U.S. District Court District of South Carolina 1977 and U.S. Court of Claims 1977. In legal practice Columbia 1981-84. Judge, South Carolina Family Court Fifth Judicial Circuit 1983 to June 30, 1988. Judge, South Carolina Circuit Court Fifth Judicial Circuit July 1, 1988 to 1993.
Assistant Attorney General South Carolina 1976-77. Assistant Public Defender 1977-80 and Deputy Public Defender 1980-81 Richland County. Member Women Judges Association.
Mailing address: P.O. Box 11629, Columbia 29211-1629.
Telephone: (803) 734-1890.
Fax: (803) 734-1829

COOPER, G. Thomas, Jr. *(Judge, South Carolina Circuit Court Fifth Judicial Circuit)*
Mailing address: P.O. Box 192, Columbia 29202-0192.
Office: 1701 Main Street, Room 323, Columbia 29202.
Telephone: (803) 576-1783.
Fax: (803) 576-1741

COOPER, Thomas W., Jr. *(Judge, South Carolina Circuit Court Third Judicial Circuit)* Elected by General Assembly Feb 5, 1992 to term beginning March 13, 1992. Reelected 1998, current term expires 2004. Born Sumter South Carolina May 20, 1941. Educated at University of South Carolina B.A. 1963 J.D. 1973, Clemson University and Coker College. In legal practice Manning 1973-92.
Member 1984-92 and Chairman 1988-92 Resolution of Fee Disputes Board Third Judicial Circuit. Member South Carolina Bar (Former Member Committee on Uniform Simplified Jury Charges) and Clarendon County Bar Association. Recipient Clarendon County Teacher of the Year 1967. English teacher and athletic coach East Clarendon High School 1963-68. Principal and assistant principal Hillcrest Junior High School 1968-69. Principal Shaw Heights Elementary School 1969-70. Past Chairman Clarendon County Unit American Cancer Society and Clarendon County Division Mental Health Association. Member South Carolina Education Association 1963-70. Member 1963-68 and Treasurer 1965-66 Clarendon County Education Association. Member 1981-2000 and Chairman 1983-97 Board of Trustees Laurence Manning Academy. Member Clarendon County Financial Advisory Committee 1983-86, South Carolina Federal Advisory Board 1987-92 and Clarendon County Election Commission 1987-92. Member Mayesville Presbyterian Church 1950-75. Former Member of Diaconate (Former Secretary and Chairman), Sunday School Teacher since 1975, Choir Member since 1975, Member of Session since 1978 and Clerk of Session Presbyterian Church at Manning. Member and Chairman Records Committee 1980-83 and Trustee Camp Harmony 1982-83 Harmony Presbytery. Commissioner to General Assembly of the Presbyterian Church USA 1984. Council Member 1987-92, Trustee 1987-92 and Personnel Committee 1987-92 Presbytery of New Harmony.
Mailing address: P.O. Drawer 699, Manning 29102-0699.
Office: 16 South Brooks Street, Manning 29102.
Telephone: (803) 435-2450.
Fax: (803) 435-2461

CREECH, Wayne M. *(Judge, South Carolina Family Court Ninth Judicial Circuit)* Reelected 2001, current term expires June 30, 2007.
Mailing address: P.O. Box 1198, Moncks Corner 29461-1198.
Office: 300-B California Avenue, Moncks Corner 29461.
Telephone: (843) 719-4462.
Fax: (843) 899-1050

CUDD, Donna P. *(Judge, Union County Probate Court)*
Mailing address: P.O. Box 447, Union 29379-0447.
Telephone: (864) 429-1625.
Fax: (864) 429-1627

CURRIE, Cameron McGowan *(Judge, United States District Court District of South Carolina)* Magistrate Judge October 1984 to July 1986. Appointed Judge for life by President Bill Clinton to term beginning March 1994. Born Florence South Carolina Oct 3, 1948. Educated at University of South Carolina B.A. 1970 and George Washington University National Law Center J.D. with honors 1975. Member Delta Delta Delta and Order of the Coif. Admitted to practice South Carolina, District of Columbia, U.S. District Courts District of South Carolina and District of Columbia, U.S. Courts of Appeals Fourth and District of Columbia Circuits and U.S. Supreme Court. In legal practice Washington D.C. 1975-78 and Columbia South Carolina July 1986 to Feb 1989.
Assistant U.S. Attorney 1978-84. Chief Deputy Attorney General and Director State Grand Jury Division Feb 1989 to March 1994. Author "The State Grand Jury" 1 No. 1 *South Carolina Lawyer* July-Aug 1989 and "A Marathon Session" 8 No. 4 *South Carolina Bar News* Feb 1997. Co-author "Sex Discrimination in the Selection and Participation of Female Jurors: A Post-*J.E.B.* Analysis" 35 No. 1 *The Judges' Journal* American Bar Association Winter 1996 and "Gender-Based Peremptory Strikes: A Post *J.E.B.* Analysis" 7 No. 4 *South Carolina Lawyer* Jan-Feb 1996. Adjunct Professor of Trial Advo-

CURRIE, CAMERON MCGOWAN—*Continued*
cacy University of South Carolina School of Law 1986-89. Member U.S. District Court Criminal Justice Act Committee 1986-89. Former Member South Carolina Defense Trial Lawyers Association, South Carolina Trial Lawyers Association, Assistant U.S. Attorneys Association and The Association of Trial Lawyers of America. Master John Belton O'Neall Chapter American Inns of Court. Member South Carolina Women Lawyers Association, District Judges Association, Federal Judges Association, The District of Columbia Bar, South Carolina Bar (CLE Committee 1986-88, Council Member Criminal Law Section 1987-88), Richland County and American (Former Member Subcommittee on Civil RICO Committee on Trial Practice Section of Litigation) Bar Associations.

Speaker "Cannabis Investigations and Asset Seizures" April 1992 and "What the Prosecutor Needs in a White Collar Crime Case" White Collar Crime School March 18, 1993 Law Enforcement Coordinating Committee, "Expert Witnesses and the Impact of *Daubert v. Merrill Dow*" Federal Practice Seminar South Carolina Bar 1995, "The Status of Admissibility of Polygraph Evidence in the Fourth Circuit After *Daubert*" Annual Conference OCDETF/VCTF 1996, "Expert Witnesses" Seminar South Carolina Trial Lawyers Association 1997, "Evidence Law" Annual Meeting South Carolina Defense Trial Attorneys Association 1998 and "Honesty and the Law" Law Enforcement CC and South Carolina Criminal Justice Academy 2000. Panel Member "The Independent Counsel Process: Is It Broken and How Should It Be Fixed?" Fourth Circuit Judicial Conference 1997 and "Women as Advocates: What Works and What Doesn't" Seminar South Carolina Women Lawyers Association 1998. Panel Member "Shifting the Paradigm: Seizing Control Over Our Professional Image" CLE South Carolina Bar 2001. Recipient Special Achievement Award from Department of Justice. Government and economics teacher Moultrie High School 1970-72. Member University of South Carolina Alumni Association.

Office: 200 Federal Building, 1100 Laurel Street, Columbia 29201.
Telephone: (803) 253-3680.

DAVIS, Edwin Malloy *(Judge, Chesterfield County Probate Court)*
Office: 200 West Main Street, Chesterfield 29709-1527.
Telephone: (843) 623-2376.
Fax: (843) 623-9886

DENNIS, R. Markley, Jr. *(Judge-at-Large, South Carolina Circuit Court)* Elected by General Assembly Feb 2, 1994 to term beginning March 31, 1994. Reelected to subsequent terms. Current term expires 2009. Born Charleston South Carolina Dec 2, 1947. Educated at University of South Carolina B.S. 1970 J.D. 1973. Member Kappa Alpha Order.

Member South Carolina Defense Trial Attorneys Association, South Carolina Trial Lawyers Association, American Judicature Society, South Carolina Bar and American Bar Association. Board of Directors Moncks Corner Rotary Club 1988-91 and Trident United Way. Member Charleston Trident Chamber of Commerce and Berkeley County Chamber of Commerce. Lay Leader Pinopolis United Methodist Church.

Mailing address: P.O. Box 1800, Moncks Corner 29461-1800.
Office: 300 B California Avenue, Moncks Corner 29461.
Telephone: (843) 719-4435.
Fax: (843) 719-4599

DOUGLAS, William R. *(Judge, Cherokee County Probate Court)*
Office: Peachtree Centre, 1434 North Limestone Street, Gaffney 29340-0022.
Telephone: (864) 487-2583.
Fax: (864) 902-8426

DUFFY, Patrick Michael *(Judge, United States District Court District of South Carolina)* Appointed for life by President Bill Clinton to term beginning 1995. Born Charleston South Carolina April 8, 1943. Educated at The Citadel B.A. 1965 and University of South Carolina School of Law J.D. 1968. In legal practice Charleston 1971-95.

Staff Attorney Neighborhood Legal Assistance Office 1968-69. Assistant County Attorney Charleston 1973-74.
Mailing address: P.O. Box 835, Charleston 29402-0835.
Telephone: (843) 579-1460.

EATON, William Kenneth *(Judge, Florence County Probate Court)*
Office: 180 N. Irby Street, MSC-L, Florence 29501.
Telephone: (843) 665-3085.
Fax: (843) 665-3068

ECKSTROM, Daniel R. *(Judge, Lexington County Probate Court)*
Office: 139 East Main Street, Room 110, Lexington 29072-3488.
Telephone: (803) 359-8324.
Fax: (803) 359-8199

EDMONDS, Deirdre *(Judge, Horry County Probate Court)*
Mailing address: P.O. Box 288, Conway 29528.
Telephone: (843) 915-5370.
Fax: (843) 915-6370

EDWARDS, Tommy B. *(Judge, South Carolina Family Court Tenth Judicial Circuit)* Term expires June 30, 2007.
Mailing address: P.O. Box 8002, Anderson 29622-8002.
Office: 100 South Main Street, Anderson 29624.
Telephone: (864) 260-4040.
Fax: (864) 224-6033

ESTRIDGE, Sandra S. *(Judge, Lancaster County Probate Court)* Elected to term beginning Jan 1, 1995. Reelected 1998 and 2002. Current term expires Dec 31, 2006.
Mailing address: P.O. Box 1809, Lancaster 29721-1809.
Office: 101 North Main Street, Lancaster 29720.
Telephone: (803) 283-3379.
Fax: (803) 283-3370
E-mail address: sestridge@lancastercountysc.net

EUBANKS, Raymond C., Jr. *(Judge, Spartanburg County Probate Court)* Appointed by Governor Richard Riley to term beginning May 1, 1980. Elected to term

EUBANKS, RAYMOND C., JR.—*Continued*

beginning Jan 1, 1983. Reelected 1986, 1990, Nov 1994, 1998 and 2002. Current term expires Dec 31, 2006. Also serves as Drug Court Judge Spartanburg County since June 2001. Born Spartanburg South Carolina Dec 18, 1933. Presbyterian. Educated at Wofford College A.B. 1956 and University of South Carolina LL.B. 1959. Member Kappa Alpha and Phi Alpha Delta. Admitted to practice South Carolina 1959. Began legal practice Spartanburg 1963.

Staff Attorney to Senator Olin D. Johnston 1959. Assistant General Counsel U.S. Senate Judiciary Subcommittee on Trading with the Enemy 1959-60. South Carolina House of Representatives 1964-68. President South Carolina Association of Probate Judges 1983-84. Member Probate Judges' Advisory Committee to South Carolina Court Administration 1985-89 and since 1994. Member Executive Board since 1998, Secretary/Treasurer since Nov 2001, Curriculum Chair Spring Conference 2002 and President Elect since Nov 2002 National College of Probate Judges. President Spartanburg County Bar Association 2001. Member South Carolina Bar. Annual Speaker July 1984-94 and Moderator July 1988 Continuing Education for Probate Judges South Carolina Supreme Court. Speaker "Basic Probate Practice" July 1987, Aug 1987 and Sept 1987 and "The South Carolina Probate Code" 1989 South Carolina Bar CLE Division, "Closing the Estate" South Carolina Committee on Continuing Lawyer Competence July 1988 and Nov 1988 and "Everything You Always Wanted to Know About Probate" 1992. Recipient Chief Justice Claude A. Taylor Distinguished Service Award from Spartanburg County Bar Association 1997. Captain USAF JAGC 1960-63. Member Planning Commission City of Spartanburg 1970-73. Board of Directors 1983-84 and since 1988, Parliamentarian since 1985, Second Vice President, First Vice President and President 1994 South Carolina Association of Counties. Moderator Presbytery of the Piedmont Presbyterian Church (USA) 1986. President Board of Directors Spartanburg County Museum of Art 2001-02. Elder Second Presbyterian Church Spartanburg. Pastel painter.

Office: 180 Magnolia Street, Room 302, Spartanburg 29306-2392.
Telephone: (864) 596-2556.
Fax: (864) 596-2011
E-mail address: reubanks@spartanburgcounty.org

FAULKNER, Debora *(Judge, Greenville County Probate Court)*
Office: 301 University Ridge, Suite 1200, Greenville 29601-3657.
Telephone: (864) 467-7170.
Fax: (864) 467-7198

FENDER, Jane D. *(Judge, South Carolina Family Court Fourteenth Judicial Circuit)* Term expires 2004.
Mailing address: P.O. Drawer 1124, Beaufort 29901-1124.
Office: 100 Ribaut Road, Suite 117, Beaufort 29902.
Telephone: (843) 470-5283.
Fax: (843) 470-5284

FEW, John C. *(Judge, South Carolina Circuit Court Thirteenth Judicial Circuit)* Currently serves as Chief Administrative Judge.
Office: 318 Greenville County Courthouse, 305 East North Street, Greenville 29601-2120.
Telephone: (864) 467-8448.
Fax: (864) 467-8504

FLOYD, Henry F. *(Judge, South Carolina Circuit Court Thirteenth Judicial Circuit)* Elected by General Assembly May 27, 1992 to term beginning June 25, 1992. Reelected 1998, current term expires 2004. Born Brevard North Carolina Nov 5, 1947. Educated at Wofford College B.A. 1970 and University of South Carolina J.D. 1973. Admitted to practice South Carolina 1973, U.S. District Court District of South Carolina, U.S. Court of Appeals Fourth Circuit and U.S. Supreme Court. In legal practice Pickens 1973-92.
Mailing address: P.O. Box 1390, Pickens 29671-1390.
Office: County Courthouse, 214 East Main Street, Pickens 29671.
Telephone: (864) 898-5790.
Fax: (864) 898-5792

FRALEY, James F., Jr. *(Judge, South Carolina Family Court Seventh Judicial Circuit)* Reelected 2001, current term expires June 30, 2007.
Office: Spartanburg County Courthouse, Second Floor, 180 Magnolia Street, Spartanburg 29306-2392.
Telephone: (864) 573-7732.
Fax: (864) 596-2463

FRIDY, Kaye W. *(Judge, Laurens County Probate Court)*
Mailing address: P.O. Box 194, Laurens 29360-0194.
Telephone: (864) 984-7315.
Fax: (864) 984-3779

GABLE, Dale Moore *(Judge, South Carolina Family Court Second Judicial Circuit)* Former Judge, Barnwell County Probate Court.
Mailing address: P.O. Box 615, Barnwell 29812-0615.
Office: 100 Main Street, Room 208, Barnwell 29812.
Telephone: (803) 541-1033.
Fax: (803) 541-1127

GAMBLE, Rudell M. *(Judge, Williamsburg County Probate Court)*
Mailing address: P.O. Box 1005, Kingstree 29556-1005.
Telephone: (843) 355-9321.
Fax: (843) 355-9305

GARFINKEL, Paul W. *(Judge, South Carolina Family Court Ninth Judicial Circuit)* Assumed office 1995. Reelected 2001, current term expires June 30, 2007.
Office: 100 Broad Street, Suite 248, Charleston 29401.
Telephone: (843) 958-4417.
Fax: (843) 958-4433

GETTYS, John P. *(Judge, York County Probate Court)*
Mailing address: P.O. Box 219, York 29745-0219.
Telephone: (803) 684-8513.
Fax: (803) 684-8536

GOLDSMITH, Brooks P. *(Judge, South Carolina Family Court Sixth Judicial Circuit)*
Mailing address: P.O. Box 2227, Lancaster 29721-2227.
Office: 201 West Dunlap Street, Lancaster 29720.
Telephone: (803) 286-6990.
Fax: (803) 286-0696

GOODE, Kenneth G. *(Judge-at-Large, South Carolina Circuit Court)*
Mailing address: P.O. Box 1175, Winnsboro 29180-1175.
Telephone: (803) 635-3946.
Fax: (803) 635-3762

GOODSTEIN, Diane Schafer *(Judge, South Carolina Circuit Court First Judicial Circuit)* Elected by General Assembly to term beginning June 1998. Term expires 2004. Born Dillon South Carolina Dec 1, 1955. Educated at University of North Carolina at Chapel Hill B.A. 1978 J.D. 1981. Admitted to practice South Carolina 1981. In legal practice Summerville 1981-98.

County Attorney Dorchester County 1986-88. Member Circuit Court Judges Advisory Committee and Commission on Judicial Conduct. Member South Carolina Bar (Former Member Professional Responsibility Committee), Dorchester County and American Bar Associations. Former Board Member Greater Summerville Chamber of Commerce, Hospice of Charleston and My Sister's House. Former Member Dorchester County Centennial Committee. Member Charleston Temple Kahal Kodosh Beth Elohim.
Office: 212 Deming Way, Box 5, Summerville 29483.
Telephone: (843) 832-0388.
Fax: (843) 832-0389

GOOLSBY, C. Tolbert, Jr. *(Associate Judge, South Carolina Court of Appeals)* Elected by General Assembly July 27, 1983 to term beginning Sept 1, 1983. Reelected Feb 20, 1985, May 3, 1989, March 21, 1995 and 2001. Current term expires June 30, 2007. Born Montgomery Alabama July 11, 1935. Presbyterian. Educated at University of Alabama 1953-54, The Citadel A.B. with general and departmental honors 1959, University of South Carolina LL.B. cum laude 1962 and University of Virginia LL.M. 1992. Member Phi Kappa Sigma, Phi Sigma Alpha, Phi Beta Kappa, Phi Alpha Delta, Citadel Honorary Society and Wig and Robe. Admitted to practice South Carolina 1962, U.S. District Court District of South Carolina 1962, U.S. Court of Appeals Fourth Circuit 1969 and U.S. Supreme Court 1974. Began legal practice Columbia 1962. In legal practice Walterboro 1972-73.

Assistant Attorney General 1962-72, Deputy Attorney General 1973-83 and Chief Deputy Attorney General 1983 South Carolina. Author Note 13 South Carolina Law Quarterly 455, 1962 and "The South Carolina Tort Claims Act: A Primer & Then Some" CLE Division South Carolina 1992. Important Decisions: Hook v. Rothstein (informed consent) 316 S.E.2d 690, 1984 S.C. App. 1984 and Ballow v. Sigma Nu General Fraternity (hazing) 352 S.E.2d 488, 1986 S.C. App. 1986. Instructor Introduction to Legal Method and Process Columbia College 1993. President The Citadel Inn of Court 1991-92. Member South Carolina Bar (Section Delegate Trial and Appellate Advocacy Section 1980-84, former Chairman Judicial Continuing Education Commission) and American Bar Association (Judicial Administration Division Representative Joint Subcommittee on Judicial Discipline). Lecturer on Tort Claims Act Jan 8, 1993, on Appellate Briefs Jan 15, 1993 and at several CLE seminars. E-3 U.S. Army 1954-56. Pepsi-Cola Route Salesman Summer 1958 and Summer 1959. Enjoys jogging and collecting fossils.
Mailing address: P.O. Box 11629, Columbia 29211-1629.
Telephone: (803) 734-1890.
Fax: (803) 734-1805

GREEN, Nancy Hand *(Judge, Bamberg County Probate Court)* Appointed by Governor Richard Riley to term beginning June 15, 1984. Elected at special election July 31, 1984. Reelected Nov 1984, 1988, 1992, 1996 and 2000. Current term expires Dec 31, 2004. Born Bamberg County South Carolina Oct 29, 1937. Member Trinity United Methodist Church. Educated at Lander College 1956-58.
Mailing address: P.O. Box 180, Bamberg 29003-0180.
Telephone: (803) 245-3008.
Fax: (803) 245-3008

GREGORY, Jackson V. *(Judge, South Carolina Circuit Court Fourteenth Judicial Circuit)*
Mailing address: P.O. Drawer 1128, Beaufort 29901-1128.
Office: 100 Ribaut Road, Beaufort 29902.
Telephone: (843) 470-5245.
Fax: (843) 522-8362

GUESS, Robert E. *(Judge, South Carolina Family Court Sixteenth Judicial Circuit)*
Mailing address: P.O. Box 547, Union 29379-0547.
Office: 210 West Main Street, Union 29379.
Telephone: (864) 429-1635.
Fax: (864) 427-0475

HARRIS, Catherine F. *(Judge, Lee County Probate Court)* Elected to term beginning Jan 5, 1993. Reelected 1996 and 2000. Current term expires Dec 31, 2004. Born Lee County South Carolina Nov 1, 1951. Baptist. Educated at Central Carolina Paralegal with honors 1995 and Limestone College B.S. with honors 1996.

Recipient Tribute to Women in Industry 1995. Sunday School Teacher and active member Cedar Creek Baptist Church. Interests include antique/classic automobiles.
Mailing address: P.O. Box 24, Bishopville 29010-0024.
Telephone: (803) 484-5341.
Fax: (803) 484-6881

HARWELL, Baxter Hicks, Jr. *(Judge, South Carolina Circuit Court Twelfth Judicial Circuit)* Elected by General Assembly June 14, 1995. Reelected 2000, current term expires June 3, 2006. Born Florence South Carolina Feb 27, 1933. Presbyterian. Educated at University of South Carolina B.A. 1958 and Cumberland School of Law of Samford University LL.B. 1960 replaced by J.D. 1969. Member Order of the Palmetto. Admitted to practice South Carolina 1961. In legal practice 1961-95.

Important Opinion: Creech v. South Carolina Wildlife and Marine Resources Department Op. No. 24677 S.C. filed Aug 11, 1997. Attended Circuit Court Annual Judicial Conferences. Recipient Distinguished Service Award 1964. Named Outstanding Young Man of the Year 1966. U.S. Army. Member House of Representatives South Carolina 1979-80 and 1989-95. National Director 1965-66 and Chief Legal Counsel 1966-67 United States

HARWELL, BAXTER HICKS, JR.—*Continued*

Jaycees. President South Carolina Jaycees 1966-67. Board of Directors County Council on Aging 1968-71. Chief Legal Counsel 1972 and President 1973-74 Lions Club. District Governor Lions International 1976-77. Advance Board Area Vocational Center Florence Public School District One. Chairman Building Commission Florence City-County Complex, Detention Center and Committee for the Expansion of Florence National Cemetery. Member Florence Jaycees 1964-65, South Carolina Commission on Aging 1970-78, Masons and Shriners. Enjoys hunting and fishing.

Office: City-County Complex, MSC-O, 180 North Irby Street, Florence 29501-3456.
Telephone: (843) 665-3020.
Fax: (843) 665-3078

HAYES, J. Mark, II *(Judge-at-Large, South Carolina Circuit Court)* Elected by General Assembly April 9, 3003 to term beginning June 2003.
Mailing address: P.O. Box 789, Gaffney 29342.
Telephone: (864) 585-5100.

HAYES, John C., III *(Judge, South Carolina Circuit Court Sixteenth Judicial Circuit)* Elected by General Assembly May 29, 1991 to term beginning Sept 3, 1991. Born Rock Hill South Carolina Oct 18, 1945. Episcopalian. Educated at University of South Carolina A.B. 1967 J.D. 1971. Law Clerk to Chief Justice Joseph R. Moss, South Carolina Supreme Court 1971-72. Member Phi Delta Phi. Admitted to practice South Carolina. In legal practice Rock Hill 1979. USAR 1968-74.

Office: Moss Justice Center, Second Floor, 1675-1H York Highway, York 29745-7434.
Telephone: (803) 628-3047.
Fax: (803) 628-3055

HEARN, Kaye G. *(Chief Judge, South Carolina Court of Appeals)* Elected by General Assembly March 21, 1995 to term beginning May 15, 1995. Born Delaware Ohio Jan 30, 1950. Educated at Bethany College B.A. magna cum laude 1972, University of South Carolina J.D. cum laude 1977 and University of Virginia School of Law LL.M. 1998. Recipient American Jurisprudence Award in Conflict of Laws. Listed in *Who's Who Among Students in American Universities and Colleges.* Law Clerk to Hon. Julius B. Ness, South Carolina Supreme Court 1977-79. Member Order of Wig and Robe. In legal practice 1979-86. Judge, South Carolina Family Court Fifteenth Judicial Circuit 1986-95.

Member Board of Bar Examiners 1984-86. Treasurer 1990-91, Vice President 1991-92 and President 1992-93 South Carolina Conference of Family Court Judges. Senior Warden St. Paul's Episcopal Church 1995-96.

Mailing address: P.O. Box 438, Conway 29528-0438.
Telephone: (843) 915-8980.
Fax: (843) 248-1824

HEATH, Mark *(Judge, Marlboro County Probate Court)*
Mailing address: P.O. Box 455, Bennettsville 29512-0455.
Telephone: (843) 479-5610.
Fax: (843) 479-5668

HENDERSON, Roger E. *(Judge, South Carolina Family Court Fourth Judicial Circuit)* Elected by General Assembly May 25, 1995 to term beginning July 1, 1995. Reelected 1998, current term expires June 30, 2004. Born Wadesboro North Carolina Oct 12, 1949. Baptist. Educated at Wofford College B.A. 1971 and University of South Carolina School of Law J.D. 1977. Member Phi Alpha Delta. Admitted to practice South Carolina 1978 and U.S. District Court District of South Carolina 1980. In legal practice Chesterfield 1978-95.

Member South Carolina Association of Criminal Defense Lawyers, South Carolina Trial Lawyers Association, South Carolina Bar and Chesterfield County Bar Association. Specialist Fourth Class USAR May 1971 to May 1977. Chairman Chesterfield County Election Commission. Member South Carolina Commission on Higher Education.

Mailing address: P.O. Box 311, Chesterfield 29709-0311.
Office: 157A West Main Street, Chesterfield 29709.
Telephone: (843) 623-3080.
Fax: (843) 623-3402

HENDRICKS, Bruce H. *(Magistrate Judge, United States District Court District of South Carolina)* Appointed by U.S. District Court judges to term beginning May 6, 2002.
Mailing address: P.O. Box 10823, Greenville 29603.
Office: 300 East Washington Street, Greenville 29601.
Telephone: (864) 239-5710.
Fax: (864) 239-5714

HERLONG, Henry M., Jr. *(Judge, United States District Court District of South Carolina)* Magistrate Judge 1986-91. Appointed Judge for life by President George Bush to term beginning 1991. Born Washington D.C. June 1, 1944. Educated at Clemson University B.A. 1967 and University of South Carolina School of Law J.D. 1970. In legal practice Edgefield 1976-83.

Assistant U.S. Attorney Criminal Division Greenville 1972-76 and Civil Division Columbia 1983-86. Legislative Assistant to U.S. Senator Strom Thurmond 1970-72.

Mailing address: P.O. Box 10469, Greenville 29603-0469.
Telephone: (864) 241-2720.

HOUCK, C. Weston *(Judge, United States District Court District of South Carolina)* Appointed for life by President Jimmy Carter to term beginning 1979. Chief Judge 1993-2000. Born Florence South Carolina April 16, 1933. Educated at University of South Carolina School of Law LL.B. 1956. In legal practice Florence 1956 and 1958-79.

State Representative South Carolina 1963-66. Chairman Florence City-County Building Commission 1968-76.

Mailing address: P.O. Box 2260, Florence 29503-2260.
Telephone: (843) 676-3800.

HOWARD, William L., Sr. *(Associate Judge, South Carolina Court of Appeals)* Elected by General Assembly April 10, 1996 to term beginning Sept 11, 1996. Born Ann Arbor Michigan Jan 19, 1948. Educated at Dickinson College B.A. 1970 and University of South Carolina J.D. 1973. In legal practice 1976-88. Judge, South Carolina Circuit Court Ninth Judicial Circuit 1988-93. Interim Judge, South Carolina Court of Appeals Aug 1994 to May 1995.

Treasurer Circuit Judges Association 1988-90. Mem-

HOWARD, WILLIAM L., SR.—*Continued*

ber South Carolina Joint Committee for Alternative Dispute Resolution.

Office: 98½ Broad Street, Second Floor, Charleston 29401-2201.

Telephone: (843) 720-7060.

Fax: (843) 720-7069

HUFF, Thomas E. *(Associate Judge, South Carolina Court of Appeals)* Elected by General Assembly Feb 14, 1996 to term beginning March 29, 1996. Reelected Feb 9, 2000, current term expires June 30, 2006. Born Augusta Georgia June 5, 1949. Educated at University of South Carolina 1969, Augusta College B.B.A. 1971 and University of South Carolina J.D. 1975.

Member House of Representatives 1979-96. Former Chairman United Way for Belvedere Committee. Vice President Augusta College Jaycees. Member Curtis Baptist Church.

Mailing address: P.O. Drawer 3247, Aiken 29802-3247.

Office: 109 Park Street, Aiken 29802.

Telephone: (803) 502-1801.

Fax: (803) 502-1808

JACOBS, Rolly W. *(Judge, South Carolina Family Court Fifth Judicial Circuit)*

Mailing address: P.O. Box 664, Camden 29020-0664.

Office: 114 Kershaw County Courthouse, Camden 29020.

Telephone: (803) 425-1500.

Fax: (803) 425-5516

JEFFERSON, Deadra L. *(Judge, South Carolina Circuit Court Ninth Judicial Circuit)* Elected by General Assembly to term beginning July 1, 2001. Term expires June 30, 2007. Educated at Converse College B.A. in English 1985 B.A. in Politics 1985 and University of South Carolina J.D. 1989. Law Clerk to Hon. Richard Earl Fields, South Carolina Circuit Court Ninth Judicial Circuit 1989-90. Admitted to practice South Carolina 1989. Judge, South Carolina Family Court Ninth Judicial Circuit April 1, 1996 to June 30, 2001.

Mailing address: P.O. Box 70219, Charleston 29415-0219.

Office: 100 Broad Street, Suite 336, Charleston 29401.

Telephone: (843) 958-5147.

Fax: (843) 958-5148

JENKINS, Robert N., Sr. *(Judge, South Carolina Family Court Thirteenth Judicial Circuit)* Term expires 2008.

Mailing address: P.O. Box 757, Greenville 29602-0757.

Office: 301 University Ridge, Greenville 29601.

Telephone: (864) 467-5854.

Fax: (864) 467-5966

JOHN, Steven H. *(Judge, South Carolina Circuit Court Fifteenth Judicial Circuit)*

Office: 1301 Second Avenue, Suite 3A30, Conway 29526-5234.

Telephone: (843) 915-6696.

Fax: (843) 915-5859

JOHNSON, Alvin D. *(Judge, South Carolina Family Court Thirteenth Judicial Circuit)* Term expires 2004.

Mailing address: P.O. Box 777, Pickens 29671-0777.

Office: 214 East Main Street, Pickens 29671.

Telephone: (864) 898-5916.

Fax: (864) 878-5398

JOHNSON, James W., Jr. *(Judge, South Carolina Circuit Court Eighth Judicial Circuit)*

Mailing address: P.O. Box 367, Laurens 29360-0367.

Office: Main Street, Laurens 29360.

Telephone: (864) 984-2076.

Fax: (864) 984-2333

JOHNSON, R. Kinard, Jr. *(Judge, South Carolina Family Court Thirteenth Judicial Circuit)* Term expires June 30, 2007.

Mailing address: P.O. Box 757, Greenville 29602-0757.

Office: 301 University Ridge, Greenville 29601.

Telephone: (864) 467-5839.

Fax: (864) 467-5845

JONES, Anne Gue *(Judge, South Carolina Family Court First Judicial Circuit)*

Mailing address: P.O. Box 2446, Orangeburg 29116-2446.

Office: 203 Courthouse, 190 Gibson Street, Orangeburg 29115.

Telephone: (803) 533-6247.

Fax: (803) 533-5888

KEESLEY, William P. *(Judge, South Carolina Circuit Court Eleventh Judicial Circuit)*

Mailing address: P.O. Box 10, Edgefield 29824-0010.

Office: 127 Courthouse Square, Edgefield 29824.

Telephone: (803) 637-4095.

Fax: (803) 637-2035

KIDD, Ronnie D. *(Judge, McCormick County Probate Court)*

Office: 133 South Mine Street, Room 101, McCormick 29835-9016.

Telephone: (864) 465-2630.

Fax: (864) 465-0071

KINARD, J. Ernest, Jr. *(Judge, South Carolina Circuit Court Fifth Judicial Circuit)*

Mailing address: P.O. Drawer 1707, Camden 29020-1707.

Office: County Courthouse, 1121 Broad Street, Camden 29020.

Telephone: (803) 576-1766.

Fax: (803) 576-1777

KING, Howard P. *(Judge, South Carolina Circuit Court Third Judicial Circuit)* Elected by General Assembly Feb 14, 1996 to term beginning March 15, 1996. Reelected July 1, 2000, current term expires 2006. Born Greenville South Carolina April 13, 1939. Methodist. Educated at The Citadel B.S. 1961 and University of South Carolina J.D. 1966. Comments Editor South Carolina Law Review 1965-66. Member Phi Delta Phi and Order of Wig and Robe. Admitted to practice South Carolina 1966, U.S. District Court District of South Carolina 1966, U.S. Court of Appeals Fourth Circuit 1970 and U.S. Supreme Court 1973. In legal practice Sumter 1966-96.

Member South Carolina Bar (President 1990-91), Sumter County and American Bar Associations. At-

KING, HOWARD P.—*Continued*

tended General Jurisdiction Course The National Judicial College April 1997 and May 1997. First Lieutenant U.S. Army 1961-63. Member Sumter Lions Club (President 1980). Enjoys golfing, reading, boating and water recreation.

Mailing address: P.O. Box 189, Sumter 29151-0189.
Office: 141 North Main Street, Suite 303, Sumter 29150-0189.
Telephone: (803) 436-2150.
Fax: (803) 436-2403

KINON, Lisa A. *(Judge, South Carolina Family Court Fifteenth Judicial Circuit)* Assumed office 1995. Term expires 2004.

Mailing address: P.O. Box 406, Conway 29528-0406.
Office: 1200 Third Avenue, Conway 29526.
Telephone: (843) 248-1344.
Fax: (843) 248-1879

KITTREDGE, John W. *(Associate Judge, South Carolina Court of Appeals)* Elected by General Assembly to term beginning June 2003. Born Greenville South Carolina Sept 28, 1956. Presbyterian. Educated at University of South Carolina B.S. summa cum laude 1979 J.D. 1982. Law Clerk to Hon. William W. Wilkins, Jr., U.S. District Court District of South Carolina 1982-84. Admitted to practice South Carolina 1982, U.S. District Court District of South Carolina 1983, U.S. Courts of Appeals Fourth 1983 and District of Columbia 1987 Circuits, U.S. Supreme Court 1986 and U.S. Court of Appeals for the Armed Forces 1987. Member Phi Beta Kappa, Order of the Coif and Order of Wig and Robe. In legal practice Greenville 1984-91. Judge, South Carolina Family Court Thirteenth Judicial Circuit July 1, 1991 to Feb 13, 1996. Judge, South Carolina Circuit Court Thirteenth Judicial Circuit 1996 to June 2003.

Attended The National Judicial College courses. Member Joint Legislative Committee on Children. Member Civil Service Commission (Chairman), Crimestoppers of Greenville (President) and Greenville Technical College Foundation (Vice President).

Office: Greenville County Courthouse, Suite 216, 305 East North Street, Greenville 29601.
Telephone: (864) 467-8593.
Fax: (864) 467-8596

KNOBEL, Barry W. *(Judge, South Carolina Family Court Tenth Judicial Circuit)* Term expires June 30, 2007.

Mailing address: P.O. Box 8002, Anderson 29622-8002.
Office: 100 South Main Street, Anderson 29624.
Telephone: (864) 260-4038.
Fax: (864) 260-4822

KONDUROS, Aphrodite K. *(Judge, South Carolina Family Court Thirteenth Judicial Circuit)*

Mailing address: P.O. Box 757, Greenville 29602.
Office: 301 University Ridge, Greenville 29601.
Telephone: (864) 467-5843.
Fax: (864) 467-5830

KORNAHRENS, Keith, Sr. *(Judge, Berkeley County Probate Court)*

Office: 300B California Avenue, Moncks Corner 29461.
Telephone: (843) 719-4519.
Fax: (843) 719-4527

KOSKO, George C. *(Magistrate Judge, United States District Court District of South Carolina)* Appointed by U.S. District Court judges to term beginning Sept 6, 2000.

Mailing address: P.O. Box 835, Charleston 29402.
Telephone: (843) 579-1486.

LANDIS, Jack Alan *(Judge, South Carolina Family Court Ninth Judicial Circuit)* Term expires 2004.

Mailing address: P.O. Box 1707, Moncks Corner 29461-1707.
Office: 300-B California Avenue, Moncks Corner 29461.
Telephone: (843) 719-4477.
Fax: (843) 719-4564

LAWSON, Marvin I. *(Judge, Darlington County Probate Court)* Acting Judge July 14, 1994 to Sept 8, 1994. Appointed Judge by Governor Carroll A. Campbell, Jr. to term beginning Sept 9, 1994. Elected Nov 1994, 1998 and 2002. Current term expires Jan 1, 2007. Born Darlington South Carolina April 5, 1956. Methodist. Educated at Francis Marion College history degree with honors 1977.

Office: 208 Courthouse, One Public Square, Darlington 29532-3213.
Telephone: (843) 398-4310.
Fax: (843) 398-4076

LEE, Alison Renee *(Judge-at-Large, South Carolina Circuit Court)* Elected by General Assembly to term beginning March 5, 1999. Reelected 2002, current term expires June 30, 2008. Born Washington D.C. Sept 17, 1958. Educated at Vassar College B.A. 1979 and Tulane University J.D. 1982. Law Clerk to Hon. Israel M. Augustine, Jr., Louisiana Court of Appeal Fourth Circuit 1982-83 and Hon. C. Tolbert Goolsby, Jr., South Carolina Court of Appeals 1983-84. Admitted to practice Texas 1982, Louisiana 1983 and South Carolina 1984. In legal practice 1984-89. Administrative Law Judge 1994-99.

Staff Counsel South Carolina Legislative Council 1989-94. Member South Carolina Women Lawyers Association. Member Planning Commission United Way of the Midlands 1986-90, St. Peter's Catholic School Board 1993-97 and St. Peter's Catholic Church Pastoral Council 1998-2002.

Mailing address: P.O. Box 192, Columbia 29202-0192.
Office: 1701 Main Street, Room 324, Columbia 29201.
Telephone: (803) 576-1765.
Fax: (803) 748-4742

LLOYD, Reginald I. *(Judge-at-Large, South Carolina Circuit Court)* Elected by General Assembly April 9, 2003.

Mailing address: P.O. Box 2766, Columbia 29202.
Telephone: (803) 252-3300.

LOCKEMY, James E. *(Judge-at-Large, South Carolina Circuit Court)* Elected by General Assembly May 3, 1989 to term beginning June 12, 1989. Reelected, current term expires 2009. Born Sept 23, 1949. Educated at The Citadel 1967-68, Pembroke State University B.A. 1971, University of South Carolina J.D. 1974, Georgetown University 1979 and University of Nevada Reno.

District Chairman Boy Scouts of America 1980-81.

LOCKEMY, JAMES E.—*Continued*

President Dillon Kiwanis Club 1982-83 and Dillon County Theatre 1995-96. Vice Commander American Legion Post 32 1982-88. Trustee East Dillon Baptist Church 1987-89.

Mailing address: P.O. Box 750, Dillon 29536-0750.

Office: One Courthouse Square, Fourth Floor, Dillon 29536.

Telephone: (843) 774-4166.

Fax: (843) 774-0788

MACAULAY, Alexander S. *(Judge, South Carolina Circuit Court Tenth Judicial Circuit)*

Mailing address: P.O. Drawer 428, Walhalla 29691-0428.

Office: 10 Short Street, Walhalla 29691.

Telephone: (864) 638-4266.

Fax: (864) 638-4267

MADDOX, J. Cordell, Jr. *(Judge, South Carolina Circuit Court Tenth Judicial Circuit)*

Mailing address: P.O. Box 8002, Anderson 29622.

Telephone: (864) 260-4636.

Fax: (864) 260-6348

MALPHRUS, Joseph N., Jr. *(Judge, Jasper County Probate Court)*

Mailing address: P.O. Box 1028, Ridgeland 29936-1028.

Telephone: (843) 726-7719.

Fax: (843) 726-7782

MANNING, L. Casey *(Judge, South Carolina Circuit Court Fifth Judicial Circuit)*

Mailing address: P.O. Box 192, Columbia 29202-0192.

Office: 1701 Main Street, Room 214, Columbia 29201.

Telephone: (803) 576-1773.

Fax: (803) 576-1744

MARCHANT, Bristow *(Magistrate Judge, United States District Court District of South Carolina)* Appointed by U.S. District Court judges Sept 1, 1992 and Sept 2000. Born Columbia South Carolina June 13, 1955. Presbyterian. Educated at College of Charleston B.A. with honors 1977 and University of South Carolina School of Law J.D. 1980. Admitted to practice South Carolina 1980, U.S. District Court District of South Carolina 1982, U.S. Court of Appeals Fourth Circuit 1982 and U.S. Supreme Court 1986. In legal practice Columbia 1983-92.

Staff Counsel Judiciary Committee U.S. Senate 1980-82. State Attorney Office of Attorney General 1982-83 and Assistant Chief Counsel Department of Highways and Public Transportation 1983 South Carolina. Member Public Defender Board Richland County 1992. Editor *The Richbar Newsletter* Richland County Bar Association 1983-90. Member Judicial Conference of the Fourth Circuit, South Carolina Bar (Insurance Committee 1985-92) and Richland County Bar Association (Secretary-Treasurer 1983-90, President Elect 1991, President 1992). Named one of Outstanding Young Men of America 1981 and 1986. State Treasurer Strom Thurmond Re-election Committee 1984. Board Member Central Midlands Regional Planning Council 1987-89. Member 1987-91 and Chairman 1988 Richland County Council. Board of Trustees Koger Center for the Arts 1987-92. Board of Visitors College of Charleston 1994-98.

Office: Federal Courthouse, 1845 Assembly Street, Columbia 29201-2431.

Telephone: (803) 765-5424.

MARING, Waldo A. *(Judge, Georgetown County Probate Court)* Elected to term beginning Jan 6, 1981. Reelected 1984, 1988, 1992, 1996 and 2000. Current term expires Jan 2005. Born Andrews South Carolina Sept 1, 1951. Southern Baptist. Educated at Columbia Junior College 1971.

Member South Carolina Association of Probate Judges (Past President) and Judicial Council of South Carolina. Republican. Charter member Georgetown Breakfast Rotary Club. Member Garden City Baptist Church.

Mailing address: P.O. Box 421270, Georgetown 29442-1270.

Telephone: (843) 527-6325.

Fax: (843) 546-4730

McCROREY, Joseph R. *(Magistrate Judge, United States District Court District of South Carolina)* Appointed by U.S. District Court judges.

Office: Federal Courthouse, 1845 Assembly Street, Columbia 29201-2431.

Telephone: (803) 765-5512.

McCULLOCH, Amy W. *(Judge, Richland County Probate Court)* Elected Nov 5, 1998 to term beginning Jan 5, 1999. Reelected 2001, current term expires Jan 2006. Born Texarkana Texas Nov 11, 1964. Methodist. Educated at University of South Carolina B.S. 1987 J.D. 1990. Law Clerk to Hon. Thomas J. Ervin, South Carolina Circuit Court Tenth Judicial Circuit 1990-91 and Magistrate Judge William M. Catoe, Jr., U.S. District Court District of South Carolina 1991. Admitted to practice South Carolina 1990 and U.S. District Court District of South Carolina 1997. In legal practice Columbia Jan 1997 to Dec 1998.

Assistant Solicitor Richland County 1991-96. Co-author "Extortion, Blackmail & Threats" *South Carolina Jurisprudence* 1991. Adjunct Professor Legal Department Midlands Technical College 1996-98 and Criminal Justice Department University of South Carolina 1997-98. Member South Carolina Women's Legal Association, South Carolina Probate Judges Association (Second Vice President), National Probate Judges Association and South Carolina Bar. Democrat. Member South Carolina Association of Counties and Rotary. Enjoys tennis and aerobics.

Mailing address: P.O. Box 192, Columbia 29202-0192.

Office: 1701 Main Street, Room 207, Columbia 29201.

Telephone: (803) 576-1961.

Fax: (803) 576-1993

E-mail address: amymcculloch@richlandonline.com

McFADDIN, George M., Jr. *(Judge, South Carolina Family Court Third Judicial Circuit)*

Mailing address: P.O. Box 1816, Sumter 29152.

Telephone: (803) 436-2373.

Fax: (803) 436-2379

McGOWAN, Joseph W., III *(Judge, South Carolina Family Court Eighth Judicial Circuit)*
Mailing address: P.O. Box 325, Laurens 29360-0325.
Office: County Courthouse Annex, 216 West Main Street, Laurens 29360.
Telephone: (864) 984-4416.
Fax: (864) 984-0508

McLIN, Nancy Chapman *(Judge, South Carolina Family Court First Judicial Circuit)* Term expires 2004.
Office: 212 Deming Way, Box 4, Summerville 29483-4707.
Telephone: (843) 832-0387.
Fax: (843) 832-0384

MILLER, Edward W. *(Judge, South Carolina Circuit Court Thirteenth Judicial Circuit)*
Office: 305 East North Street, Suite 219, Greenville 29601.
Telephone: (864) 467-8559.
Fax: (864) 233-4173

MILLING, John M. *(Judge-at-Large, South Carolina Circuit Court)* Elected by General Assembly Feb 10, 1999. Educated at Clemson University B.A. with honors 1969 and University of South Carolina J.D. 1973. Staff member South Carolina Law Review. Member Order of Wig and Robe.
Assistant Solicitor Darlington County 1977-80. Assistant Public Defender 1985. Chief Public Defender 1986-88 and 1994-97. Attorney Darlington County School District 1988-96. Town Attorney 1990-99. Member South Carolina Bar and Darlington County Bar Association. Former Board Member Darlington County Youth Home. Board of Directors Grove Hill Cemetery. Elder and Member Darlington Presbyterian Church.
Mailing address: P.O. Drawer 519, Darlington 29540-0519.
Office: 88 Public Square, Darlington 29532.
Telephone: (843) 393-4083.
Fax: (843) 393-1281

MOORE, James E. *(Associate Justice, South Carolina Supreme Court)* Elected by General Assembly May 29, 1991 to term beginning Jan 1, 1992. Reelected 1998, current term expires 2008. Born Laurens South Carolina March 13, 1936. Baptist. Educated at Duke University B.A. 1958 J.D. 1961. Awarded honorary Doctor of Humanities Lander College 1997. Member Phi Delta Phi. Admitted to practice South Carolina 1961. In legal practice Greenwood 1961-76. Judge, South Carolina Circuit Court Eighth Judicial Circuit Nov 16, 1976 to Dec 31, 1991.
South Carolina House of Representatives 1968-76. Vice Chairman Board of Commissioners on Judicial Standards 1981-91. Member ad hoc Committee on South Carolina Rules of Civil Procedure 1981-96. Chairman Advisory Committee 1984-91 and Chairman 1987-91 South Carolina Circuit Court Judges Association. Member Executive Committee National Conference of State Trial Judges American Bar Association 1989-91. Attendee 1977 and Faculty Advisor 1985 The National Judicial College. Speaker "Judicial Ethics" South Carolina Magistrates 1978, "Jury Selection and Opening Statements" CLE 1980, "New Rules of Civil Procedure" CLE Charleston, Greenville and Columbia 1985, Bench/Bar Conference on Civil Trial Advocacy 1985 and 1988, "South Carolina Rules of Civil Procedure" CLE 1986, "Trial of Death Penalty Cases" South Carolina Judicial Conference 1990 and "Alternative Dispute Resolution" Trial and Appellate Advocacy Seminar Mid-Year Meeting 1991, "Ethics and Civility in Trial and Appellate Practice" Mid-Year Meeting 1992 South Carolina Bar, "ABA Code of Judicial Conduct and ABA Model Rules of Judicial Disciplinary Enforcement Standards" South Carolina Judicial Conference 1994, "Oral Argument—A Perspective from the Supreme Court" South Carolina Bar Appellate Practice Seminar 1995 and "New Rules in South Carolina's Attorney and Judge Grievance and Disciplinary Process" South Carolina Bar CLE 1997. Panel Member "Covering the Courts" Workshop South Carolina Press Association 1988, "Judicial Ethics" South Carolina Judicial Conference 1988 and "Punitive Damages" South Carolina Defense Trial Attorneys Association 1989. Portrait Honoree South Carolina Trial Lawyers Association 1996. Enjoys golf.
Mailing address: P.O. Box 277, Greenwood 29648-0277.
Telephone: (864) 942-8559.
Fax: (864) 942-8568

MOREHEAD, A. E., III *(Judge, South Carolina Family Court Twelfth Judicial Circuit)* Elected by General Assembly to term beginning June 17, 1985. Reelected to subsequent terms. Current term expires June 30, 2007. Formerly served South Carolina Court of Appeals. Born Columbia South Carolina Sept 6, 1946. Roman Catholic. Educated at The Citadel B.A. 1968 and University of South Carolina J.D. 1973. Admitted to practice South Carolina 1973. In legal practice Columbia 1973-76 and Florence 1976-85. Lieutenant U.S. Army 1968-70.
Office: 401 City-County Complex, MSC-C, 180 North Irby Street, Florence 29501-3456.
Telephone: (843) 665-3008.
Fax: (843) 665-5275

MORRIS, Barney L. *(Judge, Clarendon County Probate Court)*
Mailing address: P.O. Box 307, Manning 29102-0307.
Telephone: (803) 435-8774.
Fax: (803) 435-8698

MURDOCK, Jamie Lee, Jr. *(Judge, South Carolina Family Court Fourth Judicial Circuit)* Term expires 2007.
Mailing address: P.O. Box 1856, Darlington 29540-1856.
Office: 402 Courthouse, One Public Square, Darlington 29532.
Telephone: (843) 398-4334.
Fax: (843) 393-7255

MYERS, Marion D. *(Judge, South Carolina Family Court Third Judicial Circuit)* Reelected 2001, current term expires June 30, 2007.
Mailing address: P.O. Box 1816, Sumter 29151-1816.
Office: 108 North Magnolia Street, Sumter 29150.
Telephone: (803) 436-2371.
Fax: (803) 436-2396

NEWMAN, Clifton *(Judge-at-Large, South Carolina Circuit Court)*
Mailing address: P.O. Box 516, Kingstree 29556-0516.
Telephone: (843) 355-9321.
Fax: (843) 355-9301

NEWTON, Martha D. *(Judge, Anderson County Probate Court)*
Mailing address: P.O. Box 8002, Anderson 29622-8002.
Telephone: (864) 260-4049.
Fax: (864) 260-4811

NICHOLSON, J. C. "Buddy", Jr. *(Judge, South Carolina Circuit Court Tenth Judicial Circuit)* Elected Judge-at-Large to term beginning Feb 26, 1999. Elected Judge by General Assembly. Born Birmingham Alabama Sept 30, 1942. Educated at The Citadel A.B. 1964 and University of South Carolina J.D. 1973. In legal practice 1973-99.

Assistant Solicitor Orangeburg County 1973-76 and Greenville County 1983. Member South Carolina Trial Lawyers, The Association of Trial Lawyers of America, South Carolina Bar (House of Delegates) and American Bar Association. Pilot USAF. Lieutenant Colonel Air National Guard (retired). Member Orangeburg County Council 1976-82. Member Rotary Club, Toastmasters Club, University of South Carolina Gamecock Club and First Presbyterian Church Anderson.
Mailing address: P.O. Box 8002, Anderson 29622-8002.
Office: 100 South Main Street, Anderson 29624.
Telephone: (864) 260-4059.
Fax: (864) 224-6320

NOBLES, Kelly Baker *(Judge, Newberry County Probate Court)*
Mailing address: P.O. Box 442, Newberry 29108-0442.
Telephone: (803) 321-2118.
Fax: (803) 321-2119

NORTON, David C. *(Judge, United States District Court District of South Carolina)* Appointed for life by President George Bush to term beginning July 13, 1990. Born Washington D.C. July 25, 1946. Episcopalian. Educated at University of the South B.A. with honors 1968 and University of South Carolina J.D. 1975. Staff member South Carolina Law Review 1973-75. Admitted to practice South Carolina 1975, U.S. District Court District of South Carolina 1975, U.S. Court of Appeals Fourth Circuit 1976 and U.S. Supreme Court 1982. In legal practice Charleston 1975-90.

Member Advisory Committee on the Rules of Evidence 1996-2002. Fourth Circuit District Court Representative Judicial Conference of the U.S. since 2002. Member South Carolina Defense Trial Attorneys Association (Executive Committee 1988-90), Fourth Circuit District Judges Association (Assistant Treasurer, Treasurer and Assistant Vice President since 2000), Judicial Conference of the Fourth Circuit, Federal Judges Association, South Carolina Bar (House of Delegates 1986-90), Charleston County (Secretary-Treasurer 1983-90) and American Bar Associations. Recipient Gedney M. Howe, Jr. Pro Bono Award from Charleston County Bar Association 1988. E-5 USN 1969-72. Enjoys hunting and playing racquetball.
Mailing address: P.O. Box 835, Charleston 29402-0835.
Telephone: (843) 579-1450.

NUESSLE, Peter R. *(Judge, South Carolina Family Court Second Judicial Circuit)* Term expires 2004.
Mailing address: P.O. Box 1275, Aiken 29802-1275.
Office: 109 Park Avenue, Aiken 29801.
Telephone: (803) 642-1729.
Fax: (803) 643-0911

ODOM, Sheila *(Judge, Hampton County Probate Court)*
Mailing address: P.O. Box 601, Hampton 29924-0601.
Telephone: (803) 943-7512.
Fax: (803) 943-7596

ORR, Sandra Burgess *(Judge, Oconee County Probate Court)*
Mailing address: P.O. Box 471, Walhalla 29691-0471.
Telephone: (864) 638-4275.
Fax: (864) 638-4278

PATTERSON, Larry R. *(Judge, South Carolina Circuit Court Thirteenth Judicial Circuit)* Former Judge, South Carolina Family Court Thirteenth Judicial Circuit.
Office: 315 Greenville County Courthouse, 301 East North Street, Greenville 29601-2113.
Telephone: (864) 467-8406.
Fax: (864) 235-3625

PEELER, Robert E. *(Judge, Edgefield County Probate Court)*
Office: 124 Courthouse Square, Edgefield 29824-1342.
Telephone: (803) 637-4076.
Fax: (803) 637-7157

PEEPLES, Rodney A. *(Judge, South Carolina Circuit Court Second Judicial Circuit)* Elected by General Assembly Feb 13, 1974 to term beginning Dec 5, 1974. Reelected to subsequent terms. Current term expires 2004. Born Hampton South Carolina Jan 8, 1940. Baptist. Member First Baptist Church. Educated at University of South Carolina B.S. 1961 J.D. 1964. Member Phi Delta Phi and Kappa Alpha Order. Admitted to practice South Carolina 1964, U.S. District Court District of South Carolina 1964 and U.S. Court of Appeals Fourth Circuit 1964. Began legal practice Barnwell 1964.

Member South Carolina Trial Lawyers Association, Judicial Conference of the Fourth Circuit, American Judicature Society (Board of Directors 1986-88), South Carolina Bar, Barnwell County and American (Task Force on Reduction of Litigation Cost and Delay Judicial Administration Division since 1987, Judicial Member-at-Large Board of Governors 1988-91) Bar Associations. Executive Committee 1981-83, Vice Chairman 1983-84, Chairman Elect 1985 and Chairman 1986 National Conference of State Trial Judges. Member Governor Edwards' Task Force on Criminal Justice Information System, Governor Riley's Task Force on Arson, Judicial Continuing Legal Education Commission, Sentencing Guidelines Commission, Circuit Court Judges Advisory Committee, Governor Campbell's Committee on Criminal Justice, Crime and Juvenile Delinquency (Chairman 1987-88) and Governor Campbell's Strategic Council on Drug Education, Enforcement and Treatment 1987-94. Vice Chairman Board of Directors State Justice Institute 1986-88. Graduate 1974 and 1976, Faculty Advisor 1978-81, Faculty member 1979 and Member since 1989 and Chairman 1992-94 Board of Trustees The National Judicial College. Recipient Distinguished Service Award from South Carolina Jaycees 1976. Board of Visitors Clemson University 1987-89. Member Western

PEEPLES, RODNEY A.—*Continued*

Carolina Higher Education Committee, Lions, Jaycees and Masons Harmony Lodge 17.
Mailing address: P.O. Box 426, Barnwell 29812-0426.
Office: 120 County Courthouse, Pechmann Street, Barnwell 29812.
Telephone: (803) 259-7022.
Fax: (803) 259-1402

PERRY, Matthew J., Jr. *(Senior Judge, United States District Court District of South Carolina)* Appointed for life by President Jimmy Carter to term beginning 1979. Assumed Senior status 1995, serves by assignment. Born Columbia South Carolina Aug 3, 1921. Educated at South Carolina State College B.S. 1948 LL.B. 1951. In legal practice Spartanburg 1951-61 and Columbia 1961-76. Judge, U.S. Court of Military Appeals 1976-79.
Office: Federal Courthouse, 1845 Assembly Street, Columbia 29201-2431.
Telephone: (803) 765-5408.

PIEPER, Daniel F. *(Judge, South Carolina Circuit Court Ninth Judicial Circuit)*
Office: 427 County Judicial Building, 100 Broad Street, Charleston 29401-2287.
Telephone: (843) 958-5142.
Fax: (843) 958-5143

PIERCE, Harriett P. *(Judge, Kershaw County Probate Court)* Elected to term beginning Jan 1, 1979. Reelected 1982, 1986, 1990, 1994, 1998 and 2002. Current term expires Dec 31, 2006. Born Camden South Carolina July 28, 1941. Methodist. Educated at Winthrop College 1961. Democrat.
Office: 1121 Broad Street, Room 302, Camden 29020-3635.
Telephone: (803) 425-1500.
Fax: (803) 425-1526

PLEICONES, Costa M. *(Associate Justice, South Carolina Supreme Court)* Elected by General Assembly to term beginning March 23, 2000. Term expires July 31, 2006. Born Greenville South Carolina Feb 29, 1944. Greek Orthodox. Educated at Wofford College A.B. 1965 and University of South Carolina J.D. 1968. Admitted to practice South Carolina 1968, U.S. District Court District of South Carolina 1968, U.S. Court of Appeals for the Armed Forces 1969, U.S. Supreme Court 1977 and U.S. Court of Appeals Fourth Circuit 1990. In legal practice Columbia 1975-91. Judge, South Carolina Circuit Court Fifth Judicial Circuit July 1, 1991 to March 22, 2000.
County Attorney Richland County Jan 1, 1979 to Jan 7, 1981. Member South Carolina Bar. Enjoys all sports except hockey. Personal Statement or Quote: "Remember where you came from."
Mailing address: P.O. Box 11330, Columbia 29211-1330.
Office: 1231 Gervais Street, Columbia 29201.
Telephone: (803) 734-1438.
Fax: (803) 734-0427
E-mail address: cpleicones@scjd.state.sc.us

PROVENCE, Tiffany *(Judge, Dorchester County Probate Court)* Appointed by Governor David M. Beasley to term beginning July 1, 1998. Reelected 2001, current term expires 2005. Born Montgomery Alabama Oct 21, 1972. Educated at University of Florida B.S. 1994, College of Charleston and University of South Carolina J.D. 1998. Member Phi Alpha Delta. Admitted to practice South Carolina 1998.
Member National Association of Women Judges, South Carolina Bar and American Bar Association. Board Member SPCA.
Office: County Courthouse, 101 Ridge Street, St. George 29477-2443.
Telephone: (843) 563-0105.
Fax: (843) 563-0222
E-mail address: dcpjudge@email.com

RENWICK, Pamela W. *(Judge, Fairfield County Probate Court)* Elected Nov 6, 1990 to term beginning Jan 1, 1991. Reelected 1994, 1998 and 2002. Current term expires Dec 31, 2006. Born Fairfield County South Carolina Oct 23, 1960. Religious Affiliation: Associate Reformed Presbyterian.
Member South Carolina Association of Probate Judges and National Association of Probate Judges.
Mailing address: P.O. Box 385, Winnsboro 29180-0385.
Office: Fairfield County Courthouse, Congress Street, Winnsboro 29180.
Telephone: (803) 712-6519.
Fax: (803) 712-6939

RIDDLE, Leslie K. *(Judge, South Carolina Family Court Fifth Judicial Circuit)* Assumed office 1995. Reelected 2001, current term expires June 30, 2007.
Mailing address: P.O. Box 192, Columbia 29202-0192.
Office: 1701 Main Street, Columbia 29201.
Telephone: (803) 576-1756.
Fax: (803) 576-1759

ROBINSON, Frederick W. *(Judge, Calhoun County Probate Court)* Elected at special election to term beginning Nov 13, 1982. Reelected to subsequent terms. Current term expires Jan 2005. Born Aiken South Carolina Feb 1, 1951. Presbyterian. Educated at University of South Carolina B.S. 1974. Member Pi Kappa Alpha.
Previously employed by St. Matthews Telephone Company. Democrat. Board Member United Way and Calhoun Mental Health Association. Enjoys golf, fishing and hunting.
Office: 302 South F.R. Huff Drive, St. Matthews 29135-1458.
Telephone: (803) 874-3514.
Fax: (803) 874-1942

RODDEY, Lois *(Judge, Chester County Probate Court)*
Mailing address: P.O. Drawer 580, Chester 29706-0580.
Telephone: (803) 385-2604.
Fax: (803) 581-5180

ROE, Sue H. *(Judge, Aiken County Probate Court)* Elected Nov 1984 to term beginning Jan 1, 1985. Reelected 1988, 1992, 1996 and 2000. Current term expires Dec 31, 2004. Born Aiken County South Carolina April 2, 1943. Baptist.
Mailing address: P.O. Box 1576, Aiken 29802.
Telephone: (803) 642-2000.
Fax: (803) 642-2007

ROGERS, Jasper G. *(Judge, Dillon County Probate Court)*
Mailing address: P.O. Box 189, Dillon 29536-0189.
Telephone: (843) 774-1423.
Fax: (843) 841-3732

ROGERS, Thomas E., III *(Magistrate Judge, United States District Court District of South Carolina)* Appointed by U.S. District Court judges to term beginning May 8, 2002.
Office: 401 West Evans Street, Florence 29501.
Telephone: (843) 676-3805.
Fax: (843) 676-3833

ROSS-BENNETT, Vivian E. *(Judge, Orangeburg County Probate Court)* Appointed by Governor David M. Beasley June 19, 1997. Elected Nov 1998 and Nov 2002. Current term expires 2006. Educated at University of Tennessee at Knoxville B.S. 1986 and University of South Carolina School of Law J.D. 1994. Admitted to practice South Carolina 1994. In legal practice 1994-97.
Adjunct Professor Claflin University since 1998. First Vice President and Curriculum Chair South Carolina Probate Judges Association 2002-03. Member Probate Judges Advisory Committee 2001-03, Commission on Alternative Dispute Resolution since 2002 and South Carolina Judicial Council since 2002. Member National College of Probate Judges, South Carolina Bar (Real Property and Probate Law Section) and American Bar Association (Chair Probate Court Committee National Conference of Special Court Judges Judicial Division 2002-03). Presenter "Civil Procedure for Probate Judges" Fall Conference South Carolina Association of Probate Judges Sept 2002, "Real Estate Issues and Probate Court" South Carolina Bar CLE Oct 4, 2002 and "General Jurisdiction and Miscellaneous Matters in Probate Court" New Probate Judges Training School Jan 10, 2003.
Mailing address: P.O. Drawer 9000, Orangeburg 29115-9000.
Telephone: (803) 533-6280.
Fax: (803) 533-6279

RUCKER, John M. *(Judge, South Carolina Family Court Eighth Judicial Circuit)* Term expires 2004.
Mailing address: P.O. Box 756, Newberry 29108-0756.
Office: 1309 College Street, Newberry 29108.
Telephone: (803) 321-2110.
Fax: (803) 276-8148

SAUNDERS, Wyatt T., Jr. *(Judge, South Carolina Circuit Court Eighth Judicial Circuit)* Former Judge, South Carolina Family Court Eighth Judicial Circuit.
Mailing address: P.O. Box 879, Greenwood 29648-0879.
Office: Monument Street, Room 210, Greenwood 29646.
Telephone: (864) 943-8020.
Fax: (864) 942-8581

SAWYER, C. David, Jr. *(Judge, South Carolina Family Court Eleventh Judicial Circuit)* Term expires June 30, 2007.
Mailing address: P.O. Box 691, Saluda 29138-0691.
Office: Lexington County Courthouse, 139 East Main Street, Lexington 29072-3456.
Telephone: (803) 359-8450.
Fax: (803) 359-8505

SEGARS-ANDREWS, Frances P. *(Judge, South Carolina Family Court Ninth Judicial Circuit)* Term expires 2004.
Office: 100 Broad Street, Suite 241, Charleston 29401.
Telephone: (843) 958-4416.
Fax: (843) 958-4415

SEYMOUR, Margaret B. *(Judge, United States District Court District of South Carolina)* Magistrate Judge 1996-98. Appointed Judge for life by President Bill Clinton to term beginning Oct 30, 1998. Born Washington D.C. Jan 17, 1947. Educated at Howard University B.A. 1969 and Washington College of Law of American University J.D. 1977. In legal practice 1988-90.
Equal Opportunity Specialist U.S. Department of Health, Education and Welfare 1972-79 and U.S. Equal Employment Opportunity Commission 1979-80. Attorney Office of Civil Rights U.S. Department of Education 1980-88. Assistant U.S. Attorney 1990-96 and Interim U.S. Attorney 1993 and 1996 District of South Carolina.
Mailing address: P.O. Box 1985, Spartanburg 29304-1985.
Telephone: (864) 582-2167.

SHORT, Paul E., Jr. *(Judge, South Carolina Circuit Court Sixth Judicial Circuit)* Judge-at-Large July 1, 1991 to Feb 9, 1999. Elected Judge by General Assembly to term beginning Feb 10, 1999. Born Gastonia North Carolina Jan 13, 1947. Presbyterian. Educated at The Citadel B.A. 1968 and University of South Carolina J.D. 1971. Admitted to practice South Carolina 1971. In legal practice Chester 1971-91.
First Lieutenant South Carolina National Guard 1972-73 and USAR. Member House of Representatives South Carolina 1983-91.
Mailing address: P.O. Box 1006, Chester 29706-1006.
Office: 158 Main Street, Room 107, Chester 29706.
Telephone: (803) 581-5011.
Fax: (803) 385-6197

SIMON, Francis M. *(Judge, Beaufort County Probate Court)* Elected Nov 1994 to term beginning Jan 3, 1995. Reelected 1998 and 2002. Current term expires Jan 1, 2007. Born Secaucus New Jersey March 27, 1928. Educated at New Jersey State Teachers College, Jersey City Junior College with honors 1949, Rutgers University School of Law J.D. 1952 and New York University Law School LL.M. 1957. Admitted to practice New York 1955, U.S. Tax Court 1965 and U.S. Supreme Court 1966. In legal practice New York City and Long Island New York 1955-89. Associate Judge Bluffton Municipal Court South Carolina 1992-94.
Author "The Keogh Act" 1963 and "Short Term Trusts" 1964 Kalb Voorhis and Co. Columnist "Estate Planning" New York Law Journal. Guest lecturer at various colleges 1959-89. Adjunct Faculty Technical College of Low Country 1991-94. Former Member New York County Lawyers Association, New York and American Bar Associations. Associate Member South Carolina Bar. Member South Carolina Probate Judges Association and National College of Probate Judges. CJLE Lecturer. Participant and Honor Graduate National Security Seminars National Defense University and Seminarian U.S. Army War College. U.S. Army and USAR 1952-60. Major General South Carolina Military Department. Former Commissioner Public Service District. Chairman Hilton Head Island Crime Prevention Task

SIMON, FRANCIS M.—*Continued*
Force. Enjoys tennis, reading, sports cars and water sports.
Mailing address: P.O. Box 1083, Beaufort 29901-1083.
Telephone: (843) 470-5319.
Fax: (843) 470-5324

SMOAK, Gerald C., Jr. *(Judge, South Carolina Family Court Fourteenth Judicial Circuit)* Term expires June 30, 2007.
Mailing address: P.O. Box 1685, Walterboro 29488-1685.
Office: 101 Hampton Street, Walterboro 29488.
Telephone: (843) 549-5060.
Fax: (843) 549-1842

SMOAK, I. A., III *(Judge, Colleton County Probate Court)* Appointed by Governor Richard Riley to term beginning July 1, 1982. Elected to term beginning Jan 1, 1983. Reelected 1986, 1990, 1994, 1998 and 2002. Current term expires Dec 31, 2006. Former Ex-Officio Master-in-Equity. Also served as Recorder, Walterboro Municipal Court 1979-82 and 1986-2000. Born Wadesboro North Carolina Sept 27, 1948. Baptist. Educated at Furman University B.A. 1970 and University of South Carolina J.D. 1973. Admitted to practice South Carolina 1973. Began legal practice Walterboro 1973.
Member South Carolina Association of Probate Judges, National College of Probate Judges and South Carolina Bar. Major South Carolina Army National Guard JAG 1970-92 (retired). Democrat. Secretary Colleton County Democratic Party 1976-79. Member National Guard Association of South Carolina, National Guard Association of the U.S. and Masons. Enjoys reading, sports and computers.
Mailing address: P.O. Box 1036, Walterboro 29488-0031.
Telephone: (843) 549-7216.
Fax: (843) 549-5571

SPEER, Carol F. *(Judge, Abbeville County Probate Court)* Appointed by Governor Carroll A. Campbell, Jr. to term beginning Aug 1990. Elected 1990, 1994, 1998 and 2002. Current term expires Dec 2006. Born Abbeville County South Carolina Sept 17, 1945. Presbyterian.
Member South Carolina Probate Judges Association and National Probate Judges Association. Democrat. Member Optimist Club and UDC. Enjoys gardening and reading.
Mailing address: P.O. Box 70, Abbeville 29620.
Office: 102 Courthouse, Abbeville 29620.
Telephone: (864) 459-4626.
Fax: (864) 459-4023

SPRUILL, James H., III *(Judge, South Carolina Family Court Fourth Judicial Circuit)* Elected by General Assembly to term beginning July 1, 1989. Reelected 1996 and 2002. Current term expires June 2008. Born Wadesboro North Carolina 1944. Educated at University of North Carolina A.B. 1965 and University of South Carolina J.D. cum laude 1970. Staff member South Carolina Law Review 1967-70. Law Clerk to Hon. Robert W. Hemphill, U.S. District Court District of South Carolina 1970-71. Member Phi Delta Phi. Admitted to practice South Carolina 1970.
Member South Carolina Bar. Lieutenant USN 1965-67.
Mailing address: P.O. Box 1492, Cheraw 29520-1492.
Office: 210 Market Street, Cheraw 29520.
Telephone: (843) 537-3123.
Fax: (843) 537-6475

STILWELL, H. Samuel *(Associate Judge, South Carolina Court of Appeals)* Elected by General Assembly Feb 14, 1996 to term beginning April 25, 1996. Born Spartanburg South Carolina Nov 6, 1935. Educated at Mars Hill Junior College A.A. 1956 and University of South Carolina A.B. 1958 LL.B. cum laude 1961.
Member South Carolina Senate 1987-95.
Mailing address: P.O. Box 26897, Greenville 29616-6897.
Office: 114 Greenville County Courthouse, Greenville 29616.
Telephone: (864) 467-8496.
Fax: (864) 467-8786

STROM, Donna S. *(Judge, South Carolina Family Court Fifth Judicial Circuit)* Term expires 2004.
Mailing address: P.O. Box 192, Columbia 29202-0192.
Office: 1701 Main Street, Room 312, Columbia 29201.
Telephone: (803) 576-1760.
Fax: (803) 576-1763

THOMAS, Paula H. *(Judge, South Carolina Circuit Court Fifteenth Judicial Circuit)* Judge-at-Large July 26, 1996 to July 6, 1998. Elected Judge by General Assembly to term beginning July 7, 1998.
Mailing address: P.O. Drawer 1270, Georgetown 29442-1270.
Office: 715 Prince Street, Georgetown 29440.
Telephone: (843) 545-3030.
Fax: (843) 545-3282

TOAL, Jean Hoefer *(Chief Justice, South Carolina Supreme Court)* Elected by General Assembly Jan 27, 1988 to term beginning March 17, 1988. Reelected 1996, current term expires July 31, 2004. Born Columbia South Carolina Aug 11, 1943. Roman Catholic. Educated at Agnes Scott College B.A. 1965 and University of South Carolina J.D. 1968. Honorary Doctor of Letters College of Charleston 1991. Honorary LL.D. Columbia College 1992, The Citadel 1999, Francis Marion University 1999 and University of South Carolina 2000. Leading Articles Editor 1966-67 and Managing Editor 1967-68 South Carolina Law Review. Member Phi Alpha Delta, Phi Beta Kappa, Mortar Board and Order of the Coif. Admitted to practice South Carolina 1968, U.S. District Court District of South Carolina 1968, U.S. Court of Appeals Fourth Circuit 1970 and U.S. Supreme Court 1981. In legal practice Greenville 1968-70 and Columbia 1970-88.
Member South Carolina Bar, Richland County and American Bar Associations. Attended Appellate Judges Seminar New York University Law School 1988. Recipient Algernon Sydney Sullivan Award from University of South Carolina 1991. Member House of Representatives South Carolina 1975-88 (Secretary House Democratic Caucus 1976-88, Chairman Constitutional Laws Subcommittee House Judiciary Committee 1977-88, Rules Committee 1982-88, Parliamentarian State Democratic Convention). Board of Visitors Clemson University 1978. Chair South Carolina Juvenile Justice Task

TOAL, JEAN HOEFER—*Continued*

Force 1992-94 and South Carolina Rhodes Scholar Selection Committee 1994. Board of Trustees Agnes Scott College since 1997. Trustee Columbia Museum of Art. Member St. Joseph's Catholic Church (Parish Council and Lector). Enjoys golf, gardening and reading.

Mailing address: P.O. Box 12456, Columbia 29211-2456.

Telephone: (803) 734-1584.

Fax: (803) 734-1167

E-mail address: jtoal@scjd.state.sc.us

TUNSTALL, Billy A., Jr. *(Judge, South Carolina Family Court Eighth Judicial Circuit)* Term expires June 30, 2007.

Office: 208 Greenwood County Courthouse, Monument Street, Greenwood 29646-2633.

Telephone: (864) 942-8643.

Fax: (864) 229-0671

TURBEVILLE, R. Wright *(Judge, South Carolina Family Court Third Judicial Circuit)* Elected by General Assembly Feb 1992 to term beginning April 1, 1992. Reelected 1995 and 2001. Current term expires June 30, 2007. Born Turbeville South Carolina Sept 27, 1944. United Methodist. Educated at Wofford College B.A. 1966, Emory University M.Div. 1969 and University of South Carolina J.D. 1977. Staff member South Carolina Law Review 1975-77. Member Order of Wig and Robe. Admitted to practice South Carolina 1977, U.S. District Court District of South Carolina 1978 and U.S. Court of Appeals Fourth Circuit 1982. In legal practice Manning 1977-92.

Former Member South Carolina Trial Lawyers Association. Member South Carolina Bar and American Bar Association. Member 1978-92 and Chairman 1988-89 Clarendon County Mental Retardation Board. Member Turbeville Puritan Club. Enjoys walking and reading.

Mailing address: P.O. Box 696, Manning 29102-0696.

Office: Boyce Street, Manning 29102.

Telephone: (803) 435-2720.

Fax: (803) 435-2560

UPCHURCH, Margaret N. *(Judge, Saluda County Probate Court)*

Office: 100 East Church Street, Saluda 29138-1444.

Telephone: (864) 445-7110.

Fax: (864) 445-9726

WAITES, John E. *(Judge, United States Bankruptcy Court District of South Carolina)* Appointed by U.S. Court of Appeals Fourth Circuit judges.

Mailing address: P.O. Box 1448, Columbia 29202-1448.

Telephone: (803) 253-3462.

WALLER, John H., Jr. *(Associate Justice, South Carolina Supreme Court)* Elected by General Assembly May 11, 1994 to term beginning July 1, 1994. Reelected 2002, current term expires July 2012. Born Mullins South Carolina Oct 31, 1937. Methodist. Educated at Wofford College B.A. 1959 and University of South Carolina School of Law J.D. 1963. Admitted to practice South Carolina 1963. In legal practice Mullins 1963-80. Judge, South Carolina Circuit Court Twelfth Judicial Circuit 1980-94. Captain U.S. Army (Armor). Member House of Representatives 1967-77 and Senate 1977-80 South Carolina.

Mailing address: P.O. Box 1059, Marion 29571-1059.

Office: 103 North Main Street, Marion 29571.

Telephone: (843) 423-8250.

Fax: (843) 423-6068

WESTBROOK, Marc H. *(Judge, South Carolina Circuit Court Eleventh Judicial Circuit)* Elected by General Assembly Feb 2, 1994 to term beginning July 1, 1994. Reelected Feb 9, 2000, current term expires June 30, 2006. Born Charleston South Carolina Oct 3, 1946. Southern Baptist. Educated at University of South Carolina B.A. 1969 J.D. 1973. Admitted to practice South Carolina 1973, U.S. District Court District of South Carolina and U.S. Court of Appeals Fourth Circuit. In legal practice West Columbia 1973-83. Judge, Springdale Municipal Court 1974-75. Judge, South Carolina Family Court Eleventh Judicial Circuit 1983-94.

Member South Carolina Bar. Attended The National Judicial College: "General Jurisdiction" Reno Nevada Sept 25, 1994 to Oct 14, 1994, "Advanced Evidence" Charleston South Carolina Nov 13-18, 1994 and "Handling Capital Cases" Orlando Florida Jan 15-20, 1995. Chairman Lexington County Council 1976-78. Member House of Representatives South Carolina 1978-83. Music Director and Deacon Springdale Baptist Church. President Midland Dixie Youth Baseball and Springdale PTA.

Office: 209 Lexington County Courthouse, 139 East Main Street, Lexington 29072-3456.

Telephone: (803) 359-8239.

Fax: (803) 359-8444

WILLIAMS, Branna Woodward *(Judge, Barnwell County Probate Court)*

Office: 108 Barnwell County Courthouse, Barnwell 29812-1899.

Telephone: (803) 541-1032.

Fax: (803) 541-1012

WILLIAMS, H. Bruce *(Judge, South Carolina Family Court Fifth Judicial Circuit)* Assumed office 1995. Term expires 2004.

Mailing address: P.O. Box 192, Columbia 29202-0192.

Office: 1701 Main Street, Columbia 29201.

Telephone: (803) 576-1752.

Fax: (803) 576-1755

WILLIAMS, James C., Jr. *(Judge, South Carolina Circuit Court First Judicial Circuit)*

Mailing address: P.O. Box 1949, Orangeburg 29116-1949.

Office: 190 Gibson Street, Room 207, Orangeburg 29115.

Telephone: (803) 535-2187.

Fax: (803) 535-2188

WOODS, Henry T. *(Judge, South Carolina Family Court Sixteenth Judicial Circuit)*

Mailing address: P.O. Box 11746, Rock Hill 29731-1746.

Office: 1070 West Heckle Boulevard, Suite 202, Rock Hill 29732.

Telephone: (803) 909-7117.

Fax: (803) 909-7118

WOOTEN, Terry L. *(Judge, United States District Court District of South Carolina)* Magistrate Judge June

WOOTEN, TERRY L.—*Continued*

1, 1999 to Dec 2001. Appointed Judge for life by President George W. Bush to term beginning Dec 3, 2001.

Office: Federal Courthouse, 401 West Evans Street, Florence 29501.

Telephone: (843) 676-3812.

WYLIE, William J., Jr. *(Judge, South Carolina Family Court First Judicial Circuit)* Term expires 2004. Former Judge, Dorchester County Probate Court.

Office: 212 Deming Way, Box 4, Summerville 29483-4707.

Telephone: (843) 832-1659.

Fax: (843) 832-0368

YOUNG, Roger M. *(Judge, South Carolina Circuit Court Ninth Judicial Circuit)* Elected by General Assembly to term beginning May 29, 2003. Term expires 2009. Born Cass City Michigan Feb 15, 1960. Educated at Charleston Southern University B.S. 1980 and University of South Carolina School of Law J.D. 1983. Judge, North Charleston Municipal Court 1988-90.

Office: 368 County Judicial Center, 100 Broad Street, Charleston 29401.

Telephone: (843) 958-2015.

Fax: (843) 958-5108

ZORN, Kathy P. *(Judge, Pickens County Probate Court)*

Office: 222 McDaniel Avenue, B-16, Pickens 29671.

Telephone: (864) 898-5903.

Fax: (864) 898-5924

SOUTH DAKOTA

Capital PIERRE

UNITED STATES DISTRICT COURT DISTRICT OF SOUTH DAKOTA

The United States District Court District of South Dakota consists of four divisions. For descriptive information refer to the United States Courts section.

Central Division includes Buffalo, Dewey, Faulk, Gregory, Haakon, Hand, Hughes, Hyde, Jerauld, Jones, Lyman, Mellette, Potter, Stanley, Sully, Todd, Tripp and Ziebach counties. The court sits at Pierre.

Northern Division includes Brown, Campbell, Clark, Codington, Corson, Day, Deuel, Edmunds, Grant, Hamlin, Marshall, McPherson, Roberts, Spink and Walworth counties. The court sits at Aberdeen.

Southern Division includes Aurora, Beadle, Bon Homme, Brookings, Brule, Charles Mix, Clay, Davison, Douglas, Hanson, Hutchinson, Kingsbury, Lake, Lincoln, McCook, Miner, Minnehaha, Moody, Sanborn, Turner, Union and Yankton counties. The court sits at Sioux Falls.

Western Division includes Bennett, Butte, Custer, Fall River, Harding, Jackson, Lawrence, Meade, Pennington, Perkins and Shannon counties. The court sits at Deadwood and Rapid City.

Chief Judge
Lawrence L. Piersol

Judges
Charles B. Kornmann
Karen E. Schreier

Senior Judges
Andrew W. Bogue
John Bailey Jones
Richard H. Battey

Clerk
Joseph A. Haas
128 U.S. Courthouse
400 South Phillips Avenue
Sioux Falls, South Dakota 57104-6851
(605) 330-4447

UNITED STATES MAGISTRATE JUDGES OF SOUTH DAKOTA

Marshall P. Young
Mark A. Moreno
John E. Simko
Myles J. Devine

UNITED STATES BANKRUPTCY COURT OF SOUTH DAKOTA

Chief Judge
Irvin N. Hoyt

Bankruptcy Clerk
Charles L. Nail, Jr.
P.O. Box 5060
Sioux Falls, South Dakota 57117-5060
(605) 330-4541

SOUTH DAKOTA SUPREME COURT

The Supreme Court is South Dakota's court of last resort. The court consists of a chief justice and four associate justices. Since passage of a constitutional amendment in 1980, vacancies are filled by the governor from nominations of the Judicial Qualifications Commission. The state is divided into five electoral districts; one justice is appointed from each electoral district and must reside in that district. After qualifying, justices serve initial three-year terms and then stand for retention at statewide elections for staggered eight-year terms. The chief justice is elected by peer vote for a four-year term. Retirement is mandatory at age seventy; however, retired justices may serve by assignment of the court.

The court has original jurisdiction in cases involving interests of the state and exclusive appellate jurisdiction over the Circuit Court. The court may render advisory opinions to the governor involving the exercise of his executive powers. The court has authority to supervise admission to the bar and the conduct of its members and has general administrative and rule-making authority over the lower courts. The court may issue writs necessary to the exercise of proper jurisdiction.

The court sits en banc at Pierre or elsewhere as required and recesses in June, July, August and December.

ELECTORAL DISTRICT ONE includes Bennett, Custer, Fall River, Lawrence, Meade, Pennington and Shannon counties.

ELECTORAL DISTRICT TWO includes Lincoln, McCook, Minnehaha and Turner counties.

ELECTORAL DISTRICT THREE includes Beadle, Brookings, Codington, Deuel, Haakon, Hamlin, Hand, Hughes, Hyde, Jerauld, Kingsbury, Lake, Miner, Moody, Sanborn, Stanley and Sully counties.

ELECTORAL DISTRICT FOUR includes Aurora, Bon Homme, Brule, Buffalo, Charles Mix, Clay, Davison, Douglas, Gregory, Hanson, Hutchinson, Jackson, Jones, Lyman, Mellette, Todd, Tripp, Union and Yankton counties.

ELECTORAL DISTRICT FIVE includes Brown, Butte, Campbell, Clark, Corson, Day, Dewey, Edmunds, Faulk, Grant, Harding, Marshall, McPherson, Perkins, Potter, Roberts, Spink, Walworth and Ziebach counties.

Chief Justice
David Gilbertson (Fifth District)

SOUTH DAKOTA SUPREME COURT—*Continued*

Associate Justices
Richard W. Sabers (Second District)
John K. Konenkamp (First District)
Steven Zinter (Third District)
Judith Meierhenry (Fourth District)

Clerk
Shirley Jameson-Fergel
500 East Capitol Avenue
Pierre, South Dakota 57501-5070
(605) 773-3511

Court Administrator
D. J. Hanson
500 East Capitol Avenue
Pierre, South Dakota 57501-5070
(605) 773-3474

SOUTH DAKOTA CIRCUIT COURTS

The Circuit Courts are South Dakota's courts of general jurisdiction. Judges are elected by the voters of their circuits on a nonpartisan ballot for eight-year terms. Vacancies are filled by the governor from nominations of the Judicial Qualifications Commission. A presiding judge in each judicial circuit is appointed by and serves at the pleasure of the chief justice to handle supervisory and administrative duties. Retirement is mandatory at age seventy; however, retired judges may serve by assignment of the court.

The courts have exclusive original jurisdiction in all felony cases and in civil cases involving disputes of title or boundary of real property; divorce or annulment of marriage; probate, guardianship and settlement of estates; juvenile proceedings; and disputes in which the amount in controversy exceeds $8,000. The courts have concurrent jurisdiction with the Magistrate Courts over misdemeanor cases and minor civil actions and appellate jurisdiction over appeals from the Magistrate Courts.

The courts sit at each county seat.

FIRST JUDICIAL CIRCUIT includes Aurora, Bon Homme, Brule, Buffalo, Charles Mix, Clay, Davison, Douglas, Hanson, Hutchinson, McCook, Turner, Union and Yankton counties. The court sits at Plankinton, Tyndall, Chamberlain, Gann Valley, Lake Andes, Vermillion, Mitchell, Armour, Alexandria, Olivet, Salem, Parker, Elk Point and Yankton.

Presiding Judge
Arthur L. Rusch

Judges
Lee Anderson
Glen W. Eng
Boyd Leiper McMurchie
Ron Miller

SECOND JUDICIAL CIRCUIT includes Lincoln and Minnehaha counties. The court sits at Canton and Sioux Falls.

Presiding Judge
Glen A. Severson

Judges
Kathleen Caldwell
Peter Lieberman
William Srstka
Gene Paul Kean
Joseph Neiles
Stuart L. Tiede

THIRD JUDICIAL CIRCUIT includes Beadle, Brookings, Clark, Codington, Deuel, Grant, Hamlin, Hand, Jerauld, Kingsbury, Lake, Miner, Moody and Sanborn counties. The court sits at Huron, Brookings, Clark, Watertown, Clear Lake, Milbank, Hayti, Miller, Wessington Springs, De Smet, Madison, Howard, Flandreau and Woonsocket.

Presiding Judge
Rodney Steele

Judges
Jon R. Erickson
David Gienapp
Ronald Roehr
Robert Timm
Tim Tucker

FOURTH JUDICIAL CIRCUIT includes Butte, Corson, Dewey, Harding, Lawrence, Meade, Perkins and Ziebach counties. The court sits at Belle Fourche, McIntosh, Timber Lake, Buffalo, Deadwood, Sturgis, Bison and Dupree.

Presiding Judge
Warren G. Johnson

Judges
John Bastian
Jerome Eckrich
Timothy Robert Johns

FIFTH JUDICIAL CIRCUIT includes Brown, Campbell, Day, Edmunds, Faulk, Marshall, McPherson, Roberts, Spink and Walworth counties. The court sits at Aberdeen, Mound City, Webster, Ipswich, Faulkton, Britton, Leola, Sisseton, Redfield and Selby.

Presiding Judge
Eugene E. Dobberpuhl

Judges
Jon Flemmer
Larry Lovrien
Jack R. Von Wald

SIXTH JUDICIAL CIRCUIT includes Bennett, Gregory, Haakon, Hughes, Hyde, Jackson, Jones, Lyman, Mellette, Potter, Stanley, Sully, Todd (attached to Tripp) and Tripp counties. The court sits at Martin, Burke, Philip, Pierre, Highmore, Kadoka, Murdo, Kennebec, White River, Gettysburg, Fort Pierre, Onida and Winner.

Presiding Judge
Max A. Gors

Judges
James Wallace Anderson
Kathleen F. Trandahl
Lori Wilbur

SEVENTH JUDICIAL CIRCUIT includes Custer, Fall River, Pennington and Shannon (attached to Fall River) counties. The court sits at Custer, Hot Springs and Rapid City.

Presiding Judge
Thomas Trimble

SOUTH DAKOTA CIRCUIT COURTS—*Continued*

Judges
Jeff W. Davis
John J. Delaney
A. Peter Fuller
Janine Kern
Merton B. Tice, Jr.

SOUTH DAKOTA MAGISTRATE COURTS

The Magistrate Courts are South Dakota's courts of limited jurisdiction and are established in each judicial circuit. Magistrates are appointed by the circuit's presiding judge upon approval of the Supreme Court. Law-trained magistrates are appointed for four-year terms; lay magistrates serve at the pleasure of the presiding judge. Retirement is mandatory at age seventy.

The courts have concurrent jurisdiction with the Circuit Courts to fix bond, to conduct preliminary hearings and to accept pleas of not guilty, nolo contendere and guilty in any criminal offense or violation of an ordinance when the punishment is a fine not exceeding $100 and/or imprisonment not exceeding thirty days. The courts hear uncontested small claims and civil actions not exceeding $8,000. Law-trained magistrates have additional concurrent jurisdiction with the Circuit Courts to act as committing magistrates in all cases and to hear misdemeanor cases and all contested civil actions not exceeding $10,000, and small claims cases not exceeding $8,000.

The circuit boundaries are the same as those of the Circuit Courts.

South Dakota Counties and County Seats

Aurora
Plankinton

Beadle
Huron

Bennett
Martin

Bon Homme
Tyndall

Brookings
Brookings

Brown
Aberdeen

Brule
Chamberlain

Buffalo
Gann Valley

Butte
Belle Fourche

Campbell
Mound City

Charles Mix
Lake Andes

Clark
Clark

Clay
Vermillion

Codington
Watertown

Corson
McIntosh

Custer
Custer

Davison
Mitchell

Day
Webster

Deuel
Clear Lake

Dewey
Timber Lake

Douglas
Armour

Edmunds
Ipswich

Fall River
Hot Springs

Faulk
Faulkton

Grant
Milbank

Gregory
Burke

Haakon
Philip

Hamlin
Hayti

Hand
Miller

Hanson
Alexandria

Harding
Buffalo

Hughes
Pierre

Hutchinson
Olivet

Hyde
Highmore

Jackson
Kadoka

Jerauld
Wessington Springs

Jones
Murdo

Kingsbury
De Smet

Lake
Madison

Lawrence
Deadwood

Lincoln
Canton

Lyman
Kennebec

Marshall
Britton

McCook
Salem

McPherson
Leola

Meade
Sturgis

Mellette
White River

Miner
Howard

Minnehaha
Sioux Falls

Moody
Flandreau

Pennington
Rapid City

Perkins
Bison

Potter
Gettysburg

Roberts
Sisseton

COUNTIES AND COUNTY SEATS—*Continued*

Sanborn
Woonsocket

Shannon
Attached to Fall River

Spink
Redfield

Stanley
Fort Pierre

Sully
Onida

Todd
Attached to Tripp

Tripp
Winner

Turner
Parker

Union
Elk Point

Walworth
Selby

Yankton
Yankton

Ziebach
Dupree

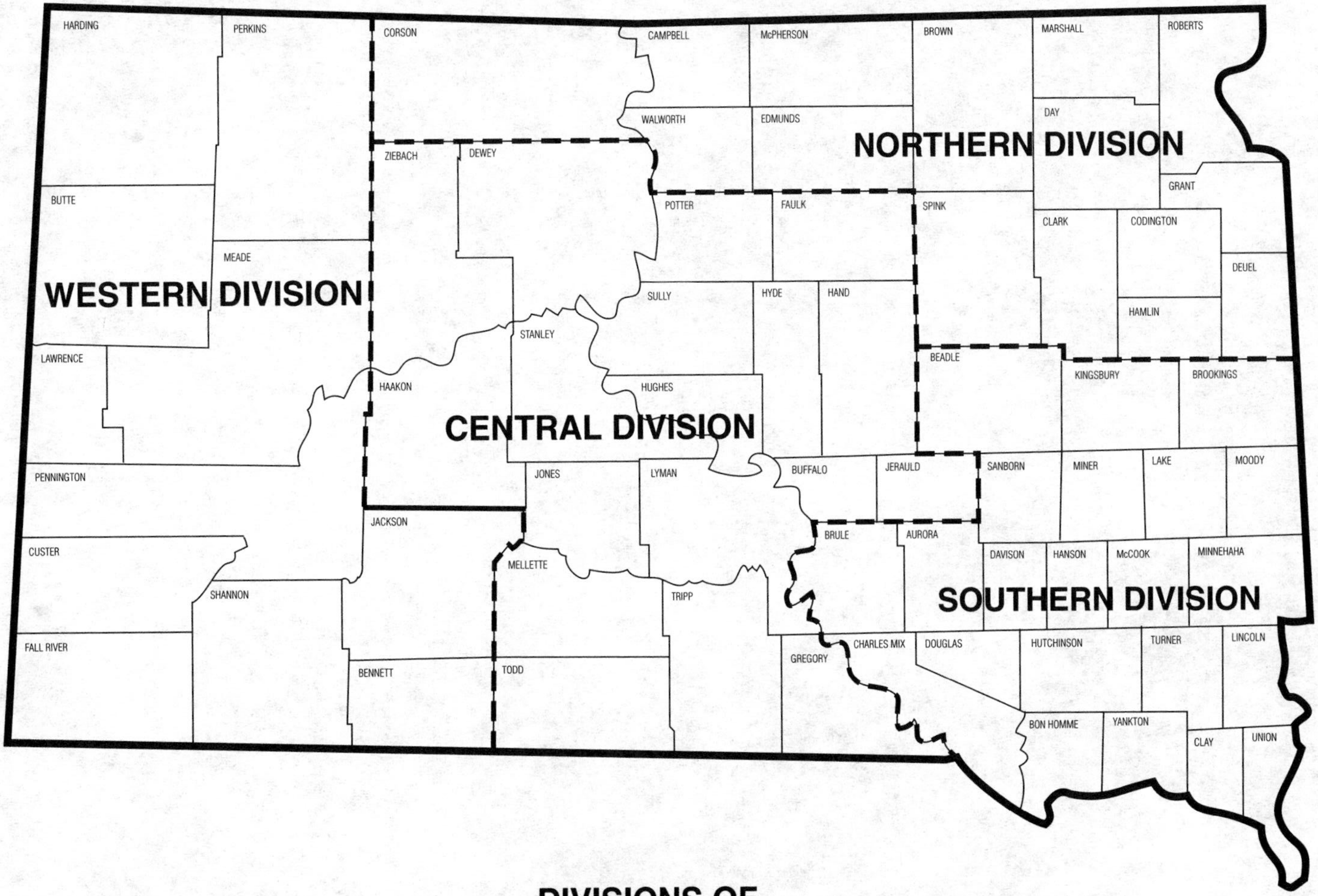
HARDING
PERKINS
CORSON
CAMPBELL
McPHERSON
BROWN
MARSHALL
ROBERTS
DAY
WALWORTH
EDMUNDS
NORTHERN DIVISION
ZIEBACH
DEWEY
GRANT
BUTTE
POTTER
FAULK
SPINK
CLARK
CODINGTON
MEADE
DEUEL
WESTERN DIVISION
SULLY
HYDE
HAND
HAMLIN
STANLEY
LAWRENCE
BEADLE
KINGSBURY
BROOKINGS
HAAKON
HUGHES
CENTRAL DIVISION
PENNINGTON
JONES
LYMAN
BUFFALO
JERAULD
SANBORN
MINER
LAKE
MOODY
JACKSON
BRULE
AURORA
CUSTER
DAVISON
HANSON
McCOOK
MINNEHAHA
MELLETTE
SHANNON
TRIPP
SOUTHERN DIVISION
FALL RIVER
CHARLES MIX
DOUGLAS
HUTCHINSON
TURNER
LINCOLN
GREGORY
BENNETT
TODD
BON HOMME
YANKTON
CLAY
UNION

DIVISIONS OF
UNITED STATES DISTRICT COURT DISTRICT OF SOUTH DAKOTA

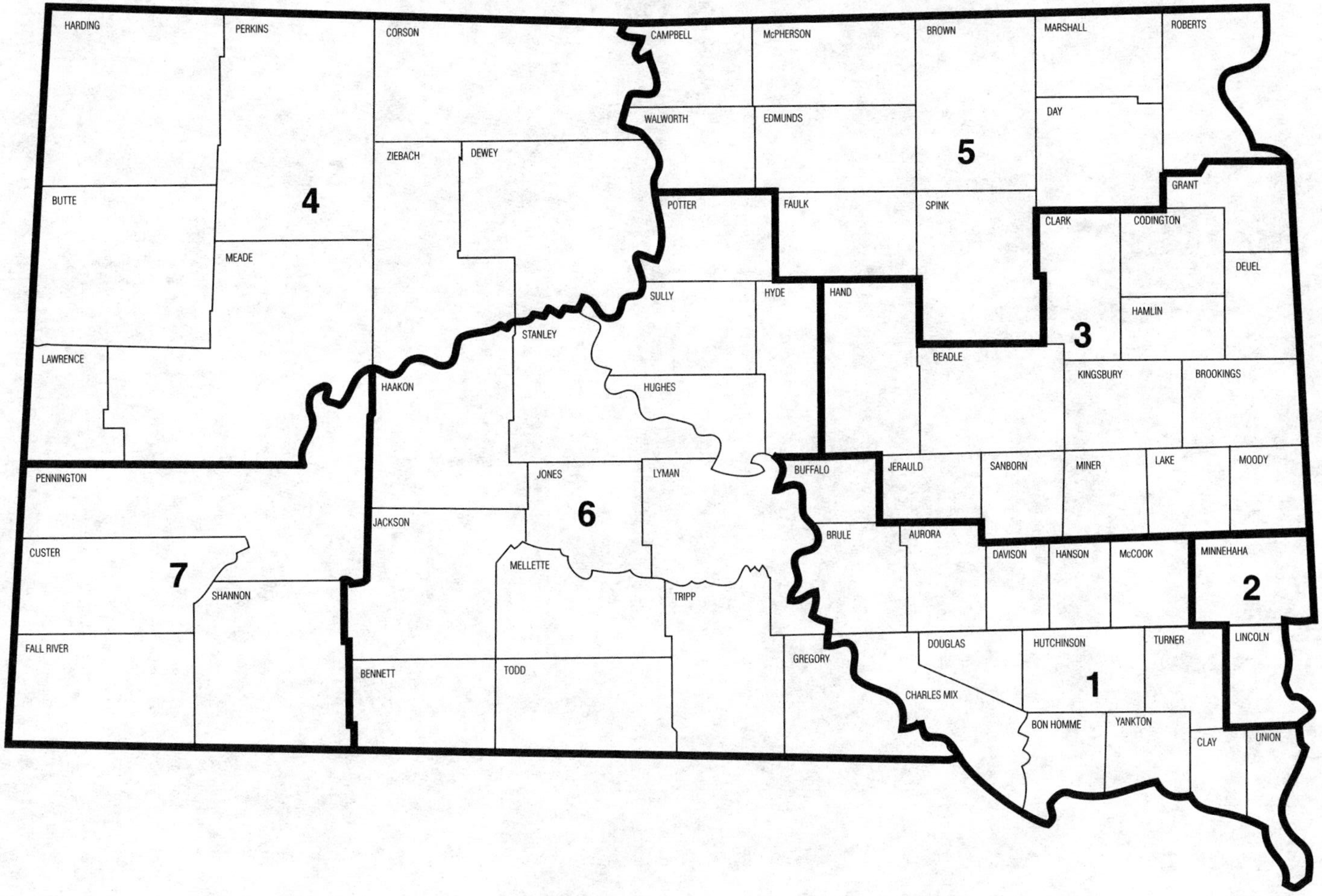
HARDING
PERKINS
CORSON
CAMPBELL
McPHERSON
BROWN
MARSHALL
ROBERTS
WALWORTH
EDMUNDS
DAY
5
ZIEBACH
DEWEY
BUTTE
4
POTTER
FAULK
SPINK
GRANT
CLARK
CODINGTON
MEADE
DEUEL
SULLY
HYDE
HAND
HAMLIN
3
STANLEY
LAWRENCE
BEADLE
KINGSBURY
BROOKINGS
HAAKON
HUGHES
PENNINGTON
JONES
LYMAN
BUFFALO
JERAULD
SANBORN
MINER
LAKE
MOODY
6
JACKSON
CUSTER
BRULE
AURORA
DAVISON
HANSON
McCOOK
MINNEHAHA
MELLETTE
7
SHANNON
TRIPP
2
FALL RIVER
DOUGLAS
HUTCHINSON
TURNER
LINCOLN
GREGORY
BENNETT
TODD
1
CHARLES MIX
BON HOMME
YANKTON
CLAY
UNION

JUDICIAL CIRCUITS OF SOUTH DAKOTA CIRCUIT COURTS

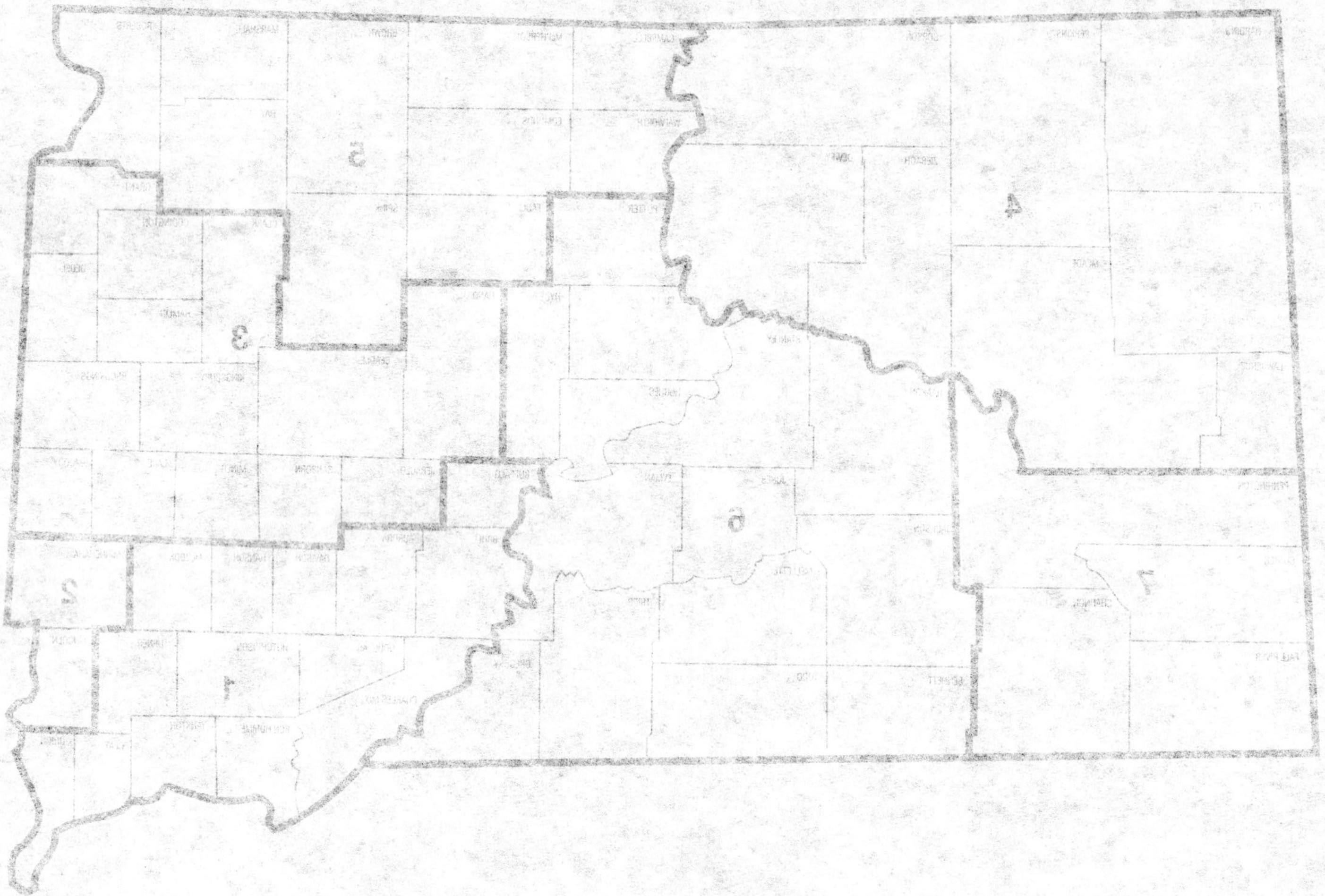
1
2
3
4
5
6
7

JUDICIAL CIRCUITS OF SOUTH DAKOTA CIRCUIT COURTS

SOUTH DAKOTA

ANDERSON, James Wallace *(Judge, South Dakota Circuit Court Sixth Judicial Circuit)* Appointed by Governor William J. Janklow Dec 1, 1981. Elected 1982, 1990 and 1998. Current term expires Jan 1, 2007. Presiding Judge Dec 1986 to July 1988. Born Philip South Dakota Oct 2, 1945. Lutheran. Educated at University of South Dakota B.A. 1967 J.D. 1974. Admitted to practice South Dakota 1975. Began legal practice Philip 1975. Magistrate, South Dakota Magistrate Court Sixth Judicial District 1977-81.

Member The State Bar of South Dakota. Captain USMC 1968-71. Enjoys reading, running, scuba diving, golf and skiing.

Mailing address: P.O. Box 1238, Pierre 57501-1238.
Telephone: (605) 773-3711.
Fax: (605) 773-6492

ANDERSON, Lee *(Judge, South Dakota Circuit Court First Judicial Circuit)*
Office: 200 East Fourth Avenue, Mitchell 57301-2692.
Telephone: (605) 995-8102.
Fax: (605) 995-8112

BASTIAN, John *(Judge, South Dakota Circuit Court Fourth Judicial Circuit)*
Mailing address: P.O. Box 237, Belle Fourche 57717-0237.
Telephone: (605) 892-2516.
Fax: (605) 892-2836

BATTEY, Richard H. *(Senior Judge, United States District Court District of South Dakota)* Appointed for life by President Ronald Reagan to term beginning 1985. Chief Judge 1994-98. Assumed Senior status Jan 1, 2000, serves by assignment. Born Aberdeen South Dakota Oct 16, 1929. Educated at University of South Dakota School of Law J.D. 1953. In legal practice Redfield 1955-85.

City Attorney Redfield 1956-63. State's Attorney Spink County 1959-65 and 1981-85. Lieutenant U.S. Army 1953-55.

Office: 318 Federal Building, 515 Ninth Street, Rapid City 57701.
Telephone: (605) 343-7784.

BOGUE, Andrew W. *(Senior Judge, United States District Court District of South Dakota)* Appointed for life by President Richard M. Nixon to term beginning 1970. Chief Judge 1980-85. Assumed Senior status July 1, 1985, serves by assignment. Born Yankton South Dakota May 23, 1919. Educated at South Dakota State College B.S. 1941 and University of South Dakota School of Law LL.B. 1947. In legal practice Parker 1947-50 and 1954-57 and Canton 1957-67.

State's Attorney Turner County 1952-54. U.S. Army Signal Corps 1943-46. Lieutenant U.S. Army JAGC 1950-52.

Office: 244 Federal Building, 515 Ninth Street, Rapid City 57701.
Telephone: (605) 343-5750.

CALDWELL, Kathleen *(Judge, South Dakota Circuit Court Second Judicial Circuit)* Former Judge, First Judicial Circuit. Assumed office Second Judicial Circuit July 1, 2000.

Office: 425 North Dakota Avenue, Sioux Falls 57104-2400.
Telephone: (605) 367-5920.

DAVIS, Jeff W. *(Judge, South Dakota Circuit Court Seventh Judicial Circuit)* Appointed to term beginning April 1, 1976. Elected to subsequent terms. Born Rapid City South Dakota Feb 12, 1948. Protestant. Educated at South Dakota School of Mines and Technology 1967 and University of South Dakota B.S. 1970 J.D. 1973. Admitted to practice South Dakota 1973. Began legal practice Rapid City 1973.

Law Clerk to South Dakota Circuit Court Seventh Judicial Circuit 1973-75. Member The State Bar of South Dakota and American Bar Association.

Mailing address: P.O. Box 230, Rapid City 57709-0230.
Telephone: (605) 394-2571.
Fax: (605) 394-6628

DELANEY, John J. *(Judge, South Dakota Circuit Court Seventh Judicial Circuit)*
Mailing address: P.O. Box 230, Rapid City 57709-0230.
Telephone: (605) 394-2571.
Fax: (605) 394-6628

DEVINE, Myles J. *(Magistrate Judge, United States District Court District of South Dakota)* Appointed by U.S. District Court judges to term beginning Jan 1, 2001.
Mailing address: P.O. Box 922, Britton 57430.
Telephone: (605) 448-2742.

DOBBERPUHL, Eugene E. *(Presiding Judge, South Dakota Circuit Court Fifth Judicial Circuit)* Elected to term beginning Jan 7, 1975. Reelected 1982, 1990 and 1998. Current term expires 2006. Born Verdon South Dakota April 9, 1933. Lutheran. Educated at South Dakota State University B.S. 1959 and University of South Dakota LL.B. 1963. Admitted to practice South Dakota 1963. In legal practice Conde 1963-64, Groton 1964-65 and Aberdeen 1965-66. Judge, Aberdeen Municipal Court 1967-77. USAF 1952-56.

Mailing address: P.O. Box 1087, Aberdeen 57402-1087.
Office: 101 Southeast First Avenue, Aberdeen 57402-4203.
Telephone: (605) 626-2450.
Fax: (605) 626-2491

ECKRICH, Jerome *(Judge, South Dakota Circuit Court Fourth Judicial Circuit)*
Mailing address: P.O. Box 939, Sturgis 57785-0939.
Telephone: (605) 347-4413.
Fax: (605) 347-3526

ENG, Glen W. *(Judge, South Dakota Circuit Court First Judicial Circuit)* Appointed by Governor William J. Janklow to term beginning Oct 6, 2000. Born Flandreau South Dakota Dec 12, 1950. Lutheran. Educated at University of South Dakota B.A. 1974 J.D. 1980. Ad-

ENG, GLEN W.—*Continued*

mitted to practice South Dakota 1981. In legal practice Flandreau 1981-2000.
State's Attorney Moody County 1985-2000.
Mailing address: P.O. Box 63, Yankton 57078-0063.
Telephone: (605) 668-3614.
Fax (605) 668-5424

ERICKSON, Jon R. *(Judge, South Dakota Circuit Court Third Judicial Circuit)* Appointed by Governor George S. Mickelson to term beginning March 1988. Elected Nov 1990 and 1998. Current term expires 2006. Born Watertown South Dakota May 10, 1950. Lutheran. Educated at University of South Dakota B.A. 1972 J.D. 1975. Admitted to practice South Dakota 1975, U.S. District Court District of South Dakota 1975, U.S. Court of Appeals Eighth Circuit 1975 and U.S. Supreme Court 1986. In legal practice Chamberlain 1975-80.
Assistant Attorney General 1980-87. Assistant U.S. Attorney 1987-88. Member Corrections Review Commission 1991. Vice Chairman South Dakota Corrections Commission 1992-93. Member Ethics Committee South Dakota Judges Association. Member The State Bar of South Dakota. Lecturer on Child Abuse Trial Tactics Wyoming Attorney General's Office CLE 1985 and Effective Advocacy Quasi-Judicial Proceedings The State Bar of South Dakota CLE 1987. Roustabout Park Department Sioux Falls 1968-75. Member 1981-85 and Chairman 1985-87 South Dakota Board of Pardons and Paroles. Enjoys sailing, cross-country skiing, bicycling, hunting, winter croquet, kayaking and reading.
Mailing address: P.O. Box 1358, Huron 57350-1358.
Telephone: (605) 353-7171.
Fax: (605) 353-7335

FLEMMER, Jon *(Judge, South Dakota Circuit Court Fifth Judicial Circuit)*
Office: 711 West First Street, Webster 57274-1359.
Telephone: (605) 626-2450.
Fax: (605) 345-3818

FULLER, A. Peter *(Judge, South Dakota Circuit Court Seventh Judicial Circuit)*
Mailing address: P.O. Box 230, Rapid City 57709-0230.
Telephone: (605) 394-2571.
Fax: (605) 394-6628

GIENAPP, David *(Judge, South Dakota Circuit Court Third Judicial Circuit)*
Office: 314 Sixth Avenue, Brookings 57006-2041.
Telephone: (605) 688-5705.
Fax: (605) 688-4838

GILBERTSON, David *(Chief Justice, South Dakota Supreme Court)* Appointed by Governor William J. Janklow to term beginning 1995. Retained by election 1998, current term expires Jan 1, 2007. Born Milwaukee Wisconsin Oct 29, 1949. Lutheran. Educated at South Dakota State University B.S. with high honors 1972 and University of South Dakota J.D. 1975. Lead Articles Editor South Dakota Law Review 1974-75. Admitted to practice South Dakota 1975, U.S. District Court District of South Dakota 1975, U.S. Court of Appeals Eighth Circuit 1984 and U.S. Supreme Court 1985. In legal practice Sisseton 1975-86. Judge, South Dakota Circuit Court Fifth Judicial Circuit 1986-95.
Office: 500 East Capitol Avenue, Pierre 57501-5070.
Telephone: (605) 773-4885.

GORS, Max A. *(Presiding Judge, South Dakota Circuit Court Sixth Judicial Circuit)* Elected Nov 6, 1990 to term beginning Jan 7, 1991. Reelected Nov 3, 1998, current term expires Jan 2006. Born Viborg South Dakota Jan 21, 1945. Lutheran. Educated at Augustana College B.A. 1967 and Drake University J.D. with honors 1970. Staff member Drake Law Review 1968-70. Member Delta Theta Phi. Admitted to practice Iowa 1970, U.S. Court of Appeals Eighth Circuit 1970, South Dakota 1971, U.S. District Court District of South Dakota 1971 and U.S. Supreme Court 1973. In legal practice Pierre South Dakota 1978-90. Magistrate Judge, South Dakota Magistrate Court Sixth Judicial Circuit 1989-91.
Assistant Attorney General Iowa and South Dakota 1970-75. Author "Criminal Pretrial Discovery in Iowa" 19 Drake L. Rev. 164, 1969, "Water Distribution" 20 Drake L. Rev. 256, 1970 and *Juvenile and Correctional Law Sourcebook* 1979-89. Instructor in Criminal Law, Procedure and Criminal Justice University of South Dakota 1975-80 and Business Law Northern University 1994-2000. Member South Dakota Judges Association (President 1997-98), The State Bar of South Dakota (Chairman Real Property, Probate and Trust Section 1988-89) and Iowa State Bar Association. Lecturer "Farm Crisis" April 25, 1986, "Legislative Update" June 22, 1989 and "South Dakota Guardianship and Conservatorship Act" June 17, 1993 The State Bar of South Dakota. Named Friend of Law Enforcement by South Dakota Peace Officers Association 1988. Recipient Satnam-Canary Award from South Dakota Corrections Association 1998 and Muriel Himrich Award from South Dakota Coin and Stamp Association 1998. Secretary of Commerce South Dakota 1975-78.
Mailing address: P.O. Box 1238, Pierre 57501-1238.
Telephone: (605) 773-3583.
Fax: (605) 773-6492
E-mail address: maxagors@aol.com

HOYT, Irvin N. *(Chief Judge, United States Bankruptcy Court District of South Dakota)*
Office: 211 U.S. Post Office & Courthouse, 225 South Pierre Street, Pierre 57501.
Telephone: (605) 224-0560.

JOHNS, Timothy Robert *(Judge, South Dakota Circuit Court Fourth Judicial Circuit)* Assumed office 1989. Born Aberdeen South Dakota July 17, 1948. Roman Catholic. Educated at Northern State College B.A. 1970 and University of South Dakota J.D. 1974. In legal practice Belle Fourche 1974-75. Magistrate, South Dakota Magistrate Court 1975-89.
Deputy States Attorney Butte County 1974-75. Attorney City of Nisland 1974-75. Member 1997-2001 and Secretary 1999-2001 South Dakota Judicial Qualifications Commission. Member South Dakota Judges Association (President 1995-96). Recipient Keyman Award from Deadwood—Lead Jaycees 1982-83. Member and President Deadwood—Lead Jaycees 1978-85. Member State Board South Dakota Special Olympics. Member Lead Kiwanis (President 2001-2002). Enjoys reading, hunting, fishing and boating.
Mailing address: P.O. Box 626, Deadwood 57732-0626.
Office: 78 Sherman Street, Deadwood 57732-1341.
Telephone: (605) 578-2044.

JOHNSON, Warren G. *(Presiding Judge, South Dakota Circuit Court Fourth Judicial Circuit)* Elected to

JOHNSON, WARREN G.—*Continued*
term beginning Jan 1, 1983. Reelected 1990 and 1998. Current term expires Dec 31, 2006. Born Flandreau South Dakota March 16, 1949. Lutheran. Educated at University of South Dakota B.A. 1971 J.D. 1974. Admitted to practice South Dakota 1974. Began legal practice Spearfish 1974.

Deputy State's Attorney Butte County April 1976 to Dec 1976 and Lawrence County Jan 1977 to Nov 1982. Member The State Bar of South Dakota. Enjoys hunting and fishing.

Mailing address: P.O. Box 626, Deadwood 57732-0626.
Telephone: (605) 578-2044.
Fax: (605) 578-3613

JONES, John Bailey *(Senior Judge, United States District Court District of South Dakota)* Appointed for life by President Ronald Reagan. Former Chief Judge. Assumed Senior status, serves by assignment. Born March 30, 1927. Methodist. Educated at University of South Dakota B.S. LL.B. Lyman County Judge 1953-56. Former Judge, South Dakota Circuit Court Sixth Judicial Circuit, appointed to term beginning 1967.

State Representative 1957 and 1959. Member American Judicature Society and The State Bar of South Dakota. USN 1945-47. Member American Legion, VFW, Elks and Lions.

Office: 303 U.S. Courthouse, 400 South Phillips Avenue, Sioux Falls 57104-6851.
Telephone: (605) 330-4563.

KEAN, Gene Paul *(Judge, South Dakota Circuit Court Second Judicial Circuit)* Former Presiding Judge.

Office: 425 North Dakota Avenue, Sioux Falls 57104-2400.
Telephone: (605) 367-5920.

KERN, Janine *(Judge, South Dakota Circuit Court Seventh Judicial Circuit)* Appointed by Governor William J. Janklow to term beginning Dec 1996. Elected 1998, current term expires Jan 2006. Born Yankton South Dakota Feb 14, 1961. Roman Catholic. Educated at Arizona State University B.S. summa cum laude 1982 and University of Minnesota J.D. cum laude 1985. Admitted to practice South Dakota 1986, U.S. District Court District of South Dakota 1986 and U.S. Court of Appeals Eighth Circuit 1986.

Assistant Attorney General 1985-93. Deputy Attorney General 1993-96.

Mailing address: P.O. Box 230, Rapid City 57709-0230.
Telephone: (605) 394-2571.
Fax: (605) 394-6628

KONENKAMP, John K. *(Associate Justice, South Dakota Supreme Court)* Appointed by Governor Walter D. Miller to term beginning 1994. Born Oct 20, 1944. Educated at University of South Dakota J.D. 1974. In legal practice 1977-84. Judge 1984-94 and Presiding Judge 1988-94, South Dakota Circuit Court Seventh Judicial Circuit, appointed by Governor William J. Janklow.

Deputy State Attorney Rapid City 1974-77. Member American Judicature Society, The State Bar of South Dakota and Pennington County Bar Association. Board Member Alternative Dispute Resolution Committee. Advisory Board Casey Family Program. Member American Legion and National CASA Association.

Office: 500 East Capitol Avenue, Pierre 57501.
Telephone: (605) 773-3511.

KORNMANN, Charles B. *(Judge, United States District Court District of South Dakota)* Appointed for life by President Bill Clinton 1995. Born Watertown South Dakota 1937. Educated at University of St. Thomas B.A. 1959 and Georgetown University Law Center LL.B. 1962. Member Phi Delta Phi. In legal practice Aberdeen 1965-95.

Part-time Assistant City Attorney Aberdeen 1970-86. Part-time Special Assistant Attorney General 1978-79. Member Judicial Elections Committee 1990. Former Member South Dakota Trial Lawyers Association, Association of Defense Trial Attorneys, Federation of Insurance and Corporate Counsel, National Chiropractic Attorneys Association and The Defense Research Institute, Inc. Member South Dakota State Bar Foundation (Director 1989-94, President 1994-95), American Board of Trial Advocates, Federal Judges Association, The State Bar of South Dakota (President 1988-89) and Brown County Bar Association. Captain South Dakota National Guard 1963-72 (retired). Policeman U.S. Capitol 1959-62. Executive Director South Dakota Democratic Party 1963-65. Delegate 1966 and 1968, Chairperson Platform Committee 1966 and Convention Chairperson 1968 South Dakota Democratic Convention. Member South Dakota Constitutional Revision Commission 1974-76. Legislative Aide to U.S. Senator George S. McGovern 1963. Campaign Assistant George S. McGovern U.S. Senate campaigns 1960 and 1962. Member South Dakota Citizens Commission on Executive Reorganization of State Government 1970-71. Member and President South Dakota Board of Charities and Corrections 1973-79. Former Member South Dakota Mining Association. Member Sacred Heart Catholic Church, Roncalli Boosters' Club, Moccasin Creek Country Club, Inc., University of St. Thomas Alumni Association and Georgetown University Alumni Association.

Office: 408 U.S. Post Office & Courthouse, 102 Fourth Avenue S.E., Aberdeen 57401.
Telephone: (605) 226-7280.
Fax: (605) 226-7478

LIEBERMAN, Peter *(Judge, South Dakota Circuit Court Second Judicial Circuit)*

Office: 425 North Dakota Avenue, Sioux Falls 57104-2400.
Telephone: (605) 367-5920.

LOVRIEN, Larry *(Judge, South Dakota Circuit Court Fifth Judicial Circuit)*

Mailing address: P.O. Box 1191, Aberdeen 57402-1191.
Telephone: (605) 626-2450.
Fax: (605) 626-2491

McMURCHIE, Boyd Leiper *(Judge, South Dakota Circuit Court First Judicial Circuit)* Elected to term beginning Jan 1975. Reelected 1982, 1990 and 1998. Current term expires Jan 5, 2007. Born Ontario Oregon July 9, 1937. Congregational United Church of Christ. Educated at University of South Dakota B.A. LL.B. Admitted to practice South Dakota 1963 and U.S. District Court District of South Dakota. In legal practice Chamberlain 1963-74. Part-time U.S. Magistrate 1965-73.

Brule County State's Attorney 1968-72. Lyman Coun-

MCMURCHIE, BOYD LEIPER—*Continued*

ty State's Attorney 1968-70. Member The State Bar of South Dakota. Member Elks, Blue Lodge, Consistory and Shriners. Enjoys reading, gardening and golf.

Office: 400 South Main Street, Parker 57053.
Telephone: (605) 297-4090.
Fax: (605) 297-2115

MEIERHENRY, Judith *(Associate Justice, South Dakota Supreme Court)* Appointed by governor. Born Burke South Dakota Jan 20, 1944. Lutheran. Educated at University of South Dakota B.A. 1966 M.A. 1968 J.D. 1977. Copy Editor University of South Dakota Law Review 1975-77. Admitted to practice South Dakota 1977 and U.S. District Court District of South Dakota 1988. In legal practice Vermillion 1977-79 and Pierre and Sioux Falls 1985-88. Former Judge and Presiding Judge, South Dakota Circuit Court Second Judicial Circuit, appointed by Governor George S. Mickelson Dec 1988.

Secretary of Labor South Dakota 1980-85. Secretary of Education and Cultural Affairs South Dakota 1984-85. Author "Teacher Dismissal" South Dakota L. Rev. 1976 and "The Due Process Right to an Unbiased Adjudicator in Administrative Proceedings" 36 South Dakota L. Rev. 551, 1991. Co-author *South Dakota Trial Handbook for Lawyers* Lawyers Cooperative Publishing 1994. Member The State Bar of South Dakota.

Office: 500 East Capitol Avenue, Pierre 57501.
Telephone: (605) 773-3511.

MILLER, Ron *(Judge, South Dakota Circuit Court First Judicial Circuit)*

Mailing address: P.O. Box 606, Plankinton 57368-0606.
Telephone: (605) 942-7729.
Fax: (605) 942-7170

MORENO, Mark A. *(Magistrate Judge, United States District Court District of South Dakota)* Appointed by U.S. District Court judges. Serves part time.

Office: 217 U.S. Post Office & Courthouse, 225 South Pierre Street, Pierre 57501.
Telephone: (605) 224-6314.

NEILES, Joseph *(Judge, South Dakota Circuit Court Second Judicial Circuit)* Appointed by Governor William J. Janklow to term beginning Aug 11, 1997. Elected Nov 3, 1998, current term expires Dec 31, 2006. Born Sioux Falls South Dakota May 21, 1951. Roman Catholic. Educated at University of South Dakota B.S. 1973 J.D. 1976. Admitted to practice South Dakota 1976, U.S. District Court District of South Dakota and U.S. Court of Appeals Eighth Circuit. In legal practice Rapid City 1976-81, Sioux Falls 1981-83 and Parker 1983-86. Magistrate Judge, South Dakota Magistrate Court Second Judicial Circuit 1986-97.

Assistant Public Defender Pennington County 1976-81. Public Defender Minnehaha County 1981-83. Member American Judicature Society, The State Bar of South Dakota (Former Chairman Criminal Law Committee and Indigent Defense Committee) and Second Circuit Bar Association.

Office: 425 North Dakota Avenue, Sioux Falls 57104.
Telephone: (605) 367-5920.
Fax: (605) 367-5979
E-mail address: joseph.neiles@ujs.state.sd.us

PIERSOL, Lawrence L. *(Chief Judge, United States District Court District of South Dakota)* Appointed for life by President Bill Clinton. Educated at University of Nebraska 1958-59 and University of South Dakota B.A. 1962 J.D. 1965. Admitted to practice South Dakota 1965.

Member The State Bar of South Dakota, Minnehaha County and American Bar Associations.

Office: 202 U.S. Courthouse, 400 South Phillips Avenue, Sioux Falls 57104-6851.
Telephone: (605) 330-4505.

ROEHR, Ronald *(Judge, South Dakota Circuit Court Third Judicial Circuit)*

Mailing address: P.O. Box 1054, Watertown 57201-1054.
Telephone: (605) 882-5090.
Fax: (605) 882-5106

RUSCH, Arthur L. *(Presiding Judge, South Dakota Circuit Court First Judicial Circuit)* Appointed by Governor Walter D. Miller to term beginning March 7, 1994. Elected 1998, current term expires Dec 31, 2006. Born Mitchell South Dakota March 16, 1946. Catholic. Educated at University of South Dakota B.S.B.A. 1968 J.D. with honors 1971. Law Clerk to Hon. Thomas Parker, South Dakota Circuit Court Seventh Judicial Circuit 1971-72. Member Phi Delta Phi. Admitted to practice South Dakota 1971 and U.S. District Court District of South Dakota 1971. In legal practice Vermillion 1972-94.

State's Attorney Clay County 1973-84. Special Assistant Attorney General South Dakota 1989-90. Author article 16 South Dakota L. Rev. 481, 1971 and *South Dakota Civil Process Manual* 1981. Important Decision: Christie v. Miller 524 N.W.2d 866, 1994. Former Member South Dakota Trial Lawyers Association. Member The State Bar of South Dakota (Trust Accounts Committee 1990-94) and American Bar Association (Section of Family Law 1992-94). Graduate Experienced Prosecutors Course National College of District Attorneys 1981, Trial Advocacy Course The Association of Trial Lawyers of America, Des Moines Iowa 1989 and General Jurisdiction Course The National Judicial College, Reno Nevada 1994. Captain U.S. Army 1968-76. Republican. Member County Executive Committee 1972-86. Delegate to State Conventions 1974, 1978, 1982 and 1986. Member Vermillion Lions Club, Vermillion Chamber of Commerce, Knights of Columbus (St. Agnes Council) and University of South Dakota Foundation. Enjoys sailing, hunting and reading.

Mailing address: P.O. Box 377, Vermillion 57069-0377.
Telephone: (605) 677-6757.
Fax: (605) 677-8885

SABERS, Richard W. *(Associate Justice, South Dakota Supreme Court)* Appointed by Governor William J. Janklow to term beginning March 1, 1986. Retained by election 1990 and 1998. Current term expires Dec 2006. Born Salem South Dakota Feb 12, 1938. Catholic. Educated at St. John's University B.A. 1960 and University of South Dakota J.D. 1966. Recipient Meisenholder Law Scholarship 1965. Editorial Board South Dakota Law Review 1965-66. Member Delta Theta Phi. Admitted to practice South Dakota 1966, U.S. District Court District of South Dakota and U.S. Court of Appeals Eighth Circuit. In legal practice Sioux Falls 1966-86.

Author "Constitutionality of the South Dakota Statute

SABERS, RICHARD W.—*Continued*

Making All Accredited High Schools Eligible for Membership in South Dakota H.S.I.A.A." 10 South Dakota L. Rev. 102 Spring 1965. Important Decisions: Hamaker v. Kenwel-Jackson (continuing corporate liability) 1986, Wells v. Billars (continuing treatment) 1986, Zacher v. Budd (open courts constitutional provision) 1986, Bego v. Gordon (sovereign immunity) 1987, Baatz v. Arrow Bar (Dram Shop constitutionality) 1988, Groseth v. Tenneco (franchise law) 410 N.W.2d 159 and Cozine v. Midwest Coast Transport (workmen's compensation law) 454 N.W.2d 548. Former member South Dakota Trial Lawyers Association. Member The State Bar of South Dakota and Second Judicial Circuit Bar Association (President 1982-83). Graduate Appellate Judges Seminar Institute of Judicial Administration New York University 1986 and 1992. Recipient Award for Outstanding Young Religious Leader (Layman) from Jaycees 1971. First Lieutenant U.S. Army Corps of Engineers 1960-62. Captain USAR 1963-69. Republican. State Representative North Dakota March of Dimes 1963. Advisory Board member St. Joseph Cathedral 1971-86. Board member East River Legal Services Corporation 1975-82. President St. John's University Alumni Association Sioux Falls area 1975-91. Board of Directors 1978-86 and Trustee 1983-86 O'Gorman Foundation. School Board member O'Gorman High School 1985-86. Member Lake Madison Development Association and Historic District Preservation Committee. Enjoys tennis, skiing, sailing, competitive sports and woodcarving.

Office: 500 East Capitol Avenue, Pierre 57501.
Telephone: (605) 773-3511.

SCHREIER, Karen E. *(Judge, United States District Court District of South Dakota)* Appointed for life by President Bill Clinton to term beginning Aug 13, 1999. Born Sioux Falls South Dakota July 29, 1956. Educated at St. Louis University A.B. 1978 J.D. 1981. Law Clerk to Hon. Francis G. Dunn, South Dakota Supreme Court 1981-82. In legal practice Sioux Falls 1982-93.

U.S. Attorney District of South Dakota 1993-99.

Office: 318 U.S. Courthouse, 515 Ninth Street, Rapid City 57701.
Telephone: (605) 343-3744.

SEVERSON, Glen A. *(Presiding Judge, South Dakota Circuit Court Second Judicial Circuit)* Appointed by Governor George S. Mickelson Nov 1992 to term beginning Feb 1, 1993. Elected 1998, current term expires Dec 31, 2006. Born Sioux Falls South Dakota March 9, 1949. Catholic. Educated at University of South Dakota B.S. 1972 J.D. 1975. Admitted to practice South Dakota 1975, Minnesota 1990, U.S. District Court District of South Dakota 1976 and U.S. Court of Appeals Eighth Circuit 1989. In legal practice Huron 1975-93.

Office: 425 North Dakota Avenue, Sioux Falls 57104-2400.
Telephone: (605) 367-5920.
Fax: (605) 367-5979

SIMKO, John E. *(Magistrate Judge, United States District Court District of South Dakota)* Appointed by U.S. District Court judges to term beginning Sept 1, 2000.

Office: 220 U.S. Courthouse, 400 South Phillips Avenue, Sioux Falls 57104.
Telephone: (605) 330-4389.

SRSTKA, William *(Judge, South Dakota Circuit Court Second Judicial Circuit)*

Office: 425 North Dakota Avenue, Sioux Falls 57104-2400.
Telephone: (605) 367-5920.
E-mail address: wjsrstka@earthlink.net

STEELE, Rodney *(Presiding Judge, South Dakota Circuit Court Third Judicial Circuit)*

Office: 314 Sixth Avenue, Brookings 57006-2041.
Telephone: (605) 688-4202.
Fax: (605) 688-4952

TICE, Merton B., Jr. *(Judge, South Dakota Circuit Court Seventh Judicial Circuit)* Elected 1974, 1982, 1990 and 1998. Current term expires 2006. Former Presiding Judge. Born Fort Benning Georgia March 31, 1943. Episcopalian. Educated at University of South Dakota B.A. 1965 LL.B. 1969. Staff member South Dakota Law Review. Law Clerk to Presiding Judge, South Dakota Supreme Court 1969-70. Member Phi Delta Phi and Phi Delta Theta. Admitted to practice South Dakota 1969 and Oklahoma 1970. In legal practice Pierre South Dakota 1969-70. Judge, Rapid City Municipal Court 1973-75.

Author "Enlightenment from Within: South Dakota's Experience with Victim's Rights" Pepperdine L. Rev. Former Deputy State's Attorney. Former City Attorney Rapid City. Member The State Bar of South Dakota and Pennington County Bar Association.

Mailing address: P.O. Box 230, Rapid City 57709-0230.
Telephone: (605) 394-2571.
Fax: (605) 394-6628

TIEDE, Stuart L. *(Judge, South Dakota Circuit Court Second Judicial Circuit)* Appointed by Governor William J. Janklow to term beginning Nov 16, 2001. Term expires Jan 1, 2007. Born Huron South Dakota Oct 9, 1948. Catholic. Educated at University of South Dakota B.A. 1970 J.D. 1975. Law Clerk to U.S. District Court District of South Dakota 1975-76. Admitted to practice South Dakota 1975, U.S. District Court District of South Dakota 1975, U.S. Courts of Appeals Eighth 1977 and Federal 1993 Circuits, U.S. Tax Court 1978 and U.S. Court of Federal Claims 1992. In legal practice Sioux Falls 1975-2001.

Former Member American Health Lawyers Association and American Bar Association. Member The State Bar of South Dakota.

Office: 425 North Dakota Avenue, Sioux Falls 57104.
Telephone: (605) 367-5920.
Fax: (605) 367-5979
E-mail address: Stuart.Tiede@ujs.state.sd.us

TIMM, Robert *(Judge, South Dakota Circuit Court Third Judicial Circuit)*

Mailing address: P.O. Box 1054, Watertown 57201-1054.
Telephone: (605) 882-5090.
Fax: (605) 882-5106

TRANDAHL, Kathleen F. *(Judge, South Dakota Circuit Court Sixth Judicial Circuit)* Appointed by Governor Walter D. Miller Dec 31, 1993 to term beginning March 4, 1994. Elected 1998, current term expires Jan 1, 2007. Born Huron South Dakota Aug 19, 1960. Catholic. Educated at Augustana College B.S. 1982 and University of South Dakota J.D. 1985. Law Clerk to Hon.

TRANDAHL, KATHLEEN F.—*Continued*

Dale Bradshaw South Dakota Circuit Court Third Judicial Circuit 1985-86. Admitted to practice South Dakota 1986 and U.S. District Court District of South Dakota 1986. In legal practice Winner 1986-94.

Deputy State's Attorney Tripp County 1986-88. Member South Dakota Trial Lawyers Association, American Judicature Society, The State Bar of South Dakota and American Bar Association. Member P.E.O. and Rotary.

Mailing address: P.O. Box 311, Winner 57580-0311.
Telephone: (605) 842-3856.
Fax: (605) 842-2267

TRIMBLE, Thomas *(Presiding Judge, South Dakota Circuit Court Seventh Judicial Circuit)* Appointed by governor.

Mailing address: P.O. Box 230, Rapid City 57709-0230.
Telephone: (605) 394-2571.
Fax: (605) 394-6628

TUCKER, Tim *(Judge, South Dakota Circuit Court Third Judicial Circuit)* Former Presiding Judge.

Mailing address: P.O. Box 507, Madison 57042-0507.
Telephone: (605) 256-5285.
Fax: (605) 256-5012

VON WALD, Jack R. *(Judge, South Dakota Circuit Court Fifth Judicial Circuit)* Appointed by Governor Walter D. Miller Dec 31, 1993 to term beginning March 7, 1994. Elected 1998, current term expires Jan 1, 2007. Born Aberdeen South Dakota Nov 2, 1943. Catholic. Educated at University of South Dakota B.S. 1965 J.D. 1967. Member Delta Theta Phi. Admitted to practice South Dakota 1967 and U.S. District Court District of South Dakota 1968. In legal practice Selby 1968-94.

Assistant Attorney General South Dakota 1967-68. Member American Judicature Society.

Mailing address: P.O. Box 328, Selby 57472-0328.
Telephone: (605) 649-7628.
Fax: (605) 649-7624

WILBUR, Lori *(Judge, South Dakota Circuit Court Sixth Judicial Circuit)*

Mailing address: P.O. Box 758, Fort Pierre 57532-0758.
Telephone: (605) 223-7777.
Fax: (605) 223-7738

YOUNG, Marshall P. *(Magistrate Judge, United States District Court District of South Dakota)* Appointed by U.S. District Court judges to term beginning June 10, 1992. Reappointed to subsequent terms. Serves part time. Born Aug 31, 1936. Educated at University of Iowa B.S.C. and University of Arizona J.D. Admitted to practice Arizona 1961 and South Dakota 1961. Began legal practice Rapid City South Dakota. Former County Judge and District County Judge. Judge 1974-92 and Presiding Judge 1979-88, South Dakota Circuit Court Seventh Judicial Circuit.

President National Council of Juvenile and Family Court Judges 1986. Faculty member National Juvenile Justice College 1970-88 and The National Judicial College 1978-87.

Office: 312 Federal Building, 515 Ninth Street, Rapid City 57701.
Telephone: (605) 343-6335.

ZINTER, Steven *(Associate Justice, South Dakota Supreme Court)* Appointed by Governor William J. Janklow April 2, 2002. Educated at University of South Dakota B.S. 1972 J.D. 1975. In legal practice Pierre 1978-86. Judge 1987-97 and Presiding Judge 1997-2002, South Dakota Circuit Court Sixth Judicial Circuit.

Office: 500 East Capitol Avenue, Pierre 57501-5070.
Telephone: (605) 773-3511.

TENNESSEE

Capital NASHVILLE

UNITED STATES DISTRICT COURTS DISTRICTS OF TENNESSEE

Within Tennessee there are three United States District Courts. For descriptive information refer to the United States Courts section.

EASTERN DISTRICT consists of four divisions.

Northeastern Division includes Carter, Cocke, Greene, Hamblen, Hancock, Hawkins, Johnson, Sullivan, Unicoi and Washington counties. The court sits at Greeneville.

Northern Division includes Anderson, Blount, Campbell, Claiborne, Grainger, Jefferson, Knox, Loudon, Monroe, Morgan, Roane, Scott, Sevier and Union counties. The court sits at Knoxville.

Southern Division includes Bledsoe, Bradley, Hamilton, Marion, McMinn, Meigs, Polk, Rhea and Sequatchie counties. The court sits at Chattanooga.

Winchester Division includes Bedford, Coffee, Franklin, Grundy, Lincoln, Moore, Van Buren and Warren counties. The court sits at Winchester.

Chief Judge
R. Allan Edgar

Judges
Curtis L. Collier
Thomas W. Phillips
Thomas A. Varlan

Senior Judges
Thomas G. Hull
James H. Jarvis, II
Leon Jordan

Clerk
Patricia L. McNutt
130 U.S. Courthouse
800 Market Street
Knoxville, Tennessee 37902
(865) 545-4228

MIDDLE DISTRICT consists of three divisions.

Columbia Division includes Giles, Hickman, Lawrence, Lewis, Marshall, Maury and Wayne counties. The court sits at Columbia.

Nashville Division includes Cannon, Cheatham, Davidson, Dickson, Houston, Humphreys, Montgomery, Robertson, Rutherford, Stewart, Sumner, Trousdale, Williamson and Wilson counties. The court sits at Nashville.

Northeastern Division includes Clay, Cumberland, DeKalb, Fentress, Jackson, Macon, Overton, Pickett, Putnam, Smith and White counties. The court sits at Cookeville.

Chief Judge
Robert L. Echols

Judges
Todd J. Campbell
Aleta A. Trauger
William J. Haynes, Jr.

Senior Judges
Thomas A. Wiseman, Jr.
John T. Nixon
Thomas A. Higgins

Clerk
Roger A. Milam
800 U.S. Courthouse
801 Broadway
Nashville, Tennessee 37203-3869
(615) 736-2364

WESTERN DISTRICT consists of two divisions.

Eastern Division includes Benton, Carroll, Chester, Crockett, Decatur, Gibson, Hardeman, Hardin, Haywood, Henderson, Henry, Lake, Madison, McNairy, Obion, Perry and Weakley counties. The Eastern Division also includes the waters of the Tennessee River to the low-water mark on the eastern shore where the river forms the boundary between the Middle and Western Districts from the north line of Alabama north to the point in Henry County, Tennessee where the south boundary of Kentucky strikes the east bank of the river. The court sits at Jackson.

Western Division includes Dyer, Fayette, Lauderdale, Shelby and Tipton counties. The court sits at Dyersburg and Memphis.

Chief Judge
James D. Todd

Judges
Jon Phipps McCalla
Bernice Bouie Donald
Samuel H. Mays, Jr.
J. Daniel Breen

Clerk
Robert R. Di Trolio
242 Federal Building
167 North Main Street
Memphis, Tennessee 38103
(901) 495-1230

UNITED STATES MAGISTRATE JUDGES OF TENNESSEE

EASTERN DISTRICT
Dennis H. Inman
William B. Mitchell Carter
C. Clifford Shirley

UNITED STATES DISTRICT COURTS DISTRICTS OF TENNESSEE—*Continued*

MIDDLE DISTRICT
Juliet Griffin
Joe B. Brown
E. Clifton Knowles

WESTERN DISTRICT
Diane K. Vescovo
Tu M. Pham

Recalled Magistrate Judge
John Y. Powers (Eastern)

UNITED STATES BANKRUPTCY COURTS OF TENNESSEE

EASTERN DISTRICT

Chief Judge
John C. Cook

Judges
Richard S. Stair, Jr.
Marcia Phillips Parsons
R. Thomas Stinnett

Recalled Judge
Ralph Houston Kelley

Bankruptcy Clerk
Ralph T. Brown
Historic U.S. Courthouse
31 East Eleventh Street
Chattanooga, Tennessee 37402-2722
(423) 752-5163

MIDDLE DISTRICT

Chief Judge
George C. Paine, II

Judges
Keith M. Lundin
Marian F. Harrison

Bankruptcy Clerk
Lloyd C. Ray, Jr.
207 Customs House
701 Broadway
Nashville, Tennessee 37203
(615) 736-5590

WESTERN DISTRICT

Chief Judge
David S. Kennedy

Judges
William Houston Brown
G. Harvey Boswell
Jennie D. Latta

Bankruptcy Clerk
Jed G. Weintraub
200 Jefferson Avenue, Suite 413
Memphis, Tennessee 38103-2328
(901) 328-3500

TENNESSEE SUPREME COURT

The Supreme Court is Tennessee's court of last resort. The court consists of a chief justice and four associate justices elected at large for eight-year terms in statewide nonpartisan elections. Vacancies are filled by the governor from a list of candidates provided by the Judicial Selection Commission. Newly appointed justices stand for retention at the next August biennial election. Not more than two justices may reside in any one of the state's three grand divisions. A chief justice is elected by peer vote to a four-year term. Senior judges may be appointed for renewable four-year terms by the Supreme Court justices. They primarily assist the Supreme Court, the Court of Appeals and the Court of Criminal Appeals and review appellate proceedings of the Workers' Compensation Panel; they may also serve in any state trial court. Retired justices may serve by assignment of the chief justice.

The court hears direct appeals from the trial courts in cases involving a question of the constitutionality of a state law or municipal ordinance, the right to hold public office and other public law issues, workers' compensation, state revenue and in certain other cases as specified by statute. The court may review decisions of the two intermediate appellate courts by writ of certiorari. The court may issue writs necessary to the exercise of proper jurisdiction and exercises rule-making and supervisory control over the lower courts and disciplinary authority over members of the bar.

EASTERN DIVISION includes Anderson, Bledsoe, Blount, Bradley, Campbell, Carter, Claiborne, Cocke, Cumberland, Grainger, Greene, Hamblen, Hamilton, Hancock, Hawkins, Jefferson, Johnson, Knox, Loudon, Marion, McMinn, Meigs, Monroe, Morgan, Polk, Rhea, Roane, Scott, Sevier, Sullivan, Unicoi, Union and Washington counties. The court sits at Knoxville.

MIDDLE DIVISION includes Bedford, Cannon, Cheatham, Clay, Coffee, Davidson, DeKalb, Dickson, Fentress, Franklin, Giles, Grundy, Hickman, Houston, Humphreys, Jackson, Lawrence, Lewis, Lincoln, Macon, Marshall, Maury, Montgomery, Moore, Overton, Perry, Pickett, Putnam, Robertson, Rutherford, Sequatchie, Smith, Stewart, Sumner, Trousdale, Van Buren, Warren, Wayne, White, Williamson and Wilson counties. The court sits at Nashville.

WESTERN DIVISION includes Benton, Carroll, Chester, Crockett, Decatur, Dyer, Fayette, Gibson, Hardeman, Hardin, Haywood, Henderson, Henry, Lake, Lauderdale, Madison, McNairy, Obion, Shelby, Tipton and Weakley counties. The court sits at Jackson.

Chief Justice
Frank F. Drowota, III

Associate Justices
E. Riley Anderson
Adolpho A. Birch, Jr.
Janice M. Holder
William M. "Mickey" Barker

Clerk
Cecil Crowson
Supreme Court Building
Nashville, Tennessee 37219-1407
(615) 741-2681

TENNESSEE SUPREME COURT—*Continued*

Chief Deputy Clerk Eastern Division
Frankie Holt
Supreme Court Building
P.O. Box 444
Knoxville, Tennessee 37901
(865) 594-6700

Chief Deputy Clerk Middle Division
Janice Rawls
Supreme Court Building
401 Seventh Avenue North
Nashville, Tennessee 37219-1407
(615) 741-2681

Chief Deputy Clerk Western Division
Susan Turner
Supreme Court Building
P.O. Box 909
Jackson, Tennessee 38302-0909
(731) 423-5840

Administrative Director
Cornelia A. Clark
600 Nashville City Center
511 Union Street
Nashville, Tennessee 37219
(615) 741-2687

TENNESSEE COURT OF APPEALS

The Court of Appeals is a Tennessee intermediate appellate court. Judges are elected for eight-year terms in statewide nonpartisan elections. Vacancies are filled by the governor from a list of candidates provided by the Judicial Selection Commission. Newly appointed judges stand for retention at the next August biennial election. Not more than four judges may reside in any one of the state's three grand divisions (see Supreme Court section). A presiding judge is elected by peer vote to a one-year term. Senior judges may be appointed for renewable four-year terms by the Supreme Court justices. They primarily assist the Supreme Court, the Court of Appeals and the Court of Criminal Appeals and review appellate proceedings of the Workers' Compensation Panel; they may also serve in any state trial court. Retired judges may serve by assignment of the chief justice.

The court has direct appellate jurisdiction over all civil cases except where the Supreme Court has exclusive jurisdiction or as provided by law. Decisions are final except when reviewed by writ of certiorari by the Supreme Court. The court may issue writs necessary to the exercise of proper jurisdiction.

The court sits en banc or in panels of three judges in the state's grand divisions (see Supreme Court section).

EASTERN DIVISION sits at Knoxville.

Judges
Houston M. Goddard
Herschel P. Franks
Charles D. Susano, Jr.
D. Michael Swiney

MIDDLE DIVISION sits at Nashville.

Judges
Patricia J. Cottrell
William Bryan Cain
Ben H. Cantrell
William Conway Koch, Jr.

WESTERN DIVISION sits at Jackson.

Judges
W. Frank Crawford
Alan E. Highers
David R. Farmer
Holly Kirby Lillard

TENNESSEE COURT OF CRIMINAL APPEALS

The Court of Criminal Appeals is a Tennessee intermediate appellate court. Judges are elected for eight-year terms in statewide nonpartisan elections. Vacancies are filled by the governor from a list of candidates provided by the Judicial Selection Commission. Newly appointed judges stand for retention at the next August biennial election. Not more than four judges may reside in any one of the state's three grand divisions (see Supreme Court section). A presiding judge is elected by peer vote to a one-year term. Senior judges may be appointed for renewable four-year terms by the Supreme Court justices. They primarily assist the Supreme Court, the Court of Appeals and the Court of Criminal Appeals and review appellate proceedings of the Workers' Compensation Panel; they may also serve in any state trial court. Retired judges may serve by assignment of the chief justice.

The court has appellate jurisdiction over felony and misdemeanor criminal cases, habeas corpus and post-conviction proceedings, criminal contempt proceedings and extradition cases. The court has no jurisdiction over cases where the sole question involves the constitutionality of a statute or ordinance. Decisions are final except when reviewed by writ of certiorari by the Supreme Court.

The court may sit en banc or in panels of three, five or seven judges in the state's grand divisions (see Supreme Court section).

EASTERN DIVISION sits at Knoxville.

Judges
Gary R. Wade
Joseph M. Tipton
Curwood Witt
Norma M. McGee Ogle

MIDDLE DIVISION sits at Nashville.

Judges
David H. Welles
Jerry Smith
Thomas T. Woodall
Robert W. Wedemeyer

WESTERN DIVISION sits at Jackson.

Judges
John Everett Williams
Joe G. Riley, Jr.
David G. Hayes
Alan E. Glenn

TENNESSEE STATE TRIAL COURTS

Effective September 1, 1984, the state's trial courts system was reorganized and divided into thirty-one judicial districts. The state trial courts consist of the Circuit Courts, the Chancery Courts and the Criminal Courts. Under the redistricting act, the Law and Equity Courts of Gibson, Montgomery and Sullivan counties became Chancery Courts and the Law and Equity Court of Dyer County became a Circuit Court.

Judges may serve in any state trial court as assigned by the presiding judge of each district. Presiding judges are selected in each judicial district from among the state trial judges to serve a one-year term. Senior judges may be appointed for renewable four-year terms by the Supreme Court justices. Although they may serve in any state trial court, they primarily assist the Supreme Court, the Court of Appeals and the Court of Criminal Appeals and review appellate proceedings of the Workers' Compensation Panel.

The courts sit at the county seats and as specified.

TENNESSEE CIRCUIT COURTS

The Circuit Courts are courts of general jurisdiction established in each of the thirty-one judicial districts in Tennessee. Judges are elected from their respective districts for eight-year terms. Vacancies may be filled by the governor. Retired judges may serve by assignment of the chief justice.

The courts have exclusive original jurisdiction of matters involving the validity of a will, mistakes in deeds of conveyance of land or land registration, application to restore citizenship, eminent domain cases, breach of duty by a county trustee or tax collector, condemnation of land for nonpayment of taxes and the Governmental Tort Liability Act. The courts also have jurisdiction over proceedings involving the seizure and destruction of intoxicating liquors when an offense against the state liquor laws has been committed, unless a Criminal Court exists in that county. The courts may also hear equity cases unless one of the parties objects. The courts have original jurisdiction over all criminal offenses unless a separate Criminal Court has been established within the judicial district. The courts have concurrent original jurisdiction with the Chancery, Criminal, General Sessions and Probate Courts in certain matters as provided by law.

The courts have concurrent appellate jurisdiction with the Chancery Courts to review actions of various administrative boards, commissions or agencies. The courts may issue writs necessary to the exercise of proper jurisdiction.

TENNESSEE CHANCERY COURTS

The Chancery Courts are courts of general equity jurisdiction established in twenty-seven of the thirty-one judicial districts in Tennessee. The chancellors are elected from their respective districts for eight-year terms. Vacancies may be filled by the governor. Retired judges may serve by assignment of the chief justice.

The courts have exclusive original jurisdiction over equity matters exceeding $50 or as provided by law and concurrent jurisdiction with the Circuit Courts of all civil cases except unliquidated damages for injuries to persons or property not resulting from a breach of contract. Concurrent jurisdiction with the Circuit Courts also includes divorce cases, workers' compensation proceedings, questions of title to estates, the validity of wills, adoptions and claims of minors. The courts' inherent jurisdiction includes cases involving injunctive relief; reformation, re-execution, surrender and recision of written instruments; receiverships; trusts; creditors' bills; and other proceedings in aid of execution. The courts also have concurrent jurisdiction with the Criminal Courts as provided by law. The courts hear boundary disputes and disagreements between the state and a corporation and may issue writs necessary to the exercise of proper jurisdiction.

The courts have concurrent appellate jurisdiction with the Circuit Courts to review actions of various administrative boards, commissions or agencies. Appeals from Chancery Courts are heard on the record in the Court of Appeals or the Supreme Court.

TENNESSEE CRIMINAL COURTS

The Criminal Courts are courts of general criminal jurisdiction established in thirteen of the thirty-one judicial districts in Tennessee. Judges are elected from their respective districts for eight-year terms. Vacancies may be filled by the governor. Retired judges may serve by assignment of the chief justice.

The courts have original jurisdiction over all criminal offenses not exclusively conferred upon another court and over certain other criminal and noncriminal matters as well as jurisdiction over all proceedings involving the seizure and destruction of intoxicating liquors when an offense against the state liquor laws has been committed. The courts have concurrent jurisdiction with the Circuit and Chancery Courts as provided by law and appellate jurisdiction over criminal suits and actions originally tried in the lower courts. In 1995, the Shelby County Drug Court, established to handle drug-related offenses, became a permanent part of the Criminal Court Thirtieth Judicial District.

FIRST JUDICIAL DISTRICT includes Carter, Johnson, Unicoi and Washington counties. The court sits at Elizabethton, Mountain City, Erwin, Johnson City and Jonesborough.

Circuit Judges
Thomas J. Seeley, Jr.
Jean A. Stanley

Chancellor
G. Richard Johnson

Criminal Judges
Lynn W. Brown
Robert E. Cupp

SECOND JUDICIAL DISTRICT includes Sullivan County. The court sits at Bristol, Blountville and Kingsport.

Circuit Judges
R. Jerry Beck
John S. McLellan, III

Chancellor
Richard E. Ladd

Criminal Judge
Phyllis H. Miller

TENNESSEE STATE TRIAL COURTS—*Continued*

THIRD JUDICIAL DISTRICT includes Greene, Hamblen, Hancock and Hawkins counties. The court sits at Greeneville, Morristown, Sneedville and Rogersville.

Circuit Judges
Kindall T. Lawson
Ben K. Wexler
John K. Wilson

Chancellor
Thomas R. Frierson, II

Criminal Judge
James E. Beckner

FOURTH JUDICIAL DISTRICT includes Cocke, Grainger, Jefferson and Sevier counties. The court sits at Newport, Rutledge, Dandridge and Sevierville.

Circuit Judges
Rex Henry Ogle
Ben W. Hooper, II
O. Duane Slone
Richard Robert Vance

Chancellor
Telford E. Forgety, Jr.

FIFTH JUDICIAL DISTRICT includes Blount County. The court sits at Maryville.

Circuit Judges
D. Kelly Thomas, Jr.
W. Dale Young

Chancellor
Telford E. Forgety, Jr.

SIXTH JUDICIAL DISTRICT includes Knox County. The court sits at Knoxville.

Circuit Judges
Wheeler Armston Rosenbalm
William K. Swann, III
Harold Wimberly
Dale C. Workman

Chancellors
Sharon J. Bell
Daryl R. Fansler
John F. Weaver

Criminal Judges
Ray L. Jenkins
Mary Beth Leibowitz
Richard R. Baumgartner

SEVENTH JUDICIAL DISTRICT includes Anderson County. The court sits at Clinton.

Circuit Judge
James B. Scott, Jr.

Chancellor
William E. Lantrip

EIGHTH JUDICIAL DISTRICT includes Campbell, Claiborne, Fentress, Scott and Union counties. The court sits at Jacksboro, Tazewell, Jamestown, Huntsville and Maynardville.

Circuit Judge
Conrad Troutman, Jr.

Chancellor
Billy Joe White

Criminal Judge
E. Shayne Sexton

NINTH JUDICIAL DISTRICT includes Loudon, Meigs, Morgan and Roane counties. The court sits at Loudon, Decatur, Wartburg and Kingston.

Circuit Judge
Russell E. Simmons, Jr.

Chancellor
Frank Vernon Williams, III

Criminal Judge
E. Eugene Eblen

TENTH JUDICIAL DISTRICT includes Bradley, McMinn, Monroe and Polk counties. The court sits at Cleveland, Athens, Madisonville, Benton and Ducktown.

Circuit Judges
John Brown Hagler
Carroll Lee Ross
Lawrence Howard Puckett

Chancellor
Jerri S. Bryant

Criminal Judge
Robert Steven Bebb

ELEVENTH JUDICIAL DISTRICT includes Hamilton County. The court sits at Chattanooga.

Circuit Judges
Samuel H. Payne
L. Marie Williams
Jacqueline E. Schulten
W. Neil Thomas, III

Chancellors
Howell N. Peoples
W. Frank Brown, III

Criminal Judges
Stephen M. Bevil
Douglas Alexander Meyer
Rebecca J. Stern

TWELFTH JUDICIAL DISTRICT includes Bledsoe, Franklin, Grundy, Marion, Rhea and Sequatchie counties. The court sits at Pikeville, Winchester, Altamont, Jasper, Dayton and Dunlap.

Circuit Judges
Thomas W. "Rusty" Graham
J. Curtis Smith
Buddy D. Perry

Chancellor
Jeffrey F. Stewart

THIRTEENTH JUDICIAL DISTRICT includes Clay, Cumberland, DeKalb, Overton, Pickett, Putnam and White counties. The court sits at Celina, Crossville, Smithville, Livingston, Byrdstown, Cookeville and Sparta.

Circuit Judges
John J. Maddux, Jr.
John A. Turnbull

TENNESSEE STATE TRIAL COURTS—*Continued*

Chancellor
Vernon Neal

Criminal Judges
Leon C. Burns, Jr.
Lillie Ann Sells

FOURTEENTH JUDICIAL DISTRICT includes Coffee County. The court sits at Manchester.

Circuit Judges
John Wiley Rollins
L. Craig Johnson

FIFTEENTH JUDICIAL DISTRICT includes Jackson, Macon, Smith, Trousdale and Wilson counties. The court sits at Gainsboro, Lafayette, Carthage, Hartsville and Lebanon.

Circuit Judges
Clara W. Byrd
John D. Wootten, Jr.

Chancellor
Charles K. "C.K." Smith

Criminal Judge
James O. Bond

SIXTEENTH JUDICIAL DISTRICT includes Cannon and Rutherford counties. The court sits at Woodbury and Murfreesboro.

Circuit Judges
Joseph S. "Steve" Daniel
James Keeble Clayton, Jr.
Don R. Ash
Royce Taylor

Chancellor
Robert Ewing Corlew, III

SEVENTEENTH JUDICIAL DISTRICT includes Bedford, Lincoln, Marshall and Moore counties. The court sits at Shelbyville, Fayetteville, Lewisburg and Lynchburg.

Circuit Judges
William Charles Lee
Franklin Lee Russell

Chancellor
James B. "J. B." Cox

EIGHTEENTH JUDICIAL DISTRICT includes Sumner County. The court sits at Gallatin.

Circuit Judge
C. L. "Buck" Rogers

Chancellor
Thomas E. Gray

Criminal Judge
Jane W. Wheatcraft

NINETEENTH JUDICIAL DISTRICT includes Montgomery and Robertson counties. The court sits at Clarksville and Springfield.

Circuit Judges
John H. Gasaway, III
Michael R. Jones
Ross H. Hicks

Chancellor
Carol Catalano

TWENTIETH JUDICIAL DISTRICT includes Davidson County. The court sits at Nashville.

Circuit Judges
Thomas White Brothers
Barbara N. Haynes
Muriel Robinson
Frank Clement, Jr.
Hamilton Gayden, Jr.
Walter C. Kurtz
Marietta M. Shipley
Carol L. Soloman

Chancellors
Irvin H. Kilcrease, Jr.
Ellen Hobbs Lyle
Carol L. McCoy

Criminal Judges
Cheryl A. Blackburn
Seth W. Norman
James Randall Wyatt, Jr.
Steve R. Dozier

TWENTY-FIRST JUDICIAL DISTRICT includes Hickman, Lewis, Perry and Williamson counties. The court sits at Centerville, Hohenwald, Linden and Franklin.

Circuit Judges
Donald P. Harris
Timothy L. Easter
Russ Heldman
Robert E. Lee Davies

TWENTY-SECOND JUDICIAL DISTRICT includes Giles, Lawrence, Maury and Wayne counties. The court sits at Pulaski, Lawrenceburg, Columbia and Waynesboro.

Circuit Judges
Jim T. Hamilton
Robert L. Jones
Stella L. Hargrove
Robert L. Holloway, Jr.

TWENTY-THIRD JUDICIAL DISTRICT includes Cheatham, Dickson, Houston, Humphreys and Stewart counties. The court sits at Ashland City, Charlotte, Erin, Waverly and Dover.

Circuit Judges
Robert E. Burch
Leonard Watson Martin
George C. Sexton

TWENTY-FOURTH JUDICIAL DISTRICT includes Benton, Carroll, Decatur, Hardin and Henry counties. The court sits at Camden, Huntingdon, Decaturville, Savannah and Paris.

Circuit Judges
C. Creed McGinley
Julian P. Guinn

Chancellor
Ron E. Harmon

TWENTY-FIFTH JUDICIAL DISTRICT includes Fayette, Hardeman, Lauderdale, McNairy and Tipton counties. The court sits at Somerville, Bolivar, Ripley, Selmer and Covington.

TENNESSEE STATE TRIAL COURTS—*Continued*

Circuit Judges
Jon Kerry Blackwood
Joseph H. Walker

Chancellors
Dewey C. Whitenton
Martha B. Brasfield

TWENTY-SIXTH JUDICIAL DISTRICT includes Chester, Henderson and Madison counties. The court sits at Henderson, Lexington and Jackson.

Circuit Judges
Donald H. Allen
Roy B. Morgan, Jr.
Roger Amos Page

Chancellor
James F. Butler

TWENTY-SEVENTH JUDICIAL DISTRICT includes Obion and Weakley counties. The court sits at Union City and Dresden.

Circuit Judge
William B. Acree, Jr.

Chancellor
W. Michael Maloan

TWENTY-EIGHTH JUDICIAL DISTRICT includes Crockett, Gibson and Haywood counties. The court sits at Alamo, Trenton, Humboldt and Brownsville.

Circuit Judge
Clayburn Peeples

Chancellor
George Robert Ellis

TWENTY-NINTH JUDICIAL DISTRICT includes Dyer and Lake counties. The court sits at Dyersburg and Tiptonville.

Circuit Judge
Russell Lee Moore, Jr.

Chancellor
J. Steven Stafford

THIRTIETH JUDICIAL DISTRICT includes Shelby County. The court sits at Memphis.

Circuit Judges

D'Army Bailey	George H. Brown, Jr.
Robert L. Childers	Robert A. Lanier
John R. McCarroll, Jr.	Kay Spalding Robilio
James F. Russell	Rita Laverne Stotts
Karen R. Williams	

Chancellors
D. J. Alissandratos
Walter L. Evans
Arnold Goldin

Criminal Judges

W. Fred Axley	Arthur Thomas Bennett
John P. Colton, Jr.	Joseph B. Dailey
Carolyn Wade Blackett	Chris Craft
Bernie Weinman	James C. Beasley, Jr.
W. Otis Higgs, Jr.	J. C. McLin

THIRTY-FIRST JUDICIAL DISTRICT includes Van Buren and Warren counties. The court sits at Spencer and McMinnville.

Circuit Judge
Larry Barton Stanley, Jr.

Chancellor
Larry Barton Stanley, Jr.

SENIOR JUDGES
John K. Byers
William H. Inman
Allen Wilson Wallace
James L. Weatherford

TENNESSEE PROBATE COURT

Shelby County Probate Court is a court of special jurisdiction in Tennessee. Judges are elected in nonpartisan elections for eight-year terms.

The court has jurisdiction in the administration of estates, probate of wills, appointment of guardians and other related matters. In other counties, probate matters are handled by the General Sessions or Chancery Courts.

The court sits at Memphis.

TENNESSEE GENERAL SESSIONS COURTS

The General Sessions Courts are courts of limited jurisdiction established in each of the ninety-five counties in Tennessee. Judges are elected from their respective counties for eight-year terms.

The courts have civil jurisdiction in cases where the amount in controversy does not exceed $15,000. In counties with populations between 68,100 and 68,400 or of more than 700,000, the amount may not exceed $25,000. The courts exercise criminal jurisdiction over misdemeanors when the punishment is a fine of $50 or less and/or a prison sentence of less than one year and may conduct preliminary felony hearings. The courts have unlimited original jurisdiction in cases of forcible entry and detainer. In several counties, the courts also handle municipal ordinance violations and probate, juvenile, mental commitment, workers' compensation and domestic relations matters. The courts may issue all warrants, set bail and issue writs necessary to the exercise of proper jurisdiction. Appeals are heard de novo by the Circuit or Criminal Courts.

The courts sit at the county seats.

TENNESSEE JUVENILE COURTS

The Juvenile Courts are courts of limited jurisdiction established in some counties in Tennessee. They are courts of record. Judges are elected to terms set by the individual municipalities or counties.

The courts have exclusive original jurisdiction over proceedings in which a child is alleged to be delinquent, unruly, dependent or neglected as well as concurrent jurisdiction with the Circuit, Chancery and Probate Courts in certain other cases. In counties without special juvenile courts, this jurisdiction is exercised by the General Sessions Courts. Appeals are heard de novo by the Circuit Courts.

TENNESSEE MUNICIPAL COURTS

Municipal Courts may be established in home-rule municipalities. In some cities, judges are nominated by the mayor and approved by the city council; they must then run in the next general election following their appointment. In other cities, judges are elected. Length of term is determined by each municipality.

The courts have jurisdiction over city ordinances and preliminary trial authority over persons charged with offenses against the state committed in the city or municipality. Other jurisdiction varies widely from court to court and may include such matters as traffic violations, issuance of warrants for escaped prisoners and summoning a jury of inquest. Several of the courts have concurrent jurisdiction with General Sessions Courts in some matters. Generally, the courts have the authority to assess fines up to $500 and may impose sentences of up to thirty days imprisonment. There are no jury trials; appeals are heard de novo by the Circuit or Criminal Courts.

There are currently more than three hundred Municipal Courts in operation throughout the state.

Tennessee Counties and County Seats

County	County Seat
Anderson	Clinton
Bedford	Shelbyville
Benton	Camden
Bledsoe	Pikeville
Blount	Maryville
Bradley	Cleveland
Campbell	Jacksboro
Cannon	Woodbury
Carroll	Huntingdon
Carter	Elizabethton
Cheatham	Ashland City
Chester	Henderson
Claiborne	Tazewell
Clay	Celina
Cocke	Newport
Coffee	Manchester
Crockett	Alamo
Cumberland	Crossville
Davidson	Nashville
Decatur	Decaturville
DeKalb	Smithville
Dickson	Charlotte
Dyer	Dyersburg
Fayette	Somerville
Fentress	Jamestown
Franklin	Winchester
Gibson	Trenton
Giles	Pulaski
Grainger	Rutledge
Greene	Greeneville
Grundy	Altamont
Hamblen	Morristown
Hamilton	Chattanooga
Hancock	Sneedville
Hardeman	Bolivar
Hardin	Savannah
Hawkins	Rogersville
Haywood	Brownsville
Henderson	Lexington
Henry	Paris
Hickman	Centerville
Houston	Erin
Humphreys	Waverly
Jackson	Gainesboro
Jefferson	Dandridge
Johnson	Mountain City
Knox	Knoxville
Lake	Tiptonville
Lauderdale	Ripley
Lawrence	Lawrenceburg
Lewis	Hohenwald
Lincoln	Fayetteville
Loudon	Loudon
Macon	Lafayette
Madison	Jackson
Marion	Jasper
Marshall	Lewisburg
Maury	Columbia
McMinn	Athens
McNairy	Selmer
Meigs	Decatur
Monroe	Madisonville
Montgomery	Clarksville
Moore	Lynchburg
Morgan	Wartburg
Obion	Union City
Overton	Livingston
Perry	Linden
Pickett	Byrdstown
Polk	Benton
Putnam	Cookeville
Rhea	Dayton
Roane	Kingston
Robertson	Springfield
Rutherford	Murfreesboro
Scott	Huntsville
Sequatchie	Dunlap
Sevier	Sevierville
Shelby	Memphis
Smith	Carthage
Stewart	Dover
Sullivan	Blountville
Sumner	Gallatin
Tipton	Covington

COUNTIES AND COUNTY SEATS—*Continued*

Trousdale
Hartsville

Unicoi
Erwin

Union
Maynardville

Van Buren
Spencer

Warren
McMinnville

Washington
Jonesborough

Wayne
Waynesboro

Weakley
Dresden

White
Sparta

Williamson
Franklin

Wilson
Lebanon

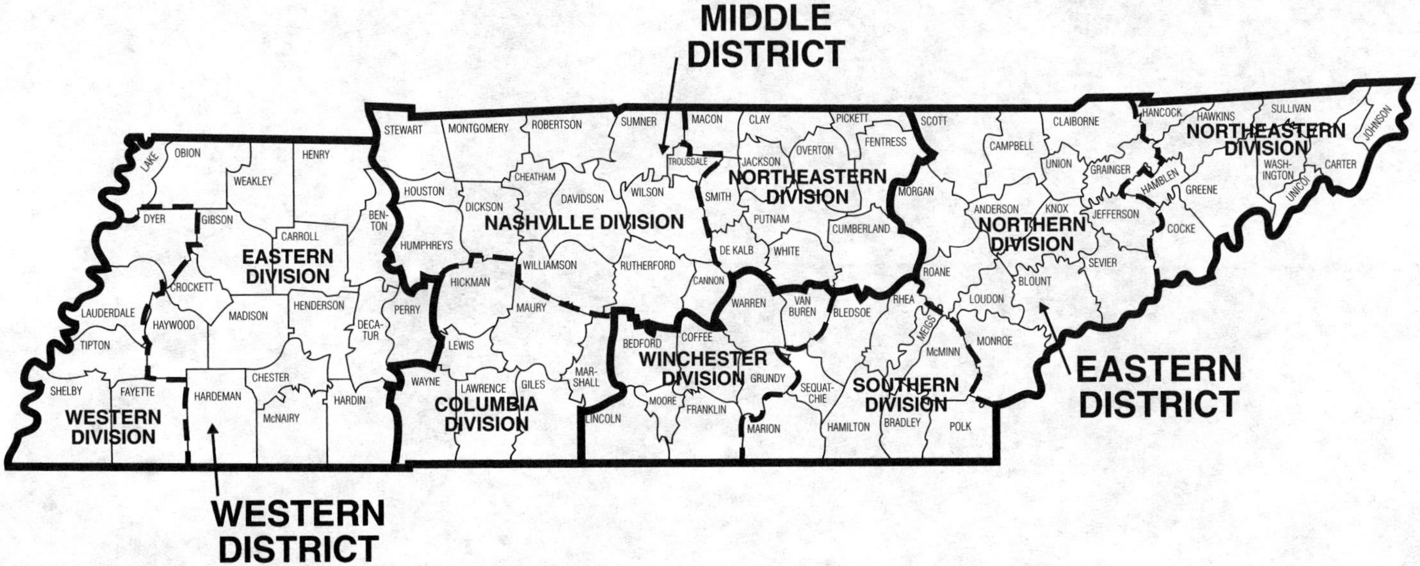
MIDDLE DISTRICT
EASTERN DISTRICT
WESTERN DISTRICT
WESTERN DIVISION
EASTERN DIVISION
NASHVILLE DIVISION
COLUMBIA DIVISION
WINCHESTER DIVISION
NORTHEASTERN DIVISION
NORTHERN DIVISION
SOUTHERN DIVISION
NORTHEASTERN DIVISION
LAKE
OBION
WEAKLEY
HENRY
DYER
GIBSON
CARROLL
BEN-TON
LAUDERDALE
CROCKETT
HAYWOOD
MADISON
HENDERSON
DECA-TUR
TIPTON
SHELBY
FAYETTE
HARDEMAN
CHESTER
McNAIRY
HARDIN
STEWART
MONTGOMERY
ROBERTSON
SUMNER
MACON
CLAY
PICKETT
HOUSTON
DICKSON
CHEATHAM
DAVIDSON
TROUSDALE
WILSON
SMITH
JACKSON
OVERTON
FENTRESS
PUTNAM
DE KALB
WHITE
CUMBERLAND
HUMPHREYS
WILLIAMSON
RUTHERFORD
CANNON
HICKMAN
PERRY
MAURY
LEWIS
WAYNE
LAWRENCE
GILES
MAR-SHALL
LINCOLN
BEDFORD
COFFEE
WARREN
VAN BUREN
BLEDSOE
MOORE
FRANKLIN
GRUNDY
SEQUAT-CHIE
MARION
HAMILTON
RHEA
MEIGS
McMINN
BRADLEY
POLK
SCOTT
MORGAN
ROANE
CAMPBELL
CLAIBORNE
UNION
ANDERSON
KNOX
LOUDON
BLOUNT
MONROE
SEVIER
GRAINGER
JEFFERSON
HAMBLEN
COCKE
HANCOCK
HAWKINS
GREENE
SULLIVAN
WASH-INGTON
UNICOI
CARTER
JOHNSON

UNITED STATES DISTRICT COURTS DISTRICTS OF TENNESSEE

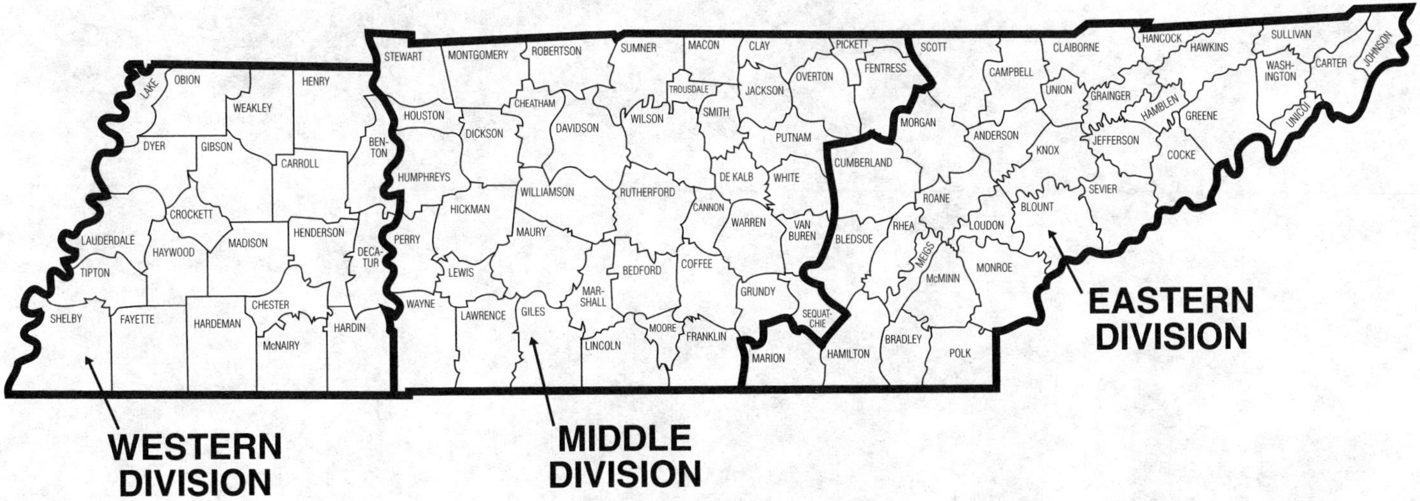
WESTERN DIVISION
MIDDLE DIVISION
EASTERN DIVISION
LAKE
OBION
HENRY
WEAKLEY
DYER
GIBSON
CARROLL
BEN-TON
LAUDERDALE
CROCKETT
HAYWOOD
MADISON
HENDERSON
DECA-TUR
TIPTON
SHELBY
FAYETTE
HARDEMAN
CHESTER
McNAIRY
HARDIN
STEWART
MONTGOMERY
ROBERTSON
SUMNER
MACON
CLAY
PICKETT
FENTRESS
OVERTON
JACKSON
TROUSDALE
SMITH
HOUSTON
CHEATHAM
DAVIDSON
WILSON
DICKSON
PUTNAM
HUMPHREYS
WILLIAMSON
RUTHERFORD
DE KALB
WHITE
CANNON
HICKMAN
WARREN
VAN BUREN
PERRY
MAURY
LEWIS
BEDFORD
COFFEE
MAR-SHALL
GRUNDY
SEQUAT-CHIE
WAYNE
LAWRENCE
GILES
LINCOLN
MOORE
FRANKLIN
MARION
SCOTT
CAMPBELL
CLAIBORNE
HANCOCK
HAWKINS
SULLIVAN
WASH-INGTON
CARTER
JOHNSON
UNICOI
UNION
GRAINGER
HAMBLEN
GREENE
MORGAN
ANDERSON
KNOX
JEFFERSON
COCKE
CUMBERLAND
ROANE
SEVIER
BLOUNT
BLEDSOE
RHEA
LOUDON
MEIGS
McMINN
MONROE
BRADLEY
POLK
HAMILTON

**GRAND DIVISIONS OF
TENNESSEE SUPREME COURT, TENNESSEE COURT OF APPEALS
AND TENNESSEE COURT OF CRIMINAL APPEALS**

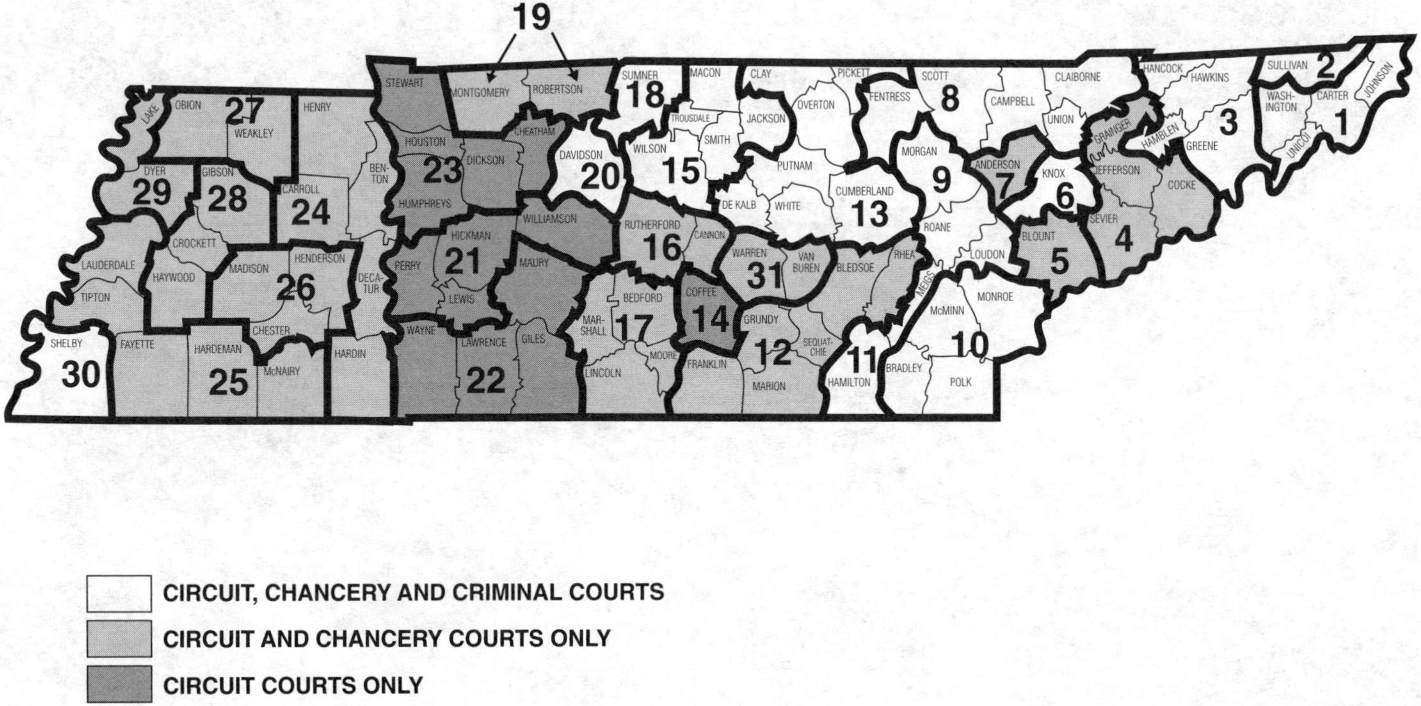
19
SHELBY
30
FAYETTE
HARDEMAN
25
McNAIRY
TIPTON
LAUDERDALE
HAYWOOD
CROCKETT
MADISON
HENDERSON
26
CHESTER
LAKE
OBION
27
WEAKLEY
DYER
29
GIBSON
28
CARROLL
24
HENRY
BEN-TON
DECA-TUR
HARDIN
STEWART
HOUSTON
23
DICKSON
HUMPHREYS
HICKMAN
21
PERRY
LEWIS
WAYNE
LAWRENCE
22
GILES
MAURY
WILLIAMSON
CHEATHAM
MONTGOMERY
ROBERTSON
DAVIDSON
20
SUMNER
18
MACON
TROUSDALE
SMITH
WILSON
15
RUTHERFORD
16
CANNON
MAR-SHALL
17
BEDFORD
MOORE
LINCOLN
COFFEE
14
FRANKLIN
CLAY
JACKSON
DE KALB
PUTNAM
WHITE
OVERTON
PICKETT
FENTRESS
CUMBERLAND
13
WARREN
31
VAN BUREN
GRUNDY
12
SEQUAT-CHIE
MARION
BLEDSOE
RHEA
11
HAMILTON
SCOTT
8
MORGAN
9
ROANE
CAMPBELL
ANDERSON
7
MEIGS
BRADLEY
McMINN
10
POLK
LOUDON
MONROE
CLAIBORNE
UNION
KNOX
6
BLOUNT
5
SEVIER
4
JEFFERSON
GRAINGER
HAMBLEN
COCKE
HANCOCK
HAWKINS
3
GREENE
SULLIVAN
2
WASH-INGTON
CARTER
1
UNICOI
JOHNSON
CIRCUIT, CHANCERY AND CRIMINAL COURTS
CIRCUIT AND CHANCERY COURTS ONLY
CIRCUIT COURTS ONLY

JUDICIAL DISTRICTS OF TENNESSEE STATE TRIAL COURTS

TENNESSEE

ACREE, William B., Jr. *(Judge, Tennessee Circuit Court Twenty-seventh Judicial District)*
Mailing address: P.O. Box 576, Union City 38281.
Office: 201 Main Street, Suite G, Union City 38261.
Telephone: (731) 884-2667.

ALISSANDRATOS, D. J. *(Chancellor, Tennessee Chancery Court Thirtieth Judicial District)*
Office: 308 Shelby County Courthouse, 140 Adams Avenue, Memphis 38103.
Telephone: (901) 545-4000.

ALLEN, Donald H. *(Judge, Tennessee Circuit Court Twenty-sixth Judicial District)*
Office: Criminal Justice Complex, Second Floor, 515 South Liberty Street, Jackson 38301.
Telephone: (731) 423-6066.

ANDERSON, E. Riley *(Associate Justice, Tennessee Supreme Court)* Elected 1990. Retained by election 1998, current term expires 2006. Chief Justice 1994-96, 1997-98 and 1998 to Aug 31, 2001. Born Chattanooga Tennessee Aug 10, 1932. Educated at University of Tennessee B.S. 1955 J.D. 1957. In legal practice Oak Ridge 1958-87. Judge, Tennessee Court of Appeals Eastern Division 1987-90.

President Tennessee Chapter American Board of Trial Advocates 1987-88 and Hamilton Burnett American Inn of Court 1988-90. Chair Tennessee Judicial Council 1990-95. Vice Chair Courts, Children and the Family Committee 1998-99 and Board of Directors 1999-2000 Conference of Chief Justices. Past President Tennessee Defense Lawyers Association and Anderson County Bar Association. Former Member Board of Delegates Tennessee Bar Association. Honorary Chair Legal Subcommittee of Character Counts!. Graduate Appellate Judges Program 1988 and Advanced Program 1999 New York University. Recipient Judge of the Year Award from American Board of Trial Advocates 1998, Vocational Service Award from Oak Ridge Rotary Club 2000 and William M. Leech, Jr. Public Service Award from Tennessee Bar Association 2002. Listed in *Who's Who in American Law* and *Who's Who in America.* Chairman Select Senate/House Committee on Court Automation Sept 1990 to 1994. Charter Commissioner Oak Ridge City 1962-64. Past President YMCA and Anderson County University of Tennessee Alumni Association. Past Vice President and Director Oak Ridge Community Art Center and Oak Ridge Chamber of Commerce. Former Chair Tennessee Medical Malpractice Review Board. Former Co-chairman March of Dimes Fund Drive. Former Member Board of Trustees Child & Family, Inc. and First Methodist Church. Advisory Board The Cornerstone Behavioral Center.
Mailing address: P.O. Box 444, Knoxville 37901-0444.
Office: 505 Main Street, Suite 200, Knoxville 37902.
Telephone: (865) 594-6400.

ASH, Don R. *(Judge, Tennessee Circuit Court Sixteenth Judicial District)*
Office: 20 Public Square North, Room 409, Murfreesboro 37130.
Telephone: (615) 898-8074.

AXLEY, W. Fred *(Judge, Tennessee Criminal Court Thirtieth Judicial District)*
Office: 519 Shelby County Justice Complex, 201 Poplar Avenue, Memphis 38103.
Telephone: (901) 545-5857.

BAILEY, D'Army *(Judge, Tennessee Circuit Court Thirtieth Judicial District)* Assumed office Sept 1, 1990. Born Nov 29, 1941. Educated at Southern University 1959-62, Clark University B.A. 1964, Boston University School of Law 1964-65 and Yale Law School LL.B. 1967. Admitted to practice California 1969 and Tennessee 1974. In legal practice Memphis Tennessee July 1974 to Aug 31, 1990.

Author "Enjoining the Enforcement of the State Criminal Statutes Which Abridge First Amendment Freedoms" Harvard Civil Rights—Civil Liberties L. Rev. Fall 1967, "Equal—But Separate?" Civil Liberties Feb 1969, "Trying to Make It (the Law) Real Compared to What?" University of Toledo L. Rev. 1971 and "Inequities of the Parole System in California" Howard University L. Jour. 1972. Staff Attorney Neighborhood Legal Assistance Foundation San Francisco California Nov 1968 to June 1970. Program Advisor Field Foundation New York City July 1970 to Oct 1971. Adjunct Professor Memphis State University 1985-86. Program Consultant Council on Legal Education Opportunity Atlanta Georgia 1969-70. Board of Directors Council on Legal Education for Professional Responsibility New York City 1969-70. Chairman Board of Directors Neighborhood Legal Services Berkeley California 1969-70. Member Steering Committee San Francisco Lawyers Committee on Urban Affairs 1969-71. President Ben F. Jones Chapter National Bar Association 1987-89. Member City Council Berkeley California April 1971 to Aug 1973. Member Equality Committee American Civil Liberties Union 1967-68 and Platform Committee National Black Political Convention Gary Indiana 1972. Legal Consultant National Committee Against Discrimination in Housing New York City 1970-71. Columnist *Commercial Appeal* Newspaper 1975-82. Board of Directors Memphis Epilepsy Foundation 1977-83 and Leadership Memphis 1979-83. Television Host Memphis Forum WPTY 1981-83. President Board of Directors Lorraine Civil Rights Museum Foundation, Inc. since 1983. Member Naegele Headliner Committee Naegele Outdoor Advertising, Inc. 1988-89 and Martin Luther King Tribute Committee April 4, 1988 to 1989. Board Commissioner Memphis Light, Gas & Water Division 1988 to Sept 1, 1990.
Office: 212 Shelby County Courthouse, 140 Adams Avenue, Memphis 38103.
Telephone: (901) 545-4022.

BARKER, William M. "Mickey" *(Associate Justice, Tennessee Supreme Court)* Born Chattanooga Tennessee. Presbyterian. Educated at University of Chattanooga B.S.

BARKER, WILLIAM M. "MICKEY"—*Continued*

1964 and University of Cincinnati J.D. 1967. Board of Editors University of Cincinnati Law Review 1966-67. Member Sigma Chi and Phi Delta Phi. Admitted to practice Tennessee 1967 and U.S. District Court Eastern District of Tennessee 1969. Began legal practice Chattanooga 1969. Former Judge, Tennessee Circuit Court Eleventh Judicial District, appointed by Governor Lamar Alexander to term beginning June 27, 1983. Former Judge, Tennessee Court of Criminal Appeals Eastern Division.

Part-time Instructor in Political Science University of Tennessee at Chattanooga. Author Legislative Note University of Cincinnati L. Rev. 1967. Member Chattanooga Trial Lawyers Association (President 1978) and Chattanooga Bar Association (Board of Governors 1976-78). Member Committee on Pattern Jury Instructions—Civil Tennessee Judicial Conference. Captain U.S. Army Medical Service 1967. Republican. Former member Hamilton County Republican Party Executive Committee. Coach Dixie Youth Baseball. Advisor Boy Scouts of America. Board of Directors Signal Mountain Playhouse. Enjoys travel and sports.

Office: 410 State Office Building, 540 McCallie Avenue, Chattanooga 37402-2096.

Telephone: (423) 634-6146.

BAUMGARTNER, Richard R. *(Judge, Tennessee Criminal Court Sixth Judicial District)*

Office: 162 City County Building, 400 Main Avenue, Knoxville 37902.

Telephone: (865) 215-2508.

BEASLEY, James C., Jr. *(Judge, Tennessee Criminal Court Thirtieth Judicial District)*

Office: 706 Criminal Justice Complex, 201 Poplar Avenue, Memphis 38103.

Telephone: (901) 545-3773.

BEBB, Robert Steven *(Judge, Tennessee Criminal Court Tenth Judicial District)* Elected to term beginning Sept 1, 1982. Reelected 1990 and 1998. Current term expires Aug 31, 2006. Born Knoxville Tennessee April 18, 1941. Methodist. Educated at Middle Tennessee State University B.S. 1964 and University of Tennessee J.D. 1973. Admitted to practice Tennessee 1973. Began legal practice Knoxville 1973. In legal practice Sweetwater eight years. Former Assistant District Attorney.

Office: 130 East Washington Avenue, Suite 7, Athens 37303.

Telephone: (423) 746-5404.

BECK, R. Jerry *(Judge, Tennessee Circuit Court Second Judicial District)*

Office: Justice Center, 200 Shelby Street, Kingsport 37660.

Telephone: (423) 224-1701.

BECKNER, James E. *(Judge, Tennessee Criminal Court Third Judicial District)* Appointed by Governor Ray Blanton to term beginning July 20, 1976. Elected to subsequent terms. Current term expires Aug 31, 2006. Born Appalachia Virginia. Baptist. Educated at Carson-Newman College B.A. cum laude 1963 and University of Tennessee J.D. 1965. Admitted to practice Tennessee 1966. Began legal practice Morristown 1966.

Instructor Morristown College 1966-67 and Walters State Community College 1973. Member Tennessee Trial Lawyers Association, The Association of Trial Lawyers of America, Hamblen County and Tennessee Bar Associations. Recipient Hamblen County Young Man of the Year Award 1970. Democrat. Board of Directors Morristown Boys Club and Morristown Theatre Guild. Enjoys tennis, motorcycling, water skiing and raising indoor plants.

Office: Hamblen County Justice Center, 510 Allison Street, Morristown 37814.

Telephone: (423) 586-8640.

BELL, Sharon J. *(Chancellor, Tennessee Chancery Court Sixth Judicial District)* Elected to term beginning Sept 1, 1986. Reelected 1990 and 1998. Current term expires Aug 31, 2006. Born Birmingham Alabama June 30, 1944. Educated at Auburn University B.S. 1966 and University of Tennessee School of Law J.D. 1969. Admitted to practice Tennessee 1970. In legal practice Knoxville 1972-82. Judge, Knox County General Sessions Court 1982-86.

Member Tennessee Trial Judges Association and Knox County Bar Association. Representative Tennessee General Assembly 1978-82.

Office: 142 City County Building, 400 Main Avenue, Knoxville 37902.

Telephone: (865) 215-2448.

BENNETT, Arthur Thomas *(Judge, Tennessee Criminal Court Thirtieth Judicial District)* Appointed by Governor Ray Blanton to term beginning Jan 9, 1976. Reappointed April 30, 1976. Elected 1990 and 1998. Current term expires Aug 31, 2006. Former Presiding Judge. Born Corapeake North Carolina Feb 3, 1933. Member Greater Middle Baptist Church (Chairman Board of Trustees). Educated at Norfolk State College 1955-57 and Howard University B.A. 1959 J.D. 1963. Member Phi Alpha Theta and Tau Kappa Alpha. Admitted to practice Tennessee 1964. In legal practice Memphis 1964. Judge, Tennessee General Sessions Court 1976.

Assistant District Attorney 1965-75. Chief Prosecutor Tennessee Criminal Court 1974. Author "An Ounce of Prevention Against Crime" 1980. Former member Juvenile Court Advisory Council and Title XX State Advisory Council Department of Human Services. Member Tennessee Judicial Conference (Secretary 1984-85), Memphis and National Bar Associations. Graduate 1972 and Faculty Advisor 1973 National College of District Attorneys. Graduate The National Judicial College 1977. Recipient Distinguished Service Award from Mallory Knights 1978, Twenty Pearl Award from Beta Epsilon Omega Chapter Alpha Kappa Alpha, Inc. 1978, Citizenship Award from Bethel Grove Community Organization 1981-82, Boy Scouts' Appreciation Award 1985 and Mock Trial Service Award from Memphis Board of Education 1985. Listed in *Who's Who Among Black Americans* 1975. U.S. Army Infantry 1953-55 and USAR 1955-62. Former Board member NAACP and P.U.S.H. Past President Fellowship Crime Prevention Committee. Former Executive Legal Director and former member Board of Directors National United Law Enforcement Officers Association. Board member Cotton Makers Jubilee, Inc. Member 33° Masons, Shriners Moolah Temple 54 and Southeast Optimist Club. Member Advisory Council and Board Memphis Skill Center. Sponsor and

BENNETT, ARTHUR THOMAS—*Continued*

Coach Little League football. Interests include judo, football, basketball and classical music.

Office: 519 Shelby County Justice Complex, 201 Poplar Avenue, Memphis 38103.

Telephone: (901) 545-5858.

Fax: (901) 545-2236

BEVIL, Stephen M. *(Judge, Tennessee Criminal Court Eleventh Judicial District)*

Office: Courts Building, 600 Market Street, Chattanooga 37402.

Telephone: (423) 209-7555.

BIRCH, Adolpho A., Jr. *(Associate Justice, Tennessee Supreme Court)* Former Chief Justice. Born Washington D.C. Sept 22, 1932. Episcopalian. Educated at Lincoln University 1952, Howard University B.A. 1956 J.D. 1956. Admitted to practice Tennessee 1957. Began legal practice Nashville 1957. Judge, Davidson County General Sessions Court 1969-78. Judge, Tennessee Criminal Court Twentieth Judicial District 1978-87. Former Judge, Tennessee Court of Criminal Appeals Middle Division.

Assistant Public Defender 1964-66. Assistant District Attorney General 1966-69. Associate Professor of Legal Medicine Meharry Medical College 1959-72. Member J. C. Napier (Past President), Nashville, National and American Bar Associations. USNR active duty 1956-58.

Office: 304 Supreme Court Building, 401 Seventh Avenue North, Nashville 37219-1407.

Telephone: (615) 741-6750.

BLACKBURN, Cheryl A. *(Judge, Tennessee Criminal Court Twentieth Judicial District)*

Office: 609 Metro Courthouse, Nashville 37201.

Telephone: (615) 862-5940.

BLACKETT, Carolyn Wade *(Judge, Tennessee Criminal Court Thirtieth Judicial District)*

Office: 519 Shelby County Justice Complex, 201 Poplar Avenue, Memphis 38103.

Telephone: (901) 545-5859.

BLACKWOOD, Jon Kerry *(Judge, Tennessee Circuit Court Twenty-fifth Judicial District)* Appointed by Governor Lamar Alexander to term beginning Nov 5, 1985. Elected 1986, 1990 and 1998. Current term expires Aug 31, 2006. Born Memphis Tennessee June 30, 1947. Methodist. Educated at Tennessee Technological University B.S. cum laude 1969 and Memphis State University School of Law J.D. 1974. Member Phi Alpha Theta. Admitted to practice Tennessee 1974. In legal practice Somerville 1974-76.

Assistant District Attorney Twenty-fifth Judicial District Tennessee Sept 1976 to Nov 1985. Member Tennessee Judicial Conference and Tennessee Bar Association. Teacher 1969-71. Political affiliation: Independent. Fayette County Board of Education 1975-76. Member St. Paul Methodist Church and Somerville Country Club. Enjoys gardening, reading and all forms of sports.

Office: 120 East Court Square, Suite 6, Somerville 38068-1493.

Telephone: (901) 465-2126.

BOND, James O. *(Judge, Tennessee Criminal Court Fifteenth Judicial District)* Elected to term beginning Sept 1, 1990. Reelected 1998, current term expires Aug 31, 2006. Born Wilson County Tennessee. Presbyterian. Educated at Middle Tennessee State University B.S. 1964 and Nashville University School of Law LL.B. 1971. Admitted to practice Tennessee 1971, U.S. Supreme Court 1976 and U.S. Court of Appeals Sixth Circuit 1982. In legal practice 1971-90.

Member Tennessee Judges Association, American Judges Association, Tennessee Trial Lawyers Association, Wilson County, Tennessee and American Bar Associations. Airman Second Class USAF 1958-60. Claim Adjuster State Farm Insurance Company 1964-71. Democrat. Member Cumberland Presbyterian Church. Enjoys sports.

Mailing address: P.O. Box 804, Lebanon 37088-0804.

Office: 108 South Cumberland Street, Lebanon 37087.

Telephone: (615) 444-9664.

BOSWELL, G. Harvey *(Judge, United States Bankruptcy Court Western District of Tennessee)* Appointed by U.S. Court of Appeals Sixth Circuit judges to term beginning Nov 16, 1993. Term expires Nov 15, 2007. Born Medina Tennessee July 8, 1947. Educated at University of Tennessee at Martin B.S. with honors 1969 and Memphis State University J.D. 1978. Member Phi Alpha Delta. Admitted to practice Tennessee 1979 and U.S. District Courts Western 1979 and Middle 1981 Districts of Tennessee and Western District of Kentucky 1981. In legal practice Humboldt Tennessee 1979-80 and Milan Tennessee 1980-93.

Assistant City Attorney Milan 1984-92. Important Decisions: In re Beare Co. (allowing assumption of executory contract as it was in the best interest of the estate and was a reasonable business judgment) 177 B.R. 879 Bankr. W.D. Tenn. 1994; In re Beare Co. (holding that oversecured creditor was entitled to market rate of interest at prime rate plus 3% risk factor) 177 B.R. 886 Bankr. W.D. Tenn. 1994; In re Beare Co. (holding that plan proposing ten year amortization of secured creditor's debt with balloon payment after five years was feasible) 177 B.R. 886 Bankr. W.D. Tenn. 1994; In re Silverstein (holding that post-judgment interest that accrued on nondischargeable support payments was not in nature of support and was dischargeable) 186 B.R. 85 Bankr. W.D. Tenn. 1995; In re Crutcher (holding that $11,000 in credit card debt that the debtor had incurred in the course of gambling was not a debt incurred through fraud and was therefore dischargeable) 215 B.R. 696 Bankr. W.D. Tenn. 1997; In re Johnson (holding that in order to declare a prepetition foreclosure sale final both the statute of frauds must be satisfied and consideration must have been tendered) 213 B.R. 134 Bankr. W.D. Tenn. 1997; and In re Lyles (holding that the proper method of determining "replacement value" in a chapter 13 valuation dispute was to average the wholesale and retail values of collateral) 226 B.R. 854 W.D. Tenn. 1998. Instructor Introduction to Law Bethel College 1981-85 and University of Memphis 1997-98. Fellow Tennessee Bar Foundation. Member National Conference of Bankruptcy Judges (Member Commercial Law League Committee 1994-97, Round Table since 1994), American Bankruptcy Institute and Tennessee Bar Association. Speaker Judge William B. Leffler Institute University of Memphis, Mid South Commercial Law Institute, Annual Bankruptcy Seminar Tennessee Bar Association, Annual Seminar Bankruptcy Section Memphis Bar Association and Workshops American Bankruptcy

BOSWELL, G. HARVEY—*Continued*

Institute. Named Outstanding Young Man of the Year by Milan Jaycees 1981-82. Enjoys fishing and hunting.

Office: 324 U.S. Courthouse, 111 South Highland Avenue, Jackson 38301.

Telephone: (731) 421-9370.

BRASFIELD, Martha B. *(Chancellor, Tennessee Chancery Court Twenty-fifth Judicial District)* Elected to term beginning Oct 1, 1998. Term expires Aug 2006. Born Covington Tennessee. Methodist. Educated at Mississippi College B.A. 1970 and Memphis State University School of Law J.D. 1975. Admitted to practice Tennessee 1975. In legal practice Covington 1975-87. Commissioner, Tennessee Claims Commission 1987-98.

Member Tennessee Lawyers' Association for Women, Tipton County and Tennessee Bar Associations. Attended General Jurisdiction Course The National Judicial College Nov 2000. Member Tennessee Supreme Court Historical Society and First United Methodist Church Covington.

Mailing address: P.O. Box 971, Covington 38019.

Office: 116 Munford, Covington 38019.

Telephone: (901) 475-2540.

BREEN, J. Daniel *(Judge, United States District Court Western District of Tennessee)* Magistrate Judge July 1, 1991 to 2003. Appointed for life by President George W. Bush to term beginning 2003. Born Jackson Tennessee July 10, 1950. Catholic. Educated at Spring Hill College B.A. with honors 1972 and University of Tennessee J.D. 1975. Research Editor University of Tennessee Law Review. Member Phi Alpha Delta. Admitted to practice Tennessee 1975, U.S. District Court Western District of Tennessee 1975, U.S. Court of Appeals Sixth Circuit 1977 and U.S. Supreme Court 1979. In legal practice Jackson 1975-91.

Member Tennessee Bar Foundation, American Bar Foundation, American Judicature Society, Federal Magistrate Judges Association, Tennessee (President 1996-97) and American Bar Associations. Board Member Jackson Madison County Health Care Foundation and Boy Scouts of America. Enjoys tennis.

Office: 345 U.S. Courthouse, 111 South Highland Avenue, Jackson 38301.

Telephone: (731) 421-9200.

Fax: (731) 421-9255

BROTHERS, Thomas White *(Judge, Tennessee Circuit Court Twentieth Judicial District)* Appointed by Governor Ned Ray McWherter to term beginning Feb 13, 1989. Elected Aug 1990 and 1998. Current term expires 2006. Presiding Judge since 1991. Born Nashville Tennessee July 16, 1951. Educated at University of Tennessee B.A. with honors 1973 and Vanderbilt University J.D. 1977. Admitted to practice Tennessee 1977 and U.S. District Court District of Tennessee. In legal practice Nashville 1978-89.

Former Secretary Tennessee Judicial Conference. Member Tennessee and American Bar Associations. Democrat.

Office: 404 Metro Courthouse, Nashville 37201.

Telephone: (615) 862-5917.

BROWN, George H., Jr. *(Judge, Tennessee Circuit Court Thirtieth Judicial District)*

Office: 212 Shelby County Courthouse, 140 Adams Avenue, Memphis 38103.

Telephone: (901) 545-4047.

BROWN, Joe B. *(Magistrate Judge, United States District Court Middle District of Tennessee)* Appointed by U.S. District Court judges to term beginning Aug 3, 1998. Term expires Aug 3, 2006. Born Louisville Kentucky Dec 9, 1940. Episcopalian. Educated at Vanderbilt University B.A. cum laude 1962 J.D. 1965. Legislation Editor Vanderbilt Law Review 1964-65. Member Order of the Coif. Admitted to practice Kentucky 1965, Tennessee 1972 and U.S. Supreme Court 1979.

U.S. Attorney Middle District of Tennessee June 1981 to Dec 1991. Member Nashville and Kentucky Bar Associations. U.S. Army JAG.

Office: U.S. Courthouse, 801 Broadway, Nashville 37203-3874.

Telephone: (615) 736-2119.

BROWN, Lynn W. *(Judge, Tennessee Criminal Court First Judicial District)* Elected to term beginning Sept 1, 1988. Reelected 1990 and 1998. Current term expires Aug 31, 2006. Born Elizabethton Tennessee Dec 27, 1950. Presbyterian. Educated at Maryville College B.A. 1973 and University of Tennessee J.D. 1976. Admitted to practice Tennessee 1977 and U.S. District Court Eastern District of Tennessee 1987. In legal practice Elizabethton 1977.

Assistant District Attorney General First Judicial District 1977-88. Member Tennessee Bar Association. Former Director and President United Way. Board of Directors Appalachian Girl Scout Council. Enjoys sailing, snow skiing, reading and hiking.

Office: 713 East Elk Avenue, Elizabethton 37643.

Telephone: (423) 543-5413.

BROWN, W. Frank, III *(Chancellor, Tennessee Chancery Court Eleventh Judicial District)*

Office: 311 Hamilton County Courthouse, 201 East Seventh Street, Chattanooga 37402.

Telephone: (423) 209-7380.

BROWN, William Houston *(Judge, United States Bankruptcy Court Western District of Tennessee)* Appointed by U.S. Court of Appeals Sixth Circuit judges to term beginning Oct 9, 1987. Reappointed Oct 2001, current term expires Oct 2015. Sitting by designation Middle District of Tennessee. Former Judge, Bankruptcy Appellate Panel Sixth Circuit. Born Union City Tennessee April 14, 1941. Baptist. Educated at Union University B.A. in English 1963, Middle Tennessee State University M.A. in History 1967 and University of Tennessee J.D. with honors 1972. Research Editor Tennessee Law Review 1971-72. Woodrow Wilson Fellow 1969-70. Member Order of Barristers and Order of the Coif. Admitted to practice Tennessee 1972, U.S. District Courts Eastern 1972 and Western 1973 Districts of Tennessee and U.S. Court of Appeals Sixth Circuit 1973. In legal practice Jackson 1973-87.

Author "The Impact of Bankruptcy on Alimony, Maintenance and Support Obligations: The Approach in the Sixth Circuit" Tennessee L. Rev. Spring 1989; "The Sixth Circuit: A Survey of Court of Appeals Decisions Under the Bankruptcy Code" *Norton Annual Survey of Bankruptcy Law* 1989; "Pleading a Core Proceeding in Bankruptcy" 3 No. 4 Memphis Bar Forum 1989; "A

BROWN, WILLIAM HOUSTON—*Continued*

Survey of Sixth Circuit Bankruptcy Decisions, 1988" *Norton Bankruptcy Adviser* Oct 1989; "A Comparison of Classification and Treatment of Family Support Obligations and Student Loans: A Case Analysis" Memphis State University L. Rev. Summer 1994; "Political and Ethical Considerations of Exemption Limitations" American Bankruptcy L. Jour. Spring 1997; and "Tolling the Three-Year Period for Discharge of Income Taxes" Mississippi College L. Rev. Spring 1998. Contributing Editor *Norton Bankruptcy Law and Practice* since 1989. Co-author *Bankruptcy Exemption Manual and Bankruptcy Jury Manual* West 1997-98. Important Decisions: In re Apple Tree Partners (negative amortization) 131 B.R. 380, 1991; In re Mark Benskin Company (trustee's rights over constructive trust claimants) 161 B.R. 644, 1993; In re The Julien Company (perfection of oral security agreement) 168 B.R. 647, 1994; and In re Tennessee-Florida Partners (revocation of Chapter 11 confirmation) 170 B.R. 946, 1994. Assistant Professor Jackson State Community College 1967-70. Associate Dean University of Tennessee College of Law 1972-73. Visiting Associate Professor of Law University of Wyoming College of Law 1984-85. Associate Professor of Law 1985-87, Director Clinical Education 1986-87 and Adjunct Professor 1987-94 University of Mississippi School of Law. Fellow Tennessee Bar Foundation and American College of Bankruptcy. Member American Inn of Court, National Conference of Bankruptcy Judges, American Bankruptcy Institute and Memphis Bar Association. Faculty Member Norton Institutes on Bankruptcy Law 1988-2001, Mid-South Commercial Law Institute 1989-2000, Southeastern Bankruptcy Law Institute 1993 and Mississippi Bankruptcy Conference. Enjoys reading, antique clocks, snow skiing and traveling.

Office: 200 Jefferson Avenue, Suite 675, Memphis 38103-2328.

Telephone: (901) 328-3530.

BRYANT, Jerri S. *(Chancellor, Tennessee Chancery Court Tenth Judicial District)* Elected to term beginning Sept 1, 1998. Term expires Sept 1, 2006. Born Maryville Tennessee Nov 26, 1961. Educated at Tennessee Wesleyan College B.A. and University of Tennessee College of Law J.D. Admitted to practice Tennessee 1987 and U.S. District Court District of Tennessee 1988. In legal practice Knoxville 1987-90 and Athens 1991-98.

Former Member McMinn County Bar Association (President 1994-98). Secretary Tennessee Trial Judges Association. Member Tennessee Judicial Conference and Tennessee Bar Association (Young Lawyers Division). Attended Tennessee Civil Mediation Training June 24-28, 1997 and Judicial Settlement and Mediation Training Sept 28-30, 1999. President Athens Kiwanis Club 2001-02. Past President H.O.P.E. Center. Former Board Member YMCA. Board of Trustees Keith Memorial United Methodist Church. Member United Way of McMinn County. Interests include her children and physical fitness.

Office: McMinn County Courthouse, 6 East Madison Avenue, Athens 37303-3697.

Telephone: (423) 746-5412.

Fax: (423) 744-2828

E-mail address: jsbryantl@yahoo.com

BURCH, Robert E. *(Judge, Tennessee Circuit Court Twenty-third Judicial District)* Appointed by Governor Lamar Alexander to term beginning Jan 29, 1980. Elected 1982, 1990 and 1998. Current term expires Aug 31, 2006. Born Memphis Tennessee March 11, 1947. Baptist. Educated at The Citadel B.A. 1969 and Vanderbilt University School of Law J.D. 1972. Admitted to practice Tennessee 1972 and U.S. Supreme Court 1975. In legal practice Dickson 1972-80. Referee, Dickson County Juvenile Court 1975-80.

Author *Trial Handbook for Tennessee Lawyers* Lawyers Co-op 1980 2nd ed. 1995. Named Tennessee Trial Judge of the Year by American Board of Trial Advocates 2002. Former Chairman Board of Directors Middle Tennessee Heart Association. Chairman Governor's Task Force on Tort Law Reform. Interests include military history and computer programming.

Mailing address: P.O. Box 158, Charlotte 37036.

Telephone: (615) 789-5699.

Fax: (615) 789-7016

E-mail address: judge@dickson.net

BURNS, Leon C., Jr. *(Judge, Tennessee Criminal Court Thirteenth Judicial District)* Appointed by Governor Ray Blanton to term beginning April 12, 1976. Elected 1978, 1982, 1990 and 1998. Current term expires Aug 31, 2006. Born Florence Alabama July 3, 1936. Church of Christ. Educated at Tennessee Technological University B.S. 1959 and University of Tennessee J.D. 1972. Admitted to practice Tennessee 1972. Began legal practice Cookeville 1972.

Member Putnam County (President 1974), Tennessee and American Bar Associations. E-4 U.S. Army 1959-61. Member Lions Club. Former member Jaycees (Past President) and Rotary Club. Former Vice President Putnam County Chamber of Commerce. Enjoys tennis, whitewater canoeing and golf.

Office: 228 East Broad Street, Suite 204, Cookeville 38501.

Telephone: (931) 528-1114.

BUTLER, James F. *(Chancellor, Tennessee Chancery Court Twenty-sixth Judicial District)* Appointed by Governor Phil Bredesen to term beginning 2003. Term expires 2004. Educated at Lambuth University B.A. 1964 and University of Tennessee College of Law J.D. 1966.

Office: 200 Madison County Courthouse, 100 East Main Street, Jackson 38301-6294.

Telephone: (731) 423-6072.

BYERS, John K. *(Senior Judge, Tennessee Appellate and Trial Courts)* Appointed Judge, Tennessee Court of Criminal Appeals by Governor Ray Blanton to term beginning June 29, 1976. Elected Aug 1976, 1982 and 1990. Appointed Senior Judge by Tennessee Supreme Court justices to term beginning 1992. Reappointed 1996 and 2000. Current term expires 2004. Serves by assignment. Born Knoxville Tennessee Sept 7, 1930. Lutheran. Educated at University of Tennessee LL.B. 1959. Admitted to practice Tennessee 1959. Began legal practice Kingsport and Bristol 1959. Judge, Tennessee Criminal Court Twenty-sixth Judicial Circuit 1967-76.

County Attorney Sullivan County 1966-76. Member Kingsport Bar Association (President 1962-63). Staff Sergeant USAF 1950-54. Judge Advocate American Legion Department of Tennessee 1963-64. Enjoys golfing.

Mailing address: P.O. Box 444, Knoxville 37901.

Telephone: (865) 594-6118.

BYRD, Clara W. *(Judge, Tennessee Circuit Court Fifteenth Judicial District)*
Mailing address: P.O. Box 788, Lebanon 37088-0788.
Office: 105½ South Cumberland Street, Lebanon 37087.
Telephone: (615) 449-7170.

CAIN, William Bryan *(Judge, Tennessee Court of Appeals Middle Division)* Appointed by Governor Don Sundquist to term beginning April 1998. Retained by election Aug 1998, current term expires Aug 2006. Born Old Hickory Tennessee Jan 30, 1932. Educated at Middle Tennessee State University and Cumberland University School of Law 1958. Judge and Presiding Judge, Tennessee Circuit Court Twenty-second Judicial District Dec 31, 1986 to April 1998.
City Attorney Columbia 1969-73. Delegate Constitutional Convention 1965. State Commander Tennessee Chapter 1969-70 and Member National Legislative Commission 1971-96 The American Legion. Member St. Peter's Episcopal Church Columbia.
Office: 215 Supreme Court Building, 401 Seventh Avenue North, Nashville 37219-1407.
Telephone: (615) 741-6491.

CAMPBELL, Todd J. *(Judge, United States District Court Middle District of Tennessee)* Appointed for life by President Bill Clinton to term beginning 1995. Born Rockford Illinois Sept 5, 1956. Educated at Vanderbilt University B.A. 1978 and University of Tennessee J.D. 1982. In legal practice Nashville 1982-93 and 1995.
Deputy Counsel to Vice President 1993, Counsel to Vice President 1993-95 and Director Administration 1993-95 Office of the Vice President of the United States. Deputy Campaign Manager for Legal Affairs and Treasurer Albert Gore, Jr. For President Committee 1987-88. Counsel to Personnel Department Clinton/Gore Presidential Transition 1992-93.
Office: A-820 U.S. Courthouse, 801 Broadway, Nashville 37203-3889.
Telephone: (615) 736-5291.

CANTRELL, Ben H. *(Judge, Tennessee Court of Appeals Middle Division)* Appointed by Governor Lamar Alexander to term beginning Sept 10, 1980. Retained by election Aug 1982, 1990 and 1998. Current term expires Aug 31, 2006. Born Palmersville Tennessee Dec 6, 1934. Methodist. Educated at Vanderbilt University B.E. 1957 and University of Tennessee J.D. 1966. Member Order of the Coif. Admitted to practice Tennessee 1966. Began legal practice Nashville 1966. Chancellor, Tennessee Chancery Court Division Seven Jan 2, 1973 to Sept 9, 1980, appointed by Governor Winfield Dunn.
Author "Due Process and the Tennessee Long Arm Statute" Tennessee L. Rev. 1966 and "Review of Administrative Agencies by Certiorari in Tennessee" Memphis State L. Rev. 1974. Instructor Nashville School of Law since 1975. Member Harry Phillips American Inn of Court, Tennessee and American Bar Associations.
Office: 211 Supreme Court Building, 401 Seventh Avenue North, Nashville 37219-1407.
Telephone: (615) 741-2206.

CARTER, William B. Mitchell *(Magistrate Judge, United States District Court Eastern District of Tennessee)* Appointed by U.S. District Court judges to term beginning July 30, 1999. Term expires July 30, 2007. Born Chattanooga Tennessee Dec 4, 1942. Presbyterian. Educated at University of North Carolina B.A. 1965, Vanderbilt University School of Law J.D. 1968 and University of Tennessee at Chattanooga M.B.A. 1972. Admitted to practice Tennessee 1968, U.S. District Court Eastern District of Tennessee 1972, U.S. Court of Appeals Sixth Circuit 1976 and U.S. Supreme Court 1985. In legal practice Chattanooga 1972-99. Municipal Judge, Lookout Mountain Municipal Court 1995-99.
Instructor in Business Law University of Tennessee at Chattanooga 1974-97 and Covenant College 1998-2001.
Mailing address: P.O. Box 11350, Chattanooga 37401.
Office: 900 Georgia Avenue, Room 102, Chattanooga 37402.
Telephone: (423) 752-5365.
Fax: (423) 752-5368
E-mail address: bill_carter@tned.uscourts.gov

CATALANO, Carol *(Chancellor, Tennessee Chancery Court Nineteenth Judicial District)*
Office: 475 Montgomery County Courts Center, Two Millennium Plaza, Clarksville 37040.
Telephone: (931) 648-7191.

CHILDERS, Robert L. *(Judge, Tennessee Circuit Court Thirtieth Judicial District)* Elected to term beginning Sept 1, 1984. Reelected 1990 and 1998. Current term expires Aug 31, 2006. Presiding Judge 1989-90 and 1997-98. Currently serves as Special Judge Workers' Compensation Panel Tennessee Supreme Court and Tennessee Court of Appeals. Born Memphis Tennessee March 12, 1948. Methodist. Educated at University of Tennessee at Martin and Memphis State University B.B.A. 1971 J.D. 1974. Member Delta Theta Phi. Admitted to practice Tennessee 1975. Began legal practice Memphis 1975.
Author "Dispositive Motions: Are You Following the Rules?" *The Memphis Bar Association Magazine* Spring 1994, "Jury Service Can Be Fun?" April 23, 1998 and "Rebuilding Public Trust in the Judicial System" Dec 23, 1999 *The Daily News.* and "New Domestic Violence Court Helping Victims" Juridicus April-May 1998. Coauthor "Tennessee Pattern Jury Instructions—Civil" *Tennessee Practice* West Publishing Co. 2nd ed. 1988 and 3rd ed. 1997. Lecturer Memphis State University School of Law. Former Member Board of Directors Family Mediation Center. Founding Member Leo Bearman, Sr. American Inn of Court. Member Executive Committee and Chair 2000 Shelby County Domestic Violence Council. Chair Tennessee Domestic Violence State Coordinating Council since 1999. Commissioner Tennessee Lawyers Assistance Program since 1999 and Commission on Lawyers Assistance Programs American Bar Association since 2000. Vice President Lawyers Helping Lawyers Committee. Member Tennessee Judicial Council (Committee on Weighted Caseload Formula 2001), Tennessee Judicial Conference (Vice President 1996-97, President 1999-2000, Executive Committee, Chairman Pattern Jury Instruction—Civil Committee), Tennessee Trial Judges Association (Past President), American Judges Association, Memphis Trial Lawyers Association (Past President), Tennessee Trial Lawyers Association (Former Member Board of Governors), American Judicature Society and Memphis Bar Association (Board of Directors 1993-95). Speaker "Comparative Fault, Questions Raised by *McIntyre vs. Balentine*" House Judiciary Subcommittee Nov 1993 and "The New Parenting Plan Legislation—How It Is Working" House Children and Family Committee Feb 2001 Tennessee General Assembly. Recipient Charles A. Rond Memorial Award for

CHILDERS, ROBERT L.—*Continued*

Outstanding Judge of the Year from Young Lawyers Division Memphis Bar Association 1986 and 1999, L. Longstreet Heiskell Memorial Award for Best Participant at Tenth Annual Bench-Bar Conference from Memphis Bar Association 1986, The Judge Wheatcraft Award from Tennessee Coalition Against Domestic and Sexual Violence Oct 19, 2001 and Distinguished Alumni Achievement Award from University of Memphis Alumni Association 2002. Named Judge of the Year by Shelby County Deputy Sheriffs Association 1990. Former President National Council Memphis State University School of Law Alumni Association. Former member Board of Directors Memphis Junior Chamber of Commerce and University of Memphis Society. Former Member Board of Visitors Memphis State University. Member Capleville Methodist Church and Variety Club of Memphis Tent 20. Enjoys music, sports and photography.

Office: 212 Shelby County Courthouse, 140 Adams Avenue, Memphis 38103.

Telephone: (901) 545-4022.

Fax: (901) 545-5659

CLAYTON, James Keeble, Jr. *(Judge, Tennessee Circuit Court Sixteenth Judicial District)* Elected to term beginning Sept 1, 1984. Reelected 1990 and 1998. Current term expires Aug 31, 2006. Born Murfreesboro Tennessee Nov 20, 1938. Presbyterian. Educated at Vanderbilt University B.A. 1960 and Nashville School of Law J.D. 1969. Admitted to practice Tennessee 1970. In legal practice Murfreesboro 1970-78. Judge, Rutherford County General Sessions Court and Rutherford County Juvenile Court 1974-84.

Executive Committee Tennessee Counsel of Juvenile Court Judges 1978-84. Secretary-Treasurer 1981 and Vice President 1982 Tennessee General Sessions Judges Conference. Member Tennessee Judicial Conference. Instructor in DUI Tennessee General Sessions Judges Conference University of Tennessee College of Law 1983. Attended The National Judicial College 1985. Lieutenant Colonel USAR 1960-88 (retired). Sales Manager Procter and Gamble 1967-71. Political Affiliation: Independent. Member Murfreesboro Rotary Club since 1963. Enjoys hunting, shooting, tennis and golf.

Office: 414 Judicial Building, Murfreesboro 37130.

Telephone: (615) 898-8001.

CLEMENT, Frank, Jr. *(Judge, Tennessee Circuit Court Twentieth Judicial District)* Former Probate Court Judge.

Office: 410 Metro Courthouse, Nashville 37201.

Telephone: (615) 862-5990.

COLLIER, Curtis L. *(Judge, United States District Court Eastern District of Tennessee)* Appointed for life by President Bill Clinton to term beginning 1995. Born Marianna Arkansas Oct 4, 1949. Educated at Tennessee State University B.S. 1971 and Duke University J.D. 1974.

Assistant U.S. Attorney Eastern District of Louisiana 1979-87 and Eastern District of Tennessee 1987-95.

Mailing address: P.O. Box 831, Chattanooga 37401-0831.

Telephone: (423) 752-5287.

COLTON, John P., Jr. *(Judge, Tennessee Criminal Court Thirtieth Judicial District)*

Office: 201 Poplar Avenue, Suite 519, Memphis 38103.

Telephone: (901) 545-5852.

COOK, John C. *(Chief Judge, United States Bankruptcy Court Eastern District of Tennessee)*

Office: Historic U.S. Courthouse, 31 East 11th Street, Chattanooga 37402-2722.

Telephone: (423) 752-5260.

CORLEW, Robert Ewing, III *(Chancellor, Tennessee Chancery Court Sixteenth Judicial District)*

Office: 304 Judicial Building, Murfreesboro 37130.

Telephone: (615) 898-8006.

COTTRELL, Patricia J. *(Judge, Tennessee Court of Appeals Middle Division)* Appointed by Governor Don Sundquist to term beginning Nov 1998. Born Memphis Tennessee Jan 15, 1947. Educated at University of Tennessee B.S. with honors 1969 J.D. 1976. Staff member Tennessee Law Review. In legal practice Nashville 1997-98.

Assistant Attorney General 1976-78 and 1981-82. Deputy Attorney General 1984-91. Chief Deputy Attorney General 1993-97. Member American Inns of Court, Nashville Bar Foundation, Tennessee Bar Foundation and Nashville Bar Association. Assistant Director Tennessee Alcoholic Beverage Commission 1979-81. Director of Law 1991-93 and Charter Revision Commission 1994-98 Metropolitan Government of Nashville and Davidson County. Member Supreme Court Historical Society.

Office: 218 Supreme Court Building, 401 Seventh Avenue North, Nashville 37219-1407.

Telephone: (615) 741-2063.

COX, James B. "J. B." *(Chancellor, Tennessee Chancery Court Seventeenth Judicial District)*

Mailing address: P.O. Box 713, Fayetteville 37334.

Office: Courthouse, 112 Main Avenue South, Fayetteville 37334.

Telephone: (931) 438-1956.

CRAFT, Chris *(Judge, Tennessee Criminal Court Thirtieth Judicial District)* Appointed by Governor Ned Ray McWherter to term beginning Dec 1, 1994. Elected 1998, current term expires 2006. Born Proctor Arkansas July 8, 1951. Educated at Vanderbilt University B.A. 1975, Memphis Theological Seminary and Memphis State University School of Law J.D. 1978. Legal Research Editor Memphis State University Law Review 1977-78. Admitted to practice Tennessee 1978. In legal practice Memphis 1978-82.

Assistant District Attorney 1982-94. Personal Statement or Quote: "Delight in the Lord, and He will give you the desires of your heart" (Psalms 37:4).

Office: 519 Shelby County Justice Complex, 201 Poplar Avenue, Memphis 38103.

Telephone: (901) 545-5858.

CRAWFORD, W. Frank *(Judge, Tennessee Court of Appeals Western Division)* Appointed by Governor Lamar Alexander to term beginning Sept 1, 1982. Retained by election 1990 and 1998. Current term expires Aug 31, 2006. Presiding Judge since Aug 1995. Born Memphis Tennessee April 2, 1927. Methodist. Educated at Memphis State University 1944, Union University 1946-48 and University of Tennessee LL.B. 1950. Board of

CRAWFORD, W. FRANK—*Continued*

Editors University of Tennessee Law Review 1950. Member Alpha Tau Omega and Phi Alpha Delta. Admitted to practice Tennessee 1951. In legal practice Memphis 1951 to Sept 1982 and Henderson 1953-54.

Lecturer on Medical Legal Jurisprudence University of Tennessee College of Medicine 1972-82. Fellow American College of Trial Lawyers and American Bar Foundation. Member American Judicature Society, Tennessee Court of the Judiciary (Presiding Judge Aug 1995-97), Memphis (Director 1959-62, President Junior Bar 1960-61), Tennessee (Vice President 1972-73) and American Bar Associations. Corporal U.S. Army (parachute infantry) 1944-46.

Office: 1414 White Station Tower, 5050 Poplar Avenue, Memphis 38157.
Telephone: (901) 537-2983.
Fax: (901) 537-2998

CUPP, Robert E. *(Judge, Tennessee Criminal Court First Judicial District)*
Office: 111 West Main Street, Suite 200, Jonesborough 37659.
Telephone: (423) 913-7001.

DAILEY, Joseph B. *(Judge, Tennessee Criminal Court Thirtieth Judicial District)*
Office: 201 Poplar Avenue, Suite 519, Memphis 38103.
Telephone: (901) 545-5857.

DANIEL, Joseph S. "Steve" *(Judge, Tennessee Circuit Court Sixteenth Judicial District)* Elected to term beginning Sept 1, 1980. Reelected to subsequent terms. Current term expires Aug 31, 2006. Currently serves as Presiding Judge. Born Milan Tennessee July 13, 1946. Church of Christ. Educated at Louisiana State University B.S. 1968 and University of Tennessee College of Law J.D. 1971. Member Sigma Alpha Epsilon. Admitted to practice Tennessee 1971. Began legal practice Knoxville 1971. In legal practice Nashville 1972 and Murfreesboro 1973.

Important Decisions: State v. Roode (authorization of helicopter searches) and Davis v. Davis (termination inter-spousal immunity). Adjunct Professor of Business Law Middle Tennessee State University since 1978. Past President Tennessee Judges Association. Former Chairman Committee on Pattern Civil Jury Instructions, Member Executive Committee and President 1994-95 Tennessee Judicial Conference. Secretary-Treasurer and Vice President since 1973 Rutherford-Cannon County Bar Association. Member National Conference of State Trial Judges and Tennessee Representative for Judiciary American Bar Association. Named Outstanding Young Man of the Year by Murfreesboro Jaycees 1981. Lieutenant Colonel USAR JAG since 1968. Democrat. Vice Chairman Board of Directors Adult Activity Center. Board of Trustees Middle Tennessee State University. Private pilot.

Office: 20 Public Square North, Murfreesboro 37130.
Telephone: (615) 898-8004.

DAVIES, Robert E. Lee *(Judge, Tennessee Circuit Court Twenty-first Judicial District)*
Mailing address: P.O. Box 1469, Franklin 37065-1469.
Office: 112 Williamson County Courthouse, 305 Public Square, Franklin 37064.
Telephone: (615) 790-5426.

DONALD, Bernice Bouie *(Judge, United States District Court Western District of Tennessee)* Appointed for life by President Bill Clinton to term beginning Dec 1995. Educated at Memphis State University B.A. 1974 J.D. 1979. Member Zeta Phi Beta. Judge, Tennessee General Sessions Criminal Court Sept 1982 to June 1988. First Black female elected judge in history of Tennessee. Former Judge, United States Bankruptcy Court Western District of Tennessee, appointed by U.S. Court of Appeals Sixth Circuit judges to term beginning June 1988. First black female in the United States to be appointed U.S. Bankruptcy Court judge.

Staff Attorney Employment Law and Economic Development Unit Memphis Area Legal Services April 1980 to Oct 1980 and Public Defender's Office Shelby County Oct 1980 to Aug 1982. Adjunct Professor in Criminal Procedure, Business Ethics, Business Management, Practical Concepts in Law and Constitutional Rights of Prisoners Shelby State Community College and in Legal Research and Writing and Professional Responsibility Memphis State University School of Law. Former Associate Member National Center for State Courts. Fellow American Bar Foundation. Member National Association of Women Judges (District Director 1983-85, Member Nominating Committee 1985, Chair Publicity Committee 1986, Treasurer 1986-87, Secretary 1987-88, Vice President 1988-89, President Elect 1989-90, President 1990-91), National Conference of Bankruptcy Judges (Elections Committee 1991, ABA Liaison Committee), American Judges Association (Court Security and Legislation Committee, Chair National Project on Domestic Violence, Delegate House of Delegates), The Association of Trial Lawyers of America, Association of Women Attorneys (President Elect 1990, President 1991), Memphis (Chair Bench Bar Conference Judiciary Practice and Procedures Committee 1990-91, Co-chair Courts Committee, Executive Director Search Committee), Tennessee, National (Former Secretary) and American (Conference Delegate National Conference of Special Court Judges Conference 1984-89, Chair Committees on Courts and the Community and Law Related Education 1985, Chair Committee on Media Relations and Fair Trial 1988-89, Secretary National Conference of Special Court Judges 1988-90, Chair Occupational Stress in the Judiciary Planning Conference since 1989, Committees on Program and Conference of Special Judges Section of National Conference of Special Court Judges, Chairperson Committee on Conference Membership Eligibility 1989-90, Committees on Literacy and the Courts 1990-93, Long Range Planning since 1991, Program and Annual Meeting 1992-93, Continuing Judicial Education 1992-93, Budget 1992-93, Coordinating and Planning 1992-93, Chair Task Force on Opportunities for Minorities in the Judicial Administration Division, Liaison Committee on Courts and Communities Judicial Administration Division and National Conference of State Trial Judges Judicial Administration Division, Member Standing Committee on Gavel Awards, Section of Criminal Justice, Vice Chair Committee on Bankruptcy Section of General Practice 1988-90) Bar Associations.

Attended General Sessions Judges Educational Conference 1982, 1983, 1984 and 1985 and Special Conference on Victims of Crimes 1985. State Judicial Leader 1984, Attended Faculty Training Conference 1985 and Special

DONALD, BERNICE BOUIE—*Continued*

Conference on Prison Overcrowding The National Judicial College. Participated in numerous panels and forums dealing with legal process and the judiciary. Lecturer on "Issues on Comparable Worth" Department of Energy; "Getting Women Elected to Office" Tennessee Women's Political Caucus; "Domestic Violence: A Blue Print for Action" American Judges Association; "Presiding in a Criminal Court, A Workshop" National Institute of Justice; and "The Automatic Stay: For Protection When You Need It Most" Federal Bar Association 1989. Recipient Young Careerist Award from Raleigh Bureau of Professional Women 1982, Community Services Award from National Conference of Christians and Jews 1986, America's Best and Brightest from *Dollars and Sense Magazine* 1988, She Knows Where She's Going Award from Girls Club of Memphis 1990, Distinguished Alumni Award from Memphis State University 1990 and Martin Luther King Community Service Award. Named Citizen of the Year by Excelsior Chapter of Eastern Star, Woman of the Year by Pentecostal Temple Church of God in Christ and one of Ten Outstanding Young Tennesseans by Memphis Jaycees 1990. Listed in Who's Who Among Memphians by *Memphis Magazine.* Former Member Lupus Foundation, Memphis Literacy Council, Criminal Justice Ministry, Tennessee Association of Women in Office (Vice President), Women in the Political Process, Family Services, Positive Mental Attitude Association, Big Brothers and Big Sisters, Inc., Memphis State University Law Alumni Association and Memphis State University Alumni Association (Representative at Large). Former Host radio programs "Studio-97" and "Lawscope." Board Member 1980-87 and President 1985-86 Memphis Street Law, Inc. Board Member 1988-92, Secretary 1989-91 and Chairman Board of Directors 1991 Midtown Health Association. Chair Leadership Memphis Crime Day 1988, 1990 and 1991. Board Member Memphis Brooks Museum of Art since 1992. Mentor Girl's Club of Memphis. Board of Directors and Chair African American Involvement Committee Memphis in May. Treasurer Tennessee Women's Forum. Advisory Panel Shelby State Community College. Member Dean Search Committee Memphis State University School of Law 1984, Calvary Street Ministry since 1992, Girl Scouts Council of Arkansas, Mississippi and Tennessee, Kiwanis (Membership Committee, Kiwanis Charities), Criminal Justice Panel, National Conference of Negro Women, Business and Professional Women Clubs and Leadership Memphis Screening Committee.

Office: 341 Federal Building, 167 North Main Street, Memphis 38103.

Telephone: (901) 495-1299.

DOZIER, Steve R. *(Judge, Tennessee Criminal Court Twentieth Judicial District)* Assumed office Dec 1997. Presiding Judge since Sept 2000. Educated at Vanderbilt University B.A. 1979 and Nashville School of Law J.D. 1984. Law Clerk to Hon. James Randall Wyatt, Jr., Tennessee Criminal Court Twentieth Judicial District Jan 1983 to Sept 1984. In legal practice June 1990 to June 1995.

Assistant District Attorney General Sept 1984 to June 1990 and June 1995 to Dec 1997. Instructor in Evidence Nashville School of Law since 2000. Member District Five Investigating Committee Tennessee Supreme Court, Harry Phillips American Inn of Court, Tennessee Judicial Conference and Nashville Bar Association (Former Chairman Criminal Justice Committee). Speaker The Third National Symposium on Child Sexual Abuse The National Children's Advocacy Center 1987 and Tennessee General Sessions Judges' Conference Sept 2000. Moderator Criminal Justice Leadership Nashville 1994. Participant Advanced Constitutional Criminal Law and Procedure 1998 and Judge As Fact Finder 2000 American Academy of Judicial Education. Member Mayor's Commission on Crack Cocaine 1997. Member Nashville's Vanderbilt Alumni Career Network, The Nashville Coalition on Child Abuse, Davidson County Child Sex Abuse Council, Governor's Alliance for Drug Free Tennessee, Fraternal Order of Police and Ducks Unlimited.

Office: 601 Metro Courthouse, Nashville 37201.

Telephone: (615) 862-5930.

DROWOTA, Frank F., III *(Chief Justice, Tennessee Supreme Court)* Elected to term beginning Sept 1, 1980. Current term expires 2006. Chief Justice Feb 1989 to Sept 1990 and since Sept 1, 2001. Born Williamsburg Kentucky July 7, 1938. Member Woodmont Christian Church. Educated at Vanderbilt University B.A. 1960 J.D. 1965. In legal practice 1965-70. Chancellor, Tennessee Chancery Court Division Seven 1970-74. Judge, Tennessee Court of Appeals Middle Division May 15, 1974 to 1980. USN 1960-62 and Commander USNR JAGC.

Office: 318 Supreme Court Building, 401 Seventh Avenue North, Nashville 37219-1407.

Telephone: (615) 741-2114.

EASTER, Timothy L. *(Judge, Tennessee Circuit Court Twenty-first Judicial District)*

Mailing address: P.O. Box 1469, Franklin 37065-1469.

Office: 305 Public Square, Room 112, Franklin 37064-2521.

Telephone: (615) 790-5426.

EBLEN, E. Eugene *(Judge, Tennessee Criminal Court Ninth Judicial District)*

Mailing address: P.O. Box 220, Kingston 37763.

Office: Roane County Courthouse, Ray Street, Kingston 37763.

Telephone: (865) 376-6573.

ECHOLS, Robert L. *(Chief Judge, United States District Court Middle District of Tennessee)* Appointed for life by President George Bush March 1992 to term beginning April 20, 1992. Chief Judge since Aug 1, 1998. Born Memphis Tennessee Jan 13, 1941. Educated at Rhodes College B.A. 1962 and University of Tennessee College of Law J.D. 1964. Listed in *Who's Who in American Colleges and Universities.* Law Clerk to Hon. Marion S. Boyd, U.S. District Court Western District of Tennessee March 1965 to Aug 1966. Member Phi Delta Phi and Sigma Alpha Epsilon. Admitted to practice Tennessee 1965. In legal practice Nashville May 1969 to April 1992. Designated Visiting Judge, U.S. Court of Appeals Sixth Circuit July 1993, 1994, 1995 and 1996.

Former Member Tennessee Trial Lawyers Association and The Association of Trial Lawyers of America. Fellow Nashville Bar Foundation, Tennessee Bar Foundation and American Bar Foundation. Member Hearing Panel Tennessee Supreme Court Disciplinary Board 1979-85. Chairman Library Committee U.S. District Court Middle District of Tennessee since 1992. Member Library Committee U.S. Court of Appeals Sixth Circuit.

ECHOLS, ROBERT L.—*Continued*

Member Tennessee State-Federal Judicial Council (Judicial Branch Committee), American College of Mortgage Attorneys, Harry Phillips American Inn of Court, Federal Judges Association, Nashville (Board of Directors 1986-90, Mentoring Program 1994, 1995, 1996 and 1997), Tennessee and American Bar Associations. Speaker Trial Practice Institute 1993 and on Excessive Force Vanderbilt Law Symposium 1993. Recipient Alumni Leadership Award 1984 and Outstanding Public Service Award 1992 University of Tennessee College of Law. U.S. Army JAGC Feb 1969 to June 1969. Arkansas National Guard Aug 1966 to Dec 1966. District of Columbia National Guard Jan 1967 to Feb 1969. Colonel Tennessee Army National Guard. Republican. Legislative Assistant to Congressman Dan Kuykendall Jan 1967 to April 1969. Member 1978-90 and Chairman 1987-90 Alumni Council, Chairman Annual Fund 1981-84 and Member Dean's Circle since 1989 University of Tennessee College of Law. Legal Counsel 1983-84 and Annual Fund Co-chairman 1981-82 Ensworth School. Board of Trustees Brentwood Academy 1984-89. Advisory Board Chairman Cordova Bank & Trust. Board of Directors McNeilly Day Home 1971-80, Investors Savings & Loan Association 1974-81, Matthew Walker Community Health Center 1979-84, American Trust Savings Bank 1980-86, Family and Children Service 1980-89, Tennessee Law Enforcement Training Academy 1983-86, Christian Leadership Concepts, Robertson County Memorial Gardens, Inc. and Montgomery Bell Academy (Capital Campaign). Member Nashville Junior Chamber of Commerce 1969-76, Cumberland Valley Girl Scouts 1979, University of Tennessee Athletics Board 1980-83, Annual Fund Committee Middle Tennessee Boy Scouts 1985, Tennessee Presidents Trust, National Guard Association of Tennessee, Reserve Officers Association, Leadership Nashville (Program Committee 1993), Leadership Nashville Alumni Association, Rhodes College Alumni Association, United Way (Allocation Panel 1977-80) and Nashville Area Chamber of Commerce.

Office: 824 U.S. Courthouse, 801 Broadway, Nashville 37203-3868.

Telephone: (615) 736-2774.

EDGAR, R. Allan *(Chief Judge, United States District Court Eastern District of Tennessee)* Appointed for life by President Ronald Reagan to term beginning April 29, 1985. Chief Judge since Nov 24, 1998. Born Munising Michigan Oct 6, 1940. Episcopalian. Educated at Davidson College B.A. 1962 and Duke University School of Law LL.B. 1965. Admitted to practice Tennessee 1965, U.S. District Court Eastern District of Tennessee 1968, U.S. Court of Appeals Sixth Circuit 1971 and U.S. Supreme Court 1980. In legal practice Chattanooga 1967-85.

Important Decisions: Lovvorn v. City of Chattanooga (drug testing, constitutional rights under Fourth, Fifth, Ninth and Fourteenth Amendments) 647 F. Supp. 875 E.D.Tenn. 1986; Mapp v. Board of Education of City of Chattanooga, Tenn. (school desegregation) 630 F. Supp. 876 E.D.Tenn. 1986 and 648 F. Supp. 876 E.D.Tenn. 1986; Broadway Books v. Roberts 642 F. Supp. 486 E.D.Tenn. 1986; and Brown v. Board of Commissioners of Chattanooga (Voting Rights Act) 722 F. Supp. 380 E.D.Tenn. 1989. Member Committee on Court Administration and Case Management Judicial Conference of the U.S. Member Chattanooga, Tennessee and Federal Bar Associations. Captain U.S. Army 1965-67. Recipient Bronze Star Medal, National Defense Service Medal, Vietnam Campaign Medal and Vietnam Service Medal. Member House of Representatives Tennessee 1971-72. Member 1979-85 and Chairman 1984-85 Tennessee Wildlife Resources Commission, appointed by Governor Lamar Alexander.

Mailing address: P.O. Box 1748, Chattanooga 37401-1748.

Telephone: (423) 752-5220.

ELLIS, George Robert *(Chancellor, Tennessee Chancery Court Twenty-eighth Judicial District)* Appointed by Governor Ned Ray McWherter to term beginning Jan 11, 1993. Elected Aug 1994 and 1998. Current term expires Sept 1, 2006. Born Dyer Tennessee Nov 14, 1948. Presbyterian. Educated at University of Tennessee B.S. 1970 and University of Memphis J.D. 1975. Member Delta Theta Phi. Admitted to practice Tennessee 1976. In legal practice Trenton 1976-78. Judge, Dyer City 1976-82. Judge, Gibson County General Sessions Court 1978-93.

Adjunct Professor Dyersburg State Community College 1993-97. Member Tennessee General Sessions Judges Conference (President), Tennessee Judicial Conference, American Judges Association and Tennessee Bar Association. Instructor Judicial Seminars on Kazakstan and Krgystan 1976 and 1977 and Seminars for the High Commercial Court of the Russian Federation Reno Nevada and Moscow Russia 1995. Facilitator The National Judicial College 1994-97. Named Presiding Judge National High School Mock Trial Championship 1997. USN 1970-72. Past President Chamber of Commerce and Lions Club. Member Rotary International and American Legion. Enjoys swimming, snow skiing and raising American quarter horses.

Office: Chancery Building, 204 North Court Square, Trenton 38382.

Telephone: (731) 855-7668.

EVANS, Walter L. *(Chancellor, Tennessee Chancery Court Thirtieth Judicial District)*

Office: 308 Shelby County Courthouse, 140 Adams Avenue, Memphis 38103.

Telephone: (901) 545-4702.

FANSLER, Daryl R. *(Chancellor, Tennessee Chancery Court Sixth Judicial District)*

Office: 125 City County Building, 400 Main Avenue, Knoxville 37902.

Telephone: (865) 215-2560.

FARMER, David R. *(Judge, Tennessee Court of Appeals Western Division)* Appointed by Governor Lamar Alexander March 14, 1986. Retained by election Aug 1986, Aug 1990 and Aug 1998. Current term expires Aug 2006. Born Springfield Missouri Dec 6, 1940. Religious affiliation: United Methodist. Educated at Memphis State University B.B.A. 1963 LL.B. 1966. Admitted to practice Tennessee 1966, Kentucky 1967 and U.S. Supreme Court 1975. In legal practice Jackson Tennessee 1968-86.

Fellow Tennessee Bar Foundation. Member Leo Bearman, Sr. American Inn of Court and Jackson-Madison County Bar Association. USAR 1966-72.

Mailing address: P.O. Box 909, Jackson 38302-0909.

Office: Supreme Court Building, Jackson 38301.

FARMER, DAVID R.—*Continued*

Telephone: (731) 423-5836.
Fax: (731) 426-0646

FORGETY, Telford E., Jr. *(Chancellor, Tennessee Chancery Court Fourth and Fifth Judicial Districts)*
Mailing address: P.O. Box 1370, Dandridge 37725-1370.
Office: 1244 Gay Street, Dandridge 37725.
Telephone: (865) 397-3497.

FRANKS, Herschel P. *(Judge, Tennessee Court of Appeals Eastern Division)* Appointed by Governor Ray Blanton to term beginning May 1978. Retained by election Aug 1978, 1982, 1990 and 1998. Current term expires Aug 31, 2006. Born Savannah Tennessee May 28, 1930. United Church of Christ. Educated at University of Maryland and University of Tennessee J.D. 1957. Recipient Bancroft-Whitney Award in Constitutional Law 1956. Admitted to practice Tennessee 1959 and U.S. Supreme Court 1968. Began legal practice Chattanooga 1959. Chancellor, Tennessee Chancery Court Division Three 1970-78 (Presiding Judge 1977-78). Special Justice, Tennessee Supreme Court 1979, 1986 and 1987.

Member Hamilton County Records Commission 1971-76. Member Chattanooga Bar Foundation and Tennessee Bar Foundation. Member Chattanooga (President 1968-69, Chairman Past President's Committee 1977-78), Tennessee (Chairman Domestic Relations Committee 1965-66 and Legal Education and Admissions to Bar Committee 1980-81) and American (Tennessee State Representative National Conference of State Trial Judges 1973-78) Bar Associations. Attended The National Judicial College 1971. Recipient Community Service Award 1971 and Foundations of Freedom Award from Chattanooga Bar Association 1986. Listed in *Who's Who in American Law* and *Who's Who in America.* USAF 1950-54. Democrat. President Optimist Club 1965. Enjoys gardening and history.

Office: 562 State Office Building, 540 McCallie Avenue, Chattanooga 37402.
Telephone: (423) 634-6344.
Fax: (423) 634-5861

FRIERSON, Thomas R., II *(Chancellor, Tennessee Chancery Court Third Judicial District)* Appointed by Governor Don Sundquist to term beginning March 8, 1996. Elected Aug 1996 and 1998. Current term expires Aug 31, 2006. Born Hamblen County Tennessee Oct 9, 1958. Methodist. Educated at University of Tennessee B.A. magna cum laude 1980 J.D. 1983. Admitted to practice Tennessee 1983 and U.S. District Court Eastern District of Tennessee 1984. In legal practice Morristown 1983-90. Judge, Hamblen County General Sessions Court 1990-96.

Member Tennessee Judicial Ethics Committee, Tennessee Trial Judges Associations and Tennessee Judicial Conference.

Office: Hamblen County Courthouse, 511 West Second North Street, Morristown 37814.
Telephone: (423) 586-9500.

GASAWAY, John H., III *(Judge, Tennessee Circuit Court Nineteenth Judicial District)* Elected to term beginning Sept 1, 1990. Reelected 1998, current term expires Aug 31, 2006. Born Atlanta Georgia Sept 11, 1947. Christian. Educated at Austin Peay State University B.S. 1969 and Nashville School of Law J.D. 1975. Admitted to practice Tennessee 1975 and U.S. District Court Middle District of Tennessee 1981. In legal practice Clarksville 1976-90.

Member American Judges Association and Tennessee Bar Association. Graduate General Jurisdiction Course The National Judicial College Aug 1992.

Office: 481 Montgomery County Court Center, Two Millennium Plaza, Clarksville 37040.
Telephone: (931) 648-5704.

GAYDEN, Hamilton, Jr. *(Judge, Tennessee Circuit Court Twentieth Judicial District)* Elected to term beginning Sept 1, 1978. Reelected 1982, 1990 and 1998. Current term expires Aug 31, 2006. Born Nashville Tennessee June 17, 1939. Baptist. Educated at Vanderbilt University B.A. 1961 LL.B. 1964. Admitted to practice Tennessee 1964. Began legal practice Franklin 1964. In legal practice Nashville 1967-74. Judge, Tennessee General Sessions Court 1974-78.

Assistant Metropolitan Attorney 1965-67. Member Unemployment Compensation Review Board 1971-74. Author *To Circle the Cross.* Member Tennessee Trial Lawyers Association, Nashville and Tennessee Bar Associations. Recipient Certificate of Merit from Red Cross 1978 and Certificate of Appreciation from Al Menah Shrine 1983. Specialist Fourth Class U.S. Army 1958-64. Employed by People's National Bank Seattle Washington 1961. Democrat. Board member Nashville Women's Club. Member Middle Tennessee Council Boy Scouts of America (Chairman Sustaining Membership Enrollment Explorer Scouts 1976), 32° Masons and Al Menah Shrine Temple. Enjoys tennis, gardening and bicycling.

Office: 502 Metro Courthouse, Nashville 37201.
Telephone: (615) 862-5901.

GLENN, Alan E. *(Judge, Tennessee Court of Criminal Appeals Western Division)* Appointed by Governor Don Sundquist to term beginning April 1999. Born Chicago Illinois Oct 3, 1942. Educated at Vanderbilt University B.A. 1965 J.D. 1968. In legal practice Memphis 1982-99.

Assistant U.S. Attorney 1970-71 and Assistant District Attorney General 1971-82. Instructor in Trial Advocacy Harvard Law School since 1986. Arbitrator 1985-99 and Board of Construction Panel 1995-99 American Arbitration Association. Lecturer National College of District Attorneys 1982-86. Vice President Theatre Memphis 1995-97. President National Ornamental Metal Museum since 1996 and Memphis Arts in the Park Festival 1997-98.

Office: 1416 White Station Tower, 5050 Poplar Avenue, Memphis 38157-1416.
Telephone: (901) 537-2980.

GODDARD, Houston M. *(Judge, Tennessee Court of Appeals Eastern Division)* Elected to term beginning 1974. Retained by election 1982, 1990 and 1998. Current term expires 2006. Presiding Judge since April 1995. Born Knoxville Tennessee Jan 1, 1927. United Methodist. Educated at University of Tennessee B.A. 1948 LL.B. 1950. Member General Assembly Tennessee 1967-72 (Minority Leader 1971-72).

Mailing address: P.O. Box 444, Knoxville 37901.
Office: 505 Main Street, Suite 202, Knoxville 37902.
Telephone: (865) 594-6707.

GOLDIN, Arnold *(Chancellor, Tennessee Chancery Court Thirtieth Judicial District)*
Office: Shelby County Courthouse, 140 Adams Avenue, Memphis 38103.
Telephone: (901) 545-4000.

GRAHAM, Thomas W. "Rusty" *(Judge, Tennessee Circuit Court Twelfth Judicial District)*
Mailing address: P.O. Box 993, Jasper 37347-0993.
Office: 210 Lawyers Building, Jasper 37347.
Telephone: (423) 942-3618.

GRAY, Thomas E. *(Chancellor, Tennessee Chancery Court Eighteenth Judicial District)* Former Judge, Sumner County General Sessions Court.
Office: 303 Courthouse, Public Square, Gallatin 37066.
Telephone: (615) 451-6004.

GRIFFIN, Juliet *(Magistrate Judge, United States District Court Middle District of Tennessee)* Appointed by U.S. District Court judges.
Office: 756 U.S. Courthouse, 801 Broadway, Nashville 37203-3874.
Telephone: (615) 736-5164.

GUINN, Julian P. *(Judge, Tennessee Circuit Court Twenty-fourth Judicial District)* Elected to term beginning Sept 1, 1984. Reelected 1990 and 1998. Current term expires Aug 31, 2006. Currently serves as Presiding Judge. Born Detroit Michigan Aug 9, 1933. Protestant. Educated at U.S. Naval Academy B.S. 1958 and University of Tennessee J.D. 1965. Admitted to practice Tennessee 1966.
Mailing address: P.O. Box 488, Paris 38242.
Office: 310 West Washington Street, Paris 38242.
Telephone: (731) 642-8956.
Fax: (731) 642-8924

HAGLER, John Brown *(Judge, Tennessee Circuit Court Tenth Judicial District)*
Mailing address: P.O. Box 846, Cleveland 37364-0846.
Office: 207 Bradley County Courthouse, Cleveland 37364.
Telephone: (423) 476-0537.

HAMILTON, Jim T. *(Judge, Tennessee Circuit Court Twenty-second Judicial District)* Elected to term beginning Sept 1, 1982. Reelected 1990 and 1998. Current term expires Aug 31, 2006. Born Selmer Tennessee June 15, 1941. Episcopalian. Educated at Middle Tennessee State University B.S. 1963 and Memphis State University J.D. 1966. Member Delta Theta Phi. Admitted to practice Tennessee 1966. In legal practice Selmer 1966-70 and Mount Pleasant 1970-82.
Mayor of Selmer 1968-70. Part-time Assistant District Attorney General 1973-82. Member Tennessee Judicial Conference and Maury County Bar Association. Democrat. Paul Harris Fellow. Member Mount Pleasant Rotary Club. Enjoys golf, reading and sports.
Mailing address: P.O. Box 413, Columbia 38402-0413.
Office: 22 Public Square, Columbia 38402.
Telephone: (931) 380-3325.

HARGROVE, Stella L. *(Judge, Tennessee Circuit Court Twenty-second Judicial District)*
Mailing address: P.O. Box 1056, Columbia 38402-1056.
Office: 14 Public Square, Columbia 38401.
Telephone: (931) 380-2543.

HARMON, Ron E. *(Chancellor, Tennessee Chancery Court Twenty-fourth Judicial District)*
Office: 802 Main Street, Savannah 38372.
Telephone: (731) 926-3360.

HARRIS, Donald P. *(Judge, Tennessee Circuit Court Twenty-first Judicial District)* Elected to term beginning Sept 1, 1986. Reelected 1990 and 1998. Current term expires Aug 31, 2006. Born Humboldt Tennessee Feb 16, 1946. Educated at University of Tennessee B.S. 1968 J.D. with honors 1973. Comments Editor Tennessee Law Review 1972-73. Member Phi Alpha Delta. Admitted to practice Tennessee 1974. In legal practice Franklin 1974-86. Judge, Franklin Municipal Court 1981-82.
Fellow Tennessee Bar Foundation. Attended General Jurisdiction Course The National Judicial College 1988. Captain U.S. Army Military Intelligence 1968-71.
Mailing address: P.O. Box 1469, Franklin 37065-1469.
Office: 305 Public Square, Room 112, Franklin 37064-2521.
Telephone: (615) 790-5426.
Fax: (615) 790-4424

HARRISON, Marian F. *(Judge, United States Bankruptcy Court Middle District of Tennessee)* Appointed by U.S. Court of Appeals Sixth Circuit judges to term beginning Dec 21, 1999. Term expires 2013.
Office: 232 Customs House, 701 Broadway, Nashville 37203.
Telephone: (615) 736-5589.

HAYES, David G. *(Judge, Tennessee Court of Criminal Appeals Western Division)* Appointed by Governor Ned Ray McWherter to term beginning April 25, 1994. Retained by election Sept 1994 and 1998. Current term expires Aug 31, 2006. Born Cookeville Tennessee Aug 22, 1943. Educated at University of Tennessee B.S. 1965 and University of Mississippi J.D. 1970. Admitted to practice Mississippi 1970, Tennessee 1971 and U.S. District Court District of Tennessee 1972. In legal practice Union City Tennessee 1972-76. Judge, Tennessee Circuit Court Twenty-seventh Judicial District, Jan 1, 1990 to April 24, 1994, appointed by Governor Ned Ray McWherter.
District Attorney Twenty-seventh Judicial District 1976-90. Corporate Attorney Exxon Corporation Houston Texas 1970-72.
Mailing address: P.O. Box 909, Jackson 38302-0909.
Office: #6 Highway 45 Bypass, Jackson 38301.
Telephone: (731) 426-0861.

HAYNES, Barbara N. *(Judge, Tennessee Circuit Court Twentieth Judicial District)* Elected to term beginning Sept 1982. Reelected 1990 and 1998. Current term expires Aug 31, 2006. Born Nashville Tennessee Sept 6, 1937. Presbyterian. Educated at University of Tennessee B.S. 1959 and Nashville School of Law J.D. 1976. Admitted to practice Tennessee 1977. In legal practice Goodlettsville 1977-82. Judge, Tennessee General Sessions Court Division I 1982-90.

HAYNES, BARBARA N.—*Continued*

Chair Tennessee Sentencing Commission since 1986. Legal Assistant to Congress. Fellow Tennessee Bar Association. Member National Association of Women Judges, Harry Phillips Inn of Court, Tennessee Trial Lawyers Association, Lawyers Association of Women, The Association of Trial Lawyers of America, Nashville (Legislative Committee), Tennessee and American Bar Associations. Attended Tennessee General Sessions Conference twice yearly 1982-90 (President 1988) and Tennessee State Trial Conference three times yearly since 1990. Taught numerous seminars for District Attorney Conference, Tennessee Bar Association and State Judicial Conferences. Recipient Freeman Award from American Civil Liberties Union 1991. Named Woman of the Year by Lawyers Association of Women. Democrat. Member League of Women Voters, Emily's List and Nashville Political Caucus. Board Member Nashville Area Chamber of Commerce. Member American Cancer Society, Muscular Dystrophy, National Conference of Christians and Jews and Family and Children's Services. Enjoys reading, gardening, basketball and football.

Office: 510 Metro Courthouse, Nashville 37201.

Telephone: (615) 862-5907.

Fax: (615) 862-5913

HAYNES, William J., Jr. *(Judge, United States District Court Middle District of Tennessee)* Magistrate Judge Dec 1984 to Nov 15, 1999. Appointed Judge for life by President Bill Clinton to term beginning Nov 16, 1999. Born Memphis Tennessee Sept 5, 1949. Catholic. Educated at College of St. Thomas B.A. 1970 and Vanderbilt University School of Law J.D. 1973. Admitted to practice Tennessee 1974 and U.S. District Court Middle District of Tennessee. In legal practice Nashville 1984.

Assistant Attorney General 1973-77, Senior Assistant Attorney General 1977-78, Deputy Attorney General Antitrust and Consumer Protection Division 1978-84 and Special Deputy Attorney General for Litigation 1984 Office of Attorney General and Reporter Tennessee. District Attorney General pro tem Shelby County 1979. Author "State Antitrust Laws" Bureau of National Affairs 1988. Contributing Author to Zeidman "Legal Aspects of Selling and Buying" Shepard's McGraw-Hill 2nd ed. 1991. Instructor Southeastern Paralegal Institute 1986-90. Lecturer on Law Vanderbilt University School of Law since 1987. Assistant to Hon. William M. Leech, Jr., former Attorney General Tennessee and Chair National Association of Attorneys General Antitrust Committee 1983-84. Member Antitrust Litigation and Training Committees National Association of Attorneys General 1982-84, Hearing Committee Tennessee Board of Professional Responsibility 1983-84. Advisory Board Corporate Practice Series Bureau of National Affairs 1989. Fellow Tennessee Bar Foundation. Member Harry Phillips Inn of Court (Master Bencher 1990-92), Napier-Looby (Board of Directors 1983), Nashville (Board of Directors 1981-83, First Vice President 1983-84), Tennessee (Commission on Women and Minorities in the Profession since 1992) and American (Vice Chair Committee on State Antitrust Enforcement Section of Antitrust Law 1989-90) Bar Associations. Speaker and Panelist New York Law Journal Press, Virginia Association of Public Purchasing Officials, National Highway Institute, National Association of Attorneys General, National Alliance of Businessmen, Practising Law Institute, Napier-Looby Bar Association, Nashville Bar Association, Tennessee Bar Association and Federal Bar Association. Named Teenager of the Year by Catholic Youth Organization 1966. Recipient Bennett Douglas Bell Award from Vanderbilt University School of Law 1973 and Black History Month Award from Middle Tennessee Federal Executives Association 1990. Former Member Williamson County Jack and Jill. Board of Directors Cumberland Museum and Science Center 1980-84. Member Tennessee Historical Society, Rotary Club of Nashville, Opportunity House (Board of Directors and Vice President 1981-83) and Children's House (Board of Directors 1982-84).

Office: 649 U.S. Courthouse, 801 Broadway, Nashville 37203-3827.

Telephone: (615) 736-7217.

HELDMAN, Russ *(Judge, Tennessee Circuit Court Twenty-first Judicial District)*

Mailing address: P.O. Box 1469, Franklin 37065-1469.

Office: 305 Public Square, Room 112, Franklin 37064.

Telephone: (615) 790-5426.

HICKS, Ross H. *(Judge, Tennessee Circuit Court Nineteenth Judicial District)* Appointed by Governor Don Sundquist Feb 11, 2002. Elected 2002. Educated at Vanderbilt University B.A. 1968 and University of Tennessee J.D. 1971.

Member Hearing Committee Panel Board of Professional Responsibility since 1999. Member Clarksville Area Chamber of Commerce, Leadership Clarksville, Clarksville-Montgomery County Metropolitan Charter Commission, Clarksville-Montgomery County Economic Development Council and Montgomery County Tourist Commission.

Office: 200 Robertson County Courthouse, Springfield 37172.

Telephone: (615) 384-6467.

HIGGINS, Thomas A. *(Senior Judge, United States District Court Middle District of Tennessee)* Appointed for life by President Ronald Reagan. Assumed Senior status, serves by assignment. Born Nashville Tennessee Aug 15, 1932. Educated at Christian Brothers College A.A. 1952, University of Tennessee B.A. 1954 and Vanderbilt University School of Law LL.B. 1957. Admitted to practice Tennessee 1957, U.S. District Court Middle District of Tennessee, U.S. Court of Military Appeals, U.S. Court of Appeals Sixth Circuit and U.S. Supreme Court.

Fellow American College of Trial Lawyers. Member Nashville (Secretary-Treasurer 1962, Director 1970-72, President 1971-72), Tennessee and American Bar Associations. First Lieutenant U.S. Army JAGC 1957-60. Recipient Army Commendation Medal with Oak Leaf Cluster. Member Cumberland Club and Cathedral of the Incarnation.

Office: A-845 U.S. Courthouse, 801 Broadway, Nashville 37203.

Telephone: (615) 736-5878.

HIGGS, W. Otis, Jr. *(Judge, Tennessee Criminal Court Thirtieth Judicial District)*

Office: 519 Shelby County Justice Complex, 201 Poplar Avenue, Memphis 38103.

Telephone: (901) 545-5850.

HIGHERS, Alan E. *(Judge, Tennessee Court of Appeals Western Division)* Appointed by Governor Lamar Alexander to term beginning Sept 1, 1982. Retained by election 1990 and 1998. Current term expires Aug 31, 2006. Born Muskogee Oklahoma July 5, 1937. Church of Christ. Educated at David Lipscomb University B.A. 1963 and Memphis State University J.D. 1968. Awarded honorary LL.D. Freed Hardeman University 1993. Admitted to practice Tennessee 1968. Began legal practice Memphis 1968. Chief Referee and Special Judge, Memphis and Shelby County Juvenile Court 1972-76. Judge, Tennessee Circuit Court Thirtieth Judicial Circuit 1977-82, appointed by Governor Ray Blanton.

Lecturer Memphis State University School of Law 1973. Board of Governors Tennessee Bar Association 1984-85. Secretary 1978-79, Vice President 1981-82 and President 1984-85 Tennessee Judicial Conference. Holds private pilot license. Enjoys photography, gardening and amateur radio.

Mailing address: P.O. Box 909, Jackson 38302.
Office: Supreme Court Building, Jackson 38301.
Telephone: (731) 423-5838.
Fax: (731) 426-0646

HOLDER, Janice M. *(Associate Justice, Tennessee Supreme Court)* Appointed by Governor Don Sundquist Dec 13, 1996. Retained by election 1998, current term expires Aug 31, 2006. Born Pennsylvania Aug 29, 1949. Catholic. Educated at University of Pittsburgh B.S. summa cum laude 1971 and Duquesne University School of Law J.D. 1975. Recent Decisions Editor Duquesne University Law Review 1974-75. Law Clerk to Senior Judge Herbert P. Sorg, U.S. District Court Western District of Pennsylvania 1975-77. Admitted to practice Pennsylvania 1975, Tennessee 1979, U.S. Supreme Court 1983, District of Columbia 1988 and U.S. District Courts Western District of Pennsylvania 1975 and Western District of Tennessee 1980. In legal practice Pittsburgh Pennsylvania 1977-79 and Memphis Tennessee 1980-90. Judge, Tennessee Circuit Court Thirtieth Judicial District 1990-96.

Editor *Memphis Bar Forum* 1987-91. Author "General Sessions Appeals: The Effect of Voluntary Nonsuit After Appeal to Circuit Court" IV No. 2 *Memphis Bar Forum* 1989, "Multiple Defendants vs. Singular Appeals" IV No. 4 *Memphis Bar Forum* 1990 and "Pattern Jury Instructions in Tennessee" Memphis State University L. Rev. 1993. Former Member Tennessee Judicial Council, Tennessee Trial Judges Association (Executive Committee 1994-96), Association of Women Attorneys (Treasurer 1989, Vice President 1991). Fellow Tennessee Bar Foundation (Trustee since 1995). Member Tennessee Lawyers Concerned for Lawyers (Executive Committee since 1989), Tennessee Judicial Conference (Vice Chair Pattern Jury Instruction—Civil Committee 1991-97, Treasurer 1993-94, Member Executive Committee 1993-96), Tennessee Lawyers Association for Women, Memphis (Board of Directors 1986-87 and 1983-94, Member Executive Committee 1986 and 1993-94, Secretary 1993, Treasurer 1994), Tennessee (House of Delegates 1989-91, Member since 1992 and Chair 1994-96 Commission on Women and Minorities) and American (Vice Chair Lawyer Impairment Project 1987, Judicial Administration Division since 1994) Bar Associations.

Speaker "Attorneys, Competence and Chemical Dependency" Tennessee Bar Association Ethics Seminar Dec 1987; "Tennessee Lawyers Concerned for Lawyers" Tennessee Judicial Conference June 1988; "Issues in Impairment Programs" Local Bar Leaders Conference Tennessee Bar Association June 1988; "Chemical Dependency in Lawyers" Ethics: Pushing the Limits Seminar Tennessee Bar Association Jan 1990; "Lawyer Impairment Program" June 1990, "Don't Let Your Emotions Lose Your Lawsuit" April 1991 and "Child Support Guidelines" April 1992 MBA Bench-Bar Conference; "A View from the Bench: Mistakes to Avoid" American Judicature Society Sidebar June 1991; "The First Amendment" Partnership for Teaching the Bill of Rights Commission on the Bicentennial of the United States Constitution June 1991; "State Employment Law in the Quad-State Area" Mid-South Management Institute on Employment Law Sept 1991; "Workers' Compensation in Tennessee: Issues and Answers" National Business Institute Oct 1991; "A View from the Bench" and "Auto Torts" Tennessee Trial Lawyers Association Feb 1992; "Jury Selection" Tennessee Judicial Conference April 1992; "To See Ourselves as Others See Us—A View from the Bench" Annual Meeting Tennessee Lawyers Association for Women June 1992; "Annual Judges Panel" Association for Women Attorneys June 1992; "Comparative Negligence" July 1992, "Litigation Tactics in Divorce—A View from the Bench" Aug 1992 and "Selecting a Favorable Jury" Dec 1992 Memphis Bar Association; "Comparative Negligence: A Review of Authorities from Other Jurisdictions" Seventeenth Annual Bench-Bar Conference Memphis Bar Association March 1993; "What Do We Do Now?—Trial of a Lawsuit Under *McIntyre*" Joint Meeting of Mississippi-Tennessee Defense Lawyers Associations April 1993; "Workers' Compensation in Tennessee, 'Issues and Answers'" National Business Institute May 1993; "The S.O.B. Litigator" Association of Women Attorneys May 1993; "Comparative Fault and Punitive Damages: Answers and Issues" General Sessions Judges Conference July 1993; "Sexual Harassment" American Association for Paralegal Education Oct 1993; "Summary Judgment" Memphis Bar Association March 1994; "Judges' Mock Trial, The Dos and Don'ts of Trial Practice" Eighteenth Annual Bench-Bar Conference Memphis Bar Association April 1994; "Judicial Panel on Comparative Negligence" Association for Women Attorneys June 1994; "Ethics for Legal Secretaries" Tennessee Association of Legal Secretaries Aug 1994; "Is It Civil or Criminal Contempt?" Domestic Relations Seminar Sept 1994 and "In the Courts: Circuit Court Practice" Nov 1994 Memphis Bar Association; "When It's Not Home Sweet Home: Stopping Domestic Violence. A Comparison of Domestic Abuse Statutes for Arkansas and Tennessee" Arkansas Bar Association Jan 1995; "Custody, Visitation and Domestic Violence" Improving Court Response to Domestic Violence Conference, SJI and Tennessee Task Force Against Domestic Violence March 1995; "Civil Pattern Jury Instruction: Malicious Prosecution" Tennessee Judicial Conference April 1995; "Domestic Violence: Creating Solutions" Veteran's Administration Hospital Oct 1995; "Ethics" St. Thomas More Catholic Lawyer's Guild of West Tennessee Oct 1995; "Mealey's Breast Implant Litigation Conference" Judicial Panel West Palm Beach Florida Nov 1995; "Mediation and the Tennessee Supreme Court's New Rule on Alternative Dispute Resolution: Ignore at Your Peril" Tennessee Bar Association Feb 1996; "Lights, Camera, Action: The Impact of Cameras in the Courtroom" Memphis Bar Association March 1996; "Celebrate Your Freedom" 1997 Regional Law Day Bristol, Kingsport, Carter County, Unicoi County

HOLDER, JANICE M.—*Continued*

and Washington County Bar Associations April 1997 and Law Day 1997 Nashville Bar Association May 1997; "Media and the Courts" Law Day 1997 Knoxville Bar Association May 1997; "Diversity in the Judiciary" American Association of University Women, East Tennessee Lawyers Association for Women, East Tennessee Women's Political Caucus, Knoxville Women's Center, League of Women Voters and Young Women's Christian Association May 1997; "Courtroom Ethics" District Attorney Generals Conference Oct 1997; and "Address to New Bar Admittees" Lawyers Association for Women Nov 1997. Recipient Sam A. Myar Award from Memphis Bar Association 1990, Charles A. Rond Memorial Award for Outstanding Jurist 1992 and Marion Griffin-Frances Loring Award from Association for Women Attorneys 1999. Named Judge of the Year by Divorce and Family Law Section Memphis Bar Association 1992. Board of Directors Alliance for the Blind and Visually Impaired 1985-94.

Office: 310 Pembroke Square, 119 South Main Street, Memphis 38103.
Telephone: (901) 543-2440.

HOLLOWAY, Robert L., Jr. *(Judge, Tennessee Circuit Court Twenty-second Judicial District)* Appointed by Governor Don Sundquist May 20, 1998. Elected to term beginning Sept 1, 1998. Term expires Aug 31, 2006. Born Florence Alabama March 4, 1952. Presbyterian. Educated at University of Tennessee at Knoxville B.A. with honors 1974 J.D. 1978. Law Clerk to Hon. James W. Parrott, Tennessee Court of Appeals Eastern Division 1978-79. Member Phi Alpha Delta. Admitted to practice Tennessee 1979. In legal practice Tennessee 1979-98.

Fellow Tennessee Bar Foundation. Member Maury County and Tennessee Bar Associations. Named Young Man of the Year by Columbia Jaycees 1991. Past President Maury County Republican Party. Past President Maury County United Way and Duck River District Boy Scouts of America. Member Kiwanis Club of Columbia (Past President). Enjoys fishing, canoeing, camping, tennis, golfing and gardening.

Mailing address: P.O. Box 1056, Columbia 38402-1056.
Office: 14 Public Square, Columbia 38401.
Telephone: (931) 380-2543.

HOOPER, Ben W., II *(Judge, Tennessee Circuit Court Fourth Judicial District)* Appointed by Governor Ned Ray McWherter to term beginning Sept 1, 1993. Elected Sept 1, 1994 and Sept 1, 1998. Current term expires Aug 31, 2006. Born Knox County Tennessee Sept 9, 1939. Baptist. Educated at University of Tennessee B.S. 1961 J.D. 1963. Member Phi Delta Phi. Admitted to practice Tennessee 1964, U.S. District Courts Northern District of Florida, Eastern District of Kentucky, Eastern District of North Carolina, Eastern District of Tennessee, Western District of Texas and Western District of Virginia, U.S. Courts of Appeals Fourth and Sixth Circuits, U.S. Tax Court and U.S. Supreme Court. In legal practice Newport 1964-93.

Local Counsel Tennessee Farmers Mutual Insurance Company since 1983. President Newport-Cocke County Bar Association 1987-88. Member Hearing Committee Tennessee Board of Professional Responsibility 1991-96. Board of Directors Federal Defender Services. Member Tennessee Trial Lawyers Association, Tennessee Criminal Defense Lawyers Association, American Judicature Society, Tennessee and American Bar Associations. Member Tennessee State Senate 1975-83 (Chairman General Welfare Committee, Member Judiciary, State and Local Government Committee, Government Operations Committee, Ethics Committee). Delegate Republican Party National Platform Committee. Member Community Corrections Program, U.S. District Courts Historical Society and Walters State's Legal Assistance Program.

Office: 130 West Broadway, Newport 37821.
Telephone: (423) 625-9440.
Fax: (423) 625-1797

HULL, Thomas G. *(Senior Judge, United States District Court Eastern District of Tennessee)* Appointed for life by President Ronald Reagan to term beginning Nov 23, 1985. Former Chief Judge. Assumed Senior status Oct 1, 2002, serves by assignment. Born May 20, 1926. Educated at Tusculum College 1947-48 and University of Tennessee J.D. 1951. Member Phi Sigma Kappa. In legal practice Greenville 1951-72. Judge, Tennessee Circuit Court Twentieth Judicial Circuit 1972-79.

General Counsel to Governor Lamar Alexander 1979-81. Important Decisions: Mozert, et al. v. Hawkins County Public Schools, et al. (religious objections to textbooks) 579 F. Supp. 1051 E.D.Tenn. 1984, 582 F. Supp. 201 E.D.Tenn. 1984, 647 F. Supp. 1194 E.D. Tenn. 1986; Floyd F. Roysden v. R. J. Reynolds Tobacco Company (first products liability action against a cigarette manufacturer in Eastern District of Tennessee) 623 F. Supp. 1189 E.D.Tenn. 1985; Donovan v. Rockford Textile Mills, Inc. (declined to adopt contrary rulings in the matter of a preliminary injunction against the sale of certain goods by a manufacturer and its secured creditor) 608 F. Supp. 215 E.D.Tenn. 1985; Larry Warren Jackson, et al. v. Sheriff Mike Gardner, et al. (1983 class action suit due to unconstitutional jail conditions) CIV-2-84-263, 1986; Burke-Parsons-Bowlby Corp. v. Appalachian Log Homes (injunctive relief against alleged trademark infringement denied) 676 F. Supp. 813 E.D.Tenn. 1987, aff'd 871 F.2d. 590 6th Cir. 1989; State Industries, Inc. v. Mor-Flo Industries, Inc. (patent infringement) CIV-2-84-276, 1988 and CIV-2-85-26, 1988; U.S. v. Davis Pipe & Metal Fabricators, Inc. (imposed the largest criminal fine against a corporation for a single disposal of hazardous waste) CR-2-89-51, 1990; Ferrari S.P.A. Esercizio v. Carl Roberts dba Roberts Motor Company (injunction against trademark infringement) CIV-2-88-73, 1990; Franklin Federal Savings Bank, et al. v. Director, Office of Thrift Supervision, et al. (permanent injunction against excluding supervisory good will from determinations of plaintiff's capitalization) CIV-2-90-116, 1990; U.S. v. Newall Charlton (first jury trial on felony destruction of an archaeological resource) CR-2-90-73, 1990; In re: Southern Industrial Banking Corp., Thomas E. DuVoisin, Liquidating Trustee v. Kennerly, Montgomery, Howard & Finley (appeal of Bankruptcy Court's findings in adversary proceeding against law firm) CIV-3-89-581; In re: Patrick F. Messing, Mostoller, Trustee v. Patrick Messing, et al. (reversal of bankruptcy court order allowing debtor to claim an exemption in proceeds from a pension benefit plan) CIV-3-90-601; and Armour v. State of Ohio (minority group would not be required to show it would constitute a majority in a redrawn district in order to pursue a voting dilution claim) 1990 WL 8710 6th Cir. (Ohio) 1990.

HULL, THOMAS G.—*Continued*

Former Member Tennessee Judicial Conference (Vice Chairman 1975). Member Tennessee Trial Lawyers Association, Greeneville (Past President), Tennessee and American Bar Associations. U.S. Army 1944-46. Former President and Member Executive Committee and Board of Trustees Tusculum College. Former President United Fund for Greene County and Greene County Chamber of Commerce. Former Board Member and Board Chairman Holston Methodist Home for Children of Greeneville. Former Chairman Greene County USO and National Association for Infantile Paralysis. Former Greene County Chairman Heart Association. Former Board Chairman Greene County Library. Member Asbury United Methodist Church, Link Hills Country Club, Moose Lodge, VFW, American Legion and Masons.

Office: 221 U.S. Courthouse, 101 Summer Street West, Greeneville 37743.

Telephone: (423) 638-1305.

INMAN, Dennis H. *(Magistrate Judge, United States District Court Eastern District of Tennessee)* Appointed by U.S. District Court judges. Former Chancellor and Presiding Judge, Tennessee Chancery Court Third Judicial District.

Office: 116 U.S. Courthouse, 101 Summer Street West, Greeneville 37743.

Telephone: (423) 638-1388.

INMAN, William H. *(Senior Judge, Tennessee Appellate and Trial Courts)* Appointed Chancellor, Tennessee Chancery Court by Governor Winfield Dunn to term beginning Sept 15, 1972. Elected 1974 and 1982. Appointed Senior Judge by Tennessee Supreme Court justices, serves by assignment. Born Morristown Tennessee Oct 3, 1926. Presbyterian. Educated at Cumberland School of Law of Samford University LL.B. 1950 replaced by J.D. 1965. Admitted to practice Tennessee 1950. Began legal practice Morristown 1950.

Counsel to Governor Lamar Alexander 1984-86. Commissioner of Commerce and Insurance 1986-87. Author *Gibson's Suits in Chancery* 6th ed. 1980 and 7th ed. 1986. President Tennessee Judicial Conference 1977-78. Presiding Judge Tennessee Court of the Judiciary 1983-86. Member International Academy of Trial Judges. USNR 1943-46. USN 1950-52.

Mailing address: P.O. Box 444, Knoxville 37901.

Telephone: (865) 594-6117.

Fax: (865) 594-5235

JARVIS, James H., II *(Senior Judge, United States District Court Eastern District of Tennessee)* Appointed for life by President Ronald Reagan to term beginning Oct 12, 1984. Chief Judge Nov 23, 1991 to Nov 23, 1998. Assumed Senior status Feb 28, 2002, serves by assignment. Born Knoxville Tennessee Feb 28, 1937. Episcopalian. Educated at University of Tennessee J.D. 1960. Member Phi Delta Phi and Sigma Chi. Admitted to practice Tennessee 1961, U.S. District Court Eastern District of Tennessee 1961 and U.S. Court of Appeals Sixth Circuit 1965. In legal practice Knoxville 1960-69 and Maryville 1970-72. Judge, Tennessee Law and Equity Court Blount County 1972-77. Judge, Tennessee Circuit Court Thirtieth Judicial Circuit 1977-84.

Former Member Tennessee Trial Judges Association (Former Member Executive Committee) and Tennessee Judicial Conference (Executive Committee 1976-78, Secretary 1977-78, Treasurer 1980-81, President 1983-84). Member Judicial Council of the Sixth Circuit (Former Member Executive Committee), Judicial Conference of the U.S. (Committee on Codes of Conduct 1994-2000), American Judicature Society, Federal Judges Association, Knoxville, Blount County, Tennessee (Board of Governors 1983-84) and American (Committee on Ethics and Professional Responsibility) Bar Associations. Republican. Former Member Board of Directors Montvale YMCA Camp, Metropolitan Knoxville YMCA, Detoxification Rehabilitation Institute and Maryville College. Board of Directors Great Smoky Mountains Conservation Association. Member ALCOA Foundation Scholarship Selection Committee and St. Andrews Episcopal Church (former member Vestry, former Chairman Finance Committee). Enjoys fishing, hunting, tennis and golf.

Office: 140 U.S. Courthouse, 800 Market Street, Knoxville 37902.

Telephone: (865) 545-4215.

JENKINS, Ray L. *(Judge, Tennessee Criminal Court Sixth Judicial District)* Elected to term beginning Sept 1, 1982. Reelected 1990 and 1998. Current term expires Aug 31, 2006. Born Knoxville Tennessee April 23, 1936. Presbyterian. Educated at University of Tennessee J.D. replaced LL.B. conferred 1959. Editor Tennessee Law Review 1959. Member Phi Kappa Phi, Phi Beta Sigma, Phi Delta Phi and Order of the Coif. Admitted to practice Tennessee 1959. Began legal practice Knoxville 1959.

Member Knoxville and Tennessee Bar Associations. Republican.

Office: 159 City County Building, 400 Main Avenue, Knoxville 37902.

Telephone: (865) 215-2509.

JOHNSON, G. Richard *(Chancellor, Tennessee Chancery Court First Judicial District)*

Office: 101 East Market Street, Johnson City 37604.

Telephone: (423) 461-1436.

JOHNSON, L. Craig *(Judge, Tennessee Circuit Court Fourteenth Judicial District)*

Office: Coffee County Executive Building, 300 Hillsboro Boulevard Box 1, Manchester 37355.

Telephone: (931) 728-2847.

JONES, Michael R. *(Judge, Tennessee Circuit Court Nineteenth Judicial District)*

Office: 460 Montgomery County Court Center, Two Millennium Plaza, Clarksville 37040.

Telephone: (931) 648-7189.

JONES, Robert L. *(Judge, Tennessee Circuit Court Twenty-second Judicial District)*

Mailing address: P.O. Box 462, Columbia 38402-0462.

Office: 20 Public Square, Columbia 38401.

Telephone: (931) 540-2458.

JORDAN, Leon *(Senior Judge, United States District Court Eastern District of Tennessee)* Appointed for life by President Ronald Reagan to term beginning Nov 15, 1988. Assumed Senior status Nov 30, 2001, serves by assignment. Religious affiliation: Church of Christ. Educated at University of Tennessee B.S. 1958 J.D. 1960. Admitted to practice Tennessee 1960. In legal practice Johnson City 1971-80. Chancellor, Tennessee Chancery Court First Judicial District 1980-88.

JORDAN, LEON—*Continued*

Member Federal Judges Association, Knoxville and Tennessee Bar Associations. U.S. Army 1954-56.

Office: 141 U.S. Courthouse, 800 Market Street, Knoxville 37902.

Telephone: (865) 545-4224.

KELLEY, Ralph Houston *(Recalled Judge, United States Bankruptcy Court Eastern District of Tennessee)* Appointed Judge by U.S. District Court judges to term beginning Jan 2, 1969. Reappointed to subsequent terms. Former Chief Judge. Appointed Recalled Judge by the Judicial Council of the Sixth Circuit. Born Chattanooga Tennessee Sept 23, 1928. Educated at University of Tennessee at Chattanooga B.A. 1952 and Vanderbilt University J.D. 1954. Admitted to practice Tennessee 1954. Began legal practice Chattanooga 1954.

Assistant Attorney General Hamilton County 1958-59. Tennessee House of Representatives 1959-61. Mayor City of Chattanooga 1963-69. Member since 1969 and President 1985-86 National Conference of Bankruptcy Judges. Member Judicial Conference of the U.S. (Committee on the Budget), Chattanooga, Tennessee Federal and American Bar Associations. Technical Sergeant USAF 1946-49. Past President Kiwanis Club. Member Christ Church Episcopal (Hamilton County Episcopal Commission). Enjoys reading, traveling and listening to jazz music.

Office: Historic U.S. Courthouse, 31 East 11th Street, Chattanooga 37402-2722.

Telephone: (423) 752-5167.

KENNEDY, David S. *(Chief Judge, United States Bankruptcy Court Western District of Tennessee)*

Office: 200 Jefferson Avenue, Suite 950, Memphis 38103-2328.

Telephone: (901) 328-3520.

KILCREASE, Irvin H., Jr. *(Chancellor, Tennessee Chancery Court Twentieth Judicial District)* Appointed by Governor Lamar Alexander to term beginning Sept 25, 1980. Elected 1982, 1990 and 1998. Current term expires 2006. Presiding Judge Sept 1, 1984 to Aug 31, 1985. Born Nashville Tennessee Nov 21, 1931. Baptist. Deacon Kayne Avenue Baptist Church. Educated at Tennessee State University and Nashville School of Law J.D. 1966. Admitted to practice Tennessee 1966. Began legal practice Nashville 1968.

Assistant Metropolitan Public Defender Aug 1969 to July 1972. Assistant U.S. Attorney and Chief of Civil Division Middle District of Tennessee July 1972 to Sept 1980. Honorary member Lawyers Association for Women. Vice Chairman Governor's Commission on the Status of Women 1973. Member since 1987 and Presiding Judge 1989-90 Tennessee Court of the Judiciary. President Tennessee Judicial Conference 2000-01. Member Tennessee Judicial Evaluation Commission since 2000. Member American Inn of Court, Napier-Looby (Board of Directors 1984-86), Nashville (Board of Directors 1982-85), Tennessee and Federal (President Nashville Chapter 1975) Bar Associations. Recipient Superior Accomplishment Award from U.S. Post Office 1966 and Award for Outstanding Contributions to the U.S. Department of Justice from U.S. Attorney General 1980. Named Federal Employee of the Year (Professional and Scientific Category) 1973 and Man of the Year by Negro Business and Professional Women's Club 1981. Corporal U.S. Army 1952-54. Democrat. Board of Directors Nashville Chapter of the Urban League 1971-72. Past member Board of Directors Middle Tennessee Diabetes Association. Advisory Board Knowles Home for the Aged, DreamMakers, Inc. and Court Appointed Special Advocate Project. Member Central Citizens' Advisory Committee for Metropolitan Nashville Schools 1974-76, American Legion (Commander Post 6 1958-59, Middle Area Commander 1959-60 and State District Commander 1961-62), Nashville Club of Frontiers International (Past President) and 33° Masons (Grand Master Masonic Grand Lodge State of Tennessee 1974-75). Enjoys drawing and reading.

Office: 401 Metro Courthouse, Nashville 37201.

Telephone: (615) 880-2597.

Fax: (615) 313-9155

KNOWLES, E. Clifton *(Magistrate Judge, United States District Court Middle District of Tennessee)* Appointed by U.S. District Court judges to term beginning July 7, 2000. Born Pensacola Florida Oct 9, 1951. Educated at Vanderbilt University B.A. magna cum laude 1973 and University of Tennessee J.D. 1977. Editor-in-Chief Tennessee Law Review 1977. Law Clerk to Hon. George Clifton Edwards, Jr., U.S. Court of Appeals Sixth Circuit 1978-79. Member Phi Beta Kappa and Order of the Coif. Admitted to practice Tennessee 1978. In legal practice Nashville 1979-99.

Office: 649 U.S. Courthouse, 801 Broadway, Nashville 37203.

Telephone: (615) 736-7344.

KOCH, William Conway, Jr. *(Judge, Tennessee Court of Appeals Middle Division)* Appointed by Governor Lamar Alexander June 18, 1984. Retained by election 1984, 1990 and 1998. Current term expires Aug 31, 2006. Born Honolulu Hawaii Sept 12, 1947. Episcopalian. Educated at Trinity College B.A. 1969, Vanderbilt University J.D. 1972 and University of Virginia School of Law LL.M. 1996. Member Delta Kappa Epsilon. Admitted to practice Tennessee 1972, U.S. District Court District of Tennessee 1972, U.S. Court of Appeals Sixth Circuit 1973 and U.S. Supreme Court 1975. Began legal practice Nashville 1972.

Assistant Attorney General Sept 1972 to Sept 1976. Senior Assistant Attorney General Oct 1976 to Aug 1977. Deputy Attorney General Sept 1977 to Dec 1978. Legal Advisor to Governor Lamar Alexander Jan 1979. Commissioner of Personnel Feb 1979 to June 1981. Counsel to the Governor July 1981 to June 1984. Author "Intermediate Appellate Court Consolidation: A Needed Reform or a Solution in Search of a Problem" Tennessee B. Jour. 10 Nov-Dec 1995 and "Reopening Tennessee's Open Courts Clause: A Historical Reconsideration of Article I, Section 17 of the Tennessee Constitution" 27 University of Memphis L. Rev. 333, 1997. Adjunct Instructor Vanderbilt University School of Law 1988-95. Instructor in Constitutional Law Nashville School of Law since 1997. Chair Committee on Compensation and Retirement Tennessee Judicial Conference since 1992. Co-chair Tennessee Supreme Court Advisory Commission on Technology. Member 1985-88 and Secretary 1997-98 Executive Committee Tennessee Judicial Conference. Member Tennessee Defense Counsel Commission 1981-84, Harry Phillips American Inns of Court (President 1990-94 and since 1995), Scribes, American Judicature Society, Nashville Bar Foundation, Tennessee Bar Foundation, Nashville (Chair Appellate Practice Committee 1990 and 1998, Tennessee and American

KOCH, WILLIAM CONWAY, JR.—*Continued*

(Judicial Administration Division) Bar Associations. Republican. Trustee Tennessee Consolidated Retirement System 1979-81. Board of Directors and Secretary United Way of Nashville and Middle Tennessee and Board of Trustees United Way of Middle Tennessee since 1980. Chair Governor's Cabinet Council on Law Enforcement 1981-84. Delegate Southeast Low-Level Radioactive Waste Compact 1982-84. Member Governor's Committee on No-Fault Legislation 1976, Tennessee Council on Pensions and Insurance 1979-81, State Board of Claims 1979-81 and State Board of Equalization 1981-84.

Office: 203 Supreme Court Building, 401 Seventh Avenue North, Nashville 37219-1407.
Telephone: (615) 741-5150.

KURTZ, Walter C. *(Judge, Tennessee Circuit Court Twentieth Judicial District)*

Office: 509 Metro Courthouse, Nashville 37201.
Telephone: (615) 862-5915.

LADD, Richard E. *(Chancellor, Tennessee Chancery Court Second Judicial District)* Assumed office April 28, 1977. Elected 1984, 1990 and 1998. Current term expires Aug 31, 2006. Former Presiding Judge. Born Oliver Springs Tennessee Jan 22, 1936. Educated at University of Tennessee B.S. 1958 J.D. 1963. Member Order of the Coif. Admitted to practice Tennessee 1964. Began legal practice Bristol 1964. Judge, Tennessee Law and Equity Court Sullivan County April 28, 1977 to Aug 31, 1984, appointed by Governor Ray Blanton.

Member Tennessee Bar Association. First Lieutenant USAF 1958-60. Enjoys tennis and fishing.

Office: Bristol Justice Center, 801 Anderson Street, Bristol 37620.
Telephone: (423) 989-4357.

LANIER, Robert A. *(Judge, Tennessee Circuit Court Thirtieth Judicial District)* Elected to term beginning Sept 1, 1982. Reelected 1990 and 1998. Current term expires Aug 31, 2006. Born Memphis Tennessee Nov 2, 1938. Baptist. Educated at Memphis State University B.S. 1960 and University of Mississippi J.D. replaced LL.B. conferred 1962. Moot Court Board. Member Phi Alpha Delta and Sigma Alpha Epsilon. Admitted to practice Mississippi 1962 and Tennessee 1963. Began legal practice Memphis Tennessee 1964.

Author "Tennessee Discovery—A Survey" Memphis State University L. Rev. Fall 1972; "The Bridge Collision" Insurance Counsel Journal Oct 1976; "Abandon Ship?" Journal of Maritime Law & Commerce Oct 1977; "History of the Memphis and Shelby County Bar" Memphis and Shelby County Bar Association 1980; "The Carmack Murder Case" Tennessee Historical Quarterly Fall 1981; "The Pauper's Oath" May 1983, "Actions for Possession of Personal Property" May-June 1987 and "Medical Records as Evidence" March-April 1988 Tennessee B. Jour.; and "The English Legal System: A Mirror for U.S.?" 19 Memphis State University L. Rev. 427 Summer 1989. Adjunct Professor of Law Memphis State University School of Law 1981-82. Member American Judicature Society, Mississippi State Bar, Tennessee and American Bar Associations. Staff Sergeant USAF Tennessee Air National Guard 1963-69. Recipient American Spirit of Honor medal 1963. Honorary Board member Memphis Humane Society (President 1974). Vice President 1982-83 and Parliamentarian West Tennessee Historical Society. Member Tennessee Historical Commission 1975-85. Co-founder Memphis Heritage, Inc. (historic preservation) and Pickwick Club & Gastronomic Society. Corresponding Carbuncle "The Giant Rats of Sumatra" Sherlock Holmes Club. Interests include history, train travel, humane causes, book collecting and binding and classic film.

Office: 212 Shelby County Courthouse, 140 Adams Avenue, Memphis 38103.
Telephone: (901) 545-4018.
Fax: (901) 545-5659

LANTRIP, William E. *(Chancellor, Tennessee Chancery Court Seventh Judicial District)* Former Presiding Judge.

Office: Anderson County Courthouse, 100 North Main, Clinton 37716.
Telephone: (865) 457-6209.

LATTA, Jennie D. *(Judge, United States Bankruptcy Court Western District of Tennessee)* Appointed by U.S. Court of Appeals Sixth Circuit judges.

Office: 200 Jefferson Avenue, Suite 650, Memphis 38103-2328.
Telephone: (901) 328-3542.

LAWSON, Kindall T. *(Judge, Tennessee Circuit Court Third Judicial District)*

Office: 4325 Highway 66, Suite 206B, Rogersville 37857.
Telephone: (423) 272-7776.

LEE, William Charles *(Judge, Tennessee Circuit Court Seventeenth Judicial District)*

Mailing address: P.O. Box 2223, Lewisburg 37092-2223.
Office: 307 Marshall County Courthouse, Lewisburg 37091.
Telephone: (931) 359-7777.

LEIBOWITZ, Mary Beth *(Judge, Tennessee Criminal Court Sixth Judicial District)* Appointed by Governor Ned Ray McWherter to term beginning Feb 15, 1989. Elected Sept 1, 1990 and 1998. Current term expires Sept 1, 2006. Born Knoxville Tennessee Sept 17, 1953. Educated at College of William & Mary A.B. 1975 and University of Dayton J.D. 1978. Associate Editor University of Dayton Law Review 1976-78. Admitted to practice Tennessee 1978.

Member Tennessee Judicial Conference, East Tennessee Lawyers Association for Women, Hamilton Burnette American Inns of Court, Knoxville and Tennessee Bar Associations. Attended The National Judicial College.

Office: M60 City-County Building, 400 Main Avenue, Knoxville 37902.
Telephone: (865) 215-2366.

LILLARD, Holly Kirby *(Judge, Tennessee Court of Appeals Western Division)* Appointed by Governor Don Sundquist 1995. Retained by election 1996 and Aug 1998. Current term expires 2006. First woman to serve on Tennessee Court of Appeals. Born Memphis Tennessee July 9, 1957. Methodist. Educated at University of Memphis B.S. magna cum laude 1979 J.D. 1982. Recipient Herff and Honors Alumni Scholarships. Notes Editor Memphis University Law Review. Law Clerk to Hon. Harry W. Wellford, U.S. Court of Appeals Sixth Circuit 1982-83. Admitted to practice Tennessee 1982. In legal practice Memphis 1983-95.

Former Member Tennessee Appellate Court Nominat-

LILLARD, HOLLY KIRBY—*Continued*

ing Commission (Chairman 1994) and Leo Bearman, Sr. American Inn of Court.

Office: 5050 Poplar Avenue, Suite 1403, Memphis 38157.

Telephone: (901) 685-3921.

LUNDIN, Keith M. *(Judge, United States Bankruptcy Court Middle District of Tennessee)* Also Judge, Bankruptcy Appellate Panel Sixth Circuit. Selected by the Judicial Council of the Sixth Circuit.

Office: 260 Customs House, 701 Broadway, Nashville 37203.

Telephone: (615) 736-5586.

LYLE, Ellen Hobbs *(Chancellor, Tennessee Chancery Court Twentieth Judicial District)*

Office: 401 Metro Courthouse, Nashville 37201.

Telephone: (615) 862-5705.

MADDUX, John J., Jr. *(Judge, Tennessee Circuit Court Thirteenth Judicial District)*

Office: 228 East Broad Street, Room 206, Cookeville 38501-3366.

Telephone: (931) 526-6692.

MALOAN, W. Michael *(Chancellor, Tennessee Chancery Court Twenty-seventh Judicial District)* Elected to term beginning Sept 1, 1990. Reelected 1998, current term expires Aug 31, 2006. Born Martin Tennessee Sept 21, 1949. Methodist. Educated at University of Tennessee at Martin B.S. 1972 and Memphis State University School of Law J.D. 1974. Member Phi Delta Phi. Admitted to practice Tennessee 1975, U.S. Supreme Court 1980 and U.S. Tax Court 1985. In legal practice Martin 1975-90. Judge, Municipal Court City of Martin 1985-90.

Instructor in Business Law University of Tennessee at Martin 1977-93. Member Tennessee Bar Association. Attended Tennessee Judicial Conference and other seminars. Lieutenant Colonel Tennessee Army National Guard since 1988.

Office: 300 Weakley County Courthouse, 116 West Main Street, Dresden 38225.

Telephone: (731) 364-3276.

Fax: (731) 364-2023

MARTIN, Leonard Watson *(Judge, Tennessee Circuit Court Twenty-third Judicial District)* Appointed by Governor Ray Blanton to term beginning Sept 1, 1976. Elected to subsequent terms. Current term expires Aug 31, 2006. Born Nashville Tennessee Aug 9, 1935. Protestant. Educated at University of Tennessee B.S. 1960 J.D. 1962. Admitted to practice Tennessee. In legal practice Knoxville 1962 and Dickson 1964-76.

Tennessee State Legislature 1969-72 (House Majority Leader 1971-72). Member Dickson County, Tennessee and American Bar Associations. Lieutenant Colonel USMCR since 1953. Democrat. Enjoys fishing, golf and hunting.

Mailing address: P.O. Box 266, Charlotte 37036.

Office: Dickson County Courthouse Annex, Charlotte 37036.

Telephone: (615) 789-7013.

MAYS, Samuel H., Jr. *(Judge, United States District Court Western District of Tennessee)* Appointed for life by President George W. Bush to term beginning June 17, 2002.

Office: 1111 Federal Building, 167 North Main Street, Memphis 38103.

Telephone: (901) 495-1200.

Fax: (901) 495-1250

McCALLA, Jon Phipps *(Judge, United States District Court Western District of Tennessee)* Appointed for life by President George Bush to term beginning Feb 1992. Born Memphis Tennessee Feb 16, 1947. Educated at University of Tennessee B.S. 1969 and Vanderbilt University School of Law J.D. 1974. Law Clerk to Hon. Bailey Brown, U.S. District Court Western District of Tennessee 1974-75. In legal practice Memphis 1975-92.

Office: 907 Federal Building, 167 North Main Street, Memphis 38103.

Telephone: (901) 495-1291.

McCARROLL, John R., Jr. *(Judge, Tennessee Circuit Court Thirtieth Judicial District)*

Office: 212 Shelby County Courthouse, 140 Adams Avenue, Memphis 38103.

Telephone: (901) 545-4022.

McCOY, Carol L. *(Chancellor, Tennessee Chancery Court Twentieth Judicial District)* Elected to term beginning Sept 1, 1996. Reelected 1998, current term expires 2006. Presiding Judge 1999-2001. Born Kingsport Tennessee Sept 4, 1947. Roman Catholic. Educated at University of South Florida B.A. with honors 1969 and Vanderbilt University School of Law J.D. 1973. Admitted to practice Tennessee 1973, Florida 1973, U.S. District Court Middle District of Tennessee 1973, U.S. Court of Appeals Sixth Circuit 1977 and U.S. Supreme Court 1978. In legal practice Nashville 1973-96.

Member Harry Phillips Inn of Court, American Judicature Society, The National Judicial College, The Florida Bar, Nashville (Board of Directors 1994-97), Tennessee and American Bar Associations. Attended annual Tennessee Judicial Seminars, The National Judicial College July 1997, Nov 2000 and Nov 2002 and LOEC Economic Institute for Judges 2001. Former Member Tennessee Commission on Status of Women and Davidson County Executive Commission. Chair Metro Action Commission. Named Woman of the Year by Business and Professional Women 1984. Recipient Athena Award 1999. Board of Directors United Way of Middle Tennessee 1982-90. Past President Crittenton Services, Tennessee Women's Political Caucus, CABLE and Metro Action Commission Head Start Program. Board of Directors Girl Scouts, YWCA, Crittenton Services, Metro Community Access Television, Leadership Nashville Alumni Association and Senior Citizens of Nashville, Inc. Enjoys family, reading, music, travel and tennis.

Office: 401 Metro Courthouse, Nashville 37201.

Telephone: (615) 862-5700.

Fax: (615) 862-5341

McGINLEY, C. Creed *(Judge, Tennessee Circuit Court Twenty-fourth Judicial District)* Appointed by Governor Ned Ray McWherter to term beginning Jan 11, 1988. Elected 1988, 1990 and 1998. Current term expires 2006. Born Tennessee Sept 15, 1950. United Methodist. Educated at University of Tennessee B.S.

MCGINLEY, C. CREED—*Continued*

1973 and University of Memphis J.D. 1976. Admitted to practice Tennessee 1976.

Assistant District Attorney General 1982-88.

Mailing address: P.O. Box 548, Savannah 38372.

Office: 166 North Guinn Street, Savannah 38372.

Telephone: (731) 925-1176.

McLELLAN, John S., III *(Judge, Tennessee Circuit Court Second Judicial District)* Appointed by Governor Ned Ray McWherter July 14, 1994. Elected Aug 1996 and 1998. Current term expires Aug 31, 2006. Born Kingsport Tennessee Jan 16, 1946. Episcopalian. Educated at University of Tennessee at Knoxville B.S. 1968 and University of Tennessee College of Law J.D. 1970. Member Phi Delta Phi. Admitted to practice Tennessee 1971, U.S. District Court Eastern District of Tennessee 1971 and U.S. Court of Appeals Sixth Circuit 1972. In legal practice Kingsport 1971-94.

County Attorney Sullivan County 1978-94. Member Tennessee Court of the Judiciary since 1999. Member Attorneys Information Exchange Group, Tennessee Judicial Conference (Secretary 1995-96, Director 1996-2002), Tennessee Trial Judges Association (Former Eastern Vice-President), American Judicature Society, Kingsport and Tennessee Bar Associations. Instructor in Ethics Annual Spring Seminar Kingsport Bar Association since 1995. Named Tennessee Jaycee President of the Year 1973 and Kingsport Legal Secretaries Boss of the Year 1977. Tennessee Jaycee State Legal Counsel 1974. Life Membership Kingsport Jaycees 1982. Honored for supporting program by Tri-Cities Chapter Tennessee Paralegal Association 1994. Member Sullivan County Democratic Party. Member Wishing Well Foundation for terminally ill children. Enjoys tennis, golf and gardening.

Office: City Hall, 225 West Center Street, Kingsport 37660.

Telephone: (423) 224-1728.

McLIN, J. C. *(Judge, Tennessee Criminal Court Thirtieth Judicial District)*

Office: Shelby County Justice Center, 201 Poplar Avenue, Memphis 38103.

Telephone: (901) 545-5858, 545-3773.

Fax: (901) 545-2237

E-mail address: MCLIN-J@CO.SHELBY.TN.US

MEYER, Douglas Alexander *(Judge, Tennessee Criminal Court Eleventh Judicial District)* Elected to term beginning Sept 1, 1982. Reelected 1990 and 1998. Current term expires Aug 31, 2006. Former Presiding Judge. Born Chattanooga Tennessee Nov 30, 1932. Episcopalian. Educated at University of Chattanooga B.A. 1954 and University of Tennessee LL.B. 1956. Member Pi Kappa Alpha and Phi Delta Phi. Admitted to practice Tennessee 1957. Began legal practice Chattanooga 1957. Judge, Chattanooga Municipal Court 1977-82.

Assistant District Attorney General 1961-65. Assistant County Attorney 1965-66. Democrat. Interested in local history and genealogy. Enjoys golf and running.

Office: Courts Building, 600 Market Street, Chattanooga 37402.

Telephone: (423) 209-7574.

MILLER, Phyllis H. *(Judge, Tennessee Criminal Court Second Judicial District)*

Mailing address: P.O. Box 585, Blountville 37617.

Office: Sullivan County Justice Center, Blountville 37617.

Telephone: (423) 279-2732.

MOORE, Russell Lee, Jr. *(Judge, Tennessee Circuit Court Twenty-ninth Judicial District)*

Office: 100 Main Avenue North, Suite 3, Dyersburg 38025-1471.

Telephone: (731) 288-8011.

MORGAN, Roy B., Jr. *(Judge, Tennessee Circuit Court Twenty-sixth Judicial District)*

Office: Criminal Justice Complex, Third Floor, 515 South Liberty, Jackson 38301.

Telephone: (731) 423-6039.

NEAL, Vernon *(Chancellor, Tennessee Chancery Court Thirteenth Judicial District)* Elected to term beginning Sept 1, 1980. Reelected 1982, 1990 and 1998. Current term expires Sept 1, 2006. Born Pickett County Tennessee Oct 10, 1931. Baptist. Educated at Tennessee Technological University B.S. 1952 and University of Tennessee College of Law J.D. 1956. Admitted to practice Tennessee 1957 and U.S. District Court Middle District of Tennessee 1958. In legal practice Cookeville March 1957 to Sept 1980.

Tennessee State Representative 1962-66. Tennessee State Senate 1966-78. Member Tennessee Judicial Conference and Tennessee Bar Association. Enjoys writing, crossword puzzles and boating.

Office: One South Jefferson Avenue, Suite 202, Cookeville 38501.

Telephone: (931) 526-2105.

NIXON, John T. *(Senior Judge, United States District Court Middle District of Tennessee)* Appointed for life by President Jimmy Carter to term beginning May 16, 1980. Assumed Senior status Aug 15, 1998, serves by assignment. Born New Orleans Louisiana Jan 9, 1933. Educated at Harvard University A.B. 1955 and Vanderbilt University LL.B. 1960. Judge, Tennessee Circuit Court Tenth Judicial Circuit 1977-78. Judge, Tennessee General Sessions Court Tenth Judicial Circuit 1978-80.

City Attorney Anniston Alabama 1962-64. Trial Attorney Civil Rights Division U.S. Department of Justice 1964-69. Staff Attorney Comptroller of the Treasury State of Tennessee 1971-76. Member Alabama State Bar, Nashville, Tennessee and American Bar Associations.

Office: 745 U.S. Courthouse, 801 Broadway, Nashville 37203-3800.

Telephone: (615) 736-5778.

NORMAN, Seth W. *(Judge, Tennessee Criminal Court Twentieth Judicial District)*

Office: 608 Metro Courthouse, Nashville 37201.

Telephone: (615) 862-5945.

OGLE, Norma M. McGee *(Judge, Tennessee Court of Criminal Appeals Eastern Division)* Appointed by Governor Don Sundquist 1998. Born Lawrenceburg Tennessee Sept 9, 1952. Methodist. Educated at University of Tennessee B.S. 1974 J.D. 1977. Admitted to practice Tennessee 1977. In legal practice 1979-98.

City Attorney Pigeon Forge 1990-98. Member Sevier County and Tennessee Bar Associations. Member Mem-

OGLE, NORMA M. MCGEE—*Continued*

phis Area Legal Services 1977-79, Local Planning Advisory Board State of Tennessee 1997-98 and Leadership Sevier Class of 1998. Chairperson 1982-94 and Member Sevier County Board of Education. Board of Directors Fort Sanders Sevier Medical Center 1982-94 and Sevier County Chapter American Heart Association 1991-94. Commissioner and Chairperson Tennessee Human Rights Commission 1995-98. Board of Directors Boys and Girls Club of the Smoky Mountains since 1995. Member Advisory Board Walter State Community College since 1997.

Mailing address: P.O. Box 444, Knoxville 37901-0444.

Office: 505 Main Street, Suite 200, Knoxville 37902.

Telephone: (865) 594-6089.

OGLE, Rex Henry *(Judge, Tennessee Circuit Court Fourth Judicial District)*

Mailing address: P.O. Box 4245, Sevierville 37864.

Office: 134 Court Avenue, Suite 207, Sevierville 37862.

Telephone: (865) 453-8385.

PAGE, Roger Amos *(Judge, Tennessee Circuit Court Twenty-sixth Judicial District)* Elected to term beginning Aug 6, 1998. Term expires Aug 31, 2006. Born Henderson Tennessee Oct 7, 1955. Southern Baptist. Educated at University of Tennessee at Martin with honors 1975 B.S. with honors 1978 and University of Memphis J.D. with honors 1984. Articles Editor University of Memphis Law Review 1982-84. Law Clerk to Hon. Julia Smith Gibbons, U.S. District Court Western District of Tennessee 1984-85. Admitted to practice Tennessee 1984, Georgia 1985 and U.S. District Courts District of Georgia and District of Tennessee. In legal practice Atlanta Georgia 1985-87 and Jackson Tennessee 1987-98.

Office: 320 Criminal Justice Complex, 515 South Liberty, Jackson 38301.

Telephone: (731) 988-3040.

E-mail address: page4@usit.net

PAINE, George C., II *(Chief Judge, United States Bankruptcy Court Middle District of Tennessee)* Appointed by U.S. Court of Appeals Sixth Circuit judges to term beginning Oct 1986. Reappointed 2000, current term expires Oct 2014.

Office: 218 Customs House, 701 Broadway, Nashville 37203.

Telephone: (615) 736-5587.

PARSONS, Marcia Phillips *(Judge, United States Bankruptcy Court Eastern District of Tennessee)* Appointed by U.S. Court of Appeals Sixth Circuit judges to term beginning Nov 23, 1993. Term expires Nov 22, 2007. Born Detroit Michigan Sept 24, 1955. Protestant. Educated at University of North Alabama B.S. with honors 1977 and University of Tennessee College of Law J.D. with honors 1980. Editorial Board Tennessee Law Review 1979-80. Law Clerk to Magistrate Judge Roger W. Dickson 1980-81. Member Phi Kappa Phi and Phi Delta Phi. Admitted to practice Tennessee 1980 and U.S. District Court Eastern District of Tennessee 1981. In legal practice Chattanooga 1981-83 and Knoxville 1983-89.

Trustee Standing Chapter 13 Knoxville 1990-93. Member American Bankruptcy Institute and Federal Bar Association.

Office: U.S. Courthouse, 220 West Depot Street, Greeneville 37743.

Telephone: (423) 638-2264.

E-mail address: marcia_parsons@tneb.uscourts.gov

PAYNE, Samuel H. *(Judge, Tennessee Circuit Court Eleventh Judicial District)* Elected to term beginning Aug 1, 1974. Reelected Aug 1981, 1990 and 1998. Current term expires Aug 31, 2006. Former Presiding Judge. Born Chattanooga Tennessee Feb 4, 1933. Educated at University of Chattanooga B.S. 1958 and University of Tennessee J.D. 1960. Member Pi Alpha Delta. Vice President Student Bar Association. In legal practice Chattanooga.

Assistant County Attorney Hamilton County eight years. Board of Trustees Chattanooga Legal Aid Society (Former Chairman). Member Chattanooga Trial Lawyers Association, Tennessee Trial Lawyers Association, Tennessee Judicial Conference, American Judicature Society, Chattanooga, Tennessee and American Bar Associations. Recipient Distinguished Alumni Award from University of Tennessee at Chattanooga Nov 1996. USAF 1950-54. Board of Directors, Treasurer and Chairman TEAM Evaluation Center for two years. Past President Rivermont P.T.O. Former Vice President St. Barnabas Apartments and St. Barnabas Nursing Home. Former Member Board of Management YMCA, Board of Family and Children's Services, Board of CADAS (Council for Alcohol and Drug Abuse) and Advisory Committee Cub Scouts. Former Member St. Peter's Episcopal Church (Curate 1979 to June 1994, Chancellor, Past Vestry and Kindergarten Board member, Senior Warden, chalice bearer, lay reader and Sunday school teacher). Vice President Hamilton County Episcopal Commission. Board of Directors Neighborhood Residential Center. Assistant St. Paul's Episcopal Church. Formed group "Jerry and the Judge" to entertain in nursing homes and retirement centers. Ordained Priest. Member Records Commission Hamilton County, American Legion and VFW. Interests include church and music.

Office: 206 Hamilton County Courthouse, 625 Georgia Avenue, Chattanooga 37402.

Telephone: (423) 209-6760.

PEEPLES, Clayburn *(Judge, Tennessee Circuit Court Twenty-eighth Judicial District)*

Office: Courthouse, One North Washington Street, Brownsville 38012.

Telephone: (731) 779-3350.

PEOPLES, Howell N. *(Chancellor, Tennessee Chancery Court Eleventh Judicial District)* Appointed by Governor Ray Blanton to term beginning May 18, 1978. Elected 1978, 1982, 1990 and 1998. Current term expires Aug 31, 2006. Born Knoxville Tennessee Sept 22, 1942. Baptist. Educated at University of Tennessee at Knoxville B.S. 1964 J.D. 1966. Admitted to practice Tennessee 1967. Began legal practice Clinton 1967. In legal practice Knoxville 1969-72 and Chattanooga 1972-75. Clerk and Master in Chancery, Tennessee Chancery Court 1975-78.

Instructor University of Tennessee Legal Clinic 1969-

PEOPLES, HOWELL N.—*Continued*

72. Member Chattanooga, Tennessee and American Bar Associations. President Civitan Club 1987-88.

Office: 311 Hamilton County Courthouse, 625 Georgia Avenue, Chattanooga 37402.

Telephone: (423) 209-7385.

Fax: (423) 209-6651

PERRY, Buddy D. *(Judge, Tennessee Circuit Court Twelfth Judicial District)*

Mailing address: P.O. Box 183, Winchester 37398-0183.

Office: 1101 Dinah Shore Boulevard, Winchester 37398.

Telephone: (931) 967-2676.

PHAM, Tu M. *(Magistrate Judge, United States District Court Western District of Tennessee)* Appointed by U.S. District Court judges.

Office: 934 Federal Building, 167 North Main Street, Memphis 38103-1814.

Telephone: (901) 495-1351.

Fax: (901) 495-1325

PHILLIPS, Thomas W. *(Judge, United States District Court Eastern District of Tennessee)* Former Magistrate Judge. Appointed for life by President George W. Bush to term beginning Nov 19, 2002.

Office: 130 U.S. Courthouse, 800 Market Street, Knoxville 37902.

Telephone: (865) 545-4255.

POWERS, John Y. *(Recalled Magistrate Judge, United States District Court Eastern District of Tennessee)* Appointed Magistrate Judge by U.S. District Court judges to term beginning Feb 21, 1984. Reappointed Feb 21, 1992. Retired July 29, 1999. Appointed Recalled Magistrate Judge by the Judicial Council of the Sixth Circuit July 30, 1999. Born Lake Orion Michigan Aug 1, 1929. Episcopalian. Educated at Union University 1947-48 and Vanderbilt University B.A. 1951 J.D. 1953. Member Alpha Tau Omega and Phi Delta Phi. Admitted to practice Tennessee 1954, U.S. Court of Military Appeals 1955, U.S. Supreme Court 1957 and U.S. District Court Eastern District of Tennessee 1966. In legal practice Chattanooga 1959-84.

With Administrative Division Department of Justice 1957-58. Member Chattanooga (Board of Governors 1969-70) and Tennessee Bar Associations. Republican. Counterintelligence Corps 1954-55 and First Lieutenant JAGC 1955-57 U.S. Army. Colonel USAR JAGC 1957-84. Previously employed by State Farm Mutual Automobile Insurance Co., Miami Florida 1958-59.

Office: 401 U.S. Courthouse, 900 Georgia Avenue, Chattanooga 37402.

Telephone: (423) 752-5230.

PUCKETT, Lawrence Howard *(Judge, Tennessee Circuit Court Tenth Judicial District)* Appointed by Governor Don Sundquist to term beginning Dec 22, 1997. Elected Sept 1, 1998, current term expires 2006. Born Bristol Virginia May 7, 1951. Protestant. Educated at Bryan College B.A. with honors 1973 and Memphis State University School of Law J.D. with honors 1979. Admitted to practice Tennessee 1980, U.S. District Court District of Tennessee and U.S. Court of Appeals Sixth Circuit 1994. In legal practice Cleveland 1980-97.

Assistant District Attorney General Tenth Judicial District. Previously worked as Admissions Counselor Bryan College. Republican. Past President College Alumni Association and Cleveland Jaycees. Trustee Bryan College since 1987. Member Farmland Community Church (Deacon and Bible Teacher). Enjoys history, genealogy and horses.

Mailing address: P.O. Box 846, Cleveland 37364.

Telephone: (423) 476-0536.

RILEY, Joe G., Jr. *(Judge, Tennessee Court of Criminal Appeals Western Division)* Appointed by Governor Don Sundquist to term beginning 1996. Retained by election Aug 1998. Born Memphis Tennessee Oct 13, 1947. Methodist. Educated at University of Tennessee B.S. with honors 1969 J.D. with honors 1972. Member Phi Beta Kappa and Order of the Coif. Admitted to practice Tennessee 1972. Began legal practice Ridgely 1972. Judge and Presiding Judge, Tennessee Circuit Court Twenty-ninth Judicial District Sept 1, 1978 to 1996.

Author "Tennessee Criminal Law Update" and of various publications concerning judicial ethics. President Tennessee Judicial Conference 1996-97. Fellow Tennessee Bar Foundation. Chair Judicial Performance Program Committee since 1995. Member Tennessee Bar Association. Enjoys hunting and fishing.

Mailing address: P.O. Box 40, Ridgely 38080-0040.

Office: 115 Lake Street, Ridgely 38080.

Telephone: (731) 264-5671.

Fax: (731) 264-9433

ROBILIO, Kay Spalding *(Judge, Tennessee Circuit Court Thirtieth Judicial District)* Elected to term beginning Sept 1, 1990. Reelected 1998, current term expires Aug 31, 2006. Born Memphis Tennessee Sept 1941. Episcopalian. Educated at Memphis State University B.A. cum laude 1973 J.D. 1980. Admitted to practice Tennessee 1980. In legal practice Memphis 1981-82. Judge, Memphis Municipal Court 1983-90.

Honorary Member Executive Committee Tennessee Judicial Conference since 2002. Member Memphis Association of Women Attorneys, Tennessee Lawyers Association for Women (President), Tennessee Trial Judges Association, American Judges Association, Memphis, Tennessee (Honorary Member Board of Governors since 2002) and American Bar Associations. Chair Committee of ADR Seminar The National Judicial College Reno Nevada. Speaker on Voir Dire and Court Room Procedure Continuing Legal Education Seminar Memphis Bar Association. Named one of the Outstanding Women in the Mid-South by Tennessee-Arkansas-Mississippi Girl Scouts 1985. Leadership Memphis Class 1988. Board Member Tennessee Association of Children and Adults With Learning Disabilities 1991. Chairperson Americans With Disabilities Act Task Force since 1993. Host "A Question of Law" monthly television program on Library Channel. Board Member Neighborhood Watch, Parenting Center and Memphis Rotary Club. Enjoys antiques, reading, playing bridge and cooking.

Office: 212 Shelby County Courthouse, 140 Adams Avenue, Memphis 38103.

Telephone: (901) 545-4024.

Fax: (901) 545-5659

ROBINSON, Muriel *(Judge, Tennessee Circuit Court Twentieth Judicial District)* Elected to term beginning Sept 1, 1982. Reelected 1990 and 1998. Current term expires Aug 31, 2006. Born Davidson County Tennessee Feb 7, 1944. Presbyterian. Educated at Nashville School of Law J.D. replaced LL.B. conferred 1969. Admitted to

ROBINSON, MURIEL—*Continued*

practice Tennessee 1969. In legal practice Nashville 1969-82.

Chairman Governor's Commission on Child Support since 1989. Instructor in Domestic Relations Nashville School of Law for 20 years. Member Lawyers Association for Women, Nashville and Tennessee Bar Associations. Democrat.

Office: 409 Metro Courthouse, Nashville 37201.

Telephone: (615) 862-5910.

ROGERS, C. L. "Buck" *(Judge, Tennessee Circuit Court Eighteenth Judicial District)*

Office: Courthouse, First Floor, 105 Public Square, Gallatin 37066.

Telephone: (615) 452-6771.

ROLLINS, John Wiley *(Judge, Tennessee Circuit Court Fourteenth Judicial District)*

Mailing address: P.O. Box 1500, Manchester 37349.

Office: 224 West Fort Street, Manchester 37355.

Telephone: (931) 728-4700.

ROSENBALM, Wheeler Armston *(Judge, Tennessee Circuit Court Sixth Judicial District)*

Office: M38 City-County Building, 400 Main Avenue, Knoxville 37902.

Telephone: (865) 215-2396.

ROSS, Carroll Lee *(Judge, Tennessee Circuit Court Tenth Judicial District)*

Mailing address: P.O. Box 1356, Athens 37371-1356.

Office: 130 Washington Avenue, Suite 3, Athens 37303.

Telephone: (423) 744-2835.

RUSSELL, Franklin Lee *(Judge, Tennessee Circuit Court Seventeenth Judicial District)*

Mailing address: P.O. Box 1005, Shelbyville 37162.

Office: 402 Belmont Avenue, Shelbyville 37160.

Telephone: (931) 684-3836.

RUSSELL, James Franklin *(Judge, Tennessee Circuit Court Thirtieth Judicial District)* Appointed by Governor Don Sundquist to term beginning Feb 24, 1997. Elected 1998, current term expires Sept 1, 2006. Born Memphis Tennessee March 21, 1945. Episcopalian. Educated at Rhodes College B.A. 1967 and University of Memphis J.D. 1970. Member Omicron Delta Kappa. Admitted to practice Tennessee 1971, U.S. Courts of Appeals Fifth, Sixth and Eighth Circuits and U.S. District Courts Western District of Tennessee, Eastern District of Arkansas and Northern District of Mississippi. In legal practice 1971-97.

Professional Mediator and Arbitrator since 1995. Co-author "The Locality Rule and Medical Malpractice: A Judicial Awakening" 1 Memphis State University L. Rev. 378. Member Tennessee Defense Lawyers Association, National Association of Railroad Trial Counsel, International Association of Defense Counsel, Tennessee Judicial Counsel, Memphis (Board of Directors 1976-78 and 1987-88, Member Board of Directors Executive Committee 1978 and 1987; Board Sponsor 1987 and Member Judicial Practice and Procedures Committee; Treasurer 1988-89, Vice President 1990, President-Elect 1991, President 1992; Chairman Committee on Law Lists, Member Membership Committee, Medico-Legal Committee, Budget Committee and Entertainment Committee), Tennessee (West Tennessee Vice President 1978 Tennessee Young Lawyers Conference, Member Membership Committee) and American (Member Judging Team and Co-chairman 1979 Awards of Achievement Committee Young Lawyers Division) Bar Associations. Attended Mediation Training Academy Dispute Management, Inc. 1995. Listed in Marquis' *Who's Who in American Law* and *Who's Who in America*. Sergeant USAR July 7, 1968 to Oct 1974. Previously worked as bookkeeper Railways Ice & Service Company and laborer Dover Elevator Corporation and Pic Walsh Truck Line. Board Member since 1985, Secretary 1991-92 and Vice Chairman since 1995 Mid-South Area Red Cross. Board Member and Treasurer 1991-92 Epilepsy Foundation of West Tennessee. 1967 Class Agent Southwestern Fund Campaign 1974. Member Whitehaven Booster Club, Whitehaven Junior Baseball Association, Southwestern Athletic Union, Inc. (Founder 1976) and Evergreen Historic District Association. President Episcopal Churchmen of Tennessee 1985. First Alternate Deputy 1985 and Deputy 1988, 1991, 1994, 1997 and 2000 Episcopal Churchmen/USA General Convention. Member Standing Committee on Constitution and Canons Diocese of Tennessee and Diocese of West Tennessee (Chairman since 1986). Vice Chancellor since 1996 Diocese of West Tennessee. Member St. John's Episcopal Church (Vestry 1975-78).

Office: 212 Shelby County Courthouse, 140 Adams Avenue, Memphis 38103.

Telephone: (901) 545-4047.

SCHULTEN, Jacqueline E. *(Judge, Tennessee Circuit Court Eleventh Judicial District)*

Office: 308 Hamilton County Courthouse, 625 Georgia Avenue, Chattanooga 37402.

Telephone: (423) 209-7393.

SCOTT, James B., Jr. *(Judge, Tennessee Circuit Court Seventh Judicial District)* Appointed by Governor Ray Blanton to term beginning May 15, 1978. Elected 1982, 1990 and 1998. Current term expires Aug 31, 2006. Born Charleston West Virginia Nov 7, 1935. Religious affiliation: Cumberland Presbyterian. Educated at University of Tennessee B.S. 1960 LL.B. 1966. Admitted to practice Tennessee 1966. Began legal practice Oak Ridge 1966.

Former Assistant District Attorney Fourth and Nineteenth Judicial Districts of Tennessee. Former District Attorney Twenty-eighth Judicial District of Tennessee. Member Tennessee Bar Association. Democrat.

Office: Anderson County Courthouse, 100 North Main, Clinton 37716.

Telephone: (865) 457-7875.

SEELEY, Thomas J., Jr. *(Judge, Tennessee Circuit Court First Judicial District)* Former Presiding Judge.

Mailing address: P.O. Box 890, Erwin 37650.

Office: Unicoi County Courthouse, Main Street, Erwin 37650.

Telephone: (423) 743-1100.

SELLS, Lillie Ann *(Judge, Tennessee Criminal Court Thirteenth Judicial District)*

Office: 228 East Broad Street, Suite 202, Cookeville 38501.

Telephone: (931) 525-1699.

SEXTON, E. Shayne *(Judge, Tennessee Criminal Court Eighth Judicial District)*
Mailing address: P.O. Box 852, Jacksboro 37757.
Office: 241 Myers Street, Jacksboro 37757.
Telephone: (423) 907-7503.

SEXTON, George C. *(Judge, Tennessee Circuit Court Twenty-third Judicial District)* Appointed by Governor Phil Bredesen Feb 12, 2003. Educated at Austin Peay State University B.S. 1978 and University of Tennessee School of Law J.D. Former Judge, Dover Municipal Court and Cumberland City Municipal Court. Judge, Stewart County General Sessions Court and Stewart County Juvenile Court 1998 to Feb 2003.
Office: Humphreys County Courthouse, 102 Thompson, Waverly 37185.
Telephone: (931) 296-4726.

SHIPLEY, Marietta M. *(Judge, Tennessee Circuit Court Twentieth Judicial District)* Elected to term beginning Sept 1990. Reelected 1998, current term expires Aug 31, 2006. Born Kansas City Kansas 1945. Lutheran. Educated at University of Kansas B.A. 1967 M.A. 1969 and Nashville School of Law J.D. with honors 1976. Law Clerk to Hon. Stephen North, Civil Court Judge, Tennessee Circuit Court Circuit Ten 1976-77. Admitted to practice Tennessee 1976 and U.S. District Court District of Tennessee 1976. In legal practice Nashville 1980-90.
Author "Prenuptial Agreements" Tennessee Practice Series 1990. Important Decisions: Jones Act Application to Workers' Compensation 1991 and Jehovah's Witnesses and Informed Consent 1992. Member Lawyers Association for Women (President 1991-92), Nashville (Chair pro bono Committee 1989-90), Tennessee (Chair Family Law Section 1990, Alternative Dispute Resolution Committee 1992-93) and American Bar Associations. Instructor in Comparative Negligence, Evaluating Settlement, Mediation and Alternative Dispute Resolution. Former high school teacher. Member Metro Social Services. Enjoys skiing, rollerblading, tennis, golf, sewing, reading and traveling.
Office: 501 Metro Courthouse, Nashville 37201.
Telephone: (615) 862-5905.

SHIRLEY, C. Clifford *(Magistrate Judge, United States District Court Eastern District of Tennessee)* Appointed by U.S. District Court judges to term beginning Feb 13, 2002.
Office: 800 Market Street, Suite 144, Knoxville 37902.
Telephone: (865) 545-4260.

SIMMONS, Russell E., Jr. *(Judge, Tennessee Circuit Court Ninth Judicial District)*
Mailing address: P.O. Box 400, Kingston 37763.
Office: 1000 Bradford Way, Suite 400, Kingston 37763.
Telephone: (865) 376-5776.

SLONE, O. Duane *(Judge, Tennessee Circuit Court Fourth Judicial District)*
Mailing address: P.O. Box 858, Dandridge 37725.
Office: 139 East Main Street, Dandridge 37725.
Telephone: (865) 397-8733.

SMITH, Charles K. "C.K." *(Chancellor, Tennessee Chancery Court Fifteenth Judicial District)*
Mailing address: P.O. Box 86, Hartsville 37074.
Office: 108 East Main Street, Hartsville 37074.
Telephone: (615) 374-2183.

SMITH, J. Curtis *(Judge, Tennessee Circuit Court Twelfth Judicial District)*
Mailing address: P.O. Box 2200, Dunlap 37327.
Office: Five Cherry Street East, Dunlap 37327.
Telephone: (423) 949-4691.

SMITH, Jerry *(Judge, Tennessee Court of Criminal Appeals Middle Division)* Appointed by Governor Don Sundquist Nov 1995. Retained by election 1996 and Aug 1998. Current term expires Aug 2006. Born Etowah Tennessee Dec 9, 1953. Episcopalian. Educated at University of Tennessee B.A. 1975 J.D. 1978. Admitted to practice Tennessee 1978. In legal practice 1978-80.
Assistant Attorney General 1980-84 and Deputy Attorney General 1984-95 Attorney General's Office. President National Association of Extradition Officials 1985-86. Attorney General's designee to Tennessee Sentencing Commission 1986-89. Member Sixth Circuit Task Force on Capital Cases 1987. Member Tennessee Judicial Conference, Nashville and Tennessee Bar Associations.
Office: 200 Supreme Court Building, 401 Seventh Avenue North, Nashville 37219-1407.
Telephone: (615) 741-3041.

SOLOMAN, Carol L. *(Judge, Tennessee Circuit Court Twentieth Judicial District)* Elected to term beginning Aug 31, 1998. Term expires Aug 31, 2006. Born Ashland Kentucky. Jewish. Educated at Vanderbilt University B.A. 1975 and Nashville School of Law J.D. 1979. Law Clerk to District Attorney's Office Seventeenth Judicial District 1975-80. Admitted to practice Tennessee 1979, U.S. District Court Middle District of Tennessee and U.S. Court of Appeals Sixth Circuit. In legal practice Nashville 1980-98.
Assistant District Attorney Seventeenth Judicial District 1979-80. Instructor Southeastern Paralegal College since 1999. Member Law Association for Women, Tennessee Judicial Association and Nashville Bar Association. Attended "Evidence" The National Judicial College. Enjoys horses, gardening and scuba diving.
Office: 301 Metro Courthouse, Nashville 37201.
Telephone: (615) 880-2591.
E-mail address: carolsoloman@jis.nashville.org

STAFFORD, J. Steven *(Chancellor, Tennessee Chancery Court Twenty-ninth Judicial District)*
Mailing address: P.O. Box 1471, Dyersburg 38025-1471.
Office: 100 Main Avenue North, Suite 4, Dyersburg 38024.
Telephone: (731) 286-8387.

STAIR, Richard S., Jr. *(Judge, United States Bankruptcy Court Eastern District of Tennessee)* Former Chief Judge.
Office: 330 U.S. Courthouse, 800 Market Street, Knoxville 37902.
Telephone: (865) 545-4284.

STANLEY, Jean A. *(Judge, Tennessee Circuit Court First Judicial District)* Elected to term beginning Sept 1998. Term expires 2006. Born Johnson City Tennessee Oct 25, 1952. Educated at East Tennessee State University B.S. cum laude 1974 and University of Tennessee J.D. 1978. Admitted to practice Tennessee, U.S. District Court District of Tennessee, U.S. Court of Appeals

STANLEY, JEAN A.—*Continued*

Sixth Circuit and U.S. Supreme Court. In legal practice Johnson City 1978-98.

General Counsel Johnson City—Washington County Chamber of Commerce 1994. Public Safety Officer Representative to Civil Service Board Johnson City. Former Member Civil Justice Reform Act Advisory Group and Bench Bar Relations Committee Tennessee Judges and Attorneys. Charter Member Tennessee Lawyers Association for Women (President 2001-02, Former Secretary and Treasurer). Guest Lecturer Tennessee Sheriff's Association, Tennessee Corrections Institute, East Tennessee State University and Washington County Sheriff's Department. Former Chair and Member Board of Zoning Appeals Johnson City. Board of Directors Girl Scouts of America. Participant Big Brothers, Big Sisters Organization. Member Annual Charity Horse Show and Equifest for Crumley House Head Injury Rehabilitation Center. Interests include breeding and selling Rocky Mountain horses.

Office: Courthouse, 101 East Market Street, Johnson City 37604.
Telephone: (423) 461-1488.
Fax: (423) 434-6445

STANLEY, Larry Barton, Jr. *(Judge, Tennessee Circuit Court Thirty-first Judicial District and Chancellor, Tennessee Chancery Court Thirty-first Judicial District)*

Office: 200 Courthouse, 111 South Court Square, McMinnville 37110.

STERN, Rebecca J. *(Judge, Tennessee Criminal Court Eleventh Judicial District)* Appointed by Governor Don Sundquist to term beginning April 1, 1997. Elected to term beginning Sept 1, 1998. Born Cleveland Tennessee Jan 23, 1957. Educated at University of Tennessee at Chattanooga B.S. magna cum laude 1980 J.D. with honors 1987. Admitted to practice Tennessee 1987. In legal practice Chattanooga 1987-89.

Assistant District Attorney 1989-97. Member Southeast Tennessee Lawyers Association for Women, National Association of Women Judges and Chattanooga Bar Association. Board Member Tennessee Preservation Trust. Enjoys reading, film and travel.

Office: Courts Building, 600 Market Street, Chattanooga 37402.
Telephone: (423) 209-7560.

STEWART, Jeffrey F. *(Chancellor, Tennessee Chancery Court Twelfth Judicial District)* Appointed by Governor Ned Ray McWherter to term beginning Oct 1, 1989. Elected Sept 1, 1990 and 1998. Current term expires Aug 31, 2006. Born Winchester Tennessee Oct 12, 1950. United Methodist. Educated at University of the South B.A. 1973 and Nashville School of Law J.D. 1977. Admitted to practice Tennessee 1977 and U.S. District Court Eastern District of Tennessee 1978. In legal practice Winchester 1978-89.

Former Member Board of Governors Tennessee Trial Lawyers. Member Tennessee Judicial Conference (Retirement and Compensation Committee, Education Committee, Benchbar Relations Committee). Attended numerous CLE programs sponsored by Tennessee Judicial Conference and Tennessee Bar Association and General Jurisdiction Course The National Judicial College. Chairman Franklin County Democratic Party 1980-89. Enjoys hunting and various other outdoor activities and sports.

Mailing address: P.O. Box 428, Winchester 37398.
Office: 102 Third Avenue S.E., Winchester 37398.
Telephone: (931) 967-2605.

STINNETT, R. Thomas *(Judge, United States Bankruptcy Court Eastern District of Tennessee)* Appointed by U.S. Court of Appeals Sixth Circuit judges.

Office: Historic U.S. Courthouse, 31 East 11th Street, Chattanooga 37402-2722.
Telephone: (423) 752-5104.

STOTTS, Rita Laverne *(Judge, Tennessee Circuit Court Thirtieth Judicial District)*

Office: 212 Shelby County Courthouse, 140 Adams Avenue, Memphis 38103.
Telephone: (901) 545-4022.

SUSANO, Charles D., Jr. *(Judge, Tennessee Court of Appeals Eastern Division)* Appointed by Governor Ned Ray McWherter to term beginning March 18, 1994. Retained by election Aug 1994 and 1998. Current term expires Aug 2006. Born Knoxville Tennessee March 24, 1936. Roman Catholic. Educated at University of Notre Dame Ph.B. in Accounting magna cum laude 1958 and University of Tennessee J.D. 1963. Staff member Tennessee Law Review 1962-63. Law Clerk to Hon. Hamilton S. Burnett, Tennessee Supreme Court 1963-64. Member Phi Delta Phi and Order of the Coif. Admitted to practice Tennessee 1964, U.S. District Court Eastern District of Tennessee 1964, U.S. Court of Appeals Sixth Circuit 1974 and U.S. Supreme Court 1977. In legal practice Knoxville 1964-94.

Assistant District Attorney General Knox County 1967-68. Author "The Action of Deceit in Tennessee" Tennessee L. Rev. 1963. Important Decision: Wyatt v. A-Best Products Co. (a subsequent amendment to the Tennessee Products Liability Act cannot be applied retroactively to revive a claim already barred by the Act's statute of repose) 924 S.W.2d Tenn. App. 1995. Former Member Advisory Committee on Civil Rules Tennessee Supreme Court. Former Member Executive Committee and Former Treasurer Tennessee Judicial Conference. Fellow Tennessee Bar Foundation and American Bar Foundation. Member Knoxville, Tennessee and American Bar Associations. Specialist Four U.S. Army Oct 1958 to Oct 1960. Democrat. Chairman Knox County Democratic Party 1972-74. Member State Democratic Executive Committee 1974-82. Member Knights of Columbus.

Mailing address: P.O. Box 444, Knoxville 37901.
Office: 505 Main Street, Suite 200, Knoxville 37902.
Telephone: (865) 594-5246.
Fax: (865) 594-5235

SWANN, William K., III *(Judge, Tennessee Circuit Court Sixth Judicial District)* Elected to term beginning Sept 1, 1982. Reelected 1990 and 1998. Current term expires Aug 31, 2006. Former Presiding Judge. Born Boston Massachusetts Sept 30, 1942. Methodist. Educated at Harvard University B.A. cum laude 1964, Yale University Ph.D. 1971 and University of Tennessee J.D. 1975. Fulbright Scholar, Austria 1964-65. Law Clerk to Hon. James W. Parrott, Tennessee Court of Appeals 1974-75. Admitted to practice Tennessee 1975. In legal practice Knoxville 1975-82.

Author "Fuer Peter Handke" *Die Zeit* European edition May 28, 1971 and North American edition June 1, 1971, "Temporary Support Hearings" 33 No. 3 Tennes-

SWANN, WILLIAM K., III—*Continued*

see Lawyer April 1984, "Cutting the Gordian Knot" 7 No. 3 *Family Advocate* American Bar Association Winter 1985, "Property Division" 22 No. 1 *Court Review* American Judges Association Winter 1985, "Setting the Benchmark" Tennessee Lawyer Jan 1985 and "Property Division in Divorce Cases" 4 No. 1 The Tennessee Trial Lawyer Winter 1985. Editorial Committee *Court Review* American Judges Association. Former Instructor Yale University. Professor of German Brown University 1970-72. Member International Society of Family Law, American Judges Association, Tennessee Judicial Conference (Treasurer 1986-87, Chairman Annual Conference 1987), Knoxville, Tennessee (Sections of General Practice and Family Law, Judge High School Moot Court Competition, former member House of Delegates) and American (Judicial Administration Division, Section of Family Law) Bar Associations. CLE Instructor Tennessee Judicial Conference, Knoxville and Tennessee Bar Associations. CME Instructor "Medical Malpractice" University of Tennessee Medical School. Faculty member Law Education Institute, Inc. since 1986. Named Man of the Year by Knoxville Area Social Workers 1985. Recipient Service Award and Membership Award from Knoxville YMCA. Board member Helen Ross McNabb Foundation (regional mental health center) and Child and Family Services of Knox County. Delegate to Association of Yale Alumni and Past President Yale Club of Knoxville. Advisory Board Knoxville Rape Crisis Center. Member Appalachian Anglers Society and Center Street United Methodist Church. Enjoys running, jogging, hiking, fishing and competing in triathlons.

Office: M44 City-County Building, 400 Main Avenue, Knoxville 37902.

Telephone: (865) 215-4241.

SWINEY, D. Michael *(Judge, Tennessee Court of Appeals Eastern Division)* Appointed by Governor Don Sundquist to term beginning July 1999. Retained by election 2000. Born Sarasota Florida May 25, 1949. Educated at University of Tennessee B.S. 1971 M.S. 1974 J.D. 1978. Member Order of the Coif. Admitted to practice Tennessee 1979. In legal practice Knoxville 1979-99.

Member Hamilton Burnette Chapter American Inns of Court.

Mailing address: P.O. Box 444, Knoxville 37901-0444.

Office: 505 Main Street, Suite 200, Knoxville 37902.

Telephone: (865) 594-6116.

TAYLOR, Royce *(Judge, Tennessee Circuit Court Sixteenth Judicial District)*

Office: 20 Public Square North, Room 505, Murfreesboro 37130.

Telephone: (615) 848-5143.

THOMAS, D. Kelly, Jr. *(Judge, Tennessee Circuit Court Fifth Judicial District)*

Office: Blount County Justice Center, 948 East Lamar Alexander Parkway, Maryville 37804.

Telephone: (865) 273-5580.

THOMAS, W. Neil, III *(Judge, Tennessee Circuit Court Eleventh Judicial District)*

Office: 206 Hamilton County Courthouse, 625 Georgia Avenue, Chattanooga 37402.

Telephone: (423) 209-6755.

TIPTON, Joseph M. *(Judge, Tennessee Court of Criminal Appeals Eastern Division)* Appointed by Governor Ned Ray McWherter Sept 1990. Retained by election Aug 1992 and Aug 1998. Current term expires 2006. Born Birmingham Alabama March 9, 1947. Episcopalian. Educated at University of Tennessee at Knoxville B.S. 1969 J.D. 1971. Member Phi Kappa Phi and Order of the Coif.

Assistant Member Tennessee Board of Law Examiners 1981-96. Adjunct Professor University of Tennessee College of Law 1983-92. Past President Tennessee Association of Criminal Defense Lawyers. Member Tennessee Judicial Conference, Knoxville and Tennessee (Former Delegate House of Delegates) Bar Associations. First recipient Outstanding Service Award from Tennessee Association of Criminal Defense Lawyers.

Mailing address: P.O. Box 444, Knoxville 37901-0444.

Office: 505 Main Street, Suite 200, Knoxville 37902.

Telephone: (865) 594-6112.

TODD, James D. *(Chief Judge, United States District Court Western District of Tennessee)* Appointed for life by President Ronald Reagan to term beginning July 11, 1985. Chief Judge since Jan 1, 2001. Born Scotts Hill Tennessee May 20, 1943. Member Forest Heights United Methodist Church. Educated at Lambuth College B.S. 1965, University of Mississippi M.C.S. 1968 and Memphis State University School of Law J.D. 1972. Admitted to practice Tennessee 1972, U.S. District Court Western District of Tennessee 1972, U.S. Court of Appeals Sixth Circuit 1973 and U.S. Supreme Court 1975. In legal practice Jackson 1972-83. Former Judge, Tennessee Circuit Court, appointed to term beginning Sept 1983.

Science teacher and Chairman Science Department Lyman High School Longwood Florida 1965-68 and Memphis University School 1968-72. Author Note 2 No. 1 Memphis State University L. Rev. Fall 1971. Former member Tennessee (Chairman Committee on Federal Practice and Procedure 1978-79) and American Bar Associations. Member Board of Professional Responsibility Hearing Committee 1983. Former member International Association of Insurance Counsel and Tennessee Defense Lawyers Association. Member Federal Judges Association and Jackson-Madison County Bar Association (Secretary-Treasurer 1973-74, Vice President 1977-78, President 1978-79, member Committee on the Judiciary 1980 and Committee on Local Rules 1983). Recipient Lifetime Achievement Award from Lambuth College 2001. President Madison County Young Republicans 1976. Chairman Madison County Committee to Re-elect Senator Baker 1978. Member Madison County Republican Executive Committee 1982. Board of Directors 1974-82 and President 1980-82 Jackson Boys Club. Chairman Goals for Jackson Committee 1976-78. Vice President Highland Park School PTA 1979-80. President Lambuth College Alumni Association 1981-82. Coach Jackson Senior League Baseball 1981-82. Treasurer Jackson Youth Baseball Association, Inc. 1982. Board of Trustees Lambuth University 1987-99.

Office: 444 U.S. Courthouse, 111 South Highland Avenue, Jackson 38301.

Telephone: (731) 421-9222.

TRAUGER, Aleta A. *(Judge, United States District Court Middle District of Tennessee)* Appointed for life by President Bill Clinton to term beginning Dec 1,

TRAUGER, ALETA A.—*Continued*

1998. Born Denver Colorado Dec 9, 1945. Methodist. Educated at Cornell College B.A. magna cum laude 1968 and Vanderbilt University M.A.T. 1972 J.D. 1976. Member Phi Beta Kappa. In legal practice Nashville 1983-91. Judge, U.S. Bankruptcy Court Middle District of Tennessee Dec 6, 1993 to Nov 30, 1998.

Assistant U.S. Attorney Middle District of Tennessee 1977-79 and 1980-82 and First Assistant and Chief of Criminal Division Northern District of Illinois 1979-80 U.S. Department of Justice. Legal Counsel College of Charleston 1984-85. Chief of Staff Mayor's Office Metropolitan Nashville 1991-92. Lecturer in Trial Advocacy Vanderbilt University School of Law 1986-88. Instructor Attorney General's Advocacy Program State of Tennessee. Former Member National Conference of Bankruptcy Judges (Chair Ethics Committee 1994-98). Member Tennessee Court of the Judiciary 1987-93 and Tennessee Supreme Court Advisory Commission on Rules of Civil and Appellate Procedure 1989-97. Master of the Bench 1990-94, Member Executive Committee 1992-94 and Chair Nominations Committee 1994 Harry Phillips American Inn of Court. Fellow Nashville Bar Foundation, Tennessee Bar Foundation and American Bar Foundation. National Member American Inns of Court since 1996. Member Marion Griffin Chapter Lawyers' Association for Women (President 1982-83, Board of Directors 1983-84 and 1986-88, Member Early Truancy Intervention Program 1995, Nominee Athena Award 1997), Tennessee Lawyers' Association for Women (Chair Committee on Elected and Appointed Positions 1988-92 and Committee on Equal Opportunity and Placement since 1997, Vice President 1988-89, President 1989-90, Board of Directors 1990-91), National Association of Women Judges (District 6 Director 1997-98, Liaison to American Bar Association Commission on Women in the Profession 2001), Federal Judges Association, Nashville (Chair Federal Court Committee 1983 and 1988, Board of Directors 1984 and 1989-91, Member Colleagues Program 1994), Tennessee, American (Vice Chair Committee on Bankruptcy Judges Judicial Division 1996) and Federal (Vice President 1983-84 and 1985-86, Co-chair Bicentennial of the Constitution Committee 1986) Bar Associations. Previously employed as teacher in England and Tennessee 1970-73. Alumni Board Vanderbilt University School of Law 1989-92. Board of Directors Nashville Institute for the Arts 1992-99 (Chair Nominations Committee 1994-96, Member Executive Committee since 1995), Miriam's Promise 1995-98 and Renewal House 1996-98. Board of Trustees Cornell College since 1998. Member International Women's Forum since 1993 (Vice President Tennessee Chapter 1996-97). Member Chancel Choir West End United Methodist Church.

Office: 825 U.S. Courthouse, 801 Broadway, Nashville 37203.

Telephone: (615) 736-7143.

TROUTMAN, Conrad, Jr. *(Judge, Tennessee Circuit Court Eighth Judicial District)*

Mailing address: P.O. Box 208, LaFollette 37766-0208.

Office: 122 West Central Avenue, LaFollette 37766.

Telephone: (423) 562-8444.

TURNBULL, John A. *(Judge, Tennessee Circuit Court Thirteenth Judicial District)*

Mailing address: P.O. Box 68, Livingston 38570.

Office: 1010 East Main Street, Livingston 38570.

Telephone: (931) 823-6453.

VANCE, Richard Robert *(Judge, Tennessee Circuit Court Fourth Judicial District)*

Mailing address: P.O. Box 6098, Sevierville 37864-6098.

Office: 303E Sevier County Courthouse, Sevierville 37864.

Telephone: (865) 453-7234.

Fax: (865) 429-7048

VARLAN, Thomas A. *(Judge, United States District Court Eastern District of Tennessee)* Appointed for life by President George W. Bush to term beginning April 5, 2003.

Office: 800 Market Street, Knoxville 37902.

Telephone: (865) 545-4762.

VESCOVO, Diane K. *(Magistrate Judge, United States District Court Western District of Tennessee)* Appointed by U.S. District Court judges.

Office: 341 Federal Building, 167 North Main Street, Memphis 38103.

Telephone: (901) 495-1307.

WADE, Gary R. *(Judge, Tennessee Court of Criminal Appeals Eastern Division)* Appointed by Governor Ned Ray McWherter Oct 29, 1987. Retained by election 1990 and 1998. Current term expires Aug 31, 2006. Born Knox County Tennessee May 31, 1948. Educated at University of Tennessee B.S. 1970 J.D. 1973. Admitted to practice Tennessee 1973. In legal practice Sevierville 1973-87.

City Attorney Pigeon Forge 1973-87. Mayor Sevierville 1977-87. Treasurer Tennessee Municipal Bond Fund 1985-87. Member Tennessee Municipal Attorneys Association 1983-87 and National Association of Municipal Law Officers 1983-87. Member American Inns of Court, Tennessee Trial Lawyers Association, Tennessee Association of Criminal Defense Lawyers (Board of Directors 1978-84), Tennessee Judicial Conference (Executive Committee since 1989), Tennessee and American Bar Associations. Recipient Service Award 1984-86 and Presidential Award 1987 from American Heart Association, Key to City Award from City of Sevierville 1987 and Service Award from Sevierville Chamber of Commerce. Named "Mover and Shaker of the Year" by *The Mountain Press* 1983, 1984 and 1985. Honored with "Gary R. Wade Boulevard" 1987. Board Chairman Sevier Title, Inc. 1975-88. Partner Kelco, Ltd. since 1986. Democrat. Chairman Sevier County Heart Association 1984, 1985 and 1986. Board of Directors Sevier County United Way 1984, 1985 and 1986. Past President Sevierville Lions Club. Member University of Tennessee Chancellor's Associates 1988-91. Finance Chairman First United Methodist Church since 1989. Eta South Province President Phi Delta Theta since 1990. Vice President East Tennessee Chapter American Heart Association. Enjoys tennis, basketball, hiking and guitar.

Mailing address: P.O. Box 444, Knoxville 37901-0444.

Office: 505 Main Street, Suite 200, Knoxville 37902.

Telephone: (865) 594-6121.

WALKER, Joseph H. *(Judge, Tennessee Circuit Court Twenty-fifth Judicial District)* Elected to term beginning Sept 1, 1990. Reelected 1998, current term expires Aug 31, 2006. Born Tennessee Sept 4, 1945. Baptist. Educated at Rhodes College B.A. 1967 and Cecil Humphries School of Law J.D. 1976. Associate Editor Memphis State University Law Review 1974-76. Admitted to practice Tennessee 1976. Began legal practice Ripley. Chancellor, Tennessee Chancery Court Ninth Judicial District 1982-83. First Lieutenant U.S. Army Infantry 1968-71.

Mailing address: P.O. Box 296, Ripley 38063.
Office: 105 Lafayette Street, Ripley 38063.
Telephone: (731) 635-0763.

WALLACE, Allen Wilson *(Senior Judge, Tennessee Trial and Appellate Courts)* Assumed office as Judge, Tennessee Circuit Court Twenty-third Judicial District. Former Presiding Judge. Retired Jan 31, 2003. Appointed Senior Judge by Tennessee Supreme Court justices, serves by assignment.

Office: 20 Humphreys County Courthouse, Waverly 37185.
Telephone: (931) 296-4726.

WEATHERFORD, James L. *(Senior Judge, Tennessee Appellate and Trial Courts)* Assumed office as Judge, Tennessee Circuit Court Twenty-second Judicial District. Former Presiding Judge. Retired Dec 31, 1996. Appointed Senior Judge by Tennessee Supreme Court justices, serves by assignment. Born Columbia Tennessee 1931. Educated at Middle Tennessee State College, Northwestern University and Cumberland University J.D. 1958. Admitted to practice Tennessee 1958.

Assistant District Attorney Twenty-second (formerly Eleventh) Judicial Circuit 1962-65. Member Lawrence County and Tennessee Bar Associations.

Mailing address: P.O. Box 411, Lawrenceburg 38464.
Telephone: (931) 762-9242.

WEAVER, John F. *(Chancellor, Tennessee Chancery Court Sixth Judicial District)*

Office: 125 City County Building, 400 Main Avenue, Knoxville 37902.
Telephone: (865) 215-2561.

WEDEMEYER, Robert W. *(Judge, Tennessee Court of Criminal Appeals Middle Division)* Appointed by Governor Don Sundquist to term beginning 2000. Retained by election 2000. Born Nashville Tennessee May 23, 1951. Educated at Vanderbilt University B.A. 1973 and University of Memphis J.D. 1976. In legal practice 1977-90. Judge, Tennessee Circuit Court Nineteenth Judicial District 1990-2000, appointed by Governor Ned Ray McWherter.

Member Tennessee Judicial Conference (Criminal Jury Instructions Committee 1992-98, Bench/Bar Relations Committee). Past President Montgomery County Chapter American Red Cross. Former Board Member Roxy Regional Theater. Former Little League Coach, Youth Soccer Coach and YMCA Basketball Coach.

Office: 220 Supreme Court Building, 401 Seventh Avenue North, Nashville 37219.
Telephone: (615) 741-2574.

WEINMAN, Bernie *(Judge, Tennessee Criminal Court Thirtieth Judicial District)* Elected to term beginning Sept 1, 1974. Reelected 1982, 1990 and 1998. Current term expires Aug 30, 2006. Born Memphis Tennessee April 24, 1934. Jewish. Educated at University of Memphis B.S. 1957 and Southern University Law Center LL.B. 1960. Admitted to practice Tennessee 1961. In legal practice Memphis 1961-65. Judge, Memphis Municipal Court 1965-74.

Author "Municipal Courts of Tennessee: A New Era" Memphis State L. Rev. 1971, Draft "Criminal Justice Mental Health Standards" American Bar Association 1984 and Memphis and Shelby County Bar Association Syllabus 1985. Important Decision: State of Tennessee v. Pervis Payne (victim impact statements allowed). Instructor Criminal Justice Department University of Memphis 1971-86. Member Leo Bearman, Sr. Chapter American Inns of Court. Attended Tennessee Judicial Conference and many CLE seminars. Instructor The National Judicial College 1972 and 1987.

Office: 519 Shelby County Justice Complex, 201 Poplar Avenue, Memphis 38103.
Telephone: (901) 545-5856.

WELLES, David H. *(Judge, Tennessee Court of Criminal Appeals Middle Division)* Appointed by Governor Ned Ray McWherter Feb 1994. Retained by election Aug 1994 and Aug 1998. Current term expires Aug 2006. Born Memphis Tennessee July 10, 1948. Methodist. Educated at University of Tennessee at Martin B.S. 1971 J.D. 1974. Member Order of the Coif. Admitted to practice Tennessee 1974. In legal practice Dresden 1974-87.

Assistant District Attorney General (part time) 1976-87. Former Member Weakly County Bar Association. Fellow Nashville Bar Foundation and Tennessee Bar Foundation. Member Tennessee Court of the Judiciary, Supreme Court Commission on Racial and Ethnic Fairness and American Bar Association. Lieutenant Colonel Tennessee Army National Guard. Chief Clerk Tennessee House of Representatives 1977-82. Legal Counsel to Governor Ned Ray McWherter 1987-94.

Office: 208 Supreme Court Building, 401 Seventh Avenue North, Nashville 37219-1407.
Telephone: (615) 532-7945.

WEXLER, Ben K. *(Judge, Tennessee Circuit Court Third Judicial District)* Elected to term beginning Sept 1, 1986. Reelected 1990 and 1998. Current term expires Aug 31, 2006. Currently serves as Presiding Judge. Born Johnson City Tennessee Feb 13, 1922. Methodist. Educated at East Tennessee State University 1949 and University of Tennessee J.D. 1960. Member Phi Alpha Delta. Admitted to practice Tennessee 1961 and U.S. District Court District of Tennessee 1966. In legal practice Greeneville 1966-86. City Judge, Greeneville 1973-80.

Assistant Attorney General 1969-76. Member Greene County and Tennessee Bar Associations. Attended Tennessee Judicial Conferences 1986-2002. Sergeant USAAC 1943-45. Previously worked for Tennessee Valley Authority and Free Service Tire Company. Republican. Chairman Greene County Republican Organization 1983-85. Enjoys hunting, fishing, sports and gardening.

Mailing address: P.O. Box 876, Greeneville 37744-0876.
Office: 116 East Depot Street, Greeneville 37743.
Telephone: (423) 639-5204.
Fax: (423) 798-1763

WHEATCRAFT, Jane W. *(Judge, Tennessee Criminal Court Eighteenth Judicial District)*
Office: Sumner County Courthouse, Second Floor, 105 Public Square, Gallatin 37066.
Telephone: (615) 452-5526.

WHITE, Billy Joe *(Chancellor, Tennessee Chancery Court Eighth Judicial District)*
Mailing address: P.O. Box 254, Tazewell 37879-0254.
Office: Claiborne County Courthouse, Tazewell 37879.
Telephone: (423) 626-5282.

WHITENTON, Dewey C. *(Chancellor, Tennessee Chancery Court Twenty-fifth Judicial District)* Appointed to term beginning 1976. Elected 1978, 1982, 1990 and 1998. Current term expires Aug 31, 2006. Currently serves as Presiding Judge. Born Bolivar Tennessee June 4, 1934. Methodist. Educated at Vanderbilt University B.A. 1956 J.D. 1959. Admitted to practice Tennessee 1959. Began legal practice Bolivar 1959.
County Attorney Hardeman County 1970-76. Chancery Representative Tennessee Judicial Council 1980-90. Editor *Directory of State Judicial Association Officers, Chief Justices and Administrators.* Member World Association of Judges, American Judges Association, Tennessee Trial Lawyers Association, The Association of Trial Lawyers of America, Tennessee Trial Judges Association (Vice President 1982-85), Hardeman County, Jackson-Madison County, Tennessee (Chairman Unauthorized Practice of Law Committee 1972-74, House of Delegates 1975-77) and American (Chairman Committee on State Judicial Associations 1994-2000 and Member Executive Committee 2000-02 and Editorial Board National Conference of State Trial Judges Judicial Administration Division) Bar Associations. Instructor Tennessee Judicial College at Vanderbilt University School of Law 1982. Recipient Award for Outstanding Service from West Tennessee Legal Services, Inc. Aug 15, 2001. Member Hardeman County Election Commission 1970-76. U.S. Army and Tennessee Army National Guard 1959-65. President Bolivar Rotary Club 1976-77 and Hardeman County Golf and Country Club 1974-75. Enjoys cooking, golf and travel.
Mailing address: P.O. Box 303, Bolivar 38008-0303.
Office: 116 Warren Street, Bolivar 38008.
Telephone: (731) 658-5373.
Fax: (731) 659-2527

WILLIAMS, Frank Vernon, III *(Chancellor, Tennessee Chancery Court Ninth Judicial District)* Elected to term beginning Sept 1, 1984. Reelected 1990 and 1998. Current term expires Aug 31, 2006. Former Presiding Judge. Born Knoxville Tennessee Feb 5, 1947. Southern Baptist. Educated at University of Tennessee B.S. 1970 J.D. 1973. Member Phi Alpha Delta. Admitted to practice Tennessee 1973, U.S. District Court Eastern District of Tennessee 1973 and U.S. Supreme Court 1974. In legal practice Rockwood 1973-80 and Kingston 1981-84.
Member Kingston Regional Planning Commission 1973-80 (Chairman 1979), Tennessee Trial Judges Association and Roane County Bar Association. Employed by Green Giant Company 1966, National Park Service 1969 and Tennessee Department of Transportation 1971. President Roane County Heritage Commission 1975-81. Member Tennessee Historical Commission since 1998. Past President Roane County Chamber of Commerce. Enjoys fishing. Interests include antiques, art and local history.
Mailing address: P.O. Box 810, Kingston 37763.
Office: 1003 Bradford Way, Kingston 37763.
Telephone: (865) 376-2193.
Fax: (865) 376-2073

WILLIAMS, John Everett *(Judge, Tennessee Court of Criminal Appeals Western Division)* Appointed by Governor Don Sundquist Nov 1998. Born Milan Tennessee Nov 11, 1953. Methodist. Educated at University of Tennessee at Martin B.S. and Cumberland School of Law of Samford University J.D. 1981. Admitted to practice Tennessee 1981. In legal practice 1981-98.
Member Tennessee Trial Lawyers Association, Carroll County (President 1981-84) and Tennessee Bar Associations. Named Outstanding Chairperson by Huntingdon Jaycee's. President Huntingdon Lion's Club 1991-92. Co-chairman Cordell Hull's Speakers' Forum and Director of Special Programs Cumberland School of Law. Member American Heart Association, American Cancer Society, American Red Cross, Carroll County Habitat for Humanity and Carroll County Ducks Unlimited.
Mailing address: P.O. Box 88, Huntingdon 38344.
Office: 115 Court Square, Huntingdon 38344.
Telephone: (731) 986-2225.
Fax: (731) 986-2226

WILLIAMS, Karen R. *(Judge, Tennessee Circuit Court Thirtieth Judicial District)*
Office: 212 Shelby County Courthouse, 140 Adams Avenue, Memphis 38103.
Telephone: (901) 545-4022.

WILLIAMS, L. Marie *(Judge, Tennessee Circuit Court Eleventh Judicial Circuit)* Appointed by Governor Don Sundquist to term beginning March 27, 1995. Elected Aug 1, 1996 and 1998. Current term expires Aug 31, 2006. Born Chattanooga Tennessee July 17, 1952. Episcopalian. Educated at University of Georgia B.A. 1974 and University of Tennessee College of Law J.D. 1976. Member Phi Alpha Delta. Admitted to practice Tennessee 1977 and U.S. District Court Eastern District of Tennessee 1977. In legal practice Chattanooga and eastern Tennessee 1977-95.
Former Member Alternative Dispute Resolution Commission Tennessee Supreme Court, Early Neutral Evaluation Panel for Federal District Court, TPI Civil Jury Instruction Committee, Tennessee Defense Lawyers Association and National Association of Railroad Trial Counsel. Chair Judicial Performance Program Committee. Member SETLAW, TLAW, Chattanooga, Tennessee and American Bar Associations. Recipient Athena Award from Tennessee Bar Foundation 1977. Board of Directors St. Barnabas Nursing Home. Vice Chancellor The Diocese of East Tennessee. Member Rotary Club of Chattanooga, Junior League of Chattanooga, Hamilton County Republican Women and UTC Chancellor's Roundtable.
Office: 308 Hamilton County Courthouse, 625 Georgia Avenue, Chattanooga 37402.
Telephone: (423) 209-6747.

WILSON, John K. *(Judge, Tennessee Circuit Court Third Judicial District)*
Mailing address: P.O. Box 625, Greeneville 37744.
Office: 101 South Main Street, Suite 401, Greeneville 37743.
Telephone: (423) 639-1731.

WIMBERLY, Harold *(Judge, Tennessee Circuit Court Sixth Judicial District)* Former Judge, Knox County General Sessions Court.
Office: M35 City-County Building, 400 Main Avenue, Knoxville 37902.
Telephone: (865) 215-2393.

WISEMAN, Thomas A., Jr. *(Senior Judge, United States District Court Middle District of Tennessee)* Appointed to serve during good behavior by President Jimmy Carter to term beginning Aug 25, 1978. Former Chief Judge. Assumed Senior status, serves by assignment. Born Tullahoma Tennessee Nov 3, 1930. Presbyterian. Educated at Vanderbilt University B.A. 1952 J.D. 1954 and University of Virginia School of Law LL.M. 1990. Associate Editor Vanderbilt Law Review 1953-54. Member Phi Delta Phi. Admitted to practice Tennessee 1954 and U.S. District Courts Eastern 1954 and Middle 1978 Districts of Tennessee. In legal practice Tullahoma 1956-71 and Nashville 1974-78.
Author "Judicial Discretion Under the New Criminal Sentencing Act of 1982" Tennessee B. Jour. Nov 1982; "Supreme Court: The Wall Come A-Tumblin' Down" *The Spire* Vanderbilt University Divinity School and Oberlin Graduate School of Theology 9 No. 2 Summer 1984; "Lawyer Voir Dire" *Litigation* American Bar Association Spring 1985; Convocation Lecture "The Church and Caesar—Rendition, Obedience, Evangelization" 175th Convocation Union Theological Seminary Richmond Virginia Sept 1985; Monograph "Education and the Separation of Church and State" Center for the Advanced Study of Educational Leadership Peabody College at Vanderbilt University Nov 1985; "Church-State Confusion: A Judicious Warning" *Church and State* 39 No. 2 Feb 1986, condensed and reprinted *The New Age* Sept 1986, reprinted *Liberty* 82 No. 4 July-Aug 1987 and *Presbyterian Survey* Nov 1987; Address "1986 Establishmentarianism: A Christian Separatist Response" Annual Religious Liberty Awards Banquet 39th National Conference Americans United for Separation of Church and State Sept 1986; "The Religious Clauses of the First Amendment" *The New Age* Sept 1987; "The Balancing Act: Public Needs vs. Individual Rights" *Exchangite* Dec 1987, revised for *Vanderbilt Lawyer* Jan 1988; Thesis "Recommendations of the Federal Courts Study Committee: A District Judge Response" Graduate Program for Judges University of Virginia School of Law April 1990; "Our Antimajoritarian Constitution" Annual Conference of Americans United for Separation of Church and State Sept 1991 Arlington Virginia; "Judging the Expert" Ohio State L. Jour. 55 No. 5, 1994; "The Case Against Bankruptcy Appellate Panels" George Mason L. Rev. 4 No. 1 Fall 1995; "Be A Clerk; Hire A Clerk" *The Vanderbilt Lawyer* 26 No. 1 Winter 1996; and "What Doth the Lord Require of Thee?" Texas Tech L. Rev. 27 No. 3 Faith and the Law Symposium 1996. Adjunct Faculty Trial Advocacy Vanderbilt University Law School since 1988. Member Advisory Committee on Bankruptcy Rules 1984-89, Chair District Judges Conference 1998 and Member 1996-2001 Judicial Conference of the U.S. Faculty Member National Institute of Trial Advocacy Boulder Colorado and Gainesville Florida 1980-91. Former Member American Inns of Court. Member Federal Judges Association (Vice President 1987-91). Recipient George Washington Honor Medal for publications from Freedom Foundation at Valley Forge 1988 and Andrew Jackson Honor Medal from the Grand Lodge Masons of Tennessee 1997. Specialist Third Class U.S. Army 1954-56. Member Tennessee House of Representatives 1964-68. Chairman Democratic Caucus 1967-68. State Treasurer Tennessee 1971-74. Consultant to Judiciary of Brcko District Bosnia Herzegovina 2002. Member Nashville Committee on Foreign Relations. Member 33° Masons and Shriners. Enjoys gourmet cooking, wine collecting and duck hunting.
Office: 777 U.S. Courthouse, 801 Broadway, Nashville 37203-3813.
Telephone: (615) 736-7013.

WITT, Curwood *(Judge, Tennessee Court of Criminal Appeals Eastern Division)* Appointed by Governor Don Sundquist to term beginning Jan 16, 1997. Retained by election 1998, current term expires Aug 31, 2006. Born Knox County Tennessee Oct 23, 1948. United Methodist. Educated at Hiwassee College A.A. with highest honors 1968, Tennessee Wesleyan College B.A. with highest honors 1970 and University of Tennessee J.D. with highest honors 1973. Staff member University of Tennessee Law Review 1971-73. Member Alpha Chi and Order of the Coif. Admitted to practice Tennessee 1973 and U.S. District Court Eastern District of Tennessee 1973. In legal practice Madisonville 1973-97. Judge, Monroe County Juvenile Court 1978-82.
School Board Attorney Monroe County 1988-97. Contributing Author 39 Tennessee L. Rev. 157, 1971 and 39 Tennessee L. Rev. 479, 1972. Member Tennessee Judicial Council 1980-88, Hearing Committee Board of Professional Responsibility 1986-92 and Tennessee Judicial Conference 1997-98. Recipient Bobbs Merrill Award 1973 and West Publishing Company 1973 from University of Tennessee Law School. Republican. President Board of Directors Boys and Girls Club of Monroe Area 1996-98. Board of Trustees Holston Conference United Methodist Church 1996-98.
Mailing address: P.O. Box 217, Madisonville 37354-0217.
Office: 138 College Street, Madisonville 37354.
Telephone: (423) 442-7430.

WOODALL, Thomas T. *(Judge, Tennessee Court of Criminal Appeals Middle Division)* Appointed by Governor Don Sundquist to term beginning Dec 1996. Retained by election Aug 1998, current term expires Aug 2006. Born Nashville Tennessee April 28, 1955. Presbyterian. Educated at Tennessee Technological University B.S. and University of Memphis J.D. Law Clerk to Hon. Mark A. Walker, Tennessee Court of Criminal Appeals 1981-82. Admitted to practice Tennessee 1981. In legal practice Shelby County 1982-84 and Dickson 1990 to Nov 1996.
Assistant District Attorney General 24th Judicial District Huntingdon 1984-90. Member Tennessee Judicial Conference, Nashville, Dickson County and Tennessee Bar Associations. Former Chairman Benton County Tennessee Unit American Heart Association. Board of Directors Dickson County Habitat for Humanity, Inc. and Dickson Help Center. Member "100 Years' Celebration" Committee City of Dickson. Sponsor Member Ducks Unlimited. Elder First Presbyterian Church of Dickson.
Office: 103 Sylvis Street, Dickson 37055.
Telephone: (615) 446-1661.

WOOTTEN, John D., Jr. *(Judge, Tennessee Circuit Court Fifteenth Judicial District)*
Mailing address: P.O. Box 112, Lafayette 37083.

WOOTTEN, JOHN D., JR.—*Continued*

Office: 200 Red Boiling Springs, Lafayette 37083.
Telephone: (615) 666-9324.

WORKMAN, Dale C. *(Judge, Tennessee Circuit Court Sixth Judicial District)*
Office: M40 City-County Building, 400 Main Avenue, Knoxville 37902.
Telephone: (865) 215-2397.

WYATT, James Randall, Jr. *(Judge, Tennessee Criminal Court Twentieth Judicial District)* Elected to term beginning Sept 1, 1982. Reelected 1990 and 1998. Current term expires Aug 31, 2006. Former Presiding Judge. Born Nashville Tennessee Dec 9, 1937. Catholic. Educated at Middle Tennessee State University B.S. 1962 and Vanderbilt University J.D. 1966. Admitted to practice Tennessee 1966. In legal practice Nashville 1968-74. Judge, Tennessee General Sessions Court 1974-82.

Special Agent FBI 1966-68. Assistant District Attorney General Davidson County 1968-74. Instructor in Criminal Law Aquinas Junior College since 1969. Member Nashville Bar Association. Attended numerous seminars conducted by The National Judicial College and American Academy of Judicial Education over the past 16 years. Sergeant USMC 1955-59. Democrat. Member Knights of Columbus.
Office: 602 Metro Courthouse, Nashville 37201.
Telephone: (615) 862-5934.

YOUNG, W. Dale *(Judge, Tennessee Circuit Court Fifth Judicial District)* Elected 1990. Reelected 1998, current term expires Aug 31, 2006. Former Presiding Judge. Born Maryville Tennessee May 12, 1938. Southern Baptist. Educated at Maryville College B.A. 1960 and University of Tennessee J.D. 1963. Member Phi Alpha Delta. Admitted to practice Tennessee 1963, U.S. District Court District of Tennessee and U.S. Supreme Court 1967. Began legal practice Maryville 1963.

Assistant District Attorney General 1965-66. Executive Assistant to Governor of Tennessee 1970-73. Member Planning Commission, Board of Zoning Appeals and Industrial Development Board City of Maryville 1980-84. Member Blount County and Tennessee Bar Associations. Employed by Tennessee National Bancshares, Inc. 1973-84. Republican. East Tennessee Republican Campaign Manager for Governor Winfield Dunn and County Campaign Manager for Senator Howard H. Baker. Enjoys photography, swimming, aerobic sports, woodworking and carpentry.
Office: Blount County Justice Center, 946 East Lamar Alexander Parkway, Maryville 37804.
Telephone: (865) 273-5550.

TEXAS

Capital AUSTIN

UNITED STATES DISTRICT COURTS DISTRICTS OF TEXAS

Within Texas there are four United States District Courts. For descriptive information refer to the United States Courts section.

EASTERN DISTRICT consists of seven divisions.

Beaumont Division includes Hardin, Jasper, Jefferson, Liberty, Newton and Orange counties. The court sits at Beaumont.

Lufkin Division includes Angelina, Houston, Nacogdoches, Polk, Sabine, San Augustine, Shelby, Trinity and Tyler counties. The court sits at Lufkin.

Marshall Division includes Camp, Cass, Harrison, Marion, Morris and Upshur counties. The court sits at Marshall.

Paris Division includes Delta, Fannin, Hopkins, Lamar and Red River counties. The court sits at Paris.

Sherman Division includes Collin, Cooke, Denton and Grayson counties. The court sits at Sherman.

Texarkana Division includes Bowie, Franklin and Titus counties. The court sits at Texarkana.

Tyler Division includes Anderson, Cherokee, Gregg, Henderson, Panola, Rains, Rusk, Smith, Van Zandt and Wood counties. The court sits at Tyler.

Chief Judge

John Hannah, Jr.

Judges

Richard A. Schell
David Folsom
Leonard E. Davis
Thad Heartfield
T. John Ward
Ronald H. Clark

Senior Judges

William Wayne Justice
William M. Steger
Howell Cobb
Paul N. Brown

Clerk

David J. Maland
106 Federal Building
211 West Ferguson Street
Tyler, Texas 75702
(903) 590-1000

NORTHERN DISTRICT consists of seven divisions.

Abilene Division includes Callahan, Eastland, Fisher, Haskell, Howard, Jones, Mitchell, Nolan, Shackelford, Stephens, Stonewall, Taylor and Throckmorton counties. The court sits at Abilene.

Amarillo Division includes Armstrong, Briscoe, Carson, Castro, Childress, Collingsworth, Dallam, Deaf Smith, Donley, Gray, Hall, Hansford, Hartley, Hemphill, Hutchinson, Lipscomb, Moore, Ochiltree, Oldham, Parmer, Potter, Randall, Roberts, Sherman, Swisher and Wheeler counties. The court sits at Amarillo.

Dallas Division includes Dallas, Ellis, Hunt, Johnson, Kaufman, Navarro and Rockwall counties. The court sits at Dallas.

Fort Worth Division includes Comanche, Erath, Hood, Jack, Palo Pinto, Parker, Tarrant and Wise counties. The court sits at Fort Worth.

Lubbock Division includes Bailey, Borden, Cochran, Crosby, Dawson, Dickens, Floyd, Gaines, Garza, Hale, Hockley, Kent, Lamb, Lubbock, Lynn, Motley, Scurry, Terry and Yoakum counties. The court sits at Lubbock.

San Angelo Division includes Brown, Coke, Coleman, Concho, Crockett, Glasscock, Irion, Menard, Mills, Reagan, Runnels, Schleicher, Sterling, Sutton and Tom Green counties. The court sits at San Angelo.

Wichita Falls Division includes Archer, Baylor, Clay, Cottle, Foard, Hardeman, King, Knox, Montague, Wichita, Wilbarger and Young counties. The court sits at Wichita Falls.

Chief Judge

A. Joe Fish

Judges

Mary Lou Robinson
Sidney A. Fitzwater
John H. McBryde
Terry R. Means
Barbara M. G. Lynn
Ed Kinkeade
Jerry Buchmeyer
Samuel R. Cummings
Jorge A. Solis
Sam A. Lindsay
David C. Godbey

Senior Judges

Eldon B. Mahon
Barefoot Sanders
Robert B. Maloney

Clerk

Karen Mitchell
14A20 U.S. Courthouse
1100 Commerce Street
Dallas, Texas 75242-1003
(214) 753-2150

SOUTHERN DISTRICT consists of seven divisions.

Brownsville Division includes Cameron and Willacy counties. The court sits at Brownsville.

Corpus Christi Division includes Aransas, Bee, Brooks, Duval, Jim Wells, Kenedy, Kleberg, Live Oak, Nueces and San Patricio counties. The court sits at Corpus Christi.

Galveston Division includes Brazoria, Chambers, Galveston and Matagorda counties. The court sits at Galveston.

UNITED STATES DISTRICT COURTS DISTRICTS OF TEXAS—*Continued*

Houston Division includes Austin, Brazos, Colorado, Fayette, Fort Bend, Grimes, Harris, Madison, Montgomery, San Jacinto, Walker, Waller and Wharton counties. The court sits at Houston.

Laredo Division includes Jim Hogg, La Salle, McMullen, Webb and Zapata counties. The court sits at Laredo.

McAllen Division includes Hidalgo and Starr counties. The court sits at McAllen.

Victoria Division includes Calhoun, De Witt, Goliad, Jackson, Lavaca, Refugio and Victoria counties. The court sits at Victoria.

Chief Judge
George P. Kazen

Judges

Hayden W. Head, Jr.	Ricardo H. Hinojosa
Lynn Nettleton Hughes	David Hittner
Kenneth M. Hoyt	Sim Lake
Melinda Harmon	John D. Rainey
Samuel B. Kent	Ewing Werlein, Jr.
Lee H. Rosenthal	Janis Graham Jack
Vanessa D. Gilmore	Nancy F. Atlas
Hilda Gloria Tagle	Keith P. Ellison
Randy Crane	Andrew S. Hanen

Senior Judge
Filemon B. Vela

Clerk
Michael N. Milby
P.O. Box 61010
Houston, Texas 77208-1010
(713) 250-5400

WESTERN DISTRICT consists of seven divisions.

Austin Division includes Bastrop, Blanco, Burleson, Burnet, Caldwell, Gillespie, Hays, Kimble, Lampasas, Lee, Llano, Mason, McCulloch, San Saba, Travis, Washington and Williamson counties. The court sits at Austin.

Del Rio Division includes Edwards, Kinney, Maverick, Terrell, Uvalde, Val Verde and Zavala counties. The court sits at Del Rio.

El Paso Division includes El Paso County. The court sits at El Paso.

Midland-Odessa Division includes Andrews, Crane, Ector, Martin, Midland and Upton counties. The court sits at Midland and may sit at Odessa at the discretion of the court when accommodations are provided at no cost to the United States.

Pecos Division includes Brewster, Culberson, Hudspeth, Jeff Davis, Loving, Pecos, Presidio, Reeves, Ward and Winkler counties. The court sits at Pecos.

San Antonio Division includes Atascosa, Bandera, Bexar, Comal, Dimmit, Frio, Gonzales, Guadalupe, Karnes, Kendall, Kerr, Medina, Real and Wilson counties. The court sits at San Antonio.

Waco Division includes Bell, Bosque, Coryell, Falls, Freestone, Hamilton, Hill, Leon, Limestone, McLennan, Milam, Robertson and Somervell counties. The court sits at Waco.

Chief Judge
James R. Nowlin

Judges

Edward C. Prado	Walter S. Smith, Jr.
Sam Sparks	Fred Biery
Orlando L. Garcia	Royal Furgeson, Jr.
David Briones	Philip Ray Martinez
Alia Moses Ludlum	

Senior Judge
Harry Lee Hudspeth

Clerk
William G. Putnicki
U.S. Courthouse
655 East Durango Boulevard
San Antonio, Texas 78206-1198
(210) 472-6550

UNITED STATES MAGISTRATE JUDGES OF TEXAS

EASTERN DISTRICT

Harry W. "Peter" McKee
Earl S. Hines
Judith K. Guthrie
Wendell C. Radford
Caroline M. Craven

NORTHERN DISTRICT

Philip R. Lane	William F. Sanderson, Jr.
Robert K. Roach	Clinton E. Averitte
Billy W. Boone	Charles Bleil
Jeff Kaplan	Nancy M. Koenig
Paul D. Stickney	
Irma C. Ramirez	

SOUTHERN DISTRICT

Calvin Botley	Marcel C. Notzon
Frances H. Stacy	Nancy K. Johnson
John Robert Froeschner	Marcia A. Crone
John William Black	Maryrose Milloy
Dorina Ramos	B. Janice Ellington
Jane Cooper-Hill	Felix Recio, Jr.
Adriana Arce-Flores	Tracy K. Caperton

WESTERN DISTRICT

Durwood Edwards	Dennis G. Green
Stephen H. Capelle	John W. Primomo
Nancy Stein Nowak	Richard P. Mesa
Michael S. McDonald	L. Stuart Platt
Pamela A. Mathy	Andrew W. Austin
Norbert J. Garney	Jeffrey C. Manske

UNITED STATES BANKRUPTCY COURTS OF TEXAS

EASTERN DISTRICT

Chief Judge
Donald R. Sharp

Judge
Bill G. Parker

UNITED STATES DISTRICT COURTS DISTRICTS OF TEXAS—*Continued*

Bankruptcy Clerk
James D. Tokoph
200 East Ferguson Street
Second Floor
Tyler, Texas 75702
(903) 590-1212

NORTHERN DISTRICT

Chief Judge
Steven A. Felsenthal

Judges
Barbara J. Houser
Robert L. Jones
Dennis Michael Lynn
Harlin DeWayne Hale

Recalled Judge
Harold C. Abramson

Bankruptcy Clerk
Tawana C. Marshall
1254 U.S. Courthouse
1100 Commerce Street
Dallas, Texas 75242-1496
(214) 753-2000

SOUTHERN DISTRICT

Chief Judge
William R. Greendyke

Judges
Manuel D. Leal
Letitia Z. Clark
Richard S. Schmidt
Karen Kennedy Brown
Wesley W. Steen

Bankruptcy Clerk
Michael N. Milby
P.O. Box 61010
Houston, Texas 77208-1010
(713) 250-5115

WESTERN DISTRICT

Chief Judge
Larry E. Kelly

Judges
Leif M. Clark
Ronald B. King
Frank R. Monroe

Bankruptcy Clerk
Lawrence T. Bick
P.O. Box 1439
San Antonio, Texas 78295-1439
(210) 472-5187

TEXAS SUPREME COURT

The Supreme Court is Texas' court of last resort for civil and juvenile cases. The court consists of a chief justice and eight justices elected in statewide partisan elections for overlapping six-year terms. Vacancies between elections are filled by the governor with the advice and consent of the Senate. Appointed justices serve until the next general election.

The court has final appellate jurisdiction over all civil and juvenile cases and authority to determine certain legal matters when no other court has jurisdiction. The court is empowered to conduct proceedings for the involuntary retirement or removal of judges and to make rules for the administration of justice including rules of civil practice and procedure. Additionally, the court has the authority to transfer cases between the Courts of Appeals. The court has original jurisdiction to issue extraordinary writs and may issue all other writs necessary to the exercise of proper jurisdiction.

The court sits at Austin.

Chief Justice
Thomas R. Phillips

Justices

Nathan L. Hecht	Craig T. Enoch
Priscilla R. Owen	Harriet O'Neill
Wallace B. Jefferson	Michael H. Schneider
Steven Wayne Smith	Dale Wainwright

Clerk
John T. Adams
Supreme Court Building
P.O. Box 12248
Austin, Texas 78711-2248
(512) 463-1312

Administrative Director
Alicia G. Key
Office of Court Administration
Tom C. Clark Building
205 West Fourteenth Street, Suite 600
P.O. Box 12066
Austin, Texas 78711-2066
(512) 463-1625

TEXAS COURT OF CRIMINAL APPEALS

The Court of Criminal Appeals is Texas' court of last resort in criminal matters. The court consists of a presiding judge and eight judges elected in statewide partisan elections for overlapping six-year terms. Vacancies between elections are filled by the governor with the advice and consent of the Senate. Appointed judges serve until the next general election.

The court has final appellate jurisdiction over all criminal cases except as provided by law and exclusive jurisdiction over automatic appeals in death penalty cases. The court is empowered to promulgate rules of evidence and rules for appellate procedure in criminal cases and may issue writs of habeas corpus and other writs necessary to the exercise of proper jurisdiction.

The court sits at Austin.

Presiding Judge
Sharon Keller

Judges

Lawrence E. Meyers	Tom Price
Paul Womack	Cheryl Johnson
Michael E. Keasler	Barbara Parker Hervey
Charles R. Holcomb	Cathy Cochran

TEXAS COURT OF CRIMINAL APPEALS—*Continued*

Clerk
Troy Bennett
Supreme Court Building
P.O. Box 12308
Austin, Texas 78711-2308
(512) 463-1551

TEXAS COURTS OF APPEALS

The Courts of Appeals are Texas' courts of intermediate appellate jurisdiction. Justices are elected from the state's fourteen districts in partisan elections for six-year terms. Vacancies between elections are filled by the governor with the advice and consent of the Senate. Each district has a chief justice who is elected to a six-year term by the voters of the district. Retired justices may serve by assignment of the chief justice of the Supreme Court.

The courts have appellate jurisdiction within their respective districts over civil and criminal cases decided in the District or County Courts. In cases of slander, divorce and certain other civil matters, the decision of the courts is usually final. The courts have limited original jurisdiction over the issuance of writs.

The counties of the first and fourteenth districts are coextensive. In addition, the counties of Brazos, Gregg, Hopkins, Hunt, Kaufman, Panola, Rusk, Upshur, Van Zandt and Wood are included in more than one district. The court sits at the cities indicated and at other locations in each district as necessary.

FIRST DISTRICT includes Austin, Brazoria, Brazos, Burleson, Chambers, Colorado, Fort Bend, Galveston, Grimes, Harris, Trinity, Walker, Waller and Washington counties. The court sits at Houston and may sit at any county seat within the district.

Chief Justice
Sherry Radack

Justices
Adele Hedges — Tim Taft
Samuel M. Nuchia — Terry Jennings
Evelyn Keyes — Elsa Alcala
George C. Hanks, Jr. — Laura Carter Higley

SECOND DISTRICT includes Archer, Clay, Cooke, Denton, Hood, Jack, Montague, Parker, Tarrant, Wichita, Wise and Young counties. The court sits at Fort Worth and may sit at any county seat within the district.

Chief Justice
John H. Cayce, Jr.

Justices
Sam Day — Terrie Livingston
Lee Ann Dauphinot — Dixon W. Holman
Anne Gardner — Sue Walker

THIRD DISTRICT includes Bastrop, Bell, Blanco, Burnet, Caldwell, Coke, Comal, Concho, Fayette, Hays, Irion, Lampasas, Lee, Llano, McCulloch, Milam, Mills, Runnels, San Saba, Schleicher, Sterling, Tom Green, Travis and Williamson counties. The court sits at Austin and may sit at any county seat within the district.

Chief Justice
W. Kenneth Law

Justices
Mack Kidd
Bea Ann Smith
Lee Yeakel
Jan Powell Patterson
David Puryear

FOURTH DISTRICT includes Atascosa, Bandera, Bexar, Brooks, Dimmit, Duval, Edwards, Frio, Gillespie, Guadalupe, Jim Hogg, Jim Wells, Karnes, Kendall, Kerr, Kimble, Kinney, La Salle, Mason, Maverick, McMullen, Medina, Menard, Real, Starr, Sutton, Uvalde, Val Verde, Webb, Wilson, Zapata and Zavala counties. The court sits at San Antonio and may sit at any county seat within the district.

Chief Justice
Alma L. López

Justices
Catherine Stone — Paul W. Green
Sarah B. Duncan — Karen Angelini
Sandee Bryan Marion — Phylis Speedlin

FIFTH DISTRICT includes Collin, Dallas, Grayson, Hunt, Kaufman, Rockwall and Van Zandt counties. The court sits at Dallas and may sit at any county seat within the district.

Chief Justice
Linda Thomas

Justices
Joseph B. Morris — Mark Whittington
Tom James — Carolyn I. Wright
James A. Moseley — David L. Bridges
Michael J. O'Neill — Kerry FitzGerald
Martin E. Richter — Molly Meredith Francis
Douglas S. Lang — vacancy

SIXTH DISTRICT includes Bowie, Camp, Cass, Delta, Fannin, Franklin, Gregg, Harrison, Hopkins, Hunt, Lamar, Marion, Morris, Panola, Red River, Rusk, Titus, Upshur and Wood counties. The court sits at Texarkana and may sit at any county seat within the district.

Chief Justice
Josh R. Morriss III

Justices
Donald Rae Ross
Jack Carter

SEVENTH DISTRICT includes Armstrong, Bailey, Briscoe, Carson, Castro, Childress, Cochran, Collingsworth, Cottle, Crosby, Dallam, Deaf Smith, Dickens, Donley, Floyd, Foard, Garza, Gray, Hale, Hall, Hansford, Hardeman, Hartley, Hemphill, Hockley, Hutchinson, Kent, King, Lamb, Lipscomb, Lubbock, Lynn, Moore, Motley, Ochiltree, Oldham, Parmer, Potter, Randall, Roberts, Sherman, Swisher, Terry, Wheeler, Wilbarger and Yoakum counties. The court sits at Amarillo.

Chief Justice
Phil Johnson

Justices
Brian P. Quinn
Don H. Reavis
James T. Campbell

EIGHTH DISTRICT includes Andrews, Brewster, Crane, Crockett, Culberson, Ector, El Paso, Gaines,

TEXAS COURTS OF APPEALS—*Continued*

Glasscock, Hudspeth, Jeff Davis, Loving, Martin, Midland, Pecos, Presidio, Reagan, Reeves, Terrell, Upton, Ward and Winkler counties. The court sits at El Paso and may sit at any county seat within the district.

Chief Justice
Richard Barajas

Justices
Susan J. Larsen
Ann Crawford McClure
David Wellington Chew

NINTH DISTRICT includes Angelina, Hardin, Jasper, Jefferson, Liberty, Montgomery, Newton, Orange, Polk, San Jacinto and Tyler counties. The court sits at Beaumont.

Chief Justice
Steve McKeithen

Justices
Don Burgess
David B. Gaultney

TENTH DISTRICT includes Bosque, Brazos, Coryell, Ellis, Falls, Freestone, Hamilton, Hill, Johnson, Leon, Limestone, Madison, McLennan, Navarro, Robertson and Somervell counties. The court sits at Waco and may sit at any county seat within the district.

Chief Justice
Rex D. Davis

Justices
William R. Vance
Thomas W. Gray

ELEVENTH DISTRICT includes Baylor, Borden, Brown, Callahan, Coleman, Comanche, Dawson, Eastland, Erath, Fisher, Haskell, Howard, Jones, Knox, Mitchell, Nolan, Palo Pinto, Scurry, Shackelford, Stephens, Stonewall, Taylor and Throckmorton counties. The court sits at Eastland.

Chief Justice
William G. "Bud" Arnot, III

Justices
Jim R. Wright
Terry McCall

TWELFTH DISTRICT includes Anderson, Cherokee, Gregg, Henderson, Hopkins, Houston, Kaufman, Nacogdoches, Panola, Rains, Rusk, Sabine, San Augustine, Shelby, Smith, Upshur, Van Zandt and Wood counties. The court sits at Tyler and may sit at any county seat within the district.

Chief Justice
James T. Worthen

Justices
Sam Griffith
Diane Vinson DeVasto

THIRTEENTH DISTRICT includes Aransas, Bee, Calhoun, Cameron, De Witt, Goliad, Gonzales, Hidalgo, Jackson, Kenedy, Kleberg, Lavaca, Live Oak, Matagorda, Nueces, Refugio, San Patricio, Victoria, Wharton and Willacy counties. The court sits at Corpus Christi and may sit at any county seat within the district.

Chief Justice
Rogelio Valdez

Justices
Federico G. Hinojosa
Linda Reyna Yañez
Nelda V. Rodriguez
Errlinda Castillo
Dori Contreras Garza

FOURTEENTH DISTRICT includes Austin, Brazoria, Brazos, Burleson, Chambers, Colorado, Fort Bend, Galveston, Grimes, Harris, Trinity, Walker, Waller and Washington counties. The court sits at Houston and may sit at any county seat within the district.

Chief Justice
Scott A. Brister

Justices

Leslie Brock Yates	John S. Anderson
J. Harvey Hudson	Wanda McKee Fowler
Richard H. Edelman	Kem Thompson Frost
Charles W. Seymore	Eva M. Guzman

TEXAS DISTRICT COURTS

The District Courts are Texas' courts of general jurisdiction. A district may consist of one or more counties, or there may be two or more District Courts in the same county. The state is currently divided into 418 judicial districts. At present each District Court is served by one judge, although a constitutional amendment in November 1985 allows the Legislature to establish more than one judge per court. Judges are elected in districtwide partisan elections for four-year terms. Vacancies between elections are filled by the governor with the advice and consent of the Senate. Retired judges may serve by assignment of the chief justice of the Supreme Court.

The courts have exclusive, appellate and original jurisdiction of all actions, proceedings and remedies, except in cases where jurisdiction is conferred on another court. Jurisdiction varies from district to district, but generally the courts have original jurisdiction over felonies, divorce, title to land, contested elections, juvenile matters and civil cases when the amount in controversy is $200 or more. In counties having statutory County Courts at Law, the District Courts usually have exclusive civil jurisdiction when the amount in controversy is $100,000 or more and concurrent jurisdiction with the County Courts at Law of amounts exceeding $500 but less than $100,000 as well as concurrent jurisdiction in specified family matters. The courts also have jurisdiction of contested probate cases in counties which lack statutory courts to hear probate matters exclusively. All matters for which a remedy is not provided by law are heard by the District Courts. The courts may issue extraordinary writs and other writs necessary to the exercise of proper jurisdiction.

Most District Courts exercise both criminal and civil jurisdiction, but in densely populated areas some courts are designated to specialize in criminal, civil or family law cases, although these courts may hear any case under District Court jurisdiction as the need arises. In 1977, the Family District Courts, formerly known as Texas Domestic Relations and Juvenile Courts, were created by the Legislature to have primary responsibility for cases involving family law matters. Districts 300 to

TEXAS DISTRICT COURTS—*Continued*

330 and District 360 are Family District Courts. Criminal District Courts are established in Dallas, Jefferson and Tarrant counties to hear criminal cases and/or cases involving divorce, dependent and neglected children, adoption and civil habeas corpus. Criminal District Courts in Dallas and Tarrant counties have concurrent criminal jurisdiction with County Courts in matters normally heard in the County Courts. In some counties various aspects of County Court jurisdiction have been transferred to the District Court; in other counties jurisdiction is concurrent in some or all matters normally heard in County Courts. Cases in which the death penalty has been assessed are appealed directly to the Court of Criminal Appeals; all other appeals are heard in the Courts of Appeals.

The courts sit at each county seat and at other places prescribed by law.

1st JUDICIAL DISTRICT includes Jasper, Newton, Sabine (County Court civil jurisdiction except probate transferred to District Court) and San Augustine (County Court civil jurisdiction except probate transferred to District Court) counties.

Judge
Joe Bob Golden

1st JUDICIAL DISTRICT A includes Jasper, Newton and Tyler counties.

Judge
Monte D. Lawlis

2nd JUDICIAL DISTRICT includes Cherokee County.

Judge
Dwight L. Phifer

3rd JUDICIAL DISTRICT includes Anderson, Henderson and Houston counties.

Judge
James N. Parsons, III

4th JUDICIAL DISTRICT includes Rusk County.

Judge
J. Clay Gossett

5th JUDICIAL DISTRICT includes Bowie (County Court jurisdiction except probate transferred to District Court) and Cass (County Court jurisdiction except probate and misdemeanor guilty pleas transferred to District Court) counties.

Judge
Ralph K. Burgess

6th JUDICIAL DISTRICT includes Fannin, Lamar and Red River (County Court civil jurisdiction except probate and all appeals from lower courts transferred to District Court; concurrent criminal jurisdiction with County Court) counties.

Judge
Jim D. Lovett

7th JUDICIAL DISTRICT includes Smith County.

Judge
Kerry L. Russell

8th JUDICIAL DISTRICT includes Delta, Franklin, Hopkins and Rains counties.

Judge
Robert E. Newsom

9th JUDICIAL DISTRICT includes Montgomery and Waller counties.

Judge
Frederick E. Edwards

10th JUDICIAL DISTRICT includes Galveston County.

Judge
David Edward Garner

11th JUDICIAL DISTRICT includes Harris County.

Judge
Mark Davidson

12th JUDICIAL DISTRICT includes Grimes, Leon, Madison and Walker counties.

Judge
William L. McAdams

13th JUDICIAL DISTRICT includes Navarro County (County Court civil jurisdiction except probate transferred to District Court).

Judge
John H. Jackson

14th JUDICIAL DISTRICT (concurrent criminal jurisdiction with County Court) includes Dallas County.

Judge
Mary Murphy

15th JUDICIAL DISTRICT includes Grayson County.

Judge
James R. Fry

16th JUDICIAL DISTRICT includes Denton County.

Judge
John Keith Narsutis

17th JUDICIAL DISTRICT includes Tarrant County.

Judge
Fred W. Davis

18th JUDICIAL DISTRICT includes Johnson and Somervell counties.

Judge
John Edward Neill

19th JUDICIAL DISTRICT includes McLennan County.

Judge
Ralph T. Strother

20th JUDICIAL DISTRICT includes Milam County.

Judge
Ed Magre

21st JUDICIAL DISTRICT includes Bastrop, Burleson, Lee and Washington counties.

TEXAS DISTRICT COURTS—*Continued*

Judge
Terry Flenniken

22nd JUDICIAL DISTRICT includes Caldwell, Comal (County Court jurisdiction except probate transferred to District Court) and Hays counties.

Judge
Charles R. Ramsay

23rd JUDICIAL DISTRICT includes Brazoria, Matagorda and Wharton counties.

Judge
Ben Hardin

24th JUDICIAL DISTRICT includes Calhoun, De Witt, Goliad, Jackson, Refugio and Victoria counties.

Judge
Joseph Patrick Kelly

25th JUDICIAL DISTRICT includes Colorado, Gonzales, Guadalupe and Lavaca counties.

Judge
Dwight E. Peschel

25th JUDICIAL DISTRICT (2nd) includes Colorado, Gonzales, Guadalupe and Lavaca counties.

Judge
Gus J. Strauss

26th JUDICIAL DISTRICT includes Williamson County.

Judge
Billy Ray Stubblefield

27th JUDICIAL DISTRICT includes Bell and Lampasas counties.

Judge
Joe Carroll

28th JUDICIAL DISTRICT includes Nueces County.

Judge
Nanette Hasette

29th JUDICIAL DISTRICT includes Palo Pinto County.

Judge
Jerry D. Ray

30th JUDICIAL DISTRICT includes Wichita County (County Court civil jurisdiction except probate transferred to District Court).

Judge
Robert P. Brotherton

31st JUDICIAL DISTRICT includes Gray, Hemphill, Lipscomb, Roberts and Wheeler counties.

Judge
Steven R. Emmert

32nd JUDICIAL DISTRICT includes Fisher, Mitchell and Nolan counties.

Judge
Glen Harrison

33rd JUDICIAL DISTRICT includes Blanco, Burnet, Llano and San Saba counties.

Judge
Guilford L. "Gil" Jones, III

34th JUDICIAL DISTRICT includes El Paso County.

Judge
William E. Moody

35th JUDICIAL DISTRICT includes Brown and Mills (County Court civil jurisdiction except probate transferred to District Court) counties.

Judge
Stephen Ellis

36th JUDICIAL DISTRICT includes Aransas, Bee, Live Oak, McMullen and San Patricio counties.

Judge
Michael E. Welborn

37th JUDICIAL DISTRICT (civil preference) includes Bexar County.

Judge
David A. Berchelmann, Jr.

38th JUDICIAL DISTRICT includes Medina, Real and Uvalde counties.

Judge
Mickey Ray Pennington

39th JUDICIAL DISTRICT includes Haskell, Kent, Stonewall and Throckmorton counties.

Judge
Charles L. Chapman

40th JUDICIAL DISTRICT includes Ellis County.

Judge
Gene Knize

41st JUDICIAL DISTRICT includes El Paso County.

Judge
Mary Anne Bramblett

42nd JUDICIAL DISTRICT includes Callahan, Coleman and Taylor counties.

Judge
John Wilson Weeks

43rd JUDICIAL DISTRICT includes Parker County.

Judge
Don Chrestman

44th JUDICIAL DISTRICT (concurrent criminal jurisdiction with County Court) includes Dallas County.

Judge
David D. Kelton

45th JUDICIAL DISTRICT (civil preference) includes Bexar County.

Judge
Barbara Hanson Nellermoe

46th JUDICIAL DISTRICT includes Foard, Hardeman and Wilbarger counties.

TEXAS DISTRICT COURTS—*Continued*

Judge
Tom A. Neely

47th JUDICIAL DISTRICT includes Armstrong, Potter and Randall counties.

Judge
Hal Miner

48th JUDICIAL DISTRICT includes Tarrant County.

Judge
Bob McCoy

49th JUDICIAL DISTRICT includes Webb (County Court jurisdiction except probate transferred to District Court) and Zapata (concurrent criminal and civil jurisdiction with County Court) counties.

Judge
Manuel R. Flores

50th JUDICIAL DISTRICT (County Court jurisdiction except probate and misdemeanor guilty pleas transferred to District Court) includes Baylor, Cottle, King and Knox counties.

Judge
David Wayne Hajek

51st JUDICIAL DISTRICT includes Coke, Irion, Schleicher, Sterling and Tom Green counties.

Judge
Barbara Lane Walther

52nd JUDICIAL DISTRICT includes Coryell County.

Judge
Phillip Zeigler

53rd JUDICIAL DISTRICT includes Travis County.

Judge
Scott H. Jenkins

54th JUDICIAL DISTRICT includes McLennan County.

Judge
George Harrison Allen

55th JUDICIAL DISTRICT includes Harris County.

Judge
Jeffrey V. Brown

56th JUDICIAL DISTRICT includes Galveston County.

Judge
Norma Venso

57th JUDICIAL DISTRICT (civil preference) includes Bexar County.

Judge
Patrick J. Boone

58th JUDICIAL DISTRICT includes Jefferson County.

Judge
James W. Mehaffy

59th JUDICIAL DISTRICT includes Grayson County.

Judge
Rayburn M. "Rim" Nall, Jr.

60th JUDICIAL DISTRICT includes Jefferson County.

Judge
James Gary Sanderson

61st JUDICIAL DISTRICT includes Harris County.

Judge
John Donovan

62nd JUDICIAL DISTRICT includes Delta, Franklin, Hopkins and Lamar counties.

Judge
Robert Scott McDowell

63rd JUDICIAL DISTRICT includes Edwards, Kinney, Terrell and Val Verde counties.

Judge
Thomas F. Lee

64th JUDICIAL DISTRICT includes Castro, Hale and Swisher counties.

Judge
Robert W. Kinkaid, Jr.

65th JUDICIAL DISTRICT includes El Paso County.

Judge
Alfredo Chavez

66th JUDICIAL DISTRICT (concurrent criminal and civil jurisdiction with County Court) includes Hill County.

Judge
F. B. "Bob" McGregor, Jr.

67th JUDICIAL DISTRICT includes Tarrant County.

Judge
Donald J. Cosby

68th JUDICIAL DISTRICT (concurrent criminal jurisdiction with County Court) includes Dallas County.

Judge
Charles Stokes

69th JUDICIAL DISTRICT includes Dallam, Hartley, Moore and Sherman counties.

Judge
Ronald E. Enns

70th JUDICIAL DISTRICT includes Ector County.

Judge
Jay Gibson

71st JUDICIAL DISTRICT includes Harrison County.

Judge
Bonnie Leggat

72nd JUDICIAL DISTRICT includes Crosby and Lubbock counties.

TEXAS DISTRICT COURTS—*Continued*

Judge
J. Blair Cherry, Jr.

73rd JUDICIAL DISTRICT (civil preference) includes Bexar County.

Judge
Andy Mireles

74th JUDICIAL DISTRICT includes McLennan County.

Judge
Alan M. Mayfield

75th JUDICIAL DISTRICT includes Liberty County.

Judge
C. T. Hight

76th JUDICIAL DISTRICT includes Camp (concurrent criminal jurisdiction with County Court), Morris (County Court civil jurisdiction except probate transferred to District Court; concurrent criminal jurisdiction with County Court) and Titus counties.

Judge
Jimmy L. White

77th JUDICIAL DISTRICT includes Freestone and Limestone counties.

Judge
Horace Dickson Black, Jr.

78th JUDICIAL DISTRICT includes Wichita County (County Court civil jurisdiction except probate transferred to District Court).

Judge
Roy T. Sparkman

79th JUDICIAL DISTRICT includes Brooks and Jim Wells counties.

Judge
Terry A. Canales

80th JUDICIAL DISTRICT includes Harris County.

Judge
Scott Link

81st JUDICIAL DISTRICT includes Atascosa, Frio, Karnes, La Salle and Wilson counties.

Judge
Donna Rayes

82nd JUDICIAL DISTRICT includes Falls and Robertson counties.

Judge
Robert Miller Stem

83rd JUDICIAL DISTRICT includes Pecos, Terrell, Upton and Val Verde counties.

Judge
Carl Pendergrass

84th JUDICIAL DISTRICT includes Hansford, Hutchinson and Ochiltree counties.

Judge
William D. Smith

85th JUDICIAL DISTRICT includes Brazos County.

Judge
J. D. Langley

86th JUDICIAL DISTRICT includes Kaufman County.

Judge
Howard Tygrett

87th JUDICIAL DISTRICT includes Anderson, Freestone, Leon and Limestone counties.

Judge
Deborah Oakes Evans

88th JUDICIAL DISTRICT includes Hardin and Tyler counties.

Judge
Earl Stover, III

89th JUDICIAL DISTRICT includes Wichita County (County Court civil jurisdiction except probate transferred to District Court).

Judge
Juanita Pavlick

90th JUDICIAL DISTRICT includes Stephens (County Court jurisdiction except probate transferred to District Court) and Young counties.

Judge
Stephen O'Neal Crawford

91st JUDICIAL DISTRICT includes Eastland County (County Court civil jurisdiction except probate transferred to District Court; concurrent criminal jurisdiction with County Court).

Judge
Steven R. Herod

92nd JUDICIAL DISTRICT includes Hidalgo County.

Judge
Edward G. Aparicio

93rd JUDICIAL DISTRICT includes Hidalgo County.

Judge
Rodolfo Delgado

94th JUDICIAL DISTRICT includes Nueces County.

Judge
Jack E. Hunter

95th JUDICIAL DISTRICT includes Dallas County (concurrent criminal jurisdiction with County Court).

Judge
Karen Johnson

96th JUDICIAL DISTRICT includes Tarrant County.

Judge
Jeff Walker

97th JUDICIAL DISTRICT includes Archer, Clay and Montague counties.

TEXAS DISTRICT COURTS—*Continued*

Judge
Roger E. Towery

98th JUDICIAL DISTRICT includes Travis County.

Judge
W. Jeanne Meurer

99th JUDICIAL DISTRICT includes Lubbock County.

Judge
Mackey K. Hancock

100th JUDICIAL DISTRICT includes Carson, Childress, Collingsworth, Donley and Hall counties.

Judge
David M. McCoy

101st JUDICIAL DISTRICT (concurrent criminal jurisdiction with County Court) includes Dallas County.

Judge
Jay Patterson

102nd JUDICIAL DISTRICT includes Bowie (County Court jurisdiction except probate transferred to District Court) and Red River (County Court civil jurisdiction except probate and all appeals from lower courts transferred to District Court; concurrent criminal jurisdiction with County Court) counties.

Judge
John F. Miller, Jr.

103rd JUDICIAL DISTRICT (civil preference) includes Cameron and Willacy counties.

Judge
Menton Murray, Jr.

104th JUDICIAL DISTRICT includes Taylor County.

Judge
Lee Hamilton

105th JUDICIAL DISTRICT (criminal preference) includes Kenedy, Kleberg and Nueces counties.

Judge
J. Manuel Banales

106th JUDICIAL DISTRICT includes Dawson, Gaines, Garza and Lynn counties.

Judge
Carter Tinsley Schildknecht

107th JUDICIAL DISTRICT (criminal preference) includes Cameron and Willacy counties.

Judge
Benjamin Euresti

108th JUDICIAL DISTRICT includes Potter County.

Judge
Abe Lopez

109th JUDICIAL DISTRICT includes Andrews, Crane and Winkler counties.

Judge
James L. Rex

110th JUDICIAL DISTRICT includes Briscoe, Dickens, Floyd and Motley counties.

Judge
John R. Hollums

111th JUDICIAL DISTRICT includes Webb County (County Court jurisdiction except probate transferred to District Court).

Judge
Raul Vasquez

112th JUDICIAL DISTRICT includes Crockett, Pecos, Reagan, Sutton and Upton counties.

Judge
Brock Jones

113th JUDICIAL DISTRICT includes Harris County.

Judge
Patricia Hancock

114th JUDICIAL DISTRICT includes Smith County.

Judge
Cynthia Stevens Kent

115th JUDICIAL DISTRICT includes Marion (County Court jurisdiction except probate transferred to District Court; concurrent jurisdiction with County Court to receive guilty pleas in misdemeanor cases) and Upshur (concurrent criminal and civil jurisdiction with County Court) counties.

Judge
Lauren L. Parish

116th JUDICIAL DISTRICT (concurrent criminal jurisdiction with County Court) includes Dallas County.

Judge
Carlos Lopez

117th JUDICIAL DISTRICT includes Nueces County.

Judge
Sandra Watts

118th JUDICIAL DISTRICT includes Glasscock (County Court civil jurisdiction except probate transferred to District Court), Howard and Martin counties.

Judge
Robert H. Moore, III

119th JUDICIAL DISTRICT includes Concho, Runnels and Tom Green counties.

Judge
Ben Woodward

120th JUDICIAL DISTRICT includes El Paso County.

Judge
Luis Aguilar

121st JUDICIAL DISTRICT includes Terry and Yoakum counties.

Judge
Kelly G. Moore

TEXAS DISTRICT COURTS—*Continued*

122nd JUDICIAL DISTRICT includes Galveston County.

Judge
John Ellisor

123rd JUDICIAL DISTRICT includes Panola and Shelby counties.

Judge
Guy William Griffin

124th JUDICIAL DISTRICT includes Gregg County.

Judge
Alvin G. Khoury

125th JUDICIAL DISTRICT includes Harris County.

Judge
John A. Coselli

126th JUDICIAL DISTRICT includes Travis County.

Judge
Darlene Byrne

127th JUDICIAL DISTRICT includes Harris County.

Judge
Sharolyn P. Wood

128th JUDICIAL DISTRICT includes Orange County.

Judge
Patrick Allen Clark

129th JUDICIAL DISTRICT includes Harris County.

Judge
S. Grant Dorfman

130th JUDICIAL DISTRICT includes Matagorda County.

Judge
Craig Estlinbaum

131st JUDICIAL DISTRICT (civil preference) includes Bexar County.

Judge
John D. Gabriel

132nd JUDICIAL DISTRICT includes Borden and Scurry counties.

Judge
Ernie B. Armstrong

133rd JUDICIAL DISTRICT includes Harris County.

Judge
Lamar McCorkle

134th JUDICIAL DISTRICT (concurrent criminal jurisdiction with County Court) includes Dallas County.

Judge
Anne Ashby

135th JUDICIAL DISTRICT includes Calhoun, De Witt, Goliad, Jackson, Refugio and Victoria counties.

Judge
Kemper Stephen Williams

136th JUDICIAL DISTRICT includes Jefferson County.

Judge
Milton Gunn Shuffield

137th JUDICIAL DISTRICT includes Lubbock County.

Judge
Cecil G. Puryear

138th JUDICIAL DISTRICT (criminal preference) includes Cameron and Willacy counties.

Judge
Robert Garza

139th JUDICIAL DISTRICT includes Hidalgo County.

Judge
Leticia Hinojosa

140th JUDICIAL DISTRICT includes Lubbock County.

Judge
Jim Bob Darnell

141st JUDICIAL DISTRICT includes Tarrant County.

Judge
Len A. Wade

142nd JUDICIAL DISTRICT includes Midland County.

Judge
George D. Gilles

143rd JUDICIAL DISTRICT includes Loving, Reeves and Ward counties.

Judge
Bob Parks

144th JUDICIAL DISTRICT (criminal preference) includes Bexar County.

Judge
Mark R. Luitjen

145th JUDICIAL DISTRICT includes Nacogdoches County.

Judge
Campbell Cox, II

146th JUDICIAL DISTRICT includes Bell County.

Judge
Rick Morris

147th JUDICIAL DISTRICT (criminal preference) includes Travis County.

Judge
Wilford Flowers

TEXAS DISTRICT COURTS—*Continued*

148th JUDICIAL DISTRICT (primary family law preference, secondary criminal preference) includes Nueces County.

Judge
Rose Vela

149th JUDICIAL DISTRICT includes Brazoria County.

Judge
Robert E. May

150th JUDICIAL DISTRICT (civil preference) includes Bexar County.

Judge
Janet P. Littlejohn

151st JUDICIAL DISTRICT includes Harris County.

Judge
Caroline E. Baker

152nd JUDICIAL DISTRICT includes Harris County.

Judge
Kenneth Price Wise

153rd JUDICIAL DISTRICT includes Tarrant County.

Judge
Kenneth Charles Curry

154th JUDICIAL DISTRICT includes Lamb County.

Judge
Felix Klein

155th JUDICIAL DISTRICT includes Austin, Fayette and Waller counties.

Judge
Dan R. Beck

156th JUDICIAL DISTRICT includes Aransas, Bee, Live Oak, McMullen and San Patricio counties.

Judge
Joel B. Johnson

157th JUDICIAL DISTRICT includes Harris County.

Judge
Randall W. Wilson

158th JUDICIAL DISTRICT includes Denton County.

Judge
Jake Collier

159th JUDICIAL DISTRICT includes Angelina County.

Judge
Paul E. White

160th JUDICIAL DISTRICT (concurrent criminal jurisdiction with County Court) includes Dallas County.

Judge
Joseph M. Cox

161st JUDICIAL DISTRICT includes Ector County.

Judge
Tryon D. Lewis

162nd JUDICIAL DISTRICT (concurrent criminal jurisdiction with County Court) includes Dallas County.

Judge
Bill Rhea

163rd JUDICIAL DISTRICT includes Orange County.

Judge
Dennis Powell

164th JUDICIAL DISTRICT includes Harris County.

Judge
Martha Hill Jamison

165th JUDICIAL DISTRICT includes Harris County.

Judge
Elizabeth Ray

166th JUDICIAL DISTRICT (civil preference) includes Bexar County.

Judge
Martha Tanner

167th JUDICIAL DISTRICT includes Travis County.

Judge
Mike F. Lynch

168th JUDICIAL DISTRICT includes El Paso County.

Judge
Guadalupe Rivera

169th JUDICIAL DISTRICT includes Bell County.

Judge
Gordon G. Adams

170th JUDICIAL DISTRICT includes McLennan County.

Judge
Jim Meyer

171st JUDICIAL DISTRICT includes El Paso County.

Judge
Bonnie Rangel

172nd JUDICIAL DISTRICT includes Jefferson County.

Judge
Donald J. Floyd

173rd JUDICIAL DISTRICT includes Henderson County.

Judge
Jack Humphrey Holland

174th JUDICIAL DISTRICT includes Harris County.

Judge
George H. Godwin

TEXAS DISTRICT COURTS—*Continued*

175th JUDICIAL DISTRICT (criminal preference) includes Bexar County.

Judge
Mary D. Roman

176th JUDICIAL DISTRICT includes Harris County.

Judge
Brian Rains

177th JUDICIAL DISTRICT includes Harris County.

Judge
Carol G. Davies

178th JUDICIAL DISTRICT includes Harris County.

Judge
William Harmon

179th JUDICIAL DISTRICT includes Harris County.

Judge
J. Michael Wilkinson

180th JUDICIAL DISTRICT includes Harris County.

Judge
Debbie Mantooth-Stricklin

181st JUDICIAL DISTRICT includes Potter and Randall counties.

Judge
John B. Board

182nd JUDICIAL DISTRICT (criminal preference) includes Harris County.

Judge
Jeannine S. Barr

183rd JUDICIAL DISTRICT (criminal preference) includes Harris County.

Judge
Joan Huffman

184th JUDICIAL DISTRICT (criminal preference) includes Harris County.

Judge
Jan Krocker

185th JUDICIAL DISTRICT (criminal preference) includes Harris County.

Judge
Susan Brown

186th JUDICIAL DISTRICT (criminal preference) includes Bexar County.

Judge
Maria Teresa "Tessa" Herr

187th JUDICIAL DISTRICT (criminal preference) includes Bexar County.

Judge
Raymond C. Angelini

188th JUDICIAL DISTRICT includes Gregg County.

Judge
David Brabham

189th JUDICIAL DISTRICT includes Harris County.

Judge
Jeff Work

190th JUDICIAL DISTRICT includes Harris County.

Judge
Jennifer Walker Elrod

191st JUDICIAL DISTRICT includes Dallas County.

Judge
Catharina Haynes

192nd JUDICIAL DISTRICT includes Dallas County.

Judge
Merrill Hartman

193rd JUDICIAL DISTRICT includes Dallas County.

Judge
David W. Evans

194th JUDICIAL DISTRICT (criminal preference) includes Dallas County.

Judge
Mary E. Miller

195th JUDICIAL DISTRICT (criminal preference) includes Dallas County.

Judge
John Nelms

196th JUDICIAL DISTRICT includes Hunt County.

Judge
Joe M. Leonard

197th JUDICIAL DISTRICT (criminal preference) includes Cameron and Willacy counties.

Judge
Midgalia Lopez

198th JUDICIAL DISTRICT includes Kerr, Kimble, Mason, McCulloch and Menard counties.

Judge
Emil Karl Prohl

199th JUDICIAL DISTRICT includes Collin County.

Judge
Robert T. Dry, Jr.

200th JUDICIAL DISTRICT includes Travis County.

Judge
Paul R. Davis, Jr.

201st JUDICIAL DISTRICT includes Travis County.

Judge
Suzanne Covington

TEXAS DISTRICT COURTS—*Continued*

202nd JUDICIAL DISTRICT (criminal preference; County Court jurisdiction except probate transferred to District Court) includes Bowie County.

Judge
Bill Peek

203rd JUDICIAL DISTRICT (criminal preference) includes Dallas County.

Judge
Lana McDaniel

204th JUDICIAL DISTRICT (criminal preference) includes Dallas County.

Judge
Mark Nancarrow

205th JUDICIAL DISTRICT (criminal preference) includes Culberson, El Paso and Hudspeth counties.

Judge
Kathleen H. Olivares

206th JUDICIAL DISTRICT includes Hidalgo County.

Judge
Rose Guerra Reyna

207th JUDICIAL DISTRICT (criminal preference) includes Caldwell (concurrent criminal jurisdiction with County Court), Comal (County Court jurisdiction except probate transferred to District Court) and Hays counties.

Judge
Jack Hollis Robison

208th JUDICIAL DISTRICT (criminal preference) includes Harris County.

Judge
Denise Collins

209th JUDICIAL DISTRICT (criminal preference) includes Harris County.

Judge
Michael Thomas McSpadden

210th JUDICIAL DISTRICT includes El Paso County.

Judge
Gonzalo Garcia

211th JUDICIAL DISTRICT includes Denton County.

Judge
L. Dee Shipman

212th JUDICIAL DISTRICT includes Galveston County.

Judge
Susan Criss

213th JUDICIAL DISTRICT includes Tarrant County.

Judge
Robert K. Gill

214th JUDICIAL DISTRICT (criminal preference) includes Nueces County.

Judge
Jose Longoria

215th JUDICIAL DISTRICT (civil preference) includes Harris County.

Judge
Levi James Benton

216th JUDICIAL DISTRICT includes Bandera, Gillespie, Kendall and Kerr counties.

Judge
Stephen B. Ables

217th JUDICIAL DISTRICT includes Angelina County.

Judge
David V. Wilson

218th JUDICIAL DISTRICT includes Atascosa, Frio, Karnes, La Salle and Wilson counties.

Judge
Stella H. Saxon

219th JUDICIAL DISTRICT includes Collin County.

Judge
Curt B. Henderson

220th JUDICIAL DISTRICT includes Bosque, Comanche and Hamilton counties.

Judge
James E. Morgan

221st JUDICIAL DISTRICT includes Montgomery County.

Judge
Suzanne Stovall

222nd JUDICIAL DISTRICT includes Deaf Smith and Oldham counties.

Judge
Roland Saul

223rd JUDICIAL DISTRICT includes Gray County.

Judge
Lee Waters

224th JUDICIAL DISTRICT (civil preference) includes Bexar County.

Judge
David Peeples

225th JUDICIAL DISTRICT (civil preference) includes Bexar County.

Judge
John J. Specia, Jr.

226th JUDICIAL DISTRICT (criminal preference) includes Bexar County.

Judge
Sid L. Harle

227th JUDICIAL DISTRICT (criminal preference) includes Bexar County.

Judge
Philip A. Kazen, Jr.

TEXAS DISTRICT COURTS—*Continued*

228th JUDICIAL DISTRICT (criminal preference) includes Harris County.

Judge
Ted Poe

229th JUDICIAL DISTRICT includes Duval, Jim Hogg and Starr counties.

Judge
Alex W. Gabert

230th JUDICIAL DISTRICT (criminal preference) includes Harris County.

Judge
Belinda Hill

231st JUDICIAL DISTRICT (family law preference) includes Tarrant County.

Judge
Randy Catterton

232nd JUDICIAL DISTRICT (criminal preference) includes Harris County.

Judge
Mary Lou Keel

233rd JUDICIAL DISTRICT (family law preference) includes Tarrant County.

Judge
William Wren Harris

234th JUDICIAL DISTRICT includes Harris County.

Judge
Bruce Oakley

235th JUDICIAL DISTRICT includes Cooke County.

Judge
Jerry W. Woodlock

236th JUDICIAL DISTRICT includes Tarrant County.

Judge
Thomas Wilson Lowe III

237th JUDICIAL DISTRICT includes Lubbock County.

Judge
Sam Medina

238th JUDICIAL DISTRICT includes Midland County.

Judge
John Gary Hyde

239th JUDICIAL DISTRICT includes Brazoria County.

Judge
Patrick E. Sebesta

240th JUDICIAL DISTRICT includes Fort Bend County.

Judge
Thomas R. Culver, III

241st JUDICIAL DISTRICT includes Smith County.

Judge
vacancy

242nd JUDICIAL DISTRICT includes Castro, Hale and Swisher counties.

Judge
Ed Self

243rd JUDICIAL DISTRICT includes El Paso County.

Judge
David C. Guaderrama

244th JUDICIAL DISTRICT includes Ector County.

Judge
Gary L. Watkins

245th JUDICIAL DISTRICT (family law preference) includes Harris County.

Judge
Annette Galik

246th JUDICIAL DISTRICT (family law preference) includes Harris County.

Judge
Jim York

247th JUDICIAL DISTRICT (family law preference) includes Harris County.

Judge
Bonnie Crane Hellums

248th JUDICIAL DISTRICT (criminal preference) includes Harris County.

Judge
Joan Campbell

249th JUDICIAL DISTRICT includes Johnson and Somervell counties.

Judge
D. Wayne Bridewell

250th JUDICIAL DISTRICT includes Travis County.

Judge
John K. Dietz

251st JUDICIAL DISTRICT includes Potter and Randall counties.

Judge
Patrick A. Pirtle

252nd JUDICIAL DISTRICT (criminal preference) includes Jefferson County.

Judge
Layne Walker

253rd JUDICIAL DISTRICT includes Chambers and Liberty counties.

Judge
Chap Cain, III

254th JUDICIAL DISTRICT (family law preference) includes Dallas County.

TEXAS DISTRICT COURTS—*Continued*

Judge
Jeffrey V. Coen

255th JUDICIAL DISTRICT (family law preference) includes Dallas County.

Judge
Craig Fowler

256th JUDICIAL DISTRICT (family law preference) includes Dallas County.

Judge
Brenda Green

257th JUDICIAL DISTRICT (family law preference) includes Harris County.

Judge
Linda Motheral

258th JUDICIAL DISTRICT includes Polk (concurrent criminal jurisdiction with County Court), San Jacinto and Trinity counties.

Judge
Elizabeth E. Coker

259th JUDICIAL DISTRICT (County Court jurisdiction except probate transferred to District Court) includes Jones and Shackelford counties.

Judge
Brooks H. Hagler

260th JUDICIAL DISTRICT includes Orange County.

Judge
Buddie J. Hahn

261st JUDICIAL DISTRICT includes Travis County.

Judge
Lora J. Livingston

262nd JUDICIAL DISTRICT (criminal preference) includes Harris County.

Judge
Mike Anderson

263rd JUDICIAL DISTRICT (criminal preference) includes Harris County.

Judge
Jim Wallace

264th JUDICIAL DISTRICT includes Bell County.

Judge
Martha Jane Trudo

265th JUDICIAL DISTRICT (criminal preference) includes Dallas County.

Judge
Keith Dean

266th JUDICIAL DISTRICT includes Erath County.

Judge
Donald Richard Jones

267th JUDICIAL DISTRICT includes Calhoun, De Witt, Goliad, Jackson, Refugio and Victoria counties.

Judge
Juergen "Skipper" Koetter

268th JUDICIAL DISTRICT includes Fort Bend County.

Judge
Brady Gifford Elliott

269th JUDICIAL DISTRICT includes Harris County.

Judge
John T. Wooldridge

270th JUDICIAL DISTRICT includes Harris County.

Judge
Brent Gamble

271st JUDICIAL DISTRICT includes Jack and Wise counties.

Judge
John H. Fostel

272nd JUDICIAL DISTRICT includes Brazos County.

Judge
Richard W. B. Davis

273rd JUDICIAL DISTRICT includes Sabine (County Court civil jurisdiction except probate transferred to District Court), San Augustine (County Court civil jurisdiction except probate transferred to District Court) and Shelby counties.

Judge
Charles R. Mitchell

274th JUDICIAL DISTRICT includes Caldwell, Comal (County Court jurisdiction except probate transferred to District Court), Guadalupe and Hays counties.

Judge
Gary L. Steel

275th JUDICIAL DISTRICT includes Hildago County.

Judge
Juan R. Partida

276th JUDICIAL DISTRICT includes Camp (concurrent criminal jurisdiction with County Court), Marion (County Court jurisdiction except probate transferred to District Court; concurrent criminal jurisdiction with County Court; concurrent jurisdiction with County Court to receive guilty pleas in misdemeanor cases), Morris (County Court civil jurisdiction except probate transferred to District Court; concurrent criminal jurisdiction with County Court) and Titus counties.

Judge
William Reed Porter

277th JUDICIAL DISTRICT includes Williamson County.

Judge
Ken Anderson

278th JUDICIAL DISTRICT includes Grimes, Leon, Madison and Walker counties.

TEXAS DISTRICT COURTS—*Continued*

Judge
Kenneth H. Keeling

279th JUDICIAL DISTRICT (family law preference) includes Jefferson County.

Judge
Thomas F. Mulvaney

280th JUDICIAL DISTRICT includes Harris County.

Judge
Tony Lindsay

281st JUDICIAL DISTRICT includes Harris County.

Judge
Jane Nenninger Bland

282nd JUDICIAL DISTRICT (criminal preference) includes Dallas County.

Judge
Karen Jane Greene

283rd JUDICIAL DISTRICT (criminal preference) includes Dallas County.

Judge
Vickers L. Cunningham, Sr.

284th JUDICIAL DISTRICT includes Montgomery County.

Judge
Olen Underwood

285th JUDICIAL DISTRICT (civil preference) includes Bexar County.

Judge
Michael Parker Peden

286th JUDICIAL DISTRICT includes Cochran and Hockley counties.

Judge
Harold Phelan

287th JUDICIAL DISTRICT includes Bailey and Parmer counties.

Judge
Gordon Houston Green

288th JUDICIAL DISTRICT (civil preference) includes Bexar County.

Judge
Frank Montalvo

289th JUDICIAL DISTRICT (primary juvenile preference, secondary criminal preference) includes Bexar County.

Judge
Carmen Kelsey

290th JUDICIAL DISTRICT (criminal preference) includes Bexar County.

Judge
Sharon MacRae

291st JUDICIAL DISTRICT (criminal preference) includes Dallas County.

Judge
Susan Hawk

292nd JUDICIAL DISTRICT (criminal preference) includes Dallas County.

Judge
Henry Wade, Jr.

293rd JUDICIAL DISTRICT includes Dimmit, Maverick and Zavala counties.

Judge
Cynthia L. Muniz

294th JUDICIAL DISTRICT (concurrent criminal and civil jurisdiction with County Courts) includes Van Zandt County.

Judge
Teresa Drum

295th JUDICIAL DISTRICT (civil preference) includes Harris County.

Judge
Tracy Christopher

296th JUDICIAL DISTRICT includes Collin County.

Judge
Betty Caton

297th JUDICIAL DISTRICT (criminal preference) includes Tarrant County.

Judge
Everett Young

298th JUDICIAL DISTRICT (civil preference) includes Dallas County.

Judge
Adolph Canales

299th JUDICIAL DISTRICT includes Travis County.

Judge
Jon Neil Wisser

300th JUDICIAL DISTRICT (family matters only) includes Brazoria County.

Judge
K. Randall Hufstetler

301st JUDICIAL DISTRICT (family matters only) includes Dallas County.

Judge
Susan Amanda Rankin

302nd JUDICIAL DISTRICT (family matters only) includes Dallas County.

Judge
Frances Ann Harris

303rd JUDICIAL DISTRICT (family matters only) includes Dallas County.

Judge
Richard Johnson

304th JUDICIAL DISTRICT (family matters only) includes Dallas County.

Judge
John Sholden

305th JUDICIAL DISTRICT (family matters only) includes Dallas County.

Judge
Cheryl Lee Shannon

306th JUDICIAL DISTRICT (family matters only) includes Galveston County.

Judge
Jan Yarbrough

307th JUDICIAL DISTRICT (family matters only) includes Gregg County.

Judge
Robin D. Sage

308th JUDICIAL DISTRICT (family matters only) includes Harris County.

Judge
Georgia Dempster

309th JUDICIAL DISTRICT (family matters only) includes Harris County.

Judge
Frank Rynd

310th JUDICIAL DISTRICT (family matters only) includes Harris County.

Judge
Lisa Millard

311th JUDICIAL DISTRICT (family matters only) includes Harris County.

Judge
Doug Warne

312th JUDICIAL DISTRICT (family matters only) includes Harris County.

Judge
James Squier

313th JUDICIAL DISTRICT (family matters only) includes Harris County.

Judge
Pat Shelton

314th JUDICIAL DISTRICT (family matters only) includes Harris County.

Judge
John F. Phillips

315th JUDICIAL DISTRICT (family matters only) includes Harris County.

Judge
"Earl" Kent Ellis

316th JUDICIAL DISTRICT (family matters only) includes Hutchinson County.

Judge
John La Grone

317th JUDICIAL DISTRICT (family matters only) includes Jefferson County.

Judge
Larry Thorne

318th JUDICIAL DISTRICT (family matters only) includes Midland County.

Judge
Dean Rucker

319th JUDICIAL DISTRICT (family matters only) includes Nueces County.

Judge
Tom Greenwell

320th JUDICIAL DISTRICT (family matters only) includes Potter County.

Judge
Don Emerson

321st JUDICIAL DISTRICT (family matters only) includes Smith County.

Judge
Carole W. Clark

322nd JUDICIAL DISTRICT (family matters only) includes Tarrant County.

Judge
Frank Walter Sullivan, III

323rd JUDICIAL DISTRICT (family matters only) includes Tarrant County.

Judge
Jean Hudson Boyd

324th JUDICIAL DISTRICT (family matters only) includes Tarrant County.

Judge
Brian Allan Carper

325th JUDICIAL DISTRICT (family matters only) includes Tarrant County.

Judge
Judith G. Wells

326th JUDICIAL DISTRICT (family matters only) includes Taylor County.

Judge
Aleta Hacker

327th JUDICIAL DISTRICT (family matters only) includes El Paso County.

Judge
Linda Chew

328th JUDICIAL DISTRICT (family matters only) includes Fort Bend County.

Judge
Ronald R. Pope

329th JUDICIAL DISTRICT (family matters only) includes Wharton County.

Judge
Daniel Richard Sklar

330th JUDICIAL DISTRICT (family matters only) includes Dallas County.

TEXAS DISTRICT COURTS—*Continued*

Judge
Marilea Whatley Lewis

331st JUDICIAL DISTRICT includes Travis County.

Judge
Robert Anton Perkins

332nd JUDICIAL DISTRICT includes Hildago County.

Judge
Mario E. Ramirez, Jr.

333rd JUDICIAL DISTRICT (civil preference) includes Harris County.

Judge
Joseph James Halbach, Jr.

334th JUDICIAL DISTRICT (civil preference) includes Harris County.

Judge
vacancy

335th JUDICIAL DISTRICT includes Bastrop, Burleson, Lee and Washington counties.

Judge
Harold Robert Towslee

336th JUDICIAL DISTRICT includes Fannin and Grayson counties.

Judge
Ray Felty Grisham

337th JUDICIAL DISTRICT (criminal preference) includes Harris County.

Judge
Don Stricklin

338th JUDICIAL DISTRICT (criminal preference) includes Harris County.

Judge
Tommy Brock Thomas, Jr.

339th JUDICIAL DISTRICT (criminal preference) includes Harris County.

Judge
Caprice Cosper

340th JUDICIAL DISTRICT includes Tom Green County.

Judge
Rae Leifeste

341st JUDICIAL DISTRICT includes Webb County (County Court jurisdiction except probate transferred to District Court).

Judge
Elma Teresa Salinas Ender

342nd JUDICIAL DISTRICT (civil preference) includes Tarrant County.

Judge
Bob McGrath

343rd JUDICIAL DISTRICT includes Aransas, Bee, Live Oak, McMullen and San Patricio counties.

Judge
Janna K. Whatley

344th JUDICIAL DISTRICT (concurrent civil and criminal jurisdiction with County Court) includes Chambers County.

Judge
Carroll E. Wilborn, Jr.

345th JUDICIAL DISTRICT (civil preference) includes Travis County.

Judge
Patrick O. Keel

346th JUDICIAL DISTRICT includes El Paso County.

Judge
Richard Abram Roman

347th JUDICIAL DISTRICT includes Nueces County.

Judge
Nelva Gonzales Ramos

348th JUDICIAL DISTRICT (civil preference) includes Tarrant County.

Judge
Dana M. Womack

349th JUDICIAL DISTRICT includes Anderson and Houston counties.

Judge
Jerry L. Calhoon

350th JUDICIAL DISTRICT includes Taylor County.

Judge
Jesse Aaron Holloway

351st JUDICIAL DISTRICT (criminal preference) includes Harris County.

Judge
Mark Kent Ellis

352nd JUDICIAL DISTRICT (civil preference) includes Tarrant County.

Judge
Bonnie Sudderth

353rd JUDICIAL DISTRICT includes Travis County.

Judge
Margaret A. Cooper

354th JUDICIAL DISTRICT includes Hunt and Rains counties.

Judge
Richard Beacom

355th JUDICIAL DISTRICT includes Hood County.

Judge
Ralph H. Walton, Jr.

356th JUDICIAL DISTRICT (concurrent civil and criminal jurisdiction with County Court) includes Hardin County.

TEXAS DISTRICT COURTS—*Continued*

Judge
Britt Plunk

357th JUDICIAL DISTRICT includes Cameron and Willacy counties.

Judge
Leonel Alejandro

358th JUDICIAL DISTRICT includes Ector County.

Judge
Bill McCoy

359th JUDICIAL DISTRICT includes Montgomery County.

Judge
Kathleen A. Hamilton

360th JUDICIAL DISTRICT (family matters only) includes Tarrant County.

Judge
Debra H. Lehrmann

361st JUDICIAL DISTRICT includes Brazos County.

Judge
Steve Smith

362nd JUDICIAL DISTRICT includes Denton County.

Judge
Bruce McFarling

363rd JUDICIAL DISTRICT (criminal preference) includes Dallas County.

Judge
Faith Johnson

364th JUDICIAL DISTRICT includes Lubbock County.

Judge
Bradley S. Underwood

365th JUDICIAL DISTRICT includes Dimmit, Maverick and Zavala counties.

Judge
Amado Abascal, III

366th JUDICIAL DISTRICT includes Collin County.

Judge
Nathan E. White, Jr.

367th JUDICIAL DISTRICT includes Denton County.

Judge
E. Lee Gabriel

368th JUDICIAL DISTRICT includes Williamson County.

Judge
Burt Carnes

369th JUDICIAL DISTRICT includes Anderson and Cherokee counties.

Judge
Bascom W. Bentley, III

370th JUDICIAL DISTRICT includes Hidalgo County.

Judge
Noé Gonzalez

371st JUDICIAL DISTRICT (criminal preference) includes Tarrant County.

Judge
James R. Wilson

372nd JUDICIAL DISTRICT (criminal preference) includes Tarrant County.

Judge
Scott Wisch

377th JUDICIAL DISTRICT (criminal preference) includes Victoria County.

Judge
Robert C. Cheshire

378th JUDICIAL DISTRICT includes Ellis County.

Judge
Roy A. "Al" Scoggins, Jr.

379th JUDICIAL DISTRICT includes Bexar County.

Judge
Robert C. "Bert" Richards

380th JUDICIAL DISTRICT includes Collin County.

Judge
Charles F. Sandoval

381st JUDICIAL DISTRICT includes Starr County.

Judge
John A. Pope, III

382nd JUDICIAL DISTRICT includes Rockwall County.

Judge
Brett Hall

383rd JUDICIAL DISTRICT includes El Paso County.

Judge
Mike Herrera

384th JUDICIAL DISTRICT includes El Paso County.

Judge
Patrick Michael Garcia

385th JUDICIAL DISTRICT includes Midland County.

Judge
Willie Bryan DuBose

386th JUDICIAL DISTRICT includes Bexar County.

Judge
Laura Parker

387th JUDICIAL DISTRICT includes Fort Bend County.

TEXAS DISTRICT COURTS—*Continued*

Judge
Robert J. Kern

388th JUDICIAL DISTRICT includes El Paso County.

Judge
Patricia A. Macias

389th JUDICIAL DISTRICT includes Hidalgo County.

Judge
Leticia Lopez

390th JUDICIAL DISTRICT includes Travis County.

Judge
Julie Harris Kocurek

391st JUDICIAL DISTRICT includes Tom Green County.

Judge
Thomas J. Gossett

392nd JUDICIAL DISTRICT includes Henderson County.

Judge
Carter William Tarrance

393rd JUDICIAL DISTRICT includes Denton County.

Judge
Vicki B. Isaacks

394th JUDICIAL DISTRICT includes Brewster, Culberson, Hudspeth, Jeff Davis and Presidio counties.

Judge
Kenneth Daly DeHart

395th JUDICIAL DISTRICT includes Williamson County.

Judge
Michael P. Jergins

396th JUDICIAL DISTRICT includes Tarrant County.

Judge
George W. Gallagher

398th JUDICIAL DISTRICT includes Hidalgo County.

Judge
Aida Salinas Flores

399th JUDICIAL DISTRICT includes Bexar County.

Judge
Juanita A. Vasquez-Gardner

400th JUDICIAL DISTRICT includes Fort Bend County.

Judge
Bradley Smith

401st JUDICIAL DISTRICT includes Collin County.

Judge
Mark Joseph Rusch

402nd JUDICIAL DISTRICT includes Wood County.

Judge
George Timothy Boswell

403rd JUDICIAL DISTRICT includes Travis County.

Judge
Brenda P. Kennedy

404th JUDICIAL DISTRICT includes Cameron and Willacy counties.

Judge
Abel C. Limas

405th JUDICIAL DISTRICT includes Galveston County.

Judge
Wayne J. Mallia

406th JUDICIAL DISTRICT includes Webb County.

Judge
Andres Reyes

407th JUDICIAL DISTRICT includes Bexar County.

Judge
Karen H. Pozza

408th JUDICIAL DISTRICT includes Bexar County.

Judge
vacancy

409th JUDICIAL DISTRICT includes El Paso County.

Judge
Sam Medrano

410th JUDICIAL DISTRICT includes Montgomery County.

Judge
K. Michael Mayes

411th JUDICIAL DISTRICT includes Polk, San Jacinto and Trinity counties.

Judge
Robert Hill Trapp

TEXAS CRIMINAL DISTRICT COURTS

County	Judge
Dallas	
No. 1	Janice L. Warder
No. 2	Cliff Stricklin
No. 3	Robert W. Francis
No. 4	John Coleman Creuzot
No. 5	Manny D. Alvarez
Jefferson	Charles Dana Carver
Tarrant	
No. 1	Sharen Wilson
No. 2	Wayne Francis Salvant
No. 3	Elizabeth Berry
No. 4	Mike Thomas

TEXAS COUNTY-LEVEL COURTS

The County Courts are courts of limited jurisdiction in Texas. There are three types of county courts: "con-

TEXAS COUNTY-LEVEL COURTS—*Continued*

stitutional" County Courts, County Courts at Law and County Probate Courts. The judges are chosen in countywide partisan elections for four-year terms. Vacancies between elections are filled by county commissioners.

The courts sit at the county seats.

TEXAS COUNTY COURTS

Generally, the "constitutional" County Courts have concurrent jurisdiction with the Justice of the Peace Courts in civil cases when the contested amount is $200 to $5,000 and with the district courts in civil cases where the matter in controversy is $500 to $5,000. The courts have general jurisdiction over uncontested probate cases unless this jurisdiction has been transferred by statute to a special Probate Court. The courts also have exclusive original jurisdiction over all misdemeanors involving a fine exceeding $500 and/or a jail sentence not exceeding one year. Unless provided by law, the courts do not have criminal jurisdiction in any county where a Criminal District Court exists. In some counties, all or part of the jurisdiction of the constitutional County Courts has been transferred to or is concurrent with the County Courts at Law or with the District Courts. The courts exercise appellate jurisdiction over decisions of Municipal and Justice of the Peace Courts; these decisions are heard by trial de novo unless the appeal is from a designated Municipal Court of Record. Appeals from original and appellate judgments of the County Courts are to the Courts of Appeal.

County	Judge
Anderson	Carey G. McKinney
Andrews	Richard H. Dolgener
Angelina	Joe R. Berry
Aransas	Glenn D. Guillory
Archer	Paul O. Wylie
Armstrong	Hugh Reed
Atascosa	Diana Bautista
Austin	Carolyn Cerny Bilski
Bailey	Marilyn Kay Cox
Bandera	Richard A. Evans
Bastrop	Ronnie McDonald
Baylor	James Coltharp
Bee	Jimmy Martinez
Bell	Jon Burrows
Bexar	Nelson W. Wolff
Blanco	Bill Guthrie
Borden	Van Lee York
Bosque	Cole Word
Bowie	James Marion Carlow
Brazoria	John G. Willy
Brazos	Randy Sims
Brewster	Val Clark Beard
Briscoe	Wayne Nance
Brooks	Joe B. Garcia
Brown	Ernest Ray West, III
Burleson	Mike Sutherland
Burnet	David L. Kithil
Caldwell	H. T. Wright
Calhoun	Michael Pfeifer
Callahan	Roger Corn
Cameron	Gilberto Hinojosa
Camp	Preston Combest
Carson	Lewis W. Powers
Cass	Charles L. McMichael
Castro	William F. Sava
Chambers	Jimmy Sylvia
Cherokee	Chris Davis
Childress	Jay Mayden
Clay	Kenneth E. Liggett
Cochran	James St. Clair
Coke	Roy Blair
Coleman	Jimmie Hobbs
Collin	Ron Harris
Collingsworth	Jim L. Forrester
Colorado	Alfred G. Jamison
Comal	Danny Scheel
Comanche	James R. Arthur
Concho	Edgar Allen Amos
Cooke	Bill Freeman
Coryell	John A. Hull
Cottle	John D. Shavor
Crane	Donnie Henderson
Crockett	John R. Jones
Crosby	Joe Heflin
Culberson	John E. Conoly
Dallam	David D. Field
Dallas	Margaret Keliher
Dawson	Sam Saleh
Deaf Smith	Tom Simons
Delta	Hugh Charles Whitney
Denton	Mary Horn
De Witt	Ben E. Prause
Dickens	Woodie McArthur, Jr.
Dimmit	Francisco G. Ponce
Donley	Jack Hall
Duval	Edmundo B. Garcia, Jr.
Eastland	Brad Stephenson
Ector	Jerry D. Caddel
Edwards	Nicholas Gallegos
Ellis	Chad Adams
El Paso	Dolores Briones
Erath	Joe "Tab" Thompson
Falls	Thomas Sehon
Fannin	Derrell Hall
Fayette	Edward F. Janecka
Fisher	Marshal Jay Bennett
Floyd	William D. Hardin
Foard	Charles Byron Bell
Fort Bend	Robert E. Hebert
Franklin	Gerald Hubbell
Freestone	Linda K. Grant
Frio	Carlos A. Garcia
Gaines	Judy House
Galveston	James D. Yarbrough
Garza	Giles W. Dalby
Gillespie	Mark Stroeher
Glasscock	Wilburn E. Bednar
Goliad	Harold F. Gleinser
Gonzales	David Bird
Gray	Richard Peet
Grayson	Tim McGraw
Gregg	Bill Stoudt
Grimes	James P. Dixon
Guadalupe	Donald L. Schraub
Hale	Bill Hollars
Hall	Jack Martin
Hamilton	Fred Cox
Hansford	Jim D. Brown
Hardeman	Kenneth D. McNabb
Hardin	Billy B. Caraway
Harris	Robert A. Eckels

TEXAS COUNTY-LEVEL COURTS—*Continued*

Harrison	Wayne McWhorter
Hartley	Ronnie Gordon
Haskell	David C. Davis
Hays	Jim Powers
Hemphill	Bob Wayne Gober
Henderson	Aubrey L. Jones Jr.
Hidalgo	Ramon Garcia
Hill	Kenneth Davis
Hockley	Larry D. Sprowls
Hood	Andy Rash
Hopkins	Cletis M. Millsap
Houston	Robert C. Von Doenhoff
Howard	Ben Allen Lockhart
Hudspeth	Becky Dean-Walker
Hunt	Joe A. Bobbitt
Hutchinson	Jack Logan Worsham
Irion	Leon Standard
Jack	Mitchell Grant Davenport
Jackson	Harrison Stafford, II
Jasper	Joe N. Folk
Jeff Davis	George E. Grubb
Jefferson	Carl R. Griffith, Jr.
Jim Hogg	Agapito Molina, Jr.
Jim Wells	L. Arnoldo Saenz
Johnson	Roger Owen Harmon
Jones	Dale Spurgin
Karnes	Alger H. Kendall, Jr.
Kaufman	James Wayne Gent
Kendall	Eddie J. Vogt
Kenedy	Joseph A. Garcia, Jr.
Kent	Jim C. White
Kerr	Pat Tinley
Kimble	Delbert Ray Roberts
King	Duane Daniel
Kinney	Herbert H. Senne, Jr.
Kleberg	Pete De La Garza
Knox	Greg Clonts
Lamar	Maurice C. Superville, Jr.
Lamb	William A. Thompson, Jr.
Lampasas	Virgil Edgar Lilley
La Salle	Jimmy P. Patterson
Lavaca	Ronald L. Leck
Lee	Evan Gonzales
Leon	Byron Ryder
Liberty	I. Lloyd Kirkham
Limestone	Elenor F. Holmes
Lipscomb	Willis V. Smith
Live Oak	Jim Huff
Llano	R. G. Floyd
Loving	Donald C. Creager
Lubbock	Thomas V. Head
Lynn	H. G. Franklin
Madison	Cecil N. Neely
Marion	Gene Seth Terry
Martin	Charles T. "Corky" Blocker
Mason	Jerry M. Bearden
Matagorda	Greg Baer Westmoreland
Maverick	Jose A. Aranda, Jr.
McCulloch	Randy Young
McLennan	Jim Lewis
McMullen	Linda Lee Henry
Medina	Jim Barden
Menard	Richard Cordes
Midland	William C. Morrow
Milam	Frank Summers
Mills	Robert E. Lindsey III
Mitchell	Currie Ray Mayo
Montague	James Orvil Kittrell
Montgomery	Alan B. Sadler
Moore	Kari Campbell
Morris	J. C. Jennings
Motley	Ed D. Smith
Nacogdoches	Sue K. Kennedy
Navarro	Alan M. Bristol
Newton	Truman Dougharty
Nolan	Tim D. Fambrough
Nueces	Terry Shamsie
Ochiltree	Kenneth Ray Donahue
Oldham	Don R. Allred
Orange	Carl K. Thibodeaux
Palo Pinto	Mickey D. West
Panola	David L. Anderson
Parker	Mark W. Riley
Parmer	Bonnie Jean Clayton
Pecos	Joe Shuster
Polk	John Paul Thompson
Potter	Arthur H. Ware
Presidio	Jerry Agan
Rains	Joe Ray Dougherty
Randall	Ernie Houdashell
Reagan	Mike B. Elkins
Real	W. B. Sansom, Jr.
Red River	Powell W. Peek
Reeves	Jimmy B. Galindo
Refugio	Roger C. Fagan
Roberts	Vernon Howard Cook
Robertson	Fred Elliott
Rockwall	Bill Bell
Runnels	Marilyn Egan
Rusk	Sandra Hodges
Sabine	Jack Leath
San Augustine	Wayne Holt
San Jacinto	William H. Law
San Patricio	Terry A. Simpson
San Saba	Byron Theodosis
Schleicher	Johnny Frank Griffin
Scurry	Rod Waller
Shackelford	Ross Elliott Montgomery
Shelby	Floyd A. Watson
Sherman	Kim Crippen
Smith	Becky Dempsey
Somervell	Walter Maynard
Starr	Eloy Vera
Stephens	Gary L. Fuller
Sterling	Robert L. Browne
Stonewall	Bobby Frank McGough
Sutton	Carla W. Garner
Swisher	Harold Keeter
Tarrant	Tom J. Vandergriff
Taylor	Victor G. Carrillo
Terrell	Leo Smith
Terry	Douglas Lee Ryburn
Throckmorton	Trey Carrington
Titus	Danny Pat Crooks
Tom Green	Michael D. Brown
Travis	Sam Biscoe
Trinity	Mark Evans
Tyler	Jerome Owens
Upshur	Dean Fowler
Upton	Vikki Bradley
Uvalde	William R. Mitchell

TEXAS COUNTY-LEVEL COURTS—*Continued*

Val Verde	Mike L. Fernandez
Van Zandt	Jeff Fisher
Victoria	Donald R. Pozzi
Walker	Robert D. Pierce
Waller	Owen Ralston
Ward	Sam G. Massey
Washington	Dorothy Morgan
Webb	Louis H. Bruni
Wharton	Lawrence E. Naiser
Wheeler	Jerry Dan Hefley
Wichita	Woodrow W. "Woody" Gossom, Jr.
Wilbarger	Gary B. Streit
Willacy	Simon Salinas
Williamson	John Christian Doerfler
Wilson	Marvin C. Quinney
Winkler	Bonnie Sue Leck
Wise	Richard R. Chase
Wood	Royce McCoy
Yoakum	Dallas Brewer
Young	Stanley H. Peavy III
Zapata	David Morales
Zavala	Joe Luna

TEXAS COUNTY COURTS AT LAW

County Courts at Law are special statutory courts created primarily in metropolitan counties to relieve the constitutional County Court of all or part of its duties. Jurisdiction varies according to statute, but some of the courts have only limited subject matter jurisdiction such as civil, criminal, probate or appellate (over Justice of the Peace or Municipal Courts). Generally, the courts have concurrent civil jurisdiction with the District Courts for amounts of at least $500 but not exceeding $100,000 as well as concurrent jurisdiction with the constitutional County Courts in other matters.

County	Judge
Anderson	Jeff Doran
Angelina	
No. 1	Lisa G. Burkhalter
No. 2	Berry Bryan
Aransas	William Adams
Austin	Gladys M. Oakley
Bastrop	Benton Eskew
Bell	
No. 1	Edward S. Johnson
No. 2	Harry John Barina, Jr.
No. 3	Gerald M. Brown
Bexar	
No. 1	Alfonso E. Alonso, Jr.
No. 2	Paul Canales
No. 3	S. "Shay" Gebhardt
No. 4	Sarah E. Garrahan
No. 5	Timothy F. Johnson
No. 6	M'Liss Christian
No. 7	Bill C. White
No. 8	Karen Crouch
No. 9	Wayne A. Christian, II
No. 10	Irene Alarcon Rios
No. 11	Jo-Ann Sylvia De Hoyos
No. 12	Michael E. Mery
Bowie	Leon F. Pesek, Jr.
Brazoria	
No. 1	Jerri Lee Mills
No. 2	Marc Holder
No. 3	James A. Blackstock
Brazos	
No. 1	Randy Michel
No. 2	Jim Locke
Brown	
No. 1	Frank Griffin
Burnet	
No. 1	Randy Savage
Caldwell	
No. 1	Edward L. Jarrett
Calhoun	Alex R. Hernandez
Cameron	
No. 1	Janet L. Leal
No. 2	Elia Cornejo-Lopez
No. 3	Daniel T. Robles
Cherokee	Daniel Boone Childs
Collin	
No. 1	Corinne Mason
No. 2	Jerry Lewis
No. 3	John O'Keefe Barry
No. 4	Ray Wheless
No. 5	Chris Oldner
Comal	Brenda Chapman
Cooke	John Morris
Coryell	Susan R. Stephens
Dallas	
No. 1	Russell Roden
No. 2	John B. Peyton
No. 3	Sally Montgomery
No. 4	W. Bruce Woody
No. 5	Mark Greenberg
No. 11	Dianne Jones
Criminal	
No. 1	Daniel Patrick Clancy
No. 2	Neil Edward Pask
No. 3	Dan L. Wyde
No. 4	Ralph Taite
No. 5	Tom Fuller
No. 6	Phil Barker
No. 7	Elizabeth Hampton Crowder
No. 8	Jane Roden
No. 9	Keith Alexander Anderson
No. 10	Lisa Fox
County Criminal Court of Appeals	
No. 1	Kristin Wade
No. 2	Lynn Burson
Denton	
No. 1	Darlene A. Whitten
No. 2	Margaret Barnes
Criminal	
No. 1	Jim Crouch
No. 2	Virgil L. Vahlenkamp, Jr.
No. 3	David Garcia
No. 4	Joe D. Bridges
No. 5	Richard Podgorski
Ector	J. A. "Jim" Bobo
No. 2	Mark D. Owens
Ellis	Bob Carroll
No. 2	A. Gene Calvert, Jr.
El Paso	
No. 1	Ricardo Herrera
No. 2	Julie Gonzalez
No. 3	Javier Alvarez

TEXAS COUNTY-LEVEL COURTS—*Continued*

No. 4	Alejandro "Alex" Gonzalez
No. 5	Carlos Villa
No. 6	M. Sue Kurita
No. 7	José J. Baca
Criminal	
No. 1	Alma Trejo
No. 2	Robert Anchondo
Erath	Bart McDougal
Fort Bend	
No. 1	Larry D. Wagenbach
No. 2	Walter S. McMeans
No. 3	Susan Griffin Lowery
No. 4	R. H. "Sandy" Bielstein
Galveston	
No. 1	Mary Nell Crapitto
No. 2	C. G. "Trey" Dibrell, III
No. 3	Roy Quintanilla
Grayson	
No. 1	James Henderson
No. 2	Carol M. Siebman
Gregg	
No. 1	Rebecca Lynn Simpson
No. 2	Alfonso Charles
Guadalupe	Linda Z. Jones
No. 2	Frank Follis
Harris	
Civil	
No. 1	Jack Cagle
No. 2	Gary Michael Block
No. 3	Lynn Bradshaw-Hull
No. 4	Cynthia M. Crowe
Criminal	
No. 1	Reagan C. Helm
No. 2	Michael Allen Peters
No. 3	Donald Wayne Jackson
No. 4	James E. Anderson
No. 5	Margaret Stewart Harris
No. 6	Larry Standley
No. 7	Pam Derbyshire
No. 8	Jay Karahan
No. 9	Analia H. Wilkerson
No. 10	Sherman A. Ross
No. 11	Diane Bull
No. 12	Jo Robin Brown
No. 13	Mark Atkinson
No. 14	Michael R. Fields
No. 15	Jean Spradling Hughes
Harrison	James Harry Ammerman, II
Hays	
No. 1	Howard S. Warner, II
No. 2	Linda A. Rodriguez
Henderson	D. Matt Livingston
Hidalgo	
No. 1	Rodolfo "Rudy" Gonzalez
No. 2	G. Jaime Garza
No. 4	Federico "Fred" Garza
No. 5	Arnoldo Cantu
Hood	Vincent Messina
Hopkins	Amy McCorkle Smith
Houston	Sarah Tunnell Clark
Hunt	Steve Henry Shipp
Jefferson	
No. 1	Alfred Sterling Gerson
No. 2	G. R. "Lupe" Flores
No. 3	John Paul Davis
Johnson	
No. 1	Robert B. Mayfield, III
No. 2	William Roy Anderson, Jr.
Kaufman	Joe Michael Parnell
Kendall	Bill R. Palmer
Kerr	Spencer Whitewood Brown
Kleberg	Martin J. Chiuminatto, Jr.
Lamar	Deane Loughmiller
Liberty	Don Taylor
Lubbock	
No. 1	Larry B. "Rusty" Ladd
No. 2	Drue Farmer
No. 3	Paula Davis Lanehart
McLennan	
No. 1	Tom Ragland
No. 2	Michael Brandon Gassaway
Medina	Watt Murrah
Midland	
No. 1	Al Walvoord
No. 2	Marvin Lee Moore
Montgomery	
No. 1	Dennis D. Watson
No. 2	Jerry Winfree
No. 3	E. Mason Martin, II
Moore	Delwin T. McGee
Nacogdoches	Jack Sinz
Nolan	Gary Harger
Nueces	
No. 1	Robert J. Vargas
No. 2	Lisa Gonzales
No. 3	Marisela Saldana
No. 4	James E. Klager
No. 5	Carl E. Lewis
Orange	Michael W. Shuff
Panola	Terry Douglas Bailey
Parker	Graham Quisenberry
Polk	Stephen Phillips
Potter	
No. 1	W. F. "Corky" Roberts
No. 2	Pamela Cook Sirmon
Randall	James W. Anderson
Reeves	Walter M. Holcombe
Rusk	Darrell Hyatt
San Patricio	Richard Hatch, III
Smith	
No. 1	Thomas Arthur Dunn
No. 2	Randall Lee Rogers
No. 3	Floyd Thomas Getz
Starr	Jesus Maria Alvarez
Tarrant	
No. 1	R. Brent Keis
No. 2	Jennifer Rymell
No. 3	Vincent G. Sprinkle
Criminal	
No. 1	Sherry L. Hill
No. 2	Mike Mitchell
No. 3	Bill D. Mills
No. 4	Debra Nekhom Harris
No. 5	Jamie Cummings
No. 6	Molly S. Jones
No. 7	Cheril S. Hardy
No. 8	Daryl R. Coffey

TEXAS COUNTY-LEVEL COURTS—*Continued*

No. 9	Brent A. Carr
No. 10	Phil A. Sorrells
Taylor	
No. 1	John Robert Harper
No. 2	Barbara B. Rollins
Tom Green	Ben Nolen
No. 2	Penny Ann Roberts
Travis	
No. 1	J. David Phillips
No. 2	Orlinda L. Naranjo
No. 3	David Crain
No. 4	Mike Denton
No. 5	Gisela D. Triana
No. 6	Jan Breland
No. 7	Elisabeth A. Earle
Val Verde	Sergio J. Gonzalez
Victoria	
No. 1	Laura Ann Weiser
No. 2	Juan Velasquez, II
Walker	Barbara Wade Hale
Waller	June Jackson
Washington	Matthew A. Reue
Webb	
No. 1	Alvino "Ben" Morales
No. 2	Jesus Garza
Wichita	
No. 1	Jim Hogan
No. 2	Thomas Hays Bacus
Williamson	
No. 1	Suzanne Brooks
No. 2	Tim Wright
No. 3	Don Higginbotham
Wise	Melton D. Cude

TEXAS COUNTY PROBATE COURTS

General probate jurisdiction is vested in either the District Courts or the constitutional County Courts, but in ten counties this jurisdiction has been vested in specialized Probate Courts. The courts' jurisdiction includes administration of estates, guardianship of minors and incompetents and mental illness matters. Proceedings are on the record and appeals are to the Courts of Appeals.

County	Judge
Bexar	
No. 1	Polly Jackson Spencer
No. 2	Tom Rickhoff
Collin	Weldon S. Copeland, Jr.
Dallas	Nikki Towry DeShazo
No. 2	Robert E. Price
No. 3	Joe Hilton Loving, Jr.
Denton	Don R. Windle
El Paso	Max D. Higgs
Galveston	Gladys B. Burwell
Harris	
No. 1	Russell Parker Austin
No. 2	Mike Wood
No. 3	Rory R. Olsen
No. 4	William C. McCulloch
Hidalgo	Homero Garza
Tarrant	
No. 1	Steve M. King
No. 2	Patrick W. Ferchill
Travis	
No. 1	Guy Herman

TEXAS MUNICIPAL COURTS

The Municipal Courts are courts of limited jurisdiction in Texas. They are created by state statute in each incorporated city in the state. Judges are appointed by the governing body of the city as provided by local charter or ordinance. Length of term varies among municipalities, but judges generally serve two-year terms.

The courts have exclusive original jurisdiction over traffic offenses and other city ordinance violations and concurrent jurisdiction with the Justice of the Peace Courts in misdemeanor cases resulting from state law violations within city limits when punishment is by fine only, and not to exceed $500. Municipal judges serve as magistrates and may issue search and arrest warrants, hold preliminary hearings, reduce testimony to writing, discharge an accused or remand the accused to jail and set bail.

Generally, Municipal Courts are not courts of record, and appeals are tried de novo in the constitutional County Courts, County Courts at Law or District Courts.

TEXAS JUSTICE OF THE PEACE COURTS

Justice of the Peace Courts are courts of limited jurisdiction in Texas. The state constitution, as amended in November 1983, provides that each county is to be divided into at least one and not more than eight justice precincts based upon population. One justice is elected from each precinct in partisan elections for four-year terms.

The courts have original jurisdiction over criminal cases when punishment is by fine only and does not exceed $500. The courts have exclusive jurisdiction over civil cases when the amount in controversy does not exceed $200 and concurrent jurisdiction with the County Courts when the amount exceeds $200 but is less than $5,000. The courts exercise jurisdiction over forcible entry and detainer cases. The courts may also issue warrants of search and arrest, conduct preliminary hearings and act as small claims courts.

Trials in these courts are not of record. Appeals are tried de novo in the constitutional County Courts, the County Courts at Law or the District Courts.

Texas Counties and County Seats

Anderson
Palestine

Andrews
Andrews

Angelina
Lufkin

Aransas
Rockport

Archer
Archer City

Armstrong
Claude

Atascosa
Jourdanton

Austin
Bellville

Bailey
Muleshoe

Bandera
Bandera

Bastrop
Bastrop

Baylor
Seymour

Bee
Beeville

Bell
Belton

Bexar
San Antonio

Blanco
Johnson City

Borden
Gail

Bosque
Meridian

Bowie
New Boston

Brazoria
Angleton

Brazos
Bryan

Brewster
Alpine

Briscoe
Silverton

Brooks
Falfurrias

Brown
Brownwood

Burleson
Caldwell

Burnet
Burnet

Caldwell
Lockhart

Calhoun
Port Lavaca

Callahan
Baird

Cameron
Brownsville

Camp
Pittsburg

Carson
Panhandle

Cass
Linden

Castro
Dimmitt

Chambers
Anahuac

Cherokee
Rusk

Childress
Childress

Clay
Henrietta

Cochran
Morton

Coke
Robert Lee

Coleman
Coleman

Collin
McKinney

Collingsworth
Wellington

Colorado
Columbus

Comal
New Braunfels

Comanche
Comanche

Concho
Paint Rock

Cooke
Gainesville

Coryell
Gatesville

Cottle
Paducah

Crane
Crane

Crockett
Ozona

Crosby
Crosbyton

Culberson
Van Horn

Dallam
Dalhart

Dallas
Dallas

Dawson
Lamesa

Deaf Smith
Hereford

Delta
Cooper

Denton
Denton

De Witt
Cuero

Dickens
Dickens

Dimmit
Carrizo Springs

Donley
Clarendon

Duval
San Diego

Eastland
Eastland

Ector
Odessa

Edwards
Rocksprings

Ellis
Waxahachie

El Paso
El Paso

Erath
Stephenville

Falls
Marlin

Fannin
Bonham

Fayette
La Grange

Fisher
Roby

Floyd
Floydada

Foard
Crowell

Fort Bend
Richmond

Franklin
Mount Vernon

Freestone
Fairfield

Frio
Pearsall

Gaines
Seminole

Galveston
Galveston

Garza
Post

Gillespie
Fredericksburg

Glasscock
Garden City

Goliad
Goliad

Gonzales
Gonzales

Gray
Pampa

Grayson
Sherman

Gregg
Longview

Grimes
Anderson

Guadalupe
Seguin

Hale
Plainview

Hall
Memphis

Hamilton
Hamilton

Hansford
Spearman

Hardeman
Quanah

Hardin
Kountze

Harris
Houston

Harrison
Marshall

Hartley
Channing

Haskell
Haskell

COUNTIES AND COUNTY SEATS—*Continued*

Hays
San Marcos

Hemphill
Canadian

Henderson
Athens

Hidalgo
Edinburg

Hill
Hillsboro

Hockley
Levelland

Hood
Granbury

Hopkins
Sulphur Springs

Houston
Crockett

Howard
Big Spring

Hudspeth
Sierra Blanca

Hunt
Greenville

Hutchinson
Stinnett

Irion
Mertzon

Jack
Jacksboro

Jackson
Edna

Jasper
Jasper

Jeff Davis
Fort Davis

Jefferson
Beaumont

Jim Hogg
Hebbronville

Jim Wells
Alice

Johnson
Cleburne

Jones
Anson

Karnes
Karnes City

Kaufman
Kaufman

Kendall
Boerne

Kenedy
Sarita

Kent
Jayton

Kerr
Kerrville

Kimble
Junction

King
Guthrie

Kinney
Brackettville

Kleberg
Kingsville

Knox
Benjamin

Lamar
Paris

Lamb
Littlefield

Lampasas
Lampasas

La Salle
Cotulla

Lavaca
Hallettsville

Lee
Giddings

Leon
Centerville

Liberty
Liberty

Limestone
Groesbeck

Lipscomb
Lipscomb

Live Oak
George West

Llano
Llano

Loving
Mentone

Lubbock
Lubbock

Lynn
Tahoka

Madison
Madisonville

Marion
Jefferson

Martin
Stanton

Mason
Mason

Matagorda
Bay City

Maverick
Eagle Pass

McCulloch
Brady

McLennan
Waco

McMullen
Tilden

Medina
Hondo

Menard
Menard

Midland
Midland

Milam
Cameron

Mills
Goldthwaite

Mitchell
Colorado City

Montague
Montague

Montgomery
Conroe

Moore
Dumas

Morris
Daingerfield

Motley
Matador

Nacogdoches
Nacogdoches

Navarro
Corsicana

Newton
Newton

Nolan
Sweetwater

Nueces
Corpus Christi

Ochiltree
Perryton

Oldham
Vega

Orange
Orange

Palo Pinto
Palo Pinto

Panola
Carthage

Parker
Weatherford

Parmer
Farwell

Pecos
Fort Stockton

Polk
Livingston

Potter
Amarillo

Presidio
Marfa

Rains
Emory

Randall
Canyon

Reagan
Big Lake

Real
Leakey

Red River
Clarksville

Reeves
Pecos

Refugio
Refugio

Roberts
Miami

Robertson
Franklin

Rockwall
Rockwall

Runnels
Ballinger

Rusk
Henderson

Sabine
Hemphill

San Augustine
San Augustine

San Jacinto
Coldspring

San Patricio
Sinton

San Saba
San Saba

Schleicher
Eldorado

Scurry
Snyder

COUNTIES AND COUNTY SEATS—*Continued*

Shackelford
Albany

Shelby
Center

Sherman
Stratford

Smith
Tyler

Somervell
Glen Rose

Starr
Rio Grande City

Stephens
Breckenridge

Sterling
Sterling City

Stonewall
Aspermont

Sutton
Sonora

Swisher
Tulia

Tarrant
Fort Worth

Taylor
Abilene

Terrell
Sanderson

Terry
Brownfield

Throckmorton
Throckmorton

Titus
Mount Pleasant

Tom Green
San Angelo

Travis
Austin

Trinity
Groveton

Tyler
Woodville

Upshur
Gilmer

Upton
Rankin

Uvalde
Uvalde

Val Verde
Del Rio

Van Zandt
Canton

Victoria
Victoria

Walker
Huntsville

Waller
Hempstead

Ward
Monahans

Washington
Brenham

Webb
Laredo

Wharton
Wharton

Wheeler
Wheeler

Wichita
Wichita Falls

Wilbarger
Vernon

Willacy
Raymondville

Williamson
Georgetown

Wilson
Floresville

Winkler
Kermit

Wise
Decatur

Wood
Quitman

Yoakum
Plains

Young
Graham

Zapata
Zapata

Zavala
Crystal City

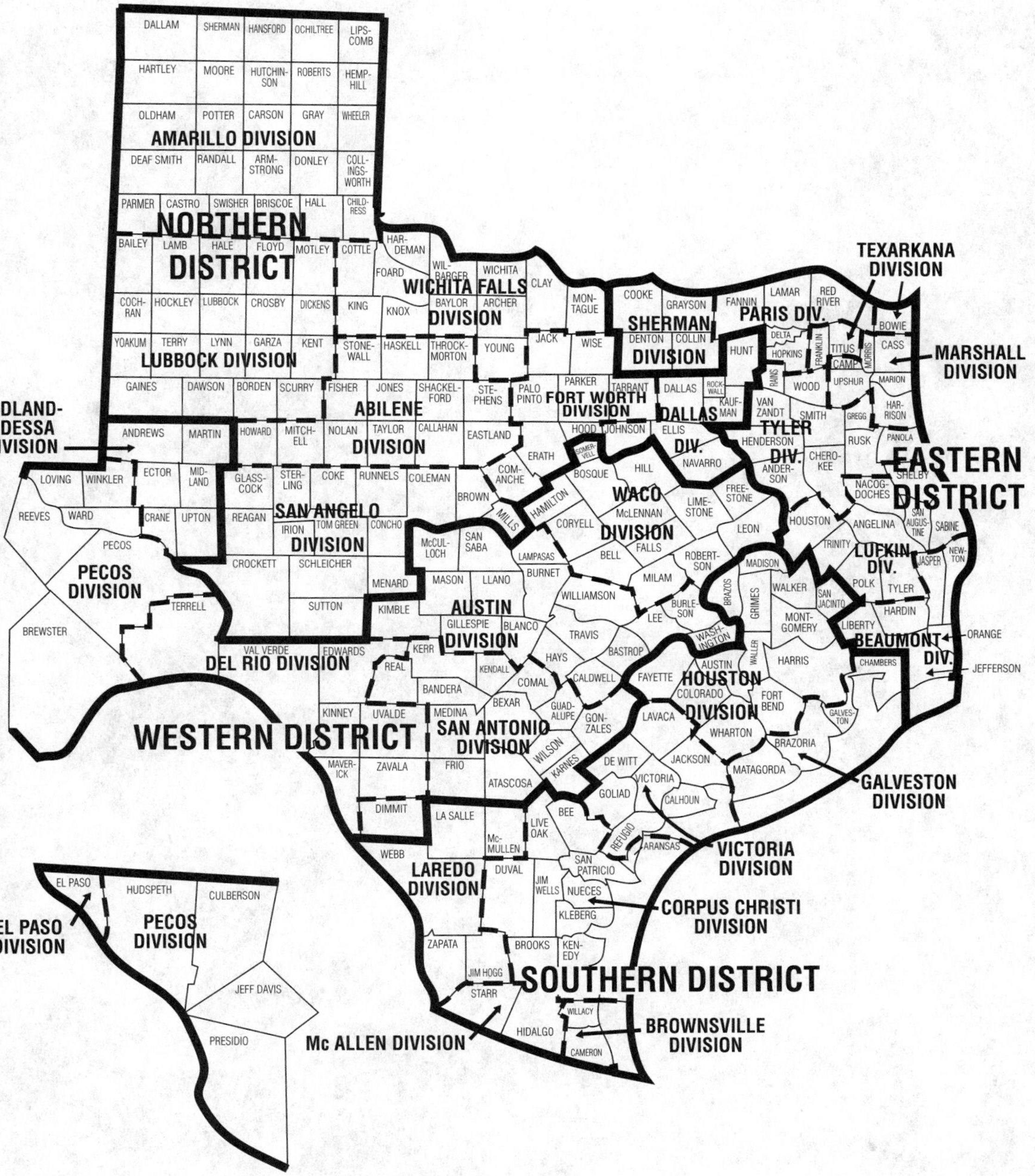

NORTHERN DISTRICT
AMARILLO DIVISION
LUBBOCK DIVISION
WICHITA FALLS DIVISION
ABILENE DIVISION
SAN ANGELO DIVISION
FORT WORTH DIVISION
DALLAS DIV.
TEXARKANA DIVISION
SHERMAN DIVISION
PARIS DIV.
MARSHALL DIVISION
TYLER DIV.
EASTERN DISTRICT
LUFKIN DIV.
BEAUMONT DIV.
MIDLAND-ODESSA DIVISION
PECOS DIVISION
WACO DIVISION
AUSTIN DIVISION
DEL RIO DIVISION
WESTERN DISTRICT
SAN ANTONIO DIVISION
HOUSTON DIVISION
GALVESTON DIVISION
VICTORIA DIVISION
CORPUS CHRISTI DIVISION
LAREDO DIVISION
SOUTHERN DISTRICT
BROWNSVILLE DIVISION
Mc ALLEN DIVISION
EL PASO DIVISION
PECOS DIVISION
DALLAM
SHERMAN
HANSFORD
OCHILTREE
LIPS-COMB
HARTLEY
MOORE
HUTCHIN-SON
ROBERTS
HEMP-HILL
OLDHAM
POTTER
CARSON
GRAY
WHEELER
DEAF SMITH
RANDALL
ARM-STRONG
DONLEY
COLL-INGS-WORTH
PARMER
CASTRO
SWISHER
BRISCOE
HALL
CHILD-RESS
BAILEY
LAMB
HALE
FLOYD
MOTLEY
COTTLE
HAR-DEMAN
FOARD
WIL-BARGER
WICHITA
CLAY
MON-TAGUE
COOKE
GRAYSON
FANNIN
LAMAR
RED RIVER
BOWIE
COCH-RAN
HOCKLEY
LUBBOCK
CROSBY
DICKENS
KING
KNOX
BAYLOR
ARCHER
YOAKUM
TERRY
LYNN
GARZA
KENT
STONE-WALL
HASKELL
THROCK-MORTON
YOUNG
JACK
WISE
DENTON
COLLIN
HUNT
DELTA
HOPKINS
FRANKLIN
TITUS
MORRIS
CASS
CAMP
RAINS
WOOD
UPSHUR
MARION
GAINES
DAWSON
BORDEN
SCURRY
FISHER
JONES
SHACKEL-FORD
STE-PHENS
PALO PINTO
PARKER
TARRANT
DALLAS
ROCK-WALL
KAUF-MAN
VAN ZANDT
SMITH
GREGG
HAR-RISON
PANOLA
ANDREWS
MARTIN
HOWARD
MITCH-ELL
NOLAN
TAYLOR
CALLAHAN
EASTLAND
HOOD
JOHNSON
ELLIS
HENDERSON
RUSK
ERATH
SOMER-VELL
NAVARRO
ANDER-SON
CHERO-KEE
SHELBY
LOVING
WINKLER
ECTOR
MID-LAND
GLASS-COCK
STER-LING
COKE
RUNNELS
COLEMAN
COM-ANCHE
BOSQUE
HILL
FREE-STONE
NACOG-DOCHES
REEVES
WARD
CRANE
UPTON
REAGAN
IRION
TOM GREEN
CONCHO
BROWN
MILLS
HAMILTON
McLENNAN
LIME-STONE
HOUSTON
SAN AUGUS-TINE
SABINE
PECOS
CORYELL
FALLS
LEON
ANGELINA
TRINITY
NEW-TON
JASPER
McCUL-LOCH
SAN SABA
LAMPASAS
BELL
ROBERT-SON
MADISON
CROCKETT
SCHLEICHER
BURNET
MILAM
BRAZOS
GRIMES
WALKER
SAN JACINTO
POLK
TYLER
MASON
LLANO
MENARD
WILLIAMSON
BURLE-SON
LEE
MONT-GOMERY
HARDIN
KIMBLE
SUTTON
TERRELL
BREWSTER
GILLESPIE
BLANCO
TRAVIS
WASH-INGTON
WALLER
LIBERTY
ORANGE
VAL VERDE
EDWARDS
KERR
HAYS
BASTROP
AUSTIN
HARRIS
CHAMBERS
JEFFERSON
REAL
KENDALL
COMAL
CALDWELL
FAYETTE
COLORADO
FORT BEND
BANDERA
BEXAR
GUAD-ALUPE
GON-ZALES
LAVACA
WHARTON
GALVES-TON
KINNEY
UVALDE
MEDINA
WILSON
BRAZORIA
KARNES
DE WITT
JACKSON
MAVER-ICK
ZAVALA
FRIO
ATASCOSA
VICTORIA
MATAGORDA
GOLIAD
CALHOUN
DIMMIT
LA SALLE
BEE
LIVE OAK
REFUGIO
ARANSAS
WEBB
Mc-MULLEN
SAN PATRICIO
DUVAL
JIM WELLS
NUECES
KLEBERG
ZAPATA
BROOKS
KEN-EDY
JIM HOGG
STARR
WILLACY
HIDALGO
CAMERON
EL PASO
HUDSPETH
CULBERSON
JEFF DAVIS
PRESIDIO

UNITED STATES DISTRICT COURTS
DISTRICTS OF TEXAS

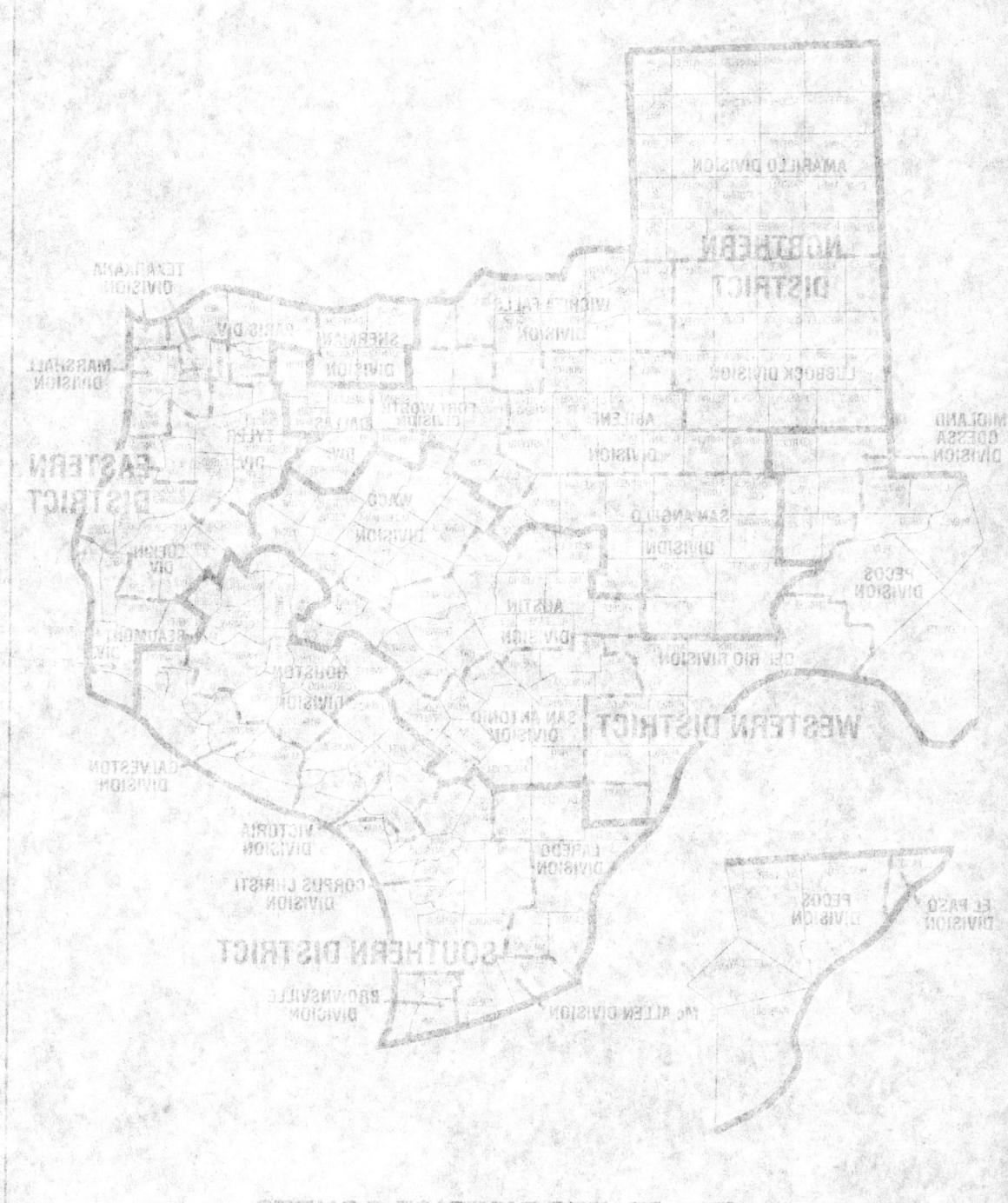

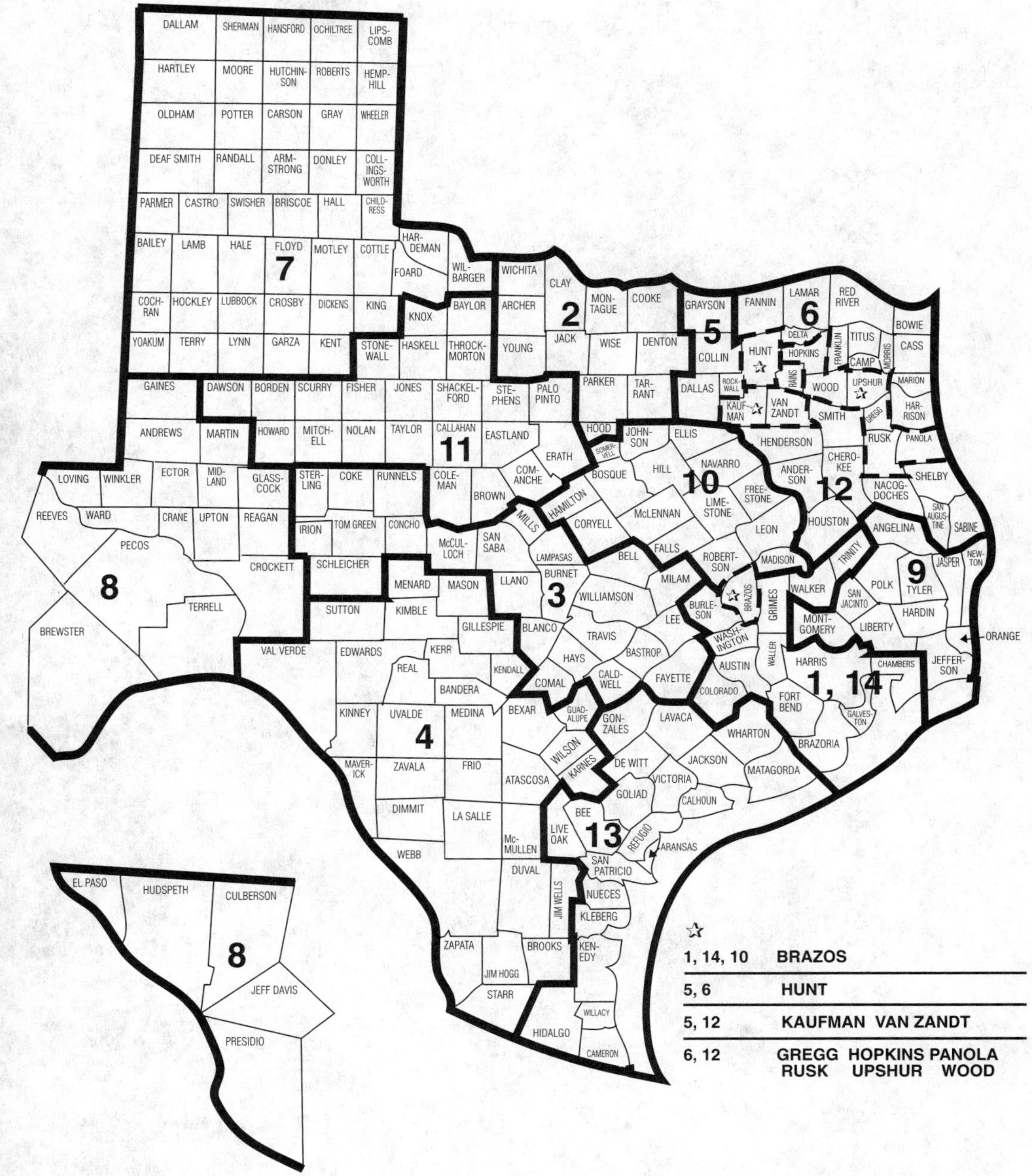
DALLAM
SHERMAN
HANSFORD
OCHILTREE
LIPS-COMB
HARTLEY
MOORE
HUTCHIN-SON
ROBERTS
HEMP-HILL
OLDHAM
POTTER
CARSON
GRAY
WHEELER
DEAF SMITH
RANDALL
ARM-STRONG
DONLEY
COLL-INGS-WORTH
PARMER
CASTRO
SWISHER
BRISCOE
HALL
CHILD-RESS
BAILEY
LAMB
HALE
FLOYD
MOTLEY
COTTLE
HAR-DEMAN
7
FOARD
WIL-BARGER
COCH-RAN
HOCKLEY
LUBBOCK
CROSBY
DICKENS
KING
KNOX
BAYLOR
YOAKUM
TERRY
LYNN
GARZA
KENT
STONE-WALL
HASKELL
THROCK-MORTON
WICHITA
CLAY
ARCHER
YOUNG
JACK
MON-TAGUE
COOKE
2
WISE
DENTON
GRAYSON
5
COLLIN
FANNIN
LAMAR
6
RED RIVER
BOWIE
DELTA
HUNT
HOPKINS
FRANKLIN
TITUS
MORRIS
CASS
CAMP
RAINS
WOOD
UPSHUR
MARION
HAR-RISON
GAINES
DAWSON
BORDEN
SCURRY
FISHER
JONES
SHACKEL-FORD
STE-PHENS
PALO PINTO
PARKER
TAR-RANT
DALLAS
ROCK-WALL
KAUF-MAN
VAN ZANDT
SMITH
GREGG
ANDREWS
MARTIN
HOWARD
MITCH-ELL
NOLAN
TAYLOR
CALLAHAN
11
EASTLAND
HOOD
JOHN-SON
ELLIS
HENDERSON
CHERO-KEE
RUSK
PANOLA
LOVING
WINKLER
ECTOR
MID-LAND
GLASS-COCK
STER-LING
COKE
RUNNELS
COLE-MAN
COM-ANCHE
ERATH
SOMER-VELL
BOSQUE
HILL
NAVARRO
10
ANDER-SON
12
SHELBY
NACOG-DOCHES
REEVES
WARD
CRANE
UPTON
REAGAN
BROWN
HAMILTON
MILLS
CORYELL
McLENNAN
LIME-STONE
FREE-STONE
HOUSTON
SAN AUGUS-TINE
SABINE
PECOS
IRION
TOM GREEN
CONCHO
McCUL-LOCH
SAN SABA
LEON
ANGELINA
CROCKETT
SCHLEICHER
LAMPASAS
BELL
FALLS
ROBERT-SON
MADISON
TRINITY
JASPER
NEW-TON
8
BURNET
MILAM
9
TYLER
MENARD
MASON
LLANO
3
WILLIAMSON
BRAZOS
GRIMES
WALKER
POLK
SAN JACINTO
TERRELL
SUTTON
KIMBLE
BURLE-SON
LEE
HARDIN
BREWSTER
GILLESPIE
BLANCO
MONT-GOMERY
LIBERTY
VAL VERDE
EDWARDS
KERR
TRAVIS
WASH-INGTON
ORANGE
HAYS
BASTROP
AUSTIN
WALLER
HARRIS
CHAMBERS
JEFFER-SON
REAL
KENDALL
CALD-WELL
FAYETTE
1, 14
COMAL
BANDERA
COLORADO
FORT BEND
GALVES-TON
KINNEY
UVALDE
MEDINA
BEXAR
GUAD-ALUPE
GON-ZALES
LAVACA
4
WHARTON
BRAZORIA
MAVER-ICK
ZAVALA
FRIO
WILSON
KARNES
DE WITT
JACKSON
MATAGORDA
ATASCOSA
VICTORIA
GOLIAD
CALHOUN
DIMMIT
LA SALLE
BEE
LIVE OAK
13
REFUGIO
ARANSAS
Mc-MULLEN
WEBB
SAN PATRICIO
DUVAL
NUECES
JIM WELLS
KLEBERG
EL PASO
HUDSPETH
CULBERSON
8
JEFF DAVIS
PRESIDIO
ZAPATA
BROOKS
KEN-EDY
JIM HOGG
STARR
WILLACY
HIDALGO
CAMERON
☆
1, 14, 10 BRAZOS
5, 6 HUNT
5, 12 KAUFMAN VAN ZANDT
6, 12 GREGG HOPKINS PANOLA RUSK UPSHUR WOOD

DISTRICTS OF TEXAS COURTS OF APPEALS

TEXAS

ABASCAL, Amado, III *(Judge, Texas District Court 365th Judicial District)*
Office: 500 Quarry Street, Box 6, Eagle Pass, 78852.
Telephone: (830) 773-1151.

ABLES, Stephen B. *(Judge, Texas District Court 216th Judicial District)* Elected to term beginning Jan 1, 1989. Reelected 1992, 1996 and 2000. Current term expires Dec 31, 2004. Presiding Judge Sixth Judicial Region since 1995. Born Dallas Texas Sept 29, 1948. Methodist. Educated at U.S. Military Academy 1967-68 and Baylor University J.D. 1973. Member Pi Alpha Delta. Admitted to practice Texas 1973. In legal practice Kerrville 1973-88.
Office: Kerr County Courthouse, Kerrville 78028-5386.
Telephone: (830) 792-2290.

ABRAMSON, Harold C. *(Recalled Judge, United States Bankruptcy Court Northern District of Texas)* Appointed Judge by U.S. Court of Appeals Fifth Circuit judges to term beginning Sept 20, 1985. Retired Sept 19, 1999. Appointed Recalled Judge by the Judicial Council of the Fifth Circuit. Born Ardmore Oklahoma Aug 18, 1928. Jewish. Member Phi Delta Phi. Admitted to practice Texas 1949, U.S. District Court Northern District of Texas and U.S. Court of Appeals Fifth Circuit. In legal practice Dallas 1949-85.
Fellow Texas Bar Foundation. Member National Conference of Bankruptcy Judges and State Bar of Texas. Personal Statement or Quote: "Be prepared."
Office: 1100 Commerce Street, Dallas 75242.
Telephone: (214) 753-2110.
Fax: (214) 753-2016

ADAMS, Chad *(Judge, Ellis County Court)* Elected to term beginning Jan 1, 2003. Educated at University of Texas at Arlington. Former Justice of the Peace, Precinct Four Ellis County.
Office: 101 West Main Street, Waxahachie 75165.
Telephone: (972) 825-5011.
Fax: (972) 825-5012
E-mail address: chad.adams@co.ellis.tx.us

ADAMS, Gordon G. *(Judge, Texas District Court 169th Judicial District)*
Mailing address: P.O. Box 747, Belton 76513-0747.
Telephone: (254) 933-5265.

ADAMS, William *(Judge, Aransas County Court at Law)* Former Judge, Aransas County Court.
Office: 301 North Live Oak, Rockport 78382-2798.
Telephone: (361) 790-0138.

AGAN, Jerry *(Judge, Presidio County Court)*
Mailing address: P.O. Box 606, Marfa 79843-0606.
Telephone: (432) 729-4452.

AGUILAR, Luis *(Judge, Texas District Court 120th Judicial District)*
Office: 500 East San Antonio Avenue, #605, El Paso 79901-2457.
Telephone: (915) 546-2103.

ALCALA, Elsa *(Justice, Texas Court of Appeals First District)* Born Kingsville Texas Feb 15, 1964. Catholic. Educated at Texas Arts & Industries University B.A. 1986 and University of Texas J.D. 1989. Recipient Order of Barristers Award 1989. Admitted to practice Texas 1989. Former Judge, Texas District Court 338th Judicial District, appointed by Governor George W. Bush to term beginning Jan 1999.
Assistant District Attorney Harris County District Attorney's Office 1989-1998. Member National Association of Women Judges, Hispanic Bar Association, State Bar of Texas, Houston and Mexican-American Bar Associations. Member Republican National Hispanic Association and Daughters of Liberty. Enjoys walking and hiking.
Office: 1307 San Jacinto, Tenth Floor, Houston 77002-7006.
Telephone: (713) 655-2700.

ALEJANDRO, Leonel *(Judge, Texas District Court 357th Judicial District)*
Office: 974 East Harrison, Brownsville 78520-7123.
Telephone: (956) 578-9522.

ALLEN, George Harrison *(Judge, Texas District Court 54th Judicial District)* Term expires Dec 31, 2006. Born Waco Texas April 16, 1937. Baptist. Educated at Texas A&M University B.S. 1960 and Baylor University J.D. 1962. Admitted to practice Texas 1963. Former Judge, McLennan County Court at Law, elected to term beginning Jan 3, 1969.
Assistant District Attorney Waco 1963. Instructor in Criminal Law and Procedures McLennan Community College 1973. Member McLennan County Bar Association and State Bar of Texas. Democrat. Member Board of Directors Waco Girls Club (Chairman 1976), Lake Air Pee Wee Football League (President 1976) and Friends of Moody Texas Ranger Memorial Library Board. Enjoys fishing and hunting.
Office: 501 Washington Avenue, Waco 76701-1380.
Telephone: (254) 757-5051.

ALLRED, Don R. *(Judge, Oldham County Court)* Elected to term beginning Jan 1, 1991. Reelected 1994, 1998 and 2002. Current term expires Dec 31, 2006. Born Amarillo Texas Nov 1, 1949. Methodist. Educated at West Texas State University.
Member Texas Association of County Judges. Previously employed with U.S. Department of Agriculture 1975-89. Democrat. Board member Vega Independent School District 1986-90 and Panhandle Regional Planning Commission since 1990. Chairman Administrative Board of Vega United Methodist Church and Oldham County Summer Youth League. Member Vega Kiwanis Club (Past President). Enjoys golf, fishing and working with youth in the community.
Mailing address: P.O. Box 195, Vega 79092-0195.
Telephone: (806) 267-2607.

ALONSO, Alfonso E., Jr. *(Judge, Bexar County Court at Law No. 1)* Appointed to term beginning March 12, 1998. Elected Nov 1998 and 2002. Current term expires Dec 31, 2006. Born Brownsville Texas Aug 6, 1938. Religious affiliation: Christian Scientist.

ALONSO, ALFONSO E., JR.—*Continued*

Educated at Trinity University B.S. 1961, St. Mary's University of San Antonio School of Law J.D. 1968 and Sam Houston State University 1981. Admitted to practice Texas 1967 and U.S. District Court Western District of Texas 1973. In legal practice San Antonio 1969-98. Justice of the Peace, Bexar County Precinct One Place Two 1995-98.

Staff Attorney Bexar County Legal Aid 1967-69. Advisory Attorney Mexican Consulate 1987-97. Member South Texas Justice of the Peace and Constable Association (Judge Advocate 1994-97), Texas Justice of the Peace and Constable Association, State Bar of Texas, Hispanic Bar Association, San Antonio, San Antonio Mexican American and Texas Mexican American Bar Associations. Recipient Child Welfare Board Award from Bexar County and Mentor and Allies Award from YMCA of San Antonio. Democrat. Board Member Ex-Offender Placement Services 1978-80, Bexar County Child Welfare 1990-92, South Town Main Street Alliance 1990-94 and General Child Support Advisory Council Office of the Attorney General 1992-94. Chairman Boy's Incorporated 1978-82 and Bexar County Volunteers in Parole 1980-82. Member Presa Community Center 1985-93. Volunteer Ford Salute to Education and Senior Citizens Council since 1990. Texas State Chairman 1991-94 and Board Member State Institutional Committee Church of Christ Scientist. Sponsor Tafolla Middle School Mentorship Program 1993-96. Executive Board Member Loving Dozen since 1996. Member Sembradores de Amistad and San Antonio Hispanic Chamber of Commerce. Enjoys tennis and chess. First judge to hold court in Texas school program. Enjoys tennis and chess.

Office: 1097 Bexar County Justice Center, 300 Dolorosa Street, San Antonio 78205-3011.
Telephone: (210) 335-2571.
E-mail address: aalonso@Txdirect.net

ALVAREZ, Javier *(Judge, El Paso County Court at Law No. 3)* Appointed to term beginning Oct 19, 1994. Elected April 1994, 1998 and 2002. Current term expires Dec 31, 2006. Born El Paso Texas Jan 1, 1950. Catholic. Educated at University of Texas at El Paso B.A. 1973 and Texas Tech University School of Law J.D. 1979. Admitted to practice Texas 1980 and U.S. District Courts Northern and Southern Districts of Texas. In legal practice Lubbock 1980-91 and El Paso since 1991. Enjoys hunting and fishing.

Office: 500 East San Antonio, Room 1001, El Paso 79901.
Telephone: (915) 546-2183.

ALVAREZ, Jesus Maria *(Judge, Starr County Court at Law)*
Office: 501 North Britton Avenue, Rio Grande City 78582.
Telephone: (956) 487-4871.

ALVAREZ, Manny D. *(Judge, Texas Criminal District Court No. 5 Dallas County)*
Office: LB 42 Frank Crowley Courts Building, 133 North Industrial Boulevard, Dallas 75207-4313.
Telephone: (214) 653-5942.

AMMERMAN, James Harry, II *(Judge, Harrison County Court at Law)*
Office: 263 Harrison County Courthouse, Marshall 75670.
Telephone: (903) 935-4838.

AMOS, Edgar Allen *(Judge, Concho County Court)*
Mailing address: P.O. Box 158, Paint Rock 76866-0158.
Telephone: (325) 732-4321.

ANCHONDO, Robert *(Judge, El Paso County Criminal Court at Law No. 2)*
Office: 500 East San Antonio, El Paso 79907.
Telephone: (915) 834-8232.

ANDERSON, David L. *(Judge, Panola County Court)*
Office: 110 South Sycamore Street, Room 216-A, Carthage 75633.
Telephone: (903) 693-0391.

ANDERSON, James E. *(Judge, Harris County Criminal Court at Law No. 4)* Elected to term beginning Jan 1, 1987. Reelected 1990, 1994, 1998 and 2002. Current term expires Dec 31, 2006.
Office: 1201 Franklin, Room 8136, Houston 77002.
Telephone: (713) 755-6192.

ANDERSON, James W. *(Judge, Randall County Court at Law)*
Office: 501 Sixteenth Street, Canyon 79015-3850.
Telephone: (806) 468-5551.

ANDERSON, John S. *(Justice, Texas Court of Appeals Fourteenth District)* Term expires Dec 31, 2006. Born Texas Aug 2, 1946. Educated at Washington & Lee University B.A. 1968 and University of Texas J.D. 1971. Admitted to practice Texas 1972 and District of Columbia 1974.

Board of Directors 1982-84 and Treasurer 1984-85 Houston Bar Association. Fellow Texas Bar Foundation. Member College of the State Bar of Texas.

Office: 1307 San Jacinto, 11th Floor, Houston 77002-7006.
Telephone: (713) 655-2800.

ANDERSON, Keith Alexander *(Judge, Dallas County Criminal Court at Law No. 9)*
Office: LB 23 Frank Crowley Courts Bldg., 133 North Industrial Boulevard, Dallas 75207-4313.
Telephone: (214) 653-5687.

ANDERSON, Ken *(Judge, Texas District Court 277th Judicial District)*
Office: 405 South Martin Luther King Blvd., Box 6, Georgetown 78626-0405.
Telephone: (512) 943-1277.

ANDERSON, Mike *(Judge, Texas District Court 262nd Judicial District)*
Office: 1201 Franklin, Room 15144, Houston 77002.
Telephone: (713) 755-6961.

ANDERSON, William Roy, Jr. *(Judge, Johnson County Court at Law No. 2)*
Office: Two North Main Street, Cleburne 76031-5584.
Telephone: (817) 556-6395.

ANGELINI, Karen *(Justice, Texas Court of Appeals Fourth District)* Appointed by Governor George W. Bush to term beginning Jan 2, 1997. Elected Nov 1998

ANGELINI, KAREN—*Continued*

and 2000. Current term expires Dec 31, 2006. Born Austin Texas March 3, 1951. Methodist. Educated at University of Texas at Austin B.A. with honors 1972 and St. Mary's University School of Law J.D. 1979. Associate Editor St. Mary's University Law Review. Law Clerk to Hon. Fred Klingeman, Texas Court of Civil Appeals Fourth Supreme Judicial District 1980-81. Admitted to practice Texas 1980 and U.S. District Courts Southern and Western Districts of Texas. In legal practice San Antonio 1981-91.

Law Clerk to Hon. Edward C. Prado, U.S. District Court Western District of Texas 1991-92 and Hon. Robert B. O'Connor, U.S. District Court Western District of Texas 1993-96. Former Member San Antonio Young Lawyers Association (Former Vice President) and Federal Bar Association (Former Chairperson Admissions Committee). Member Texas Bar Foundation, State Bar of Texas, San Antonio (Director since 1995) and Bexar County Women's (Advisory Board since 1997) Bar Associations. Republican. Member Alamo City Republican Women's Club, Bexar County Republican Women's Club and Hispanic Republican Women's Club. Former Member Board of Trustees Southwestern Texas Methodist Church Conference and Advisory Board Metropolitan Methodist Hospital. Former Board Member Methodist Healthcare Ministries. Member Advisory Board Christian Assistance Ministry, San Antonio District Methodist Board of Laity and St. Mary's Law School Alumni Association.

Office: 3200 Bexar County Justice Center, 300 Dolorosa Street, San Antonio 78205-3037.
Telephone: (210) 335-2589.

ANGELINI, Raymond C. *(Judge, Texas District Court 187th Judicial District)*
Office: 2129 Bexar County Justice Center, 300 Dolorosa Street, San Antonio 78205-3028.
Telephone: (210) 335-2517.

APARICIO, Edward G. *(Judge, Texas District Court 92nd Judicial District)*
Office: 100 North Closner, Second Floor, Edinburg 78539.
Telephone: (956) 318-2250.

ARANDA, Jose A., Jr. *(Judge, Maverick County Court)* Elected to term beginning Jan 2003.
Office: 500 Quarry Street, Box 3, Eagle Pass 78852-4528.
Telephone: (830) 773-3824.
Fax: (830) 773-6450

ARCE-FLORES, Adriana *(Magistrate Judge, United States District Court Southern District of Texas)* Appointed by U.S. District Court judges to term beginning Oct 10, 2000.
Mailing address: P.O. Box 6238, Laredo 78042.
Telephone: (956) 790-1750.

ARMSTRONG, Ernie B. *(Judge, Texas District Court 132nd Judicial District)*
Office: 1806 25th Street, Suite 404, Snyder 79549.
Telephone: (325) 573-5371.

ARNOT, William G. "Bud", III *(Chief Justice, Texas Court of Appeals Eleventh District)* Former Justice. Born Austin Texas April 13, 1950. Baptist. Educated at Washington and Lee University, University of Texas B.B.A. 1972, Baylor University J.D. 1975 and University of Virginia LL.M. 1992. Admitted to practice Texas 1975 and U.S. District Courts Northern 1976 and Western 1981 Districts of Texas. In legal practice Abilene 1975-86.

Member State Bar of Texas, Abilene and Eastland Bar Associations.

Mailing address: P.O. Box 271, Eastland 76448-0271.
Telephone: (254) 629-2638.

ARTHUR, James R. *(Judge, Comanche County Court)*
Office: Comanche County Courthouse, 101 West Central, Comanche 76442-3297.
Telephone: (325) 356-2466.

ASHBY, Anne *(Judge, Texas District Court 134th Judicial District)* Appointed by Governor William P. Clements to term beginning Jan 1990. Elected Dec 1990, 1994, 1998 and 2002. Current term expires Dec 31, 2006. Born Dallas Texas Feb 17, 1953. Christian. Educated at University of Texas B.B.A. 1975 and South Texas College of Law J.D. 1979. Law Clerk to Hon. Jim Scanlan, Harris County Probate Court No. 3, 1978-79. Admitted to practice Texas 1979 and U.S. District Court Northern District of Texas. In legal practice Dallas 1986. Master/Referee, Texas District Court 304th Judicial District 1982-86. Judge, Dallas County Court at Law No. 3, 1987-89.
Office: George Allen Sr. Courts Building, Fourth Floor, 600 Commerce Street, Dallas 75202-4606.
Telephone: (214) 653-6995.

ATKINSON, Mark *(Judge, Harris County Criminal Court at Law No. 13)*
Office: 1201 Franklin, Room 11032, Houston 77002.
Telephone: (713) 755-7950.

ATLAS, Nancy F. *(Judge, United States District Court Southern District of Texas)* Appointed for life by President Bill Clinton to term beginning Aug 22, 1995. Born New York New York May 20, 1949. Educated at Tufts University B.S. magna cum laude 1971 B.S. cum laude 1971 and New York University School of Law J.D. 1974. Managing Editor Annual Survey of American Law 1973-74. Law Clerk to Hon. Dudley B. Bonsal, U.S. District Court Southern District of New York Sept 1974 to Sept 1976. Member Phi Beta Kappa. Admitted to practice New York 1975, U.S. District Courts Eastern 1975 and Southern 1975 Districts of New York and Southern 1982 and Northern 1989 Districts of Texas, U.S. Courts of Appeals Second 1975 and Fifth 1982 Circuits, U.S. Supreme Court 1980 and Texas 1982. In legal practice New York New York Nov 1976 to Dec 1978 and Houston Texas July 1982 to Aug 1995.

Assistant U.S. Attorney Civil Division Southern District of New York Feb 1979 to June 1982. Co-author "Alternative Dispute Resolution in Bankruptcy" American Bar Association Bankruptcy and Insolvency Committee Newsletter May 1994 and "The DTPA in the Courts—An Empirical Study" 21 St. Mary's L. Jour. 609, 1990, revised *Houston Lawyer* July-Aug 1990. Co-Editor *The Advocate's Handbook on ADR* American Bar Association Section of Litigation 1999. Life Fellow Houston Bar Foundation. Fellow Texas Bar Foundation and American Bar Foundation. Arbitrator Securities Arbitration American Arbitration Association 1993. Member since 1992 and Chair since 1995 Alternate Dispute Resolution Panel U.S. District Court Southern District of

ATLAS, NANCY F.—*Continued*

Texas. Member Working Group on Alternative Dispute Resolution and Law Practice since 1997 and Working Group on Ethics of Advocates in Alternative Dispute Resolution 1998-99 CPR Institute for Dispute Resolution. Member Association of Attorney-Mediators, Inc., State Bar of Texas (Co-chair Quality of Practice Committee and Task Force on Quality and Credentialing for ADR Providers 1993-95 and Council Member 1992-95 Alternative Dispute Resolution Section, Member 1991-92 and Co-chair 1992-93 Rules and Legislative Committee), Houston, Federal and American (Task Force on Judicial System Section of Litigation 1994-95, Chair Alternate Dispute Resolution Working Group and Member since 1994 Joint Task Force on Bankruptcy Procedure Section of Business Law and Section of Litigation, Co-chair Bylaws, Resolutions and Blanket Authority Committee 1998-99 and Council Member since 1998 Section of Litigation) Bar Associations. Author/Lecturer "Bankruptcy and Workouts in the Context of Litigation Involving Financially Troubled Defendants or Co-Defendants" University of Houston Law Center/American Corporate Counsel Association March 1987; "A One Way or a Round Trip Ticket?" CLE Seminar Removal and Remand Feb 14, 1997 and "Confidentiality on ADR Procedures: What Does It Mean and Is It Enforceable?" Alternative Dispute Resolution Seminar April 10, 1997 Houston Bar Association; "Practical Tips for Pretrial Litigation/Trial in Employment Cases" National Employment Lawyers Association April 8, 1998; "Types of ADR Processes: Choosing Who and What" Insurance Seminar April 30, 1998; and "Implementing the ADR Act of 1998" Workshop for District Judges Federal Judicial Center June 2-4, 1999. Lecturer "All About Federal Courts" Kiwanis Club of Houston Sept 15, 1999. Recipient Woman on the Move Award from *The Houston Post*, KPRC-TV and Texas Executive Women 1994 and Justice Frank G. Evans Award for Outstanding Service to Alternative Dispute Resolution from State Bar of Texas June 1997. Board Member Roberta Stokes Dance Company 1984-89 and Texas Appellate Resource Center 1988-93. Board Member 1985-93, Treasurer 1990 and Vice President 1991 American Jewish Committee. Advisory Board Children's Museum of Houston 1988-92. Member Texas Attorney General's Hospital Task Force Houston Region 1989. Co-chair Cattle Baron's Ball American Cancer Society 1991. Board of Advisors University of Texas Center for Public Policy Dispute Resolution 1993-95. Member since 1984 and Membership Committee 1991-92 Congregation Emanu El.

Office: 9015 U.S. Courthouse, 515 Rusk Avenue, Houston 77002.

Telephone: (713) 250-5990.

AUSTIN, Andrew W. *(Magistrate Judge, United States District Court Western District of Texas)* Appointed by U.S. District Court judges to term beginning Nov 22, 1999. Term expires Nov 21, 2007. Born Cincinnati Ohio Oct 6, 1960. Educated at University of Virginia B.A. with honors 1982, University of Texas School of Law J.D. with honors 1985 and Cambridge University, England M.Phil. 1990. Law Clerk to Hon. James R. Nowlin, U.S. District Court Western District of Texas 1986-87. Member Phi Beta Kappa. Admitted to practice Texas 1985, U.S. District Courts Eastern, Northern Southern and Western Districts of Texas and U.S. Court of Appeals Fifth Circuit. In legal practice Austin 1988-99.

Author "Faith and the Constitutional Definition of Religion" 22 Cumberland L. Rev. 1, 1991. Adjunct Professor University of Texas School of Law Spring 1987 and Spring 1989. Member State Bar of Texas and Travis County Bar Association.

Office: 200 West Eighth Street, Austin 78701.

Telephone: (512) 916-5744.

AUSTIN, Russell Parker *(Judge, Harris County Probate Court No. 1)*

Office: Family Law Center Building, Sixth Floor, 1115 Congress Street, Houston 77002.

Telephone: (713) 755-6084.

AVERITTE, Clinton E. *(Magistrate Judge, United States District Court Northern District of Texas)* Appointed by U.S. District Court judges to term beginning 1987. Born 1948. Educated at University of Texas B.S. 1971 and Southern Methodist University J.D. 1974.

Assistant Attorney General Texas 1974-77. Assistant District Attorney and Chief Business Crimes Division Lubbock County 1979-80. Assistant U.S. Attorney Northern District of Texas 1980-87. Fellow Texas Bar Foundation. Member Federal Magistrate Judges Association and Amarillo Bar Association.

Office: Federal Building, Box 13246, 205 East Fifth Avenue, Amarillo 79101.

Telephone: (806) 324-2335.

BACA, José J. *(Judge, El Paso County Court at Law No. 7)* Elected to term beginning Jan 1, 2003. Term expires Dec 31, 2006. Born Ciudad Juarez Mexico Dec 26, 1934. Roman Catholic. Educated at junior college N.M.M.I. 1956, University of Colorado B.S. 1958 and St. Mary's University of San Antonio J.D. 1972. Member Phi Alpha Delta and Delta Sigma Phi. Admitted to practice Texas 1972. Began legal practice El Paso 1973. Justice of the Peace 1979-82. Judge, Texas District Court 346th Judicial District Sept 1, 1983 to Dec 31, 2002, appointed by Governor Mark White.

Assistant County Attorney El Paso County 1973-75. Member State Bar of Texas (District 17 Chairman Character Committee) and Mexican-American Bar Association (President). Captain U.S. Army 1958-65. Democrat.

Office: 500 East San Antonio, Room 902, El Paso 79901.

Telephone: (915) 543-3877.

Fax: (915) 543-3883

BACUS, Thomas Hays *(Judge, Wichita County Court at Law No. 2)* Appointed to term beginning Jan 1, 1986. Elected 1986, 1990, 1994, 1998 and 2002. Current term expires Dec 31, 2006. Born Fort Worth Texas June 4, 1946. Southern Baptist. Educated at Texas Christian University B.A. 1968 and Texas Tech University J.D. 1973. Member Phi Alpha Delta. Admitted to practice Texas 1973, U.S. District Court Northern District of Texas 1973 and U.S. Court of Appeals Fifth Circuit 1977. In legal practice Wichita Falls 1973-78. Judge, Wichita County Court 1979-85.

President Texas County Court at Law Judges Association 1988-89. Director 1989-90 and Chairman 1989 Texas Center for the Judiciary. Member Citizens Commission on the Texas Judicial System 1992-93, Supreme Court Education Committee 1992-93, Funding Parity Task Force Texas Commission on Judicial Efficiency 1995-96, Strategic Planning Group Texas Office of

BACUS, THOMAS HAYS—*Continued*

Court Administration 1997-98 and Texas Supreme Court and Court of Criminal Appeals Committee on Court Funding 1996 and 1998. Member State Bar of Texas (Judicial Liaison to Board of Directors 1989-90, Task Force on Delivery of Legal Services to the Poor 1992-93 and Chairman 1989-90, Director 1989-91, Nominating Committee 1992-93 and Secretary-Treasurer since 1991 Judicial Section) and Wichita County Bar Association. Instructor Texas County Judges School CLE 1986 and 1987 and Texas County and District Clerks Association School 1988. Faculty Regional Judicial Conferences 1989-92 and College for New Judges 1989-92. Named Official of the Year by West Texas County Judges and Commissioners Association 1984-85. E-5 USNR 1968-74. Member Wichita County Teen Court Advisory Board 1998-99. Enjoys fishing and woodworking.

Office: 353 Wichita County Courthouse, Wichita Falls 76301-2440.

Telephone: (940) 766-8111.

BAILEY, Terry Douglas *(Judge, Panola County Court at Law)* Elected Nov 1998 to term beginning Jan 1, 1999. Reelected 2002, current term expires Dec 31, 2006. Born Logansport Louisiana. Christian. Educated at University of North Texas B.A. 1970 and South Texas College of Law J.D. 1974. Lead Articles Editor South Texas Law Journal 1973-74. Member Order of Lytae. Admitted to practice Texas 1974, U.S. District Court Eastern District of Texas 1974, U.S. Courts of Appeals Fifth 1974 and Eleventh 1978 Circuits and U.S. Supreme Court 1984. In legal practice Carthage 1974-98.

Member State Bar of Texas (District One Grievance Committee) and Panola County Bar Association. Member Masons and Order of the Eastern Star. Participates in youth activities. Enjoys hunting, fishing and golf.

Office: 205 Panola County Courthouse, Carthage 75633.

Telephone: (903) 693-0396.

E-mail address: TBailey@theNett.Com

BAKER, Caroline E. *(Judge, Texas District Court 151st Judicial District)*

Office: 604 Civil Courts Building, 301 Fannin Street, Houston 77002.

Telephone: (713) 755-6289.

BANALES, J. Manuel *(Judge, Texas District Court 105th Judicial District)* Term expires Dec 31, 2006.

Office: 901 Leopard, Suite 802, Corpus Christi 78401.

Telephone: (361) 595-8533.

BARAJAS, Richard *(Chief Justice, Texas Court of Appeals Eighth District)* Justice 1991-93. Appointed Chief Justice by Governor Ann W. Richards Jan 1, 1994. Elected 1994 and 2000. Current term expires Dec 31, 2006. First Hispanic elected to Texas Court of Appeals Eighth District. Chief Justice since Jan 1, 1994. Born El Paso Texas Aug 2, 1953. Educated at Baylor University B.A. 1974 J.D. 1977. Admitted to practice Texas 1977. Began legal practice Fort Stockton.

District Attorney 83rd Judicial District 1988-91. Important Decisions: In re Thoma 873 S.W.2d 477, Tex. Rev. Trib. 1994; Cap Rock Elec. Co-op., Inc. v. Texas Utilities Elec. Co. 874 S.W.2d 92, Tex. App.—El Paso 1994; Contico Intern., Inc. v. Alvarez 910 S.W.2d 29, Tex. App.—El Paso 1995; Escobar v. Sutherland 917 S.W.2d 399, Tex. App.—El Paso 1996; and In re J.B.K., Attorney 1996 WL 113252, Tex. App.—El Paso 1996. Chair Appellate Court Technology Committee. Member Texas Commission on Judicial Efficiency, Texas Committee on Judicial Funding and Texas Center for the Judiciary. Member National Association of Latino Elected Officials, Mexican-American Bar Association of Texas, National Hispanic Bar Association and State Bar of Texas (Judicial Ethics Committee, Committee on Victims and Witnesses). Lecturer on the proper balancing of the constitutional rights between the criminal defendant and the intended victim. Recipient Presidential Award for Victim Services from President George Bush 1992. Lieutenant Commander USN JAGC.

Office: 500 East San Antonio Avenue, Suite 1203, El Paso 79901-2421.

Telephone: (915) 546-2240.

BARDEN, Jim *(Judge, Medina County Court)*

Office: 1100 Sixteenth Street, Room 101, Hondo 78861-1846.

Telephone: (830) 741-6020.

BARINA, Harry John, Jr. *(Judge, Bell County Court at Law No. 2)*

Mailing address: P.O. Box 485, Belton 76513.

Telephone: (254) 933-5125.

BARKER, Phil *(Judge, Dallas County Criminal Court at Law No. 6)* Elected to term beginning Jan 1, 1991. Reelected 1994, 1998 and 2002. Current term expires Dec 31, 2006. Born Salem West Virginia Feb 20, 1941. Methodist. Educated at Salem International University B.S. 1964 and Southern Methodist University J.D. 1971. Admitted to practice Texas 1971, U.S. District Court Northern District of Texas 1972 and U.S. Court of Appeals Fifth Circuit 1972. In legal practice Dallas 1971-90. Judge, DeSoto Municipal Court 1977-80 and Lancaster Municipal Court 1980-85.

Instructor in Evidence and Criminal Law El Centro College 1974-76. Staff Sergeant E-6 Texas National Guard 1965-71.

Office: LB 20 Frank Crowley Courts Bldg., 133 North Industrial Boulevard, Dallas 75207-4313.

Telephone: (214) 653-5657.

Fax: (214) 653-5777

E-mail address: pbarker@dallascounty.org

BARNES, Margaret *(Judge, Denton County Court at Law No. 2)*

Office: 1450 East McKinney Street, Denton 76209-4524.

Telephone: (940) 349-2120.

BARR, Jeannine S. *(Judge, Texas District Court 182nd Judicial District)*

Office: 1201 Franklin, Room 18032, Houston 77002.

Telephone: (713) 755-6350.

BARRY, John O'Keefe *(Judge, Collin County Court at Law No. 3)*

Office: 1800 North Graves, Suite 145, McKinney 75069.

Telephone: (972) 548-3830.

BAUTISTA, Diana *(Judge, Atascosa County Court)*

Office: Circle Drive, Room 41, Jourdanton 78026.

Telephone: (830) 769-3093.

BEACOM, Richard *(Judge, Texas District Court 354th Judicial District)*
Mailing address: P.O. Box 1097, Greenville 75403-1097.
Telephone: (903) 408-4194.

BEARD, Val Clark *(Judge, Brewster County Court)*
Mailing address: P.O. Box 1630, Alpine 79831-1630.
Telephone: (432) 837-2412.

BEARDEN, Jerry M. *(Judge, Mason County Court)* Elected Nov 4, 2002 to term beginning Jan 2, 2003. Born Colorado City Texas Sept 29, 1946. Lutheran. Educated at Sam Houston State University B.S. 1968 M.S. 1976.

Republican. Member School Fair Committee and State Livestock Show Committee. Enjoys hunting, farming and ranching. Personal Statement or Quote: "Keep it short and to the point!"
Mailing address: P.O. Box 1726, Mason 76856.
Telephone: (325) 347-5556.
Fax: (325) 347-6868
E-mail address: masonjdg@tstar.net

BECK, Dan R. *(Judge, Texas District Court 155th Judicial District)* Former Judge, Fayette County Court.
Office: County Courthouse, La Grange 78945-2657.
Telephone: (979) 968-8500.

BEDNAR, Wilburn E. *(Judge, Glasscock County Court)* Elected to term beginning Jan 1, 1987. Reelected 1990, 1994, 1998 and 2002. Current term expires Dec 31, 2006. Born Tom Green County Texas Nov 22, 1934. Church of Christ. Educated at Texas Tech University. U.S. Army 1957-59. Member local school board and various local committees.
Mailing address: P.O. Box 67, Garden City 79739-0067.
Telephone: (915) 354-2382.

BELL, Bill *(Judge, Rockwall County Court)*
Office: 1101 Ridge Road, Suite 206, Rockwall 75087.
Telephone: (972) 882-0240.

BELL, Charles Byron *(Judge, Foard County Court)* Assumed office March 1978. Elected to subsequent terms.
Mailing address: P.O. Box 660, Crowell 79227-0660.
Telephone: (940) 684-1424.

BENNETT, Marshal Jay *(Judge, Fisher County Court)* Elected to term beginning Jan 1, 1979. Reelected to subsequent terms.
Mailing address: P.O. Box 306, Roby 79543-0306.
Telephone: (325) 776-2151.

BENTLEY, Bascom W., III *(Judge, Texas District Court 369th Judicial District)* Appointed by Governor William P. Clements to term beginning Sept 1, 1989. Elected 1990, 1994, 1998 and 2002. Current term expires Dec 31, 2006. Born Fairfield Texas March 27, 1951. Religious affiliation: Disciples of Christ. Educated at University of Texas at Austin B.B.A. 1974 and University of Houston J.D. 1976. Admitted to practice Texas 1977 and U.S. District Court Eastern District of Texas. Judge, Anderson County Court at Law 1982-89.

City Attorney Palestine 1977-80. County Attorney Anderson County 1980-81. Instructor Trinity Valley Community College. Member State Bar of Texas and Anderson County Bar Association. Member United Way and Salvation Army. Enjoys hunting.
Mailing address: P.O. Box 221, Palestine 75802-0221.
Telephone: (903) 723-7415.

BENTON, Levi James *(Judge, Texas District Court 215th Judicial District)*
Office: 301 Fannin, Sixth Floor, Houston 77002.
Telephone: (713) 755-6382.

BERCHELMANN, David A., Jr. *(Judge, Texas District Court 37th Judicial District)* Born San Antonio Texas July 14, 1947. Educated at St. Mary's University of San Antonio B.A. 1970 J.D. 1973. Admitted to practice Texas 1973, U.S. District Court Western District of Texas, U.S. Court of Appeals Fifth Circuit and U.S. Supreme Court. In legal practice 1980-81. Judge, Texas District Court 290th Judicial District Oct 1981 to Dec 1988, appointed by Governor William P. Clements. Former Judge, Texas Court of Criminal Appeals, appointed to term beginning Jan 1, 1989.

Assistant District Attorney and Lead Felony Prosecutor Bexar County 1973-80. Former Member San Antonio Young Lawyers Association. President Catholic Lawyers Guild. Member Texas District and County Attorneys Association, State Bar of Texas (Judicial Section) and San Antonio Bar Association. Named one of Outstanding Young Men of America by Jaycees 1982. Honored by Mayor Henry Cisneros for instituting first community service program in San Antonio with the week of Aug 18, 1983 proclaimed Community Service Restitution Week. Board of Directors Alamo Kiwanis.
Office: 209 Bexar County Courthouse, 100 Dolorosa Street, San Antonio 78205-3028.
Telephone: (210) 335-2515.

BERRY, Elizabeth *(Judge, Texas Criminal District Court No. 3 Tarrant County)*
Office: Tarrant County Justice Center, 401 West Belknap, Fort Worth 76196-0215.
Telephone: (817) 884-1356.

BERRY, Joe R. *(Judge, Angelina County Court)*
Mailing address: P.O. Box 908, Lufkin 75902-0908.
Telephone: (936) 634-5413.

BIELSTEIN, R. H. "Sandy" *(Judge, Fort Bend County Court at Law No. 4)* Elected Nov 2000. Reelected 2002, current term expires Jan 1, 2007. Born Houston Texas March 30, 1945. Educated at University of Houston B.A. 1977 and South Texas College of Law J.D. with honors 1989. Admitted to practice Texas 1989, U.S. District Court Southern District of Texas 1990 and U.S. Court of Appeals Fifth Circuit 1993. In legal practice Richmond Nov 1989 to Dec 2000.
Office: 301 Jackson, Room 101, Richmond 77469-3108.
Telephone: (281) 341-4501.
Fax: (281) 238-3377

BIERY, Fred *(Judge, United States District Court Western District of Texas)* Appointed for life by President Bill Clinton March 11, 1994. Born McAllen Texas Nov 11, 1947. Methodist. Educated at Texas Lutheran College B.A. 1970 and Southern Methodist University J.D. 1973. Hatton Sumners Scholar. Member Order of the Coif. Admitted to practice Texas 1973. Began legal practice San Antonio 1973. Judge, Bexar County Court at Law No. 2, 1979-82. Judge, Texas District Court

BIERY, FRED—*Continued*

150th Judicial District 1983-88. Justice, Texas Court of Appeals Fourth District Jan 1, 1989 to 1994.

Member State Bar of Texas, San Antonio (President 1987-88) and American Bar Associations. Board of Regents Texas Lutheran College since 1971. E-4 USAR 1970-76. Democrat.

Office: U.S. Courthouse, 655 East Durango Boulevard, San Antonio 78206-1198.

Telephone: (210) 472-6505.

BILSKI, Carolyn Cerny *(Judge, Austin County Court)*

Office: One East Main, Bellville 77418-1598.

Telephone: (979) 865-5911.

BIRD, David *(Judge, Gonzales County Court)* Elected Nov 3, 1998 to term beginning Jan 1, 1999. Reelected 2002, current term expires Dec 31, 2006. Born Camp Roberts California Oct 3, 1953. Methodist. Educated at Texas A&M University B.S. 1976 and Southwest Texas State University M.S. 2000.

Democrat. Member Lions Club and Gonzales Economic Development Oversight Committee. Enjoys polo, music and his children's sports.

Mailing address: P.O. Box 80, Gonzales 78629-0080.

Telephone: (830) 672-2327.

BISCOE, Sam *(Judge, Travis County Court)*

Mailing address: P.O. Box 1748, Austin 78767-1748.

Telephone: (512) 854-9555.

BLACK, Horace Dickson, Jr. *(Judge, Texas District Court 77th Judicial District)* Term expires Dec 31, 2004. Former Judge, Freestone County Court.

Mailing address: P.O. Box 230, Groesbeck 76642.

Telephone: (254) 729-3206.

BLACK, John William *(Magistrate Judge, United States District Court Southern District of Texas)* Appointed by U.S. District Court judges.

Office: 204 Federal Building, 600 East Harrison Street, Brownsville 78520.

Telephone: (956) 548-2570.

BLACKSTOCK, James A. *(Judge, Brazoria County Court at Law No. 3)*

Office: 111 East Locust Street, Room 404, Angleton 77515-4678.

Telephone: (979) 864-1603.

BLAIR, Roy *(Judge, Coke County Court)*

Mailing address: P.O. Box 52, Robert Lee 76945.

Telephone: (325) 453-2641.

BLAND, Jane Nenninger *(Judge, Texas District Court 281st Judicial District)* Appointed by Governor George W. Bush to term beginning Dec 5, 1997. Elected Nov 1998 and Nov 2002. Current term expires Dec 31, 2006. Born St. Louis Missouri June 1, 1965. Roman Catholic. Educated at University of Texas at Austin B.B.A. with highest honors 1987 J.D. with high honors 1990. Associate Editor Texas Law Review 1988-90. Law Clerk to Hon. Thomas Gibbs Gee, U.S. Court of Appeals Fifth Circuit 1990-91. Member Chancellors and Order of the Coif. Admitted to practice Texas 1990, U.S. District Court Southern District of Texas, U.S. Courts of Appeals Fifth and Federal Circuits and U.S. Supreme Court. Board Certified—Civil Trial Law and Civil Appellate Law—Texas Board of Legal Specialization. In legal practice Houston 1990-97.

Member American Judicature Society, College of the State Bar of Texas, State Bar of Texas, Houston and Fifth Circuit Bar Associations.

Office: 212A Civil Courts Building, 301 Fannin Street, Houston 77002.

Telephone: (713) 755-5506.

BLEIL, Charles *(Magistrate Judge, United States District Court Northern District of Texas)* Appointed by U.S. District Court judges to term beginning 1996. Born 1942. Educated at Texas Tech University B.B.A. 1966, University of Texas School of Law J.D. 1966 and University of Virginia LL.M. 1990. In legal practice Texarkana 1971-78. Judge, Texas District Court Fifth Judicial District Oct 6, 1978 to 1981. Justice, Texas Court of Appeals Sixth District 1981-96.

Life Fellow Texas Bar Foundation. Member State Bar of Texas and Tarrant County Bar Association.

Office: 520 U.S. Courthouse, 501 West Tenth Street, Fort Worth 76102-3643.

Telephone: (817) 850-6670.

BLOCK, Gary Michael *(Judge, Harris County Civil Court at Law No. 2)*

Office: 301 Civil Courts Building, 301 Fannin Street, Houston 77002.

Telephone: (713) 755-5785.

BLOCKER, Charles T. "Corky" *(Judge, Martin County Court)* Elected Nov 3, 1998 to term beginning Jan 1, 1999. Reelected Nov 5, 2002, current term expires Dec 31, 2006. Born Midland Texas Sept 5, 1937. Religious affiliation: Church of Christ. Educated at Texas Tech University B.S. 1963. Specialist 5 U.S. Army 1960-62.

Mailing address: P.O. Box 1330, Stanton 79782.

Office: 301 North St. Peter, Stanton 79782.

Telephone: (915) 756-2231.

Fax: (915) 756-2992

BOARD, John B. *(Judge, Texas District Court 181st Judicial District)*

Office: 501 South Fillmore Street, Suite 3-B, Amarillo 79101-2444.

Telephone: (806) 379-2360.

BOBBITT, Joe A. *(Judge, Hunt County Court)*

Mailing address: P.O. Box 1097, Greenville 75403-1097.

Telephone: (903) 408-4146.

BOBO, J. A. "Jim" *(Judge, Ector County Court at Law)* Elected Nov 8, 1990 to term beginning Jan 1, 1991. Reelected Nov 8, 1994, 1998 and 2002. Current term expires Dec 31, 2006. Administrative Judge and Juvenile Judge since 1991. Born Ohio Aug 19, 1945. Lutheran. Educated at Tarleton State University B.A. 1967 and Texas Tech University J.D. 1970. Admitted to practice Texas 1970. In legal practice 1973-89. Magistrate, U.S. District Court Western District of Texas 1976-78.

Assistant Attorney District Attorney's Office 1970-72 and County Attorney's Office 1973 Ector County. President Texas Association for Board Certified Specialist Criminal Law 1986-87. Former Member Texas Criminal Defense Lawyers Association (President 1989-90). Member State Bar of Texas. Attended National Prosecutor's College 1972 and Advanced Criminal Law Seminar

BOBO, J. A. "JIM"—*Continued*

1978-89. Recipient Hutton Humanitarian Award (for contribution to assistance of abused children and prevention of child abuse) 1995 and Everett Berry Service Award (for dedicated service to the citizens of Ector County) 1996. Named Outstanding Young Man of Odessa 1975 and Most Outstanding Judge of the Year by CASA 1994. Republican. Member Republican Men of Ector County. President Odessa Jaycees 1975-76. Board Member Big Brothers/Big Sisters and Dy-Fy-It. Board of Directors YMCA. Member Leadership Odessa 1988-89 and Mayor's Drug Task Force.

Office: 300 North Grant, Room 234, Odessa 79761.
Telephone: (432) 498-4110.

BOONE, Billy W. *(Magistrate Judge, United States District Court Northern District of Texas)* Appointed by U.S. District Court judges to term beginning 1987. Serves part time. Born 1955. Educated at Texas Tech University B.B.A. 1977 J.D. cum laude 1980. In legal practice since 1980.

Member Federal Magistrate Judges Association, State Bar of Texas, Abilene and American Bar Associations.
Office: 104 Pine Street, Suite 705, Abilene 79601.
Telephone: (915) 695-7460.

BOONE, Patrick J. *(Judge, Texas District Court 57th Judicial District)*
Office: 410 Bexar County Courthouse, 100 Dolorosa Street, San Antonio 78205-3028.
Telephone: (210) 335-2531.

BOSWELL, George Timothy *(Judge, Texas District Court 402nd Judicial District)* Appointed by Governor George W. Bush to term beginning Sept 1, 1999. Elected 2000, current term expires Dec 31, 2004. Born Houston Texas July 12, 1942. Episcopalian. Educated at University of Texas B.A. 1965, Texas Christian University M.A. 1967 Ph.D. 1972 and Baylor University J.D. 1977. Admitted to practice Texas 1977.

Republican. Member 1978-86 and President 1982-83 Board Waco Independent School District. Enjoys sailing.
Mailing address: P.O. Box 1707, Quitman 75783-1707.
Telephone: (903) 763-2332.
Fax: (903) 763-1511

BOTLEY, Calvin *(Magistrate Judge, United States District Court Southern District of Texas)* Appointed by U.S. District Court judges to term beginning Oct 31, 1979. Reappointed to subsequent terms. Born Pineville Louisiana Dec 2, 1944. Baptist. Educated at Grambling State University B.A. with honors 1966 and Texas Southern University J.D. 1972. Recipient American Jurisprudence Awards 1972. Member Sigma Rho Sigma and Phi Alpha Delta (Justice 1972). Admitted to practice Texas 1972, U.S. District Courts Southern, Northern, Eastern and Western Districts of Texas 1972-76, U.S. Courts of Appeals Fifth 1973 and Eleventh 1983 Circuits and U.S. Supreme Court 1975. Began legal practice Houston 1972. In legal practice Austin 1973-74.

Assistant District Attorney Harris County 1972-73. Assistant Attorney General Texas 1973-78. Assistant U.S. Attorney 1978-79. Member Committee on Sentencing, Probation and Pretrial Services Federal Judicial Center and Committee on Court Security Judicial Conference of the U.S. Member American Judicature Society, Council of U.S. Magistrates, College of the State Bar of Texas, State Bar of Texas and American Bar Association. Recipient Outstanding Member and Outstanding Achievement Awards from Phi Alpha Delta 1973. Sergeant U.S. Army 1966-69. Recipient Army Commendation Medal, Army Commendation with oak leaf cluster, Vietnam Service Medal and National Defense Medal. Member Houston Council on Human Relations (Director since 1978). Enjoys skeet and trap shooting, reading and boating.

Office: 7720 U.S. Courthouse, 515 Rusk Avenue, Houston 77002.
Telephone: (713) 250-5757.

BOYD, Jean Hudson *(Judge, Texas Family District Court 323rd Judicial District)*
Office: 2701 Kimbo Road, Fort Worth 76111.
Telephone: (817) 838-4600.

BRABHAM, David *(Judge, Texas District Court 188th Judicial District)*
Office: 101 East Methvin, Suite 408, Longview 75601-7236.
Telephone: (903) 237-2588.

BRADLEY, Vikki *(Judge, Upton County Court)* Appointed to term beginning April 27, 1992. Elected Nov 3, 1992, 1994, 1998 and 2002. Current term expires Dec 31, 2006.
Mailing address: P.O. Box 482, Rankin 79778.
Telephone: (432) 693-2321.

BRADSHAW-HULL, Lynn *(Judge, Harris County Civil Court at Law No. 3)*
Office: 512 Civil Courts Building, 301 Fannin Street, Houston 77002.
Telephone: (713) 755-5788.

BRAMBLETT, Mary Anne *(Judge, Texas District Court 41st Judicial District)* Term expires Dec 31, 2004.
Office: 500 East San Antonio Avenue, #1006, El Paso 79901-2457.
Telephone: (915) 546-2149.

BRELAND, Jan *(Judge, Travis County Court at Law No. 6)* Elected Nov 1998 to term beginning Jan 1, 1999. Reelected 2002, current term expires Dec 31, 2006. Born Seymour Texas March 15, 1949. Christian. Educated at Tarleton State University B.A. with honors 1971 and Texas Tech University M.Ed. with honors 1977 J.D. with honors 1980. Staff member Texas Tech Law Review 1979-80. Law Clerk to Hon. Leon Douglas and Hon. Marvin Teague, Texas Court of Criminal Appeals 1980-81. Member Phi Alpha Delta. Admitted to practice Texas 1980. Justice of the Peace, Travis County Court Precinct Two 1989-98.

Assistant County Attorney Travis County 1981-85. Legal Counsel Texas Department of Public Safety 1985-89.
Mailing address: P.O. Box 1748, Austin 78767-1748.
Telephone: (512) 854-9677.

BREWER, Dallas *(Judge, Yoakum County Court)*
Mailing address: P.O. Box 456, Plains 79355.
Telephone: (806) 456-7491.

BRIDEWELL, D. Wayne *(Judge, Texas District Court 249th Judicial District)* Former Judge, Johnson County Court, assumed office 1985.
Office: Two North Main Street, Second Floor, Cleburne 76031-5573.
Telephone: (817) 556-6825.

BRIDGES, David L. *(Justice, Texas Court of Appeals Fifth District)* Elected to term beginning Jan 1, 1997. Reelected Nov 2002, current term expires Dec 31, 2008.

Office: 200 George Allen Sr. Courts Building, 600 Commerce Street, Dallas 75202.

Telephone: (214) 712-3412.

BRIDGES, Joe D. *(Judge, Denton County Criminal Court at Law No. 4)*

Office: 127 North Woodrow Lane, Denton 76205.

Telephone: (940) 349-2380.

BRIONES, David *(Judge, United States District Court Western District of Texas)* Appointed for life by President Bill Clinton to term beginning Oct 17, 1994. Born El Paso Texas Feb 26, 1943. Roman Catholic. Educated at University of Texas at El Paso B.A. 1969 and University of Texas School of Law J.D. 1971. Admitted to practice Texas 1971, U.S. District Court Western District of Texas 1973 and U.S. Court of Appeals Fifth Circuit 1990. In legal practice El Paso 1971-91. Judge, El Paso County Court at Law No. 1, 1991-94.

Member Mexican-American Bar Association of El Paso (President 1982), Mexican-American Bar Association of Texas, State Bar of Texas and El Paso Bar Association. Attended Course on Advanced Evidence The National Judicial College Reno Nevada Aug 1993. Named Outstanding Jurist of El Paso by El Paso Young Lawyers Association 1997-98. E-4 U.S. Army 1964-66.

Office: U.S. Courthouse, 511 East San Antonio Avenue, El Paso 79901-2401.

Telephone: (915) 534-6744.

BRIONES, Dolores *(Judge, El Paso County Court)*

Office: 500 East San Antonio, #301, El Paso 79901.

Telephone: (915) 546-2098.

BRISTER, Scott A. *(Chief Justice, Texas Court of Appeals Fourteenth District)* Appointed Justice First District 2001. Appointed Chief Justice by Governor Rick Perry 2001. Born Waco Texas Jan 8, 1955. Educated at Duke University A.B. summa cum laude 1977 and Harvard Law School J.D. cum laude 1980. Member Phi Beta Kappa and Sigma Phi Epsilon. Briefing Attorney to Chief Justice Joe R. Greenhill, Texas Supreme Court 1980-81. Admitted to practice Texas 1980, U.S. District Court Southern District of Texas 1981, U.S. Court of Appeals Fifth Circuit 1981, U.S. Tax Court 1983 and U.S. Supreme Court 1986. Board Certified—Civil Trial Law—Texas Board of Legal Specialization. Former Judge, Texas District Court 234th Judicial District, appointed by Governor William P. Clements to term beginning Oct 17, 1989.

Author "Proving Up Attorney's Fees at Trial" 28 *The Houston Lawyer* Sept-Oct 1990. Fellow Texas Bar Foundation. Member Texas Supreme Court Task Force on Sanctions 1991, College of the State Bar of Texas, State Bar of Texas, Houston (Continuing Legal Education Committee) and American Bar Associations. Speaker "The Establishment Clause" Rice University Oct 8, 1985, University of Houston Law Center April 27, 1987 and South Texas College of Law Sept 26, 1989, "Medical Malpractice Law" Rice University Pre-Medical and Pre-Law Societies March 20, 1989, "Discovery Developments—An Insurance Perspective" Sheinfeld, Maley & Kay May 9, 1990, "The New Texas Rules of Civil Procedure" Fulbright & Jaworski Aug 8, 1990, Family Law Section Houston Bar Association Sept 5, 1990, Weil, Gotshal & Manges Sept 12, 1990 and Houston Bar Association Sept 14, 1990 and "The Damages We Create—Proving Up Attorney's Fees at Trial" Litigation Section Houston Bar Association April 5, 1990. Program Chair and Moderator "Discovery: A Serialized Institute" Houston Bar Association Sept 1989 to Nov 1989. Moderator "Personal Injury and Wrongful Death" State Bar Professional Development Program March 16, 1990, "Handling Insurance and Tort Claims" University of Houston Law Center Sept 13, 1990 and "Second Annual Medical Malpractice Conference" South Texas College of Law Oct 12, 1990. Delegate State Republican Convention 1982. Alternate Senatorial District Republican Convention 1988. Chairman Harris County Republican Judicial Qualifications Screening Committee 1991. Member Admissions Interviewing Committee Duke University since 1982. Community Associate Hanszen College Rice University since 1990. Advisory Board Intervarsity Christian Fellowship since 1990. Big Brother Depelchin Children's Center 1982-87. Member Grace Covenant Church.

Office: 1307 San Jacinto, Eleventh Floor, Houston 77002-7006.

Telephone: (713) 655-2800.

BRISTOL, Alan M. *(Judge, Navarro County Court)*

Office: 300 West Third Street, Suite 102, Corsicana 75110.

Telephone: (903) 654-3025.

BROOKS, Suzanne *(Judge, Williamson County Court at Law No. 1)*

Office: 405 South Martin Luther King Blvd., Box 5, Georgetown 78262.

Telephone: (512) 943-1200.

BROTHERTON, Robert P. *(Judge, Texas District Court 30th Judicial District)*

Office: 900 Seventh Street, Room 360, Wichita Falls 76301.

Telephone: (940) 766-8180.

BROWN, Gerald M. *(Judge, Bell County Court at Law No. 3)* Elected Nov 1998 to term beginning Jan 1, 1999. Reelected Nov 2002, current term expires Dec 31, 2006. Presbyterian. Educated at Texas A&M University B.A. 1963, University of Texas School of Law LL.B. 1966 and St. Mary's University of San Antonio M.A. 1986. Member Phi Alpha Delta. Admitted to practice Texas 1966, U.S. Court of Appeals for the Armed Forces 1969, U.S. Supreme Court 1977 and U.S. District Court Western District of Texas. Board Certified—Criminal Law—Texas Board of Legal Specialization. In legal practice Temple 1972-98.

Assistant County Attorney Travis County 1971-72. Life Fellow Texas Bar Foundation. Member State Bar of Texas and Bell-Lampasas-Mills Counties Bar Association (President 1986-87). U.S. Army 1963-71 and Colonel USAR JAGC 1971-93. Republican. Member Kiwanis Club of Temple (President 2000-01).

Mailing address: P.O. Box 365, Belton 76513.

Office: Courthouse Annex, 550 East Second Street, Belton 76513.

Telephone: (254) 933-5789.

Fax: (254) 933-5792

BROWN, Jeffrey V. *(Judge, Texas District Court 55th Judicial District)*
Office: 615A Civil Courts Building, 301 Fannin Street, Houston 77002.
Telephone: (713) 755-6255.

BROWN, Jim D. *(Judge, Hansford County Court)*
Mailing address: P.O. Box 367, Spearman 79081-0367.
Telephone: (806) 659-4100.

BROWN, Jo Robin *(Judge, Harris County Criminal Court at Law No. 12)*
Office: 1201 Franklin, Room 10040, Houston 77002.
Telephone: (713) 755-7738.

BROWN, Karen Kennedy *(Judge, United States Bankruptcy Court Southern District of Texas)* Appointed by U.S. Court of Appeals Fifth Circuit judges to term beginning April 2, 1990. Term expires April 2, 2004. Born Houston Texas May 23, 1947. Episcopalian. Educated at University of Pennsylvania B.A. 1970 and University of Houston J.D. 1973. Moot Court. Law Clerk to Hon. John R. Brown, U.S. Court of Appeals Fifth Circuit 1973-75 and Hon. Woodrow B. Seals, U.S. District Court Southern District of Texas 1975-76. Member Order of Barons. Admitted to practice Texas 1974, U.S. Court of Appeals Fifth Circuit 1974, U.S. District Courts Southern 1975 and Western 1978 Districts of Texas and U.S. Supreme Court 1979. Began legal practice Houston 1974. Magistrate, United States District Court Southern District of Texas March 12, 1984 to March 31, 1990.

Assistant Federal Public Defender 1976-82. Author "The Clean Air Financing Act—A New Direction for the Texas Bond Market" Houston L. Rev. July 1974. Important Decisions: Synair Corp. v. American Industrial Tire, Inc. (Patent) 645 F. Supp. 1080, 1986, Chaplin v. Exxon (Toxic Tort) 25 E.R.C. 2009, 1986 and Gas Reclamation Inc. v. Jones, et al. (Rule 11) 113 F.R.D. 1, 1986. Member American Judicature Society, National Conference of Bankruptcy Judges, State Bar of Texas, Houston, Federal and American Bar Associations. Worked as clerk-typist 1964-65, cashier 1965, secretary 1966 and student research assistant 1973. Enjoys sailing and reading.
Office: 10501 U.S. Courthouse, 515 Rusk Avenue, Houston 77002.
Telephone: (713) 250-5250.

BROWN, Michael D. *(Judge, Tom Green County Court)*
Office: 112 West Harris, San Angelo 76903-5877.
Telephone: (325) 653-3318.

BROWN, Paul N. *(Senior Judge, United States District Court Eastern District of Texas)* Appointed for life by President Ronald Reagan to term beginning Nov 8, 1985. Assumed Senior status April 1, 2001, serves by assignment. Born Grayson County Texas. Presbyterian. Educated at University of Texas at Austin 1947 J.D. 1950. Admitted to practice Texas 1950. USN July 1944 to June 1946 and Aug 1950 to Nov 1951.
Office: 216 Federal Building, 101 East Pecan Street, Sherman 75090.
Telephone: (903) 892-9405.

BROWN, Spencer Whitewood *(Judge, Kerr County Court at Law)*
Office: 700 Main Street, Room 123, Kerrville 78028-5389.
Telephone: (830) 792-2207.

BROWN, Susan *(Judge, Texas District Court 185th Judicial District)*
Office: 1201 Franklin, Room 17136, Houston 77002.
Telephone: (713) 755-6362.

BROWNE, Robert L. *(Judge, Sterling County Court)*
Mailing address: P.O. Box 819, Sterling City 76951-0819.
Telephone: (325) 378-3481.

BRUNI, Louis H. *(Judge, Webb County Court)*
Office: 1000 Houston Street, Third Floor, Laredo 78042.
Telephone: (956) 523-4600.

BRYAN, Berry *(Judge, Angelina County Court at Law No. 2)*
Mailing address: P.O. Box 908, Lufkin 75902-0908.
Telephone: (936) 634-8984.

BUCHMEYER, Jerry *(Judge, United States District Court Northern District of Texas)* Appointed for life by President Jimmy Carter to term beginning Dec 17, 1979. Former Chief Judge. Born Overton Texas Sept 5, 1933. Educated at University of Texas B.A. LL.B. Member Phi Delta Phi. Admitted to practice Texas 1957. Began legal practice Dallas 1958.

Important Decisions: Terrazas v. Clements 537 F. Supp. 514, N.D. Tex. 1982; Baker v. Wade (holding that State of Texas homosexual conduct statute was unconstitutional) 553 F. Supp. 1121, N.D. Tex. 1982, 106 F.R.D. 526, N.D. Tex. 1985, reversed 769 F.2d 289, 5th Cir. en banc 1985; Wagner v. Thomas (pro se prisoner case involving "dirty books" and "dirty looks") 608 F. Supp. 1095, N.D. Tex. 1985; Walker v. United States Department of Housing & Urban Development, et al. (Walker I: holding that Dallas Housing Authority violated consent decree by failing to correct racial discrimination in low income public housing in Dallas) 734 F. Supp. 1231, N.D. Tex. 1989; Walker v. United States Department of Housing & Urban Development, et al. (Walker II: holding that prohibition of use of federal funds for demolition of vacant and uninhabitable housing units at Dallas' West Dallas Housing Project was unconstitutional) 734 F. Supp. 1273, N.D. Tex. 1989; Walker v. United States Department of Housing & Urban Development, et al. (Walker II: holding the City of Dallas liable for deliberate racial segregation and discrimination in low income public housing in Dallas) 734 F. Supp. 1289, N.D. Tex. 1989; Williams v. City of Dallas (holding that "at-large" system for election of some members of the Dallas City Council violated §2 of the Voting Rights Act because it dilutes the votes of political cohesive blacks and Hispanics in Dallas) 734 F. Supp. 1317, N.D. Tex. 1990; and issued an order intended to force mostly white suburbs of Dallas to accept public housing 1996. Member State Bar of Texas (Chairman Grievance Committee 1975-78, Board of Directors 1982-83), Dallas (President 1979) and American Bar Associations. Former member Board of Directors

BUCHMEYER, JERRY—*Continued*

Dallas Legal Services. Member First Community Church.

Office: 15D28A U.S. Courthouse, 1100 Commerce Street, Dallas 75242-1003.
Telephone: (214) 753-2295.

BULL, Diane *(Judge, Harris County Criminal Court at Law No. 11)*
Office: 1201 Franklin, Room 10144, Houston 77002.
Telephone: (713) 755-7780.

BURGESS, Don *(Justice, Texas Court of Appeals Ninth District)* Elected to term beginning Nov 28, 1984. Reelected 1986, 1992 and 1998. Current term expires Dec 31, 2004. Born Beaumont Texas Oct 28, 1946. Episcopalian. Educated at Sam Houston State University 1964, University of Texas at Austin B.A. 1968, University of Houston J.D. 1971 and University of Virginia LL.M. 1992. Admitted to practice Texas 1971, U.S. District Court Eastern District of Texas 1972, U.S. Court of Appeals Fifth Circuit 1972, U.S. Supreme Court 1976 and U.S. Court of Military Appeals 1983. Began legal practice Orange 1972. In legal practice Bridge City 1975. Judge, Texas District Court 260th Judicial District Jan 1, 1978 to Nov 27, 1984, appointed by Governor Dolph Briscoe.

Assistant County Attorney Orange County 1972-74. Adjunct Instructor Lamar State College Fall 1993, Spring 1994, Fall 1996, Fall 1999, Spring 2000 and Fall 2000. Member State Bar of Texas, Orange County, Jefferson County and American Bar Associations. Colonel USAR JAG (retired). Democrat.

Office: 1001 Pearl, Suite 330, Beaumont 77701-3552.
Telephone: (409) 835-8403.
Fax: (409) 835-8497

BURGESS, Ralph K. *(Judge, Texas District Court 5th Judicial District)*
Office: 100 North State Line, Box 10, Texarkana 75501.
Telephone: (903) 798-3004.

BURKHALTER, Lisa G. *(Judge, Angelina County Court at Law No. 1)*
Mailing address: P.O. Box 908, Lufkin 75902-0908.
Telephone: (936) 639-2204.

BURROWS, Jon *(Judge, Bell County Court)* Elected Nov 1998. Reelected Nov 2002, current term expires Dec 31, 2006. Born Frederick Oklahoma July 12, 1946. Baptist. Educated at University of Oklahoma B.M.E. 1968 M.M.E. 1969 and University of Texas J.D. 1976. Admitted to practice Texas 1976 and U.S. District Court Western District of Texas 1978. In legal practice Temple 1976-97.

Member State Bar of Texas and American Bar Association. Republican.

Mailing address: P.O. Box 768, Belton 76513.
Telephone: (254) 933-5105.
Fax: (254) 933-5179

BURSON, Lynn *(Judge, Dallas County Criminal Court of Appeals No. 2)*
Office: LB 10 Frank Crowley Courts Bldg., 133 North Industrial Boulevard, Dallas 75207-4313.
Telephone: (214) 653-5717.

BURWELL, Gladys B. *(Judge, Galveston County Probate Court)*
Office: 722 Moody, Room 305, Galveston 77550.
Telephone: (409) 766-2251.

BYRNE, Darlene *(Judge, Texas District Court 126th Judicial District)* Elected Nov 2000 to term beginning Jan 1, 2001. Term expires Dec 31, 2004. Born Marietta Georgia Jan 24, 1960. Christian. Educated at Jacksonville State University B.A. with special honors and distinction 1981 and University of Houston Law Center J.D. magna cum laude 1987. Legal Development Editor Houston Law Review 1986-87. Admitted to practice Texas 1987 and U.S. District Courts Eastern, Northern, Southern and Western Districts of Texas. In legal practice Houston 1987-91 and Austin 1991 and 1996-2000.

Assistant County Attorney Travis County 1992-96. Member Travis County Women's Lawyers Association, American Judges Association, Travis County Hispanic Bar Association and Travis County Bar Association (Judicial Affairs Committee 2001). Member Travis County Women's Political Caucus and Finance Committee Travis County Democratic Party. Graduate Leadership Austin 1997. Volunteer Austin Rape Crisis Center (Board Member/Treasurer 1993-95), Ballet Austin (Former Chairman), Meals on Wheels and Big Brothers/Big Sisters. Den Leader Boy Scouts of America. Enjoys golf, snow skiing, working out, reading and spending time with her kids. Personal Statement or Quote: "Learn to play well with others."

Mailing address: P.O. Box 1748, Austin 78767-1748.
Telephone: (512) 854-9313.
E-mail address: darlene.byrne@co.travis.tx.us

CADDEL, Jerry D. *(Judge, Ector County Court)*
Office: 300 North Grant, Room 227, Odessa 79761.
Telephone: (432) 498-4100.

CAGLE, Jack *(Judge, Harris County Civil Court at Law No. 1)*
Office: 509 Civil Courts Building, 301 Fannin Street, Houston 77002.
Telephone: (713) 755-5783.

CAIN, Chap, III *(Judge, Texas District Court 253rd Judicial District)* Former Judge, Liberty County Court at Law.
Office: 1923 Sam Houston, Liberty 77575-4800.
Telephone: (936) 336-4668.

CALHOON, Jerry L. *(Judge, Texas District Court 349th Judicial District)*
Office: 500 North Church Street, Palestine 75801.
Telephone: (903) 723-7415.

CALVERT, A. Gene, Jr. *(Judge, Ellis County Court at Law No. 2)*
Office: 1201 North Highway 77, Suite B, Waxahachie 75165.
Telephone: (972) 825-5066.

CAMPBELL, James T. *(Justice, Texas Court of Appeals Seventh District)*
Mailing address: P.O. Box 9540, Amarillo 79105-9540.
Telephone: (806) 342-2650.

CAMPBELL, Joan *(Judge, Texas District Court 248th Judicial District)*
Office: 1201 Franklin, Room 16144, Houston 77002.
Telephone: (713) 755-7094.

CAMPBELL, Kari *(Judge, Moore County Court)* Elected to term beginning Jan 1, 1999. Reelected Nov 5, 2002, current term expires Dec 31, 2006. Born Littlefield Texas Jan 22, 1966. Catholic.
Office: 715 Dumas Avenue, Room 202, Dumas 79029.
Telephone: (806) 935-5588.
Fax: (806) 935-5697
E-mail address: mcjudge@moorecountytexas.com

CANALES, Adolph *(Judge, Texas District Court 298th Judicial District)* Elected to term beginning Jan 1, 1987. Reelected Nov 1990, 1994, 1998 and 2002. Current term expires Dec 31, 2006. Born Houston Texas 1939. Educated at Southern Methodist University B.A. 1961 and Georgetown University Law Center J.D. 1968. Member Phi Delta Phi. Admitted to practice District of Columbia 1968 and Texas 1968.
Member State Bar of Texas, Bar Association of the District of Columbia and Dallas Bar Association. Attended Evidence Workshop Professional Education Systems, Inc. 1992. U.S. Army Military Intelligence USAR. Enjoys reading, music, chess and personal computers.
Office: 600 Commerce, Sixth Floor, Dallas 75202-4606.
Telephone: (214) 653-6781.

CANALES, Paul *(Judge, Bexar County Court at Law No. 2)*
Office: 2.11 Bexar County Courthouse, 100 Dolorosa Street, San Antonio 78205-3066.
Telephone: (210) 335-2573.

CANALES, Terry A. *(Judge, Texas District Court 79th Judicial District)* Term expires Dec 31, 2004.
Mailing address: P.O. Box 1375, Alice 78333-1375.
Telephone: (361) 325-5604.

CANTU, Arnoldo *(Judge, Hidalgo County Court at Law No. 5)*
Office: 100 North Closner, Second Floor, Edinburg 78539.
Telephone: (956) 318-2460.

CAPELLE, Stephen H. *(Magistrate Judge, United States District Court Western District of Texas)* Appointed by U.S. District Court judges.
Office: U.S. Courthouse, 200 West Eighth Street, Austin 78701.
Telephone: (512) 916-5679.

CAPERTON, Tracy K. *(Magistrate Judge, United States District Court Southern District of Texas)* Appointed by U.S. District Court judges to term beginning April 8, 2002.
Office: 1701 West Business Highway 83, McAllen 78501.
Telephone: (956) 618-8080.

CARAWAY, Billy B. *(Judge, Hardin County Court)*
Office: 300 Monroe Street, Kountze 77625.
Telephone: (409) 246-5120.

CARLOW, James Marion *(Judge, Bowie County Court)*
Mailing address: P.O. Box 248, New Boston 75570.
Telephone: (903) 628-6719.

CARNES, Burt *(Judge, Texas District Court 368th Judicial District)* Appointed by Governor William P. Clements to term beginning Sept 1, 1989. Elected Jan 1991, Jan 1995, Jan 1999 and 2002. Current term expires Dec 31, 2006. Born 1949. Roman Catholic. Educated at University of Texas at Austin B.A. 1972 J.D. 1976. Admitted to practice Texas 1976. In legal practice Taylor 1979-89.
Assistant District Attorney Dallas County 1976-77 and Travis County 1977-79. USMCR Feb 1, 1969 to Jan 31, 1975.
Office: 405 South Martin Luther King Blvd., Box 8, Georgetown 78626-0405.
Telephone: (512) 943-1368.

CARPER, Brian Allan *(Judge, Texas Family District Court 324th Judicial District)* Term expires Dec 31, 2006.
Office: 100 North Houston Street, Fort Worth 76196-0232.
Telephone: (817) 884-1431.

CARR, Brent A. *(Judge, Tarrant County Criminal Court at Law No. 9)*
Office: Tarrant County Justice Center, Eighth Floor, 401 West Belknap, Fort Worth 76196-7678.
Telephone: (817) 884-3410.

CARRILLO, Victor G. *(Judge, Taylor County Court)*
Office: 300 Oak Street, Abilene 79602.
Telephone: (325) 674-1235.

CARRINGTON, Trey *(Judge, Throckmorton County Court)*
Mailing address: P.O. Box 700, Throckmorton 76483.
Telephone: (940) 849-3081.

CARROLL, Bob *(Judge, Ellis County Court at Law)*
Office: 1201 North Highway 77, Suite B, Waxahachie 75165.
Telephone: (972) 825-5066.

CARROLL, Joe *(Judge, Texas District Court 27th Judicial District)* Term expires Dec 31, 2004.
Mailing address: P.O. Box 747, Belton 76513-0747.
Telephone: (254) 933-5261.

CARTER, Jack *(Justice, Texas Court of Appeals Sixth District)* Former Judge, Texas District Court 5th Judicial District.
Office: Bi-State Justice Building, 100 North State Line No. 20, Texarkana 75501-5666.
Telephone: (903) 798-3046.

CARVER, Charles Dana *(Judge, Texas Criminal District Court Jefferson County)*
Mailing address: P.O. Box 3707, Beaumont 77704-3707.
Telephone: (409) 835-8432.

CASTILLO, Errlinda *(Justice, Texas Court of Appeals Thirteenth District)* Elected to term beginning Jan 2001. Term expires Dec 31, 2006. Born Sinton Texas. Educated at Texas Arts & Industries University B.S. 1976 and University of Texas at Austin School of Law J.D. 1984. Admitted to practice Texas, U.S. District Courts Eastern, Northern, Southern and Western Districts of Texas, U.S. Court of Appeals Fifth Circuit and U.S. Supreme Court. In legal practice 1991 to Jan 2001.
Office: 901 Leopard, Tenth Floor, Corpus Christi 78401.
Telephone: (361) 888-0605.

CATON, Betty *(Judge, Texas District Court 296th Judicial District)* Appointed by Governor George W.

CATON, BETTY—*Continued*
Bush December 5, 1996 to term beginning Jan 2, 1997. Elected 1998 and 2002. Current term expires Dec 31, 2006. Born Wichita Falls Texas Oct 13, 1941. Protestant. Educated at North Texas State University B.A. with honors 1972 and Southern Methodist University J.D. 1974. Admitted to practice Texas 1975. In legal practice McKinney 1975-96.

President Collin County Bar Association 1989-90. Sustaining Life Fellow Texas Bar Foundation since 1991. Member State Bar of Texas (Pro Bono College 1994).

Office: 210 South McDonald, Suite 424, McKinney 75069.

Telephone: (972) 548-4409.

CATTERTON, Randy *(Judge, Texas District Court 231st Judicial District)*

Office: 100 West Weatherford Street, Fort Worth 76196-0226.

Telephone: (817) 884-1763.

CAYCE, John H., Jr. *(Chief Justice, Texas Court of Appeals Second District)* Elected to term beginning Jan 1, 1995. Reelected to subsequent term. Current term expires Dec 31, 2006. Educated at University of Texas at Arlington summa cum laude and St. Mary's University of San Antonio School of Law J.D. 1982. Editor-in-Chief St. Mary's Law Journal. Briefing Attorney Texas Supreme Court 1982. Board Certified—Civil Appellate Law—Texas Board of Legal Specialization. Began legal practice Fort Worth 1983.

Chair Council of Chief Justices of Texas 1996-97. Member Rules Advisory Committee Texas Supreme Court. Deacon Richland Hills Church of Christ.

Office: 9000 Tarrant County Justice Center, 401 West Belknap, Fort Worth 76196.

Telephone: (817) 884-2170.

CHAPMAN, Brenda *(Judge, Comal County Court at Law)*

Office: 100 Main Plaza, Suite 203, New Braunfels 78130-5166.

Telephone: (830) 620-5583.

CHAPMAN, Charles L. *(Judge, Texas District Court 39th Judicial District)* Appointed by Governor Mark White to term beginning March 29, 1985. Elected 1986, 1990, 1994, 1998 and 2002. Current term expires Dec 31, 2006. Born Fort Worth Texas Jan 2, 1946. Presbyterian. Educated at Texas Christian University B.B.A. 1968 and Baylor University J.D. 1971. Member Kappa Sigma and Phi Alpha Delta. Admitted to practice Texas 1971 and U.S. District Court Northern District of Texas 1978. In legal practice Haskell 1971-85.

County Attorney Haskell County Jan 1, 1973 to March 29, 1985. Board Member Judicial Section State Bar of Texas Sept 2000 to Sept 2003. Past President 39th Judicial District Bar Association. Chairman 39th Judicial District Juvenile Board. Attended Texas College for New Judges 1985. E-5 USAR 1968-74. Democrat.

Mailing address: P.O. Box 966, Haskell 79521-0966.

Telephone: (940) 864-2661.

CHARLES, Alfonso *(Judge, Gregg County Court at Law No. 2)*

Office: 101 East Methvin, Suite 303, Longview 75601.

Telephone: (903) 234-3110.

CHASE, Richard R. *(Judge, Wise County Court)*

Mailing address: P.O. Box 393, Decatur 76234.

Telephone: (940) 627-5743.

CHAVEZ, Alfredo *(Judge, Texas District Court 65th Judicial District)*

Office: 500 East San Antonio Avenue, #1105, El Paso 79901-2457.

Telephone: (915) 546-2102.

CHERRY, J. Blair, Jr. *(Judge, Texas District Court 72nd Judicial District)* Appointed by Governor William P. Clements to term beginning Sept 13, 1988. Elected Nov 1988, 1992, 1996 and 2000. Current term expires Dec 31, 2004. Born Austin Texas June 2, 1939. Christian. Educated at University of Texas at Austin B.A. 1962 J.D. 1964. Admitted to practice Texas 1964, U.S. District Court Northern District of Texas 1969 and U.S. Court of Appeals Fifth Circuit 1970. In legal practice Midland 1964-66 and Lubbock 1966-88.

District Attorney 72nd Judicial District 1969-72. Member State Bar of Texas and Lubbock County Bar Association. Attended General Jurisdiction Course The National Judicial College 1988. Republican. Enjoys golf, fishing and gardening.

Mailing address: P.O. Box 10536, Lubbock 79408-3536.

Telephone: (806) 775-1023.

CHESHIRE, Robert C. *(Judge, Texas District Court 377th Judicial District)*

Office: 101 North Bridge Street, Victoria 77901-6544.

Telephone: (361) 578-8756.

CHEW, David Wellington *(Justice, Texas Court of Appeals Eighth District)* Elected 1994 to term beginning Jan 1, 1995. Reelected 2000, current term expires Dec 31, 2006. Born El Paso Texas Sept 29, 1947. Educated at University of Texas at El Paso, U.S. Naval Academy B.S. 1971 and Southern Methodist University School of Law J.D. 1978. Board Certified—Immigration and Nationality Law—Texas Board of Legal Specialization. Began legal practice El Paso 1978.

Important Decisions: Jose Parra v. Larchmont Farms, Inc. WL 755557 1995, Tex. App.—El Paso writ pending 1995; General Dynamics, Material Service Corp. and El Paso Sand, Inc. v. Louis Torres 915 S.W.2d 45, Tex. App.—El Paso writ denied 1995; Sherri Henderson v. The State of Texas 906 S.W.2d 589, Tex. App.—El Paso pet. ref'd 1995; Petro Stopping Centers, Inc. v. Owens-Corning Fiberglas Corp. 906 S.W.2d 618, Tex. App.—El Paso no writ 1995; and Pride Petroleum Services, Inc. v. Jerry Criswell 924 S.W.2d 720, Tex. App.—El Paso writ denied 1996. Listed in *The Best Lawyers in America* 1994-95 and 1995-96. Served to Lieutenant Commander USN. West-Central City Representative El Paso City Council 1989-91.

Office: 500 East San Antonio Avenue, Suite 1203, El Paso 79901-2421.

Telephone: (915) 546-2240.

CHEW, Linda *(Judge, Texas Family District Court 327th Judicial District)*

Office: 500 East San Antonio Avenue, #606, El Paso 79901-2457.

Telephone: (915) 546-2032.

CHILDS, Daniel Boone *(Judge, Cherokee County Court at Law)*
Office: County Courthouse, Rusk 75785.
Telephone: (903) 683-6497.

CHIUMINATTO, Martin J., Jr. *(Judge, Kleberg County Court at Law)* Elected to term beginning Jan 1, 1987. Reelected Nov 1990, 1994, 1998 and 2002. Current term expires Dec 31, 2006. Born Kingsville Texas Nov 20, 1948. Episcopalian. Educated at Texas Arts and Industries University B.S. 1970 and St. Mary's University of San Antonio J.D. 1975. Staff member St. Mary's Law Journal Spring 1974. Member Kappa Sigma and Phi Delta Phi. Admitted to practice Texas 1975, U.S. District Courts Western 1976 and Southern 1979 Districts of Texas and U.S. Court of Appeals Fifth Circuit 1976. Board Certified—Family Law—Texas Board of Legal Specialization 1988. In legal practice Kingsville 1980-86.
Assistant City Attorney El Paso 1975-78. City Attorney Kingsville 1978-83. Member College of the State Bar of Texas, Texas Bar Foundation, Texas City Attorneys Association, State Bar of Texas and Kleberg-Kenedy Counties Bar Association (President 1980-81). Graduate 1986 and Faculty Member 1990-92 College for New Judges and Director since 1990 Texas Center for the Judiciary, Inc. Commander USNR since 1974 (active duty 1970-72). Member Kingsville Rotary Club (President 1983-84), Coastal Bend Alumni Association of Kappa Sigma (President since 1978), Kleberg County Family Guidance Services, Mental Health Mental Retardation Advisory Council, Brookshire Foundation, Kingsville Chamber of Commerce, Epiphany School Foundation, Kingsville Action Network and Church of the Epiphany.
Mailing address: P.O. Box 1556, Kingsville 78364-1556.
Telephone: (361) 595-8565.

CHRESTMAN, Don *(Judge, Texas District Court 43rd Judicial District)* Appointed by Governor George W. Bush to term beginning Nov 2000. Elected 2000, current term expires Dec 31, 2004. Born Sinton Texas July 5, 1942. Baptist. Educated at Baylor University B.B.A. 1965 J.D. 1970. Admitted to practice Texas 1970, U.S. District Court District of Texas 1982 and U.S. Supreme Court 1992. In legal practice Weatherford Texas 1980-2000.
City Councilman Weatherford. Personal Statement or Quote: ". . . with liberty and justice for all."
Office: 117 Fort Worth Highway, Weatherford 76086-4302.
Telephone: (817) 594-7343.
E-mail address: judgedmc@hotmail.com

CHRISTIAN, M'Liss *(Judge, Bexar County Court at Law No. 6)* Elected Nov 1998 to term beginning Jan 1, 1999. Reelected 2002, current term expires Dec 31, 2006. Born San Antonio Texas March 26, 1960. Educated at University of Arizona B.A. and St. Mary's University School of Law J.D. Member Phi Alpha Delta. Admitted to practice Texas 1988 and U.S. District Court Western District of Texas 1992. In legal practice San Antonio 1998-99.
Assistant Criminal District Attorney Bexar County 1991-98. Fellow San Antonio Bar Foundation. Member National Association of Women Judges, Bexar County Women's, San Antonio and Mexican-American Bar Associations. Republican. Member Alamo City Republican Women, Bexar County Republican Women, Bexar County Republican Men, Hispanic Republican Women and Republican Business Women.
Office: 1045 Bexar County Justice Center, 300 Dolorosa Street, San Antonio 78205-3013.
Telephone: (210) 335-2156.

CHRISTIAN, Wayne Anthony, II *(Judge, Bexar County Court at Law No. 9)*
Office: 2191 Bexar County Justice Center, 300 Dolorosa Street, San Antonio 78205-3020.
Telephone: (210) 335-2008.

CHRISTOPHER, Tracy *(Judge, Texas District Court 295th Judicial District)* Elected Nov 1994 to term beginning Jan 1, 1995. Reelected 1998 and 2002. Current term expires Dec 31, 2006. Born Kansas City Missouri July 17, 1956. Catholic. Educated at University of Notre Dame B.A. with honors 1978 and University of Texas at Austin J.D. with honors 1981. Staff member Review of Litigation 1979-91. Member Board of Advocates. Admitted to practice Texas 1981, U.S. Court of Appeals Fifth Circuit 1981 and U.S. District Court Southern District of Texas 1982. Board Certified—Civil Trial Law—Texas Board of Legal Specialization. In legal practice Houston 1981-94.
Fellow and Member State Bar of Texas and Houston Bar Association. Member Association of Civil, Trial and Appellate Specialists and College of the State Bar of Texas. Speaker and Moderator at various CLE seminars for lawyers, legal assistants and accountants. Republican. Leader Girl Scouts of America. Enjoys camping, swimming and bike riding.
Office: 301 Fannin, Houston 77002.
Telephone: (713) 755-5541.

CLANCY, Daniel Patrick *(Judge, Dallas County Criminal Court at Law No. 1)* Elected 1998 to term beginning Jan 1, 1999. Reelected 2002, current term expires Dec 31, 2006. Born Dallas Texas June 10, 1965. Catholic. Educated at Southwest Texas State University B.A. 1988 and Mississippi College School of Law J.D. 1991. Admitted to practice Texas 1992. In legal practice 1997-99.
Assistant District Attorney Dallas County 1992-97.
Office: 133 North Industrial Boulevard, LB 14, Dallas 75207-4313.
Telephone: (214) 653-5605.

CLARK, Carole W. *(Judge, Texas Family District Court 321st Judicial District)*
Office: 100 North Broadway, First Floor, Tyler 75702-7236.
Telephone: (903) 535-0590.

CLARK, Leif M. *(Judge, United States Bankruptcy Court Western District of Texas)* Appointed by U.S. Court of Appeals Fifth Circuit judges to term beginning Aug 3, 1987. Reappointed 2001, current term expires Aug 2015. Born Washington D.C. Nov 12, 1947. Lutheran. Educated at University of Maryland B.A. with honors 1968, Trinity Lutheran Seminary M.Div. with honors 1972 and University of Houston Law Center J.D. with honors 1980. Associate Editor Houston Law Review 1978-80. Member Phi Delta Phi. Admitted to practice Texas 1980, U.S. District Courts Western 1981 and Southern 1982 Districts of Texas and U.S. Court of Appeals Fifth Circuit 1983. In legal practice San Antonio 1980-87.

CLARK, LEIF M.—*Continued*

Author "Church Lobbying" Houston L. Rev. 1980 and "Technology Transfers" St. Mary's L. Jour. 1989. Important Decisions: Greystone III Joint Venture 1989 and Komet 1989. Instructor in American Constitutional Law International Law Program McGeorge School of Law, Salzburg Austria since 1989. Member Commercial Law League of America, National Conference of Bankruptcy Judges and American Bar Association. Speaker at numerous seminars for State Bar of Texas and University of Texas. Republican. Director Housing for Exceptional People, Inc. 1973-75. Interim campus pastor University of Houston. Member St. John's Lutheran Church and Texas Bach Choir. Enjoys choral singing, theatre, cycling, golf and mountain climbing.

Mailing address: P.O. Box 1439, San Antonio 78295-1439.

Telephone: (210) 472-5181.

CLARK, Letitia Z. *(Judge, United States Bankruptcy Court Southern District of Texas)* Former Chief Judge.

Office: 4013 U.S. Courthouse, 515 Rusk Avenue, Houston 77002.

Telephone: (713) 250-5782.

CLARK, Patrick Allen *(Judge, Texas District Court 128th Judicial District)* Appointed by Governor William P. Clements Feb 1980. Elected 1980, 1984, 1988, 1992, 1996 and 2000. Current term expires Dec 31, 2004. Born Port Arthur Texas May 16, 1945. Catholic. Educated at Wharton County Junior College 1963-64, Lamar State College of Technology B.S. 1967 and University of Texas J.D. 1970. Admitted to practice Texas 1970. Judge, Orange County Court at Law 1978-80.

With District Attorney's Office 1974-78. Former member American Bar Association. Member State Bar of Texas and Orange County (Secretary-Treasurer 1978, Vice President 1979, President 1980) Bar Association. Captain U.S. Army JAGC 1970-74. Democrat. Board member Orange County Credit Union. Former Board Member and President Orange Camp Fire Board. Eucharistic Minister and former CCD Instructor St. Mary's Church. Member Knights of Columbus since 1975 and St. Mary's School Foundation. Enjoys family activities and sports.

Office: 801 West Division, Orange 77630-6353.

Telephone: (409) 882-7085.

CLARK, Ronald H. *(Judge, United States District Court Eastern District of Texas)* Appointed for life by President George W. Bush to term beginning Nov 22, 2002. Born Caripito Venezuela Jan 5, 1953. Educated at University of Connecticut B.A. 1973 M.A. 1974 and University of Texas J.D. 1979. Admitted to practice Texas 1979. In legal practice 1982-93.

Office: 300 Willow, Beaumont 77701.

Telephone: (409) 654-4301.

CLARK, Sarah Tunnell *(Judge, Houston County Court at Law)*

Office: 401 East Houston Avenue, Crockett 75835.

Telephone: (936) 544-3255.

CLAYTON, Bonnie Jean *(Judge, Parmer County Court)*

Mailing address: P.O. Box 506, Farwell 79325-0506.

Telephone: (806) 481-3383.

CLONTS, Greg *(Judge, Knox County Court)*

Mailing address: P.O. Box 77, Benjamin 79505-0077.

Telephone: (940) 459-2191.

COBB, Howell *(Senior Judge, United States District Court Eastern District of Texas)* Appointed for life by President Ronald Reagan to term beginning May 17, 1985. Assumed Senior status, serves by assignment. Born Atlanta Georgia Dec 7, 1922. Episcopalian. Educated at St. John's College, Annapolis and University of Virginia LL.B. 1948. Member Kappa Alpha Order. Admitted to practice Georgia 1948, Texas 1949, U.S. District Courts Eastern and Southern Districts of Texas, U.S. Court of Appeals Fifth Circuit and U.S. Supreme Court. In legal practice Houston 1949-54 and Beaumont 1954-85.

Former member Texas Association of Defense Counsel and International Association of Insurance Counsel. Member American Board of Trial Advocates, State Bar of Texas (Committee member 1972 and Chairman 1972 District 2A Grievance Committee), Jefferson County (Secretary 1960) and American Bar Associations. First Lieutenant USMC PTO 1942-45. Republican. Former Member Board of Directors Beaumont Art Museum (Past President), Former Member Board of Trustees All Saints Episcopal School and Vestry St. Stephen's Episcopal Church.

Mailing address: P.O. Box 632, Beaumont 77704-0632.

Telephone: (409) 654-2830.

COCHRAN, Cathy *(Judge, Texas Court of Criminal Appeals)* Appointed by Governor Rick Perry 2001. Educated at Stanford University B.A. with distinction 1966 and University of Houston Law Center J.D. summa cum laude 1984. Editor-in-Chief Houston Law Review. Member Order of the Coif and Order of Barons. Board Certified—Criminal Law—Texas Board of Legal Specialization.

Mailing address: P.O. Box 12308, Austin 78711-2308.

Office: Supreme Court Building, Austin 78701.

Telephone: (512) 463-1570.

COEN, Jeffrey V. *(Judge, Texas District Court 254th Judicial District)*

Office: George Allen Sr. Courts Building, Fifth Floor, 600 Commerce Street, Dallas 75202-4606.

Telephone: (214) 653-6136.

COFFEY, Daryl R. *(Judge, Tarrant County Criminal Court at Law No. 8)* Elected to term beginning Sept 1, 1991. Reelected to subsequent terms. Current term expires Dec 31, 2006. Presiding Criminal Judge pro tem 1997. Presiding Criminal Judge 1998. Born Glasgow Kentucky Nov 1, 1956. Educated at Western Kentucky University B.S. 1978 and University of Louisville J.D. 1981. Admitted to practice Kentucky 1982, Texas 1983, U.S. District Court Northern District of Texas 1987, U.S. Court of Appeals Fifth Circuit 1987 and U.S. Supreme Court 1987. In legal practice Burkesville 1982 and Fort Worth Texas 1988 to Sept 1991.

Assistant District Attorney Jan 4, 1984 to Feb 1998. Special Prosecutor Eighth Administrative Judicial Region 1988. Author "Lawyer Contempt: An Overview" Summer Seminar Tarrant County Trial Lawyers Association 1991 and 1992. Secretary/Treasurer Texas Center for the Judiciary, Inc. 1997-98. Member Tarrant County Trial Lawyers Association, Texas Criminal Defense Lawyers Association, The Association of Trial Lawyers of Ameri-

COFFEY, DARYL R.—*Continued*

ca, Texas Association of County Judges, Texas Association for Court Administration, State Bar of Texas (Judicial Section), Tarrant County, Kentucky and Mexican-American Bar Associations. Attended College for New Judges Texas Center for the Judiciary, Inc. 1990. Guest Lecturer Tarrant County Bar Association and Tarrant County Criminal Defense Lawyers Association. Named "2001 Best Elected Official" by *Fort Worth Weekly*. Chair Community Justice Plan of Tarrant County 1999. Member Fort Worth Civic Leader Association and Tarrant County Citizens Crime Commission.

Office: 300 West Belknap, Second Floor, Fort Worth 76196.
Telephone: (817) 884-3400.
E-mail address: dcoffey@tarrantcounty.com

COKER, Elizabeth E. *(Judge, Texas District Court 258th Judicial District)* Elected April 1998 to term beginning Jan 1, 1999. Reelected 2002, current term expires Dec 31, 2006. Born Conroe Texas Aug 28, 1966. Southern Baptist. Educated at Baylor University B.A. 1989 J.D. 1992. Admitted to practice Texas 1992.
Mailing address: P.O. Box 1115, Groveton 75845-1115.
Office: 162 West First Street, Groveton 75845.
Telephone: (936) 642-2512.
Fax: (936) 642-2312

COLLIER, Jake *(Judge, Texas District Court 158th Judicial District)*
Office: 1450 East McKinney Street, Suite 3325, Denton 76209-4524.
Telephone: (940) 349-2320.

COLLINS, Denise *(Judge, Texas District Court 208th Judicial District)*
Office: 1201 Franklin, Room 17040, Houston 77002.
Telephone: (713) 755-6374.

COLTHARP, James *(Judge, Baylor County Court)*
Office: 119 East McLain, Seymour 76380.
Telephone: (940) 888-3553.

COMBEST, Preston *(Judge, Camp County Court)*
Office: 126 Church Street, Room 303, Pittsburg 75686.
Telephone: (903) 856-3845.

CONOLY, John E. *(Judge, Culberson County Court)*
Mailing address: P.O. Box 747, Van Horn 79855.
Telephone: (432) 283-2059.

COOK, Vernon Howard *(Judge, Roberts County Court)*
Mailing address: P.O. Box 478, Miami 79059-0478.
Telephone: (806) 868-3721.

COOPER, Margaret A. *(Judge, Texas District Court 353rd Judicial District)*
Mailing address: P.O. Box 1748, Austin 78767-1748.
Telephone: (512) 854-9380.

COOPER-HILL, Jane *(Magistrate Judge, United States District Court Southern District of Texas)* Appointed by U.S. District Court judges.
Office: U.S. Courthouse, 1133 North Shoreline Boulevard, Corpus Christi 78401.
Telephone: (361) 888-3550.

COPELAND, Weldon S., Jr. *(Judge, Collin County Probate Court)* Born El Paso Texas. Baptist. Educated at University of Texas B.B.A. 1973 and Texas Tech University School of Law J.D. 1976. Member Phi Delta Phi. Admitted to practice Texas 1977, New Mexico 1978, U.S. District Court Western District of Texas 1978 and U.S. Court of Appeals 1979. Judge, Plano Municipal Court 1985-88. Former Judge, Collin County Court at Law No. 1, appointed to term beginning Sept 1988. Enjoys racquetball.
Office: 1800 North Graves, Suite 125, McKinney 75069.
Telephone: (972) 548-3810.

CORDES, Richard *(Judge, Menard County Court)*
Mailing address: P.O. Box 1038, Menard 76859-1038.
Telephone: (325) 396-4789.

CORN, Roger *(Judge, Callahan County Court)*
Office: 104 West Fourth Street, Suite 200, Baird 79504-5323.
Telephone: (325) 854-1155.

CORNEJO-LOPEZ, Elia *(Judge, Cameron County Court at Law No. 2)*
Office: 974 East Harrison, Brownsville 78520.
Telephone: (956) 544-0856.

COSBY, Donald J. *(Judge, Texas District Court 67th Judicial District)* Appointed by Governor George W. Bush to term beginning Oct 2000. Elected 2000, current term expires Dec 31, 2004. Born Fort Worth Texas Feb 12, 1955. Educated at Tulane University B.A. 1977 and St. Mary's University of San Antonio School of Law J.D. 1980. Admitted to practice Texas 1980.
Office: Tarrant County Justice Center, Eighth Floor, 401 West Belknap, Fort Worth 76196-0121.
Telephone: (817) 884-1452.
E-mail address: dcosby@tarrantcounty.com

COSELLI, John A. *(Judge, Texas District Court 125th Judicial District)*
Office: Civil Courts Building, 301 Fannin Street, Houston 77002.
Telephone: (713) 755-5577.

COSPER, Caprice *(Judge, Texas District Court 339th Judicial District)*
Office: 1201 Franklin, Room 14136, Houston 77002.
Telephone: (713) 755-7784.

COVINGTON, Suzanne *(Judge, Texas District Court 201st Judicial District)*
Mailing address: P.O. Box 1748, Austin 78767-1748.
Telephone: (512) 854-9305.

COX, Campbell, II *(Judge, Texas District Court 145th Judicial District)*
Office: 101 West Main Street, Room 217, Nacogdoches 75961.
Telephone: (936) 560-7799.

COX, Fred *(Judge, Hamilton County Court)*
Office: County Courthouse, Hamilton 76531-1897.
Telephone: (254) 386-3815.

COX, Joseph M. *(Judge, Texas District Court 160th Judicial District)*
Office: George Allen Sr. Courts Building, Fourth Floor, 600 Commerce Street, Dallas 75202-4606.
Telephone: (214) 653-7273.

COX, Marilyn Kay *(Judge, Bailey County Court)*
Office: 300 South First Street, Suite 100, Muleshoe 79347-4217.
Telephone: (806) 272-3077.

CRAIN, David *(Judge, Travis County Court at Law No. 3)* Appointed Feb 1992 to term beginning March 1992. Elected Nov 1992, Nov 1994, 1998 and 2002. Current term expires Dec 31, 2006. Born Houston Texas Feb 16, 1952. Educated at University of Texas B.A. 1974 LL.B. 1981. Admitted to practice Texas 1982 and U.S. District Court District of Texas 1984. Justice of the Peace Precinct Five Travis County 1985-91.
Mailing address: P.O. Box 1748, Austin 78767-1748.
Telephone: (512) 854-9243.

CRANE, Randy *(Judge, United States District Court Southern District of Texas)* Appointed for life by President George W. Bush to term beginning March 27, 2002. Born Houston Texas 1965. Educated at University of Texas B.A. 1985 J.D. 1987. In legal practice McAllen 1988-2002.
Office: 1701 West Business Highway 83, McAllen 78501.
Telephone: (956) 618-8065.

CRAPITTO, Mary Nell *(Judge, Galveston County Court at Law No. 1)*
Office: 722 Moody, Room 301, Galveston 77550.
Telephone: (409) 766-2233.

CRAVEN, Caroline M. *(Magistrate Judge, United States District Court Eastern District of Texas)* Appointed by U.S. District Court judges.
Office: U.S. Courthouse, 500 North State Line Avenue, Texarkana 75501.
Telephone: (903) 792-6424.

CRAWFORD, Stephen O'Neal *(Judge, Texas District Court 90th Judicial District)*
Office: 516 Fourth Street, Room 203, Graham 76450-2964.
Telephone: (940) 549-0091.

CREAGER, Donald C. *(Judge, Loving County Court)*
Mailing address: P.O. Box 193, Mentone 79754-0193.
Telephone: (432) 377-2362.

CREUZOT, John Coleman *(Judge, Texas Criminal District Court No. 4 Dallas County)*
Office: LB 41 Frank Crowley Courts Building, 133 North Industrial Boulevard, Dallas 75207-4313.
Telephone: (214) 653-5930.

CRIPPEN, Kim *(Judge, Sherman County Court)*
Mailing address: P.O. Box 165, Stratford 79084.
Telephone: (806) 366-2021.

CRISS, Susan *(Judge, Texas District Court 212th Judicial District)*
Office: 722 Moody, Fifth Floor, Galveston 77550.
Telephone: (409) 766-2266.

CRONE, Marcia A. *(Magistrate Judge, United States District Court Southern District of Texas)* Appointed by U.S. District Court judges to term beginning Aug 7, 1992. Reappointed Aug 8, 2000, current term expires Aug 7, 2008. Born Dallas Texas Dec 12, 1952. Methodist. Educated at University of Texas B.A. with honors 1973 and University of Houston J.D. with honors 1978. Member Phi Beta Kappa. Admitted to practice Texas 1979, U.S. District Courts Eastern 1979, Northern 1979, Southern 1979 and Western 1979 Districts of Texas, District of Columbia 1982, U.S. Courts of Appeals Fifth, Ninth, Eleventh and District of Columbia Circuits and U.S. Supreme Court. In legal practice Houston 1978-92 and Washington D.C. 1981-83.
Fellow Houston Bar Foundation and Texas Bar Foundation. Board of Directors since 1993 and President Houston Chapter 1996-97 Federal Bar Association. Board of Directors since 1994 and Counselor since 1998 Inns of Court. Member The District of Columbia Bar, State Bar of Texas and Houston Bar Association. Member St. Luke's United Methodist Church. Enjoys reading and traveling.
Office: 7509 U.S. Courthouse, 515 Rusk Avenue, Houston 77002.
Telephone: (713) 250-5840.

CROOKS, Danny Pat *(Judge, Titus County Court)*
Office: 100 West First Street, Suite 200, Mount Pleasant 75455.
Telephone: (903) 577-6791.

CROUCH, Jim *(Judge, Denton County Criminal Court at Law No. 1)* Appointed to term beginning Sept 1995. Elected 1996, 1998 and 2002. Current term expires Dec 31, 2006. Born Eastland Texas June 28, 1959. Southern Baptist. Educated at Baylor University B.S. in Education 1980 J.D. 1983. Admitted to practice Texas 1983 and U.S. District Court Eastern District of Texas 1984.
Assistant District Attorney Smith County 1983-84 and Denton County 1984-95. Member State Bar of Texas, Alliance and Denton County Bar Associations. Republican.
Office: 1450 East McKinney Street, Suite 1419, Denton 76209.
Telephone: (940) 349-2160.

CROUCH, Karen *(Judge, Bexar County Court at Law No. 8)*
Office: 1083 Bexar County Justice Center, 300 Dolorosa Street, San Antonio 78205-3012.
Telephone: (210) 335-2005.

CROWDER, Elizabeth Hampton *(Judge, Dallas County Criminal Court at Law No. 7)*
Office: LB 21 Frank Crowley Courts Bldg., 133 North Industrial Boulevard, Dallas 75207-4313.
Telephone: (214) 653-5667.

CROWE, Cynthia M. *(Judge, Harris County Civil Court at Law No. 4)* Elected Nov 4, 1994 to term beginning Jan 1, 1995. Reelected 1998 and 2002. Current term expires Dec 31, 2006. Born Springfield Massachusetts June 4, 1958. Presbyterian. Educated at Loyola University B.A. 1980 and Vermont Law School J.D. 1983. Admitted to practice Texas 1983, U.S. District Courts Eastern, Northern, Southern and Western Districts of Texas and U.S. Court of Appeals Fifth Circuit. In legal practice Houston 1983-94.
Member Houston Bar Association.
Office: 250 Family Law Center Building, 1115 Congress Street, Houston 77002.
Telephone: (713) 755-5791.

CUDE, Melton D. *(Judge, Wise County Court at Law)*
Mailing address: P.O. Box 901, Decatur 76234.
Telephone: (940) 627-5005.

CULVER, Thomas R., III *(Judge, Texas District Court 240th Judicial District)* Appointed by Governor William P. Clements to term beginning Jan 1, 1991. Elected to term beginning Jan 1, 1995. Reelected Nov 1998 and 2002. Current term expires Dec 31, 2006. Born Abilene Texas March 30, 1949. Baptist. Educated at Baylor University B.B.A. 1971 J.D. 1973. Admitted to practice Texas 1973, U.S. District Court Southern District of Texas 1980, U.S. Courts of Appeals Fifth 1980 and Eleventh 1980 Circuits and U.S. Supreme Court 1980. In legal practice Rosenberg 1973-76. Judge, Fort Bend County Court at Law No. 1, 1981-90.

First Assistant District Attorney Fort Bend County 1977-81. Chairman Fort Bend County Juvenile Board since 1981 and Unauthorized Practice of Law Subcommittee since 1988. Member Fort Bend County Board of Judges, Purchasing Agent Board and Board of District Judges, College of the State Bar of Texas, State Bar of Texas and Fort Bend County Bar Association.

Office: County Courthouse, Richmond 77469-3110.
Telephone: (281) 341-8600.

CUMMINGS, Jamie *(Judge, Tarrant County Criminal Court at Law No. 5)*
Office: Tarrant County Justice Center, Sixth Floor, 401 West Belknap, Fort Worth 76196-0243.
Telephone: (817) 884-2727.

CUMMINGS, Samuel R. *(Judge, United States District Court Northern District of Texas)* Appointed for life by President Ronald Reagan to term beginning 1987. Born 1944. Educated at Texas Tech University B.B.A. with high honors 1967 and Baylor University School of Law J.D. cum laude 1970. Board Certified—Civil Trial Law—Texas Board of Legal Specialization. In legal practice Amarillo 1970-87.

Fellow Texas Bar Foundation. Member State Bar of Texas.

Office: C-210 U.S. Courthouse, 1205 Texas Avenue, Lubbock 79401.
Telephone: (806) 472-7459.

CUNNINGHAM, Vickers L., Sr. *(Judge, Texas District Court 283rd Judicial District)* Born Dallas County Texas 1962. Baptist. Educated at Southern Methodist University B.B.A. 1984 J.D. 1988. Admitted to practice Texas 1988. In legal practice 1994. Former Judge, Dallas County Criminal Court at Law No. 8, elected to term beginning Jan 1, 1995.

Assistant District Attorney Dallas County 1988-94. Member American Judicature Society, Dallas and American Bar Associations.

Office: LB 33 Frank Crowley Courts Bldg., 133 North Industrial Boulevard, Dallas 75207-4313.
Telephone: (214) 653-5860.

CURRY, Kenneth Charles *(Judge, Texas District Court 153rd Judicial District)*
Office: Tarrant County Justice Center, 401 West Belknap, Fort Worth 76196-0225.
Telephone: (817) 884-1489.

DALBY, Giles W. *(Judge, Garza County Court)* Elected Nov 1970 to term beginning Jan 1, 1971. Reelected 1974, 1978, 1982, 1986, 1990, 1994, 1998 and 2002. Current term expires Dec 31, 2006. Born Lubbock Texas Sept 1, 1932. Presbyterian. Educated at Texas Tech University and Kennedy Western University B.S.

Member County Judges and Commissioners Association of Texas (Director, Past President), West Texas County Judges and Commissioners Association (President 1978) and Texas Association of Counties (Past President). Instructor County Judges Seminar 1991 and Chairman Continuing Education Committee Texas County Judges Association. Named Outstanding County Judge by West Texas County Judges and Commissioners Association 1975. Recipient John Ben Shepperd Form Award 1988 and Citizen of the Year 1988. Director Chamber of Commerce 1972-75, First National Bank since 1973 and Plains National Bank Lubbock. Board of Trustees Post Independent School District (President 1964-72) and Methodist Hospital Lubbock. Trustee since 1984 and Chairman since 1990 Texas County and District Retirement System. President Texas Association of Counties. Drive Chairman Boy Scouts of America. Member West Texas Boys Ranch, Red Raider Club, Texas Alcoholism Council, President's Council Texas Tech University and First Presbyterian Church (Elder). Enjoys reading, riding and radios.

Office: 300 West Main, Post 79356.
Telephone: (806) 495-4405.

DANIEL, Duane *(Judge, King County Court)*
Mailing address: P.O. Box 127, Guthrie 79236-0127.
Telephone: (806) 596-4411.

DARNELL, Jim Bob *(Judge, Texas District Court 140th Judicial District)*
Mailing address: P.O. Box 10536, Lubbock 79408-3536.
Telephone: (806) 775-1128.

DAUPHINOT, Lee Ann *(Justice, Texas Court of Appeals Second District)* Elected to term beginning Jan 1, 1995. Reelected 2000, current term expires Dec 31, 2006. Educated at Texas Christian University B.A., Stanford University M.A. and Southern Methodist University J.D. 1978. Fulbright Fellow, Woodrow Wilson Fellow and Hatton Sumners Scholar. Board Certified—Criminal Law—Texas Board of Legal Specialization. Judge, Texas Criminal District Court No. 2 Tarrant County 1990-95.

Member Texas Judicial Council, College of the State Bar of Texas and National Association of Women Judges. Elder St. Stephen Presbyterian Church.

Office: 9000 Tarrant County Justice Center, 401 West Belknap, Fort Worth 76196.
Telephone: (817) 884-2173.

DAVENPORT, Mitchell Grant *(Judge, Jack County Court)*
Office: 100 Main Street, Jacksboro 76458.
Telephone: (940) 567-2241.

DAVIDSON, Mark *(Judge, Texas District Court 11th Judicial District)* Tax Master-in-Chancery 1987-88. Elected Judge to term beginning Jan 1, 1989. Reelected Nov 3, 1992, 1996 and 2000. Current term expires Dec 31, 2004. Born Arlington Virginia July 23, 1953. Roman Catholic. Educated at University of Texas B.A. 1973 and University of Houston J.D. 1977. Member Phi Alpha Delta. Admitted to practice Texas 1978, U.S. District Court Southern District of Texas 1978 and U.S. Court of Appeals Fifth Circuit 1978. In legal practice Houston 1978-88.

Office: 211 Civil Courts Building, 301 Fannin Street, Houston 77002.
Telephone: (713) 755-6250.

DAVIES, Carol G. *(Judge, Texas District Court 177th Judicial District)*
Office: 1201 Franklin, Room 19136, Houston 77002.
Telephone: (713) 755-6332.

DAVIS, Chris *(Judge, Cherokee County Court)*
Office: 502 North Main Street, Rusk 75785.
Telephone: (903) 683-2324.

DAVIS, David C. *(Judge, Haskell County Court)*
Office: One Avenue D, Haskell 79521.
Telephone: (940) 864-2851.

DAVIS, Fred W. *(Judge, Texas District Court 17th Judicial District)* Elected to term beginning Jan 1, 1989. Reelected 1992, 1996 and 2000. Current term expires Dec 31, 2004. Local Administrative Judge Tarrant County 1995-96. Born San Angelo Texas Jan 16, 1938. Presbyterian. Educated at Sul Ross State College B.S. and Baylor University School of Law J.D. Admitted to practice Texas 1962 and U.S. District Court Northern District of Texas 1963. In legal practice Arlington 1962-88.

Instructor University of Texas at Arlington 1964-65. Member State Bar of Texas, Arlington and Tarrant County Bar Associations. Republican.

Office: Tarrant County Justice Center, 401 West Belknap, Fort Worth 76196-0220.
Telephone: (817) 884-1460.

DAVIS, John Paul *(Judge, Jefferson County Court at Law No. 3)* Appointed to term beginning Dec 22, 1989. Elected 1990, 1994, 1998 and 2002. Current term expires Dec 31, 2006. Born Bay City Texas Nov 9, 1939. Baptist. Educated at Prairie View A and M University B.S. 1963 and University of Houston J.D. 1972. Member Phi Alpha Delta and Omega Psi Phi. Admitted to practice Texas 1972, U.S. District Court Eastern District of Texas 1974 and U.S. Court of Appeals Fifth Circuit 1975. In legal practice Beaumont 1976-89. Judge, Beaumont Municipal Court 1980-89.

Assistant Criminal District Attorney Jefferson County 1973-76. Member State Bar of Texas. Member Texas Center for the Judiciary, Inc. U.S. Army Vietnam 1963-65. Life Member NAACP.

Office: 1001 Pearl Street, Beaumont 77701.
Telephone: (409) 835-8697.

DAVIS, Kenneth *(Judge, Hill County Court)* Elected Dec 1, 1998. Reelected Nov 5, 2002, current term expires Dec 31, 2006. Born Itasca Texas May 28, 1941. Baptist. Educated at Baylor University B.B.A. 1965 and Prairie View A and M University 1980.

Democrat. County Commissioner Precinct 4 Hill County 1971-89. Secretary 2001, Vice President 2002, Lead CEO 2002-03 and President 2003 Executive Board Heart of Texas Council of Governments. Chairman of Deacons 1983-85 and 2000-01 and Finance Committee 2000-01 and Deacon First Baptist Church. Member Pontiac-Oakland Club International for 28 years. Interests include playing steel guitar and collecting classic cars. Personal Statement or Quote: "Follow the Bible's teachings—always treat others as you would like to be treated."

Mailing address: P.O. Box 457, Hillsboro 76645.
Office: #1 Courthouse Square, Hillsboro 76645.
Telephone: (254) 582-4020.
Fax: (254) 582-4028
E-mail address: countyjudge@hillsboro.net

DAVIS, Leonard E. *(Judge, United States District Court Eastern District of Texas)* Appointed for life by President George W. Bush to term beginning May 15, 2002. Educated at University of Texas at Arlington B.A., Texas Christian University M.M.S. and Baylor University School of Law J.D. cum laude 1976. Recipient American Jurisprudence Awards in Contracts and Federal Courts. Editor-in-Chief Baylor Law Review. Moot Court. Admitted to practice U.S. District Courts Eastern, Northern and Southern Districts of Texas, U.S. Court of Appeals Fifth Circuit and U.S. Supreme Court. Chief Justice, Texas Court of Appeals Twelfth District July 9, 2000 to May 2002.

Member State Bar of Texas.

Office: 211 West Ferguson Street, Suite 318, Tyler 75702.
Telephone: (903) 590-1084.

DAVIS, Paul R., Jr. *(Judge, Texas District Court 200th Judicial District)* Appointed by Governor Mark White to term beginning Oct 3, 1983. Elected 1984, 1988, 1992, 1996 and 2000. Current term expires Dec 31, 2004. Born Pittsburgh Pennsylvania Nov 10, 1945. Educated at University of Tulsa B.A. 1967 and University of Texas School of Law J.D. 1970. Editor Texas Law Forum. Member Phi Delta Phi and Kappa Sigma. Admitted to practice Texas 1970. Began legal practice Austin 1970.

Co-author with James Farris "Legislative Changes to the Family Code" 1977 and 1981 and with John Sampson "A Brief, Expurgated History of the Recommendations of the Child Support Advisory Committee" Family Law Section Report No. 1 State Bar of Texas 1987. Author "Visitation Guidelines: A Judge's Perspective" Family Law Section Report No. 6 State Bar of Texas 1987 and "The Balanced Approach for Juvenile Justice—A Challenge from the Bench" 39 No. 3 Juvenile and Family Court Journal 51, 1988. Director 1973-74 and Secretary-Treasurer 1974-75 Austin Junior Bar Association. Director Court Appointed Special Advocates of Travis County 1986-92. Member Texas Multidisciplinary Task Force on Children's Justice 1989-93. Member Drafting Committee, Child Support Guidelines Advisory Committee and Education Committee since 1991 Texas Supreme Court, Metropolitan Courts Judges Committee and Substance Abuse Committee National Council of Juvenile and Family Law Judges and Judicial Education Executive Committee since 1991. Member Texas Trial Lawyers Association (Director 1975-80, Assistant Family Law Legislative Coordinator 1978-81), State Bar of Texas (Member and Secretary District 9 Grievance Committee 1978-81) and Travis County Bar Association (Chairman Committee on Admissions 1973-74, Director 1987-89).

Speaker "Contempt—Getting 'Em Out of Jail" Texas Trial Lawyers Association Family Law Seminar Oct 1977; "Jurisdiction, Venue & Transfer in Family Law Cases" SMU Symposium on Family Law 1979; "Jurisdiction, Conflicts and Transfers" Travis County Bar Association Family Law Symposium 1979; "The Use of the Expert Witness in the Trial of Divorce Custody Cases" SMU Symposium for Specialists on Texas Family Law and Community Property 1980; Family Law State Bar Convention Nuts & Bolts Course 1982; "Division and Disposition of the Marital Estate" State Bar of Texas Divorce Seminar 1984; "Survey of New Family Law Legislation" Fall 1987 and "Review of the Application of the Texas Child Support Guidelines" Fall 1987

DAVIS, PAUL R., JR.—*Continued*

Texas Annual Judicial Section Conference; "Evidentiary Problems: Similar Events, Business Records, Medical Records and Government Records" Advanced College of Trial Advocacy The Association of Trial Lawyers of America Aug 1987; "A Balanced Approach to Juvenile Justice" Southern Legislators Conference on Children and Youth Nov 15-18, 1987; "Contempt: A Walk Through the Maze" Texas Regional Judicial Conferences Spring 1988; "Judicial Responsibility: Abuse of the System and Authority of the Court" Families in Court: A National Symposium The National Judicial College May 1989; "Missing and Exploited Children" Tennessee Joint Conference on Juvenile Justice Memphis Aug 1989; and "Mirrors, Resolutions and Contempts—An Analysis of the Roles and Enforcement Powers of the Court" Reno 1989. Panelist "Judges and Restitution Programs: What Have We Done for Each Other Lately?" The Second Annual Conference on Juvenile Restitution May 1988. Faculty Texas College for New Judges since 1992. Director Child and Family Service of Austin 1985-87, Pebble Project and Child Assault Prevention Program 1988-90 and New Life Institute since 1993. Board Member United Way/Capital Area 1991-92. Convener and Chairman Travis County Runaway Task Force. Member Steering Committee Institute for Community Family Treatment. Advisory Committee University of Texas Legal Assistant Certificate Program since 1991. Former Vice President West Austin Optimist Little League (coached Little League baseball, football and soccer).

Mailing address: P.O. Box 1748, Austin 78767-1748.
Telephone: (512) 854-9306.

DAVIS, Rex D. *(Chief Justice, Texas Court of Appeals Tenth District)* Appointed by Governor George W. Bush to term beginning May 31, 1996. Elected Nov 1996 to term beginning Jan 1, 1997. Reelected Nov 2000, current term expires Dec 31, 2006. Born Brenham Texas Aug 23, 1950. Educated at Temple Junior College, University of Texas at Austin and Baylor University School of Law J.D. cum laude 1974. Recipient American Jurisprudence Award in Constitutional Law. Admitted to practice Texas 1974. In legal practice McLennan County 1974-96. Justice pro tem, Texas Supreme Court 1998.

President Waco-McLennan County Bar Association 1990-91. Former Chair Council of Intermediate Chief Justices. Fellow Texas Bar Foundation. Charter Member Abner V. McCall American Inn of Court. Member College of the State Bar of Texas. Lecturer Baylor University School of Law and Hankamer School of Business Baylor University 1999-2003. Former Board Member D.A.R.E. of McLennan County and Heart of Texas Chapter Services American Red Cross. Past President Rotary Club of Northwest Waco. Member and Chairman Planning and Zoning Commission City of Woodway 1983-89. Member and Vice President Board of Trustees Midway Independent School District 1992-96. Coach Midway Little League. Member, Teacher, Former Deacon Chairman and Former Department Director Columbus Avenue Baptist Church. Enjoys jogging, reading, hunting, fishing and sports.

Mailing address: P.O. Box 1606, Waco 76703-1606.
Telephone: (254) 757-5200.

DAVIS, Richard W. B. *(Judge, Texas District Court 272nd Judicial District)* Elected to term beginning Jan 1, 2001. Term expires Dec 31, 2004. Born Nov 30, 1963. Christian. Educated at Texas A&M University B.S.M.E. 1986 and University of Houston J.D. Member Phi Eta Sigma. Admitted to practice Texas 1992. In legal practice Bryan July 1992 to Dec 1998. Judge, Brazos County Court at Law No. 2 Jan 1, 1999 to Jan 30, 2000.

Member Texas Army National Guard for ten years. Enjoys raising six kids and running marathons. Personal Statement or Quote: "Let honor be your guiding star with your fellows, your superiors, with all."

Office: 300 East 26th Street, Suite 204, Bryan 77803.
Telephone: (979) 361-4220.
Fax: (979) 361-4517
E-mail address: rdavis@co.brazos.tx.us

DAY, Sam *(Justice, Texas Court of Appeals Second District)* Assumed office 1990. Elected to subsequent terms. Current term expires Dec 31, 2006. Educated at University of Texas B.A. J.D. Admitted to practice Texas.

Sustaining Life Fellow Texas Bar Foundation. Member American Board of Trial Advocates and American Inns of Court.

Office: 9000 Tarrant County Justice Center, 401 West Belknap, Fort Worth 76196.
Telephone: (817) 884-1900.

DEAN, Keith *(Judge, Texas District Court 265th Judicial District)* Former Judge, Dallas County Criminal Court No. 5.

Office: LB 30 Frank Crowley Courts Building, 133 North Industrial Boulevard, Dallas 75207-4313.
Telephone: (214) 653-5840.

DEAN-WALKER, Becky *(Judge, Hudspeth County Court)*

Mailing address: P.O. Box 68, Sierra Blanca 79851-0068.
Telephone: (915) 369-2321.

DeHART, Kenneth Daly *(Judge, Texas District Court 394th Judicial District)*

Mailing address: P.O. Box 1410, Alpine 79831-1410.
Telephone: (432) 837-5831.

DE HOYOS, Jo-Ann Sylvia *(Judge, Bexar County Court at Law No. 11)*

Office: B50 Bexar County Courthouse, 100 Dolorosa Street, San Antonio 78205.
Telephone: (210) 335-2023.

DE LA GARZA, Pete *(Judge, Kleberg County Court)*

Mailing address: P.O. Box 752, Kingsville 78364-0752.
Telephone: (361) 595-8585.

DELGADO, Rodolfo *(Judge, Texas District Court 93rd Judicial District)*

Office: 100 North Closner, Second Floor, Edinburg 78539.
Telephone: (956) 318-2255.

DEMPSEY, Becky *(Judge, Smith County Court)*
Office: 100 North Broadway, #304, Tyler 75702-7236.
Telephone: (903) 535-0583.

DEMPSTER, Georgia *(Judge, Texas Family District Court 308th Judicial District)*
Office: Family Law Center Building, Third Floor, 1115 Congress Street, Houston 77002.
Telephone: (713) 755-6230.

DENTON, Mike *(Judge, Travis County Court at Law No. 4)*
Mailing address: P.O. Box 1748, Austin 78767-1748.
Telephone: (512) 854-9896.

DERBYSHIRE, Pam *(Judge, Harris County Criminal Court at Law No. 7)* Elected Nov 1998 to term beginning Jan 1, 1999. Reelected Nov 2002, current term expires Dec 31, 2006. Born Detroit Michigan Nov 11, 1957. Educated at University of South Florida 1979 and South Texas College of Law J.D. 1982. Admitted to practice Texas 1982. In legal practice Houston 1991-98.
Assistant District Attorney 1983-90. Assistant U.S. Attorney 1990-91. Member Association of Women Attorneys and Houston Bar Association. Republican.
Office: 1201 Franklin, Room 9144, Houston 77002.
Telephone: (713) 755-6204.
E-mail address: Pam_Derbyshire@ccl.co.harris.tx.us

DeSHAZO, Nikki Towry *(Judge, Dallas County Probate Court)* Elected 1982 to term beginning Jan 1, 1983. Reelected 1986, 1990, 1994, 1998 and 2002. Current term expires Dec 31, 2006. Presiding Judge Statutory Probate Judges of Texas 1993-97. Born Tahlequah Oklahoma July 12, 1944. Presbyterian. Educated at Northwestern University of Louisiana B.S.N. 1966 and Southern Methodist University School of Law J.D. 1976. Admitted to practice Texas 1976. Began legal practice Dallas 1976.
Co-author three-volume set *Probate Texas Practice Guide* West Publishing. Fellow Texas Bar Foundation. Member Texas College of Probate Judges, National College of Probate Judges (Executive Council 1993-2000, President 1998-99), State Bar of Texas (President Women and Law Section 1986-87, Council member Real Estate, Probate and Trust Section 1987-91) and Dallas Bar Association (Chairman Mock Trial Committee 1986 and All States Mock Trial Committee 1988). Instructor in Advanced Estate Planning courses Texas College of Probate Judges Annual Workshops and Seminars and Wills and Probate courses The National Judicial College. Second Lieutenant (flight nurse) USAFR 1966-68. Republican. President Executive Women of Dallas 1992 and Leadership Dallas 1991. Member Westminster Presbyterian Church. Enjoys running, reading and traveling.
Office: 501 Main Street, Dallas 75202-3513.
Telephone: (214) 653-7236.

DeVASTO, Diane Vinson *(Justice, Texas Court of Appeals Twelfth District)* Born Fort Worth Texas April 19, 1951. Baptist. Educated at Baylor University B.A. 1972 J.D. 1974. Admitted to practice Texas 1974. In legal practice Tyler. Judge, Tyler Municipal Court 1983-94. Judge, Smith County Court at Law No. 1 1994-95. Former Judge, Texas District Court 241st Judicial District, appointed by Governor George W. Bush to term beginning Dec 22, 1995.
Assistant City Attorney 1974-76. Instructor University of Texas at Tyler 1978-80. Member State Bar of Texas and Smith County Bar Association.
Office: 1517 Front Street, Suite 354, Tyler 75702-7854.
Telephone: (903) 593-8471.

DIBRELL, C. G. "Trey", III *(Judge, Galveston County Court at Law No. 2)*
Office: 722 Moody, Room 601, Galveston 77550.
Telephone: (409) 766-2405.

DIETZ, John K. *(Judge, Texas District Court 250th Judicial District)*
Mailing address: P.O. Box 1748, Austin 78767-1748.
Telephone: (512) 854-9312.

DIXON, James P. *(Judge, Grimes County Court)* Elected to term beginning Jan 1, 2003. Born Houston Texas April 24, 1932. Personal Statement or Quote: "Tell the truth."
Mailing address: P.O. Box 160, Anderson 77830.
Telephone: (936) 873-2111.

DOERFLER, John Christian *(Judge, Williamson County Court)*
Office: Williamson County Courthouse, Second Floor, Georgetown 78626.
Telephone: (512) 943-1550.

DOLGENER, Richard H. *(Judge, Andrews County Court)*
Office: 104 Courthouse, Andrews 79714.
Telephone: (432) 524-1401.

DONAHUE, Kenneth Ray *(Judge, Ochiltree County Court)*
Office: 511 South Main, Perryton 79070-3154.
Telephone: (806) 435-8031.

DONOVAN, John *(Judge, Texas District Court 61st Judicial District)*
Office: Civil Courts Building, Fifth Floor, 301 Fannin Street, Houston 77002.
Telephone: (713) 755-6258.

DORAN, Jeff *(Judge, Anderson County Court at Law)*
Office: 500 North Church Street, Palestine 75801.
Telephone: (903) 723-7469.

DORFMAN, S. Grant *(Judge, Texas District Court 129th Judicial District)*
Office: 1019 Congress Street, Sixteenth Floor, Houston 77002.
Telephone: (713) 755-6279.

DOUGHARTY, Truman *(Judge, Newton County Court)*
Office: P.O. Drawer J, Newton 75966.
Telephone: (409) 379-5691.

DOUGHERTY, Joe Ray *(Judge, Rains County Court)*
Mailing address: P.O. Box 158, Emory 75440-0158.
Telephone: (903) 473-2555.

DRUM, Teresa *(Judge, Texas District Court 294th Judicial District)*
Office: 121 East Dallas, Room 301, Canton 75103-1604.
Telephone: (903) 567-4422.

DRY, Robert T., Jr. *(Judge, Texas District Court 199th Judicial District)*
Office: 210 South McDonald, Suite 534, McKinney 75069.
Telephone: (972) 548-4415.

DuBOSE, Willie Bryan *(Judge, Texas District Court 385th Judicial District)*

Office: 200 West Wall, Suite 401, Midland 79701-4557.

Telephone: (432) 688-1835.

DUNCAN, Sarah B. *(Justice, Texas Court of Appeals Fourth District)* Elected Nov 1994 to term beginning Jan 1, 1995. Reelected Nov 2000, current term expires Dec 31, 2006. Born Waco Texas May 23, 1955. Educated at Smith College 1973-75, University of Texas at Austin B.A. with honors 1977 J.D. with honors 1984. Staff member Texas Law Review 1982-84. Admitted to practice Texas 1984. Board Certified—Civil Appellate Law—Texas Board of Legal Specialization. In legal practice Austin, Houston and San Antonio 1984-94.

Co-author chapters on Stay of Execution and Original Proceedings *Revised Texas Appellate Practice Manual* State Bar of Texas 2nd ed. 1993. Member Rules Committee Appellate Practice and Advocacy Section State Bar of Texas since 1989. Member Supreme Court Advisory Committee on the Rules of Civil Procedure since 1993. Author and Speaker "Other Aspects of Tort Reform" St. Mary's Tenth Annual Procedural Law Institute—Tort Reform 1988, "Foreclosing on a Wraparound Note" St. Mary's Eleventh Annual Procedural Law Institute—Foreclosure Litigation 1989, "Enforcement of Judgments and Supersedeas" Advanced Appellate Practice Course State Bar of Texas 1990, "The Use of Expert Witnesses to Establish Legal Malpractice" St. Mary's Twelfth Annual Procedural Law Institute—Malpractice Litigation 1990, "Charge Submission After Tort Reform" Appellate and Advocacy Section Meeting State Bar of Texas Annual Meeting June 21, 1991, "Briefing the Argument" Advanced Civil Appellate Practice Course State Bar of Texas 1992, "Preparing the Jury Charge" Advanced Civil Trial Short Course Southern Methodist University School of Law 1993, "The Charge—A Rebuttal" Tenth Annual Litigation Update Institute State Bar of Texas 1994 and "Rules Changes" Appellate Practice for Lawyers and Legal Assistants State Bar of Texas 1995. Speaker on "Big Quake or Little Shake (The Upcoming Rules Changes)" Appellate Practice and Advocacy Section Meeting State Bar of Texas Annual Meeting June 24, 1994.

Office: 3200 Bexar County Justice Center, 300 Dolorosa Street, San Antonio 78205-3037.

Telephone: (210) 335-3919.

E-mail address: sarah.duncan@courts.state.tx.us

DUNN, Thomas Arthur *(Judge, Smith County Court at Law No. 1)*

Office: 100 North Broadway Avenue, Second Floor, Tyler 75702-7236.

Telephone: (903) 535-0606.

EARLE, Elisabeth A. *(Judge, Travis County Court at Law No. 7)*

Office: P.O. Box 1748, Austin 78767-1748.

Telephone: (512) 854-9679.

ECKELS, Robert A. *(Judge, Harris County Court)* Elected Nov 1994 to term beginning Jan 1, 1995. Reelected Nov 1998 and 2002. Current term expires Dec 31, 2006. Born Houston Texas March 14, 1957. Presbyterian. Educated at University of Houston B.A. 1980 and South Texas College of Law J.D. 1993. Admitted to practice Texas 1993 and Colorado 1995.

Senior Fellow American Leadership Forum. Member State Bar of Texas, Houston and Colorado Bar Associations. Named Outstanding Young Houstonian by Greater Houston Chamber of Commerce and Houston Junior Chamber of Commerce 1995 and Statesman of the Year by Texas Asian Republican Caucus 1996. Republican. Member House of Representatives Texas 1983-94. Board of Directors 1985-90 and Vice President 1990-94 National Republican Legislators Association. Board of Directors National Conference of Republican County Officials since 1995 and National Council of Elected County Officials since 1996. Delegate British-American Project 1996. Chairman Tax and Fiscal Policy Committee National Association of Counties since 1996. Chairman Harris County Juvenile Board. Board Member Houston Livestock Show and Rodeo, I-69 Mid-Continent Highway Coalition, Inc., Houston-Galveston Area Council and Gulf Coast Community Service Association. Executive Board Greater Houston Convention and Visitors Bureau.

Office: 1001 Preston, Suite 911, Houston 77002.

Telephone: (713) 755-4000.

EDELMAN, Richard H. *(Justice, Texas Court of Appeals Fourteenth District)* Elected Nov 1994 to term beginning Jan 1, 1995. Reelected Nov 2000, current term expires Dec 31, 2006. Born Baton Rouge Louisiana April 8, 1955. Educated at University of Texas B.B.A. with honors 1976 J.D. with honors 1981. Admitted to practice Texas 1981. In legal practice Houston 1981-87 and 1990-94.

Panel of Arbitrators American Arbitration Association 1991-94. Chairman Federal Practice Section Houston Bar Association 1993-94. Member State Bar College of Texas, Houston Bar Foundation and Texas Bar Foundation. Accountant 1976-78.

Office: 1307 San Jacinto, 11th Floor, Houston 77002-7006.

Telephone: (713) 655-2800.

EDWARDS, Durwood *(Magistrate Judge, United States District Court Western District of Texas)* Appointed by U.S. District Court judges.

Office: U.S. Courthouse, 803 North Second Street, Alpine 79830-3123.

Telephone: (915) 837-9740.

EDWARDS, Frederick E. *(Judge, Texas District Court 9th Judicial District)*

Office: 301 North Thompson, Suite 110, Conroe 77301-2505.

Telephone: (936) 539-7866.

EGAN, Marilyn *(Judge, Runnels County Court)* Appointed Sept 1, 1995. Elected 1996, Nov 1998 and 2002. Current term expires Dec 31, 2006. Born Norton Texas Oct 15, 1941. Baptist. Enjoys reading.

Office: 613 Courthouse Square, Ballinger 76821-5727.

Telephone: (325) 365-2633.

ELKINS, Mike B. *(Judge, Reagan County Court)*

Mailing address: P.O. Box 100, Big Lake 76932.

Telephone: (325) 884-2665.

ELLINGTON, B. Janice *(Magistrate Judge, United States District Court Southern District of Texas)* Appointed by U.S. District Court judges.

Office: U.S. Courthouse, 1133 North Shoreline Boulevard, Corpus Christi 78401.

Telephone: (361) 888-3291.

ELLIOTT, Brady Gifford *(Judge, Texas District Court 268th Judicial District)* Term expires Dec 31, 2006.

Office: 301 South Jackson, Room 101, Richmond 77469-3108.

Telephone: (281) 341-8610.

ELLIOTT, Fred *(Judge, Robertson County Court)*

Mailing address: P.O. Box 427, Franklin 77856.

Telephone: (979) 828-3542.

ELLIS, "Earl" Kent *(Judge, Texas Family District Court 315th Judicial District)*

Office: Family Law Center Building, Fourth Floor, 1115 Congress Street, Houston 77002.

Telephone: (713) 755-6480.

ELLIS, Mark Kent *(Judge, Texas District Court 351st Judicial District)*

Office: 1201 Franklin, Room 14032, Houston 77002.

Telephone: (713) 755-5620.

ELLIS, Stephen *(Judge, Texas District Court 35th Judicial District)* Elected Nov 5, 1996 to term beginning Jan 1, 1997. Reelected 2000, current term expires Dec 31, 2004. Born Silver City New Mexico Nov 21, 1951. Baptist. Educated at Baylor University B.A. 1973 J.D. 1976. Member Omicron Delta Kappa (President Baylor Circle 1973). Admitted to practice Texas 1976 and U.S. District Court Northern District of Texas 1980. In legal practice Brownwood 1976-96.

Assistant District Attorney 1976-80 and District Attorney 1981-88, 35th District of Texas. Member American Judicature Society, American Judges Association, State Bar of Texas (Section of Judiciary) and Brown County Bar Association (President 1978). Named Texas CASA Judge of the Year 2002. Democrat. Sunday School Teacher since 1976, Deacon since 1980 and Chairman of Deacons 1997 First Baptist Church Brownwood. Cubmaster Cub Scout Pack 14, 1992-97 and Scout Master Troop 14 1997-2002 Comanche Trail Council Boy Scouts of America. Former Director and Campaign Volunteer Brown County United Way. Life Member Baylor University Alumni Association. Member Brownwood Kiwanis Club (President 1981-82), Brown County Chamber of Commerce and Baylor University School of Law Alumni Association. Enjoys ranching, backpacking, hunting, camping, art, music, theater and Civil War history.

Office: 200 South Broadway, Brownwood 76801-3192.

Telephone: (915) 646-1987.

ELLISON, Keith P. *(Judge, United States District Court Southern District of Texas)* Appointed for life by President Bill Clinton to term beginning Aug 2, 1999. Born 1950. Educated at Harvard University A.B. 1972, Oxford University, England B.A. 1974 and Yale University J.D. 1976. Rhodes Scholar. Editor Yale Law Journal. Law Clerk to Hon. J. Skelly Wright, U.S. Court of Appeals District of Columbia Circuit 1976-77 and Hon. Harry A. Blackmun, U.S. Supreme Court 1977-78. In legal practice Tulsa Oklahoma 1978-84 and Houston Texas 1985-99.

Member Council on Foreign Relations, American Bankruptcy Institute, The American Law Institute, State Bar of Texas, Houston and New York State Bar Associations. Board of Directors American-South African Scholarship Association and Harry A. Blackmun Scholarship Foundation. Secretary District VII Rhodes Scholarship Selection Committee.

Mailing address: P.O. Box 6065, Laredo 78042.

Office: 103 U.S. Courthouse Annex, 904 Juarez Avenue, Laredo 78040-4951.

Telephone: (956) 726-2242.

Fax: (956) 794-1035

E-mail address: Keith_Ellison@txs.uscourts.gov

ELLISOR, John *(Judge, Texas District Court 122nd Judicial District)*

Office: 722 Moody, #603, Galveston 77550.

Telephone: (409) 766-2275.

ELROD, Jennifer Walker *(Judge, Texas District Court 190th Judicial District)*

Office: 1310 Prairie, Eleventh Floor, Houston 77002.

Telephone: (713) 755-6370.

EMERSON, Don *(Judge, Texas Family District Court 320th Judicial District)* Assumed office 1985. Elected 1986, 1990, 1994, 1998 and 2002. Current term expires Dec 31, 2006.

Office: 501 South Fillmore Street, Suite 4-B, Amarillo 79101-2444.

Telephone: (806) 379-2370.

EMMERT, Steven R. *(Judge, Texas District Court 31st Judicial District)* Elected to term beginning Jan 1, 1999. Reelected 2002, current term expires Dec 31, 2006. Born Pauls Valley Oklahoma June 13, 1957. Methodist. Educated at West Texas State University B.S. 1980 and Oklahoma City University School of Law J.D. 1985. Admitted to practice Texas 1986 and Oklahoma 1986. In legal practice Wheeler Texas 1986-99.

County Attorney Wheeler County Texas 1990-98. Member College of the State Bar of Texas, State Bar of Texas and Oklahoma Bar Association. Republican. Enjoys ranching.

Mailing address: P.O. Box 766, Wheeler 79096.

Telephone: (806) 826-5501.

Fax: (806) 826-5503

ENDER, Elma Teresa Salinas *(Judge, Texas District Court 341st Judicial District)* Term expires Dec 31, 2004.

Mailing address: P.O. Box 1598, Laredo 78042-1598.

Telephone: (956) 523-4329.

ENNS, Ronald E. *(Judge, Texas District Court 69th Judicial District)*

Office: 715 South Dumas Avenue, No. 302, Dumas 79029-4326.

Telephone: (806) 935-2700.

ENOCH, Craig T. *(Justice, Texas Supreme Court)* Elected to term beginning Jan 1, 1993. Reelected 1998, current term expires Dec 31, 2004. Born Wichita Kansas 1950. Educated at Southern Methodist University B.A. 1972 J.D. 1975 and University of Virginia School of Law LL.M. 1992. Admitted to practice Texas 1975. Judge, Texas District Court 101st Judicial District 1981-87. Chief Justice, Texas Court of Appeals Fifth District 1987-92.

Supreme Court Liaison to State Bar of Texas. Chair Appellate Judges Conference Judicial Division American Bar Association.

Mailing address: P.O. Box 12248, Austin 78711-2248.

Telephone: (512) 463-1340.

ESKEW, Benton *(Judge, Bastrop County Court at Law)* Appointed to term beginning Aug 1, 1994. Elected Nov 8, 1994, 1998 and 2002. Current term expires Dec 31, 2006. Born Bastrop Texas Sept 2, 1961. Baptist. Educated at Baylor University B.B.A. with honors 1984 J.D. with honors 1986. Member Delta Theta Phi. Admitted to practice Texas 1986 and U.S. District Courts Northern 1988 and Western 1988 Districts of Texas. In legal practice Austin 1986-91 and Bastrop 1991-94.

Co-author "Default Judgments: Procedure(s) for Alleging or Controverting Facts on the Conscious Indifference Issue" 40 Baylor L. Rev. 59, 1987. Member Austin Young Lawyers Association (Co-chair Athletics Committee 1990-91), State Bar of Texas, Bastrop County (Treasurer 1993) and American Bar Associations. Board of Directors Boys and Girls Club of Bastrop. Member Calvary Baptist Church.

Office: 804 Pecan Street, Bastrop 78602.
Telephone: (512) 332-7290.

ESTLINBAUM, Craig *(Judge, Texas District Court 130th Judicial District)* Elected Nov 2000 to term beginning Jan 1, 2001. Term expires Dec 31, 2004. Born Bay City Texas March 25, 1962. Educated at Texas A&M University B.S. 1984 M.AGR. 1985 and South Texas College of Law J.D. magna cum laude 1994. Editor-in-Chief South Texas Law Review 1993-94. Admitted to practice Texas 1994 and U.S. District Court Southern District of Texas 1995.

Office: 1700 Seventh Street, Room 317, Bay City 77414.
Telephone: (979) 244-7635.
Fax: (979) 245-6478

EURESTI, Benjamin *(Judge, Texas District Court 107th Judicial District)* Elected to term beginning Jan 1, 1991. Reelected 1994, 1998 and 2002. Current term expires Dec 31, 2006. Born Brownsville Texas June 18, 1949. Presbyterian. Educated at Texas Southmost College 1969, University of Houston B.A. 1975 and Thurgood Marshall School of Law J.D. 1979. Admitted to practice Texas 1979. In legal practice Brownsville 1982-84 and 1990.

Assistant District Attorney 1981-82 and District Attorney 1985-90 Cameron County. Important Decisions: League of United Latin American Citizens (LULAC) et al. v. Ann Richards et al. (ruled the $1.3 billion system of higher education is unconstitutional and gave the legislature until May 1993 to fix it) 1991. Member Criminal Justice Council State Bar of Texas 1988. Former Member Texas District and County Attorneys Association and American Bar Association. Member Cameron County Bar Association. Attended Texas College for New Judges Dec 3, 1990, Regional Judicial Conferences March 6, 1991 and March 13, 1992, Criminal Justice Conference May 16, 1991, Judicial Section Annual Conference Sept 25, 1991 Texas Center for the Judiciary, Anatomy of a Personal Injury Trial State Bar of Texas Dec 13, 1991, Criminal Defense Skills Course Criminal Defense Lawyers April 16, 1992, Virginia Judicial Conference July 19-31, 1992 and El Paso Judicial Conference Sept 21-25, 1992. Democrat. Member Brownsville Planning and Zoning Committee, Brownsville Local Development Corporation, Brownsville Citizens Advisory Committee and Brownsville Rotary Club. Enjoys golf.

Office: 974 East Harrison Street, Brownsville 78520-7123.
Telephone: (956) 544-0845.

EVANS, David W. *(Judge, Texas District Court 193rd Judicial District)* Former Judge, Dallas County Court at Law No. 1.

Office: George Allen Sr. Courts Building, Fourth Floor, 600 Commerce Street, Dallas 75202-4606.
Telephone: (214) 653-6998.

EVANS, Deborah Oakes *(Judge, Texas District Court 87th Judicial District)*
Mailing address: P.O. Box 722, Fairfield 75840-0722.
Telephone: (903) 723-7415.

EVANS, Mark *(Judge, Trinity County Court)*
Mailing address: P.O. Box 457, Groveton 75845.
Telephone: (936) 642-1746.

EVANS, Richard A. *(Judge, Bandera County Court)*
Mailing address: P.O. Box 877, Bandera 78003-0877.
Telephone: (830) 796-3781.

FAGAN, Roger C. *(Judge, Refugio County Court)*
Office: 808 Commerce, Room 104, Refugio 78377.
Telephone: (361) 526-4434.

FAMBROUGH, Tim D. *(Judge, Nolan County Court)*
Office: 100 East Third, Suite 105, Sweetwater 79556-4546.
Telephone: (325) 235-2263.
Fax: (325) 236-9416

FARMER, Drue *(Judge, Lubbock County Court at Law No. 2)*
Mailing address: P.O. Box 10536, Lubbock 79408-3536.
Telephone: (806) 775-1301.

FELSENTHAL, Steven A. *(Chief Judge, United States Bankruptcy Court Northern District of Texas)* Chief Judge since April 15, 2002.

Office: 12A24 U.S. Courthouse, 1100 Commerce Street, Dallas 75242-1496.
Telephone: (214) 753-2040.

FERCHILL, Patrick W. *(Judge, Tarrant County Probate Court No. 2)* Assumed office 1981. Elected 1982, 1986, 1990, 1994, 1998 and 2002. Current term expires Dec 31, 2006. Born Longview Texas June 29, 1946. Episcopalian. Educated at Southern Methodist University B.B.A. 1968 and University of Texas School of Law J.D. 1972. Admitted to practice Texas 1971. Judge, Fort Worth Municipal Court No. 2, 1976-77. Chief Judge, Fort Worth Municipal Court No. 1, 1977-78. Judge, Tarrant County Court at Law No. 1, 1978-81.

Board Member National Guardianship Association. Trustee National Guardianship Foundation.

Office: 100 West Weatherford, Room 220A, Fort Worth 76196-7752.
Telephone: (817) 884-1415.

FERNANDEZ, Mike L. *(Judge, Val Verde County Court)*
Mailing address: P.O. Box 4250, Del Rio 78841.
Telephone: (830) 774-7501.

FIELD, David D. *(Judge, Dallam County Court)* Appointed to term beginning March 1, 1986. Elected 1986, 1990, 1994, 1998 and 2002. Current term expires Dec 31, 2006. Born Lubbock Texas July 24, 1950. Baptist. Educated at Texas Tech University B.S. 1973 M.S. 1975.

Previously employed as engineering consultant, farm

FIELD, DAVID D.—*Continued*

and ranch owner and high school and junior college teacher. Deacon Baptist Church. Member Rotary Club. Enjoys sports, skiing, remodeling, antiques and classic cars.

Mailing address: P.O. Box 9395, Dalhart 79022.

Telephone: (806) 244-2450.

FIELDS, Michael R. *(Judge, Harris County Criminal Court at Law No. 14)*

Office: 1201 Franklin, Room 11040, Houston 77002.

Telephone: (713) 755-5683.

FISH, A. Joe *(Chief Judge, United States District Court Northern District of Texas)* Appointed for life by President Ronald Reagan to term beginning March 11, 1983. Chief Judge since Jan 1, 2002. Born Los Angeles California Nov 12, 1942. Episcopalian. Educated at Yale University B.A. with honors 1965 LL.B. 1968. Member Phi Beta Kappa. Admitted to practice Texas 1968, U.S. Court of Appeals Fifth Circuit 1968, U.S. District Court Northern District of Texas 1971 and U.S. Supreme Court 1976. Began legal practice Dallas 1968. Judge, Texas District Court 95th Judicial District 1980-81. Associate Justice, Texas Court of Appeals Fifth Supreme Judicial District 1981-83.

Important Decisions: Wilson v. Southwest Airlines 98 FRD 725 (N.D. Tex. 1983); In re Cumpton 30 BR 49 (N.D. Tex. 1983); Wells v. Dallas Independent School District 576 F. Supp. 497 (N.D. Tex. 1984); Commerce Publishing Corp. v. U.S. Postal Service 579 F. Supp. 1402 (N.D. Tex. 1984); Hunt v. BP Exploration Co. (Libya) Ltd. 580 F. Supp. 304 (N.D. Tex. 1984); Shermco Industries v. Secretary of the Air Force 584 F. Supp. 76 (N.D. Tex. 1984); Gibb v. Delta Drilling Co. 104 FRD 59 (N.D. Tex. 1984); Bartholow v. Garner 43 BR 463 (N.D. Tex. 1984); Maurice Pierce & Associates, Inc. v. Computerage, Inc. 608 F. Supp. 173 (N.D. Tex. 1985); McBirney v. Autrey 106 FRD 240 (N.D. Tex. 1985); Worlds of Wonder, Inc. v. Veritel Learning Systems, Inc. 658 F. Supp. 351 (N.D. Tex. 1986); Procter & Gamble Co. v. Kimberly Clark Corp. 684 F. Supp. 1403 (N.D. Tex. 1987); Farzad v. Chandler 670 F. Supp. 690 (N.D. Tex. 1987); and In re Brio Refining, Inc. 86 BR 487 (N.D. Tex. 1988). Life Fellow Texas Bar Foundation. Member State Bar of Texas, Dallas and American Bar Associations. Staff Sergeant USAR 1968-74. Republican.

Office: 1528 U.S. Courthouse, 1100 Commerce Street, Dallas 75242-1003.

Telephone: (214) 753-2310.

FISHER, Jeff *(Judge, Van Zandt County Court)*

Office: 121 East Dallas, Room 201, Canton 75103.

Telephone: (903) 567-4071.

FitzGERALD, Kerry *(Justice, Texas Court of Appeals Fifth District)* Appointed by Governor George W. Bush to term beginning Oct 21, 1999. Elected 2000. Reelected 2002, current term expires Dec 31, 2008. Educated at Georgetown University 1959-61, Southern Methodist University B.B.A. 1963 and University of Texas School of Law J.D. 1966. Board Certified—Criminal Law—Texas Board of Legal Specialization. Admitted to practice Texas, U.S. Court of Appeals Fifth Circuit and U.S. Supreme Court. Associate Judge, Dallas Municipal Court 1994-99.

Assistant District Attorney 1966-69 and Chief Appellate Section District Attorney's Office Dallas County. Significant Decisions Report Editor 1980-86 and Editor 1986-94 *Voice for the Defense* Texas Criminal Defense Lawyers Association. Author "The 1980-81 Term: Significant Decisions of the Texas Court of Criminal Appeals" 33 Baylor L. Rev. 877, 1981; "Criminal Procedure: Pre-Trial, Trial and Appeal" 45 Southwestern L. Jour. 1593, 1992 and 46, 1261, 1993 and 52, 937, 1999 Southern Methodist University L. Rev.; "Criminal Law" 51 Southern Methodist University L. Rev. 881, 1998; and "Ethics, The Private Practitioner and the Grievance Committee Process in Texas" Dallas Bar Association, Trans Pecos Association and Dallas County District Attorney's Office. President Texas Association of Certified Specialists in Criminal Law 1995-96. Chair Fee Disputes Subcommittee 1997-99 and Former Chair Criminal Law Section Dallas Bar Association. Former Member Dallas Merit Selection Panel, Texas District and County Attorney's Association and Grievance Committee State Bar of Texas. Member Knights of Columbus and Masons.

Office: George Allen Sr. Courts Building, 600 Commerce Street, Dallas 75202-4658.

Telephone: (214) 712-3405.

FITZWATER, Sidney A. *(Judge, United States District Court Northern District of Texas)* Appointed for life by President Ronald Reagan March 19, 1986. Born Olney Maryland Sept 22, 1953. Baptist. Educated at Baylor University B.A. 1975 J.D. 1976. Associate Editor Baylor Law Review 1976. Member Omicron Delta Kappa, Phi Alpha Delta, Harris Honor Society and National Order of Barristers. Admitted to practice Texas 1977, U.S. Court of Appeals Fifth Circuit 1977, U.S. District Court Northern District of Texas 1979 and U.S. Supreme Court 1981. Began legal practice Houston 1977. In legal practice Dallas 1978-82. Judge, Texas District Court 298th Judicial District 1982-86, appointed by Governor William P. Clements.

Author "Reexamining the Special Exception" 37 Southwestern L. Jour. 789 Nov 1983 and "Toward a Renaissance of Professionalism in Trial Advocacy" 20 Texas Tech L. Rev. 787, 1989. Fellow Texas Bar Foundation. Member Fifth Circuit District Judges Association, State Bar of Texas and Dallas Bar Association. Instructor externship seminar course Southern Methodist University Law School 1984-85. Recipient Award of Merit 1983 and Outstanding Young Alumnus Award 1985 from Baylor University and Distinguished Alumni Award from Fort Worth Independent School District 1986. Director Dallas Services for Visually Impaired Children 1980-85 and Lakehill Preparatory School 1984-85.

Office: 15A3 U.S. Courthouse, 1100 Commerce Street, Dallas 75242-1003.

Telephone: (214) 753-2333.

FLENNIKEN, Terry *(Judge, Texas District Court 21st Judicial District)*

Office: 100 East Main, Suite 305, Brenham 77833-3782.

Telephone: (979) 277-6200.

FLORES, Aida Salinas *(Judge, Texas District Court 398th Judicial District)* Elected to term beginning Jan 1, 2001. Born Aug 4, 1950. Catholic. Educated at University of Texas Pan Am B.A. 1970 and University of Texas at Austin J.D. 1977. Admitted to practice Texas 1977 and U.S. District Court Southern District of Texas

FLORES, AIDA SALINAS—*Continued*
1982. In legal practice Mission 1977-99. Judge, Alton Municipal Court 1998-99.

Assistant District Attorney Hidalgo County 1977-80. Member National Association of Women Judges, American Judges Association, State Bar of Texas and Hidalgo County Bar Association. Member HWNT Chamber of Commerce.

Office: 100 North Closner, Second Floor, Edinburg 78539.
Telephone: (956) 318-2470.
Fax: (956) 318-2475
E-mail address: aida398@aol.com

FLORES, G. R. "Lupe" *(Judge, Jefferson County Court at Law No. 2)*
Office: 1001 Pearl Street, Beaumont 77701.
Telephone: (409) 835-8429.

FLORES, Manuel R. *(Judge, Texas District Court 49th Judicial District)* Elected to term beginning Jan 1, 1987. Reelected 1990, 1994, 1998 and 2002. Current term expires Dec 31, 2006. Former Judge, Webb County Court at Law.
Office: 1110 Victoria, Suite 304, Laredo 78042.
Telephone: (956) 523-4237.

FLOWERS, Wilford *(Judge, Texas District Court 147th Judicial District)* Elected to term beginning Jan 1, 1991. Reelected 1994, 1998 and 2002. Current term expires Dec 31, 2006. Born Port Arthur Texas June 13, 1950. Baptist. Educated at Lamar University B.B.A. 1972 and University of Texas J.D. 1976. Admitted to practice Texas 1977. Judge, Travis County Court at Law No. 6, 1987-90.
Mailing address: P.O. Box 1748, Austin 78767-1748.
Telephone: (512) 854-9311.

FLOYD, Donald J. *(Judge, Texas District Court 172nd Judicial District)* Appointed by Governor William P. Clements, Jr. to term beginning Dec 15, 1989. Elected 1990, 1994, 1998 and 2002. Current term expires Dec 31, 2006. Born Port Arthur Texas Oct 1, 1943. Educated at Dillard University B.A. with honors 1966 and Thurgood Marshall School of Law Texas Southern University J.D. with honors 1972. Recipient United Negro College Fund Scholarship Dillard University, Ford Foundation Scholarship Thurgood Marshall School of Law and American Jurisprudence Awards in Legal Bibliography, Property Law, Introduction to Poverty Law, Survey of Law and Conflict of Laws. Chairman Constitutional Committee Student Bar Association 1970-71 (recipient Service Award). Member Phi Alpha Delta (recipient Theodore Greener Chapter Officers Award). Admitted to practice Texas, U.S. District Courts Eastern District of Texas and District of Columbia, U.S. Courts of Appeals Fifth and District of Columbia Circuits, U.S. Court of Military Appeals, U.S. Tax Court, U.S. Court of Claims, U.S. Customs Court, U.S. Court of Customs and Patent Appeals, U.S. Court of International Trade and U.S. Supreme Court. In legal practice Port Arthur 1974-82. Judge, Port Arthur Municipal Court Sept 1982 to Dec 1983. Judge, Jefferson County Court at Law No. 3, 1983-89.

Trial Attorney Civil Rights Division U.S. Department of Justice Washington D.C. 1972-74. Member State Bar of Texas, The District of Columbia Bar, Port Arthur (President 1979-80), Jefferson County, National and American Bar Associations. Listed in *Who's Who Among Black Americans* 1976-77. Recipient Award of Appreciation from Boy Scouts of America 1977, U.S. Jaycees Outstanding Young Men of America Award 1978, Achievement Award from Port Arthur Chapter Kappa Alpha Psi 1981, Royalist Civic and Social Club Outstanding Achievement Award 1982, Man of the Year Award from Golden Gate Civic and Social Club of Port Arthur 1983, Outstanding Community Service Award from Mary Alphin District of Federated Clubs 1983, Port Arthur Branch NAACP Freedom Award 1983 and Lincoln High School Class of 1962 Outstanding Achievement Award 1983. Charter member Golden Triangle Coalition of Black Democrats and member Texas Coalition of Black Democrats. Vice President Washington D.C. Chapter Dillard University Alumni Association 1973-74. President Parish Council Assumption Catholic Church Washington D.C. 1973-74. President Port Arthur Chapter Kappa Alpha Psi Fraternity 1977-83. Board of Directors East Texas Legal Services Corporation 1977-79, Opportunities Industrialization Center of Southeast Texas, Sacred Heart Children's World, Kiwanis Club of Port Arthur, Greater Port Arthur Chamber of Commerce and Allied Merchants Bank of Port Arthur. Vice President Board of Trustees Port Arthur Independent School District 1982-83. Chairman of Advancement Beauchamp District Three Rivers Council Boy Scouts of America. Member Royalist Social Club of Port Arthur, Port Arthur Branch NAACP and St. Mary's Catholic Church.
Office: 1001 Pearl Street, Beaumont 77701-3707.
Telephone: (409) 835-8485.

FLOYD, R. G. *(Judge, Llano County Court)*
Office: 801 Ford Street, Room 101, Llano 78643-1919.
Telephone: (325) 247-5054.

FOLK, Joe N. *(Judge, Jasper County Court)*
Office: 121 North Austin, Room 106, Jasper 75951.
Telephone: (409) 384-2612.

FOLLIS, Frank *(Judge, Guadalupe County Court at Law No. 2)*
Office: 101 East Court Street, Seguin 78155-5742.
Telephone: (830) 303-4188.

FOLSOM, David *(Judge, United States District Court Eastern District of Texas)* Appointed for life by President Bill Clinton to term beginning 1995. Born Murfreesboro Arkansas March 12, 1947. Educated at University of Arkansas B.A. 1969 J.D. 1974. In legal practice Texarkana 1974-95.

Deputy Prosecuting Attorney Lafayette County Arkansas 1978-81.
Office: 309 U.S. Courthouse, 500 North State Line Avenue, Texarkana 75501.
Telephone: (903) 794-4067.

FORRESTER, Jim L. *(Judge, Collingsworth County Court)*
Office: Courthouse, Second Floor, 800 West Avenue, Wellington 79095-3039.
Telephone: (806) 447-5408.

FOSTEL, John H. *(Judge, Texas District Court 271st Judicial District)*
Mailing address: P.O. Box 805, Decatur 76234.
Telephone: (940) 627-3200.

FOWLER, Craig *(Judge, Texas District Court 255th Judicial District)*
Office: George Allen Sr. Courts Building, Fifth Floor, 600 Commerce Street, Dallas 75202-4606.
Telephone: (214) 653-6159.

FOWLER, Dean *(Judge, Upshur County Court)*
Mailing address: P.O. Box 730, Gilmer 75644.
Telephone: (903) 843-4003.

FOWLER, Wanda McKee *(Justice, Texas Court of Appeals Fourteenth District)* Assumed office 1995. Elected to subsequent term. Current term expires Dec 31, 2006. Educated at Baylor University B.A. 1978 and Southern Methodist University School of Law J.D. 1981. Briefing Attorney to Chief Justice Tom F. Coleman and Hon. Arthur D. Dyess, Texas Court of Appeals First District 1981-83. In legal practice 1983-85 and 1988-94.
Staff Attorney Texas Court of Appeals First District 1985-86. In-House Counsel GTE Mobilnet 1986-88. Fellow Houston Bar Foundation and Texas Bar Foundation. Member Institute of Judicial Administration, Inc., College of the State Bar of Texas, State Bar of Texas and Houston Bar Association. Administrative Board, Children's Sunday School Teacher, Member Pastor-Parish Relations Committee and Choir St. Paul's United Methodist Church.
Office: 1307 San Jacinto, 11th Floor, Houston 77002-7006.
Telephone: (713) 655-2800.

FOX, Lisa *(Judge, Dallas County Criminal Court at Law No. 10)*
Office: LB 24 Frank Crowley Courts Bldg., 133 North Industrial Boulevard, Dallas 75207-4313.
Telephone: (214) 653-5697.

FRANCIS, Molly Meredith *(Justice, Texas Court of Appeals Fifth District)* Term expires Dec 31, 2008. Former Judge, Dallas County Criminal Court No. 9. Former Judge, Texas District Court 283rd Judicial District.
Office: George Allen Sr. Courts Building, 600 Commerce Street, Dallas 75202-4658.
Telephone: (214) 712-3411.

FRANCIS, Robert W. *(Judge, Texas Criminal District Court No. 3 Dallas County)* Elected Nov 1996 to term beginning Jan 1, 1997. Reelected 2000, current term expires Dec 31, 2004. Born Louisville Kentucky Oct 3, 1959. Lutheran. Educated at University of Texas B.B.S. 1982 and South Texas College of Law J.D. 1985. Admitted to practice Texas 1985, U.S. District Courts Northern 1986 and Eastern 1995 Districts of Texas and U.S. Court of Appeals Fifth Circuit 1992.
Assistant District Attorney Dallas 1985-90. Past President Dallas Criminal Defense Lawyers Association. Member State Bar of Texas, Dallas and American Bar Associations. Member Lions Club of Coppell and YMCA (Indian Princess). Enjoys backpacking, hunting and golfing.
Office: LB 40 Frank Crowley Courts Building, 133 North Industrial Boulevard, Dallas 75207-4313.
Telephone: (214) 653-5922.

FRANKLIN, H. G. *(Judge, Lynn County Court)*
Mailing address: P.O. Box 1167, Tahoka 79373-1167.
Telephone: (806) 561-4222.

FREEMAN, Bill *(Judge, Cooke County Court)*
Office: 110 County Courthouse, Gainesville 76240.
Telephone: (940) 668-5435.

FROESCHNER, John Robert *(Magistrate Judge, United States District Court Southern District of Texas)* Appointed by U.S. District Court judges Jan 25, 1991. Born St. Louis Missouri March 19, 1950. Educated at Elmhurst College B.A. 1972 and University of Missouri-Columbia J.D. 1976. Admitted to practice Texas 1976. In legal practice 1977-91.
Office: 508A U.S. Courthouse, 601 25th Street, Galveston 77550-1738.
Telephone: (409) 766-3729.

FROST, Kem Thompson *(Justice, Texas Court of Appeals Fourteenth District)* Appointed by Governor George W. Bush Jan 1999 to term beginning April 1, 1999. Elected 2000 and 2002. Current term expires Dec 31, 2008. Educated at University of Texas at Austin B.A./B.B.A. with honors 1980 and Texas Tech University School of Law J.D. with honors 1983. Recipient American Jurisprudence Awards in Contracts and Criminal Law. Staff member Texas Tech Law Review. Member Delta Theta Phi. Admitted to practice Texas, U.S. District Courts Eastern, Northern, Southern and Western Districts of Texas, U.S. Court of Appeals Fifth Circuit and U.S. Supreme Court. In legal practice 1983-99.
Life Fellow Texas Bar Foundation. Member State Bar of Texas, Houston, Fifth Circuit and American Bar Associations.
Office: 1307 San Jacinto, 11th Floor, Houston 77002-7006.
Telephone: (713) 655-2800.

FRY, James R. *(Judge, Texas District Court 15th Judicial District)* Elected to term beginning Jan 1, 1985. Reelected 1988, 1992, 1996 and 2000. Current term expires Dec 31, 2004. Born Paris Texas Dec 29, 1946. Presbyterian. Educated at Baylor University J.D. 1970. Member Phi Alpha Delta. Admitted to practice Texas 1970, U.S. District Court Eastern District of Texas 1971, U.S. Court of Appeals Fifth Circuit 1972 and U.S. Supreme Court 1973. In legal practice Sherman 1970-84.
Part-time Instructor Paralegal Program Grayson College 1981-86. Member State Bar of Texas and Grayson County Bar Association (President 1975-76). Staff Sergeant Texas National Guard 1971-77. Democrat. Former Board of Directors Sherman Boys Club and Campfire Girls. Former member Sherman Optimist Club and Jaycees. Member Sherman Rotary Club. Enjoys golf, racquetball, snow skiing and cooking.
Office: 200 South Crockett, Suite 217A, Sherman 75090.
Telephone: (903) 813-4303.

FULLER, Gary L. *(Judge, Stephens County Court)*
Office: Stephens County Courthouse, Breckenridge 76424.
Telephone: (254) 559-2190.

FULLER, Tom *(Judge, Dallas County Criminal Court at Law No. 5)*
Office: LB 18 Frank Crowley Courts Bldg., 133 North Industrial Boulevard, Dallas 75207-4313.
Telephone: (214) 653-5640.

FURGESON, Royal, Jr. *(Judge, United States District Court Western District of Texas)* Appointed for life by President Bill Clinton July 1993 to term beginning

FURGESON, ROYAL, JR.—*Continued*

March 11, 1994. Born Lubbock Texas Dec 9, 1941. Jewish. Educated at Texas Technological College B.A. with honors 1964 and University of Texas School of Law J.D. with honors 1967. Associate Editor Texas Law Review 1965-67. Law Clerk to Hon. Halbert O. Woodward, U.S. District Court Northern District of Texas 1969-70. Member Phi Delta Phi. Admitted to practice Texas 1970. In legal practice El Paso 1970-94.

Fellow American College of Trial Lawyers. Member The American Law Institute, State Bar of Texas and American Bar Association. Recipient Faculty Award and Community Service Award from University of Texas School of Law. Captain U.S. Army 1967-69.

Office: 301 Federal Building, 200 East Wall Street, Midland 79701.

Telephone: (915) 686-4040.

GABERT, Alex W. *(Judge, Texas District Court 229th Judicial District)* Former Judge, Starr County Court at Law No. 1.

Mailing address: P.O. Box 726, Rio Grande City 78582.

Telephone: (956) 487-2636.

GABRIEL, E. Lee *(Judge, Texas District Court 367th Judicial District)*

Office: 1450 East McKinney Street, Suite 3426, Denton 76209-4524.

Telephone: (940) 349-2350.

GABRIEL, John D. *(Judge, Texas District Court 131st Judicial District)* Elected to term beginning Jan 1, 1993. Reelected Nov 1996 and 2000. Current term expires Dec 31, 2004. Born San Antonio Texas April 26, 1953. Educated at University of Texas at Austin B.A. 1974 J.D. 1976. Admitted to practice Texas 1977.

Office: 202 Bexar County Courthouse, 100 Dolorosa Street, San Antonio 78205-3028.

Telephone: (210) 335-2521.

GALIK, Annette *(Judge, Texas District Court 245th Judicial District)* Elected to term beginning Jan 2, 1995. Reelected 1998 and 2002. Current term expires Dec 31, 2006. Born Mississippi Jan 25, 1949. Christian. Educated at University of Houston B.S. cum laude 1987 J.D. 1989. Republican.

Office: Family Law Center Building, Third Floor, 1115 Congress Avenue, Houston 77002.

Telephone: (713) 755-6935.

GALINDO, Jimmy B. *(Judge, Reeves County Court)*

Office: 100 East Fourth, Third Floor, Pecos 79772.

Telephone: (432) 445-5418.

GALLAGHER, George W. *(Judge, Texas District Court 396th Judicial District)*

Office: Tarrant County Justice Center, 401 West Belknap, Fort Worth 76196-0215.

Telephone: (817) 884-2495.

GALLEGOS, Nicholas *(Judge, Edwards County Court)*

Mailing address: P.O. Box 348, Rocksprings 78880-0348.

Telephone: (830) 683-6122.

GAMBLE, Brent *(Judge, Texas District Court 270th Judicial District)*

Office: 301 Fannin, Sixth Floor, Houston 77002.

Telephone: (713) 755-5509.

GARCIA, Carlos A. *(Judge, Frio County Court)*

Office: 500 East San Antonio Street, Box 7, Pearsall 78061-3145.

Telephone: (830) 334-2154.

GARCIA, David *(Judge, Denton County Criminal Court at Law No. 3)*

Office: 1450 East McKinney Street, Denton 76209.

Telephone: (940) 347-2180.

GARCIA, Edmundo B., Jr. *(Judge, Duval County Court)*

Mailing address: P.O. Box 189, San Diego 78384.

Telephone: (361) 279-3322.

GARCIA, Gonzalo *(Judge, Texas District Court 210th Judicial District)*

Office: 500 East San Antonio Avenue, #1005, El Paso 79901-2457.

Telephone: (915) 546-2130.

GARCIA, Joe B. *(Judge, Brooks County Court)*

Mailing address: P.O. Box 515, Falfurrias 78355-0515.

Telephone: (361) 325-5604.

GARCIA, Joseph Alexander, Jr. *(Judge, Kenedy County Court)*

Mailing address: P.O. Box 37, Sarita 78385.

Telephone: (361) 294-5224.

GARCIA, Orlando L. *(Judge, United States District Court Western District of Texas)* Appointed for life by President Bill Clinton to term beginning 1994. Born Jim Wells County Texas Nov 18, 1952. Educated at University of Texas at Austin B.A. 1975 J.D. 1978. In legal practice San Antonio 1978-90. Justice, Texas Court of Appeals Fourth District Jan 1, 1991 to 1992.

Member Texas House of Representatives 1983-91.

Office: U.S. Courthouse, 655 East Durango Boulevard, San Antonio 78206-1198.

Telephone: (210) 472-6565.

GARCIA, Patrick Michael *(Judge, Texas District Court 384th Judicial District)*

Office: 500 East San Antonio Avenue, Suite 906, El Paso 79901-2457.

Telephone: (915) 546-2134.

GARCIA, Ramon *(Judge, Hidalgo County Court)* Elected to term beginning Jan 1, 2003. Born McAllen Texas July 20, 1948. Educated at Pan American University B.A. 1970 and University of Houston College of Law J.D. with honors 1972. Member Phi Alpha Delta and Order of Barons. Admitted to practice Texas 1972, U.S. District Court Southern District of Texas 1973, U.S. Courts of Appeals Fifth 1974 and Federal 1986 Circuits and U.S. Supreme Court 1976.

Member Texas Association of School Board Attorneys, Texas Trial Lawyers Association (Board of Directors), Attorney Information Exchange Group, Inc., The Association of Trial Lawyers of America, State Bar of Texas (District 12-B Grievance Committee 1986-92, Texas Disciplinary Rules of Professional Conduct Committee), Hidalgo County, Hispanic National, Federal (Board of Directors) and American Bar Associations.

GARCIA, RAMON—*Continued*

Chairman Hidalgo County Democratic Party 1994-2000. Member Roundtable Texas Democratic Party and Business Leadership Council National Democratic Party. Board of Regents Pan American University 1983-87. Advisory Board Rio Grande Valley Historical Collection. Member Hidalgo County Historical Museum and University of Texas/Pan American University Alumni Association.

Mailing address: P.O. Box 1356, Edinburg 78540.

Office: 100 East Cano, Second Floor, Edinburg 78539.

Telephone: (956) 318-2600.

Fax: (956) 318-2699

GARDNER, Anne *(Justice, Texas Court of Appeals Second District)* Appointed by Governor George W. Bush to term beginning Jan 1, 2000. Elected Nov 7, 2000, current term expires Dec 31, 2004. Born Corpus Christi Texas. Educated at University of Texas 1964 J.D. 1966. Associate Editor Texas Law Review. Law Clerk to Hon. Leo Brewster, U.S. District Court Northern District of Texas 1967-71. Board Certified—Civil Appellate Law—Texas Board of Legal Specialization. In legal practice 1971 to Dec 31, 1999.

Author Chapter 71 "Liability Insurance" *Texas Torts and Remedies* Matthew-Bender 1987, "Summary Judgements" *The Advocate* Litigation Section State Bar of Texas 1991, "Insurer Insolvency—'Due Diligence' of the Surplus Lines Broker" *CPCU Symposium* 1993, "Ambiguity—and Other Contract Issues in Insurance Coverage Disputes" Ultimate Insurance Seminar State Bar of Texas 1993, "Mandamus Proceedings" Texas Association of Defense Counsel Fall Meeting 1995 and "Persuasive Brief Writing" Appellate Section Seminar Tarrant County Bar Association 1997. Co-author "Practicing Under the New Texas Rules of Appellate Procedure" 49 Baylor L. Rev. 867, 1998. Past President, Director 1977-79 and 1982-84 and Vice President 1984-85 Tarrant County Bar Association. Director Texas Association of Defense Counsel 1988-91, 1991-94 and 1997-99. Chairman Advisory Commission on Appellate Civil Law Texas Board of Legal Specialization 1993. Member Advisory Committee Texas Supreme Court 1993-98. Emeritus Master of the Bench and Founding Member Eldon Mahon Inn of Court. Life Fellow Texas Bar Foundation. Charter Fellow Tarrant County Bar Foundation. Member State Bar College of Texas and American Bar Association.

Office: 9000 Tarrant County Justice Center, 401 West Belknap, Fort Worth 76196.

Telephone: (817) 884-2175.

GARNER, Carla W. *(Judge, Sutton County Court)* Assumed office 1985. Elected to subsequent terms.

Mailing address: P.O. Box 1212, Sonora 76950.

Telephone: (325) 387-2711.

GARNER, David Edward *(Judge, Texas District Court 10th Judicial District)*

Office: 722 Moody, Room 503, Galveston 77550.

Telephone: (409) 766-2232.

GARNEY, Norbert J. *(Magistrate Judge, United States District Court Western District of Texas)* Appointed by U.S. District Court judges to term beginning Sept 11, 2000.

Office: 511 East San Antonio Avenue, El Paso 79901.

Telephone: (915) 534-6980.

GARRAHAN, Sarah E. *(Judge, Bexar County Court at Law No. 4)* Elected to term beginning Jan 1, 1987. Reelected Nov 1990, Nov 8, 1994, 1998 and 2002. Current term expires Dec 31, 2006. Born Wilson County Texas Nov 2, 1936. Educated at University of Texas at San Antonio B.B.A. 1977 and St. Mary's University of San Antonio School of Law J.D. 1981. In legal practice San Antonio 1983-86.

Adjunct Professor of Trial Advocacy St. Mary's University of San Antonio School of Law 1990-91. Member American Judicature Society, State Bar of Texas, San Antonio and Bexar County Women's Bar Associations. Named Alumnus of the Year by University of Texas at San Antonio 1986 and San Antonio College 1989. Republican. Enjoys reading.

Office: 2090 Bexar County Justice Center, 300 Dolorosa Street, San Antonio 78205-3018.

Telephone: (210) 335-2426.

GARZA, Dori Contreras *(Justice, Texas Court of Appeals Thirteenth District)*

Office: Hidalgo County Administrative Bldg., Fifth Floor, 100 East Cano, Edinburgh 78539.

Telephone: (956) 318-2405.

GARZA, Federico "Fred" *(Judge, Hidalgo County Court at Law No. 4)*

Office: 100 North Closner, Third Floor, Edinburg 78539.

Telephone: (956) 318-2390.

GARZA, G. Jaime *(Judge, Hidalgo County Court at Law No. 2)* Assumed office Jan 1, 1981. Elected 1982, 1986, 1990, 1994, 1998 and 2002. Current term expires Dec 31, 2006. Born McAllen Texas March 12, 1948. Catholic. Educated at Texas Arts & Industries University B.A. 1970 and University of Texas School of Law J.D. 1973. Admitted to practice Texas 1974. Began legal practice Edinburg 1975. Democrat.

Office: 100 North Closner, Third Floor, Edinburg 78539.

Telephone: (956) 318-2380.

GARZA, Homero *(Judge, Hidalgo County Probate Court)* Former Judge, Hidalgo County Court at Law No. 3.

Office: 100 North Closner, Third Floor, Edinburg 78539.

Telephone: (956) 318-2385.

GARZA, Jesus *(Judge, Webb County Court at Law No. 2)*

Office: 1110 Victoria, Suite 404, Laredo 78040.

Telephone: (956) 718-8640.

GARZA, Robert *(Judge, Texas District Court 138th Judicial District)* Elected to term beginning Jan 1, 1985. Reelected Nov 1988, Nov 1992, 1996 and 2000. Current term expires Dec 31, 2004. Local Administrative Judge Cameron and Willacy Counties 1991. Currently serves as Acting Presiding Judge Fifth Administrative Judicial Region. Born Brownsville Texas May 25, 1953. Catholic. Educated at Texas Southmost College A.A. 1973, Pan American University B.A. 1975 and Thurgood Marshall School of Law J.D. 1979. Admitted to practice Texas 1979 and U.S. District Court Southern District of Texas 1980. In legal practice Brownsville 1979-84.

Former Member Texas Criminal Defense Lawyers Association, The Association of Trial Lawyers of America and American Bar Association. Board Member Judicial

GARZA, ROBERT—*Continued*
Education Committee Texas Supreme Court. Chairman Cameron County Juvenile Board. Member Texas Association of Court Administration, Texas Corrections Association, Citizens Commission on the Texas Judicial System, American Judicature Society, American Judges Association, State Bar of Texas (Board Member Juvenile Section) and Cameron County Bar Association. Attended New Judges Conference Nov 1984 and courses in the Judiciary since Jan 1985, General Jurisdiction The National Judicial College Sept 14, 1986 to Oct 3, 1986, "Juvenile Detention Issues for the 90's" National Juvenile Detention Association June 24-27, 1990 and Advanced Seminar on Anglo-American Jurisprudence Wadham College, Oxford England July 7-20, 1991. Named Outstanding Young Man of America 1985 and Distinguished Alumnus in Arts and Sciences by Pan American University 1985. Listed in *Who's Who in Texas Today* 1987. Employed as farmer 1960-75 and secondary level teacher Brownsville Independent School District Aug 1975 to Aug 1976. Democrat. Former Member Brownsville Civitan Club, Toastmasters International and St. Mary's Church Men's Club. Former Member Board of Directors American Red Cross. Member Brownsville Sunrise Rotary Club, Knights of Columbus of Brownsville and Parent-Teacher Association of Lincoln Park School and St. Mary's School. District Chairman Tip-o-Tex Boy Scouts. Enjoys running, fishing, basketball and baseball.

Office: 974 East Harrison Street, Brownsville 78520-7123.

Telephone: (956) 544-0877.

GASSAWAY, Michael Brandon *(Judge, McLennan County Court at Law No. 2)* Elected 1982 to term beginning Jan 1, 1983. Reelected 1986, 1990, 1994, 1998 and 2002. Current term expires Dec 31, 2006. Born Waco Texas May 11, 1952. Methodist. Educated at Baylor University J.D. 1975. Member Delta Theta Phi. Admitted to practice Texas 1976. Began legal practice West 1976. Judge, West Municipal Court 1976-82.

Member State Bar of Texas (Judicial Section) and McLennan County Bar Association. Graduate Texas College of the Judiciary and The National Judicial College. Democrat. Enjoys skiing and water sports.

Office: 501 Washington Avenue, Room 207, Waco 76701.

Telephone: (254) 757-5030.

GAULTNEY, David B. *(Justice, Texas Court of Appeals Ninth District)* Elected to term beginning Jan 1, 2001. Term expires Dec 31, 2006. Born Eku Nigeria Oct 20, 1954. Educated at Southwest Texas State University B.A. with highest honors 1976, University of Texas J.D. with honors 1979 and University of Houston LL.M. 1993. Board Certified—Civil Appellate Law, Civil Trial Law, Personal Injury Trial Law—Texas Board of Legal Specialization. In legal practice for 21 years.

Life Fellow Texas Bar Foundation.

Office: 1001 Pearl, Suite 330, Beaumont 77701-3552.

Telephone: (409) 835-8404.

GEBHARDT, S. "Shay" *(Judge, Bexar County Court at Law No. 3)* Elected Nov 2, 1990 to term beginning Jan 1, 1991. Reelected Nov 2, 1994, Nov 2, 1996 and 2001. Current term expires 2005. Born Sequin Texas. Catholic. Educated at Texas Eastern School of Nursing R.N. 1968, University of Texas at Tyler B.S. 1981 and St. Mary's University of San Antonio School of Law J.D. 1984. Admitted to practice Texas 1984. In legal practice Austin 1984-85 and San Antonio 1985-90.

Member Bexar County Womens Bar Association, State Bar of Texas and San Antonio Bar Association. Attended judicial conferences on Family Law, Evidence and Mediation Certification National College for Judges and numerous CLE courses. Republican. Enjoys design, reading and traveling.

Office: 1.23 Bexar County Courthouse, 100 Dolorosa Street, San Antonio 78205-3067.

Telephone: (210) 335-2575.

GENT, James Wayne *(Judge, Kaufman County Court)*

Office: 100 West Mulberry, Kaufman 75142.

Telephone: (972) 932-4331.

GERSON, Alfred Sterling *(Judge, Jefferson County Court at Law No. 1)*

Office: 1149 Pearl Street, Beaumont 77701.

Telephone: (409) 835-8470.

GETZ, Floyd Thomas *(Judge, Smith County Court at Law No. 3)*

Office: 100 North Broadway, Third Floor, Tyler 75702-7236.

Telephone: (903) 535-0566.

GIBSON, Jay *(Judge, Texas District Court 70th Judicial District)* Appointed by Governor Ann W. Richards to term beginning June 1, 1992. Elected Nov 1992, 1994, 1998 and 2002. Current term expires Dec 2006. Born Philadelphia Pennsylvania June 9, 1950. Educated at University of Texas at Austin B.A. 1972 and Southern Methodist University J.D. 1975. Admitted to practice Texas 1975 and U.S. District Court Western District of Texas 1977. In legal practice Odessa 1975-92.

State Representative Texas 1978-84. Democrat.

Office: 300 North Grant Avenue, Room 331, Odessa 79761-5158.

Telephone: (432) 498-4270.

GILL, Robert K. *(Judge, Texas District Court 213th Judicial District)* Elected Nov 3, 1992 to term beginning Jan 1, 1993. Reelected 1996 and 2000. Current term expires Dec 31, 2004. Born Omaha Nebraska Dec 30, 1955. Christian. Educated at University of Illinois B.A. 1978 and Southern Illinois University J.D. 1981. Admitted to practice Texas 1981 and U.S. District Court Northern District of Texas.

Co-author *Texas Criminal Lawyers Handbook* James Publishing 2000. Member State Bar of Texas and Tarrant County Bar Association. Republican.

Office: Tarrant County Justice Center, 401 West Belknap, Fort Worth 76196-0217.

Telephone: (817) 884-1529.

GILLES, George D. *(Judge, Texas District Court 142nd Judicial District)* Elected Nov 1992 to term beginning Jan 1, 1993. Reelected Nov 1996 and Nov 2000. Current term expires Dec 31, 2004. Educated at Texas Tech University B.B.A. 1973 J.D. 1976. Admitted to practice Texas 1976. In legal practice Midland 1976-93.

Office: 200 West Wall, Suite 300, Midland 79701-4557.

Telephone: (432) 688-1134.

GILMORE, Vanessa D. *(Judge, United States District Court Southern District of Texas)* Appointed for life by President Bill Clinton to term beginning June 9, 1994. Born St. Albans New York Oct 26, 1956. Educated at Hampton University B.S. 1977 and University of Houston J.D. 1981. In legal practice Houston 1981-94.

Office: 9513 U.S. Courthouse, 515 Rusk Avenue, Houston 77002.

Telephone: (713) 250-5931.

GLEINSER, Harold F. *(Judge, Goliad County Court)*

Mailing address: P.O. Box 677, Goliad 77963-0677.

Telephone: (361) 645-3337.

GOBER, Bob Wayne *(Judge, Hemphill County Court)* Elected 1978 to term beginning Jan 1, 1979. Reelected 1982, 1986, 1990, 1994, 1998 and 2002. Current term expires Dec 31, 2006.

Mailing address: P.O. Box 536, Canadian 79014-0536.

Telephone: (806) 323-6521.

GODBEY, David C. *(Judge, United States District Court Northern District of Texas)* Appointed for life by President George W. Bush to term beginning Aug 7, 2002. Born Temple Texas Sept 17, 1957. Methodist. Educated at Southern Methodist University B.S.E.E. magna cum laude 1978 and Harvard University J.D. magna cum laude 1982. Staff member Harvard Law Review 1980-82. Law Clerk to Hon. Irving L. Goldberg, U.S. Court of Appeals Fifth Circuit. Admitted to practice Texas 1982 and U.S. Patent and Trademark Office. Board Certified—Civil Appellate Law—Texas Board of Legal Specialization. Judge, Texas District Court 160th Judicial District Jan 1, 1995 to Aug 6, 2002.

Instructor in Legal Protection of Computer Software Southern Methodist University School of Law 1987-91. Member Dallas (Chairman Appellate Section 1996) and American Bar Associations. Republican. Enjoys tae kwon do, computers, bridge and science fiction.

Office: 1100 Commerce Street, Room 1358, Dallas 75242.

Telephone: (214) 753-2700.

GODWIN, George H. *(Judge, Texas District Court 174th Judicial District)* Term expires Dec 31, 2004.

Office: 1201 Franklin, Room 19144, Houston 77002.

Telephone: (713) 755-6324.

GOLDEN, Joe Bob *(Judge, Texas District Court 1st Judicial District)* Elected to term beginning Jan 1, 1989. Reelected 1992, 1996 and 2000. Current term expires Dec 31, 2004. Born Texas. Methodist. Educated at University of Texas B.B.A. 1954 J.D. 1960. Law Clerk to Hon. Joe Jefferson Fisher, U.S. District Court Eastern District of Texas. Member Phi Alpha Delta. Admitted to practice Texas 1960, U.S. District Court Eastern District of Texas 1960, U.S. Court of Appeals Fifth Circuit 1962 and U.S. Supreme Court 1965. Began legal practice Jasper.

Board of Regents Stephen F. Austin State University 1968-80. First Lieutenant USAF.

Mailing address: P.O. Box 1290, Jasper 75951-1290.

Telephone: (409) 384-3792.

GONZALES, Evan *(Judge, Lee County Court)*

Mailing address: P.O. Box 390, Giddings 78942.

Telephone: (979) 542-3178.

GONZALES, Lisa *(Judge, Nueces County Court at Law No. 2)*

Office: 901 Leopard, Suite 702, Corpus Christi 78401.

Telephone: (361) 888-0596.

GONZALES RAMOS, Nelva *(Judge, Texas District Court 347th Judicial District)* Elected to term beginning Jan 1, 2001. Term expires Dec 31, 2004. Born Port Lavaca Texas Aug 22, 1965. Educated at Southwest Texas State University B.S. 1987 and University of Texas J.D. with honors 1991. Admitted to practice Texas 1991. In legal practice Sept 1991 to June 1997. Judge, Texas Municipal Court June 30, 1997 to Aug 31, 1999.

Member Nueces County Juvenile Board, State Bar of Texas and Corpus Christi Bar Association. Member National Conference for Community and Justice.

Office: 901 Leopard, Suite 804, Corpus Christi 78401.

Telephone: (361) 888-0593.

GONZALEZ, Alejandro "Alex" *(Judge, El Paso County Court at Law No. 4)* Elected to term beginning Jan 1, 1999. Reelected Nov 5, 2002, current term expires Dec 31, 2006. Born El Paso Texas Nov 8, 1958. Catholic. Educated at University of Texas at El Paso B.B.A. 1981 and University of Texas School of Law J.D. Staff member American Journal of Criminal Law 1983-84. Admitted to practice Texas 1985, U.S. District Court Western District of Texas, U.S. Court of Appeals Fifth Circuit and U.S. Supreme Court. In legal practice El Paso 1992-99. Former Associate Judge, El Paso Municipal Court.

Assistant County Attorney El Paso County. Assistant Public Defender Western District of Texas. Member State Bar of Texas (Leaders Committee), El Paso, Federal and Mexican American Bar Associations. Member El Paso Democratic Party, Tejano Democrats and Texas Democratic Party. Member El Paso Historical Society and Conference Reporting Advisory Committee El Paso Community College.

Office: 500 East San Antonio, Room 805, El Paso 79901.

Telephone: (915) 546-2190.

Fax: (915) 546-2191

E-mail address: agonza4521@aol.com

GONZALEZ, Julie *(Judge, El Paso County Court at Law No. 2)*

Office: 500 East San Antonio, #801, El Paso 79901.

Telephone: (915) 546-2145.

GONZALEZ, Noé *(Judge, Texas District Court 370th Judicial District)*

Office: 100 North Closner, Second Floor, Edinburg 78539.

Telephone: (956) 318-2280.

GONZALEZ, Rodolfo "Rudy" *(Judge, Hidalgo County Court at Law No. 1)*

Office: 100 North Closner, Third Floor, Edinburg 78539.

Telephone: (956) 318-2375.

GONZALEZ, Sergio J. *(Judge, Val Verde County Court at Law)*

Mailing address: P.O. Box 1431, Del Rio 78840-1431.

Telephone: (830) 774-7575.

GORDON, Ronnie *(Judge, Hartley County Court)* Appointed to term beginning June 12, 1993. Elected

GORDON, RONNIE—*Continued*

Nov 8, 1994, 1998 and 2002. Current term expires Dec 31, 2006. Born Hartley County Texas April 18, 1959. Baptist.

Mailing address: P. O. Box G, Channing 79018.
Telephone: (806) 235-3442.

GOSSETT, J. Clay *(Judge, Texas District Court 4th Judicial District)*
Office: 115 North Main, Suite 303, Henderson 75652.
Telephone: (903) 657-0358.

GOSSETT, Thomas J. *(Judge, Texas District Court 391st Judicial District)*
Office: 112 West Beauregard, San Angelo 76903-5850.
Telephone: (325) 659-6571.

GOSSOM, Woodrow W. "Woody", Jr. *(Judge, Wichita County Court)* Elected Nov 1998 to term beginning Jan 1, 1999. Reelected 2002, current term expires Dec 31, 2006. Born St. Louis Missouri. Presbyterian. Educated at Midwestern State University B.A. 1967 and University of Denver M.A. 1969.

Honorary Member Wichita County Bar Association. Member Texas Association of Counties and West Texas County Judge and Commissioners Association. Colonel U.S. Army (retired). Republican. Member University Kiwanis, Arts Council, YMCA Board. Enjoys racquetball and hunting.

Office: 900 Seventh Street, Suite 202, Wichita Falls 76301-2440.
Telephone: (940) 766-8101.
E-mail address: county.judge@co.wichita.tx.us

GRANT, Linda K. *(Judge, Freestone County Court)*
Office: 118 East Commerce, Room 201, Fairfield 75840.
Telephone: (903) 389-3335.

GRAY, Thomas W. *(Justice, Texas Court of Appeals Tenth District)* Elected to term beginning Jan 1, 1999. Term expires Dec 31, 2004. Born Madisonville Texas 1956. Educated at Sam Houston State University B.B.A. cum laude 1978, Texas A&M University M.B.A. 1979 and Baylor University School of Law J.D. cum laude 1985. Admitted to practice Texas 1985. In legal practice Corsicana 1985-88 and Dallas 1988-98. Judge, Rice Municipal Court 1998.

Member State Bar of Texas.
Mailing address: P.O. Box 1606, Waco 76703-1606.
Telephone: (254) 757-5200.

GREEN, Brenda *(Judge, Texas District Court 256th Judicial District)*
Office: George Allen Sr. Courts Building, Sixth Floor, 600 Commerce Street, Dallas 75202-4606.
Telephone: (214) 653-6449.

GREEN, Dennis G. *(Magistrate Judge, United States District Court Western District of Texas)* Appointed by U.S. District Court judges to term beginning Dec 13, 1985. Reappointed 1993 and 2001. Current term expires 2009. Born Cushing Oklahoma Oct 23, 1944. Protestant. Educated at Syracuse University 1962-64, Central State University B.A. 1966 and South Texas College of Law J.D. 1970. Member Delta Theta Phi. Admitted to practice Texas 1972, U.S. District Courts Districts of Texas 1976 and U.S. Courts of Appeals Fifth 1976 and District of Columbia 1978 Circuits. In legal practice Houston 1972-82 and Waco since 1983.

Assistant District Attorney Houston 1972-75 and 1976-79 and Waco 1983. Assistant U.S. Attorney Southern District of Texas 1975-76. Trial Counsel Shell Oil Company Houston 1979-83. Author "Possession of Marihuana in Texas" South Texas L. Jour. 1972. Assistant Editor-in-Chief South Texas L. Jour. 1972. Member State Bar of Texas (President 1972) and American Bar Association. U.S. Army 1967-69.

Office: U.S. Courthouse, 111 East Broadway, Del Rio 78840.
Telephone: (830) 703-2050.

GREEN, Gordon Houston *(Judge, Texas District Court 287th Judicial District)*
Office: 300 South First Street, Suite 287, Muleshoe 79347.
Telephone: (806) 272-5460.

GREEN, Paul W. *(Justice, Texas Court of Appeals Fourth District)* Elected Nov 1994 to term beginning Jan 1, 1995. Reelected 2000, current term expires Dec 31, 2006. Born San Antonio Texas 1952. Educated at University of Texas at Austin B.B.A. 1974 and St. Mary's University J.D. 1977. In legal practice San Antonio 1977-94.

President San Antonio Bar Association 1991-92. House of Delegates American Bar Association 1991-93. Director State Bar of Texas 1993-94. Fellow San Antonio Bar Foundation and Texas Bar Foundation.

Office: 3200 Bexar County Justice Center, 300 Dolorosa Street, San Antonio 78205-3037.
Telephone: (210) 335-2692.

GREENBERG, Mark *(Judge, Dallas County Court at Law No. 5)*
Office: 500 Main Street, Fourth Floor, Dallas 75202-3513.
Telephone: (214) 653-6441.

GREENDYKE, William R. *(Chief Judge, United States Bankruptcy Court Southern District of Texas)* Chief Judge since Jan 1, 2002.
Office: 4202 U.S. Courthouse, 515 Rusk Avenue, Houston 77002.
Telephone: (713) 250-5470.

GREENE, Karen Jane *(Judge, Texas District Court 282nd Judicial District)*
Office: LB 32 Frank Crowley Courts Building, 133 North Industrial Boulevard, Dallas 75207-4313.
Telephone: (214) 653-5852.

GREENWELL, Tom *(Judge, Texas Family District Court 319th Judicial District)*
Office: 901 Leopard, Suite 801, Corpus Christi 78401.
Telephone: (361) 888-0533.

GRIFFIN, Frank *(Judge, Brown County Court at Law No. 1)*
Office: 200 South Broadway, Brownwood 76801-3192.
Telephone: (325) 646-5859.

GRIFFIN, Guy William *(Judge, Texas District Court 123rd Judicial District)* Elected Nov 1996 to term beginning Jan 1, 1997. Reelected Nov 2000, current term expires Dec 31, 2004. Born Houston Texas July 13, 1952. Methodist. Educated at University of Texas at Austin B.B.A. 1973 and South Texas College of Law

GRIFFIN, GUY WILLIAM—*Continued*

J.D. 1978. Admitted to practice Texas 1978, U.S. District Court Eastern District of Texas and U.S. Court of Appeals Fifth Circuit. In legal practice Center 1978-96.

Fellow Texas Bar Foundation. Member American Bar Association.

Office: 200 San Augustine, Suite 3, Center 75935.

Telephone: (936) 598-9928.

GRIFFIN, Johnny Frank *(Judge, Schleicher County Court)* Elected 1978 to term beginning Jan 1, 1979. Reelected 1982, 1986, 1990, 1994, 1998 and 2002. Current term expires Dec 31, 2006.

Mailing address: P.O. Box 536, Eldorado 76936-0536.

Telephone: (325) 853-2766.

GRIFFITH, Carl R., Jr. *(Judge, Jefferson County Court)* Elected March 1996 to term beginning Nov 12, 1996. Reelected 1998 and 2002. Current term expires Dec 31, 2006. Born Beaumont Texas Feb 21, 1955. Baptist. Educated at Lamar University Criminal Justice degree 1983 Counseling degree 1987.

Recipient A World of Difference Award from Anti-Defamation League of B'nai B'rith 1991, Community Builder Award (highest award given to non-mason) from Masons Grand Lodge of Texas April 1995, Outstanding Political Service Award from Texas Public Workers Association 1996, Executive of the Year Award from Sales and Marketing Executives Club of Southeast Texas March 1997, Hometown Hero Service Industry Award from Beaumont Convention and Visitors Bureau 2000 and Frances K. Monk "Regional Leadership" Award 2003. Named Texas Outstanding Law Enforcement Administrator by Combined Law Enforcement Association of Texas (CLEAT) 1992 and Free Enterprise Person of the Year by Associated Builders & Contractors of Southeast Texas 1999. Sheriff Jefferson County 1989-96. Private Pilot. Enjoys scuba diving, hunting and fishing.

Office: 1149 Pearl Street, Fourth Floor, Beaumont 77701.

Telephone: (409) 835-8466.

GRIFFITH, Sam *(Justice, Texas Court of Appeals Twelfth District)* Elected to term beginning Jan 1, 2001. Born Sept 8, 1951. Educated at Stephen F. Austin State University B.S. 1975 M.S. 1978 and St. Mary's University of San Antonio School of Law J.D. 1986. Admitted to practice Texas, U.S. District Courts Eastern and Northern Districts of Texas, U.S. Court of Appeals Fifth Circuit and U.S. Supreme Court. In legal practice Tyler 1987 to July 1997. Judge, Smith County Court at Law No. 3 Aug 1997 to Dec 1998.

Member State Bar of Texas (Committee on Legal Related Education) and Smith County Bar Association.

Office: 1517 West Front, Suite 354, Tyler 75702-7854.

Telephone: (903) 593-8471.

GRISHAM, Ray Felty *(Judge, Texas District Court 336th Judicial District)* Term expires Dec 31, 2004.

Office: 200 South Crockett, Suite 231A, Sherman 75090.

Telephone: (903) 813-4309.

GRUBB, George E. *(Judge, Jeff Davis County Court)*

Mailing address: P.O. Box 836, Fort Davis 79734.

Telephone: (432) 426-3968.

GUADERRAMA, David C. *(Judge, Texas District Court 243rd Judicial District)*

Office: 500 East San Antonio Avenue, #901, El Paso 79901-2457.

Telephone: (915) 546-2168.

GUILLORY, Glenn D. *(Judge, Aransas County Court)*

Office: 301 North Live Oak, Rockport 78382-2798.

Telephone: (361) 790-0100.

GUTHRIE, Bill *(Judge, Blanco County Court)*

Mailing address: P.O. Box 471, Johnson City 78636-0471.

Telephone: (830) 868-4266.

GUTHRIE, Judith K. *(Magistrate Judge, United States District Court Eastern District of Texas)* Appointed by U.S. District Court judges to term beginning May 16, 1986. Reappointed 1994 and 2002. Current term expires May 16, 2010. Born Chicago Illinois July 13, 1948. Presbyterian. Educated at Arizona State University 1966-68, St. Mary's College B.A. 1971 and University of Houston J.D. cum laude 1980. Law Clerk to Chief Justice J. W. Summers, Texas Court of Appeals Twelfth Supreme Judicial District 1981-82. Admitted to practice Texas 1981. In legal practice Houston 1980-81 and Tyler 1982-86.

Instructor Legal Assistant Program Tyler Junior College. Member Federal Magistrate Judges Association, State Bar of Texas, Smith County, Fifth Circuit and American Bar Associations. Lecturer Advanced Criminal Law Seminar State Bar of Texas. Named one of Outstanding Young Women of America 1977. Previously worked as Editor American Council on Education Washington D.C., Executive Assistant and EEO Coordinator Texas House of Representatives Austin and Legal Assistant Bracewell & Patterson Houston and Austin. Former County Chairman Democratic Party. Former Democratic Precinct Chairman Smith County. Board of Directors Texas Foundation for Women's Resources. Member Advisory Committee Tyler Junior College. Enjoys traveling, sailing and gardening.

Office: 300 Federal Building, 211 West Ferguson Street, Tyler 75702.

Telephone: (903) 590-1077.

GUZMAN, Eva M. *(Justice, Texas Court of Appeals Fourteenth District)* Former Judge, Texas Family District Court 309th Judicial District.

Office: 1307 San Jacinto, Eleventh Floor, Houston 77002-7006.

Telephone: (713) 655-2800.

HACKER, Aleta *(Judge, Texas Family District Court 326th Judicial District)* Term expires Dec 31, 2006.

Office: 300 Oak Street, Abilene 79602-1521.

Telephone: (325) 674-1325.

HAGLER, Brooks H. *(Judge, Texas District Court 259th Judicial District)*

Mailing address: P.O. Box 429, Anson 79501-0429.

Telephone: (325) 823-2721.

HAHN, Buddie J. *(Judge, Texas District Court 260th Judicial District)* Term expires Dec 31, 2006.

Office: 801 West Division, Orange 77630-6353.

Telephone: (409) 882-7095.

HAJEK, David Wayne *(Judge, Texas District Court 50th Judicial District)* Elected 1984 to term beginning

HAJEK, DAVID WAYNE—*Continued*

Jan 1, 1985. Reelected 1988, 1992, 1996 and 2000. Current term expires Dec 31, 2004. Currently serves as Local Administrative Judge. Born Seymour Texas Jan 28, 1951. Catholic. Educated at Texas Tech University B.B.A. 1972 J.D. 1976. Member Phi Alpha Delta. Admitted to practice Texas 1976. In legal practice Seymour 1976-84.

County Attorney Baylor County 1978-81 and 1983-84. Member College of the State Bar of Texas and State Bar of Texas.

Mailing address: P.O. Box 508, Seymour 76380-0508.

Telephone: (940) 889-2852.

HALBACH, Joseph James, Jr. *(Judge, Texas District Court 333rd Judicial District)*

Office: 510 Civil Courts Building, 301 Fannin Street, Houston 77002.

Telephone: (713) 755-7760.

HALE, Barbara Wade *(Judge, Walker County Court at Law)*

Office: 1100 University Avenue, Suite 101, Huntsville 77340.

Telephone: (936) 436-4919.

HALE, Harlin DeWayne *(Judge, United States Bankruptcy Court Northern District of Texas)* Appointed by U.S. Court of Appeals Fifth Circuit judges to term beginning Nov 7, 2002.

Office: 1254 U.S. Courthouse, 1100 Commerce Street, Dallas 75242-1496.

Telephone: (214) 753-2016.

HALL, Brett *(Judge, Texas District Court 382nd Judicial District)*

Office: 1101 Ridge Road, Suite 203, Rockwall 75087.

Telephone: (972) 882-0270.

HALL, Derrell *(Judge, Fannin County Court)*

Office: 101 East Sam Rayburn Drive, Suite 101, Bonham 75418-4346.

Telephone: (903) 583-7455.

HALL, Jack *(Judge, Donley County Court)*

Mailing address: P.O. Box 909, Clarendon 79226-0909.

Telephone: (806) 874-3625.

HAMILTON, Kathleen A. *(Judge, Texas District Court 359th Judicial District)*

Office: 300 North Main, Room 217, Conroe 77301-2874.

Telephone: (936) 539-7900.

HAMILTON, Lee *(Judge, Texas District Court 104th Judicial District)* Former Judge, Taylor County Court.

Office: 300 Oak Street, Abilene 79602.

Telephone: (325) 674-1313.

HANCOCK, Mackey K. *(Judge, Texas District Court 99th Judicial District)* Former Judge, Lubbock County Court at Law No. 3.

Mailing address: P.O. Box 10536, Lubbock 79408-3536.

Telephone: (806) 775-1124.

HANCOCK, Patricia *(Judge, Texas District Court 113th Judicial District)* Elected Nov 1994 to term beginning Jan 1, 1995. Reelected Nov 1998 and Nov 2002. Current term expires Dec 31, 2006. Born Houston Texas July 24, 1947. Catholic. Educated at University of Texas at Austin B.A. 1971 and South Texas College of Law J.D. 1984. Editor-in-Chief South Texas Law Review 1982-83. Law Clerk to Justice F. Lee Duggan, Texas Court of Appeals First District 1984-85. Admitted to practice Texas 1984, U.S. District Court Southern District of Texas 1984, U.S. Court of Appeals Fifth 1984 and Eleventh 1984 Circuits and U.S. Supreme Court 1994. In legal practice Houston Texas 1984-94.

Fellow Texas Bar Foundation. Member State Bar of Texas and Houston Bar Association.

Office: Civil Courts Building, Second Floor, 301 Fannin Street, Houston 77002.

Telephone: (713) 755-6294.

HANEN, Andrew S. *(Judge, United States District Court Southern District of Texas)* Appointed for life by President George W. Bush to term beginning June 7, 2002. Born Elgin Illinois Dec 10, 1953. Educated at Denison University B.A. cum laude 1975 and Baylor University School of Law J.D. summa cum laude 1978. Editorial Board Baylor Law Review 1977-78. Briefing Attorney to Chief Justice Joe R. Greenhill, Texas Supreme Court Aug 1978 to Aug 1979. Moot Court Society. Member Delta Theta Phi and Beta Theta Pi. Admitted to practice Texas 1978, U.S. District Courts Eastern, Northern, Southern and Western Districts of Texas, U.S. Courts of Appeals Fifth and Eleventh Circuits and U.S. Supreme Court. Board Certified—Civil Trial Law—Texas Board of Legal Specialization. In legal practice Houston 1979-2002.

Member Magistrate Judge Merit Review Panel Southern District of Texas 1995. Life Fellow Houston Bar Foundation and Texas Bar Foundation. Charter Fellow Houston Young Lawyers Foundation. Member Houston Volunteer Lawyers Program, Houston Young Lawyers Association (President 1988-89), State Bar of Texas (Board of Directors 2000-02) and Houston Bar Association (President 1999-2000). Presenter "Ethical Considerations in Federal Court Practice" Federal Court Practice Institute Dec 1992 to Feb 1993, "Shoes for the Shoemaker's Children: A Practical Guide and Suggested Forms to Address Ethical Issues" Advanced Real Estate Course July 1998, "Ethical Issues Encountered in a Federal Court Practice" Federal Court Practice 1999 Nov 1999 and "Disqualification of a Lawyer" Advanced Expert Witness Course Feb 2001 State Bar of Texas; "In Pursuit of a Physician: The Professional Liability Claim" 95th Annual Convention and Scientific Seminar Texas Osteopathic Medical Association June 1994; "Ethical Considerations and Malpractice Prevention in Litigation" How to Offer and Exclude Evidence March 1995 and March 1996 and Litigation and Trial Tactics Dec 2000 University of Houston Law Foundation; "Practical and Ethical Considerations of Relationships with Treating Physicians in Mass Tort Settings" Drug and Medical Device Seminar The Defense Research Institute, Inc. May 1997; "Current Issues in Legal Ethics" Matagorda County Bar Association March 2000; "Delivery of Legal Services to the Disadvantaged" Equal Justice Conference American Bar Association April 2000; "Multidisciplinary Practice and the ABA Proposal" Hispanic Bar Association May 2000; "Legal Ethics and Malpractice" Houston Bar Association CLE Feb 2001; "Disqualification in the Age of Lawyer Mobility" Ethics and Procedure for the Bench and Bar Texas Association of Defense Counsel Nov 2001; "Multidisciplinary Practice" Waco-McLennan County Bar Association Dec 2001; and "Ethical Consid-

HANEN, ANDREW S.—*Continued*

erations and Malpractice Prevention in Litigation" Brazoria County Bar Association May 2002. Named Outstanding Young Lawyer of Texas by State Bar of Texas and Texas Young Lawyers Association 1989-90. Recipient President's Award for Outstanding Service to Houston Bar Association 1984-85, 1989-90 and 1995-96, Outstanding Young Alumnus Award from Baylor University Alumni Association 1990 and Professionalism Award from College of the State Bar of Texas 2000. Member Leadership Houston since 1991. Former Vice Chairman Board of Directors Sunshine Kinds Foundation. Volunteer Habitat for Humanity and American Red Cross. Charter Member Texas Supreme Court Historical Society. Life Member Baylor University Alumni Association. Member South Main Baptist Church.

Office: 600 East Harrison Street, Suite 301, Brownsville 78520.

Telephone: (956) 548-2591.

Fax: (956) 548-2612

HANKS, George C., Jr. *(Justice, Texas Court of Appeals First District)* Appointed by Governor Rick Perry to term beginning Dec 31, 2002. Term expires Jan 1, 2004. Born Breaux Bridge Louisiana Sept 25, 1964. Catholic. Educated at University of Wales, Swansea Sept 1985 to July 1986, Louisiana State University B.A. summa cum laude 1986 and Harvard Law School J.D. 1989. Law Clerk to Hon. Sim Lake, U.S. District Court Southern District of Texas 1989-91. Member Phi Kappa Phi, Mu Sigma Rho, Phi Eta Sigma and Mortar Board. Admitted to practice Texas 1989, U.S. District Courts Southern District of Texas 1992 and District of Arizona 1994 and U.S. Court of Appeals Fifth Circuit 1993. In legal practice Houston Sept 1991 to Jan 7, 2002. Judge, Texas District Court 157th Judicial District Jan 8, 2001 to Dec 30, 2002.

Special Disciplinary Counsel Commission for Lawyer Discipline State Bar of Texas 1994-96. Author "How to Exclude Inadmissible Evidence: The Use of Motions in Limine, Objections, Limiting Instructions, Motions to Strike and Instructions to Disregard at Trial" 1996 and "Preserving Privileges in Claims Investigation and Insurance Litigation" 1998 University of Houston Law Foundation, "When Sticks & Stones May Break Your Bones: An Overview of Texas Premise Liability Law for Business Owners" Texas B. Jour. 1997, "Landowner Liability for the Criminal Acts of Third Parties" 12 No. 2 *The Letter of the Law* Texas Real Estate Center April 1998 and "When Sovereign Immunity Is Not Enough: The Rise of Premise Liability Claims Against Governmental Entities" *Houston Lawyer* Sept-Oct 1998. Former Member Texas Association of Defense Counsel. Fellow Houston Bar Foundation. Member 1994-99 and Chairman 1998-99 District 4F Grievance Committee State Bar of Texas. Member Houston Lawyers Association, Houston Young Lawyers Association, College of the State Bar of Texas, Houston (Editorial Board), Fifth Circuit and National Bar Associations. Speaker "How to Offer and Exclude Evidence" March 1995 and March 1996, "Insurance Law for Agents, Adjusters and Attorneys" Dec 1997, "Advanced Business Litigation" Sept 1999 and Aug 2000 and "Advanced Civil Litigation Under the New Rules" April 2000 University of Houston Law Foundation and "Civil Trial Tactics: Tips from the Experts" Houston Young Lawyers Association May 2001. Republican. Mentor Galena Park High School and Galena Park Middle School 1993-96. Board of Directors and Volunteer Big Brothers and Big Sisters of Houston 1995-97. Board of Directors Sheltering Arms 1997, Ensemble Theatre 1997-98 and American Red Cross of Houston. Coordinator of Liturgical Ministries and Member St. Albert Catholic Church. Member Harvard Club of Houston. Interests include ice hockey, general aviation, World War II aviation and scuba diving. Personal Statement or Quote: "You cannot teach what you do not know and you cannot lead where you have not been."

Office: 1307 San Jacinto, Tenth Floor, Houston 77002.

Telephone: (713) 655-2700.

Fax: (713) 752-2304

E-mail address: ghanks@prodigy.net

HANNAH, John, Jr. *(Chief Judge, United States District Court Eastern District of Texas)* Appointed for life by President Bill Clinton to term beginning 1994. Chief Judge since June 17, 2001. Born Nacogdoches County Texas June 30, 1939. Educated at Sam Houston State University B.S. 1966, South Texas College of Law and University of Houston Law Center. In legal practice Lufkin 1971-73, 1975-77 and 1981-91.

District Attorney Angelina County 1973-75. Legal Counsel Common Cause of Texas 1975. U.S. Attorney Eastern District of Texas 1977-81. Member Texas House of Representatives Fifth District 1967-73. Secretary of State Texas 1991-94.

Office: 100 U.S. Courthouse, 221 West Ferguson Street, Tyler 75702.

Telephone: (903) 590-1091.

HARDIN, Ben *(Judge, Texas District Court 23rd Judicial District)*

Office: 111 East Locust, Room 402, Angleton 77515-4678.

Telephone: (979) 864-1205.

HARDIN, William D. *(Judge, Floyd County Court)* Appointed to term beginning Dec 1, 1986. Elected 1988, 1990, 1994, 1998 and 2002. Current term expires Dec 31, 2006. Born McAdoo Texas Nov 15, 1927. Baptist. Educated at Lippert's Business College 1950.

Staff Sergeant U.S. Army 1946-47. Court Reporter Texas District Court 110th Judicial District 1952-77. Previously worked as farmer. Democrat. Member Rotary Club. Enjoys jogging.

Office: 105 Floyd County Courthouse, Floydada 79235.

Telephone: (806) 983-4905.

HARDY, Cheril S. *(Judge, Tarrant County Criminal Court at Law No. 7)* Elected to term beginning Nov 9, 1996. Reelected 1998 and 2002. Current term expires Dec 31, 2006. Presiding Judge since 1998. Presiding Judge Board of Criminal Judges 1999. Born Welasco Texas. Religious affiliation: Disciples of Christ. Educated at Texas Christian University B.S. 1972, North Texas State University M.A. in Education 1973 and Southern Methodist University J.D. 1983. Admitted to practice Texas 1983. In legal practice Arlington, Bedford, Euless, Fort Worth and Hurst 1983-96.

Instructor Texas Wesleyan School of Law 1998-99. Fellow Tarrant County Bar Foundation and Texas Bar Foundation. Member Texas Association of Judges, Family Law Bar Association of Tarrant County (President, Director), College of the State Bar of Texas, State Bar of Texas and Tarrant County Bar Association. Attended

HARDY, CHERIL S.—*Continued*

Advanced Family Law 1986-96, Advanced Criminal Law 1996-99, Rusty Duncan Short Course (Criminal) 1996-99, numerous CLE courses, College of Advanced Judicial Studies 1996-99, Criminal Justice DWI Conference 1998 and Issues in Criminal Justice 1999. Republican.

Office: Tarrant County Justice Center, Seventh Floor, 401 West Belknap, Fort Worth 76196-0276.

Telephone: (817) 884-2969.

E-mail address: Cherilshardy@tarrantcounty.com

HARGER, Gary *(Judge, Nolan County Court at Law)*

Office: 100 East Third, Suite 107, Sweetwater 79556-4547.

Telephone: (325) 235-2353.

HARLE, Sid L. *(Judge, Texas District Court 226th Judicial District)* Term expires Dec 31, 2006.

Office: 2081 Bexar County Justice Center, 300 Dolorosa Street, San Antonio 78205-3028.

Telephone: (210) 335-2446.

HARMON, Melinda *(Judge, United States District Court Southern District of Texas)* Appointed for life by President George Bush to term beginning Aug 12, 1989. Born Port Arthur Texas Nov 1, 1946. Educated at Radcliffe College A.B. 1969 and University of Texas School of Law J.D. 1972. Law Clerk to Hon. John V. Singleton, Jr., U.S. District Court Southern District of Texas 1973-75. Judge, Texas District Court 280th Judicial District 1988-89.

Trial Attorney Litigation Section Exxon Company 1975-88.

Office: 9114 U.S. Courthouse, 515 Rusk Avenue, Houston 77002.

Telephone: (713) 250-5194.

HARMON, Roger Owen *(Judge, Johnson County Court)*

Office: Two North Main Street, Cleburne 76031.

Telephone: (817) 556-6360.

HARMON, William *(Judge, Texas District Court 178th Judicial District)* Term expires Dec 31, 2004.

Office: 1201 Franklin, Room 19032, Houston 77002.

Telephone: (713) 755-6336.

HARPER, John Robert *(Judge, Taylor County Court at Law No. 1)* Elected Nov 5, 2002 to term beginning Jan 1, 2003. Term expires Dec 31, 2006. Born Fort Worth Texas Feb 18, 1968. Religious affiliation: Church of Christ. Educated at Abilene Christian University B.S. with honors 1990 and Texas Tech University School of Law 1992. Admitted to practice Texas 1993.

Assistant District Attorney Feb 1994 to Dec 2002. Member State Bar of Texas. Republican. Member Lions Club. Enjoys hunting.

Office: Taylor County Courthouse, 300 Oak, Abilene 79602.

Telephone: (325) 674-1323.

Fax: (325) 738-8528

E-mail address: harperr@taylorcountytexas.org

HARRIS, Debra Nekhom *(Judge, Tarrant County Criminal Court at Law No. 4)*

Office: Tarrant County Justice Center, Fifth Floor, 401 West Belknap, Fort Worth 76196-0239.

Telephone: (817) 884-1426.

HARRIS, Frances Ann *(Judge, Texas Family District Court 302nd Judicial District)* Elected 1982 to term beginning Jan 1, 1983. Reelected 1986, 1990, 1994, 1998 and 2002. Current term expires Dec 31, 2006. Born Fort Worth Texas March 2, 1951. Baptist. Educated at University of Texas B.A. 1972 and Baylor University J.D. 1974. Member Order of Barristers and Phi Delta Theta. Admitted to practice Texas 1974, U.S. District Courts Northern 1978 and Eastern 1978 Districts of Texas and U.S. Court of Appeals Fifth Circuit 1978. Began legal practice Garland 1974. Master in Chancery, Texas Family District Courts 1980-82.

Board of Directors Northeast Texas Family Law Specialists since 1983. Life Fellow Texas Bar Foundation. Member State Bar of Texas (Adjunct Member Family Law Council since 1983), Garland (President 1980) and Dallas (Board of Directors Family Law Section 1981) Bar Associations. Republican. Board of Directors Galaxy Center. Co-founder Operation Kindness Humane Society. Member Garland Women's Activities Building Council (First Vice President, Board of Directors 1978) and Soroptimist International of Garland (President 1979).

Office: George Allen Sr. Courts Building, Fifth Floor, 600 Commerce Street, Dallas 75202-4606.

Telephone: (214) 653-7375.

HARRIS, Margaret Stewart *(Judge, Harris County Criminal Court at Law No. 5)*

Office: 1201 Franklin, Room 9040, Houston 77002.

Telephone: (713) 755-6196.

HARRIS, Ron *(Judge, Collin County Court)*

Office: 210 South McDonald, Suite 626, McKinney 75069.

Telephone: (972) 548-4635.

HARRIS, William Wren *(Judge, Texas District Court 233rd Judicial District)*

Office: 100 North Houston, Fort Worth 76196-0227.

Telephone: (817) 884-1794.

HARRISON, Glen *(Judge, Texas District Court 32nd Judicial District)* Born Pecos Texas Sept 13, 1961. Southern Baptist. Educated at Texas Tech University B.A. cum laude 1984 J.D. 1986. Admitted to practice Texas 1987 and U.S. District Court Northern District of Texas 1987. Former Judge, Nolan County Court at Law, appointed to term beginning 1989.

Member Texas Judicial Ethics Committee 1993-95. Member Executive Committee Judicial Section State Bar of Texas since 1996.

Office: 100 East Third, Suite 204A, Sweetwater 79556-4572.

Telephone: (325) 235-3133.

HARTMAN, Merrill *(Judge, Texas District Court 192nd Judicial District)* Term expires Dec 31, 2006.

Office: George Allen Sr. Courts Building, Fourth Floor, 600 Commerce Street, Dallas 75202-4606.

Telephone: (214) 653-7709.

HASETTE, Nanette *(Judge, Texas District Court 28th Judicial District)* Elected Nov 1996 to term beginning Jan 1, 1997. Reelected Nov 2000, current term expires Dec 31, 2004. Born Corpus Christi Texas Sept 26, 1960. Catholic. Educated at University of Texas at El Paso B.S. 1984 and South Texas College of Law J.D. 1988. Admitted to practice Texas 1988 and U.S. District Court Southern District of Texas 1996.

Assistant County Attorney 1989-91. Past President

HASETTE, NANETTE—*Continued*

Coastal Bend Women Lawyers Association. Member State Bar of Texas (Former Board Member, Women in the Law Section) and Corpus Christi Bar Association.

Office: 901 Leopard Street, Room 803, Corpus Christi 78401.

Telephone: (361) 888-0506.

HATCH, Richard, III *(Judge, San Patricio County Court at Law)*

Office: 400 West Sinton Street, Room B-15, Sinton 78387-2450.

Telephone: (361) 364-6142.

HAWK, Susan *(Judge, Texas District Court 291st Judicial District)*

Office: LB 34 Frank Crowley Courts Building, 133 North Industrial Boulevard, Dallas 75207-4313.

Telephone: (214) 653-5870.

HAYNES, Catharina *(Judge, Texas District Court 191st Judicial District)* Elected Nov 1998 to term beginning Jan 1, 1999. Reelected Nov 2002, current term expires Dec 31, 2006. Born Melbourne Florida Nov 1963. Presbyterian. Educated at Florida Institute of Technology B.S. with highest honors 1983 and Emory University School of Law J.D. with distinction 1986. Notes and Comments Editor Emory Law Journal 1985-86. Member Order of the Coif. Admitted to practice Texas 1986, U.S. District Courts Eastern, Northern and Western Districts of Texas, U.S. Courts of Appeal Fifth and Tenth Circuits and U.S. Supreme Court. Board Certified—Consumer Law—Texas Board of Legal Specialization. In legal practice Dallas 1986-98.

Author "Federal Civil Procedures and Evidence During Trial" *Lawyers Cooperative Federal Practice Guide* 1998. Co-author Chapter 17 "Posttrial Motions" *Fifth Circuit Edition.* At-large Director Dallas Bar Association 2001. Member National Association of Women Judges and American Bar Association. Recipient JoAnna Moreland Outstanding Committee Chair Award from Dallas Bar Association 1996 and 2002. Republican.

Office: 600 Commerce Street, Room 343, Dallas 75201.

Telephone: (214) 653-6609.

E-mail address: chaynes777@aol.com

HEAD, Hayden W., Jr. *(Judge, United States District Court Southern District of Texas)* Appointed for life by President Ronald Reagan to term beginning Oct 26, 1981. Born Sherman Texas Nov 12, 1944. Educated at University of Texas B.A. 1966 LL.B. 1968. In legal practice Corpus Christi 1968-69 and 1972-81.

Office: U.S. Courthouse, 1133 North Shoreline Boulevard, Corpus Christi 78401.

Telephone: (361) 888-3148.

HEAD, Thomas V. *(Judge, Lubbock County Court)*

Mailing address: P.O. Box 10536, Lubbock 79408-3536.

Telephone: (806) 775-1086.

HEARTFIELD, Thad *(Judge, United States District Court Eastern District of Texas)* Appointed for life by President Bill Clinton to term beginning 1995. Born Port Arthur Texas Sept 10, 1940. Educated at St. Mary's University B.A. 1962 J.D. 1965. In legal practice Beaumont 1966-69 and 1973-95.

Assistant District Attorney Jefferson County 1965-66. City Attorney Beaumont 1969-73. Director Lower Neches Valley Authority 1983-94.

Mailing address: P.O. Box 949, Beaumont 77704-0949.

Telephone: (409) 654-2860.

HEBERT, Robert E. *(Judge, Fort Bend County Court)*

Office: 301 Jackson, Suite 719, Richmond 77469-3108.

Telephone: (281) 341-8608.

HECHT, Nathan L. *(Justice, Texas Supreme Court)* Elected to term beginning Jan 1, 1989. Reelected 1994 and 2000. Current term expires Dec 31, 2006. Born Clovis New Mexico Aug 15, 1949. Christian. Educated at Yale University B.A. in Philosophy with honors 1971 and Southern Methodist University School of Law J.D. cum laude 1974. Articles Editor Southwestern Law Journal 1972-74. Law Clerk to Hon. Roger Robb, U.S. Court of Appeals District of Columbia Circuit 1974-75. Member Delta Theta Phi, Order of the Coif and Barristers. Admitted to practice Texas 1974, District of Columbia 1975, U.S. District Courts Northern and Western Districts of Texas and District of Columbia, U.S. Courts of Appeals Fifth and District of Columbia Circuits and U.S. Supreme Court. In legal practice Dallas 1976-81. Judge, Texas District Court 95th Judicial District Sept 1, 1981 to 1986. Justice, Texas Court of Appeals Fifth Supreme Judicial District 1986-88.

Author Comment "The Death Penalty: A Cruel and Unusual Punishment" 27 Southwestern L. Jour. 298, 1973 and note " 'Property' Under Due Process—Non-Tenured Teachers' Right to Re-Employment" 27 Southwestern L. Jour. 398, 1973. Fellow American Bar Foundation and Texas Bar Foundation. Member American Law Institute, State Bar of Texas, The District of Columbia Bar, Dallas (CLE Education Committee and clinic speaker 1982, Judiciary Committee 1982-84, Courthouse Committee 1983, Chairman Subcommittee on Dallas Local Court Rules 1983-84) and American Bar Associations. Recipient Most Outstanding Young Lawyer Award from Dallas Association of Young Lawyers 1984. Lieutenant USNR JAGC 1971-79. Republican. Board of Trustees Children's Medical Center Hospital since 1983. Board of Visitors Southern Methodist University School of Law since 1983. Member Valley View Christian Church (Chairman of Elders and Missions Committee, Sunday School teacher, pianist, organist). Enjoys piano and organ.

Mailing address: P.O. Box 12248, Austin 78711-2248.

Telephone: (512) 463-1348.

HEDGES, Adele *(Justice, Texas Court of Appeals First District)* Assumed office Nov 19, 1992. Elected to subsequent terms. Current term expires Dec 31, 2006. Born Orange Texas Feb 4, 1947. Educated at University of Houston B.A. 1968 J.D. summa cum laude 1994 and Rice University M.A. 1971 Ph.D. 1972. Articles Editor Houston Law Review. State Moot Court Team. Admitted to practice Texas 1974. In legal practice 1974-77 and 1985-92.

General Counsel Champion Realty Corporation 1978 and Republic Bank of Houston 1981-85. Member Garden Club of Houston.

Office: 1307 San Jacinto, Tenth Floor, Houston 77002-7006.

Telephone: (713) 655-2700.

HEFLEY, Jerry Dan *(Judge, Wheeler County Court)* Mailing address: P.O. Box 486, Wheeler 79096-0486.
Telephone: (806) 826-5961.

HEFLIN, Joe *(Judge, Crosby County Court)* Office: 201 West Aspen, Suite 104, Crosbyton 79322-0104.
Telephone: (806) 675-2011.

HELLUMS, Bonnie Crane *(Judge, Texas District Court 247th Judicial District)* Elected Nov 8, 1994 to term beginning Jan 1, 1995. Reelected Nov 1998 and 2002. Current term expires Dec 31, 2006. Born Chicago Illinois June 12, 1943. Methodist. Educated at Southern Methodist University B.A. 1965, University of Illinois M.Ed. 1966, South Texas College of Law J.D. 1981 and University of Nevada-Reno. Recipient American Jurisprudence Award for Excellence in Legal Studies. Admitted to practice Texas 1983, U.S. District Court Southern District of Texas 1984 and U.S. Supreme Court 1985. In legal practice Houston 1983-95. Former Special Master, Texas District Court 309th Judicial District.

Guest Lecturer on Trial Advocacy since 1995 and Speaker on Mediation since 1995 South Texas College of Law. Member Board of Juvenile Court Volunteers 1993, Judicial Advisory Board Child Advocates, Inc. 1995-99 and Supreme Court Ad Hoc Committee on Expert Witnesses 1997-99. Chair Committee on Judicial Liaison Harris County 1998. Fellow Houston Bar Foundation and Texas Bar Foundation. Member Task Force 2000, American Inns of Court, Houston Volunteer Lawyers Association (Board 1995, Secretary since 1998), State Bar of Texas, Houston and American (Family Law Trial Advocacy Institute 1991) Bar Associations. Panelist Advanced Family Law Seminar San Antonio 1996. Moderator Family Law Practice Seminar 1996-99 and "AIDS and the Law" CLE Houston Bar Association 1997. Speaker North Harris County Bar Association 1996; "Family Violence" Spring Shadows Glen 1996; "Family Violence" Judicial Section Meeting Corpus Christi Sept 1996, "Family Law Changes" Advanced Judicial Training Houston March 1997 and "Significant Decisions" Judicial Section Meeting Fort Worth Sept 1997 Texas Judicial Conference; and "Legal Aspects of Being Single Again" Greater Houston Women's Foundation 1997. Faculty Member Family Law Trial Advocacy Training Institute American Bar Association 1997, 1998, 1999 and 2000 and National Judicial College 1998, 1999 and 2000. Presenter March Madness presentation on Family Law Houston Bar Association 1998 and 1999.

Recipient Community Partnership Award from Houston Area Marriage and Family Therapists 1997, Lifetime Achievement Award Texas Businesswoman of the Year from Exhibit Hope 1998 and Texas Leader Award from Leadership Houston 1999. Named one of "Women on the Move" by Houston Post, Texas Executive Women and Foley's 1991. Listed in *Who's Who of American Women in Law, Who's Who of American Women* and *Who's Who of Women in the World.* Women's Counselor University of Houston 1968-69. Assistant Dean of Students and Foreign Student Advisor 1969-74 and Director of Student Activities, Counseling and Foreign Student Advisor (functional equivalent of Dean) 1974-83 Rice University. Republican. Sustaining Member Republican National Committee 1991. Member Magic Circle Republican Women.

Local Arrangements Chairman 1983, Parliamentarian 1984-85, Secretary 1986-88, President Elect 1988-89, President 1989-90 and Immediate Past President 1990-91 National Association of Women Deans, Administrators and Counselors. Vice President 1987-88 and President 1988-89 Women's Executive Forum. Member Class VIII 1989-90, Board of Directors 1995-96 and Board of Leadership 1995-97 Leadership Houston. Board of Directors Advocates for Incest Survivors 1992. President Eye-Openers Breakfast Network 1992. Attorney Chair Greater Houston Women's Foundation 1992. Clinical Member American Association for Marriage and Family Therapists 1993. Member American Leadership Forum since 2000. Former Member Development Board Houston Achievement Place, Houston Taipei Society and Texas Executive Women's Mentoring Project for Girls at Risk. President and Program Chair Family Mediation Network. Vice President West University Little League Auxiliary. Board of Directors St. Agnes Academy. Youth Director Palmer Memorial Episcopal Church. Consultant and Guest Lecturer Parkside of Katy Treatment Center for Alcohol and Substance Abuse Issues. Co-leader Girl Scout Troop. Model Arthritis Foundation. Member Ronald McDonald House, Texas Association of College and University Student Personnel Administrators, American Association of Sex Educators, Counselors and Therapists, St. Luke's United Methodist Church (Administrative Board, President Voyager's Class, Chairman Committee on Hospice Care, Member Executive Committee, Finance Committee, Long Range Planning Committee and Youth Group Sponsor), Judicial Outreach for Literacy Training and Houston Works Board (Member since 1993, Vice Chair since 1999).

Office: Family Law Center Building, Second Floor, 1115 Congress Avenue, Houston 77002.
Telephone: (713) 755-6246.
E-mail address: Bonnie.Hellums@dca.co.harris.tx.us

HELM, Reagan C. *(Judge, Harris County Criminal Court at Law No. 1)*
Office: 1201 Franklin, Room 8040, Houston 77002.
Telephone: (713) 755-6180.

HENDERSON, Curt B. *(Judge, Texas District Court 219th Judicial District)* Appointed by Governor William P. Clements to term beginning Aug 1988. Elected 1988, 1990, 1994, 1998 and 2002. Current term expires Dec 31, 2006. Educated at Texas A&M University B.A. 1975 and Baylor University School of Law J.D. 1977. Admitted to practice Texas 1978. Judge, Collin County Court at Law 1986-88.

Assistant Criminal District Attorney 1979-86.

Office: 210 South McDonald, Suite 414, McKinney 75069.
Telephone: (972) 548-4402.
Fax: (972) 548-4456
E-mail address: chenderson@co.collin.tx.us

HENDERSON, Donnie *(Judge, Crane County Court)* Mailing address: P.O. Box 457, Crane 79731-0457.
Telephone: (432) 558-1100.

HENDERSON, James *(Judge, Grayson County Court at Law No. 1)*
Office: 200 South Crockett, Sherman 75090-5958.
Telephone: (903) 813-4380.

HENRY, Linda Lee *(Judge, McMullen County Court)*
Mailing address: P.O. Box 237, Tilden 78072.
Telephone: (361) 274-3341.

HERMAN, Guy *(Judge, Travis County Probate Court No. 1)* Born Yokohama Japan Feb 10, 1949. Educated at University of Texas B.A. 1972 J.D. 1977. Admitted to practice Texas 1977. In legal practice Austin 1978-80. Justice of the Peace Precinct 5, 1980-85. Former Judge, Travis County Court at Law No. 4, appointed to term beginning June 1, 1985. Democrat.
Mailing address: P.O. Box 1748, Austin 78767-1748.
Telephone: (512) 854-9258.

HERNANDEZ, Alex R. *(Judge, Calhoun County Court at Law)*
Office: 211 South Ann Street, Port Lavaca 77979.
Telephone: (361) 553-8451.

HEROD, Steven R. *(Judge, Texas District Court 91st Judicial District)*
Office: 100 West Main, Suite 302, Eastland 76448.
Telephone: (254) 629-1797.

HERR, Maria Teresa "Tessa" *(Judge, Texas District Court 186th Judicial District)*
Office: 3097 Bexar County Justice Center, 300 Dolorosa Street, San Antonio 78205-3028.
Telephone: (210) 335-2505.

HERRERA, Mike *(Judge, Texas District Court 383rd Judicial District)*
Office: 500 East San Antonio, El Paso 79901-2457.
Telephone: (915) 546-2132.

HERRERA, Ricardo *(Judge, El Paso County Court at Law No. 1)*
Office: 500 East San Antonio, #802, El Paso 79901.
Telephone: (915) 546-2011.

HERVEY, Barbara Parker *(Judge, Texas Court of Criminal Appeals)* Elected Nov 2000 to term beginning Jan 1, 2001. Term expires Dec 31, 2006. Educated at University of North Carolina at Greensboro B.A. 1975 and St. Mary's University J.D. 1979. Began legal practice San Antonio.
Assistant Criminal District Attorney Appellate Section Bexar County 1984-2000. Member State Bar of Texas and Bexar County Women's Bar Association. Member Bexar County Republican Women.
Mailing address: P.O. Box 12308, Austin 78711-2308.
Office: Supreme Court Building, Austin 78701.
Telephone: (512) 463-1575.

HIGGINBOTHAM, Don *(Judge, Williamson County Court at Law No. 3)*
Office: 405 South Martin Luther King Boulevard, No. 16, Georgetown 78626.
Telephone: (512) 943-1160.

HIGGS, Max D. *(Judge, El Paso County Probate Court)*
Office: 500 East San Antonio, #1003, El Paso 79901.
Telephone: (915) 546-2161.

HIGHT, C. T. *(Judge, Texas District Court 75th Judicial District)*
Mailing address: P.O. Box 10148, Liberty 77575-0148.
Telephone: (936) 336-4678.

HIGLEY, Laura Carter *(Justice, Texas Court of Appeals First District)*
Office: 1307 San Jacinto, Tenth Floor, Houston 77002-7006.
Telephone: (713) 655-2700.

HILL, Belinda *(Judge, Texas District Court 230th Judicial District)*
Office: 1201 Franklin, Room 16040, Houston 77002.
Telephone: (713) 755-6782.

HILL, Sherry L. *(Judge, Tarrant County Criminal Court at Law No. 1)* Elected to term beginning Jan 1, 1991. Reelected 1994, 1998 and 2002. Current term expires Dec 31, 2006.
Office: Tarrant County Justice Center, Fifth Floor, 401 West Belknap, Fort Worth 76196-0236.
Telephone: (817) 884-1337.

HINES, Earl S. *(Magistrate Judge, United States District Court Eastern District of Texas)* Appointed by U.S. District Court judges. Born Port Arthur Texas Oct 18, 1943. United Methodist. Educated at University of Texas at Austin B.A. with honors 1965 J.D. 1967. Law Clerk to Hon. Joe J. Fisher, U.S. District Court Eastern District of Texas 1967-68. Member Phi Beta Kappa, Phi Delta Phi and Phi Eta Sigma. Admitted to practice Texas 1967. In legal practice Beaumont 1971-83.
Assistant Attorney General Texas 1969-70. Member State Bar of Texas, Jefferson County and American Bar Associations.
Office: 234 U.S. Courthouse, 300 Willow Street, Beaumont 77701.
Telephone: (409) 654-2815.

HINOJOSA, Federico G. *(Justice, Texas Court of Appeals Thirteenth District)* Appointed by Governor Ann W. Richards to term beginning Nov 4, 1991. Elected 1992, 1994 and 2000. Current term expires Dec 31, 2006. Born Edinburg Texas April 16, 1947. Educated at Pan American University B.A. 1969 and University of Houston Law Center J.D. 1977. Admitted to practice Texas 1977. Began legal practice Houston. In legal practice McAllen 1984-91.
Child Support Attorney Texas Department of Human Resources 1981-83. Assistant Criminal District Attorney Hidalgo County 1983-84. Member American Judicature Society, Mexican American Bar Association of Texas, State Bar of Texas, Cameron County and Hidalgo County Bar Associations.
Office: Hidalgo County Administration Bldg., Fifth Floor, 100 East Cano, Edinburg 78539.
Telephone: (956) 318-2405.

HINOJOSA, Gilberto *(Judge, Cameron County Court)* Former Judge, Texas District Court 107th Judicial District. Former Judge, Cameron County Court at Law No. 2. Former Justice, Texas Court of Appeals Thirteenth District, elected to term beginning Jan 1, 1991.
Office: 964 East Harrison, Brownsville 78520.
Telephone: (956) 544-0830.

HINOJOSA, Leticia *(Judge, Texas District Court 139th Judicial District)* Born Brownsville Texas. Catholic. Educated at University of Texas B.A. magna cum laude 1978 J.D. 1981. Member Phi Alpha Delta. Admitted to practice Texas 1981 and U.S. District Court Southern District of Texas 1984. Former Judge, Hidalgo

HINOJOSA, LETICIA—*Continued*

County Court at Law No. 4, appointed to term beginning Sept 15, 1989.

Member State Bar of Texas and Hidalgo County Bar Association. Attended Advanced Estate Law Seminar June 13, 1990 and Advanced Probate Course June 13, 1991. Named Outstanding Professional Woman by Business and Professional Womens Club of McAllen. Recipient Certificate of Appreciation from Juvenile Court 1989 and 1990. Democrat. Delegate to Texas State Democratic Convention 1984. Enjoys antique collecting, crafts, films and travel.

Office: 100 North Closner, Second Floor, Edinburg 78539.

Telephone: (956) 318-2260.

HINOJOSA, Ricardo H. *(Judge, United States District Court Southern District of Texas)* Appointed for life by President Ronald Reagan to term beginning May 5, 1983. Born Rio Grande Texas Jan 24, 1950. Educated at University of Texas at Austin B.A. 1972 and Harvard Law School J.D. 1975. Law Clerk to Texas Supreme Court 1975-76. In legal practice McAllen 1976-83.

Mailing address: P.O. Box 5007, McAllen 78502-5007.

Telephone: (956) 618-8100.

HITTNER, David *(Judge, United States District Court Southern District of Texas)* Appointed for life by President Ronald Reagan to term beginning June 9, 1986. Born Schenectady New York July 10, 1939. Educated at New York University B.S. 1961 J.D. 1964. Admitted to practice New York 1964, Texas 1967 and U.S. Supreme Court 1969. Began legal practice Houston 1967. Judge, Texas District Court 133rd Judicial District 1978-86, appointed by Governor Dolph Briscoe.

Author "Legal Ethics" 55 ABA Journal 663, "Summary Judgments" 54 Baylor L. Rev. 1, "Default Judgments" 37 Southwestern L. Jour. 421, "A Judge's View of Jury Service" 47 Texas B. Jour. 227, "Frivolous Appeals in Texas" 50 Texas B. Jour. 358, "Post Judgment Procedures" 45 Texas B. Jour. 417 and *Federal Civil Procedure Before Trial* Fifth Circuit Edition. Contributing Author *Texas Civil Trial Handbook* and *Texas Collections Manual.* Member The American Law Institute, State Bar of Texas, Houston and New York State Bar Associations. Lecturer and Chairman State Bar of Texas CLE programs. Recipient President's Award from State Bar of Texas and Special Award of Merit from American Bar Association. Infantry Captain and Paratrooper U.S. Army 1965-66. Member American Canoe Association (Past national officer), American Legion and Masons. National committee member Boy Scouts of America and Girl Scouts of the U.S.A.

Office: 8509 U.S. Courthouse, 515 Rusk Avenue, Houston 77002.

Telephone: (713) 250-5711.

HOBBS, Jimmie *(Judge, Coleman County Court)*

Office: 100 West Live Oak Street, Coleman 76834.

Telephone: (325) 625-2889.

HODGES, Sandra *(Judge, Rusk County Court)* Elected to term beginning Jan 1, 1987. Reelected Nov 6, 1990, 1994, 1998 and 2002. Current term expires Dec 31, 2006. Born Houston Texas Nov 5, 1939. Methodist. Educated at Kilgore Junior College 1957-59. Previously worked as legal secretary.

Office: 115 North Main, Suite 104, Henderson 75652.

Telephone: (903) 657-0302.

HOGAN, Jim *(Judge, Wichita County Court at Law No. 1)*

Office: 900 Seventh Street, Room 201, Wichita Falls 76301-2440.

Telephone: (940) 766-8107.

HOLCOMB, Charles R. *(Judge, Texas Court of Criminal Appeals)* Elected to term beginning Jan 1, 2001. Term expires Dec 31, 2006. Born 1933. Educated at Lee College, Lamar University and South Texas School of Law J.D. 1958. In legal practice 1972-81. Judge, Orange County Court at Law 1966-72. Justice, Texas Court of Appeals Twelfth District 1993-98.

City Attorney Deer Park and Orange 1959-66. County Attorney 1974-81 and District Attorney 1981-91 Cherokee County.

Mailing address: P.O. Box 12308, Austin 78711-2308.

Telephone: (512) 463-1551.

HOLCOMBE, Walter M. *(Judge, Reeves County Court at Law)*

Office: 100 East Fourth, Box 749, Pecos 79772.

Telephone: (432) 445-5497.

HOLDER, Marc *(Judge, Brazoria County Court at Law No. 2)*

Office: 111 East Locust, 300A, Angleton 77515-4678.

Telephone: (979) 864-1571.

HOLLAND, Jack Humphrey *(Judge, Texas District Court 173rd Judicial District)* Term expires Dec 31, 2006.

Office: Henderson County Courthouse, Athens 75751.

Telephone: (903) 675-6107.

HOLLARS, Bill *(Judge, Hale County Court)*

Office: 500 Broadway, Room 100, Plainview 79072-8050.

Telephone: (806) 291-5214.

HOLLOWAY, Jesse Aaron *(Judge, Texas District Court 350th Judicial District)* Former Judge, Taylor County Court, assumed office 1985.

Office: 300 Oak Street, Abilene 79602-1521.

Telephone: (325) 674-1242.

HOLLUMS, John R. *(Judge, Texas District Court 110th Judicial District)*

Office: 100 Main Street, Floydada 79235-2758.

Telephone: (806) 983-3384.

HOLMAN, Dixon W. *(Justice, Texas Court of Appeals Second District)* Term expires Dec 31, 2008. Former Judge, Texas District Court 141st Judicial District. Former Judge, Texas District Court 48th Judicial District, assumed office Jan 1, 1993.

Office: 9000 Tarrant County Justice Center, 401 West Belknap, Fort Worth 76196.

Telephone: (817) 884-2176.

HOLMES, Elenor F. *(Judge, Limestone County Court)*

Mailing address: P.O. Box 469, Groesbeck 76642-0469.

Telephone: (254) 729-3810.

HOLT, Wayne *(Judge, San Augustine County Court)* Office: 100 West Columbia, Room 203, San Augustine 75972-1904.
Telephone: (936) 275-2762.

HORN, Mary *(Judge, Denton County Court)* Office: 110 West Hickory Street, Denton 76201.
Telephone: (940) 349-2820.

HOUDASHELL, Ernie *(Judge, Randall County Court)*
Office: 400 Sixteenth Street, Canyon 79015-3850.
Telephone: (806) 468-5500.

HOUSE, Judy *(Judge, Gaines County Court)* Mailing address: P.O. Box 847, Seminole 79360-4341.
Telephone: (432) 758-5411.

HOUSER, Barbara J. *(Judge, United States Bankruptcy Court Northern District of Texas)* Appointed by U.S. Court of Appeals Fifth Circuit judges to term beginning Jan 20, 2000. Term expires Jan 20, 2014. Educated at University of Nebraska 1975 and Southern Methodist University J.D. 1978. Staff member Southern Methodist University Law Review. Admitted to practice Texas and U.S. Supreme Court. In legal practice Dallas 1978 to Jan 19, 2000.

Contributing Author *Collier on Bankruptcy* 15th ed. and *Collier Bankruptcy Manual* 3rd ed. Former Chairman Committee on Bankruptcy and Corporate Reorganization Dallas Bar Association. Member National Bankruptcy Conference, American College of Bankruptcy, State Bar of Texas and American Bar Association.

Office: 12A24 U.S. Courthouse, 1100 Commerce Street, Dallas 75242-1496.
Telephone: (214) 753-2055.

HOYT, Kenneth M. *(Judge, United States District Court Southern District of Texas)* Appointed for life by President Ronald Reagan to term beginning April 1, 1988. Born San Augustine Texas March 2, 1948. Baptist. Educated at Texas Southern University A.B. J.D. Editor Texas Southern University Law Review. Member Sigma Pi Phi. Admitted to practice Texas 1972, U.S. District Court Southern District of Texas and U.S. Court of Appeals Fifth Circuit. In legal practice Houston 1972-84. Judge, Texas District Court 125th Judicial District 1981-82. Justice, Texas Court of Appeals First Supreme Judicial District 1985-88.

Author articles Texas Southern L. Rev. 1970, Texas Tech L. Rev. 1986 and South Texas L. Rev. 1999. Adjunct Professor Thurgood Marshall School of Law.

Office: 11144 U.S. Courthouse, 515 Rusk Avenue, Houston 77002.
Telephone: (713) 250-5613.

HUBBELL, Gerald *(Judge, Franklin County Court)* Mailing address: P.O. Box 577, Mount Vernon 75457-0577.
Telephone: (903) 537-2342.

HUDSON, J. Harvey *(Justice, Texas Court of Appeals Fourteenth District)* Elected to term beginning Jan 1, 1995. Reelected 2000, current term expires Dec 31, 2006. Born Houston Texas Sept 20, 1949. Educated at Texas A&M University B.S. 1972 and South Texas College of Law J.D. magna cum laude 1979. Recipient American Jurisprudence Awards in Contracts, Constitutional Law and Civil Procedure. Senior Lead Articles Editor South Texas Law Journal. Member Order of Lytae.

Assistant District Attorney Trial Bureau 1979-81 and Consumer Fraud Division 1981-83 and Chief Appellate Division 1983-84 Harris County. Member College of the State Bar of Texas, State Bar of Texas and Houston Bar Association.

Office: 1307 San Jacinto, 11th Floor, Houston 77002-7006.
Telephone: (713) 655-2800.

HUDSPETH, Harry Lee *(Senior Judge, United States District Court Western District of Texas)* Magistrate July 8, 1977 to Nov 26, 1979. Appointed Judge for life by President Jimmy Carter to term beginning Nov 27, 1979. Former Chief Judge. Assumed Senior status June 30, 2001, serves by assignment. Born Dallas Texas Dec 28, 1935. Religious affiliation: Disciples of Christ. Educated at University of Texas B.A. with high honors 1955 J.D. 1958. Member Phi Beta Kappa, Chancellors and Order of the Coif. Admitted to practice Texas 1958. Board Certified—Criminal Law—Texas Board of Legal Specialization.

Member Texas Criminal Defense Lawyers Association (Director 1972-77), El Paso Trial Lawyers Association (President 1972) and El Paso Bar Association (Director 1971-74). Democrat.

Office: 350 Judicial Building, 903 San Jacinto Boulevard, Austin 78701.
Telephone: (512) 916-5038.

HUFF, Jim *(Judge, Live Oak County Court)* Elected to term beginning Jan 1, 1987. Reelected 1990, 1994, 1998 and 2002. Current term expires Dec 31, 2006. Born San Antonio Texas Nov 20, 1954. Roman Catholic. Educated at Texas A&M University B.S. 1977, St. Mary's University B.A. 1978 and Sam Houston State University.

Attended judicial conference Lubbock Texas Feb 2, 1987. Previously worked as Assistant Chief Deputy Live Oak County Sheriff's Department. Member Sheriff's Mounted Posse, St. Vincent DePaul Service Organization, Sacred Heart Catholic Church, Lions Club and Knights of Columbus. Enjoys ranching.

Mailing address: P.O. Box 487, George West 78022.
Telephone: (361) 449-2733.

HUFFMAN, Joan *(Judge, Texas District Court 183rd Judicial District)*
Office: 1201 Franklin, Room 18136, Houston 77002.
Telephone: (713) 755-6354.

HUFSTETLER, K. Randall *(Judge, Texas Family District Court 300th Judicial District)*
Office: 111 East Locust, Angleton 77515-4678.
Telephone: (281) 756-1227.

HUGHES, Jean Spradling *(Judge, Harris County Criminal Court at Law No. 15)*
Office: 1201 Franklin, Room 11136, Houston 77002.
Telephone: (713) 755-4760.

HUGHES, Lynn Nettleton *(Judge, United States District Court Southern District of Texas)* Appointed to serve during good behavior by President Ronald Reagan to term beginning Dec 17, 1985. Born Houston Texas Sept 9, 1941. Educated at University of Alabama B.A. 1963, University of Texas J.D. 1968 and University of Virginia LL.M. 1992. Admitted to practice Texas 1966. In legal practice Houston 1966-79. Judge, Texas District

HUGHES, LYNN NETTLETON—*Continued*

Court 165th Judicial District 1979-80. Judge, Texas District Court 189th Judicial District 1981-85.

Consultant European Community 1989. Advisor Republic of Moldova 1993, Albania 1995 and 1998 and Ukraine 1996. Author "The Legal Implications of the Consulting Relationship" *Environmental Geology* 1980; "A Note on the UEFJA in Harris County" 20 Houston Lawyer 52, 1982; "Judicial Notice and Presumptions in Civil Cases" *Texas Rules of Evidence Benchbook* 1983; "Individual Dockets for the Civil District Courts" 22 Houston Lawyer 22, 1985; "Shipowners' Right to a Limitation of Liability Adrift on a Sea of Tort Changes" 4 *Lloyd's Maritime and Commercial Law Quarterly* 517, 1988; "Mass and Complex Case Management" 8 *The Advocate* 21, 1989; "Charters for Plain Language" 31 New Mexico Bar Bulletin 17, 1992; "Floating Back & Forth With Federalism: Removal & Remand for the Proctor" 18 Houston Journal of International Law 803, 1996; "Principle and Pragmatism" 21 Tulane Maritime L. Jour. 1, 1997; "Don't Make a Federal Case Out of It" 25 American Journal of Criminal Law 151, 1997; "Neo-Scholasticism" 37 Houston L. Rev. 321, 2000; "Contracts, Custom, and Courts in Cyberspace" 96 Northwestern L. Rev 1599, 2002; and "Realism Intrudes: Law, Politics, and War" Houston Journal of International Law 2003. Advisory Director Houston Journal of International Law since 1980 (Chairman 1989-99). Important Decisions: Xerox Corporation v. County of Harris (state taxation of foreign commerce) 103 S. Ct. 523, 1982 and Southdown, Inc. v. Moore McCormick Resources, Inc. (hostile corporate defenses invalidated) 686 F. Supp. 595, 1988. Adjunct Professor South Texas College of Law since 1973 and University of Texas School of Law 1990-91 and 2000-01. Master Bencher American Inn of Court XV (President 1986-92). Consultant Texas Judicial Budget Board 1984. Member Texas Supreme Court Task Force on Revision of the Rules of Civil Procedure 1991-95. Member Supreme Court Historical Society, American Society for Legal History, The Maritime Law Association of the U.S., The American Law Institute, American Judicature Society, State Bar of Texas (Nominations Committee Judicial Section since 1966, Committee on the Texas Constitution 1981-85, Member 1981-85 and Vice Chairman 1982-83 Committee on Selection, Compensation and Tenure of State Judges, Member 1981-91 and Vice Chairman 1984-86 Committee on Court Cost, Delay and Efficiency, Member Committee for Liaison with Law Schools 1987-92, Plain Language Committee 1989-96), Houston, Federal (Director Houston Chapter 1985-89) and American Bar Associations. Lecturer Texas Judicial College 1983. Texas Delegate to National Conference of State Trial Judges 1983-85. Trustee Rift Valley Research Mission since 1978. Member Judicial Advisory Board Law and Economics Center George Mason University School of Law since 1999. Member American Anthropological Association, Houston Philosophical Society, Houston World Affairs Council (Director since 1997, Co-chairman 1999-2000), American Field Service, Council on Foreign Relations and St. Martin's Episcopal Church. Sailor.

Office: 11122 U.S. Court House, 515 Rusk Avenue, Houston 77002-2605.
Telephone: (713) 250-5900.

HULL, John A. *(Judge, Coryell County Court)*
Office: 620 East Main, Gatesville 76528-1334.
Telephone: (254) 865-5911.

HUNTER, Jack E. *(Judge, Texas District Court 94th Judicial District)* Term expires Dec 31, 2006.
Office: 901 Leopard, Suite 901, Corpus Christi 78401.
Telephone: (361) 888-0320.

HYATT, Darrell *(Judge, Rusk County Court at Law)*
Office: 115 North Main, Suite 201, Henderson 75652.
Telephone: (903) 657-0344.

HYDE, John Gary *(Judge, Texas District Court 238th Judicial District)*
Office: 200 West Wall, Suite 400, Midland 79701-4557.
Telephone: (915) 688-1142.

ISAACKS, Vicki B. *(Judge, Texas District Court 393rd Judicial District)*
Office: 1450 East McKinney Street, Second Floor, Denton 76209-4524.
Telephone: (940) 349-2360.

JACK, Janis Graham *(Judge, United States District Court Southern District of Texas)* Appointed for life by President Bill Clinton to term beginning March 14, 1994. Born Los Angeles California May 28, 1946. Educated at University of Baltimore B.A. in Sociology 1974 and South Texas College of Law J.D. summa cum laude 1981. Member Phi Alpha Delta and Order of Lytae. Admitted to practice Texas 1981 and U.S. District Court Southern District of Texas. In legal practice Corpus Christi 1981-94.

Certified Mediator Texas 1992. Former Member Committee for the Establishment of Rape Examination Nurse Program for the City of Corpus Christi Nueces County Medical Society and CLE Committee and Medical-Legal Committee Corpus Christi Bar Association. Fellow Texas Bar Foundation. Judicial Member The Maritime Law Association of the U.S. Member National Association of Women Judges, Fifth Circuit District Judges Association, Federal Judges Association, State Bar of Texas (Former Council Member Women and the Law Section) and American Bar Association. Director Family Law Seminar Corpus Christi Bar Association 1990. Listed in *Dictionary of International Biography* 24th ed. and *Who's Who in American Law* 9th ed. Licensed as Registered Nurse Texas. Former Board Member and Officer League of Women Voters of Corpus Christi and Corpus Christi Area Women's Political Caucus. Former Delegate Coastal Bend Council of Governments. Former Coordinator Nueces County Texans for ERA. Vice Chair for Membership 1977 and Vice Chair for Legislation 1978 Texas Women's Political Caucus. Member Membership Committee National Women's Political Caucus 1977-78. Board of Equalization City of Corpus Christi 1978. Former Member Board of Directors South Texas College of Law. Former Board Member Y.W.C.A. of Corpus Christi, Planning Council United Way of Coastal Bend, Teen Court of Nueces County and Nueces County Juvenile Citizen Advisory Board. Former Board Member, Officer and Legal Counsel Planned Parenthood of South Texas. Former Local Co-chair United Negro College Fund Telethon. Former Honorary Trustee Coastal Bend Council for the Deaf. Former Committee Member Humana Hospital Institutional Review Board. Former Member Leadership Corpus Christi and Superintendent's

JACK, JANIS GRAHAM—*Continued*

Advisory Committee on School Integration Corpus Christi Independent School District. Member The Philosophical Society of Texas.

Office: 1133 North Shoreline Boulevard, Corpus Christi 78401.

Telephone: (361) 888-3525.

Fax: (361) 888-3530

JACKSON, Donald Wayne *(Judge, Harris County Criminal Court at Law No. 3)*

Office: 1201 Franklin, Seventh Floor, Houston 77002.

Telephone: (713) 755-6188.

JACKSON, John H. *(Judge, Texas District Court 13th Judicial District)* Elected Nov 6, 1996 to term beginning Jan 1, 1997. Reelected 2000, current term expires Dec 31, 2004. Born Navarro County Texas Oct 27, 1950. Presbyterian. Educated at Texas A&M University B.A. 1973 and South Texas College of Law J.D. 1976. Admitted to practice Texas 1977, U.S. District Court Northern District of Texas 1977, U.S. Court of Appeals Fifth Circuit 1977 and U.S. Court of Claims 1977. Board Certified—Criminal Law—Texas Board of Legal Specialization.

First Assistant Criminal District Attorney 1978-96. President Navarro County Bar Association 1982-84. Member State Bar of Texas. Democrat. Enjoys outdoor sports.

Mailing address: P.O. Box 333, Corsicana 75151-0333.

Telephone: (903) 654-3020.

JACKSON, June *(Judge, Waller County Court at Law)*

Office: 836 Austin Street, Room 216, Hempstead 77445.

Telephone: (979) 826-7762.

JAMES, Tom *(Justice, Texas Court of Appeals Fifth District)* Term expires Dec 31, 2006.

Office: George Allen Sr. Courts Building, 600 Commerce Street, Dallas 75202-4658.

Telephone: (214) 712-3409.

JAMISON, Alfred G. *(Judge, Colorado County Court)*

Mailing address: P.O. Box 236, Columbus 78934.

Telephone: (979) 732-2604.

JAMISON, Martha Hill *(Judge, Texas District Court 164th Judicial District)* Appointed by Governor George W. Bush to term beginning Dec 24, 1999. Elected 2000, current term expires Dec 31, 2004. Born Houston Texas 1952. United Methodist. Educated at University of Texas B.J. 1973 J.D. 1977. Admitted to practice Texas 1978 and U.S. District Courts Eastern and Southern Districts of Texas.

Fellow Houston Bar Foundation and Texas Bar Foundation. Member Houston and American Bar Associations. Republican.

Office: 1019 Congress Street, Sixteenth Floor, Houston 77002.

Telephone: (713) 755-6316.

JANECKA, Edward F. *(Judge, Fayette County Court)*

Office: 151 North Washington, Suite 304, La Grange 78945.

Telephone: (979) 968-6469.

JARRETT, Edward L. *(Judge, Caldwell County Court at Law No. 1)* Currently serves as Administrative Judge.

Office: 102 Courthouse, 110 South Main Street, Lockhart 78644.

Telephone: (512) 398-6527.

JEFFERSON, Wallace B. *(Justice, Texas Supreme Court)* Appointed by Governor Rick Perry to term beginning March 14, 2001. Elected Nov 2002, current term expires Dec 2006. Educated at Michigan State University and University of Texas School of Law. Board Certified—Civil Appellate Law—Texas Board of Legal Specialization. In legal practice San Antonio 1988-91.

Mailing address: P.O. Box 12248, Austin 78711-2248.

Telephone: (512) 463-7899.

JENKINS, Scott H. *(Judge, Texas District Court 53rd Judicial District)*

Mailing address: P.O. Box 1748, Austin 78767-1748.

Telephone: (512) 854-9308.

JENNINGS, J. C. *(Judge, Morris County Court)*

Office: 500 Broadnax Street, Daingerfield 75638-1337.

Telephone: (903) 645-3691.

JENNINGS, Terry *(Justice, Texas Court of Appeals First District)* Elected to term beginning Jan 1, 2001. Term expires Dec 31, 2006. Educated at University of Texas at Austin B.A. and University of Houston Law Center J.D. Associate Editor Houston Law Review. Member Pi Sigma Alpha.

With Trial Bureau 1990-94 and Special Crimes Bureau Harris County District Attorney's Office. Member Texas District and County Attorneys Association. Lector Holy Rosary Church. Member Council 11023 Knights of Columbus, Friends of the Houston Public Library and Friends of the Library-Kingwood.

Office: 1307 San Jacinto, Tenth Floor, Houston 77002-7006.

Telephone: (713) 655-2716.

JERGINS, Michael P. *(Judge, Texas District Court 395th Judicial District)*

Office: 405 South Martin Luther King Blvd., Box 15, Georgetown 78626-0405.

Telephone: (512) 943-1395.

JOHNSON, Cheryl *(Judge, Texas Court of Criminal Appeals)* Elected Nov 1998 to term beginning Jan 1, 1999. Term expires Dec 31, 2003. Born Aurora Illinois Sept 30, 1946. Methodist. Educated at The Ohio State University B.S. 1968, University of Illinois M.S. 1970 and John Marshall Law School J.D. with high honors 1983. Staff member 1981-83 and Executive Editor Aug 1982 to June 1983 Student Publications. Law Clerk to Hon. Sam D. Johnson, U.S. Court of Appeals Fifth Circuit 1983-84. Admitted to practice Illinois 1984, Texas 1984, U.S. Court of Appeals Seventh Circuit 1986 and U.S. District Court Western District of Texas 1991. In legal practice Austin Texas 1984-98. Republican.

Mailing address: P.O. Box 12308, Austin 78711-2308.

Telephone: (512) 463-1560.

E-mail address: cheryl.johnson@cca.courts.state.tx.us

JOHNSON, Edward S. *(Judge, Bell County Court at Law No. 1)* Elected to term beginning Jan 5, 1987. Reelected 1990, 1994, 1998 and 2002. Current term expires Dec 31, 2006. Born Temple Texas May 29, 1944. Episcopalian. Educated at Texas Arts & Industries Uni-

JOHNSON, EDWARD S.—*Continued*
versity B.B.A. 1966 and Baylor University Law School J.D. 1969. Member Phi Alpha Delta. Admitted to practice Texas 1969, U.S. District Court Western District of Texas 1977, U.S. Supreme Court 1977 and U.S. Court of Appeals Fifth Circuit 1978. In legal practice Texas 1969-79.

City Attorney Rogers 1973-79. Assistant District Attorney 1979-86. Former member Texas Association of Bank Counsel, Central Texas Criminal Defense Lawyers Association, Texas Criminal Defense Lawyers Association, Texas District and County Attorneys Association, Central Texas Peace Officers Association and American Bar Association. Member State Bar of Texas and Bell-Lampasas-Mills Counties Bar Association. Attended Career Prosecutors Course National College of District Attorneys 1983, Texas College for New Judges 1986 and Texas Center for the Judiciary Inc.

Mailing address: P.O. Box 781, Belton 76513.
Telephone: (254) 933-5127.

JOHNSON, Faith *(Judge, Texas District Court 363rd Judicial District)*

Office: LB 36 Frank Crowley Courts Building, 133 North Industrial Boulevard, Dallas 75207-4313.
Telephone: (214) 653-5890.

JOHNSON, Joel B. *(Judge, Texas District Court 156th Judicial District)* Elected Nov 1994 to term beginning Jan 1, 1995. Reelected 1998 and 2002. Current term expires Dec 31, 2006. Born Rockport Texas Dec 10, 1953. Educated at Baylor University B.B.A. 1976 J.D. 1978. Admitted to practice Texas 1978 and U.S. District Court Southern District of Texas 1982. Board Certified—Criminal Law—Texas Board of Legal Specialization. In legal practice Sinton 1982-94.

Assistant County Attorney 1978-79. Assistant District Attorney 1979-82. Fellow Texas Bar Foundation. Member College of the State Bar of Texas, State Bar of Texas, Nueces County and San Patricio County Bar Associations.

Mailing address: P.O. Box 700, Sinton 78387.
Telephone: (361) 364-6200.
Fax: (361) 364-6155

JOHNSON, Karen *(Judge, Texas District Court 95th Judicial District)*

Office: George Allen Sr. Courts Building, Third Floor, 600 Commerce Street, Dallas 75202-4606.
Telephone: (214) 653-6361.

JOHNSON, Nancy K. *(Magistrate Judge, United States District Court Southern District of Texas)* Appointed by U.S. District Court judges.

Office: 7019 U.S. Courthouse, 515 Rusk Avenue, Houston 77002.
Telephone: (713) 250-5375.

JOHNSON, Phil *(Chief Justice, Texas Court of Appeals Seventh District)* Former Justice. Educated at Texas Tech University B.A. 1965 J.D. with honors 1975. Associate Editor Texas Tech Law Review 1974-75. Member Phi Delta Phi. Admitted to practice Texas 1975, U.S. District Courts Northern and Western Districts of Texas, U.S. Court of Appeals Fifth Circuit and U.S. Supreme Court. In legal practice Lubbock 1975-98.

Captain USAF 1965-72. Republican.

Mailing address: P.O. Box 9540, Amarillo 79105-9540.
Telephone: (806) 342-2650.

JOHNSON, Richard *(Judge, Texas Family District Court 303rd Judicial District)* Elected to term beginning Jan 1, 1995. Reelected 1998 and 2002. Current term expires Dec 31, 2006. Born Los Angeles California. Educated at University of Texas B.B.A. 1966 J.D. 1967. Admitted to practice Texas 1967, U.S. Supreme Court 1980, U.S. District Court Northern District of Texas and U.S. Court of Appeals Fifth Circuit. Board Certified—Family Law—Texas Board of Legal Specialization. In legal practice Dallas Sept 1967 to Oct 31, 1992. Judge, County Court at Law Nov 1, 1992 to Dec 31, 1994.

Member Texas Association of Family Law Specialists and American Academy of Matrimonial Lawyers.

Office: 600 Commerce Street, #560, Dallas 75202.
Telephone: (214) 653-7611.
Fax: (214) 653-6699
E-mail address: RJohnson@dallascounty.org

JOHNSON, Timothy F. *(Judge, Bexar County Court at Law No. 5)* Elected Nov 4, 1986 to term beginning Jan 1, 1987. Reelected Nov 6, 1990, 1994, Nov 1998 and 2002. Current term expires Dec 31, 2006. Born Ottawa Illinois June 23, 1950. Catholic. Educated at Illinois State University B.S. 1972 and St. Mary's University J.D. 1978. Member Phi Delta Phi. Admitted to practice Texas 1978. In legal practice San Antonio.

Assistant District Attorney Bexar County 1978-80. Vice President and General Counsel Newell Recycling Company 1980-86. Instructor Southwest Texas State University 1979 and San Antonio College since 1989. Member State Bar of Texas, San Antonio and American Bar Associations. Board of Managers YMCA. Advisory Director San Antonio Safety Council. AACOG Criminal Justice Commission.

Office: 2162 Bexar County Justice Center, 300 Dolorosa Street, San Antonio 78205-3019.
Telephone: (210) 335-2567.

JONES, Aubrey L., Jr. *(Judge, Henderson County Court)*

Office: 206-A North Murchison, Athens 75751.
Telephone: (903) 675-6120.

JONES, Brock *(Judge, Texas District Court 112th Judicial District)* Appointed by Governor Mark White to term beginning April 16, 1984. Elected Nov 6, 1984, Nov 6, 1986, Nov 6, 1990, Nov 6, 1994, Nov 1998 and 2002. Current term expires Dec 31, 2006. Born Houston Texas Dec 22, 1937. Christian. Educated at University of Texas at Austin B.A. 1960 LL.B. 1967. Member Pi Alpha Delta. Admitted to practice Texas 1967. Judge, Travis County Court at Law No. 1, 1974-82.

Assistant Attorney General Texas 1967-68. Member State Bar of Texas. Democrat.

Mailing address: P.O. Drawer C, Ozona 76943.
Telephone: (325) 392-5225.

JONES, Dianne *(Judge, Dallas County Court at Law No. 11)*

Office: Frank Crowley Courts Bldg., 133 North Industrial Boulevard, Dallas 75207.
Telephone: (214) 712-5068.

JONES, Donald Richard *(Judge, Texas District Court 266th Judicial District)* Term expires Dec 31, 2006.

Mailing address: P.O. Box 1427, Stephenville 76401.
Telephone: (254) 965-1485.

JONES, Guilford L. "Gil", III *(Judge, Texas District Court 33rd Judicial District)*

Office: 220 South Pierce Street, Burnet 78611-3136.
Telephone: (512) 756-5436.

JONES, John R. *(Judge, Crockett County Court)*
Mailing address: P.O. Box 1857, Ozona 76943-1857.
Telephone: (325) 392-2965.

JONES, Linda Z. *(Judge, Guadalupe County Court at Law)*

Office: 101 East Court Street, Seguin 78155-5742.
Telephone: (830) 303-4188.

JONES, Molly S. *(Judge, Tarrant County Criminal Court at Law No. 6)*

Office: Tarrant County Justice Center, Eighth Floor, 401 West Belknap, Fort Worth 76196-0275.
Telephone: (817) 884-2745.

JONES, Robert L. *(Judge, United States Bankruptcy Court Northern District of Texas)* Appointed by U.S. Court of Appeals Fifth Circuit judges to term beginning April 4, 2000. Term expires April 4, 2014.

Office: 312 U.S. Courthouse, 1205 Texas Avenue, Lubbock 79401-4002.
Telephone: (806) 472-5020.

JUSTICE, William Wayne *(Senior Judge, United States District Court Eastern District of Texas)* Appointed for life by President Lyndon B. Johnson to term beginning June 29, 1968. Chief Judge April 16, 1980 to Feb 23, 1990. Assumed Senior status, serves Western District of Texas by assignment. Born Athens Texas Feb 25, 1920. Educated at University of Texas LL.B. 1942. Member Order of the Coif. Admitted to practice Texas 1942. In legal practice Athens 1946-61. Sat by designation with U.S. Court of Appeals District of Columbia Circuit 1975 and 1976.

Part-time City Attorney Athens 1948-50 and 1952-58. U.S. Attorney Eastern District of Texas 1961-68. Former member Joint Committee on the Code of Judicial Conduct and Judicial Ethics Committee Judicial Conference of the U.S. Recipient Outstanding Federal Trial Judge Award from The Association of Trial Lawyers of America 1982. First Lieutenant Field Artillery U.S. Army 1942-46. Democrat. State Vice President Young Democrats of Texas 1947 and member Advisory Council Democratic National Committee 1954. Alternate delegate Democratic National Convention 1956. Presidential Elector 1960. Commander Taylor Commandery 1954. Member VFW (Commander Athens Post 7013, 1952-53), Athens Rotary Club (President 1960) and Masons (Master Athens Lodge 1959).

Office: 310 Judicial Building, 903 San Jacinto Boulevard, Austin 78701.
Telephone: (512) 916-5283.

KAPLAN, Jeff *(Magistrate Judge, United States District Court Northern District of Texas)* Appointed by U.S. District Court judges to term beginning June 1, 1994. Reappointed 1994, current term expires June 1, 2010. Born Morristown New Jersey June 28, 1956. Educated at Vanderbilt University B.A. cum laude 1978 and Southern Methodist University School of Law J.D. 1981. Law Clerk to Hon. James K. Allen, Texas Court of Appeals Fifth District 1981-82. Admitted to practice Texas 1981, U.S. District Courts Northern 1982 and Southern 1991 Districts of Texas and U.S. Court of Appeals Fifth Circuit 1982. Board Certified—Civil Trial Law and Civil Appellate Law—Texas Board of Legal Specialization. In legal practice Dallas 1982-91 and 1992-94. Justice, Texas Court of Appeals Fifth District 1991-92.

Instructor in Legal Research and Writing Southern Methodist University School of Law 1983-87. Certified Civil Trial Specialist National Board of Trial Advocacy. Member State Bar of Texas, Dallas and Federal Bar Associations.

Office: 16F41 U.S. Courthouse, 1100 Commerce Street, Dallas 75242-1003.
Telephone: (214) 753-2400.

KARAHAN, Jay *(Judge, Harris County Criminal Court at Law No. 8)*

Office: 1201 Franklin, Room 9136, Houston 77002.
Telephone: (713) 755-6208.

KAZEN, George P. *(Chief Judge, United States District Court Southern District of Texas)* Appointed for life by President Jimmy Carter to term beginning May 11, 1979. Born Laredo Texas Feb 29, 1940. Roman Catholic. Educated at University of Texas B.B.A. 1960 J.D. with honors 1961. Cadet Commander USAF ROTC and Regional Commander Arnold Air Society. Recipient Delta Sigma Pi Award as outstanding B.B.A. graduate 1960. Teaching Quizmaster University of Texas School of Law. Case Note Editor Texas Law Review 1960-61. Briefing Attorney to Texas Supreme Court 1961-62. Member Order of the Coif, Chancellors, Phi Delta Phi, Beta Gamma Sigma and Friars Club. Admitted to practice Texas 1961, U.S. District Court Southern District of Texas, U.S. Court of Appeals Fifth Circuit, U.S. Court of Claims and U.S. Supreme Court. In legal practice Laredo 1965-79.

Official Representative of Fifth Circuit to testify before U.S. Sentencing Commission regarding proposed sentencing guidelines in federal criminal cases Dec 3, 1986. Author Case Notes 38 Texas L. Rev. 120, 39 Texas L. Rev. 237 and 39 Texas L. Rev. 243 and Comment 40 Texas L. Rev. 137, reprinted 12 No. 5 Monthly Digest of Tax Articles 51. Contributing Editor *Texas Estate Administration* State Bar of Texas 1975. Co-author *Federal Civil Procedure Before Trial—5th Circuit* Lawyers Co-op Publishing Co. 1996. Instructor Adjunct Professor of Law St. Mary's University of San Antonio School of Law since 1990. Member 1990-99 and Chair 1996-99 Judicial Conference Committee on Criminal Law. Fellow Texas Bar Foundation. Charter member Texas Criminal Defense Lawyers Association and Texas Association of Bank Counsel. Member Laredo Legal Aid Society (Founder and First President 1966-69), Fifth Circuit District Judges Criminal Pattern Jury Charges Committee, Texas Association of Defense Counsel, Fifth Circuit District Judges Association (Secretary-Treasurer 1983-84, Vice President 1984-85, President Elect 1985-86, President 1986-88), Judicial Council of the Fifth Circuit, State Bar of Texas (Chairman Grievance Committee District 12-A, Vice Chairman Admissions Committee District 12), Laredo (President 1976-77) and American Bar Associations. Lecturer State Bar seminars on real estate and federal evidence. Panelist "The Future and the Courts Conference" State Justice Institute American Ju-

KAZEN, GEORGE P.—*Continued*

dicature Society May 1990, "The Future of Litigation in the Federal Courts" American Bar Association Section of Litigation June 1990 and "Techniques for Processing Criminal Cases" Workshop for Judges of the Seventh Circuit Oct 1990. Named Outstanding Young Lawyer by Laredo Jaycees 1970. Recipient Volunteer of the Year Award Diocese of Corpus Christi Department of Catholic Schools. Captain (legal officer) USAF 1962-65. Recipient Air Force Commendation Medal 1965. Director, Vice President and President Economic Opportunities Development Corporation 1968-70. Board of Trustees Laredo Junior College 1972-79. Director Laredo Chamber of Commerce 1975-76 and University of Texas School of Law Alumni Association 1976-77. Former Director City National Bank of Laredo and D. D. Hachar Foundation. Former President Laredo Civic Music Association. Lifetime Chairman, Board member and President St. Augustine-Ursuline Consolidated (School Board 1976-89). Lifetime Director Boys' Club of Laredo (President 1980). Member Blessed Sacrament Parish.

Mailing address: P.O. Box 1060, Laredo 78042-1060.
Telephone: (956) 726-2237.

KAZEN, Philip A., Jr. *(Judge, Texas District Court 227th Judicial District)*

Office: 2123 Bexar County Justice Center, 300 Dolorosa Street, San Antonio 78205-3028.
Telephone: (210) 335-2304.

KEASLER, Michael E. *(Judge, Texas Court of Criminal Appeals)* Elected 1998 to term beginning Jan 1, 1999. Term expires Dec 31, 2004. Born Dallas Texas Aug 16, 1942. Episcopalian. Educated at University of Texas at Austin B.A. 1964 LL.B. 1967. Admitted to practice Texas 1967, U.S. District Court Northern District of Texas 1968, U.S. Court of Appeals Fifth Circuit 1969 and U.S. Supreme Court 1975. In legal practice Dallas 1967-69. Judge, Texas District Court 292nd Judicial District 1981-98. Presiding Local Administrative Judge Dallas County 1988.

Assistant District Attorney Dallas County 1969-81. Author "Ethical Standards for Judges" *The National Judicial College Alumni Magazine* Winter 1995 and "The Ethics of Electing Judges" *The Long Term View* Massachusetts School of Law Summer 1997. Fellow Texas Bar Foundation. Member The American Law Institute, American Judicature Society, State Bar of Texas (Chair Judicial Section 1996-97) and American Bar Association (Chair Ethics Committee 1997-98 and Member National Conference of State Trial Judges 1981-98 and Appellate Judges Conference since 1999 Judicial Administration Division). Dean Regional Judicial Conferences Texas 1990-97 and Texas College of Advanced Judicial Studies 1993-97. Faculty The National Judicial College since 1992. Instructor in Legal Ethics programs for state judges Texas, Alabama, Arizona, Arkansas, Florida, Louisiana, Nevada, New Hampshire, New York, North Dakota, Ohio, Oregon, South Dakota and Tennessee. Presenter Judicial Ethics program U.S. Immigration Judges. Republican. Board of Directors Dallas Republican Men's Club 1982. President Republicans of Grand Prairie Texas 1988-89. Chair Dallas County Juvenile Board 1985-86. Member Rotary and Scottish Rite. Enjoys reading, teaching and running.

Mailing address: P.O. Box 12308, Austin 78711-2308.
Office: Supreme Court Building, Austin 78701.
Telephone: (512) 463-1555.
E-mail address: michael.keasler@cca.courts.state.tx.us

KEEL, Mary Lou *(Judge, Texas District Court 232nd Judicial District)* Elected Nov 1994 to term beginning Jan 1, 1995. Reelected 1998 and 2002. Current term expires Dec 31, 2006. Born Austin Texas Jan 5, 1961. Educated at University of Texas B.A. 1982 and University of Houston J.D. 1985. Law Clerk to Hon. Murry B. Cohen, Texas Court of Appeals First District 1985-86. Admitted to practice Texas 1985. Board Certified—Criminal Law—Texas Board of Legal Specialization 1990.

Assistant District Attorney Harris County 1986-94. Republican.

Office: 1201 Franklin, Room 16136, Houston 77002.
Telephone: (713) 755-6778.

KEEL, Patrick O. *(Judge, Texas District Court 345th Judicial District)*

Mailing address: P.O. Box 1748, Austin 78767-1748.
Telephone: (512) 854-9374.

KEELING, Kenneth H. *(Judge, Texas District Court 278th Judicial District)*

Office: 1100 University Avenue, Suite 303, Huntsville 77340-4642.
Telephone: (936) 436-4916.

KEETER, Harold *(Judge, Swisher County Court)*

Office: 119 South Maxwell, Tulia 79088.
Telephone: (806) 995-3504.
Fax: (806) 995-2214
E-mail address: harold.keeter@swisher-tx.net

KEIS, R. Brent *(Judge, Tarrant County Court at Law No. 1)* Appointed to term beginning March 3, 1989. Elected Nov 1990, 1994, 1998 and 2002. Current term expires Dec 31, 2006. Administrative Judge Tarrant County Courts 1993-96. Born Weatherford Texas June 3, 1952. Episcopalian. Educated at University of Texas at Austin B.A. with honors 1973 J.D. with honors 1976. Member Phi Delta Phi and Phi Beta Kappa. Admitted to practice Texas 1976, U.S. Court of Military Appeals 1977 and U.S. District Court Northern District of Texas 1980. In legal practice Fort Worth 1979-89.

Author "The Discovery Process: Have We Misdiagnosed the Disease?" 56 Texas B. Jour. 16, 1993. Contributor *Benchbook for Texas Judiciary* 1993-95. Managing Editor *Tarrant County Bench Book* 1995. Fellow Texas Bar Foundation. Member Judicial PEER Committee Texas Center for the Judiciary 1991-96. Member Fort Worth-Tarrant County Young Lawyers Association (Director 1981-82), State Bar of Texas and Tarrant County Bar Association. Faculty Member Texas College for New Judges 1993. Lieutenant USNR JAGC 1976-79. Republican.

Office: 100 West Weatherford, Room 440A, Fort Worth 76196-0240.
Telephone: (817) 884-1457.

KELIHER, Margaret *(Judge, Dallas County Court)* Former Judge, Texas District Court 44th Judicial District.

Office: Administration Building, 411 Elm Street, Dallas 75202-3513.
Telephone: (214) 653-7555.

KELLER, Sharon *(Presiding Judge, Texas Court of Criminal Appeals)* Elected Nov 1994 to term beginning Jan 1, 1995. Reelected Nov 2000, current term expires Dec 31, 2006. Presiding Judge since 2000. Born Dallas Texas. Catholic. Educated at Rice University B.A. 1975 and Southern Methodist University School of Law J.D. 1978. Admitted to practice Texas 1978.

Assistant District Attorney 1987-94. Republican.

Mailing address: P.O. Box 12308, Austin 78711.

Telephone: (512) 463-1551.

KELLY, Joseph Patrick *(Judge, Texas District Court 24th Judicial District)* Appointed by Governor Ann W. Richards to term beginning Aug 9, 1993. Elected Nov 1994, Nov 1996 and Nov 2000. Current term expires Dec 31, 2004. Born Pecos Texas March 5, 1940. Catholic. Educated at University of Notre Dame B.B.A. 1961 and University of Texas School of Law J.D. 1963. Member Phi Alpha Delta. Admitted to practice Texas 1963, U.S. Supreme Court 1966, U.S. Court of Appeals for the Armed Forces, U.S. Tax Court, U.S. Court of Federal Claims. In legal practice Victoria 1963-64 and 1967-93.

Author *Of Client Confidences* 1985. Life Fellow Texas Bar Foundation. Member Texas Center for the Judiciary, Inc. and State Bar of Texas (Judicial Section). Attended Texas New Judges School 1993 and General Jurisdiction course The National Judicial College 1994. USMCR 1963-73 (active duty 1964-67). Trial Counsel Second Marine Air Wing and Counsel to Commandant USMC 1965-67. Special Counsel to Secretary of the Navy 1965-67. Democrat. County Chairman Democratic Party 1983-85. Board of Directors 1970-79 and 1985-93 and Chairman 1983 and 1993 Guadalupe-Blanco River Authority. Former Jaycee. Member Victoria Rotary Club, Marine Corps League and Marine Corps Association. Enjoys reading, hunting, fishing, golf and spectator sports.

Mailing address: P.O. Box 1457, Victoria 77902-1457.

Telephone: (361) 575-3172.

KELLY, Larry E. *(Chief Judge, United States Bankruptcy Court Western District of Texas)* Chief Judge since March 1, 2002.

Office: 332 Judicial Building, 903 San Jacinto Boulevard, Austin 78701-2450.

Telephone: (512) 916-5875.

KELSEY, Carmen *(Judge, Texas District Court 289th Judicial District)*

Office: 600 Mission Road, San Antonio 78210-3851.

Telephone: (210) 531-1180.

KELTON, David D. *(Judge, Texas District Court 44th Judicial District)*

Office: 600 Commerce Street, Dallas 75202-4606.

Telephone: (214) 653-6996.

KENDALL, Alger H., Jr. *(Judge, Karnes County Court)*

Office: 101 North Panna Maria Street, Karnes City 78118-2998.

Telephone: (830) 780-3732.

KENNEDY, Brenda P. *(Judge, Texas District Court 403rd Judicial District)* Former Judge, Travis County Court at Law No. 7.

Mailing address: P.O. Box 1748, Austin 78767-1748.

Telephone: (512) 854-9679.

KENNEDY, Sue K. *(Judge, Nacogdoches County Court)*

Office: 101 West Main, Suite 130, Nacogdoches 75961.

Telephone: (936) 560-7755.

KENT, Cynthia Stevens *(Judge, Texas District Court 114th Judicial District)* Term expires Dec 31, 2004. Former Judge, Smith County Court at Law No. 2, assumed office 1985.

Office: 100 North Broadway, Second Floor, Tyler 75702-7236.

Telephone: (903) 535-0613.

KENT, Samuel B. *(Judge, United States District Court Southern District of Texas)* Appointed for life by President George Bush to term beginning Oct 1, 1990. Born Denver Colorado June 22, 1949. Educated at University of Texas B.A. 1971 J.D. 1975. In legal practice Galveston 1975-90.

Office: 613 U.S. Courthouse, 601 25th Street, Galveston 77550-1738.

Telephone: (409) 766-3551.

KERN, Robert J. *(Judge, Texas District Court 387th Judicial District)*

Office: 301 Jackson, Suite 211, Richmond 77469-3110.

Telephone: (281) 238-3290.

KEYES, Evelyn *(Justice, Texas Court of Appeals First District)*

Office: 1307 San Jacinto, Tenth Floor, Houston 77002-7006.

Telephone: (713) 655-2700.

KHOURY, Alvin G. *(Judge, Texas District Court 124th Judicial District)* Elected Nov 1980 to term beginning Jan 1, 1981. Reelected 1984, 1988, 1992, 1996 and 2000. Current term expires Dec 31, 2004. Born Longview Texas Oct 15, 1936. Catholic. Educated at Southern Methodist University B.A. 1957 LL.B. 1959. Member Delta Theta Phi. Admitted to practice Texas 1959. In legal practice Longview 1959-71.

Assistant District Attorney Gregg County Jan 1972 to Dec 1980. Member State Bar of Texas and Gregg County Bar Association. Attended The National Judicial College 1985 and 1986. Named Knight of the Year by Knights of Columbus. Republican. Member Gregg County Republican Men's Club. Past Grand Knight Council 2771 and Past Faithful Navigator 4° Knights of Columbus. Past President Longview Jaycees. Chairman Gregg County Fair, Lions Club, Kiwanis Club and Elks Lodge. Enjoys high school football and fishing.

Office: 101 East Methvin, Suite 447, Longview 75601-7213.

Telephone: (903) 236-0265.

KIDD, Mack *(Justice, Texas Court of Appeals Third District)* Elected Nov 1990 to term beginning Jan 1, 1991. Reelected 1994 and 2000. Current term expires Dec 31, 2006. Born Jan 18, 1941. Educated at University of Texas at Austin B.B.A. 1962 J.D. 1964. Admitted to practice Texas 1964. Board Certified—Personal Injury Trial Law—Texas Board of Legal Specialization. In legal practice Austin 1964-90.

Former Member Task Force on Judicial Ethics Texas Supreme Court. Life Fellow Texas Bar Foundation. Member Gender Fairness Task Force Texas Supreme Court, Systematic Issues Committee Texas Access to

KIDD, MACK—*Continued*

Justice Commission, Texas Trial Lawyers Association (Past President), The Association of Trial Lawyers of America (Past Governor Board of Governors), American Board of Trial Advocates (Former Director), College of the State Bar of Texas, State Bar of Texas (Committee of Women in the Profession, Committee on Professionalism, Chair Judicial Ethics Committee Judicial Section), Travis County, Federal and American Bar Associations. Frequent speaker and lecturer State Bar of Texas.

Mailing address: P.O. Box 12547, Capitol Station, Austin 78711-2547.

Office: Price Daniel Sr. Building, 209 West 14th Street, Austin 78701.

Telephone: (512) 463-1733.

Fax: (512) 477-3330

KING, Ronald B. *(Judge, United States Bankruptcy Court Western District of Texas)* Appointed by U.S. Court of Appeals Fifth Circuit judges to term beginning Oct 1, 1988. Reappointed 2002, current term expires Sept 30, 2016. Born San Antonio Texas Aug 16, 1953. Presbyterian. Educated at Southern Methodist University B.A. with high honors 1974 and University of Texas School of Law J.D. with high honors 1977. Law Clerk to Hon. James G. Denton, Texas Supreme Court 1977-78. Member Phi Beta Kappa, Phi Delta Phi and Order of the Coif. Admitted to practice Texas 1977, U.S. District Court Western District of Texas, U.S. Court of Appeals Fifth Circuit and U.S. Tax Court. In legal practice San Antonio 1978-88.

Member National Conference of Bankruptcy Judges, State Bar of Texas and San Antonio Bankruptcy Bar Association.

Mailing address: P.O. Box 1439, San Antonio 78295-1439.

Telephone: (210) 472-6609.

KING, Steve M. *(Judge, Tarrant County Probate Court No. 1)*

Office: 100 East Weatherford, Room 260A, Fort Worth 76196-0241.

Telephone: (817) 884-1200.

KINKAID, Robert W., Jr. *(Judge, Texas District Court 64th Judicial District)*

Office: 500 Broadway, Room 240, Plainview 79072-8050.

Telephone: (806) 291-5234.

KINKEADE, Ed *(Judge, United States District Court Northern District of Texas)* Appointed for life by President George W. Bush to term beginning Nov 18, 2002. Born 1951. Educated at Baylor University B.A. 1973 J.D. 1974 and University of Virginia LL.M. 1998. In legal practice 1974-80. Judge, Dallas County Criminal Court at Law No. 10, 1981. Judge, Texas District Court 194th Judicial District 1981-88. Justice, Texas Court of Appeals Fifth District 1988-2002.

Author *Kinkeade & McColloch's Texas Penal Code Annotated* and *A Practical Guide to Texas Evidence.* Adjunct Professor of Law Texas Wesleyan University.

Office: 1100 Commerce Street, Room 1625, Dallas 75242-1103.

Telephone: (214) 753-2720.

Fax: (214) 753-2727

KIRKHAM, I. Lloyd *(Judge, Liberty County Court)*

Office: 1923 Sam Houston, Room 201, Liberty 77575.

Telephone: (936) 336-4665.

KITHIL, David L. *(Judge, Burnet County Court)*

Office: 220 South Pierce Street, Burnet 78611-3136.

Telephone: (512) 756-5404.

KITTRELL, James Orvil *(Judge, Montague County Court)*

Mailing address: P.O. Box 475, Montague 76251-0475.

Telephone: (940) 894-2401.

KLAGER, James E. *(Judge, Nueces County Court at Law No. 4)* Appointed to term beginning May 31, 1985. Elected to subsequent terms. Current term expires Dec 31, 2006. Born Chanute Kansas June 17, 1930. Presbyterian. Educated at University of Texas B.A. 1956 and Baylor University LL.B. 1959. Admitted to practice Texas 1959, U.S. District Court Southern District of Texas and U.S. Tax Court. In legal practice Corpus Christi 1959-85. Associate Judge, Municipal Court 1957-85.

Director Texas Center for the Judiciary 1989-92 and Judicial Section 1999-2000 and Criminal Justice Section 1999-2000 State Bar of Texas. Member State Bar of Texas and Corpus Christi Bar Association. USN/USMC FMF 1950-54.

Office: 901 Leopard, Suite 704, Corpus Christi 78401.

Telephone: (361) 888-0237.

KLEIN, Felix *(Judge, Texas District Court 154th Judicial District)* Elected Nov 1994 to term beginning Jan 1, 1995. Reelected 1998 and 2002. Current term expires Dec 31, 2006.

Office: 100 Sixth Street, Room 211, Littlefield 79339-3366.

Telephone: (806) 385-4222.

E-mail address: FelixKlein@HOTMAIL.COM

KNIZE, Gene *(Judge, Texas District Court 40th Judicial District)* Term expires Dec 31, 2006.

Office: 305 East Franklin Street, Waxahachie 75165-3700.

Telephone: (972) 923-5060.

KOCUREK, Julie Harris *(Judge, Texas District Court 390th Judicial District)*

Mailing address: P.O. Box 1748, Austin 78767-1748.

Telephone: (512) 854-4885.

KOENIG, Nancy M. *(Magistrate Judge, United States District Court Northern District of Texas)* Appointed by U.S. District Court judges to term beginning December 28, 1998. Term expires Dec 2006. Born 1951. Educated at University of Texas at Austin B.A. 1972 M.A. 1975 and Texas Tech University J.D. 1982. Law Clerk to Chief Judge Halbert O. Woodward, U.S. District Court Northern District of Texas 1982-83 and 1984.

Assistant General Counsel State Bar of Texas 1983-84. Assistant U.S. Attorney Northern District of Texas 1984-98. Fellow Texas Bar Foundation. Member State Bar of Texas and American Bar Association.

Office: C-115 U.S. Courthouse, 1205 Texas Avenue, Lubbock 79401-4001.

Telephone: (806) 472-7380.

KOETTER, Juergen "Skipper" *(Judge, Texas District Court 267th Judicial District)*
Office: 115 North Bridge Street, Second Floor, Victoria 77901-6544.
Telephone: (361) 578-1998.

KROCKER, Jan *(Judge, Texas District Court 184th Judicial District)* Elected to term beginning Jan 1, 1995. Reelected 1998 and 2002. Current term expires Dec 31, 2006. Born Washington D.C. 1949. Presbyterian. Educated at University of Texas at Austin B.J. 1971 and University of Texas School of Law J.D. 1980. Admitted to practice Texas 1981. Board Certified—Criminal Law—Texas Board of Legal Specialization. In legal practice Houston 1990-94.
Assistant District Attorney Harris County 1981-90. Special Prosecutor Polk County 1990-91. Member Garland Walker Inns of Court, Harris County District Judges Association (Legislative Committee), College of the State Bar of Texas and State Bar of Texas (Grievance Committee, Judicial Task Force on Mental Health). Speaker on mentally ill defendants and the criminal courts Coordinated Houston Seminar on Mentally Ill Defendants Fall 2002. Republican. Member Republican National Convention 1992.
Office: 1201 Franklin, Seventeenth Floor, Houston 77002.
Telephone: (713) 755-6358.
Fax: (713) 755-8973

KURITA, M. Sue *(Judge, El Paso County Court at Law No. 6)*
Office: 500 East San Antonio, #1106, El Paso 79901.
Telephone: (915) 543-3868.

LADD, Larry B. "Rusty" *(Judge, Lubbock County Court at Law No. 1)*
Mailing address: P.O. Box 10536, Lubbock 79408-3536.
Telephone: (806) 775-1305.

LA GRONE, John *(Judge, Texas Family District Court 316th Judicial District)*
Mailing address: P.O. Box 1181, Stinnett 79083-1181.
Telephone: (806) 878-4019.

LAKE, Sim *(Judge, United States District Court Southern District of Texas)* Appointed for life by President Ronald Reagan to term beginning Sept 2, 1988. Educated at Texas A&M University B.A. with honors 1966 and University of Texas at Austin J.D. with high honors 1969. Associate Editor Texas Law Review 1968-69. Member Chancellors and Order of the Coif. Admitted to practice Texas 1969, U.S. District Court Southern District of Texas 1969, U.S. Court of Appeals Fifth Circuit 1969 and U.S. Supreme Court 1976. In legal practice Houston 1969-70 and 1972-88.
Member Houston Bar Foundation, Texas Bar Foundation, The American Law Institute, State Bar of Texas and Houston Bar Association. Captain U.S. Army 1970-71.
Office: 9535 U.S. Courthouse, 515 Rusk Avenue, Houston 77002.
Telephone: (713) 250-5177.

LANE, Philip R. *(Magistrate Judge, United States District Court Northern District of Texas)* Appointed by U.S. District Court judges to term beginning Feb 22, 1971. Reappointed to subsequent terms. Serves part time. Born San Angelo Texas Feb 12, 1939. Educated at U.S. Air Force Academy B.S. with honors 1961 and University of Texas J.D. with honors 1968. Admitted to practice Texas 1969. Began legal practice San Angelo 1969.
Member State Bar of Texas and Tom Green County Bar Association. Captain USAF 1961-65 and 1968-69.
Office: 1100 Commerce Street, Fifteenth Floor, Dallas 75242.
Telephone: (214) 753-2393.

LANEHART, Paula Davis *(Judge, Lubbock County Court at Law No. 3)* Elected Nov 1994. Reelected 1998 and 2002. Current term expires Dec 31, 2006. Born Dallas Texas July 3, 1950. Methodist. Educated at Texas Tech University B.B.A. 1973 J.D. 1977. Admitted to practice Texas 1977 and U.S. District Court Northern District of Texas 1980. In legal practice Lubbock 1977-87. Associate Judge, Lubbock County 1987-94.
Board of Directors Texas Center for Judiciary since 1996. Member State Bar of Texas (Member Child Abuse and Neglect Committee 1987-92, Member 1990-96 and Chair 1994-95 Local Bar Services Committee) and Lubbock County Bar Association (President 1989). Recipient Woman of Excellence Award in Government 1995. Republican. Board of Directors Lakeridge Country Club. Member Lubbock Lions Club (President 1995). Enjoys golf and watching Texas Tech University basketball.
Mailing address: P.O. Box 10536, Lubbock 79408-3536.
Telephone: (806) 775-1309.

LANG, Douglas S. *(Justice, Texas Court of Appeals Fifth District)*
Office: George Allen Sr. Courts Building, 600 Commerce Street, Dallas 75202-4658.
Telephone: (214) 712-3400.

LANGLEY, J. D. *(Judge, Texas District Court 85th Judicial District)* Elected to term beginning Jan 1, 1991. Reelected 1994, 1998 and 2002. Current term expires Dec 31, 2006. Born Greenville Texas Aug 13, 1952. Methodist. Educated at Texas A&M University B.S. 1974 and South Texas College of Law J.D. 1983. Member Order of the Lytae. Admitted to practice Texas 1983 and U.S. District Court Southern District of Texas 1983. In legal practice College Station 1983-84. Judge, Brazos County Court at Law No. 2, 1986-90.
Assistant District Attorney Brazos County 1984-85. Part-time Instructor in Texas State and Local Government Blinn College. Member State Bar of Texas (Treasurer 1987-88, Chairman Elect 1988-89, Chairman 1989-90 and Immediate Past Chairman 1990-91 Juvenile Law Section). Lecturer "Discovery in Juvenile Cases" Feb 1990 and "Nuts and Bolts of Juvenile Practice" Feb 1991 Juvenile Law Conference State Bar of Texas. Captain USMC 1974-79. Republican.
Office: 300 East 26th Street, Suite 224, Bryan 77803-5360.
Telephone: (979) 361-4270.
Fax: (979) 361-4276
E-mail address: jlangley@co.brazos.tx.us

LARSEN, Susan J. *(Justice, Texas Court of Appeals Eighth District)* Appointed by Governor Ann W. Richards April 1992. Elected to subsequent terms. Current term expires Dec 31, 2004. First woman to serve Texas Court of Appeals Eighth District. Born Bakersfield California June 10, 1955. Educated at California State Uni-

LARSEN, SUSAN J.—*Continued*

versity at Fullerton and College of William & Mary Marshall-Wythe School of Law J.D. 1981. Board Certified—Civil Appellate Law—Texas Board of Legal Specialization. Began legal practice Nacogdoches.

Staff Attorney El Paso Legal Assistant Society. Important Decisions: Gem Homes, Inc. v. Contreras 861 S.W.2d 449, Tex. App.—El Paso writ denied 1993; In re Betty Brock Bell 894 S.W.2d 119, Tex. Spec. Ct. R. 1995; Bejarano v. Hunter 899 S.W.2d 346, Tex. App.—El Paso orig. proceeding 1995; Ector County v. Hollmann 901 S.W.2d 687, Tex. App.—El Paso no writ 1995; Beneficial Personnel Services of Texas, Inc. v. Rey No. 08-95-00185-CV 1996 WL 354416, Tex. App.—El Paso n.w.h. June 27, 1996; and Beneficial Personnel Services of Texas, Inc. v. Porras No. 08-94-00169-CV 1996 WL 354542, Tex. App.—El Paso n.w.h. June 27, 1996. Past President El Paso Women's Bar Association. Chair Regional Gender Bias Committee Eighth Judicial Region. Member Gender Bias Task Force Committee. Private Pilot. Enjoys backpacking and snow skiing.

Office: 500 East San Antonio Avenue, Suite 1203, El Paso 79901-2421.

Telephone: (915) 546-2240.

LAW, W. Kenneth *(Chief Justice, Texas Court of Appeals Third District)* Elected 2002 to term beginning Jan 1, 2003. Educated at Baylor University School of Law 1973. In legal practice Bell County.

Mailing address: P.O. Box 12547, Austin 78711-2547.

Telephone: (512) 463-1733.

LAW, William H. *(Judge, San Jacinto County Court)*

Office: One State Highway 150, Room 5, Coldspring 77331.

Telephone: (936) 653-4331.

LAWLIS, Monte D. *(Judge, Texas District Court 1st Judicial District A)* Appointed by Governor Dolph Briscoe to term beginning Sept 1, 1977. Elected 1978, 1982, 1986, 1990, 1994, 1998 and 2002. Current term expires Dec 31, 2006. Born Huntsville Texas June 21, 1937. Baptist. Educated at Baylor University B.A. 1959 LL.B. 1960. Associate Editor Baylor Law Review 1959-60. Admitted to practice Texas 1960. Began legal practice Baytown 1964. In legal practice Jasper 1967-77.

City Attorney Kirbyville 1972-77. Assistant District Attorney 1st Judicial District 1976-77. Member State Bar of Texas and 1st Judicial District Bar Association. Attended Texas College for the Judiciary 1977 and annual judicial conferences 1977-90. Recipient United States of America Legion of Merit Award for service as a member of the USAFR Oct 1990. Captain USAF 1960-63 and Colonel USAFR (retired). Trustee Jasper Independent School District 1972-77. Former member Executive Board Baptist General Convention of Texas. Boy Scout Merit Badge Counselor. Enjoys woodworking, furniture refinishing and photography.

Mailing address: P.O. Box 1299, Jasper 75951-1299.

Telephone: (409) 384-5474.

LEAL, Janet L. *(Judge, Cameron County Court at Law No. 1)*

Office: 974 East Harrison, Brownsville 78520.

Telephone: (956) 544-0855.

LEAL, Manuel D. *(Judge, United States Bankruptcy Court Southern District of Texas)* Former Chief Judge.

Office: 6202 U.S. Courthouse, 515 Rusk Avenue, Houston 77002.

Telephone: (713) 250-5780.

LEATH, Jack *(Judge, Sabine County Court)* Appointed by Governor George W. Bush to term beginning Feb 1996. Elected to term beginning Jan 1999. Reelected 2002, current term expires Dec 31, 2006. Born Henderson Texas Aug 6, 1933. Methodist. Educated at Stephen F. Austin University B.S. 1957 M.Ed. 1960.

Mailing address: P.O. Box 716, Hemphill 75948.

Telephone: (409) 787-3543.

Fax: (409) 787-2044

LECK, Bonnie Sue *(Judge, Winkler County Court)*

Mailing address: P.O. Drawer Y, Kermit 79745.

Telephone: (432) 586-6658.

LECK, Ronald L. *(Judge, Lavaca County Court)*

Mailing address: P.O. Box 243, Hallettsville 77964-0243.

Telephone: (361) 798-2301.

LEE, Thomas F. *(Judge, Texas District Court 63rd Judicial District)*

Mailing address: P.O. Drawer 1089, Del Rio 78841-1089.

Telephone: (830) 774-7523.

LEGGAT, Bonnie *(Judge, Texas District Court 71st Judicial District)* Term expires Dec 31, 2004.

Office: 200 West Houston, Room 219, Marshall 75670.

Telephone: (903) 935-4896.

LEHRMANN, Debra H. *(Judge, Texas Family District Court 360th Judicial District)* Appointed by Governor George W. Bush to term beginning Sept 2000. Elected 2000, current term expires Dec 31, 2004. Born Corpus Christi Texas Nov 16, 1956. Educated at University of Texas B.A. magna cum laude 1979 J.D. 1982. Member Phi Beta Kappa. In legal practice 1986-87. IV-D Master, Tarrant County Family Law Courts July 1987 to Jan 1991.

Lead Attorney 1983-84 and Director of Enforcement 1984-85 Domestic Relations Office Tarrant County. Author "Evaluating the Probative Value of Child Custody Evaluations" Juvenile & Family Court Journal Spring 2002 and "Who Are We Protecting?" 2000 and "The Child's Voice—An Analysis of the Methodology Used to Involve Children in Custody Litigation" Nov 2002 Texas B. Jour. Instructor "Domestic Violence—The Tragic Facts" Texas Christian University March 2001 and "Attorneys as Ad Litems" Texas Wesleyan University School of Law 2002. Member Family Law Task Force Tarrant County 1987-88. Charter Member Tarrant County Bar Foundation. Fellow Texas Bar Foundation. Member Tarrant County Women Lawyers, Association of Family and Conciliatory Courts (President Elect), State Bar of Texas (Judicial Section), Tarrant County, Tarrant County Family and American (Committee to Develop Standards for Representatives of Children in Custody and Access Litigation Section of Family Law since 2000) Bar Associations. Lecturer "Ad Litems in Peril?" Advanced Family Law Course Aug 2000, "Judicial Intent and Ad Litem Appointments" Tarrant County Child Protective Services Sept 2000, "The 360th District Court—Access Facilitation" Tarrant County Family Law

LEHRMANN, DEBRA H.—*Continued*

Bar Association 2000, "Access Facilitation—A Tool for Families in Conflict" Arlington Bar Association Feb 2001, "Listening to Children" Conference Section of Family Law American Bar Association 2001, "Conciliatory Law" Tarrant County Bench Bar Conference 2002 and "Who Are We Listening to?" Advanced Family Law Seminar Aug 2002. Named Outstanding Young Lawyer of Tarrant County 1990. Recipient National Amazing Woman Award 2001. Republican. Board of Directors 1984-85 and Member Task Force 1984-85 Texas Association of Domestic Relations Offices. Board of Directors Tarrant County Parents United 1985-86. Judge Teen Court Tarrant County 1987-88. Advisory Board Dispute Resolution Services of Tarrant County since 2001. Member Network for Executive Women. Personal Statement or Quote: "A soft answer turneth away wrath, but grievous words stir up anger" (Proverbs 15:1).

Office: Civil Courts Building, Second Floor, 100 North Houston, Fort Worth 76196-0282.
Telephone: (817) 884-2708.
Fax: (817) 884-3360
E-mail address: dlehrmann@tarrantcounty.com

LEIFESTE, Rae *(Judge, Texas District Court 340th Judicial District)*
Office: 112 West Beauregard, San Angelo 76903-5850.
Telephone: (325) 659-6569.

LEONARD, Joe M. *(Judge, Texas District Court 196th Judicial District)* Former Judge, Hunt County Court at Law, assumed office 1985.
Mailing address: P.O. Box 1097, Greenville 75403-1097.
Telephone: (903) 408-4190.

LEWIS, Carl E. *(Judge, Nueces County Court at Law No. 5)*
Office: 2310 Gollihar Road, Corpus Christi 78415.
Telephone: (361) 561-6056.

LEWIS, Jerry *(Judge, Collin County Court at Law No. 2)*
Office: 1800 North Graves, Suite 140, McKinney 75069.
Telephone: (972) 548-3820.

LEWIS, Jim *(Judge, McLennan County Court)*
Mailing address: P.O. Box 1728, Waco 76703.
Telephone: (254) 757-5049.

LEWIS, Marilea Whatley *(Judge, Texas Family District Court 330th Judicial District)*
Office: 529 George Allen Sr. Courts Building, 600 Commerce, Dallas 75202-4606.
Telephone: (214) 653-7207.

LEWIS, Tryon D. *(Judge, Texas District Court 161st Judicial District)* Term expires Dec 31, 2004.
Office: 300 North Grant, Room 335, Odessa 79761-5158.
Telephone: (432) 498-4260.

LIGGETT, Kenneth E. *(Judge, Clay County Court)*
Office: 100 North Bridge, Henrietta 76365-2898.
Telephone: (940) 538-4651.

LILLEY, Virgil Edgar *(Judge, Lampasas County Court)*
Mailing address: P.O. Box 231, Lampasas 76550-0231.
Telephone: (512) 556-8271.

LIMAS, Abel C. *(Judge, Texas District Court 404th Judicial District)*
Office: 974 East Harrison, Brownsville 78520-7123.
Telephone: (956) 544-0837.

LINDSAY, Sam A. *(Judge, United States District Court Northern District of Texas)* Appointed for life by President Bill Clinton to term beginning Sept 1, 1998. Born 1951. Educated at St. Mary's University of San Antonio B.A. 1974 and University of Texas School of Law J.D. 1977.

With Dallas City Attorney's Office 1979-92. City Attorney Dallas 1992-98. Member Dallas Legal Association and State Bar of Texas.

Office: U.S. Courthouse, 1100 Commerce Street, Dallas 75242-1003.
Telephone: (214) 753-2365.

LINDSAY, Tony *(Judge, Texas District Court 280th Judicial District)*
Office: 600 Civil Courts Building, 301 Fannin Street, Houston 77002.
Telephone: (713) 755-5518.

LINDSEY, Robert E., III *(Judge, Mills County Court)*
Mailing address: P.O. Box 483, Goldthwaite 76844.
Telephone: (325) 648-2222.

LINK, Scott *(Judge, Texas District Court 80th Judicial District)*
Office: 1019 Congress Street, Sixteenth Floor, Houston 77002.
Telephone: (713) 755-6774.

LITTLEJOHN, Janet P. *(Judge, Texas District Court 150th Judicial District)*
Office: 401 Bexar County Courthouse, 100 Dolorosa Street, San Antonio 78205-3028.
Telephone: (210) 335-2533.

LIVINGSTON, D. Matt *(Judge, Henderson County Court at Law)*
Office: Henderson County Courthouse, Athens 75751.
Telephone: (903) 675-6162.

LIVINGSTON, Lora J. *(Judge, Texas District Court 261st Judicial District)*
Mailing address: P.O. Box 1748, Austin 78767-1748.
Telephone: (512) 854-9309.

LIVINGSTON, Terrie *(Justice, Texas Court of Appeals Second District)* Elected to term beginning Dec 16, 1994. Reelected to subsequent terms. Current term expires Dec 31, 2008. Born Atlanta Georgia March 9, 1955. Educated at Texas Tech University B.A. with distinction and honors 1977 and University of Texas School of Law J.D. 1980. In legal practice Texas 1980-94.

Author and Lecturer "Practice Basics in the Second Court of Appeals" Tarrant County Bar Association 1995 and Dallas County Bar Association 1995, "Summary Judgements: How Appealing Are They?" Tarrant County Probate Bar Association 1996 and "Review of the Not So New Significant Changes to Texas Rules of Appel-

LIVINGSTON, TERRIE—*Continued*

late Procedure" Dallas and Tarrant County Trial Lawyers' Association 1998. Member Texas Bar Foundation, College of the State Bar of Texas, State Bar of Texas, Tarrant County Women's (President 1992), Tarrant County Appellate, Tarrant County Probate, Parker County, Tarrant County (Secretary-Treasurer 1992, Vice President 1993) and American (Appellate Judges Conference Judicial Administration Division 1995) Bar Associations. Member Fort Worth Professional Women's Organization, Commercial Real Estate Women of Tarrant County, Business and Estate Council, Circle "T" Girl Scout Council (Director 1986-92, Advisory Director since 1997), League of Women Voters, Downtown Fort Worth, Inc. Retail Council, Harris Health Exchange, Women's Club of Fort Worth, Delta Delta Delta Alumnae Association, First United Methodist Church of Fort Worth, Fort Worth Zoo Association.

Office: 9000 Tarrant County Justice Center, 401 West Belknap, Fort Worth 76196.

Telephone: (817) 884-1900.

Fax: (817) 884-1932

LOCKE, Jim *(Judge, Brazos County Court at Law No. 2)* Appointed. Elected to term beginning Jan 1, 2001. Reelected 2002, current term expires Dec 31, 2006. Born Bryan Texas Feb 16, 1953. Methodist. Educated at Texas A&M University B.S. 1975 and Baylor University School of Law J.D. 1978. Admitted to practice Texas 1978.

President Brazos County Bar Association 2002-03.

Office: 300 East 26th Street, Suite 203, Bryan 77803.

Telephone: (979) 361-4260.

Fax: (979) 361-4514

E-mail address: jlocke@co.brazos.tx.us

LOCKHART, Ben Allen *(Judge, Howard County Court)*

Office: 207 Howard County Courthouse, 300 Main, Big Spring 79720.

Telephone: (432) 264-2202.

LONGORIA, Jose *(Judge, Texas District Court 214th Judicial District)*

Office: 901 Leopard, Suite 902, Corpus Christi 78401.

Telephone: (361) 888-0463.

LOPEZ, Abe *(Judge, Texas District Court 108th Judicial District)* Term expires Dec 31, 2004.

Office: 501 South Fillmore Street, Suite 4-A, Amarillo 79101-2444.

Telephone: (806) 379-2355.

LÓPEZ, Alma L. *(Chief Justice, Texas Court of Appeals Fourth District)* Justice Oct 1993 to Dec 31, 2002, appointed by Governor Ann W. Richards. Elected Chief Justice Nov 2002. Term expires Dec 31, 2008. Born Laredo Texas Aug 17, 1943. Educated at St. Mary's University B.B.A. 1965 J.D. 1968.

Board Member Bexar County Women's Bar Association since 1996 and Texas Women Lawyers Association since 1997. Member Democratic Women of Texas. Board Member Family Violence Prevention Services, Inc. since 1996, St. Mary's Hispanic Law Alumni Association since 1996, Texas Migrant Council since 1999, South Texas Higher Education Agency since 1999 and Kids Exchange since 1999.

Office: 3200 Bexar County Justice Center, 300 Dolorosa Street, San Antonio 78205-3037.

Telephone: (210) 335-2658.

LOPEZ, Carlos *(Judge, Texas District Court 116th Judicial District)* Former Judge, Dallas County Court at Law No. 2.

Office: 600 Commerce, Sixth Floor, Dallas 75202-4606.

Telephone: (214) 653-6015.

LOPEZ, Leticia *(Judge, Texas District Court 389th Judicial District)*

Office: 100 North Closner, Second Floor, Edinburg 78539.

Telephone: (956) 318-2080.

LOPEZ, Midgalia *(Judge, Texas District Court 197th Judicial District)* Former Judge, Cameron County Court at Law No. 2.

Office: 974 East Harrison Street, Brownsville 78520-7123.

Telephone: (956) 574-8150.

LOUGHMILLER, Deane *(Judge, Lamar County Court at Law)*

Office: 119 North Main Street, Paris 75460-9465.

Telephone: (903) 737-2430.

LOVETT, Jim D. *(Judge, Texas District Court 6th Judicial District)*

Mailing address: P.O. Box 904, Clarksville 75426.

Telephone: (903) 427-2274.

LOVING, Joe Hilton, Jr. *(Judge, Dallas County Probate Court No. 3)*

Office: 500 Main Street, Suite 209, Dallas 75202-3500.

Telephone: (214) 653-7595.

LOWE, Thomas Wilson, III *(Judge, Texas District Court 236th Judicial District)*

Office: Tarrant County Justice Center, 401 West Belknap, Fort Worth 76196-0228.

Telephone: (817) 884-1709.

LOWERY, Susan Griffin *(Judge, Fort Bend County Court at Law No. 3)* Elected to term beginning Nov 1996. Reelected Nov 1998 and 2002. Current term expires Dec 31, 2006. Born Houston Texas Aug 8, 1943. Episcopalian. Educated at Baylor University B.A. 1965 and South Texas College of Law J.D. 1983. Admitted to practice Texas 1984, U.S. District Court Southern District of Texas 1984 and U.S. Court of Appeals Fifth Circuit 1984. In legal practice Wharton 1984-87 and Richmond 1992-96.

Assistant District Attorney Fort Bend County 1987-92.

Office: 301 Jackson Street, Suite 420, Richmond 77469-3108.

Telephone: (281) 341-4430.

E-mail address: lowersus@co.fort-bend.tx.us

LUDLUM, Alia Moses *(Judge, United States District Court Western District of Texas)* Former Magistrate Judge. Appointed Judge for life by President George W. Bush to term beginning Nov 18, 2002.

Office: A-202 U.S. Courthouse, 111 East Broadway Street, Del Rio 78840.

Telephone: (830) 703-2038.

LUITJEN, Mark R. *(Judge, Texas District Court 144th Judicial District)* Elected Nov 3, 1998 to term beginning Jan 1, 1999. Reelected Nov 5, 2002, current term expires Dec 31, 2006. Born McAllen Texas July 30, 1955. Christian. Educated at Trinity University B.A. cum laude 1976 and St. Mary's University J.D. 1980. Admitted to practice Texas 1980 and U.S. District Court Western District of Texas 1992. In legal practice San Antonio 1980-82.

With District Attorney's Office Bexar County 1982-98. Former Member Texas District and County Attorneys Association, Texas Criminal Defense Lawyers Association and Association of Government Attorneys in Capital Litigation. Member State Bar of Texas and San Antonio Bar Association. Lecturer on "Capital Murder Punishment Phase—State's Perspective" 1994 and "Changes to Indigent Appointments" 2001 Advanced Criminal Law Course State Bar of Texas, "Debunking the Myths of Capital Punishment" 17th Annual Conference Association of Government Attorneys 1996 and New York Prosecutor's Training Institute 2001 and "Pleading Your Client Guilty" Annual Criminal Law Institute San Antonio Bar Association 1997. Recipient Distinguished Service Award from San Antonio Police Officers Association Oct 24, 2000. Republican. Enjoys antique map collecting, hunting, fishing and music.

Office: 3054 Bexar County Justice Center, 300 Dolorosa Street, San Antonio 78205-3023.
Telephone: (210) 335-2511.
Fax: (210) 335-2503

LUNA, Joe *(Judge, Zavala County Court)*
Mailing address: P.O. Box 5008, Crystal City 78839.
Telephone: (830) 374-3810.

LYNCH, Mike F. *(Judge, Texas District Court 167th Judicial District)*
Mailing address: P.O. Box 1748, Austin 78767-1748.
Telephone: (512) 854-9310.

LYNN, Barbara M. G. *(Judge, United States District Court Northern District of Texas)* Appointed for life by President Bill Clinton to term beginning Feb 14, 2000. Born Binghamton New York Sept 19, 1952. Educated at University of Virginia B.A. with highest distinction 1973 and Southern Methodist University J.D. summa cum laude 1976. Leading Articles Editor Southwestern Law Journal 1975-76. Member Delta Theta Phi, Phi Beta Kappa, Barristers and Order of the Coif. Admitted to practice Texas 1976. In legal practice Dallas 1976-99.

Board of Directors Dallas Bar Association 1984-88. Chair Dallas Association of Defense Counsel 1997 and Section of Litigation American Bar Association 1998-99. Master Patrick E. Higginbotham Inn of Court. Fellow Dallas Bar Foundation, Texas Bar Foundation, American Bar Foundation, American College of Trial Lawyers and The American Law Institute. Research Fellow Southwestern Legal Foundation. Member Dallas Chapter American Inns of Court. Instructor National Institute of Trial Advocacy since 1978 and Southern Methodist University Dedmon School of Law 2002. Executive Board Southern Methodist University Dedmon School of Law 1990-94 and since 1998.

Office: 1100 Commerce Street, Fifteenth Floor, Dallas 75242.
Telephone: (214) 753-2420.

LYNN, Dennis Michael *(Judge, United States Bankruptcy Court Northern District of Texas)* Appointed by U.S. Court of Appeals Fifth Circuit judges to term beginning Sept 18, 2001. Term expires Sept 17, 2015.

Office: 147 U.S. Courthouse, 501 West Tenth Street, Fort Worth 76102.
Telephone: (817) 333-6021.

MACIAS, Patricia A. *(Judge, Texas District Court 388th Judicial District)*
Office: 500 East San Antonio, #706, El Paso 79901-2457.
Telephone: (915) 543-3850.

MacRAE, Sharon *(Judge, Texas District Court 290th Judicial District)* Term expires Dec 31, 2006.
Office: 3102 Bexar County Justice Center, 300 Dolorosa Street, San Antonio 78205-3028.
Telephone: (210) 335-2696.

MAGRE, Ed *(Judge, Texas District Court 20th Judicial District)*
Mailing address: P.O. Box 728, Cameron 76520-0728.
Telephone: (254) 697-7010.

MAHON, Eldon B. *(Senior Judge, United States District Court Northern District of Texas)* Appointed for life by President Richard M. Nixon to term beginning July 3, 1972. Assumed Senior status, serves by assignment. Born Loraine Texas April 9, 1918. Methodist. Educated at McMurry College B.A. 1939 and University of Texas LL.B. 1942. Law Clerk to Texas Supreme Court 1945-46. Admitted to practice Texas 1942. In legal practice Abilene 1964-68. Judge, Texas District Court 1960-63.

County Attorney Mitchell County 1947. District Attorney 32nd Judicial District of Texas 1948-60. U.S. Attorney Northern District of Texas 1968. Member American Judicature Society, State Bar of Texas, Fort Worth-Tarrant County, Federal and American Bar Associations. Named an outstanding Texas prosecutor by Texas Law Enforcement Foundation 1957. USAAC 1942-45. Vice President Texas Electric Service Company 1963-64. Former Trustee McMurry College. Fort Worth President West Texas Council of Girl Scouts 1966-68.

Office: 502 U.S. Courthouse, 501 West Tenth Street, Fort Worth 76102.
Telephone: (817) 850-6640.

MALLIA, Wayne J. *(Judge, Texas District Court 405th Judicial District)* Educated at University of Texas B.A. 1983 and St. Mary's University School of Law J.D. 1987.

Assistant Criminal District Attorney and First Assistant Criminal District Attorney Galveston County. Former Treasurer Galveston County Young Lawyers Association and Galveston County Bar Association. Chairman Law Library Committee for two years. Former Member Board of Directors Operation D.A.R.E. Galveston, Women's Resource and Crisis Center and Galveston Alliance of Island Neighborhoods. Former Advisor Law Explorer Post Boy Scouts of America. Former Member Galveston Jaycees. President San Jacinto Neighborhood Association. Founding Advisory Board Member Teen Court Galveston.

Office: 722 Moody, Sixth Floor, Galveston 77550.
Telephone: (409) 765-2688.

MALONEY, Robert B. *(Senior Judge, United States District Court Northern District of Texas)* Appointed for life by President Ronald Reagan to term beginning 1986. Assumed Senior status Aug 31, 2000, serves by

MALONEY, ROBERT B.—*Continued*
assignment. Born 1933. Educated at Southern Methodist University B.B.A. 1956 J.D. 1960. In legal practice 1962-84. Justice, Texas Court of Appeals Fifth District 1983-85.

Assistant District Attorney Dallas County 1961-62. Fellow Texas Bar Foundation. Member State Bar of Texas and Dallas Bar Association. Member Texas House of Representatives 1973-82.

Office: 15E26 U.S. Courthouse, 1100 Commerce Street, Dallas 75242-1003.

Telephone: (214) 753-2320.

MANSKE, Jeffrey C. *(Magistrate Judge, United States District Court Western District of Texas)* Appointed by U.S. District Court judges to term beginning Aug 1, 2001.

Office: 901 Washington Avenue, Waco 76701.

Telephone: (254) 750-1545.

MANTOOTH-STRICKLIN, Debbie *(Judge, Texas District Court 180th Judicial District)*

Office: 1201 Franklin, Room 18144, Houston 77002.

Telephone: (713) 755-6344.

MARION, Sandee Bryan *(Justice, Texas Court of Appeals Fourth District)* Appointed by Governor Rick Perry to term beginning Jan 2002. Born San Antonio Texas 1956. Educated at University of Texas at Austin B.A. with honors 1977 and St. Mary's University School of Law 1980. Board Certified—Family Law—Texas Board of Legal Specialization. In legal practice Boerne 1980-86. Judge, Bexar County Probate Court No. 2 1992-2002.

Office: 3200 Bexar County Justice Center, 300 Dolorosa Street, San Antonio 78205-3037.

Telephone: (210) 335-2629.

MARTIN, E. Mason, II *(Judge, Montgomery County Court at Law No. 3)* Appointed to term beginning Jan 1, 1986. Elected Nov 1986, Nov 1990, 1994, 1998 and 2002. Current term expires Dec 31, 2006. Born Conroe Texas Dec 24, 1943. Church of Christ. Educated at Abilene Christian University B.S. 1967, Roosevelt University M.A. 1971 and Pepperdine University School of Law J.D. 1977. Admitted to practice Texas 1977 and U.S. District Court Southern District of Texas. In legal practice Conroe 1977-85.

Member College of the State Bar of Texas, County Court at Law Judges Association, State Bar of Texas (Judicial Section) and Montgomery County Bar Association. Corporal USMC 1969-71. Assistant Dean Carl Sandburg High School 1971-74. Republican. Enjoys jogging and mountain climbing.

Office: 210 West Davis, Suite 250, Conroe 77301-2549.

Telephone: (936) 539-7973.

MARTIN, Jack *(Judge, Hall County Court)*

Office: 512 Main Street, Suite 7, Memphis 79245-3343.

Telephone: (806) 259-2511.

MARTINEZ, Jimmy *(Judge, Bee County Court)*

Office: 105 West Corpus Christi Street, #105, Beeville 78102.

Telephone: (361) 362-3260.

MARTINEZ, Philip Ray *(Judge, United States District Court Western District of Texas)* Appointed for life by President George W. Bush to term beginning Feb 15, 2002. Born El Paso Texas July 13, 1957. Catholic. Educated at University of Texas at El Paso B.S. with high honors 1979 and Harvard Law School J.D. 1982. Recipient Joseph M. Ray Award 1979. Admitted to practice Texas 1982, U.S. Court of Appeals Fifth Circuit 1982 and U.S. District Court Western District of Texas 1984. In legal practice El Paso 1982-90. Judge, El Paso County Court at Law No. 1 Jan 1, 1991 to Oct 23, 1991. Judge, Texas Family District Court 327th Judicial District Oct 23, 1991 to Feb 2002, appointed by Governor Ann W. Richards.

Author "Freedom of Expression: Constitutional History" Texas Young Lawyers Association 1991 and *Juvenile Justice: El Paso County* 1992. Fellow Texas Bar Foundation since 1988. Director 1985-87 and 1990-92 and Chairman of the Board 1986-87 El Paso Legal Assistance Society. Member El Paso Young Lawyers Association, Texas Young Lawyers Association (Director 1992), Texas Center for the Judiciary, State Bar of Texas (Sections: Litigation, Consumer Law, Antitrust, Judicial, Juvenile Law, Liaison with Law Schools Committee 1984-86, Legal Services to the Poor in Civil Matters Committee 1988-91), El Paso Mexican-American, El Paso (Director 1989-92, Treasurer 1992) and American Bar Associations. Author and Speaker "Defending a D.T.P.A. Claim" D.T.P.A. Seminar University of Texas 1989-90, D.T.P.A. Seminar Texas Tech University 1990, "Rule 76a: Sealing of the Court Record" Advanced Civil Trial Course State Bar of Texas 1991 and "Issues in Juvenile Justice" MABA of Texas Conference 1992. Speaker "The Sentencing Dilemma" Northwest Region Texas Corrections Association Conference 1992, "New Developments in Juvenile Justice" Texas Association of County Judges and Commissioners Annual Conference 1992 and "Texas Discovery" The Rutter Group of Texas 1992-93. Recipient Outstanding Achievement Award from El Paso Young Lawyers Association 1989-90. Named Young Lawyer of the Year by El Paso Bar Association 1992. Democrat. Member Mexican-American Democrats since 1986 and El Paso County Democratic Party (Gold Star Member since 1990). Westside Coordinator Unity 90 Democratic Rally 1990. Volunteer Unity 92 Democratic Rally 1992. Delegate to Democratic State Convention 1992. Director National Conference of Christians and Jews 1987-89 and 1990-92 (Co-chairman 1988-89), El Paso Cancer Treatment Center 1987-92, Rio Grande Council of Governments Alternative Dispute Resolution Center 1988, El Paso Service and Education Labor Force, Inc. 1990-92, Stop the Violence Coalition 1992 (Co-chairman 1992) and El Paso Chamber of Commerce 1992 (Chairman Leadership Council). Member El Paso County Commissioners' Court (Redistricting Committee 1978, Member 1984-86 and Chairman 1985-86 Parks Board, Member 1985-92 and Chairman 1990-91 Ascarate Golf Course Advisory Board) and Sunset Commission City of El Paso 1989-90. Chairman El Paso County Juvenile Board since Oct 23, 1991. Director 1978-79 and 1983-90 and President 1983-89 Ascarate Junior Golf Tournament, Inc. Member Harvard Schools and Scholarship Committee 1988-92 (Chairman 1991). Director Boy Scouts of America Yucca Council 1991-92, University of Texas at El Paso Alumni Association 1992 and University of Texas at El Paso Miner Foundation 1992.

Office: 511 East San Antonio Avenue, El Paso 79901.

Telephone: (915) 534-6736.

MASON, Corinne *(Judge, Collin County Court at Law No. 1)*
Office: 1800 North Graves, Suite 135, McKinney 75069.
Telephone: (972) 548-3860.

MASSEY, Sam G. *(Judge, Ward County Court)* Elected Nov 1990 to term beginning Jan 1, 1991. Reelected 1994, 1998 and 2002. Current term expires Dec 31, 2006. Born Pecos Texas Sept 13, 1946. Educated at Sul Ross State University. Graduate The National Judicial College.
Office: 400 South Allen Street, Monahans 79756-4600.
Telephone: (915) 943-3200.

MATHY, Pamela A. *(Magistrate Judge, United States District Court Western District of Texas)* Appointed by U.S. District Court judges to term beginning June 8, 1998. Term expires June 7, 2006. Born 1952. Educated at Marquette University B.A. magna cum laude 1973, University of Texas at Austin M.A. 1976, University of Wisconsin-Madison J.D. cum laude 1978 and Georgetown University LL.M. 1982. Article Editor Wisconsin Law Review. Law Clerk and Staff Attorney to Hon. Walter J. Cummings, U.S. Court of Appeals Seventh Circuit 1978-80. Member Phi Beta Kappa and Order of the Coif. Admitted to practice Wisconsin 1978, District of Columbia 1979, Illinois 1979, Texas 1985 and California 1996. In legal practice Washington D.C. 1980-81.
Senior Staff Attorney U.S. Court of Appeals Seventh Circuit 1981-83. Assistant U.S. Attorney 1983-98. Member State Bar of Texas, San Antonio, Bexar County Women's, Federal and American Bar Associations. Member Rotary.
Office: U.S. Courthouse, 655 East Durango Boulevard, San Antonio 78206.
Telephone: (210) 472-6350.
Fax: (210) 472-6354

MAY, Robert E. *(Judge, Texas District Court 149th Judicial District)* Appointed by Governor William P. Clements to term beginning June 1, 1990. Elected Nov 1990, 1994, 1998 and 2002. Current term expires Dec 31, 2006. Born Velasco Texas Dec 14, 1947. Baptist. Educated at Texas A&M University B.A. 1970 and Baylor University J.D. 1975. Admitted to practice Texas, U.S. District Court Southern District of Texas, U.S. Court of Appeals Fifth Circuit and U.S. Supreme Court. In legal practice Odessa 1976-77 and Lake Jackson 1978-90. Associate Judge, Lake Jackson City Court 1978-90.
Assistant Criminal District Attorney Angleton 1976-78. Second Lieutenant USAR. Previously employed as school teacher Reicher Catholic High School and Westchester Senior High School. Republican. Member Board of Junior Achievement, His Love Christian Counseling Service and Consumer Credit Counseling Service. Enjoys authoring children's books.
Office: 111 East Locust, Angleton 77515-4678.
Telephone: (979) 864-1261.

MAYDEN, Jay *(Judge, Childress County Court)*
Office: County Courthouse, Box 1, Childress 79201.
Telephone: (940) 937-2221.

MAYES, K. Michael *(Judge, Texas District Court 410th Judicial District)* Elected 1996 to term beginning Jan 1, 1997. Reelected 2000, current term expires Dec 31, 2004. Administrative District Judge 2000-02. Pretrial Judge, Rule 11 Region 2 for all Ford/Firestone Litigation since Feb 2001. Educated at Southern Methodist University B.A. magna cum laude 1974 and University of Houston J.D. summa cum laude 1977. Member Phi Delta Phi. Admitted to practice Texas 1977, Hawaii 1977, U.S. District Courts Eastern, Northern and Southern Districts of Texas and District of Hawaii, U.S. Court of Appeals Fifth Circuit and U.S. Supreme Court.
Co-author "Vicarious Liability and the Operating Room Surgeon" 17 South Texas L. Jour. 367, 1976. Author "42 U.S.C. Section 1983 Litigation" State Bar of Texas CLE 1986 and "High-Tech Times" 28 No. 2 *In Chambers* Summer 2001 and 101 No. 3 *The Texas Record* Sept 2001. Member State Bar of Texas (Judicial Section), Montgomery County and Hawaii State Bar Associations. Speaker "Governmental Liability," "Summary Judgment: The Realities of Granting or Denying One," "Local Rules of Court" and "Technology in the Courtroom" Continuing Legal Education State Bar of Texas. Volunteer Conroe Area Youth Baseball League, Oak Ridge/The Woodlands Area Little League and Oak Ridge/The Woodlands Montgomery YMCA. Elder Woodlands Christian Church. Life Member Montgomery County Fair Association. Member Advisory Committee Child Advocates of Montgomery County, Conroe Chamber of Commerce and South Montgomery County/Woodlands Chamber of Commerce.
Office: 300 North Main, Room 200, Conroe 77301.
Telephone: (936) 539-7860.
E-mail address: mmayes@co.montgomery.tx.us

MAYFIELD, Alan M. *(Judge, Texas District Court 74th Judicial District)*
Office: 501 Washington Avenue, Room 307, Waco 76701-1380.
Telephone: (254) 757-5075.

MAYFIELD, Robert B., III *(Judge, Johnson County Court at Law No. 1)*
Office: Two North Main Street, #301, Cleburne 76031-5584.
Telephone: (817) 556-6354.

MAYNARD, Walter *(Judge, Somervell County Court)*
Mailing address: P.O. Box 851, Glen Rose 76043.
Telephone: (254) 897-2322.

MAYO, Currie Ray *(Judge, Mitchell County Court)*
Office: 349 Oak Street, Room 200, Colorado City 79512.
Telephone: (325) 728-8439.

McADAMS, William L. *(Judge, Texas District Court 12th Judicial District)* Elected Nov 1988 to term beginning Jan 1, 1989. Reelected Nov 1992, Nov 1996 and Nov 2000. Current term expires Dec 31, 2004. Born Huntsville Texas July 20, 1953. United Methodist. Educated at Texas A&M University B.B.A. 1975 and Baylor University J.D. 1979. Member Delta Theta Phi. Admitted to practice Texas 1979, U.S. District Court Southern District of Texas 1985, U.S. Court of Appeals Fifth Circuit 1985 and U.S. Supreme Court 2000. In legal practice Washington D.C. 1979-80 and Huntsville Texas 1980-88.
Member Texas Association for Court Administration, American Judges Association, State Bar of Texas (Dis-

MCADAMS, WILLIAM L.—*Continued*

trict 5-A Grievance Committee 1987-88, Judicial Section), Grimes County and Walker County (President 1985-86) Bar Associations. Recipient Distinguished Director Service Award Huntsville-Walker County Chamber of Commerce 1988 and Gavel Award from Walker County Bar Association and East Texas Legal Services, Inc. 1992. Democrat. Member 1983-86 and Vice Chairman 1984-86 Huntsville Planning Commission. President Huntsville A&M Club 1982-84 and Huntsville Leadership Institute Alumni Association 1984-85. Director Walker County United Way 1986-88 and Huntsville High School Ex-students Association 1987-90. Trustee First United Methodist Church of Huntsville since 1986. Member Advisory Committee Texas Prison Museum 1986-91. Board of Directors East Texas Legal Services, Inc. 1987-89. Committeeman Houston Livestock Show and Rodeo since 1996. Life Member Walker County Fair Association. Member Walker County Unit Committee American Cancer Society.

Office: 1100 University Avenue, Suite 202, Huntsville 77340-4642.

Telephone: (936) 436-4915.

McARTHUR, Woodie, Jr. *(Judge, Dickens County Court)*

Mailing address: P.O. Box 179, Dickens 79229-0179.

Telephone: (806) 623-5532.

McBRYDE, John H. *(Judge, United States District Court Northern District of Texas)* Appointed for life by President George Bush to term beginning 1990. Born 1931. Educated at Texas Christian University B.S. 1953 and University of Texas School of Law LL.B. 1956. In legal practice Fort Worth 1956-90.

Fellow American College of Trial Lawyers. Member Texas Bar Foundation, American Bar Foundation and State Bar of Texas.

Office: 401 U.S. Courthouse, 501 West Tenth Street, Fort Worth 76102.

Telephone: (817) 850-6650.

McCALL, Terry *(Justice, Texas Court of Appeals Eleventh District)* Elected to term beginning Jan 1, 1999. Term expires Dec 31, 2004.

Mailing address: P.O. Box 271, Eastland 76448-0271.

Telephone: (254) 629-2638.

McCLURE, Ann Crawford *(Justice, Texas Court of Appeals Eighth District)* Elected Nov 8, 1994 to term beginning Jan 1, 1995. Reelected 2000, current term expires Dec 31, 2006. Born Cincinnati Ohio Sept 5, 1953. Presbyterian. Educated at Texas Christian University B.F.A. magna cum laude 1974 and University of Houston J.D. 1979. Board Certified—Family Law and Civil Appellate Law—Texas Board of Legal Specialization. In legal practice Houston 1979-83 and El Paso 1983-94.

Former Editor *The Family Law Forum.* Former Articles Editor State Bar Section Reports—Family Law. Contributing Editor "Law West of the Pecos" El Paso Bar Bulletin and *Texas Family Law Service* Bancroft-Whitney. Author "A Child's Bill of Rights" Public School Presentations. Important Decisions: Columbia Universal Life Ins. Co. v. Miles 923 S.W.2d 803, Tex. App.—El Paso writ req'd 1996; Gibson v. State 921 S.W.2d 747, Tex. App.—El Paso petition filed 1996; Feldman v. Kohler 918 S.W.2d 615, Tex. App.—El Paso writ denied 1996; Parallax Corp. v. City of El Paso 910 S.W.2d 86, Tex. App.—El Paso writ denied 1996; and Dechon v. Dechon 909 S.W.2d 950, Tex. App.—El Paso no writ 1996. Member Editorial Committee Texas Family Law Practice Manual 1982-93 and Family Law Specialization Exam Commission 1989-93. Former Member Texas Board of Law Examiners and Board of Disciplinary Appeals. Executive Member Family Law Council of Community Property States, Texas Academy of Family Law Specialists (Former Director), College of the State Bar of Texas, State Bar of Texas (Director 1987-91, CLE Liaison 1991-93, Treasurer 1993-94, Secretary 1994-95, Vice Chair 1995-96, Chair Elect 1996-97 and Chair 1997-98 Family Law Section, Ex-Officio Member Professional Development Program Committee 1990-94, Vice Chair CLE Committee 1990-94, Director 1991-95 and Treasurer 1996-97 Appellate and Advocacy Section, Former Co-chair Small Cities CLE Subcommittee, Sections: Judicial, Litigation, Criminal Law, Women and the Law), El Paso (Director since 1996), Midland, Ector County, Trans-Pecos (President since 1995) and American (Section of Family Law, Judicial Administration Division) Bar Associations.

Instructor "Interference with Custody and Possession of Children, Or, How to Make the Hurting Stop" 1985, "A Serious Immediate Question Concerning the Welfare of the Child: Just How Serious Does It Have to Be?" 1986, "Appellate Practice and Procedure: A Second Chance at 'Winning'?" 1988, "When Solution is the Goal: Alternatives to Formal Litigation" 1991, "Objections and Preservation of Error" 1992, "Malpractice and the Bermuda Triangle: Negligence, Breach of Contract and the DTPA" 1993, "Evidence Can Be 'Appealing'" 1995 and "It Might Be Malpractice If . . ." 1996 Advanced Family Law Seminar; "Appellate Practice and Procedure: The New Specialization" 1987, "Laying the Predicate for Appeal: Preservation of Error in the Trial Court" 1989, "Coping With Stress in the Family Law Practitioner" Spousal Presentation 1991 and "Ten Ways to Lose Your Appeal" 1993 Marriage Dissolution Seminar; "Ethics, Malpractice and Frivolous Appeals" 1990, "Appeals from Non-Jury Trials" 1991, "Making Non-Jury Trials More 'Appealing'" 1994, "Appellate Justices Panel" 1995 and "Non-Jury Trials Revisited" 1996 Advanced Civil Appellate Practice Seminar; "Getting It In and Keeping It Out" The Ultimate Trial Notebook III Annual Convention State Bar of Texas 1991; "Women in Family Law" 1991, "Surviving the Silent Killer" 1993 and "Gender Issues in the Every Day Practice of Law—Is the Gap Narrowing?" 1996 Women and the Law Seminar; "Findings of Fact and Conclusions of Law—Don't Leave the Courthouse Without Them" 1994 and "Appeals from Non-Jury Trials" 1996 Family Law Seminar El Paso Bar Association; "Evidence Can Be 'Appealing'" 1995 and "Appellate Procedure Update: Just When You Thought You Knew All the Answers, the Courts Changed All the Questions" 1996 Annual Conference on State and Federal Appeals University of Texas School of Law; "Reflections . . . A Review of the Eighth Court of Appeals' Significant Opinions in Criminal Law" El Paso Criminal Law Seminar 1996; and "Evidence Can Be 'Appealing'" Advanced Evidence and Discovery 1996. Course Director Family Law for the Experienced Non-Specialist 1989, Law and Tactics Seminar 1991 and Marriage Dissolution Seminar 1995. Assistant Course Director Advanced Family Law Seminar 1990. Co-Course Director Ultimate Trial Notebook Annual Meeting State Bar of Texas 1994. Speaker on

MCCLURE, ANN CRAWFORD—*Continued*

"The Oral Argument and Its Preparation: A Demonstration" Advanced Civil Appellate Practice Seminar 1993, "The Great Debate: Divisibility of Goodwill at Divorce" Advanced Family Law Seminar 1994 and "Conflicts of Interest and Attorney Disqualification" Advanced Personal Injury Seminar 1996.

Listed in *Best Lawyers in America* 1989-90, 1991-92 and 1993-94, *Who's Who in America, Who's Who in American Law, Who's Who Among American Women, Who's Who in the South and Southwest* and *International Who's Who of Professionals.*

Office: 500 East San Antonio, Suite 1203, El Paso 79901-2421.

Telephone: (915) 546-2240.

McCORKLE, Lamar *(Judge, Texas District Court 133rd Judicial District)* Elected to term beginning Jan 1, 1987. Reelected 1988, 1992, 1996 and 2000. Current term expires Dec 31, 2004. Born Pennsylvania May 15, 1951. Episcopalian. Educated at University of Arizona and South Texas College of Law J.D. 1980. Law Clerk to Hon. David Hittner, Texas District Court 133rd Judicial District and Chief Justice Tom F. Coleman, Texas Court of Appeals First Supreme Judicial District. Admitted to practice Texas 1980. In legal practice Houston since 1980.

Office: 521 Civil Courts Building, 301 Fannin Street, Houston 77002.

Telephone: (713) 755-6266.

McCOY, Bill *(Judge, Texas District Court 358th Judicial District)* Appointed by Governor Mark White to term beginning Sept 1, 1985. Elected Nov 1986, 1990, 1994, 1998 and 2002. Current term expires Dec 31, 2006. Currently serves as Administrative Judge. Born Archer City Texas Jan 12, 1938. Educated at University of Texas at El Paso B.B.A. 1962 and Baylor University J.D. 1966. Member Phi Delta Phi. Admitted to practice Texas 1966, U.S. Supreme Court 1981 and U.S. District Court Western District of Texas. In legal practice Odessa 1976-85.

Assistant District Attorney 1966-68. County Attorney Ector County 1968-76. Member State Bar of Texas and Ector County Bar Association. Democrat. Enjoys ranching and flying.

Office: 300 North Grant, Room 322, Odessa 79761-5158.

Telephone: (432) 498-4250.

McCOY, Bob *(Judge, Texas District Court 48th Judicial District)* Appointed by Governor George W. Bush to term beginning Oct 1995. Elected Nov 1996 and 2000. Current term expires Dec 31, 2004. Born Tyler Texas March 12, 1947. Church of Christ. Educated at Texas Tech University B.S. 1970 M.S. 1972 and University of Houston J.D. with honors 1981. Law Clerk to Hon. James P. Wallace, Texas Supreme Court 1982-83. Member Phi Delta Phi. Admitted to practice Texas 1982, U.S. District Courts Southern 1982, Northern 1983, Eastern 1988 and Western 1988 Districts of Texas and Western District of Oklahoma 1994, U.S. Court of Appeals Fifth Circuit 1986 and U.S. Supreme Court 1996. Board Certified—Personal Injury Trial Law—Texas Board of Legal Specialization. In legal practice Fort Worth Texas 1983-95.

Office: 401 West Belknap, Fort Worth 76196.

Telephone: (817) 884-2690.

McCOY, David M. *(Judge, Texas District Court 100th Judicial District)*

Office: County Courthouse, Box 7, Childress 79201-3721.

Telephone: (940) 937-3541.

McCoy, Royce *(Judge, Wood County Court)*

Mailing address: P.O. Box 938, Quitman 75783-0938.

Telephone: (903) 763-2716.

McCULLOCH, William C. *(Judge, Harris County Probate Court No. 4)* Appointed to term beginning Sept 1, 1985. Elected Nov 1986, 1990, 1994, 1998 and 2002. Current term expires Dec 31, 2006. Born Dallas Texas Jan 29, 1940. Presbyterian. Educated at University of Texas B.A. 1963 LL.B. 1964. Member Phi Delta Phi. Admitted to practice Texas 1964. In legal practice Dallas 1967-70 and Houston 1970-76.

With Trust Department Texas Commerce Bank 1976-85. Adjunct Professor of Law South Texas College of Law. Fellow Houston Bar Foundation, Texas Bar Foundation and College of the State Bar of Texas. Member Texas College of Probate Judges, National College of Probate Judges, State Bar of Texas and Houston Bar Association (Past Chairman Wills, Probate and Trust Section). Speaker Wills and Probate Institutes of State Bar of Texas, University of Houston Law Center, South Texas College of Law and Houston Bar Association. Captain USAR 1965-67. Republican.

Office: Family Law Center Building, Fifth Floor, 1115 Congress Street, Houston 77002.

Telephone: (713) 755-5959.

McDANIEL, Lana *(Judge, Texas District Court 203rd Judicial District)* Elected Nov 1994 to term beginning Jan 1, 1995. Reelected 1998 and 2002. Current term expires Dec 31, 2006. Presiding Judge Dallas County Criminal District Courts for three years. Currently serves as Local Administrative Judge Dallas County. Born Dallas Texas Aug 14, 1954. Educated at Baylor University B.F.A. magna cum laude 1976 J.D. 1981. Admitted to practice Texas 1982, U.S. District Court Northern District of Texas 1989, U.S. Court of Appeals Fifth Circuit 1989 and U.S. Supreme Court 1989. In legal practice 1994-95.

Assistant District Attorney Dallas 1982-94. Life Fellow Dallas Bar Foundation. Founding Fellow Dallas Association of Young Lawyers. Member Dallas Bar Association (Member Criminal Justice Committee). President Coppell Republican Club 1998-2000. Member Dallas Republican Career Women (Former Treasurer, Former Legislative Chair) and Southwest Dallas County Republican Club (Second Vice President 1995 and 1996, Secretary). Co-Vice Chair and Chair Texas High School Mock Trial Committee since 1999. Board of Directors and Chair Community Service Restitution Committee Volunteer Center of Dallas County. Member Baylor University Women's Council of Dallas and Dallas County Juvenile Board. Enjoys gardening, drawing, painting and collecting antiques.

Office: LB 28 Frank Crowley Courts Building, 133 North Industrial Boulevard, Dallas 75207-4313.

Telephone: (214) 653-5822.

McDONALD, Michael S. *(Magistrate Judge, United States District Court Western District of Texas)* Appointed by U.S. District Court judges.

Office: 206 U.S. Courthouse, 511 East San Antonio Avenue, El Paso 79901-2401.

Telephone: (915) 534-6005.

McDONALD, Ronnie *(Judge, Bastrop County Court)*

Office: 804 Pecan Street, Bastrop 78602.

Telephone: (512) 332-7201.

McDOUGAL, Bart *(Judge, Erath County Court at Law)* Elected Nov 1992 to term beginning Feb 1993. Reelected Nov 1994, 1998 and 2002. Current term expires Dec 31, 2006. Born Comanche Texas April 28, 1959. Christian. Educated at Tarleton State University B.S. with high honors 1981 and Texas Tech University J.D. 1983. Admitted to practice Texas 1984. In legal practice Stephenville and Hamilton 1984-92.

Important Decisions: In re S.D.J. (admissibility of statement by juvenile leading to discovery of physical evidence; competency to stand trial) 879 S.W.2d 370, 1994. Member Texas Association of County Court at Law Judges and State Bar of Texas (Judicial Section).

Office: 100 West Washington Street, Stephenville 76401.

Telephone: (254) 965-1417.

McDOWELL, Robert Scott *(Judge, Texas District Court 62nd Judicial District)*

Office: 119 North Main Street, Paris 75460-4267.

Telephone: (903) 737-2433.

McFARLING, Bruce *(Judge, Texas District Court 362nd Judicial District)* Elected to term beginning Jan 1, 2001. Term expires Dec 31, 2004. Born Richardson Texas May 11, 1966. Educated at Texas Tech University B.B.A. cum laude 1988 J.D. magna cum laude 1994. Admitted to practice Texas 1994 and U.S. District Court Eastern District of Texas 1999.

Assistant District Attorney Denton County Nov 1994 to Dec 2000. Special Assistant U.S. Attorney Eastern District of Texas June 1998 to Dec 2000. Republican.

Office: 1450 East McKinney Street, Third Floor, Denton 76209.

Telephone: (940) 349-2340.

E-mail address: bruce.mcfarling@co.denton.tx.us

McGEE, Delwin T. *(Judge, Moore County Court at Law)* Elected Nov 6, 1990 to term beginning Jan 1, 1991. Reelected 1994, 1998 and 2002. Current term expires Dec 31, 2006. Born Lubbock Texas Dec 21, 1953. Baptist. Educated at Texas Tech University B.B.A. 1978 J.D. 1983. Member Delta Theta Phi. Admitted to practice Texas 1984. In legal practice Dumas 1984-91.

Member The Association of Trial Lawyers of America, State Bar of Texas, 69th Judicial District (Treasurer) and American Bar Associations.

Office: 715 South Dumas Avenue, Room 206, Dumas 79029-4326.

Telephone: (806) 935-2440.

McGOUGH, Bobby Frank *(Judge, Stonewall County Court)* Elected to term beginning Jan 1, 1991. Reelected 1994, 1998 and 2002. Current term expires Dec 31, 2006. Born Peacock Texas Nov 19, 1939. Baptist. Educated at Texas Tech University B.B.A. 1961 and Auburn University M.S. 1974. Colonel USAF 1962-87 (retired).

Mailing address: P.O. Box 366, Aspermont 79502-0366.

Telephone: (940) 989-3393.

McGRATH, Bob *(Judge, Texas District Court 342nd Judicial District)*

Office: Tarrant County Justice Center, 401 West Belknap, Fort Worth 76196-0280.

Telephone: (817) 884-2710.

McGRAW, Tim *(Judge, Grayson County Court)*

Office: 100 West Houston Street, Suite 15, Sherman 75090-5958.

Telephone: (903) 813-4228.

McGREGOR, F. B. "Bob", Jr. *(Judge, Texas District Court 66th Judicial District)*

Mailing address: P.O. Box 284, Hillsboro 76645-0284.

Telephone: (254) 582-4045.

McKEE, Harry W. "Peter" *(Magistrate Judge, United States District Court Eastern District of Texas)* Appointed by U.S. District Court judges to term beginning Aug 6, 1982. Reappointed 1990 and 1998. Current term expires Aug 2006. Born Mandan North Dakota Oct 21, 1940. Educated at University of North Dakota Ph.B. 1963 and George Washington University LL.B. 1966. Admitted to practice North Dakota 1966 and Texas 1980. Began legal practice Washington D.C. 1966. In legal practice Beaumont Texas 1979.

Trial Attorney 1966-79, Special Assistant 1979 and Assistant U.S. Attorney 1979-82 U.S. Department of Justice. Member State Bar of Texas, Smith County and American Bar Associations.

Office: 210 Federal Building, 211 West Ferguson Street, Tyler 75702.

Telephone: (903) 590-1164.

McKEITHEN, Steve *(Chief Justice, Texas Court of Appeals Ninth District)* Elected to term beginning Jan 1, 2003. Term expires Dec 31, 2008. Born Harris County Texas March 17, 1952. Catholic. Educated at University of Houston B.A. 1976 and South Texas College of Law J.D. 1984. Admitted to practice Texas 1984, U.S. District Court Southern District of Texas 1989, U.S. Court of Appeals Fifth Circuit 1991 and U.S. Supreme Court 1996. In legal practice Conroe Jan 1985 to Jan 1989 and July 1998 to Dec 2002. Judge, Montgomery Municipal Court 1992-98.

Assistant County Attorney Montgomery County Feb 1989 to July 1998. Member Montgomery County Bar Association (Board of Directors 1996). Enjoys shooting and traveling.

Office: 1001 Pearl, Suite 330, Beaumont 77701-3552.

Telephone: (409) 835-8405.

E-mail address: steve.mckeithen@courts.state.tx.us

McKINNEY, Carey G. *(Judge, Anderson County Court)*

Office: 500 North Church Street, Palestine 75801.

Telephone: (903) 723-7406.

McMEANS, Walter S. *(Judge, Fort Bend County Court at Law No. 2)*

Office: 301 Jackson, Suite 323, Richmond 77469-3108.

Telephone: (281) 341-4446.

McMICHAEL, Charles L. *(Judge, Cass County Court)*
Mailing address: P.O. Box 825, Linden 75563.
Telephone: (903) 756-5181.

McNABB, Kenneth D. *(Judge, Hardeman County Court)* Elected Nov 1986 to term beginning Jan 1, 1987. Reelected 1990, 1994, 1998 and 2002. Current term expires Dec 31, 2006. Born Quanah Texas June 14, 1937. Methodist. Educated at North Texas State University in Business 1959.
Texas Air National Guard 1960-66. Previously worked as farmer. Democrat.
Mailing address: P.O. Box 30, Quanah 79252.
Telephone: (940) 663-2911.

McSPADDEN, Michael Thomas *(Judge, Texas District Court 209th Judicial District)* Appointed by Governor William P. Clements to term beginning Jan 1, 1982. Elected Nov 1982, 1986, 1990, 1994, 1998 and 2002. Current term expires Dec 31, 2006. Born Borger Texas July 24, 1944. Presbyterian. Educated at University of Oklahoma B.A. 1966 J.D. 1973. Member Phi Alpha Delta and Beta Theta Pi. Admitted to practice Texas 1977 and U.S. District Court Southern District of Texas 1977. Began legal practice Houston 1977.
Former Assistant District Attorney Harris County. Author numerous guest newspaper editorials 1984-90 and two articles *Houston Lawyer* 1988-89. Fellow Houston Bar Foundation and Texas Bar Foundation. Member State Bar of Texas, Houston and American Bar Associations. Frequent speaker at legal associations 1982-96. Guest Lecturer "Saturday Morning in Court" 1984-94. Highest rated criminal court judge by Judicial Qualifications Poll Houston Bar Association since 1986. Named State District Judge of the Year by Houston Police Officer's Association 1987 and by Harris County Sheriff's Association 1990 and Champion of Crime Stoppers by Bay Area Crime Stoppers Organization 1989. Honored in recognition and appreciation for the compassion shown to victims of crimes during Victims' Rights Week 1989. Corporal USMC 1969-71. Republican. Past President Houston Racquet Club and George Hermann Society. Board member and advisor to numerous victims' rights and charitable organizations. Enjoys hunting, fishing and playing tennis.
Office: 1201 Franklin, Room 17032, Houston 77002.
Telephone: (713) 755-6378.

McWHORTER, Wayne *(Judge, Harrison County Court)*
Office: 200 West Houston, Suite 315, Marshall 75670.
Telephone: (903) 935-4805.

MEANS, Terry R. *(Judge, United States District Court Northern District of Texas)* Appointed for life by President George Bush to term beginning Nov 5, 1991. Born Roswell New Mexico July 3, 1948. Baptist. Educated at Southern Methodist University B.A. with distinction 1971 J.D. 1974. Admitted to practice Texas 1974, U.S. District Courts Eastern, Northern and Western Districts of Texas and U.S. Court of Appeals Fifth Circuit. In legal practice Corsicana 1974-89. Justice, Texas Court of Appeals Tenth District Jan 1, 1989 to Jan 1991, appointed by Governor William P. Clements.
Master American Inn of Court. Member State Bar of Texas. Attended Orientation for New Judges Washington D.C. 1992, Fifth Circuit Judges Conferences 1992-2002, Religion in America FJC Seminar Washington D.C. 1994 and Financial Statements in Courtroom workshop San Diego 1994. Republican. Texas State Chairman "Students for Bush" George Bush's 1970 U.S. Senate Campaign. Chairman Republican Party of Navarro County 1976-80 and 1981-89. Presidential Elector State of Texas 1980. Republican nominee for State Representative Ellis and Navarro counties 1980 and Republican nominee for Justice Texas Court of Appeals Tenth District 1990. Enjoys racquetball and soccer.
Office: 201 U.S. Courthouse, 501 West Tenth Street, Fort Worth 76102.
Telephone: (817) 850-6670.

MEDINA, Sam *(Judge, Texas District Court 237th Judicial District)* Former Judge, Lubbock County Court at Law No. 1.
Mailing address: P.O. Box 10536, Lubbock 79408-3536.
Telephone: (806) 775-1027.

MEDRANO, Sam *(Judge, Texas District Court 409th Judicial District)*
Office: 500 East San Antonio, Room 700, El Paso 79901-2457.
Telephone: (915) 834-8209.

MEHAFFY, James W. *(Judge, Texas District Court 58th Judicial District)* Elected March 1994 to term beginning June 24, 1994. Reelected 1998 and 2002. Current term expires Dec 31, 2006. Born Houston Texas Nov 23, 1940. Episcopalian. Educated at University of Texas B.A. 1962 and University of Washington J.D. 1965. Member Phi Delta Phi. Admitted to practice Texas 1965, U.S. District Courts Eastern, Southern and Western Districts of Texas, U.S. Court of Appeals Fifth Circuit, U.S. Court of Federal Claims and U.S. Supreme Court. Board Certified—Personal Injury Trial Law—Texas Board of Legal Specialization. In legal practice Beaumont 1965-94.
Editor Jefferson County B. Jour. 1989-93. Adjunct Professor of Business Law Lamar University-Beaumont 1992-93. Board of Directors Texas Lawyers' Assistance Program. Life Member Texas Bar Foundation. Member Mass Tort Litigation Committee Conference of Chief Justices, Information Technology Task Force Texas Commission on Judicial Efficiency, Michelle F. Mehaffy Inn of Court (President), Texas Center for Legal Ethics and Professionalism, College of the State Bar of Texas, State Bar of Texas (Judicial Section) and Jefferson County Bar Association (Director 1968-70 and 1989-91, President 1992-93). Democrat. Former Board of Trustees All Saints' Episcopal School. Former Member Friendship Beaumont and Vestry St. Marks Episcopal Church. Director Mickey Mehaffy Children's Advocacy Program and CASA (Court Appointed Special Advocates) of Southeast Texas. Enjoys spending time with his family.
Office: 1001 Pearl Street, Room 201, Beaumont 77701-3707.
Telephone: (409) 835-8434.

MERY, Michael E. *(Judge, Bexar County Court at Law No. 12)*
Office: 3.22 Bexar County Courthouse, 100 Dolorosa Street, San Antonio 78205.
Telephone: (210) 335-2783.

MESA, Richard P. *(Magistrate Judge, United States District Court Western District of Texas)* Appointed by U.S. District Court judges.
Office: 409 U.S. Courthouse, 511 East San Antonio Avenue, El Paso 79901-2401.
Telephone: (915) 534-6732.

MESSINA, Vincent *(Judge, Hood County Court at Law)*
Office: 100 East Pearl, Room 6, Granbury 76048.
Telephone: (817) 408-3408.

MEURER, W. Jeanne *(Judge, Texas District Court 98th Judicial District)* Elected Nov 1988 to term beginning Jan 1, 1989. Reelected 1992, 1996 and 2000. Current term expires Dec 31, 2004. Born McAllen Texas June 20, 1953. Catholic. Educated at Sam Houston State University B.S. with honors 1975 and University of Texas J.D. 1977. Admitted to practice Texas 1977. In legal practice Austin 1977-79. Master/Referee, Travis County District Courts 1984-89.
Member Travis County Young Lawyers, Travis County Child Abuse Task Force, American Inns of Court, American Judicature Society, State Bar of Texas and Travis County Bar Association. Member Texas Association of Domestic Relations Officials since 1984, CASA of Travis County since 1985, Child and Family Services (Board of Directors 1989-90), Austin Women's Center (Board of Directors 1991), St. Mary's School (Board of Directors) and Travis County Juvenile Board (Chairman since 1991).
Mailing address: P.O. Box 1748, Austin 78767-1748.
Telephone: (512) 854-9307.

MEYER, Jim *(Judge, Texas District Court 170th Judicial District)*
Office: County Courthouse, Waco 76701-1380.
Telephone: (254) 757-5045.

MEYERS, Lawrence E. *(Judge, Texas Court of Criminal Appeals)* Elected Nov 8, 1992 to term beginning Jan 1, 1993. Reelected to subsequent term. Current term expires Dec 31, 2004. Educated at Southern Methodist University B.A. 1970 and University of Kansas J.D. 1973. Member Sigma Alpha Epsilon. In legal practice Fort Worth 1975-88. Justice, Texas Court of Appeals Second District 1989-1992. Substitute Judge, Fort Worth Municipal Court for three years.
Assistant District Attorney Montgomery County Kansas. Member State Bar of Texas, Tarrant County and Kansas Bar Associations. Member Parish Council St. Mary's of the Assumption Catholic Church.
Mailing address: P.O. Box 12308, Austin 78711-2308.
Office: Supreme Court Building, Austin 78701.
Telephone: (512) 463-1580.

MICHEL, Randy *(Judge, Brazos County Court at Law No. 1)* Elected Nov 1998 to term beginning Jan 1, 1999. Reelected 2002, current term expires Dec 31, 2006. Born Meridian Mississippi May 21, 1949. Christian. Educated at Baylor University B.A. 1971, University of Oklahoma M.S. 1972 and University of Kentucky J.D. 1979. Member Omicron Delta Kappa and Phi Eta Sigma. Admitted to practice Kentucky 1980, Texas 1983, U.S. District Courts Western District of Kentucky and Eastern, Southern and Western Districts of Texas and U.S. Courts of Appeals Fifth and Sixth Circuits. Board Certified—Civil Trial Law—Texas Board of Legal Specialization. In legal practice Bowling Green Kentucky 1980-83 and Bryan Texas 1983-90. Judge Jan 1992 to 1998 and Presiding Judge May 1995 to Jan 1997, College Station Municipal Court.
Certified Mediator National Mediation Arbitration Services, Inc. and American Arbitration Association 1991-98. Mediator Southern District of Texas 1992-98. Author "Should Jurors Be Allowed to Pose Written Questions to Witnesses During Trial?" 55 No. 11 Texas B. Jour. Nov 1992, "To Certify or Not to Certify: A Question Among Mediators" *Alternative Resolutions* Alternative Dispute Resolution Section State Bar of Texas 1994, *Justice Gone Awry: The Arrest and Trials of Jesus Christ* WinePress Publishing 1995 and "A Refresher on 'Undue Influence' " 28 No. 3 *In Chambers* 10-11 Winter 2001. Life Fellow Texas Bar Foundation. Member Academy of Family Mediators, American Arbitration Association, The Association of Trial Lawyers of America, The Defense Research Institute, Inc., American Judges Association, American Judicature Society, State Bar of Texas, Brazos County (President 1996-97), Kentucky and American (Sections: Dispute Resolution, Litigation) Bar Associations. Instructor-Trainer in Mediation National Mediation Academy. Recipient Barbara Weathers Walker Pro Bono Award from Brazos County Bar Association June 29, 1990 and Oct 25, 1999. Named "Distinguished Volunteer Citizen" by African-American National Heritage Society Jan 2002. Board of Directors Local Chapter American Diabetes Association 1984-85, Brazos Food Bank 1990-96 and Brazos County Civil Legal Aid, Inc. 1990-95. Commissioner Planning and Zoning Commission City of College Station 1988-92. Coach Little League baseball and flag football 1988-92. Board of Elders Grace Bible Church since 1999.
Office: 300 East 26th Street, Suite 210, Bryan 77803.
Telephone: (979) 361-4250.
Fax: (979) 361-4519
E-mail address: rmichel@co.brazos.tx.us

MILLARD, Lisa *(Judge, Texas Family District Court 310th Judicial District)*
Office: Family Law Center Building, Third Floor, 1115 Congress Street, Houston 77002.
Telephone: (713) 755-6238.

MILLER, John F., Jr. *(Judge, Texas District Court 102nd Judicial District)*
Office: 100 North State Line, Box 10, Texarkana 75501.
Telephone: (903) 798-3004.

MILLER, Mary E. *(Judge, Texas District Court 194th Judicial District)*
Office: LB 26 Frank Crowley Courts Building, 133 North Industrial Boulevard, Dallas 75207-4313.
Telephone: (214) 653-5800.

MILLOY, Maryrose *(Magistrate Judge, United States District Court Southern District of Texas)* Appointed by U.S. District Court judges.
Office: 7007 U.S. Courthouse, 515 Rusk Avenue, Houston 77002.
Telephone: (713) 250-5860.

MILLS, Bill D. *(Judge, Tarrant County Criminal Court at Law No. 3)* Elected at special election to term beginning April 22, 1976. Reelected to subsequent terms. Current term expires Dec 31, 2006. Born Marshall Texas Jan 9, 1931. Baptist. Educated at University

MILLS, BILL D.—*Continued*
of Texas B.B.A. 1956 and Southern Methodist University J.D. 1964. Admitted to practice Texas 1964.

Formerly with Tarrant County District Attorney's Office. Member State Bar of Texas (Judicial Section) and Tarrant County Bar Association. Airman First Class USAF 1950-54. Republican.

Office: Tarrant County Justice Center, Seventh Floor, 401 West Belknap, Fort Worth 76196-0238.

Telephone: (817) 884-1374.

MILLS, Jerri Lee *(Judge, Brazoria County Court at Law No. 1)* Elected Nov 8, 1994 to term beginning Jan 1, 1995. Reelected Nov 1998 and 2002. Current term expires Dec 31, 2006. Born Freeport Texas May 14, 1951. Church of Christ. Educated at University of Houston B.S. 1983 and South Texas College of Law J.D. 1987. Admitted to practice Texas 1988. Board Certified—Family Law—Texas Board of Legal Specialization 1994. In legal practice Lake Jackson 1988-94.

Director Brazoria County Women's Bar Association since 1992. President Brazoria County Bar Association 1994-95. Republican. Board of Directors The Boys and Girls Club of Brazoria County. Member American Business Womens Association and American Association of University Women. Enjoys reading and traveling.

Office: 111 East Locust Street, Room 206A, Angleton 77515-4678.

Telephone: (979) 864-1260.

MILLSAP, Cletis M. *(Judge, Hopkins County Court)* Elected Nov 3, 1998 to term beginning Jan 1, 1999. Reelected Nov 5, 2002, current term expires Dec 31, 2006. Born Sulphur Springs Texas Dec 9, 1949. Baptist. Educated at Richland College A.A.S. 1974. Justice of the Peace, Precinct One Hopkins County 1987-98.

Chairman Budget and Oversight Justice Court Training Center 1997-98. President Justice of the Peace and Constable Association of Texas 1998. Democrat. Councilman Garland City 1977-78. Member Sulphur Springs Lodge No. 221 Ancient Free and Accepted Masons of Texas. Interests include reading and studying American history.

Mailing address: P.O. Box 288, Sulphur Springs 75483.

Office: County Courthouse, Sulphur Springs 75482.

Telephone: (903) 438-4006.

Fax: (903) 438-9007

E-mail address: judge@hopkinscountytx.org

MINER, Hal *(Judge, Texas District Court 47th Judicial District)*

Office: 501 South Filmore Street, Suite 3-A, Amarillo 79101-2449.

Telephone: (806) 379-2350.

MIRELES, Andy *(Judge, Texas District Court 73rd Judicial District)* Term expires Dec 31, 2004.

Office: 401 Bexar County Courthouse, 100 Dolorosa Street, San Antonio 78205-3028.

Telephone: (210) 335-2523.

MITCHELL, Charles R. *(Judge, Texas District Court 273rd Judicial District)*

Office: 202 Courthouse, San Augustine 75972.

Telephone: (936) 275-9634.

MITCHELL, Mike *(Judge, Tarrant County Criminal Court at Law No. 2)* Appointed to term beginning April 12, 1990. Elected Nov 1990, Nov 1994, 1998 and 2002. Current term expires Dec 31, 2006. Born Dothan Alabama Nov 29, 1954. Religious affiliation: Christian. Educated at University of Texas at Austin B.A. with honors 1975 J.D. 1978. Admitted to practice Texas 1978 and U.S. District Court Northern District of Texas 1979. In legal practice Fort Worth 1978-81 and Arlington 1986-90. Judge, Fort Worth Municipal Court 1982-85.

Assistant City Attorney Fort Worth 1981-82. Member State Bar of Texas. Republican. Enjoys reading, music and railroads.

Office: Tarrant County Justice Center, Sixth Floor, 401 West Belknap, Fort Worth 76196-0237.

Telephone: (817) 884-1338.

MITCHELL, William R. *(Judge, Uvalde County Court)* Elected Nov 1986 to term beginning Jan 1, 1987. Reelected 1990, 1994, 1998 and 2002. Current term expires Dec 31, 2006. Born Uvalde Texas June 21, 1948. Presbyterian. Educated at Southwest Texas State University B.A. 1970. Former Justice of the Peace, Precinct One, Uvalde County.

Lieutenant U.S. Army 1971-77. Past President, Secretary and Lieutenant Governor Kiwanis International. Past President Uvalde Youth Baseball. Chairman United Way Fund. State officer American Cancer Society. Elder First Presbyterian Church. Volunteer Uvalde County EMS. High school football and basketball official. Enjoys ranching, hunting and all outdoor sports.

Office: Courthouse Square, Box 3, Uvalde 78801-5239.

Telephone: (830) 278-3216.

MOLINA, Agapito "Cuate", Jr. *(Judge, Jim Hogg County Court)*

Mailing address: P.O. Box 729, Hebbronville 78361-0729.

Telephone: (361) 527-3015.

MONROE, Frank R. *(Judge, United States Bankruptcy Court Western District of Texas)* Appointed by U.S. Court of Appeals Fifth Circuit judges. Chief Judge June 6, 2001 to March 1, 2002.

Office: 326 Judicial Building, 903 San Jacinto Boulevard, Austin 78701-2450.

Telephone: (512) 916-5800.

MONTALVO, Frank *(Judge, Texas District Court 288th Judicial District)*

Office: 406 Bexar County Courthouse, 100 Dolorosa Street, San Antonio 78205-3028.

Telephone: (210) 335-2663.

MONTGOMERY, Ross Elliott *(Judge, Shackelford County Court)*

Mailing address: P.O. Box 1614, Albany 76430-0161.

Telephone: (325) 762-2232.

MONTGOMERY, Sally *(Judge, Dallas County Court at Law No. 3)*

Office: Records Building, Sixth Floor, Dallas 75202-3513.

Telephone: (214) 653-7595.

MOODY, William E. *(Judge, Texas District Court 34th Judicial District)* Appointed by Governor Mark White Dec 1, 1986. Elected Nov 8, 1988, Nov 1992, 1996 and 2000. Current term expires Dec 31, 2004. Presiding Judge Sixth Administrative Region Feb 1991 to April 1995. Born Auburn Indiana Feb 26, 1950. Catho-

MOODY, WILLIAM E.—*Continued*
lic. Educated at University of Texas at El Paso B.A. with honors 1972 and Texas Tech University J.D. 1975. Member Phi Alpha Delta. Admitted to practice Texas 1975.

Assistant District Attorney Texas District Court 34th Judicial District 1975-86. Member State Bar of Texas and El Paso Bar Association. Attended New Judges Course 1986, Regional Judicial Conference 1988 and State Judicial Conference 1988. Captain USAR 1972-80. Previously worked as Assistant Manager pizza parlor, Property Appraiser El Paso County Tax Office and Legislative Assistant for State Representative Luther Jones. Democrat. Precinct Chairman 1972-74. Delegate Democratic State Conventions 1972, 1974, 1976, 1978, 1980, 1984 and 1988. Campaign Manager for District Attorney S. Simmons 1976, 1980 and 1984 and for Governor Mark White El Paso County 1982 and 1986. President Local Chapter 1977-78 and Regional Vice President Texas 1979-80 and 1987-88 Association for Retarded Citizens. Board of Directors Life Management Center 1988-89. Enjoys golf, jogging and reading.

Office: 905 El Paso County Courthouse, 500 East San Antonio Avenue, El Paso 79901-2457.
Telephone: (915) 546-2101.

MOORE, Kelly G. *(Judge, Texas District Court 121st Judicial District)* Appointed by Governor George W. Bush to term beginning Oct 3, 1995. Elected Nov 1996 and 2000. Current term expires Dec 31, 2004.

Office: 500 West Main, Room 302W, Brownfield 79316.
Telephone: (806) 637-7742.

MOORE, Marvin Lee *(Judge, Midland County Court at Law No. 2)*

Office: 200 West Wall, Suite 6, Midland 79701-4547.
Telephone: (432) 688-1151.

MOORE, Robert H., III *(Judge, Texas District Court 118th Judicial District)*

Mailing address: P.O. Box 528, Big Spring 79721-0528.
Telephone: (432) 264-2225.

MORALES, Alvino "Ben" *(Judge, Webb County Court at Law No. 1)* Elected to term beginning 1999. Reelected 2002, current term expires Dec 31, 2006. Born Taylor Texas March 18, 1950. Catholic. Educated at Southwest Texas State University B.S. 1976 and Texas Southern University School of Law J.D. 1979. Admitted to practice Texas 1979, U.S. District Courts Southern 1980 and Western 1982 Districts of Texas and U.S. Court of Appeals Fifth Circuit 1981. In legal practice Laredo 1979-99. Assistant Judge and Judge, Laredo Municipal Court 1990-98.

Assistant County Attorney Webb County 1985-88. Enjoys reading and sports.

Office: 1110 Victoria, Suite 303, Laredo 78040.
Telephone: (956) 523-4340.
Fax: (956) 523-5058
E-mail address: bmorales@webbcounty.com

MORALES, David *(Judge, Zapata County Court)*
Mailing address: P.O. Box 99, Zapata 78076-0099.
Telephone: (956) 765-9920.

MORGAN, Dorothy *(Judge, Washington County Court)* Elected Nov 6, 1990 to term beginning Jan 1, 1991. Reelected Nov 8, 1994, 1998 and 2002. Current term expires Dec 31, 2006. Born Bleiblerville Texas Oct 29, 1946. Catholic.

Mayor Brenham 1982-90. Member Texas Municipal League (President, Director, member Legislative Policy Committee on Finance and General Municipal Affairs, Resolutions Committee). Recipient Outstanding Young Woman of America Award. Listed in *Who's Who of Outstanding Southern Women* and *Who's Who of American Teachers.* Moderator Texas Municipal League State Annual Conference and Texas Council of Mayors, Councilmen and Commissioners. Teacher Brenham Independent School District for fourteen years. Keynote speaker Republican State Convention 1990. Chairman Sesquicentennial Committee of Brenham/Washington County and Brazos Valley Development Council Regional Review Committee. Director Brenham/Washington County Arts Council, Brenham State School Volunteer Services, 4-H Council, Brazos Valley Development Council, Brenham Outreach Advisory Council and Texas Public Power Association. Vice President Board of Directors Mental Health/Mental Retardation of Brazos Valley. Trustee and Secretary Texas Council of Community Health and Mental Retardation Centers, Inc.

Office: 100 East Main, Suite 104, Brenham 77833.
Telephone: (979) 277-6200.

MORGAN, James E. *(Judge, Texas District Court 220th Judicial District)* Elected to term beginning Jan 1, 1983. Reelected 1986, 1990, 1994, 1998 and 2002. Current term expires Dec 31, 2006. Born Gorman Texas May 21, 1948. Methodist. Educated at Tarleton State University B.S. with honors 1970, Texas A&M University M.S. 1973 and University of Texas J.D. 1976. Admitted to practice Texas 1976, U.S. Supreme Court 1980 and U.S. District Court Northern District of Texas 1981. In legal practice De Leon 1976-78 and 1980-81 and Comanche 1980-81.

Administrative Assistant and General Counsel for Congressman Charles Stenholm 1979-80. Assistant Professor of Business Administration Law Tarleton State University 1976-78. Member Judicial College of the State Bar of Texas since 1986.

Office: County Courthouse, Comanche 76442.
Telephone: (325) 356-5202.

MORRIS, John *(Judge, Cooke County Court at Law)*
Office: 100 South Dixon, Gainesville 76240.
Telephone: (940) 668-5491.

MORRIS, Joseph B. *(Justice, Texas Court of Appeals Fifth District)* Term expires Dec 31, 2006. Former Judge, Texas District Court 101st Judicial District.

Office: George Allen Sr. Courts Building, 600 Commerce Street, Dallas 75202-4658.
Telephone: (214) 712-3407.

MORRIS, Rick *(Judge, Texas District Court 146th Judicial District)* Appointed by Governor William P. Clements to term beginning May 18, 1989. Elected Nov 1990, Nov 1992 and 1996 and Nov 2000. Current term expires Dec 31, 2004. Local Administrative District Judge Bell County. Born Gatesville Texas Sept 20, 1950. Church of Christ. Educated at University of Texas B.B.A. 1973 and Baylor University School of Law J.D. 1975. Member Phi Alpha Delta. Admitted to practice Texas 1975 and U.S. District Court Western District of Texas. In legal practice Killeen 1975-89.

Assistant U.S. Attorney Southern District of Texas

MORRIS, RICK—*Continued*
March 1989 to April 1989. Director Texas Center for the Judiciary, Inc. 1994-97. Member Advisory Committee on Child Support and Visitation Guidelines Texas Supreme Court 1992-93. Member Texas Bar Foundation, College of the State Bar of Texas, State Bar of Texas (Grievance Committee District B-C 1982-89) and Bell-Lampasas Counties (President 1982-83) Bar Association.
Mailing address: P.O. Box 747, Belton 76513-0747.
Telephone: (254) 933-5261.
Fax: (254) 933-5358

MORRISS, Josh R., III *(Chief Justice, Texas Court of Appeals Sixth District)* Appointed by Governor Rick Perry June 2002. Elected Nov 2002. Educated at Southern Methodist University B.S. M.B.A.
Office: Bi-State Justice Building, 100 North State Line No. 20, Texarkana 75501-5666.
Telephone: (903) 798-3046.

MORROW, William C. *(Judge, Midland County Court)*
Office: 200 West Wall, Suite 6, Midland 79701-4547.
Telephone: (915) 688-1147.

MOSELEY, James A. *(Justice, Texas Court of Appeals Fifth District)* Term expires Dec 31, 2006.
Office: George Allen Sr. Courts Building, 600 Commerce Street, Dallas 75202-4658.
Telephone: (214) 712-3413.

MOTHERAL, Linda *(Judge, Texas District Court 257th Judicial District)*
Office: Family Law Center Building, Sixth Floor, 1115 Congress Avenue, Houston 77002.
Telephone: (713) 755-6950.

MULVANEY, Thomas F. *(Judge, Texas District Court 279th Judicial District)* Elected Nov 1998. Reelected 2002, current term expires Dec 31, 2006. Born Louisville Kentucky June 24, 1950. Roman Catholic. Educated at University of Houston B.A. 1972 J.D. 1975. Member Phi Delta Phi and Order of Barons. Admitted to practice Texas 1975, U.S. District Court Eastern District of Texas 1978 and U.S. Supreme Court 1978. In legal practice Beaumont 1978-98.
Assistant Criminal District Attorney 1975-78.
Office: 1149 Pearl Street, Beaumont 77701-3707.
Telephone: (409) 835-8655.
E-mail address: mulvaney@co.jefferson.tx.us

MUNIZ, Cynthia L. *(Judge, Texas District Court 293rd Judicial District)*
Mailing address: P.O. Drawer 4360, Eagle Pass 78853-4360.
Office: 500 Quarry Street, Eagle Pass, 78852.
Telephone: (830) 758-1730.

MURPHY, Mary *(Judge, Texas District Court 14th Judicial District)*
Office: George Allen Sr. Courts Building, Third Floor, 600 Commerce Street, Dallas 75202-4606.
Telephone: (214) 653-6000.

MURRAH, Watt *(Judge, Medina County Court at Law)*
Office: County Courthouse, Hondo 78861.
Telephone: (830) 741-6061.

MURRAY, Menton, Jr. *(Judge, Texas District Court 103rd Judicial District)* Elected to term beginning Dec 8, 1988. Reelected 1990, 1994, 1998 and 2002. Current term expires Dec 31, 2006. Local Administrative Judge Cameron and Willacy Counties 1997-2000. Born Harlingen Texas Feb 21, 1942. Catholic. Educated at University of Texas B.A. 1964 J.D. 1966. Member Phi Alpha Delta. Admitted to practice Texas 1966 and U.S. District Court Southern District of Texas 1968. In legal practice Harlingen 1968-80 and Brownsville 1987-88. Judge, Cameron County Court at Law No. 2, 1980-84. Judge, Texas District Court 357th Judicial District 1985-86.
Assistant Attorney General Texas 1966-68. Assistant District Attorney Cameron County 1970-73. Adjunct Professor Reynaldo Garza School of Law 1984-85. Member State Bar of Texas and Cameron County Bar Association. Democrat.
Office: 974 East Harrison Street, Brownsville 78520.
Telephone: (956) 544-0844.

NAISER, Lawrence E. *(Judge, Wharton County Court)*
Office: 103 South Fulton, Wharton 77488.
Telephone: (979) 532-4612.

NALL, Rayburn M. "Rim", Jr. *(Judge, Texas District Court 59th Judicial District)*
Office: 200 South Crockett, Suite 218A, Sherman 75090.
Telephone: (903) 813-4305.

NANCARROW, Mark *(Judge, Texas District Court 204th Judicial District)*
Office: LB 29 Frank Crowley Courts Building, 133 North Industrial Boulevard, Dallas 75207-4313.
Telephone: (214) 653-5830.

NANCE, Wayne *(Judge, Briscoe County Court)* Elected to term beginning Jan 1, 2003. Born Tulia Texas Sept 22, 1946.
Mailing address: P.O. Box 153, Silverton 79257.
Telephone: (806) 823-2131.

NARANJO, Orlinda L. *(Judge, Travis County Court at Law No. 2)*
Mailing address: P.O. Box 1748, Austin 78767-1748.
Telephone: (512) 854-9242.

NARSUTIS, John Keith *(Judge, Texas District Court 16th Judicial District)* Elected Nov 1984 to term beginning Jan 1, 1985. Reelected Nov 8, 1988, Nov 1992, 1996 and 2000. Current term expires Dec 31, 2004. Born Oak Park Illinois March 23, 1948. Baptist. Educated at Baylor University B.A. 1970 J.D. 1972. Admitted to practice Texas 1972. In legal practice Denton 1975-84. Judge, Texas District Court 158th Judicial District 1982-84.
Assistant City Attorney Denton 1973-75. Author "Procedural Aspects of Restraining the Real Estate Foreclosure Sale" Dec 1988 and "Review of Contempt Rulings by Appellate Courts in Texas" April 1989 Texas B. Jour., "District Court Relationship to County Government" *County Progress* 1990 and "Alibi in Texas Courts" 1990 and "Boutwell and the Rodriguez Dilemma" 1991 Texas B. Jour. Instructor Texas Woman's University 1976. Named Outstanding Republican Volunteer Denton County 1986. Past President Dentex Title Company. Republican. Chairman President Ford Campaign 1976, Denton County Republican Party 1977 and Will Garwood for Supreme Court Campaign. Steering Committee Dick Armey for Congress 1984. Board of Directors and Executive Board Texas Area 5 Health

NARSUTIS, JOHN KEITH—*Continued*

Systems Agency 1976-77. Coach first and second grade YMCA football 1978 and second and third grade YMCA baseball 1988. President University Drive Kiwanis 1980. Chairman Denton County Juvenile Board 1986. Member Denton United Way (Budget and Admissions Committee 1978-80). Co-chairman Denton County Family Violence Task Force 1985. Youth soccer coach 1993-95. Enjoys reading, writing, athletics and music.

Office: 1450 East McKinney Street, Suite 3330, Denton 76209-4524.

Telephone: (940) 349-2310.

NEELY, Cecil N. *(Judge, Madison County Court)* Elected Nov 8, 1994 to term beginning Jan 1, 1995. Reelected 1998 and 2002. Current term expires Dec 31, 2006. Born Navasota Texas Nov 23, 1933. Methodist. Educated at University of Nebraska B.G.S. 1970 and Sam Houston State University M.A. 1971.

Brigadier General U.S. Army (retired). Past President Madisonville Sidewalk Cattlemen's Association and Madison County Historical Commission. Director Madison County Economic Development Corporation. Director and Former Chairman Brazos Valley Council of Governments. Enjoys hunting, fishing and golfing.

Office: 101 West Main, Room 110, Madisonville 77864-1990.

Telephone: (936) 348-2670.

Fax: (936) 348-2690

E-mail address: general@madisoncountytx.org

NEELY, Tom A. *(Judge, Texas District Court 46th Judicial District)*

Office: 1700 Wilbarger Street, Room 34A, Vernon 76384-4749.

Telephone: (940) 552-7051.

NEILL, John Edward *(Judge, Texas District Court 18th Judicial District)*

Office: Two North Main Street, Second Floor, Cleburne 76031-5573.

Telephone: (817) 556-6820.

NELLERMOE, Barbara Hanson *(Judge, Texas District Court 45th Judicial District)*

Office: 402 Bexar County Courthouse, 100 Dolorosa Street, San Antonio 78205-3028.

Telephone: (210) 335-2507.

NELMS, John *(Judge, Texas District Court 195th Judicial District)* Elected to term beginning Nov 18, 1992. Reelected Nov 8, 1994, Nov 1998 and 2002. Current term expires Dec 31, 2006. Born Dallas Texas Nov 16, 1934. Roman Catholic. Educated at Texas A&M University B.A. 1956 and University of Texas LL.B. 1963. Member Delta Theta Phi. Admitted to practice Texas 1963 and U.S. District Court Northern District of Texas 1965. In legal practice Dallas 1965-88.

Assistant District Attorney Dallas County 1963-65 and 1988-92. Member Texas District and County Attorneys Association, Texas Criminal Defense Lawyers Association, State Bar of Texas, Dallas Criminal and Dallas Bar Associations. Attended The National Judicial College 1993. First Lieutenant USAF 1957-60. Republican.

Office: LB 27 Frank Crowley Courts Building, 133 North Industrial Boulevard, Dallas 75207-4313.

Telephone: (214) 653-5812.

NEWSOM, Robert E. *(Judge, Texas District Court 8th Judicial District)* Elected March 14, 1996 to term beginning Jan 1, 1997. Reelected 2000, current term expires Dec 31, 2004. Born Mount Vernon Texas June 25, 1951. Protestant. Educated at East Texas State University B.S.B.A. 1974 and Texas Tech University School of Law J.D. 1986. Admitted to practice Texas 1987. In legal practice Sulphur Springs 1987-97.

Assistant District Attorney 1987-92. County Attorney 1992-96. Member State Bar of Texas and Northeast Texas Bar Association.

Office: Hopkins County Courthouse, Third Floor, Sulphur Springs 75482.

Telephone: (903) 438-4022.

NOLEN, Ben *(Judge, Tom Green County Court at Law)*

Office: 122 West Harris, San Angelo 76903.

Telephone: (915) 659-6559.

NOTZON, Marcel C. *(Magistrate Judge, United States District Court Southern District of Texas)* Appointed by U.S. District Court judges.

Mailing address: P.O. Box 1241, Laredo 78042-1241.

Telephone: (956) 726-2209.

NOWAK, Nancy Stein *(Magistrate Judge, United States District Court Western District of Texas)* Appointed by U.S. District Court judges to term beginning June 19, 1989. Served part time. Reappointed 1993 and 2001. Current term expires 2009. Born Des Moines Iowa Sept 17, 1952. Presbyterian. Educated at Drake University B.A. 1974 M.A. 1976 and George Washington University J.D. 1980. Staff member Journal of International Law and Economics 1979-80. Law Clerk to Hon. Edward C. Prado and Hon. Jamie C. Boyd, U.S. District Court Western District of Texas and Hon. James D. Hodges, Jr., U.S. District Court Northern District of Iowa 1981-87. Admitted to practice District of Columbia 1980, U.S. Claims Court 1981, U.S. Tax Court 1981, Iowa 1982, Texas 1986, U.S. District Courts District of Columbia 1981, Northern District of Iowa 1982 and Western District of Texas 1985 and U.S. Courts of Appeals District of Columbia 1981 and Eighth 1982 Circuits. In legal practice District of Columbia 1980-81.

Assistant U.S. Trustee 1988-89 and Assistant U.S. Attorney 1987-88 Western District of Texas U.S. Department of Justice. Author "Trade Agreements Act of 1979" 14 Journal of International Law and Economics 63, 1979 and "Managerial Restructuring" 56 *Notre Dame Lawyer* 120, 1980. Board of Editors Federal Courts Law Review. Member Bexar County Women's Bar Association and San Antonio Bar Association (Chairperson Decision Annotations Committee since 1987). Attended Mediation training Attorney-Mediators Institute 1992. Recipient Young Alumni Achievement Award Drake University 1990. Member Leadership San Antonio 1990-91.

Office: U.S. Courthouse, 655 H. F. Garcia Boulevard, San Antonio 78206-1198.

Telephone: (210) 472-6363.

NOWLIN, James R. *(Chief Judge, United States District Court Western District of Texas)* Appointed for life by President Ronald Reagan to term beginning Nov 6, 1981. Chief Judge since Dec 1, 2000. Born San Antonio Texas Nov 21, 1937. Presbyterian. Educated at Trinity University B.A. 1959 M.A. 1962 and University of Texas at Austin J.D. 1963. Admitted to practice Texas

NOWLIN, JAMES R.—*Continued*

1963, U.S. District Courts District of Columbia 1966 and Western District of Texas 1971, U.S. Court of Claims 1969, U.S. Supreme Court 1969 and Colorado 1993. Began legal practice San Antonio Texas 1963.

Instructor in U.S. History and U.S. Government San Antonio College 1964 and 1971-73. Member U.S. District Judges Association, State Bar of Texas, San Antonio, Travis County, Colorado and American Bar Associations. Captain USAR 1959-68 (active duty 1959-60). Associate Legal Counsel Labor and Public Welfare Committee U.S. Senate 1965-66. Member House of Representatives Texas 1967-71 and 1973-81.

Office: U.S. Courthouse, 200 West Eighth Street, Austin 78701.

Telephone: (512) 916-5675.

NUCHIA, Samuel M. *(Justice, Texas Court of Appeals First District)* Elected to term beginning Jan 1, 1997. Reelected 2002, current term expires Dec 31, 2008.

Office: 1307 San Jacinto, Tenth Floor, Houston 77002-7006.

Telephone: (713) 655-2700.

OAKLEY, Bruce *(Judge, Texas District Court 234th Judicial District)*

Office: 1310 Prairie, Eleventh Floor, Houston 77002.

Telephone: (713) 755-6263.

OAKLEY, Gladys M. *(Judge, Austin County Court at Law)* Appointed to term beginning Jan 1, 1986. Elected 1986, 1990, 1994, 1998 and 2002. Current term expires Dec 31, 2006. Born Bleiblerville Texas Aug 15, 1926. Lutheran. Educated at University of Houston B.B.A. 1951 J.D. 1957. Member Kappa Beta Pi. Admitted to practice Texas 1957. In legal practice Bellville 1969-86.

Board of Directors Texas Center for the Judiciary 1999-2002. Member State Bar of Texas and Austin County Bar Association (Past President, Past Secretary, Treasurer). Secretary Houston Transit Company 1944-50 and Transcontinental Gas Pipeline Corporation 1950-57. Assistant Corporate Secretary Transco 1957-69. Republican. Democratic Precinct Chairman Houston 1960-68. Republican Precinct Chairman 1970-86. Board of Directors Bellville General Hospital 1989-95, Bellville Hospital Foundation and Boys and Girls Club of Bellville. Board of Trustees St. Mary's Episcopal Church Day School. Advisory Board Raising Academic Performance. Member Bluebonnet Society, Friends of Lifeline, Bellville Golf and Recreation Club and United Daughters of the Confederacy. Enjoys gardening and bridge.

Office: One East Main, Bellville 77418-1598.

Telephone: (979) 865-5911.

OLDNER, Chris *(Judge, Collin County Court at Law No. 5)*

Office: 1800 North Graves, Suite 130, McKinney 75069.

Telephone: (972) 548-3850.

OLIVARES, Kathleen H. *(Judge, Texas District Court 205th Judicial District)*

Office: 500 East San Antonio Avenue, Room 1002, El Paso 79901-2457.

Telephone: (915) 546-2107.

OLSEN, Rory R. *(Judge, Harris County Probate Court No. 3)*

Office: Family Law Center Building, Fifth Floor, 1115 Congress Street, Houston 77002.

Telephone: (713) 755-6953.

O'NEILL, Harriet *(Justice, Texas Supreme Court)* Elected Nov 1998 to term beginning Jan 1, 1999. Term expires Dec 31, 2004. Educated at University College Oxford, England, Converse College B.A. with honors 1978 and University of South Carolina J.D. 1982. Member Society of Wig and Robe. Admitted to practice Texas 1982. In legal practice Houston 1982-92. Judge, Texas District Court 152nd Judicial District 1993-95. Justice, Texas Court of Appeals Fourteenth District 1995-98, appointed by Governor George W. Bush.

Co-author with M. Cotham "The DTPA Letter: A Potential Pitfall and Ally" *The Houston Lawyer* Jan-Feb 1986; with Kelly Kirkland "Through a Glass Darkly: The Statutory Injunction in Texas" Texas B. Jour. Jan 1989; with B. Keeling "Damages: Evidentiary Requirements and Proof Techniques" *How to Offer and Exclude Evidence* University of Houston CLE March 1995, March 1996 and Feb 1997, "Actual and Punitive Damages" 20th Annual Advanced Civil Trial Course State Bar of Texas Fall 1997 and "Damages Update" Litigation Update Institute State Bar of Texas Jan 15-16, 1999; and with L. Coe "Recent Cases and Developing Issues in Tort and Insurance Law" Law Update Seminar for Insurance and Risk Management Professionals May 8, 1996. Author *Appealing Damage Awards* HYLA Pocket Parts Jan 1996, "Appealing Summary Judgments" *The Texas Law Reporter* Jan 1996 and "Trial Tactics and Common Errors" Medical Malpractice Conference Texas Trial Lawyers Association 1997. Advisory Board *Advocacy in Mediation* The CLE Institute Oct 1996. Guest Speaker Thurgood Marshall School of Law Lecture Series April 1997. Panelist "Nuts and Bolts of Administering a Mediation Docket" Texas Center for Advanced Judicial Studies Austin 1993.

Mailing address: P.O. Box 12248, Austin 78711-2248.

Telephone: (512) 463-1320.

O'NEILL, Michael J. *(Justice, Texas Court of Appeals Fifth District)* Elected to term beginning Jan 1, 1999. Term expires Dec 31, 2004. Born Tyler Texas March 7, 1939. Roman Catholic. Educated at Massachusetts Institute of Technology B.S. 1961, University of Kansas Ph.D. with honors in Mathematics 1969, Northwestern University 1971 and University of Notre Dame Law School J.D. 1976. Admitted to practice Texas 1976 and U.S. District Court Northern District of Texas 1980. In legal practice Dallas 1976-85. Judge, Dallas County Court at Law No. 1, 1985-89. Judge, Texas District Court 193rd Judicial District 1989-99.

Instructor University of Kansas 1963-69. Professor of Mathematics Northwestern University 1970-72 and University of Notre Dame 1972-75. Charter Member William "Mac" Taylor American Inn of Court. Member College of the State Bar of Texas, State Bar of Texas (Member since 1987 and Chairman Computer Subcommittee 1988 P.E.E.R. Committee) and Dallas Bar Association. Alternate Delegate 1982 and Delegate 1984 and 1986 Republican State Conventions. Volunteer GOP National Convention 1984. Participant Dallas County Republican Party Voter Registration Drive 1982-86. Member Greater Dallas Community Relations Committee (Chairman Education Committee 1980-82, Commissioner

O'NEILL, MICHAEL J.—*Continued*

1980-84, Chairman Justice Committee 1982-84), The Institute for Advanced Study, Dallas Women's Education and Employment, Inc. (Board of Directors, Vice Chairman of the Board 1980-84), Sons of the American Revolution, St. Patrick's Church (President Men's Club 1983-84, Treasurer Parent Teacher Association 1984-85), Boy Scouts of America Pack 719 (Commissioner 1984-85, Treasurer 1985-86) and Texas Fund Raising Board 1984-85 Massachusetts Institute of Technology.

Office: George Allen Sr. Courts Building, 600 Commerce Street, Dallas 75202.
Telephone: (214) 712-3406.

OWEN, Priscilla R. *(Justice, Texas Supreme Court)* Elected 1994 to term beginning Jan 1, 1995. Reelected 2000, current term expires Dec 31, 2006. Born Palacios Texas Oct 4, 1954. Episcopalian. Educated at Baylor University B.A. with honors 1976 J.D. with honors 1977. Staff member Baylor Law Review. Admitted to practice Texas 1978 and U.S. Courts of Appeals Fourth, Fifth, Eighth and Eleventh Circuits. In legal practice Houston 1978-94.

Fellow Houston Bar Foundation and American Bar Foundation. Member The American Law Institute, American Judicature Society and Houston Bar Association. Named Young Lawyer of the Year and Outstanding Young Alumna by Baylor University. Republican. Board Member Texas Hearing and Service Dogs.

Mailing address: P.O. Box 12248, Austin 78711-2248.
Telephone: (512) 463-1344.

OWENS, Jerome *(Judge, Tyler County Court)*
Office: 100 West Bluff, Room 102, Woodville 75979-5245.
Telephone: (409) 283-2141.

OWENS, Mark D. *(Judge, Ector County Court at Law No. 2)* Elected March 1994 to term beginning Jan 1, 1995. Reelected 1998 and 2002. Current term expires Dec 31, 2006. Born Monroe Louisiana March 21, 1961. Protestant. Educated at University of Texas B.B.A. 1983 and South Texas College of Law J.D. 1986. Admitted to practice Texas 1987, U.S. District Courts Northern 1987 and Western 1991 Districts of Texas, U.S. Court of Appeals Fifth Circuit 1988 and U.S. Court of Federal Claims 1988. In legal practice Dallas and Odessa.

Member Texas Trial Lawyers Association, The Association of Trial Lawyers of America, Texas Association of County Court at Law Judges (Secretary-Treasurer 1996-97), U.S. Court of Federal Claims Bar Association, State Bar of Texas and American Bar Association. Republican.

Office: 300 North Grant, Room 235, Odessa 79761.
Telephone: (432) 498-4120.

PALMER, Bill R. *(Judge, Kendall County Court at Law)*
Office: 201 East San Antonio, Suite 201, Boerne 78006.
Telephone: (830) 249-9343.

PARISH, Lauren L. *(Judge, Texas District Court 115th Judicial District)*
Mailing address: P.O. Box 1052, Gilmer 75644-1052.
Telephone: (903) 843-2836.

PARKER, Bill G. *(Judge, United States Bankruptcy Court Eastern District of Texas)* Appointed by U.S. Court of Appeals Fifth Circuit judges to term beginning Oct 30, 1998. Term expires Oct 2012.

Office: 200 East Ferguson Street, First Floor, Tyler 75702.
Telephone: (903) 590-1212.

PARKER, Laura *(Judge, Texas District Court 386th Judicial District)* Appointed by Governor George W. Bush to term beginning Sept 1999. Elected 2000, current term expires Dec 2004. Born Austin Texas March 7, 1965. Episcopalian. Educated at Vassar College B.A. 1987 and St. Mary's University of San Antonio School of Law J.D. cum laude 1992. Recipient American Jurisprudence Awards in Labor Law, Jurisprudence and Wills and Estates. Member Phi Delta Phi. Admitted to practice Texas 1992.

Assistant District Attorney Bexar County Jan 1993 to Sept 1999. Member Texas Center for the Judiciary, Inc., American Inns of Court, National Council of Juvenile and Family Court Judges, National Association of Women Judges, Bexar County Women's Bar Association, State Bar of Texas and San Antonio Bar Association. Guest Lecturer Sexual Assault Nurse Examiner's Course 1997 and 1998, Juvenile Law Institute Aug 1998 and Healthy Families Association March 2001. Member Alamo Heights Board of Adjustment June 1996 to Sept 1999. Board of Directors Rape Crisis Center June 1998 to Sept 1999 and Communities in Schools since April 2001. Member Rotary Club of San Antonio and Women's Leadership Council United Way. Enjoys playing tennis.

Office: 235 East Mitchell, San Antonio 78210.
Telephone: (210) 531-1055.

PARKS, Bob *(Judge, Texas District Court 143rd Judicial District)* Assumed office July 21, 1986. Elected 1986, 1988, 1992, 1996 and 2000. Current term expires Dec 31, 2004.

Mailing address: P.O. Box 205, Monahans 79756-0205.
Telephone: (915) 943-2749.

PARNELL, Joe Michael *(Judge, Kaufman County Court at Law)*
Office: 100 West Mulberry, Kaufman 75142.
Telephone: (972) 932-4331.

PARSONS, James N., III *(Judge, Texas District Court 3rd Judicial District)*
Office: 500 North Church Street, Palestine 75801.
Telephone: (903) 723-7415.

PARTIDA, Juan R. *(Judge, Texas District Court 275th Judicial District)* Elected to term beginning Dec 9, 1988. Reelected 1990, 1994, 1998 and 2002. Current term expires Dec 31, 2006. Born Edinburg Texas. Educated at University of Texas B.A. 1974 J.D. 1977. Admitted to practice Texas 1977. Judge, Hidalgo County Court at Law No. 1, 1986-88.

Chairman Hidalgo County Bail Bond Board May 1989 to May 1991. Member College of the State Bar of Texas, Texas Center for the Judiciary, Inc., State Bar of Texas and Hidalgo County Bar Association. Attended Texas College for New Judges Texas Judicial College 1986 and Advanced Evidence Course The National Judi-

PARTIDA, JUAN R.—*Continued*

cial College July 1989. Democrat. Enjoys tennis, jogging, swimming and football.

Office: 100 North Closner, Second Floor, Edinburg 78539.

Telephone: (956) 318-2270.

PASK, Neil Edward *(Judge, Dallas County Criminal Court at Law No. 2)*

Office: LB 15 Frank Crowley Courts Building, 133 North Industrial Boulevard, Dallas 75207-4313.

Telephone: (214) 653-5617.

PATTERSON, Jan Powell *(Justice, Texas Court of Appeals Third District)* Elected Nov 1998 to term beginning Jan 1, 1999. Term expires Dec 31, 2004. Born Austin Texas. Educated at University of Texas B.A. J.D. Law Clerk to Hon. Harold R. Tyler, Jr., U.S. District Court Southern District of New York. Admitted to practice Texas 1973, New York 1973 and U.S. District Courts Eastern, Northern and Western Districts of Texas and Eastern, Northern and Southern Districts of New York. In legal practice New York and Austin Texas.

Former Assistant U.S. Attorney Southern District of New York and Western District of Texas. Former Senior Special Prosecutor. Visiting Professor and Adjunct Professor University of Texas. Past President Litigation Section State Bar of Texas. Trustee Texas Center for Legal Ethics and Professionalism. Member Supreme Court Advisory Committee.

Mailing address: P.O. Box 12547, Austin 78711-2547.

Office: 209 West Fourteenth Street, Austin 78701.

Telephone: (512) 463-1688.

Fax: (512) 463-1685

PATTERSON, Jay *(Judge, Texas District Court 101st Judicial District)*

Office: George Allen Sr. Courts Building, Fourth Floor, 600 Commerce Street, Dallas 75202-4606.

Telephone: (214) 653-6937.

PATTERSON, Jimmy P. *(Judge, La Salle County Court)*

Office: 105 Courthouse Square, Cotulla 78014.

Telephone: (830) 879-4430.

PAVLICK, Juanita *(Judge, Texas District Court 89th Judicial District)*

Office: 900 Seventh Street, Room 300, Wichita Falls 76301.

Telephone: (940) 766-8184.

PEAVY, Stanley H., III *(Judge, Young County Court)*

Office: 5160 Fourth Street, Room 108, Graham 76450.

Telephone: (940) 549-2030.

PEDEN, Michael Parker *(Judge, Texas District Court 285th Judicial District)* Appointed by Governor William P. Clements to term beginning Feb 3, 1989. Elected Nov 1989, Nov 19, 1994, 1998 and 2002. Current term expires Dec 31, 2006. Born San Antonio Texas Feb 10, 1950. Methodist. Educated at Texas Tech University B.A. 1972 and St. Mary's University J.D. 1975. Admitted to practice Texas 1975. Justice of the Peace Precinct 3, 1983-85. Judge, Bexar County Court at Law No. 8 June 1, 1985 to Feb 2, 1989.

Member San Antonio Bar Association.

Office: Bexar County Courthouse, 100 Dolorosa Street, San Antonio 78205-3028.

Telephone: (210) 335-2086.

PEEK, Bill *(Judge, Texas District Court 202nd Judicial District)*

Office: 100 North State Line, Box 10, Texarkana 75501.

Telephone: (903) 798-3004.

PEEK, Powell W. *(Judge, Red River County Court)*

Office: 200 North Walnut Street, Clarksville 75426.

Telephone: (903) 427-2680.

PEEPLES, David *(Judge, Texas District Court 224th Judicial District)* Elected to term beginning Jan 1, 1995. Reelected Nov 1998 and Nov 2002. Current term expires Dec 31, 2006. Presiding Judge, Fourth Administrative Judicial Region since 1996. Born Fort Worth Texas Nov 6, 1945. Presbyterian. Educated at Austin College B.A. 1967 and University of Texas M.A. 1970 J.D. 1974. Note and Comment Editor Texas Law Review 1973-74. Admitted to practice Texas 1974. Board Certified—Civil Trial Law—Texas Board of Legal Specialization. Began legal practice Houston 1974. In legal practice San Antonio 1977. Judge, Texas District Court 285th Judicial District 1981-88, appointed by Governor William P. Clements. Justice, Texas Court of Appeals Fourth District Nov 29, 1988 to Dec 31, 1994.

Member National Conference of Commissioners on Uniform State Laws 1987-99 and Texas Supreme Court Advisory Committee on Rules since 1993. Member State Bar of Texas (CLE Committee 1980-83, Administration of Justice Committee 1988-91, Chairman 1989-90) and San Antonio Bar Association (Fee Dispute Committee 1979-81). Republican. Enjoys carpentry, hiking, reading and children.

Office: 400 Bexar County Courthouse, 100 Dolorosa Street, San Antonio 78205-3028.

Telephone: (210) 335-2132.

PEET, Richard *(Judge, Gray County Court)*

Office: 315 North Ballard Street, Pampa 79065-6541.

Telephone: (806) 669-8007.

PENDERGRASS, Carl *(Judge, Texas District Court 83rd Judicial District)*

Mailing address: P.O. Box 1860, Del Rio 78841-1860.

Telephone: (830) 774-7654.

PENNINGTON, Mickey Ray *(Judge, Texas District Court 38th Judicial District)* Term expires Dec 31, 2004.

Office: 17 County Courthouse, Uvalde 78801-5239.

Telephone: (830) 278-3913.

PERKINS, Robert Anton *(Judge, Texas District Court 331st Judicial District)* Appointed by Governor William P. Clements to term beginning Sept 1, 1982. Elected 1982, 1986, 1990, 1994, 1998 and 2002. Current term expires Dec 31, 2006. Born Laredo Texas Oct 27, 1947. Catholic. Educated at University of Texas B.A. 1970 J.D. 1973. Admitted to practice Texas 1973. Began legal practice Austin 1973. Justice of the Peace, Precinct 4 Travis County 1975-80. Judge, Travis County Court at Law No. 2, 1980-82.

Member College of the State Bar of Texas, State Bar

PERKINS, ROBERT ANTON—*Continued*

of Texas (Judicial Section since 1982) and Travis County Bar Association. Author and Lecturer on Texas Criminal Jury Charges. Democrat. Active in Tejano Democrats of Texas. Board of Directors Pan American Recreation Center 1975-82 and Center for Battered Women of Austin 1978-80. Member Austin Human Relations Commission 1977-79.

Mailing address: P.O. Box 1748, Austin 78767-1748.
Telephone: (512) 854-9443.

PESCHEL, Dwight E. *(Judge, Texas District Court 25th Judicial District)*

Office: 101 East Court Street, Room 203, Seguin 78155-5742.
Telephone: (830) 303-4188.

PESEK, Leon F., Jr. *(Judge, Bowie County Court at Law)*

Mailing address: P.O. Box 248, New Boston 75570-0248.
Telephone: (903) 628-6835.

PETERS, Michael Allen *(Judge, Harris County Criminal Court at Law No. 2)* Elected to term beginning Jan 1, 1991. Reelected 1994, 1998 and 2002. Current term expires Dec 31, 2006. Born Fairfield Ohio Feb 5, 1945. Roman Catholic. Educated at St. Thomas University B.A. 1967 and University of Houston Law Center J.D. 1973. In legal practice Texas Sept 1973 to Dec 1991.

Member Association of County Court Judges of Texas and American Judges Association. Participant The National Judicial College. Speaker Advanced Evidence Course State Bar of Texas, Certification Course for Court Appointed Lawyers Harris County and Advanced Criminal Law Seminar. Recipient Presidential Award from Harris County Criminal Defense Lawyers 1994. Named County Criminal Court Judge of the Year by P.O.L.I.C.E. Organization 1997. First Lieutenant U.S. Army Nov 1967 to Aug 1970. Republican. Former Board Member Wood Forest Civic Association. Former Volunteer Children's Miracle Telethon. Former Member Lions Club. Board of Directors Santa Maria Hostel. Cofounder OCS 514 Vietnam Veterans Group. Volunteer Mentor Program Houston Bar Association and Houston Trial Lawyers Foundation for JFK Elementary School Project. Keynote Speaker Veteran's Day Program Spring Forest Middle School. Member Houston Council on Drugs and Alcohol and St. Cecilia Catholic Community. Interests include Harley Davidson motorcycles. Personal Statement or Quote: "No whining."

Office: 1201 Franklin, Houston 77002.
Telephone: (713) 755-6184.
Fax: (832) 467-9966
E-mail address: judgeuno@aol.com

PEYTON, John B. *(Judge, Dallas County Court at Law No. 2)*

Office: Records Building, Third Floor, Dallas 75202-3513.
Telephone: (214) 653-7366.

PFEIFER, Michael *(Judge, Calhoun County Court)*

Office: 211 South Ann Street, Third Floor, Port Lavaca 77979.
Telephone: (361) 553-4600.

PHELAN, Harold *(Judge, Texas District Court 286th Judicial District)*

Office: 802 Houston Street, Suite 315, Levelland 79336-4545.
Telephone: (806) 894-8240.

PHIFER, Dwight L. *(Judge, Texas District Court 2nd Judicial District)* Elected Nov 7, 2000 to term beginning Jan 1, 2001. Term expires Dec 31, 2004. Born Jacksonville Texas March 15, 1951. Methodist. Educated at Southwest Texas State University B.A. 1972 and University of Texas J.D. 1976. Law Clerk to Hon. Tom Coleman, Texas Court of Civil Appeals First District 1976-77. Member Phi Delta Phi. Admitted to practice Texas 1976, U.S. District Court Eastern District of Texas 1978, U.S. Court of Appeals Fifth Circuit 1983 and U.S. Supreme Court 1991. In legal practice Jacksonville 1979-2000.

Member State Bar of Texas. Democrat.
Mailing address: P.O. Box 287, Rusk 75785-0287.
Telephone: (903) 683-2236.

PHILLIPS, J. David *(Judge, Travis County Court at Law No. 1)* Elected March 8, 1988 to term beginning April 15, 1988. Reelected 1990, 1994, 1998 and 2002. Current term expires Dec 31, 2006. Born Southwest City Missouri Sept 2, 1950. Educated at Oklahoma State University B.A. 1972 and University of Texas J.D. 1975. Admitted to practice Texas 1975. In legal practice Austin 1975-79. Associate Judge 1979-82 and Presiding Judge 1982-88 Austin Municipal Court.

Master Robert W. Calvert Inn by American Inns of Court since 2000. Life Fellow Texas Bar Foundation. Member State Bar of Texas (Judicial, Litigation, American Indian Law Sections) and Travis County Bar Association. Recipient "Pride of the City" Award 1986. Democrat. Sustaining Member South Austin Democrats. Board Member 1981-86 and President 1984-86 American Institute for Learning. Member Travis Audubon Society and Leadership Austin.

Mailing address: P.O. Box 1748, Austin 78767-1748.
Telephone: (512) 473-9241.
E-mail address: judge.phillips@co.travis.tx.us

PHILLIPS, John F. *(Judge, Texas Family District Court 314th Judicial District)*

Office: Family Law Center Building, Fourth Floor, 1115 Congress Street, Houston 77002.
Telephone: (713) 755-6475.

PHILLIPS, Stephen *(Judge, Polk County Court at Law)*

Office: 101 West Church Street, Second Floor, Livingston 77351-9401.
Telephone: (936) 327-6856.

PHILLIPS, Thomas R. *(Chief Justice, Texas Supreme Court)* Assumed office 1988. Elected 1990, 1996 and 2002. Current term expires Dec 31, 2008. Born Dallas Texas Oct 23, 1949. Educated at Baylor University B.A. in Political Science summa cum laude 1971 and Harvard Law School J.D. 1974. Honorary LL.D. Texas Tech University 1997. Honorary D.H.L. St. Edward's University 1998. Named Outstanding Political Science Student 1971. Staff member Harvard Journal on Legislation 1972-73. Briefing Attorney to Hon. Ruel C. Walker, Texas Supreme Court 1974-75. Member Delta Theta Phi. Admitted to practice Texas 1974, U.S. District Court Southern District of Texas 1977 and U.S. Court

PHILLIPS, THOMAS R.—*Continued*
of Appeals Fifth Circuit 1977. Board Certified—Civil Trial Law—Texas Board of Legal Specialization. In legal practice Houston 1975-81. Judge, Texas District Court 280th Judicial District 1981-88, appointed by Governor William P. Clements.

Director Center for American and International Law (formerly Southwestern Legal Foundation) since 1992. Chair National Mass Tort Conference Planning Committee 1993-94. Board of Directors 1995-99 and Chair 1997-98 National Center for State Courts. Fellow Houston Bar Foundation, Texas Bar Foundation and American Bar Foundation. Member Administrative Conference of the U.S. (State-Federal Relations Committee 1990-96), The American Law Institute (Advisor Federal Judicial Code Project 1996-2001), American Judicature Society (Director since 1989), National Conference of Chief Justices (President 1997-98), State Bar of Texas (Member Committee on Judicial Selection, Tenure and Compensation 1981-84, Committee on Administration of Rules of Evidence 1983-88, Chairman Committee on Pattern Jury Charges 1985-88 and Vice-Chairman Committee on Administration of Justice 1986-88), Houston, Bastrop County, Travis County and American (Task Force on Lawyers' Political Contributions 1997-98, Committee on Judicial Selection and Judicial Campaign since 2001) Bar Associations. Recipient Outstanding Young Lawyer of Houston Award 1985-86, Award of Merit from Houston Bar Association 1986-87, Outstanding Texas Leader Award from John Ben Shepperd Public Leadership Forum 1989, Award of Excellence in Government from Texas Chamber of Commerce 1992 and Distinguished Service Award from National Center for State Courts 1999. Inducted into Woodrow Wilson High School Hall of Fame 1989. Named Outstanding Young Alumnus 1989 and Distinguished Alumnus 1998 Baylor University and Appellate Judge of the Year by Texas Association of Civil Trial and Appellate Specialists 1992-93. Advisory Director Review of Litigation since 1990 and Director Institute for Transnational Law since 2000 University of Texas School of Law.

Mailing address: P.O. Box 12248, Austin 78711-2248.
Telephone: (512) 463-1316.

PIERCE, Robert D. "Danny" *(Judge, Walker County Court)*
Office: 1100 University Avenue, Suite 204, Huntsville 77340.
Telephone: (936) 436-4910.

PIRTLE, Patrick A. *(Judge, Texas District Court 251st Judicial District)* Appointed by Governor William P. Clements to term beginning Jan 1, 1989. Elected to subsequent terms. Current term expires Dec 31, 2006. Born Lubbock Texas Aug 28, 1952. Christian. Educated at Texas Tech University B.B.A. with honors 1974 and Texas Tech University J.D. 1977. Member Phi Alpha Delta. Admitted to practice Texas 1974, U.S. District Court Northern District of Texas 1978 and U.S. Court of Appeals Fifth Circuit 1985. In legal practice Amarillo 1977-88. Associate Justice, Texas Court of Appeals Seventh District 1988.

Instructor in Real Estate Law West Texas A&M University 1997. Member State Bar of Texas, Amarillo and American Bar Associations. Republican. Enjoys church and family.

Office: 501 South Fillmore Street, Suite 4-C, Amarillo 79101-2444.
Telephone: (806) 379-2365.
E-mail address: PirtleP@co.potter.tx.us

PLATT, L. Stuart *(Magistrate Judge, United States District Court Western District of Texas)* Appointed by U.S. District Court judges to term beginning Sept 1996. Term expires Sept 2004. Born San Antonio Texas Nov 14, 1952. Christian. Educated at Texas A&M University B.A. 1974, Trinity University M.S. 1977 and St. Mary's University of San Antonio School of Law J.D. 1979. Admitted to practice Texas 1980, U.S. District Court Eastern District of Texas 1981, U.S. Court of Appeals Fifth Circuit 1985, U.S. Supreme Court 1985 and U.S. Army Court of Military Review 1992. In legal practice Greenville 1980-86.

Assistant U.S. Attorney Eastern District of Texas 1986-94 and Eastern District of Tennessee 1994-96. USAR.

Office: 200 East Wall Street, Room 219, Midland 79701.
Telephone: (915) 570-4439.
Fax: (915) 570-4619

PLUNK, Britt *(Judge, Texas District Court 356th Judicial District)* Elected May 5, 1984 to term beginning Jan 1, 1985. Reelected 1988, 1992, 1996 and 2000. Current term expires Dec 31, 2004. Born Beaumont Texas May 10, 1947. Methodist. Educated at Lamar University B.S. 1969 and South Texas College of Law J.D. 1973. Member Phi Alpha Delta. Admitted to practice Texas 1973. In legal practice Silsbee 1973-77.

Assistant District Attorney 88th Judicial District 1977-81. County Attorney Hardin County 1981-85. Member American Judges Association, State Bar of Texas and Hardin County Bar Association. Attended numerous advanced seminars in criminal, family and personal injury law State Bar of Texas. Democrat. Enjoys hunting and cattle ranching.

Mailing address: P.O. Box 640, Kountze 77625-0640.
Telephone: (409) 246-5155.

PODGORSKI, Richard *(Judge, Denton County Criminal Court at Law No. 5)*
Office: 1450 East McKinney Street, Denton 76209.
Telephone: (940) 349-2190.

POE, Ted *(Judge, Texas District Court 228th Judicial District)* Term expires Dec 31, 2006.
Office: 1201 Franklin, Room 16032, Houston 77002.
Telephone: (713) 755-6650.

PONCE, Francisco G. *(Judge, Dimmit County Court)*
Office: 103 North Fifth Street, Carrizo Springs 78834.
Telephone: (830) 876-2323.

POPE, John A., III *(Judge, Texas District Court 381st Judicial District)*
Office: County Courthouse, Third Floor, Rio Grande City 78582.
Telephone: (956) 487-8665.

POPE, Ronald R. *(Judge, Texas Family District Court 328th Judicial District)*
Office: 301 Jackson, Suite 307, Richmond 77469-3110.
Telephone: (281) 341-4406.

PORTER, William Reed *(Judge, Texas District Court 276th Judicial District)* Appointed by Governor William P. Clements to term beginning June 1, 1981. Elected 1982, 1986, 1990, 1994, 1998 and 2002. Current term expires Dec 31, 2006. Born Naples Texas Feb 16, 1942. Baptist. Educated at North Texas State University B.A. 1964 and University of Texas LL.B. 1967. Administrative and Review Editor Texas Law Review 1966-67. Member Phi Delta Phi. Admitted to practice Texas 1967 and California 1971. Began legal practice Daingerfield Texas 1972.

County Attorney Morris County 1974-81. Member State Bar of California, State Bar of Texas and Northeast Texas Bar Association (President 1984-85). Captain USMC 1967-71. Certified as Military Judge by USN JAG 1969. Democrat. Past President Daingerfield Chamber of Commerce and Daingerfield Chapter of Kiwanis International. Enjoys gun, stamp and coin collecting, hunting and fishing.

Mailing address: P.O. Box 480, Daingerfield 75638-0480.

Telephone: (903) 645-2506.

POWELL, Dennis *(Judge, Texas District Court 163rd Judicial District)* Elected to term beginning Jan 1, 2001. Term expires Dec 31, 2004. Born Hope Arkansas Aug 9, 1955. Christian. Educated at Lamar University B.S. with highest honors 1977 and University of Houston J.D. with high honors 1981. Associate Editor Houston Law Review. Member Phi Delta Phi and Board of Advocates. Admitted to practice Texas 1982, U.S. District Court Eastern District of Texas and U.S. Court of Appeals Fifth Circuit. In legal practice Orange 1982-2000.

Member State Bar of Texas and Orange County Bar Association. Teacher and Board Member Community Church.

Office: 801 West Division, Orange 77630-6353.

Telephone: (409) 882-7090.

E-mail address: dpowell@co.orange.tx.us

POWERS, Jim *(Judge, Hays County Court)*

Office: 111 East San Antonio Street, Suite 300, San Marcos 78666.

Telephone: (512) 393-2205.

POWERS, Lewis W. *(Judge, Carson County Court)*

Mailing address: P.O. Box 369, Panhandle 79068.

Telephone: (806) 537-3622.

POZZA, Karen H. *(Judge, Texas District Court 407th Judicial District)* Elected to term beginning Jan 1, 2001. Term expires Dec 31, 2004. Born Azores Sept 28, 1965. Educated at Baylor University B.B.A. 1986 and St. Mary's University of San Antonio J.D. 1991. Recipient American Jurisprudence Awards in Evidence I and Advanced Trial Advocacy. Associate Editor St. Mary's Law Journal. Member Phi Delta Phi and Delta Sigma Pi. Admitted to practice Texas 1991, U.S. District Court Western District of Texas 1992 and U.S. Supreme Court 1996. In legal practice San Antonio 1991-2000.

Author Comment "The Stagnation of Texas Ground Water Law, A Political v. Environmental Stalemate" 22 St. Mary's L. Jour. 493, 1990. Member San Antonio Young Lawyers Association (Director 1992-93, Treasurer 1993-95), Texas Young Lawyers Association (Director 1994-96), William S. Sessions American Inn of Court, San Antonio Bar Foundation, Texas Bar Foundation, Bexar County Women's Bar Association, College of the State Bar of Texas, State Bar of Texas (Personal Injury Practice Manual Committee 1996-2000, Texas Pattern Jury Charge Committee 1998-2001) and San Antonio Bar Association (Director 1997-99, Member Bench Bar Conference Committee 1998-2000, Pro-Bono Committee 1998-2003, Treasurer 1999-2000, Secretary 2000-01, Vice President 2001-02, President Elect 2002-03). Board Member Child Guidance Center 2001-03 and Bexar County Dispute Resolution Center 2001-03.

Office: Bexar County Courthouse, 100 Dolorosa Street, San Antonio 78205.

Telephone: (210) 335-2462.

Fax: (210) 335-1217

E-mail address: kpozza@co.bexar.tx.us

POZZI, Donald R. *(Judge, Victoria County Court)*

Office: 101 North Bridge, Room 102, Victoria 77901-6544.

Telephone: (361) 575-4558.

PRADO, Edward C. *(Judge, United States District Court Western District of Texas)* Appointed for life by President Ronald Reagan to term beginning 1984. Born San Antonio Texas June 7, 1947. Educated at University of Texas B.A. 1969 J.D. 1972. Judge, Texas District Court 187th Judicial District 1980.

Assistant District Attorney Bexar County 1972-76. Assistant Public Defender 1976-80 and U.S. Attorney 1981-84 Western District of Texas.

Office: U.S. Courthouse, 655 East Durango Boulevard, San Antonio 78206-1198.

Telephone: (210) 472-4060.

PRAUSE, Ben E. *(Judge, De Witt County Court)*

Office: 307 North Gonzales, Cuero 77954-2970.

Telephone: (361) 275-2116.

PRICE, Robert E. *(Judge, Dallas County Probate Court No. 2)* Appointed 1986. Elected 1986, 1990, 1994, 1998 and 2002. Current term expires Dec 31, 2006. Born Waco Texas Jan 13, 1931. Episcopalian. Educated at Texas A&M College 1949, Southern Methodist University B.A. 1952 LL.B. 1954 LL.M. 1972 and Air War College 1976. Editor-in-Chief Southwestern Law Journal 1953-54. Member Phi Eta Sigma, Phi Alpha Delta and Phi Delta Theta. Admitted to practice Texas 1954, U.S. District Court Northern District of Texas, U.S. Court of Federal Claims, U.S. Court of Military Appeals and U.S. Supreme Court. In legal practice Dallas 1956-86.

Co-author "Rights of a Beneficiary Witness in Texas" Southwestern L. Jour. 1953. Lecturer Southern Methodist University School of Law 1972-73. Member 1976-82 and Chairman 1978-82 and Vice Chairman 1980-82 Legislative and Legal Awareness Subcommittee 1978-82 Texas Governor's Committee on Employment of the Handicapped. Fellow The American College of Trust and Estate Counsel (State Membership Committee 1982-90, Fiduciary Litigation Committee 1991-2002) and Texas Bar Foundation. Member State Bar of Texas, Dallas and American (National Conference of Special Court Judges Judicial Administration Division 1992, Committee on Probate and Surrogate's Courts 1992-96, Committee on Dispute Resolution since 1997 Judicial Administration Division) Bar Associations. Faculty Member Texas College of Probate Judges and National College of Probate Judges. Lecturer Practice Skills Course State Bar of Texas, Legal Assistants Program Southern Methodist University School of Continuing Education and

PRICE, ROBERT E.—*Continued*
Texas Practical Probate Seminar Professional Education Systems, Inc. Colonel USAFR JAGC 1953-82 (active duty 1954-56; retired). Republican. Trustee St. Michael and All Angels Foundation 1984-88. Board of Directors Downtown Episcopal Ministry Diocese of Dallas 1986-88.
Office: 509 Main Street, Suite 211, Dallas 75202-3513.
Telephone: (214) 653-7138.

PRICE, Tom *(Judge, Texas Court of Criminal Appeals)* Elected to term beginning Jan 1, 1997. Reelected 2002, current term expires Dec 31, 2008. Born Des Moines Iowa March 13, 1945. Presbyterian. Educated at East Texas State University B.S. 1968 and Baylor University J.D. 1970. Admitted to practice Texas 1970. Began legal practice Dallas 1970. Former Judge, Dallas County Criminal Court No. 5, elected to term beginning Jan 1, 1975. Former Judge, Texas District Court 282nd Judicial District.
Member State Bar of Texas (Judicial Section), Dallas and Dallas County Criminal Bar Associations. Private First Class USMCR 1963-64. Democrat. Enjoys politics.
Mailing address: P.O. Box 12308, Austin 78711-2308.
Office: Supreme Court Building, Austin 78701.
Telephone: (512) 463-1565.

PRIMOMO, John W. *(Magistrate Judge, United States District Court Western District of Texas)* Appointed by U.S. District Court judges.
Office: U.S. Courthouse, 655 East Durango Boulevard, San Antonio 78206-1198.
Telephone: (210) 472-6357.

PROHL, Emil Karl *(Judge, Texas District Court 198th Judicial District)* Elected Nov 6, 1990 to term beginning Jan 1, 1991. Reelected 1994, 1998 and 2002. Current term expires Dec 31, 2006. Juvenile Judge for Kimble, Mason, Menard and McCulloch counties. Born Fort Worth Texas March 25, 1940. Presbyterian. Educated at North Texas State University B.A. 1963, Boston University M.S. 1965 and Texas Tech University School of Law J.D. 1972. Member Delta Theta Phi. Admitted to practice Texas 1973. In legal practice Kerrville 1973-90.
Member Texas Supreme Court Task Force on Judicial Ethics 1992. Former Director Texas Center for the Judiciary, Inc. Former Chairman Legislative Committee of Judicial Funding. Chairman 198th and 216th Judicial Districts Criminal Justice Advisory Boards. Life Fellow Texas Bar Foundation. Member American Judicature Society, College of the State Bar of Texas, State Bar of Texas (Judicial Ethics Committee) and Kerr County Bar Association. Faculty Member Texas College for New Judges and Alamo Area Law Enforcement Academy. Lecturer Criminal Justice Conferences and Texas Judicial Regional Conferences. First Lieutenant U.S. Army 1965-68.
Office: 700 Main Street, Kerrville 78028.
Telephone: (830) 792-2290.
Fax: (830) 792-2294
E-mail address: kprohl@ktc.com

PURYEAR, Cecil G. *(Judge, Texas District Court 137th Judicial District)* Elected to term beginning Jan 1, 1987. Reelected 1990, 1994, 1998 and 2002. Current term expires Dec 31, 2006. Born Lubbock Texas Nov 3, 1944. Methodist. Educated at Texas Tech University B.A. 1967 J.D. 1970. Member Phi Alpha Delta. Admitted to practice Texas 1970. In legal practice Lubbock 1970-79. Presiding Judge, Lubbock Municipal Court 1979-82. Judge, Lubbock County Court at Law No. 1 1983-87.
Counsel Small Business Administration 1970-71. Assistant County Attorney and Assistant City Attorney Lubbock County 1971-72. Assistant District Counsel U.S. Small Business Administration Lubbock 1972-79. Member State Bar of Texas and Lubbock County Bar Association. Member Lubbock Lions Club (Former President, Former Director) and Executive Board South Plains Council Boy Scouts of America (Adult Leader, District Commissioner). Enjoys scouting, restoring classic cars and outdoor activities.
Mailing address: P.O. Box 10536, Lubbock 79408-3536.
Telephone: (806) 775-1022.

PURYEAR, David *(Justice, Texas Court of Appeals Third District)* Elected Nov 2000 to term beginning Jan 1, 2001. Term expires Dec 31, 2006. Educated at Texas Tech University School of Law J.D. 1983. Judge, Travis County Court at Law No. 6 1990-1998.
Assistant County Attorney Travis County 1983-90. Assistant Attorney General 1999-2000.
Mailing address: P.O. Box 12547, Austin 78711-2547.
Telephone: (512) 463-1733.

QUINN, Brian P. *(Justice, Texas Court of Appeals Seventh District)* Assumed office 1995. Elected to subsequent term. Current term expires Dec 31, 2006. Educated at University of Texas at El Paso B.A. 1978 and Texas Tech University School of Law J.D. 1981. Law Clerk to Hon. George P. Kazen, U.S. District Court Southern District of Texas. Admitted to practice Texas 1981.
Member State Bar of Texas, Amarillo and Lubbock County Bar Associations.
Mailing address: P.O. Box 9540, Amarillo 79105-9540.
Telephone: (806) 342-2650.

QUINNEY, Marvin C. *(Judge, Wilson County Court)*
Office: 1420 Third Street, Room 102, Floresville 78114.
Telephone: (830) 393-7303.

QUINTANILLA, Roy *(Judge, Galveston County Court at Law No. 3)*
Office: 722 Moody, #229A, Galveston 77550.
Telephone: (409) 621-7920.

QUISENBERRY, Graham *(Judge, Parker County Court at Law)* Elected Nov 1994 to term beginning Jan 1995. Reelected 1998 and 2002. Current term expires Dec 31, 2006. Born Seymour Texas July 22, 1955. Educated at Texas A&M University B.A. 1977 and St. Mary's University J.D. 1981. Admitted to practice Texas 1981 and U.S. District Court Northern District of Texas. In legal practice Fort Worth 1981-95.
Sustaining Life Fellow Texas Bar Foundation. Fellow College of the State Bar of Texas. Member Fort Worth-Tarrant County Young Lawyers Association (Director 1987-88, Secretary 1988, President 1989), Texas Young Lawyers Association (Director District Twelve 1990-91), State Bar of Texas, Parker County and Tarrant County (Board Member Spring 1989) Bar Associations. Board

QUISENBERRY, GRAHAM—*Continued*

Member and Second Vice President East Parker County Chamber of Commerce. Member Lake Worth Area Chamber of Commerce (Vice President 1991-92, President 1992-93) and Aledo Parent-Teacher Organization (Second Vice President 1993-94, President 1994-95). Enjoys running and hunting.

Office: 117 Fort Worth Highway, Weatherford 76086-4302.

Telephone: (817) 598-6179.

RADACK, Sherry *(Chief Justice, Texas Court of Appeals First District)* Justice 2001 to Dec 2002. Appointed Chief Justice by Governor Rick Perry Dec 23, 2002. Educated at Rice University B.A. and University of Houston Law Center J.D. Former Judge, Texas District Court 55th Judicial District.

Office: 1307 San Jacinto, Tenth Floor, Houston 77002-7006.

Telephone: (713) 655-2708.

RADFORD, Wendell C. *(Magistrate Judge, United States District Court Eastern District of Texas)* Appointed by U.S. District Court judges.

Mailing address: P.O. Box 607, Beaumont 77704-0607.

Telephone: (409) 654-2845.

RAGLAND, Tom *(Judge, McLennan County Court at Law No. 1)*

Office: 501 Washington Avenue, Room 210, Waco 76701.

Telephone: (254) 757-5030.

RAINEY, John D. *(Judge, United States District Court Southern District of Texas)* Appointed for life by President George Bush to term beginning May 14, 1990. Born Freeport Texas Feb 10, 1945. Methodist. Educated at Southern Methodist University B.B.A. 1967 J.D. 1972. Member Phi Alpha Delta. Admitted to practice Texas 1972. In legal practice Dallas 1972-79 and Angleton 1979-86. Judge, Texas District Court 149th Judicial District 1987-90.

Fellow Texas Bar Foundation. Specialist Five U.S. Army 1969-70.

Office: 312 Main Street, Room 406, Victoria 77901.

Telephone: (361) 788-5030.

RAINS, Brian *(Judge, Texas District Court 176th Judicial District)* Term expires Dec 31, 2004.

Office: 1201 Franklin, Room 19040, Houston 77002.

Telephone: (713) 755-6328.

RALSTON, Owen *(Judge, Waller County Court)*

Office: 836 Austin Street, Room 203, Hempstead 77445.

Telephone: (979) 826-7700.

RAMIREZ, Irma C. *(Magistrate Judge, United States District Court Northern District of Texas)* Appointed by U.S. District Court judges to term beginning Sept 9, 2002.

Office: 1100 Commerce, Fifteenth Floor, Dallas 75242.

Telephone: (214) 753-2393.

RAMIREZ, Mario E., Jr. *(Judge, Texas District Court 332nd Judicial District)* Term expires Dec 31, 2004.

Office: 100 North Closner, Second Floor, Edinburg 78539.

Telephone: (956) 318-2275.

RAMOS, Dorina *(Magistrate Judge, United States District Court Southern District of Texas)* Appointed by U.S. District Court judges.

Mailing address: P.O. Box 4569, McAllen 78502-4569.

Telephone: (956) 618-8060.

RAMSAY, Charles R. *(Judge, Texas District Court 22nd Judicial District)* Term expires Dec 31, 2004. Former Judge, Hays County Court at Law.

Office: 110 East Martin Luther King Drive, Room 108A, San Marcos 78666-5542.

Telephone: (512) 393-7700.

RANGEL, Bonnie *(Judge, Texas District Court 171st Judicial District)*

Office: 500 East San Antonio Avenue, #601, El Paso 79901-2457.

Telephone: (915) 546-2100.

RANKIN, Susan Amanda *(Judge, Texas Family District Court 301st Judicial District)*

Office: George Allen Sr. Courts Building, Fifth Floor, 600 Commerce Street, Dallas 75202-4606.

Telephone: (214) 653-7385.

RASH, Andy *(Judge, Hood County Court)*

Office: 100 East Pearl Street, Granbury 76048-2499.

Telephone: (817) 579-3200.

RAY, Elizabeth *(Judge, Texas District Court 165th Judicial District)* Appointed by Governor Ann W. Richards to term beginning Oct 1992. Elected Nov 1992, 1996 and 2000. Current term expires Dec 31, 2004. Born Dallas Texas July 10, 1952. Baptist. Educated at Texas Tech University B.A. 1975 and Baylor University School of Law J.D. 1978. Law Clerk to Magistrate Alexander H. McGlinchey, U.S. District Court Northern District of Texas Dec 1979 to Jan 1981. Member Phi Alpha Delta. Admitted to practice Texas 1979, U.S. District Courts Northern 1979, Southern 1980 and Eastern 1984 Districts of Texas, U.S. Court of Appeals Fifth Circuit 1980 and U.S. Supreme Court 1984. Board Certified—Civil Trial Law—Texas Board of Legal Specialization. In legal practice Clear Lake City 1981-82 and Houston 1982-92.

Important Decisions: Scheffey v. CNA Insurance Co. (libel) 89-28406A, 1993; Pena v. GreatWestern (breach of contract) 92-04968, 1993; and Turner v. Dolcefino (libel) 92-32914, 1996. Adjunct Professor of Civil Pretrial Advocacy South Texas College of Law since 1997. Fellow Houston Bar Foundation, Texas Bar Foundation and College of the State Bar of Texas. Member Board of Civil District Judges (Policies and Procedures Committee 1995, Alternative Dispute Resolution 1995-96, Rules Committee 1996 and Mass Torts Committee 1996, Chair Special Dockets Committee 1996), Houston (Pictorial Directory Committee 1985-86, AIDS Committee 1989, Combined Committee of Administration of Justice, Appellate Judiciary and Courts and Courthouse Facilities 1989-91, Planning Committee for Bench-Bar Conference 1994-95, Chairman Section of Litigation 1991-92) and American Bar Associations. Speaker Women's Legal Fo-

RAY, ELIZABETH—*Continued*
rum South Texas College of Law Spring 1988 and 1989, "How to Deal Effectively with Outside Counsel" Aramco Oil Co. Legal Staff Sept 1989, "Business and Consumer Law" Fort Bend Independent School District Houston Bar Association Nov 1989, "How to Deal Effectively with Outside Counsel" Dec 1989 and "Trial Tactics" 1991 Legal Staff Conoco Oil Co., "A True Story About Sanctions and Its Evil Twin Mandamus" South Texas College of Law 1994, 1995 and 1996 and Ad Litem Seminar Houston Bar Association 1995 and 1996. Member Planning Committee Motion Advocacy—Trial and Techniques Seminar South Texas College of Law 1991. Attended Mediation Training Attorney's Mediation Institute 1992. Counselor for the profoundly retarded 1973-74 and Music Supervisor 1974-75 Lubbock State School for the Mentally Retarded. Owner and Manager Cotton Club 1974-75. Realtor Kodiak Realtors 1975-76. Member Ticket Sale Committee Houston Livestock and Rodeo 1985-87. Fellow Baylor Law School Alumni Association. Member American Red Cross (Host Committee) and West University Baptist Church (Budget Committee 1994-96).

Office: 312 Civil Courts Building, 301 Fannin Street, Houston 77002.

Telephone: (713) 755-6320.

RAY, Jerry D. *(Judge, Texas District Court 29th Judicial District)* Elected to term beginning Jan 1, 2001. Term expires Dec 31, 2004. Born Beaumont Texas July 27, 1946. Educated at University of Texas at Austin B.B.A. 1969 J.D. 1973. Member Delta Theta Phi. Admitted to practice Texas 1973. In legal practice Mineral Wells 1973-92.

District Attorney 29th Judicial District Jan 1, 1993 to Dec 31, 2000. Fellow Texas Bar Foundation. Member State Bar of Texas and Palo Pinto County Bar Association.

Mailing address: P.O. Box 187, Palo Pinto 76484-0187.

Telephone: (940) 659-1225.

RAYES, Donna *(Judge, Texas District Court 81st Judicial District)*

Mailing address: P.O. Box 161, Jourdanton 78026-0161.

Telephone: (830) 769-3572.

REAVIS, Don H. *(Justice, Texas Court of Appeals Seventh District)* Assumed office 1996. Elected to subsequent term. Current term expires Dec 31, 2006. Educated at McMurry College B.A. and University of Texas School of Law LL.B. Admitted to practice Texas 1959, U.S. District Court Northern District of Texas and U.S. Court of Appeals Fifth Circuit. In legal practice 1960-96.

President Amarillo Bar Association 1978. Director State Bar of Texas 1981-84. Fellow Texas Bar Foundation. Member American Bar Association.

Mailing address: P.O. Box 9540, Amarillo 79105-9540.

Telephone: (806) 342-2650.

RECIO, Felix, Jr. *(Magistrate Judge, United States District Court Southern District of Texas)* Appointed by U.S. District Court judges to term beginning March 22, 1999. Term expires March 22, 2007.

Office: 203 U.S. Courthouse, 600 East Harrison Street, Brownsville 78520-7152.

Telephone: (956) 548-2564.

REED, Hugh *(Judge, Armstrong County Court)*

Mailing address: P.O. Box 189, Claude 79019-0189.

Telephone: (806) 226-3221.

REUE, Matthew A. *(Judge, Washington County Court at Law)*

Office: 100 East Main, Suite 203, Brenham 77833.

Telephone: (979) 277-6200.

REX, James L. *(Judge, Texas District Court 109th Judicial District)*

Office: 201 County Courthouse, Andrews 79714-6517.

Telephone: (432) 524-1419.

REYES, Andres *(Judge, Texas District Court 406th Judicial District)*

Office: 1110 Victoria, Suite 402, Laredo 78042.

Telephone: (956) 523-4957.

REYNA, Rose Guerra *(Judge, Texas District Court 206th Judicial District)* Elected Nov 1998 to term beginning Jan 1, 1999. Reelected 2002, current term expires Dec 31, 2006. Born McAllen Texas Aug 1, 1960. Catholic. Educated at Pan American University B.A. with honors 1981 and University of Texas at Austin J.D. with honors 1983. Admitted to practice Texas 1984, U.S. District Court Southern District of Texas 1984, U.S. Court of Appeals Fifth Circuit 1992 and U.S. Supreme Court 1994. In legal practice Edinburg 1984-85 and McAllen 1985-98.

Member Texas Young Lawyers Association (Former Board of Directors) Texas Rural Legal Aid (Former Board of Directors), Texas Association of State Judges, National Association of Women Judges, State Bar of Texas (District 12B Grievance Committee 1989-91) and Hidalgo County Bar Association (Former Director, Past President). Lecturer on "New Rules of Procedures" Jan 15, 1999, "Guardian Ad Litem Guardianship and Guardian Ad Litem Duties and Ethics" Nov 12, 1999, and "Guardian Ad Litems" Hidalgo County Bar Association; "Jury Charge" Advanced Civil Trial Seminar State Bar of Texas Sept 1999; and "Motions for Summary Judgement" Nueces County Bar Association. Recipient Distinguished Young Leadership Award. Named Notable Women of Texas and Outstanding Women of America. Listed in *Who's Who in American Law* 11th ed. Enjoys jogging, swimming and reading.

Office: 100 North Closner, Second Floor, Edinburg 78539.

Telephone: (956) 318-2265.

E-mail address: RGR206@aol.com

RHEA, Bill *(Judge, Texas District Court 162nd Judicial District)*

Office: George Allen Sr. Courts Building, Sixth Floor, 600 Commerce Street, Dallas 75202-4606.

Telephone: (214) 653-7348.

RICHARDS, Robert C. "Bert" *(Judge, Texas District Court 379th Judicial District)*

Office: 3060 Bexar County Justice Center, 300 Dolorosa Street, San Antonio 78205-3028.

Telephone: (210) 335-2911.

RICHTER, Martin E. *(Justice, Texas Court of Appeals Fifth District)* Term expires Dec 31, 2006. Former Judge, Dallas County Court at Law No. 2. Former Judge, Texas District Court 116th Judicial District.

Office: George Allen Sr. Courts Building, 600 Commerce Street, Dallas 75202-4658.

Telephone: (214) 712-3404.

RICKHOFF, Tom *(Judge, Bexar County Probate Court No. 2)* Born Farragut Idaho July 13, 1944. Catholic. Educated at St. Mary's University B.A. 1966 J.D. 1966. Admitted to practice Texas 1969. Former Judge, Texas District Court 289th Judicial District, appointed by Governor William P. Clements to term beginning Sept 1, 1981. First Republican ever elected in county-wide election (1982). Former Justice, Texas Court of Appeals Fourth District.

Former District Clerk Bexar County. Former Special Trial Attorney-Prosecutor and Chief of Special Crimes U.S. Attorney's Office. With Organized Crime Strike Force Department of Justice 1974-81. Member State Bar of Texas. Named Politician of the Year by *The San Antonio Light* 1979. Lieutenant Colonel U.S. Army 1968-70 and JAG 1970-74. Recipient Vietnamese Cross of Gallantry 1970 and Bronze Star. Loan Officer Landmark State Bank 1967-69. Republican. Enjoys playing tennis.

Office: 100 Dolorosa Street, #2.06, San Antonio 78205-3028.

Telephone: (210) 335-2504.

RILEY, Mark W. *(Judge, Parker County Court)*

Office: 123 North Main, Weatherford 76086-4302.

Telephone: (817) 599-5607.

RIOS, Irene Alarcon *(Judge, Bexar County Court at Law No. 10)*

Office: 3.26 Bexar County Courthouse, 100 Dolorosa Street, San Antonio 78205.

Telephone: (210) 335-2948.

RIVERA, Guadalupe *(Judge, Texas District Court 168th Judicial District)*

Office: 500 East San Antonio Avenue, #602, El Paso 79901-2457.

Telephone: (915) 546-2141.

ROACH, Robert K. *(Magistrate Judge, United States District Court Northern District of Texas)* Appointed by U.S. District Court judges to term beginning April 1, 1980. Reappointed to subsequent terms. Serves part time. Born Kansas City Missouri Jan 1, 1943. Religious affiliation: Disciples of Christ. Educated at Stanford University 1961-63, University of Oklahoma B.A. 1965 and University of Texas LL.B. 1968. Law Clerk to Hon. Halbert O. Woodward, U.S. District Court Northern District of Texas 1968-69. Member Kappa Sigma. Admitted to practice Texas 1968, U.S. District Court Northern District of Texas 1968 and U.S. Courts of Appeals Tenth 1972 and Fifth 1976 Circuits. Began legal practice Fort Worth 1969. In legal practice Wichita Falls 1970.

House Counsel United Services Management, Inc. 1971-75. Member State Bar of Texas (Director Construction Law Section 1990-92), Wichita County (President 1992-93) and American Bar Associations. Board of Directors Big Brothers & Big Sisters of Wichita County 1980-85 and Red River Lyric Theatre. Chairman Board of Trustees Wichita Falls Firemen's Pension Board since 1981. District Chairman Wichita District Boy Scouts 1982-85. Member North Texas Field & Stream Association and church choir. Enjoys playing golf, snow skiing, fishing, guitar and computer programming.

Office: 912 City National Building, 807 Eighth Street, Wichita Falls 76301.

Telephone: (940) 322-7856.

ROBERTS, Delbert Ray *(Judge, Kimble County Court)*

Office: 501 Main Street, Junction 76849-4763.

Telephone: (325) 446-2724.

ROBERTS, Penny Ann *(Judge, Tom Green County Court at Law No. 2)*

Office: 112 West Harris, San Angelo 76903-5877.

Telephone: (325) 659-6506.

ROBERTS, W. F. "Corky" *(Judge, Potter County Court at Law No. 1)*

Office: 500 South Fillmore, Room 407, Amarillo 79101-2437.

Telephone: (806) 379-2375.

ROBINSON, Mary Lou *(Judge, United States District Court Northern District of Texas)* Appointed for life by President Jimmy Carter to term beginning 1979. Born Aug 25, 1926. Educated at Amarillo Junior College and University of Texas B.A. LL.B. Honorary member Delta Kappa Gamma. Began legal practice Amarillo 1950. Judge, Potter County Court at Law 1955-60. Judge, Texas District Court 108th Judicial District 1960-73. Associate Justice 1973-77 and Chief Justice 1977-79, Texas Court of Civil Appeals Seventh Supreme Judicial District.

Member National Association of Women Lawyers, State Bar of Texas (Former member Executive Committee Judicial Section), Amarillo and American Bar Associations. Named Texas Woman of the Year by Texas Federation of Business and Professional Women 1973, one of Ten Outstanding Panhandle Women by West Texas State University 1976 and one of Four Valiant Women by United Church Women. Listed in *Who's Who of American Women* and *Who's Who in the South and Southwest.* Organizer Opportunity House, Inc., an organization furnishing a temporary home for troubled youngsters (Board President 1975). Chairman Amarillo Presbyterian Community 1974. Member Advisory Committee Department of Continuing Education for Women Amarillo College, Advisory Committee YWCA Board, Amarillo Business and Professional Women's Club (President 1974-75), Texas Business and Professional Women's Federation (Former Chairman Wills and Estates, former Equal Legal Rights Consultant and Legal Advisor 1971-72), Advisory Council Juvenile Corrections Master Plan for Texas, Amarillo Comprehensive Alcoholism Treatment Center Advisory Committee, League of Women Voters, American Association of University Women and Amarillo Club of Zonta International (Past President). Former member Board of Directors Kairos House (Drug Treatment Center), Llano Estacado Council Boy Scouts of America (Vice President 1974-76), United Fund (Citizens Budget Committee), Potter-Randall Citizens Committee, Governor's Commission on Status of Women and Solicitations Review Board. Member Westminster Presbyterian Church (Elder and Deacon).

Office: Federal Building, Box F13248, 205 East Fifth Avenue, Amarillo 79101-1559.

Telephone: (806) 324-2354.

ROBISON, Jack Hollis *(Judge, Texas District Court 207th Judicial District)*
Office: 150 North Seguin, Suite 317, New Braunfels 78130-5159.
Telephone: (830) 620-5562.

ROBLES, Daniel T. *(Judge, Cameron County Court at Law No. 3)* Elected Nov 17, 1998 to term beginning Jan 1, 1999. Reelected 2002, current term expires Dec 31, 2006. Born San Benito Texas Jan 14, 1963. Catholic. Educated at Pan American University B.A. 1986 and Thurgood Marshall School of Law J.D. with honors 1989. Member Phi Delta Phi. Admitted to practice Texas 1989. In legal practice Harlingen.
Assistant District Attorney Cameron County 1989-91. Member State Bar of Texas, Cameron County and Hidalgo County Bar Associations. Attended College for New Judges CLE Dec 11, 1998, Regional Conference CLE March 3, 2000, Civil Practice and Litigation Techniques in Federal and State Courts Course ALI-ABA April 13, 2000 and Products Liability Course ALI-ABA Aug 17, 2000. Enjoys spending time with family and golfing.
Office: 974 East Harrison, Brownsville 78520.
Telephone: (956) 574-8136.
E-mail address: drobles@co.cameron.tx.us

RODEN, Jane *(Judge, Dallas County Criminal Court at Law No. 8)*
Office: LB 22 Frank Crowley Courts Bldg., 133 North Industrial Boulevard, Dallas 75207-4313.
Telephone: (214) 653-5677.

RODEN, Russell *(Judge, Dallas County Court at Law No. 1)*
Office: 500 Main Street, Suite 410, Dallas 75202-3513.
Telephone: (214) 653-7556.

RODRIGUEZ, Linda A. *(Judge, Hays County Court at Law No. 2)* Elected Nov 6, 1990 to term beginning Jan 1, 1991. Reelected Nov 1994, 1998 and 2002. Current term expires Dec 31, 2006. Born Edinburg Texas Nov 15, 1955. Catholic. Educated at University of Texas at Austin B.A. in Journalism with honors 1978 J.D. 1982. Admitted to practice Texas 1982. In legal practice San Marcos 1982-90 and Lockhart 1988-90.
Prosecutor (First Female and First Hispanic) Hays and Caldwell counties. Member State Bar of Texas (District Admissions Committee) and Hays County Bar Association (Past President). Attended Advanced Criminal Law Course 1986 and 1997, Advanced Family Law Course 1986, Texas Criminal and District Attorneys Association Conference 1988, "Family Law for Experienced Non-Specialist" seminar 1989, Annual Probate and Estate Planning seminar Oct 1990, Texas College for New Judges Dec 1990, Advanced Judicial Studies 1999-2000 and Juvenile Law Conferences. Previously employed as news editor and journalist. Former Board Member Hays County Womens Center. Member and Past President Gary Job Corps Community Relations Council. Member Hays CISD District Leadership Team and Bond Review Task Force. Enjoys reading, writing and playing the piano.
Office: 110 East Martin Luther King Drive, San Marcos 78666-5541.
Telephone: (512) 393-7625.

RODRIGUEZ, Nelda V. *(Justice, Texas Court of Appeals Thirteenth District)* Elected to term beginning Jan 1, 1995. Reelected to subsequent term. Current term expires Dec 31, 2006. Born Kingsville Texas Feb 12, 1954. Educated at Texas A&M University and Thurgood Marshall School of Law J.D. Former Judge, Corpus Christi Municipal Court.
Member Coastal Bend Women Lawyer's Association, Texas Bar Foundation, College of the State Bar of Texas and State Bar of Texas. Member League of Women Voters, Tejano Democrats and Mexican American Democrats. Parliamentarian and State Delegate Hispanic Women's Network of Texas. Co-founder and Director Fighting to Rid Gangs in America Foundation. Member Communities in Schools Mentor Program.
Office: 901 Leopard, Tenth Floor, Corpus Christi 78401.
Telephone: (361) 888-0786.

ROGERS, Randall Lee *(Judge, Smith County Court at Law No. 2)* Appointed to term beginning Jan 1, 1988. Elected 1988, 1990, 1994, 1998 and 2002. Current term expires Dec 31, 2006. Born Fort Worth Texas May 2, 1949. Methodist. Educated at Texas Tech University B.B.A. 1971 J.D. 1974. Member Phi Alpha Delta. Admitted to practice Texas 1974, U.S. District Courts Eastern 1976, Northern 1976 and Southern 1976 Districts of Texas and U.S. Courts of Appeals Fifth 1976 and Eleventh 1976 Circuits. In legal practice Fort Worth 1974-76. Judge, Smith County Court 1987. City Councilman Forest Hill 1974-76.
Prosecutor McLennan County 1976-83. District Attorney Smith County 1983-87. Instructor in Advanced Juvenile Law Texas Judicial College 1996. Republican. Treasurer Youth Alternatives 1990-97. Member International Order of Oddfellows (Noble and Grand 1995). Enjoys camping.
Office: 100 North Broadway, Room 104, Tyler 75702-7236.
Telephone: (903) 535-0618.
E-mail address: CCL2@co.smith.tx.us

ROLLINS, Barbara B. *(Judge, Taylor County Court at Law No. 2)* Appointed to term beginning April 1, 1988. Elected 1990, 1994, Nov 1998 and 2002. Current term expires Dec 31, 2006. Born Bryan Texas Jan 22, 1947. United Methodist. Educated at McMurry College B.S. with honors 1969, Scarritt College M.A. 1972 and University of Texas J.D. with honors 1978. Admitted to practice Texas 1979.
Office: 300 Oak Street, Abilene 79602.
Telephone: (325) 674-1208.

ROMAN, Mary D. *(Judge, Texas District Court 175th Judicial District)*
Office: 2199 Bexar County Justice Center, 300 Dolorosa Street, San Antonio 78205-3028.
Telephone: (210) 335-2527.

ROMAN, Richard Abram *(Judge, Texas District Court 346th Judicial District)*
Office: 500 East San Antonio Avenue, #902, El Paso 79901-2457.
Telephone: (915) 546-2119.

ROSENTHAL, Lee H. *(Judge, United States District Court Southern District of Texas)* Appointed for life by President George Bush to term beginning May 13, 1992. Born Richmond Indiana Nov 30, 1952. Educated at University of Chicago B.A. 1974 J.D. 1977. Topics and Comments Editor University of Chicago Law Review.

ROSENTHAL, LEE H.—*Continued*

Law Clerk to Chief Judge John R. Brown, U.S. Court of Appeals Fifth Circuit 1977-78. In legal practice Houston 1978-92.

Board of Editors *Manual for Complex Litigation* Federal Judicial Center since 1998. Member Advisory Committee for the Federal Rules of Civil Procedure Texas Judicial Conference since 1996. Chair Subcommittee on Class Actions Federal Rules Committee since 1999. Member Committee on Transnational Rules of Civil Procedure, The American Law Institute, State Bar of Texas, Houston and American Bar Associations.

Office: 11535 U.S. Courthouse, 515 Rusk Avenue, Houston 77002.

Telephone: (713) 250-5980.

ROSS, Donald Rae *(Justice, Texas Court of Appeals Sixth District)* Elected to term beginning Dec 7, 1996. Reelected 2000, current term expires Dec 31, 2006. Born Rusk County Texas March 8, 1939. Educated at Baylor University B.A. 1961 M.A. 1963 and Southern Methodist University J.D. 1970. Admitted to practice Texas 1971. Began legal practice Henderson 1971. Judge, Texas District Court 4th Judicial District Dec 11, 1982 to Dec 1996.

County and District Attorney Rusk County 1973-82. Member Texas Bar Foundation, College of the State Bar of Texas, State Bar of Texas, Texarkana and Northeast Texas Bar Associations. Democrat. Peace Corps Volunteer Thailand 1963-65. Member Kiwanis Club and United Methodist Church. Interests include Sacred Harp singing.

Office: Bi-State Justice Building, 100 North State Line No. 20, Texarkana 75501-5666.

Telephone: (903) 798-3046.

ROSS, Sherman A. *(Judge, Harris County Criminal Court at Law No. 10)*

Office: 1201 Franklin, Room 10136, Houston 77002.

Telephone: (713) 755-6216.

RUCKER, Dean *(Judge, Texas Family District Court 318th Judicial District)* Term expires Dec 31, 2006.

Office: 200 West Wall, Suite 200, Midland 79701-4557.

Telephone: (915) 688-1144.

RUSCH, Mark Joseph *(Judge, Texas District Court 401st Judicial District)* Former Judge, Collin County Court at Law No. 4.

Office: 210 South McDonald, Suite 226, McKinney 75069.

Telephone: (972) 548-4241.

RUSSELL, Kerry L. *(Judge, Texas District Court 7th Judicial District)*

Office: 100 North Broadway, Second Floor, Tyler 75702-7236.

Telephone: (903) 535-0625.

RYBURN, Douglas Lee *(Judge, Terry County Court)*

Office: 500 West Main, Room 102, Brownfield 79316-4335.

Telephone: (806) 637-6421.

RYDER, Byron *(Judge, Leon County Court)*

Mailing address: P.O. Box 429, Centerville 75833.

Telephone: (903) 536-2331.

RYMELL, Jennifer *(Judge, Tarrant County Court at Law No. 2)*

Office: 100 West Weatherford, Room 240A, Fort Worth 76196-0234.

Telephone: (817) 884-1813.

RYND, Frank *(Judge, Texas Family District Court 309th Judicial District)*

Office: Family Law Center Building, Seventh Floor, 1115 Congress Street, Houston 77002.

Telephone: (713) 755-6234.

SADLER, Alan B. *(Judge, Montgomery County Court)*

Office: 301 North Thompson, Suite 210, Conroe 77301-2883.

Telephone: (936) 539-7812.

SAENZ, L. Arnoldo *(Judge, Jim Wells County Court)* Elected to term beginning Jan 1, 1995. Reelected 1998 and 2002. Current term expires Dec 31, 2006. Born Premont Texas April 30, 1952. Catholic. Educated at Texas Arts & Industries University B.B.A. 1977. Democrat.

Office: 200 North Almond Street, Alice 78332.

Telephone: (361) 668-5706.

Fax: (361) 668-8671

E-mail address: lasaenz@thei.net

SAGE, Robin D. *(Judge, Texas Family District Court 307th Judicial District)* Elected Nov 1990 to term beginning Jan 1, 1991. Reelected 1994, 1998 and 2002. Current term expires Dec 31, 2006. Christian. Educated at Baylor University B.A. 1980 J.D. 1981. Associate Editor Baylor Law Review 1979-81. Member Phi Delta Theta. Admitted to practice Texas 1981 and U.S. District Court Eastern District of Texas 1982. In legal practice Longview 1981-90.

Office: 101 East Methvin, Suite 463, Longview 75601-7234.

Telephone: (903) 237-2534.

ST. CLAIR, James *(Judge, Cochran County Court)*

Office: 105 Cochran County Courthouse, Morton 79346-2598.

Telephone: (806) 266-5508.

SALDANA, Marisela *(Judge, Nueces County Court at Law No. 3)*

Office: 901 Leopard, Suite 703.03, Corpus Christi 78401.

Telephone: (361) 888-0466.

SALEH, Sam *(Judge, Dawson County Court)*

Mailing address: P.O. Drawer 1268, Lamesa 79331-1268.

Telephone: (806) 872-7544.

SALINAS, Simon *(Judge, Willacy County Court)*

Office: Willacy County Courthouse Annex, Raymondville 78580-1999.

Telephone: (956) 689-3393.

SALVANT, Wayne Francis *(Judge, Texas Criminal District Court No. 2 Tarrant County)*

Office: Tarrant County Justice Center, 401 West Belknap, Fort Worth 76196-0214.

Telephone: (817) 884-1349.

SANDERS, Barefoot *(Senior Judge, United States District Court Northern District of Texas)* Appointed for life by President Jimmy Carter to term beginning 1979.

SANDERS, BAREFOOT—*Continued*

Former Chief Judge. Assumed Senior status, serves by assignment. Born Dallas Texas Feb 5, 1925. Educated at University of Texas A.B. 1949 LL.B. 1950. President Students Association 1948-49. Admitted to practice Texas 1950. In legal practice Dallas 1951-61 and 1969-79.

U.S. Attorney Northern District of Texas 1961-65. Assistant Deputy Attorney General 1965-66 and Assistant Attorney General Civil Division 1966-67 U.S. Department of Justice. Fellow Dallas Bar Foundation and Texas Bar Foundation. Chair National Conference of Federal Trial Judges American Bar Association 1988-89. Fifth Circuit District Judge Representative to Judicial Conference of the U.S. 1989-92. President Fifth Circuit District Judges Association 1990-92. Judicial Panel on Multidistrict Litigation 1992-2000. Member Dallas (Director 1975-78) and American Bar Associations. Lieutenant j.g. USNR 1943-46. Member House of Representatives Texas 1952-58. Legislative Counsel to President Lyndon B. Johnson 1967-69. Democratic nominee for U.S. Senator from Texas 1972. Member Northaven Methodist Church.

Office: 15E6C U.S. Courthouse, 1100 Commerce Street, Dallas 75242-1003.

Telephone: (214) 753-2375.

SANDERSON, James Gary *(Judge, Texas District Court 60th Judicial District)* Term expires Dec 31, 2004.

Mailing address: P.O. Box 3707, Beaumont 77704-3707.

Telephone: (409) 835-8472.

SANDERSON, William F., Jr. *(Magistrate Judge, United States District Court Northern District of Texas)* Appointed by U.S. District Court judges March 19, 1979. Reappointed to subsequent terms. Born Battlecreek Michigan July 26, 1943. Educated at Vanderbilt University B.A. 1965 and University of Texas School of Law J.D. 1968. Member Phi Alpha Delta. Admitted to practice Texas 1968, U.S. District Courts Northern 1969 and Western 1977 Districts of Texas, U.S. Court of Appeals Fifth Circuit 1970 and U.S. Tax Court 1978. Began legal practice Dallas 1968. In legal practice Midland 1977-79.

Assistant U.S. Attorney Northern District of Texas 1969-77. Author "Outline of Habeas Corpus Proceedings in Federal Court" *Voice for the Defense* Texas Criminal Defense Lawyers Association 9-10 Fall/Winter 1975. Member NorthPark Presbyterian Church.

Office: 14A20 U.S. Courthouse, 1100 Commerce Street, Dallas 75242-1003.

Telephone: (214) 753-2385.

SANDOVAL, Charles F. *(Judge, Texas District Court 380th Judicial District)*

Office: 210 South McDonald, Suite 434, McKinney 75069.

Telephone: (972) 548-4762.

SANSOM, W. B., Jr. *(Judge, Real County Court)*

Mailing address: P.O. Box 446, Leakey 78873.

Telephone: (830) 232-5304.

SAUL, Roland *(Judge, Texas District Court 222nd Judicial District)*

Office: 235 East Third, Room 305, Hereford 79045-5593.

Telephone: (806) 364-7222.

SAVA, William F. *(Judge, Castro County Court)*

Office: 100 East Bedford, Room 111, Dimmitt 79027.

Telephone: (806) 647-4451.

SAVAGE, Randy *(Judge, Burnet County Court at Law No. 1)*

Office: 220 South Pierce, Burnet 78611.

Telephone: (512) 756-5449.

SAXON, Stella H. *(Judge, Texas District Court 218th Judicial District)*

Office: 101 North Panna Maria, #2, Karnes City 78118-2930.

Telephone: (830) 780-3089.

SCHEEL, Danny *(Judge, Comal County Court)*

Office: 199 Main Plaza, New Braunfels 78130-5166.

Telephone: (830) 620-5569.

SCHELL, Richard A. *(Judge, United States District Court Eastern District of Texas)* Appointed for life by President Ronald Reagan June 6, 1988 to term beginning Aug 15, 1988. Former Chief Judge. Born Dallas Texas March 10, 1950. Methodist. Educated at Southern Methodist University B.A. in Economics with distinction 1972 J.D. 1975. Briefing Attorney to Texas Court of Civil Appeals 1974-75. Admitted to practice Texas 1975. In legal practice McKinney Jan 1977 to Dec 1981. Judge, Collin County Court at Law No. 1, 1982-86. Judge, Texas District Court 219th Judicial District 1986-88, appointed by Governor Mark White.

Assistant District Attorney Collin County 1976-77. Instructor in Legal Writing and Research Methods Southern Methodist University Law School 1975-76. Member State Bar of Texas and Plano Bar Association (President 1978-79).

Mailing address: P.O. Box 1470, Beaumont 77704-1470.

Telephone: (409) 654-2880.

SCHILDKNECHT, Carter Tinsley *(Judge, Texas District Court 106th Judicial District)* Appointed by Governor Rick Perry July 26, 2001 to term beginning Aug 31, 2001. Elected Nov 5, 2002, current term expires Dec 31, 2006. Born Neosho Missouri April 29, 1941. Presbyterian. Educated at Stephens College A.A. with honors 1961, Texas Tech University B.S. with honors 1963 J.D. 1992. Member Phi Delta Phi. Admitted to practice Texas 1992. In legal practice Lamesa 1992-2001.

President Lamesa Bar Association 1995-97. Fellow Texas Bar Foundation. Member Texas Association of District Judges, National Association of Women Judges, College of the State Bar of Texas, State Bar of Texas (Judicial Section) and American Bar Association. Republican. President Lamesa Club of Rotary 1997-98, United Way 1998 and 2000 and Lamesa Area Chamber of Commerce 1999. Enjoys spending time with family.

Mailing address: P.O. Box 1268, Lamesa 79331.

Office: Dawson County Courthouse, Lamesa 79331.

Telephone: (806) 872-3740.

Fax: (806) 872-7810

SCHMIDT, Richard S. *(Judge, United States Bankruptcy Court Southern District of Texas)* Former Chief Judge.

Office: U.S. Courthouse, 1133 North Shoreline Boulevard, Corpus Christi 78401.
Telephone: (361) 888-3207.

SCHNEIDER, Michael H. *(Justice, Texas Supreme Court)* Appointed by Governor Rick Perry. Elected 2002, current term expires Dec 31, 2008. Born San Antonio Texas Jan 6, 1943. United Methodist. Educated at Stephen F. Austin State University B.S. 1965, University of Houston J.D. 1971 and University of Virginia LL.M. 2001. Admitted to practice Texas 1971. Former Presiding Judge, Texas District Court 157th Judicial District, elected Nov 3, 1990 to term beginning Jan 1, 1991. Former Justice and Chief Justice, Texas Court of Appeals First District, appointed by Governor George W. Bush.

Assistant District Attorney Harris County 1971-75. General Solicitor Union Pacific Railroad. Member State Bar of Texas and Houston Bar Association. Named Trial Judge of the Year 1995 and Appellate Judge of the Year 2000 by Texas Association of Civil Trial and Appellate Specialists. Republican.

Mailing address: P.O. Box 12248, Austin 78711-2248.
Telephone: (512) 463-1336.

SCHRAUB, Donald L. *(Judge, Guadalupe County Court)*

Office: 307 West Court Street, Suite 200, Seguin 78155.
Telephone: (830) 303-4188.

SCOGGINS, Roy A. "Al", Jr. *(Judge, Texas District Court 378th Judicial District)* Born Pine Bluff Arkansas July 22, 1955. Baptist. Educated at Baylor University B.B.A. 1977 J.D. 1979. Member Delta Theta Pi and Lambda Chi Alpha. Admitted to practice Texas 1979. Began legal practice Ennis 1979. Former Judge, Ellis County Court at Law, appointed to term beginning March 1, 1985.

Member State Bar of Texas, Ellis County (President 1987) and American Bar Associations. Enjoys playing tennis and golf and snow skiing.

Office: 200 East Main Street, Suite 330, Waxahachie 75165-3706.
Telephone: (972) 923-5014.

SEBESTA, Patrick E. *(Judge, Texas District Court 239th Judicial District)* Born Wharton Texas Jan 26, 1963. Educated at Sam Houston State University B.A.T. 1985 and South Texas College of Law LL.B. 1993. Admitted to practice Texas 1993. In legal practice Angleton 1994-99. Former Judge, Brazoria County Court at Law No. 2, elected to term beginning Jan 1999.

Republican. Den Leader Boy Scouts of America. Member Angleton Noon Lions Club and Little League. Enjoys playing golf.

Office: 111 East Locust Street, Angleton 77515-4678.
Telephone: (979) 864-1571.
E-mail address: pesebesta@hotmail.com

SEHON, Thomas *(Judge, Falls County Court)*
Mailing address: P.O. Box 338, Marlin 76661-0458.
Telephone: (254) 883-1426.

SELF, Ed *(Judge, Texas District Court 242nd Judicial District)*

Office: 500 Broadway, Room 340, Plainview 79072-8050.
Telephone: (806) 291-5254.

SENNE, Herbert H., Jr. *(Judge, Kinney County Court)*

Mailing address: P.O. Box 348, Brackettville 78832.
Office: 501 South Ann Street, Brackettville 78832.
Telephone: (830) 563-2401.

SEYMORE, Charles W. *(Justice, Texas Court of Appeals Fourteenth District)* Elected to term beginning Jan 1, 2001. Term expires Dec 31, 2006. Born Searcy Arkansas July 22, 1947. Educated at Southern Nazarene University B.A. 1972 and University of Houston J.D. 1983. Admitted to practice Texas 1983 and Colorado 1992. In legal practice 1983-2000.

Member American Judges Association, State Bar of Texas, Houston, Fort Bend County and Colorado Bar Associations.

Office: 1307 San Jacinto, Eleventh Floor, Houston 77002-7006.
Telephone: (713) 655-2800.

SHAMSIE, Terry *(Judge, Nueces County Court)*
Office: 901 Leopard, Suite 301, Corpus Christi 78401.
Telephone: (361) 888-0444.

SHANNON, Cheryl Lee *(Judge, Texas Family District Court 305th Judicial District)*
Office: 2600 Lone Star Drive, Dallas 75212-6307.
Telephone: (214) 698-4924.

SHARP, Donald R. *(Chief Judge, United States Bankruptcy Court Eastern District of Texas)* Appointed by U.S. Court of Appeals Fifth Circuit judges.

Office: 300A First Interstate Bank Bldg., 660 North Central Expressway, Plano 75074.
Telephone: (972) 509-1250.

SHAVOR, John D. *(Judge, Cottle County Court)*
Mailing address: P.O. Box 729, Paducah 79248-0729.
Telephone: (806) 492-3613.

SHELTON, Pat *(Judge, Texas Family District Court 313th Judicial District)* Elected Nov 8, 1994 to term beginning Jan 1, 1995. Reelected 1998 and 2002. Current term expires Dec 31, 2006. Born Kermit Texas Nov 11, 1951. Educated at University of Texas B.S. with honors 1973 M.Ed. 1975 and University of Houston J.D. 1982. Admitted to practice Texas 1983. Board Certified—Criminal Law and Juvenile Law—Texas Board of Legal Specialization.

Assistant District Attorney Harris County 1983-86. Republican.

Office: Family Law Center Building, Fourth Floor, 1115 Congress Street, Houston 77002.
Telephone: (713) 755-6470.

SHIPMAN, L. Dee *(Judge, Texas District Court 211th Judicial District)* Elected 1994 to term beginning Jan 1, 1995. Reelected 1998 and 2002. Current term expires Dec 31, 2006. Born Cleburne Texas April 26, 1955. Educated at University of Texas at Arlington B.B.A. 1978 and Texas Tech University School of Law J.D. 1983. Member Phi Delta Phi, Beta Alpha Psi and Alpha Chi. Board Certified—Criminal Law—Texas Board of Legal Specialization. In legal practice Aug 1983 to Jan 1984 and Jan 1988 to Jan 1991.

SHIPMAN, L. DEE—*Continued*

Assistant District Attorney Trial Section Dallas County Jan 1984 to Jan 1988. First Assistant District Attorney Denton County Jan 1991 to Dec 1994. Member Denton County Community Criminal Justice Committee 1991-92. Member College of the State Bar of Texas, State Bar of Texas and Denton County Bar Association. Certified Public Accountant Texas 1980. Sustaining Member Denton County Republican Party.

Office: 1450 East McKinney Street, Suite 2325, Denton 76209-4524.

Telephone: (940) 349-2330.

SHIPP, Steve Henry *(Judge, Hunt County Court at Law)*

Mailing address: P.O. Box 1097, Greenville 75403-1097.

Telephone: (903) 408-4200.

SHOLDEN, John *(Judge, Texas Family District Court 304th Judicial District)*

Office: 2600 Lone Star Drive, Dallas 75212-6307.

Telephone: (214) 698-4936.

SHUFF, Michael W. *(Judge, Orange County Court at Law)*

Office: 801 West Division, Orange 77630-6353.

Telephone: (409) 882-7084.

SHUFFIELD, Milton Gunn *(Judge, Texas District Court 136th Judicial District)* Appointed by Governor George W. Bush June 1995 to term beginning July 1995. Elected Nov 1996 and Nov 2000. Current term expires Dec 31, 2004. Born Littlerock Arkansas June 19, 1953. Episcopalian. Educated at University of Texas at Austin B.S. 1976 and University of Dayton J.D. 1981. Admitted to practice Texas 1981, Ohio 1981, U.S. District Court Eastern District of Texas 1983, U.S. Court of Appeals Fifth Circuit 1985 and U.S. Supreme Court 1988. In legal practice Beaumont Texas 1981-83 and 1985-95 and Hamilton Ohio 1983-85.

Corporate Counsel Ohio Casualty Insurance 1983-85. Author "20 Suggestions to Increase Courtroom Effectiveness of the Inexperienced Trial Attorney" Texas B. Jour. May 1995 and West Legal News and Pittsburgh Legal Journal Dec 1996. Past President Mickey Mehaffy Inns of Court. Former Member The Defense Research Institute, Inc. and International Association of Defense Counsel. Fellow Texas Bar Foundation. Member State Bar of Texas, Jefferson County, Ohio State (inactive), Fifth Circuit and American Bar Associations. Named "Best Judge" in Jefferson County by *Lawscapes* 1999 and highest ranking civil district judge in Jefferson County by Jefferson County Bar Association 1999 and 2001. Board Member Jefferson County Juvenile Board, Jefferson County Alternative School (boot camp), The Selwyn School and All Saints School. Commissioner Civil Service Commission. Member Three Rivers Council. Enjoys soccer, music and golf.

Mailing address: P.O. Box 3707, Beaumont 77704.

Office: 1001 Pearl Street, Room 204, Beaumont 77701-3707.

Telephone: (409) 835-8481.

Fax: (409) 784-5814

SHUSTER, Joe *(Judge, Pecos County Court)*

Office: 103 West Callaghan, Fort Stockton 79735.

Telephone: (432) 336-8724.

SIEBMAN, Carol M. *(Judge, Grayson County Court at Law No. 2)*

Office: 200 South Crockett, Sherman 75090-5958.

Telephone: (903) 813-4381.

SIMONS, Tom *(Judge, Deaf Smith County Court)*

Office: 235 East Third, Room 201, Hereford 79045-5542.

Telephone: (806) 363-7000.

SIMPSON, Rebecca Lynn *(Judge, Gregg County Court at Law No. 1)*

Office: 101 East Methvin, Suite 416, Longview 75601.

Telephone: (903) 236-8445.

SIMPSON, Terry A. *(Judge, San Patricio County Court)*

Office: 400 West Sinton, Room 109, Sinton 78387-2450.

Telephone: (361) 364-6120.

SIMS, Randy *(Judge, Brazos County Court)*

Office: 300 East 26th Street, Suite 114, Bryan 77803.

Telephone: (979) 361-4102.

SINZ, Jack *(Judge, Nacogdoches County Court at Law)*

Office: 101 West Main, Room 204, Nacogdoches 75961.

Telephone: (936) 560-7744.

SIRMON, Pamela Cook *(Judge, Potter County Court at Law No. 2)* Elected to term beginning Jan 1999. Reelected 2002, current term expires Dec 2006. Born Amarillo Texas Aug 1961. Methodist. Educated at Texas Tech University B.S. 1983 M.A. 1985 J.D. 1989. Admitted to practice Texas 1989 and U.S. District Court Northern District of Texas 1992. In legal practice Amarillo 1998.

Assistant County Attorney Potter County 1989-97. Member State Bar of Texas (Judicial Section) and Amarillo Bar Association. Republican. Board Member High Plains Food Bank and Women's Forum.

Office: 500 South Fillmore, Room 301, Amarillo 79101-2437.

Telephone: (806) 379-2380.

SKLAR, Daniel Richard *(Judge, Texas Family District Court 329th Judicial District)* Term expires Dec 31, 2006. Former Judge, Wharton County Court.

Office: Wharton County Courthouse, Wharton 77488.

Telephone: (979) 532-1514.

SMITH, Amy McCorkle *(Judge, Hopkins County Court at Law)*

Mailing address: P.O. Box 288E, Sulphur Springs 75482-0288.

Telephone: (903) 438-4004.

SMITH, Bea Ann *(Justice, Texas Court of Appeals Third District)* Appointed by Governor William P. Clements to term beginning Feb 1, 1991. Elected Nov 1992, 1994 and 2000. Current term expires Dec 31, 2006. Born Oklahoma 1943. Episcopalian. Educated at University of Texas at Austin B.A. with honors 1965 J.D. with honors 1975 and Brandeis University M.A. 1967. Associate Editor Texas Law Review 1973-75. Law Clerk to Hon. Thomas Gibbs Gee, U.S. Court of Appeals Fifth Circuit 1976-77. Member Order of the Coif. Admitted to practice Texas 1976, U.S. District

SMITH, BEA ANN—*Continued*

Court Western District of Texas 1977 and U.S. Court of Appeals Fifth Circuit 1977. In legal practice Austin 1977-91.

Author "Prophylactic Due Process: Constitutional Infirmities of the Texas Lower Court System" 53 Texas L. Rev. 1005, 1975; "The Partnership Theory of Marriage: A Borrowed Solution Fails" 68 Texas L. Rev. 689, 1990; "Why the Community Property System Fails Divorced Women and Children" 7 Texas Journal of Women and Law 235, 1998; "Alarming Attacks on Judges: Time to Defend Our Constitutional Trusteed" 80 Oregon L. Rev. 2001; and "An Independent Judiciary: Trustee of Our Constitutional Rights" 2 Studi Senesi, tome CXIII 237-269, 2001. Adjunct Professor University of Texas School of Law 1983-88 and since 1991. Faculty Institute of Judicial Administration New York University School of Law since 1996. President Elect National Association of Women Judges. Fellow Texas Bar Foundation. Member State Bar of Texas and American Bar Association. Democrat.

Mailing address: P.O. Box 12547, Austin 78711-2547.
Telephone: (512) 463-1733.
E-mail address: bea.smith@3rd.coa.courts.state.tx.us

SMITH, Bradley *(Judge, Texas District Court 400th Judicial District)*
Office: 301 Jackson, Richmond 77469.
Telephone: (281) 341-4422.

SMITH, Ed D. *(Judge, Motley County Court)*
Mailing address: P.O. Box 719, Matador 79244-0719.
Telephone: (806) 347-2334.

SMITH, Leo *(Judge, Terrell County Court)* Elected to term beginning Jan 1, 2003. Term expires Dec 31, 2006. Born Abilene Texas Aug 19, 1960. Baptist.

Board of Directors PBRPC. Member Terrell County Fair Board.

Mailing address: P.O. Box 4810, Sanderson 79848.
Telephone: (432) 345-2421.
Fax: (432) 345-2653
E-mail address: co.judge@co.terrell.tx.us

SMITH, Steve *(Judge, Texas District Court 361st Judicial District)* Born San Antonio Texas April 19, 1952. Religious affiliation: Christian. Educated at Abilene Christian University B.M.Ed. with high honors 1974 and University of Texas School of Law J.D. 1977. Admitted to practice Texas 1977 and U.S. District Courts Southern 1979 and Western 1980 Districts of Texas. In legal practice Bryan 1977-88 and College Station 1988-94. Judge, College Station Municipal Court 1988-94. Former Judge, Brazos County Court at Law No. 1, elected to term beginning Jan 1, 1995.

Adjunct Professor of State Government Blinn College. President 1998 Texas Association of County Court at Law Judges. Member American Judges Association, State Bar of Texas (Judicial Section) and American Bar Association (Former Chair National Conference of Special Court Judges Judicial Division). Board Member Texas Center for the Judiciary since 1998. Attended The National Judicial College and numerous CLE courses. Recipient Charles Plum Distinguished Non-Student Award from Texas A&M University. Enjoys golf.

Office: 300 East 26th Street, Suite 305, Bryan 77803-5361.
Telephone: (979) 361-4380.

SMITH, Steven Wayne *(Justice, Texas Supreme Court)*
Mailing address: P.O. Box 12248, Austin 78711-2248.
Telephone: (512) 463-1336.

SMITH, Walter S., Jr. *(Judge, United States District Court Western District of Texas)* Magistrate Feb 7, 1983 to Oct 5, 1984. Appointed Judge for life by President Ronald Reagan to term beginning Oct 6, 1984. Born Marlin Texas Oct 26, 1940. Presbyterian. Educated at Baylor University B.A. 1964 J.D. 1966. Editorial Board Baylor Law Review 1965-66. Member Phi Delta Phi. Admitted to practice Texas 1966, U.S. District Court Western District of Texas 1968 and U.S. Supreme Court 1970. Began legal practice Waco 1966. Judge, Texas District Court 54th Judicial District 1980-83.

Mailing address: P.O. Box 1908, Waco 76703-1908.
Telephone: (254) 750-1519.

SMITH, William D. *(Judge, Texas District Court 84th Judicial District)*
Mailing address: P.O. Box 489, Spearman 79081-0489.
Telephone: (806) 659-4160.

SMITH, Willis V. *(Judge, Lipscomb County Court)*
Mailing address: P.O. Box 69, Lipscomb 79056-0069.
Telephone: (806) 862-4131.

SOLIS, Jorge A. *(Judge, United States District Court Northern District of Texas)* Appointed for life by President George Bush to term beginning 1991. Born 1951. Educated at McMurry College B.A. 1973 and University of Texas School of Law J.D. 1976. In legal practice Abilene 1981-82 and 1988. Judge, Texas District Court 350th Judicial District 1989-91.

Assistant Criminal District Attorney Abilene 1976-81. Criminal District Attorney Taylor County 1983-87. Special Prosecutor West Central Narcotics Task Force Abilene 1988.

Office: 13B31 U.S. Courthouse, 1100 Commerce Street, Dallas 75242-1003.
Telephone: (214) 753-2342.

SORRELLS, Phil A. *(Judge, Tarrant County Criminal Court at Law No. 10)*
Office: Tarrant County Justice Center, Sixth Floor, 401 West Belknap, Fort Worth 76196-7679.
Telephone: (817) 884-3420.

SPARKMAN, Roy T. *(Judge, Texas District Court 78th Judicial District)*
Office: 900 Seventh Street, Suite 314, Wichita Falls 76301.
Telephone: (940) 766-8182.

SPARKS, Sam *(Judge, United States District Court Western District of Texas)* Appointed for life by President George Bush to term beginning Nov 7, 1991. Born Austin Texas Sept 27, 1939. Educated at University of Texas B.A. J.D. Law Clerk to Hon. Homer Thornberry, U.S. District Court District of Texas 1963-65. Former Foreman Texas Cowboys. Former Treasurer and Vice President Delta Tau Delta. Admitted to practice Texas 1963, U.S. Courts of Appeals Fifth 1963 and Tenth 1984 Circuits, U.S. District Court Western District of Texas 1965 and U.S. Supreme Court 1978. In legal practice El Paso 1966-91.

Important Decisions: Steve Jackson Games v. U.S. Secret Service 1991; Hopwood v. State of Texas 1992;

SPARKS, SAM—*Continued*

Faulder v. Texas Board of Pardons and Paroles, et al. A 98 CA 801, 1998; Barber v. Texas Board of Pardons and Paroles, et al. A 98 CA 803, 1998; Hamilton, et al. v. The City of Austin, Bruce Babbitt, Secretary of the Department of the Interior, et al. A 98 CA 317, 1998; Atwater, et al. v. City of Lago Vista, et al. 121 S.Ct. 1536, 2001; United States v. David Roland Waters A 00 CR 211, 2001; and Spiller, et al. v. Walker, et al. A 98 CA 255. Member Texas Supreme Court Advisory Commission 1978-91. Advocate American Board of Trial Advocates 1986. Member Texas State-Federal Judicial Council 1993-94. Board of Directors and Vice President Texas Association of Defense Counsel. President and Board of Directors El Paso Bar Association. President El Paso Chapter American Board of Trial Advocates. Fellow American College of Trial Lawyers.

Office: 100 U.S. Courthouse, 200 West Eighth Street, Austin 78701-2333.

Telephone: (512) 916-5230.

SPECIA, John J., Jr. *(Judge, Texas District Court 225th Judicial District)* Term expires Dec 31, 2006.

Office: 200 Bexar County Courthouse, 100 Dolorosa Street, San Antonio 78205-3028.

Telephone: (210) 335-2233.

SPEEDLIN, Phylis J. *(Judge, Texas Court of Appeals Fourth District)* Appointed by Governor Rick Perry to term beginning March 19, 2003. Born Pittsburgh Pennsylvania March 7, 1949. Methodist. Educated at Pittsburgh Presbyterian University R.N. 1970, Incarnate Word College B.S.N. with honors 1975, Trinity University M.S. with honors 1977 and St. Mary's University J.D. with honors 1983. Member John M. Harlan Society. Staff Writer St. Mary's Law Journal 1982-83. Admitted to practice Texas 1983, U.S. District Courts Western 1984 and Southern Districts of Texas and U.S. Supreme Court 1988. Board Certified Personal Injury Trial Law Texas Board of Legal Specialization. In legal practice San Antonio 1983-99. Judge, Texas District Court 408th Judicial District Jan 1, 2000 to March 18, 2003, appointed by Governor George W. Bush.

Author Case Note "Telecommunication—Right of Access" 13 St. Mary's L. Jour. 692, 1982. Co-author with Kathleen Silber *Dear Birthmother* Corona Publishers 1983. Member Association of Attorney Mediators (Treasurer 1998-99), American Board of Trial Advocates (San Antonio Chapter), William S. Sessions American Inn of Court, State Bar of Texas (Pattern Jury Committee Volume 3 1993-95) and San Antonio Bar Association (Medical-Legal Liaison Committee 1988-90, District Courts Committee 1997-99, Continuing Legal Education Committee 2000, Vice Chair Program Committee 2000). Author and Speaker "Liability for Patient Dumping" Medical Malpractice Conference Texas Tech University School of Law and St. Mary's University School of Law 1990. Speaker "Mock Trial/Tips on Giving a Deposition" South Central Texas Society of Gastrointestinal Nurses and Associates 1991, "Anatomy of a Lawsuit" Perinatal Conference 1992 and "Nurse's Role in Malpractice" Fourth Annual Perinatal Connection 1994 University of Texas Health Science Center, "Legal Issues Involving the Neonate" National Perinatal Nurses Association 1995, "Legal Aspects of Nursing Practice" University of Texas Health Science Center School of Nursing 1998 and "Medical Malpractice Suits Against the Advanced Practice Nurse" and "Advanced Nurse Practitioner—Contractual Relationships" Eleventh Annual Texas Nurse Practitioners Conference 1999. Author *Statute of Limitation in Health Care Litigation* TADC Fall Meeting Sept 1997. U.S. Army Nurse Corp 1970-75. Assistant Hospital Administrator 1977-80. Republican. Founder and Director San Antonio Adoption Awareness Center 1979. Board Member San Antonio Young Life 1992-95 and 2000. Member Rotary Club of San Antonio, Business and Professional Women's Club Inc. of San Antonio and Altrusa International Inc. of San Antonio.

Office: 3200 Bexar County Justice Center, 300 Dolorosa Street, San Antonio 78205-3037.

Telephone: (210) 335-2693.

SPENCER, Polly Jackson *(Judge, Bexar County Probate Court No. 1)* Appointed to term beginning July 16, 1990. Elected 1994, 1998 and 2002. Current term expires Dec 31, 2006. Born Jan 13, 1948. Presbyterian. Educated at Duke University B.A. 1970 and St. Mary's University of San Antonio School of Law J.D. 1976. Member Phi Delta Phi. Admitted to practice Texas 1977. Board Certified—Estate Planning and Probate Law—Texas Board of Legal Specialization. In legal practice Houston 1977-78 and San Antonio 1978-90.

Member Supreme Court Task Force on Judicial Appointments 1993. Fellow San Antonio Bar Foundation and Texas Bar Foundation. Member San Antonio Estate Planners Council, Texas College of Probate Judges, National College of Probate Judges, State Bar of Texas, San Antonio and American Bar Associations. Speaker on matters relating to probate, estate planning and guardianships State Bar of Texas Professional Development Program Texas College of Probate Judges' and San Antonio Bar Association presentations. Chair Bexar County Mental Health and Substance Abuse Advisory Committee.

Office: 123 Bexar County Courthouse, 100 Dolorosa Street, San Antonio 78205-3041.

Telephone: (210) 335-2678.

SPRINKLE, Vincent G. *(Judge, Tarrant County Court at Law No. 3)*

Office: 100 West Weatherford, Room 290A, Fort Worth 76196-0270.

Telephone: (817) 884-1917.

SPROWLS, Larry D. *(Judge, Hockley County Court)* Elected March 5, 1994 to term beginning Jan 1, 1995. Reelected 1998 and 2002. Current term expires Dec 31, 2006.

Office: 802 Houston Street, Suite 101, Levelland 79336-4545.

Telephone: (806) 894-6856.

SPURGIN, Dale *(Judge, Jones County Court)*

Mailing address: P.O. Box 148, Anson 79501-0148.

Telephone: (325) 823-3741.

SQUIER, James *(Judge, Texas Family District Court 312th Judicial District)*

Office: Family Law Center Building, Second Floor, 1115 Congress Street, Houston 77002.

Telephone: (713) 755-6941.

STACY, Frances H. *(Magistrate Judge, United States District Court Southern District of Texas)* Appointed by U.S. District Court judges to term beginning Feb 20, 1990. Reappointed 1998, current term expires 2006. Born Sumter South Carolina Jan 9, 1955. Catholic. Edu-

STACY, FRANCES H.—*Continued*
cated at Baylor University B.A. 1977 J.D. 1979. Notes and Comments Editor Baylor Law Review 1978-79. Admitted to practice Texas 1979 and U.S. District Court Southern District of Texas.

Assistant U.S. Attorney Southern District of Texas May 1980 to Feb 1990 (Criminal Division May 1980 to Oct 1980, Civil Rights Division Oct 1980 to June 1981, Land Use and Natural Resources Division June 1981 to Aug 1986, Civil Division Aug 1986 to June 1987 and Appeals Division June 1987 to Dec 1989). Author "Practice Notes: Rule 16 Conferences" LIX No. 6 *Pocket Parts* Newsletter Houston Young Lawyers Association Nov 1995, Chapter 7 *Federal Civil Procedure Before Trial: 5th Circuit* Lawyers Cooperative Publishing 1996, "The Public Interest Law Firm: Greater Bar Support is Needed" 30 Baylor L. Rev. 797, "Time for Appeal of Termination of the Parent-Child Relationship in a Joint Proceeding for Termination and Adoption" 31 Baylor L. Rev. 360 and "Age Discrimination by Local Government Employers—The Defense of a Bona Fide Occupational Qualification" 31 Baylor L. Rev. 527. Important Decisions: Maritrend, Inc. v. The Galveston Wharves 152 F.R.D. 543 S.D. Texas 1993, J.M. Huber Corporation v. Positive Action Tool, et al. 881 F. Supp. 279 S.D. Texas 1995, Southwest Mobile Systems Corp. v. Stewart & Stevenson H92-0386 S.D. Texas 1995, Beldya L. Mitchell and Geraldine Savoy v. St. Elizabeth H4-3674 S.D. Texas 1995, E.E.O.C. v. Texas Bus Lines H95-3981 S.D. Texas 1996, Becerra v. Asher 921 F. Supp. 1538 S.D. Texas 1996 and Marine Indemnity Ins. v. Lockwood Warehouse & Storage WL 211796 S.D. Texas 1996. Member Texas Bar Foundation, American Inns of Court, U.S. Magistrate Judges Association, State Bar of Texas, Houston, Federal and American Bar Associations. Participant Video Seminar on 1993 Changes to Federal Rules of Civil Procedure State Bar of Texas. Recipient Commendation from U.S. Attorney Daniel K. Hedges 1984, Commendation from U.S. Postal Service 1984 and Commendation from Federal Bureau of Investigation 1987. Named Younger Federal Lawyer of the Year 1985.

Office: 7727 U.S. Courthouse, 515 Rusk Avenue, Houston 77002.
Telephone: (713) 250-5681.

STAFFORD, Harrison, II *(Judge, Jackson County Court)* Elected Nov 6, 1990 to term beginning Jan 1, 1991. Reelected 1994, 1998 and 2002. Current term expires Dec 31, 2006. Born Houston Texas April 25, 1941. Episcopalian. Educated at University of Texas B.B.A. 1963 LL.B. 1966 and Wharton School of Finance and Commerce University of Pennsylvania M.B.A. 1968. Admitted to practice Texas 1966.

Co-auditor Jackson County Sept 1, 1972 to Dec 31, 1990. Member Edna Lions Club, Jackson County Chamber of Commerce and Texana Museum and Library Association.

Office: 115 West Main, Room 207, Edna 77957-2799.
Telephone: (361) 782-2352.
E-mail address: jcjudge@ykc.com

STANDARD, Leon *(Judge, Irion County Court)*
Mailing address: P.O. Box 770, Mertzon 76941-0770.
Telephone: (325) 835-4361.

STANDLEY, Larry *(Judge, Harris County Criminal Court at Law No. 6)*
Office: 1201 Franklin, Room 9032, Houston 77002.
Telephone: (713) 755-6200.

STEEL, Gary L. *(Judge, Texas District Court 274th Judicial District)*
Office: 101 East Court Street, Room 205, Seguin 78155-5779.
Telephone: (830) 303-4188, 401-0606.

STEEN, Wesley W. *(Judge, United States Bankruptcy Court Southern District of Texas)*
Office: 4505 U.S. Courthouse, 515 Rusk Avenue, Houston 77002.
Telephone: (713) 250-5153.

STEGER, William M. *(Senior Judge, United States District Court Eastern District of Texas)* Appointed for life by President Richard M. Nixon to term beginning Dec 29, 1970. Assumed Senior status Jan 1, 1988, serves by assignment. Born Dallas Texas Aug 22, 1920. Baptist. Educated at Baylor University and Southern Methodist University LL.B. 1950. Member Delta Theta Phi. Admitted to practice Texas 1951, U.S. District Court Eastern District of Texas 1953, U.S. Court of Appeals Fifth Circuit 1953 and U.S. Supreme Court 1954. In legal practice Longview 1951-53 and Tyler 1959-70.

U.S. District Attorney Eastern District of Texas 1953-59. Important Decisions: Greco v. Orange Memorial Hospital Corp. aff'd 513 F.2d 873, 1975 and U.S.A. v. Cauble, rehearing denied, 706 5th Cir. F.2d 1322, 714 5th Cir. F.2d 137, 1983, cert. denied, 104 S.Ct. 996, 1984. Member State Bar of Texas. Captain USAAC 1942-47. Republican. State Chairman Republican Party of Texas 1969-70. Enjoys fishing.

Mailing address: P.O. Box 1109, Tyler 75710-1109.
Telephone: (903) 590-1176.

STEM, Robert Miller *(Judge, Texas District Court 82nd Judicial District)* Appointed by Governor Mark White to term beginning Sept 1985. Elected Nov 1986, 1990, 1994, 1998 and 2002. Current term expires Dec 31, 2006. Born Waco Texas Sept 20, 1953. Baptist. Educated at Baylor University B.A. 1976 J.D. 1977. Admitted to practice Texas 1978. Began legal practice Marlin.

District Attorney Falls County 1980. Member State Bar of Texas. Attended Judicial Section Conference. Enjoys hunting, fishing and ranching.

Mailing address: P.O. Box 75, Marlin 76661-0075.
Telephone: (254) 883-1421.

STEPHENS, Susan R. *(Judge, Coryell County Court at Law)*
Office: 620 East Main, Gatesville 76528-1334.
Telephone: (254) 865-5911.

STEPHENSON, Brad *(Judge, Eastland County Court)* Elected Nov 1998 to term beginning Jan 1, 1999. Born Sweetwater Texas June 16, 1957. Baptist. Educated at Texas Tech University B.B.A. 1980 and Texas Wesleyan School of Law J.D. 1997. Admitted to practice Texas 1997. In legal practice Eastland Texas 1997-99.

Member State Bar of Texas and American Bar Association. Republican.

Mailing address: P.O. Box 327, Eastland 76448-0327.
Telephone: (254) 629-1263.
E-mail address: ecjudge@eastlandcountytexas.com

STICKNEY, Paul D. *(Magistrate Judge, United States District Court Northern District of Texas)* Appointed by U.S. District Court judges to term beginning March 2, 1998. Term expires 2006. Born 1953. Educated at University of South Dakota B.S. 1978 J.D. 1981. In legal practice 1981-90.

First Assistant Federal Public Defender 1990-98. Member Dallas County and Tarrant County Bar Associations.

Office: 15A28 U.S. Courthouse, 1100 Commerce Street, Dallas 75242-1003.

Telephone: (214) 753-2410.

STOKES, Charles *(Judge, Texas District Court 68th Judicial District)* Born Dallas Texas 1951. Methodist. Educated at Midwestern State University B.A. 1974 M.A. 1976 and Washburn University of Topeka J.D. 1982. Admitted to practice Texas 1982, U.S. District Court Northern District of Texas 1982, U.S. Court of Appeals Fifth Circuit 1986 and U.S. Supreme Court 1988. In legal practice Garland and Dallas 1982-90. Judge, Garland Municipal Court 1986-87. Judge, Roulett Municipal Court 1990. Former Judge, Dallas County Court at Law No. 5, elected Nov 1990 to term beginning Jan 1, 1991.

Member Garland and Dallas County Bar Associations. Republican.

Office: George Allen Sr. Courts Building, Third Floor, 600 Commerce, Dallas 75202-4606.

Telephone: (214) 653-6510.

STONE, Catherine *(Justice, Texas Court of Appeals Fourth District)* Appointed by Governor Ann W. Richards to term beginning March 24, 1994. Elected Nov 1994, current term expires Dec 31, 2006. Born Biddeford Maine Nov 28, 1953. Educated at Assumption College B.A. magna cum laude and St. Mary's University of San Antonio School of Law J.D. 1982. Briefing Attorney to Hon. James Baskin and Hon. Pete Tijerina, Texas Court of Appeals Fourth District 1982-83. Board Certified—Civil Appellate Law—Texas Board of Legal Specialization.

Office: 3200 Bexar County Justice Center, 300 Dolorosa Street, San Antonio 78205-3037.

Telephone: (210) 335-2281.

STOUDT, Bill *(Judge, Gregg County Court)*

Office: 101 East Methvin, Suite 300, Longview 75601-7214.

Telephone: (903) 236-8420.

STOVALL, Suzanne *(Judge, Texas District Court 221st Judicial District)* Born Athens Georgia March 28, 1943. Catholic. Educated at Trinity University B.S. 1964 and University of Texas 1969. In legal practice Plainview 1969-80 and Woodlands 1982-86. Former Judge, Montgomery County Court at Law No. 1, elected to term beginning Jan 1, 1987.

Member State Bar of Texas and Montgomery County Bar Association (Board of Directors 1990-91). Participant Summer 1987 and Faculty Advisor Summer 1989 General Jurisdiction Course The National Judicial College. Named Woman of the Year by YWCA 1987 and Lawyer of the Year by Montgomery County Bar Association 1992. Republican. Board of Directors Salvation Army of Montgomery County and YWCA of Montgomery County.

Office: 300 North Main, Conroe 77301-2874.

Telephone: (936) 539-7808.

STOVER, Earl, III *(Judge, Texas District Court 88th Judicial District)*

Mailing address: P.O. Box 607, Kountze 77625-0607.

Telephone: (409) 246-5151.

STRAUSS, Gus J. *(Judge, Texas District Court 2nd 25th Judicial District)* Term expires Dec 31, 2004.

Mailing address: P.O. Box 511, Hallettsville 77964.

Telephone: (361) 798-2607.

STREIT, Gary B. *(Judge, Wilbarger County Court)*

Office: 1700 Wilbarger Street, Room 12, Vernon 76384-4747.

Telephone: (940) 553-2300.

STRICKLIN, Cliff *(Judge, Texas Criminal District Court No. 2 Dallas County)*

Office: LB 39 Frank Crowley Courts Building, 133 North Industrial Boulevard, Dallas 75207-4313.

Telephone: (214) 653-5912.

STRICKLIN, Don *(Judge, Texas District Court 337th Judicial District)*

Office: 1201 Franklin, Room 15032, Houston 77002.

Telephone: (713) 755-7746.

STROEHER, Mark *(Judge, Gillespie County Court)* Elected to term beginning Jan 1, 1995. Reelected 1998 and Nov 2002. Current term expires Dec 31, 2006. Born Fredericksburg Texas April 6, 1956. Lutheran. Educated at University of Texas at Austin B.B.A. 1978 and St. Mary's University of San Antonio J.D. 1981. Member Phi Alpha Delta. Admitted to practice Texas 1981. In legal practice Fredericksburg 1981-94. Republican.

Office: 101 West Main Street, Unit 9, Fredericksburg 78624.

Telephone: (830) 997-7502.

Fax: (830) 997-9958

STROTHER, Ralph T. *(Judge, Texas District Court 19th Judicial District)* Appointed by Governor George W. Bush to term beginning Feb 24, 1999. Elected Nov 7, 2000, current term expires Dec 31, 2004. Born Groesbeck Texas May 12. Baptist. Educated at Baylor University B.A. 1965 M.A. 1967 J.D. 1982. Admitted to practice Texas 1983 and U.S. District Court Western District of Texas 1987. In legal practice Waco 1982-99 and Colorado City and Sweetwater 1984-85.

First Assistant District Attorney McLennan County 1988-91. General Counsel Texas State Technical College 1993-99. Member State Bar of Texas and McLennan County Bar Association. Republican. Former Member Waco School Board. Board of Directors Crime Stoppers. Member Rotary Club of Waco and Historic Waco Foundation. Enjoys running, dancing and reading.

Office: 501 Washington Avenue, Room 303, Waco 76701-1380.

Telephone: (254) 757-5081.

E-mail address: 19th@co.mclennan.tx.us

STUBBLEFIELD, Billy Ray *(Judge, Texas District Court 26th Judicial District)* Elected Nov 3, 1992 to term beginning Jan 1, 1993. Reelected Nov 5, 1996 and Nov 7, 2000. Current term expires Dec 31, 2004. Born Fort Stockton Texas Feb 17, 1949. Methodist. Educated at Southwestern University B.A. 1971 and University of Texas at Austin J.D. 1978. Southwestern Scholar. Member Delta Theta Phi. Admitted to practice Texas 1976, U.S. District Court Western District of Texas, U.S.

STUBBLEFIELD, BILLY RAY—*Continued*

Court of Appeals Fifth Circuit and U.S. Supreme Court. In legal practice Georgetown 1976-92.

County Attorney Williamson County 1977-92. Former Member Texas District and County Attorneys Association (Founding Member Civil Section). Member State Bar of Texas (Judicial Section) and Williamson County Bar Association. Member Rotary Club (Past President). Interests include sailing, photography, traveling and Civil War history.

Office: 405 South Martin Luther King Boulevard, Box 2, Georgetown 78626-0405.

Telephone: (512) 943-1226.

SUDDERTH, Bonnie *(Judge, Texas District Court 352nd Judicial District)* Appointed by Governor George W. Bush to term beginning April 1, 1996. Elected Nov 1996 and Nov 2000. Current term expires Dec 31, 2004. Born Brownwood Texas Sept 2, 1959. Presbyterian. Educated at University of Southern California B.S. magna cum laude 1982, University of Exeter, England 1984 and University of Texas School of Law J.D. 1985. Admitted to practice Texas 1986, U.S. District Court Northern District of Texas 1986 and U.S. Court of Appeals Fifth Circuit 1988. In legal practice Fort Worth 1986-90. Judge 1990 and Chief Judge 1990-96, Fort Worth Municipal Court.

Author "The Community Service Alternative" 3 No. 4 *Municipal Court Recorder* 1993 and "The Patriot Movement: Paper Warriors and Common Law Courts" *Court Review Magazine* Fall/Winter 1997. Adjunct Professor Texas Wesleyan University Law School since 1999. Commissioner Texas Commission on Judicial Conduct 1991-96. Officer 1991-94 and President 1995-96 Texas Municipal Courts Association. Officer 1992-96 and Chair 1994-95 Municipal Judges Section State Bar of Texas. Member Task Force Staff Diversity Committee Texas Commission on Judicial Efficiency 1996. Governor 1992-98, First Vice President 1999-2000, President Elect 2000-01 and President 2001-02 American Judges Association. Fellow Texas Bar Foundation and College of the State Bar of Texas. Charter Fellow Tarrant County Bar Association. Faculty Member Texas Municipal Courts Education Center 1991-96. Presenter "Courts Under Attack: The Paper War" Sept 1997 and "Scientific Evidence in the Courts: Concepts and Controversies" Aug 1998 Annual Educational Conference American Judges Association. Named Outstanding Woman of Fort Worth by Fort Worth Commission on the Status of Women 1995 and one of Tarrant County's Most Influential Women 1997. Republican. Board Member Fort Worth Teen Court, Inc. 1990-96. Regional Director Committee for Employer Support of the Guard and Reserve U.S. Department of Defense since 1992. Participant Cinderella Conference American Association of University Women and Circle T Girl Scout Association since 1995.

Office: Tarrant County Justice Center, 401 West Belknap, Fort Worth 76196-7283.

Telephone: (817) 884-2731.

E-mail address: bsudderth@tarrantcounty.com

SULLIVAN, Frank Walter, III *(Judge, Texas Family District Court 322nd Judicial District)* Appointed by Governor Mark White to term beginning Nov 2, 1983. Elected 1984, 1986, 1990, 1994, 1998 and 2002. Current term expires Dec 31, 2006. Born Fort Worth Texas. Episcopalian. Educated at University of Texas at Austin B.A. 1970 and Texas Tech University J.D. 1973. Admitted to practice Texas 1973, U.S. Supreme Court 1977 and U.S. District Court Northern District of Texas. Board Certified—Family Law—Texas Board of Legal Specialization. In legal practice Fort Worth 1973-83.

Director Texas Academy of Family Law Specialists. Member State Bar of Texas and Tarrant County Bar Association. Faculty Member Advanced Family Law Course 1988-94, Marriage Dissolution Course Texas College for New Judges and The National Judicial College. Republican.

Office: Tarrant County Justice Center, 401 West Belknap, Fort Worth 76196-0230.

Telephone: (817) 884-1427.

SUMMERS, Frank *(Judge, Milam County Court)* Mailing address: P.O. Box 1008, Cameron 76520.

Telephone: (254) 697-7000.

SUPERVILLE, Maurice Charles, Jr. *(Judge, Lamar County Court)* Appointed to term beginning Dec 5, 1995. Elected 1996. Reelected 1998 and Nov 2002. Current term expires Dec 31, 2006. Born Houston Texas Sept 28, 1957. Catholic. Educated at University of Texas at Austin B.B.A. in Accounting 1984 J.D. 1989. Admitted to practice Texas 1989.

Assistant County Attorney Lamar County 1989-95. Member State Bar of Texas, Lamar County and Northeast Texas Bar Associations. CPA May 1986. Corporate Tax Accountant and Financial Auditor 1984-86. Consumer bankruptcy and tax accountant 1989. Democrat. Member Lamar County Grassroots Democrats. Member Rotary Club. Enjoys reading and dining out with good friends.

Office: 119 North Main Street, Room 201, Paris 75460.

Telephone: (903) 737-2410.

Fax: (903) 785-3858

E-mail address: countyjudge_lamar_tx@yahoo.com

SUTHERLAND, Mike *(Judge, Burleson County Court)*

Office: 100 West Buck, Suite 306, Caldwell 77836.

Telephone: (979) 567-2333.

SYLVIA, Jimmy *(Judge, Chambers County Court)*

Mailing address: P.O. Box 939, Anahuac 77514.

Telephone: (409) 267-8295.

E-mail address: jsylvia@chambers.lib.tx.us

TAFT, Tim *(Justice, Texas Court of Appeals First District)* Elected Nov 1994 to term beginning Jan 1, 1995. Reelected Nov 2000, current term expires Dec 31, 2006. Born Seattle Washington March 14, 1946. Religious affiliation: Christian. Educated at Washington State University B.S. in Psychology 1968 and University of Houston Law Center J.D. 1978. Admitted to practice Texas 1978.

Assistant District Attorney Harris County 1979-94. Member Houston Bar Association. Specialist 5 U.S. Army Vietnam 1969-70. Staff Sergeant Texas Airborne National Guard 1974-80. Republican.

Office: 1307 San Jacinto, Tenth Floor, Houston 77002-7006.

Telephone: (713) 655-2709.

TAGLE, Hilda Gloria *(Judge, United States District Court Southern District of Texas)* Appointed for life by President Bill Clinton to term beginning March 27, 1998. Born Corpus Christi Texas Dec 18, 1946. Reli-

TAGLE, HILDA GLORIA—*Continued*

gious affiliation: Disciples of Christ. Educated at Del Mar College A.A. 1967, East Texas State University B.A. 1969, North Texas State University M.L.S. 1971 and University of Texas School of Law J.D. 1977. Member Alpha Chi and Alpha Lambda Sigma. Admitted to practice Texas 1977, U.S. District Court Southern District of Texas 1989 and U.S. Supreme Court. In legal practice Corpus Christi 1981-85. Judge, Nueces County Court at Law No. 3 July 1, 1985 to Dec 31, 1994. Judge, Texas District Court 148th Judicial District Jan 1, 1995 to March 1998.

Assistant City Attorney Corpus Christi 1977. Assistant County Attorney 1978-79 and Assistant District Attorney 1979-81 Nueces County. Instructor in Legal Assistant Program Del Mar College 1981-85. Member State Commission on Judicial Conduct 1989-94. Member Board of Law Examiners Character and Fitness Division, District 11 Committee on Admissions and Judicial Education Executive Committee 1988-89 Texas Supreme Court. Fellow Texas Bar Foundation since 1992 (Vice Chair Law Focused Education Committee 1994). Founding Member Mexican American Bar Association of the Coastal Bend. Charter Member and Past Chair Women Lawyers of the Coastal Bend. Member Nueces County Bail Bond Board (Secretary-Treasurer 1988), State Bar of Texas (Resolutions Committee 1988 and 1990 and Bylaws Revision Committee 1989 Judicial Section, Secretary Women and the Law Section Council 1989-90, Opportunities for Minorities Committee 1990-91, Continuing Legal Education Committee 1991-92, Co-chair 1992 Annual Meeting Planning Committee) and Corpus Christi Bar Association (Chair Lawyers for Literacy Committee 1988-89). Presenter "Setting, Revoking and Forfeiting Bail Bonds" Regional Judicial Conference Texas Center for the Judiciary Inc. 1987, "Literacy and the Courts" Judicial Section Annual Conference 1989, "Probating a Simple Will" Coastal Bend Mexican American Bar Association 1992, "Incompetency, Insanity and Mental Illness" Annual Meeting Mexican American Bar Association of Texas 1994. Recipient Good Gals Award Texas Women's Political Caucus 1990, United Married Couples Award 1991 and Y Women in Careers Award 1992. Member National Women's Political Caucus (Chair Judicial/Dispute Resolution Committee 1994), Leadership Corpus Christi Class X 1981-82 and Class XX (Chair Selection Committee), Southern Regional Council, Governor's Commission for Women and Spanish American Genealogical Association. Founding Member Hispanic Women's Network of Texas. Deacon South Shore Christian Church.

Office: 306 U.S. Courthouse, 600 East Harrison Street, Brownsville 78520.

Telephone: (956) 548-2510.

TAITE, Ralph *(Judge, Dallas County Criminal Court at Law No. 4)* Appointed to term beginning Feb 8, 1988. Elected Nov 1988, Nov 1990, Nov 1994, 1998 and 2002. Current term expires Dec 31, 2006. Born Houston Texas Sept 17, 1942. Christian. Educated at Southern Methodist University B.A. 1964 J.D. 1966. Member Phi Alpha Delta. Admitted to practice Texas 1966. In legal practice Dallas 1968-83. District Attorney Dallas County 1966-68. Chief Public Defender Dallas County 1983-88.

Office: LB 17 Frank Crowley Courts Bldg., 133 North Industrial Boulevard, Dallas 75207-4313.

Telephone: (214) 653-5637.

TANNER, Martha *(Judge, Texas District Court 166th Judicial District)* Appointed by Governor Ann W. Richards April 29, 1992. Elected Nov 5, 1992, Nov 1996 and 2000. Current term expires Dec 31, 2004. Born Houston Texas. Episcopalian. Educated at St. Mary's University of San Antonio School of Law LL.B. Admitted to practice Texas 1968. In legal practice San Antonio 1968-92.

Member American Inns of Court, State Bar of Texas and San Antonio Bar Association. Democrat. Enjoys cooking, swimming, reading and walking.

Office: 405 Bexar County Courthouse, 100 Dolorosa Street, San Antonio 78205-3028.

Telephone: (210) 335-2501.

TARRANCE, Carter William *(Judge, Texas District Court 392nd Judicial District)*

Office: 109 West Corsicana, Suite 101, Athens 75751.

Telephone: (903) 675-6110.

TAYLOR, Don *(Judge, Liberty County Court at Law)*

Office: 1923 Sam Houston, Liberty 77575.

Telephone: (936) 336-4662.

TERRY, Gene Seth *(Judge, Marion County Court)*

Office: 102 West Austin Street, Room 205, Jefferson 75657-2266.

Telephone: (903) 665-3261.

THEODOSIS, Byron *(Judge, San Saba County Court)*

Office: 500 East Wallace Street, San Saba 76877-0001.

Telephone: (325) 372-3635.

THIBODEAUX, Carl K. *(Judge, Orange County Court)*

Office: 801 West Division, Orange 77630-6353.

Telephone: (409) 882-7070.

THOMAS, Linda *(Chief Justice, Texas Court of Appeals Fifth District)* Term expires Dec 31, 2006. Former Judge, Texas District Court 256th Judicial District, elected to term beginning Jan 1, 1979.

Office: George Allen Sr. Courts Building, 600 Commerce Street, Dallas 75202-4658.

Telephone: (214) 712-3401.

THOMAS, Mike *(Judge, Texas Criminal District Court No. 4 Tarrant County)*

Office: Tarrant County Justice Center, 401 West Belknap, Fort Worth 76196-0216.

Telephone: (817) 884-1362.

THOMAS, Tommy Brock, Jr. *(Judge, Texas District Court 338th Judicial District)*

Office: 1201 Franklin, Room 15040, Houston 77002.

Telephone: (713) 755-7774.

THOMPSON, Joe "Tab" *(Judge, Erath County Court)*

Office: 100 West Washington, Stephenville 76401.

Telephone: (254) 965-1452.

THOMPSON, John Paul *(Judge, Polk County Court)* Office: 101 West Church Street, Third Floor, Livingston 77351-9401.
Telephone: (936) 327-6813.

THOMPSON, William A., Jr. *(Judge, Lamb County Court)*
Office: 100 Sixth Street, Room 101, Littlefield 79339.
Telephone: (806) 385-4222.

THORNE, Larry *(Judge, Texas Family District Court 317th Judicial District)*
Office: County Courthouse, Beaumont 77701-3707.
Telephone: (409) 835-8588.

TINLEY, Pat *(Judge, Kerr County Court)*
Office: 700 Main Street, Kerrville 78028-5389.
Telephone: (830) 792-2211.

TOWERY, Roger E. *(Judge, Texas District Court 97th Judicial District)*
Mailing address: P.O. Box 530, Henrietta 76365-0530.
Telephone: (940) 538-4314.

TOWSLEE, Harold Robert *(Judge, Texas District Court 335th Judicial District)* Term expires Dec 31, 2004.
Mailing address: P.O. Box 648, Caldwell 77836-0648.
Telephone: (979) 567-2335.

TRAPP, Robert Hill *(Judge, Texas District Court 411th Judicial District)*
Office: One State Highway 150, Room 23, Coldspring 77331.
Telephone: (936) 653-5470.

TREJO, Alma *(Judge, El Paso County Criminal Court at Law No. 1)*
Office: 500 East San Antonio, El Paso 79907.
Telephone: (915) 546-8421.

TRIANA, Gisela D. *(Judge, Travis County Court at Law No. 5)*
Mailing address: P.O. Box 1748, Austin 78767-1748.
Telephone: (512) 854-9676.

TRUDO, Martha Jane *(Judge, Texas District Court 264th Judicial District)* Elected Nov 5, 1994 to term beginning Jan 1, 1995. Reelected 1998 and 2002. Current term expires Dec 31, 2006. Born San Antonio Texas. Christian. Educated at St. Mary's University of San Antonio B.A. 1968 J.D. 1970. Admitted to practice Texas 1971 and U.S. District Court Western District of Texas. In legal practice Killeen 1982-94.
Member Texas District Judges Association, State Bar of Texas and Bell-Lampasas-Mills Bar Association. Colonel USAR JAG 1982-2003 (active duty 1973-82; retired). Member Rotary. Enjoys reading, playing tennis and ranching.
Mailing address: P.O. Box 747, Belton 76513-0747.
Telephone: (254) 933-5261.

TYGRETT, Howard *(Judge, Texas District Court 86th Judicial District)*
Mailing address: P.O. Box 621, Kaufman 75142-0621.
Telephone: (972) 932-4331.

UNDERWOOD, Bradley S. *(Judge, Texas District Court 364th Judicial District)* Appointed by Governor William P. Clements to term beginning Oct 16, 1989. Elected 1990, 1994, Nov 1998 and 2002. Current term expires Dec 31, 2006. Born Bonham Texas Aug 2, 1954. Protestant. Educated at Midwestern State University B.B.A. summa cum laude 1977 and Texas Tech University J.D. 1980. Admitted to practice Texas 1980 and U.S. District Court Northern District of Texas 1982. Judge, Lubbock County Court at Law No. 2, 1986-89.
Member Lubbock County Young Lawyers Association (Director 1988-89), State Bar of Texas (Judicial Section) and Lubbock County Bar Association (Director 1993-95). Attended School for New Judges Texas Center for the Judiciary Sam Houston State University Dec 1-5, 1986, Annual Conference State Bar of Texas Judicial Section 1987-92, West Texas Judicial Conference 1987-94 and Criminal Justice Conference Texas Center for Judiciary 1987-94. Lecturer Creditor's Rights Seminar State Bar of Texas Spring 1990 and "All in a Day's Work" Seminar Lubbock County Bar Association Spring 1991. Moderator Stay Abreast of Law Seminar Texas Tech School of Law Fall 1990. Attended seminars for judges Texas Center for the Judiciary 1991-94. Republican. Interests include computers, golf and reading.
Mailing address: P.O. Box 10536, Lubbock 79408-3536.
Telephone: (806) 775-1021.

UNDERWOOD, Olen *(Judge, Texas District Court 284th Judicial District)* Appointed by Governor William P. Clements to term beginning May 1, 1981. Elected 1982, 1986, 1990, 1994, 1998 and 2002. Current term expires Dec 31, 2006. Presiding Judge Second Administrative Judicial Region since May 1, 1996. Born Polk County Texas May 25, 1942. Baptist. Educated at University of Texas B.B.A. 1965 and University of Houston J.D. 1970. Member Phi Delta Phi and Order of the Barons. Admitted to practice Texas 1970. Began legal practice Houston 1970. In legal practice Conroe 1975.
President Southern Juvenile and Family Court Judges 1991-92. Member American Judges Association, State Bar of Texas (Secretary District 5-A Grievance Committee 1979-81), Montgomery County (President 1980) and American Bar Associations. Attended Texas College of the Judiciary 1981. Named Outstanding Citizen of the Year by Knights of Columbus 1989 and Texas CASA Judge of the Year 2001. Founder Specialized Treatment and Rehabilitation and Crimestoppers of Montgomery County.
Office: 301 North Main, Suite 201, Conroe 77301.
Telephone: (936) 538-8176.
Fax: (936) 538-8167

VAHLENKAMP, Virgil L., Jr. *(Judge, Denton County Criminal Court at Law No. 2)* Born Abilene Texas July 7, 1958. Christian. Educated at University of North Texas B.B.A. cum laude 1980 and Texas Tech University School of Law J.D. 1983. Member Phi Alpha Delta. Admitted to practice Texas 1983. Former Judge, Denton County Court at Law No. 2, appointed to term beginning Dec 13, 1988.
Assistant District Attorney Denton 1983-88. Member State Bar of Texas, Denton County and American Bar Associations. Republican.
Office: 1450 East McKinney Street, Denton 76209.
Telephone: (940) 349-2170.

VALDEZ, Rogelio *(Chief Justice, Texas Court of Appeals Thirteenth District)* Elected Nov 7, 2000. Term expires Dec 31, 2006. First Hispanic person elected to Chief Justice of Thirteenth District. Born Raymondville Texas Dec 20, 1951. Educated at Texas Arts & Industries University 1976 and Texas Southern University

VALDEZ, ROGELIO—*Continued*

J.D. 1979. Judge, Cameron County Court at Law No. 1 1983-86. Judge 1987-2000 and Presiding Judge 1991-2000, Texas District Court 357th Judicial District.

Office: Hidalgo County Administrative Bldg., Fifth Floor, 100 East Cano, Edinburg 78539.

Telephone: (956) 318-2405.

VANCE, William R. *(Justice, Texas Court of Appeals Tenth District)* Elected to term beginning Jan 1, 1991. Reelected 1996 and 2002. Current term expires Dec 31, 2008. Born Bryan Texas Dec 19, 1939. Educated at Texas A&M University B.A., University of Texas School of Law J.D. 1963 and University of Virginia School of Law LL.M. in Judicial Process 1995. Admitted to practice Texas 1963, U.S. Supreme Court 1971, U.S. Court of Appeals Fifth Circuit 1981 and U.S. District Courts Northern, Southern and Western Districts of Texas. In legal practice 1979-90. Judge, Brazos County Court 1967-78.

Assistant County Attorney Brazos County 1964-67. District Director Board of Directors State Bar of Texas 1985. Sustaining Life Fellow Texas Bar Foundation. Member Brazos County (President 1968), Waco-McLennan County and American Bar Associations. Past President Texas Association of Regional Councils. Former Chairman Board of Trustees Brazos Valley Mental Health-Mental Retardation. Former Director and Chairman Board Brazos Valley Development Council.

Mailing address: P.O. Box 1606, Waco 76703-1606.

Telephone: (254) 757-5200.

VANDERGRIFF, Tom J. *(Judge, Tarrant County Court)*

Office: 100 East Weatherford, Room 501, Fort Worth 76196-0101.

Telephone: (817) 884-1991.

VARGAS, Robert J. *(Judge, Nueces County Court at Law No. 1)*

Office: 901 Leopard, Suite 701, Corpus Christi 78401.

Telephone: (361) 888-0344.

VASQUEZ, Raul *(Judge, Texas District Court 111th Judicial District)* Former Judge, Webb County Court at Law.

Office: 1110 Victoria, Suite 301, Laredo 78042.

Telephone: (956) 523-4223.

VASQUEZ-GARDNER, Juanita A. *(Judge, Texas District Court 399th Judicial District)*

Office: Bexar County Justice Center, 300 Dolorosa Street, San Antonio 78205-3028.

Telephone: (210) 335-3667.

VELA, Filemon B. *(Senior Judge, United States District Court Southern District of Texas)* Appointed for life by President Jimmy Carter to term beginning June 18, 1980. Assumed Senior status May 1, 2000, serves by assignment. Born Harlingen Texas May 1, 1935. Catholic. Educated at Texas Southmost College 1954-56, University of Texas 1956-57 and St. Mary's University of San Antonio J.D. 1962. Admitted to practice Texas 1962. Began legal practice 1962. Judge, Texas District Court 107th Judicial District, elected to term beginning Jan 1, 1975.

Instructor Law Enforcement College. Member State Bar of Texas. Attended Texas College of the Judiciary and National College of the State Judiciary. Speaker Bi-National Judicial Conference, Puebla Mexico May 6, 1992, U.S. Customs Money Laundering and Asset Forfeiture Conference, Santiago Chile July 1994 and Lima Peru March 1995, Judicial Seminar Drug Enforcement Administration, Caracas Venezuela Oct 31, 1995, on controlled deliveries Venezuelan Authorities Nov 1, 1995, on Assets Forfeiture Regional Drug Enforcement Seminar, San Jose Costa Rica May 15, 1996 and Instituto Nacional de Ciencias Penales, Mexico City Mexico Sept 28-29, 1996. Participant Constitutional Bicentennial Presentations World-Net TV Argentina, Venezuela and Guatemala, U.S.I.A. Tours Mexico and Ecuador and State and Valley schools and organizations. Co-recipient Outstanding Jurist Award from Texas Bar Foundation 1993. Filemon B. Vela Middle School dedicated Jan 19, 1992. Private First Class USAS 1957-59. Democrat. Former City Commissioner Brownsville. Charter President Esperanza Home for Boys. Chairman Emeritus Rio Grande Marine Institute (Home for Youth). Conductor "Despacho Juridico" Spanish Radio Legal Information Program Valley Bar Association KGBT-Radio since 1972. Co-sponsor 220 Spanish Radio programs "Enriquezca Su Vida, Termine Sus Estudios (Enrich Your Life, Complete Your Studies)." Member Dropout Prevention/Literacy Committee Texas Young Lawyers Association. Member Brownsville Independent School District Task Force (student drop-out program).

Office: 600 East Harrison Street, Room 3058, Brownsville 78520.

Telephone: (956) 548-2595.

VELA, Rose *(Judge, Texas District Court 148th Judicial District)*

Office: 901 Leopard, Suite 903, Corpus Christi 78401-3688.

Telephone: (361) 888-0333.

VELASQUEZ, Juan, II *(Judge, Victoria County Court at Law No. 2)*

Office: 115 North Bridge, Room 127, Victoria 77901-6544.

Telephone: (361) 575-7195.

VENSO, Norma *(Judge, Texas District Court 56th Judicial District)* Elected Nov 1996 to term beginning Jan 1, 1997. Reelected Nov 2000, current term expires Dec 31, 2004. Born Fort Worth Texas June 22, 1953. Methodist. Educated at University of Texas B.A. with honors 1974 J.D. 1977. Admitted to practice Texas 1978 and U.S. District Courts Western 1978 and Southern 1982 Districts of Texas.

President Galveston County Mediation Association 1995. Member College of the State Bar of Texas and Texas Bar Foundation. Democrat.

Office: 722 Moody, Sixth Floor, Galveston 77550.

Telephone: (409) 766-2226.

VERA, Eloy *(Judge, Starr County Court)*

Office: 203 Starr County Courthouse, Rio Grande City 78582.

Telephone: (956) 487-8015.

VILLA, Carlos *(Judge, El Paso County Court at Law No. 5)*

Office: 500 East San Antonio, #806, El Paso 79901.

Telephone: (915) 546-2004.

VOGT, Eddie J. *(Judge, Kendall County Court)* Office: 201 East San Antonio Street, Suite 120, Boerne 78006-2049.
Telephone: (830) 249-9343.

VON DOENHOFF, Robert Christopher *(Judge, Houston County Court)*
Mailing address: P.O. Box 370, Crockett 75835.
Office: 401 East Houston, Crockett 75835.
Telephone: (936) 544-3255.

WADE, Henry, Jr. *(Judge, Texas District Court 292nd Judicial District)* Born Dallas Texas July 27, 1955. Educated at Southern Methodist University B.B.A. 1977 and Texas Tech University J.D. 1988. Associate Editor Texas Tech Law Review 1987-88. Member Order of the Coif. Admitted to practice Texas 1988 and U.S. District Court Northern District of Texas 1990. In legal practice Dallas 1991-94. Former Judge, Dallas County Criminal Court No. 1, assumed office Jan 1, 1995.
Assistant District Attorney Dallas County 1987-90 and Bell County 1990-91. Member Dallas Bar Association. Captain USAF 1978-85.
Office: LB 35 Frank Crowley Courts Building, 133 North Industrial Boulevard, Dallas 75207-4313.
Telephone: (214) 653-5880.

WADE, Kristin *(Judge, Dallas County Criminal Court of Appeals No. 1)* Elected to term beginning Jan 1999. Reelected 2002, current term expires Jan 2007. Born Houston Texas April 27, 1962. Methodist. Educated at Trinity University B.A. 1984 and Southern Methodist University J.D. 1988. Admitted to practice Texas 1988.
Assistant District Attorney 1988-92. Member State Bar of Texas (Treasurer Criminal Justice Section) and Dallas Bar Association. Member Junior League of Dallas.
Office: LB 9 Frank Cowley Courts Bldg., 133 North Industrial Boulevard, Dallas 75207-4313.
Telephone: (214) 653-5707.

WADE, Len A. *(Judge, Texas District Court 141st Judicial District)*
Office: Tarrant County Justice Center, 401 West Belknap, Fort Worth 76196-0224.
Telephone: (817) 884-1992.

WAGENBACH, Larry D. *(Judge, Fort Bend County Court at Law No. 1)*
Office: 301 Jackson, Suite 323, Richmond 77469-3108.
Telephone: (281) 341-4415.

WAINWRIGHT, Dale *(Justice, Texas Supreme Court)* Former Judge, Texas District Court 334th Judicial District.
Mailing address: P.O. Box 12248, Austin 78711-2248.
Telephone: (512) 463-1332.

WALKER, Jeff *(Judge, Texas District Court 96th Judicial District)* Term expires Dec 31, 2004.
Office: Tarrant County Justice Center, 401 West Belknap, Fort Worth 76196-0223.
Telephone: (817) 884-1450.

WALKER, Layne *(Judge, Texas District Court 252nd Judicial District)*
Mailing address: P.O. Box 3707, Beaumont 77704-3707.
Telephone: (409) 835-8597.

WALKER, Sue *(Justice, Texas Court of Appeals Second District)*
Office: 9000 Tarrant County Justice Center, 401 West Belknap, Fort Worth 76196.
Telephone: (817) 884-2174.

WALLACE, Jim *(Judge, Texas District Court 263rd Judicial District)*
Office: 1201 Franklin, Room 15136, Houston 77002.
Telephone: (713) 755-6944.

WALLER, Rod *(Judge, Scurry County Court)*
Office: 1806 25th Street, Snyder 79549.
Telephone: (325) 573-8576.

WALTHER, Barbara Lane *(Judge, Texas District Court 51st Judicial District)*
Office: 112 West Beauregard, San Angelo 76903-5835.
Telephone: (325) 659-6571.

WALTON, Ralph H., Jr. *(Judge, Texas District Court 355th Judicial District)*
Office: 100 East Pearl Street, Room 20, Granbury 76048.
Telephone: (817) 579-3233.

WALVOORD, Al *(Judge, Midland County Court at Law No. 1)* Elected 1990 to term beginning Jan 1, 1991. Reelected 1994, 1998 and 2002. Current term expires Dec 31, 2006. Born Monroe Louisiana March 15, 1938. Educated at Baylor University B.A. 1959 and Northwestern University J.D. 1962. Member Phi Alpha Delta. Admitted to practice Texas 1962 and U.S. District Courts Northern and Western Districts of Texas. In legal practice Midland 1970-91.
Prosecutor Dallas, Dallas and Ector counties 1963-70. Member Texas Bar Foundation, State Bar of Texas and Midland Bar Association.
Office: 200 West Wall, Suite 6, Midland 79701-4547.
Telephone: (432) 688-1149.

WARD, T. John *(Judge, United States District Court Eastern District of Texas)* Appointed for life by President Bill Clinton to term beginning Sept 24, 1999. Educated at Texas Tech University B.A. 1964 and Baylor University School of Law LL.B. 1967. Admitted to practice Texas 1967, U.S. District Courts Eastern, Northern, Southern and Western Districts of Texas, U.S. Court of Appeals Fifth Circuit and U.S. Supreme Court. In legal practice Lubbock 1968, Henderson 1968-69, Longview 1969-90 and 1993-99 and Houston 1991-93.
Advocate American Board of Trial Advocates since 1989. Board of Governors Fifth Circuit Bar Association 1987-91 and 1996-99. Life Fellow Texas Bar Foundation. Fellow American College of Trial Lawyers (Judicial Fellow since 1999). Member Bar Association for U.S. District Court Eastern District of Texas, State Bar of Texas and American Bar Association.
Office: 100 East Houston, Marshall 75670.
Telephone: (903) 935-3868.
Fax: (903) 935-2295

WARDER, Janice L. *(Judge, Texas Criminal District Court No. 1 Dallas County)* Elected Nov 1992 to term beginning Dec 1, 1992. Reelected 1994, 1998 and 2002. Current term expires Dec 31, 2006. Born Morgantown West Virginia Aug 1, 1950. Methodist. Educated at West Virginia University B.S. M.A. with honors 1976 and Southern Methodist University J.D. 1980. Admitted

WARDER, JANICE L.—*Continued*

to practice Texas 1980 and U.S. District Court Northern District of Texas 1980.

Assistant District Attorney 1980-92. Faculty Member Justice of the Peace Training Center Southwest Texas State University since 1984. Member Texas Bar Foundation, College of the State Bar of Texas, American Inns of Court, State Bar of Texas and Dallas Bar Association. Instructor Texas District Attorneys Association, State Judicial Conference, Nevada Judicial Conference and various police academies. Named Judge of Competent Jurisdiction and Wiretap Judge for First Judicial Region. Republican. Board Member Texas Federation of Republican Women. Presiding Judge, Dallas County DIVERT Drug Treatment Court. Certified Disciple Bible Instructor. Enjoys snow skiing, kayaking and traveling.

Office: LB 38 Frank Crowley Courts Building, 133 North Industrial Boulevard, Dallas 75207-4313.

Telephone: (214) 653-5900.

Fax: (214) 653-5927

E-mail address: warderct@aol.com

WARE, Arthur H. *(Judge, Potter County Court)* Elected Nov 6, 1990 to term beginning Jan 1, 1991. Reelected 1994, 1998 and 2002. Current term expires Dec 31, 2006. Born Amarillo Texas Nov 13, 1949.

Office: 500 South Fillmore, Room 101, Amarillo 79101-2437.

Telephone: (806) 379-2250.

WARNE, Doug *(Judge, Texas Family District Court 311th Judicial District)*

Office: Family Law Center Building, Seventh Floor, 1115 Congress Street, Houston 77002.

Telephone: (713) 755-6242.

WARNER, Howard S., II *(Judge, Hays County Court at Law No. 1)*

Office: 110 East Martin Luther King Drive, Room 177, San Marcos 78666-5541.

Telephone: (512) 393-7625.

WATERS, Lee *(Judge, Texas District Court 223rd Judicial District)* Elected Nov 6, 1990 to term beginning Jan 1, 1991. Reelected 1994, 1998 and 2002. Current term expires Dec 31, 2006. Born Pampa Texas Sept 12, 1950. Southern Baptist. Educated at University of Texas B.B.A. 1973 J.D. 1975. Member Delta Theta Phi. Admitted to practice Texas 1976, U.S. District Courts Northern District of Texas 1977 and Western District of Oklahoma 1986 and U.S. Supreme Court 1985. Board Certified—Civil Trial Law—Texas Board of Legal Specialization. In legal practice Pampa 1976-90.

Life Fellow Texas Bar Foundation. Member College of the State Bar of Texas, State Bar of Texas (Juror Education Committee, Minimum Continuing Legal Education Task Force and Alternative Dispute Resolution Committee) and Gray County Bar Association (Vice President 1989, President 1992). Paul Harris Fellow Rotary International. Named one of the Outstanding Young Men of America 1981 and Optimist of the Month by Pampa Optimist Club Feb 1985. Director 1981-87 and President 1985-86 Pampa Rotary Club. Director 1981-87 and Chairman 1985-86 Gray County Chapter American Red Cross. Director 1986-89 and Vice President 1988-89 Pampa Chamber of Commerce.

Mailing address: P.O. Box 2160, Pampa 79066-2160.

Telephone: (806) 669-8014.

WATKINS, Gary L. *(Judge, Texas District Court 244th Judicial District)* Elected to term beginning Jan 1, 1999. Reelected 2002, current term expires Dec 31, 2006. Born Crane Texas Dec 12, 1946. Catholic. Educated at University of Texas at Austin B.A. 1969 J.D. 1973. Admitted to practice Texas 1973. In legal practice Odessa Texas 1973-99. Judge, Ector County Court 1977-82.

Member House of Representatives Texas 1987-93.

Office: 300 North Grant, Room 324, Odessa 79761-5158.

Telephone: (432) 498-4240.

WATSON, Dennis D. *(Judge, Montgomery County Court at Law No. 1)*

Office: 210 West Davis, Suite 201, Conroe 77301-2884.

Telephone: (936) 539-7831.

WATSON, Floyd A. *(Judge, Shelby County Court)*

Office: 200 San Augustine, Box 6, Center 75735-3954.

Telephone: (936) 598-3863.

WATTS, Sandra *(Judge, Texas District Court 117th Judicial District)*

Office: 901 Leopard, Suite 904, Corpus Christi 78401.

Telephone: (361) 888-0436.

WEEKS, John Wilson *(Judge, Texas District Court 42nd Judicial District)*

Office: 300 Oak Street, Abilene 79602-1521.

Telephone: (325) 674-1314.

WEISER, Laura Ann *(Judge, Victoria County Court at Law No. 1)* Appointed to term beginning June 1, 1990. Elected 1990, 1994, 1998 and 2002. Current term expires Dec 31, 2006. Born Denver Colorado Feb 6, 1959. Methodist. Educated at Houston Baptist University B.A. with honors 1981 and University of Houston Law Center J.D. 1985. Admitted to practice Texas 1986. In legal practice Victoria 1986-90.

Adjunct Professor Victoria College and University of Houston. Board Member Texas Center for the Judiciary, Inc. Member State Bar of Texas (Juvenile Law Committee Judicial Section) and Victoria County Bar Association. Attended Special Court Jurisdiction Advanced Course June 1991, Drinking Driver Course 1993 and Criminal Procedure 2000 The National Judicial College and Texas Judicial College Jan 1990. Instructor Victoria Police Academy. Recipient Friend of Education Award from Victoria Classroom Teacher's Association 1990-91 and South Texas Woman Award 1998. Teacher Houston 1981 and Alief 1982-85. Democrat. Member Victoria Democrats Club. Chairman Victoria County Juvenile Board 1990-99. Board of Directors Youth Home of Victoria. Member Junior League of Victoria, Inc. and Child Study Clinic. Enjoys music and literature.

Mailing address: P.O. Box 2474, Victoria 77902-2474.

Telephone: (361) 575-4550.

E-mail address: lweiser@victoriacountytx.org

WELBORN, Michael E. *(Judge, Texas District Court 36th Judicial District)* Elected to term beginning Jan 1, 2003. Term expires Dec 31, 2006. Born Aransas Pass Texas March 7, 1948. Methodist. Educated at Texas Arts & Industries University B.A. 1973 and South Texas College of Law J.D. 1984. Member Order of Barristers. Admitted to practice Texas 1984. In legal practice Sin-

WELBORN, MICHAEL E.—*Continued*
ton 1984-86. Judge, San Patricio County Court at Law 1992-2002.

Assistant District Attorney 36th Judicial District 1986-92. Member Rotary. Enjoys sailing and fishing.
Mailing address: P.O. Box 700, Sinton 78387.
Telephone: (361) 364-6200.
Fax: (361) 364-6155
E-mail address: mwelborn@go.com

WELLS, Judith G. *(Judge, Texas Family District Court 325th Judicial District)*
Office: 100 North Houston Street, Fourth Floor, Fort Worth 76196-0233.
Telephone: (817) 884-1587.

WERLEIN, Ewing, Jr. *(Judge, United States District Court Southern District of Texas)* Appointed for life by President George Bush to term beginning May 22, 1992. Born Houston Texas Sept 14, 1936. Educated at Southern Methodist University B.A. with honors 1958 and University of Texas School of Law LL.B. with honors 1961. Case Note Editor Texas Law Review. Member Phi Beta Kappa, Phi Delta Phi (Chapter President 1960-61) and Order of the Coif. Admitted to practice Texas, U.S. District Courts Eastern and Southern Districts of Texas, U.S. Courts of Appeals Fifth and Tenth Circuits, U.S. Tax Court, U.S. Court of Federal Claims and U.S. Supreme Court. In legal practice 1964-92.

Fellow Houston Bar Foundation (Ex Officio Director 1988-89), Texas Bar Foundation, American Bar Foundation, American College of Trial Lawyers and International Society of Barristers. Member State Bar of Texas (Director 1990-93, Member Texas Lawyer's Creed Committee 1994-95) and Houston Bar Association (President 1988-89). Recipient Life Membership Award from Houston Chamber of Commerce 1966. Captain USAF JAG 1961-64. Member 1974-84 and Chair 1980-84 General Board of Publication and Chancellor Texas Annual Conference since 1977 United Methodist Church. Trustee Southern Methodist University 1976-92 and Asbury Theological Seminary since 1989. Advisory Trustee Free Enterprise Education Center 1977-91. Member 1981-93 and Treasurer 1991-93 World Methodist Council. Board of Governors The Forum Club of Houston since 1988. Director The Methodist Hospital Houston since 1990. Member Sons of the American Revolution.
Office: 9136 U.S. Courthouse, 515 Rusk Avenue, Houston 77002.
Telephone: (713) 250-5920.

WEST, Ernest Ray, III *(Judge, Brown County Court)*
Office: 200 South Broadway, Brownwood 76801-3192.
Telephone: (325) 643-2828.

WEST, Mickey D. *(Judge, Palo Pinto County Court)*
Mailing address: P.O. Box 190, Palo Pinto 76484-0190.
Telephone: (940) 659-1253.

WESTMORELAND, Greg Baer *(Judge, Matagorda County Court)*
Office: 1700 Seventh Street, Room 301, Bay City 77414-5034.
Telephone: (979) 244-7605.

WHATLEY, Janna K. *(Judge, Texas District Court 343rd Judicial District)* Elected Nov 7, 2000 to term beginning Jan 1, 2001. Term expires Dec 31, 2004. Born Sinton Texas July 5, 1963. United Methodist. Educated at Texas A&M University B.S. with honors 1985 and Baylor University School of Law J.D. 1987. Admitted to practice Texas 1987, U.S. District Court Southern District of Texas 1987 and U.S. Court of Appeals Fifth Circuit. In legal practice Sinton, Beeville, Rockport, George West, Tilden and Corpus Christi 1987-2000.

Member State Bar of Texas, Aransas County and San Patricio County Bar Associations. Past President Sinton Rotary Club.
Mailing address: P.O. Box 700, Sinton 78387.
Office: San Patricio County Courthouse, Sinton 78387.
Telephone: (361) 364-6200.
Fax: (361) 364-6155

WHELESS, Ray *(Judge, Collin County Court at Law No. 4)*
Office: 1800 North Graves, Suite 160, McKinney 75069.
Telephone: (972) 548-3840.

WHITE, Bill C. *(Judge, Bexar County Court at Law No. 7)*
Office: 2121 Bexar County Justice Center, 300 Dolorosa Street, San Antonio 78205-3013.
Telephone: (210) 335-2002.

WHITE, Jim C. *(Judge, Kent County Court)*
Mailing address: P.O. Box 6, Jayton 79528-0006.
Telephone: (806) 237-3373.

WHITE, Jimmy L. *(Judge, Texas District Court 76th Judicial District)*
Mailing address: P.O. Box 1306, Mount Pleasant 75456-1306.
Telephone: (903) 577-6736.

WHITE, Nathan E., Jr. *(Judge, Texas District Court 366th Judicial District)* Appointed by Governor William P. Clements to term beginning Aug 29, 1989. Elected Nov 1990, Nov 1994, 1998 and 2002. Current term expires Dec 31, 2006. Born Dallas Texas Nov 28, 1941. Church of Jesus Christ of Latter-Day Saints. Educated at Southern Methodist University B.B.A. 1964 J.D. 1972. Member Phi Alpha Delta. Admitted to practice Texas 1972. In legal practice Plano 1972-89. Judge, Collin County Commissioners Court 1974-82.

Past President Plano and Collin County Bar Associations. Member State Bar of Texas. Named Citizen of the Year by City of Plano 1982. Lieutenant s.g. USN 1966-71. Republican County Chairman 1971-74. Member State Republican Executive Committee 1980-82. District Governor Rotary Dallas Area 1979-80. President Texas Society Sons of the American Revolution 2001-02. Interests include golf, photography and genealogy.
Office: 210 South McDonald, Suite 514, McKinney 75069.
Telephone: (972) 548-4570.

WHITE, Paul E. *(Judge, Texas District Court 159th Judicial District)*
Mailing address: P.O. Box 908, Lufkin 75902-0908.
Telephone: (936) 639-3913.

WHITNEY, Hugh Charles *(Judge, Delta County Court)*
Office: 200 West Dallas Avenue, Cooper 75432.
Telephone: (903) 395-4400.

WHITTEN, Darlene A. *(Judge, Denton County Court at Law No. 1)*
Office: 210 South Woodrow Lane, Denton 76205.
Telephone: (940) 349-2520.

WHITTINGTON, Mark *(Justice, Texas Court of Appeals Fifth District)* Term expires Dec 31, 2008. Former Judge, Dallas County Court at Law No. 3. Former Judge, Texas District Court 160th Judicial District.
Office: George Allen Sr. Courts Building, 600 Commerce Street, Dallas 75202-4658.
Telephone: (214) 712-3408.

WILBORN, Carroll E., Jr. *(Judge, Texas District Court 344th Judicial District)* Appointed by Governor Mark White to term beginning Sept 1, 1983. Elected 1984, 1988, 1992, 1996 and 2000. Current term expires Dec 31, 2004. Born San Antonio Texas Aug 28, 1945. Episcopalian. Educated at Southern Methodist University B.B.A. 1968 and University of Houston J.D. 1971. Member Sigma Alpha Epsilon and Phi Alpha Delta. Admitted to practice Texas 1971. Began legal practice Anahuac 1971.
Assistant County Attorney Chambers County 1972-73. Assistant District Attorney 1973-77 and District Attorney 1977-83 Liberty-Chambers Counties. Member Judicial Advisory Council Texas Board of Criminal Justice. Chairman Criminal Law Section State Bar of Texas.
Mailing address: P.O. Box 490, Anahuac 77514-0490.
Telephone: (409) 267-8264.

WILKERSON, Analia H. *(Judge, Harris County Criminal Court at Law No. 9)*
Office: 1201 Franklin, Room 10032, Houston 77002.
Telephone: (713) 755-6212.

WILKINSON, J. Michael *(Judge, Texas District Court 179th Judicial District)* Term expires Dec 31, 2004.
Office: 1201 Franklin, Room 18040, Houston 77002.
Telephone: (713) 755-6340.

WILLIAMS, Kemper Stephen *(Judge, Texas District Court 135th Judicial District)* Appointed by Governor George W. Bush to term beginning Jan 1, 1996. Elected 1996 and 2000. Current term expires Dec 31, 2004. Born Victoria Texas Sept 27, 1959. Catholic. Educated at St. Mary's University of San Antonio B.A. magna cum laude and Baylor University J.D. 1985. Admitted to practice Texas 1985. In legal practice Victoria 1985-95.
Member State Bar of Texas (Judicial Section) and Victoria County Bar Association. Republican.
Office: 115 North Bridge Street, Third Floor, Victoria 77901-6544.
Telephone: (361) 575-2412.

WILLY, John G. *(Judge, Brazoria County Court)*
Office: 111 East Locust Street, Suite 504A, Angleton 77515-4678.
Telephone: (979) 864-1595.

WILSON, David V. *(Judge, Texas District Court 217th Judicial District)* Appointed by Governor Dolph Briscoe to term beginning April 1, 1977. Elected 1978, 1982, 1986, 1990, 1994, 1998 and 2002. Current term expires Dec 31, 2006. Born Temple Texas March 13, 1940. Educated at Baylor University, Southwestern University B.A. 1964 and South Texas College of Law J.D. 1969. Admitted to practice Texas 1969 and U.S. District Court Eastern District of Texas 1972. In legal practice Houston 1970 and Lufkin 1971. Justice of the Peace, Angelina County Jan 1973 to Oct 1975.
Assistant District Attorney Oct 1975 to March 1977. Instructor Angelina College 1977. Former member Angelina County Junior Bar Association (President 1975). Member State Bar of Texas and Angelina County Bar Association (Secretary-Treasurer 1972). Recipient Outstanding Lion Award from Hudson Lions Club 1973. Chairman Attorneys Division United Fund 1976. Member Hudson Lions Club (Secretary 1973, Newsletter Editor 1973 and President 1977-78), Angelina County Youth Advisory Council (President 1979), Angelina College Human Services Advisory Committee and First United Methodist Church of Lufkin (President Chancel Choir 1978, Trustee, Administration Board).
Mailing address: P.O. Box 908, Lufkin 75902-0908.
Telephone: (936) 639-3914.

WILSON, James R. *(Judge, Texas District Court 371st Judicial District)* Elected Nov 1994 to term beginning Jan 1, 1995. Reelected 1998 and Nov 2002. Current term expires Dec 31, 2006. Born Fort Worth Texas Dec 8, 1955. Episcopalian. Educated at University of Texas as Arlington B.A. 1978 and California Western School of Law J.D. 1989. Admitted to practice Texas 1989 and U.S. District Court Northern District of Texas 1990. In legal practice Fort Worth 1989-95.
Member State Bar of Texas and Tarrant County Bar Association. Republican. Board of Directors Texas Girls Choir. Member "You Ol' Goat" Committee. Enjoys woodworking.
Office: Tarrant County Justice Center, 401 West Belknap, Fort Worth 76196-7118.
Telephone: (817) 884-2985.

WILSON, Randall W. *(Judge, Texas District Court 157th Judicial District)* Appointed by Governor Rick Perry to term beginning March 26, 2003.
Office: Harris County Courthouse, Eleventh Floor, 1310 Prairie, Houston 77002.
Telephone: (713) 755-6270.

WILSON, Sharen *(Judge, Texas Criminal District Court No. 1 Tarrant County)* Appointed by Governor William P. Clements to term beginning May 2, 1990. Elected Nov 1990, 1994, 1998 and 2002. Current term expires Dec 31, 2006. Born Amarillo Texas Sept 24, 1956. Baptist. Educated at Amarillo College A.S. with honors 1976, Texas Tech University B.A. with honors 1978 and Texas Tech University School of Law J.D. 1980. Admitted to practice Texas 1981. Board Certified—Criminal Law—Texas Board of Legal Specialization. In legal practice Fort Worth 1988-90.
With Tarrant County District Attorney's Office 1980-88. Fellow Texas Bar Foundation. Member College of the State Bar of Texas and State Bar of Texas. Named Outstanding Young Leader of Fort Worth Texas by Fort Worth Jaycees 1991. Republican. Member Rotary Club of Fort Worth since 1991 and Forum Fort Worth, Inc.
Office: Tarrant County Justice Center, 401 West Belknap, Fort Worth 76196-0213.
Telephone: (817) 884-1350.

WINDLE, Don R. *(Judge, Denton County Probate Court)* Assumed office 1995. Elected Nov 1998 and

WINDLE, DON R.—*Continued*

Nov 2002. Current term expires Dec 31, 2006. Born Wichita Falls Texas June 25, 1948. United Methodist. Educated at University of North Texas B.A. 1970 and Texas Tech University School of Law J.D. 1973. Member Delta Theta Phi. Admitted to practice Texas 1973, Arkansas 1973, U.S. Courts of Appeals Eighth 1973, Fifth 1982 and Federal 1983 Circuits, U.S. Supreme Court 1978 and U.S. Court of Appeals for the Armed Forces 1983. Board Certified—Civil Trial Law and Commercial, Residential and Farm and Ranch Real Estate Law—Texas Board of Legal Specialization. In legal practice Denton 1973-92. Associate Judge, Denton Municipal Court 1990-92. Judge, Denton County Court at Law No. 3 March 15, 1992 to 1995.

Civil County Attorney Denton County 1984-86. Commissioner Texas Advisory Commission on Intergovernmental Relations 1987-91. Author "The Subdivision of Land and Its Regulations—A Review of Texas Laws and Regulatory Issues" Texas Advisory Commission on Intergovernmental Relations 1989. President Texas Association of County Courts at Law since 1992. Fellow Texas Bar Foundation. Member American Arbitration Association, National College of Probate Judges, American Judicature Society (Administrative Division), State Bar of Texas (Judicial Section) and American Bar Association. Participant The National Judicial College since 1994. Attends 40 to 50 hours CLE College of the State Bar of Texas and regional and state Judicial conferences annually. USCG Auxiliary. Lieutenant Colonel USAF Auxiliary. Auxiliary Aviator since 1998. Republican. Key Member Republican Party of Texas 1986. Member Denton County Republican Mens Club. Life Member Sons of the Republic of Texas. Member Boy Scouts of America Longhorn Council (Sustaining Member Eagle Scouts), Navy League of the U.S., Air Force Association, Aircraft Owners and Pilots Association and Cessna Pilots Association. Interests include Texas history and politics and aviation.

Office: 1450 East McKinney Street, #2412, Denton 76209-4524.

Telephone: (940) 349-2140.

Fax: (940) 349-2141

E-mail address: don.windle@co.denton.tx.us

WINFREE, Jerry *(Judge, Montgomery County Court at Law No. 2)* Appointed to term beginning Jan 1, 1982. Elected 1986, 1990, 1994, 1998 and 2002. Current term expires Dec 31, 2006. Born Texas Sept 27, 1940. Educated at University of Texas B.S. 1965 and University of Houston J.D. 1970. Admitted to practice Texas 1970.

Assistant County Attorney Harris County 1970-73. Assistant County Attorney 1973-75 and Assistant District Attorney 1975-81 Montgomery County.

Office: 210 West Davis, Suite 300, Conroe 77301-2836.

Telephone: (936) 539-7832.

WISCH, Scott *(Judge, Texas District Court 372nd Judicial District)*

Office: Tarrant County Justice Center, 401 West Belknap, Fort Worth 76196-7119.

Telephone: (817) 884-2992.

WISE, Kenneth Price *(Judge, Texas District Court 152nd Judicial District)*

Office: 1019 Congress Street, Sixteenth Floor, Houston 77002.

Telephone: (713) 755-6282.

WISSER, Jon Neil *(Judge, Texas District Court 299th Judicial District)* Appointed by Governor William P. Clements to term beginning Sept 1, 1982. Elected 1982, 1986, 1990, 1994, 1998 and 2002. Current term expires Dec 31, 2006. Born New York New York July 21, 1945. Educated at University of Texas at Austin B.A. 1967 J.D. 1972. Member Phi Delta Phi. Admitted to practice Texas 1972. Began legal practice Austin 1972. Justice of the Peace, Travis County Justice Court Precinct 3, 1975-77. Judge, Travis County Court at Law No. 3 July 1, 1977 to Aug 31, 1982.

Member State Bar of Texas and Travis County Bar Association. Captain U.S. Army 1967-69. Democrat. Past President Lions Club and South Austin Civic Club. Enjoys playing tennis, running and reading.

Mailing address: P.O. Box 1748, Austin 78767-1748.

Telephone: (512) 854-9442.

WOLFF, Nelson W. *(Judge, Bexar County Court)*

Office: 101 Bexar County Courthouse, 100 Dolorosa Street, San Antonio 78205-3028.

Telephone: (210) 335-2626.

WOMACK, Dana M. *(Judge, Texas District Court 348th Judicial District)* Elected Nov 1996 to term beginning Jan 1, 1997. Reelected 2000, current term expires Dec 31, 2004. Born Dallas Texas Aug 18, 1960. Baptist. Educated at Baylor University B.A. 1982 J.D. 1983. Member Delta Theta Phi. Admitted to practice Texas 1984 and U.S. District Courts Northern 1984, Western 1985 and Eastern 1989 Districts of Texas. Board Certified—Civil Appellate Law and Civil Trial Law—Texas Board of Legal Specialization.

Assistant County Attorney Ector County 1984-85. Assistant District Attorney Tarrant County 1985-96. Member State Bar of Texas and Tarrant County Bar Association.

Office: Tarrant County Justice Center, 401 West Belknap, Fort Worth 76196-0281.

Telephone: (817) 884-2715.

WOMACK, Paul *(Judge, Texas Court of Criminal Appeals)* Elected to term beginning Jan 1, 1997. Reelected 2002, current term expires Dec 31, 2008. Born Shreveport Louisiana April 1, 1947. Educated at Louisiana State University B.S. 1970 and University of Texas School of Law J.D. 1975. Admitted to practice Texas 1976, U.S. District Courts Southern and Western Districts of Texas, U.S. Courts of Appeals Fifth and Eleventh Circuits and U.S. Supreme Court. In legal practice San Antonio Sept 1, 1977 to Jan 31, 1979.

Assistant District Attorney 53rd Judicial District of Texas Nov 15, 1982 to Feb 28, 1987. First Assistant District Attorney 26th Judicial District of Texas Aug 1, 1987 to Dec 31, 1996.

Mailing address: P.O. Box 12308, Austin 78711-2308.

Office: Supreme Court Building, Austin 78701.

Telephone: (512) 463-1595.

WOOD, Mike *(Judge, Harris County Probate Court No. 2)*
Office: Family Law Center Building, Sixth Floor, 1115 Congress Street, Houston 77002.
Telephone: (713) 755-6090.

WOOD, Sharolyn P. *(Judge, Texas District Court 127th Judicial District)* Elected to term beginning Jan 1, 1985. Reelected 1988, 1992, 1996 and 2000. Current term expires Dec 31, 2004. Born Denton Texas Nov 7, 1947. Methodist. Educated at Rice University B.A. 1970 and University of Texas School of Law J.D. 1973. Member Phi Delta Phi. Admitted to practice Texas 1973. In legal practice Houston 1973-81 and 1983-84. Judge, Texas District Court 295th Judicial District 1981-82, appointed by Governor William P. Clements.
Office: 205 Civil Courts Building, 301 Fannin Street, Houston 77002.
Telephone: (713) 755-6274.

WOODLOCK, Jerry W. *(Judge, Texas District Court 235th Judicial District)* Elected Nov 1988 to term beginning Jan 1, 1989. Reelected Nov 1992, Nov 1996 and Nov 2000. Current term expires Dec 31, 2004. Born Fort Worth Texas Dec 18, 1944. Methodist. Educated at University of Texas at Arlington B.A. 1967 and University of Texas at Austin J.D. 1970. Member Phi Alpha Delta. Admitted to practice Texas 1970. In legal practice Gainesville 1970-89.
County Attorney Cooke County 1971-74. District Attorney 235th Judicial District 1974-79. Member College of the State Bar of Texas, State Bar of Texas and Cooke County Bar Association.
Office: Cooke County Courthouse, Gainesville 76240-4796.
Telephone: (940) 668-5401.

WOODWARD, Ben *(Judge, Texas District Court 119th Judicial District)* Appointed by Governor George W. Bush to term beginning July 1, 1999. Elected Nov 2000, current term expires Dec 31, 2004. Born Coleman Texas Dec 14, 1953. Methodist. Educated at University of Texas B.B.A. 1976 and Texas Tech University J.D. with honors 1979. Business Editor Texas Tech Law Review 1977-79. Law Clerk to Hon. Zollie Steakley, Texas Supreme Court 1979-80. Member Order of the Coif. Admitted to practice Texas 1979, U.S. District Courts Northern and Western Districts of Texas and U.S. Court of Appeals Fifth Circuit. In legal practice San Angelo 1980-99.
Office: 112 West Beauregard, San Angelo 76903-5850.
Telephone: (325) 659-6570.
E-mail address: B.Woodward@alumni.utexas.net

WOODY, W. Bruce *(Judge, Dallas County Court at Law No. 4)*
Office: Records Building, Third Floor, Dallas 75202-3513.
Telephone: (214) 653-7466.

WOOLDRIDGE, John T. *(Judge, Texas District Court 269th Judicial District)* Appointed by Governor George W. Bush to term beginning 1997. Elected 1998 and 2002. Current term expires Dec 31, 2006. Educated at Texas Christian University B.F.A. 1981, St. Mary's University of San Antonio School of Law J.D. 1987 and Tulane University School of Law LL.M. 1991. Admitted to practice Texas 1987.
Office: 304 Civil Courts Building, 301 Fannin Street, Houston 77002.
Telephone: (713) 755-5516.
E-mail address: judge@269th.com

WORD, Cole *(Judge, Bosque County Court)*
Mailing address: P.O. Box 647, Meridian 76665-0647.
Telephone: (254) 435-2382.

WORK, Jeff *(Judge, Texas District Court 189th Judicial District)*
Office: Civil Courts Building, Sixth Floor, 301 Fannin Street, Houston 77002.
Telephone: (713) 755-6366.

WORSHAM, Jack Logan *(Judge, Hutchinson County Court)* Appointed Oct 20, 1995. Elected Nov 3, 1996 and 1998. Reelected Nov 12, 2002, current term expires Dec 31, 2006. Born Amarillo Texas May 27, 1929. Methodist. Educated at West Texas A&M University B.S. 1950.
Mailing address: P.O. Box 790, Stinnett 79083-0790.
Telephone: (806) 878-4000.

WORTHEN, James T. *(Chief Justice, Texas Court of Appeals Twelfth District)* Justice Jan 1, 1999 to Dec 31, 2002. Elected Chief Justice to term beginning Jan 1, 2003. Term expires Dec 31, 2008.
Office: 1517 West Front Street, Suite 354, Tyler 75702-7854.
Telephone: (903) 593-8471.

WRIGHT, Carolyn I. *(Justice, Texas Court of Appeals Fifth District)* Term expires Dec 31, 2004. Former Judge, Texas District Court 256th Judicial District.
Office: George Allen Sr. Courts Building, 600 Commerce Street, Dallas 75202-4658.
Telephone: (214) 712-3410.

WRIGHT, H. T. *(Judge, Caldwell County Court)*
Office: Courthouse, Second Floor, 110 South Main Street, Lockhart 78644.
Telephone: (512) 398-1809.

WRIGHT, Jim R. *(Justice, Texas Court of Appeals Eleventh District)* Term expires Dec 31, 2008. Former Judge, Texas District Court 91st Judicial District.
Mailing address: P.O. Box 271, Eastland 76448-0271.
Telephone: (254) 629-2638.

WRIGHT, Tim *(Judge, Williamson County Court at Law No. 2)*
Office: 405 South Martin Luther King Blvd., Box 4, Georgetown 78626.
Telephone: (512) 943-1410.

WYDE, Dan L. *(Judge, Dallas County Criminal Court at Law No. 3)* Appointed to term beginning May 20, 1997. Elected Nov 1997. Reelected 2001. Current term expires Dec 31, 2005. Born Port Arthur Texas Dec 7, 1962. Jewish. Educated at University of Texas at Austin B.B.A. and University of Houston Law Center J.D. Admitted to practice Texas 1990.
Assistant District Attorney Dallas County 1990-97. Member State Bar of Texas and Dallas Bar Association.

WYDE, DAN L.—*Continued*

Moderator in Evidence and Trial Tactics various CLE seminars. Republican.

Office: LB 16 Frank Crowley Courts Bldg., 133 North Industrial Boulevard, Dallas 75207-4313.

Telephone: (214) 653-5627.

E-mail address: dwyde@dallascounty.org

WYLIE, Paul O. *(Judge, Archer County Court)* Mailing address: P.O. Box 458, Archer City 76351-0458.

Telephone: (940) 574-2581.

YAÑEZ, Linda Reyna *(Justice, Texas Court of Appeals Thirteenth District)* Appointed by Governor Ann W. Richards to term beginning 1993. Elected to subsequent term. Current term expires Dec 31, 2004. First Hispanic woman to serve on Texas Court of Appeals. Educated at Pan American University B.A. 1970, Texas Southern University School of Law J.D. 1976 and University of Virginia School of Law LL.M. 1998. Admitted to practice Texas and Illinois.

Consulting Attorney Mexican Consul Generals Boston Massachusetts and Brownsville Texas. Regional Counsel Mexican American Legal Defense and Education Fund Chicago Illinois. Member Legal Advisory Committee United Nations High Commissioner for Refugees. Member State Bar of Texas, Illinois State, Massachusetts and American Bar Associations.

Office: Hidalgo County Administrative Bldg., Fifth Floor, 100 East Cano, Edinburg 78539.

Telephone: (956) 318-2405.

YARBROUGH, James D. *(Judge, Galveston County Court)*

Office: 722 Moody, Suite 200, Galveston 77550.

Telephone: (409) 766-2244.

YARBROUGH, Jan *(Judge, Texas Family District Court 306th Judicial District)*

Office: 722 Moody, #507, Galveston 77550.

Telephone: (409) 766-2255.

YATES, Leslie Brock *(Justice, Texas Court of Appeals Fourteenth District)* Assumed office 1994. Elected to subsequent term. Current term expires Dec 31, 2004. Educated at University of Florida B.A. 1980 and University of Houston School of Law J.D. 1984.

Former Member College of the State Bar of Texas. Member Texas Bar Foundation, Texas Association of State Judges and Houston Bar Association. Advisory Board Child Advocates 1996-98. Member Campaign for the Homeless since 1998.

Office: 1307 San Jacinto, 11th Floor, Houston 77002-7006.

Telephone: (713) 655-2800.

YEAKEL, Lee *(Justice, Texas Court of Appeals Third District)* Appointed by Governor George W. Bush to term beginning Dec 10, 1998. Elected 2000, current term expires Dec 31, 2006. Born Oklahoma City Oklahoma April 18, 1945. Episcopalian. Educated at University of Texas B.A. 1966 J.D. 1969 and University of Virginia LL.M. 2001. Admitted to practice Texas 1969, U.S. District Court Western District of Texas 1970, U.S. Court of Appeals Fifth Circuit 1972 and U.S. Supreme Court 1975. In legal practice Austin 1969-1998.

Member Commission on Uniform State Laws and The American Law Institute. Republican. Member State Republican Executive Committee 1988-90. Chairman Travis County Republican Party 1990-92.

Mailing address: P.O. Box 12547, Austin 78711-2547.

Telephone: (512) 463-1733.

YORK, Jim *(Judge, Texas District Court 246th Judicial District)*

Office: Family Law Center Building, Seventh Floor, 1115 Congress Street, Houston 77002.

Telephone: (713) 755-6938.

YORK, Van Lee *(Judge, Borden County Court)*

Mailing address: P.O. Box 156, Gail 79738.

Telephone: (806) 756-4391.

YOUNG, Everett *(Judge, Texas District Court 297th Judicial District)* Term expires Dec 31, 2006.

Office: Tarrant County Justice Center, 401 West Belknap, Fort Worth 76196-0229.

Telephone: (817) 884-1906.

YOUNG, Randy *(Judge, McCulloch County Court)* Appointed to term beginning Dec 5, 1989. Elected Nov 1990, 1994, 1998 and 2002. Current term expires Dec 31, 2006. Born Brady Texas Dec 5, 1957. Church of Christ. Educated at Angelo State University B.S. Owner Brady Automotive Supply and BAS Publications.

Office: 202 McCulloch County Courthouse, Brady 76825.

Telephone: (325) 597-0733.

ZEIGLER, Phillip *(Judge, Texas District Court 52nd Judicial District)* Appointed by Governor Ann W. Richards to term beginning Jan 29, 1991. Elected 1992, 1996 and 2000. Current term expires Dec 31, 2004. Born Gatesville Texas. Educated at Texas Tech University B.A. 1967 and University of Texas J.D. 1972. Admitted to practice Texas 1972. In legal practice Gatesville and Houston.

District Attorney 52nd Judicial District 1983-91. Member State Bar of Texas. Lieutenant j.g. USNR 1969-70. Democrat.

Mailing address: P.O. Box 19, Gatesville 76528.

Telephone: (254) 865-5911.

UTAH

Capital SALT LAKE CITY

UNITED STATES DISTRICT COURT DISTRICT OF UTAH

United States District Court District of Utah consists of two divisions. For descriptive information refer to the United States Courts section.

Central Division includes Beaver, Carbon, Daggett, Duchesne, Emery, Garfield, Grand, Iron, Juab, Kane, Millard, Piute, Salt Lake, San Juan, Sanpete, Sevier, Summit, Tooele, Uintah, Utah, Wasatch, Washington and Wayne counties. The court sits at Provo, St. George and Salt Lake City.

Northern Division includes Box Elder, Cache, Davis, Morgan, Rich and Weber counties. The court sits at Ogden and Salt Lake City.

Chief Judge
Dee V. Benson

Judges
Tena Campbell
Dale A. Kimball
Brian T. Stewart
Paul G. Cassell

Senior Judges
Bruce S. Jenkins
David K. Winder
J. Thomas Greene
David Sam

Clerk
Markus B. Zimmer
150 U.S. Courthouse
350 South Main Street
Salt Lake City, Utah 84101-2180
(801) 524-6100

UNITED STATES MAGISTRATE JUDGES OF UTAH

F. Bennion Redd
Samuel Alba
David Nuffer
Clark B. Allred

UNITED STATES BANKRUPTCY COURT OF UTAH

Chief Judge
Glen E. Clark

Judges
Judith A. Boulden
William T. Thurman

Bankruptcy Clerk
William C. Stillgebauer
361 U.S. Courthouse
350 South Main Street
Salt Lake City, Utah 84101
(801) 524-6687

UTAH SUPREME COURT

The Supreme Court is Utah's court of last resort. The court consists of five justices. Justices are initially appointed by the governor upon recommendation of a Judicial Nominating Commission and run unopposed for retention at the first general election occurring more than three years after appointment. Retention elections are held every ten years. The chief justice is elected by peer vote to a four-year term. The associate chief justice is elected by peer vote to a two-year term. Retired justices may serve as senior judges in any court other than the Supreme Court.

The court has exclusive appellate jurisdiction over first degree and capital felony convictions from the District Court and civil judgments other than domestic relations, cases where the Court of Appeals does not have jurisdiction and over some administrative agencies. The court may review decisions of the Court of Appeals by writ of certiorari and may issue other writs necessary to the exercise of proper jurisdiction. The court has original jurisdiction over questions of state law certified from federal court and extraordinary writs. The court exercises constitutional rule-making authority over procedure and evidence and regulates admission to the bar and the conduct of its members.

The court sits en banc at Salt Lake City but may sit at other locations. The court holds session all year.

Chief Justice
Christine Meaders Durham

Associate Chief Justice
Matthew B. Durrant

Justices
Michael J. Wilkins
Jill N. Parrish
Ronald E. Nehring

Clerk
Pat H. Bartholomew
450 South State
P.O. Box 140210
Salt Lake City, Utah 84114-0210
(801) 238-7974

Court Administrator
Marilyn Branch
450 South State
P.O. Box 140241
Salt Lake City, Utah 84114-1241
(801) 578-3834

UTAH COURT OF APPEALS

The Court of Appeals, implemented January 1, 1987, is Utah's court of intermediate appellate jurisdiction. The court consists of a presiding judge and six judges. Judges are initially appointed by the governor upon recommendation of a Judicial Nominating Commission and run unopposed for retention at the first general election occurring more than three years after appointment. Retention elections are held every six years. The presiding judge is elected by peer vote to a two-year term. The associate presiding judge is elected by peer vote to a one-year term. Retired judges may serve as senior judges in any court other than the Supreme Court.

The court exercises appellate jurisdiction over cases from the District Court and the Juvenile Court, domestic relations cases, felony cases except those appealed directly to the Supreme Court and over cases from those administrative agencies which are not appealed directly to the Supreme Court. The court also has jurisdiction to hear cases transferred to it by the Supreme Court, which are limited by statute to appeals of civil cases from the District Court.

The court sits in rotating panels of three judges and is prohibited from sitting en banc. The court sits at Salt Lake City; however, it holds court four times a year in different geographic regions of the state.

Presiding Judge
Norman H. Jackson

Judges
Russell W. Bench
Judith M. Billings
James Z. Davis
Pamela T. Greenwood
Gregory K. Orme
William A. Thorne, Jr.

UTAH DISTRICT COURT

The District Court is Utah's court of general jurisdiction and consists of eight judicial districts. On January 1, 1992, the fifth, sixth, seventh and eighth judicial districts of the Circuit Court consolidated with the District Court. The remaining four districts consolidated on July 1, 1996. Judges are initially appointed by the governor upon recommendation of a Judicial Nominating Commission and run unopposed for retention at the first general election occurring more than three years after appointment. Retention elections are held every six years. A presiding judge is elected by peer vote in each district to a two-year term. In a district having more than two judges, the judges may elect an associate presiding judge by peer vote to a two-year term. Retired judges may serve as senior judges in any court other than the Supreme Court.

The court has original jurisdiction over all civil and criminal matters except where exclusive jurisdiction is conferred upon another court. The court has concurrent criminal jurisdiction with the Juvenile Court in cases involving traffic offenses by juveniles. The court exercises exclusive criminal jurisdiction in felony cases and may also hear cases involving juveniles who have been certified by Juvenile Court to stand trial as adults for felonies. The court may issue writs necessary to the exercise of proper jurisdiction.

The court sits at each county seat and in other municipalities designated by the Judicial Council.

FIRST JUDICIAL DISTRICT includes Box Elder, Cache and Rich counties. The court sits at Brigham City, Logan and Randolph.

Associate Presiding Judge
Gordon J. Low

Judges
Ben H. Hadfield
Clint S. Judkins
Thomas L. Willmore

SECOND JUDICIAL DISTRICT includes Davis, Morgan and Weber counties. The court sits at Farmington, Morgan and Ogden.

Presiding Judge
W. Brent West

Judges
Michael G. Allphin
Parley R. Baldwin
Glen R. Dawson
Roger S. Dutson
Scott M. Hadley
Darwin Hansen
Pamela G. Heffernan
Ernest W. Jones
Thomas L. Kay
Michael D. Lyon
Jon M. Memmott
Rodney S. Page

THIRD JUDICIAL DISTRICT includes Salt Lake, Summit and Tooele counties. The court sits at Salt Lake City, Coalville and Tooele.

Presiding Judge
Sandra N. Peuler

Judges
Judith S. H. Atherton
William W. Barrett
William B. Bohling
Ann Boyden
Pat B. Brian
Michael K. Burton
Terry L. Christiansen
L. A. Dever
Joseph C. Fratto, Jr.
J. Dennis Frederick
Dennis M. Fuchs
Timothy R. Hanson
Stephen L. Henriod
Robert K. Hilder
Glenn K. Iwasaki
Leslie A. Lewis
Denise P. Lindberg
Bruce C. Lubeck
Paul G. Maughan
Sheila K. McCleve
Tyrone E. Medley
Frank G. Noel
Anthony Quinn
Robin W. Reese
Steven Roth
Randall N. Skanchy
vacancy
vacancy
vacancy

FOURTH JUDICIAL DISTRICT includes Juab, Millard, Utah and Wasatch counties. The court sits at Nephi, Fillmore, Provo and Heber City.

Presiding Judge
Gary D. Stott

Judges
John C. Backlund
Guy R. Burningham
Lynn W. Davis
Donald J. Eyre, Jr.
Steven L. Hansen
Fred D. Howard
Claudia Laycock
Howard H. Maetani
Anthony W. Schofield
James R. Taylor
vacancy

FIFTH JUDICIAL DISTRICT includes Beaver, Iron and Washington counties. The court sits at Beaver, Parowan and St. George.

Presiding Judge
J. Philip Eves

UTAH DISTRICT COURT—*Continued*

Judges
G. Rand Beacham
James L. Shumate
vacancy

SIXTH JUDICIAL DISTRICT includes Garfield, Kane, Piute, Sanpete, Sevier and Wayne counties. The court sits at Panguitch, Kanab, Junction, Manti, Richfield and Loa.

Presiding Judge
K. L. McIff

Judge
David L. Mower

SEVENTH JUDICIAL DISTRICT includes Carbon, Emery, Grand and San Juan counties. The court sits at Price, Castle Dale, Moab and Monticello.

Presiding Judge
Bryce K. Bryner

Judges
Lyle R. Anderson
Bruce K. Halliday

EIGHTH JUDICIAL DISTRICT includes Daggett, Duchesne and Uintah counties. The court sits at Manila, Duchesne and Vernal.

Presiding Judge
A. Lynn Payne, Jr.

Judge
John R. Anderson

UTAH JUVENILE COURT

The Juvenile Court is a court of limited jurisdiction and consists of eight districts. Judges are initially appointed by the governor upon recommendation by a Juvenile Court Nominating Commission and run unopposed for retention at the first general election occurring more than three years after appointment. Retention elections are held every six years. A presiding judge is elected in each district to a two-year term. Retired judges may serve as senior judges in any court other than the Supreme Court.

The court exercises jurisdiction over criminal law violations by juveniles; limited status offenses, such as truancy, curfew and ungovernability; abuse, neglect or dependency of children and termination of the parent-child relationship; judicial consent for marriage and employment when required by law; support obligations by parents; and resolution of custody disputes involving juveniles under continuing jurisdiction of the court. The court exercises concurrent jurisdiction with other courts to try adults for offenses such as contributing to the delinquency, abuse or neglect of juveniles and with the District Court and Justice Courts over traffic offenses committed by juveniles. In some cases which would be felonies if committed by adults, the court may, after appropriate hearing, transfer juveniles to the District Court for trial as adults. Appeals are to the Court of Appeals.

The court sits at each county seat and in other municipalities designated by the Judicial Council.

FIRST JUDICIAL DISTRICT includes Box Elder, Cache and Rich counties. The court sits at Brigham City, Logan and Randolph.

Presiding Judge
Jeffrey "R" Burbank

Judge
Larry Jones

SECOND JUDICIAL DISTRICT includes Davis, Morgan and Weber counties. The court sits at Farmington, Morgan and Ogden.

Presiding Judge
Diane W. Wilkins

Judges
J. Mark Andrus
L. Kent Bachman
Kathleen Nelson
Stephen A. Van Dyke

THIRD JUDICIAL DISTRICT includes Salt Lake, Summit and Tooele counties. The court sits at Salt Lake City, Coalville and Tooele.

Presiding Judge
Frederic M. Oddone

Judges
Joseph W. Anderson
Kimberly K. Hornak
Sharon P. McCully
Robert S. Yeates
Charles Behrens
Elizabeth Lindsley
Andrew A. Valdez

FOURTH JUDICIAL DISTRICT includes Juab, Millard, Utah and Wasatch counties. The court sits at Nephi, Fillmore, Provo and Heber City.

Presiding Judge
Kay A. Lindsay

Judges
Leslie D. Brown
Mary T. Noonan
Sterling B. Sainsbury

FIFTH JUDICIAL DISTRICT includes Beaver, Iron and Washington counties. The court sits at Beaver, Parowan and St. George.

Presiding Judge
Hans Q. Chamberlain

Judge
Thomas M. Higbee

SIXTH JUDICIAL DISTRICT includes Garfield, Kane, Piute, Sanpete, Sevier and Wayne counties. The court sits at Panguitch, Kanab, Junction, Manti, Richfield and Loa.

Presiding Judge
Paul D. Lyman

SEVENTH JUDICIAL DISTRICT includes Carbon, Emery, Grand and San Juan counties. The court sits at Price, Castle Dale, Moab and Monticello.

Presiding Judge
Scott Johansen

Judge
Mary Manley

UTAH JUVENILE COURT—*Continued.*

EIGHTH JUDICIAL DISTRICT includes Daggett, Duchesne and Uintah counties. The court sits at Manila, Duchesne and Vernal.

Presiding Judge
Larry A. Steele

UTAH JUSTICE COURTS

Justice Courts are courts of limited jurisdiction in Utah. There are two types of Justice Courts in the state. Municipal Justice Courts may be established in any city or town. County (precinct) Justice Courts are found in every county in the state except Cache County. Within precincts, judges are appointed for four-year terms by the County Commission. Within cities or towns, judges are appointed by the city council for four-year terms.

In cities or towns where Justice Courts are established, the courts have exclusive jurisdiction in all cases involving municipal ordinance violations and Class B and C misdemeanors, infractions and small claims matters involving less than $5,000 occurring within the municipality. County Justice Courts have jurisdiction over all Class B and C misdemeanors and infractions committed within the counties but not within a municipality with a District Court or Municipal Justice Court. Justice Courts have concurrent jurisdiction with the Juvenile Court and District Court over minors charged with traffic offenses.

Judges need not be attorneys, but they are required to attend at least one training seminar sponsored by the Judicial Council each year.

Utah Counties and County Seats

Beaver
Beaver

Box Elder
Brigham City

Cache
Logan

Carbon
Price

Daggett
Manila

Davis
Farmington

Duchesne
Duchesne

Emery
Castle Dale

Garfield
Panguitch

Grand
Moab

Iron
Parowan

Juab
Nephi

Kane
Kanab

Millard
Fillmore

Morgan
Morgan

Piute
Junction

Rich
Randolph

Salt Lake
Salt Lake City

San Juan
Monticello

Sanpete
Manti

Sevier
Richfield

Summit
Coalville

Tooele
Tooele

Uintah
Vernal

Utah
Provo

Wasatch
Heber City

Washington
St. George

Wayne
Loa

Weber
Ogden

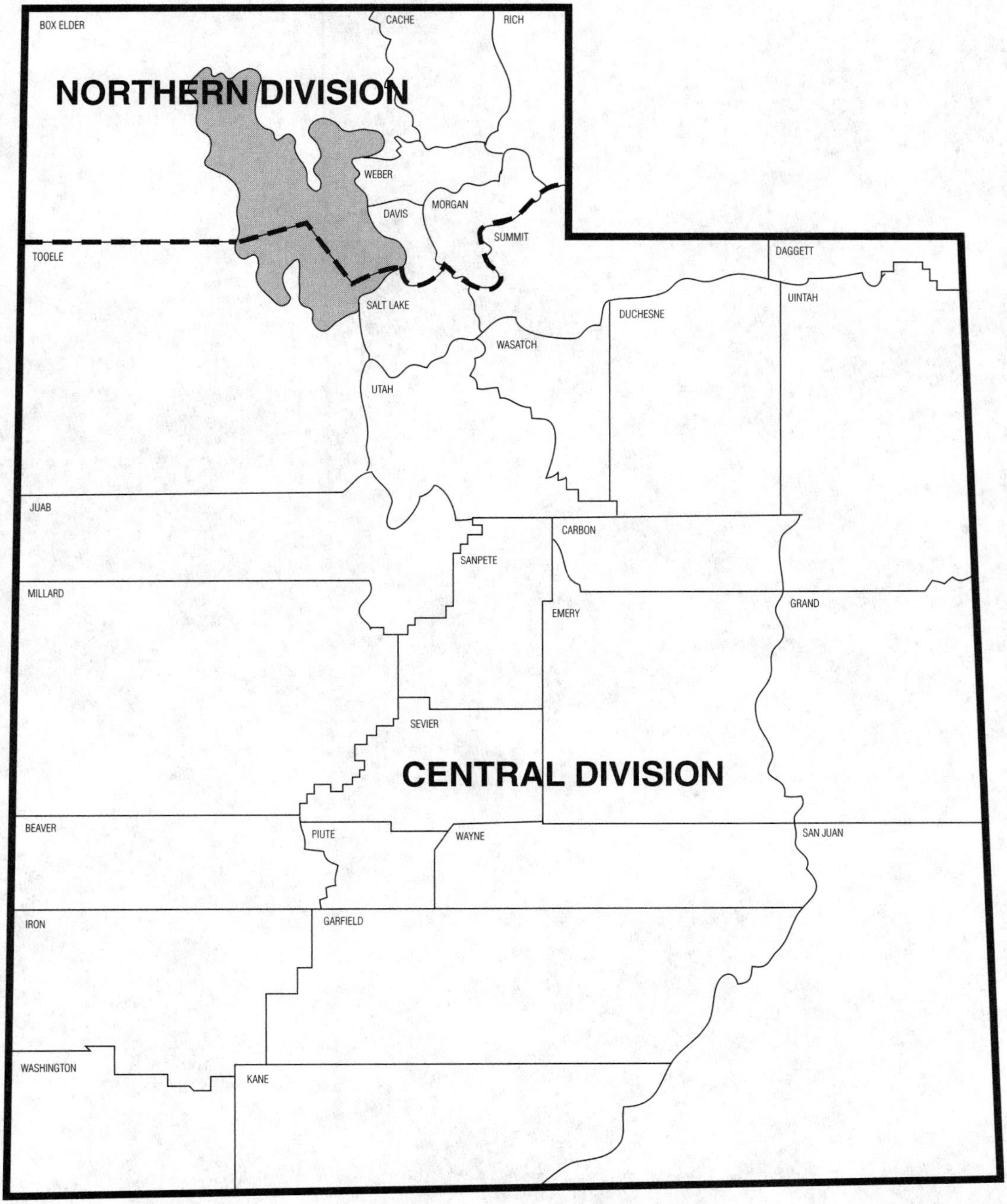
NORTHERN DIVISION
CENTRAL DIVISION
BOX ELDER
CACHE
RICH
WEBER
MORGAN
DAVIS
SUMMIT
TOOELE
DAGGETT
UINTAH
SALT LAKE
DUCHESNE
WASATCH
UTAH
JUAB
CARBON
SANPETE
MILLARD
GRAND
EMERY
SEVIER
BEAVER
PIUTE
WAYNE
SAN JUAN
IRON
GARFIELD
WASHINGTON
KANE

DIVISIONS OF UNITED STATES DISTRICT COURT DISTRICT OF UTAH

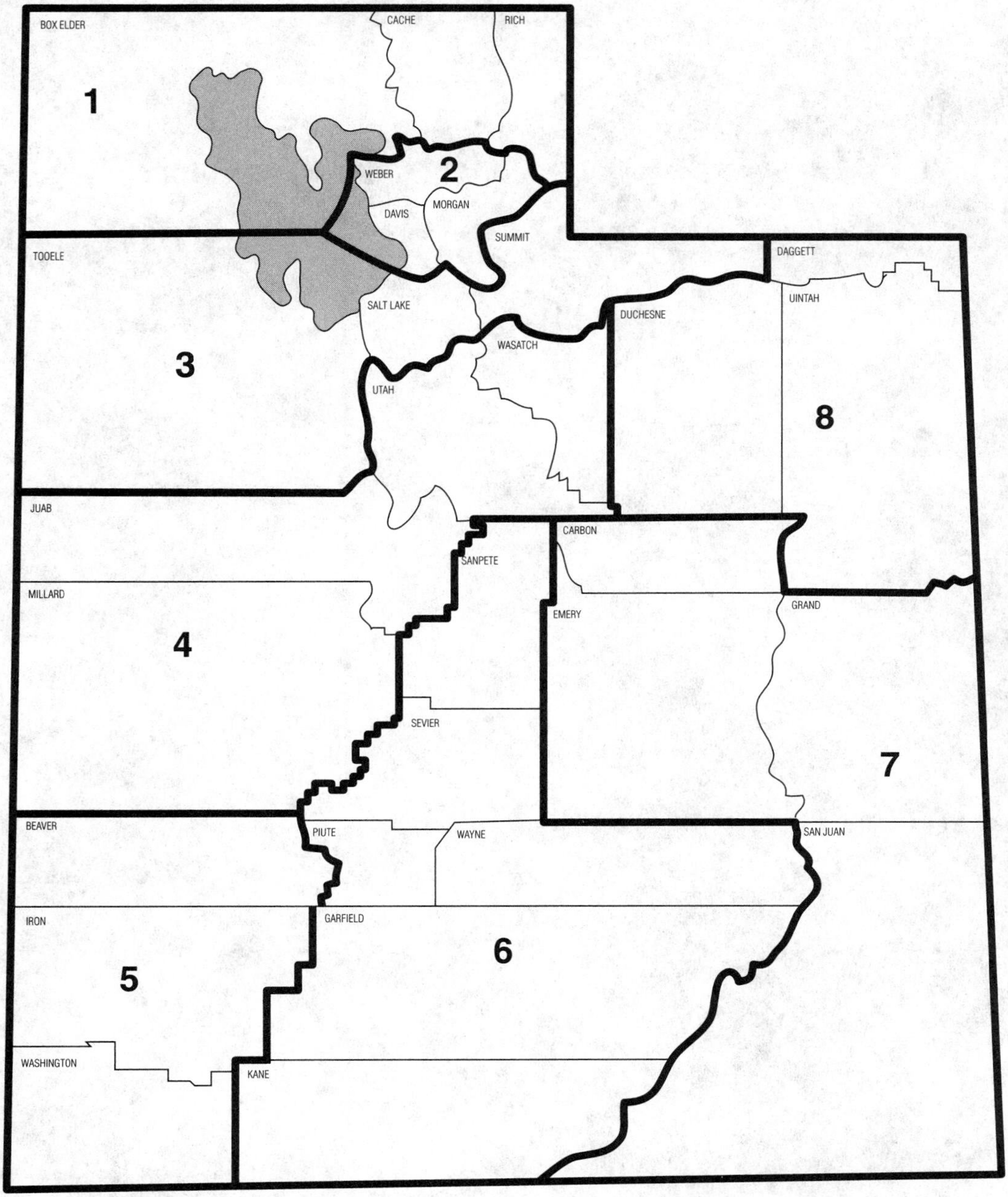
BOX ELDER
CACHE
RICH
1
WEBER
2
DAVIS
MORGAN
SUMMIT
TOOELE
DAGGETT
SALT LAKE
UINTAH
DUCHESNE
WASATCH
3
UTAH
8
JUAB
CARBON
SANPETE
MILLARD
GRAND
EMERY
4
SEVIER
7
BEAVER
PIUTE
WAYNE
SAN JUAN
IRON
GARFIELD
6
5
WASHINGTON
KANE

JUDICIAL DISTRICTS OF UTAH DISTRICT COURT AND JUVENILE COURT

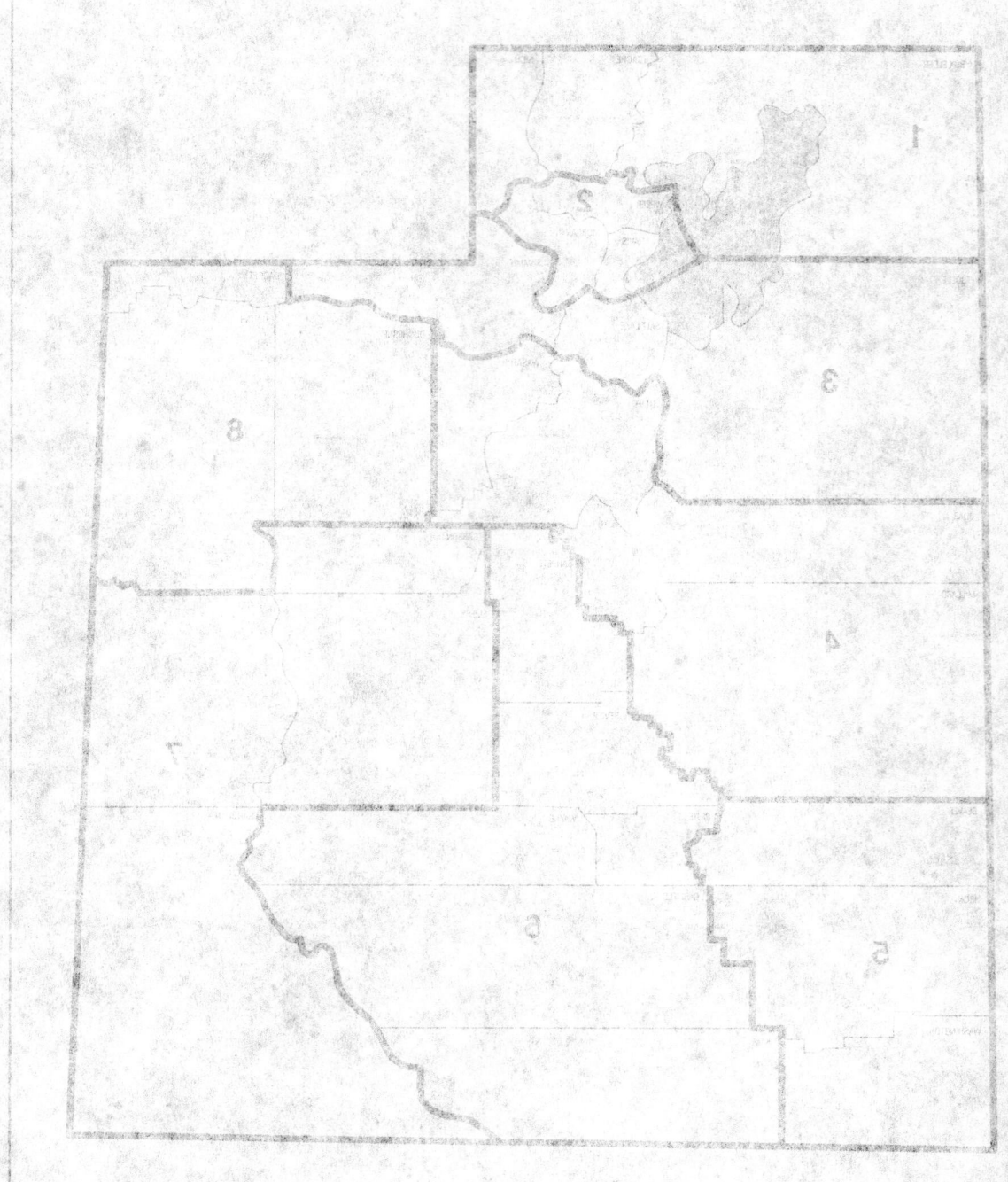

UTAH

ALBA, Samuel *(Magistrate Judge, United States District Court District of Utah)* Appointed by U.S. District Court judges.
Office: 260 U.S. Courthouse, 350 South Main Street, Salt Lake City 84101.
Telephone: (801) 524-6155.

ALLPHIN, Michael G. *(Judge, Utah District Court Second Judicial District)* Appointed by governor. Former Presiding Judge.
Mailing address: P.O. Box 769, Farmington 84025.
Office: 800 West State Street, Farmington 84025.
Telephone: (801) 447-3850.
Fax: (801) 447-3880

ALLRED, Clark B. *(Magistrate Judge, United States District Court District of Utah)* Appointed by U.S. District Court judges. Serves part time.
Office: 121 West Main Street, Vernal 84078-2503.
Telephone: (435) 789-4908.

ANDERSON, John R. *(Judge, Utah District Court Eighth Judicial District)* Appointed by governor. Former Presiding Judge.
Office: 920 East Highway 40, Vernal 84078-2803.
Telephone: (435) 781-9300.
Fax: (435) 789-0564

ANDERSON, Joseph W. *(Judge, Utah Juvenile Court Third Judicial District)* Appointed by Governor Michael O. Leavitt June 9, 1995 to term beginning Aug 7, 1995. Retained by election 1998, current term expires 2004. Currently serves Third District Court. Born Murray Utah Dec 20, 1945. Church of Jesus Christ of Latter-Day Saints. Educated at University of Utah B.A. cum laude 1971 M.A. 1974 J.D. 1974. Law Clerk to Hon. Robert Earl Maxwell, U.S. District Court Northern District of West Virginia 1974-75. Member Society of Bar and Gavel. Admitted to practice Utah 1974, West Virginia 1977 and U.S. Court of Appeals Fourth 1979 and Tenth 1982 Circuits. In legal practice Salt Lake City Utah 1975-79.
Assistant U.S. Attorney Northern District of West Virginia 1979-82 and Utah 1982-95. Author "This is Not 'Kiddie' Court" Voir Dire issue Utah B. Jour. 1997 and "Act Well Thy Part" II No. 5 Utah B. Jour. June 1998. Important Decisions: In re C.K. and S.K. (Upheld decision not to terminate mother's parental rights, even though she was unfit parent, where father was given custody) Utah App. Lexis 4, Utah App. 011, 2000 and State v. M.L.C.(Juvenile is not entitled to bail) 933 P.2d 380 S. Ct. Utah 1997. Member Utah State Bar, The West Virginia State Bar and Federal Bar Association. Instructor Utah State Judicial Conference on Evidence 1998 and Utah Juvenile Court Conference on Evidence 1997 and 1998 and on Rules of Discovery 2000. Utah Army National Guard. Enjoys outdoor sports, gardening and crafts.
Mailing address: P.O. Box 140431, Salt Lake City 84114-0431.
Office: 450 South State, Second Floor, Salt Lake City 84111.
Telephone: (801) 238-7760.
Fax: (801) 238-7771
E-mail address: jjwander@email.utcourts.gov

ANDERSON, Lyle R. *(Judge, Utah District Court Seventh Judicial District)* Appointed by governor. Former Presiding Judge.
Office: 125 East Center Street, Moab 84532.
Telephone: (435) 259-1350.
Fax: (435) 259-4081

ANDRUS, J. Mark *(Judge, Utah Juvenile Court Second Judicial District)* Appointed by governor. Former Presiding Judge.
Office: 444 26th Street, Ogden 84401.
Telephone: (801) 626-3800.
Fax: (801) 626-3827

ATHERTON, Judith S. H. *(Judge, Utah District Court Third Judicial District)* Currently serves Third Juvenile Court.
Mailing address: P.O. Box 1860, Salt Lake City 84110.
Office: 450 South State, Salt Lake City 84111.
Telephone: (801) 238-7326.
Fax: (801) 238-7074

BACHMAN, L. Kent *(Judge, Utah Juvenile Court Second Judicial District)* Appointed by Governor Scott M. Matheson to term beginning Aug 1977. Retained by election. Former Presiding Judge. Born Ogden Utah Oct 10, 1939. Educated at University of Utah College of Law J.D. 1968. Referee First District Juvenile Court 1969-71.
Former Deputy Attorney Weber County. Former Chief Deputy City Attorney Ogden City. Member Utah Judicial Council and Utah Board of Juvenile Court Judges.
Office: 444 26th Street, Ogden 84401.
Telephone: (801) 626-3800.
Fax: (801) 626-3827

BACKLUND, John C. *(Judge, Utah District Court Fourth Judicial District)* Assumed office July 1, 1996. Retained by election 2000, current term expires Dec 31, 2006. Born Torrance California Dec 13, 1946. Church of Jesus Christ of Latter-Day Saints. Educated at El Camino Junior College 1964-65, Brigham Young University B.A. 1971 and University of Utah J.D. 1974. Admitted to practice Utah 1974. Began legal practice Pleasant Grove 1974. In legal practice Provo 1979. Judge, Utah Circuit Court Fourth Judicial District July 1, 1983 to June 30, 1996, appointed by Governor Scott M. Matheson.
City Attorney Pleasant Grove 1976-83, Alpine 1976-83 and Lindon 1977-82. Instructor Utah Technical College 1975. Member Utah State Bar.
Office: 97 East Center, Orem 84057.
Telephone: (801) 764-5870.
Fax: (801) 226-5244

BALDWIN, Parley R. *(Judge, Utah District Court Second Judicial District)* Assumed office July 1, 1996. Born Afton Wyoming Jan 25, 1946. Educated at University of Utah College of Law J.D. 1972. Judge and Pre-

BALDWIN, PARLEY R.—*Continued*

siding Judge, Utah Circuit Court Second Judicial District June 1987 to June 30, 1996, appointed by Governor Norman H. Bangerter.

Former Assistant Corporate Counsel City of Ogden.
Office: 2525 Grant Avenue, Ogden 84401.
Telephone: (801) 395-1146.
Fax: (801) 395-1182

BARRETT, William W. *(Judge, Utah District Court Third Judicial District)* Appointed by governor.
Mailing address: P.O. Box 1860, Salt Lake City 84110.
Office: 450 South State, Salt Lake City 84111.
Telephone: (801) 238-7357.
Fax: (801) 238-7074

BEACHAM, G. Rand *(Judge, Utah District Court Fifth Judicial District)* Appointed by governor. Former Presiding Judge.
Office: Washington County Hall of Justice, 220 North 200 East, St. George 84770.
Telephone: (435) 986-5700.
Fax: (435) 986-5723

BEHRENS, Charles *(Judge, Utah Juvenile Court Third Judicial District)* Appointed by Governor Michael O. Leavitt. Former Presiding Judge.
Office: 210 West 10000 South, Sandy 84070.
Telephone: (801) 565-5753.
Fax: (801) 565-5747

BENCH, Russell W. *(Judge, Utah Court of Appeals)* Appointed by Governor Norman H. Bangerter to term beginning Jan 17, 1987. Retained by election Nov 1990, Nov 1996 and Nov 2002. Current term expires Jan 2009. Former Associate Presiding Judge and Presiding Judge. Born Roosevelt Utah May 12, 1950. Educated at University of Utah B.A. with honors 1973 J.D. 1976 and Brigham Young University M.P.A. with honors 1985. Law Clerk to Chief Justice, Utah Supreme Court 1977-80. Admitted to practice Utah 1976. In legal practice Salt Lake City 1976-86.

Special Assistant Utah Attorney General 1976-77. Central Staff Attorney Utah Supreme Court 1981-86. Previously worked for Western Airlines. Enjoys music, sports and travel.
Office: 450 South State, Salt Lake City 84111.
Telephone: (801) 578-3950.
Fax: (801) 238-7981

BENSON, Dee V. *(Chief Judge, United States District Court District of Utah)* Appointed for life by President George Bush to term beginning 1991. Chief Judge since Nov 2, 1999. Born Sandy Utah Aug 25, 1948. Educated at Brigham Young University B.A. 1973 J.D. 1976. In legal practice Salt Lake City 1976-84.

Associate Deputy U.S. Attorney General 1988-89 and U.S. Attorney 1989-91 District of Utah. Counsel to U.S. Senate Committee on the Judiciary Subcommittee on the Constitution 1984-86 and Congressional Investigating Committee on Iran-Contra 1987. Chief of Staff to U.S. Senator Orrin Hatch 1986-88.
Office: 246 U.S. Courthouse, 350 South Main Street, Salt Lake City 84101.
Telephone: (801) 524-6160.

BILLINGS, Judith M. *(Judge, Utah Court of Appeals)* Appointed by Governor Norman H. Bangerter to term beginning Feb 1, 1987. Retained by election. Former Presiding Judge. Currently serves as Associate Presiding Judge. Born April 22, 1943. Educated at University of Utah College of Law J.D. 1977. In legal practice Salt Lake City 1977-86. Former Judge, Utah District Court Third Judicial District.

Adjunct Professor University of Utah College of Law. Former Chairman Child Support Task Force Utah Judicial Council. Chair Task Force on Child Support Guidelines National Association of Women Judges. Member Utah Board of Appellate Court Judges (Judicial Performance Evaluation Committee).
Office: 450 South State, Salt Lake City 84111.
Telephone: (801) 238-3900.

BOHLING, William B. *(Judge, Utah District Court Third Judicial District)* Appointed by governor.
Mailing address: P.O. Box 1860, Salt Lake City 84110.
Office: 450 South State, Salt Lake City 84111.
Telephone: (801) 238-7507.
Fax: (801) 238-7542

BOULDEN, Judith A. *(Judge, United States Bankruptcy Court District of Utah)* Appointed by U.S. District Court judges. Reappointed by U.S. Court of Appeals Tenth Circuit judges. Also Judge, Bankruptcy Appellate Panel Tenth Circuit. Selected by the Judicial Council of the Tenth Circuit.
Office: 330 U.S. Courthouse, 350 South Main Street, Salt Lake City 84101.
Telephone: (801) 524-5749.

BOYDEN, Ann *(Judge, Utah District Court Third Judicial District)* Appointed by Governor Michael O. Leavitt.
Mailing address: P.O. Box 1860, Salt Lake City 84110.
Office: 450 South State Street, Salt Lake City 84111.
Telephone: (801) 238-7337.
Fax: (801) 238-7076

BRIAN, Pat B. *(Judge, Utah District Court Third Judicial District)* Appointed by Governor Norman H. Bangerter to term beginning May 1987. Retained by election. Born Loa Utah March 17, 1938. Educated at College of Southern Utah A.A. in Business 1958, Brigham Young University B.S. 1962 and Vanderbilt University J.D. 1965.

Former Deputy District Attorney Orange County California (Chief Deputy-in-Charge Drug Task Force and Homicide Detail). Former Assistant U.S. Attorney Alaska. Adjunct Professor of Criminal Evidence and Police Science Saddleback College 1972-74, Criminal Law and Procedure Pepperdine Law School 1974-76 and Torts, Legal Writing and Trial Practice Brigham Young University Law School since 1986. Member State Grand Jury Commission since 1990. Member Utah State D.U.I. Revision Commission, Utah State Victim Restitution Commission, Child Abuse Task Force and Jury Instruction Revision Committee (Criminal). Member Inns of Court (Master), California Trial Lawyers Association, The Association of Trial Lawyers of America, National District Attorneys Association, American Judges Association, State Bar of California, Utah State Bar (Arbitration Commission), Orange County, Los Angeles County

BRIAN, PAT B.—*Continued*
and American Bar Associations. Faculty member National Center for State Courts.
Office: 3636 Constitution Boulevard, West Valley City 84119.
Telephone: (801) 238-7354.
Fax: (801) 238-7076

BROWN, Leslie D. *(Judge, Utah Juvenile Court Fourth Judicial District)* Appointed by Governor Scott M. Matheson to term beginning July 1, 1979. Retained by election. Former Presiding Judge. Also served Eighth Judicial District. Born Benson Arizona June 4, 1945. Church of Jesus Christ of Latter-Day Saints. Educated at Brigham Young University B.A. 1969 and University of Utah J.D. 1972. Law Clerk to Hon. F. Henri Henriod, Utah Supreme Court 1972. Admitted to practice Utah 1972. Began legal practice Duchesne 1972. In legal practice Provo 1976.
County Attorney Duchesne County 1975-77. Adjunct Professor of Social Work and Instructor in Family Law Brigham Young University since 1981. Member Governor's Commission on Criminal and Juvenile Justice 1983-87, National Council of Juvenile and Family Court Judges and Utah State Bar. Sergeant U.S. Army National Guard 1968-74. Owner Northeastern Utah Title Company. Democrat. President Utah State Young Democrats 1968-69. Vice Chairman County Democrats 1977. President Duchesne Area Chamber of Commerce. Enjoys family and youth sports programs.
Office: 99 East Center Street, Orem 84057.
Telephone: (801) 764-5833.
Fax: (801) 764-5859

BRYNER, Bryce K. *(Presiding Judge, Utah District Court Seventh Judicial District)* Assumed office Jan 1, 1992. Born Jan 18, 1944. Educated at University of Utah College of Law J.D. 1971. Judge, Utah Circuit Court Seventh Judicial District Dec 1988 to Dec 31, 1991, appointed by Governor Norman H. Bangerter.
Former City Attorney Price and Helper City. Public Defender Carbon County 1979.
Office: 149 East 100 South, Price 84501.
Telephone: (435) 636-3400.
Fax: (435) 637-7349

BURBANK, Jeffrey "R" *(Presiding Judge, Utah Juvenile Court First Judicial District)* Appointed by governor. Also serves as Presiding Judge First District Court.
Office: 61 East 100 North, Logan 84321-4505.
Telephone: (435) 750-1260.

BURNINGHAM, Guy R. *(Judge, Utah District Court Fourth Judicial District)* Appointed by Governor Norman H. Bangerter Oct 28, 1992 to term beginning Dec 4, 1992. Retained by election 1998 and 2002. Presiding Judge 1997-98. Born Salt Lake City Utah Nov 22, 1944. Church of Jesus Christ of Latter-Day Saints. Educated at University of Utah B.S. 1971 J.D. 1973. Admitted to practice Utah 1973, U.S. District Court District of Utah 1973, U.S. Supreme Court 1981 and U.S. Court of Appeals Tenth Circuit. In legal practice Salt Lake City 1973-77.
Utah County Attorney (Chief Civil Division) Provo 1977-92. Instructor in Commercial Law Brigham Young University 1979-87. Former Member 1994-99 and Chairman 1998-99 Utah Board of District Court Judges. Member A. Sherman Christensen Chapter American Inn of Court (Master of the Bench since 1992, President 1998-99). Attended and instructed numerous conferences, seminars and CLE at The National Judicial College, Center for State Courts and Utah State Bar. USAR. Active involvement in church assignments. Enjoys scouting with Boy Scouts of America, reading, golf, skiing and family.
Office: 125 North 100 West, Provo 84601.
Telephone: (801) 429-1062.
Fax: (801) 429-1160
E-mail: jburning@provo.ut.courts.gov

BURTON, Michael K. *(Judge, Utah District Court Third Judicial District)* Assumed office July 1, 1996. Born Salt Lake City Utah Feb 22, 1948. Educated at University of Utah B.A. in English 1972 and Brigham Young University J.D. 1976. Judge, Utah Circuit Court July 1983 to June 30, 1996, appointed by Governor Scott M. Matheson.
Prosecutor and City Attorney Sandy City 1973-82. Deputy County Attorney Salt Lake County 1982-83.
Office: 5022 South State Street, Murray 84107.
Telephone: (801) 238-7501.
Fax: (801) 238-7542

CAMPBELL, Tena *(Judge, United States District Court District of Utah)* Appointed for life by President Bill Clinton to term beginning 1995. Born Wendell Idaho Dec 11, 1944. Educated at University of Idaho B.A. 1967 and Arizona State University M.A. 1970 J.D. 1977. In legal practice Salt Lake City 1977-81.
Deputy County Attorney Salt Lake County 1981. Assistant U.S. Attorney District of Utah 1981-95.
Office: 235 U.S. Courthouse, 350 South Main Street, Salt Lake City 84101.
Telephone: (801) 524-6170.

CASSELL, Paul G. *(Judge, United States District Court District of Utah)* Appointed for life by President George W. Bush to term beginning May 17, 2002.
Office: 112 U.S. Courthouse, 350 South Main Street, Salt Lake City 84101.
Telephone: (801) 524-3005.

CHAMBERLAIN, Hans Q. *(Presiding Judge, Utah Juvenile Court Fifth Judicial District)* Appointed by governor.
Office: 220 North 200 East, St. George 84770.
Telephone: (435) 586-9832.
Fax: (435) 586-4801

CHRISTIANSEN, Terry L. *(Judge, Utah District Court Third Judicial District)* Appointed by Governor Michael O. Leavitt.
Office: 3636 Constitution Boulevard, West Valley City 84119.
Telephone: (801) 982-2400.
Fax: (801) 967-9857

CLARK, Glen E. *(Chief Judge, United States Bankruptcy Court District of Utah)* Appointed by U.S. District Court judges to term beginning July 1, 1982. Reappointed by U.S. Court of Appeals Tenth Circuit judges. Also Judge, Bankruptcy Appellate Panel Tenth Circuit. Selected by the Judicial Council of the Tenth Circuit. Born Cedar Rapids Iowa Nov 23, 1943. Educated at University of Iowa B.A. 1966 and University of Utah College of Law J.D. 1971. Articles Editor Utah Law Review 1970-71. Member Order of the Coif. Admitted to practice Utah 1971, U.S. District Court District of

CLARK, GLEN E.—*Continued*
Utah 1971 and U.S. Court of Appeals Tenth Circuit 1972. Began legal practice Salt Lake City 1971.
Office: 365 U.S. Courthouse, 350 South Main Street, Salt Lake City 84101.
Telephone: (801) 524-6549.

DAVIS, James Z. *(Judge, Utah Court of Appeals)* Appointed by Governor Michael O. Leavitt Nov 1993. Former Presiding Judge and Former Associate Presiding Judge. Educated at University of Utah College of Law J.D. 1968. In legal practice 1971-93.
Deputy County Attorney Weber County and Legal Advisor Weber County Police 1973-82. President Utah State Bar 1991-92.
Office: 450 South State, Salt Lake City 84111.
Telephone: (801) 238-3900.

DAVIS, Lynn W. *(Judge, Utah District Court Fourth Judicial District)* Appointed by governor. Former Presiding Judge. Born Riverside California June 14, 1947. Church of Jesus Christ of Latter-Day Saints. Educated at University of California at Riverside 1966, Brigham Young University B.S. with honors 1971 and J. Reuben Clark Law School J.D. 1976. Honorary member Phi Delta Phi. Member J. Reuben Clark Law Society. Admitted to practice Utah 1977, U.S. District Court District of Utah 1977, U.S. Court of Appeals Tenth Circuit 1981 and U.S. Supreme Court 1983. In legal practice Provo 1977-79. Former Judge, Utah Circuit Court Fourth Judicial District, appointed by Governor Norman H. Bangerter to term beginning May 17, 1987.
Deputy County Attorney Civil Division Utah County 1979-87. Instructor in Introduction to Commercial Law Brigham Young University 1983-85. Adjunct Faculty and Director Trial Advocacy Program J. Reuben Clark Law School 1993-94. Master of the Bench American Inns of Court I 1992-95. Peer Review Consultant National Institute of Justice since 1994. Chairman Utah Board of District Court Judges 1996-97. Member Utah State Bar (Bar Examiner Committee, Chairman Criminal Law Section). Chairman Utah State Court Interpreter and Translator Committee since 1989. Frequent Instructor legal and judicial seminars and conferences. Faculty member Office of State Court Administrator for Law and Literature Conferences. Recipient Award for Exceptional Services from Utah State Bar Constitutional Bicentennial Committee 1987 and 1988 and Utah State Trial Judge of the Year Award 1999. Listed in *Who's Who in American Law* and *Oxford Who's Who.*
Office: 125 North 100 West, Provo 84601.
Telephone: (801) 429-1063.
Fax: (801) 429-1137

DAWSON, Glen R. *(Judge, Utah District Court Second Judicial District)* Appointed by governor.
Office: 805 South Main, Bountiful 84010.
Telephone: (801) 397-7028.
Fax: (801) 397-7010

DEVER, L. A. *(Judge, Utah District Court Third Judicial District)* Appointed by governor.
Mailing address: P.O. Box 1860, Salt Lake City 84110.
Office: 450 South State, Salt Lake City 84111.
Telephone: (801) 238-7464.
Fax: (801) 238-7074

DURHAM, Christine Meaders *(Chief Justice, Utah Supreme Court)* Appointed by Governor Scott M. Matheson to term beginning Feb 3, 1982. Retained by election. Former Associate Chief Justice. Born Los Angeles California Aug 3, 1945. Church of Jesus Christ of Latter-Day Saints. Educated at Wellesley College A.B. with high honors 1967 and Duke University School of Law J.D. 1971. Honorary Doctor of Humanities Weber State College 1993 and Salt Lake Community College 1997. Honorary LL.D. University of Utah 1998. Admitted to practice North Carolina 1971 and Utah 1974. In legal practice Durham North Carolina 1971-73 and Salt Lake City Utah 1974-78. Judge 1978-81 and Presiding Judge 1981-82, Utah District Court Third Judicial District.
Instructor in Legal Medicine Duke University 1971-73 and University of Utah 1974-76. Adjunct Professor of Law Brigham Young University 1974-78. Adjunct Professor State Constitutional Law Seminar University of Utah College of Law. Co-founder Women Lawyers of Utah 1980. President Utah District Judges Association 1980-81, National Association of Women Judges 1986-87 and Women Judges' Fund for Justice 1987-88. Charter Member and Bencher American Inn of Court I 1980-82. Board of Directors American Judicature Society 1986-89. Former Member Governor's Task Force on Implementation of Revised Judicial Article Utah Constitution and Utah Judicial Council (Committee on Judicial Performance Evaluation 1988-91, Chair Standing Committee on Judicial Branch Education 1990-92). Former Member Board of Directors National Center for State Courts. Fellow American Bar Foundation. Board of Trustees American Inns of Court Foundation. Member Utah Constitutional Revision Commission, Advisory Committee on Federal Rules of Civil Procedure Federal Judicial Conference, The American Law Institute (Council Member), and American Bar Association (Committee on Education 1984-95 and Executive Committee 1995-98 Appellate Judges Conference Judicial Administration Division, Commission on Women in the Profession). Chair Advisory Board and Faculty Member Leadership Institute for Judicial Education 1990-98. Recipient Woman Lawyer of the Year Award from Women Lawyers of Utah 1986, Alumna Achievement Award from Wellesley College 1987, Distinguished Service Award from Utah State University 1990, Outstanding Achievement Award from YWCA 1992, Award for Service to Women in the Profession from Utah State Bar 1995 and Charles A. Murphy Award for Public Service from Duke Law School Alumni Association 1996. Named Appellate Judge of the Year by Utah State Bar 1990 and Honoree of the Year by National Association of Women Judges 1997. Member Advisory Council Department of Family and Consumer Affairs University of Utah 1974-77. Board of Directors Odyssey Institute, Inc. 1974-78. Board of Trustees Legal Services for the Developmentally Disabled 1977-78, Salt Lake County Legal Aid Society 1980-82, Duke University and Utah Easter Seal Foundation. Governing Board Developmental Disabilities, Inc. 1980-82. Former Member Emeritus Duke University Law School Board of Visitors. Board of Overseers The Institute for Civil Justice.
Office: 450 South State, Salt Lake City 84111.
Telephone: (801) 238-3900.

DURRANT, Matthew B. *(Associate Chief Justice, Utah Supreme Court)* Appointed by Governor Michael O. Leavitt Jan 2000. Educated at Harvard Law School J.D. 1984. Law Clerk to Hon. Monroe G. McKay, U.S.

DURRANT, MATTHEW B.—*Continued*

Court of Appeals Tenth Circuit. In legal practice Salt Lake City. Judge, Utah District Court Third Judicial District July 1997 to Jan 2000, appointed by Governor Michael O. Leavitt.

Office: 450 South State, Salt Lake City 84111.
Telephone: (801) 238-3900.

DUTSON, Roger S. *(Judge, Utah District Court Second Judicial District)* Assumed office July 1, 1996. Retained by election 1998, current term expires 2004. Born Roberts Idaho Aug 5, 1937. Church of Jesus Christ of Latter-Day Saints. Educated at Utah State University B.S. 1962 and George Washington University J.D. 1965. Member Blue Key and Alpha Sigma Nu. Admitted to practice Virginia 1965, Utah 1968, U.S. District Court District of Utah 1968 and U.S. Court of Appeals Tenth Circuit 1968. In legal practice Ogden Utah 1968-80. Judge, Utah Circuit Court Second Judicial District March 1988 to June 30, 1996 appointed by Governor Norman H. Bangerter.

City Attorney, Assistant City Manager and Director Redevelopment Agency Roy City 1980-88. Member Utah State Bar, Weber County and American Bar Associations. Lieutenant Commander USN Defense Counsel JAGC 1965-68. Member Kiwanis International (Past President, Former Lieutenant Governor). Leader Boy Scouts of America. Enjoys reading, outdoor activities and sports.

Office: 2525 Grant Avenue, Ogden 84401.
Telephone: (801) 395-1156.
Fax: (801) 395-1182

EVES, J. Philip *(Presiding Judge, Utah District Court Fifth Judicial District)* Appointed by Governor Norman H. Bangerter to term beginning April 1987. Retained by election. Born Aug 27, 1941. Educated at University of California at Davis J.D. 1973. Former Judge, Utah Circuit Court Ninth Circuit.

Deputy District Attorney Ventura County (California) 1973-78. Former Deputy Attorney Iron County. Former City Attorney Parowan and Enoch City.

Mailing address: P.O. Box 608, Parowan 84761.
Telephone: (435) 477-8695.
Fax: (435) 477-8766

EYRE, Donald J., Jr. *(Judge, Utah District Court Fourth Judicial District)* Appointed by governor. Former Presiding Judge.

Office: 125 North 100 West, Provo 84601.
Telephone: (801) 429-1180.

FRATTO, Joseph C., Jr. *(Judge, Utah District Court Third Judicial District)* Appointed by governor.

Mailing address: P.O. Box 1860, Salt Lake City 84110.
Office: 450 South State, Salt Lake City 84111.
Telephone: (801) 238-7392.
Fax: (801) 238-7542

FREDERICK, J. Dennis *(Judge, Utah District Court Third Judicial District)* Appointed by Governor Scott M. Matheson to term beginning Oct 29, 1982. Retained by election. Born Salt Lake City Utah July 12, 1940. Educated at University of Tulsa, University of Arkansas and University of Utah B.S. in Psychology 1964 J.D. 1966. Recipient Scholarship from National Office Management Association University of Tulsa 1958-59 and Dean's Scholarship from University of Utah 1961-62. Member Phi Alpha Delta. Admitted to practice Utah 1966, U.S. District Court District of Utah 1966, U.S. Courts of Appeals Tenth 1971 and Ninth 1977 Circuits and U.S. Supreme Court 1973. In legal practice Salt Lake City 1966-82.

Deputy District Attorney 1968-71. National Claims Counsel Advisory Board Commercial Union Assurance Company Boston Massachusetts 1979-81. Author *Utah Redbook—Summary of Utah Landlord/Tenant Law* 1979 and supplement 1981 Apartment Association of Utah. Trial Advocacy Program University of Utah 1983-84. Master of the Bench Sutherland Inn of Court II 1986-91. Former member Federation of Insurance Counsel. Member Fifth Circuit Court Nominating Committee 1974, The Defense Research Institute, Inc. 1975-82, Utah State Division of Corrections Recodification Committee Task Force 1984-85, American Board of Trial Advocates, International Association of Insurance Counsel, Utah Insurance Law Revision Commission (Advisory Committee 1980-81), Utah Judicial Council (Vice Chair Executive Committee), Utah Commission on Administration of Justice in the District Courts, Utah State Bar (Examinations Committee 1978-84, Courts and Judges Committee 1984 and Judiciary Committee 1985), Salt Lake County (Executive Committee 1980-83) and American Bar Associations. Listed in *Who's Who in American Law*. Recipient Utah Bar Foundation Achievement Award 1987 and District Court Judge of the Year Award from Utah State Bar 1988. Utah Air National Guard 1967-70. Captain USAR JAGC 1970-74. Legal Counsel The Children's Center Salt Lake City 1968. President, Vice President and Advisor Cosgriff Home & School Association St. Ambrose Parish 1982-85. Charter member University of Utah College of Law Alumni Association since 1980. Enjoys music, skiing, tennis and golf.

Mailing address: P.O. Box 1860, Salt Lake City 84110.
Office: 450 South State, Salt Lake City 84111.
Telephone: (801) 238-7509.
Fax: (801) 238-7542

FUCHS, Dennis M. *(Judge, Utah District Court Third Judicial District)* Assumed office July 1, 1996. Born New York New York March 31, 1947. Educated at Boston University School of Law J.D. 1973. Judge, Utah Circuit Court Third Judicial District Dec 1986 to June 30, 1996, appointed by Governor Norman H. Bangerter.

Deputy County Attorney Salt Lake County 1975-79. Chairperson Utah State Board of Pardons 1983-86. Member Utah Supreme Court Advisory Committee on Criminal Procedure and Corrections Task Force.

Mailing address: P.O. Box 1860, Salt Lake City 84110.
Office: 450 South State, Salt Lake City 84111.
Telephone: (801) 238-7324.
Fax: (801) 238-7076

GREENE, J. Thomas *(Senior Judge, United States District Court District of Utah)* Appointed for life by President Ronald Reagan to term beginning May 6, 1985. Assumed Senior status, serves by assignment. Born Salt Lake City Utah Nov 28, 1929. Church of Jesus Christ of Latter-Day Saints. Educated at University of Utah B.A. with high honors 1952 LL.B. magna cum laude 1955 replaced by J.D. Note Editor Utah Law Review 1953-55. Law Clerk to Hon. J. Allan Crockett,

GREENE, J. THOMAS—*Continued*

Utah Supreme Court 1954-56. Member Phi Eta Sigma, Phi Beta Kappa, Phi Delta Phi, Pi Kappa Alpha and Order of the Coif. Admitted to practice Utah 1955, U.S. District Court District of Utah 1955, U.S. Court of Appeals Tenth Circuit 1957 and U.S. Supreme Court 1957. In legal practice Salt Lake City 1955-85.

Life Fellow American Bar Foundation. Director American Judicature Society 1975-85. Member Judicial Conference Committee on Court Administration and Case Management 1990-99. Life Member The American Law Institute. Member Utah State Bar (President 1970-71, Chairman Judiciary Committee 1970 and Post Law School Education Committee 1985-87) and American Bar Association (House of Delegates 1975-93, member Special Committee on Delivery of Legal Services 1980-83, Chairman Standing Committee on Environmental Law 1970-79) and Standing Committee on Judicial Selection, Tenure and Compensation 1986-88, member Board of Governors 1988-91, Council member Section of Natural Resources, Energy and Environmental Law and Section of General Practice). Lecturer and Panelist on Banking Law, Negotiable Instruments, Letters of Credit and Bank Transactions ALI-ABA and "Restatement of Law on Lawyers" The American Law Institute. Recipient Merit of Honor Award from University of Utah Emeritus 1994 and Distinguished Service Award from Utah Chapter Federal Bar Association 1997. Named Judge of the Year by Utah State Bar 1995. President Salt Lake County Community Services Council 1972-75. Chairman Utah State Building Authority 1983-87. Regent Utah State Board of Regents 1983-86. Enjoys reading, travel and tennis.

Office: 220 U.S. Courthouse, 350 South Main Street, Salt Lake City 84101.
Telephone: (801) 524-6180.

GREENWOOD, Pamela T. *(Judge, Utah Court of Appeals)* Appointed by Governor Norman H. Bangerter to term beginning Jan 1987. Retained by election. Former Presiding Judge. Born Brigham City Utah Sept 8, 1943. Educated at University of Utah B.S. 1967 and University of Utah College of Law J.D. 1972. Admitted to practice Utah 1972 and U.S. District Court District of Utah 1972. In legal practice Salt Lake City.

General Counsel and Vice President First Interstate Bank 1980-87. Fellows State Chair (Utah) American Bar Association. Member Sutherland Inn of Court, Utah Board of Appellate Court Judges (Gender and Justice Task Force) and Utah State Bar (Counsel 1977-80, President 1990-91). Board of Trustees University of Utah Alumni Association. Enjoys classical and jazz music.

Office: 450 South State, Salt Lake City 84111.
Telephone: (801) 578-3950.
Fax: (801) 238-7981

HADFIELD, Ben H. *(Judge, Utah District Court First Judicial District)* Appointed by governor.

Mailing address: P.O. Box 873, Brigham City 84302-0873.
Office: 43 North Main, Brigham City 84302.
Telephone: (435) 734-4600.

HADLEY, Scott M. *(Judge, Utah District Court Second Judicial District)* Appointed by Governor Michael O. Leavitt.

Office: 2525 Grant Avenue, Ogden 84401.
Telephone: (801) 395-1131.
Fax: (801) 395-1182

HALLIDAY, Bruce K. *(Judge, Utah District Court Seventh Judicial District)* Assumed office Jan 1, 1992. Born Salt Lake City Utah Sept 8, 1938. Educated at University of Utah College of Law J.D. 1965. In legal practice 1965-79. Judge and Presiding Judge, Utah Circuit Court Seventh Judicial District Feb 1987 to Dec 31, 1991, appointed by Governor Norman H. Bangerter.

County Attorney San Juan County 1979-1987.
Office: 149 East 100 South, Price 84501.
Telephone: (435) 636-3400.
Fax: (435) 637-7349

HANSEN, Darwin *(Judge, Utah District Court Second Judicial District)* Appointed by Governor Michael O. Leavitt.

Mailing address: P.O. Box 769, Farmington 84025.
Office: 800 West State Street, Farmington 84025.
Telephone: (801) 447-3840.
Fax: (801) 447-3880

HANSEN, Steven L. *(Judge, Utah District Court Fourth Judicial District)* Appointed by governor. Former Presiding Judge.

Office: 125 North 100 West, Provo 84601.
Telephone: (801) 429-1008.
Fax: (801) 429-1020

HANSON, Timothy R. *(Judge, Utah District Court Third Judicial District)* Appointed by Governor Scott M. Matheson to term beginning Oct 1982. Retained by election Nov 1988, Nov 1994 and Nov 2000. Current term expires Dec 31, 2006. Born Salt Lake City Utah Dec 23, 1942. Educated at University of Utah B.S. 1967 J.D. 1970. Admitted to practice Utah 1970, U.S. District Court District of Utah 1970, U.S. Court of Appeals Tenth Circuit 1972 and U.S. Supreme Court 1974. In legal practice Salt Lake City 1970-82.

Former Member American Bar Association. Member Standing Committee on Civil and Appellate Procedure 1984-87 and Advisory Committee on Rules of Evidence 1987-89. Member Utah State Judicial Council (Chairman Information Committee 1985-88, District Court Representative 1985-90, Capitol Facilities Task Force 1986-87, Gender and Justice Task Force 1987-90, Gender and Justice Implementation Committee since 1990), Utah State Bar (Judicial Member Judicial Conduct Commission 1990-2000) and Salt Lake County Bar Association. First Lieutenant USAR 1962-72.

Mailing address: P.O. Box 1860, Salt Lake City 84110.
Office: 450 South State, Salt Lake City 84111.
Telephone: (801) 238-7515.
Fax: (801) 238-7542

HEFFERNAN, Pamela G. *(Judge, Utah District Court Second Judicial District)* Assumed office July 1, 1996. Retained by election. Former Judge, Utah Circuit Court Second Judicial District.

Office: 2525 Grant Avenue, Ogden 84401.
Telephone: (801) 395-1151.
Fax: (801) 395-1182

HENRIOD, Stephen L. *(Judge, Utah District Court Third Judicial District)* Appointed by governor.

Mailing address: P.O. Box 1860, Salt Lake City 84110.

HENRIOD, STEPHEN L.—*Continued*

Office: 450 South State, Salt Lake City 84111.
Telephone: (801) 238-7021.
Fax: (801) 238-7076

HIGBEE, Thomas M. *(Judge, Utah Juvenile Court Fifth Judicial District)* Appointed by Governor Michael O. Leavitt.
Office: 220 North 200 East, St. George 84770.
Telephone: (435) 986-5730.
Fax: (435) 986-5739

HILDER, Robert K. *(Judge, Utah District Court Third Judicial District)* Appointed by Governor Michael O. Leavitt.
Mailing address: P.O. Box 1860, Salt Lake City 84110.
Office: 450 South State, Salt Lake City 84111.
Telephone: (801) 238-7383.
Fax: (801) 238-7404

HORNAK, Kimberly K. *(Judge, Utah Juvenile Court Third Judicial District)* Appointed by governor.
Office: 210 West 10000 South, Sandy 84070.
Telephone: (801) 565-5751.
Fax: (801) 565-5747

HOWARD, Fred D. *(Judge, Utah District Court Fourth Judicial District)* Appointed by governor. Former Presiding Judge.
Office: 125 North 100 West, Provo 84601.
Telephone: (801) 429-1054.
Fax: (801) 429-1020

IWASAKI, Glenn K. *(Judge, Utah District Court Third Judicial District)* Appointed by governor.
Mailing address: P.O. Box 1860, Salt Lake City 84110.
Office: 450 South State, Salt Lake City 84111.
Telephone: (801) 238-7505.
Fax: (801) 238-7542

JACKSON, Norman H. *(Presiding Judge, Utah Court of Appeals)* Appointed by Governor Norman H. Bangerter to term beginning Jan 20, 1987. Retained by election 1990, 1996 and 2002. Current term expires Jan 2009. Former Associate Presiding Judge. Born Kanab Utah April 14, 1933. Church of Jesus Christ of Latter-Day Saints. Educated at Brigham Young University B.S. 1958 M.S. 1959 and University of Utah J.D. 1962. Recipient Faculty Senior Award for Outstanding Contributions to the College of Law and Faculty Award for Highest Grade in Contracts. Editor-in-Chief The Summation. Member Three-Student National Moot Court Team, Order of Artus and Blue Key. Admitted to practice Utah 1962. In legal practice Richfield 1962-87.

County Attorney Garfield County 1973-74. Board of Directors Utah Legal Services Corporation 1977-82. Board of Commissioners Utah Air Travel Commission 1983-91. Member Utah Information Technology Commission since 1994. Member Utah Board of Appellate Judges since 1987, Utah Bar Foundation (Board of Trustees 1982-93, Vice President 1984-91, President 1991-93), American Inns of Court I (Executive Committee 1989-92, President 1991-92) and Utah State Bar (Commissioner 1970-73, member Committees on Long Range Planning, Legislative, Law Office Management and Legal Services to the Poor). First Lieutenant USAF 1959-60. State Legal Counsel Utah Jaycees 1966-68. Board of Visitors Brigham Young University J. Reuben Clark Law School 1980-83.
Office: 450 South State, Salt Lake City 84111.
Telephone: (801) 238-3900.

JENKINS, Bruce S. *(Senior Judge, United States District Court District of Utah)* Appointed for life by President Jimmy Carter to term beginning 1978. Former Chief Judge. Assumed Senior status 1994. Born Salt Lake City Utah. Educated at University of Utah B.A. magna cum laude 1949 J.D. 1952. Board of Editors Utah Law Review. Member National Honorary Debate Society, Skull and Bones, Owl and Key, Phi Beta Kappa, Phi Kappa Phi, Phi Eta Sigma, Tau Kappa Alpha and Order of the Coif. Research Clerk Utah Supreme Court. Admitted to practice Utah 1952, U.S. District Court District of Utah 1952, U.S. Court of Appeals Tenth Circuit and U.S. Supreme Court. In legal practice 1952-65. Bankruptcy Judge, U.S. District Court District of Utah 1965-78.

Assistant State Attorney General and Deputy Prosecutor Salt Lake County. Author "Causation and the Judicial Equation" 1 Courts, Health, Science & The Law 320, 1991 and 4 Utah B. Jour. 24 Nov 1991; "The First Thing We Do . . . ." 6 Utah Bar Jour. 31, Oct 1993; "Is That a Fact?" 12 No. 4 Utah B. Jour. April 1999; "For Thinking Press 1, For Compassion Press 2, For Judgment Press 3" LXVIII No. 7 *Vital Speeches* 2002; and Chapter 26 "Problems of Discretion and Responsibility: The Debate Over Tort Liability" *Handbook of Public Law and Public Administration.* Important Decisions and Opinions: Topaz Beryllium Co. v. United States 479 F. Supp. 309 D. Utah 1979 aff'd 649 F.2d 775 10th Cir. 1981, Hackford v. First Security Bank of Utah 521 F. Supp. 541 D. Utah 1981, Ute Indian Tribe v. State of Utah 521 F. Supp. 1072 D. Utah 1981, Home Box Office v. Wilkinson 531 F. Supp. 987 D. Utah 1981, Community TV v. Roy City 555 F. Supp. 1164 D. Utah 1982, Allen, et al. v. United States 588 F. Supp. 247 D. Utah 1984, Hartford Acc. & Idem. Corp. v. United States Fidelity and Guar. Co. 765 F. Supp. 677 D. Utah 1991, Quaker State Minit-Lube, Inc. v. Fireman's Fund Insurance Company 868 F. Supp. 1278 D. Utah 1994, Meyers By and Through Meyers v. Board of Education of San Juan School District 935 F. Supp. 1473 D. Utah 1996, Ute Indian Tribe v. State of Utah 935 F. Supp. 1473 D. Utah 1996, Tyler v. City of Manhattan (dissenting) 118 F.3d 1400 10th Cir. 1997, United States v. Webb (concurring) 115 F.3d 711 9th Cir. 1997, Weaver v. Nebo School Dist. 29 F. Supp.2d 1279 D. Utah 1998, United States v. Phillips 59 F. Supp.2d 1178 D. Utah 1999, East High Gay-Straight Alliance v. Bd. of Educ. 81 F. Supp.2d 1166 D. Utah 1999 and United States v. Garfield County 122 F. Supp.2d 1201 D. Utah 2000. Former member Utah State Senate (Former Minority Leader, former Senate President and former Vice Chairman Commission on the Reorganization of the Executive Branch). Honorary member Federal Bar Association. Lecturer Cultural Exchange Program Africa. Listed in *Who's Who in America.* Advisory Council Utah Technical College 1967-72. Named Alumnus of the Year by University of Utah College of Law Alumni Association 1985 and Judge of the Year by Utah State Bar 1993. Recipient George Washington Honor Medal from Valley Forge Utah Chapter Freedoms Foundation 1993, Distinguished Judicial Service Award from Federal Bar Association Dec 1993 and Emeritus Merit of Honor Award from University of Utah Alumni Association 1997. Insti-

JENKINS, BRUCE S.—*Continued*

tutional Council Utah State University 1976-77. Board of Trustees University of Utah College of Law Alumni Association. Member Salt Lake Committee on Foreign Relations (Former President), International Platform Association, Utah Association for the United Nations and American Inns of Court 1. Honorary member Salt Lake Kiwanis. Interested in photography, history and collecting books.

Office: 462 U.S. Courthouse, 350 South Main Street, Salt Lake City 84101.
Telephone: (801) 524-5167.

JOHANSEN, Scott *(Presiding Judge, Utah Juvenile Court Seventh Judicial District)* Appointed by Governor Norman H. Bangerter to term beginning Jan 1991. Retained by election 1996 and 2002. Current term expires 2008. Born Utah 1950. Church of Jesus Christ of Latter-Day Saints. Educated at Snow College A.S. 1970 and Brigham Young University B.A. 1974 J.D. 1977. Admitted to practice Utah 1977. In legal practice Price and Castle Dale 1977-91.

County Attorney Emery County 1979-91. Corporate Counsel Emery Telephone 1990. Chairman Board of Juvenile Judges 1995-96. Former Member Utah Judicial Council (Chairman Policy and Planning Executive Committee 2000-01). Member Utah State Bar.

Office: 149 East 100 South, Price 84501.
Telephone: (435) 636-3434.
Fax: (435) 637-2102
E-mail address: jjohanse@email.utcourts.gov

JONES, Ernest W. *(Judge, Utah District Court Second Judicial District)* Appointed by Governor Michael O. Leavitt.

Office: 2525 Grant Avenue, Ogden 84401.
Telephone: (801) 395-1176.
Fax: (801) 395-1182

JONES, Larry *(Judge, Utah Juvenile Court First Judicial District)* Appointed by Governor Michael O. Leavitt.

Office: 61 West 100 North, Logan 84321-4505.
Telephone: (435) 750-1260.

JUDKINS, Clint S. *(Judge, Utah District Court First Judicial District)* Assumed office July 1, 1996. Former Presiding Judge. Born Aug 27, 1945. Educated at Utah State University B.A. in History 1969 and University of Utah College of Law J.D. 1972. Judge and Presiding Judge, Utah Circuit Court First Judicial District 1988 to June 30, 1996, appointed by Governor Norman H. Bangerter. Former City Attorney Tremonton City.

Office: 140 North 100 West, Logan 84321.
Telephone: (435) 750-1300.
Fax: (435) 750-1355

KAY, Thomas L. *(Judge, Utah District Court Second Judicial District)* Appointed by Governor Michael O. Leavitt to term beginning July 1, 1998. Retained by election Nov 2002. Current term expires Jan 1, 2009. Born Clearfield Utah Feb 17, 1952. Church of Jesus Christ of Latter-Day Saints. Educated at University of Utah B.A. magna cum laude 1976 and Brigham Young University J. Reuben Clark Law School J.D. cum laude 1979. Note and Comment Editor Brigham Young University Law Review 1977-79. Law Clerk to Hon. David K. Winder, U.S. District Court District of Utah 1980-81. Member Phi Beta Kappa and Phi Kappa Phi. Admitted to practice Utah 1979. In legal practice 1981-98.

Mediator U.S. District Court District of Utah. Author "Should Legal Malpractice Insurance Be Mandatory" Brigham Young University L. Rev. 102, 1978; "Legal Malpractice in Utah" 1993, "Ways to Avoid Being the Target 1993 and "Avoiding Legal Malpractice in Utah" 1994-96 Utah State Bar CLE; and "Practical Legal Ethics" National Business Institute 1997. Co-author "Legal Malpractice Jury Instructions" Model Utah Jury Instructions 1993. Master of the Bench Rex E. Lee Inn of Court and American Inn of Court I. Member Advisory Committee on the Rules of Evidence and Advisory Committee on the Rules of Professional Conduct Utah Supreme Court. Member Association of Ski Defense Attorneys, Utah Defense Association, The Defense Research Institute, Inc., Utah State Bar, Davis County, Salt Lake County and American Bar Associations. Presenter Utah State Bar CLE since 1990 and "Who Wants to Be a Prisoner?" various school and youth groups. Attended The National Judicial College 1999. Delegate to County and State Political Conventions 1974-80. Baseball Coach since 1988. Author ten volumes of poetry since 1993. Member Davis County Domestic Violence Victims' Project.

Office: 425 North Wasatch Drive, Layton 84041.
Telephone: (801) 444-4310.
Fax: (801) 444-4309
E-mail address: tkay@email.utcourts.gov

KIMBALL, Dale A. *(Judge, United States District Court District of Utah)* Appointed for life by President Bill Clinton Nov 24, 1997. Born Provo Utah Nov 28, 1939. Educated at Brigham Young University B.S. magna cum laude 1964 and University of Utah J.D. 1967. Case Note Editor Utah Law Review. Member Phi Kappa Phi and Order of the Coif. In legal practice Salt Lake City 1967-74 and 1975 to Nov 23, 1997.

Author Case Note "Appropriation of Name, Likeness and Personality—Relatives and Administratrix Held to Have No Claim Under Privacy or Property Theories" 9 Utah L. Rev. 999, 1964-65; Note "The Constitutional Convention, Its Nature and Powers—And the Amending Procedure" Utah L. Rev. 390, 1966; Note "'Like Grade and Quality' Under Section 2(a) of the Robinson-Patman Act" Utah L. Rev. 251, 1967; "Compulsion Without Protection or Recourse: The Case for No-Fault Accident Insurance for School Children" Utah L. Rev. 925, 1975; and Chapter 204 "Liens" *American Law of Mining* 2nd ed. Co-author "Acquisition of Non-Mineral Land for Mine Related Purposes" *23rd Annual Rocky Mountain Mining Law Institute* 595. Professor of Law Brigham Young University J. Reuben Clark Law School 1974-76. Former Chairman Ethics and Discipline Committee, Committee on the Unauthorized Practice of Law Utah State Bar and Judicial Performance Evaluation Committee. Former Master of the Bench American Inns of Court. Former Member Mediation/Arbitration Panels U.S. District Court District of Utah. Counselor to the Inn American Inns of Court I. Board Member Salt Lake Chapter J. Reuben Clark Law Society and Salt Lake Chapter Federal Bar Association. Fellow American Bar Foundation. Presenter various seminars Federal and American Bar Associations. Recipient Distinguished Lawyer of the Year Award from Utah State Bar 1996. Former Chairman and Member Pioneer Theatre Board. Former Member Board of Governors Alta View Hospital

KIMBALL, DALE A.—*Continued*

and Jordan Education Foundation Board. Trustee Alumni Board University of Utah College of Law.

Office: 220 U.S. Courthouse, 350 South Main Street, Salt Lake City 84101.

Telephone: (801) 524-6610.

E-mail address: Dale_Kimball@utd.uscourts.gov

LAYCOCK, Claudia *(Judge, Utah District Court Fourth Judicial District)* Appointed by Governor Michael O. Leavitt.

Office: 125 North 100 West, Provo 84601.

Telephone: (801) 429-1064.

Fax: (801) 429-1160

LEWIS, Leslie A. *(Judge, Utah District Court Third Judicial District)* Appointed by Governor Norman H. Bangerter to term beginning Jan 14, 1991. Retained by election. Former Presiding Judge. Born Palo Alto California Dec 3, 1948. Episcopalian. Educated at Tulane University, H. Sophie Newcomb Memorial College B.A. 1971 and University of Utah J.D. 1974. Admitted to practice Utah 1974 and California 1991. In legal practice Salt Lake City Utah 1974-78 and 1988-91.

Prosecutor May 1978 to Aug 1988 and Trial Team Leader Special Victim's Prosecution Unit Oct 1985 to July 1988 Salt Lake County Attorney's Office. Author Judicial Benchbook 1993. Former Member Governor's Council on Victims. Member Divorce, Child Custody and Visitation Task Force 1991-92, Juvenile Court Reorganization Task Force, Prison Population Growth Task Force, Governor's Task Force on Child Abuse (Member Executive Committee, Chair Subcommittee I), Standing Committee on Judicial Branch Education, Standing Committee for Model Utah Civil Jury Instructions, Inmate Services Committee, Utah Board of District Court Judges (Chairperson), Sutherland II Inn (President), Inns of Court (Master), Women Lawyers of Utah, National Association of Women Judges (Former Chair), Utah State Bar, State Bar of California, Salt Lake County (Executive Committee) and American (Executive Committee National Conference of State Trial Judges Judicial Administration Division) Bar Associations. Team Leader State Team Domestic Violence Conference San Francisco March 1993. Presented "Children in Court—Striking a Balance Between the Rights of a Child and a Defendant" and "Effective Sentencing of Youthful Offenders" National Conference Tacoma Washington March 1993. Presented program on Courtroom Technology (Computer-integrated Courtroom) April 1993. Conducted Mock Trials for law school students, high school students and girl scouts. Instituted Law Clerk/Bailiff Program Salt Lake County 1992. Prosecutor of the Year 1985. Founded "Booked" volunteer literary program for people in jail 1992. Former Member Advisory Board Assistance League of Salt Lake City. Former Board Member Rape Crisis Center, Center for Family Development, Salt Lake Acting Company and Westminster College Woman's Board. Chair and Founder "Booked" Advisory Board. Member Board Odyssey House. Member Utah Women's Forum, Utah Chapter National Child Abuse Prevention Association (Honorary Board Member), National Federation of Business and Professional Women of U.S.A., and Gateway League Business and Professional Women's Club (President 1984).

Mailing address: P.O. Box 1860, Salt Lake City 84110.

Office: 450 South State, Salt Lake City 84111.

Telephone: (801) 238-7513.

Fax: (801) 238-7542

LINDBERG, Denise Posse-Blanco *(Judge, Utah District Court Third Judicial District)* Appointed by Governor Michael O. Leavitt Sept 10, 1998 to term beginning Nov 20, 1998. Born Cuba. Educated at Brigham Young University B.A. 1970 J.D. magna cum laude 1988 and University of Utah M.S. 1973 M.S.W. 1979 Ph.D. 1980. Articles Editor Brigham Young University Law Review. Law Clerk to Hon. Monroe G. McKay, U.S. Court of Appeals Tenth Circuit 1988-89 and Hon. Sandra Day O'Connor, U.S. Supreme Court 1990-91. Member Order of the Coif. Admitted to practice Utah 1988, District of Columbia 1989, U.S. District Court District of Utah 1988, U.S. Court of Appeals Tenth Circuit 1989 and U.S. Supreme Court 1991. In legal practice Washington D.C. 1989-94 and Salt Lake City 1998.

General Counsel and Corporate Secretary Human Affairs International 1994-97. Member Committee on Improving Jury Service Utah Judicial Council 2001. Master of the Bench A. Sherman Christensen American Inn of Court I. Member The American Law Institute (Advisor ALI Model Penal Code Sentencing Project since 2001) and Utah State Bar (Member Courts and Judges Committee 1994-2000, Co-chair Legal/Healthcare Committee 1997-2000, Member Ethics Advisory Opinion Committee since 2001). Rehabilitation Counselor Utah State Office of Rehabilitation Services 1971-72. Treatment Specialist Utah State Division of Alcohol and Drugs 1974-76. Social work intern University of Utah Medical Center 1977-78. Consultant-mental health and substance abuse training Interwest Regional Medical Education Center Veteran's Administration Regional Medical Center 1978-79. Forecasting and long range planner, policy analyst and community organization specialist Utah State Office of Education 1980-85.

Office: 210 West 10000 South, Sandy 84070.

Telephone: (801) 565-5722.

Fax: (801) 565-5747

LINDSAY, Kay A. *(Presiding Judge, Utah Juvenile Court Fourth Judicial District)* Appointed by governor. Formerly served Eighth Judicial District. Presiding Judge since July 1998.

Office: 2021 South State Street, Provo 84606.

Telephone: (801) 354-7251.

Fax: (801) 373-6579

LINDSLEY, Elizabeth *(Judge, Utah Juvenile Court Third Judicial District)* Appointed by Governor Michael O. Leavitt.

Office: 210 West 10000 South, Sandy 84070.

Telephone: (801) 565-5757.

Fax: (801) 565-5747

LOW, Gordon J. *(Associate Presiding Judge, Utah District Court First Judicial District)* Appointed by Governor Norman H. Bangerter to term beginning 1987. Former Presiding Judge. Born Logan Utah June 27, 1945. Educated at Arizona State University College of Law J.D. 1973.

Former member Judicial Performance Evaluation Committee and Judicial Article Task Force. Commis-

LOW, GORDON J.—*Continued*

sioner Utah State Bar. Member Utah Supreme Court Advisory Committee on Evidence.
Office: 140 North 100 West, Logan 84321.
Telephone: (435) 750-1300.
Fax: (435) 750-1355

LUBECK, Bruce C. *(Judge, Utah District Court Third Judicial District)* Appointed by Governor Michael O. Leavitt.
Office: 6300 North Silver Creek Drive, Park City 84098.
Telephone: (435) 615-4300.
Fax: (435) 615-4907

LYMAN, Paul D. *(Presiding Judge, Utah Juvenile Court Sixth Judicial District)* Appointed by Governor Michael O. Leavitt to term beginning July 2000. Term expires July 2005. Born Oakland California April 28, 1953. Educated at Brigham Young University B.S. in Economics magna cum laude 1976 and University of Chicago J.D. 1979. Admitted to practice Colorado 1979 and Utah 1985. In legal practice Richfield Utah July 1985 to July 2000.
Deputy County Attorney Sevier County July 1985 to June 2000. County Attorney Wayne County Jan 1996 to June 2000. USAF JAG 1980-85. Mayor Richfield 1994-97. Member Richfield City Council 1989-94.
Office: 895 East 300 North, Richfield 84701.
Telephone: (435) 896-2700.
Fax: (435) 896-8047

LYON, Michael D. *(Judge, Utah District Court Second Judicial District)* Appointed by governor. Former Presiding Judge.
Office: 2525 Grant Avenue, Ogden 84401.
Telephone: (801) 395-1171.
Fax: (801) 395-1182

MAETANI, Howard H. *(Judge, Utah District Court Fourth Judicial District)* Appointed by governor.
Office: 75 East 80 North, American Fork 84003.
Telephone: (801) 756-9654.
Fax: (801) 763-0153

MANLEY, Mary *(Judge, Utah Juvenile Court Seventh Judicial District)* Appointed by Governor Michael O. Leavitt.
Mailing address: P.O. Box 635, Castle Dale 84513.
Telephone: (435) 381-5311.

MAUGHAN, Paul G. *(Judge, Utah District Court Third Judicial District)* Appointed by Governor Michael O. Leavitt.
Mailing address: P.O. Box 1860, Salt Lake City 84110.
Office: 450 South State, Salt Lake City 84111.
Telephone: (801) 238-7127.
Fax: (801) 238-7542

McCLEVE, Sheila K. *(Judge, Utah District Court Third Judicial District)* Assumed office July 1, 1996. Retained by election 2000, current term expires Dec 31, 2006. Born Salt Lake City Utah Dec 2, 1949. Church of Jesus Christ of Latter-Day Saints. Educated at Brigham Young University B.A. cum laude 1973 J.D. 1976 and Oxford University, England 1983. Member Women's Academic Council and Phi Kappa Phi. Admitted to practice Utah 1977 and U.S. Supreme Court 1987. In legal practice Salt Lake City 1977-78. Administrative Law Judge, Public Service Commission May 1980 to Aug 1981. Judge, Utah Circuit Court Third Judicial District March 5, 1984 to June 30, 1996, appointed by Governor Scott M. Matheson.
Deputy County Attorney Civil Division Salt Lake County 1978-79. Assistant City Prosecutor Salt Lake City June 1979 to May 1980. Senior Research Attorney for Hon. Richard C. Howe, Utah Supreme Court Aug 1981 to March 1984. Former Chairman Circuit Judges Sentencing Guidelines Committee. Former member Criminal and Juvenile Justice Sentencing Guidelines Committee, Assessing the Need for Judicial Resources Committee, National Association of Women Judges, Women Lawyers of Utah, Young Lawyers of Utah, Judicial Ethics Advisory Committee, Child Abuse Coordinating Committee, Salt Lake County and American Bar Associations. Member Utah Board of Circuit Court Judges. Attended courses in Evidence and Administrative Procedure 1980 and Courts of Limited Jurisdiction 1984 The National Judicial College and Search and Seizure Questions and Evidence Problems American Judicial Academy 1988. Named Brigham Young University Honored Alumnus by J. Reuben Clark College of Law 1986. Board of Visitors Brigham Young University J. Reuben Clark School of Law 1986-88. Former Chairman South Salt Lake Community Development Committee.
Mailing address: P.O. Box 1860, Salt Lake City 84110.
Office: 450 South State, Salt Lake City 84111.
Telephone: (801) 238-7370.
Fax: (801) 238-7076

McCULLY, Sharon P. *(Judge, Utah Juvenile Court Third Judicial District)* Appointed by Governor Scott M. Matheson to term beginning July 1, 1983. Retained by election Nov 1986, 1992 and 1998. Current term expires 2004. Former Presiding Judge. Born Price Utah May 18, 1954. Church of Jesus Christ of Latter-Day Saints. Educated at Brigham Young University B.A. 1975 and University of Utah J.D. 1978. Admitted to practice Utah 1978. Began legal practice Salt Lake City 1978.
Former Assistant State Attorney General. Member Utah Judicial Council, Utah Board of Juvenile Court Judges, National Council of Juvenile and Family Court Judges, National Association of Women Judges and Utah State Bar. Enjoys sports and camping.
Mailing address: P.O. Box 140431, Salt Lake City 84114.
Office: 450 South State, Salt Lake City 84111.
Telephone: (801) 238-7700.

McIFF, K. L. *(Presiding Judge, Utah District Court Sixth Judicial District)* Appointed by governor.
Office: 895 East 300 North, Richfield 84701.
Telephone: (435) 896-2700.
Fax: (435) 896-8047

MEDLEY, Tyrone E. *(Judge, Utah District Court Third Judicial District)* Appointed by governor. Born Dec 29, 1951. Educated at University of Utah College of Law J.D. 1977. Former Judge, Utah Circuit Court Third Judicial District, appointed by Governor Scott M. Matheson to term beginning July 1984.
Former Deputy Attorney Salt Lake County. Member Advisory Committee on Criminal Procedure and Adviso-

MEDLEY, TYRONE E.—*Continued*

ry Committee on Alternative Dispute Resolution Utah Supreme Court.

Mailing address: P.O. Box 1860, Salt Lake City 84110.

Office: 450 South State, Salt Lake City 84111.

Telephone: (801) 238-7503.

Fax: (801) 238-7542

MEMMOTT, Jon M. *(Judge, Utah District Court Second Judicial District)* Appointed by governor. Former Presiding Judge.

Mailing address: P.O. Box 769, Farmington 84025.

Office: 800 West State Street, Farmington 84025.

Telephone: (801) 447-3870.

Fax: (801) 447-3880

MOWER, David L. *(Judge, Utah District Court Sixth Judicial District)* Assumed office Jan 1, 1992. Former Presiding Judge. Born Salt Lake City Utah May 2, 1947. Educated at University of Utah College of Law J.D. 1974. In legal practice Utah 1974-86. Judge and Presiding Judge, Utah Circuit Court Sixth Judicial District Dec 1986 to Dec 31, 1991, appointed by Governor Norman H. Bangerter.

County Attorney Garfield County 1974-78. Member Sentencing Guidelines Committee and Forms Committee.

Office: 895 East 300 North, Richfield 84701.

Telephone: (435) 896-2700.

Fax: (435) 896-8047

NEHRING, Ronald E. *(Justice, Utah Supreme Court)* Appointed by Governor Michael O. Leavitt to term beginning May 2003. Former Judge and Presiding Judge, Utah District Court Third Judicial District.

Office: 450 South State, Salt Lake City 84111.

Telephone: (801) 238-3900.

NELSON, Kathleen *(Judge, Utah Juvenile Court Second Judicial District)* Appointed by Governor Michael O. Leavitt.

Office: 444 26th Street, Ogden 84401.

Telephone: (801) 626-3800.

Fax: (801) 626-3827

NOEL, Frank G. *(Judge, Utah District Court Third Judicial District)* Appointed by Governor Norman H. Bangerter to term beginning Oct 1, 1986. Retained by election. Former Presiding Judge. Born Ogden Utah Feb 21, 1943. Church of Jesus Christ of Latter-Day Saints. Educated at Weber State College A.S. 1965, Utah State University B.S. 1967 M.S. 1968 and University of Utah J.D. 1972. Assistant Comment Editor Utah Law Review 1971-72. Admitted to practice Utah 1972 and U.S. Court of Appeals Tenth Circuit 1976. In legal practice Salt Lake City 1972-83. Judge, Utah Circuit Court Fifth Circuit 1983-86.

Member Salt Lake County and American Bar Associations.

Mailing address: P.O. Box 1860, Salt Lake City 84110.

Office: 450 South State, Salt Lake City 84111.

Telephone: (801) 238-7057.

Fax: (801) 238-7076

NOONAN, Mary T. *(Judge, Utah Juvenile Court Fourth Judicial District)* Appointed by Governor Michael O. Leavitt.

Office: 2021 South State, Provo 84601.

Telephone: (801) 354-7241.

Fax: (801) 373-6579

NUFFER, David *(Magistrate Judge, United States District Court District of Utah)* Appointed part-time Magistrate Judge by U.S. District Court judges May 1, 1995. Appointed full-time Magistrate Judge to term beginning Jan 17, 2003. Current term expires Jan 2011. Born Portland Oregon Feb 28, 1952. Church of Jesus Christ of Latter-Day Saints. Educated at Brigham Young University B.A. 1975 J.D. 1978. Admitted to practice Utah 1978 and Arizona 1989. In legal practice St. George Utah 1979.

Member Utah State Bar (Commissioner 1994-2000, President 2000-01) and State Bar of Arizona.

Mailing address: P.O. Box 2379, St. George 84771-2379.

Telephone: (801) 524-6100.

ODDONE, Frederic M. *(Presiding Judge, Utah Juvenile Court Third Judicial District)* Appointed by governor.

Mailing address: P.O. Box 140431, Salt Lake City 84114.

Office: 450 South State, Salt Lake City 84111.

Telephone: (801) 238-7753.

Fax: (801) 238-7747

ORME, Gregory K. *(Judge, Utah Court of Appeals)* Appointed by Governor Norman H. Bangerter Oct 25, 1986 to term beginning Feb 2, 1987. Retained by election 1990, 1996 and 2002. Current term expires Jan 2009. Former Presiding Judge. Born Boston Massachusetts Dec 14, 1953. Educated at University of Utah B.A. magna cum laude 1975 and George Washington University J.D. with high honors 1978. Law Clerk to Hon. Monroe G. McKay, U.S. Court of Appeals Tenth Circuit 1978-79. Member Phi Beta Kappa and Order of the Coif. Admitted to practice Utah 1978, U.S. District Court District of Utah 1978 and U.S. Court of Appeals Tenth Circuit 1979. In legal practice Salt Lake City 1979-87.

Author "Tucker Act Jurisdiction Over Breach of Trust Claims" Brigham Young University L. Rev. 855, 1979. Judicial Advisor Utah Bar Journal since 1999. Former Member Utah Judicial Council. Member American Judicature Society and Utah State Bar (Chairman Constitutional Bicentennial Committee 1986-89, Executive Council Administrative Practice Section 1987-89). Named Outstanding Young Lawyer of the Year 1986.

Mailing address: P.O. Box 140230, Salt Lake City 84114-0230.

Office: 450 South State, Salt Lake City 84111.

Telephone: (801) 578-3950.

PAGE, Rodney S. *(Judge, Utah District Court Second Judicial District)* Appointed by Governor Scott M. Matheson to term beginning March 1984. Retained by election. Former Presiding Judge. Born Ogden Utah May 24, 1940. Educated at University of Utah College of Law J.D. 1969.

County Attorney Davis County 1978-84. Former Member Utah Supreme Court Sentencing Guidelines

PAGE, RODNEY S.—*Continued*

Committee. Member Utah Judicial Council and Utah Supreme Court Advisory Committee on Civil Procedure.
Mailing address: P.O. Box 769, Farmington 84025-0769.
Telephone: (801) 447-3860.
Fax: (801) 447-3880

PARRISH, Jill N. *(Justice, Utah Supreme Court)* Appointed by Governor Michael O. Leavitt to term beginning March 2003.
Office: 450 South State, Salt Lake City 84111.
Telephone: (801) 238-3900.

PAYNE, A. Lynn, Jr. *(Presiding Judge, Utah District Court Eighth Judicial District)* Assumed office Jan 1, 1992. Born Delta Utah April 21, 1946. Educated at University of Utah College of Law J.D. 1975. In legal practice Vernal 1982-87. Judge and Presiding Judge, Utah Circuit Court Eighth Judicial District 1987 to Dec 31, 1991, appointed by Governor Norman H. Bangerter.
City Prosecutor Salt Lake City 1975-78. County Attorney Salt Lake County 1978-81.
Office: 920 East Highway 40, Vernal 84078-2803.
Telephone: (435) 781-9300.
Fax: (435) 789-0564

PEULER, Sandra N. *(Presiding Judge, Utah District Court Third Judicial District)* Appointed by governor.
Mailing address: P.O. Box 1860, Salt Lake City 84110.
Office: 450 South State, Salt Lake City 84111.
Telephone: (801) 238-7051.
Fax: (801) 238-7076

QUINN, Anthony *(Judge, Utah District Court Third Judicial District)* Appointed by Governor Michael O. Leavitt.
Mailing address: P.O. Box 1860, Salt Lake City 84110.
Office: 450 South State, Salt Lake City 84111.
Telephone: (801) 238-7035.
Fax: (801) 238-7064

REDD, F. Bennion *(Magistrate Judge, United States District Court District of Utah)* Appointed by U.S. District Court judges to term beginning March 29, 1979. Reappointed March 27, 1987 and to subsequent terms. Serves part time. Born Blanding Utah Sept 16, 1921. Church of Jesus Christ of Latter-Day Saints. Educated at University of Utah B.S. 1949 B.S.L. 1950 J.D. 1951. Member Phi Delta Phi, Kappa Sigma and Delta Phi. Admitted to practice Utah 1951. Began legal practice Monticello 1951.
County Attorney San Juan County 1951-78. Member Utah State Bar and Southeastern Utah Bar Association. First Lieutenant U.S. Army Infantry 1944-46.
Office: 132 South Main Street, Monticello 84535.
Telephone: (435) 587-2424.
Fax: (435) 587-2244

REESE, Robin W. *(Judge, Utah District Court Third Judicial District)* Assumed office July 1, 1996. Born Salt Lake City Utah March 3, 1954. Educated at University of Utah College of Law J.D. 1980. In legal practice Salt Lake City 1980-81. Judge and Presiding Judge, Utah Circuit Court Third Judicial District March 1987 to June 30, 1996, appointed by Governor Norman H. Bangerter.
County Attorney Salt Lake County 1981-87. Member Sentencing Guidelines Committee.
Mailing address: P.O. Box 1860, Salt Lake City 84110.
Office: 450 South State, Salt Lake City 84111.
Telephone: (801) 238-7365.
Fax: (801) 238-7074

ROTH, Stephen *(Judge, Utah District Court Third Judicial District)* Appointed by Governor Michael O. Leavitt.
Mailing address: P.O. Box 1860, Salt Lake City 84110.
Office: 450 South State, Salt Lake City 84111.
Telephone: (801) 238-7326.
Fax: (801) 238-7076

SAINSBURY, Sterling B. *(Judge, Utah Juvenile Court Fourth Judicial District)* Appointed by governor. Formerly served Eighth Judicial District.
Office: 99 East Center Street, Orem 84057.
Telephone: (801) 764-5832.
Fax: (801) 764-5859

SAM, David *(Senior Judge, United States District Court District of Utah)* Appointed for life by President Ronald Reagan. Chief Judge June 1997 to Nov 1, 1999. Assumed Senior status Nov 1, 1999, serves by assignment. Born Hobart Indiana Aug 12, 1933. Church of Jesus Christ of Latter-Day Saints. Educated at Brigham Young University B.S. 1957 and University of Utah J.D. 1960. Admitted to practice Utah 1960. Began legal practice Duchesne 1963. Former Judge, Utah District Court Fourth Judicial District, appointed by Governor Calvin Rampton to term beginning July 1, 1976.
County Attorney 1966-71 and County Commissioner 1973-74 Duchesne County. Part-time Instructor Brigham Young University 1976-84. President Utah District Judges Association 1982. Chairman Utah State Judicial Conference 1982. Member Advisory Committee on Codes of Conduct Judicial Conference of the U.S. 1987-91 and Judicial Council of the Tenth Circuit 1991-93. Counselor American Inns of Court. Member American Judicature Society and Utah State Bar. Named Judge of the Year by Utah State Bar 1999. Captain USAF 1961-63. Republican. Member Advisory Board for Uintah Basin Utah State University 1972-77, Utah Board of Water Resources 1973-77, Utah Technical College Advisory Board 1984-85 and U.S. Delegation to Romania Aug 1991. Honorary Member Order of the Coif J. Reuben Clark Chapter Brigham Young University April 1996. Member Supreme Court Historical Society. Enjoys beekeeping, sports and reading.
Office: 441 U.S. Courthouse, 350 South Main Street, Salt Lake City 84101.
Telephone: (801) 524-6190.

SCHOFIELD, Anthony W. *(Judge, Utah District Court Fourth Judicial District)* Appointed by Governor Michael O. Leavitt to term beginning Aug 1993. Retained by election 1996 and 2002. Current term expires Dec 31, 2008. Born Farmington New Mexico March 5, 1949. Church of Jesus Christ of Latter-Day Saints. Educated at Brigham Young University B.A. 1973 J.D. cum laude 1976. Staff member Brigham Young University Law Review 1974-76. Law Clerk to Hon. A. Sherman Christensen, U.S. District Court District of Utah 1976-77. Admitted to practice Utah 1976, U.S. Courts of Appeals Seventh 1977 and Tenth 1977 Circuits and Guam

SCHOFIELD, ANTHONY W.—*Continued*
1997. In legal practice Salt Lake City Utah 1980-81 and Provo Utah 1981-93.

Instructor in Insurance Law Brigham Young University 1997. President Central Utah Bar Association 1985 and 1992. Member Utah State Bar. Member American Fork Planning Commission 1981-86. Board of Trustees American Fork Hospital 1984-93. Bishop 1985-88 and Stake President 1991-94 Church of Jesus Christ of Latter-Day Saints.

Office: 125 North 100 West, Provo 84601.
Telephone: (801) 429-1045.
Fax: (801) 429-1160

SHUMATE, James L. *(Judge, Utah District Court Fifth Judicial District)* Assumed office Jan 1, 1992. Former Presiding Judge. Former Judge, Utah Circuit Court Fifth Judicial District.

Office: Washington County Hall of Justice, 220 North 200 East, St. George 84770.
Telephone: (435) 986-5700.
Fax: (435) 986-5723

SKANCHY, Randall N. *(Judge, Utah District Court Third Judicial District)* Appointed by Governor Michael O. Leavitt.

Mailing address: P.O. Box 1860, Salt Lake City 84110.
Office: 450 South State, Salt Lake City 84111.
Telephone: (801) 238-7412.
Fax: (801) 238-7074

STEELE, Larry A. *(Presiding Judge, Utah Juvenile Court Eighth Judicial District)* Appointed by governor.

Office: 920 East Highway 40, Vernal 84078-2803.
Telephone: (435) 781-9335.
Fax: (435) 789-0564

STEWART, Brian T. *(Judge, United States District Court District of Utah)* Appointed for life by President Bill Clinton to term beginning Nov 15, 1999. Born Logan Utah Aug 19, 1948. Educated at Utah State University B.S. 1972 and University of Utah J.D. In legal practice Salt Lake City 1974-80.

Assistant to Senator Orrin G. Hatch 1980. Administrative Assistant to U.S. Representative James V. Hansen 1981-85. Commissioner Public Service Commission 1985-92. Executive Director Department of Commerce 1992 and Department of Natural Resources 1993-98 Utah. Chief of Staff to Governor Michael O. Leavitt 1998-99.

Office: 148 U.S. Courthouse, 350 South Main Street, Salt Lake City 84101.
Telephone: (801) 524-6617.

STOTT, Gary D. *(Presiding Judge, Utah District Court Fourth Judicial District)* Appointed by governor.

Office: 125 North 100 West, Provo 84601.
Telephone: (801) 429-1065.
Fax: (801) 429-1137

TAYLOR, James R. *(Judge, Utah District Court Fourth Judicial District)* Appointed by Governor Michael O. Leavitt.

Office: 125 North 100 West, Provo 84601.
Telephone: (801) 429-1066.
Fax: (801) 429-1137

THORNE, William A., Jr. *(Judge, Utah Court of Appeals)* Appointed by Governor Michael O. Leavitt. Born Lakeport California Nov 11, 1952. Educated at Stanford University Law School J.D. 1977. In legal practice Salt Lake City 1977-86. Former Judge, Utah Circuit Court Third Judicial District, appointed by Governor Norman H. Bangerter to term beginning Oct 1986. Former Judge, Utah District Court Third Judicial District.

Former Chairman Utah Juvenile Justice Task Force Commission on Criminal and Juvenile Justice. Chairman Bail Bonding Committee.

Office: 450 South State, Salt Lake City 84111.
Telephone: (801) 238-3900.

THURMAN, William T. *(Judge, United States Bankruptcy Court District of Utah)* Appointed by U.S. Court of Appeals Tenth Circuit judges to term beginning Sept 4, 2001. Term expires Sept 3, 2015.

Office: 358 U.S. Courthouse, 350 South Main Street, Salt Lake City 84101.
Telephone: (801) 524-6572.

VALDEZ, Andrew A. *(Judge, Utah Juvenile Court Third Judicial District)* Appointed by governor.

Mailing address: P.O. Box 140431, Salt Lake City 84114.
Office: 450 South State, Salt Lake City 84111.
Telephone: (801) 238-7787.
Fax: (801) 238-7771

VAN DYKE, Stephen A. *(Judge, Utah Juvenile Court Second Judicial District)* Appointed by Governor Norman H. Bangerter to term beginning July 1, 1985. Retained by election Nov 8, 1988, 1994 and 2000. Current term expires Dec 31, 2006. Former Presiding Judge. Born Ogden Utah Nov 15, 1941. Church of Jesus Christ of Latter-Day Saints. Educated at Brigham Young University B.S. 1966 M.A. 1967, Bowling Green State University Ph.D. 1976 and Brigham Young University J. Reuben Clark Law School J.D. 1980. Associate Editor Brigham Young University Law Review 1979. Admitted to practice Utah 1981. In legal practice Salt Lake City 1980-82 and Layton 1982-85. Mental Health Commissioner, Utah Second Judicial District 1983-85.

Author Case Note "Reverse Discrimination" Brigham Young University L. Rev. 1979. Assistant Professor of Communications Southern Utah State College 1970-78. Adjunct Professor of Business Law Weber State College 1984-85. Former Member Utah Judicial Council. Member Utah State Task Force on Judicial Master Plan, Utah Commission on Juvenile Justice and Delinquency Prevention, State Advisory Committee on Juvenile Court Rules of Procedure, Utah Board of Juvenile Court Judges, National Council of Juvenile and Family Court Judges (Advisory Committee on Legislation), Utah State Bar and Davis County Bar Association (Vice President 1983-84, President 1984-85). Enjoys hunting, fishing and writing.

Mailing address: P.O. Box 325, Farmington 84025.
Office: 800 West State Street, Farmington 84025.
Telephone: (801) 451-4900.
Fax: (801) 451-4950

WEST, W. Brent *(Presiding Judge, Utah District Court Second Judicial District)* Assumed office July 1, 1996. Retained by election, current term expires Jan 2006. Born Salt Lake City Utah May 17, 1951. Educated at University of Utah B.S. with honors 1973 and Southern Methodist University J.D. 1975. Member Delta Theta Phi. Admitted to practice Utah 1976 and U.S.

WEST, W. BRENT—*Continued*
District Court District of Utah 1976. Began legal practice Ogden 1976. Judge and Presiding Judge, Utah Circuit Court Second Judicial District April 5, 1984 to June 30, 1996, appointed by Governor Scott M. Matheson. Presiding Judge, Third Circuit Court Board of Judges 1985-88 and Second Circuit Court Board of Judges 1988-90.

Assistant City Attorney 1977-81 and Chief Prosecutor 1981-84 Ogden. Member 1986-88 and Chair 1989-91 Utah Board of Circuit Court Judges. Vice Chair Warrant's Task Force 1987. Chair Collections/Warrants Ad Hoc Committee 1996-98. Former Member Appellate Operations Task Force, Utah Task Force on Gender and Justice, Audio-Video Technology Evaluation Committee, Common Court Boundaries Committee, Statewide Transition Committee, Weber County Criminal Justice Advisory Council and Utah Judicial Council (Management Committee 1991-94). Fellow The Association of Trial Lawyers of America. Chair Uniform Bail Schedule Committee 1987-91 and since 1998. Member Utah Task Force on Racial and Ethnic Fairness, Rex E. Lee Inn of Courts, Utah State Bar (Bench and Bar Committee 1994-96, Fee Arbitration Committee since 1997) and Weber County Bar Association (Treasurer 1977-79). Listed in *Who's Who in the West* 1989. Named Circuit Court Judge of the Year 1989 and Judge of the Year 1997. Recipient Outstanding Young Men in America Award 1989, Outstanding Service Award from Exchange Club of Ogden 1990, Friend of the Court Award by Justice Court 1991 and Medal of Honor from Business Leaders Against Crime 1998. Director 1977-90, Treasurer 1978-80 and Vice President 1987-89 Children's Aide Society. Director 1979-86 and President 1980-86 Ogden City School Volunteer's Association. MOWEDA Board of Directors 1985-87. Group Leader Parent's United 1986. Director Your Community Connection 1992-95. Coach Utah State Mock Trials Weber High School 1996-97. Director The Family Summit Foundation since 1995. Former Member Weber/Morgan Counties Child Abuse Coordination Council. Member Ogden Unit American Contract Bridge League (Director 1978-80 and 1987-89, President 1980, 1987 and 1988), Community Relations Committee Department of Corrections Northern Utah Community Correction's Center, Ogden High Alumni Association and Crimson Club. Enjoys golf, bridge and watching Dallas Cowboys.

Office: 269 State Courts Building, 2525 Grant Avenue, Ogden 84401.
Telephone: (801) 395-1135.

WILKINS, Diane W. *(Presiding Judge, Utah Juvenile Court Second Judicial District)* Appointed by governor.

Mailing address: P.O. Box 325, Farmington 84025.
Office: 800 West State Street, Farmington 84025.
Telephone: (801) 451-4900.
Fax: (801) 451-4950

WILKINS, Michael J. *(Justice, Utah Supreme Court)* Appointed by Governor Michael O. Leavitt Jan 2000. Educated at University of Utah College of Law J.D. 1977. In legal practice Salt Lake City 1977-94. Judge, Presiding Judge and Associate Presiding Judge, Utah Court of Appeals Aug 1994 to Jan 2000, appointed by Governor Michael O. Leavitt.

Former Member Legislative Compensation Commission, Board of Appellate Judges Supreme Court Task Force on Video in the Courtroom, and Courts Complex Steering Commission. Chair Standing Committee on Technology Utah Judicial Council. Member Utah Information Technology Commission and Utah Substance Abuse and Anti-violence Coordinating Council.

Office: 450 South State, Salt Lake City 84111.
Telephone: (801) 238-3900.

WILLMORE, Thomas L. *(Judge, Utah District Court First Judicial District)* Appointed by Governor Michael O. Leavitt.

Office: 140 North 100 West, Logan 84321.
Telephone: (435) 750-1300.
Fax: (435) 750-1355

WINDER, David K. *(Senior Judge, United States District Court District of Utah)* Appointed for life by President Jimmy Carter to term beginning Dec 6, 1979. Former Chief Judge. Assumed Senior status, serves by assignment. Born Salt Lake City Utah June 8, 1932. Educated at University of Utah B.A. 1955 and Stanford University J.D. 1958. Admitted to practice Utah 1958 and California 1958. Began legal practice Salt Lake City Utah 1958. In legal practice Utah 1958-76. Judge, Utah District Court Third Judicial District 1977-79.

Member Utah State Bar and State Bar of California. Sergeant USAF 1950-52. Political affiliation: Independent. Enjoys golf, tennis, hiking and reading.

Office: 102 U.S. Courthouse, 350 South Main Street, Salt Lake City 84101.
Telephone: (801) 524-6600.

YEATES, Robert S. *(Judge, Utah Juvenile Court Third Judicial District)* Appointed by governor.

Mailing address: P.O. Box 140431, Salt Lake City 84114.
Office: 450 South State, Salt Lake City 84111.
Telephone: (801) 238-7755.
Fax: (801) 238-7747

VERMONT

Capital MONTPELIER

UNITED STATES DISTRICT COURT DISTRICT OF VERMONT

The court sits at Bennington, Brattleboro, Burlington, Montpelier, Rutland, St. Johnsbury and Windsor. For descriptive information refer to the United States Courts section.

Chief Judge
William K. Sessions III

Judge
J. Garvan Murtha

Clerk
Richard P. Wasko
507 Federal Building
P.O. Box 945
Burlington, Vermont 05402-0945
(802) 951-6301

UNITED STATES MAGISTRATE JUDGE OF VERMONT

Jerome J. Niedermeier

UNITED STATES BANKRUPTCY COURT OF VERMONT

Judge
Colleen A. Brown

Bankruptcy Clerk
Thomas J. Hart
P.O. Box 6648
Rutland, Vermont 05702-6648
(802) 776-2000

VERMONT SUPREME COURT

The Supreme Court is Vermont's court of last resort. The court consists of a chief justice and four associate justices initially appointed for six-year terms by the governor with the advice and consent of the Senate from a list of nominees submitted by the Judicial Nominating Board. Thereafter, justices are subject to retention votes by the General Assembly for six-year terms. The governor appoints the chief justice; if that position becomes vacant, the justice who has served longest assumes the duties of chief justice until an appointment is made. Retirement is mandatory at age seventy; however, retired justices may serve by assignment of the chief justice.

The court has appellate jurisdiction over the Superior, District and Family Courts and over the Probate Court when a question of law is involved as well as appellate jurisdiction over certain administrative agency proceedings. The court has administrative control over all courts, admittance to the bar and the regulation of the practice of law and disciplinary control over judges and attorneys. In addition, the court may issue writs necessary to the exercise of proper jurisdiction.

The court sits en banc at Montpelier.

Chief Justice
Jeffrey L. Amestoy

Associate Justices
John A. Dooley
Denise R. Johnson
Marilyn S. Skoglund
vacancy

Clerk and Court Administrator
Lee Suskin
109 State Street
Montpelier, Vermont 05609-0701
(802) 828-3278

VERMONT TRIAL COURTS

The Trial Courts consist of the Superior Court, the District Court and the Family Court. Judges may serve any or all of the Trial Courts and may be rotated at six-month intervals as determined by the administrative judge for Trial Courts. The administrative judge is appointed by the Supreme Court to serve an indefinite term. In order to ascertain the current court assignment of a particular judge, the office of the administrative judge should be contacted.

Administrative Judge for Trial Courts
Francis B. McCaffrey
255 North Main Street, Suite 4
Barre, Vermont 05641
(802) 476-4797

VERMONT SUPERIOR COURT

The Superior Court is Vermont's court of general jurisdiction. Judges are initially appointed for six-year terms by the governor with the advice and consent of the Senate from a list of qualified attorneys submitted by the Judicial Nominating Board. Thereafter, judges are subject to retention votes by the General Assembly for six-year terms. Each county is served by two assistant judges, who are elected in county elections for four-year terms. Retirement is mandatory at age seventy; however, retired judges may serve upon designation of the chief justice and assignment of the administrative judge for Trial Courts.

The court has jurisdiction in civil cases and small claims cases. The court also has jurisdiction over real estate and hears appeals de novo from the Probate Court.

The court sits at each county seat.

VERMONT TRIAL COURTS—*Continued*

VERMONT DISTRICT COURT

The District Court is a statewide court of general criminal jurisdiction and limited civil jurisdiction in Vermont. The court is divided into three multi-county units subdivided into circuits, each comprising one county. Judges are initially appointed for six-year terms by the governor with the advice and consent of the Senate from a list of candidates submitted by the Judicial Nominating Board. Thereafter, judges are subject to retention votes by the General Assembly for six-year terms. Retirement is mandatory at age seventy; however, retired judges may serve upon designation of the chief justice and assignment of the administrative judge for Trial Courts.

The court has criminal jurisdiction in felonies, misdemeanors and violations of municipal ordinances.

UNIT ONE includes all towns, villages and cities in the counties of Orange, Windham and Windsor circuits. The principal office of the District Court for territorial Unit No. 1 is located in the town of Hartford.

UNIT TWO includes all towns, villages and cities in the counties of Addison, Bennington, Chittenden and Rutland circuits. The principal office of the District Court for territorial Unit No. 2 is located in the city of Burlington.

UNIT THREE includes all towns, villages and cities in the counties of Caledonia, Essex, Franklin, Grand Isle, Lamoille, Orleans and Washington circuits. The principal office of the District Court for territorial Unit No. 3 is located in the city of Barre.

VERMONT FAMILY COURT

The Family Court, established October 1, 1990, is a court of statewide jurisdiction in Vermont. Judges and assistant judges from the Superior Court and judges from the District Court are assigned to sit on the Family Court. The court is also served by magistrates, whose method of selection is similar to the judges for Trial Courts. The administrative judge for Trial Courts may appoint temporary magistrates.

The court has exclusive jurisdiction over proceedings involving desertion and support; parentage actions; rights of married women; enforcement of support; annulment and divorce; grandparents' visitation rights; uniform child custody; protective services and care for retarded persons; mental health proceedings; involuntary sterilization; and abuse prevention, as well as juvenile and family and child cases. Magistrates have jurisdiction to hear and dispose of proceedings for the establishment, modification and enforcement of child support and over cases arising under the Uniform Interstate Support Act, as well as jurisdiction over child support in parentage cases after parentage has been established. The Family Court is a court of record and has all of the equitable and other powers of the Superior Court as to civil matters within its jurisdiction except as specifically limited by statute.

The court sits at the county seats and as determined by the Supreme Court.

Trial Court Judges

Brian L. Burgess	Karen R. Carroll
Edward J. Cashman	William D. Cohen
Alan W. Cook	Nancy Corsones
Geoffrey W. Crawford	James R. Crucitti
Amy M. Davenport	Theresa S. DiMauro
Jane G. Dimotsis	Katherine A. Hayes
David A. Howard	David A. Jenkins
Ben W. Joseph	Matthew I. Katz
Mark J. Keller	Michael S. Kupersmith
Linda Levitt	M. Kathleen Manley
Walter M. Morris, Jr.	Richard W. Norton
Dennis R. Pearson	Dean B. Pineles
David T. Suntag	Mary Miles Teachout
Helen M. Toor	Howard VanBenthuysen
John P. Wesley	M. Patricia Zimmerman
vacancy	

County	Assistant Judge
Addison	Wayne Heath Frank Broughton
Bennington	Wesley Mook James Colvin
Caledonia	Roy Carroll Vance William P. Kennedy
Chittenden	Elizabeth Gretkowski Thomas Crowley
Essex	Allen D. Hodgdon Calvin Colby
Franklin	Teresa Manahan Roberta "Bobbie" Allard
Grand Isle	Sherri Potvin B. Kevin Steady
Lamoille	Richard Dillon Joanne Batchelder
Orange	Prudence Pease Russell Hotchkiss
Orleans	Kenneth Magoon William Gilding
Rutland	Marlene R. Burke Jean Coloutti
Washington	Cynthia Cyr Karl Barney Bloom
Windham	Trish Hain Mary Ann Clarkson
Windsor	William M. Boardman Ken Cooper

Family Court Magistrates

Douglas P. Cohn	Thomas J. Devine
Shelley J. Gartner	Christine Hoyt
Patricia Whalen	Barb Zander

VERMONT PROBATE COURT

The Probate Court is a court of special jurisdiction in Vermont. The court is divided into eighteen districts with some counties consisting of more than one district. Judges are elected from their respective districts for four-year terms. Retirement is mandatory at age seventy.

The court has jurisdiction over the probate of wills; administration of estates, trusts and guardianships; name changes; and uniform gifts to minors. Appeals are to the Superior Court.

ADDISON DISTRICT includes Addison County. The court sits at Middlebury.

Judge
Amy B. Douglas

VERMONT PROBATE COURT—*Continued*

BENNINGTON DISTRICT includes the towns of Bennington, Glastenbury, Pownal, Readsboro, Searsburg, Shaftsbury, Stamford and Woodford. The court sits at Bennington.

Judge
Doris S. Buchanan

CALEDONIA DISTRICT includes Caledonia County. The court sits at St. Johnsbury.

Judge
Ernest T. Balivet

CHITTENDEN DISTRICT includes Chittenden County. The court sits at Burlington.

Judge
Susan L. Fowler

ESSEX DISTRICT includes Essex County. The courts sits at Island Pond.

Judge
Marilyn W. Maxwell

FAIR HAVEN DISTRICT includes the towns of Benson, Castleton, Fair Haven, Hubbardton, Pawlet, Poultney, Sudbury, Wells and West Haven. The court sits at Fair Haven.

Judge
Christopher Howe

FRANKLIN DISTRICT includes Franklin County. The court sits at St. Albans.

Judge
Robert Cronin

GRAND ISLE DISTRICT includes Grand Isle County. The court sits at North Hero.

Judge
George Spear

HARTFORD DISTRICT includes the towns of Barnard, Bethel, Bridgewater, Hartford, Hartland, Norwich, Pomfret, Rochester, Royalton, Sharon, Stockbridge and Woodstock. The court sits at Woodstock.

Judge
Joanne M. Ertel

LAMOILLE DISTRICT includes Lamoille County. The court sits at Hyde Park.

Judge
Philip J. Fitzpatrick

MANCHESTER DISTRICT includes the towns of Arlington, Dorset, Landgrove, Manchester, Peru, Rupert, Sandgate, Sunderland and Winhall. The court sits at Manchester.

Judge
Sally Cook

MARLBORO DISTRICT includes the towns of Brattleboro, Dover, Dummerston, Gilford, Halifax, Marlboro, Newfane, Stratton, Somerset, Vernon, Wardsboro, Whitingham and Wilmington. The court sits at Brattleboro.

Judge
Robert M. Pu

ORANGE DISTRICT includes Orange County. The court sits at Chelsea.

Judge
Bernard M. Lewis

ORLEANS DISTRICT includes Orleans County. The court sits at Newport.

Judge
John P. Monette

RUTLAND DISTRICT includes the towns of Brandon, Chittenden, Clarendon, Danby, Ira, Mendon, Middletown Springs, Mount Holly, Mount Tabor, Pittsfield, Pittsford, Proctor, Rutland Town, Rutland City, Sherburne, Shrewsbury, Tinmouth, Wallingford and West Rutland. The court sits at Rutland City.

Judge
Kevin Candon

WASHINGTON DISTRICT includes Washington County. The court sits at Montpelier.

Judge
George K. Belcher

WESTMINSTER DISTRICT includes the towns of Athens, Bellows Falls, Brookline, Grafton, Jamaica, Londonderry, Putney, Rockingham, Townshend, Westminster and Windham. The court sits at Bellows Falls.

Judge
Edward M. Goutas

WINDSOR DISTRICT includes the towns of Andover, Baltimore, Cavendish, Chester, Ludlow, North Springfield, Plymouth, Reading, Springfield, Weathersfield, West Windsor, Weston and Windsor. The court sits at North Springfield.

Judge
Sarah E. Vail

VERMONT ENVIRONMENTAL COURT

The Environmental Court, established in 1989, is a court of record of statewide jurisdiction in Vermont. The court consists of one judge initially appointed by the governor with the advice and consent of the Senate from a list of qualified attorneys submitted by the Judicial Nominating Board. Thereafter, the judge is subject to retention votes by the General Assembly for six-year terms.

The court hears all matters arising under chapter 201 of Title 10 and under 24 V.S.A. chapter 61, subchapter 12. Any acts which are potentially harmful to the environment, such as violations of the Land Use Development Law, operations conducted without proper permits and illegal sewage dumping, are subject to enforcement actions by the Agency of Natural Resources. These violation orders may be brought before the Environmental Court to be affirmed or reversed. The Environmental Court also hears appeals of municipal zoning board and planning commission decisions. Appeals are to the Supreme Court.

The court sits at Montpelier.

VERMONT ENVIRONMENTAL COURT—*Continued*

Judge
Merideth Wright

VERMONT JUDICIAL BUREAU

The Traffic and Municipal Ordinance Bureau was established on May 29, 1990. The name was changed to Vermont Judicial Bureau in 1998. The bureau consists of four hearing officers appointed by the Administrative Judge for the Trial Courts.

The bureau has jurisdiction over traffic violations, littering violations, civil municipal ordinance violations and fish and wildlife violations. Appeals are to the District Courts.

Hearings are held at each county seat.

Vermont Counties and County Seats

Addison
Middlebury

Bennington
Bennington
Manchester

Caledonia
St. Johnsbury

Chittenden
Burlington

Essex
Guildhall

Franklin
St. Albans

Grand Isle
North Hero

Lamoille
Hyde Park

Orange
Chelsea

Orleans
Newport

Rutland
Rutland

Washington
Montpelier

Windham
Newfane

Windsor
Woodstock

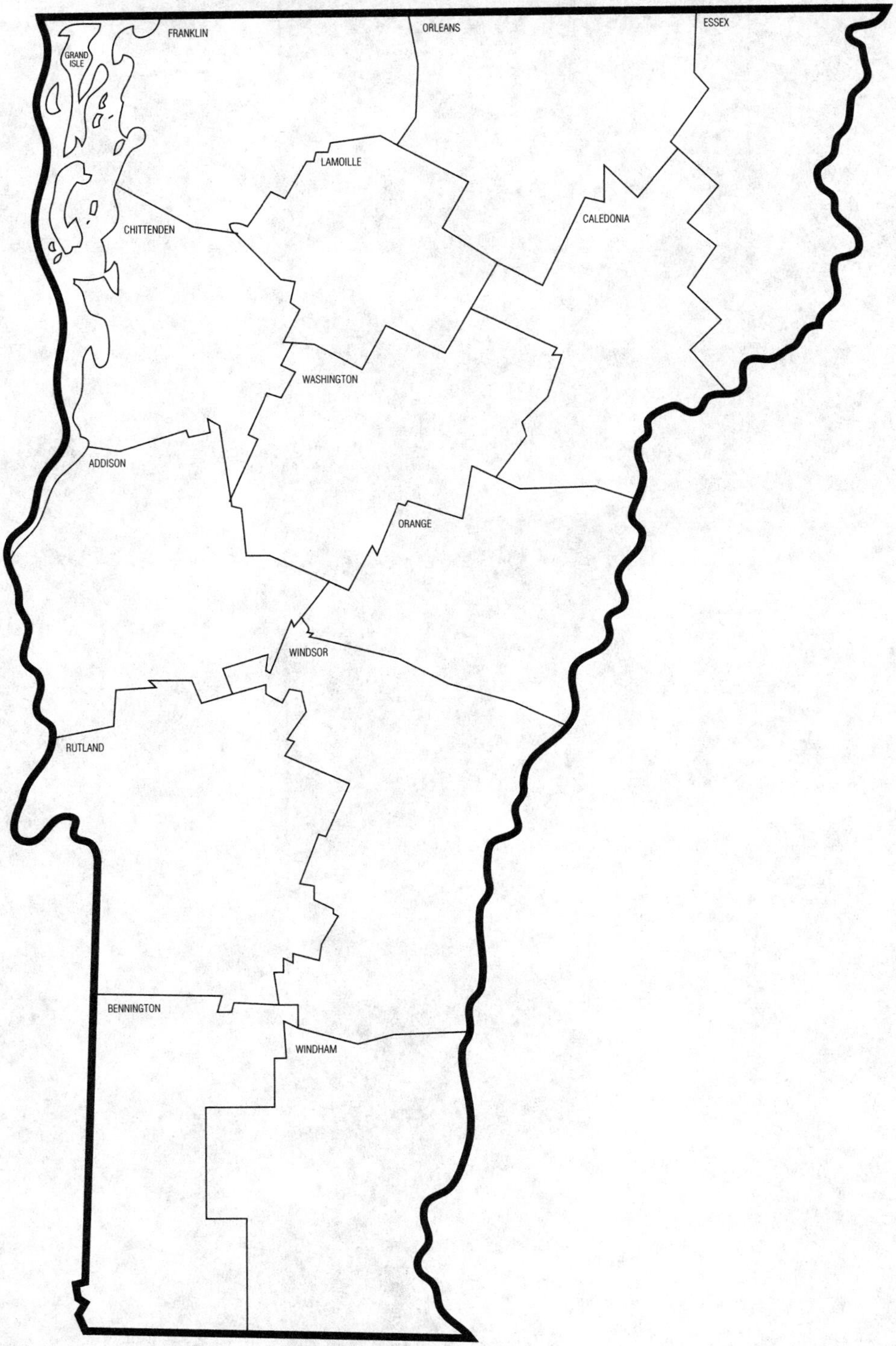
FRANKLIN
ORLEANS
ESSEX
GRAND ISLE
LAMOILLE
CHITTENDEN
CALEDONIA
WASHINGTON
ADDISON
ORANGE
WINDSOR
RUTLAND
BENNINGTON
WINDHAM

UNITED STATES DISTRICT COURT DISTRICT OF VERMONT

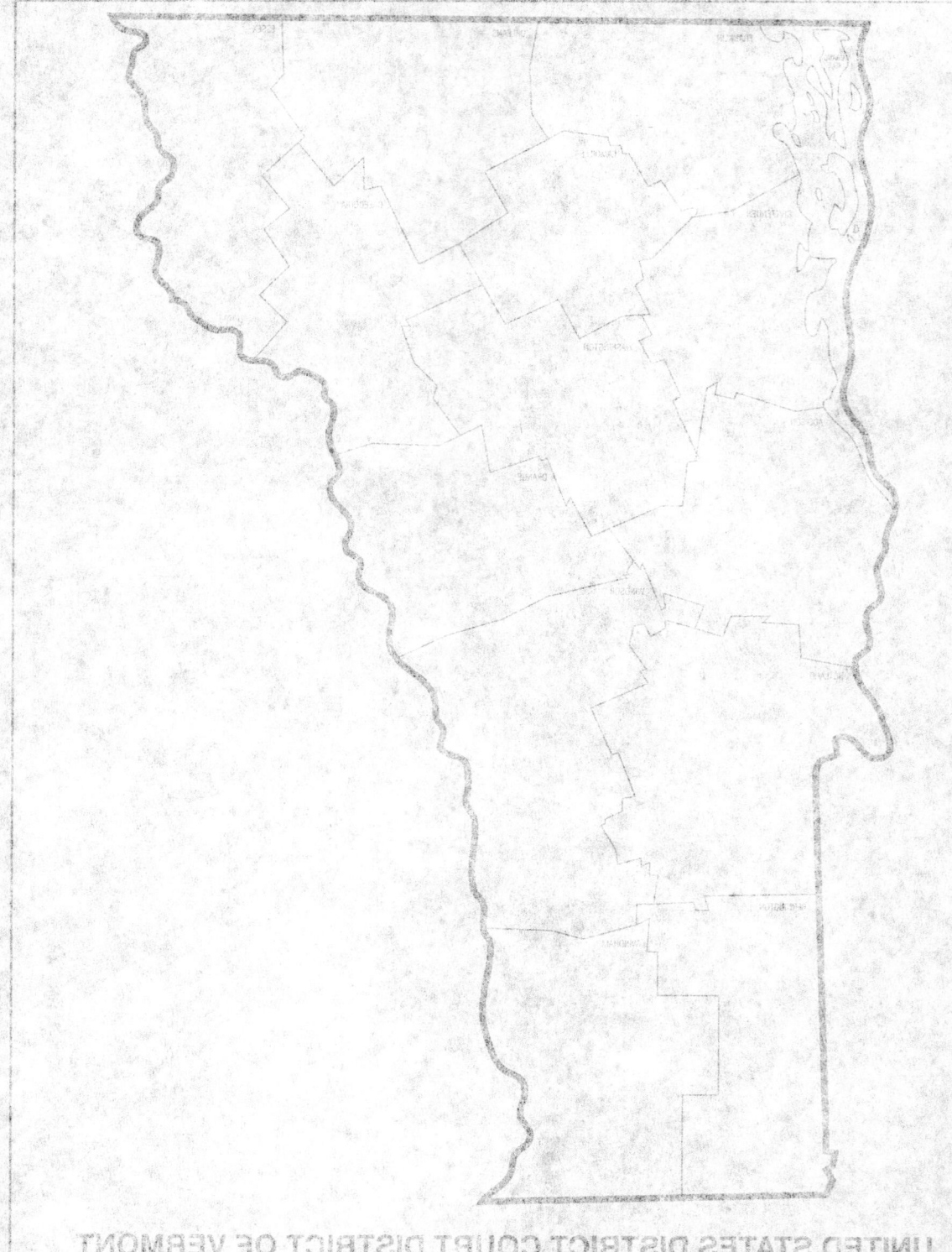

VERMONT

ALLARD, Roberta "Bobbie" *(Assistant Judge, Vermont Trial Court Franklin County)* Elected to term beginning Feb 1999. Reelected 2002, current term expires Feb 2007. Born St. Albans Vermont March 4, 1945. Catholic.

Member Vermont Association of County Judges and National Association of Judges. Attended National Association Convention June 1999 and The National Judicial College Aug 2000. Democrat. Member Franklin County Democratic Committee. Member St. Albans City Planning Commission 1985-87. Enjoys reading and puzzles.

Mailing address: P.O. Box 808, St. Albans 05478-0808.

Office: 36 Lake Street, St. Albans 05478.

Telephone: (802) 524-7997.

Fax: (802) 524-7946

AMESTOY, Jeffrey L. *(Chief Justice, Vermont Supreme Court)* Appointed by Governor Howard Dean to term beginning Feb 1, 1997. Retained by General Assembly 2003, current term expires 2009. Born Rutland Vermont July 24, 1946. Educated at Hobart College B.A. 1968, University of California Hastings College of the Law J.D. 1972 and Harvard University John F. Kennedy School of Government M.P.A. 1982.

Assistant Attorney General 1977-78, Chief Prosecutor Attorney General's Medicaid Fraud Division 1978-81 and Attorney General 1985-97 Vermont. Counsel Governor's Commission on Administration of Justice 1974-76. Commissioner Labor and Industry 1982-84.

Office: 109 State Street, Montpelier 05609-0801.

Telephone: (802) 828-3278.

BALIVET, Ernest T. *(Judge, Caledonia District Probate Court)* Formerly served Bennington District.

Mailing address: P.O. Box 406, St. Johnsbury 05819.

Telephone: (802) 748-6605.

BATCHELDER, Joanne *(Assistant Judge, Vermont Trial Court Lamoille County)*

Mailing address: P.O. Box 490, Hyde Park 05655.

Telephone: (802) 888-2207.

BELCHER, George K. *(Judge, Washington District Probate Court)* Elected to term beginning Feb 1, 1991. Reelected 1994, 1998 and 2002. Current term expires Jan 31, 2007. Born Pensacola Florida July 1, 1949. Educated at Kansas University B.A. 1971 and Vermont Law School J.D. cum laude 1977. Note Contributor and Note Editor Vermont Law Review 1975-77. Admitted to practice Vermont 1978 and U.S. District Court District of Vermont 1978. In legal practice Montpelier 1978-80 and Barre 1981-91.

Instructor in Business Law Vermont College 1978-81. Member Washington County (President 1995), Vermont and American Bar Associations. Lieutenant j.g. USNR 1971-74.

Office: 10 Elm Street #2, Montpelier 05602-0015.

Telephone: (802) 828-3405.

BLOOM, Karl Barney *(Assistant Judge, Vermont Trial Court Washington County)* Elected to term beginning Feb 1, 1999. Reelected 2002, current term expires Jan 31, 2007. Currently serves Washington County Superior, Traffic and Family Courts. Born Xenia Ohio July 15, 1943. Jewish. Educated at University of Cincinnati B.A. 1964 and University of Hawaii M.A. 1967.

Listed in *Who's Who in the East* 25th ed. Democrat. Peace Corps 1973-75.

Office: 65 State Street, Montpelier 05602.

Telephone: (802) 828-2091.

BOARDMAN, William M. *(Assistant Judge, Vermont Trial Court Windsor County)* Elected to term beginning Feb 1, 1991. Reelected 1994, 1998 and 2002. Current term expires Jan 31, 2007. Born New York New York May 8, 1938. Educated at Yale College B.A. 1960 M.F.A. 1964.

Member Vermont Association of County Judges and National Judges Association. Currently employed with Panther News Service (multi-media satire and journalism). Member Dramatists Guild and Writers Guild of America East. Personal Statement or Quote: "You can't step in the same river twice" (Heraclitus).

Office: Windsor County Superior Court, 12 The Green, Woodstock 05091.

Telephone: (802) 457-2121.

Fax: (802) 457-3446

BROUGHTON, Frank *(Assistant Judge, Vermont Trial Court Addison County)*

Office: Seven Mahady Court, Middlebury 05753.

Telephone: (802) 388-7741.

BROWN, Colleen A. *(Judge, United States Bankruptcy Court District of Vermont)* Appointed by U.S. Court of Appeals Second Circuit judges to term beginning April 10, 2000. Term expires April 2014.

Mailing address: P.O. Box 6648, Rutland 05702-6648.

Telephone: (802) 770-5806.

BUCHANAN, Doris S. *(Judge, Bennington District Probate Court)* Elected Nov 8, 1990 to term beginning Jan 1, 1991. Reelected Nov 1994, Nov 1998 and Nov 2002. Current term expires Jan 31, 2007. Born Bennington Vermont. Catholic.

Clerk Vermont Trial Court Feb 1, 1959 to Sept 30, 1990. Member Vermont Probate Judges Association. Enjoys spending time with family.

Mailing address: P.O. Box 65, Bennington 05201-0065.

Office: 207 South Street, Bennington 05201.

Telephone: (802) 447-2705.

Fax: (802) 447-2703

E-mail address: bnprobat@mail.state.vt.us

BURGESS, Brian L. *(Judge, Vermont Trial Court)* Appointed by governor.

Office: 32 Cherry Street, Suite 300, Burlington 05401.

Telephone: (802) 651-1800.

BURKE, Marlene R. *(Assistant Judge, Vermont Trial Court Rutland County)*

Office: 83 Center Street, Suite 3, Rutland 05701.

Telephone: (802) 775-4394.

CANDON, Kevin *(Judge, Rutland District Probate Court)*
Mailing address: P.O. Box 339, Rutland 05702.
Office: 83 Center Street, Rutland 05701.
Telephone: (802) 775-0114.

CARROLL, Karen R. *(Judge, Vermont Trial Court)* Appointed by governor.
Office: 30 Putney Road, Second Floor, Brattleboro 05301.
Telephone: (802) 257-2800.

CASHMAN, Edward J. *(Judge, Vermont Trial Court)* Appointed by governor.
Mailing address: P.O. Box 490, Hyde Park 05655.
Telephone: (802) 888-2207.

CLARKSON, Mary Ann *(Assistant Judge, Vermont Trial Court Windham County)* Elected to term beginning Feb 1, 2003.
Mailing address: P.O. Box 207, Newfane 05345.
Telephone: (802) 365-7979.

COHEN, William D. *(Judge, Vermont Trial Court)* Appointed by governor.
Office: 83 Center Street, Rutland 05701.
Telephone: (802) 786-5856.

COHN, Douglas P. *(Magistrate, Vermont Trial Court)* Appointed by governor.
Office: 32 Cherry Street, Suite 200, Burlington 05401.
Telephone: (802) 651-1800.

COLBY, Calvin *(Assistant Judge, Vermont Trial Court Essex County)* Elected to term beginning Feb 1, 2003.
Mailing address: P.O. Box 75, Guildhall 05905.
Telephone: (802) 676-3910.

COLOUTTI, Jean *(Assistant Judge, Vermont Trial Court Rutland County)*
Office: 83 Center Street, Suite 3, Rutland 05701.
Telephone: (802) 775-4394.

COLVIN, James *(Assistant Judge, Vermont Trial Court Bennington County)*
Mailing address: P.O. Box 4157, Bennington 05201.
Telephone: (802) 447-2700.

COOK, Alan W. *(Judge, Vermont Trial Court)* Appointed by Governor Richard A. Snelling to term beginning July 6, 1978. Retained by General Assembly 1984, 1990, 1996 and 2002. Current term expires Jan 31, 2009. Born New Bedford Massachusetts Nov 29, 1941. Protestant. Educated at Norwich University B.A. 1963 and Boston University J.D. 1966 M.A. 1968. Admitted to practice Massachusetts 1966 and Vermont 1972. In legal practice Barre Vermont 1971-73.

State Assistant Attorney General 1973-78. Acting State Commissioner of Mental Health 1976-77. Colonel USAR (retired).
Mailing address: P.O. Box 458, Woodstock 05091.
Telephone: (802) 457-2121.

COOK, Sally *(Judge, Manchester District Probate Court)*
Mailing address: P.O. Box 446, Manchester 05254.
Telephone: (802) 362-1410.

COOPER, Ken *(Assistant Judge, Vermont Trial Court Windsor County)*
Mailing address: P.O. Box 458, Woodstock 05091.
Telephone: (802) 457-2121.

CORSONES, Nancy *(Judge, Vermont Trial Court)* Appointed by governor.
Office: 92 State Street, Rutland 05701.
Telephone: (802) 786-5880.

CRAWFORD, Geoffrey W. *(Judge, Vermont Trial Court)* Appointed by governor.
Mailing address: Box 207, Newfane 05345.
Telephone: (802) 365-7979.

CRONIN, Robert *(Judge, Franklin District Probate Court)*
Office: 17 Church Street, St. Albans 05478.
Telephone: (802) 524-7948.

CROWLEY, Thomas *(Assistant Judge, Vermont Trial Court Chittenden County)*
Mailing address: P.O. Box 187, Burlington 05402-0187.
Office: 175 Main Street, Burlington 05401.
Telephone: (802) 863-3467.

CRUCITTI, James R. *(Judge, Vermont Trial Court)* Appointed by governor.
Office: 32 Cherry Street, Suite 300, Burlington 05401.
Telephone: (802) 651-1800.

CYR, Cynthia *(Assistant Judge, Vermont Trial Court Washington County)*
Office: 65 State Street, Montpelier 05602.
Telephone: (802) 828-2091.

DAVENPORT, Amy M. *(Judge, Vermont Trial Court)* Appointed by governor.
Office: 82 Railroad Row, White River Junction 05001.
Telephone: (802) 295-8838.

DEVINE, Thomas J. *(Magistrate, Vermont Trial Court)* Appointed by Governor Howard Dean Nov 1994. Retained by General Assembly 1997, current term expires Jan 31, 2004. Born Boston Massachusetts Oct 12, 1960. Catholic. Educated at Boston University B.A. 1982 and George Washington University J.D. 1985. Admitted to practice Massachusetts 1985 and Vermont 1991.

Tax Counsel Massachusetts Department of Revenue 1986-90. Supervising Attorney Vermont Office of Child Support 1990-94. Important Decisions: OLS Ex rel. Degolier v. Crane 21 Fam. L. Rep. 1422 Vermont 1995. Chair Advisory Committee on Rules for Family Proceedings. Member Vermont Trial Court Judges Association, Vermont (Family Law Committee) and Massachusetts Bar Associations.
Office: 32 Cherry Street, Suite 200, Burlington 05401.
Telephone: (802) 651-1800.

DILLON, Richard *(Assistant Judge, Vermont Trial Court Lamoille County)*
Mailing address: P.O. Box 490, Hyde Park 05655.
Telephone: (802) 888-2207.

DiMAURO, Theresa S. *(Judge, Vermont Trial Court)* Appointed by governor.
Office: 82 Railroad Row, White River Junction 05001.
Telephone: (802) 295-8865.

DIMOTSIS, Jane G. *(Judge, Vermont Trial Court)* Appointed by governor.
Office: 255 North Main Street, Suite 3, Barre 05641.
Telephone: (802) 479-4205.

DOOLEY, John A. *(Associate Justice, Vermont Supreme Court)* Appointed by Governor Madeleine M. Kunin to term beginning June 12, 1987. Retained by General Assembly 1993 and 1999. Current term expires 2005. Born Nashua New Hampshire April 10, 1944. Methodist. Educated at Union College B.E.E. 1965 and Boston College Law School LL.B. cum laude 1968. Legislation Editor Boston College Law Review 1966-68. Law Clerk to Hon. Bernard J. Leddy, U.S. District Court District of Vermont 1968-69. Admitted to practice Vermont 1968, U.S. District Court District of Vermont 1968, U.S. Court of Appeals Second Circuit 1971 and U.S. Supreme Court 1974. In legal practice Burlington 1981-84. Magistrate, U.S. District Court District of Vermont 1971-75.
Deputy Director 1969-72 and Director 1972-78 Vermont Legal Aid, Inc. Consultant Legal Services Corporation 1978-81. Legal Counsel to Governor Madeleine M. Kunin 1984-85. Secretary of Administration Vermont 1985-87. Author *Legal Problems of the Poor* Little-Brown 1975. Member Vermont Bar Association (President 1988-89).
Office: 109 State Street, Montpelier 05609-0801.
Telephone: (802) 828-3278.

DOUGLAS, Amy B. *(Judge, Addison District Probate Court)* Elected Nov 1998 to term beginning Feb 1, 1999. Reelected 2002, current term expires Jan 31, 2007. Born Middlebury Vermont Jan 18, 1949. Educated at Kalamazoo College B.A. 1971, Arizona State University M.B.A. 1982 and Whittier College School of Law J.D. 1993. Admitted to practice Vermont 1994. In legal practice Orwell 1996-98.
Member Vermont and American Bar Associations. Enjoys birding and reading.
Office: Seven Mahady Court, Middlebury 05753.
Telephone: (802) 388-2612.

ERTEL, Joanne M. *(Judge, Hartford District Probate Court)* Formerly served Caledonia District.
Mailing address: P.O. Box 275, Woodstock 05091.
Telephone: (802) 457-1503.

FITZPATRICK, Philip J. *(Judge, Lamoille District Probate Court)* Elected to term beginning Feb 1, 1998. Reelected 2002, current term expires 2006. Born Bronxville New York Aug 21, 1945. Educated at Georgetown University B.A. cum laude 1967 and Boston University School of Law J.D. cum laude 1973. Admitted to practice Vermont 1974. Began legal practice Jeffersonville 1974.
Mailing address: P.O. Box 102, Hyde Park 05655-0102.
Telephone: (802) 888-3306.

FOWLER, Susan L. *(Judge, Chittenden District Probate Court)* Elected Nov 8, 1994 to term beginning Feb 1, 1995. Reelected Nov 8, 1998 and 2002. Current term expires Jan 31, 2007. Born Middletown Connecticut March 13, 1953. Episcopalian. Educated at Boston University B.A. cum laude 1975 and Vermont Law School J.D. 1980. Law Clerk to Vermont Trial Court 1980-81. Admitted to practice Connecticut 1981, Vermont 1981 and U.S. Court of Appeals Second Circuit 1991. In legal practice Burlington Vermont 1984-95.
Assistant District Attorney White River Junction 1981 and Burlington 1981-84. Member American Academy of Adoption Attorneys and Vermont Bar Association. Democrat. Interests include Morgan horses, family, gardening and sports.
Mailing address: P.O. Box 511, Burlington 05402.
Telephone: (802) 651-1518.

GARTNER, Shelley J. *(Magistrate, Vermont Trial Court)* Appointed by governor.
Office: 83 Center Street, Rutland 05701.
Telephone: (802) 786-5856.

GILDING, William *(Assistant Judge, Vermont Trial Court Orleans County)*
Office: 247 Main Street, Suite 1, Newport 05855.
Telephone: (802) 334-3344.

GOUTAS, Edward M. *(Judge, Westminster District Probate Court)* Appointed by Governor Richard A. Snelling to term beginning June 13, 1979. Elected 1982, 1986, 1990, 1994, 1998 and 2002. Current term expires Jan 31, 2007. Also serves as Justice of the Peace since 1976. Born Bellows Falls Vermont Sept 12, 1942. Roman Catholic. Educated at St. Michael's College B.A. 1964 and St. John's University J.D. 1968. St. Thomas More Scholar 1968. Admitted to practice New York 1968 and Vermont 1970. Began legal practice Brattleboro Vermont 1969. In legal practice Bellows Falls Vermont since 1973.
Trustee Bellows Falls Village Corporation 1973-75. Member Advisory Committee on Vermont Rules of Probate Procedure since 1986. Member Windham County (President 1994-95), Vermont and American Bar Associations. Democrat. Former Director Community House of Brattleboro and American Red Cross. Board of Directors Bellows Falls Country Club and Youth Services, Inc. Life Master Duplicate Bridge. Executive Committee Vermont Golf Association since 1994. Enjoys golf, spectator sports and philately.
Mailing address: P.O. Box 47, Bellows Falls 05101.
Telephone: (802) 463-3019.

GRETKOWSKI, Elizabeth *(Assistant Judge, Vermont Trial Court Chittenden County)*
Mailing address: P.O. Box 187, Burlington 05402-0187.
Office: 175 Main Street, Burlington 05401.
Telephone: (802) 863-3467.

HAIN, Trish *(Assistant Judge, Vermont Trial Court Windham County)*
Mailing address: P.O. Box 207, Newfane 05345.
Telephone: (802) 365-7979.

HAYES, Katherine A. *(Judge, Vermont Trial Court)* Appointed by governor.
Office: 255 North Main Street, Suite 3, Barre 05641.
Telephone: (802) 479-4205.

HEATH, Wayne *(Assistant Judge, Vermont Trial Court Addison County)*
Office: Seven Mahady Court, Middlebury 05753.
Telephone: (802) 388-7741.

HODGDON, Allen D. *(Assistant Judge, Vermont Trial Court Essex County)* Elected to term beginning Feb 1, 1991. Reelected 1994, 1998 and 2002. Current term expires Jan 31, 2007. Born April 18, 1952. Con-

HODGDON, ALLEN D.—*Continued*
gregationalist. Educated at University of Illinois B.A. with honors 1974.

Republican. Former School Board Director. Former Chairman Guidhall Planning Commission. Former Member Vermont Philharmonic Orchestra. Enjoys collecting antiques.

Mailing address: P.O. Box 75, Guildhall 05905.
Telephone: (802) 676-3910.

HOTCHKISS, Russell *(Assistant Judge, Vermont Trial Court Orange County)* Elected to term beginning Feb 1, 2003.

Office: Five Court Street, Chelsea 05038.
Telephone: (802) 685-4610.

HOWARD, David A. *(Judge, Vermont Trial Court)* Appointed by Governor Howard Dean to term beginning Feb 1, 1998. Term expires Jan 31, 2004. Educated at University of Vermont B.A. 1973 and Boston College Law School J.D. 1976. Admitted to practice Vermont 1976, U.S. District Court District of Vermont 1978, Massachusetts 1979 and U.S. Court of Appeals Second Circuit.

Office: One Veterans Memorial Drive, Bennington 05201.
Telephone: (802) 447-2727.

HOWE, Christopher *(Judge, Fair Haven District Probate Court)*

Office: Three North Park Place, Fair Haven 05743.
Telephone: (802) 265-3380.

HOYT, Christine *(Magistrate, Vermont Trial Court)* Appointed by governor.

Office: 82 Railroad Row, White River Junction 05001.
Telephone: (802) 295-8838.

JENKINS, David A. *(Judge, Vermont Trial Court)* Appointed by Governor Richard A. Snelling to term beginning Nov 3, 1981. Retained by General Assembly. Born Springfield Massachusetts Feb 6, 1935. Educated at Dartmouth College A.B. 1957 and University of Connecticut School of Law J.D. 1965. Admitted to practice Vermont 1965 and Connecticut 1965. Judge, District Court of Vermont 1979-81.

Mailing address: c/o Court Administrator, 109 State Street, Montpelier 05609-0701.
Telephone: (802) 828-3278.

JOHNSON, Denise R. *(Associate Justice, Vermont Supreme Court)* Appointed by Governor Madeleine M. Kunin to term beginning Dec 3, 1990. Retained by General Assembly. Born Wyandotte Michigan July 13, 1947. Educated at Wayne State University A.B. 1969 and University of Connecticut School of Law J.D. 1974.

Assistant Attorney General and Chief Public Protection Division 1980-88. Chair Vermont Human Rights Commission 1988-90.

Office: 109 State Street, Montpelier 05609-0801.
Telephone: (802) 828-3278.

JOSEPH, Ben W. *(Judge, Vermont Trial Court)* Appointed by governor.

Office: 32 Cherry Street, Suite 300, Burlington 05401.
Telephone: (802) 651-1800.

KATZ, Matthew I. *(Judge, Vermont Trial Court)* Appointed by Governor Madeleine M. Kunin to term beginning 1985. Retained by General Assembly. Born New York New York Aug 6, 1946. Jewish. Educated at Trinity College B.A. 1967 and Rutgers University J.D. 1970. Admitted to practice Vermont 1970. In legal practice Burlington 1970-85.

Mailing address: P.O. Box 187, Burlington 05402-0187.
Telephone: (802) 863-3467.

KELLER, Mark J. *(Judge, Vermont Trial Court)* Appointed by governor.

Office: 1126 Main Street, Suite 1, St. Johnsbury 05819.
Telephone: (802) 748-6600.

KENNEDY, William P. *(Assistant Judge, Vermont Trial Court Caledonia County)* Elected to term beginning Feb 1, 1999. Reelected 2002, current term expires Jan 31, 2007. Born Bennington Vermont Nov 13, 1939. Congregationalist.

Member Vermont Association of County Judges and National Judges Association (Chaplin 2001-02). Attended The National Judicial College 1999. Recipient Citizen of the Year Award from St. Johnsbury Community 1987, Sister Beatrice Award 1987 and Recognition Award from Masonic Community 1989. U.S. Army RFA 1957-66. Manager Hovey's Men's Shops for twenty-nine years. Owner Bill Kennedy Sales Clothing since 1995. Distinguished Lieutenant Governor Kiwanis New England District 1977-78 and 1985-86. Founder and Former Chairman Board of Directors Northeast Kingdom Crime Stoppers. Former Trustee Northeast Kingdom Chamber of Commerce. Volunteer and Thresholds/Decisions Teacher Vermont Department of Corrections. Board Member Court Reparative Services in St. Johnsbury. Member St. Johnsbury Kiwanis Club (President 1974-75), South Congregationalist Church and B.O.P. Elks Lodge 1343.

Office: 1126 Main Street, Suite 1, St. Johnsbury 05819.
Telephone: (802) 748-6600.

KUPERSMITH, Michael S. *(Judge, Vermont Trial Court)* Appointed by governor.

Office: 36 Lake Street, St. Albans 05478.
Telephone: (802) 524-7997.

LEVITT, Linda *(Judge, Vermont Trial Court)* Appointed by governor.

Office: 32 Cherry Street, Suite 200, Burlington 05401.
Telephone: (802) 651-1800.

LEWIS, Bernard M. *(Judge, Orange District Probate Court)* Elected to term beginning Feb 1, 2003.

Office: Five Court Street, Chelsea 05038.
Telephone: (802) 685-4610.

MAGOON, Kenneth *(Assistant Judge, Vermont Trial Court Orleans County)*

Office: 247 Main Street, Suite 1, Newport 05855.
Telephone: (802) 334-3344.

MANAHAN, Teresa *(Assistant Judge, Vermont Trial Court Franklin County)*

Mailing address: P.O. Box 808, St. Albans 05478-0808.
Office: 17 Church Street, St. Albans 05478.
Telephone: (802) 524-7993.

MANLEY, M. Kathleen *(Judge, Vermont Trial Court)* Former Magistrate. Appointed by governor.
Mailing address: P.O. Box 75, Guildhall 05905.
Telephone: (802) 676-3910.

MAXWELL, Marilyn W. *(Judge, Essex District Probate Court)* Elected to term beginning Feb 1, 1983. Reelected 1986, 1990, 1994, 1998 and 2002. Current term expires Jan 31, 2007. Born Barton Vermont April 8, 1946. Protestant.
Mailing address: P.O. Box 426, Island Pond 05846-0426.
Telephone: (802) 723-4770.

McCAFFREY, Francis B. *(Administrative Judge, Vermont Trial Court)* Appointed by governor.
Office: 255 North Main Street, Second Floor, Barre 05641.
Telephone: (802) 476-4797.

MONETTE, John P. *(Judge, Orleans District Probate Court)* Appointed by Governor Madeleine M. Kunin to term beginning May 23, 1986. Elected 1986, 1990, 1994, 1998 and 2002. Current term expires Jan 31, 2007. Educated at Harvard College A.B. cum laude 1976 and University of Maine School of Law J.D. 1979. Admitted to practice Vermont 1979 and U.S. District Court District of Vermont 1980. In legal practice Newport since 1979.
Member Vermont Probate Judges Association, Orleans County, Vermont and American Bar Associations. Board of Directors North County Union High School 1980-86 (Chairman 1985-86) and Northeast Kingdom Mental Health Service, Inc. 1982-86.
Office: 247 Main Street, Newport 05855.
Telephone: (802) 334-3366.

MOOK, Wesley *(Assistant Judge, Vermont Trial Court Bennington County)*
Mailing address: P.O. Box 4157, Bennington 05201.
Telephone: (802) 447-2700.

MORRIS, Walter M., Jr. *(Judge, Vermont Trial Court)* Appointed by governor.
Office: 247 Main Street, Newport 05855.
Telephone: (802) 334-3355.

MURTHA, J. Garvan *(Judge, United States District Court District of Vermont)* Appointed for life by President Bill Clinton to term beginning 1995. Chief Judge 1995 to June 30, 2002. Born Hartford Connecticut March 3, 1941. Educated at Yale University B.A. 1963, University of Connecticut School of Law LL.B. 1968 and Georgetown University Law Center LL.M. 1970. In legal practice Brattleboro 1973-95.
Deputy State's Attorney Windham County 1970-73.
Mailing address: P.O. Box 760, Brattleboro 05302-0760.
Telephone: (802) 258-4413.

NIEDERMEIER, Jerome J. *(Magistrate Judge, United States District Court District of Vermont)* Appointed by U.S. District Court judges to term beginning April 23, 1982. Reappointed April 23, 1990 and 1998, current term expires 2006. Born Bridgeport Connecticut July 18, 1943. Catholic. Educated at Boston College B.A. with honors 1967 and Georgetown University J.D. 1972. Admitted to practice District of Columbia 1973, Connecticut 1973 and Vermont 1976. Began legal practice Washington D.C. 1973. In legal practice Vermont 1976.
Former Assistant U.S. Attorney. Member The District of Columbia Bar, Connecticut, Vermont and American Bar Associations.
Mailing address: P.O. Box 836, Burlington 05402-0836.
Telephone: (802) 951-6308.

NORTON, Richard W. *(Judge, Vermont Trial Court)* Appointed by governor.
Office: 83 Center Street, Rutland 05701.
Telephone: (802) 775-4394.

PEARSON, Dennis R. *(Judge, Vermont Trial Court)* Appointed by governor.
Mailing address: P.O. Box 808, St. Albans 05478.
Telephone: (802) 524-3863.

PEASE, Prudence *(Assistant Judge, Vermont Trial Court Orange County)* Elected to term beginning Feb 1, 2003.
Office: Five Court Street, Chelsea 05038.
Telephone: (802) 685-4610.

PINELES, Dean B. *(Judge, Vermont Trial Court)* Appointed by governor.
Office: 32 Cherry Street, Suite 200, Burlington 05401.
Telephone: (802) 651-1800.

POTVIN, Sherri *(Assistant Judge, Vermont Trial Court Grand Isle County)* Elected to term beginning Feb 1991. Reelected to subsequent terms. Current term expires Nov 2006. Born Montpelier Vermont Feb 11, 1959. Educated at Champlain College A.S. 1990.
Member State Association of County Judges and National Lay Judges Association. Enjoys walking and the outdoors.
Mailing address: P.O. Box 7, North Hero 05474.
Telephone: (802) 372-8350.

PU, Robert M. *(Judge, Marlboro District Probate Court)* Elected to term beginning Feb 1, 1987. Reelected 1990, 1994, 1998 and 2002. Current term expires Jan 31, 2007. Born Rockville Centre New York July 26, 1950. Congregationalist. Educated at Columbia University B.A. 1971 and Boston University J.D. 1975. Admitted to practice Vermont 1976, U.S. District Court District of Vermont 1977, U.S. Court of Appeals Second Circuit 1981 and U.S. Supreme Court 1982. In legal practice Brattleboro 1975-80 and since 1985. Brattleboro Town Attorney 1980-86.
Mailing address: P.O. Box 523, Brattleboro 05302.
Office: West River Road, Brattleboro 05302.
Telephone: (802) 257-2898.

SESSIONS, William K., III *(Chief Judge, United States District Court District of Vermont)* Appointed for life by President Bill Clinton to term beginning 1995. Chief Judge since July 1, 2002. Born Hartford Connecticut Feb 9, 1947. Educated at Middlebury College B.A. 1969 and George Washington University National Law Center J.D. 1972. Law Clerk to Hon. Hilton Dier, Addison District Probate Court 1973. Member Phi Delta Phi. In legal practice Middlebury 1978-95.
Public Defender Addison County 1974-78. Adjunct Professor Vermont Law School 1978-95. Member Civil Justice Reform Act Advisory Committee 1991-95 and Early Neutral Evaluation Panel District of Vermont 1994-95. Commissioner and Vice Chair U.S. Sentencing Commission since 1999. Former Member Vermont Association of Criminal Defense Lawyers. Member Judicial

SESSIONS, WILLIAM K., III—*Continued*

Council of the Second Circuit, Judicial Conference of the U.S. (Judicial Branch Committee) and Vermont Bar Association (Judicial Nominating Board 1981-86, Rule of Law Project Russia since 1992). Teacher Department of Corrections District of Columbia 1969. Chair Addison County Democratic Party 1985-91. Campaign Manager Leahy for U.S. Senate Campaign 1992. Executive Director Youth Services Bureau Addison County 1973-74. Board of Directors Vermont Chapter ACLU 1977-80 and Children's Art Exchange 1990-93. Chair Cornwall Planning Commission 1979-80 and 1981-85. Member Friends of the Children's Art Exchange since 1993. Trustee Vermont Law School 1995-2000. Chairman Vermont State Committee of Selection of the Rhodes Scholarship Trust 2001 and 2002.

Mailing address: P.O. Box 928, Burlington 05402-0928.

Office: U.S. Courthouse, 11 Elmwood Avenue, Burlington 05401.

Telephone: (802) 951-6350.

Fax: (802) 951-6785

SKOGLUND, Marilyn S. *(Associate Justice, Vermont Supreme Court)* Appointed by Governor Howard Dean to term beginning Aug 27, 1997. Born Chicago Illinois Aug 1946. Educated at Southern Illinois University B.A. 1971. Former Judge, Vermont Trial Court, appointed by Governor Howard Dean 1994.

Special Assistant Attorney General 1978-81, Assistant Attorney General 1981-89 and Chief Civil Law Division 1989-93 and Public Protection Division 1993-94 Office of the Attorney General.

Office: 109 State Street, Montpelier 05609-0801.

Telephone: (802) 828-3278.

SPEAR, George *(Judge, Grand Isle District Probate Court)*

Mailing address: P.O. Box 7, North Hero 05474.

Telephone: (802) 372-3522.

STEADY, B. Kevin *(Assistant Judge, Vermont Trial Court Grand Isle County)* Elected to term beginning Feb 1, 2003.

Mailing address: P.O. Box 7, North Hero 05474.

Telephone: (802) 372-8350.

SUNTAG, David T. *(Judge, Vermont Trial Court)* Appointed by governor.

Office: One Veterans Memorial Drive, Box 4, Bennington 05201.

Telephone: (802) 447-2729.

TEACHOUT, Mary Miles *(Judge, Vermont Trial Court)* Appointed by governor.

Office: 65 State Street, Montpelier 05602.

Telephone: (802) 828-2091.

TOOR, Helen M. *(Judge, Vermont Trial Court)* Appointed by Governor Howard Dean to term beginning June 7, 1999. Term expires March 2004. Born Pittsburgh Pennsylvania July 21, 1956. Educated at University of Vermont B.A. 1978 and University of Chicago Law School J.D. 1982. Admitted to practice New York 1983, U.S. District Courts Southern District of New York 1983 and District of Vermont 1989, U.S. Court of Appeals Second Circuit 1987 and Vermont 1990. In legal practice New York New York Sept 1982 to Jan 1987.

Assistant U.S. Attorney Southern District of New York Jan 1987 to Sept 1989. Chief Civil Division U.S. Attorney's Office Vermont Sept 1989 to June 1999. Member Chittenden County and Vermont Bar Associations.

Office: Seven Mahady Court, Middlebury 05753.

Telephone: (802) 388-7741.

VAIL, Sarah E. *(Judge, Windsor District Probate Court)*

Mailing address: P.O. Box 402, North Springfield 05150.

Telephone: (802) 886-2284.

VanBENTHUYSEN, Howard *(Judge, Vermont Trial Court)* Appointed by Governor Howard Dean to term beginning Aug 22, 1997. Retained by General Assembly 2003, current term expires 2009. Born Burlington Vermont. Educated at University of Vermont B.A. cum laude 1973, Colorado State University M.Ed. 1976 and Albany Law School of Union University J.D. cum laude 1982. Editor Albany Law Review 1980-82. Admitted to practice Vermont 1982, U.S. District Court District of Vermont, U.S. Court of Appeals Second Circuit and U.S. Supreme Court. In legal practice Burlington 1982-85 and St. Albans 1995-97.

State's Attorney Franklin County 1985-95. Member Chittenden County, Franklin County and Vermont Bar Associations. Vermont Army National Guard since 1986.

Office: 36 Lake Street, St. Albans 05478.

Telephone: (802) 524-7997.

VANCE, Roy Carroll *(Assistant Judge, Vermont Trial Court Caledonia County)* Elected to term beginning Feb 1, 1987. Reelected 1990, 1994, 1998 and 2002. Current term expires Jan 31, 2007. Born St. Johnsbury Vermont April 15, 1943. Protestant. Educated at New England School of Barbering 1963.

President National Judges Association 2001-02. Master Barber 1963-73. Employed by New England Telephone Company, Washington Electric and other utilities and in private tree removal and construction 1973-81. President and Supervisor Vance Tree Contractor Inc. since 1981. Republican. Member Vermont General Assembly 1973-80. Board of Selectmen Danville 1981-87 (Chairman 1984). Board of Directors N.V.D.A. 1973-83 and Caledonia County Fair 1976-87. Board of Trustees Vermont College 1975-83. President Danville Village Improvement Association 1983-87. Member Prudential Committee Danville Fire District 1973-87 (Chairman 1983-87), St. Johnsbury Baseball 1984-87 (Vice President 1985-86, Formed Senior Babe Ruth League 1986), Danville Fire Department (dispatcher), Danville Rescue Squad, Danville Chamber of Commerce (President 1978 and 1979, Trustee since 1980), Knights of Pythias (Chancellor Commander 1979, Grand Chancellor State of Vermont since 1980), St. Johnsbury Rotary (Paul Harris Fellow 1983, President 1985-86, Vermont Delegate to National Convention Kansas City 1985), Damon Lodge 16 Masons (Treasurer 1985), Mount Sinai Temple Montpelier (Order of Shrine since 1984, in charge of northern Vermont Shrine Football Game fund raising 1985-86, Fire Brigade since 1984, Chief 1985, Potentate 1994), Royal Order of Jesters, New England Draft Horse Association, St. Johnsbury Country Club (Director 1978-80) and Northeastern Vermont Baseball and Softball Umpires

VANCE, ROY CARROLL—*Continued*

Association. Coach Danville High School Junior Varsity Basketball since 1983.
Office: 1126 Main Street, Suite 1, St. Johnsbury 05819.
Telephone: (802) 748-6600.

WESLEY, John P. *(Judge, Vermont Trial Court)* Appointed by governor.
Office: 36 Putney Road, First Floor, Brattleboro 05301.
Telephone: (802) 257-2830.

WHALEN, Patricia *(Magistrate, Vermont Trial Court)* Appointed by Governor Madeleine M. Kunin to term beginning Oct 1, 1990. Retained by General Assembly Oct 1, 1996 and Oct 1, 2002. Current term expires Oct 1, 2008. Born Philadelphia Pennsylvania May 27, 1947. Educated at College Misericordia B.A. 1969 and Vermont Law School J.D. 1979. Staff member Vermont Law Review 1979-81. Admitted to practice Vermont 1981.
Staff Attorney Vermont Legal Aid 1981-90. Member Vermont Trial Court Judges Association (President 1999-2000), National Association of Women Judges, International Association of Women Judges and Vermont Bar Association.
Office: Six Putney Road, Brattleboro 05301.
Telephone: (802) 257-2830.
E-mail address: whalen@mail.crt.state.vt.us

WRIGHT, Merideth *(Judge, Vermont Environmental Court)* Appointed by governor.
Office: 255 North Main Street, Barre 05641.
Telephone: (802) 479-4486.

ZANDER, Barb *(Magistrate, Vermont Trial Court)* Appointed by governor.
Office: 255 North Main Street, Second Floor, Barre 05641.
Telephone: (802) 479-4205.

ZIMMERMAN, M. Patricia *(Judge, Vermont Trial Court)* Appointed by governor.
Office: 255 North Main Street, Barre 05641.
Telephone: (802) 479-4252.

VIRGINIA

Capital RICHMOND

UNITED STATES DISTRICT COURTS DISTRICTS OF VIRGINIA

Within Virginia there are two United States District Courts. For descriptive information refer to the United States Courts section.

EASTERN DISTRICT includes Accomack, Amelia, Arlington, Brunswick, Caroline, Charles City, Chesterfield, Dinwiddie, Essex, Fairfax, Fauquier, Gloucester, Goochland, Greensville, Hanover, Henrico, Isle of Wight, James City, King and Queen, King George, King William, Lancaster, Loudoun, Lunenburg, Mathews, Mecklenburg, Middlesex, New Kent, Northampton, Northumberland, Nottoway, Powhatan, Prince Edward, Prince George, Prince William, Richmond, Southampton, Spotsylvania, Stafford, Surry, Sussex, Westmoreland and York counties and the cities of Norfolk, Suffolk, Virginia Beach and Warwick. The court sits at Alexandria, Newport News, Norfolk and Richmond.

Chief Judge
Claude M. Hilton

Judges
James Randolph Spencer
Rebecca Beach Smith
Robert E. Payne
Leonie M. Brinkema
Jerome B. Friedman
Henry E. Hudson
Thomas S. Ellis, III
Henry Coke Morgan, Jr.
Raymond Alvin Jackson
Gerald Bruce Lee

Senior Judges
Albert V. Bryan, Jr.
J. Calvitt Clarke, Jr.
Richard L. Williams
James C. Cacheris
Robert G. Doumar

Clerk
Elizabeth Paret
U.S. Courthouse
401 Courthouse Square
Alexandria, Virginia 22314-5798
(703) 299-2107

WESTERN DISTRICT includes Albemarle, Alleghany, Amherst, Appomattox, Augusta, Bath, Bedford, Bland, Botetourt, Buchanan, Buckingham, Campbell, Carroll, Charlotte, Clarke, Craig, Culpeper, Cumberland, Dickenson, Floyd, Fluvanna, Franklin, Frederick, Giles, Grayson, Greene, Halifax, Henry, Highland, Lee, Louisa, Madison, Montgomery, Nelson, Orange, Page, Patrick, Pittsylvania, Pulaski, Rappahannock, Roanoke, Rockbridge, Rockingham, Russell, Scott, Shenandoah, Smyth, Tazewell, Warren, Washington, Wise and Wythe counties. The court sits at Abingdon, Big Stone Gap, Charlottesville, Danville, Harrisonburg, Lynchburg and Roanoke.

Chief Judge
Samuel Grayson Wilson

Judges
James Parker Jones
Norman K. Moon

Senior Judges
James Clinton Turk
Glen Morgan Williams
James Harry Michael, Jr.
Jackson L. Kiser

Clerk
John F. Corcoran
P.O. Box 1234
Roanoke, Virginia 24006-1234
(540) 857-5100

UNITED STATES MAGISTRATE JUDGES OF VIRGINIA

EASTERN DISTRICT
David G. Lowe
James E. Bradberry
Thomas R. Jones, Jr.
Dennis W. Dohnal
Liam O'Grady
Tommy E. Miller
Barry R. Poretz
Theresa Carroll Buchanan
F. Bradford Stillman

WESTERN DISTRICT
Glen E. Conrad
B. Waugh Crigler
Pamela Meade Sargent

Recalled Magistrate Judge
William T. Prince (Eastern)

UNITED STATES BANKRUPTCY COURTS OF VIRGINIA

EASTERN DISTRICT

Chief Judge
Douglas O. Tice, Jr.

Judges
David H. Adams
Stephen S. Mitchell
Stephen C. St. John
Robert G. Mayer

Bankruptcy Clerk
William C. Redden
310 U.S. Courthouse Annex
1100 East Main Street
Richmond, Virginia 23219-3515
(804) 916-2400

WESTERN DISTRICT

Chief Judge
Ross W. Krumm

UNITED STATES DISTRICT COURTS DISTRICTS OF VIRGINIA—*Continued*

Judges
William E. Anderson
William F. Stone, Jr.

Bankruptcy Clerk
John W. L. Craig II
P.O. Box 2390
Roanoke, Virginia 24010-2390
(540) 857-2391

SUPREME COURT OF VIRGINIA

The Supreme Court is Virginia's court of last resort. The court consists of a chief justice and six justices elected for twelve-year terms by majority vote of the General Assembly. Interim appointments are made by the governor subject to election by the General Assembly at the next regular session. The chief justice is selected by a vote of the seven justices of the Court.

The court has appellate jurisdiction over decisions of the lower courts. Except in cases involving the death penalty, the disbarment of an attorney or the State Corporation Commission, the court exercises discretionary review. The court has original jurisdiction in matters filed by the Judicial Inquiry and Review Commission relating to judicial censure, retirement and removal of judges. The court exercises administrative control over the lower courts and may issue writs necessary to the exercise of proper jurisdiction.

The court sits at Richmond en banc or in divisions, as prescribed by law.

Chief Justice
Leroy Rountree Hassell

Justices
Elizabeth B. Lacy
Lawrence L. Koontz, Jr.
Donald W. Lemons
Barbara Milano Keenan
Cynthia D. Kinser
G. Steven Agee

Clerk
Patricia Harrington Krueger
Supreme Court Building, Fifth Floor
100 North Ninth Street
Richmond, Virginia 23219
(804) 786-2251

Executive Secretary
Robert N. Baldwin
Supreme Court Building, Third Floor
100 North Ninth Street
Richmond, Virginia 23219-2334
(804) 786-6455

COURT OF APPEALS OF VIRGINIA

The Court of Appeals, which began operation January 1, 1985, is Virginia's court of intermediate appellate jurisdiction. The court consists of a chief judge and ten judges elected for eight-year terms by majority vote of the General Assembly. Interim appointments are made by the governor subject to election by the General Assembly at the next regular session. A chief judge is elected by peer vote to a four-year term.

The court exercises appellate jurisdiction over decisions of the Circuit Courts in traffic infractions and in criminal cases except when a sentence of death has been imposed, decisions involving domestic relations matters and appeals from administrative agencies. The court also hears appeals from the Workers' Compensation Commission. Except in noncapital criminal and traffic infraction cases, all appeals are a matter of right. The court may issue writs necessary to the exercise of proper jurisdiction.

Judges sit en banc and in panels of three. The court sits at such locations as the chief judge designates.

Chief Judge
Johanna L. Fitzpatrick

Judges
James W. Benton, Jr.
Rosemarie P. Annunziata
Robert P. Frank
Robert J. Humphreys
Walter S. Felton, Jr.
Elizabeth A. McClanahan
Larry G. Elder
Rudolph Bumgardner, III
Jean Harrison Clements
D. Arthur Kelsey

Clerk
Cynthia L. McCoy
109 North Eighth Street
Richmond, Virginia 23219-2321
(804) 371-8428

VIRGINIA CIRCUIT COURTS

The Circuit Courts are Virginia's trial courts of general jurisdiction. The state is divided into thirty-one judicial circuits. Judges are elected to eight-year terms by majority vote of the General Assembly. Interim appointments are made by the governor subject to election by the General Assembly at the next regular session. A chief judge is elected in each circuit by peer vote to a two-year term. Magistrates are appointed by the chief judge of each circuit and may issue warrants, set bail and perform other duties as prescribed by law. Retired judges may serve by special assignment of the chief justice.

The courts have concurrent jurisdiction with the District Courts in civil cases in which the amount in controversy is between $3,000 and $15,000. The courts exercise exclusive jurisdiction in civil cases in which the amount exceeds $15,000 and in equity matters such as adoptions, divorces and land title disputes. The courts have original jurisdiction over felony cases and misdemeanor charges which originate from grand jury indictment. The courts also hear probate cases and any case for which jurisdiction has not been specified in the Code of Virginia. Appeals from the lower courts are heard de novo in the Circuit Courts. The courts may issue writs necessary to the exercise of proper jurisdiction.

The courts sit at each county seat and independent city.

FIRST JUDICIAL CIRCUIT includes the city of Chesapeake.

Chief Judge
V. Thomas Forehand, Jr.

Judges
Frederick Hillary Creekmore, Sr.
Samuel Bernard Goodwyn
Bruce H. Kushner

VIRGINIA CIRCUIT COURTS—*Continued*

SECOND JUDICIAL CIRCUIT includes the city of Virginia Beach and the counties of Accomack and Northampton. The court sits at Virginia Beach, Accomac and Eastville.

Chief Judge
Thomas S. Shadrick

Judges
Andrew J. Canada, Jr.
Edward W. Hanson, Jr.
Frederick B. Lowe
Stephen C. Mahan
Henry T. Padrick, Jr.
Alan E. Rosenblatt
A. Bonwill Shockley
Glen Allen Tyler
Patricia L. West

THIRD JUDICIAL CIRCUIT includes the city of Portsmouth.

Chief Judge
Dean W. Sword, Jr.

Judges
James A. Cales, Jr.
Mark S. Davis
Johnny E. Morrison

FOURTH JUDICIAL CIRCUIT includes the city of Norfolk.

Chief Judge
Marc Jacobson

Judges
Junius P. Fulton, III
Charles D. Griffith, Jr.
Jerome James
Joseph A. Leafe
Everett A. Martin, Jr.
John C. Morrison, Jr.
Charles Evans Poston
Lydia Calvert Taylor

FIFTH JUDICIAL CIRCUIT includes the cities of Franklin and Suffolk and the counties of Isle of Wight and Southampton. The court sits at Franklin, Suffolk, Isle of Wight and Courtland.

Chief Judge
Westbrook J. Parker

Judges
Rodham T. Delk, Jr.
Carl E. Eason, Jr.

SIXTH JUDICIAL CIRCUIT includes the cities of Emporia and Hopewell and the counties of Brunswick, Greensville, Prince George, Surry and Sussex. The court sits at Emporia, Hopewell, Lawrenceville, Prince George, Surry and Sussex.

Chief Judge
Robert G. O'Hara, Jr.

Judge
vacancy

SEVENTH JUDICIAL CIRCUIT includes the city of Newport News.

Chief Judge
H. Vincent Conway, Jr.

Judges
Edward Lewis Hubbard
David F. Pugh
Charles P. Tench
Randolph T. West

EIGHTH JUDICIAL CIRCUIT includes the city of Hampton.

Chief Judge
Christopher W. Hutton

Judges
William Chapman Andrews, III
Louis R. Lerner
Wilford Taylor, Jr.

NINTH JUDICIAL CIRCUIT includes the cities of Poquoson and Williamsburg and the counties of Charles City, Gloucester, James City, King and Queen, King William, Mathews, Middlesex, New Kent and York. The court sits at Poquoson, Williamsburg, Charles City, Gloucester, King and Queen Court House, King William, Mathews, Saluda, New Kent and Yorktown.

Chief Judge
Thomas B. Hoover

Judges
Samuel T. Powell, III
William H. Shaw, III
Prentis Smiley, Jr.

TENTH JUDICIAL CIRCUIT includes the city of South Boston and the counties of Appomattox, Buckingham, Charlotte, Cumberland, Halifax, Lunenburg, Mecklenburg and Prince Edward. The court sits at South Boston, Appomattox, Buckingham, Charlotte Court House, Cumberland, Halifax, Lunenburg, Boydton and Farmville.

Chief Judge
William Lindley Wellons

Judges
Richard S. Blanton
Leslie M. Osborn

ELEVENTH JUDICIAL CIRCUIT includes the city of Petersburg and the counties of Amelia, Dinwiddie, Nottoway and Powhatan. The court sits at Petersburg, Amelia Court House, Dinwiddie, Nottoway and Powhatan.

Chief Judge
Thomas V. Warren

Judges
Pamela S. Baskervill
James F. D'Alton, Jr.

TWELFTH JUDICIAL CIRCUIT includes the city of Colonial Heights and Chesterfield County. The court sits at Colonial Heights and Chesterfield.

Chief Judge
Michael Coghlan Allen

Judges
Herbert Cogbill Gill, Jr.
Timothy J. Hauler
Cleo Elaine Powell
Frederick Gore Rockwell, III

THIRTEENTH JUDICIAL CIRCUIT includes the city of Richmond.

Chief Judge
Melvin R. Hughes, Jr.

VIRGINIA CIRCUIT COURTS—*Continued*

Judges

Bradley B. Cavedo
Randall G. Johnson
Theodore J. Markow
Beverly W. Snukals
Margaret Poles Spencer
Walter W. Stout, III
Richard D. Taylor, Jr.

FOURTEENTH JUDICIAL CIRCUIT includes Henrico County. The court sits at Richmond.

Chief Judge

Lee A. Harris, Jr.

Judges

Catherine Currin Hammond
Gary A. Hicks
George F. Tidey

FIFTEENTH JUDICIAL CIRCUIT includes the city of Fredericksburg and the counties of Caroline, Essex, Hanover, King George, Lancaster, Northumberland, Richmond, Spotsylvania, Stafford and Westmoreland. The court sits at Fredericksburg, Bowling Green, Tappahannock, Hanover, King George, Lancaster, Heathsville, Warsaw, Spotsylvania, Stafford and Montross.

Chief Judge

John Richard Alderman

Judges

James W. Haley, Jr.
William H. Ledbetter, Jr.
Horace A. Revercomb III
John Whittier Scott, Jr.
Ann Hunter Simpson
Harry T. Taliaferro, III

SIXTEENTH JUDICIAL CIRCUIT includes the city of Charlottesville and the counties of Albemarle, Culpeper, Fluvanna, Goochland, Greene, Louisa, Madison and Orange. The court sits at Charlottesville, Culpeper, Palmyra, Goochland, Stanardsville, Louisa, Madison and Orange.

Chief Judge

Daniel R. Bouton

Judges

John R. Cullen
Edward L. Hogshire
Paul M. Peatross, Jr.
Timothy K. Sanner

SEVENTEENTH JUDICIAL CIRCUIT includes the city of Falls Church and Arlington County. The court sits at Falls Church and Arlington.

Chief Judge

Paul F. Sheridan

Judges

Joanne F. Alper
Benjamin N. A. Kendrick
William T. Newman, Jr.

EIGHTEENTH JUDICIAL CIRCUIT includes the city of Alexandria.

Chief Judge

Donald M. Haddock

Judges

John E. Kloch
Alfred D. Swersky

NINETEENTH JUDICIAL CIRCUIT includes the city of Fairfax and Fairfax County. The court sits at Fairfax.

Chief Judge

Michael P. McWeeny

Judges

Leslie M. Alden
Randy I. Bellows
Gaylord L. Finch, Jr.
Martin Langhorne Keith
Stanley P. Klein
Kathleen H. MacKay
R. Terrence Ney
Jane Marum Roush
Dennis J. Smith
David T. Stitt
Jonathan C. Thacher
Arthur B. Vieregg, Jr.
Marcus D. Williams
Robert Wooldridge, Jr.

TWENTIETH JUDICIAL CIRCUIT includes Fauquier, Loudoun and Rappahannock counties. The court sits at Warrenton, Leesburg and Washington.

Chief Judge

Thomas D. Horne

Judges

James H. Chamblin
Burke F. McCahill
Jeffrey W. Parker

TWENTY-FIRST JUDICIAL CIRCUIT includes the city of Martinsville and the counties of Henry and Patrick. The court sits at Martinsville and Stuart.

Chief Judge

David Victor Williams

Judges

Martin F. Clark, Jr.
Charles M. Stone

TWENTY-SECOND JUDICIAL CIRCUIT includes the city of Danville and the counties of Franklin and Pittsylvania. The court sits at Danville, Rocky Mount and Chatham.

Chief Judge

William N. Alexander, II

Judges

Joseph Walton Milam, Jr.
Charles J. Strauss

TWENTY-THIRD JUDICIAL CIRCUIT includes the cities of Roanoke and Salem and Roanoke County. The court sits at Roanoke and Salem.

Chief Judge

Robert P. Doherty, Jr.

Judges

Jonathan M. Apgar
William D. Broadhurst
Charles N. Dorsey
James R. Swanson
Clifford R. Weckstein

TWENTY-FOURTH JUDICIAL CIRCUIT includes the cities of Bedford and Lynchburg and the counties of Amherst, Bedford, Campbell and Nelson. The court sits at Bedford, Lynchburg, Amherst, Rustburg and Lovingston.

Chief Judge

J. Leyburn Mosby, Jr.

VIRGINIA CIRCUIT COURTS—*Continued*

Judges
J. Michael Gamble
J. Samuel Johnston, Jr.
Mosby Garland Perrow, III
James W. Updike, Jr.

TWENTY-FIFTH JUDICIAL CIRCUIT includes the cities of Buena Vista, Clifton Forge, Covington, Lexington, Staunton and Waynesboro and the counties of Alleghany, Augusta, Bath, Botetourt, Craig, Highland and Rockbridge. The court sits at Buena Vista, Clifton Forge, Covington, Lexington, Staunton, Waynesboro, Warm Springs, Fincastle, New Castle and Monterey.

Chief Judge
Duncan M. Byrd, Jr.

Judges
Humes J. Franklin, Jr.
George E. Honts, III
Thomas H. Wood

TWENTY-SIXTH JUDICIAL CIRCUIT includes the cities of Harrisonburg and Winchester and the counties of Clarke, Frederick, Page, Rockingham, Shenandoah and Warren. The court sits at Harrisonburg, Winchester, Berryville, Luray, Woodstock and Front Royal.

Chief Judge
John E. Wetsel, Jr.

Judges
Dennis Lee Hupp
James V. Lane
John J. McGrath, Jr.
John R. Prosser

TWENTY-SEVENTH JUDICIAL CIRCUIT includes the cities of Galax and Radford and the counties of Bland, Carroll, Floyd, Giles, Grayson, Montgomery, Pulaski and Wythe. The court sits at Galax, Radford, Bland, Hillsville, Floyd, Pearisburg, Independence, Christiansburg, Pulaski and Wytheville.

Chief Judge
Robert M. D. Turk

Judges
J. Colin Campbell, Sr.
Brett L. Geisler
Colin R. Gibb
Ray Wilson Grubbs

TWENTY-EIGHTH JUDICIAL CIRCUIT includes the city of Bristol and the counties of Smyth and Washington. The court sits at Bristol, Marion and Abingdon.

Chief Judge
Charles B. Flannagan, II

Judge
C. Randall Lowe

TWENTY-NINTH JUDICIAL CIRCUIT includes Buchanan, Dickenson, Russell and Tazewell counties. The court sits at Grundy, Clintwood, Lebanon and Tazewell.

Chief Judge
Keary R. Williams

Judges
Michael Lee Moore
Henry A. Vanover

THIRTIETH JUDICIAL CIRCUIT includes the city of Norton and the counties of Lee, Scott and Wise. The court sits at Norton, Jonesville, Gate City and Wise.

Chief Judge
John Robert Stump

Judges
Birg E. Sergent
vacancy

THIRTY-FIRST JUDICIAL CIRCUIT includes the cities of Manassas and Manassas Park and Prince William County. The court sits at Manassas and Manassas Park.

Chief Judge
William D. Hamblen

Judges
Rossie D. Alston, Jr.
LeRoy F. Millette, Jr.
Richard B. Potter
Herman A. Whisenant, Jr.

VIRGINIA GENERAL DISTRICT COURTS

The General District Courts are courts of limited jurisdiction in Virginia. They are not courts of record. The state is divided into thirty-two judicial districts. Judges are elected for six-year terms by majority vote of the General Assembly. Interim appointments are made by the circuit judges of the corresponding circuit. A chief judge is elected in each district by peer vote to a two-year term. Retired judges may serve by special assignment of the chief justice.

The courts have exclusive jurisdiction in civil cases in which the amount in question does not exceed $3,000 and concurrent jurisdiction with the Circuit Courts in cases in which the amount does not exceed $15,000. The courts exercise jurisdiction over criminal cases involving ordinances, laws and by-laws of the county or city and all misdemeanors punishable by one year in jail and/or a $2,500 fine. Jurisdiction of the courts extends to all adult traffic offenses. The courts may hold preliminary felony hearings. Appeals are heard de novo in the Circuit Courts.

The courts sit at all county seats and independent cities.

FIRST JUDICIAL DISTRICT includes the city of Chesapeake.

Chief Judge
Colon H. Whitehurst

Judges
Robert R. Carter
David L. Williams
Timothy S. Wright

SECOND JUDICIAL DISTRICT includes the city of Virginia Beach.

Chief Judge
Robert L. Simpson, Jr.

VIRGINIA GENERAL DISTRICT COURTS—*Continued*

Judges

Albert D. Alberi	Thomas M. Ammons, III
J. Dale Bimson	Virginia Ladd Cochran
W. Edward Hudgins, Jr.	Pamela E. Hutchens

SECOND JUDICIAL DISTRICT A includes Accomack and Northampton counties. The court sits at Accomac and Eastville.

Chief Judge
Robert B. Phillips

THIRD JUDICIAL DISTRICT includes the city of Portsmouth.

Chief Judge
S. Lee Morris

Judges
Archie Elliott, Jr.
Morton V. Whitlow

FOURTH JUDICIAL DISTRICT includes the city of Norfolk.

Chief Judge
Gwendolyn Jones Jackson

Judges
Ray Wilbur Dezern, Jr.
Louis A. Sherman
Norman A. Thomas
Alfred M. Tripp
Bruce A. Wilcox

FIFTH JUDICIAL DISTRICT includes the cities of Franklin and Suffolk and the counties of Isle of Wight and Southampton. The court sits at Franklin, Suffolk, Isle of Wight and Courtland.

Chief Judge
Robert B. Edwards

Judges
G. Blair Harry
James A. Moore

SIXTH JUDICIAL DISTRICT includes the cities of Emporia and Hopewell and the counties of Brunswick, Greensville, Prince George, Surry and Sussex. The court sits at Emporia, Hopewell, Lawrenceville, Prince George, Surry and Sussex.

Chief Judge
J. Larry Palmer

Judges
Theodore J. Burr, Jr.
Kenneth Wilson Nye
Gammiel Gray Poindexter

SEVENTH JUDICIAL DISTRICT includes the city of Newport News.

Chief Judge
Timothy S. Fisher

Judges
Alfred O. Masters, Jr.
Gary A. Mills
Joan T. Morris

EIGHTH JUDICIAL DISTRICT includes the city of Hampton.

Chief Judge
Albert W. Patrick, III

Judges
Bonnie L. Jones
C. Edward Knight, III

NINTH JUDICIAL DISTRICT includes the cities of Poquoson and Williamsburg and the counties of Charles City, Gloucester, James City, King and Queen, King William, Mathews, Middlesex, New Kent and York. The court sits at Poquoson, Williamsburg, Charles City, Gloucester, James City, King and Queen Court House, King William, Mathews, Saluda, New Kent and Yorktown.

Chief Judge
R. Bruce Long

Judges
Merlin M. Renne
J. R. Zepkin

TENTH JUDICIAL DISTRICT includes the city of South Boston and the counties of Appomattox, Buckingham, Charlotte, Cumberland, Halifax, Lunenburg, Mecklenburg and Prince Edward. The court sits at South Boston, Appomattox, Buckingham, Charlotte Court House, Cumberland, Halifax, Lunenburg, Boydton and Farmville.

Chief Judge
Robert G. Woodson, Jr.

Judges
Joel C. Cunningham
Charles H. Warren

ELEVENTH JUDICIAL DISTRICT includes the city of Petersburg and the counties of Amelia, Dinwiddie, Nottoway and Powhatan. The court sits at Petersburg, Amelia Court House, Dinwiddie, Nottoway and Powhatan.

Chief Judge
G. Richard Beck

Judge
Garland L. Bigley

TWELFTH JUDICIAL DISTRICT includes the city of Colonial Heights and Chesterfield County. The court sits at Colonial Heights and Chesterfield.

Chief Judge
Philip V. Daffron

Judges
Robert D. Laney
Thomas Leroy Murphey
Thomas L. Vaughn

THIRTEENTH JUDICIAL DISTRICT includes the city of Richmond.

Chief Judge
Thomas O. Jones

Judges

David Eugene Cheek, Sr.	Barbara J. Gaden
Birdie H. Jamison	Robert A. Pustilnik

VIRGINIA GENERAL DISTRICT COURTS—*Continued*

Ralph B. Robertson
Gregory L. Rupe
Joi Jeter Taylor

FOURTEENTH JUDICIAL DISTRICT includes Henrico County. The court sits at Richmond.

Chief Judge
L. Neil Steverson

Judges
John A. Garrett
Burnett Miller, III
Archer L. Yeatts, III

FIFTEENTH JUDICIAL DISTRICT includes the city of Fredericksburg and the counties of Caroline, Essex, Hanover, King George, Lancaster, Northumberland, Richmond, Spotsylvania, Stafford and Westmoreland. The court sits at Fredericksburg, Bowling Green, Tappahannock, Hanover, King George, Lancaster, Heathsville, Warsaw, Spotsylvania, Stafford and Montross.

Chief Judge
John R. Stevens

Judges
H. Harrison Braxton, Jr.
George Mason III
Peter L. Trible
Gordon F. Willis

SIXTEENTH JUDICIAL DISTRICT includes the city of Charlottesville and the counties of Albemarle, Culpeper, Fluvanna, Goochland, Greene, Louisa, Madison and Orange. The court sits at Charlottesville, Culpeper, Palmyra, Goochland, Stanardsville, Louisa, Madison and Orange.

Chief Judge
Roger L. Morton

Judges
William G. Barkley
Robert H. Downer, Jr.
William A. Talley, Jr.

SEVENTEENTH JUDICIAL DISTRICT includes the city of Falls Church and Arlington County. The court sits at Falls Church and Arlington.

Chief Judge
Thomas J. Kelley, Jr.

Judges
Dorothy H. Clarke
Karen Anne Henenberg
Richard J. McCue

EIGHTEENTH JUDICIAL DISTRICT includes the city of Alexandria.

Chief Judge
E. Robert Giammittorio

Judge
Becky J. Moore

NINETEENTH JUDICIAL DISTRICT includes the city of Fairfax and Fairfax County. The court sits at Fairfax.

Chief Judge
Richard T. Horan

Judges
Michael Joseph Cassidy
Stewart P. Davis
Thomas E. Gallahue
Donald P. McDonough
William J. Minor Jr.
Lorraine Nordlund
Ian Michael O'Flaherty
Mark C. Simmons
Robert J. Smith

TWENTIETH JUDICIAL DISTRICT includes Fauquier, Loudoun and Rappahannock counties. The court sits at Warrenton, Leesburg and Washington.

Chief Judge
Charles B. Foley

Judges
Julia Taylor Cannon
Dean S. Worcester

TWENTY-FIRST JUDICIAL DISTRICT includes the city of Martinsville and the counties of Henry and Patrick. The court sits at Martinsville and Stuart.

Chief Judge
Robert Morgan Armstrong

Judge
J. Frank Greenwalt, Jr.

TWENTY-SECOND JUDICIAL DISTRICT includes the city of Danville and the counties of Franklin and Pittsylvania. The court sits at Danville, Rocky Mount and Chatham.

Chief Judge
George A. Jones, Jr.

Judge
M. Lee Stilwell, Jr.

TWENTY-THIRD JUDICIAL DISTRICT includes the cities of Roanoke and Salem and Roanoke County. The court sits at Roanoke and Salem.

Chief Judge
Julian H. Raney, Jr.

Judges
George W. Harris, Jr.
Vincent Austin Lilley
Jacqueline F. Ward Talevi

TWENTY-FOURTH JUDICIAL DISTRICT includes the cities of Bedford and Lynchburg and the counties of Amherst, Bedford, Campbell and Nelson. The court sits at Bedford, Lynchburg, Amherst, Rustburg and Lovingston.

Chief Judge
Joseph Michael Serkes

Judges
Harold A. Black
R. Edwin Burnette, Jr.
Jesse C. Crumbley, III

TWENTY-FIFTH JUDICIAL DISTRICT includes the cities of Buena Vista, Clifton Forge, Covington, Lexington, Staunton and Waynesboro and the counties of Alleghany, Augusta, Bath, Botetourt, Craig, Highland and Rockbridge. The court sits at Buena Vista, Clifton Forge, Covington, Lexington, Staunton, Waynesboro, Warm Springs, Fincastle, New Castle and Monterey.

Chief Judge
Louis K. Campbell

VIRGINIA GENERAL DISTRICT COURTS—*Continued*

Judges
William D. Heatwole
Joseph E. Hess
A. Lee McGratty
John Gregory Mooney

TWENTY-SIXTH JUDICIAL DISTRICT includes the cities of Harrisonburg and Winchester and the counties of Clarke, Frederick, Page, Rockingham, Shenandoah and Warren. The court sits at Harrisonburg, Winchester, Berryville, Luray, Woodstock and Front Royal.

Chief Judge
W. Dale Houff

Judges
Norman deVere Morrison
John A. Paul
David Shaw Whitacre

TWENTY-SEVENTH JUDICIAL DISTRICT includes the cities of Galax and Radford and the counties of Bland, Carroll, Floyd, Giles, Grayson, Montgomery, Pulaski and Wythe. The court sits at Galax, Radford, Bland, Hillsville, Floyd, Pearisburg, Independence, Christiansburg, Pulaski and Wytheville.

Chief Judge
Daniel Woodrow Bird, Jr.

Judges
John C. Quigley, Jr.
Edward M. Turner, III
Gino W. Williams

TWENTY-EIGHTH JUDICIAL DISTRICT includes the city of Bristol and the counties of Smyth and Washington. The court sits at Bristol, Marion and Abingdon.

Chief Judge
Joseph Scott Tate

Judge
Isaac St. C. Freeman

TWENTY-NINTH JUDICIAL DISTRICT includes Buchanan, Dickenson, Russell and Tazewell counties. The court sits at Grundy, Clintwood, Lebanon and Tazewell.

Chief Judge
Frederick H. Combs

Judge
Patrick Reynolds Johnson

THIRTIETH JUDICIAL DISTRICT includes the city of Norton and the counties of Lee, Scott and Wise. The court sits at Norton, Jonesville, Gate City and Wise.

Chief Judge
Suzanne Kuczko Fulton

Judge
R. Larry Lewis

THIRTY-FIRST JUDICIAL DISTRICT includes the cities of Manassas and Manassas Park and Prince William County. The court sits at Manassas and Manassas Park.

Chief Judge
Peter W. Steketee

Judges
Lon Edward Farris
Charles F. Sievers
Wenda Kavanagh Travers

VIRGINIA JUVENILE AND DOMESTIC RELATIONS DISTRICT COURTS

The Juvenile and Domestic Relations District Courts are courts of limited and special jurisdiction in Virginia. They are not courts of record. The judges are elected to six-year terms by majority vote of the General Assembly. Interim appointments are made by the circuit judges of the corresponding circuit subject to election by the General Assembly at the next regular session. A chief judge is elected in each district by peer vote to a two-year term. Retired judges may serve by special assignment of the chief justice.

The courts have exclusive original jurisdiction over juvenile and domestic relations proceedings involving delinquents; juveniles accused of traffic offenses; children in need of supervision; children who have been abused, neglected or abandoned; adults accused of child abuse or offenses against family members; adults involved in disputes concerning the visitation, support or custody of children; foster care and entrustment agreements; court ordered rehabilitation services; and court consent for certain medical treatment. Appeals are heard de novo in the Circuit Courts.

The courts sit at all county seats and independent cities.

FIRST JUDICIAL DISTRICT includes the city of Chesapeake.

Chief Judge
Rufus A. Banks, Jr.

Judges
Eileen Anita Olds
Larry D. Willis

SECOND JUDICIAL DISTRICT includes the city of Virginia Beach.

Chief Judge
Deborah Louise Rawls

Judges
Randall M. Blow
Ronald Harris Marks
Ramona D. Taylor
Woodrow Lewis, Jr.
Deborah M. Paxson
Winship C. Tower

SECOND JUDICIAL DISTRICT A includes Accomack and Northampton counties. The court sits at Accomac and Eastville.

Chief Judge
B. Bryan Milbourne

THIRD JUDICIAL DISTRICT includes the city of Portsmouth.

Chief Judge
Alotha Carol Willis

Judges
Joel Pierson Crowe
William S. Moore, Jr.

VIRGINIA JUVENILE AND DOMESTIC RELATIONS DISTRICT COURTS—*Continued*

FOURTH JUDICIAL DISTRICT includes the city of Norfolk.

Chief Judge
M. Randolph Carlson, II

Judges
William O. Hawkins
Joseph P. Massey
Joan C. Skeppstrom
William P. Williams

FIFTH JUDICIAL DISTRICT includes the cities of Franklin and Suffolk and the counties of Isle of Wight and Southampton. The court sits at Franklin, Suffolk, Isle of Wight and Courtland.

Chief Judge
William R. Moore, Jr.

Judge
Alfreda Talton-Harris

SIXTH JUDICIAL DISTRICT includes the cities of Emporia and Hopewell and the counties of Brunswick, Greensville, Prince George, Surry and Sussex. The court sits at Emporia, Hopewell, Lawrenceville, Prince George, Surry and Sussex.

Chief Judge
Charles A. Perkinson, Jr.

Judge
Samuel E. Campbell

SEVENTH JUDICIAL DISTRICT includes the city of Newport News.

Chief Judge
Ronald E. Bensten

Judges
Aundria Deloris Foster
Judith Anne Kline

EIGHTH JUDICIAL DISTRICT includes the city of Hampton.

Chief Judge
Nelson T. Durden

Judges
Jay Edward Dugger
Robert B. Wilson, V

NINTH JUDICIAL DISTRICT includes the cities of Poquoson and Williamsburg and the counties of Charles City, Gloucester, James City, King and Queen, King William, Mathews, Middlesex, New Kent and York. The court sits at Poquoson, Williamsburg, Charles City, Gloucester, James City, King and Queen Court House, King William, Mathews, Saluda, New Kent and Yorktown.

Chief Judge
Isabel Hall Atlee

Judges
George C. Fairbanks, IV
James H. Smith

TENTH JUDICIAL DISTRICT includes the city of South Boston and the counties of Appomattox, Buckingham, Charlotte, Cumberland, Halifax, Lunenburg, Mecklenburg and Prince Edward. The court sits at South Boston, Appomattox, Buckingham, Charlotte Court House, Cumberland, Halifax, Lunenburg, Boydton and Farmville.

Chief Judge
Michael Miller Rand

Judges
William S. Kerr
S. Anderson Nelson

ELEVENTH JUDICIAL DISTRICT includes the city of Petersburg and the counties of Amelia, Dinwiddie, Nottoway and Powhatan. The court sits at Petersburg, Amelia Court House, Dinwiddie, Nottoway and Powhatan.

Chief Judge
James E. Hume

Judge
Valentine W. Southall, Jr.

TWELFTH JUDICIAL DISTRICT includes the city of Colonial Heights and Chesterfield County. The court sits at Colonial Heights and Chesterfield.

Chief Judge
Harold W. Burgess, Jr.

Judges
Lynn S. Brice
Bonnie C. Davis
Jerry Hendrick, Jr.
Edward A. Robbins Jr.

THIRTEENTH JUDICIAL DISTRICT includes the city of Richmond.

Chief Judge
Anne B. Holton

Judges
J. Stephen Buis
Clarence N. Jenkins Jr.
Kimberly B. O'Donnell
Angela Edwards Roberts

FOURTEENTH JUDICIAL DISTRICT includes Henrico County. The court sits at Richmond.

Chief Judge
Denis F. Soden

Judges
William G. Boice
Anna Elisabeth Oxenham
Sharon B. Will

FIFTEENTH JUDICIAL DISTRICT includes the city of Fredericksburg and the counties of Caroline, Essex, Hanover, King George, Lancaster, Northumberland, Richmond, Spotsylvania, Stafford and Westmoreland. The court sits at Fredericksburg, Bowling Green, Tappahannock, Hanover, King George, Lancaster, Heathsville, Warsaw, Spotsylvania, Stafford and Montross.

Chief Judge
J. Maston Davis

VIRGINIA JUVENILE AND DOMESTIC RELATIONS DISTRICT COURTS—*Continued*

Judges
J. Martin Bass
Joseph J. Ellis
Larry E. Gilman
J. Dean Lewis
David F. Peterson

SIXTEENTH JUDICIAL DISTRICT includes the city of Charlottesville and the counties of Albemarle, Culpeper, Fluvanna, Goochland, Greene, Louisa, Madison and Orange. The court sits at Charlottesville, Culpeper, Palmyra, Goochland, Stanardsville, Louisa, Madison and Orange.

Chief Judge
Edward DeJarnette Berry

Judges
Dwight D. Johnson
Frank W. Somerville
Susan L. Whitlock

SEVENTEENTH JUDICIAL DISTRICT includes the city of Falls Church and Arlington County. The court sits at Falls Church and Arlington.

Chief Judge
George D. Varoutsos

Judge
Esther L. Wiggins

EIGHTEENTH JUDICIAL DISTRICT includes the city of Alexandria.

Chief Judge
Stephen W. Rideout

Judge
Nolan Boyd Dawkins

NINETEENTH JUDICIAL DISTRICT includes the city of Fairfax and Fairfax County. The court sits at Fairfax.

Chief Judge
Charles James Maxfield

Judges
Gayl Branum Carr
Jane Pritchard Delbridge
David Stanford Schell
Kimberly J. Daniel
Teena D. Grodner
Michael J. Valentine

TWENTIETH JUDICIAL DISTRICT includes Fauquier, Loudoun and Rappahannock counties. The court sits at Warrenton, Leesburg and Washington.

Chief Judge
H. Dudley Payne, Jr.

Judge
Avelina S. Jacob

TWENTY-FIRST JUDICIAL DISTRICT includes the city of Martinsville and the counties of Henry and Patrick. The court sits at Martinsville and Stuart.

Chief Judge
Susan N. Deatherage

Judge
Junius P. Warren

TWENTY-SECOND JUDICIAL DISTRICT includes the city of Danville and the counties of Franklin and Pittsylvania. The court sits at Danville, Rocky Mount and Chatham.

Chief Judge
David A. Melesco

Judges
Stacey W. Moreau
Dale M. Wiley

TWENTY-THIRD JUDICIAL DISTRICT includes the cities of Roanoke and Salem and Roanoke County. The court sits at Roanoke and Salem.

Chief Judge
Joseph Phillips Bounds

Judges
Joseph M. Clarke, II
John B. Ferguson
Philip Trompeter

TWENTY-FOURTH JUDICIAL DISTRICT includes the cities of Bedford and Lynchburg and the counties of Amherst, Bedford, Campbell and Nelson. The court sits at Bedford, Lynchburg, Amherst, Rustburg and Lovingston.

Chief Judge
Kenneth W. Farrar

Judges
Lawrence Janow
William R. Light
Philip Arthur Wallace
A. Ellen White

TWENTY-FIFTH JUDICIAL DISTRICT includes the cities of Buena Vista, Clifton Forge, Covington, Lexington, Staunton and Waynesboro and the counties of Alleghany, Augusta, Bath, Botetourt, Craig, Highland and Rockbridge. The court sits at Buena Vista, Clifton Forge, Covington, Lexington, Staunton, Waynesboro, Warm Springs, Fincastle, New Castle and Monterey.

Chief Judge
Dudley J. Emick, Jr.

Judges
Anita D. Filson
Victor V. Ludwig
Paul A. Tucker

TWENTY-SIXTH JUDICIAL DISTRICT includes the cities of Harrisonburg and Winchester and the counties of Clarke, Frederick, Page, Rockingham, Shenandoah and Warren. The court sits at Harrisonburg, Winchester, Berryville, Luray, Woodstock and Front Royal.

Chief Judge
William W. Sharp

Judges
Carle F. Germelman, Jr.
Marvin C. Hillsman, Jr.
William H. Logan, Jr.

TWENTY-SEVENTH JUDICIAL DISTRICT includes the cities of Galax and Radford and the counties of Bland, Carroll, Floyd, Giles, Grayson, Montgomery, Pulaski and Wythe. The court sits at Galax, Radford,

VIRGINIA JUVENILE AND DOMESTIC RELATIONS DISTRICT COURTS—*Continued*

Bland, Hillsville, Floyd, Pearisburg, Independence, Christiansburg, Pulaski and Wytheville.

Chief Judge
Robert C. Viar, Jr.

Judges
Howard Lee Chitwood
James L. Tompkins, III

TWENTY-EIGHTH JUDICIAL DISTRICT includes the city of Bristol and the counties of Smyth and Washington. The court sits at Bristol, Marion and Abingdon.

Chief Judge
Eugene E. Lohman

Judge
Charles F. Lincoln

TWENTY-NINTH JUDICIAL DISTRICT includes Buchanan, Dickenson, Russell and Tazewell counties. The court sits at Grundy, Clintwood, Lebanon and Tazewell.

Chief Judge
Teresa M. Chafin

Judge
John M. Farmer

THIRTIETH JUDICIAL DISTRICT includes the city of Norton and the counties of Lee, Scott and Wise. The court sits at Norton, Jonesville, Gate City and Wise.

Chief Judge
Elizabeth S. Wills

Judge
James Michael Shull

THIRTY-FIRST JUDICIAL DISTRICT includes the cities of Manassas and Manassas Park and Prince William County. The court sits at Manassas and Manassas Park.

Chief Judge
James Bailey Robeson

Judges
William A. Becker
Janice Justina Brice
Paul F. Gluchowski
Mary Grace O'Brien

Virginia Counties and County Seats

Accomack
Accomac

Albemarle
Charlottesville

Alleghany
Covington

Amelia
Amelia C. H.

Amherst
Amherst

Appomattox
Appomattox

Arlington
Arlington

Augusta
Staunton

Bath
Warm Springs

Bedford
Bedford

Bland
Bland

Botetourt
Fincastle

Brunswick
Lawrenceville

Buchanan
Grundy

Buckingham
Buckingham

Campbell
Rustburg

Caroline
Bowling Green

Carroll
Hillsville

Charles City
Charles City

Charlotte
Charlotte C. H.

Chesterfield
Chesterfield

Clarke
Berryville

Craig
New Castle

Culpeper
Culpeper

Cumberland
Cumberland

Dickenson
Clintwood

Dinwiddie
Dinwiddie

Essex
Tappahannock

Fairfax
Fairfax

Fauquier
Warrenton

Floyd
Floyd

Fluvanna
Palmyra

Franklin
Rocky Mount

Frederick
Winchester

Giles
Pearisburg

Gloucester
Gloucester

Goochland
Goochland

Grayson
Independence

Greene
Stanardsville

Greensville
Emporia

Halifax
Halifax

Hanover
Hanover

COUNTIES AND COUNTY SEATS—*Continued*

Henrico
Richmond
Henry
Martinsville
Highland
Monterey
Isle of Wight
Isle of Wight
James City
Williamsburg
King and Queen
King and Queen C. H.
King George
King George
King William
King William
Lancaster
Lancaster
Lee
Jonesville
Loudoun
Leesburg
Louisa
Louisa
Lunenburg
Lunenburg
Madison
Madison
Mathews
Mathews
Mecklenburg
Boydton
Middlesex
Saluda
Montgomery
Christiansburg
Nelson
Lovingston
New Kent
New Kent
Northampton
Eastville
Northumberland
Heathsville
Nottoway
Nottoway
Orange
Orange
Page
Luray
Patrick
Stuart
Pittsylvania
Chatham
Powhatan
Powhatan
Prince Edward
Farmville
Prince George
Prince George
Prince William
Manassas
Pulaski
Pulaski
Rappahannock
Washington
Richmond
Warsaw
Roanoke
Salem
Rockbridge
Lexington
Rockingham
Harrisonburg
Russell
Lebanon
Scott
Gate City
Shenandoah
Woodstock
Smyth
Marion
Southampton
Courtland
Spotsylvania
Spotsylvania
Stafford
Stafford
Surry
Surry
Sussex
Sussex
Tazewell
Tazewell
Warren
Front Royal
Washington
Abingdon
Westmoreland
Montross
Wise
Wise
Wythe
Wytheville
York
Yorktown

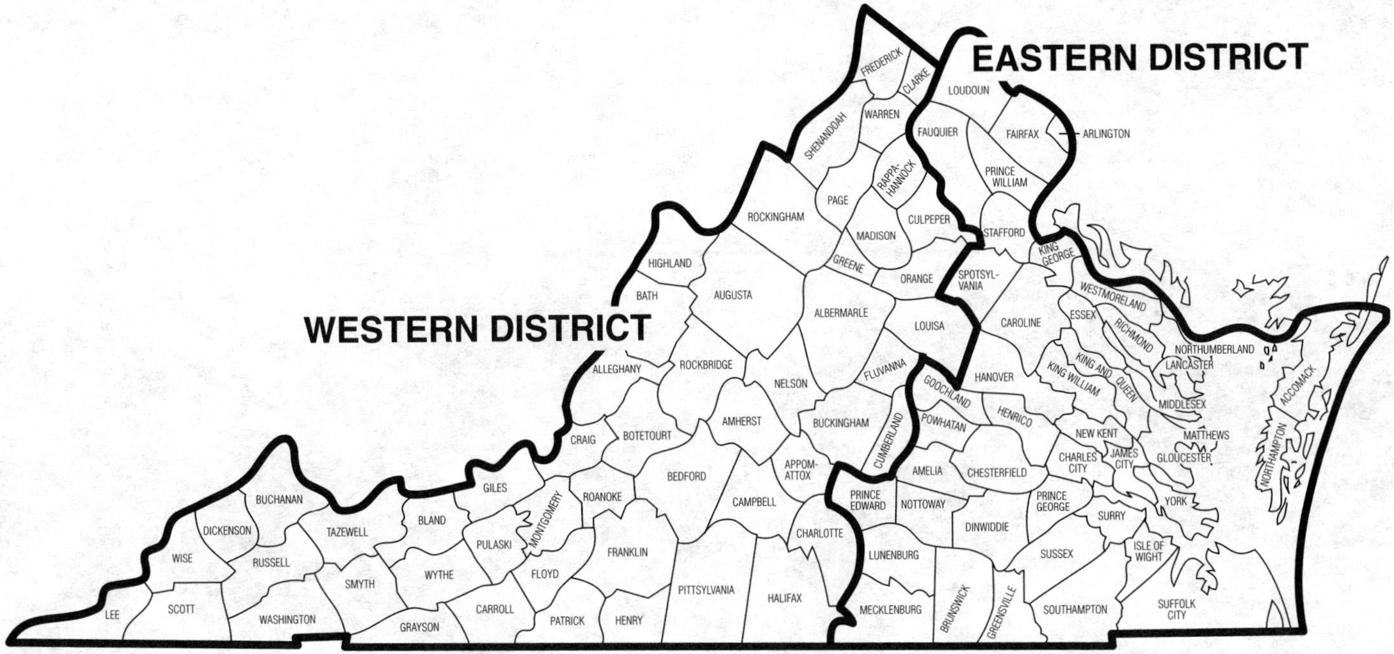
EASTERN DISTRICT
WESTERN DISTRICT
FREDERICK
CLARKE
LOUDOUN
WARREN
SHENANDOAH
FAUQUIER
FAIRFAX
ARLINGTON
PRINCE WILLIAM
RAPPA-HANNOCK
PAGE
ROCKINGHAM
CULPEPER
MADISON
STAFFORD
GREENE
KING GEORGE
HIGHLAND
ORANGE
SPOTSYL-VANIA
BATH
AUGUSTA
ALBERMARLE
WESTMORELAND
LOUISA
CAROLINE
ESSEX
RICHMOND
NORTHUMBERLAND
LANCASTER
ALLEGHANY
ROCKBRIDGE
NELSON
FLUVANNA
HANOVER
KING AND QUEEN
KING WILLIAM
ACCOMACK
MIDDLESEX
AMHERST
BUCKINGHAM
GOOCHLAND
HENRICO
POWHATAN
CRAIG
BOTETOURT
CUMBERLAND
NEW KENT
MATTHEWS
NORTHAMPTON
APPOM-ATTOX
CHARLES CITY
JAMES CITY
GLOUCESTER
AMELIA
CHESTERFIELD
BEDFORD
GILES
ROANOKE
BUCHANAN
PRINCE EDWARD
NOTTOWAY
PRINCE GEORGE
MONTGOMERY
CAMPBELL
YORK
SURRY
BLAND
DINWIDDIE
DICKENSON
TAZEWELL
CHARLOTTE
PULASKI
FRANKLIN
LUNENBURG
SUSSEX
ISLE OF WIGHT
WISE
RUSSELL
WYTHE
FLOYD
SMYTH
PITTSYLVANIA
HALIFAX
BRUNSWICK
GREENSVILLE
SUFFOLK CITY
LEE
SCOTT
CARROLL
MECKLENBURG
SOUTHAMPTON
WASHINGTON
PATRICK
HENRY
GRAYSON

UNITED STATES DISTRICT COURTS DISTRICTS OF VIRGINIA

VIRGINIA

ADAMS, David H. *(Judge, United States Bankruptcy Court Eastern District of Virginia)* Appointed by U.S. Court of Appeals Fourth Circuit judges.
Office: U.S. Courthouse, 600 Granby Street, Norfolk 23510-1915.
Telephone: (757) 222-7470.

AGEE, G. Steven *(Justice, Supreme Court of Virginia)* Term expires March 1, 2015. Former Judge, Court of Appeals of Virginia, assumed office Jan 1, 2001.
Office: 100 North Ninth Street, Fifth Floor, Richmond 23219.
Telephone: (804) 786-2251.

ALBERI, Albert D. *(Judge, Virginia General District Court Second Judicial District)* Assumed office July 1, 1998. Term expires June 30, 2004.
Office: 2425 Nimmo Parkway, Virginia Beach 23456-9057.
Telephone: (757) 427-8783.
Fax: (757) 426-5672

ALDEN, Leslie M. *(Judge, Virginia Circuit Court Nineteenth Judicial Circuit)* Term expires July 31, 2004.
Office: 4110 Chain Bridge Road, Fairfax 22030.
Telephone: (703) 246-4111, 691-7320.

ALDERMAN, John Richard *(Chief Judge, Virginia Circuit Court Fifteenth Judicial Circuit)* Term expires Jan 31, 2008.
Mailing address: P.O. Box 39, Hanover 23069-0039.
Office: 7507 Library Drive, Hanover 23069.
Telephone: (804) 537-6150.

ALEXANDER, William N., II *(Chief Judge, Virginia Circuit Court Twenty-second Judicial Circuit)* Term expires March 15, 2010. Born Roanoke Virginia Oct 2, 1944. Methodist. Educated at Davidson College B.A. 1966 and University of Virginia J.D. 1971. Admitted to practice Virginia 1971 and U.S. Court of Appeals Fourth Circuit. Former Judge, Virginia General District Court Twenty-second Judicial District, elected by General Assembly to term beginning Sept 1, 1984.
Commonwealth's Attorney Franklin County 1976-84. Captain USAR.
Mailing address: P.O. Box 601, Rocky Mount 24151.
Office: 275 South Main Street, Suite 212, Rocky Mount 24151.
Telephone: (540) 483-3075.

ALLEN, Michael Coghlan *(Chief Judge, Virginia Circuit Court Twelfth Judicial Circuit)* Elected by General Assembly to term beginning April 1, 2000. Term expires March 31, 2008.
Mailing address: P.O. Box 57, Chesterfield 23832.
Office: 9500 Courthouse Road, Chesterfield 23832.
Telephone: (804) 748-1241.

ALPER, Joanne F. *(Judge, Virginia Circuit Court Seventeenth Judicial Circuit)* Elected by General Assembly to term beginning June 1, 1998. Term expires May 31, 2006. Judge July 1, 1991 to May 31, 1998 and Former Chief Judge, Virginia Juvenile and Domestic Relations District Court Seventeenth Judicial District.
Office: 1425 North Courthouse Road, Arlington 22201.
Telephone: (703) 228-7010.

ALSTON, Rossie D., Jr. *(Judge, Virginia Circuit Court Thirty-first Judicial Circuit)* Assumed office Feb 1, 2001. Term expires Jan 31, 2009. Judge, Virginia Juvenile and Domestic Relations District Court Thirty-first Judicial District Feb 1, 1999 to Jan 31, 2001.
Office: 9311 Lee Avenue, Manassas 20110.
Telephone: (703) 792-6010.

AMMONS, Thomas M., III *(Judge, Virginia General District Court Second Judicial District)* Term expires Jan 31, 2008. Former Chief Judge.
Office: 2425 Nimmo Parkway, Virginia Beach 23456-9057.
Telephone: (757) 427-8783.
Fax: (757) 426-5672

ANDERSON, William E. *(Judge, United States Bankruptcy Court Western District of Virginia)* Former Chief Judge.
Mailing address: P.O. Box 442, Lynchburg 24505-0442.
Telephone: (434) 846-3118.

ANDREWS, William Chapman, III *(Judge, Virginia Circuit Court Eighth Judicial Circuit)* Term expires March 31, 2004. Former Judge and Chief Judge, Virginia General District Court Eighth Judicial District.
Mailing address: P.O. Box 40, Hampton 23669-0040.
Office: 101 King's Way Mall, Hampton 23669.
Telephone: (757) 727-6106.

ANNUNZIATA, Rosemarie P. *(Judge, Court of Appeals of Virginia)* Elected by General Assembly to term beginning June 1, 1995. Reelected 2003, current term expires 2011. Born Newark New Jersey Nov 8. Educated at Elmira College B.A. cum laude 1962, Yale University M.A. 1967 and Washington College of Law of American University J.D. 1978. Member Phi Beta Kappa. Admitted to practice Virginia 1978 and U.S. Supreme Court 1978. In legal practice Fairfax 1978-86 and Vienna 1986-89. Hearing Officer, Commonwealth of Virginia 1979-86. Hearing Officer, Fairfax County Civil Service Commission 1980-89. Commissioner in Chancery, Fairfax Virginia Circuit Court 1988-89. Judge, Virginia Circuit Court Nineteenth Judicial Circuit 1989-95.
Co-author with William O. P. Snead, III *Handbook on Malpractice* Virginia Trial Lawyers Association 1983. Author "Loss of Earning Capacity—Can the Infant Plaintiff Recover?" Virginia Trial Lawyers Association Law Letter and Journal Oct 1985. Important Decisions: Theisman v. Theisman (concurring in part and dissenting in part) 22 Va. App. 557, 574, 1996; Rahbaran v. Rahbaran 20 Va. App. 195, 1997; Barker v. Barker 27 Va. App. 519, 1998; Parish v. Spaulding 26 Va. App. 566, 1998; Pavlick v. Commonwealth 27 Va. App. 219, 1998; Alliance to Save the Mattaponi v. Commonwealth of Virginia, ex rel. State Water Control Board 30 Va.

ANNUNZIATA, ROSEMARIE P.—*Continued*

App. 690, 1999; Anderson v. Anderson 209 Va. App. 673, 1999; Kelln v. Kelln 30 Va. App. 113, 1999 and 29 Va. App. 119, 1999; and Rusty's Welding Service, Inc. v. Gibson 209 Va. App. 673, 1999. Adjunct Professor of Law, Legal Writing and Research George Mason University School of Law 1988-90. Member Judicial Education Committee Judicial Conference of Virginia, Virginia State Bar Council, Virginia Women Attorneys Association, National Association of Women Judges, American Judicature Association, American Judges Association, International Association of Women Judges (Board of Managerial Trustees), Virginia State Bar (Board of Governors Family Law Section), Virginia and American Bar Associations. Speaker Office of Citizen Exchanges Program in Egypt, Jordan and Syria U.S. Information Agency June 1996. Preliminary Speaker to an address by Justice Antonin J. Scalia U.S. Supreme Court Dec 6, 1996. Guest Speaker for Senegalese jurists and officials U.S. Information Service, Dakar Senegal Feb 3, 1997. Panelist Third U.S.—France Conference on the American Justice System, Quantico Virginia April 1999. Participant Fourth Annual Franco-American Judicial Conference Office of International Affairs U.S. Department of Justice, Paris France May 2000. Recipient Special Achievement Award from Fairfax County Commission for Women 1981 and Human Rights Award from Fairfax County Human Rights Commission 1997. Listed in *Who's Who in American Law.* Member since 1995 and President 1999-2001 Women's Advisory Board and Member Committee on College of Arts and Sciences since 1999 George Mason University. Volunteer Christ House shelter for the homeless. Member Dean's Advisory Council Washington College of Law of American University. Enjoys theatre, art and travel.

Office: 10201 Main Street, Suite 200, Fairfax 22030-2403.

Telephone: (703) 359-1194.

APGAR, Jonathan M. *(Judge, Virginia Circuit Court Twenty-third Judicial Circuit)* Term expires March 31, 2005.

Mailing address: P.O. Box 211, Roanoke 24010-0211.

Office: 315 West Church Avenue, Roanoke 24016-5029.

Telephone: (540) 853-2436.

ARMSTRONG, Robert Morgan *(Chief Judge, Virginia General District Court Twenty-first Judicial District)* Term expires June 30, 2007.

Office: 3160 Kings Mountain Road, Suite A, Martinsville 24112.

Telephone: (276) 634-4815.

ATLEE, Isabel Hall *(Chief Judge, Virginia Juvenile and Domestic Relations District Court Ninth Judicial District)* Assumed office Feb 1, 1997. Elected by General Assembly 2003, current term expires Jan 2009.

Mailing address: P.O. Box 630, Gloucester 23061-0630.

Office: Courthouse, Gloucester 23061.

Telephone: (804) 693-4850.

BANKS, Rufus A., Jr. *(Chief Judge, Virginia Juvenile and Domestic Relations District Court First Judicial District)* Assumed office July 1, 1999. Term expires June 30, 2005.

Office: 301 Albemarle Drive, Second Floor, Chesapeake 23322-5501.

Telephone: (757) 382-8100.

BARKLEY, William G. *(Judge, Virginia General District Court Sixteenth Judicial District)* Assumed office May 1, 1990. Elected by General Assembly 1996 and 2002. Current term expires April 30, 2008. Former Chief Judge.

Mailing address: P.O. Box 2489, Charlottesville 22902.

Office: 501 East Jefferson Street, Suite 138, Charlottesville 22902-5110.

Telephone: (434) 972-4005.

BASKERVILL, Pamela S. *(Judge, Virginia Circuit Court Eleventh Judicial Circuit)* Assumed office April 1, 2001. Term expires March 31, 2009.

Office: Seven Courthouse Avenue, Petersburg 23803.

Telephone: (804) 733-2367.

BASS, J. Martin *(Judge, Virginia Juvenile and Domestic Relations District Court Fifteenth Judicial District)* Term expires May 15, 2007. Former Chief Judge.

Mailing address: P.O. Box 400, Stafford 22555-0400.

Office: The Judicial Center, 1300 Courthouse Road, Stafford 22554.

Telephone: (540) 658-8775.

BECK, G. Richard *(Chief Judge, Virginia General District Court Eleventh Judicial District)* Assumed office July 1, 1992. Elected by General Assembly to term beginning July 1, 1998, current term expires June 30, 2004.

Office: 35 East Tabb Street, Petersburg 23803.

Telephone: (804) 733-2374.

BECKER, William A. *(Judge, Virginia Juvenile and Domestic Relations District Court Thirty-first Judicial District)* Elected by General Assembly to term beginning July 1, 1987. Reelected 1993 and 1999. Current term expires June 30, 2005. Chief Judge July 1990 to July 1992. Born Alexandria Virginia May 20, 1948. Educated at Lawrence University B.A. cum laude 1970 and Washington University School of Law J.D. 1973. Admitted to practice Virginia 1973. Captain USAF 1966-74.

Office: 9311 Lee Avenue, Manassas 20110.

Telephone: (703) 792-6160.

BELLOWS, Randy I. *(Judge, Virginia Circuit Court Nineteenth Judicial Circuit)* Term expires Feb 2011.

Office: 4110 Chain Bridge Road, Fairfax 22030.

Telephone: (703) 246-4111, 691-7320.

BENSTEN, Ronald E. *(Chief Judge, Virginia Juvenile and Domestic Relations District Court Seventh Judicial District)* Elected by General Assembly to term beginning March 1, 1992. Reelected 1998, current term expires Jan 31, 2004. Born Virginia April 21, 1945. Presbyterian. Educated at College of William & Mary A.B. with honors 1967 and Yale Law School J.D. 1973. Admitted to practice Virginia 1973.

Office: 2501 Huntington Avenue, Newport News 23607.

Telephone: (757) 926-3603.

BENTON, James W., Jr. *(Judge, Court of Appeals of Virginia)* Elected by General Assembly to term beginning Jan 4, 1985. Reelected to term beginning Jan 1,

BENTON, JAMES W., JR.—*Continued*
1992 and Jan 2000. Current term expires Dec 31, 2007. Born Norfolk Virginia Sept 16, 1944. Educated at Temple University A.B. 1966, Northwestern University and University of Virginia J.D. 1970. Admitted to practice Virginia 1970. In legal practice Richmond 1970-85.

Member Old Dominion Bar Association. Attended Appellate Judges Seminar Institute of Judicial Administration.

Office: 109 North Eighth Street, Richmond 23219-2321.

Telephone: (804) 786-6176.

BERRY, Edward DeJarnette *(Chief Judge, Virginia Juvenile and Domestic Relations District Court Sixteenth Judicial District)* Assumed office Feb 1, 1994. Elected by General Assembly to term beginning Feb 1, 2000, current term expires Jan 31, 2006.

Office: Juvenile Court Building, 411 East High Street, Charlottesville 22901.

Telephone: (434) 979-7165.

BIGLEY, Garland L. *(Judge, Virginia General District Court Eleventh Judicial District)* Elected by General Assembly to term beginning Aug 1, 2001. Term expires July 31, 2007. Born Newport Rhode Island Nov 28, 1946. Presbyterian. Educated at University of Virginia Diploma 1967 and University of Richmond T. C. Williams School of Law J.D. cum laude 1992. Moot Court Board 1990-92. Member McNeill Law Society. Admitted to practice Virginia 1992. In legal practice Richmond Aug 1992 to Oct 1994.

Senior Assistant Attorney General Virginia Office of Attorney General Oct 1994 to July 31, 2001. Member Richmond and Virginia Bar Associations. City Councilman Petersburg 1986-92. President Medical Society of Virginia Alliance 1984-85. Board of Visitors Virginia State University 1994-2001. Enjoys reading and gardening.

Mailing address: P.O. Box 280, Dinwiddie 23841-0280.

Office: Dinwiddie Courthouse, Dinwiddie 23841.

Telephone: (804) 469-4533.

BIMSON, J. Dale *(Judge, Virginia General District Court Second Judicial District)* Elected by General Assembly to term beginning July 1, 1989. Reelected July 1, 1995 and July 1, 2001. Current term expires June 30, 2007. Former Chief Judge. Born Richmond Virginia July 4, 1936. Baptist. Educated at Virginia Commonwealth University B.S. 1961, George Washington University 1962 and University of Richmond J.D. 1965. Member Phi Alpha Delta. Admitted to practice Virginia 1965, U.S. Supreme Court 1972 and U.S. Court of Appeals Fourth Circuit 1974. In legal practice Virginia Beach 1965-89. Hearing Officer Virginia Commonwealth 1975-89.

City Attorney Virginia Beach 1965-89. Adjunct Professor Virginia Wesleyan College since 1980 and in Labor Law and Public Administration Troy State University since 1989. President Virginia Beach Bar Association 1986-87. Commander USNR 1956-68.

Office: 2425 Nimmo Parkway, Virginia Beach 23456-9057.

Telephone: (757) 427-8783.

Fax: (757) 426-5672

BIRD, Daniel Woodrow, Jr. *(Chief Judge, Virginia General District Court Twenty-seventh Judicial District)* Assumed office Feb 1, 1992. Elected by General Assembly Feb 1, 1998, current term expires Jan 31, 2004.

Office: 245 South Fourth Street, Suite 205, Wytheville 24382.

Telephone: (276) 223-6075.

BLACK, Harold A. *(Judge, Virginia General District Court Twenty-fourth Judicial District)* Assumed office April 1, 1998. Term expires March 31, 2004.

Office: 123 East Main Street, Suite 202, Bedford 24523-2034.

Telephone: (540) 586-7637.

BLANTON, Richard S. *(Judge, Virginia Circuit Court Tenth Judicial Circuit)* Term expires March 2011.

Mailing address: P.O. Box 304, Farmville 23901-0304.

Office: Courthouse Building, North Main Street, Farmville 23901.

Telephone: (434) 392-5171.

Fax: (434) 392-5171

BLOW, Randall M. *(Judge, Virginia Juvenile and Domestic Relations District Court Second Judicial District)* Assumed office April 1, 2001. Term expires March 31, 2007.

Office: 2425 Nimmo Parkway, Building 10, Virginia Beach 23456.

Telephone: (757) 427-4391.

BOICE, William G. *(Judge, Virginia Juvenile and Domestic Relations District Court Fourteenth Judicial District)* Term expires April 30, 2007. Former Chief Judge.

Mailing address: P.O. Box 27032, Richmond 23273-0732.

Office: Juvenile Courts Building, 4201 East Parham Road, Richmond 23273.

Telephone: (804) 501-4688.

BOUNDS, Joseph Phillips *(Chief Judge, Virginia Juvenile and Domestic Relations District Court Twenty-third Judicial District)* Assumed office July 1, 1994. Elected by General Assembly to term beginning July 1, 2000, current term expires June 30, 2006.

Mailing address: P.O. Box 986, Roanoke 24005-0986.

Office: 315 West Church Avenue S.W., First Floor, Roanoke 24016.

Telephone: (540) 853-2389.

BOUTON, Daniel R. *(Chief Judge, Virginia Circuit Court Sixteenth Judicial Circuit)* Elected by General Assembly to term beginning April 1, 2000. Term expires March 31, 2008.

Mailing address: P.O. Box 230, Orange 22960.

Office: 127 Belleview Avenue, Orange 22960.

Telephone: (540) 672-4030.

BRADBERRY, James E. *(Magistrate Judge, United States District Court Eastern District of Virginia)* Appointed by U.S. District Court judges.

Office: 344 U.S. Courthouse, 600 Grandby Street, Norfolk 23510.

Telephone: (757) 222-7012.

BRAXTON, H. Harrison, Jr. *(Judge, Virginia General District Court Fifteenth Judicial District)* Term expires June 30, 2008.

Mailing address: P.O. Box 940, Stafford 22555-0940.

Office: The Judicial Center, 1300 Courthouse Road, Stafford 22554.

Telephone: (540) 658-8766.

BRICE, Janice Justina *(Judge, Virginia Juvenile and Domestic Relations District Court Thirty-first Judicial District)* Assumed office July 1, 1990. Elected by General Assembly 1996. Reelected to term beginning July 1, 2002, current term expires June 30, 2008. Former Chief Judge.

Office: 9311 Lee Avenue, Manassas 20110.

Telephone: (703) 792-6160.

BRICE, Lynn S. *(Judge, Virginia Juvenile and Domestic Relations District Court Twelfth Judicial District)* Assumed office July 1, 2001. Term expires June 30, 2007.

Mailing address: P.O. Box 520, Chesterfield 23832-0520.

Office: 7000 Lucy Corr Boulevard, Chesterfield 23832.

Telephone: (804) 748-1379.

BRINKEMA, Leonie M. *(Judge, United States District Court Eastern District of Virginia)* Magistrate Judge 1985-93. Appointed Judge for life by President Bill Clinton to term beginning 1993. Born Teaneck New Jersey June 26, 1944. Educated at Rutgers University B.A. 1966 M.L.S. 1970 and Cornell Law School J.D. 1976. In legal practice Alexandria 1984-85.

Trial Attorney Public Integrity Section 1976-77 and Office of International Affairs 1983-84 Criminal Division U.S. Department of Justice. Assistant U.S. Attorney Eastern District of Virginia 1977-83.

Office: U.S. Courthouse, 401 Courthouse Square, Alexandria 22314-5799.

Telephone: (703) 229-2116.

BROADHURST, William D. *(Judge, Virginia Circuit Court Twenty-third Judicial Circuit)* Former Judge, Virginia General District Court Twenty-third Judicial District, assumed office July 16, 1994.

Mailing address: P.O. Box 2610, Roanoke 24010-2610.

Office: 315 West Church Avenue, Roanoke 24016.

Telephone: (540) 853-6702.

BRYAN, Albert V., Jr. *(Senior Judge, United States District Court Eastern District of Virginia)* Appointed for life by President Richard M. Nixon to term beginning Aug 9, 1971. Former Chief Judge. Assumed Senior status, serves by assignment. Born Alexandria Virginia Nov 8, 1926. Episcopalian. Educated at Virginia Military Institute 1943-44, George Washington University 1946-47 and University of Virginia LL.B. 1950. Admitted to practice Virginia 1949. Began legal practice Alexandria 1949. Judge, Virginia Circuit Court 1962-71.

Member Virginia State Bar, Alexandria and American Bar Associations. E-3 USMC 1944-46. Democrat.

Office: U.S. Courthouse, 401 Courthouse Square, Alexandria 22314-5799.

Telephone: (703) 299-2111.

BUCHANAN, Theresa Carroll *(Magistrate Judge, United States District Court Eastern District of Virginia)* Appointed by U.S. District Court judges.

Office: U.S. Courthouse, 401 Courthouse Square, Alexandria 22314-5799.

Telephone: (703) 299-2120.

BUIS, J. Stephen *(Judge, Virginia Juvenile and Domestic Relations District Court Thirteenth Judicial District)* Assumed office Sept 1, 2001. Term expires Aug 31, 2007.

Office: C181 Oliver Hill Courts Bldg., 1600 North Seventeenth Street, Richmond 23219-1214.

Telephone: (804) 646-2942.

BUMGARDNER, Rudolph, III *(Judge, Court of Appeals of Virginia)* Elected by the General Assembly Nov 28, 1997 to term beginning Feb 1, 1998. Term expires Jan 31, 2006. Former Judge and Chief Judge, Virginia Circuit Court Twenty-fifth Judicial Circuit.

Mailing address: P.O. Box 388, Staunton 24402-0388.

Office: 2-14 West Beverley Street, Staunton 24401-0657.

Telephone: (540) 332-8926.

BURGESS, Harold W., Jr. *(Chief Judge, Virginia Juvenile and Domestic Relations District Court Twelfth Judicial District)* Assumed office Feb 1, 1997. Elected by General Assembly 2003, current term expires Jan 2009.

Mailing address: P.O. Box 520, Chesterfield 23832-0520.

Office: 7000 Lucy Corr Boulevard, Chesterfield 23832.

Telephone: (804) 748-1379.

BURNETTE, R. Edwin, Jr. *(Judge, Virginia General District Court Twenty-fourth Judicial District)* Assumed office Aug 1, 2001. Term expires July 31, 2007. Born Lynchburg Virginia Sept 25, 1953. Educated at College of William & Mary B.A. 1975 J.D. 1978. In legal practice Virginia July 1978 to July 2001.

Adjunct Professor of Law College of William & Mary Marshall-Wythe School of Law since 1995. Task Force Member Commission for the Future of Virginia's Judicial System 1987-89. Member Virginia Commission on Women and Minorities in the Legal System 1992-94 and Ad Hoc Committee on Local Rules Supreme Court of Virginia 1999-2000. Fellow Virginia Law Foundation and American Bar Foundation. Member Boyd-Graves Conference (Steering Committee), Virginia Association of Defense Attorneys, Virginia Trial Lawyers Association, Virginia State Bar (Chair Alternative Dispute Resolution Committee 1985-89 and Resolutions Committee 1994-96, Council Member representing Twenty-fourth Judicial Circuit 1985-95, Vice Chair Standing Committee on Legal Ethics 1988-89, Member Executive Committee 1990-95, President 1993-94, Member Task Force on Public Access to Attorney Disciplinary Process 2000), Lynchburg (President 1991-92), Virginia and American (House of Delegates 1986-88) Bar Associations.

Lecturer Professionalism Course 1988-93 and "Professionalism for Law Students" Seminar 2001 Virginia State Bar, "Professional Ethics for Virginia Lawyers" Seminar Committee on Continuing Legal Education Virginia Law Foundation 1991-92, "Ethics for Virginia Lawyers" Seminar 1996 and "Virginia's New Scheduling Order" Seminar 2000 Virginia Continuing Legal Education, "Ethics & Professionalism" Seminar Lynchburg Bar

BURNETTE, R. EDWIN, JR.—*Continued*

Association 2000 and "Ethics" Seminar Annual Statewide Legal Aid Conference 2000. Recipient The Citizen-Lawyer Award from William & Mary Law School Association 1992, The Pro Bono Award from Lynchburg Bar Association and Virginia Legal Aid Society 1992, The Public Service Award from Lynchburg Bar Association 1993 and St. George Tucker Outstanding Adjunct Professor of Law Award from College of William & Mary School of Law 2000-01. Inducted into American Legion Boys State Hall of Fame. Honored by Young Lawyers Conference Virginia State Bar with the creation of R. Edwin Burnette, Jr. Young Lawyer of the Year Award. Past President Lynchburg Symphony Orchestra and Kaleidoscope Festival. Former Board Member United Way of Central Virginia. Sunday School Teacher and Church Moderator Peakland Baptist Church. President William & Mary Law School Association. Member Executive Committee and Former Board Member Centra Health, Inc.

Office: 905 Court Street, Lynchburg 24504.
Telephone: (434) 847-1560, 847-1639.

BURR, Theodore J., Jr. *(Judge, Virginia General District Court Sixth Judicial District)* Assumed office July 1, 2001. Term expires June 30, 2007.

Office: 315 South Main Street, Emporia 23847.
Telephone: (434) 634-5400.

BYRD, Duncan M., Jr. *(Chief Judge, Virginia Circuit Court Twenty-fifth Judicial Circuit)* Elected by General Assembly to term beginning July 1, 1974. Reelected 1982, 1990 and 1998. Current term expires April 30, 2006. Born Hot Springs Virginia April 27, 1943. Presbyterian. Educated at Virginia Military Institute B.S. in Civil Engineering 1965 and T. C. Williams School of Law University of Richmond LL.B. 1968. Admitted to practice Virginia 1968. Began legal practice Bath County 1968. Judge, Bath County Court and Bath County Juvenile and Domestic Relations District Court May 1971 to July 1974.

Member Virginia State Bar. Captain U.S. Army 1968-70.

Mailing address: P.O. Box 670, Covington 24426-0670.
Office: Courthouse, 266 West Main Street, Covington 24426.
Telephone: (540) 965-1738.
Fax: (540) 965-1737

CACHERIS, James C. *(Senior Judge, United States District Court Eastern District of Virginia)* Appointed for life by President Ronald Reagan to term beginning Dec 18, 1981. Former Chief Judge. Assumed Senior status March 30, 1998. Educated at University of Pennsylvania B.S. 1955 and George Washington University J.D. with honors 1960. Associate Editor George Washington University Law Review 1959-60. Member Sigma Chi and Phi Delta Phi. Admitted to practice District of Columbia 1960 and Virginia 1962. In legal practice Washington D.C. 1960-71 and Alexandria Virginia 1962-71. Judge, Virginia Circuit Court Nineteenth Judicial Circuit 1971-81.

Assistant Corporation Counsel Washington D.C. 1960-62. Lecturer on Law George Washington University National Law Center 1983-84.

Office: U.S. Courthouse, 401 Courthouse Square, Alexandria 22314-5799.
Telephone: (703) 299-2110.

CALES, James A., Jr. *(Judge, Virginia Circuit Court Third Judicial Circuit)* Term expires Jan 31, 2005. Former Chief Judge. Former Judge and Chief Judge, Virginia General District Court Third Judicial District.

Mailing address: P.O. Box 1217, Portsmouth 23705-1217.
Office: 601 Crawford Parkway, Portsmouth 23704.
Telephone: (757) 393-8671.

CAMPBELL, J. Colin, Sr. *(Judge, Virginia Circuit Court Twenty-seventh Judicial Circuit)* Term expires April 2011. Former Chief Judge.

Mailing address: P.O. Box 130, Independence 24348-0130.
Office: 129 Davis Street, Independence 24348.
Telephone: (276) 773-2231.

CAMPBELL, Louis K. *(Chief Judge, Virginia General District Court Twenty-fifth Judicial District)* Elected by General Assembly Feb 1988 to term beginning July 1, 1988. Reelected 1994 and 2000. Current term expires June 30, 2006. Chief Judge since July 1996. Born Arlington Virginia July 8, 1950. Methodist. Educated at College of William & Mary A.B. 1972 J.D. 1975. Staff member William and Mary Law Review 1972-75. Admitted to practice Virginia 1975, U.S. District Court Western District of Virginia and U.S. Supreme Court. In legal practice Botetourt County 1975-88. Substitute Judge, Virginia General District Court 1983-88.

Member American Judges Association, Virginia Judges Association, Virginia State Bar and Virginia Bar Association. First Lieutenant U.S. Army 1975. Secretary Botetourt County Electoral Board 1980-82. Advisor Order of DeMolay Roanoke Valley Chapter. Interests include golf and community involvement in youth services.

Mailing address: P.O. Box 858, Fincastle 24090-0858.
Office: Back Street, Fincastle 24090.
Telephone: (540) 473-8244.

CAMPBELL, Samuel E. *(Judge, Virginia Juvenile and Domestic Relations District Court Sixth Judicial District)* Term expires Feb 28, 2006. Former Chief Judge.

Office: 100 East Broadway, Hopewell 23860.
Telephone: (804) 541-2257.

CANADA, Andrew Joseph, Jr. *(Judge, Virginia Circuit Court Second Judicial Circuit)* Elected by General Assembly to term beginning April 16, 2000. Term expires April 15, 2008. Former Judge, Virginia Juvenile and Domestic Relations District Court Second Judicial District. Born May 8, 1939. Educated at Hampden-Sydney College B.A. and University of Richmond LL.B.

Prosecutor and Assistant Commonwealth's Attorney Virginia Beach. Adjunct Professor Regent University Law School. Member Reagan Task Force for Criminal Justice. Named Outstanding Legislator of America and Outstanding Young Man of Virginia Beach. Listed in *Who's Who in the South.* State Senator Virginia Beach sixteen years. Former Member Board of Directors American Council of Young Political Leaders. Past President Princess Anne Lion's Club. Former Chairman Fund

CANADA, ANDREW JOSEPH, JR.—*Continued*

Raising for St. Jude's Hospital Virginia Beach. Former Member Board of Directors Virginia Council of Alcoholism and Drug Dependence, Inc. Secretary and Legal Counsel Virginia Beach Jaycees. Founding Member Virginia Beach Chapter Big Brothers/Big Sisters. Member Virginia Beach Boy's Club.
Office: Building Ten, Fourth Floor, 2425 Nimmo Parkway, Virginia Beach 23456-9017.
Telephone: (757) 427-4181.

CANNON, Julia Taylor *(Judge, Virginia General District Court Twentieth Judicial District)* Assumed office April 1, 1992. Elected by General Assembly April 1, 1998, current term expires March 31, 2004.
Office: 18 East Market Street, Leesburg 20176.
Telephone: (703) 777-0312.

CARLSON, M. Randolph, II *(Chief Judge, Virginia Juvenile and Domestic Relations District Court Fourth Judicial District)* Assumed office Jan 1, 2000. Term expires Dec 31, 2006.
Office: 800 East City Hall Avenue, Norfolk 23510.
Telephone: (757) 664-7340.

CARR, Gayl Branum *(Judge, Virginia Juvenile and Domestic Relations District Court Nineteenth Judicial District)* Term expires July 31, 2006.
Office: 4000 Chain Bridge Road, Fairfax 22030.
Telephone: (703) 246-3367.

CARTER, Robert R. *(Judge, Virginia General District Court First Judicial District)* Term expires Feb 2009. Former Chief Judge.
Office: Civic Center, 307 Albemarle Drive, Chesapeake 23322-5571.
Telephone: (757) 382-3111, 382-3150.

CASSIDY, Michael Joseph *(Judge, Virginia General District Court Nineteenth Judicial District)* Assumed office June 19, 1998. Elected by General Assembly to term beginning Feb 1, 1999. Current term expires Jan 31, 2005.
Office: 4110 Chain Bridge Road, Fairfax 22030.
Telephone: (703) 246-2153.

CAVEDO, Bradley B. *(Judge, Virginia Circuit Court Thirteenth Judicial Circuit)* Term expires Feb 2011.
Office: Courts Building, 400 North Ninth Street, Richmond 23219.
Telephone: (804) 646-6505.

CHAFIN, Teresa M. *(Chief Judge, Virginia Juvenile and Domestic Relations District Court Twenty-ninth Judicial District)* Elected to term beginning April 1, 2002. Term expires March 31, 2008.
Mailing address: P.O. Box 65, Lebanon 24266.
Office: Main Street, Lebanon 24266.
Telephone: (276) 889-8051, 889-8052.

CHAMBLIN, James H. *(Judge, Virginia Circuit Court Twentieth Judicial Circuit)* Elected by General Assembly Jan 1987 to term beginning March 6, 1987. Reelected 1995 and 2003. Current term expires Feb 2011. Former Chief Judge. Born Leesburg Virginia Sept 9, 1946. United Methodist. Educated at Hampden-Sydney College B.A. summa cum laude 1968 and University of Richmond School of Law J.D. 1971. Executive Editor University of Richmond Law Review 1970-71. Member Phi Alpha Delta, Omicron Delta Kappa and Phi Beta Kappa. Admitted to practice Virginia 1971. In legal practice Leesburg 1971-87.
Mailing address: P.O. Box 550, Leesburg 20178.
Office: 18 East Market Street, Leesburg 20178.
Telephone: (703) 777-0464.
Fax: (703) 777-0676.

CHEEK, David Eugene, Sr. *(Judge, Virginia General District Court Thirteenth Judicial District)* Assumed office July 1, 1992. Elected by General Assembly July 1, 1998, current term expires June 30, 2004.
Office: Safety Health & Welfare Building, 501 North Ninth Street, Richmond 23219.
Telephone: (804) 646-6677.

CHITWOOD, Howard Lee *(Judge, Virginia Juvenile and Domestic Relations District Court Twenty-seventh Judicial District)* Assumed office May 16, 1999. Elected by General Assembly to term beginning Feb 1, 2000, current term expires Jan 31, 2006.
Office: 45 Third Street N.W., Suite 103, Pulaski 24301.
Telephone: (540) 980-3822.

CLARK, Martin F., Jr. *(Judge, Virginia Circuit Court Twenty-first Judicial Circuit)* Term expires April 2011. Former Judge, Virginia Juvenile and Domestic Relations District Court Twenty-first Judicial District.
Mailing address: P.O. Box 762, Stuart 24171.
Office: Main Street, Stuart 24171.
Telephone: (276) 694-3775.

CLARKE, Dorothy H. *(Judge, Virginia General District Court Seventeenth Judicial District)* Elected by General Assembly to term beginning March 1997. Reelected 2003, current term expires Feb 2009. Educated at Georgetown University B.S. 1966 J.D. 1981. Editorial Board American Criminal Law Review 1978-81. Admitted to practice Virginia 1982, U.S. District Court Eastern District of Virginia and U.S. Court of Appeals Fourth Circuit. In legal practice Arlington 1982-97. Former State Administrative Hearing Officer (Administrative Law Judge).
Co-author "White Collar Crime: A Survey of Law" American Criminal L. Rev. Member Virginia Mediation Network, Virginia Women Attorneys Association (Founding Member Northern Virginia Chapter), Association of Family and Conciliation Courts, National Association of Women Judges (Secretary Virginia Chapter), American Academy of Family Mediators, Virginia State Bar (Domestic Relations Section), Arlington (Chair Alternative Dispute Resolution Section and Task Force on Mediation, Member Courts Committee and Continuing Legal Education Committee, Law Day Volunteer, County Fair Volunteer, Family Law Section), Fairfax (Committee on Juvenile and Domestic Relations Court, Family Law Section), Virginia (Commission on the Needs of Children, Family Law Section) and American (Committee on Mediation Section of Dispute Resolution, Section of Family Law) Bar Associations. Speaker Family Law Seminar 1994, Alternative Dispute Resolution Seminars 1995 and 1996 and Divorce Seminar 1997 Arlington Bar Association and Pro Bono Conference Virginia Trial Lawyers Association 1996. Listed in *Who's Who in American Law* and *Who's Who of American Women.* Named Arlington Woman of the Year. Coordinator Arlington Democratic Mass Meetings 1976 and 1978. Delegate Democratic National Convention 1988. Member Emily's List, Democratic State Central Committee,

CLARKE, DOROTHY H.—*Continued*

Tenth Congressional District Democratic Committee, Arlington Democratic Steering Committee and Arlington Democratic Campaign Committee. Former Vice Chair Northern Virginia Regional Juvenile Detention Commission. Member Advisory Board Virginia Department for Children 1980-88 (Chair 1986-88), Arlington County School Board 1984-92 (Chairman 1986-87 and 1991-92) and Arlington Committee of 100. Board of Directors Virginia School Boards Association 1985-91 and American Association of University Women (Past Local President, Former Member State Board of Directors). Former Member Board of Directors Friends of Argus and Aurora House. Former Member Arlington Human Services Commission, Women's Advisory Board Girls Scouts of the National Capital Area, United Way of National Capital Area Trustees Assembly, Arlington YMCA Committee of Management, Arlington County Civic Federation, Arlington Commission on the Status of Women, Service League of Northern Virginia and Friends of TACTS. Life Member Virginia PTA.

Office: 1425 North Courthouse Road, Suite 2500, Arlington 22201.

Telephone: (703) 228-4490.

CLARKE, J. Calvitt, Jr. *(Senior Judge, United States District Court Eastern District of Virginia)* Appointed for life by President Gerald R. Ford to term beginning Jan 2, 1975. Assumed Senior status 1991, serves by assignment. Born Harrisburg Pennsylvania Aug 9, 1920. Presbyterian. Educated at University of Virginia B.S. 1944 J.D. 1944. Member Delta Theta Phi. Admitted to practice Virginia 1944. In legal practice Richmond 1944-75.

Member Judicial Conference of the Fourth Circuit, American Judicature Society, International Association of Defense Counsel, The Defense Research Institute, Inc., Virginia State Bar, Richmond, Norfolk-Portsmouth, Virginia and American Bar Associations.

Office: U.S. Courthouse, 600 Granby Street, Norfolk 23510-1915.

CLARKE, Joseph M., II *(Judge, Virginia Juvenile and Domestic Relations District Court Twenty-third Judicial District)* Appointed by Twenty-third Circuit judges to term beginning Oct 1, 1988. Elected by General Assembly 1989. Reelected 1995 and 2001. Current term expires Jan 31, 2007. Former Chief Judge. Born Roanoke Virginia Sept 27, 1952. Methodist. Educated at Virginia Commonwealth University B.S. 1974 and University of Richmond J.D. 1978. Admitted to practice Virginia 1978, U.S. District Court Western District of Virginia 1978 and U.S. Court of Appeals Fourth Circuit 1983. In legal practice Roanoke 1978-88. Substitute Judge, Virginia General District Court Twenty-third Judicial District 1987-88.

Author *Virginia Criminal Law Case Finder* The Michie Company 1987. Member The Association of Trial Lawyers of America, Virginia Trial Lawyers Association, Virginia and American Bar Associations. Recipient Outstanding Young Men of America Award 1985. Board of Directors 1979-84 and Vice President 1984 Roanoke Valley Safety Council. Big Brother 1979-84, Board of Directors 1981-86 and President 1985 Big Brothers/Big Sisters of Roanoke Valley. Professional Advisory Committee Parents Anonymous 1980-84. President Fraternal Order of Police Associates 1982. Enjoys family, church, sports, music and reading.

Mailing address: P.O. Box 986, Roanoke 24005.

Office: 315 West Church Avenue S.W., First Floor, Roanoke 24016.

Telephone: (540) 853-2389.

CLEMENTS, Jean Harrison *(Judge, Court of Appeals of Virginia)* Assumed office July 1, 2000. Term expires June 30, 2008. Former Judge and Chief Judge, Virginia Juvenile and Domestic Relations District Court Twentieth Judicial District. Judge, Virginia Circuit Court Twentieth Judicial Circuit July 1, 1998 to June 30, 2000.

Office: 209-A Gibson Street N.W., Leesburg 20176-2114.

Telephone: (703) 737-7114.

COCHRAN, Virginia Ladd *(Judge, Virginia General District Court Second Judicial District)* Term expires June 30, 2006.

Office: 2425 Nimmo Parkway, Virginia Beach 23456-9057.

Telephone: (757) 427-8783.

Fax: (757) 426-5672

COMBS, Frederick H. *(Chief Judge, Virginia General District Court Twenty-ninth Judicial District)* Term expires Jan 2009. Born Hampton Virginia March 22, 1946. Presbyterian. Educated at University of Richmond B.S.B.A. 1968 LL.B 1973. Admitted to practice Virginia 1973.

Mailing address: P.O. Box 566, Tazewell 24651-0566.

Office: Main Street, Tazewell 24651.

Telephone: (276) 988-9057.

CONRAD, Glen E. *(Magistrate Judge, United States District Court Western District of Virginia)* Appointed by U.S. District Court judges to term beginning May 23, 1976. Reappointed 1981, 1989 and 1997. Current term expires 2005. Born Radford Virginia June 29, 1949. Educated at College of William & Mary A.B. 1971 J.D. 1974. Admitted to practice Virginia 1974.

Member Roanoke, Virginia, Federal and American Bar Associations.

Mailing address: P.O. Box 2822, Roanoke 24001-2822.

Telephone: (540) 857-5124.

CONWAY, H. Vincent, Jr. *(Chief Judge, Virginia Circuit Court Seventh Judicial Circuit)* Term expires Jan 31, 2008.

Office: Courthouse Building, 2500 Washington Avenue, Newport News 23607-4307.

Telephone: (757) 926-8561.

CREEKMORE, Frederick Hillary, Sr. *(Judge, Virginia Circuit Court First Judicial Circuit)* Elected by General Assembly to term beginning Aug 1, 1998. Term expires July 31, 2006. Educated at University of Richmond B.A. 1960 LL.B. 1963. Member Omicron Delta Kappa. Admitted to practice Virginia 1963. Judge, Virginia Juvenile and Domestic Relations District Court First Judicial District Aug 1, 1990 to July 31, 1998.

Office: 307 Albemarle Drive, Suite 400A, Chesapeake 23322-5580.

Telephone: (757) 382-3050.

CRIGLER, B. Waugh *(Magistrate Judge, United States District Court Western District of Virginia)* Ap-

CRIGLER, B. WAUGH—*Continued*

pointed by U.S. District Court judges to term beginning Oct 1, 1981. Reappointed 1989 and 1997. Current term expires 2005. Born Charlottesville Virginia July 17, 1948. Educated at Washington and Lee University B.A. 1970 and University of Tennessee J.D. 1973. Staff member University of Tennessee Law Review 1971-72. Law Clerk to Hon. Robert L. Taylor, U.S. District Court Eastern District of Tennessee 1973-74. Member Order of the Coif, Phi Gamma Delta, Phi Kappa Phi and Phi Alpha Delta. Admitted to practice Tennessee 1973, Virginia 1974 and District of Columbia 1975. Began legal practice Culpeper Virginia 1974.

Instructor Germanna Community College 1977-78 and University of Virginia School of Law since 1986. Member Criminal Rules Advisory Committee 1991-97 and State-Federal Judicial Council 1992-99. Member Thomas Jefferson American Inn of Court (President 1991-92), Virginia State Bar (Professionalism Committee since 1999, Chair Subcommittee on Professionalism for Law Students since 1999), The District of Columbia Bar, Tennessee, Virginia (Chairman Criminal Law Committee Young Lawyers Division 1978-79) and American (Chairman Criminal Law Committee Young Lawyers Division 1979-80) Bar Associations. Member United Way 1974-75 and Torch Club 1984-88. Enjoys antiques, gardening, landscaping and woodworking.

Office: 328 U.S. Courthouse, 255 West Main Street, Charlottesville 22902.

Telephone: (434) 296-7779.

CROWE, Joel Pierson *(Judge, Virginia Juvenile and Domestic Relations District Court Third Judicial District)* Assumed office July 1, 1998. Elected by General Assembly to term beginning Feb 1, 2000, current term expires Jan 31, 2006. Former Chief Judge.

Mailing address: P.O. Box 1073, Portsmouth 23705-1073.

Office: Civic Center, 603 Crawford Street, Portsmouth 23705.

Telephone: (757) 393-8851.

CRUMBLEY, Jesse C., III *(Judge, Virginia General District Court Twenty-fourth Judicial District)* Term expires Jan 31, 2007. Former Chief Judge.

Mailing address: P.O. Box 97, Rustburg 24588-0097.

Office: 732 Village Highway, Rustburg 24588.

Telephone: (434) 332-9546.

CULLEN, John R. *(Judge, Virginia Circuit Court Sixteenth Judicial Circuit)* Term expires June 30, 2010. Former Chief Judge. Former Judge and Chief Judge, Virginia Juvenile and Domestic Relations District Court Sixteenth Judicial District.

Office: 135 West Cameron Street, Culpeper 22701.

Telephone: (540) 727-3440.

Fax: (540) 727-7535

CUNNINGHAM, Joel C. *(Judge, Virginia General District Court Tenth Judicial District)* Assumed office April 16, 1998. Term expires April 15, 2004.

Mailing address: P.O. Box 458, Halifax 24558-0458.

Office: Eight South Main Street, Suite 134B, Halifax 24558.

Telephone: (434) 476-3385.

DAFFRON, Philip V. *(Chief Judge, Virginia General District Court Twelfth Judicial District)* Term expires March 31, 2006.

Mailing address: P.O. Box 144, Chesterfield 23832-0144.

Office: Chesterfield Courthouse, 9500 Courthouse Road, Chesterfield 23832.

Telephone: (804) 748-1231.

D'ALTON, James F., Jr. *(Judge, Virginia Circuit Court Eleventh Judicial Circuit)* Appointed by Governor L. Douglas Wilder to term beginning July 1, 1992. Elected by General Assembly to term beginning July 1, 2000, current term expires June 30, 2008. Judge, Virginia General District Court Twelfth Judicial District Feb 1, 1976 to June 30, 1992.

Office: Seven Courthouse Avenue, Petersburg 23803.

Telephone: (804) 733-2367.

DANIEL, Kimberly J. *(Judge, Virginia Juvenile and Domestic Relations District Court Nineteenth Judicial District)* Assumed office July 1, 2001. Term expires June 30, 2007.

Office: 4000 Chain Bridge Road, Fairfax 22030.

Telephone: (703) 246-3367.

DAVIS, Bonnie C. *(Judge, Virginia Juvenile and Domestic Relations District Court Twelfth Judicial District)* Elected by General Assembly Feb 1993 to term beginning July 1, 1993. Reelected 1999, current term expires June 30, 2005. Former Chief Judge. Born Petersburg Virginia July 13, 1949. Baptist. Educated at Longwood College B.A. 1971 and University of Richmond J.D. 1980. Admitted to practice Virginia 1980, U.S. District Court Eastern District of Virginia 1980 and U.S. Court of Appeals Fourth Circuit 1980. In legal practice Richmond 1980-83.

Assistant Commonwealth Attorney Chesterfield County 1983-93. Co-author *Juvenile Law and Practice in Virginia* Virginia Law Foundation 1994. Instructor in Business Law Richard Bland College 1983-93. Member Virginia State Bar, Metropolitan Richmond Women's and Virginia Bar Associations. Instructor Juvenile Law and Practice in Virginia CLE Committee Virginia Law Foundation. Recipient Women of Achievement Award from Metropolitan Richmond Women's Bar Association. Listed in *Who's Who of American Women, Who's Who of Emerging Leaders in America* and *Who's Who in American Law.* Enjoys photography.

Mailing address: P.O. Box 520, Chesterfield 23832-0520.

Office: 7000 Lucy Corr Boulevard, Chesterfield 23832.

Telephone: (804) 748-1379.

DAVIS, J. Maston *(Chief Judge, Virginia Juvenile and Domestic Relations District Court Fifteenth Judicial District)* Term expires Feb 28, 2007.

Mailing address: P.O. Box 1000, Warsaw 22572-1000.

Office: 101 Court Circle, Warsaw 22572.

Telephone: (804) 333-4616.

DAVIS, Mark S. *(Judge, Virginia Circuit Court Third Judicial Circuit)*

Mailing address: P.O. Box 1217, Portsmouth 23705-1217.

Office: 601 Crawford Parkway, Portsmouth 23704.

Telephone: (757) 393-8671.

DAVIS, Stewart P. *(Judge, Virginia General District Court Nineteenth Judicial District)* Term expires March 14, 2006.
Office: 4110 Chain Bridge Road, Fairfax 22030.
Telephone: (703) 246-2153.

DAWKINS, Nolan Boyd *(Judge, Virginia Juvenile and Domestic Relations District Court Eighteenth Judicial District)* Assumed office July 1, 1994. Elected by General Assembly to term beginning July 1, 2000, current term expires June 30, 2006.
Mailing address: P.O. Box 21461, Alexandria 22320.
Office: 520 King Street, Alexandria 22314.
Telephone: (703) 838-4141.

DEATHERAGE, Susan N. *(Chief Judge, Virginia Juvenile and Domestic Relations District Court Twenty-first Judicial District)* Term expires April 30, 2007.
Office: 3160 Kings Mountain Road, Second Floor, Suite C, Martinsville 24112-0751.
Telephone: (276) 634-4830.

DELBRIDGE, Jane Pritchard *(Judge, Virginia Juvenile and Domestic Relations District Court Nineteenth Judicial District)* Term expires Feb 28, 2007. Former Chief Judge.
Office: 4000 Chain Bridge Road, Fairfax 22030.
Telephone: (703) 246-3367.

DELK, Rodham T., Jr. *(Judge, Virginia Circuit Court Fifth Judicial Circuit)* Assumed office March 16, 1993. Elected by General Assembly to term beginning March 16, 2001, current term expires March 15, 2009.
Mailing address: P.O. Box 1814, Suffolk 23439-1814.
Office: Courts Building, 150 North Main Street, Suffolk 23434.
Telephone: (757) 923-2271.

DEZERN, Ray Wilbur, Jr. *(Judge, Virginia General District Court Fourth Judicial District)* Term expires Dec 31, 2007.
Office: 811 East City Hall Avenue, Room 284, Norfolk 23510-2772.
Telephone: (757) 664-4915, 664-4916.

DOHERTY, Robert P., Jr. *(Chief Judge, Virginia Circuit Court Twenty-third Judicial Circuit)* Term expires Feb 2011.
Office: Two East Calhoun Street, Salem 24153.
Telephone: (540) 375-3067.

DOHNAL, Dennis W. *(Magistrate Judge, United States District Court Eastern District of Virginia)* Appointed by U.S. District Court judges to term beginning Jan 31, 2000. Term expires Jan 2008.
Office: U.S. Courthouse, 1000 East Main Street, Richmond 23219.
Telephone: (804) 916-2220.

DORSEY, Charles N. *(Judge, Virginia Circuit Court Twenty-third Judicial Circuit)* Elected by General Assembly to term beginning July 1, 2002. Term expires June 30, 2010.
Mailing address: P.O. Box 2610, Roanoke 24010-2610.
Office: 315 West Church Avenue, Roanoke 24016.
Telephone: (540) 853-6702.

DOUMAR, Robert G. *(Senior Judge, United States District Court Eastern District of Virginia)* Appointed for life by President Ronald Reagan to term beginning Jan 4, 1982. Assumed Senior status, serves by assignment. Born Norfolk Virginia Feb 17, 1930. Roman Catholic. Educated at University of Virginia B.A. 1951 LL.B. 1953. Editorial Board Virginia Law Review 1952-53. Member Phi Delta Phi, Order of the Coif and Raven Society. Admitted to practice Virginia 1952. In legal practice Norfolk 1955-81.

Co-author "Actions for Defective Products" Virginia State Bar 1974. Fellow International Society of Barristers. Member Virginia Trial Lawyers Association, American Association of Defense Attorneys, The Defense Research Institute, Inc., The Association of Trial Lawyers of America, Virginia Conference of Local Bar Associations (President 1980-81), Virginia State Bar, Norfolk and Portsmouth (President 1976), Virginia and American Bar Associations. Lecturer on Products Liability 1974 and Virginia Procedure 1977 Virginia CLE and Medical Malpractice 1974 and Products Liability 1979 Virginia Trial Lawyers Association. Recipient Brotherhood Award from National Conference of Christians and Jews 1982 and Outstanding Citizen Award from Knights of Columbus Council 367, 1985. Major U.S. Army JAGC (active duty June 1953 to April 1955, inactive reserve 1955-70). Chairman Republican Party City of Norfolk 1959-63 and 1966-80. Member Republican State Central Committee 1966-80. Delegate Republican National Conventions 1968, 1972 and 1976. Member Norfolk Rotary Club, Knights of Columbus Council 367, American Legion Post 35 and Elks Lodge 38.
Office: 344 U.S. Courthouse, 600 Granby Street, Norfolk 23510-1915.
Telephone: (757) 222-7006.

DOWNER, Robert H., Jr. *(Judge, Virginia General District Court Sixteenth Judicial District)* Assumed office June 1, 2001. Term expires May 31, 2007.
Mailing address: P.O. Box 2677, Charlottesville 22902-2677.
Office: 606 East Market Street, Charlottesville 22902-5304.
Telephone: (434) 970-3388.

DUGGER, Jay Edward *(Judge, Virginia Juvenile and Domestic Relations District Court Eighth Judicial District)* Assumed office July 1, 2001. Term expires June 30, 2007.
Mailing address: P.O. Box 69104, Hampton 23669-9404.
Office: 220 North King Street, Hampton 23669.
Telephone: (757) 727-6147, 727-6742.

DURDEN, Nelson T. *(Chief Judge, Virginia Juvenile and Domestic Relations District Court Eighth Judicial District)* Elected by General Assembly to term beginning Aug 1, 1973. Reelected to subsequent terms. Current term expires Jan 31, 2004. Born Baltimore Maryland Nov 3, 1936. Episcopalian. Educated at Hampden-Sydney College B.A. 1960 and University of Virginia School of Law Bachelor of Laws 1963 J.D. 1970. Member Phi Alpha Delta. Admitted to practice Virginia 1963. In legal practice Hampton 1963-73. Substitute Judge, Hampton Municipal Court 1968-73.

Alternate Member State Management Team Comprehensive Services Act. Member Virginia Trial Lawyers Association, Virginia Council of Juvenile Court Judges (President 1997-99), National Council of Juvenile and Family Court Judges, District Court Judges Association,

DURDEN, NELSON T.—*Continued*

Virginia State Bar, Hampton, Virginia and American Bar Associations. Attends two state conferences each year.
Mailing address: P.O. Box 69104, Hampton 23669-9404.
Office: 220 North King Street, Hampton 23669.
Telephone: (757) 727-6147, 727-6742.

EASON, Carl E., Jr. *(Judge, Virginia Circuit Court Fifth Judicial Circuit)* Term expires Feb 2011.
Mailing address: P.O. Box 1604, Suffolk 23439-1604.
Office: Courts Building, 150 North Main Street, Suffolk 23434.
Telephone: (757) 923-2251.

EDWARDS, Robert B. *(Chief Judge, Virginia General District Court Fifth Judicial District)* Elected by General Assembly to term beginning April 1, 1968. Reelected to subsequent terms. Current term expires June 30, 2004. Born Knoxville Tennessee Nov 7, 1937. Baptist. Educated at University of Richmond B.A. with honors 1958 and University of Virginia LL.B. 1962. Member Lambda Chi Alpha and Sigma Nu Phi. Admitted to practice Virginia 1962 and U.S. Court of Military Appeals 1963. Captain U.S. Army JAGC 1962-66.
Mailing address: P.O. Box 122, Isle of Wight 23397.
Office: Isle of Wight Courthouse, Isle of Wight 23397.
Telephone: (757) 365-6244.

ELDER, Larry G. *(Judge, Court of Appeals of Virginia)* Elected by General Assembly to term beginning May 1, 1991. Reelected 1999, current term expires April 2007. Former Judge and Chief Judge, Virginia Juvenile and Domestic Relations District Court Eleventh Judicial District.
Office: 101 North Eighth Street, Richmond 23219-2306.
Telephone: (804) 786-6735.

ELLIOTT, Archie, Jr. *(Judge, Virginia General District Court Third Judicial District)* Term expires June 2009. Former Chief Judge.
Mailing address: P.O. Box 129, Portsmouth 23705-0129.
Office: 711 Crawford Street, Portsmouth 23704-3809.
Telephone: (757) 393-8681, 393-8506, 393-8624.

ELLIS, Joseph J. *(Judge, Virginia Juvenile and Domestic Relations District Court Fifteenth Judicial District)* Assumed office July 1, 1999. Term expires June 30, 2005.
Mailing address: P.O. Box 400, Stafford 22555-0400.
Office: The Judicial Center, 1300 Courthouse Road, Stafford 22554.
Telephone: (540) 658-8775.

ELLIS, Thomas S., III *(Judge, United States District Court Eastern District of Virginia)* Appointed for life by President Ronald Reagan to term beginning 1987. Born May 15, 1940. Episcopalian. Educated at Princeton University B.S.E. 1961, Harvard University J.D. magna cum laude 1969 and Magdalen College Oxford University, England Diploma in Law 1970. Recipient Lecture Award Institute of Aeronautic Sciences Princeton University 1961. Knox Fellow Harvard University 1969-70. In legal practice 1969-87.
Author "In Defense of In Pari Delicto" 56 American Bar Association Journal 1970; "A Survey of Government Control of Mergers in the United Kingdom" Part I No. 3 and Part II No. 4, 22 Northern Ireland Legal Quarterly 1971; "Initial Requests Under the Freedom of Information Act" Virginia B. Jour. Spring 1979; "Legal Aspects of SIDS" 15 Medical College of Virginia Quarterly No. 4, 1980; "A Primer on Settling Uncertified Class Actions" Virginia B. Jour. Spring 1980; "Letting Defective Babies Die: Who Decides?" American Journal of Law and Medicine 4 Winter 1982; "Infant Brain Death: Some Comments" 2 Notre Dame Journal of Law, Ethics and Public Policy 661, 1986; and "Student-Edited and Faculty-Edited Journals in the Marketplace of Legal Ideas: A Reply to Professor Dekanal" 57 University of Missouri-Kansas City L. Rev. 246, 1989. Co-author with William F. Young *Antitrust Law, The Virginia Law—A Basic Handbook* 1981, with Tom O'Brien "A Case for the Abolition of Jury Exemptions in Virginia" 20 University of Richmond L. Rev. 971, 1986, and with Karen Adams chapters in *Evidence in America: The Federal Rules in the States* 1987. Lecturer on Law College of William & Mary 1981-83. Former Member National Panel of Arbitrators American Arbitration Association. Former Member Boyd-Graves Conference, Virginia Trial Lawyers Association, Bar Association of the City of Richmond, The District of Columbia Bar, Virginia State Bar, Virginia, Federal and American Bar Associations. Member Committee on Rules of Practice and Procedure Judicial Conference of the U.S. Temporary Member Senior Common Room Oxford University, England 1984. Lieutenant USN 1961-66. Member Advisory Council Department of Astrophysics Princeton University since 1984. Former Vice President Princeton Association of Virginia. Former member Board of Directors Virginia Poverty Law Center, Science Museum of Virginia and American Lung Association of Virginia. Former member Vietnamese Resettlement Committee and St. Paul's Church.
Office: U.S. Courthouse, 401 Courthouse Square, Alexandria 22314-5799.
Telephone: (703) 299-2114.

EMICK, Dudley J., Jr. *(Chief Judge, Virginia Juvenile and Domestic Relations District Court Twenty-fifth Judicial District)* Assumed office Feb 1, 1994. Elected by General Assembly to term beginning Feb 1, 2000, current term expires Jan 31, 2006.
Mailing address: P.O. Box 858, Fincastle 24090-0858.
Office: Back Street, Fincastle 24090.
Telephone: (540) 473-8244.

FAIRBANKS, George C., IV *(Judge, Virginia Juvenile and Domestic Relations District Court Ninth Judicial District)* Assumed office Feb 1, 1998. Term expires Jan 31, 2004.
Office: 5201 Monticello Avenue, Suite 3, Williamsburg 23188-8218.
Telephone: (757) 564-2200.

FARMER, John M. *(Judge, Virginia Juvenile and Domestic Relations District Court Twenty-ninth Judicial District)* Elected by General Assembly to term beginning April 1, 2002. Term expires March 31, 2008.
Mailing address: P.O. Box 128, Clintwood 24228.
Office: Main Street, Clintwood 24228.
Telephone: (276) 926-1630.

FARRAR, Kenneth W. *(Chief Judge, Virginia Juvenile and Domestic Relations District Court Twenty-fourth Judicial District)* Elected by General Assembly to

FARRAR, KENNETH W.—*Continued*

term beginning July 1, 1999. Term expires June 30, 2005. Born Lynchburg Virginia March 11, 1948. Baptist. Educated at Virginia Polytechnic Institute and State University B.S. 1970 and University of Baltimore J.D. 1974. Admitted to practice Virginia 1974, U.S. Court of Appeals Fourth Circuit and U.S. Tax Court. In legal practice Lovingston 1974-99.

Member Virginia Trial Lawyers Association, Amhearst/Nelson, Virginia and American Bar Associations. Member School Board Holy Cross Regional School. Member Christmas in April. Enjoys golfing, sailing, hunting and fishing. Personal Statement or Quote: "If I knew where I was going to die I never would go near that place."

Mailing address: P.O. Box 59, Lovingston 22949.
Telephone: (434) 847-1580.
E-mail address: farrarkw@ci.lynchburg.va.us

FARRIS, Lon Edward *(Judge, Virginia General District Court Thirty-first Judicial District)* Assumed office June 1, 1991. Elected by General Assembly 1997 and 2003. Current term expires May 2009.

Office: 9311 Lee Avenue, Manassas 20110.
Telephone: (703) 792-6141.

FELTON, Walter S., Jr. *(Judge, Court of Appeals of Virginia)* Elected by General Assembly Feb 28, 2002 to term beginning Sept 1, 2002. Term expires 2010. Educated at University of Richmond B.A. 1966 J.D. 1969.

Office: 3917 Midlands Road, Building 1, Suite B, Williamsburg 23188.
Telephone: (757) 253-4147.
Fax: (757) 253-4231
E-mail address: MManey@courts.state.va.us

FERGUSON, John B. *(Judge, Virginia Juvenile and Domestic Relations District Court Twenty-third Judicial District)* Assumed office Feb 1, 1994. Elected by General Assembly to term beginning Feb 1, 2000, current term expires Jan 31, 2006. Former Chief Judge.

Mailing address: P.O. Box 986, Roanoke 24005-0986.
Office: 315 West Church Avenue S.W., First Floor, Roanoke 24016.
Telephone: (540) 853-2389.

FILSON, Anita D. *(Judge, Virginia Juvenile and Domestic Relations District Court Twenty-fifth Judicial District)* Assumed office April 1, 2001. Term expires March 31, 2007.

Office: 150 South Main Street, Lexington 24450.
Telephone: (540) 463-3631, 463-3855.

FINCH, Gaylord L., Jr. *(Judge, Virginia Circuit Court Nineteenth Judicial Circuit)* Assumed office July 1, 2001. Term expires June 30, 2009. Former Judge and Chief Judge, Virginia Juvenile and Domestic Relations District Court Nineteenth Judicial District.

Office: 4110 Chain Bridge Road, Fairfax 22030.
Telephone: (703) 246-4111, 691-7320.

FISHER, Timothy S. *(Chief Judge, Virginia General District Court Seventh Judicial District)* Assumed office July 1, 1999. Elected by General Assembly to term beginning Feb 1, 2000, current term expires Jan 31, 2006.

Office: 2500 Washington Avenue, Newport News 23607-4307.
Telephone: (757) 926-3520.

FITZPATRICK, Johanna L. *(Chief Judge, Court of Appeals of Virginia)* Elected by General Assembly to term beginning Sept 1, 1992. Reelected Sept 1, 2000, current term expires Aug 31, 2008. Former Judge, Virginia Circuit Court Nineteenth Judicial Circuit.

Office: 300 North Lee Street, Suite 503, Alexandria 22314.
Telephone: (703) 518-8069.

FLANNAGAN, Charles B., II *(Chief Judge, Virginia Circuit Court Twenty-eighth Judicial Circuit)* Elected by General Assembly March 19, 1982. Reelected March 1990 and March 1998. Current term expires March 14, 2006. Born Bristol Virginia Aug 7, 1943. Protestant. Educated at East Tennessee State University B.S. 1965 and Vanderbilt University School of Law J.D. 1968. Admitted to practice Tennessee 1968 and Virginia 1969. In legal practice Bristol Virginia 1968-82.

Office: City Hall, 497 Cumberland Street, Bristol 24201.
Telephone: (276) 645-7351.

FOLEY, Charles B. *(Chief Judge, Virginia General District Court Twentieth Judicial District)* Term expires March 15, 2004.

Office: Six Court Street, Warrenton 20186-3299.
Telephone: (540) 347-8627.

FOREHAND, V. Thomas, Jr. *(Chief Judge, Virginia Circuit Court First Judicial Circuit)* Term expires June 2011. Former Judge, Virginia General District Court First Judicial District.

Office: 307 Albemarle Drive, Suite 400A, Chesapeake 23322-5579.
Telephone: (757) 382-3050.

FOSTER, Aundria Deloris *(Judge, Virginia Juvenile and Domestic Relations District Court Seventh Judicial District)* Assumed office July 1, 1991. Elected by General Assembly July 1, 1997 and 2003. Current term expires June 2009. Former Chief Judge.

Office: 2501 Huntington Avenue, Newport News 23607.
Telephone: (757) 926-3603.

FRANK, Robert P. *(Judge, Court of Appeals of Virginia)* Elected by General Assembly to term beginning March 16, 1999. Term expires March 15, 2007. Born Newport News Virginia March 16, 1944. Educated at University of Virginia B.A. with honors 1965 J.D. 1968. Admitted to practice Virginia 1968. In legal practice Newport News 1968-86. Judge, Virginia Juvenile and Domestic Relations District Court Seventh Judicial District Oct 6, 1986 to June 30, 1991. Former Judge and Chief Judge, Virginia Circuit Court Seventh Judicial Circuit, elected by General Assembly to term beginning July 1, 1991.

Adjunct Professor College of William & Mary School of Law.

Office: One Old Oyster Point Road, Newport News 23602-0687.
Telephone: (757) 249-4159.

FRANKLIN, Humes J., Jr. *(Judge, Virginia Circuit Court Twenty-fifth Judicial Circuit)* Assumed office Feb 13, 1998. Term expires Feb 12, 2006.

Mailing address: P.O. Box 1286, Staunton 24402-1286.
Office: 113 East Beverley Street, Staunton 24401.
Telephone: (540) 332-3870.

FREEMAN, Isaac St. C. *(Judge, Virginia General District Court Twenty-eighth Judicial District)*
Office: Courthouse, East Main and Court Streets, Abingdon 24210.
Telephone: (276) 676-6279, 676-6281.

FRIEDMAN, Jerome B. *(Judge, United States District Court Eastern District of Virginia)* Appointed for life by President Bill Clinton to term beginning Nov 25, 1997. Born Newark New Jersey Feb 19, 1943. Jewish. Educated at Old Dominion University B.S. 1965 and Wake Forest University J.D. 1969. Member Phi Alpha Delta. Admitted to practice Virginia 1969. In legal practice Norfolk and Virginia Beach 1970-85. Judge and Chief Judge, Virginia Juvenile and Domestic Relations District Court Second Judicial District 1985-91. Former Judge and Chief Judge, Virginia Circuit Court Second Judicial Circuit, elected by General Assembly to term beginning Jan 4, 1991.
Member Federal Judges Association, Virginia State Bar, Norfolk and Portsmouth, Virginia Beach, Virginia and Federal Bar Associations. Former Member Rotary Club. Enjoys golf.
Office: U.S. Courthouse, 600 Granby Street, Norfolk 23510-1915.
Telephone: (757) 222-7004.

FULTON, Junius P., III *(Judge, Virginia Circuit Court Fourth Judicial Circuit)* Term expires Jan 31, 2005.
Office: 100 St. Paul's Boulevard, Norfolk 23510.
Telephone: (757) 664-4380.

FULTON, Suzanne Kuczko *(Chief Judge, Virginia General District Court Thirtieth Judicial District)* Term expires Jan 31, 2007. Former Judge, Virginia Juvenile and Domestic Relations District Court Thirtieth Judicial District.
Mailing address: P.O. Box 829, Wise 24293-0829.
Office: Courthouse, Wise 24293.
Telephone: (276) 328-3426, 328-8296.

GADEN, Barbara J. *(Judge, Virginia General District Court Thirteenth Judicial District)* Assumed office April 16, 2001. Term expires April 15, 2007.
Office: 203 John Marshall Courts Building, 400 North Ninth Street, Richmond 23219.
Telephone: (804) 646-6461.

GALLAHUE, Thomas E. *(Judge, Virginia General District Court Nineteenth Judicial District)* Assumed office April 1, 1998. Term expires March 31, 2004.
Office: 4110 Chain Bridge Road, Fairfax 22030.
Telephone: (703) 246-2153.

GAMBLE, J. Michael *(Judge, Virginia Circuit Court Twenty-fourth Judicial Circuit)* Assumed office March 1, 1991. Elected by General Assembly, current term expires Feb 28, 2007.
Mailing address: P.O. Box 462, Amherst 24521.
Office: 113 Taylor Street, Amherst 24521.
Telephone: (434) 946-9321.

GARRETT, John A. *(Judge, Virginia General District Court Fourteenth Judicial District)* Elected by General Assembly to term beginning Aug 1, 2002. Term expires July 31, 2008.
Mailing address: P.O. Box 27032, Richmond 23273-7032.
Office: 4301 East Parham Road, Richmond 23228.
Telephone: (804) 501-4723, 501-4727.

GEISLER, Brett L. *(Judge, Virginia Circuit Court Twenty-seventh Judicial Circuit)*
Mailing address: P.O. Box 218, Hillsville 24343-0218.
Office: 605 Pine Street, Hillsville 24343.
Telephone: (276) 728-3117.

GERMELMAN, Carle F., Jr. *(Judge, Virginia Juvenile and Domestic Relations District Court Twenty-sixth Judicial District)* Elected by General Assembly to term beginning Sept 1, 1968. Reelected 1974, 1980, 1986, 1992 and 1998. Current term expires Jan 31, 2004. Former Chief Judge. Born Richmond Virginia Jan 17, 1936. Episcopalian. Educated at University of Richmond LL.B. 1960. Member McNeill Law Society. Admitted to practice Virginia 1960. Began legal practice Winchester 1963.
Adjunct Professor Lord Fairfax Community College 1977. Member Virginia State Bar and Virginia Bar Association. Captain U.S. Army JAGC 1960-63. Enjoys fly fishing, fly tying, amateur magic and rock collecting.
Office: Judicial Center, Five North Kent Street, Winchester 22601.
Telephone: (540) 667-5770.

GIAMMITTORIO, E. Robert *(Chief Judge, Virginia General District Court Eighteenth Judicial District)* Assumed office May 1, 1992. Elected by General Assembly May 1, 1998, current term expires April 30, 2004.
Mailing address: P.O. Box 20206, Alexandria 22320-1206.
Office: Courthouse, Second Floor, 520 King Street, Alexandria 22314.
Telephone: (703) 838-4010.

GIBB, Colin R. *(Judge, Virginia Circuit Court Twenty-seventh Judicial Circuit)* Assumed office July 1, 1994. Elected by General Assembly to term beginning July 1, 2002, current term expires June 30, 2010. Former Chief Judge.
Office: 45 Third Street N.W., Suite 101, Pulaski 24301.
Telephone: (540) 980-7825.

GILL, Herbert Cogbill, Jr. *(Judge, Virginia Circuit Court Twelfth Judicial Circuit)* Elected by General Assembly to term beginning Sept 1, 1987. Reelected Sept 1, 1995 and 2003. Current term expires Aug 2011. Former Chief Judge. Born Chesterfield Virginia Aug 8, 1943. United Methodist. Educated at Hampden-Sydney College B.A. 1965 and University of Richmond T.C. Williams School of Law J.D. 1971. Admitted to practice Virginia 1971. In legal practice Chesterfield 1971-87.
Assistant Commonwealth Attorney 1971-79. Instructor John Tyler Community College 1978. Member American Judicature Society, American Judges Association, Virginia State Bar, Chesterfield-Colonial Heights (President 1978) and American Bar Associations. Attended courses in General Jurisdiction 1988, Evidence 1989 and Handling Capital Cases 1990. Recipient Award of Merit from Chesterfield County Board of Supervisors 1987. Teacher Gill School 1965-66. With U.S. Department of Defense 1966-68. Member American Red Cross (Vice Chairman), Boy Scouts of America (District Chairman) and Lions Club.
Mailing address: P.O. Box 57, Chesterfield 23832.

GILL, HERBERT COGBILL, JR.—*Continued*

Office: 9500 Courthouse Road, Chesterfield 23832.
Telephone: (804) 748-1241.

GILMAN, Larry E. *(Judge, Virginia Juvenile and Domestic Relations District Court Fifteenth Judicial District)* Assumed office April 1, 1998. Term expires March 31, 2004.
Mailing address: P.O. Box 86, Hanover 23069-0086.
Office: 7515 Library Drive, Second Floor, Hanover 23069.
Telephone: (804) 365-6200.

GLUCHOWSKI, Paul F. *(Judge, Virginia Juvenile and Domestic Relations District Court Thirty-first Judicial District)* Assumed office July 1, 1993. Elected by General Assembly July 1, 1999, current term expires June 30, 2005. Former Chief Judge.
Office: 9311 Lee Avenue, Manassas 20110.
Telephone: (703) 792-6160.

GOODWYN, Samuel Bernard *(Judge, Virginia Circuit Court First Judicial Circuit)* Assumed office July 1, 1997. Term expires June 30, 2005. Former Judge, Virginia General District Court First Judicial District.
Office: 307 Albemarle Drive, Suite 400A, Chesapeake 23322-5579.
Telephone: (757) 382-3050.

GREENWALT, J. Frank, Jr. *(Judge, Virginia General District Court Twenty-first Judicial District)* Elected by General Assembly to term beginning July 1, 1978. Reelected to subsequent terms. Current term expires June 30, 2008. Former Chief Judge. Born Front Royal Virginia July 5, 1942. Baptist. Educated at University of Richmond B.A. 1964 J.D. 1970. Williams Scholar 1964. Member Sigma Phi Epsilon and Phi Delta Phi. Admitted to practice Virginia 1970. Began legal practice Stuart 1970.
Member Virginia State Bar (Chairman Fifth District Committee 1975-78), Patrick and Martinsville-Henry County Bar Associations. Sergeant U.S. Army 1964-66. Member Stuart Rotary (President 1978). Packmaster Cub Scouts. Sunday School teacher Stuart Baptist Church. Director ANCHOR (juvenile group home), Alcohol Treatment Board and VASAP Board. Enjoys sports.
Mailing address: P.O. Box 149, Stuart 24171-0149.
Office: 318 Administration Building, 106 Rucker Street, Stuart 24171.
Telephone: (276) 694-7258.

GRIFFITH, Charles D., Jr. *(Judge, Virginia Circuit Court Fourth Judicial Circuit)* Elected by General Assembly to term beginning May 1, 2000. Term expires April 30, 2008.
Office: 100 St. Paul's Boulevard, Norfolk 23510.
Telephone: (757) 664-4380.

GRODNER, Teena D. *(Judge, Virginia Juvenile and Domestic Relations District Court Nineteenth Judicial District)* Assumed office April 16, 1998. Term expires April 15, 2004.
Office: 4000 Chain Bridge Road, Fairfax 22030.
Telephone: (703) 246-3367.

GRUBBS, Ray Wilson *(Judge, Virginia Circuit Court Twenty-seventh Judicial Circuit)* Assumed office March 1, 1994. Elected by General Assembly to term beginning March 1, 2002, current term expires Feb 28, 2010. Former Chief Judge. Former Judge, Virginia General District Court Twenty-seventh Judicial District.
Mailing address: P.O. Box 389, Christiansburg 24068-0389.
Office: One East Main Street, Room 418, Christiansburg 24073-3027.
Telephone: (540) 382-2222.

HADDOCK, Donald M. *(Chief Judge, Virginia Circuit Court Eighteenth Judicial Circuit)* Term expires Jan 31, 2009.
Office: Courthouse, 520 King Street, Alexandria 22314.
Telephone: (703) 838-4044.

HALEY, James W., Jr. *(Judge, Virginia Circuit Court Fifteenth Judicial Circuit)* Assumed office Feb 1, 1990. Elected by General Assembly to term beginning Feb 1, 1998, current term expires Jan 31, 2006. Former Chief Judge. Former Judge and Chief Judge, Virginia General District Court Fifteenth Judicial District.
Mailing address: P.O. Box 69, Stafford 22555-0069.
Office: 1300 Courthouse Road, Stafford 22554.
Telephone: (540) 658-8750.

HAMBLEN, William D. *(Chief Judge, Virginia Circuit Court Thirty-first Judicial Circuit)* Elected by General Assembly to term beginning July 1, 1990. Reelected July 1, 1998, current term expires June 30, 2006. Former Chief Judge. Born Houston Texas Sept 20, 1947. Educated at Virginia Polytechnic Institute and State University B.A. 1971 and College of William & Mary J.D. 1974. Admitted to practice Virginia 1974. In legal practice Manassas 1974-80. Judge, Virginia General District Court Thirty-first Judicial District 1986-90.
Assistant Commonwealth Attorney Prince William County 1980-86. Lieutenant U.S. Army 1967-70.
Office: 9311 Lee Avenue, Manassas 20110.
Telephone: (703) 792-6015.

HAMMOND, Catherine Currin *(Judge, Virginia Circuit Court Fourteenth Judicial Circuit)* Assumed office May 4, 1999. Elected by General Assembly to term beginning Feb 1, 2000, current term expires Jan 31, 2008. Educated at Denison University B.F.A. 1975 and University of Virginia School of Law J.D. 1984. Law Clerk to Hon. Charles L. Brieant, Jr., U.S. District Court Southern District of New York 1984-85. Admitted to practice Virginia 1985 and New York 1985.
Mailing address: P.O. Box 27032, Richmond 23273-7032.
Office: 4301 East Parham Road, Richmond 23273.
Telephone: (804) 501-4707.

HANSON, Edward W., Jr. *(Judge, Virginia Circuit Court Second Judicial Circuit)* Term expires Feb 15, 2009. Former Judge, Virginia General District Court First Judicial District.
Office: Building Ten, Fourth Floor, 2425 Nimmo Parkway, Virginia Beach 23456-9017.
Telephone: (757) 427-4181.

HARRIS, George W., Jr. *(Judge, Virginia General District Court Twenty-third Judicial District)* Appointed by Governor Charles Robb to term beginning April 16, 1985. Elected by General Assembly 1991, 1997 and 2003. Current term expires April 2009. Born Lynchburg Virginia Dec 20, 1936. Methodist. Educated at Virginia Union University B.S. 1963 and North Carolina Central University J.D. 1967. Admitted to practice Virginia

HARRIS, GEORGE W., JR.—*Continued*

1967, U.S. District Courts Eastern and Western Districts of Virginia and U.S. Court of Appeals Fourth Circuit. In legal practice Roanoke 1967-85.

Member Old Dominion Bar, Virginia State Bar, Virginia, National and American Bar Associations. Attended Special Court Course The National Judicial College April 10, 1987. Recipient Diploma of Judicial Skills American Academy of Judicial Education July 28, 1989.

Mailing address: P.O. Box 997, Salem 24153-0997.
Office: Courthouse, 305 East Main Street, Salem 24153.
Telephone: (540) 387-6168.

HARRIS, Lee A., Jr. *(Chief Judge, Virginia Circuit Court Fourteenth Judicial Circuit)* Term expires July 31, 2006.

Mailing address: P.O. Box 27032, Richmond 23273-7032.
Office: 4301 East Parham Road, Richmond 23273.
Telephone: (804) 501-4708.

HARRY, G. Blair *(Judge, Virginia General District Court Fifth Judicial District)* Term expires Feb 29, 2008.

Mailing address: P.O. Box 1648, Suffolk 23434-1648.
Office: 150 North Main Street, Suffolk 23434.
Telephone: (757) 923-2281.

HASSELL, Leroy Rountree *(Chief Justice, Supreme Court of Virginia)* Assumed office Dec 28, 1989. Elected by General Assembly to term beginning Feb 1, 1990. Reelected 2002, current term expires Jan 31, 2014. Born Norfolk Virginia Aug 17, 1955. Educated at University of Virginia B.A. 1977 and Harvard Law School J.D. 1980. Admitted to practice Virginia 1980.

Fellow American Bar Foundation. Member Virginia State Bar, Richmond and Virginia Bar Associations. Former Chairman Richmond School Board. Former Director Richmond Renaissance, Inc., American Red Cross, Carpenter Center for the Performing Arts and Legal Aid of Central Virginia. Director Massey Cancer Center. Member University of Virginia Alumni Association and Trinity Baptist Church.

Mailing address: P.O. Box 1315, Richmond 23218-1315.
Office: 100 North Ninth Street, Richmond 23219.
Telephone: (804) 786-6404.

HAULER, Timothy J. *(Judge, Virginia Circuit Court Twelfth Judicial Circuit)* Appointed by Governor L. Douglas Wilder to term beginning July 1, 1993. Elected by General Assembly to term beginning July 1, 2001, current term expires June 30, 2009. Former Chief Judge. Born Cleveland Ohio Jan 29, 1946. Roman Catholic. Educated at University of Notre Dame B.B.A. 1968 and Case Western Reserve University J.D. 1971. Moot Court Board 1970-71. Member Phi Alpha Delta. Admitted to practice Ohio 1971 and Virginia 1975. In legal practice Cleveland Ohio 1971-72 and Colonial Heights Virginia 1976-86. Judge and Chief Judge, Virginia General District Court Twelfth Judicial District May 1, 1986 to June 30, 1993, appointed by Governor Gerald L. Baliles.

Member American Judges Association, Virginia Trial Lawyers Association, Virginia State Bar, Ohio State and American Bar Associations. Captain U.S. Army JAGC 1972-1976. Colonel USAR 1986-95 (retired). Military Judge, U.S. Army Legal Services Agency Trial Judiciary 1987-95. Chairman Colonial Heights School Board 1984-85. Enjoys aviation, dressage and classical music.

Mailing address: P.O. Box 57, Chesterfield 23832.
Office: 9500 Courthouse Road, Chesterfield 23832.
Telephone: (804) 748-1241.

HAWKINS, William O. *(Judge, Virginia Juvenile and Domestic Relations District Court Fourth Judicial District)* Assumed office July 1, 1998. Term expires June 30, 2004.

Office: 800 East City Hall Avenue, Norfolk 23510.
Telephone: (757) 664-7340.

HEATWOLE, William D. *(Judge, Virginia General District Court Twenty-fifth Judicial District)* Assumed office July 1, 1993. Elected by General Assembly to term beginning July 1, 1999, current term expires June 30, 2005.

Mailing address: P.O. Box 1028, Waynesboro 22980.
Office: 250 South Wayne Avenue, Waynesboro 22980.
Telephone: (540) 942-6636, 942-6637, 942-6674.

HENDRICK, Jerry, Jr. *(Judge, Virginia Juvenile and Domestic Relations District Court Twelfth Judicial District)* Assumed office Feb 1, 1990. Elected by General Assembly 1996 and 2002. Current term expires Jan 31, 2008. Former Chief Judge.

Mailing address: P.O. Box 520, Chesterfield 23832-0520.
Office: 7000 Lucy Corr Boulevard, Chesterfield 23832.
Telephone: (804) 748-1379.

HENENBERG, Karen Anne *(Judge, Virginia General District Court Seventeenth Judicial District)* Term expires Feb 28, 2007. Former Chief Judge.

Office: 1425 North Courthouse Road, Second Floor, Suite 2400, Arlington 22201.
Telephone: (703) 228-7900.

HESS, Joseph E. *(Judge, Virginia General District Court Twenty-fifth Judicial District)* Elected by General Assembly to term beginning Feb 1, 1975. Reelected to subsequent terms. Current term expires Jan 31, 2005. Former Chief Judge.

Office: 2039 Sycamore Avenue, Buena Vista 24416.
Telephone: (540) 261-8632.

HICKS, Gary A. *(Judge, Virginia Circuit Court Fourteenth Judicial Circuit)* Assumed office Aug 1, 1999. Elected by General Assembly to term beginning Feb 1, 2000, current term expires Jan 31, 2008. Judge, Virginia General District Court Fourteenth Judicial District July 1, 1993 to July 31, 1999.

Mailing address: P.O. Box 27032, Richmond 23273-7032.
Office: 4301 East Parham Road, Richmond 23273.
Telephone: (804) 501-4202.

HILLSMAN, Marvin C., Jr. *(Judge, Virginia Juvenile and Domestic Relations District Court Twenty-sixth Judicial District)* Assumed office Feb 1, 1999. Term expires Jan 31, 2005.

Office: 53 Court Square, Room 161, Harrisonburg 22801.
Telephone: (540) 564-3370.

HILTON, Claude M. *(Chief Judge, United States District Court Eastern District of Virginia)* Appointed for life by President Ronald Reagan to term beginning

HILTON, CLAUDE M.—*Continued* 1985. Chief Judge since Dec 3, 1997. Born Scott County Virginia Dec 8, 1940. Educated at The Ohio State University B.S. 1963 and Washington College of Law of American University J.D. 1966. In legal practice Arlington 1968-73 and 1976-85. Commissioner in Chancery, Virginia Circuit Court Seventeenth Judicial Circuit 1976-85.

Assistant Commonwealth's Attorney Arlington 1967-68. Commonwealth's Attorney 1974-75.

Office: U.S. Courthouse, 401 Courthouse Square, Alexandria 22314-5799.

Telephone: (703) 299-2112.

HOGSHIRE, Edward L. *(Judge, Virginia Circuit Court Sixteenth Judicial Circuit)* Assumed office May 1, 1998. Term expires April 30, 2006. Former Chief Judge.

Office: 315 East High Street, Charlottesville 22901.

Telephone: (434) 970-3766.

HOLTON, Anne B. *(Chief Judge, Virginia Juvenile and Domestic Relations District Court Thirteenth Judicial District)* Assumed office July 1, 1998. Term expires June 30, 2004.

Office: C181 Oliver Hill Courts Bldg., 1600 North Seventeenth Street, Richmond 23219-1214.

Telephone: (804) 646-2942.

HONTS, George E., III *(Judge, Virginia Circuit Court Twenty-fifth Judicial Circuit)* Elected by General Assembly to term beginning July 1, 1983. Reelected July 1, 1991 and July 1, 1999. Current term expires June 30, 2007. Born Eagle Rock Virginia Feb 20, 1940. Episcopalian. Educated at Washington and Lee University B.A. 1962 J.D. 1968 and University of Nevada Reno M.J.S. 1988. Member Omicron Delta Kappa, Phi Alpha Delta and Delta Tau Delta. Admitted to practice Virginia 1968. In legal practice Fincastle 1968-83. Substitute Judge, Virginia General District Court 1972-83.

Commissioner of Accounts Virginia Circuit Court Twenty-fifth Judicial Circuit Botetourt County 1970-83. Board of Directors Virginia National Bank 1976-83. Chairman Judicial Compensation Committee 1984-91 and Member Judicial Sentencing Guidelines Committee since 1990 Judicial Conference of Virginia. Member Virginia State Bar and American Bar Association 1968-81. Member American Judicature Society. Attended The National Judicial College 1984. Faculty Advisor General Jurisdiction Course The National Judicial College 1990. Board of Visitors Radford University 1982-83. First Lieutenant USAR 1964-66.

Mailing address: P.O. Box 219, Fincastle 24090-0219.

Office: Courthouse, Main Street, Fincastle 24090.

Telephone: (540) 473-8274.

HOOVER, Thomas B. *(Chief Judge, Virginia Circuit Court Ninth Judicial Circuit)* Assumed office Feb 1, 1998. Term expires Jan 31, 2006. Judge July 1, 1993 to Jan 31, 1998 and Former Chief Judge, Virginia Juvenile and Domestic Relations District Court Ninth Judicial District.

Mailing address: P.O. Box 98, New Kent 23124-0098.

Office: Courthouse, 12001 Courthouse Circle, New Kent 23124.

Telephone: (804) 966-9520.

HORAN, Richard T. *(Chief Judge, Virginia General District Court Nineteenth Judicial District)* Term expires Jan 31, 2004.

Office: 4110 Chain Bridge Road, Fairfax 22030.

Telephone: (703) 246-2153.

HORNE, Thomas D. *(Chief Judge, Virginia Circuit Court Twentieth Judicial Circuit)* Elected by General Assembly to term beginning July 1, 1982. Reelected 1990 and 1998. Current term expires June 30, 2006. Born Baltimore Maryland Oct 15, 1943. Episcopalian. Educated at Muhlenberg College A.B. 1965 and College of William & Mary J.D. 1969. Assistant Editor College of William & Mary Law Review. Member Alpha Tau Omega, Phi Alpha Theta, Phi Delta Phi and Omicron Delta Kappa. Admitted to practice Virginia 1969 and U.S. Court of Military Appeals 1971. In legal practice Leesburg 1972.

Assistant Commonwealth's Attorney and Commonwealth's Attorney 1972-82. Member Virginia State Bar and American Bar Association. Captain USMC 1969-72.

Mailing address: P.O. Box 550, Leesburg 20178.

Office: 18 East Market Street, Leesburg 20178.

Telephone: (703) 777-0464.

Fax: (703) 777-0676

HOUFF, W. Dale *(Chief Judge, Virginia General District Court Twenty-sixth Judicial District)* Elected by General Assembly to term beginning April 16, 2000. Term expires April 15, 2006.

Office: 116 South Court Street, Suite B, Luray 22835.

Telephone: (540) 743-5705, 743-5334.

HUBBARD, Edward Lewis *(Judge, Virginia Circuit Court Seventh Judicial Circuit)* Assumed office July 1, 1998. Term expires June 30, 2006. Judge July 1, 1990 to June 30, 1998 and Former Chief Judge, Virginia Juvenile and Domestic Relations District Court Seventh Judicial District.

Office: Courthouse Building, 2500 Washington Avenue, Newport News 23607-4307.

Telephone: (757) 926-8561.

HUDGINS, W. Edward, Jr. *(Judge, Virginia General District Court Second Judicial District)* Elected by General Assembly to term beginning April 1, 2000. Term expires May 31, 2006.

Office: 2425 Nimmo Parkway, Virginia Beach 23456-9057.

Telephone: (757) 427-8783.

Fax: (757) 426-5672

HUDSON, Henry E. *(Judge, United States District Court Eastern District of Virginia)* Appointed for life by President George W. Bush to term beginning Sept 3, 2002. Born Washington D.C. 1947. Educated at American University B.A. 1969 J.D. 1974. In legal practice 1979, 1991-92 and 1994-98. Judge, Virginia Circuit Court Nineteenth Judicial Circuit Feb 1, 1999 to 2002.

Office: U.S. Courthouse, 1000 East Main Street, Richmond 23219.

HUGHES, Melvin R., Jr. *(Chief Judge, Virginia Circuit Court Thirteenth Judicial Circuit)* Term expires Jan 31, 2009. Former Judge, Virginia General District Court Thirteenth Judicial District.

Office: John Marshall Courts Building, 400 North Ninth Street, Richmond 23219.

Telephone: (804) 646-6505.

HUME, James E. *(Chief Judge, Virginia Juvenile and Domestic Relations District Court Eleventh Judicial District)* Assumed office May 1, 1991. Elected by General Assembly 1997 and 2003. Current term expires April 2009.
Office: 27 East Tabb Street, Petersburg 23803.
Telephone: (804) 733-2372.

HUMPHREYS, Robert J. *(Judge, Court of Appeals of Virginia)* Assumed office April 16, 2000. Term expires April 15, 2008.
Office: 300 Pinehurst Centre, 477 Viking Drive, Virginia Beach 23452.
Telephone: (757) 431-3468.

HUPP, Dennis Lee *(Judge, Virginia Circuit Court Twenty-sixth Judicial Circuit)* Elected by General Assembly March 6, 1992 to term beginning Aug 1, 1992. Reelected to term beginning Aug 1, 2000, current term expires July 31, 2008. Born Winchester Virginia April 24, 1951. Religious Affiliation: Disciples of Christ. Educated at James Madison University B.A. 1973 and Cumberland School of Law J.D. 1977. Member Delta Theta Phi. Admitted to practice Virginia 1977. In legal practice Woodstock 1977-92.
Commonwealth's Attorney Shenandoah County 1984-91. Member Virginia State Bar and Virginia Bar Association. Attended Judicial Institute University of Virginia 1992, General Jurisdiction course The National Judicial College 1994 and annual meetings Judicial Conference of Virginia Spring and Fall. Former Democrat. Former Shenandoah County Chair Virginia State Central Committee. Elder and Sunday school teacher Strasburg Christian Church. Member Sons of Confederate Veterans and Strasburg Museum. Interests include Civil War, history and golf.
Mailing address: P.O. Box 406, Woodstock 22664-0406.
Office: 112 South Main Street, Woodstock 22664.
Telephone: (540) 459-6150.

HUTCHENS, Pamela E. *(Judge, Virginia General District Court Second Judicial District)* Assumed office April 1, 1997. Elected by General Assembly 2003, current term expires March 2009.
Office: 2425 Nimmo Parkway, Virginia Beach 23456-9057.
Telephone: (757) 427-8783.
Fax: (757) 426-5672

HUTTON, Christopher W. *(Chief Judge, Virginia Circuit Court Eighth Judicial Circuit)* Term expires Aug 2011.
Mailing address: P.O. Box 40, Hampton 23669-0040.
Office: 101 King's Way Mall, Hampton 23669.
Telephone: (757) 727-6106.

JACKSON, Gwendolyn Jones *(Chief Judge, Virginia General District Court Fourth Judicial District)* Elected by General Assembly to term beginning March 22, 1991. Reelected 1997 and 2003. Current term expires Feb 2009. Born Norfolk Virginia. Baptist. Educated at Hampton University B.S. cum laude 1969 and University of Virginia School of Law J.D. 1972. Member Delta Sigma Theta. Admitted to practice Virginia 1972. In legal practice Richmond 1972-74 and Norfolk 1978-91.
Member Association of District Court Judges of Virginia, American Judges Association and American Bar Association (National Conference of Special Court Judges Judicial Administration Division). Attended Traffic Court Seminar American Bar Association Oct 1992. Recipient Woman of the Year Excellence Award from Bachelor Benedict Club 1980, pro bono Award from Legal Defense and Educational Fund, Inc. NAACP 1987 and Constance Baker Motley Law Award. Member Vocational Education Advisory Committee Norfolk Public Schools, The Links, Inc. and Woman's Club of Norfolk. Interests include reading, collecting biographies and drafting historical outlines.
Office: 811 East City Hall Avenue, Room 284, Norfolk 23510-2772.
Telephone: (757) 664-4913, 664-4914.

JACKSON, Raymond Alvin *(Judge, United States District Court Eastern District of Virginia)* Appointed for life by President Bill Clinton to term beginning 1993. Born Sussex Virginia August 3, 1949. Educated at Norfolk State University B.A. 1970 and University of Virginia School of Law J.D. 1973.
Assistant U.S. Attorney Eastern District of Virginia 1977-93.
Office: 307 U.S. Courthouse, 600 Granby Street, Norfolk 23510-1915.
Telephone: (757) 222-7003.

JACOB, Avelina S. *(Judge, Virginia Juvenile and Domestic Relations District Court Twentieth Judicial District)* Assumed office Feb 10, 2001. Term expires Feb 9, 2007.
Office: 18 East Market Street, Leesburg 20176-0950.
Telephone: (703) 777-0300.

JACOBSON, Marc *(Chief Judge, Virginia Circuit Court Fourth Judicial Circuit)* Term expires March 2011. Former Judge, Virginia General District Court Fourth Judicial District.
Office: 100 St. Paul's Boulevard, Norfolk 23510.
Telephone: (757) 664-4380.

JAMES, Jerome *(Judge, Virginia Circuit Court Fourth Judicial Circuit)* Term expires Jan 31, 2008. Former Chief Judge.
Office: 100 St. Paul's Boulevard, Norfolk 23510.
Telephone: (757) 664-4380.

JAMISON, Birdie Hairston *(Judge, Virginia General District Court Thirteenth Judicial District)* Assumed office Dec 1, 1991. Elected by General Assembly Dec 1, 1997 and 2003. Current term expires Nov 2009. Former Chief Judge.
Office: 209 John Marshall Courts Building, 400 North Ninth Street, Richmond 23219-1508.
Telephone: (804) 646-6437.

JANOW, Lawrence *(Judge, Virginia Juvenile and Domestic Relations District Court Twenty-fourth Judicial District)* Elected by General Assembly to term beginning July 1, 1979. Reelected to subsequent terms. Current term expires Jan 31, 2004. Former Chief Judge. Born Newport News Virginia Sept 13, 1942. Jewish. Educated at University of Virginia B.A. in Psychology 1964 and University of Oklahoma J.D. 1968. Member Phi Alpha Delta and Zeta Beta Tau. Admitted to practice Virginia 1968. In legal practice Amherst 1968-79. Specialist USAR.
Mailing address: P.O. Box 178, Amherst 24521.
Office: 113 Taylor Street, Amherst 24521.
Telephone: (434) 946-9355.

JENKINS, Clarence N., Jr. *(Judge, Virginia Juvenile and Domestic Relations District Court Thirteenth Judicial District)* Term expires Feb 2009.
Office: C181 Oliver Hill Courts Bldg., 1600 North Seventeenth Street, Richmond 23219-1214.
Telephone: (804) 646-2942.

JOHNSON, Dwight D. *(Judge, Virginia Juvenile and Domestic Relations District Court Sixteenth Judicial District)* Assumed office Feb 1, 2001. Term expires Jan 31, 2007.
Office: Juvenile Court Building, 411 East High Street, Charlottesville 22901.
Telephone: (434) 979-7165.

JOHNSON, Patrick Reynolds *(Judge, Virginia General District Court Twenty-ninth Judicial District)* Term expires March 31, 2007.
Mailing address: P.O. Box 654, Grundy 24614-0654.
Office: Main and Walnut Streets, Grundy 24614.
Telephone: (276) 935-6526.

JOHNSON, Randall G. *(Judge, Virginia Circuit Court Thirteenth Judicial Circuit)* Appointed by Governor Gerald L. Baliles Oct 22, 1987. Elected by General Assembly 1988 and 1996. Current term expires Jan 31, 2004. Former Chief Judge. Born Richmond Virginia June 5, 1947. Presbyterian. Educated at Howard University B.A. 1968 J.D. cum laude 1974. Admitted to practice Virginia 1974. In legal practice Richmond 1974-87.
Office: John Marshall Courts Building, 400 North Ninth Street, Richmond 23219.
Telephone: (804) 646-6515.

JOHNSTON, J. Samuel, Jr. *(Judge, Virginia Circuit Court Twenty-fourth Judicial Circuit)* Term expires Feb 28, 2005. Former Chief Judge. Former Judge, Virginia General District Court Twenty-fourth Judicial District.
Mailing address: P.O. Box 7, Rustburg 24588-0007.
Office: 732 Village Highway, Rustburg 24588.
Telephone: (434) 592-9517.

JONES, Bonnie L. *(Judge, Virginia General District Court Eighth Judicial District)* Term expires March 31, 2008. Former Chief Judge.
Mailing address: P.O. Box 70, Hampton 23669-0070.
Office: 236 North King Street, Hampton 23669.
Telephone: (757) 727-6260.

JONES, George A., Jr. *(Chief Judge, Virginia General District Court Twenty-second Judicial District)* Assumed office April 1, 1994. Elected by General Assembly to term beginning April 1, 2000, current term expires March 31, 2006.
Mailing address: P.O. Box 695, Chatham 24531-0695.
Office: 11 Bank Street, Suite 201, Chatham 24531.
Telephone: (434) 432-7879.

JONES, James Parker *(Judge, United States District Court Western District of Virginia)* Appointed for life by President Bill Clinton to term beginning 1996. Born Tampa Florida July 3, 1940. Educated at Duke University A.B. 1962 and University of Virginia School of Law LL.B. 1965. Law Clerk to Hon. Clement Haynsworth, U.S. Court of Appeals Fourth Circuit 1966-68. In legal practice Abingdon 1968-71 and Bristol 1971-95.
Assistant Commonwealth Attorney General Virginia 1965-66. Member Virginia State Board of Education 1990-96. State Senator Virginia 1983-88.
Mailing address: P.O. Box 669, Abingdon 24212-0669.
Telephone: (276) 628-4080.

JONES, Thomas O. *(Chief Judge, Virginia General District Court Thirteenth Judicial District)* Term expires Jan 31, 2004.
Office: 209 John Marshall Courts Building, 400 North Ninth Street, Richmond 23219-1508.
Telephone: (804) 646-6439.

JONES, Thomas Rawles, Jr. *(Magistrate Judge, United States District Court Eastern District of Virginia)* Appointed by U.S. District Court judges to term beginning March 1, 1994. Reappointed 2002, current term expires 2010. Born Suffolk Virginia June 12, 1948. Educated at University of Virginia B.A. 1970 J.D. 1973. Law Clerk to Hon. Albert V. Bryan, Jr., U.S. District Court Eastern District of Virginia 1973-74. Admitted to practice Virginia 1974. In legal practice Alexandria 1974-94.
Assistant Commonwealth's Attorney 1974-82.
Office: U.S. Courthouse, 401 Courthouse Square, Alexandria 22314-5799.
Telephone: (703) 299-2122.

KEENAN, Barbara Milano *(Justice, Supreme Court of Virginia)* Assumed office July 1, 1991. Elected by General Assembly 2003, current term expires June 2015. Former Judge, Virginia Circuit Court Nineteenth Judicial Circuit. Former Judge, Court of Appeals of Virginia.
Office: 100 North Ninth Street, Fifth Floor, Richmond 23219.
Telephone: (804) 786-2251.

KEITH, Martin Langhorne *(Judge, Virginia Circuit Court Nineteenth Judicial Circuit)* Elected by General Assembly to term beginning March 15, 1995. Reelected 2003, current term expires March 2011. Born Washington D.C. Nov 4, 1936. Educated at University of Virginia B.A. 1958 J.D. 1970. Member Order of the Coif. Managing Editor Virginia Law Review 1968-70. Admitted to practice Virginia 1970. In legal practice Washington D.C. 1970-95.
County Attorney Fairfax County 1972-73. President Virginia Bar Association 1994. Member Virginia State Bar.
Office: 4110 Chain Bridge Road, Fairfax 22030.
Telephone: (703) 246-2221.
Fax: (703) 385-4432

KELLEY, Thomas J., Jr. *(Chief Judge, Virginia General District Court Seventeenth Judicial District)* Elected by General Assembly to term beginning Feb 10, 1995. Reelected 2001, current term expires Jan 31, 2007. Born Washington D.C. May 24, 1956. Religious Affiliation: Disciples of Christ. Educated at University of Richmond B.A. 1978 B.S. 1981. Admitted to practice Virginia 1981. In legal practice Arlington 1982-95.
Member Virginia State Bar and Arlington County Bar Association.
Office: 1425 North Courthouse Road, Suite 12200, Arlington 22201.
Telephone: (703) 228-4490.

KELSEY, D. Arthur *(Judge, Court of Appeals of Virginia)* Term expires Feb 2011. Educated at Old Dominion University B.A. magna cum laude 1982 and Col-

KELSEY, D. ARTHUR—*Continued* lege of William & Mary Marshall-Wythe School of Law J.D. 1985. Law Clerk to Chief Judge John A. MacKenzie, U.S. District Court Eastern District of Virginia 1985-86. Member Order of the Coif. Former Judge, Virginia Circuit Court Fifth Judicial Circuit, elected by General Assembly to term beginning April 16, 2000.

Co-author with Hughes "Toxic & Environmental Torts Within Admiralty" 62 Tulane L. Rev. 405, 1988; with Cohen Chapter 3 *The Virginia Lawyer* Lexis Law Publishing 1998; and with Holloway "Mistaken LHWCA Compensation Payments: Subrogation Lien or Third Party Credit?" 30 Journal of Maritime Law and Commerce 1, 1999. Author "In Rem Liens & Ship Repair Contracts" Shipping Finance Annual 1996. Contributing Author *ABA Antitrust Law Developments* 4th ed. 1997 and Supplement 1998. Associate Editor *American Maritime Cases* 1999-2000. Important Decisions: Commonwealth v. Beverly 52 Va. Cir. 255, 2000 WL 765084 Va. Cir. Ct. May 18, 2000 and 52 Va. Cir. 255, 2000 WL 981926 Va. Circ. Ct. July 7, 2000; Commonwealth v. Wilkins 52 Va. Cir. 500, 2000 WL 1137748 Va. Cir. Ct. Aug 10, 2000; Dogwood Realty, Inc. v. Virginia Department of Social Services 53 Va. Cir. 236, 2000 WL 1342494 Va. Cir. Ct. Sept 1, 2000; Commonwealth v. Hoverstadt 53 Va. Cir. 271, 2000 WL 1336667 Va. Cir. Ct. Sept 15, 2000; Commonwealth v. Wiggins 53 Va. Cir. 357, 2000 WL 1520314 Va. Cir. Ct. Oct 10, 2000; Denson v. Virginia Retirement Sys. 43 Va. Cir. 386, 2000 WL 1573089 Va. Cir. Ct. Oct 23, 2000; Commonwealth v. Ridley 53 Va. Cir. 410, 2000 WL 1663351 Va. Cir. Ct. Oct 27, 2000; Commonwealth v. Brown 53 Va. Cir. 448, 2000 WL 1725060 Va. Cir. Ct. Nov 15, 2000; Commonwealth v. Graham 2000 WL 1810020 Va. Cir. Ct. Dec 11, 2000; Commonwealth v. Hodge 2000 WL 33233620 Va. Cir. Ct. Dec 12, 2000; Commonwealth v. Jordan 2000 WL 1875859 Va. Cir. Ct. Dec 22, 2000; Commonwealth v. Vick 2001 WL 92380 Va. Cir. Ct. Jan 29, 2001; Gay v. Luihn Food Systems, Inc. 2001 WL 43095 Va. Cir. Ct. Feb 7, 2001; Commonwealth v. Norton 2000 WL 243906 Va. Cir. Ct. March 13, 2001; Commonwealth v. Potter 2001 WL 283143 Va. Cir. Ct. March 20, 2001; Commonwealth v. Evans 2001 WL 474422 Va. Cir. Ct. May 7, 2001; Kirk Timber & Farming Co. v. Union Camp Corp. 2001 WL 920837 Va. Cir. Ct. Aug 15, 2001; Nuckles v. Nuckles 2001 WL 1079619 Va. Cir. Ct. Sept 17, 2001; and Commonwealth v. Foulks 2001 WL 1112976 Va. Cir. Ct. Sept 24, 2001. Council Member Civil Litigation Section Virginia Bar Association. Barrister James Kent American Inn of Court. Member Boyd-Graves Conference.

Office: 109 North Eighth Street, Richmond 23219-2321.

Telephone: (804) 371-8428.

KENDRICK, Benjamin N. A. *(Judge, Virginia Circuit Court Seventeenth Judicial Circuit)* Term expires Feb 15, 2009.

Office: 1425 North Courthouse Road, Arlington 22201.

Telephone: (703) 228-7010.

KERR, William S. *(Judge, Virginia Juvenile and Domestic Relations District Court Tenth Judicial District)* Term expires Jan 31, 2008. Former Chief Judge.

Mailing address: P.O. Box 26, Appomattox 24522-0026.

Office: County Office Building, Morton Lane, Appomattox 24522.

Telephone: (434) 352-8225.

KINSER, Cynthia D. *(Justice, Supreme Court of Virginia)* Assumed office July 1, 1997. Elected by General Assembly to term beginning Feb 1, 1998, current term expires Jan 31, 2010. Former Magistrate Judge, U.S. District Court Western District of Virginia.

Mailing address: P.O. Box 457, Pennington Gap 24277.

Office: 602 West Morgan Avenue, Suite 7, Pennington Gap 24277.

Telephone: (276) 546-4563, 546-4573.

KISER, Jackson L. *(Senior Judge, United States District Court Western District of Virginia)* Appointed for life by President Ronald Reagan Dec 3, 1981 to term beginning Jan 12, 1982. Former Chief Judge. Assumed Senior status April 30, 1997, serves by assignment. Born Welch West Virginia June 24, 1929. Educated at Concord College B.A. 1951 and Washington and Lee University LL.B. magna cum laude 1952. Member Order of the Coif.

U.S. Commissioner 1956-58 and Assistant U.S. Attorney 1958-61 Western District of Virginia. Fellow American College of Trial Lawyers. Member Judicial Council of the Fourth Circuit, Judicial Conference of the Fourth Circuit (Former Member Committee on Space and Facilities Judicial Conference), Virginia Trial Lawyers Association, Virginia State Bar, Martinsville-Henry County, Virginia and American Bar Associations. U.S. Army JAGC 1952-55. Captain USAR 1955-61.

Mailing address: P.O. Box 3326, Danville 24543-3326.

Telephone: (434) 799-8700.

KLEIN, Stanley P. *(Judge, Virginia Circuit Court Nineteenth Judicial Circuit)* Assumed office July 1, 1992. Elected by General Assembly to term beginning July 1, 2000, current term expires June 30, 2008.

Office: 4110 Chain Bridge Road, Fairfax 22030.

Telephone: (703) 246-4111, 691-7320.

KLINE, Judith Anne *(Judge, Virginia Juvenile and Domestic Relations District Court Seventh Judicial District)*

Office: 2501 Huntington Avenue, Newport News 23607.

Telephone: (757) 926-3603.

KLOCH, John E. *(Judge, Virginia Circuit Court Eighteenth Judicial Circuit)* Term expires Jan 31, 2005.

Office: Courthouse, 520 King Street, Alexandria 22314.

Telephone: (703) 838-4044.

KNIGHT, C. Edward, III *(Judge, Virginia General District Court Eighth Judicial District)* Term expires April 30, 2008. Former Chief Judge.

Mailing address: P.O. Box 70, Hampton 23669-0070.

Office: 236 North King Street, Hampton 23669.

Telephone: (757) 727-6260.

KOONTZ, Lawrence L., Jr. *(Justice, Supreme Court of Virginia)* Elected by General Assembly to term beginning 1995. Term expires Aug 15, 2007. Born Roanoke Virginia Jan 25, 1940. Presbyterian. Educated at Virginia Polytechnic University B.S. 1962 and University of Richmond LL.B. 1965. Admitted to practice Virginia 1965. Judge, Virginia Juvenile and Domestic Relations District Court Jan 1968 to Dec 1976. Judge, Virginia Circuit Court Twenty-third Judicial Circuit 1976-85. Judge and Chief Judge, Court of Appeals of Virginia 1985-95.

Assistant Commonwealth's Attorney Roanoke 1967-68. Instructor in Police Science Virginia Western Community College since 1974. Member Virginia State Bar, Roanoke and American Bar Associations. President Virginia Juvenile Judges Association 1975-76. President Roanoke Valley Mental Health Association. Member Big Brothers Association and 4-H Association. Enjoys tennis, fishing and reading.

Mailing address: P.O. Box 687, Salem 24153-0687.

Office: 305 East Main Street, Second Floor, Salem 24153.

Telephone: (540) 387-6082.

KRUMM, Ross W. *(Chief Judge, United States Bankruptcy Court Western District of Virginia)* Appointed by U.S. Court of Appeals Fourth Circuit judges to term beginning Dec 29, 1986. Reappointed 2000, current term expires Dec 29, 2014.

Mailing address: P.O. Box 191, Harrisonburg 22801-0191.

Telephone: (540) 434-6747.

KUSHNER, Bruce H. *(Judge, Virginia Circuit Court First Judicial Circuit)* Assumed office May 1, 1999. Term expires April 30, 2007. Judge, Virginia Juvenile and Domestic Relations District Court First Judicial District Aug 1, 1998 to April 30, 1999.

Office: 307 Albemarle Drive, Suite 400A, Chesapeake 23322-5579.

Telephone: (757) 382-3050.

LACY, Elizabeth B. *(Justice, Supreme Court of Virginia)* Assumed office Jan 4, 1989. Elected by General Assembly to term beginning Feb 1, 1989. Reelected Feb 2001, current term expires Jan 31, 2013.

Mailing address: P.O. Box 1315, Richmond 23218-1315.

Office: 100 North Ninth Street, Richmond 23219.

Telephone: (804) 786-9980.

LANE, James V. *(Judge, Virginia Circuit Court Twenty-sixth Judicial Circuit)* Assumed office March 1, 2001. Term expires Feb 28, 2009.

Office: Courthouse, Court Square, Harrisonburg 22801.

Telephone: (540) 564-3111.

LANEY, Robert D. *(Judge, Virginia General District Court Twelfth Judicial District)* Term expires April 30, 2008. Former Chief Judge.

Mailing address: P.O. Box 144, Chesterfield 23832-0144.

Office: Chesterfield Courthouse, 9500 Courthouse Road, Chesterfield 23832.

Telephone: (804) 748-1231.

LEAFE, Joseph A. *(Judge, Virginia Circuit Court Fourth Judicial Circuit)* Assumed office March 16, 1998. Term expires March 15, 2006.

Office: 100 St. Paul's Boulevard, Norfolk 23510.

Telephone: (757) 664-4380.

LEDBETTER, William H., Jr. *(Judge, Virginia Circuit Court Fifteenth Judicial Circuit)* Elected by General Assembly to term beginning April 1, 1987. Reelected 1995 and 2003. Current term expires Feb 2011. Former Chief Judge. Born Macon Georgia Aug 22, 1941. Episcopalian. Educated at Campbell College B.A. with honors 1963, Duke University 1963, University of Richmond LL.B. with honors 1966 and Yale University Law School LL.M. 1967. Member Phi Delta Phi. Admitted to practice Virginia 1966 and U.S. Supreme Court 1973. In legal practice Fredericksburg 1971. Substitute Judge, Virginia General District Court Fifteenth Judicial District 1974-87.

Author "Criminal Defense in South Carolina" South Carolina Bar CLE 1970. Instructor University of South Carolina School of Law 1967-71, University of Richmond School of Law 1968 and Mary Washington College 1980-83. Member Fifteenth Judicial Circuit Bar (President 1983), Virginia and American Bar Associations. Member Fredericksburg Industrial Development Authority 1978-81.

Mailing address: P.O. Box 96, Spotsylvania 22553-0096.

Office: 9113 Courthouse Road, Spotsylvania 22553.

Telephone: (540) 582-7229.

Fax: (540) 582-7973

LEE, Gerald Bruce *(Judge, United States District Court Eastern District of Virginia)* Appointed for life by President Bill Clinton to term beginning Oct 9, 1998. Born Washington D.C. Feb 9, 1952. Educated at American University B.A. 1973 J.D. 1976. In legal practice Fairfax County 1976-92. Judge, Virginia Circuit Court Nineteenth Judicial Circuit 1992-98.

Office: U.S. Courthouse, 401 Courthouse Square, Alexandria 22314.

Telephone: (703) 299-2117.

LEMONS, Donald W. *(Justice, Supreme Court of Virginia)* Term expires March 16, 2012. Former Judge, Virginia Circuit Court Thirteenth Judicial Circuit. Former Judge, Court of Appeals of Virginia.

Mailing address: P.O. Box 1315, Richmond 23218-1315.

Office: 100 North Ninth Street, Richmond 23219.

Telephone: (804) 225-2183.

LERNER, Louis R. *(Judge, Virginia Circuit Court Eighth Judicial Circuit)* Assumed office April 1, 2001. Term expires March 31, 2009. Former Judge and Chief Judge, Virginia Juvenile and Domestic Relations District Court Eighth Judicial District.

Mailing address: P.O. Box 40, Hampton 23669-0040.

Office: 101 King's Way Mall, Hampton 23669.

Telephone: (757) 727-6106.

LEWIS, J. Dean *(Judge, Virginia Juvenile and Domestic Relations District Court Fifteenth Judicial District)* Elected by General Assembly to term beginning 1986. Reelected 1992 and 1998. Current term expires June 30, 2004. Chief Judge July 1990 to July 1992. Born Alexandria Virginia May 6, 1948. Educated at Mary Washington College B.A. 1970 and College of

LEWIS, J. DEAN—*Continued*

William & Mary Marshall-Wythe School of Law J.D. 1973. Admitted to practice Virginia 1973. Commissioner in Chancery 1976 and Substitute Judge 1985, Virginia District Court Fifteenth Judicial District.

Member Forms Advisory Committee Virginia Supreme Court 1992-2000. Member Governor's Commission on Violent Crime 1992-93. Superintendent of Schools Juvenile Court Judges Liaison Committee Oct 1995 to 1998. Board of Directors 1998-2003 and Co-chair Standards Committee since 2000 National Court Appointed Special Advocates Association. Member Virginia Trial Lawyers Association, National Council of Juvenile and Family Court Judges (Board of Trustees July 1990 to July 1993, Chairman Alcohol and Substance Abuse Committee 1991-93, Secretary 1993-94, Treasurer 1994-96, Vice President 1996-97, President Elect 1997-98, President 1998-99), Association of Family and Conciliation Courts, Virginia State Bar, Virginia and American (Advisory Panel on Reasonable Efforts April 1995) Bar Associations. Participant White House Leadership Conference on Youth, Drug Use and Violence March 1996. Faculty Member Pre-Bench Orientation of New Juvenile and Domestic Relations Judges Office of the Executive Secretary Supreme Court of Virginia 1992-2000. Recipient Certificate of Appreciation Award from Governor's Council on Child Abuse and Neglect Prevention 1989, Prince B. Woodard Citizenship Award from Fredericksburg/Stafford/Spotsylvania Chamber of Commerce 1989, Fredericksburg District PTA/PTSA award for dedication to youth in the 16th Planning District 1990, Alcohol and Drug Abuse Distinguished Service Award from Rappahannock Area Community Services Board 1990 and Distinguished Service Award for dedication in promoting a drug-free environment from Commonwealth Alliance for Drug Rehabilitation and Education (CADRE) 1991. Named National CASA Judge of the Year by the National Court Appointed Special Advocate Association 1997. Convener 16th Planning District Youth Drug and Alcohol Task Force since 1989. Advisor Police Executive Research Forum 1994-99.

Mailing address: P.O. Box 157, Spotsylvania 22553-0157.

Office: 9113 Courthouse Road, Second Floor, Spotsylvania 22553.

Telephone: (540) 582-7131.

LEWIS, R. Larry *(Judge, Virginia General District Court Thirtieth Judicial District)* Term expires Feb 2009. Former Chief Judge.

Mailing address: P.O. Box 306, Jonesville 24263-0306.

Office: Lee County Courthouse, Main Street, Jonesville 24263.

Telephone: (276) 346-7729, 346-7735.

LEWIS, Woodrow, Jr. *(Judge, Virginia Juvenile and Domestic Relations District Court Second Judicial District)* Assumed office May 1, 1992. Elected by General Assembly 1998, current term expires April 30, 2004.

Office: 2425 Nimmo Parkway, Building 10, Virginia Beach 23456.

Telephone: (757) 427-4391.

LIGHT, William R. *(Judge, Virginia Juvenile and Domestic Relations District Court Twenty-fourth Judicial District)*

Mailing address: P.O. Box 757, Lynchburg 24505-0757.

Office: 901 Church Street, First Floor, Lynchburg 24504.

Telephone: (434) 847-1580.

LILLEY, Vincent Austin *(Judge, Virginia General District Court Twenty-third Judicial District)* Assumed office July 1, 1994. Elected by General Assembly to term beginning July 1, 2000, current term expires June 30, 2006.

Mailing address: P.O. Box 997, Salem 24153-0997.

Office: Courthouse, 305 East Main Street, Salem 24153.

Telephone: (540) 387-6168.

LINCOLN, Charles F. *(Judge, Virginia Juvenile and Domestic Relations District Court Twenty-eighth Judicial District)* Assumed office March 9, 1999. Elected by General Assembly to term beginning Feb 2000, current term expires 2006.

Office: 109 West Main Street, Marion 24354.

Telephone: (276) 782-4052.

LOGAN, William H., Jr. *(Judge, Virginia Juvenile and Domestic Relations District Court Twenty-sixth Judicial District)* Assumed office July 1, 1999. Term expires June 30, 2005.

Office: 114 West Court Street, Woodstock 22664.

Telephone: (540) 459-6130.

LOHMAN, Eugene E. *(Chief Judge, Virginia Juvenile and Domestic Relations District Court Twenty-eighth Judicial District)* Elected by General Assembly to term beginning July 1, 1982. Reelected 1988, 1994 and 2000. Current term expires June 30, 2006. Born Saltville Virginia Aug 19, 1943. Educated at Emory and Henry College B.A. 1969 and University of Virginia School of Law J.D. 1972. Recipient Merit Scholarship to Virginia-Maryland Banking School University of Virginia 1968 and Best Memo Award from University of Virginia Legal Research Group 1971. Member Phi Alpha Delta. Admitted to practice Virginia 1972, U.S. District Court Eastern District of Virginia 1972, U.S. Courts of Appeals Fourth Circuit 1977 and District of Columbia Circuit 1977 and U.S. Supreme Court 1978. Began legal practice Marion 1972. In legal practice Abingdon 1975-79 and Bristol 1979-82.

Staff Attorney 1972-74 and Executive Director 1974-75 Smyth-Bland Legal Aid Society (Board of Directors, member Probation and Parole Committee). Member Highlands Juvenile Detention Center Commission, National Council of Juvenile and Family Court Judges, Virginia Association of District Court Judges, Virginia Association of Juvenile and Domestic Relations Court Judges, Virginia Trial Lawyers Association (District Vice President 1977-78), Virginia State Bar, Bristol, Washington County, Smyth County and American Bar Associations. Completed Basic Course in Juvenile Justice National Council of Juvenile and Family Court Judges Nov 1983. Recipient Certificate of Appreciation from Emory and Henry College Internship Program 1984. E-5 U.S. Army 1961-64 (helicopter mechanic and crew chief). Apprentice cabinetmaker Contempo Associates 1964-66. Assistant cost accountant Olin Mathieson Chemical Corp. 1967-69. Board of Directors Eastern Lit-

LOHMAN, EUGENE E.—*Continued*
tle League Bristol 1976-82. Enjoys tennis, golf, music, jogging, woodworking, photography, swimming, traveling and flying.
Office: Courthouse, 187 East Main Street, Abingdon 24210.
Telephone: (276) 676-6282, 676-6283, 676-6266.

LONG, R. Bruce *(Chief Judge, Virginia General District Court Ninth Judicial District)* Assumed office June 1, 1998. Elected by General Assembly Feb 1, 1999, current term expires Jan 31, 2005. Born Newport News Virginia. Methodist. Educated at University of Richmond B.A. 1967 and College of William & Mary Marshall-Wythe School of Law J.D. 1974. Member Phi Alpha Delta. Admitted to practice Virginia 1974, U.S. District Court Eastern District of Virginia 1976 and U.S. Court of Appeals Fourth Circuit 1988. In legal practice Gloucester County 1974-98.
Member Tidewater Area Judges Association and Virginia State Bar (Disciplinary Board 1993-98). Attended Constitutional and Criminal Law Seminar American Academy of Judicial Education 1999. Listed in *Who's Who in South and Southwest* 1982 and *Who's Who in American Law* 1998. Recipient Virginia Citizens Planning Association Award 1984. USAF 1969-72. Member 1980-84 and Chairman Gloucester County Board of Supervisors. Member Rotary and Lions. Enjoys golfing and boating.
Mailing address: P.O. Box 873, Gloucester 23061-0873.
Telephone: (804) 693-4860.
Fax: (804) 693-6669

LOWE, C. Randall *(Judge, Virginia Circuit Court Twenty-eighth Judicial Circuit)* Assumed office Feb 1, 2001. Term expires Jan 31, 2009.
Mailing address: P.O. Box 289, Abingdon 24212-0289.
Office: 189 East Main Street, Abingdon 24212.
Telephone: (276) 676-6224.

LOWE, David G. *(Magistrate Judge, United States District Court Eastern District of Virginia)* Appointed by U.S. District Court judges.
Office: U.S. Courthouse, 1000 East Main Street, Richmond 23205.
Telephone: (804) 916-2280.

LOWE, Frederick B. *(Judge, Virginia Circuit Court Second Judicial Circuit)* Assumed office Feb 1, 1991. Elected by General Assembly to term beginning Feb 1, 1999, current term expires Jan 31, 2007.
Office: Building Ten, Fourth Floor, 2425 Nimmo Parkway, Virginia Beach 23456-9017.
Telephone: (757) 427-4181.

LUDWIG, Victor V. *(Judge, Virginia Juvenile and Domestic Relations District Court Twenty-fifth Judicial District)*
Mailing address: P.O. Box 1028, Waynesboro 22980-1028.
Office: 250 South Wayne Street, Waynesboro 22980.
Telephone: (540) 942-6633.

MacKAY, Kathleen H. *(Judge, Virginia Circuit Court Nineteenth Judicial Circuit)* Assumed office Feb 13, 1998. Term expires Feb 12, 2006. Former Judge, Virginia Juvenile and Domestic Relations District Court Nineteenth Judicial District.
Office: 4110 Chain Bridge Road, Fairfax 22030.
Telephone: (703) 246-4111, 691-7320.

MAHAN, Stephen C. *(Judge, Virginia Circuit Court Second Judicial Circuit)*
Office: Building Ten, Fourth Floor, 2425 Nimmo Parkway, Virginia Beach 23456-9017.
Telephone: (757) 427-4181.

MARKOW, Theodore J. *(Judge, Virginia Circuit Court Thirteenth Judicial Circuit)* Appointed by Governor Gerald L. Baliles to term beginning Feb 1, 1987. Elected by General Assembly 1995 and 2003. Current term expires Jan 2011. Former Chief Judge. Born Richmond Virginia June 9, 1939. Catholic. Educated at Medical College of Virginia B.S. in Pharmacy 1961 and University of Richmond LL.B. 1968. Member Phi Delta Phi. Admitted to practice Virginia 1968. In legal practice Richmond 1968-86.
Member Bar Association of the City of Richmond, Virginia State Bar and Virginia Bar Association.
Office: John Marshall Courts Building, 400 North Ninth Street, Richmond 23219.
Telephone: (804) 646-6515.

MARKS, Ronald Harris *(Judge, Virginia Juvenile and Domestic Relations District Court Second Judicial District)* Appointed by Governor Gerald L. Baliles March 18, 1986 to term beginning July 3, 1986. Elected by General Assembly 1992 and 1998. Current term expires June 30, 2004. Former Chief Judge. Born New York New York Jan 7, 1944. Educated at Otterbein College B.A. 1965 and Washington and Lee University J.D. 1968. Admitted to practice Virginia 1968. In legal practice Virginia Beach and Norfolk 1968-86.
Member Virginia Trial Lawyers Association, The Association of Trial Lawyers of America, Virginia State Bar and Virginia Bar Association.
Office: 2425 Nimmo Parkway, Building 10, Virginia Beach 23456.
Telephone: (757) 427-4391.

MARTIN, Everett A., Jr. *(Judge, Virginia Circuit Court Fourth Judicial Circuit)* Term expires March 2011. Born Norfolk Virginia Oct 14, 1952. Presbyterian. Educated at Washington and Lee University B.A. with honors 1974 J.D. 1977 and New York University LL.M. 1980. Law Clerk to Hon. Richard B. Kellam, U.S. District Court Eastern District of Virginia 1977-78. Admitted to practice Virginia 1977. Former Judge, Virginia Juvenile and Domestic Relations District Court Fourth Judicial District, elected by General Assembly to term beginning July 9, 1990.
Office: 100 St. Paul's Boulevard, Norfolk 23510.
Telephone: (757) 664-4380.

MASON, George, III *(Judge, Virginia General District Court Fifteenth Judicial District)*
Mailing address: P.O. Box 688, Montross 22520.
Office: 111 Polk Street, Montross 22520.
Telephone: (804) 493-0105.

MASSEY, Joseph P. *(Judge, Virginia Juvenile and Domestic Relations District Court Fourth Judicial District)* Appointed by Fourth Circuit judges to term beginning Sept 26, 1997. Elected by General Assembly Feb 7, 1998, current term expires Feb 7, 2004. Former Chief Judge. Born Norfolk Virginia Dec 10, 1950. Presbyteri-

MASSEY, JOSEPH P.—*Continued*

an. Educated at Duke University B.A. 1973 and University of Richmond J.D. with honors 1977. Law Clerk to Chief Judge Richard B. Kellam, U.S. District Court Eastern District of Virginia Aug 1977 to Aug 1978. Member McNeill Law Society. Admitted to practice Virginia 1977. In legal practice Portsmouth 1978-97.

Town Attorney Surry County 1995-97. Member Hoffman-Hanson American Inn of Court, Southeastern Virginia Juvenile Judges Association, National Council of Juvenile and Family Court Judges, Virginia State Bar and Norfolk-Portsmouth Bar Association. Member Planning Council Edmarc Hospice for Children. Enjoys boating, golfing and reading.

Office: 800 East City Hall Avenue, Norfolk 23510.
Telephone: (757) 664-7340.

MASTERS, Alfred O., Jr. *(Judge, Virginia General District Court Seventh Judicial District)*

Office: 2500 Washington Avenue, Newport News 23607-4307.
Telephone: (757) 926-3520.

MAXFIELD, Charles James *(Chief Judge, Virginia Juvenile and Domestic Relations District Court Nineteenth Judicial District)* Assumed office May 16, 1994. Elected by General Assembly to term beginning May 16, 2000, current term expires May 15, 2006.

Office: 4000 Chain Bridge Road, Fairfax 22030.
Telephone: (703) 246-3367.

MAYER, Robert G. *(Judge, United States Bankruptcy Court Eastern District of Virginia)* Appointed by U.S. Court of Appeals Fourth Circuit judges to term beginning Oct 15, 1999. Educated at Massachusetts Institute of Technology S.B. 1972 and University of Virginia J.D. 1975. Law Clerk to Supreme Court of Virginia 1975-76. Admitted to practice Virginia 1975.

Office: U.S. Courthouse, 200 South Washington Street, Alexandria 22314-5405.
Telephone: (703) 258-1280.

McCAHILL, Burke F. *(Judge, Virginia Circuit Court Twentieth Judicial Circuit)* Elected by General Assembly to term beginning July 1, 2000. Term expires June 30, 2008. Born Lynn Massachusetts Nov 3, 1942. Educated at University of Notre Dame A.B. magna cum laude 1964 and Georgetown University Law Center J.D. summa cum laude 1967. Articles Editor Georgetown Law Review 1966-67. Admitted to practice New York 1967, Virginia 1987 and District of Columbia. In legal practice 1968-96 Former Judge, Virginia Juvenile and Domestic Relations Court Twentieth Judicial District.

Past President Page County Bar Association. Lieutenant USN JAGC 1967-70. Member Virginia Board of Corrections 1994-96.

Mailing address: P.O. Box 9, Leesburg 20178.
Office: Market and King Streets, Leesburg 20178.
Telephone: (703) 777-0464.
Fax: (703) 777-0676

McCLANAHAN, Elizabeth A. *(Judge, Court of Appeals of Virginia)*

Office: 109 North Eighth Street, Richmond 23219-2321.
Telephone: (804) 371-8428.

McCUE, Richard J. *(Judge, Virginia General District Court Seventeenth Judicial District)* Assumed office July 1, 2001. Term expires June 30, 2007.

Office: 1425 North Courthouse Road, Second Floor, Suite 2400, Arlington 22201.
Telephone: (703) 228-7900.

McDONOUGH, Donald Patrick *(Judge, Virginia General District Court Nineteenth Judicial District)* Term expires June 30, 2006.

Office: 4110 Chain Bridge Road, Fairfax 22030.
Telephone: (703) 246-2153.

McGRATH, John J., Jr. *(Judge, Virginia Circuit Court Twenty-sixth Judicial Circuit)* Elected by General Assembly July 1, 1996. Reelected Feb 1, 1997, current term expires Jan 31, 2005. Born Lynn Massachusetts Nov 3, 1942. Educated at University of Notre Dame A.B. magna cum laude 1964 and Georgetown University Law Center J.D. summa cum laude 1967. Articles Editor Georgetown Law Review 1966-67. Admitted to practice New York 1967, Virginia 1987 and District of Columbia. In legal practice New York, Washington D.C. and Luray Virginia 1968-96.

Lieutenant USN JAGC 1967-70. Past President Page County Bar Association. Member Virginia Board of Corrections 1994-96.

Office: Courthouse Square, Harrisonburg 22801.
Telephone: (540) 564-3123.
E-mail address: jmcgrath@rockinghamcountyva.gov

McGRATTY, A. Lee *(Judge, Virginia General District Court Twenty-fifth Judicial District)* Assumed office Feb 1, 1997. Elected by General Assembly 2003, current term expires Jan 2009.

Office: 113 East Beverley Street, First Floor, Staunton 24401-4390.
Telephone: (540) 332-3878.

McWEENY, Michael P. *(Chief Judge, Virginia Circuit Court Nineteenth Judicial Circuit)* Elected by General Assembly to term beginning March 14, 1988. Reelected 1996, current term expires Feb 29, 2004. Born Williamsburg Virginia Feb 20, 1947. Catholic. Educated at Washington and Lee University B.A. 1969 and University of Notre Dame J.D. 1972. Admitted to practice Virginia 1972, U.S. District Court Eastern District of Virginia 1974 and U.S. Supreme Court 1975. In legal practice Fairfax 1972-85. Judge, Virginia General District Court Nineteenth Judicial District 1985-88.

Member Virginia Trial Lawyers Association, The Association of Trial Lawyers of America, Fairfax County and American Bar Associations. Captain USAR.

Office: 4110 Chain Bridge Road, Fairfax 22030.
Telephone: (703) 246-4111, 691-7320.

MELESCO, David A. *(Chief Judge, Virginia Juvenile and Domestic Relations District Court Twenty-second Judicial District)* Assumed office July 1, 1994. Elected by General Assembly to term beginning July 1, 2000, current term expires June 30, 2006.

Office: 3 Courthouse, 275 South Main Street, Rocky Mount 24151.
Telephone: (540) 483-3055.

MICHAEL, James Harry, Jr. *(Senior Judge, United States District Court Western District of Virginia)* Appointed for life by President Jimmy Carter to term beginning Oct 20, 1980. Assumed Senior status 1996. Born Charlottesville Virginia Oct 17, 1918. Episcopalian.

MICHAEL, JAMES HARRY, JR.—*Continued*

Educated at University of Virginia B.S. 1940 LL.B. 1942. Staff member University of Virginia Law Review. Member Sigma Nu Phi. Admitted to practice Virginia 1942. Began legal practice Charlottesville 1946. Associate Judge, Virginia Juvenile and Domestic Relations District Court Sixteenth Judicial District 1954-67. Special Master in patent cases, U.S. District Court Western District of Virginia 1960-70.

Lecturer University of Virginia 1947-54. Former Chairman Virginia Code Commission. Fellow American Bar Foundation since 1989. Member Council of State Governments 1968-80 (Chairman 1976), Virginia Trial Lawyers Association, American Judicature Society, Virginia State Bar, Charlottesville-Albemarle County (President 1966-67), Virginia (Vice President 1956-57) and American Bar Associations. Recipient Distinguished Service Award Virginia Trial Lawyers Association 1993. Commander USN 1942-46 and USNR since 1946. Founding member Charlottesville-Albemarle Rescue Squad 1950-80. Member 1951-62, Vice Chairman 1961 and Special Counsel 1966-80 Charlottesville Public School Board. Member Senate Virginia 1967-80. Board of Trustees Emeritus Church Schools Diocese of Virginia. Member Christ Episcopal Church (lay reader, former vestryman and Senior Warden). President Civic League of Charlottesville and Albemarle County 1964-65.

Office: 320 U.S. Courthouse, 255 West Main Street, Charlottesville 22902.

Telephone: (434) 295-3148.

MILAM, Joseph Walton, Jr. *(Judge, Virginia Circuit Court Twenty-second Judicial Circuit)* Elected by General Assembly to term beginning Feb 1, 2001. Term expires Jan 31, 2009. Born Danville Virginia June 3, 1956. Episcopalian. Educated at Emory University B.S. 1978 and University of Richmond J.D. 1983. Associate Editor University of Richmond Law Review 1982-83. Member Omicron Delta Kappa. Admitted to practice Virginia 1983 and U.S. District Court Western District of Virginia 1983. In legal practice Roanoke and Danville 1983-2001.

Member Virginia State Bar, Virginia and American Bar Associations.

Mailing address: P.O. Box 3300, Danville 24543.
Office: 401 Patton Street, Danville 24543.
Telephone: (434) 799-5171.
Fax: (434) 792-2741
E-mail address: milamjw@ci.danville.va.us

MILBOURNE, B. Bryan *(Chief Judge, Virginia Juvenile and Domestic Relations District Court Second Judicial District A)* Assumed office July 1, 1994. Elected by General Assembly to term beginning July 1, 2000, current term expires June 30, 2006.

Mailing address: P.O. Box 299, Accomac 23301-0299.
Office: 23371 Front Street, Accomac 23301-1558.
Telephone: (757) 787-0920.

MILLER, Burnett, III *(Judge, Virginia General District Court Fourteenth Judicial District)* Term expires May 31, 2006. Former Chief Judge.

Mailing address: P.O. Box 27032, Richmond 23273-7032.
Office: 4301 East Parham Road, Richmond 23228-2745.
Telephone: (804) 501-4723, 501-4727.

MILLER, Tommy E. *(Magistrate Judge, United States District Court Eastern District of Virginia)* Appointed by U.S. District Court judges.

Office: 173 U.S. Courthouse, 600 Granby Street, Norfolk 23510-1915.
Telephone: (757) 222-7007.

MILLETTE, LeRoy F., Jr. *(Judge, Virginia Circuit Court Thirty-first Judicial Circuit)* Assumed office July 1, 1993. Elected by General Assembly July 1, 2001, current term expires June 30, 2009. Former Chief Judge. Judge and Chief Judge, Virginia General District Court Thirty-first Judicial District July 1, 1990 to June 30, 1993.

Office: 9311 Lee Avenue, Manassas 20110.
Telephone: (703) 792-6015.

MILLS, Gary A. *(Judge, Virginia General District Court Seventh Judicial District)*

Office: 2500 Washington Avenue, Newport News 23607-4307.
Telephone: (757) 926-3520.

MINOR, William J., Jr. *(Judge, Virginia General District Court Nineteenth Judicial District)* Term expires July 31, 2008.

Office: 4110 Chain Bridge Road, Fairfax 22030.
Telephone: (703) 246-2153.

MITCHELL, Stephen S. *(Judge, United States Bankruptcy Court Eastern District of Virginia)* Appointed by U.S. Court of Appeals Fourth Circuit judges.

Office: 300 U.S. Courthouse, 200 South Washington Street, Alexandria 22314-5405.
Telephone: (703) 258-1240.

MOON, Norman K. *(Judge, United States District Court Western District of Virginia)* Appointed for life by President Bill Clinton to term beginning Nov 25, 1997. Born Lynchburg Virginia Nov 4, 1936. Educated at University of Virginia B.A. 1959 J.D. 1962 LL.M. Judicial 1988. Member Phi Alpha Delta. Admitted to practice Virginia 1962, U.S. District Courts Western 1962 and Eastern 1962 Districts of Virginia, U.S. Court of Appeals Fourth Circuit 1962 and U.S. Supreme Court 1966. In legal practice Lynchburg 1962-74. Judge 1974-85 and Chief Judge 1983-85, Virginia Circuit Court Twenty-fourth Judicial Circuit. Judge 1985-93 and Chief Judge 1993-97, Court of Appeals of Virginia.

Lecturer on Trial Advocacy University of Virginia School of Law 1975-98. Chairman Sixth District Committee on Professional Ethics 1972-74. Member Institute of Judicial Administration, American Judges Association, National Council of Chief Judges (Secretary 1995, Treasurer 1996, President Elect 1997), Virginia State Bar, Virginia and American Bar Associations. Attended The National Judicial College and Appellate Judges Seminar Institute of Judicial Administration.

Mailing address: P.O. Box 657, Lynchburg 24505-0657.
Telephone: (434) 845-4891.

MOONEY, John Gregory *(Judge, Virginia General District Court Twenty-fifth Judicial District)* Term expires Feb 15, 2007.

Mailing address: P.O. Box 139, Covington 24426-0139.
Office: 266 West Main Street, Covington 24426.
Telephone: (540) 965-1720.

MOORE, Becky J. *(Judge, Virginia General District Court Eighteenth Judicial District)* Assumed office Feb 1, 1998. Term expires Jan 31, 2004.
Mailing address: P.O. Box 20206, Alexandria 22320-1206.
Office: Courthouse, Second Floor, 520 King Street, Alexandria 22314.
Telephone: (703) 838-4010.

MOORE, James A. *(Judge, Virginia General District Court Fifth Judicial District)* Assumed office July 1, 2001. Term expires June 30, 2007.
Mailing address: P.O. Box 1648, Suffolk 23434-1648.
Office: 150 North Main Street, Suffolk 23434.
Telephone: (757) 923-2281.

MOORE, Michael Lee *(Judge, Virginia Circuit Court Twenty-ninth Judicial Circuit)* Elected by General Assembly to term beginning April 1, 2002. Term expires March 31, 2010. Former Judge and Chief Judge, Virginia Juvenile and Domestic Relations District Court Twenty-ninth Judicial District.
Mailing address: P.O. Box 968, Tazewell 24651-0968.
Office: Courthouse, 101 Main Street, Tazewell 24651.
Telephone: (276) 988-1222.

MOORE, William R., Jr. *(Chief Judge, Virginia Juvenile and Domestic Relations District Court Fifth Judicial District)* Term expires Feb 28, 2007.
Mailing address: P.O. Box 81, Isle of Wight 23397.
Office: Courthouse, Isle of Wight 23397.
Telephone: (757) 365-6237.

MOORE, William S., Jr. *(Judge, Virginia Juvenile and Domestic Relations District Court Third Judicial District)* Term expires Jan 31, 2004. Former Chief Judge.
Mailing address: P.O. Box 1073, Portsmouth 23705-1073.
Office: Civic Center, 603 Crawford Street, Portsmouth 23705.
Telephone: (757) 393-8851.

MOREAU, Stacey W. *(Judge, Virginia Juvenile and Domestic Relations District Court Twenty-second Judicial District)*
Mailing address: P.O. Box 270, Chatham 24531-0270.
Office: Courthouse Addition, Third Floor, Five Bank Street, Chatham 24531.
Telephone: (434) 432-7861.

MORGAN, Henry Coke, Jr. *(Judge, United States District Court Eastern District of Virginia)* Appointed for life by President George Bush to term beginning May 1, 1992. Born Norfolk Virginia Feb 8, 1935. Episcopalian. Educated at Washington and Lee University B.S. 1957 J.D. 1960 and University of Virginia LL.M. in Judicial Process 1998. Staff member Washington and Lee Law Review 1956-58. Member Sigma Nu and Phi Alpha Delta. Moot Court Team. Admitted to practice Virginia 1960. In legal practice 1960-92.

Assistant City Attorney City of Norfolk 1960-63. Member Commonwealth Law Group, Ltd. (Founder and First President), Virginia State Bar, Norfolk-Portsmouth (Chair Joint Committee on Continuing Legal Education of the Virginia State Bar and Virginia Bar Association 1978-82), Virginia Beach (President 1981), Virginia and Federal (President Tidewater Chapter 1988-89) Bar Associations. U.S. Army June 1958 to Dec 1958. Teacher City of Norfolk School Board 1959. Enjoys golf, tennis and contemporary literature.
Office: 183 U.S. Courthouse, 600 Granby Street, Norfolk 23510.
Telephone: (757) 222-7002.

MORRIS, Joan T. *(Judge, Virginia General District Court Seventh Judicial District)* Assumed office May 12, 1989. Elected by General Assembly 1990, 1996 and 2002. Current term expires Jan 31, 2008. Former Chief Judge.
Office: 2500 Washington Avenue, Newport News 23607-4307.
Telephone: (757) 926-3520.

MORRIS, S. Lee *(Chief Judge, Virginia General District Court Third Judicial District)* Term expires Jan 2009.
Mailing address: P.O. Box 129, Portsmouth 23705-0129.
Office: 711 Crawford Street, Portsmouth 23704-3809.
Telephone: (757) 393-8681, 393-8506, 393-8624.

MORRISON, John C., Jr. *(Judge, Virginia Circuit Court Fourth Judicial Circuit)* Term expires March 31, 2004. Former Chief Judge. Former Judge and Chief Judge, Virginia Juvenile and Domestic Relations District Court Fourth Judicial District.
Office: 100 St. Paul's Boulevard, Norfolk 23510.
Telephone: (757) 664-4380.

MORRISON, Johnny E. *(Judge, Virginia Circuit Court Third Judicial Circuit)* Assumed office Feb 1, 1991. Elected by General Assembly to term beginning Feb 1, 1999, current term expires Jan 31, 2007. Former Chief Judge.
Mailing address: P.O. Box 1217, Portsmouth 23705-1217.
Office: 601 Crawford Parkway, Portsmouth 23704.
Telephone: (757) 393-8671.

MORRISON, Norman deVere *(Judge, Virginia General District Court Twenty-sixth Judicial District)* Elected by General Assembly to term beginning July 1, 1985. Reelected 1991, 1997 and 2003. Current term expires June 2009. Former Chief Judge. Born Winchester Virginia Oct 17, 1947. Episcopalian. Educated at Hampden-Sydney College B.A. 1969 and University of Richmond J.D. 1973. Member Phi Alpha Delta. Admitted to practice Virginia 1973. In legal practice Berryville 1973-85.

Member Virginia Trial Lawyers Association, Association of District Court Judges of Virginia, Virginia State Bar, Clarke County (Secretary 1973-80, President 1980-84), Frederick County and Virginia Bar Associations. Completed Special Courts course The National Judicial College. Captain JAG Virginia Army National Guard 1969-90. Member Clarke County Lions Club and Grace Episcopal Church. Enjoys hiking, camping, biking, fishing and reading.
Mailing address: P.O. Box 612, Berryville 22611.
Office: 104 North Church Street, Berryville 22611.
Telephone: (540) 955-5128.

MORTON, Roger L. *(Chief Judge, Virginia General District Court Sixteenth Judicial District)* Assumed office Feb 1, 1999. Term expires Jan 31, 2005.
Office: 135 West Cameron Street, Culpeper 22701.
Telephone: (540) 727-3417.

MOSBY, J. Leyburn, Jr. *(Chief Judge, Virginia Circuit Court Twenty-fourth Judicial Circuit)* Appointed by Governor James S. Gilmore, III to term beginning April 1, 2001. Term expires March 31, 2009. Educated at Washington and Lee University B.S. 1962 J.D. 1965. Admitted to practice Virginia 1965. Substitute Judge, Virginia General District Court Twenty-fourth Judicial District 1973-2000.

Member Virginia Trial Lawyers Association, Virginia State Bar, Virginia and American Bar Associations.

Mailing address: P.O. Box 4, Lynchburg 24505-0004.
Office: 900 Court Street, Lynchburg 24504.
Telephone: (434) 847-1490.
Fax: (434) 847-1864
E-mail address: jlmosbyjr@aol.com

MURPHEY, Thomas Leroy *(Judge, Virginia General District Court Twelfth Judicial District)* Assumed office July 1, 1994. Elected by General Assembly to term beginning July 1, 2000, current term expires June 30, 2006. Former Chief Judge.

Mailing address: P.O. Box 144, Chesterfield 23832-0144.
Office: Chesterfield Courthouse, 9500 Courthouse Road, Chesterfield 23832.
Telephone: (804) 748-1231.

NELSON, S. Anderson *(Judge, Virginia Juvenile and Domestic Relations District Court Tenth Judicial District)*

Mailing address: P.O. Box 340, Boydton 23917-0340.
Office: 1294 Jefferson Street, Boydton 23917.
Telephone: (434) 738-6191.

NEWMAN, William T., Jr. *(Judge, Virginia Circuit Court Seventeenth Judicial Circuit)* Assumed office March 1, 1993. Elected by General Assembly to term beginning March 1, 2001, current term expires Feb 28, 2009.

Office: 1425 North Courthouse Road, Arlington 22201.
Telephone: (703) 228-7010.

NEY, R. Terrence *(Judge, Virginia Circuit Court Nineteenth Judicial Circuit)* Appointed by Governor James S. Gillmore, III to term beginning Jan 10, 1999. Elected by General Assembly to term beginning Feb 28, 1999. Term expires Feb 28, 2007. Born Pensacola Florida July 18, 1944. Episcopalian. Educated at Harvard College B.A. 1966 and University of Texas J.D. 1969. Member Phi Delta Phi. Admitted to practice Virginia 1970. In legal practice Fairfax, McLean and Richmond 1969-99.

Editor and Chapter Author *Appellate Practice* Virginia Federal Courts 1986, 1992 and 2001. Member Executive Council National Conference of Bar Presidents 1995-98. Fellow American College of Trial Lawyers, American Academy of Appellate Lawyers and Virginia Law Foundation. Member The American Law Institute, Fairfax, Virginia (President 1995) and American (Member House of Delegates since 1998) Bar Associations.

Office: 4110 Chain Bridge Road, Fairfax 22030.
Telephone: (703) 246-2221.
Fax: (703) 385-4432
E-mail address: RTNEY@FAIRFAXCOUNTY.GOV

NORDLUND, Lorraine *(Judge, Virginia General District Court Nineteenth Judicial District)* Term expires July 31, 2008.

Office: 4110 Chain Bridge Road, Fairfax 22030.
Telephone: (703) 246-2153.

NYE, Kenneth Wilson *(Judge, Virginia General District Court Sixth Judicial District)* Term expires June 30, 2007.

Office: 100 East Broadway, Hopewell 23860.
Telephone: (804) 541-2257.

O'BRIEN, Mary Grace *(Judge, Virginia Juvenile and Domestic Relations District Court Thirty-first Judicial District)* Assumed office Feb 1, 2001. Term expires Jan 31, 2007. Educated at LeMoyne College B.A. cum laude 1980 and Washington and Lee University School of Law J.D. 1983.

Office: 9311 Lee Avenue, Manassas 20110.
Telephone: (703) 792-6160.

O'DONNELL, Kimberly B. *(Judge, Virginia Juvenile and Domestic Relations District Court Thirteenth Judicial District)* Term expires Sept 30, 2006. Former Chief Judge.

Office: C181 Oliver Hill Courts Building, 1600 North Seventeenth Street, Richmond 23219-1214.
Telephone: (804) 646-2942.

O'FLAHERTY, Ian Michael *(Judge, Virginia General District Court Nineteenth Judicial District)* Assumed office July 1, 1990. Elected by General Assembly 1996 and 2002. Current term expires June 30, 2008.

Office: 4110 Chain Bridge Road, Fairfax 22030.
Telephone: (703) 246-2153.

O'GRADY, Liam *(Magistrate Judge, United States District Court Eastern District of Virginia)* Appointed by U.S. District Court judges to term beginning Feb 19, 2003.

Office: U.S. Courthouse, 401 Courthouse Square, Alexandria 22314.
Telephone: (703) 299-2100.

O'HARA, Robert G., Jr. *(Chief Judge, Virginia Circuit Court Sixth Judicial Circuit)* Term expires Jan 31, 2010.

Mailing address: P.O. Box 631, Emporia 23847-0631.
Office: 337 South Main Street, Emporia 23847.
Telephone: (434) 348-4215.

OLDS, Eileen Anita *(Judge, Virginia Juvenile and Domestic Relations District Court First Judicial District)* Term expires June 30, 2007. Former Chief Judge.

Office: 301 Albemarle Drive, Second Floor, Chesapeake 23322-5501.
Telephone: (757) 382-8100.

OSBORN, Leslie M. *(Judge, Virginia Circuit Court Tenth Judicial Circuit)* Elected by General Assembly to term beginning April 1, 2000. Term expires March 31, 2008. Born Farmville Virginia May 18, 1953. Baptist. Educated at University of Richmond B.A. cum laude 1975 J.D. 1978. Member Omicron Delta Kappa. Admitted to practice Virginia 1978 and U.S. Court of Appeals Fourth Circuit 1978. In legal practice Kenbridge 1978-2000.

Town Attorney Kenbridge 1989-2000. Member Lunenburg County (Chairman Family Law Section) and Vir-

OSBORN, LESLIE M.—*Continued*
ginia Bar Associations. President Lions Club and Kenbridge Chamber of Commerce.
Mailing address: P.O. Box 520, Boydton 23917.
Office: 393 Washington Street, Boydton 23917.
Telephone: (434) 738-6191.
Fax: (434) 738-0492
E-mail address: losborn@courts.state.va.us

OXENHAM, Anna Elisabeth *(Judge, Virginia Juvenile and Domestic Relations District Court Fourteenth Judicial District)* Assumed office July 1, 1994. Elected by General Assembly to term beginning July 1, 2000, current term expires June 30, 2006. Former Chief Judge.
Mailing address: P.O. Box 27032, Richmond 23273-0732.
Office: Juvenile Courts Building, 4201 East Parham Road, Richmond 23273.
Telephone: (804) 501-4688.

PADRICK, Henry Thomas, Jr. *(Judge, Virginia Circuit Court Second Judicial Circuit)* Assumed office Feb 13, 1998. Term expires Feb 12, 2006. Judge, Virginia Juvenile and Domestic Relations District Court Second Judicial District April 16, 1992 to Feb 12, 1998.
Office: Building Ten, Fourth Floor, 2425 Nimmo Parkway, Virginia Beach 23456-9017.
Telephone: (757) 427-4181.

PALMER, J. Larry *(Chief Judge, Virginia General District Court Sixth Judicial District)* Elected by General Assembly to term beginning April 1, 2000. Term expires March 31, 2006.
Office: 100 East Broadway, Hopewell 23860.
Telephone: (804) 541-2257.

PARKER, Jeffrey W. *(Judge, Virginia Circuit Court Twentieth Judicial Circuit)* Assumed office May 1, 2001. Term expires April 30, 2009.
Office: 40 Culpeper Street, Warrenton 20186-3298.
Telephone: (540) 347-8610.

PARKER, Westbrook J. *(Chief Judge, Virginia Circuit Court Fifth Judicial Circuit)* Current term expires June 30, 2010.
Mailing address: P.O. Box 190, Courtland 23837-0190.
Office: 22350 Main Street, Courtland 23837.
Telephone: (757) 653-2200.

PATRICK, Albert W., III *(Chief Judge, Virginia General District Court Eighth Judicial District)* Term expires Jan 31, 2008.
Mailing address: P.O. Box 70, Hampton 23669-0070.
Office: 236 North King Street, Hampton 23669.
Telephone: (757) 727-6260.

PAUL, John A. *(Judge, Virginia General District Court Twenty-sixth Judicial District)* Elected by General Assembly to term beginning July 1, 1973. Reelected to subsequent terms. Current term expires Jan 31, 2004. Former Chief Judge. Born Panama City Panama March 22, 1938. Episcopalian. Educated at Washington and Lee University B.A. magna cum laude 1959 LL.B. magna cum laude 1962 replaced by J.D. Member Order of the Coif and Phi Beta Kappa. Editor Washington and Lee Law Review. Admitted to practice Virginia 1962. Began legal practice Harrisonburg 1962.
Adjunct Associate Professor of Political Science James Madison University 1966-80. Member Virginia Association of District Court Judges (President 1983). Captain U.S. Army 1963-66.
Office: 53 Court Square, Room 132, Harrisonburg 22801.
Telephone: (540) 564-3130.

PAXSON, Deborah M. *(Judge, Virginia Juvenile and Domestic Relations District Court Second Judicial District)* Elected by General Assembly to term beginning April 1, 2000. Term expires March 31, 2006.
Office: 2425 Nimmo Parkway, Building 10, Virginia Beach 23456.
Telephone: (757) 427-4391.

PAYNE, H. Dudley, Jr. *(Chief Judge, Virginia Juvenile and Domestic Relations District Court Twentieth Judicial District)* Term expires April 30, 2007.
Office: 14 Main Street, Warrenton 20186.
Telephone: (540) 347-8739.

PAYNE, Robert E. *(Judge, United States District Court Eastern District of Virginia)* Appointed for life by President George Bush to term beginning May 28, 1992. Born Mount Sterling Kentucky May 7, 1941. Episcopalian. Educated at Washington and Lee University B.S. 1963 LL.B. magna cum laude 1967. Comments Editor Washington and Lee Law Review 1966-67. Member Phi Alpha Delta and Order of the Coif. Admitted to practice Virginia 1967, U.S. District Courts Eastern 1967 and Western 1967 Districts of Virginia, U.S. Court of Appeals for the Armed Forces 1967, U.S. Courts of Appeals Fourth 1973, District of Columbia 1978 and Eighth 1983 Circuits and U.S. Supreme Court 1974. In legal practice Richmond 1971-92.
Author "Limiting Instructions in Joint Criminal Trials" 22 Washington and Lee L. Rev. 285, 1965 and "Lawyer Counsel in Special Courts-Martial" 23 Washington and Lee L. Rev. 142, 1966. Member Virginia Association of Defense Attorneys (Chairman Commercial Litigation Section 1989-91), District Judges Association, Federal Judges Association, Virginia State Bar, Virginia (Chairman Commercial Litigation Committee Civil Litigation Section 1989) and American (Section of Litigation) Bar Associations. Captain JAGC U.S. Army 1967-71.
Office: U.S. Courthouse, 1000 East Main Street, Richmond 23219-3525.
Telephone: (804) 916-2260.

PEATROSS, Paul M., Jr. *(Judge, Virginia Circuit Court Sixteenth Judicial Circuit)* Term expires Jan 31, 2007. Former Chief Judge. Former Judge, Virginia General District Court Sixteenth Judicial District.
Office: Albemarle County Courthouse, 501 East Jefferson Street, Charlottesville 22902.
Telephone: (434) 972-4083, 972-4085.

PERKINSON, Charles A., Jr. *(Chief Judge, Virginia Juvenile and Domestic Relations District Court Sixth Judicial District)* Elected by General Assembly to term beginning March 1, 1970. Reelected to subsequent terms. Current term expires June 30, 2004. Born Richmond Virginia Dec 13, 1938. Methodist. Educated at Virginia Commonwealth University B.S. 1962 and University of Richmond J.D. 1965. Admitted to practice Virginia 1965. Began legal practice Lawrenceville 1965. Judge, Virginia General District Court Sixth Judicial District March 1, 1970 to June 30, 1980.
Member Virginia State Bar, Brunswick County and

PERKINSON, CHARLES A., JR.—*Continued*

Sixth Judicial District Bar Associations. Enjoys hunting and gardening.

Mailing address: P.O. Box 66, Lawrenceville 23868.

Office: Courthouse, 202 North Main Street, Lawrenceville 23868.

Telephone: (434) 848-2315.

PERROW, Mosby Garland, III *(Judge, Virginia Circuit Court Twenty-fourth Judicial Circuit)* Term expires June 30, 2005. Former Chief Judge.

Mailing address: P.O. Box 4, Lynchburg 24505-0004.

Office: 900 Court Street, Lynchburg 24504.

Telephone: (434) 847-1590.

PETERSON, David F. *(Judge, Virginia Juvenile and Domestic Relations District Court Fifteenth Judicial District)* Appointed by Governor James S. Gilmore, III June 10, 1999. Elected by General Assembly to term beginning July 1, 1999. Term expires June 30, 2005. Also serves as Presiding Judge, Rappahannock Regional Drug Treatment Court Juvenile Division. Born Des Moines Iowa Sept 25, 1944. Presbyterian. Educated at Coe College B.A. 1967 and Duke University J.D. 1973. Admitted to practice Virginia 1974 and U.S. District Court Eastern District of Virginia 1975. In legal practice Fredericksburg 1974-99. Substitute Judge, Virginia General District Court Fifteenth Judicial District 1987-99.

Member Fredericksburg (Former Chairman Bench-Bar Committee, Member Family Law Committee), Virginia and American Bar Associations. Private First Class U.S. Army 1968-69. Former Chairman Fredericksburg Parks and Recreation, Rappahannock Goodwill, Inc., Rappahannock Legal Services and Rappahannock Area Community Services Board. Board Member Rappahannock Mediation Center. Enjoys camping, hiking, canoeing and swimming.

Office: 701 Princess Anne Street, Fredericksburg 22401.

Telephone: (540) 372-1072.

Fax: (540) 372-1164

PHILLIPS, Robert B. *(Chief Judge, Virginia General District Court Second Judicial District A)* Term expires June 30, 2006. Former Chief Judge, Virginia Juvenile and Domestic Relations District Court Second Judicial District A.

Mailing address: P.O. Box 276, Accomac 23301.

Office: 23371 Front Street, Accomac 23301.

Telephone: (757) 787-0923.

POINDEXTER, Gammiel Gray *(Judge, Virginia General District Court Sixth Judicial District)* Elected by General Assembly Feb 1, 1995 to term beginning Sept 1, 1995. Reelected 2001, current term expires Aug 31, 2007. Former Chief Judge. Born Baton Rouge Louisiana Sept 22, 1944. Baptist. Educated at Indiana University A.B. 1965 and Louisiana State University J.D. 1968. Member Alpha Kappa Alpha. Admitted to practice District of Columbia 1969, Louisiana 1969, Virginia 1972 and U.S. Court of Appeals Fourth Circuit 1972. In legal practice Surry County 1976-95.

Commonwealth's Attorney 1976-95. Member American Judges Association, Old Dominion (President 1980-82) and National Bar Associations. Attended Basic Judicial Training 1996 and Leader Basic Evidence 1998 Reno Nevada. Member and County Chair Democratic Central Committee. Delegate Democratic National Convention four times. Member Link, Inc., Business of Professional Women and NAACP. Enjoys reading, sewing and studying piano.

Mailing address: P.O. Box 187, Prince George 23875-0187.

Office: 6601 Courts Drive, Prince George 23875.

Telephone: (804) 733-2781, 733-2783.

PORETZ, Barry R. *(Magistrate Judge, United States District Court Eastern District of Virginia)* Appointed by U.S. District Court judges.

Office: U.S. Courthouse, 401 Courthouse Square, Alexandria 22314-5799.

Telephone: (703) 299-2119.

POSTON, Charles Evans *(Judge, Virginia Circuit Court Fourth Judicial Circuit)* Assumed office June 1, 1994. Elected by General Assembly to term beginning June 1, 2002. Term expires May 31, 2010. Former Chief Judge. Former Judge and Chief Judge, Virginia Juvenile and Domestic Relations District Court Fourth Judicial District.

Office: 100 St. Paul's Boulevard, Norfolk 23510.

Telephone: (757) 664-4380.

POTTER, Richard B. *(Judge, Virginia Circuit Court Thirty-first Judicial Circuit)* Elected by General Assembly to term beginning June 1, 1991. Reelected 1999, current term expires May 31, 2007. Former Chief Judge. Born Washington D.C. Jan 17, 1947. Baptist. Educated at College of William & Mary A.B. 1969 J.D. 1972. Member Phi Alpha Delta. Admitted to practice Virginia 1972, U.S. District Court Eastern District of Virginia 1976 and U.S. Supreme Court 1976. In legal practice Manassas 1972-85. Judge and Chief Judge, Virginia General District Court Thirty-first Judicial District 1988 to May 31, 1991.

Instructor in Business Law and White Collar Crime Strayer Junior College of Finance and Nova University 1981-93. Member American Judicature Society, Virginia State Bar and American Bar Association (Committee on Ethics and Professional Responsibility). Recipient Lieutenant Governor Award from Kiwanis International. U.S. Army Military Intelligence 1972-78 (retired). Chapter President S.A.R.

Office: 9311 Lee Avenue, Manassas 20110.

Telephone: (703) 792-6015.

POWELL, Cleo Elaine *(Judge, Virginia Circuit Court Twelfth Judicial Circuit)* Elected by General Assembly to term beginning July 1, 2000. Term expires June 30, 2008. Born Brunswick County Virginia Jan 12, 1957. Educated at University of Virginia B.A. with honors 1979 J.D. 1982. Admitted to practice Virginia 1982. In legal practice 1982-93. Judge, Virginia General District Court Twelfth Judicial District 1993-2000.

With Office of the Attorney General 1986-89. With Virginia Power 1989-93. Member ASAP, John Tyler Policy Board, John Marshall Inn of Court, Virginia Association of Black Women Attorneys, Virginia Association of Women Judges, Bar Association of the City of Richmond, Metropolitan Richmond Women's, Chesterfield/Colonial Heights, Old Dominion, Virginia, National and American Bar Associations. Member First Baptist Church South Richmond.

Mailing address: P.O. Box 57, Chesterfield 23832.

Office: 9500 Courthouse Road, Chesterfield 23832.

Telephone: (804) 717-6369.

POWELL, CLEO ELAINE—*Continued*

Fax: (804) 751-4173
E-mail address: PowellC@co.chesterfield.va.us

POWELL, Samuel T., III *(Judge, Virginia Circuit Court Ninth Judicial Circuit)* Assumed office July 1, 1993. Elected by General Assembly to term beginning July 1, 2001, current term expires June 30, 2009. Former Chief Judge. Former Judge and Chief Judge, Virginia Juvenile and Domestic Relations District Court Ninth Judicial District.
Office: 5201 Monticello Avenue, Suite 6, Williamsburg 23188-8218.
Telephone: (757) 564-2242.

PRINCE, William T. *(Recalled Magistrate Judge, United States District Court Eastern District of Virginia)* Appointed Magistrate Judge by U.S. District Court judges to term beginning March 1, 1990. Retired Sept 30, 2000. Appointed Recalled Magistrate Judge by the Judicial Council of the Fourth Circuit. Served District of New Mexico March 25, 2000 to May 3, 2002, Western District of Pennsylvania Sept 30 2002 to Nov 15, 2002 and Eastern District of Tennessee March 2003 to April 11, 2003. Born Norfolk Virginia Oct 3, 1929. Catholic. Educated at College of William & Mary A.B. 1955 B.C.L. 1957 M.L.T. 1959. Member Phi Alpha Delta. Admitted to practice Virginia 1957, U.S. District Court Eastern District of Virginia 1959, U.S. Court of Appeals Fourth Circuit 1960 and U.S. Supreme Court 1975. In legal practice Norfolk 1959-90.
Fellow Virginia Law Foundation, American Bar Foundation and American College of Trial Lawyers. Member American Inns of Court XXVII (President 1987-89), Virginia Association of Defense Attorneys, American Judicature Society (Board of Directors 1984-88), American Counsel Association, National Association of Railroad Trial Counsel, Virginia State Bar (President 1978-79), Norfolk and Portsmouth, Virginia and American (Delegate House of Delegates 1984-90) Bar Associations. Sergeant First Class U.S. Army 1948-49 and 1950-52.
Office: 340 U.S. Courthouse, 600 Granby Street, Norfolk 23510-1915.
Telephone: (757) 222-7046.

PROSSER, John R. *(Judge, Virginia Circuit Court Twenty-sixth Judicial Circuit)* Term expires Feb 12, 2006.
Office: Five North Kent Street, Winchester 22601.
Telephone: (540) 667-5770.

PUGH, David F. *(Judge, Virginia Circuit Court Seventh Judicial Circuit)* Former Judge and Chief Judge, Virginia General District Court Seventh Judicial District, assumed office April 1, 1990.
Office: Courthouse Building, 2500 Washington Avenue, Newport News 23607-4307.
Telephone: (757) 926-8561.

PUSTILNIK, Robert A. *(Judge, Virginia General District Court Thirteenth Judicial District)* Elected by General Assembly to term beginning May 1, 2002. Term expires April 30, 2008. Serves Civil Division.
Office: 203 John Marshall Courts Building, 400 North Ninth Street, Richmond 23219.
Telephone: (804) 646-6815.

QUIGLEY, John C., Jr. *(Judge, Virginia General District Court Twenty-seventh Judicial District)* Assumed office April 1, 1994. Elected by General Assembly to term beginning 2000, current term expires March 31, 2006. Born Montgomery County Virginia July 15, 1945. Methodist. Educated at Radford University B.S. 1974 and University of Richmond T.C. Williams School of Law J.D. 1979. Member Phi Alpha Delta. Admitted to practice Virginia 1979 and U.S. Supreme Court. In legal practice Montgomery County 1979-94. E-5 USMC 1965-69.
Office: One East Main Street, Suite 201, Christiansburg 24073.
Telephone: (540) 394-2085.

RAND, Michael Miller *(Chief Judge, Virginia Juvenile and Domestic Relations District Court Tenth Judicial District)* Assumed office Feb 1, 1994. Elected by General Assembly to term beginning Feb 1, 2000, current term expires Jan 31, 2006.
Mailing address: P.O. Box 430, Halifax 24558-0430.
Office: Courthouse Building, Second Floor, Halifax 24558.
Telephone: (434) 476-3388, 476-3389.

RANEY, Julian H., Jr. *(Chief Judge, Virginia General District Court Twenty-third Judicial District)* Term expires March 14, 2008.
Office: 315 West Church Avenue S.W., Second Floor, Roanoke 24016-5007.
Telephone: (540) 853-2511.

RAWLS, Deborah Louise *(Chief Judge, Virginia Juvenile and Domestic Relations District Court Second Judicial District)* Assumed office March 1, 1991. Elected by General Assembly 1997 and 2003. Current term expires Feb 2009.
Office: Building 10, 2425 Nimmo Parkway, Virginia Beach 23456.
Telephone: (757) 427-4391.

RENNE, Merlin M. *(Judge, Virginia General District Court Ninth Judicial District)* Elected by General Assembly to term beginning July 1, 1990. Reelected to terms beginning July 1, 1996 and July 1, 2002. Current term expires June 30, 2008. Former Chief Judge. Born Vineland New Jersey Jan 10, 1945. Episcopalian. Educated at Brown University A.B. 1966 and College of William & Mary Marshall-Wythe School of Law J.D. 1975. Admitted to practice Virginia 1975. In legal practice Yorktown 1975-79.
Assistant Commonwealth's Attorney 1975-80 and Commonwealth's Attorney 1980-90 York County and Poquoson Virginia. Member Commission on the Future of Virginia's Judiciary System 1987-90. Member 1980-90 and President 1986-87 Virginia Association of Commonwealth's Attorneys. Member Tidewater Area General District Court Judges Association, Virginia State Bar (Board of Governors 1989-90, Criminal Law Section) and York-Poquoson Bar Association (Chairman 1984-86). USN 1966-69. Captain USNR 1971-90 (retired). Previously employed as teacher Kempsville High School Virginia Beach. Member 1977-90 and Chairman 1980-83 York County Democratic Committee. Legal Advisor York-Gloucester Fourth of July Celebration Committee 1979-83.
Mailing address: P.O. Box 316, Yorktown 23690-0316.
Office: 300 Ballard Street, Yorktown 23690.
Telephone: (757) 890-3450, 890-3451, 890-3461.

REVERCOMB, Horace A., III *(Judge, Virginia Circuit Court Fifteenth Judicial Circuit)* Elected by General Assembly to term beginning July 1, 1999. Term expires June 30, 2007. Former Chief Judge. Judge, Virginia General District Court Fifteenth Judicial District July 1, 1990 to June 30, 1999.
Mailing address: P.O. Box 917, Bowling Green 22427-0917.
Office: Courthouse Lane, Bowling Green 22427.
Telephone: (804) 633-4541.

RIDEOUT, Stephen W. *(Chief Judge, Virginia Juvenile and Domestic Relations District Court Eighteenth Judicial District)* Term expires Feb 28, 2007.
Mailing address: P.O. Box 21461, Alexandria 22320.
Office: 520 King Street, Alexandria 22314.
Telephone: (703) 838-4141.

ROBBINS, Edward A., Jr. *(Judge, Virginia Juvenile and Domestic Relations District Court Twelfth Judicial District)* Term expires Feb 2009.
Mailing address: P.O. Box 520, Chesterfield 23832.
Office: 7000 Lucy Corr Boulevard, Chesterfield 23832.
Telephone: (804) 748-1379.

ROBERTS, Angela Edwards *(Judge, Virginia Juvenile and Domestic Relations District Court Thirteenth Judicial District)* Assumed office March 1, 1990. Elected by General Assembly to term beginning March 1, 1996. Reelected to term beginning March 1, 2002, current term expires Feb 29, 2008. Former Chief Judge.
Office: C181 Oliver Hill Courts Bldg., 1600 North Seventeenth Street, Richmond 23219-1214.
Telephone: (804) 646-2942.

ROBERTSON, Ralph B. *(Judge, Virginia General District Court Thirteenth Judicial District)* Term expires Feb 2009. Former Chief Judge.
Office: Safety Health & Welfare Building, 501 North Ninth Street, Richmond 23219.
Telephone: (804) 646-6677.

ROBESON, James Bailey *(Chief Judge, Virginia Juvenile and Domestic Relations District Court Thirty-first Judicial District)* Assumed office July 1, 1997. Elected by General Assembly 2003, current term expires June 2009.
Office: 9311 Lee Avenue, Manassas 20110.
Telephone: (703) 792-6160.

ROCKWELL, Frederick Gore, III *(Judge, Virginia Circuit Court Twelfth Judicial Circuit)* Assumed office May 1, 2002. Term expires April 30, 2010. Judge, Virginia Juvenile and Domestic Relations District Court Twelfth Judicial District April 1, 1994 to April 30, 2002.
Mailing address: P.O. Box 57, Chesterfield 23832.
Office: 9500 Courthouse Road, Chesterfield 23832.
Telephone: (804) 748-1241.

ROSENBLATT, Alan E. *(Judge, Virginia Circuit Court Second Judicial Circuit)* Term expires March 15, 2010.
Office: Building Ten, Fourth Floor, 2425 Nimmo Parkway, Virginia Beach 23456-9017.
Telephone: (757) 427-4181.

ROUSH, Jane Marum *(Judge, Virginia Circuit Court Nineteenth Judicial Circuit)* Assumed office July 1, 1993. Elected by General Assembly to term beginning July 1, 2001, current term expires June 30, 2009.
Office: 4110 Chain Bridge Road, Fairfax 22030.
Telephone: (703) 246-4111, 691-7320.

RUPE, Gregory L. *(Judge, Virginia General District Court Thirteenth Judicial District)* Term expires Jan 2009.
Office: 905 Decatur Street, Richmond 23224.
Telephone: (804) 646-8990.

ST. JOHN, Stephen C. *(Judge, United States Bankruptcy Court Eastern District of Virginia)* Appointed by U.S. Court of Appeals Fourth Circuit judges.
Office: 473 U.S. Courthouse, 600 Granby Street, Norfolk 23510-1915.
Telephone: (757) 222-7480.

SANNER, Timothy K. *(Judge, Virginia Circuit Court Sixteenth Judicial Circuit)*
Office: 100 West Main Street, Box 37, Louisa 23093-0037.
Telephone: (540) 967-5300.

SARGENT, Pamela Meade *(Magistrate Judge, United States District Court Western District of Virginia)* Appointed by U.S. District Court judges to term beginning Dec 15, 1997. Term expires 2005. Born Norton Virginia Sept 30, 1961. Educated at Virginia Polytechnic Institute and State University B.A. magna cum laude 1983 and University of South Carolina School of Law J.D. cum laude 1988. Staff member South Carolina Law Review. Managing Editor Journal of Law and Education. Law Clerk to Hon. H. Emory Widener, Jr., U.S. Court of Appeals Fourth Circuit 1988-89. Winner J. Woodrow Lewis Moot Court Competition. Member Omicron Delta Kappa, Order of the Coif and Order of Wig and Robe. Admitted to practice Virginia 1988, U.S. District Court Western District of Virginia, U.S. Court of Appeals Fourth Circuit and U.S. Supreme Court. In legal practice Abingdon 1989-97.

Faculty Member University of Virginia Trial Advocacy Institute since 1999. Member Character and Fitness Committee Virginia Board of Bar Examiners 1995-97. Member Drafting Committee on Revision of Uniform Certification of Questions of Law Act since 1994 and Drafting Committee on Electronic Transactions Act since 1996. Commissioner National Conference of Commissioners on Uniform State Laws. Member John Belton O'Neill Chapter Inns of the Court, Virginia State Bar (Nominating Committee 1994 and 1997, Long-Range Planning Committee 1994-96 and Board of Governors 1995-97 Young Lawyers' Conference, Judicial Nominations Committee 1996-97, Law Office Management Assistance Program Committee 1996-97), Virginia (Western District Judicial Committee 1995-97) and American Bar Associations. Presenter "Public Forum on Certificate Authorities and Digital Signatures: Enhancing Global Electronic Commerce" U.S. Department of Commerce July 24, 1997, "Judicial Involvement in Local Bar Activities" Virginia State Bar Conference of Local Bar Association's Bar Leaders Institute March 16, 1998, "Can We Navigate the Ship of Professionalism and Ethics Through the Ice of Gamesmanship? A Titanic Question" Virginia State Bar Annual Meeting June 19, 1998, "The Electronics Transactions Act" The 32nd Annual Uniform Commercial Code Institute Oct 23, 1998, "Roundtable Discussion: Relationships with Other Attorneys and Obligations to the Profession and the Community" Virginia

SARGENT, PAMELA MEADE—*Continued*

State Bar Professionalism Course Aug 12, 1999, "Trying Federal Cases in the Western District of Virginia" Virginia CLE Course Sept 29, 1999 and "How Do I Prepare for the New Electronic Transactions Act?" The 33rd Annual Uniform Commercial Code Institute Nov 5, 1999. Attended Workshop for U.S. Magistrate Judges Federal Judicial Center Sept 23-25, 1998 and Nov 8-10, 1999. Faculty Member Virginia State Bar Professionalism Course since 1999. Childcare Volunteer Parents Helping Parents 1992-95. Board of Directors 1993-97, Secretary 1994-95 and Chairman 1995-97 Bristol Regional Speech and Hearing Center. Graduate Russell County Chamber of Commerce Leadership Development Program 1993. Member Virginia Board of Medical Assistance Services 1996-97, Economic Development Task Force Russell County Vision Project 1997 and Community Heights Baptist Church. Coach Lebanon High School Mock Trial Team since 1994.

Mailing address: P.O. Box 846, Abingdon 24212-0846.

Telephone: (276) 628-6021.

SCHELL, David Stanford *(Judge, Virginia Juvenile and Domestic Relations District Court Nineteenth Judicial District)* Assumed office April 5, 1991. Elected by General Assembly 1997 and 2003. Current term expires April 2009. Former Chief Judge.

Office: 4000 Chain Bridge Road, Fairfax 22030.

Telephone: (703) 246-3367.

SCOTT, John Whittier, Jr. *(Judge, Virginia Circuit Court Fifteenth Judicial Circuit)* Term expires June 30, 2004. Former Chief Judge. Former Judge, Virginia General District Court Fifteenth Judicial District.

Mailing address: P.O. Box 7326, Fredericksburg 22404-7326.

Telephone: (540) 372-1171.

Fax: (540) 372-1174

SERGENT, Birg E. *(Judge, Virginia Circuit Court Thirtieth Judicial Circuit)* Appointed by Governor James S. Gilmore, III to term beginning July 1, 1998. Elected by General Assembly to term beginning Feb 1, 1999, current term expires Jan 31, 2007. Born Lee County Virginia May 27, 1937. Methodist. Educated at Union College A.B. 1957 and University of Richmond LL.B. 1959. In legal practice Lee and Scott Counties 1959-98.

Assistant U.S. Attorney Western District of Virginia 1969-73.

Mailing address: P.O. Box 326, Jonesville 24263-0326.

Office: Main Street, Jonesville 24263.

Telephone: (276) 346-7763.

Fax: (276) 346-3440

SERKES, Joseph Michael *(Chief Judge, Virginia General District Court Twenty-fourth Judicial District)* Appointed by Twenty-fourth Circuit judges to term beginning April 1993. Elected by General Assembly 1994 and 2000. Current term expires Jan 31, 2006.

Mailing address: P.O. Box 514, Lovingston 22949.

Office: 84 Courthouse Square, Lovingston 22949.

Telephone: (434) 263-7040.

SHADRICK, Thomas S. *(Chief Judge, Virginia Circuit Court Second Judicial Circuit)* Term expires June 30, 2005.

Office: Building Ten, Fourth Floor, 2425 Nimmo Parkway, Virginia Beach 23456-9017.

Telephone: (757) 427-4181.

SHARP, William W. *(Chief Judge, Virginia Juvenile and Domestic Relations District Court Twenty-sixth Judicial District)* Appointed by Twenty-sixth Circuit judges April 1994 to term beginning July 1, 1994. Elected by General Assembly Jan 1995 and 2001. Current term expires Feb 2007. Born Baltimore Maryland Feb 4, 1953. Episcopalian. Educated at Yale College B.A. 1974 and College of William & Mary School of Law J.D. 1977. Admitted to practice Virginia 1977. In legal practice Front Royal 1977-94.

Assistant Town Attorney Front Royal 1977-85. Assistant Commonwealth's Attorney Warren County 1980-83. Treasurer Virginia Council of Juvenile and Domestic Relations Judges. Member Judicial Conference of Virginia for District Court Judges (Law Revision Committee) and Virginia Bar Association (Judicial Section). Member Front Royal Rotary Club.

Mailing address: P.O. Box 1618, Front Royal 22630.

Office: One Court Square, Front Royal 22630.

Telephone: (540) 635-4107.

Fax: (540) 635-8207

E-mail address: wsharp@courts.state.va.us

SHAW, William H., III *(Judge, Virginia Circuit Court Ninth Judicial Circuit)* Assumed office March 16, 1998. Term expires March 15, 2006. Judge, Virginia General District Court Ninth Judicial District March 1, 1994 to March 15, 1998.

Mailing address: P.O. Box 2118, Gloucester 23061-2118.

Office: 6489 Main Street, Gloucester 23061.

Telephone: (804) 693-2502.

SHERIDAN, Paul F. *(Chief Judge, Virginia Circuit Court Seventeenth Judicial Circuit)* Current term expires Jan 31, 2010.

Office: 1425 North Courthouse Road, Arlington 22201.

Telephone: (703) 228-7010.

SHERMAN, Louis A. *(Judge, Virginia General District Court Fourth Judicial District)* Elected by General Assembly to term beginning April 1, 1995. Reelected April 1, 2001, current term expires March 31, 2007. Born New York New York Sept 28, 1946. Educated at West Virginia University B.A. with honors 1968 and University of Virginia School of Law J.D. 1971. Law Clerk to Hon. Joseph H. Young, U.S. District Court District of Maryland 1971-72. Member Phi Alpha Delta and Phi Beta Kappa. Admitted to practice Virginia 1971 and District of Columbia 1972. In legal practice Richmond 1972-77 and Norfolk 1977-95.

President Tidewater Area General District Court Judges Association 1998-2001. First Vice President Association of District Court Judges of Virginia since April 2000. Member American Judges Association, Norfolk, Portsmouth, Virginia (Judicial Division) and American (Judicial Division) Bar Associations. Attended Virginia Judicial Institute 1995-2000. Participant Advanced Special Court Judges Training National Judicial College March 1996 and "No Reversals—Correct Rulings: Evidence in Action" American Academy of Judicial Educa-

SHERMAN, LOUIS A.—*Continued*

tion Aug 2000. Executive Director Tidewater Legal Aid Society 1977-82. Board of Directors Family Services of Tidewater and Ohef Sholom Temple. Member Operation Understanding Hampton Roads. Enjoys reading, traveling, walking and baseball.

Office: 811 East City Hall Avenue, Room 284, Norfolk 23510-2772.

Telephone: (757) 664-4913, 664-4914.

SHOCKLEY, A. Bonwill *(Judge, Virginia Circuit Court Second Judicial Circuit)* Elected by General Assembly to term beginning March 16, 1992. Reelected to term beginning March 16, 2000, current term expires March 15, 2008. Former Judge, Virginia Juvenile and Domestic Relations District Court Second Judicial District.

Office: Building Ten, Fourth Floor, 2425 Nimmo Parkway, Virginia Beach 23456-9017.

Telephone: (757) 427-4181.

SHULL, James Michael *(Judge, Virginia Juvenile and Domestic Relations District Court Thirtieth Judicial District)*

Office: 9 Courthouse, 104 East Jackson Street, Gate City 24251-3417.

Telephone: (276) 386-7341.

SIEVERS, Charles F. *(Judge, Virginia General District Court Thirty-first Judicial District)* Assumed office July 1, 1993. Elected by General Assembly to term beginning July 1, 1999, current term expires June 30, 2005. Former Chief Judge.

Office: 9311 Lee Avenue, Manassas 20110.

Telephone: (703) 792-6141.

SIMMONS, Mark C. *(Judge, Virginia General District Court Nineteenth Judicial District)* Elected by General Assembly to term beginning April 1, 2000. Term expires March 31, 2006.

Office: 4110 Chain Bridge Road, Fairfax 22030.

Telephone: (703) 246-2153.

SIMPSON, Ann Hunter *(Judge, Virginia Circuit Court Fifteenth Judicial Circuit)* Elected by General Assembly to term beginning July 1, 1999. Term expires June 30, 2007. Former Judge, Virginia Juvenile and Domestic Relations District Court Fifteenth Judicial District.

Mailing address: P.O. Box 895, Stafford 22555-0895.

Office: 1300 Courthouse Road, Stafford 22554.

Telephone: (540) 658-4840.

SIMPSON, Robert L., Jr. *(Chief Judge, Virginia General District Court Second Judicial District)* Term expires Feb 2009.

Office: 2425 Nimmo Parkway, Virginia Beach 23456-9057.

Telephone: (757) 427-8783.

Fax: (757) 426-5672

SKEPPSTROM, Joan C. *(Judge, Virginia Juvenile and Domestic Relations District Court Fourth Judicial District)* Term expires March 31, 2007. Former Chief Judge.

Office: 800 East City Hall Avenue, Norfolk 23510.

Telephone: (757) 664-7340.

SMILEY, Prentis, Jr. *(Judge, Virginia Circuit Court Ninth Judicial Circuit)* Elected by General Assembly to term beginning April 1, 1995. Reelected 2003, current term expires March 2011. Former Chief Judge. Born Bristol Virginia June 6, 1938. Christian. Educated at Lynchburg College B.A. 1960 and College of William & Mary Marshall-Wythe School of Law J.D. 1964. Member Phi Alpha Delta. Admitted to practice Virginia 1964. In legal practice Yorktown and Williamsburg 1964-95.

Mailing address: P.O. Box 371, Yorktown 23690-0371.

Office: 300 Ballard Street, Yorktown 23690.

Telephone: (757) 890-3350.

SMITH, Dennis J. *(Judge, Virginia Circuit Court Nineteenth Judicial Circuit)* Elected by General Assembly to term beginning June 1, 1995. Reelected 2003, current term expires May 2011. Born Brooklyn New York. Educated at Brooklyn College B.A. 1975 and American University Washington College of Law J.D. 1978. Admitted to practice District of Columbia 1978 and Virginia 1978. In legal practice Fairfax 1979-95.

Office: 4110 Chain Bridge Road, Fairfax 22030.

Telephone: (703) 246-4111, 691-7320.

SMITH, James H. *(Judge, Virginia Juvenile and Domestic Relations District Court Ninth Judicial District)* Assumed office April 1, 1994. Elected by General Assembly to term beginning 2000, current term expires Sept 30, 2006. Former Chief Judge.

Mailing address: P.O. Box 357, Yorktown 23690-0357.

Office: 300 Ballard Street, Yorktown 23690.

Telephone: (757) 890-3470.

SMITH, Rebecca Beach *(Judge, United States District Court Eastern District of Virginia)* Magistrate Judge 1985-89. Appointed Judge for life by President George Bush to term beginning 1989. Born Hopewell Virginia May 25, 1949. Educated at College of William & Mary B.A. 1971 J.D. 1979 and University of Virginia M.A. 1973. Law Clerk to Hon. J. Calvitt Clarke, Jr., U.S. District Court Eastern District of Virginia 1979-80. In legal practice Norfolk 1980-85.

Office: 358 U.S. Courthouse, 600 Granby Street, Norfolk 23510-1915.

Telephone: (757) 222-7001.

SMITH, Robert J. *(Judge, Virginia General District Court Nineteenth Judicial District)* Assumed office Feb 1, 1991. Elected by General Assembly 1997 and 2003. Current term expires Jan 2009.

Office: 4110 Chain Bridge Road, Fairfax 22030.

Telephone: (703) 246-2153.

SNUKALS, Beverly W. *(Judge, Virginia Circuit Court Thirteenth Judicial Circuit)* Elected by General Assembly to term beginning April 1, 2002. Term expires March 31, 2010. Judge, Virginia General District Court Thirteenth Judicial District Aug 1, 1998 to March 31, 2002.

Office: John Marshall Courts Building, 400 North Ninth Street, Richmond 23219.

Telephone: (804) 646-6505.

SODEN, Denis F. *(Chief Judge, Virginia Juvenile and Domestic Relations District Court Fourteenth Judicial District)* Elected by General Assembly to term be-

SODEN, DENIS F.—*Continued*

ginning July 2001. Term expires June 30, 2006. Served Twelfth Judicial District July 1, 2000 to July 1, 2001.
Mailing address: P.O. Box 27032, Richmond 23273-0732.
Office: Juvenile Courts Building, 4201 East Parham Road, Richmond 23228.
Telephone: (804) 501-4688.

SOMERVILLE, Frank W. *(Judge, Virginia Juvenile and Domestic Relations District Court Sixteenth Judicial District)* Assumed office July 1, 1994. Elected by General Assembly to term beginning July 1, 2000, current term expires June 30, 2006. Former Chief Judge.
Mailing address: P.O. Box 821, Orange 22960.
Office: 107/109 North Madison Road, Orange 22960.
Telephone: (540) 672-3150.

SOUTHALL, Valentine W., Jr. *(Judge, Virginia Juvenile and Domestic Relations District Court Eleventh Judicial District)* Term expires Sept 30, 2006. Former Chief Judge.
Mailing address: P.O. Box 24, Amelia 23002-0024.
Office: 16441 Court Street, Amelia 23002-4870.
Telephone: (804) 561-2456.

SPENCER, James Randolph *(Judge, United States District Court Eastern District of Virginia)* Appointed for life by President Ronald Reagan to term beginning Sept 24, 1986. Born Florence South Carolina March 25, 1949. Educated at Clark College A.B. magna cum laude 1971, Harvard Law School J.D. cum laude 1974 and Howard University Divinity School M.Div. 1985. Member Omega Psi Phi, Phi Beta Kappa and Alpha Kappa Mu. Admitted to practice Georgia 1974, District of Columbia and Virginia.
Staff Attorney Atlanta Legal Aid Society 1974-75. Assistant U.S. Attorney District of Columbia 1978-83 and Eastern District of Virginia 1983 to Sept 1986. Adjunct Professor of Law University of Virginia since 1987. Member Black Assistant U.S. Attorneys Association, Judge Advocate General's Association, Old Dominion Bar Association, The District of Columbia Bar, Virginia State Bar, State Bar of Georgia, Washington, National, Federal and American Bar Associations. Honor Graduate Judge Advocate General's School 1975. Prosecutor U.S. Army JAGC 1975-78. Military Judge USAR. Ordained by National Baptist Convention. Associate Pastor Third Union Baptist Church. Member Big Brothers of America, NAACP and United States Tennis Association. Author book of poems *Rage and Romance.*
Office: U.S. Courthouse, 1000 East Main Street, Richmond 23219-3525.
Telephone: (804) 916-2250.

SPENCER, Margaret Poles *(Judge, Virginia Circuit Court Thirteenth Judicial Circuit)* Assumed office Aug 1, 1998. Term expires July 31, 2006. Former Chief Judge.
Office: Manchester Courthouse, Tenth and Hull Streets, Richmond 23224-0129.
Telephone: (804) 646-8470.

STEKETEE, Peter W. *(Chief Judge, Virginia General District Court Thirty-first Judicial District)* Assumed office July 1, 1999. Term expires June 30, 2005.
Office: 9311 Lee Avenue, Manassas 20110.
Telephone: (703) 792-6141.

STEVENS, John R. *(Chief Judge, Virginia General District Court Fifteenth Judicial District)* Term expires March 31, 2006.
Mailing address: P.O. Box 180, Fredericksburg 22404-0180.
Office: 615 Princess Anne Street, Fredericksburg 22401-5914.
Telephone: (540) 372-1044.

STEVERSON, L. Neil *(Chief Judge, Virginia General District Court Fourteenth Judicial District)* Elected by General Assembly to term beginning Feb 1, 2000. Term expires Jan 31, 2006.
Mailing address: P.O. Box 27032, Richmond 23273-7032.
Office: 4301 East Parham Road, Richmond 23228-2745.
Telephone: (804) 501-4727.

STILLMAN, F. Bradford *(Magistrate Judge, United States District Court Eastern District of Virginia)* Appointed by U.S. District Court judges to term beginning Oct 1, 2000.
Office: U.S. Courthouse, 600 Granby Street, Norfolk 23510.
Telephone: (757) 222-7201.

STILWELL, M. Lee, Jr. *(Judge, Virginia General District Court Twenty-second Judicial District)* Assumed office March 1, 1998. Term expires Feb 29, 2004.
Mailing address: P.O. Box 3300, Danville 24543-3300.
Office: 401 Patton Street, Danville 24541-1215.
Telephone: (434) 799-5179.

STITT, David T. *(Judge, Virginia Circuit Court Nineteenth Judicial Circuit)* Term expires June 2011.
Office: 4110 Chain Bridge Road, Fairfax 22030.
Telephone: (703) 246-4111, 691-7320.

STONE, Charles M. *(Judge, Virginia Circuit Court Twenty-first Judicial Circuit)* Term expires June 2011. Former Judge and Chief Judge, Virginia General District Court Twenty-first Judicial District.
Mailing address: P.O. Box 1347, Martinsville 24114.
Office: 55 West Church Street, Martinsville 24112.
Telephone: (276) 656-5106.

STONE, William F., Jr. *(Judge, United States Bankruptcy Court Western District of Virginia)* Appointed by U.S. Court of Appeals Fourth Circuit judges to term beginning July 23, 1999. Term expires July 23, 2013. Born Martinsville Virginia Aug 21, 1946. Presbyterian. Educated at Washington and Lee University B.A. 1968 J.D. summa cum laude 1970. Lead Articles Editor Washington and Lee Law Review 1969-70. Law Clerk to Hon. Ted Dalton, U.S. District Court Western District of Virginia 1970-71. Member Omicron Delta Kappa and Order of the Coif. Admitted to practice Virginia 1970. In legal practice Martinsville 1971-99.
Member Virginia State Bar, Virginia and American Bar Associations.
Mailing address: P.O. Box 2389, Roanoke 24010-2389.
Office: Commonwealth of Virginia Building, 210 Church Avenue S.W., Roanoke 24010.
Telephone: (540) 857-2394.
Fax: (540) 857-2095
E-mail address: william_stone@vawb.uscourts.gov

STOUT, Walter W., III *(Judge, Virginia Circuit Court Thirteenth Judicial Circuit)* Elected by General Assembly to term beginning Aug 1, 1994. Reelected to term beginning Aug 1, 2002, current term expires July 31, 2010. Former Chief Judge. Born Plainfield New Jersey April 21, 1941. Presbyterian. Educated at College of William & Mary B.A. 1964 and University of Richmond J.D. 1967. Member Phi Delta Phi. Admitted to practice Virginia 1967 and U.S. Court of Appeals Fourth Circuit 1967. In legal practice Richmond 1967-84. Judge and Chief Judge, Virginia General District Court Thirteenth Judicial District April 11, 1984 to July 1994.

Member Richmond and Virginia Bar Associations. Captain U.S. Army 1967-69.

Office: John Marshall Courts Building, 400 North Ninth Street, Richmond 23219.

Telephone: (804) 646-6505.

STRAUSS, Charles J. *(Judge, Virginia Circuit Court Twenty-second Judicial Circuit)* Assumed office March 16, 1998. Term expires March 15, 2006.

Office: Three North Main Street, Drawer 31, Chatham 24531.

Telephone: (434) 432-7887.

STUMP, John Robert *(Chief Judge, Virginia Circuit Court Thirtieth Judicial Circuit)* Elected by General Assembly to term beginning July 1, 1981. Reelected 1989 and 1997. Current term expires June 30, 2005. Born Norton Virginia June 4, 1939. Episcopalian. Educated at Hampden-Sydney College B.A. 1961 and University of Richmond LL.B. 1964. Law Clerk to Hon. A. C. Buchanan, Supreme Court of Virginia 1964-66. Member Phi Delta Phi. Admitted to practice Virginia 1964. Began legal practice Norton 1966. Substitute Judge, Virginia Juvenile and Domestic Relations District Court and Virginia General District Court 1974-81.

Member Virginia Trial Lawyers Association, The Association of Trial Lawyers of America, Wise County (President 1973) and American Bar Associations. Enjoys golf, reading, writing and walking.

Mailing address: P.O. Box 1248, Wise 24293-1248.

Office: 206 East Main Street, Wise 24293.

Telephone: (276) 328-6111.

SWANSON, James R. *(Judge, Virginia Circuit Court Twenty-third Judicial Circuit)* Assumed office April 1, 2001. Term expires March 31, 2009.

Mailing address: P.O. Box 1126, Salem 24153-1126.

Office: 305 East Main Street, Salem 24153.

Telephone: (540) 387-6205.

SWERSKY, Alfred D. *(Judge, Virginia Circuit Court Eighteenth Judicial Circuit)* Term expires Jan 31, 2010.

Office: Courthouse, 520 King Street, Alexandria 22314.

Telephone: (703) 838-4044.

SWORD, Dean W., Jr. *(Chief Judge, Virginia Circuit Court Third Judicial Circuit)* Elected by General Assembly Jan 29, 1999 to term beginning July 1, 1999. Term expires June 30, 2007. Born Portsmouth Virginia Dec 9, 1943. Catholic. Educated at Belmont Abbey College A.B. 1966 and University of Richmond LL.B. 1967. Member Delta Theta Phi. Admitted to practice Virginia 1967, U.S. District Court District of Virginia 1967, U.S. Supreme Court 1971 and U.S. Court of Appeals Fourth Circuit 1988. In legal practice Portsmouth 1967-99. Assistant Commonwealth's Attorney Portsmouth 1970-71. Member Virginia Trial Lawyers Association, Portsmouth and Virginia Bar Associations.

Mailing address: P.O. Box 1217, Portsmouth 23705-1217.

Office: 601 Crawford Parkway, Portsmouth 23704.

Telephone: (757) 393-8635.

E-mail address: dsword@courts.state.va.us

TALEVI, Jacqueline F. Ward *(Judge, Virginia General District Court Twenty-third Judicial District)* Term expires Jan 2009.

Office: 315 West Church Avenue S.W., Second Floor, Roanoke 24016-5007.

Telephone: (540) 853-2511.

TALIAFERRO, Harry T., III *(Judge, Virginia Circuit Court Fifteenth Judicial Circuit)* Assumed office May 1, 2001. Term expires April 30, 2009.

Mailing address: P.O. Box 69, Warsaw 22572-0069.

Office: 101 Court Circle, Warsaw 22572-0956.

Telephone: (804) 333-5568.

TALLEY, William A., Jr. *(Judge, Virginia General District Court Sixteenth Judicial District)* Term expires March 31, 2008. Former Chief Judge.

Mailing address: P.O. Box 417 Palmyra 22963-0417.

Office: Courthouse, Main Street, Palmyra 22963.

Telephone: (434) 591-1980.

TALTON-HARRIS, Alfreda *(Judge, Virginia Juvenile and Domestic Relations District Court Fifth Judicial District)* Assumed office April 16, 1992. Elected by General Assembly to term beginning April 16, 1998, current term expires April 15, 2004.

Mailing address: P.O. Box 1648, Suffolk 23434.

Office: 150 North Main Street, Second Floor, Suffolk 23434.

Telephone: (757) 923-2300.

TATE, Joseph Scott *(Chief Judge, Virginia General District Court Twenty-eighth Judicial District)* Assumed office Sept 1, 1992. Elected by General Assembly to term beginning Sept 1, 1998, current term expires Aug 31, 2004.

Office: 109 West Main Street, Marion 24354.

Telephone: (276) 782-4047.

TAYLOR, Joi Jeter *(Judge, Virginia General District Court Thirteenth Judicial District)* Assumed office April 16, 1998. Term expires April 15, 2004.

Office: 203 John Marshall Courts Building, 400 North Ninth Street, Richmond 23219.

Telephone: (804) 646-6461.

TAYLOR, Lydia Calvert *(Judge, Virginia Circuit Court Fourth Judicial Circuit)* Elected by General Assembly to term beginning April 1, 1988. Reelected 1996, current term expires March 31, 2004. Former Chief Judge. Born Norfolk Virginia Jan 10, 1940. Roman Catholic. Educated at Sweet Briar College B.A. 1962, University of Chile, Santiago 1968-69, Old Dominion University M.A. with highest honors 1973 and Marshall-Wythe School of Law College of William & Mary J.D. with highest honors 1980. Fulbright Scholar 1968-69. Recipient West Publishing Company Award for Outstanding Academic Achievement 1977-78. Davis Y. Pascal Fellow 1979-80. Research Editor William & Mary Law Review. Law Clerk to Hon. Walter E. Hoffman, U.S. District Court Eastern District of Virginia

TAYLOR, LYDIA CALVERT—*Continued*

1980-81. Member Order of the Coif. Admitted to practice Virginia 1980, U.S. District Court Eastern District of Virginia 1980, U.S. Court of Appeals Fourth Circuit 1980 and U.S. Supreme Court 1983. Judge, Virginia General District Court Fourth Judicial District July 1, 1985 to March 31, 1988.

Assistant City Attorney Norfolk 1981-85. Author "*United States v. Chicago:* Standard of Proof of Employment Discrimination by Governmental Employers Under Title VII" William and Mary L. Rev. Spring 1979. Fulbright Visiting Professor of American Law Chile Summer 1989. Member Virginia State Bar, Norfolk-Portsmouth, Virginia and American Bar Associations. Attended U.S. Law Week's Constitutional Law Seminar Bureau of National Affairs, Washington D.C. Sept 1984, 1987 and 1989-90; Press and Court Relations National Center for State Courts Williamsburg Virginia Spring 1985; Trial Advocacy course The Association of Trial Lawyers of America Richmond Virginia Fall 1985; and The National Judicial College Reno Nevada Spring 1986. Faculty Advisor General Jurisdiction Course Summer 1990 and Faculty "Juries" General Jurisdiction Course April 1991 The National Judicial College. Recipient Outstanding Service by an Assistant City Attorney Award from National Institute of Municipal Law Officers 1984. Reporter for Washington Post 1962-65. Freelance translator Spanish/English 1971-72. Textbook editor University of Texas 1973-77. Board of Directors Norfolk Forum 1980-87, Cultural Alliance of Greater Hampton Roads since 1983, Junior League of Norfolk-Virginia Beach 1984-85, Virginia Opera since 1989, Worker Connection 1990-95, Kids Vote-America and National Conference of Christians and Jews since 1995. Founding Board Child Abuse Center of Hampton Roads since 1993. Enjoys travel and reading.

Office: 100 St. Paul's Boulevard, Norfolk 23510.
Telephone: (757) 664-4380.

TAYLOR, Ramona D. *(Judge, Virginia Juvenile and Domestic Relations District Court Second Judicial District)* Elected by General Assembly to term beginning April 16, 2000. Term expires April 15, 2006.

Office: 2425 Nimmo Parkway, Building 10, Virginia Beach 23456.
Telephone: (757) 427-4391.

TAYLOR, Richard D., Jr. *(Judge, Virginia Circuit Court Thirteenth Judicial Circuit)* Appointed by Governor Mark R. Warner to term beginning July 2002. Elected by General Assembly Jan 2003, current term expires 2011. Born Norfolk Virginia Dec 21, 1957. Baptist. Educated at Georgetown University B.A. 1979 J.D. 1982. Judge and Chief Judge, Virginia Juvenile and Domestic Relations District Court Thirteenth Judicial District 1993-2002.

Office: 303F John Marshall Courts Building, 400 North Ninth Street, Richmond 23219.
Telephone: (804) 646-6516.
Fax: (804) 646-0316
E-mail address: taylorrd@ci.richmond.va.us

TAYLOR, Wilford, Jr. *(Judge, Virginia Circuit Court Eighth Judicial Circuit)* Term expires June 2011. Former Chief Judge. Former Judge and Chief Judge, Virginia General District Court Eighth Judicial District.

Mailing address: P.O. Box 40, Hampton 23669-0040.
Office: 101 King's Way Mall, Hampton 23669.
Telephone: (757) 727-6106.

TENCH, Charles P. *(Judge, Virginia Circuit Court Seventh Judicial Circuit)* Former Judge, Virginia Juvenile and Domestic Relations District Court Seventh Judicial District, assumed office July 1, 1998.

Office: Courthouse Building, 2500 Washington Avenue, Newport News 23607-4307.
Telephone: (757) 926-8561.

THACHER, Jonathan Cooper *(Judge, Virginia Circuit Court Nineteenth Judicial Circuit)* Assumed office May 1, 1998. Term expires April 30, 2006. Born Boston Massachusetts March 23, 1947. Educated at University of Miami B.A. 1970 and George Mason University School of Law J.D. with honors 1980. Admitted to practice Virginia 1970, U.S. District Court Eastern District of Virginia 1970, U.S. Court of Appeals Fourth Circuit 1970 and U.S. Supreme Court 1975. In legal practice Fairfax 1970-94. Judge, Virginia General District Court Nineteenth Judicial District March 1994 to April 30, 1998.

Adjunct Faculty George Mason University School of Law since 1990. Captain U.S. Army 1970-75. Head Coach freshman boys basketball Paul VI Catholic High School. Enjoys competitive water skiing and coaching high school basketball.

Office: 4110 Chain Bridge Road, Fairfax 22030.
Telephone: (703) 246-4111, 691-7320.

THOMAS, Norman A. *(Judge, Virginia General District Court Fourth Judicial District)* Assumed office April 1, 2001. Term expires March 31, 2007. Born Norfolk Virginia Sept 18, 1956. Educated at University of Virginia B.A. with distinction 1978 and College of William & Mary Marshall-Wythe School of Law J.D. 1981. Admitted to practice Virginia 1981.

Member American Judges Association, Norfolk and Portsmouth and American Bar Associations.

Office: 811 East City Hall Avenue, Room 284, Norfolk 23510-2772.
Telephone: (757) 664-4915, 664-4916.

TICE, Douglas O., Jr. *(Chief Judge, United States Bankruptcy Court Eastern District of Virginia)* Appointed by U.S. Court of Appeals Fourth Circuit judges to term beginning Sept 3, 1987. Reappointed 2001, current term expires Sept 3, 2015. Chief Judge since Feb 10, 1999. Born Lexington North Carolina May 2, 1933. Educated at University of North Carolina at Chapel Hill B.S. 1955 J.D. 1957. Board of Student Editors North Carolina Law Review 1956-57. Admitted to practice North Carolina 1957, U.S. Tax Court 1961, Virginia 1970, U.S. Court of Appeals Fourth Circuit 1970 and U.S. District Court Eastern District of Virginia 1976. In legal practice Raleigh North Carolina 1959-61 and Richmond Virginia 1975-87.

Attorney Office of Regional Counsel Internal Revenue Service 1961-70. Corporate Counsel Carlton Industries, Inc. 1970-75. Author "Bread or Blood, The Richmond Bread Riot" *Civil War Times Illustrated* March 1973. Co-author *Monument & Boulevard, Richmond's Grand Avenues* 1996. Bankruptcy Editorial Consultant *The Accountant's Business Manual* American Institute of Certified Public Accountants 1987. Instructor Legal Assistants Program J. Sargeant Reynolds Community College 1976-85 and University of Richmond 1977. Executive Secretary North Carolina Judicial Council 1958-59. Member

TICE, DOUGLAS O., JR.—*Continued*

National Conference of Bankruptcy Judges, American Bankruptcy Institute, Richmond and Virginia Bar Associations. Captain USAR 1959-67. Executive Council The Richmond Forum 1979-86. Enjoys hiking and American history.
Office: 310 U.S. Courthouse Annex, 1100 East Main Street, Richmond 23219-3515.
Telephone: (804) 916-2460.

TIDEY, George F. *(Judge, Virginia Circuit Court Fourteenth Judicial Circuit)* Term expires April 30, 2004. Former Chief Judge. Born Mount Carmel Pennsylvania Jan 11, 1933. Methodist. Educated at University of Richmond B.S. 1955 LL.B. 1962. Admitted to practice Virginia 1962. In legal practice Richmond Oct 1, 1962 to March 31, 1985. Former Judge, Virginia General District Court Fourteenth Judicial District, elected to term beginning April 1, 1985. First Lieutenant USAF 1956-59.
Mailing address: P.O. Box 27032, Richmond 23273-7032.
Office: 4301 East Parham Road, Richmond 23273.
Telephone: (804) 501-5252.

TOMPKINS, James L., III *(Judge, Virginia Juvenile and Domestic Relations District Court Twenty-seventh Judicial District)* Term expires June 30, 2005. Former Chief Judge.
Mailing address: P.O. Box 698, Hillsville 24343-0698.
Office: Government Center, 605-13 Pine Street, Hillsville 24343-1463.
Telephone: (276) 728-7751, 728-7741.

TOWER, Winship C. *(Judge, Virginia Juvenile and Domestic Relations District Court Second Judicial District)* Assumed office July 1, 2000. Term expires June 30, 2006.
Office: 2425 Nimmo Parkway, Building 10, Virginia Beach 23456.
Telephone: (757) 427-4391.

TRAVERS, Wenda Kavanagh *(Judge, Virginia General District Court Thirty-first Judicial District)* Assumed office Oct 1, 1990. Elected by General Assembly to term beginning Oct 1, 1996. Reelected 2002, current term expires Sept 2008. Former Chief Judge.
Office: 9311 Lee Avenue, Manassas 20110.
Telephone: (703) 792-6141.

TRIBLE, Peter L. *(Judge, Virginia General District Court Fifteenth Judicial District)* Elected by General Assembly to term beginning July 1, 1999. Term expires July 1, 2005. Born Hagerstown Maryland Oct 9, 1942. Educated at Virginia Military Institute B.A. 1965 and University of South Carolina J.D. 1971. Admitted to practice Virginia 1973, U.S. District Court Eastern District of Virginia 1976 and U.S. Court of Appeals Fourth Circuit 1980. In legal practice Richmond 1987-99.
Assistant Attorney General Virginia 1973-75. City Attorney Colonial Heights 1975-78. County Attorney Hanover County 1978-87. Major USAR 1966-81.
Mailing address: P.O. Box 511, Bowling Green 22427-0511.
Office: 108 Courthouse Lane, Bowling Green 22427.
Telephone: (804) 633-5720.

TRIPP, Alfred M. *(Judge, Virginia General District Court Fourth Judicial District)*
Office: 811 East City Hall Avenue, Room 284, Norfolk 23510-2772.
Telephone: (757) 664-4911, 664-4912.

TROMPETER, Philip *(Judge, Virginia Juvenile and Domestic Relations District Court Twenty-third Judicial District)* Term expires April 2009. Former Chief Judge.
Mailing address: P.O. Box 986, Roanoke 24005-0986.
Office: 315 West Church Avenue S.W., First Floor, Roanoke 24016.
Telephone: (540) 853-2389.

TUCKER, Paul A. *(Judge, Virginia Juvenile and Domestic Relations District Court Twenty-fifth Judicial District)* Assumed office July 1, 1999. Term expires June 30, 2005.
Mailing address: P.O. Box 1336, Staunton 24402-1336.
Office: Six East Johnson Street, First Floor, Staunton 24401-4303.
Telephone: (540) 245-5306.

TURK, James Clinton *(Senior Judge, United States District Court Western District of Virginia)* Appointed for life by President Richard M. Nixon Aug 17, 1972 to term beginning Oct 28, 1972. Chief Judge Oct 28, 1973 to May 1994. Assumed Senior status Nov 1, 2002, serves by assignment. Born Roanoke County Virginia May 3, 1923. Educated at Roanoke College A.B. cum laude 1949 and Washington and Lee University LL.B. summa cum laude 1952 replaced by J.D. 1972. Member Phi Beta Kappa, Omicron Delta Kappa, Pi Kappa Phi, Phi Alpha Delta and Order of the Coif. Admitted to practice Virginia 1951. In legal practice 1952-72.
State Senator General Assembly 1959-72 (Minority Leader 1965-72). Fellow American College of Trial Lawyers. Member American College of Trial Lawyers, American Judicature Society, Virginia State Bar, Virginia and American Bar Associations. U.S. Army 1943-46. Member First Baptist Church of Redford.
Office: Federal Building, 246 Franklin Road S.W., Roanoke 24011-2214.
Telephone: (540) 857-5122.

TURK, Robert M. D. *(Chief Judge, Virginia Circuit Court Twenty-seventh Judicial Circuit)* Assumed office July 1, 2000. Term expires June 30, 2008.
Mailing address: P.O. Box 6309, Christiansburg 24068-6309.
Office: One East Main Street, Suite B-5, Christiansburg 24073-3036.
Telephone: (540) 382-5760.

TURNER, Edward M., III *(Judge, Virginia General District Court Twenty-seventh Judicial District)* Assumed office March 1, 1992. Elected by General Assembly to term beginning March 1, 1998, current term expires Feb 28, 2004.
Mailing address: P.O. Box 698, Hillsville 24343-0698.
Office: Government Center, 605-13 Pine Street, Hillsville 24343-1463.
Telephone: (276) 728-7751, 728-7741.

TYLER, Glen Allen *(Judge, Virginia Circuit Court Second Judicial Circuit)* Assumed office April 1, 1992.

TYLER, GLEN ALLEN—*Continued*

Elected by General Assembly to term beginning April 1, 2000, current term expires March 31, 2008.
Mailing address: P.O. Box 126, Accomac 23301-0126.
Office: Courthouse Road, Accomac 23301.
Telephone: (757) 787-5776.

UPDIKE, James W., Jr. *(Judge, Virginia Circuit Court Twenty-fourth Judicial Circuit)* Assumed office April 1, 1998. Term expires March 31, 2006. Former Chief Judge. Former Judge, Virginia General District Court Twenty-fourth Judicial District.
Office: 123 East Main Street, Suite 301, Bedford 24523.
Telephone: (540) 586-7632.

VALENTINE, Michael J. *(Judge, Virginia Juvenile and Domestic Relations District Court Nineteenth Judicial District)* Term expires June 30, 2004. Former Chief Judge.
Office: 4000 Chain Bridge Road, Fairfax 22030.
Telephone: (703) 246-3367.

VANOVER, Henry A. *(Judge, Virginia Circuit Court Twenty-ninth Judicial Circuit)* Elected by General Assembly to term beginning April 1, 2002. Term expires March 31, 2010.
Office: Main Street, Box 190, Clintwood 24228-0190.
Telephone: (276) 926-1616.

VAROUTSOS, George D. *(Chief Judge, Virginia Juvenile and Domestic Relations District Court Seventeenth Judicial District)* Substitute Judge 1986-98. Elected Judge by General Assembly to term beginning March 16, 1998. Term expires March 15, 2004. Chief Judge since March 1998. Born Jan 17, 1949. Educated at University of Richmond B.A. 1970 J.D. 1973. Law Clerk to U.S. District Court Eastern District of Virginia 1973-74. Admitted to practice Virginia 1973, District of Columbia 1976, U.S. District Courts Eastern 1973 and Western 1990 Districts of Virginia, U.S. Court of Appeals Fourth Circuit 1974 and U.S. Supreme Court 1982. In legal practice Arlington Virginia 1974-98.
Member Virginia Medical Malpractice Review Panel 1985-98. Former Member George Mason Inn of Court. Director and Trustee Arlington Bar Foundation since 1991. Founding Member The Plaintiff's Bar. Member Arlington Criminal Justice Coordinating Council, Judicial Conference of the Fourth Circuit, Virginia Trial Lawyers Association, The Association of Trial Lawyers of America, National Council of Juvenile and Family Court Judges, Virginia State Bar (Seminar Committee 1989-93, Member 1989-96 and Vice Chair 1994-96 Personal Insurance Committee, Council Member since 1989), Alexandria and Arlington County (Board of Directors 1980-87, President 1988-89, Chair Bar Facilities 1990-94, Judicial Selection Committee) Bar Associations. Chair Abuse and Neglect Seminar CLE Committee Oct 1996. Moderator Bench and Bar Dialogue Courts Committee. Recipient President's Award from Arlington County Bar Association 1992 and Alumni Achievement Award from University of Richmond 1996. Parish Council St. Katherine's Church 1978-86. President University of Richmond Law School Association 1994-96. Director National Marrow Foundation since 1994 and Arlington County Courthouse Law Library since 1994. Chair Ad Hoc Baseball Stadium Advisory Committee 1996-98. Project Director Training for Juvenile Drivers Licensing Ceremony since 1997.
Mailing address: P.O. Box 925, Arlington 22216.
Office: 4100 Arlington County Justice Center, 1425 North Courthouse Road, Arlington 22201.
Telephone: (703) 228-4495.

VAUGHN, Thomas L. *(Judge, Virginia General District Court Twelfth Judicial District)* Assumed office July 1, 2000. Term expires June 30, 2006.
Mailing address: P.O. Box 144, Chesterfield 23832-0144.
Office: Chesterfield Courthouse, 9500 Courthouse Road, Chesterfield 23832-6684.
Telephone: (804) 748-1231.

VIAR, Robert C., Jr. *(Chief Judge, Virginia Juvenile and Domestic Relations District Court Twenty-seventh Judicial District)* Term expires April 2009.
Office: 305 Courthouse, One East Main Street, Christiansburg 24073.
Telephone: (540) 382-6999.

VIEREGG, Arthur B., Jr. *(Judge, Virginia Circuit Court Nineteenth Judicial Circuit)* Assumed office March 1, 1993. Elected by General Assembly to term beginning March 1, 2001, current term expires Feb 28, 2009. Born St. Louis Missouri Jan 31, 1943. Educated at Duke University A.B. 1964 J.D. 1967. Admitted to practice Virginia 1970.
Office: 4110 Chain Bridge Road, Fairfax 22030.
Telephone: (703) 246-4111, 691-7320.

WALLACE, Philip Arthur *(Judge, Virginia Juvenile and Domestic Relations District Court Twenty-fourth Judicial District)* Assumed office July 1, 1991. Elected by General Assembly 1997 and 2003. Current term expires June 2009. Former Chief Judge.
Office: 123 East Main Street, Suite 101, Bedford 24523.
Telephone: (540) 586-7641.

WARREN, Charles H. *(Judge, Virginia General District Court Tenth Judicial District)* Assumed office April 16, 1998. Term expires April 15, 2004.
Mailing address: P.O. Box 306, Boydton 23917-0306.
Office: Courthouse, Jefferson Street, Boydton 23917.
Telephone: (434) 738-6191.

WARREN, Junius P. *(Judge, Virginia Juvenile and Domestic Relations District Court Twenty-first Judicial District)* Term expires Jan 31, 2008. Former Chief Judge.
Mailing address: P.O. Drawer 751, Martinsville 24114.
Office: Municipal Building, 55 West Church Street, Martinsville 24112-6209.
Telephone: (276) 656-5168.

WARREN, Thomas V. *(Chief Judge, Virginia Circuit Court Eleventh Judicial Circuit)* Term expires Jan 31, 2010.
Mailing address: P.O. Box 25, Nottoway 23955-0025.
Telephone: (434) 645-9043.

WECKSTEIN, Clifford R. *(Judge, Virginia Circuit Court Twenty-third Judicial Circuit)* Elected by General Assembly to term beginning Feb 24, 1987. Reelected 1995 and 2003. Current term expires Jan 2011. Former Chief Judge. Born Cincinnati Ohio March 30, 1949. Jewish. Educated at University of Virginia B.A. 1971

WECKSTEIN, CLIFFORD R.—*Continued*

and Marshall-Wythe School of Law College of William & Mary J.D. 1974. Editor *Amicus Curiae* 1973-74. Member Omicron Delta Kappa and Phi Alpha Delta. Admitted to practice Virginia 1974, U.S. District Courts Eastern 1975 and Western 1975 Districts of Virginia, U.S. Court of Appeals Fourth Circuit 1976 and U.S. Supreme Court 1977. In legal practice Roanoke 1974-87. Substitute Judge, Virginia General District Court Twenty-third Judicial District and Virginia Juvenile and Domestic Relations District Court Twenty-third Judicial District 1980-87.

Member Virginia Women Attorneys Association, American Judges Association, American Judicature Society, Virginia Trial Lawyers Association, The Association of Trial Lawyers of America, Virginia State Bar (Chairman Sixth District Ethics Committee 1984-86, Board of Governors Criminal Law Section 1984-87 and Family Law Section 1988-1992), Roanoke (Director 1982-84, Chairman Courts, Judicial Endorsements and By-Laws Committee 1983-85 and Public Service Committee 1986-87), Virginia and American Bar Associations. Lecturer and outline author "Defense of Drunk Driving Cases" 1982, "Federal Court Civil Practice" 1984 and "Trying the Equitable Distribution Case" 1985 Virginia CLE Committee. Named Boss of the Year by Roanoke Valley Legal Secretaries Association 1983. Intern reporter 1969-70 and copy editor 1971 *Roanoke World News*. Board member 1980-87, Vice President 1980-84 and President 1984-87 Legal Aid Society of the Roanoke Valley.

Mailing address: P.O. Box 2610, Roanoke 24010-2610.

Office: 315 West Church Avenue, Roanoke 24016-5029.

Telephone: (540) 853-6702.

WELLONS, William Lindley *(Chief Judge, Virginia Circuit Court Tenth Judicial Circuit)* Assumed office July 1, 1993. Elected by General Assembly to term beginning July 1, 2001, current term expires June 30, 2009. Born Port Maria Jamaica Nov 7, 1942. Baptist. Educated at College of William & Mary B.A. 1965 J.D. 1968. Admitted to practice Virginia 1968. Began legal practice Courtland 1969. In legal practice Victoria 1971-83. Judge, Virginia Juvenile and Domestic Relations District Court Tenth Judicial District April 9, 1983 to June 30, 1993.

Member American Judicature Society, Virginia State Bar (Council member 1978-83), Lunenburg County, Tenth Judicial Circuit, Virginia and American Bar Associations.

Office: Courthouse, Lunenburg 23952.

Telephone: (434) 696-2230.

WEST, Patricia L. *(Judge, Virginia Circuit Court Second Judicial Circuit)* Assumed office July 1, 2000. Term expires June 30, 2008. Judge, Virginia Juvenile and Domestic Relations District Court Second Judicial District Feb 1, 1998 to June 30, 2000.

Office: Building Ten, Fourth Floor, 2425 Nimmo Parkway, Virginia Beach 23456-9017.

Telephone: (757) 427-4181.

WEST, Randolph T. *(Judge, Virginia Circuit Court Seventh Judicial Circuit)* Elected by General Assembly to term beginning March 1, 1990. Reelected 1998, current term expires Feb 28, 2006. Former Chief Judge. Born Nottoway County Virginia Sept 7, 1934. Protestant. Educated at University of Richmond B.A. in Political Science 1961 and T. C. Williams School of Law University of Richmond J.D. 1964. Admitted to practice Virginia 1964. Began legal practice Newport News 1964. Judge and Chief Judge, Virginia General District Court Seventh Judicial District, Nov 1, 1973 to Feb 28, 1990.

Member Virginia State Bar and Newport News Bar Association. Sergeant U.S. Army 1953-55.

Office: Courthouse Building, 2500 Washington Avenue, Newport News 23607-4307.

Telephone: (757) 926-8561.

WETSEL, John E., Jr. *(Chief Judge, Virginia Circuit Court Twenty-sixth Judicial Circuit)* Assumed office July 1, 1991. Elected by General Assembly to term beginning July 1, 1999, current term expires June 30, 2007.

Office: Five North Kent Street, Winchester 22601.

Telephone: (540) 667-5770.

WHISENANT, Herman A., Jr. *(Judge, Virginia Circuit Court Thirty-first Judicial Circuit)* Elected by General Assembly to term beginning Aug 1, 1980. Reelected 1988 and 1996. Current term expires July 31, 2004. Former Chief Judge. Born Bessemer Alabama July 1, 1941. Administrative Board Grace Methodist Church. Educated at Virginia Military Institute B.A. 1963 and T. C. Williams School of Law University of Richmond LL.B. 1966. Admitted to practice Virginia 1966. In legal practice Manassas 1970-73. Judge, Virginia Juvenile and Domestic Relations District Court Thirty-first Judicial District 1973-80.

Instructor University of Maryland Far East Division 1969. Member Virginia Trial Lawyers Association, Virginia District Court Judges Association, National Council of Juvenile and Family Court Judges, American Judges Association, The Association of Trial Lawyers of America, Virginia State Bar, Prince William County and American Bar Associations. Captain USAF 1963-73 (Judge Advocate 1966-70). Member Manassas Volunteer Fire Company, Kiwanis Club and Masons.

Office: 9311 Lee Avenue, Manassas 20110.

Telephone: (703) 792-6015.

WHITACRE, David Shaw *(Judge, Virginia General District Court Twenty-sixth Judicial District)* Assumed office April 1, 1991. Elected by General Assembly 1997 and 2003. Current term expires March 2009. Former Chief Judge.

Office: Judicial Center, Five North Kent Street, Winchester 22601-5037.

Telephone: (540) 722-7208.

WHITE, A. Ellen *(Judge, Virginia Juvenile and Domestic Relations District Court Twenty-fourth Judicial District)* Assumed office July 1, 1994. Elected by General Assembly to term beginning Feb 1, 2001, current term expires Jan 31, 2007.

Mailing address: P.O. Box 220, Rustburg 24588-0220.

Office: 732 Village Highway, Second Floor, Rustburg 24588.

Telephone: (434) 332-9555.

WHITEHURST, Colon H. *(Chief Judge, Virginia General District Court First Judicial District)* Assumed office Aug 1, 1990. Elected by General Assembly to

WHITEHURST, COLON H.—*Continued*
term beginning Aug 1, 1996, current term expires July 31, 2002.
Office: Civic Center, 307 Albemarle Drive, Chesapeake 23322-5571.
Telephone: (757) 382-3111, 382-3150.

WHITLOCK, Susan L. *(Judge, Virginia Juvenile and Domestic Relations District Court Sixteenth Judicial District)* Assumed office July 1, 1999. Term expires June 30, 2005. Former Chief Judge.
Mailing address: P.O. Box 452, Louisa 23093-0452.
Office: Cunningham Building, 314 West Main Street, Louisa 23093-9451.
Telephone: (540) 967-5330.

WHITLOW, Morton V. *(Judge, Virginia General District Court Third Judicial District)* Assumed office Feb 1, 1998. Term expires Jan 31, 2004. Former Chief Judge.
Mailing address: P.O. Box 129, Portsmouth 23705-0129.
Office: 711 Crawford Street, Portsmouth 23704-3809.
Telephone: (757) 393-8681, 393-8506, 393-8624.

WIGGINS, Esther L. *(Judge, Virginia Juvenile and Domestic Relations District Court Seventeenth Judicial District)* Assumed office Feb 1, 1999. Term expires Jan 31, 2005.
Mailing address: P.O. Box 925, Arlington 22216.
Office: 4100 Arlington County Justice Center, 1425 North Courthouse Road, Arlington 22201-2622.
Telephone: (703) 228-4495.

WILCOX, Bruce A. *(Judge, Virginia General District Court Fourth Judicial District)*
Office: 811 East City Hall Avenue, Room 284, Norfolk 23510-2772.
Telephone: (757) 664-4911, 664-4912.

WILEY, Dale M. *(Judge, Virginia Juvenile and Domestic Relations District Court Twenty-second Judicial District)* Assumed office July 1, 1998. Term expires June 30, 2004.
Mailing address: P.O. Box 3300, Danville 24543-3300.
Office: 401 Patton Street, Danville 24541-1215.
Telephone: (434) 799-5173, 799-5174.

WILL, Sharon B. *(Judge, Virginia Juvenile and Domestic Relations District Court Fourteenth Judicial District)* Assumed office April 16, 1998. Term expires April 15, 2004. Former Chief Judge.
Mailing address: P.O. Box 27032, Richmond 23273-0732.
Office: Juvenile Courts Building, 4201 East Parham Road, Richmond 23228.
Telephone: (804) 501-4688.

WILLIAMS, David L. *(Judge, Virginia General District Court First Judicial District)* Assumed office July 1, 1997. Elected by General Assembly 2003, current term expires June 2009.
Office: Civic Center, 307 Albemarle Drive, Chesapeake 23322-5571.
Telephone: (757) 382-3111, 382-3150.

WILLIAMS, David Victor *(Chief Judge, Virginia Circuit Court Twenty-first Judicial Circuit)* Assumed office March 1, 1990. Elected by General Assembly to term beginning March 1, 1998, current term expires Feb 28, 2006.
Office: 3160 Kings Mountain Road, Suite B, Martinsville 24112-1049.
Telephone: (276) 634-4850.

WILLIAMS, Gino W. *(Judge, Virginia General District Court Twenty-seventh Judicial District)*
Office: One East Main Street, Suite 201, Christiansburg 24073.
Telephone: (540) 394-2085.

WILLIAMS, Glen Morgan *(Senior Judge, United States District Court Western District of Virginia)* U.S. Commissioner and Magistrate 1963-75. Appointed Judge for life by President Gerald R. Ford to term beginning Oct 12, 1976. Assumed Senior status, serves by assignment. Born Lee County Virginia Feb 17, 1920. Christian. Educated at Milligan College A.B. magna cum laude 1940 and University of Virginia J.D. with honors 1948. Editorial Board Virginia Law Review. Member Order of the Coif, Honor Council and Raven Society. Listed in *Who's Who in American Colleges and Universities.* Admitted to practice Virginia 1947, U.S. Court of Appeals Fourth Circuit 1947, U.S. District Court Western District of Virginia 1953 and U.S. Supreme Court 1966. In legal practice Jonesville 1947-76.
Commonwealth's Attorney Lee County 1948-51. Important Decisions: Phillips v. Harris (Social Security grids) 488 F. Supp. 1161, 1980 and A&E Supply v. Nationwide Insurance (bad faith insurance claim) 589 F. Supp. 428, 1984; 612 F. Supp. 760, 1985; rev'd 798 F.2d 669, 1986; cert. denied 479 U.S. 1091, 1987. Member Virginia State Bar (Judicial Ethics Committee, Committee for Selection of Justices of Supreme Court of Virginia and Council member), Lee County, Virginia and American Bar Associations. Attended Law and Economics and Antitrust Seminars Judicial Conference of the Fourth Circuit. Recipient Distinguished Alumnus Award from Milligan College 1980 and Distinguished Service Award from Virginia Trial Lawyers Association April 1991. Lieutenant s.g. USN 1942-46. Recipient Atlantic Theater Ribbon, Mediterranean Ribbon with two stars, Pacific Theater Ribbon with one star and a citation from Commander Minecraft, Pacific Fleet. Republican. Member State Senate Virginia 1953-55. Member Lee County School Board, American Legion, the 40 and 8, Powell Valley Shrine Club, Cyrene Commandery 21, Royal Arch Masons, Lions, Lee Players, PTA and First Christian Church. Enjoys swimming, reading, tennis, golf and history.
Mailing address: P.O. Box 339, Abingdon 24212-0339.
Telephone: (276) 628-8147.

WILLIAMS, Keary R. *(Chief Judge, Virginia Circuit Court Twenty-ninth Judicial Circuit)* Term expires Feb 15, 2011. Former Judge and Chief Judge, Virginia General District Court Twenty-ninth Judicial District.
Mailing address: P.O. Box 849, Grundy 24614.
Office: Courthouse, Grundy 24614.
Telephone: (276) 935-6565, 935-6564.
Fax: (276) 935-8516
E-mail address: judgew@buchanancounty.org

WILLIAMS, Marcus D. *(Judge, Virginia Circuit Court Nineteenth Judicial Circuit)* Appointed by Governor L. Douglas Wilder to term beginning Oct 12, 1990. Elected by General Assembly 1991 and 1999. Current

WILLIAMS, MARCUS D.—*Continued*

term expires Jan 31, 2007. Born Nashville Tennessee Oct 24, 1952. Methodist. Educated at Fisk University B.A. with honors 1973 and Catholic University of America J.D. 1977. Member Phi Alpha Delta. Admitted to practice Virginia 1977, District of Columbia 1978, U.S. Courts of Appeals District of Columbia 1978 and Fourth 1980 Circuits and U.S. District Court Eastern District of Virginia 1979. Judge, Virginia General District Court Nineteenth Judicial District 1987-90.

Assistant Commonwealth's Attorney April 1978 to March 1980 and Assistant County Attorney April 1980 to June 1987 Fairfax County. Author *Instructor's Manual to Accompany the Legal Environment of Business: Government Regulation and Public Policy Analysis* South-Western Publishing Company 1987; "European Antitrust Law and Its Application to American Corporations and Their Subsidiaries" 9 Whittier L. Rev. 517, 1987; "Regulatory Options and Legal Standards for Cancelled Electric Utility Plants" 6 Midwest L. Rev. 109, 1988; "Arbitration of International Commercial Contracts: Securities and Antitrust Claims" 37 Virginia Lawyer 23 May 1989; "Lawyer, Judge, Solicitor General, Educator: A Tribute to Wade H. McCree, Jr." 12 National Black L. Jour. 1, 1990; and "Judicial Review: Guardian of Civil Liberties and Civil Rights" 1 George Mason Civil Rights L. Jour. 1991. Lecturer on Business Legal Studies School of Business Administration 1980-95 and on Law, School of Law Fall 1987 George Mason University. Former Member Association of District Court Judges. Fellow Thomas J. Watson Foundation 1977-78. Vice Chairman CLE Committee Fairfax Bar Association. Member American Judges Association and American Bar Association (Virginia Delegate National Conference of Special Court Judges Judicial Administration Division 1990). Lecturer on "Civil and Criminal Practice in the General District Court" Virginia Law Foundation 1988, 1989 and 1990; "U.S. Supreme Court Decisions 1988-89 Term" Nov 1989 and "Appropriate Trial Advocacy: Ethical Considerations and Beyond" 1991 CLE seminar The Old Dominion Bar Association Jamaica Nov 1989; and "Recent Decisions in Commercial Law" Spring Convention Fairfax Bar Association 1992, 1993 and 1994. Faculty member General Jurisdiction Course and Faculty Advisor Special Jurisdiction Course The National Judicial College June 1991 and May 1992. Lectured on judicial review, judicial selection and alternative dispute resolution American Participant Program Lectures U.S. Information Agency Liberia, Botswana and Zambia March 1990. Presented paper "All in the Corporate Family: Is the Intra-Enterprise Conspiracy Doctrine a Dead Letter?" American Business Law Association Conference Toronto Canada Aug 1990. Organized and Hosted Metropolitan Washington Regional Judicial Conference on Family Violence and Child Sexual Abuse for trial judges in Virginia, Washington D.C. and Maryland March 15, 1996. Recipient Commendation for Services as Assistant County Attorney from Fairfax County Board of Supervisors 1987 and Certificate of Appreciation for Outstanding and Dedicated Service 1990 and Otis M. Smith Award March 22, 1997 and Outstanding Achievement Service Award April 2001 from Black Law Students Association The Catholic University of America. Board of Associates Saint Paul's College 1986-87. Flunkbusters Mentor Program Herndon High School 1987. Board of Visitors Catholic University of America Columbus School of Law since 1999. Musician (guitar, bass guitar, keyboard, saxophone). Enjoys jazz, blues and classical music.

Office: 4110 Chain Bridge Road, Fairfax 22030.
Telephone: (703) 246-4111.

WILLIAMS, Richard L. *(Senior Judge, United States District Court Eastern District of Virginia)* Appointed for life by President Jimmy Carter to term beginning Oct 28, 1980. Assumed Senior status May 1, 1992. Born Morrisville Virginia April 6, 1923. Educated at University of Virginia LL.B. 1951. Admitted to practice Virginia 1951. Began legal practice Richmond 1951. Judge, Virginia Circuit Court Thirteenth Judicial Circuit 1972-76.

Instructor University of Virginia School of Law 1973-76. Fellow American College of Trial Lawyers. Second Lieutenant USAAC 1940-45. Enjoys fishing and hunting.

Office: U.S. Courthouse, 1000 East Main Street, Richmond 23219-3525.
Telephone: (804) 916-2240.

WILLIAMS, William P. *(Judge, Virginia Juvenile and Domestic Relations District Court Fourth Judicial District)* Assumed office June 1, 1994. Elected by General Assembly to term beginning June 1, 2000, current term expires May 31, 2006.

Office: 800 East City Hall Avenue, Norfolk 23510.
Telephone: (757) 664-7340.

WILLIS, Alotha Carol *(Chief Judge, Virginia Juvenile and Domestic Relations District Court Third Judicial District)* Term expires Feb 15, 2007.

Mailing address: P.O. Box 1073, Portsmouth 23705-1073.
Office: Civic Center, 603 Crawford Street, Portsmouth 23705.
Telephone: (757) 393-8851.

WILLIS, Gordon F. *(Judge, Virginia General District Court Fifteenth Judicial District)*

Mailing address: P.O. Box 339, Spotsylvania 22553-0339.
Office: Judicial Center, First Floor, 9111 Courthouse Road, Spotsylvania 22553.
Telephone: (540) 582-7110.

WILLIS, Larry D. *(Judge, Virginia Juvenile and Domestic Relations District Court First Judicial District)* Assumed office May 1, 1999. Term expires April 30, 2005.

Office: 301 Albemarle Drive, Second Floor, Chesapeake 23322-5501.
Telephone: (757) 382-8100.

WILLS, Elizabeth S. *(Chief Judge, Virginia Juvenile and Domestic Relations District Court Thirtieth Judicial District)* Term expires Jan 31, 2007.

Mailing address: P.O. Box 2320, Wise 24293.
Office: Courthouse, Main Street, Wise 24293.
Telephone: (276) 328-4486.

WILSON, Robert B., V *(Judge, Virginia Juvenile and Domestic Relations District Court Eighth Judicial District)* Assumed office April 1, 2001. Term expires March 31, 2007.

Mailing address: P.O. Box 69104, Hampton 23669-9404.
Office: 220 North King Street, Hampton 23669.
Telephone: (757) 727-6147, 727-6742.

WILSON, Samuel Grayson *(Chief Judge, United States District Court Western District of Virginia)* Magistrate 1976-81. Appointed Judge for life by President George Bush to term beginning 1990. Chief Judge since 1997. Born Norfolk Virginia July 31, 1949. Educated at University of Richmond B.A. 1971 and Wake Forest University School of Law J.D. 1974. In legal practice Roanoke 1981-90.

Assistant Commonwealth's Attorney Roanoke 1974-76. Assistant U.S. Attorney Western District of Virginia 1976.

Mailing address: P.O. Box 2421, Roanoke 24010-2421.

Telephone: (540) 857-5120.

WOOD, Thomas H. *(Judge, Virginia Circuit Court Twenty-fifth Judicial Circuit)* Term expires March 14, 2008. Former Judge, Virginia General District Court Twenty-fifth Judicial District.

Mailing address: P.O. Box 689, Staunton 24402-0689.

Office: Augusta County Courthouse, One East Johnson Street, Staunton 24401.

Telephone: (540) 245-5321.

WOODSON, Robert G., Jr. *(Chief Judge, Virginia General District Court Tenth Judicial District)* Term expires May 31, 2007.

Mailing address: P.O. Box 24, Cumberland 23040-0024.

Office: Courthouse, Cumberland 23040.

Telephone: (804) 492-4848.

WOOLDRIDGE, Robert W., Jr. *(Judge, Virginia Circuit Court Nineteenth Judicial Circuit)* Elected by General Assembly to term beginning Sept 1992. Reelected 2000, current term expires Aug 31, 2008. Born Pittsburgh Pennsylvania Oct 12, 1949. Educated at College of William & Mary B.A. 1972 J.D. 1979 and University of Virginia M.A. 1976. Admitted to practice Virginia 1979, U.S. District Court Eastern District of Virginia and U.S. Court of Appeals Fourth Circuit. In legal practice Fairfax 1979-84 and McLean 1984-92.

Member Virginia State Bar (Bar Council 1990-92), Fairfax County (President 1989-90) and Virginia Bar Associations. Virginia National Guard 1972-78.

Office: 4110 Chain Bridge Road, Fairfax 22030.

Telephone: (703) 246-4111, 691-7320.

WORCESTER, Dean S. *(Judge, Virginia General District Court Twentieth Judicial District)* Elected by General Assembly to term beginning March 1, 2002. Term expires Feb 29, 2008.

Office: 18 East Market Street, Leesburg 20176.

Telephone: (703) 777-0312.

WRIGHT, Timothy S. *(Judge, Virginia General District Court First Judicial District)* Assumed office July 1, 1997. Elected by General Assembly 2003, current term expires June 2009.

Office: Civic Center, 307 Albemarle Drive, Chesapeake 23322-5571.

Telephone: (757) 382-3111, 382-3150.

YEATTS, Archer L., III *(Judge, Virginia General District Court Fourteenth Judicial District)* Term expires June 30, 2007.

Mailing address: P.O. Box 27032, Richmond 23273-7032.

Office: 4301 East Parham Road, Richmond 23228-2745.

Telephone: (804) 501-4727.

ZEPKIN, J. R. *(Judge, Virginia General District Court Ninth Judicial District)* Elected by General Assembly to term beginning July 1, 1974. Reelected to subsequent terms. Current term expires June 30, 2004. Former Chief Judge.

Office: 5201 Monticello Avenue, Suite 2, Williamsburg 23188-8218.

Telephone: (757) 564-2400.

WASHINGTON

Capital OLYMPIA

UNITED STATES DISTRICT COURTS DISTRICTS OF WASHINGTON

Within Washington there are two United States District Courts. For descriptive information refer to the United States Courts section.

EASTERN DISTRICT includes Adams, Asotin, Benton, Chelan, Columbia, Douglas, Ferry, Franklin, Garfield, Grant, Kittitas, Klickitat, Lincoln, Okanogan, Pend Oreille, Spokane, Stevens, Walla Walla, Whitman and Yakima counties. The court sits at Richland, Spokane, Walla Walla and Yakima.

Chief Judge
Fred Van Sickle

Judges
Wm. Fremming Nielsen
Robert H. Whaley
Edward F. Shea

Senior Judges
Justin L. Quackenbush
Alan A. McDonald

Clerk
James R. Larsen
P.O. Box 1493
Spokane, Washington 99210-1493
(509) 353-2150

WESTERN DISTRICT includes Clallam, Clark, Cowlitz, Grays Harbor, Island, Jefferson, King, Kitsap, Lewis, Mason, Pacific, Pierce, San Juan, Skagit, Skamania, Snohomish, Thurston, Wahkiakum and Whatcom counties. The court sits at Bellingham, Seattle and Tacoma.

Chief Judge
John C. Coughenour

Judges
Barbara J. Rothstein
Franklin D. Burgess
Marsha J. Pechman
Thomas S. Zilly
Robert S. Lasnik
Ronald B. Leighton

Senior Judges
Walter T. McGovern
Jack E. Tanner
Carolyn R. Dimmick
Robert J. Bryan

Clerk
Bruce Rifkin
215 U.S. Courthouse
1010 Fifth Avenue
Seattle, Washington 98104-1130
(206) 553-5598

UNITED STATES MAGISTRATE JUDGES OF WASHINGTON

EASTERN DISTRICT
Cynthia Imbrogno
Lonny Ray Suko

WESTERN DISTRICT
John L. Weinberg
Ira J. Uhrig
Ricardo S. Martinez
Karen L. Strombom
Gilbert H. Kleweno
J. Kelley Arnold
Monica J. Benton

Recalled Magistrate Judge
Philip Kerner Sweigert (Western)

UNITED STATES BANKRUPTCY COURTS OF WASHINGTON

EASTERN DISTRICT

Chief Judge
Patricia C. Williams

Judge
John A. Rossmeissl

Recalled Judge
John M. Klobucher

Bankruptcy Clerk
Theodore S. McGregor
P.O. Box 2164
Spokane, Washington 99210-2164
(509) 353-2404

WESTERN DISTRICT

Chief Judge
Philip H. Brandt

Judges
Samuel J. Steiner
Thomas T. Glover
Karen A. Overstreet
Paul B. Snyder

Bankruptcy Clerk
Mark L. Hatcher
315 Park Place Building
1200 Sixth Avenue
Seattle, Washington 98101-3122
(206) 553-7545

WASHINGTON SUPREME COURT

The Supreme Court is Washington's court of last resort. The court consists of a chief justice and eight justices elected in statewide nonpartisan elections to staggered six-year terms. Vacancies are filled by the governor. Newly appointed justices run for election on nonpartisan ballots at the next general election to complete

WASHINGTON SUPREME COURT—*Continued*

the unexpired term. The chief justice is elected to a four-year term by a vote of the court. The court's senior judge holds the title of associate chief justice, the court's second-in-command. Retirement is mandatory at age seventy-five; however, retired justices may serve pro tem.

The court may permit direct review of cases in which a statute authorizes direct review; the trial court holds invalid a statute, ordinance, tax, impost, assessment or toll upon the ground that is repugnant to the United States Constitution, the Washington State Constitution, a statute of the United States or a treaty; a conflict arises among decisions of the Court of Appeals or an inconsistency arises in the decisions of the Supreme Court; a fundamental and urgent issue of broad public import requires prompt and ultimate determination; the death penalty is declared; or an action is brought against a state officer in the nature of quo warranto, prohibition, injunction or mandamus. The court has discretionary review of decisions from the Court of Appeals. The court exercises supervisory control over lower courts and disciplinary control over judges and attorneys. The court has original jurisdiction to issue writs necessary to the exercise of proper jurisdiction. The court may answer questions of law certified to it by a federal court.

The court sits en banc for all reviews and in two departments of five each on motion days with the chief justice presiding at both departments. The court sits at Olympia or at such other locations as may be determined by the court.

Chief Justice
Gerry L. Alexander

Associate Chief Justice
Charles W. Johnson

Justices

Bobbe J. Bridge	Tom Chambers
Mary B. Fairhurst	Faith Ireland
Barbara A. Madsen	Susan Owens
Richard B. Sanders	

Clerk
C. J. Merritt
415 Twelfth Avenue S.W.
P.O. Box 40929
Olympia, Washington 98504-0929
(360) 357-2077

Court Administrator
Mary C. McQueen
1206 Quince Street S.E.
P.O. Box 41170
Olympia, Washington 98504-1170
(360) 357-2121

WASHINGTON COURT OF APPEALS

The Court of Appeals is Washington's intermediate appellate court and consists of three divisions. Judges are elected on a nonpartisan ballot by the voters in their respective divisions for staggered six-year terms. Vacancies are filled by the governor. Newly appointed judges run for election on nonpartisan ballots at the next general election to complete the unexpired term. A presiding chief judge is elected by peer vote to a one-year term. The judges of each division elect a chief judge and an acting chief judge for two-year terms. The acting chief judge is second-in-command. Retirement is mandatory at age seventy-five; however, retired judges may serve pro tem.

The court has exclusive appellate jurisdiction except in those cases which are to be appealed directly to the Supreme Court and those over which the Supreme Court has asserted jurisdiction.

Presiding Chief Judge
John A. Schultheis

DIVISION I includes Island, King, San Juan, Skagit, Snohomish and Whatcom counties. The court sits at Seattle and may also sit at Bellingham and Everett.

Chief Judge
Mary Kay Becker

Acting Chief Judge
Ronald E. Cox

Judges

Susan R. Agid	Marlin J. Appelwick
William W. Baker	H. Joseph Coleman
Anne L. Ellington	C. Kenneth Grosse
Faye Kennedy	Ann Schindler

DIVISION II includes Clallam, Clark, Cowlitz, Grays Harbor, Jefferson, Kitsap, Lewis, Mason, Pacific, Pierce, Skamania, Thurston and Wahkiakum counties. The court sits at Tacoma and may also sit at Vancouver or at other such locations as may be determined by the court.

Chief Judge
J. Robin Hunt

Acting Chief Judge
Christine J. Quinn-Brintnall

Judges
David Armstrong
C. C. Bridgewater
Elaine Houghton
J. Dean Morgan
Karen Goodman Seinfeld

DIVISION III includes Adams, Asotin, Benton, Chelan, Columbia, Douglas, Ferry, Franklin, Garfield, Grant, Kittitas, Klickitat, Lincoln, Okanogan, Pend Oreille, Spokane, Stevens, Walla Walla, Whitman and Yakima counties. The court sits at Spokane and may also sit at Richland, Walla Walla, Wenatchee and Yakima.

Chief Judge
Stephen M. Brown

Acting Chief Judge
Kenneth H. Kato

Judges
Frank L. Kurtz
John A. Schultheis
Dennis J. Sweeney

WASHINGTON SUPERIOR COURT

The Superior Court is Washington's court of general jurisdiction. There are thirty-one judicial districts comprised of one or more counties. Judges are elected from each district on nonpartisan ballots for four-year terms. Vacancies are filled by the governor. Newly appointed

WASHINGTON SUPERIOR COURT—*Continued*

judges run for election on nonpartisan ballots at the next general election to complete the unexpired term. Retirement is mandatory at age seventy-five; however, retired judges may serve pro tem.

The court has exclusive original jurisdiction over all civil matters in which the amount in controversy exceeds $50,000 and over cases involving title or possession of real property and legality of tax, impost, assessment or toll. The court's criminal jurisdiction includes felony cases and all other criminal cases not otherwise provided for by law. The court has exclusive jurisdiction in probate, domestic and juvenile matters. The court also has appellate jurisdiction over the District and Municipal Courts. Appeals are tried de novo or on the record for error of law.

The court sits at each county seat.

County	Judge
Adams	Richard W. Miller
Asotin-Columbia-Garfield	William D. Acey
Benton-Franklin	Carolyn A. Brown
	Craig Jay Matheson
	Robert G. Swisher
	Vic L. VanderSchoor
	Dennis D. Yule
Chelan	Lesley A. Allan
	John E. Bridges
	T. W. "Chip" Small
Clallam	Kenneth Day Williams
	George L. Wood
Clark	Roger A. Bennett
	Robert L. Harris
	Barbara D. Johnson
	John F. Nichols
	Edwin L. Poyfair
	James E. Rulli
	Diane M. Woolard
	John P. Wulle
Columbia	See Asotin-Columbia-Garfield
Cowlitz	Jill Johanson
	James J. Stonier
	James Edgar F. X. Warme
	Stephen M. Warning
Douglas	John Hotchkiss
Ferry-Pend Oreille-Stevens	Rebecca M. Baker
	Larry M. Kristianson
Franklin	See Benton-Franklin
Garfield	See Asotin-Columbia-Garfield
Grant	John M. Antosz
	Kenneth L. Jorgensen
	Evan Eugene Sperline
Grays Harbor	David E. Foscue
	Gordon L. Godfrey
	F. Mark McCauley
Island-San Juan	Vickie I. Churchill
	Alan R. Hancock
Jefferson	Thomas J. Majhan
King	Robert H. Alsdorf
	Sharon Armstrong
	Suzanne M. Barnett
	Greg Canova
	Cheryl Carey
King—Cont.	James Cayce
	Patricia Clark
	James A. Doerty
	William L. Downing
	Joan DuBuque
	Richard D. Eadie
	John Erlick
	Deborah Fleck
	Michael J. Fox
	Brian D. Gain
	Steven Charles Gonzalez
	Donald D. Haley
	Glenna Hall
	Helen L. Halpert
	Michael Hayden
	Michael Heavey
	Bruce W. Hilyer
	Philip G. Hubbard, Jr.
	Laura Inveen
	Richard A. Jones
	Paris Kallas
	Ronald Kessler
	Linda Lau
	Terence Lukens
	Dean S. Lum
	Nicole MacInnes
	George Tauno Mattson
	Douglas McBroom
	Harry McCarthy
	LeRoy McCullough
	Richard McDermott
	Charles W. Mertel
	Laura Gene Middaugh
	Douglass North
	Dale B. Ramerman
	Jeffrey M. Ramsdell
	Palmer Robinson
	Carol Schapira
	Steven Scott
	Catherine Shaffer
	Michael S. Spearman
	Julie Spector
	Michael Trickey
	Anthony P. Wartnik
	Jay V. White
	Mary Yu
Kitsap	Leonard W. Costello
	M. Karlynn Haberly
	Russell W. Hartman
	Anna M. Laurie
	Terry K. McCluskey
	Leila Mills
	Jay B. Roof
Kittitas	Michael E. Cooper
Klickitat-Skamania	E. Thompson Reynolds
Lewis	Richard L. Brosey
	David R. Draper
	H. John Hall
Lincoln	Philip W. Borst
Mason	James B. Sawyer, II
	Toni A. Sheldon
Okanogan	Jack Burchard
Pacific-Wahkiakum	Joel Morris Penoyar
Pend Oreille	See Ferry-Pend Oreille-Stevens
Pierce	Stephanie A. Arend
	Sergio Armijo

WASHINGTON SUPERIOR COURT—*Continued*

Pierce—Cont.	Rosanne Buckner
	Bryan E. Chushcoff
	Bruce W. Cohoe
	Ron Culpepper
	Frank Cuthbertson
	Thomas Felnagle
	Frederick W. Fleming
	Vicki L. Hogan
	Thomas P. Larkin
	John A. McCarthy
	Kathryn J. Nelson
	James R. Orlando
	D. Gary Steiner
	Katherine M. Stolz
	Brian Tollefson
	Marywave Van Deren
	Kitty-Ann van Doorninck
	Lisa R. Worswick
San Juan	See Island-San Juan
Skagit	Susan K. Cook
	John M. Meyer
	Michael E. Rickert
Skamania	See Klickitat-Skamania
Snohomish	James H. Allendoerfer
	George N. Bowden
	Ronald L. Castleberry
	Kenneth L. Cowsert
	Ellen J. Fair
	Anita L. Farris
	Charles S. French
	David F. Hulbert
	Gerald L. Knight
	Linda C. Krese
	Larry E. McKeeman
	Joseph A. Thibodeau
	Richard J. Thorpe
	Thomas J. Wynne
Spokane	Robert D. Austin
	Paul A. Bastine
	Ellen K. Clark
	Salvatore F. Cozza
	Tari S. Eitzen
	Jerome Leveque
	Maryann Moreno
	Kathleen M. O'Connor
	Neal Q. Rielly
	Richard J. Schroeder
	Greg D. Sypolt
	Linda G. Tompkins
Stevens	See Ferry-Pend Oreille-Stevens
Thurston	Daniel J. Berschauer
	Paula Casey
	Richard D. Hicks
	Wm. Thomas McPhee
	Christine A. Pomeroy
	Richard A. Strophy
	Gary Tabor
Wahkiakum	See Pacific-Wahkiakum
Walla Walla	Donald W. Schacht
	Robert L. Zagelow
Whatcom	Michael F. Moynihan
	Steven J. Mura
	David A. Nichols
Whitman	David J. Frazier
Yakima	F. James Gavin
	Robert N. Hackett, Jr.
	Susan L. Hahn
	James P. Hutton
	Michael W. Leavitt
	C. James Lust
	Michael E. Schwab
	Heather K. Van Nuys

WASHINGTON COURTS OF LIMITED JURISDICTION

Washington has two types of courts of limited jurisdiction. District Courts have jurisdiction over state and county matters. There is at least one District Court established by statute in each county, but the governing body of the county has the option of dividing the county into as many District Courts as deemed necessary. Municipal Courts have jurisdiction over municipal matters. Any city may establish a Municipal Department of the District Court, or a Municipal Court may be established as a separate court by ordinance in cities or towns with populations of up to 20,000 or more than 400,000.

WASHINGTON DISTRICT COURTS

Judges are elected from their respective districts in nonpartisan elections to four-year terms. A presiding judge may be selected in each district for a term of not less than two years. Magistrates may be appointed by and serve at the pleasure of the governing body of the county.

The courts have jurisdiction over criminal matters in which the penalty does not exceed a $5,000 fine and/or one year imprisonment. The courts have civil jurisdiction in cases in which the amount in controversy does not exceed $50,000 and in small claims cases not exceeding $2,500. The courts also have jurisdiction over traffic matters and may conduct felony preliminary hearings. Appeals are to the Superior Court.

The courts sit at each county seat and at other locations throughout the state.

---

*Also Municipal Judge

ADAMS COUNTY has two District Courts.

Othello District Court sits at Othello.

Judge

Gary John Brueher

Ritzville District Court sits at Ritzville.

Judge

Adalia Hille

ASOTIN COUNTY has one District Court.

Asotin District Court sits at Asotin.

Judge

Ray D. Lutes

BENTON COUNTY has one District Court with one branch.

Benton District Court sits at Kennewick.

WASHINGTON COURTS OF LIMITED JURISDICTION—*Continued*

Judges
Holly A. Hollenbeck
Jacki Lahtinen
Eugene Franklin Pratt, III

Benton District Court Prosser Branch sits at Prosser.

Judge
Robert J. Ingvalson

CHELAN COUNTY has one District Court.

Chelan District Court sits at Wenatchee.

Judges
Alicia H. Nakata
Thomas C. Warren

CLALLAM COUNTY has two District Courts.

Clallam District Court No. 1 sits at Port Angeles.

Judge
Rick Porter

Clallam District Court No. 2 sits at Forks.

Judge
Erik S. Rohrer

CLARK COUNTY has one District Court.

Clark District Court sits at Vancouver.

Judges
Scott S. Anders*
Kenneth R. Eiesland*
Randal Brandt Fritzler*
Vernon L. Schreiber*
Darvin J. Zimmerman*

COLUMBIA COUNTY has one District Court.

Columbia District Court sits at Dayton.

Judge
Scott G. Marinello*

COWLITZ COUNTY has one District Court.

Cowlitz District Court sits at Kelso.

Judges
David R. Koss
Edward J. Putka*

DOUGLAS COUNTY has one District Court with one branch.

Douglas District Court sits at East Wenatchee. Court may also sit at Bridgeport.

Judge
Judith L. McCauley

FERRY COUNTY has one District Court.

Ferry District Court sits at Republic.

Judge
Lynda C. Eaton

FRANKLIN COUNTY has one District Court.

Franklin District Court sits at Pasco.

Judge
Jerry Roach

GARFIELD COUNTY has one District Court.

Garfield District Court sits at Pomeroy.

Judge
G. Paul Miller

GRANT COUNTY has one District Court.

Grant District Court sits at Ephrata.

Judges
Richard C. Fitterer*
Janis Whitener-Moberg*

GRAYS HARBOR COUNTY has two District Courts.

Grays Harbor District Court No. 1 sits at Montesano.

Judge
Stephen E. Brown

Grays Harbor District Court No. 2 sits at Aberdeen.

Judge
Thomas A. Copland

ISLAND COUNTY has one District Court.

Island District Court sits at Oak Harbor.

Judge
Peter H. Strow

JEFFERSON COUNTY has one District Court.

Jefferson District Court sits at Port Townsend.

Judge
Mark Huth

KING COUNTY has one District Court with three divisions.

King District Court East Division sits at Bellevue, Issaquah, Redmond and Shoreline.

Judges

David S. Admire	Janet E. Garrow
Linda Jacke	Peter Nault
Mary Ann Ottinger	J. Wesley Saint Clair
Douglas Joseph Smith	David A. Steiner
Robert A. Wacker	Fred L. Yeatts

King District Court South Division sits at Burien and Kent.

Judges

Rick Bathum	David Christie
Charles Delaurenti, II	D. Mark Eide
Judith R. Eiler	Corinna Harn
Robert E. McBeth	Darrell E. Phillipson
Victoria Seitz	Elizabeth D. Stephenson
Linda G. Thompson	

King District Court West Division sits at Seattle.

Judges
Arthur Chapman
Mark C. Chow
Eileen A. Kato
Barbara Linde
Mariane Spearman

WASHINGTON COURTS OF LIMITED JURISDICTION—*Continued*

KITSAP COUNTY has one District Court with two branches.

Kitsap District Court sits at Port Orchard. Court may also sit at Poulsbo and Silverdale.

Judges
Marilyn Paja
W. Daniel Phillips
James M. Riehl

KITTITAS COUNTY has two District Courts.

Lower Kittitas District Court sits at Ellensburg.

Judge
Thomas A. Haven

Upper Kittitas District Court sits at Cle Elum.

Judge
Darrel R. Ellis*

KLICKITAT COUNTY has two District Courts.

East District Court sits at Goldendale.

Judge
Brian Altman

West District Court sits at White Salmon.

Judge
Robert Douglas Weisfield

LEWIS COUNTY has one District Court.

Lewis District Court sits at Chehalis.

Judges
Lew Hutchinson
Michael P. Roewe

LINCOLN COUNTY has one District Court.

Lincoln District Court sits at Davenport.

Judge
Joshua F. Grant

MASON COUNTY has one District Court.

Mason District Court sits at Shelton.

Judge
Victoria Meadows

OKANOGAN COUNTY has one District Court.

Okanogan District Court sits at Okanogan.

Judges
Christopher E. Culp
David S. Edwards

PACIFIC COUNTY has two District Courts.

North District Court sits at South Bend.

Judge
Elizabeth Penoyar*

South District Court sits at Ilwaco.

Judge
Douglas Goelz

PEND OREILLE COUNTY has one District Court.

Pend Oreille District Court sits at Newport.

Judge
Philip J. Van de Veer

PIERCE COUNTY has one District Court.

Pierce District Court sits at Tacoma.

Judges

Karla Buttorff	James R. Heller
Judy Rae Jasprica	David M. Kenworthy
Jack F. Nevin	Pat O'Malley
Margaret V. Ross	

SAN JUAN COUNTY has one District Court.

San Juan District Court sits at Friday Harbor.

Judge
Stewart R. Andrew

SKAGIT COUNTY has one District Court.

Skagit District Court sits at Mount Vernon.

Judges
Stephen R. Skelton*
David A. Svaren*

SKAMANIA COUNTY has one District Court.

Skamania District Court sits at Stevenson.

Judge
Ronald Reynier, Jr.

SNOHOMISH COUNTY has one District Court with four divisions.

Snohomish District Court Cascade Division sits at Arlington.

Judge
Jay F. Wisman

Snohomish District Court Everett Division sits at Everett.

Judges
Roger M. Fisher
Thomas E. Kelly

Snohomish District Court Evergreen Division sits at Monroe.

Judges
Steve M. Clough
Patricia Lyon

Snohomish District Court South Division sits at Lynnwood.

Judges
Stephen J. Dwyer
Carol A. McRae
Timothy P. Ryan

SPOKANE COUNTY has one District Court.

Spokane District Court sits at Spokane.

Judges

Harold D. Clarke III*	Patti Connolley Walker*
Sara Derr*	Mike Padden*
Vance W. Peterson*	Annette S. Plese*
Gregory J. Tripp*	Richard B. White*
Donna Wilson*	vacancy

STEVENS COUNTY has one District Court.

Stevens District Court sits at Colville.

WASHINGTON COURTS OF LIMITED JURISDICTION—*Continued*

Judge
Pamela F. Payne

THURSTON COUNTY has one District Court.

Thurston District Court sits at Olympia.

Judges
Susan A. Dubuisson
Clifford L. Stilz, Jr.

WAHKIAKUM COUNTY has one District Court.

Wahkiakum District Court sits at Cathlamet.

Judge
William J. Faubion

WALLA WALLA COUNTY has one District Court.

Walla Walla District Court sits at Walla Walla.

Judges
John O. Knowlton
Jerry A. Votendahl

WHATCOM COUNTY has one District Court.

Whatcom District Court sits at Bellingham.

Judges
Edward B. Ross
Ira J. Uhrig

WHITMAN COUNTY has one District Court with one branch.

Whitman District Court sits at Colfax. Court may also sit at Pullman.

Judge
Douglas B. Robinson

YAKIMA COUNTY has one District Court.

Yakima District Court sits at Yakima.

Judges
Rod Fitch
Michael G. McCarthy
Ruth Reukauf
Kevin M. Roy

WASHINGTON MUNICIPAL COURTS

In municipalities with full-time judicial officers, judges are elected from their respective municipalities in nonpartisan elections to four-year terms. In other municipalities judges are appointed by the local governing body. Magistrates may be appointed by and serve at the pleasure of the local governing body.

The courts have exclusive original jurisdiction over municipal ordinances and may impose penalties not to exceed a fine of $5,000 and/or one year imprisonment. The courts may conduct preliminary hearings. In cities with populations over 400,000, jurisdiction is concurrent with the Superior and District Courts over all matters within the jurisdiction of the District Courts. Appeals are to the Superior Court.

---

*Also District Judge
†Magistrate

Municipality	Judge
Aberdeen	Paul D. Conroy
Airway Heights	Charlie Rohr
Albion	Scott J. Bergstedt
Algona	See Auburn Municipal Court
Anacortes	Stephen R. Skelton*
	David A. Svaren*
Auburn	Patrick R. Burns
Bainbridge Island	Stephen J. Holman
Battle Ground	George L. W. Brintnall
Bellingham	Debra Lev
Black Diamond	Robert E. West, Jr.
Blaine	Michael Bobbink
Bonney Lake	James J. Helbling
Bothell	John W. Rusden
Bremerton	James Docter
Brewster	John R. Harmon
Bridgeport	John R. Harmon
Buckley	Marjorie Tedrick
Bucoda	See Tenino Municipal Court
Burlington	Stephen R. Skelton*
	David A. Svaren*
Camas-Washougal	Scott S. Anders*
	Kenneth R. Eiesland*
	Randal Brandt Fritzler*
	Vernon L. Schreiber*
	Darvin J. Zimmerman*
Cashmere	J. Kirk Bromiley
Castle Rock	Evelyn Wooster
Cathlamet	Dennis P. Maher
Centralia	Merle R. Krouse
Chehalis	Steven R. Buzzard
Chelan	Jill R. Wise
Cheney	Gregory J. Tripp*
Cle Elum	Darrel R. Ellis*
Clyde Hill	See Kirkland Municipal Court
Colfax	Scott J. Bergstedt
College Place	Richard G. Wernette
Colton	Scott Gallina
Connell	Alan B. Gunter
Cosmopolis	John D. Schumacher
Coulee City	Richard C. Fitterer*
	Janis Whitener-Moberg*
Dayton	Scott G. Marinello*
Deer Park	Sara Derr*
Des Moines	Colleen A. Hartl
East Wenatchee	Jeffrey Barker
Eatonville	A'Lan S. Hutchinson
Edmonds	James L. White
Electric City	Richard C. Fitterer*
	Janis Whitener-Moberg*
Elma	David S. Hatch
Elmer City	Howard Stewart
Enumclaw	David A. Berner
Everett	David C. Mitchell
	Timothy B. Odell
Everson-Nooksack	Michael Bobbink
Federal Way	David Tracy
Ferndale	Terrance G. Lewis
Fife	Kevin G. Ringus
Fircrest	John A. Miller
Gig Harbor	Michael A. Dunn
Grand Coulee	Richard C. Fitterer*
	Janis Whitener-Moberg*

WASHINGTON COURTS OF LIMITED JURISDICTION—*Continued*

Grandview	Rickey C. Kimbrough
Granger	William C. Murphy
Hoquiam	William Stewart
Hunts Point	See Kirkland Municipal Court
Ilwaco	Elizabeth Penoyar*
Kahlotus	Mike Ayers
Kent	Robert McSeveney
	Glenn Phillips
Kirkland	Albert M. Raines
Kittitas	Mark A. Chmelewski
LaCenter	See Battle Ground Municipal Court
Lake Forest Park	Linda S. Portnoy
Lake Stevens	See Marysville Municipal Court
Lakewood	Ernest A. Heller
Langley	Carolyn Cliff
Leavenworth	J. Kirk Bromiley
Long Beach	Elizabeth Penoyar*
Lynden	Terrence G. Lewis
Lynnwood	Stephen E. Moore
Maple Valley	L. Stephen Rochon
Marysville	Larry M. Trivett
Mattawa	Richard C. Fitterer*
	Janis Whitener-Moberg*
McCleary	Arthur A. Blauvelt, III
Medical Lake	Richard B. Kayne
Medina	See Kirkland Municipal Court
Milton	William Wood
Montesano	Arthur A. Blauvelt, III
Moses Lake	Richard C. Fitterer*
	Janis Whitener-Moberg*
Mount Vernon	Stephen R. Skelton*
	David A. Svaren*
Moxee City	Susan C. Arb
Napavine	Steven R. Buzzard
North Bonneville	William A. Nix
Oakville	Kyle L. Imler
Ocean Shores	Paul L. Stritmatter
Olympia	Lee Creighton
Omak	Henry A. Rawson
Orting	Jeffrey K. Day
Pacific	L. Stephen Rochon
Pasco	Mary Berndt Ramirez
Pateros	See Brewster Municipal Court
Port Orchard	Tarrell Decker
Poulsbo	Jeff Tolman
Prescott	John P. Junke
Puyallup	Stephen R. Shelton
Quincy	Richard C. Fitterer*
	Janis Whitener-Moberg*
Rainier	Craig Hanson
Raymond	Elizabeth Penoyar*
Renton	Terry L. Jurado
Ridgefield	See Battle Ground Municipal Court
Riverside	Henry A. Rawson
Roslyn	Darrel R. Ellis*
Roy	Thomas Ellington
Royal City	Richard C. Fitterer*
	Janis Whitener-Moberg*
Ruston	Sandra L. Allen
SeaTac	Paul J. Codd
Seattle	Fred Bonner
	Theresa Doyle
	Judith Hightower
	George W. Holifield
	Michael S. Hurtado
	C. Kimi Kondo
	Ron A. Mamiya
	Jean Rietschel
	Paul Beighle†
	Francis deVilla†
	Charles Duffey†
	Debbie Hankins†
	Shirley Wilson†
Sedro-Woolley	Brian L. Stiles
Selah	Lauri McIntire Boyd
Shelton	Amber L. Finlay
South Bend	Elizabeth Penoyar*
South Prairie	Robert W. Hamilton
Spokane	Harold D. Clarke III*
	Patti Connolly Walker*
	Sara Derr*
	Mike Padden*
	Vance W. Peterson*
	Annette S. Plese*
	Gregory J. Tripp*
	Richard B. White*
	Donna Wilson*
Steilacoom	Spirro Damis
Stevenson	Robert K. Leick
Sumas	Michael Bobbink
Sumner	Stephen R. Shelton
Sunnyside	Steven L. Michels
Tacoma	Jack Emery
	David B. Ladenburg
	Elizabeth Verhey
Tekoa	Stephen Bishop
Tenino	John V. Lyman
Tonasket	Roger A. Castelda
Toppenish	Ramon P. Reid
Tukwila	vacancy
Tumwater	John V. Lyman
Twisp	David Ebenger
Union Gap	William C. Murphy
Uniontown	Scott Gallina
Vader	Steven R. Buzzard
Wapato	Ramon P. Reid
Warden	Richard C. Fitterer*
	Janis Whitener-Moberg*
Westport	Stephen J. Hyde
Wilkeson	Robert W. Hamilton
Winlock	Steven R. Buzzard
Winthrop	David Ebenger
Woodland	Edward J. Putka*
Yakima	Jonathan H. Martin
	Susan J. Woodard
Yarrow Point	See Kirkland Municipal Court
Yelm	Thomas L. Meyer
Zillah	Debbie Mendoza

Washington Counties and County Seats

Adams
Ritzville

Asotin
Asotin

Benton
Prosser

Chelan
Wenatchee

Clallam
Port Angeles

Clark
Vancouver

Columbia
Dayton

Cowlitz
Kelso

Douglas
Waterville

Ferry
Republic

Franklin
Pasco

Garfield
Pomeroy

Grant
Ephrata

Grays Harbor
Montesano

Island
Coupeville

Jefferson
Port Townsend

King
Seattle

Kitsap
Port Orchard

Kittitas
Ellensburg

Klickitat
Goldendale

Lewis
Chehalis

Lincoln
Davenport

Mason
Shelton

Okanogan
Okanogan

Pacific
South Bend

Pend Oreille
Newport

Pierce
Tacoma

San Juan
Friday Harbor

Skagit
Mount Vernon

Skamania
Stevenson

Snohomish
Everett

Spokane
Spokane

Stevens
Colville

Thurston
Olympia

Wahkiakum
Cathlamet

Walla Walla
Walla Walla

Whatcom
Bellingham

Whitman
Colfax

Yakima
Yakima

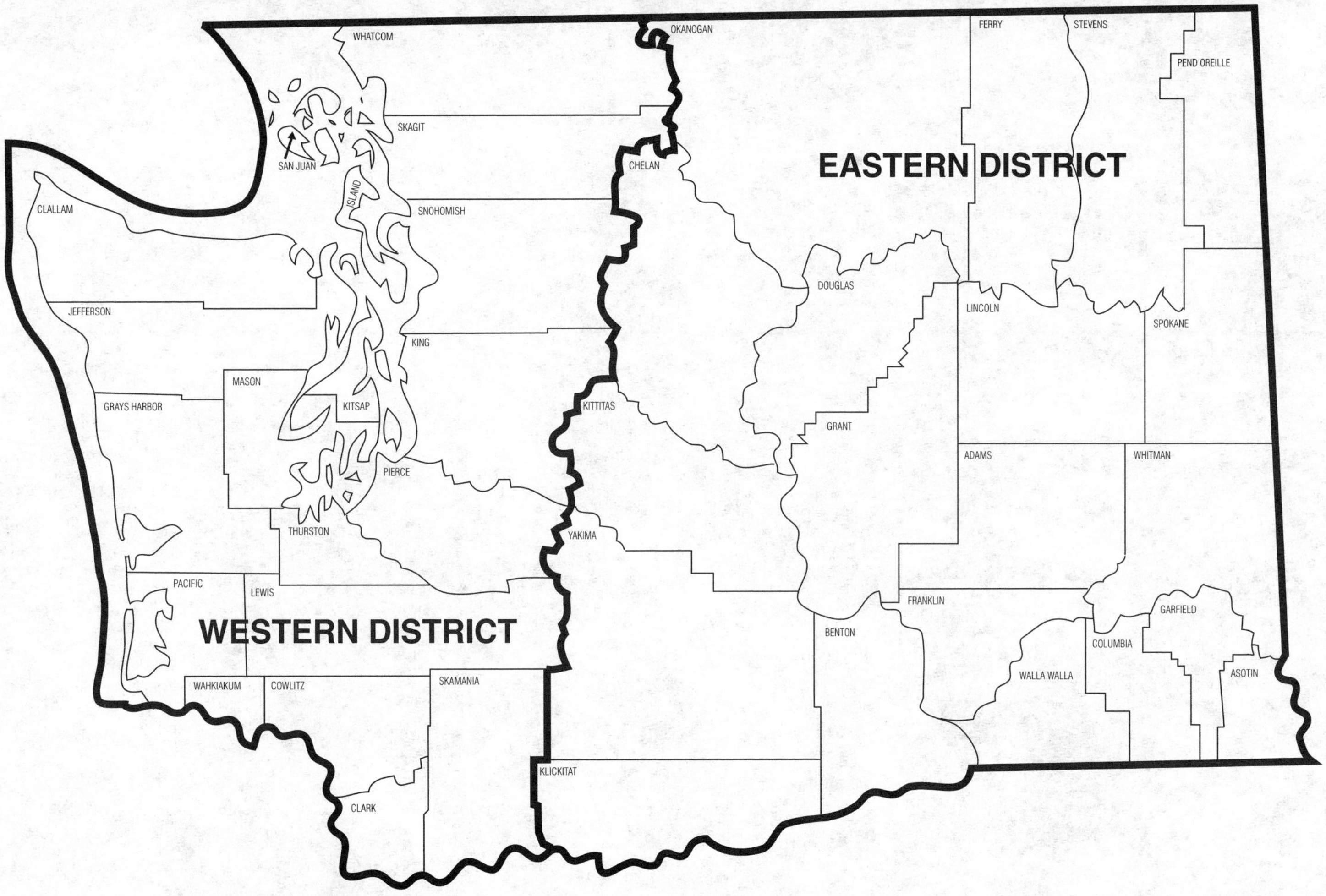
EASTERN DISTRICT
WESTERN DISTRICT
WHATCOM
OKANOGAN
FERRY
STEVENS
PEND OREILLE
SKAGIT
SAN JUAN
CHELAN
ISLAND
CLALLAM
SNOHOMISH
DOUGLAS
LINCOLN
SPOKANE
JEFFERSON
KING
MASON
KITSAP
KITTITAS
GRAYS HARBOR
GRANT
ADAMS
WHITMAN
PIERCE
THURSTON
YAKIMA
PACIFIC
LEWIS
FRANKLIN
GARFIELD
BENTON
COLUMBIA
WALLA WALLA
ASOTIN
WAHKIAKUM
COWLITZ
SKAMANIA
KLICKITAT
CLARK

UNITED STATES DISTRICT COURTS DISTRICTS OF WASHINGTON

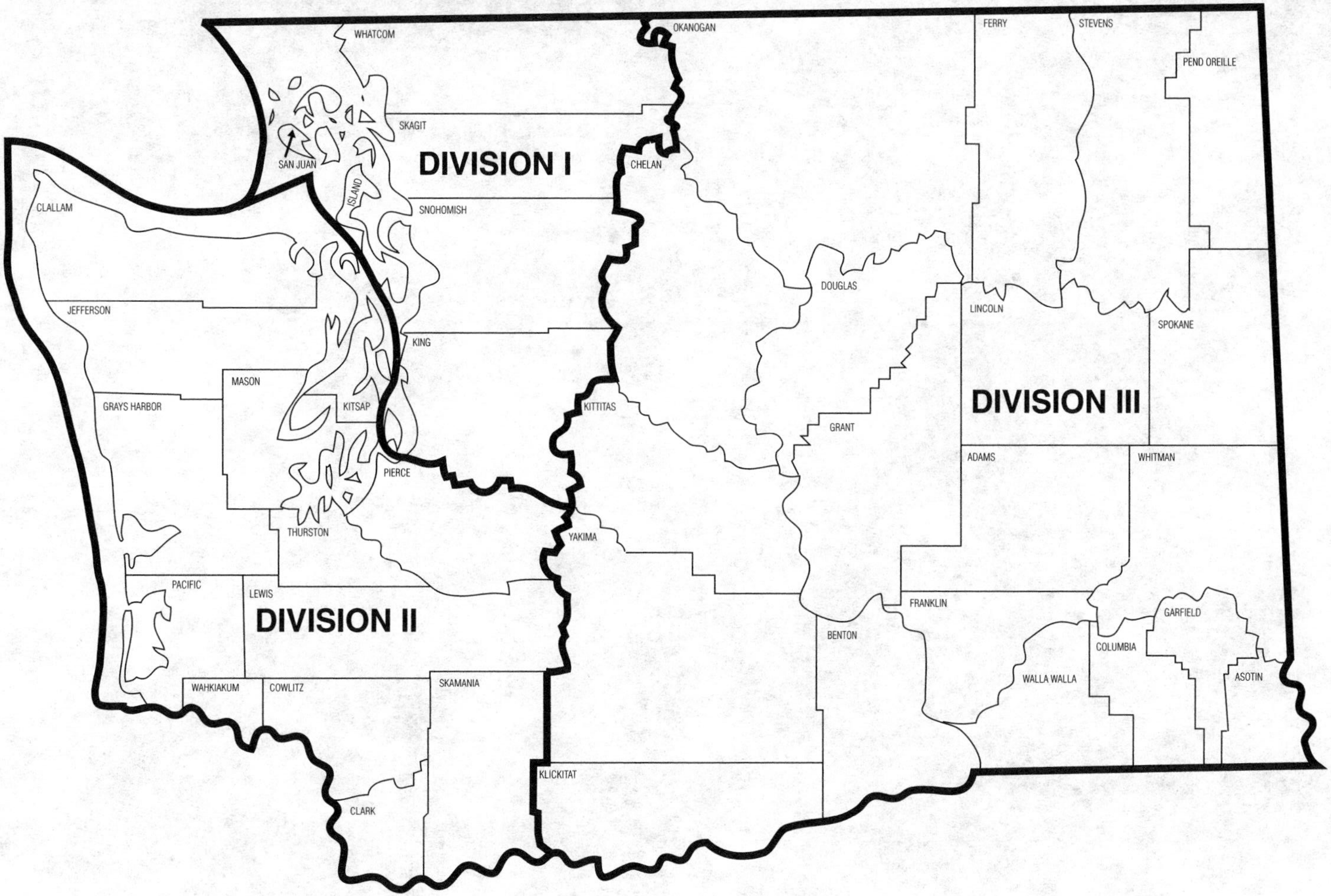
WHATCOM
OKANOGAN
FERRY
STEVENS
PEND OREILLE
SKAGIT
SAN JUAN
DIVISION I
CHELAN
ISLAND
CLALLAM
SNOHOMISH
DOUGLAS
LINCOLN
SPOKANE
JEFFERSON
KING
MASON
GRAYS HARBOR
KITSAP
KITTITAS
DIVISION III
GRANT
ADAMS
WHITMAN
PIERCE
THURSTON
YAKIMA
PACIFIC
LEWIS
DIVISION II
FRANKLIN
GARFIELD
BENTON
COLUMBIA
WAHKIAKUM
COWLITZ
SKAMANIA
WALLA WALLA
ASOTIN
KLICKITAT
CLARK

DIVISIONS OF WASHINGTON COURT OF APPEALS

WASHINGTON

ACEY, William D. *(Judge, Washington Superior Court Asotin-Columbia-Garfield Counties)* Elected Sept 19, 2000, term expires Jan 2005. Born Seattle Washington Aug 22, 1951. Educated at Mercer University B.A. 1973 and Walter F. George School of Law J.D. 1976. Admitted to practice Georgia 1976 and Washington 1982. Judge, Asotin District Court Asotin County Jan 5, 1988 to Jan 7, 2001.

Member Washington State Superior Court Judges Association and State Bar of Georgia (inactive).

Mailing address: P.O. Box 159, Asotin 99402-0159.

Office: Asotin County Courthouse, Asotin 99402.

Telephone: (509) 243-2082.

ADMIRE, David S. *(Judge, King District Court East Division King County)* Elected to term beginning Jan 10, 1983. Reelected 1986, 1990, 1994, 1998 and 2002. Current term expires Jan 2007. Currently serves as Presiding Judge East Division. Born Pasco Washington Feb 11, 1949. Protestant. Educated at Columbia Basin College A.A. 1969, University of Washington B.A. 1971 and Catholic University of America J.D. 1974. Admitted to practice Washington 1974, U.S. District Court Western District of Washington and U.S. Court of Appeals Ninth Circuit. Began legal practice Walla Walla 1974. In legal practice Seattle 1975.

Professor of Criminal Law and Procedure Seattle University 1977-97. Member King County District Court Judges Association, Washington State Magistrates Association and Seattle-King County Bar Association. Former Legislative Assistant to U.S. Senator Henry M. Jackson. Redmond City Council 1980-83.

Office: 8601-160th Avenue N.E., Redmond 98052-3548.

Telephone: (206) 296-3667.

AGID, Susan R. *(Judge, Washington Court of Appeals Division I)* Appointed by Governor Booth Gardner to term beginning Jan 7, 1991. Elected 1993 and 1999. Current term expires Jan 1, 2005. Former Acting Chief Judge and Chief Judge. Born Chicago Illinois Oct 26, 1941. Educated at University of Pennsylvania B.A. cum laude 1965 and Columbia University Law School J.D. with honors 1975. Harlan Fiske Stone Scholar 1974 and 1975. Admitted to practice Washington 1975 and U.S. District Court Western District of Washington 1975. In legal practice Seattle 1975-78 and 1983-86. Judge, Washington Superior Court King County 1986-91, appointed by Governor Booth Gardner.

Senior Deputy Prosecutor Civil Division King County 1978-83. Author *Fair Employment Litigation Manual: Procedural Guide and Sample Documents* New York Equal Employment Opportunity Commission 1975; *Fair Employment Litigation: Proving and Defending a Title VII Case* 2nd ed. New York Practising Law Institute 1979; "Platting, State Environmental Policy Act, Growth Management Fees and Challenges to Restrictions" CLE Manual *Land Use Regulation* Washington State Association of Prosecuting Attorneys 1982; "Employee Privacy Rights and Public Disclosure" Council on Management Seminar 1983; "It All Comes Back to Advocacy" Administrative Law Section Washington State Bar Association Convention 1983; "Investigating Employee Misconduct" Council on Management Annual Seminar 1984; "Current Developments in Land Use Law" Environmental and Land Use Law Section Mid-Year Seminar Washington State Bar Association 1984; "Miscellaneous Labor Law Statutes: The Occupational Safety and Health Act, Employment of Aliens and the Vietnam Era Veterans Readjustment Act" Annual Labor Law Seminar Washington State Bar Association 1985; "The Exclusionary Rule and the Good Faith Exception" Crime, the Court and the Constitution Seminar University of Washington Continuing Legal Education Nov 14, 1987; "Pretrial Practice in Civil Litigation" Washington Women Lawyers Litigation Seminar May 19, 1989; "Evidence Law Update" Washington Association of Prosecuting Attorneys Convention June 22, 1989; "Washington Employment Litigation and Recent Developments" Professional Education Systems Seminar Sept 29, 1989; and "Depositions and the SOB Litigator" University of Washington School of Law Continuing Legal Education March 3, 1990. Adjunct Professor University of Puget Sound Law School 1978-82. Member Seattle-King County, Washington State (Board Member Environmental and Land Use Law Section 1981-84) and American (Judicial Administration Division) Bar Associations. Administrator Food Research and Action Center 1968-71 and Action Center on Social Welfare Policy and Law 1968-71. Board member The Bertschi School. Enjoys cooking, travel and languages.

Office: One Union Square, 600 University Street, Seattle 98101-1176.

Telephone: (206) 464-6047.

Fax: (206) 389-2614

ALEXANDER, Gerry L. *(Chief Justice, Washington Supreme Court)* Elected to term beginning Jan 1995. Reelected 2000, current term expires Jan 2007. Chief Justice since Jan 2001. Born Aberdeen Washington April 28, 1936. Presbyterian. Educated at University of Washington B.A. 1958 J.D. 1964. Admitted to practice Washington 1964. Began legal practice Olympia 1964. Judge, Washington Superior Court Mason-Thurston Counties July 1973 to Jan 1985. Judge, Washington Court of Appeals Division II Jan 1985 to Jan 1995.

Member American Inns of Court, American Judges Association, Thurston-Mason County (President 1973), Washington State and American Bar Associations. First Lieutenant U.S. Army 1958-61.

Mailing address: P.O. Box 40929, Olympia 98504-0929.

Office: 415 Twelfth Avenue S.W., Olympia 98504.

Telephone: (360) 357-2029.

ALLAN, Lesley A. *(Judge, Washington Superior Court Chelan County)*

Mailing address: P.O. Box 880, Wenatchee 98807-0880.

Office: 401 Washington Street, Wenatchee 98801.

Telephone: (509) 667-6210.

E-mail address: Lesley.Allan@co.chelan.wa.us

ALLEN, Sandra L. *(Judge, Ruston Municipal Court)*
Office: 5117 North Winnifred Street, Tacoma 98407-6512.
Telephone: (253) 759-3544.

ALLENDOERFER, James H. *(Judge, Washington Superior Court Snohomish County)* Appointed by Governor Booth Gardner to term beginning Jan 1, 1991. Elected 1992, 1996 and 2000. Current term expires Jan 1, 2005. Born Bryn Mawr Pennsylvania March 15, 1943. Episcopalian. Educated at Carleton College B.A. 1964 and University of Washington J.D. 1967. Associate Editor Washington Law Review 1966-67. Law Clerk to Hon. Orris L. Hamilton, Washington Supreme Court 1967-68. Admitted to practice Washington 1967 and U.S. District Court Western District of Washington 1976. In legal practice Snohomish 1973-91.
City Attorney Marysville 1973-91. Member Snohomish County, Washington State and American Bar Associations. Member Boy Scouts of America, Exchange Club and Everett Symphony Association. Enjoys hiking and skiing.
Office: 3000 Rockefeller Avenue, Everett 98201-4046.
Telephone: (425) 388-3777.
E-mail address: judge@co.snohomish.wa.us

ALSDORF, Robert H. *(Judge, Washington Superior Court King County)*
Office: 516 Third Avenue, Room C203, Seattle 98104-2381.
Telephone: (206) 296-9203.
E-mail address: robert.alsdorf@metrokc.gov

ALTMAN, Brian *(Judge, East District Court Klickitat County)*
Office: 205 South Columbus Avenue, Goldendale 98620-9279.
Telephone: (509) 773-4670.
E-mail address: briana@co.klickitat.wa.us

ANDERS, Scott S. *(Judge, Clark District Court Clark County and Judge, Camas-Washougal Municipal Court)*
Mailing address: P.O. Box 9806, Vancouver 98666-8806.
District Court office: 1200 Franklin Street, Vancouver 98660-2812.
Municipal Court office: 89 C Street, Washougal 98671-2142.
Telephone: (360) 397-2199.

ANDREW, Stewart R. *(Judge, San Juan District Court San Juan County)*
Mailing address: P.O. Box 127, Friday Harbor 98250-0127.
Office: Second and Court Streets, Friday Harbor 98250.
Telephone: (360) 378-4017.

ANTOSZ, John M. *(Judge, Washington Superior Court Grant County)*
Mailing address: P.O. Box 37, Ephrata 98823-0037.
Office: 35 C Street N.W., Ephrata 98823.
Telephone: (509) 754-2011.

APPELWICK, Marlin J. *(Judge, Washington Court of Appeals Division I)* Assumed office 1998. Educated at Mankato State University B.A. 1976 B.S. 1976 and University of Washington School of Law J.D. 1979. In legal practice Lake City 18 years.
Washington Commissioner National Conference of Commissioners on Uniform State Laws since 1985. Co-chair Council on Public Legal Education. Member Domestic Relations Committee Board for Judicial Administration. Recipient President's Award of Merit from Washington State District and Municipal Court Judges Association 1991, Lifetime Achievement Award from Washington State Trial Lawyers Association 1994 and Commendation Award from National Commission Against Drunk Driving 1994. Member Washington State Legislature 16 years. Enjoys baseball.
Office: One Union Square, 600 University Street, Seattle, 98101-1176.
Telephone: (206) 389-3926.
Fax: (206) 389-2614

ARB, Susan C. *(Judge, Moxee City Municipal Court)*
Office: 128 North Second Street, Room 329, Yakima 98901-2631.
Telephone: (509) 575-8851.

AREND, Stephanie A. *(Judge, Washington Superior Court Pierce County)*
Office: 930 Tacoma Avenue South, Room 534, Tacoma 98402-2108.
Telephone: (253) 798-7562.
E-mail address: SUPCRTDEPT12@co.pierce.wa.us

ARMIJO, Sergio *(Judge, Washington Superior Court Pierce County)* Former Judge, Tacoma Municipal Court.
Office: 930 Tacoma Avenue South, Room 534, Tacoma 98402-2108.
Telephone: (253) 798-3655.
E-mail address: SUPCRTDEPT9@co.pierce.wa.us

ARMSTRONG, David *(Judge, Washington Court of Appeals Division II)* Elected Nov 1995 to term beginning Jan 1996. Reelected Nov 2000, current term expires Jan 2007. Former Acting Chief Judge and Chief Judge. Educated at University of Washington 1961 and University of California Hastings College of the Law 1964. Staff member Hastings Law Review. Admitted to practice California and Washington. Began legal practice Kitsap County Washington 1970.
Deputy Prosecuting Attorney San Bernardino County California. Member Kitsap County and Washington State Bar Associations. Enjoys Christian service, charitable and educational activities, playing the piano, reading and family activities.
Office: 950 Broadway, Suite 300, Tacoma 98402-4454.
Telephone: (253) 593-2207.
Fax: (253) 593-2060

ARMSTRONG, Sharon *(Judge, Washington Superior Court King County)* Assumed office July 1985.
Office: 516 Third Avenue, Room C203, Seattle 98104-2381.
Telephone: (206) 296-9363.
E-mail address: sharon.armstrong@metrokc.gov

ARNOLD, J. Kelley *(Magistrate Judge, United States District Court Western District of Washington)* Appointed by U.S. District Court judges to term beginning Oct 28, 1994. Reappointed 2002, current term expires Oct 27, 2010. Born Lewiston Idaho Oct 3, 1937. Presbyterian. Educated at Washington State University and University of Idaho J.D. 1961. Member Kappa Sigma and Phi Alpha Delta. Admitted to practice Washington 1961, U.S. Court of Military Appeals 1962 and U.S.

ARNOLD, J. KELLEY—*Continued*

District Court District of Washington 1965. Began legal practice Tacoma 1963. Judge and Presiding Judge, Washington Superior Court Pierce County, April 1, 1982 to Oct 27, 1994, appointed by Governor John Spellman.

Former Deputy Prosecuting Attorney. Member Tacoma Chapter American Inns of Court (President 1988-89), Washington State Superior Court Judges Association (Chairman Family and Juvenile Law Committee 1984-85), Tacoma-Pierce County (President 1977-78), Washington State and American Bar Associations. Recipient Liberty Bell Award from Tacoma-Pierce County Young Lawyers Association 1987 and 1999 and Outstanding Jurist of the Year Award from Washington Chapter American Board of Trial Advocates 1996. Captain USAS JAGC 1961-63. Member Tacoma Narrows Rotary Club (President 1972).

Office: 3409 U.S. Courthouse, 1717 Pacific Avenue, Tacoma 98402-3226.
Telephone: (253) 593-6751.

AUSTIN, Robert D. *(Judge, Washington Superior Court Spokane County)*
Office: West 1116 Broadway Avenue, Spokane 99260-0350.
Telephone: (509) 477-4709.
E-mail address: raustin@spokanecounty.org

AYERS, Mike *(Judge, Kahlotus Municipal Court)*
Mailing address: P.O. Box 100, Kahlotus 99335-0100.
Office: 130 East Weston Street, Kahlotus 99335.
Telephone: (509) 282-3372.

BAKER, Rebecca M. *(Judge, Washington Superior Court Ferry-Pend Oreille-Stevens Counties)* Elected to term beginning Jan 13, 1997. Reelected 2000, current term expires Jan 2005.
Office: 215 South Oak, Room 209, Colville 99114-2862.
Telephone: (509) 684-7520.
E-mail address: rbaker@co.stevens.wa.us

BAKER, William W. *(Judge, Washington Court of Appeals Division I)* Appointed to term beginning Jan 1990. Former Chief Judge. Former Presiding Chief Judge. Educated at Stanford University and University of Washington School of Law. Law Clerk to Washington Supreme Court. In legal practice Everett 23 years.

Former Vice Chair special commission reviewing Washington judicial selection and retention procedures. Former Member Gender and Justice Commission and Minority and Justice Commission. Chair Planning Committee Washington Court of Appeals. President Washington State Chapter American Judicature Society.

Office: One Union Square, 600 University Street, Seattle 98101-1176.
Telephone: (206) 464-7423.
Fax: (206) 389-2614

BARKER, Jeffrey *(Judge, East Wenatchee Municipal Court)*
Office: 271 Ninth Street N.E., East Wenatchee 98802-4438.
Telephone: (509) 884-0680.

BARNETT, Suzanne M. *(Judge, Washington Superior Court King County)* Elected to term beginning Jan 1996. Reelected 2000, current term expires Dec 2004. Born Roanoke Virginia Feb 13, 1949. Educated at College of William & Mary A.B. 1971 and Washington and Lee University J.D. 1981. Note and Comment Editor Washington and Lee Law Review 1980. Law Clerk to Hon. Henry Clyde Pearson, U.S. Bankruptcy Court Western District of Virginia 1981-82. Admitted to practice Virginia 1981, Washington 1982 and Texas 1987.
Office: 516 Third Avenue, Room C203, Seattle 98104-2381.
Telephone: (206) 296-9213.
E-mail address: suzanne.barnett@metrokc.gov

BASTINE, Paul A. *(Judge, Washington Superior Court Spokane County)*
Office: West 1116 Broadway Avenue, Spokane 99260-0350.
Telephone: (509) 477-5717.
E-mail address: pbastine@spokanecounty.org

BATHUM, Rick *(Judge, King District Court South Division King County)* Appointed to term beginning July 13, 2000. Elected Nov 2, 2000 and 2002. Current term expires Dec 31, 2006. Born Enumclaw Washington Dec 1, 1951. Educated at Western Washington University B.A. with honors 1974 and University of Puget Sound J.D. 1977. Admitted to practice Washington 1978. In legal practice Enumclaw 1978-2000 and Auburn since 1982. Magistrate, Aukeen District Court King County 1979-82. Judge, Buckley Municipal Court Sept 1, 1986 to July 12, 2000, appointed by Mayor Gene Robertson.

Assistant City Attorney Enumclaw 1978-80, Black Diamond 1978-80 and Kent 1983-84. Author *District and Municipal Court Practice* Washington State Bar Association 1983. Member Washington State District and Municipal Court Judges Association (Education Committee since 2000), King County and Washington State Bar Associations. President Community Hospital Memorial Foundation 1990. Board Member Enumclaw Community Hospital 1990-2000. Interests include football, cattle ranching and hiking.

Mailing address: P.O. Box 397, Enumclaw 98022.
Office: Regional Justice Center, Fourth Avenue and James, Kent 98031.
Telephone: (206) 296-7758.

BECKER, Mary Kay *(Chief Judge, Washington Court of Appeals Division I)* Appointed by Governor Mike Lowry to term beginning Jan 1994. Elected 1994 and 2000. Current term expires Jan 2007. Former Acting Chief Judge. Born Aberdeen Washington. Educated at Stanford University and University of Washington School of Law J.D. 1982.

Former Paralegal Northwest Washington Legal Services. Former Member Whatcom County Council. Member House of Representatives Washington 1975-83. Former Chair Board of Trustees Western Washington University.

Office: One Union Square, 600 University Street, Seattle 98101-1176.
Telephone: (206) 464-7656.
Fax: (206) 389-2614

BEIGHLE, Paul *(Magistrate, Seattle Municipal Court)*
Office: 600 Fifth Avenue, Seattle 98104.
Telephone: (206) 684-5607.
E-mail address: Paul.Beighle@seattle.gov

BENNETT, Roger A. *(Judge, Washington Superior Court Clark County)*
Mailing address: P.O. Box 5000, Vancouver 98666-5000.
Office: 1200 Franklin Street, Vancouver 98660-2812.
Telephone: (360) 397-2315.
E-mail address: Roger.Bennett@clark.wa.gov

BENTON, Monica J. *(Magistrate Judge, United States District Court Western District of Washington)* Appointed by U.S. District Court Judges to term beginning Feb 28, 2000. Term expires Feb 28, 2008. Former Judge, King District Court Seattle Division King County.
Office: U.S. Courthouse, 1010 Fifth Avenue, Seattle 98104.
Telephone: (206) 553-4463.

BERGSTEDT, Scott J. *(Judge, Albion and Colfax Municipal Courts)*
Mailing address: P.O. Box 38, Albion 99102-0038.
Office: Third and F Streets, Albion 99102.
Telephone: (509) 332-8001.

BERNER, David A. *(Judge, Enumclaw Municipal Court)*
Office: 1339 Griffin Avenue, Enumclaw 98022-3011.
Telephone: (360) 825-7771.

BERSCHAUER, Daniel J. *(Judge, Washington Superior Court Thurston County)* Assumed office Oct 19, 1984. Elected to subsequent terms. Former Judge, Thurston District Court Thurston County.
Office: 2000 Lakeridge Drive S.W., Building 2, Olympia 98502-6001.
Telephone: (360) 709-3052.
E-mail address: berschd@co.thurston.wa.us

BISHOP, Stephen *(Judge, Tekoa Municipal Court)*
Mailing address: P.O. Box 337, Garfield 99130-0337.
Office: Third and California, Garfield 99130.
Telephone: (509) 635-1551.

BLAUVELT, Arthur A., III *(Judge, McCleary and Montesano Municipal Courts)* Appointed to McCleary Municipal Court by Mayor Gary Dent to term beginning July 30, 1990. Reappointed Jan 1, 1991. Appointed to Montesano Municipal Court by Mayor Doug George to term beginning July 30, 1996. Judge pro tem, Washington Superior Court Grays Harbor County since 1993. Born Oceanside New York Feb 22, 1951. Educated at Western Washington University B.A. 1973 and University of Puget Sound J.D. 1977. Admitted to practice Washington 1977 and U.S. District Court Western District of Washington 1977. In legal practice Tacoma 1977-80 and Aberdeen since 1980. Judge, Elma Municipal Court Jan 1, 1987 to May 1995, appointed by Mayor William E. Eaton.
Member Washington State Trial Lawyers Association, The Association of Trial Lawyers of America, Grays Harbor (President 1989-90) and Washington State Bar Associations. Named Boss of the Year by Grays Harbor Legal Professionals 1984. Previously employed by McDonalds, Inc., Torrance California; Wakefield Seafoods, Inc., Bellingham Washington; and University of Puget Sound, Tacoma Washington. Board of Directors Timberland Opportunities Association. Trustee Timberland Regional Libraries since July 1990 (Representative Grays Harbor). Volunteer American Heart Association. Interests include work and family.
Mailing address: P.O. Box 1106, Aberdeen 98520-0223.
Office: 100 South Third Street, McCleary 98557-9652.
Telephone: (360) 533-2865.

BOBBINK, Michael *(Judge, Blaine, Everson-Nooksack and Sumas Municipal Courts)*
Office: 344 H Street, Blaine 98230-4109.
Telephone: (360) 332-8311.
E-mail address: mbobbink@ci.blaine.wa.us

BONNER, Fred *(Judge, Seattle Municipal Court)*
Office: 600 Fifth Avenue, Seattle 98104.
Telephone: (206) 684-8709.
E-mail address: Fred.Bonner@seattle.gov

BORST, Philip W. *(Judge, Washington Superior Court Lincoln County)* Elected Sept 20, 1988 to term beginning Jan 9, 1989. Reelected 1992, 1996 and 2000. Current term expires Jan 2005. Born Grand Coulee Washington Jan 27, 1941. Educated at University of Washington B.A. 1963 J.D. 1966. Admitted to practice Washington 1967, U.S. District Courts Eastern and Western Districts of Washington and U.S. Court of Appeals Ninth Circuit. In legal practice Wilbur 1967-89.
Prosecuting Attorney Adams County 1967-72 and Lincoln County 1971-89. President Washington Association of Prosecuting Attorneys 1984-85. Board of Trustees Washington State Superior Court Judges Association 1996-98.
Mailing address: P.O. Box 396, Davenport 99122-0396.
Office: 450 Logan Street, Davenport 99122.
Telephone: (509) 725-3081.

BOWDEN, George N. *(Judge, Washington Superior Court Snohomish County)* Appointed by Governor Gary Locke to term beginning Jan 1998. Elected 1998 and 2000. Current term expires Jan 2005. Born East Orange New Jersey Nov 21, 1946. Educated at Bowdoin College B.A. 1971 and University of Maine School of Law J.D. 1974. Admitted to practice Washington 1974, Maine 1975, U.S. District Court Western District of Washington 1978, U.S. Court of Appeals Ninth Circuit 1980 and U.S. Supreme Court 1982. In legal practice Everett Washington 1979-97.
Assistant County Attorney Lincoln County Maine 1974. Deputy Prosecuting Attorney Grays Harbor, King and Snohomish counties Washington 1974-79. Member Washington Association of Prosecuting Attorneys, Washington Association of Criminal Defense Lawyers, National Association of Criminal Defense Lawyers, National District Attorneys Association, The Association of Trial Lawyers of America, Snohomish County and Washington State Bar Associations. Member Rotary and Everett Symphony.
Office: 3000 Rockefeller Avenue, Everett 98201-4046.
Telephone: (425) 388-3532.
Fax: (425) 388-3110
E-mail address: george.bowden@co.snohomish.wa.us

BOYD, Lauri McIntire *(Judge, Selah Municipal Court)* Judge pro tem 1992-95. Appointed by Mayor John Sweesy to term beginning Jan 3, 1995. Reappointed Jan 1, 1998, 2000 and 2003. Current term expires Dec 31, 2007. Also serves as Arbitrator since 1992 and Court Commissioner pro tem since 1996, Washing-

BOYD, LAURI MCINTIRE—*Continued*

ton Superior Court Yakima County. Born Bremerton Washington Oct 10, 1958. Lutheran. Educated at Western Washington University B.A. cum laude 1982 and University of Puget Sound School of Law J.D. 1986. Admitted to practice Washington 1987 and U.S. Supreme Court 1999. In legal practice Tacoma 1986-88.

Deputy Prosecuting Attorney 1989-91 and Appellate Division since 1995 Yakima County. Assistant City Prosecutor City of Yakima 1991-95. Chair Mandatory Continuing Legal Education Board 1993-94. Former Member American Inns of Court. Member Yakima County and Washington State (Court Rules and Procedures Committee 1991-95 and Law Examiners Committee since 1999) Bar Associations. Enjoys reading, travel and skiing.

Office: 128 North Second Street, Room 329, Yakima 98901-2631.

Telephone: (509) 698-7331.

BRANDT, Philip H. *(Chief Judge, United States Bankruptcy Court Western District of Washington)* Appointed by U.S. Court of Appeals Ninth Circuit judges to term beginning 1991. Term expires 2005. Chief Judge Bankruptcy Court since Oct 1, 2001. Also Judge, Bankruptcy Appellate Panel Ninth Circuit. Selected by the Judicial Council of the Ninth Circuit January 1998. Educated at Harvard University B.A. in Economics 1966 and University of Washington J.D. 1972. In legal practice Tacoma 1976-91.

Attorney Department of Justice 1973 and Federal Maritime Commission 1973. Deputy Prosecutor Pierce County 1974. Important Decisions: In re Wallaert 149 B.R. 665, Bankr. W.D. Wash. Nov 30, 1992 (No. 92-32032, 92-33117); In re Ford 159 B.R. 930, 29 Bankr. Cas. 2d (Collier) 1580, Bankr. W.D. Wash. 1983 (No. 93-32649); In re Orris 166 B.R. 935 Bankr. W.D. Wash. May 3, 1994 (No. 92-35604, 93-31676, 92-34171); In re Steffen 181 B.R. 981, Bankr. W.D. Wash. 1995 (No. 94-33752); In re Ehrle 189 B.R. 771, 28 U.C.C. Rep. Serv. 2d 691, 95 Daily Journal D.A.R 16,837, Bankr. 9th Cir. Cal. Nov 21, 1995 (No. CC-94-2546-BHO, SA93-14904-JB, SA93-1621-JB); In re Sheldon 196 B.R. 551 Bankr. W.D. Wash. April 4, 1996 (No. 95-34508); In re Penberthy 211 B.R. 391, 31 Bankr. Ct. Dec. (LRP) 503, Bankr. W.D. Wash. July 24, 1997 (No. 94-08427); In re Fernandez 227 B.R. 174, 98 Cal. Daily Op. Serv. 8485, 98 Daily Journal D.A.R. 11,825, 2 Cal. Bankr. Ct. Rep. 31, Bankr. 9th Cir. Cal. Nov 5, 1998 (No. CC-97-1628-BKME, LA97-02372-TD, CC-97-1863-BKME, LA97-25043-TD); In re Hough 239 B.R. 412 Bankr. L. Rep. (CCH) P78,012, 99 Cal. Daily Op. Serv. 8158, 1999 Daily Journal D.A.R. 10,453, 3 Cal. Bankr. Ct. Rep. 69 Bankr. 9th Cir. Idaho Sept 10, 1999 (No. ID-99-1092-BRP, 98-01101, 98-6172); In re Reinertson 241 B.R. 451, 1999 Daily Journal D.A.R. 11,953 Bankr. 9th Cir. Mont. Nov 2, 1999 (No. MT-98-1674-BHAP); and In re Foross 1999 WL 1270364, Bankr. 9th Cir. Cal. Nov 30, 1999 (No. EC-98-1832-BMAR, 97-25921-A-13, 98-2325-A). Director Standards Project Governor's Committee on Law and Justice 1975-76. Member National Conference on Bankruptcy Judges, Tacoma-Pierce County, Washington State and American (Member Joint ad hoc Committee on Bankruptcy Court Structure and Insolvency Processes, National Conference of Federal Trial Judges Judicial Division) Bar Associations. USN 1966-69. Captain USNR 1989 (retired). Former Board Member Whatcom Chamber of Commerce and Industry (Former Chairman Industrial/Port Committee). Member Economic Development Task Force Whatcom County Council 1982 and Bellingham School Board 1985. Former Board Member Martin Luther King Center. Former Member City Club of Tacoma and Tacoma-Pierce County Chamber of Commerce.

Office: 2100 U.S. Courthouse, 1717 Pacific Avenue, Tacoma 98402-3233.

Telephone: (253) 593-6310.

BRIDGE, Bobbe J. *(Justice, Washington Supreme Court)* Appointed by Governor Gary Locke to term beginning Jan 5, 2000. Elected 2000, current term expires Jan 2007. Born Seattle Washington Oct 16, 1944. Jewish. Educated at University of Washington B.A. 1966 J.D. 1976 and University of Michigan Ph.C. 1970. Editor University of Washington Law Review. Admitted to practice Washington 1976. In legal practice Seattle 1976-90. Judge, Washington Superior Court King County Jan 27, 1990 to Jan 4, 2000, appointed by Governor Booth Gardner.

Lecturer on Society and Justice University of Washington 1975-76. Chair Judicial Information System Committee. Member Washington State Superior Court Judges Association and Washington State Bar Association. Instructor in Family and Juvenile Law for newly appointed judges and commissioners. Recipient Edward F. Stern Human Relations Award from American Jewish Committee 1982, Community Catalyst Award from Mothers Against Violence in America 1997 and Hannah G. Solomon Award 1996. Board Member Phi Beta Kappa and Center for Career Alternatives. Member Seattle Children's Home and Families for Kids.

Mailing address: P.O. Box 40929, Olympia 98504-0929.

Office: 415 Twelfth Avenue S.W., Olympia 98504.

Telephone: (360) 357-2049.

E-mail address: J_B.BRIDGE@COURTS.WA.GOV

BRIDGES, John E. *(Judge, Washington Superior Court Chelan County)*

Mailing address: P.O. Box 880, Wenatchee 98807-0880.

Office: 401 Washington Street, Wenatchee 98801.

Telephone: (509) 667-6210.

BRIDGEWATER, C. C. *(Judge, Washington Court of Appeals Division II)* Appointed by Governor Mike Lowry to term beginning Nov 1, 1994. Elected Nov 1995 and 2001. Current term expires Jan 2008. Former Acting Chief Judge and Chief Judge. Educated at Stanford University B.A. 1966 and University of Texas at Austin J.D. 1969. Began legal practice Washington 1975.

Former Attorney Federal Trade Commission Kansas City Missouri. Prosecuting Attorney 1986-94 and Former Deputy Prosecuting Attorney Cowlitz County. Member Washington Association of Prosecuting Attorneys, Washington Hospital Attorneys and Cowlitz County Bar Association. Chair Cancer Society Jail and Bail. Board Member YMCA of S.W. Washington, Little League, KLTV and Health Care Foundation. Member Hospital Institutional Review Board and Rotary.

Office: 950 Broadway, Suite 300, Tacoma 98402-4454.

Telephone: (253) 593-2204.

Fax: (253) 593-2060

BRINTNALL, George L. W. *(Judge, Battle Ground Municipal Court)*
Mailing address: P.O. Box 2347, Battle Ground 98604-2347.
Office: 505 S.W. First Street, Battle Ground 98604.
Telephone: (360) 342-5150.

BROMILEY, J. Kirk *(Judge, Cashmere and Leavenworth Municipal Courts)* Born Wenatchee Washington April 26, 1949. Educated at Gonzaga University B.A. 1971 J.D. 1974. Admitted to practice Washington 1974. Began legal practice Wenatchee 1974. Former Judge, Douglas District Court Douglas County, appointed to term beginning March 14, 1977.
Member Chelan-Douglas Counties and Washington State Bar Associations.
Mailing address: P.O. Box 1688, Wenatchee 98807-1688.
Office: 2600 Chester Kimm Road, Wenatchee 98801.
Telephone: (509) 662-3685.

BROSEY, Richard L. *(Judge, Washington Superior Court Lewis County)* Former Court Commissioner. Former Judge, Chehalis Municipal Court.
Mailing address: P.O. Box 357, Chehalis 98532-0357.
Office: 345 West Main, Fourth Floor, Chehalis 98532-1921.
Telephone: (360) 740-1172.

BROWN, Carolyn A. *(Judge, Washington Superior Court Benton-Franklin Counties)*
Office: 7320 West Quinault Avenue, Kennewick 99336-7665.
Telephone: (509) 736-3071.

BROWN, Stephen E. *(Judge, Grays Harbor District Court No. 1 Grays Harbor County)* Elected Nov 1986 to term beginning Jan 1, 1987. Reelected 1990, 1994, 1998 and 2002. Current term expires Jan 2007. Born Aberdeen Washington Aug 24, 1955. Episcopalian. Educated at Stanford University B.A. 1977 and University of Washington J.D. 1980. Admitted to practice Washington 1980 and U.S. District Court Western District of Washington 1982. In legal practice Montesano 1981-83 and Elma 1983-86. Judge, Elma Municipal Court 1984-86. Deputy Prosecuting Attorney Grays Harbor County 1980-81.
Office: 102 Broadway Avenue West, Room 202A, Montesano 98563-3621.
Telephone: (360) 249-3441.

BROWN, Stephen M. *(Chief Judge, Washington Court of Appeals Division III)* Former Acting Chief Judge. Former Judge, Washington Superior Court Yakima County.
Mailing address: P.O. Box 2159, Spokane 99210-2159.
Office: 500 North Cedar Street, Spokane 99201-1987.
Telephone: (509) 456-3920.

BRUEHER, Gary John *(Judge, Othello District Court Adams County)*
Office: 165 North First Avenue, Othello 99344-1003.
Telephone: (509) 488-3935.

BRYAN, Robert J. *(Senior Judge, United States District Court Western District of Washington)* Appointed for life by President Ronald Reagan to term beginning June 2, 1986. Assumed Senior status Nov 1, 2000, serves by assignment. Born Bremerton Washington Oct 29, 1934. Educated at University of Washington B.A. 1956 J.D. 1958. Admitted to practice Washington 1959 and U.S. District Court Western District of Washington 1959. In legal practice Bremerton and Seattle 1959-67 and 1984-86. Judge, Washington Superior Court Kitsap County 1967-84.
President-Judge Washington State Superior Court Judges Association 1978-79. Chair Ninth Circuit Committee on Jury Instructions 1991-92. President Ninth Circuit District Judges Association since 2000. Board of Directors Federal Judicial Center since 2000. Major USAR Infantry.
Office: 4427 U.S. Courthouse, 1717 Pacific Avenue, Tacoma 98402-3226.
Telephone: (253) 593-6591.

BUCKNER, Rosanne *(Judge, Washington Superior Court Pierce County)* Assumed office Jan 14, 1985.
Office: 930 Tacoma Avenue South, Room 534, Tacoma 98402-2108.
Telephone: (253) 798-7502.
E-mail address: SUPCRTDEPT6@co.pierce.wa.us

BURCHARD, Jack *(Judge, Washington Superior Court Okanogan County)*
Mailing address: P.O. Box 112, Okanogan 98840-0112.
Office: 149 Third North, Okanogan 98840.
Telephone: (509) 422-7130.
E-mail address: jburchard@co.okanogan.wa.us

BURGESS, Franklin D. *(Judge, United States District Court Western District of Washington)* Magistrate Judge 1981-93. Appointed Judge for life by President Bill Clinton to term beginning 1994. Born Eudora Arkansas March 9, 1935. Educated at Gonzaga University B.A. 1965 J.D. 1966. In legal practice Tacoma 1969-80.
Legal Intern U.S. Atomic Energy Commission 1966-67. Assistant City Attorney Tacoma 1967-69. Regional Counsel U.S. Department of Housing and Urban Development Seattle 1980-81. Airman USAF 1954-58.
Office: 3124 U.S. Courthouse, 1717 Pacific Avenue, Tacoma 98402-3226.
Telephone: (253) 593-6307.

BURNS, Patrick R. *(Judge, Auburn Municipal Court)* Elected to term beginning Jan 1, 1997. Reelected Nov 2001, current term expires Dec 31, 2005. Born Fort Collins Colorado 1951. Roman Catholic. Educated at University of Washington B.A. with honors 1975 and University of Puget Sound J.D. 1978. Admitted to practice Washington 1978 and U.S. District Court District of Western Washington 1978. In legal practice Auburn 1978-96.
Prosecuting Attorney City of Pacific 1982-86. Member South King County, King County, Washington State and American Bar Associations. Participant 1997 and Instructor 2000 Washington State Judicial College. Attended "Courts of Limited Jurisdiction" The National Judicial College 1999 and Traffic Court Seminar American Bar Association 1999. Member Auburn City Council 1982-94 and King County Metropolitan Regional Planning Committee 1992-94. Past President and Board Member Pediatric Interim Care Center. Board Member Suburban Cities Association 1990-94 and Auburn Youth

BURNS, PATRICK R.—*Continued*
Resources. Enjoys reading, hiking, swimming and running.
Office: 3 First Street N.W., Suite A, Auburn 98801-4938.
Telephone: (253) 931-3076.
E-mail address: pburns@ci.auburn.wa.us

BUTTORFF, Karla *(Judge, Pierce District Court Pierce County)*
Office: 930 Tacoma Avenue South, Room 601, Tacoma 98402-2115.
Telephone: (253) 798-6288.
E-mail address: kbuttor@co.pierce.wa.us

BUZZARD, Steven R. *(Judge, Chehalis, Napavine, Vader and Winlock Municipal Courts)* Assumed office Chehalis Municipal Court 1998. Appointed to Napavine Municipal Court 2001. Appointed to Vader Municipal Court 2001. Appointed to Winlock Municipal Court to term beginning 1983. Also serves as Judge pro tem, Washington Superior Court Lewis County and Judge pro tem, Lewis District Court Lewis County. Educated at Central Washington University B.A. in Political Science 1971 B.A. in Social Science 1971 and University of Puget Sound J.D. 1975. Admitted to practice Washington 1975, U.S. District Court Western District of Washington 1976, U.S. Supreme Court 1979 and U.S. Tax Court 1983. Began legal practice Bremerton 1975. In legal practice Centralia 1978. Judge, Centralia Municipal Court 1980-84.
Former City Attorney Bucoda, Mossyrock and Vader. Instructor Centralia College 1988-89. Trustee Washington State Government Lawyers Bar Association 1991-98. Member Guardian Ad Litem Advisory Board Lewis County Juvenile Court. Member Washington State Trial Lawyers Association, The Association of Trial Lawyers of America, Washington State District and Municipal Court Judges Association, Lewis County and American (Committee on Rural Courts Judicial Administration Division) Bar Associations. Listed in *Who's Who in American Law* 1987-88 and 1996-97, *Who's Who of Emerging Leaders in America* 1991-92 and *Who's Who Business Leaders* 1997-98. USCG 1967-71. U.S. Merchant Marine. Former Chairman Lewis County Community Services Board and Reliable Enterprises for the Developmentally Disabled. Former Member Executive Board Lewis County United Way. Founding Member and Former Treasurer Centralia Dollars for Scholars. Instructor Centralia Police Department and Chehalis Police Department. Advisor Lewis County Children with Special Needs. Member Commander's Club Disabled American Veterans Association. Judge Washington State High School Mock Trial Program, YMCA Mock Trial Championship Competition and University of Puget Sound School of Law Mock Trial Program. Team Sponsor Chehalis Youth Soccer and Centralia Youth Soccer. Volunteer Umpire Little League. Volunteer Lewis County Legal Aid and Salvation Army. Participant New York City Marathon, San Francisco Marathon, Mount Whitney 2001 and Seattle to Portland Bicycle Ride. Member American Legion, Association for Retarded Citizens, Kiwanis (Past Distinguished President) and Elks (Trustee).
Mailing address: P.O. Box 59, Centralia 98531-0059.
Office: 314 Harrison Avenue, Centralia 98531.
Telephone: (360) 736-1108.
Fax: (360) 330-2078

CANOVA, Greg *(Judge, Washington Superior Court King County)*
Office: 516 Third Avenue, Room C203, Seattle 98104-2381.
Telephone: (206) 296-9290.
E-mail address: gregory.canova@metrokc.gov

CAREY, Cheryl *(Judge, Washington Superior Court King County)*
Office: 516 Third Avenue, Room C203, Seattle 98104-2381.
Telephone: (206) 296-9120.
E-mail address: cheryl.carey@metrokc.gov

CASEY, Paula *(Judge, Washington Superior Court Thurston County)* Assumed office Dec 18, 1984. Elected to subsequent terms.
Office: 2000 Lakeridge Drive S.W., Building 2, Olympia 98502-6001.
Telephone: (360) 786-5557.

CASTELDA, Roger A. *(Judge, Tonasket Municipal Court)*
Mailing address: P.O. Box 487, Tonasket 98855-0487.
Office: 209 Whitcomb Avenue South, Tonasket 98855.
Telephone: (509) 486-2132.

CASTLEBERRY, Ronald L. *(Judge, Washington Superior Court Snohomish County)*
Office: 3000 Rockefeller Avenue, Everett 98201-4046.
Telephone: (425) 388-3356.
E-mail address: judge@co.snohomish.wa.us

CAYCE, James *(Judge, Washington Superior Court King County)* Former Judge, Auburn Municipal Court. Former Judge, King District Court Aukeen Division King County. Former Presiding Judge King County District Court.
Office: 401 Fourth Avenue North, Room 2D, Kent 98032-4429.
Telephone: (206) 296-9120.
E-mail address: james.cayce@metrokc.gov

CHAMBERS, Tom *(Justice, Washington Supreme Court)* Educated at Yakima Valley Community College, Washington State University and University of Washington J.D. 1969.
President Washington State Bar Association 1996-97. Past President Damages Attorney Roundtable, Washington State Trial Lawyers Association and Washington Chapter American Board of Trial Advocates. Former Member Board of Governors The Association of Trial Lawyers of America. Member American College of Trial Lawyers and Lawyer-Pilots Bar Association (Former Chair Washington State Chapter). Named Trial Lawyer of the Year by American Board of Trial Advocates 1996. Board Member United Way of King County and Rise 'n' Shine Foundation.
Mailing address: P.O. Box 40929, Olympia 98504-0929.
Office: 415 Twelfth Avenue S.W., Olympia 98504.
Telephone: (360) 357-2045.

CHAPMAN, Arthur *(Judge, King District Court West Division King County)* Former Judge, Seattle Municipal Court.
Office: E327 Seattle Courthouse, 516 Third Avenue, Seattle 98104-3273.

CHAPMAN, ARTHUR—*Continued*

Telephone: (206) 296-3610.
E-mail address: arthur.chapman@metrokc.gov

CHMELEWSKI, Mark A. *(Judge, Kittitas Municipal Court)*
Mailing address: P.O. Box 719, Kittitas 98934-0719.
Office: 207 Main, Kittitas 98934.
Telephone: (509) 968-0220.

CHOW, Mark C. *(Judge, King District Court West Division King County)* Currently serves as Presiding Judge West Division.
Office: E327 Seattle Courthouse, 516 Third Avenue, Seattle 98104-3273.
Telephone: (206) 296-3620.
E-mail address: mark.chow@metrokc.gov

CHRISTIE, David *(Judge, King District Court South Division King County)*
Office: GD Regional Justice Center Office, 401 Fourth Avenue North, Kent 98032.
Telephone: (206) 205-9200.
E-mail address: david.christie@metrokc.gov

CHURCHILL, Vickie I. *(Judge, Washington Superior Court Island-San Juan Counties)* Elected Sept 17, 1996 to term beginning Jan 12, 1997. Reelected 2000, current term expires Jan 11, 2005. Born Texas Oct 10, 1946. Episcopalian. Educated at University of Missouri B.J. cum laude 1969 and University of Puget Sound School of Law J.D. cum laude 1986. Admitted to practice Washington 1987. In legal practice Oak Harbor 1987-96.
Member Washington State Superior Court Judges Association, Washington State and American Bar Associations.
Mailing address: P.O. Box 5000, Coupeville 98239-5000.
Office: 101 N.E. Sixth, Coupeville 98239.
Telephone: (360) 679-7361.
E-mail address: vickiec@co.island.wa.us

CHUSHCOFF, Bryan E. *(Judge, Washington Superior Court Pierce County)*
Office: 930 Tacoma Avenue South, Room 534, Tacoma 98402-2108.
Telephone: (253) 798-7574.
E-mail address: SUPCRTDEPT4@co.pierce.wa.us

CLARK, Ellen K. *(Judge, Washington Superior Court Spokane County)*
Office: West 1116 Broadway Avenue, Spokane 99260-0350.
Telephone: (509) 477-6006.
E-mail address: dept12@spokanecounty.org

CLARK, Patricia *(Judge, Washington Superior Court King County)*
Office: 516 Third Avenue, Room C203, Seattle 98104-2381.
Telephone: (206) 296-9190.
E-mail address: patricia.clark@metrokc.gov

CLARKE, Harold D., III *(Judge, Spokane District Court Spokane County and Judge, Spokane Municipal Court)* Elected Nov 3, 1998 to term beginning Jan 11, 1999. Reelected 2002, current term expires Dec 31, 2006. Born Spokane Washington July 8, 1954. Educated at Washington State University B.S. 1976 and Gonzaga University School of Law J.D. 1979. Admitted to practice Washington 1980 and Idaho 1992. In legal practice Spokane Washington 1980-98.
Office: 1100 West Mallon Avenue, Spokane 99260-2043.
Telephone: (509) 477-2963.
E-mail address: hdclarke@spokanecounty.org

CLIFF, Carolyn *(Judge, Langley Municipal Court)*
Mailing address: P.O. Box 366, Langley 98260-0366.
Office: 112 Second Street, Langley 98260.
Telephone: (360) 221-4246.

CLOUGH, Steve M. *(Judge, Snohomish District Court Evergreen Division Snohomish County)*
Office: 14414-179th Avenue S.E., Monroe 98272-1149.
Telephone: (360) 805-6776.

CODD, Paul J. *(Judge, SeaTac Municipal Court)*
Office: 4800 South 188th Street, SeaTac 98188.
Telephone: (206) 973-4610.

COHOE, Bruce W. *(Judge, Washington Superior Court Pierce County)*
Office: 930 Tacoma Avenue South, Room 534, Tacoma 98402-2108.
Telephone: (253) 798-3646.
E-mail address: SUPCRTDEPT14@co.pierce.wa.us

COLEMAN, H. Joseph *(Judge, Washington Court of Appeals Division I)* Appointed by Governor John Spellman to term beginning July 27, 1984. Elected 1984, 1990, 1996 and 2002. Current term expires Jan 2009. Former Chief Judge Division I. Former Presiding Chief Judge. Born Yakima Washington Dec 3, 1940. Presbyterian. Educated at University of Washington B.A. 1962 J.D. 1965. Law Clerk to Hon. Matthew W. Hill, Washington Supreme Court 1965-66. Member Theta Xi. Admitted to practice Washington 1965. Began legal practice Seattle 1966. Judge, Washington Superior Court King County Jan 1977 to July 1984.
Legal Counsel Seattle Police Department 1970-76. Instructor in Administration of Justice North Seattle Community College 1971-75. Chairman Gender and Justice Task Force Oct 1987 to Aug 1989. Member Washington State Sentencing Guidelines Commission 1981-84 and Judicial Conduct Commission 1990-99. Member King County, Washington State and American Bar Associations.
Office: One Union Square, 600 University Street, Seattle 98101-4170.
Telephone: (206) 464-7657.
Fax: (206) 389-2614

CONNOLLEY WALKER, Patti *(Judge, Spokane District Court Spokane County and Judge, Spokane Municipal Court)*
Office: 1100 West Mallon Avenue, Spokane 99260-2043.
Telephone: (509) 477-2971.
E-mail address: pwalker@spokanecounty.org

CONROY, Paul D. *(Judge, Aberdeen Municipal Court)*
Office: 210 East Market Street, Aberdeen 98520-5242.
Telephone: (360) 533-5411.

COOK, Susan K. *(Judge, Washington Superior Court Skagit County)*
Office: 205 West Kincaid Street, Suite 202, Mount Vernon 98273-4225.
Telephone: (360) 336-9320.

COOPER, Michael E. *(Judge, Washington Superior Court Kittitas County)* Elected Sept 20, 1988 to term beginning Jan 9, 1989. Reelected Sept 1992, Sept 1996 and Sept 2000. Current term expires Jan 2005. Born New York New York July 23, 1945. Christian. Educated at Washington State University B.A. in History 1967 and University of Montana J.D. 1970. Admitted to practice Washington 1970, Montana 1970 and U.S. District Courts District of Montana 1970 and Eastern District of Washington 1977. In legal practice Ellensburg 1978-89.
Special Assistant to Montana Attorney General 1971-73. Assistant City Attorney Tacoma 1973-77. City Attorney Pasco 1977-78, Ellensburg 1984-89 and Roslyn 1985-89. Member Washington State Superior Court Judges Association, State Bar of Montana, Washington State and American Bar Associations. Attended general jurisdiction course The National Judicial College. First Lieutenant U.S. Army 1970-71. Political affiliation: nonpartisan.
Office: 205 West Fifth Avenue, Suite 207, Ellensburg 98926-2887.
Telephone: (509) 962-7533.
E-mail address: SCCooper@co.kittitas.wa.us

COPLAND, Thomas A. *(Judge, Grays Harbor District Court No. 2 Grays Harbor County)*
Mailing address: P.O. Box 142, Aberdeen 98520-0035.
Office: 2109 Sumner Avenue, Room 201, Aberdeen 98520.
Telephone: (360) 532-7061.

COSTELLO, Leonard W. *(Judge, Washington Superior Court Kitsap County)*
Office: 614 Division Street, Port Orchard 98366-4683.
Telephone: (360) 337-7140.
E-mail address: lcostello@co.kitsap.wa.us

COUGHENOUR, John C. *(Chief Judge, United States District Court Western District of Washington)* Appointed for life by President Ronald Reagan to term beginning Sept 28, 1981. Born Pittsburg Kansas July 27, 1941. Educated at Kansas State College B.S. 1963 and University of Iowa J.D. 1966. Board of Editors Iowa Law Review 1965-66. Member Order of the Coif. Admitted to practice Washington 1966 and Iowa 1966. Began legal practice Seattle Washington 1966.
Visiting Assistant Professor University of Washington School of Law 1970-73. Member Iowa State, Washington State and American Bar Associations.
Office: 609 U.S. Courthouse, 1010 Fifth Avenue, Seattle 98104-1130.
Telephone: (206) 553-4424.

COWSERT, Kenneth L. *(Judge, Washington Superior Court Snohomish County)*
Office: 3000 Rockefeller Avenue, Everett 98201-4046.
Telephone: (425) 388-3039.
E-mail address: judge@co.snohomish.wa.us

COX, Ronald E. *(Acting Chief Judge, Washington Court of Appeals Division I)* Elected 1994 to term beginning Jan 1995. Reelected 2000, current term expires Jan 2007. Educated at U.S. Military Academy 1966 and University of Washington School of Law 1973.
Past President King County Bar Foundation. Former Member Judicial Screening Committee, Judicial Evaluation Committee, Judicial Election Reform Task Force, Court Congestion and Delay Reduction Task Force. Mentor to high school and law school students. Volunteer with organizations promoting education and welfare of children.
Office: One Union Square, 600 University Street, Seattle 98101-1176.
Telephone: (206) 464-7654.
Fax: (206) 389-2614

COZZA, Salvatore "Sam" F. *(Judge, Washington Superior Court Spokane County)* Elected Nov 1996 to term beginning Jan 1997. Reelected 2000, current term expires Jan 2005. Born Spokane Washington March 15, 1955. Roman Catholic. Educated at Gonzaga University B.A. with honors 1977 and University of Washington J.D. 1980. Member Phi Alpha Delta. Admitted to practice Washington 1981, U.S. District Courts Eastern and Western Districts of Washington and U.S. Court of Appeals Ninth Circuit. Judge, Spokane District Court Spokane County and Spokane Municipal Court Jan 1991 to Jan 1997.
Deputy Prosecutor Spokane County 1981-90. Member Washington State District and Municipal Court Judges Association.
Office: West 1116 Broadway Avenue, Spokane 99260-0350.
Telephone: (509) 477-4795.
E-mail address: dept6@spokanecounty.org

CREIGHTON, Lee *(Judge, Olympia Municipal Court)*
Mailing address: P.O. Box 1967, Olympia 98507-1967.
Office: 909 Eighth Avenue S.E., Olympia 98501.
Telephone: (360) 753-8312.

CULP, Christopher E. *(Judge, Okanogan District Court Okanogan County)* Also serves as Court Commissioner, Washington Superior Court Okanogan County. Former Judge, Coulee Dam and Tonasket Municipal Court.
Mailing address: P.O. Box 980, Okanogan 98840-0980.
Office: 149 Third North, Okanogan 98840.
Telephone: (509) 422-7170.

CULPEPPER, Ron *(Judge, Washington Superior Court Pierce County)* Former Judge, Pierce District Court No. 1 Pierce County
Office: 930 Tacoma Avenue South, Room 534, Tacoma 98402-2108.
Telephone: (253) 798-6640.
E-mail address: SUPCRTDEPT17@co.pierce.wa.us

CUTHBERTSON, Frank *(Judge, Washington Superior Court Pierce County)*
Office: 930 Tacoma Avenue South, Room 534, Tacoma 98402-2108.
Telephone: (253) 798-7625.
E-mail address: SUPCRTDEPT21@co.pierce.wa.us

DAMIS, Spirro *(Judge, Steilacoom Municipal Court)* Former Judge, DuPont and Milton Municipal Courts.
Office: 1030 Roe Street, Steilacoom 98388-4010.
Telephone: (253) 581-1910.

DAY, Jeffrey K. *(Judge, Orting Municipal Court)*
Mailing address: P.O. Box 489, Orting 98360-0489.
Office: 120 Washington Avenue North, Orting 98360.
Telephone: (360) 893-3160.
E-mail address: jkday@msn.com

DECKER, Tarrell *(Judge, Port Orchard Municipal Court)*
Office: 216 Prospect Street, Port Orchard 98366-5326.
Telephone: (360) 876-1701.

DELAURENTI, Charles J., II *(Judge, King District Court South Division King County)* Appointed to term beginning Feb 8, 1982. Elected Nov 1982, 1986, 1990, 1994, 1998 and 2002. Current term expires Dec 2006. Born Seattle Washington May 25, 1943. Catholic. Educated at Seattle University B.A. 1965 and Gonzaga University J.D. 1969. Law Clerk to Chief Justice Robert T. Hunter, Washington Supreme Court 1969-70. Member Phi Alpha Delta. Admitted to practice Washington 1969, U.S. District Court Western District of Washington 1972, U.S. Court of Appeals Ninth Circuit 1972 and U.S. Supreme Court 1973. Began legal practice Seattle 1970.

Former Prosecutor King County. Member South King County and Washington State Bar Associations. Enjoys reading, walking and model railroads.

Office: GD Regional Justice Center Office, 401 Fourth Avenue North, Kent 98032.
Telephone: (206) 205-9200.
E-mail address: charles.delaurenti@metrokc.gov

DERR, Sara *(Judge, Spokane District Court Spokane County and Judge, Deer Park and Spokane Municipal Courts)*
Office: 1100 West Mallon Avenue, Spokane 99260-2043.
Telephone: (509) 477-2959.
E-mail address: sderr@spokanecounty.org

deVILLA, Francis *(Magistrate, Seattle Municipal Court)*
Office: 600 Fifth Avenue, Seattle 98104.
Telephone: (206) 684-5607.
E-mail address: Francis.deVilla@seattle.gov

DIMMICK, Carolyn R. *(Senior Judge, United States District Court Western District of Washington)* Appointed for life by President Ronald Reagan to term beginning 1985. Former Chief Judge. Assumed Senior status, serves by assignment. Born Seattle Washington Oct 24, 1929. Protestant. Educated at University of Washington B.A. 1951 J.D. 1953. Awarded honorary LL.D. Gonzaga University 1982. Admitted to practice Washington 1953. In legal practice Seattle 1959-60 and 1962-65. Judge, Northeast District Court King County 1965-75. Judge, Washington Superior Court King County 1976-80. Justice, Washington Supreme Court 1981-84.

Assistant Attorney General Washington 1953-54. Deputy Prosecuting Attorney King County 1955-59 and 1960-62. Editor and Contributor *Washington State Manual for Justice Courts* Washington State Magistrates Association 1971. Member Public Defenders Advisory Committee to draft King County "Public Defenders Ordinance" 1969-70, Committee on Court Services for Children and Families Washington Council of National Council on Crime and Delinquency 1970-71 and Executive Committee 1977-79, Criminal Justice Committee and Family Law Committee Washington Superior Court King County. Chairman Audit Committee Superior Court Judges Association 1979. Member Rules Committee since 1981 and Chairman Board for Judiciary Education since 1983 Washington Supreme Court. Member Washington State Magistrates Association (Chairman Judicial Ethics Committee 1970-75, member Board of Governors 1975-76), American Judicature Society, National Association of Women Judges (Charter member 1979, Chairman Judicial Qualifications Committee 1981, member Program Committee 1983), American Judges Association (Board of Governors 1974-76 and 1978-81, member Executive Committee 1975-76, Chairman Judicial Qualifications Committee 1977-79 and 1982-83, member Court of Appeals since 1983), Judicial Conference of the U.S. (Member since 1988 and Chairman 1990 and 1993 Judicial Resource Committee), Seattle-King County (Ex officio member Judicial Administration Section 1970), Washington State and American (Committee on Plans and Development National Conference of Special Court Judges Judicial Administration Division 1975-76, Advisory Committee on Implementation of Standards on Jury Management National Conference of State Trial Judges 1978, Appellate Judges Conference since 1981) Bar Associations. Named Honorary Member Order of the Coif 1989. Member Visiting Committee University of Washington School of Law since 1982 and University of Washington School of Law Foundation since 1988.

Office: 407 U.S. Courthouse, 1010 Fifth Avenue, Seattle 98104-1130.
Telephone: (206) 553-2469.

DOCTER, James *(Judge, Bremerton Municipal Court)*
Office: 239 Fourth Street, Bremerton 98337-1875.
Telephone: (360) 478-5989.
E-mail address: JDocter@ci.bremerton.wa.us

DOERTY, James A. *(Judge, Washington Superior Court King County)*
Office: 516 Third Avenue, Room C203, Seattle 98104-2381.
Telephone: (206) 296-9250.
E-mail address: james.doerty@metrokc.gov

DOWNING, William L. *(Judge, Washington Superior Court King County)* Appointed by Governor Booth Gardner to term beginning July 1, 1989. Elected Nov 1992, 1996 and 2000. Current term expires Jan 2005. Born Albany New York Aug 8, 1949. Educated at Vassar College B.A. 1971 and University of Washington J.D. 1978. Admitted to practice Washington 1978, U.S. District Court Western District of Washington 1984, U.S. Court of Appeals Ninth Circuit 1984 and U.S. Supreme Court 1984.

Deputy Prosecuting Attorney King County 1978-89. Member Washington Supreme Court Committee on Jury Instructions since 1984. Previously worked as a deckhand on tugboats and fishing boats. Organized high school mock trial competition.

Office: 516 Third Avenue, Room C203, Seattle 98104-2381.
Telephone: (206) 296-9362.
E-mail address: william.downing@metrokc.gov

DOYLE, Theresa *(Judge, Seattle Municipal Court)*
Office: 600 Fifth Avenue, Seattle 98104.
Telephone: (206) 684-8709.
E-mail address: Theresa.Doyle@seattle.gov

DRAPER, David R. *(Judge, Washington Superior Court Lewis County)* Elected to term beginning Jan 12, 1981. Reelected 1984, 1988, 1992, 1996 and 2000. Current term expires Jan 2005. Born Seattle Washington Nov 10, 1944. Educated at Seattle Pacific College 1963-65, University of Washington B.A. with honors 1967 and Cornell Law School J.D. 1972. Admitted to practice Washington 1972 and U.S. District Court District of Washington 1972. In legal practice Chehalis 1972-75 and 1977-80 and Centralia 1975-77.

Former Member Lewis County (President 1974) and Washington State Bar Associations. Member Washington State Superior Court Judges Association (Board of Trustees 1989-91). Specialist Five U.S. Army 1968-70. Enjoys farming, hunting and fishing.

Mailing address: P.O. Box 357, Chehalis 98532-0357.
Office: 345 West Main, Fourth Floor, Chehalis 98532.
Telephone: (360) 740-1170.

DUBUISSON, Susan A. *(Judge, Thurston District Court Thurston County)*
Office: 2000 Lakeridge Drive S.W., Building 3, Olympia 98502-6001.
Telephone: (360) 786-5562.

DuBUQUE, Joan *(Judge, Washington Superior Court King County)*
Office: 516 Third Avenue, Room C203, Seattle 98104-2381.
Telephone: (206) 296-9255.
E-mail address: joan.dubuque@metrokc.gov

DUFFEY, Charles *(Magistrate, Seattle Municipal Court)*
Office: 600 Fifth Avenue, Seattle 98104.
Telephone: (206) 684-5607.
E-mail address: Charles.Duffey@seattle.gov

DUNN, Michael A. *(Judge, Gig Harbor Municipal Court)*
Office: 3150 Grandview Street, Gig Harbor 98335-1252.
Telephone: (253) 851-7808.

DWYER, Stephen J. *(Judge, Snohomish District Court South Division Snohomish County)*
Office: 20520-68th Avenue West, Lynnwood 98036-7406.
Telephone: (425) 774-8803.

EADIE, Richard D. *(Judge, Washington Superior Court King County)*
Office: 516 Third Avenue, Room C203, Seattle 98104-2381.
Telephone: (206) 296-9095.
E-mail address: richard.eadie@metrokc.gov

EATON, Lynda C. *(Judge, Ferry District Court Ferry County)* Elected 1994 to term beginning Jan 13, 1995. Reelected 1998 and 2002. Current term expires Dec 2006. Also serves as Court Commissioner, Washington Superior Court Ferry County. Born Columbus Montana. Educated at University of Montana B.A. and Gonzaga University J.D. Admitted to practice Washington 1991. In legal practice Leavenworth 1991-93 and Republic since 1994.

Office: 350 East Delaware Avenue, Suite 6, Republic 99166-9747.
Telephone: (509) 775-5244.

EBENGER, David *(Judge, Twisp and Winthrop Municipal Courts)*
Mailing address: P.O. Box 278, Twisp 98856-0278.
Office: 118 South Glover Street, Twisp 98856.
Telephone: (509) 997-6112.

EDWARDS, David S. *(Judge, Okanogan District Court Okanogan County)* Also serves as Court Commissioner, Washington Superior Court Okanogan County. Former Judge, Coulee Dam Municipal Court.
Mailing address: P.O. Box 980, Okanogan 98840-0980.
Office: 149 Third North, Okanogan 98840.
Telephone: (509) 422-7170.

EIDE, D. Mark *(Judge, King District Court South Division King County)*
Office: GD Regional Justice Center Office, 401 Fourth Avenue North, Kent 98032.
Telephone: (206) 205-9200.
E-mail address: mark.eide@metrokc.gov

EIESLAND, Kenneth R. *(Judge, Clark District Court Clark County and Judge, Camas-Washougal Municipal Court)*
Mailing address: P.O. Box 9806, Vancouver 98666-8806.
District Court office: 1200 Franklin Street, Vancouver 98660-2812.
Municipal Court office: 89 C Street, Washougal 98671-2142.
Telephone: (360) 397-2198.

EILER, Judith R. *(Judge, King District Court South Division King County)*
Office: GD Regional Justice Center Office, 401 Fourth Avenue North, Kent 98032.
Telephone: (206) 205-9200.
E-mail address: judith.eiler@metrokc.gov

EITZEN, Tari S. *(Judge, Washington Superior Court Spokane County)*
Office: West 1116 Broadway Avenue, Spokane 99260-0350.
Telephone: (509) 477-4704.
E-mail address: teitzen@spokanecounty.org

ELLINGTON, Anne L. *(Judge, Washington Court of Appeals Division I)* Assumed office May 1995. Born Pensacola Florida. Educated at University of Colorado B.A. 1969 and University of Washington School of Law 1974. Law Clerk to Hon. Orris Hamilton, Washington Supreme Court. Judge 1984 to May 1995, Assistant Presiding Judge 1989-94 and Presiding Judge 1994-95, Washington Superior Court King County.

Assistant Attorney General 1975-78. Member National Commission on Trial Court Performance Standards. Member Governor's Community Protection Task Force. Board of Trustees University of Washington School of Law Alumni.

Office: One Union Square, 600 University Street, Seattle 98101-1176.
Telephone: (206) 464-6046.
Fax: (206) 389-2614

ELLINGTON, Thomas *(Judge, Roy Municipal Court)*
Mailing address: P.O. Box 700, Roy 98580-0700.
Office: 107 South Warren Street, Roy 98580.
Telephone: (253) 843-0463.

ELLIS, Darrel R. *(Judge, Upper Kittitas District Court Kittitas County and Judge, Cle Elum and Roslyn Municipal Courts)*
Office: 700 East First Street, Cle Elum 98922.
Telephone: (509) 674-5533.

EMERY, Jack *(Judge, Tacoma Municipal Court)*
Office: 930 Tacoma Avenue South, Room 841, Tacoma 98402-2181.
Telephone: (253) 591-5259.

ERLICK, John *(Judge, Washington Superior Court King County)*
Office: 516 Third Avenue, Room C203, Seattle 98104-2381.
Telephone: (206) 296-9345.
E-mail address: john.erlick@metrokc.gov

FAIR, Ellen J. *(Judge, Washington Superior Court Snohomish County)* Former Judge, Snohomish District Court South Division Snohomish County.
Office: 3000 Rockefeller Avenue, Everett 98201-4046.
Telephone: (425) 388-3014.
E-mail address: judge@co.snohomish.wa.us

FAIRHURST, Mary B. *(Justice, Washington Supreme Court)*
Mailing address: P.O. Box 40929, Olympia 98504-0929.
Office: 415 Twelfth Avenue S.W., Olympia 98504.
Telephone: (360) 357-2053.

FARRIS, Anita L. *(Judge, Washington Superior Court Snohomish County)*
Office: 3000 Rockefeller Avenue, Everett 98201-4046.
Telephone: (425) 388-3449.
E-mail address: judge@co.snohomish.wa.us

FAUBION, William J. *(Judge, Wahkiakum District Court Wahkiakum County)* Also serves as Court Commissioner, Washington Superior Court Wahkiakum County. Former Judge, Cathlamet Municipal Court.
Mailing address: P.O. Box 144, Cathlamet 98612-0144.
Office: 64 Main Street, Cathlamet 98612.
Telephone: (360) 795-3461.

FELNAGLE, Thomas *(Judge, Washington Superior Court Pierce County)*
Office: 930 Tacoma Avenue South, Room 534, Tacoma 98402-2108.
Telephone: (253) 798-3966.
E-mail address: SUPCRTDEPT15@co.pierce.wa.us

FINLAY, Amber L. *(Judge, Shelton Municipal Court)* Also serves as Court Commissioner, Washington Superior Court Mason County.
Mailing address: P.O. Box 1277, Shelton 98584-0900.
Office: Civil Center, 525 West Cota Street, Shelton 98584.
Telephone: (360) 426-9772.

FISHER, Roger M. *(Judge, Snohomish District Court Everett Division Snohomish County)*
Office: 3000 Rockefeller Avenue, Everett 98201-4046.
Telephone: (425) 388-3331.

FITCH, Rod *(Judge, Yakima District Court Yakima County)*
Office: 128 North Second Street, Suite 225, Yakima 98901-2639.
Telephone: (509) 574-1783.
E-mail address: rod.fitch@co.yakima.wa.us

FITTERER, Richard C. *(Judge, Grant District Court Grant County and Judge, Coulee City, Electric City, Grand Coulee, Mattawa, Moses Lake, Quincy, Royal City and Warden Municipal Courts)* Elected Sept 1994 to term beginning Jan 1, 1995. Reelected 1998 and 2002. Current term expires Jan 2007. Born Ellensburg Washington Jan 22, 1946. Roman Catholic. Educated at Seattle University B.C.S. 1968 J.D. 1975. Admitted to practice Washington 1976 and U.S. District Courts Western 1976 and Eastern 1977 Districts of Washington. In legal practice Moses Lake 1976-95.
City Attorney Soap Lake 1980-95. City Attorney Mattawa 1985-95. Member Washington State District and Municipal Court Judges Association (Board Member, Chair Court Rules Committee), Washington State Trial Lawyers Association, The Association of Trial Lawyers of America, American Judges Association, Grant County (Past President) and Washington State Bar Associations.
Mailing address: P.O. Box 37, Ephrata 98823-0037.
Office: 35 C Street N.W., Ephrata 98823.
Telephone: (509) 754-2011.

FLECK, Deborah *(Judge, Washington Superior Court King County)*
Office: 401 Fourth Avenue North, Room 2D, Kent 98032-4429.
Telephone: (206) 296-9273.
E-mail address: deborah.fleck@metrokc.gov

FLEMING, Frederick W. *(Judge, Washington Superior Court Pierce County)*
Office: 930 Tacoma Avenue South, Room 534, Tacoma 98402-2108.
Telephone: (253) 798-7568.
E-mail address: SUPCRTDEPT7@co.pierce.wa.us

FOSCUE, David E. *(Judge, Washington Superior Court Grays Harbor County)* Appointed by Governor Booth Gardner to term beginning Jan 2, 1986. Elected Sept 1986, Sept 1988, 1992, 1996 and 2000. Current term expires Jan 2005. Born Pittsfield Massachusetts March 7, 1944. Educated at College of Wooster B.A. 1966 and Duke University School of Law J.D. 1969. Admitted to practice Washington 1969 and U.S. District Court Western District of Washington 1971. In legal practice Aberdeen 1969-71.
Deputy Prosecuting Attorney 1971-76. Corporation Counsel Aberdeen 1976-85. President Pacific Crest Trail Association 1999-2000.
Office: 102 Broadway Avenue West, Montesano 98563-3621.
Telephone: (360) 249-6363.

FOX, Michael J. *(Judge, Washington Superior Court King County)* Appointed by Governor Booth Gardner Feb 1, 1988. Elected Nov 8, 1988, 1992, 1996 and 2000. Current term expires Jan 2005. Born New London Connecticut July 7, 1944. Educated at Cornell University A.B. with honors 1966 and University of Virginia LL.B. 1969. Admitted to practice Connecticut 1969, Washington 1970, U.S. District Courts District of Connecticut 1969 and Western 1970 and Eastern 1971 Districts of Washington, U.S. Court of Appeals Ninth Circuit 1971, District of Columbia 1973 and U.S. Supreme Court 1973. In legal practice Seattle 1981-88.
Attorney Seattle Legal Services 1969-73. National

FOX, MICHAEL J.—*Continued*

Counsel United Farm Workers of America 1973. Attorney Northwest Labor and Employment Law Office 1973-77 and Evergreen Legal Services 1977-81. Author "Some Rules for Community Lawyers" Clearinghouse Review Feb 1980 and "Planning and Conducting a Coordinated Discovery Program" *Litigation* April 1981. Attended Trial Judge Academy American Academy of Judicial Education July 1988. Recipient Silver Gavel Award from Washington State Hispanic Bar Association 1990. Secretary 1986-87 and Vice President 1987-88 Legal Foundation of Washington. Fluent in Spanish. Enjoys bicycling, running, skiing and modern American history.

Office: 516 Third Avenue, Room C203, Seattle 98104-2381.
Telephone: (206) 296-9180.
E-mail address: michael.fox@metrokc.gov

FRAZIER, David J. *(Judge, Washington Superior Court Whitman County)* Former Court Commissioner. Born Walla Walla Washington March 6, 1951. Protestant. Educated at Washington State University B.A. in Political Science 1973 and Gonzaga University School of Law LL.B. 1976. Member Alpha Kappa Lambda. Admitted to practice Washington 1976 and U.S. District Court Eastern District of Washington 1979. Began legal practice Tekoa 1976. Former Judge, Whitman District Court Whitman County, elected to term beginning Jan 10, 1983.

City Attorney Tekoa 1976-83. Deputy Prosecuting Attorney Whitman County 1981. Member Washington District and Municipal Court Judges Association, Whitman County, Washington State and American Bar Associations.

Mailing address: P.O. Box 679, Colfax 99111-0679.
Office: 404 North Main Street, Colfax 99111.
Telephone: (509) 397-6244.
E-mail address: frazier@co.whitman.wa.us

FRENCH, Charles S. *(Judge, Washington Superior Court Snohomish County)*

Office: 3000 Rockefeller Avenue, Everett 98201-4046.
Telephone: (425) 388-3075.
E-mail address: judge@co.snohomish.wa.us

FRITZLER, Randal Brandt *(Judge, Clark District Court Clark County and Judge, Camas-Washougal Municipal Court)* Elected to term beginning Jan 15, 1987. Reelected 1990, 1994, 1998 and 2002. Current term expires Jan 2007. Presiding Judge, Clark County Domestic Violence Court since Jan 1998. Born Hollywood California Dec 14, 1943. Educated at University of Nebraska B.A. 1966 and University of Puget Sound J.D. 1974. Admitted to practice Washington 1975 and U.S. District Court Western District of Washington 1976. In legal practice Vancouver 1975-86. Court Commissioner, Washington Superior Court Clark County 1997-98.

Director Washington Arbitration Services Southwest Washington 1983-86. Author "Creating a Domestic Violence Court—Combat in the Trenches" 37 No. 1 Court Review Spring 2000 and "The Development of a Specialized Domestic Violence Court in Vancouver, Washington Utilizing Innovative Judicial Paradigms" 69 No. 1 University of Missouri at Kansas City L. Rev. Dec 2000. Instructor Clark College 1978-79 and 1988-91. Board of Governors 1994-97 and Education Committee since 2000 Washington District and Municipal Court Judges Association. Chair Portability and Specialization Subcommittee 2000-01 and Member Jurisdiction and Portability Workgroup Project 2001 and Best Practices Committee since Dec 2000 Washington State Board for Judicial Administration. Member C.C.J./C.O.S.C.A. Therapeutic Courts Task Force since 2000. Member American Judicature Society (Board of Governors and House of Delegates since 2000), American Judges Association and American Bar Association. Founder Clark County Domestic Violence Court Jan 1998. Attended Executive Component of Court 1987 and Trial Court Judicial Leadership Program Oct 21-23, 1999 Institute for Court Management National Center for State Courts, Advanced Seminar in Anglo-American Jurisprudence Wadham College Oxford University 1988, American Academy of Judicial Education 1989, General Jurisdiction Course 1990 and Special Court Jurisdiction Advanced Course 1996 The National Judicial College, Conference on Domestic Violence 1993 and 1995, National Court Technology Conference National Center for State Courts 1994 and 1997 and Traffic Court Seminar American Bar Association 1997. Faculty Washington State Judicial Orientation Program 1990. Presenter and Panelist Southwest Washington Access to Justice Conference Kelso Washington March 1998, "The Many Faces of Domestic Violence" Soroptimist International Jan 30, 1999, Joint Conference of American Psychology and Law Society and European Association of Psychology and Law Trinity College Dublin Ireland July 6-9, 1999 and "Domestic Violence Courts: Court Innovation" Annual Meeting American Society of Criminology Toronto Ontario Nov 17-20, 1999. Presenter "Domestic Violence Courts" 50th Annual Meeting American Society of Criminology Nov 14, 1998; "Preventing Intimate Violence; Have Law and Public Policy Failed?" University of Missouri School of Law April 3-4, 2000; Therapeutic Jurisprudence 2000 project American Judges Association San Juan, Puerto Rico May 4-6, 2000; on application of therapeutic jurisprudence in specialized courts joint conference of the Washington State District and Municipal Court Judge's Association and the Washington State Court Manager's Association May 6-10, 2000; "Therapeutic Jurisprudence, Preventive Law and Restorative Justice: Viewing Specialized Therapeutic Courts in the United States as a Paradigm Shift in the Jurisprudence and Practice of Law and Judging" XXVth Anniversary Congress of the International Academy of Law and Mental Health Sienna, Italy July 9-15, 2000; and "Dissolutions and Domestic Violence Court" CLE Seminar Washington State Bar Association Oct 26, 2000. Speaker "Violence Towards Women" The Criminal Justice Student Association and Criminal Justice 403 Washington State University Guest Speaker Series Feb 8, 1999 and 5th Annual Correctional Options Workshop Washington Association of Sheriffs and Police Chiefs Leavenworth, Washington Sept 7, 2000. Speaker and Workshop Leader Sixteenth Annual Summer Institute for the Gifted Pacific Lutheran University Aug 2, 1999. Co-Presenter with Justice Barbara A. Madsen "Domestic Violence: Improving the Judicial Response" Access to Justice Conference II Ocean Shores Washington Sept 17-18, 1999.

Recipient Certificate of Distinction from University of Puget Sound 1984 and Award for Promotion of Professionalism in Corrections 1997 and Outstanding Judge Award 1998 from Washington State Misdemeanant Corrections Association. Listed in *Who's Who in American Law* 5th ed. 1987-88 and *Who's Who of Emerging*

FRITZLER, RANDAL BRANDT—*Continued*

Leaders in America 2nd ed. 1989-90. Engineer's aide Nebraska Department of Roads Oct 1962 to Sept 1966. Social studies teacher secondary schools 1966-71. Instructor/Curriculum Writer Omaha Public Schools and Unified School District #223 Sept 1966 to Aug 1973. Part-time political science and history teacher junior college 1971-73. Participant Judges in the Classroom Judicial Education program for High Schools Washington since 1992. Judge YWCA Annual Mock Trial Competition 1994-99.

Mailing address: P.O. Box 9806, Vancouver 98666-9806.

District Court office: 1200 Franklin Street, Vancouver 98660-2812.

Municipal Court office: 89 C Street, Washougal 98671-2142.

Telephone: (360) 397-2199.

GAIN, Brian D. *(Judge, Washington Superior Court King County)* Elected Sept 15, 1992 to term beginning Jan 11, 1993. Reelected 1996 and 2000. Current term expires Jan 2005. Born Escondido California Feb 14, 1946. Roman Catholic. Educated at Seattle University B.A. 1967 and Loyola University of Los Angeles J.D. 1972. Admitted to practice Washington 1972, U.S. District Court Western District of Washington 1972, U.S. Court of Appeals Ninth Circuit 1972 and U.S. Supreme Court 1980. Judge, Bellevue District Court King County July 1981 to Jan 10, 1993. First Lieutenant U.S. Army 1967-69.

Office: Regional Justice Center, 401 Fourth Avenue North, Kent 98032.

Telephone: (206) 296-9170.

E-mail address: brian.gain@metrokc.gov

GALLINA, Scott *(Judge, Colton and Uniontown Municipal Courts)*

Mailing address: P.O. Box 157, Colton 99113-0157.

Office: 706 Broadway, Colton 99113.

Telephone: (509) 229-3887.

GARROW, Janet E. *(Judge, King District Court East Division King County)* Elected Nov 1998 to term beginning Jan 11, 1999. Reelected 2002, current term expires Jan 2007. Born Wisconsin 1953. Educated at Marquette University B.A. 1975, Purdue University M.S. 1977 and University of Puget Sound J.D. 1981. Admitted to practice Washington 1981, U.S. District Courts Eastern and Western Districts of Washington and U.S. Court of Appeals Ninth Circuit. In legal practice Seattle 1990-99.

Staff Attorney Eastside Defender Association (Seattle and Bellevue) 1981-84. Assistant City Attorney Bellevue 1984-87. Member Washington State District and Municipal Court Judges Association and Washington State Bar Association.

Office: Bellevue Courthouse, 585-112th Avenue S.E., Bellevue 98004.

Telephone: (206) 205-9200.

E-mail address: janet.garrow@metrokc.gov

GAVIN, F. James *(Judge, Washington Superior Court Yakima County)*

Office: 128 North Second Street, Yakima 98901-2639.

Telephone: (509) 574-2710.

E-mail address: james.gavin@co.yakima.wa.us

GLOVER, Thomas T. *(Judge, United States Bankruptcy Court Western District of Washington)* Former Chief Judge.

Office: 315 Park Place Building, 1200 Sixth Avenue, Seattle 98101-3122.

Telephone: (206) 553-1626.

GODFREY, Gordon L. *(Judge, Washington Superior Court Grays Harbor County)* Appointed by Governor Booth Gardner to term beginning July 1, 1992. Elected Nov 1992, 1996 and 2000. Current term expires Dec 31, 2004. Born Aberdeen Washington Nov 30, 1947. Episcopalian. Educated at Wayne State College B.S. magna cum laude 1973 and Gonzaga University LL.D. 1976. Admitted to practice Washington 1976. In legal practice Aberdeen 1976-92.

Member Washington State Bar Association. USN 1967-69. Enjoys youth baseball and golf.

Office: 102 Broadway Avenue West, Montesano 98563-3621.

Telephone: (360) 249-6363.

GOELZ, Douglas *(Judge, South District Court Pacific County)* Also serves as Court Commissioner, Washington Superior Court Pacific County.

Mailing address: P.O. Box 794, Ilwaco 98624-0794.

Telephone: (360) 642-9417.

GONZALEZ, Steven Charles *(Judge, Washington Superior Court King County)*

Office: 516 Third Avenue, Room C203, Seattle 98104-2381.

Telephone: (206) 296-9145.

E-mail address: steven.gonzales@metrokc.gov

GRANT, Joshua F. *(Judge, Lincoln District Court Lincoln County)* Appointed by Lincoln County Commissioners to term beginning Jan 1, 2000. Elected Nov 2000 and Nov 2002. Current term expires Dec 31, 2006. Born Spokane Washington March 25, 1949. Educated at Washington State University B.A. 1971 and Willamette University College of Law J.D. 1975. Admitted to practice Washington 1975 and U.S. District Courts Eastern 1983 and Western 1984 Districts of Washington.

Prosecuting Attorney Garfield County 1975-89. Deputy Prosecuting Attorney Lincoln County 1989-99.

Mailing address: P.O. Box 329, Davenport 99122-0329.

Office: 406 Sinclair, Davenport 99122.

Telephone: (509) 725-2281.

Fax: (509) 725-6481

GROSSE, C. Kenneth *(Judge, Washington Court of Appeals Division I)* Assumed office Jan 1985. Former Acting Chief Judge and Chief Judge Division I. Former Presiding Chief Judge. Educated at University of Washington B.A. 1966 J.D. 1968.

Vice Chair Judicial Information System Committee since 1986. Former Member Washington Courts 2000 Commission. Member Judicial Council and Board for Judicial Administration.

Office: One Union Square, 600 University Street, Seattle 98101-1176.

Telephone: (206) 464-7655.

Fax: (206) 389-2614

GUNTER, Alan B. *(Judge, Connell Municipal Court)*

Mailing address: P.O. Box 187, Connell 99326-0187.

Office: 104 East Adams, Connell 99326.

Telephone: (509) 234-6581.

HABERLY, M. Karlynn *(Judge, Washington Superior Court Kitsap County)*
Office: 614 Division Street, Port Orchard 98366-4683.
Telephone: (360) 337-7140.
E-mail address: mhaberly@co.kitsap.wa.us

HACKETT, Robert N., Jr. *(Judge, Washington Superior Court Yakima County)* Elected Sept 15, 1988 to term beginning Jan 8, 1989. Reelected to subsequent terms. Current term expires Jan 2005. Born Salt Lake City Utah July 9, 1942. Educated at Whitman College B.A. 1964 and University of Oregon J.D. 1967. Admitted to practice Washington 1968 and U.S. District Court Eastern District of Washington.
Chief Deputy Prosecuting Attorney Yakima County 1973-89. E-4 U.S. Army 1968-69.
Office: 128 North Second Street, Yakima 98901-2639.
Telephone: (509) 574-2710.
E-mail address: robert.hackett@co.yakima.wa.us

HAHN, Susan L. *(Judge, Washington Superior Court Yakima County)*
Office: 128 North Second Street, Yakima 98901-2639.
Telephone: (509) 574-2710.
E-mail address: susan.hahn@co.yakima.wa.us

HALEY, Donald D. *(Judge, Washington Superior Court King County)* Appointed by Governor John Spellman to term beginning Jan 5, 1983. Elected Nov 1983, 1984, 1988, 1992, 1996 and 2000. Current term expires Jan 2005. Born Roanoke Louisiana Nov 25, 1932. Baptist. Educated at University of Washington B.A. in Political Science 1955 LL.B. 1958. Member Phi Alpha Delta. Law Clerk-Bailiff to Hon. Eugene A. Wright, Washington Superior Court 1959. In legal practice Seattle 1959-63. Hearing Examiner Washington Board of Industrial Insurance Appeals 1963-68. Judge pro tem, Seattle Municipal Court 1982.
Chair Audit Committee and Member Human Relations Committee, Courts and Community Committee, Jury Committee and Juvenile Court Committee Washington Superior Court King County. Member Washington State Superior Court Judges Association (President Elect, Member Board of Trustees, Representative to Bench-Bar Press Liaison Committee "Fire Brigade" Bench-Bar Press Committee of Washington), Loren Miller, Seattle-King County (Internal and Client Relations Subcommittee 1969-71, Member Speakers Subcommittee 1973 and Chairperson 1980 Public Information Committee, Member Judiciary and Courts Committee 1972-73, Criminal Law Section 1974-82, Bench-Bar Press Special Conference 1975, Advertising Subcommittee Delivery of Legal Services Committee 1976-78, Organization Committee Family Law Section 1977-82 and Nominating Committee 1978), Washington State (Committees on Trial Practice Seminar and Rules and Instructions 1974-76), National and American (Liaison to Committees on Education and Ethics and Professional Responsibility and Member Executive Committee and Member Committee on Membership, Bylaws, Credentials and Communications National Conference of State Trial Judges, Member Task Force on Opportunities for Minorities in the JAD and Committee on the Elderly and Persons with Disability Judicial Administration Division) Bar Associations. Member Neighborhood Council Operation Equality Seattle Urban League 1960-62 and Central Area Committee on Civil Rights 1969. Advisory Board Haller Lake Community Study 1964-65. Board member Seattle-King County Economic Opportunity Board, Inc. 1969-74, Washington State International Trade Fair 1971-73, Seattle-King County Legal Services Center 1971-74 and Local Board No. 2, 1972-76 and Local Board No. 19 since 1982 Selective Service System. Member 1971-81 and Chairman 1973, 1976 and 1978 Seattle Civil Service Commission. Chairman East Branch Advisory Council Seattle Model City Program 1972-74. Board member 1959, President Credit Union 1966-68, President Seattle Branch 1969-72, Chairman West Coast Region 1971-72 and President Northwest Area Conference 1977-81 NAACP. President Haller Lake Elementary PTA 1967-68.
Office: 516 Third Avenue, Room C203, Seattle 98104-2381.
Telephone: (206) 296-9165.
E-mail address: donald.haley@metrokc.gov

HALL, Glenna *(Judge, Washington Superior Court King County)*
Office: 401 Fourth Avenue North, Room 2D, Kent 98032-4429.
Telephone: (206) 296-9220.
E-mail address: glenna.hall@metrokc.gov

HALL, H. John *(Judge, Washington Superior Court Lewis County)*
Mailing address: P.O. Box 357, Chehalis 98532-0357.
Office: 345 West Main Street, Fourth Floor, Chehalis 98532.
Telephone: (360) 740-1174.

HALPERT, Helen L. *(Judge, Washington Superior Court King County)* Former Judge and Presiding Judge, Seattle Municipal Court.
Office: 516 Third Avenue, Room C203, Seattle 98104-2381.
Telephone: (206) 296-9235.
E-mail address: helen.halpert@metrokc.gov

HAMILTON, Robert W. *(Judge, South Prairie and Wilkeson Municipal Courts)*
Mailing address: P.O. Box C, Wilkeson 98396.
Office: 540 Church Street, Wilkeson 98396.
Telephone: (360) 829-0171.

HANCOCK, Alan R. *(Judge, Washington Superior Court Island-San Juan Counties)* Elected Sept 1988 to term beginning Jan 9, 1989. Reelected Sept 1992, Sept 1996 and Sept 2000. Current term expires Jan 2005. Born Coupeville Washington Jan 8, 1951. Educated at Western Washington University B.A. magna cum laude 1973 and University of Washington J.D. 1976. Admitted to practice Washington 1976 and U.S. District Court Western District of Washington 1977. In legal practice Oak Harbor 1985-88.
Deputy Prosecuting Attorney 1976-84. Member Island County, Washington State and American Bar Associations. Recipient Outstanding Judge Award for Washington State from Washington State Bar Association 1996.
Mailing address: P.O. Box 5000, Coupeville 98239-5000.
Office: Sixth and Main, Coupeville 98239.
Telephone: (360) 679-7361.

HANKINS, Debbie *(Magistrate, Seattle Municipal Court)*
Office: 600 Fifth Avenue, Seattle 98104.
Telephone: (206) 684-5607.
E-mail address: Debbie.Hankins@seattle.gov

HANSON, Craig *(Judge, Rainier Municipal Court)*
Mailing address: P.O. Box 258, Rainier 98576-0258.
Office: 102 Rochester Street, Rainier 98576.
Telephone: (360) 867-9390.

HARMON, John R. *(Judge, Brewster and Bridgeport Municipal Courts)* Court Commissioner, Douglas District Court Bridgeport Branch Douglas County since June 2002. Former Judge, Douglas District Court Bridgeport Branch Douglas County.
Mailing address: P.O. Box 730, Bridgeport 98813-0730.
Douglas County office: 1206 Columbia Avenue, Bridgeport 98813.
Telephone: (509) 686-2034.
Okanogan County office: 105 Third Street, Brewster 98812.
Telephone: (509) 689-2756.

HARN, Corinna *(Judge, King District Court South Division King County)* Currently serves as Assistant Presiding Judge King County District Court. Former Judge, Renton Municipal Court.
Office: 516 Third Avenue, Room W-1034, Seattle 98104-2385.
Telephone: (206) 205-9200.
E-mail address: corinna.harn@metrokc.gov

HARRIS, Robert L. *(Judge, Washington Superior Court Clark County)* Appointed by Governor Dixy Lee Ray to term beginning Sept 1, 1979. Elected 1984, 1988, 1992, 1996 and 2000. Current term expires Jan 2005. Presiding Judge since 1997. Born Spokane Washington Oct 3, 1934. Educated at Washington State University B.A. 1955 and University of Washington J.D. 1958. Law Clerk to Hon. Frank Weaver, Washington Supreme Court 1958-59. Member Theta Chi and Phi Delta Phi. Admitted to practice Washington 1958. In legal practice Vancouver 1959-79.
Deputy Prosecutor Clark County 1959-70. Important Decisions: Van Vonno, et al. v. The Hertz Corp. (establishing Hertz as an insurance company) 1989; State v. Dodd (death penalty) 1990; State v. Hazen (death penalty); and State v. Stevenson (death penalty). Member Washington State Superior Court Judges Association (Chairman Criminal Law Committee 1991, Board of Trustees 1997-2000, Executive Committee Project 2001 Board of Judicial Administration 1999-2002, President Elect 2000-01, President 2001-02), Clark County (President 1973) and Washington State (Bar Examiner 1969-70) Bar Associations. Attended National Drug Conference for Judges The National Judicial College and U.S. Department of Justice 1989 and Death Penalty Seminar The National Judicial College 1990. Airman Second Class USAF 1959-65. President St. Joseph Community Hospital 1967-74. Board member YMCA. Enjoys coaching youth sports.
Mailing address: P.O. Box 5000, Vancouver 98666-5000.
Office: 1200 Franklin Street, Vancouver 98660.
Telephone: (360) 397-2017.
E-mail address: robert.harris@clark.wa.gov

HARTL, Colleen A. *(Judge, Des Moines Municipal Court)*
Office: 21630 Eleventh Avenue South, Suite C, Des Moines 98198-6317.
Telephone: (206) 870-6517.
E-mail address: chartl@cityofdesmoines.com

HARTMAN, Russell W. *(Judge, Washington Superior Court Kitsap County)*
Office: 614 Division Street, Port Orchard 98366-4683.
Telephone: (360) 337-7140.
E-mail address: rhartman@co.kitsap.wa.us

HATCH, David S. *(Judge, Elma Municipal Court)*
Mailing address: P.O. Box 2013, Elma 98541-2013.
Office: 108 North Second Street, Elma 98541.
Telephone: (360) 482-2603.

HAVEN, Thomas A. *(Judge, Lower Kittitas District Court Kittitas County)* Former Court Commissioner, Washington Superior Court Kittitas County.
Office: 205 West Fifth Avenue, Suite 180, Ellensburg 98926-2887.
Telephone: (509) 962-7511.

HAYDEN, Michael *(Judge, Washington Superior Court King County)*
Office: 516 Third Avenue, Room C203, Seattle 98104-2381.
Telephone: (206) 296-9230.
E-mail address: michael.hayden@metrokc.gov

HEAVEY, Michael *(Judge, Washington Superior Court King County)*
Personal Statement or Quote: "You have not lived a perfect day until you have done something for someone who will never be able to repay you."
Office: 401 Fourth Avenue North, Room 2D, Kent 98032-4429.
Telephone: (206) 296-9280.
E-mail address: michael.heavey@metrokc.gov

HELBLING, James J. *(Judge, Bonney Lake Municipal Court)* Appointed by mayor to term beginning Jan 19, 1986. Reappointed Jan 1990, Jan 1994, Jan 1998 and Jan 2002. Current term expires Jan 2006. Born Mandan North Dakota May 8, 1939. Roman Catholic. Educated at University of Puget Sound B.A. 1966 and Gonzaga University School of Law J.D. 1973. Admitted to practice Washington 1973 and U.S. District Court Western District of Washington 1973. In legal practice Tacoma since 1973. Former Judge, Buckley Municipal Court.
Member Washington State Trial Lawyers Association, The Association of Trial Lawyers of America, Tacoma-Pierce County and Washington State Bar Associations. U.S. Army 1961-63.
Mailing address: P.O. Box 7380, Bonney Lake 98390-0944.
Office: 19306 Bonney Lake Boulevard, Bonney Lake 98390.
Telephone: (253) 862-6606.
E-mail address: JHelbling@citybonneylake.org

HELLER, Ernest A. *(Judge, Lakewood Municipal Court)*
Office: 6000 Main Street S.W., Lakewood 98499.
Telephone: (253) 512-2258.
E-mail address: eheller@ci.lakewood.wa.us

HELLER, James R. *(Judge, Pierce District Court Pierce County)*
Office: 930 Tacoma Avenue South, Room 601, Tacoma 98402-2115.
Telephone: (253) 798-7485.
E-mail address: jheller@co.pierce.wa.us

HICKS, Richard D. *(Judge, Washington Superior Court Thurston County)*
Office: 2000 Lakeridge Drive S.W., Building 2, Olympia 98502-6001.
Telephone: (360) 754-4405.
E-mail address: hicksr@co.thurston.wa.us

HIGHTOWER, Judith *(Judge, Seattle Municipal Court)*
Office: 600 Fifth Avenue, Seattle 98104.
Telephone: (206) 684-8709.
E-mail address: Judith.Hightower@seattle.gov

HILLE, Adalia *(Judge, Ritzville District Court Adams County)*
Office: 210 West Broadway Avenue, Ritzville 99169-1860.
Telephone: (509) 659-3265.

HILYER, Bruce W. *(Judge, Washington Superior Court King County)* Appointed by Governor Gary Locke to term beginning July 1, 2000. Elected 2000, current term expires Jan 2005. Born Seattle Washington April 4, 1951. Educated at Cornell University B.A. 1973 and University of Washington J.D. with high honors 1979. Member Order of the Coif. Admitted to practice Washington and U.S. District Courts Western District of Washington, Eastern District of Oregon and Southern District of West Virginia. In legal practice Seattle Washington 1985-2000.
Deputy Prosecutor King County 1979-81. Legal Counsel to Mayor Seattle 1981-84. Chair Washington State Parks and Recreation Commission. Enjoys flying, hiking, skiing, hunting and fishing.
Office: 516 Third Avenue, Room C203, Seattle 98104-2381.
Telephone: (206) 296-9096.
E-mail address: bruce.hilyer@metrokc.gov

HOGAN, Vicki L. *(Judge, Washington Superior Court Pierce County)*
Office: 930 Tacoma Avenue South, Room 534, Tacoma 98402-2108.
Telephone: (253) 798-7566.
E-mail address: SUPCRTDEPT5@co.pierce.wa.us

HOLIFIELD, George W. *(Judge, Seattle Municipal Court)*
Office: 600 Fifth Avenue, Seattle 98104.
Telephone: (206) 684-8709.
E-mail address: George.Holifield@seattle.gov

HOLLENBECK, Holly A. *(Judge, Benton District Court Benton County)*
Office: 7320 West Quinault Avenue, Kennewick 99336-7665.
Telephone: (509) 735-8476.

HOLMAN, Stephen J. *(Judge, Bainbridge Island Municipal Court)* Appointed by Bainbridge Island City Council to term beginning Jan 1, 1990. Reappointed Jan 1, 1994, Jan 1, 1998 and Jan 1, 2002. Current term expires Dec 31, 2005. Court Commissioner, Kitsap District Court Kitsap County since Jan 1, 1990. Born New York New York March 5, 1950. Educated at University of California at San Diego B.S. 1972 and University of Santa Clara J.D. magna cum laude 1977. Admitted to practice California 1977, Washington 1978 and U.S. District Court Western District of Washington 1978. In legal practice Bainbridge Island Washington 1978-81, Port Orchard Washington 1983-90 and Silverdale Washington 1983-90.
Mailing address: P.O. Box 151, Rolling Bay 98061.
Office: 10255 Valley Road N.E., Rolling Bay 98061.
Telephone: (206) 842-5641.
E-mail address: sholman@ci.bainbridge-isl.wa.us

HOTCHKISS, John *(Judge, Washington Superior Court Douglas County)*
Mailing address: P.O. Box 488, Waterville 98858-0488.
Office: 203 South Rainier, Waterville 98858.
Telephone: (509) 745-9063.
E-mail address: jhotchkiss@co.douglas.wa.us

HOUGHTON, Elaine *(Judge, Washington Court of Appeals Division II)* Appointed by governor to term beginning 1993. Elected 1993, 1996 and 2002. Current term expires Jan 2009. Former Chief Judge. Born Seattle Washington. Educated at University of Puget Sound School of Law 1979. In legal practice Alaska and Washington.
Member Washington State Minority and Justice Commission (Chair Work Force Diversity Subcommittee) and Tacoma-Pierce County Bar Association. Enjoys fly fishing and kayaking in Washington and Alaska.
Office: 950 Broadway, Suite 300, Tacoma 98402-4454.
Telephone: (253) 593-2817.
Fax: (253) 593-2060

HUBBARD, Philip G., Jr. *(Judge, Washington Superior Court King County)* Elected Nov 1996 to term beginning Jan 1997. Reelected Nov 2000, current term expires Jan 2004. Born Iowa City Iowa Oct 17, 1946. Protestant. Educated at University of Iowa B.A. with honors 1969 and University of Michigan J.D. 1972. Admitted to practice Washington 1973, U.S. District Courts Eastern 1980 and Western 1980 Districts of Washington and U.S. Court of Appeals Ninth Circuit 1980. In legal practice Seattle 1984-93.
Office: Regional Justice Center Room 2D, 401 Fourth Avenue North, Kent 98032-4429.
Telephone: (206) 296-9175.
E-mail address: phil.hubbard@metrokc.gov

HULBERT, David F. *(Judge, Washington Superior Court Snohomish County)*
Office: 3000 Rockefeller Avenue, Everett 98201-4046.
Telephone: (425) 388-3608.
E-mail address: judge@co.snohomish.wa.us

HUNT, J. Robin *(Chief Judge, Washington Court of Appeals Division II)* Elected Nov 1996 to term beginning Jan 13, 1997. Reelected Nov 2002, current term expires Jan 2009. Former Acting Chief Judge. Chief Judge since April 1, 2002. Born Worcester Massachusetts May 16, 1948. Educated at Smith College A.B. 1970 and Wayne State University Law School J.D. cum laude 1973. Law Clerk to Hon. Cornelia G. Kennedy, U.S. District Court Eastern District of Michigan 1973-74. Admitted to practice Alaska 1974, Washington 1975, U.S. District Courts District of Alaska 1974 and Western District of Washington 1975, U.S. Court of Appeals Ninth Circuit 1979 and U.S. Supreme Court 1979. In legal practice Alaska 1974-75 and Seattle Washington 1975-76. Judge pro tem 1982-94 and Hearing Examiner 1984-96, Bainbridge Island and Winslow Municipal Courts.

HUNT, J. ROBIN—*Continued*

Deputy and Senior Deputy Prosecutor King County 1976-83. Member Kitsap County Women Lawyers Association, Kitsap County, Washington State and American (Council of Chief Judges Appellate Judges Conference Judicial Division) Bar Associations. Attended Conference for New Appellate Judges New York University July 1997. Former Director Bainbridge Island School Board. Member Eagle Harbor Congregational Church. Enjoys music, theatre, swimming, kayaking and hiking.
Office: 950 Broadway, Suite 300, Tacoma 98402-4454.
Telephone: (253) 593-2976.
Fax: (253) 593-2060

HURTADO, Michael S. *(Judge, Seattle Municipal Court)*
Office: 600 Fifth Avenue, Seattle 98104.
Telephone: (206) 684-8709.
E-mail address: Michael.Hurtado@seattle.gov

HUTCHINSON, A'Lan S. *(Judge, Eatonville Municipal Court)* Former Judge, Pierce District Court No. 3 Pierce County.
Mailing address: P.O. Box 309, Eatonville 98328-0309.
Office: 201 Center Street East, Eatonville 98328.
Telephone: (360) 832-3361.

HUTCHINSON, Lew *(Judge, Lewis District Court Lewis County)*
Mailing address: P.O. Box 336, Chehalis 98532-0336.
Office: 345 West Main Street, Chehalis 98532.
Telephone: (360) 740-1200.

HUTH, Mark *(Judge, Jefferson District Court Jefferson County)* Also serves as Court Commissioner, Washington Superior Court Jefferson County.
Mailing address: P.O. Box 1220, Port Townsend 98368-0920.
Office: 1820 Jefferson Street, Port Townsend 98368.
Telephone: (360) 385-9135.

HUTTON, James P. *(Judge, Washington Superior Court Yakima County)* Elected Nov 25, 1996 to term beginning Jan 13, 1997. Reelected Sept 2000, current term expires Jan 2005. Presiding Administrative Judge 2000. Born Seattle Washington March 7, 1949. Educated at University of Washington B.A. 1972 and Gonzaga University School of Law J.D. 1976. Admitted to practice Washington 1977, U.S. District Court Eastern District of Washington 1977, U.S. Court of Appeals Ninth Circuit 1977 and U.S. Court of Federal Claims 1977. In legal practice Yakima Washington 1977-97.
Member Washington State Superior Court Judges Association (Secretary 1998-99), Yakima County and Washington State Bar Associations. Enjoys snow skiing.
Office: 128 North Second Street, Yakima 98901-2639.
Telephone: (509) 574-2710.
Fax: (509) 574-2701
E-mail address: james.hutton@co.yakima.wa.us

HYDE, Stephen J. *(Judge, Westport Municipal Court)*
Mailing address: P.O. Box 1208, Westport 98595-1208.
Office: 506 North Montesano Street, Westport 98595.
Telephone: (360) 538-0175.

IMBROGNO, Cynthia *(Magistrate Judge, United States District Court Eastern District of Washington)* Appointed by U.S. District Court judges.
Mailing address: P.O. Box 263, Spokane 99210-0263.
Telephone: (509) 353-0660.

IMLER, Kyle L. *(Judge, Oakville Municipal Court)*
Mailing address: P.O. Box D, Oakville 98568-0078.
Office: 204 East Main, Oakville 98568.
Telephone: (360) 273-5531.

INGVALSON, Robert J. *(Judge, Benton District Court Prosser Branch Benton County)*
Office: 620 Market Street, Prosser 99350-1300.
Telephone: (509) 786-5480.

INVEEN, Laura *(Judge, Washington Superior Court King County)* Former Judge, Seattle District Court King County.
Office: 516 Third Avenue, Room C203, Seattle 98104-2381.
Telephone: (206) 296-9268.
E-mail address: laura.inveen@metrokc.gov

IRELAND, Faith *(Justice, Washington Supreme Court)* Elected 1998 to term beginning Jan 11, 1999. Term expires Jan 2005. Born Seattle Washington 1942. Educated at University of Washington B.A., Willamette University School of Law 1969 and Golden Gate University LL.M. in Taxation. Began legal practice Seattle 1970. Judge, Washington Superior Court King County 1984-98, appointed by Governor John Spellman.
Former Board Member Washington State Superior Court Judges Association (President 1996-97). Vice Chair Board for Judicial Administration 1996-98. Former Board Member Washington State Trial Lawyers Association. Chair Supreme Court Education Committee. Member Board for Court Education. Founding Member Washington Women Lawyers Association. Former Dean Washington Judicial College.
Mailing address: P.O. Box 40929, Olympia 98504-0929.
Office: 415 Twelfth Avenue S.W., Olympia 98504.
Telephone: (360) 357-2033.

JACKE, Linda *(Judge, King District Court East Division King County)*
Office: Bellevue Courthouse, 585-112th Avenue S.E., Bellevue 98004.
Telephone: (206) 205-9200.
E-mail address: linda.jacke@metrokc.gov

JASPRICA, Judy Rae *(Judge, Pierce District Court Pierce County)*
Office: 930 Tacoma Avenue South, Room 601, Tacoma 98402-2115.
Telephone: (253) 798-3313.
E-mail address: jjaspri@co.pierce.wa.us

JOHANSON, Jill *(Judge, Washington Superior Court Cowlitz County)*
Office: 312 S.W. First Avenue, Kelso 98626-1739.
Telephone: (360) 577-3085.

JOHNSON, Barbara D. *(Judge, Washington Superior Court Clark County)*
Mailing address: P.O. Box 5000, Vancouver 98666-5000.
Office: 1200 Franklin Street, Vancouver 98660-2812.
Telephone: (360) 397-2005.
E-mail address: Barbara.Johnson@clark.wa.gov

JOHNSON, Charles W. *(Associate Chief Justice, Washington Supreme Court)* Elected 1990 to term beginning Jan 14, 1991. Reelected 1996 and 2002. Current term expires Jan 2009. One of the youngest judges in history to serve on Washington Supreme Court. Educated at University of Puget Sound School of Law 1976. Admitted to practice Washington and U.S. District Court Western District of Washington.

Member Puget Sound Chapter American Inns of Court, Tacoma-Pierce County and Washington State Bar Associations. Board of Directors Washington Association for Children and Parents. Board of Visitors Seattle University School of Law. Enjoys sailing, downhill skiing, cycling and other outdoor activities.

Mailing address: P.O. Box 40929, Olympia 98504-0929.

Office: 415 Twelfth Avenue S.W., Olympia 98504.

Telephone: (360) 357-2020.

JONES, Richard A. *(Judge, Washington Superior Court King County)* Appointed by Governor Mike Lowry to term beginning July 25, 1994. Elected Sept 1994, Sept 1996 and 2000. Current term expires Dec 31, 2004. Born Seattle Washington Sept 5, 1950. Educated at Seattle University B.A. 1972 and University of Washington School of Law J.D. 1975. In legal practice 1983-87.

Deputy Prosecuting Attorney King County 1975-78. Staff Attorney Port of Seattle 1978-83. Assistant U.S. Attorney 1988 to July 1994. Chair Thanksgiving Food Drive 1987-94 and President 1987-90 Loren Miller Bar Association. Member Municipal Court Judicial Screening Committee 1988-89, Judicial Screening Committee 1988-92 and Judicial Screening Task Force 1991-93 King County Bar Association and Washington State Minority Justice Commission since 1991. Co-chair Opportunities for Minorities in the Legal Profession Committee Washington State Bar Association 1991-92. Instructor "Advanced Crime Scene Investigation," "Search and Seizure" and "Advanced Narcotics Investigations" Washington State Criminal Justice Training Center. Instructor EEO Counselor and Investigator Training Workshop Executive Office for U.S. Attorneys July 1991 and Criminal Trial Advocacy Course Attorney General's Advocacy Institute April 1992. Lecturer National Association of Law Placement National Conference 1993. Recipient V.A. Inspector General Special Recognition for Prosecution of Equity Skimming Cases 1988, Affirmative Action Award from King County Bar Association 1991, Special Recognition Award for Furthering Equal Opportunity from Washington State Bar Association 1991, Special Achievement Awards for Sustained Superior Performance of Duty from Department of Justice 1991 and 1992, Resolution and Commendation for Outstanding Service as Co-chair Opportunities for Minorities in the Legal Profession Committee from Board of Governors Washington State Bar Association 1992 and Director's Award for Superior Achievement in Furthering Equal Employment Opportunity from U.S. Attorney's Office 1993. President Central Area Group Homes Program 1979-80. Board of Directors University Preparatory Academy 1985-91 and Fairhaven College Law and Diversity since 1991. Co-chair Northwest Minority Job Fair since 1987. Mentor Program University of Washington School of Law since 1991. Trustee 1990-93, Chair Diversity Enrichment Committee 1991-93 and President 1994-95 University of Washington School of Law Alumni Association. Trustee/Secretary 1990-92, Chair Community Campaign 1991-92, Vice President 1992-97 YMCA of Greater Seattle. Member Seattle Police Department Chief Selection Committee 1994. Board of Regents Seattle University since 1996. Dean Washington State Judicial College since 1998. Trustee University of Washington School of Law Foundation Board.

Office: 516 Third Avenue, Room C203, Seattle 98104-2381.

Telephone: (206) 296-9260.

E-mail address: richard.jones@metrokc.gov

JORGENSEN, Kenneth L. *(Judge, Washington Superior Court Grant County)*

Mailing address: P.O. Box 37, Ephrata 98823-0037.

Office: 35 C Street N.W., Ephrata 98823.

Telephone: (509) 754-2011.

JUNKE, John P. *(Judge, Prescott Municipal Court)* Former Judge, Walla Walla Municipal Court. Former Judge, Walla Walla District Court Walla Walla County.

Mailing address: P.O. Box 994, Walla Walla 99362-0020.

Telephone: (509) 529-3923.

JURADO, Terry L. *(Judge, Renton Municipal Court)*

Office: 1055 South Grady Way, Renton 98055-3232.

Telephone: (425) 430-6550.

KALLAS, Paris *(Judge, Washington Superior Court King County)*

Office: 516 Third Avenue, Room C203, Seattle 98104-2381.

Telephone: (206) 296-9105.

E-mail address: paris.kallas@metrokc.gov

KATO, Eileen A. *(Judge, King District Court West Division King County)* Assumed office June 1994. Judge pro tem, Washington Superior Court King County since May 1993. Educated at San Jose State University B.S. 1976 M.B.A. 1977 and University of Santa Clara School of Law J.D. 1980. Business Editor Santa Clara Law Review. In legal practice 1989 to June 1994. Judge pro tem, Seattle Municipal Court May 1992 to June 1994.

Special Trial Attorney Office of District Counsel Internal Revenue Service 1980-89. Special Assistant to U.S. Attorney Western District of Washington 1984-89. Instructor in Business Law and Accounting South Seattle Community College 1988-94. Member Executive Committee King County District Court 1999-2000 and 2001-02. Member Washington Women Lawyers, Washington State District and Municipal Court Judges Association (Vice President 2002-03), American Judicature Society, Asian Bar Association of Washington, National Asian Pacific American and American (Judicial Division) Bar Associations. Panelist "How to Become a Judge" 1995 and "The Impact of Women in the Legal Profession" 1996 National Asian Pacific American Bar Association, "Choice in Law Practice" University of Washington School of Law CLE 1997, "Access to Justice—Immigrants in the Courts" Spring Conference Washington State District and Municipal Court Judges Association May 1998, "Access to Justice—Judges and Litigants: Communication is a Two-Way Street" Superior Court Judges' Spring Conference April 1999 and "Evolution of the Young Lawyer—Advancing the Cause of Professionalism" Annual Conference Young Lawyers Division Washington State Bar Association May 2000. Speaker "District Court: The Court for All Reasons—Proposed Uniform Local Civil Rules" 1996, "District Court Civil Practice" Dec 1999 and "Civility and Pro-

KATO, EILEEN A.—*Continued*
fessionalism" Dec 2000, 2001 and 2002 King County Bar Association CLE; "Try It in District Court—The Limits are Higher and the Rules are Changing" Roundtable Meeting Washington State Trial Lawyers Association Oct 1997; "Access to Justice—The Judicial Role in Ensuring Justice: Ethical Mandates and Constraints" Spring Conference Washington State District and Municipal Court Judges Association May 1999; and "Civility and Professionalism" Washington State Bar Association Feb 2001 and Feb 2002. Dean Emeritus Washington State Judicial College 1998-2000. Faculty Member Advanced Program National Judicial Leadership Institute on Education June 1998 and The National Judicial College since 2001. Member since 2000 and Secretary since 2000 Washington State Board for Court Education. Member Japanese American Citizens League since 1988 and Seattle Foundation since 1996. Judge Moot Court, Mock Trial and Client Counseling Competitions since 1989 and Mentor First-Year Minority Mentorship Program since 1990 University of Washington School of Law. Board of Directors Empty Space Theatre 1992-98, New Beginnings Shelter for Battered Women and Children 1993-94, Northwest Minority Law Student Job Fair since 1993 and Nikkei Concerns since 1998. Founder and Participant Juvenile Justice Roundtable Asian Pacific Islander Task Force on Youth 1996-2001.

Office: 516 Third Avenue, Suite E301, Seattle 98104.
Telephone: (206) 296-3615.

KATO, Kenneth H. *(Acting Chief Judge, Washington Court of Appeals Division III)* Appointed by Governor Gary Locke to term beginning 1997. Elected 1998 and 2002. Current term expires Jan 2008. Educated at University of Washington B.A. 1971 J.D. 1975. In legal practice Spokane 1975-88. Commissioner, Washington Court of Appeals Division III 1988-96. Judge, Washington Superior Court Spokane County 1996-97.

Member Washington State Minority and Justice Commission (Chairperson Research Subcommittee), Asian Bar Association of Washington, National Asian Pacific American Bar Association, Spokane County and Washington State Bar Associations. Named Judge of the Year by Asian Bar Association of Washington 1998. Recipient Trailblazer Award from National Asian Pacific American Bar Association 2000. Member Washington Junior Golf Association.

Mailing address: P.O. Box 2159, Spokane 99210-2159.
Office: 500 North Cedar Street, Spokane 99201-1987.
Telephone: (509) 456-4032.
Fax: (509) 456-4287

KAYNE, Richard B. *(Judge, Medical Lake Municipal Court)*

Mailing address: P.O. Box 369, Medical Lake 99022-0369.
Office: 124 South Lefevre Street, Medical Lake 99022.
Telephone: (509) 565-5000.
E-mail address: rkayne@medical-lake.org

KELLY, Thomas E. *(Judge, Snohomish District Court Everett Division Snohomish County)* Elected Nov 1978 to term beginning Jan 8, 1979. Reelected 1982, 1986, 1990, 1994, 1998 and 2002. Current term expires Jan 2007. Born Spokane Washington May 13, 1940. Catholic. Educated at Gonzaga University J.D. 1966. Admitted to practice Washington 1966. Began legal practice Olympia.

With Attorney General's Office Washington 1966-69. Member Washington State Magistrates Association. Honorary member Snohomish County and Washington State Bar Associations.

Office: 3000 Rockefeller Avenue, Everett 98201-4046.
Telephone: (425) 388-3331.

KENNEDY, Faye *(Judge, Washington Court of Appeals Division I)* Elected Nov 1990 to term beginning Jan 1991. Reelected 1996 and 2002. Current term expires Jan 2009. Former Acting Chief Judge and Chief Judge. Educated at University of Idaho College of Law J.D. 1967. Law Clerk to Chief Justice Robert Finley, Washington Supreme Court 1967-68. Admitted to practice Washington 1967. In legal practice Everett 1974 to Nov 1990. Judge, Snohomish District Court Everett Division Snohomish County 1970-74.

Deputy Prosecuting Attorney Snohomish County 1968-70. Author two chapters *Washington Family Law Deskbook.* Past President Snohomish County Bar Association. Former Member Board of Directors Washington Trial Lawyers Association. Fellow American Academy of Matrimonial Lawyers. Member Washington State Gender and Justice Commission and Washington State Domestic Relations Commission. Named Family Law Attorney of the Year 1990. Board Member Snohomish County United Way, Snohomish County Mental Health Services and Everett Area Chamber of Commerce.

Office: One Union Square, 600 University Street, Seattle 98101-1176.
Telephone: (206) 464-7658.
Fax: (206) 389-2614

KENWORTHY, David M. *(Judge, Pierce District Court Pierce County)* Elected to term beginning Jan 9, 1995. Reelected 1998 and 2002. Current term expires Jan 2007. Born Lucas County Iowa April 22, 1938. Educated at Iowa State University B.S. 1961, University of Puget Sound M.B.A. M.P.A. 1980 and Georgetown University J.D. 1970. Admitted to practice Washington 1971, U.S. District Court Western District of Washington 1972 and U.S. Supreme Court 1992.

Deputy Reporter of Decisions Washington Supreme Court 1971-94. Member Washington State Bar Association. Colonel USMC 1961-91.

Office: 930 Tacoma Avenue South, Room 601, Tacoma 98402-2115.
Telephone: (253) 798-6627.
Fax: (253) 798-6616
E-mail address: dkenwor@co.pierce.wa.us

KESSLER, Ronald *(Judge, Washington Superior Court King County)* Born Philadelphia Pennsylvania May 6, 1947. Educated at Washington and Lee University B.A. 1969 and Villanova University J.D. 1972. Admitted to practice Washington 1973, Pennsylvania 1973, U.S. District Court Western District of Washington 1974 and U.S. Court of Appeals Ninth Circuit 1974. In legal practice 1973-85. Former Judge, Seattle Municipal Court, appointed by Mayor Charles Royer to term beginning Jan 1985.

With Seattle Legal Services (VISTA) 1972-73. Staff Attorney Seattle-King County Public Defender Associa-

KESSLER, RONALD—*Continued*
tion 1976-85. Instructor University of Washington 1980-81.

Office: 401 Fourth Avenue North, Room 2D, Kent 98032-4429.
Telephone: (206) 296-9113.
E-mail address: ronald.kessler@metrokc.gov

KIMBROUGH, Rickey C. *(Judge, Grandview Municipal Court)*
Office: 207 West Second Street, Grandview 98930-1360.
Telephone: (509) 882-9202.

KLEWENO, Gilbert H. *(Magistrate Judge, United States District Court Western District of Washington)* Appointed by U.S. District Court judges to term beginning Feb 15, 1987. Reappointed 1991, 1995, 1999 and 2003. Current term expires March 2007. Serves part time.
Mailing address: P.O. Box 938, Vancouver 98666-0938.
Telephone: (360) 696-0401.

KLOBUCHER, John M. *(Recalled Judge, United States Bankruptcy Court Eastern District of Washington)* Appointed Judge by U.S. District Court judges to term beginning Dec 7, 1981. Reappointed by U.S. Court of Appeals Ninth Circuit judges Aug 25, 1986. Former Chief Judge. Appointed Recalled Judge by the Judicial Council of the Ninth Circuit July 13, 1997. Born Spokane Washington July 12, 1932. Roman Catholic. Educated at Washington State University 1952 and Gonzaga University J.D. 1960. Law Clerk to Hon. Charles Powell, U.S. District Court Eastern District of Washington 1960-61. Admitted to practice Washington 1960. Began legal practice Spokane 1961.

Deputy Prosecuting Attorney Criminal Division Spokane County 1961-63. Member Spokane County (President 1981) and Washington State Bar Associations. Corporal U.S. Army 1953-54. Member Inland Empire Fly Fishing Club (President 1977). Enjoys fly fishing.
Mailing address: P.O. Box 2164, Spokane 99210-2164.
Telephone: (509) 353-2404.

KNIGHT, Gerald L. *(Judge, Washington Superior Court Snohomish County)*
Office: 3000 Rockefeller Avenue, Everett 98201-4046.
Telephone: (425) 388-3571.
E-mail address: judge@co.snohomish.wa.us

KNOWLTON, John O. *(Judge, Walla Walla District Court Walla Walla County)* Former Court Commissioner, Washington Superior Court Walla Walla County. Former Judge, College Place Municipal Court.
Office: 317 West Rose, Walla Walla 99362.
Telephone: (509) 527-3236.

KONDO, C. Kimi *(Judge, Seattle Municipal Court)* Former Presiding Judge.
Office: 600 Fifth Avenue, Seattle 98104.
Telephone: (206) 684-8709.
E-mail address: Kimi.Kondo@seattle.gov

KOSS, David R. *(Judge, Cowlitz District Court Cowlitz County)* Also serves as Court Commissioner, Washington Superior Court Cowlitz County.
Office: 312 S.W. First Avenue, Room 207, Kelso 98626-1797.
Telephone: (360) 577-3073.
E-mail address: KossD@co.cowlitz.wa.us

KRESE, Linda C. *(Judge, Washington Superior Court Snohomish County)*
Office: 3000 Rockefeller Avenue, Everett 98201-4046.
Telephone: (425) 388-3954.
E-mail address: judge@co.snohomish.wa.us

KRISTIANSON, Larry M. *(Judge, Washington Superior Court Ferry-Pend Oreille-Stevens Counties)* Former Judge, Stevens District Court Stevens County.
Office: 215 South Oak, Room 209, Colville 99114-2862.
Telephone: (509) 684-7520.

KROUSE, Merle R. *(Judge, Centralia Municipal Court)*
Mailing address: P.O. Box 609, Centralia 98531-0609.
Office: 118 West Maple Street, Centralia 98531.
Telephone: (360) 330-7667.

KURTZ, Frank L. *(Judge, Washington Court of Appeals Division III)* Appointed by Governor Mike Lowry Aug 1996. Former Acting Chief Judge and Chief Judge. Educated at Creighton University and Gonzaga University.
Mailing address: P.O. Box 2159, Spokane 99210-2159.
Office: 500 North Cedar Street, Spokane 99201-1987.
Telephone: (509) 625-5159.
Fax: (509) 456-4287

LADENBURG, David B. *(Judge, Tacoma Municipal Court)*
Office: 930 Tacoma Avenue South, Room 841, Tacoma 98402-2181.
Telephone: (253) 591-5259.

LAHTINEN, Jacki *(Judge, Benton District Court Benton County)* Currently serves as Presiding Judge.
Office: 7320 West Quinault Avenue, Kennewick 99336-7665.
Telephone: (509) 735-8476.
E-mail address: jacki.lahtinen@co.benton.wa.us

LARKIN, Thomas P. *(Judge, Washington Superior Court Pierce County)* Former Judge, Pierce District Court No. 1 Pierce County.
Office: 930 Tacoma Avenue South, Room 534, Tacoma 98402-2108.
Telephone: (253) 798-7565.
E-mail address: SUPCRTDEPT3@co.pierce.wa.us

LASNIK, Robert S. *(Judge, United States District Court Western District of Washington)* Appointed for life by President Bill Clinton to term beginning Dec 2, 1998. Born Staten Island New York Jan 27, 1951. Educated at Brandeis University A.B. 1972, Northwestern University M.S. 1973 M.A. 1974 and University of Washington School of Law J.D. 1978. Judge, Washington Superior Court King County 1990-98.

LASNIK, ROBERT S.—*Continued*

Deputy Prosecutor 1978-81, Senior Deputy Prosecutor 1981-83 and Chief of Staff 1983-90 King County.

Office: 911 U.S. Courthouse, 1010 Fifth Avenue, Seattle 98104-1186.

Telephone: (206) 553-2673.

LAU, Linda *(Judge, Washington Superior Court King County)* Former Judge, Seattle District Court King County.

Office: 516 Third Avenue, Room C203, Seattle 98104-2381.

Telephone: (206) 296-9242.

E-mail address: linda.lau@metrokc.gov

LAURIE, Anna M. *(Judge, Washington Superior Court Kitsap County)*

Office: 614 Division Street, Port Orchard 98366-4683.

Telephone: (360) 337-7140.

E-mail address: alaurie@co.kitsap.wa.us

LEAVITT, Michael W. *(Judge, Washington Superior Court Yakima County)*

Office: 128 North Second Street, Yakima 98901-2639.

Telephone: (509) 574-2710.

E-mail address: michael.leavitt@co.yakima.wa.us

LEICK, Robert K. *(Judge, Stevenson Municipal Court)*

Mailing address: P.O. Box 371, Stevenson 98648-0371.

Office: 150 N.W. Loop Road, Stevenson 98648.

Telephone: (509) 427-5970.

LEIGHTON, Ronald B. *(Judge, United States District Court Western District of Washington)* Appointed for life by President George W. Bush to term beginning Nov 26, 2002.

Office: U.S. Courthouse, 1717 Pacific Avenue, Tacoma 98402.

Telephone: (253) 593-6449.

LEV, Debra *(Judge, Bellingham Municipal Court)*

Office: 2014 C Street, Bellingham 98225-4019.

Telephone: (360) 676-6978.

E-mail address: dlev@cob.org

LEVEQUE, Jerome *(Judge, Washington Superior Court Spokane County)*

Office: West 1116 Broadway Avenue, Spokane 99260-0350.

Telephone: (509) 477-5784.

E-mail address: jleveque@spokanecounty.org

LEWIS, Terrance G. *(Judge, Ferndale and Lynden Municipal Courts)*

Mailing address: P.O. Box 291, Ferndale 98248-0291.

Office: 2095 Main Street, Ferndale 98248.

Telephone: (360) 384-2827.

LINDE, Barbara *(Judge, King District Court West Division King County)* Elected Nov 1994 to term beginning Jan 1995. Reelected Nov 1998 and 2002. Current term expires Jan 2007. Presiding Judge 1998. Born Seattle Washington Oct 6, 1955. Educated at University of Washington B.A. 1977 and Seattle University J.D. cum laude 1980. Associate Editor Seattle University Law Review 1978-80. Admitted to practice Washington 1980.

Senior Deputy Prosecuting Attorney King County 1980-94. Board of Governors Washington State District and Municipal Court Judges Association 1997-99. Former Member Core Mission of the Courts Subcommittee Commission on Justice, Efficiency, and Accountability. Member Washington Jury Commission since 1999.

Office: E327 Seattle Courthouse, 516 Third Avenue, Seattle 98104-3273.

Telephone: (206) 296-3625.

E-mail address: barbara.linde@metrokc.gov

LUKENS, Terence *(Judge, Washington Superior Court King County)*

Office: 516 Third Avenue, Room C203, Seattle 98104-2381.

Telephone: (206) 296-9140.

E-mail address: terence.lukens@metrokc.gov

LUM, Dean S. *(Judge, Washington Superior Court King County)*

Office: 401 Fourth Avenue North, Room 2D, Kent 98032-4429.

Telephone: (206) 296-9295.

E-mail address: dean.lum@metrokc.gov

LUST, C. James *(Judge, Washington Superior Court Yakima County)*

Office: 128 North Second Street, Yakima 98901-2639.

Telephone: (509) 574-2710.

E-mail address: james.lust@co.yakima.wa.us

LUTES, Ray D. *(Judge, Asotin District Court Asotin County)* Also serves as Court Commissioner, Washington Superior Court Asotin County.

Mailing address: P.O. Box 429, Asotin 99402-0429.

Office: Asotin County Courthouse, Asotin 99402.

Telephone: (509) 243-2029.

LYMAN, John V. *(Judge, Tenino and Tumwater Municipal Courts)* Former Judge, Ranier Municipal Court.

Mailing address: P.O. Box 4019, Tenino 98589-4019.

Office: 358 McClellan Street S.E., Tenino 98589.

Telephone: (360) 264-4157.

LYON, Patricia *(Judge, Snohomish District Court Evergreen Division Snohomish County)*

Office: 14414-179th Avenue S.E., Monroe 98272-1149.

Telephone: (360) 805-6776.

MacINNES, Nicole *(Judge, Washington Superior Court King County)* Former Judge, Seattle Municipal Court.

Office: 516 Third Avenue, Room C203, Seattle 98104-2381.

Telephone: (206) 296-9210.

E-mail address: nicole.macinnes@metrokc.gov

MADSEN, Barbara A. *(Justice, Washington Supreme Court)* Elected to term beginning Jan 11, 1993. Reelected 1998, current term expires Jan 2005. Born Renton Washington. Educated at University of Washington B.A. 1974 and Gonzaga University School of Law J.D. Court Commissioner, Seattle Municipal Court 1985-88. Former Judge and Presiding Judge, Seattle Municipal Court, appointed by Mayor Charles Royer 1988.

Staff Attorney 1982-84 and Special Prosecutor 1984-88 Seattle City Attorney's Office. Member American Judges Association and National Association of Women Judges. Judge Annual Moot Court Competition Gonzaga

MADSEN, BARBARA A.—*Continued*

University School of Law. Volunteer in Tacoma and Thurston County public schools.

Mailing address: P.O. Box 40929, Olympia 98504-0929.

Office: 415 Twelfth Avenue S.W., Olympia 98504.

Telephone: (360) 357-2037.

MAHER, Dennis P. *(Judge, Cathlamet Municipal Court)*

Mailing address: P.O. Box 68, Cathlamet 98612-0068.

Office: 100 Main Street, Cathlamet 98612.

Telephone: (360) 795-3203.

MAJHAN, Thomas J. *(Judge, Washington Superior Court Jefferson County)*

Mailing address: P.O. Box 1220, Port Townsend 98368-0920.

Office: 1820 Jefferson Street, Port Townsend 98368.

Telephone: (360) 385-9125.

MAMIYA, Ron A. *(Judge, Seattle Municipal Court)* Former Presiding Judge.

Office: 600 Fifth Avenue, Seattle 98104.

Telephone: (206) 684-8709.

E-mail address: Ron.Mamiya@seattle.gov

MARINELLO, Scott G. *(Judge, Columbia District Court Columbia County and Judge, Dayton Municipal Court)*

Office: 341 East Main Street, Dayton 99328-1361.

Telephone: (509) 382-4812.

MARTIN, Jonathan H. *(Judge, Yakima Municipal Court)*

Office: 200 South Third Street, Yakima 98901-2830.

Telephone: (509) 575-3050.

E-mail address: jmartin@ci.yakima.wa.us

MARTINEZ, Ricardo S. *(Magistrate Judge, United States District Court Western District of Washington)* Appointed by U.S. District Court judges.

Office: 304 U.S. Courthouse, 1010 Fifth Avenue, Seattle 98104-1130.

Telephone: (206) 553-1396.

MATHESON, Craig Jay *(Judge, Washington Superior Court Benton-Franklin Counties)* Born Pasco Washington Feb 6, 1951. Educated at Northwestern University B.A. 1973 and Gonzaga University J.D. 1976. Member Sigma Alpha Epsilon. Admitted to practice Washington 1976. In legal practice Kennewick 1978-84. Former Judge, Benton District Court Benton County, appointed by County Commissioners to term beginning April 15, 1987.

Legal Counsel Washington Public Power Supply System. Deputy Prosecuting Attorney Benton County 1976-78. Former member Benton-Franklin County, Washington State and American Bar Associations. Member Washington State District and Municipal Court Judges Association. Member United Way, Kennewick Citizens for a New Stadium and Toastmasters. Enjoys snow skiing, water skiing, coaching and reading.

Office: 7320 West Quinault Avenue, Kennewick 99336-7665.

Telephone: (509) 736-3071.

MATTSON, George Tauno *(Judge, Washington Superior Court King County)* Appointed by Governor Dixy Lee Ray Jan 1, 1981. Elected to subsequent terms. Current term expires Jan 2005. Born Seattle Washington Dec 7, 1942. Roman Catholic. Educated at University of Washington B.A. 1964 LL.B. 1966. Admitted to practice Washington 1966 and U.S. District Court Western District of Washington 1966. In legal practice Seattle 1966 and 1970-71. Judge, Renton District Court King County 1971-81.

Staff Attorney Legal Services Center Oct 15, 1966 to Dec 31, 1967. Deputy Prosecuting Attorney King County Jan 1, 1968 to June 15, 1970. Honorary member Seattle-King County and Washington State Bar Associations. Member 1971-80, Secretary 1973-74, Vice President 1974-76 and President 1976-77 Washington State Magistrates Association. Member Washington State Superior Court Judges Association. Co-Dean Washington Judicial College 1984-88.

Office: 401 Fourth Avenue North, Room 2D, Kent 98032-4429.

Telephone: (206) 296-9215.

E-mail address: george.mattson@metrokc.gov

McBETH, Robert E. *(Judge, King District Court South Division King County)* Appointed by King County Council to term beginning Jan 1, 1981. Elected 1981, 1982, 1986, 1990, 1994, 1998 and 2002. Current term expires Dec 2006. Born Spokane Washington June 9, 1943. Methodist. Educated at Washington State University B.A. 1965 and University of Washington J.D. 1968. Member Phi Alpha Delta. Admitted to practice Washington 1968 and U.S. District Court Western District of Washington 1968. In legal practice Renton 1970-80.

President King County District Court Judges Association 1984. Attended "Courts of Limited Jurisdiction—General" 1981 and "Evidence" 1983 The National Judicial College. Captain U.S. Army 1968-70. Legal Counsel Democratic Caucus Washington State House of Representatives 1971. City Councilman Renton 1976. Board of Directors Renton Rotary Club. President Renton Jaycees. State Legal Counsel Washington Jaycees. Enjoys tennis and scuba diving.

Office: GD Regional Justice Center Office, 401 Fourth Avenue North, Kent 98032.

Telephone: (206) 205-9200.

E-mail address: robert.mcbeth@metrokc.gov

McBROOM, Douglas *(Judge, Washington Superior Court King County)*

Office: 516 Third Avenue, Room C203, Seattle 98104-2381.

Telephone: (206) 296-9285.

E-mail address: douglas.mcbroom@metrokc.gov

McCARTHY, Harry *(Judge, Washington Superior Court King County)*

Office: 401 Fourth Avenue North, Room 2D, Kent 98032-4429.

Telephone: (206) 296-9205.

E-mail address: harry.mccarthy@metrokc.gov

McCARTHY, John A. *(Judge, Washington Superior Court Pierce County)* Former Judge, Pierce District Court No. 1 Pierce County.

Office: 930 Tacoma Avenue South, Room 534, Tacoma 98402-2108.

Telephone: (253) 798-7571.

E-mail address: SUPCRTDEPT11@co.pierce.wa.us

McCARTHY, Michael G. *(Judge, Yakima District Court Yakima County)* Former Judge, Union Gap Municipal Court.

Office: 128 North Second Street, Suite 225, Yakima 98901-2639.
Telephone: (509) 574-1784.
E-mail address: michael.mccarthy@co.yakima.wa.us

McCAULEY, F. Mark *(Judge, Washington Superior Court Grays Harbor County)*

Office: 102 Broadway Avenue West, Montesano 98563-3621.
Telephone: (360) 249-6363.

McCAULEY, Judith L. *(Judge, Douglas District Court Douglas County)* Also serves as Court Commissioner, Washington Superior Court Douglas County.

Office: 110 Third Street N.E., Suite Two, East Wenatchee 98802-4879.
Telephone: (509) 884-3536.

McCLUSKEY, Terry K. *(Judge, Washington Superior Court Kitsap County)* Elected Sept 17, 1996 to term beginning Jan 13, 1997. Reelected 2000, current term expires Jan 2005. Born Oak Park Illinois Nov 4, 1943. Catholic. Educated at Loras College B.A. 1965 and University of Illinois College of Law J.D. 1968. Admitted to practice Illinois 1968 and Washington 1972. In legal practice Bremerton Washington 1972-96.

City Attorney Bremerton 1972-82 and Port Orchard 1972-96. Instructor in Law and Banking Olympic College 1975-76. USMC 1968-72. Judge Special Courts Martials 1971-72.

Office: 614 Division Street, Port Orchard 98366-4683.
Telephone: (360) 337-7140.
E-mail address: tmccluskey@co.kitsap.wa.us

McCULLOUGH, LeRoy *(Judge, Washington Superior Court King County)*

Office: 516 Third Avenue, Room C203, Seattle 98104-2381.
Telephone: (206) 296-9245.
E-mail address: leroy.mccullough@metrokc.gov

McDERMOTT, Richard *(Judge, Washington Superior Court King County)*

Office: 401 Fourth Avenue North, Room 2D, Kent 98032-4429.
Telephone: (206) 296-9115.
E-mail address: richard.mcdermott@metrokc.gov

McDONALD, Alan A. *(Senior Judge, United States District Court Eastern District of Washington)* Appointed for life by President Ronald Reagan to term beginning Sept 17, 1985. Assumed Senior status, serves by assignment. Born Harrah Washington Dec 13, 1927. Religious affiliation: Disciples of Christ. Educated at Whitman College 1946 and University of Washington B.S. 1950 LL.B. 1952. Board of Editors University of Washington Law Review 1950-52. Admitted to practice Washington 1952 and U.S. District Court Eastern District of Washington 1952. In legal practice Yakima 1954-85.

President Yakima County Bar Association. Fellow American College of Trial Lawyers. Member Royal Duck Club.

Mailing address: P.O. Box 2706, Yakima 98907-2706.
Telephone: (509) 575-5839.

McGOVERN, Walter T. *(Senior Judge, United States District Court Western District of Washington)* Appointed for life by President Richard M. Nixon to term beginning May 14, 1971. Chief Judge 1975-87. Assumed Senior status, serves by assignment. Born Seattle Washington May 24, 1922. Roman Catholic. Educated at University of Santa Clara, Gonzaga University and University of Washington B.A. 1948 LL.B. 1950. Admitted to practice Washington 1950. Began legal practice Seattle 1950. Judge, Seattle Municipal Court 1959-65. Judge, Washington Superior Court King County 1965-68. Justice, Washington Supreme Court 1968-71.

Member Judicial Conference of the U.S. (Member 1981-87 and Chairman Subcommittee on Supporting Personnel 1983-87 Committee on Court Administration; Chairman Committee on Judicial Resources 1987-90), Seattle-King County (Former Treasurer), Washington State and American Bar Associations. Captain USNR.

Office: 508 U.S. Courthouse, 1010 Fifth Avenue, Seattle 98104-1130.
Telephone: (206) 553-5410.

McKEEMAN, Larry E. *(Judge, Washington Superior Court Snohomish County)*

Office: 3000 Rockefeller Avenue, Everett 98201-4046.
Telephone: (425) 388-3435.
E-mail address: judge@co.snohomish.wa.us

McPHEE, Wm. Thomas *(Judge, Washington Superior Court Thurston County)*

Office: 2000 Lakeridge Drive S.W., Building 2, Olympia 98502-6001.
Telephone: (360) 786-5557.
E-mail address: mcpheet@co.thurston.wa.us

McRAE, Carol A. *(Judge, Snohomish District Court South Division Snohomish County)*

Office: 20520-68th Avenue West, Lynnwood 98036-7406.
Telephone: (425) 774-8803.

McSEVENEY, Robert *(Judge, Kent Municipal Court)*

Office: 1220 Central Avenue South, Kent 98032-7426.
Telephone: (253) 856-5730.
E-mail address: rmcseveney@ci.kent.wa.us

MEADOWS, Victoria *(Judge, Mason District Court Mason County)* Elected Nov 3, 1994 to term beginning Jan 1995. Reelected 1998 and 2002. Current term expires Dec 31, 2006. Born Inglewood California Sept 27, 1958. Educated at Seattle University B.S. cum laude 1979 and Seattle University School of Law J.D. 1982. Admitted to practice Washington 1982 and U.S. District Court Western District of Washington 1982. In legal practice Shelton 1993-94. Judge, Washington Superior Court Mason County July 1, 1992 to Nov 18, 1992, appointed by Governor Booth Gardner.

Deputy Prosecutor Pierce County 1982-83. Chief Deputy Prosecutor Mason County 1984-92. Member Washington State District and Municipal Court Judges Association and Washington State Bar Association (inactive). Attended Washington State Judicial College Jan 1994, The National Judicial College March 1996 and Annual State Conference Training Office of the Administrator of the Courts. Former Instructor Mason County Sheriff Reserve Academy and on Domestic Violence for law enforcement and victims' advocates. Member Rotary,

MEADOWS, VICTORIA—*Continued*

Oysterfest and Shelton Yacht Club. Enjoys gardening, photography and skiing.
Mailing address: P.O. Box O, Shelton 98584-0090.
Office: 419 North Fourth Street, First Floor, Shelton 98584.
Telephone: (360) 427-9670.
Fax: (360) 427-7776

MENDOZA, Debbie *(Judge, Zillah Municipal Court)*
Mailing address: P.O. Box 388, Zillah 98953-0388.
Office: 111 Seventh Street, Zillah 98953.
Telephone: (509) 829-3543.

MERTEL, Charles W. *(Judge, Washington Superior Court King County)*
Office: 516 Third Avenue, Room C203, Seattle 98104-2381.
Telephone: (206) 296-9135.
E-mail address: charles.mertel@metrokc.gov

MEYER, John M. *(Judge, Washington Superior Court Skagit County)* Assumed office 1997. Elected to subsequent term. Educated at University of Washington B.A. 1968 B.S. 1968 and University of California Hastings College of the Law J.D. 1971. In legal practice Mount Vernon 1975-97. Former Judge, Mount Vernon Municipal Court. Judge, Skagit District Court Skagit County 1995-97.
Staff Attorney Federal Power Commission 1973-75. Trustee Washington State Trial Lawyers Association 1986-90. President Skagit County Bar Association 1993-94. Member Education Committee since 1999 and Treasurer since 2000 Washington State Superior Court Judges Association. Trustee Skagit Valley College 1993-97. Past President University of Washington Alumni Association, Skagit Valley College Foundation, Skagit Valley Family YMCA, Kiwanis Club of Mount Vernon and Salem Lutheran Church. Chair Skagit Homeless Youth Task Force.
Office: 205 West Kincaid Street, Suite 202, Mount Vernon 98273-4225.
Telephone: (360) 336-9320.
E-mail address: sjmmeyer@aol.com

MEYER, Thomas L. *(Judge, Yelm Municipal Court)*
Mailing address: P.O. Box 479, Yelm 98597-0479.
Office: 105 Yelm Avenue West, Yelm 98597.
Telephone: (360) 458-3242.

MICHELS, Steven L. *(Judge, Sunnyside Municipal Court)* Appointed by City Council to term beginning Jan 1, 1986. Reappointed 1990, 1994, 1998 and 2002. Current term expires Dec 31, 2006. Born Sunnyside Washington May 20, 1949. Episcopalian. Educated at Whitman College B.A. in Political Science 1971 and Lewis & Clark College School of Law J.D. 1974. Member Phi Alpha Delta. Admitted to practice Washington 1975. In legal practice Sunnyside since 1975.
Member Yakima Indian Nation and Yakima County Bar Associations.
Office: 401 Homer Street, Sunnyside 98944-1354.
Telephone: (509) 839-4427.

MIDDAUGH, Laura Gene *(Judge, Washington Superior Court King County)*
Office: 401 Fourth Avenue North, Room 2D, Kent 98032-4429.
Telephone: (206) 296-9225.
E-mail address: laura.middaugh@metrokc.gov

MILLER, G. Paul *(Judge, Garfield District Court Garfield County)* Also serves as Court Commissioner, Washington Superior Court Garfield County.
Mailing address: P.O. Box 817, Pomeroy 99347-0817.
Office: 789 Main Street, Pomeroy 99347.
Telephone: (509) 843-1002.
E-mail address: gpmiller@co.garfield.wa.us

MILLER, John A. *(Judge, Fircrest Municipal Court)*
Office: 115 Ramsdell Street, Fircrest 98466-6912.
Telephone: (253) 564-8922.

MILLER, Richard W. *(Judge, Washington Superior Court Adams County)*
Mailing address: P.O. Box 126, Ritzville 99169-0126.
Office: 210 West Broadway Avenue, Ritzville 99169.
Telephone: (509) 659-3272.
E-mail address: RichardM@co.adams.wa.us

MILLS, Leila *(Judge, Washington Superior Court Kitsap County)*
Office: 614 Division Street, Port Orchard 98366-4683.
Telephone: (360) 337-7140.
E-mail address: lmills@co.kitsap.wa.us

MITCHELL, David C. *(Judge, Everett Municipal Court)* Appointed by Mayor William Moore to term beginning Jan 1, 1987. Reappointed by Mayor Pete Kinch Jan 1, 1990 and by mayor Jan 1, 1994. Elected to term beginning Jan 1, 1998. Reelected 2001, current term expires Dec 31, 2005. Born Bremerton Washington June 22, 1944. Educated at University of Washington B.A. 1966 J.D. 1969. Staff member Washington Law Review 1967-68. Admitted to practice Washington 1969, U.S. Court of Military Appeals 1969 and U.S. District Court Western District of Washington 1977. Began legal practice Everett.
Member Washington State Bar Association (Legislative Committee 1979-87). U.S. Army active duty 1969-73. Lieutenant Colonel USAR Judge Advocate (retired).
Office: 3028 Wetmore Avenue, Everett 98201-4018.
Telephone: (425) 257-8778.
E-mail address: dmitchell@ci.everett.wa.us

MOORE, Stephen E. *(Judge, Lynnwood Municipal Court)* Appointed by Mayor Tina Roberts-Martinez to term beginning Jan 1, 2001. Reappointed Jan 1, 2002, current term expires Dec 31, 2005. Educated at Washington State University B.A. with distinction 1973 M.A. 1974 and University of Washington J.D. 1977. Admitted to practice Washington 1977. USN.
Mailing address: P.O. Box 5008, Lynnwood 98046-5008.
Office: 19321-44th Avenue West, Lynnwood 98046.
Telephone: (425) 670-6668.
E-mail address: smoore@ci.lynnwood.wa.us

MORENO, Maryann *(Judge, Washington Superior Court Spokane County)*
Office: West 1116 Broadway Avenue, Spokane 99260-0350.
Telephone: (509) 477-4712.
E-mail address: dept7@spokanecounty.org

MORGAN, J. Dean *(Judge, Washington Court of Appeals Division II)* Assumed office 1990. Elected to subsequent terms. Born Berkeley California Sept 3, 1942. Educated at University of California at Berkeley B.A.

MORGAN, J. DEAN—*Continued*

1964 and Hastings College of the Law J.D. 1968. Member Order of the Coif. Admitted to practice Washington 1968 and California 1969. In legal practice Seattle Washington 1968-72. Judge, Washington Superior Court Clark County 1977-90.

Public Defender Clark County 1972-77. Member State Bar of California, Clark County, Washington State and American Bar Associations.

Office: 950 Broadway, Suite 300, Tacoma 98402-4454.
Telephone: (253) 593-2974.
Fax: (253) 593-2060

MOYNIHAN, Michael F. *(Judge, Washington Superior Court Whatcom County)* Elected to term beginning Jan 1, 1989. Reelected 1992, 1996 and 2000. Current term expires Jan 2005. Born Seattle Washington Nov 10, 1940. Catholic. Educated at Seattle University 1964 and University of Washington LL.B. 1967. Admitted to practice Washington 1968. Began legal practice Seattle 1968. In legal practice Lynnwood 1968-71 and Bellingham since 1974. Court Commissioner, Whatcom District Court Whatcom County 1976-79. Former Judge, Bellingham Municipal Court. Judge, Blaine, Everson-Nooksack, Ferndale, Lynden and Sumas Municipal Courts, Jan 1, 1979 to Dec 31, 1988.

Former member King County and Snohomish County Bar Associations. Honorary member Whatcom County and Washington State Bar Associations. Board Member Catholic Community Services.

Office: 311 Grand Avenue, Room 301, Bellingham 98225-4048.
Telephone: (360) 676-6725.
E-mail address: mmoyniha@co.whatcom.wa.us

MURA, Steven J. *(Judge, Washington Superior Court Whatcom County)* Former Magistrate Judge, U.S. District Court Western District of Washington, appointed by U.S. District Court judges.

Office: 311 Grand Avenue, Room 301, Bellingham 98225-4048.
Telephone: (360) 676-6793.
E-mail address: smura@co.whatcom.wa.us

MURPHY, William C. *(Judge, Granger and Union Gap Municipal Courts)*

Mailing address: P.O. Box 960, Granger 98932-1100.
Office: 102 Main Street, Granger 98903.
Telephone: (509) 854-2656.

NAKATA, Alicia H. *(Judge, Chelan District Court Chelan County)*

Mailing address: P.O. Box 2182, Wenatchee 98807-2182.
Office: 350 Orondo Avenue, Fourth Floor, Wenatchee 98801-2885.
Telephone: (509) 667-6600.
E-mail address: Alicia.Nakata@co.chelan.wa.us

NAULT, Peter *(Judge, King District Court East Division King County)*

Office: Redmond Courthouse, 8601-160th Avenue N.E., Redmond 98052.
Telephone: (206) 205-9200.
E-mail address: peter.nault@metrokc.gov

NELSON, Kathryn J. *(Judge, Washington Superior Court Pierce County)*

Office: 930 Tacoma Avenue South, Room 534, Tacoma 98402-2108.
Telephone: (253) 798-7564.
E-mail address: SUPCRTDEPT13@co.pierce.wa.us

NEVIN, Jack F. *(Judge, Pierce District Court Pierce County)*

Office: 930 Tacoma Avenue South, Room 601, Tacoma 98402-2115.
Telephone: (253) 798-3314.
E-mail address: jnevin@co.pierce.wa.us

NICHOLS, David A. *(Judge, Washington Superior Court Whatcom County)* Assumed office Jan 14, 1985. Elected to subsequent terms.

Office: 311 Grand Avenue, Room 301, Bellingham 98225-4048.
Telephone: (360) 676-6795.
E-mail address: dnichols@co.whatcom.wa.us

NICHOLS, John F. *(Judge, Washington Superior Court Clark County)* Former Judge, Camas-Washougal Municipal Court. Former Judge, Clark District Court Clark County.

Mailing address: P.O. Box 5000, Vancouver 98666-5000.
Office: 1200 Franklin Street, Vancouver 98660-2812.
Telephone: (360) 397-2260.
E-mail address: John.Nichols@clark.wa.gov

NIELSEN, Wm. Fremming *(Judge, United States District Court Eastern District of Washington)* Appointed for life by President George Bush to term beginning May 1991. Former Chief Judge. Born Seattle Washington Aug 8, 1934. Episcopalian. Educated at University of Washington B.S. 1956 LL.B. 1963. Law Clerk to Hon. Charles L. Powell, U.S. District Court Eastern District of Washington 1963-64. Member Phi Delta Phi. Admitted to practice Washington 1963, U.S. District Court Eastern District of Washington, U.S. Court of Appeals Ninth Circuit and U.S. Supreme Court. In legal practice Spokane 1964-91.

Fellow American College of Trial Lawyers. Member Spokane County (President 1981) and Washington State Bar Associations. Lieutenant Colonel USAF (retired).

Mailing address: P.O. Box 2208, Spokane 99210-2208.
Telephone: (509) 353-3163.

NIX, William A. *(Judge, North Bonneville Municipal Court)* Appointed by North Bonneville Municipal Council to term beginning Dec 2, 1987. Reappointed to term beginning Jan 1, 1991, Jan 1, 1995, Jan 1, 1999 and 2003. Current term expires Dec 31, 2006. Born Portland Oregon Aug 25, 1949. Educated at Washington State University B.A. 1977.

MA1 USN since June 1, 1968. Police Sergeant White Salmon 1980-89. Enjoys philately and antique collections.

Mailing address: P.O. Box 7, North Bonneville 98639-0007.
Office: City Hall, Cascade Drive, North Bonneville 98639.
Telephone: (509) 427-8182.

NORTH, Douglass *(Judge, Washington Superior Court King County)*
Office: 516 Third Avenue, Room C203, Seattle 98104-2381.
Telephone: (206) 296-9110.
E-mail address: douglass.north@metrokc.gov

O'CONNOR, Kathleen M. *(Judge, Washington Superior Court Spokane County)*
Office: West 1116 Broadway Avenue, Spokane 99260-0350.
Telephone: (509) 477-4707.
E-mail address: dept4@spokanecounty.org

ODELL, Timothy B. *(Judge, Everett Municipal Court)*
Office: 3028 Wetmore Avenue, Everett 98201-4018.
Telephone: (425) 257-8778.
E-mail address: todell@ci.everett.wa.us

O'MALLEY, Pat *(Judge, Pierce District Court Pierce County)*
Office: 930 Tacoma Avenue South, Room 601, Tacoma 98402-2115.
Telephone: (253) 798-6332.
E-mail address: pomalle@co.pierce.wa.us

ORLANDO, James R. *(Judge, Washington Superior Court Pierce County)*
Office: 930 Tacoma Avenue South, Room 534, Tacoma 98402-2108.
Telephone: (253) 798-7578.
E-mail address: SUPCRTDEPT1@co.pierce.wa.us

OTTINGER, Mary Ann *(Judge, King District Court East Division King County)*
Office: Issaquah Courthouse, 5415-220th Avenue S.E., Issaquah 98029-6839.
Telephone: (206) 205-9200.
E-mail address: maryann.ottinger@metrokc.gov

OVERSTREET, Karen A. *(Judge, United States Bankruptcy Court Western District of Washington)* Appointed by U.S. Court of Appeals Ninth Circuit judges.
Office: 315 Park Place Building, 1200 Sixth Avenue, Seattle 98101-3122.
Telephone: (206) 553-1624.

OWENS, Susan *(Justice, Washington Supreme Court)* Born North Carolina Aug 19, 1949. Presbyterian. Educated at Duke University B.A. 1971 and University of North Carolina at Chapel Hill J.D. 1975. Admitted to practice Oregon 1975 and Washington 1976. Began legal practice Port Angeles Washington 1976. Former Judge, Clallam District Court No. 2 Clallam County, appointed to term beginning July 1, 1981. Chief Judge, Quileute Tribe 1987-92. Chief Judge, Lower Elwha S'klallam Tribe 1994-2000.
Instructor City College of Seattle 1979-80. Co-chair Rural Courts Committee 1991-93. Board of Governors Washington District and Municipal Court Judges Association since 1993. Member Oregon State Bar and Washington State Bar Association (Civil Rights Committee 1978-80). Graduate The National Judicial College. President National Organization for Women Clallam County 1979-80. Charter Member Soroptimists International of Olympic Rain Forest.
Mailing address: P.O. Box 40929, Olympia 98504-0929.
Telephone: (360) 357-2041.

PADDEN, Mike *(Judge, Spokane District Court Spokane County and Judge, Spokane Municipal Court)*
Office: 1100 West Mallon Avenue, Spokane 99260-2043.
Telephone: (509) 477-2960.
E-mail address: mpadden@spokanecounty.org

PAJA, Marilyn *(Judge, Kitsap District Court Kitsap County)* Former Judge, Gig Harbor Municipal Court.
Office: 614 Division Street, Port Orchard 98366-4684.
Telephone: (360) 337-7033.

PAYNE, Pamela F. *(Judge, Stevens District Court Stevens County)* Also serves as Court Commissioner, Washington Superior Court Stevens County.
Office: 215 South Oak Street, Room 213, Colville 99114-2862.
Telephone: (509) 684-5249.
E-mail address: ppayne@co.stevens.wa.us

PECHMAN, Marsha J. *(Judge, United States District Court Western District of Washington)* Appointed for life by President Bill Clinton to term beginning October 5, 1999. Born Salem Oregon Feb 6, 1951. Educated at Cornell University B.A. 1973 and Boston University J.D. 1976. Admitted to practice Washington 1976. In legal practice Seattle 1981-87. Judge pro tem, District Court King County 1980-87 and Washington Superior Court King County 1980-87. Judge, Washington Superior Court King County Jan 1, 1988 to October 4, 1999, appointed by Governor Booth Gardner.
Deputy Prosecuting Attorney King County 1976-79. Staff Attorney Criminal Law Clinical Internship Program University of Washington 1979-81. Author "Subrogation, or the Right to Be Paid Back" 1987, "The Art of Advocacy—Expert Witnesses" 1987 and "The Struck Jury System: How It Works and How to Work It" *Trial News* Washington State Trial Lawyers Association 1991. Adjunct Faculty Member for Trial Advocacy University of Washington School of Law 1979-87. Professor of Law and Director of Law Practice Clinic University of Puget Sound School of Law 1986-87. Member State of Washington Judicial Ethics Advisory Committee 1994-99 and and Jury Instruction Committee Ninth Circuit since 2002. Member Superior Court Judges Association (Education Committee 1991-99, Dean Judicial Orientation 1992). Faculty Member National Institute for Trial Advocacy since 1980. Enjoys skiing, reading and theater.
Office: 502 U.S. Courthouse, 1010 Fifth Avenue, Seattle 98104-1130.
Telephone: (206) 553-2671.

PENOYAR, Elizabeth *(Judge, North District Court Pacific County and Judge, Ilwaco, Long Beach, Raymond and South Bend Municipal Courts)*
Mailing address: P.O. Box 134, South Bend 98586-0134.
Office: 300 Memorial Avenue, Second Floor, South Bend 98586.
Telephone: (360) 875-9354.

PENOYAR, Joel Morris *(Judge, Washington Superior Court Pacific-Wahkiakum Counties)* Elected to term beginning Dec 8, 1988. Reelected 1992, 1996 and 2000. Current term expires Dec 31, 2004. Born April 12, 1948. Educated at University of Michigan B.A. 1970 and University of Oregon J.D. 1975. Admitted to practice Oregon 1975 and Washington 1976. In legal practice South Bend Washington 1976-88. Judge, Raymond

PENOYAR, JOEL MORRIS—*Continued*
Municipal Court 1976-83. Judge, North Pacific District Court Pacific County 1976-88.

City Attorney South Bend since 1976. Author Noise Control Ordinance Eugene Oregon 1975. Important Decisions: Lapinski v. Johnson 1977 and State v. Steve Nelson (does Washington have concurrent jurisdiction with Oregon over waters of Columbia River?). Washington State Board of Bar Examiners 1979-87. Member Oregon State Bar and Washington State Bar Association. Heavyweight Fours National Champion 1968. Member Pacific County Historical Society (Past President), Lions and Chamber of Commerce. Enjoys hunting, canoeing, sports, gardening and children.

Mailing address: P.O. Box 67, South Bend 98586-0067.

Office: 300 Memorial Avenue, Second Floor, South Bend 98586.

Telephone: (360) 875-9326.

E-mail address: jpenoyar@co.pacific.wa.us

PETERSON, Vance W. *(Judge, Spokane District Court Spokane County and Judge, Spokane Municipal Court)*

Office: 1100 West Mallon Avenue, Spokane 99260-2043.

Telephone: (509) 477-2964.

E-mail address: vpeterson@spokanecounty.org

PHILLIPS, Glenn *(Judge, Kent Municipal Court)*

Office: 1220 Central Avenue South, Kent 98032-7426.

Telephone: (253) 856-5730.

E-mail address: gphillips@ci.kent.wa.us

PHILLIPS, W. Daniel *(Judge, Kitsap District Court Kitsap County)* Assumed office Jan 1, 1982. Elected 1982, 1986, 1990, 1994, 1998 and 2002. Current term expires Jan 2007. Presiding Judge 1983-86 and 1992. Born Spokane Washington Oct 31, 1944. Educated at University of Washington B.A. 1967 J.D. 1970. Admitted to practice Washington 1970 and U.S. Supreme Court 1976. Began legal practice Port Orchard 1971.

Member Washington District and Municipal Court Judges Association (President 1989-90) and American Bar Association. Recipient Washington State Judge of the Year Award from State Probation Officer Association 1999-2000. President Rotary Club 1990-91.

Office: 614 Division Street, Port Orchard 98366-4684.

Telephone: (360) 337-7033.

PHILLIPSON, Darrell E. *(Judge, King District Court South Division King County)* Judge pro tem 1976-83. Magistrate 1977-79. Elected Judge to term beginning Jan 7, 1983. Reelected 1986, 1990, 1994, 1998 and 2002. Current term expires Jan 2007. Presiding Judge 1988-89. Currently serves as Presiding Judge South Division. Born Spokane Washington April 7, 1947. Lutheran. Educated at Eastern Washington University B.A. with honors 1969 and University of California Boalt Hall School of Law J.D. 1972. Admitted to practice Washington 1972. Began legal practice Kent 1972. In legal practice Tukwila 1975-83. Judge pro tem, Federal Way District Court 1975.

Counsel King County Rape Relief 1976-83. Author *Model Local Rules for District and Municipal Courts* 1986 and *Criminal Rules for Courts of Limited Jurisdiction* 1987 West Publishing Company. Important Decision: State v. Redwing, et al. (Women's Peace Camp trespass case) 1984. Instructor Highline Community College 1978-81 and Shoreline Community College 1982-83. Chairman Kent Juvenile Court Conference Committee 1973-78. Member American Judges Association, Washington State Magistrates Association (Chairman Rules Committee 1983-88), Washington State (Rules Committee 1984-88) and American Bar Associations. Recipient Distinguished Citizen Award from Lions Club 1965 and Distinguished Service Award from King County Juvenile Court 1979. Treasurer Valley Cities Mental Health since 1976. Member Lake Fenwick Park Committee 1977 and Kent Planning Commission 1977-79. Vice Chairman Kent Drunk Driving Task Force 1983-87. Enjoys hydroplane racing, auto racing and sailing.

Office: GD Regional Justice Center Office, 401 Fourth Avenue North, Kent 98032.

Telephone: (206) 205-9200.

E-mail address: Darrell.Phillipson@metrokc.gov

PLESE, Annette S. *(Judge, Spokane District Court Spokane County and Judge, Spokane Municipal Court)*

Office: 1100 West Mallon Avenue, Spokane 99260-2043.

Telephone: (509) 477-2958.

E-mail address: aplese@spokanecounty.org

POMEROY, Christine A. *(Judge, Washington Superior Court Thurston County)* Former Judge, Olympia and Tumwater Municipal Courts.

Office: 2000 Lakeridge Drive S.W., Building 2, Olympia 98502-6001.

Telephone: (360) 709-3232.

PORTER, Rick *(Judge, Clallam District Court No. 1 Clallam County)*

Office: 223 East Fourth Street, Suite 10, Port Angeles 98362-3015.

Telephone: (360) 417-2560.

PORTNOY, Linda S. *(Judge, Lake Forest Park Municipal Court)*

Office: 17425 Ballinger Way N.E., Lake Forest Park 98155.

Telephone: (206) 364-7711.

E-mail address: lportnoy@ci.lake-forest-park.wa.us

POYFAIR, Edwin L. *(Judge, Washington Superior Court Clark County)*

Mailing address: P.O. Box 5000, Vancouver 98666-5000.

Office: 1200 Franklin Street, Vancouver 98660-2812.

Telephone: (360) 397-2354.

E-mail address: Edwin.Poyfair@clark.wa.gov

PRATT, Eugene Franklin, III *(Judge, Benton District Court Benton County)* Appointed to term beginning Nov 17, 1979. Elected to subsequent terms. Current term expires Dec 2006. Born Ontario Oregon Feb 4, 1947. Christian. Educated at University of Oregon B.S. 1971 and University of Idaho J.D. 1974. Admitted to practice Washington 1974. Began legal practice Richland 1974. In legal practice Kennewick 1977.

County Prosecutor Benton County 1979. E-5 U.S. Army 1966-69. Republican. Active in Christian activities. Enjoys vocation, family activities, sports, hunting and fishing.

Office: 7320 West Quinault Avenue, Kennewick 99336-7665.

Telephone: (509) 735-8476.

PUTKA, Edward J. *(Judge, Cowlitz District Court Cowlitz County and Judge, Woodland Municipal Court)* Also serves as Court Commissioner, Washington Superior Court Cowlitz County.

Mailing address: P.O. Box 9, Woodland 98674-0100.
District Court office: 312 S.W. First Avenue, Room 207, Kelso 98626-1797.
Municipal Court office: 100 Davidson Avenue, Woodland 98674.
Telephone: (360) 577-3073.
E-mail address: putkae@co.cowlitz.wa.us

QUACKENBUSH, Justin L. *(Senior Judge, United States District Court Eastern District of Washington)* Appointed for life by President Jimmy Carter to term beginning June 27, 1980. Former Chief Judge. Assumed Senior status, serves by assignment. Born Spokane Washington Oct 3, 1929. Episcopalian. Educated at University of Illinois 1947-49, University of Idaho B.A. 1951 and Gonzaga University LL.B. cum laude 1957. Member Phi Delta Theta and Phi Alpha Delta. Admitted to practice Washington 1957, U.S. District Court District of Washington 1957, U.S. Court of Appeals Ninth Circuit 1960 and U.S. Supreme Court 1967. In legal practice 1960-80.

Deputy Prosecuting Attorney 1957-60. Adjunct Professor of Law Gonzaga University School of Law 1960-67. Member Spokane County (Board of Trustees 1976-78), Washington State and American Bar Associations. Lieutenant USN 1951-54. Chairman Spokane County Planning Commission 1969-73. Board of Trustees Spokane Chamber of Commerce 1978-79. Enjoys golf.

Mailing address: P.O. Box 1432, Spokane 99210-1432.
Telephone: (509) 353-2180.

QUINN-BRINTNALL, Christine J. *(Acting Chief Judge, Washington Court of Appeals Division II)* Elected Nov 2000 to term beginning Dec 6, 2000. Educated at The Evergreen State College B.A. and University of Puget Sound J.D. with honors 1980. Staff member University of Puget Sound Law Review. Law Clerk to Hon. James A. Andersen, Washington Court of Appeals Division I.

Former Deputy Prosecuting Attorney King County. Chief Criminal Deputy 1983-86, Senior Criminal Prosecutor and Head of Appeals Unit 1986-94 and Member Civil Division 1994-2000 Pierce County. Board Member and Past President Tacoma Youth Symphony. Volunteer reading tutor Tacoma public schools. Enjoys folk dancing and playing flute and piano.

Office: 950 Broadway, Suite 300, Tacoma 98402-4454.
Telephone: (253) 593-5447.
Fax: (253) 593-2060

RAINES, Albert M. *(Judge, Kirkland Municipal Court)* Former Judge, Des Moines Municipal Court.

Mailing address: P.O. Box 678, Kirkland 98083-0678.
Office: 410 Sixth Street South, Kirkland 98033-6718.
Telephone: (425) 803-1924.

RAMERMAN, Dale B. *(Judge, Washington Superior Court King County)*

Office: 516 Third Avenue, Room C203, Seattle 98104-2381.
Telephone: (206) 296-9240.
E-mail address: dale.ramerman@metrokc.gov

RAMIREZ, Mary Berndt *(Judge, Pasco Municipal Court)*

Office: 1016 North Fourth, Pasco 99301.
Telephone: (509) 545-3492.

RAMSDELL, Jeffrey M. *(Judge, Washington Superior Court King County)* Elected Nov 1996 to term beginning Jan 1997. Reelected Nov 2000, current term expires Jan 2005. Born Neptune New Jersey Dec 4, 1955. Educated at Gettysburg College B.A. cum laude with department honors 1979 and University of Toledo College of Law J.D. magna cum laude 1985. Staff member University of Toledo Law Review 1983-85. Law Clerk to Hon. Solie M. Ringold, Washington Court of Appeals Division I 1985-86. Member Order of the Coif. Admitted to practice Washington 1985 and U.S. District Court Western District of Washington. Judge pro tem, Seattle Municipal Court 1994-96.

Deputy Prosecuting Attorney King County 1987-89. Staff Attorney Washington Court of Appeals Division I 1990-96. Adjunct Professor of Legal Writing University of Puget Sound School of Law 1989-91. Member Task Force to Evaluate the Policies and Practices of the Fair Campaign Practice Committee King County Bar Association 1997-98. Member Bench-Bar Press Committee since 1999. Member Courts and Community Committee and Technology Committee King County Superior Court. Member Washington State Superior Court Judges Association (Trustee 1997-2000.) Club Leader and Instructor Everett Mountaineers. Enjoys carpentry, mountaineering and bicycling.

Office: 516 Third Avenue, Room C203, Seattle 98104-2381.
Telephone: (206) 296-9125.
E-mail address: jeffrey.ramsdell@metrokc.gov

RAWSON, Henry A. *(Judge, Omak and Riverside Municipal Courts)*

Mailing address: P.O. Box 72, Omak 98841-0072.
Office: Two North Ash, Omak 98841.
Telephone: (509) 826-2971.

REID, Ramon P. *(Judge, Toppenish and Wapato Municipal Courts)* Appointed to Toppenish Municipal Court by mayor 1964. Reappointed to subsequent terms. Appointed to Wapato Municipal Court 1996. Born Chehalis Washington Nov 15, 1929. Educated at Seattle University B.A. 1953 and University of Washington J.D. 1956. Admitted to practice Washington 1956. Began legal practice Granger 1956. In legal practice Sunnyside 1960 and Toppenish 1964.

Member Yakima County and Washington State Bar Associations. Member Rotary and Toppenish Mural Society (President 2002-03). Interests include traveling, reading and art.

Office: 21 West First Avenue, Toppenish 98948-1524.
Telephone: (509) 865-3011.

REUKAUF, Ruth *(Judge, Yakima District Court Yakima County)*

Office: 128 North Second Street, Suite 225, Yakima 98901-2639.
Telephone: (509) 574-1785.
E-mail address: ruth.reukauf@co.yakima.wa.us

REYNIER, Ronald, Jr. *(Judge, Skamania District Court Skamania County)*
Mailing address: P.O. Box 790, Stevenson 98648-0790.
Office: 240 Vancouver Avenue, Stevenson 98648.
Telephone: (509) 427-9430.

REYNOLDS, E. Thompson *(Judge, Washington Superior Court Klickitat-Skamania Counties)* Appointed by Governor Mike Lowry June 1995. Elected Nov 1995, 1996 and 2000. Current term expires Jan 2005. Born Lancaster Pennsylvania July 3, 1944. Protestant. Educated at Grove City College B.A. 1966 and Gonzaga University School of Law J.D. 1977. Admitted to practice Washington 1977. In legal practice White Salmon 1977-83.
City Attorney White Salmon 1983-95. Member Washington State Superior Court Judges Association (Trustee 1999-2002) and Washington State Bar Association. Attended Washington State Judicial College 1996. Member Law and Justice Planning Council Klickitat and Skamania Counties. Captain USAF 1966-70. Captain Pennsylvania National Guard 1972-74. Commissioner Klickitat Hospital District No. 2 1989-95. Member Rotary and Elks. Enjoys running, bicycling, skiing and reading.
Office: 205 South Columbus Avenue, Goldendale 98620-9279.
Telephone: (509) 773-5755.

RICKERT, Michael E. *(Judge, Washington Superior Court Skagit County)* Elected Nov 3, 1992 to term beginning Jan 11, 1993. Reelected Nov 1996 and 2000. Current term expires Jan 2005. Born Fort Lewis Washington June 30, 1952. Protestant. Educated at Washington State University B.A. 1975 and University of Puget Sound J.D. cum laude 1983. Admitted to practice Washington 1993 and U.S. Court of Appeals Ninth Circuit 1993. In legal practice Mount Vernon 1983-86.
Prosecuting Attorney Skagit County 1986-92. Board of Directors Washington Association of Prosecuting Attorneys 1990-92. Member Governors Advisory Council on Criminal Justice 1989-96. Attended The National Judicial College 1992. Named Paul Harris Fellow by Rotary. Captain U.S. Army Counterintelligence 1975-80. Enjoys athletics, mountain climbing and boating.
Office: 205 West Kincaid Street, Suite 202, Mount Vernon 98273-4225.
Telephone: (360) 336-9320.

RIEHL, James M. *(Judge, Kitsap District Court Kitsap County)*
Office: 614 Division Street, Port Orchard 98366-4684.
Telephone: (360) 337-7033.

RIELLY, Neal Q. *(Judge, Washington Superior Court Spokane County)*
Office: West 1116 Broadway Avenue, Spokane 99260-0350.
Telephone: (509) 477-5713.
E-mail address: nrielly@spokanecounty.org

RIETSCHEL, Jean *(Judge, Seattle Municipal Court)* Former Presiding Judge.
Office: 600 Fifth Avenue, Seattle 98104.
Telephone: (206) 684-8709.
E-mail address: Jean.Rietschel@seattle.gov

RINGUS, Kevin G. *(Judge, Fife Municipal Court)*
Office: 3737 Pacific Highway East, Fife 98424-1135.
Telephone: (253) 922-6635.

ROACH, Jerry *(Judge, Franklin District Court Franklin County)*
Office: 1016 North Fourth Avenue, Pasco 99301-3706.
Telephone: (509) 545-3597.
E-mail address: jroach@co.franklin.wa.us

ROBINSON, Douglas B. *(Judge, Whitman District Court Whitman County)* Also serves as Court Commissioner, Washington Superior Court Whitman County. Former Court Commissioner, Whitman District Court Whitman County. Former Judge, Colfax, Colton, Garfield and Palouse Municipal Courts.
Mailing address: P.O. Box 230, Colfax 99111-0230.
Office: 404 North Main Street, Colfax 99111.
Telephone: (509) 397-6260.

ROBINSON, Palmer *(Judge, Washington Superior Court King County)*
Office: 516 Third Avenue, Room C203, Seattle 98104-2381.
Telephone: (206) 296-9103.
E-mail address: palmer.robinson@metrokc.gov

ROCHON, L. Stephen *(Judge, Maple Valley and Pacific Municipal Courts)*
Office: 1339 Griffin Avenue, Enumclaw 98022-3011.
Telephone: (888) 688-4916.

ROEWE, Michael P. *(Judge, Lewis District Court Lewis County)* Also serves as Court Commissioner, Washington Superior Court Lewis County. Former Judge, Chehalis Municipal Court.
Mailing address: P.O. Box 336, Chehalis 98532-0336.
Office: 345 West Main Street, Chehalis 98532.
Telephone: (360) 740-1200.

ROHR, Charlie *(Judge, Airway Heights Municipal Court)* Also serves as Court Commissioner, Spokane District Court Spokane County and Spokane Municipal Court.
Mailing address: P.O. Box 969, Airway Heights 99001-0969.
Office: 1208 South Lundstrom, Airway Heights 99001.
Telephone: (509) 244-5578.
E-mail address: crohr@spokanecounty.org

ROHRER, Erik S. *(Judge, Clallam District Court No. 2 Clallam County)* Also serves as Court Commissioner, Washington Superior Court Clallam County.
Office: 502 East Division Street, Forks 98331-8618.
Telephone: (360) 374-6383.

ROOF, Jay B. *(Judge, Washington Superior Court Kitsap County)* Born Chicago Illinois Sept 30, 1943. Educated at University of Houston B.A. 1965 and University of Washington J.D. 1968. Admitted to practice Washington 1968. In legal practice Poulsbo since 1970. Former Judge, Poulsbo Municipal Court, appointed to term beginning Jan 1974.
Prosecuting Attorney Kitsap County Port Orchard 1968. Member The Association of Trial Lawyers of America, American Judicature Society, Kitsap County (President 1973-75) and American Bar Associations. USAR 1968-74.
Office: 614 Division Street, Port Orchard 98366-4683.
Telephone: (360) 337-7140.
E-mail address: jroof@co.kitsap.wa.us

ROSS, Edward B. *(Judge, Whatcom District Court Whatcom County)* Elected to term beginning Jan 8, 1979. Reelected 1982, 1986, 1990, 1994, 1998 and 2002. Current term expires Jan 2007. Born Kansas City Missouri Sept 22, 1942. Educated at Kansas City Junior College A.A. 1962, Brandeis University B.A. 1965 and University of California Hastings College of the Law J.D. 1971. Admitted to practice Washington 1971. Began legal practice Bellingham 1971. In legal practice Ferndale 1974.

Assistant City Attorney Bellingham 1971-74. Member Washington State Bar Association 1971. Specialist 5 U.S. Army 1966-68.

Office: 311 Grand Avenue, Suite 401, Bellingham 98225-4046.

Telephone: (360) 676-6770.

ROSS, Margaret V. *(Judge, Pierce District Court Pierce County)*

Office: 930 Tacoma Avenue South, Room 601, Tacoma 98402-2115.

Telephone: (253) 798-3312.

E-mail address: mross@co.pierce.wa.us

ROSSMEISSL, John A. *(Judge, United States Bankruptcy Court Eastern District of Washington)* Former Chief Judge.

Office: 200 The Chinook Tower Building, 402 East Yakima Avenue, Yakima 98901-2760.

Telephone: (509) 454-5633.

ROTHSTEIN, Barbara Jacobs *(Judge, United States District Court Western District of Washington)* Appointed for life by the President. Chief Judge 1987-94. Born Brooklyn New York Feb 3, 1939. Educated at Cornell University B.A. 1960 and Harvard University LL.B. 1966. Member Phi Beta Kappa. Admitted to practice Massachusetts 1966 and Washington 1969. Began legal practice Boston Massachusetts 1966. Former Judge, Washington Superior Court King County, appointed by Governor Dixy Lee Ray to term beginning Nov 1, 1977.

With Office of Washington Attorney General Seattle 1969. Instructor University of Washington School of Law 1975-77. Member Judicial Conference Committee on State and Federal Relations, American Judicature Society, Seattle-King County, Washington State and American Bar Associations.

Office: 705 U.S. Courthouse, 1010 Fifth Avenue, Seattle 98104-1187.

Telephone: (206) 553-2740.

ROY, Kevin M. *(Judge, Yakima District Court Yakima County)*

Office: 128 North Second Street, Suite 225, Yakima 98901-2639.

Telephone: (509) 574-1797.

E-mail address: kevin.roy@co.yakima.wa.us

RULLI, James E. *(Judge, Washington Superior Court Clark County)*

Mailing address: P.O. Box 5000, Vancouver 98666-5000.

Office: 1200 Franklin Street, Vancouver 98660-2812.

Telephone: (360) 397-6133.

E-mail address: James.Rulli@clark.wa.gov

RUSDEN, John W. *(Judge, Bothell Municipal Court)*

Office: 10116 N.E. 183rd Street, Bothell 98011-3416.

Telephone: (425) 487-5587.

RYAN, Timothy P. *(Judge, Snohomish District Court South Division Snohomish County)*

Office: 20520-68th Avenue West, Lynnwood 98036-7406.

Telephone: (425) 774-8803.

SAINT CLAIR, J. Wesley *(Judge, King District Court East Division King County)* Former Magistrate. Currently serves as Presiding Judge King County District Court.

Office: 516 Third Avenue, Room W-1034, Seattle 98104-2385.

Telephone: (206) 205-2820.

E-mail address: Wesley.SaintClair@metrokc.gov

SANDERS, Richard B. *(Justice, Washington Supreme Court)* Elected at special election to term beginning Dec 12, 1995. Reelected 1998, current term expires Jan 2005. Born Tacoma Washington. Educated at University of Washington B.A. J.D. 1969. Eagle Scout.

Mailing address: P.O. Box 40929, Olympia 98504-0929.

Office: 415 Twelfth Avenue S.W., Olympia 98504.

Telephone: (360) 357-2067.

SAWYER, James B., II *(Judge, Washington Superior Court Mason County)* Former Court Commissioner. Former Judge, Mason District Court Mason County. Former Judge, Shelton Municipal Court.

Mailing address: P.O. Box X, Shelton 98584-0078.

Office: 419 North Fourth Street, Second Floor, Shelton 98584.

Telephone: (360) 427-9670.

SCHACHT, Donald W. *(Judge, Washington Superior Court Walla Walla County)* Elected to term beginning Jan 9, 1989. Reelected 1992, 1996 and 2000. Current term expires Jan 2005. Educated at Washington State University B.A. 1969 and Willamette University College of Law J.D. 1972.

Mailing address: P.O. Box 836, Walla Walla 99362-0259.

Office: 315 West Main Street, Walla Walla 99362.

Telephone: (509) 527-3229.

SCHAPIRA, Carol *(Judge, Washington Superior Court King County)* Elected to term beginning 1989. Reelected 1992, 1996 and 2000. Current term expires Jan 2005. Born New York March 28, 1948. Jewish. Educated at Hofstra University B.A. cum laude 1969 and Harvard University J.D. 1972. Admitted to practice Washington 1973, U.S. District Courts Western District of Washington and District of South Dakota and U.S. Court of Appeals Ninth Circuit.

With Equal Employment Opportunity Commission 1982-87. Former Treasurer Washington State Superior Court Judges Association. Former Trustee Young Lawyers Section Seattle-King County Bar Association. Board Member Metrocenter YMCA. Member Herzl Nertamid Synagogue, Therapeutic Health Services and Jewish Family Services.

Office: 516 Third Avenue, Room C203, Seattle 98104-2381.

Telephone: (206) 296-9150.

E-mail address: carol.schapira@metrokc.gov

SCHINDLER, Ann *(Judge, Washington Court of Appeals Division I)* Appointed by Governor Gary Locke to term beginning Jan 2002. Educated at University of San Francisco B.A. and University of Washington School of

SCHINDLER, ANN—*Continued*

Law J.D. In legal practice 1978-82. Judge, Washington Superior Court King County 1991-2002, appointed by Governor Booth Gardner.

Office: One Union Square, 600 University Street, Seattle 98104-1176.

Telephone: (206) 464-7659.

Fax: (206) 389-2614

SCHREIBER, Vernon L. *(Judge, Clark District Court Clark County and Judge, Camas-Washougal Municipal Court)* Former Magistrate.

Mailing address: P.O. Box 9806, Vancouver 98666-8806.

District Court office: 1200 Franklin Street, Vancouver 98660-2812.

Municipal Court office: 89 C Street, Washougal 98671-2142.

Telephone: (360) 397-2198.

SCHROEDER, Richard J. *(Judge, Washington Superior Court Spokane County)* Appointed by Governor Booth Gardner Sept 1990 to term beginning Oct 29, 1990. Elected Sept 1991, Sept 1992, Sept 1996 and Sept 2000. Current term expires Jan 2005. Born Minneapolis Minnesota Aug 2, 1931. Catholic. Educated at University of South Dakota 1949-52, Washington State University 1955-58 and Gonzaga University J.D. 1963. Admitted to practice Washington 1963 and U.S. District Courts Eastern 1964 and Western 1964 Districts of Washington. In legal practice Spokane 1967-90.

Assistant Attorney General 1963-64. Deputy Prosecuting Attorney 1964-67.

Office: West 1116 Broadway Avenue, Spokane 99260-0350.

Telephone: (509) 477-4766.

E-mail address: rschroeder@spokanecounty.org

SCHULTHEIS, John A. *(Presiding Chief Judge, Washington Court of Appeals and Judge, Washington Court of Appeals Division III)* Elected to term beginning 1993. Reelected 1998, current term expires Jan 2005. Former Acting Chief Judge and Chief Judge. Born Colton Washington Jan 12, 1934. Roman Catholic. Educated at Washington State University 1952-54 and 1956-57 and Gonzaga University LL.B. J.D. 1962. Admitted to practice Washington 1962. In legal practice Spokane 1962-74. Judge 1974-83 and Presiding Judge 1978-79, Spokane County District Court. Judge Dec 19, 1983 to 1993 and Presiding Judge 1992-93, Washington Superior Court Spokane County, appointed by Governor John Spellman.

Deputy Prosecuting Attorney Spokane County 1963-65 and City Assistant Corporation Counsel 1972-74. Adjunct Professor Gonzaga University School of Law 1965-71. President Washington State District and Municipal Court Judges Association 1982-83. Member Washington State Board for Judicial Administration 1981-83. Alternate member Judicial Qualifications Commission 1981-83 and since 1997. Member Board of Trustees since 1965 and President 1969-73 Spokane Junior Livestock Show. Board of Directors since 1971 and President 1979-81 Merry Glen School (parents cooperative society for the handicapped).

Mailing address: P.O. Box 2159, Spokane 99210-2159.

Office: 500 North Cedar Street, Spokane 99201-1987.

Telephone: (509) 456-3944.

Fax: (509) 456-4287

SCHUMACHER, John D. *(Judge, Cosmopolis Municipal Court)*

Mailing address: P.O. Box 478, Cosmopolis 98537-0478.

Office: 1101 First Street, Cosmopolis 98537.

Telephone: (360) 533-5233.

SCHWAB, Michael E. *(Judge, Washington Superior Court Yakima County)*

Office: 128 North Second Street, Yakima 98901-2639.

Telephone: (509) 574-2710.

E-mail address: michael.schwab@co.yakima.wa.us

SCOTT, Steven *(Judge, Washington Superior Court King County)* Appointed by Governor Booth Gardner to term beginning Jan 1, 1988. Elected Nov 1988, Nov 1992, Nov 1996 and 2000. Current term expires Dec 31, 2004. Born San Mateo California. Methodist. Educated at Stanford University B.A. with great distinction 1970 and University of Pennsylvania J.D. 1974. Law Clerk to Hon. Jacob Tanzer, Oregon Court of Appeals 1974-75. Admitted to practice Oregon 1974, Washington 1977, U.S. District Courts Eastern 1978 and Western 1979 Districts of Washington and U.S. Court of Appeals Ninth Circuit 1980. In legal practice Seattle Washington 1986-88.

Director Evergreen Legal Services 1985-86. Director Institutional Legal Services 1978-81. Author "The Failure of Overincarceration and the Need for an Alternative Approach in Corrections" Washington State Bar News Feb 1981. Adjunct Faculty Member University of Washington School of Law 1978-79. Member King County Corrections Advisory Committee 1981-83 and Washington State Sentencing Guidelines Commission 1981-84. Member Seattle-King County and Washington State Bar Associations. President and Board of Directors University Temple Day Care 1987. Board of Directors Washington Council on Crime and Delinquency 1987. Enjoys basketball, skiing, tennis, hiking and family activities.

Office: 516 Third Avenue, Room C203, Seattle 98104-2381.

Telephone: (206) 296-9111.

E-mail address: steven.scott@metrokc.gov

SEINFELD, Karen Goodman *(Judge, Washington Court of Appeals Division II)* Court Commissioner 1985-87. Assumed office as Judge 1992. Former Chief Judge. Former Presiding Chief Judge. Born Los Angeles California Oct 12, 1939. Educated at Stanford University B.A. 1961 and University of Puget Sound Law School J.D. cum laude 1977. Recipient American Jurisprudence Award in Torts 1976. Admitted to practice Washington 1978, U.S. District Court Western District of Washington 1979 and U.S. Supreme Court 1982. Judge, Washington Superior Court Pierce County April 1, 1987 to 1992, appointed by Governor Booth Gardner.

Deputy Prosecuting Attorney 1978-82. General Counsel Pierce County Council 1983-85. Author "Appealability A Matter of Substance, Not Form" Washington State Bar News April 1987. Member Washington Women Lawyers Association, Puget Sound Inn of Court (Past President), Washington State Judges Association, Pierce County and Washington State Bar Associations. Delegate Democratic National Convention 1984. Former Trustee and Chair Tacoma Public Library Board. Former Governor A+ for Public Education. Former Member Charter

SEINFELD, KAREN GOODMAN—*Continued*
Review Commission City of Tacoma. Former Board Member League of Women Voters. Sustaining Member and Community Advisory Board Junior League of Tacoma. Chair Board of Visitors Seattle University Law School. Board Member City Club of Tacoma. Member Sunrise Rotary. Interested in historical preservation, art education and gardening.
Office: 950 Broadway, Suite 300, Tacoma 98402-4454.
Telephone: (253) 593-2975.
Fax: (253) 593-2060

SEITZ, Victoria *(Judge, King District Court South Division King County)*
Office: GD Regional Justice Center Office, 401 Fourth Avenue North, Kent 98032.
Telephone: (206) 205-9200.
E-mail address: victoria.seitz@metrokc.gov

SHAFFER, Catherine *(Judge, Washington Superior Court King County)* Appointed by Governor Gary Locke to term beginning Nov 27, 2000. Elected Nov 7, 2000 to term beginning Jan 8, 2001, current term expires Jan 2005. Born Brooklyn New York June 15, 1958. Jewish. Educated at Wellesley College B.A. 1980 and Columbia University School of Law J.D. 1986. Wellesley Scholar, James Kent Scholar and Harlan Fiske Stone Scholar. Staff member Columbia Law Review 1984-86. Law Clerk to Hon. Eugene H. Nickerson, U.S. District Court Eastern District of New York. Admitted to practice Washington 1987. In legal practice Sept 1987 to July 1990. Judge pro tem, Des Moines Municipal Court Jan 1999 to Nov 26, 2000.
Deputy Prosecuting Attorney King County July 1990 to Nov 2000.
Office: 401 Fourth Avenue North, Room 2D, Kent 98032-4429.
Telephone: (206) 296-9185.
E-mail address: catherine.shaffer@metrokc.gov

SHEA, Edward F. *(Judge, United States District Court Eastern District of Washington)* Appointed for life by President Bill Clinton to term beginning 1998. Born Malden Massachusetts June 6, 1942. Educated at Boston State College B.S.Ed. 1965 and Georgetown University Law Center J.D. 1970. Law Clerk to Hon. Harold J. Petrie, Washington Court of Appeals Division II 1970-71. In legal practice 1971-98.
Office: 190 Federal Building, 825 Jadwin Avenue, Richland 99352-3562.
Telephone: (509) 376-7261.

SHELDON, Toni A. *(Judge, Washington Superior Court Mason County)*
Mailing address: P.O. Box X, Shelton 98584-0078.
Office: 419 North Fourth Street, Second Floor, Shelton 98584.
Telephone: (360) 427-9670.

SHELTON, Stephen R. *(Judge, Puyallup and Sumner Municipal Courts)* Appointed to Puyallup Municipal Court by city manager Jan 1, 1994. Reappointed by city manager Jan 1, 1998 and Jan 1, 2002. Current term expires Dec 31, 2005. Born Tacoma Washington Nov 6, 1948. Educated at University of Washington 1973 and Seattle University School of Law 1981. Admitted to practice Washington 1982. Former Judge, Ruston Municipal Court, appointed by mayor May 1, 1996.
Deputy Prosecuting Attorney Pierce County 1983-90. City Attorney Auburn 1990-93. Mayor and Councilmember Fircrest 1988-93. Enjoys golf.
Office: 202 West Pioneer Avenue, Puyallup 98371-5372.
Telephone: (253) 841-5450.
E-mail address: steves@ci.puyallup.wa.us

SKELTON, Stephen R. *(Judge, Skagit District Court Skagit County and Judge, Anacortes, Burlington and Mount Vernon Municipal Courts)*
Mailing address: P.O. Box 340, Mount Vernon 98273-0340.
Office: 600 South Third Street, Mount Vernon 98273.
Telephone: (360) 336-9319.
E-mail address: stephens@co.skagit.wa.us

SMALL, T. W. "Chip" *(Judge, Washington Superior Court Chelan County)* Appointed by Governor Booth Gardner to term beginning June 27, 1991. Elected Fall 1991, Fall 1992, Fall 1996 and Fall 2000. Current term expires Dec 31, 2004. Born Mineola New York Jan 3, 1953. Roman Catholic. Educated at Bradley University B.A. with honors 1973 and University of Washington J.D. 1978. Former Magister Phi Delta Phi. Member Phi Kappa Phi. Admitted to practice Washington 1978 and U.S. District Courts Eastern 1978 and Western 1978 Districts of Washington. In legal practice Wenatchee 1978-91 and Moses Lake 1989-91. Judge pro tem, District Court Douglas County 1985-88.
Member Public Trust and Confidence Committee Board of Judicial Administration since 2000. Member Washington State Trial Lawyers Association, The Defense Research Institute, Inc., Superior Court Judges Association, American Judges Association, Chelan-Douglas County, Washington State and American Bar Associations. Attended General Jurisdiction Course and Ethics for Judges Course The National Judicial College. Instructor of numerous Continuing Legal Education courses on real estate, notary public, ethics and professionalism. Trustee Wenatchee Valley College 1985-90. Board Member 1991-94 and President 1994 Legal Foundation of Washington. Member Ethics Advisory Committee since 1995. Board Member since 1997 and Chair since 1999 Access to Justice. Enjoys golf and horseback riding.
Mailing address: P.O. Box 880, Wenatchee 98807-0880.
Office: 401 Washington Street, Wenatchee 98801.
Telephone: (509) 667-6210.
E-mail address: Chip.Small@co.chelan.wa.us

SMITH, Douglas Joseph *(Judge, King District Court East Division King County)* Magistrate Shoreline and Mercer Island District Courts 1985-91. Elected Nov 6, 1990 to term beginning Jan 14, 1991. Reelected 1994, 1998 and 2002. Current term expires Jan 2007. Born San Francisco California April 17, 1947. Roman Catholic. Educated at Seattle University B.A. 1969 and University of San Francisco J.D. 1973. Admitted to practice Washington 1973, U.S. District Court Western District of Washington 1978 and U.S. Court of Appeals Ninth Circuit 1978. In legal practice Bellevue 1978-90. Former Judge, Lake Forest Park Municipal Court, appointed to term beginning Jan 6, 1990.
Deputy Prosecuting Attorney King County 1973-78. Assistant City Attorney Seattle 1988-90. Supervising Attorney Eastside Defender Association 1974-78. Member Washington State Trial Lawyers Association, East King

SMITH, DOUGLAS JOSEPH—*Continued*
County, Seattle-King County and Washington State Bar Associations. USAR 1968. Accountant Oroweat Baking Company 1970-73. President Shorecrest High Boosters Club. Member Lake Forest Park Rotary Club. Enjoys running, tennis and coaching youth sports.

Office: Shoreline Courthouse, 18050 Meridian Avenue North, Shoreline 98133.
Telephone: (206) 205-9200.
E-mail address: douglas.smith@metrokc.gov

SNYDER, Paul B. *(Judge, United States Bankruptcy Court Western District of Washington)* Appointed by U.S. Court of Appeals Ninth Circuit judges.

Office: 2209 U.S. Courthouse, 1717 Pacific Avenue, Tacoma 98402-3233.
Telephone: (253) 593-6342.

SPEARMAN, Mariane *(Judge, King District Court West Division King County)* Former Judge, Kirkland Municipal Court.

Office: E327 Seattle Courthouse, 516 Third Avenue, Seattle 98104-3273.
Telephone: (206) 296-3630.
E-mail address: mariane.spearman@metrokc.gov

SPEARMAN, Michael S. *(Judge, Washington Superior Court King County)* Appointed by Governor Mike Lowry to term beginning July 1, 1993. Elected Nov 2, 1993, Nov 5, 1996 and 2000. Current term expires Jan 2005. Born Lawrence Kansas Nov 26, 1952. Educated at Brown University B.A. 1974 and New York University J.D. 1981. Admitted to practice District of Columbia 1981, Washington 1984, U.S. District Court Western District of Washington and U.S. Court of Appeals District of Columbia Circuit. In legal practice District of Columbia 1981-83 and Seattle Washington 1983-93.

Public Defender King County 1983-86 and 1988-93. Public Defender U.S. District Court Western District of Washington Feb 1993 to May 1993.

Office: 516 Third Avenue, Room C203, Seattle 98104-2381.
Telephone: (206) 296-9211.
E-mail address: michael.spearman@metrokc.gov

SPECTOR, Julie *(Judge, Washington Superior Court King County)*

Office: 401 Fourth Avenue North, Room 2D, Kent 98032-4429.
Telephone: (206) 296-9160.
E-mail address: julie.spector@metrokc.gov

SPERLINE, Evan Eugene *(Judge, Washington Superior Court Grant County)* Appointed by Governor John Spellman to term beginning Dec 12, 1983. Elected 1984, 1988, 1992, 1996 and 2000. Current term expires Jan 2005. Born Wenatchee Washington Aug 19, 1949. Lutheran (ELCA). Educated at Washington State University B.A. with honors 1971 and University of Washington J.D. 1974. Member Sigma Nu. Admitted to practice Washington 1974 and U.S. District Court Eastern District of Washington 1980. In legal practice East Wenatchee 1974-78 and Moses Lake 1979-83.

Instructor in Business Law Wenatchee Valley Junior College 1976. Member Commission on Judicial Conduct 1989-91, The Association of Trial Lawyers of America (Judicial Member), American Judicature Society, Washington State Superior Court Judges Association (Chair Civil Law and Rules Committee 1986-89, Secretary 1991-93, President Elect 1993-94, President 1994-95), American Judges Association, Washington State (Chair Public Relations Committee 1981) and American (Judicial Administration Division) Bar Associations. Attended General Jurisdiction Course 1985 and Judicial Writing Course 1989 The National Judicial College. Lecturer "Consumer Protection Act" Litigation Section 1987 and Judge "Jury Voir Dire" Mock Jury Selection 1988 Washington State Bar Association. Lecturer "Jury Voir Dire" 1987 and Instructor "Drafting Instructions" Jury Instruction Seminar 1989 Washington State Superior Court Judges Association. Instructor in Jury Management Class Washington State Judges Orientation 1991-92. Member City Council East Wenatchee 1977-78. President Chief Moses Junior High PTA. Board of Directors Moses Lake Chamber of Commerce and Moses Lake United Way. Interests include guitar, athletics and church activities.

Mailing address: P.O. Box 37, Ephrata 98823-0037.
Office: 35 C Street N.W., Ephrata 98823.
Telephone: (509) 754-2011.

STEINER, D. Gary *(Judge, Washington Superior Court Pierce County)* Former Judge, Pierce District Court Pierce County. Former Judge, Eatonville Municipal Court.

Office: 930 Tacoma Avenue South, Room 534, Tacoma 98402-2108.
Telephone: (253) 798-7572.
E-mail address: SUPCRTDEPT10@co.pierce.wa.us

STEINER, David A. *(Judge, King District Court East Division King County)* Former Presiding Judge King County District Court.

Office: Redmond Courthouse, 8601-160th Avenue N.E., Redmond 98052.
Telephone: (206) 205-9200.
E-mail address: david.steiner@metrokc.gov

STEINER, Samuel J. *(Judge, United States Bankruptcy Court Western District of Washington)* Former Chief Judge.

Office: 315 Park Place Building, 1200 Sixth Avenue, Seattle 98101-3122.
Telephone: (206) 553-1628.

STEPHENSON, Elizabeth D. *(Judge, King District Court South Division King County)*

Office: GD Regional Justice Center Office, 401 Fourth Avenue North, Kent 98032.
Telephone: (206) 205-9200.
E-mail address: elizabeth.stephenson@metrokc.gov

STEWART, Howard *(Judge, Elmer City Municipal Court)*

Mailing address: P.O. Box 179, Elmer City 99124-0179.
Office: 505 Seaton Avenue, Elmer City 99124.
Telephone: (509) 633-2872.

STEWART, William *(Judge, Hoquiam Municipal Court)* Appointed by Mayor Phyllis Shramyer to term beginning 1990. Elected to subsequent terms. Serves part time. Born Aberdeen Washington. Educated at University of Puget Sound J.D. 1982. Member Phi Delta Phi. Admitted to practice Washington 1982 and U.S. District Court Western District of Washington. In legal practice Montesano since 1982.

Member Washington District and Municipal Court Judges Association. Attended Washington State Judicial

STEWART, WILLIAM—*Continued*

College. Member Montesano Lions Club, Montesano Community Education, American and Washington Tree Farm Program and Washington Farm Forestry Association. Interests include tree farming, canoeing and boating.

Mailing address: P.O. Box 300, Hoquiam 98550-0300.
Office: 609 Eighth Street, Hoquiam 98550.
Telephone: (360) 532-5524.

STILES, Brian L. *(Judge, Sedro-Woolley Municipal Court)*

Office: 220A Woodworth Street, Sedro-Woolley 98284-1433.
Telephone: (360) 855-0131.
E-mail address: brian@stileslaw.com

STILZ, Clifford L., Jr. *(Judge, Thurston District Court Thurston County)* Appointed by Thurston County Board of Commissioners to term beginning Jan 1, 1985. Elected Nov 1986, 1990, 1994, 1998 and 2002. Current term expires Jan 2007. Born Olympia Washington July 7, 1944. Episcopalian. Educated at Willamette University B.A. 1966, University of California at Los Angeles M.P.A. 1967 and University of Washington J.D. 1970. Managing Editor Washington Law Review 1969-70. Law Clerk to Hon. Robert C. Finley, Washington Supreme Court 1970-71. Member Kappa Sigma and Phi Alpha Delta. Admitted to practice Washington 1970, U.S. District Court Western District of Washington 1971, U.S. Court of Appeals Ninth Circuit 1973 and U.S. Supreme Court 1978. In legal practice Olympia 1971-84.

Member Thurston County, Washington State (Chairman Bench, Bar, Press Committee) and American Bar Associations. Past Chairman Advisory Board Olympia Corps Salvation Army. Past President Olympus Council of Camp Fire and Kiwanis Club of Olympia.

Mailing address: P.O. Box 40947, Olympia 98504-0947.
Office: 2000 Lakeridge Drive S.W., Building 3, Olympia 98502.
Telephone: (360) 786-5562.
E-mail address: kip.stilz@courts.wa.gov

STOLZ, Katherine M. *(Judge, Washington Superior Court Pierce County)*

Office: 930 Tacoma Avenue South, Room 534, Tacoma 98402-2108.
Telephone: (253) 798-7573.
E-mail address: SUPCRTDEPT2@co.pierce.wa.us

STONIER, James J. *(Judge, Washington Superior Court Cowlitz County)*

Office: 312 S.W. First Avenue, Kelso 98626-1739.
Telephone: (360) 577-3085.
E-mail address: StonierJ@co.cowlitz.wa.us

STRITMATTER, Paul L. *(Judge, Ocean Shores Municipal Court)* Appointed to term beginning June 1, 1972. Reappointed to subsequent terms. Born Aberdeen Washington April 23, 1943. Educated at University of Washington B.A. 1966 and Willamette University School of Law J.D. magna cum laude 1969. Law Clerk to Hon. Matthew Hill, Washington Supreme Court 1969 and Hon. Charles F. Stafford, Washington Supreme Court 1970. Admitted to practice Washington 1969, U.S. District Court Western District of Washington 1973 and U.S. Supreme Court 1988. In legal practice Hoquiam since 1970.

Author "Presumptions in the Washington Supreme Court" 5 Gonzaga L. Rev. 198, 1970; chapter for *Washington Community Property Deskbook* 1977; "Roadside Hazards" III Washington State Trial Lawyers Association L. Jour. 69, 1979; "Cross-Examination" Trial Aug 1986; chapter "Highway Design, Abutting Landowners and Public Utilities" *Washington Auto Accident Deskbook* 1987 and 2001; "Trial Talk, The Psychology of Cross-Examination" Colorado Trial Lawyers Association May 1987; "The Psychology of Cross-Examination" Wyoming Trial Lawyers Association Summer 1987; "Tactical Decisions in a Personal Injury Case" The Association of Trial Lawyers of America Monograph Series 1988; chapter "Entry of Judgment" *Washington Civil Procedure Deskbook* 1992 and 2001. Co-author chapter "Trial Preparation and Trial: Effective Voir Dire/Jury Selection" *Washington Civil Procedure Deskbook* 1998.

Member Washington Pattern Jury Instruction Committee 1985-90. Fellow American College of Trial Lawyers. Member Washington State Trial Lawyers Association (Secretary 1977, Board of Directors 1978-82 and 1986-96, Vice President 1983, President Elect 1984, President 1984-85), Washington State Trial Lawyers Association Foundation (Board of Directors since 2000), Damage Attorneys Round Table (President 1989-92), Trial Lawyers for Public Justice (Founder 1982, Board of Directors since 1983, Treasurer 1985-87 and 1998-2000, Vice President 2000-01, President Elect 2001, President 2002-03), American Society of Barristers, The College of Master Advocates and Barristers, American Bar Foundation, American Board of Trial Advocates, The Association of Trial Lawyers of America (Advisory Task Force to States 1985-86, Circuit Key Men Committee 1985-86, State Development Fund Board 1985-86, Public Affairs Committee 1985-87, State Delegate 1986-90, Committee on Ethics 1987-93, Board of Governors 1990-93), International Academy of Trial Lawyers (Board of Directors since 1998), International Society of Barristers, American Judicature Society, Washington State (Board of Governors 1987-90, President 1993-94) and American Bar Associations.

Lecturer Washington State Bar Association 1976-98, Washington State Trial Lawyers Association 1977-2000, Pacific Northwest College of Advocacy June 1979, Idaho Trial Lawyers Association May 1982, The Association of Trial Lawyers of America 1983-2000, Western Trial Lawyers Association June 1984, Oregon Trial Lawyers Association March 1985, Washington Association of Defense Counsel July 1985, University of Washington School of Law Sept 1986, Poulsbo CLE Aug 1988 and Aug 1990 and Washington Attorney General's Conference Sept 1997. Presiding Judge Willamette College of Trial Advocacy Nov 1979. Recipient "Boss of the Year" Award from Grays Harbor Legal Secretaries Association 1977-78, Justice Brandeis Award 1982 and Trial Lawyer of the Year Award 1987 from Washington State Trial Lawyers Association, Special Award of Honor 1990 and Award of Merit 1995 from Washington State Bar Association, Distinguished Alumni Award in Law from Willamette University 1994, Alvin Anderson Award from Washington State Trial Lawyers Association 2000 and Pursuit of Justice Award from American Bar Association 2003. Named to Grizzly Alumni Honor Roll by Hoquiam High School 1986. Listed in *Who's Who in American Law* since 1986, *Who's Who in American Society* since 1986, *Who's Who of Emerging Leaders in America* since 1988 and *The Best Lawyers in*

STRITMATTER, PAUL L.—*Continued*

America since 1989. Board of Directors Washington State Head Injury Foundation 1990-93. Board Member and Officer since 1990 Legal Aid for Washington Fund. Chair Access to Justice Board 1994-98 and Northwest Justice Project 1996-97.

Office: 413 Eighth Street, Hoquiam 98550-3692.
Telephone: (360) 533-2710.
Fax: (360) 532-8032
E-mail address: pauls@skwwc.com

STROMBOM, Karen L. *(Magistrate Judge, United States District Court Western District of Washington)* Appointed by U.S. District Court judges to term beginning April 4, 2003. Former Judge, Washington Superior Court Pierce County.

Office: U.S. Courthouse, 1717 Pacific Avenue, Tacoma 98402.
Telephone: (253) 593-6313.

STROPHY, Richard A. *(Judge, Washington Superior Court Thurston County)* Assumed office Jan 14, 1985. Elected to subsequent terms. Former Judge, Thurston District Court Thurston County.

Office: 2000 Lakeridge Drive S.W., Building 2, Olympia 98502-6001.
Telephone: (360) 709-3052.

STROW, Peter H. *(Judge, Island District Court Island County)*

Office: 800 S.E. Eighth Avenue, Oak Harbor 98277-2998.
Telephone: (360) 679-3993.
E-mail address: PeterS@co.island.wa.us

SUKO, Lonny Ray *(Magistrate Judge, United States District Court Eastern District of Washington)* Appointed by U.S. District Court judges Aug 1, 1995. Term expires July 31, 2003. Born Spokane Washington Oct 12, 1943. Protestant. Educated at Washington State University B.A. with distinction 1965 and University of Idaho J.D. 1968. Law Clerk to Hon. Charles L. Powell, U.S. District Court Eastern District of Washington 1968-69. Member Phi Beta Kappa and Phi Alpha Delta. Admitted to practice Washington 1968, U.S. District Courts Eastern 1968 and Western 1978 Districts of Washington and U.S. Court of Appeals Ninth Circuit 1978. In legal practice Yakima 1969-95.

Mailing address: P.O. Box 2726, Yakima 98907-2726.
Office: 25 South Third Street, Yakima 98901.
Telephone: (509) 454-5635.
Fax: (509) 454-5794

SVAREN, David A. *(Judge, Skagit District Court Skagit County and Judge, Anacortes, Burlington and Mount Vernon Municipal Courts)* Appointed to term beginning May 27, 1999. Elected Nov 7, 2000 and Nov 5, 2002. Current term expires Dec 31, 2006. Born Billings Montana July 3, 1955. Lutheran. Educated at Pacific Lutheran University B.A. 1978 and Willamette University J.D. 1981. Admitted to practice Washington 1981, U.S. District Court Western District of Washington 1982 and U.S. Court of Appeals Ninth Circuit 1993. In legal practice Burlington 1981-99.

Assistant City Attorney (part time) 1981-84 and City Attorney (part time) 1984-99 Burlington. Important Decision: Halvorsen v. Skagit County (flood damage liability) 139 Wash. 2d 1, 1999. Member Washington State Trial Lawyers Association, Skagit County and Washington State Bar Associations. Youth Baseball Coach YMCA. Chair Skagit County People's Law School (twice). Member Kiwanis. Enjoys backpacking, skiing, wood working, antique automobiles and gardening.

Office: 600 South Third Street, Mount Vernon 98273.
Telephone: (360) 336-9319.
Fax: (360) 336-9318
E-mail address: dsvaren@co.skagit.wa.us

SWEENEY, Dennis J. *(Judge, Washington Court of Appeals Division III)* Elected 1991. Chief Judge Division III 1995-97. Presiding Chief Judge 1998-99. Born New London Connecticut. Educated at Gonzaga University School of Law J.D. 1972 and University of Virginia LL.M. 1995. In legal practice Pasco for 19 years.

Author "An Analysis of Harmless Error in Washington—A Principled Process" 31 Gonzaga L. Rev. 277 Fall 1995, *The Judges Role in Making a Record: Exercising Judicial Discretion* Board for Trial Court Education Washington State Superior Court Judges Association 2nd ed. June 1996, *Judicial Discretion in Washington* Board for Court Education 1996 and *The Work of Appellate Judges and Judicature* Fall 2001. Fellow American College of Trial Lawyers since 1990. Associate American Board of Trial Advocates since 1991. Member Task Force to Review Judicial Conduct. Member Washington Society of Certified Public Accountants and American Institute of Certified Public Accountants. Presenter "Keeping the Lid on Damages—The Journey Back to Reality" Washington State Bar Association Continuing Legal Education Program Nov 16, 1990, "Dealing with Soft Tissue Injuries" Washington State Trial Lawyers Legal Education Seminar May 17, 1991, "Effective Appellate Court Representation—American College of Trial Lawyers Greatest Hits" University of Washington Law School Foundation Continuing Legal Education 1994, "Judicial Discretion—Making the Record" 1994 and "Harmless Error in Washington" 1996 Washington State Fall Judicial Conference, "Judicial Discretion in Washington" Washington State Superior Court Judges Association Spring Conference 1996, Seminars for Legal Aid Benton Franklin Bar Association 1996-99 and "Access to Justice" Washington State Judicial College 1998-99. Recipient Appellate Judge of the Year Award from Washington State Trial Lawyers Association 1998. CPA Washington. Certified Flight Instructor 1988-90. Commercial Pilot's License 1990.

Mailing address: P.O. Box 2159, Spokane 99210-2159.
Office: North 500 Cedar, Spokane 99201-1987.
Telephone: (509) 456-3922.

SWEIGERT, Philip Kerner *(Recalled Magistrate Judge, United States District Court Western District of Washington)* Appointed by U.S. District Court judges to term beginning Aug 1, 1977. Reappointed 1985 and 1993. Appointed Recalled Magistrate Judge by the Judicial Council of the Ninth Circuit. Born San Francisco California June 6, 1933. Educated at Stanford University B.A. 1956 and Hastings College of the Law J.D. 1961. Member Order of the Coif and Thurston Honor Society. Recipient Outstanding Law Graduate Award 1961. Admitted to practice California 1962 and Washington 1963. Began legal practice Los Angeles California 1962. In legal practice Seattle Washington 1963-77.

Member American Bar Association. Honorary member

SWEIGERT, PHILIP KERNER—*Continued*

King County and Washington State Bar Associations. U.S. Army 1956-58.
Office: 215 U.S. Courthouse, 1010 Fifth Avenue, Seattle 98104-1130.
Telephone: (206) 553-5598.

SWISHER, Robert G. *(Judge, Washington Superior Court Benton-Franklin Counties)*
Office: 7320 West Quinault Avenue, Kennewick 99336-7665.
Telephone: (509) 736-3071.

SYPOLT, Greg D. *(Judge, Washington Superior Court Spokane County)*
Office: West 1116 Broadway Avenue, Spokane 99260-0350.
Telephone: (509) 477-6373.
E-mail address: gsypolt@spokanecounty.org

TABOR, Gary *(Judge, Washington Superior Court Thurston County)*
Office: 2000 Lakeridge Drive S.W., Building 2, Olympia 98502-6001.
Telephone: (360) 786-5217.

TANNER, Jack E. *(Senior Judge, United States District Court Western District of Washington)* Appointed for life by President Jimmy Carter to Eastern District of Washington to term beginning 1978. Reassigned to Western District of Washington Nov 8, 1978. Assumed Senior status Jan 28, 1991, serves by assignment. Born Tacoma Washington Jan 28, 1919. Educated at University of Washington School of Law LL.B. 1955. In legal practice Tacoma 1955-78. U.S. Army 1943-45.
Office: 3144 U.S. Courthouse, 1717 Pacific Avenue, Tacoma 98402-3226.
Telephone: (253) 593-6542.

TEDRICK, Marjorie *(Judge, Buckley Municipal Court)*
Mailing address: P.O. Box 1452, Buckley 98321-1452.
Office: 811 Main Street, Buckley 98321.
Telephone: (253) 859-8262.

THIBODEAU, Joseph A. *(Judge, Washington Superior Court Snohomish County)*
Office: 3000 Rockefeller Avenue, Everett 98201-4046.
Telephone: (425) 388-3607.
E-mail address: judge@co.snohomish.wa.us

THOMPSON, Linda G. *(Judge, King District Court South Division King County)* Elected Nov 1994 to term beginning Jan 9, 1995. Reelected Nov 1998 and 2002. Current term expires Jan 2007. Born Wenatchee Washington Oct 8, 1948. Protestant. Educated at University of Texas at Arlington B.A. 1982 and College of William & Mary J.D. 1988. Law Clerk to Hon. Theodor vonBrand, Department of Labor Office of Administrative Law Judges 1988-90. Admitted to practice Virginia 1988 and Washington 1990. In legal practice Seattle Washington 1991-94.
Member Washington State District and Municipal Court Judges Association, American Judges Association, Virginia and Washington State Bar Associations. Attended numerous CJE courses and judicial conferences since 1995, The National Judicial College 1996 and Washington State Judicial College 1996.
Office: 1210 South Central Avenue, Kent 98032.
Telephone: (206) 205-2070.
E-mail address: Linda.Thompson@Metrokc.goc

THORPE, Richard J. *(Judge, Washington Superior Court Snohomish County)*
Office: 3000 Rockefeller Avenue, Everett 98201-4046.
Telephone: (425) 388-3408.
E-mail address: judge@co.snohomish.wa.us

TOLLEFSON, Brian *(Judge, Washington Superior Court Pierce County)*
Office: 930 Tacoma Avenue South, Room 534, Tacoma 98402-2108.
Telephone: (253) 798-7565.
E-mail address: SUPCRTDEPT8@co.pierce.wa.us

TOLMAN, Jeff *(Judge, Poulsbo Municipal Court)*
Mailing address: P.O. Box 98, Poulsbo 98370-0098.
Office: 19050 Jensen Way N.E., Poulsbo 98370.
Telephone: (360) 779-9846.

TOMPKINS, Linda G. *(Judge, Washington Superior Court Spokane County)*
Office: West 1116 Broadway Avenue, Spokane 99260-0350.
Telephone: (509) 477-5792.
E-mail address: ltompkins@spokanecounty.org

TRACY, David *(Judge, Federal Way Municipal Court)*
Mailing address: P.O. Box 9717, Federal Way 98063-9717.
Office: 34004 Ninth Avenue South, Suite A2, Federal Way 98003.
Telephone: (253) 835-3000.
E-mail address: david.tracy@ci.federal-way.wa.us

TRICKEY, Michael *(Judge, Washington Superior Court King County)*
Office: 516 Third Avenue, Room C203, Seattle 98104-2381.
Telephone: (206) 296-9265.
E-mail address: michael.trickey@metrokc.gov

TRIPP, Gregory J. *(Judge, Spokane District Court Spokane County and Judge, Cheney and Spokane Municipal Courts)* Appointed by Spokane County Commissioners Jan 14, 1997 to term beginning March 1, 1997. Born Bismarck North Dakota Nov 25, 1948. Protestant. Educated at University of Washington B.A. 1970 and Willamette University J.D. 1973. Member Phi Delta Phi. Admitted to practice Washington 1973 and U.S. District Courts Eastern and Western Districts of Washington. In legal practice Seattle and Spokane.
Deputy Prosecuting Attorney 1973-75. Member Washington State District and Municipal Court Judges Association.
Office: 1100 West Mallon Avenue, Spokane 99260-2043.
Telephone: (509) 477-2965.
E-mail address: gtripp@spokanecounty.org

TRIVETT, Larry M. *(Judge, Marysville Municipal Court)*
Office: 1635 Grove Street, Marysville 98270-4301.
Telephone: (360) 651-5035.

UHRIG, Ira J. *(Magistrate Judge, United States District Court Western District of Washington and Judge, Whatcom District Court Whatcom County)* Appointed

UHRIG, IRA J.—*Continued*

Magistrate Judge by U.S. District Court judges. Serves part time.
Office: Whatcom County Courthouse, Fourth Floor, 311 Grand Avenue, Bellingham 98225-4046.
Telephone: (360) 738-2512.

VAN DEREN, Marywave *(Judge, Washington Superior Court Pierce County)*
Office: 930 Tacoma Avenue South, Room 534, Tacoma 98402-2108.
Telephone: (253) 798-7735.
E-mail address: SUPCRTDEPT19@co.pierce.wa.us

VanderSCHOOR, Vic L. *(Judge, Washington Superior Court Benton-Franklin Counties)*
Office: 7320 West Quinault Avenue, Kennewick 99336-7665.
Telephone: (509) 736-3071.

VAN de VEER, Philip J. *(Judge, Pend Oreille District Court Pend Oreille County)* Also serves as Court Commissioner, Washington Superior Court Pend Oreille County.
Mailing address: P.O. Box 5030, Newport 99156.
Office: 229 South Garden Avenue, Newport 99156.
Telephone: (509) 447-4110.
E-mail address: philip.vandeveer@courts.wa.gov

van DOORNINCK, Kitty-Ann *(Judge, Washington Superior Court Pierce County)*
Office: 930 Tacoma Avenue South, Room 534, Tacoma 98402-2108.
Telephone: (253) 798-6098.
E-mail address: SUPCRTDEPT20@co.pierce.wa.us

VAN NUYS, Heather K. *(Judge, Washington Superior Court Yakima County)* Appointed by Governor Booth Gardner to term beginning Aug 1, 1988. Elected Sept 1988, Sept 1992, Sept 1996 and 2000. Current term expires Jan 2005. Born Yakima Washington. Methodist. Educated at University of Washington B.A. 1977 and Willamette University J.D. 1980. Admitted to practice Washington 1980, U.S. District Court Western District of Washington 1980 and U.S. Supreme Court 1989. In legal practice Seattle 1980-81 and Yakima 1981-82. Judge, Yakima District Court Yakima County 1983-88.
Member John Gavin Inn American Inns of Court, National Association of Women Judges (Board Member 1992-94) and American Bar Association.
Office: 128 North Second Street, Yakima 98901-2639.
Telephone: (509) 574-2710.
E-mail address: heather.vannuys@co.yakima.wa.us

VAN SICKLE, Fred *(Chief Judge, United States District Court Eastern District of Washington)* Appointed for life by President George Bush to term beginning 1991. Chief Judge since Sept 1, 2000. Born Superior Wisconsin Jan 31, 1943. Educated at University of Wisconsin B.S. 1965 and University of Washington School of Law J.D. 1968. In legal practice Washington 1970-75. Judge, Washington Superior Court Douglas-Grant Counties 1975-79. Judge, Washington Superior Court Chelan-Douglas Counties 1979-91.
Prosecuting Attorney Douglas County 1971-75. First Lieutenant U.S. Army JAGC 1968-70.
Mailing address: P.O. Box 2209, Spokane 99210-2209.
Telephone: (509) 353-3224.

VERHEY, Elizabeth *(Judge, Tacoma Municipal Court)*
Office: 930 Tacoma Avenue South, Room 841, Tacoma 98402-2181.
Telephone: (253) 591-5259.

VOTENDAHL, Jerry A. *(Judge, Walla Walla District Court Walla Walla County)*
Office: 317 West Rose, Walla Walla 99362.
Telephone: (509) 527-3236.

WACKER, Robert A. *(Judge, King District Court East Division King County)* Elected to term beginning Jan 1975. Reelected 1978, 1982, 1986, 1990, 1994, 1998 and 2002. Current term expires Jan 2007. Born Boston Massachusetts Nov 16, 1933. Protestant. Educated at University of Washington B.A. 1960 LL.B. 1964. Admitted to practice Washington 1964. In legal practice Seattle 1964-75.
Office: Shoreline Courthouse, 18050 Meridian Avenue North, Shoreline 98133.
Telephone: (206) 205-9200.
E-mail address: robert.wacker@metrokc.gov

WARME, James Edgar F. Xavier *(Judge, Washington Superior Court Cowlitz County)*
Office: 312 S.W. First Avenue, Kelso 98626-1739.
Telephone: (360) 577-3085.
E-mail address: WarmeJ@co.cowlitz.wa.us

WARNING, Stephen M. *(Judge, Washington Superior Court Cowlitz County)*
Office: 312 S.W. First Avenue, Kelso 98626-1739.
Telephone: (360) 577-3085.
E-mail address: WarningS@co.cowlitz.wa.us

WARREN, Thomas C. *(Judge, Chelan District Court Chelan County)* Appointed by Chelan County Commissioners to term beginning Feb 1, 1986. Elected to term beginning Jan 9, 1987. Reelected Nov 1990, Nov 1994, Nov 1998 and 2002. Current term expires Jan 2007. Born Wenatchee Washington Jan 1, 1941. Methodist. Educated at University of Washington B.A. 1963 LL.B. 1966. Associate Editor University of Washington Law Review 1964-66. Admitted to practice Washington 1966, U.S. District Court Western District of Washington 1966 and U.S. Court of Appeals for the Armed Forces 1967. In legal practice Wenatchee 1971-86. Judge, Cashmere and Leavenworth Municipal Courts 1980-86.
Editor "Gavel Babble" Newsletter Washington District and Municipal Court Judges Association since 1993. Member Executive Committee since 1992 and Chair 2000-01 National Conference of Special Court Judges Judicial Administration Division American Bar Association. President Washington District and Municipal Court Judges Association 1993-94. Captain U.S. Army JAGC 1967-71.
Mailing address: P.O. Box 2182, Wenatchee 98807-2182.
Office: 350 Orondo Avenue, Fourth Floor, Wenatchee 98801-2885.
Telephone: (509) 667-6600.
E-mail address: Thomas.Warren@co.chelan.wa.us

WARTNIK, Anthony P. *(Judge, Washington Superior Court King County)* Appointed by Governor Dixy Lee Ray to term beginning April 1, 1980. Elected Nov 1980, 1984, 1988, 1992, 1996 and 2000. Current term expires Jan 2005. Born Los Angeles California May 10, 1938. Jewish. Educated at University of Washington

WARTNIK, ANTHONY P.—*Continued*

B.A. 1961 J.D. 1963. Member Zeta Beta Tau and Phi Alpha Delta. Admitted to practice Washington 1963. Began legal practice Seattle 1963. Judge, Bellevue District Court King County 1971-80.

Author address to Washington Alcohol and Drug Institute, "Court Review" American Judges Association 1977. Co-author "The New Child Support Guidelines" 46 No. 1 Washington State Bar News Jan 1992. Chair Governor's Advisory Panel on Fetal Alcohol Syndrome 1995. Member Washington State Child Support Commission 1987-90, American Judges Association (Board of Governors 1972-78, Court of Appeals 1979-84), American Judges Foundation (President 1974-77, Board Chairman 1977-82), Seattle-King County, East King County (Secretary-Treasurer 1973-78) and Washington State Bar Associations. Faculty Advisor National College of State Courts 1973 and Washington Judicial College 1977. Named Outstanding Young Man of the Year State of Washington by Junior Chamber of Commerce 1972. Former member and officer PTA, community associations and swim club. Enjoys boating, fishing, golf, tennis and racquetball.

Office: 516 Third Avenue, Room C203, Seattle 98104-2381.

Telephone: (206) 296-9270.

E-mail address: anthony.wartnik@metrokc.gov

WEINBERG, John L. *(Magistrate Judge, United States District Court Western District of Washington)* Appointed by U.S. District Court judges 1973. Reappointed 1981, 1989 and 1997. Current term expires Nov 11, 2005. Born Chicago Illinois April 24, 1941. Educated at Swarthmore College B.A. 1962 and University of Chicago J.D. 1965. Law Clerk to Hon. Henry L. Burman, Illinois Appellate Court; Hon. Walter V. Schaefer, Illinois Supreme Court; and Hon. William T. Beeks, U.S. District Court Western District of Washington. Admitted to practice Illinois 1966 and Washington 1967. In legal practice Seattle Washington 1968-73.

Member American Judicature Society, Federal Magistrate Judge Association (National President 1982-83), Seattle-King County, Washington State and American Bar Associations. Hobbies include tennis, duplicate bridge, swimming and softball.

Office: 304 U.S. Courthouse, 1010 Fifth Avenue, Seattle 98104-1192.

Telephone: (206) 553-5774.

WEISFIELD, Robert Douglas *(Judge, West District Court Klickitat County)* Appointed by Klickitat County Board of Commissioners to term beginning Jan 3, 1978. Elected Nov 1978, 1982, 1986, 1990, 1994, 1998 and 2002. Current term expires Dec 2006. Born Seattle Washington Oct 18, 1946. Jewish. Educated at University of Washington B.A. 1968 and University of Oregon J.D. 1971. Member Zeta Beta Tau. Admitted to practice Washington 1972. Began legal practice Tacoma 1972. In legal practice Bigen since 1984.

Assistant City Attorney Tacoma 1972-75. Instructor in Evidence Clark College 1987. Member Washington State Magistrates Association and Washington State Bar Association. Attended The National Judicial College Fall 1978 and Fall 1981. First Lieutenant USAR 1968-76. President White Salmon Rotary Club 1987. Enjoys ranching.

Mailing address: P.O. Box 435, White Salmon 98672-0435.

Office: 180 N.W. Lincoln Street, White Salmon 98672.

Telephone: (509) 493-1190.

WERNETTE, Richard G. *(Judge, College Place Municipal Court)*

Office: 625 South College Avenue, College Place 99324-1516.

Telephone: (509) 529-1200.

WEST, Robert E., Jr. *(Judge, Black Diamond Municipal Court)*

Mailing address: P.O. Box 599, Black Diamond 98010-0599.

Office: 25510 Lawson Street, Black Diamond 98010.

Telephone: (360) 886-7784.

WHALEY, Robert H. *(Judge, United States District Court Eastern District of Washington)* Appointed for life by President Bill Clinton to term beginning July 12, 1995. Born Huntington West Virginia April 5, 1943. Educated at Princeton University A.B. 1965 and Emory University J.D. 1968. Associate Editor Journal of Public Law 1967-68. Admitted to practice Georgia 1968, Colorado 1970 and Washington 1971. In legal practice Atlanta Georgia 1968-69 and Spokane Washington 1972-92. Judge, Washington Superior Court Spokane County 1992-95.

Trial Attorney Land and Natural Resources Division Department of Justice 1969-71. Assistant U.S. Attorney Eastern District of Washington 1971-72. Contributing author Georgia State B. Jour. 1968; 22 No. 1 Gonzaga L. Rev. 1987; and 59 Antitrust L. Jour. 575, 1990. Adjunct Professor of Remedies, Federal Jurisdiction and Antitrust Gonzaga University School of Law 1974. Fellow American College of Trial Lawyers. Former Member State Bar of Georgia, Colorado and Washington State (Bar Examiner) Bar Associations. Member Washington State Judicial Recommendation Committee, Washington State Trial Lawyers Association (President and Board of Directors 1974-81), Washington Association of Criminal Trial Lawyers (President and Board Member 1987-91), Federal (Judicial Recommendation Committee) and American Bar Associations. Attends Judicial Education Programs Federal Judicial Center. Named Trial Lawyer of the Year by Washington State Trial Lawyers Association 1985. Enjoys hunting and fishing.

Mailing address: P.O. Box 283, Spokane 99210-0283.

Telephone: (509) 353-2170.

WHITE, James L. *(Judge, Edmonds Municipal Court)*

Office: 250 Fifth Avenue North, Edmonds 98020-3146.

Telephone: (425) 771-0211.

WHITE, Jay V. *(Judge, Washington Superior Court King County)*

Office: 401 Fourth Avenue North, Room 2D, Kent 98032-4429.

Telephone: (206) 296-9251.

E-mail address: jay.white@metrokc.gov

WHITE, Richard B. *(Judge, Spokane District Court Spokane County and Judge, Spokane Municipal Court)*
Office: 1100 West Mallon Avenue, Spokane 99260-2043.
Telephone: (509) 477-2961.
E-mail address: rwhite@spokanecounty.org

WHITENER-MOBERG, Janis *(Judge, Grant District Court Grant County and Judge, Coulee City, Electric City, Grand Coulee, Mattawa, Moses Lake, Quincy, Royal City and Warden Municipal Courts)* Elected to term beginning Jan 1, 1991. Reelected 1994, 1998 and 2002. Current term expires Dec 2006. Born Wenatchee Washington Jan 11, 1958. Educated at Washington State University B.A. 1980 and Gonzaga University J.D. 1985. Admitted to practice Washington 1986.
Mailing address: P.O. Box 37, Ephrata 98823-0037.
Office: 35 C Street N.W., Ephrata 98823.
Telephone: (509) 754-2011.

WILLIAMS, Kenneth Day *(Judge, Washington Superior Court Clallam County)* Elected Sept 11, 1992 to term beginning Jan 13, 1993. Reelected Sept 17, 1996 and Nov 2000. Current term expires Jan 2005. Born Seattle Washington June 4, 1946. Educated at Washington State University B.A. with honors 1968 and University of Washington J.D. 1974. Admitted to practice Washington 1974, U.S. District Court Western District of Washington 1977 and U.S. Court of Appeals Ninth Circuit 1981. In legal practice Port Angeles 1974-92. Judge pro tem, Clallam District Court Clallam County 1980-92. Judge pro tem, Washington Court of Appeals Oct 2000.
City Attorney Sequim 1974-92. Instructor "The Law of Surveying" Peninsula College 1990-91. Board Member and Vice President 2003 Washington State Association of Drug Court Professionals. Member Clallam County Bar Association (President 1989-90). E-4 U.S. Army Vietnam War 1968-70. President 2002 and Board Member Boys and Girls Club. Board of Directors Pro Bono Lawyers. Member Pioneer Dance Board, Lauridson Trust Board and First Book.
Mailing address: P.O. Box 863, Port Angeles 98362-0149.
Office: 223 East Fourth Street, Port Angeles 98362.
Telephone: (360) 417-2386.

WILLIAMS, Patricia C. *(Chief Judge, United States Bankruptcy Court Eastern District of Washington)* Appointed by U.S. Court of Appeals Ninth Circuit judges 1997. Term expires 2011. Chief Judge since June 15, 1999. Educated at Park College B.A. 1969 and Gonzaga University J.D. 1975. Admitted to practice Washington 1975 and Idaho 1988. Board Certified Business Bankruptcy Law American Bankruptcy Board of Certification. Member Idaho State Bar.
Mailing address: P.O. Box 2164, Spokane 99210-2164.
Telephone: (509) 353-2404.

WILSON, Donna *(Judge, Spokane District Court Spokane County and Judge, Spokane Municipal Court)*
Office: 1100 West Mallon Avenue, Spokane 99260-2043.
Telephone: (509) 477-2957.
E-mail address: dwilson@spokanecounty.org

WILSON, Shirley *(Magistrate, Seattle Municipal Court)*
Office: 600 Fifth Avenue, Seattle 98104.
Telephone: (206) 684-5607.
E-mail address: Shirley.Wilson@seattle.gov

WISE, Jill R. *(Judge, Chelan Municipal Court)*
Mailing address: P.O. Box 1669, Chelan 98816-1669.
Office: 143 Johnson Avenue, Chelan 98816.
Telephone: (509) 682-8044.

WISMAN, Jay F. *(Judge, Snohomish District Court Cascade Division Snohomish County)* Former Judge, Marysville Municipal Court.
Office: 415 East Burke Avenue, Arlington 98223-1010.
Telephone: (360) 652-9552.

WOOD, George L. *(Judge, Washington Superior Court Clallam County)*
Office: 223 East Fourth Street, Suite 8, Port Angeles 98362-3015.
Telephone: (360) 417-2386.

WOOD, William *(Judge, Milton Municipal Court)*
Office: 1000 Laurel Street, Milton 98354-8850.
Telephone: (253) 922-7625.

WOODARD, Susan J. *(Judge, Yakima Municipal Court)*
Office: 200 South Third Street, Yakima 98901-2830.
Telephone: (509) 575-3050.

WOOLARD, Diane M. *(Judge, Washington Superior Court Clark County)* Appointed by Governor Gary Locke to term beginning July 1, 2000. Elected 2000, current term expires Dec 30, 2004. Born Ketchikan Alaska. Educated at University of Washington B.A. 1967 and Northwestern University School of Law J.D. 1985. Admitted to practice Washington 1986. In legal practice Vancouver 1987-2000.
Deputy Prosecuting Attorney Clark County 1986-87.
Mailing address: P.O. Box 5000, Vancouver 98666-5000.
Office: 1200 Franklin Street, Vancouver 98660.
Telephone: (360) 397-2068.
E-mail address: diane.woolard@clark.wa.gov

WOOSTER, Evelyn *(Judge, Castle Rock Municipal Court)*
Mailing address: P.O. Box 515, Castle Rock 98611-0515.
Office: 141 A Street, Castle Rock 98611.
Telephone: (360) 274-8181.

WORSWICK, Lisa R. *(Judge, Washington Superior Court Pierce County)* Former Judge, Roy Municipal Court. Former Court Commissioner, Pierce District Court No. 1 Pierce County.
Office: 930 Tacoma Avenue South, Room 534, Tacoma 98402-2108.
Telephone: (253) 798-6630.
E-mail address: lworswi@co.pierce.wa.us

WULLE, John P. *(Judge, Washington Superior Court Clark County)* Former Judge, Clark District Court Clark County. Former Judge, Camas-Washougal Municipal Court.
Mailing address: P.O. Box 5000, Vancouver 98666-5000.

WULLE, JOHN P.—*Continued*

Office: 1200 Franklin Street, Vancouver 98660-2812.
Telephone: (360) 397-2248.
E-mail address: John.Wulle@clark.wa.gov

WYNNE, Thomas J. *(Judge, Washington Superior Court Snohomish County)* Elected Sept 15, 1992 to term beginning Jan 11, 1993. Reelected Sept 1996 and Sept 2000. Current term expires Jan 2005. Born Everett Washington April 22, 1943. Protestant. Educated at University of Washington B.A. 1965 J.D. 1968. Admitted to practice Washington 1968 and U.S. District Court Western District of Washington 1975. Began legal practice Seattle 1968. In legal practice Everett 1972-78. Judge, South District Court Snohomish County Jan 8, 1979 to Jan 10, 1993.

Deputy Prosecuting Attorney Snohomish County 1972-78. Member Judicial Information Systems Committee, Technology Committee Washington State Superior Court Judges Association, Snohomish County and Washington State Bar Associations. Captain U.S. Army 1969-71 and Lieutenant Colonel USAR (retired). Member Lynnwood Rotary.

Office: 3000 Rockefeller Avenue, M/S 502, Everett 98201-4060.
Telephone: (425) 388-3418.
E-mail address: judge@co.snohomish.wa.us

YEATTS, Fred L. *(Judge, King District Court East Division King County)*

Office: Bellevue Courthouse, 585-112th Avenue S.E., Bellevue 98004-6426.
Telephone: (206) 296-3650.

YU, Mary *(Judge, Washington Superior Court King County)*

Office: 516 Third Avenue, Room C203, Seattle 98104-2381.
Telephone: (206) 296-9275.
E-mail address: mary.yu@metrokc.gov

YULE, Dennis D. *(Judge, Washington Superior Court Benton-Franklin Counties)* Appointed by Governor Booth Gardner to term beginning March 17, 1986. Elected Nov 4, 1986, Nov 8, 1988, Nov 3, 1992, Nov 1996 and Nov 2000. Current term expires Dec 31, 2004. Born Shelton Washington April 11, 1943. Educated at Seattle Pacific University B.A. 1964 and Duke University J.D. 1967.

Office: 7320 West Quinault Avenue, Kennewick 99336-7665.
Telephone: (509) 736-3071.

ZAGELOW, Robert L. *(Judge, Washington Superior Court Walla Walla County)* Assumed office 1997. Elected to subsequent term. Born June 8, 1944. Educated at Washington State University B.A. with distinction 1966 M.A. 1968 and University of Idaho J.D. 1971. Editor-in-Chief Idaho Law Review. Member Phi Kappa Phi, Phi Sigma Alpha and Omicron Delta Epsilon. Admitted to practice Washington, U.S. District Court Eastern District of Washington, U.S. Bankruptcy Court Eastern District of Washington and U.S. Court of Appeals Ninth Circuit. In legal practice Walla Walla 1971-96. Judge, Walla Walla District Court Walla Walla County 1995.

Author Note "Automobile Dealership Fraud: Punitive Damages" 7 No. 1 Idaho L. Rev. 117-123, 1970. Co-author with Ken D. Duft *Agribusiness Management, Co-operative Director Liability Exposure: Issues and Resolutions* 1989. Chairman Agricultural Subcommittee 1993 and Member Executive Committee Section of Corporations, Business and Banking Washington State Bar Association. Member Joint Committee Concerning Judicial Elections and Judicial Pamphlets King County Bar Association and Washington State Bar Association since 1995. Member American College of Real Estate Lawyers, American Arbitration Association, Washington State Superior Court Judges Association (Rural Courts Committee 1997), Federal Bar Association of the Eastern District of Washington, Walla Walla County (Past President, Chairman Task Force to Establish Pro Bono Services) and American Bar Associations. Board of Governors since 1990 and Vice President Walla Walla Community College Foundation. Member Walla Walla Regional Advisory Council Washington State Long-Term Care Ombudsman Program since 1990. Member Convention Center Task Force since 1991 and Former Member Board of Directors Walla Walla Chamber of Commerce. Board of Directors Blue Mountain Area Foundation since 1993, Goodwill Industries of Walla Walla since 1993 and Walla Walla Valley Estate Planning Council since 1995. Former Member Board of Directors Walla Walla United Way, Walla Walla Chapter Association of Retarded Citizens, Children's Home Society of Washington and Bank of the West. Board of Trustees and Former Chairman First Congregational Church.

Mailing address: P.O. Box 836, Walla Walla 99362-0259.
Office: 315 West Main Street, Walla Walla 99362.
Telephone: (509) 527-3228.
E-mail address: rzagelow@co.walla-walla.wa.us

ZILLY, Thomas S. *(Judge, United States District Court Western District of Washington)* Appointed for life by President Ronald Reagan to term beginning April 30, 1988. Born Detroit Michigan Jan 1, 1935. Catholic. Educated at University of Michigan B.A. 1956 and Cornell University Law School LL.B. 1962. Managing Editor Cornell Law Quarterly 1961-62. Recipient First Place Frazer Prize and Constitutional Law Award from Cornell Law School. Admitted to practice Washington 1962, U.S. District Courts Eastern 1962 and Western 1962 Districts of Washington, U.S. Court of Appeals Ninth Circuit 1962 and U.S. Supreme Court 1976. In legal practice Seattle 1962-88.

Author Note "Eminent Domain: Fee Simple Determinable and Possibility of Reverter—Distribution of Award" 46 Cornell Law Quarterly 631, 1961; Note "Real Property: Covenants—Affirmative Covenants Which Run With the Land" Cornell Law Quarterly 349, 1961; Note "Torts: Landowner's Common Law and Statutory Liability to Firemen for Negligent Maintenance of Premises" 47 Cornell Law Quarterly 119, 1961, reprinted in *Personal Injury Annual 1962* 523 Frumer & Friedman; "Recent Developments in Legal Malpractice" 31 Washington State Bar News 8 June 1977; "Recent Developments in Legal Malpractice Litigation" 6 Journal of the Section of Litigation 8 American Bar Association Fall 1979; and Column "Dicta" Seattle-King County Bar Bulletin Jan 1986 to Dec 1987. Co-author Chapter 12 *Legal Malpractice, Professional Responsibility, A Guide for Attorneys* American Bar Association Professional Education Publication 1976. Important Decisions: Northern Spotted Owl v. Hodel (ruled the Fish and Wildlife Service acted arbitrarily and capriciously in deciding not to list the northern spotted owl as endangered or threatened

ZILLY, THOMAS S.—*Continued*

under the Endangered Species Act) 716 F. Supp. 479, 1988; Multicare Medical Center v. Washington (ruled Medicaid payments to hospitals by Washington State are unreasonably low and constitute a "hidden tax" on non-Medicaid patients who must pay more to make up the difference) 768 F. Supp. 1349, W.D. Wash. 1991; and Greene v. Lujan (ruled that the Samish Indian Tribe's status as a recognized tribe could not be taken away without due process of law) No. C89-645Z, W.D. Wash. Feb 25, 1992.

Member Ninth Circuit Jury Committee since 1993 and Executive Committee Ninth Circuit Conference 1994-97. Member Ninth Circuit District Judges Association, Federal Judges Association (Board of Directors since 1998), Seattle-King County (President 1986-87), Washington State (Bar Examiner 1975-85), Federal and American (Committee on Technology National Conference of Federal Trial Judges Judicial Administration Division) Bar Associations. Attended Seminar for New Judges 1988, Ninth Circuit Judicial Conference since 1988, Ninth Circuit Workshop for Judges since 1989, Ninth Circuit Sentencing Institute 1991, Case Management Skills Development Seminar July 1992 and Fiscal Year 1993 National Workshop for Federal District Judges May 1993 Federal Judicial Center; Liberty Fund Colloquium Aug 1990; and Basic Economics Institute George Mason University April 1993. Instructor/Speaker "Oral Advocacy Skills for the Experienced Trial Lawyer" Washington State Bar Association Oct 1989, "Depositions—Tactics, Strategies and Problems" University of Washington School of Law and Washington Law School Foundation March 3, 1990, "View from the Bench" Washington State Trial Lawyers Association Nov 1991, "Effective Use of Arbitration, Mediation and Settlement" Washington State Bar Association Nov 18, 1994, "Trials Viewed from the Bench 'What We See'" Federal Bar Association Dec 5, 1994, "Technology and Exhibits in the Courtroom" A View From the Bench Washington State Bar Association March 26, 1997, "Discovery Abuses" Judges Meeting Federal Bar Association Sept 18, 1998, North West Alternative Dispute Resolution Conference Washington State Bar Association May 1, 1999, "Ethics, Professionalism" CLE Washington State Bar Association Sept 24, 1999 and "Early Mediation" CLE Alternative Dispute Resolution Committee Federal Bar Association Oct 22, 1999. Recipient Tuahku District Service to Youth Award from Chief Seattle Council Boy Scouts of America 1983. Lieutenant USNR Aug 1956 to June 1962 (active duty Aug 1956 to Aug 1959). Scoutmaster Troop 15 Thunderbird (Tuahku) District Seattle 1976-84. Hobbies include family, wine making, boating, playing squash and downhill and cross-country skiing.

Office: 410 U.S. Courthouse, 1010 Fifth Avenue, Seattle 98104-1124.

Telephone: (206) 553-1469.

ZIMMERMAN, Darvin J. *(Judge, Clark District Court Clark County and Judge, Camas-Washougal Municipal Court)*

Mailing address: P.O. Box 9806, Vancouver 98666-8806.

District Court office: 1200 Franklin Street, Vancouver 98660-2812.

Municipal Court office: 89 C Street, Washougal 98671-2142.

Telephone: (360) 397-2199.

WEST VIRGINIA

Capital CHARLESTON

UNITED STATES DISTRICT COURTS DISTRICTS OF WEST VIRGINIA

Within West Virginia there are two United States District Courts. For descriptive information refer to the United States Courts section.

NORTHERN DISTRICT includes Barbour, Berkeley, Braxton, Brooke, Calhoun, Doddridge, Gilmer, Grant, Hampshire, Hancock, Hardy, Harrison, Jefferson, Lewis, Marion, Marshall, Mineral, Monongalia, Morgan, Ohio, Pendleton, Pleasants, Pocahontas, Preston, Randolph, Ritchie, Taylor, Tucker, Tyler, Upshur, Webster and Wetzel counties. The court sits at Clarksburg, Elkins, Fairmont, Martinsburg and Wheeling.

Chief Judge
Irene M. Keeley

Judges
Frederick P. Stamp, Jr.
W. Craig Broadwater

Senior Judge
Robert Earl Maxwell

Clerk
Dr. Wally Edgell
P.O. Box 2857
Clarksburg, West Virginia 26302-2857
(304) 622-8513

SOUTHERN DISTRICT includes Boone, Cabell, Clay, Fayette, Greenbrier, Jackson, Kanawha, Lincoln, Logan, Mason, McDowell, Mercer, Mingo, Monroe, Nicholas, Putnam, Raleigh, Roane, Summers, Wayne, Wirt, Wood and Wyoming counties. The court sits at Beckley, Bluefield, Charleston, Huntington, Lewisburg and Parkersburg.

Chief Judge
David A. Faber

Judges
Charles H. Haden, II
John T. Copenhaver, Jr.
Joseph R. Goodwin
Robert C. Chambers

Senior Judges
Robert J. Staker
Elizabeth Virginia Hallanan

Clerk
Ronald D. Lawson
P.O. Box 3869
Charleston, West Virginia 25338-3869
(304) 347-3086

UNITED STATES MAGISTRATE JUDGES OF WEST VIRGINIA

NORTHERN DISTRICT
James E. Seibert
John S. Kaull
David J. Joel

SOUTHERN DISTRICT
Maurice G. Taylor, Jr.
Mary E. Stanley
R. Clarke Vandervort

UNITED STATES BANKRUPTCY COURTS OF WEST VIRGINIA

NORTHERN DISTRICT

Judge
L. Edward Friend, II

Bankruptcy Clerk
Michael D. Sturm
P.O. Box 70
Wheeling, West Virginia 26003-0008
(304) 233-1655

SOUTHERN DISTRICT

Judge
Ronald G. Pearson

Bankruptcy Clerk
Samuel L. Kay
P.O. Box 3924
Charleston, West Virginia 25339-3924
(304) 347-3000

WEST VIRGINIA SUPREME COURT OF APPEALS

The Supreme Court of Appeals is West Virginia's court of last resort. The court consists of a chief justice and four justices elected in statewide partisan elections for twelve-year terms. Vacancies are filled by the governor pending the next general election. The chief justice position rotates annually among the justices. Retired justices may serve on a recall basis with their consent and the approval of the court.

The court has appellate jurisdiction in criminal cases when there has been a conviction for a felony or misdemeanor in Circuit Courts or when a conviction has been made in any court of limited jurisdiction and affirmed in a Circuit Court. The court has appellate jurisdiction in civil cases in equity, in controversies concerning titles or boundaries of land, in cases involving freedom or the constitutionality of a law and in other controversies as specified by law. The court may issue any writs necessary to the exercise of proper jurisdiction and has ad-

WEST VIRGINIA SUPREME COURT OF APPEALS—*Continued*

ministrative authority over the Circuit and Magistrates Courts.

Three justices constitute a quorum. The court sits en banc at Charleston and any other location the court may designate and recesses from mid-December through early January and during the month of August.

Chief Justice
Larry Victor Starcher

Justices
Robin Jean Davis
Elliott E. Maynard
Warren R. McGraw
Joseph P. Albright

Clerk
Rory L. Perry
Supreme Court of Appeals
E-317 State Capitol
1900 Kanawha Boulevard East
Charleston, West Virginia 25305
(304) 558-2601

Interim Administrative Director
James M. Albert
Supreme Court of Appeals
Administrative Office
E100 State Capitol
1900 Kanawha Boulevard East
Charleston, West Virginia 25305-0830
(304) 558-0145

WEST VIRGINIA CIRCUIT COURTS

The Circuit Courts are West Virginia's courts of general jurisdiction. The state is divided into thirty-one circuits. Judges are elected in partisan elections in their respective circuits for eight-year terms. Vacancies are filled by the governor pending the next general election. A chief judge is elected by peer vote to a term agreed upon by the judges in each circuit. If there is no agreement, the Supreme Court of Appeals has established that the term will be for four years. Retired judges may serve on a recall basis with their consent and the approval of the Supreme Court of Appeals.

The courts have original jurisdiction over criminal cases and civil jurisdiction over equity matters and cases at law. Except where jurisdiction is conferred upon another court, the courts have appellate jurisdiction in civil and criminal cases from courts of limited jurisdiction. The courts may issue any writs necessary to the exercise of proper jurisdiction.

The courts sit at the county seats within each circuit.

FIRST JUDICIAL CIRCUIT includes Brooke, Hancock and Ohio counties. The court sits at Wellsburg, New Cumberland and Wheeling.

Chief Judge
Ronald E. Wilson

Judges
Arthur M. Recht
Martin J. Gaughan
James P. Mazzone

SECOND JUDICIAL CIRCUIT includes Marshall, Tyler and Wetzel counties. The court sits at Moundsville, Middlebourne and New Martinsville.

Chief Judge
Mark A. Karl

Judge
John T. Madden

THIRD JUDICIAL CIRCUIT includes Doddridge, Pleasants and Ritchie counties. The court sits at West Union, St. Marys and Harrisville.

Chief Judge
Robert L. Holland, Jr.

FOURTH JUDICIAL CIRCUIT includes Wirt and Wood counties. The court sits at Elizabeth and Parkersburg.

Chief Judge
Robert A. Waters

Judges
Jeffrey B. Reed
George W. Hill

FIFTH JUDICIAL CIRCUIT includes Calhoun, Jackson, Mason and Roane counties. The court sits at Grantsville, Ripley and Spencer.

Chief Judge
David Nibert

Judge
Thomas C. Evans, III

SIXTH JUDICIAL CIRCUIT includes Cabell County. The court sits at Huntington.

Chief Judge
Dan P. O'Hanlon

Judges
John L. Cummings
David M. Pancake
Alfred E. Ferguson

SEVENTH JUDICIAL CIRCUIT includes Logan County. The court sits at Logan.

Chief Judge
Roger L. Perry

Judge
Eric H. O'Briant

EIGHTH JUDICIAL CIRCUIT includes McDowell County. The court sits at Welch.

Chief Judge
Rudolph J. Murensky, II

Judge
Booker T. Stephens

NINTH JUDICIAL CIRCUIT includes Mercer County. The court sits at Princeton.

Chief Judge
Derek C. Swope

Judge
John R. Frazier

WEST VIRGINIA CIRCUIT COURTS—*Continued*

TENTH JUDICIAL CIRCUIT includes Raleigh County. The court sits at Beckley.

Chief Judge
John A. Hutchison

Judges
Harry L. Kirkpatrick, III
Robert A. Burnside, Jr.

ELEVENTH JUDICIAL CIRCUIT includes Greenbrier and Pocahontas counties. The court sits at Lewisburg and Marlinton.

Chief Judge
Frank E. Jolliffe

Judge
James J. Rowe

TWELFTH JUDICIAL CIRCUIT includes Fayette County. The court sits at Fayetteville.

Chief Judge
Charles M. Vickers

Judge
John W. Hatcher, Jr.

THIRTEENTH JUDICIAL CIRCUIT includes Kanawha County. The court sits at Charleston.

Chief Judge
Tod J. Kaufman

Judges
Irene C. Berger
Louis H. Bloom
Jennifer Bailey Walker
Charles E. King
James C. Stucky
Paul Zakaib, Jr.

FOURTEENTH JUDICIAL CIRCUIT includes Braxton, Clay, Gilmer and Webster counties. The court sits at Sutton, Clay, Glenville and Webster Springs.

Chief Judge
Richard A. Facemire

Judge
Jack Alsop

FIFTEENTH JUDICIAL CIRCUIT includes Harrison County. The court sits at Clarksburg.

Chief Judge
J. Lewis Marks, Jr.

Judges
Thomas A. Bedell
James A. Matish

SIXTEENTH JUDICIAL CIRCUIT includes Marion County. The court sits at Fairmont.

Chief Judge
Fred L. Fox, II

Judge
David R. Janes

SEVENTEENTH JUDICIAL CIRCUIT includes Monongalia County. The court sits at Morgantown.

Chief Judge
Russell M. Clawges, Jr.

Judge
Robert B. Stone

EIGHTEENTH JUDICIAL CIRCUIT includes Preston County. The court sits at Kingwood.

Chief Judge
Lawrance S. Miller, Jr.

NINETEENTH JUDICIAL CIRCUIT includes Barbour and Taylor counties. The court sits at Philippi and Grafton.

Chief Judge
Alan D. Moats

TWENTIETH JUDICIAL CIRCUIT includes Randolph County. The court sits at Elkins.

Chief Judge
John L. Henning, Jr.

TWENTY-FIRST JUDICIAL CIRCUIT includes Grant, Mineral and Tucker counties. The court sits at Petersburg, Keyser and Parsons.

Chief Judge
Andrew N. Frye, Jr.

Judge
Philip B. Jordan, Jr.

TWENTY-SECOND JUDICIAL CIRCUIT includes Hampshire, Hardy and Pendleton counties. The court sits at Romney, Moorefield and Franklin.

Chief Judge
Donald H. Cookman

TWENTY-THIRD JUDICIAL CIRCUIT includes Berkeley, Jefferson and Morgan counties. The court sits at Martinsburg, Charles Town and Berkeley Springs.

Chief Judge
David H. Sanders

Judges
Christopher C. Wilkes
Thomas W. Steptoe, Jr.
Gray Silver, III

TWENTY-FOURTH JUDICIAL CIRCUIT includes Wayne County. The court sits at Wayne.

Chief Judge
Darrell Pratt

TWENTY-FIFTH JUDICIAL CIRCUIT includes Boone and Lincoln counties. The court sits at Madison and Hamlin.

Chief Judge
Jay M. Hoke

Judge
E. Lee Schlaegel

TWENTY-SIXTH JUDICIAL CIRCUIT includes Lewis and Upshur counties. The court sits at Weston and Buckhannon.

Chief Judge
Thomas Howard Keadle

TWENTY-SEVENTH JUDICIAL CIRCUIT includes Wyoming County. The court sits at Pineville.

WEST VIRGINIA CIRCUIT COURTS—*Continued*

Chief Judge
John S. Hrko

TWENTY-EIGHTH JUDICIAL CIRCUIT includes Nicholas County. The court sits at Summersville.

Chief Judge
Gary L. Johnson

TWENTY-NINTH JUDICIAL CIRCUIT includes Putnam County. The court sits at Point Pleasant and Winfield.

Chief Judge
N. Edward Eagloski, II

Judge
O. C. Spaulding

THIRTIETH JUDICIAL CIRCUIT includes Mingo County. The court sits at Williamson.

Chief Judge
Michael Thornsbury

THIRTY-FIRST JUDICIAL CIRCUIT includes Monroe and Summers counties. The court sits at Union and Hinton.

Chief Judge
Robert A. Irons

WEST VIRGINIA COURT OF CLAIMS

The Court of Claims is an arm of the Legislature. The court consists of three judges appointed for six-year terms by the President of the Senate and the Speaker of the House of Delegates. One judge is appointed to serve as presiding judge.

The court has jurisdiction of money damage claims in contract and tort otherwise barred by governmental immunity except certain types of claims specifically listed. The court also has jurisdiction of claims made under the state's Crime Victims Compensation Act. The court renders advisory opinions to state agencies upon request.

The court sits at Charleston.

Presiding Judge
David M. Baker

Judges
Benjamin Hays Webb, II
Franklin L. Gritt, Jr.

WEST VIRGINIA COUNTY COMMISSIONS

County Commissions, formerly known as County Courts, are established in each county and serve primarily administrative functions. Three commissioners are elected by the voters of their respective counties for six-year terms, except in Jefferson and Preston counties, where the terms are five and eight years respectively. A president is elected by peer vote in each county for a one-year term.

The commissioners exercise judicial jurisdiction over all matters of probate, mental commitments, the appointment and qualification of guardians, committees, curators and the settlement of accounts. Commissioners are also responsible for the superintendence and administration of internal police and fiscal affairs of their county.

Any two commissioners constitute a quorum except in Ohio County, where a board of commissioners administers police and fiscal affairs.

WEST VIRGINIA FAMILY COURTS

The Family Court is West Virginia's court of special jurisdiction. A constitutional amendment passed by the voters in November 2000 allowed the Legislature to create a unified family court system, which, in October 2001, was changed again to a system of 35 family court judges serving 26 realigned family court circuits. These new family court judges were appointed by the governor to serve a one-year term ending December 31, 2002, with elections for six-year terms occurring in 2002. Subsequent terms will be eight years.

Family court judges have the authority to make final rulings on family law and related matters. Their jurisdiction includes matters of divorce, annulment, separate maintenance, paternity, grandparent visitation, domestic violence final hearings, and child custody and family support proceedings, except those incidental to child abuse and neglect proceedings. Family court judges may also perform marriages. Until June 30, 2005 appeals are to the circuit courts, unless both parties agree to appeal directly to the Supreme Court. At that time the Legislature will reevaluate the family court appeals process.

The court sits at a county seat within each circuit.

FAMILY COURT CIRCUIT ONE includes Brooke, Hancock and Ohio counties. The court sits at Wheeling.

Judges
Joyce Chernenko
William Sinclair

FAMILY COURT CIRCUIT TWO includes Marshall, Tyler and Wetzel counties. The court sits at New Martinsville.

Judge
Robert C. Hicks

FAMILY COURT CIRCUIT THREE includes Pleasants, Ritchie, Wirt and Wood counties. The court sits at Parkersburg.

Judges
Annette Fantasia
C. Darren Tallman

FAMILY COURT CIRCUIT FOUR includes Calhoun, Doddridge, Gilmer and Roane counties. The court sits at Spencer.

Judge
Larry S. Whited

FAMILY COURT CIRCUIT FIVE includes Jackson and Mason counties. The court sits at Point Pleasant.

Judge
Deloris J. Nibert

FAMILY COURT CIRCUIT SIX includes Cabell County. The court sits at Huntington.

Judges
Ronald Anderson
Patricia Keller

WEST VIRGINIA FAMILY COURTS—*Continued*

FAMILY COURT CIRCUIT SEVEN includes Wayne County. The court sits at Wayne.

Judge
Stephen Lewis

FAMILY COURT CIRCUIT EIGHT includes Mingo County. The court sits at Williamson.

Judge
Robert Calfee

FAMILY COURT CIRCUIT NINE includes Logan County. The court sits at Logan.

Judge
Kelly Gilmore Codispoti

FAMILY COURT CIRCUIT TEN includes Boone and Lincoln counties. The court sits at Madison.

Judge
Cynthia J. Jarrell

FAMILY COURT CIRCUIT ELEVEN includes Kanawha County. The court sits at Charleston.

Judges
Jane Charnock
Mike Kelly
Robert Montgomery
D. Mark Snyder

FAMILY COURT CIRCUIT TWELVE includes McDowell and Mercer counties. The court sits at Welch and Princeton.

Judges
Kimber Radcliffe Warner
Edwin B. Wiley

FAMILY COURT CIRCUIT THIRTEEN includes Raleigh and Wyoming counties. The court sits at Beckley.

Judges
H. Suzanne McGraw
Louise Staton

FAMILY COURT CIRCUIT FOURTEEN includes Fayette and Summers counties. The court sits at Fayetteville.

Judge
Janet F. Steele

FAMILY COURT CIRCUIT FIFTEEN includes Greenbrier and Monroe counties. The court sits at Lewisburg.

Judge
Joseph Pomponio

FAMILY COURT CIRCUIT SIXTEEN includes Clay, Nicholas and Webster counties. The court sits at Summersville.

Judge
Timothy Ruckman

FAMILY COURT CIRCUIT SEVENTEEN includes Braxton, Lewis and Upshur counties. The court sits at Sutton.

Judge
Robert Sowa

FAMILY COURT CIRCUIT EIGHTEEN includes Harrison County. The court sits at Clarksburg.

Judge
M. Drew Crislip

FAMILY COURT CIRCUIT NINETEEN includes Marion County. The court sits at Fairmont.

Judge
David P. Born

FAMILY COURT CIRCUIT TWENTY includes Monongalia County. The court sits at Morgantown.

Judge
J. Jeffrey Culpepper

FAMILY COURT CIRCUIT TWENTY-ONE includes Barbour, Preston and Taylor counties. The court sits at Philippi.

Judge
Beth Longo

FAMILY COURT CIRCUIT TWENTY-TWO includes Grant, Randolph and Tucker counties. The court sits at Elkins.

Judge
Jaymie Godwin Wilfong

FAMILY COURT CIRCUIT TWENTY-THREE includes Hampshire, Mineral and Morgan counties. The court sits at Romney.

Judge
Charles Parsons

FAMILY COURT CIRCUIT TWENTY-FOUR includes Berkeley and Jefferson counties. The court sits at Martinsburg and Charles Town.

Judges
Sally Jackson
William Wertman

FAMILY COURT CIRCUIT TWENTY-FIVE includes Hardy, Pendleton and Pocahontas counties. The court sits at Marlinton.

Judge
David Arrington

FAMILY COURT CIRCUIT TWENTY-SIX includes Putnam County. The court sits at Winfield.

Judge
William M. "Chip" Watkins

WEST VIRGINIA MAGISTRATE COURTS

Magistrate Courts are courts of limited countywide jurisdiction in West Virginia. The courts replaced West Virginia Justice of the Peace Courts by 1974 judicial amendment. Magistrates are elected in partisan elections by the voters of their respective counties for four-year terms. A chief magistrate may be chosen by the chief judge of the Circuit Court.

The courts have original criminal jurisdiction to conduct preliminary felony examinations as well as jurisdiction over most misdemeanors as prescribed by law. The courts have original civil jurisdiction in cases when the amount in controversy does not exceed $5,000, except

WEST VIRGINIA MAGISTRATE COURTS—*Continued*

for matters excluded from their jurisdiction as provided by law. Jurisdiction also extends to cases involving unlawful entry or detainer of real property, or wrongful occupation of residential real property as long as title to said property is not in dispute. Appeals are to the Circuit Courts.

The courts sit at each county seat.

WEST VIRGINIA MUNICIPAL COURTS

The Municipal Courts are courts of limited jurisdiction in West Virginia. Judges are elected and serve terms as designated by the ordinance or charter of the municipality. In smaller towns, the mayor may serve as judge.

The courts have jurisdiction over violations of municipal ordinances.

West Virginia Counties and County Seats

Barbour
Philippi

Berkeley
Martinsburg

Boone
Madison

Braxton
Sutton

Brooke
Wellsburg

Cabell
Huntington

Calhoun
Grantsville

Clay
Clay

Doddridge
West Union

Fayette
Fayetteville

Gilmer
Glenville

Grant
Petersburg

Greenbrier
Lewisburg

Hampshire
Romney

Hancock
New Cumberland

Hardy
Moorefield

Harrison
Clarksburg

Jackson
Ripley

Jefferson
Charles Town

Kanawha
Charleston

Lewis
Weston

Lincoln
Hamlin

Logan
Logan

Marion
Fairmont

Marshall
Moundsville

Mason
Point Pleasant

McDowell
Welch

Mercer
Princeton

Mineral
Keyser

Mingo
Williamson

Monongalia
Morgantown

Monroe
Union

Morgan
Berkeley Springs

Nicholas
Summersville

Ohio
Wheeling

Pendleton
Franklin

Pleasants
St. Marys

Pocahontas
Marlinton

Preston
Kingwood

Putnam
Winfield

Raleigh
Beckley

Randolph
Elkins

Ritchie
Harrisville

Roane
Spencer

Summers
Hinton

Taylor
Grafton

Tucker
Parsons

Tyler
Middlebourne

Upshur
Buckhannon

Wayne
Wayne

Webster
Webster Springs

Wetzel
New Martinsville

Wirt
Elizabeth

Wood
Parkersburg

Wyoming
Pineville

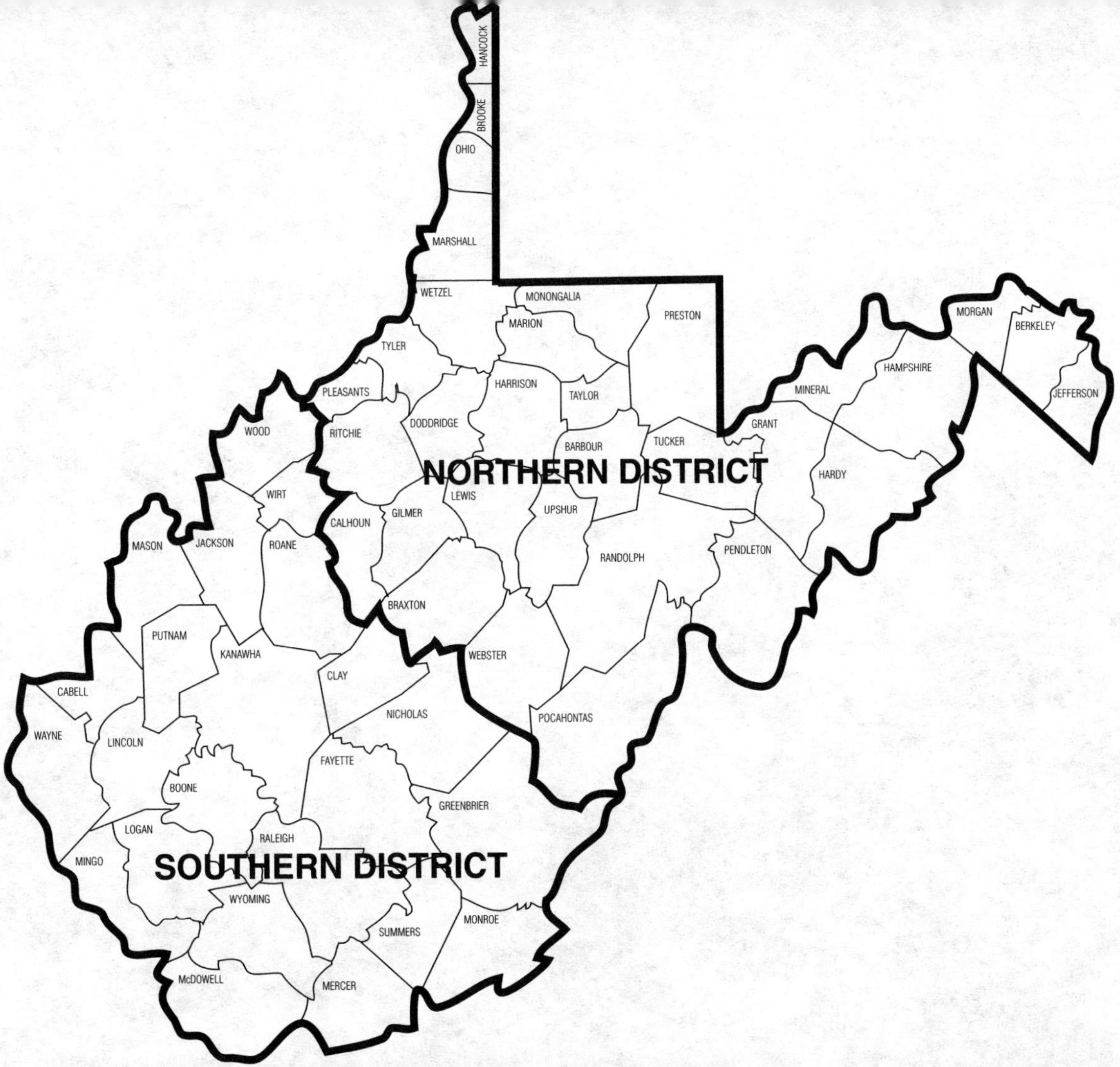
NORTHERN DISTRICT
SOUTHERN DISTRICT
HANCOCK
BROOKE
OHIO
MARSHALL
WETZEL
MONONGALIA
MARION
PRESTON
TYLER
PLEASANTS
HARRISON
TAYLOR
MORGAN
BERKELEY
JEFFERSON
HAMPSHIRE
MINERAL
GRANT
HARDY
RITCHIE
DODDRIDGE
BARBOUR
TUCKER
WOOD
WIRT
LEWIS
CALHOUN
GILMER
UPSHUR
PENDLETON
RANDOLPH
MASON
JACKSON
ROANE
BRAXTON
PUTNAM
KANAWHA
CLAY
WEBSTER
CABELL
NICHOLAS
POCAHONTAS
WAYNE
LINCOLN
FAYETTE
BOONE
GREENBRIER
LOGAN
RALEIGH
MINGO
WYOMING
SUMMERS
MONROE
McDOWELL
MERCER

UNITED STATES DISTRICT COURTS DISTRICTS OF WEST VIRGINIA

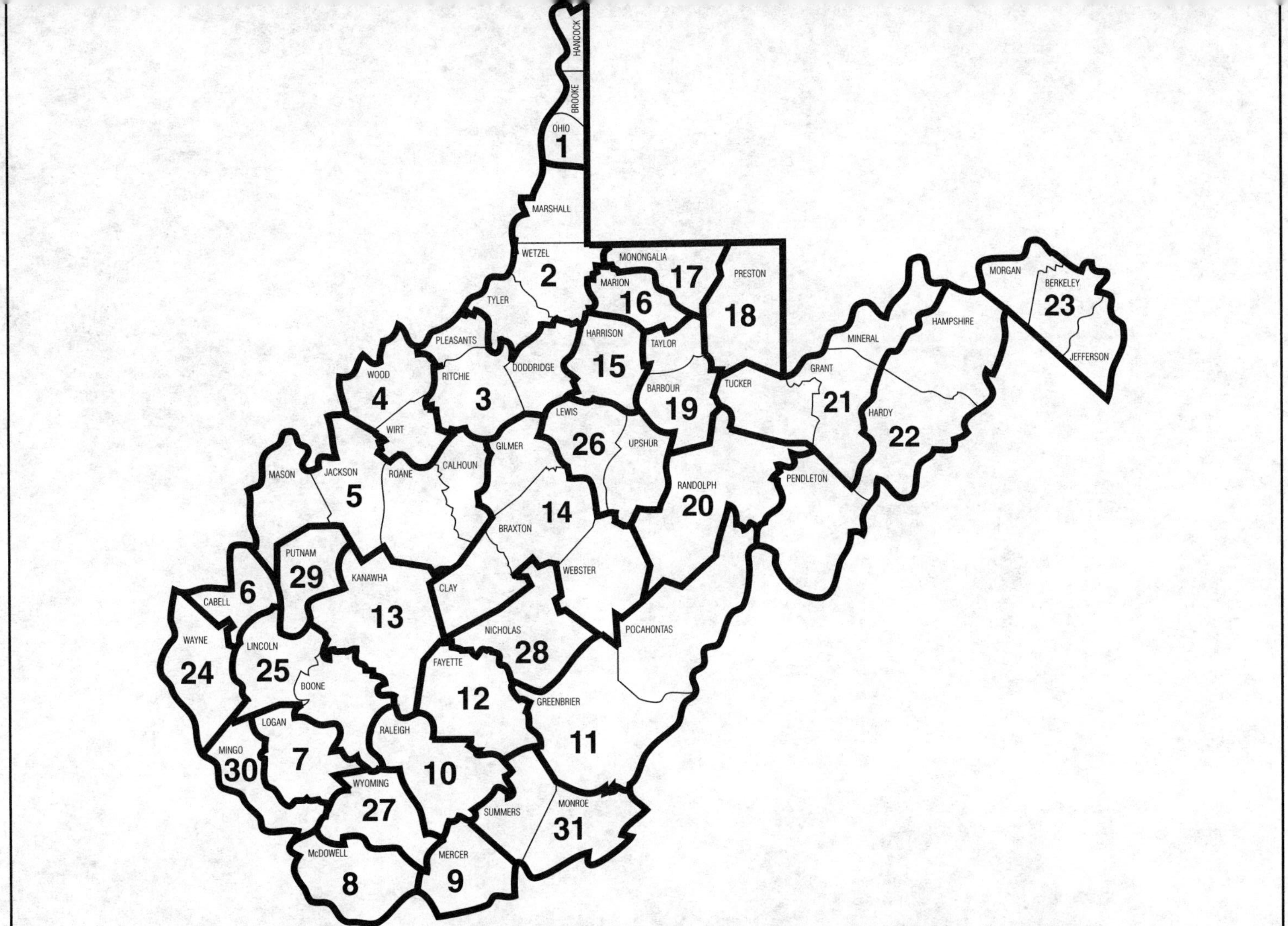
HANCOCK
BROOKE
OHIO
1
MARSHALL
WETZEL
2
TYLER
MONONGALIA
MARION
17
16
PRESTON
18
HARRISON
TAYLOR
15
BARBOUR
19
TUCKER
PLEASANTS
RITCHIE
DODDRIDGE
3
WOOD
4
WIRT
LEWIS
26
UPSHUR
GILMER
MASON
JACKSON
5
ROANE
CALHOUN
BRAXTON
14
RANDOLPH
20
PENDLETON
GRANT
21
MINERAL
HARDY
22
HAMPSHIRE
MORGAN
BERKELEY
23
JEFFERSON
PUTNAM
29
KANAWHA
13
CLAY
WEBSTER
CABELL
6
WAYNE
24
LINCOLN
25
BOONE
NICHOLAS
28
POCAHONTAS
FAYETTE
12
GREENBRIER
11
LOGAN
7
MINGO
30
RALEIGH
10
WYOMING
27
SUMMERS
MONROE
31
McDOWELL
8
MERCER
9

JUDICIAL CIRCUITS OF WEST VIRGINIA CIRCUIT COURTS

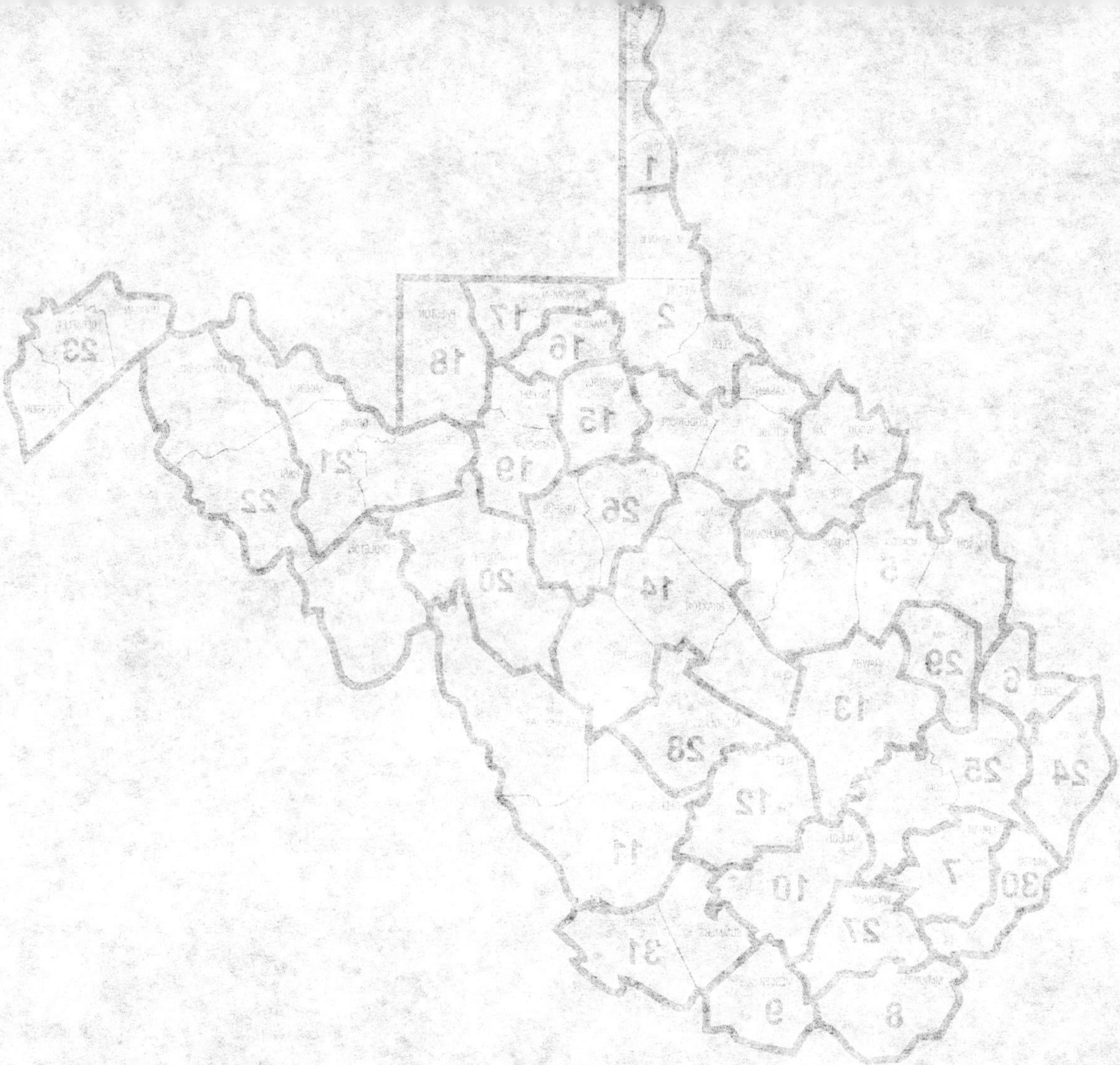

JUDICIAL CIRCUITS OF WEST VIRGINIA CIRCUIT COURTS

© Forster-Long, Inc. THE AMERICAN BENCH: Judges of the Nation

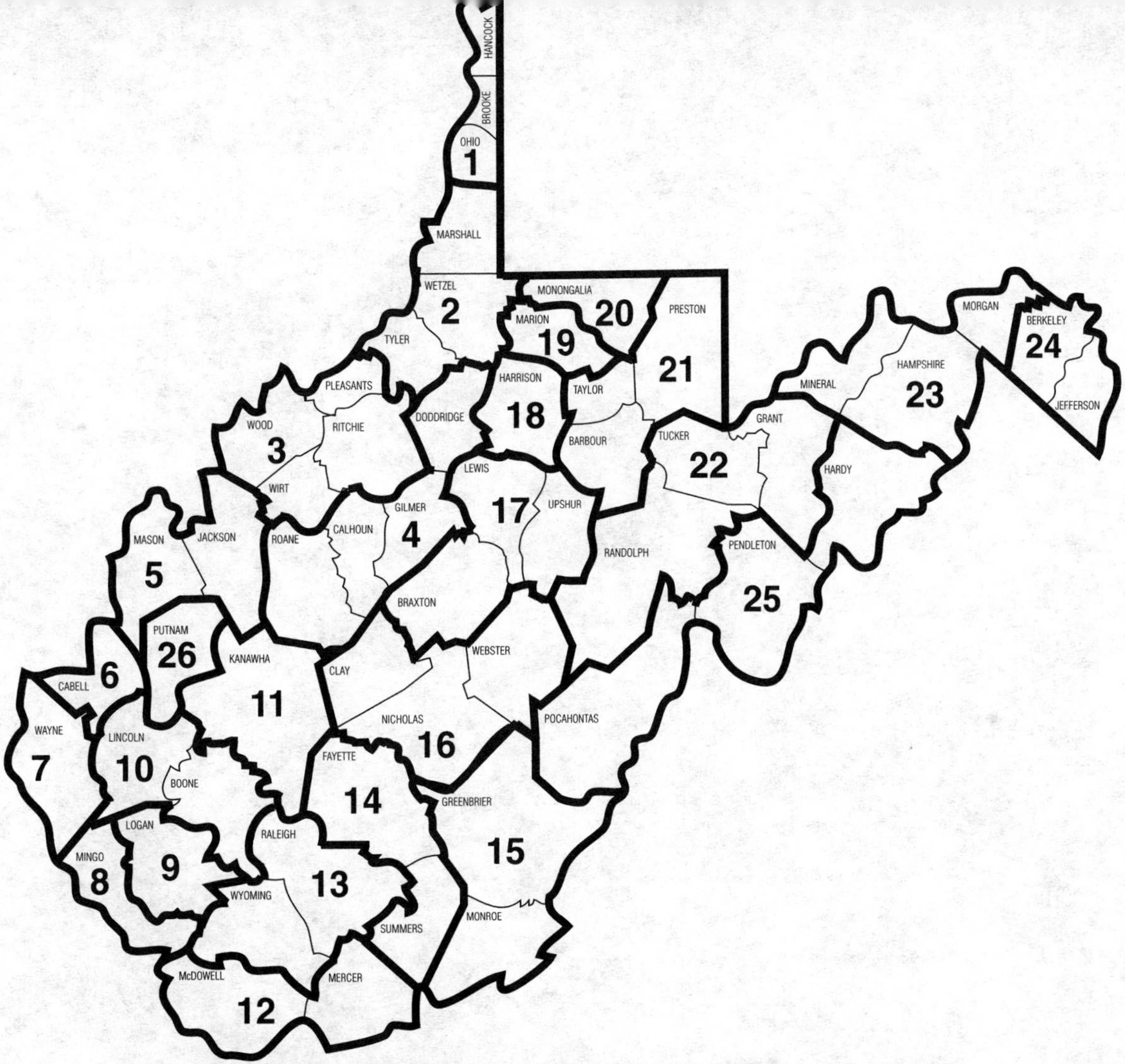
HANCOCK
BROOKE
OHIO
1
MARSHALL
WETZEL
2
TYLER
MONONGALIA
20
MARION
19
PRESTON
21
PLEASANTS
WOOD
3
RITCHIE
WIRT
DODDRIDGE
HARRISON
18
TAYLOR
BARBOUR
TUCKER
22
GRANT
MINERAL
HAMPSHIRE
23
MORGAN
BERKELEY
24
JEFFERSON
HARDY
LEWIS
17
UPSHUR
GILMER
4
CALHOUN
ROANE
JACKSON
MASON
5
RANDOLPH
PENDLETON
25
BRAXTON
PUTNAM
26
KANAWHA
11
CLAY
WEBSTER
CABELL
6
WAYNE
7
LINCOLN
10
BOONE
NICHOLAS
16
POCAHONTAS
FAYETTE
14
GREENBRIER
15
LOGAN
9
MINGO
8
RALEIGH
13
WYOMING
SUMMERS
MONROE
McDOWELL
12
MERCER

CIRCUITS OF WEST VIRGINIA FAMILY COURTS

WEST VIRGINIA

ALBRIGHT, Joseph P. *(Justice, West Virginia Supreme Court of Appeals)* Elected Nov 2000 to term beginning Jan 1, 2001. Term expires Dec 31, 2012. Born Wood County West Virginia Nov 8, 1938. Educated at University of Notre Dame B.S.B.A. cum laude J.D. Recipient Webber Prize for Appellate Advocacy. Staff member Notre Dame Law Review. In legal practice Parkersburg 1962 to Sept 1995 and 1997-2000 and Parkersburg and Charleston 1997-2000. Justice, West Virginia Supreme Court of Appeals Sept 1995 to Dec 1996, appointed by Governor Gaston Caperton.

Former Assistant Prosecuting Attorney Wood County. Former City Attorney Parkersburg. Officer and Director Albright's of Belpre, Inc. since 1959. Member 1970-72 and 1974-86 and Speaker 1985-86 House of Delegates West Virginia Legislature. Charter Board Parkersburg 1969-70.

Office: E308 State Capitol, Charleston 25305.
Telephone: (304) 558-2605.
E-mail address: albrighj@mail.wvnet.edu

ALSOP, Jack *(Judge, West Virginia Circuit Court Fourteenth Judicial Circuit)* Former Chief Judge.

Office: Webster County Courthouse, 2 Court Square, Webster Springs 26288.
Telephone: (304) 847-5062.

ANDERSON, Ronald *(Judge, West Virginia Family Court Circuit Six)* Appointed by Governor Bob Wise to term beginning Jan 1, 2002. Elected 2002, current term expires Dec 31, 2008.

Office: 303 Cabell County Courthouse, 750 Fifth Avenue, Huntington 25702.
Telephone: (304) 528-5519.
Fax: (304) 528-5717

ARRINGTON, David *(Judge, West Virginia Family Court Circuit Twenty-five)* Appointed by Governor Bob Wise to term beginning Jan 1, 2002. Elected 2002, current term expires Dec 31, 2008.

Mailing address: P.O. Box 237, Marlinton 24954.
Office: 818C Tenth Avenue, Marlinton 24954.
Telephone: (304) 799-4084.
Fax: (304) 799-0571

BAKER, David M. *(Presiding Judge, West Virginia Court of Claims)* Appointed April 10, 1990. Reappointed July 1, 1993 and July 1, 1999. Current term expires June 30, 2005. Born Clarksburg West Virginia Oct 11, 1923. Educated at West Virginia University A.B. 1948 J.D. 1950.

President Cabell County Bar Association 1972-73 and Lawyer-Pilots Bar Association 1986-88. U.S. Army 1943-46. Former Member 51st and 53rd Legislatures House of Delegates.

Office: 1900 Kanawha Boulevard East, Room W-334, Charleston 25305-0610.
Telephone: (304) 347-4851.

BEDELL, Thomas A. *(Judge, West Virginia Circuit Court Fifteenth Judicial Circuit)* Elected Nov 1992 to term beginning Jan 1, 1993. Reelected Nov 2000, current term expires Dec 31, 2008. Former Chief Judge. Born Clarksburg West Virginia May 7, 1956. Methodist. Educated at Salem College B.S. 1977 and West Virginia University J.D. 1981. Admitted to practice West Virginia 1981, U.S. District Court Northern District of West Virginia and U.S. Court of Appeals Fourth Circuit. In legal practice Clarksburg 1983-92.

Member West Virginia Judicial Association and West Virginia Bar Association. Democrat.

Office: Harrison County Courthouse, 301 West Main Street, Clarksburg 26301.
Telephone: (304) 624-8630.

BERGER, Irene C. *(Judge, West Virginia Circuit Court Thirteenth Judicial Circuit)*

Office: Kanawha County Judicial Annex, 111 Court Street, Charleston 25301.
Telephone: (304) 357-0361.

BLOOM, Louis H. *(Judge, West Virginia Circuit Court Thirteenth Judicial Circuit)*

Office: Kanawha County Judicial Annex, 111 Court Street, Charleston 25301.
Telephone: (304) 357-0365.

BORN, David P. *(Judge, West Virginia Family Court Circuit Nineteen)* Appointed by Governor Bob Wise to term beginning Jan 1, 2002. Elected 2002, current term expires Dec 31, 2008.

Office: Marion County Courthouse, Third Floor, 219 Adams Street, Fairmont 26554-2833.
Telephone: (304) 367-2760.
Fax: (304) 367-2782

BROADWATER, W. Craig *(Judge, United States District Court Northern District of West Virginia)* Appointed for life by President Bill Clinton. Born Elk City Oklahoma Aug 8, 1950. Methodist. Educated at West Virginia University B.A. magna cum laude 1972 J.D. 1977. Staff member West Virginia University Law Review 1976-77. Admitted to practice West Virginia 1977. Began legal practice Wheeling 1977. Hearing Examiner, West Virginia Workers' Compensation Fund 1979-81. Judge and Chief Judge, West Virginia Circuit Court First Judicial Circuit, appointed by Governor John D. Rockefeller IV to term beginning Oct 31, 1983.

Member The West Virginia State Bar, Ohio County and American Bar Associations. Recipient Diploma of Judicial Skills American Academy of Judicial Education July 15, 1988. Recipient Trial Judge of the Year from West Virginia Trial Lawyers Association 1986-87. Second Lieutenant U.S. Army 1972-74. Major West Virginia Army National Guard 1976-88. Member Ohio County Democratic Executive Committee 1981-83. Member Reserve Officers Association, National Guard Association of the United States, Elm Grove VFW Post 4442 and American Legion Wheeling Post 1.

Office: 214 Federal Building, 217 West King Street, Martinsburg 25401-3211.
Telephone: (304) 267-7027.

BURNSIDE, Robert A., Jr. *(Judge, West Virginia Circuit Court Tenth Judicial Circuit)* Elected Nov 8, 1988 to term beginning Dec 22, 1988. Reelected 1992

BURNSIDE, ROBERT A., JR.—*Continued*

and 2000. Current term expires Dec 31, 2008. Former Chief Judge. Born Montgomery West Virginia Sept 19, 1948. Episcopalian. Educated at Concord College B.A. 1970 and West Virginia University J.D. 1977. Admitted to practice West Virginia 1977 and U.S. District Court Southern District of West Virginia 1977. In legal practice Beckley 1977-88.

Instructor in Business Law and Litigation Mountain State University. Member West Virginia Judicial Association and The West Virginia State Bar (inactive). Democrat. Member Rotary.

Office: Raleigh County Courthouse, 215 Main Street, Beckley 25801.
Telephone: (304) 255-9128.
E-mail address: burnsr@mail.wvnet.edu

CALFEE, Robert *(Judge, West Virginia Family Court Circuit Eight)* Appointed by Governor Bob Wise to term beginning Jan 1, 2002. Elected 2002, current term expires Dec 31, 2008.

Mailing address: P.O. Box 258, Williamson 25661.
Office: 327 Mingo County Courthouse, Williamson 25661.
Telephone: (304) 235-6007.
Fax: (304) 235-6032

CHAMBERS, Robert C. *(Judge, United States District Court Southern District of West Virginia)* Appointed for life by President Bill Clinton. Born Matewan West Virginia Aug 27, 1952. Educated at Marshall University A.B. 1975 and West Virginia University College of Law J.D. 1978. Admitted to practice West Virginia 1978. In legal practice Charleston and Huntington 1978-97.

Member West Virginia Trial Lawyers Association (Board of Governors). Speaker House of Delegates West Virginia 1986-96.

Mailing address: P.O. Box 1570, Huntington 25716-1570.
Office: 845 Fifth Avenue, Huntington 25701.
Telephone: (304) 528-7583.
Fax: (304) 528-7585

CHARNOCK, Jane *(Judge, West Virginia Family Court Circuit Eleven)* Appointed by Governor Bob Wise to term beginning Jan 1, 2002. Elected 2002, current term expires Dec 31, 2008. Born Charleston West Virginia. Educated at West Virginia University B.S.J. cum laude 1982 J.D. 1986. Member Phi Alpha Delta. Admitted to practice West Virginia 1986, U.S. District Court Southern District of West Virginia, U.S. Court of Appeals Fourth Circuit and U.S. Supreme Court. In legal practice Charleston May 1986 to June 30, 1997.

Assistant Prosecuting Attorney Kanawha County July 1, 1997 to Sept 30, 1999. Family Law Master Thirteenth Judicial Circuit Oct 1, 1999 to Dec 31, 2001. Member National Council of Juvenile and Family Court Judges and The West Virginia State Bar.

Mailing address: P.O. Box 75117, Charleston 25375.
Telephone: (304) 558-0497.
Fax: (304) 558-4237

CHERNENKO, Joyce *(Judge, West Virginia Family Court Circuit One)* Appointed by Governor Bob Wise to term beginning Jan 1, 2002. Elected 2002, current term expires Dec 31, 2008.

Office: Courthouse Annex, Second Floor, 51 Sixteenth Street, Wheeling 26003.
Telephone: (304) 238-1051.
Fax: (304) 238-1000

CLAWGES, Russell M., Jr. *(Chief Judge, West Virginia Circuit Court Seventeenth Judicial Circuit)* Appointed by Governor Gaston Caperton to term beginning Jan 13, 1997. Elected 1998 and Nov 2000. Current term expires Dec 31, 2008. Born Morgantown West Virginia Jan 30, 1950. Religious affiliation: Christian and Missionary Alliance. Educated at West Virginia University B.A. 1971 J.D. 1974. Member Order of the Coif. Admitted to practice West Virginia 1974, U.S. District Court Northern District of West Virginia 1974 and U.S. Court of Appeals for the Armed Forces 1975. In legal practice Morgantown 1978-97.

Adjunct Lecturer on Trial Advocacy West Virginia University College of Law 1986-96. Member The West Virginia State Bar, West Virginia and American Bar Associations. Captain USAF JAG 1974-78. Democrat. Enjoys golf.

Office: Monongalia County Courthouse, 243 High Street, Morgantown 26505.
Telephone: (304) 291-7216.

CODISPOTI, Kelly Gilmore *(Judge, West Virginia Family Court Circuit Nine)* Appointed by Governor Bob Wise to term beginning Jan 1, 2002. Elected 2002, current term expires Dec 31, 2008.

Office: 420 Main Street, Logan 25601.
Telephone: (304) 792-7038.
Fax: (304) 792-7112

COOKMAN, Donald H. *(Chief Judge, West Virginia Circuit Court Twenty-second Judicial Circuit)* Elected to term beginning Jan 1, 1993. Reelected 2000, current term expires Dec 31, 2008. Born Cumberland Maryland June 4, 1945. Presbyterian. Educated at West Virginia University B.S. 1967 J.D. 1971. Admitted to practice West Virginia 1971. In legal practice Romney 1971-92.

Prosecuting Attorney Hampshire County 1973-92.
Mailing address: P.O. Box 856, Romney 26757.
Telephone: (304) 822-7442.
E-mail address: cookmanj@mountain.net

COPENHAVER, John T., Jr. *(Judge, United States District Court Southern District of West Virginia)* Bankruptcy Judge 1958-76. Appointed Judge for life by President Gerald R. Ford to term beginning 1976. Born Charleston West Virginia Sept 29, 1925. Educated at West Virginia University A.B. 1947 LL.B. 1950. Member Scribes. Law Clerk to Hon. Ben Moore, U.S. District Court District of West Virginia 1950-51. Began legal practice Charleston 1951.

Adjunct Professor of Law West Virginia University College of Law 1970-76. Member National Bankruptcy Conference since 1970, The West Virginia State Bar, Kanawha County, West Virginia and American (Chairman Consumer Bankruptcy Committee and member Business Bankruptcy Committee Section of Corporation, Banking and Business Law) Bar Associations. President Legal Aid Society of Charleston 1954. Past President National Conference of Bankruptcy Judges. Former Faculty Chairman Desk Book for Bankruptcy Judges on Rules of Bankruptcy Procedure. Faculty member Federal Judicial Center 1972-76. Recipient Gavel Award from

COPENHAVER, JOHN T., JR.—*Continued*

West Virginia University College of Law 1971. Chairman and President West Virginia Housing Development Fund 1969-72. President Charleston Municipal Planning Commission 1964.

Mailing address: P.O. Box 2546, Charleston 25329-2546.

Telephone: (304) 347-3146.

CRISLIP, M. Drew *(Judge, West Virginia Family Court Circuit Eighteen)* Appointed by Governor Bob Wise to term beginning Jan 1, 2002. Elected 2002, current term expires Dec 31, 2008.

Office: 423 Harrison County Courthouse, 301 West Main Street, Clarksburg 26301.

Telephone: (304) 627-2148.

Fax: (304) 627-2186

CULPEPPER, J. Jeffrey *(Judge, West Virginia Family Court Circuit Twenty)* Appointed by Governor Bob Wise to term beginning Jan 1, 2002. Elected 2002, current term expires Dec 31, 2008. Born St. Louis Missouri Jan 10, 1963. Religious affiliation: Church of Christ. Educated at West Virginia University B.S. 1989 J.D. 1993. Dean's List. Law Clerk to Hon. Robert B. Stone, West Virginia Circuit Court Seventeenth Judicial Circuit. Admitted to practice West Virginia 1994. In legal practice Morgantown 1994-97.

Personal Statement or Quote: "The only ones who never fail are the ones who never try."

Office: 271 Spruce Street, Morgantown 26501.

Telephone: (304) 285-3228.

Fax: (304) 285-3161

E-mail address: culpepj@mail.wvnet.edu

CUMMINGS, John L. *(Judge, West Virginia Circuit Court Sixth Judicial Circuit)* Former Chief Judge.

Office: Cabell County Courthouse, 750 Fifth Avenue, Huntington 25701.

Telephone: (304) 526-8606.

DAVIS, Robin Jean *(Justice, West Virginia Supreme Court of Appeals)* Elected 1996 to term beginning Jan 1, 1997. Reelected Nov 2000, current term expires Dec 31, 2012. Chief Justice 1998 and 2002. Born Boone County West Virginia April 6, 1956. Educated at West Virginia Wesleyan College B.S. 1978 and West Virginia University M.A. 1982 J.D. 1982. In legal practice 1982-84.

Author "A Tribute to Franklin D. Cleckley: A Compendium of Essential Legal Principles from His Opinions as Justice of the W.Va. Supreme Court of Appeals" West Virginia L. Rev. Member West Virginia Board of Law Examiners 1991-96. Creator West Virginia Trial Court Rules. Recipient Distinguished West Virginian Award from Governor Cecil H. Underwood 2000.

Office: E301 State Capitol, Charleston 25305.

Telephone: (304) 558-4811.

E-mail address: davisro@mail.wvnet.edu

EAGLOSKI, N. Edward, II *(Chief Judge, West Virginia Circuit Court Twenty-ninth Judicial Circuit)*

Office: Putnam County Courthouse, 3389 Winfield Road, Winfield 25213.

Telephone: (304) 586-0209.

EVANS, Thomas C., III *(Judge, West Virginia Circuit Court Fifth Judicial Circuit)* Former Chief Judge.

Mailing address: P.O. Box 800, Ripley 25271.

Office: Jackson County Courthouse, Ripley 25271.

Telephone: (304) 373-2310.

FABER, David A. *(Chief Judge, United States District Court Southern District of West Virginia)* Appointed for life by the President. Chief Judge since Dec 20, 2002.

Mailing address: P.O. Box 5009, Beckley 25801.

Telephone: (304) 253-2438.

FACEMIRE, Richard A. *(Chief Judge, West Virginia Circuit Court Fourteenth Judicial Circuit)* Elected to term beginning Jan 1, 2001. Term expires Jan 1, 2009. Born Sutton West Virginia June 17, 1955. Methodist. Educated at West Virginia Wesleyan College B.A. 1978, Marshall University M.A. 1979 and Antioch School of Law J.D. 1982. Law Clerk to U.S. District Court Southern District of West Virginia May 1982 to April 1, 1985. Admitted to practice West Virginia 1983, U.S. District Court District of West Virginia 1983, U.S. Court of Appeals Fourth Circuit and U.S. Supreme Court. In legal practice Clay and Sutton 1985 to Jan 2001.

Assistant Attorney General West Virginia March 1985 to Aug 4, 1985. Prosecuting Attorney Clay County Aug 5, 1985 to Sept 1, 1992. Member West Virginia Bar Association. Trustee Gassaway Methodist Church. Member Lions Club, Rotary Club, Masons and Boy Scouts of America. Interests include genealogy. Enjoys running and jogging.

Office: Braxton County Courthouse, 300 Main Street, Sutton 26601.

Telephone: (304) 765-2807.

Fax: (304) 765-5496

FANTASIA, Annette *(Judge, West Virginia Family Court Circuit Three)* Appointed by Governor Bob Wise to term beginning Jan 1, 2002. Elected 2002, current term expires Dec 31, 2008.

Office: 208 Avery Street, Parkersburg 26101.

Telephone: (304) 420-4533.

Fax: (304) 424-1769

FERGUSON, Alfred E. *(Judge, West Virginia Circuit Court Sixth Judicial Circuit)* Appointed by Governor John D. Rockefeller IV to term beginning July 1, 1977. Elected 1978, 1984, 1992 and 2000. Current term expires Dec 31, 2008. Former Chief Judge. Born Huntington West Virginia July 14, 1937. Religious affiliation: Christ Temple. Educated at Marshall University A.B. 1959 and West Virginia University LL.B. 1962. Admitted to practice West Virginia 1962. Began legal practice Huntington 1962.

Former Member Governor's Committee on Crime and Delinquency. Member Judicial Investigation Commission, West Virginia Judicial Association, Cabell County Bar Association (Former Vice President) and The West Virginia State Bar. E-3 West Virginia Air National Guard 1962-67. Democrat. Former Member Board of Directors Local American Red Cross Center. Enjoys fishing and hunting.

Office: Cabell County Courthouse, 750 Fifth Avenue, Huntington 25701.

Telephone: (304) 526-8608.

FOX, Fred L., II *(Chief Judge, West Virginia Circuit Court Sixteenth Judicial Circuit)* Elected to term beginning Nov 1970. Reelected to subsequent terms. Born Charleston West Virginia Aug 12, 1938. Presbyterian.

FOX, FRED L., II—*Continued*

Educated at Davis & Elkins College A.B. 1960 and West Virginia University College of Law J.D. 1967. Member Order of the Coif and Tau Kappa Epsilon. Admitted to practice West Virginia 1967 and U.S. District Courts Southern 1967 and Northern 1967 Districts of West Virginia. Began legal practice Fairmont 1967.

Instructor West Virginia University College of Law 1974-75 and Fairmont State College 1975-84. Member West Virginia Judicial Association (President 1987-88), The West Virginia State Bar, Marion County and West Virginia Bar Associations. Recipient Law Enforcement Award from Fraternal Order of Police 1975. Captain USMC 1960-69. Recipient two Bronze Stars, Cross of Gallantry and Purple Heart. Democrat. Enjoys running, golf, country music and reading.

Mailing address: P.O. Box 629, Fairmont 26555.

Office: Marion County Courthouse, Fairmont 26554.

Telephone: (304) 367-5390.

FRAZIER, John R. *(Judge, West Virginia Circuit Court Ninth Judicial Circuit)* Appointed by Governor John D. Rockefeller IV to term beginning Nov 21, 1981. Elected 1982, 1984, 1992 and 2000. Current term expires Dec 31, 2008. Former Chief Judge. Born Charleston West Virginia Aug 2, 1945. Protestant. Member Princeton Presbyterian Church. Educated at Concord College B.S. 1967 and West Virginia University School of Law J.D. with honors 1972. Associate Editor West Virginia Law Review. Member Order of the Coif and Sigma Tau Gamma. Admitted to practice West Virginia 1972. Began legal practice Princeton 1972.

West Virginia House of Delegates 19th Delegate District 65th Legislature 1981-82 (Judiciary Committee, Constitutional Revision Committee and Joint Enrolled Bills Committee). Former Cost Accountant Monsanto Company. Member Mercer County and West Virginia Bar Associations. Personnel Specialist E-5 U.S. Army 1967-69 Vietnam 1968-69. Former Member Princeton Jaycees, West Virginia Jaycees, Mercer County Fellowship Home, Bluestone Health Clinic, Mercer County Opportunity Workshop for the Handicapped, Princeton/Athens United Way and Princeton Recreation Center. Enjoys sports and politics.

Office: Mercer County Courthouse, 1501 West Main Street, Princeton 24740.

Telephone: (304) 487-8347.

FRIEND, L. Edward, II *(Judge, United States Bankruptcy Court Northern District of West Virginia)* Appointed by U.S. Court of Appeals Fourth Circuit judges to term beginning 1985. Educated at West Virginia University B.S. 1963 LL.B. 1968 and Akron University M.B.A. 1968. In legal practice Morgantown 15 years.

Former Assistant U.S. Attorney Northern District of West Virginia.

Mailing address: P.O. Box 70, Wheeling 26003-0008.

Telephone: (304) 233-1655.

FRYE, Andrew N., Jr. *(Chief Judge, West Virginia Circuit Court Twenty-first Judicial Circuit)*

Mailing address: P.O. Box 446, Petersburg 26847-0446.

Office: Grant County Courthouse, Petersburg 26847.

Telephone: (304) 257-1112.

GAUGHAN, Martin J. *(Judge, West Virginia Circuit Court First Judicial Circuit)* Former Chief Judge.

Mailing address: P.O. Box 474, Wellsburg 26070.

Office: Brooke County Courthouse, 632 Main Street, Wellsburg 26070.

Telephone: (304) 737-1400.

GOODWIN, Joseph R. *(Judge, United States District Court Southern District of West Virginia)* Appointed for life by President Bill Clinton to term beginning 1995. Born Ripley West Virginia Dec 23, 1942. Educated at West Virginia University B.S. 1965 J.D. 1970. Editor-in-Chief West Virginia Law Review. Admitted to practice West Virginia 1970. In legal practice Charleston 1970-95. Judge, Ripley Municipal Court 1972-73.

City Attorney Ripley 1971-72.

Mailing address: P.O. Box 2546, Charleston 25329-2546.

Office: 300 Virginia Street East, Suite 5009, Charleston 25301.

Telephone: (304) 347-3192.

Fax: (304) 347-3193.

E-mail address: judge-goodwin@wvsd.uscourts.gov

GRITT, Franklin L., Jr. *(Judge, West Virginia Court of Claims)* Appointed.

Office: 1900 Kanawha Boulevard East, Room W-334, Charleston 25305-0610.

Telephone: (304) 347-4851.

HADEN, Charles H., II *(Judge, United States District Court Southern District of West Virginia)* Appointed for life by President Gerald R. Ford to term beginning Dec 19, 1975. Former Chief Judge. Born Morgantown West Virginia April 16, 1937. Protestant. Educated at West Virginia University B.S.B.A. 1958 J.D. with honors 1961. Board of Editors West Virginia Law Review 1959-61. Recipient Outstanding Graduate Award from West Virginia University College of Commerce 1957. Admitted to practice West Virginia 1961. In legal practice Morgantown 1961-69. Justice 1972-75 and Chief Justice 1975, West Virginia Supreme Court of Appeals.

Member West Virginia House of Delegates 1963-64. Board of Education Monongalia County 1967-68. State Tax Commissioner 1969-72. Important Decisions: State v. Thomas 203 S.E.2d 445 (1974), Long v. City of Weirton 214 S.E.2d 832 (1975) and Beverlin v. Board of Education 216 S.E.2d 554 (1975) 78 ALR 3d. 73. Assistant Professor West Virginia University College of Law 1967-68. President Fourth Circuit District Judges Association 1993-95. Fellow American Bar Foundation. Member Judicial Council of the Fourth Circuit 1986-91 and since 1996, Judicial Conference of the U.S., West Virginia Judicial Association, Monongalia County, Kanawha County, West Virginia and American Bar Associations. Recipient Gavel Award from West Virginia University College of Law 1973, Special Award for Outstanding Judicial Service Award 1975 and Outstanding Trial Judge in West Virginia Award 1982 from West Virginia Trial Lawyers Association and Outstanding Alumnus of West Virginia University Award 1986. Republican. President West Virginia University Alumni Association 1982-83. Former Member Visiting Committees College of Law and School of Medicine West Virginia University. Board of Directors West Virginia Uni-

HADEN, CHARLES H., II—*Continued*

versity Foundation. Enjoys tennis, bird watching and the outdoors.

Mailing address: P.O. Box 351, Charleston 25322-0351.

Telephone: (304) 347-3100.

HALLANAN, Elizabeth Virginia *(Senior Judge, United States District Court Southern District of West Virginia)* Appointed for life by President Ronald Reagan to term beginning Nov 30, 1983. Assumed Senior status, serves by assignment. Born Charleston West Virginia Jan 10, 1925. Educated at Morris Harvey College (now University of Charleston) A.B. and West Virginia University College of Law J.D. Awarded honorary LL.D. Morris Harvey College 1971. Judge, West Virginia Juvenile Court July 1, 1959 to Jan 1, 1961. First woman judge of a court of record in West Virginia.

Member West Virginia Board of Education 1955-57 (House of Delegates 1956, Assistant Commissioner of Public Institutions 1957). Executive Director West Virginia Association of Colleges and Universities May 1, 1961 to March 4, 1969. Chairman West Virginia Public Service Commission 1969-75. President Great Lakes Conference of Public Utilities Commissioners Aug 1973 to July 1974 (first woman president). Second Vice President National Association of Regulatory Utility Commissioners since 1973 (first woman office holder). Member White House Conference on Children and Youth, Governor's Committee on Crime, Delinquency and Corrections, Governor's Advisory Committee on Mental Health and Governor's ad hoc Commission of Inquiry into the Buffalo Creek Flood. Chairman West Virginia Council on Crime and Delinquency. Member Kanawha County Bar Association (Charter member Board of Directors Legal Aid Society). Recipient special citation for Meritorious Service to Community from *Charleston Gazette* 1959, special citation for Meritorious Service to Community from the Junior Department of Charleston Women's Club 1959 and Morris Harvey Alumni Key Award 1968. Republican candidate for State Senate Kanawha County 1957. Board of Directors Columbia Gas System Wilmington Delaware May 1975 to Oct 1983, Charleston National Bank May 1975 to Oct 1983, Committee of One Hundred, Family Service Travelers Aid (Treasurer) and Goodwill Industries of Kanawha Valley, Inc. President Charleston Business and Professional Women's Club. Chairman Public Affairs Committee Altrusa Club of Charleston. Board of Trustees Morris Harvey College, Laird Foundation, Inc. and YMCA of Kanawha County. Board member West Virginia Rehabilitation Center Foundation, AAY (Education Committee) and Education Foundation, Inc. (Secretary). Advisory Board West Virginia College for Graduate Studies. Member Human Rights Commission City of Charleston, Morris Harvey College Alumni Council, Project Finding Committee Junior League of Charleston, Wheeling Diocesan Commission for Religious Unity and Wheeling Diocesan Pastorial Council. President Sacred Heart Parish Council.

Mailing address: P.O. Box 2546, Charleston 25329-2546.

Telephone: (304) 347-3217.

HATCHER, John W., Jr. *(Judge, West Virginia Circuit Court Twelfth Judicial Circuit)* Appointed by Governor Gaston Caperton to term beginning Jan 4, 1991. Elected Nov 3, 1992 and 2000. Current term expires Dec 31, 2008. Former Chief Judge. Born Oak Hill West Virginia May 25, 1944. Baptist. Educated at West Virginia University A.B. with honors 1966 J.D. 1969. Student Editor West Virginia Law Review 1968-69. Member Phi Alpha Delta. Admitted to practice West Virginia 1969, U.S. Court of Military Appeals 1969 and U.S. Supreme Court 1972. In legal practice Fayetteville 1973-90.

Attended Medical, Scientific and Forensic Evidence class Aug 1992 and General Jurisdiction Course 1993 The National Judicial College. Captain U.S. Army Vietnam 1969-73. Democrat. Member West Virginia House of Delegates 1981-90 (Chairman House Judiciary Committee 1987-90). Member Fayetteville Rotary Club (Past President). Enjoys hunting and reading.

Mailing address: P.O. Drawer 90, Fayetteville 25840.

Office: Fayette County Courthouse, 100 Court Street, Fayetteville 25840.

Telephone: (304) 574-3838.

HENNING, John L., Jr. *(Chief Judge, West Virginia Circuit Court Twentieth Judicial Circuit)* Appointed by Governor Gaston Caperton Aug 1, 1991. Elected Nov 1992 and 2000. Current term expires Dec 31, 2008. Born Canton Ohio Nov 20, 1945. Protestant. Educated at Northeastern Oklahoma A&M Junior College A.A. 1965, Morehead State University B.S. 1968 and University of Baltimore J.D. 1975. Admitted to practice West Virginia 1975, Maryland 1975, U.S. District Court Northern District of West Virginia 1975, U.S. Court of Appeals Fourth Circuit 1978 and U.S. Supreme Court 1979. In legal practice Elkins West Virginia 1975-91.

Lieutenant USN 1968-72. Board of Directors Sheltered Workshop. Member Rotary, United Way and YMCA. Enjoys wilderness canoeing.

Office: Randolph County Courthouse, 2 Randolph Avenue, Elkins 26241.

Telephone: (304) 636-3815.

HICKS, Robert C. *(Judge, West Virginia Family Court Circuit Two)* Appointed by Governor Bob Wise to term beginning Jan 1, 2002. Elected 2002, current term expires Dec 31, 2008.

Mailing address: P.O. Box 490, New Martinsville 26155.

Telephone: (304) 455-5191.

Fax: (304) 455-1131

HILL, George W. *(Judge, West Virginia Circuit Court Fourth Judicial Circuit)* Elected to term beginning Dec 17, 1988. Reelected 1992 and 2000. Current term expires Dec 31, 2008. Born Fairmont West Virginia July 11, 1930. Episcopalian. Educated at Yale University B.A. 1952 and West Virginia University J.D. 1958. Associate Editor West Virginia Law Review 1956-58. Law Clerk to Hon. Herbert S. Boreman, U.S. District Court Northern District of West Virginia and U.S. Court of Appeals Fourth Circuit 1958-59. Admitted to practice West Virginia 1958, U.S. District Court Northern District of West Virginia 1958 and U.S. Court of Appeals Fourth Circuit 1959. In legal practice Parkersburg 1959-88.

Member West Virginia Judicial Association, American Judges Association and The West Virginia State Bar. Recipient Diploma of Judicial Skills Harvard Law School and University of Virginia School of Law American Academy of Judicial Education July 1989. Lieuten-

HILL, GEORGE W.—*Continued*
ant Commander USNR June 1952 to May 1955 (retired). Democrat.

Office: 421 Wood County Judicial Building, 2 Government Square, Parkersburg 26101-5353.

Telephone: (304) 424-1756.

HOKE, Jay M. *(Chief Judge, West Virginia Circuit Court Twenty-fifth Judicial Circuit)*

Mailing address: P.O. Box 605, Hamlin 25523.

Office: 8000 Court Street, Hamlin 25523.

Telephone: (304) 824-7919.

HOLLAND, Robert L., Jr. *(Chief Judge, West Virginia Circuit Court Third Judicial Circuit)*

Office: Doddridge County Courthouse, 118 East Court Street, West Union 26456.

Telephone: (304) 873-1565.

HRKO, John S. *(Chief Judge, West Virginia Circuit Court Twenty-seventh Judicial Circuit)* Elected Nov 1984 to term beginning Jan 1, 1985. Reelected 1992 and 2000. Current term expires Dec 31, 2008. Born Eccles West Virginia Sept 20, 1944. Educated at Marshall University A.B. 1969 and West Virginia University J.D. 1972. Staff member West Virginia University Law Review 1971-72. Admitted to practice West Virginia 1972 and U.S. District Court Southern District of West Virginia 1972. In legal practice Mullens 1972-85.

Assistant Prosecuting Attorney 1974-76 and 1980-85. Member West Virginia Judicial Association (Treasurer, Secretary, Vice President, President since 1997), The West Virginia State Bar, Wyoming County (President), and American Bar Associations. Attended "Common Errors" West Virginia Trial Lawyers Association 1995, CLE Cabell County Bar Association 1996 and "Burden of Proof" West Virginia University College of Law 1999. Democrat. Enjoys golf and travel.

Mailing address: P.O. Box 581, Pineville 24874.

Office: Wyoming County Courthouse, Main and Bank Streets, Pineville 24874.

Telephone: (304) 732-8000.

E-mail address: hrkoj@wvnvm.wvnet.edu

HUTCHISON, John A. *(Chief Judge, West Virginia Circuit Court Tenth Judicial Circuit)* Appointed by Governor Gaston Caperton to term beginning July 7, 1995. Elected 1996 and 2000. Current term expires Dec 31, 2008. Born Beckley West Virginia July 17, 1950. Methodist. Educated at Davis & Elkins College B.A. 1972 and West Virginia University College of Law J.D. 1980. Admitted to practice West Virginia 1980, U.S. District Court Southern District of West Virginia 1980, U.S. Tax Court 1982 and U.S. Supreme Court 1989. In legal practice Beckley 1980-91 and Charleston 1991-95.

Member West Virginia Judicial Association and West Virginia Bar Association. Attended General Jurisdiction, Advanced Evidence and Criminal Sentencing Courses The National Judicial College. Soccer Official FEFA. Official U.S. Swimming. Soccer and Swimming Official West Virginia Secondary Schools Activities Commission. Enjoys woodworking, hunting, fishing, soccer and golf.

Office: Raleigh County Courthouse, 215 Main Street, Beckley 25801.

Telephone: (304) 255-9132.

E-mail address: Hutchj@inetone.net

IRONS, Robert A. *(Chief Judge, West Virginia Circuit Court Thirty-first Judicial Circuit)*

Mailing address: P.O. Box 648, Union 24983.

Office: Monroe County Courthouse, Union 24983.

Telephone: (304) 772-3459.

JACKSON, Sally *(Judge, West Virginia Family Court Circuit Twenty-four)* Appointed by Governor Bob Wise to term beginning Jan 1, 2002. Elected 2002, current term expires Dec 31, 2008.

Office: 110 North George Street, Second Floor, Charles Town 25414.

Telephone: (304) 724-6253 (Jefferson County), 267-0044 (Berkeley County).

Fax: (304) 724-6258 (Jefferson County), 267-0072 (Berkeley County)

JANES, David R. *(Judge, West Virginia Circuit Court Sixteenth Judicial Circuit)* Elected to term beginning Jan 1, 2001. Term expires Dec 31, 2008. Former Chief Judge. Born Chicago Illinois Aug 22, 1951. Episcopalian. Educated at West Virginia University B.A. 1973 and Vanderbilt University J.D. 1977. Admitted to practice West Virginia 1977. In legal practice Fairmont 1977-2000.

Mailing address: P.O. Box 1611, Fairmont 26555-1611.

Office: Marion County Courthouse, Fairmont 26554.

Telephone: (304) 367-5395.

JARRELL, Cynthia J. *(Judge, West Virginia Family Court Circuit Ten)* Appointed by Governor Bob Wise to term beginning Jan 1, 2002. Elected 2002, current term expires Dec 31, 2008.

Office: 102 Boone County Courthouse, 206 Court Street, Madison 25130.

Telephone: (304) 369-7357 (Boone County), 824-7990 (Lincoln County).

Fax: (304) 369-7841

JOEL, David J. *(Magistrate Judge, United States District Court Northern District of West Virginia)* Appointed by U.S. District Court judges to term beginning Oct 9, 2001. Term expires Oct 8, 2005. Serves part time.

Office: 217 West King Street, Martinsburg 25401.

Telephone: (304) 267-8225.

JOHNSON, Gary L. *(Chief Judge, West Virginia Circuit Court Twenty-eighth Judicial Circuit)* Elected Nov 3, 1992 to term beginning Jan 1, 1993. Reelected 2000, current term expires Dec 31, 2008. Born Richwood West Virginia July 1, 1951. Roman Catholic. Educated at West Virginia University B.A. 1973 M.P.A. 1974 J.D. 1980. Admitted to practice West Virginia 1980 and U.S. District Courts Southern 1980 and Northern Districts of West Virginia. In legal practice Richwood 1982-92. Municipal Judge, Richwood Municipal Court 1980-84 and Administrative Judge, West Virginia Department of Employment Security 1981-84.

Prosecuting Attorney Nicholas County 1985-89. Instructor in Business Law Glenville State College 1989-92. Member West Virginia Judicial Association, The West Virginia State Bar and Nicholas County Bar Association. Democrat. Member Richwood Lions Club.

Office: 216 Nicholas County Courthouse, 700 Main Street, Summersville 26651.

Telephone: (304) 872-7840.

JOLLIFFE, Frank E. *(Chief Judge, West Virginia Circuit Court Eleventh Judicial Circuit)* Appointed by Governor John D. Rockefeller IV July 1, 1979. Elected 1980, 1984, 1992 and 2000. Current term expires Dec 31, 2008. Born Morgantown West Virginia April 4, 1943. Presbyterian. Educated at West Virginia University A.B. 1966 J.D. with honors 1969. Staff member West Virginia Law Review. Member Order of the Coif. Admitted to practice West Virginia 1969, U.S. District Court Southern District of West Virginia 1969 and U.S. Court of Appeals Fourth Circuit 1974. In legal practice Lewisburg 1969-74 and 1978-79 and Morgantown 1977-78.

Assistant U.S. Attorney Southern District of West Virginia 1974-77. Democrat. Member House of Delegates West Virginia 1973-74.

Mailing address: P.O. Box 926, Lewisburg 24901.

Office: Greenbrier County Courthouse, 200 North Court Street, Lewisburg 24901.

Telephone: (304) 647-6621.

JORDAN, Philip B., Jr. *(Judge, West Virginia Circuit Court Twenty-first Judicial Circuit)* Former Chief Judge.

Mailing address: P.O. Box 150, Keyser 26726.

Office: Mineral County Courthouse, Keyser 26726.

Telephone: (304) 788-5150.

KARL, Mark A. *(Chief Judge, West Virginia Circuit Court Second Judicial Circuit)*

Office: Marshall County Courthouse, Seventh Street, Moundsville 26041.

Telephone: (304) 845-1727.

KAUFMAN, Tod J. *(Chief Judge, West Virginia Circuit Court Thirteenth Judicial Circuit)* Elected to term beginning 1988. Reelected 1992 and 2000. Current term expires Dec 31, 2008. Born Charleston West Virginia Oct 15, 1952. Educated at London School of Economics and Political Science, England 1973-74, Tufts University B.A. cum laude 1975 and West Virginia University College of Law 1980. Law Clerk to U.S. Tax Court Summer 1979. Admitted to practice West Virginia 1980, U.S. District Courts Northern 1980 and Southern 1980 Districts of West Virginia, U.S. Supreme Court 1989 and U.S. Court of Appeals Fourth Circuit. In legal practice Charleston 1980-88.

Legislator West Virginia State Senate 1982-88. Member West Virginia Judicial Association, American Judicature Society, The West Virginia State Bar and American Bar Association (National Conference of State Trial Judges Judicial Administration Division).

Office: Kanawha County Judicial Annex, 111 Court Street, Charleston 25301.

Telephone: (304) 357-0363.

KAULL, John S. *(Magistrate Judge, United States District Court Northern District of West Virginia)* Appointed by U.S. District Court judges.

Mailing address: P.O. Box 2857, Clarksburg 26302.

Office: 500 West Pike Street, Clarksburg 26301.

Telephone: (304) 622-1516.

Fax: (304) 624-5866

KEADLE, Thomas Howard *(Chief Judge, West Virginia Circuit Court Twenty-sixth Judicial Circuit)* Elected to term beginning Jan 1, 1985. Reelected 1992 and 2000. Current term expires Dec 31, 2008. Born Alderson West Virginia Jan 23, 1938. Catholic. Educated at West Virginia University A.B. with honors 1971 J.D. 1974. Admitted to practice West Virginia 1974. Began legal practice Romney 1974. In legal practice Buckhannon 1981.

Trooper West Virginia State Police 1960-68. Sergeant USMC 1955-59. Democrat. Enjoys hunting.

Mailing address: P.O. Box 57, Buckhannon 26201.

Office: Upshur County Courthouse, 40 West Main Street, Buckhannon 26201.

Telephone: (304) 472-5556.

KEELEY, Irene M. *(Chief Judge, United States District Court Northern District of West Virginia)* Appointed for life by President George Bush to term beginning 1992. Chief Judge since 2001. Born Brooklyn New York Jan 17, 1944. Educated at College of Notre Dame of Maryland B.A. 1965 and West Virginia University M.A. 1977 J.D. 1980. In legal practice Clarksburg 1980-92.

Mailing address: P.O. Box 2808, Clarksburg 26302-2808.

Telephone: (304) 624-5850.

KELLER, Patricia *(Judge, West Virginia Family Court Circuit Six)* Appointed by Governor Bob Wise to term beginning Jan 1, 2002. Elected 2002, current term expires Dec 31, 2008.

Office: 750 Fifth Avenue, Room 309, Huntington 25701.

Telephone: (304) 528-5521.

Fax: (304) 528-5850

KELLY, Mike *(Judge, West Virginia Family Court Circuit Eleven)* Appointed by Governor Bob Wise to term beginning Jan 1, 2002. Elected 2002, current term expires Dec 31, 2008.

Mailing address: P.O. Box 246, Charleston 25321.

Telephone: (304) 558-5801.

Fax: (304) 558-5803

KING, Charles E. *(Judge, West Virginia Circuit Court Thirteenth Judicial Circuit)* Former Chief Judge.

Office: Kanawha County Judicial Annex, 111 Court Street, Charleston 25301.

Telephone: (304) 357-0367.

KIRKPATRICK, Harry L., III *(Judge, West Virginia Circuit Court Tenth Judicial Circuit)* Former Chief Judge.

Office: Raleigh County Courthouse, 215 Main Street, Beckley 25801.

Telephone: (304) 255-9130.

LEWIS, Stephen *(Judge, West Virginia Family Court Circuit Seven)*

Mailing address: P.O. Box 429, Wayne 25570.

Office: 211 South Court Street, Wayne 25570.

Telephone: (304) 272-5828.

Fax: (304) 272-5126

LONGO, Beth *(Judge, West Virginia Family Court Circuit Twenty-one)* Appointed by Governor Bob Wise to term beginning Jan 1, 2002. Elected 2002, current term expires Dec 31, 2008.

Mailing address: P.O. Box 454, Philippi 26416.

Office: 209 South Main Street, Philippi 26416.

Telephone: (304) 457-3483.

Fax: (304) 457-6500

MADDEN, John T. *(Judge, West Virginia Circuit Court Second Judicial Circuit)* Appointed by Governor

MADDEN, JOHN T.—*Continued*

Gaston Caperton to term beginning May 31, 1990. Elected Nov 7, 2000, current term expires Dec 31, 2008. Former Chief Judge. Born Glen Dale West Virginia July 13, 1932. Episcopalian. Educated at Lafayette College A.B. 1954 and West Virginia University College of Law LL.B. 1958. Member Phi Delta Phi. Admitted to practice West Virginia 1958, U.S. District Court Northern District of West Virginia and U.S. Court of Appeals Fourth Circuit. In legal practice Wheeling 1958-60 and Moundsville 1960-90.

Member The West Virginia State Bar, Marshall County and West Virginia Bar Associations. Democrat. Member West Virginia House of Delegates 1963-66.

Office: Marshall County Courthouse, Seventh Street, Moundsville 26041.

Telephone: (304) 845-3505.

MARKS, J. Lewis, Jr. *(Chief Judge, West Virginia Circuit Court Fifteenth Judicial Circuit)*

Office: Harrison County Courthouse, 301 West Main Street, Clarksburg 26301.

Telephone: (304) 624-8620.

MATISH, James A. *(Judge, West Virginia Circuit Court Fifteenth Judicial Circuit)* Elected to term beginning Jan 1, 2001. Term expires Dec 31, 2008. Born Clarksburg West Virginia Nov 22, 1953. Catholic. Educated at West Virginia University B.S. magna cum laude 1975 J.D. 1978. Moot Court Board. In legal practice Clarksburg May 1978 to Dec 2000.

Instructor in Real Estate Law Salem International University. Vice President 1996, President 1997 and Former Board Member Harrison County Bar Association. Founder and Past President West Virginia Society for Criminal Justice, Inc. Member West Virginia Trial Lawyers Association, West Virginia Judicial Association and The West Virginia State Bar. Instructor CLE seminars West Virginia University College of Law. Democrat. Member 1988 to March 1997, Former Treasurer and Former Chairman Harrison County Building Commission. Former Member Board of Directors The Heritage Bank of Harrison County and The Sacred Heart Children's Center, Inc. Former Solicitor for Funds United Way of Harrison County. Former Trial Judge and Appellate Judge Moot Court West Virginia University College of Law. Lector and Former Member Finance Committee St. Ann's Catholic Church.

Office: 301 West Main Street, Suite 116, Clarksburg 26301.

Telephone: (304) 624-8593.

Fax: (304) 624-8592

E-mail address: jamesmatish@courtswv.org

MAXWELL, Robert Earl *(Senior Judge, United States District Court Northern District of West Virginia)* Appointed for life by President Lyndon B. Johnson to term beginning Sept 13, 1965. Former Chief Judge. Assumed Senior status, serves by assignment. Born South Bend Indiana. Catholic. Educated at Davis & Elkins College 1946 and West Virginia University LL.B. 1949. Admitted to practice West Virginia 1949, U.S. District Court Northern District of West Virginia 1949, U.S. Supreme Court 1954 and U.S. Court of Appeals Fourth Circuit 1961. Former Judge, Temporary Emergency Court of Appeals of the U.S., appointed by U.S. Supreme Court Chief Justice Warren Earl Burger.

Prosecuting Attorney Randolph County 1953-61. U.S. Attorney Northern District of West Virginia 1961-64. Member Fourth Circuit District Judges Association (Past President), Judicial Conference of the U.S. (Former Chairman Budget Committee), The West Virginia State Bar, Randolph County, West Virginia and American Bar Associations. Democrat.

Mailing address: P.O. Box 1275, Elkins 26241-1275.

Telephone: (304) 636-5198.

MAYNARD, Elliott E. *(Justice, West Virginia Supreme Court of Appeals)* Elected Nov 1996 to term beginning Jan 1, 1997. Term expires Dec 31, 2008. Chief Justice 2000. Born Williamson West Virginia Dec 8, 1942. Educated at Florida Southern College B.S. 1967 and West Virginia University J.D. 1974. In legal practice Williamson 1974-81. Judge and Chief Judge, West Virginia Circuit Court Thirtieth Judicial Circuit 1981-96, appointed by Governor John D. Rockefeller IV.

Prosecuting Attorney Mingo County 1976-81. Former Member National District Attorneys Association. Member American Judges Association, American Judicature Society, The West Virginia State Bar and American Bar Association. Managing Director Tug Valley Chamber of Commerce 1968-70. Member Charleston Rotary Club.

Office: E306 State Capitol, Charleston 25305.

Telephone: (304) 558-2606.

E-mail address: spike@mail.wvnet.edu

MAZZONE, James P. *(Judge, West Virginia Circuit Court First Judicial Circuit)*

Office: Ohio County Courthouse, 1500 Chapline Street, City/County Building, Wheeling 26003.

Telephone: (304) 234-3620.

McGRAW, H. Suzanne *(Judge, West Virginia Family Court Circuit Thirteen)* Appointed by Governor Bob Wise to term beginning Jan 1, 2002. Elected 2002, current term expires Dec 31, 2008.

Office: 115 Prince Street, Suite B, Beckley 25801.

Telephone: (304) 254-2908 (Raleigh County), 732-6119 (Wyoming County).

Fax: (304) 250-6579

McGRAW, Warren R. *(Justice, West Virginia Supreme Court of Appeals)* Elected Nov 1998 to term beginning Jan 1, 1999. Chief Justice 2001. Born Wyoming County West Virginia May 10, 1939. Educated at Morris Harvey College A.B. 1960, West Virginia University and Wake Forest University J.D. 1963. Admitted to practice West Virginia 1963.

Former Prosecuting Attorney Wyoming County. Member Raleigh County and Wyoming County Bar Associations. Member House of Delegates 1968-72 and State Senate 1972-84 (President 1980-84) West Virginia. Delegate to Democratic National Convention West Virginia 1972-74. Former Delegate State Democratic Judicial Convention and State Democratic Convention. Former Chairman Democratic Executive Committee Wyoming County. Past President Jaycees. Former Member Wyoming County Board of Education, Heart Fund and Wyoming County Cancer Fund Member Rotary International.

Office: E302 State Capitol, Charleston 25305.

Telephone: (304) 558-2602.

E-mail address: mcgraw@mail.wvnet.edu

MILLER, Lawrance S., Jr. *(Chief Judge, West Virginia Circuit Court Eighteenth Judicial Circuit)*
Office: Preston County Courthouse, 101 West Main Street, Kingwood 26537.
Telephone: (304) 329-0066.

MOATS, Alan D. *(Chief Judge, West Virginia Circuit Court Nineteenth Judicial Circuit)*
Office: Taylor County Courthouse, 214 West Main Street, Grafton 26354.
Telephone: (304) 265-3474.

MONTGOMERY, Robert *(Judge, West Virginia Family Court Circuit Eleven)*
Office: 100 Judicial Annex, 111 Court Street, Charleston 25301.
Telephone: (304) 558-0554.
Fax: (304) 558-4237

MURENSKY, Rudolph J., II *(Chief Judge, West Virginia Circuit Court Eighth Judicial Circuit)*
Mailing address: P.O. Box 768, Welch 24801.
Office: McDowell County Courthouse, Wyoming Street, Welch 24801.
Telephone: (304) 436-8512.

NIBERT, David *(Chief Judge, West Virginia Circuit Court Fifth Judicial Circuit)*
Office: Mason County Courthouse, 200 Sixth Street, Point Pleasant 25550.
Telephone: (304) 675-3480.

NIBERT, Deloris J. *(Judge, West Virginia Family Court Circuit Five)* Appointed by Governor Bob Wise to term beginning Jan 1, 2002. Elected 2002, current term expires Dec 31, 2008. Born Logansport Indiana May 18, 1957. United Methodist. Educated at Fairmont State College B.S. magna cum laude 1991 and West Virginia University J.D. 1995. Admitted to practice West Virginia 1996. In legal practice West Virginia 1995-2001.
Member West Virginia and American Bar Associations.
Office: Mason County Courthouse, 200 Sixth Street, Point Pleasant 25550.
Telephone: (304) 675-0884 (Mason County), 373-2301 (Jackson County).
Fax: (304) 675-5986 (Mason County), 372-7951 (Jackson County)

O'BRIANT, Eric H. *(Judge, West Virginia Circuit Court Seventh Judicial Circuit)* Former Chief Judge.
Office: Logan County Courthouse, 300 Stratton Street, Logan 25601.
Telephone: (304) 792-8570.

O'HANLON, Dan P. *(Chief Judge, West Virginia Circuit Court Sixth Judicial Circuit)*
Office: Cabell County Courthouse, 750 Fifth Avenue, Huntington 25701.
Telephone: (304) 526-8603.

PANCAKE, David M. *(Judge, West Virginia Circuit Court Sixth Judicial Circuit)* Former Chief Judge.
Office: Cabell County Courthouse, 750 Fifth Avenue, Huntington 25701.
Telephone: (304) 526-8612.

PARSONS, Charles *(Judge, West Virginia Family Court Circuit Twenty-three)* Appointed by Governor Bob Wise to term beginning Jan 1, 2002. Elected 2002, current term expires Dec 31, 2008.
Mailing address: P.O. Box 921, Romney 26757.
Office: 82 West Main Street, Romney 26757.
Telephone: (304) 822-7012.
Fax: (304) 822-7778

PEARSON, Ronald G. *(Judge, United States Bankruptcy Court Southern District of West Virginia)* Appointed by U.S. District Court judges. Born Fairmont West Virginia June 15, 1942. Presbyterian. Educated at West Virginia University B.S. in Industrial Engineering 1965 J.D. 1968. Admitted to practice West Virginia 1968, U.S. District Courts Northern 1968 and Southern 1968 Districts of West Virginia and U.S. Court of Appeals Fourth Circuit 1968.
Attorney Legal Aid Society 1968-70. Instructor in State and Local Tax Law West Virginia University 1977. Board of Governors National Conference of Bankruptcy Judges 1994-96. Member The West Virginia State Bar. Attended and lectured at numerous State Bar seminars and other educational programs. Director Local Government Relations Division State Tax Department West Virginia 1971-73. Commissioner West Virginia Department of Finance and Administration 1973-75. Comptroller Carbon Industries 1977-79. Republican. Treasurer State of West Virginia 1975-76. Trustee National Youth Science Foundation. Interests include coin collecting, music, skiing and tennis.
Office: 6408 U.S. Courthouse, 300 Virginia Street East, Charleston 25301-2523.
Telephone: (304) 347-3238.

PERRY, Roger L. *(Chief Judge, West Virginia Circuit Court Seventh Judicial Circuit)*
Office: Logan County Courthouse, 300 Stratton Street, Logan 25601.
Telephone: (304) 792-8580.

POMPONIO, Joseph *(Judge, West Virginia Family Court Circuit Fifteen)* Appointed by Governor Bob Wise to term beginning Jan 1, 2002. Elected 2002, current term expires Dec 31, 2008.
Office: 106 South Court Street, Lewisburg 24901.
Telephone: (304) 647-7406.
Fax: (304) 647-7427

PRATT, Darrell *(Chief Judge, West Virginia Circuit Court Twenty-fourth Judicial Circuit)* Appointed by Governor Gaston Caperton Jan 10, 1997. Elected Nov 1998, current term expires Dec 31, 2006. Born Radnor West Virginia Jan 5, 1954. Protestant. Educated at Marshall University B.A. 1975 and West Virginia University College of Law J.D. 1981. Admitted to practice West Virginia 1981 and U.S. District Court Southern District of West Virginia 1981. In legal practice Wayne 1981-93.
Prosecuting Attorney Wayne County 1984-97.
Mailing address: P.O. Box 68, Wayne 25570.
Office: Wayne County Courthouse, Court Street, Wayne 25570.
Telephone: (304) 272-5486.
E-mail address: dpratt01@earthlink.net

RECHT, Arthur M. *(Judge, West Virginia Circuit Court First Judicial Circuit)* Former Chief Judge. Former Justice, West Virginia Supreme Court of Appeals.
Office: Ohio County Courthouse, 1500 Chapline Street, City/County Building, Wheeling 26003.
Telephone: (304) 234-3794.

REED, Jeffrey B. *(Judge, West Virginia Circuit Court Fourth Judicial Circuit)* Former Chief Judge.
Office: 221 Wood County Judicial Building, 2 Government Square, Parkersburg 26101-5353.
Telephone: (304) 424-1721.

ROWE, James J. *(Judge, West Virginia Circuit Court Eleventh Judicial Circuit)* Appointed by Gaston Caperton to term beginning Jan 1, 1997. Elected Nov 2000, current term expires Dec 31, 2008. Former Chief Judge. Born Bedford Virginia Aug 2, 1950. Presbyterian. Educated at West Virginia University B.A. 1972 and George Mason University J.D. 1977. Admitted to practice Virginia 1977 and West Virginia 1978. In legal practice Lewisburg West Virginia 1978-96.
Member Fourth Circuit Judicial Association, West Virginia Judicial Association, American Judicature Society, The West Virginia State Bar, Virginia State Bar, West Virginia and American Bar Associations. Member Lewisburg Rotary.
Mailing address: P.O. Box 751, Lewisburg 24901.
Office: Greenbrier County Courthouse, 200 North Court Street, Lewisburg 24901.
Telephone: (304) 647-6619.
E-mail address: jamesrowe@courtswv.org

RUCKMAN, Timothy *(Judge, West Virginia Family Court Circuit Sixteen)* Appointed by Governor Bob Wise to term beginning Jan 1, 2002. Elected 2002, current term expires Dec 31, 2008.
Office: 300 Courthouse Annex, 511 Church Street, Summersville 26651.
Telephone: (304) 872-9618.
Fax: (304) 872-9621

SANDERS, David H. *(Chief Judge, West Virginia Circuit Court Twenty-third Judicial Circuit)*
Office: Berkeley County Courthouse, 100 West King Street, Martinsburg 25401.
Telephone: (304) 264-1947.

SCHLAEGEL, E. Lee *(Judge, West Virginia Circuit Court Twenty-fifth Judicial Circuit)* Former Chief Judge.
Office: Boone County Courthouse, 200 State Street, Madison 25130.
Telephone: (304) 369-7350.

SEIBERT, James E. *(Magistrate Judge, United States District Court Northern District of West Virginia)* Appointed by U.S. District Court judges to term beginning March 24, 1999.
Mailing address: P.O. Box 471, Wheeling 26003-0060.
Telephone: (304) 233-1348.

SILVER, Gray, III *(Judge, West Virginia Circuit Court Twenty-third Judicial Circuit)*
Mailing address: P.O. Box 5129, Martinsburg 25402.
Office: 110 North Maple Avenue, Suite 200, Martinsburg 25401.
Telephone: (304) 263-4100.

SINCLAIR, William *(Judge, West Virginia Family Court Circuit One)* Appointed by Governor Bob Wise to term beginning Jan 1, 2002. Elected 2002, current term expires Dec 31, 2008.
Office: Courthouse Annex, Second Floor, 51 Sixteenth Street, Wheeling 26003.
Telephone: (304) 238-1012.
Fax: (304) 238-1020

SNYDER, D. Mark *(Judge, West Virginia Family Court Circuit Eleven)* Appointed by Governor Bob Wise to term beginning Jan 1, 2002. Elected 2002, current term expires Dec 31, 2008.
Office: 100 Judicial Annex, 111 Court Street, Charleston 25301.
Telephone: (304) 558-0536.
Fax: (304) 558-4237

SOWA, Robert *(Judge, West Virginia Family Court Circuit Seventeen)* Appointed by Governor Bob Wise to term beginning Jan 1, 2002. Elected 2002, current term expires Dec 31, 2008.
Office: 300 Main Street, Suite 202, Sutton 26601.
Telephone: (304) 765-0302 (Braxton County), 765-3219 (Lewis County).
Fax: (304) 765-3641

SPAULDING, O. C. *(Judge, West Virginia Circuit Court Twenty-ninth Judicial Circuit)* Former Chief Judge.
Office: Putnam County Judicial Building, 3389 Winfield Road, Winfield 25213.
Telephone: (304) 586-0262.

STAKER, Robert J. *(Senior Judge, United States District Court Southern District of West Virginia)* Appointed for life by President Jimmy Carter to term beginning Sept 1979. Assumed Senior status, serves by assignment. Born Kermit West Virginia Feb 14, 1925. Presbyterian. Educated at Marshall University and West Virginia University College of Law LL.B. 1952. Admitted to practice West Virginia 1952 and U.S. District Court Southern District of West Virginia. In legal practice Williamson 1952-69. Judge, West Virginia Circuit Court Thirtieth Judicial Circuit 1969-79.
Member Federal Judges Association. Attended The National Judicial College 1970 and various seminars sponsored by West Virginia Judicial Association. USN Aug 3, 1943 to April 1946. Democrat.
Mailing address: P.O. Box 1570, Huntington 25716-1570.
Telephone: (304) 529-5500.

STAMP, Frederick P., Jr. *(Judge, United States District Court Northern District of West Virginia)* Appointed by President George Bush. Former Chief Judge. Born Wheeling West Virginia 1934. Educated at Washington and Lee University B.A. 1956 and University of Richmond LL.B. 1959. Admitted to practice West Virginia 1959.
Fellow American College of Trial Lawyers and American Bar Foundation. Member National Conference of Commissioners on Uniform State Laws, Judicial Conference of the United States (Chairman Committee on Federal—State Jurisdiction), The West Virginia State Bar,

STAMP, FREDERICK P., JR.—*Continued*

Ohio County, West Virginia and American Bar Associations.

Mailing address: P.O. Box 791, Wheeling 26003-0100.

Telephone: (304) 233-1120.

STANLEY, Mary E. *(Magistrate Judge, United States District Court Southern District of West Virginia)* Appointed by U.S. District Court judges Oct 22, 1992 and Oct 2000. Born Washington D.C. March 7, 1948. Episcopalian. Educated at Mount Holyoke College A.B. 1970 and University of Virginia J.D. 1973. Law Clerk to Hon. Dennis R. Knapp, U.S. District Court Southern District of West Virginia 1976-77. Admitted to practice West Virginia 1973, U.S District Court Southern District of West Virginia 1976 and U.S. Court of Appeals Fourth Circuit 1977.

Assistant U.S. Attorney Southern District of West Virginia 1977-92. Member The West Virginia State Bar.

Office: 5408 U.S. Courthouse, 300 Virginia Street East, Charleston 25301.

Telephone: (304) 347-3279.

STARCHER, Larry Victor *(Chief Justice, West Virginia Supreme Court of Appeals)* Elected Nov 1996 to term beginning Jan 1, 1997. Term expires Dec 31, 2011. Born Rocksdale West Virginia Sept 25, 1942. Methodist. Educated at West Virginia University A.B. cum laude 1964 J.D. 1967. President Mountain Honorary Society and Helvetia Honorary Society. Member Beta Theta Pi, Phi Delta Phi, Phi Alpha Theta and Pi Sigma Alpha. Admitted to practice West Virginia 1967. Began legal practice Morgantown 1967. Former Judge and Chief Judge, West Virginia Circuit Court Seventeenth Judicial Circuit, elected to term beginning Jan 1, 1977.

Director North Central West Virginia Legal Aid Society 1969-76. Author "Cameras in Court—A Revival in West Virginia and the Nation" West Virginia L. Rev. 1982, "Bail—Alternatives" West Virginia Trial Lawyers Association 1983 and "Choosing West Virginia's Judges" *The West Virginia Lawyer* Oct 1998 and *QLR* Spring 2001. Important Decision: Nobles v. Gregory et al. (major prison condition case) Feb 1985. Former Instructor in Law, Public Administration and History West Virginia University. Fellow Harvard University summer 1978. Member The Association of Trial Lawyers of America, American Correctional Association, West Virginia Judicial Association, National Conference of Chief Judges, The West Virginia State Bar, Kanawha County and Monongalia County Bar Associations. Attended The National Judicial College, West Virginia Judicial Association CLE and West Virginia Trial Lawyers Association CLE. Contract Administrator 1966-67 and Assistant to Vice President 1967-69 West Virginia University. Member City Council Morgantown 1971-72. Former member Young Democrats. Member West Virginia Martin Luther King Holiday Commission. Interests include carpentry, gardening and skiing.

Office: E307 State Capitol, Charleston 25305.

Telephone: (304) 558-2604.

Fax: (304) 558-4308

E-mail address: larrystarcher@courtswv.org

STATON, Louise *(Judge, West Virginia Family Court Circuit Thirteen)* Appointed by Governor Bob Wise to term beginning Jan 1, 2002. Elected 2002, current term expires Dec 31, 2008.

Office: 115 Prince Street, Suite B, Beckley 25801.

Telephone: (304) 256-6749 (Raleigh County), 732-6119 (Wyoming County).

Fax: (304) 256-6811 (Raleigh County), 732-7309 (Wyoming County)

STEELE, Janet F. *(Judge, West Virginia Family Court Circuit Fourteen)* Appointed by Governor Bob Wise to term beginning Jan 1, 2002. Elected 2002, current term expires Dec 31, 2008.

Office: 213 North Court Street, Fayetteville 25840.

Telephone: (304) 574-3393.

Fax: (304) 574-2599

STEPHENS, Booker T. *(Judge, West Virginia Circuit Court Eighth Judicial Circuit)* Elected to term beginning Jan 1, 1985. Reelected 1992 and 2000. Current term expires Dec 31, 2008. Former Chief Judge. Born Bluefield West Virginia Nov 3, 1944. Missionary Baptist. Educated at West Virginia State College B.A. 1966 and Howard University School of Law J.D. 1972. Member Delta Theta Phi and Alpha Phi Alpha. Admitted to practice West Virginia 1973. Began legal practice Charleston 1973. In legal practice Welch 1975. Special Justice, West Virginia Supreme Court of Appeals Feb 1985 and Nov 1988.

Assistant Prosecuting Attorney McDowell County 1977. West Virginia House of Delegates 1978-82 (Chairman House Committee on Political Subdivisions 1980-81). Instructor West Virginia University College of Law 1974-76 and Bluefield State College 1976-77. Member West Virginia, Mountain State, National and American Bar Associations. Recipient Diploma of Judicial Skills American Academy of Judicial Education July 1986. Recipient Earl Warren Fellowship Award from NAACP 1972. Specialist Five U.S. Army 1966-68. Democrat. Life member NAACP. 32° Mason (Past Master Excelsior Lodge 22). Member Mount Chapel Baptist Church and Shriners (Kanawha Consistory 73 and Salaam Temple 83). Enjoys sports, music and reading.

Mailing address: P.O. Box 310, Welch 24801.

Office: McDowell County Courthouse, Wyoming Street, Welch 24801.

Telephone: (304) 436-8531.

STEPTOE, Thomas W., Jr. *(Judge, West Virginia Circuit Court Twenty-third Judicial Circuit)* Elected Nov 8, 1984 to term beginning Jan 1, 1985. Reelected Nov 8, 1991 and 2000. Current term expires Dec 31, 2008. Former Chief Judge. Born Charleston West Virginia April 25, 1951. Episcopalian. Educated at University of Virginia B.A. with honors 1974 and West Virginia University College of Law J.D. 1977. Admitted to practice West Virginia 1977. In legal practice Charles Town 1977-85.

Important Decisions: Oakley v. Gainer 175 W. Va. 115, 331 S.E.2d 846, 1985. Democrat. Member Jamestowne Society, Clan Wallace Society, Northern Neck of Virginia Historical Society and Jefferson County Historical Society.

Office: Jefferson County Courthouse, 100 East Washington Street, Charles Town 25414.

Telephone: (304) 728-3201.

STONE, Robert B. *(Judge, West Virginia Circuit Court Seventeenth Judicial Circuit)* Former Chief Judge.

Office: Monongalia County Courthouse, 243 High Street, Morgantown 26505.

Telephone: (304) 291-7265.

STUCKY, James C. *(Judge, West Virginia Circuit Court Thirteenth Judicial Circuit)* Former Chief Judge.

Office: Kanawha County Judicial Annex, 111 Court Street, Charleston 25301.

Telephone: (304) 357-0364.

SWOPE, Derek C. *(Chief Judge, West Virginia Circuit Court Ninth Judicial Circuit)*

Office: Mercer County Courthouse, 1501 West Main Street, Princeton 24740.

Telephone: (304) 487-8346.

TALLMAN, C. Darren *(Judge, West Virginia Family Court Circuit Three)*

Office: 208 Avery Street, Parkersburg 26101.

Telephone: (304) 420-4533.

Fax: (304) 424-1769

TAYLOR, Maurice G., Jr. *(Magistrate Judge, United States District Court Southern District of West Virginia)* Appointed by U.S. District Court judges.

Mailing address: P.O. Box 2807, Huntington 25727-2807.

Telephone: (304) 529-5709.

THORNSBURY, Michael *(Chief Judge, West Virginia Circuit Court Thirtieth Judicial Circuit)*

Mailing address: P.O. Box 1198, Williamson 25661.

Office: Mingo County Courthouse, 75 East Second Avenue, Williamson 25661.

Telephone: (304) 235-0340.

VANDERVORT, R. Clarke *(Magistrate Judge, United States District Court Southern District of West Virginia)* Appointed by U.S. District Court judges to term beginning Dec 20, 2001. Term expires Dec 19, 2009.

Mailing address: P.O. Box 4190, Bluefield 24701.

Office: 601 Federal Street, Bluefield 24701.

Telephone: (304) 327-0376.

VICKERS, Charles M. *(Chief Judge, West Virginia Circuit Court Twelfth Judicial Circuit)*

Mailing address: P.O. Box 599, Fayetteville 25840.

Office: Fayette County Courthouse, 100 Church Street, Fayetteville 25840.

Telephone: (304) 574-1600.

WALKER, Jennifer Bailey *(Judge, West Virginia Circuit Court Thirteenth Judicial Circuit)*

Office: Kanawha County Judicial Annex, 111 Court Street, Charleston 25301.

Telephone: (304) 357-0366.

WARNER, Kimber Radcliffe *(Judge, West Virginia Family Court Circuit Twelve)*

Mailing address: P.O. Box 427, Welch 24801.

Office: McDowell County Courthouse, Welch 24801.

Telephone: (304) 436-6943.

Fax: (304) 436-2817

WATERS, Robert A. *(Chief Judge, West Virginia Circuit Court Fourth Judicial Circuit)*

Office: 321 Wood County Judicial Building, 2 Government Square, Parkersburg 26101-5353.

Telephone: (304) 424-1746.

WATKINS, William M. "Chip" *(Judge, West Virginia Family Court Circuit Twenty-six)*

Office: Putnam County Judicial Building, 3389 Winfield Road, Winfield 25213.

Telephone: (304) 586-0242.

Fax: (304) 586-0228

WEBB, Benjamin Hays, II *(Judge, West Virginia Court of Claims)* Appointed March 17, 1993. Reappointed July 1, 1997 and 2003. Current term expires 2009. Born Huntington West Virginia Oct 2, 1920. Educated at Marshall College A.B. 1942 and West Virginia University College of Law LL.B. 1948.

Past President Marion County and West Virginia Bar Associations. Life Member American Law Institute. Permanent Delegate Judicial Conference of the Fourth Circuit. Member West Virginia Law Institute.

Office: 1900 Kanawha Boulevard East, Room W-334, Charleston 25305-0610.

Telephone: (304) 347-4851.

WERTMAN, William *(Judge, West Virginia Family Court Circuit Twenty-four)* Appointed by Governor Bob Wise to term beginning Jan 1, 2002. Elected 2002, current term expires Dec 31, 2008.

Office: 105 South Spring Street, Martinsburg 25401.

Telephone: (304) 267-0051.

Fax: (304) 267-0072

WHITED, Larry S. *(Judge, West Virginia Family Court Circuit Four)* Appointed by Governor Bob Wise to term beginning Jan 1, 2002. Elected 2002, current term expires Dec 31, 2008. Born Roane County West Virginia Nov 12, 1946. Methodist. Educated at West Virginia University B.A. 1987 and Memphis State University J.D. 1990. Admitted to practice West Virginia 1990. In legal practice Grantsville Jan 1, 1991 to Dec 31, 1996.

Prosecuting Attorney Roane County Jan 1, 1997 to Sept 30, 1999. USAF 1965-69. Republican.

Office: Roane County Courthouse, Second Floor, 200 Main Street, Spencer 25276.

Telephone: (304) 927-0973.

Fax: (304) 927-2676

E-mail address: whitela@mail.wvnet.edu

WILEY, Edwin B. *(Judge, West Virginia Family Court Circuit Twelve)* Appointed by Governor Bob Wise to term beginning Jan 1, 2002. Elected 2002, current term expires Dec 31, 2008.

Office: 130 Scott Street, Princeton 24740.

Telephone: (304) 425-0537.

Fax: (304) 431-2642

WILFONG, Jaymie Godwin *(Judge, West Virginia Family Court Circuit Twenty-two)*

Office: Seven Randolph Avenue, Elkins 26241.

Telephone: (304) 637-0212.

Fax: (304) 637-0244

WILKES, Christopher C. *(Judge, West Virginia Circuit Court Twenty-third Judicial Circuit)* Elected Nov 3, 1992 to term beginning Jan 1, 1993. Reelected 2000, current term expires Dec 31, 2008. Former Chief Judge. Born Annapolis Maryland April 12, 1956. Educated at West Virginia University B.S. 1980 and Ohio Northern University J.D. 1983. Member Phi Kappa Phi and Willis Society. Admitted to practice West Virginia 1983, U.S. District Courts Southern 1983 and Northern 1986 Districts of West Virginia and U.S. Supreme Court 1988. In

WILKES, CHRISTOPHER C.—*Continued*

legal practice Martinsburg 1983-93. Judge, Martinsburg and Ranson Municipal Courts 1985-92.

Member West Virginia Judicial Association, American Judges Association, The West Virginia State Bar and Berkeley County Bar Association. Attended General Jurisdiction Course The National Judicial College July 1994. Republican.

Office: Berkeley County Courthouse, 110 West King Street, Martinsburg 25401.

Telephone: (304) 264-1992.

WILSON, Ronald E. *(Chief Judge, West Virginia Circuit Court First Judicial Circuit)*

Mailing address: P.O. Box 428, New Cumberland 26047.

Office: Hancock County Courthouse, New Cumberland 26047.

Telephone: (304) 564-3311, 234-3621.

ZAKAIB, Paul, Jr. *(Judge, West Virginia Circuit Court Thirteenth Judicial Circuit)* Former Chief Judge.

Office: Kanawha County Judicial Annex, 111 Court Street, Charleston 25301.

Telephone: (304) 357-0362.

WISCONSIN

Capital MADISON

UNITED STATES DISTRICT COURTS DISTRICTS OF WISCONSIN

Within Wisconsin there are two United States District Courts. For descriptive information refer to the United States Courts section.

EASTERN DISTRICT includes Brown, Calumet, Dodge, Door, Florence, Fond du Lac, Forest, Green Lake, Kenosha, Kewaunee, Langlade, Manitowoc, Marinette, Marquette, Menominee, Milwaukee, Oconto, Outagamie, Ozaukee, Racine, Shawano, Sheboygan, Walworth, Washington, Waukesha, Waupaca, Waushara and Winnebago counties. The court sits at Green Bay, Milwaukee and Oshkosh.

Chief Judge
Rudolph T. Randa

Judges
J. P. Stadtmueller
Charles N. Clevert, Jr.
Lynn Adelman
William C. Griesbach

Senior Judge
Thomas J. Curran

Clerk
Sofron B. Nedilsky
362 U.S. Courthouse
517 East Wisconsin Avenue
Milwaukee, Wisconsin 53202
(414) 297-3372

WESTERN DISTRICT includes Adams, Ashland, Barron, Bayfield, Buffalo, Burnett, Chippewa, Clark, Columbia, Crawford, Dane, Douglas, Dunn, Eau Claire, Grant, Green, Iowa, Iron, Jackson, Jefferson, Juneau, La Crosse, Lafayette, Lincoln, Marathon, Monroe, Oneida, Pepin, Pierce, Polk, Portage, Price, Richland, Rock, Rusk, St. Croix, Sauk, Sawyer, Taylor, Trempealeau, Vernon, Vilas, Washburn and Wood counties. The court sits at Eau Claire, La Crosse, Madison, Superior and Wausau.

Chief Judge
Barbara B. Crabb

Judge
John C. Shabaz

Clerk
Joseph W. Skupniewitz
P.O. Box 432
Madison, Wisconsin 53701-0432
(608) 264-5156

UNITED STATES MAGISTRATE JUDGES OF WISCONSIN

EASTERN DISTRICT
Aaron E. Goodstein
James R. Sickel
Patricia J. Gorence
William E. Callahan, Jr.

WESTERN DISTRICT
Joseph W. Skupniewitz
Stephen L. Crocker

UNITED STATES BANKRUPTCY COURTS OF WISCONSIN

EASTERN DISTRICT

Chief Judge
Russell A. Eisenberg

Judges
James Edward Shapiro
Margaret Dee McGarity

Bankruptcy Clerk
Christopher L. Austin
126 U.S. Courthouse
517 East Wisconsin Avenue
Milwaukee, Wisconsin 53202
(414) 297-3291

WESTERN DISTRICT

Chief Judge
Robert D. Martin

Judge
Thomas S. Utschig

Bankruptcy Clerk
Marcia M. Anderson
P.O. Box 548
Madison, Wisconsin 53701-0548
(608) 261-5750

WISCONSIN SUPREME COURT

The Supreme Court is Wisconsin's court of last resort. The court consists of a chief justice and six justices elected at large in nonpartisan elections for staggered ten-year terms. Vacancies occurring between terms are filled by the governor. The justice with the greatest seniority serves as chief justice. Retired justices may serve as reserve judges in the Court of Appeals and the Circuit Courts.

The court exercises appellate jurisdiction over all courts and may hear original actions and proceedings. The court may review judgments of, may remove cases from and may accept certification by the Court of Appeals. The court has general superintending control over

WISCONSIN SUPREME COURT—*Continued*

all lower courts and may hear, determine and issue any writ relevant to its jurisdiction.

Four justices constitute a quorum. The court sits en banc at Madison.

Chief Justice
Shirley Schlanger Abrahamson

Justices

Jon P. Wilcox	Ann Walsh Bradley
N. Patrick Crooks	David T. Prosser, Jr.
Diane S. Sykes	Patience D. Roggensack

Clerk
Cornelia G. Clark
110 East Main Street
Suite 215
P.O. Box 1688
Madison, Wisconsin 53701-1688
(608) 266-1880

Interim Director of State Courts
A. John Voelker
16 East State Capitol
P.O. Box 1688
Madison, Wisconsin 53701-1688
(608) 266-6828

WISCONSIN COURT OF APPEALS

The Court of Appeals is Wisconsin's primary court of appellate jurisdiction. The court is divided into four districts. Three judges from District Three, four judges from Districts One and Two and five judges from District Four are elected at large for staggered six-year terms. Vacancies occurring between terms are filled by the governor. A chief judge is appointed by the Supreme Court for a three-year term to serve as administrative head of the court. Presiding judges are appointed in each district by the chief judge to serve a two-year term. Retired judges may be appointed to serve temporary duty as reserve judges.

The court has appellate jurisdiction of all final judgments and orders from Circuit Courts and has original jurisdiction to issue all prerogative writs. The court's decisions may be reviewed by the Supreme Court at its discretion, but there is no automatic appeal process. The court exercises supervisory control over the lower courts.

The court sits in panels of three judges, but certain cases may be disposed of by one judge.

Chief Judge
Thomas Cane

DISTRICT ONE includes Milwaukee County. The court sits at Milwaukee.

Presiding Judge
Ted E. Wedemeyer, Jr.

Judges
Ralph Adam Fine
Charles B. Schudson
Patricia S. Curley

DISTRICT TWO includes Calumet, Fond du Lac, Green Lake, Kenosha, Manitowoc, Ozaukee, Racine, Sheboygan, Walworth, Washington, Waukesha and Winnebago counties. The court sits at Waukesha. Secondary court locations are at Fond du Lac and Racine.

Presiding Judge
Neal P. Nettesheim

Judges
Richard S. Brown
Daniel P. Anderson
Harry G. Snyder

DISTRICT THREE includes Ashland, Barron, Bayfield, Brown, Buffalo, Burnett, Chippewa, Door, Douglas, Dunn, Eau Claire, Florence, Forest, Iron, Kewaunee, Langlade, Lincoln, Marathon, Marinette, Menominee, Oconto, Oneida, Outagamie, Pepin, Pierce, Polk, Price, Rusk, St. Croix, Sawyer, Shawano, Taylor, Trempealeau, Vilas and Washburn counties. The court sits at Wausau. Secondary court locations are at Eau Claire, Green Bay and Superior.

Presiding Judge
Michael W. Hoover

Judges
Thomas Cane
Gregory A. Peterson

DISTRICT FOUR includes Adams, Clark, Columbia, Crawford, Dane, Dodge, Grant, Green, Iowa, Jackson, Jefferson, Juneau, La Crosse, Lafayette, Marquette, Monroe, Portage, Richland, Rock, Sauk, Vernon, Waupaca, Waushara and Wood counties. The court sits at Madison. Secondary court locations are at La Crosse and Stevens Point.

Presiding Judge
Margaret J. Vergeront

Judges
Charles P. Dykman
David G. Deininger
Paul G. Lundsten
vacancy

WISCONSIN CIRCUIT COURTS

The Circuit Courts are Wisconsin's trial courts of general jurisdiction. The County Courts merged with the Circuit Courts August 1, 1978. The state is divided into sixty-nine circuits. Each circuit consists of one county except the combined county circuits of Buffalo-Pepin, Forest-Florence and Shawano-Menominee. For administrative purposes, the circuits are combined into ten judicial administrative districts. A chief judge is appointed in each district by the Supreme Court to serve a two-year term. Judges are elected in nonpartisan elections for six-year terms. Vacancies occurring between terms are filled by the governor. Retired judges may be appointed to serve temporary duty as reserve judges.

The courts have original jurisdiction of all civil and criminal matters in the circuit except where exclusive jurisdiction has been given to another court. The courts hear administrative reviews of state administrative agency decisions and have appellate jurisdiction of all cases from Municipal Courts.

The courts sit at each county seat except where otherwise indicated.

Circuit	Judge
Adams	Charles A. Pollex
Ashland	Robert E. Eaton
Barron	James C. Babler
	Edward R. Brunner

WISCONSIN CIRCUIT COURTS—*Continued*

Bayfield	John P. Anderson
Brown	William M. Atkinson
	Sue E. Bischel
	Richard J. Dietz
	Kendall M. Kelley
	J. D. McKay
	Peter Joseph Naze
	Mark A. Warpinski
	Donald R. Zuidmulder
Buffalo-Pepin Court sits at Alma and Durand	Dane F. Morey
Burnett	Michael J. Gableman
Calumet	Donald A. Poppy
Chippewa	Roderick A. Cameron
	Thomas J. Sazama
Clark	Jon M. Counsell
Columbia	Daniel S. George
	James Otto Miller
	Richard L. Rehm
Crawford	Michael Kirchman
Dane	John C. Albert
	Angela Gina Baldi Bartell
	Robert A. DeChambeau
	Steven D. Ebert
	Patrick J. Fiedler
	David T. Flanagan
	C. William Foust
	Shelley Gaylord
	Paul B. Higginbotham
	Moria Krueger
	Daniel R. Moeser
	Gerald C. Nichol
	Diane M. Nicks
	Michael Nowakowski
	Sarah B. O'Brien
	Stuart A. Schwartz
	Maryann Sumi
Dodge	Andrew P. Bissonnette
	Daniel W. Klossner
	John R. Storck
Door	Peter C. Diltz
	D. Todd Ehlers
Douglas	George L. Glonek
	Michael T. Lucci
Dunn	Rod W. Smeltzer
	William C. Stewart, Jr.
Eau Claire	William M. Gabler
	Paul J. Lenz
	Benjamin D. Proctor
	Lisa Kay Stark
	Eric J. Wahl
Florence	See Forest-Florence
Fond du Lac	Dale L. English
	Peter L. Grimm
	Richard James Nuss
	Steven W. Weinke
	Robert J. Wirtz
Forest-Florence Court sits at Crandon and Florence	Robert A. Kennedy, Jr.
Grant	George S. Curry
	Robert P. Van De Hey
Green	James R. Beer
Green Lake	William M. McMonigal
Iowa	William D. Dyke
Iron	Patrick J. Madden
Jackson	Gerald W. Laabs
Jefferson	Jackie R. Erwin
	William F. Hue
	Randy R. Koschnick
	John M. Ullsvik
Juneau	Dennis C. Schuh
Kenosha	David Mark Bastianelli
	Michael S. Fisher
	Barbara A. Kluka
	Bruce E. Schroeder
	Mary K. Wagner
	Wilbur W. Warren
	S. Michael Wilk
Kewaunee	Dennis J. Mleziva
La Crosse	Ramona A. Gonzalez
	Dennis G. Montabon
	Michael J. Mulroy
	Dale T. Pasell
	John J. Perlich
Lafayette	William D. Johnston
Langlade	James P. Jansen
Lincoln	Glenn H. Hartley
	J. Michael Nolan
Manitowoc	Darryl W. Deets
	Fred H. Hazlewood
	Patrick L. Willis
Marathon	Dorothy L. Bain
	Patrick Michael Brady
	Gregory E. Grau
	Vincent K. Howard
	Raymond F. Thums
Marinette	Tim A. Duket
	David G. Miron
Marquette	Richard O. Wright
Menominee	See Shawano-Menominee
Milwaukee Court also sits at Wauwatosa	Dominic S. Amato
	Carl Ashley
	David L. Borowski
	William W. Brash, III
	Kitty K. Brennan
	Michael Brian Brennan
	Louis B. Butler, Jr.
	Karen E. Christenson
	Jeffrey A. Conen
	Thomas R. Cooper
	Jean W. DiMotto
	John J. DiMotto
	M. Joseph Donald
	Thomas P. Donegan
	Timothy G. Dugan
	Michael J. Dwyer
	Clare L. Fiorenza
	Mel Flanagan
	Christopher R. Foley
	John Franke
	Bonnie L. Gordon
	Michael D. Guolee
	David A. Hansher
	Charles F. Kahn, Jr.
	Daniel L. Konkol
	Jeffrey A. Kremers
	Mary M. Kuhnmuench
	Elsa C. Lamelas

WISCONSIN CIRCUIT COURTS—*Continued*

Milwaukee—Cont.	Michael G. Malmstadt
	Victor Manian
	Kevin E. Martens
	John E. McCormick
	Patricia D. McMahon
	Dennis P. Moroney
	Marshall B. Murray
	Daniel A. Noonan
	Richard J. Sankovitz
	Jacqueline Schellinger
	John Siefert
	William Sosnay
	Michael P. Sullivan
	Jeffrey A. Wagner
	Joseph R. Wall
	Francis T. Wasielewski
	Lee Edward Wells
	Maxine A. White
	Timothy M. Witkowiak
Monroe	Steven Luse Abbott
	Michael J. McAlpine
Oconto	Richard D. Delforge
	Larry L. Jeske
Oneida	Robert E. Kinney
	Mark A. Mangerson
Outagamie	James T. Bayorgeon
	John A. Des Jardins
	Dee Rule Dyer
	Harold V. Froehlich
	Michael W. Gage
	Dennis C. Luebke
	Joseph M. Troy
Ozaukee	Paul V. Malloy
	Joseph D. McCormack
	Thomas R. Wolfgram
Pepin	See Buffalo-Pepin
Pierce	Robert W. Wing
Polk	Molly E. GaleWyrick
	Robert H. Rasmussen
Portage	John V. Finn
	Frederic W. Fleishauer
	Thomas T. Flugaur
Price	Douglas T. Fox
Racine	Dennis J. Barry
	Charles H. Constantine
	Faye M. Flancher
	Richard J. Kreul
	Wayne J. Marik
	Emily S. Mueller
	Gerald Paul Ptacek
	Stephen A. Simanek
	Allan "Pat" Torhorst
	Emmanuel J. Vuvunas
Richland	Edward E. Leineweber
Rock Court also sits at Beloit	Michael J. Byron
	James P. Daley
	Daniel T. Dillon
	John H. Lussow
	John W. Roethe
	James E. Welker
	Richard T. Werner
Rusk	Frederick A. Henderson
St. Croix	Eric J. Lundell
	Scott R. Needham
	Edward F. Vlack III
Sauk	James Evenson
	Guy D. Reynolds
	Patrick J. Taggart
Sawyer	Norman L. Yackel
Shawano-Menominee Court sits at Shawano and Keshena	Thomas G. Grover
	James Roy Habeck
Sheboygan	James J. Bolgert
	Terence Bourke
	Gary J. Langhoff
	L. Edward Stengel
	Timothy M. Van Akkeren
Taylor	Gary L. Carlson
Trempealeau	John A. Damon
Vernon	Michael J. Rosborough
Vilas	James B. Mohr
Walworth	James L. Carlson
	Michael S. Gibbs
	Robert J. Kennedy
	John R. Race
Washburn	Eugene D. Harrington
Washington	Patrick J. Faragher
	Andrew Thomas Gonring
	David C. Resheske
	Annette K. Ziegler
Waukesha	Michael O. Bohren
	Mac Davis
	Lee S. Dreyfus
	Kathryn W. Foster
	Mark S. Gempeler
	Donald J. Hassin
	Patrick C. Haughney
	James Robert Kieffer
	Robert G. Mawdsley
	Ralph M. Ramirez
	Paul F. Reilly
	Linda Van De Water
Waupaca	John P. Hoffmann
	Raymond S. Huber
	Philip M. Kirk
Waushara	Lewis R. Murach
Winnebago	William H. Carver
	Thomas J. Gritton
	Robert A. Haase
	Robert A. Hawley
	Barbara Hart Key
	Bruce K. Schmidt
Wood	James M. Mason
	Gregory J. Potter
	Edward F. Zappen, Jr.

RESERVE CIRCUIT COURT JUDGES

Thomas H. Barland	Michael J. Barron
John G. Bartholomew	Richard T. Becker
Michael W. Brennan	John P. Buckley
Henry B. Buslee	Louis J. Ceci
Dennis D. Conway	Dennis D. Costello
William E. Crane	Edwin C. Dahlberg
William J. Duffy	William F. Eich
James R. Erickson	Mark J. Farnum, Jr.
John A. Fiorenza	Dennis J. Flynn
John F. Foley	Thomas J. Gallagher
Richard D. Galstad	William D. Gardner
Raymond E. Gieringer	Laurence C. Gram
Richard G. Greenwood	William J. Haese
Charles D. Heath	Kent C. Houck
Robert A. P. Kennedy	John D. Koehn

WISCONSIN CIRCUIT COURTS—*Continued*

Charles E. Kuehn
Robert W. Landry
Howard W. Latton
Eugene F. McEssey
John W. Mickiewicz
Roger P. Murphy
Hugh F. Nelson
Robert J. Parins
Robert F. Pfiffner
James W. Rice
Leo F. Schlaefer
Earl W. Schmidt
Patrick T. Sheedy
Russell W. Stamper
Walter J. Swietlik
Leah M. Lampone
Daniel L. LaRocque
Patrick John Madden
Robert McGraw
Robert J. Miech
Gordon Myse
Peter G. Pappas
Robert R. Pekowsky
Robert W. Radcliffe
Conrad A. Richards
Gary B. Schlosstein
Arnold K. Schumann
Richard H. Stafford
Donald W. Steinmetz
James H. Taylor
Louise Tesmer
Timothy Louis Vocke
Joseph E. Wimmer
Phillip P. Todryk
Thomas S. Williams
Virginia A. Wolfe

WISCONSIN MUNICIPAL COURTS

Municipal Courts are courts of limited jurisdiction in Wisconsin and may be established in any city, town or village. The judges are elected for two to four-year terms as determined by the municipality.

The courts have exclusive jurisdiction of local ordinances when legal relief only is sought. If equitable relief is demanded, the Circuit Courts have jurisdiction. Appeals are to the Circuit Courts.

There are currently over two hundred Municipal Courts in operation throughout the state.

Wisconsin Counties and County Seats

Adams
Friendship

Ashland
Ashland

Barron
Barron

Bayfield
Washburn

Brown
Green Bay

Buffalo
Alma

Burnett
Grantsburg

Calumet
Chilton

Chippewa
Chippewa Falls

Clark
Neillsville

Columbia
Portage

Crawford
Prairie du Chien

Dane
Madison

Dodge
Juneau

Door
Sturgeon Bay

Douglas
Superior

Dunn
Menomonie

Eau Claire
Eau Claire

Florence
Florence

Fond du Lac
Fond du Lac

Forest
Crandon

Grant
Lancaster

Green
Monroe

Green Lake
Green Lake

Iowa
Dodgeville

Iron
Hurley

Jackson
Black River Falls

Jefferson
Jefferson

Juneau
Mauston

Kenosha
Kenosha

Kewaunee
Kewaunee

La Crosse
La Crosse

Lafayette
Darlington

Langlade
Antigo

Lincoln
Merrill

Manitowoc
Manitowoc

Marathon
Wausau

Marinette
Marinette

Marquette
Montello

Menominee
Keshena

Milwaukee
Milwaukee

Monroe
Sparta

Oconto
Oconto

Oneida
Rhinelander

Outagamie
Appleton

Ozaukee
Port Washington

Pepin
Durand

Pierce
Ellsworth

Polk
Balsam Lake

Portage
Stevens Point

Price
Phillips

Racine
Racine

Richland
Richland Center

Rock
Janesville

Rusk
Ladysmith

St. Croix
Hudson

Sauk
Baraboo

Sawyer
Hayward

Shawano
Shawano

Sheboygan
Sheboygan

Taylor
Medford

Trempealeau
Whitehall

Vernon
Viroqua

Vilas
Eagle River

Walworth
Elkhorn

Washburn
Shell Lake

Washington
West Bend

Waukesha
Waukesha

Waupaca
Waupaca

Waushara
Wautoma

Winnebago
Oshkosh

Wood
Wisconsin Rapids

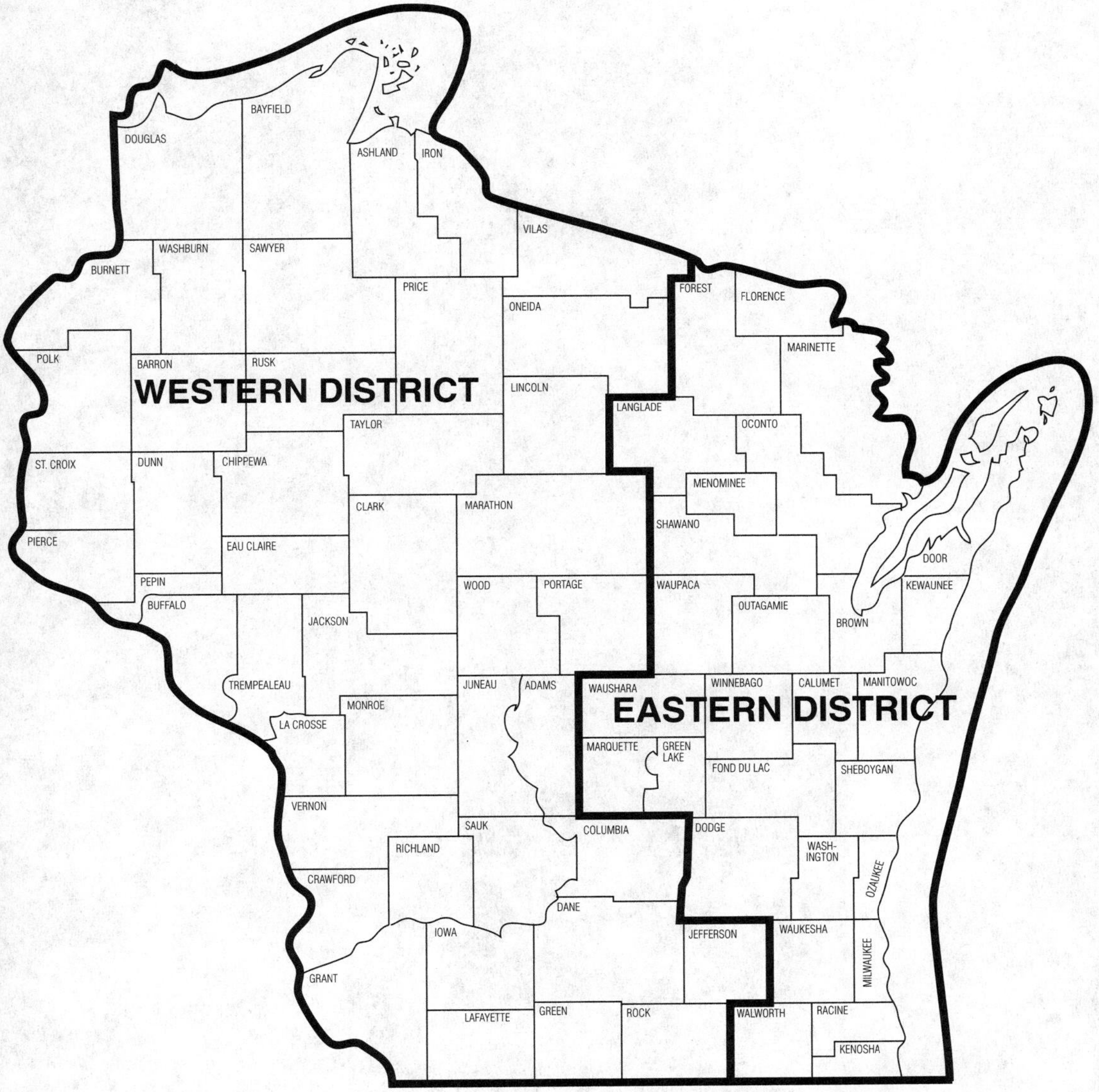
WESTERN DISTRICT
EASTERN DISTRICT
DOUGLAS
BAYFIELD
ASHLAND
IRON
VILAS
WASHBURN
SAWYER
BURNETT
PRICE
ONEIDA
FOREST
FLORENCE
POLK
BARRON
RUSK
MARINETTE
LINCOLN
LANGLADE
TAYLOR
OCONTO
ST. CROIX
DUNN
CHIPPEWA
MENOMINEE
CLARK
MARATHON
SHAWANO
PIERCE
EAU CLAIRE
DOOR
PEPIN
WOOD
PORTAGE
WAUPACA
KEWAUNEE
BUFFALO
OUTAGAMIE
JACKSON
BROWN
TREMPEALEAU
JUNEAU
ADAMS
WAUSHARA
WINNEBAGO
CALUMET
MANITOWOC
MONROE
LA CROSSE
MARQUETTE
GREEN LAKE
FOND DU LAC
SHEBOYGAN
VERNON
SAUK
COLUMBIA
DODGE
RICHLAND
WASH-INGTON
CRAWFORD
OZAUKEE
DANE
IOWA
JEFFERSON
WAUKESHA
MILWAUKEE
GRANT
LAFAYETTE
GREEN
ROCK
WALWORTH
RACINE
KENOSHA

UNITED STATES DISTRICT COURTS
DISTRICTS OF WISCONSIN

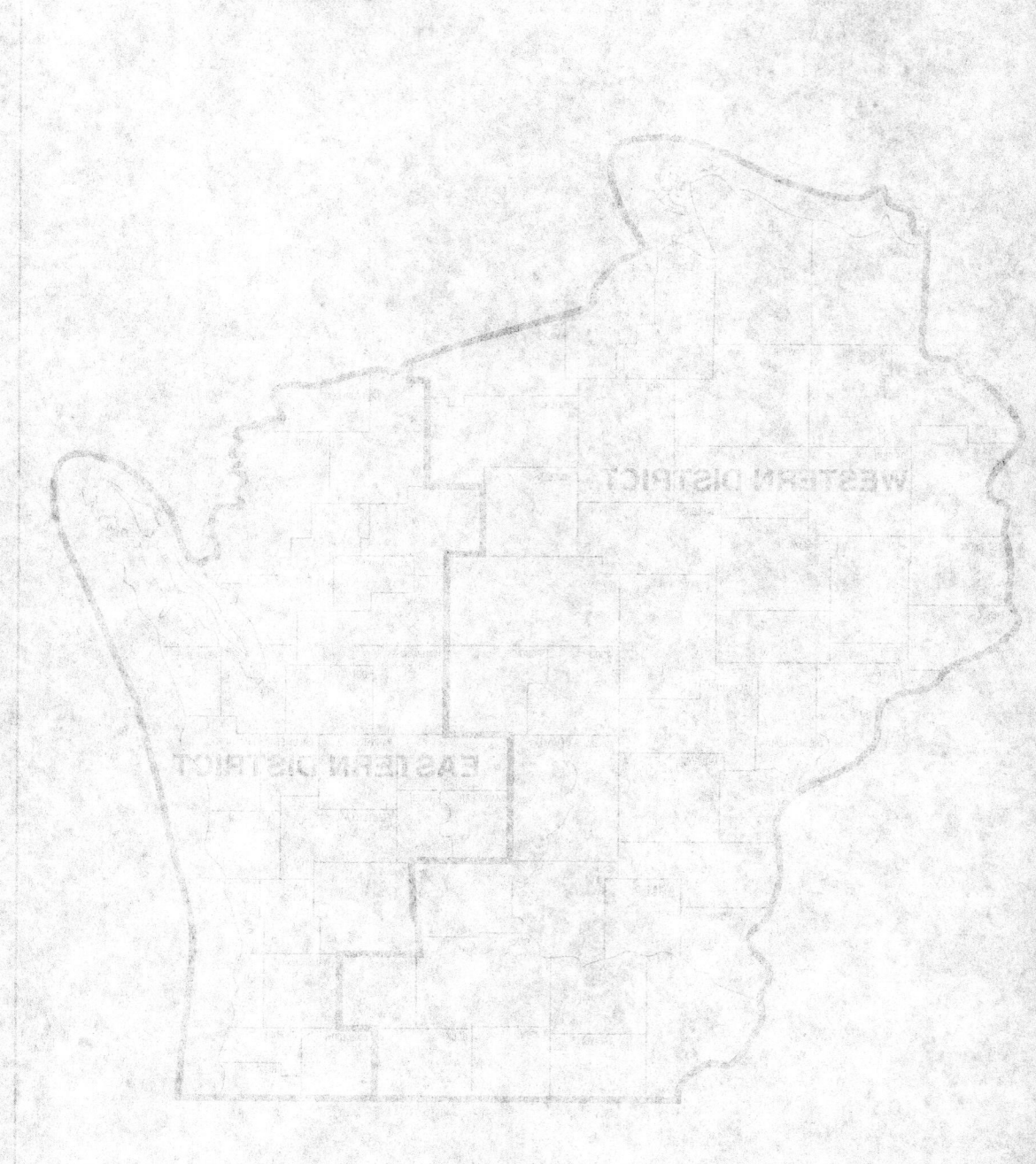

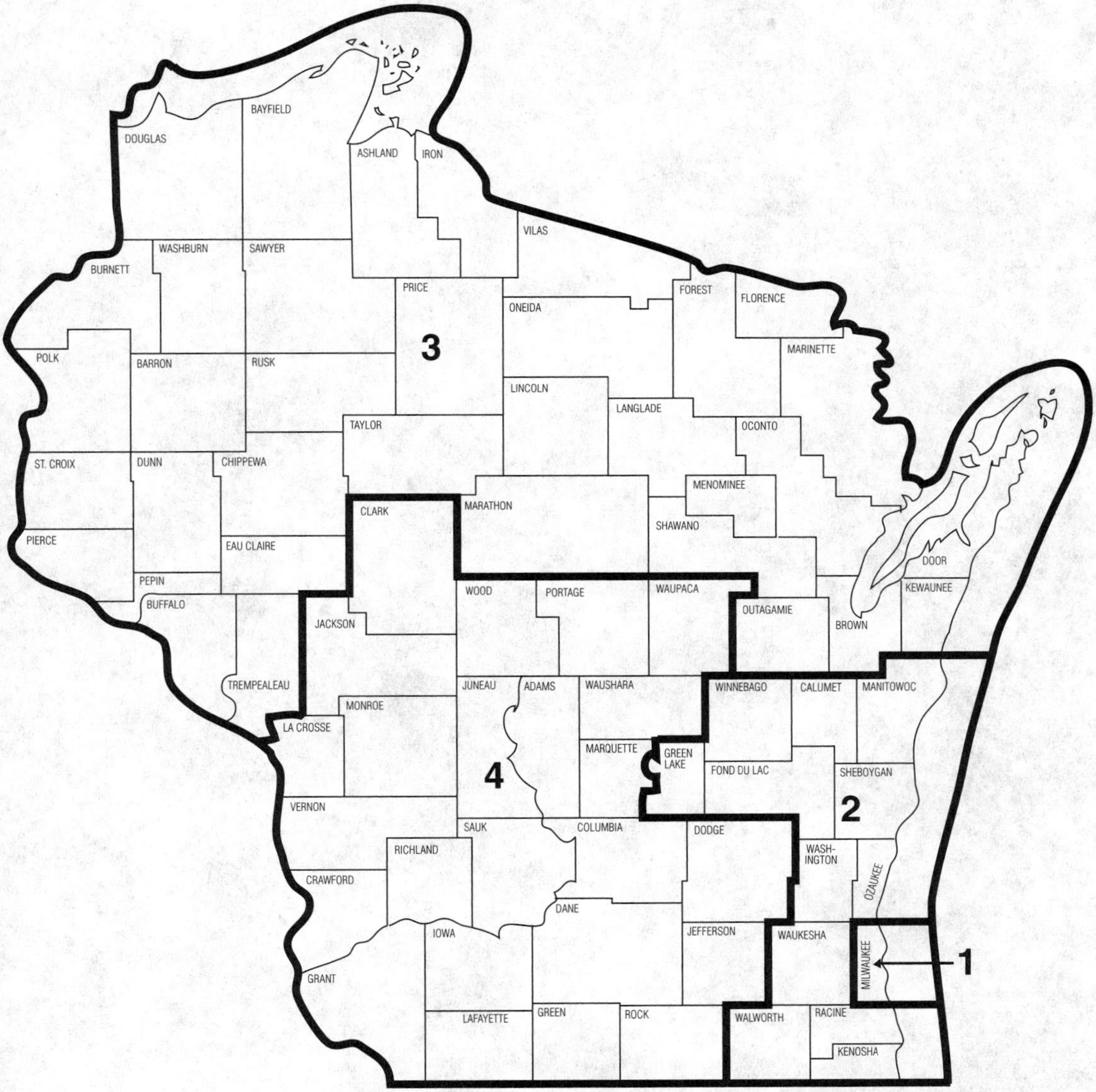
BAYFIELD
DOUGLAS
ASHLAND
IRON
VILAS
WASHBURN
SAWYER
BURNETT
PRICE
FOREST
FLORENCE
ONEIDA
3
POLK
BARRON
RUSK
MARINETTE
LINCOLN
LANGLADE
TAYLOR
OCONTO
ST. CROIX
DUNN
CHIPPEWA
MENOMINEE
CLARK
MARATHON
SHAWANO
PIERCE
EAU CLAIRE
DOOR
PEPIN
WOOD
PORTAGE
WAUPACA
KEWAUNEE
BUFFALO
OUTAGAMIE
JACKSON
BROWN
TREMPEALEAU
JUNEAU
ADAMS
WAUSHARA
WINNEBAGO
CALUMET
MANITOWOC
MONROE
LA CROSSE
MARQUETTE
GREEN LAKE
FOND DU LAC
SHEBOYGAN
4
2
VERNON
SAUK
COLUMBIA
DODGE
RICHLAND
WASH-INGTON
OZAUKEE
CRAWFORD
DANE
IOWA
JEFFERSON
WAUKESHA
MILWAUKEE
1
GRANT
LAFAYETTE
GREEN
ROCK
WALWORTH
RACINE
KENOSHA

DISTRICTS OF WISCONSIN COURT OF APPEALS

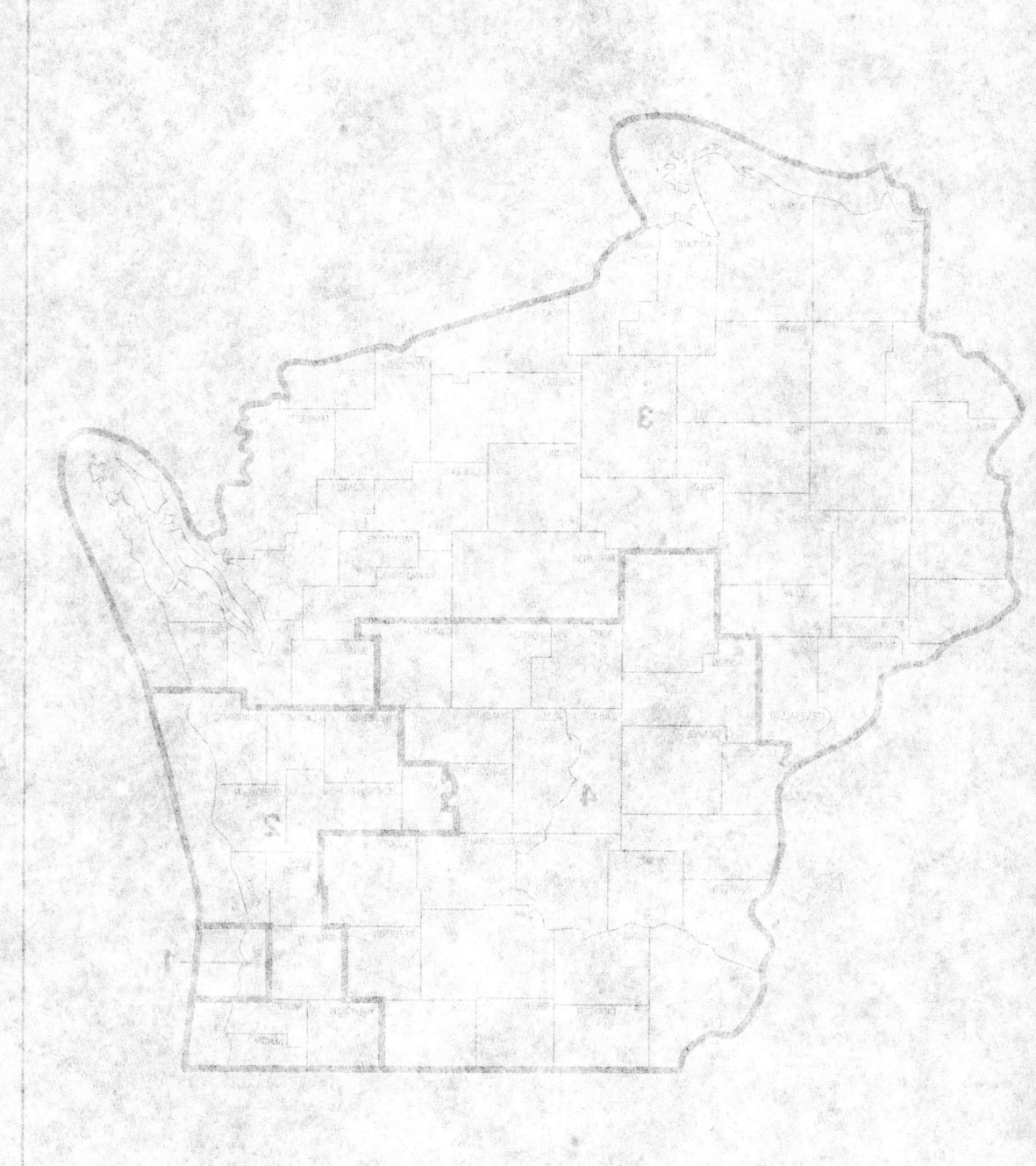

WISCONSIN

ABBOTT, Steven Luse *(Judge, Wisconsin Circuit Court Monroe Circuit)* Elected to term beginning June 28, 1995. Reelected 2001, current term expires 2007. Born St. Paul Minnesota Nov 19, 1939. Episcopalian. Educated at University of Wisconsin B.S. 1961 and University of California Hastings College of the Law LL.B. 1964. Admitted to practice Wisconsin 1965 and U.S. District Court Western District of Wisconsin 1965. U.S. Army.

Office: 301 Monroe County Courthouse, 112 South Court Street, Sparta 54656-1765.

Telephone: (608) 269-8700.

ABRAHAMSON, Shirley Schlanger *(Chief Justice, Wisconsin Supreme Court)* Appointed by Governor Patrick J. Lucey Aug 6, 1976. Elected to term beginning Aug 1, 1979. Reelected April 1989 and April 1999. Current term expires July 31, 2009. Born New York New York Dec 1933. Educated at New York University A.B. magna cum laude 1953, Indiana University School of Law J.D. with high distinction 1956 and University of Wisconsin School of Law S.J.D. 1962. Awarded honorary LL.D. Willamette University 1978, Ripon College 1981, Beloit College 1982, Capital University 1983, John Marshall Law School 1984, Northeastern University 1985, Indiana University 1986, Hamline University 1988, Northland College 1988, University of Notre Dame 1993, Suffolk University 1994, DePaul University 1996, Marian College 1998 and Lawrence University 1998.. Articles and Book Review Editor Indiana Law Journal. Member Phi Beta Kappa and Order of the Coif. Admitted to practice Indiana 1956, New York 1961 and Wisconsin 1962. In legal practice Madison Wisconsin 1962-76.

Staff Attorney for Clinical Legal Education Center for Public Representation Inc. 1974-75. Editor *Constitutions of the United States: National and State* 2 Volumes 1962. Author "How Tootsie the Goldfish Is Teaching People to Think Like a Judge" 21 No. 2 The Judges' Journal Spring 1982, reprinted in *Handbook for Judges* 1984; "Reincarnation of State Courts" 36 No. 4 Southwestern L. Jour. Nov 1982; "Are Judges Too Lenient?" 22 No. 2 The Judges' Journal Spring 1983, reprinted in *Understanding the Law* Peck and White, eds. ABA 1983; "The Value of Humanities for Judges" *Making Connections I: Humanities and the Criminal Justice System* 1984; "Demystifying the Judicial Process: How Can Judges and Journalists Really Help?" 67 *Judicature* 448-57, 1984; "Judicial Review and Constitutional Limitations" 14 No. 3 Golden Gate University L. Rev. Fall 1984; "The Woman Has Robes: Four Questions" 14 No. 3 Golden Gate University L. Rev. Fall 1984; "Paradoxes of the 80's" 60 No. 2 Chicago-Kent L. Rev. 1984; "Homegrown Justice: The State Constitutions" Chapter 11 *Developments in State Constitutional Law: The Williamsburg Conference* West Publishing 1985; "Looking Toward the 21st Century: Lawyer Testing and the Bar Admission Process in the Year 2000" 54 No. 1 Bar Examiner Feb 1985; "Some Enlightenment on Crime" 83 No. 4 Michigan L. Rev. Feb 1985; "Redefining Roles: The Victims' Rights Movement" No. 3 Utah L. Rev. 1985; "Criminal Law and State Constitutions: The Emergence of State Constitutional Law" 63 Nos. 6-7 Texas L. Rev. March/April 1985; "Justice and Juror" 20 No. 2 Georgia L. Rev. 1986; "A View from the Other Side of the Bench" 69 No. 4 Marquette L. Rev. 1986; "State Constitutional Law" *Encyclopedia of the American Judicial System* 1987; Chapter "The State and Federal Courts of the United States as Guardians of Individual Rights" *Law, Justice and the Judiciary: Transnational Trends* 1988; Chapter "The Living Constitution: A View from the Bench" *The United States Constitution: Its Birth, Growth and Influence in Asia* 1988; and "The Consumer and the Courts" 74 No. 2 *Judicature* Aug/Sept 1990. Co-author with Diane Gutmann "New Federalism: State Constitutions and State Courts" *A Workable Government? The Constitution After 200 Years* 1987, reprinted 71 No. 2 *Judicature* Aug/Sept 1987 and with Charles G. Curtis, Jr. "Rule of Reason" and "Understanding Test" *Oxford Companion to the Supreme Court of the United States.* Editorial Board The Judges' Journal 1983-86.

Fellow 1957-58, Assistant Director Legislative Drafting Research Fund 1958-60 and Consultant 1960-64 Columbia University School of Law. Professor University of Wisconsin Law School since 1966. Lecturer Political Science Department and Research Associate School of Law University of Wisconsin Sept 1961 to June 1962. Lecturer Marquette University School of Law 1977-81. Guest Lecturer "Reincarnation of the State Courts" Roy R. Ray Lecture Southern Methodist University School of Law March 5, 1982, "Redefining Roles" William H. Leary Lecture University of Utah College of Law Nov 15, 1984, "Criminal Provisions in State Constitutions" Tom Sealy Lecture University of Texas School of Law Jan 24, 1985, "Justice and Juror" Edith House Lecture University of Georgia Law School March 7, 1985, "Judges, Legislators and Lawyers: Strained Benchfellows" Frank Rowe Kenison Lecture Franklin Pierce Law Center Feb 13, 1986, East China Institute of Politics and Law Willamette University Law School Summer Program 1986, "The Original Understanding" Cleveland-Marshall College of Law Cleveland State University Feb 19, 1987, "The Court as Guardian of the Constitution" Fourth International Appellate Judges Conference 1987, "Shall We Dance? Steps for Legislators and Judges in Statutory Interpretation" William B. Lockhart Lecture University of Minnesota Law School March 29, 1990 and "Divided We Stand: State Constitutions in a More Perfect Union" Mathew O. Tobriner Lecture Hastings College of the Law Nov 14, 1990.

Fellow American Bar Foundation. Member Advisory Board National Institute of Justice 1980-81, Commission on Accreditation for Law Enforcement Agencies 1983-86, Advisory Board Project on Judicial Peremptory Challenge Procedure U.S. Department of Justice 1985-86, Council Fund for Research on Dispute Resolution Ford Foundation since 1987, Advisory Board State Constitutional Law Developments Clearinghouse Project National Association of Attorneys General 1987-89, Study Group Program of Research on Mental Health and the Law John D. and Catherine T. MacArthur Foundation

ABRAHAMSON, SHIRLEY SCHLANGER—*Continued*

since 1988 and Planning Committee Fifth International Appellate Judges Conference of 1990. Member The American Law Institute (Council member since 1985), Wisconsin Judicial Council 1987-89, The Foundation for Women Judges (Board of Directors since 1983), American Judicature Society (Board of Directors 1983-90, Executive Committee 1986-90), State Bar of Wisconsin (Director Criminal Law Section 1977-78), Dane County (Former member Legal Referral Committee, Legal Aid Committee and Public Speaker Committee), Indiana State, New York State and American (State and Local Vice Chair Attorneys' Employment and Practice Committee Section of Administrative Law 1979-82; Council member 1976-86 and Chair Standards Review Committee 1981-83 Section of Legal Education and Admissions to the Bar; Council member Special Committee on Youth Education for Citizenship 1982-88; member Lawyers Competency Committee 1982-84, Victims Committee since 1986 and Task Force Standards on Prosecution Function, Defense Function and Providing Defense Services 1988-90 Section of Criminal Justice, Action Commission to Improve the Tort Liability System 1985-87 and Executive Committee Appellate Judges' Conference Judicial Administration Division 1986-89) Bar Associations. Member Advisory Committee Civil Litigation Research Project University of Wisconsin Disputes Processing Research Program and University of Southern California Program for Justice System Research 1979-82. Participant summer 1982 and Moderator summer 1983 Seminar on Justice and Society Aspen Institute for Humanistic Studies. Guest Lecturer "Coming to Judgment" Roger G. Traynor Lecture California Judicial College July 18, 1984. Listed in *Who's Who in America* since 1972. Recipient Freedom of Information Award from Society of Professional Journalists Sigma Delta Chi Milwaukee Chapter 1982, Writer's Cup from Women in Communications, Inc. Madison Chapter 1984 and Thomas Jefferson Award from Texas Press Association 1987. Board of Visitors Indiana University School of Law, Bloomington since 1972, University of Miami School of Law since 1982, J. Reuben Clark Law School Brigham Young University 1986-88, University of Chicago Law School since 1988 and Northwestern University School of Law since 1989. Member The University of Wisconsin Foundation since 1980. Board of Directors Foundations of the American Constitutional System, Inc. Department of History University of Wisconsin-Madison 1981-84. Fellow Wisconsin Academy of Sciences, Arts and Letters since 1982. Member Academy of Law Alumni Fellows Indiana University School of Law, Bloomington 1985. Member American Philosophical Society and American Academy of Arts & Sciences.

Mailing address: P.O. Box 1688, Madison 53701-1688.

Office: 16 East State Capitol, Madison 53702.

Telephone: (608) 266-1885.

ADELMAN, Lynn *(Judge, United States District Court Eastern District of Wisconsin)* Appointed for life by President Bill Clinton Dec 1997. Born Milwaukee Wisconsin Oct 1, 1939. Jewish. Educated at Princeton University A.B. with honors 1961 and Columbia University School of Law LL.B. with honors 1965. Admitted to practice New York 1967, Wisconsin 1972, U.S. District Courts Southern District of New York 1967 and Eastern District of Wisconsin 1972, U.S. Court of Appeals Seventh Circuit 1972 and U.S. Supreme Court 1992. In legal practice New York City New York 1967-72 and Milwaukee Wisconsin 1973-97.

Author "Departures from the Uniform Marital Property Act Contained in the Wisconsin Marital Property Act" 68 Marquette L. Rev. 390, 1985; "The Presumption of Release in Bail Decisions" *Wisconsin Lawyer* July 1989; "Should Wisconsin Lower the Blood Alcohol Content to .08 for Driving Under the Influence? Yes" *Wisconsin Counties Magazine* May 1992; "Wisconsin Should Not Reverse 140 Years of History by Reinstating the Death Penalty" *Wisconsin Lawyer* May 1993; "Bad Laws Make Hard Cases: Hate Crime Laws and the Supreme Court's Opinion in *Wisconsin v. Mitchell*" 29 Gonzaga L. Rev. 1, 1994; "Campaign Finance Reform" Wisconsin Medical Journal May 1997; and "Rewriting Crime Laws is a Precondition of 'Truth in Sentencing'" *Wisconsin Lawyer* June 1997. Recipient Freedom of Information Award from Wisconsin Society of Professional Journalists 1990, Conservationist of the Year from Waukesha County Conservation Alliance 1991, Eunice Edgar Award from Wisconsin Chapter American Civil Liberties Union 1994, Outstanding Pro Bono Publico Service Award from Legal Action of Wisconsin 1994 and Lifetime Achievement Award from Mothers Against Drunk Driving 1995. State Senator Wisconsin 1977-97.

Office: 204 U.S. Courthouse, 517 East Wisconsin Avenue, Milwaukee 53202.

Telephone: (414) 297-1285.

ALBERT, John C. *(Judge, Wisconsin Circuit Court Dane Circuit)*

Office: 204 City-County Building, 210 Martin Luther King Jr. Boulevard, Madison 53703.

Telephone: (608) 266-4235.

AMATO, Dominic S. *(Judge, Wisconsin Circuit Court Milwaukee Circuit)* Appointed by Governor Tommy G. Thompson to term beginning 1988. Elected to subsequent terms. Current term expires July 31, 2007. Serves Civil Division. Educated at University of Arizona College of Law J.D. 1972. Law Clerk to Chief Justice Bruce F. Beilfuss, Wisconsin Supreme Court 1972-73. In legal practice 1973-88. Court Commissioner, Milwaukee County 1984-88. Substitute Judge, Milwaukee Municipal Court 1985-88. Judge, Village of Brown Deer Municipal Court 1985-88.

Former Arbitrator American Arbitration Association. Former Member Family Bench and Bar Committee and Bench and Bar Committee Wisconsin Court of Appeals District One and Milwaukee County Judicial Substitution Study Committee. Former Member Wisconsin Academy of Trial Lawyers, Wisconsin Trial Judges Association, Wisconsin Municipal Judges Association and American Bar Association. Member State Bar of Arizona, State Bar of Wisconsin and Milwaukee Bar Association. Former Member Board of Directors Sacred Heart Rehabilitation Hospital, Blind Children, Inc., Milwaukee County Home Improvement Council and Brown Deer Little League Baseball. Former Member Advisory Committee on School Safety for Milwaukee Metropolitan Area. Personal Statement or Quote: "The paramount rule of this branch is: Fundamental fairness and the opportunity to be heard."

Office: 414 Milwaukee County Courthouse, 901 North Ninth Street, Milwaukee 53233-1425.

Telephone: (414) 278-4484.

ANDERSON, Daniel P. *(Judge, Wisconsin Court of Appeals District Two)* Elected to term beginning Aug 1, 1990. Reelected April 1995 and 2001. Current term expires July 31, 2007. Former Presiding Judge. Born Plymouth Wisconsin Jan 1, 1945. Roman Catholic. Educated at University of Wisconsin-Madison B.S. 1967 J.D. cum laude 1973 and University of Southern California 1967-69. Admitted to practice Wisconsin 1974 and U.S. District Courts Eastern 1974 and Western 1974 Districts of Wisconsin. Began legal practice Plymouth 1974. Former Judge, Wisconsin County Court Sheboygan County, appointed by Governor Martin J. Schreiber to term beginning Jan 9, 1978. Former Judge, Wisconsin Circuit Court Sheboygan Circuit, elected to term beginning Aug 1, 1979.

Editorial Board *Judicial Benchbook, Civil Law Volume* Wisconsin ATS/CLE 1983-84. Member Information Technology Strategic Planning Committee since 1994 and e-Filing Committee and Chair e-Signature Committee 2000 Wisconsin Court System. Member Planning and Policy Advisory Committee since 1997 Wisconsin Supreme Court (Ad hoc Committee on Alternative Dispute Resolution since 1997, Planning Subcommittee). Member Wisconsin Judicial Conference (Member and Secretary Sections on Civil Law 1983-84, member Section on Criminal Law and Ad Hoc Committee on Sentencing Guidelines), Wisconsin Judicial Council (Chair Committee on Improving Jury Communications 1980 and ad hoc Committee on Evidence and Civil Procedure 1993-97), American Judicature Society, State Bar of Wisconsin, Waukesha and Sheboygan County Bar Associations. Instructor "Criminal Motions" and "Civil Jury Problems" 1981-84, "Forensic Economics" Civil Law Seminar 1982, "Computers and the Courts" Annual Meeting 1983 and "1984 Civil Law Update" Annual Meeting 1984 Wisconsin Judicial Conference, "Trial Techniques" State Bar of Wisconsin ATS/CLE 1983-84 and "CD-ROM Legal Research" Professional Education Systems. Faculty Member Wisconsin Judicial College 1984-90 and "Criminal Evidence," "Word Processing for Judges," "Introduction to Personal Computers in the Courts" and "Essential Computer Skills for Appellate Judges" The National Judicial College 1989-95. Volunteer Faculty Member The National Judicial College since 1989. Recipient Faculty Recognition Award Wisconsin Judicial College 1983. Captain USAF 1967-71. Trustee Plymouth Public Library 1973-78. Board of Directors American Red Cross 1979-82. Enjoys personal computers, photography and suspense novels.

Office: 2727 North Grandview Boulevard, Suite 300, Waukesha 53188-1672.

Telephone: (262) 521-5372.

ANDERSON, John P. *(Judge, Wisconsin Circuit Court Adams Circuit)* Elected April 2003.

Office: Courthouse, 117 East Fifth Street, Washburn 54891-9464.

Telephone: (715) 373-6118.

ASHLEY, Carl *(Judge, Wisconsin Circuit Court Milwaukee Circuit)* Elected April 6, 1999 to term beginning Aug 2, 1999. Term expires Aug 2, 2005. Born Milwaukee Wisconsin May 27, 1956. Catholic. Educated at Marquette University B.S. 1979 J.D. 1983. Staff Writer Marquette Law Review 1982-83. Admitted to practice Wisconsin 1983, U.S. District Courts Eastern 1983 and Western 1983 Districts of Wisconsin and U.S. Court of Appeals Seventh Circuit 1993. In legal practice Milwaukee 1990-99. Administrative Law Judge, Milwaukee 1997-99.

Public Defender Wisconsin 1983-90. Past President Milwaukee Association of Minority Attorneys. Board of Directors Legal Action of Wisconsin. Member Supreme Court Commission on Judicial Elections and Ethics. Member State Bar of Wisconsin, Milwaukee (Board of Directors), National and American Bar Associations. Named Volunteer of the Year by Metropolitan Fair Housing Council. Recipient Excellence in Community Service Award from Career Youth Development and Black Excellence Award. Co-recipient Educational Lawyer of the Year Award from State Bar of Wisconsin 1999. Election Commissioner NAACP 1996. Former Member Board of Directors Metropolitan Fair Housing Council. Member Alumni Board of Directors and Former Member Multicultural Advisory Committee Marquette University Law School. Board of Directors Catholic Archdiocese and Wild Space. Coordinator WAMA High School Mock Trial Program.

Office: 515 Milwaukee County Courthouse, 901 North Ninth Street, Milwaukee 53233-1425.

Telephone: (414) 278-4472.

E-mail address: Carl.Ashley-@milwaukee.courts.state.wi.us

ATKINSON, William M. *(Judge, Wisconsin Circuit Court Brown Circuit)* Elected April 2, 1991 to term beginning Aug 1, 1991. Reelected April 2, 1997 and 2003. Current term expires July 31, 2009. Educated at University of Wisconsin-Oshkosh B.B.A. and University of Nebraska J.D. Judge, Green Bay Municipal Court 1985-91.

Mailing address: P.O. Box 23600, Green Bay 54305-3600.

Office: Brown County Courthouse, 100 South Jefferson Street, Green Bay 54301.

Telephone: (920) 448-4129.

BABLER, James C. *(Judge, Wisconsin Circuit Court Barron Circuit)* Appointed by Governor Jim Doyle to term beginning March 2003.

Office: 218 Courthouse, 330 East La Salle Avenue, Barron 54812-1540.

Telephone: (715) 537-6260.

BAIN, Dorothy L. *(Judge, Wisconsin Circuit Court Marathon Circuit)*

Office: Marathon County Courthouse, 500 Forest Street, Wausau 54403-5568.

Telephone: (715) 261-1335.

BARLAND, Thomas H. *(Reserve Judge, Wisconsin Circuit Court)* Assumed office 1976. Retired 2000. Assumed Reserve status, serves by assignment. Born San Francisco California March 3, 1930. Presbyterian. Educated at University of Wisconsin-Madison B.A. with honors 1951 LL.B. with honors 1956. Staff member Wisconsin Law Review. Member Order of the Coif, Artus and Phi Kappa Phi. Admitted to practice Wisconsin 1956. Began legal practice Eau Claire 1956. County Judge 1967-76.

Private Mediator and Arbitrator. Co-author "The Wisconsin Rules of Evidence: A Courtroom Handbook" Wisconsin State Bar ATS/CLE 1982. Former Member Wisconsin Council on Criminal Justice. Chair Wisconsin Judicial Conduct Advisory Committee. Fellow American Bar Foundation and The American College of Trust and Estate Counsel. Member American Judicature Society, State Bar of Wisconsin, Eau Claire County and Ameri-

BARLAND, THOMAS H.—*Continued*

can (Delegate National Conference of State Trial Judges Judicial Administration Division) Bar Associations. Former Faculty Member The National Judicial College. Lecturer 1970-88 and Associate Dean 1987-93 Wisconsin Judicial College. Named Outstanding Young Man by Wisconsin Jaycees 1963 and Judge of the Year by State Bar of Wisconsin 1997. Recipient Judicial Excellence Award from National Conference of State Trial Judges Judicial Division American Bar Association 2000. First Lieutenant USAS 1953-55. Member Wisconsin Assembly 1961-67 (Caucus Chairman 1963-64). Board of Directors Eau Claire County Dispute Settlement Center. Member Wisconsin State Historical Society (President 1967-70, Member Board of Curators).

Mailing address: 1617 Drummond Street, Eau Claire 54701-4052.

BARRON, Michael J. *(Reserve Judge, Wisconsin Circuit Court)* Elected to term beginning Aug 1, 1973. Reelected 1979, 1986, 1992 and 1998. Retired. Assumed Reserve status, serves by assignment. Born Milwaukee Wisconsin Dec 18, 1933. Roman Catholic. Educated at University of Wisconsin-Milwaukee B.S. 1956, Marquette University J.D. 1959 and John Marshall Law School 1966-67. President Marquette University Student Bar Association 1958-59. Member Phi Delta Phi. Admitted to practice Wisconsin 1959. Began legal practice Milwaukee 1959.

Member Wisconsin Assembly 1961-64 and Milwaukee County Board of Supervisors 1964-73. Author "Heifetz and Collateral Source Rule" Wisconsin Bar Bulletin June 1975. Important Decisions: Wisconsin State Bankers Association v. Mutual Savings and Loan Association 1976 and Mercury Records et al. v. Heilman 1974-79. Instructor in Economics Milwaukee Area Technical College 1960-61. Instructor in Business Law Marquette University School of Business 1961-62. Member Wisconsin Judicial Council 1980-88. Member since 1982 and Chairman 1994-98 Wisconsin Civil Jury Instructions Committee. Delegate National Conference of State Trial Judges 1982-85. Chairman Civil Law Section Wisconsin Judicial Conference 1982-83. Member American Judicature Society, State Bar of Wisconsin (Board of Directors Negligence Section 1969-70), Milwaukee (Board of Directors 1984-87) and American (Delegate National Conference of State Trial Judges Judicial Administration Division 1982-85) Bar Associations. Board of Directors Wisconsin Academy of Trial Lawyers 1968-69. Deputy Chief Judge 1976-86 and Chief Judge 1986-90 Milwaukee County Board of Judges. Board of Directors since 1987, President 1991-92 and Secretary-Chief Financial Officer since 1994 National Conference of Metropolitan Courts. Recipient Outstanding Young Man Award from Milwaukee Jaycees 1965. Named Distinguished Alumnus of 1987 by University of Wisconsin-Milwaukee. President East Side Businessmen's Association 1963-64. President Milwaukee Convention and Visitors' Bureau, Inc. 1968-69. President Milwaukee Archdiocesan School Board 1982-83. President University of Wisconsin-Milwaukee Alumni Association 1982-84. Member Friends of Art. Enjoys water skiing and snow skiing.

Mailing address: 3027 North Lake Drive, Milwaukee 53211.

BARRY, Dennis J. *(Judge, Wisconsin Circuit Court Racine Circuit)* Appointed by Governor Lee Dreyfus to term beginning Aug 1, 1980. Elected 1981, 1987, 1993 and 1999. Current term expires August 1, 2005. Born Racine Wisconsin April 4, 1947. Educated at Lawrence University B.A. 1969 and Marquette University Law School J.D. 1973. Admitted to practice Wisconsin 1973, U.S. District Court Eastern District of Wisconsin 1973 and Arizona 1990. In legal practice Racine Wisconsin 1974-78.

Deputy Assistant District Attorney Kenosha County 1973-74. District Attorney Racine County 1979-80. Contributor Wisconsin Juvenile Justice Code 1995. Important Decisions: State v. Matzker (first Wisconsin sexual predator case) 1994 and State v. Zimmerman (fetal alcohol case) 1996. Chairman Wisconsin Juvenile Justice Committee 1994-95. Member Wisconsin Sentencing Commission, Justinian Law Society, State Bar of Wisconsin (Board of Governors since 2002), State Bar of Arizona and Racine County Bar Association. Named State Judge of the Year by State Bar of Wisconsin 1997. U.S. Army 1969-70. Member Racine Rotary Club (Past President).

Office: Racine County Courthouse, 730 Wisconsin Avenue, Racine 53403.

Telephone: (262) 636-3550.

Fax: (262) 636-3341

BARTELL, Angela Gina Baldi *(Judge, Wisconsin Circuit Court Dane Circuit)* Assumed office Jan 3, 1978. Elected 1979, 1985, 1991, 1997 and 2003. Current term expires July 31, 2009. Chief Judge, Administrative District Five 1982-88. Born Milwaukee Wisconsin Jan 25, 1946. Educated at University of Wisconsin-Madison B.A. with honors 1969 J.D. magna cum laude 1971. Articles Editor Wisconsin Law Review 1970-71. Member Order of the Coif, Phi Beta Kappa, Sigma Epsilon Sigma and Crucible. Law Clerk to Judge James E. Doyle, U.S. District Court Western District of Wisconsin 1971-72. Admitted to practice Wisconsin 1972. In legal practice Madison 1973-77. Former Judge, Wisconsin County Court Dane County Jan 3 to Aug 1, 1978, appointed by Governor Martin J. Schreiber.

Author Comment "Wisconsin Post Conciliation Remedies-Habeas Corpus: Past, Present and Future" 1145 Wisconsin L. Rev. 1970. Editor Wisconsin Judicial Benchbook Project 1980-82. Instructor in Real Estate and Alternatives to Probate (practice course) 1977-78, Trial of a Civil Case 1978-79 and Decision Making 1988 University of Wisconsin. Member Wisconsin Criminal Jury Instructions Committee since 1992. Fellow American Bar Foundation. Member Legal Association for Women, Voluntary Association of Trial Court Judges, The American Law Institute, State Bar of Wisconsin (President Young Lawyers Section 1974-75, Vice Chair Criminal Law Section 1978-79), Dane County and American Bar Associations. Member Board of Bar Commissioners 1976-77 and Board of Attorneys Professional Responsibility 1977. Associate Dean Wisconsin Judicial College since 1999. Recipient Joseph E. Davis Prize 1969-70, Salmon Dalberg Award 1970-71 and Daniel Grady Award 1971. Listed in *Who's Who in America* 2001. Trustee Wisconsin Trust Account Foundation 1993-97. Member since 1995 and Chairman 2000-01 Board of Directors Dane County United Way. President Elect Rotary Club of Madison.

Office: 329 City-County Building, 210 Martin Luther King Jr. Blvd., Madison 53703.

Telephone: (608) 266-4460.

BARTHOLOMEW, John G. *(Reserve Judge, Wisconsin Circuit Court)* Elected to term beginning Jan 1979. Reelected 1986. Retired June 1, 1989. Assumed Reserve status, serves by assignment. Born Lodi Wisconsin July 28, 1919. Lutheran. Educated at University of Wisconsin-Madison B.A. 1942 and Marquette University J.D. 1947. Admitted to practice Wisconsin 1947. In legal practice Durand 1947-63. Judge, Pepin County Court 1963-68. Judge, Wisconsin Circuit Court Circuit Eight (St. Croix, Pierce, Dunn, Buffalo and Pepin counties) 1968-78.

District Attorney Pepin County 1948-56. Member Wisconsin Jury Instruction Committee 1976-89. Staff Sergeant U.S. Army 1942-45.

Mailing address: 1312 Wisconsin Street, #322, Hudson 54016.

BASTIANELLI, David Mark *(Judge, Wisconsin Circuit Court Kenosha Circuit)* Appointed by Governor Anthony S. Earl to term beginning Jan 27, 1985. Elected 1985, 1991, 1997 and 2003. Current term expires July 31, 2009. Born Kenosha Wisconsin Oct 23, 1950. Educated at University of Wisconsin-Madison B.B.A. 1972 and University of Kentucky J.D. 1976. Admitted to practice Wisconsin 1976. Began legal practice Kenosha 1976. Municipal Judge, City of Kenosha 1980-84.

Assistant District Attorney 1976-79. Instructor in Business Law Gateway Technical Institute 1979-80. Member The Association of Trial Lawyers of America, Kenosha and American Bar Associations. Former Member Board of Directors March of Dimes. Board of Directors Italian American Society.

Office: 205 Kenosha County Courthouse, 912 56th Street, Kenosha 53140-3747.

Telephone: (262) 653-2581.

BAYORGEON, James T. *(Judge, Wisconsin Circuit Court Outagamie Circuit)* Appointed by Governor Anthony S. Earl Oct 14, 1983. Elected 1984, 1990, 1996 and April 2002. Current term expires July 31, 2008. Born Kaukauna Wisconsin May 7, 1935. Catholic. Educated at Marquette University undergraduate degree 1955 J.D. 1958. Associate Editor Marquette Law Review. Law Clerk to Hon. F. Ryan Duffy, Sr., U.S. Court of Appeals Seventh Circuit 1961-62. Member Delta Theta Phi. Admitted to practice Wisconsin 1958, U.S. District Court Eastern District of Wisconsin 1958, U.S. Court of Military Appeals 1958 and U.S. Court of Appeals Seventh Circuit 1961. Began legal practice Appleton 1962.

Member State Bar of Wisconsin, Outagamie County and American Bar Associations. First Lieutenant USAR JAGC 1958-61.

Office: Justice Center, 320 South Walnut Street, Appleton 54911-5991.

Telephone: (920) 832-5152.

BECKER, Richard T. *(Reserve Judge, Wisconsin Circuit Court)* Elected 1977 to term beginning Jan 2, 1978. Reelected 1984, 1990 and 1996. Retired. Assumed Reserve status, serves by assignment. Born Hartford Wisconsin July 24, 1935. Roman Catholic. Educated at Marquette University B.S. 1957 LL.B. 1959. Admitted to practice Wisconsin 1959. Began legal practice Hartford 1960.

District Attorney 1961-67. Instructor Northwestern University 1959-60. Chairman Criminal Law Section Wisconsin Judicial Conference 1986-87. Member Criminal Jury Instruction Committee 1984-94, State Bar of Wisconsin and Washington County Bar Association.

Mailing address: 827 North Main Street, Hartford 53027.

BEER, James R. *(Judge, Wisconsin Circuit Court Green Circuit)* Appointed by Governor Tommy G. Thompson to term beginning Oct 14, 1996. Elected April 1, 1997 and April 2003. Current term expires July 30, 2009. Born Monroe Wisconsin Nov 3, 1946. Protestant. Educated at University of Wisconsin at Madison B.S. 1969 and Marquette University Law School J.D. 1972. Member Phi Alpha Delta. Admitted to practice Wisconsin 1972 and U.S. District Court Western District of Wisconsin 1972. In legal practice Monroe 1972-96. Court Commissioner 1988-96 and Family Court Commissioner 1993-96.

District Attorney Green County 1975-77. Acting Corporation Counsel Green County 1986-90. Member State Bar of Wisconsin and Green County Bar Association. Attended National Prosecutors School Northwestern University 1975. Member Moose Lodge of Monroe, Green County Conservation League, Kiwanis Club, Zor Shrine and Smith Masonic Lodge. Interests include archaeology.

Office: Green County Courthouse, 1016 16th Avenue, Monroe 53566.

Telephone: (608) 328-9420.

BISCHEL, Sue E. *(Judge, Wisconsin Circuit Court Brown Circuit)* Elected to term beginning May 1, 1992. Reelected to subsequent term. Born Little Chute Wisconsin Sept 25, 1952. Catholic. Educated at University of Wisconsin-Eau Claire B.A. with high honors 1974 and University of Minnesota J.D. 1978. Admitted to practice Wisconsin 1978, U.S. District Court Eastern District of Wisconsin 1978 and U.S. Supreme Court 1978. In legal practice Green Bay 1980-83.

Staff Attorney Legal Services of Northeastern Wisconsin 1978-80. Assistant District Attorney Brown County 1983-92. Member Wisconsin Attorney General's Law Enforcement Advisory Committee 1987-90. Member Wisconsin District Attorneys Association (Executive Committee 1987-90), State Bar of Wisconsin (Prosecutorial Systems Committee 1988-89) and Brown County Bar Association (President 1988). Recipient ZONTA Award for outstanding woman in government and human services 1992 and Optimist Award for outstanding contribution to law enforcement 1992. Junior high school English teacher 1974-75. Member St. Matthew Parish. Enjoys sailing, piano playing, singing, exercise and raising four children.

Mailing address: P.O. Box 23600, Green Bay 54305-3600.

Office: Brown County Courthouse, 100 South Jefferson Street, Green Bay 54301.

Telephone: (920) 448-4115.

BISSONNETTE, Andrew P. *(Judge, Wisconsin Circuit Court Dodge Circuit)* Appointed by Governor Tommy G. Thompson to term beginning June 9, 1989. Elected 1989, 1995 and 2001. Current term expires July 31, 2007.

Office: Dodge County Justice Facility, 210 West Center Street, Juneau 53039-1091.

Telephone: (920) 386-3805.

BOHREN, Michael O. *(Judge, Wisconsin Circuit Court Waukesha Circuit)* Appointed by Governor Tommy G. Thompson to term beginning April 3, 2000.

BOHREN, MICHAEL O.—*Continued*

Elected April 2001, current term expires July 31, 2007. Born Appleton Wisconsin Feb 27, 1947. Educated at Ripon College A.B. cum laude 1969 and Marquette University J.D. 1975. Admitted to practice Wisconsin 1975, U.S. Supreme Court 1978 and U.S. Courts of Appeals Fifth and Seventh Circuits. In legal practice Milwaukee and Waukesha 1975-2000.

Member State Bar of Wisconsin and Waukesha County Bar Association. Political affiliation: Nonpartisan. Member Kettle Moraine School Board 1982-2000. Board of Directors Waukesha Symphony since 1997 and Waukesha Kiwanis since 2000.

Office: Waukesha County Courthouse, 515 West Moreland Boulevard, Waukesha 53188-2428.

Telephone: (262) 548-7482.

BOLGERT, James J. *(Judge, Wisconsin Circuit Court Sheboygan Circuit)*

Office: Sheboygan County Courthouse, 615 North Sixth Street, Sheboygan 53081-4692.

Telephone: (920) 459-3085.

BOROWSKI, David L. *(Judge, Wisconsin Circuit Court Milwaukee Circuit)* Elected April 2003.

Office: Milwaukee County Courthouse, 901 North Ninth Street, Milwaukee 53233-1425.

Telephone: (414) 278-5116.

BOURKE, Terence *(Judge, Wisconsin Circuit Court Sheboygan Circuit)* Elected April 2003.

Office: Sheboygan County Courthouse, 615 North Sixth Street, Sheboygan 53081-4692.

Telephone: (920) 459-0393.

BRADLEY, Ann Walsh *(Justice, Wisconsin Supreme Court)* Elected to term beginning 1995. Term expires July 31, 2005. Born Richland Center Wisconsin. Educated at Webster College B.A. 1972 and University of Wisconsin Law School J.D. 1976. Former Judge, Wisconsin Circuit Court Marathon Circuit.

Mailing address: P.O. Box 1688, Madison 53701-1688.

Office: 16 East State Capitol, Madison 53702.

Telephone: (608) 266-1886.

BRADY, Patrick Michael *(Judge, Wisconsin Circuit Court Marathon Circuit)*

Office: Marathon County Courthouse, 500 Forest Street, Wausau 54403-5568.

Telephone: (715) 261-1381.

BRASH, William W., III *(Judge, Wisconsin Circuit Court Milwaukee Circuit)* Appointed by Governor Scott McCallum to term beginning Nov 2001. Elected April 2002, current term expires July 31, 2008. Municipal Judge, Village of Fox Point 1984-97. Reserve Municipal Judge, Milwaukee 1997-2001.

Office: 629 Milwaukee County Courthouse, 901 North Ninth Street, Milwaukee 53233-1425.

Telephone: (414) 278-4564.

BRENNAN, Kitty K. *(Judge, Wisconsin Circuit Court Milwaukee Circuit)*

Office: 206 Milwaukee County Courthouse, 901 North Ninth Street, Milwaukee 53233-1425.

Telephone: (414) 278-4506.

BRENNAN, Michael Brian *(Judge, Wisconsin Circuit Court Milwaukee Circuit)* Appointed by Governor Tommy G. Thompson to term beginning Jan 1, 2000. Elected April 1, 2001. Born Milwaukee Wisconsin Oct 24, 1963. Roman Catholic. Educated at University of Notre Dame B.A. cum laude 1986 and Northwestern University School of Law J.D. 1989. Coordinating Note and Comment Editor Northwestern Law Review 1988-89. Admitted to practice Wisconsin 1989 and Illinois 1990.

Instructor Marquette University Law School 1994. Member State Bar of Wisconsin.

Office: 313 Safety Building, 821 West State Street, Milwaukee 53233.

Telephone: (414) 278-4772.

Fax: (414) 223-1262

E-mail address: michael.brennan-@milwaukee.courts.state.wi.us

BRENNAN, Michael W. *(Reserve Judge, Wisconsin Circuit Court)* Assumed office Aug 1, 1978. Elected 1979, 1985, 1991 and 1997. Retired. Assumed Reserve status, serves by assignment. Former Judge, Wisconsin County Court Clark County.

Mailing address: 305 South Lincoln Avenue, Marshfield 54449.

BROWN, Richard S. *(Judge, Wisconsin Court of Appeals District Two)* Elected to term beginning Aug 1, 1978. Reelected 1982, 1988, 1994 and 2000. Current term expires July 31, 2006. Presiding Judge 1984-90 and 1998-2001. Born Racine Wisconsin March 31, 1946. Educated at Miami University A.B. 1968, University of Wisconsin J.D. 1971 and University of Virginia LL.M. 1984. Member Phi Delta Phi. Admitted to practice Wisconsin 1971. Began legal practice Racine 1971. In legal practice Oshkosh 1973-78.

Author "Allocation of Cases in a Two-Tiered Appellate Structure: The Wisconsin Experience and Beyond" Marquette L. Rev. 1984-85 and "Proposal for a Modified Merit Selection Plan for Wisconsin" 20 Quinnipiac L. Rev. 651, 2001. Member Wisconsin Judicial Conference, American Judicature Society (Board of Directors), Institute for Judicial Administration, State Bar of Wisconsin, Waukesha County and American (Judicial Administration Division, Section of Individual Rights and Responsibilities) Bar Associations. Faculty Member The National Judicial College since 1991. Vice Chairperson Prop, Inc. (structured help to juveniles in need) 1975-78. Executive Vice President Oshkosh Symphony Orchestra 1976-78. President Oakwood Parent Association 1978. Enjoys running, skiing and golf.

Office: 2727 North Grandview Boulevard, Suite 300, Waukesha 53188-1672.

Telephone: (262) 521-5232.

BRUNNER, Edward R. *(Judge, Wisconsin Circuit Court Barron Circuit)* Elected to term beginning Aug 1, 1988. Reelected April 5, 1994 and 2000. Current term expires July 31, 2006. Currently serves as Chief Judge Administrative District Ten. Born Akron Ohio Feb 18, 1948. Roman Catholic. Educated at St. Charles Borromeo College 1966-67, Marquette University B.A. 1970 and University of Akron Law Center J.D. 1974. Admitted to practice Ohio 1974, Wisconsin 1977 and U.S. District Court Western District of Wisconsin 1978. In legal practice Rice Lake Wisconsin 1977-88.

City Attorney Rice Lake Wisconsin 1980-87. Guest Lecturer University of Wisconsin. Director Executive Committee and Member Planning Committee and Criminal Benchbook Committee Wisconsin Judicial Confer-

BRUNNER, EDWARD R.—*Continued*

ence. Member State Bar of Wisconsin, Ohio State and American Bar Associations. Instructor Case Law Update Juvenile Law Seminar Wisconsin Judicial Education 1991 and Case Law Update Probate and Mental Health Wisconsin Judicial Conference 1992. Attended The National Judicial College. Recipient Judicial Education Pettit Scholarship from The National Judicial College 1992. Administrator Ohio Youth Commission Akron Ohio 1971-74. Executive Director Youth Services, Inc. Lorain Ohio 1974-77.

Office: 218 Barron County Courthouse, 330 East LaSalle Avenue, Barron 54812-1540.

Telephone: (715) 537-6399.

BUCKLEY, John P. *(Reserve Judge, Wisconsin Circuit Court)* Retired. Assumed Reserve status, serves by assignment.

Mailing address: 2962-A Madison Street, Waukesha 53188.

BUSLEE, Henry B. *(Reserve Judge, Wisconsin Circuit Court)* Appointed by Governor Lee Dreyfus to term beginning Oct 8, 1979. Elected 1980, 1986, 1992 and 1998. Retired 2002. Assumed Reserve status, serves by assignment. Born Oak Park Illinois July 12, 1924. Lutheran. Educated at St. Olaf College B.A. 1949 and University of Wisconsin J.D. Member Gamma Eta Gamma. Admitted to practice Wisconsin 1952. Began legal practice Madison 1952. In legal practice Fond du Lac since 1960.

Assistant City Attorney Madison 1955-60. City Attorney 1960-66 and City Manager 1966-68 Fond du Lac. Member State Bar of Wisconsin. Retired as Lieutenant Colonel U.S. Army 1975.

Mailing address: Six Ridgewood Court, Fond du Lac 54935.

BUTLER, Louis B., Jr. *(Judge, Wisconsin Circuit Court Milwaukee Circuit)* Elected April 2002 to term beginning Aug 1, 2002. Term expires July 31, 2008. Educated at Lawrence University 1973 and University of Wisconsin Law School J.D. 1997. Former Judge, Milwaukee Municipal Court, appointed to term beginning June 1992.

President Wisconsin Municipal Judges Association. Faculty Member The National Judicial College. Board of Directors Milwaukee Access Telecommunications Authority.

Office: 622 Milwaukee County Courthouse, 901 North Ninth Street, Milwaukee 53233-1425.

Telephone: (414) 278-4517.

BYRON, Michael J. *(Judge, Wisconsin Circuit Court Rock Circuit)* Appointed by Governor Tommy G. Thompson to term beginning May 1, 1991. Elected April 7, 1992 and April 1998. Current term expires July 1, 2004. Born Milwaukee Wisconsin Nov 1, 1941. Roman Catholic. Educated at College of the Holy Cross B.S. 1963 and University of Wisconsin J.D. 1966. Admitted to practice Wisconsin 1966 and U.S. District Court Western District of Wisconsin 1966. In legal practice Beloit 1968-91.

Assistant District Attorney Rock County 1966-68. Member State Bar of Wisconsin.

Office: Rock County Courthouse, 51 South Main Street, Janesville 53545-3978.

Telephone: (608) 743-2249.

CALLAHAN, William E., Jr. *(Magistrate Judge, United States District Court Eastern District of Wisconsin)* Appointed by U.S. District Court judges.

Office: 449 U.S. Courthouse, 517 East Wisconsin Avenue, Milwaukee 53202-4507.

Telephone: (414) 297-1664.

CAMERON, Roderick A. *(Judge, Wisconsin Circuit Court Chippewa Circuit)* Appointed by Governor Anthony S. Earl to term beginning April 1, 1983. Elected 1984, 1990, 1996 and April 2002. Current term expires July 31, 2008. Born Rice Lake Wisconsin Dec 29, 1949. Educated at Trinity College, Connecticut B.S. 1972 and University of Wisconsin J.D. 1974. Admitted to practice Wisconsin 1975 and U.S. District Court Western District of Wisconsin 1975. Began legal practice Chippewa Falls 1975. In legal practice Stanley 1976.

Assistant District Attorney Chippewa County 1975-76. City Attorney Stanley 1976-83. Member Special Functions Subcommittee Circuit Court Automation Project since 1991. Member Decorum Study Committee since 1992. Member Wisconsin Trial Judges Association, State Bar of Wisconsin and Chippewa County Bar Association (President 1978-79). Interested in genealogy and highland piping.

Office: Chippewa County Courthouse, 711 North Bridge Street, Chippewa Falls 54729-1876.

Telephone: (715) 726-7781.

CANE, Thomas *(Chief Judge, Wisconsin Court of Appeals and Judge, Wisconsin Court of Appeals District Three)* Assumed office as Judge 1981. Elected to subsequent terms. Former Presiding Judge. Former Deputy Chief Judge. Chief Judge since 1998. Born Ontonagon Michigan March 28, 1939. Roman Catholic. Educated at University of Michigan B.B.A. 1961, Marquette University J.D. 1964 and University of Virginia LL.M. 1986. Admitted to practice Wisconsin 1964. In legal practice Kaukauna 1967-69. Judge, Wisconsin Circuit Court Outagamie Circuit 1972-81.

Deputy District Attorney Outagamie County 1969-72. Instructor in Business Law University of Maryland (overseas program) 1965-67 and North Central Technical Institute, in Police Science Fox Valley Technical Institute 1969-72 and in CPA Review and Business Law University of Wisconsin-Green Bay 1971. Former Member Wisconsin Judicial Planning Committee. Member Wisconsin Administrative Committee of Courts, Wisconsin Judicial Education Committee, Wisconsin Judicial Commission, State Bar of Wisconsin and Outagamie County Bar Association. Director and Officer Wisconsin Board of County Judges. Named Wisconsin's Outstanding Young Man 1974. Captain USAF JAGC 1964-67. Former Member Board of Directors Marathon County Civic Corporation, Appleton YMCA and Fox River Valley Big Brothers. Former Member VFW, Kiwanis and Knights of Columbus. Board of Directors Wausau Country Club. Member American Legion, and Rotary International. Enjoys golfing, camping, fishing and upland hunting.

Office: 2100 Stewart Avenue, Suite 310, Wausau 54401.

Telephone: (715) 845-6404.

CARLSON, Gary L. *(Judge, Wisconsin Circuit Court Taylor Circuit)* Term expires July 31, 2004.

Office: Taylor County Courthouse, 224 South Second Street, Medford 54451-1899.

Telephone: (715) 748-1435.

CARLSON, James L. *(Judge, Wisconsin Circuit Court Walworth Circuit)* Term expires July 31, 2004.

Mailing address: P.O. Box 1001, Elkhorn 53121-1001.

Office: Walworth County Courthouse, Elkhorn 53121.

Telephone: (262) 741-4224.

CARVER, William H. *(Judge, Wisconsin Circuit Court Winnebago Circuit)* Assumed office Aug 1, 1978. Elected 1980, 1986, 1992 and 1998. Current term expires July 31, 2004. Born Oshkosh Wisconsin Jan 27, 1938. Educated at University of Wisconsin B.B.A. 1960 LL.B. 1965. Admitted to practice Wisconsin 1965. Began legal practice Oshkosh 1965. Judge, Wisconsin County Court Winnebago County Jan 7, 1974 to July 31, 1978.

Assistant District Attorney 1966-70. District Attorney 1971-73.

Mailing address: P.O. Box 2808, Oshkosh 54903-2808.

Office: Winnebago County Courthouse, 415 Jackson Drive, Oshkosh 54901-4751.

Telephone: (920) 236-4866.

CECI, Louis J. *(Reserve Judge, Wisconsin Circuit Court)* Retired. Assumed Reserve status, serves by assignment. Born New York New York Sept 10, 1927. Educated at Marquette University Ph.B. 1951 J.D. 1954. Member Phi Alpha Delta. Admitted to practice Wisconsin 1954 and U.S. District Courts Eastern 1954 and Western 1987 Districts of Wisconsin. In legal practice Milwaukee 1954-68. Judge, Wisconsin County Court Milwaukee County 1968-73. Judge, Wisconsin Circuit Court Br. 1 1974-82. Justice, Wisconsin Supreme Court April 26, 1982 to Sept 4, 1993.

Assistant City Attorney Milwaukee 1958-63. Legislator Wisconsin State Assembly 1965-66. Certified as Mediator for all civil cases by Florida Supreme Court. Member State Bar of Wisconsin and Waukesha County Bar Association. Lecturer Wisconsin Judicial Conferences 1970-79. Attended New York University Appellate Judges Institute of Judicial Administration 1982. Recipient Wisconsin Civic Recognition Award from PLAV Milwaukee 1970, Community Improvement Award 1971 and Community-Judiciary Award 1982 from Pompeii Men's Club Milwaukee and Good Government Award from Milwaukee Jaycees 1973. RM Third Class USN 1945-46. Lecturer Badger Boys State at Ripon 1961 and 1982-84. Assistant District Commissioner Boy Scouts of America Milwaukee 1962. Commander American Legion Post Milwaukee 1962-63.

Mailing address: 4737 Dolphin Cay Lane South, Suite 301, St. Petersburg, Florida 33711-4671.

CHRISTENSON, Karen E. *(Judge, Wisconsin Circuit Court Milwaukee Circuit)* Elected April 7, 1998 to term beginning Aug 1, 1998. Term expires Aug 1, 2004. Educated at University of Wisconsin B.A. M.A. and Marquette University J.D. Staff member Marquette Law Review. Admitted to practice Wisconsin 1978 and U.S. District Court Eastern District of Wisconsin 1978. In legal practice Milwaukee 1978-85.

Assistant District Attorney Milwaukee County 1985-98.

Office: 502 Safety Building, 821 West State Street, Milwaukee 53233.

Telephone: (414) 278-4563.

E-mail address: Karen.Christenson-@milwaukee.courts.state.wi.us

CLEVERT, Charles N., Jr. *(Judge, United States District Court Eastern District of Wisconsin)* Appointed to serve during good behavior by President Bill Clinton. Born Richmond Virginia. Educated at Davis & Elkins College B.A. 1969 and Georgetown University J.D. 1972. Admitted to practice Wisconsin 1972, U.S. District Court Eastern District of Wisconsin 1974 and U.S. Court of Appeals Seventh Circuit 1975. Former Judge and Chief Judge, United States Bankruptcy Court Eastern District of Wisconsin, appointed by U.S. District Court judges Nov 1977.

Assistant District Attorney Milwaukee County. Assistant U.S. Attorney Eastern District of Wisconsin. Special Assistant U.S. Attorney Northern District of Illinois. Instructor University of Wisconsin Law School 1987-89. Past President National Conference of Bankruptcy Judges. Board of Directors American Judicature Society and American Bankruptcy Institute. Member Wisconsin Association of Minority Attorneys, Seventh Circuit National (Judicial Council) and American (Chair Elect National Conference of Federal Trial Judges Judicial Administration Division) Bar Associations. Enjoys playing golf and bridge.

Office: 208 U.S. Courthouse, 517 East Wisconsin Avenue, Milwaukee 53202.

Telephone: (414) 297-1585.

CONEN, Jeffrey A. *(Judge, Wisconsin Circuit Court Milwaukee Circuit)*

Office: 310 Safety Building, 821 West State Street, Milwaukee 53233-1427.

Telephone: (414) 278-4470.

CONSTANTINE, Charles H. *(Judge, Wisconsin Circuit Court Racine Circuit)* Term expires July 31, 2008.

Office: 703 Racine County Courthouse, 730 Wisconsin Avenue, Racine 53403-1274.

Telephone: (262) 636-3132.

CONWAY, Dennis D. *(Reserve Judge, Wisconsin Circuit Court)* Appointed by Governor Martin J. Schreiber to term beginning Aug 8, 1977. Elected 1978, 1985, 1991 and 1997. Retired Sept 1, 2001. Assumed Reserve status, serves by assignment. Former Chief Judge, Administrative District Six (Chair Committee of Chief Judges 1996-98). Born Wisconsin Rapids Wisconsin July 22, 1936. Catholic. Educated at University of Notre Dame B.A. cum laude 1958 and University of Wisconsin LL.B. 1964. Admitted to practice Wisconsin 1964 and U.S. District Courts Eastern 1964 and Western 1964 Districts of Wisconsin. In legal practice Elkhorn 1964-67 and Wisconsin Rapids 1967-77.

Member Wisconsin Judicial Ethics Reform Committee 1985-91, Wisconsin Board of Bar Examiners 1985-91 (Chairman 1990-91), State Bar of Wisconsin, Wood County and American Bar Associations. U.S. Army Security Agency 1959-61. Member McMillan Library Board 1970-77 (President 1975-76). Member South Wood County Historical Corporation since 1967 (Presi-

CONWAY, DENNIS D.—*Continued*
dent 1974) and Riverview Hospital Association Board 1986-88 (Executive Board 1988).

Mailing address: 585 Third Street South, Wisconsin Rapids 54495-8095.

COOPER, Thomas R. *(Judge, Wisconsin Circuit Court Milwaukee Circuit)*

Office: 208 Milwaukee County Courthouse, 901 North Ninth Street, Milwaukee 53233-1425.

Telephone: (414) 278-4582.

COSTELLO, Dennis D. *(Reserve Judge, Wisconsin Circuit Court)* Elected April 6, 1978. Retired Aug 1, 1985. Served Racine County. Assumed Reserve status 1985, serves by assignment. Born Racine Wisconsin. Educated at Marquette University B.S. 1964 J.D.S. 1967. Admitted to practice Wisconsin 1967. In legal practice Racine 1967-78.

Corporation Counsel Door County Jan 1, 1988 to Oct 4, 1996 and Walworth County Oct 7, 1996 to Dec 31, 2002. Member The Association of Trial Lawyers of America, Wisconsin Association of Trial Judges (Board of Directors), Wisconsin Reserve Judges Association (Past President), Wisconsin Judicial Conference, State Bar of Wisconsin and American Bar Association. Lecturer Wisconsin Judicial Seminar. Graduate Wisconsin Judicial College and The National Judicial College. Enjoys scuba diving, skiing, windsurfing and fishing.

Mailing address: 342 Pierce Drive, Williams Bay 53191.

COUNSELL, Jon M. *(Judge, Wisconsin Circuit Court Clark Circuit)*

Office: Clark County Courthouse, 517 Court Street, Neillsville 54456-1904.

Telephone: (715) 743-5172.

CRABB, Barbara B. *(Chief Judge, United States District Court Western District of Wisconsin)* Magistrate 1971-79. Appointed Judge for life by President Jimmy Carter to term beginning Nov 26, 1979. Chief Judge 1980-96 and since June 26, 2001. Born Green Bay Wisconsin March 17, 1939. Educated at University of Wisconsin B.A. with honors 1960 J.D. with honors 1962. Editorial Board Wisconsin Law Review 1961-62. Member Kappa Alpha Theta, Phi Beta Kappa, Mortar Board and Order of the Coif. Admitted to practice Wisconsin 1963. Began legal practice Madison 1963.

Member State Bar of Wisconsin, Dane County and American Bar Associations.

Mailing address: P.O. Box 591, Madison 53701-0591.

Telephone: (608) 264-5447.

CRANE, William E. *(Reserve Judge, Wisconsin Circuit Court)* Retired. Assumed Reserve status, serves by assignment.

Mailing address: 2354 Wisconsin Street, Oshkosh 54901.

CROCKER, Stephen L. *(Magistrate Judge, United States District Court Western District of Wisconsin)* Appointed by U.S. District Court judges.

Mailing address: P.O. Box 591, Madison 53701-0591.

Telephone: (608) 264-5153.

CROOKS, N. Patrick *(Justice, Wisconsin Supreme Court)* Elected March 1996 to term beginning Aug 1, 1996. Term expires Aug 1, 2006. Born Green Bay Wisconsin May 16, 1938. Educated at St. Norbert College B.A. in History magna cum laude 1960 and University of Notre Dame J.D. 1963. Staff member 1961-63 and Book Review Editor 1962-63 Notre Dame Lawyer. Member Delta Epsilon Sigma and Alpha Phi Omega (Vice President). Listed in *Who's Who in American Colleges and Universities.* Admitted to practice Wisconsin, U.S. Supreme Court, U.S. Court of Military Appeals and U.S. District Court Eastern District of Wisconsin. In legal practice Green Bay 1963 and 1966-77. Judge, Wisconsin County Court Brown County Sept 16, 1977 to July 31, 1978, appointed by Governor Martin J. Schreiber. Judge, Wisconsin Circuit Court Brown Circuit Aug 1, 1978 to July 31, 1996.

With Internal Security Division Department of Justice June 1962 to Sept 1962. Author "Federal Rules of Criminal Procedure-Arrest—State Law Governs Propriety of Arrest Made Under Federal Warrant Where Federal Rules Are Silent" 36 Notre Dame Lawyer 432, 1961; Sections on Obscenity, Sunday Closing Laws and Clerical Privilege in "Church-State Religious Institutions and Values: A Legal Survey 1960-62" 37 Notre Dame Lawyer 649, 1962; "Management Prerogatives No Longer Include Right to Make Unilateral Decision to Subcontract" 38 Notre Dame Lawyer 288, 1963; Sections on Conferences, Motion Practice and Closing Arguments in "View from the Bench" State Bar of Wisconsin Oct 1988; and Sections on Waiver to Adult Court and Custody Hearing "Family, Probate and Juvenile Volume" 3 *Wisconsin Judicial Benchbook.* Instructor in Business Law University of Wisconsin-Green Bay 1970-72. Member Wisconsin Law Foundation (Board member and Executive Committee), Wisconsin Academy of Trial Lawyers, State Bar of Wisconsin, Brown County (Secretary-Treasurer 1971-73, President 1977), Dane County, Federal 1964-65 and American (Judicial Administration Division) Bar Associations. Recipient Human Rights Award from Baha'i Community Green Bay 1971, United Community Council Community Services Award for involvement in establishing Brown County Youth Home 1971, St. Norbert College Award for Distinguished Achievement in Social Science 1977, University of Notre Dame Award of the Year 1978, Service Award from Brown County Vandalism Prevention Association 1982, W. Heraly MacDonald Award from Brown County United Way 1983, St. Joseph Academy Award for Community Service 1989 and Alma Mater Award from St. Norbert College 1992. Captain U.S. Army JAGC 1963-66. Recipient Army Commendation Medal from Judge Advocate General 1966. Member Northeast Regional Criminal Justice Coordinating Council 1973-85 and St. Norbert College Priorities Campaign Steering Committee 1974. Civic Co-chairman Brotherhood Week 1968-69. Chairman County Heart Fund Campaign 1969, Brown County Community Relations Social Development Commission 1970-73, Legal Aid Inc. 1971-73 and Town of Allouez Ethics Board 1975-80. President St. Matthew Parish Council 1973-74, United Way of Brown County 1976-78 (Campaign Chairman 1973) and St. Joseph Academy School Board 1987-89. Member St. Norbert College President's Green Bay Task Force. Enjoys watching sporting events, boating and reading.

Mailing address: P.O. Box 1688, Madison 57301-1688.

Office: 16 East State Capitol, Madison 53702.

Telephone: (608) 266-1883.

CURLEY, Patricia S. *(Judge, Wisconsin Court of Appeals District One)* Assumed office 1996. Elected

CURLEY, PATRICIA S.—*Continued*

April 2002, current term expires July 31, 2008. Born Milwaukee Wisconsin Oct 25, 1946. Educated at Marquette University J.D. 1973. Judge, Wisconsin Circuit Court Milwaukee Circuit 1978-96.

Assistant District Attorney Milwaukee County 1973-78. Co-Author *Trial By Jury* Franklin Watts, Inc. and "Representing the Best Interests of Children: The Wisconsin Experience" Journal of American Academy of Matrimonial Lawyers. Author "The Ethics of Judicial Political and Campaign Practices" Wisconsin Lawyer. Fellow American Academy of Matrimonial Lawyers. Former Member Wisconsin Judicial Commission. Founding Member L. J. Foley Inns of Courts.

Office: 633 West Wisconsin Avenue, Suite 1400, Milwaukee 53203-1908.

Telephone: (414) 227-4682.

CURRAN, Thomas J. *(Senior Judge, United States District Court Eastern District of Wisconsin)* Appointed for life by President Ronald Reagan to term beginning 1983. Assumed Senior status Jan 1, 1997, serves by assignment. Born Mauston Wisconsin April 30, 1924. Educated at Marquette University B.N.S. 1945 LL.B. 1948. In legal practice Mauston 1948-83.

Office: 250 U.S. Courthouse, 517 East Wisconsin Avenue, Milwaukee 53202.

Telephone: (414) 297-4167.

CURRY, George S. *(Judge, Wisconsin Circuit Court Grant Circuit)*

Mailing address: P.O. Box 149, Lancaster 53813-0149.

Office: Grant County Courthouse, 130 West Maple Street, Lancaster 53813.

Telephone: (608) 723-6576.

DAHLBERG, Edwin C. *(Reserve Judge, Wisconsin Circuit Court)* Assumed office Aug 1, 1978. Elected 1984, 1990 and 1996. Retired. Assumed Reserve status, serves by assignment. Born Beloit Wisconsin April 22, 1923. Lutheran. Educated at University of Wisconsin Ph.B. 1947 LL.B. 1949. Admitted to practice Wisconsin 1949. Began legal practice Beloit 1950. Judge, Beloit Municipal Court 1960-63. Judge, Wisconsin County Court Rock County 1963-78.

Mailing address: 2226 Park Avenue, Beloit 53511.

DALEY, James P. *(Judge, Wisconsin Circuit Court Rock Circuit)* Term expires July 31, 2008.

Office: Rock County Courthouse, Fifth Floor, 51 South Main Street, Janesville 53545-3978.

Telephone: (608) 743-2261.

DAMON, John A. *(Judge, Wisconsin Circuit Court Trempealeau Circuit)* Elected April 1995 to term beginning Aug 1, 1995. Reelected 2001, current term expires July 31, 2007. Born Milwaukee Wisconsin June 7, 1954. Greek Orthodox. Educated at Macalester College B.A. 1976 and Marquette University J.D. 1983. Admitted to practice Wisconsin 1983 and U.S. District Courts Eastern 1983 and Western 1983 Districts of Wisconsin. In legal practice Osseo 1983-95.

City Attorney Osseo, Eleva and Strum 1985-95. Member Tri-County Bar Association.

Mailing address: P.O. Box 67, Whitehall 54773-0067.

Office: Trempealeau County Courthouse, Whitehall 54773.

Telephone: (715) 538-2311.

E-mail address: john.damon-@trempealeau.courts.state.wi.us

DAVIS, Mac *(Judge, Wisconsin Circuit Court Waukesha Circuit)* Elected April 1990 to term beginning Aug 1, 1990. Reelected April 1997 and 2003. Current term expires July 31, 2009. Born Washington D.C. April 5, 1952. Religious affiliation: United Church of Christ. Educated at University of Wisconsin at Madison B.A. with honors 1973 and University of Michigan J.D. cum laude 1976. Law Clerk to Hon. William E. Gramling, Wisconsin Circuit Court Waukesha County 1972. Admitted to practice Wisconsin 1976 and U.S. District Court Eastern District of Wisconsin 1977. In legal practice Waukesha 1976-90.

Member State Bar of Wisconsin and Waukesha County Bar Association. Instructor Wisconsin Judicial College and The National Judicial College. Member State Senate Wisconsin 1983-90. Member Kiwanis, United Way and Mental Health Association.

Office: Waukesha County Courthouse, 515 West Moreland Boulevard, Waukesha 53188-2428.

Telephone: (262) 548-7548.

DeCHAMBEAU, Robert A. *(Judge, Wisconsin Circuit Court Dane Circuit)* Elected April 1987 to term beginning May 18, 1987. Reelected April 1993 and April 1999. Current term expires July 31, 2005. Born Marinette Wisconsin Oct 11, 1938. Educated at University of Wisconsin-Oshkosh B.S. 1961 and University of Wisconsin Law School J.D. 1965. Admitted to practice Wisconsin 1965 and U.S. District Courts Eastern 1965 and Western 1965 Districts of Wisconsin. In legal practice Green Bay 1969-70 and Madison 1972-73.

Assistant District Attorney 1965-69 and Deputy District Attorney 1973-87. Instructor University of Wisconsin Law School 1980-95. Member State Bar of Wisconsin and Dane County Bar Association.

Office: 223 City-County Building, 210 Martin Luther King Jr. Blvd., Madison 53703-3343.

Telephone: (608) 266-4231.

DEETS, Darryl W. *(Judge, Wisconsin Circuit Court Manitowoc Circuit)* Appointed by Governor Tommy G. Thompson to term beginning April 4, 1988. Elected April 1989, 1995 and 2001. Current term expires July 31, 2007. Born Freeport Illinois May 19, 1951. Presbyterian. Educated at Illinois Wesleyan University B.A. magna cum laude 1973 and University of Illinois J.D. 1976. Recipient Trial Advocacy Award from International Academy of Trial Lawyers 1976. Admitted to practice Wisconsin 1976 and U.S. District Court Eastern District of Wisconsin 1976. In legal practice Manitowoc 1976-88.

Village Attorney Whitelaw 1980-88 and Valders 1981-88. City Attorney Two Rivers 1987-88. Member State Bar of Wisconsin and American Bar Association. Enjoys downhill and cross country skiing, playing tennis and biking.

Mailing address: P.O. Box 2000, Manitowoc 54221-2000.

Office: Manitowoc County Courthouse, 1010 South Eighth Street, Manitowoc 54220-5392.

Telephone: (920) 683-4042.

DEININGER, David G. *(Judge, Wisconsin Court of Appeals District Four)* Appointed by Governor Tommy G. Thompson June 30, 1996 to term beginning Aug 1,

DEININGER, DAVID G.—*Continued*

1996. Elected to term beginning Aug 1, 1997, current term expires July 31, 2003. Born Monroe Wisconsin July 9, 1947. Protestant. Educated at U.S. Naval Academy B.S. with honors 1969 and University of Wisconsin Law School J.D. with honors 1978. Member Order of the Coif. Admitted to practice Illinois 1978, Wisconsin 1978 and U.S. District Court Western District of Wisconsin 1978. In legal practice Monroe Wisconsin 1978-94. Judge, Wisconsin Circuit Court Green Circuit 1994-96.

Corporation Counsel Green County 1980-84. Important Decisions: Jackson v. Benson (constitutionality of private school choice legislation) 213 Wis. 2d 1, 570 N.W.2d 407 (Ct. App.) 1997; and Dairyland Greyhound Park v. McCallum (Indian tribes not indispensable parties in suit to enjoin governor from extending gaming compacts) 259 Wis.2d 2002. Instructor Blackhawk Technical College 1982-85 and in Municipal Law General Practice University of Wisconsin Law School 1985-86. Member State Bar of Wisconsin. Lieutenant USN 1969-75. Member Wisconsin State Assembly 1986-94 (Chair Minority Caucus and Ranking Member Judiciary Committee). Member Monroe Theater Guild. Enjoys boating, cross-country skiing and bridge.

Office: 10 East Doty Street, Suite 700, Madison 53703-3330.

Telephone: (608) 266-9338.

Fax: (608) 267-0432

DELFORGE, Richard D. *(Judge, Wisconsin Circuit Court Oconto Circuit)*

Office: Oconto County Courthouse, 301 Washington Street, Oconto 54153-1621.

Telephone: (920) 834-6837.

Des JARDINS, John A. *(Judge, Wisconsin Circuit Court Outagamie Circuit)*

Office: Justice Center, 320 South Walnut Street, Appleton 54911-5991.

Telephone: (920) 832-4727.

DIETZ, Richard J. *(Judge, Wisconsin Circuit Court Brown Circuit)* Appointed by Governor Tommy G. Thompson to term beginning Aug 1, 1988. Elected 1989, 1995 and 2001. Current term expires July 31, 2007. Born Milwaukee Wisconsin 1944. Educated at Marquette University B.A. 1967 J.D. 1969. Admitted to practice Wisconsin 1969 and U.S. District Court Eastern District of Wisconsin 1969. In legal practice Green Bay 1972-78 and DePere 1978-88.

Assistant District Attorney Brown County 1969-72. Member Wisconsin Juvenile Jury Instructions Committee 1994-98 and Wisconsin Civil Jury Instructions Committee since 1998. Member Robert J. Parins Chapter American Inns of Court and State Bar of Wisconsin. Recipient Respect for Law Award from Optimist Club 1993.

Mailing address: P.O. Box 23600, Green Bay 54305-3600.

Office: Brown County Courthouse, 100 South Jefferson Street, Green Bay 54301.

Telephone: (920) 448-4121.

DILLON, Daniel T. *(Judge, Wisconsin Circuit Court Rock Circuit)*

Office: Rock County Courthouse, Fifth Floor, 51 South Main Street, Janesville 53545-3978.

Telephone: (608) 743-2242.

DILTZ, Peter C. *(Judge, Wisconsin Circuit Court Door Circuit)* Elected April 5, 1994 to term beginning Aug 1, 1994. Reelected 2000, current term expires July 31, 2006. Born Evanston Illinois June 7, 1945. Educated at University of Arizona B.A. 1968 and University of Wisconsin J.D. 1972. Admitted to practice Wisconsin 1972. In legal practice Sister Bay 1972-74 and Sturgeon Bay 1974-94. Commissioner Family Court Door County 1976-94.

Member 1976-94 and President 1993 Wisconsin Family Court Commissioners Association. Member Wisconsin Trial Judges Association. Graduate Wisconsin Judicial College 1994 and General Jurisdiction Course The National Judicial College 1995. USAR 1969-75. President Door County Chamber of Commerce 1993-94 and Door Community Auditorium 2000-01. Enjoys kayaking, boating, traveling and reading.

Mailing address: P.O. Box 670, Sturgeon Bay 54235-0670.

Office: Door County Courthouse, 421 Nebraska Street, Sturgeon Bay 54235.

Telephone: (920) 746-2280.

DiMOTTO, Jean W. *(Judge, Wisconsin Circuit Court Milwaukee Circuit)* Elected to term beginning Aug 1, 1997.

Office: 423 Safety Building, 821 West State Street, Milwaukee 53233-1427.

Telephone: (414) 278-4523.

DiMOTTO, John J. *(Judge, Wisconsin Circuit Court Milwaukee Circuit)* Elected to term beginning Aug 1, 1990. Reelected 1996 and April 2002. Current term expires July 31, 2008. Born Milwaukee Wisconsin Feb 9, 1950. Roman Catholic. Educated at Marquette University B.A. with honors 1972 and University of Wisconsin J.D. 1974. Member Phi Delta Phi. Admitted to practice Wisconsin 1975 and U.S. District Courts Western 1975 and Eastern 1984 Districts of Wisconsin.

Assistant District Attorney Milwaukee County 1975-90. Member Justinian Law Society, Association for Women Lawyers, Milwaukee and American Bar Associations. Attended Wisconsin Judicial College Aug 1990. Instructor in Sentencing Wisconsin Judicial College Aug 1991 and 1992. Recipient Justice for Women Award from Milwaukee Women's Center May 1992. Member Milwaukee Chapter UNICO. Enjoys reading and sports.

Office: 512 Milwaukee County Courthouse, 901 North Ninth Street, Milwaukee 53233-1425.

Telephone: (414) 278-4366.

DONALD, M. Joseph *(Judge, Wisconsin Circuit Court Milwaukee Circuit)*

Office: 620 Safety Building, 821 West State Street, Milwaukee 53233-1427.

Telephone: (414) 278-4775.

DONEGAN, Thomas P. *(Judge, Wisconsin Circuit Court Milwaukee Circuit)*

Office: 402 Milwaukee County Courthouse, 901 North Ninth Street, Milwaukee 53233-1425.

Telephone: (414) 278-5291.

DREYFUS, Lee S. *(Judge, Wisconsin Circuit Court Waukesha Circuit)* Term expires July 31, 2008.

Office: Waukesha County Courthouse, 515 West Moreland Boulevard, Waukesha 53188-2428.

Telephone: (262) 548-7541.

DUFFY, William J. *(Reserve Judge, Wisconsin Circuit Court)* Elected to term beginning June 4, 1968. Reelected 1974, 1980 and 1986. Chief Judge Administrative District Eight 1982-88. Retired Dec 1991. Assumed Reserve status, serves by assignment. Born North Branch Minnesota Oct 29, 1916. Catholic. Educated at St. Norbert College B.A. 1938 and University of Wisconsin LL.B. 1941. Admitted to practice Wisconsin 1941 and U.S. Supreme Court 1959. Began legal practice Green Bay 1945.

Member Wisconsin Assembly 1949-51. Instructor in Labor Law ad hoc University of Wisconsin-Green Bay 1972-77. Member State Bar of Wisconsin and American Bar Association. Captain USAAC 1941-45. Democrat. First President Green Bay Voluntary Commission on Human Rights. Member Governor's Commission on Human Rights 1959-65.

Mailing address: 1181 Division Street, Green Bay 54303.

DUGAN, Timothy G. *(Judge, Wisconsin Circuit Court Milwaukee Circuit)*

Office: 404 Milwaukee County Courthouse, 901 North Ninth Street, Milwaukee 53233-1425.

Telephone: (414) 278-4496.

DUKET, Tim A. *(Judge, Wisconsin Circuit Court Marinette Circuit)* Elected to term beginning Aug 1, 1990. Reelected 1996 and April 2002. Current term expires July 31, 2008. Born Marinette Wisconsin Oct 14, 1954. Educated at University of Wisconsin-Eau Claire B.A. with honors 1977 and University of Wisconsin-Madison J.D. 1979. Admitted to practice Wisconsin 1980.

District Attorney Marinette County 1981-90.

Office: Marinette County Courthouse, 1926 Hall Avenue, Marinette 54143-1717.

Telephone: (715) 732-7470.

DWYER, Michael J. *(Judge, Wisconsin Circuit Court Milwaukee Circuit)* Elected to term beginning Aug 1, 1997. Reelected 2003, current term expires July 31, 2009. Born Milwaukee Wisconsin June 12, 1950. Educated at University of Wisconsin B.A. 1972 and Georgetown University Law Center J.D. 1975. Admitted to practice Wisconsin 1975 and U.S. District Court Eastern District of Wisconsin 1975. In legal practice Milwaukee 1975-97.

Member National Council of Juvenile and Family Court Judges, State Bar of Wisconsin and Milwaukee Bar Association.

Office: 508 Milwaukee County Courthouse, 901 North Ninth Street, Milwaukee 53233-1425.

Telephone: (414) 278-4488.

E-mail address: Michael.Dwyer-@milwaukee.courts.state.wi.us

DYER, Dee Rule *(Judge, Wisconsin Circuit Court Outagamie Circuit)*

Office: Justice Center, 320 South Walnut Street, Appleton 54911-5991.

Telephone: (920) 832-6038.

DYKE, William D. *(Judge, Wisconsin Circuit Court Iowa Circuit)* Assumed office Jan 2, 1997. Elected 1998, current term expires July 31, 2004. Born Princeton Illinois April 25, 1930. Educated at DePauw University B.A. 1953 and University of Wisconsin-Madison J.D. 1960. Admitted to practice Wisconsin 1960. Began legal practice Jefferson 1960.

Member Wisconsin Law Foundation and State Bar of Wisconsin. Mayor Madison 1969-73.

Office: Iowa County Courthouse, 222 North Iowa Street, Dodgeville 53533-1548.

Telephone: (608) 935-0347.

DYKMAN, Charles P. *(Judge, Wisconsin Court of Appeals District Four)* Elected April 1978 to term beginning Aug 1, 1978. Reelected 1980, 1986, 1992 and 1998. Current term expires 2004. Former Presiding Judge. Educated at University of Wisconsin-Madison B.S. 1961 J.D. 1965. In legal practice 1965-78.

Member Legal Association for Women, Wisconsin Judicial Conference (Commission on Judicial Elections and Ethics, Executive Committee, Planning Committee), Wisconsin Judicial Commission, National Association of Women Judges, Dane County and Seventh Circuit Bar Associations. Teaches seed starting and canning classes. Enjoys sailing and gardening.

Office: 10 East Doty Street, Suite 700, Madison 53703-3397.

Telephone: (608) 266-9362.

EATON, Robert E. *(Judge, Wisconsin Circuit Court Ashland Circuit)*

Office: Ashland County Courthouse, 201 Main Street West, Ashland 54806-1652.

Telephone: (715) 682-7013.

EBERT, Steven D. *(Judge, Wisconsin Circuit Court Dane Circuit)*

Office: 214 City-County Building, 210 Martin Luther King Jr. Blvd., Madison 53703.

Telephone: (608) 266-4351.

EHLERS, D. Todd *(Judge, Wisconsin Circuit Court Door Circuit)* Commissioner 1998-2000. Elected Judge to term beginning Aug 1, 2000. Born Sturgeon Bay Wisconsin Sept 13, 1957. Educated at St. Norbert College B.A. cum laude 1978 and Marquette University J.D. 1982. Admitted to practice Wisconsin 1982 and U.S. District Courts Eastern 1982 and Western 1982 Districts of Wisconsin. In legal practice Marshfield 1982-84 and Sturgeon Bay 1984-2000.

Assistant Corporate Counsel Door County 1984-86. Member Wisconsin Trial Judges Association, State Bar of Wisconsin, Door-Kewaunee and Door County Bar Associations.

Mailing address: P.O. Box 670, Sturgeon Bay 54235.

Office: 421 Nebraska Street, Sturgeon Bay 54235.

Telephone: (920) 746-2204.

Fax: (920) 746-2470

EICH, William F. *(Reserve Judge, Wisconsin Circuit Court)* Retired. Assumed Reserve status, serves by assignment. Born Chicago Illinois Aug 14, 1938. Educated at Beloit College B.A. 1960 and University of Wisconsin LL.B. 1963. Law Clerk to Wisconsin Supreme Court 1963-64. Admitted to practice Wisconsin 1963. In legal practice Madison 1964-65. Judge, Wisconsin County Court Dane County 1975-78. Judge, Wisconsin Circuit Court Dane Circuit 1978-85. Former Judge, Wisconsin Court of Appeals District Four, appointed by Governor Tommy G. Thompson to term beginning April 1995. Former Chief Judge, Wisconsin Court of Appeals.

Assistant Attorney General and Deputy Attorney General Wisconsin 1965-71. Chairman Wisconsin Public

EICH, WILLIAM F.—*Continued*
Service Commission 1971-75. Author various law review articles. Lecturer University of Wisconsin School of Law. Member State Bar of Wisconsin.
Mailing address: 840 Farwell Drive, Madison 53704.

EISENBERG, Russell A. *(Chief Judge, United States Bankruptcy Court Eastern District of Wisconsin)* Chief Judge since June 1, 2000.
Office: 162 U.S. Courthouse, 517 East Wisconsin Avenue, Milwaukee 53202.
Telephone: (414) 297-3291.

ENGLISH, Dale L. *(Judge, Wisconsin Circuit Court Fond du Lac Circuit)* Elected March 19, 1996 to term beginning Aug 1, 1996. Reelected April 2002, current term expires July 31, 2008. Born Madison Wisconsin Nov 12, 1956. Lutheran. Educated at Luther College B.A. cum laude 1979 and Marquette University Law School J.D. 1982. Member Omicron Delta Epsilon. Admitted to practice Wisconsin 1982, U.S. District Courts Eastern 1982 and Western 1982 Districts of Wisconsin, U.S. Court of Appeals Seventh Circuit 1986 and U.S. Supreme Court 1988. In legal practice Fond du Lac 1982-94 and Appleton 1994-96.
Important Decision: State ex rel. Peckham v. Krenke 229 Wis. 2d 778 Wis. Ct. App. 1999. Member Employee Ethics Advisory Committee 1996-97. Member Wisconsin Trial Judges Association, American Judges Association, State Bar of Wisconsin, Fond du Lac County (Treasurer 1984-85, President Elect 2000, President 2001) and American (National Conference of State Trial Judges Judicial Administration Division since 1997) Bar Associations. Participated in Judicial Exchange Program 1999. Listed in *Who's Who in American Law* 1986-87, 1996-97 and 1998-99. Board of Directors 1983-85, Legal Counsel 1983-85, State Director 1983-84 Fond du Lac Jaycees. Volunteer Big Brothers/Big Sisters of Fond du Lac 1983-87. Member Planning Commission City of Fond du Lac 1986-95. Board of Directors 1988-95 and 1997-2001, Secretary 1989, Vice President 1990-91, President Elect 1992, President 1993, Past President 1994 Fond du Lac YMCA. Board of Directors D.A.R.E. of Fond du Lac, Inc. 1990-96. Volunteer coach youth baseball and football since 1989. Enjoys weight training, softball, tennis, sports, music and family activities.
Mailing address: P.O. Box 1355, Fond du Lac 54936-1355.
Office: City-County Government Center, 160 South Macy Street, Fond du Lac 54935.
Telephone: (920) 929-3072.
Fax: (920) 929-3933

ERICKSON, James R. *(Reserve Judge, Wisconsin Circuit Court)* Elected to term beginning 1984. Reelected 1990 and 1996. Retired. Assumed Reserve status, serves by assignment.
Mailing address: P.O. Box 400, Balsam Lake 54810-9071.

ERWIN, Jackie R. *(Judge, Wisconsin Circuit Court Jefferson Circuit)*
Office: Jefferson County Courthouse, 320 South Main Street, Jefferson 53549-1799.
Telephone: (920) 674-7210.

EVENSON, James *(Judge, Wisconsin Circuit Court Sauk Circuit)* Elected April 1, 1986 to term beginning Aug 1, 1986. Reelected 1992 and 1998. Current term expires July 31, 2004. Currently serves as Chief Judge Administrative District Six. Born Baraboo Wisconsin April 14, 1946. Educated at University of Wisconsin-Madison B.A. 1969 J.D. 1973. Admitted to practice Wisconsin 1973. In legal practice Baraboo 1973-86.
Office: Sauk County Courthouse, 515 Oak Street, Baraboo 53913-2496.
Telephone: (608) 355-3218.

FARAGHER, Patrick J. *(Judge, Wisconsin Circuit Court Washington Circuit)*
Mailing address: P.O. Box 1986, West Bend 53095-7986.
Office: Washington County Courthouse, 432 East Washington Street, West Bend 53095-2500.
Telephone: (262) 335-4348.

FARNUM, Mark J., Jr. *(Reserve Judge, Wisconsin Circuit Court)* Assumed office Aug 1, 1978. Elected 1985. Retired. Assumed Reserve status, serves by assignment. Born Janesville Wisconsin Sept 17, 1926. Catholic. Educated at Milton College B.S. 1949 and University of Wisconsin LL.B. 1952. Admitted to practice Wisconsin 1952. Began legal practice Janesville 1952. Judge, Wisconsin County Court Rock County July 1, 1962 to July 31, 1978.
Assistant District Attorney 1954-58 and District Attorney 1958-62 Rock County. Member Wisconsin Judicial Council (Chairman Committee Drafting Wisconsin Code of Evidence, Wisconsin Video Tape Rule and Wisconsin Criminal Code 1972), Wisconsin Board of Criminal Court Judges, Wisconsin Board of County Court Judges since 1968, Wisconsin Civil Jury Instructions Committee since 1979, Wisconsin Judicial Commission, State Bar of Wisconsin and Rock County Bar Association. Radioman Second Class USN 1944-46. Member local fraternal organizations. Enjoys golf.
Mailing address: 3005 South Lexington Court, Beloit 53511.

FIEDLER, Patrick J. *(Judge, Wisconsin Circuit Court Dane Circuit)* Appointed by Governor Tommy G. Thompson to term beginning Nov 24, 1993. Elected 1994 and 2000. Current term expires July 31, 2006. Born Milwaukee Wisconsin July 24, 1953. Roman Catholic. Educated at University of Wisconsin-Milwaukee B.B.A. 1977 and Marquette University J.D. 1980. Member Tau Epsilon Rho. Admitted to practice Wisconsin 1980, U.S. District Courts Eastern 1980 and Western 1980 Districts of Wisconsin and U.S. Court of Appeals Seventh Circuit 1987. In legal practice Dodgeville 1985-87.
Assistant District Attorney Waukesha 1980-84. U.S. Attorney Western District of Wisconsin 1987-91. Member Wisconsin Trial Judges Association, State Bar of Wisconsin and Dane County Bar Association. Member Kiwanis.
Office: 316 City-County Building, 210 Martin Luther King Jr. Blvd., Madison 53703.
Telephone: (608) 266-4325.

FINE, Ralph Adam *(Judge, Wisconsin Court of Appeals District One)* Assumed office 1988. Elected to subsequent terms. Born 1941. Educated at Tufts University A.B. 1962 and Columbia University School of Law LL.B. 1965. Law Clerk to U.S. District Court District of New York. Admitted to practice New York 1965, Wisconsin 1973, U.S. Supreme Court, U.S. Courts of Appeals Third, Fourth, Fifth, Sixth, Seventh, Ninth, Tenth

FINE, RALPH ADAM—*Continued*

and District of Columbia Circuits and U.S. District Courts Eastern and Southern Districts of New York and Eastern and Western Districts of Wisconsin. Judge, Wisconsin Circuit Court Milwaukee Circuit 1979-88.

Appellate Attorney Civil Division U.S. Department of Justice Washington D.C. Author *Mary Jane versus Pennsylvania* McCall 1970; *The Great Drug Deception* Stein & Day 1972; *Escape of the Guilty* Dodd, Mead & Co. 1986; *The "How-to-Win Trial" Manual* Juris 1998; *The "How-to-Win" Appeal Manual* Juris 2000; and *Fine's Wisconsin Evidence* Juris supplemented annually. Contributor chapter on the Eighth Amendment *A Time for Choices* First Amendment Congress 1991; *Emerging Problems Under the Federal Rules of Evidence* West 2nd ed. 1991 and Lexis 3rd ed. 1998; and *Criminal Justice?* edited by Robert James Bidinotto, Foundation for Economic Education 1994-95. Reporter *Evidence in America* Lexis. Professorial Lecturer on Law and Trial Advocacy George Washington University National Law Center Fall 1992. Member The American Law Institute. Presiding Judge PBS *Frontline* "Inside the Jury Room" (first time jury deliberations in a criminal trial were filmed and broadcast). Recipient Hon. William J. Brennan, Jr., Award from University of Virginia School of Law Jan 1995. Television show host *A Fine Point* 1975-78 and Investigative reporter WITI-TV May 1974 to Dec 1975.

Office: 633 West Wisconsin Avenue, Suite 1400, Milwaukee 53203-1908.

Telephone: (414) 227-4683.

FINN, John V. *(Judge, Wisconsin Circuit Court Portage Circuit)* Appointed by Governor Tommy G. Thompson to term beginning April 11, 1988. Elected April 1989, 1995 and 2001. Current term expires July 31, 2007. Born New York New York July 20, 1945. Educated at Marquette University B.A. 1967 and St. John's University School of Law J.D. 1970. Admitted to practice New York 1970 and Wisconsin 1976. In legal practice New York New York 1975-76 and Stevens Point Wisconsin 1976-88.

Assistant District Attorney Bronx 1970-74. Instructor University of Wisconsin-Stevens Point 1977-81. Member State Bar of Wisconsin and Portage County Bar Association.

Office: Portage County Courthouse, 1516 Church Street, Stevens Point 54481-3598.

Telephone: (715) 346-1360.

FIORENZA, Clare L. *(Judge, Wisconsin Circuit Court Milwaukee Circuit)*

Office: 113 Safety Building, 821 West State Street, Milwaukee 53233-1427.

Telephone: (414) 278-4486.

FIORENZA, John A. *(Reserve Judge, Wisconsin Circuit Court)* Retired. Assumed Reserve status, serves by assignment. Born Rockford Illinois March 13, 1932. Educated at Marquette University B.S. 1953 J.D. 1956. Member St. Thomas More Society. Admitted to practice Wisconsin, U.S. District Courts Eastern and Western Districts of Wisconsin, U.S. Court of Appeals Seventh Circuit, U.S. Tax Court and U.S. Supreme Court. In legal practice 1956-66 and since 1972 Milwaukee County. Judge, Milwaukee County Court, appointed by Governor Warren Perley Knowles to term beginning June 1966 to 1972. Former Court Commissioner, Milwaukee County.

Referee Board of Attorneys Professional Responsibility. Member American Arbitration Association, American Justinian Society of Jurists, Board of Milwaukee County Judges (Former Chairman), American Judicature Society, Milwaukee Bar Association Foundation, Inc. (Director 1987-94, President 1993-94), State Bar of Wisconsin (Board of Governors 1975-78, 1982-85, 1987-90 and 1992-96), Milwaukee (President 1981-82) and American Bar Associations. Attended National College of State Trial Judges 1967. Former Director Wisconsin Judicial College. Recipient Distinguished Law Alumnus Award from Marquette University Law School Alumni Association 1992, Award of Excellence from Marquette Club of Milwaukee 1993 and Distinguished Service Award from Brown Deer Jaycees. Named Alumnus of the Year by Marquette University 1995. Director 1986-91 and President 1988-90 Marquette National Alumni Association. Past President and Director Wisconsin Club. Past President Brown Deer Jaycees. Founder and Director Woolsack Society Marquette University Law School.

Mailing address: 10532 North Port Washington Road, Mequon 53092.

Telephone: (262) 240-4612.

Fax: (262) 240-4414

FISHER, Michael S. *(Judge, Wisconsin Circuit Court Kenosha Circuit)* Assumed office Aug 1, 1978. Elected to subsequent terms. Current term expires July 31, 2005. Former Judge, Wisconsin County Court Kenosha County.

Office: 117 Kenosha County Courthouse, 912 56th Street, Kenosha 53140-3747.

Telephone: (262) 653-2791.

FLANAGAN, David T. *(Judge, Wisconsin Circuit Court Dane Circuit)*

Office: 313 City-County Building, 210 Martin Luther King Jr. Boulevard, Madison 53703.

Telephone: (608) 266-4194.

FLANAGAN, Mel *(Judge, Wisconsin Circuit Court Milwaukee Circuit)* Appointed by Governor Tommy G. Thompson to term beginning March 1993. Elected April 1994 and 2000. Current term expires July 31, 2006. Born St. Louis Missouri March 11, 1952. Educated at University of Hawaii B.A. 1980 and University of Wisconsin J.D. 1984. Admitted to practice Wisconsin 1984.

Assistant District Attorney Milwaukee 1984-86 and 1988-93. Deputy District Attorney Madison 1986-88. Member Association for Women Lawyers, National Association of Women Judges, State Bar of Wisconsin and Milwaukee Bar Association.

Office: 413 Milwaukee County Courthouse, 901 North Ninth Street, Milwaukee 53233-1425.

Telephone: (414) 278-4474.

FLANCHER, Faye M. *(Judge, Wisconsin Circuit Court Racine Circuit)* Appointed by Governor Scott McCallum to term beginning Feb 6, 2002. Elected April 2003, current term expires July 31, 2009.

Office: 703 Racine County Courthouse, 730 Wisconsin Avenue, Racine 53403-1274.

Telephone: (262) 636-3435.

FLEISHAUER, Frederic W. *(Judge, Wisconsin Circuit Court Portage Circuit)* Elected to term beginning Jan 5, 1981. Reelected 1986, 1992 and 1998. Current term expires July 31, 2004. Born Baraboo Wisconsin Aug 4, 1944. Lutheran. Member Trinity Lutheran

FLEISHAUER, FREDERIC W.—*Continued*

Church Stevens Point (Past President). Educated at University of Wisconsin-Madison B.A. with honors 1966 J.D. 1973. Admitted to practice Wisconsin 1973 and U.S. District Courts Western 1973 and Eastern 1977 Districts of Wisconsin. In legal practice Madison 1973-74 and Stevens Point 1977-78.

Assistant District Attorney 1974-77, Condemnation Commissioner 1977-78 and District Attorney 1978-81 Portage County. Guest Lecturer on Natural Resources Law Enforcement 1978-80 and Political Science and Sociology 1981-91 University of Wisconsin-Stevens Point. Instructor Midstate Technical Institute 1977-78. Member Criminal Jury Instructions Committee, Supreme Court Committee on Judicial Ethics Code, Circuit Court Automation Project, Judicial Education Committee of Supreme Court, State Bar of Wisconsin, Portage County and American Bar Associations. Lieutenant USNR 1966-69. Past President Community Industries, Inc. (vocational rehabilitation center). Past Chairman Portage County Highway Safety Commission. Member Izaak Walton League, Health Committee Stevens Point Area Foundation and University of Wisconsin-Stevens Point Academy of Letters and Science (Past President). Enjoys breeding and raising Spanish Arabian horses, hunting, fishing, gardening and photography.

Office: Portage County Courthouse, 1516 Church Street, Stevens Point 54481-3598.

Telephone: (715) 346-1355.

FLUGAUR, Thomas T. *(Judge, Wisconsin Circuit Court Portage Circuit)*

Office: Portage County Courthouse, 1516 Church Street, Stevens Point 54481-3598.

Telephone: (715) 346-1244.

FLYNN, Dennis J. *(Reserve Judge, Wisconsin Circuit Court)* Assumed office Aug 1, 1978. Elected to subsequent terms. Retired Jan 1, 2002. Assumed Reserve status, serves by assignment. Born Racine Wisconsin Jan 14, 1942. Roman Catholic. Educated at Georgetown School of Foreign Service B.S.F.S. 1964 and Marquette University 1967. Admitted to practice Wisconsin, U.S. District Court Eastern District of Wisconsin 1967, U.S. Supreme Court 1967 and U.S. Court of Appeals Seventh Circuit 1972. Began legal practice Racine 1967. Judge, Wisconsin County Court Racine County July 1, 1976 to July 31, 1978.

Racine County Corporation Counsel 1971-76. Member Racine County Bar Association (Board of Governors 1974-76).

Mailing address: 5535 River Hills Road, Racine 53403.

FOLEY, Christopher R. *(Judge, Wisconsin Circuit Court Milwaukee Circuit)* Term expires July 31, 2004.

Office: 1410 Children's Court Center, 10201 West Watertown Plank Road, Milwaukee 53226-3532.

Telephone: (414) 454-4216.

FOLEY, John F. *(Reserve Judge, Wisconsin Circuit Court)* Retired. Assumed Reserve status, serves by assignment.

Mailing address: 609 North 115th Street, Milwaukee 53226.

FOSTER, Kathryn W. *(Judge, Wisconsin Circuit Court Waukesha Circuit)* Currently serves as Chief Judge Administrative District Three.

Office: Waukesha County Courthouse, 515 West Moreland Boulevard, Waukesha 53188-2428.

Telephone: (262) 548-7210.

FOUST, C. William *(Judge, Wisconsin Circuit Court Dane Circuit)*

Office: 207 City-County Building, 210 Martin Luther King Jr. Blvd., Madison 53703.

Telephone: (608) 266-4200.

FOX, Douglas T. *(Judge, Wisconsin Circuit Court Price Circuit)* Elected to term beginning Aug 1, 1984. Reelected 1990, 1996 and April 2002. Current term expires July 31, 2008. Born Phillips Wisconsin Sept 24, 1952. Presbyterian. Educated at University of Wisconsin-Milwaukee B.A. magna cum laude 1975 J.D. 1978. Member Phi Beta Kappa and Phi Kappa Phi. Admitted to practice Wisconsin 1978. In legal practice Phillips 1978-84. Commissioner, Price County Court 1982-84.

Member District Eleven Professional Responsibility Committee 1983-85, Wisconsin Judicial Conference (Chairman Probate and Mental Health Section 1990-91), Wisconsin Judicial Council (ad hoc Committee on Family Court Commissioners 1990), State Bar of Wisconsin and Price-Taylor County Bar Association (Treasurer 1981-82, Secretary 1982-84). Attended Wisconsin Judicial College 1984 and General Jurisdiction Course The National Judicial College 1988. Board of Trustees Phillips Public Library 1983-93. Vice Chairman Headwaters District Boy Scouts of America 1986-88. Member Masons and MENSA. Enjoys tree farming, hunting and fishing.

Office: Price County Courthouse, 126 Cherry Street, Phillips 54555-1249.

Telephone: (715) 339-3315.

FRANKE, John *(Judge, Wisconsin Circuit Court Milwaukee Circuit)* Elected to term beginning Aug 1, 1987. Reelected 1993 and 1999. Current term expires July 31, 2005.

Office: G55-A Criminal Justice Facility, 949 North Ninth Street, Milwaukee 53233-1425.

Telephone: (414) 278-4955.

FROEHLICH, Harold V. *(Judge, Wisconsin Circuit Court Outagamie Circuit)* Assumed office Sept 1981. Elected to term beginning Aug 1, 1982. Reelected 1988, 1994 and 2000. Current term expires July 31, 2006. Chief Judge Administrative District Eight 1988-94. Born Appleton Wisconsin May 12, 1932. Educated at University of Wisconsin B.B.A. in Accounting 1959 B.B.L. 1962. Member Phi Alpha Delta and Phi Kappa Phi. Admitted to practice Wisconsin 1962. In legal practice 1962-81. Commissioner Family Court 1975-78.

Member American Institute of Certified Public Accountants 1962-97. Former Member Wisconsin Institute of Certified Public Accountants. Secretary Wisconsin Judicial Conference 1991-97. Chair State Committee of Chief Judges 1992-94. Member Wisconsin Trial Judges Association (Secretary 1985-91, President 1991-2000), American Judges Association (Chair Budget Committee since 1999, Member Executive Committee since 1999, Treasurer since 1999), State Bar of Wisconsin, Outagamie County and American Bar Associations. Attended numerous seminars State Bar of Wisconsin 1962-80. Named one of Wisconsin's Five Outstanding Men by

FROEHLICH, HAROLD V.—*Continued*

Wisconsin Jaycees and Wisconsin Newsmaker of the Year 1969. Listed in *Who's Who in the Midwest* and *Who's Who in America.* Petty Officer First Class USN 1951-55. Part-time bakery employee 1947-48. Millworker Fox Valley Knitting Mill 1949-50 (part-time) and Kimberly-Clark Corporation 1950-51. Employee Ruschlein & Stortroen C.P.A. 1958-62. CPA Wisconsin since 1962. Real Estate Broker Wisconsin since 1965. Vice President Black Creek Improvement Corporation since 1973 and Development of Black Creek, Inc. 1980-86. Member State Assembly Wisconsin 1963-73 (Speaker 1965-71, Republican Minority Leader 1971-73). Member U.S. House of Representatives (Wisconsin) 1973-75. Delegate to State Republican Conventions 1956-80 and National Republican Conventions 1972-76. Vice Chairman 1968-69 and Chairman 1969-70 Midwest Council of State Governments. Presidential Elector 1968 and 1972. Member Appleton's 19th Ward Republican Precinct Committee 1955-63, Outagamie County Young Republican Organization 1955-62 (Chairman, Treasurer 1959-60), Outagamie County Republican Party 1955-81 (Chairman Statutory Committee 1958-60), Eighth District Young Republican Organization 1957-59 (Chairman 1957-59) and Executive Committee Wisconsin Republican Party 1965-69 and 1975-76. Chairman Eighth District Republican Party 1975-76. Board of Regents Fox Valley Lutheran High School 1990-93. Former Member Optimist Club, Lions Club and Jaycees. Member American Legion, VFW and Mount Olive Evangelical Lutheran Church (Past Congregational President).

Office: Justice Center, 320 South Walnut Street, Appleton 54911-5991.

Telephone: (920) 832-5602.

GABLEMAN, Michael J. *(Judge, Wisconsin Circuit Court Burnett Circuit)* Appointed by Governor Scott McCallum to term beginning Sept 2002. Elected April 2003.

Mailing address: P.O. Box 115, Siren 54872-9043.

Office: Government Center, 7410 County Road K, Siren 54872.

Telephone: (715) 349-2149.

GABLER, William M. *(Judge, Wisconsin Circuit Court Eau Claire Circuit)*

Office: Eau Claire County Courthouse, 721 Oxford Avenue, Eau Claire 54703-5481.

Telephone: (715) 839-4812.

GAGE, Michael W. *(Judge, Wisconsin Circuit Court Outagamie Circuit)* Elected to term beginning Aug 1, 1985. Reelected 1991, 1997 and 2003. Current term expires July 31, 2009. Born Appleton Wisconsin June 19, 1949. Catholic. Educated at Princeton University B.A. 1974 and William Mitchell College of Law J.D. 1978. Admitted to practice Wisconsin 1978. In legal practice Kaukauna 1978-80.

District Attorney Outagamie County Jan 1981 to June 1985. Member State Bar of Wisconsin and American Bar Association.

Office: Justice Center, 320 South Walnut Street, Appleton 54911-5991.

Telephone: (920) 832-1550.

GaleWYRICK, Molly E. *(Judge, Wisconsin Circuit Court Polk Circuit)* Elected April 2002 to term beginning Aug 1, 2002. Term expires July 31, 2008. Educated at Hamline University School of Law J.D. In legal practice Osceola 14 years.

Former Board Member Polk and Burnett County Community Referral Agency. President Board of Directors Polk County Kinship. Director St. Croix Valley Community Foundation. Chair Alternate Education Committee Amery School District.

Office: 240 Polk County Courthouse, 100 Polk County Plaza, Balsam Lake 54810-9071.

Telephone: (715) 485-9293.

GALLAGHER, Thomas J. *(Reserve Judge, Wisconsin Circuit Court)* Former Chief Judge Administrative District Ten. Retired. Assumed Reserve status, serves by assignment.

Mailing address: 46075 Krafts Point Road, Cable 54821.

GALSTAD, Richard D. *(Reserve Judge, Wisconsin Circuit Court)* Appointed by Governor Anthony S. Earl to term beginning July 1, 1983. Elected 1984 and 1990. Retired. Assumed Reserve status, serves by assignment. Born La Crosse Wisconsin April 9, 1930. Lutheran. Educated at University of Wisconsin B.S. 1952 J.D. 1957. Member Phi Gamma Delta and Phi Delta Phi. Admitted to practice Wisconsin 1957. Began legal practice Osseo 1957.

Chairman Wisconsin Mining Investment and Local Impact Fund Board 1980-83. Member American Judicature Society, State Bar of Wisconsin, Tri-County (President 1978) and American Bar Associations. Lieutenant USNR 1947-64 (active duty 1952-54). President Osseo-Fairchild Board of Education 1962-83. Former District Judge Advocate American Legion. Enjoys hunting and travel.

Mailing address: P.O. Box 335, Osseo 54758-0335.

GARDNER, William D. *(Reserve Judge, Wisconsin Circuit Court)* Elected to term beginning Aug 1, 1979. Reelected April 1985 and April 1991. Retired. Assumed Reserve status, serves by assignment. Born Wisconsin Rapids Wisconsin May 21, 1933. Catholic. Educated at St. Francis Seminary and Marquette University J.D. 1960. Admitted to practice Wisconsin 1960 and U.S. District Court Eastern District of Wisconsin 1960. In legal practice Milwaukee 1960-62.

Secretary and General Counsel Data Retrieval Corporation of America 1966-68. Deputy District Attorney Milwaukee County 1969-79. Member State Bar of Wisconsin. Instructor in Juvenile Juries, Termination of Parental Rights and Traffic Laws and Penalties Wisconsin Judicial Conference. E-3 U.S. Army 1955-57. Liability Claims Manager West Bend Mutual Insurance Company 1962-68. Moot Court Judge Marquette University. Member Explorers. Enjoys reading and fishing.

Mailing address: 4930 South 18th Street, Milwaukee 53221.

GAYLORD, Shelley *(Judge, Wisconsin Circuit Court Dane Circuit)* Elected April 2003.

Office: City-County Building, 210 Martin Luther King Jr. Blvd., Madison 53703.

Telephone: (608) 266-4321.

GEMPELER, Mark S. *(Judge, Wisconsin Circuit Court Waukesha Circuit)* Appointed by Governor Anthony S. Earl to term beginning March 8, 1983. Elected 1984, 1990, 1996 and 2002. Current term expires July 31, 2008. Acting Chief Judge 1992 and Chief Judge

GEMPELER, MARK S.—*Continued*

1994-2000 Administrative District Three. Born Sparta Wisconsin Jan 3, 1949. Methodist. Educated at Northern Illinois University B.A. in History 1971 and Marquette University Law School J.D. 1974. Member Phi Alpha Theta. Admitted to practice Wisconsin 1974.

Assistant U.S. Attorney 1978-79. Assistant District Attorney 1974-77. Corporation Counsel 1980-83. Chair Committee of Chief Judges 1998. Member Wisconsin Judicial Conference (Criminal Jury Instructions Committee since 1988, Chairman Criminal Law Section 1990). Attended The National Judicial College since 1985. Associate Dean and Faculty Member Wisconsin Judicial College.

Office: Waukesha County Courthouse, 515 West Moreland Boulevard, Waukesha 53188-2428.

Telephone: (262) 548-7481.

GEORGE, Daniel S. *(Judge, Wisconsin Circuit Court Columbia Circuit)* Elected April 1991 to term beginning Aug 1, 1991. Reelected 1997 and 2003. Current term expires July 31, 2009. Born Madison Wisconsin Dec 24, 1951. Educated at University of Wisconsin at Madison B.A. with honors 1974 and Marquette University J.D. 1977. Member Phi Delta Phi. Admitted to practice Wisconsin 1977 and U.S. District Courts Eastern 1977 and Western 1977 Districts of Wisconsin. In legal practice Milwaukee 1977-79 and Columbus 1980-81.

Assistant District Attorney and District Attorney Dodge County 1981-87. Corporation Counsel Columbia County 1987-91.

Mailing address: P.O. Box 368, Portage 53901.

Office: Administration Building, 400 DeWitt Street, Portage 53901-0587.

Telephone: (608) 742-9619.

GIBBS, Michael S. *(Judge, Wisconsin Circuit Court Walworth Circuit)* Elected April 7, 1992 to term beginning Aug 3, 1992. Elected 1998, current term expires July 31, 2004. Born Toledo Ohio July 9, 1952. Christian. Educated at University of Colorado B.A. 1974 and John Marshall Law School J.D. 1978. Member Phi Delta Phi. Admitted to practice Wisconsin 1978 and U.S. District Court Eastern District of Wisconsin 1979. In legal practice Lake Geneva 1978-92.

Director Wisconsin Trial Judges Association. Member American Judges Association, State Bar of Wisconsin and Walworth County Bar Association. Attended Wisconsin Judicial College and The National Judicial College. Enjoys reading, golfing, bicycling, cross country skiing, fishing, hunting and family activities.

Mailing address: P.O. Box 1001, Elkhorn 53121-1001.

Office: Walworth County Courthouse, Elkhorn 53121.

Telephone: (262) 741-4224.

GIERINGER, Raymond E. *(Reserve Judge, Wisconsin Circuit Court)* Assumed office Aug 1, 1978. Elected 1979, 1985 and 1991. Retired 1991. Assumed Reserve status 1992, serves by assignment. Born Milwaukee Wisconsin Oct 31, 1925. Christian Scientist. Educated at Marquette University B.M.E. 1946 LL.B. 1948. Member Sigma Phi Delta and Pi Tau Sigma. Admitted to practice Wisconsin 1948. In legal practice Milwaukee 1948-51 and Adams County 1959-72. Judge, Wisconsin County Court Adams County 1972-78.

District Attorney Adams County 1960-66. City Attorney Adams 1962-70. Member Criminal Justice Planning Council Northeast District Region II since 1983. Member Criminal Jury Instructions Committee, Wisconsin District Attorney Association (Life Member), Voluntary Association of Trial Judges of Wisconsin, Wisconsin Judicial Conference (Chairman Family and Children's Law Section 1986, Member Legislative Committee since 1985 and Executive Committee 1986, Representative to Judicial Council 1986-91), State Bar of Wisconsin (Media Law Relations Committee) and American Bar Association (Judicial Administration Division). Attended State College of Judiciary and National College of the Judiciary. USNR 1944-46. Previously worked as Comptroller and Chief Executive Office in industry. Past Master Winneconnie Lodge 186 Masons. Member Adams Lodge and AAONMS Tripoli Shrine. Pilot. Enjoys hunting, fishing and boating activities.

Mailing address: P.O. Box 462, Friendship 53934.

GLONEK, George L. *(Judge, Wisconsin Circuit Court Douglas Circuit)*

Office: Douglas County Courthouse, 1313 Belknap Street, Superior 54880-2769.

Telephone: (715) 395-1207.

GONRING, Andrew Thomas *(Judge, Wisconsin Circuit Court Washington Circuit)*

Mailing address: P.O. Box 1986, West Bend 53095-7986.

Office: Washington County Courthouse, 432 East Washington Street, West Bend 53095-2500.

Telephone: (262) 335-4351.

GONZALEZ, Ramona A. *(Judge, Wisconsin Circuit Court La Crosse Circuit)* Assumed office 1995. Elected to subsequent term.

Office: County Law Enforcement Center, 333 Vine Street, La Crosse 54601-3296.

Telephone: (608) 785-5840.

GOODSTEIN, Aaron E. *(Magistrate Judge, United States District Court Eastern District of Wisconsin)* Appointed by U.S. District Court judges to term beginning Nov 1, 1979. Reappointed Nov 1, 1987 and 1995. Current term expires 2003. Born Sheboygan Wisconsin April 28, 1942. Educated at University of Wisconsin-Madison B.A. 1964 J.D. 1967. Staff member Wisconsin Law Review 1965-67. Law Clerk to Hon. Myron L. Gordon, U.S. District Court Eastern District of Wisconsin 1967-68. Member Order of the Coif. Admitted to practice Wisconsin 1967 and U.S. Court of Appeals Seventh Circuit 1968. Began legal practice Milwaukee 1968.

Co-author "Wisconsin Criminal Procedure" Wisconsin L. Rev. 430, 1966, "The Legislative Development of Public Assistance" Wisconsin L. Rev. 414, 1968, "Playing By the Rules in Federal Court" The Milwaukee Lawyer Winter 1984 and "Complaints, Warrants for Arrest and Search Warrants" Program 1 Federal Judicial Center Video Orientation Series for U.S. Magistrate Judges 1992. Board of Directors Milwaukee Legal Aid Society 1974-79. Chairperson Magistrate Judges Education Committee Federal Judicial Center 1990-98. Member Committee on Administration of the Magistrate Judges System Judicial Conference of the U.S. 1993-99. Officer Federal Magistrate Judges Association since 2000. Member Milwaukee Young Lawyers Association (President 1976-77), State Bar of Wisconsin (President Young Lawyers Division 1975-76, Board of Governors 1975-77), Milwaukee (Executive Board 1978-79, Secretary 1979-82) and American (Gavel Awards Standing Com-

GOODSTEIN, AARON E.—*Continued*

mittee 1981-87, Chairperson Magistrate Judges Committee National Conference of Federal Trial Judges 1990-94) Bar Associations. Faculty Member, Panelist and Speaker on topics covering federal criminal and civil procedure for the Federal Judicial Center, Milwaukee Bar Association, Judicial Conference of Seventh Circuit, Corporate Practice Institute Seminar Marquette University Law School and U.S. District Courts Eastern and Western Districts of Wisconsin. Recipient Pro Bono Award from Gene and Ruth Posner Foundation 1988. Board of Directors University of Wisconsin Law School Alumni Association 1989-98.

Office: 258 U.S. Courthouse, 517 East Wisconsin Avenue, Milwaukee 53202.

Telephone: (414) 297-3963.

Fax: (414) 297-1129

GORDON, Bonnie L. *(Judge, Wisconsin Circuit Court Milwaukee Circuit)*

Office: 513 Milwaukee County Courthouse, 901 North Ninth Street, Milwaukee 53233-1425.

Telephone: (414) 278-5153.

GORENCE, Patricia J. *(Magistrate Judge, United States District Court Eastern District of Wisconsin)* Appointed by U.S. District Court Chief Judge Terence T. Evans to term beginning April 1, 1994. Reappointed 2002, current term expires April 1, 2010. Born Sheboygan Wisconsin March 16, 1943. Roman Catholic. Educated at Marquette University B.A. 1965 J.D. 1977 and University of Wisconsin-Madison M.A. 1968. Contributing member Marquette Law Review 1976-77. Law Clerk to Hon. Robert W. Warren, U.S. District Court Eastern District of Wisconsin 1977-79. Member Alpha Sigma Nu. Admitted to practice Wisconsin 1977, U.S. District Courts Eastern 1977 and Western 1977 Districts of Wisconsin, U.S. Court of Appeals Seventh Circuit 1979 and U.S. Supreme Court 1980. In legal practice Milwaukee 1993-94.

Assistant U.S. Attorney 1979-84 and 1988-90, First Assistant U.S. Attorney 1984-87 and 1989-91 and U.S. Attorney 1987-88 Eastern District of Wisconsin. Deputy Attorney General Wisconsin Department of Justice 1991-93. Author "Women's Name Rights" Marquette L. Rev. 1978. Instructor in General Practice University of Wisconsin Law School 1992 and 1994. Member Association of Women Lawyers, The American Law Institute, National Association of Women Judges, American Judicature Society, State Bar of Wisconsin (Chair Professional Committee, Vice Chair Legal Education Commission), Seventh Circuit and American Bar Associations. Instructor Civil and Criminal Trial Advocacy Course U.S. Department of Justice 1984-90. Recipient Special Commendation Award from U.S. Department of Justice 1986 and from Internal Revenue Service 1988 and President's Award from State Bar of Wisconsin 1995. Named Prosecutor of the Year by Milwaukee Bar Association 1990. Treasurer University of Wisconsin-Milwaukee-Slovenian Arts Council. Board Member Professional Dimensions and Bottomless Closet-Milwaukee.

Office: 264 U.S. Courthouse, 517 East Wisconsin Avenue, Milwaukee 53202-4507.

Telephone: (414) 297-4165.

GRAM, Laurence C. *(Reserve Judge, Wisconsin Circuit Court)* Assumed office Aug 1, 1978. Elected to subsequent terms. Retired. Assumed Reserve status, serves by assignment. Former Judge, Wisconsin County Court Milwaukee County.

Mailing address: N22 West 29150 Elmhurst Drive, Pewaukee 53072.

GRAU, Gregory E. *(Judge, Wisconsin Circuit Court Marathon Circuit)* Assumed office 1995. Elected to subsequent term.

Office: Marathon County Courthouse, 500 Forest Street, Wausau 54403-5568.

Telephone: (715) 261-1370.

GREENWOOD, Richard G. *(Reserve Judge, Wisconsin Circuit Court)* Appointed by Governor Martin J. Schreiber Aug 1, 1977 to term beginning Sept 1, 1977. Elected 1979, 1985 and 1991. Retired. Assumed Reserve status, serves by assignment. Born Green Bay Wisconsin Nov 4, 1927. Roman Catholic. Educated at U.S. Naval Academy B.S. 1949 and Marquette University J.D. 1958. Board of Editors Marquette Law Review 1956-58. Member Delta Theta Phi and Alpha Sigma Nu. Admitted to practice Wisconsin 1958, U.S. Court of Claims 1959 and U.S. Supreme Court 1967. Began legal practice Green Bay 1958.

Assistant District Attorney 1960-62. Assistant City Attorney Green Bay 1962-71. City Attorney Green Bay 1971-77. Author "Assumption of Risk in Automobile Negligence Cases in Wisconsin" Marquette L. Rev. 1959. Member State Bar of Wisconsin, Brown County and American Bar Associations. Lecturer on Punitive Damages Wisconsin Judicial Education 1981-82. Attended Trial Judges Academy University of Virginia 1980, Jurisprudence and Humanities courses Washington and Lee University 1981 and Fact Finding and Judicial Administration courses University of Virginia 1983. Received Diploma of Judicial Skills American Academy of Judicial Education 1984. Member Wisconsin Civil Jury Instructions Committee 1984. Lieutenant USN as Carrier Pilot 1945-55. Enjoys philately, skiing and flying private planes.

Mailing address: P.O. Box 23600, Green Bay 54305-3600.

GRIESBACH, William C. *(Judge, United States District Court Eastern District of Wisconsin)* Appointed for life by President George W. Bush to term beginning May 17, 2002. Born Jan 24, 1954. Educated at Marquette University B.A. 1976 J.D. 1979. Law Clerk to Chief Justice Bruce B. Beilfuss, Wisconsin Supreme Court 1979-80. In legal practice Green Bay 1982-87. Judge, Wisconsin Circuit Court Brown Circuit 1995-2002, appointed by Governor Tommy G. Thompson.

Staff Attorney U.S. Court of Appeals Seventh Circuit 1980-82. Assistant District Attorney Brown County 1987-95.

Mailing address: P.O. Box 22370, Green Bay 54305-2370.

Office: Jefferson Court Building, 125 South Jefferson Street, Green Bay 54301.

Telephone: (920) 884-7775.

GRIMM, Peter L. *(Judge, Wisconsin Circuit Court Fond du Lac Circuit)* Assumed office 1991. Elected to subsequent term.

Mailing address: P.O. Box 1355, Fond du Lac 54936-1355.

Office: Fond du Lac County Courthouse, 160 South Macy Street, Fond du Lac 54935-4241.

Telephone: (920) 929-3071.

GRITTON, Thomas J. *(Judge, Wisconsin Circuit Court Winnebago Circuit)* Elected to term beginning Aug 1, 2000. Term expires July 31, 2006.
Mailing address: P.O. Box 2808, Oshkosh 54903-2808.
Office: Winnebago County Courthouse, 415 Jackson Drive, Oshkosh 54901-4751.
Telephone: (920) 236-4808.

GROVER, Thomas G. *(Judge, Wisconsin Circuit Court Shawano-Menominee Circuit)* Assumed office Aug 1, 1978. Elected 1983, 1989, 1995 and 2001. Current term expires July 31, 2007. Born Dec 15, 1944. Lutheran. Educated at Marquette University B.S.B.A. 1968 J.D. 1972. Admitted to practice Wisconsin 1972. In legal practice Hudson 1972-74 and Shawano 1974-75. Judge, Wisconsin County Court Shawano-Menominee Counties Jan 1976 to July 1978.
Member Shawano County Bar Association and State Bar of Wisconsin. Political affiliation: Independent. Member Shawano Area United Way (President Board of Directors), Mielke Theatre Board of Governors (President), Shawano County Arts Council (Vice President), Shawano Optimist Club (Board of Directors) and Shawano Rotary Club.
Mailing address: P.O. Box 279, Keshena 54135-0279.
Keshena office: Menominee County Courthouse, Keshena 54135.
Shawano office: Shawano County Courthouse, 311 North Main Street, Shawano 54166-2198.
Telephone: (715) 526-9328.

GUOLEE, Michael D. *(Judge, Wisconsin Circuit Court Milwaukee Circuit)* Assumed office Aug 1, 1978. Elected 1984, 1990, 1996 and April 2002. Current term expires July 31, 2008. Former Judge, Wisconsin County Court Milwaukee County.
Office: 412 Milwaukee County Courthouse, 901 North Ninth Street, Milwaukee 53233-1425.
Telephone: (414) 278-4480.

HAASE, Robert A. *(Judge, Wisconsin Circuit Court Winnebago Circuit)* Term expires July 31, 2006. Former Chief Judge Administrative District Four.
Mailing address: P.O. Box 2808, Oshkosh 54903-2808.
Office: Winnebago County Courthouse, 415 Jackson Drive, Oshkosh 54901-4751.
Telephone: (920) 236-4828.

HABECK, James Roy *(Judge, Wisconsin Circuit Court Shawano-Menominee Circuit)* Family and Court Commissioner 1983-2002. Elected Judge April 2002 to term beginning Aug 1, 2002. Term expires July 31, 2008. Educated at Marquette University Law School J.D. In legal practice Shawano.
Legal Counsel Wisconsin Towns Association 1987-2002. Prosecutor Shawano County District Attorney's Office. Director Wisconsin Family Court Commissioners Association. Director Shawano Area Chamber of Commerce.
Mailing address: P.O. Box 279, Keshena 54135-0279.
Keshena office: Menominee County Courthouse, Keshena 54135.
Shawano office: Shawano County Courthouse, 311 North Main Street, Shawano 54166-2198.
Telephone: (715) 526-9352.

HAESE, William J. *(Reserve Judge, Wisconsin Circuit Court)* Retired. Assumed Reserved status, serves by assignment.
Mailing address: 7433 North Beach Court, Fox Point 53217-3656.

HANSHER, David A. *(Judge, Wisconsin Circuit Court Milwaukee Circuit)* Elected April 6, 1991 to term beginning Aug 1, 1991. Reelected April 6, 1997 and 2003. Current term expires July 31, 2009. Born Milwaukee Wisconsin March 13, 1944. Educated at University of Wisconsin-Madison B.S. 1965 J.D. 1968. Member Phi Alpha Delta. Admitted to practice Wisconsin 1968, U.S. Court of Appeals Seventh Circuit 1970 and U.S. Supreme Court 1974. In legal practice Milwaukee 1972-91.
Assistant City Attorney Milwaukee 1968-72. Board of Directors Milwaukee Bar Foundation. Member Policy and Planning Committee Wisconsin Supreme Court and Judicial Ethics Committee State of Wisconsin. Member State Bar of Wisconsin and Milwaukee Bar Association. Enjoys reading and caber tossing.
Office: 632 Milwaukee County Courthouse, 901 North Ninth Street, Milwaukee 53233-1425.
Telephone: (414) 278-5340.

HARRINGTON, Eugene D. *(Judge, Wisconsin Circuit Court Washburn Circuit)* Elected to term beginning Aug 1, 1997.
Mailing address: P.O. Box 458, Shell Lake 54871-0458.
Office: Washburn County Courthouse, 110 West Fourth Avenue, Shell Lake 54871.
Telephone: (715) 468-4680.

HARTLEY, Glenn H. *(Judge, Wisconsin Circuit Court Lincoln Circuit)*
Office: Lincoln County Courthouse, 1110 East Main Street, Merrill 54452-2579.
Telephone: (715) 536-0416.

HASSIN, Donald J. *(Judge, Wisconsin Circuit Court Waukesha Circuit)*
Office: Waukesha County Courthouse, 515 West Moreland Boulevard, Waukesha 53188-2428.
Telephone: (262) 548-7538.

HAUGHNEY, Patrick C. *(Judge, Wisconsin Circuit Court Waukesha Circuit)* Term expires July 31, 2008.
Office: Waukesha County Courthouse, 515 West Moreland Boulevard, Waukesha 53188-2428.
Telephone: (262) 970-4768.

HAWLEY, Robert A. *(Judge, Wisconsin Circuit Court Winnebago Circuit)* Term expires July 31, 2006.
Mailing address: P.O. Box 2808, Oshkosh 54903-2808.
Office: Winnebago County Courthouse, 415 Jackson Drive, Oshkosh 54901-4751.
Telephone: (920) 236-4868.

HAZLEWOOD, Fred H. *(Judge, Wisconsin Circuit Court Manitowoc Circuit)* Term expires July 31, 2005.
Mailing address: P.O. Box 2000, Manitowoc 54221-2000.
Office: Manitowoc County Courthouse, 1010 South Eighth Street, Manitowoc 54220-5392.
Telephone: (920) 683-4022.

HEATH, Charles D. *(Reserve Judge, Wisconsin Circuit Court)* Elected April 1977 to term beginning Jan 1, 1978. Appointed by governor Aug 1, 1977. Elected

HEATH, CHARLES D.—*Continued*

1984, 1990 and 1996. Retired. Assumed Reserve status, serves by assignment. Born Menominee Michigan Sept 28, 1938. Episcopalian. Educated at University of Wisconsin B.S. 1964 J.D. 1967. Admitted to practice Wisconsin 1967. Began legal practice Fond du Lac 1967. In legal practice Marinette 1970.

District Attorney Marinette County 1975-77.

Mailing address: P.O. Box 706, Marinette 54143.

HENDERSON, Frederick A. *(Judge, Wisconsin Circuit Court Rusk Circuit)* Term expires July 31, 2004.

Office: Rusk County Courthouse, 311 Miner Avenue East, Ladysmith 54848-1862.

Telephone: (715) 532-2150.

HIGGINBOTHAM, Paul B. *(Judge, Wisconsin Circuit Court Dane Circuit)*

Office: 323 City-County Building, 210 Martin Luther King Jr. Blvd., Madison 53703.

Telephone: (608) 266-4986.

HOFFMANN, John P. *(Judge, Wisconsin Circuit Court Waupaca Circuit)* Appointed by Governor Anthony S. Earl to term beginning Feb 14, 1985. Elected 1986, 1992 and 1998. Current term expires July 31, 2004. Born New London Wisconsin May 5, 1945. Educated at University of Notre Dame B.B.A. 1967 and University of Wisconsin J.D. cum laude 1972. Staff member University of Wisconsin Law Review 1968-69 and 1971-72. Admitted to practice Wisconsin 1972. Began legal practice Madison 1972. In legal practice Manawa 1977.

Member State Bar of Wisconsin and Waupaca County Bar Association. Specialist Five USMC 1969-71.

Office: Waupaca County Courthouse, 811 Harding Street, Waupaca 54981-2087.

Telephone: (715) 258-6425.

HOOVER, Michael W. *(Presiding Judge, Wisconsin Court of Appeals District Three)* Assumed office 1997. Born Milwaukee Wisconsin Dec 21, 1951. Educated at University of Wisconsin-Madison B.A. 1974 J.D. 1978. Judge, Wisconsin Circuit Court Marathon Circuit 1988-97.

Assistant District Attorney Marathon County 1978-80. Assistant City Attorney Wausau 1980-88. Author/Editor *Wisconsin Criminal Law Benchbook.* Former Faculty Mount Senario College. Instructor/Speaker on Judicial Education and the State Bar. Enjoys golf.

Office: 2100 Stewart Avenue, Suite 310, Wausau 54401.

Telephone: (715) 845-6634.

HOUCK, Kent C. *(Reserve Judge, Wisconsin Circuit Court)* Assumed office Aug 1, 1978. Elected 1979, 1985 and 1991. Retired. Assumed Reserve status, serves by assignment. Former Judge, Wisconsin County Court Richland County.

Mailing address: 22889 Hansberry Lane, Richland Center 53581.

HOWARD, Vincent K. *(Judge, Wisconsin Circuit Court Marathon Circuit)* Assumed office June 7, 1992. Elected April 2002, current term expires July 31, 2008. Presiding Judge 1994-98. Born Chicago Illinois May 7, 1947. United Methodist. Educated at University of Wisconsin-Madison B.B.A. 1969 and Marquette University Law School J.D. 1972. Staff member Marquette Law Review. Member Phi Alpha Delta. Admitted to practice Wisconsin 1972 and U.S. District Courts Eastern 1972 and Western 1972 Districts of Wisconsin. Began legal practice Wausau 1972.

Director Wisconsin Voluntary Judges Association. Member State Judicial Benchbook Committee, State Bar of Wisconsin and Marathon County Bar Association. Chairman Marathon County Republican Party 1975-81. Candidate State Assembly Representative 1976 and 1978. Board of Trustees First United Methodist Church 1977-80.

Office: Marathon County Courthouse, 500 Forest Street, Wausau 54403-5568.

Telephone: (715) 261-1360.

HUBER, Raymond S. *(Judge, Wisconsin Circuit Court Waupaca Circuit)* Elected to term beginning Aug 1, 2000. Term expires July 31, 2006. Born Clintonville Wisconsin March 13, 1957. Methodist. Educated at Carroll College B.S. cum laude 1978 and University of Wisconsin Law School J.D. with honors 1982. Admitted to practice Wisconsin 1982 and U.S. District Courts Eastern 1982 and Western 1982 Districts of Wisconsin. In legal practice Clintonville 1982-2000.

City Attorney Clintonville 1987-2000. Member State Bar of Wisconsin and Waupaca County Bar Association (President 1998-99).

Office: Waupaca County Courthouse, 811 Harding Street, Waupaca 54981-2087.

Telephone: (715) 258-6437.

HUE, William F. *(Judge, Wisconsin Circuit Court Jefferson Circuit)* Assumed office 1995. Elected to subsequent term.

Office: Jefferson County Courthouse, 320 South Main Street, Jefferson 53549-1799.

Telephone: (920) 674-7151.

JANSEN, James P. *(Judge, Wisconsin Circuit Court Langlade Circuit)* Elected to term beginning Aug 1, 1981. Reelected 1987, 1993 and 1999. Current term expires July 31, 2005. Born Manitowoc Wisconsin Feb 5, 1944. Catholic. Educated at Michigan Technological University B.S. 1966 and Valparaiso University J.D. 1973. Admitted to practice Wisconsin 1973. Began legal practice Antigo 1973.

Office: Langlade County Courthouse, 800 Clermont Street, Antigo 54409-1985.

Telephone: (715) 627-6221.

JESKE, Larry L. *(Judge, Wisconsin Circuit Court Oconto Circuit)* Elected to term beginning Aug 1, 1993. Reelected 1999, current term expires July 31, 2005.

Office: Oconto County Courthouse, 301 Washington Street, Oconto 54153-1621.

Telephone: (920) 834-6837.

JOHNSTON, William D. *(Judge, Wisconsin Circuit Court Lafayette Circuit)*

Office: Lafayette County Courthouse, 626 Main Street, Darlington 53530-1396.

Telephone: (608) 776-4811.

KAHN, Charles F., Jr. *(Judge, Wisconsin Circuit Court Milwaukee Circuit)*

Office: 503 Milwaukee County Courthouse, 901 North Ninth Street, Milwaukee 53233-1425.

Telephone: (414) 278-4521.

KELLEY, Kendall M. *(Judge, Wisconsin Circuit Court Brown Circuit)* Appointed by Governor Scott McCallum 2002. Elected April 2003.

Mailing address: P.O. Box 23600, Green Bay 54305-3600.

Office: Brown County Courthouse, 100 South Jefferson Street, Green Bay 54301.

Telephone: (920) 448-4116.

KENNEDY, Robert A., Jr. *(Judge, Wisconsin Circuit Court Forest-Florence Circuit)* Elected April 2002 to term beginning Aug 1, 2002. Current term expires July 31, 2008. Educated at University of Wisconsin-Oshkosh and University of Wisconsin Law School J.D. 1980. In legal practice Crandon.

District Attorney Florence County.

Mailing address: P.O. Box 410, Florence 54121-0410.

Office: Florence County Courthouse, 501 Lake Avenue, Florence 54121.

Telephone: (715) 528-3205.

Crandon office: Forest County Courthouse, 200 East Madison Street, Crandon 54520-1414.

Telephone: (715) 478-2329.

KENNEDY, Robert A. P. *(Reserve Judge, Wisconsin Circuit Court)* Appointed by Governor Tommy G. Thompson to term beginning May 22, 1989. Elected 1990 and 1996. Retired. Assumed Reserve status, serves by assignment.

Mailing address: 208 East Polk Street, Crandon 54520-1414.

KENNEDY, Robert J. *(Judge, Wisconsin Circuit Court Walworth Circuit)*

Mailing address: P.O. Box 1001, Elkhorn 53121-1001.

Office: Walworth County Courthouse, Elkhorn 53121.

Telephone: (262) 741-4224.

KEY, Barbara Hart *(Judge, Wisconsin Circuit Court Winnebago Circuit)*

Mailing address: P.O. Box 2808, Oshkosh 54903-2808.

Office: Winnebago County Courthouse, 415 Jackson Drive, Oshkosh 54901-4751.

Telephone: (920) 236-4835.

KIEFFER, James Robert *(Judge, Wisconsin Circuit Court Waukesha Circuit)* Elected April 2, 1985 to term beginning Aug 1, 1985. Reelected 1991, 1997 and 2003. Current term expires July 31, 2009. Served Juvenile Court Aug 1, 1985 to July 31, 1988, Criminal Court Aug 1, 1988 to July 31, 1993 and Family Court from Aug 1, 1993 to Jan 31, 1997. Former Presiding Judge Family Division. Presiding Judge Civil Division since Feb 1, 1997. Born Milwaukee Wisconsin June 12, 1951. Roman Catholic. Educated at Marquette University B.A. 1973 J.D. 1976. Member Tau Epsilon Rho. Admitted to practice Wisconsin 1976 and U.S. District Courts Eastern 1976 and Western 1976 Districts of Wisconsin. In legal practice Milwaukee 1976-78.

Assistant District Attorney Waukesha County 1978-85. Member State Bar of Wisconsin and Waukesha County Bar Association (President 1991-92). Instructor Wisconsin Judicial College 1988. Named one of Ten Outstanding Young Wisconsinites by Wisconsin Jaycees 1986. Member Waukesha Kiwanis Club and St. John Newmann Catholic Church. Enjoys spending time with family, camping, coaching youth sports, reading and weight lifting. Avid fan of Milwaukee Brewers, Green Bay Packers, Milwaukee Bucks, Wisconsin Badgers and Marquette Golden Eagles.

Office: Waukesha County Courthouse, 515 West Moreland Boulevard, Waukesha 53188-2428.

Telephone: (262) 548-7476.

KINNEY, Robert E. *(Judge, Wisconsin Circuit Court Oneida Circuit)* Assumed office Aug 1, 1978. Elected 1984, 1990, 1996 and April 2002. Current term expires July 31, 2008. Born Eau Claire Wisconsin Aug 17, 1947. Educated at University of Wisconsin-Eau Claire B.S. magna cum laude 1969 and University of Wisconsin-Madison J.D. 1971. Law Clerk to Wisconsin Department of Justice Dane County. Admitted to practice Wisconsin 1971 and U.S. District Courts Eastern 1971 and Western 1971 Districts of Wisconsin. Began legal practice Madison 1971. In legal practice Wausau 1972-74 and Rhinelander 1974-76. Judge, Wisconsin County Court Oneida County June 26, 1976 to July 31, 1978, appointed by Governor Patrick J. Lucey.

Instructor in Police Science Associate Degree Program Nicolet College 1975-76. Member Voluntary Association of Trial Judges of Wisconsin, State Bar of Wisconsin and Tri-County Bar Association. Lecturer Wisconsin Juvenile Court Judges Seminar 1982. Enjoys racquetball and water skiing.

Mailing address: P.O. Box 400, Rhinelander 54501-0400.

Office: Oneida County Courthouse, One Courthouse Square, Rhinelander 54501.

Telephone: (715) 369-6157.

KIRCHMAN, Michael *(Judge, Wisconsin Circuit Court Crawford Circuit)* Assumed office Aug 1, 1978. Elected to subsequent terms. Current term expires July 31, 2007. Former Judge, Wisconsin County Court Crawford County.

Office: Crawford County Courthouse, 220 North Beaumont Road, Prairie du Chien 53821-1405.

Telephone: (608) 326-0205.

KIRK, Philip M. *(Judge, Wisconsin Circuit Court Waupaca Circuit)* Appointed by Governor Lee Dreyfus June 1, 1981. Elected 1981, 1987, 1993 and 1999. Current term expires July 31, 2005. Former Chief Judge Administrative District Eight. Born Urbana Illinois Jan 27, 1947. Educated at University of Wisconsin-Madison 1970 and Illinois Institute of Technology, Chicago-Kent College of Law 1973. Admitted to practice Wisconsin 1975 and Illinois 1975. Began legal practice Waupaca Wisconsin 1976.

Member American Judicature Society, State Bar of Wisconsin, Waupaca County and American Bar Associations.

Office: Waupaca County Courthouse, 811 Harding Street, Waupaca 54981-2087.

Telephone: (715) 258-6430.

KLOSSNER, Daniel W. *(Judge, Wisconsin Circuit Court Dodge Circuit)* Term expires July 31, 2008.

Office: Dodge County Justice Facility, 210 West Center Street, Juneau 53039-1091.

Telephone: (920) 386-3540.

KLUKA, Barbara A. *(Judge, Wisconsin Circuit Court Kenosha Circuit)* Elected to term beginning Aug 1, 1989. Reelected 1995 and 2001. Current term expires July 31, 2007. Currently serves as Chief Judge Administrative District Two. Born Kenosha Wisconsin Nov 30,

KLUKA, BARBARA A.—*Continued*

1944. Catholic. Educated at Alverno College B.A. with honors 1962, University of Wisconsin-Milwaukee M.A. 1973 and Marquette University J.D. 1978. Admitted to practice Wisconsin 1978 and U.S. District Courts Eastern 1978 and Western 1978 Districts of Wisconsin. In legal practice Kenosha and Southeast Wisconsin 1980-89.

Assistant District Attorney Kenosha County 1978-80. Member Women Lawyers Association, National Association of Women Judges, State Bar of Wisconsin, Kenosha County and American Bar Associations. Attended General Jurisdiction course The National Judicial College 1991. Recipient Outstanding Alumna Award from Alverno College 1989 and Empowering Women in Politics Award from University of Wisconsin-Parkside 1990. High school teacher Kenosha and Port Washington Wisconsin 1966-75. Board of Trustees St. Joseph High School. Advisory Board Boy Scouts of America. Member Kenosha County Historical Society. Enjoys reading, mystery novels, history, walking, bicycling, bowling, cooking and travel.

Office: 305 Kenosha County Courthouse, 912 56th Street, Kenosha 53140-3747.

Telephone: (262) 653-2663.

KOEHN, John D. *(Reserve Judge, Wisconsin Circuit Court)* Retired. Assumed Reserve status, serves by assignment.

Mailing address: 6350 Sawgrass, Chandler, Arizona 85249.

KONKOL, Daniel L. *(Judge, Wisconsin Circuit Court Milwaukee Circuit)* Elected April 1992 to term beginning Aug 1, 1992. Elected 1998, current term expires July 31, 2004. Served Misdemeanor and Traffic Division 1992-96 and since Aug 1, 2002, Juvenile Division 1996-98 and Felony Division 1998-2002. Born Milwaukee Wisconsin July 17, 1951. Educated at Marquette University B.A. 1973 J.D. 1976. Member Phi Delta Phi. Admitted to practice Wisconsin 1976. Assistant Commissioner, Family Court Milwaukee County 1985-92.

Assistant District Attorney Racine County 1976-84. Author "The New Paternity Law: Law and Procedures" The Milwaukee Lawyer 1988 and "Civil Restraining Orders: Distinguishing Domestic Abuse and Harassment" Wisconsin Lawyer 1990. Member State Bar of Wisconsin and Milwaukee Bar Association.

Office: 501 Courthouse, 901 North Ninth Street, Milwaukee 53233.

Telephone: (414) 278-4551.

KOSCHNICK, Randy R. *(Judge, Wisconsin Circuit Court Jefferson Circuit)*

Office: Jefferson County Courthouse, 320 South Main Street, Jefferson 53549-1799.

Telephone: (920) 674-7217.

KREMERS, Jeffrey A. *(Judge, Wisconsin Circuit Court Milwaukee Circuit)*

Office: 401 Milwaukee County Courthouse, 901 North Ninth Street, Milwaukee 53233-1425.

Telephone: (414) 278-4498.

KREUL, Richard J. *(Judge, Wisconsin Circuit Court Racine Circuit)* Elected to term beginning Aug 1994. Reelected April 2000, current term expires July 31, 2006. Born Racine Wisconsin. Educated at University of Notre Dame B.S. 1959 and Georgetown University J.D. 1962. Admitted to practice Wisconsin 1962. In legal practice Milwaukee 1962-67 and Racine 1967-94.

Office: 703 Racine County Courthouse, 730 Wisconsin Avenue, Racine 53403-1274.

Telephone: (262) 636-3661.

KRUEGER, Moria *(Judge, Wisconsin Circuit Court Dane Circuit)* Assumed office Aug 1, 1978. Elected 1979, 1985, 1991, 1997 and 2003. Current term expires July 31, 2009. Judge, Wisconsin County Court Dane County Sept 19, 1977 to July 31, 1978.

Office: 330 City-County Building, 210 Martin Luther King Jr. Blvd., Madison 53703.

Telephone: (608) 266-4700.

KUEHN, Charles E. *(Reserve Judge, Wisconsin Circuit Court)* Retired. Assumed Reserve status, serves by assignment.

Mailing address: 344 Miramar Drive, Green Bay 54301.

KUHNMUENCH, Mary M. *(Judge, Wisconsin Circuit Court Milwaukee Circuit)*

Office: 316 Safety Building, 821 West State Street, Milwaukee 53233-1427.

Telephone: (414) 278-4596.

LAABS, Gerald W. *(Judge, Wisconsin Circuit Court Jackson Circuit)* Elected April 2002 to term beginning Aug 1, 2002. Term expires July 31, 2008. Educated at University of Wisconsin Law School J.D. In legal practice Jackson County thirty-two years. Court Commissioner 1975-2002 and Former Family Court Commissioner, Jackson County.

Assistant District Attorney Jackson County. Past President and Former Secretary Tri-County Bar Association.

Office: Jackson County Courthouse, 307 Main Street, Black River Falls 54615-0609.

Telephone: (715) 284-0213.

LAMELAS, Elsa C. *(Judge, Wisconsin Circuit Court Milwaukee Circuit)* Appointed by Governor Tommy G. Thompson to term beginning Nov 8, 1993. Elected April 1994 and 2000. Current term expires July 31, 2006. Born Havana Cuba April 13, 1951. Roman Catholic. Educated at Dominican College B.A. magna cum laude 1973 and University of Michigan J.D. 1978. Admitted to practice Michigan 1979, Wisconsin 1983, U.S. District Court Eastern District of Wisconsin and U.S. Court of Appeals Seventh Circuit.

Trial Attorney U.S. Department of Justice 1979-83. Assistant District Attorney Milwaukee County 1983-84. Assistant U.S. Attorney 1984-93 and Chief Criminal Division 1993 U.S. Attorney's Office. Chair Intensive Sanctions Review Panel 1997-98 and Committee to Improve Court Interpretation in Wisconsin since 1999. Member Criminal Penalties Study Committee (Chair Sentencing Guidelines Subcommittee 1998-99) and Enhanced Probation Task Force 1999. Member Association of Women Lawyers, Hispanic Bar Association of Wisconsin, State Bar of Wisconsin and Milwaukee Bar Association. Recipient Special Achievement Award 1979 and Special Commendation for Outstanding Service 1983 from U.S. Department of Justice, Community Leader Award from University of Milwaukee and Milwaukee Public Schools 1996 and Women Who Have Put Their Stamp on Milwaukee Award U.S. Postal Service 1999. Named Citizen of the Year by Greater Milwaukee Legal Auxiliary 1995 and Outstanding Woman of

LAMELAS, ELSA C.—*Continued*

Achievement by YWCA 2001. Board Member Project Benjamin (Milwaukee Archdiocese), Notre Dame Middle School for Girls, Aurora Weier House and Latino Arts Board.

Office: 634 Milwaukee County Courthouse, 901 North Ninth Street, Milwaukee 53233-1425.

Telephone: (414) 278-4554.

LAMPONE, Leah M. *(Reserve Judge, Wisconsin Circuit Court)* Retired. Assumed Reserve status, serves by assignment.

Mailing address: 9516 West Brookside Drive, Greenfield 53228.

LANDRY, Robert W. *(Reserve Judge, Wisconsin Circuit Court)* Appointed 1959. Elected to subsequent terms. Retired. Assumed Reserve status, serves by assignment. Born Madison Wisconsin June 22, 1922. United Methodist. Educated at University of Chicago A.B. 1946 and University of Wisconsin LL.B. 1949. Admitted to practice Wisconsin 1949. Began legal practice Milwaukee 1949. Judge, Milwaukee Civil Court 1954-59.

Instructor in Law and Society Lafarge Learning Institute. Captain USNR (retired). State Legislator 1951-54.

Mailing address: 1B Needle Rush Point, 17119 Perdido Key Drive, Pensacola, Florida 32507.

LANGHOFF, Gary J. *(Judge, Wisconsin Circuit Court Sheboygan Circuit)* Elected to term beginning Aug 1, 1987. Reelected 1993 and 1999. Current term expires July 31, 2005.

Office: Sheboygan County Courthouse, 615 North Sixth Street, Sheboygan 53081-4692.

Telephone: (920) 459-0308.

LaROCQUE, Daniel L. *(Reserve Judge, Wisconsin Circuit Court)* Retired. Assumed Reserve status, serves by assignment. Born Sault Ste. Marie Michigan July 11, 1936. Catholic. Educated at Marquette University J.D. 1962. Member Phi Delta Phi. Admitted to practice Wisconsin 1962 and U.S. District Courts Eastern 1962 and Western 1962 Districts of Wisconsin. In legal practice Wasau 1962-64. Judge, Wisconsin County Court Marathon County Jan 2, 1978 to July 31, 1978. Judge, Wisconsin Circuit Court Marathon Circuit Aug 1, 1978 to 1984. Chief Judge, Wisconsin Circuit Court Ninth Judicial Administrative District 1983-84. Former Judge, Wisconsin Court of Appeals District Three, appointed by Governor Anthony A. Earl to term beginning Jan 1, 1985.

Corporation Counsel Marathon County 1964-69. District Attorney Marathon County 1965-76. President Wisconsin District Attorneys Association 1975-76. Member State Bar of Wisconsin. Attended The National Judicial College 1979 and Institute of Judicial Administration New York University Law School 1985. Lecturer on Civil and Criminal Jury Trials Wisconsin Judicial College 1981-85. Previously worked as ironworker American Bridge Company.

Mailing address: 211 West Main Street, Sun Prairie 53590.

LATTON, Howard W. *(Reserve Judge, Wisconsin Circuit Court)* Elected to term beginning Aug 6, 1973. Elected to subsequent terms. Retired April 9, 1984. Assumed Reserve status, serves by assignment. Born Medford Wisconsin April 27, 1916. United Methodist. Educated at University of Wisconsin B.A. 1938 J.D. 1941. Admitted to practice Wisconsin 1941.

District Attorney Columbia County 1953-58. USAAC 1942-45.

Mailing address: 316 Knottwood Court, Sun City Center, Florida 33573.

LEINEWEBER, Edward E. *(Judge, Wisconsin Circuit Court Richland Circuit)* Elected April 1997 to term beginning Aug 1, 1997. Reelected 2003, current term expires July 31, 2009. Born Chicago Illinois Feb 13, 1949. Catholic. Educated at University of Notre Dame B.B.A. cum laude 1971 and University of Wisconsin J.D. 1976. Editor Wisconsin Law Review 1975-76. Admitted to practice Wisconsin 1976 and U.S. District Court Western District of Wisconsin 1976. In legal practice Richland Center 1976-97.

District Attorney Richland County 1987-93. City Attorney Richland Center 1994-97. Member Wisconsin Trial Judges Association and State Bar of Wisconsin. Member Kiwanis and Church Council. Interests include aviation and travel.

Office: Richland County Courthouse, 181 West Seminary Street, Richland Center 53581-2356.

Telephone: (608) 647-2626.

LENZ, Paul J. *(Judge, Wisconsin Circuit Court Eau Claire Circuit)*

Office: Eau Claire County Courthouse, 721 Oxford Avenue, Eau Claire 54703-5481.

Telephone: (715) 839-4815.

LUCCI, Michael T. *(Judge, Wisconsin Circuit Court Douglas Circuit)* Elected to term beginning Aug 1, 1985. Reelected 1991, 1997 and 2003. Current term expires July 31, 2009. Born Milwaukee Wisconsin Dec 30, 1942. Catholic. Educated at University of Wisconsin-Milwaukee B.A. 1966 and Marquette University Law School J.D. 1973. Admitted to practice Wisconsin 1973 and U.S. District Courts Eastern 1973 and Western 1973 Districts of Wisconsin. In legal practice Superior June 1973 to July 31, 1985.

Member Volunteer Association of Wisconsin Judges, State Bar of Wisconsin and Douglas County Bar Association. Attended Wisconsin Judicial College Aug 1985. E-5 U.S. Army 1967-69. Previously employed as factory assembler, brewery worker, camp counselor, research assistant for history department, sacker and stocker in grocery stores, house painter, janitor and maintenance worker. Member Douglas County Democratic Party 1980 to July 31, 1985 (Board of Directors). Past President Jaycees. Junior Achievement Adviser. Member Parish Council, United Way Board, Elks Club, Mental Health Board, Children's Shelter Board and Fish and Game League. Enjoys reading, fishing, sports and coaching Little League.

Office: Douglas County Courthouse, 1313 Belknap Street, Superior 54880-2769.

Telephone: (715) 395-1358.

LUEBKE, Dennis C. *(Judge, Wisconsin Circuit Court Outagamie Circuit)* Appointed by Governor Anthony S. Earl to term beginning Nov 19, 1984. Elected 1985, 1991 and 1997 and April 2003. Current term expires July 31, 2009. Born Neenah Wisconsin July 25, 1945. Lutheran. Educated at University of Wisconsin B.S. 1967 J.D. 1970. Member Phi Eta Sigma and Phi Kappa Phi. Admitted to practice Wisconsin 1970. Began legal prac-

LUEBKE, DENNIS C.—*Continued*

tice Racine 1970. In legal practice Little Chute and Appleton 1973-84.

Former Member Wisconsin Academy of Trial Lawyers and The Association of Trial Lawyers of America. Vice Chair Wisconsin Judicial Conference. Member State Bar of Wisconsin, Outagamie County and American Bar Associations. Faculty Member Wisconsin Judicial College. Lecturer judicial and bar association seminars. Former Director and President Legal Service of Northeastern Wisconsin, Outagamie County Alcohol and Other Drug Abuse Prevention Commission, Outagamie County Domestic Abuse Task Force Committee and Outagamie County Legal Aid Society. Chair Outagamie County Security Committee. Member Outagamie County Committee on Jail Alternatives, Outagamie County Restorative Justice Project and Tri-County Huber Facility Study Committee. Enjoys hunting and skiing.

Office: Justice Center, 320 South Walnut Street, Appleton 54911-5991.

Telephone: (920) 832-5153.

LUNDELL, Eric J. *(Judge, Wisconsin Circuit Court St. Croix Circuit)* Appointed by Governor Tommy G. Thompson to term beginning July 1, 1989. Elected April 1990, 1996 and April 2002. Current term expires July 31, 2008. Born St. Paul Minnesota Oct 29, 1947. Methodist. Educated at University of Wisconsin-Eau Claire B.S. 1970 and University of Minnesota J.D. 1973. Admitted to practice Wisconsin 1973 and U.S. District Court Western District of Wisconsin 1977. In legal practice New Richmond 1973-74.

District Attorney St. Croix County 1976-89. Instructor in Economics University of Wisconsin-Eau Claire 1987. Former Member American Bar Association. Member State Bar of Wisconsin. Attended "Managing Complex Cases" The National Judicial College 1992. USAF 1966-71. Enjoys rock hunting, fishing, hunting, golf and camping.

Office: Government Center, 1101 Carmichael Street, Hudson 54016-7710.

Telephone: (715) 386-4613.

LUNDSTEN, Paul G. *(Judge, Wisconsin Court of Appeals District Four)* Appointed by Governor Tommy G. Thompson to term beginning Nov 6, 2000. Born La Crosse Wisconsin Aug 11, 1955. Educated at University of Wisconsin-Madison B.A. 1980 J.D. cum laude 1983.

Assistant Attorney General Wisconsin Department of Justice 1983-2000.

Office: 10 East Doty Street, Suite 700, Madison 53703-3397.

Telephone: (608) 266-9361.

LUSSOW, John H. *(Judge, Wisconsin Circuit Court Rock Circuit)* Elected to term beginning May 2, 1979. Reelected April 1, 1986, April 7, 1992 and April 1998. Current term expires July 31, 2004. Former Presiding Judge. Born Detroit Michigan Jan 23, 1941. Catholic. Educated at Beloit College B.A. 1963 and University of Wisconsin-Madison J.D. 1966. Member Phi Alpha Delta. Admitted to practice Wisconsin 1966, U.S. District Court Northern District of Illinois 1968 and U.S. Court of Appeals Seventh Circuit. In legal practice Beloit 1968-79.

Member State Bar of Wisconsin and Rock County Bar Association. Attended The National Judicial College Reno Nevada.

Office: Rock County Courthouse, 51 South Main Street, Janesville 53545-3978.

Telephone: (608) 743-2254.

MADDEN, Patrick J. *(Judge, Wisconsin Circuit Court Iron Circuit)* Appointed by Governor Tommy G. Thompson to term beginning July 14, 1986. Elected 1987, 1993 and 1999. Current term expires July 31, 2005. Born Green Bay Wisconsin Jan 31, 1950. Catholic. Educated at University of Wisconsin-Green Bay B.S. magna cum laude 1971, University of Wisconsin-Madison M.A. 1974 J.D. 1976 and University of Nevada M.J.S. 1994. Admitted to practice Wisconsin 1976 and U.S. Supreme Court 1988.

Member American Judges Association, State Bar of Wisconsin and American Bar Association. Listed in *Who's Who in American Law* 1985.

Office: Iron County Courthouse, 300 Taconite Street, Hurley 54534-1546.

Telephone: (715) 561-3434.

MADDEN, Patrick John *(Reserve Judge, Wisconsin Circuit Court)* Assumed office Aug 1, 1978. Elected 1984 and 1990. Retired July 31, 1996. Assumed Reserve status, serves by assignment. Born Milwaukee Wisconsin May 21, 1926. Roman Catholic. Educated at Marquette University B.S. 1947 LL.B. 1950 and Georgetown University LL.M. 1956. Admitted to practice Wisconsin 1950, U.S. Supreme Court 1955 and U.S. Court of Military Appeals 1955. Judge, Wisconsin County Court Milwaukee County Jan 3, 1972 to July 31, 1978.

Lecturer on Criminal Law University of Wisconsin-Milwaukee School of Social Welfare 1974-77. Instructor Marquette University Law School 1977-78. Member State Bar of Wisconsin and Milwaukee Bar Association. Commander USNR 1944-78 (retired).

Mailing address: 7916 North Links Circle, Fox Point 53217.

MALLOY, Paul V. *(Judge, Wisconsin Circuit Court Ozaukee Circuit)* Appointed by Governor Scott McCallum to term beginning March 2002. Elected April 2003. Term expires July 31, 2009. Educated at University of Wisconsin-Milwaukee B.S.B.A. 1981 and John Marshall Law School J.D. 1985. In legal practice 1987-2002.

Member State Bar of Wisconsin (Board of Governors). Member Republican Party of Ozaukee County. Member Wisconsin Lawyer's Assistance Program, Grafton Lion's Club, American Legion and Ozaukee County 4-H.

Mailing address: P.O. Box 994, Port Washington 53074-0994.

Office: Ozaukee County Courthouse, 1201 South Spring Street, Port Washington 53074-2491.

Telephone: (262) 284-8357.

MALMSTADT, Michael G. *(Judge, Wisconsin Circuit Court Milwaukee Circuit)*

Office: 2421 Children's Court Center, 10201 West Watertown Plank Road, Milwaukee 53226-3532.

Telephone: (414) 257-7150.

MANGERSON, Mark A. *(Judge, Wisconsin Circuit Court Oneida Circuit)* Elected to term beginning Aug 1, 1988. Reelected 1994 and 2000. Current term expires July 31, 2006. Deputy Chief Judge Ninth Judicial District 1990-96. Born Rhinelander Wisconsin. Educated at

MANGERSON, MARK A.—*Continued*

Valparaiso University B.A. 1971 J.D. 1974. National Moot Court Team 1973-74. Admitted to practice Wisconsin 1974 and U.S. District Courts Western 1974 and Eastern 1976 Districts of Wisconsin.

District Attorney Vilas County 1974-76 and Oneida County 1976-80. Instructor in Arrest, Search and Seizure Nicolet Area Technical College 1978-79. Member Chief Judges Subcommittee on Child Support 1990-97 and Wisconsin Criminal Jury Instructions Committee since 1998. Member Wisconsin Association of Trial Judges and State Bar of Wisconsin. Faculty Wisconsin Judicial College 1996-99.

Mailing address: P.O. Box 400, Rhinelander 54501-0400.

Office: Oneida County Courthouse, One Courthouse Square, Rhinelander 54501.

Telephone: (715) 369-6200.

MANIAN, Victor *(Judge, Wisconsin Circuit Court Milwaukee Circuit)* Elected to term beginning Jan 2, 1976. Reelected 1982, 1988, 1994 and 2000. Current term expires July 31, 2006. Chief Judge Dec 15, 1979 to July 31, 1986. Born Milwaukee Wisconsin Oct 21, 1929. Lutheran (Wisconsin Synod). Educated at University of Wisconsin-Milwaukee 1953-56 and Marquette University LL.B. 1960. Admitted to practice Wisconsin 1960. Began legal practice at Milwaukee 1960. Judge, Milwaukee County Court Jan 2, 1973 to Jan 2, 1976.

Author "Principles and Cases of the Law and of Arrest, Search and Seizure" McGraw-Hill 1974 and "Readings and Cases in Criminal Law" West 1975. Instructor Milwaukee Area Technical College 1969-72 and University of Wisconsin-Milwaukee 1974-78. Adjunct Professor of Law Marquette University Law School 1982-86. Member Executive Committee Wisconsin Judicial Administrative District One, Board of Directors National Conference of Metropolitan Courts 1984-86, Criminal Jury Instructions Committee Wisconsin Supreme Court, Milwaukee Bar Association and State Bar of Wisconsin. U.S. Army 1948-49. Former Board of Regents Wisconsin Lutheran College and Board of Directors Milwaukee Federation of Wisconsin Evangelical Lutheran Churches. Member Board for Parish Services Wisconsin Evangelical Lutheran Synod.

Office: 608 Milwaukee County Courthouse, 901 North Ninth Street, Milwaukee 53233-1425.

Telephone: (414) 278-5338.

MARIK, Wayne J. *(Judge, Wisconsin Circuit Court Racine Circuit)* Elected to term beginning Aug 1, 1985. Reelected 1991, 1997 and 2003. Current term expires July 31, 2009.

Office: 703 Racine County Courthouse, 730 Wisconsin Avenue, Racine 53403-1274.

Telephone: (262) 636-3865.

MARTENS, Kevin E. *(Judge, Wisconsin Circuit Court Milwaukee Circuit)* Appointed by Governor Scott McCallum to term beginning July 23, 2001. Elected April 2002 to term beginning Aug 1, 2002. Term expires July 31, 2008. Educated at Marquette University B.S. summa cum laude 1990 and Harvard Law School J.D. cum laude 1993. Law Clerk to Senior Judge Robert W. Warren, U.S. District Court Eastern District of Wisconsin. In legal practice Milwaukee 1995-97.

Assistant U.S. Attorney Eastern District of Wisconsin March 1997 to 2002. Author "Fair or Foul? The Survival of Small-Market Teams in Major League Baseball" 4 Marquette Sports L. Jour. 324 Spring 1994. Associate Lecturer University of Wisconsin Law School 1999-2001. Member Wisconsin Hispanic Lawyers Association, State Bar of Wisconsin and Milwaukee Bar Association. Board of Directors Southwest Branch YMCA of Metropolitan Milwaukee and Betty Brinn Children's Museum.

Office: 1411 Children's Court Center, 10201 West Watertown Plank Road, Milwaukee 53226-3532.

Telephone: (414) 257-7277.

MARTIN, Robert D. *(Chief Judge, United States Bankruptcy Court Western District of Wisconsin)* Appointed by U.S. District Court judges to term beginning June 1, 1978. Term extended by congressional action. Reappointed by U.S. Court of Appeals Seventh Circuit judges June 1, 1988 and June 1, 2002. Current term expires 2016. Born Iowa City Iowa Oct 7, 1944. Educated at Cornell College A.B. 1966 and University of Chicago J.D. 1969. Law Clerk summers of 1967 and 1968. Admitted to practice Wisconsin, U.S. District Courts Eastern and Western Districts of Wisconsin, U.S. Court of Appeals Seventh Circuit and U.S. Supreme Court. In legal practice Madison since 1969.

Author forms manual for Ginsberg's *Bankruptcy* Prentice Hall Law & Business 1st ed. 1985 and supplement 1988 and 2nd ed. 1992 and supplements, "Chapter 12 After Almost One Year in the Bankruptcy Courts" 37 Drake L. Rev. 211, 1987-88 and *Bankruptcy; Annotated Forms* 1 and 2 Prentice Hall Law & Business 1989. Coauthor with Richard Jacobson Chapter 16 "Bankruptcy" *Construction Law* Matthew Bender 1986 and supplement 1988 and with John K. Pearson *Secured Transactions Handbook for Wisconsin Lawyers and Lenders* University of Wisconsin Law School 1990. Contributing Author *Norton Bankruptcy Law and Practice* and *Norton Bankruptcy Law Adviser* Callaghan since 1988. Instructor Debtor-Creditor Section General Practice Course Sept 1974, March 1976, Feb 1977, 1980 and Spring 2001 and Lecturer Debtor-Creditor Law Course 1981, 1983, 1985 and 1987 and Farm Credit Law Seminar 1985 University of Wisconsin. Member National Conference of Bankruptcy Judges (Governor Seventh Circuit 1988-91, Secretary 1993-94, Vice President 1994-95, President 1995-96), American College of Bankruptcy, American Judicature Society, State Bar of Wisconsin and Dane County Bar Association. Co-chair "Financial and Business Planning for Agriculture" ALI-ABA Stanford University June 1979. Instructor Annual Bankruptcy Update Seminar ATS-CLE since 1979, Norton Bankruptcy Litigation Institutes since 1987 and Advanced Bankruptcy Seminar School for Newly Appointed Bankruptcy Judges Federal Judicial Center 1989. Chair Annual Debtor/Creditor Law Conference CLEW University of Wisconsin since 1980.

Mailing address: P.O. Box 548, Madison 53701-0548.

Telephone: (608) 264-5188.

MASON, James M. *(Judge, Wisconsin Circuit Court Wood Circuit)* Term expires July 31, 2004.

Mailing address: P.O. Box 8095, Wisconsin Rapids 54495-8095.

Office: Wood County Courthouse, 400 Market Street, Wisconsin Rapids 54494-4825.

Telephone: (715) 421-8518.

MAWDSLEY, Robert G. *(Judge, Wisconsin Circuit Court Waukesha Circuit)*
Office: Waukesha County Courthouse, 515 West Moreland Boulevard, Waukesha 53188-2428.
Telephone: (262) 548-7503.

McALPINE, Michael J. *(Judge, Wisconsin Circuit Court Monroe Circuit)*
Office: 302 Monroe County Courthouse, 112 South Court Street, Sparta 54656-1765.
Telephone: (608) 269-8926.

McCORMACK, Joseph D. *(Judge, Wisconsin Circuit Court Ozaukee Circuit)* Term expires July 31, 2009.
Mailing address: P.O. Box 994, Port Washington 53074-0994.
Office: Ozaukee County Courthouse, 1201 South Spring Street, Port Washington 53074-2491.
Telephone: (262) 284-8362.

McCORMICK, John E. *(Judge, Wisconsin Circuit Court Milwaukee Circuit)* Term expires July 31, 2005.
Office: 634 Milwaukee County Courthouse, 901 North Ninth Street, Milwaukee 53233-1425.
Telephone: (414) 278-4476.

McESSEY, Eugene F. *(Reserve Judge, Wisconsin Circuit Court)* Retired. Assumed Reserve status, serves by assignment.
Mailing address: W3935 Silica Road, Fond du Lac 54935-9559.

McGARITY, Margaret Dee *(Judge, United States Bankruptcy Court Eastern District of Wisconsin)*
Office: 162 U.S. Courthouse, 517 East Wisconsin Avenue, Milwaukee 53202.
Telephone: (414) 297-3291.

McGRAW, Robert *(Reserve Judge, Wisconsin Circuit Court)* Assumed office Aug 1, 1978. Elected to subsequent terms. Retired. Assumed Reserve status, serves by assignment. Born Wichita Kansas March 10, 1920. Catholic. Educated at Marquette University Ph.B. 1940 LL.B. 1943. Graduated first in law school class. Member Alpha Sigma Nu. Admitted to practice Wisconsin 1943. Began legal practice Waukesha 1943. Judge, Wisconsin County Court Waukesha County July 1, 1972 to July 31, 1978.
Instructor in Search and Seizure 1970-74. Member Waukesha County Bar Association (President) and State Bar of Wisconsin (Grievance Committee).
Mailing address: 3139 Madison Street, Waukesha 53188.

McKAY, J. D. *(Judge, Wisconsin Circuit Court Brown Circuit)* Appointed by Governor Tommy G. Thompson to term beginning Aug 15, 1996. Elected to term beginning Aug 1, 1997. Reelected 2003, current term expires July 31, 2009. Born Des Moines Iowa April 19, 1941. Lutheran. Educated at University of Wisconsin B.S. 1964 J.D. 1968. Admitted to practice Wisconsin 1968 and U.S. District Courts Eastern and Western Districts of Wisconsin. In legal practice Green Bay 1968-96.
Member Wisconsin Trial Judges Association, American Judges Association, State Bar of Wisconsin and Brown County Bar Association.
Mailing address: P.O. Box 23600, Green Bay 54305-3600.
Office: Brown County Courthouse, 100 South Jefferson Street, Green Bay 54301.
Telephone: (920) 448-4120.

McMAHON, Patricia D. *(Judge, Wisconsin Circuit Court Milwaukee Circuit)* Appointed by Governor Anthony S. Earl to term beginning Jan 10, 1986. Elected April 1987, 1993 and 1999. Current term expires July 31, 2005. Former Presiding Judge Civil Division. Currently serves as Presiding Judge Misdemeanor Division. Born Houston Texas July 12, 1943. Educated at College of William & Mary B.S. 1965 and Emory University J.D. with honors 1968. Associate Editor Journal of Public Law 1967-68. Admitted to practice Wisconsin 1968, Georgia 1968, U.S. District Courts Eastern 1968 and Western 1977 Districts of Wisconsin, U.S. Court of Appeals Seventh Circuit 1971 and U.S. Supreme Court 1972. In legal practice Milwaukee Wisconsin 1968-85.
Staff Attorney 1970-75, Managing Attorney 1975-77, Executive Director 1977-1983 and Associate Director 1983-85 Legal Action of Wisconsin, Inc. Board of Directors State Public Defender Program 1984-85 and Milwaukee Bar Foundation. Member Long-range Planning Committee, Courthouse Security Task Force, Grant Application Committee, Computer Committee and Library Committee Milwaukee County Judiciary. Chair Affirmative Action Committee. Presiding Judge of Three Judge Panel appointed by Chief Judge Sheedy to conduct an investigation into the resources allocated to the courts. Member Special Functions Subcommittee Circuit Court Automation Project. Member Milwaukee Young Lawyers Association, Wisconsin Judges Association (Board of Directors), Association of Women Lawyers, National Association of Women Judges, State Bar of Wisconsin (Legal Assistance Committee, Council Member and Former Chairperson Individual Rights Section), State Bar of Georgia, Milwaukee (Legal Aid to Indigents Committee, Judicial Selection Committee, Board of Directors), and American Bar Associations. Attended State Justice Institute Advisory Committee to Review Continuing Education Materials on State Court Litigation 1983. Board of Directors Wisconsin Trust Account Foundation, Inc. and Migrant Legal Action Program, Inc.
Office: 504 Milwaukee County Courthouse, 901 North Ninth Street, Milwaukee 53233-1425.
Telephone: (414) 278-4525.

McMONIGAL, William M. *(Judge, Wisconsin Circuit Court Green Lake Circuit)* Appointed by Governor Tommy G. Thompson Feb 23, 1992 to term beginning April 24, 1992. Elected April 1993 and April 1999. Current term expires July 31, 2005. Born Berlin Wisconsin Aug 30, 1946. Roman Catholic. Educated at Marquette University B.S. 1968 J.D. 1971. Member Delta Theta Phi. Admitted to practice Wisconsin 1971 and U.S. District Courts Eastern 1971 and Western 1971 Districts of Wisconsin. In legal practice Berlin 1971-92.
Member State Bar of Wisconsin and Green Lake County Bar Association.
Mailing address: P.O. Box 3188, Green Lake 54941-3188.
Office: Green Lake County Courthouse, 492 Hill Street, Green Lake 54941.
Telephone: (920) 294-4042.

MICKIEWICZ, John W. *(Reserve Judge, Wisconsin Circuit Court)* Appointed by Governor Lee Dreyfus to term beginning Jan 13, 1983. Elected 1984 and 1990. Retired July 31, 1996. Assumed Reserve status, serves by assignment. Born Two Rivers Wisconsin July 13, 1937. Educated at University of Wisconsin-Madison B.S. 1959 J.D. 1962. Member Sigma Nu. Admitted to practice Wisconsin 1962. Began legal practice Fond du Lac 1962.

Member State Bar of Wisconsin. Past President Fond du Lac Exchange Club. Former Director Fond du Lac Chamber of Commerce. Enjoys sporting clays.

Mailing address: 77 Eastbrook Lane, Fond du Lac 54935.

MIECH, Robert J. *(Reserve Judge, Wisconsin Circuit Court)* Assumed office Aug 1, 1978. Elected 1979, 1985 and 1991. Retired. Assumed Reserve status, serves by assignment. Former Judge, Wisconsin County Court Milwaukee County.

Mailing address: 315 Hemlock Court, South Milwaukee 53172.

MILLER, James Otto *(Judge, Wisconsin Circuit Court Columbia Circuit)* Elected to term beginning Aug 1, 1999. Term expires July 31, 2005. Born Portage Wisconsin July 8, 1945. Presbyterian. Educated at Lawrence University B.A. magna cum laude 1967 and University of Wisconsin-Madison J.D. 1971. Admitted to practice Wisconsin 1971 and U.S. District Court Western District of Wisconsin 1971. In legal practice Portage Feb 1971 to July 31, 1999.

Certified Mediator U.S. Arbitration and Mediation of Wisconsin, Inc. 1994 to July 31, 1999. Instructor in Military Law University of Wisconsin, Marquette University and Ripon College. Vice Chairman Board of Attorneys Professional Responsibility District 7 Committee 1979-94. Board of Directors Civil Trial Counsel of Wisconsin Oct 1998 to July 31, 1999. Chairman Guidelines Formulation Committee Sixth Judicial District OAS/OAR. Member Family Law Seminar Planning Committee. Member State Bar of Wisconsin (State Bar Communications Committee 1972-77, Journalist/Lawyers Joint Interest Committee 1976-77, Fee Arbitration Panel 1995 to July 31, 1999), Columbia County (Secretary/Treasurer 1972-74, Vice President 1975-76) and American Bar Associations. Captain USAR JAGC 1968-80 (retired).

Mailing address: P.O. Box 181, Portage 53901.

Office: Administration Building, 400 DeWitt Street, Portage 53901-0587.

Telephone: (608) 742-9653.

Fax: (608) 742-9601

E-mail address: James.Miller-@columbia.courts.state.wi.us

MIRON, David G. *(Judge, Wisconsin Circuit Court Marinette Circuit)* Appointed by Governor Tommy G. Thompson to term beginning Jan 5, 2001. Elected April 2002, current term expires July 31, 2008. Educated at Marquette University Law School J.D. 1983.

District Attorney Marinette County 1990-2001. Past President Marinette County Bar Association. Member Marinette County Courthouse Security Committee.

Office: Marinette County Courthouse, 1926 Hall Avenue, Marinette 54143-1717.

Telephone: (715) 732-7465.

MLEZIVA, Dennis J. *(Judge, Wisconsin Circuit Court Kewaunee Circuit)*

Office: Kewaunee County Courthouse, 613 Dodge Street, Kewaunee 54216-1398.

Telephone: (920) 388-7142.

MOESER, Daniel R. *(Judge, Wisconsin Circuit Court Dane Circuit)* Elected 1979. Reelected to subsequent terms. Current term expires July 31, 2009. Former Chief Judge Administrative District Five.

Office: 308 City-County Building, 210 Martin Luther King Jr. Blvd., Madison 53703.

Telephone: (608) 266-4377.

Fax: (608) 266-4151

MOHR, James B. *(Judge, Wisconsin Circuit Court Vilas Circuit)* Term expires July 31, 2008. Currently serves as Chief Judge Administrative District Nine.

Office: Vilas County Courthouse, 330 Court Street, Eagle River 54521.

Telephone: (715) 479-3638.

MONTABON, Dennis G. *(Judge, Wisconsin Circuit Court La Crosse Circuit)* Appointed by Governor Martin J. Schreiber Aug 1, 1978. Elected 1979, 1985, 1991, 1997 and 2003. Current term expires July 31, 2009. Presiding Judge La Crosse County since 1995. Born Tomahawk Wisconsin Sept 30, 1943. Catholic. Educated at University of Wisconsin-Madison B.S. 1965 and John Marshall Law School J.D. 1972. Recipient American Jurisprudence Award. Admitted to practice Wisconsin 1972 and Illinois 1972. Began legal practice Tomahawk Wisconsin 1972. In legal practice La Crosse Wisconsin 1976-78.

Inspector General Bureau of Alcohol, Tobacco and Firearms U.S. Department of the Treasury Chicago Illinois 1966-72. District Attorney Lincoln County 1973-76. Hearing Officer Myterle Werth Hospital Application Menominee 1977-78. Instructor in Criminal Procedure Nicolet College 1975-76. Member Northeast Criminal Justice Planning Council 1975-76, Wisconsin Council on Criminal Justice 1975-76, Lower West Central Justice Planning Council 1977-78 and Supreme Court Committees on Special Bail Study 1979-81, Wisconsin Court Information System-USER 1982-98, ad hoc Committee on the Administrative Committee of the Courts 1988-90 and Legislative Committee since 2002. Member Jail Study 1983-86, Sentencing Strategies Committee since 1994 and Criminal Justice Management Council since 2001 La Crosse County. Member Steering Committee since 1989, Advisory Committee since 1989 and Chairman Special Function Committee 1990-98 Wisconsin Circuit Court Automation Project. Life member Wisconsin District Attorneys Association. Member Wisconsin Trial Judges Association (Board of Directors since 1984, Vice President 1992-2000), Wisconsin Judicial Conference (Legislative Committee 1982-88, Panelist Court Security 1989, Facilitator 1990), State Bar of Wisconsin, Lincoln County (Former Vice President) and La Crosse County Bar Associations. Panel member Wisconsin Supreme Court Judicial Education Family Law Seminar Dec 1983. Former Democrat. Chairman Lincoln County Democratic Party 1975-76. Secretary Home and School Association 1979-80 and Member 1980-86 and President 1983-84 School Board Cathedral Catholic School. Member Merrill Optimist Club 1973-76, La Crosse County Executive Committee 1977-78, Kiwanis Club 1978-93, La Crosse County Alcohol and Youth Task Force (Steering Committee 1979-82), Riverland Girl Scout

MONTABON, DENNIS G.—*Continued*

Council (Board of Directors 1980-89, Chairman Finance Committee 1986-99) and Cathedral Church. Enjoys traveling, gardening, his grandchild and Green Bay Packers.

Office: County Law Enforcement Center, 333 Vine Street, La Crosse 54601-3296.

Telephone: (608) 785-9773.

E-mail address: Dennis.Montabon-@lacrossecourts.state.wi.us

MOREY, Dane F. *(Judge, Wisconsin Circuit Court Buffalo-Pepin Circuit)* Appointed by Governor Tommy G. Thompson to term beginning Jan 18, 1990. Elected April 1990, April 1996 and April 2002. Current term expires July 31, 2008. Born Trego Wisconsin Sept 4, 1932. Methodist. Educated at University of Wisconsin Law School J.D. 1959. Admitted to practice Wisconsin 1959. In legal practice Mauston 1959-62 and Durand 1962-90.

District Attorney Juneau County 1960-61. Member Voluntary Judges Association, American Judicature Society, State Bar of Wisconsin, Tri-County and American Bar Associations. Sergeant E-5 U.S. Army Sept 1952 to June 1955. Korean Language Linguist. Member Lions and United Methodist Church. Enjoys skiing, camping, woodworking, bowling and golf.

Mailing address: P.O. Box 39, Durand 54736-0039.

Office: Government Center, 740 Seventh Avenue West, Durand 54736-1635.

Telephone: (715) 672-8859.

Office: Buffalo County Courthouse, 407 Second Street South, Alma 54610-9753.

Telephone: (608) 685-6202.

MORONEY, Dennis P. *(Judge, Wisconsin Circuit Court Milwaukee Circuit)* Appointed by Governor Tommy G. Thompson to term beginning Nov 8, 1993. Elected April 1994 and 2000. Current term expires July 31, 2006. Born Milwaukee Wisconsin April 16, 1947. Catholic. Educated at Regis University B.A. 1969 and Marquette University J.D. 1973. Member Delta Theta Phi. Admitted to practice Wisconsin 1973 and U.S. District Courts Eastern 1973 and Western 1973 Districts of Wisconsin. In legal practice Milwaukee 1973-93.

Fellow American Bar Association. Representative Jury Summit 2001. President St. Thomas More Society 2000-01. Member Milwaukee Young Lawyers Association, Association of Women Lawyers, State Bar of Wisconsin and Milwaukee Bar Association. Graduate Wisconsin Judicial College 1994 and The National Judicial College 1995. Named Pro Bono Lawyer of the Year 1990. Recipient Image Award from Career Youth Development. Past President Civitan Club of Milwaukee. Vice President and Board Member Metropolitan Milwaukee Civic Alliance. Enjoys sports and family activities.

Office: 502 Milwaukee County Courthouse, 901 North Ninth Street, Milwaukee 53233-1425.

Telephone: (414) 278-4504.

E-mail address: dennis.moroney-@milwaukee.courts.state.wi.us

MUELLER, Emily S. *(Judge, Wisconsin Circuit Court Racine Circuit)*

Office: 703 Racine County Courthouse, 730 Wisconsin Avenue, Racine 53403-1274.

Telephone: (262) 636-3869.

MULROY, Michael J. *(Judge, Wisconsin Circuit Court La Crosse Circuit)* Elected to term beginning Aug 1, 1983. Reelected April 1989, 1995 and 2001. Current term expires July 31, 2007. Born Stevens Point Wisconsin June 14, 1941. Educated at St. Norbert College B.A. 1963 and Marquette University J.D. 1971. Admitted to practice Wisconsin 1971. Began legal practice La Crosse 1971.

District Attorney La Crosse County 1977-83. President Wisconsin District Attorneys Association 1982. Captain U.S. Army 1963-68. Enjoys running.

Office: County Law Enforcement Center, 333 Vine Street, La Crosse 54601-3296.

Telephone: (608) 785-9587.

MURACH, Lewis R. *(Judge, Wisconsin Circuit Court Waushara Circuit)* Elected to term beginning Aug 1, 1993. Reelected 1999, current term expires July 31, 2005.

Mailing address: P.O. Box 508, Wautoma 54982-0508.

Office: Waushara County Courthouse, 209 St. Marie Street, Wautoma 54982.

Telephone: (920) 787-0448.

MURPHY, Roger P. *(Reserve Judge, Wisconsin Circuit Court)* Appointed by Governor Lee S. Dreyfus to term beginning April 1, 1980. Elected 1981, 1987 and 1993. Retired. Assumed Reserve status, serves by assignment. Born Lancaster Wisconsin Oct 17, 1923. Protestant. Educated at University of Wisconsin-Madison B.S. 1948 LL.B. 1951. Member Chi Phi. Admitted to practice Wisconsin 1951. Began legal practice Waukesha 1956. In legal practice Elm Grove 1971-80.

District Attorney Waukesha County 1961-71. Member State Bar of Wisconsin, Waukesha County and American Bar Associations. Lieutenant USAAC 1942-45. State Senator 33rd Senate District of Wisconsin 1971-80. Past Exalted Ruler Waukesha Elks Lodge 400.

Mailing address: 1012 Hawthorn Circle, Waukesha 53188-2923.

MURRAY, Marshall B. *(Judge, Wisconsin Circuit Court Milwaukee Circuit)*

Office: 2414 Children's Court Center, 10201 West Watertown Plank Road, Milwaukee 53226-3532.

Telephone: (414) 257-7121.

MYSE, Gordon *(Reserve Judge, Wisconsin Circuit Court)* Retired. Assumed Reserve status, serves by assignment. Born Kaukauna Wisconsin. Educated at Beloit College B.A. 1957 and University of Michigan Law School LL.B. 1960. Admitted to practice Wisconsin 1960, U.S. District Court Eastern District of Wisconsin 1960 and U.S. Supreme Court 1971. In legal practice Appleton 1964-72 and 1983-86. Commissioner, Family Court Outagamie County 1965-66. Judge, Wisconsin Circuit Court Outagamie Circuit Aug 1, 1972 to Sept 6, 1983. Former Judge, Wisconsin Court of Appeals District Three, appointed by Governor Tommy Thompson Aug 1986.

Contributor 60 No. 3 Marquette L. Rev. Spring 1977. Former Director Wisconsin Trial Lawyers Academy. Member 1973-80 and Chairman Jury Communications Committee 1983 Judicial Commission of Wisconsin. Chairman ad hoc Committee to Study Judicial Discipline 1979-83 and Judicial Conference Study Group concerning elimination of preliminary hearings 1980-83. Member Wisconsin Jury Instructions Committee 1978-83,

MYSE, GORDON—*Continued*

Benchbook Committee 1980-83, Wisconsin Judicial Council, Wisconsin Voluntary Judges Association, State Bar of Wisconsin, Outagamie County and American Bar Associations. Faculty Member 1976-83 and Participant in numerous educational CLEW programs Wisconsin Judicial College. Faculty Advisor The National Judicial College 1980, 1981 and 1985. USNR 1961-64.

Mailing address: 4394 Glidden Drive, Sturgeon Bay 54235.

NAZE, Peter Joseph *(Judge, Wisconsin Circuit Court Brown Circuit)* Elected to term beginning Aug 1, 1987. Reelected 1993 and 1999. Current term expires July 31, 2005.

Mailing address: P.O. Box 23600, Green Bay 54305-3600.

Office: Brown County Courthouse, 100 South Jefferson Street, Green Bay 54301.

Telephone: (920) 448-4118.

NEEDHAM, Scott R. *(Judge, Wisconsin Circuit Court St. Croix Circuit)* Elected April 7, 1994 to term beginning Aug 1, 1994. Reelected 2000, current term expires July 31, 2006. Born Marshfield Wisconsin May 22, 1953. Lutheran. Educated at Carthage College B.A. with honors 1975 and University of Wisconsin J.D. with honors 1978. Admitted to practice Wisconsin 1978 and U.S. District Court Western District of Wisconsin 1978. In legal practice New Richmond 1978-94.

Member Planning Committee Wisconsin Judicial Conference, Wisconsin Judicial Education Committee, Criminal Jury Instruction Committee and State Bar of Wisconsin. Attended Wisconsin Judicial College and The National Judicial College. Enjoys family travel, golf and reading.

Office: Government Center, 1101 Carmichael Road, Hudson 54016-7710.

Telephone: (715) 386-4611.

Fax: (715) 381-4401

NELSON, Hugh F. *(Reserve Judge, Wisconsin Circuit Court)* Elected to term beginning Jan 7, 1980. Reelected 1986. Retired. Assumed Reserve status, serves by assignment. Born Kaukauna Wisconsin. Educated at Westminster College 1945, St. Norbert College 1946-49 and University of Wisconsin-Madison 1953. Member Phi Alpha Delta. Admitted to practice Wisconsin 1953. Began legal practice Menasha 1954. In legal practice Appleton 1954-79.

Member State Bar of Wisconsin, Outagamie County (President 1973, former member Grievance Committee), Calumet County and American Bar Associations. V-5 Program USN 1945-46. Former Director Outagamie County Public Defender Program and High Cliff Forest Park Association. Member American Legion and Elks. Enjoys reading, gardening, home projects, travel and tennis.

Mailing address: W6615 Firelane 6, Menasha 54952-9420.

NETTESHEIM, Neal P. *(Presiding Judge, Wisconsin Court of Appeals District Two)* Term expires July 31, 2008. Born Milwaukee Wisconsin Jan 8, 1942. Educated at Northwestern University B.A. 1963 and Marquette University J.D. 1966. Staff member Marquette Law Review. Admitted to practice Wisconsin 1966. Began legal practice Waukesha 1966. Former Judge, Wisconsin County Court Waukesha County, elected to term beginning July 1975.

Member State Bar of Wisconsin and Waukesha County Bar Association. Enjoys sports and music.

Office: 2727 North Grandview Boulevard, Suite 300, Waukesha 53188-1672.

Telephone: (262) 521-5234.

NICHOL, Gerald C. *(Judge, Wisconsin Circuit Court Dane Circuit)*

Office: 213 City-County Building, 210 Martin Luther King Jr. Blvd., Madison 53703.

Telephone: (608) 266-4009.

NICKS, Diane M. *(Judge, Wisconsin Circuit Court Dane Circuit)*

Office: 328 City-County Building, 210 Martin Luther King Jr. Blvd., Madison 53703.

Telephone: (608) 266-9095.

NOLAN, J. Michael *(Judge, Wisconsin Circuit Court Lincoln Circuit)*

Office: Lincoln County Courthouse, 1110 East Main Street, Merrill 54452-2579.

Telephone: (715) 536-0343.

NOONAN, Daniel A. *(Judge, Wisconsin Circuit Court Milwaukee Circuit)* Term expires July 31, 2008.

Office: 409 Milwaukee County Courthouse, 901 North Ninth Street, Milwaukee 53233-1425.

Telephone: (414) 278-4548.

NOWAKOWSKI, Michael *(Judge, Wisconsin Circuit Court Dane Circuit)* Elected to term beginning Aug 1, 1985. Reelected 1991, 1997 and 2003. Current term expires July 31, 2009. Chief Judge Administrative District Five since Aug 1, 2001. Born Milwaukee Wisconsin April 15, 1948. Educated at University of Wisconsin B.S. with honors 1971 J.D. with honors 1974. Member Phi Kappa Phi and Order of the Coif. Admitted to practice Wisconsin 1974. In legal practice Madison 1974-85.

Member State Bar of Wisconsin, Dane County and American Bar Associations. Instructor State Bar of Wisconsin CLE 1979-92. Member Board of Supervisors Dane County 1976-80.

Office: 225 City-County Building, 210 Martin Luther King Jr. Blvd., Madison 53703.

Telephone: (608) 266-4186.

NUSS, Richard James *(Judge, Wisconsin Circuit Court Fond du Lac Circuit)* Appointed by Governor Scott McCallum to term beginning 2002. Educated at Marquette University J.D. 1972. In legal practice Wisconsin 1972-94. Commissioner, Fond du Lac County Family Court 1994-2002.

Captain USMC. Former Exalted Ruler Fond du Lac Elks Lodge 57. Past President Kiwanis Club. Member Youth Service Bureau and American Legion.

Mailing address: P.O. Box 1355, Fond du Lac 54936-1355.

Office: Fond du Lac County Courthouse, 160 South Macy Street, Fond du Lac 54935-4241.

Telephone: (920) 929-3067.

O'BRIEN, Sarah B. *(Judge, Wisconsin Circuit Court Dane Circuit)*

Office: 306 City-County Building, 210 Martin Luther King Jr. Blvd., Madison 53703.

Telephone: (608) 267-1565.

PAPPAS, Peter G. *(Reserve Judge, Wisconsin Circuit Court)* Retired. Assumed Reserve status, serves by assignment. Former Chief Judge Administrative District Seven.

Mailing address: 2545 Madison Place, La Crosse 54601-5142.

PARINS, Robert J. *(Reserve Judge, Wisconsin Circuit Court)* Elected to term beginning Jan 1968. Reelected 1974 and 1980. Resigned June 1, 1982 to become President of the Green Bay Packers, Inc. Assumed Reserve status 1982, serves by assignment. Born Green Bay Wisconsin Aug 23, 1918. Catholic. Educated at University of Wisconsin B.A. 1940 LL.B. 1942. Admitted to practice Wisconsin 1942. Began legal practice Green Bay 1944.

Brown County District Attorney 1949-50. President Green Bay Packers, Inc. 1982-89. Member Wisconsin Board of Circuit Judges (Civil Jury Instructions Committee), Wisconsin Board of Attorneys Professional Competence 1976-78, State Bar of Wisconsin and American Bar Association. Instructor Wisconsin Judicial College 1974-76. Faculty Advisor The National Judicial College 1976.

Mailing address: 1027 South Van Buren Street, Green Bay 54301.

PASELL, Dale T. *(Judge, Wisconsin Circuit Court La Crosse Circuit)*

Office: County Law Enforcement Center, 333 Vine Street, La Crosse 54601-3296.

Telephone: (608) 785-5880.

PEKOWSKY, Robert R. *(Reserve Judge, Wisconsin Circuit Court)* Assumed office Jan 3, 1977. Elected 1978, 1984, 1990 and 1996. Retired. Assumed Reserve status, serves by assignment. Chief Judge Administrative District Five Aug 1, 1988 to July 31, 1994. Born Springfield Wisconsin May 28, 1937. Educated at University of Wisconsin B.S. LL.B. Cited for excellence in Estate Planning by Wisconsin Trustee Association. Chairman Legal Aid. Admitted to practice Wisconsin 1964. Began legal practice Madison 1964. Judge, Wisconsin County Court Dane County Jan 1, 1977 to July 31, 1978, appointed by Governor Patrick J. Lucey.

Assistant Vice President and Trust Officer First Wisconsin National Bank of Madison 1966-72. Dane County Register in Probate at Madison 1972-76. Important Decisions: Guardianship of Peter Christian Hatleberg 6-53-1672, Aug 12, 1977 and Temporary Guardianship of an Incompetent (individual rights protected by statute) 6-402-1685, Sept 30, 1977. Instructor in Estate Planning at University of Wisconsin Law School 1973-76. Author "Layman's Guide to Probate" Dane County 1973, "Handbook for Personal Representatives in Informal Probate" Dane County 1973, "Guide to Probate in Wisconsin" Dane County 1977 and thirty-six weekly articles on Probate in Madison Capital Times. Instructor in Estate Planning University of Wisconsin Law School 1973-76. Member Wisconsin Sentencing Commission 1989-95. Past President Wisconsin Registers in Probate Association. Former member State Trial Court Operations Study Committee and Board of Directors Legal Services Center of Dane County, Inc. Chairman Probate and Mental Health Section 1979 and Second Vice Chair since 1994 Wisconsin Judicial Conference. Member State Bar of Wisconsin and Dane County Bar Association (Treasurer 1975-76, Former Chairman Law for the Public). Named state winner in Civic and Governmental Affairs Program by Jaycees. Recipient Law Enforcement Award 1994. Former Counsel Wisconsin Association for Sudden Infant Death. Former Co-President (with wife) Huegel Elementary School PTA. President and Director Mt. Horeb Area Historical Society, Inc. Ex-Officio Director Dane County Historical Society. Member Madison Jaycees (Former Vice President and Director and former Chairman Corporate Gifts for Children's Zoo, program to collect railroad car full of food, clothing and supplies for Vietnamese and committee to draft Jaycee position on open housing in Madison) and Wesley United Methodist Church at Madison (Former Representative to Wisconsin Protestant Legislative Council, Chairman Social Christians Concern and Missions and member Building Committee). Enjoys antique collections.

Mailing address: 77 Oak Creek Trail, Madison 53717.

PERLICH, John J. *(Judge, Wisconsin Circuit Court La Crosse Circuit)* Elected to term beginning Aug 1, 1985. Reelected 1991, 1997 and 2003. Current term expires July 31, 2009. Born Hancock Michigan Jan 8, 1948. Catholic. Educated at Iowa State University B.S. 1970 and Drake University J.D. 1973. Admitted to practice Wisconsin 1973 and Iowa 1973. In legal practice La Crosse Wisconsin 1973-85. Judge, La Crosse Municipal Court 1983-85. Enjoys boating and hunting.

Office: County Law Enforcement Center, 333 Vine Street, La Crosse 54601-3296.

Telephone: (608) 785-9851.

PETERSON, Gregory A. *(Judge, Wisconsin Court of Appeals District Three)* Assumed office 1999. Born Minneapolis Minnesota Aug 24, 1946. Educated at University of Wisconsin-Madison B.A. 1969 J.D. 1973. Admitted to practice Wisconsin 1973. In legal practice Eau Claire 1973-83. Judge, Wisconsin Circuit Court Eau Claire Circuit Aug 1, 1983 to 1999, appointed by Governor Anthony S. Earl. Former Chief Judge, Administrative District Ten.

Member Wisconsin Criminal Jury Instruction Committee since 1990. Member Wisconsin Trial Judges Association, State Bar of Wisconsin and Eau Claire County Bar Association.

Office: 2100 Stewart Avenue, Suite 310, Wausau 54401.

Telephone: (715) 845-4664.

E-mail address: Gregory.Peterson@courts.state.wi.us

PFIFFNER, Robert F. *(Reserve Judge, Wisconsin Circuit Court)* Retired. Assumed Reserve status, serves by assignment.

Mailing address: 709 Miles Street, Chippewa Falls 54729.

POLLEX, Charles A. *(Judge, Wisconsin Circuit Court Adams Circuit)* Elected April 2003.

Mailing address: P.O. Box 200, Friendship 53934-0200.

Office: Adams County Courthouse, 402 Main Street, Friendship 53934.

Telephone: (608) 339-4215.

POPPY, Donald A. *(Judge, Wisconsin Circuit Court Calumet Circuit)* Family Court Commissioner 1979-92. Elected Judge to term beginning Aug 1, 1992. Reelected 1998, current term expires July 31, 2004. Born Eau Claire Wisconsin March 20, 1949. Educated at University of Wisconsin B.B.A. summa cum laude 1971 J.D. 1974. Admitted to practice Wisconsin 1974 and U.S.

POPPY, DONALD A.—*Continued*

District Courts Western 1974 and Eastern 1985 Districts of Wisconsin. In legal practice Brillian 1974-90.
District Attorney 1975-92. Member Wisconsin Trial Judges Association, State Bar of Wisconsin and Calumet County Bar Association. Attended The National Judicial College Reno Nevada 1993. Enjoys skiing, boating, archery, hunting, fishing and reading.
Office: Calumet County Courthouse, 206 Court Street, Chilton 53014-1198.
Telephone: (920) 849-2361.

POTTER, Gregory J. *(Judge, Wisconsin Circuit Court Wood Circuit)* Term expires July 31, 2008.
Mailing address: P.O. Box 8095, Wisconsin Rapids 54495-8095.
Office: Wood County Courthouse, 400 Market Street, Wisconsin Rapids 54494-4825.
Telephone: (715) 421-8520.

PROCTOR, Benjamin D. *(Judge, Wisconsin Circuit Court Eau Claire Circuit)*
Office: Eau Claire County Courthouse, 721 Oxford Avenue, Eau Claire 54703-5481.
Telephone: (715) 839-6170.

PROSSER, David T., Jr. *(Justice, Wisconsin Supreme Court)* Appointed by Governor Tommy G. Thompson to term beginning 1998. Elected 2001, current term expires July 31, 2011. Born Chicago Illinois. Educated at DePauw University B.A. 1965 and University of Wisconsin Law School J.D. 1968. Former Member Wisconsin Tax Appeals Commission.
District Attorney Outagamie County. Attorney/Advisor Office of Criminal Justice U.S. Department of Justice. Legislative Member National Conference of Commissioners on Uniform State Laws. Administrative Assistant to Congressman Harold Froehlich. Member State Assembly Wisconsin 1979-96 (Assembly Minority Leader six years, Assembly Speaker two years).
Mailing address: P.O. Box 1688, Madison 53701-1688.
Office: 16 East State Capitol, Madison 53702.
Telephone: (608) 266-1882.

PTACEK, Gerald Paul *(Judge, Wisconsin Circuit Court Racine Circuit)* Term expires July 31, 2007.
Office: 703 Racine County Courthouse, 730 Wisconsin Avenue, Racine 53403-1274.
Telephone: (262) 636-3333.

RACE, John R. *(Judge, Wisconsin Circuit Court Walworth Circuit)* Appointed by Governor Anthony S. Earl to term beginning Aug 1, 1984. Elected 1985, 1991, 1997 and 2003. Current term expires July 31, 2009. Born Racine Wisconsin Oct 6, 1934. Educated at University of Wisconsin-Madison B.S. 1956 J.D. 1960. Member Phi Delta Phi. Admitted to practice Wisconsin 1960. Began legal practice Racine 1960. In legal practice Milwaukee 1962-67 and Elkhorn 1967-84.
Mailing address: P.O. Box 1001, Elkhorn 53121-1001.
Office: Walworth County Courthouse, Elkhorn 53121.
Telephone: (262) 741-4224.

RADCLIFFE, Robert W. *(Reserve Judge, Wisconsin Circuit Court)* Elected to term beginning Aug 1, 1984. Reelected 1990 and 1996. Former Chief Judge Administrative District Seven. Retired. Assumed Reserve status, serves by assignment. Born Jackson County Wisconsin July 16, 1934. Educated at University of Wisconsin LL.B. 1962. Admitted to practice Wisconsin 1962. Began legal practice Black River Falls 1962.
District Attorney 1963-75. Member State Bar of Wisconsin, Tri-County and American Bar Associations. Lieutenant USN 1954-58.
Mailing address: P.O. Box 607, Black River Falls 54615-0609.

RAMIREZ, Ralph M. *(Judge, Wisconsin Circuit Court Waukesha Circuit)*
Office: Waukesha County Courthouse, 515 West Moreland Boulevard, Waukesha 53188-2428.
Telephone: (262) 548-7454.

RANDA, Rudolph T. *(Chief Judge, United States District Court Eastern District of Wisconsin)* Appointed for life by President George Bush to term beginning 1992. Chief Judge since Sept 1, 2002. Born Milwaukee Wisconsin July 25, 1940. Educated at University of Wisconsin-Milwaukee B.S. 1963 and University of Wisconsin Law School J.D. 1966. In legal practice Milwaukee 1966-67. Judge, Milwaukee Municipal Court 1975-79. Judge, Wisconsin Circuit Court Milwaukee Circuit 1979-81 and 1982-92. Judge, Wisconsin Court of Appeals District One 1981-82. Judge, Wisconsin Court of Appeals District Four 1983-85.
Attorney U.S. Attorney General's Office 1969. Assistant City Attorney 1970-73 and Principal City Attorney 1973-75 Milwaukee.
Office: 310 U.S. Courthouse, 517 East Wisconsin Avenue, Milwaukee 53202.
Telephone: (414) 297-3071.

RASMUSSEN, Robert H. *(Judge, Wisconsin Circuit Court Polk Circuit)* Elected April 2, 1991 to term beginning Aug 1, 1991. Reelected 1997 and 2003. Current term expires July 31, 2009. Born La Crosse Wisconsin Oct 19, 1947. United Church of Christ. Educated at University of Wisconsin-River Falls B.S. 1969 and University of Wisconsin-Madison J.D. 1972. Admitted to practice Wisconsin 1972 and U.S. District Court Western District of Wisconsin 1972. In legal practice Phillips 1972-74 and Amery 1979-91.
District Attorney Polk County 1975-79. City Attorney Amery 1981-91. Member Wisconsin Trial Judges Association and State Bar of Wisconsin. Attended General Jurisdiction Course The National Judicial College Fall 1992. Member Amery Youth Hockey Association. Enjoys hunting, fishing, snowmobiling and youth activities.
Office: 280 Polk County Courthouse, 100 Polk County Plaza, Balsam Lake 54810-9071.
Telephone: (715) 485-9233.

REHM, Richard L. *(Judge, Wisconsin Circuit Court Columbia Circuit)* Assumed office 1991. Elected 1997 and 2003. Current term expires July 31, 2009.
Mailing address: P.O. Box 333, Portage 53901.
Office: Administration Building, 400 DeWitt Street, Portage 53901-0587.
Telephone: (608) 742-9633.

REILLY, Paul F. *(Judge, Wisconsin Circuit Court Waukesha Circuit)* Elected April 2003.
Office: Waukesha County Courthouse, 515 West Moreland Boulevard, Waukesha 53188-2428.
Telephone: (262) 548-7540.

RESHESKE, David C. *(Judge, Wisconsin Circuit Court Washington Circuit)* Appointed by Governor

RESHESKE, DAVID C.—*Continued*

Tommy G. Thompson to term beginning July 9, 1999. Elected Jan 1, 2000, current term expires Dec 31, 2006. Born Fond du Lac Wisconsin Jan 13, 1947. Educated at Ripon College B.A. 1971 and Marquette University Law School LL.B. 1974. Admitted to practice Wisconsin 1974 and U.S. District Courts Eastern 1974 and Western 1974 Districts of Wisconsin. In legal practice West Bend 1988-95.

District Attorney Washington County 1981-88 and 1995-99. Enjoys golf, travel and Green Bay Packers football.

Office: Washington County Courthouse, 432 East Washington Street, West Bend 53095.

Telephone: (262) 335-4358.

Fax: (262) 335-4776

E-mail: david.resheske@washington.courts.state.wi.us

REYNOLDS, Guy D. *(Judge, Wisconsin Circuit Court Sauk Circuit)* Elected to term beginning Aug 1, 2000. Term expires July 31, 2006.

Office: Sauk County Courthouse, 515 Oak Street, Baraboo 53913-2496.

Telephone: (608) 355-3222.

RICE, James W. *(Reserve Judge, Wisconsin Circuit Court)* Assumed office Aug 1, 1978. Elected to subsequent terms. Retired. Assumed Reserve status, serves by assignment. Former Judge, Wisconsin County Court Monroe County.

Mailing address: 216 North Spring Street, Sparta 54656.

RICHARDS, Conrad A. *(Reserve Judge, Wisconsin Circuit Court)* Elected to term beginning Aug 1, 1989. Reelected 1995. Retired. Assumed Reserve status, serves by assignment.

Mailing address: 1729 Golf View Circle, Hudson 54016.

ROETHE, John W. *(Judge, Wisconsin Circuit Court Rock Circuit)*

Office: Rock County Courthouse, Fifth Floor, 51 South Main Street, Janesville 53545-3978.

Telephone: (608) 743-2237.

ROGGENSACK, Patience D. *(Justice, Wisconsin Supreme Court)* Elected April 2003 to term beginning Aug 1, 2003. Term expires July 31, 2013. Born Joliet Illinois July 7, 1940. Educated at Drake University B.A. 1962 and University of Wisconsin Law School J.D. 1980. In legal practice 1980-96. Judge, Wisconsin Court of Appeals District Four 1996 to July 31, 2003.

Fellow American Bar Foundation. Member National Association of Women Judges. Lecturer University of Wisconsin Law School and Madison Area Technical College.

Mailing address: P.O. Box 1688, Madison 53701-1688.

Office: 16 East State Capitol, Madison 53702.

Telephone: (608) 266-1888.

ROSBOROUGH, Michael J. *(Judge, Wisconsin Circuit Court Vernon Circuit)* Appointed June 2, 1986. Elected to term beginning Aug 1, 1987. Reelected 1993 and 1999. Current term expires July 31, 2005. Chief Judge Administrative District Seven since Aug 1, 2001.

Mailing address: P.O. Box 448, Viroqua 54665-0448.

Office: Vernon County Courthouse, Viroqua 54665.

Telephone: (608) 637-5364.

SANKOVITZ, Richard J. *(Judge, Wisconsin Circuit Court Milwaukee Circuit)* Appointed by Governor Tommy G. Thompson Sept 1996. Elected April 1, 1997 and 2003. Current term expires July 31, 2009. Presiding Judge Misdemeanor Division 1998-2000. Currently serves General Felony Court. Born Denver Colorado Aug 13, 1958. Roman Catholic. Educated at Marquette University B.A. summa cum laude 1980 and Harvard University Law School J.D. 1983. Law Clerk to Hon. Terence T. Evans, U.S. District Court Eastern District of Wisconsin 1983-84. Member Phi Beta Kappa and Alpha Sigma Nu. Admitted to practice Illinois 1984, U.S. District Courts Northern District of Illinois 1984 and Eastern 1986 and Western 1986 Districts of Wisconsin, U.S. Court of Appeals Seventh Circuit 1985, Wisconsin 1986 and U.S. Supreme Court 1995. In legal practice Chicago Illinois 1984-86 and Milwaukee Wisconsin 1986-96.

Contributing Author "Contract Law in Wisconsin" State Bar of Wisconsin CLE Books 2nd ed. 2000. Adjunct Professor of Business Ethics Marquette University 1990-92 and of Negotiation Milwaukee School of Education 1993-95. Former Member Committee for a Diverse Judiciary. State Delegate to National Conference of State Trial Court Judges. Member Planning Subcommittee Planning and Policy Advisory Committee Wisconsin Supreme Court. Master Thomas E. Fairchild American Inns of Court. Member Association for Women Lawyers, State Bar of Wisconsin (Former Chair Bench/Bar and Judicial Independence Committees, Member Legal Education Commission), Milwaukee (Former Chair Courts Committee, Former Member Judicial Selection Committee, Member Legal Services to the Indigent Committee), Seventh Circuit and American (Sections: Litigation, Antitrust Law, Judicial Division) Bar Associations. Named one of Best Lawyers in Milwaukee by *Milwaukee Magazine* 1990. Recipient Award for Outstanding Pro Bono Services by an Individual Attorney from MYLA/LAW Volunteer Lawyers Project 1992, Outstanding Service Award from State Bar of Wisconsin 1994, Forty Under Forty Award from *The Business Journal* 1997 and Outstanding Pro Bono Service Award from Association for Women Lawyers 2001. Former Chair Board of Directors St. Coletta of Wisconsin, Inc. Enjoys running, biking, sailing and woodworking.

Office: 506 Safety Building, 821 West State Street, Milwaukee 53233-1427.

Telephone: (414) 278-4490.

SAZAMA, Thomas J. *(Judge, Wisconsin Circuit Court Chippewa Circuit)* Former Magistrate Judge, U.S. District Court Western District of Wisconsin.

Office: Chippewa County Courthouse, 711 North Bridge Street, Chippewa Falls 54729-1876.

Telephone: (715) 726-7783.

SCHELLINGER, Jacqueline *(Judge, Wisconsin Circuit Court Milwaukee Circuit)*

Office: 514 Milwaukee County Courthouse, 901 North Ninth Street, Milwaukee 53233-1425.

Telephone: (414) 278-5316.

SCHLAEFER, Leo F. *(Reserve Judge, Wisconsin Circuit Court)* Retired. Assumed Reserve status, serves by assignment.

Mailing address: 1350 Bobolink, West Bend 53095.

SCHLOSSTEIN, Gary B. *(Reserve Judge, Wisconsin Circuit Court)* Assumed office Aug 1, 1978. Subsequently elected. Retired Jan 15, 1990. Assumed Reserve status, serves by assignment. Born Winona Minnesota Jan 11, 1928. Lutheran. Educated at University of Wisconsin B.S. 1951 LL.B. 1953 J.D. 1966. Admitted to practice Wisconsin 1953. Began legal practice Cochrane 1953. Judge, Wisconsin County Courts Buffalo and Pepin Counties Sept 1, 1958 to July 31, 1978.

District Attorney Buffalo County 1954-58. Member Cochrane City Council 1953-58. Member Tri-County Bar Association (Secretary 1956, President 1975). Chairman Wisconsin Judicial Council 1976-79 and Wisconsin Board of Juvenile Court Judges 1969. Attended National College of Trial Judges 1966 and National College of Juvenile Judges 1975. Instructor Wisconsin Judicial College 1969-74. U.S. Army ETO 1945-47. Member Masons (Past Master).

Mailing address: W1586 County Route KK, Alma 54610-8404.

SCHMIDT, Bruce K. *(Judge, Wisconsin Circuit Court Winnebago Circuit)* Assumed office 1991. Elected to subsequent term.

Mailing address: P.O. Box 2808, Oshkosh 54903-2808.

Office: Winnebago County Courthouse, 415 Jackson Drive, Oshkosh 54901-4751.

Telephone: (920) 236-4918.

SCHMIDT, Earl William *(Reserve Judge, Wisconsin Circuit Court)* Elected to term beginning Aug 1, 1984. Reelected 1990 and 1996. Former Chief Judge, Administrative District Nine. Retired. Assumed Reserve status, serves by assignment. Born Birnamwood Wisconsin March 11, 1936. Lutheran. Educated at University of Wisconsin B.S. in Political Science with honors 1962 M.S. in Agricultural Economics 1964 M.S. in Public Administration 1964 J.D. 1972. Admitted to practice Wisconsin 1972. Began legal practice Wittenberg 1972.

District Attorney Shawano-Menominee Counties 1973-74. Wisconsin State Representative 1975-82. Former Member Wisconsin District Attorneys Association. Member Voluntary Association of Trial Judges, State Bar of Wisconsin and Shawano County Bar Association. Previously worked as dairy farmer and development economist in Venezuela, Dominican Republic and Brazil. Member Rotary Club and Elks. Enjoys reading, hunting, fishing and woodworking.

Mailing address: N9827 Whippoorwill Drive, Birnamwood 54414.

SCHROEDER, Bruce E. *(Judge, Wisconsin Circuit Court Kenosha Circuit)* Commissioner 1978-83. Appointed Judge by Governor Anthony S. Earl to term beginning May 25, 1983. Elected 1984, 1990, 1996 and 2002. Current term expires July 31, 2008. Born Milwaukee Wisconsin Nov 16, 1945. Roman Catholic. Educated at Marquette University B.A. 1967 J.D. 1970. Admitted to practice Wisconsin 1971, U.S. District Court Eastern District of Wisconsin 1971 and U.S. Court of Appeals Seventh Circuit 1981. Began legal practice Kenosha 1971. In legal practice 1976-83.

Assistant District Attorney 1971-72 and District Attorney 1972-76 Kenosha County. Member State Bar of Wisconsin and Kenosha County Bar Association.

Office: 209 Kenosha County Courthouse, 912 56th Street, Kenosha 53140-3747.

Telephone: (262) 653-2579.

SCHUDSON, Charles B. *(Judge, Wisconsin Court of Appeals District One)* Elected to term beginning 1992. Reelected 1998, current term expires July 31, 2004. Born Milwaukee Wisconsin Jan 30, 1950. Jewish. Educated at Dartmouth College B.A. magna cum laude 1972 and University of Wisconsin Law School J.D. 1974. Fulbright Fellow 1974. Member University of Wisconsin Law Review 1973-74. Member Phi Beta Kappa. Admitted to practice Wisconsin 1975. Judge, Wisconsin Circuit Court Milwaukee Circuit July 1, 1982 to 1992, appointed by Governor Lee S. Dreyfus.

Assistant District Attorney Milwaukee County 1975-82. Special Assistant U.S. Attorney Eastern District of Wisconsin 1977-79. Wisconsin Special Assistant Attorney General 1978-79. Author "The Criminal Justice System as Family: Trying the Impossible for Battered Women" U.S. Commission on Civil Rights 1978 and "What Children Can't Tell Us and Why" *Family Advocate* American Bar Association 1996. Co-author "Nailing an Omelet to the Wall: Prosecuting Nursing Home Homicide" in *Corporations as Criminals* Sage 1984 and *On Trial: America's Courts and Their Treatment of Sexually Abused Children* Beacon Press 1st ed. 1989, 2nd ed. 1991. Faculty Member Wisconsin Law School Program for Latin American Attorneys 1974, University of Wisconsin-Milwaukee Department of Criminal Justice 1978-86 and University of Wisconsin Law School 1999-2001. Consultant/Faculty American Academy of Pediatrics. Lecturer U.S. Department of Justice seminars for white collar crime investigators and prosecutors 1977-79. Member State Bar of Wisconsin. Lecturer judicial colleges and conferences in approximately forty states, Canada, Iceland, Israel and Russia. Faculty Member National Council of Juvenile and Family Court Judges and The National Judicial College 1985-2001. Recipient Award for Superior Performance from U.S. Department of Justice 1980, Certificate of Special Achievement as person in Wisconsin legal profession who provided outstanding service to children from Wisconsin Committee for Prevention of Child Abuse 1986, Judge of the Year Award from Career Youth Development 1995, Human Rights Leadership Award from Freedom Magazine 1998 and Foundation for Improvement of Justice Award 2000. Honorary Curator of American History Milwaukee County Museum. Enjoys music, sports, theatre and collecting presidential campaign memorabilia.

Office: 633 West Wisconsin Avenue, Suite 1400, Milwaukee 53203-1908.

Telephone: (414) 227-4684.

SCHUH, Dennis C. *(Judge, Wisconsin Circuit Court Juneau Circuit)* Appointed by Governor Jim Doyle June 2003.

Office: Juneau County Justice Center, 200 Oak Street, Mauston 53948.

Telephone: (608) 847-9351.

SCHUMANN, Arnold K. *(Reserve Judge, Wisconsin Circuit Court)* Assumed office June 25, 1982. Elected 1983 and April 1989. Retired July 31, 1995. Assumed Reserve status, serves by assignment. Born Watertown Wisconsin Oct 6, 1931. Lutheran. Educated at University

SCHUMANN, ARNOLD K.—*Continued*

of Wisconsin B.S. 1957 J.D. 1966. Admitted to practice Wisconsin 1966. In legal practice Watertown 1966.

Member State Bar of Wisconsin and Jefferson County Bar Association (Past President). Corporal U.S. Army 1952-54. President Watertown Rotary Club. Former Member Board of Directors M & I Bank of Watertown. Board of Control Northwestern College Watertown. Sports participant and fan. Enjoys racquetball, golf, swimming, travel and writing.

Mailing address: 537 South Fischer Avenue, Jefferson 53549-2129.

SCHWARTZ, Stuart A. *(Judge, Wisconsin Circuit Court Dane Circuit)*

Office: 231 City-County Building, 210 Martin Luther King Jr. Blvd., Madison 53703.

Telephone: (608) 267-2517.

SHABAZ, John C. *(Judge, United States District Court Western District of Wisconsin)* Appointed by President Ronald Reagan to term beginning Jan 19, 1982. Former Chief Judge. Born Milwaukee Wisconsin June 25, 1931. Educated at University of Wisconsin B.S. and Marquette University J.D. Admitted to practice Wisconsin. Began legal practice West Allis 1957.

Member State Bar of Wisconsin and Dane County Bar Association. Captain U.S. Army 1953-64. State Representative Wisconsin Legislature 1965-81.

Mailing address: P.O. Box 591, Madison 53701-0591.

Telephone: (608) 264-5504.

SHAPIRO, James Edward *(Judge, United States Bankruptcy Court Eastern District of Wisconsin)* Appointed by U.S. District Court judges to term beginning Feb 2, 1982. Reappointed by U.S. Court of Appeals Seventh Circuit judges 1986 and 2000. Current term expires March 31, 2014. Chief Judge September 18, 1996 to May 31, 2000. Born Chicago Illinois May 28, 1930. Jewish. Educated at University of Wisconsin B.S. 1951 and Harvard Law School J.D. 1954. Admitted to practice Wisconsin 1956, U.S. District Court Eastern District of Wisconsin 1956, U.S. Court of Appeals Seventh Circuit 1962 and U.S. Supreme Court 1971. In legal practice Milwaukee 1956-82. Court Commissioner, Milwaukee County 1969-78.

Board of Appeals Village of Bayside 1969-77. Director Legal Aid Society of Milwaukee 1969-77. Member State Bar of Wisconsin (Director Bankruptcy, Insolvency and Creditors' Rights Section 1984-85) and Milwaukee Bar Association (Past Chairman Bankruptcy Section). First Lieutenant U.S. Army Military Police 1954-56. Enjoys tennis.

Office: 140 U.S. Courthouse, 517 East Wisconsin Avenue, Milwaukee 53202.

Telephone: (414) 297-3291.

SHEEDY, Patrick T. *(Reserve Judge, Wisconsin Circuit Court)* Elected to term beginning Jan 7, 1980. Reelected 1986 and 1992. Chief Judge Administrative District One 1990-98. Retired. Assumed Reserve status, serves by assignment. Born Green Bay Wisconsin Oct 31, 1921. Catholic. Educated at Marquette University B.S. 1943 J.D. 1948 and John Marshall Law School LL.M. 1972. Member Alpha Sigma Nu and Delta Sigma Rho. Admitted to practice Wisconsin 1948. In legal practice Milwaukee 1948-80.

Instructor Marquette University 1948-54. Member State Bar of Wisconsin (President 1974-75, Board of Governors), Milwaukee (Executive Board) and American (House of Delegates since 1974, Board of Governors 1985-88) Bar Associations. Colonel U.S. Army JAGC 1942-72. President Marquette Law Alumni and Exchange Club. Chairman Milwaukee Archdiocesan School Board. Member Kiwanis.

Mailing address: 107 East Foxdale Road, Glendale 53217.

SICKEL, James R. *(Magistrate Judge, United States District Court Eastern District of Wisconsin)* Appointed by U.S. District Court judges. Serves part time.

Office: 101 Jefferson Court Building, 125 South Jefferson Street, Green Bay 54301-4500.

Telephone: (920) 432-7716.

SIEFERT, John *(Judge, Wisconsin Circuit Court Milwaukee Circuit)* Elected April 1999 to term beginning Aug 1, 1999. Term expires July 31, 2005. Born Racine Wisconsin April 14, 1949. Roman Catholic. Educated at University of Chicago B.A. 1971 and University of Wisconsin J.D. 1974. Admitted to practice Wisconsin 1974. Municipal Judge, Milwaukee 1979-83 and 1993-99.

Instructor in Police Science Milton College 1978-79. Adjunct Faculty Mt. Senario College. Member State Bar of Wisconsin. Police Officer Milwaukee 1976-79 and 1983-89. Milwaukee County Treasurer (two terms). Member Wisconsin Law Enforcement Officer's Association.

Office: 615 Milwaukee County Courthouse, 901 North Ninth Street, Milwaukee 53233-1425.

Telephone: (414) 278-4764.

E-mail address: jsiefert@wi.rr.com

SIMANEK, Stephen A. *(Judge, Wisconsin Circuit Court Racine Circuit)* Term expires July 31, 2004. Former Chief Judge Administrative District Two.

Office: 703 Racine County Courthouse, 730 Wisconsin Avenue, Racine 53403-1274.

Telephone: (262) 636-3150.

SKUPNIEWITZ, Joseph W. *(Magistrate Judge, United States District Court Western District of Wisconsin)* Appointed by U.S. District Court judges Dec 26, 1972. Reappointed to subsequent terms. Serves part time. Also serves as Clerk of Court.

Mailing address: P.O. Box 432, Madison 53701-0432.

Telephone: (608) 264-5156.

SMELTZER, Rod W. *(Judge, Wisconsin Circuit Court Dunn Circuit)* Elected to term beginning Aug 1, 1997.

Office: 1300 Judicial Center, 615 Stokke Parkway, Menomonie 54751.

Telephone: (715) 232-1449.

SNYDER, Harry G. *(Judge, Wisconsin Court of Appeals District Two)* Assumed office 1991. Former Presiding Judge. Born Davenport Iowa Feb 11, 1938. Educated at Ripon College 1956-58, University of Wisconsin-Madison B.S. 1961 and Marquette University Law School J.D. 1964. In legal practice 1970-80.

Assistant District Attorney Waukesha County 1968-69. Former Member Legislative Committee Wisconsin Judicial Conference. USAF 1964-67. State Representative

SNYDER, HARRY G.—*Continued*

84th District State Assembly Wisconsin 1975-80. Enjoys travel.

Office: 2727 North Grandview Boulevard, Suite 300, Waukesha 53188-1672.

Telephone: (262) 521-5233.

SOSNAY, William *(Judge, Wisconsin Circuit Court Milwaukee Circuit)*

Office: 509 Milwaukee County Courthouse, 901 North Ninth Street, Milwaukee 53233-1425.

Telephone: (414) 278-4514.

STADTMUELLER, J. P. *(Judge, United States District Court Eastern District of Wisconsin)* Appointed for life by President Ronald Reagan to term beginning 1987. Chief Judge 1995 to Aug 31, 2002. Born Oshkosh Wisconsin Jan 28, 1942. Educated at Marquette University B.A. 1964 J.D. 1967. In legal practice Milwaukee 1968-69 and 1975-76.

Assistant U.S. Attorney 1969-74 and 1977-78, First Assistant U.S. Attorney 1974-75, Deputy U.S. Attorney 1978-81 and U.S. Attorney 1981-87 Eastern District of Wisconsin.

Office: U.S. Courthouse, 517 East Wisconsin Avenue, Milwaukee 53202.

Telephone: (414) 297-1122.

STAFFORD, Richard H. *(Reserve Judge, Wisconsin Circuit Court)* Appointed by Governor Martin J. Schreiber to term beginning Aug 1, 1978. Elected 1979, 1985 and 1991. Retired. Assumed Reserve status, serves by assignment. Born Chippewa Falls Wisconsin April 13, 1928. Presbyterian. Educated at University of Wisconsin-Madison B.S. LL.B. Admitted to practice Wisconsin 1953. Began legal practice Chippewa Falls 1955.

Member Association of Trial Judges, State Bar of Wisconsin and Chippewa County Bar Association. Corporal U.S. Army 1953-55. Enjoys fishing, hunting and other outdoor activities.

Mailing address: 804 West Columbia Street, Chippewa Falls 54729.

STAMPER, Russell Wright *(Reserve Judge, Wisconsin Circuit Court)* Appointed by Governor Anthony S. Earl to term beginning April 30, 1983. Elected 1984 and 1990. Retired July 31, 1996. Assumed Reserve status, serves by assignment. Born Buffalo New York Sept 26, 1944. Baptist. Educated at State University of New York at Buffalo B.S. 1967 J.D. 1973. Member Alpha Phi Alpha and Phi Alpha Delta. Admitted to practice Wisconsin 1973, U.S. District Court Eastern District of Wisconsin 1976 and U.S. Court of Appeals Seventh Circuit 1976. Began legal practice Milwaukee 1973.

Lecturer on Administration of Justice Milwaukee Area Technical College 1975-76. Member State Bar of Wisconsin and Milwaukee Bar Association. Listed in *Who's Who in American Law* 1977. E-2 U.S. Army 1969. Previously worked as teacher. President Wisconsin Black Lawyers Association 1982-83. Interests include history, theology and travel.

Mailing address: 1217 West Clarke Street, Milwaukee 53206.

STARK, Lisa Kay *(Judge, Wisconsin Circuit Court Eau Claire Circuit)* Elected to term beginning Aug 1, 2000. Term expires July 31, 2006.

Office: Eau Claire County Courthouse, 721 Oxford Avenue, Eau Claire 54703-5481.

Telephone: (715) 839-4809.

STEINMETZ, Donald W. *(Reserve Judge, Wisconsin Circuit Court)* Elected to term beginning Aug 1. 1080. Reelected 1990. Retired. Assumed Reserve status, serves by assignment. Born Milwaukee Wisconsin Sept 19, 1924. Catholic. Educated at University of Wisconsin-Madison B.A. 1949 J.D. 1951. In legal practice 1951-58. Judge 1966-78 and Deputy Presiding Judge 1977-78, Wisconsin County Court Milwaukee County. Judge, Wisconsin Circuit Court 1978-80.

Assistant Milwaukee City Attorney 1958-60. First Assistant District Attorney Milwaukee County 1960-65. Special Assistant Attorney General of Wisconsin 1965-66. Author "Disparity in Sentencing" Trial Judges Journal Jan 1968. Member American Judicature Society. Wisconsin Administrative Committee of Courts, Wisconsin Judicial Planning Committee, Voluntary Association of Trial Judges (Executive Board 1979-80), State Bar of Wisconsin, Milwaukee and American Bar Associations. President Wisconsin Board of County Judges. Instructor National College of the State Judiciary 1966 and in Small Claims, Temporary Restraining Orders, Contempt and Gag Rule at Wisconsin Judicial Education College 1974-78. Participant Humanities Seminar sponsored by National Endowment for the Humanities University of Wisconsin 1974 and Institute of Judicial Administration Senior Appellate Judges Seminar 1981. Secretary Executive Board Milwaukee Board of Judges 1967-70. Member Judicial Election and Selection Committee 1967-68, Law Library Committee 1968, Court Reorganization Committee 1969, Committee to Recommend Rules on Use of Sound Camera Equipment in the Courtroom 1969-70, Judicial Code of Ethics Committee 1973-74, Administrative Committee of Courts 1976-79, Career Criminal Committee 1977, State Judicial Planning Committee 1977, Criminal Jury Instructions Committee 1978-80,Wisconsin Council on Criminal Justice 1979-80, State Court Reporters Compensation and Qualifications Committee 1979-80 and State Board of Criminal Court Judges (Secretary). Second Lieutenant Bombardier-Navigator U.S. Army Air Corps 1943-45. President South Division High School Old Timers. Life Member Wisconsin Alumni Association and National "W" Club. Member Centurions of St. Joseph's Hospital and American Legion.

Mailing address: N53 West 34356 Road Q, Okauchee 53069.

STENGEL, L. Edward *(Judge, Wisconsin Circuit Court Sheboygan Circuit)* Elected to term beginning Aug 1, 1985. Reelected 1991, 1997 and 2003. Current term expires July 31, 2009. Chief Judge Administrative District Four since April 9, 2001. Born Springfield Illinois Dec 16, 1948. Educated at University of Notre Dame B.A. 1971 and Marquette University J.D. 1975. District Attorney Sheboygan County 1977-85.

Office: Sheboygan County Courthouse, 615 North Sixth Street, Sheboygan 53081-4692.

Telephone: (920) 459-0308.

STEWART, William C., Jr. *(Judge, Wisconsin Circuit Court Dunn Circuit)*
Office: 1300 Judicial Center, 615 Stokke Parkway, Menomonie 54751.
Telephone: (715) 232-1449.

STORCK, John R. *(Judge, Wisconsin Circuit Court Dodge Circuit)* Appointed by Governor Tommy G. Thompson Sept 2, 1994 to term beginning Oct 7, 1994. Elected 1995 and 2001. Current term expires July 31, 2007. Born Beaver Dam Wisconsin June 27, 1954. United Methodist. Educated at University of Wisconsin-Madison B.B.A. 1976 and Harvard Law School J.D. cum laude 1979. Admitted to practice Wisconsin 1979. In legal practice Mayville 1979-94.
Member State Bar of Wisconsin and Dodge County Bar Association.
Office: Dodge County Justice Facility, 210 West Center Street, Juneau 53039-1091.
Telephone: (920) 386-3550.
E-mail address: John.Storck@dodge.courts.state.wi.us

SULLIVAN, Michael P. *(Judge, Wisconsin Circuit Court Milwaukee Circuit)* Assumed office Jan 2, 1978. Elected 1984, 1990, 1996 and April 2002. Current term expires July 31, 2008. Born Chicago Illinois Jan 4, 1944. Educated at Marquette University 1965 and University of Michigan 1968. Admitted to practice Wisconsin 1970. Judicial Court Commissioner Milwaukee County 1972-77.
Assistant City Attorney Milwaukee 1970-72. Member State Bar of Wisconsin and Milwaukee Bar Association.
Office: 415 Milwaukee County Courthouse, 901 North Ninth Street, Milwaukee 53233-1425.
Telephone: (414) 278-4500.
E-mail: michael.sullivan@milwaukee.courts.state.wi.us

SUMI, Maryann *(Judge, Wisconsin Circuit Court Dane Circuit)*
Office: 215 City-County Building, 210 Martin Luther King Jr. Blvd., Madison 53703.
Telephone: (608) 266-4233.

SWIETLIK, Walter J. *(Reserve Judge, Wisconsin Circuit Court)* Appointed by Governor Martin J. Schreiber to term beginning Aug 9, 1978. Elected 1979, 1985, 1991 and 1997. Retired March 2002. Assumed Reserve status, serves by assignment. Born Milwaukee Wisconsin April 20, 1935. Catholic. Educated at Marquette University B.S. 1957 LL.B. 1960. Admitted to practice Wisconsin 1960 and U.S. District Court District of Wisconsin 1960. Began legal practice Port Washington 1960. In legal practice Cedarburg 1971-78.
Ozaukee County District Attorney 1963-71. Member State Bar of Wisconsin and Ozaukee County Bar Association.
Mailing address: 4260 Blueberry Road, Fredonia 53021.

SYKES, Diane S. *(Justice, Wisconsin Supreme Court)* Born Milwaukee Wisconsin Dec 23, 1957. Catholic. Educated at Northwestern University B.S. 1980 and Marquette University J.D. Staff member Marquette Law Review 1982-84. Law Clerk to Hon. Terence T. Evans, U.S. District Court Eastern District of Wisconsin 1984-85. Admitted to practice Wisconsin 1984. In legal practice Milwaukee 1985-92. Former Judge, Wisconsin Circuit Court Milwaukee Circuit.
Faculty Member Wisconsin Judicial College.
Mailing address: P.O. Box 1688, Madison 53701-1688.
Office: 16 East State Capitol, Madison 53702.
Telephone: (608) 266-1884.

TAGGART, Patrick J. *(Judge, Wisconsin Circuit Court Sauk Circuit)* Appointed by Governor Tommy G. Thompson to term beginning July 30, 1993. Elected 1999, current term expires July 31, 2005.
Office: Sauk County Courthouse, 515 Oak Street, Baraboo 53913-2496.
Telephone: (608) 355-3214.

TAYLOR, James H. *(Reserve Judge, Wisconsin Circuit Court)* Retired. Assumed Reserve status, serves by assignment.
Mailing address: 4573 Sand Point Road, Webster 54893.

TESMER, Louise *(Reserve Judge, Wisconsin Circuit Court)* Elected to term beginning Aug 1, 1989. Reelected 1995. Retired. Assumed Reserve status, serves by assignment.
Mailing address: 8875 Woodbridge Drive, Greendale 53129.

THUMS, Raymond F. *(Judge, Wisconsin Circuit Court Marathon Circuit)* Term expires July 31, 2007.
Office: Marathon County Courthouse, 500 Forest Street, Wausau 54403-5568.
Telephone: (715) 261-1350.

TODRYK, Phillip P. *(Reserve Judge, Wisconsin Circuit Court)* Retired. Assumed Reserve status, serves by assignment.
Mailing address: P.O. Box 779, Hudson 54016.

TORHORST, Allan "Pat" *(Judge, Wisconsin Circuit Court Racine Circuit)* Elected to term beginning Aug 1, 1991. Reelected 1997 and 2003. Current term expires July 31, 2009. Born Waukegan Illinois March 7, 1941. Educated at University of Wisconsin B.S. 1963 J.D. 1966. Admitted to practice Wisconsin 1966.
Office: 703 Racine County Courthouse, 730 Wisconsin Avenue, Racine 53403-1274.
Telephone: (262) 636-3304.

TROY, Joseph M. *(Judge, Wisconsin Circuit Court Outagamie Circuit)* Elected to term beginning Aug 1, 1987. Reelected 1993 and 1999. Current term expires July 31, 2005. Currently serves as Chief Judge Administrative District Eight.
Office: Justice Center, 320 South Walnut Street, Appleton 54911-5991.
Telephone: (920) 832-5245.

ULLSVIK, John M. *(Judge, Wisconsin Circuit Court Jefferson Circuit)*
Office: Jefferson County Courthouse, 320 South Main Street, Jefferson 53549-1799.
Telephone: (920) 674-7178.

UTSCHIG, Thomas S. *(Judge, United States Bankruptcy Court Western District of Wisconsin)*
Mailing address: P.O. Box 5009, Eau Claire 54702-5009.
Telephone: (715) 839-2985.

VAN AKKEREN, Timothy M. *(Judge, Wisconsin Circuit Court Sheboygan Circuit)* Elected to term beginning Aug 1, 1989. Reelected 1995 and 2001. Current term expires July 31, 2007.

Office: Sheboygan County Courthouse, 615 North Sixth Street, Sheboygan 53081-4692.

Telephone: (920) 459-0393.

VAN DE HEY, Robert P. *(Judge, Wisconsin Circuit Court Grant Circuit)* Appointed by Governor Tommy G. Thompson Nov 1998. Elected April 1999, current term expires July 31, 2005. Born Eau Claire Wisconsin Dec 8, 1959. Educated at University of Wisconsin-Madison B.S. 1982 J.D. 1985. Admitted to practice Wisconsin 1985. In legal practice Lancaster 1986-98.

Village Attorney Tennyson and Potosi 1986-95. City Attorney Lancaster 1996-98. Board of Attorneys Professional Responsibility District Twelve Committee 1996-98. Member District Five Committee 1993-96, Probate/Benchbook Committee 2002 and Planning Committee Wisconsin Judicial Conference 2003. Member State Bar of Wisconsin and Grant County Bar Association.

Mailing address: P.O. Box 89, Lancaster 53813.

Office: Grant County Courthouse, 130 West Maple Street, Lancaster 53813.

Telephone: (608) 723-7826.

E-mail address: Robert.vandehey-@grant.courts.state.wi.us

VAN DE WATER, Linda *(Judge, Wisconsin Circuit Court Waukesha Circuit)* Elected to term beginning May 5, 2003.

Office: Juvenile Center, 521 Riverview, Waukesha 53188-3636.

Telephone: (262) 548-7543.

VERGERONT, Margaret J. *(Presiding Judge, Wisconsin Court of Appeals District Four)* Elected April 1994 to term beginning Aug 1, 1994. Reelected 2000, current term expires July 31, 2006. Born Madison Wisconsin May 6, 1946. Educated at University of Wisconsin B.A. with honors 1968 M.A. in English 1969 J.D. with honors 1975. Law Clerk to Hon. James E. Doyle, U.S. District Court Western District of Wisconsin 1975-76. Member Phi Beta Kappa and Phi Kappa Phi. Admitted to practice Wisconsin 1975, U.S. District Courts Eastern 1976 and Western 1976 Districts of Wisconsin and U.S. Court of Appeals Seventh Circuit. In legal practice Madison 1984-94.

Member Board of Legal Action of Wisconsin 1986-90 and Judicial Education Committee since 2000. Member Legal Association of Women, National Association of Women Judges, American Judicature Society, State Bar of Wisconsin (Delivery of Legal Services Committee 1989-91, Board of Governors 1992-94, Diversity Outreach Committee since 1995), Dane County (Delivery of Legal Services Committee 1982-95; Executive Board 1986-88, 1989-90 and 1991-92; President 1990-91; Trustee Pro Bono Trust Fund 1992-94) and American (Appellate Judges Conference Judicial Administration Division) Bar Associations. Recipient Pro Bono Awards from State Bar of Wisconsin 1988 and Dane County Bar Association 1988. Mentor Franklin-Randall Mentor Program since 1994. Enjoys gardening, traveling and reading.

Office: 10 East Doty Street, Suite 700, Madison 53703-3397.

Telephone: (608) 267-3100.

E-mail address: margaret.vergeront@courts.state.wi.us

VLACK, Edward F., III *(Judge, Wisconsin Circuit Court St. Croix Circuit)* Elected Nov 2000 to term beginning Aug 1, 2001. Term expires July 31, 2007.

Office: Government Center, 1101 Carmichael Street, Hudson 54016-7710.

Telephone: (715) 386-4612.

VOCKE, Timothy Louis *(Reserve Judge, Wisconsin Circuit Court)* Elected to term beginning Jan 2, 1979. Retired Jan 4, 1983. Assumed Reserve status, serves by assignment. Born Berwyn Illinois April 13, 1948. Lutheran. Educated at University of Kansas B.A. 1970 and University of Wisconsin J.D. 1973. Admitted to practice Wisconsin 1973, U.S. District Courts Eastern 1973 and Western 1987 Districts of Wisconsin and U.S. Supreme Court 1983. Began legal practice Racine 1973. In legal practice Eagle River 1976-79 and Rhinelander since 1983.

Assistant District Attorney 1973-76 and District Attorney 1976-79. Important Decisions: Noranda Exploration, Inc. v. M. E. Ostrum, Bronson C. LaFollette and Anthony S. Earl (constitutionality of §107.15 Wisconsin Statutes) Dec 18, 1980; and Thomas H. Barland et al. v. Eau Claire County et al. (inherent powers of circuit courts) 95 CV 765 May 3, 1996, aff'd Wis Sup Ct. Reserve Judge Representative to Executive Committee Wisconsin Judicial Conference since 1997. Member Legislative Council's Special Committee on Pretrial Release 1980-81, Code of Professional Responsibility Review Committee Wisconsin Supreme Court 1984-85, Judicial Independence Committee 1987-93 (Chairman 1991-92) and Bench/Bar Committee since 1996. Former Member Racine County Bar Association. Member Civil Trial Council of Wisconsin, Wisconsin Reserve Judges Association, Wisconsin Judicial Council, State Bar of Wisconsin and Tri-County Bar Association. Attended Wisconsin Judicial College 1978 and General Jurisdiction Course 1979 and Civil Litigation Graduate Session The National Judicial College. Midshipman NROTC 1966-69. Former Member Board of Directors Northwoods Hospital. District Chairman Boy Scouts of America 1984-87. Certified Combat Hapkido Instructor. Reactive Self Defense Instructor Wisconsin Conservation Corps, Rhinelander School District and State Judiciary. Member North Central Black Belt Instructors Federation. Participates in Sam Dan, Taekwon-do, Cho Dan, Kyuki-do and Sam Dan Combat Hapkido.

Mailing address: 540 Spring Lake Road, Rhinelander 54501.

VUVUNAS, Emmanuel J. *(Judge, Wisconsin Circuit Court Racine Circuit)* Appointed by Governor Lee Dreyfus to term beginning Aug 1, 1979. Elected 1980, 1986, 1992 and 1998. Current term expires July 31, 2004. Born Milwaukee Wisconsin March 13, 1942. Greek Orthodox. Educated at University of Wisconsin B.S. 1965 J.D. 1967. Admitted to practice Wisconsin 1967. Began legal practice Racine 1968.

Member State Bar of Wisconsin and Racine Bar Association. Member Kiwanis.

Office: 703 Racine County Courthouse, 730 Wisconsin Avenue, Racine 53403-1274.

Telephone: (262) 636-3804.

WAGNER, Jeffrey A. *(Judge, Wisconsin Circuit Court Milwaukee Circuit)*
Office: 500 Milwaukee County Courthouse, 901 North Ninth Street, Milwaukee 53233-1425.
Telephone: (414) 278-5393.

WAGNER, Mary K. *(Judge, Wisconsin Circuit Court Kenosha Circuit)*
Office: 336 Kenosha County Courthouse, 912 56th Street, Kenosha 53140-3747.
Telephone: (262) 653-2712.

WAHL, Eric J. *(Judge, Wisconsin Circuit Court Eau Claire Circuit)* Elected to term beginning Aug 1, 1993. Reelected 1999, current term expires July 31, 2005. Born St. Johns Michigan June 14, 1942. Educated at University of Wisconsin-Madison B.S. 1964 J.D. 1967 and George Washington University National Law Center LL.M. 1971. Admitted to practice Wisconsin 1967, U.S. District Court Western District of Wisconsin, U.S. Court of Appeals Seventh Circuit and U.S. Supreme Court. In legal practice Madison 1974-76 and Eau Claire 1976-93.
Assistant U.S. Attorney Western District of Wisconsin 1971-74. Special Agent FBI 1967-71.
Office: Eau Claire County Courthouse, 721 Oxford Avenue, Eau Claire 54703-5481.
Telephone: (715) 839-4806.

WALL, Joseph R. *(Judge, Wisconsin Circuit Court Milwaukee Circuit)* Elected Nov 2000 to term beginning Aug 1, 2001. Term expires July 31, 2007.
Office: 1410 Children's Court Center, 10201 West Watertown Plank Road, Milwaukee 53226-3532.
Telephone: (414) 257-6937.

WARPINSKI, Mark A. *(Judge, Wisconsin Circuit Court Brown Circuit)*
Mailing address: P.O. Box 23600, Green Bay 54305-3600.
Office: Brown County Courthouse, 100 South Jefferson Street, Green Bay 54301.
Telephone: (920) 448-4112.

WARREN, Wilbur W. *(Judge, Wisconsin Circuit Court Kenosha Circuit)*
Office: 124 Kenosha County Courthouse, 912 56th Street, Kenosha 53140-3747.
Telephone: (262) 653-2739.

WASIELEWSKI, Francis T. *(Judge, Wisconsin Circuit Court Milwaukee Circuit)* Appointed by Governor Anthony S. Earl to term beginning Oct 1, 1983. Elected 1984, 1990, 1996 and April 2002. Current term expires July 31, 2008. Born Milwaukee Wisconsin Sept 21, 1942. Catholic. Educated at Marquette University B.S. 1964 and University of Wisconsin J.D. 1968. Member Phi Delta Phi. Admitted to practice Wisconsin 1968. In legal practice Milwaukee 1968-70 and 1975-83.
Assistant City Attorney Milwaukee 1970-75. Commissioner 1977-83 and Chairman 1982-83 Metropolitan Sewage District Milwaukee. Chairman Administrative Review Appeals Board City of Milwaukee 1978-83. Member Wisconsin Association of Trial Judges, State Bar of Wisconsin and American Bar Association. Member Rotary Club and Milwaukee Chamber Music Society. Enjoys reading, piano, skiing and jogging.
Office: 2410 Children's Court Center, 10201 West Watertown Plank Road, Wauwatosa 53226-3532.
Telephone: (414) 454-4220.

WEDEMEYER, Ted E., Jr. *(Presiding Judge, Wisconsin Court of Appeals District One)* Born Milwaukee Wisconsin Aug 30, 1932. Roman Catholic. Educated at College of the Holy Cross A.B. 1954, Marquette University LL.B. 1957 and John Marshall Law School LL.M. 1961. Admitted to practice Wisconsin 1957. Began legal practice Milwaukee 1957. Judge, Municipal Court 1975-77. Former Judge, Wisconsin Circuit Court Circuit Two, appointed by Governor Martin J. Schreiber to term beginning Oct 28, 1977.
Member State Bar of Wisconsin, Milwaukee and American Bar Associations. Director Milwaukee Criminal Justice Council. Airman Second Class USAF 1957-58. Board of Trustees Milwaukee Library. Chairman Board of Zoning Appeals. Chairman of Board Metro-Kickers Soccer Club. Board of Directors Milwaukee Christian Center, Easter Seals and Volunteers of America. Planning Committee DePaul Rehabilitation Center.
Office: 633 West Wisconsin Avenue, Suite 1400, Milwaukee 53203-1908.
Telephone: (414) 227-5160.

WEINKE, Steven W. *(Judge, Wisconsin Circuit Court Fond du Lac Circuit)* Elected to term beginning Aug 1, 1986. Reelected 1992 and 1998, current term expires July 31, 2004. Born Fond du Lac Wisconsin May 2, 1939. Educated at University of Wisconsin B.S. 1961 J.D. 1966. Admitted to practice Wisconsin 1966. Began legal practice Fond du Lac 1966.
Member State Bar of Wisconsin and Fond du Lac County Bar Association.
Mailing address: P.O. Box 1355, Fond du Lac 54936-1355.
Office: Fond du Lac County Courthouse, 160 South Macy Street, Fond du Lac 54935.
Telephone: (920) 929-3069.

WELKER, James E. *(Judge, Wisconsin Circuit Court Rock Circuit)* Elected to term beginning Aug 1, 1988. Reelected 1994 and 2000. Current term expires July 31, 2006. Born Richland Center Wisconsin May 24, 1936. Congregational. Educated at University of Wisconsin B.A. 1959 J.D. 1969. Member Phi Alpha Delta. Admitted to practice Wisconsin 1969 and U.S. District Courts Eastern 1969 and Western 1969 Districts of Wisconsin. In legal practice Janesville 1969-88.
Author "Paternity Judgments: Who Is a Necessary Party?" Wisconsin Journal of Family Law 1991. Instructor in Legal Writing 1967-69 and Legal Practice 1974-76 University of Wisconsin. Member State Bar of Wisconsin (Chairperson Family Law Section 1989-90), Rock County and American Bar Associations. Instructor in Family Law for numerous seminars State Bar of Wisconsin 1974-90. English speech instructor 1959-66. President Congregational Church 1988. Interests include community theater and research in World War I Eastern Front.
Office: Rock County Courthouse, Fifth Floor, 51 South Main Street, Janesville 53545-3978.
Telephone: (608) 743-2233.

WELLS, Lee Edward *(Judge, Wisconsin Circuit Court Milwaukee Circuit)* Appointed by Governor Lee S. Dreyfus to term beginning Aug 31, 1981. Elected 1982, 1988, 1994 and 2000. Current term expires July 31, 2006. Born Milwaukee Wisconsin Sept 4, 1941. Ed-

WELLS, LEE EDWARD—*Continued*
ucated at Marquette University B.A. cum laude 1963 and University of Wisconsin Law School J.D. with honors 1966. Staff member Wisconsin Law Review. Member Phi Alpha Delta. Admitted to practice Wisconsin 1966, U.S. District Court Eastern District of Wisconsin 1970 and U.S. Court of Appeals Seventh Circuit 1972. Began legal practice Milwaukee 1966.

Assistant District Attorney 1969-72 and Deputy District Attorney 1976-81 Milwaukee County. Associate Professor of Law Marquette University Law School 1972-75. Member State Bar of Wisconsin.

Office: 712 Milwaukee County Courthouse, 901 North Ninth Street, Milwaukee 53233-1425.

Telephone: (414) 278-4560.

WERNER, Richard T. *(Judge, Wisconsin Circuit Court Rock Circuit)*

Office: Rock County Courthouse, Fifth Floor, 51 South Main Street, Janesville 53545-3978.

Telephone: (608) 743-2229.

WHITE, Maxine A. *(Judge, Wisconsin Circuit Court Milwaukee Circuit)*

Office: 403 Milwaukee County Courthouse, 901 North Ninth Street, Milwaukee 53233-1425.

Telephone: (414) 278-4482.

WILCOX, Jon P. *(Justice, Wisconsin Supreme Court)* Appointed by Governor Tommy G. Thompson to term beginning Sept 1, 1992. Elected 1997, current term expires 2007. Born Berlin Wisconsin Sept 5, 1936. Lutheran. Educated at Ripon College A.B. 1958 and University of Wisconsin J.D. 1965. Member Phi Alpha Delta. Admitted to practice Wisconsin and U.S. District Court Western District of Wisconsin. In legal practice La Crosse and Wautoma 1965-79. Commissioner Waushara County Family Court 1978-79. Judge, Wisconsin Circuit Court Waushara Circuit Aug 1, 1979 to Aug 31, 1992. Chief Judge, Wisconsin Circuit Court Sixth Judicial Administrative District 1985-92.

Contributor *Wisconsin News Reporters Handbook* (Wisconsin Courts and Court Procedures) 1987. Member District Board of Attorneys Professional Responsibility 1976-79. Governor Appointee 1984, Vice Chairperson and Chairperson 1987-92 Wisconsin Sentencing Commission. Chairperson Wisconsin Chief Judges Association 1990-92. Member State-Federal Judicial Council 1992-99. Member Judicial Legislative Committee 1981-87, Wisconsin Felony Sentencing Guideline Committee 1982-84, Judicial Clerk Utilization Committee 1986-87 and Wisconsin Judicial Council 1992-98. Board of Directors Wisconsin Law Foundation since 1995. Fellow American Bar Foundation. Member State Bar of Wisconsin (Media and Law Relations Committee since 1982, Judicial Substitution Committee 1986-87, Bench/Bar Committee since 1993, Co-chairperson Outstanding Jurist Award Subcommittee since 1995 and Commission on Co-Equal Branch of Government since 1995), Dane County, Tri-County and American (Committee on Continuing Appellate Education Appellate Judges Conference Judicial Administration Division since 1995) Bar Associations. Lecturer various seminars Wisconsin Judicial Education Committee since 1980. Faculty Member Wisconsin Judicial College 1985-96. Presenter *Judicial Discretion and Sentencing* National Institute of Justice Conference 1987. Recipient Outstanding Jaycee Award 1974 and Distinguished Alumni Award from Ripon College 1993. First Lieutenant Military Police Branch U.S. Army 1959-61. Member State Legislature Wisconsin 1969-75 (Insurance and Banking Committee, Judiciary Committee, State Building Commission, State Bond Board, Transportation Committee, Legislative Council's Special Committee on Criminal Penalties, Governor's Highway Safety Task Force, Governor's Commission on Reapportionment, Elections Committee, Taxation and Joint Interim Committee, Legislative Council's Age of Majority Study Committee, Remedial Legislation Committee). Member Wisconsin Conservation Congress 1975-80 and Prison Overcrowding Task Force 1988-90. Board of Visitors University of Wisconsin Law School 1970-76. Member Rotary, Trout Unlimited, Ruffed Grouse Society and Ducks Unlimited.

Mailing address: P.O. Box 1688, Madison 53701-1688.

Office: 16 East State Capitol, Madison 53702.

Telephone: (608) 266-1881.

WILK, S. Michael *(Judge, Wisconsin Circuit Court Kenosha Circuit)*

Office: 100 Kenosha County Courthouse, 912 56th Street, Kenosha 53140-3747.

Telephone: (262) 653-2469.

WILLIAMS, Thomas S. *(Reserve Judge, Wisconsin Circuit Court)* Assumed office Aug 1, 1978. Elected 1980, 1986 and 1992. Deputy Chief Judge 1982-84 and 1990 and Former Chief Judge Administrative District Four. Retired. Assumed Reserve status 1998, serves by assignment. Born Oshkosh Wisconsin July 3, 1933. Educated at Carleton College B.A. in Psychology cum laude 1955, Harvard University 1955-56 and University of Wisconsin J.D. magna cum laude 1958. Editor Wisconsin Law Review 1957-58. Member Phi Beta Kappa, Phi Delta Phi and Order of the Coif. Admitted to practice Wisconsin 1958 and U.S. District Court Eastern District of Wisconsin 1958. In legal practice Oshkosh 1958-74. Judge, Wisconsin County Court Winnebago County Jan 6, 1974 to July 31, 1978.

Member 1981-89 and Chairman 1986-89 Wisconsin Judicial Council. Member State Bar of Wisconsin, Winnebago County and American (Delegate 1981-83 and since 1988 and Member Executive Committee 1984-87 and 1994-96 National Conference of State Trial Judges Judicial Administration Division) Bar Associations. Past President Wisconsin Bowhunters Association and Big Brothers of the Fox Valley Region. Past Council Commissioner Twin Lakes Council Boy Scouts of America.

Mailing address: 1212 Goss Court, Oshkosh 54901.

WILLIS, Patrick L. *(Judge, Wisconsin Circuit Court Manitowoc Circuit)*

Mailing address: P.O. Box 2000, Manitowoc 54221-2000.

Office: Manitowoc County Courthouse, 1010 South Eighth Street, Manitowoc 54220-5392.

Telephone: (920) 683-2758.

WIMMER, Joseph E. *(Reserve Judge, Wisconsin Circuit Court)* Retired. Assumed Reserve status, serves by assignment.
Mailing address: 1020 Downing Drive, Waukesha 53186.

WING, Robert W. *(Judge, Wisconsin Circuit Court Pierce Circuit)* Commissioner 1979-84. Appointed Judge by Governor Anthony S. Earl to term beginning Jan 2, 1985. Elected April 1, 1986, 1992 and 1998. Current term expires July 31, 2004. Born Milwaukee Wisconsin March 17, 1947. Educated at University of Wisconsin-Madison B.A. with honors 1969 J.D. cum laude 1974. Admitted to practice Wisconsin 1974. Began legal practice River Falls 1974. In legal practice River Falls and Prescott 1979-84.
District Attorney Pierce County 1975-79. Specialist Four U.S. Army 1969-71. Member Kiwanis.
Office: Pierce County Courthouse, 414 West Main Street, Ellsworth 54011.
Telephone: (715) 273-3531.

WIRTZ, Robert J. *(Judge, Wisconsin Circuit Court Fond du Lac Circuit)* Elected April 6, 1999 to term beginning Aug 1, 1999. Term expires July 31, 2005. Born Waukesha Wisconsin 1958. Educated at University of Wisconsin-Madison B.A. 1979 and University of Missouri at Kansas City J.D. with distinction 1984. Staff member University of Missouri Kansas City Law Review 1983-84. Cases and Statutes Editor The Urban Lawyer 1983-84. Admitted to practice Wisconsin 1984. In legal practice Fond du Lac 1985-99.
Member State Bar of Wisconsin.
Mailing address: P.O. Box 1355, Fond du Lac 54936-1355.
Office: Fond du Lac County Courthouse, 160 South Macy Street, Fond du Lac 54935.
Telephone: (920) 929-7053.

WITKOWIAK, Timothy M. *(Judge, Wisconsin Circuit Court Milwaukee Circuit)*
Office: 2425 Children's Court Center, 10201 West Watertown Plank Road, Milwaukee 53226-3532.
Telephone: (414) 257-7098.

WOLFE, Virginia A. *(Reserve Judge, Wisconsin Circuit Court)* Family Court Commissioner 1986-88. Elected Judge to term beginning Aug 1, 1988. Reelected 1994. Retired. Assumed Reserve status, serves by assignment. Born Milwaukee Wisconsin 1942. Episcopalian. Educated at University of Wisconsin-Madison B.A. 1963 J.D. 1971 and Lehigh University M.Ed. 1967. Admitted to practice Wisconsin 1971 and U.S. District Courts Eastern 1971 and Western 1971 Districts of Wisconsin. In legal practice Milwaukee 1971-73, Jefferson 1973-77 and Baraboo 1977-86.
Instructor General Practice Seminar University of Wisconsin Law School 1976, 1977 and 1991. Second Vice President Wisconsin Judicial Conference 1991-94. Director Wisconsin Trial Judges Association. Member James Doyle American Inn of Court, State Bar of Wisconsin and Sauk County Bar Association. President Rotary Club 1991-92. Board of Directors Milwaukee Diocese Haiti Project. Enjoys scuba diving.
Mailing address: P.O. Box 44070, Madison 53744-4070.

WOLFGRAM, Thomas R. *(Judge, Wisconsin Circuit Court Ozaukee Circuit)* Appointed by Governor Tommy G. Thompson Sept 9, 1994. Elected Aug 1, 1995 and 2001. Current term expires July 31, 2007. Born Milwaukee Wisconsin Jan 27, 1952. Educated at University of Wisconsin-Oshkosh B.S. magna cum laude 1974 and Marquette University J.D. 1977. Member Phi Delta Phi. Admitted to practice Wisconsin 1977 and U.S. District Courts Eastern 1977 and Western 1977 Districts of Wisconsin. In legal practice Cedarburg 1987-94.
Deputy District Attorney Washington County 1979-84. District Attorney Ozaukee County 1984-86. Member State Bar of Wisconsin. Attended Wisconsin Judicial College 1995. Enjoys fishing, boating, travel, reading and cooking.
Mailing address: P.O. Box 994, Port Washington 53074-0994.
Office: Ozaukee County Courthouse, 1201 South Spring Street, Port Washington 53074-2491.
Telephone: (262) 284-8415.

WRIGHT, Richard O. *(Judge, Wisconsin Circuit Court Marquette Circuit)* Elected to term beginning 1995. Reelected 2001, current term expires July 31, 2007. Born Fort Wayne Indiana Jan 16, 1942. Christian. Educated at University of Wisconsin-Madison B.S. 1964 J.D. 1967. Admitted to practice Wisconsin 1967, U.S. District Courts Western 1967 and Eastern 1968 Districts of Wisconsin and Illinois 1972. In legal practice Oxford Wisconsin 1974-95.
District Attorney Marquette County Jan 1975 to Dec 1982. Author *Whose FBI* Open Court 1974. President Marquette County Big Brothers Big Sisters.
Mailing address: P.O. Box 749, Montello 53949-0749.
Office: Marquette County Courthouse, 77 West Park Street, Montello 53949-9366.
Telephone: (608) 297-9105.
E-mail address: richard.wright-@marquette.courts.state.wi.us

YACKEL, Norman L. *(Judge, Wisconsin Circuit Court Sawyer Circuit)* Appointed by Governor Tommy G. Thompson to term beginning March 1991. Elected to subsequent terms.
Mailing address: P.O. Box 447, Hayward 54843-0447.
Office: Sawyer County Courthouse, 10610 Main, Hayward 54843-6595.
Telephone: (715) 634-4886.

ZAPPEN, Edward F., Jr. *(Judge, Wisconsin Circuit Court Wood Circuit)* Elected to term beginning Aug 1, 1985. Reelected 1991, 1997 and 2003. Current term expires July 31, 2009.
Mailing address: P.O. Box 8095, Wisconsin Rapids 54495-8095.
Office: Wood County Courthouse, 400 Market Street, Wisconsin Rapids 54494-4825.
Telephone: (715) 421-8415.

ZIEGLER, Annette K. *(Judge, Wisconsin Circuit Court Washington Circuit)* Appointed by Governor Tommy T. Thompson to term beginning April 21, 1997.
Mailing address: P.O. Box 1986, West Bend 53095-7986.
Office: Washington County Courthouse, 432 East Washington Street, West Bend 53095-2500.
Telephone: (262) 335-4345.

ZUIDMULDER, Donald R. *(Judge, Wisconsin Circuit Court Brown Circuit)* Assumed office Aug 1, 1997. Born Green Bay Wisconsin May 2, 1942. United Meth-

ZUIDMULDER, DONALD R.—*Continued*

odist. Educated at University of Wisconsin at Madison B.S. 1964 J.D. 1968. Admitted to practice Wisconsin 1968, U.S. District Courts Eastern 1968 and Western 1968 Districts of Wisconsin, U.S. Court of Appeals Seventh Circuit 1990 and U.S. Supreme Court 1990. In legal practice Green Bay 1975-97.

Assistant Attorney General Wisconsin 1968-70. District Attorney Brown County 1971-75. Member State Bar of Wisconsin (Board of Governors 1990-94) and Brown County Bar Association.

Mailing address: P.O. Box 23600, Green Bay 54305-3600.

Office: Brown County Courthouse, 100 South Jefferson Street, Green Bay 54301.

Telephone: (920) 448-4110.

WYOMING

Capital CHEYENNE

UNITED STATES DISTRICT COURT DISTRICT OF WYOMING

Within Wyoming, including those portions of Yellowstone National Park situated in Idaho and Montana, there is one United States District Court. The court sits at Casper, Cheyenne, Evanston, Jackson, Lander and Sheridan. For descriptive information refer to the United States Courts section.

Chief Judge
William F. Downes

Judges
Clarence A. Brimmer
Alan Bond Johnson

Clerk
Betty A. Griess
2141 Federal Building
2120 Capitol Avenue
Cheyenne, Wyoming 82001
(307) 433-2120

UNITED STATES MAGISTRATE JUDGES OF WYOMING

Richard D. Gist
Timothy J. Bommer
William C. Beaman
Scott W. Skavdahl
Robert W. Connor, Jr.
Stephen E. Cole
Karen L. Marty

UNITED STATES BANKRUPTCY COURT OF WYOMING

Judge
Peter J. McNiff

Bankruptcy Clerk
Joyce W. Harris
6004 Federal Building
2120 Capitol Avenue
Cheyenne, Wyoming 82001
(307) 433-2200

WYOMING SUPREME COURT

The Supreme Court is Wyoming's court of last resort. The court consists of a chief justice and four justices each initially appointed by the governor from a list of three nominees submitted by the Judicial Nominating Commission and subject to retention vote one year after appointment. If retained, a justice serves for the remainder of the eight-year term. Subsequent eight-year terms are by retention election. The chief justice is elected by peer vote to serve a two-year term. Retirement is mandatory at age seventy; however, retired justices may serve by assignment of the chief justice.

The court has final appellate jurisdiction over all cases from the District Courts and original jurisdiction to issue extraordinary writs. The court exercises superintending control over inferior courts, regulates admission to the bar and the practice of law and may issue writs necessary to the exercise of proper jurisdiction.

The court sits en banc at Cheyenne and recesses during July.

Chief Justice
William U. Hill

Justices
Thomas Michael Golden
Marilyn S. Kite
Larry L. Lehman
Barton R. Voigt

Clerk
Judy Pacheco
Supreme Court Building
2301 Capitol Avenue
Cheyenne, Wyoming 82002
(307) 777-7316

Court Administrator
Holly A. Hansen
233 Supreme Court Building
2301 Capitol Avenue
Cheyenne, Wyoming 82002
(307) 777-7480

WYOMING DISTRICT COURTS

The District Courts are Wyoming's courts of general jurisdiction. Judges are appointed by the governor from a list of three nominees submitted by the Judicial Nominating Commission and are subject to retention vote in their districts one year after appointment. If retained, a judge serves for the remainder of the six-year term. Subsequent six-year terms are by retention election. Retirement is mandatory at age seventy; however, retired judges may serve by assignment of the chief justice.

The courts have original jurisdiction over all civil and criminal cases including equity, probate and juvenile matters and appellate jurisdiction over the Municipal Courts and over administrative boards and commissions. The courts may issue extraordinary writs and any writ necessary to the exercise of proper jurisdiction.

The courts sit at the county seats in each district.

FIRST JUDICIAL DISTRICT includes Laramie County. The court sits at Cheyenne.

Judges
Edward Grant
Nicholas Kalokathis
James Burke

SECOND JUDICIAL DISTRICT includes Albany and Carbon counties. The court sits at Laramie and Rawlins.

WYOMING DISTRICT COURTS—*Continued*

Judges
Kenneth Stebner
Jeffrey Donnell

THIRD JUDICIAL DISTRICT includes Lincoln, Sweetwater and Uinta counties. The court sits at Kemmerer, Green River and Evanston.

Judges
Dennis L. Sanderson
Jere Ryckman
Nena R. James

FOURTH JUDICIAL DISTRICT includes Johnson and Sheridan counties. The court sits at Buffalo and Sheridan.

Judge
John C. Brackley

FIFTH JUDICIAL DISTRICT includes Big Horn, Hot Springs, Park and Washakie counties. The court sits at Basin, Thermopolis, Cody and Worland.

Judges
Gary P. Hartman
Hunter H. Patrick

SIXTH JUDICIAL DISTRICT includes Campbell, Crook and Weston counties. The court sits at Gillette, Sundance and Newcastle.

Judges
Dan R. Price II
John Perry

SEVENTH JUDICIAL DISTRICT includes Natrona County. The court sits at Casper.

Judges
David B. Park
Thomas Sullins

EIGHTH JUDICIAL DISTRICT includes Converse, Goshen, Niobrara and Platte counties. The court sits at Douglas, Torrington, Lusk and Wheatland.

Judges
Keith G. Kautz
John Brooks

NINTH JUDICIAL DISTRICT includes Fremont, Sublette and Teton counties. The court sits at Lander, Pinedale and Jackson.

Judges
Nancy Guthrie
Norman E. Young

WYOMING CIRCUIT COURTS

Circuit Courts are courts of limited jurisdiction in Wyoming. Effective July 1, 2000, County Courts became Circuit Courts. All twenty-three counties are organized into nine districts. Judges are appointed by the governor from a list of three names submitted by the Judicial Nominating Commission and are subject to retention vote one year after appointment. If retained, a judge serves for the remainder of the four-year term. Subsequent four-year terms are by retention election. Judges may also serve as Municipal Court judges. Magistrates may be appointed by the county commissioner to assist the judges. They are not required to be law trained. The magistrates' authority is limited by statute, but in the absence of the judge and with permission, a law-trained magistrate may perform all the duties of the judge.

The courts have conclusive jurisdiction over civil cases when the amount in controversy does not exceed $7,000. The courts exercise jurisdiction over all misdemeanors, may exercise jurisdiction over ordinance violations at the request of a municipality and may set bail and conduct felony preliminary hearings.

The courts sit at the county seats in each district.

---

*Also Municipal Court Judge

FIRST JUDICIAL DISTRICT includes Laramie County. The court sits at Cheyenne.

County	Judge
Laramie	Robert W. "Yogi" Allen
	Denise Nau
	Thomas Campbell

SECOND JUDICIAL DISTRICT includes Albany and Carbon counties. The court sits at Laramie and Rawlins.

County	Judge
Albany	Robert Castor
Carbon	Wade Waldrip*

THIRD JUDICIAL DISTRICT includes Lincoln, Sweetwater and Uinta counties. The court sits at Kemmerer, Green River and Evanston.

County	Judge
Lincoln	Frank J. Zebre
Sweetwater	Samuel A. Soulé
	Victoria Schofield
Uinta	Thomas F. Mealey, Jr.

FOURTH JUDICIAL DISTRICT includes Johnson and Sheridan counties. The court sits at Buffalo and Sheridan.

County	Judge
Johnson	J. John Sampson
Sheridan	J. John Sampson

FIFTH JUDICIAL DISTRICT includes Big Horn, Hot Springs, Park and Washakie counties. The court sits at Basin, Thermopolis, Cody and Worland.

County	Judge
Big Horn	Robert Skar
Hot Springs	Robert Skar
Park	Bruce Waters
Washakie	Robert Skar

SIXTH JUDICIAL DISTRICT includes Campbell, Crook and Weston counties. The court sits at Gillette, Sundance and Newcastle.

County	Judge
Campbell	William S. Edwards
	Terrill Tharp
Crook	Fred R. Dollison
Weston	Fred R. Dollison

SEVENTH JUDICIAL DISTRICT includes Natrona County. The court sits at Casper.

County	Judge
Natrona	Steven Brown
	Michael Huber
	Michael N. Patchen

WYOMING CIRCUIT COURTS—*Continued*

EIGHTH JUDICIAL DISTRICT includes Converse, Goshen, Niobrara and Platte counties. The court sits at Douglas, Torrington, Lusk and Wheatland.

County	Judge
Converse	I. Vincent Case, Jr.
Goshen	Randal R. Arp
Niobrara	I. Vincent Case, Jr.
	Randal R. Arp
Platte	I. Vincent Case, Jr.
	Randal R. Arp

NINTH JUDICIAL DISTRICT includes Fremont, Sublette and Teton counties. The court sits at Lander, Pinedale and Jackson.

County	Judge
Fremont	Robert Brim Denhardt*
	Donald Hall
Sublette	John V. Crow
Teton	Timothy Charles Day

WYOMING JUSTICE COURTS

Justice Courts were courts of limited jurisdiction in Wyoming. The courts operated in counties where there was no Circuit Court. As of January 1, 2003, all remaining Justice Courts merged with Circuit Courts.

WYOMING MUNICIPAL COURTS

Municipal Courts are courts of limited jurisdiction in Wyoming. The courts are established in incorporated cities or towns. Judges are appointed by the mayor with consent of the council for terms set by the municipality. Circuit Court judges may also serve as Municipal Court judges.

The courts have exclusive jurisdiction over all offenses against city ordinances but may not impose fines exceeding $750 and/or imprisonment exceeding six months.

†Also Circuit Court Judge

City	Judge
Afton	Alvin Robinson
Alpine	A. Deland Lainhart
Baggs	Agnes Stocks
Bairoil	David Clark
Bar Nunn	David Drell
Basin	T. A. Trammell
Buffalo	Christopher Wages
Burns	Bernard Pitts
Casper	Robert J. Hand, Jr.
	Keith Nachbar
	Richard Wilking
Cheyenne	Paul Galeotos
	Mark Moran
Chugwater	Vicki Mickelsen
Cody	C. Edward Webster, II
Cokeville	Charles Powell
Dayton	Tyler Vanerhoef
Diamondville	Wanda Newman
Dixon	Agnes Stocks
	Wade Waldrip†
Douglas	Frank Peasley
Dubois	Robert Brim Denhardt†
East Thermopolis	Louis L. Walrath
Edgerton	Patrick Busskohl
Encampment	Janet Herring
Evanston	Richard Lavery
Evansville	Forrest E. "Skip" Gillum
Fort Laramie	Lois Paules
Fremont	Robert Brim Denhardt†
Gillette	J. Stan Wolfe
	James Edwards
Glendo	C. Robert Goetz
Glenrock	Mike Roy
Green River	Peggy J. Beckum
Greybull	Randy Royal
Guernsey	William M. Conner
Hartville	William M. Conner
Hudson	M. L. Barton
Hulett	Dave Wolfskili
Jackson	Thomas H. Jordan
Kemmerer	J. Michael Lamp
La Barge	J. Michael Lamp
Lander	Teresa McKee
Laramie	Ronald D. Copenhaver
Lingle	Earl Cross
Lovell	Sylvia Gams
Lusk	Doyle Davies
Lyman	Richard Lavery
Marbleton	J. Michael Lamp
Medicine Bow	Theresa J. Archer
Meeteetse	J. W. Yetter
Midwest	Patrick Busskohl
Mills	Richard H. Peek
Moorcroft	Mary B. Garman
Mountain View	Richard Lavery
Newcastle	Theodore Greenwood
Opal	J. Michael Lamp
Pine Bluffs	Bernard Pitts
Pinedale	Ruth Neely
Pine Haven	Robert Hegge II
Powell	James S. Allison
Ranchester	Stuart S. Healy
Rawlins	David Erickson
Riverside	Janet Herring
Rock Springs	Daniel Erramouspe
Rolling Hills	Thomas Reese
Sheridan	Stuart S. Healy
Shoshoni	Becky Zent
Sinclair	David Clark
Sundance	Mary B. Garman
Superior	Ed Risha
Ten Sleep	Richard Hopkinson
Thayne	A. Deland Lainhart
Thermopolis	Jerry Williams
Torrington	Chuck Lowry
Upton	Mary B. Garman
Wamsutter	Daniel Massey
Wheatland	Vicki Mickelsen
Worland	G. Albert Sinn
Wright	C. John Cotton

Wyoming Counties and County Seats

Albany
Laramie

Big Horn
Basin

Campbell
Gillette

Carbon
Rawlins

Converse
Douglas

Crook
Sundance

Fremont
Lander

Goshen
Torrington

Hot Springs
Thermopolis

Johnson
Buffalo

Laramie
Cheyenne

Lincoln
Kemmerer

Natrona
Casper

Niobrara
Lusk

Park
Cody

Platte
Wheatland

Sheridan
Sheridan

Sublette
Pinedale

Sweetwater
Green River

Teton
Jackson

Uinta
Evanston

Washakie
Worland

Weston
Newcastle

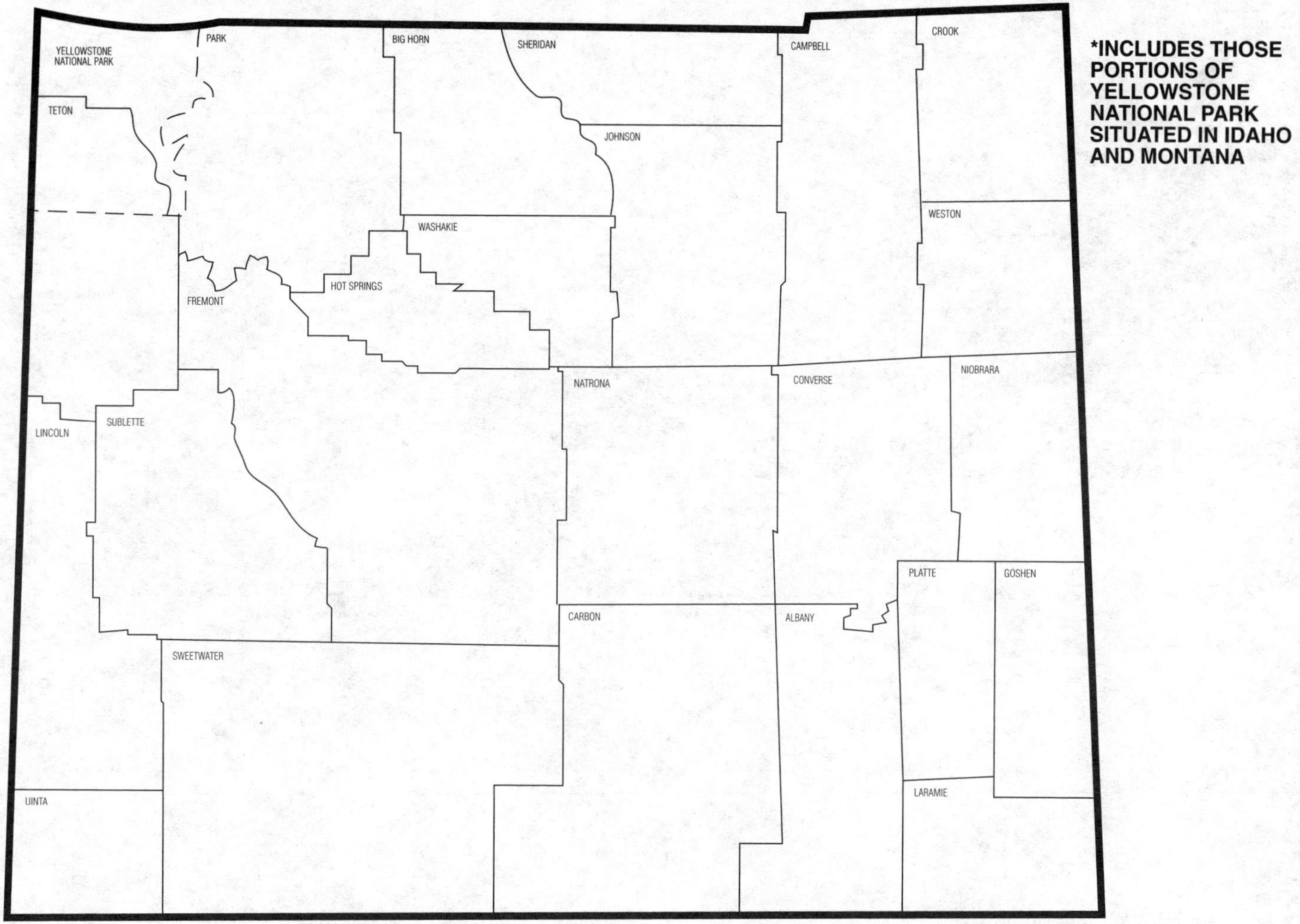
YELLOWSTONE NATIONAL PARK
PARK
BIG HORN
SHERIDAN
CAMPBELL
CROOK
TETON
JOHNSON
WESTON
WASHAKIE
HOT SPRINGS
FREMONT
NATRONA
CONVERSE
NIOBRARA
LINCOLN
SUBLETTE
PLATTE
GOSHEN
CARBON
ALBANY
SWEETWATER
UINTA
LARAMIE
*INCLUDES THOSE PORTIONS OF YELLOWSTONE NATIONAL PARK SITUATED IN IDAHO AND MONTANA

UNITED STATES DISTRICT COURT DISTRICT OF WYOMING*

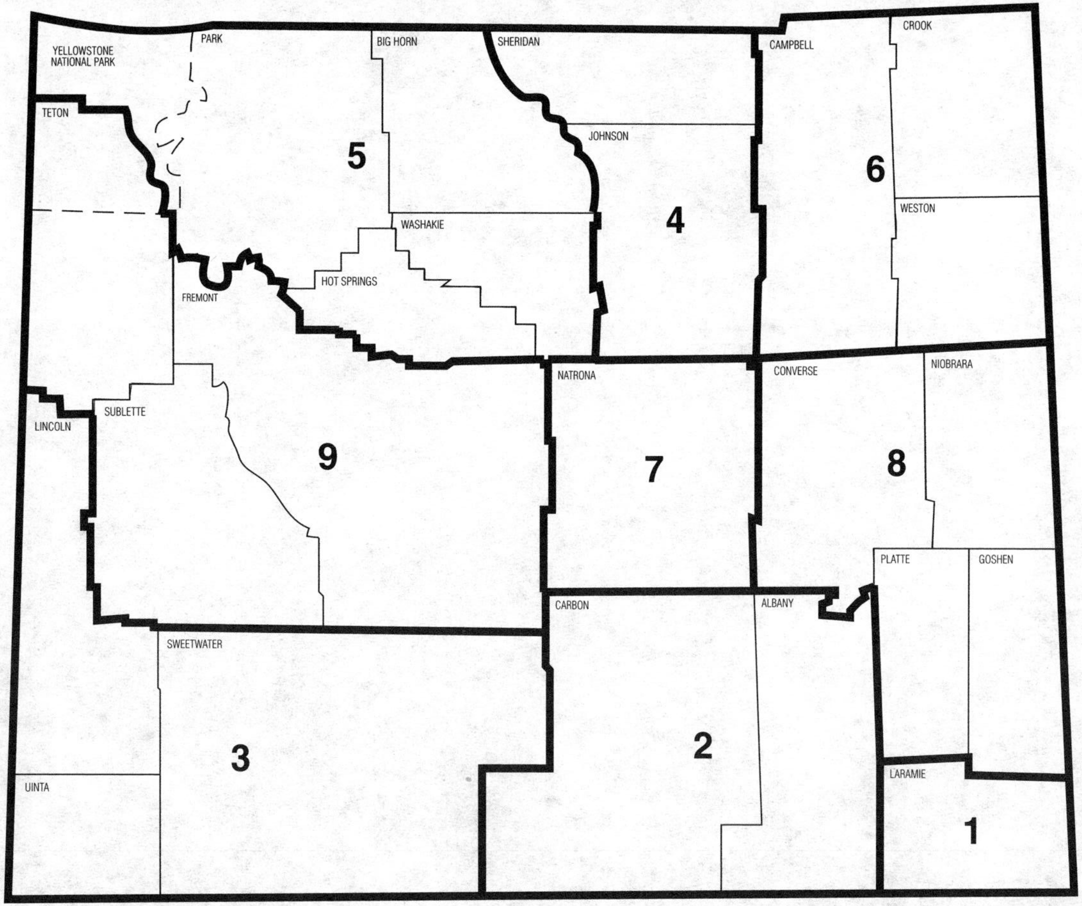
YELLOWSTONE NATIONAL PARK
PARK
BIG HORN
SHERIDAN
CAMPBELL
CROOK
TETON
JOHNSON
5
6
4
WESTON
WASHAKIE
HOT SPRINGS
FREMONT
NATRONA
CONVERSE
NIOBRARA
LINCOLN
SUBLETTE
9
7
8
PLATTE
GOSHEN
CARBON
ALBANY
SWEETWATER
3
2
LARAMIE
UINTA
1

JUDICIAL DISTRICTS OF WYOMING DISTRICT COURTS AND WYOMING CIRCUIT COURTS

WYOMING

ALLEN, Robert W. "Yogi" *(Judge, Wyoming Circuit Court First Judicial District, Laramie County)* Assumed office July 1, 2000. Retained by election 2000, current term expires Jan 2005. Born Cheyenne Wyoming April 21, 1946. Methodist. Educated at University of Wyoming B.A. 1968 J.D. 1974. Admitted to practice Wyoming 1974. Justice of the Peace, Laramie County Justice Court 1977-78. Judge, Wyoming County Court Laramie County Jan 1, 1979 to June 30, 2000, appointed by Governor Ed Herschler.

Assistant City Attorney Cheyenne 1974-77. Instructor in Business Law Community College since 1975. Member Wyoming State Bar. Lieutenant U.S. Army 1968-70. Political affiliation: Independent. Member Masons, Shriners, Kiwanis, Elks, Legion, VFW and University of Wyoming Booster Club.

Office: 2300 Laramie County Complex, 309 West 20th Street, Cheyenne 82001-3691.

Telephone: (307) 633-4326.

Fax: (307) 633-4392

ALLISON, James S. *(Judge, Powell Municipal Court)* Appointed to term beginning Feb 1, 1981. Reappointed Jan 1984. Born Greybull Wyoming Aug 29, 1947. Presbyterian. Educated at Northwest Community College A.A. with honors 1968 and University of Wyoming B.S. with honors 1970 J.D. with honors 1974. Admitted to practice Wyoming 1975. In legal practice Powell since 1975. Former Justice of the Peace, Park County Justice Court, appointed to term beginning Aug 23, 1988.

Member Wyoming Association of Judges of Courts of Limited Jurisdiction (Bench Book Committee since 1985), Wyoming State Bar, Park County (President 1976-77) and American Bar Associations. Attends Annual Seminar for Judges of Courts of Limited Jurisdiction Wyoming Association of Judges of Courts of Limited Jurisdiction. Recipient Distinguished Service Award from Powell Jaycees 1978, Citation for Meritorious Service from Governor's Committee for the Employment of the Handicapped 1982 and Certificate of Commendation from Wyoming School Board Association 1984. Named one of Outstanding Young Men of America by U.S. Jaycees 1981 and 1982. Listed in *Who's Who in American Law* 1987-88. Republican Precinct Committee Man 1988. Vice President Powell Jaycees 1976-77. Board Member Union Presbyterian Church Powell (Board of Deacons 1977-80, Board of Elders 1983-85), Northwest Board of Cooperative Services 1977-82, Park County School District #1 1977-83, Northwest Civic Orchestra 1979-82, Big Horn Enterprises 1982-86 and Powell Valley Chamber of Commerce 1985-88 (Treasurer 1986, President 1987). Member Powell Rotary Club since 1976 (Board Member and President 1980-81), Mayor's Committee on the Disabled Powell since 1985, State Planning Council on Developmental Disabilities 1986-87 and Powell Hospital (Long Range Planning Committee 1988-90). Enjoys geology and computers.

Mailing address: P.O. Box 1008, Powell 82435.

Office: 270 North Clark, Powell 82435.

ARCHER, Theresa J. *(Judge, Medicine Bow Municipal Court)*

Mailing address: P.O. Box 156, Medicine Bow 82329-0156.

Office: 319 Pine Street, Medicine Bow 82329.

ARP, Randal R. *(Judge, Wyoming Circuit Court Eighth Judicial District, Goshen, Niobrara and Platte Counties)*

Mailing address: P.O. Drawer BB, Torrington 82240.

Telephone: (307) 532-2938.

Fax: (307) 532-5101

BARTON, M. L. *(Judge, Hudson Municipal Court)*

Mailing address: P.O. Box 56, Hudson 82515.

Office: 333 South Main, Hudson 82515.

BEAMAN, William C. *(Magistrate Judge, United States District Court District of Wyoming)* Appointed by U.S. District Court judges to term beginning Jan 1975. Reappointed to subsequent terms. Born Cheyenne Wyoming Oct 25, 1945. Episcopalian. Educated at Arizona State University B.A. 1967 and University of Wyoming J.D. 1971. Law Clerk to Hon. Ewing T. Kerr, U.S. District Court District of Wyoming 1971-73. Admitted to practice Wyoming 1971. Began legal practice Cheyenne 1973.

Past Member Cheyenne Board of Adjustments. Member Wyoming Trial Lawyers Association, Wyoming State Bar, Laramie County (Secretary-Treasurer 1975) and American Bar Associations. Staff Sergeant Wyoming Air National Guard 1967-73. Member Elks and Rotary Club. Enjoys snow and water skiing, tennis, fishing and bird hunting.

Office: 2117 Federal Building, 2120 Capitol Avenue, Cheyenne 82001.

Telephone: (307) 433-2180.

BECKUM, Peggy J. *(Judge, Green River Municipal Court)* Appointed to term beginning Jan 1, 1979. Born Buffalo Wyoming Jan 6, 1946. Episcopalian. Educated at Casper College B.S. in Political Science 1992 M.S. in Political Science 1993. Justice of the Peace, Sweetwater County Justice Court 1977-81.

Member Wyoming Municipal Courts Association, Wyoming Association of Judges of Courts of Limited Jurisdiction, National Judges Association and American Bar Association (Associate member). Recipient Judicial Career Education Achievement Award 1985 and Judicial Education Achievement Award since 1987 The National Judicial College.

Office: 50 East Second North, Green River 82935.

BOMMER, Timothy J. *(Magistrate Judge, United States District Court District of Wyoming)* Appointed by U.S. District Court judges to term beginning 1976. Reappointed to subsequent terms. Serves part time. Born Columbus Ohio Dec 9, 1940. Educated at Wisconsin State University and University of Wyoming B.A. 1963 J.D. 1970. Admitted to practice Wyoming 1970 and Colorado 1970.

Deputy County and Prosecuting Attorney Teton County 1970-74. Regional Director Governor's Planning

BOMMER, TIMOTHY J.—*Continued*

Committee on Criminal Administration 1973-74. Chairman Character and Fitness Committee Board of Law Examiners since 1997. Member Judicial Nominating Commission 1984-88, Wyoming Trial Lawyers Association (Board of Directors 1976-79), The Association of Trial Lawyers of America, American Board of Trial Advocates, Wyoming State Bar (Ethics Committee 1975-79, Fee Arbitration Committee 1978-84 and Chairman 1980-84) and Teton County Bar Association (President 1981). Captain USAF 1963-67.
Mailing address: P.O. Box 1728, Jackson 83001-1728.
Telephone: (307) 733-3515.

BRACKLEY, John C. *(Judge, Wyoming District Court Fourth Judicial District)* Appointed by Governor Michael J. Sullivan to term beginning Jan 22, 1993. Retained by election Nov 1994 and 2000. Current term expires Jan 2007.
Office: B11J Sheridan County Courthouse, 224 South Main Street, Sheridan 82801.
Telephone: (307) 674-4478.
Fax: (307) 674-4470

BRIMMER, Clarence A. *(Judge, United States District Court District of Wyoming)* Appointed for life by President Gerald R. Ford to term beginning Sept 26, 1975. Former Chief Judge. Born Rawlins Wyoming July 11, 1922. Educated at University of Michigan B.A. 1944 J.D. 1947. Admitted to practice Wyoming 1948. Began legal practice Rawlins 1948. Judge, Rawlins Municipal Court 1948-54.
Wyoming Attorney General 1971-74. Author "Mining Partnerships" Rocky Mountain Mineral Law Institute 1969 and "A Rancher's Subservient Surface Estate" Land and Water L. Rev. 1970. Member Judicial Conference of the U.S. (Executive Committee 1996-99), Judicial Panel on Multidistrict Litigation, Wyoming Judicial Conference, Wyoming State Bar and American Bar Association. U.S. Army 1945-46. Republican. Republican State Chairman 1967-71. Gubernatorial Candidate 1974. Member National Advisory Board BLM 1969-71.
Mailing address: P.O. Box 985, Cheyenne 82003-0985.
Telephone: (307) 772-2463.

BROOKS, John *(Judge, Wyoming District Court Eighth Judicial District)* Appointed by Governor Jim Geringer. Former Magistrate Judge, United States District Court District of Wyoming.
Office: 107 North Fifth, Douglas 82633.
Telephone: (307) 358-5693.
Fax: (307) 358-6343

BROWN, Steven *(Judge, Wyoming Circuit Court Seventh Judicial District, Natrona County)* Assumed office July 1, 2000. Retained by election Nov 2000, current term expires Jan 2005. Judge, Wyoming County Court Natrona County 1998 to June 30, 2001, appointed by Governor Jim Geringer.
Office: 201 North David, Casper 82601.
Telephone: (307) 235-9266.
Fax: (307) 235-9331

BURKE, James *(Judge, Wyoming District Court First Judicial District)* Appointed by Governor Jim Geringer.
Office: 3300 Laramie County Complex, 309 West Twentieth Street, Cheyenne 82001.
Telephone: (307) 633-4533.

BUSSKOHL, Patrick *(Judge, Edgerton and Midwest Municipal Courts)*
Edgarton mailing address: P.O. Box 407, Edgerton 82635.
Edgarton office: 311 North Second, Edgerton 82635.
Midwest office: 531 Peake Street, Midwest 82643.
Telephone: (307) 437-6763.

CAMPBELL, Thomas *(Judge, Wyoming Circuit Court First Judicial District, Laramie County)* Appointed by Governor Jim Geringer. Former Judge, Superior Municipal Court.
Office: 2300 Laramie County Complex, 309 West 20th Street, Cheyenne 82001-3691.
Telephone: (307) 633-4298.
Fax: (307) 633-4392

CASE, I. Vincent, Jr. *(Judge, Wyoming Circuit Court Eighth Judicial District, Converse, Niobrara and Platte Counties)* Assumed office July 1, 2000. Retained by election Nov 2000, current term expires Jan 2005. Born Walsenburg Colorado June 17, 1950. Educated at University of Wyoming B.S. 1972 J.D. 1975. Admitted to practice Wyoming 1976 and U.S. District Court District of Wyoming 1976. In legal practice Douglas 1975-93. Judge, Douglas Municipal Court Jan 1977 to Jan 12, 1994. Judge, Wyoming County Court Converse County Jan 13, 1994 to June 30, 2000, appointed by Governor Michael J. Sullivan.
Converse County Deputy and Prosecuting Attorney 1978-79. Glenrock Town Attorney 1976-82. Instructor in Business Law Eastern Wyoming College 1984-93. Member Wyoming Conference of Special Court Judges, Wyoming State Bar and Converse County Bar Association (President 1977-78 and 1990-91, Secretary 1984-89). Former Member Kiwanis (Secretary 1977-78, President 1982-83). Member Douglas Community Club and Loyal Order of Moose. Enjoys fishing, hunting, golf, skiing, carpentry, auto repair and piano.
Mailing address: P.O. Box 45, Douglas 82633.
Office: Converse County Courthouse, Douglas 82633.
Telephone: (307) 358-2196.
Fax: (307) 358-2501

CASTOR, Robert *(Judge, Wyoming Circuit Court Second Judicial District, Albany County)* Assumed office July 1, 2000. Retained by election 2002, current term expires Jan 2007. Judge, Wyoming County Court Albany County July 1, 1984 to June 30, 2000, appointed by Governor Ed Herschler.
Office: 105 Albany County Courthouse, 525 Grand Avenue, Laramie 82070.
Telephone: (307) 742-5747.
Fax: (307) 742-5610

CLARK, David *(Judge, Bairoil and Sinclair Municipal Courts)*
Bairoil mailing address: P.O. Box 58, Bairoil 82322.
Bairoil office: 1101 Antelope Drive, Bairoil 82322.
Sinclair office: 300 Lincoln, Sinclair 82334.

COLE, Stephen E. *(Magistrate Judge, United States District Court District of Wyoming)* Appointed by U.S. District Court judges to term beginning Feb 1, 1975. Reappointed to subsequent terms, current term expires 2006. Born Powell Wyoming April 18, 1947. Educated at Arizona State University 1965-66 and University of Wyoming B.A. 1969 J.D. 1974. Member Sigma Nu. Admitted to practice Wyoming 1974. Began legal practice

COLE, STEPHEN E.—*Continued*

Worland 1974. Judge, Worland Municipal Court 1975-81. Judge, Ten Sleep Municipal Court 1977-81. Justice of the Peace, Washakie County Justice Court 1977-81.

Former Member Washakie County Bar. Member Federal Magistrate Judges Association and Wyoming State Bar. Enjoys cross-country skiing, fly fishing, music and reading.

Mailing address: P.O. Box 387, Yellowstone National Park 82190.
Telephone: (307) 344-2169.
Fax: (307) 344-2195
E-mail address: Stephen_Cole@wyd.uscourts.gov

CONNER, William M. *(Judge, Guernsey and Hartville Municipal Courts)* Appointed to Guernsey Municipal Court to term beginning March 1, 1990. Reappointed Jan 1, 1991, Jan 1, 1993, Jan 1, 1995, Jan 1, 1997, Jan 1, 1999, Jan 1, 2001 and Jan 1, 2003. Current term expires Dec 31, 2004. Born York Pennsylvania Nov 18, 1958. Roman Catholic. Educated at University of Wyoming.

State Director National Judges Association. Member Wyoming Judges Association. Security Officer State of Wyoming. Republican. Enjoys hunting, fishing, athletics and shooting sports.

Guernsey mailing address: P.O. Box 667, Guernsey 82214.
Guernsey office: 81 West Whalen, Guernsey 82214.
Telephone: (307) 836-2335.
Hartville office: 136 West Main, Hartville 82215.
Telephone: (307) 836-2288.

CONNOR, Robert W., Jr. *(Magistrate Judge, United States District Court District of Wyoming)* Appointed by U.S. District Court judges to term beginning Feb 1977. Reappointed to subsequent terms. Serves part time. Born Hannibal Missouri Dec 30, 1942. Member St. Peters Episcopal Church. Educated at University of Wyoming B.S. 1967 J.D. 1971. Admitted to practice Wyoming 1971 and U.S. District Court District of Wyoming 1972. Began legal practice Sheridan 1971. Former Judge, Sheridan Municipal Court.

Member Wyoming State Bar, Sheridan County (Past President, Vice President and Secretary-Treasurer) and American Bar Associations. First Lieutenant USAS JAGC. Republican. Enjoys golf and hunting.

Mailing address: P.O. Box 607, Sheridan 82801-0607.
Telephone: (307) 672-2491.

COPENHAVER, Ronald D. *(Judge, Laramie Municipal Court)* Assistant Judge 1979-82. Appointed Judge to term beginning Jan 1, 1982. Also serves as Commissioner, Wyoming County Court Albany County since 1991. Born Laramie Wyoming July 8, 1949. Lutheran. Educated at University of Wyoming B.A. 1975 J.D. 1978. Admitted to practice Wyoming 1979. Began legal practice Laramie 1979.

Member Wyoming Conference of Special Court Judges (President) and Wyoming State Bar. E-5 U.S. Army 1969-72. Previously worked in oil fields. Republican. Active in church. Enjoys skiing, gardening, fishing, golf, boating and black powder shooting.

Mailing address: P.O. Box C, Laramie 82070.
Office: 406 Ivinson, Laramie 82073.
Telephone: (307) 721-5205.
Fax: (307) 721-5211

COTTON, C. John *(Judge, Wright Municipal Court)*
Mailing address: P.O. Box 70, Wright 82732-0070.
Office: 201 Wright Boulevard, Wright 82732.

CROSS, Earl *(Judge, Lingle Municipal Court)*
Mailing address: P.O. Box 448, Lingle 82223.
Office: 220 Main street, Lingle 82223.
Telephone: (307) 837-2422.
Fax: (307) 837-2148

CROW, John V. *(Judge, Wyoming Circuit Court Ninth Judicial District, Sublette County)* Assumed office July 1, 2000. Retained by election 2000, current term expires Jan 2005. Judge, Wyoming County Court Sublette County Jan 1, 1995 to June 30, 2000, appointed by Governor Michael J. Sullivan.

Mailing address: P.O. Box 1796, Pinedale 82941.
Telephone: (307) 367-2556.
Fax: (307) 367-2658

DAVIES, Doyle *(Judge, Lusk Municipal Court)*
Mailing address: P.O. Box 390, Lusk 82225.
Office: 201 East Third Street, Lusk 82225.
Telephone: (307) 334-3612.
Fax: (307) 334-2154

DAY, Timothy Charles *(Judge, Wyoming Circuit Court Ninth Judicial District, Teton County)* Appointed by governor.

Mailing address: P.O. Box 2906, Jackson 83001.
Office: 172 North Center Street, Jackson 83001.
Telephone: (307) 733-7713.
Fax: (307) 733-8694

DENHARDT, Robert Brim *(Judge, Wyoming Circuit Court Ninth Judicial District, Fremont County and Judge, Dubois and Fremont Municipal Courts)* Assumed office July 1, 2000. Retained by election 2000, current term expires Jan 2005. Born Sulphur Springs Texas Sept 4, 1944. Baptist. Educated at University of California at Santa Barbara B.A. 1967 and University of Denver J.D. 1972. Admitted to practice Wyoming 1972. Began legal practice Lander 1972. Judge, Lander Municipal Court 1981-82. Judge, Wyoming County Court Fremont County Jan 3, 1983 to June 30, 2000, appointed by Governor Ed Herschler.

Director Wind River Legal Services 1974-75. Assistant Public Defender 1975-77. Secretary-Treasurer Wyoming Association of Judges of Courts of Limited Jurisdiction 1985-87. Member Wyoming State Bar and Fremont County Bar Association. First Lieutenant U.S. Army 1967-69. Former Vice President Democratic Central Committee Fremont County. Political affiliation: Independent. Member Lions International. Coach Little League baseball. Enjoys hunting, fishing, camping and outdoor activities.

Circuit Court office: 230 Fremont County Courthouse, 450 North Second Street, Lander 82520.
Municipal Court office: 712 Meckem Street, Dubois 82513.
Telephone: (307) 332-3239.
Fax: (307) 332-1152

DOLLISON, Fred R. *(Judge, Wyoming Circuit Court Sixth Judicial District, Crook and Weston Counties)* Appointed by governor.

Mailing address: P.O. Box 650, Sundance 82729.
Office: 309 Cleveland, Sundance 82729.
Telephone: (307) 283-2929.
Fax: (307) 283-2931

DONNELL, Jeffrey *(Judge, Wyoming District Court Second Judicial District)* Appointed by Governor Jim Geringer to term beginning Oct 21, 1996. Retained by election Nov 1998, current term expires Jan 2005.
Mailing address: P.O. Box 1106, Laramie 82073-1106.
Telephone: (307) 745-3337.
Fax: (307) 742-0210

DOWNES, William F. *(Chief Judge, United States District Court District of Wyoming)* Appointed for life by President Bill Clinton to term beginning 1994. Chief Judge since July 12, 1999. Born Boston Massachusetts July 24, 1946. Educated at University of Texas B.A. 1968 and University of Houston J.D. 1974. In legal practice Green River 1975-78 and Casper 1978-94.
Attorney Underwriter's Services, Inc. 1974-75. Captain USMC 1968-71.
Office: 210 U.S. Courthouse, 111 South Wolcott Street, Casper 82601.
Telephone: (307) 261-5441.

DRELL, David *(Judge, Bar Nunn Municipal Court)*
Office: 4820 North Wardwell Industrial Avenue, Bar Nunn 82601.

EDWARDS, James *(Judge, Gillette Municipal Court)*
Mailing address: P.O. Box 3003, Gillette 82717-3003.
Office: 201 East Fifth Street, Gillette 82717.
Telephone: (307) 686-5253.

EDWARDS, William S. *(Judge, Wyoming Circuit Court Sixth Judicial District, Campbell County)* Assumed office July 1, 2000. Retained by election Nov 7, 2000, current term expires Jan 2005. Born Abilene Texas Jan 26, 1944. Educated at University of New Mexico B.B.A. 1972 and University of Wyoming J.D. 1978. Admitted to practice Wyoming 1979 and U.S. District Court District of Wyoming 1979. In legal practice Gillette 1979-87. Judge, Wyoming County Court Campbell County March 4, 1991 to June 30, 2000, appointed by Governor Michael J. Sullivan.
Deputy County Attorney Campbell County 1987-91. U.S. Army active duty Feb 1964 to Jan 1970.
Office: 500 South Gillette Avenue, Suite 300, Gillette 82716.
Telephone: (307) 682-2190.
Fax: (307) 687-6214

ERICKSON, David *(Judge, Rawlins Municipal Court)*
Mailing address: P.O. Box 953, Rawlins 82301.
Office: 521 West Cedar Street, Rawlins 82301.
Telephone: (307) 328-4535.
Fax: (307) 328-4555

ERRAMOUSPE, Daniel *(Judge, Rock Springs Municipal Court)*
Office: 212 D Street, Rock Springs 82901.
Telephone: (307) 352-1550.

GALEOTOS, Paul *(Judge, Cheyenne Municipal Court)*
Office: 2101 O'Neil Avenue, Cheyenne 82001.

GAMS, Sylvia *(Judge, Lovell Municipal Court)*
Mailing address: P.O. Box 188, Lovell 82431.ffice: 336 Nevada Avenue, Lovell 82431.

GARMAN, Mary B. *(Judge, Moorcroft, Sundance and Upton Municipal Courts)*
Mailing address: P.O. Box 398, Sundance 82729.
Telephone: (307) 283-2535.

GILLUM, Forrest E. "Skip" *(Judge, Evansville Municipal Court)* Appointed to term beginning Jan 3, 1975. Born Casper Wyoming Sept 21, 1945. Educated at Chadron State College B.A. 1975 and University of Wyoming M.P.A. 1981.
Instructor in Criminal Justice Department Casper College since 1972 and Wyoming Law Enforcement Academy since 1980. Republican. Member Casper Kiwanis Club and Casper Civil Service Commission.
Mailing address: P.O. Drawer 158, Evansville 82636.
Office: 235 Curtis Street, Evansville 82636.
Telephone: (307) 235-1282.
Fax: (307) 266-5109

GIST, Richard D. *(Magistrate Judge, United States District Court District of Wyoming)* Appointed by U.S. District Court judges to term beginning Jan 1, 1971. Reappointed to subsequent terms. Current term expires Jan 1, 2007. Serves part time. Born Bairoil Wyoming Feb 6, 1940. Protestant. Educated at University of Wyoming B.S. in Engineering 1963 J.D. 1965. Member Sigma Xi. Admitted to practice Wyoming 1966, U.S. District Court District of Wyoming 1966 and U.S. Court of Military Appeals 1967. Began legal practice Casper 1966. In legal practice Lander since 1970. Former Alternate Judge, Lander Municipal Court. Former Commissioner, Wyoming District Court Ninth Judicial District.
Member Trial Lawyers Association, Wyoming State Bar and Fremont County Bar Association (Vice President 1971-72). Captain U.S. Army JAGC 1966-70. Republican. Member Wyoming Lodge No. 2 AF & AM, Lander Scottish Rite, Lander Shrine Club and Olivet Chapter 3 OES. Enjoys hunting, fishing, leather work, woodworking and golf.
Office: 150 North Third Street, Lander 82520.
Telephone: (307) 332-2757.

GOETZ, C. Robert *(Judge, Glendo Municipal Court)* Former Judge, Chugwater and Wheatland Municipal Courts.
Mailing address: P.O. Box 396, Glendo 82213.
Office: 204 South Yellowstone, Glendo 82213.
Telephone: (307) 735-4242.

GOLDEN, Thomas Michael *(Justice, Wyoming Supreme Court)* Appointed by Governor Michael J. Sullivan to term beginning June 30, 1988. Retained by election Nov 7, 1990 and 1998. Current term expires Jan 2007. Former Chief Justice. Born Enid Oklahoma Sept 30, 1942. Protestant. Educated at University of Wyoming B.A. 1964 J.D. 1967 and University of Virginia LL.M. 1992. Editor-in-Chief Land and Water Law Review 1966-67. Member Omicron Delta Kappa and Delta Theta Phi. Admitted to practice Wyoming 1967, U.S. District Court District of Wyoming 1967, U.S. Court of Appeals Tenth Circuit 1967 and U.S. Supreme Court 1970. In legal practice Rawlins 1971-83 and Casper 1983-88.
Member State Board of Law Examiners Wyoming 1977-81 and 1986-88. Important Decisions: Billis v. State 800 P.2d 401 Wyo. 1990, Nulle v. Gillette-Campbell County Joint Powers Fire Board 797 P.2d 1171 Wyo. 1990, Dellapenta v. Dellapenta 838 P.2d 1153 Wyo. 1992, Tortolito v. State 885 P.2d 864 Wyo.

GOLDEN, THOMAS MICHAEL—*Continued*

1995, Ortega v. Flaim 902 P.2d 199 Wyo. 1995, Campbell County School District v. State of Wyoming 907 P.2d 1238 Wyo. 1995, Loghry v. Unicover Corp. 927 P.2d 706 Wyo. 1996 and Johnson v. State 930 P.2d 358 Wyo. 1996. Member Tenth Circuit Select Committee to appoint successor to Hon. James Barrett, U.S. Court of Appeals Tenth Circuit. Member Wyoming State Bar. Captain U.S. Army JAGC 1967-71.

Office: Supreme Court Building, Cheyenne 82002.
Telephone: (307) 777-7421.

GRANT, Edward *(Judge, Wyoming District Court First Judicial District)* Appointed by Governor Ed Herschler to term beginning Feb 14, 1986. Retained by election Nov 1988, Nov 1994 and 2000. Current term expires Jan 2007.

Office: 3300 Laramie County Complex, 309 West 20th Street, Cheyenne 82001.
Telephone: (307) 633-4291.
Fax: (307) 633-4465

GREENWOOD, Theodore *(Judge, Newcastle Municipal Court)*

Office: Ten West Warwick, Newcastle 82701.

GUTHRIE, Nancy *(Judge, Wyoming District Court Ninth Judicial District)* Appointed by Governor Michael J. Sullivan Nov 2, 1994 to term beginning Jan 4, 1995. Retained by election Nov 1996 and 2002. Current term expires Jan 2009.

Mailing address: P.O. Box 1036, Jackson 83001-1036.
Telephone: (307) 733-1461.
Fax: (307) 734-8954

HALL, Donald *(Judge, Wyoming Circuit Court Ninth Judicial District, Fremont County)* Assumed office July 1, 2000. Retained by election 2000, current term expires Jan 2005. Judge, Wyoming County Court Fremont County June 8, 1982 to June 30, 2000, appointed by Governor Ed Herschler.

Office: 818 South Federal Boulevard, Riverton 82501.
Telephone: (307) 856-7259.
Fax: (307) 857-3635

HAND, Robert J., Jr. *(Judge, Casper Municipal Court)*

Office: 200 North David, Casper 82601.
Telephone: (307) 235-8267.
Fax: (307) 234-9387

HARTMAN, Gary P. *(Judge, Wyoming District Court Fifth Judicial District)* Appointed by Governor Ed Herschler to term beginning Aug 5, 1983. Retained by election Nov 1984, Nov 1990, Nov 1996 and 2002. Current term expires Jan 2009. Born Basin Wyoming Aug 11, 1941. Educated at University of Wyoming B.A. 1968 J.D. 1972. Admitted to practice Wyoming 1972 and Colorado 1973. Former Justice of the Peace, Big Horn County Justice Court, elected to term beginning Jan 1, 1975. Former Judge, Greybull Municipal Court.

Sergeant USAF 1962-66. Member American Legion, Rotary Club and Volunteer Fire Department. Enjoys flying.

Mailing address: P.O. Box 408, Worland 82401-0408.
Telephone: (307) 347-2331.
Fax: (307) 347-6428

HEALY, Stuart S. *(Judge, Ranchester and Sheridan Municipal Courts)* Appointed by mayor Sept 1, 1989. Reappointed to subsequent terms. Current term expires Jan 2005. Born Casper Wyoming Sept 19, 1944. Catholic. Educated at University of Wyoming B.A. 1967 M.A. 1972 J.D. 1975. Admitted to practice Wyoming 1975, U.S. District Court Eastern District of Montana 1984, U.S. Courts of Appeals Ninth 1984 and Tenth Circuits and U.S. Supreme Court 1992. In legal practice Sheridan Wyoming since 1975.

Member Wyoming State Bar. Attended General Jurisprudence I and II The National Judicial College. Captain U.S. Army 1968-71. Enjoys athletics and especially golf.

Office: 45 West Twelfth Street, Sheridan 82801.
Telephone: (307) 672-3188.

HEGGE, Robert, II *(Judge, Pine Haven Municipal Court)*

Office: 24 Waters Drive, Pine Haven 82721-9761.

HERRING, Janet *(Judge, Encampment and Riverside Municipal Courts)*

Encampment mailing address: P.O. Box 5, Encampment 82325.
Encampment office: 622 Rankin, Encampment 82325.
Telephone: (307) 327-5501.
Riverside office: 207 West Welton, Riverside 82325.

HILL, William U. *(Chief Justice, Wyoming Supreme Court)* Appointed by Governor Jim Geringer Nov 3, 1998. Retained by election 2000, current term expires Jan 2009. Chief Justice since July 1, 2002. Born Montgomery Alabama. Educated at University of Wyoming B.A. 1970 J.D. 1974. In legal practice Riverton and Cheyenne Wyoming and Seattle Washington.

Assistant U.S. Attorney, Assistant Attorney General and Attorney General March 1995 to Nov 1998 Wyoming. Chief of Staff and Chief Counsel to Senator Malcolm Wallop Washington D.C.

Office: Supreme Court Building, 2301 Capitol Avenue, Cheyenne 82002.
Telephone: (307) 777-7571.

HOPKINSON, Richard *(Judge, Ten Sleep Municipal Court)*

Mailing address: P.O. Box 5, Ten Sleep 82442.
Office: 415 Fifth Street, Ten Sleep 82442.
Telephone: (307) 366-2265.

HUBER, Michael *(Judge, Wyoming Circuit Court Seventh Judicial District, Natrona County)* Assumed office July 1, 2000. Retained by election 2000, current term expires Jan 2005. Judge, Wyoming County Court Natrona County Jan 4, 1982 to June 30, 2000, appointed by Governor Ed Herschler.

Office: 201 North David, Casper 82601.
Telephone: (307) 235-9266.
Fax: (307) 235-9331

JAMES, Nena R. *(Judge, Wyoming District Court Third Judicial District)* Appointed by Governor Jim Geringer. Born Thermopolis Wyoming April 5, 1950. Educated at University of Wyoming B.A. 1971 J.D. 1974. Admitted to practice Wyoming 1974. In legal practice Rock Springs since 1974. Justice of the Peace 1975-81. Former Judge, Rock Springs Municipal Court, appointed to term beginning July 7, 1987.

Instructor in Criminal Law Western Wyoming College 1975. Member Wyoming State Bar, Sweetwater County and American (Section of Family Law, Judicial Administration Division) Bar Associations. Attended four

JAMES, NENA R.—*Continued*

courses at The National Judicial College. Enjoys needlework, music, cooking, gardening and golf.

Mailing address: P.O. Box 310, Green River 82935-0310.

Telephone: (307) 872-3228.

Fax: (307) 872-6494

JOHNSON, Alan Bond *(Judge, United States District Court District of Wyoming)* Appointed for life by President Ronald Reagan 1986. Former Chief Judge. Born Cheyenne Wyoming Jan 14, 1939. Presbyterian. Educated at Vanderbilt University B.A. 1961 and University of Wyoming J.D. 1964. Admitted to practice Wyoming 1964. In legal practice Cheyenne 1968-75. Magistrate, U.S. District Court District of Wyoming 1971-75. Part-time Judge, Cheyenne Municipal Court 1972. Judge, Wyoming District Court First Judicial District 1974-86, appointed by Governor Stanley Hathaway.

Chairman City Police Civil Service Commission 1972-74. Author Casenotes University of Wyoming L. Jour. 1968. Member Wyoming State Bar, Laramie County (Treasurer 1969 and 1970) and American Bar Associations. Secretary Wyoming Judicial Conference 1977. Captain USAF 1964-67. Member Wyoming Air National Guard. Listed in *Who's Who in American Law* 1976 and 1977. Vice President Laramie County Cancer Society 1969-71. Member Cheyenne Frontier Days Committee (Chairman Indian Committee since 1976). Trustee Laramie County Arts Council 1972-74. Treasurer Cheyenne Symphony and Choral Society 1973. Board Member Cheyenne Little Theatre 1970-72. Member Rotary Club and Greater Cheyenne Chamber of Commerce. Enjoys tennis, fishing and hiking.

Office: 2242 Federal Building, 2120 Capitol Avenue, Cheyenne 82001.

Telephone: (307) 433-2170.

JORDAN, Thomas H. *(Judge, Jackson Municipal Court)* Appointed to term beginning Jan 5, 1988. Born Duluth Minnesota Jan 14, 1946. Christian. Educated at Northern Arizona University B.S. 1968 M.S. 1980. Member Alpha Phi Sigma.

Director Criminal Justice Department 1980-83. Member Wyoming Conference of Special Court Judges (President) and National Judges Association. Attended Judicial Training course at The National Judicial College 1988. E-5 U.S. Army 1969-71. Recipient Bronze Star 1970. Previously employed in law enforcement nine years and as a college instructor four years. Member Rotary Club. Enjoys outdoor sports.

Mailing address: P.O. Box 1687, Jackson 83001.

Office: 150 East Pearl, Jackson 83001.

Telephone: (307) 733-4809.

Fax: (307) 739-0919

KALOKATHIS, Nicholas *(Judge, Wyoming District Court First Judicial District)* Appointed by Governor Michael J. Sullivan to term beginning July 6, 1987. Retained by election Nov 1988, Nov 1994 and 2000. Current term expires Jan 2007.

Office: 3300 Laramie County Complex, 309 West 20th Street, Cheyenne 82001.

Telephone: (307) 633-4290.

KAUTZ, Keith G. *(Judge, Wyoming District Court Eighth Judicial District)* Appointed by Governor Michael J. Sullivan to term beginning Jan 4, 1993. Retained by election Nov 1994 and 2000. Current term expires Jan 2007. Born Torrington Wyoming March 27, 1954. Baptist. Educated at University of Wyoming B.S. with honors 1975 J.D. 1978. Member Phi Beta Kappa. Admitted to practice Wyoming 1978, U.S. District Court District of Wyoming 1978 and U.S. Court of Appeals Tenth Circuit 1978. In legal practice Sheridan 1978-79 and Torrington 1980-92.

Member Christian Legal Society, Wyoming Trial Lawyers Association (Board of Directors 1988-92, Secretary-Treasurer 1992-93), The Association of Trial Lawyers of America and Wyoming State Bar (Fee Arbitration Committee 1988-92). Republican. Board Member Goshen County Fair and Southeast Wyoming Mental Health Center. Member Torrington Rotary Club and Torrington Community Hospital Foundation. Enjoys horsemanship, hunting, fishing, bicycling and flying.

Mailing address: P.O. Box 1055, Torrington 82240-1055.

Telephone: (307) 532-3004.

Fax: (307) 532-2563

KITE, Marilyn S. *(Justice, Wyoming Supreme Court)* Appointed by Governor Jim Geringer to term beginning June 2, 2000. Retained by election Nov 2002, current term expires Jan 2011. Educated at University of Wyoming B.A. with honors 1970 and University of Wyoming College of Law J.D. 1974. In legal practice 1979-2000.

Senior Assistant Attorney General Wyoming 1974-78. Faculty Member Western Trial Advocacy University of Wyoming. Board of Trustees Rocky Mountain Mineral Law Foundation. Board of Litigation Mountain States Legal Foundation. Advisory Board Tenth Circuit Court of Appeals. Member Wyoming Judicial Nominating Commission. Faculty Member Denver Regional National Institute for Trial Advocacy.

Office: Supreme Court Building, Cheyenne 82002.

Telephone: (307) 777-7422.

LAINHART, A. Deland *(Judge, Alpine and Thayne Municipal Courts)* Former Judge, Afton Municipal Court.

Alpine mailing address: P.O. Box 3070, Alpine 83128.

Alpine office: 121 Highway 89, Alpine 83128.

Thayne office: 115 Petersen Parkway, Thayne 83127.

LAMP, J. Michael *(Judge, Kemmerer, La Barge, Marbleton and Opal Municipal Courts)* Former Judge, Big Piney Municipal Court.

La Barge mailing address: P.O. Box 327, La Barge 83123.

La Barge office: 228 South La Barge Street, La Barge 83123.

Kemmerer office: 220 Wyoming Highway 233, Kemmerer 83101-9700.

LAVERY, Richard *(Judge, Evanston, Lyman and Mountain View Municipal Courts)*

Lyman mailing address: P.O. Box 300, Lyman 82937.

Lyman office: 100 East Sage Street, Lyman 82937.

Evanston office: 1200 Main Street, Evanston 82930-3396.

Telephone: (307) 783-6300.

Fax: (307) 783-6390

LEHMAN, Larry L. *(Justice, Wyoming Supreme Court)* Appointed by Governor Michael J. Sullivan to

LEHMAN, LARRY L.—*Continued*

term beginning July 8, 1994. Retained by election Nov 1996. Term expires Jan 2005. Chief Justice July 1, 1998 to June 30, 2002. Born Iowa City Iowa. Educated at University of Wyoming College of Law J.D. 1976. In legal practice Evanston. Judge, Wyoming County Court Uinta County March 18, 1985 to March 3, 1988. Judge, Wyoming District Court Second Judicial District March 4, 1988 to July 7, 1994.

Office: Supreme Court Building, Cheyenne 82002.
Telephone: (307) 777-7557.

LOWRY, Chuck *(Judge, Torrington Municipal Court)*

Mailing address: P.O. Box 250, Torrington 82240.
Office: 2017 East A, Torrington 82240.
Telephone: (307) 532-4213.
Fax: (307) 532-2010

MARTY, Karen L. *(Magistrate Judge, United States District Court District of Wyoming)* Appointed by U.S. District Court judges to term beginning July 1, 1999. Reappointed 2003, current term expires June 30, 2007. Serves part time.

Office: 20 East Flaming Gorge Way, Green River 82935-4210.
Telephone: (307) 875-3235.

MASSEY, Daniel *(Judge, Wamsutter Municipal Court)* Former Judge, Hanna Municipal Court.

Mailing address: P.O. Box 6, Wamsutter 82336.
Office: 231 McCormick, Wamsutter 82336.

McKEE, Teresa *(Judge, Lander Municipal Court)*

Office: 240 Lincoln Street, Lander 82520-2848.

McNIFF, Peter J. *(Judge, United States Bankruptcy Court District of Wyoming)* Appointed by U.S. Court of Appeals Tenth Circuit judges.

Office: Federal Building, 2120 Capitol Avenue, Cheyenne 82001.
Telephone: (307) 433-2250.

MEALEY, Thomas F., Jr. *(Judge, Wyoming Circuit Court Third Judicial District, Uinta County)* Assumed office July 1, 2000. Retained by election 2002, current term expires Jan 6, 2007. Born Worcester Massachusetts Oct 8, 1937. Educated at Utah State University B.S. 1965, Fordham University M.S.W. 1968 and New England School of Law J.D. 1975. Recipient American Jurisprudence Awards in Criminal Law 1972 and Legal Writing 1973. Admitted to practice Wyoming 1979 and U.S. District Court District of Wyoming 1979. In legal practice Evanston 1980-88. Judge, Evanston Municipal Court 1984-88. Judge, Wyoming County Court Uinta County May 2, 1988 to June 30, 2000, appointed by Governor Michael J. Sullivan.

Deputy County Attorney 1980-81 and Assistant Public Defender 1982-84 Uinta County. Member Wyoming Trial Lawyers, Wyoming State Bar(Active 1979-88 and Honorary since May 1988) and Uinta County Bar Association. Specialist E-5 U.S. Army 1961-64. Personal Statement or Quote: "Wisdom can't be told."

Office: 225 Ninth Street, Evanston 82930.
Telephone: (307) 789-2471.
Fax: (307) 789-5062
E-mail address: tfm@courts.state.wy.us

MICKELSEN, Vicki *(Judge, Chugwater and Wheatland Municipal Courts)*

Chugwater mailing address: P.O. Box 243, Chugwater 82210.
Chugwater office: 248 Second Street, Chugwater 82210.
Wheatland office: 600 Ninth Street, Wheatland 82201.
Telephone: (307) 322-4929.
Fax: (307) 322-2968

MORAN, Mark *(Judge, Cheyenne Municipal Court)* Former Judge, Burns and Pine Bluffs Municipal Courts.

Office: 2101 O'Neil Avenue, Cheyenne 82001.

NACHBAR, Keith *(Judge, Casper Municipal Court)*

Office: 200 North David, Casper 82601.

NAU, Denise *(Judge, Wyoming Circuit Court First Judicial District, Laramie County)* Assumed office July 1, 2000. Retained by election 2002, current term expires Jan 2007. Judge, Wyoming County Court Laramie County April 19, 1996 to June 30, 2000, appointed by Governor Jim Geringer.

Office: 2300 Laramie County Complex, 309 West 20th Street, Cheyenne 82001-3691.
Telephone: (307) 633-4298.
Fax: (307) 633-4392

NEELY, Ruth *(Judge, Pinedale Municipal Court)*

Mailing address: P.O. Box 709, Pinedale 82941.
Office: 210 West Pine Street, Pinedale 82941.

NEWMAN, Wanda *(Judge, Diamondville Municipal Court)*

Mailing address: P.O. Box 281, Diamondville 83116.
Office: 20 US 30/189, Diamondville 83116.
Telephone: (307) 877-6251.
Fax: (307) 877-6709

PARK, David B. *(Judge, Wyoming District Court Seventh Judicial District)* Appointed by Governor Jim Geringer Jan 1999. Judge, Wyoming County Court Natrona County March 1, 1991 to 1998.

Office: 214 Natrona County Courthouse, 200 North Center Street, Casper 82601.
Telephone: (307) 235-9253.
Fax: (307) 235-9493

PATCHEN, Michael N. *(Judge, Wyoming Circuit Court Seventh Judicial District, Natrona County)* Magistrate June 1996 to Sept 2001. Appointed Judge by Governor Jim Geringer Sept 2001. Retained by election Nov 2002, current term expires Jan 6, 2007. Appointed to Municipal Court to term beginning Feb 1991. Reappointed to subsequent terms. Born Portland Oregon July 8, 1952.Religious affiliation: Evangelical Free. Educated at Utah State University B.S. 1974 and University of Wyoming J.D. 1987. Admitted to practice Wyoming 1987, U.S. District Court District of Wyoming 1987 and U.S. Court of Appeals Tenth Circuit 1987. In legal practice Gillette Aug 1987 to Sept 2001. Judge, Wright Municipal Court Feb 1991 to Sept 2001.

Member Christian Legal Society, Wyoming State Bar and American Bar Association. Enjoys sports card collecting.

Mailing address: P.O. Box 1339, Casper 82602.
Office: 201 North David, Casper 82601.
Telephone: (307) 235-9266.
Fax: (307) 235-9331
E-mail address: mnp@courts.state.wy.us

PATRICK, Hunter H. *(Judge, Wyoming District Court Fifth Judicial District)* Appointed by Governor Michael J. Sullivan to term beginning July 22, 1988. Retained by election 1990, 1996 and 2002. Current term expires Jan 2009. Born Gasville Arkansas Aug 19, 1939. Presbyterian. Educated at University of Wyoming B.A. 1961 J.D. 1966. Member Delta Sigma Rho (President) and Phi Kappa Delta. Named Outstanding Varsity Debater of the Year. Admitted to practice Wyoming 1966 and Colorado 1967. In legal practice Powell Wyoming 1966-88. Judge, Powell Municipal Court 1967-68. Justice of the Peace, Park County Justice Court 1971-88.

Powell City Attorney 1968-88. Instructor in Business Law Northwest Community College 1968-1998. Vice Chair 1994-95 and Chair 1995-96 District Judges Conference Wyoming. Fellow American Bar Association. Member Wyoming Association of Judges (President 1973-80), Wyoming Judicial Planning Commission March 1979 to Jan 1987, Wyoming Commission on Judicial Conduct and Ethics since 1997, American Judicature Society (Board of Directors since 2002), Wyoming State Bar, Park County (Past President), Colorado and American (Executive Committee Delegate for Wyoming, Utah, Colorado and New Mexico National Association of Special Court Judges Judicial Administration Division 1987, Wyoming State Delegate House of Delegates 1994-2001, Executive Committee Delegate for Wyoming, Colorado, Kansas and Nebraska National Conference of Trial Court Judges 1997-2000, and Board of Governors since 2001) Bar Associations. Attended The National Judicial College 1976, 1978, 1979, 1980, 1982, 1984, 1988, 1989, 1990, 1991, 1992, 1993, 1995, 1996, 1997 and 1999 (Faculty Advisor 1978, 1980, 1982, 1991, 1993, 1997, 1999 and 2002). Recipient Public Service Award from American Bar Association Law Day Program 1990 and 1992, Annual Public Service Award from Wyoming State Bar 1999 and Judicial Award from Wyoming Crime Victims' Compensation Fund. Democrat. Chairman Courts Section Wyoming Girls State 1982-84 and 1988-99. Member Rotary Club (Past President), International Order of Odd Fellows Lodge and Powell Elks Lodge. Enjoys photography, fishing, hiking, gardening, bicycling, public speaking and court-community relations.

Mailing address: P.O. Box 1868, Cody 82414.
Office: Park County Courthouse, Cody 82414.
Telephone: (307) 527-8670.

PAULES, Lois *(Judge, Fort Laramie Municipal Court)*
Mailing address: P.O. Box 177, Fort Laramie 82212.
Office: 100 East Bliss Street, Fort Laramie 82212.

PEASLEY, Frank *(Judge, Douglas Municipal Court)*
Mailing address: P.O. Box 1030, Douglas 82633.
Office: 101 North Fourth, Douglas 82633.

PEEK, Richard H. *(Judge, Mills Municipal Court)* Appointed to term beginning Sept 1975. Born Ogden Utah April 5, 1950. Educated at Casper College A.S. 1970 and University of Wyoming B.S. with honors 1972 J.D. 1975. Admitted to practice Wyoming 1975. Began legal practice Casper 1975.

Casper Assistant City Attorney since 1975. Member The Association of Trial Lawyers of America, Wyoming State Bar, Natrona County and American Bar Associations. Republican.

Mailing address: P.O. Box 789, Mills 82644.
Office: 704 Fourth Street, Mills 82644.

PERRY, John *(Judge, Wyoming District Court Sixth Judicial District)* Appointed by Governor Jim Geringer.
Office: 328 Campbell County Courthouse, 500 South Gillette Avenue, Gillette 82716.
Telephone: (307) 686-8517.
Fax: (307) 687-6426

PITTS, Bernard *(Judge, Burns and Pine Bluffs Municipal Courts)*
Burns mailing address: P.O. Box 66, Burns 82053.
Burns office: 102 First Street, Burns 82053.
Pine Bluffs office: 220 Main Street, Pine Bluffs 82082.

POWELL, Charles *(Judge, Cokeville Municipal Court)*
Mailing address: P.O. Box 99, Cokeville 83114.
Office: 110 Pine Street, Cokeville 83114.

PRICE, Dan R., II *(Judge, Wyoming District Court Sixth Judicial District)* Appointed by Governor Michael J. Sullivan to term beginning Nov 16, 1990. Retained by election Nov 1992 and Nov 1998. Current term expires Jan 2005. Born Pueblo Colorado Oct 6, 1949. Educated at University of Wyoming B.S. 1971 J.D. 1974. Admitted to practice Wyoming 1974 and U.S. District Court District of Wyoming 1979. In legal practice Gillette 1974-90.

Deputy County Attorney Campbell County 1974-76.
Office: 500 South Gillette Avenue, Gillette 82716.
Telephone: (307) 686-8517.
Fax: (307) 687-6426
E-mail address: drp@courts.state.wy.us

REESE, Thomas *(Judge, Rolling Hills Municipal Court)*
Office: 38 South Badger, Rolling Hills 82637.

RISHA, Ed *(Judge, Superior Municipal Court)*
Mailing address: P.O. Box 40, Superior 82945.
Office: 27 Front Street, Superior 82945.
Telephone: (307) 362-8273.
Fax: (307) 362-8173

ROBINSON, Alvin *(Judge, Afton Municipal Court)*
Mailing address: P.O. Box 310, Afton 83110.
Office: 416 Washington Street, Afton 83110.

ROY, Mike *(Judge, Glenrock Municipal Court)* Former Alternate Judge.
Mailing address: P.O. Box 417, Glenrock 82637.
Office: 219 South Third, Glenrock 82637.
Telephone: (307) 436-9441.
Fax: (307) 436-5753

ROYAL, Randy *(Judge, Greybull Municipal Court)*
Mailing address: P.O. Box 271, Greybull 82426.
Office: 24 South Fifth Street, Greybull 82426.
Telephone: (307) 765-9431.

RYCKMAN, Jere *(Judge, Wyoming District Court Third Judicial District)* Appointed by Governor Michael J. Sullivan to term beginning Sept 26, 1988. Retained

RYCKMAN, JERE—*Continued*

by election Nov 1990, Nov 1996 and 2002. Current term expires Jan 2009.
Mailing address: P.O. Box 1210, Green River 82935-1210.
Telephone: (307) 872-6344.
Fax: (307) 872-6494

SAMPSON, J. John *(Judge, Wyoming Circuit Court Fourth Judicial District, Johnson and Sheridan Counties)* Assumed office July 1, 2000. Retained by election 2000, current term expires Jan 2005. Judge, Wyoming County Court Sheridan County Nov 1, 1991 to June 30, 2000, appointed by Governor Michael J. Sullivan.
Office: B-7 Sheridan County Courthouse, 224 South Main Street, Sheridan 82801.
Telephone: (307) 674-2940.
Fax: (307) 674-2944

SANDERSON, Dennis L. *(Judge, Wyoming District Court Third Judicial District)* Appointed by Governor Jim Geringer.
Mailing address: P.O. Box 2077, Evanston 82931-2077.
Telephone: (307) 789-7002.
Fax: (307) 783-0400

SCHOFIELD, Victoria *(Judge, Wyoming Circuit Court Third Judicial District, Sweetwater County)* Assumed office July 1, 2000. Former Judge, Wyoming County Court Sweetwater County, appointed by Governor Jim Geringer.
Mailing address: P.O. Drawer 1720, Green River 82935.
Telephone: (307) 872-6460.
Fax: (307) 872-6375

SINN, G. Albert *(Judge, Worland Municipal Court)*
Mailing address: P.O. Box 226, Worland 82401.
Office: 829 Big Horn Avenue, Worland 82401.
Telephone: (307) 347-4255.

SKAR, Robert *(Judge, Wyoming Circuit Court Fifth Judicial District, Big Horn, Hot Springs and Washakie Counties)* Assumed office Big Horn County July 1, 2000. Former Judge, Wyoming County Court Big Horn County, appointed by Governor Jim Geringer.
Mailing address: P.O. Box 749, Basin 82410.
Office: Big Horn County Courthouse, Basin 82410.
Telephone: (307) 568-2367.
Fax: (307) 568-3873
Office: 417 Arapahoe Street, Thermopolis 82443.
Telephone: (307) 864-5161.
Fax: (307) 864-5116

SKAVDAHL, Scott W. *(Magistrate Judge, United States District Court District of Wyoming)* Appointed by U.S. District Court judges to term beginning Dec 4, 2001. Serves part time.
Mailing address: P.O. Box 10700, Casper 82602.
Telephone: (307) 265-0700.
Fax: (307) 266-2306

SOULÉ, Samuel A. *(Judge, Wyoming Circuit Court Third Judicial District, Sweetwater County)* Assumed office July 1, 2000. Retained by election, current term expires Dec 31, 2006. Born Hampton Virginia July 5, 1936. Baptist. Educated at Wofford College A.B. 1959 and University of Wyoming J.D. 1971. Admitted to practice Wyoming 1972, U.S. District Court District of Wyoming 1972 and U.S. Supreme Court 1981. In legal practice Laramie 1972-75. Judge, Wyoming County Court Sweetwater County July 2, 1981 to June 30, 2000, appointed by Governor Ed Herschler.
Staff Member Office of Attorney General Wyoming April 1, 1975 to July 2, 1981. Former Senior Assistant Attorney General. State DPASS Attorney Council 1984-90. Important Decision: State v. Walters, et al. (constitutionality of state obscenity statute; resulted in complete revision of statutes) 1981. Member 1972-81 and honorary member since 1981 Wyoming State Bar. Attended General Jurisdiction 1981, Legal Writing 1982 and Search and Seizure 1984 The National Judicial College and Western Trial Advocacy course University of Wyoming College of Law 1985. E-4 U.S. Army. Junior high school teacher Spartanburg South Carolina 1963-65. Social worker Rawlins 1965-67. Landman American Nuclear Corporation Laramie 1971-72. Political affiliation: Independent. Member Wyoming Jaycees 1966-73, Cowboy Joe Boosters 1977-79 and Rock Springs Tennis Association 1983-85. Member Governor's Advisory Council for Department of Public Assistance and Social Services 1984-90 (Chairman 1986). Chairman Finance Committee School District #1 Aug 1989 to Jan 1990. Board of Directors Wyoming Tennis Association 1985-87. Advisory Council BLM Rock Springs 1990-93. Enjoys guitar, riding, team roping and steer roping.
Mailing address: P.O. Box 2028, Rock Springs 82902.
Telephone: (307) 352-6817.
Fax: (307) 352-6758

STEBNER, Kenneth *(Judge, Wyoming District Court Second Judicial District)* Appointed by Governor Michael J. Sullivan to term beginning Aug 30, 1994. Retained by election Nov 1996 and 2002, current term expires Jan 2009. Judge, Wyoming County Court Carbon County Jan 1, 1983 to Aug 29, 1994, appointed by Governor Ed Herschler. Former Judge, Wamsutter Municipal Court.
Office: 201 Carbon County Courthouse, 415 West Pine Street, Rawlins 82301.
Telephone: (307) 328-2683.
Fax: (307) 328-2728

STOCKS, Agnes *(Judge, Baggs and Dixon Municipal Courts)*
Baggs mailing address: P.O. Box 300, Baggs 82321.
Baggs office: 130 Penland Street, Baggs 82321.
Dixon office: 975 Fourth Street, Dixon 82323.

SULLINS, Thomas *(Judge, Wyoming District Court Seventh Judicial District)* Appointed by Governor Jim Geringer to term beginning Oct 6, 1995. Retained by election Nov 1996 and 2002. Current term expires Jan 2009.
Office: 214 Natrona County Courthouse, 200 North Center Street, Casper 82601.
Telephone: (307) 235-9253.
Fax: (307) 235-9493

THARP, Terrill *(Judge, Wyoming Circuit Court Sixth Judicial District, Campbell County)* Assumed office July 1, 2000. Retained by election 2000, current term expires Jan 2005. Judge, Wyoming County Court Campbell County Sept 1, 1994 to June 30, 2000, appointed by Governor Michael J. Sullivan.
Office: 500 South Gillette Avenue, Suite 301, Gillette 82716.

THARP, TERRILL—*Continued*

Telephone: (307) 682-2190.
Fax: (307) 687-6214

TRAMMELL, T. A. *(Judge, Basin Municipal Court)*
Mailing address: P.O. Box 599, Basin 82410.
Office: 209 South Fourth Street, Basin 82410.

VANERHOEF, Tyler *(Judge, Dayton Municipal Court)*
Mailing address: P.O. Box 100, Dayton 82836.
Office: 608 Broadway, Dayton 82836.

VOIGT, Barton R. *(Justice, Wyoming Supreme Court)* Appointed by Governor Jim Geringer to term beginning March 29, 2001. Retained by election Nov 2002, current term expires Jan 2011. Born Thermopolis Wyoming. Educated at University of Wyoming B.A. M.A. J.D. In legal practice Thermopolis ten years. Judge, Wyoming District Court Eighth Judicial District April 7, 1993 to April 22, 2001, appointed by Governor Michael J. Sullivan. Former Judge, Wyoming County Court Gillette County.
Former County Attorney Hot Springs County.
Office: Supreme Court Building, Cheyenne 82002.
Telephone: (307) 777-7573.

WAGES, Christopher *(Judge, Buffalo Municipal Court)*
Office: 46 North Main Street, Buffalo 82834.
Telephone: (307) 684-5566.

WALDRIP, Wade *(Judge, Wyoming Circuit Court Second Judicial District, Carbon County and Judge, Dixon Municipal Court)*
Circuit Court office: Carbon County Courthouse, 415 West Pine Street, Rawlins 82301.
Municipal Court office: 975 Fourth Street, Dixon 82323.
Telephone: (307) 324-6655.
Fax: (307) 324-9465

WALRATH, Louis L. *(Judge, East Thermopolis Municipal Court)* Former Judge, Thermopolis Municipal Court. Born Billings Montana Aug 22, 1940. Baptist. Educated at University of Colorado B.A. 1962 and University of Wyoming J.D. 1965. Admitted to practice Wyoming 1965, U.S. District Court District of Wyoming 1965, U.S. Court of Appeals Tenth Circuit 1976 and U.S. Tax Court 1985. In legal practice Thermopolis 1965-93. Former Justice of the Peace, Hot Springs County Justice Court, appointed to term beginning May 1966.
Town Attorney Thermopolis 1966-81 and 1983-84. Member Wyoming State Bar. Attended courses on "Advanced Evidence" 1988, "Law, Ethics and Justice" 1989, "Sentencing Misdemeanants" 1991 and "Introduction to Personal Computers in the Courts" The National Judicial College. E-5 Wyoming National Guard 1966-72. Republican. Chairman Hot Springs Republican Party 1973-74. Member Hospital Board, Thermopolis Improvement Corp. and Chamber of Commerce. Enjoys flying and gardening.
Office: 112 East Warren Street, East Thermopolis 82443.
Telephone: (307) 864-9221.

WATERS, Bruce *(Judge, Wyoming Circuit Court Fifth Judicial District, Park County)* Appointed by Governor Jim Geringer April 13, 2001.
Office: 206 Park County Courthouse, 1002 Sheridan Avenue, Cody 82414.
Telephone: (307) 527-8590.
Fax: (307) 527-8596

WEBSTER, C. Edward, II *(Judge, Cody Municipal Court)*
Mailing address: P.O. Box 2200, Cody 82414.
Office: 1338 Rumsey Avenue, Cody 82414.

WILKING, Richard *(Judge, Casper Municipal Court)*
Office: 200 North David, Casper 82601.

WILLIAMS, Jerry *(Judge, Thermopolis Municipal Court)*
Mailing address: P.O. Box 603, Thermopolis 82443.
Office: 420 Broadway Street, Thermopolis 82443.

WOLFE, J. Stan *(Judge, Gillette Municipal Court)*
Mailing address: P.O. Box 3003, Gillette 82717-3003.
Office: 201 East Fifth Street, Gillette 82717.
Telephone: (307) 686-5253.

WOLFSKILI, Dave *(Judge, Hulett Municipal Court)*
Mailing address: P.O. Box 278, Hulett 82720.
Office: 123 Hill Street, Hulett 82720.

YETTER, J. W. *(Judge, Meeteetse Municipal Court)*
Mailing address: P.O. Box 38, Meeteetse 82433-0388.
Office: 910 Park Avenue, Meeteetse 82433.
Telephone: (307) 868-2278.

YOUNG, Norman E. *(Judge, Wyoming District Court Ninth Judicial District)* Appointed by governor.
Office: Fremont County Courthouse, 450 North Second Street, Lander 82520.
Telephone: (307) 332-4592.
Fax: (307) 332-4059

ZEBRE, Frank J. *(Judge, Wyoming Circuit Court Third Judicial District, Lincoln County)* Assumed office July 1, 2000. Retained by election Nov 2002, current term expires Jan 2007. Born Kemmerer Wyoming Oct 7, 1954. Catholic. Educated at University of Wyoming B.S. 1977 J.D. 1980. Admitted to practice Wyoming 1980. In legal practice Kemmerer 1980-84. Judge, Wyoming County Court Lincoln County July 1, 1984 to June 30, 2000, appointed by Governor Ed Herschler.
Mailing address: P.O. Box 949, Kemmerer 83101.
Telephone: (307) 877-4431.
Fax: (307) 877-4936

ZENT, Becky *(Judge, Shoshoni Municipal Court)*
Mailing address: P.O. Box 267, Shoshoni 82649.
Office: 102 East Second, Shoshoni 82649.
Telephone: (307) 876-2515.

GLOSSARY

Accretion Increase or extension of the boundaries of land by action of natural forces, as out of the sea or river.

Ad hoc For this purpose alone; special.

Ad litem For the purposes of a suit; pending a suit.

Ancillary Subordinate; attendant upon; in addition to another proceeding which is considered "principal."

Appeal To take a case to a higher court for review.

Assumpsit An action on contract to recover damages for a breach of contract.

Certiorari Discretionary writ issued from the U.S. Supreme Court or a state supreme court to an inferior court ordering the lower court to prepare the records of a case and to send them up for review.

Committing magistrate An inferior judicial officer vested with the authority to conduct preliminary criminal hearings.

Concurrent Having the same authority, e.g., concurrent jurisdiction.

Courts of Record Courts in which the proceedings are recorded and which have power to fine or imprison for contempt.

De Novo A completely new trial, conducted as if no previous trial had been held.

Eminent Domain Power to take private property for public use.

En Banc A session of court held by all the judges, as distinguished from sessions of the same court presided over by a single judge.

Et Seq. And the following.

Ex Officio By virtue of office or position.

Ex Relatione (Ex Rel.) Legal proceedings instituted by the state at the instigation of an individual.

Forcible Entry and Detainer Summary proceeding to restore possession of land to one who is wrongfully kept out or has been wrongfully deprived of possession.

Habeas Corpus A writ to inquire whether a person is lawfully imprisoned or detained.

Injunction A court order enjoining or prohibiting a party from a specific course of action.

In re Referring to judicial proceedings where there are no adversaries, but rather where a matter itself requires judicial actions.

Interlocutory Temporary; not final or definitive.

Jurisdiction The right and power to interpret and apply the law.

Court of Appellate Jurisdiction—A court having jurisdiction of appeal and review, with original jurisdiction conferred only in special cases.

Court of General Jurisdiction—A trial court of unlimited jurisdiction in civil and/or criminal cases.

Court of Limited or Special Jurisdiction—A trial court whose legal jurisdiction covers only a particular class of cases, e.g., probate, juvenile, traffic, or cases where the amount in controversy is below a prescribed sum or which is subject to specific exceptions.

Court of Original Jurisdiction—A court having jurisdiction in the first instance to try a case and pass judgment upon the law and facts, as distinguished from a court of appellate jurisdiction; includes both courts of general jurisdiction and courts of limited or special jurisdiction.

Mandamus A writ issued from a superior court directing a lower court or other authority to perform a particular act.

Nolo contendre A plea meaning that the defendant does not contest the charges but does not admit guilt.

Preliminary hearing The examination of a person charged with a crime before a magistrate or a judge.

Pro bono For the public good.

Pro hac vice For this one particular occasion.

Pro tempore (Pro tem) For the time being; temporarily.

Quid pro quo Giving one valuable thing for another.

Quorum A majority of the entire body; the number of members who must be present in order to conduct business.

Quo Warranto A writ to prevent a continued exercise of unlawfully asserted authority.

Replevin An action to recover personal property unlawfully taken, or a writ to initiate such action.

Retention Vote An election in which a judge stands unopposed on his judicial record.

Summary Proceeding A simple proceeding held before a judge without the usual full hearing.

Tort A wrongful act other than a breach of contract for which a civil action results.

Venue The locality where a crime is committed, where a cause of action occurs, from which a jury must be called, or in which a trial must be held.

Vicinage Neighborhood; places which are adjoining or near.

Voir dire The preliminary examination a court may make when a witness or juror's interest, competency, etc. is questioned; also refers to the oath itself.

Writ A written court order commanding the designated recipient to perform or not perform acts specified in the order.